P9-EFJ-740

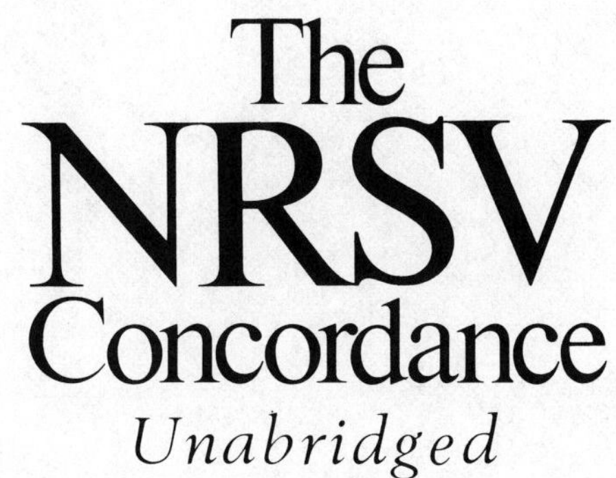
The
NRSV
Concordance
Unabridged

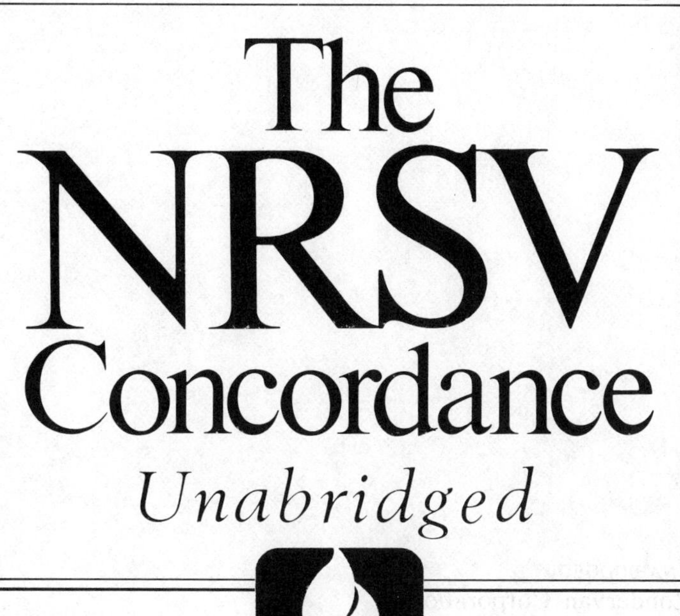

The NRSV Concordance

Unabridged

Including the Apocryphal / Deuterocanonical Books

John R. Kohlenberger III

ZondervanPublishingHouse
Academic and Professional Books
Grand Rapids, Michigan
A Division of HarperCollins*Publishers*

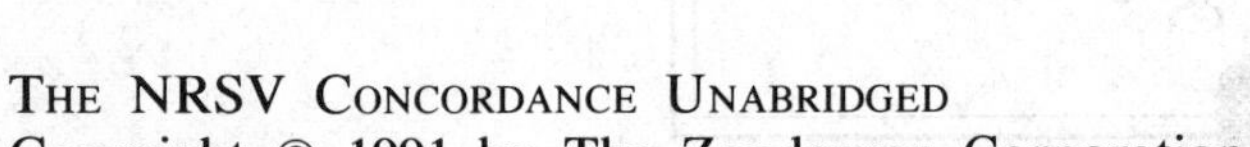

Requests for information should be addressed to:
Zondervan Publishing House
Academic and Professional Books
1415 Lake Drive S.E.
Grand Rapids, Michigan 49506

Library of Congress Cataloging-in-Publication Data

Kohlenberger, John R.
The NRSV concordance unabridged : including the apocryphal/deuterocanonical books / John R. Kohlenberger III.
p. cm.
Includes bibliographical references and indexes.
ISBN 0-310-53910-2 (alk. paper)
1. Bible—Concordances, English—New Revised Standard. I. Title.
BS425.K645 1991
220.5'20433—dc20 91-12197
CIP

Printed in the United States of America

91 92 93 94 95 96 / AK / 10 9 8 7 6 5 4 3 2 1

This edition is printed on acid-free paper and meets the American National Standards Institute Z39.48 standard.

CONTENTS

ACKNOWLEDGMENTS

Having just completed a decade's labor on the *NIV Exhaustive Concordance*, the concept of another major concordance project was initially met with fear and trembling. However, the incredible cooperation and encouragement of a handful of people helped make *The NRSV Concordance Unabridged* a reality in a brief, though intense, seven-month period.

Stan Gundry, General Manager, Zondervan Publishing House/Publisher, Academic and Professional Books, and Bruce Ryskamp, Corporate Vice President/Book, Bible and Electronic Group Executive, initiated the project and allowed me a free hand in design and production. Zondervan's Chief Executive Officer Jim Buick showed great interest and support. Imprint Editor Ed van der Maas was involved in all aspects of design, proofreading, and production and, as usual, was a source of great encouragement to me and my family.

The National Council of Churches, copyright holder of the New Revised Standard Version, granted Zondervan Publishing House the publishing rights for this first concordance to the NRSV. Dr. Arthur O. Van Eck, Associate General Secretary, Division of Education and Ministry, kept me up to date on changes to the NRSV database. Dr. Bruce M. Metzger, Chair of the NRSV Translation Committee, responded quickly and graciously to my questions regarding the NRSV text and footnotes.

Dennis Thomas developed original software to analyze, sort, and set contexts for the main concordance. He and his wife Carole regularly entertained me in their home during late evenings of data crunching.

Doug Johnston was in charge of the production for Zondervan and put in a great deal of extra effort on the book. Jan Ortiz provided valuable editorial assistance. Laura Weller and Connie Van Dyke did a great job of proofreading the main concordance. Verlyn D. Verbrugge compiled the Topical Index to the NRSV. Tim Beals edited the KJV to NRSV cross-references and proofread the Index to NRSV Footnotes.

Larry and Cyndi Stone and Aaron Jarrard of OmniTek Computers in Portland, Oregon provided technical assistance and allowed me generous use of their hardware.

The staff of Multnomah Graphics, particularly its director, Eric Weber, permitted me 24-hour access to their offices and equipment. Typesetters Brian Davis, Marty and Rachel Bogan, and art director Bruce DeRoos provided valuable mechanical assistance, often after hours.

Two special women deserve special recognition for their sacrificial involvement. Carolyn Kohlenberger took valuable time from her own writing schedule to proofread all sections of the concordance, particularly the phrase indexes and contexts of the main concordance. She and our children, Sarah and Joshua, also showed great patience with the too-busy author. Lisa Hill proofread the related-words list and edited much of the unique and complex Index to NRSV Footnotes—all while finishing seminary and beginning a short-term mission.

Through the talents of these individuals, *The NRSV Concordance Unabridged* is a far better book than the author alone could have made it. However, the author does accept full responsibility for any shortcomings or errors found in the book.

DEDICATION

This is the first concordance I have edited on my own, but it could not have been accomplished without the skills developed as a student and colleague of Dr. Edward W. Goodrick. While I was a student at Multnomah School of the Bible, Dr. Goodrick introduced me to the biblical languages and, incidentally, to the original Revised Standard Version. It was my pleasure to introduce him to the New Revised Standard Version on its publication. And it is now my privilege to dedicate to him *The NRSV Concordance Unabridged.*

To Edward W. Goodrick
with profound gratitude and great affection

PREFACE

The first concordance to the English Bible was compiled by John Marbeck, a church musician who nearly lost his life for his labors. Sentenced to the stake for heresy in 1544, he was saved through the intervention of Bishop Stephen Gardiner, who dearly loved Marbeck's music. His life was spared, but his work destroyed. Yet six years later, in 1550, his concordance was published—a mere fourteen years after the publication of the Great Bible upon which it was based.

The most influential English Bible translation to date is the King James, or Authorized, Version. Its most famous concordance was created by Alexander Cruden, who nearly lost his sanity for his labors. Cruden's first edition appeared in 1737, 126 years after the publication of the KJV. The third and definitive edition came out in 1769 and is the fountainhead from which have flowed dozens of abridged and reprint editions. *Cruden's Unabridged Concordance* contained references to both the canonical and apocryphal books of the KJV and was last published by Baker in 1980.

The concordance is an essential tool for basic Bible study. Consequently, the explosion of Bible translations in the twentieth century was followed by an explosion of Bible concordances, such as those to the American Standard Version (1922), Moffatt (1950), Revised Standard Version (1957), New American Standard (1981), New International Version (1981), Good News Bible (1983), and New King James Version (1983).

Previously Published Concordances to the Revised Standard Version

The Revised Standard Version New Testament was published in 1946, the Old Testament in 1952. Five years later the first edition of *Nelson's Complete Concordance of the RSV* appeared. Edited by John W. Ellison, it was the first computer-assisted Bible concordance ever produced. It indexes 310,000 contexts to most of the vocabulary of the 66 canonical books; 131 words were omitted, 5 were partially concorded. The second edition of 1972 is still published by Nelson.

This English-only concordance to the canonical books was supplemented in 1983 by the release of Eerdmans' *A Concordance to the Apocrypha/Deuterocanonical Books of the RSV*, computer generated by the Abbey of Maredsous. This volume covers the 18 deuterocanonical books of the RSV. It lists 72,639 contexts; 74 words are omitted, 3 are partially indexed. Frequency counts are given for each word, but no verbal or conceptual cross-references.

An Analytical Concordance to the RSV of the New Testament, by Clinton Morrison (Westminster: 1979) was the first multilingual concordance to the RSV. Based on the format of Young's *Analytical Concordance*, each English entry is subdivided according to Greek vocabulary. It claims to index every Greek word in the NT except those translated as "the," "and," "but," and "self, he, she, it." But many common words are indexed without contexts, e.g., BE, I, and SAY.

The Eerdmans Analytical Concordance to the RSV, edited by Richard Whitaker, was published in 1988 and remains the definitive concordance to the RSV and the only concordance to date to apply the format of Young's *Analytical Concordance* to a modern translation of the whole Bible. This volume indexes all 84 books of the RSV; 27 words and "all personal pronouns" are omitted; 12 are partially listed; ALL, UPON, WHAT and "other very frequent words" are indexed without contexts. Proper names are indexed separately from the main concordance. No frequency statistics are offered.

A Brief History of the NRSV Concordance Unabridged

The New Revised Standard Version was published in May of 1990. In the fall of that same year, the National Council of Churches granted Zondervan Publishing House publishing rights to the first concordance to the NRSV. The editorial and typesetting work was completed within seven months, and *The NRSV Concordance Unabridged* was released on May 1, 1991, within a year of the original publication of the NRSV!

The NRSV Concordance Unabridged is the first exhaustive concordance to any edition of the Revised Standard Version. It indexes all 84 of the NRSV, the 66 (proto-)canonical books and the 18 deuterocanonical books, as well as all 906,953 words of the NRSV. (It is not, however, called "exhaustive" in its title; in Bible concordances "exhaustive" implies the inclusion of indexes to the original biblical languages; see the introduction, page ix.)

The NRSV Concordance Unabridged again teamed biblical scholar John R. Kohlenberger III and computer programmer Dennis B. Thomas in their fifth concordance project. Unique to this project were the inclusion of the deuterocanonical books, a body of literature nearly as large as the New Testament, and the development of the phrase-index code system (see the introduction, pages x, xi, xiii).

The 31-megabyte database which comprises *The NRSV Concordance Unabridged* was typeset by John R. Kohlenberger III, using Ventura Publisher 3.0 and WordPerfect 5.0. Auto-Graphics Inc. of Pomona, California, typeset the Topical Index to the NRSV.

INTRODUCTION

A concordance is an index to a book. It is usually arranged in alphabetical order and shows the location of each word in the book. In addition, it often supplies several words of the context in which each word is found.

The NRSV Concordance Unabridged (*NRSVCU*) is unabridged in two senses. First, it is unabridged in terms of the books of the New Revised Standard Version. It covers all 84 books contained in the NRSV: the 66 (proto-)canonical books of the Old and New Testaments as well as 18 books received as apocryphal or deuterocanonical by the Roman Catholic and Eastern Orthodox Churches.

Second, the *NRSVCU* is unabridged in terms of vocabulary. All 906,953 words of the NRSV are indexed. In this the *NRSVCU* is truly an exhaustive concordance. However, we have avoided using the term "exhaustive" in the title because all previous exhaustive concordances—*Strong's Exhaustive Concordance* (1890), *The Exhaustive Concordance to the NAS* (Holman, 1981), and *The NIV Exhaustive Concordance* (Zondervan, 1990)—also indexed the English text to the original biblical languages: Hebrew, Aramaic, and Greek. The *NRSVCU* is an exhaustive English index but contains no index to the biblical languages. Therefore we have preferred the title "unabridged" to the potentially misleading title "exhaustive."

FEATURES OF THE NRSV CONCORDANCE UNABRIDGED

The *NRSVCU* is divided into three major sections: (1) the Main Concordance, (2) the Index of Articles, Conjunctions, Particles, Prepositions, and Pronouns, (3) the Index to NRSV Footnotes. In addition, it contains a Topical Index to the NRSV.

THE MAIN CONCORDANCE

Below is a typical entry from the Main Concordance:

AARON‡ (339) [AARON'S]
A. DESCENDANT[S] OF AARON (23)
B. SONS OF AARON (20)
C. AARON THE PRIEST (17)
D. SON OF AARON (14)

Ex 4: 14 "What of your brother, **A** the Levite?
Lev 6: 14 The sons of **A** shall offer it before the LORD, B

The heading consists of:

(1) the indexed word: **AARON**;
(2) the double dagger (‡) follows the indexed word in 2204 headings to indicate that the word is also found in the Index to NRSV Footnotes;
(3) the frequency count in parentheses: (339);
(4) the list of related words in brackets: [AARON'S];
(5) The letters A, B, C, D indicate special phrases that are indexed in the context lines. These subheadings are found under 280 headings.

The context lines consist of:

(1) the book-chapter-verse reference;
(2) the context for the indexed word;
(3) for more than 39,000 lines, a phrase-index code letter (in this case, B).

Headings

There are four kinds of headings: (1) NRSV word headings, (2) phrase-index subheadings, (3) NRSV "See" references, and (4) KJV "See" references.

NRSV Word Headings

The NRSV contains a total of 906,953 words, with a vocabulary of 16,529 words. The *NRSVCU* is an exhaustive alphabetic index to every word of the NRSV.

The simplest heading is a word and its frequency count:

ABBA (3)

If the heading word is followed by a double dagger, as in the case of **AARON**‡, this indicates that this word also appears in the Index to Footnotes (see below, pp. xiii-xiv).

The frequency count lists the total number of times the word appears in the NRSV, which is also the number of contexts listed in the concordance. The *NRSVCU* is the first English-only concordance to provide this information.

The headings show the indexed words exactly as they are spelled in the NRSV. (The sole exceptions are two headings apiece for GOD, LORD, and LORD'S; see the last paragraph in this section.) If the word occurs in other forms or spellings, these words appear in square brackets following the frequency count:

ABIDE (42) [ABIDES, ABIDING, ABODE]

ABIDES (18) [ABIDE]

ABIDING (3) [ABIDE]

ABODE (9) [ABIDE]

Rather than listing all related words after each indexed word, the editor chose one indexed word to act as the "group heading." All related words are listed after the group heading, and each of the related word headings points back to the group heading. In the example above, ABIDE serves as the group heading for ABIDES, ABIDING, and ABODE.

The headings also group together words that share common elements. For example:

ABASE (193) [ABASED, SELF-ABASEMENT]

Place and proper names composed of more than one word in the original languages are usually hyphenated in the NRSV, for example, Abel-beth-maacah, Baal-zebub, and Beth-horon. If individual components of these compound names occur in the biblical text, they are cross-referenced. For example:

BAAL-MEON (3) [BETH-BAAL-MEON, BETH-MEON]

Compound or double names that are *not* hyphenated in the NRSV are *not* given a separate heading. However, the components are cross-referenced. For example, there is no reference for SIMON PETER, but each of these names refers to the other:

PETER (157) [=CEPHAS, PETER'S, =SIMON]

SIMON (154) [=PETER, =SIMEON, SIMON'S, =THASSI]

These examples also show another feature unique to the *NRSVCU*. When a person or place is known by more than one name in the biblical text, the cross-reference indicates this by using the equal sign (=). This does *not* mean that Peter is always the same individual as Simon, for there are twelve men named Simon in the NRSV. If there is uncertainty as to the identity of two names, the cross-reference is followed by a question mark:

BARTHOLOMEW (4) [=NATHANAEL?]

As mentioned above, there are two headings apiece for GOD, LORD, and LORD'S. †LORD and †LORD'S represent the proper name of God, *Yahweh*, which is typeset in the NRSV as "LORD" and "LORD's." This distinguishes "LORD" from "Lord" and "lord," which are indexed under the heading *LORD, and "LORD's" from "Lord's" and "lord's," indexed under *LORD'S. In contexts where the Hebrew words for "Lord" (*Adonay*) and "LORD" (*Yahweh*) appear as a compound name, the NRSV translates Lord GOD. Therefore the heading †GOD is used for "GOD" and *GOD for "God" and "god."

Phrase-Index Subheadings

Unique to the *NRSVCU* is the indexing of 630 important phrases involving 280 key words. The key words were selected from the 828 words that occur more than 100 times in the NRSV. The key words were then analyzed in their contexts to determine important phrases and combinations in which they appear. Usually the phrases had to occur ten times or more in order to be indexed. There were exceptions for such phrases as "day of the Lord" and "book of life," each of which occurs only seven times.

Phrase-index subheadings immediately follow the NRSV word heading and are arranged in descending order of frequency:

GLORY (468) [GLORIES, GLORIFIED, GLORIFIES, GLORIFY, GLORIFYING, GLORIOUS, GLORIOUSLY, VAINGLORY]
A. HIS GLORY (50)
B. GLORY OF THE †LORD (35)
C. YOUR GLORY (34)
D. GLORY OF ... *GOD (25)
E. MY GLORY (20)
F. GAVE/GIVE/GIVING GLORY (19)
G. GLORY OF THE *LORD (6)

The frequency count (in parentheses) indicates the number of times each phrase occurs in the NRSV. The letter code that precedes each phrase appears at the end of every context line in which the phrase is found:

Dt	5:24	"Look, the LORD our God has shown us his **g**	A
Ps	19: 1	The heavens are telling the **g** of God;	D
Eze	8: 4	And the **g** of the God of Israel was there,	D

An ellipsis (...) in the phrase allows for variations in wording. For example, GLORY OF ... *GOD accounts for "glory of God," "glory of the God," and "glory of our great God." If there is only one variation in wording, the variable word is enclosed in brackets, as in FEAR [YOUR] GOD. The front slash (/) separates different forms of a word used in the phrase, as in GAVE/GIVE/GIVING GLORY.

NRSV "See" References

87 words occur a total of 480,027 times—more than half the bulk of the NRSV! These words are exhaustively indexed in their own section: the Index of Articles, Conjunctions, Particles, Prepositions, and Pronouns (see p. xiii). These words are also represented by headings in the Main Concordance, with a message referring to this special index:

A (10838) [AN] See Index of Articles Etc.

Ten of these 87 words have a selected listing of contexts in the Main Concordance.

HAD, HAS, HAVE, and HAVING are usually used as auxiliary verbs to indicate the English perfect tense, as in the clause "everything I **have** commanded you." When used as auxiliary verbs, these words are not indexed in the Main Concordance. But these words also occur as verbs in their own right, expressing the idea of ownership, "He **had** so many flocks," or causing action, "God **had** me wander." In these latter cases, the words are indexed in the Main Concordance: HAD, 607 of 3470 occurrences; HAS, 332 of 2937; HAVE, 1180 of 5723; HAVING, 64 of 172.

Neither I nor AM is indexed in the Main Concordance, but many important passages containing the self-revelation of God contain the phrase I AM, such as Exodus 3:14, "**I AM WHO I AM**," and John 8:58, "before Abraham was, **I am**!" 61 highly significant verses have been selected from the 1036 occurrences of the phrase I AM for the Main Concordance.

MINE is indexed in the Main Concordance when it is not a pronoun (2 of 85 occurrences). When ON is used as a proper name (5 of 5394), it is indexed in the Main Concordance, as is SO (1 of 3960). When WILL is used in the sense of volition, as in the "will of God" or "will of man" (114 of 7473 occurrences), it is indexed in the Main Concordance. For more information on the Index of Articles Etc., see below p. xiii.

A second type of NRSV "See" reference points to the Index to NRSV Footnotes. The NRSV footnotes contain 298 words in alternate translations, added verses and phrases, and transliterations that do not appear in the text of the NRSV. Each of these words is listed as a heading in the Main Concordance with a reference to the Index to Footnotes:

BABOONS See Index to Footnotes

KJV "See" References

The King James, or Authorized, Version has been the dominant English Bible translation from the early seventeenth century to the latter half of the twentieth century. Because of this, the KJV has had profound impact on the language of both the church and English-speaking society. To help users familiar with KJV vocabulary find the proper NRSV terms, 1730 KJV words appear in 1515 KJV "See" references, pointing to 2675 NRSV words. These include such headings as:

CARNAL (KJV) See FLESH, HUMAN, MATERIAL

COMFORTER (KJV) See also ADVOCATE

[HOLY] GHOST (KJV) See [HOLY] SPIRIT

Note that multiple-word "see" references, such as HOLY SPIRIT, do *not* refer to a multiple-word heading. Rather, they direct the user to look for that *combination* of words under the heading for *any* of the words in the multiple-word reference.

Context Lines

Concordances are word indexes. At the very least, they index the book, chapter, and verse in which each word is located. Most concordances also show each word within a brief phrase or clause: a context. This gives a better idea of the use of the word and helps to locate a specific verse that contains that word.

Most concordances limit their contexts to a single line. This is generally true of the *NRSVCU*; however, it has many multiple line contexts. These longer contexts help give a better glimpse into a word's function in the English text, and can also show multiple uses of a word in a single verse.

The purpose of context lines in a concordance is simply to help the reader recognize or locate a specific verse in the Bible. For word study—or any kind of Bible study—the context offered by a concordance is rarely enough to go on. Nevertheless, sometimes a short sentence or a whole verse fits on one line, as in the case of John 11:35, "Jesus began to weep." Under the heading PRAISE, the *NRSVCU* was able to present the entirety of Psalm 150 on thirteen consecutive lines!

Taken by themselves, context lines can and do misrepresent the teaching of Scripture by taking statements out of the larger context. "There is no God" is a context taken straight from Psalm 14:1. Of course the Bible does not teach this; it is what "Fools say in their hearts"! Similarly, a context for Leviticus 24:16 might read, "the LORD shall be put to death" while the text actually says, "One who blasphemes the name of the LORD shall be put to death."

Great care has been taken by the editor, programmer, and proofreaders of the *NRSVCU* to create contexts that are informative and accurate. But the reader should always check word contexts by looking them up in the NRSV itself. "The Wicked Bible," a KJV edition of 1631, accidentally omitted the word "not" from the seventh commandment, for which the printers were fined 300 pounds sterling! Though there are no longer such fines for misleading contexts, the editor and publisher are still deeply concerned that the *NRSVCU* be used discerningly.

Context Lines: General Format

The simplest context line presents three items of information. First, the location of the indexed word by book, chapter, and verse. Second, the context line. Third, within the context line, the indexed word is abbreviated by its first letter and is *usually* in bold type (special typefaces are discussed below). If a word occurs more than once in a context, it is abbreviated each time. For example, under the heading HOLY:

Rev 4: 8 they sing, **"H, h, h,** the Lord God the Almighty,
6: 10 Sovereign Lord, **h** and true,

A table of book abbreviations precedes page 1 of the Main Concordance. Special chapter and verse designations are discussed in the following section.

Special Typefaces. Some words and verses are set in italic type in the NRSV. These include *Selah* and *Higgaion* throughout the Psalms and Habakkuk 3, the titles to the Psalms, and two added sections in Sirach, 26:19-27 and 51:12b. In addition to GOD and LORD (see above, p. x), the NRSV uses small caps for words in Exodus 3:14; Daniel 5:25-28; and Sirach 18:30; 20:27; 23:7; 24:1; 30:1, 18; 44:1; 51:1. These typefaces are reflected in the context lines, as under the heading SON:

Sir 51: 1 PRAYER OF JESUS S OF SIRACH

Ps 3: T *A Psalm of David, when he fled from his s Absalom.*

Double Brackets. Five passages of the New Testament are enclosed in double brackets (⟦ ⟧) to point out that most ancient authorities lack these verses. They are the traditional "longer ending" of Mark (16:9-20), the "shorter ending" of Mark (designated as 16:S in the *NRSVCU*), Luke 22:43-44; 23:34a; and John 7:53-8:11. All contexts from these verses are enclosed in double brackets to reflect the NRSV, as under the heading JESUS:

Mk 16: 19 ⟦So then the Lord **J**, after he had spoken to them,⟧

Jn 8: 6 ⟦**J** bent down and wrote with his finger⟧

Context Lines: Special Chapter and Verse Designations

Books of One Chapter. Five canonical books have only one chapter: Obadiah, Philemon, 2 John, 3 John, and Jude. Therefore some reference books refer only to the verse number (e.g., Jude 1). In the *NRSVCU* all contexts from these books refer to chapter 1 in addition to the verse number (e.g., Jude 1:1).

Six deuterocanonical books have one chapter: The Letter of Jeremiah, The Prayer of Azariah, Susanna, Bel and the Dragon, The Prayer of Manasseh, and Psalm 151.

The Prayer of Azariah and The Prayer of Manasseh are both indexed by chapter 1 in the *NRSVCU*. The Letter of Jeremiah is also chapter 6 of Baruch. The *NRSVCU* reflects the NRSV by using 6 as its chapter number. Susanna is chapter 13 of the Greek version of Daniel, but its chapter number is 1 in the NRSV and therefore also in the *NRSVCU*. Bel and the Dragon is chapter 14 of the Greek version of Daniel, but its chapter number is 1 in the NRSV and therefore also in the *NRSVCU*. Psalm 151 is not a canonical Psalm, so its book abbreviation differs from that of the Psalms (Pm versus Ps), while 151 is used as its chapter number.

Prologues, Superscripts, and Titles. Of the canonical Psalms, 116 have superscripts or titles that are not numbered as verses in the NRSV, as does Psalm 151. The letter "T" is used as the verse designation for these titles.

The book of Sirach (or Ecclesiasticus) has a three-paragraph prologue preceding chapter 1. The abbreviation "Pr" is used as the "chapter" number of the prologue; the numbers 1, 2, and 3 are used as "verse" designations for the three paragraphs.

The Shorter Ending of Mark. The NRSV is one of the few translations to include the "shorter ending" of Mark. However, it places this ending in the text between Mark 16:8 and the traditional "longer ending," verses 9 to 20. Rather than index this passage as part of verse 8, the letter "S" is used as the verse designation for the "shorter ending."

Two Verses Translated as One. James 1:7,8 and Tobit 14:8,9 were each translated as a single unit with a double verse number. The *NRSVCU* follows the NRSV by indexing these verses with both numbers, separated by a comma.

Double Versification in 2 Esdras 7. Between verses 35 and 36 of 2 Esdras 7, the NRSV (and the RSV before it) inserts a 70-verse section. The inserted verses are italicized (*36-140*), while the traditional verses are in Roman type. Thus, there are Roman verses 36-70 as well as italic verses *36-70*. Further, the traditional verses 36-70 are also numbered *106-140* (e.g., 2 Esdras 7:36 *106*).

The *NRSVCU* uses the italicized number as the verse designation for *36-105*. For verses *106-140* = 36-70, the italicized number appears first, followed by the traditional number in brackets at the beginning of the context line, as under the heading ANSWERED:

2Es 7:17 Then I **a** and said, "O sovereign Lord,
7:*102* I **a** and said, "If I have found favor in your sight,
7:*106* [36] I **a** and said, "How then do we find

Transposed Chapters and Verses. In the canonical books, the NRSV rearranges verses 2-4 in Exodus 22 in the order 4, 2, 3 and transposes verses 23 and 22 in Judges 20. In the Apocrypha, Tobit 9 transposes verses 3 and 4. Sirach splits and transposes 28:24-25 and 43:16-17. A larger problem of sequence relates to the chapters in the Additions to Esther, which has the chapter order 11:2-12; 12; 1; 2; 3:1-13; 13:1-7; 3:14-15; 4; 13:8-18; 14; 15; 5; 6; 7; 8:1-12; 16; 8:13-17; 9; 10; 11:1. (This resulted from arranging the additions in the original Greek order while retaining the KJV versification.)

The *NRSVCU* arranges all contexts in strict numerical chapter/verse order, rather than in the NRSV's transposed order. This makes the location of verses easier in the Concordance, and should present no great incovenience with regard to the few transposed passages.

Context Lines: Phrase-Index Code Letters

As mentioned above (p. x), the *NRSVCU* is unique in the indexing of 630 important phrases and word combinations involving 280 key words. More than 39,000 context lines end with phrase-index code letters:

JESUS (994) [JESUS']
A. JESUS CHRIST (138)
B. *LORD JESUS (103)
C. CHRIST JESUS (86)
D. JESUS OF NAZARETH (15)
E. NAME OF JESUS (11)

Ac 9:17 "Brother Saul, the Lord **J**, who appeared to you B
9:27 he had spoken boldly in the name of **J**. E
9:34 Peter said to him, "Aeneas, **J** Christ heals you; A
15:26 risked their lives for the sake of our Lord **J** Christ. AB
16:18 "I order you in the name of **J** Christ to come out AE

Occasionally indexed phrases intersect, resulting in a compound phrase and two code letters at the end of the context line. In the examples above, "AB" indicates the compound phrase LORD JESUS CHRIST and "AE" NAME OF JESUS CHRIST.

THE INDEX OF ARTICLES, CONJUNCTIONS, PARTICLES, PREPOSITIONS, AND PRONOUNS

The Main Concordance indexes 429,293 references to 16,452 NRSV words. The Index of Articles, Conjunctions, Particles, Prepositions, and Pronouns indexes 480,027 references to 87 NRSV words. These include 65 words that appear more than 1,000 times each, such as "I," "me," and "my," and 22 less frequent words that are related to them, such as "myself" and "mine." This index makes the *NRSVCU* the first truly exhaustive English-only concordance.

The format of the Index of Articles Etc. is very simple. Each of the 87 words has its own heading, followed by a frequency count:

A (10838)

The eight words that are partially indexed in the Main Concordance (AM, HAD, HAS, HAVE, HAVING, I, MINE, ON, SO, and WILL, see above page xi) are exhaustively indexed here, and also have the message "See also selected list in the Main Concordance."

The 87 words of this section are indexed without contexts, since providing contexts would be of little benefit to the reader and would more than double the size of the *NRSVCU*! Book, chapter, and verse references appear in biblical order. Books and chapters are set in bold print for easy location. If the indexed word occurs more than once in a verse, the total number of occurrences is indicated by a raised number:

Jer 1:5, 6, 7, 11, 13^2, 18^2; **2:**2^2, 6^3, 7, 10, 11, 14^2,

This example from the indefinite article "A" shows that the article appears twice in Jeremiah 1:13, 1:18, 2:2, and 2:14, and three times in 2:6. Note too that book and chapter references appear just once. Verses within the same chapter are set off by commas. The final verse of the chapter is followed by a semicolon.

INDEX TO NRSV FOOTNOTES

The NRSV has 6,266 footnotes. Most offer alternate or "literal" translations, or discuss alternate readings in ancient texts and versions. The *NRSVCU* is the first English concordance to index such footnotes.

Unlike the Main Concordance, the Index to Footnotes does not index every occurrence of every word in the notes. Only words that differ from the NRSV text are indexed. Whenever a footnote states that ancient texts or versions "add" or "lack" a phrase, the words of the addition or omission are indexed. When an alternate translation is offered, following key terms such as "or," "Heb," "Gk," and "cn," the words that differ from the NRSV text are indexed. In all, 2,502 words are represented by 6,686 contexts in the Index to NRSV Footnotes.

For example, in Mark 9:29, following the sentence "This kind can come out only through prayer." the footnote states "Other ancient authorities add *and fasting*." The word "fasting" is indexed and the heading FASTING‡ in the Main Concordance notes this by use of the double dagger. Similarly, the phrase "you shall deny yourselves" in Leviticus 16:29, 31; 23:27 and 23:32 is footnoted "Or *shall fast*." All four verses are in the Index to Footnotes, and in the Main Concordance the heading FAST‡ has the double dagger. (Like the Main Concordance, the Index to NRSV Footnotes does not index any occurrences of the 87 words found in the Index to Articles Etc. See preceding section.)

The format of the Index to NRSV Footnotes is similar to that of the Main Concordance:

FASTING (2)
Mt 17: 20 + v.21 *But this kind does not come out except by prayer and **fasting***
Mk 9: 29 out only through prayer." {Other ancient authorities add *and **fasting***}

Each heading is followed by a frequency count. This frequency count represents the number of occurrences of the word in the Index, not the total number of occurrences of the word in the footnotes. The context line usually shows a phrase from the NRSV text, followed by the footnote enclosed within braces { }. The indexed word is fully spelled out in bold italic. When a footnote contains an entire added verse, such as in Matthew 17:20 above, this is indicated by the plus sign (+), the added verse number (v.21), and the text of the addition. In such cases, the "plus verse" reference substitutes for the explanatory text "Other ancient authorities add verse . . . ".

Ellipses (...) and angle brackets (< >) are used to indicate abbreviations of NRSV and footnote text. For example, under the heading ALL:

Ac 8: 36 baptized?" {Other ancient authorities add all or most of verse 37, *And Philip said, "If you believe with all your heart, you may."* >}
Sir 13: 13 + v.14 < *During **all** your life love the Lord,* >
42: 15 and all ... will. {Syr Compare Heb: most Gk witnesses lack *and **all** ... will*}
2Es 14: 48 did so. {Syr adds ... *after he had written **all** these things.* >}

In Acts 8:36, the right angle bracket (>) indicates that further text *follows* in the cited footnote. In Sirach 13:14, the left angle bracket (<) indicates there is more footnote text *preceeding* the cited context and the right angle bracket indicates further text *follows*. In 42:15, the ellipses (...) mark omissions *within* both the NRSV and footnote texts. In 2 Esdras 14:48 the ellipsis marks the omission of text *within* the footnote and the right angle bracket notes that additional footnote text follows.

A table of abbreviations used in NRSV footnotes precedes page 1 of the Index to NRSV Footnotes.

TOPICAL INDEX TO THE NRSV

A 76-page Topical Index to the NRSV was prepared for the *NRSVCU* by Verlyn Verbrugge. Its thematic analysis of key words provides a useful supplement to the straightforward vocabulary index of the Main Concordance.

The following is a typical entry:

ADULTERY
-Sexual unfaithfulness to one's spouse
A. Old Testament perspective
1. Laws against adultery
-In the Ten Commandments ...... Ex 20:14
Dt 5:18
-Various laws on adultery .... Lev 20:10
Nu 5:12-31
Dt 22:22-24

Indexed words are often defined (in italics). Articles are organized in an A, B, C, 1, 2, 3 outline. Dashes (-) itemize information under topics and subtopics. Verse references follow topical information. Multiple references to single items are listed in columns.

THE NRSV CONCORDANCE UNABRIDGED

FEATURES OF THE MAIN CONCORDANCE

NRSV WORD HEADING
The indexed word as spelled in the NRSV; a double dagger (‡) indicates the word is also in the Index to NRSV Footnotes (see the introduction, page x).

FREQUENCY COUNT
Total number of occurrences of the word in the NRSV (see introduction, page x).

RELATED WORD LIST
Other spellings and related words in the NRSV (see the introduction, page x).

DAY‡ (1750) [BIRTHDAY, DAILY, DAY'S, DAYBREAK, DAYLIGHT, DAYS, DAYS', DAYTIME]
A. ON THAT DAY (146)

PHRASE-INDEX CODE
Identifies a special phrase indexed in the context lines (see introduction, pp. x, xi).

FREQUENCY COUNT
Total number of occurrences of the phrase in the NRSV (see introduction, page xi).

Ex 8: 22 But on that **d** I will set apart the land of Goshen, A

PHRASE-INDEX CODE
Indicates the occurrence of a special phrase in the context (intro., pp. xi, xiii).

INDEXED WORD
Abbreviated by its first letter, usually in **bold** type (see the introduction, page x).

BIBLICAL REFERENCE
See the abbreviations in the table below.

Ps 92: T *A Song for the Sabbath* ***D.***

ITALIC TYPEFACE
Italicized text in the NRSV is reflected in the context lines (see introduction, p. xii).

Mk 16: 9 ⟦after he rose early on the first **d** of the week,⟧

DOUBLE BRACKETS ⟦ ⟧
Passages bracketed as textually doubtful in the NRSV have their contexts in double brackets (see the introduction, page xii).

A (10838) [AN] See Index of Articles Etc.

NRSV "See" REFERENCES
Refers to an index in another location (see introduction, page xi).

ANATHEMA (KJV) See ACCURSED

KJV "See" REFERENCES
Cross-references key words to NRSV vocabulary (introduction, p. xi).

ABBREVIATIONS FOR THE BOOKS OF THE BIBLE

CANONICAL BOOKS

1Ch . . . . 1 Chronicles
1Co . . . 1 Corinthians
1Jn . . . . 1 John
1Ki . . . . 1 Kings
1Pe . . . . 1 Peter
1Sa . . . . 1 Samuel
1Th . 1 Thessalonians
1Ti . . . . . . 1 Timothy
2Ch . . . . 2 Chronicles
2Co . . . 2 Corinthians
2Jn . . . . 2 John
2Ki . . . . 2 Kings
2Pe . . . . 2 Peter
2Sa . . . . 2 Samuel
2Th . . 2 Thessalonians
2Ti . . . . . . 2 Timothy
3Jn . . . . 3 John
Ac . . . . Acts
Am . . . . Amos
Col . . . . . . Colossians
Da . . . . Daniel
Dt . . . . Deuteronomy
Ecc . . . . . Ecclesiastes
Eph . . . . . . Ephesians
Est . . . . Esther
Ex . . . . Exodus
Eze . . . . Ezekiel
Ezr . . . . Ezra
Gal . . . . Galatians
Ge . . . . Genesis
Hab . . . . . . Habakkuk
Hag . . . . Haggai
Heb . . . . . . Hebrews
Hos . . . . Hosea
Isa . . . . Isaiah
Jas . . . . James
Jdg . . . . Judges
Jer . . . . Jeremiah
Jn . . . . John
Jnh . . . . Jonah
Job . . . . Job
Joel . . . . Joel
Jos . . . . Joshua
Jude . . . . Jude
La . . . . Lamentations
Lev . . . . Leviticus
Lk . . . . Luke
Mal . . . . Malachi
Mic . . . . Micah
Mk . . . . Mark
Mt . . . . Matthew
Na . . . . Nahum
Ne . . . . . . Nehemiah
Nu . . . . Numbers
Ob . . . . Obadiah
Phm . . . . . . Philemon
Php . . . . . Philippians
Pr . . . . Proverbs
Ps . . . . Psalms
Rev . . . . . Revelation
Ro . . . . Romans
Ru . . . . Ruth
SS . . . Song of Songs
Tit . . . . Titus
Zec . . . . . . Zechariah
Zep . . . . . Zephaniah

APOCRYPHA

1Es . . . . 1 Esdras
1Mc . . . 1 Maccabees
2Es . . . . 2 Esdras
2Mc . . . 2 Maccabees
3Mc . . . 3 Maccabees
4Mc . . . 4 Maccabees
AdE . . . . Additions to Esther
Aza . . . . . . Prayer of Azariah
Bar . . . . Baruch
Bel . . . . Bel and the Dragon
Jdt . . . . Judith
LtJ . . . . Letter of Jeremiah
Man . . . . . . Prayer of Manasseh
Pm . . . . . . Psalm 151
Sir . . . . Sirach
Sus . . . . Susanna
Tob . . . . Tobit
Wis . . . . Wisdom

OTHER

S . . . Shorter Ending of Mark
T . . . . . . Psalm Titles
Pr: . . Sirach Prologue

THE NRSV CONCORDANCE UNABRIDGED

A

A (10838) [AN] See Index of Articles Etc.

AARON‡ (339) [AARON'S]

A. DESCENDANT[S] OF AARON (23)
B. SONS OF AARON (20)
C. AARON THE PRIEST (17)
D. SON OF AARON (14)

Ex 4:14 "What of your brother A, the Levite?
4:27 The LORD said to A, "Go into the wilderness
4:28 Moses told A all the words of the LORD
4:29 and A went and assembled all the elders of
4:30 A spoke all the words that the LORD had spoken
5: 1 Afterward Moses and A went to Pharaoh and said,
5: 4 But the king of Egypt said to them, "Moses and A,
5:20 they came upon Moses and A who were waiting
6:13 Thus the LORD spoke to Moses and A,
6:20 and she bore him A and Moses,
6:23 A married Elisheba, daughter of Amminadab
6:26 It was this same A and Moses to whom
6:27 the Israelites out of Egypt, the same Moses and A.
7: 1 and your brother A shall be your prophet.
7: 2 and your brother A shall tell Pharaoh to let
7: 6 Moses and A did so; they did just
7: 7 and A eighty-three when they spoke to Pharaoh.
7: 8 The LORD said to Moses and A,
7: 9 'Perform a wonder,' then you shall say to A,
7:10 So Moses and A went to Pharaoh and did as
7:10 A threw down his staff before Pharaoh
7:19 The LORD said to Moses, "Say to A,
7:20 Moses and A did just as the LORD commanded.
8: 5 And the LORD said to Moses, "Say to A,
8: 6 A stretched out his hand over the waters of Egypt;
8: 8 Then Pharaoh called Moses and A, and said,
8:12 Then Moses and A went out from Pharaoh;
8:16 Then the LORD said to Moses, "Say to A,
8:17 A stretched out his hand with his staff and struck
8:25 Then Pharaoh summoned Moses and A, and said,
9: 8 Then the LORD said to Moses and A,
9:27 Then Pharaoh summoned Moses and A,
10: 3 So Moses and A went to Pharaoh, and said to him,
10: 8 So Moses and A were brought back to Pharaoh,
10:16 Pharaoh hurriedly summoned Moses and A
11:10 Moses and A performed all these wonders
12: 1 LORD said to Moses and A in the land of Egypt:
12:28 as the LORD had commanded Moses and A.
12:31 Then he summoned Moses and A in the night,
12:43 The LORD said to Moses and A:
12:50 as the LORD had commanded Moses and A.
16: 2 of the Israelites complained against Moses and A
16: 6 So Moses and A said to all the Israelites,
16: 9 to A, "Say to the whole congregation of
16:10 And as A spoke to the whole congregation of
16:33 And Moses said to A, "Take a jar,
16:34 so A placed it before the covenant,
17:10 and fought with Amalek, while Moses, A,
17:12 A and Hur held up his hands, one on one side,
18:12 and A came with all the elders of Israel
19:24 "Go down, and come up bringing A with you;
24: 1 "Come up to the LORD, you and A, Nadab,
24: 9 Then Moses and A, Nadab, and Abihu,

Ex 24:14 for A and Hur are with you;
27:21 A and his sons shall tend it from evening
28: 1 Then bring near to you your brother A,
28: 1 A and Aaron's sons, Nadab and Abihu,
28: 2 for the glorious adornment of your brother A.
28: 4 for your brother A and his sons to serve me
28:12 and A shall bear their names before the LORD
28:29 So A shall bear the names of the sons of Israel in
28:30 thus A shall bear the judgment of the Israelites
28:35 A shall wear it when he ministers,
28:38 and A shall take on himself any guilt incurred in
28:41 You shall put them on your brother A,
28:43 A and his sons shall wear them when they go into
29: 4 You shall bring A and his sons to the entrance of
29: 5 and put on A the tunic and the robe of the ephod,
29: 9 You shall then ordain A and his sons.
29:10 A and his sons shall lay their hands on the head of
29:15 and A and his sons shall lay their hands on
29:19 and A and his sons shall lay their hands on
29:21 and sprinkle it on A and his vestments and
29:24 and you shall place all these on the palms of A and
29:27 from that which belonged to A and his sons.
29:28 These things shall be a perpetual ordinance for A
29:29 The sacred vestments of A shall be passed on
29:32 and A and his sons shall eat the flesh of the ram
29:35 Thus you shall do to A and to his sons,
29:44 A also and his sons I will consecrate,
30: 7 A shall offer fragrant incense on it;
30: 8 and when A sets up the lamps in the evening,
30:10 Once a year A shall perform the rite of atonement
30:19 the water A and his sons shall wash their hands
30:30 You shall anoint A and his sons,
31:10 for the priest A and the vestments of his sons,
32: 1 the people gathered around A, and said to him,
32: 2 A said to them, "Take off the gold rings that are
32: 3 from their ears, and brought them to A.
32: 5 When A saw this, he built an altar before it;
32: 5 and A made proclamation and said,
32:21 Moses said to A, "What did this people do to you
32:22 A said, "Do not let the anger of my lord burn hot;
32:25 (for A had let them run wild,
32:35 because they made the calf—the one that A made.
34:30 When A and all the Israelites saw Moses,
34:31 and A and all the leaders of the congregation
35:19 the holy vestments for the priest A,
38:21 under the direction of Ithamar son of the priest A.
39: 1 they made the sacred vestments for A;
39:27 woven of fine linen, for A and his sons,
39:41 the sacred vestments for the priest A,
40:12 Then you shall bring A and his sons to
40:13 and put on A the sacred vestments,
40:31 and A and his sons washed their hands
Lev 1: 7 The sons of the priest A shall put fire on the altar
2: 3 of the grain offering shall be for A and his sons,
2:10 of the grain offering shall be for A and his sons;
3:13 sons of A shall dash its blood against all sides B
6: 9 Command A and his sons, saying:
6:14 The sons of A shall offer it before the LORD, B
6:16 A and his sons shall eat what is left of it;
6:18 Every male among the descendants of A shall A
6:20 This is the offering that A and his sons shall offer
6:25 Speak to A and his sons, saying:
7:10 shall belong to all the sons of A equally. B
7:31 but the breast shall belong to A and his sons.
7:33 one among the sons of A who offers the blood B
7:34 have given them to A the priest and to his sons, C
7:35 This is the portion allotted to A and to his sons
8: 2 Take A and his sons with him, the vestments,
8: 6 Then Moses brought A and his sons forward,
8:14 and A and his sons laid their hands upon the head
8:18 A and his sons laid their hands on the head of
8:22 A and his sons laid their hands on the head of

Lev 8:27 on the palms of A and on the palms of his sons,
8:30 that was on the altar and sprinkled them on A
8:30 Thus he consecrated A and his vestments,
8:31 And Moses said to A and his sons,
8:31 as I was commanded, 'A and his sons shall eat it';
8:36 A and his sons did all the things that
9: 1 the eighth day Moses summoned A and his sons
9: 2 to A, "Take a bull calf for a sin offering and a ram
9: 7 Then Moses said to A, "Draw near to the altar
9: 8 A drew near to the altar,
9: 9 The sons of A presented the blood to him, B
9:21 the right thigh A raised as an elevation offering
9:22 A lifted his hands toward the people
9:23 Moses and A entered the tent of meeting,
10: 3 to A, "This is what the LORD meant
10: 3 be glorified.' " And A was silent.
10: 4 sons of Uzziel the uncle of A, and said to them,
10: 6 to A and to his sons Eleazar and Ithamar, "Do
10: 8 And the LORD spoke to A:
10:12 Moses spoke to A and to his remaining sons,
10:19 And A spoke to Moses, "See,
11: 1 LORD spoke to Moses and A, saying to them:
13: 1 The LORD spoke to Moses and A, saying:
13: 2 to A the priest or to one of his sons the priests. C
14:33 The LORD spoke to Moses and A, saying:
15: 1 The LORD spoke to Moses and A, saying:
16: 1 to Moses after the death of the two sons of A, B
16: 2 Tell your brother A not to come just at any time
16: 3 Thus shall A come into the holy place:
16: 6 A shall offer the bull as a sin offering for himself,
16: 8 and A shall cast lots on the two goats,
16: 9 A shall present the goat on which the lot fell for
16:11 A shall present the bull as a sin offering
16:21 Then A shall lay both his hands on the head of
16:23 Then A shall enter the tent of meeting,
17: 2 to A and his sons and to all the people of Israel
21: 1 Speak to the priests, the sons of A, B
21:17 Speak to A and say: No one of your
21:21 descendant of A the priest who has a blemish AC
21:24 to A and to his sons and to all the people of Israel.
22: 2 Direct A and his sons to deal carefully with
22:18 to A and his sons and all the people of Israel
24: 3 A shall set it up in the tent of meeting,
24: 8 Every sabbath day A shall set them in order before
24: 9 They shall be for A and his descendants,
Nu 1: 3 You and A shall enroll them,
1:17 and A took these men who had been designated
1:44 whom Moses and A enrolled with the help of
2: 1 The LORD spoke to Moses and A, saying:
3: 1 This is the lineage of A and Moses at the time
3: 2 These are the names of the sons of A: B
3: 3 these are the names of the sons of A, B
3: 4 as priests in the lifetime of their father A.
3: 6 and set them before A the priest, C
3: 9 the Levites to A and his descendants;
3:10 a register of A and his descendants;
3:32 Eleazar son of A the priest was to be chief CD
3:38 were Moses and A and Aaron's sons,
3:39 of the Levites whom Moses and A enrolled at
3:48 Give to A and his sons the money by which
3:51 and Moses gave the redemption money to A
4: 1 The LORD spoke to Moses and A, saying:
4: 5 A and his sons shall go in and take down
4:15 When A and his sons have finished covering
4:16 Eleazar son of A the priest shall have charge CD
4:17 Then the LORD spoke to Moses and A, saying:
4:19 A and his sons shall go in and assign each to
4:27 the command of A and his sons, in all that they are
4:28 the oversight of Ithamar son of A the priest. CD
4:33 under the hand of Ithamar son of A the priest. CD
4:34 and A and the leaders of the congregation enrolled
4:37 and A enrolled according to the commandment of

Nu 4:41 and A enrolled according to the commandment of
4:45 and A enrolled according to the commandment of
4:46 and A and the leaders of Israel enrolled,
6:23 to A and his sons, saying, Thus you shall bless
7: 8 the direction of Ithamar son of A the priest. CD
8: 2 Speak to A and say to him:
8: 3 A did so; he set up its
8:11 and A shall present the Levites before the LORD
8:13 Then you shall have the Levites stand before A
8:19 I have given the Levites as a gift to A and his sons
8:20 Moses and A and the whole congregation of
8:21 then A presented them as an elevation offering
8:21 and A made atonement for them to cleanse them.
8:22 of meeting in attendance on A and his sons.
9: 6 They came before Moses and A on that day,
10: 8 sons of A, the priests, shall blow the trumpets; B
12: 1 Miriam and A spoke against Moses because of
12: 4 Suddenly the LORD said to Moses, A,
12: 5 and called A and Miriam;
12:10 And A turned towards Miriam and saw
12:11 Then A said to Moses, "Oh, my lord,
13:26 and A and to all the congregation of the Israelites
14: 2 the Israelites complained against Moses and A;
14: 5 and A fell on their faces before all the assembly of
14:26 And the LORD spoke to Moses and to A, saying:
15:33 A, and to the whole congregation.
16: 3 They assembled against Moses and against A,
16:11 What is A that you rail against him?"
16:16 before the LORD, you and they and A;
16:17 you also, and A, each his censer."
16:18 of the tent of meeting with Moses and A.
16:20 the LORD spoke to Moses and to A, saying:
16:37 Eleazar son of A the priest to take the censers CD
16:40 who is not of the descendants of A, A
16:41 against Moses and against A,
16:42 Moses and A turned toward the tent of meeting;
16:43 Then Moses and A came to the front of the tent
16:46 Moses said to A, "Take your censer,
16:47 So A took it as Moses had ordered,
16:50 A returned to Moses at the entrance of the tent
17: 6 and the staff of A was among theirs.
17: 8 the staff of A for the house of Levi had sprouted.
17:10 "Put back the staff of A before the covenant,
18: 1 The LORD said to A: You and your sons
18: 8 The LORD spoke to A: I have given you charge of
18:20 Then the LORD said to A: You shall have no
18:28 the LORD's offering to the priest A.
19: 1 The LORD spoke to Moses and A, saying:
20: 2 against Moses and against A.
20: 6 Then Moses and A went away from the assembly
20: 8 you and your brother A, and command the rock
20:10 Moses and A gathered the assembly together
20:12 But the LORD said to Moses and A,
20:23 the LORD said to Moses and A at Mount Hor,
20:24 "Let A be gathered to his people.
20:25 Take A and his son Eleazar,
20:26 strip A of his vestments, and put them
20:26 But A shall be gathered to his people,
20:28 Moses stripped A of his vestments,
20:28 and A died there on the top of the mountain.
20:29 When all the congregation saw that A had died,
20:29 all the house of Israel mourned for A thirty days.
25: 7 Phinehas son of Eleazar, son of A the priest, CD
25:11 son of A the priest, has turned back my wrath CD
26: 1 to Moses and to Eleazar son of A the priest, CD
26: 9 who rebelled against Moses and A in the company
26:59 A, Moses, and their sister Miriam.
26:60 To A were born Nadab, Abihu, Eleazar,
26:64 of those enrolled by Moses and A the priest, C
27:13 be gathered to your people, as your brother A was,
33: 1 under the leadership of Moses and A.
33:38 A the priest went up Mount Hor at the command C
33:39 A was one hundred twenty-three years old
Dt 9:20 so angry with A that he was ready to destroy him,
9:20 I interceded also on behalf of A at that same time.
10: 6 There A died, and there he was buried;
32:50 as your brother A died on Mount Hor
Jos 21: 4 descendants of A the priest received by lot AC
21:10 which went to the descendants of A, A
21:13 descendants of A the priest they gave Hebron, AC
21:19 The towns of the descendants of A— A
24: 5 Then I sent Moses and A,
24:33 Eleazar son of A died; D
Jdg 20:28 son of A, ministered before it in those days), D
1Sa 12: 6 and A and brought your ancestors up out of
12: 8 to the LORD and the LORD sent Moses and A,
1Ch 6: 3 The children of Amram: A, Moses, and Miriam.
6: 3 sons of A: Nadab, Abihu, Eleazar, and Ithamar. B
6:49 But A and his sons made offerings on the altar
6:50 These are the sons of A: B
6:54 to the sons of A of the families of Kohathites— B
6:57 To the sons of A they gave the cities of refuge: B
12:27 Jehoiada, leader of the house of A,
15: 4 the descendants of A and the Levites: A
23:13 The sons of Amram: A and Moses.
23:13 A was set apart to consecrate the most holy things,
23:28 to assist the descendants of A for the service of A
23:32 and shall attend the descendants of A, A
24: 1 divisions of the descendants of A were these. A
24: 1 sons of A: Nadab, Abihu, Eleazar, and Ithamar. B
24:19 for them by their ancestor A,
24:31 to their kindred, the descendants of A, in A
27:17 for Levi, Hashabiah son of Kemuel; for A, Zadok;
2Ch 13: 9 the descendants of A, and the Levites, A
13:10 to the LORD who are descendants of A, A
26:18 but for the priests the descendants of A, A
29:21 the descendants of A to offer them on the altar A
2Ch 31:19 And for the descendants of A, the priests, A
35:14 the descendants of A were occupied in offering A
35:14 and for the priests, the descendants of A. A
Ezr 7: 5 son of Eleazar, son of the chief priest A—
Ne 10:38 And the priest, the descendant of A, A
12:47 that which was for the descendants of A. A
Ps 77:20 like a flock by the hand of Moses and A.
99: 6 Moses and A were among his priests,
105:26 and A whom he had chosen.
106:16 and of A, the holy one of the LORD.
115:10 O house of A, trust in the LORD!
115:12 he will bless the house of A;
118: 3 Let the house of A say,
133: 2 on the beard of A, running down over the collar
135:19 O house of A, bless the LORD!
Mic 6: 4 and I sent before you Moses, A, and Miriam.
Lk 1: 5 His wife was a descendant of A, A
Ac 7:40 to A, 'Make gods for us who will lead the way
Heb 5: 4 when called by God, just as A was.
7:11 rather than one according to the order of A?
Tob 1: 7 I would give these to the priests, the sons of A, B
Sir 45: 6 He exalted A, a holy man
45:20 He added glory to A and gave him a heritage;
45:25 so the heritage of A is for his descendants alone.
50:13 the sons of A in their splendor held the Lord's B
50:16 Then the sons of A shouted; B
1Mc 7:14 "A priest of the line of A has come with the army,
1Es 1:13 and for their kindred the priests, the sons of A, B
1:14 and for their kindred the priests, the sons of A. B
5: 5 the descendants of Phinehas son of A; D
8: 2 Abishua son of Phineas son of Eleazar son of A D
2Es 1: 3 son of A, of the tribe of Levi, who was a captive D
1:13 I gave you Moses as leader and A as priest;
4Mc 7:11 For just as our father A, armed with the censer,
7:12 so the descendant of A, Eleazar, though being A

AARON'S (30) [AARON]

A. AARON'S SONS (15)

Ex 6:25 A son Eleazar married one of the daughters
7:12 but A staff swallowed up theirs.
15:20 Then the prophet Miriam, A sister,
28: 1 Aaron and A sons, Nadab and Abihu, A
28: 3 that they make A vestments to consecrate him
28:30 be on A heart when he goes in before the LORD;
28:38 It shall be on A forehead, and Aaron shall take
28:40 For A sons you shall make tunics and sashes A
29:20 of its blood and put it on the lobe of A right ear
29:26 the breast of the ram of A ordination and raise it
Lev 1: 5 and A sons the priests shall offer the blood, A
1: 8 A sons the priests shall arrange the parts, A
1:11 and A sons the priests shall dash its blood A
2: 2 and bring it to A sons the priests. A
3: 2 and A sons the priests shall dash the blood A
3: 5 A sons shall turn these into smoke on the altar, A
3: 8 and A sons shall dash its blood against all sides A
6:22 from among A descendants as a successor,
8:12 of the anointing oil on A head and anointed him,
8:13 And Moses brought forward A sons, A
8:23 of A right ear and on the thumb of his right hand
8:24 After A sons were brought forward, A
9:12 A sons brought him the blood, A
9:18 A sons brought him the blood, A
10: 1 Now A sons, Nadab and Abihu, A
10:16 A remaining sons, and said,
22: 4 of A offspring who has a leprous disease or
Nu 3:38 were Moses and Aaron and A sons, A
17: 3 and write A name on the staff of Levi.
Heb 9: 4 A rod that budded, and the tablets of the covenant;

AARONITES (KJV) See AARON

ABADDON (7) [=APOLLYON]

Job 26: 6 Sheol is naked before God, and A has no covering.
28:22 A and Death say, 'We have heard a rumor of it
31:12 for that would be a fire consuming down to A,
Ps 88:11 or your faithfulness in A?
Pr 15:11 Sheol and A lie open before the LORD,
27:20 Sheol and A are never satisfied,
Rev 9:11 his name in Hebrew is A,

ABAGTHA (1)

Est 1:10 Harbona, Bigtha and A, Zethar and Carkas,

ABANA (1)

2Ki 5:12 Are not A and Pharpar, the rivers of Damascus,

ABANDON (24) [ABANDONED, ABANDONING, ABANDONS]

Nu 32:15 he will again a them in the wilderness;
Dt 4:31 he will neither a you nor destroy you;
Jos 10: 6 saying, "Do not a your servants;
1Ki 8:57 may he not leave us or a us,
1Ch 28: 9 but if you forsake him, he will a you forever.
2Ch 15: 2 but if you a him, he will a you.
Ps 37:33 The LORD will not a them to their power,
94:14 he will not a his heritage;
Mk 7: 8 You a the commandment of God and hold
Ac 2:27 For you will not a my soul to Hades,
7:19 and forced our ancestors to a their infants so
Heb 10:35 Do not, therefore, a that confidence of yours;
Jude 1:11 and a themselves to Balaam's error for the sake
Tob 4: 3 Honor your mother and do not a her all the days
Tob 14: 6 They will all a their idols,
Sir 9:10 Do not a old friends, for new ones cannot equal
13: 4 but if you are in need he will a you.
16:27 and they do not a their tasks.
23: 1 do not a me to their designs,
LtJ 6:41 they themselves cannot perceive this and a them,
3Mc 2:32 a courageous spirit and did not a their religion;
4Mc 7: 9 and you did not a the holiness that you praised,
18: 5 to become pagans and to a their ancestral customs,

ABANDONED‡ (44) [ABANDON]

Dt 29:25 "It is because they a the covenant of the LORD,
32:15 He a God who made him,
Jdg 2:12 and they a the LORD, the God
2:13 They a the LORD, and worshiped Baal and
10: 6 Thus they a the LORD, and did not worship him.
10:10 because we have a our God and have worshiped
10:13 Yet you have a me and worshiped other gods;
2Sa 5:21 The Philistines a their idols there,
2Ki 7: 7 So they fled away in the twilight and a their tents,
21:22 he a the LORD, the God of his ancestors, and did
22:17 Because they have a me and have made offerings
1Ch 10: 7 they a their towns and fled;
14:12 They a their gods there,
2Ch 7:22 'Because they a the LORD the God
12: 1 he a the law of the LORD,
12: 5 You a me, so I have a you to the hand of Shishak."
13:10 us, the LORD is our God, and we have not a him.
13:11 of the LORD our God, but you have a him.
24:18 They a the house of the LORD,
24:24 because they had a the LORD,
28: 6 because they had a the LORD,
Ne 9:28 and you a them to the hands of their enemies,
Job 20:19 For they have crushed and a the poor,
Ps 78:60 He a his dwelling at Shiloh,
Isa 54: 7 For a brief moment I a you,
Jer 12: 7 I have forsaken my house, I have a my heritage;
22: 9 they a the covenant of the LORD their God,
Ac 2:31 'He was not a to Hades, nor did his flesh
7:21 when he was a, Pharaoh's daughter adopted him
27:20 all hope of our being saved was at last a.
Eph 4:19 and have a themselves to licentiousness,
Rev 2: 4 that you have a the love you had at first.
Jdt 5: 8 Since they had a the ways of their ancestors,
Wis 18: 5 and one child had been a and rescued,
Sir 49: 4 for they a the law of the Most High;
1Mc 1:15 and removed the marks of circumcision, and a
2Mc 10:13 because he had a Cyprus,
3Mc 1:19 for marriage a the bridal chambers prepared
1:20 Mothers and nurses a even newborn children here
2Es 8:56 of his law, and a his ways.
10:32 I said, "It was because you a me.
4Mc 2:10 so that virtue is not a for their sakes.
10: 7 they a the instruments and scalped him

ABANDONING (1) [ABANDON]

1Mc 2:19 everyone of them a the religion of their ancestors,

ABANDONS (1) [ABANDON]

Sir 29:17 and the ungrateful person a his rescuer.

ABARIM‡ (5) [IYE-ABARIM]

Nu 27:12 "Go up this mountain of the A range,
33:47 and camped in the mountains of A,
33:48 They set out from the mountains of A and camped
Dt 32:49 the A, Mount Nebo, which is in the land of Moab,
Jer 22:20 cry out from A, for all your lovers are crushed.

ABASE (2) [ABASED, SELF-ABASEMENT]

Job 40:11 and look on all who are proud, and a them.
Eze 21:26 Exalt that which is low, a that which is high.

ABASE, ABASED, ABASING (KJV) See also HUMBLE, IN NEED, LOW, TERRIFIED

ABASED (3) [ABASE]

2Sa 6:22 and I will be a in my own eyes;
Ps 44: 9 Yet you have rejected us and a us,
Mal 2: 9 I make you despised and a before all the people,

ABASHED (1) [ABASHMENT]

Isa 24:23 Then the moon will be a, and the sun ashamed;

ABASHMENT (1) [ABASHED]

Sir 41:16 nor is every kind of a to be approved.

ABATAZA (1)

AdE 1:10 Bazan, Tharra, Boraze, Zatholtha, A, and Tharaba,

ABATE (2) [ABATED]

Ge 8: 5 The waters continued to a until the tenth month;
2Mc 9:18 But when his sufferings did not in any way a,

ABATED (12) [ABATE]

Ge 8: 3 of one hundred fifty days the waters had a;
Lev 13: 6 the disease has a and the disease has not spread in
13:21 nor is it deeper than the skin but has a,
13:26 and it is no deeper than the skin but has a,
13:28 the skin but has a, it is a swelling from the burn,
13:56 and the disease has a after it is washed,
Nu 11: 2 and Moses prayed to the LORD, and the fire a.

Dt 34: 7 his sight was unimpaired and his vigor had not a.
Est 2: 1 when the anger of King Ahasuerus had a,
7:10 Then the anger of the king a.
AdE 2: 1 After these things, the king's anger a,
7:10 With that the anger of the king a.

ABATED (KJV) See also RECEDED, REDUCED, SUBSIDED

ABBA (3)
Mk 14:36 "A, Father, for you all things are possible;
Ro 8:15 received a spirit of adoption. When we cry, "A!
Gal 4: 6 the Spirit of his Son into our hearts, crying, "A!

ABBREVIATING (1)
2Mc 2:26 For us who have undertaken the toil of a,

ABDA (2)
1Ki 4: 6 and Adoniram son of A was in charge of
Ne 11:17 A son of Shammua son of Galal son of Jeduthun.

ABDEEL (1)
Jer 36:26 and Seraiah son of Azriel and Shelemiah son of A

ABDI (4)
1Ch 6:44 Ethan son of Kishi, son of A, son of Malluch,
2Ch 29:12 and of the sons of Merari, Kish son of A,
Ezr 10:26 Mattaniah, Zechariah, Jehiel, A, Jeremoth,
1Es 9:27 Mattaniah and Zecharias, Jezrielus and A,

ABDIEL (1)
1Ch 5:15 Ahi son of A, son of Guni, was chief in their clan;

ABDON (8)
Jos 21:30 with its pasture lands, A with its pasture lands,
Jdg 12:13 him A son of Hillel the Pirathonite judged Israel.
12:15 Then A son of Hillel the Pirathonite died,
1Ch 6:74 with its pasture lands, A with its pasture lands,
8:23 A, Zichri, Hanan,
8:30 His firstborn son: A, then Zur, Kish, Baal, Nadab,
9:36 His firstborn son was A, then Zur, Kish, Baal,
2Ch 34:20 Ahikam son of Shaphan, A son of Micah,

ABDUCTED (1)
Jdg 21:23 for each of them from the dancers whom they a.

ABEDNEGO (15) [=AZARIAH]
Da 1: 7 he called Meshach, and Azariah he called A.
2:49 and A over the affairs of the province of Babylon.
3:12 Shadrach, Meshach, and A.
3:13 Meshach, and A be brought in;
3:14 "Is it true, O Shadrach, Meshach, and A,
3:16 Shadrach, Meshach, and A answered the king,
3:19 Meshach, and A that his face was distorted.
3:20 and A and to throw them into the furnace
3:22 the men who lifted Shadrach, Meshach, and A.
3:23 But the three men, Shadrach, Meshach, and A,
3:26 and A, servants of the Most High God, come out!
3:26 Shadrach, Meshach, and A came out from the fire.
3:28 be the God of Shadrach, Meshach, and A,
3:29 Meshach, and A shall be torn limb from limb,
3:30 Meshach, and A in the province of Babylon.

ABEL (16)
Ge 4: 2 Next she bore his brother A.
4: 2 Now A was a keeper of sheep,
4: 4 A for his part brought of the firstlings of his flock,
4: 4 And the LORD had regard for A and his offering,
4: 8 Cain said to his brother A,
4: 8 Cain rose up against his brother A, and killed him.
4: 9 LORD said to Cain, "Where is your brother A?"
4:25 for me another child instead of A,
2Sa 20:14 Sheba passed through all the tribes of Israel to A
20:15 Joab's forces came and besieged him in A
20:18 to say in the old days, 'Let them inquire at A';
Mt 23:35 of righteous A to the blood of Zechariah son
Lk 11:51 from the blood of A to the blood of Zechariah,
Heb 11: 4 By faith A offered to God
12:24 that speaks a better word than the blood of A.
4Mc 18:11 He read to you about A slain by Cain,

ABEL-BETH-MAACAH (2) [MAACAH]
1Ki 15:20 He conquered Ijon, Dan, A, and all Chinneroth,
2Ki 15:29 A, Janoah, Kedesh, Hazor, Gilead, and Galilee,

ABEL-KERAMIM (1)
Jdg 11:33 twenty towns, and as far as A.

ABEL-MAIM (1)
2Ch 16: 4 They conquered Ijon, Dan, A,

ABEL-MEHOLAH (3)
Jdg 7:22 as far as the border of A, by Tabbath.
1Ki 4:12 and from Beth-shean to A,
19:16 and you shall anoint Elisha son of Shaphat of A

ABEL-MIZRAIM (1)
Ge 50:11 the place was named A; it is beyond the Jordan.

ABEL-SHITTIM (1)
Nu 33:49 by the Jordan from Beth-jeshimoth as far as A in

ABETTED (1)
3Mc 2:25 in Egypt, he increased in his deeds of malice, a by

ABEZ (KJV) See EBEZ

ABHOR (21) [ABHORRED, ABHORRENCE, ABHORRENT, ABHORS]
Lev 26:11 and I shall not a you.
26:15 if you spurn my statutes, and a my ordinances,
26:30 of your idols. I will a you.
26:44 or a them so as to destroy them utterly
Dt 7:26 You must utterly detest and a it,
23: 7 You shall not a any of the Edomites,
23: 7 You shall not a any of the Egyptians,
Job 9:31 and my own clothes will a me.
19:19 All my intimate friends a me,
30:10 They a me, they keep aloof from me;
Ps 22:24 not despise or a the affliction of the afflicted;
119:163 I hate and a falsehood, but I love your law.
Am 5:10 and they a the one who speaks the truth.
6: 8 I a the pride of Jacob and hate his strongholds;
Mic 3: 9 who a justice and pervert all equity,
Ro 2:22 You that a idols, do you rob temples?
AdE 14:15 the wicked and a the bed of the uncircumcised and
14:16 that I a the sign of my proud position,
14:16 I a it like a filthy rag,
2Es 16:50 so righteousness shall a iniquity,
4Mc 5: 8 why should you a eating the very excellent meat

ABHORRED (9) [ABHOR]
Lev 20:23 Because they did all these things, I a them.
26:43 to spurn my ordinances, and they a my statutes.
Ps 106:40 against his people, and he a his heritage;
Pr 24:24 will be cursed by peoples, a by nations;
Isa 49: 7 to one deeply despised, a by the nations,
Eze 16: 5 for you were a on the day you were born.
Jdt 9: 4 with zeal for you and a the pollution of their blood
2Mc 5: 8 and a as the executioner of his country
3Mc 2:33 they a those who separated themselves from them,

ABHORRENCE (2) [ABHOR]
Isa 66:24 and they shall be an a to all flesh.
3Mc 2:31 with an obvious a of the price to be exacted

ABHORRENT (20) [ABHOR]
Ge 46:34 because all shepherds are a to the Egyptians."
Dt 7:25 for it is a to the LORD your God.
7:26 Do not bring an a thing into your house,
12:31 because every a thing that
13:14 that such an a thing has been done among you,
14: 3 You shall not eat any a thing.
17: 1 for that is a to the LORD your God.
17: 4 that such an a thing has occurred in Israel,
18: 9 you must not learn to imitate the a practices
18:12 For whoever does these things is a to the LORD;
18:12 it is because of such a practices that
20:18 that they may not teach you to do all the a things
22: 5 for whoever does such things is a to
23:18 for both of these are a to the LORD your God.
24: 4 for that would be a to the LORD,
25:16 are a to the LORD your God.
27:15 anything a to the LORD, the work of an artisan,
32:16 with a things they provoked him.
1Sa 27:12 "He has made himself utterly a
1Ch 21: 6 for the king's command was a to Joab.

ABHORS (3) [ABHOR]
Ps 5: 6 the LORD a the bloodthirsty and deceitful.
Sir 17:26 and hate intensely what he a.
2Es 16:49 a respectable and virtuous woman a a prostitute,

ABI (1)
2Ki 18: 2 His mother's name was A daughter of Zechariah.

ABI-ALBON (1)
2Sa 23:31 A the Arbathite; Azmaveth of Bahurim;

ABIA, ABIAH (KJV) See ABIJAH

ABIASAPH (1)
Ex 6:24 The sons of Korah: Assir, Elkanah, and A;

ABIATHAR‡ (31) [ABIATHAR'S]
1Sa 22:20 named A, escaped and fled after David.
22:21 A told David that Saul had killed the priests of
22:22 David said to A, "I knew on that day,
23: 6 A son of Ahimelech fled to David at Keilah,
23: 9 he said to the priest A, "Bring the ephod here."
30: 7 David said to the priest A son of Ahimelech,
30: 7 So A brought the ephod to David.
2Sa 8:17 of Ahitub and Ahimelech son of A were priests;
15:24 A came up, and Zadok also, with all the Levites,
15:27 "Look, go back to the city in peace, you and A,
15:27 Ahimaaz your son, and Jonathan son of A.
15:29 and A carried the ark of God back to Jerusalem,
15:35 The priests Zadok and A will be with you there.
15:35 tell it to the priests Zadok and A.
17:15 Then Hushai said to the priests Zadok and A,
19:11 to the priests Zadok and A,
20:25 Sheva was secretary; Zadok and A were priests;
1Ki 1: 7 with Joab son of Zeruiah and with the priest A,
1:19 the priest A, and Joab the commander of the army;
1:25 Joab the commander of the army, and the priest A,
1:42 Jonathan son of the priest A arrived.
2:22 also for the priest A and for Joab son of Zeruiah!"
2:26 The king said to the priest A, "Go to Anathoth,
2:27 So Solomon banished A from being priest to
2:35 the king put the priest Zadok in the place of A.
4: 4 Zadok and A were priests;
1Ch 15:11 David summoned the priests Zadok and A,
18:16 of Ahitub and Ahimelech son of A were priests;
24: 6 and Zadok the priest, and Ahimelech son of A,
27:34 Ahithophel came Jehoiada son of Benaiah, and A.
Mk 2:26 the house of God, when A was high priest, and ate

ABIATHAR'S (1) [ABIATHAR]
2Sa 15:36 Zadok's son Ahimaaz and A son Jonathan;

ABIB (6)
Ex 13: 4 Today, in the month of A, you are going out.
23:15 at the appointed time in the month of A,
34:18 at the time appointed in the month of A;
34:18 for in the month of A you came out from Egypt.
Dt 16: 1 Observe the month of A by keeping the passover
16: 1 of A the LORD your God brought you out

ABIDA (2)
Ge 25: 4 sons of Midian were Ephah, Epher, Hanoch, A,
1Ch 1:33 Ephah, Epher, Hanoch, A, and Eldaah.

ABIDAH (KJV) See ABIDA

ABIDAN (5)
Nu 1:11 From Benjamin, A son of Gideoni.
2:22 of the Benjaminites shall be A son of Gideoni,
7:60 On the ninth day A son of Gideoni,
7:65 This was the offering of A son of Gideoni.
10:24 the company of the tribe of Benjamin was A son

ABIDE‡ (42) [ABIDES, ABIDING, ABODE]
Ge 6: 3 "My spirit shall not a in mortals forever,
Jdg 5:17 and Dan, why did he a with the ships?
Ps 15: 1 who may a in your tent?
25:13 They will a in prosperity,
37:18 and their heritage will a forever;
37:27 and do good; so you shall a forever.
49:12 Mortals cannot a in their pomp;
49:20 Mortals cannot a in their pomp;
61: 4 Let me a in your tent forever,
91: 1 who a in the shadow of the Almighty,
Pr 2:21 For the upright will a in the land,
Isa 32:16 and righteousness a in the fruitful field.
32:18 My people will a in a peaceful habitation,
Zec 5: 4 and it shall a in that house and consume it,
14:11 Jerusalem shall a in security.
Jn 6:56 Those who eat my flesh and drink my blood a
15: 4 A in me as I a in you.
15: 4 neither can you unless you a in me.
15: 5 Those who a in me and I in them bear much fruit,
15: 6 Whoever does not a in me is thrown away like
15: 7 If you a in me, and my words a in you,
15: 9 so I have loved you; a in my love.
15:10 you will a in my love,
15:10 as I have kept my Father's commandments and a
1Co 13:13 And now faith, hope, and love a, these three;
1Jn 2: 6 "I a in him," ought to walk just as he walked.
2:24 Let what you heard from the beginning a in you.
2:24 then you will a in the Son and in the Father.
2:27 and just as it has taught you, a in him.
2:28 And now, little children, a in him,
3:17 How does God's love a in anyone who has
3:24 All who obey his commandments a in him,
4:13 By this we know that we a in him and he in us,
4:15 that Jesus is the Son of God, and they a in God.
4:16 God is love, and those who a in love a in God,
2Jn 1: 9 Everyone who does not a in the teaching
Wis 3: 9 and the faithful will a with him in love,
Sir 1:15 and among their descendants she will a faithfully.
24: 7 in whose territory should I a?

ABIDE, ABIDETH, ABIDING (KJV) See also ENDURE, KEEP, LIVE, REMAIN, STAND, STAY

ABIDES‡ (18) [ABIDE]
Job 41:22 In its neck a strength, and terror dances before it.
Ps 26: 8 and the place where your glory a.
125: 1 which cannot be moved, but a forever.
Hag 2: 5 My spirit a among you; do not fear.
Jn 14:17 You know him, because he a with you,
15: 4 as the branch cannot bear fruit by itself unless it a
1Jn 2:14 you are strong and the word of God a in you,
2:24 If what you heard from the beginning a in you,
2:27 the anointing that you received from him a in you,
3: 6 No one who a in him sins;
3: 9 because God's seed a in them;
3:14 Whoever does not love a in death.
3:24 commandments abide in him, and he a in them.
3:24 And by this we know that he a in us,

1Jn 4:15 God **a** in those who confess that Jesus is the Son
4:16 in love abide in God, and God **a** in them.
2Jn 1:2 the truth that **a** in us and will be with us forever:
1:9 whoever **a** in the teaching has both the Father and

ABIDING (3) [ABIDE]
Ps 68:18 against the LORD God's **a** there.
Jn 5:38 and you do not have his word **a** in you,
1Jn 3:15 that murderers do not have eternal life **a** in them.

ABIEL (3)
1Sa 9:1 of **A** son of Zeror son of Becorath son of Aphiah,
14:51 and Ner the father of Abner was the son of **A**.
1Ch 11:32 Hurai of the wadis of Gaash, **A** the Arbathite,

ABIEZER (6) [ABIEZRITE, ABIEZRITES]
Jos 17:2 **A**, Helek, Asriel, Shechem, Hepher, and Shemida;
Jdg 8:2 of Ephraim better than the vintage of **A**?
2Sa 23:27 **A** of Anathoth; Mebunnai the Hushathite;
1Ch 7:18 And his sister Hammolecheth bore Ishhod, **A**,
11:28 Ira son of Ikkesh of Tekoa, **A** of Anathoth,
27:12 Ninth, for the ninth month, was **A** of Anathoth,

ABIEZRITE (1) [ABIEZER]
Jdg 6:11 which belonged to Joash the **A**,

ABIEZRITES (3) [ABIEZER]
Jdg 6:24 at Ophrah, which belongs to the **A**.
6:34 and the **A** were called out to follow him.
8:32 in the tomb of his father Joash at Ophrah of the **A**.

ABIGAIL (16) [ABIGAL]
1Sa 25:3 and the name of his wife **A**.
25:14 But one of the young men told **A**, Nabal's wife,
25:18 Then **A** hurried and took two hundred loaves,
25:23 When **A** saw David, she hurried and alighted from
25:32 David said to **A**, "Blessed be the LORD,
25:36 **A** came to Nabal; he was holding a feast in his
25:39 David sent and wooed **A**, to make her his wife.
25:40 When David's servants came to **A** at Carmel,
25:42 **A** got up hurriedly and rode away on a donkey;
27:3 Ahinoam of Jezreel, and **A** of Carmel,
30:5 and **A** the widow of Nabal of Carmel.
2Sa 2:2 and **A** the widow of Nabal of Carmel.
3:3 Chileab, of **A** the widow of Nabal of Carmel;
1Ch 2:16 and their sisters were Zeruiah and **A**.
2:17 **A** bore Amasa, and the father of Amasa was Jether
3:1 the second Daniel, by **A** the Carmelite;

ABIGAL (1) [ABIGAIL]
2Sa 17:25 who had married **A** daughter of Nahash,

ABIHAIL (6)
Nu 3:35 of the clans of Merari was Zuriel son of **A**;
1Ch 2:29 The name of Abishur's wife was **A**,
5:14 These were the sons of **A** son of Huri,
2Ch 11:18 and of **A** daughter of Eliab son of Jesse.
Est 2:15 the turn came for Esther daughter of **A** the uncle
9:29 Queen Esther daughter of **A**,

ABIHU (12)
Ex 6:23 and she bore him Nadab, **A**, Eleazar, and Ithamar.
24:1 Nadab, and **A**, and seventy of the elders of Israel,
24:9 Then Moses and Aaron, Nadab, and **A**,
28:1 Aaron and Aaron's sons, Nadab and **A**,
Lev 10:1 Now Aaron's sons, Nadab and **A**,
Nu 3:2 Nadab the firstborn, and **A**, Eleazar, and Ithamar;
3:4 Nadab and **A** died before the LORD
26:60 To Aaron were born Nadab, **A**, Eleazar,
26:61 and **A** died when they offered illicit fire before
1Ch 6:3 sons of Aaron: Nadab, **A**, Eleazar, and Ithamar.
24:1 sons of Aaron: Nadab, **A**, Eleazar, and Ithamar.
24:2 But Nadab and **A** died before their father,

ABIHUD (1)
1Ch 8:3 And Bela had sons: Addar, Gera, **A**,

ABIJAH (28) [ABIJAM]
1Sa 8:2 **A**; they were judges in Beer-sheba.
1Ki 14:1 At that time **A** son of Jeroboam fell sick.
1Ch 2:24 **A** wife of Hezron bore him Ashhur,
3:10 Rehoboam, **A** his son, Asa his son,
6:28 sons of Samuel: Joel his firstborn, the second **A**.
7:8 Eliezer, Elioenai, Omri, Jeremoth, **A**, Anathoth,
24:10 the seventh to Hakkoz, the eighth to **A**,
2Ch 11:20 who bore him **A**, Attai, Ziza, and Shelomith.
11:22 Rehoboam appointed **A** son of Maacah
12:16 and his son **A** succeeded him.
13:1 **A** began to reign over Judah.
13:2 Now there was war between **A** and Jeroboam.
13:3 **A** engaged in battle, having an army
13:4 Then **A** stood on the slope of Mount Zemaraim
13:15 God defeated Jeroboam and all Israel before **A**
13:17 **A** and his army defeated them
13:19 **A** pursued Jeroboam, and took cities from him:
13:20 not recover his power in the days of **A**;
13:21 But **A** grew strong. He took fourteen wives,
13:22 The rest of the acts of **A**,
14:1 So **A** slept with his ancestors,
29:1 His mother's name was **A** daughter of Zechariah.
Ne 10:7 Meshullam, **A**, Mijamin,
12:4 Iddo, Ginnethoi, **A**,
12:17 of **A**, Zichri; of Miniamin, of Moadiah, Piltai;
Mt 1:7 and Rehoboam the father of **A**, and **A** the father of
Lk 1:5 who belonged to the priestly order of **A**.

ABIJAM (5) [ABIJAH]
1Ki 14:31 His son **A** succeeded him.
15:1 **A** began to reign over Judah.
15:7 The rest of the acts of **A**, and all that he did,
15:7 There was war between **A** and Jeroboam.
15:8 **A** slept with his ancestors,

ABILENE (1)
Lk 3:1 and Trachonitis, and Lysanias ruler of **A**,

ABILITY (11) [ABLE]
Ex 28:3 And you shall speak to all who have **a**,
31:3 with **a**, intelligence, and knowledge in every kind
1Ch 26:6 for they were men of great **a**.
26:30 one thousand seven hundred men of **a**,
26:31 and men of great **a** among them were found
26:32 two thousand seven hundred men of **a**,
Mt 25:15 to another one, to each according to his **a**.
Ac 2:4 as the Spirit gave them **a**.
11:29 The disciples determined that according to their **a**,
Sir 29:20 Assist your neighbor to the best of your **a**,
1Es 5:44 vowed that, to the best of their **a**,

ABIMAEL (2)
Ge 10:28 Obal, **A**, Sheba,
1Ch 1:22 Ebal, **A**, Sheba,

ABIMELECH (63) [ABIMELECH'S]
Ge 20:2 And King **A** of Gerar sent and took Sarah.
20:3 But God came to **A** in a dream by night,
20:4 Now **A** had not approached her;
20:8 So **A** rose early in the morning,
20:9 Then **A** called Abraham, and said to him,
20:10 And **A** said to Abraham, "What were you thinking
20:14 Then **A** took sheep and oxen,
20:15 **A** said, "My land is before you;
20:17 Then Abraham prayed to God; and God healed **A**,
20:18 the wombs of the house of **A** because of Sarah,
21:22 At that time **A**, with Phicol the commander
21:25 When Abraham complained to **A** about a well
21:26 **A** said, "I do not know who has done this;
21:27 and oxen and gave them to **A**,
21:29 And **A** said to Abraham, "What is the meaning
21:32 When they had made a covenant at Beer-sheba, **A**,
26:1 Isaac went to Gerar, to King **A** of the Philistines.
26:8 King **A** of the Philistines looked out of a window
26:9 **A** called for Isaac, and said, "So she is your wife!
26:10 **A** said, "What is this you have done to us?
26:11 So **A** warned all the people, saying,
26:16 And **A** said to Isaac, "Go away from us;
26:26 Then **A** went to him from Gerar,
Jdg 8:31 also bore him a son, and he named him **A**.
9:1 Now **A** son of Jerubbaal went to Shechem
9:3 and their hearts inclined to follow **A**, for they said,
9:4 of Baal-berith with which **A** hired worthless
9:6 and they went and made **A** king,
9:16 when you made **A** king, and if you have dealt well
9:18 and have made **A**, the son of his slave woman,
9:19 then rejoice in **A**, and let him also rejoice in you;
9:20 let fire come out from **A**, and devour the lords
9:20 and from Beth-millo, and devour **A**."
9:21 where he remained for fear of his brother **A**.
9:22 **A** ruled over Israel three years.
9:23 an evil spirit between **A** and the lords of Shechem;
9:23 the lords of Shechem dealt treacherously with **A**.
9:24 and their blood be laid on their brother **A**,
9:25 and it was reported to **A**.
9:27 ate and drank, and ridiculed **A**.
9:28 Gaal son of Ebed said, "Who is **A**,
9:29 under my command! Then I would remove **A**;
9:31 He sent messengers to **A** at Arumah, saying,
9:34 So **A** and all the troops with him got up by night
9:35 **A** and the troops with him rose from the ambush.
9:38 'Who is **A**, that we should serve him?'
9:39 of the lords of Shechem, and fought with **A**.
9:40 **A** chased him, and he fled before him.
9:41 So **A** resided at Arumah;
9:42 went out into the fields. When **A** was told,
9:44 **A** and the company that was with him rushed
9:45 **A** fought against the city all that day;
9:47 **A** was told that all the lords of the Tower of
9:48 So **A** went up to Mount Zalmon,
9:48 **A** took an ax in his hand,
9:49 and following **A** put it against the stronghold,
9:50 Then **A** went to Thebez, and encamped
9:52 **A** came to the tower, and fought against it,
9:55 When the Israelites saw that **A** was dead,
9:56 Thus God repaid **A** for the crime he committed
10:1 After **A**, Tola son of Puah son of Dodo,
2Sa 11:21 Who killed **A** son of Jerubbaal?
Ps 34:T *Of David, when he feigned madness before* **A**,

ABIMELECH'S (2) [ABIMELECH]
Ge 21:25 about a well of water that **A** servants had seized,
Jdg 9:53 an upper millstone on **A** head,

ABINADAB (11)
1Sa 7:1 and brought it to the house of **A** on the hill.
16:8 Jesse called **A**, and made him pass before Samuel.
17:13 and next to him **A**, and the third Shammah.
31:2 Philistines killed Jonathan and **A** and Malchishua,
2Sa 6:3 and brought it out of the house of **A**,
6:3 Uzzah and Ahio, the sons of **A**,
1Ch 2:13 **A** the second, Shimea the third,
8:33 Saul of Jonathan, Malchishua, **A**, and Esh-baal;
9:39 Saul of Jonathan, Malchishua, **A**, and Esh-baal;
10:2 Philistines killed Jonathan and **A** and Malchishua,
13:7 the ark of God on a new cart, from the house of **A**,

ABINOAM (4)
Jdg 4:6 and summoned Barak son of **A** from Kedesh
4:12 that Barak son of **A** had gone up to Mount Tabor,
5:1 Deborah and Barak son of **A** sang on that day,
5:12 Barak, lead away your captives, O son of **A**.

ABIRAM (13)
Nu 16:1 along with Dathan and **A** sons of Eliab,
16:12 Moses sent for Dathan and **A** sons of Eliab;
16:24 from the dwellings of Korah, Dathan, and **A**.
16:25 So Moses got up and went to Dathan and **A**;
16:27 from the dwellings of Korah, Dathan, and **A**;
16:27 and **A** came out and stood at the entrance
26:9 The descendants of Eliab: Nemuel, Dathan, and **A**.
26:9 These are the same Dathan and **A**,
Dt 11:6 to Dathan and **A**, sons of Eliab son of Reuben,
1Ki 16:34 he laid its foundation at the cost of **A** his firstborn,
Ps 106:17 and covered the faction of **A**.
Sir 45:18 and **A** and their followers and the company
4Mc 2:17 When Moses was angry with Dathan and **A**,

ABISHAG (5)
1Ki 1:3 and found **A** the Shunammite,
1:15 **A** the Shunammite was attending the king.
2:17 to give me **A** the Shunammite as my wife."
2:21 "Let **A** the Shunammite be given
2:22 why do you ask **A** the Shunammite for Adonijah?

ABISHAI (25)
1Sa 26:6 and to Joab's brother **A** son of Zeruiah,
26:6 **A** said, "I will go down with you."
26:7 So David and **A** went to the army by night;
26:8 **A** said to David, "God has given your enemy
26:9 But David said to **A**, "Do not destroy him;
2Sa 2:18 The three sons of Zeruiah were there, Joab, **A**,
2:24 But Joab and **A** pursued Abner.
3:30 So Joab and his brother **A** murdered Abner
10:10 of his men he put in the charge of his brother **A**,
10:14 they likewise fled before **A**, and entered the city.
16:9 Then **A** son of Zeruiah said to the king,
16:11 David said to **A** and to all his servants,
18:2 one third under the command of **A** son of Zeruiah,
18:5 The king ordered Joab and **A** and Ittai, saying,
18:12 for in our hearing the king commanded you and **A**
19:21 **A** son of Zeruiah answered,
20:6 David said to **A**, "Now Sheba son
20:10 Then Joab and his brother **A** pursued Sheba son
21:17 But **A** son of Zeruiah came to his aid,
23:18 Now **A** son of Zeruiah, the brother of Joab,
1Ch 2:16 The sons of Zeruiah: **A**, Joab, and Asahel, three.
11:20 **A**, the brother of Joab, was chief of the Thirty.
18:12 **A** son of Zeruiah killed eighteen thousand Edomites
19:11 of his troops he put in the charge of his brother **A**,
19:15 they likewise fled before **A**, Joab's brother,

ABISHALOM (2)
1Ki 15:2 His mother's name was Maacah daughter of **A**.
15:10 His mother's name was Maacah daughter of **A**.

ABISHUA (7)
1Ch 6:4 the father of Phinehas, Phinehas of **A**,
6:5 **A** of Bukki, Bukki of Uzzi,
6:50 Eleazar his son, Phinehas his son, **A** his son,
8:4 **A**, Naaman, Ahoah,
Ezr 7:5 son of **A**, son of Phinehas, son of Eleazar, son of
1Es 8:2 of Amariah son of Uzzi son of Bukki son of **A** son
2Es 1:2 of Borith son of **A** son of Phinehas son of Eleazar

ABISHUR (1) [ABISHUR'S]
1Ch 2:28 The sons of Shammai: Nadab and **A**.

ABISHUR'S (1) [ABISHUR]
1Ch 2:29 The name of **A** wife was Abihail,

ABITAL (2)
2Sa 3:4 the fifth, Shephatiah son of **A**;
1Ch 3:3 the fifth Shephatiah, by **A**;

ABITUB (1)
1Ch 8:11 He also had sons by Hushim: **A** and Elpaal.

ABIUD (2)
Mt 1:13 and Zerubbabel the father of **A**, and **A** the father of

ABJECTS (KJV) See RUFFIANS

ABLAZE (6) [BLAZE]
Dt 9:15 while the mountain was **a**;
Ps 58:9 whether green or **a**, may he sweep them away!
83:14 as the flame sets the mountains **a**,

Jas 3: 5 How great a forest is set a by a small fire!
2Pe 3:12 of which the heavens will be set a and dissolved,
1Mc 6:39 the hills were a with them and gleamed

ABLE (193) [ABILITY, ABLE-BODIED, ENABLE, ENABLED, ENABLES, ENABLING]

Ge 15: 5 if you are a to count them."
Ex 10: 5 so that no one will be a to see the land.
18:21 You should also look for a men among all
18:23 then you will be a to endure,
18:25 Moses chose a men from all Israel
40:35 Moses was not a to enter the tent of meeting
Lev 5: 1 though a to testify as one who has seen or learned
Nu 1: 3 everyone in Israel a to go to war.
1:20 everyone a to go to war:
1:22 everyone a to go to war:
1:24 everyone a to go to war:
1:26 everyone a to go to war:
1:28 everyone a to go to war:
1:30 everyone a to go to war:
1:32 everyone a to go to war:
1:34 everyone a to go to war:
1:36 everyone a to go to war:
1:38 everyone a to go to war:
1:40 everyone a to go to war:
1:42 everyone a to go to war:
1:45 everyone a to go to war in Israel—
5:28 be immune and be a to conceive children.
11:14 I am not a to carry all this people alone,
13:30 for we are well a to overcome it."
13:31 "We are not a to go up against this people,
14:16 because the LORD was not a to bring this people
22: 6 perhaps I shall be a to defeat them and drive them
22:11 be a to fight against them and drive them out.' "
22:37 Am I not a to honor you?"
24:13 be a to go beyond the word of the LORD, to do
26: 2 everyone in Israel a to go to war."
Dt 7:22 you will not be a to make a quick end of them,
7:24 no one will be a to stand against you,
9:28 'Because the LORD was not a to bring them into
11:25 No one will be a to stand against you;
16:17 all shall give as they are a,
31: 2 I am no longer a to get about,
Jos 1: 5 No one shall be a to stand against you all the days
23: 9 no one has been a to withstand you to this day.
Jdg 8: 3 what have I been a to do in comparison
1Sa 6:20 "Who is a to stand before the LORD,
17: 9 If he is a to fight with me and kill me,
17:33 "You are not a to go against this Philistine to fight
2Sa 24: 9 there were eight hundred thousand soldiers a
1Ki 3: 9 a to discern between good and evil;
11:28 The man Jeroboam was very a,
2Ki 3:21 all who were a to put on armor,
18:23 if you are a on your part to set riders on them.
18:29 for he will not be a to deliver you out of my hand.
1Ch 26: 7 whose brothers were a men, Elihu and Semachiah.
26: 8 were a men qualified for the service;
26: 9 Meshelemiah had sons and brothers, a men,
29: 2 so far as I was a, the gold for the things of gold,
29:14 that we should be a to make this freewill offering?
2Ch 2: 6 But who is a to build him a house, since heaven,
20: 6 so that no one is a to withstand you.
20:37 And the ships were wrecked and were not a to go
22: 9 And the house of Ahaziah had no one a to rule
25: 5 a to handle spear and shield.
25: 9 LORD is a to give you much more than this."
32:13 Were the gods of the nations of those lands at all a
32:14 that my ancestors utterly destroyed was a to save
32:14 your God should be a to save you from my hand?
32:15 for no god of any nation or kingdom has been a
Ne 5: 8 "As far as we were a,
Ps 18:38 so that they were not a to rise;
76: 5 none of the troops was a to lift a hand.
Pr 27: 4 but who is a to stand before jealousy?
Ecc 6:10 not a to dispute with those who are stronger.
Isa 19:15 will be a to do anything for Egypt,
36: 8 if you are a on your part to set riders on them.
36:14 for he will not be a to deliver you.
47:11 which you will not be a to ward off;
47:12 perhaps you may be a to succeed,
Jer 49:10 and he is not a to conceal himself.
La 4:14 that no one was a to touch their garments.
Eze 33:12 be a to live by their righteousness when they sin.
Da 2:26 "Are you a to tell me the dream that I have seen
2:47 for you have been a to reveal this mystery!"
3:17 If our God whom we serve is a to deliver us from
3:29 for there is no other god who is a to deliver
4:18 You are a, however, for you are endowed with
4:37 and he is a to bring low those who walk in pride.
5:15 but they were not a to give the interpretation of
5:16 Now if you are a to read the writing
6:20 has your God whom you faithfully serve been a
Hos 5:13 But he is not a to cure you or heal your wound.
Am 7:10 the land is not a to bear all his words.
Zep 1:18 nor their gold will be a to save them on the day of
Mt 3: 9 for I tell you, God is a from these stones to raise
9:28 "Do you believe that I am a to do this?"
20:22 Are you a to drink the cup that I am about
20:22 They said to him, "We are a."
22:46 No one was a to give him an answer,
26:61 'I am a to destroy the temple of God and
Mk 3:25 that house will not be a to stand.
4:33 as they were a to hear it;
9:22 but if you are a to do anything,
Mk 9:23 Jesus said to him, "If you are a!—
9:27 and he was a to stand.
9:39 in my name will be a soon afterward to speak evil
10:38 Are you a to drink the cup that I drink,
10:39 They replied, "We are a."
Lk 3: 8 for I tell you, God is a from these stones to raise
12:26 If then you are not a to do so small a thing as that,
13:24 many, I tell you, will try to enter and will not be a.
14:29 he has laid a foundation and is not a to finish,
14:30 'This fellow began to build and was not a
14:31 will not sit down first and consider whether he is a
20:26 And they were not a in the presence of the people
21:15 that none of your opponents will be a to withstand
Jn 9: 7 Then he went and washed and came back a to see.
18:28 so as to avoid ritual defilement and to be a to eat
21: 6 not a to haul it in because there were
Ac 5:39 you will not be a to overthrow them—
15:10 that neither our ancestors nor we have been a
20:32 a message that is a to build you up and to give you
24: 8 By examining him yourself you will be a to learn
27:16 of a small island called Cauda we were scarcely a
Ro 4:21 that God was a to do what he had promised.
8:39 will be a to separate us from the love of God
14: 4 for the Lord is a to make them stand.
15:14 and a to instruct one another.
16:25 Now to God who is a to strengthen you according
1Co 10:13 also provide the way out so that you may be a
2Co 1: 4 be a to console those who are in any affliction
5:12 so that you may be a to answer those who boast
9: 8 And God is a to provide you with every blessing
Eph 3:20 to him who by the power at work within us is a
6:11 so that you may be a to stand against the wiles of
6:13 so that you may be a to withstand on that evil day,
6:16 be a to quench all the flaming arrows of
2Ti 1:12 and I am sure that he is a to guard until
2: 2 to faithful people who will be a to teach others
3:15 the sacred writings that are a to instruct you
Tit 1: 9 be a both to preach with sound doctrine and
Heb 2:18 he is a to help those who are being tested.
4:12 it is a to judge the thoughts and intentions of
5: 2 He is a to deal gently with the ignorant
5: 7 to the one who was a to save him from death,
7:25 Consequently he is a for all time
11:19 the fact that God is a even to raise someone from
Jas 3: 2 a to keep the whole body in check with a bridle.
4:12 There is one lawgiver and judge who is a to save
2Pe 1:15 that after my departure you may be a at any time
Jude 1:24 Now to him who is a to keep you from falling,
Rev 3: 8 which no one is a to shut.
5: 3 on earth or under the earth was a to open the scroll
6:17 and who is a to stand?"
Jdt 10:19 for if we let them go they will be a to beguile
11:18 and not one of them will be a to withstand you.
AdE 6:13 You will not be a to defend yourself,
Wis 17: 5 And no power of fire was a to give light,
Sir Pr: 1 also as lovers of learning be a through the spoken
LtJ 6:34 they will not be a to repay it.
6:35 Likewise they are not a to give either wealth
6:40 as though Bel were a to understand!
6:58 and they will not be a to help themselves.
6:64 for they are not a either to decide a case or
1Mc 3:38 a men among the Friends of the king,
3:53 How will we be a to withstand them,
5:40 we will not be a to resist him,
6:27 and you will not be a to stop them."
10:73 be a to withstand my cavalry and such an army in
2Mc 8:18 who is a with a single nod to strike
9:10 Because of his intolerable stench no one was a
1Es 9:11 and we are not a to stand in the open air.
3Mc 4:16 that are not a even to communicate or to come
4:17 that they were no longer a to take the census of
2Es 2:28 but they shall not be a to do anything against you,
4:27 be a to bring the things that have been promised to
5:38 "O sovereign Lord, who is a
5:45 be a to support all of them present at one time."
7:*102* the righteous will be a to intercede for the ungodly
7:*115* [45] Therefore no one will then be a to have mercy
8: 6 the likeness of a human being may be a to live
8:47 of being a to love my creation more than I love it.
9: 7 It shall be that all who will be saved and will be a
12:38 whose hearts you know are a to comprehend
13:47 so that they may be a to cross over.
14:22 so that people may be a to find the path,
15:17 and shall not be a to do so.
4Mc 1:33 Is it not because reason is a to rule over appetites?
2: 6 I could prove to you all the more that reason is a
2:18 the temperate mind is a to get the better of
4:24 he had not been a in any way to put an end to
7:18 these alone are a to control the passions of
7:22 be a to overcome the emotions through godliness?
8: 6 as I am a to punish those who disobey my orders,
10: 7 they were not a in any way to break his spirit,
11:25 not been a to persuade us to change our mind or
14:17 If they are not a to keep the intruder away,
18: 5 Since in no way whatever was he a to compel

ABLE-BODIED (2) [ABLE, BODY]

Jdg 3:29 all strong, a men; no one escaped.
Jdt 14: 2 and let every a man go out of the town;

ABNER (61) [ABNER'S]

1Sa 14:50 of the commander of his army was A son of Ner,
14:51 and Ner the father of A was the son of Abiel.
17:55 he said to A, the commander of the army, "A,
17:55 A said, "As your soul lives, O king,
17:57 A took him and brought him before Saul,
1Sa 20:25 Jonathan stood, while A sat by Saul's side;
26: 5 with A son of Ner, the commander of his army.
26: 7 and A and the army lay around him.
26:14 called to the army and to A son of Ner, saying, "A!
26:14 A replied, "Who are you that calls to the king?"
26:15 David said to A, "Are you not a man?
2Sa 2: 8 But A son of Ner, commander of Saul's army,
2:12 A son of Ner, and the servants of Ishbaal son
2:14 A said to Joab, "Let the young men come forward
2:17 and A and the men of Israel were beaten by
2:19 Asahel pursued A, turning neither to the right nor
2:20 Then A looked back and said, "Is it you, Asahel?"
2:21 A said to him, "Turn to your right or to your left,
2:22 A said again to Asahel, "Turn away
2:23 So A struck him in the stomach with the butt
2:24 But Joab and Abishai pursued A.
2:25 The Benjaminites rallied around A and formed
2:26 Then A called to Joab, "Is the sword
2:29 A and his men traveled all that night through
2:30 Joab returned from the pursuit of A;
3: 6 A was making himself strong in the house of Saul.
3: 7 And Ishbaal said to A, "Why have you gone in
3: 8 The words of Ishbaal made A very angry;
3: 9 So may God do to A and so may he add to it!
3:11 And Ishbaal could not answer A another word,
3:12 A sent messengers to David at Hebron, saying,
3:16 Then A said to him, "Go back home!"
3:17 A sent word to the elders of Israel, saying,
3:19 A also spoke directly to the Benjaminites;
3:19 then A went to tell David at Hebron all that Israel
3:20 A came with twenty men to David at Hebron,
3:20 David made a feast for A and the men who were
3:21 A said to David, "Let me go and rally all Israel
3:21 David dismissed A, and he went away in peace.
3:22 But A was not with David at Hebron,
3:23 it was told Joab, "A son of Ner came to the king,
3:24 "What have you done? A came to you;
3:25 You know that A son of Ner came to deceive you,
3:26 he sent messengers after A,
3:27 When A returned to Hebron,
3:28 before the LORD for the blood of A son of Ner.
3:30 So Joab and his brother Abishai murdered A
3:31 and put on sackcloth, and mourn over A."
3:32 They buried A at Hebron.
3:32 up his voice and wept at the grave of A,
3:33 The king lamented for A, saying, "Should A die as
3:37 the king had no part in the killing of A son of Ner.
4: 1 When Saul's son Ishbaal heard that A had died
4:12 of Ishbaal they took and buried in the tomb of A
1Ki 2: 5 A son of Ner, and Amasa son of Jether,
2:32 A son of Ner, commander of the army of Israel,
1Ch 26:28 and Saul son of Kish, and A son of Ner,
27:21 for Benjamin, Jaasiel son of A;

ABNER'S (1) [ABNER]

2Sa 2:31 of Benjamin three hundred sixty of A men.

ABOARD (1)

Jn 21:11 So Simon Peter went a and hauled the net ashore,

ABODE (9) [ABIDE]

Ex 15:13 you guided them by your strength to your holy a.
15:17 that you made your a, the sanctuary, O LORD,
Dt 33:28 untroubled is Jacob's a in a land of grain
Ps 68:16 at the mount that God desired for his a,
76: 2 His a has been established in Salem,
104:13 From your lofty a you water the mountains;
Pr 3:33 but he blesses the a of the righteous.
Isa 34:13 It shall be the haunt of jackals, an a for ostriches.
Jer 31:23 "The LORD bless you, O a of righteousness,

ABODEST (KJV) See TARRY

ABOLISH (6) [ABOLISHED, ABOLISHES, ABOLISHING]

Da 11:31 They shall a the regular burnt offering and set up
Hos 2:18 and I will a the bow, the sword,
Mt 5:17 "Do not think that I have come to a the law or
5:17 I have come not to a but to fulfill.
AdE 14: 9 to a what your mouth has ordained,
2Es 15:60 a part of your land and a a portion of your glory,

ABOLISHED (6) [ABOLISH]

La 2: 6 the LORD has a in Zion festival and sabbath,
Eph 2:15 He has a the law with its commandments
2Ti 1:10 who a death and brought life and immortality
1Mc 6:59 of their laws that we a that they became angry
2Mc 2:22 re-established the laws that were about to be a,
4Mc 4:20 but also the temple service was a.

ABOLISHES (1) [ABOLISH]

Heb 10: 9 He a the first in order to establish the second.

ABOLISHING (1) [ABOLISH]

1Mc 3:29 and disaster that he had caused in the land by a

ABOMINABLE (31) [ABOMINATION]

1Ki 15:13 because she had made an a image for Asherah;
2Ki 16: 3 according to the a practices of the nations whom
21: 2 following the a practices of the nations that
2Ch 15: 8 and put away the a idols from all the land of Judah
15:16 because she had made an a image for Asherah.

2Ch 28: 3 according to the a practices of the nations whom
33: 2 according to the a practices of the nations whom
Job 15:16 how much less one who is a and corrupt,
Ps 14: 1 They are corrupt, they do a deeds;
53: 1 They are corrupt, they commit a acts;
Isa 65: 4 with broth of a things in their vessels;
Jer 44: 4 "I beg you not to do this a thing that I hate!"
Eze 7:20 they made their a images, their detestable things;
16:36 and because of all your a idols,
16:50 They were haughty, and did a things before me;
18:13 He has done all these a things;
18:24 and commit iniquity and do the same a things that
22: 2 Then declare to it all its a deeds.
23:36 Then declare to them their a deeds.
36:31 for your iniquities and your a deeds.
Sir 41: 5 The children of sinners are a children,
1Mc 1:48 to make themselves a by everything unclean
2Mc 6: 5 with a offerings that were forbidden by the laws.
9:13 Then the a fellow made a vow to the Lord,
15: 5 he did not succeed in carrying out his a design.
3Mc 6: 9 who are being outrageously treated by the a
4Mc 9:15 "Most a tyrant, enemy of heavenly justice, savage
9:17 "You a lackeys, your wheel is not so powerful as
9:32 You will not escape, you most a tyrant,
10:10 most a tyrant, are suffering because
10:17 and utterly a Antiochus gave orders

ABOMINABLY (2) [ABOMINATION]

1Ki 21:26 He acted most a in going after idols,
Eze 16:52 of your sins in which you acted more a than they,

ABOMINATE (1) [ABOMINATION]

3Mc 3:23 both by speech and by silence they a those few

ABOMINATION (53) [ABOMINABLE, ABOMINABLY, ABOMINATE, ABOMINATIONS]

Ge 43:32 for that is an a to the Egyptians.
Lev 7:18 it shall be an a, and the one who eats
11:13 They shall not be eaten; they are an a:
18:22 with a woman; it is an a.
19: 7 If it is eaten at all on the third day, it is an a;
20:13 both of them have committed an a;
20:25 not bring a on yourselves by animal or by bird or
1Ki 11: 5 and Milcom the a of the Ammonites.
11: 7 a high place for Chemosh the a of Moab, and for
Molech the a of the Ammonites,
2Ki 23:13 Astarte the a of the Sidonians, for Chemosh the a
of Moab, and for Milcom the a of the Ammonites.
Pr 3:32 for the perverse are an a to the LORD,
6:16 seven that are an a to him:
8: 7 wickedness is an a to my lips.
11: 1 A false balance is an a to the LORD,
11:20 Crooked minds are an a to the LORD,
12:22 Lying lips are an a to the LORD,
13:19 but to turn away from evil is an a to fools.
15: 8 The sacrifice of the wicked is an a to the LORD,
15: 9 The way of the wicked is an a to the LORD,
15:26 Evil plans are an a to the LORD,
16: 5 All those who are arrogant are an a to the LORD;
16:12 It is an a to kings to do evil,
17:15 the righteous are both alike an a to the LORD.
20:10 and diverse measures are both alike an a to
20:23 Differing weights are an a to the LORD,
21:27 The sacrifice of the wicked is an a;
24: 9 and the scoffer is an a to all.
28: 9 even one's prayers are an a.
29:27 The unjust are an a to the righteous,
29:27 but the upright are an a to the wicked.
Isa 1:13 incense is an a to me.
41:24 whoever chooses you is an a.
44:19 Now shall I make the rest of it an a?
Jer 2: 7 and made my heritage an a.
6:15 They acted shamefully, they committed a;
8:12 They acted shamefully, they committed a;
32:35 did it enter my mind that they should do this a,
Eze 18:12 lifts up his eyes to the idols, commits a,
22:11 One commits a with his neighbor's wife;
Da 9:27 and in their place shall be an a that desolates,
11:31 the regular burnt offering and set up the a
12:11 the regular burnt offering is taken away and the a
Mal 2:11 a has been committed in Israel and in Jerusalem;
Lk 16:15 for what is prized by human beings is an a in
Rev 21:27 nor anyone who practices a or falsehood,
Wis 14:11 an a, snares for human souls and a trap for the feet
Sir 1:25 but godliness is an a to a sinner.
13:20 Humility is an a to the proud;
13:20 likewise the poor are an a to the rich.
1Mc 6: 7 the a that he had erected on the altar in Jerusalem;

ABOMINATIONS (66) [ABOMINATION]

Lev 18:26 and my ordinances and commit none of these a,
18:27 who were before you, committed all of these a,
18:29 of these a shall be cut off from their people.
18:30 So keep my charge not to commit any of these a
1Ki 14:24 the a of the nations that the LORD drove out
2Ki 21:11 of Judah has committed these a,
23:24 and all the a that were seen in the land of Judah
2Ch 34:33 Josiah took away all the a from all the territory
36: 8 rest of the acts of Jehoiakim, and the a that he did,
36:14 following all the a of the nations;
Ezr 9: 1 from the peoples of the lands with their a,
9:11 of the peoples of the lands, with their a.
9:14 with the peoples who practice these a?
Pr 26:25 for there are seven a concealed within;
Isa 66: 3 and in their a they take delight;
Jer 4: 1 if you remove your a from my presence,
7:10 only to go on doing all these a?
7:30 they have set their a in the house that is called
13:27 I have seen your a, your adulteries and neighings,
16:18 and have filled my inheritance with their a.
32:34 up their a in the house that bears my name,
44:22 the a that you committed;
Eze 5: 9 And because of all your a,
5:11 all your detestable things and with all your a—
6: 9 the evils that they have committed, for all their a.
6:11 Alas for all the vile a of the house of Israel!
7: 3 I will punish you for all your a.
7: 4 while your a are among you.
7: 8 and punish you for all your a.
7: 9 while your a are among you.
8: 6 the great a that the house
8: 6 Yet you will see still greater a."
8: 9 and see the vile a that they are committing here."
8:13 "You will see still greater a
8:15 You will see still greater a than these."
8:17 that the house of Judah commits the a done here?
9: 4 and groan over all the a that are committed in it."
11:18 from it all its detestable things and all its a.
11:21 after their detestable things and their a,
12:16 that they may tell of all their a among the nations
14: 6 and turn away your faces from all your a.
16: 2 Mortal, make known to Jerusalem her a,
16:22 And in all your a and your whorings you did
16:43 not committed lewdness beyond all your a?
16:47 and acted according to their a;
16:51 you have committed more a than they,
16:51 by all the a that you have committed.
16:58 the penalty of your lewdness and your a,
20: 4 Then let them know the a of their ancestors,
33:26 You depend on your swords, you commit a,
33:29 because of all their a that they have committed.
43: 8 they were defiling my holy name by their a
44: 6 O house of Israel, let there be an end to all your a
44: 7 You have broken my covenant with all your a.
44:13 consequences of the a that they have committed.
Zec 9: 7 and its a from between its teeth;
Rev 17: 4 holding in her hand a golden cup full of a and
17: 5 mother of whores and of earth's a."
Wis 12:23 you tormented through their own a.
Sir 10:13 and the one who clings to it pours out a.
15:13 The Lord hates all a; such things are
27:30 Anger and wrath, these also are a,
49: 2 and removing the wicked a.
1Es 7:13 all those who had separated themselves from the a
Man 1:10 setting up a and multiplying offenses.
3Mc 2:18 as the houses of the a are trampled down.'

ABOUND (17) [ABOUNDED, ABOUNDING, ABOUNDS]

Ge 8:17 so that they may a on the earth,
9: 7 a on the earth and multiply in it."
Dt 28:11 The LORD will make you a in prosperity,
Ps 4: 7 when their grain and wine a.
72: 7 In his days may righteousness flourish and peace a,
Pr 28:20 The faithful will a with blessings,
Ro 6: 1 in sin in order that grace may a?
15:13 so that you may a in hope by the power of
2Co 3: 9 much more does the ministry of justification a
1Th 3:12 And may the Lord make you increase and a in love
3:12 just as we a in love for you.
Sir 11:12 who lack strength and a in poverty;
23: 3 be multiplied, and my sins may a, and I may fall
2Es 3:33 the nations and have seen that they a in wealth,
7:*51* while the ungodly a, hear the explanation for this.
7:*136* [66] because he makes his compassions a more
7:*137* [67] for if he did not make them a, the world

ABOUNDED (2) [ABOUND]

Ro 5:15 Jesus Christ, a for the many.
5:20 but where sin increased, grace a all the more,

ABOUNDETH (KJV) See ABUNDANT

ABOUNDING (11) [ABOUND]

Ex 34: 6 and a in steadfast love and faithfulness,
Nu 14:18 to anger, and a in steadfast love, forgiving iniquity
Ne 9:17 slow to anger and a in steadfast love,
Ps 86: 5 a in steadfast love to all who call on you.
86:15 to anger and a in steadfast love and faithfulness.
103: 8 slow to anger and a in steadfast love.
145: 8 slow to anger and a in steadfast love.
Pr 8:24 when there were no springs a with water.
Joel 2:13 slow to anger, and a in steadfast love,
Jnh 4: 2 slow to anger, and a in steadfast love,
Col 2: 7 just as you were taught, a in thanksgiving.

ABOUNDS (1) [ABOUND]

Ro 3: 7 my falsehood God's truthfulness a to his glory,

ABOUT‡ (785)

Ge 3:17 have eaten of the tree a which I commanded you,
12:11 When he was a to enter Egypt,
13:10 Lot looked a him, and saw that the plain of
18:17 "Shall I hide from Abraham what I am a to do,
18:19 so that the LORD may bring a for Abraham
19:13 For we are a to destroy this place,
19:14 for the LORD is a to destroy the city."
20: 3 "You are a to die because of
21:14 and wandered a in the wilderness of Beer-sheba.
21:16 a the distance of a bowshot;
21:25 When Abraham complained to Abimelech a
24:28 and told her mother's household a these things.
25:32 Esau said, "I am a to die;
26: 7 When the men of the place asked him a his wife,
26:32 and told him a the well that they had dug,
29:13 Laban heard the news a his sister's son Jacob,
31:34 Laban felt all a in the tent, but did not find them.
31:37 Although you have felt a through all my goods,
31:43 what can I do today a these daughters of mine, or
a their children whom they have borne?
38:24 A three months later Judah was told,
39: 8 my master has no concern a anything in the house,
41:25 God has revealed to Pharaoh what he is a to do.
41:28 God has shown to Pharaoh what he is a to do.
41:32 and God will shortly bring it a.
42: 9 the dreams that he had dreamed a them.
43: 7 "The man questioned us carefully a ourselves
43:27 He inquired a their welfare, and said,
43:30 and he was a to weep.
48:21 Then Israel said to Joseph, "I am a to die,
49:29 "I am a to be gathered to my people.
50: 5 he said, 'I am a to die.
50:24 Then Joseph said to his brothers, "I am a to die;
Ex 11: 4 A midnight I will go out through Egypt.
12:37 a six hundred thousand men on foot,
21:13 but came a by an act of God,
32:14 And the LORD changed his mind a the disaster
32:28 and a three thousand of the people fell on that day.
32:34 lead the people to the place a which I have spoken
Lev 4: 2 in any of the LORD's commandments a things
6: 3 or have found something lost and lied a it—
6: 5 or anything else a which you have sworn falsely,
10:16 Moses made inquiry a the goat of the sin offering,
Nu 11: 1 in the hearing of the LORD a their misfortunes,
11:31 a a day's journey on this side and a day's journey
11:31 a two cubits deep on the ground.
14:15 then the nations who have heard a you will say,
14:36 against him by bringing a bad report a the land—
14:37 an unfavorable report a the land died by a plague
Dt 2: 4 You are a to pass through the territory
3:21 to all the kingdoms into which you are a to cross.
4: 5 in the land that you are a to enter and occupy.
4:14 in the land that you are a to cross into and occupy.
4:32 For ask now a former ages, long before your own,
6: 1 in the land that you are a to cross into and occupy,
6: 7 to your children and talk a them when you are
7: 1 into the land that you are a to enter and occupy,
9: 1 You are a to cross the Jordan today,
11:10 For the land that you are a to enter to occupy is
11:19 talking a them when you are at home and
12: 2 the places where the nations whom you are a
12:29 before you the nations whom you are a to enter
13:12 If you hear it said a one of the towns that
18:14 that you are a to dispossess do give heed
23:20 in all your undertakings in the land that you are a
24: 1 because he finds something objectionable a her,
27: 4 a which I am commanding you today,
28:29 you shall grope a at noon as blind people grope
31: 2 I am no longer able to get a,
Jos 3: 4 a distance of a two thousand cubits;
4:13 A forty thousand armed for war crossed over
7: 3 a two or three thousand men should go up
7: 4 So a three thousand of the people went up there;
7: 5 The men of Ai killed a thirty-six of them,
8:12 Taking a five thousand men,
10:13 and did not hurry to set for a a whole day.
18: 3 be slack a going in and taking possession of
23:14 "And now I am a to go the way of all the earth,
Jdg 3:29 At that time they killed a ten thousand of
8:10 a fifteen thousand men, all who were left of all
8:15 a whom you taunted me, saying,
8:18 "What a the men whom you killed at Tabor?"
9:49 a a thousand men and women.
9:54 so people will not say a me,
16:27 and on the roof there were a three thousand men
17: 2 a which you uttered a curse,
20: 3 "Tell us, how did this criminal act come a?"
20:31 killing a thirty men of Israel.
20:39 to inflict casualties on the Israelites, killing a
Ru 1: 4 When they had lived there a ten years,
2:17 and it was a an ephah of barley.
1Sa 3:11 I am a to do something in Israel that will make
3:13 that I am a to punish his house forever,
4: 2 who killed a four thousand men on the field
4:19 was pregnant, a to give birth.
4:20 As she was a to die,
9: 5 will stop worrying a the donkeys and worry a us."
9: 6 perhaps he will tell us a the journey
9:16 "Tomorrow a this time I will send to you a man
9:22 of whom there were a thirty.
10: 2 stopped worrying a them and is worrying a you,
10: 2 What shall I do a my son?'
10:16 But a the matter of the kingship,
11: 1 A a month later, Nahash the Ammonite went up
13:15 the people who were present with him, a
14: 2 that were with him were a six hundred men,
14:14 killed a twenty men within an area a half a furrow
14:23 and the troops with Saul numbered altogether a
19: 1 with his son Jonathan and with all his servants a
19: 3 and I will speak to my father a you;
19: 5 the LORD brought a a great victory for all Israel.
20:12 a this time tomorrow, or on the third day,
20:23 As for the matter a which you and I have spoken,

1Sa 21: 2 'No one must know anything of the matter **a**
22: 2 Those who were with him numbered **a**
23: 13 Then David and his men, who were **a** six hundred,
25: 13 and **a** four hundred men went up after David,
25: 38 **A** ten days later the LORD struck Nabal,
27: 11 thinking, "They might tell **a** us, and say,
28: 9 then are you laying a snare for my life to bring **a**
2Sa 3: 18 then bring it **a**; for the LORD has promised David:
3: 26 but David did not know **a** it.
4: 4 the news **a** Saul and Jonathan came from Jezreel.
4: 5 and **a** the heat of the day they came to the house
5: 17 David heard **a** it and went down to the stronghold.
7: 6 I have been moving **a** in a tent and a tabernacle.
7: 7 Wherever I have moved **a** among all the people
11: 2 and was walking **a** on the roof of the king's house,
11: 3 David sent someone to inquire **a** the woman.
11: 18 Then Joab sent and told David all the news **a**
11: 19 the king all the news **a** the fighting,
13: 35 as your servant said, so it has come **a.**"
15: 20 and shall I today make you wander **a** with us,
18: 3 For if we flee, they will not care **a** us.
18: 3 If half of us die, they will not care **a** us.
19: 10 Now therefore why do you say nothing **a** bringing
19: 18 as he was **a** to cross the Jordan,
23: 10 The LORD brought **a** a great victory that day.
23: 12 and the LORD brought **a** a great victory.
1Ki 1: 27 Has this thing been brought **a** by my lord the king
2: 2 "I am **a** to go the way of all the earth.
2: 15 kingdom has turned **a** and become my brother's,
6: 29 of the house all around **a** with carved engravings
11: 29 **A** that time, when Jeroboam was leaving
11: 31 the God of Israel, "See, I am **a** to tear the kingdom
12: 15 because it was a turn of affairs brought **a** by
18: 26 They limped **a** the altar that they had made.
19: 11 for the LORD is **a** to pass by."
20: 6 to you tomorrow **a** this time,
21: 27 lay in the sackcloth, and went **a** dejectedly.
22: 6 **a** four hundred of them, and said to them,
22: 8 for he never prophesies anything favorable **a** me,
22: 18 that he would not prophesy anything favorable **a**
22: 36 Then **a** sunset a shout went through the army,
2Ki 2: 1 the LORD was **a** to take Elijah up to heaven by
3: 20 The next day, **a** the time of the morning offering,
7: 1 the LORD, Tomorrow **a** this time a measure
7: 18 **a** this time tomorrow in the gate of Samaria,"
9: 23 Then Joram reined **a** and fled, saying to Ahaziah,
11: 1 she set **a** to destroy all the royal family.
11: 2 from among the king's children who were **a** to
19: 20 to me **a** King Sennacherib of Assyria.
1Ch 12: 1 not move **a** freely because of Saul son of Kish;
17: 6 Wherever I have moved **a** among all Israel,
19: 5 When David was told **a** the men,
21: 15 but when he was **a** to destroy it,
2Ch 2: 4 I am now **a** to build a house for the name of
2: 5 The house that I am **a** to build will be great,
2: 9 house I am **a** to build will be great and wonderful.
10: 15 because it was a turn of affairs brought **a** by God
18: 7 for he never prophesies anything favorable **a** me,
18: 17 that he would not prophesy anything favorable **a**
22: 7 of Ahaziah should come **a** through his going
22: 10 she set **a** to destroy all the royal family of
22: 11 from among the king's children who were **a** to
25: 9 "But what shall we do **a** the hundred talents
29: 36 for the thing had come **a** suddenly.
31: 9 Hezekiah questioned the priests and the Levites **a**
32: 31 to him to inquire **a** the sign that had been done in
Ezr 7: 14 and his seven counselors to make inquiries **a**
Ne 1: 2 and I asked them **a** the Jews that survived,
1: 2 who had escaped the captivity, and **a** Jerusalem.
Est 6: 2 how Mordecai had told **a** Bigthana and Teresh,
6: 4 the king **a** having Mordecai hanged on the gallows
9: 1 king's command and edict were **a** to be executed,
9: 29 confirming this second letter **a** Purim.
Job 24: 10 They go **a** naked, without clothing;
30: 22 and you toss me **a** in the roar of the storm.
30: 28 I go **a** in sunless gloom;
36: 33 Its crashing tells **a** him; he is jealous with anger
38: 41 and wander **a** for lack of food?
Ps 22: 30 future generations will be told **a** the Lord,
35: 11 they ask me **a** things I do not know.
35: 14 I went **a** as one who laments for a mother,
39: 6 Surely everyone goes **a** like a shadow.
41: 7 All who hate me whisper together **a** me;
42: 9 Why must I walk **a** mournfully because
43: 2 Why must I walk **a** mournfully because of
48: 12 Walk **a** Zion, go all around it, count its towers,
59: 6 howling like dogs and prowling **a** the city.
59: 14 howling like dogs and prowling **a** the city.
59: 15 They roam **a** for food, and growl if they do
64: 9 they will tell what God has brought **a,**
69: 12 and the drunkards make songs **a** me.
109: 10 May his children wander **a** and beg;
143: 5 I think **a** all your deeds,
Pr 1: 2 For learning **a** wisdom and instruction,
11: 13 A gossip goes **a** telling secrets,
27: 1 Do not boast **a** tomorrow,
Ecc 4: 15 I saw all the living who, moving **a** under the sun,
12: 5 and the mourners will go **a** the streets;
SS 3: 2 "I will rise now and go **a** the city,
3: 3 The sentinels found me, as they went **a** in the city.
Isa 22: 17 The LORD is **a** to hurl you away violently,
23: 5 they will be in anguish over the report **a** Tyre.
23: 15 to Tyre as in the song **a** the prostitute:
23: 16 go **a** the city, you forgotten prostitute!
24: 1 Now the LORD is **a** to lay waste the earth
27: 2 On that day: A pleasant vineyard, sing **a** it!
30: 11 let us hear no more **a** the Holy One of Israel."
Isa 30: 13 and **a** to collapse, whose crash comes suddenly,
43: 19 I am **a** to do a new thing;
45: 11 Will you question me **a** my children,
45: 20 those who carry **a** their wooden idols,
47: 15 they all wander **a** in their own paths;
54: 11 I am **a** to set your stones in antimony,
65: 17 For I am **a** to create new heavens and a new earth;
65: 18 for I am **a** to create Jerusalem as a joy,
Jer 2: 36 How lightly you gad **a,** changing your ways!
6: 28 all stubbornly rebellious, going **a** with slanders;
12: 14 I am **a** to pluck them up from their land,
13: 13 I am **a** to fill all the inhabitants of this land—
15: 5 Who will turn aside to ask **a** your welfare?
18: 8 I will change my mind **a** the disaster
18: 10 then I will change my mind **a** the good
26: 3 that I may change my mind **a** the disaster
26: 13 the LORD will change his mind **a** the disaster
26: 19 not the LORD change his mind **a** the disaster
26: 19 But we are **a** to bring great disaster on ourselves!"
36: 8 the prophet Jeremiah ordered him **a** reading from
40: 3 and now the LORD has brought it **a,**
40: 16 for you are telling a lie **a** Ishmael."
46: 2 Concerning Egypt, **a** the army of Pharaoh Neco,
46: 13 that the LORD spoke to the prophet Jeremiah **a**
50: 11 though you frisk **a** like a heifer on the grass,
La 3: 7 He has walled me **a** so that I cannot escape;
3: 39 Why should any who draw breath complain **a**
Eze 8: 16 the porch and the altar, were **a** twenty-five men,
12: 22 what is this proverb of yours **a** the land of Israel,
16: 6 and saw you flailing **a** in your blood.
16: 22 when you were naked and bare, flailing **a**
16: 44 everyone who uses proverbs will use this proverb **a**
16: 52 for you have brought **a** for your sisters
21: 23 to remembrance, bringing **a** their capture.
24: 16 with one blow I am **a** to take away from you
32: 2 you thrash **a** in your streams,
33: 30 your people who talk together **a** you by the walls,
36: 22 O house of Israel, that I am **a** to act,
37: 19 I am **a** to take the stick of Joseph (which is in
Da 2: 13 and the wise men were **a** to be executed;
5: 31 being **a** sixty-two years old.
8: 27 then I arose and went **a** the king's business.
Joel 1: 18 of cattle wander **a** because there is no pasture
Am 8: 8 and be tossed **a** and sink again,
Jnh 3: 10 God changed his mind **a** the calamity
4: 6 so Jonah was very happy **a** the bush.
4: 9 "Is it right for you to be angry **a** the bush?"
4: 10 the LORD said, "You are concerned **a** the bush,
4: 11 And should I not be concerned **a** Nineveh,
Mic 2: 11 someone were to go **a** uttering empty falsehoods,
Na 3: 19 All who hear the news **a** you clap their hands
Hab 2: 6 with mocking riddles, say **a** them,
Hag 2: 21 saying, I am **a** to shake the heavens and the earth,
2: 22 I am **a** to destroy the strength of the kingdoms of
Zec 12: 2 I am **a** to make Jerusalem a cup of reeling for all
Mal 3: 14 or by going **a** as mourners before the LORD
Mt 2: 13 Herod is **a** to search for the child, to destroy him."
6: 25 "Therefore I tell you, do not worry **a** your life,
6: 25 or **a** your body, what you will wear.
6: 28 And why do you worry **a** clothing?
6: 34 "So do not worry **a** tomorrow,
8: 33 they told the whole story **a** what had happened to
9: 31 and spread the news **a** him throughout that district.
9: 35 Then Jesus went **a** all the cities and villages,
10: 19 not worry **a** how you are to speak or what you are
11: 7 Jesus began to speak to the crowds **a** John:
11: 10 This is the one **a** whom it is written, 'See,
14: 1 At that time Herod the ruler heard reports **a** Jesus;
14: 21 And those who ate were **a** five thousand men,
15: 7 Isaiah prophesied rightly **a** you when he said:
16: 8 why are you talking **a** having no bread?
16: 11 to perceive that I was not speaking **a** bread?
17: 9 "Tell no one **a** the vision until after the Son
17: 12 also the Son of Man is **a** to suffer at their hands."
17: 13 that he was speaking to them **a** John the Baptist.
18: 19 if two of you agree on earth **a** anything you ask,
19: 17 "Why do you ask me **a** what is good?
20: 3 When he went out **a** nine o'clock,
20: 5 he went out again **a** noon and about three o'clock,
20: 5 he went out again about noon and **a** three o'clock,
20: 6 And **a** five o'clock he went out
20: 9 When those hired **a** five o'clock came,
20: 22 Are you able to drink the cup that I am **a**
21: 45 they realized that he was speaking **a** them.
24: 36 "But **a** that day and hour no one knows,
26: 70 saying, "I do not know what you are talking **a.**"
27: 1 against Jesus in order to bring **a** his death.
27: 19 a great deal because of a dream **a** him."
27: 46 And **a** three o'clock Jesus cried with a loud voice,
Mk 1: 30 and they told him **a** her at once.
4: 10 along with the twelve asked him **a** the parables.
5: 13 and the herd, numbering **a** two thousand,
5: 27 She had heard **a** Jesus, and came up behind him in
5: 30 Jesus turned **a** in the crowd and said,
5: 42 immediately the girl got up and began to walk **a**
6: 6 Then he went **a** among the villages teaching.
6: 29 When his disciples heard **a** it,
6: 52 for they did not understand **a** the loaves,
6: 55 and rushed **a** that whole region and began to bring
7: 6 "Isaiah prophesied rightly **a** you hypocrites,
7: 17 his disciples asked him **a** the parable.
7: 25 an unclean spirit immediately heard **a** him,
8: 9 Now there were **a** four thousand people.
8: 17 "Why are you talking **a** having no bread?
8: 30 he sternly ordered them not to tell anyone **a** him.
9: 9 to tell no one **a** what they had seen,
9: 12 How then is it written **a** the Son of Man,
Mk 9: 13 as it is written **a** him."
9: 16 "What are you arguing **a** with them?"
9: 20 and he fell on the ground and rolled **a,**
9: 33 "What were you arguing **a** on the way?"
10: 10 Then in the house the disciples asked him again **a**
12: 26 in the story **a** the bush, how God said to him,
13: 4 and what will be the sign that all these things are **a**
13: 11 do not worry beforehand **a** what you are to say;
13: 32 "But **a** that day or hour no one knows,
14: 68 not know or understand what you are talking **a.**"
14: 71 "I do not know this man you are talking **a.**"
Lk 1: 4 the things **a** which you have been instructed.
1: 56 And Mary remained with her **a** three months and
1: 65 and all these things were talked **a** throughout
2: 17 they made known what had been told them **a**
2: 33 and mother were amazed at what was being said **a**
2: 38 and began to praise God and to speak **a** the child
3: 23 Jesus was **a** thirty years old
4: 14 and a report **a** him spread through all
4: 37 And a report **a** him began to reach every place in
4: 38 and they asked him **a** her.
5: 15 more than ever the word **a** Jesus spread abroad;
7: 3 When he heard **a** Jesus, he sent some Jewish elders
7: 17 This word **a** him spread throughout Judea and all
7: 24 Jesus began to speak to the crowds **a** John:
7: 27 This is the one **a** whom it is written, 'See,
8: 42 **a** twelve years old, who was dying.
9: 7 Herod the ruler heard **a** all that had taken place,
9: 9 but who is this **a** whom I hear such things?"
9: 11 the crowds found out **a** it, they followed him;
9: 11 and spoke to them **a** the kingdom of God,
9: 14 For there were **a** five thousand men.
9: 14 "Make them sit down in groups of **a** fifty each."
9: 28 Now **a** eight days after these sayings Jesus took
9: 31 which he was **a** to accomplish at Jerusalem.
9: 45 And they were afraid to ask him **a** this saying.
10: 7 Do not move **a** from house to house.
11: 53 and to cross-examine him **a** many things,
12: 11 do not worry **a** how you are to defend yourselves
12: 22 "Therefore I tell you, do not worry **a** your life,
12: 22 or **a** your body, what you will wear.
12: 26 why do you worry **a** the rest?
13: 1 very time there were some present who told him **a**
16: 2 'What is this that I hear **a** you?
18: 1 a parable **a** their need to pray always and not
18: 31 and everything that is written **a** the Son of Man by
18: 34 But they understood nothing **a** all these things;
20: 37 in the story **a** the bush,
21: 5 When some were speaking **a** the temple,
21: 7 what will be the sign that this is **a** to take place?"
22: 4 the chief priests and officers of the temple police **a**
22: 37 indeed what is written **a** me is being fulfilled."
22: 41 Then he withdrew from them **a** a stone's throw,
22: 59 Then **a** an hour later still another kept insisting,
22: 60 "Man, I do not know what you are talking **a!**"
23: 8 because he had heard **a** him and was hoping
23: 44 It was now **a** noon, and darkness came over
24: 4 While they were perplexed **a** this,
24: 13 **a** seven miles from Jerusalem,
24: 14 and talking with each other **a** all these things
24: 19 They replied, "The things **a** Jesus of Nazareth,
24: 27 to them the things **a** himself in all the scriptures.
24: 36 While they were talking **a** this,
24: 44 that everything written **a** me in the law of Moses,
Jn 1: 22 What do you say **a** yourself?"
1: 39 It was **a** four o'clock in the afternoon.
1: 45 "We have found him **a** whom Moses in the law
2: 25 and needed no one to testify **a** anyone;
3: 12 If I have told you **a** earthly things and you do
3: 12 can you believe if I tell you **a** heavenly things?
3: 25 Now a discussion **a** purification arose
3: 31 of the earth belongs to the earth and speaks **a**
4: 6 by the well. It was **a** noon.
4: 32 "I have food to eat that you do not know **a.**"
5: 31 "If I testify **a** myself, my testimony is not true.
5: 46 you would believe me, for he wrote **a** me.
6: 10 so they sat down, **a** five thousand in all,
6: 15 that they were **a** to come and take him by force
6: 19 When they had rowed **a** three or four miles,
6: 41 Jews began to complain **a** him because he said,
6: 61 being aware that his disciples were complaining **a**
6: 66 of his disciples turned back and no longer went **a**
7: 1 After this Jesus went **a** in Galilee.
7: 1 to go **a** in Judea because the Jews were looking
7: 12 And there was considerable complaining **a** him
7: 13 Yet no one would speak openly **a** him for fear of
7: 14 **A** the middle of the festival Jesus went up into
7: 32 the crowd muttering such things **a** him,
7: 39 Now he said this **a** the Spirit,
8: 26 I have much to say **a** you and much to condemn;
8: 27 not understand that he was speaking to them **a**
9: 17 "What do you say **a** him?
10: 41 but everything that John said **a** this man was true."
11: 13 Jesus, however, had been speaking **a** his death,
11: 19 and Mary to console them **a** their brother.
11: 51 that year he prophesied that Jesus was **a** to die for
11: 54 Jesus therefore no longer walked **a** openly among
12: 4 of his disciples (the one who was **a** to betray him),
12: 6 (He said this not because he cared **a** the poor,
12: 41 because he saw his glory and spoke **a** him.
12: 49 a commandment **a** what to say and what to speak.
16: 4 that I told you **a** them.
16: 8 the world wrong **a** sin and righteousness
16: 9 **a** sin, because they do not believe in me;
16: 10 **a** righteousness, because I am going to the Father
16: 11 **a** judgment, because the ruler of this world
16: 18 We do not know what he is talking **a.**"

Jn 18:19 the high priest questioned Jesus a his disciples and a his teaching.
18:34 or did others tell you a me?"
19:14 for the Passover; and it was a noon.
19:39 weighing a a hundred pounds.
21: 8 only a a hundred yards off.
21:21 he said to Jesus, "Lord, what a him?"
Ac 1: 1 I wrote a all that Jesus did and taught from
1: 3 during forty days and speaking a the kingdom
1:15 the believers (together the crowd numbered a
2:11 in our own languages we hear them speaking a
2:41 and that day a three thousand persons were added.
3: 3 he saw Peter and John a to go into the temple,
4: 4 and they numbered a five thousand.
4:20 from speaking a what we have seen and heard."
5: 7 After an interval of a three hours his wife came in,
5:20 and tell the people the whole message a this life."
5:24 they were perplexed a them,
5:36 and a number of men, a four hundred, joined him;
8:12 the good news a the kingdom of God and
8:34 The eunuch asked Philip, "A whom,
8:34 the prophet say this, a himself or a someone else?"
8:35 he proclaimed to him the good news a Jesus.
9:13 "Lord, I have heard from many a this man,
10: 3 One afternoon at a three o'clock he had a vision
10: 9 A noon the next day, as they were on their journey
10:17 while Peter was greatly puzzled a what to make of
10:19 While Peter was still thinking a the vision,
10:38 how he went a doing good
10:43 All the prophets testify a him
12: 1 A that time King Herod laid violent hands
13:11 and he went a groping for someone to lead him by
13:12 for he was astonished at the teaching a the Lord.
13:18 For a forty years he put up with them in
13:20 for a four hundred fifty years.
13:22 In his testimony a him he said,
13:29 that was written a him, they took him down from
13:42 to speak a these things again the next sabbath.
16:25 A midnight Paul and Silas were praying
16:27 he drew his sword and was a to kill himself,
17:18 (This was because he was telling the good news a
17:32 but others said, "We will hear you again a this."
18:14 Just as Paul was a to speak,
18:15 but since it is a matter of questions a words
19: 7 altogether there were a twelve of them.
19: 8 and argued persuasively a the kingdom of God.
19:23 A that time no little disturbance broke out
19:34 for a two hours all of them shouted in unison,
20: 3 He was a to set sail for Syria when
20:21 as I testified to both Jews and Greeks a repentance
20:25 among whom I have gone a proclaiming
21:21 They have been told a you that you teach all
21:24 that there is nothing in what they have been told a
21:37 Just as Paul was a to be brought into the barracks,
22: 5 and the whole council of elders can testify a me.
22: 6 a noon a great light from heaven suddenly shone a
22:18 they will not accept your testimony a me.'
22:26 "What are you a to do?
22:29 Immediately those who were a to examine him
23:16 Now the son of Paul's sister heard a the ambush;
23:27 This man was seized by the Jews and was a to
24:21 'It is a the resurrection of the dead that I am
24:22 Felix, who was rather well informed a the Way,
25: 5 and if there is anything wrong a the man,
25:15 and the elders of the Jews informed me a him
25:19 with him a their own religion and a a certain Jesus,
25:24 you see this man a whom the whole Jewish
25:26 to write to our sovereign a him.
26:26 Indeed the king knows a these things,
27: 2 on a ship of Adramyttium that was a to set sail to
27:27 a midnight the sailors suspected
28:10 and when we were a to sail,
28:21 "We have received no letters from Judea a you,
28:21 or spoken anything evil a you.
28:23 the kingdom of God and trying to convince them a
28:31 proclaiming the kingdom of God and teaching a
Ro 1: 5 and apostleship to bring a the obedience of faith
1:19 For what can be known a God is plain to them,
1:25 the truth a God for a lie and worshiped and served
4: 2 he has something to boast a, but not before God.
4:19 which was already as good as dead (for he was a
8:18 not worth comparing with the glory a to
8:31 What then are we to say a these things?
9: 9 "A this time I will return and Sarah shall have
15:14 I myself feel confident a you,
16:26 to bring a the obedience of faith—
1Co 1:18 For the message a the cross is foolishness
3:21 So let no one boast a human leaders.
7: 1 Now concerning the matters a which you wrote:
7:21 Do not be concerned a it.
7:32 The unmarried man is anxious a the affairs of
7:33 married man is anxious a the affairs of the world,
7:34 the unmarried woman and the virgin are anxious a
7:34 but the married woman is anxious a the affairs of
11:34 A the other things I will give instructions
2Co 2: 3 for I am confident a all of you,
5:12 but giving you an opportunity to boast a us,
7: 4 I often boast a you; I have great pride in you;
7: 7 by the consolation with which he was consoled a
7:14 if I have been somewhat boastful a you to him,
8: 1 a the grace of God that has been granted to
8:20 that no one should blame us a this generous gift
8:24 of your love and of our reason for boasting a you.
9: 1 not necessary for me to write you a the ministry to
9: 2 of my boasting a you to the people of Macedonia,
9: 3 the brothers in order that our boasting a you may
11:12 be recognized as our equals in what they boast a.

2Co 12: 8 Three times I appealed to the Lord a this,
Gal 4:20 for I am perplexed a you.
5:10 I am confident a you in the Lord that you will
6:13 to be circumcised so that they may boast a
Eph 4:14 to and fro and blown a by every wind of doctrine,
4:21 you have heard a him and were taught in him,
Php 1: 7 It is right for me to think this way a all of you,
1:27 and see you or am absent and hear a you,
3:15 and if you think differently a anything,
4: 6 not worry a anything, but in everything by prayer
4: 8 and if there is anything worthy of praise, think a
Col 4: 7 Tychicus will tell you all the news a me;
4: 9 They will tell you a everything here.
1Th 1: 8 so that we have no need to speak a it.
1: 9 the people of those regions report a us what kind
3: 5 I sent to find out a your faith;
3: 7 and persecution we have been encouraged a you
4:13 brothers and sisters, a those who have died,
1Ti 1: 7 or the things a which they make assertions.
1:18 in accordance with the prophecies made earlier a
5:13 gadding a from house to house;
6: 4 for controversy and for disputes a words.
6:15 which he will bring a at the right time—
2Ti 1: 8 of the testimony a our Lord or of me his prisoner,
Tit 3: 9 genealogies, dissensions, and quarrels a the law,
Phm 1:19 I say nothing a your owing me
Heb 2: 5 a which we are speaking, to angels.
4: 4 For in one place it speaks a the seventh day
4: 8 God would not speak later a another day.
5:11 A this we have much to say that is hard to explain,
6: 1 leaving behind the basic teaching a Christ,
6: 2 instruction a baptisms, laying on
7:14 in connection with that tribe Moses said nothing a
8: 5 for Moses, when he was a to erect the tent,
11: 7 warned by God a events as yet unseen,
11:22 the exodus of the Israelites and gave instructions a
11:37 they went a in skins of sheep and goats, destitute,
13: 9 not by regulations a food,
1Pe 1:11 inquiring a the person or time that the Spirit
2Pe 3: 9 The Lord is not slow a his promise,
1Jn 2:27 But as his anointing teaches you a all things,
5:16 I do not say that you should pray a that.
3Jn 1:12 Everyone has testified favorably a Demetrius,
Jude 1: 3 while eagerly preparing to write to you a
1: 9 with the devil and disputed a the body of Moses,
1:14 It was also a these that Enoch,
Rev 2:10 Do not fear what you are a to suffer.
2:10 the devil is a to throw some of you into prison so
3:16 I am a to spit you out of my mouth.
8: 1 there was silence in heaven for a half an hour.
8:13 of the other trumpets that the three angels are a
10: 4 the seven thunders had sounded, I was a to write,
10:11 "You must prophesy again a many peoples
12: 4 the dragon stood before the woman who was a
14:20 for a distance of a two hundred miles.
16:15 not going a naked and exposed to shame.")
16:21 each weighing a a hundred pounds,
17: 8 and is a to ascend from the bottomless pit and go
Tob 1:19 of the Ninevites went and informed the king a me,
1:19 the king knew a me and that I was being searched
2:14 These things are known a you!"
4: 2 and explain to him a the money before I die?"
5: 9 so that I may learn a his family and
5:14 because I wanted to be sure a your ancestry.
6:13 tonight I will speak to her father a the girl,
6:16 brother, and say no more a this demon.
6:18 Now when you are a to go to bed with her,
10: 8 to your father Tobit and they will inform him a
10:12 may I hear a good report a you as long as I live."
14: 3 When he was a to die, he called his son Tobias
14: 4 for I believe the word of God that Nahum spoke a
Jdt 2: 1 a carrying out his revenge on the whole region,
5: 5 and I will tell you the truth a this people that lives
6:16 and Uzziah questioned him a what had happened.
7:14 the sword reaches them they will be strewn a in
8: 1 Now in those days Judith heard a these things:
8:32 I am a to do something that will go down
8:34 not tell you until I have finished what I am a
10:12 for they are a to be handed over to you to
10:18 waiting until they told him a her.
11:11 by which they are a to provoke their God to anger
11:16 the whole world wherever people shall hear a
AdE 2: 1 and he no longer was concerned a Vashti
4: 7 into the royal treasury to bring a the destruction of
5: 5 both came to the dinner that Esther had spoken a.
5:11 And he told them a his riches and the honor that
6: 2 He found the words written a Mordecai,
6: 2 the king a the two royal eunuchs who were
6: 4 the king was inquiring a the goodwill shown
6: 4 to the king a hanging Mordecai on the gallows
9:29 and gave full authority to the letter a Purim.
11: 1 to Egypt the preceding Letter a Purim,
13: 4 that we honorably intend cannot be brought a.
Wis 6:16 because she goes a seeking those worthy of her,
8:18 I went a seeking how to get her for myself.
12:14 nor can any king or monarch confront you a
13:17 When he prays a possessions and his marriage
14: 1 to sail and a to voyage over raging waves calls
14:22 not enough for them to err a the knowledge
14:30 because they thought wrongly a God
17:20 and went a its work unhindered,
Sir 9: 7 or wander a in its deserted sections.
9:15 and let all your discussion be a the law of
11: 4 Do not boast a wearing fine clothes,
11: 9 Do not argue a a matter that does not concern you,
13:13 for you are walking a with your own downfall.
29:18 and has tossed them a like waves of the sea;

Sir 29:28 It is hard for a sensible person to bear scolding a
31: 1 and anxiety a it drives away sleep.
33: 2 but the one who is hypocritical a it is like a boat in
34: 9 with much experience knows what he is talking a.
37:11 Do not consult with a woman a her rival or with a coward a war,
37:11 a merchant a business or with a buyer a selling,
37:11 with miser a generosity or with the merciless a kindness,
37:11 with an idler a any work or with a seasonal laborer a completing his work,
37:11 with a lazy servant a a big task—
38:25 and whose talk is a bulls?
38:26 and he is careful a fodder for the heifers.
41: 1 who has nothing to worry a and is prosperous
41: 2 worn down by age and anxious a everything;
51: 3 from grinding teeth a to devour me,
Bar 3:31 or is concerned a the path to her.
Sus 1: 8 to see her, going in and walking a, and they began
1:27 for nothing like this had ever been said a Susanna.
Bel 1:12 otherwise Daniel will, who is telling lies a us."
1:28 When the Babylonians heard a it,
1:35 and I know nothing a the den."
1Mc 3:34 and gave him orders a all that he wanted done.
3:48 the book of the law to inquire into those matters a
3:56 or were a to be married,
4:44 They deliberated what to do a the altar
5:13 and have destroyed a a thousand persons there."
7:32 A five hundred of the army of Nicanor fell,
9:49 a one thousand of Bacchides' men fell that day.
9:61 And Jonathan's men seized a fifty of the men of
10:19 We have heard a you, that you are
10:35 from them or annoy any of them a any matter.
10:63 that no one is to bring charges against him a
11: 4 and its suburbs destroyed, and the corpses lying a,
11:29 and wrote a letter to Jonathan a all these things;
11:47 they killed on that day a one hundred thousand.
11:53 But he broke his word a all that he had promised;
13:14 and that he was a to join battle with him,
13:29 erecting a them great columns,
14:21 to our people have told us a your glory and honor,
16:10 and a two thousand of them fell.
16:18 a report a these things and sent it to the king,
2Mc 2:13 that he founded a library and collected the books a
2:13 and letters of kings a votive offerings.
2:16 therefore, we are a to celebrate the purification,
2:22 that were a to be abolished, while the Lord
3: 2 it came a that the kings themselves honored
3: 4 with the high priest a the administration of
3: 7 of the money a which he had been informed.
3: 9 he told a the disclosure that had been made
3:15 toward heaven upon him who had given the law a
3:18 the holy place was a to be brought into dishonor.
3:38 there is certainly some power of God a the place.
4: 1 who had informed a the money
4:40 Lysimachus armed a three thousand men
4:43 Charges were brought against Menelaus a
5: 1 A this time Antiochus made his second invasion
5:27 But Judas Maccabeus, with a nine others,
6:30 When he was a to die under the blows,
7:18 And when he was a to die, he said,
7:42 a the eating of sacrifices and the extreme tortures.
8: 1 and so they gathered a six thousand.
8: 3 that was being destroyed and a to be leveled to
8:11 from the Almighty that was a to overtake him.
9: 1 A that time, as it happened,
9: 7 And so it came a that he fell out of his chariot
11: 2 gathered a eighty thousand infantry
11: 5 a fortified place a five stadia from Jerusalem,
11:17 and have asked a the matters indicated in it.
12: 1 and the Jews went a their farming.
13: 7 By such a fate it came a that Menelaus
14: 4 in a the one hundred fifty-first year,
14: 5 and was asked a the attitude and intentions of
14:41 When the troops were a to capture the tower
1Es 1:42 But the things that are reported a Jehoiakim,
2:22 in the annals what has been written a them,
4:33 and he began to speak a truth:
8:53 And again we prayed to our Lord a these things,
8:86 that has happened to us has come a because
8:93 Let us take an oath to the Lord a this,
3Mc 1: 5 it came a that the enemy was routed in the action,
3: 7 instead they gossiped a the differences in worship
4:19 he was clearly convinced a the matter
5:10 to report to the king a these preparations.
5:37 must I give you orders a these things?
5:42 the changes of mind that had come a within him
5:46 entered at a dawn into the courtyard—
2Es 4: 6 that you should ask me a such things?"
4: 9 But now I have asked you only a fire and wind
4: 9 and you have given me no answer a them."
4:23 For I did not wish to inquire a the ways above,
4:23 but a those things that we daily experience:
4:25 It is a these things that I have asked."
4:28 For the evil a which you ask me has been sown,
4:35 the souls of the righteous in their chambers ask a
4:52 "Concerning the signs a which you ask me,
6:20 seal is placed upon the age that is a to pass away,
6:21 and these shall live and leap a.
6:46 and you commanded them to serve humankind, a
7:80 but shall immediately wander a in torments,
8:15 A all humankind you know best;
8:15 but I will speak a your people,
8:16 and a your inheritance, for whom I lament,
8:16 and a Israel, for whom I am sad,
8:16 and a the seed of Jacob, for whom I am troubled.
8:38 indeed I will not concern myself a the fashioning

2Es 8:38 or **a** their death, their ju[illegible]
8:55 [illegible] ask any more questions **a** the great number
9: 2 that it is the very time when the Most High is **a**
9:13 to be curious **a** how the ungodly will be punished;
9:34 and when it comes **a** that what was sown
10:38 and tell you **a** the things that you fear;
10:43 and who told you **a** the misfortune of her son—
13:22 As for what you said **a** those who survive,
13:46 and now, when they are **a** to come again,
13:53 And you alone have been enlightened **a** this,
14:25 be put out until what you are **a** to write is finished.
15:53 and clapping your hands and talking **a** their death
4Mc 1: 1 that I am **a** to discuss is most philosophical,
4:13 although otherwise he had scruples **a** doing so,
6:26 When he was now burned to his very bones and **a**
8: 4 grouped **a** their mother as though a chorus,
8:27 But the youths, though **a** to be tortured,
10: 9 When he was **a** to die, he said,
12:15 Then because he too was **a** to die, he said,
17: 1 Some of the guards said that when she also was **a**
18:11 He read to you **a** Abel slain by Cain,
18:11 as a burnt offering, and **a** Joseph in prison.
18:12 and he taught you **a** Hananiah, Azariah,

ABOVE‡ (178)

Ge 1: 7 the dome from the waters that were **a** the dome.
1:20 and let birds fly **a** the earth across the dome of
6:16 Make a roof for the ark, and finish it to a cubit **a;**
7:17 and bore up the ark, and it rose high **a** the earth.
7:20 the waters swelled **a** the mountains,
49:25 with blessings of heaven **a,**
Ex 20: 4 in the form of anything that is in heaven **a,**
25:20 The cherubim shall spread out their wings **a,**
25:22 and from **a** the mercy seat,
28:27 at its joining **a** the decorated band of the ephod.
30: 6 You shall place it in front of the curtain that is **a**
37: 9 The cherubim spread out their wings **a,**
39:20 at its joining **a** the decorated band of the ephod.
39:31 to fasten it on the turban **a;**
40:20 and set the mercy seat **a** the ark;
Lev 11:21 that have jointed legs **a** their feet,
21:10 The priest who is exalted **a** his fellows,
Nu 3:46 over and **a** the number of the Levites,
3:49 from those who were over and **a** those redeemed
7:89 to him from **a** the mercy seat that was on the ark
16: 3 then do you exalt yourselves **a** the assembly of
Dt 4:39 to heart that the LORD is God in heaven **a** and on
5: 8 in the form of anything that is in heaven **a,**
11:21 as long as the heavens are **a** the earth.
17:20 neither exalting himself **a** other members of
26:19 to set you high **a** all nations that he has made,
28: 1 the LORD your God will set you high **a** all
28:43 among you shall ascend **a** you higher and higher,
33:13 with the choice gifts of heaven **a,**
Jos 2:11 The LORD your God is indeed God in heaven **a**
3:13 of the Jordan flowing from **a** shall be cut off;
3:16 the waters flowing from **a** stood still,
1Sa 9: 2 he stood head and shoulders **a** everyone else.
2Sa 22:49 you exalted me **a** my adversaries,
1Ki 7:11 There were costly stones **a,** cut to measure,
7:18 to cover the capitals that were **a** the pomegranates;
7:20 and also **a** the rounded projection that was beside
7:29 both **a** and below the lions and oxen,
8: 7 cherubim made a covering **a** the ark and its poles.
8:23 like you in heaven **a** or on earth beneath,
14: 9 but you have done evil **a** all those who were
2Ki 19:15 who are enthroned **a** the cherubim, you are God,
25:28 a seat **a** the other seats of the kings who were
1Ch 16:25 he is to be revered **a** all gods.
29:11 O LORD, and you are exalted as head **a** all.
2Ch 5: 8 cherubim made a covering **a** the ark and its poles.
24:20 he stood **a** the people and said to them,
34: 4 he demolished the incense altars that stood **a**
Ne 3:28 **A** the Horse Gate the priests made repairs,
8: 5 for he was standing **a** all the people;
9: 5 which is exalted **a** all blessing and praise."
12:37 at the ascent of the wall, **a** the house of David,
12:38 **a** the Tower of the Ovens, to the Broad Wall,
12:39 and **a** the Gate of Ephraim, and by the Old Gate,
Est 3: 1 and set his seat **a** all the officials who were
5:11 and how he had advanced him **a** the officials and
Job 3: 4 May God **a** not seek it, or light shine on it.
18: 6 and the lamp **a** them is put out.
18:16 and their branches wither **a.**
28:18 the price of wisdom is **a** pearls.
31: 2 What would be my portion from God **a,**
31:28 for I should have been false to God **a.**
Ps 8: 1 You have set your glory **a** the heavens.
18:48 indeed, you exalted me **a** my adversaries;
27: 6 my head is lifted up **a** my enemies all around me,
50: 4 He calls to the heavens **a** and to the earth,
57: 5 Be exalted, O God, **a** the heavens.
57:11 Be exalted, O God, **a** the heavens.
78:23 Yet he commanded the skies **a,**
89: 7 great and awesome **a** all that are around him?
95: 3 and a great King **a** all gods.
96: 4 he is to be revered **a** all gods.
97: 9 you are exalted far **a** all gods.
103:11 For as the heavens are high **a** the earth,
104: 6 the waters stood **a** the mountains.
108: 5 Be exalted, O God, **a** the heavens,
113: 4 The LORD is high **a** all nations,
113: 4 and his glory **a** the heavens.
135: 5 our Lord is **a** all gods.
137: 6 if I do not set Jerusalem **a** my highest joy.
138: 2 for you have exalted your name and your word **a**
Ps 148: 4 and you waters **a** the heavens!
148:13 his glory is **a** earth and heaven.
Pr 8:28 when he made firm the skies **a,**
Isa 2: 2 and shall be raised **a** the hills;
6: 2 Seraphs were in attendance **a** him;
8: 7 it will rise **a** all its channels
14:13 I will raise my throne **a** the stars of God;
37:16 God of Israel, who are enthroned **a** the cherubim,
40:22 It is he who sits **a** the circle of the earth,
45: 8 Shower, O heavens, from **a,**
Jer 4:28 and the heavens **a** grow black;
17: 9 The heart is devious **a** all else;
31:37 If the heavens **a** can be measured,
35: 4 **a** the chamber of Maaseiah son of Shallum,
43:10 and he will set his throne **a** these stones
52:32 a seat **a** the seats of the other kings who were
Eze 1:11 Their wings were spread out **a;**
1:22 shining like crystal, spread out **a** their heads.
1:25 a voice from **a** the dome over their heads;
1:26 And **a** the dome over their heads
1:26 and seated **a** the likeness of a throne
8: 2 be its loins it was fire, and **a** the loins it was like
10: 1 and **a** the dome that was over the heads of
10: 1 of the cherubim there appeared **a** them something
10:18 from the threshold of the house and stopped **a**
10:19 and the glory of the God of Israel was **a** them.
11:22 and the glory of the God of Israel was **a** them.
29:15 and never again exalt itself **a** the nations;
31: 5 So it towered high **a** all the trees of the field;
32: 8 the shining lights of the heavens I will darken **a**
41:17 to the space **a** the door,
41:20 from the floor to the area **a** the door,
Da 6: 3 Soon Daniel distinguished himself **a** all
Am 2: 9 I destroyed his fruit **a,** and his roots beneath.
Mic 4: 1 and shall be raised up **a** the hills.
Hag 1:10 the heavens **a** you have withheld the dew,
Mt 10:24 "A disciple is not **a** the teacher, nor a slave **a** the master;
Mk 2: 4 they removed the roof **a** him;
Lk 6:40 A disciple is not **a** the teacher,
Jn 3: 3 the kingdom of God without being born from **a."**
3: 7 'You must be born from **a.'**
3:31 The one who comes from **a** is **a** all;
3:31 The one who comes from heaven is **a** all.
8:23 "You are from below, I am from **a;**
19:11 over me unless it had been given you from **a;**
Ac 2:19 And I will show portents in the heaven **a** and signs
Gal 4:26 the other woman corresponds to the Jerusalem **a;**
Eph 1:21 far **a** all rule and authority and power and dominion, and **a** every name that is named,
3: 3 as I wrote **a** in a few words,
4: 6 who is **a** all and through all and in all.
4:10 the same one who ascended far **a** all the heavens,
Php 2: 9 and gave him the name that is **a** every name,
Col 3: 1 seek the things that are **a,** where Christ is,
3: 2 Set your minds on things that are **a,**
3:14 **A** all, clothe yourselves with love,
2Th 2: 4 and exalts himself **a** every so-called god or object
1Ti 3: 2 Now a bishop must be **a** reproach,
5: 7 so that they may be **a** reproach.
2Ti 4:13 also the books, and **a** all the parchments.
Heb 7:26 separated from sinners, and exalted **a** the heavens.
9: 5 **a** it were the cherubim of glory overshadowing
10: 8 When he said **a,** "You have neither desired
Jas 1:17 is from **a,** coming down from the Father of lights,
3:15 Such wisdom does not come down from **a,**
3:17 But the wisdom from **a** is first pure,
5:12 **A** all, my beloved, do not swear,
1Pe 4: 8 **A** all, maintain constant love for one another,
Tob 1: 2 **a** Asher toward the west, and north of Phogor.
Jdt 13:18 by the Most High God **a** all other women on earth;
AdE 13:14 But I did this so that I might not set human glory **a**
Sir 3: 2 For the Lord honors a father **a** his children,
15: 5 She will exalt him **a** his neighbors,
27:24 I have hated many things, but him **a** all;
30:16 and no gladness **a** joy of heart.
32:13 But **a** all bless your Maker,
37:15 But **a** all pray to the Most High
40:11 and what is from **a** returns **a.**
49: 8 which God showed him **a** the chariot of
49:16 but **a** every other created living being was Adam.
LtJ 6:63 And the fire sent from **a** to consume mountains
6:73 such a person will be far **a** reproach.
Aza 1:24 flames poured out **a** the furnace forty-nine cubits,
1:38 Bless the Lord, all you waters **a** the heavens;
2Mc 15: 2 and hallowed **a** other days,"
1Es 3:12 but **a** all things truth is victor."
3Mc 3:30 The letter was written in the **a** form.
2Es 4: 7 or how many streams are **a** the firmament,
4:21 and he who is **a** the heavens can understand what is **a** the height of the heavens."
4:23 For I did not wish to inquire about the ways **a,**
8: 6 O Lord **a** us, grant to your servant
8:45 Surely not, O Lord **a!**
15:59 Unhappy **a** all others, you shall come

ABRAHAM‡ (266) [ABRAHAM'S, =ABRAM, =ABRAM'S]

A. *GOD OF ABRAHAM (18)
B. FATHER ABRAHAM (13)
C. DESCENDANT[S] OF ABRAHAM (8)
D. SON OF ABRAHAM (3)

Ge 17: 5 but your name shall be **A;**
17: 9 God said to **A,** "As for you,
17:15 God said to **A,** "As for Sarai your wife,
Ge 17:17 Then **A** fell on his face and laughed,
17:18 And **A** said to God, "O that Ishmael might live
17:22 finished talking with him, God went up from **A.**
17:23 Then **A** took his son Ishmael and all
17:24 **A** was ninety-nine years old
17:26 very day **A** and his son Ishmael were circumcised;
18: 1 The LORD appeared to **A** by the oaks of Mamre,
18: 6 And **A** hastened into the tent to Sarah, and said,
18: 7 **A** ran to the herd, and took a calf,
18:11 Now **A** and Sarah were old, advanced in age;
18:13 The LORD said to **A,** "Why did Sarah laugh,
18:16 and **A** went with them to set them on their way.
18:17 "Shall I hide from **A** what I am about to do,
18:18 that **A** shall become a great and mighty nation,
18:19 about for **A** what he has promised him."
18:22 while **A** remained standing before the LORD.
18:23 Then **A** came near and said,
18:27 **A** answered, "Let me take it upon myself to speak
18:33 when he had finished speaking to **A;**
18:33 and **A** returned to his place.
19:27 **A** went early in the morning to the place
19:29 the Plain, God remembered **A,** and sent Lot out of
20: 1 From there **A** journeyed toward the region of
20: 2 **A** said of his wife Sarah,
20: 9 Then Abimelech called **A,** and said to him,
20:10 And Abimelech said to **A,**
20:11 **A** said, "I did it because I thought,
20:14 and male and female slaves, and gave them to **A,**
20:17 Then **A** prayed to God;
21: 2 Sarah conceived and bore **A** a son in his old age,
21: 3 **A** gave the name Isaac to his son
21: 4 And **A** circumcised his son Isaac
21: 5 **A** was a hundred years old when his son Isaac
21: 7 to **A** that Sarah would nurse children?
21: 8 and **A** made a great feast on the day
21: 9 whom she had borne to **A,** playing with her son
21:10 to **A,** "Cast out this slave woman with her son;
21:11 The matter was very distressing to **A** on account
21:12 to **A,** "Do not be distressed because of the boy and
21:14 So **A** rose early in the morning,
21:22 with Phicol the commander of his army, said to **A,**
21:24 And **A** said, "I swear it."
21:25 When **A** complained to Abimelech about a well
21:27 So **A** took sheep and oxen and gave them
21:28 **A** set apart seven ewe lambs of the flock.
21:29 And Abimelech said to **A,**
21:33 **A** planted a tamarisk tree in Beer-sheba,
21:34 And **A** resided as an alien many days in the land
22: 1 After these things God tested **A.**
22: 1 He said to him, **"A!"**
22: 3 So **A** rose early in the morning,
22: 4 On the third day **A** looked up and saw
22: 5 Then **A** said to his young men,
22: 6 **A** took the wood of the burnt offering and laid it
22: 7 Isaac said to his father **A,** "Father!" B
22: 8 **A** said, "God himself will provide the lamb for
22: 9 **A** built an altar there and laid the wood in order.
22:10 Then **A** reached out his hand and took the knife
22:11 to him from heaven, and said, **"A, A!"**
22:13 And **A** looked up and saw a ram,
22:13 **A** went and took the ram and offered it up as
22:14 So **A** called that place "The LORD will provide";
22:15 The angel of the LORD called to **A** a second time
22:19 So **A** returned to his young men,
22:19 and **A** lived at Beer-sheba.
22:20 Now after these things it was told **A,**
23: 2 **A** went in to mourn for Sarah and to weep for her.
23: 3 **A** rose up from beside his dead,
23: 5 The Hittites answered **A,**
23: 7 **A** rose and bowed to the Hittites,
23:10 and Ephron the Hittite answered **A** in the hearing
23:12 **A** bowed down before the people of the land.
23:14 Ephron answered **A,**
23:16 **A** agreed with Ephron;
23:16 and **A** weighed out for Ephron the silver
23:18 to **A** as a possession in the presence of the Hittites,
23:19 **A** buried Sarah his wife in the cave of the field
24: 1 Now **A** was old, well advanced in years;
24: 1 and the LORD had blessed **A** in all things.
24: 2 **A** said to his servant, the oldest of his house,
24: 6 **A** said to him, "See to it that you do
24: 9 under the thigh of **A** his master and swore to him
24:12 And he said, "O LORD, God of my master **A,**
24:12 and show steadfast love to my master **A.**
24:27 "Blessed be the LORD, the God of my master **A,**
24:42 and said, 'O LORD, the God of my master **A,**
24:48 and blessed the LORD, the God of my master **A,**
25: 1 **A** took another wife, whose name was Keturah.
25: 5 **A** gave all he had to Isaac.
25: 6 But to the sons of his concubines **A** gave gifts,
25: 8 **A** breathed his last and died in a good old age,
25:10 the field that **A** purchased from the Hittites.
25:10 There **A** was buried, with his wife Sarah.
25:11 After the death of **A** God blessed his son Isaac.
25:12 Sarah's slave-girl, bore to **A.**
25:19 **A** was the father of Isaac,
26: 1 that had occurred in the days of **A.**
26: 3 will fulfill the oath that I swore to your father **A.** B
26: 5 because **A** obeyed my voice and kept my charge,
26:15 in the days of his father **A.)** B
26:18 that had been dug in the days of his father **A;** B
26:18 had stopped them up after the death of **A;**
26:24 "I am the God of your father **A;** B
28: 4 May he give to you the blessing of **A,**
28: 4 land that God gave to **A."**
28:13 the God of **A** your father and the God of Isaac; A
31:42 the God of **A** and the Fear of Isaac, A

Ge 31:53 May the God of A and the God of Nahor"— A
32: 9 of my father A and God of my father Isaac, B
35:12 land that I gave to A and Isaac I will give to you,
35:27 Hebron), where A and Isaac had resided as aliens.
48:15 before whom my ancestors A and Isaac walked,
48:16 and the name of my ancestors A and Isaac;
49:30 the field that A bought from Ephron the Hittite as
49:31 There A and his wife Sarah were buried;
50:13 which A bought as a burial site from Ephron
50:24 up out of this land to the land that he swore to A,
Ex 2:24 and God remembered his covenant with A, Isaac,
3: 6 "I am the God of your father, the God of A, A
3:15 the God of your ancestors, the God of A, A
3:16 the God of your ancestors, the God of A, A
4: 5 the God of their ancestors, the God of A, A
6: 3 to A, Isaac, and Jacob as God Almighty,
6: 8 into the land that I swore to give to A, Isaac,
32:13 Remember A, Isaac, and Israel, your servants,
33: 1 and go to the land of which I swore to A, Isaac,
Lev 26:42 with Isaac and also my covenant with A,
Nu 32:11 shall see the land that I swore to give to A,
Dt 1: 8 to A, to Isaac, and to Jacob,
6:10 to A, to Isaac, and to Jacob, to give you—
9: 5 to A, to Isaac, and to Jacob.
9:27 Remember your servants, A, Isaac, and Jacob;
29:13 to A, to Isaac, and to Jacob.
30:20 to A, to Isaac, and to Jacob.
34: 4 "This is the land of which I swore to A, to Isaac,
Jos 24: 2 Terah and his sons A and Nahor—
24: 3 Then I took your father A from beyond the River B
1Ki 18:36 "O LORD, God of A, Isaac, and Israel, A
2Ki 13:23 because of his covenant with A, Isaac, and Jacob,
1Ch 1:27 Abram, that is, A.
1:28 The sons of A: Isaac and Ishmael.
1:34 A became the father of Isaac.
16:16 the covenant that he made with A,
29:18 O LORD, the God of A, Isaac, and Israel, A
2Ch 20: 7 to the descendants of your friend A?
30: 6 return to the LORD, the God of A, Isaac, A
Ne 9: 7 of Ur of the Chaldeans and gave him the name A;
Ps 47: 9 peoples gather as the people of the God of A. A
105: 6 O offspring of his servant A,
105: 9 the covenant that he made with A,
105:42 For he remembered his holy promise, and A,
Isa 29:22 Therefore thus says the LORD, who redeemed A,
41: 8 Jacob, whom I have chosen, the offspring of A,
51: 2 Look to A your father and to Sarah who bore you;
63:16 though A does not know us and Israel does
Jer 33:26 as rulers over the offspring of A,
Eze 33:24 "A was only one man, yet he got possession of
Mic 7:20 to Jacob and unswerving loyalty to A,
Mt 1: 1 the son of David, the son of A. D
1: 2 A was the father of Isaac,
1:17 from A to David are fourteen generations;
3: 9 'We have A as our ancestor';
3: 9 from these stones to raise up children to A.
8:11 and west and will eat with A and Isaac and Jacob
22:32 'I am the God of A, A
Mk 12:26 how God said to him, 'I am the God of A, A
Lk 1:55 to A and to his descendants forever."
1:73 the oath that he swore to our ancestor A,
3: 8 'We have A as our ancestor';
3: 8 from these stones to raise up children to A.
3:34 son of A, son of Terah, son of Nahor, D
13:16 of A whom Satan bound for eighteen long years,
13:28 be weeping and gnashing of teeth when you see A
16:22 and was carried away by the angels to be with A.
16:23 up and saw A far away with Lazarus by his side.
16:24 He called out, 'Father A, have mercy on me, B
16:25 But A said, 'Child, remember that
16:29 A replied, 'They have Moses and the prophets;
16:30 He said, 'No, father A; B
19: 9 because he too is a son of A. D
20:37 where he speaks of the Lord as the God of A, A
Jn 8:33 descendants of A and have never been slaves C
8:37 I know that you are descendants of A; C
8:39 They answered him, "A is our father."
8:39 you would be doing what A did,
8:40 This is not what A did.
8:52 A died, and so did the prophets;
8:53 Are you greater than our father A, who died? B
8:56 Your ancestor A rejoiced
8:57 not yet fifty years old, and have you seen A?"
8:58 "Very truly, I tell you, before A was, I am."
Ac 3:13 The God of A, the God of Isaac, A
3:25 to A, 'And in your descendants all the families of
7: 2 of glory appeared to our ancestor A when he was
7: 8 And so A became the father of Isaac
7:16 in the tomb that A had bought for a sum of silver
7:17 of the promise that God had made to A,
7:32 the God of A, Isaac, and Jacob.' A
Ro 4: 1 What then are we to say was gained by A,
4: 2 For if A was justified by works,
4: 3 "A believed God, and it was reckoned to him
4: 9 "Faith was reckoned to A as righteousness."
4:12 the example of the faith that our ancestor A had
4:13 the world did not come to A or to his descendants
4:16 but also to those who share the faith of A (for he is
11: 1 I myself am an Israelite, a descendant of A, C
2Co 11:22 Are they descendants of A? C
Gal 3: 6 as A "believed God, and it was reckoned to him
3: 7 those who believe are the descendants of A. C
3: 8 declared the gospel beforehand to A, saying,
3: 9 who believe are blessed with A who believed.
3:14 that in Christ Jesus the blessing of A might come
3:16 the promises were made to A and to his offspring;
3:18 but God granted it to A through the promise.
Gal 4:22 For it is written that A had two sons,
Heb 2:16 come to help angels, but the descendants of A. C
6:13 When God made a promise to A,
6:15 And thus A, having patiently endured,
7: 1 met A as he was returning from defeating
7: 2 to him A apportioned "one-tenth of everything."
7: 4 A the patriarch gave him a tenth of the spoils.
7: 5 though these also are descended from A.
7: 6 from A and blessed him who had received
7: 9 who receives tithes, paid tithes through A,
11: 8 By faith A obeyed when he was called to set out
11:17 By faith A, when put to the test, offered up Isaac.
Jas 2:21 Was not our ancestor A justified by works
2:23 that says, "A believed God, and it was reckoned
1Pe 3: 6 Thus Sarah obeyed A and called him lord.
Tob 4:12 Remember, my son, that Noah, A, Isaac,
14: 7 and live in safety forever in the land of A,
Jdt 8:26 Remember what he did with A,
AdE 13:15 And now, O Lord God and King, God of A, A
14:18 except in you, O Lord God of A. A
Sir 44:19 A was the great father of a multitude of nations,
44:22 the same assurance for the sake of his father A. B
51:12 *Give thanks to the shield of A,*
Bar 2:34 to A, Isaac, and Jacob, and they will rule over it;
Aza 1:12 for the sake of A your beloved and for the sake
1Mc 2:52 Was not A found faithful when tested,
12:21 that they are brothers and are of the family of A.
2Mc 1: 2 and may he remember his covenant with A
Man 1: 1 of A and Isaac and Jacob and
1: 8 for A and Isaac and Jacob,
3Mc 6: 3 look upon the descendants of A, C
2Es 1:39 to them I will give as leaders A,
3:13 for yourself one of them, whose name was A;
6: 8 He said to me, "From A to Isaac,
7:*106* [36] do we find that first A prayed for the people
4Mc 6:17 the children of A, think so basely that out
6:22 O children of A, die nobly for your religion!
7:19 like our patriarchs A and Isaac and Jacob,
9:21 the courageous youth, worthy of A, did not groan,
13:17 we so die, A and Isaac and Jacob will welcome us,
14:20 she was of the same mind as A.
15:28 of God-fearing A she remembered his fortitude.
16:20 For his sake also our father A was zealous B
16:25 as do A and Isaac and Jacob and all the patriarchs.
17: 6 children were true descendants of father A. BC
18: 1 O Israelite children, offspring of the seed of A,
18:20 of the daughter of A to the catapult and back again
18:23 But the sons of A with their

ABRAHAM'S (18) [ABRAHAM]

Ge 17:23 every male among the men of A house,
20:18 the house of Abimelech because of Sarah, A wife.
22:23 These eight Milcah bore to Nahor, A brother.
23:20 in it passed from the Hittites into A possession as
24:15 the wife of Nahor, A brother,
24:34 So he said, "I am A servant.
24:52 When A servant heard their words,
24:59 and her nurse along with A servant and his men.
25: 7 This is the length of A life,
25:12 These are the descendants of Ishmael, A son,
25:19 These are the descendants of Isaac, A son:
26:24 your offspring numerous for my servant A sake."
28: 9 and took Mahalath daughter of A son Ishmael,
1Ch 1:32 The sons of Keturah, A concubine:
Jn 8:39 Jesus said to them, "If you were A children,
Ac 13:26 "My brothers, you descendants of A family,
Ro 9: 7 and not all of A children are his true descendants;
Gal 3:29 if you belong to Christ, then you are A offspring,

ABRAM‡ (54) [=ABRAHAM]

Ge 11:26 he became the father of A, Nahor, and Haran.
11:27 Terah was the father of A, Nahor, and Haran;
11:29 A and Nahor took wives; the name of Abram's
11:31 Terah took his son A and his grandson Lot son
12: 1 Now the LORD said to A,
12: 4 So A went, as the LORD had told him;
12: 4 A was seventy-five years old when he departed
12: 5 A took his wife Sarai and his brother's son Lot,
12: 6 A passed through the land to the place
12: 7 Then the LORD appeared to A, and said,
12: 9 And A journeyed on by stages toward the Negeb.
12:10 A went down to Egypt to reside there as an alien,
12:14 When A entered Egypt the Egyptians saw that
12:16 And for her sake he dealt well with A;
12:18 So Pharaoh called A, and said,
13: 1 So A went up from Egypt, he and his wife,
13: 2 A was very rich in livestock, in silver, and in gold.
13: 4 and there A called on the name of the LORD.
13: 5 Now Lot, who went with A,
13: 8 Then A said to Lot, "Let there be no strife
13:12 A settled in the land of Canaan,
13:14 The LORD said to A, after Lot had separated
13:18 So A moved his tent, and came and settled by
14:13 Then one who had escaped came and told A
14:13 of Aner; these were allies of A.
14:14 A heard that his nephew had been taken captive,
14:19 "Blessed be A by God Most High,
14:20 And A gave him one tenth of everything.
14:21 Then the king of Sodom said to A,
14:22 But A said to the king of Sodom,
14:23 so that you might not say, 'I have made A rich.'
15: 1 came to A in a vision, "Do not be afraid, A,
15: 2 But A said, "O Lord GOD,
15: 3 And A said, "You have given me no offspring,
15:11 down on the carcasses, A drove them away.
15:12 the sun was going down, a deep sleep fell upon A,
Ge 15:13 Then the LORD said to A,
15:18 On that day the LORD made a covenant with A,
16: 2 to A, "You see that the LORD has prevented me
16: 2 And A listened to the voice of Sarai.
16: 3 after A had lived ten years in the land of Canaan,
16: 3 and gave her to her husband A as a wife.
16: 5 Then Sarai said to A, "May the wrong done to me
16: 6 A said to Sarai, "Your slave-girl is in your power;
16:15 Hagar bore A a son; and A named his son,
16:16 A was eighty-six years old
17: 1 When A was ninety-nine years old, the LORD appeared to A, and said to him,
17: 3 Then A fell on his face; and God said to him,
17: 5 No longer shall your name be A,
1Ch 1:27 A, that is, Abraham.
Ne 9: 7 the God who chose A and brought him out of Ur

ABRAM'S (7) [=ABRAHAM]

Ge 11:29 the name of A wife was Sarai,
11:31 and his daughter-in-law Sarai, his son A wife,
12:17 with great plagues because of Sarai, A wife.
13: 7 between the herders of A livestock and the herders
14:12 the son of A brother, who lived in Sodom,
16: 1 Now Sarai, A wife, bore him no children.
16: 3 A wife, took Hagar the Egyptian, her slave-girl,

ABREK See Index to Footnotes

ABROAD (23)

Ge 10:18 Afterward the families of the Canaanites spread a.
10:32 from these the nations spread a on the earth after
11: 4 otherwise we shall be scattered a upon the face of
11: 8 So the LORD scattered them a from there over
11: 9 and from there the LORD scattered them a over
28:14 and you shall spread a to the west and to the east
Lev 18: 9 whether born at home or born a.
1Sa 2:24 that I hear the people of the LORD spreading a.
1Ch 13: 2 let us send a to our kindred who remain in all
Job 15:23 They wander a for bread, saying, 'Where is it?'
Ps 41: 6 when they go out, they tell it a.
68: 9 Rain in abundance, O God, you showered a;
Pr 5:16 Should your springs be scattered a,
SS 4:16 that its fragrance may be wafted a.
Isa 16: 8 their shoots once spread a and crossed over
Zec 2: 6 I have spread you a like the four winds of heaven,
Lk 5:15 more than ever the word about Jesus spread a;
2Co 9: 9 it is written, "He scatters a, he gives to the poor;
Rev 16:14 who go a to the kings of the whole world,
Wis 18:10 for their children was spread a.
Sir Pr: 3 for those living a who wished to gain learning
2Mc 4:39 and when report of them had spread a,
3Mc 5:26 The rays of the sun were not yet shed a,

ABROGATION (1)

Heb 7:18 the a of an earlier commandment

ABRON (1)

Jdt 2:24 the fortified towns along the brook A,

ABRONAH (2)

Nu 33:34 They set out from Jotbathah and camped at A.
33:35 They set out from A and camped at Ezion-geber.

ABSALOM‡ (108) [ABSALOM'S]

2Sa 3: 3 the third, A son of Maacah,
13: 1 A had a beautiful sister whose name was Tamar;
13:20 Her brother A said to her,
13:22 But A spoke to Amnon neither good nor bad; for A hated Amnon,
13:23 two full years A had sheepshearers at Baal-hazor,
13:23 and A invited all the king's sons.
13:24 A came to the king, and said,
13:25 But the king said to A, "No, my son,
13:26 Then A said, "If not, please let my brother Amnon
13:27 But A pressed him until he let Amnon and all
13:27 A made a feast like a king's feast.
13:28 Then A commanded his servants,
13:29 servants of A did to Amnon as A had commanded.
13:30 to David that A had killed all the king's sons,
13:32 by A from the day Amnon raped his sister Tamar.
13:34 But A fled. When the young man who kept watch
13:37 But A fled, and went to Talmai son of Ammihud,
13:38 A, having fled to Geshur, stayed there three years.
13:39 the heart of the king went out, yearning for A;
14: 1 that the king's mind was on A.
14:21 go, bring back the young man A."
14:23 went to Geshur, and brought A to Jerusalem.
14:24 So A went to his own house,
14:25 to be praised so much for his beauty as A;
14:27 There were born to A three sons,
14:28 So A lived two full years in Jerusalem,
14:29 Then A sent for Joab to send him to the king;
14:31 Then Joab rose and went to A at his house,
14:32 A answered Joab, "Look, I sent word to you:
14:33 and told him; and he summoned A.
14:33 before the king; and the king kissed A.
15: 1 After this A got himself a chariot and horses,
15: 2 A used to rise early and stand beside the road into
15: 2 A would call out and say,
15: 3 A would say, "See, your claims are good
15: 4 A said moreover, "If only I were judge in the land!
15: 6 Thus A did to every Israelite who came to the king
15: 6 so A stole the hearts of the people of Israel.

2Sa 15: 7 At the end of four years A said to the king,
15:10 But A sent secret messengers throughout all
15:10 A has become king at Hebron!"
15:11 Two hundred men from Jerusalem went with A;
15:12 While A was offering the sacrifices,
15:12 and the people with A kept increasing.
15:13 "The hearts of the Israelites have gone after A."
15:14 or there will be no escape for us from A.
15:31 among the conspirators with A.
15:34 But if you return to the city and say to A,
15:37 just as A was entering Jerusalem.
16: 8 the kingdom into the hand of your son A.
16:15 Now A and all the Israelites came to Jerusalem;
16:16 Hushai the Archite, David's friend, came to A,
16:16 Hushai said to A, "Long live the king!
16:17 A said to Hushai, "Is this your loyalty
16:18 Hushai said to A, "No;
16:20 Then A said to Ahithophel, "Give us your counsel;
16:21 to A, "Go in to your father's concubines,
16:22 So they pitched a tent for A upon the roof;
16:22 and A went in to his father's concubines in
16:23 both by David and by A.
17: 1 Moreover Ahithophel said to A,
17: 4 The advice pleased A and all the elders of Israel.
17: 5 Then A said, "Call Hushai the Archite also,
17: 6 When Hushai came to A, A said to him,
17: 7 Then Hushai said to A, "This time the counsel
17: 9 a slaughter among the troops who follow A.'
17:14 A and all the men of Israel said,
17:14 so that the LORD might bring ruin on A.
17:15 and so did Ahithophel counsel A and the elders
17:18 But a boy saw them, and told A;
17:24 A crossed the Jordan with all the men of Israel.
17:25 Now A had set Amasa over the army in the place
17:26 Israelites and A encamped in the land of Gilead.
18: 5 "Deal gently for my sake with the young man A."
18: 5 to all the commanders concerning A.
18: 9 A happened to meet the servants of David.
18: 9 A was riding on his mule,
18:10 and told Joab, "I saw A hanging in an oak."
18:12 For my sake protect the young man A!
18:14 and thrust them into the heart of A,
18:15 surrounded A and struck him, and killed him.
18:17 They took A, threw him into a great pit in
18:18 Now A in his lifetime had taken and set up
18:29 The king said, "Is it well with the young man A?"
18:32 "Is it well with the young man A?"
18:33 he said, "O my son A, my son, my son A!
18:33 Would I had died instead of you, O A, my son,
19: 1 "The king is weeping and mourning for A."
19: 4 "O my son A, O A, my son, my son!"
19: 6 that if A were alive and all of us were dead today,
19: 9 and now he has fled out of the land because of A.
19:10 A, whom we anointed over us, is dead in battle.
20: 6 Sheba son of Bichri will do us more harm than A;
1Ki 1: 6 and he was born next after A.
2: 7 when I fled from your brother A.
2:28 though he had not supported A—
1Ch 3: 2 the third A, son of Maacah, daughter
2Ch 11:20 After her he took Maacah daughter of A,
11:21 of A more than all his other wives
Ps 3: T *A Psalm of David, when he fled from his son A.*
1Mc 11:70 of them was left except Mattathias son of A
13:11 He sent Jonathan son of A to Joppa,
2Mc 11:17 John and A, who were sent by you,

ABSALOM'S (5) [ABSALOM]

2Sa 13: 4 "I love Tamar, my brother A sister."
13:20 a desolate woman, in her brother A house.
14:30 So A servants set the field on fire.
17:20 When A servants came to the woman at the house,
18:18 It is called A Monument to this day.

ABSENCE (2) [ABSENT]

1Co 16:17 because they have made up for your a;
Php 2:12 but much more now in my a,

ABSENT (9) [ABSENCE]

Ge 31:49 when we are a one from the other.
1Co 5: 3 For though a in body, I am present in spirit;
2Co 10:11 that what we say by letter when a,
13: 2 and I warn them now while a,
Php 1:27 whether I come and see you or am a and hear
Col 2: 5 For though I am a in body,
Wis 11:11 Whether a or present, they were equally distressed,
14:17 so that by their zeal they might flatter the a one as
1Mc 4: 4 while the division was still a from the camp.

ABSHAI See Index to Footnotes

ABSOLUTE (1)

1Ti 5: 2 to younger women as sisters—with a purity.

ABSOLVE (1) [ABSOLVED]

Dt 21: 8 A, O LORD, your people Israel,

ABSOLVED (1) [ABSOLVE]

Dt 21: 8 Then they will be a of bloodguilt.

ABSTAIN (12) [ABSTINENCE]

Ac 15:20 to them to a only from things polluted by idols
15:29 that you a from what has been sacrificed to idols
21:25 that they should a from what has been sacrificed
Ro 14: 3 Those who eat must not despise those who a, and
those who a must not pass judgment
14: 6 while those who a, a in honor of the Lord
1Th 4: 3 that you a from fornication;
5:22 a from every form of evil.
1Pe 2:11 to a from the desires of the flesh that wage war
4Mc 1:33 that when we are attracted to forbidden foods we a
1:34 we a because of domination by reason.

ABSTINENCE (2) [ABSTAIN]

Zec 7: 3 "Should I mourn and practice a in the fifth month,
1Ti 4: 3 They forbid marriage and demand a from foods,

ABUBUS (2)

1Mc 16:11 of A had been appointed governor over the plain
16:15 The son of A received them treacherously in

ABUNDANCE (79) [ABUNDANT, ABUNDANTLY]

Ge 41:49 So Joseph stored up grain in such a—
Dt 28:47 and with gladness of heart for the a of everything,
33:15 and the a of the everlasting hills;
1Ki 1:19 fatted cattle, and sheep in a,
1:25 fatted cattle, and sheep in a,
1Ch 22:15 You have an a of workers:
29: 2 all sorts of precious stones, and marble in a.
29:16 all this a that we have provided for building you
29:21 and sacrifices in a for all Israel;
2Ch 2: 9 to prepare timber for me in a,
14:15 and carried away sheep and goats in a,
18: 2 Ahab slaughtered an a of sheep and oxen for him
20:25 the booty, because of its a.
24:11 they did day after day, and collected money in a.
31: 5 people of Israel gave in a the first fruits of grain,
32: 4 the Assyrian kings come and find water in a?"
32: 5 and made weapons and shields in a.
32:29 and flocks and herds in a;
Ne 5:18 and every ten days skins of wine in a;
9:25 vineyards, olive orchards, and fruit trees in a;
Job 36:31 by these he governs peoples; he gives food in a.
Ps 5: 7 But I, through the a of your steadfast love,
36: 8 They feast on the a of your house,
37:16 a little that the righteous person has than the a
37:19 in the days of famine they have a.
49: 6 those who trust in their wealth and boast of the a
68: 9 Rain in a, O God, you showered abroad;
69:13 O God, in the a of your steadfast love, answer me.
72:16 May there be a of grain in the land;
78:25 he sent them food in a.
105:40 and gave them food from heaven in a.
106: 7 not remember the a of your steadfast love,
106:45 and showed compassion according to the a
Pr 11:14 but in an a of counselors there is safety.
20:15 There is gold, and a of costly stones;
21: 5 The plans of the diligent lead surely to a,
24: 6 and in a of counselors there is victory.
Isa 7:22 and will eat curds because of the a of milk
15: 7 the a they have gained and what they have laid
30:33 and wide, with fire and wood in a;
33: 6 a of salvation, wisdom, and knowledge;
33:23 Then prey and spoil in a will be divided;
60: 5 because the a of the sea shall be brought to you,
63: 7 according to the a of his steadfast love.
Jer 33: 6 I will heal them and reveal to them a of prosperity
40:12 they gathered wine and summer fruits in great a.
La 3:32 he will have compassion according to the a
Eze 7:11 None of them shall remain, not their a,
27:12 Tarshish did business with you out of the a
28:16 the a of your trade you were filled with violence,
Na 2: 9 An a of every precious thing!"
Zec 14:14 gold, silver, and garments in great a.
Mt 12:34 For out of the a of the heart the mouth speaks.
13:12 more will be given, and they will have an a;
25:29 more will be given, and they will have an a;
Mk 12:44 For all of them have contributed out of their a;
Lk 6:45 it is out of the a of the heart that the mouth speaks.
12:15 for one's life does not consist in the a
21: 4 for all of them have contributed out of their a,
Ro 5:17 surely will those who receive the a of grace and
2Co 8:14 your present a and their need, so that their a may
be for your need,
9: 8 to provide you with every blessing in a,
1Pe 1: 2 May grace and peace be yours in a.
2Pe 1: 2 and peace be yours in a in the knowledge of God
Jude 1: 2 May mercy, peace, and love be yours in a.
Tob 2: 2 the table was set for me and an a of food placed
Sir 45:20 and prepared bread of first fruits in a;
1Mc 10:21 and equipped them with arms in a.
1Es 8:20 a hundred baths of wine, and salt in a.
3Mc 5: 2 maddened by the lavish a of drink,
5:10 a great a of wine and satiated with frankincense,
6: 4 Pharaoh with his a of chariots,
2Es 1:20 not split the rock so that waters flowed in a?
2:27 but you shall rejoice and have a.
6:44 Immediately fruit came forth in endless a and
6:56 and you have compared their a to a drop from
7:*123* [53] and in which are a and healing,
15:41 and all the streams shall be filled with the a

ABUNDANT‡ (48) [ABUNDANCE]

Nu 24: 7 and his seed shall have a water,
1Ch 12:40 a provisions of meal, cakes of figs,
2Ch 11:23 he gave them a provisions,
Job 37:23 and a righteousness he will not violate.
Ps 31:19 O how a is your goodness that you have laid up
37:11 and delight themselves in a prosperity.
51: 1 to your a mercy blot out my transgressions.
52: 7 trusted in a riches, and sought refuge in wealth!"
69:16 according to your a mercy, turn to me.
145: 7 They shall celebrate the fame of your a goodness,
147: 5 Great is our Lord, and a in power;
Pr 3: 2 and years of life and a welfare they will give you.
14: 4 a crops come by the strength of the ox.
Isa 23:18 but her merchandise will supply a food
Eze 17: 5 A plant by a waters, he set it like a willow twig.
17: 8 to good soil by a waters, so that it might produce
19:10 fruitful and full of branches from a water.
27:16 with you because of your a goods;
27:18 Damascus traded with you for your a goods—
27:33 with your a wealth and merchandise you enriched
31: 5 from a water in its shoots.
31: 7 for its roots went down to a water.
32:13 I will destroy all its livestock from beside a waters;
36:29 and make it a and lay no famine upon you.
36:30 the fruit of the tree and the produce of the field a,
Da 4: 1 May you have a prosperity!
4:12 Its foliage was beautiful, its fruit a,
4:21 and its fruit a, and which provided food for all,
6:25 "May you have a prosperity!
11:13 with a great army and a supplies.
Joel 2:23 he has poured down for you a rain,
Jn 3:23 at Aenon near Salim because water was a there;
2Co 1: 5 For just as the sufferings of Christ are a for us, so
also our consolation is a through Christ.
2: 4 but to let you know the a love that I have for you.
8: 2 for during a severe ordeal of affliction, their a joy
AdE 1: 7 There was a sweet wine, such as
10: 6 and there was light and sun and a water—
11:10 there came a great river, with a water;
Wis 11: 7 you gave them a water unexpectedly,
Sir 14:18 Like a leaves on a spreading tree that sheds some
24:17 and my blossoms become glorious and a fruit.
24:29 For her thoughts are more a than the sea,
Aza 1:19 deal with us in your patience and in your a mercy.
1Mc 6: 6 the arms, supplies, and a spoils that they had taken
2Es 7:*56* but silver is more a than gold,
7:*57* those that are a or those that are rare?"
7:*136* [66] and a in compassion,

ABUNDANTLY (19) [ABUNDANCE]

Ge 30:30 before I came, and it has increased a;
41:47 the seven plenteous years the earth produced a.
Nu 20:11 water came out a, and the congregation
Dt 30: 9 the LORD your God will make you a prosperous
2Ch 31: 5 and they brought in a the tithe of everything.
Job 36:28 the skies pour down and drop upon mortals a.
Ps 31:23 but a repays the one who acts haughtily.
65:10 You water its furrows a, settling its ridges,
78:15 and gave them drink a as from the deep.
104:16 The trees of the LORD are watered a,
132:15 I will a bless its provisions;
Isa 35: 2 it shall blossom a, and rejoice with joy
55: 7 and to our God, for he will a pardon.
Lk 12:16 "The land of a rich man produced a.
Jn 10:10 I came that they may have life, and have it a.
2Co 9: 8 you may share a in every good work.
Eph 3:20 to accomplish a far more than all we can ask
Php 1:26 that I may share a in your boasting in Christ Jesus
2Th 1: 3 as is right, because your faith is growing a,

ABUSE (19) [ABUSED, ABUSIVE]

Ex 22:22 You shall not a any widow or orphan.
22:23 If you do a them, when they cry out to me,
Pr 9: 7 Whoever corrects a scoffer wins a;
22:10 quarreling and a will cease.
Jer 38:19 be handed over to them and they would a me."
Lk 6:28 pray for those who a you.
Heb 10:33 sometimes being publicly exposed to a
11:26 He considered a suffered for the Christ to
13:13 the camp and bear the a he endured.
1Pe 2:23 When he was abused, he did not return a;
3: 9 Do not repay evil for evil or a for a;
3:16 those who a you for your good conduct
Sir 7:20 Do not a slaves who work faithfully,
19:25 there are people who a favors to gain a verdict.
27:15 and their a is grievous to hear.
27:21 and there is reconciliation after a,
27:28 Mockery and a issue from the proud,
2Es 10:22 our children have suffered a,

ABUSED (5) [ABUSE]

Dt 28:29 and you shall be continually a and robbed,
28:33 you shall be continually a and crushed,
Jdg 19:25 and a her all through the night until the morning.
1Pe 2:23 When he was a, he did not return abuse;
2Es 9: 9 those who have now a my ways shall be amazed,

ABUSIVE (6) [ABUSE]

Eze 35:12 have heard all the a speech that you uttered
Col 3: 8 malice, slander, and a language from your mouth.
2Ti 3: 2 a, disobedient to their parents, ungrateful, unholy,
Sir 18:18 A fool is ungracious and a,
23:15 to using a language will never become disciplined
41:22 of a words, before friends—do not be insulting

ABYSS (9)

Lk 8:31 not to order them to go back into the a.
Ro 10: 7 "or 'Who will descend into the a?' "

Tob 13: 2 and he brings up from the great a,
Sir 1: 3 height of heaven, the breadth of the earth, the a,
16:18 the a and the earth, tremble at his visitation!
24: 5 of heaven and traversed the depths of the a.
24:29 and her counsel deeper than the great a.
42:18 He searches out the a and the human heart;
2Es 16:57 He searches the a and its treasures;

ACACIA (28)

Ex 25: 5 tanned rams' skins, fine leather, a wood,
25:10 They shall make an ark of a wood;
25:13 You shall make poles of a wood,
25:23 You shall make a table of a wood,
25:28 You shall make the poles of a wood,
26:15 You shall make upright frames of a wood for
26:26 You shall make bars of a wood,
26:32 You shall hang it on four pillars of a overlaid
26:37 You shall make for the screen five pillars of a,
27: 1 You shall make the altar of a wood,
27: 6 poles of a wood, and overlay them with bronze;
30: 1 you shall make it of a wood.
30: 5 You shall make the poles of a wood,
35: 7 tanned rams' skins, and fine leather; a wood,
35:24 and everyone who possessed a wood of any use in
36:20 the upright frames for the tabernacle of a wood.
36:31 He made bars of a wood,
36:36 For it he made four pillars of a,
37: 1 Bezalel made the ark of a wood;
37: 4 He made poles of a wood,
37:10 He also made the table of a wood,
37:15 He made the poles of a wood to carry the table,
37:25 He made the altar of incense of a wood,
37:28 And he made the poles of a wood,
38: 1 the altar of burnt offering also of a wood;
38: 6 he made the poles of a wood,
Dt 10: 3 So I made an ark of a wood,
Isa 41:19 I will put in the wilderness the cedar, the a,

ACCAD (1)

Ge 10:10 Erech, and A, all of them in the land of Shinar.

ACCENT (1)

Mt 26:73 also one of them, for your a betrays you."

ACCEPT (91) [ACCEPTABLE, ACCEPTANCE, ACCEPTED, ACCEPTING, ACCEPTS]

Ge 21:30 "These seven ewe lambs you shall a
23:13 a it from me, so that I may bury my dead there."
32:20 I shall see his face; perhaps he will a me."
33:10 then a my present from my hand;
33:11 Please a my gift that is brought to you,
Ex 22:11 the owner shall a the oath,
Lev 22:25 nor shall you a any such animals from a foreigner
Nu 3:12 I hereby a the Levites from among the Israelites
3:41 But you shall a the Levites for me—
3:45 A the Levites as substitutes for all the firstborn
3:47 you shall a five shekels apiece,
7: 5 A these from them, that they may be used in doing
35:31 Moreover you shall a no ransom for the life of
35:32 Nor shall you a ransom for one who has fled to
Dt 16:19 and you must not a bribes,
33:11 his substance, and a the work of his hands;
1Sa 2:15 he will not a boiled meat from you, but only raw."
10: 4 which you shall a from them.
26:19 up against me, may he a an offering;
1Ki 2:42 And you said to me, 'The sentence is fair; I a.'
2Ki 5:15 please a a present from your servant."
5:16 whom I serve, I will a nothing!"
5:16 He urged him to a, but he refused.
5:23 Naaman said, "Please a two talents."
5:26 Is this a time to a money and to a clothing,
12: 7 Now therefore do not a any more money
12: 8 that they would neither a more money from
Est 4: 4 but he would not a them.
Job 21:29 and do you not a their testimony,
42: 8 for you, for I will a his prayer not to deal with you
Ps 50: 9 I will not a a bull from your house,
119:108 A my offerings of praise, O LORD,
Pr 2: 1 if you a my words and treasure
4:10 Hear, my child, and a my words,
6:35 He will a no compensation,
17:23 The wicked a a concealed bribe to pervert
19:20 Listen to advice and a instruction,
Ecc 5:19 to a their lot and find enjoyment in their toil—
Isa 29:24 and those who grumble will a instruction.
Jer 7:28 of the LORD their God, and did not a discipline;
14:10 therefore the LORD does not a them,
14:12 and grain offering, I do not a them;
25:28 they refuse to a the cup from your hand to drink,
32:33 they would not listen and a correction.
Eze 20:40 in the land; there I will a them,
20:41 As a pleasing odor I will a you,
43:27 and I will a you, says the Lord GOD.
Hos 8:13 though they eat flesh, the LORD does not a them.
14: 2 a that which is good, and we will offer
Am 5:22 and grain offerings, I will not a them;
Zep 3: 7 "Surely the city will fear me, it will a correction;
Mal 1:10 and I will not a an offering from your hands.
1:13 Shall I a that from your hand?
Mt 11:14 and if you are willing to a it,
19:11 "Not everyone can a this teaching,
19:12 Let anyone a this who can."
Mk 4:20 they hear the word and a it and bear fruit,
Lk 14:18 and see it; please a my regrets.'
14:19 to try them out; please a my regrets.'
Jn 1:11 and his own people did not a him.
5:34 Not that I a such human testimony,
5:41 I do not a glory from human beings.
5:43 come in my Father's name, and you do not a me;
5:43 if another comes in his own name, you will a him.
5:44 when you a glory from one another and do
6:60 "This teaching is difficult; who can a it?"
8:43 It is because you cannot a my word.
Ac 22:18 because they will not a your testimony about me.'
24:15 a hope that they themselves also a—
2Co 6: 1 we urge you also not to a the grace of God in vain.
11:16 but if you do, then a me as a fool,
1Ti 5:19 Never a any accusation against an elder except on
Heb 11:35 Others were tortured, refusing to a a release,
1Pe 2:13 For the Lord's sake a the authority
2:18 a the authority of your masters with all deference,
3: 1 in the same way, a the authority of your husbands,
5: 5 you who are younger must a the authority of
Jdt 11: 5 Judith answered him, "A the words of your slave,
Sir 2: 4 A whatever befalls you, and in times
6:23 Listen, my child, and a my judgment;
7: 9 an offering to the Most High God, he will a it."
18:14 He has compassion on those who a his discipline
32:14 The one who seeks God will a his discipline,
35:14 Do not offer him a bribe, for he will not a it;
36:26 A woman will a any man as a husband,
1Mc 10:46 they did not believe or a them,
15:20 And it has seemed good to us to a the shield
2Mc 1:26 A this sacrifice on behalf of all your people Israel
7:29 A death, so that in God's mercy I may get you
4Mc 8:17 and exhorted us to a kind treatment

ACCEPTABLE (37) [ACCEPT]

Lev 1: 4 it shall be a in your behalf as atonement for you.
7:18 it shall not be a, nor shall it be credited to
19: 5 offer it in such a way that it is a on your behalf.
19: 7 it is an abomination; it will not be a.
22:19 to be a in your behalf it shall be a male
22:20 for it will not be a in your behalf.
22:21 to be a it must be perfect;
22:27 on it shall be a as the LORD's offering by fire.
22:29 you shall sacrifice it so that it may be a
Ps 19:14 of my mouth and the meditation of my heart be a
51:17 The sacrifice a to God is a broken spirit;
69:13 At an a time, O God, in the abundance
Pr 10:32 The lips of the righteous know what is a,
21: 3 and justice is more a to the LORD than sacrifice.
Isa 58: 5 Will you call this a fast, a day a to the LORD?
60: 7 they shall be a on my altar,
Jer 6:20 Your burnt offerings are not a,
Da 4:27 Therefore, O king, may my counsel be a to you:
Ac 10:35 and does what is right is a to him.
Ro 12: 1 as a living sacrifice, holy and a to God,
12: 2 what is good and a and perfect.
14:18 The one who thus serves Christ is a to God
15:16 so that the offering of the Gentiles may be a,
15:31 my ministry to Jerusalem may be a to the saints,
2Co 6: 2 For he says, "At an a time I have listened to you,
6: 2 now is the a time; see, now is the day of salvation!
8:12 the gift is a according to what one has—
Php 4:18 a sacrifice a and pleasing to God.
Col 3:20 for this is your a duty in the Lord.
1Ti 2: 3 and is a in the sight of God our Savior,
Heb 11: 4 to God a more a sacrifice than Cain's.
12:28 to God an a worship with reverence and awe;
1Pe 2: 5 to offer spiritual sacrifices a to God
Wis 9:12 Then my works will be a,
Sir 2: 5 For gold is tested in the fire, and those found a,
34:22 the gifts of the lawless are not a.
35: 9 The sacrifice of the righteous is a,

ACCEPTANCE‡ (5) [ACCEPT]

Lev 1: 3 for a in your behalf before the LORD.
23:11 the sheaf before the LORD, that you may find a;
Ro 11:15 what will their a be but life from the dead!
1Ti 1:15 The saying is sure and worthy of full a,
4: 9 The saying is sure and worthy of full a.

ACCEPTED‡ (31) [ACCEPT]

Ge 4: 7 If you do well, will you not be a?
Lev 22:23 but it will not be a for a vow.
22:25 they shall not be a in your behalf.
Dt 33: 3 they marched at your heels, a direction from you.
Jdg 13:23 not have a a burnt offering and a grain offering
18:20 Then the priest a the offer.
Est 9:27 the Jews established and a as a custom
Job 33:26 Then he prays to God, and is a by him,
42: 9 and the LORD a Job's prayer.
Isa 56: 7 their burnt offerings and their sacrifices will be a
Jer 2:30 down your children; they a no correction.
Zep 3: 2 It has listened to no voice; it has a no correction.
Lk 4:24 no prophet is a in the prophet's hometown.
Jn 3:33 Whoever has a his testimony has certified this,
Ac 8:14 the apostles at Jerusalem heard that Samaria had a
11: 1 that the Gentiles had also a the word of God.
2Co 8:17 For he not only a our appeal,
11: 4 or a different gospel from the one you a,
1Th 2:13 you a it not as a human word but
Heb 10:34 and you cheerfully a the plundering
AdE 9:23 So the Jews a what Mordecai had written to them
Wis 3: 6 and like a sacrificial burnt offering he a them.
Sir 35:20 to the Lord will be a,
Aza 1:16 a contrite heart and a humble spirit may we be a,
1Mc 1:43 All the Gentiles a the command of the king.
6:60 to the Jews an offer of peace, and they a it.
9:31 So Jonathan a the leadership at that time in place
14:47 So Simon a and agreed to be high priest,
2Mc 12: 4 When they a, because they wished
3Mc 3:17 They a our presence by word,
6:26 toward us and often have a willingly the worst

ACCEPTING (7) [ACCEPT]

2Ki 5:20 that Aramean Naaman off too lightly by not a
Isa 33:15 who wave away a bribe instead of a it,
Ac 18:14 be justified in a the complaint of you Jews;
2Co 11: 8 I robbed other churches by a support from them
1Pe 3: 5 to adorn themselves by a the authority
3Jn 1: 7 a no support from non-believers.
Wis 12:24 a as gods those animals that

ACCEPTS (6) [ACCEPT]

Dt 20:11 If it a your terms of peace and surrenders to you,
Ps 6: 9 has heard my supplication; the LORD a my prayer.
Mal 2:13 because he no longer regards the offering or a it
Jn 3:32 yet no one a his testimony.
Heb 12: 6 and chastises every child whom he a."
Sir 3:17 then you will be loved by those whom God a.

ACCESS (9)

Est 1:14 who had a to the king, and sat first in
Pr 18:16 A gift opens doors; it gives a to the great.
Zec 3: 7 the right of a among those who are standing here.
Ro 5: 2 through whom we have obtained a to this grace
Eph 2:18 him both of us have a in one Spirit to the Father.
3:12 in whom we have a to God in boldness
2Mc 12:21 and difficult of a because of the narrowness of all
14: 3 to be safe or to have a again to the holy altar,
1Es 2:24 you will no longer have a to Coelesyria

ACCESSION (1)

Ezr 4: 6 In the reign of Ahasuerus, in his a year,

ACCESSORIES (1)

Nu 3:36 the bars, the pillars, the bases, and all their a—

ACCLAIMED (1)

Nu 23:21 a as a king among them.

ACCHO (KJV) See ACCO

ACCO (1)

Jdg 1:31 Asher did not drive out the inhabitants of A,

ACCOMMODATED (1)

3Mc 3:20 a ourselves to their folly and did as was proper,

ACCOMPANIED (14) [ACCOMPANY]

2Ch 29:27 a by the instruments of King David of Israel.
30:21 a by loud instruments for the LORD.
Mk 16:20 ⟦and confirmed the message by the signs that a it.⟧
Ac 1:21 of the men who have a us during all the time that
10:23 and some of the believers from Joppa a him.
11:12 These six brothers also a me,
15:38 in Pamphylia and had not a them in the work.
18:18 and sailed for Syria, a by Priscilla and Aquila.
20: 4 He was a by Sopater son of Pyrrhus from Beroea,
27: 2 we put to sea, a by Aristarchus,
1Co 9: 5 not have the right to be a by a believing wife,
Jdt 10:10 they had done this, Judith went out, a by her maid.
1Mc 12:47 while one thousand a him.
4Mc 4: 5 to our country a by the accursed Simon and

ACCOMPANIMENT (1) [ACCOMPANY]

3Mc 6:35 to the a of joyous thanksgiving and psalms.

ACCOMPANY (8) [ACCOMPANIED, ACCOMPANIMENT, ACCOMPANYING]

Mk 16:17 ⟦And these signs will a those who believe:⟧
Ac 16: 3 Paul wanted Timothy to a him;
1Co 16: 4 that I should go also, they will a me.
Tob 5:10 Can you a him and guide him?
5:17 my son, a you both for your safety."
5:22 For a good angel will a him;
Jdt 10:17 from their number a hundred men to a her
2Mc 3:24 as to a him were astounded by the power of God,

ACCOMPANYING (1) [ACCOMPANY]

Nu 6:17 the priest also shall make the a grain offering

ACCOMPLISH‡ (15) [ACCOMPLISHED, ACCOMPLISHES, ACCOMPLISHING, ACCOMPLISHMENTS]

Ex 14:13 and see the deliverance that the LORD will a
2Sa 3: 9 has sworn to David, that will I a for him,
Job 35: 6 If you have sinned, what do you a against him?
37:12 to a all that he commands them on the face of
Isa 55:11 but it shall a that which I purpose,
60:22 in its time I will a it quickly.
Eze 17:24 I the LORD have spoken; I will a it.
Lk 9:31 which he was about to a at Jerusalem.
Eph 3:20 to a abundantly far more than all we can ask
Jdt 2:12 what I have spoken I will a by my own hand.

Jdt 10: 9 to be opened for me so that I may go out and **a**
11: 6 God will **a** something through you,
11:16 to **a** with you things that will astonish
2Mc 14:29 for an opportunity to **a** this by a stratagem.
3Mc 6:15 of their enemies did I neglect them,' so **a** it,

ACCOMPLISHED (25) [ACCOMPLISH]

1Sa 14:45 who has **a** this great victory in Israel?
2Ch 7:11 and in his own house he successfully **a.**
8:16 Thus all the work of Solomon was **a** from the day
Ezr 1: 1 the LORD by the mouth of Jeremiah might be **a,**
Ne 6:16 for they perceived that this work had been **a** with
Ps 31:19 and **a** for those who take refuge in you,
Jer 23:20 until he has executed and **a** the intents of his mind.
30:24 until he has executed and **a** the intents of his mind.
39:16 and they shall be **a** in your presence on that day.
44:25 and your wives have **a** in deeds what you declared
La 4:22 is **a,** he will keep you in exile no longer;
Da 12: 7 all these things would be **a.**
Mt 5:18 will pass from the law until all is **a.**
Mk 13: 4 be the sign that all these things are about to be **a?"**
Lk 18:31 about the Son of Man by the prophets will be **a.**
Ac 19:21 Now after these things had been **a,**
Ro 15:18 of anything except what Christ has **a** through me
AdE 13: 3 I asked my counselors how this might be **a,**
16: 7 "What has been wickedly **a** through
2Mc 10:38 When they had **a** these things,
1Es 1:17 with the sacrifices to the Lord were **a** that day:
2: 1 of the Lord by the mouth of Jeremiah might be **a—**
3Mc 7: 4 be firmly established until this was **a,**
2Es 6:38 and your word **a** the work.
4Mc 8: 3 handsome, modest, noble, and **a** in every way—

ACCOMPLISHES (2) [ACCOMPLISH]

Eph 1:11 to the purpose of him who **a** all things according
Tob 14:11 So now, my children, see what almsgiving **a,**

ACCOMPLISHING (2) [ACCOMPLISH]

2Mc 12:18 for he had by then left there without **a** anything,
4Mc 9:12 without **a** anything, they placed him upon

ACCOMPLISHMENTS (2) [ACCOMPLISH]

1Ki 10: 6 in my own land of your **a** and of your wisdom,
2Ch 9: 5 in my own land of your **a** and of your wisdom,

ACCORD (23) [ACCORDANCE, ACCORDING, ACCORDINGLY]

Nu 16:28 it has not been of my own **a:**
Dt 31: 5 to you and you shall deal with them in full **a** with
Jos 9: 2 they gathered together with one **a** to fight Joshua
1Ki 22:13 the words of the prophets with one **a** are favorable
2Ch 18:12 the words of the prophets with one **a** are favorable
Ps 83: 5 They conspire with one **a;**
Zep 3: 9 the name of the LORD and serve him with one **a.**
Jn 10:18 but I lay it down of my own **a.**
Ac 8: 6 with one **a** listened eagerly to what was said
12:10 It opened for them of its own **a,**
2Co 8:17 he is going to you of his own **a.**
Php 2: 2 being in full **a** and of one mind.
Jdt 13:17 and said with one **a,** "Blessed are you our God,
15: 5 with one **a** they fell upon the enemy,
15: 9 they all blessed her with one **a** and said to her,
Wis 10:20 and praised with one **a** your defending hand;
18: 9 and with one **a** agreed to the divine law,
1Mc 10:64 in **a** with the proclamation,
2Mc 6:19 went up to the rack of his own **a,**
1Es 9:38 with one **a** in the open square before the east gate
3Mc 5:21 and joyfully with one **a** gave their approval,
5:50 they prostrated themselves with one **a** on
4Mc 11: 3 I have come of my own **a,**

ACCORDANCE (82) [ACCORD]

Ge 44:10 He said, "Even so; in **a** with your words, let it be:
Ex 24: 8 that the LORD has made with you in **a**
25: 9 In **a** with all that I show you concerning
34:27 in **a** with these words I have made a covenant
36: 1 in the construction of the sanctuary shall work in **a**
Lev 27:16 be in **a** with its seed requirements:
Nu 6:21 to the LORD must be in **a** with the nazirite vow,
6:21 in **a** with whatever vow they take,
29:18 as prescribed in **a** with their number;
29:21 as prescribed in **a** with their number;
29:24 as prescribed in **a** with their number;
29:27 as prescribed in **a** with their number;
29:30 as prescribed in **a** with their number;
29:33 as prescribed in **a** with their number;
29:37 as prescribed in **a** with their number;
35:24 in **a** with these ordinances;
Dt 26:13 the widows, in **a** with your entire commandment
29:21 in **a** with all the curses of the covenant written
Jos 1: 7 being careful to act in **a** with all the law
1: 8 be careful to act in **a** with all that is written in it.
2Sa 3:39 the one who does wickedly in **a**
7:17 In **a** with all these words and with all this vision,
2Ki 9:26 in **a** with the word of the LORD."
10:30 in **a** with all that was in my heart have dealt with
16:11 in **a** with all that King Ahaz had sent
17:13 in **a** with all the law that I sent to you
1Ch 17:15 In **a** with all these words and all this vision,
2Ch 6:23 by rewarding them in **a** with their righteousness.
10:14 to them in **a** with the advice of the young men,
30:19 not in **a** with the sanctuary's rules of cleanness."
31:21 and in **a** with the law and the commandments,
34:31 to act in **a** with all that is written in this book."
35:26 in **a** with what is written in the law of the LORD,
Jer 9:13 and have not obeyed my voice, or walked in **a**
32: 8 in **a** with the word of the LORD, and said to me,
Eze 36:19 **a** with their conduct and their deeds I judged
Mt 22:16 and teach the way of God in **a** with truth,
Mk 12:14 but teach the way of God in **a** with truth.
Lk 20:21 but teach the way of God in **a** with truth.
Ro 2: 2 on those who do such things is in **a** with truth."
15: 5 to live in harmony with one another, in **a**
1Co 15: 3 Christ died for our sins in **a** with the scriptures,
15: 4 and that he was raised on the third day in **a** with
2Co 4:13 the same spirit of faith that is in **a** with scripture—
Eph 3:11 This was in **a** with the eternal purpose
1Ti 1:18 in **a** with the prophecies made earlier about you,
6: 3 and the teaching that is in **a** with godliness,
Tit 1: 1 and the knowledge of the truth that is in **a**
1: 9 the word that is trustworthy in **a** with the teaching,
Heb 9:19 to all the people by Moses in **a** with the law,
11: 7 an heir to the righteousness that is in **a** with faith.
1Pe 4:19 in **a** with God's will entrust themselves to
2Pe 3:13 But, in **a** with his promise,
Tob 3: 5 and have not walked in **a** with truth before you.
4: 6 in **a** with truth will prosper in all their activities.
7:11 to you in **a** with the decree in the book of Moses,
7:12 be your wife in **a** with the law and decree written
AdE 1:19 in **a** with the laws of the Medes and Persians so
3:12 and in **a** with Haman's instructions they wrote in
Sir 16:14 everyone receives in **a** with one's deeds.
Bar 2: 2 in **a** with the threats that were written in the law
Aza 1:20 Deliver us in **a** with your marvelous works,
Sus 1:62 Acting in **a** with the law of Moses,
1Mc 7:16 in **a** with the word that was written,
14:46 the right to act in **a** with these decisions.
1Es 1: 5 in **a** with the directions of King David of Israel
4:52 in **a** with the commandment
5:49 in **a** with the directions in the book of Moses
7: 9 for the services of the Lord God of Israel in **a** with
8:10 In **a** with my gracious decision,
8:12 in **a** with what is in the law of the Lord,
8:16 perform it in **a** with the will of your God;
9: 4 in **a** with the decision of the ruling elders,
9:15 And those who had returned from exile acted in **a**
3Mc 3:23 in **a** with their infamous way of life,
7: 6 and in **a** with the clemency that we have
7:17 in **a** with the common desire, for seven days.
7:22 of their property, in **a** with the registration,
4Mc 2: 8 soon as one adopts a way of life in **a** with the law,
6:18 be irrational if having lived in **a** with truth up
6:18 up to old age and having maintained in **a** with law
8: 1 a philosophy in **a** with devout reason,

ACCORDING‡ (569) [ACCORD]

Ge 1:26 in our image, **a** to our likeness;
5: 3 **a** to his image, and named him Seth.
6:20 Of the birds **a** to their kinds, and of the animals **a** to their kinds, of every creeping thing of the ground **a** to its kind,
10:32 **a** to their genealogies, in their nations;
18:21 down and see whether they have done altogether **a**
23:16 **a** to the weights current among the merchants.
25:16 twelve princes **a** to their tribes.
33:14 **a** to the pace of the cattle that are before me and **a** to the pace of the children,
36:40 **a** to their families and their localities
36:43 **a** to their settlements in the land that they held.
41:12 giving an interpretation to each **a** to his dream.
43:33 the firstborn **a** to his birthright and the youngest **a** to his youth,
45:21 Joseph gave them wagons **a** to the instruction
47:12 **a** to the number of their dependents.
Ex 6:16 The following are the names of the sons of Levi **a**
6:19 the families of the Levites **a** to their genealogies.
16:16 an omer to a person **a** to the number of persons,
21:31 the owner shall be dealt with **a** to this same rule.
25:40 see that you make them **a** to the pattern for them,
26:30 Then you shall erect the tabernacle **a** to the plan
30:13 half a shekel **a** to the shekel of the sanctuary
30:37 When you make incense **a** to this composition,
39: 6 **a** to the names of the sons of Israel.
Lev 5:10 the second he shall offer for a burnt offering **a** to
9:16 and sacrificed it **a** to regulation.
11:22 Of them you may eat: the locust **a** to its kind, the bald locust **a** to its kind, the cricket **a** to its kind, and the grasshopper **a** to its kind.
11:29 weasel, the mouse, the great lizard **a** to its kind,
25:52 **a** to the years involved they shall make payment
27: 8 the priest shall assess them **a** to what each one
27:12 **a** to the assessment of the priest, so it shall be.
27:18 the price for it **a** to the years that remain until
Nu 1: 2 by ancestral houses, **a** to the number of names,
1:18 **a** to the number of names from twenty years old
1:20 **a** to the number of names, individually,
1:22 **a** to the number of names, individually,
1:24 **a** to the number of the names,
1:26 **a** to the number of names,
1:28 **a** to the number of names,
1:30 **a** to the number of names,
1:32 **a** to the number of names,
1:34 **a** to the number of names,
1:36 **a** to the number of names,
1:38 **a** to the number of names,
1:40 **a** to the number of names,
1:42 **a** to the number of names,
2:34 everyone by clans, **a** to ancestral houses.
3:16 Moses enrolled them **a** to the word of the LORD,
Nu 3:51 **a** to the word of the LORD,
4:37 and Aaron enrolled **a** to the commandment of
4:41 and Aaron enrolled **a** to the commandment of
4:45 and Aaron enrolled **a** to the commandment of
4:49 **A** to the commandment of the LORD
7: 5 to each **a** to his service.
7: 7 and four oxen he gave to the Gershonites, **a** to their
7: 8 and eight oxen he gave to the Merarites, **a** to their
7:13 **a** to the shekel of the sanctuary,
7:19 **a** to the shekel of the sanctuary,
7:25 **a** to the shekel of the sanctuary,
7:31 **a** to the shekel of the sanctuary,
7:37 **a** to the shekel of the sanctuary,
7:43 **a** to the shekel of the sanctuary,
7:49 **a** to the shekel of the sanctuary,
7:55 **a** to the shekel of the sanctuary,
7:61 **a** to the shekel of the sanctuary,
7:67 **a** to the shekel of the sanctuary,
7:73 **a** to the shekel of the sanctuary,
7:79 **a** to the shekel of the sanctuary,
7:85 the vessels two thousand four hundred shekels **a**
7:86 weighing ten shekels apiece **a** to the shekel of
8: 4 **a** to the pattern that the LORD had shown Moses,
9: 3 **a** to all its statutes and all its regulations you shall
9:12 **a** to all the statute for the passover
9:14 to keep the passover to the LORD shall do so **a** to
9:14 the statute of the passover and **a** to its regulation;
9:20 and **a** to the command of the LORD
9:20 then **a** to the command of the LORD
13: 3 **a** to the command of the LORD,
14:19 the iniquity of this people **a** to the greatness
14:34 **A** to the number of the days
15:12 **A** to the number that you offer,
15:24 with its grain offering and its drink offering, **a** to
17: 6 one for each leader, **a** to their ancestral houses,
18:16 **a** to the shekel of the sanctuary (that is,
26:35 the descendants of Ephraim **a** to their clans:
26:53 the land shall be apportioned for inheritance **a** to
26:54 be given its inheritance **a** to its enrollment.
26:55 **a** to the names of their ancestral tribes they shall
26:56 be apportioned **a** to lot between the larger and
29: 6 **a** to the ordinance for them, a pleasing odor,
30: 2 he shall do **a** to all that proceeds out of his mouth.
33: 2 and these are their stages **a** to their starting places.
33:54 You shall apportion the land by lot **a**
33:54 **a** to your ancestral tribes you shall inherit.
36: 5 Then Moses commanded the Israelites **a** to
Dt 12: 8 all of us **a** to our own desires,
12:15 within any of your towns, **a** to the blessing that
16:17 **a** to the blessing of the LORD your God
32: 8 the boundaries of the peoples **a** to the number of
Jos 2:21 She said, "**A** to your words, so be it."
4: 8 **a** to the number of the tribes of the Israelites,
4:10 **a** to all that Moses had commanded Joshua.
8:27 **a** to the word of the LORD that he had issued
8:34 **a** to all that is written in the book of the law.
11:23 **a** to all that the LORD had spoken to Moses;
11:23 an inheritance to Israel **a** to their tribal allotments.
12: 7 of Israel as a possession **a** to their allotments,
13:15 an inheritance to the tribe of the Reubenites **a**
13:23 **a** to their families with their towns and villages.
13:24 also to the tribe of the Gadites, **a** to their families.
13:28 the inheritance of the Gadites **a** to their clans,
13:29 it was allotted to the half-tribe of the Manassites **a**
13:31 of Machir son of Manasseh **a** to their clans—
15: 1 of Judah **a** to their families reached southward to
15:12 the boundary surrounding the people of Judah **a**
15:13 **A** to the commandment of the LORD to Joshua,
15:20 the tribe of the people of Judah **a** to their families.
17: 4 So **a** to the commandment of
18:11 of the tribe of Benjamin **a** to its families came up,
18:20 **a** to its families, boundary by boundary all around.
18:21 of Benjamin **a** to their families were Jericho,
18:28 This is the inheritance of the tribe of Benjamin **a**
19: 1 for the tribe of Simeon, **a** to its families;
19: 8 This was the inheritance of the tribe of Simeon **a**
19:10 The third lot came up for the tribe of Zebulun, **a**
19:16 **a** to its families—these towns with their villages,
19:17 for the tribe of Issachar, **a** to its families.
19:23 **a** to its families—the towns with their villages.
19:24 The fifth lot came out for the tribe of Asher **a**
19:31 This is the inheritance of the tribe of Asher **a**
19:32 for the tribe of Naphtali, **a** to its families.
19:39 This is the inheritance of the tribe of Naphtali **a**
19:40 The seventh lot came out for the tribe of Dan, **a**
19:48 of the tribe of Dan, **a** to their families—
21: 7 The Merarites **a** to their families received twelve
Jdg 11:36 do to me **a** to what has gone out of your mouth,
11:39 who did with her **a** to the vow he had made.
1Sa 2:35 who shall do **a** to what is in my heart and
6: 4 **a** to the number of the lords of the Philistines;
6:18 **a** to the number of all the cities of
25:30 the LORD has done to my lord **a** to all the good
2Sa 7:21 Because of your promise, and **a** to your own heart,
7:22 **a** to all that we have heard with our ears.
9:11 "**A** to all that my lord the king commands
22:21 The LORD rewarded me **a** to my righteousness;
22:21 **a** to the cleanness of my hands he recompensed me
22:25 Therefore the LORD has recompensed me **a**
22:25 **a** to my cleanness in his sight.
1Ki 2: 6 Act therefore **a** to your wisdom,
3:12 I now do **a** to your word.
4:28 the horses and swift steeds, each **a** to his charge.
6:38 and **a** to all its specifications.
7: 9 cut **a** to measure, sawed with saws,
8:32 and vindicating the righteous by rewarding them **a**
8:39 **a** to all their ways, for only you know what is

1Ki 8:43 and do **a** to all that the foreigner calls to you,
8:56 who has given rest to his people Israel **a** to all
9: 4 doing **a** to all that I have commanded you,
12:14 to them **a** to the advice of the young men,
12:24 **a** to the word of the LORD.
13: 5 **a** to the sign that the man of God had given by
13:26 to the lion, which has torn him and killed him **a** to
14:18 **a** to the word of the LORD,
15:29 not one that breathed, until he had destroyed it, **a**
16:12 **a** to the word of the LORD,
16:34 **a** to the word of the LORD,
17: 5 So he went and did **a** to the word of the LORD;
17:16 **a** to the word of the LORD that he spoke
18:31 **a** to the number of the tribes of the sons of Jacob,
22:38 **a** to the word of the LORD that he had spoken.
2Ki 1:17 So he died **a** to the word of the LORD
2:22 **a** to the word that Elisha spoke.
4:44 and had some left, **a** to the word of the LORD.
5:14 **a** to the word of the man of God;
7:16 **a** to the word of the LORD.
8: 2 So the woman got up and did **a** to the word of
10:17 **a** to the word of the LORD that he spoke
11: 9 The captains did **a** to all that
11:14 **a** to custom, with the captains and the trumpeters
14: 6 **a** to what is written in the book of the law
14:25 **a** to the word of the LORD, the God of Israel,
16: 3 **a** to the abominable practices of the nations whom
21: 8 to do **a** to all that I have commanded them,
21: 8 and **a** to all the law that my servant Moses
22:13 to do **a** to all that is written concerning us."
23:16 and burned them on the altar, and defiled it, **a** to
23:25 and with all his might, **a** to all the law of Moses;
23:35 from all **a** to their assessment,
24: 2 he sent them against Judah to destroy it, **a** to
1Ch 5: 1 not enrolled in the genealogy **a** to the birthright;
5:13 And their kindred **a** to their clans:
6:19 the clans of the Levites **a** to their ancestry.
6:49 **a** to all that Moses the servant
6:54 These are their dwelling places **a**
6:62 To the Gershomites **a** to their families
6:63 To the Merarites **a** to their families
7: 4 by their generations, **a** to their ancestral houses,
7: 9 by genealogies, **a** to their generations, as heads
7:11 of Jediael **a** to the heads of their ancestral houses,
8:28 **a** to their generations, chiefs.
9: 9 and their kindred **a** to their generations,
9: 9 of families **a** to their ancestral houses.
9:34 of the Levites, **a** to their generations;
11: 3 **a** to the word of the LORD by Samuel.
11:10 **a** to the word of the LORD concerning Israel.
12:23 **a** to the word of the LORD.
15:15 as Moses had commanded **a** to the word of
15:20 and Benaiah were to play harps **a** to Alamoth;
15:21 and Azaziah were to lead with lyres **a** to
16:40 **a** to all that is written in the law of the LORD
17:19 O LORD, and **a** to your own heart,
17:20 **a** to all that we have heard with our ears.
23:24 of families as they were enrolled **a** to the number
23:27 for **a** to the last words of David these were
23:31 **a** to the number required of them,
24: 3 David organized them **a** to the appointed duties
24:19 in their service to enter the house of the LORD **a**
24:30 the sons of the Levites **a** to their ancestral houses.
25: 5 **a** to the promise of God to exalt him;
28:15 **a** to the use of each in the service,
2Ch 6:30 to all whose heart you know, **a** to all their ways,
7:17 doing **a** to all that I have commanded you
8:13 offering **a** to the commandment of Moses for
8:14 **A** to the ordinance of his father David,
17: 4 and not **a** to the ways of Israel.
23: 8 The Levites and all Judah did **a** to all that
23:18 **a** to the order of David.
25: 4 **a** to what is written in the law,
26:11 in divisions **a** to the numbers in the muster made
28: 3 **a** to the abominable practices of the nations whom
29:25 **a** to the commandment of David and of Gad
30:16 They took their accustomed posts **a** to the law
31: 2 division by division, everyone **a** to his service,
31:16 for their service **a** to their offices,
31:17 of the priests was **a** to their ancestral houses;
31:17 from twenty years old and upwards was **a**
32:25 not respond **a** to the benefit done to him,
33: 2 **a** to the abominable practices of the nations whom
34:32 of Jerusalem acted **a** to the covenant of God,
35: 5 Take position in the holy place **a** to the groupings
35: 6 acting **a** to the word of the LORD by Moses."
35:10 in their divisions **a** to the king's command.
35:12 that they might distribute them **a** to the groupings
35:13 the passover lamb with fire **a** to the ordinance;
35:15 were in their place **a** to the command of David,
35:16 **a** to the command of King Josiah.
Ezr 2:69 **A** to their resources they gave to
3: 4 and offered the daily burnt offerings by number **a**
3: 7 **a** to the grant that they had from King Cyrus
3:10 **a** to the directions of King David of Israel;
6:13 Then, **a** to the word sent by King Darius, Tattenai,
6:17 **a** to the number of the tribes of Israel.
7:14 to make inquiries about Judah and Jerusalem **a** to
7:18 you may do, **a** to the will of your God.
7:25 Ezra, **a** to the God-given wisdom you possess,
10: 3 **a** to the counsel of my lord and
10: 3 and let it be done **a** to the law.
10:16 heads of families, **a** to their families,
Ne 4:13 I stationed the people **a** to their families,
6: 6 and **a** to this report you wish to become their king.
6: 7 it will be reported to the king **a** to these words.
6:14 O my God, **a** to these things that they did,
Ne 8:18 on the eighth day there was a solemn assembly, **a**
9:27 to you and you heard them from heaven, and **a**
9:28 many times you rescued them **a** to your mercies.
12:24 **a** to the commandment of David the man of God,
12:45 **a** to the command of David and his son Solomon.
13:22 spare me **a** to the greatness of your steadfast love.
Est 1: 7 and the royal wine was lavished **a** to the bounty of
1:15 "**A** to the law, what is to be done to Queen Vashti
3:12 and an edict, **a** to all that Haman commanded,
8: 9 **a** to all that Mordecai commanded,
9:13 in Susa be allowed tomorrow also to do **a** to
Job 1: 5 in the morning and offer burnt offerings **a** to
34:11 For **a** to their deeds he will repay them,
34:11 and **a** to their ways he will make it befall them.
42: 8 for I will accept his prayer not to deal with you **a** to
Ps 6: T *with stringed instruments;* ***a*** *to The Sheminith.*
7: 8 judge me, O LORD, **a** to my righteousness and
7: 8 to my righteousness and **a** to the integrity that is
8: T *To the leader:* ***a*** *to the Gittith.*
9: T *To the leader:* ***a*** *to Muth-labben.*
12: T *To the leader:* ***a*** *to the Sheminith.*
18:20 The LORD rewarded me **a** to my righteousness;
18:20 **a** to the cleanness of my hands he recompensed me
18:24 Therefore the LORD has recompensed me **a** to
18:24 **a** to the cleanness of my hands in his sight.
22: T *To the leader:* ***a*** *to The Deer of the Dawn.*
25: 7 **a** to your steadfast love remember me,
28: 4 Repay them **a** to their work,
28: 4 and **a** to the evil of their deeds;
28: 4 repay them **a** to the work of their hands;
35:24 O LORD, my God, **a** to your righteousness,
45: T *To the leader:* ***a*** *to Lilies.*
46: T *Of the Korahites.* ***A*** *to Alamoth. A Song.*
51: 1 O God, **a** to your steadfast love; **a** to your
abundant mercy blot out my transgressions.
53: T *To the leader:* ***a*** *to Mahalath.*
56: T *the leader:* ***a*** *to The Dove on Far-off Terebinths.*
60: T *To the leader:* ***a*** *to the Lily of the Covenant.*
62: T *To the leader:* ***a*** *to Jeduthun.*
62:12 For you repay to all **a** to their work.
69: T *To the leader:* ***a*** *to Lilies. Of David.*
69:16 **a** to your abundant mercy, turn to me.
77: T *To the leader:* ***a*** *to Jeduthun. Of Asaph.*
78:10 but refused to walk **a** to his law.
79:11 **a** to your great power preserve those doomed
81: T *To the leader:* ***a*** *to The Gittith. Of Asaph.*
84: T *To the leader:* ***a*** *to The Gittith. Of the Korahites.*
88: T *To the leader:* ***a*** *to Mahalath Leannoth.*
89:30 If his children forsake my law and do not walk **a** to
103:10 He does not deal with us **a** to our sins,
103:10 nor repay us **a** to our iniquities.
106:45 and showed compassion **a** to the abundance
109:26 Save me **a** to your steadfast love.
110: 4 a priest forever **a** to the order of Melchizedek."
119: 9 By guarding it **a** to your word.
119:25 revive me **a** to your word.
119:28 strengthen me **a** to your word.
119:41 O LORD, your salvation **a** to your promise.
119:58 be gracious to me **a** to your promise.
119:65 O LORD, **a** to your word.
119:76 Let your steadfast love become my comfort **a** to
119:107 give me life, O LORD, **a** to your word.
119:116 Uphold me **a** to your promise, that I may live,
119:124 Deal with your servant **a** to your steadfast love,
119:133 Keep my steps steady **a** to your promise,
119:154 give me life **a** to your promise.
119:156 give me life **a** to your justice.
119:159 preserve my life **a** to your steadfast love.
119:169 give me understanding **a** to your word.
119:170 deliver me **a** to your promise.
150: 2 praise him **a** to his surpassing greatness!
Pr 24:12 And will he not repay all **a** to their deeds?
26: 4 Do not answer fools **a** to their folly,
26: 5 Answer fools **a** to their folly,
Ecc 8:14 that there are righteous people who are treated **a** to
8:14 and there are wicked people who are treated **a** to
Isa 21:16 Within a year, **a** to the years of a hired worker,
59:18 **A** to their deeds, so will he repay;
63: 7 of Israel that he has shown them **a** to his mercy,
63: 7 **a** to the abundance of his steadfast love.
Jer 13: 2 I bought a loincloth **a** to the word of the LORD,
17:10 to give to all **a** to their ways,
17:10 **a** to the fruit of their doings.
18:12 and each of us will act **a** to the stubbornness
21:14 I will punish you **a** to the fruit of your doings,
25:14 and I will repay them **a** to their deeds and
32:19 rewarding all **a** to their ways and **a** to the fruit of
34:16 whom you had set free **a** to their desire,
42: 5 and faithful witness against us if we do not act **a**
50:29 Repay her **a** to her deeds;
La 3:32 he will have compassion **a** to the abundance
3:64 O LORD, **a** to the work of their hands!
Eze 5: 7 but have acted **a** to the ordinances of the nations
7: 3 I will judge you **a** to your ways,
7: 8 I will judge you **a** to your ways,
7: 9 I will punish you **a** to your ways,
7:27 **A** to their way I will deal with them;
7:27 **a** to their own judgments I will judge them.
11:12 but you have acted **a** to the ordinances of
16:47 and acted **a** to their abominations;
18:30 all of you **a** to your ways, says the Lord GOD.
20:44 not **a** to your evil ways, or corrupt deeds,
22: 6 princes of Israel in you, everyone **a** to his power,
23:24 and they shall judge you **a** to their ordinances.
24:14 **A** to your ways and your doings I will judge you,
25:14 shall act in Edom **a** to my anger and **a** to my wrath;
33:20 I will judge all of you **a** to your ways!
Eze 35:11 with you **a** to the anger and envy that you showed
39:24 I dealt with them **a** to their uncleanness
44:24 and they shall decide it **a** to my judgments.
45: 8 the house of Israel have the land **a** to their tribes.
47:21 So you shall divide this land among you **a** to
Da 1:13 deal with your servants **a** to what you observe."
6: 8 **a** to the law of the Medes and the Persians,
6:12 **a** to the law of the Medes and Persians,
9: 2 **a** to the word of the LORD to the prophet Jeremiah,
11: 4 nor **a** to the dominion with which he ruled;
Hos 7:12 I will discipline them **a** to the report made
12: 2 and will punish Jacob **a** to his ways,
12: 2 and repay him **a** to his deeds.
13: 2 idols of silver made **a** to their understanding,
Jnh 3: 3 **a** to the word of the LORD.
Hab 3: 1 prayer of the prophet Habakkuk **a** to Shigionoth.
Hag 2: 5 **a** to the promise that I made you
Zec 1: 6 of hosts has dealt with us **a** to our ways and deeds,
5: 3 for everyone who steals shall be cut off **a** to
5: 3 and everyone who swears falsely shall be cut off **a**
Mt 2:16 **a** to the time that he had learned from
8:13 let it be done for you **a** to your faith."
9:29 "**A** to your faith let it be done to you."
25:15 to another one, to each **a** to his ability.
Mk 7: 5 "Why do your disciples not live **a** to the tradition
15: 8 to ask Pilate to do for them **a** to his custom.
Lk 1: 6 living blamelessly **a** to all the commandments
1: 9 **a** to the custom of the priesthood,
1:38 let it be with me **a** to your word."
1:55 **a** to the promise he made to our ancestors,
2:22 the time came for their purification **a** to the law
2:24 and they offered a sacrifice **a** to what is stated in
2:29 now you are dismissing your servant in peace, **a**
23:56 On the sabbath they rested **a** to the commandment.
Jn 8:44 When he lies, he speaks **a** to his own nature,
18:31 "Take him yourselves and judge him **a** to your law.
19: 7 and **a** to that law he ought to die
19:40 **a** to the burial custom of the Jews.
Ac 2:23 to you **a** to the definite plan and foreknowledge
7:44 to make it **a** to the pattern he had seen.
11:29 The disciples determined that **a** to their ability,
15: 1 you are circumcised **a** to the custom of Moses,
22: 3 educated strictly **a** to our ancestral law,
22:12 a devout man **a** to the law and well spoken of
23: 3 Are you sitting there to judge me **a** to the law,
23:31 So the soldiers, **a** to their instructions,
24:14 But this I admit to you, that **a** to the Way,
24:14 down **a** to the law or written in the prophets.
Ro 1: 3 who was descended from David **a** to the flesh
1: 4 and was declared to be Son of God with power **a**
2: 6 For he will repay **a** to each one's deeds:
2:16 **a** to my gospel, God, through Jesus Christ,
4: 1 our ancestor **a** to the flesh?
4:18 "the father of many nations," **a** to what was said,
8: 4 who walk not **a** to the flesh but **a** to the Spirit.
8: 5 For those who live **a** to the flesh set their minds on
8: 5 but those who live **a** to the Spirit set their minds
8:12 not to the flesh, to live **a** to the flesh—
8:13 for if you live **a** to the flesh, you will die;
8:27 Spirit intercedes for the saints **a** to the will of God.
8:28 who are called **a** to his purpose.
9: 3 my kindred **a** to the flesh.
9: 5 **a** to the flesh, comes the Messiah, who is over all,
12: 3 each **a** to the measure of faith
12: 6 We have gifts that differ **a** to the grace given
16:25 Now to God who is able to strengthen you **a** to my
16:25 **a** to the revelation of the mystery
16:26 **a** to the command of the eternal God,
1Co 3: 3 and behaving **a** to human inclinations?
3: 8 and each will receive wages **a** to the labor of each.
3:10 **A** to the grace of God given to me,
12: 8 the utterance of knowledge **a** to the same Spirit,
2Co 1:17 Do I make my plans **a** to ordinary human standards
8: 3 they voluntarily gave **a** to their means,
8:11 be matched by completing it **a** to your means.
8:12 the gift is acceptable **a** to what one has—
8:12 not **a** to what one does not have.
10: 2 to oppose those who think we are acting **a**
10: 3 but we do not wage war **a** to human standards;
11:18 since many boast **a** to human standards,
Gal 1: 4 **a** to the will of our God and Father,
3:29 then you are Abraham's offspring, heirs **a** to
4:23 the child of the slave, was born **a** to the flesh;
4:29 at that time the child who was born **a** to the flesh
persecuted the child who was born **a** to the Spirit,
Eph 1: 5 **a** to the good pleasure of his will,
1: 7 **a** to the riches of his grace
1: 9 **a** to his good pleasure that he set forth in Christ,
1:11 having been destined **a** to the purpose of him who
accomplishes all things **a** to his counsel
1:19 **a** to the working of his great power.
3: 7 Of this gospel I have become a servant **a** to
3:16 I pray that, **a** to the riches of his glory,
4: 7 But each of us was given grace **a** to the measure
4:24 created **a** to the likeness of God
Php 3:17 and observe those who live **a** to the example
4:19 of yours **a** to his riches in glory in Christ Jesus.
Col 1:25 I became its servant **a** to God's commission
2: 8 deceit, **a** to human tradition, **a** to the elemental
spirits of the universe, and not **a** to Christ.
3:10 which is being renewed in knowledge **a** to
2Th 1:12 **a** to the grace of our God and the Lord Jesus
3: 6 from believers who are living in idleness and not **a**
2Ti 1: 9 not **a** to our works but **a** to his own purpose
2: 5 no one is crowned without competing **a** to
Tit 3: 5 but **a** to his mercy, through the water of rebirth
3: 7 we might become heirs **a** to the hope

Heb 2: 4 and by gifts of the Holy Spirit, distributed **a**
5: 6 **a** to the order of Melchizedek."
5: 10 having been designated by God a high priest **a** to
6: 20 having become a high priest forever **a** to the order
7: 11 to speak of another priest arising **a** to the order
7: 11 rather than one **a** to the order of Aaron?
7: 17 **a** to the order of Melchizedek."
8: 4 since there are priests who offer gifts **a** to the law.
8: 5 "See that you make everything **a** to the pattern
10: 8 and sin offerings" (these are offered **a** to the law),
Jas 2: 8 if you really fulfill the royal law **a** to the scripture,
1Pe 1: 17 the one who judges all people impartially **a**
2Pe 2: 22 It has happened to them **a** to the true proverb,
3: 15 So also our beloved brother Paul wrote to you **a** to
1Jn 5: 14 that if we ask anything **a** to his will, he hears us.
2Jn 1: 6 this is love, that we walk **a** to his commandments;
Rev 20: 12 And the dead were judged **a** to their works,
20: 13 and all were judged **a** to what they had done.
22: 12 to repay **a** to everyone's work.
Tob 1: 8 and we would eat it **a** to the ordinance decreed
1: 8 of Moses and **a** to the instructions of Deborah,
4: 8 do not be afraid to give **a** to the little you have.
6: 13 the penalty of death **a** to the decree of the book
7: 13 to him as wife **a** to the decree of the law of Moses.
8: 16 but you have dealt with us **a** to your great mercy.
AdE 1: 8 The drinking was not **a** to a fixed rule;
Wis 2: 20 for, **a** to what he says, he will be protected."
6: 4 or keep the law, or walk **a** to the purpose of God,
9: 9 and what is right **a** to your commandments.
16: 25 **a** to the desire of those who had need,
Sir Pr: 1 even greater progress in living **a** to the law.
Pr: 3 to gain learning and are disposed to live **a** to
1: 10 upon all the living **a** to his gift;
11: 26 of death to reward individuals **a** to their conduct.
14: 11 My child, treat yourself well, **a** to your means,
16: 12 he judges a person **a** to one's deeds.
29: 11 Lay up your treasure **a** to the commandments of
32: 17 and will find a decision **a** to his liking.
35: 24 until he repays mortals **a** to their deeds,
35: 24 and the works of all **a** to their thoughts;
36: 22 **a** to your goodwill toward your people,
50: 22 and deals with us **a** to his mercy.
51: 18 For I resolved to live **a** to wisdom,
Sus 1: 3 had trained their daughter **a** to the law of Moses.
1Mc 1: 14 a gymnasium in Jerusalem, **a** to Gentile custom,
1: 60 **A** to the decree, they put to death
2: 23 **a** to the king's command.
3: 56 he told to go home again, **a** to the law.
7: 42 and judge him **a** to this wickedness."
13: 46 treat us **a** to our wicked acts but **a** to your mercy."
15: 21 so that he may punish them **a** to their law."
2Mc 6: 23 and moreover **a** to the holy God-given law,
11: 25 to them and that they shall live **a** to the customs
12: 38 they purified themselves **a** to the custom,
1Es 1: 2 having placed the priests **a** to their divisions,
1: 5 Stand in order in the temple **a** to the groupings of
1: 6 and keep the passover **a** to the commandment of
1: 10 stood in proper order **a** to kindred
1: 15 were in their place **a** to the arrangement made
1: 18 **a** to the command of King Josiah.
3: 9 the victory shall be given **a** to what is written."
5: 1 up, **a** to their tribes, with their wives and sons
5: 4 **a** to their ancestral houses in the tribes,
5: 55 **a** to the decree that they had in writing
5: 60 **a** to the directions of King David of Israel;
7: 6 did **a** to what was written in the book of Moses.
7: 8 **a** to the number of the twelve leaders of the tribes
7: 9 **a** to kindred, for the services of the Lord God
8: 23 "And you, Ezra, **a** to the wisdom of God,
8: 28 **a** to their ancestral houses and their groups,
Man 1: 7 Lord, **a** to your great goodness you have promised
1: 14 you will save me **a** to your great mercy,
3Mc 3: 14 it was brought to conclusion, **a** to plan,
5: 29 "O king, **a** to your eager purpose."
7: 2 the great God guiding our affairs **a** to our desire.
2Es 2: 18 **A** to their counsel I have consecrated and prepared
8: 37 and it will turn out **a** to your words.
10: 13 but it is with the earth **a** to the way of the earth—
4Mc 5: 11 philosophize **a** to the truth of what is beneficial,
11: 5 of all things and live **a** to his virtuous law?
15: 3 the religion that preserves them for eternal life **a**

ACCORDINGLY (12) [ACCORD]

Nu 8: 20 of the Israelites did with the Levites **a;**
Ne 8: 2 **A,** the priest Ezra brought the law before
Da 3: 8 **A,** at this time certain Chaldeans came forward
Jn 11: 5 **A,** though Jesus loved Martha and her sister
Ro 7: 3 **A,** she will be called an adulteress if she lives
Heb 7: 22 **a** Jesus has also become the guarantee of
AdE 16: 24 not act **a** shall be destroyed in wrath with spear
Sir 3: 1 act **a,** that you may be kept in safety.
1Mc 12: 23 that our envoys report to you **a."**
2Mc 11: 25 **A,** since we choose that this nation also should
3Mc 6: 31 **A** those disgracefully treated and near to death,
4Mc 1: 13 **a,** is whether reason is sovereign over

ACCOS (1)

1Mc 8: 17 So Judas chose Eupolemus son of John son of **A,**

ACCOUNT‡ (91) [ACCOUNTABLE, ACCOUNTED, ACCOUNTING, ACCOUNTS]

Ge 12: 13 and that my life may be spared on your **a."**
21: 11 The matter was very distressing to Abraham on **a**
Ex 3: 7 I have heard their cry on **a** of their taskmasters.
Dt 1: 37 Even with me the LORD was angry on your **a,**
3: 26 But the LORD was angry with me on your **a**
15: 10 for on this **a** the LORD your God will bless you
28: 20 on **a** of the evil of your deeds,
31: 18 On that day I will surely hide my face on **a** of all
Jdg 6: 7 When the Israelites cried to the LORD on **a** of
18: 12 On this **a** that place is called Mahaneh-dan
1Sa 23: 10 to destroy the city on my **a.**
1Ki 9: 15 This is the **a** of the forced labor
1Ch 11: 11 This is an **a** of David's mighty warriors:
16: 19 When they were few in number, of little **a,**
16: 21 he rebuked kings on their **a,**
27: 24 for this, and the number was not entered into the **a**
Ezr 4: 15 On that **a** this city was laid waste.
10: 14 the fierce wrath of our God on this **a** is averted
Ne 13: 26 Did not King Solomon of Israel sin on **a**
Est 10: 2 and the full **a** of the high honor of Mordecai,
Job 31: 37 I would give him an **a** of all my steps;
40: 4 I am of small **a;** what shall I answer you?
Ps 10: 13 and say in their hearts, "You will not call us to **a"?**
105: 12 When they were few in number, of little **a,**
105: 14 he rebuked kings on their **a,**
106: 32 and it went ill with Moses on their **a;**
Isa 2: 22 for of what **a** are they?
53: 3 and we held him of no **a.**
Jer 15: 15 know that on your **a** I suffer insult.
29: 22 And on **a** of them this curse shall be used by all
Eze 12: 19 on **a** of the violence of all those who live in it.
16: 14 Your fame spread among the nations on **a**
16: 61 but not on **a** of my covenant with you.
Da 6: 2 to these the satraps gave **a,**
7: 28 Here the **a** ends. As for me,
Joel 3: 2 on **a** of my people and my heritage Israel,
Am 8: 8 Shall not the land tremble on this **a,**
Jnh 1: 7 on whose **a** this calamity has come upon us."
1: 14 do not let us perish on **a** of this man's life.
Mt 1: 1 An **a** of the genealogy of Jesus the Messiah,
5: 11 of evil against you falsely on my **a.**
12: 36 on the day of judgment you will have to give an **a**
13: 21 trouble or persecution arises on **a** of the word,
14: 3 and put him in prison on **a** of Herodias,
Mk 4: 17 trouble or persecution arises on **a** of the word,
6: 17 and put him in prison on **a** of Herodias,
Lk 1: 1 an orderly **a** of the events that have been fulfilled
1: 3 to write an orderly **a** for you,
6: 22 and defame you on **a** of the Son of Man.
19: 3 but on **a** of the crowd he could not,
Jn 12: 11 on **a** of him that many of the Jews were deserting
15: 21 But they will do all these things to you on **a**
Ac 26: 6 And now I stand here on trial on **a** of my hope in
1Co 14: 24 by all and called to **a** by all.
2Co 7: 12 it was not on **a** of the one who did the wrong, nor on **a** of the one who was wronged,
Php 4: 17 but I seek the profit that accumulates to your **a.**
Col 3: 6 On **a** of these the wrath of God is coming
Phm 1: 18 or owes you anything, charge that to my **a.**
Heb 4: 13 the eyes of the one to whom we must render an **a.**
13: 17 over your souls and will give an **a.**
1Jn 2: 12 because your sins are forgiven on **a** of his name.
Rev 1: 7 and on his **a** all the tribes of the earth will wail.
AdE 9: 19 On this **a** then the Jews who are scattered around
12: 4 and Mordecai wrote an **a** of them.
Wis 3: 17 Even if they live long they will be held of no **a,**
6: 15 and one who is vigilant on her **a** will soon be free
Sir 10: 8 Sovereignty passes from nation to nation on **a**
16: 8 whom he loathed on **a** of their arrogance.
28: 1 for he keeps a strict **a** of their sins.
40: 10 and on their **a** the flood came.
1Mc 6: 59 for it was on **a** of their laws that we abolished
2Mc 2: 14 also collected all the books that had been lost on **a**
3: 6 that they did not belong to the **a** of the sacrifices,
4: 28 the two of them were summoned by the king on **a**
6: 22 and be treated kindly on **a** of his old friendship
7: 18 For we are suffering these things on our own **a,**
8: 35 by opponents whom he regarded as of the least **a,**
11: 4 He took no **a** whatever of the power of God,
12: 43 taking **a** of the resurrection.
3Mc 2: 17 or call us to **a** for this profanation,
5: 15 and he gave him an **a** of the situation.
5: 42 took no **a** of the changes of mind that had come
7: 7 into **a** the friendly and firm goodwill that they had
2Es 4: 39 on **a** of us that the time of threshing is delayed for
4: 39 on **a** of the sins of those who inhabit the earth."
9: 7 and will be able to escape on **a** of their works,
9: 7 or on **a** of the faith by which they have believed,
12: 48 to this place to pray on **a** of the desolation of Zion,
12: 48 of Zion, and to seek mercy on **a** of the humiliation
4Mc 9: 8 and shall be with God, on whose **a** we suffer;

ACCOUNTABLE (5) [ACCOUNT]

Ge 43: 9 you can hold me **a** for him.
Dt 18: 19 in my name, I myself will hold **a.**
Ro 3: 19 and the whole world may be held **a** to God.
14: 12 So then, each of us will be **a** to God.
Jas 2: 10 but fails in one point has become **a** for all of it.

ACCOUNTED (10) [ACCOUNT]

Ps 44: 22 and **a** as sheep for the slaughter.
Isa 40: 15 and are **a** as dust on the scales;
40: 17 they are **a** by him as less than nothing
53: 4 yet we **a** him stricken, struck down by God,
Da 4: 35 All the inhabitants of the earth are **a** as nothing,
Ro 8: 36 we are **a** as sheep to be slaughtered."
Wis 7: 8 and I **a** wealth as nothing in comparison with her.
7: 9 and silver will be **a** as clay before her.
Sir 40: 19 but a blameless wife is **a** better than either.
2Es 12: 7 and if I have been **a** righteous before you

ACCOUNTING (5) [ACCOUNT]

2Ki 12: 15 an **a** from those into whose hand they delivered
22: 7 But no **a** shall be asked from them for the money
Lk 16: 2 Give me an **a** of your management,
1Pe 3: 15 to anyone who demands from you an **a** for
4: 5 an **a** to him who stands ready to judge the living

ACCOUNTS‡ (7) [ACCOUNT]

1Ch 29: 30 with **a** of all his rule and his might and of
2Ch 24: 27 **A** of his sons, and of the many oracles
Mt 18: 23 to a king who wished to settle **a** with his slaves.
25: 19 of those slaves came and settled **a** with them.
Tob 1: 21 the son of my brother Hanael over all the **a**
1: 22 of the **a** under King Sennacherib of Assyria;
Sir 42: 3 of keeping **a** with a partner or

ACCRUED (4)

Eze 18: 8 does not take advance or **a** interest,
18: 13 takes advance or **a** interest;
18: 17 takes no advance or **a** interest,
22: 12 you take both advance interest and **a** interest,

ACCUMULATE (1) [ACCUMULATES]

2Ti 4: 3 they will **a** for themselves teachers

ACCUMULATES (1) [ACCUMULATE]

Php 4: 17 but I seek the profit that **a** to your account.

ACCURACY (1) [ACCURATE]

Sir 42: 4 of **a** with scales and weights,

ACCURATE (4) [ACCURACY, ACCURATELY]

Pr 11: 1 but an **a** weight is his delight.
AdE 4: 5 and ordered him to get **a** information for her
Sir 31: 24 and their testimony to his stinginess is **a.**
32: 3 for it is your right, but with **a** knowledge,

ACCURATELY (3) [ACCURATE]

Ac 18: 25 with burning enthusiasm and taught **a** the things
18: 26 and explained the Way of God to him more **a.**
Sir 16: 25 and declare knowledge **a.**

ACCURSED (22) [CURSE]

Ps 119: 21 You rebuke the insolent, **a** ones,
Isa 65: 20 of a hundred will be considered **a.**
Jer 48: 10 **A** is the one who is slack in doing the work of
48: 10 and **a** is the one who keeps back the sword
Mic 6: 10 and the scant measure that is **a?**
Mt 25: 41 'You that are **a,** depart from me into
Jn 7: 49 not know the law—they are **a."**
Ro 9: 3 For I could wish that I myself were **a** and cut off
1Co 16: 22 Let anyone be **a** who has no love for the Lord.
Gal 1: 8 to what we proclaimed to you, let that one be **a!**
1: 9 contrary to what you received, let that one be **a!**
2Pe 2: 14 They have hearts trained in greed. **A** children!
Rev 22: 3 Nothing **a** will be found there any more.
Wis 3: 13 their offspring are **a.**
12: 11 For they were an **a** race from the beginning,
14: 8 But the idol made with hands is **a,**
Sir 23: 26 behind an **a** memory and her disgrace will never
2Mc 7: 9 he was at his last breath, he said, "You **a** wretch,
12: 35 wishing to take the **a** man alive,
4Mc 4: 5 to our country accompanied by the **a** Simon and
9: 24 to our nation and take vengeance on the **a** tyrant."
18: 22 and will pursue the **a** tyrant.

ACCUSATION (9) [ACCUSE]

Ezr 4: 6 they wrote an **a** against the inhabitants of Judah
Lk 3: 14 from anyone by threats or false **a,**
6: 7 so that they might find an **a** against him.
23: 4 "I find no basis for an **a** against this man."
Jn 18: 29 "What **a** do you bring against this man?"
Ac 24: 19 they ought to be here before you to make an **a,**
1Ti 5: 19 Never accept any **a** against an elder except on
Sir 26: 5 and false **a**— all these are worse than death.
1Mc 7: 6 They brought to the king this **a** against the people:

ACCUSATIONS (3) [ACCUSE]

Mt 27: 13 not hear how many **a** they make against you?"
Ac 26: 2 I am to make my defense today against all the **a** of
2Mc 14: 27 provoked by the false **a** of that depraved man,

ACCUSE (21) [ACCUSATION, ACCUSATIONS, ACCUSED, ACCUSER, ACCUSERS, ACCUSES, ACCUSING]

Dt 19: 16 a malicious witness comes forward to **a** someone
Ps 69: 4 my enemies who **a** me falsely.
103: 9 He will not always **a,**
109: 4 In return for my love they **a** me,
Isa 43: 26 **A** me, let us go to trial;
57: 16 For I will not continually **a,**
Jer 2: 9 Therefore once more I **a** you, says the LORD,
2: 9 says the LORD, and I **a** your children's children.
Hos 4: 4 Yet let no one contend, and let none **a,**
Zec 3: 1 and Satan standing at his right hand to **a** him.
Mt 12: 10 so that they might **a** him.

Mk 3: 2 so that they might a him.
Lk 23: 2 They began to a him, saying,
Jn 5:45 Do not think that I will a you before the Father;
Ac 24: 2 Tertullus began to a him, saying:
24: 8 concerning everything of which we a him."
25: 5 about the man, let them a him."
Ro 2:15 and their conflicting thoughts will a
Wis 12:12 Who will a you for the destruction of nations
1Mc 10:61 renegades, gathered together against him to a him;
2Es 16:50 and shall a her to her face

ACCUSED (15) [ACCUSE]
Da 6:24 and those who had a Daniel were brought
Mt 27:12 But when he was a by the chief priests and elders,
Mk 15: 3 Then the chief priests a him of many things.
Ac 22:30 Since he wanted to find out what Paul was being a
23:28 I wanted to know the charge for which they a him,
23:29 that he was a concerning questions of their law,
25:16 before the a had met the accusers face to face
26: 7 your Excellency, that I am a by Jews!
Tit 1: 6 not a of debauchery and not rebellious.
Wis 10:14 Those who a him she showed to be false,
Sir 46:19 And no one a him.
2Mc 5: 8 A before Aretas the ruler of the Arabs,
10:13 As a result he was a before Eupator by
10:21 and a these men of having sold their kindred
14:38 he had been a of Judaism,

ACCUSER‡ (7) [ACCUSE]
Job 9:15 I must appeal for mercy to my a.
Ps 109: 6 let an a stand on his right.
Mt 5:25 Come to terms quickly with your a while you are
5:25 or your a may hand you over to the judge,
Lk 12:58 when you go with your a before a magistrate,
Jn 5:45 before the Father; your a is Moses,
Rev 12:10 for the a of our comrades has been thrown down,

ACCUSERS‡ (10) [ACCUSE]
Ps 71:13 Let my a be put to shame and consumed;
109:20 May that be the reward of my a from the LORD,
109:25 I am an object of scorn to my a;
109:29 May my a be clothed with dishonor;
Ac 23:30 ordering his a also to state
23:35 "I will give you a hearing when your a arrive."
25:16 over anyone before the accused had met the a face
25:18 the a stood up, they did not charge him with any
1Mc 10:64 When his a saw the honor that was paid him,
2Es 16:65 and your own iniquities shall stand as your a on

ACCUSES (2) [ACCUSE]
Rev 12:10 who a them day and night before our God.
Wis 2:12 and a us of sins against our training.

ACCUSING (2) [ACCUSE]
Lk 23:10 and the scribes stood by, vehemently a him.
2Mc 4: 5 a his compatriots but having in view the welfare,

ACCUSTOM (2) [CUSTOM]
Sir 23: 9 Do not a your mouth to oaths,
23:13 Do not a your mouth to coarse, foul language,

ACCUSTOMED (10) [CUSTOM]
Ex 21:29 If the ox has been a to gore in the past,
21:36 it was known that the ox was a to gore in the past,
Jdg 14:10 a feast there as the young men were a to do.
2Ch 30:16 They took their a posts according to the law
Jer 13:23 Then also you can do good who are a to do evil.
Mt 27:15 Now at the festival the governor was a to release
1Co 8: 7 Since some have become so a to idols until now,
Jdt 13:10 as they were a to do for prayer.
Sir 23:15 Those who are a to using abusive language
1Mc 6:30 and thirty-two elephants a to war.

ACELDAMA (KJV) See HAKELDAMA

ACHAIA (10)
Ac 18:12 But when Gallio was proconsul of A,
18:27 And when he wished to cross over to A,
19:21 in the Spirit to go through Macedonia and A,
Ro 15:26 and A have been pleased to share their resources
1Co 16:15 of Stephanas were the first converts in A,
2Co 1: 1 including all the saints throughout A:
9: 2 saying that A has been ready since last year;
11:10 of mine will not be silenced in the regions of A.
1Th 1: 7 to all the believers in Macedonia and in A.
1: 8 from you not only in Macedonia and in A,

ACHAICUS (1)
1Co 16:17 and Fortunatus and A, because they have made up

ACHAN (7) [ACHAR]
Jos 7: 1 A son of Carmi son of Zabdi son of Zerah,
7:18 and A son of Carmi son of Zabdi son of Zerah,
7:19 Then Joshua said to A, "My son,
7:20 And A answered Joshua, "It is true;
7:24 and all Israel with him took A son of Zerah,
22:20 Did not A son of Zerah break faith in the matter of
2Es 7:*107* [37] Joshua after him for Israel in the days of A,

ACHAR (1) [ACHAN]
1Ch 2: 7 The sons of Carmi: A, the troubler of Israel,

ACHAZ (KJV) See AHAZ

ACHBOR (7)
Ge 36:38 and Baal-hanan son of A succeeded him as king.
36:39 Baal-hanan son of A died,
2Ki 22:12 Ahikam son of Shaphan, A son of Micaiah,
22:14 So the priest Hilkiah, Ahikam, A, Shaphan,
1Ch 1:49 Shaul died, Baal-hanan son of A succeeded him.
Jer 26:22 Then King Jehoiakim sent Elnathan son of A
36:12 Elnathan son of A, Gemariah son of Shaphan,

ACHIEVE (3) [ACHIEVEMENT, ACHIEVEMENTS]
Job 5:12 so that their hands a no success.
Ac 27:13 they thought they could a their purpose;
Jdt 11: 6 and my lord will not fail to a his purposes.

ACHIEVEMENT (1) [ACHIEVE]
Job 21:16 Is not their prosperity indeed their own a?

ACHIEVEMENTS (1) [ACHIEVE]
1Mc 16:23 of the walls that he completed, and his a,

ACHIM (2)
Mt 1:14 and Zadok the father of A,
1:14 and A the father of Eliud,

ACHIOR (12) [ACHIOR'S]
Jdt 5: 5 Then A, the leader of all the Ammonites,
5:22 When A had finished saying these things,
6: 1 to A in the presence of all the foreign contingents:
6: 2 A and you mercenaries of Ephraim,
6: 5 "As for you, A, you Ammonite mercenary,
6:10 to seize A and take him away to Bethulia
6:13 they bound A and left him lying at the foot of
6:16 They set A in the midst of all their people,
6:20 Then they reassured A, and praised him highly.
14: 5 bring A the Ammonite to me so that he may see
14: 6 So they summoned A from the house of Uzziah.
14:10 When A saw all that the God of Israel had done,

ACHIOR'S (1) [ACHIOR]
Jdt 11: 9 "Now as for A speech in your council,

ACHISH (21)
1Sa 21:10 he went to King A of Gath.
21:11 The servants of A said to him,
21:12 and was very much afraid of King A of Gath.
21:14 A said to his servants, "Look,
27: 2 to King A son of Maoch of Gath.
27: 3 David stayed with A at Gath, he and his troops,
27: 5 Then David said to A, "If I have found favor
27: 6 So that day A gave him Ziklag;
27: 9 the camels, and the clothing, and came back to A.
27:10 When A asked, "Against whom have you made
27:12 A trusted David, thinking,
28: 1 A said to David, "You know, of course,
28: 2 David said to A, "Very well,
28: 2 A said to David, "Very well,
29: 2 and his men were passing on in the rear with A,
29: 3 A said to the commanders of the Philistines,
29: 6 Then A called David and said to him,
29: 8 David said to A, "But what have I done?
29: 9 A replied to David, "I know that you are
1Ki 2:39 of Shimei's slaves ran away to King A son
2:40 and went to A in Gath, to search for his slaves;

ACHMETHA (KJV) See ECBATANA

ACHOR (5)
Jos 7:24 and they brought them up to the Valley of A.
7:26 that place to this day is called the Valley of A.
15: 7 from the Valley of A, and so northward, turning
Isa 65:10 and the Valley of A a place for herds to lie down,
Hos 2:15 and make the Valley of A a door of hope.

ACHSAH (5)
Jos 15:16 to him I will give my daughter A as wife."
15:17 and he gave him his daughter A as wife.
Jdg 1:12 I will give him my daughter A as wife."
1:13 and he gave him his daughter A as wife.
1Ch 2:49 and the daughter of Caleb was A.

ACHSHAPH (3)
Jos 11: 1 to the king of Shimron, to the king of A,
12:20 the king of Shimron-meron one the king of A one
19:25 Its boundary included Helkath, Hali, Beten, A,

ACHZIB (4)
Jos 15:44 A, and Mareshah: nine towns with their villages.
19:29 and it ends at the sea; Mahalab, A,
Jdg 1:31 or the inhabitants of Sidon, or of Ahlab, or of A,
Mic 1:14 the houses of A shall be a deception to the kings

ACKNOWLEDGE (38) [ACKNOWLEDGED, ACKNOWLEDGES, ACKNOWLEDGING]
Dt 4:35 To you it was shown so that you would a that
4:39 So a today and take to heart that
11: 2 but it is you who must a his greatness,
21:17 He must a as firstborn the son of
33: 9 he ignored his kin, and did not a his children.
Job 40:14 Then I will also a to you
Pr 3: 6 In all your ways a him,
Isa 26:13 but we a your name alone.
33:13 and you who are near, a my might.
61: 9 all who see them shall a that they are a people
63:16 not know us and Israel does not a us;
Jer 3:13 Only a your guilt, that you have rebelled against
14:20 We a our wickedness, O LORD,
Da 11:39 Those who a him he shall make more wealthy,
Hos 5:15 until they a their guilt and seek my face.
Mt 10:32 I also will a before my Father in heaven;
Lk 12: 8 Son of Man also will a before the angels of God;
Ac 23: 8 but the Pharisees a all three.)
Ro 1:28 And since they did not see fit to a God,
1Co 14:37 must a that what I am writing to you is
3Jn 1: 9 to put himself first, does not a our authority.
Tob 12: 6 and a him in the presence of all the living for
12: 6 Do not be slow to a him.
12: 7 but to a and reveal the works of God,
12: 7 and with fitting honor to a him.
12:20 So now get up from the ground, and a God.
13: 3 A him before the nations, O children of Israel;
13: 6 a him at the top of your voice.
13: 6 In the land of my exile I a him,
13: 8 of his majesty, and a him in Jerusalem.
13:10 A the Lord, for he is good,
13:16 to see your glory and a the King of heaven.
Wis 15: 2 because we know that you a us as yours.
Man 1:12 O Lord, I have sinned, and I a my transgressions.
2Es 9:10 For as many as did not a me in their lifetime,
9:12 these must in torment a it after death.
10:16 For if you a the decree of God to be just,
4Mc 6:34 to a the dominance of reason when it masters

ACKNOWLEDGED (11) [ACKNOWLEDGE]
Ge 38:26 Then Judah a them and said,
Ps 32: 5 I a my sin to you, and I did not hide my iniquity;
Lk 7:29 including the tax collectors, a the justice of God,
Gal 2: 2 in a private meeting with the a leaders) the gospel
2: 6 those who were supposed to be a leaders
2: 9 and John, who were a pillars, recognized the grace
Tob 11:17 Tobit a that God had been merciful to him
12:22 and they a God for these marvelous deeds of his,
Wis 18:13 they a your people to be God's child.
Sir 44:23 he a him with his blessings,
2Es 8:28 but remember those who have willingly a that you

ACKNOWLEDGES (2) [ACKNOWLEDGE]
Mt 10:32 "Everyone therefore who a me before others,
Lk 12: 8 "And I tell you, everyone who a me before others,

ACKNOWLEDGING (1) [ACKNOWLEDGE]
Tob 14: 2 and continually blessing God and a God's majesty.

ACQUAINTANCE (2) [ACQUAINTANCES, ACQUAINTED]
2Mc 6:21 the man aside because of their long a with him,
4Mc 6:13 partly out of sympathy from their a with him,

ACQUAINTANCES (4) [ACQUAINTANCE]
Job 19:13 and my a are wholly estranged from me.
Ps 31:11 an object of dread to my a;
Lk 23:49 all his a, including the women who had followed
Sir 30: 2 and will boast of him among a.

ACQUAINTED (7) [ACQUAINTANCE]
Dt 8: 3 with which neither you nor your ancestors were a,
Job 24:13 who are not a with its ways,
Ps 139: 3 and are a with all my ways.
Isa 53: 3 a man of suffering and a with infirmity;
Tob 5: 4 someone who was a with the way.
5: 6 I am a with it and know all the roads.
2Mc 14: 9 Since you are a, O king, with the details

ACQUIRE (14) [ACQUIRED, ACQUIRES, ACQUIRING]
Lev 25:44 from the nations around you that you may a male
25:45 also a them from among the aliens residing
Dt 17:16 Even so, he must not a many horses for himself,
17:16 the people to Egypt in order to a more horses,
17:17 And he must not a many wives for himself,
17:17 also silver and gold he must not a in great quantity
Ru 4: 5 "The day you a the field from the hand of Naomi,
4: 8 the next-of-kin said to Boaz, "A it for yourself,"
Pr 1: 5 and the discerning a skill,
8: 5 a intelligence, you who lack it.
Jdt 8:22 and a disgrace in the eyes of those who a us.
Sir 16:24 Listen to me, my child, and a knowledge,
51:25 A wisdom for yourselves without money.
51:28 and through me you will a silver and gold.

ACQUIRED‡ (15) [ACQUIRE]
Ge 12: 5 and the persons whom they had a in Haran;
31:18 in his possession that he had a in Paddan-aram,
36: 6 all the property he had a in the land of Canaan;
46: 6 the goods that they had a in the land of Canaan,
Ex 15:16 passed by, until the people whom you a passed by.
Dt 3:14 the Manassite a the whole region of Argob as far
Ru 4: 9 "Today you are witnesses that I have a from

Ru 4:10 I have also **a** Ruth the Moabite,
Ne 5:16 to the work on this wall, and **a** no land;
Ps 74: 2 Which you **a** long ago, which you redeemed to be
Pr 20:21 An estate quickly **a** in the beginning will not
Ecc 1:16 I said to myself, "I have **a** great wisdom,
Ac 1:18 (Now this man **a** a field with the reward
Sir Pr: 1 and had **a** considerable proficiency in them,
14:15 and what you **a** by toil to be divided by lot?

ACQUIRES (4) [ACQUIRE]
Lev 22:11 a priest **a** anyone by purchase, the person may eat
Pr 18:15 An intelligent mind **a** knowledge,
Sir 34:11 but he that has traveled **a** much cleverness.
36:29 He who **a** a wife gets his best possession,

ACQUIRING (4) [ACQUIRE]
Ru 4: 5 you are also **a** Ruth the Moabite,
Eze 38:12 who are **a** cattle and goods,
Jdt 15: 6 and plundered it, **a** great riches.
Sir 42: 4 and of **a** much or little;

ACQUIT (7) [ACQUITTAL, ACQUITTED, ACQUITTING]
Ex 20: 7 LORD will not **a** anyone who misuses his name.
23: 7 for I will not **a** the guilty.
Dt 5:11 LORD will not **a** anyone who misuses his name.
Job 10:14 you watch me, and do not **a** me of my iniquity.
Isa 5:23 who **a** the guilty for a bribe,
Sir 10:29 Who will **a** those who condemn themselves?
42: 2 and of rendering judgment to **a** the ungodly;

ACQUITTAL (1) [ACQUIT]
Ps 69:27 may they have no **a** from you.

ACQUITTED (4) [ACQUIT]
Job 23: 7 and I should be **a** forever by my judge.
1Co 4: 4 but I am not thereby **a**.
2Mc 4:47 he **a** of the charges against him,
3Mc 7: 7 we justly have **a** them of every charge

ACQUITTING (1) [ACQUIT]
Sus 1:53 condemning the innocent and **a** the guilty,

ACRE (1) [ACRES]
1Sa 14:14 an area about half a furrow long in an **a** of land.

ACRES (1) [ACRE]
Isa 5:10 For ten **a** of vineyard shall yield but one bath,

ACROSS (34)
Ge 1:20 and let birds fly above the earth **a** the dome of
32:23 He took them and sent them **a** the stream,
Nu 22: 1 in the plains of Moab **a** the Jordan from Jericho.
Dt 32:49 which is in the land of Moab, **a** from Jericho,
Jos 7: 7 Why have you brought this people **a** the Jordan
1Sa 10:27 the Israelites **a** the Jordan whose right eye Nahash,
1Ki 6: 3 **a** the width of the house.
6:21 then he drew chains of gold **a**,
1Ch 6:78 and **a** the Jordan from Jericho, on the east side of
2Ch 3: 4 **a** the width of the house;
Job 1:19 and suddenly a great wind came **a** the desert,
Isa 9: 4 yoke of their burden, and the bar **a** their shoulders,
Jer 25:22 and the kings of the coastland **a** the sea;
Eze 42: 3 **A** the twenty cubits that belonged to
Da 8: 5 coming **a** the face of the whole earth
Jnh 3: 3 an exceedingly large city, a three days' walk **a**.
Mt 4:15 **a** the Jordan, Galilee of the Gentiles—
Mk 4:35 he said to them, "Let us go **a** to the other side."
8:13 he went **a** to the other side.
Lk 8:22 "Let us go **a** to the other side of the lake."
Jn 1:28 This took place in Bethany **a** the Jordan
3:26 "Rabbi, the one who was with you **a** the Jordan,
6:17 and started **a** the sea to Capernaum.
10:40 He went away again **a** the Jordan to the place
18: 1 he went out with his disciples **a** the Kidron valley
Ac 27: 5 After we had sailed **a** the sea that is off Cilicia
27:27 as we were drifting **a** the sea of Adria,
Rev 1:13 clothed with a long robe and with a golden sash **a**
15: 6 with golden sashes **a** their chests.
Jdt 15: 2 and fled by every path **a** the plain and through
1Mc 5:39 and they are encamped **a** the stream,
9:48 with him leaped into the Jordan and swam **a** to
2Mc 8:35 and made his way alone like a runaway slave **a**
2Es 13:40 he took them **a** the river,

ACT‡ (109) [ACTED, ACTING, ACTION, ACTIONS, ACTIVATED, ACTIVATES, ACTIVE, ACTIVITIES, ACTIVITY, ACTS]
Ge 19: 7 "I beg you, my brothers, do not **a** so wickedly.
Ex 1:16 "When you **a** as midwives to the Hebrew women,
21:13 but came about by an **a** of God,
23: 1 You shall not join hands with the wicked to **a** as
Nu 5:13 against her since she was not caught in the **a**;
31:16 the Israelites **a** treacherously against the LORD
Dt 4:16 not **a** corruptly by making an idol for yourselves,
4:25 if you **a** corruptly by making an idol in the form
12: 8 You shall not **a** as we are acting here today,
17:13 and will not **a** presumptuously again.
22:21 because she committed a disgraceful **a** in Israel
22:28 and they are caught in the **a**,
25:16 For all who do such things, all who **a** dishonestly,
Dt 31:29 that after my death you will surely **a** corruptly,
Jos 1: 7 being careful to **a** in accordance with all the law
1: 8 that you may be careful to **a** in accordance with all
Jdg 14: 4 for he was seeking a pretext to **a** against
16:28 so that with this one **a** of revenge I may pay back
19:23 "No, my brothers, do not **a** so wickedly.
20: 3 "Tell us, how did this criminal **a** come about?"
Ru 3:13 if he will **a** as next-of-kin for you, good;
3:13 If he is not willing to **a** as next-of-kin for you,
3:13 I will **a** as next-of-kin for you.
1Sa 14: 6 it may be that the LORD will **a** for us;
14:24 Now Saul committed a very rash **a** on that day.
1Ki 2: 6 **A** therefore according to your wisdom,
8:32 and **a**, and judge your servants,
8:39 **a**, and render to all whose hearts you know—
1Ch 28:10 as the sanctuary; be strong, and **a**."
28:20 "Be strong and of good courage, and **a**.
2Ch 6:23 and **a**, and judge your servants,
19: 9 He charged them: "This is how you shall **a**:
24: 5 and see that you **a** quickly."
24: 5 But the Levites did not **a** quickly.
25: 8 Rather, go by yourself and **a**;
34:21 the word of the LORD, to **a** in accordance
Ne 13:18 Did not your ancestors **a** in this way,
13:27 and do all this great evil and **a** treacherously
Ps 36: 3 they have ceased to **a** wisely and do good.
37: 5 trust in him, and he will **a**.
109:21 **a** on my behalf for your name's sake;
119:126 It is time for the LORD to **a**,
Pr 12:22 but those who **a** faithfully are his delight.
13: 5 but the wicked **a** shamefully and disgracefully.
Ecc 7:16 Do not be too righteous, and do not **a** too wise;
Jer 6:28 they are bronze and iron, all of them **a** corruptly.
7: 5 if you truly **a** justly one with another,
9:24 I **a** with steadfast love, justice,
14: 7 Although our iniquities testify against us, **a**,
17: 4 By your own **a** you shall lose the heritage
18:12 of us will **a** according to the stubbornness
22: 3 **A** with justice and righteousness,
42: 5 against us if we do not **a** according to everything
Eze 8:18 Therefore I will **a** in wrath;
24:14 the time is coming, I will **a**.
25:14 and they shall **a** in Edom according to my anger
36:22 O house of Israel, that I am about to **a**,
36:32 It is not for your sake that I will **a**,
37:14 have spoken and will **a**," says the LORD.
44: 8 but you have appointed foreigners to **a** for you
44:24 In a controversy they shall **a** as judges,
Da 9:19 O Lord, listen and **a** and do not delay!
11:23 he shall **a** deceitfully and become strong with
11:36 "The king shall **a** as he pleases.
12:10 but the wicked shall continue to **a** wickedly.
Mal 3:17 my special possession on the day when I **a**,
4: 3 on the day when I **a**, says the LORD of hosts.
Mt 7:26 of mine and does not **a** on them will be like
Lk 6:49 and does not **a** is like a man who built a house on
Jn 8: 4 ⟦in the very **a** of committing adultery.⟧
Ro 5:18 so one man's **a** of righteousness leads
14:23 because they do not **a** from faith;
2Co 3:12 we have such a hope, we **a** with great boldness,
8: 9 you know the generous **a** of our Lord Jesus Christ,
Heb 13:18 desiring to **a** honorably in all things.
Jas 1:17 Every generous **a** of giving,
1:25 being not hearers who forget but doers who **a**—
2:12 and so **a** as those who are to be judged by the law
Tob 4: 6 for those who **a** in accordance
7:11 and the Lord will **a** on behalf of you both."
Jdt 11:15 the response reaches them and they **a** upon it,
AdE 8:11 and to **a** as they wished against their opponents
16:24 that does not **a** accordingly shall be destroyed
Wis 12:18 for you have power to **a** whenever you choose.
18:21 a blameless man was quick to **a** as their champion;
Sir 3: 1 **a** accordingly, that you may be kept in safety.
8:15 for they will **a** as they please,
15:15 and to **a** faithfully is a matter of your own choice.
16:14 He makes room for every **a** of mercy;
32: 9 Among the great do not **a** as their equal;
32:23 Guard yourself in every **a**,
1Mc 7: 3 But when this **a** became known to him, he said,
8:25 of the Jews shall **a** as their allies wholeheartedly,
8:27 the Romans shall willingly **a** as their allies,
10: 4 "Let us **a** first to make peace with him
14:46 All the people agreed to grant Simon the right to **a**
16:17 an **a** of great treachery and returned evil for good.
2Mc 4:31 a man of high rank, to **a** as his deputy.
5:18 from his rash **a** as soon as he came forward,
3Mc 4:21 But this was an **a** of the invincible providence
5:28 This was the **a** of God who rules over all things,
2Es 3:30 and have spared those who **a** wickedly,
6:34 then you will not **a** hastily in the last times.' "
8:27 of the endeavors of those who **a** wickedly,
4Mc 2: 8 one is forced to **a** contrary to natural ways and
2:13 so that one rebukes friends when they **a** wickedly.
5:24 so that in all our dealings we **a** impartially,
5:33 as to break the ancestral law by my own **a**.
11: 4 what **a** of ours are you destroying us in this way?

ACTED (46) [ACT]
Ex 32: 7 up out of the land of Egypt, have **a** perversely;
Dt 9:12 from Egypt have **a** corruptly.
Jos 7:11 they have stolen, they have **a** deceitfully,
9: 4 they on their part **a** with cunning:
Jdg 9:16 if you **a** in good faith and honor
9:19 you have **a** in good faith and honor with Jerubbaal
1Ki 8:47 and have done wrong; we have **a** wickedly';
21:26 He **a** most abominably in going after idols,
2Ch 6:37 and have done wrong; we have **a** wickedly';
34:32 of Jerusalem **a** according to the covenant of God,
Ne 9:10 that they **a** insolently against our ancestors.
9:16 "But they and our ancestors **a** presumptuously
9:29 Yet they **a** presumptuously and did
9:33 you have dealt faithfully and we have **a** wickedly;
Jer 6:15 They **a** shamefully, they committed abomination;
8:12 They **a** shamefully, they committed abomination;
38: 9 these men have **a** wickedly in all they did to
Eze 5: 7 or kept my ordinances, but have **a** according to
11:12 but you have **a** according to the ordinances of
15: 8 because they have **a** faithlessly,
16:47 and **a** according to their abominations;
16:52 in which you **a** more abominably than they,
20: 9 But I **a** for the sake of my name,
20:14 But I **a** for the sake of my name,
20:22 and **a** for the sake of my name,
25:12 Because Edom **a** revengefully against the house
25:15 Because with unending hostilities the Philistines **a**
Da 5:20 and his spirit was hardened so that he **a** proudly,
8:11 Even against the prince of the host it **a** arrogantly;
9: 5 and done wrong, **a** wickedly and rebelled,
Hos 2: 5 she who conceived them has **a** shamefully.
Mic 3: 4 because they have **a** wickedly.
Lk 16: 8 the dishonest manager because he had **a** shrewdly;
Ac 3:17 now, friends, I know that you **a** in ignorance,
1Ti 1:13 But I received mercy because I had **a** ignorantly
AdE 8: 7 and have hanged him on a tree because he **a**
10: 3 Mordecai **a** with authority on behalf
Sir 32:19 but when you have **a**, do not regret it.
2Mc 3:30 they praised the Lord who had **a** marvelously
6:29 a little before had **a** toward him with goodwill
12:43 In doing this he **a** very well and honorably,
1Es 1:24 concerning those who sinned and **a** wickedly
9:15 And those who had returned from exile **a**
3Mc 2: 5 and sulfur the people of Sodom who **a** arrogantly,
2:32 But the majority **a** firmly with a courageous spirit
2Es 8:35 those who have been born who has not **a** wickedly;

ACTING‡ (15) [ACT]
Nu 10:25 **a** as the rear guard of all the camps, set out,
Dt 12: 8 You shall not act as we are **a** here today,
2Ki 10:19 But Jehu was **a** with cunning in order to destroy
2Ch 35: 6 **a** according to the word of the LORD by Moses."
Ne 6:13 to intimidate me and make me sin by **a**
Eze 14:13 when a land sins against me by **a** faithlessly,
18: 9 to observe my ordinances, **a** faithfully—
24:19 that you are **a** this way?"
Ac 17: 7 They are all **a** contrary to the decrees of
2Co 10: 2 to oppose those who think we are **a** according
Gal 2:14 when I saw that they were not **a** consistently with
Tob 12:18 when I was with you, I was not **a** on my own will,
AdE 13: 2 but always **a** reasonably and with kindness),
Sus 1:62 **A** in accordance with the law of Moses,
2Mc 7: 2 One of them, **a** as their spokesman, said,

ACTION (21) [ACT]
Ezr 10: 4 Take **a**, for it is your duty, and we are with you;
Da 11: 3 who shall rule with great dominion and take **a**
11: 7 and he shall take **a** against them and prevail.
11:30 be enraged and take **a** against the holy covenant.
11:32 to their God shall stand firm and take **a**.
Lk 12:35 "Be dressed for **a** and have your lamps lit;
23:51 had not agreed to their plan and **a**.
Ac 5:17 Then the high priest took **a**;
2Co 10:15 that, as your faith increases, our sphere of **a**
10:16 in someone else's sphere of **a**.
1Pe 1:13 Therefore prepare your minds for **a**;
1Jn 3:18 not in word or speech, but in truth and **a**.
Sir 15:19 and he knows every human **a**.
Sus 1:61 And they took **a** against the two elders,
1Mc 4:34 of Lysias five thousand men; they fell in **a**.
2Mc 15:28 the **a** was over and they were returning with joy,
1Es 8:95 Rise up and take **a**, for it is your task,
3Mc 1: 5 it came about that the enemy was routed in the **a**,
3:19 and are unwilling to regard any **a** as sincere.
5:12 the **a** of the Lord he was overcome by so pleasant
5:26 that what the king desired was ready for **a**.

ACTIONS (12) [ACT]
Jdg 9:16 and have done to him as his **a** deserved—
1Sa 2: 3 and by him **a** are weighed.
Isa 65: 7 into their laps full payment for their **a**.
Da 11:16 against him shall take the **a** he pleases,
Ro 7:15 I do not understand my own **a**.
Tit 1:16 but they deny him by their **a**.
Wis 2:12 he is inconvenient to us and opposes our **a**;
9:11 and she will guide me wisely in my **a**
19: 1 for God knew in advance even their future **a**:
Sir 11:31 and to worthy **a** they attach blame.
3Mc 6:27 begging pardon for your former **a**!
2Es 12:25 up his wickedness and perform his last **a**.

ACTIVATED (1) [ACT]
1Co 12:11 All these are **a** by one and the same Spirit,

ACTIVATES (1) [ACT]
1Co 12: 6 it is the same God who **a** all of them in everyone.

ACTIVE (4) [ACT]
Heb 4:12 Indeed, the word of God is living and **a**,
Jas 2:22 You see that faith was **a** along with his works,
Wis 8: 5 the **a** cause of all things?
15:11 with **a** souls and breathed a living spirit into them.

ACTIVITIES (3) [ACT]

1Co 12: 6 and there are varieties of **a**,
Tob 4: 6 in accordance with truth will prosper in all their **a**.
Sir 11:10 if you multiply **a**, you will not be held blameless.

ACTIVITY (1) [ACT]

Wis 7:17 to know the structure of the world and the **a** of

ACTS (103) [ACT]

Ex 6: 6 with an outstretched arm and with mighty **a**
7: 4 out of the land of Egypt by great **a** of judgment.
Nu 15:29 you shall have the same law for anyone who **a**
15:30 But whoever **a** high-handedly,
Dt 3:24 or on earth can perform deeds and mighty **a**
1Ki 11:41 Now the rest of the **a** of Solomon,
11:41 not written in the Book of the **A** of Solomon?
14:19 Now the rest of the **a** of Jeroboam,
14:29 Now the rest of the **a** of Rehoboam,
15: 7 The rest of the **a** of Abijam, and all that he did,
15:23 Now the rest of all the **a** of Asa, all his power,
15:31 Now the rest of the **a** of Nadab, and all that he did,
16: 5 Now the rest of the **a** of Baasha, what he did,
16:14 Now the rest of the **a** of Elah, and all that he did,
16:20 Now the rest of the **a** of Zimri,
16:27 Now the rest of the **a** of Omri that he did,
22:39 Now the rest of the **a** of Ahab, and all that he did,
22:45 Now the rest of the **a** of Jehoshaphat,
2Ki 1:18 Now the rest of the **a** of Ahaziah that he did,
8:23 Now the rest of the **a** of Joram, and all that he did,
10:34 Now the rest of the **a** of Jehu, all that he did,
12:19 Now the rest of the **a** of Joash, and all that he did,
13: 8 the rest of the **a** of Jehoahaz and all that he did,
13:12 Now the rest of the **a** of Joash, and all that he did,
14:15 Now the rest of the **a** that Jehoash did, his might,
14:28 Now the rest of the **a** of Jeroboam,
15: 6 Now the rest of the **a** of Azariah,
15:31 Now the rest of the **a** of Pekah, and all that he did,
15:36 Now the rest of the **a** of Jotham,
16:19 Now the rest of the **a** of Ahaz that he did,
21:17 Now the rest of the **a** of Manasseh, all that he did,
21:25 Now the rest of the **a** of Amon that he did,
23:28 Now the rest of the **a** of Josiah, and all that he did,
1Ch 29:29 Now the **a** of King David, from first to last,
2Ch 9:29 Now the rest of the **a** of Solomon,
12:15 Now the **a** of Rehoboam, from first to last,
13:22 The rest of the **a** of Abijah,
16:11 The **a** of Asa, from first to last,
20:34 Now the rest of the **a** of Jehoshaphat,
26:22 Now the rest of the **a** of Uzziah, from first to last,
27: 7 Now the rest of the **a** of Jotham,
28:26 Now the rest of his **a** and all his ways,
32: 1 After these things and these **a** of faithfulness,
32:32 Now the rest of the **a** of Hezekiah,
33:18 Now the rest of the **a** of Manasseh,
35:26 the rest of the **a** of Josiah and his faithful deeds
35:27 and his **a**, first and last, are written in the Book of
36: 8 Now the rest of the **a** of Jehoiakim,
Est 10: 2 All the **a** of his power and might,
Job 40:19 "It is the first of the great **a** of God—
Ps 31:23 but abundantly repays the one who **a** haughtily.
53: 1 They are corrupt, they commit abominable **a**;
71:15 My mouth will tell of your righteous **a**,
103: 7 his **a** to the people of Israel.
106:39 Thus they became unclean by their **a**,
145: 4 and shall declare your mighty **a**.
Pr 8:22 the first of his **a** of long ago.
14:17 One who is quick-tempered **a** foolishly,
14:35 but his wrath falls on one who **a** shamefully.
17: 2 over a child who **a** shamefully,
20:11 Even children make themselves known by their **a**,
21:24 named "Scoffer," **a** with arrogant pride.
Isa 63: 7 the praiseworthy **a** of the LORD,
Jer 5: 1 who **a** justly and seeks truth—
Eze 14:21 upon Jerusalem my four deadly **a** of judgment,
23:43 but they carry on their sexual **a** with her.
30:14 and will execute **a** of judgment on Thebes.
30:19 Thus I will execute **a** of judgment on Egypt.
Da 9:16 O Lord, in view of all your righteous **a**,
Mic 6: 5 that you may know the saving **a** of the LORD."
Mt 7:24 then who hears these words of mine and **a**
Lk 6:47 hears my words, and **a** on them.
Jn 7: 4 no one who wants to be widely known **a** in secret.
Ac 9:36 She was devoted to good works and **a** of charity.
Ro 1:27 Men committed shameless **a** with men
Jas 2: 1 do you with your **a** of favoritism really believe
1Pe 2: 9 in order that you may proclaim the mighty **a**
Tob 1: 3 I performed many **a** of charity for my kindred
1:16 In the days of Shalmaneser I performed many **a**
2:14 she replied to me, "Where are your **a** of charity?
Wis 19:13 for they justly suffered because of their wicked **a**;
Sir 10: 6 and do not resort to **a** of insolence.
16:22 Who is to announce his **a** of justice?
22: 4 but one who **a** shamefully is a grief to her father.
26:24 *shameless woman constantly* **a** *disgracefully*,
31:11 and the assembly will proclaim his **a** of charity.
1Mc 9:22 Now the rest of the **a** of Judas,
13:46 "Do not treat us according to our wicked **a** but
14:45 Whoever **a** contrary to these decisions
16:23 of the **a** of John and his wars and the brave deeds
2Mc 4:33 When Onias became fully aware of these **a**,
4:39 When many **a** of sacrilege had been committed in
8:18 "For they trust to arms and **a** of daring," he said,
1Es 1:25 After all these **a** of Josiah,
1:33 and every one of the **a** of Josiah, and his splendor,
1:49 of the people and the priests committed many **a**
1:52 because of their ungodly **a** he gave command
3Mc 6:24 and life by secretly devising **a** of no advantage to
7: 6 But we very severely threatened them for these **a**,
7: 9 and inescapably as an antagonist to avenge such **a**.
2Es 15: 8 be silent no longer concerning their ungodly **a**
4Mc 4:21 The divine justice was angered by these **a**
9:15 or as one who **a** impiously,

ACTUALLY‡ (9)

Dt 1:28 We **a** saw there the offspring of the Anakim!' "
Jer 26:19 of Judah and all Judah **a** put him to death?
29:28 For he has **a** sent to us in Babylon, saying,
Ac 21:28 that, he has **a** brought Greeks into the temple
Ro 5: 7 for a good person someone might **a** dare to die.
1Co 5: 1 It is **a** reported that there is sexual immorality
Gal 2: 6 (what they **a** were makes no difference to me;
2:10 which was **a** what I was eager to do.
Php 1:12 that what has happened to me has **a** helped

ACUB, ACUM See Index to Footnotes

ACUPH (1)

1Es 5:31 the descendants of **A**, the descendants

ADADAH (1)

Jos 15:22 Kinah, Dimonah, **A**,

ADAH (8)

Ge 4:19 the name of the one was **A**,
4:20 **A** bore Jabal; he was the ancestor of those
4:23 "**A** and Zillah, hear my voice;
36: 2 **A** daughter of Elon the Hittite,
36: 4 **A** bore Eliphaz to Esau; Basemath bore Reuel;
36:10 Eliphaz son of **A** the wife of Esau;
36:12 These were the sons of **A**, Esau's wife.
36:16 they are the sons of **A**.

ADAIAH (10)

2Ki 22: 1 His mother's name was Jedidah daughter of **A**
1Ch 6:41 son of Ethni, son of Zerah, son of **A**,
8:21 **A**, Beraiah, and Shimrath were the sons
9:12 and **A** son of Jeroham, son of Pashhur, son
2Ch 23: 1 Maaseiah son of **A**, and Elishaphat son of Zichri.
Ezr 10:29 Meshullam, Malluch, **A**, Jashub, Sheal,
10:39 Shelemiah, Nathan, **A**,
Ne 11: 5 of **A** son of Joiarib son of Zechariah son of
11:12 and **A** son of Jeroham son of Pelaliah son
1Es 9:30 Olamus, Mamuchus, **A**, Jashub,

ADALIA (1)

Est 9: 8 Poratha, **A**, Aridatha,

ADAM‡ (30) [ADAM'S]

Ge 4:25 **A** knew his wife again, and she bore a son
5: 1 This is the list of the descendants of **A**.
5: 3 When **A** had lived one hundred thirty years,
5: 4 The days of **A** after he became the father
5: 5 that **A** lived were nine hundred thirty years;
Jos 3:16 rising up in a single heap far off at **A**,
1Ch 1: 1 **A**, Seth, Enosh;
Hos 6: 7 But at **A** they transgressed the covenant;
Lk 3:38 son of Enos, son of Seth, son of **A**, son of God.
Ro 5:14 Yet death exercised dominion from **A** to Moses,
5:14 not like the transgression of **A**,
1Co 15:22 as all die in **A**, so all will be made alive in Christ.
15:45 Thus it is written, "The first man, **A**, became a
15:45 the last **A** became a life-giving spirit.
1Ti 2:13 For **A** was formed first, then Eve;
2:14 and **A** was not deceived, but the woman was
Jude 1:14 in the seventh generation from **A**, prophesied,
Tob 8: 6 You made **A**, and for him you made his wife Eve
Sir 40: 1 and a heavy yoke is laid on the children of **A**,
49:16 but above every other created living being was **A**.
2Es 3: 5 and it gave you **A**, a lifeless body?
3:10 just as death came upon **A**,
3:21 For the first **A**, burdened with an evil heart,
3:26 as **A** and all his descendants had done,
6:54 and over these you placed **A**, as ruler over all
6:56 for the other nations that have descended from **A**,
7:11 and when **A** transgressed my statutes,
7:*70* the world and **A** and all who have come from him,
7:*116* [46] if the earth had not produced **A**,
7:*118* [48] O **A**, what have you done?

ADAM'S (1) [ADAM]

2Es 4:30 For a grain of evil seed was sown in **A** heart from

ADAMAH‡ (1)

Jos 19:36 **A**, Ramah, Hazor,

ADAMANT (2)

Zec 7:12 They made their hearts **a** in order not to hear
4Mc 16:13 a mind like **a** and giving rebirth for immortality to

ADAMANT (KJV) See also FLINT

ADAMI-NEKEB (1)

Jos 19:33 from the oak in Zaanannim, and **A**, and Jabneel,

ADAR (25)

Ezr 6:15 on the third day of the month of **A**,
Est 3: 7 of the twelfth month, which is the month of **A**.
3:13 which is the month of **A**,
8:12 which is the month of **A**.
9: 1 in the twelfth month, which is the month of **A**,
9:15 also on the fourteenth day of the month of **A**
9:17 This was on the thirteenth day of the month of **A**,
9:19 hold the fourteenth day of the month of **A** as a day
9:21 of the month **A** and also the fifteenth day of
AdE 2:16 which is **A**, in the seventh year of his reign.
3: 7 lot fell on the fourteenth day of the month of **A**.
3:13 which is **A**, and to plunder their goods.
8:12 the thirteenth of the twelfth month, which is **A**,
9: 1 which is **A**, the decree written by the king arrived.
9:19 the country outside Susa keep the fourteenth of **A**
9:19 the fifteenth day of **A** as their joyful holiday,
9:21 the fourteenth and fifteenth days of **A**,
9:22 The whole month (namely, **A**),
10:13 So they will observe these days in the month of **A**,
13: 6 on the fourteenth day of the twelfth month, **A**,
16:20 that on the thirteenth day of the twelfth month, **A**,
1Mc 7:43 in battle on the thirteenth day of the month of **A**.
7:49 be celebrated each year on the thirteenth day of **A**.
2Mc 15:36 which is called **A** in the Aramaic language—
1Es 7: 5 by the twenty-third day of the month of **A**,

ADASA (2)

1Mc 7:40 Judas encamped in **A** with three thousand men.
7:45 from **A** as far as Gazara,

ADBEEL (2)

Ge 25:13 of Ishmael; and Kedar, **A**,
1Ch 1:29 of Ishmael, Nebaioth; and Kedar, **A**,

ADD (33) [ADDED, ADDING, ADDITION, ADDITIONAL, ADDS]

Ge 30:24 saying, "May the LORD **a** to me another son!"
Lev 2:15 You shall **a** oil to it and lay frankincense on it;
5:16 and shall **a** one-fifth to it and give it to the priest.
6: 5 the principal amount and shall **a** one-fifth to it.
6:12 Every morning the priest shall **a** wood to it,
22:14 he shall **a** one-fifth of its value to it,
27:31 they must **a** one-fifth to them.
Dt 4: 2 You must neither **a** anything
12:32 do not **a** to it or take anything from it.
19: 9 then you shall **a** three more cities to these three,
2Sa 3: 9 So may God do to Abner and so may he **a** to it!
1Ki 12:11 a heavy yoke, I will **a** to your yoke.
12:14 made your yoke heavy, but I will **a** to your yoke;
2Ki 20: 6 I will **a** fifteen years to your life.
1Ch 22:14 To these you must **a** more.
2Ch 10:11 a heavy yoke, I will **a** to your yoke.
10:14 made your yoke heavy, but I will **a** to it;
Ps 69:27 **A** guilt to their guilt; may they have no acquittal
Pr 30: 6 Do not **a** to his words, or else he will rebuke you,
Isa 5: 8 you who join house to house, who **a** field to field,
29: 1 **A** year to year; let the festivals run their round.
38: 5 I will **a** fifteen years to your life.
Jer 7:21 **A** your burnt offerings to your sacrifices,
Mt 6:27 by worrying **a** a single hour to your span of life?
Lk 12:25 by worrying **a** a single hour to your span of life?
Rev 22:18 if anyone adds to them, God will **a** to that person
Tob 5:16 and I will **a** something to your wages."
Sir 4: 3 Do not **a** to the troubles of the desperate,
5: 5 not be so confident of forgiveness that you **a** sin
13: 3 poor person suffers wrong, and must **a** apologies.
1Mc 8:30 in effect both parties shall determine to **a**
11: 1 of Alexander's kingdom by trickery and **a** it
2Es 7:*52* will you **a** to them lead and clay?"

ADDAN (2)

Ezr 2:59 Tel-harsha, Cherub, **A**, and Immer,
1Es 5:36 under the leadership of Cherub, **A**, and Immer,

ADDAR (2) [HAZAR-ADDAR]

Jos 15: 3 along by Hezron, up to **A**, makes a turn to Karka,
1Ch 8: 3 And Bela had sons: **A**, Gera, Abihud,

ADDED‡ (39) [ADD]

Ge 24:25 She **a**, "We have plenty of straw and fodder and
Lev 27:13 one-fifth must be **a** to the assessment.
27:15 one-fifth shall be **a** to its assessed value,
27:19 then one-fifth shall be **a** to its assessed value,
27:27 be ransomed at its assessment, with one-fifth **a**;
Nu 19:17 and running water shall be **a** in a vessel;
36: 3 from the inheritance of our ancestors and **a** to
36: 4 then their inheritance will be **a** to the inheritance
Dt 5:22 and the thick darkness, and he **a** no more.
1Sa 12:19 for we have **a** to all our sins the evil of demanding
26:18 And he **a**, "Why does my lord pursue his servant?
2Sa 12: 8 had been too little, I would have **a** as much more.
19:35 Why then should your servant be an **a** burden
Est 5:12 Haman **a**, "Even Queen Esther let no one
Pr 9:11 and years will be **a** to your life.
Ecc 3:14 nothing can be **a** to it, nor anything taken from it;
Jer 36:32 and many similar words were **a** to them.
45: 3 The LORD has **a** sorrow to my pain;
Da 4:36 and still more greatness was **a** to me.
Lk 3:20 **a** to them all by shutting up John in prison.
Ac 1:26 and he was **a** to the eleven apostles.
2:41 and that day about three thousand persons were **a**.
2:47 And day by day the Lord **a** to their number

Ac 5:14 Yet more than ever believers were **a** to the Lord,
12:17 he **a,** "Tell this to James and to the believers."
Gal 3:19 It was **a** because of transgressions,
Heb 2: 4 while God **a** his testimony by signs and wonders
10: 9 then he **a,** "See, I have come
Tob 5:15 Then he **a,** "I will pay you a drachma a day
7: 5 And Tobias **a,** "He is my father!"
Sir 42:21 Nothing can be **a** or taken away,
45:20 He **a** glory to Aaron and gave him a heritage;
1Mc 1:50 He **a,** "And whoever does not obey the command
10:30 the three districts **a** to it from Samaria and Galilee,
10:38 the three districts that have been **a** to Judea from
11:34 were **a** to Judea from Samaria.
14:15 and **a** to the vessels of the sanctuary.
1Es 2: 7 besides the other things **a** as votive offerings for
3Mc 5:20 "but," he **a,** "tomorrow without delay prepare

ADDER (4) [ADDER'S, ADDERS, ADDERS']
Ps 58: 4 like the deaf **a** that stops its ear,
91:13 You will tread on the lion and the **a,**
Pr 23:32 the last it bites like a serpent, and stings like an **a.**
Isa 14:29 from the root of the snake will come forth an **a,**

ADDER'S (1) [ADDER]
Isa 11: 8 the weaned child shall put its hand on the **a** den.

ADDERS (1) [ADDER]
Jer 8:17 **a** that cannot be charmed, and they shall bite you,

ADDERS (KJV) See also VIPERS

ADDERS' (1) [ADDER]
Isa 59: 5 They hatch **a** eggs, and weave the spider's web;

ADDI (2)
Lk 3:28 son of **A,** son of Cosam, son of Elmadam,
1Es 9:31 Of the descendants of **A:** Naathus

ADDICTED (1)
Tit 1: 7 not be arrogant or quick-tempered or **a** to wine

ADDING (5) [ADD]
Nu 5: 7 for the wrong, **a** one fifth to it, and giving it to
Ecc 7:27 **a** one thing to another to find the sum,
Isa 30: 1 but against my will, **a** sin to sin;
Sir 31:30 reducing his strength and **a** wounds.
2Mc 2:32 without **a** any more to what has already been said;

ADDITION (34) [ADD]
Ge 28: 9 to be his wife in **a** to the wives he had.
31:50 or if you take wives in **a** to my daughters,
Lev 9:17 in **a** to the burnt offering of the morning.
Nu 5: 8 in **a** to the ram of atonement
28:10 in **a** to the regular burnt offering
28:15 it shall be offered in **a** to the regular burnt offering
28:23 You shall offer these in **a** to the burnt offering of
28:24 it shall be offered in **a** to the regular burnt offering
28:31 In **a** to the regular burnt offering
29: 6 in **a** to the burnt offering of the new moon
29:11 in **a** to the sin offering of atonement,
29:16 in **a** to the regular burnt offering,
29:19 in **a** to the regular burnt offering
29:22 in **a** to the regular burnt offering
29:25 in **a** to the regular burnt offering,
29:28 in **a** to the regular burnt offering
29:31 in **a** to the regular burnt offering,
29:38 in **a** to the regular burnt offering
29:39 in **a** to your votive offerings
31: 8 in **a** to others who were slain by them;
35: 6 and in **a** to them you shall give forty-two towns.
Dt 29: 1 in **a** to the covenant that he had made with them
1Ch 29: 3 in **a** to all that I have provided for the holy house,
2Ch 28:13 the LORD in **a** to our present sins and guilt,
2Co 7:13 In **a** to our own consolation,
Tob 2:14 "It was given to me as a gift in **a** to my wages."
1Mc 8:30 and any **a** or deletion that they may make shall
2Mc 4: 9 In **a** to this he promised
9:17 and in **a** to all this he also would become a Jew
12: 2 and in **a** to these Nicanor the governor of Cyprus,
3Mc 1:22 In **a,** the bolder of the citizens would not tolerate
4:10 and in **a** they were confined under a solid deck,
2Es 2: 5 as a witness in **a** to the mother of the children,
4Mc 1: 2 in **a** it includes the praise of the highest virtue—

ADDITIONAL (3) [ADD]
Ge 43:22 Moreover we have brought down with us **a** money
1Mc 10:41 the **a** funds that the government officials have
1Es 4:52 and an **a** ten talents a year for burnt offerings to

ADDON (1)
Ne 7:61 Tel-harsha, Cherub, **A,** and Immer,

ADDRESS (6) [ADDRESSED, ADDRESSES, ADDRESSING]
Dt 20: 5 Then the officials shall **a** the troops, saying,
20: 8 The officials shall continue to **a** the troops, saying,
Ps 45: 1 I **a** my verses to the king;
Ac 12:21 and delivered a public **a** to them.
Wis 13:17 he is not ashamed to **a** a lifeless thing.
4Mc 5:15 he began to **a** the people as follows:

ADDRESSED (13) [ADDRESS]
Ge 50: 4 Joseph **a** the household of Pharaoh,
Dt 32:48 On that very day the LORD **a** Moses as follows:
Ezr 10: 2 of the descendants of Elam, **a** Ezra, saying,
Job 21: 4 As for me, is my complaint **a** to mortals?
Ps 18: T *who **a** the words of this song to the LORD,*
Lk 23:20 Pilate, wanting to release Jesus, **a** them again;
Ac 2:14 raised his voice and **a** them,
3:12 When Peter saw it, he **a** the people,
21:40 he **a** them in the Hebrew language, saying:
Rev 7:13 Then one of the elders **a** me, saying,
AdE 3:12 the governors were **a** each in his own language.
1Mc 14:40 that the Jews were **a** by the Romans as friends
2Mc 15:15 and as he gave it he **a** him thus:

ADDRESSES (1) [ADDRESS]
Heb 12: 5 And you have forgotten the exhortation that **a** you

ADDRESSING (3) [ADDRESS]
Dt 5: 1 statutes and ordinances that I am **a** to you today;
20: 9 When the officials have finished **a** the troops,
Ac 22: 2 When they heard him **a** them in Hebrew,

ADDS‡ (10) [ADD]
Job 34:37 For he **a** rebellion to his sin;
Pr 10:22 and he **a** no sorrow with it.
16:23 and **a** persuasiveness to their lips.
Gal 3:15 no one **a** to it or annuls it.
Heb 10:17 he also **a,** "I will remember their sins
Rev 22:18 if anyone **a** to them, God will add to that person
Sir 3:27 and the sinner **a** sin to sins.
13: 3 A rich person does wrong, and even **a** insults;
21:15 he praises it and **a** to it;
26:15 A modest wife **a** charm to charm,

ADDUS (1)
1Es 5:34 the descendants of **A,** the descendants of Subas,

ADER (KJV) See EDER

ADHERE (1) [ADHERED, ADHERENTS]
Ne 10:28 the peoples of the lands to **a** to the law of God,

ADHERED (1) [ADHERE]
1Mc 1:57 or anyone who **a** to the law,

ADHERENTS (3) [ADHERE]
Ac 12:24 the word of God continued to advance and gain **a.**
Ro 4:14 If it is the **a** of the law who are to be the heirs,
4:16 to the **a** of the law but also to those who share

ADIDA (2)
1Mc 12:38 Simon also built **A** in the Shephelah;
13:13 Simon encamped in **A,** facing the plain.

ADIEL (3)
1Ch 4:36 Jaakobah, Jeshohaiah, Asaiah, **A,** Jesimiel,
9:12 son of Malchijah, and Maasai son of **A,**
27:25 the king's treasuries was Azmaveth son of **A.**

ADIN (6)
Ezr 2:15 Of **A,** four hundred fifty-four.
8: 6 Of the descendants of **A,** Ebed son of Jonathan,
Ne 7:20 Of **A,** six hundred fifty-five.
10:16 Adonijah, Bigvai, **A,**
1Es 5:14 The descendants of **A,** four hundred fifty-four.
8:32 Of the descendants of **A,** Obed son of Jonathan,

ADINA (1)
1Ch 11:42 **A** son of Shiza the Reubenite,

ADITHAIM (1)
Jos 15:36 **A,** Gederah, Gederothaim:

ADJOINING (16) [JOIN]
Eze 48: 2 **A** the territory of Dan, from the east side to
48: 3 **A** the territory of Asher, from the east side to
48: 4 **A** the territory of Naphtali,
48: 5 **A** the territory of Manasseh,
48: 6 **A** the territory of Ephraim,
48: 7 **A** the territory of Reuben,
48: 8 **A** the territory of Judah, from the east side to
48:12 a most holy place, **a** the territory of the Levites.
48:24 **A** the territory of Benjamin,
48:25 **A** the territory of Simeon,
48:26 **A** the territory of Issachar,
48:27 **A** the territory of Zebulun,
48:28 And **a** the territory of Gad to the south,
Sus 1: 4 and had a fine garden **a** his house;
1Mc 10:39 Ptolemais and the land **a** it I have given as a gift to
2Mc 12:16 so that the **a** lake, a quarter of a mile wide,

ADJOURNED (1)
Ac 24:22 **a** the hearing with the comment,

ADJURATION (1) [ADJURE]
Lev 5: 1 in that you have heard a public **a** to testify and—

ADJURE (8) [ADJURATION]
1Ki 2:42 and solemnly **a** you, saying,
SS 2: 7 I **a** you, O daughters of Jerusalem,
3: 5 I **a** you, O daughters of Jerusalem,
5: 8 I **a** you, O daughters of Jerusalem,
5: 9 more than another beloved, that you thus **a** us?
8: 4 I **a** you, O daughters of Jerusalem,
Mk 5: 7 I **a** you by God, do not torment me."
Ac 19:13 "I **a** you by the Jesus whom Paul proclaims."

ADJURE (KJV) See also SWEAR

ADLAI (1)
1Ch 27:29 the herds in the valleys was Shaphat son of **A.**

ADMAH (5)
Ge 10:19 and in the direction of Sodom, Gomorrah, **A,**
14: 2 King Shinab of **A,** King Shemeber of Zeboiim,
14: 8 the king of Gomorrah, the king of **A,**
Dt 29:23 **A** and Zeboiim, which the LORD destroyed
Hos 11: 8 How can I make you like **A?**

ADMATHA (1)
Est 1:14 **A,** Tarshish, Meres, Marsena, and Memucan,

ADMIN (1)
Lk 3:33 son of **A,** son of Arni, son of Hezron,

ADMINISTER (1) [ADMINISTERED, ADMINISTERING, ADMINISTRATION, ADMINISTRATIONS, ADMINISTRATORS]
Sus 1: 9 to Heaven or remembering their duty to **a** justice.

ADMINISTERED (4) [ADMINISTER]
1Sa 7:17 he **a** justice there to Israel,
2Sa 8:15 and David **a** justice and equity to all his people.
1Ch 18:14 and he **a** justice and equity to all his people.
Heb 11:33 **a** justice, obtained promises,

ADMINISTERING (2) [ADMINISTER]
2Co 8:19 with us while we are **a** this generous undertaking
8:20 about this generous gift that we are **a,**

ADMINISTRATION (3) [ADMINISTER]
Tob 1:21 and he had authority over the entire **a.**
AdE 16: 5 of friends who have been entrusted with the **a**
2Mc 3: 4 with the high priest about the **a** of the city market.

ADMINISTRATIONS (1) [ADMINISTER]
Tob 1:22 of **a** of the accounts under King Sennacherib

ADMINISTRATORS (2) [ADMINISTER]
AdE 8: 9 in writing to the **a** and governors of the provinces
4Mc 7: 8 Such should be those who are **a** of the law,

ADMIRABLE (1) [ADMIRE]
2Mc 7:20 The mother was especially **a** and worthy

ADMIRATION (1) [ADMIRE]
4Mc 6:13 partly out of **a** for his endurance,

ADMIRE‡ (2) [ADMIRABLE, ADMIRATION, ADMIRED, ADMIRES]
4Mc 8: 5 with favorable feelings I **a** each and every one
17:16 not **a** the athletes of the divine legislation?

ADMIRED (6) [ADMIRE]
Est 2:15 Now Esther was **a** by all who saw her.
Jdt 10:19 They marveled at her beauty and **a** the Israelites,
Wis 8:11 and in the sight of rulers I shall be **a.**
Sir 38: 3 and in the presence of the great they are **a.**
2Mc 4:16 and those whose ways of living they **a** and wished
4Mc 18: 3 the sake of religion were not only **a** by mortals,

ADMIRES (1) [ADMIRE]
Sir 27:23 his mouth is all sweetness, and he **a** your words;

ADMIT (3) [ADMITS, ADMITTED, ADMITTEDLY, ADMITTING]
Ex 40:15 and their anointing shall **a** them to a perpetual
Ac 24:14 But this I **a** to you, that according to the Way,
LtJ 6:56 then must anyone **a** or think that they are gods?

ADMITS (1) [ADMIT]
Sir 20: 3 the one who **a** his fault will be kept from failure.

ADMITTED (8) [ADMIT]
Dt 23: 1 or whose penis is cut off shall be **a** to
23: 2 of an illicit union shall not be **a** to the assembly of
23: 2 of their descendants shall be **a** to the assembly of
23: 3 or Moabite shall be **a** to the assembly of
23: 3 of their descendants shall be **a** to the assembly of
23: 8 that are born to them may be **a** to the assembly of
Eze 44: 5 and mark well those who may be **a** to the temple
4Mc 16: 1 it must be **a** that devout reason is sovereign over

ADMITTEDLY (1) [ADMIT]
4Mc 6:31 A, then, devout reason is sovereign over

ADMITTING (2) [ADMIT]
Eze 44: 7 in a foreigners, uncircumcised in heart and flesh,
3Mc 7:12 a and approving the truth of what they said,

ADMONISH (7) [ADMONITION]
Ps 81: 8 O my people, while I a you;
1Co 4:14 but to a you as my beloved children.
Col 3:16 teach and a one another in all wisdom;
1Th 5:12 and have charge of you in the Lord and a you;
5:14 And we urge you, beloved, to a the idlers,
Jdt 8:27 to him in order to a them."
2Es 7:*49* and I will instruct you, and will a you once more.

ADMONITION (5) [ADMONISH]
Pr 15: 5 but the one who heeds a is prudent.
15:31 The ear that heeds wholesome a will lodge among
15:32 but those who heed a gain understanding.
22:20 Have I not written for you thirty sayings of a
Tit 3:10 After a first and second a,

ADNA (2)
Ezr 10:30 A, Chelal, Benaiah, Maaseiah, Mattaniah, Bezalel,
Ne 12:15 of Harim, A; of Meraioth, Helkai;

ADNAH (2)
1Ch 12:20 A, Jozabad, Jediael, Michael, Jozabad, Elihu,
2Ch 17:14 of the thousands: A the commander,

ADO (KJV) See COMMOTION

ADONI-BEZEK (3)
Jdg 1: 5 They came upon A at Bezek,
1: 6 A fled; but they pursued him,
1: 7 A said, "Seventy kings with their thumbs

ADONI-ZEDEK (2)
Jos 10: 1 When King A of Jerusalem heard
10: 3 So King A of Jerusalem sent a message

ADONIJAH (26)
2Sa 3: 4 the fourth, A son of Haggith;
1Ki 1: 5 Now A son of Haggith exalted himself, saying,
1: 7 with the priest Abiathar, and they supported A.
1: 8 and David's own warriors did not side with A.
1: 9 A sacrificed sheep, oxen, and fatted cattle by
1:11 not heard that A son of Haggith has become king
1:13 Why then is A king?'
1:18 But now suddenly A has become king,
1:24 have you said, 'A shall succeed me as king,
1:25 and saying, 'Long live King A!'
1:41 A and all the guests who were with him heard it
1:42 A said, "Come in, for you are a worthy man and
1:43 Jonathan answered A, "No,
1:49 of A got up trembling and went their own ways.
1:50 A, fearing Solomon, got up and went to grasp
1:51 "A is afraid of King Solomon;
2:13 Then A son of Haggith came to Bathsheba,
2:19 to speak to him on behalf of A.
2:21 the Shunammite be given to your brother A
2:22 why do you ask Abishag the Shunammite for A?
2:23 A has devised this scheme at the risk of his life!
2:24 today A shall be put to death."
2:28 for Joab had supported A though he had
1Ch 3: 2 the fourth A, son of Haggith;
2Ch 17: 8 Zebadiah, Asahel, Shemiramoth, Jehonathan, A,
Ne 10:16 A, Bigvai, Adin,

ADONIKAM (5)
Ezr 2:13 Of A, six hundred sixty-six.
8:13 Of the descendants of A, those who came later,
Ne 7:18 Of A, six hundred sixty-seven.
1Es 5:14 The descendants of A, six hundred sixty-seven.
8:39 Of the descendants of A, the last ones,

ADONIRAM (2)
1Ki 4: 6 A son of Abda was in charge of the forced labor.
5:14 A was in charge of the forced labor.

ADOPT (4) [ADOPTED, ADOPTING, ADOPTION, ADOPTS]
Isa 44: 5 "The LORD's," and a the name of Israel.
Ac 16:21 not lawful for us as Romans to a or observe."
2Mc 6: 8 to the neighboring Greek cities that they should a
4Mc 5:11 a a mind appropriate to your years,

ADOPTED (6) [ADOPT]
2Ch 7:22 and they a other gods, and worshiped them
Est 2: 7 Mordecai a her as his own daughter.
2:15 who had a her as his own daughter,
9:23 the Jews a as a custom what they had begun to do,
Ac 7:21 Pharaoh's daughter a him and brought him up
1Mc 1:43 Many even from Israel gladly a his religion;

ADOPTING (1) [ADOPT]
4Mc 8: 8 Enjoy your youth by a the Greek way of life and

ADOPTION (6) [ADOPT]
Ro 8:15 but you have received a spirit of a.
8:23 groan inwardly while we wait for a,
9: 4 They are Israelites, and to them belong the a,
Gal 4: 5 so that we might receive a as children.
Eph 1: 5 for a as his children through Jesus Christ,
2Mc 4:13 Hellenization and increase in the a of foreign ways

ADOPTS (1) [ADOPT]
4Mc 2: 8 as one a a way of life in accordance with the law,

ADORA (1)
1Mc 13:20 and he circled around by the way to A.

ADORAIM (1)
2Ch 11: 9 A, Lachish, Azekah,

ADORAM (2) [=HADORAM]
2Sa 20:24 A was in charge of the forced labor;
1Ki 12:18 When King Rehoboam sent A,

ADORES (1)
2Es 7:*78* first of all it a the glory of the Most High.

ADORN‡ (5) [ADORNED, ADORNMENT, ADORNS]
1Pe 3: 3 not a yourselves outwardly by braiding your hair,
3: 5 to a themselves by accepting the authority
AdE 14: 2 every part that she loved to a she covered
2Mc 9:16 he would a with the finest offerings;
2Es 16:47 the more they a their cities,

ADORNED (17) [ADORN]
2Ki 9:30 she painted her eyes, and a her head,
2Ch 3: 6 He a the house with settings of precious stones.
Pr 14:18 The simple are a with folly,
Eze 16:11 I a you with ornaments: I put bracelets on your
16:13 You were a with gold and silver,
Lk 21: 5 how it was a with beautiful stones
Rev 17: 4 and a with gold and jewels and pearls,
18:16 in purple and scarlet, a with gold, with jewels,
21: 2 prepared as a bride a for her husband.
21:19 of the wall of the city are a with every jewel;
AdE 1: 6 which was a with curtains of fine linen and cotton,
15: 2 majestically a, after invoking the aid of
Sir 45:12 a delight to the eyes, richly a.
48:11 Happy are those who saw you and were a
3Mc 3: 5 since they a their style of life with the good deeds
6: 1 a ripe old age and throughout his life had been a
4Mc 6: 2 he remained a with the gracefulness of his piety.

ADORNMENT (7) [ADORN]
Ex 28: 2 for the glorious a of your brother Aaron.
28:40 you shall make them for their glorious a.
Pr 3:22 they will be life for your soul and a for your neck.
1Pe 3: 4 let your a be the inner self with the lasting beauty
1Mc 2:11 All her a has been taken away;
2Mc 2: 2 on seeing the gold and silver statues and their a.
2:29 to consider only what is suitable for its a,

ADORNS (2) [ADORN]
Ps 149: 4 he a the humble with victory.
Isa 61:10 and as a bride a herself with her jewels.

ADRAMMELECH (3)
2Ki 17:31 in the fire to A and Anammelech,
19:37 his sons A and Sharezer killed him with
Isa 37:38 his sons A and Sharezer killed him with

ADRAMYTTIUM (1)
Ac 27: 2 a ship of A that was about to set sail to the ports

ADRIA (1)
Ac 27:27 as we were drifting across the sea of A,

ADRIEL (2)
1Sa 18:19 she was given to A the Meholathite as a wife.
2Sa 21: 8 of Saul, whom she bore to A son of Barzillai

ADRIFT (2) [DRIFT]
Ac 27:32 soldiers cut away the ropes of the boat and set it a.
2Co 11:25 for a night and a day I was a at sea;

ADUEL (1)
Tob 1: 1 of Hananiel son of A son of Gabael son

ADULLAM (9) [ADULLAMITE]
Jos 12:15 the king of Libnah one the king of A one
15:35 Jarmuth, A, Socoh, Azekah,
1Sa 22: 1 David left there and escaped to the cave of A;
2Sa 23:13 down to join David at the cave of A,
1Ch 11:15 down to the rock to David at the cave of A,
2Ch 11: 7 Beth-zur, Soco, A,
Ne 11:30 A, and their villages, Lachish and its fields,
Mic 1:15 the glory of Israel shall come to A.
2Mc 12:38 and went to the city of A.

ADULLAMITE (3) [ADULLAM]
Ge 38: 1 near a certain A whose name was Hirah.
38:12 he and his friend Hirah the A.
38:20 When Judah sent the kid by his friend the A,

ADULT (1) [ADULTS]
1Co 13:11 I became an a, I put an end to childish ways.

ADULTERER (3) [ADULTERY]
Lev 20:10 both the a and the adulteress shall be put to death.
Job 24:15 The eye of the a also waits for the twilight,
Isa 57: 3 you offspring of an a and a whore.

ADULTERERS (10) [ADULTERY]
Ps 50:18 and you keep company with a.
Jer 9: 2 For they are all a, a band of traitors.
23:10 For the land is full of a;
Hos 7: 4 They are all a; they are like a
Mal 3: 5 against the a, against those who swear falsely,
Lk 18:11 thieves, rogues, a, or even like this tax collector.
1Co 6: 9 Fornicators, idolaters, a, male prostitutes,
Heb 13: 4 for God will judge fornicators and a.
Jas 4: 4 A! Do you not know that friendship with the
Wis 3:16 But children of a will not come to maturity,

ADULTERESS (10) [ADULTERY]
Lev 20:10 both the adulterer and the a shall be put to death.
Pr 2:16 from the a with her smooth words,
5:20 and embrace the bosom of an a?
6:24 from the smooth tongue of the a.
7: 5 from the a with her smooth words.
23:27 For a prostitute is a deep pit; an a is a narrow well.
30:20 This is the way of an a:
Hos 3: 1 "Go, love a woman who has a lover and is an a,
Ro 7: 3 be called an a if she lives with another man while
7: 3 and if she marries another man, she is not an a.

ADULTERESSES (1) [ADULTERY]
Eze 23:45 because they are a and blood is on their hands.

ADULTERIES (3) [ADULTERY]
Jer 3: 8 She saw that for all the a of that faithless one,
13:27 your a and neighings, your shameless prostitutions
Eze 23:43 Then I said, Ah, she is worn out with a,

ADULTEROUS (4) [ADULTERY]
Eze 16:32 A wife, who receives strangers instead
Mt 12:39 "An evil and a generation asks for a sign,
16: 4 An evil and a generation asks for a sign,
Mk 8:38 and of my words in this a and sinful generation,

ADULTERY‡ (44) [ADULTERER, ADULTERERS, ADULTERESS, ADULTERESSES, ADULTERIES, ADULTEROUS]
Ex 20:14 You shall not commit a.
Lev 20:10 If a man commits a with the wife of his neighbor,
Dt 5:18 Neither shall you commit a.
Pr 6:32 But he who commits a has no sense;
Jer 3: 9 committing a with stone and tree.
5: 7 they committed a and trooped to the houses
7: 9 Will you steal, murder, commit a, swear falsely,
23:14 they commit a and walk in lies;
29:23 and have committed a with their neighbors' wives,
Eze 16:38 I will judge you as women who commit a
23:37 For they have committed a,
23:37 with their idols they have committed a;
23:45 But righteous judges shall declare them guilty of a
Hos 2: 2 and her a from between her breasts,
4: 2 lying, and murder, and stealing and a break out;
4:13 and your daughters-in-law commit a.
4:14 nor your daughters-in-law when they commit a;
Mt 5:27 'You shall not commit a.'
5:28 has already committed a with her in his heart.
5:32 the ground of unchastity, causes her to commit a;
5:32 whoever marries a divorced woman commits a.
15:19 out of the heart come evil intentions, murder, a,
19: 9 and marries another commits a."
19:18 not murder; You shall not commit a;
Mk 7:22 a, avarice, wickedness, deceit,
10:11 and marries another commits a against her;
10:12 and marries another, she commits a."
10:19 'You shall not murder; You shall not commit a;
Lk 16:18 divorces his wife and marries another commits a,
16:18 a woman divorced from her husband commits a.
18:20 'You shall not commit a;
Jn 8: 3 ⟦a woman who had been caught in a;⟧
8: 4 ⟦in the very act of committing a.⟧
Ro 2:22 You that forbid a, do you commit a?
13: 9 The commandments, "You shall not commit a;
Jas 2:11 For the one who said, "You shall not commit a,"
2:11 Now if you do not commit a but if you murder,
2Pe 2:14 They have eyes full of a, insatiable for sin.
Rev 2:22 and those who commit a with her I am throwing
Wis 14:24 or grieve one another by a,
14:26 sexual perversion, disorder in marriages, a,
Sir 23:23 through her fornication she has committed a
25: 2 and an old fool who commits a.

ADULTS (1) [ADULT]
1Co 14:20 rather, be infants in evil, but in thinking be a.

ADUMMIM (2)
Jos 15: 7 which is opposite the ascent of A,
18:17 which is opposite the ascent of A;

ADVANCE (21) [ADVANCED, ADVANCEMENT, ADVANCES, ADVANCING]
Lev 25:36 not take interest in a or otherwise make a profit
25:37 not lend them your money at interest taken in a,
Jer 46: 3 Prepare buckler and shield, and a for battle!
46: 9 A, O horses, and dash madly, O chariots!
49:28 Rise up, a against Kedar! Destroy the people
49:31 Rise up, a against a nation at ease,
Eze 18: 8 does not take a or accrued interest,
18:13 takes a or accrued interest;
18:17 takes no a or accrued interest,
22:12 you take both a interest and accrued interest,
38: 9 You shall a, coming on like a storm;
Da 11:10 which shall a like a flood and pass through,
11:13 and after some years he shall a with a great army
11:40 He shall a against countries and pass through like
Lk 21:14 up your minds not to prepare your defense in a;
Ac 12:24 word of God continued to a and gain adherents.
2Co 9: 5 in a for this bountiful gift that you have promised,
1Pe 1:11 when it testified in a to the sufferings destined
Jdt 2:10 and seize all their territory for me in a.
9: 6 For all your ways are prepared in a,
Wis 19: 1 for God knew in a even their future actions:

ADVANCED‡ (31) [ADVANCE]
Ge 18:11 Now Abraham and Sarah were old, a in age;
24: 1 Now Abraham was old, well a in years;
Jos 13: 1 Now Joshua was old and a in years;
13: 1 LORD said to him, "You are old and a in years,
23: 1 and Joshua was old and well a in years,
23: 2 "I am now old and well a in years;
Jdg 20:24 So the Israelites a against the Benjaminites
1Sa 17:12 In the days of Saul the man was already old and a
1Ki 1: 1 King David was old and a in years;
2Ki 20: 9 the shadow has now a ten intervals;
1Ch 19:14 So Joab and the troops who were with him a
Est 2: 9 a her and her maids to the best place in the harem.
3: 1 and a him and set his seat above all
5:11 and how he had a him above the officials and
10: 2 to which the king a him,
Gal 1:14 I a in Judaism beyond many among my people of
AdE 5:11 how he had a him to be the first in the kingdom.
1Mc 1: 3 He a to the ends of the earth,
6:40 and they a steadily and in good order.
6:42 But Judas and his army a to the battle,
9:12 the phalanx a to the sound of the trumpets;
10:77 At the same time he a into the plain,
2Mc 4:40 a man a in years and no less a in folly.
6:18 a man now a in age and of noble presence,
10:27 up their arms and a a considerable distance from
11:10 They a in battle order, having their heavenly ally,
13:19 He a against Beth-zur, a strong fortress of
15:25 and his troops a with trumpets and battle songs,
4Mc 5: 4 learned in the law, a in age,
16: 1 a woman, a in years and mother of seven sons,

ADVANCEMENT (1) [ADVANCE]
AdE 2:21 were angry because of Mordecai's a,

ADVANCES (1) [ADVANCE]
Sir 20:27 The wise person a himself by his words,

ADVANCING (2) [ADVANCE]
Ex 14:10 and there were the Egyptians a on them.
AdE 3: 1 a him and granting him precedence over all

ADVANTAGE (26) [ADVANTAGEOUS, ADVANTAGES]
Dt 30: 7 and on the adversaries who took a of you.
2Sa 11:23 "The men gained an a over us
Job 35: 3 If you ask, 'What a have I?
Ecc 3:19 and humans have no a over the animals;
5: 9 But all things considered, this is an a for a land:
6: 8 For what a have the wise over fools?
7:11 an a to those who see the sun.
7:12 and the a of knowledge is that wisdom gives life
10:11 there is no a in a charmer.
Da 11:17 but it shall not succeed or be to his a.
Jn 16: 7 it is to your a that I go away,
Ro 3: 1 Then what a has the Jew?
6:21 So what a did you then get from the things
6:22 the a you get is sanctification.
1Co 10:24 Do not seek your own a, but that of the other.
10:33 not seeking my own a, but that of many,
2Co 7: 2 we have taken a of no one.
11:20 or preys upon you, or takes a of you,
12:17 Did I take a of you through any
12:18 Titus did not take a of you, did he?
Jude 1:16 flattering people to their own a.
Sir 19:27 but when no one notices, he will take a of you.
30:23 and no a ever comes from it.
37:22 If a person is wise to his own a,
3Mc 6:24 by secretly devising acts of no a to the kingdom.
4Mc 1:17 and human affairs to our a.

ADVANTAGEOUS (1) [ADVANTAGE]
2Mc 8: 7 He found the nights most a for such attacks.

ADVANTAGES (1) [ADVANTAGE]
Bar 4: 3 or your a to an alien people.

ADVERSARIES (49) [ADVERSARY]
Ex 15: 7 of your majesty you overthrew your a;
Dt 30: 7 on your enemies and on the a who took advantage
32:27 for their a might misunderstand and say,
32:41 I will take vengeance on my a,
32:43 and take vengeance on his a;
33: 7 and be a help against his a.
33:11 crush the loins of his a, of those that hate him,
Jos 5:13 "Are you one of us, or one of our a?"
Jdg 2: 3 but they shall become a to you,
1Sa 2:10 The LORD! His a shall be shattered;
2Sa 22:49 you exalted me above my a,
1Ch 12:17 but if you have come to betray me to my a,
Ezr 4: 1 When the a of Judah and Benjamin heard that
Job 22:20 'Surely our a are cut off, and what they left,
Ps 17: 7 O savior of those who seek refuge from their a
18:48 indeed, you exalted me above my a;
27: 2 my a and foes—they shall stumble and fall.
27:12 Do not give me up to the will of my a,
31:11 I am the scorn of all my a,
38:20 for good are my a because I follow after good.
42:10 with a deadly wound in my body, my a taunt me,
55:12 it is not a who deal insolently with me—
74:23 the uproar of your a that goes up continually.
78:66 He put his a to rout;
97: 3 and consumes his a on every side.
106:11 waters covered their a; not one of them was left.
119:157 Many are my persecutors and my a,
143:12 and destroy all my a, for I am your servant.
Isa 9:11 So the LORD raised a against them,
26:11 Let the fire for your a consume them.
50: 8 Who are my a? Let them confront me.
59:18 wrath to his a, requital to his enemies;
63:18 now our a have trampled down your sanctuary.
64: 2 to make your name known to your a,
Jer 18:19 O LORD, and listen to what my a say!
Eze 30:16 and Memphis face a by day.
39:23 from them and gave them into the hand of their a,
Mic 5: 9 Your hand shall be lifted up over your a,
Na 1: 2 the LORD takes vengeance on his a and rages
1: 8 He will make a full end of his a,
1Co 16: 9 to me, and there are many a.
Heb 10:27 and a fury of fire that will consume the a.
Wis 2:18 and will deliver him from the hand of his a.
Sir 23: 3 and I may fall before my a,
47: 7 and annihilated his a the Philistines;
51: 2 In the face of my a you have been my helper
2Mc 10:26 to their enemies and an adversary to their a,
15:16 with which you will strike down your a."
1Es 8:51 and an escort to keep us safe from our a;

ADVERSARY‡ (20) [ADVERSARIES, ADVERSE, ADVERSITIES, ADVERSITY]
Nu 10: 9 in your land against the a who oppresses you,
22:22 of the LORD took his stand in the road as his a.
22:32 I have come out as an a,
1Sa 29: 4 or else he may become an a to us in the battle.
2Sa 19:22 that you should today become an a to me?
1Ki 5: 4 there is neither a nor misfortune.
11:14 Then the LORD raised up an a against Solomon,
11:23 God raised up another a against Solomon,
11:25 He was an a of Israel all the days of Solomon,
Job 16: 9 my a sharpens his eyes against me.
19:11 and counts me as his a.
31:35 Oh, that I had the indictment written by my a!
Am 3:11 An a shall surround the land,
Na 1: 9 He will make an end; no a will rise up twice.
1Ti 5:14 so as to give the a no occasion to revile us.
1Pe 5: 8 Like a roaring lion your a the devil prowls around,
Sir 21:27 an ungodly person curses an a, he curses himself.
36: 9 destroy the a and wipe out the enemy.
1Mc 1:36 an evil a of Israel at all times.
2Mc 10:26 to their enemies and an a to their adversaries,

ADVERSE (1) [ADVERSARY]
Mk 6:48 at the oars against an a wind,

ADVERSITIES (3) [ADVERSARY]
Ps 31: 7 you have taken heed of my a,
2Es 10:20 for how many are the a of Zion?—
15:56 and will hand you over to a.

ADVERSITIES (KJV) See also CALAMITIES

ADVERSITY (16) [ADVERSARY]
Nu 20:14 You know all the a that has befallen us:
Dt 30:15 before you today life and prosperity, death and a.
2Sa 4: 9 who has redeemed my life out of every a,
1Ki 1:29 who has saved my life from every a,
Job 36:15 and opens their ear by a.
Ps 10: 6 throughout all generations we shall not meet a."
Pr 17:17 and kinsfolk are born to share a.
24:10 If you faint in the day of a,
Ecc 7:14 and in the day of a consider;
Isa 30:20 Though the Lord may give you the bread of a and
48:10 I have tested you in the furnace of a.
Sir 11:25 In the day of prosperity, a is forgotten,
11:25 and in the day of a, prosperity is not remembered.
12: 8 nor is an enemy hidden in a.
12: 9 but in a even one's friend disappears.
Sir 20: 9 There may be good fortune for a person in a,

ADVERTISE (KJV) See ADVISE, TELL

ADVICE (30) [ADVISE]
Nu 31:16 These women here, on Balaam's a, made the
Jdg 20: 7 all of you, give your a and counsel here."
2Sa 17: 4 The a pleased Absalom and all the elders of Israel.
1Ki 1:12 Now therefore come, let me give you a,
12: 8 he disregarded the a that the older men gave him,
12:13 the a that the older men had given him
12:14 to them according to the a of the young men,
2Ch 10: 8 But he rejected the a that the older men gave him,
10:13 King Rehoboam rejected the a of the older men;
10:14 he spoke to them in accordance with the a of
22: 5 He even followed their a,
25:16 you have done this and have not listened to my a."
Est 1:21 This a pleased the king and the officials,
5:14 This a pleased Haman, and he had
Job 26: 3 one who has no wisdom, and given much good a!
Ps 1: 1 who do not follow the a of the wicked,
Pr 8:14 I have good a and sound wisdom;
12: 5 the a of the wicked is treacherous.
12:15 but the wise listen to a.
12:26 The righteous gives good a to friends,
13:10 but wisdom is with those who take a.
19:20 Listen to a and accept instruction,
20:18 Plans are established by taking a;
Ecc 4:13 who will no longer take a.
Jer 38:15 And if I give you a, you will not listen to me."
2Co 8:10 And in this matter I am giving my a:
Tob 4:18 Seek a from every wise person and do
AdE 5:14 This a pleased Haman,
Sir 37:11 pay no attention to any a they give.
4Mc 5:12 on your old age by honoring my humane a?

ADVISABLE (1) [ADVISE]
1Co 16: 4 If it seems a that I should go also,

ADVISE (9) [ADVICE, ADVISABLE, ADVISED, ADVISER, ADVISERS, ADVISES]
Nu 24:14 let me a you what this people will do
1Ki 12: 6 "How do you a me to answer this people?"
12: 9 He said to them, "What do you a
2Ch 10: 6 "How do you a me to answer this people?"
10: 9 He said to them, "What do you a
2Mc 7:25 the mother to him and urged her to a the youth
4Mc 1: 1 to a you to pay earnest attention to philosophy.
5: 6 I would a you to save yourself by eating pork,
8: 5 Not only do I a you not to display

ADVISED (3) [ADVISE]
Est 2:15 who had charge of the women, a.
Jn 18:14 the one who had a the Jews that it was better
Ac 27: 9 even the Fast had already gone by, Paul a them,

ADVISER (1) [ADVISE]
Ge 26:26 with Ahuzzath his a and Phicol the commander

ADVISERS (3) [ADVISE]
Est 6:13 his a and his wife Zeresh said to him,
Pr 15:22 plans go wrong, but with many a they succeed.
Sir 6: 6 but let your a be one in a thousand.

ADVISES (1) [ADVISE]
2Sa 17: 6 shall we do as he a?

ADVOCATE (6) [ADVOCATES, ADVOCATING]
Jn 14:16 and he will give you another A,
14:26 But the A, the Holy Spirit,
15:26 "When the A comes, whom I will send to you
16: 7 the A will not come to you;
1Jn 2: 1 if anyone does sin, we have an a with the Father,
Wis 12:12 Or who will come before you to plead as an a for

ADVOCATES (1) [ADVOCATE]
4Mc 15:25 of her own soul she saw mighty a—

ADVOCATING (1) [ADVOCATE]
Ac 16:21 and are a customs that are not lawful for us

AENEAS (2)
Ac 9:33 There he found a man named A,
9:34 Peter said to him, "A, Jesus Christ heals you;

AENON (1)
Jn 3:23 John also was baptizing at A near Salim

AESORA (1)
Jdt 4: 4 and to Choba and A, and the valley of Salem.

AFFAIR (6) [AFFAIRS]
Nu 16:49 besides those who died in the a of Korah.
25:18 the trickery with which they deceived you in the a
25:18 and in the a of Cozbi, the daughter of a leader
31:16 against the LORD in the a of Peor,
Est 2:23 When the a was investigated and found to be so,

AdE 9:26 because of what they had experienced in this a

AFFAIRS (34) [AFFAIR]

2Sa 14:20 the course of a your servant Joab did this.
19:29 "Why speak any more of your a?
1Ki 12:15 because it was a turn of a brought about by
1Ch 26:32 for everything pertaining to God and for the a of
2Ch 10:15 because it was a turn of a brought about by God
Ps 112: 5 who conduct their a with justice.
Isa 58:13 your own interests, or pursuing your own a;
Da 2:49 Abednego over the a of the province of Babylon.
3:12 over the a of the province of Babylon:
1Co 7:32 unmarried man is anxious about the a of the Lord,
7:33 married man is anxious about the a of the world,
7:34 and the virgin are anxious about the a of the Lord,
7:34 but the married woman is anxious about the a of
1Th 4:11 to mind your own a, and to work with your hands,
2Ti 2: 4 in the army gets entangled in everyday a;
Jdt 8:12 up in the place of God in human a?
12:11 the eunuch who had charge of his personal a,
14:13 to the steward in charge of all his personal a,
AdE 13: 6 who is in charge of a and is our second father,
16: 5 with the administration of public a,
1Mc 3:32 in charge of the king's a from the river Euphrates
6:57 and the a of the kingdom press urgently on us.
2Mc 3: 7 who was in charge of his a,
4: 6 the king's attention public a could not again reach
4:30 While such was the state of a,
7:24 for his Friend and entrust him with public a.
9:20 If you and your children are well and your a are
11:23 be undisturbed in caring for their own a.
11:26 and go on happily in the conduct of their own a."
11:29 to return home and look after your own a.
1Es 4:11 and no one may go away to attend to his own a,
3Mc 3:21 and the myriad a liberally entrusted to them from
7: 2 great God guiding our a according to our desire.
4Mc 1:17 and human a to our advantage.

AFFECT (1) [AFFECTS]

2Es 8:50 for many miseries will a those who inhabit

AFFECTION‡ (12) [AFFECTIONS]

Ge 43:30 because he was overcome with a for his brother,
Eze 24:25 the delight of their eyes and their heart's a,
Ro 12:10 love one another with mutual a;
2Pe 1: 7 godliness with mutual a, and mutual a with love.
2Mc 9:21 I remember with a your esteem and goodwill.
3Mc 5:32 not for an a arising from our nurture in common
4Mc 2:10 For the law prevails even over a for parents,
13:19 You are not ignorant of the a of family ties,
13:23 sympathy and brotherly a had been so established,
13:27 and virtuous habits had augmented the a
15:13 O sacred nature and a of parental love,

AFFECTIONS (1) [AFFECTION]

2Co 6:12 There is no restriction in our a, but only in yours.

AFFECTS (1) [AFFECT]

Job 35: 8 Your wickedness a others like you,

AFFINITY (KJV) See ALLIANCE, INTERMARRY

AFFIRM (1) [REAFFIRM]

Eph 4:17 Now this I a and insist on in the Lord:

AFFLICT‡ (13) [AFFLICTED, AFFLICTION, AFFLICTIONS, AFFLICTS]

Nu 24:24 from Kittim and shall a Asshur and Eber;
Dt 28:22 The LORD will a you with consumption, fever,
28:27 The LORD will a you with the boils of Egypt,
28:28 The LORD will a you with madness, blindness,
2Sa 7:10 and evildoers shall a them no more, as formerly,
Ps 94: 5 O LORD, and a your heritage.
Isa 3:17 the Lord will a with scabs the heads of
Jer 19: 9 and those who seek their life a them.
La 3:33 for he does not willingly a or grieve anyone.
Am 5:12 you who a the righteous, who take a bribe,
Na 1:12 Though I have afflicted you, I will a you no more.
2Th 1: 6 of God to repay with affliction those who a you,
Tob 13: 5 He will a you for your iniquities,

AFFLICTED‡ (38) [AFFLICT]

Ge 12:17 But the LORD a Pharaoh and his house
Ex 9:11 boils a the magicians as well as all the Egyptians.
Dt 26: 6 When the Egyptians treated us harshly and a us,
29:22 the afflictions with which the LORD has a it—
2Ch 15: 5 for great disturbances a all the inhabitants of
Job 34:28 and he heard the cry of the a—
36: 6 but gives the a their right.
36:15 He delivers the a by their affliction,
Ps 9:12 he does not forget the cry of the a.
22:24 he did not despise or abhor the affliction of the a;
25:16 for I am lonely and a.
35:13 I wore sackcloth; I a myself with fasting.
44: 2 you a the peoples, but them you set free;
90:15 Make us glad as many days as you have a us,
102: T *A prayer of one a, when faint and pleading*
116:10 I kept my faith, even when I said, "I am greatly a";
119:107 I am severely a; give me life,
Pr 22:22 or crush the a at the gate;
31: 5 and will pervert the rights of all the a.
Isa 53: 4 struck down by God, and a.
53: 7 He was oppressed, and he was a,
54:11 O a one, storm-tossed, and not comforted,
58:10 to the hungry and satisfy the needs of the a,
Am 2: 7 and push the a out of the way;
Mic 4: 6 and those whom I have a.
Na 1:12 Though I have a you, I will afflict you no more.
Mt 4:24 those who were a with various diseases and pains,
2Co 1: 6 If we are being a, it is for your consolation
4: 8 We are a in every way, but not crushed;
7: 5 but we were a in every way—
2Th 1: 7 and to give relief to the a as well as to us,
1Ti 5:10 washed the saints' feet, helped the a,
Tob 6: 8 in the presence of a man or woman a by a demon
11:15 Though he a me, he has had mercy upon me.
13: 9 he a you for the deeds of your hands,
Jdt 5:12 and he a the whole land of Egypt
Wis 19:16 with festal celebrations, afterward a with terrible
Sir 30:14 healthy, and fit than rich and a in body.

AFFLICTION (37) [AFFLICT]

Ge 16:11 for the LORD has given heed to your a.
29:32 "Because the LORD has looked on my a;
31:42 God saw my a and the labor of my hands,
Dt 16: 3 eat unleavened bread with it—the bread of a—
26: 7 the LORD heard our voice and saw our a,
28:61 Every other malady and a,
Job 10:15 for I am filled with disgrace and look upon my a.
30:16 days of a have taken hold of me.
30:27 days of a come to meet me.
36: 8 in fetters and caught in the cords of a,
36:15 He delivers the afflicted by their a,
36:21 because of that you have been tried by a.
Ps 22:24 he did not despise or abhor the a of the afflicted;
25:18 Consider my a and my trouble,
31: 7 because you have seen my a;
38:11 and companions stand aloof from my a,
44:24 Why do you forget our a and oppression?
107:17 and because of their iniquities endured a;
Isa 30:20 the bread of adversity and the water of a,
La 1: 7 in the days of her a and wandering,
1: 9 "O LORD, look at my a,
3: 1 I am one who has seen a under the rod
3:19 of my a and my homelessness is wormwood
Hab 3: 7 I saw the tents of Cushan under a;
2Co 1: 4 who consoles us in all our a, so that we may be able to console those who are in any a with
1: 8 of the a we experienced in Asia;
4:17 For this slight momentary a is preparing us for
7: 4 I am overjoyed in all our a.
8: 2 for during a severe ordeal of a,
2Th 1: 6 of God to repay with a those who afflict you,
Rev 2: 9 "I know your a and your poverty,
2:10 and for ten days you will have a.
Tob 6: 8 and every a will flee away and never remain with
AdE 11: 8 a and great tumult on the earth!
14:12 make yourself known in this time of our a,
Bar 5: 1 Take off the garment of your sorrow and a,

AFFLICTIONS (12) [AFFLICT]

Dt 28:59 and lasting a and grievous and lasting maladies.
29:22 and the a with which the LORD has afflicted it—
1Ki 8:38 all knowing the a of their own hearts so
Ps 34:19 Many are the a of the righteous,
Ac 7:10 and rescued him from all his a,
2Co 6: 4 through great endurance, in a, hardships,
Col 1:24 in Christ's a for the sake of his body,
2Th 1: 4 and faith during all your persecutions and the a
Tob 13:14 with you because of your a;
2Es 8:27 of those who have kept your covenants amid a.
4Mc 6:24 that he was so courageous in the face of the a,
18:15 who said, 'Many are the a of the righteous.'

AFFLICTS (1) [AFFLICT]

Tob 13: 2 For he a, and he shows mercy;

AFFLUENCE (1)

Dt 33:19 the a of the seas and the hidden treasures of

AFFORD‡ (12)

Lev 5: 7 But if you cannot a a sheep,
5:11 if you cannot a two turtledoves or two pigeons,
12: 8 If she cannot a a sheep,
14:21 But if he is poor and cannot a so much,
14:22 as he can a, one for a sin offering and the other
14:30 of the turtledoves or pigeons such as he can a,
14:32 who cannot a the offerings for his cleansing.
27: 8 If any cannot a the equivalent,
27: 8 according to what each one making a vow can a.
Nu 6:21 apart from what else they can a.
Sir 35:12 and as generously as you can a.
38:11 as much as you can a.

AFFORDED (1)

2Es 9:26 and the nourishment they a satisfied me.

AFFORDING See Index to Footnotes

AFFRIGHT (KJV) See TERRIFY

AFFRONT (1) [AFFRONTS]

Pr 17: 9 One who forgives an a fosters friendship,

AFFRONTS (1) [AFFRONT]

Nu 15:30 whether a native or an alien, a the LORD,

AFLAME‡ (4) [FLAME]

Pr 29: 8 Scoffers set a city a, but the wise turn away wrath.
Isa 13: 8 at one another; their faces will be a.
1Co 7: 9 For it is better to marry than to be a with passion.
2Mc 14:45 Still alive and a with anger, he rose,

AFOREHAND (KJV) See BEFOREHAND

AFOREMENTIONED (2) [MENTION]

3Mc 5:47 grievous and pitiful destruction of the a people.
6:35 the a choral group and passed the time in feasting

AFORESAID (3) [SAY]

2Mc 3:28 this man who had just entered the a treasury with
3Mc 1:26 determined to bring the a plan to a conclusion.
6:36 they instituted the observance of the a days as

AFRAID‡ (217) [FEAR]

Ge 3:10 and I was a, because I was naked;
15: 1 "Do not be a, Abram, I am your shield;
18:15 saying, "I did not laugh"; for she was a.
19:30 for he was a to stay in Zoar;
20: 8 and the men were very much a.
21:17 "What troubles you, Hagar? Do not be a;
26: 7 for he was a to say, "My wife," thinking,
26:24 do not be a, for I am with you and will bless you
28:17 he was a, and said, "How awesome is this place!
31:31 Jacob answered Laban, "Because I was a,
32: 7 Then Jacob was greatly a and distressed;
32:11 from the hand of Esau, for I am a of him;
35:17 the midwife said to her, "Do not be a;
43:18 Now the men were a because they were brought
43:23 He replied, "Rest assured, do not be a;
46: 3 do not be a to go down to Egypt,
50:19 But Joseph said to them, "Do not be a!
Ex 2:14 Then Moses was a and thought,
3: 6 Moses hid his face, for he was a to look at God.
14:13 But Moses said to the people, "Do not be a,
20:18 they were a and trembled and stood at a distance,
20:20 Moses said to the people, "Do not be a;
34:30 and they were a to come near him.
Lev 26: 6 and no one shall make you a;
Nu 12: 8 not a to speak against my servant Moses?"
21:34 the LORD said to Moses, "Do not be a of him;
Dt 2: 4 They will be a of you, so,
5: 5 for you were a because of the fire and did not go
7:18 do not be a of them.
7:19 the same to all the peoples of whom you are a.
9:19 For I was a that the anger that the LORD bore
13:11 Then all Israel shall hear and be a,
17:13 All the people will hear and be a,
19:20 The rest shall hear and be a,
20: 1 you shall not be a of them;
20: 3 Do not lose heart, or be a, or panic,
20: 8 saying, "Is anyone a or disheartened?
21:21 and all Israel will hear, and be a.
28:10 and they shall be a of you.
Jos 10:25 Joshua said to them, "Do not be a or dismayed;
11: 6 the LORD said to Joshua, "Do not be a of them,
Jdg 6:27 but because he was too a of his family and
8:20 But the boy did not draw his sword, for he was a,
Ru 3:11 And now, my daughter, do not be a,
1Sa 3:15 Samuel was a to tell the vision to Eli.
4: 7 the Philistines were a;
4:20 the women attending her said to her, "Do not be a,
7: 7 of Israel heard of it they were a of the Philistines.
12:20 And Samuel said to the people, "Do not be a;
17:11 they were dismayed and greatly a.
17:24 fled from him and were very much a.
18:12 Saul was a of David, because the LORD was
18:29 Saul was still more a of David.
21:12 and was very much a of King Achish of Gath.
22:23 Stay with me, and do not be a;
23: 3 "Look, we are a here in Judah;
23:17 He said to him, "Do not be a;
28: 5 Saul saw the army of the Philistines, he was a,
2Sa 1:14 "Were you not a to lift your hand to destroy
6: 9 David was a of the LORD that day;
9: 7 David said to him, "Do not be a,
10:19 So the Arameans were a to help
12:18 And the servants of David were a to tell him that
13:28 Do not be a; have I not myself commanded you?
14:15 the king because the people have made me a;
1Ki 1:51 "Adonijah is a of King Solomon;
17:13 Elijah said to her, "Do not be a;
19: 3 Then he was a; he got up and
2Ki 1:15 do not be a of him."
6:16 He replied, "Do not be a,
19: 6 not be a because of the words that you have heard,
25:24 "Do not be a because of the Chaldean officials;
25:26 for they were a of the Chaldeans.
1Ch 13:12 David was a of God that day;
21:30 he was a of the sword of the angel of the LORD.
22:13 Do not be a or dismayed.
28:20 Do not be a or dismayed;
2Ch 20: 3 Jehoshaphat was a; he set himself to seek
32: 7 not be a or dismayed before the king of Assyria
Ezr 4: 4 and made them a to build,
Ne 2: 2 Then I was very much a.
4:14 "Do not be a of them.
6:14 the rest of the prophets who wanted to make me a.

Ne 6:16 all the nations around us were **a** and fell greatly
Job 6:21 you see my calamity, and are **a.**
9:28 I become **a** of all my suffering,
11:19 You will lie down, and no one will make you **a;**
19:29 be **a** of the sword, for wrath brings the punishment
32:6 I was timid and **a** to declare my opinion to you.
41:25 When it raises itself up the gods are **a;**
Ps 3:6 I am not **a** of ten thousands
27:1 of whom shall I be **a?**
49:16 Do not be **a** when some become rich,
56:3 when I am **a,** I put my trust in you.
56:4 I am not **a;** what can flesh do to me?
56:11 in God I trust; I am not **a.**
77:16 O God, when the waters saw you, they were **a;**
78:53 He led them in safety, so that they were not **a;**
112:7 They are not **a** of evil tidings;
112:8 Their hearts are steady, they will not be **a;**
119:120 and I am **a** of your judgments.
Pr 3:24 If you sit down, you will not be **a;**
3:25 Do not be **a** of sudden panic,
31:21 She is not **a** for her household when it snows,
Ecc 12:5 one is **a** of heights, and terrors are in the road;
Isa 10:24 not be **a** of the Assyrians when they beat you with
12:2 I will trust, and will not be **a,**
17:2 and no one will make them **a.**
33:14 The sinners in Zion are **a;**
37:6 not be **a** because of the words that you have heard,
41:5 The coastlands have seen and are **a,**
41:10 for I am with you, do not be **a,** for I am your God;
41:23 or do harm, that we may be **a** and terrified.
44:8 Do not fear, or be **a;** have I not told you
51:12 then are you **a** of a mere mortal who must die,
Jer 1:8 Do not be **a** of them,
10:5 Do not be **a** of them, for they cannot do evil,
22:25 into the hands of those of whom you are **a,**
26:21 he was **a** and fled and escaped to Egypt.
30:10 and no one shall make him **a.**
38:19 "I am **a** of the Judeans who have deserted to
40:9 saying, "Do not be **a** to serve the Chaldeans.
41:18 for they were **a** of them,
42:11 Do not be **a** of the king of Babylon,
42:11 do not be **a** of him, says the LORD,
46:27 and no one shall make him **a.**
Eze 2:6 And you, O mortal, do not be **a** of them,
2:6 and do not be **a** of their words,
2:6 do not be **a** of their words,
27:35 and their kings are horribly **a,**
34:28 and no one shall make them **a.**
39:26 in their land with no one to make them **a,**
Da 10:11 "I am **a** of my lord the king;
Am 3:6 and the people are not **a?**
Jnh 1:5 the mariners were **a,** and each cried to his god.
1:10 Then the men were even more **a,** and said to him,
Mic 4:4 and no one shall make them **a;**
Zep 3:13 and no one shall make them **a.**
Zec 8:13 Do not be **a,** but let your hands be strong.
8:15 to the house of Judah; do not be **a.**
9:5 Ashkelon shall see it and be **a;**
Mt 1:20 do not be **a** to take Mary as your wife,
2:22 he was **a** to go there.
8:26 And he said to them, "Why are you **a,**
10:31 So do not be **a;** you are of more
14:27 it is I; do not be **a."**
17:7 saying, "Get up and do not be **a."**
21:26 we say, 'Of human origin,' we are **a** of the crowd;
25:25 so I was **a,** and I went and hid your talent in
28:5 But the angel said to the women, "Do not be **a;**
28:10 Then Jesus said to them, "Do not be **a;**
Mk 4:40 He said to them, "Why are you **a?**
5:15 man who had had the legion; and they were **a.**
6:50 it is I; do not be **a."**
9:32 not understand what he was saying and were **a**
10:32 and those who followed were **a.**
11:18 for they were **a** of him,
11:32 they were **a** of the crowd,
16:8 and they said nothing to anyone, for they were **a.**
Lk 1:13 But the angel said to him, "Do not be **a,**
1:30 The angel said to her, "Do not be **a,** Mary,
2:10 But the angel said to them, "Do not be **a;**
5:10 Then Jesus said to Simon, "Do not be **a;**
8:25 They were **a** and amazed, and said to one another,
8:35 in his right mind. And they were **a.**
9:45 And they were **a** to ask him about this saying.
12:7 of your head are all counted. Do not be **a;**
12:32 "Do not be **a,** little flock,
19:21 for I was **a** of you, because you are a harsh man;
22:2 for they were **a** of the people.
Jn 6:20 But he said to them, "It is I; do not be **a."**
9:22 His parents said this because they were **a** of
12:15 "Do not be **a,** daughter of Zion.
14:27 and do not let them be **a.**
19:8 when Pilate heard this, he was more **a** than ever.
Ac 5:26 for they were **a** of being stoned by the people.
9:26 and they were all **a** of him,
16:38 and they were **a** when they heard
18:9 "Do not be **a,** but speak and do not be silent;
22:29 and the tribune also was **a,**
27:24 and he said, 'Do not be **a,** Paul;
Ro 13:4 But if you do what is wrong, you should be **a,**
2Co 11:3 But I am **a** that as the serpent deceived Eve
Gal 4:11 I am **a** that my work for you may have been wasted
1Th 3:5 was **a** that somehow the tempter had tempted you
Heb 11:23 and they were not **a** of the king's edict.
13:6 "The Lord is my helper; I will not be **a.**
2Pe 2:10 they are not **a** to slander the glorious ones,
Rev 1:17 on me, saying, "Do not be **a;**
Tob 1:19 I was **a** and ran away.
Tob 2:8 my neighbors laughed and said, "Is he still not **a?**
4:8 not be **a** to give according to the little you have.
4:21 Do not be **a,** my son,
6:15 I am **a** that I may die and bring my father's
6:18 Do not be **a,** for she was set apart for you before
12:16 they fell face down, for they were **a.**
12:17 he said to them, "Do not be **a;** peace be with you.
Jdt 1:11 for they were not **a** of him,
5:23 They said, "We are not **a** of the Israelites;
11:1 woman, and do not be **a** in your heart,
Wis 8:15 dread monarchs will be **a** of me when they hear
Sir 22:16 after due reflection will not be **a** in a crisis.
1Mc 3:22 as for you, do not be **a** of them."
4:8 not fear their numbers or be **a** when they charge.
7:30 he was **a** of him and would not meet him again.
10:76 people of the city became **a** and opened the gates,
12:28 they were **a** and were terrified at heart;
12:42 he was **a** to raise his hand against him.
14:12 and there was none to make them **a.**
16:6 that the soldiers were **a** to cross the stream,
2Es 6:33 'Believe and do not be **a!**
10:27 I was **a,** and cried with a loud voice and said,
10:55 do not be **a,** and do not let your heart be terrified;
15:18 be destroyed, and people shall be **a.**
16:10 He will flash lightning, and who will not be **a?**
4Mc 8:14 "Be **a,** young fellows; whatever justice you revere
8:15 not only were they not **a,**

AFRESH (KJV) See AGAIN

AFTER‡ (906) [AFTERWARD, AFTERWARDS]

Ge 4:17 and named it Enoch **a** his son Enoch.
5:4 The days of Adam **a** he became the father
5:7 Seth lived **a** the birth of Enosh
5:10 Enosh lived **a** the birth of Kenan
5:13 Kenan lived **a** the birth of Mahalalel
5:16 Mahalalel lived **a** the birth of Jared
5:19 Jared lived **a** the birth of Enoch
5:22 Enoch walked with God **a** the birth of Methuselah
5:26 Methuselah lived **a** the birth Lamech
5:30 Lamech lived **a** the birth of Noah
5:32 **A** Noah was five hundred years old,
7:10 And **a** seven days the waters of the flood came on
9:9 with you and your descendants **a** you,
9:28 **A** the flood Noah lived three hundred fifty years.
10:1 children were born to them **a** the flood.
10:32 the nations spread abroad on the earth **a** the flood.
11:10 he became the father of Arpachshad two years **a**
11:11 and Shem lived **a** the birth of Arpachshad
11:13 and Arpachshad lived **a** the birth of Shelah
11:15 and Shelah lived **a** the birth of Eber
11:17 and Eber lived **a** the birth of Peleg
11:19 and Peleg lived **a** the birth of Reu
11:21 and Reu lived **a** the birth of Serug
11:23 and Serug lived **a** the birth of Nahor
11:25 and Nahor lived **a** the birth of Terah
13:14 **a** Lot had separated from him,
14:17 **A** his return from the defeat of Chedorlaomer and
15:1 **A** these things the word of the LORD came
16:3 **a** Abram had lived ten years in the land
16:13 "Have I really seen God and remained alive **a**
17:7 your offspring **a** you throughout their generations,
17:7 to be God to you and to your offspring **a** you.
17:8 I will give to you, and to your offspring **a** you,
17:9 you and your offspring **a** you
17:10 between me and you and your offspring **a** you:
17:19 as an everlasting covenant for his offspring **a** him.
18:5 and **a** that you may pass on—
18:11 it had ceased to be with Sarah **a** the manner
18:12 "**A** I have grown old, and my husband is old,
18:19 and his household **a** him to keep the way of
19:6 of the door to the men, shut the door **a** him,
19:31 and there is not a man on earth to come in to us **a**
22:1 **A** these things God tested Abraham.
22:20 Now **a** these things it was told Abraham,
23:19 **A** this, Abraham buried Sarah his wife in the cave
24:55 at least ten days; **a** that she may go."
24:67 So Isaac was comforted **a** his mother's death.
25:11 **A** the death of Abraham God blessed his son Isaac.
26:18 for the Philistines had stopped them up **a** the death
35:12 and I will give the land to your offspring **a** you."
37:17 So Joseph went **a** his brothers,
39:7 And **a** a time his master's wife cast her eyes
39:10 And although she spoke to Joseph day **a** day,
40:1 Some time **a** this, the cupbearer of the king
41:1 **A** two whole years, Pharaoh dreamed
41:3 ugly and thin, came up out of the Nile **a** them,
41:6 and blighted by the east wind, sprouted **a** them.
41:19 Then seven other cows came up **a** them, poor,
41:23 and blighted by the east wind, sprouting **a** them;
41:27 The seven lean and ugly cows that came up **a**
41:30 **A** them there will arise seven years of famine,
44:4 Joseph said to his steward, "Go, follow **a** the men;
45:15 and **a** that his brothers talked with him.
48:1 **A** this Joseph was told, "Your father is ill."
48:4 and will give this land to your offspring **a** you for
48:6 offspring born to you **a** them, they shall be yours.
50:14 **A** he had buried his father,
Ex 2:11 One day, **a** Moses had grown up,
2:23 **A** a long time the king of Egypt died.
3:20 **a** that he will let you go.
7:25 Seven days passed **a** the LORD had struck
10:5 They shall devour the last remnant left you **a**
11:8 **A** that I will leave."
Ex 12:44 of it **a** he has been circumcised;
14:17 of the Egyptians so that they will go in **a** them;
14:23 Egyptians pursued, and went into the sea **a** them,
15:20 the women went out **a** her with tambourines and
16:1 of the second month **a** they had departed from
18:2 **A** Moses had sent away his wife Zipporah,
18:7 each asked **a** the other's welfare,
19:1 the third new moon **a** the Israelites had gone out
19:9 when I speak with you and so trust you ever **a."**
22:3 but if it happens **a** sunrise, bloodguilt is incurred.
28:43 for him and for his descendants **a** him.
29:29 of Aaron shall be passed on to his sons **a** him;
Lev 2:2 **A** taking from it a handful of the choice flour
6:10 The priest shall put on his linen vestments **a**
8:21 And **a** the entrails and the legs were washed
8:24 **A** Aaron's sons were brought forward,
9:22 and he came down **a** sacrificing the sin offering,
13:3 **a** the priest has examined him he shall pronounce
13:7 in the skin **a** he has shown himself to the priest
13:35 in the skin **a** he was pronounced clean,
13:55 The priest shall examine the diseased article **a**
13:56 and the disease has abated **a** it is washed,
14:8 **A** that he shall come into the camp,
14:43 **a** he has taken out the stones and scraped
14:48 not spread in the house **a** the house was plastered,
15:28 and **a** that she shall be clean.
16:1 to Moses **a** the death of the two sons of Aaron,
23:11 on the day **a** the sabbath the priest shall raise it.
23:15 And from the day **a** the sabbath,
23:16 until the day **a** the seventh sabbath, fifty days;
25:46 as a possession for your children **a** you,
25:48 **a** they have sold themselves they shall have
27:18 but if the field is consecrated **a** the jubilee,
Nu 1:1 in the second year **a** they had come out of the land
4:15 **a** that the Kohathites shall come to carry these,
6:19 **a** they have shaved the consecrated head.
6:20 **A** that the nazirites may drink wine.
7:88 the dedication offering for the altar, **a**
9:1 of the second year **a** they had come out of the land
12:14 and **a** that she may be brought in again."
12:16 **A** that the people set out from Hazeroth,
15:18 **A** you come into the land
25:8 he went **a** the Israelite man into the tent,
25:13 for him and for his descendants **a** him a covenant
26:1 **A** the plague the LORD said to Moses and
30:15 But if he nullifies them some time **a** he has heard
32:22 then **a** that you may return and be free
32:42 and renamed it Nobah **a** himself.
33:3 on the day **a** the passover
33:38 in the fortieth year **a** the Israelites had come out of
35:28 but **a** the death of the high priest
Dt 1:4 This was **a** he had defeated King Sihon of
1:8 to give to them and to their descendants **a** them."
1:46 **A** you had stayed at Kadesh as many days
3:14 **a** himself, Havvoth-jair, as it is to this day.)
4:29 if you search **a** him with all your heart and soul.
4:37 he chose their descendants **a** them.
4:40 and that of your descendants **a** you,
10:15 their descendants **a** them, out of all the peoples,
11:12 a land that the LORD your God looks **a.**
12:25 all may go well with you and your children **a** you,
12:28 with you and with your children **a** you forever,
12:30 **a** they have been destroyed before you:
21:13 **a** that you may go in to her and be her husband,
22:13 but **a** going in to her,
24:4 is not permitted to take her again to be his wife **a**
29:22 next generation, your children who rise up **a** you,
31:27 how much more **a** my death!
31:29 that **a** my death you will surely act corruptly,
Jos 1:1 **A** the death of Moses the servant of the LORD,
5:4 the wilderness **a** they had come out of Egypt.
5:5 the wilderness **a** they had come out of Egypt had
5:11 On the day **a** the passover, on that very day,
6:9 the rear guard came **a** the ark,
6:13 and the rear guard came **a** the ark of the LORD,
8:6 They will come out **a** us
8:17 not a man left in Ai or Bethel who did not go out **a**
9:16 But when three days had passed **a** they had made
19:47 and **a** capturing it and putting it to the sword,
19:47 calling Leshem, Dan, **a** their ancestor Dan.
22:27 and between the generations **a** us,
24:20 and consume you, **a** having done you good."
24:29 **A** these things Joshua son of Nun,
Jdg 1:1 **A** the death of Joshua, the Israelites inquired of
2:10 and another generation grew up **a** them,
2:17 they lusted **a** other gods and bowed down to them.
3:22 the hilt also went in **a** the blade, and the fat closed
3:24 **A** he had gone, the servants came.
3:28 He said to them, "Follow **a** me;
3:28 So they went down **a** him,
3:31 **A** him came Shamgar son of Anath,
4:1 in the sight of the LORD, **a** Ehud died.
6:29 **A** searching and inquiring, they were told,
7:16 **A** he divided the three hundred men
7:23 and they pursued **a** the Midianites.
10:1 **A** Abimelech, Tola son of Puah son of Dodo,
10:3 **A** him came Jair the Gileadite,
11:4 **A** a time the Ammonites made war against Israel.
12:8 **A** him Ibzan of Bethlehem judged Israel.
12:11 **A** him Elon the Zebulunite judged Israel;
12:13 **A** him Abdon son of Hillel
14:8 **A** a while he returned to marry her,
15:1 **A** a while, at the time of the wheat harvest,
16:4 **A** this he fell in love with a woman in the valley
16:16 **a** she had nagged him with her words day **a** day,
16:22 But the hair of his head began to grow again **a**
18:7 **a** the manner of the Sidonians,

Jdg 18:29 They named the city Dan, a their ancestor Dan,
19: 3 Then her husband set out a her,
19: 5 with a bit of food, and a that you may go."
Ru 1:15 return a your sister-in-law."
2:18 what was left over a she herself had been satisfied.
3:10 you have not gone a young men,
4: 4 to you to redeem it, and I come a you."
1Sa 1: 9 A they had eaten and drunk at Shiloh,
5: 9 But a they had brought it to Gath,
6: 6 A he had made fools of them,
6:12 and the lords of the Philistines went a them as far
7: 2 and all the house of Israel lamented a the LORD.
8: 3 not follow in his ways, but turned aside a gain;
10: 5 A that you shall come to Gibeath-elohim,
11: 7 "Whoever does not come out a Saul and Samuel,
12:21 not turn aside a useless things that cannot profit
13:14 the LORD has sought out a man a his own heart;
14:12 to his armor-bearer, "Come up a me;
14:13 with his armor-bearer following a him.
14:13 and his armor-bearer, coming a him, killed them.
14:22 they too followed closely a them in the battle.
14:31 A they had struck down the Philistines that day
14:36 down a the Philistines by night and despoil them
14:37 "Shall I go down a the Philistines?
15:31 So Samuel turned back a Saul;
17:35 I went a it and struck it down, rescuing the lamb
20:19 On the day a tomorrow, you shall go
20:27 But on the second day, the day a the new moon,
20:37 Jonathan called a the boy and said,
20:38 Jonathan called a the boy, "Hurry, be quick,
22:20 named Abiathar, escaped and fled a David.
24: 8 also rose up and went out of the cave and called a
24:21 that you will not cut off my descendants a me,
25:13 and about four hundred men went up a David,
25:19 "Go on ahead of me; I am coming a you."
25:42 She went a the messengers of David
26: 3 When he learned that Saul came a him into
2Sa 1: 1 A the death of Saul, when David had returned
1:10 for I knew that he could not live a he had fallen.
2: 1 A this David inquired of the LORD,
3:26 he sent messengers a Abner,
5:13 In Jerusalem, a he came from Hebron,
7:12 I will raise up your offspring a you,
11: 4 (Now she was purifying herself a her period.)
13: 4 why are you so haggard morning a morning?
13:17 and bolt the door a her."
13:18 his servant put her out, and bolted the door a her.
13:23 A two full years Absalom had sheepshearers
13:37 David mourned for his son day a day.
15: 1 A this Absalom got himself a chariot and horses,
15:13 hearts of the Israelites have gone a Absalom."
15:16 behind to look a the house.
16:21 the ones he has left to look a the house;
17:21 A they had gone, the men came up out of the well,
18:22 "Come what may, let me also run a the Cushite."
20: 3 the ten concubines whom he had left to look a
20: 7 Joab's men went out a him,
20:13 all the people went on a Joab to pursue Sheba son
21: 1 year a year; and David inquired of the LORD.
21:14 A that, God heeded supplications for the land.
21:18 A this a battle took place with the Philistines,
1Ki 1: 6 and he was born next a Absalom.
1:14 I will come in a you and confirm your words."
1:20 on the throne of my lord the king a him.
1:27 on the throne of my lord the king a him?"
3:12 before you and no one like you shall arise a you.
3:18 Then on the third day a I gave birth,
6: 1 In the four hundred eightieth year a
11: 4 his wives turned away his heart a other gods;
11:24 of a marauding band, a the slaughter by David;
13:14 He went a the man of God,
13:23 A the man of God had eaten food and had drunk,
13:31 A he had buried him, he said to his sons,
13:33 Even a this event Jeroboam did not turn
15: 4 up his son a him, and establishing Jerusalem;
16:24 a the name of Shemer, the owner of the hill.
17: 7 But a a while the wadi dried up,
17:17 A this the son of the woman,
18: 1 A many days the word of the LORD came
19:11 and a the wind an earthquake,
19:12 and a the earthquake a fire, but the LORD was
19:12 and a the fire a sound of sheer silence.
19:20 He left the oxen, ran a Elijah, and said,
20:15 a them he mustered all the people of Israel,
20:27 A the Israelites had been mustered
21:26 He acted most abominably in going a idols,
2Ki 1: 1 A the death of Ahab, Moab rebelled against Israel.
5:20 I will run a him and get something out of him."
5:21 So Gehazi went a Naaman.
5:21 When Naaman saw someone running a him,
6:23 a they ate and drank, he sent them on their way,
7:14 and the king sent them a the Aramean army,
7:15 So they went a them as far as the Jordan;
11:20 the city was quiet a Athaliah had been killed with
14:17 of Joash of Judah lived fifteen years a the death
14:19 they sent a him to Lachish, and killed him there.
14:22 a King Amaziah slept with his ancestors.
17:15 They went a false idols and became false;
17:33 a the manner of the nations from
18: 5 like him among all the kings of Judah a him,
23:25 nor did any like him arise a him.
1Ch 2:24 A the death of Hezron, in Caleb-ephrathah,
6:31 a the ark came to rest there.
8: 8 And Shaharaim had sons in the country of Moab a
14:14 God said to him, "You shall not go up a them;
17:11 I will raise up your offspring a you,
20: 4 A this, war broke out with the Philistines at Gezer;
1Ch 27: 1 month a month throughout the year,
27: 7 for the fourth month, and his son Zebadiah a him;
27:34 A Ahithophel came Jehoiada son of Benaiah,
28: 8 for an inheritance to your children a you forever.
2Ch 1:12 and none a you shall have the like."
2:17 a the census that his father David had taken;
5:10 with the people of Israel a they came out of Egypt.
11:16 of Israel came a them from all the tribes of Israel
11:20 A her he took Maacah daughter of Absalom,
18: 2 A some years he went down to Ahab in Samaria.
20: 1 A this the Moabites and Ammonites,
20:35 A this King Jehoshaphat of Judah joined
21:15 until your bowels come out, day a day,
21:18 A all this the LORD struck him in his bowels
22: 4 a the death of his father they were his counselors,
23:21 the city was quiet a Athaliah had been killed with
24:11 So they did day a day,
24:17 Now a the death of Jehoiada the officials
25:14 Now a Amaziah came from the slaughter of
25:25 lived fifteen years a the death of King Joash son
25:27 they sent a him to Lachish, and killed him there.
26: 2 a the king slept with his ancestors.
26:17 But the priest Azariah went in a him,
32: 1 A these things and these acts of faithfulness,
32: 9 A this, while King Sennacherib of Assyria was
35:20 A all this, when Josiah had set the temple in order,
Ezr 3: 5 and a that the regular burnt offerings,
3: 8 the second year a their arrival at the house of God
7: 1 A this, in the reign of King Artaxerxes of Persia,
9: 1 A these things had been done,
9:10 "And now, our God, what shall we say a this?
9:13 A all that has come upon us for our evil deeds and
Ne 3:16 A him Nehemiah son of Azbuk,
3:17 A him the Levites made repairs:
3:18 A him their kin made repairs:
3:20 A him Baruch son of Zabbai
3:21 A him Meremoth son of Uriah son
3:22 A him the priests, the men of the surrounding area,
3:23 A them Benjamin and Hasshub made repairs
3:23 A them Azariah son of Maaseiah son
3:24 A him Binnui son of Henadad
3:25 A him Pedaiah son of Parosh
3:27 A him the Tekoites repaired another section
3:29 A them Zadok son of Immer
3:29 A him Shemaiah son of Shecaniah,
3:30 A him Hananiah son of Shelemiah
3:30 A him Meshullam son of Berechiah made repairs
3:31 A him Malchijah, one of the goldsmiths,
4:14 A I looked these things over,
5: 7 A thinking it over, I brought charges against
9:28 But a they had rest, they again did evil before you,
12:32 and a them went Hoshaiah and half the officials
13: 6 A some time I asked leave of the king
13:19 that they should not be opened until a the sabbath.
Est 2: 1 A these things, when the anger
2:12 a being twelve months under the regulations for
3: 1 A these things King Ahasuerus promoted Haman
3: 4 to him day a day and he would not listen to them,
4:16 A that I will go to the king,
Job 3: 1 A this Job opened his mouth and cursed the day
5: 5 and the thirsty pant a their wealth.
19:26 and a my skin has been thus destroyed,
20:21 There was nothing left a they had eaten;
21: 3 then a I have spoken, mock on.
21:21 For what do they care for their household a them,
21:33 everyone will follow a, and those who went
29:22 A I spoke they did not speak again,
30: 5 people shout a them as a a thief.
37: 4 A it his voice roars; he thunders with his
39: 8 and it searches a every green thing.
39:10 or will it harrow the valleys a you?
42: 7 A the LORD had spoken these words to Job,
42:16 A this Job lived one hundred and forty years,
Ps 4: 2 long will you love vain words, and seek a lies?
14: 2 if there are any who are wise, who seek a God.
27: 4 of the LORD, that will I seek a:
35: 4 be put to shame and dishonor who seek a my life.
38:20 for good are my adversaries because I follow a
40: 4 to those who go astray a false gods.
49:17 their wealth will not go down a them.
51: T *came to him, a he had gone in to Bathsheba.*
53: 2 if there are any who are wise, who seek a God.
61: 8 as I pay my vows day a day.
68:30 Trample under foot those who lust a tribute;
Pr 19: 7 When they call a them, they are not there.
20:25 and begin to reflect only a making a vow.
24:27 and a that build your house.
Ecc 1:11 of people yet to come by those who come a them.
1:14 and see, all is vanity and a chasing a wind.
1:17 I perceived that this also is but a chasing a wind.
2:11 and again, all was vanity and a chasing a wind,
2:12 for what can the one do who comes a the king?
2:17 for all is vanity and a chasing a wind.
2:18 seeing that I must leave it to those who come a me
2:26 This also is vanity and a chasing a wind.
3:22 who can bring them to see what will be a them?
4: 4 This also is vanity and a chasing a wind.
4: 6 with toil, and a chasing a wind.
4:16 Surely this also is vanity and a chasing a wind.
6: 9 this also is vanity and a chasing a wind.
6:12 For who can tell them what will be a them under
7:14 not find out anything that will come a them.
9: 3 and a that they go to the dead.
11: 1 for a many days you will get it back.
SS 1: 4 Draw me a you, let us make haste.
Isa 1:23 Everyone loves a bribe and runs a gifts.
24:22 and a many days they will be punished.
Isa 38: 9 a he had been sick and had recovered
43:10 nor shall there be any a me.
48: 2 For they call themselves a the holy city,
58: 2 Yet day a day they seek me and delight
64:12 A all this, will you restrain yourself, O LORD?
Jer 2: 5 and went a worthless things,
2: 8 and went a things that do not profit.
2:23 "I am not defiled, I have not gone a the Baals"?
2:25 for I have loved strangers, and a them I will go."
3: 7 "A she has done all this she will return to me";
3:15 I will give you shepherds a my own heart,
7: 6 if you do not go a other gods to your own hurt,
7: 9 and go a other gods that you have not known,
7:25 the prophets to them, day a day;
9:14 and have gone a the Baals,
9:16 and I will send the sword a them,
11:10 they have gone a other gods to serve them;
12: 6 they are in full cry a you;
12:15 And a I have plucked them up,
13: 6 And a many days the LORD said to me,
13:10 and have gone a other gods to serve them
16:11 and have gone a other gods and have served
24: 1 This was a King Nebuchadrezzar
25: 6 do not go a other gods to serve and worship them,
25:12 Then a seventy years are completed,
25:26 far and near, one a another,
25:26 And a them the king of Sheshach shall drink.
28:12 Sometime a the prophet Hananiah had broken
29: 2 This was a King Jeconiah, and the queen mother,
31:19 For a I had turned away I repented;
31:19 and a I was discovered, I struck my thigh;
31:33 the house of Israel a those days, says the LORD:
32:16 A I had given the deed of purchase to Baruch son
32:18 the guilt of parents into the laps of their children a
32:39 and the good of their children a them.
34: 8 a King Zedekiah had made a covenant with all
35:15 and do not go a other gods to serve them,
36:27 a the king had burned the scroll with the words
39:12 look a him well and do him no harm,
40: 1 from the LORD a Nebuzaradan the captain of
41: 4 On the day a the murder of Gedaliah,
41:16 from Mizpah a he had slain Gedaliah son
42:16 that you dread shall follow close a you into Egypt;
49:37 I will send the sword a them,
Eze 5: 2 and I will unsheathe the sword a them.
5:12 to every wind and will unsheathe the sword a
6: 9 and their wanton eyes that turned a their idols.
7: 5 Thus says the Lord GOD: Disaster a disaster!
9: 5 "Pass through the city a him, and kill;
11:21 But as for those whose heart goes a their detestable
16:23 A all your wickedness (woe, woe to you!
20:16 for their heart went a their idols.
20:30 defile yourselves a the manner of your ancestors
20:30 and go astray a their detestable things?
23: 5 she lusted a her lovers the Assyrians,
23:12 She lusted a the Assyrians,
23:16 When she saw them she lusted a them,
23:17 and a she defiled herself with them,
23:20 and lusted a her paramours there,
38: 8 A many days you shall be mustered;
40: 1 in the fourteenth year a the city was struck down,
44:10 from me a their idols when Israel went astray,
44:26 A he has become clean, they shall count seven
46:12 and a he has gone out the gate shall be closed.
48:31 gates of the city being named a the tribes of Israel.
Da 2:39 A you shall arise another kingdom inferior
4: 8 he who was named Belteshazzar a the name
7: 6 A this, as I watched, another appeared,
7: 7 A this I saw in the visions by night a fourth beast,
7:24 and another shall arise a them.
8: 1 Daniel, a the one that had appeared to me at first.
9:26 A the sixty-two weeks, an anointed one shall
11: 6 A some years they shall make an alliance,
11:13 and a some years he shall advance with
11:23 And a an alliance is made with him,
Hos 2: 5 For she said, "I will go a my lovers;
2:13 and went a her lovers, and forgot me,
5:11 because he was determined to go a vanity.
6: 2 A two days he will revive us;
11:10 They shall go a the LORD, who roars like a lion;
14: 8 It is I who answer and look a you.
Joel 2: 2 nor will be again a them in ages to come.
2: 3 but a them a desolate wilderness,
Am 2: 4 by the same lies a which their ancestors walked.
4:10 among you a pestilence a the manner of Egypt;
7: 1 the latter growth a the king's mowings).
Mic 7: 1 a the summer fruit has been gathered,
7: 1 a the vintage has been gleaned,
Zec 2: 8 the LORD of hosts (a his glory sent me) regarding
6: 5 a presenting themselves before the LORD of all
14:16 against Jerusalem shall go up year a year
Mt 1:12 And a the deportation to Babylon:
2: 1 a Jesus was born in Bethlehem of Judea,
2:13 Now a they had left, an angel of
2:22 And a being warned in a dream,
3:11 one who is more powerful than I is coming a me;
5: 1 and a he sat down, his disciples came to him.
5:15 No one a lighting a lamp puts it under
9: 1 And a getting into a boat he crossed the sea
9:32 A they had gone away, a demoniac who was mute
14:23 And a he had dismissed the crowds,
14:35 A the people of that place recognized him,
15:23 "Send her away, for she keeps shouting a us."
15:29 A Jesus had left that place,
15:36 and a giving thanks he broke them and gave them
15:39 A sending away the crowds,
17: 9 the vision until a the Son of Man has been raised

Mt 20: 2 **A** agreeing with the laborers for the usual daily
21:32 and even **a** you saw it,
24:29 "Immediately **a** the suffering of those days
25:19 **A** a long time the master of those slaves came
26: 2 that **a** two days the Passover is coming,
26:22 and began to say to him one **a** another,
26:26 and **a** blessing it he broke it,
26:27 and **a** giving thanks he gave it to them, saying,
26:32 But **a** I am raised up, I will go ahead of you
26:55 Day **a** day I sat in the temple teaching,
26:73 **A** a little while the bystanders came up and said
27: 7 **A** conferring together, they used them to buy
27:17 So **a** they had gathered, Pilate said to them,
27:26 and **a** flogging Jesus, he handed him over to
27:29 and **a** twisting some thorns into a crown,
27:31 **A** mocking him, they stripped him of the robe
27:53 **A** his resurrection they came out of the tombs
27:62 The next day, that is, **a** the day of Preparation,
27:63 'A three days I will rise again.'
28: 1 **A** the sabbath, as the first day of the week
28:12 **A** the priests had assembled with the elders,
Mk 1: 7 one who is more powerful than I is coming **a** me;
1:14 Now **a** John was arrested, Jesus came to Galilee,
1:43 **A** sternly warning him he sent him away at once,
2: 1 When he returned to Capernaum **a** some days,
2: 4 and **a** having dug through it,
6:46 **A** saying farewell to them,
8: 6 and **a** giving thanks he broke them and gave them
8: 7 and **a** blessing them, he ordered
8:31 and be killed, and **a** three days rise again.
9: 9 until **a** the Son of Man had risen from the dead.
9:26 **A** crying out and convulsing him terribly,
9:31 and three days **a** being killed, he will rise again."
10:34 and **a** three days he will rise again."
12:34 **A** that no one dared to ask him any question.
13:24 "But in those days, **a** that suffering,
14:19 to be distressed and to say to him one **a** another,
14:22 and **a** blessing it he broke it, gave it to them,
14:23 and **a** giving thanks he gave it to them,
14:28 **a** I am raised up, I will go before you to Galilee."
14:49 Day **a** day I was with you in the temple teaching,
14:70 **a** a little while the bystanders again said to Peter,
15:15 and **a** flogging Jesus, he handed him over to
15:17 and **a** twisting some thorns into a crown,
15:20 **A** mocking him, they stripped him of the purple
16: 9 ⟦Now **a** he rose early on the first day of the week,⟧
16:12 ⟦**A** this he appeared in another form to two of⟧
16:14 ⟦not believed those who saw him **a** he had risen.⟧
16:19 ⟦So then the Lord Jesus, **a** he had spoken to them,⟧
Lk 1: 3 **a** investigating everything carefully from
1:24 **A** those days his wife Elizabeth conceived,
1:59 were going to name him Zechariah **a** his father.
2:21 **A** eight days had passed, it was time to circumcise
2:36 with her husband seven years **a** her marriage,
2:46 **A** three days they found him in the temple,
4:38 **A** leaving the synagogue he entered Simon's house
5:27 **A** this he went out and saw a tax collector
5:39 And no one **a** drinking old wine desires new wine,
6:10 **A** looking around at all of them, he said to him,
7: 1 **A** Jesus had finished all his sayings in the hearing
8: 4 and people from town **a** town came to him, he said
8:16 "No one **a** lighting a lamp hides it under a jar,
9:28 Now about eight days **a** these sayings Jesus took
10: 1 **A** this the Lord appointed seventy others
11: 1 and **a** he had finished, one of his disciples said
11:33 "No one **a** lighting a lamp puts it in a cellar,
12: 4 and **a** that can do nothing more.
12: 5 fear him who, **a** he has killed,
12:30 For it is the nations of the world that strive **a** all
13:22 Jesus went through one town and village **a** another,
15: 4 the ninety-nine in the wilderness and go **a** the one
18:33 **A** they have flogged him, they will kill him,
19:14 of his country hated him and sent a delegation **a**
19:28 **A** he had said this, he went on ahead,
19:35 and **a** throwing their cloaks on the colt,
21: 8 Do not go **a** them.
22:17 Then he took a cup, and **a** giving thanks he said,
22:20 And he did the same with the cup **a** supper,
22:53 When I was with you day **a** day in the temple,
Jn 1:15 'He who comes **a** me ranks ahead of me
1:27 the one who is coming **a** me;
1:30 '**A** me comes a man who ranks ahead of me
2:10 the inferior wine **a** the guests have become drunk.
2:12 **A** this he went down to Capernaum
2:22 **A** he was raised from the dead,
3: 4 "How can anyone be born **a** having grown old?
3:22 **A** this Jesus and his disciples went into
4:54 that Jesus did **a** coming from Judea to Galilee.
5: 1 **A** this there was a festival of the Jews,
6: 1 **A** this Jesus went to the other side of the Sea
6:23 near the place where they had eaten the bread **a**
7: 1 **A** this Jesus went about in Galilee.
7: 9 **A** saying this, he remained in Galilee.
7:10 But **a** his brothers had gone to the festival,
11: 6 **a** having heard that Lazarus was ill,
11: 7 Then **a** this he said to the disciples,
11:11 **A** saying this, he told them,
12:19 Look, the world has gone **a** him!"
12:36 **A** Jesus had said this, he departed and hid
13:12 **A** he had washed their feet, had put on his robe,
13:21 **A** saying this Jesus was troubled in spirit,
13:27 **A** he received the piece of bread,
13:30 So, **a** receiving the piece of bread,
17: 1 **A** Jesus had spoken these words,
18: 1 **A** Jesus had spoken these words,
18:38 **A** he had said this, he went out to the Jews again
19:28 **A** this, when Jesus knew that all was now finished,
Jn 19:38 **A** these things, Joseph of Arimathea,
20:20 **A** he said this, he showed them his hands
21: 1 **A** these things Jesus showed himself again to
21: 4 Just **a** daybreak, Jesus stood on the beach;
21:14 to the disciples **a** he was raised from the dead.
21:19 **A** this he said to him, "Follow me."
Ac 1: 2 **a** giving instructions through the Holy Spirit to
1: 3 **A** his suffering he presented himself alive to them
3:24 from Samuel and those **a** him,
4:21 **A** threatening them again, they let them go,
4:23 **A** they were released, they went to their friends
5: 4 And **a** it was sold, were not the proceeds
5: 7 **A** an interval of about three hours his wife came
5:37 **A** him Judas the Galilean rose up at the time of
7: 4 **A** his father died, God had him move from there
7: 5 to him as his possession and to his descendants **a**
7: 7 'and **a** that they shall come out and worship me
8: 3 the church by entering house **a** house;
8:13 **A** being baptized, he stayed constantly with Philip
8:25 Now **a** Peter and John had testified and spoken
9:19 and **a** taking some food, he regained his strength.
9:23 **A** some time had passed, the Jews plotted
10: 8 and **a** telling them everything,
10:37 in Galilee **a** the baptism that John announced:
10:41 and who ate and drank with him **a** he rose from
12: 3 **A** he saw that it pleased the Jews,
12: 4 to bring him out to the people **a** the Passover.
12:10 **A** they had passed the first and the second guard,
12:20 and **a** winning over Blastus,
12:25 Then **a** completing their mission Barnabas
13: 3 Then **a** fasting and praying they laid their hands
13:15 **A** the reading of the law and the prophets,
13:19 **A** he had destroyed seven nations in the land
13:20 **A** that he gave them judges until the time of
13:22 son of Jesse, to be a man **a** my heart,
13:25 No, but one is coming **a** me;
13:36 **a** he had served the purpose of God
14:21 **A** they had proclaimed the good news to that city
14:23 And **a** they had appointed elders for them
15: 2 And **a** Paul and Barnabas had no small dissension
15: 7 **A** there had been much debate,
15:13 **A** they finished speaking, James replied,
15:16 '**A** this I will return, and I will rebuild
15:33 **A** they had been there for some time,
15:36 **A** some days Paul said to Barnabas, "Come,
16:23 **A** they had given them a severe flogging,
16:40 **A** leaving the prison they went to Lydia's home;
17: 1 **A** Paul and Silas had passed through Amphipolis
17: 9 **a** they had taken bail from Jason and the others,
17:15 and **a** receiving instructions to have Silas
18: 1 **A** this Paul left Athens and went to Corinth.
18:18 **A** staying there for a considerable time,
18:23 **A** spending some time there he departed and went
19: 4 to believe in the one who was to come **a** him,
19:21 Now **a** these things had been accomplished,
19:21 He said, "**A** I have gone there,
20: 1 **A** the uproar had ceased, Paul sent for
20: 1 and **a** encouraging them and saying farewell,
20: 6 from Philippi **a** the days of Unleavened Bread,
20:11 and **a** he had broken bread and eaten,
20:15 and the day **a** that we came to Miletus.
20:29 I know that **a** I have gone,
21:15 **A** these days we got ready and started to go up
21:19 **A** greeting them, he related one by one the things
22:17 "**A** I had returned to Jerusalem and
24:17 Now **a** some years I came to bring alms
24:27 **A** two years had passed, Felix was succeeded
25: 1 Three days **a** Festus had arrived in the province,
25: 6 **A** he had stayed among them not more than eight
25:12 Then Festus, **a** he had conferred with his council,
25:13 **A** several days had passed,
25:26 King Agrippa, so that, **a** we have examined him,
26:19 "**A** that, King Agrippa, I was not disobedient to
27: 5 **A** we had sailed across the sea that is off Cilicia
27:17 **A** hoisting it up they took measures to undergird
27:35 **A** he had said this, he took bread;
27:38 **A** they had satisfied their hunger,
28: 1 **A** we had reached safety, we then learned that
28: 6 but **a** they had waited **a** long time and saw
28: 9 **A** this happened, the rest of the people on
28:13 **A** one day there a south wind sprang up,
28:23 **A** they had set a day to meet with him,
Ro 4:10 Was it before or **a** he had been circumcised?
4:10 It was not **a**, but before he was circumcised.
1Co 9:27 so that **a** proclaiming to others I myself should not
11:25 In the same way he took the cup also, **a** supper,
14:25 **A** the secrets of the unbeliever's heart are disclosed
15:24 **a** he has destroyed every ruler and every authority
16: 5 I will visit you **a** passing through Macedonia—
Gal 1:18 Then **a** three years I did go up to Jerusalem
2: 1 Then **a** fourteen years I went up again
2:12 But **a** they came, he drew back
Php 2:27 so that I would not have one sorrow **a** another.
Tit 3:10 **A** a first and second admonition,
Heb 7:27 he has no need to offer sacrifices day **a** day,
8:10 the house of Israel **a** those days, says the Lord:
9:25 as the high priest enters the Holy Place year **a** year
9:27 for mortals to die once, and **a** that the judgment,
10: 1 that are continually offered year **a** year,
10: 3 sacrifices there is a reminder of sin year **a** year.
10:11 And every priest stands day **a** day at his service,
10:15 the Holy Spirit also testifies to us, for **a** saying,
10:16 "This is the covenant that I will make with them **a**
10:26 For if we willfully persist in sin **a** having received
10:32 **a** you had been enlightened,
11:23 for three months **a** his birth, because they saw that
11:30 the walls of Jericho fell **a** they had been encircled
1Pe 5:10 And **a** you have suffered for a little while,
2Pe 1:15 that **a** my departure you may be able at any time
2: 8 living among them day **a** day,
2:20 **a** they have escaped the defilements of the world
2:21 of righteousness than, **a** knowing it, to turn back
Rev 1:19 what is, and what is to take place **a** this.
4: 1 **A** this I looked, and there in heaven
4: 1 and I will show you what must take place **a** this."
7: 1 **A** this I saw four angels standing at
7: 9 **A** this I looked, and there was a great multitude
11:11 But **a** the three and a half days,
12:15 the serpent poured water like a river **a** the woman,
15: 5 **A** this I looked, and the temple of the tent
18: 1 **A** this I saw another angel coming down
19: 1 **A** this I heard what seemed to be the loud voice of
20: 3 **A** that he must be let out for a little while.
Tob 1:10 **A** I was carried away captive to Assyria and came
1:21 and his son Esar-haddon reigned **a** him.
6: 6 So **a** cutting open the fish
8:19 **A** this he asked his wife to bake many loaves
13:11 Generation **a** generation will give joyful praise
14: 2 and **a** regaining it he lived in prosperity,
14: 5 **A** this they all will return from their exile
Jdt 4: 3 the altar and the temple had been consecrated **a**
8: 9 to surrender the town to the Assyrians **a** five days,
8:33 the days **a** which you have promised to surrender
11: 3 You will live tonight and ever **a**.
12: 8 **A** bathing, she prayed the Lord God of Israel
16:21 **A** this they all returned home
16:22 the days of her life **a** her husband Manasseh died
16:25 or for a long time **a** her death.
AdE 1: 1 It was **a** this that the following things happened in
1: 4 **A** this, when he had displayed to them the riches
2: 1 **A** these things, the king's anger abated,
2:12 Now the period **a** which a girl was to go to
3: 1 **A** these events King Artaxerxes promoted Haman
3: 4 Day **a** day they spoke to him,
4:16 **A** that I will go to the king, contrary to the law,
11:12 and **a** he awoke he had it on his mind,
12: 3 and **a** they had confessed it,
15: 2 **a** invoking the aid of the all-seeing God
Wis 4:18 **A** this they will become dishonored corpses,
8:13 an everlasting remembrance to those who come **a**
15: 8 of earth a short time before and **a** a little while go
16: 3 while your people, **a** suffering want a short time,
19: 8 **a** gazing on marvelous wonders.
Sir 7:22 Do you have cattle? Look **a** them;
22:16 the mind firmly resolved **a** due reflection will not
27:17 but if you betray his secrets, do not follow **a** him.
27:20 Do not go **a** him, for he is too far off,
27:21 and there is reconciliation **a** abuse,
31: 8 and who does not go **a** gold.
34:30 If one washes **a** touching a corpse,
41: 3 before you and those who will come **a**.
41:22 and do not be insulting **a** making a gift.
44: 9 they and their children **a** them.
44:14 but their name lives on generation **a** generation.
46:20 Even **a** he had fallen asleep,
47: 1 **A** him Nathan rose up to prophesy in the days
47:12 **A** him a wise son rose up who because
Bar 1: 9 **a** King Nebuchadnezzar of Babylon
LtJ 6: 3 **a** that I will bring you away from there in peace.
6:47 and reproach for those who come **a**.
Sus 1:12 Day **a** day they watched eagerly to see her.
Bel 1:14 **A** they had gone out, the king set out the food
1Mc 1: 1 **A** Alexander son of Philip, the Macedonian,
1: 5 **A** this he fell sick and perceived
1: 7 **a** Alexander had reigned twelve years, he died.
1: 9 They all put on crowns **a** his death,
1: 9 so did their descendants **a** them for many years;
1:20 **A** subduing Egypt, Antiochus returned in
1:58 against those who were found month **a** month in
3:55 **A** this Judas appointed leaders of the people,
5:37 **A** these things Timothy gathered another army
7:33 **A** these events Nicanor went up to Mount Zion.
8: 7 and decreed that he and those who would reign **a**
8:30 If **a** these terms are in effect
9:23 **A** the death of Judas, the renegades emerged
9:37 **A** these things it was reported to Jonathan
9:42 **A** they had fully avenged the blood
10:34 and the three days before a festival and the three **a**
11:54 **A** this Trypho returned, and with him
13:20 **A** this Trypho came to invade the country
14:24 **A** this Simon sent Numenius to Rome with
16: 6 when his troops saw him, they crossed over **a** him.
16:24 the time that he became high priest **a** his father.
2Mc 1: 7 in those years **a** Jason and his company revolted
1:20 But **a** many years had passed,
1:31 **A** the materials of the sacrifice had been consumed
2: 2 and that the prophet, **a** giving them the law,
4:14 the unlawful proceedings in the wrestling arena **a**
4:23 **A** a period of three years Jason sent Menelaus,
4:25 **A** receiving the king's orders he returned,
4:26 who **a** supplanting his own brother was supplanted
6: 1 Not long **a** this, the king sent an Athenian senator
7: 7 **A** the first brother had died in this way,
7:10 **A** him, the third was the victim of their sport.
7:13 **A** he too had died, they maltreated and tortured
7:18 **A** him they brought forward the sixth.
7:26 **A** much urging on his part,
7:36 For our brothers **a** enduring
7:41 Last of all, the mother died, **a** her sons.
8:25 **A** pursuing them for some distance,
8:28 **A** the sabbath they gave some of the spoils
10: 3 they offered sacrifices, **a** a lapse of two years,
10:16 **a** making solemn supplication and imploring God
11: 1 Very soon **a** this, Lysias, the king's guardian

2Mc 11:29 to return home and look a your own affairs.
12:11 A a hard fight, Judas and his companions,
12:12 and a receiving his pledges they went back
12:20 of the divisions, and hurried a Timothy, who had
12:27 A the rout and destruction of these,
12:32 A the festival called Pentecost,
13:13 A consulting privately with the elders,
1Es 1:25 A all these acts of Josiah,
1:31 and a he was brought back to Jerusalem he died,
5: 1 A this the heads of ancestral houses were chosen
5:56 In the second year a their coming to the temple
5:57 the second month in the second year a they came
6:20 Then this Sheshbazzar, a coming here,
7:10 the fourteenth day of the first month, a the priests
8: 1 A these things, when Artaxerxes,
8:68 A these things had been done,
Pm 151: T *a he had fought in single combat with Goliath.*
3Mc 1: 9 A he had arrived in Jerusalem,
1:12 Even a the law had been read to him,
2:24 A a while he recovered,
4:15 to an end a forty days but still uncompleted.
4:17 But a the previously mentioned interval of time
4:19 A he had threatened them severely,
5:16 The king, a considering this,
5:18 A the party had been going on for some time,
5:37 A summoning Hermon he said in
6:33 a convening a great banquet
7:20 a inscribing them as holy on a pillar
2Es 3: 1 In the thirtieth year a the destruction of the city,
3: 8 And every nation walked a its own will;
4:49 And a this a cloud full of water passed before me
5: 4 you shall see it thrown into confusion a
5:21 A seven days the thoughts
5:41 or we, ourselves, or those who come a us?"
5:46 'If you bear ten children, why one a another?'
5:55 those who come a you will be smaller than you,
6:25 be that whoever remains a all that I have foretold
6:35 Now a this I wept again and fasted seven days in
7:29 A those years my son the Messiah shall die,
7:31 A seven days the world that is not yet awake shall
7:*66* of any torment or salvation promised to them a
7:*69* if a death we were not to come into judgment,
7:*75* whether a death, as soon as everyone of us yields
7:*100* a they have been separated from the bodies,
7:*107* [37] Joshua a him for Israel in the days of Achan,
7:*117* [47] sorrow now and expect punishment a death?
7:*126* [56] not consider what we should suffer a death."
7:*130* [60] did not believe him or the prophets a him,
9:12 these must in torment acknowledge it a death.
9:27 A seven days, while I lay on the grass,
9:45 And a thirty years God heard your servant,
10:46 a three thousand years Solomon built the city,
11:13 And a a time its reign came to an end,
11:17 A you no one shall rule as long as you have ruled,
11:19 they wielded power one a another and
11:22 And a this I looked and saw that the twelve wings
11:33 A this I looked again and saw the head in
12:14 And twelve kings shall reign in it, one a another.
12:49 and a these days I will come to you."
13: 1 A seven days I dreamed a dream in the night.
13: 5 A this I looked and saw that
13: 8 A this I looked and saw
13:12 A this I saw the same man come down from
13:56 that a three more days I will tell you other things,
14:30 which you also have transgressed a them.
14:34 and a death you shall obtain mercy.
14:35 For a death the judgment will come,
15:38 A that, heavy storm clouds shall be stirred up from
15:47 who have always lusted a you.
4Mc 1:23 Fear precedes pain and sorrow comes a.
4:23 and a he had plundered them he issued a decree
6: 3 A they had tied his arms
6: 8 to kick him in the side to make him get up again a
6:30 A he said this, the holy man died nobly
8: 2 any who ate defiling food would be freed a eating,
9:26 the guards brought in the next eldest, and a fitting
11: 1 When he too died, a being cruelly tortured,
12:19 A he had uttered these imprecations,
13:21 When they were born a an equal time of gestation,
16: 6 A bearing seven children,
17: 5 a lighting the way of your star-like seven sons
18: 5 both punished on earth and is being chastised a

AFTERBIRTH (1) [BEAR]

Dt 28:57 the a that comes out from between her thighs,

AFTERGROWTH (2) [GROW]

Lev 25: 5 not reap the a of your harvest or gather the grapes
25:11 you shall not sow, or reap the a,

AFTERNOON‡ (9) [NOON]

2Sa 11: 2 late one a, when David rose from his couch
Mt 27:45 over the whole land until three in the a.
Mk 15:33 over the whole land until three in the a.
Lk 23:44 over the whole land until three in the a,
Jn 1:39 It was about four o'clock in the a.
4:52 "Yesterday at one in the a the fever left him."
Ac 3: 1 at three o'clock in the a.
10: 3 One a at about three o'clock he had a vision
1Mc 10:80 at his men from early morning until late a.

AFTERWARD (63) [AFTER]

Ge 6: 4 in those days—and also a—
10:18 A the families of the Canaanites spread abroad.
15:14 and a they shall come out with great possessions.
25:26 A his brother came out, with his
38:30 A his brother came out with the crimson thread
Ex 5: 1 A Moses and Aaron went to Pharaoh and said,
34:32 A all the Israelites came near,
Lev 14:19 A he shall slaughter the burnt offering;
14:36 and a the priest shall go in to inspect the house.
16:26 and a may come into the camp.
16:28 and a may come into the camp.
22: 7 and a he may eat of the sacred donations,
Nu 5:26 and a shall make the woman drink the water.
31: 2 a you shall be gathered to your people."
31:24 a you may come into the camp."
Dt 17: 7 and a the hands of all the people.
Jos 2:16 then a you may go your way."
8:34 And a he read all the words of the law,
10:26 A Joshua struck them down and put them to death,
23: 1 A long time a, when the LORD had given rest
Jdg 1: 9 A the people of Judah went down to fight against
7:11 and a your hands shall be strengthened to attack
1Sa 9:13 a those eat who are invited.
24: 5 A David was stricken to the heart
2Sa 3:28 A, when David heard of it, he said,
8: 1 Some time a, David attacked the Philistines
10: 1 Some time a, the king of the Ammonites died,
24:10 But a, David was stricken to the heart
1Ch 2:21 A Hezron went in to the daughter of Machir father
18: 1 Some time a, David attacked the Philistines
19: 1 Some time a, King Nahash of
2Ch 24: 4 Some time a Joash decided to restore the house of
33:14 A he built an outer wall for the city of David west
35:14 A they made preparations for themselves and for
Ps 73:24 and a you will receive me with honor.
Pr 20:17 but a the mouth will be full of gravel.
28:23 person will a find more favor than one who flatters
Isa 1:26 A you shall be called the city of righteousness,
Jer 16:16 and a I will send for many hunters,
21: 7 A, says the LORD, I will give King Zedekiah
34:11 But a they turned around and took back the male
46:26 A Egypt shall be inhabited as in the days of old,
49: 6 But a I will restore the fortunes of the Ammonites,
Da 11:18 A he shall turn to the coastlands,
Hos 3: 5 A the Israelites shall return and seek
Joel 2:28 Then a I will pour out my spirit on all flesh;
Mk 9:39 a deed of power in my name will be able soon a
16: S ⟦And a Jesus himself sent out through them,⟧
Jn 13:36 you cannot follow me now; but you will follow a."
Jude 1: 5 a destroyed those who did not believe.
Jdt 13: 9 Soon a she went out and gave Holofernes' head
Wis 5:11 and a no sign of its coming is found there;
19:11 A they saw also a new kind of birds,
19:16 with festal celebrations, a afflicted
Sir 17:23 A he will rise up and repay them,
Bar 3:37 A she appeared on earth and lived
LtJ 6:50 it will a be known that they are false.
1Mc 4:18 and a seize the plunder boldly."
2Mc 5:20 the nation and a participated in its benefits;
6:15 on us a when our sins have reached their height.
1Es 1:13 A they prepared the passover for themselves and
3Mc 2: 5 an example to those who should come a.
2Es 10:56 and a you will hear as much as your ears can hear.

AFTERWARDS‡ (16) [AFTER]

Ge 30:21 A she bore a daughter, and named her Dinah.
32:20 and a I shall see his face;
Ex 11: 1 a he will let you go from here;
Nu 19: 7 and a he may come into the camp;
Dt 13: 9 and a the hand of all the people.
Jos 24: 5 and a I brought you out.
24: 7 A you lived in the wilderness a long time.
1Sa 24: 8 A David also rose up and went out of the cave
1Ki 17:13 and a make something for yourself and your son.
Mt 4: 2 and forty nights, and a he was famished.
Lk 7:11 Soon a he went to a town called Nain,
8: 1 Soon a he went on through cities and villages,
Gal 1:17 and a I returned to Damascus.
Sir 13: 7 Should he see you a, he will pass you by
2Es 7:*101* and a they shall be gathered in their habitations."
8:11 and a you will still guide it in your mercy.

AGABUS (2)

Ac 11:28 One of them named A stood up and predicted by
21:10 a prophet named A came down from Judea.

AGAG (8) [AGAGITE]

Nu 24: 7 his king shall be higher than A,
1Sa 15: 8 He took King A of the Amalekites alive,
15: 9 Saul and the people spared A,
15:20 I have brought A the king of Amalek,
15:32 "Bring A king of the Amalekites here to me."
15:32 And A came to him haltingly.
15:32 A said, "Surely this is the bitterness of death."
15:33 And Samuel hewed A in pieces before the LORD

AGAGITE (5) [AGAG]

Est 3: 1 the A, and advanced him and set his seat above all
3:10 and gave it to Haman son of Hammedatha the A,
8: 3 with him to avert the evil design of Haman the A
8: 5 by Haman son of Hammedatha the A,
9:24 Haman son of Hammedatha the A,

AGAIN‡ (543)

Ge 4:25 Adam knew his wife a, and she bore a son
8:10 and a he sent out the dove from the ark;
8:21 "I will never a curse the ground because
8:21 nor will I ever a destroy every living creature
9:11 that never a shall all flesh be cut off by the waters
9:11 never a shall there be a flood to destroy the earth."
9:15 and the waters shall never a become a flood
18:29 A he spoke to him, "Suppose forty are found there.
24:20 into the trough and ran a to the well to draw,
26:18 Isaac dug a the wells of water that had been dug in
28:21 so that I come a to my father's house in peace,
29:33 She conceived a and bore a son, and said,
29:34 A she conceived and bore a son, and said,
29:35 She conceived a and bore a son, and said,
30: 7 Rachel's maid Bilhah conceived a and bore Jacob
30:19 Leah conceived a, and she bore Jacob a sixth son.
30:31 I will a feed your flock and keep it:
35: 9 to Jacob a when he came from Paddan-aram,
38: 4 A she conceived and bore
38: 5 Yet a she bore a son, and she named him Shelah.
38:26 And he did not lie with her a.
43: 2 "Go a, buy us a little more food."
43:13 and be on your way a to the man;
44:25 And when our father said, 'Go a,
46: 4 and I will also bring you up a;
48:21 and will bring you a to the land of your ancestors.
Ex 4: 6 A, the LORD said to him,
5:22 Then Moses turned a to the LORD and said,
8:29 not let Pharaoh a deal falsely by not letting
10:14 as had never been before, nor ever shall be a.
10:28 Take care that you do not see my face a,
10:29 I will never see your face a."
11: 6 such as has never been or will ever be a.
14:13 whom you see today you shall never see a.
24:14 "Wait here for us, until we come to you a;
34:35 and Moses would put the veil on his face a,
Lev 13: 6 priest shall examine him a on the seventh day,
13: 7 he shall appear a before the priest.
13:16 But if the raw flesh a turns white,
13:57 If it appears a in the garment, in warp or woof,
14:39 The priest shall come a on the seventh day
14:43 If the disease breaks out a in the house,
Nu 11: 4 and the Israelites also wept a, and said,
11:25 But they did not do so a.
12:14 and after that she may be brought in a."
12:15 on the march until Miriam had been brought in a.
18: 5 that wrath may never a come upon the Israelites.
22:15 Once a Balak sent officials,
22:25 Balaam's foot against the wall; so he struck it a.
24:23 A he uttered his oracle, saying:
32:15 he will a abandon them in the wilderness;
Dt 3:26 Never speak to me of this matter a!
10:10 And once a the LORD listened to me.
13:11 and never a do any such wickedness.
17:13 and will not act presumptuously a.
17:16 "You must never return that way a."
18:16 or ever a see this great fire, I will die."
19:20 a crime such as this shall never a be committed
24: 4 is not permitted to take her a to be his wife
28:68 by a route that I promised you would never see a;
30: 3 gathering you a from all the peoples among whom
30: 8 Then you shall a obey the LORD,
30: 9 the LORD will a take delight in prospering you,
33:11 of those that hate him, so that they do not rise a.
Jos 2:23 the two men came down a from the hill country.
Jdg 3:12 The Israelites a did what was evil in the sight of
4: 1 The Israelites a did what was evil in the sight of
9:37 Gaal spoke a and said, "Look,
10: 6 The Israelites a did what was evil in the sight of
11: 9 "If you bring me home a to fight with
11:14 Once a Jephthah sent messengers to the king of
13: 1 The Israelites a did what was evil in the sight of
13: 8 to us a and teach us what we are to do concerning
13: 9 the angel of God came a to the woman as she sat
13:21 of the LORD did not appear a to Manoah
16:22 But the hair of his head began to grow a
19: 7 until he spent the night there a.
20:22 and a formed the battle line in the same place
20:23 and they inquired of the LORD, "Shall we a draw
Ru 1:14 Then they wept aloud a.
1Sa 3: 5 But he said, "I did not call; lie down a."
3: 6 The LORD called a, "Samuel!"
3: 6 But he said, "I did not call, my son; lie down a."
3: 8 The LORD called Samuel a, a third time.
7:13 the Philistines were subdued and did not a enter
9: 8 The boy answered Saul a, "Here,
10:22 So they inquired a of the LORD,
15:35 not see Saul a until the day of his death,
17:30 and the people answered him a as before.
19: 8 A there was war, and David went out to fight
19:21 Saul sent messengers a the third time,
20:17 Jonathan made David swear a by his love for him;
23: 4 Then David inquired of the LORD a.
26:21 my son David, for I will never harm you a,
2Sa 2:22 Abner said a to Asahel, "Turn away
3:34 And all the people wept over him a.
5:22 Once a the Philistines came up,
6: 1 David a gathered all the chosen men of Israel,
12:23 Can I bring him back a?
14:10 bring him to me, and he shall never touch you a."
14:13 the king does not bring his banished one home a.
18:22 Then Ahimaaz son of Zadok said a to Joab,
21:15 The Philistines went to war a with Israel,
21:20 There was a war at Gath, where there was a man
24: 1 A the anger of the LORD was kindled
1Ki 2:30 Then Benaiah brought the king word a, saying,
8:33 are defeated before an enemy but turn a to you,
8:34 and bring them a to the land that you gave
10:10 never a did spices come in such quantity as
12: 5 "Go away for three days, then come a to me."

1Ki 12:12 "Come to me **a** the third day."
12:24 the word of the LORD and went home **a,**
12:27 the heart of this people will turn **a** to their master,
13:33 for the high places **a** from among all the people;
17:21 let this child's life come into him **a."**
17:22 life of the child came into him **a,** and he revived.
18:34 **A** he said, "Do it a third time";
18:43 Then he said, "Go **a** seven times."
19: 6 He ate and drank, and lay down **a.**
19:20 Then Elijah said to him, "Go back **a;**
20: 5 The messengers came **a** and said:
20: 9 The messengers left and brought him word **a.**
2Ki 1:11 **A** the king sent to him another captain of fifty
1:13 **A** the king sent the captain of a third fifty
4:22 to the man of God and come back **a."**
4:35 then got up **a** and bent over him;
9:20 **A** the sentinel reported, "He reached them,
13:25 of Jehoahaz took **a** from Ben-hadad son of Hazael
19: 9 he sent messengers **a** to Hezekiah, saying,
19:30 of the house of Judah shall **a** take root downward,
24: 7 The king of Egypt did not come **a** out of his land,
1Ch 9: 2 Now the first to live **a** in their possessions
13: 3 Then let us bring **a** the ark of our God to us;
14:13 Once **a** the Philistines made a raid in the valley.
14:14 When David **a** inquired of God, God said to him,
20: 5 **A** there was war with the Philistines;
20: 6 **A** there was war at Gath, where there was a man
2Ch 6:24 are defeated before an enemy but turn **a** to you,
6:25 and bring them **a** to the land that you gave to them
10: 5 He said to them, "Come to me **a** in three days."
10:12 "Come to me **a** the third day."
19: 4 then he went out **a** among the people,
25:10 to him from Ephraim, letting them go home **a.**
28:17 the Edomites had **a** invaded and defeated Judah,
30: 6 so that he may turn **a** to the remnant
33: 8 I will never **a** remove the feet of Israel from
33:13 restored him **a** to Jerusalem and to his kingdom.
Ezr 9:14 shall we break your commandments **a**
Ne 9:28 But after they had rest, they **a** did evil before you,
13:21 If you do so **a,** I will lay hands on you."
Est 1:19 Vashti is never **a** to come before King Ahasuerus;
2:14 she did not go in to the king **a,**
7: 2 the king **a** said to Esther, "What is your petition,
8: 3 Then Esther spoke **a** to the king;
Job 7: 5 my skin hardens, then breaks out **a.**
7: 7 my eye will never **a** see good.
10: 9 and will you turn me to dust **a?**
14: 7 if it is cut down, that it will sprout **a,**
14:12 so mortals lie down and do not rise **a;**
14:14 If mortals die, will they live **a?**
16:14 He bursts upon me **a** and **a;**
20:15 They swallow down riches and vomit them up **a;**
27: 1 Job **a** took up his discourse and said:
29: 1 Job **a** took up his discourse and said:
29:22 After I spoke they did not speak **a,**
41: 8 you will not do it **a!**
Ps 3: 5 I wake **a,** for the LORD sustains me.
37:36 **A** I passed by, and they were no more;
39:13 Turn your gaze away from me, that I may smile **a,**
41: 8 that I will not rise **a** from where I lie.
42: 5 Hope in God; for I shall **a** praise him,
42:11 for I shall **a** praise him, my help and my God.
43: 5 for I shall **a** praise him, my help and my God.
49:19 who will never **a** see the light.
71:20 and calamities will revive me **a;**
71:20 the depths of the earth you will bring me up **a.**
71:21 increase my honor, and comfort me once **a.**
77: 7 and never **a** be favorable?
78:39 a wind that passes and does not come **a.**
78:41 They tested God **a** and **a,**
80:14 Turn **a,** O God of hosts;
85: 4 Restore us **a,** O God of our salvation,
85: 6 Will you not revive us **a,**
104: 9 so that they might not **a** cover the earth.
Pr 3:28 Do not say to your neighbor, "Go, and come **a,**
19:19 you effect a rescue, you will only have to do it **a.**
24:16 for though they fall seven times, they will rise **a;**
Ecc 2: 1 But **a,** this also was vanity.
2:11 and **a,** all was vanity and a chasing after wind,
3:20 all are from the dust, and all turn to dust **a.**
4: 1 **A** I saw all the oppressions that are practiced
4: 7 **A,** I saw vanity under the sun:
4:11 **A,** if two lie together, they keep warm;
5:15 so they shall go **a,** naked as they came;
9: 6 never **a** will they have any share in all
9:11 **A** I saw that under the sun the race is not to
SS 5: 3 how could I put it on **a?**
Isa 6:13 if a tenth part remain in it, it will be burned **a,**
7:10 **A** the LORD spoke to Ahaz, saying,
8: 5 The LORD spoke to me **a:**
14: 1 and will **a** choose Israel, and will set them
21:12 If you will inquire, inquire; come back **a."**
24:20 and it falls, and will not rise **a.**
29:14 so I will **a** do amazing things with this people,
37:31 of the house of Judah shall **a** take root downward,
54: 9 that the waters of Noah would never **a** go over
62: 8 not **a** give your grain to be food for your enemies,
Jer 6: 9 pass your hand **a** over its branches.
8: 4 When people fall, do they not get up **a?**
10:20 there is no one to spread my tent **a,**
12:15 I will **a** have compassion on them,
12:15 and I will bring them **a** to their heritage
22:12 and he shall never see this land **a.**
22:30 on the throne of David, and ruling **a** in Judah.
31: 4 **A** I will build you, and you shall be built,
31: 4 **A** you shall take your tambourines,
31: 5 **A** you shall plant vineyards on the mountains
Jer 31:12 and they shall never languish **a.**
31:40 It shall never **a** be uprooted or overthrown.
32:15 Houses and fields and vineyards shall **a** be bought
33:12 or animals, and in all its towns there shall **a**
33:13 flocks shall **a** pass under the hands of
34:10 so that they would not be enslaved **a;**
34:11 and brought them **a** into subjection as slaves.
34:16 and you brought them **a** into subjection to
50:39 she shall never **a** be peopled,
La 3: 3 against me alone he turns his hand, **a** and **a,**
Eze 3:20 **A,** if the righteous turn from their righteousness
5: 4 From these, **a,** you shall take some,
5: 9 and the like of which I will never do **a.**
16: 8 I passed by you **a** and looked on you;
16:63 never open your mouth **a** because of your shame,
18:27 **A,** when the wicked turn away from
20:27 In this **a** your ancestors blasphemed me,
21: 5 it shall not be sheathed **a.**
24:13 not be cleansed until I have satisfied my fury
26:14 You shall never **a** be rebuilt,
26:21 though sought for, you will never be found **a,**
29:15 and never **a** exalt itself above the nations;
29:15 that they will never **a** rule over the nations.
29:16 The Egyptians shall never **a** be the reliance of
33:14 **A,** though I say to the wicked,
36:30 that you may never **a** suffer the disgrace of famine
37:22 Never **a** shall they be two nations,
37:22 never **a** shall they be divided into two kingdoms.
37:23 They shall never **a** defile themselves
39:29 and I will never **a** hide my face from them,
47: 4 **A** he measured one thousand,
47: 4 **A** he measured one thousand,
47: 5 **A** he measured one thousand,
Da 9:25 for sixty-two weeks it shall be built **a** with streets
10:18 **A** one in human form touched me
11:10 and **a** shall carry the war as far as his fortress.
11:13 For the king of the north shall **a** raise a multitude,
Hos 1: 6 She conceived **a** and bore a daughter.
3: 1 The LORD said to me **a,** "Go,
5:15 I will return **a** to my place
11: 9 I will not **a** destroy Ephraim;
12: 9 I will make you live in tents **a,**
14: 7 They shall **a** live beneath my shadow,
Joel 2: 2 nor will be **a** after them in ages to come.
2:26 And my people shall never **a** be put to shame.
2:27 And my people shall never **a** be put to shame.
3:17 and strangers shall never **a** pass through it.
Am 7: 8 I will never **a** pass them by;
7:13 but never **a** prophesy at Bethel,
8: 2 I will never **a** pass them by.
8: 8 and be tossed about and sink **a,**
8:14 they shall fall, and never rise **a.**
9: 5 and all of it rises like the Nile, and sinks **a,**
9:15 and they shall never **a** be plucked up out of
Jnh 2: 4 how shall I look **a** upon your holy temple?'
Mic 1: 7 as the wages of a prostitute they shall **a** be used.
1:15 I will **a** bring a conqueror upon you,
7:19 He will **a** have compassion upon us;
Na 1:15 for never **a** shall the wicked invade you;
Hag 2: 6 For thus says the LORD of hosts: Once **a,**
Zec 1:17 My cities shall **a** overflow with prosperity;
1:17 LORD will **a** comfort Zion and **a** choose Jerusalem.
2:12 and will **a** choose Jerusalem.
4: 1 The angel who talked with me came **a,**
5: 1 **A** I looked up and saw a flying scroll.
6: 1 And **a** I looked up and saw four chariots coming
8: 4 Old men and old women shall **a** sit in the streets
8:15 so **a** I have purposed in these days to do good
9: 8 no oppressor shall **a** overrun them,
12: 6 while Jerusalem shall **a** be inhabited in its place,
13: 3 And if any prophets appear **a,**
14:11 for never **a** shall it be doomed to destruction;
Mt 4: 7 Jesus said to him, "**A** it is written,
4: 8 **A,** the devil took him to a very high mountain
5:33 "**A,** you have heard that it was said to those
13:45 "**A,** the kingdom of heaven is like a merchant
13:47 "**A,** the kingdom of heaven is like a net
18:19 **A,** truly I tell you, if two of you agree on earth
19:24 **A** I tell you, it is easier for a camel to go through
20: 5 he went out **a** about noon and about three o'clock,
21:19 he said to it, "May no fruit ever come from you **a!"**
21:36 **A** he sent other slaves, more than the first;
22: 4 **A** he sent other slaves, saying,
23:39 For I tell you, you will not see me **a** until you say,
26:29 I will never **a** drink of this fruit of the vine until
26:42 **A** he went away for the second time and prayed,
26:43 **A** he came and found them sleeping,
26:44 So leaving them **a,** he went away and prayed for
26:72 **A** he denied it with an oath,
27:21 The governor **a** said to them,
27:50 Then Jesus cried **a** with a loud voice
27:63 'After three days I will rise **a.'**
Mk 2:13 Jesus went out **a** beside the sea;
3: 1 **A** he entered the synagogue,
3:20 and the crowd came together **a,**
4: 1 **A** he began to teach beside the sea.
4:12 so that they may not turn **a** and be forgiven.' "
5:21 Jesus had crossed **a** in the boat to the other side,
7:14 Then he called the crowd **a** and said to them,
8: 1 when there was **a** a great crowd without anything
8:13 And he left them, and getting into the boat **a,**
8:25 Then Jesus laid his hands on his eyes **a;**
8:31 and be killed, and after three days rise **a.**
9:25 come out of him, and never enter him **a!"**
9:31 and three days after being killed, he will rise **a."**
10: 1 And crowds **a** gathered around him; and, as was his custom, he **a** taught them.
Mk 10:10 Then in the house the disciples asked him **a**
10:24 But Jesus said to them **a,** "Children,
10:32 He took the twelve aside **a** and began
10:34 and after three days he will rise **a."**
10:51 blind man said to him, "My teacher, let me see **a."**
11:14 "May no one ever eat fruit from you **a."**
11:27 **A** they came to Jerusalem.
12: 4 And **a** he sent another slave to them;
14:25 I will never **a** drink of the fruit of the vine until
14:39 And **a** he went away and prayed,
14:61 **A** the high priest asked him,
14:69 on seeing him, began **a** to say to the bystanders,
14:70 But **a** he denied it. Then after a little while the bystanders **a** said to Peter,
15: 4 Pilate asked him **a,** "Have you no answer?
15:12 to them **a,** "Then what do you wish me to do with
Lk 6:30 do not ask for them **a.**
6:34 Even sinners lend to sinners, to receive as much **a.**
6:43 nor **a** does a bad tree bear good fruit;
13:20 And **a** he said, "To what should I compare
15:24 for this son of mine was dead and is alive **a;**
18:33 and on the third day he will rise **a."**
18:41 He said, "Lord, let me see **a."**
23:20 wanting to release Jesus, addressed them **a;**
24: 7 and be crucified, and on the third day rise **a."**
Jn 1:35 The next day John **a** was standing with two
4:13 of this water will be thirsty **a,**
4:46 Then he came **a** to Cana in Galilee
6:15 he withdrew **a** to the mountain by himself.
8: 2 ⟦Early in the morning he came **a** to the temple.⟧
8: 8 ⟦once **a** he bent down and wrote on the ground.⟧
8:11 ⟦Go your way, and from now on do not sin **a."**⟧
8:12 **A** Jesus spoke to them, saying,
8:21 **A** he said to them, "I am going away,
9:17 So they said **a** to the blind man,
9:27 Why do you want to hear it **a?**
10: 7 So **a** Jesus said to them, "Very truly, I tell you,
10:17 because I lay down my life in order to take it up **a.**
10:18 and I have power to take it up **a.**
10:19 **A** the Jews were divided because of these words.
10:31 The Jews took up stones **a** to stone him.
10:39 Then they tried to arrest him **a,**
10:40 He went away **a** across the Jordan to the place
11: 7 this he said to the disciples, "Let us go to Judea **a."**
11: 8 and are you going there **a?"**
11:23 Jesus said to her, "Your brother will rise **a."**
11:24 "I know that he will rise **a** in the resurrection on
11:38 Then Jesus, **a** greatly disturbed, came to the tomb.
12:28 "I have glorified it, and I will glorify it **a."**
14: 3 I will come **a** and will take you to myself,
16:16 and you will no longer see me, and **a** a little while,
16:17 and you will no longer see me, and **a** a little while,
16:19 and you will no longer see me, and **a** a little while,
16:22 but I will see you **a,** and your hearts will rejoice,
16:28 **a,** I am leaving the world and am going to
18: 7 **A** he asked them, "Whom are you looking for?"
18:27 **A** Peter denied it, and at that moment
18:33 Then Pilate entered the headquarters **a,**
18:38 he went out to the Jews **a** and told them,
19: 4 Pilate went out **a** and said to them, "Look,
19: 9 He entered his headquarters **a** and asked Jesus,
19:37 And **a** another passage of scripture says,
20:21 Jesus said to them **a,** "Peace be with you.
20:26 A week later his disciples were **a** in the house,
21: 1 After these things Jesus showed himself **a** to
Ac 4:21 After threatening them **a,** they let them go,
10:15 The voice said to him **a,** a second time,
11:10 then everything was pulled up **a** to heaven.
13:42 to speak about these things **a** the next sabbath.
17:32 but others said, "We will hear you **a** about this."
20:25 will ever see my face **a.**
20:38 that they would not see him **a.**
27:28 a little farther on they took soundings **a**
Ro 6: 9 being raised from the dead, will never die **a;**
10:19 **A** I ask, did Israel not understand?
11:23 for God has the power to graft them in **a.**
14: 9 For to this end Christ died and lived **a,**
15:10 **a** he says, "Rejoice, O Gentiles, with his people";
15:11 and **a,** "Praise the Lord, all you Gentiles,
15:12 and **a** Isaiah says, "The root of Jesse shall come,
1Co 3:20 and **a,** "The Lord knows the thoughts of the wise,
7: 5 and then come together **a,**
12:21 nor **a** the head to the feet, "I have no need of you."
2Co 1:10 that he will rescue us **a,**
1:23 to spare you that I did not come **a** to Corinth.
3: 1 Are we beginning to commend ourselves **a?**
5:12 We are not commending ourselves to you **a,**
12:21 I fear that when I come **a,**
13: 2 that if I come **a,** I will not be lenient—
Gal 2: 1 Then after fourteen years I went up **a** to Jerusalem
2:18 I build up **a** the very things that I once tore down,
4: 9 how can you turn back **a** to the weak
4: 9 How can you want to be enslaved to them **a?**
4:19 for whom I am **a** in the pain of childbirth
5: 1 and do not submit **a** to a yoke of slavery.
5: 3 Once **a** I testify to every man who lets himself
Eph 6: 8 we will receive the same **a** from the Lord,
Php 1:26 in Christ Jesus when I come to you **a.**
2:28 in order that you may rejoice at seeing him **a,**
4: 4 Rejoice in the Lord always; **a** I will say, Rejoice.
1Th 2:18 certainly I, Paul, wanted to **a** and **a—**
4:14 For since we believe that Jesus died and rose **a,**
Heb 1: 5 **a,** "I will be his Father, and he will be my Son"?
1: 6 And **a,** when he brings the firstborn into
2:13 And **a,** "I will put my trust in him."
2:13 And **a,** "Here am I and the children whom God
4: 5 And **a** in this place it says,

Heb 4: 7 a he sets a certain day—"today"—saying
5:12 to teach you a the basic elements of the oracles
6: 1 and not laying a the foundation:
6: 4 For it is impossible to restore a to repentance
6: 6 on their own they are crucifying a the Son of God
9:25 Nor was it to offer himself a and a,
9:26 then he would have had to suffer a and a since
10:11 offering a and a the same sacrifices
10:30 And a, "The Lord will judge his people."
Jas 5:18 Then he prayed a, and the heaven gave rain and
2Pe 2:20 they are a entangled in them and overpowered,
Rev 10: 8 voice that I had heard from heaven spoke to me a,
10:11 "You must prophesy a about many peoples
18:14 to you, never to be found a!"
Tob 2: 8 yet here he is a burying the dead!"
10: 7 and mother do not believe that they will see me a.
13: 5 but he will a show mercy on all of you.
13: 9 will a have mercy on the children of the righteous.
14: 5 "But God will a have mercy on them,
Jdt 6: 5 you shall not see my face a from this day
7:30 the Lord our God will turn his mercy to us a,
16:25 No one ever a spread terror among the Israelites
AdE 2:14 in to the king a unless she is summoned by name.
5:12 and I am invited a tomorrow.
8: 3 Then she spoke once a to the king and,
Wis 10: 4 wisdom a saved it, steering the righteous man by
13: 8 Yet a, not even they are to be excused;
14: 1 A, one preparing to sail and about to voyage
16:13 down to the gates of Hades and back a.
Sir 4:18 Then she will come straight back to them a
17: 1 and makes them return to it a.
19:13 or if he did, so that he may not do it a.
24:32 I will a make instruction shine forth like the dawn,
24:33 I will a pour out teaching like prophecy,
27:19 and will not catch him a.
33: 1 in trials such a one will be rescued a and a.
34:30 a corpse, and touches it a, what has been gained
34:31 and goes a and does the same things,
44:18 that all flesh should never a be blotted out by
46:12 the names of those who have been honored live a
Bar 2:34 I will bring them a into the land that I swore
2:35 and I will never a remove my people Israel from
Sus 1:14 But turning back, they met a;
1Mc 3:15 Once a a strong army of godless men went up
3:56 he told to go home a, according to the law.
4:35 to invade Judea a with an even larger army.
7:30 he was afraid of him and would not meet him a.
8:32 If now they appeal a for help against you,
9:72 and did not come a into their territory.
2Mc 2: 7 until God gathers his people together a
3:33 the same young men appeared a
4: 6 not a reach a peaceful settlement,
5: 7 and fled a into the country of the Ammonites.
5:20 the Almighty was restored a in all its glory when
7:11 and from him I hope to get them back a."
7:14 to cherish the hope God gives of being raised a
7:23 in his mercy give life and breath back to you a,
7:29 so that in God's mercy I may get you back a along
7:33 he will a be reconciled with his own servants.
10: 4 and implored the Lord that they might never a fall
12: 7 to come a and root out the whole community
12:44 that those who had fallen would rise a,
13:19 was turned back, attacked a, and was defeated.
14: 3 to be safe or to have access a to the holy altar,
14:46 of life and spirit to give them back to him a.
15:39 For just as it is harmful to drink wine alone, or, a,
1Es 3: 3 he went to sleep, but woke up a.
6:18 these King Cyrus took out a from the temple
8:53 And a we prayed to our Lord about these things,
8:87 but we turned back a to transgress your law
3Mc 5:13 and a implored him who is easily reconciled
5:25 the supreme God to help them a at once.
5:40 and a revoking your decree in the matter?
2Es 2:40 Take a your full number, O Zion,
3: 9 But a, in its time you brought the flood upon
3:12 and peoples and many nations, and a they began
5:13 and if you pray a, and weep as you do now,
5:21 of my heart were very grievous to me a.
5:36 and make the withered flowers bloom a for me;
6:31 you will pray a and fast a for seven days,
6:31 I will a declare to you greater things than these,
6:35 Now after this I wept a and fasted seven days in
6:36 within me a, and I began to speak in the presence
6:41 "A, on the second day, you created the spirit of
7: 1 to me on the former nights was sent to me a.
7:78 the body to return a to him who gave it,
8: 9 the womb gives up a what has been created in it,
9:15 and I say now, and will say it a:
9:27 my heart was troubled a as it was before.
10:19 So I spoke a to her, and said,
10:24 so that the Mighty One may be merciful to you a,
11:10 I looked a and saw that the voice did not come
11:19 after another and then were never seen a.
11:33 After this I looked a and saw the head in
12: 3 When I looked a, they were already vanishing.
13:46 and now, when they are about to come a,
13:47 Most High will stop the channels of the river a,
14:35 the judgment will come, when we shall live a;
16:67 and forget your iniquities, never to commit them a;
4Mc 6: 8 in the side to make him get up a after he fell.
7:13 his sinews feeble, he became young a
18:20 to the catapult and back a to more tortures,

AGAINST‡ (1802)

Ge 4: 8 Cain rose up a his brother Abel, and killed him.
13:13 of Sodom were wicked, great sinners a the LORD.
14: 9 and King Arioch of Ellasar, four kings a five.
14:15 He divided his forces a them by night,
15:10 laying each half over a the other;
16:12 his hand a everyone, and everyone's hand a him;
18:20 "How great is the outcry a Sodom and Gomorrah
19: 9 Then they pressed hard a the man Lot,
19:13 because the outcry a its people has become great
20: 6 furthermore it was I who kept you from sinning a
20: 9 How have I sinned a you,
27:45 until your brother's anger a you turns away,
32:25 When the man saw that he did not prevail a Jacob,
34:25 took their swords and came a the city unawares,
34:30 and if they gather themselves a me and attack me,
39: 9 could I do this great wickedness, and sin a God?"
41:36 a reserve for the land a the seven years of famine
50:15 a grudge a us and pays us back in full for all
Ex 1:10 join our enemies and fight a us and escape from
2:19 "An Egyptian helped us a the shepherds;
4:14 of the LORD was kindled a Moses and he said,
7: 5 when I stretch out my hand a Egypt and bring
9:17 You are still exalting yourself a my people,
10:16 "I have sinned a the LORD your God, and a you.
14:25 for the LORD is fighting for them a Egypt."
14:31 Israel saw the great work that the LORD did a
15:24 And the people complained a Moses, saying,
16: 2 of the Israelites complained a Moses and Aaron in
16: 7 he has heard your complaining a the LORD.
16: 7 For what are we, that you complain a us?"
16: 8 the complaining that you utter a him—
16: 8 Your complaining is not a us but a the LORD
17: 3 and the people complained a Moses and said,
19:22 or the LORD will break out a them."
19:24 otherwise he will break out a them."
20:16 You shall not bear false witness a your neighbor.
23:21 do not rebel a him, for he will
23:27 and will throw into confusion all the people a
23:29 and the wild animals would multiply a you.
23:33 or they will make you sin a me;
24: 6 and half of the blood he dashed a the altar.
29:16 and shall take its blood and dash it a all sides of
29:20 dash the rest of the blood a all sides of the altar.
32:10 so that my wrath may burn hot a them
32:11 "why does your wrath burn hot a your people,
32:33 "Whoever has sinned a me I will blot out
Lev 1: 5 the blood, dashing the blood a all sides of the altar
1:11 and Aaron's sons the priests shall dash its blood a
1:15 and its blood shall be drained out a the side of
3: 2 and Aaron's sons the priests shall dash the blood a
3: 8 and Aaron's sons shall dash its blood a all sides of
3:13 the sons of Aaron shall dash its blood a all sides
6: 2 and commit a trespass a the LORD by deceiving
7: 2 its blood shall be dashed a all sides of the altar.
8:19 Moses dashed the blood a all sides of the altar.
8:24 and Moses dashed the rest of the blood a all sides
9:12 and he dashed it a all sides of the altar.
9:18 which he dashed a all sides of the altar,
17: 6 the blood a the altar of the LORD at the entrance
17:10 I will set my face a that person who eats blood,
19:18 You shall not take vengeance or bear a grudge a
20: 3 I myself will set my face a them,
20: 5 I myself will set my face a them and a their family,
20: 6 I will set my face a them,
26:17 I will set my face a you,
26:22 I will let loose wild animals a you,
26:25 I will bring the sword a you,
26:33 and I will unsheathe the sword a you;
26:37 you shall have no power to stand a your enemies.
26:40 in that they committed treachery a me and,
Nu 5:13 and there is no witness a her since she was
10: 9 in your land a the adversary who oppresses you,
11: 1 Then the fire of the LORD burned a them,
11: 3 because the fire of the LORD burned a them.
11:33 the anger of the LORD was kindled a the people,
12: 1 Miriam and Aaron spoke a Moses because of
12: 8 not afraid to speak a my servant Moses?"
12: 9 And the anger of the LORD was kindled a them,
13:31 "We are not able to go up a this people,
14: 2 all the Israelites complained a Moses and Aaron;
14: 9 Only, do not rebel a the LORD;
14:27 shall this wicked congregation complain a me?
14:27 which they complain a me.
14:29 who have complained a me,
14:35 to all this wicked congregation gathered together a
14:36 and made all the congregation complain a him
16: 3 They assembled a Moses and a Aaron,
16:11 and all your company have gathered together a
16:11 What is Aaron that you rail a him?"
16:19 Then Korah assembled the whole congregation a
16:41 the Israelites rebelled a Moses and a Aaron,
16:42 when the congregation had assembled a them,
17: 5 of the Israelites that they continually make a you.
17:10 you may make an end of their complaints a me,
20: 2 they gathered together a Moses and a Aaron.
20:18 or we will come out with the sword a you."
20:20 And Edom came out a them with a large force,
20:24 because you rebelled a my command at the waters
21: 1 he fought a Israel and took some of them captive.
21: 5 The people spoke a God and a Moses,
21: 7 We have sinned by speaking a the LORD and a you;
21:23 and went out a Israel to the wilderness;
21:23 he came to Jahaz, and fought a Israel.
21:26 who had fought a the former king of Moab
21:33 and King Og of Bashan came out a them,
22:11 be able to fight a them and drive them out.' "
22:25 it scraped a the wall, and scraped Balaam's foot
22:25 and scraped Balaam's foot a the wall;
23:23 no enchantment a Jacob, no divination a Israel;
Nu 24:10 Then Balak's anger was kindled a Balaam,
25: 3 and the LORD's anger was kindled a Israel.
26: 9 who rebelled a Moses and Aaron in the company
26: 9 when they rebelled a the LORD,
27: 3 of those who gathered themselves together a
27:14 because you rebelled a my word in the wilderness
31: 3 so that they may go a Midian,
31: 7 They did battle a Midian,
31:16 made the Israelites act treacherously a the LORD
32:13 And the LORD's anger was kindled a Israel,
32:14 to increase the LORD's fierce anger a Israel!
32:23 you do not do this, you have sinned a the LORD;
33: 4 LORD executed judgments even a their gods.
Dt 1:26 You rebelled a the command of the LORD
1:41 "We have sinned a the LORD!
1:43 You rebelled a the command of the LORD
1:44 then came out a you and chased you as bees do.
2:15 Indeed, the LORD's own hand was a them,
2:32 So when Sihon came out a us,
3: 1 King Og of Bashan came out a us,
4:26 I call heaven and earth to witness a you today
5:20 Neither shall you bear false witness a your
6:15 be kindled a you and he would destroy you from
6:22 awesome signs and wonders a Egypt, a Pharaoh
7: 4 the anger of the LORD would be kindled a you,
7:20 LORD your God will send the pestilence a them,
7:24 no one will be able to stand a you,
9: 7 you have been rebellious a the LORD from
9:16 Then I saw that you had indeed sinned a
9:19 the anger that the LORD bore a you was so fierce
9:23 you rebelled a the command of
9:24 You have been rebellious a the LORD as long
11:17 then the anger of the LORD will be kindled a you
11:25 No one will be able to stand a you;
13: 5 be put to death for having spoken treason a
13: 9 your own hand shall be first a them
15: 2 every creditor shall remit the claim that is held a
15: 9 your neighbor might cry to the LORD a you,
17: 7 the witnesses shall be the first raised a the person
19:18 having testified falsely a another,
20: 1 When you go out to war a your enemies,
20: 3 Today you are drawing near to do battle a
20: 4 to fight for you a your enemies,
20:10 When you draw near to a town to fight a it,
20:12 but makes war a you, then you shall besiege it;
20:18 and you thus sin a the LORD your God.
20:19 making war a it in order to take it,
20:19 you must not destroy its trees by wielding an ax a
20:20 in building siegeworks a the town that makes war
21:10 When you go out to war a your enemies,
22:14 and makes up charges a her, slandering her
22:17 now he has made up charges a her,
23: 4 and because they hired a you Balaam son of Beor,
23: 9 When you are encamped a your enemies you shall guard a any impropriety.
24: 8 Guard a an outbreak of a leprous skin disease
24:15 otherwise they might cry to the LORD a you,
28: 7 The LORD will cause your enemies who rise a
28: 7 they shall come out a you one way,
28:25 you shall go out a them one way and flee
28:48 your enemies whom the LORD will send a you,
29: 7 of Heshbon and King Og of Bashan came out a us
29:20 LORD's anger and passion will smoke a them.
29:27 the anger of the LORD was kindled a that land,
30:19 and earth to witness a you today that I have set
31:17 My anger will be kindled a them in that day.
31:19 in order that this song may be a witness for me a
31:26 let it remain there as a witness a you.
31:28 and call heaven and earth to witness a them.
32:23 upon them, spend my arrows a them:
32:24 The teeth of beasts I will send a them,
32:46 to heart all the words that I am giving in witness a
33: 7 and be a help a his adversaries.
34:11 a Pharaoh and all his servants and his entire land,
Jos 1: 5 No one shall be able to stand a you all the days
1:18 Whoever rebels a your orders
7: 1 the anger of the LORD burned a the Israelites.
7:20 the one who sinned a the LORD God of Israel.
8: 2 Set an ambush a the city, behind it."
8: 3 and all the fighting men set out to go up a Ai.
8: 4 "You shall lie in ambush a the city, behind it;
8: 5 When they come out a us, as before,
8:14 not know that there was an ambush a him behind
8:20 to the wilderness turned back a the pursuers.
8:22 And the others came out from the city a them;
9:18 Then all the congregation murmured a the leaders.
10: 5 and camped a Gibeon, and made war a it.
10: 6 in the hill country are gathered a us."
10:18 "Roll large stones a the mouth of the cave,
10:21 no one dared to speak a any of the Israelites.
10:25 for thus the LORD will do to all the enemies a
10:27 they set large stones a the mouth of the cave,
10:29 to Libnah, and fought a Libnah.
11:20 to harden their hearts so that they would come a
15: 8 that lies over a the valley of Hinnom, on the west,
15:15 From there he went up a the inhabitants of Debir;
19:47 the Danites went up and fought a Leshem,
22:12 of the Israelites gathered at Shiloh, to make war a
22:16 'What is this treachery that you have committed a
22:16 an altar today in rebellion a the LORD?
22:18 If you rebel a the LORD today,
22:19 only do not rebel a the LORD, or rebel a us
22:29 be it from us that we should rebel a the LORD,
22:31 because you have not committed this treachery a
22:33 and spoke no more of making war a them,
23:16 the anger of the LORD will be kindled a you,
24: 9 set out to fight a Israel.

Jos 24:11 the citizens of Jericho fought **a** you,
24:22 "You are witnesses **a** yourselves
24:27 "See, this stone shall be a witness **a** us;
24:27 therefore it shall be a witness **a** you,
Jdg 1: 1 "Who shall go up first for us **a** the Canaanites, to fight **a** them?"
1: 3 that we may fight **a** the Canaanites;
1: 5 and fought **a** him, and defeated the Canaanites and
1: 8 people of Judah fought **a** Jerusalem and took it.
1: 9 down to fight **a** the Canaanites who lived in
1:10 Judah went **a** the Canaanites who lived in Hebron
1:11 From there they went **a** the inhabitants of Debir
1:22 The house of Joseph also went up **a** Bethel;
2:14 So the anger of the LORD was kindled **a** Israel,
2:15 of the LORD was **a** them to bring misfortune,
2:20 So the anger of the LORD was kindled **a** Israel;
3: 8 the anger of the LORD was kindled **a** Israel,
3:12 the LORD strengthened King Eglon of Moab **a**
3:28 and seized the fords of the Jordan **a** the Moabites,
5:13 the people of the LORD marched down for him **a**
5:20 from their courses they fought **a** Sisera.
5:23 to the help of the LORD **a** the mighty.
6: 3 and the people of the east would come up **a** them.
6: 4 They would encamp **a** them and destroy
6:31 But Joash said to all who were arrayed **a** him,
6:32 that is to say, "Let Baal contend **a** him,"
6:39 "Do not let your anger burn **a** me,
7:22 the LORD set every man's sword **a** his fellow and **a** all the army;
7:24 "Come down **a** the Midianites and seize the waters **a** them,
8: 1 when you went to fight **a** the Midianites?"
8: 3 When he said this, their anger **a** him subsided.
9:18 up **a** my father's house this day,
9:31 and they are stirring up the city **a** you.
9:33 and the troops that are with him come out **a** you,
9:34 and lay in wait **a** Shechem in four companies.
9:43 he rose **a** them and killed them.
9:45 Abimelech fought **a** the city all that day;
9:49 and following Abimelech put it **a** the stronghold,
9:50 and encamped **a** Thebez, and took it.
9:52 Abimelech came to the tower, and fought **a** it,
9:56 for the crime he committed **a** his father
10: 7 So the anger of the LORD was kindled **a** Israel,
10: 9 to fight **a** Judah and **a** Benjamin and **a** the house of Ephraim;
10:10 saying, "We have sinned **a** you,
10:18 "Who will begin the fight **a** the Ammonites?
11: 4 After a time the Ammonites made war **a** Israel.
11: 5 And when the Ammonites made war **a** Israel,
11:12 that you have come to me to fight **a** my land?"
11:27 It is not I who have sinned **a** you,
11:32 over to the Ammonites to fight **a** them;
11:36 LORD has given you vengeance **a** your enemies,
12: 1 "Why did you cross over to fight **a**
12: 3 and crossed over **a** the Ammonites,
12: 3 then have you come up to me this day, to fight **a**
12: 5 Then the Gileadites took the fords of the Jordan **a**
14: 4 he was seeking a pretext to act **a** the Philistines.
15:10 "Why have you come up **a** us?"
16:26 so that I may lean **a** them."
16:29 and he leaned his weight **a** them,
18: 9 They said, "Come, let us go up **a** them;
19:24 but **a** this man do not do such a vile thing."
20: 5 The lords of Gibeah rose up **a** me,
20: 9 we will go up **a** it by lot.
20:11 So all the men of Israel gathered **a** the city,
20:14 to go out to battle **a** the Israelites.
20:18 "Which of us shall go up first to battle **a**
20:19 up in the morning, and encamped **a** Gibeah.
20:20 The Israelites went out to battle **a** Benjamin;
20:20 Israelites drew up the battle line **a** them at Gibeah.
20:23 "Shall we again draw near to battle **a** our kinsfolk
20:23 And the LORD said, "Go up **a** them."
20:24 So the Israelites advanced **a** the Benjaminites
20:25 Benjamin moved out **a** them from Gibeah
20:28 to battle **a** our kinsfolk the Benjaminites,
20:30 Then the Israelites went up **a** the Benjaminites on
20:30 and set themselves in array **a** Gibeah, as before.
20:31 When the Benjaminites went out **a** the army,
20:34 There came **a** Gibeah ten thousand picked men
20:36 to the troops in ambush that they had stationed **a**
20:48 the Israelites turned back **a** the Benjaminites,
Ru 1:13 because the hand of the LORD has turned **a** me."
1Sa 2:25 If one person sins **a** another,
2:25 but if someone sins **a** the LORD,
3:12 that day I will fulfill **a** Eli all that I have spoken
4: 1 In those days the Philistines mustered for war **a**
4: 1 and Israel went out to battle **a** them;
4: 2 The Philistines drew up in line **a** Israel,
5: 9 the hand of the LORD was **a** the city,
7: 6 and said, "We have sinned **a** the LORD."
7: 7 the lords of the Philistines went up **a** Israel.
7:10 with a mighty voice that day **a** the Philistines
7:13 the hand of the LORD was **a** the Philistines all
12: 3 testify **a** me before the LORD and
12: 3 Testify **a** me and I will restore it to you."
12: 5 He said to them, "The LORD is witness **a** you,
12: 9 of Moab; and they fought **a** them.
12:12 that King Nahash of the Ammonites came **a** you,
12:14 not rebel **a** the commandment of the LORD,
12:15 but rebel **a** the commandment of the LORD,
12:15 hand of the LORD will be **a** you and your king.
12:23 from me that I should sin **a** the LORD by ceasing
14:20 and every sword was **a** the other,
14:33 the troops are sinning **a** the LORD by eating with
14:34 not sin **a** the LORD by eating with the blood.' "

1Sa 14:47 fought **a** all his enemies on every side—**a** Moab, **a** the Ammonites, **a** Edom, **a** the kings of Zobah, and **a** the Philistines;
14:52 There was hard fighting **a** the Philistines all
15:18 and fight **a** them until they are consumed.'
17: 2 and formed ranks **a** the Philistines.
17: 9 but if I prevail **a** him and kill him,
17:21 the Philistines drew up for battle, army **a** army.
17:28 and Eliab's anger was kindled **a** David.
17:33 not able to go **a** this Philistine to fight with him;
17:35 and if it turned **a** me, I would catch it by the jaw,
17:55 When Saul saw David go out **a** the Philistine,
18:17 For Saul thought, "I will not raise a hand **a** him;
18:21 and that the hand of the Philistines may be **a** him."
19: 4 "The king should not sin **a** his servant David, ecause he has not sinned **a** you,
19: 5 why then will you sin **a** an innocent person
20: 1 And what is my sin **a** your father that he is trying
20:30 Then Saul's anger was kindled **a** Jonathan.
22: 8 Is that why all of you have conspired **a** me?
22: 8 that my son has stirred up my servant **a** me,
22:13 Saul said to him, "Why have you conspired **a** me,
22:13 so that he has risen **a** me, to lie in wait,
23: 1 "The Philistines are fighting **a** Keilah,
23: 3 if we go to Keilah **a** the armies of the Philistines?"
23: 9 David learned that Saul was plotting evil **a** him,
23:28 and went **a** the Philistines;
24: 6 the LORD's anointed, to raise my hand **a** him;
24:10 I said, 'I will not raise my hand **a** my lord;
24:11 I have not sinned **a** you,
24:12 but my hand shall not be **a** you.
24:13 but my hand shall not be **a** you.
24:14 **A** whom has the king of Israel come out?
24:15 and plead my cause, and vindicate me **a** you."
25:17 for evil has been decided **a** our master and **a** all his
26: 9 who can raise his hand **a** the LORD's anointed,
26:11 The LORD forbid that I should raise my hand **a**
26:19 If it is the LORD who has stirred you up **a** me,
26:23 not raise my hand **a** the LORD's anointed.
27:10 "**A** whom have you made a raid today?" David would say, "**A** the Negeb of Judah," or "**A** the Negeb of the Jerahmeelites," or, "**A** the Negeb of
28: 1 gathered their forces for war, to fight **a** Israel.
28:15 for the Philistines are warring **a** me,
28:18 and did not carry out his fierce wrath **a** Amalek,
29: 8 and fight **a** the enemies of my lord the king?"
31: 1 Now the Philistines fought **a** Israel;
2Sa 1:16 for your own mouth has testified **a** you, saying,
5: 6 and his men marched to Jerusalem **a** the Jebusites,
5:19 "Shall I go up **a** the Philistines?
5:20 LORD has burst forth **a** my enemies before me,
6: 7 The anger of the LORD was kindled **a** Uzzah;
8:10 and to congratulate him because he had fought **a**
10: 9 When Joab saw that the battle was set **a** him both
10: 9 and arrayed them **a** the Arameans;
10:10 and he arrayed them **a** the Ammonites.
10:13 with him moved forward into battle **a**
10:14 Joab returned from fighting **a** the Ammonites,
10:17 The Arameans arrayed themselves **a** David
11:23 and came out **a** us in the field;
12: 5 David's anger was greatly kindled **a** the man.
12:11 up trouble **a** you from within your own house;
12:13 "I have sinned **a** the LORD."
12:26 Now Joab fought **a** Rabbah of the Ammonites,
12:27 and said, "I have fought **a** Rabbah;
12:28 and encamp **a** the city, and take it;
12:29 and fought **a** it and took it.
14: 7 Now the whole family has risen **a** your servant.
14:13 then have you planned such a thing **a** the people
17:21 for thus and so has Ahithophel counseled **a** you."
18: 6 So the army went out into the field **a** Israel;
18:12 I would not raise my hand **a** the king's son;
18:13 if I had dealt treacherously **a** his life
18:28 up the men who raised their hand **a** my lord
18:31 from the power of all who rose up **a** you."
20:15 they threw up a siege ramp **a** the city,
20:15 and it stood **a** the rampart.
20:21 has lifted up his hand **a** King David;
21:15 They fought **a** the Philistines,
23: 8 wielded his spear **a** eight hundred whom he killed
23:18 With his spear he fought **a** three hundred men
23:21 but Benaiah went **a** him with a staff,
24: 1 the anger of the LORD was kindled **a** Israel, and he incited David **a** them, saying, "Go,
24: 4 But the king's word prevailed **a** Joab and
24:17 I pray, be **a** me and **a** my father's house."
1Ki 6: 5 He also built a structure **a** the wall of the house,
6:10 He built the structure **a** the whole house,
8:31 "If someone sins **a** a neighbor and is given an oath
8:33 "When your people Israel, having sinned **a** you,
8:35 up and there is no rain because they have sinned **a**
8:44 "If your people go out to battle **a** their enemy,
8:46 "If they sin **a** you—for there is no one who does
8:50 and forgive your people who have sinned **a** you,
8:50 that they have committed **a** you;
11:14 the LORD raised up an adversary **a** Solomon,
11:23 God raised up another adversary **a** Solomon,
11:26 a widow, rebelled **a** the king.
11:27 following was the reason he rebelled **a** the king.
12:19 in rebellion **a** the house of David to this day.
12:21 to fight **a** the house of Israel,
12:24 up or fight **a** your kindred the people of Israel.
13: 2 proclaimed **a** the altar by the word of the LORD,
13: 4 the king heard what the man of God cried out **a**
13: 4 But the hand that he stretched out **a** him withered
13:32 that he proclaimed by the word of the LORD **a**
13:32 and **a** all the houses of the high places that are in

1Ki 14:25 King Shishak of Egypt came up **a** Jerusalem;
15:17 King Baasha of Israel went up **a** Judah,
15:20 and sent the commanders of his armies **a** the cities
15:27 of the house of Issachar, conspired **a** him;
16: 1 the LORD came to Jehu son of Hanani **a** Baasha,
16: 7 by the prophet Jehu son of Hanani **a** Baasha
16: 9 commander of half his chariots, conspired **a** him.
16:12 which he spoke **a** Baasha by the prophet Jehu—
16:15 Now the troops were encamped **a** Gibbethon,
17:18 She then said to Elijah, "What have you **a** me,
20: 1 He marched **a** Samaria, laid siege to it,
20:12 And they took their positions **a** the city.
20:22 the spring the king of Aram will come up **a** you."
20:23 but let us fight **a** them in the plain,
20:25 then we will fight **a** them in the plain,
20:26 the Arameans and went up to Aphek to fight **a**
21:10 and have them bring a charge **a** him, saying,
21:13 and the scoundrels brought a charge **a** Naboth,
22: 6 "Shall I go to battle **a** Ramoth-gilead,
22:32 So they turned to fight **a** him;
2Ki 1: 1 After the death of Ahab, Moab rebelled **a** Israel.
3: 5 the king of Moab rebelled **a** the king of Israel.
3: 7 "The king of Moab has rebelled **a** me;
3: 7 will you go with me to battle **a** Moab?"
3:21 that the kings had come up to fight **a** them,
3:26 king of Moab saw that the battle was going **a** him,
6:18 When the Arameans came down **a** him,
6:24 he marched **a** Samaria and laid siege to it.
6:32 that you shut the door and hold it closed **a** him.
7: 6 the Hittites and the kings of Egypt to fight **a** us."
7:12 the Arameans have prepared **a** us.
8:20 In his days Edom revolted **a** the rule of Judah,
8:22 So Edom has been in revolt **a** the rule of Judah
8:28 He went with Joram son of Ahab to wage war **a**
8:29 when he fought **a** King Hazael of Aram.
9:14 of Jehoshaphat son of Nimshi conspired **a** Joram.
9:14 at Ramoth-gilead **a** King Hazael of Aram;
9:15 when he fought **a** King Hazael of Aram.
9:25 how the LORD uttered this oracle **a** him:
10: 9 It was I who conspired **a** my master
12:17 Aram went up, fought **a** Gath, and took it.
12:17 when Hazael set his face to go up **a** Jerusalem,
13: 3 The anger of the LORD was kindled **a** Israel,
13:12 the might with which he fought **a** King Amaziah
14:19 They made a conspiracy **a** him in Jerusalem,
15:10 Shallum son of Jabesh conspired **a** him,
15:19 King Pul of Assyria came **a** the land;
15:25 conspired **a** him with fifty of the Gileadites,
15:30 Then Hoshea son of Elah made a conspiracy **a**
15:37 of Aram and Pekah son of Remaliah **a** Judah.
16: 9 the king of Assyria marched up **a** Damascus,
16:13 the blood of his offerings of well-being **a** the altar.
16:15 then dash **a** it all the blood of the burnt offering,
17: 3 King Shalmaneser of Assyria came up **a** him;
17: 7 of Israel had sinned **a** the LORD their God,
17: 9 of Israel secretly did things that were not right **a**
18: 7 He rebelled **a** the king of Assyria and would
18: 9 King Shalmaneser of Assyria came up **a** Samaria,
18:13 King Sennacherib of Assyria came up **a** all
18:20 that you have rebelled **a** me?
18:25 is it without the LORD that I have come up **a**
18:25 The LORD said to me, Go up **a** this land,
19: 8 and found the king of Assyria fighting **a** Libnah;
19: 9 "See, he has set out to fight **a** you,"
19:22 **A** whom have you raised your voice
19:22 **A** the Holy One of Israel!
19:27 and coming in, and your raging **a** me.
19:28 Because you have raged **a** me
19:32 or cast up a siege ramp **a** it.
21:23 The servants of Amon conspired **a** him,
21:24 of the land killed all those who had conspired **a**
22:13 the wrath of the LORD that is kindled **a** us,
22:17 therefore my wrath will be kindled **a** this place,
22:19 when you heard how I spoke **a** this place,
22:19 and **a** its inhabitants, that they should become
23:17 and predicted these things that you have done **a**
23:26 by which his anger was kindled **a** Judah,
24: 1 then he turned and rebelled **a** him.
24: 2 The LORD sent **a** him bands of the Chaldeans,
24: 2 he sent them **a** Judah to destroy it,
24:20 Zedekiah rebelled **a** the king of Babylon.
25: 1 with all his army **a** Jerusalem, and laid siege to it;
25: 1 they built siegeworks **a** it all around.
1Ch 5:20 and when they received help **a** them,
5:25 But they transgressed **a** the God of their ancestors,
10: 1 Now the Philistines fought **a** Israel;
11:11 wielded his spear **a** three hundred whom he killed
11:20 With his spear he fought **a** three hundred
11:23 but Benaiah went **a** him with a staff,
12:19 when he came with the Philistines for the battle **a**
12:21 They helped David **a** the band of raiders,
13:10 The anger of the LORD was kindled **a** Uzzah;
13:11 because the LORD had burst out **a** Uzzah;
14: 8 and David heard of it and went out **a** them.
14:10 "Shall I go up **a** the Philistines?
14:11 "God has burst out **a** my enemies by my hand,
15:13 the LORD our God burst out **a** us,
18:10 he had fought **a** Hadadezer and defeated him.
19:10 the line of battle was set **a** him both in front and in
19:10 of the picked men of Israel and arrayed them **a**
19:11 and they were arrayed **a** the Ammonites.
19:17 came to them, and drew up his forces **a** them.
19:17 David set the battle in array **a** the Arameans,
21: 1 Satan stood up **a** Israel, and incited David to count
21: 4 But the king's word prevailed **a** Joab.
21:17 my God, be **a** me and **a** my father's house;
2Ch 6:22 "If someone sins **a** another and is required to take

2Ch 6:24 “When your people Israel, having sinned **a** you,
6:26 up and there is no rain because they have sinned **a**
6:34 “If your people go out to battle **a** their enemies,
6:36 “If they sin **a** you—for there is no one who does
6:39 and forgive your people who have sinned **a** you.
10:19 in rebellion **a** the house of David to this day.
11: 1 the house of Judah and Benjamin to fight **a** Israel,
11: 4 You shall not go up or fight **a** your kindred.
11: 4 the LORD and turned back from the expedition **a**
12: 2 King Shishak of Egypt came up **a** Jerusalem
12: 9 So King Shishak of Egypt came up **a** Jerusalem;
13: 3 and Jeroboam drew up his line of battle **a** him
13: 6 rose up and rebelled **a** his lord;
13:12 to sound the call to battle **a** you.
13:12 O Israelites, do not fight **a** the LORD,
14: 9 the Ethiopian came out **a** them with an army of
14:11 and in your name we have come **a** this multitude.
14:11 let no mortal prevail **a** you.”
15: 6 nation **a** nation and city **a** city,
16: 1 King Baasha of Israel went up **a** Judah,
16: 4 and sent the commanders of his armies **a** the cities
17: 1 and strengthened himself **a** Israel.
17:10 and they did not make war **a** Jehoshaphat.
18: 2 and induced him to go up **a** Ramoth-gilead.
18: 5 “Shall we go to battle **a** Ramoth-gilead,
18:31 So they turned to fight **a** him;
19: 2 wrath has gone out **a** you from the LORD.
20: 1 came **a** Jehoshaphat for battle.
20: 2 “A great multitude is coming **a** you from Edom,
20:12 powerless **a** this great multitude that is coming **a** us
20:16 Tomorrow go down **a** them;
20:17 tomorrow go out **a** them, and the LORD will be
20:22 the LORD set an ambush **a** the Ammonites,
20:22 who had come **a** Judah, so that they were routed.
20:29 the LORD had fought **a** the enemies of Israel.
20:37 of Dodavahu of Mareshah prophesied **a**
21: 8 In his days Edom revolted **a** the rule of Judah
21:10 So Edom has been in revolt **a** the rule of Judah
21:10 At that time Libnah also revolted **a** his rule,
21:16 The LORD aroused **a** Jehoram the anger of
21:17 They came up **a** Judah, invaded it,
22: 5 of King Ahab of Israel to make war **a** King Hazael
24:19 they testified **a** them, but they would not listen.
24:21 But they conspired **a** him,
24:23 the end of the year the army of Aram came up **a**
24:25 his servants conspired **a** him because of the blood
24:26 Those who conspired **a** him were Zabad son
24:27 and of the many oracles **a** him,
25:27 from the LORD they made a conspiracy **a** him
26: 6 He went out and made war **a** the Philistines,
26: 7 God helped him **a** the Philistines, **a** the Arabs who lived in Gur-baal, and **a** the Meunites.
26:13 to help the king **a** the enemy.
27: 5 the king of the Ammonites and prevailed **a** them.
28:10 But what have you except sins **a**
28:12 stood up **a** those who were coming from the war,
28:13 for you propose to bring on us guilt **a** the LORD
28:13 and there is fierce wrath **a** Israel.”
28:20 So King Tilgath-pilneser of Assyria came **a** him,
29:22 priests received the blood and dashed it **a** the altar;
29:22 the rams and their blood was dashed **a** the altar;
29:22 the lambs and their blood was dashed **a** the altar.
32: 1 and invaded Judah and encamped **a**
32: 2 that Sennacherib had come and intended to fight **a**
32:16 more **a** the Lord GOD and **a** his servant Hezekiah.
32:17 the LORD the God of Israel and to speak **a** him,
33:11 the LORD brought **a** them the commanders of
33:24 His servants conspired **a** him and killed him
33:25 of the land killed all those who had conspired **a**
34:27 before God when you heard his words **a** this place
35:20 and Josiah went out **a** him.
35:21 I am not coming **a** you today,
35:21 but **a** the house with which I am at war;
36: 6 **A** him King Nebuchadnezzar of Babylon came up,
36: 8 and what was found **a** him,
36:13 He also rebelled **a** King Nebuchadnezzar,
36:13 and hardened his heart **a** turning to the LORD,
36:16 until the wrath of the LORD **a** his people became
36:17 he brought up **a** them the king of the Chaldeans,
Ezr 4: 6 they wrote an accusation **a** the inhabitants
4: 8 and Shimshai the scribe wrote a letter **a** Jerusalem
4:19 and discovered that this city has risen **a** kings
8:22 and cavalry to protect us **a** the enemy on our way,
8:22 his power and his wrath are **a** all who forsake him.
Ne 1: 6 which we have sinned **a** you.
2:19 Are you rebelling **a** the king?”
4: 8 and fight **a** Jerusalem and to cause confusion in it.
4: 9 set a guard as a protection **a** them day and night.
4:12 the places where they live they will come up **a**
5: 1 of the people and of their wives **a** their Jewish kin.
5: 7 I brought charges **a** the nobles and the officials;
6:12 but he had pronounced the prophecy **a** me
9:10 and wonders **a** Pharaoh and all his servants and all
9:10 that they acted insolently **a** our ancestors.
9:26 and rebelled **a** you and cast your law
9:29 but sinned **a** your ordinances,
12:24 with their associates over **a** them,
13: 2 but hired Balaam **a** them to curse them—
13:15 and I warned them at that time **a** selling food.
13:27 and do all this great evil and act treacherously **a**
Est 1:18 of the queen's behavior will rebel **a**
2: 1 and what had been decreed **a** her.
4:16 that I will go to the king, though it is **a** the law;
6:13 is of the Jewish people, you will not prevail **a** him,
8: 3 the Agagite and the plot that he had devised **a**
9:24 had plotted **a** the Jews to destroy them,
9:25 that he had devised **a** the Jews should come

Job 1:12 only do not stretch out your hand **a** him!”
2: 3 although you incited me **a** him,
6: 4 the terrors of God are arrayed **a** me.
8: 4 If your children sinned **a** him,
8:15 If one leans **a** its house, it will not stand;
10: 2 let me know why you contend **a** me.
10:16 you repeat your exploits **a** me.
10:17 You renew your witnesses **a** me,
10:17 you bring fresh troops **a** me.
13:26 For you write bitter things **a** me,
14:20 You prevail forever **a** them, and they pass away;
15: 6 your own lips testify **a** you.
15:13 so that you turn your spirit **a** God,
15:24 they prevail **a** them, like a king prepared
15:25 Because they stretched out their hands **a** God,
15:26 running stubbornly **a** him with
16: 4 I could join words together **a** you,
16: 8 he has shriveled me up, which is a witness **a** me;
16: 8 my leanness has risen up **a** me,
16: 9 my adversary sharpens his eyes **a** me.
16:10 they mass themselves together **a** me.
17: 8 and the innocent stir themselves up **a** the godless.
19: 5 If indeed you magnify yourselves **a** me,
19: 5 and make my humiliation an argument **a** me,
19:11 He has kindled his wrath **a** me,
19:12 they have thrown up siegeworks **a** me,
19:18 when I rise, they talk **a** me.
19:19 and those whom I loved have turned **a** me.
20:27 and the earth will rise up **a** them.
24:13 “There are those who rebel **a** the light,
30:24 “Surely one does not turn **a** the needy,
31:13 when they brought a complaint **a** me;
31:21 if I have raised my hand **a** the orphan,
31:38 “If my land has cried out **a** me,
32:14 He has not directed his words **a** me,
33:10 Look, he finds occasions **a** me,
33:13 Why do you contend **a** him, saying,
34:37 and multiplies his words **a** God.”
35: 6 you have sinned, what do you accomplish **a** him?
36:33 he is jealous with anger **a** iniquity.
40:23 it is confident though Jordan rushes **a** its mouth.
42: 7 “My wrath is kindled **a** you and **a** your two friends;
Ps 2: 2 **a** the LORD and his anointed, saying,
3: 1 how many are my foes! Many are rising **a** me;
3: 6 of people who have set themselves **a**
5:10 for they have rebelled **a** you.
7: 6 lift yourself up **a** the fury of my enemies;
15: 3 nor take up a reproach **a** their neighbors;
15: 5 and do not take a bribe **a** the innocent.
21:11 If they plan evil **a** you, if they devise mischief,
27: 3 an army encamp **a** me, my heart shall not fear;
27: 3 though war rise up **a** me, yet I will be confident.
27:12 for false witnesses have risen **a** me,
31:13 as they scheme together **a** me,
31:18 Let the lying lips be stilled that speak insolently **a**
34:16 The face of the LORD is **a** evildoers,
35: 1 fight **a** those who fight **a** me!
35: 3 Draw the spear and javelin **a** my pursuers;
35: 4 be turned back and confounded who devise evil **a**
35:15 they gathered together **a** me;
35:20 but they conceive deceitful words **a**
35:21 They open wide their mouths **a** me;
35:26 let those who exalt themselves **a** me be clothed
37:12 The wicked plot **a** the righteous,
38:16 those who boast **a** me when my foot slips.”
41: 4 heal me, for I have sinned **a** you.”
41: 9 who ate of my bread, has lifted the heel **a** me.
43: 1 O God, and defend my cause **a** an ungodly people;
50: 7 and I will speak, O Israel, I will testify **a** you.
50:20 You sit and speak **a** your kin;
51: 4 **A** you, you alone, have I sinned,
52: 1 O mighty one, of mischief done **a** the godly?
54: 3 insolent have risen **a** me, the ruthless seek my life;
55: 3 and in anger they cherish enmity **a** me.
55:18 for many are arrayed **a** me.
56: 2 on me all day long, for many fight **a** me.
56: 5 all their thoughts are **a** me for evil.
59: 1 protect me from those who rise up **a** me.
59: 3 the mighty stir up strife **a** me.
60:11 O grant us help **a** the foe,
61: 3 a strong tower **a** the enemy.
68:18 even from those who rebel **a**
73: 9 They set their mouths **a** heaven,
74: 1 Why does your anger smoke **a** the sheep
78:17 Yet they sinned still more **a** him,
78:17 rebelling **a** the Most High in the desert.
78:19 They spoke **a** God, saying,
78:21 a fire was kindled **a** Jacob,
78:21 his anger mounted **a** Israel,
78:31 of God rose **a** them and he killed the strongest
78:40 How often they rebelled **a** him in the wilderness
78:56 Yet they tested the Most High God, and rebelled **a**
79: 8 not remember **a** us the iniquities of our ancestors;
81:14 and turn my hand **a** their foes.
83: 3 They lay crafty plans **a** your people;
83: 3 they consult together **a** those you protect.
83: 5 **a** you they make a covenant—
86:14 O God, the insolent rise up **a** me;
89:38 you are full of wrath **a** your anointed.
91:12 so that you will not dash your foot **a** a stone.
94:16 Who rises up for me **a** the wicked?
94:16 Who stands up for me **a** evildoers?
94:21 They band together **a** the life of the righteous,
105:16 When he summoned famine **a** the land,
105:28 they rebelled **a** his words.
106: 7 but rebelled **a** the Most High at the Red Sea.
106:40 the anger of the LORD was kindled **a** his people,

Ps 107:11 for they had rebelled **a** the words of God,
108:12 O grant us help **a** the foe,
109: 2 For wicked and deceitful mouths are opened **a** me,
109: 2 speaking **a** me with lying tongues.
109: 6 They say, “Appoint a wicked man **a** him;
109:20 of those who speak evil **a** my life.
119:11 so that I may not sin **a** you.
119:23 Even though princes sit plotting **a** me,
124: 3 when their anger was kindled **a** us;
129: 2 yet they have not prevailed **a** me.
135: 9 O Egypt, **a** Pharaoh and all his servants.
137: 7 **a** the Edomites the day of Jerusalem's fall,
137: 9 be who take your little ones and dash them **a**
138: 7 you preserve me **a** the wrath of my enemies;
139:20 and lift themselves up **a** you for evil!
139:21 And do I not loathe those who rise up **a** you?
141: 5 for my prayer is continually **a** their wicked deeds.
Pr 3:29 Do not plan harm **a** your neighbor
17:11 but a cruel messenger will be sent **a** them.
19: 3 yet the heart rages **a** the LORD.
21:22 One wise person went up **a** a city of warriors
21:30 no counsel, can avail **a** the LORD.
23:11 he will plead their cause **a** you.
24:15 in wait like an outlaw **a** the home of the righteous;
24:28 not be a witness **a** your neighbor without cause,
25:18 or a sharp arrow is one who bears false witness **a**
28: 4 but those who keep the law struggle **a** them.
Ecc 4:12 And though one might prevail **a** another,
8:11 sentence **a** an evil deed is not executed speedily,
9:14 A great king came **a** it and besieged it,
9:14 building great siegeworks **a** it.
10: 4 If the anger of the ruler rises **a** you,
Isa 1: 2 but they have rebelled **a** me.
1:25 I will turn my hand **a** you;
2: 4 nation shall not lift up sword **a** nation,
2:12 the LORD of hosts has a day **a** all that is proud
2:12 **a** all that is lifted up and high;
2:13 **a** all the cedars of Lebanon, lofty and lifted up;
2:13 and **a** all the oaks of Bashan;
2:14 **a** all the high mountains, and **a** all the lofty hills;
2:15 **a** every high tower, and **a** every fortified wall;
2:16 **a** all the ships of Tarshish,
2:16 and **a** all the beautiful craft.
3: 8 their speech and their deeds are **a** the LORD,
3: 9 The look on their faces bears witness **a** them;
5:25 the anger of the LORD was kindled **a** his people,
5:25 he stretched out his hand **a** them and struck them;
7: 1 but could not mount an attack **a** it.
7: 5 has plotted evil **a** you, saying,
7: 6 up **a** Judah and cut off Jerusalem and conquer it
8: 7 up **a** it the mighty flood waters of the River,
8:14 He will become a sanctuary, a stone one strikes **a**;
9: 8 The Lord sent a word **a** Jacob, and it fell on Israel;
9:11 So the LORD raised adversaries **a** them,
9:21 and together they were **a** Judah.
10: 6 **A** a godless nation I send him,
10: 6 and **a** the people of my wrath I command him,
10:15 the saw magnify itself **a** the one who handles it?
10:24 and lift up their staff **a** you as the Egyptians did.
10:26 The LORD of hosts will wield a whip **a** them,
11:14 They shall put forth their hand **a** Edom and Moab,
13:17 See, I am stirring up the Medes **a** them,
14: 4 you will take up this taunt **a** the king of Babylon:
14:22 I will rise up **a** them, says the LORD of hosts,
19: 2 I will stir up Egyptians **a** Egyptians,
19: 2 one **a** the other, neighbor **a** neighbor,
19: 2 city **a** city, kingdom **a** kingdom;
19:12 the LORD of hosts has planned **a** Egypt.
19:16 before the hand that the LORD of hosts raises **a**
19:17 of the plan that the LORD of hosts is planning **a**
20: 1 came to Ashdod and fought **a** it and took it—
20: 3 for three years as a sign and a portent **a** Egypt
23: 8 Who has planned this **a** Tyre,
27: 4 I will march to battle **a** it.
27: 8 By expulsion, by exile you struggled **a** them;
29: 3 And like David I will encamp **a** you;
29: 3 with towers and raise siegeworks **a** you.
29: 7 the multitude of all the nations that fight **a** Ariel,
29: 7 all that fight **a** her and her stronghold,
29: 8 the multitude of all the nations be that fight **a**
30: 1 who make an alliance, but **a** my will,
31: 2 but will rise **a** the house of the evildoers,
31: 2 and **a** the helpers of those who work iniquity.
31: 4 when a band of shepherds is called out **a** it—
34: 2 For the LORD is enraged **a** all the nations,
34: 2 and furious **a** all their hoards;
36: 1 King Sennacherib of Assyria came up **a** all
36: 5 that you have rebelled **a** me?
36:10 is it without the LORD that I have come up **a**
36:10 The LORD said to me, Go up **a** this land,
37: 8 and found the king of Assyria fighting **a** Libnah;
37: 9 “He has set out to fight **a** you.”
37:23 **A** whom have you raised your voice
37:23 **A** the Holy One of Israel!
37:28 and coming in, and your raging **a** me.
37:29 Because you have raged **a** me
37:33 or cast up a siege ramp **a** it.
41:11 all who are incensed **a** you shall be ashamed
41:11 those who strive **a** you shall be as nothing
41:12 those who war **a** you shall be as nothing at all.
42:13 he shows himself mighty **a** his foes.
42:24 Was it not the LORD, **a** whom we have sinned,
43:27 and your interpreters transgressed **a** me.
45:24 all who were incensed **a** him shall come to him
48:14 and his arm shall be **a** the Chaldeans.
54:17 No weapon that is fashioned **a** you shall prosper,
54:17 and you shall confute every tongue that rises **a**

Isa 57: 4 **A** whom do you open your mouth wide
59:12 and our sins testify **a** us.
63:10 he himself fought **a** them.
66:14 and his indignation is **a** his enemies.
66:24 the dead bodies of the people who have rebelled **a**
Jer 1:15 **a** all its surrounding walls and against all the cities
1:15 against all its surrounding walls and **a** all the cities
1:16 And I will utter my judgments **a** them,
1:18 and a bronze wall, **a** the whole land—
1:18 **a** the kings of Judah, its princes, its priests,
1:19 They will fight **a** you;
1:19 but they shall not prevail **a** you, for I am with you,
2: 8 the rulers transgressed **a** me;
2:15 lions have roared **a** him, they have roared loudly.
2:29 Why do you complain **a** me?
2:29 You have all rebelled **a** me, says the LORD.
3:13 that you have rebelled **a** the LORD your God,
3:25 for we have sinned **a** the LORD our God,
4:12 Now it is I who speak in judgment **a** them.
4:16 Proclaim **a** Jerusalem, "Besiegers come from
4:16 they shout **a** the cities of Judah.
4:17 because she has rebelled **a** me, says the LORD.
5: 6 A leopard is watching **a** their cities;
6: 3 Shepherds with their flocks shall come **a** her.
6: 4 "Prepare war **a** her; up, and let us attack at noon!"
6: 6 cast up a siege ramp **a** Jerusalem.
6:12 for I will stretch out my hand **a** the inhabitants of
6:21 I am laying before this people stumbling blocks **a**
6:23 equipped like a warrior for battle, **a** you,
8:14 because we have sinned **a** the LORD.
11:17 who planted you, has pronounced evil **a** you,
11:19 not know it was **a** me that they devised schemes,
12: 1 O LORD, when I lay charges **a** you;
12: 8 she has lifted up her voice **a** me—
13:14 And I will dash them one **a** another,
14: 7 Although our iniquities testify **a** us, act,
14: 7 and we have sinned **a** you.
14:20 for we have sinned **a** you.
15: 6 so I have stretched out my hand **a** you
15: 8 I have brought **a** the mothers of youths a destroyer
15:20 they will fight **a** you, but they shall not prevail
16:10 the LORD pronounced all this great evil **a** us?
16:10 that we have committed **a** the LORD our God?"
18:11 shaping evil **a** you and devising a plan **a** you.
18:18 they said, "Come, let us make plots **a** Jeremiah—
18:18 Come, let us bring charges **a** him,
19:15 the disaster that I have pronounced **a** it,
20:10 and we can prevail **a** him,
21: 2 of Babylon is making war **a** us;
21: 4 with which you are fighting **a** the king of Babylon
21: 4 and **a** the Chaldeans who are besieging you
21: 5 I myself will fight **a** you with outstretched hand
21:10 For I have set my face **a** this city for evil and not
21:13 See, I am **a** you, O inhabitant of the valley,
21:13 you who say, "Who can come down **a** us,
22: 7 I will prepare destroyers **a** you,
23:30 See, therefore, I am **a** the prophets,
23:31 See, I am **a** the prophets, says the LORD,
23:32 See, I am **a** those who prophesy lying dreams,
25: 9 I will bring them **a** this land and its inhabitants,
25: 9 and **a** all these nations around;
25:13 upon that land all the words that I have uttered **a**
25:13 which Jeremiah prophesied **a** all the nations.
25:29 for I am summoning a sword **a** all the inhabitants
25:30 therefore, shall prophesy **a** them all these words,
25:30 he will roar mightily **a** his fold, and shout,
25:30 **a** all the inhabitants of the earth.
25:31 for the LORD has an indictment **a** the nations;
26:11 the sentence of death because he has prophesied **a**
26:12 the LORD who sent me to prophesy **a** this house
26:13 about the disaster that he has pronounced **a** you.
26:19 about the disaster that he had pronounced **a** them?
26:20 He prophesied **a** this city and **a** this land
28: 8 pestilence **a** many countries and great kingdoms.
28:16 because you have spoken rebellion **a** the LORD."
29:32 for he has spoken rebellion **a** the LORD.
31:20 As often as I speak **a** him, I still remember him.
32: 5 you fight **a** the Chaldeans, you shall not succeed?"
32:24 siege ramps have been cast up **a** the city to take it,
32:24 into the hands of the Chaldeans who are fighting **a**
32:29 Chaldeans who are fighting **a** this city shall come,
33: 4 a defense **a** the siege ramps and before the sword:
33: 8 I will cleanse them from all the guilt of their sin **a**
33: 8 the guilt of their sin and rebellion **a** me.
34: 1 the peoples under his dominion were fighting **a**
34: 7 the king of Babylon was fighting **a** Jerusalem and
34: 7 and **a** all the cities of Judah that were left, Lachish
34:22 and they will fight **a** it, and take it,
35:11 when King Nebuchadrezzar of Babylon came up **a**
35:17 that I have pronounced **a** them;
36: 2 on it all the words that I have spoken to you **a**
36: 7 that the LORD has pronounced **a** this people."
37: 8 the Chaldeans shall return and fight **a** this city;
37:10 the whole army of Chaldeans who are fighting **a**
37:19 'The king of Babylon will not come **a** you and
37:19 of Babylon will not come against you and **a**
38: 5 for the king is powerless **a** you."
39: 1 and all his army came **a** Jerusalem and besieged it;
39:16 I am going to fulfill my words **a** this city for evil
40: 3 because all of you sinned **a** the LORD and did
41: 9 that King Asa had made for defense **a**
41:12 and went to fight **a** Ishmael son of Nethaniah.
42: 5 be a true and faithful witness **a** us if we do not act
43: 3 but Baruch son of Neriah is inciting you **a** us,
44:23 because you sinned **a** the LORD and did not obey
44:29 that my words **a** you will surely be carried out:
46:12 for warrior has stumbled **a** warrior;
Jer 46:22 and come **a** her with axes,
47: 7 **A** Ashkelon and **a** the seashore—
48: 2 In Heshbon they planned evil **a** her:
48:18 For the destroyer of Moab has come up **a** you;
48:26 because he magnified himself **a** the LORD;
48:40 and spread his wings **a** Moab;
48:42 because he magnified himself **a** the LORD.
49: 2 when I will sound the battle alarm **a** Rabbah of
49:14 "Gather yourselves together and come **a** her,
49:19 a lion coming up from the thickets of the Jordan **a**
49:20 the LORD has made **a** Edom and the purposes
49:20 the purposes that he has formed **a** the inhabitants
49:22 and spread his wings **a** Bozrah,
49:28 Thus says the LORD: Rise up, advance **a** Kedar!
49:30 made a plan **a** you and formed a purpose **a** you.
49:31 Rise up, advance **a** a nation at ease,
49:32 and I will bring calamity **a** them from every side,
50: 3 For out of the north a nation has come up **a** her;
50: 7 because they have sinned **a** the LORD,
50: 9 and bring **a** Babylon a company of great nations
50: 9 and they shall array themselves **a** her;
50:14 spare no arrows, for she has sinned **a** the LORD.
50:15 Raise a shout **a** her from all sides,
50:21 Go up to the land of Merathaim; go up **a** her,
50:26 Come **a** her from every quarter;
50:29 Summon archers **a** Babylon,
50:31 I am **a** you, O arrogant one,
50:35 A sword **a** the Chaldeans, says the LORD,
50:35 says the LORD, and **a** the inhabitants of Babylon,
50:35 and **a** her officials and her sages!
50:36 A sword **a** the diviners,
50:36 A sword **a** her warriors
50:37 A sword **a** her horses and **a** her chariots,
50:37 and **a** all the foreign troops in her midst,
50:37 A sword **a** all her treasures,
50:38 A drought **a** her waters, that they may be dried up!
50:42 set in array as a warrior for battle, **a** you,
50:44 a lion coming up from the thickets of the Jordan **a**
50:45 the LORD has made **a** Babylon, and the purposes
50:45 and the purposes that he has formed **a** the land of
51: 1 a destructive wind **a** Babylon and **a** the inhabitants
51: 2 when they come **a** her from every side on the day
51:12 Raise a standard **a** the walls of Babylon;
51:25 I am **a** you, O destroying mountain,
51:25 I will stretch out my hand **a** you,
51:27 prepare the nations for war **a** her,
51:27 summon **a** her the kingdoms, Ararat, Minni,
51:27 appoint a marshal **a** her, bring up horses
51:28 Prepare the nations for war **a** her,
51:29 for the LORD's purposes **a** Babylon stand,
51:46 rumors of violence in the land and of ruler **a** ruler.
51:48 the destroyers shall come **a** them out of the north,
51:56 for a destroyer has come **a** her, **a** Babylon;
52: 3 Zedekiah rebelled **a** the king of Babylon.
52: 4 with all his army **a** Jerusalem, and they laid siege
52: 4 they built siegeworks **a** it all around.
La 1:15 a time **a** me to crush my young men;
1:17 the LORD has commanded **a** Jacob
1:18 for I have rebelled **a** his word;
2:16 All your enemies open their mouths **a** you;
3: 3 **a** me alone he turns his hand,
3:46 All our enemies have opened their mouths **a** us;
3:60 You have seen all their malice, all their plots **a** me.
3:61 O LORD, all their plots **a** me.
3:62 The whispers and murmurs of my assailants are **a**
Eze 2: 3 to a nation of rebels who have rebelled **a** me;
2: 3 they and their ancestors have transgressed **a** me
3: 8 See, I have made your face hard **a** their faces,
3: 8 and your forehead hard **a** their foreheads.
3:13 of the wings of the living creatures brushing **a**
4: 2 put siegeworks **a** it, and build a siege wall **a** it,
4: 2 and cast up a ramp **a** it;
4: 2 set camps also **a** it, and plant battering rams **a** it all
4: 3 be in a state of siege, and press the siege **a** it.
4: 7 and with your arm bared you shall prophesy **a** it.
5: 4 from there a fire will come out **a** all the house
5: 6 she has rebelled **a** my ordinances and my statutes,
5: 8 I, I myself, am coming **a** you;
5:16 when I loose **a** you my deadly arrows of famine,
5:17 I will send famine and wild animals **a** you,
6: 2 toward the mountains of Israel, and prophesy **a**
6:14 I will stretch out my hand **a** them,
7: 6 It has awakened **a** you; see, it comes!
7: 8 I will spend my anger **a** you.
11: 4 Therefore prophesy **a** them; prophesy, O mortal."
13: 2 prophesy **a** the prophets of Israel
13: 8 I am **a** you, says the Lord GOD.
13: 9 be **a** the prophets who see false visions
13:17 set your face **a** the daughters of your people,
13:17 out of their own imagination; prophesy **a** them
13:20 I am **a** your bands with which you hunt lives;
14: 8 I will set my face **a** them;
14: 9 and I will stretch out my hand **a** him,
14:13 when a land sins **a** me by acting faithlessly,
14:13 and I stretch out my hand **a** it,
15: 7 I will set my face **a** them;
15: 7 when I set my face **a** them.
16:27 Therefore I stretched out my hand **a** you,
16:37 I will gather them **a** you from all around,
16:40 They shall bring up a mob **a** you,
17:15 But he rebelled **a** him by sending ambassadors
17:20 with him there for the treason he has committed **a**
18:22 that they have committed shall be remembered **a**
18:31 the transgressions that you have committed **a** me,
19: 4 The nations sounded an alarm **a** him;
20: 8 But they rebelled **a** me and would not listen to me;
20: 8 and spend my anger **a** them in the midst of
Eze 20:13 house of Israel rebelled **a** me in the wilderness;
20:21 But the children rebelled **a** me;
20:21 and spend my anger **a** them in the wilderness.
20:38 and those who transgress **a** me;
20:46 set your face toward the south, preach **a** the south,
20:46 and prophesy **a** the forest land in the Negeb;
21: 2 toward Jerusalem and preach **a** the sanctuaries;
21: 2 prophesy **a** the land of Israel
21: 3 I am coming **a** you, and will draw my sword out
21: 4 therefore my sword shall go out of its sheath **a**
21:12 Cry and wail, O mortal, for it is **a** my people;
21:12 **a** all Israel's princes; they are thrown to the sword,
21:22 to set battering rams **a** the gates, to cast up ramps,
23:22 I will rouse **a** you your lovers
23:22 and I will bring them **a** you from every side:
23:24 They shall come **a** you from the north
23:24 they shall set themselves **a** you on every side
23:25 I will direct my indignation **a** you,
23:46 Bring up an assembly **a** them,
25: 2 toward the Ammonites and prophesy **a** them.
25: 6 with all the malice within you **a** the land of Israel,
25: 7 therefore I have stretched out my hand **a** you,
25:12 Because Edom acted revengefully **a** the house
25:13 I will stretch out my hand **a** Edom,
25:16 I will stretch out my hand **a** the Philistines,
26: 3 I am **a** you, O Tyre! I will hurl many nations **a** you,
26: 7 I will bring **a** Tyre from the north
26: 8 He shall set up a siege wall **a** you,
26: 8 cast up a ramp **a** you,
26: 8 and raise a roof of shields **a** you.
26: 9 He shall direct the shock of his battering rams **a**
28: 7 I will bring strangers **a** you,
28: 7 they shall draw their swords **a** the beauty
28:21 set your face toward Sidon, and prophesy **a** it,
28:22 I am **a** you, O Sidon, and I will gain glory
28:23 by the sword that is **a** it on every side.
29: 2 set your face **a** Pharaoh king of Egypt,
29: 2 and prophesy **a** him and **a** all Egypt;
29: 3 I am **a** you, Pharaoh king of Egypt,
29:10 I am **a** you, and **a** your channels,
29:18 of Babylon made his army labor hard **a** Tyre;
29:18 to pay for the labor that he had expended **a** it.
30:11 and they shall draw their swords **a** Egypt,
30:22 I am **a** Pharaoh king of Egypt,
30:25 He shall stretch it out **a** the land of Egypt,
32:11 sword of the king of Babylon shall come **a** you.
33:16 that they have committed shall be remembered **a**
34: 2 prophesy **a** the shepherds of Israel:
34:10 the Lord GOD, I am **a** the shepherds;
35: 2 set your face **a** Mount Seir, and prophesy **a** it,
35: 3 am **a** you, Mount Seir; I stretch out my hand **a** you
35:11 that you showed because of your hatred **a** them;
35:12 that you uttered **a** the mountains of Israel,
35:13 you magnified yourselves **a** me with your mouth,
35:13 and multiplied your words **a** me; I heard it.
36: 5 jealousy **a** the rest of the nations, and **a** all Edom,
38: 2 prince of Meshech and Tubal. Prophesy **a** him
38: 3 I am **a** you, O Gog, chief prince of Meshech
38: 8 in the latter years you shall go **a** a land restored
38:11 "I will go up **a** the land of unwalled villages;
38:16 you will come up **a** my people Israel,
38:16 In the latter days I will bring you **a** my land,
38:17 for years that I would bring you **a** them?
38:18 On that day, when Gog comes **a** the land of Israel,
38:21 the sword **a** Gog in all my mountains,
38:21 the swords of all will be **a** their comrades.
39: 1 And you, mortal, prophesy **a** Gog, and say:
39: 1 I am **a** you, O Gog, chief prince of Meshech
39: 2 and lead you **a** the mountains of Israel.
39:26 and all the treachery they have practiced **a** me,
43:18 upon it and for dashing blood **a** it,
Da 3:19 Then Nebuchadnezzar was so filled with rage **a**
3:29 that utters blasphemy **a** the God of Shadrach,
4:33 the sentence was fulfilled **a** Nebuchadnezzar.
5:23 You have exalted yourself **a** the Lord of heaven!
6: 4 the satraps tried to find grounds for complaint **a**
6: 5 not find any ground for complaint **a** this Daniel
7:25 He shall speak words **a** the Most High,
8: 7 It was enraged **a** it and struck the ram,
8:11 Even **a** the prince of the host it acted arrogantly;
8:25 and shall even rise up **a** the Prince of princes.
9: 7 of the treachery that they have committed **a** you.
9: 8 and our ancestors, because we have sinned **a** you.
9: 9 for we have rebelled **a** him,
9:11 because we have sinned **a** you.
9:12 which he spoke **a** us and **a** our rulers,
9:12 that what has been done **a** Jerusalem has never
10:20 Now I must return to fight **a** the prince of Persia,
10:21 There is no one with me who contends **a**
11: 2 he shall stir up all **a** the kingdom of Greece.
11: 7 He shall come **a** the army and enter the fortress of
11: 7 and he shall take action **a** them and prevail.
11:11 the king of the south shall go out and do battle **a**
11:14 "In those times many shall rise **a** the king of
11:16 But he who comes **a** him shall take
11:24 He shall devise plans **a** strongholds,
11:25 and determination **a** the king of the south with
11:25 for plots shall be devised **a** him
11:28 but his heart shall be set **a** the holy covenant.
11:30 For ships of Kittim shall come **a** him,
11:30 be enraged and take action **a** the holy covenant.
11:36 shall speak horrendous things **a** the God of gods.
11:40 He shall advance **a** countries and pass through like
11:42 He shall stretch out his hand **a** the countries,
Hos 2: 6 and I will build a wall **a** her,
4: 1 for the LORD has an indictment **a** the inhabitants
4: 7 more they increased, the more they sinned **a** me;

Hos 5: 5 Israel's pride testifies a him;
7:10 Israel's pride testifies a him;
7:13 Destruction to them, for they have rebelled a me!
7:13 I would redeem them, but they speak lies a me.
7:14 and wine; they rebel a me.
7:15 yet they plot evil a me.
8: 5 My anger burns a them.
10:10 I will come a the wayward people to punish them;
10:10 be gathered a them when they are punished
10:14 the tumult of war shall rise a your people,
12: 2 The LORD has an indictment a Judah,
13:16 because she has rebelled a her God;
Joel 2:25 and the cutter, my great army, which I sent a you.
Am 1: 8 I will turn my hand a Ekron,
1:14 So I will kindle a fire a the wall of Rabbah,
3: 1 Hear this word that the LORD has spoken a you,
3: 1 a the whole family that I brought up out of
3:13 Hear, and testify a the house of Jacob,
5: 6 he will break out a the house of Joseph like fire,
5: 9 who makes destruction flash out a the strong,
5:19 went into the house and rested a hand a the wall,
6:14 Indeed, I am raising up a you a nation,
7: 9 and I will rise a the house of Jeroboam with
7:10 "Amos has conspired a you in the very center of
7:16 You say, 'Do not prophesy a Israel,
7:16 and do not preach a the house of Isaac.'
Ob 1: 1 Let us rise a it for battle!"
1: 7 your confederates have prevailed a you;
1:15 For the day of the LORD is near a all the nations.
Jnh 1: 2 that great city, and cry out a it;
1:13 for the sea grew more and more stormy a them.
Mic 1: 2 and let the Lord GOD be a witness a you,
2: 3 Now, I am devising a this family an evil
2: 4 On that day they shall take up a taunt song a you,
2: 8 But you rise up a my people as an enemy;
3: 5 war a those who put nothing into their mouths.
4: 3 nation shall not lift up sword a nation,
4:11 Now many nations are assembled a you, saying,
5: 1 with a wall; siege is laid a us;
5: 5 we will raise a them seven shepherds
7: 6 the daughter rises up a her mother,
7: 6 the daughter-in-law a her mother-in-law;
7: 9 because I have sinned a him,
Na 1: 2 on his adversaries and rages a his enemies.
1: 9 Why do you plot a the LORD?
1:11 From you one has gone out who plots evil a
2: 1 A shatterer has come up a you.
2:13 See, I am a you, says the LORD of hosts,
3: 5 I am a you, says the LORD of hosts, and will lift
Hab 3: 8 Was your wrath a the rivers, O LORD?
3: 8 Or your anger a the rivers,
3: 8 or your rage a the sea,
Zep 1: 4 I will stretch out my hand a Judah,
1: 4 and a all the inhabitants of Jerusalem;
1:16 a the fortified cities and a the lofty battlements.
1:17 because they have sinned a the LORD,
2: 5 The word of the LORD is a you, O Canaan,
2: 8 and made boasts a their territory.
2:10 because they scoffed and boasted a the people of
2:11 The LORD will be terrible a them;
2:13 And he will stretch out his hand a the north,
3:11 of all the deeds by which you have rebelled a me;
3:15 The LORD has taken away the judgments a you,
Zec 1:21 the horns of the nations that lifted up their horns a
2: 9 See now, I am going to raise my hand a them,
7:10 do not devise evil in your hearts a one another.
8:10 and I set them all a one other.
8:17 do not devise evil in your hearts a one another,
9: 1 the LORD is a the land of Hadrach and will rest
9:13 I will arouse your sons, O Zion, a your sons,
10: 3 My anger is hot a the shepherds,
12: 2 it will be a Judah also in the siege a Jerusalem.
12: 3 all the nations of the earth shall come together a it.
12: 9 to destroy all the nations that come a Jerusalem.
13: 7 "Awake, O sword, a my shepherd, a the man who
is my associate,"
13: 7 I will turn my hand a the little ones.
14: 2 I will gather all the nations a Jerusalem to battle,
14: 3 the LORD will go forth and fight a those nations
14:12 the peoples that wage war a Jerusalem:
14:13 and the hand of the one will be raised a the hand
14:16 of the nations that have come a Jerusalem shall go
Mal 3: 5 I will be swift to bear witness a the sorcerers, a the
adulterers, a those who swear falsely, a those who
oppress the hired workers in their wages,
3: 5 a those who thrust aside the alien,
3:13 You have spoken harsh words a me,
3:13 Yet you say, "How have we spoken a you?"
Mt 4: 6 so that you will not dash your foot a a stone.' "
5:11 and persecute you and utter all kinds of evil a
5:23 that your brother or sister has something a you,
7:27 and the winds blew and beat a that house,
10:21 and children will rise a parents and have them put
10:35 For I have come to set a man a his father, and a
daughter a her mother, and a daughter-in-law a
her mother-in-law;
12:14 But the Pharisees went out and conspired a him,
12:25 "Every kingdom divided a itself is laid waste,
12:25 and no city or house divided a itself will stand.
12:26 If Satan casts out Satan, he is divided a himself;
12:30 Whoever is not with me is a me,
12:31 but blasphemy a the Spirit will not be forgiven.
12:32 Whoever speaks a word a the Son of Man will
12:32 but whoever speaks a the Holy Spirit will not
14:24 was far from the land, for the wind was a them.
16:18 and the gates of Hades will not prevail a it.
18:15 "If another member of the church sins a you,
Mt 18:21 "Lord, if another member of the church sins a me,
20:11 they received it, they grumbled a the landowner,
23:31 Thus you testify a yourselves
24: 7 nation will rise a nation, and kingdom a kingdom,
26:59 looking for false testimony a Jesus
26:62 What is it that they testify a you?"
27: 1 the elders of the people conferred together a Jesus
27:13 not hear how many accusations they make a
27:37 Over his head they put the charge a him,
Mk 3: 6 and immediately conspired with the Herodians a
3:24 If a kingdom is divided a itself,
3:25 And if a house is divided a itself,
3:26 And if Satan has risen up a himself and is divided,
3:29 but whoever blasphemes a the Holy Spirit
6:11 the dust that is on your feet as a testimony a
6:19 And Herodias had a grudge a him,
6:48 When he saw that they were straining at the oars a
9:40 Whoever is not a us is for us.
10:11 and marries another commits adultery a her;
11:25 forgive, if you have anything a anyone;
12:12 they realized that he had told this parable a them,
13: 8 nation will rise a nation, and kingdom a kingdom;
13:12 and children will rise a parents and have them put
14:55 whole council were looking for testimony a Jesus
14:56 For many gave false testimony a him,
14:57 Some stood up and gave false testimony a him,
14:60 What is it that they testify a you?"
15: 4 See how many charges they bring a you."
15:26 The inscription of the charge a him read,
15:46 He then rolled a stone a the door of the tomb.
Lk 4:11 so that you will not dash your foot a a stone.' "
6: 7 so that they might find an accusation a him.
6:48 the river burst a that house but could not shake it,
6:49 When the river burst a it, immediately it fell,
9: 5 the dust off your feet as a testimony a them."
9:50 for whoever is not a you is for you."
10:11 we wipe off in protest a you.
11:17 "Every kingdom divided a itself becomes a desert,
11:18 If Satan also is divided a himself,
11:23 Whoever is not with me is a me,
11:51 Yes, I tell you, it will be charged a this generation.
12:10 everyone who speaks a word a the Son of Man
12:10 but whoever blasphemes a the Holy Spirit will not
12:15 Be on your guard a all kinds of greed;
12:52 three a two and two a three;
12:53 father a son and son a father, mother a daughter
and daughter a mother, mother-in-law a her
daughter-in-law and daughter-in-law a
14:31 what king, going out to wage war a another king,
14:31 with ten thousand to oppose the one who comes a
15:18 "Father, I have sinned a heaven and before you;
15:21 'Father, I have sinned a heaven and before you;
17: 4 if the same person sins a you seven times a day,
18: 3 'Grant me justice a my opponent.'
20:19 that he had told this parable a them,
21:10 Nation will rise a nation, and kingdom a kingdom;
21:23 be great distress on the earth and wrath a
23: 4 "I find no basis for an accusation a this man."
23:14 not found this man guilty of any of your charges a
Jn 7: 7 because I testify a it that its works are evil.
8: 6 ⟦that they might have some charge to bring a him.⟧
11:38 It was a cave, and a stone was lying a it.
13:18 one who ate my bread has lifted his heel a me.'
18:29 "What accusation do you bring a this man?"
18:38 "I find no case a him.
19: 4 to you to let you know that I find no case a him."
19: 6 I find no case a him."
19:12 Everyone who claims to be a king sets himself a
Ac 4:26 gathered together a the Lord and a his Messiah.'
4:27 gathered together a your holy servant Jesus,
5:39 that case you may even be found fighting a God!"
6: 1 the Hellenists complained a the Hebrews
6:11 "We have heard him speak blasphemous words a
6:13 "This man never stops saying things a
7:57 and with a loud shout all rushed together a him.
7:60 "Lord, do not hold this sin a them."
8: 1 That day a severe persecution began a the church
9: 1 still breathing threats and murder a the disciples
13:11 And now listen—the hand of the Lord is a you,
13:50 and stirred up persecution a Paul and Barnabas,
13:51 they shook the dust off their feet in protest a them,
14: 2 up the Gentiles and poisoned their minds a
19:38 the artisans with him have a complaint a anyone,
19:38 let them bring charges there a one another.
20: 3 about to set sail for Syria when a plot was made a
21:28 the man who is teaching everyone everywhere a
22:24 to find out the reason for this outcry a him.
23:30 When I was informed that there would be a plot a
23:30 also to state before you what they have a him."
24: 1 they reported their case a Paul to the governor.
24:13 to you the charge that they now bring a me.
24:19 if they have anything a me.
25: 2 the leaders of the Jews gave him a report a Paul.
25: 3 as a favor to them a Paul,
25: 7 bringing many serious charges a him,
25: 8 "I have in no way committed an offense a the law
of the Jews, or a the temple, or a the emperor."
25:11 but if there is nothing to their charges a me,
25:15 about him and asked for a sentence a him.
25:16 an opportunity to make a defense a the charge.
25:27 to send a prisoner without indicating the charges a
26: 2 to make my defense today a all the accusations of
26: 9 that I ought to do many things a the name of Jesus
26:10 the saints in prison, but I also cast my vote a them
26:14 It hurts you to kick a the goads.'
27: 4 because the winds were a us.
27: 7 and as the wind was a us,
Ac 28:17 though I had done nothing a our people or
28:19 even though I had no charge to bring a my nation.
28:22 that everywhere it is spoken a."
Ro 1:18 of God is revealed from heaven a all ungodliness
2:21 While you preach a stealing, do you steal?
4: 8 the one a whom the Lord will not reckon sin."
4:18 Hoping a hope, he believed that he would become
8:31 If God is for us, who is a us?
8:33 Who will bring any charge a God's elect?
11: 2 how he pleads with God a Israel?
1Co 4: 4 I am not aware of anything a myself,
4: 6 of you will be puffed up in favor of one a another.
6: 1 When any of you has a grievance a another,
6: 6 but a believer goes to court a a believer—
6:18 but the fornicator sins a the body itself.
8:12 But when you thus sin a members of your family,
8:12 when it is weak, you sin a Christ.
11:29 eat and drink judgment a themselves.
2Co 1:23 But I call on God as witness a me:
5:19 not counting their trespasses a them,
8: 8 but I am testing the genuineness of your love a
10: 5 and every proud obstacle raised up a
13: 8 For we cannot do anything a the truth,
Gal 5:23 There is no law a such things.
5:26 competing a one another, envying one another.
Eph 6:11 you may be able to stand a the wiles of the devil.
6:12 struggle is not a enemies of blood and flesh, but a
the rulers, a the authorities, a the cosmic powers
of this present darkness, a the spiritual forces of
Col 2:14 the record that stood a us with its legal demands.
3:13 if anyone has a complaint a another,
1Ti 5:19 Never accept any accusation a an elder except on
2Ti 4:16 May it not be counted a them!
Heb 12: 3 Consider him who endured such hostility a
12: 4 In your struggle a sin you have not yet resisted to
Jas 4:11 Do not speak evil a one another,
4:11 Whoever speaks evil a another or judges another,
4:11 speaks evil a the law and judges the law;
5: 3 and their rust will be evidence a you,
5: 9 Beloved, do not grumble a one another,
1Pe 2:11 the desires of the flesh that wage war a the soul.
3:12 But the face of the Lord is a those who do evil."
2Pe 2: 3 Their condemnation, pronounced a them long ago,
2:11 do not bring a them a slanderous judgment from
3Jn 1:10 to what he is doing in spreading false charges a
Jude 1: 9 not dare to bring a condemnation of slander a him,
1:15 that ungodly sinners have spoken a him."
Rev 2: 4 But I have this a you,
2:14 But I have a few things a you:
2:16 to you soon and make war a them with the sword
2:20 But I have this a you:
7: 1 so that no wind could blow on earth or sea or a
12: 7 Michael and his angels fought a the dragon.
13: 4 "Who is like the beast, and who can fight a it?"
13: 6 It opened its mouth to utter blasphemies a God,
18:20 For God has given judgment for you a her."
19:19 make war a the rider on the horse and a his army.
Tob 2: 6 the prophecy of Amos, how he said a Bethel,
2:14 I became flushed with anger a her over this.
3: 3 before you. They sinned a you,
4: 9 a good treasure for yourself a the day of necessity.
13:12 Cursed are all who speak a harsh word a you;
Jdt 1: 5 Then King Nebuchadnezzar made war a
1:13 In the seventeenth year he led his forces a
2: 6 March out a all the land to the west,
2: 7 for I am coming a them in my anger,
5:17 as they did not sin a their God they prospered,
5:20 in this people and they sin a their God
6: 2 and tell us not to make war a the people of Israel
6:17 and all that Holofernes had boasted he would do a
7: 1 to break camp and move a Bethulia,
7:11 my lord, do not fight a them in regular formation,
7:28 to witness a you heaven and earth and our God,
8: 9 the harsh words spoken by the people a the ruler,
9:13 planned cruel things a your covenant, and a your
sacred house, and a Mount Zion, and a the house
11: 2 I would never have lifted my spear a them.
11:10 nor can the sword prevail a them,
11:10 unless they sin a their God.
13: 5 to destroy the enemies who have risen up a us."
13:11 still showing his power in Israel and his strength a
14: 2 down to the plain a the Assyrian outpost;
14:13 the slaves have been so bold as to come down a us
16:17 Woe to the nations that rise up a my people!
AdE 3:10 the decree that was to be written a the Jews.
4: 8 has spoken a us and demands our death.
8: 3 to avert all the evil that Haman had planned a
8: 7 and have hanged him on a tree because he acted a
8:11 as they wished a their opponents and enemies
8:13 and let all the Jews be ready on that day to fight a
9:24 of Hammedatha, the Macedonian, fought a them,
9:25 but the wicked plot he had devised a the Jews
11: 7 to fight a the righteous nation.
14:11 but turn their plan a them,
14:11 and make an example of him who began this a us.
14:13 turn his heart to hate the man who is fighting a us,
16: 3 even undertake to scheme a their own benefactors.
16:20 they may defend themselves a those who attack
16:23 a reminder of destruction for those who plot a us.
Wis 2:12 he reproaches us for sins a the law,
2:12 and accuses us of sins a our training.
3:10 the righteous and rebelled a the Lord;
3:14 who has not devised wicked things a the Lord;
4: 6 of evil a their parents when God examines them.
5:20 and creation will join with him to fight a
5:22 the water of the sea will rage a them,
5:23 a mighty wind will rise a them,

Wis 7:30 but a wisdom evil does not prevail.
16:18 not consume the creatures sent a the ungodly,
Sir 3:14 and will be credited to you a your sins;
4:25 Never speak a the truth, but be ashamed
6:12 they turn a you, and hide themselves from you.
7: 7 Commit no offense a the public,
7:12 Do not devise a lie a your brother,
8:11 or they may lie in ambush a your words.
8:14 Do not go to law a a judge,
12:11 take care to be on your guard a him.
13: 2 The pot will strike a it and be smashed.
18:27 when sin is all around, one guards a wrongdoing.
22:18 Fences set on a high place will not stand firm a
22:18 a fool's resolve will not stand firm a any fear.
22:21 Even if you draw your sword a a friend,
22:22 If you open your mouth a your friend,
23:18 one who sins a his marriage bed says to himself,
23:23 she has committed an offense a her husband;
26:11 Be on guard a her impudent eye,
26:11 and do not be surprised if she sins a you.
28: 3 Does anyone harbor anger a another,
28:23 It will be sent out a them like a lion;
29:13 it will fight for you a the enemy.
30: 6 He has left behind him an avenger a his enemies,
34:19 a guard a stumbling and a help a falling.
35:19 as she cries out a the one who causes them to fall?
36: 3 Lift up your hand a foreign nations
37: 4 but in time of trouble they are a him.
37: 8 He may cast the lot a you
37:31 but the one who guards a it prolongs his life.
38:15 He who sins a his Maker,
40:29 and well instructed guards a that.
45:18 Outsiders conspired a him,
45:19 he performed wonders a them to consume them
46: 1 to take vengeance on the enemies that rose a
46: 2 and brandished his sword a the cities!
48:18 he shook his fist a Zion, and made great boasts
50: 4 and fortified the city a siege.
51:10 when there is no help a the proud.
Bar 1:13 for we have sinned a the Lord our God,
2: 1 So the Lord carried out the threat he spoke a us:
2: 1 a our judges who ruled Israel, and a our kings
2: 5 because our nation sinned a the Lord our God,
2:12 O Lord our God, a all your ordinances.
3: 7 the iniquity of our ancestors who sinned a you.
4:15 For he brought a distant nation a them,
LtJ 6:18 on every side a anyone who has offended a king,
Sus 1:21 we will testify a you that a young man was
1:24 and the two elders shouted a her.
1:43 that these men have given false evidence a me.
1:43 the wicked things that they have charged a me!"
1:49 for these men have given false evidence a her."
1:61 And they took action a the two elders,
Bel 1: 9 because he has spoken blasphemy a Bel."
1:28 they were very indignant and conspired a the king,
1Mc 1:20 He went up a Israel and came to Jerusalem with
1:36 for the citadel became an ambush a the sanctuary,
1:58 They kept using violence a Israel,
1:58 a those who were found month after month in
2:26 just as Phinehas did a Zimri son of Salu.
2:32 and prepared for battle a them on the sabbath day.
2:41 "Let us fight a anyone who comes to attack us on
2:66 the army for you and fight the battle a the peoples.
3:10 and a large force from Samaria to fight a Israel.
3:17 fight a so great and so strong a multitude?
3:20 They come a us in great insolence and lawlessness
3:23 he rushed suddenly a Seron and his army,
3:35 to send a force a them to wipe out and destroy
3:52 the Gentiles are assembled a us to destroy us;
3:52 you know what they plot a us.
3:58 to fight with these Gentiles who have assembled a
4:12 the foreigners looked up and saw them coming a
4:18 But stand now a our enemies and fight them,
4:41 to fight a those in the citadel until he had cleansed
5: 5 and he encamped a them,
5: 9 Now the Gentiles in Gilead gathered together a
5:15 had gathered together a them "to annihilate us."
5:21 to Galilee and fought many battles a the Gentiles,
5:35 and fought a it and took it;
5:39 ready to come and fight a you."
5:43 Then he crossed over a them first,
5:50 he fought a the town all that day and all the night,
5:58 of the forces that were with them and marched a
6:25 It is not a us alone
6:26 today they have encamped a the citadel
6:31 through Idumea and encamped a Beth-zur,
6:48 of the king's army went up to Jerusalem a them,
6:57 the place a which we are fighting is strong,
6:63 but he fought a him, and took the city by force.
7: 6 They brought to the king this accusation a
7:25 to the king and brought malicious charges a them.
7:42 that Nicanor has spoken wickedly a the sanctuary,
8: 4 They also subdued the kings who came a them
8: 5 and the others who rose up a them.
8: 6 to fight a them with one hundred twenty elephants
8:10 a general a the Greeks and attacked them.
8:32 If now they appeal again for help a you,
9: 2 by the road that leads to Gilgal and encamped a
9: 3 one hundred fifty-second year they encamped a
9: 8 "Let us get up and go a our enemies.
9:29 like him to go a our enemies and Bacchides,
9:64 Then he came and encamped a Bethbasi;
9:64 he fought a it for many days and made machines
10: 4 with him before he makes peace with Alexander a
10:61 renegades, gathered together a him to accuse him;
10:63 and proclaim that no one is to bring charges a him
10:69 and he assembled a large force and encamped a
1Mc 10:70 "You are the only one to rise up a us,
10:70 Why do you assume authority a us in
10:76 So they fought a it, and the people of
10:86 Then Jonathan left there and encamped a Askalon,
11: 8 and he kept devising wicked designs a Alexander.
11:15 Alexander heard of it, he came a him in battle.
11:20 and he built many engines of war to use a it.
11:25 of his nation kept making complaints a him,
11:39 that all the troops were grumbling a Demetrius.
11:41 for they kept fighting a Israel.
11:50 make the Jews stop fighting a us and our city."
11:55 they fought a Demetrius, and he fled
11:65 Simon encamped before Beth-zur and fought a it
11:68 they had set an ambush a him in the mountains,
11:72 Then he turned back to the battle a the enemy
12:13 the kings around us have waged war a us.
12:24 a larger force than before, to wage war a him.
12:31 So Jonathan turned aside a
12:39 and to raise his hand a King Antiochus.
12:42 he was afraid to raise his hand a him.
13:16 so that when released he will not revolt a us,
13:43 In those days Simon encamped a Gazara
13:47 an agreement with them and stopped fighting a
14: 1 so that he could make war a Trypho.
15: 4 a landing in the country so that I may proceed a
15:13 So Antiochus encamped a Dor,
15:19 not seek their harm or make war a them
15:19 or make alliance with those who war a them.
15:25 continually throwing his forces a it
15:39 He commanded him to encamp a Judea,
16: 4 and they marched a Cendebeus and camped for
16: 6 Then he and his army lined up a them.
16:13 and made treacherous plans a Simon and his sons,
16:16 in a Simon in the banquet hall and killed him
2Mc 1:11 for taking our side a the king,
1:12 for he drove out those who fought a the holy city.
2:20 and further the wars a Antiochus Epiphanes
3:38 or plotter a your government, send him there,
4: 1 who had informed about the money a
4: 2 as a plotter a the government the man who was
4:38 where he had committed the outrage a Onias,
4:39 the populace gathered a Lysimachus,
4:43 Charges were brought a Menelaus
4:47 he acquitted of the charges a him,
4:50 having become the chief plotter a his compatriots.
5: 8 pursued by everyone, hated as a rebel a the laws,
7: 6 as Moses declared in his song that bore witness a
7:18 because of our sins a our own God.
7:19 for having tried to fight a God!"
7:31 who have contrived all sorts of evil a
7:34 you raise your hand a the children of heaven.
8: 4 and the blasphemies committed a his name;
8:16 of Gentiles who were wickedly coming a them,
8:17 that the Gentiles had committed a the holy place,
8:18 to strike down those who are coming a us,
8:20 of the battle a the Galatians that took place
9: 7 breathing fire in his rage a the Jews,
10:21 for money by setting their enemies free to fight a
10:36 around a the defenders and set fire to the towers;
11: 2 and all his cavalry and came a the Jews.
11:11 They hurled themselves like lions a the enemy,
12:10 on their march a Timothy,
12:15 calling a the great Sovereign of the world,
12:26 Then Judas marched a Carnaim and the temple
12:27 he marched also a Ephron,
12:32 festival called Pentecost, they hurried a Gorgias,
12:37 then he charged a Gorgias's troops
13: 1 with a great army a Judea,
13: 4 of kings aroused the anger of Antiochus a
13: 8 because he had committed many sins a
13:19 He advanced a Beth-zur, a strong fortress of
14:26 he had appointed that conspirator a the kingdom,
15:24 of your arm may these blasphemers who come a
15:32 which had been boastfully stretched out a
1Es 1:25 and Josiah went out a him.
1:27 I was not sent a you by the Lord God,
1:29 and the commanders came down a King Josiah.
1:40 King Nebuchadnezzar of Babylon came up a him;
1:52 until in his anger a his people because of their
1:52 he gave command to bring a them the kings of
2:16 a those who were living in Judea and Jerusalem:
2:26 that this city from of old has fought a kings,
4: 4 and if he sends them out a the enemy, they go,
6:15 But when our ancestors sinned a the Lord
8:92 and said to Ezra, "We have sinned a the Lord,
Man 1: 7 and forgiveness to those who have sinned a you,
1: 8 who did not sin a you,
3Mc 3: 1 not only was he enraged a those Jews who lived
3: 2 a hostile rumor was circulated a the Jewish nation
3:11 in his same purpose, wrote this letter a them:
3:24 if a sudden disorder later arises a us,
4:16 and uttering improper words a the supreme God.
5: 8 that he avert with vengeance the evil plot a them
5:43 and would also march a Judea and rapidly level it
6: 5 the whole world by the spear and was lifted up a
6: 6 the fiery furnace with dew and turning the flame a
7: 9 For you should know that if we devise any evil a
7:10 the Jewish nation who had willfully transgressed a
2Es 1: 5 the iniquities that they have committed a me,
2:28 but they shall not be able to do anything a you,
4:14 'Come, let us go and make war a the sea,
7:22 they were not obedient, and spoke a him;
8: 5 and a your will you depart,
8:34 that you are so bitter a it?
11: 6 and no one spoke a it—
13: 5 from the four winds of heaven to make war a
13: 8 and saw that all who had gathered together a him,
2Es 13:31 They shall plan to make war a one another,
13:31 city a city, place a place, people a people, and kingdom a kingdom.
13:33 and the warfare that they have a one another;
15: 3 Do not fear the plots a you,
15:15 and nation shall rise up to fight a nation,
15:16 growing strong a one another,
15:26 For God knows all who sin a him;
15:27 because you have sinned a him.
15:35 They shall clash a one another and shall pour out
16:70 be a great uprising a those who fear the Lord.
4Mc 2:17 he did nothing a them in anger,
3:21 that time certain persons attempted a revolution a
4:22 For when he was warring a Ptolemy in Egypt,
4:22 He speedily marched a them,
8:24 not struggle a compulsion or take hollow pride
11:12 they are splendid favors that you grant us a
14:19 for making honeycombs defend themselves a
17: 3 you held firm and unswerving a the earthquake of
18: 5 he left Jerusalem and marched a the Persians.

AGAPE (1)

1Es 4:31 At this the king would gaze at her with mouth **a.**

AGAR (KJV) See HAGAR

AGATE (3)

Ex 28:19 and the third row a jacinth, an **a**, and an amethyst;
39:12 a jacinth, an **a**, and an amethyst;
Rev 21:19 first was jasper, the second sapphire, the third **a**,

AGATES (KJV) See RUBIES

AGE‡ (123) [AGED, AGES, AGING, WELL-AGED]

A. OLD AGE (41)
B. THIS AGE (17)
C. END OF THE/THIS AGE (10)
D. AGE TO COME (7)

Ge 15:15 you shall be buried in a good old **a.** A
18:11 Abraham and Sarah were old, advanced in **a;**
21: 2 and bore Abraham a son in his old **a,** A
21: 7 Yet I have borne him a son in his old **a."** A
25: 8 and died in a good old **a,** A
37: 3 because he was the son of his old **a;** A
44:20 and a young brother, the child of his old **a.** A
48:10 Now the eyes of Israel were dim with **a,**
Lev 27: 3 of **a** the equivalent shall be fifty shekels of silver
27: 5 If the **a** is from five to twenty years of age,
27: 5 If the age is from five to twenty years of **a,**
27: 6 If the **a** is from one month to five years,
Nu 8:25 and from the **a** of fifty years they shall retire from
18:16 reckoned from one month of **a,**
Jdg 2: 8 died at the **a** of one hundred ten years.
8:32 Then Gideon son of Joash died at a good old **a,** A
Ru 4:15 a restorer of life and a nourisher of your old **a;** A
1Sa 2:31 so that no one in your family will live to old **a.** A
2:32 no one in your family shall ever live to old **a.** A
1Ki 14: 4 for his eyes were dim because of his **a.**
15:23 But in his old **a** he was diseased in his feet. A
1Ch 27:23 not count those below twenty years of **a,**
29:28 He died in a good old **a,** full of days, riches, A
Job 5:26 You shall come to your grave in ripe old **a,** A
21: 7 Why do the wicked live on, reach old **a,** A
Ps 71: 9 Do not cast me off in the time of old **a;** A
71:18 So even to old **a** and gray hairs, O God, A
92:14 In old **a** they still produce fruit; A
Isa 46: 4 even to your old **a** I am he, A
60:15 a joy from **a** to **a.**
Eze 16: 8 you were at the **a** for love.
Da 1:10 the other young men of your own **a,**
2:20 "Blessed be the name of God from **a** to age,
2:20 "Blessed be the name of God from age to **a,**
Zec 8: 4 each with staff in hand because of their great **a**
Mt 12:32 either in this **a** or in the age to come. B
12:32 either in this age or in the **a** to come. D
13:39 the harvest is the end of the **a,** C
13:40 so will it be at the end of the **a.** C
13:49 So it will be at the end of the **a.** C
24: 3 sign of your coming and of the end of the **a?"** C
28:20 I am with you always, to the end of the **a."** C
Mk 5:42 to walk about (she was twelve years of **a).**
10:30 will not receive a hundredfold now in this **a—** B
10:30 and in the **a** to come eternal life. D
Lk 1:36 your relative Elizabeth in her old **a** has A
2:36 She was of a great **a,**
2:37 then as a widow to the **a** of eighty-four.
16: 8 the children of this **a** are more shrewd in dealing B
18:30 who will not get back very much more in this **a,** B
18:30 and in the **a** to come eternal life." D
20:34 "Those who belong to this **a** marry and B
20:35 of a place in that **a** and in the resurrection from
Jn 9:21 Ask him; he is of **a.**
9:23 Therefore his parents said, "He is of **a;** ask him."
1Co 1:20 Where is the debater of this **a?** B
2: 6 it is not a wisdom of this **a** or of the rulers B
2: 6 a wisdom of this age or of the rulers of this **a,** B
2: 8 None of the rulers of this **a** understood this; B
3:18 If you think that you are wise in this **a,** B
Gal 1: 4 for our sins to set us free from the present evil **a,**
1:14 beyond many among my people of the same **a,**
Eph 1:21 not only in this **a** but also in the age to come. B
1:21 not only in this age but also in the **a** to come. D

1Ti 6:17 As for those who in the present **a** are rich,
Tit 2:12 the present **a** to live lives that are self-controlled,
Heb 6: 5 word of God and the powers of the **a** to come, D
9:26 at the end of the **a** to remove sin by the sacrifice C
Tob 3:10 And I shall bring my father in his old **a** down A
14:13 with great respect in their old **a**, A
14:14 at the **a** of one hundred seventeen years.
Jdt 16:23 reaching the **a** of one hundred five.
Wis 3:17 and finally their old **a** will be without honor. A
4: 8 For old **a** is not honored for length of time, A
4: 9 and a blameless life is ripe old **a**. A
4:16 the prolonged old **a** of the unrighteous. A
Sir 3:12 My child, help your father in his old **a**, A
25: 3 how can you find anything in your old **a**? A
30:24 and anxiety brings on premature old **a**. A
41: 2 worn down by **a** and anxious about everything;
46: 9 which remained with him in his old **a**, A
47:13 Solomon reigned in an **a** of peace,
2Mc 6:18 a man now advanced in **a** and of noble presence,
6:23 the dignity of his old **a** and the gray hairs A
6:25 while I defile and disgrace my old **a**. A
6:27 I will show myself worthy of my old **a** A
1Es 5:41 All those of Israel, twelve or more years of **a**,
5:58 or more years of **a** to have charge of the work of
3Mc 4: 5 sluggish and bent with **a**, was being led away,
6: 1 who had attained a ripe old **a** and A
2Es 2:34 at the end of the **a** is close at hand. C
2:36 Flee from the shadow of this **a**, B
2:39 of this **a** have received glorious garments from B
4:26 because the **a** is hurrying swiftly to its end.
4:27 because this **a** is full of sadness and infirmities. B
4:36 for he has weighed the **a** in the balance,
5:50 Or is she now approaching old **a**?" A
5:53 from those born during the time of old **a**, A
6: 7 Or when will be the end of the first **a** and C
6: 7 and the beginning of the **a** that follows?"
6: 9 Now Esau is the end of this **a**, BC
6: 9 and Jacob is the beginning of the **a** that follows.
6:20 When the seal is placed upon the **a** that is about
7:*113* [43] day of judgment will be the end of this **a** BC
7:*113* [43] the beginning of the immortal **a** to come, D
8:52 the **a** to come is prepared, plenty is provided, D
9:13 the **a** belongs and for whose sake the **a** was made."
9:18 in this **a** when I was preparing for those who B
14:10 The **a** has lost its youth,
14:11 For the **a** is divided into twelve parts,
14:17 the weaker the world becomes through old **a**, A
4Mc 5: 4 learned in the law, advanced in **a**,
5: 7 for I respect your **a** and your gray hairs.
5:12 on your old **a** by honoring my humane advice? A
5:33 not so pity my old **a** as to break the ancestral law A
5:36 not defile the honorable mouth of my old **a**, A
6:12 At that point, partly out of pity for his old **a**, A
6:18 if having lived in accordance up to old **a** A
7:15 O man of blessed **a** and of venerable gray hair
8:20 and have compassion on our mother's **a**;
11:14 "I am younger in **a** than my brothers,

AGED (33) [AGE]

Lev 19:32 You shall rise before the **a**, and defer to the old;
2Sa 19:32 Barzillai was a very **a** man, eighty years old.
2Ch 36:17 the **a** or the feeble; he gave them all into his hand.
Job 12:12 Is wisdom with the **a**, and understanding in length
15:10 The gray-haired and the **a** are on our side,
29: 8 and the **a** rose up and stood;
32: 6 "I am young in years, and you are **a**;
32: 9 nor the **a** that understand what is right.
Ps 119:100 I understand more than the **a**,
Pr 17: 6 Grandchildren are the crown of the **a**,
20:29 but the beauty of the **a** is their gray hair.
Isa 47: 6 on the **a** you made your yoke exceedingly heavy.
Jer 6:11 the old folk and the very **a**.
Joel 2:16 Sanctify the congregation; assemble the **a**;
Wis 2:10 the widow or regard the gray hairs of the **a**.
Sir 8: 9 Do not ignore the discourse of the **a**,
9:10 when it has **a**, you can drink it with pleasure.
25: 4 and for the **a** to possess good counsel!
25: 5 How attractive is wisdom in the **a**,
25: 6 Rich experience is the crown of the **a**,
25:20 A sandy ascent for the feet of the **a**—
42: 8 or the **a** who are guilty of sexual immorality.
Bar 4:15 which had no respect for the **a** and no pity for
2Mc 8:30 and also to the **a**, shares equal to their own.
4Mc 7:10 O **a** man, more powerful than tortures;
7:16 of piety an **a** man despised tortures even to death,
8: 2 to compel an **a** man to eat defiling foods,
8: 3 before him along with their **a** mother.
9: 6 And if the **a** men of the Hebrews because
9: 6 which our **a** instructor also overcame.
16:17 while an **a** man endures such agonies for the sake
17: 9 "Here lie buried an **a** priest and an **a** woman

AGEE (1)

2Sa 23:11 Next to him was Shammah son of **A**, the Hararite.

AGENTS (1)

2Mc 4: 3 by one of Simon's approved **a**,

AGES‡ (28) [AGE]

Dt 4:32 For ask now about former **a**,
Ps 135:13 your renown, O LORD, throughout all **a**.
Pr 8:23 **A** ago I was set up, at the first,
Ecc 1:10 It has already been, in the **a** before us.
Isa 64: 4 From **a** past no one has heard,
Joel 2: 2 nor will be again after them in **a** to come.
Ro 16:25 of the mystery that was kept secret for long **a**
1Co 2: 7 which God decreed before the **a** for our glory.
10:11 on whom the ends of the **a** have come.
Eph 2: 7 so that in the **a** to come he might show
3: 9 the plan of the mystery hidden for **a**
Col 1:26 the mystery that has been hidden throughout the **a**
1Ti 1:17 To the King of the **a**, immortal, invisible,
2Ti 1: 9 to us in Christ Jesus before the **a** began,
Tit 1: 2 who never lies, promised before the **a** began—
1Pe 1:20 but was revealed at the end of the **a** for your sake.
Tob 11:14 be blessed throughout all the **a**.
13: 1 because his kingdom lasts throughout all **a**.
13: 6 and exalt the King of the **a**.
13:10 for he is good, and bless the King of the **a**,
13:13 and will praise the Lord of the **a**.
13:16 For Jerusalem will be built as his house for all **a**.
Sir 24: 9 Before the **a**, in the beginning, he created me,
24: 9 and for all the **a** I shall not cease to be.
36:22 that you are the Lord, the God of the **a**.
1Es 4:40 and the power and the majesty of all the **a**.
2Es 11:44 and his **a** have reached completion.
13:26 for many **a**, who will himself deliver his creation;

AGGRESSIVE (1)

Pr 11:16 The timid become destitute, but the **a** gain riches.

AGHAST (1)

Isa 13: 8 They will look **a** at one another;

AGIA (2)

1Es 5:34 of **A**, the descendants of Pochereth-hazzebaim,
5:38 the descendants of Jaddus who had married **A**,

AGILE (1)

Ge 49:24 and his arms were made **a** by the hands of

AGING (1) [AGE]

2Es 5:55 as born of a creation that already is **a** and passing

AGITATED‡ (5) [AGITATION, AGITATOR]

Mt 26:37 and began to be grieved and **a**.
Mk 14:33 and began to be distressed and **a**.
AdE 15:16 Then the king was **a**, and all his servants tried
3Mc 1:17 those who remained behind in the city were **a**
2Es 3: 3 My spirit was greatly **a**, and I began

AGITATION (1) [AGITATED]

Job 20: 2 because of the **a** within me.

AGITATOR (1) [AGITATED]

Ac 24: 5 an **a** among all the Jews throughout the world,

AGO‡ (46)

Jos 24: 2 Long **a** your ancestors—Terah and his sons
1Sa 9:20 As for your donkeys that were lost three days **a**,
30:13 behind because I fell sick three days **a**.
2Ki 19:25 Have you not heard that I determined it long **a**?
Ezr 4:15 and that sedition was stirred up in it from long **a**.
4:19 that this city has risen against kings from long **a**,
5:11 the house that was built many years **a**,
Ne 12:46 in the days of David and Asaph long **a** there was
Ps 74: 2 which you acquired long **a**,
77: 5 and remember the years of long **a**.
102:25 Long **a** you laid the foundation of the earth,
119:152 Long **a** I learned from your decrees
Pr 8:22 the first of his acts of long **a**.
8:23 Ages **a** I was set up, at the first,
Ecc 1:11 The people of long **a** are not remembered,
9: 7 for God has long **a** approved what you do.
Isa 22:11 or have regard for him who planned it long **a**.
37:26 Have you not heard that I determined it long **a**?
45:21 Who told this long **a**? Who declared it of old?
48: 3 The former things I declared long **a**,
48: 5 I declared them to you from long **a**,
48: 7 They are created now, not long **a**;
51: 9 as in days of old, the generations of long **a**!
52: 4 For thus says the Lord GOD: Long **a**,
Jer 2:20 long **a** you broke your yoke and burst your bonds,
La 2:17 as he ordained long **a**, he has demolished
3: 6 in darkness like the dead of long **a**.
Eze 26:20 to the people of long **a**,
32:27 not lie with the fallen warriors of long **a** who went
Mt 11:21 they would have repented long **a** in sackcloth
Lk 10:13 they would have repented long **a**,
Ac 3:21 that God announced long **a**
5:36 For some time **a** Theudas rose up,
10:30 Cornelius replied, "Four days **a** at this very hour,
15:18 known from long **a**.'
2Co 12: 2 in Christ who fourteen years **a** was caught up to
Heb 1: 1 Long **a** God spoke to our ancestors in many
1Pe 3: 5 in this way long **a** the holy women who hoped
2Pe 2: 3 pronounced against them long **a**,
3: 5 that by the word of God heavens existed long **a**
Jude 1: 4 people who long **a** were designated
Wis 12: 3 Those who lived long **a** in your holy land
1Es 6:14 The house was built many years **a** by a king
3Mc 4: 1 for the inveterate enmity that had long **a** been
2Es 10:41 The woman who appeared to you a little while **a**,
4Mc 9: 5 a short time **a** you learned nothing from Eleazar.

AGONE (KJV) See AGO

AGONIES (13) [AGONY]

2Es 5:34 for every hour I suffer **a** of heart,
12:26 one of the kings shall die in his bed, but in **a**.
4Mc 3:18 it can overthrow bodily **a** even
6: 7 because his body could not endure the **a**,
6:34 of reason when it masters even external **a**.
6:35 I have proved not only that reason has mastered **a**,
8:28 of the emotions and sovereign over **a**,
13: 5 in those who were not turned back by fiery **a**?
14: 1 so that they not only despised their **a**,
14: 9 and in **a** of fire at that.
14:11 the mind of woman despised even more diverse **a**,
15:19 in his tortures gazing boldly at the same **a**,
16:17 aged man endures such **a** for the sake of religion,

AGONY (9) [AGONIES]

2Ch 21:19 and he died in great **a**.
Isa 13: 8 Pangs and **a** will seize them;
Eze 30:16 Pelusium shall be in great **a**;
Lk 16:24 for I am in **a** in these flames.'
16:25 but now he is comforted here, and you are in **a**.
Rev 12: 2 in the **a** of giving birth.
16:10 people gnawed their tongues in **a**,
1Mc 9:56 And Alcimus died at that time in great **a**.
4Mc 9:28 But he steadfastly endured this **a** and said,

AGORA See Index to Footnotes

AGREE (14) [AGREEABLE, AGREED, AGREEING, AGREEMENT, AGREEMENTS, AGREES]

Ge 34:22 on this condition will they **a** to live among us,
34:23 Only let us **a** with them,
Job 22:21 "**A** with God, and be at peace;
Mt 18:19 if two of you **a** on earth about anything you ask,
20:13 did you not **a** with me for the usual daily wage?
Mk 14:56 and their testimony did not **a**.
14:59 But even on this point their testimony did not **a**.
Ro 7:16 if I do what I do not want, I **a** that the law is good.
2Co 13:11 listen to my appeal, **a** with one another,
1Ti 6: 3 Whoever teaches otherwise and does not **a** with
1Jn 5: 8 and the water and the blood, and these three **a**.
AdE 14:13 that there may be an end of him and those who **a**
1Mc 6:59 Let us **a** to let them live by their laws
4Mc 9:16 "**A** to eat so that you may be released from

AGREEABLE (1) [AGREE]

Lev 10:19 would it have been **a** to the LORD?"

AGREED‡ (27) [AGREE]

Ge 23:16 Abraham **a** with Ephron;
37:27 our brother, our own flesh." And his brothers **a**.
42:20 And they **a** to do so.
Ex 2:21 Moses **a** to stay with the man,
Lev 10:20 And when Moses heard that, he **a**.
Jdg 17:11 The Levite **a** to stay with the man;
2Ki 12: 8 So the priests **a** that they would neither accept
1Ch 13: 4 The whole assembly **a** to do so,
2Ch 30:23 the whole assembly **a** together to keep the festival
Da 1:14 he **a** to this proposal and tested them for ten days.
2: 9 You have **a** to speak lying and misleading words
6: 7 the governors are **a** that the king should establish
Lk 22: 5 They were greatly pleased and **a**
23:51 had not **a** to their plan and action.
Jn 9:22 for the Jews had already **a** that anyone who
Ac 5: 9 that you have **a** together to put the Spirit of
23:20 "The Jews have **a** to ask you to bring Paul down
Wis 18: 9 and with one accord **a** to the divine law,
1Mc 9:71 He **a**, and did as he said;
14:46 All the people **a** to grant Simon the right to act
14:47 So Simon accepted and **a** to be high priest,
2Mc 11:15 **a** to all that Lysias urged.
11:18 and he has **a** to what was possible.
12:12 **a** to make peace with them;
14:20 that they were of one mind, they **a** to
4Mc 4:17 Jason **a** that if the office were conferred
14: 6 **a** to go to death for its sake.

AGREEING (3) [AGREE]

Mt 20: 2 After **a** with the laborers for the usual daily wage,
Gal 2: 9 **a** that we should go to the Gentiles and they to
Rev 17:17 into their hearts to carry out his purpose by **a**

AGREEMENT (20) [AGREE]

Dt 26:17 Today you have obtained the LORD's **a**:
26:18 Today the LORD has obtained your **a**:
Jdg 20:38 the **a** between the main body of Israel and the men
Ne 9:38 Because of all this we make a firm **a** in writing,
Isa 28:15 and with Sheol we have an **a**;
28:18 and your **a** with Sheol will not stand;
Da 11: 6 to the king of the north to ratify the **a**.
1Co 1:10 be in **a** and that there be no divisions among you,
7: 5 Do not deprive one another except perhaps by **a**
2Co 6:15 What **a** does Christ have with Beliar?
6:16 What **a** has the temple of God with idols?
Wis 10: 5 the nations in wicked **a** had been put to confusion,
Sir 11:20 Stand by your **a** and attend to it,
25: 1 **a** among brothers and sisters,
41:19 Be ashamed of breaking an oath or **a**,
1Mc 7:18 for they have violated the **a** and the oath
10:26 Since you have kept your **a** with us
13:47 an **a** with them and stopped fighting against them.

2Mc 12: 1 When this **a** had been reached,
14:28 to annul their **a** when the man had done no wrong.

AGREEMENTS (1) [AGREE]
1Mc 15:27 broke all the **a** he formerly had made with Simon,

AGREES (1) [AGREE]
Ac 15:15 This **a** with the words of the prophets,

AGRIPPA (11)
Ac 25:13 King **A** and Bernice arrived at Caesarea
25:22 **A** said to Festus, "I would like to hear
25:23 the next day **A** and Bernice came with great pomp,
25:24 Festus said, "King **A** and all here present with us,
25:26 King **A**, so that, after we have examined him,
26: 1 **A** said to Paul, "You have permission to speak
26: 2 King **A**, I am to make my defense today
26:19 "After that, King **A**, I was not disobedient to
26:27 King **A**, do you believe the prophets?
26:28 **A** said to Paul, "Are you so quickly persuading me
26:32 **A** said to Festus, "This man could have been set

AGROUND (2)
Ac 27:26 But we will have to run **a** on some island."
27:41 But striking a reef, they ran the ship **a**;

AGUE (KJV) See FEVER

AGUR (1)
Pr 30: 1 The words of **A** son of Jakeh.

AH (42) [AHA]
Ge 27:27 "**A**, the smell of my son is like the smell of a field
Jos 7: 7 Joshua said, "**A**, Lord GOD!
SS 1:15 **A**, you are beautiful, my love;
1:15 **a**, you are beautiful; your eyes are doves.
1:16 **A**, you are beautiful, my beloved, truly lovely.
Isa 1: 4 **A**, sinful nation, people laden with iniquity,
1:24 **A**, I will pour out my wrath on my enemies,
5: 8 **A**, you who join house to house,
5:11 **A**, you who rise early in the morning in pursuit
5:18 **A**, you who drag iniquity along with cords
5:20 **A**, you who call evil good and good evil,
5:21 **A**, you who are wise in your own eyes,
5:22 **A**, you who are heroes in drinking wine
10: 1 **A**, you who make iniquitous decrees,
10: 5 **A**, Assyria, the rod of my anger—
17:12 **A**, the thunder of many peoples,
17:12 **A**, the roar of nations, they roar like the roaring of
18: 1 **A**, land of whirring wings beyond the rivers
28: 1 **A**, the proud garland of the drunkards of Ephraim,
29: 1 **A**, Ariel, Ariel, the city where David encamped!
33: 1 **A**, you destroyer, who yourself have
44:16 He also warms himself and says, "**A**, I am warm,
Jer 1: 6 Then I said, "**A**, Lord GOD!
4:10 Then I said, "**A**, Lord GOD,
14:13 Then I said: "**A**, Lord GOD!
32:17 **A** Lord GOD! It is you who made the heavens
47: 6 **A**, sword of the LORD!
La 2:16 **A**, this is the day we longed for;
Eze 4:14 Then I said, "**A** Lord GOD!
9: 8 on my face and cried out, "**A** Lord GOD!
11:13 cried with a loud voice, and said, "**A** Lord GOD!
20:49 Then I said, "**A** Lord GOD!
21:12 **A**! Strike the thigh!
21:15 **A**! It is made for flashing,
23:43 Then I said, **A**, she is worn out with adulteries,
34: 2 **A**, you shepherds of Israel who have been feeding
Da 9: 4 saying, "**A**, Lord, great and awesome God,
Hos 12: 8 Ephraim has said, "**A**, I am rich,
Am 5: 7 **A**, you that turn justice to wormwood,
Na 3: 1 **A**! City of bloodshed, utterly deceitful,
Zep 2: 5 **A**, inhabitants of the seacoast,
3: 1 **A**, soiled, defiled, oppressing city!

AHA (12) [AH]
Job 39:25 When the trumpet sounds, it says '**A**!'
Ps 35:21 they say, "**A**, **A**, our eyes have seen it."
35:25 Do not let them say to themselves, "**A**,
40:15 because of their shame who say to me, "**A**, **A**!"
70: 3 Let those who say, "**A**, **A**!"
Eze 25: 3 Thus says the Lord GOD, Because you said, "**A**!"
26: 2 because Tyre said concerning Jerusalem, "**A**,
36: 2 Because the enemy said of you, "**A**!"
Mk 15:29 shaking their heads and saying, "**A**!

AHAB (92) [AHAB'S]
1Ki 16:28 in Samaria; his son **A** succeeded him.
16:29 **A** son of Omri began to reign over Israel;
16:29 **A** son of Omri reigned over Israel
16:30 **A** son of Omri did evil in the sight of the LORD
16:33 **A** also made a sacred pole.
16:33 **A** did more to provoke the anger of the LORD,
17: 1 Elijah the Tishbite, of Tishbe in Gilead, said to **A**,
18: 1 saying, "Go, present yourself to **A**;
18: 2 So Elijah went to present himself to **A**.
18: 3 **A** summoned Obadiah, who was in charge of
18: 5 Then **A** said to Obadiah, "Go through the land
18: 6 **A** went in one direction by himself,
18: 9 that you would hand your servant over to **A**,
18:12 when I come and tell **A** and he cannot find you,
18:16 So Obadiah went to meet **A**, and told him;
18:16 and **A** went to meet Elijah.
18:17 When **A** saw Elijah, **A** said to him, "Is it you,
18:20 So **A** sent to all the Israelites,
18:41 Elijah said to **A**, "Go up, eat and drink;
18:42 So **A** went up to eat and to drink.
18:44 Then he said, "Go say to **A**,
18:45 **A** rode off and went to Jezreel.
18:46 up his loins and ran in front of **A** to the entrance
19: 1 **A** told Jezebel all that Elijah had done,
20: 2 into the city to King **A** of Israel, and said to him:
20:13 a certain prophet came up to King **A** of Israel
20:14 **A** said, "By whom?" He said,
21: 1 beside the palace of King **A** of Samaria.
21: 2 And **A** said to Naboth, "Give me your vineyard,
21: 3 But Naboth said to **A**, "The LORD forbid
21: 4 **A** went home resentful and sullen because
21:15 to **A**, "Go, take possession of the vineyard
21:16 As soon as **A** heard that Naboth was dead,
21:16 **A** set out to go down to the vineyard of Naboth
21:18 to meet King **A** of Israel, who rules in Samaria;
21:20 **A** said to Elijah, "Have you found me,
21:21 and will cut off from **A** every male, bond or free,
21:24 Anyone belonging to **A** who dies in the city
21:25 (Indeed, there was no one like **A**,
21:27 When **A** heard those words,
21:29 "Have you seen how **A** has humbled himself
22:20 And the LORD said, 'Who will entice **A**,
22:39 Now the rest of the acts of **A**, and all that he did,
22:40 So **A** slept with his ancestors;
22:41 over Judah in the fourth year of King **A** of Israel.
22:49 Then Ahaziah son of **A** said to Jehoshaphat,
22:51 of **A** began to reign over Israel in Samaria in
2Ki 1: 1 After the death of **A**, Moab rebelled against Israel.
3: 1 Jehoram son of **A** became king over Israel
3: 5 when **A** died, the king of Moab rebelled against
8:16 In the fifth year of King Joram son of **A** of Israel,
8:18 as the house of **A** had done, for the daughter of **A** was his wife.
8:25 the twelfth year of King Joram son of **A** of Israel,
8:27 He also walked in the way of the house of **A**,
8:27 as the house of **A** had done, for he was son-in-law to the house of **A**.
8:28 of **A** to wage war against King Hazael of Aram
8:29 of Judah went down to see Joram son of **A**
9: 7 You shall strike down the house of your master **A**,
9: 8 For the whole house of **A** shall perish;
9: 8 I will cut off from **A** every male, bond or free,
9: 9 the house of **A** like the house of Jeroboam son
9:25 and I rode side by side behind his father **A** how
9:29 In the eleventh year of Joram son of **A**,
10: 1 Now **A** had seventy sons in Samaria.
10: 1 and to the guardians of the sons of **A**, saying,
10:10 the LORD spoke concerning the house of **A**;
10:11 So Jehu killed all who were left of the house of **A**
10:17 he killed all who were left to **A** in Samaria,
10:18 "**A** offered Baal small service;
10:30 in my heart have dealt with the house of **A**,
21: 3 made a sacred pole, as King **A** of Israel had done,
21:13 and the plummet for the house of **A**;
2Ch 18: 1 and he made a marriage alliance with **A**.
18: 2 After some years he went down to **A** in Samaria.
18: 2 **A** slaughtered an abundance of sheep and oxen
18: 3 King **A** of Israel said to King Jehoshaphat
18:19 LORD said, 'Who will entice King **A** of Israel,
21: 6 as the house of **A** had done; for the daughter of **A** was his wife.
21:13 as the house of **A** led Israel into unfaithfulness,
22: 3 He also walked in the ways of the house of **A**,
22: 4 as the house of **A** had done;
22: 5 with Jehoram son of King **A** of Israel to make war
22: 6 of Judah went down to see Joram son of **A**
22: 7 to destroy the house of **A**.
22: 8 Jehu was executing judgment on the house of **A**,
Jer 29:21 concerning **A** son of Kolaiah and Zedekiah son
29:22 "The LORD make you like Zedekiah and **A**,
Mic 6:16 of Omri and all the works of the house of **A**,

AHAB'S (1) [AHAB]
1Ki 21: 8 So she wrote letters in **A** name and sealed them

AHAR See Index to Footnotes

AHARAH (1)
1Ch 8: 1 Ashbel the second, **A** the third,

AHARHEL (1)
1Ch 4: 8 Zobebah, and the families of **A** son of Harum.

AHASAI (KJV) See AHZAI

AHASBAI (1)
2Sa 23:34 Eliphelet son of **A** of Maacah;

AHASHTARI See Index to Footnotes

AHASUERUS‡ (30)
Ezr 4: 6 In the reign of **A**, in his accession year,
Est 1: 1 happened in the days of **A**, the same **A** who ruled
1: 2 In those days when King **A** sat on his royal throne
1: 9 a banquet for the women in the palace of King **A**.
1:15 not performed the command of King **A** conveyed
1:16 in all the provinces of King **A**.
1:17 'King **A** commanded Queen Vashti to be brought
1:19 that Vashti is never again to come before King **A**;
2: 1 when the anger of King **A** had abated,
2:12 The turn came for each girl to go in to King **A**,
2:16 to King **A** in his royal palace in the tenth month,
2:21 and conspired to assassinate King **A**.
3: 1 After these things King **A** promoted Haman son
3: 6 throughout the whole kingdom of **A**.
3: 7 in the twelfth year of King **A**, they cast Pur—
3: 8 Then Haman said to King **A**,
3:12 it was written in the name of King **A** and sealed
6: 2 and who had conspired to assassinate King **A**.
7: 5 Then King **A** said to Queen Esther, "Who is he,
8: 1 that day King **A** gave to Queen Esther the house
8: 7 Then King **A** said to Queen Esther and to
8:10 He wrote letters in the name of King **A**,
8:12 throughout all the provinces of King **A**,
9: 2 throughout all the provinces of King **A**
9:20 the Jews who were in all the provinces of King **A**,
9:30 provinces of the kingdom of **A**,
10: 1 King **A** laid tribute on the land and on the islands
10: 3 For Mordecai the Jew was next in rank to King **A**,
Da 9: 1 In the first year of Darius son of **A**,

AHAVA (3)
Ezr 8:15 I gathered them by the river that runs to **A**,
8:21 Then I proclaimed a fast there, at the river **A**,
8:31 the river **A** on the twelfth day of the first month,

AHAZ‡ (45)
2Ki 15:38 his ancestor; his son **A** succeeded him.
16: 1 King **A** son of Jotham of Judah began to reign.
16: 2 **A** was twenty years old when he began to reign;
16: 5 they besieged **A** but could not conquer him.
16: 7 **A** sent messengers to King Tiglath-pileser
16: 8 **A** also took the silver and gold found in the house
16:10 When King **A** went to Damascus
16:10 King **A** sent to the priest Uriah a model of
16:11 with all that King **A** had sent from Damascus,
16:11 before King **A** arrived from Damascus.
16:15 King **A** commanded the priest Uriah, saying,
16:16 Uriah did everything that King **A** commanded.
16:17 Then King **A** cut off the frames of the stands,
16:19 Now the rest of the acts of **A** that he did,
16:20 **A** slept with his ancestors,
17: 1 In the twelfth year of King **A** of Judah,
18: 1 Hezekiah son of King **A** of Judah began to reign.
20:11 by which the sun had declined on the dial of **A**.
23:12 The altars on the roof of the upper chamber of **A**,
1Ch 3:13 **A** his son, Hezekiah his son, Manasseh his son,
8:35 The sons of Micah: Pithon, Melech, Tarea, and **A**.
8:36 **A** became the father of Jehoaddah;
9:41 Pithon, Melech, Tahrea, and **A**;
9:42 and **A** became the father of Jarah, and Jarah
2Ch 27: 9 and his son **A** succeeded him.
28: 1 **A** was twenty years old when he began to reign;
28:16 At that time King **A** sent to the king of Assyria
28:19 the LORD brought Judah low because of King **A**
28:21 For **A** plundered the house of the LORD and
28:22 yet more faithless to the LORD—this same King **A**.
28:24 **A** gathered together the utensils of the house
28:27 **A** slept with his ancestors,
29:19 that King **A** repudiated during his reign
Isa 1: 1 Jotham, **A**, and Hezekiah, kings of Judah.
7: 1 In the days of **A** son of Jotham son of Uzziah,
7: 2 the heart of **A** and the heart of his people shook as
7: 3 Then the LORD said to Isaiah, Go out to meet **A**,
7:10 Again the LORD spoke to **A**, saying,
7:12 But **A** said, I will not ask,
14:28 In the year that King **A** died this oracle came:
38: 8 on the dial of **A** turn back ten steps."
Hos 1: 1 in the days of Kings Uzziah, Jotham, **A**,
Mic 1: 1 **A**, and Hezekiah of Judah,
Mt 1: 9 the father of **A**, and **A** the father of Hezekiah,

AHAZIAH (36) [AHAZIAH'S]
1Ki 22:40 and his son **A** succeeded him.
22:49 Then **A** son of Ahab said to Jehoshaphat,
22:51 **A** son of Ahab began to reign over Israel
2Ki 1: 2 **A** had fallen through the lattice
1:17 of Jehoshaphat of Judah, because **A** had no son.
1:18 Now the rest of the acts of **A** that he did,
8:24 of David; his son **A** succeeded him.
8:25 **A** son of King Jehoram of Judah began to reign.
8:26 **A** was twenty-two years old when he began
8:29 King **A** son of Jehoram of Judah went down
9:16 King **A** of Judah had come down to visit Joram.
9:21 King Joram of Israel and King **A** of Judah set out,
9:23 and fled, saying to **A**, "Treason, **A**!"
9:27 When King **A** of Judah saw this,
9:29 **A** began to reign over Judah.
10:13 Jehu met relatives of King **A** of Judah and said,
10:13 They answered, "We are kin of **A**;
11: 2 Ahaziah's sister, took Joash son of **A**,
12:18 Jehoram, and **A**, his ancestors, the kings of Judah,
13: 1 In the twenty-third year of King Joash son of **A**
14:13 son of **A**, at Beth-shemesh;
1Ch 3:11 Joram his son, **A** his son, Joash his son,
2Ch 20:35 of Judah joined with King **A** of Israel,
20:37 saying, "Because you have joined with **A**,
22: 1 of Jerusalem made his youngest son **A** king
22: 1 So **A** son of Jehoram reigned as king of Judah.
22: 2 **A** was forty-two years old when he began to reign;
22: 6 And **A** son of King Jehoram of Judah went down
22: 7 by God that the downfall of **A** should come about
22: 8 who attended **A**, and he killed them.

2Ch 22: 9 for **A,** who was captured while hiding in Samaria
22: 9 house of **A** had no one able to rule the kingdom.
22: 11 the king's daughter, took Joash son of **A,**
22: 11 because she was a sister of **A—**
25: 23 son of Joash, son of **A,** at Beth-shemesh;

AHAZIAH'S (4) [AHAZIAH]

2Ki 11: 1 Now when Athaliah, **A** mother,
11: 2 But Jehosheba, King Joram's daughter, **A** sister,
2Ch 22: 8 the officials of Judah and the sons of **A** brothers,
22: 10 Now when Athaliah, **A** mother,

AHBAN (1)

1Ch 2: 29 and she bore him **A** and Molid.

AHEAD (75)

Ge 32: 16 and said to his servants, "Pass on **a** of me,
32: 17 And whose are these **a** of you?'
32: 20 "I may appease him with the present that goes **a**
32: 21 So the present passed on **a** of him;
33: 3 He himself went on **a** of them,
33: 14 Let my lord pass on **a** of his servant,
46: 28 Israel sent Judah **a** to Joseph to lead the way
48: 20 So he put Ephraim **a** of Manasseh.
Ex 17: 5 LORD said to Moses, "Go on **a** of the people,
Nu 22: 26 Then the angel of the LORD went **a,**
Dt 1: 22 "Let us send men **a** of us to explore the land for us
Jos 6: 5 and all the people shall charge straight **a.**"
6: 20 so the people charged straight **a** into the city
24: 12 I sent the hornet **a** of you,
1Sa 9: 12 They answered, "Yes, there he is just **a** of you.
10: 8 And you shall go down to Gilgal **a** of me;
23: 24 So they set out and went to Ziph **a** of Saul.
25: 19 "Go on **a** of me; I am coming after you."
30: 20 which were driven **a** of the other cattle;
2Sa 15: 1 and fifty men to run **a** of him.
19: 17 rushed down to the Jordan **a** of the king,
1Ki 19: 19 There were twelve yoke of oxen **a** of him,
2Ki 4: 31 Gehazi went on **a** and laid the staff on the face of
Ps 105: 17 he had sent a man **a** of them,
Pr 15: 21 but a person of understanding walks straight **a.**
Eze 1: 9 each of them moved straight **a,**
1: 12 moved straight **a;** wherever the spirit would go,
10: 22 Each one moved straight **a.**
12: 27 "The vision that he sees is for many years **a;**
46: 9 but shall go out straight **a.**
Am 4: 3 in the wall you shall leave, each one straight **a;**
Mt 2: 9 there, **a** of them, went the star that they had seen
11: 10 'See, I am sending my messenger **a** of you,
14: 22 the disciples get into the boat and go on **a** to
21: 2 "Go into the village **a** of you,
21: 9 The crowds that went **a** of him and
21: 31 into the kingdom of God **a** of you.
26: 32 after I am raised up, I will go **a** of you to Galilee."
28: 7 and indeed he is going **a** of you to Galilee;
Mk 1: 2 "See, I am sending my messenger **a** of you,
6: 33 on foot from all the towns and arrived **a** of them.
6: 45 into the boat and go on **a** to the other side,
10: 32 and Jesus was walking **a** of them;
11: 2 "Go into the village **a** of you,
11: 9 Then those who went **a** and those who followed
16: 7 and Peter that he is going **a** of you to Galilee;
Lk 7: 27 'See, I am sending my messenger **a** of you,
9: 52 And he sent messengers **a** of him.
10: 1 and sent them on **a** of him in pairs to every town
19: 4 he ran **a** and climbed a sycamore tree to see him,
19: 28 After he had said this, he went on **a,**
19: 30 "Go into the village **a** of you,
24: 28 he walked **a** as if he were going on.
Jn 1: 15 'He who comes after me ranks **a** of me
1: 30 'After me comes a man who ranks **a** of me
3: 28 but I have been sent **a** of him.'
5: 7 someone else steps down **a** of me."
10: 4 he has brought out all his own, he goes **a** of them,
Ac 20: 5 They went **a** and were waiting for us in Troas;
20: 13 We went **a** to the ship and set sail for Assos,
1Co 11: 21 each of you goes **a** with your own supper,
2Co 9: 5 to urge the brothers to go on **a** to you,
Php 3: 13 behind and straining forward to what lies **a,**
Heb 11: 26 for he was looking **a** to the reward.
Tob 11: 3 Let us run **a** of your wife and prepare the house
Jdt 2: 19 to go **a** of King Nebuchadnezzar and to cover
5: 24 Therefore let us go **a,** Lord Holofernes,
11: 22 "God has done well to send you **a** of the people,
12: 15 Her maid went **a** and spread for her on the ground
Sir 12: 17 you will find him there **a** of you;
32: 10 Lightning travels **a** of the thunder,
1Mc 9: 11 the slingers and the archers went **a** of the army,
10: 23 Alexander has gotten **a** of us in forming
16: 21 But someone ran **a** and reported to John at Gazara
2Mc 8: 8 he was pushing **a** with more frequent successes,

AHER (1)

1Ch 7: 12 the sons of Ir, Hushim the son of **A.**

AHI (2)

1Ch 5: 15 **A** son of Abdiel, son of Guni, was chief
7: 34 sons of Shemer: **A,** Rohgah, Hubbah, and Aram.

AHIAH (1)

Ne 10: 26 **A,** Hanan, Anan,

AHIAM (2)

2Sa 23: 33 **A** son of Sharar the Hararite;
1Ch 11: 35 **A** son of Sachar the Hararite, Eliphal son of Ur,

AHIAN (1)

1Ch 7: 19 The sons of Shemida were **A,** Shechem, Likhi,

AHIEZER (6)

Nu 1: 12 From Dan, **A** son of Ammishaddai.
2: 25 of the Danites shall be **A** son of Ammishaddai,
7: 66 On the tenth day **A** son of Ammishaddai,
7: 71 This was the offering of **A** son of Ammishaddai.
10: 25 the whole company was **A** son of Ammishaddai.
1Ch 12: 3 The chief was **A,** then Joash,

AHIHUD (2)

Nu 34: 27 And of the tribe of the Asherites a leader, **A** son
1Ch 8: 7 Heglam, who became the father of Uzza and **A.**

AHIJAH (25)

1Sa 14: 3 along with **A** son of Ahitub,
14: 18 Saul said to **A,** "Bring the ark of God here."
1Ki 4: 3 Elihoreph and **A** sons of Shisha were secretaries;
11: 29 the prophet **A** the Shilonite found him on the road.
11: 29 **A** had clothed himself with a new garment.
11: 30 **A** laid hold of the new garment he was wearing
12: 15 which the LORD had spoken by **A** the Shilonite
14: 2 for the prophet **A** is there,
14: 4 and came to the house of **A.**
14: 4 Now **A** could not see, for his eyes were dim
14: 5 But the LORD said to **A,**
14: 6 But when **A** heard the sound of her feet,
14: 18 which he spoke by his servant the prophet **A.**
15: 27 Baasha son of **A,** of the house of Issachar,
15: 29 that he spoke by his servant **A** the Shilonite—
15: 33 Baasha son of **A** began to reign over all Israel
21: 22 and like the house of Baasha son of **A,**
2Ki 9: 9 and like the house of Baasha son of **A.**
1Ch 2: 25 Ram his firstborn, Bunah, Oren, Ozem, and **A.**
8: 7 **A,** and Gera, that is, Heglam,
11: 36 Hepher the Mecherathite, **A** the Pelonite,
26: 20 **A** had charge of the treasuries of the house of God
2Ch 9: 29 and in the prophecy of **A** the Shilonite,
10: 15 by **A** the Shilonite to Jeroboam son of Nebat.
2Es 1: 2 son of **A** son of Phinehas son of Eli son

AHIKAM (20)

2Ki 22: 12 **A** son of Shaphan, Achbor son of Micaiah,
22: 14 So the priest Hilkiah, **A,** Achbor, Shaphan,
25: 22 He appointed Gedaliah son of **A** son of Shaphan
2Ch 34: 20 the king commanded Hilkiah, **A** son of Shaphan,
Jer 26: 24 the hand of **A** son of Shaphan was with Jeremiah
39: 14 They entrusted him to Gedaliah son of **A** son
40: 5 then return to Gedaliah son of **A** son of Shaphan,
40: 6 Jeremiah went to Gedaliah son of **A** at Mizpah,
40: 7 Gedaliah son of **A** governor in the land,
40: 9 Gedaliah son of **A** son of Shaphan swore to them
40: 11 in Judah and had appointed Gedaliah son of **A** son
40: 14 But Gedaliah son of **A** would not believe them.
40: 16 Gedaliah son of **A** said to Johanan son of Kareah,
41: 1 came with ten men to Gedaliah son of **A,**
41: 2 down Gedaliah son of **A** son of Shaphan with
41: 6 he said to them, "Come to Gedaliah son of **A.**"
41: 10 had committed to Gedaliah son of **A.**
41: 16 from Mizpah after he had slain Gedaliah son of **A**
41: 18 of Nethaniah had killed Gedaliah son of **A,**
43: 6 of the guard had left with Gedaliah son of **A** son

AHIKAR‡ (9)

Tob 1: 21 He appointed **A,** the son of my brother Hanael
1: 22 **A** interceded for me, and I returned to Nineveh.
1: 22 Now **A** was chief cupbearer, keeper of the signet,
2: 10 and **A** took care of me for two years
11: 18 **A** and his nephew Nadab were also present
14: 10 my son, what Nadab did to **A** who had reared him.
14: 10 **A** came out into the light,
14: 10 because he tried to kill **A.**
14: 10 **A** escaped the fatal trap that Nadab had set

AHILUD (5)

2Sa 8: 16 Jehoshaphat son of **A** was recorder;
20: 24 Jehoshaphat son of **A** was the recorder;
1Ki 4: 3 Jehoshaphat son of **A** was recorder;
4: 12 Baana son of **A,** in Taanach, Megiddo,
1Ch 18: 15 Jehoshaphat son of **A** was recorder;

AHIMAAZ (15)

1Sa 14: 50 name of Saul's wife was Ahinoam daughter of **A.**
2Sa 15: 27 you and Abiathar, with your two sons, **A** your son,
15: 36 Zadok's son **A** and Abiathar's son Jonathan;
17: 17 Jonathan and **A** were waiting at En-rogel;
17: 20 they said, "Where are **A** and Jonathan?"
18: 19 Then **A** son of Zadok said, "Let me run,
18: 22 Then **A** son of Zadok said again to Joab,
18: 23 Then **A** ran by the way of the Plain,
18: 27 of the first one is like the running of **A** son
18: 28 Then **A** cried out to the king, "All is well!"
18: 29 **A** answered, "When Joab sent your servant,
1Ki 4: 15 **A,** in Naphtali (he had taken Basemath,
1Ch 6: 8 Ahitub of Zadok, Zadok of **A,**
6: 9 **A** of Azariah, Azariah of Johanan,
6: 53 Zadok his son, **A** his son.

AHIMAN (4)

Nu 13: 22 **A,** Sheshai, and Talmai, the Anakites, were there.
Jos 15: 14 Sheshai, **A,** and Talmai, the descendants of Anak.
Jdg 1: 10 and they defeated Sheshai and **A** and Talmai.
1Ch 9: 17 Shallum, Akkub, Talmon, **A;**

AHIMELECH (18)

1Sa 21: 1 David came to Nob to the priest **A.**
21: 1 **A** came trembling to meet David, and said to him,
21: 2 David said to the priest **A,**
21: 8 David said to **A,** "Is there no spear or sword here
22: 9 of Jesse coming to Nob, to **A** son of Ahitub;
22: 11 The king sent for the priest **A** son of Ahitub and
22: 14 Then **A** answered the king,
22: 16 The king said, "You shall surely die, **A,**
22: 20 But one of the sons of **A** son of Ahitub,
23: 6 When Abiathar son of **A** fled to David at Keilah,
26: 6 Then David said to **A** the Hittite,
30: 7 David said to the priest Abiathar son of **A,**
2Sa 8: 17 of Ahitub and **A** son of Abiathar were priests;
1Ch 18: 16 of Ahitub and **A** son of Abiathar were priests;
24: 3 and **A** of the sons of Ithamar,
24: 6 and Zadok the priest, and **A** son of Abiathar,
24: 31 in the presence of King David, Zadok, **A,**
Ps 52: T *"David has come to the house of* **A.**"

AHIMOTH (1)

1Ch 6: 25 The sons of Elkanah: Amasai and **A,**

AHINADAB (1)

1Ki 4: 14 **A** son of Iddo, in Mahanaim;

AHINOAM (7)

1Sa 14: 50 name of Saul's wife was **A** daughter of Ahimaaz.
25: 43 David also married **A** of Jezreel;
27: 3 and David with his two wives, **A** of Jezreel,
30: 5 **A** of Jezreel, and Abigail the widow of Nabal
2Sa 2: 2 along with his two wives, **A** of Jezreel,
3: 2 his firstborn was Amnon, of **A** of Jezreel;
1Ch 3: 1 the firstborn Amnon, by **A** the Jezreelite;

AHIO (6)

2Sa 6: 3 Uzzah and **A,** the sons of Abinadab,
6: 4 and **A** went in front of the ark.
1Ch 8: 14 and **A,** Shashak, and Jeremoth.
8: 31 Gedor, **A,** Zecher,
9: 37 Gedor, **A,** Zechariah, and Mikloth;
13: 7 and Uzzah and **A** were driving the cart.

AHIRA (5)

Nu 1: 15 From Naphtali, **A** son of Enan.
2: 29 leader of the Naphtalites shall be **A** son of Enan,
7: 78 On the twelfth day **A** son of Enan,
7: 83 This was the offering of **A** son of Enan.
10: 27 the company of the tribe of Naphtali was **A** son

AHIRAM (1) [AHIRAMITES]

Nu 26: 38 of **A,** the clan of the Ahiramites;

AHIRAMITES (1) [AHIRAM]

Nu 26: 38 of Ahiram, the clan of the **A;**

AHISAMACH (3)

Ex 31: 6 I have appointed with him Oholiab son of **A,**
35: 34 both him and Oholiab son of **A,**
38: 23 and with him was Oholiab son of **A,**

AHISHAHAR (1)

1Ch 7: 10 Ehud, Chenaanah, Zethan, Tarshish, and **A.**

AHISHAR (1)

1Ki 4: 6 **A** was in charge of the palace;

AHITHOPHEL (20)

2Sa 15: 12 he sent for **A** the Gilonite, David's counselor,
15: 31 David was told that **A** was among the conspirators
15: 31 I pray you, turn the counsel of **A** into foolishness."
15: 34 then you will defeat for me the counsel of **A.**
16: 15 to Jerusalem; **A** was with him.
16: 20 Then Absalom said to **A,** "Give us your counsel;
16: 21 **A** said to Absalom, "Go in to your father's
16: 23 Now in those days the counsel that **A** gave was as
16: 23 so all the counsel of **A** was esteemed,
17: 1 Moreover **A** said to Absalom,
17: 6 Absalom said to him, "This is what **A** has said;
17: 7 "This time the counsel that **A** has given is
17: 14 the Archite is better than the counsel of **A.**"
17: 14 to defeat the good counsel of **A,**
17: 15 so did **A** counsel Absalom and the elders of Israel;
17: 21 for thus and so has **A** counseled against you."
17: 23 When **A** saw that his counsel was not followed,
23: 34 Eliam son of **A** the Gilonite;
1Ch 27: 33 **A** was the king's counselor,
27: 34 **A** came Jehoiada son of Benaiah, and Abiathar.

AHITUB (18)

1Sa 14: 3 along with Ahijah son of **A,**
22: 9 of Jesse coming to Nob, to Ahimelech son of **A;**
22: 11 The king sent for the priest Ahimelech son of **A**
22: 12 Saul said, "Listen now, son of **A.**"

1Sa 22:20 But one of the sons of Ahimelech son of **A**,
2Sa 8:17 of **A** and Ahimelech son of Abiathar were priests;
1Ch 6: 7 Meraioth of Amariah, Amariah of **A**,
6: 8 **A** of Zadok, Zadok of Ahimaaz,
6:11 the father of Amariah, Amariah of **A**,
6:12 **A** of Zadok, Zadok of Shallum,
6:52 Meraioth his son, Amariah his son, **A** his son,
9:11 son of **A**, the chief officer of the house of God;
18:16 of **A** and Ahimelech son of Abiathar were priests;
Ezr 7: 2 son of Shallum, son of Zadok, son of **A**,
Ne 11:11 of Zadok son of Meraioth son of **A**,
Jdt 8: 1 of **A** son of Elijah son of Hilkiah son of Eliab son
1Es 8: 2 of Zadok son of **A** son of Amariah son of Uzzi son
2Es 1: 1 of Hilkiah son of Shallum son of Zadok son of **A**

AHLAB (1)
Jdg 1:31 or the inhabitants of Sidon, or of **A**, or of Achzib,

AHLAI (2)
1Ch 2:31 The son of Sheshan: **A**.
11:41 Uriah the Hittite, Zabad son of **A**,

AHOAH (1)
1Ch 8: 4 Abishua, Naaman, **A**,

AHOHI (1) [AHOHITE]
2Sa 23: 9 three warriors was Eleazar son of Dodo son of **A**.

AHOHITE (4) [AHOHI]
2Sa 23:28 Zalmon the **A**; Maharai of Netophah;
1Ch 11:12 the three warriors was Eleazar son of Dodo, the **A**.
11:29 Sibbecai the Hushathite, Ilai the **A**,
27: 4 Dodai the **A** was in charge of the division of

AHOLAH (KJV) See OHOLAH

AHOLIAB (KJV) See OHOLIAB

AHOLIBAH (KJV) See OHOLIBAH

AHOLIBAMAH (KJV) See OHOLIBAMAH

AHUMAI (1)
1Ch 4: 2 and Jahath became the father of **A** and Lahad.

AHUZZAM (1)
1Ch 4: 6 Naarah bore him **A**, Hepher, Temeni,

AHUZZATH (1)
Ge 26:26 with **A** his adviser and Phicol the commander

AHZAI (1)
Ne 11:13 of Azarel son of **A** son of Meshillemoth son

AI (37)
Ge 12: 8 with Bethel on the west and **A** on the east;
13: 3 at the beginning, between Bethel and **A**,
Jos 7: 2 Joshua sent men from Jericho to **A**,
7: 2 And the men went up and spied out **A**.
7: 3 or three thousand men should go up and attack **A**.
7: 4 and they fled before the men of **A**.
7: 5 The men of **A** killed about thirty-six of them,
8: 1 the fighting men with you, and go up now to **A**.
8: 1 over to you the king of **A** with his people,
8: 2 You shall do to **A** and its king as you did
8: 3 and all the fighting men set out to go up against **A**.
8: 9 and lay between Bethel and **A**, to the west of **A**;
8:10 with the elders of Israel, before the people to **A**.
8:11 and camped on the north side of **A**,
8:11 with a ravine between them and **A**.
8:12 he set them in ambush between Bethel and **A**,
8:14 When the king of **A** saw this,
8:17 There was not a man left in **A** or Bethel who did
8:18 the sword that is in your hand toward **A**;
8:20 So when the men of **A** looked back,
8:21 they turned back and struck down the men of **A**.
8:23 king of **A** was taken alive and brought to Joshua.
8:24 the inhabitants of **A** in the open wilderness
8:24 the sword, all Israel returned to **A**, and attacked it
8:25 was twelve thousand—all the people of **A**.
8:26 he had utterly destroyed all the inhabitants of **A**.
8:28 So Joshua burned **A**, and made it forever a heap
8:29 he hanged the king of **A** on a tree until evening;
9: 3 heard what Joshua had done to Jericho and to **A**,
10: 1 Jerusalem heard how Joshua had taken **A**,
10: 1 doing to **A** and its king as he had done to Jericho
10: 2 like one of the royal cities, and was larger than **A**,
12: 9 the king of Jericho one the king of **A**,
Ezr 2:28 Of Bethel and **A**, two hundred twenty-three.
Ne 7:32 Of Bethel and **A**, one hundred twenty-three.
Jer 49: 3 Wail, O Heshbon, for **A** is laid waste!

AIAH (6)
Ge 36:24 These are the sons of Zibeon: **A** and Anah;
2Sa 3: 7 concubine whose name was Rizpah daughter of **A**.
21: 8 king took the two sons of Rizpah daughter of **A**,
21:10 Then Rizpah the daughter of **A** took sackcloth,
21:11 When David was told what Rizpah daughter of **A**,
1Ch 1:40 The sons of Zibeon: **A** and Anah.

AIATH (1)
Isa 10:28 he has come to **A**; he has passed

AID (16) [AIDE, AIDED, AIDING]
2Sa 21:17 But Abishai son of Zeruiah came to his **a**,
Ps 22:19 O my help, come quickly to my **a**!
Eze 16:49 but did not **a** the poor and needy.
29:16 when they turned to them for **a**.
AdE 15: 2 invoking the **a** of the all-seeing God and Savior,
Wis 13:18 **a** he entreats a thing that is utterly inexperienced;
1Mc 11:47 So the king called the Jews to his **a**,
12:15 the help that comes from Heaven for our **a**,
16:18 to send troops to **a** him and to turn over to him
2Mc 3:39 over that place himself and brings it **a**,
8: 8 to come to the **a** of the king's government.
11: 7 to risk their lives with him to **a** their kindred.
3Mc 1:16 the supreme God to **a** in the present situation and
5: 6 that the Jews were left without any **a**,
5:35 since this also was his **a** that they had received.
4Mc 13:26 with the **a** of their religion.

AIDE (1) [AID]
2Ki 9:25 Jehu said to his **a** Bidkar, "Lift him out,

AIDED (2) [AID]
Ezr 1: 6 All their neighbors **a** them with silver vessels,
6:22 so that he **a** them in the work on the house of God,

AIDING (1) [AID]
3Mc 4:21 of the invincible providence of him who was **a**

AIJA (1)
Ne 11:31 at Michmash, **A**, Bethel and its villages,

AIJALON (10)
Jos 10:12 and Moon, in the valley of **A**."
19:42 Shaalabbin, **A**, Ithlah,
21:24 **A** with its pasture lands, Gath-rimmon
Jdg 1:35 The Amorites continued to live in Har-heres, in **A**,
12:12 and was buried at **A** in the land of Zebulun.
1Sa 14:31 from Michmash to **A**, the troops were very faint;
1Ch 6:69 **A** with its pasture lands, Gath-rimmon
8:13 of **A**, who put to flight the inhabitants of Gath);
2Ch 11:10 **A**, and Hebron, fortified cities that are in Judah
28:18 and had taken Beth-shemesh, **A**, Gederoth,

AILMENT (1) [AILMENTS]
Lk 13:12 "Woman, you are set free from your **a**."

AILMENTS (1) [AILMENT]
1Ti 5:23 for the sake of your stomach and your frequent **a**.

AIM (8) [AIMED, AIMLESSLY]
Ps 21:12 you will **a** at their faces with your bows.
64: 3 who **a** bitter words like arrows,
2Co 5: 9 we make it our **a** to please him.
1Ti 1: 5 the **a** of such instruction is love that comes from
2Ti 2: 4 the soldier's **a** is to please the enlisting officer.
3:10 my conduct, my **a** in life, my faith, my patience,
Wis 5:21 Shafts of lightning will fly with true **a**,
Sir 9:14 As much as you can, **a** to know your neighbors,

AIMED (1) [AIM]
2Mc 2:25 we have **a** to please those who wish to read,

AIMLESSLY (2) [AIM]
Ex 14: 3 'They are wandering **a** in the land;
1Co 9:26 So I do not run **a**, nor do I box as though beating

AIN (5)
Nu 34:11 from Shepham to Riblah on the east side of **A**;
Jos 15:32 Shilhim, **A**, and Rimmon:
19: 7 **A**, Rimmon, Ether, and Ashan—
21:16 **A** with its pasture lands, Juttah
1Ch 4:32 And their villages were Etam, **A**, Rimmon,

AIR‡ (81) [AIRS]
Ge 1:26 and over the birds of the **a**, and over the cattle,
1:28 the **a** and over every living thing that moves upon
1:30 and to every bird of the **a**,
2:19 the field and every bird of the **a**, and brought them
2:20 and to the birds of the **a**,
6: 7 and creeping things and birds of the **a**,
7: 3 and seven pairs of the birds of the **a** also,
7:23 and creeping things and birds of the **a**;
9: 2 and on every bird of the **a**,
Ex 9: 8 let Moses throw it in the **a** in the sight of Pharaoh.
9:10 and Moses threw it in the **a**,
Dt 4:17 the likeness of any winged bird that flies in the **a**,
28:26 Your corpses shall be food for every bird of the **a**
1Sa 17:44 and I will give your flesh to the birds of the **a** and
17:46 to the birds of the **a** and to the wild animals of
2Sa 21:10 not allow the birds of the **a** to come on the bodies
1Ki 14:11 the birds of the **a** shall eat;
16: 4 in the field the birds of the **a** shall eat."
21:24 in the open country the birds of the **a** shall eat."
Job 2:12 they tore their robes and threw dust in the **a**
12: 7 the birds of the **a**, and they will tell you;
28:21 and concealed from the birds of the **a**.
35:11 and makes us wiser than the birds of the **a**?'
Job 41:16 near to another that no **a** can come between them.
Ps 8: 8 of the **a**, and the fish of the sea, whatever passes
50:11 I know all the birds of the **a**,
79: 2 the bodies of your servants to the birds of the **a**
104:12 the streams the birds of the **a** have their habitation;
Ecc 10:20 for a bird of the **a** may carry your voice,
Jer 4:25 and all the birds of the **a** had fled.
7:33 the birds of the **a**, and for the animals of the earth;
9:10 both the birds of the **a** and the animals have fled
14: 6 they pant for **a** like jackals;
15: 3 the birds of the **a** and the wild animals of the earth
16: 4 for the birds of the **a** and for the wild animals of
19: 7 to the birds of the **a** and to the wild animals of
34:20 for the birds of the **a** and the wild animals of
Eze 29: 5 the earth and to the birds of the **a** I have given you
31: 6 the birds of the **a** made their nests in its boughs;
31:13 On its fallen trunk settle all the birds of the **a**,
32: 4 will cause all the birds of the **a** to settle on you,
38:20 and the birds of the **a**, and the animals of the field,
Da 2:38 the birds of the **a**, and whom he has established
4:12 the birds of the **a** nested in its branches,
4:21 in whose branches the birds of the **a** had nests—
Hos 2:18 of the **a**, and the creeping things of the ground;
4: 3 with the wild animals and the birds of the **a**,
7:12 I will bring them down like birds of the **a**;
Zep 1: 3 I will sweep away the birds of the **a** and the fish of
Mt 6:26 Look at the birds of the **a**;
8:20 "Foxes have holes, and birds of the **a** have nests;
13:32 birds of the **a** come and make nests in its branches.
Mk 4:32 that the birds of the **a** can make nests in its shade."
Lk 8: 5 and the birds of the **a** ate it up.
9:58 "Foxes have holes, and birds of the **a** have nests;
13:19 and the birds of the **a** made nests in its branches."
Ac 10:12 and reptiles and birds of the **a**.
11: 6 beasts of prey, reptiles, and birds of the **a**.
22:23 and tossing dust into the **a**,
1Co 9:26 nor do I box as though beating the **a**;
14: 9 For you will be speaking into the **a**.
Eph 2: 2 following the ruler of the power of the **a**,
1Th 4:17 with them to meet the Lord in the **a**;
Rev 9: 2 the sun and the **a** were darkened with the smoke
16:17 The seventh angel poured his bowl into the **a**,
Jdt 11: 7 and the cattle and the birds of the **a** will live,
Wis 2: 3 and the spirit will dissolve like empty **a**.
5:11 when a bird flies through the **a**,
5:11 the light **a**, lashed by the beat of its pinions
5:12 the **a**, thus divided, comes together at once,
7: 3 I was born, I began to breathe the common **a**,
13: 2 they supposed that either fire or wind or swift **a**,
17:10 refusing to look even at the **a**,
Bar 3:17 of the birds of the **a**, and who hoarded up silver
Aza 1:58 Bless the Lord, all birds of the **a**;
2Mc 4:24 extolled him with an **a** of authority,
5: 2 the **a**, in companies fully armed with lances
1Es 9:11 and we are not able to stand in the open **a**.
2Es 6: 4 and before the heights of the **a** were lifted up,
7:*40* or wind or water or **a**,
8:20 and whose upper chambers are in the **a**,

AIRS (1) [AIR]
2Co 11:20 or puts on **a**, or gives you a slap in the face.

AJAH (KJV) See AIAH

AJALON (KJV) See AIJALON

AKAN‡ (1)
Ge 36:27 These are the sons of Ezer: Bilhan, Zaavan, and **A**.

AKKUB (11)
1Ch 3:24 Hodaviah, Eliashib, Pelaiah, **A**, Johanan, Delaiah,
9:17 Shallum, **A**, Talmon, Ahiman;
Ezr 2:42 of Shallum, of Ater, of Talmon, of **A**, of Hatita,
2:45 Lebanah, Hagabah, **A**,
Ne 7:45 descendants of Shallum, of Ater, of Talmon, of **A**,
8: 7 Also Jeshua, Bani, Sherebiah, Jamin, **A**,
11:19 The gatekeepers, **A**, Talmon and their associates,
12:25 and **A** were gatekeepers standing guard at
1Es 5:28 the descendants of Talmon, the descendants of **A**,
5:30 the descendants of **A**, the descendants of Uthai,
9:48 Jeshua and Anniuth and Sherebiah, Jadinus, **A**,

AKRABATTENE (1)
1Mc 5: 3 at **A**, because they kept lying in wait for Israel.

AKRABBIM (3)
Nu 34: 4 your boundary shall turn south of the ascent of **A**,
Jos 15: 3 it goes out southward of the ascent of **A**,
Jdg 1:36 border of the Amorites ran from the ascent of **A**,

ALABASTER (4)
SS 5:15 His legs are **a** columns, set upon bases of gold.
Mt 26: 7 to him with an **a** jar of very costly ointment,
Mk 14: 3 with an **a** jar of very costly ointment of nard,
Lk 7:37 brought an **a** jar of ointment.

ALAMMELECH (KJV) See ALLAMMELECH

ALAMOTH (2)
1Ch 15:20 and Benaiah were to play harps according to **A**;
Ps 46: T *Of the Korahites. According to **A**. A Song.*

ALARM (18) [ALARMED, ALARMS]
Nu 10: 5 an a, the camps on the east side shall set out;
10: 6 when you blow a second a,
10: 6 An a is to be blown whenever they are to set out.
10: 7 you shall blow, but you shall not sound an a.
10: 9 you shall sound an a with the trumpets,
31: 6 the sanctuary and the trumpets for sounding the a
Ps 31:22 I had said in my a,
Jer 4:19 for I hear the sound of the trumpet, the a of war.
20:16 let him hear a cry in the morning and an a at noon,
36:16 they turned to one another in a,
49: 2 when I will sound the battle a against Rabbah of
Eze 19: 4 The nations sounded an a against him;
Da 11:44 reports from the east and the north shall a him,
Hos 5: 8 Sound the a at Beth-aven;
Joel 2: 1 sound the a on my holy mountain!
2Co 7:11 what indignation, what a, what longing,
1Pe 3: 6 as you do what is good and never let fears a you.
AdE 15: 8 and in a he sprang from his throne and took her

ALARMED (11) [ALARM]
Jer 36:24 was a, nor did they tear their garments.
Mt 24: 6 see that you are not a;
Mk 13: 7 you hear of wars and rumors of wars, do not be a;
16: 5 on the right side; and they were a.
16: 6 But he said to them, "Do not be a;
Ac 20:10 and said, "Do not be a, for his life is in him."
2Th 2: 2 not to be quickly shaken in mind or a,
Jdt 4: 2 they were a both for Jerusalem and for the temple
14: 7 every nation those who hear your name will be a.
Wis 17: 3 terribly a, and appalled by specters.
1Mc 10: 8 They were greatly a when they heard that

ALARMS (1) [ALARM]
SS 3: 8 with his sword at his thigh because of a by night.

ALAS (51)
Ge 42:21 They said to one another, "A,
48: 7 For when I came from Paddan, Rachel, a,
Ex 32:31 So Moses returned to the LORD and said, "A,
Nu 24:23 "A, who shall live when God does this?
Jdg 11:35 he saw her, he tore his clothes, and said, "A,
2Sa 14: 5 She answered, "A, I am a widow;
1Ki 13:30 they mourned over him, saying, "A, my brother!"
2Ki 3:10 Then the king of Israel said, "A!
6: 5 into the water; he cried out, "A,
6:15 His servant said, "A, master!
Ecc 10:16 A for you, O land, when your king is a servant,
Isa 31: 1 A for those who go down to Egypt for help
Jer 22:18 for him, saying, "A, my brother!" or "A, sister!"
22:18 for him, saying, "A, lord!" or "A, his majesty!"
30: 7 A! that day is so great there is none like it;
34: 5 for you and lament for you, saying, "A, lord!"
48: 1 A for Nebo, it is laid waste!
50:27 A for them, their day has come,
Eze 6:11 Clap your hands and stamp your foot, and say, A
13: 3 Thus says the Lord GOD, A for
30: 2 Thus says the Lord GOD: Wail, "A for the day!"
Joel 1:15 A for the day! For the day of the
Am 5:16 and in all the streets they shall say, "A! a!"
5:18 A for you who desire the day of the LORD!
6: 1 A for those who are at ease in Zion,
6: 4 A for those who lie on beds of ivory,
Mic 2: 1 A for those who devise wickedness and evil deeds
Hab 2: 6 "A for you who heap up what is not your own!"
2: 9 "A for you who get evil gain for your houses,
2:12 "A for you who build a town by bloodshed,
2:15 "A for you who make your neighbors drink,
2:19 A for you who say to the wood, "Wake up!"
Rev 18:10 "A, a, the great city, Babylon, the mighty city!
18:16 "A, a, the great city, clothed in fine linen,
18:19 "A, a, the great city, where all who had ships at sea
1Mc 2: 7 and said, "A! Why was I born to see
2Es 13:16 a for those who will be left in those days!
13:16 And still more, a for those who are not left!
13:19 But a for those also who are left,
15:14 A for the world and for those who live in it!
15:24 A for those who sin and do not observe
16:17 A for me! A for me! Who will deliver me in those
4Mc 16: 9 A for my children, some unmarried,
16:10 A, I who had so many and beautiful children am

ALCIMUS (16)
1Mc 7: 5 they were led by A, who wanted to be high priest.
7: 9 He sent him, and with him he sent the ungodly A,
7:12 a group of scribes appeared in a body before A
7:15 A spoke peaceable words to them
7:20 He placed A in charge of the country and left
7:21 A struggled to maintain his high priesthood,
7:23 the wrongs that A and those with him had done
7:25 When A saw that Judas and those
9: 1 he sent Bacchides and A into the land of Judah
9:54 A gave orders to tear down the wall of
9:55 for at that time A was stricken
9:56 And A died at that time in great agony.
9:57 When Bacchides saw that A was dead,
2Mc 14: 3 a certain A, who had formerly been high priest
14:13 and to install A as high priest of the great temple.
14:26 when A noticed their goodwill for one another,

ALEMA‡ (1)
1Mc 5:26 in A and Chaspho, Maked and Carnaim"—

ALEMETH (4)
1Ch 6:60 with its pasture lands, A with its pasture lands,
7: 8 Omri, Jeremoth, Abijah, Anathoth, and A.
8:36 and Jehoaddah became the father of A, Azmaveth,
9:42 and Jarah of A, Azmaveth, and Zimri;

ALERT (14)
Jos 8: 4 not go very far from the city, but all of you stay a.
2Sa 5:24 in the tops of the balsam trees, then be on the a;
2Ki 6:10 a place so that it was on the a.
Isa 29:20 all those a to do evil shall be cut off—
Mk 13:23 But be a; I have already told you everything.
13:33 keep a; for you do not know
Lk 12:37 Blessed are those slaves whom the master finds a
21:36 Be a at all times, praying that you may have
Ac 20:31 be a, remembering that for three years I did
1Co 16:13 Keep a, stand firm in your faith, be courageous,
Eph 6:18 To that end keep a and always persevere
Col 4: 2 keeping a in it with thanksgiving.
1Pe 5: 8 Discipline yourselves, keep a.
1Mc 12:27 to be a and to keep their arms at hand so as to

ALEXANDER (31) [ALEXANDER'S]
Mk 15:21 the father of A and Rufus.
Ac 4: 6 with Annas the high priest, Caiaphas, John, and A,
19:33 Some of the crowd gave instructions to A,
19:33 And A motioned for silence and tried to make
1Ti 1:20 among them are Hymenaeus and A,
2Ti 4:14 A the coppersmith did me great harm;
1Mc 1: 1 After A son of Philip, the Macedonian,
1: 7 And after A had reigned twelve years, he died.
6: 2 and weapons left there by A son of Philip,
10: 1 In the one hundred sixtieth year A Epiphanes,
10: 4 before he makes peace with A against us,
10:15 Now King A heard of all the promises
10:18 "King A to his brother Jonathan, greetings.
10:23 A has gotten ahead of us in forming a friendship
10:47 They favored A, because he had been the first
10:48 Now King A assembled large forces
10:49 and A pursued him and defeated them.
10:51 Then A sent ambassadors to Ptolemy king
10:58 King A met him, and Ptolemy gave him
10:59 King A wrote to Jonathan to come and meet him.
10:68 When King A heard of it,
10:88 When King A heard of these things,
11: 2 for King A had commanded them to meet him,
11: 8 and he kept devising wicked designs against A.
11:11 on A because he coveted his kingdom.
11:12 He was estranged from A,
11:14 Now King A was in Cilicia at that time,
11:15 When A heard of it, he came against him in battle.
11:16 So A fled into Arabia to find protection there,
11:17 Zabdiel the Arab cut off the head of A and sent it
11:39 up Antiochus, the young son of A,

ALEXANDER'S (4) [ALEXANDER]
1Mc 11: 1 and he tried to get possession of A kingdom
11: 2 since he was A father-in-law.
11: 9 in marriage my daughter who was A wife,
11:39 Trypho had formerly been one of A supporters;

ALEXANDRIA (2) [ALEXANDRIAN, ALEXANDRIANS]
Ac 18:24 to Ephesus a Jew named Apollos, a native of A.
3Mc 3: 1 in A, but was still more bitterly hostile

ALEXANDRIAN (3) [ALEXANDRIA]
Ac 27: 6 an A ship bound for Italy and put us on board.
28:11 A ship with the Twin Brothers as its figurehead.
3Mc 3:21 both to deem them worthy of A citizenship and

ALEXANDRIANS (2) [ALEXANDRIA]
Ac 6: 9 A, and others of those from Cilicia and Asia,
3Mc 2:30 they shall have equal citizenship with the A."

ALGUM (3) [ALMUG]
2Ch 2: 8 cypress, and a timber from Lebanon,
9:10 from Ophir brought a wood and precious stones.
9:11 the a wood, the king made steps for the house

ALIAH (1) [=ALVAH]
1Ch 1:51 The clans of Edom were: clans Timna, A, Jetheth,

ALIAN (1) [=ALVAN]
1Ch 1:40 A, Manahath, Ebal, Shephi, and Onam.

ALIEN‡ (79) [ALIEN'S, ALIENS]
Ge 12:10 down to Egypt to reside there as an a,
17: 8 the land where you are now an a,
19: 9 And they said, "This fellow came here as an a,
20: 1 While residing in Gerar as an a,
21:23 and with the land where you have resided as an a."
21:34 as an a many days in the land of the Philistines.
23: 4 "I am a stranger and an a residing among you;
26: 3 Reside in this land as an a, and I will be with you,
28: 4 of the land where you now live as an a—
32: 4 'I have lived with Laban as an a,
37: 1 in the land where his father had lived as an a,
Ex 2:22 "I have been an a residing in a foreign land."
12:19 whether an a or a native of the land.
12:48 If an a who resides with you wants to celebrate
Ex 12:49 be one law for the native and for the a who resides
18: 3 "I have been an a in a foreign land"),
20:10 your livestock, or the a resident in your towns.
22:21 You shall not wrong or oppress a resident a,
23: 9 You shall not oppress a resident a;
23: 9 you know the heart of an a,
23:12 and your homeborn slave and the resident a may
Lev 16:29 the citizen nor the a who resides among you.
17:12 nor shall any a who resides among you eat blood.
18:26 either the citizen or the a who resides among you
19:10 you shall leave them for the poor and the a:
19:33 When an a resides with you in your land,
19:33 you shall not oppress the a.
19:34 The a who resides with you shall be to you as
19:34 you shall love the a as yourself,
23:22 you shall leave them for the poor and for the a:
24:22 You shall have one law for the a and for
25:47 with one of them and sell themselves to an a,
25:50 from the year when they sold themselves to the a
Nu 9:14 Any a residing among you who wishes to keep
9:14 you shall have one statute for both the resident a
15:14 An a who lives with you,
15:15 for both you and the resident a a single statute,
15:15 you and the a shall be alike before the LORD.
15:16 You and the a who resides with you shall have
15:29 the native among the Israelites and the a residing
15:30 whether a native or an a, affronts the LORD,
19:10 the Israelites and for the a residing among them.
35:15 for the resident or transient a among them,
Dt 1:16 whether citizen or resident a.
5:14 or the resident a in your towns,
23: 7 because you were an a residing in their land.
24:17 not deprive a resident a or an orphan of justice;
24:19 it shall be left for the a, the orphan,
24:20 it shall be for the a, the orphan, and the widow.
24:21 it shall be for the a, the orphan, and the widow.
26: 5 he went down into Egypt and lived there as an a,
27:19 "Cursed be anyone who deprives the a,
Jos 8:33 All Israel, a as well as citizen,
2Sa 1:13 He answered, "I am the son of a resident a,
Job 19:15 I have become an a in their eyes.
Ps 39:12 For I am your passing guest, an a,
69: 8 an a to my mother's children.
105:23 Jacob lived as an a in the land of Ham.
119:19 I live as an a in the land;
120: 5 Woe is me, that I am an a in Meshech,
Pr 5:10 and your labors will go to the house of an a;
Isa 17:10 and set out slips of an a god,
28:11 and with a tongue he will speak to this people,
28:21 and to work his work—a is his work!
Jer 7: 6 if you do not oppress the a,
22: 3 And do no wrong or violence to the a, the orphan,
Eze 22: 7 the a residing within you suffers extortion;
22:29 and have extorted from the a without redress.
Zec 7:10 the orphan, the a, or the poor;
Mal 3: 5 against those who thrust aside the a,
Ac 7:29 Moses fled and became a resident a in the land
Jdt 4:10 and every resident a and hired laborer
AdE 14:15 the bed of the uncircumcised and of any a.
16:10 a Macedonian (really an a to the Persian blood,
Wis 12:15 deeming it a to your power
Bar 4: 3 or your advantages to an a people.
2Mc 6:24 in his ninetieth year had gone over to an a religion,
1Es 8:69 not put away from themselves the a peoples of
8:70 the holy race has been mixed with the a peoples of

ALIEN'S (2) [ALIEN]
Lev 25:47 or to a branch of the a family,
25:53 by the year they shall be under the a authority,

ALIENATE (2) [ALIENATED]
Pr 17: 9 but one who dwells on disputes will a a friend.
1Ti 5:11 for when their sensual desires a them from Christ,

ALIENATED (3) [ALIENATE]
Eph 4:18 a from the life of God because of their ignorance
3Mc 4:16 a mind a from truth and with a profane mouth,
2Es 7:48 which has a us from God,

ALIENS‡ (59) [ALIEN]
Ge 15:13 your offspring shall be a in a land that is not theirs,
35:27 where Abraham and Isaac had resided as a.
47: 4 "We have come to reside as a in the land;
Ex 6: 4 the land in which they resided as a.
22:21 for you were a in the land of Egypt.
23: 9 for you were a in the land of Egypt.
Lev 17: 8 or of the a who reside among them who offers
17:10 or of the a who reside among them eats any blood,
17:13 or of the a who reside among them,
17:15 All persons, citizens or a,
19:34 for you were a in the land of Egypt:
20: 2 or of the a who reside in Israel,
22:18 or of the a residing in Israel presents an offering,
24:16 A as well as citizens, when they blaspheme
25:23 with me you are but a and tenants.
25:35 they shall live with you as though resident a.
25:45 the a residing with you, and from their families
25:47 If resident a among you prosper,
Nu 15:26 as well as the a residing among them,
Dt 14:21 you may give it to a residing in your towns
14:29 as well as the resident a, the orphans,
24:14 or a who reside in your land in one of your towns.
26:11 with the Levites and the a who reside among you,
26:12 giving it to the Levites, the a, the orphans,
26:13 and I have given it to the Levites, the resident a,

Dt 28:43 **A** residing among you shall ascend
29:11 your women, and the **a** who are in your camp,
31:12 as well as the **a** residing in your towns—
Jos 8:35 and the **a** who resided among them.
20: 9 and for the **a** residing among them,
2Sa 4: 3 to Gittaim and are there as resident **a** to this day).
1Ch 22: 2 to gather together the **a** who were residing in
29:15 For we are **a** and transients before you,
2Ch 2:17 of all the **a** who were residing in the land of Israel,
15: 9 and Simeon who were residing as **a** with them,
30:25 the resident **a** who came out of the land of Israel,
30:25 and the resident **a** who lived in Judah, rejoiced.
Ps 144: 7 from the mighty waters, from the hand of **a**,
144:11 and deliver me from the hand of **a**,
Isa 1: 7 in your very presence **a** devour your land;
14: 1 and **a** will join them and attach themselves to
25: 2 the palace of **a** is a city no more,
25: 5 of **a** like heat in a dry place, you subdued the heat
52: 4 down into Egypt to reside there as **a**;
Jer 51:51 for **a** have come into the holy places of the LORD's
La 5: 2 turned over to strangers, our homes to **a**.
Eze 14: 7 or of the **a** who reside in Israel,
20:38 of the land where they reside as **a**,
47:22 for yourselves and for the **a** who reside
47:23 In whatever tribe **a** reside,
Ac 7: 6 be resident **a** in a country belonging to others,
Eph 2:12 being **a** from the commonwealth of Israel,
2:19 So then you are no longer strangers and **a**,
1Pe 2:11 as **a** and exiles to abstain from the desires of
1Mc 2: 7 the sanctuary given over to **a**?
3:36 settle **a** in all their territory,
3:45 The sanctuary was trampled down, and **a** held
1Es 8:83 of is a land polluted with the pollution of the **a** of
2Es 14:29 At first our ancestors lived as **a** in Egypt,

ALIGHT (1) [ALIGHTED, ALIGHTING]

LtJ 6:22 swallows, and birds **a** on their bodies and heads;

ALIGHTED (1) [ALIGHT]

1Sa 25:23 she hurried and **a** from the donkey,

ALIGHTING (2) [ALIGHT]

Mt 3:16 the Spirit of God descending like a dove and **a**
Sir 43:17 and its descent is like locusts **a**.

ALIKE (36) [LIKE]

Ex 8:17 and gnats came on humans and animals **a**;
Nu 15:15 you and the alien shall be **a** before the LORD.
Dt 1:17 hear out the small and the great **a**;
12:22 the unclean and the clean **a** may eat it.
15:22 the unclean and the clean **a**,
29:19 (thus bringing disaster on moist and dry **a**)—
32:25 for young man and woman **a**,
1Sa 30:24 by the baggage; they shall share **a**."
1Ki 7:37 all of them were cast **a**,
1Ch 16: 3 every person in Israel—man and woman **a**—
24: 5 They organized them by lot, all **a**,
25: 8 small and great, teacher and pupil **a**.
26:13 small and great **a**, for their gates.
2Ch 31:15 old and young **a**, by divisions,
Est 1:20 to their husbands, high and low **a**."
4:11 all **a** are to be put to death.
Job 21:26 They lie down **a** in the dust,
Ps 14: 3 They have all gone astray, they are all **a** perverse;
36: 6 you save humans and animals **a**, O LORD.
53: 3 They have all fallen away, they are all **a** perverse;
87: 7 Singers and dancers **a** say,
148:12 Young men and women **a**,
Pr 17:15 and one who condemns the righteous are both **a**
20:10 and diverse measures are both **a** an abomination to
27:15 on a rainy day and a contentious wife are **a**;
Ecc 11: 6 this or that, or whether both **a** will be good.
Isa 46: 5 and compare me, as though we were **a**?
Jer 5: 5 But they all **a** had broken the yoke,
Eze 10:10 And as for their appearance, the four looked **a**,
Lk 14:18 But they all **a** began to make excuses.
Ro 14: 5 while others judge all days to be **a**.
1Co 15:39 Not all flesh is **a**, but there is one flesh
AdE 1:20 to their husbands, rich and poor **a**."
Wis 6: 7 and he takes thought for all **a**.
15: 7 and those for contrary uses, making all **a**;
18: 9 so that the saints would share **a** the same things,

ALIVE‡ (129) [LIVE]

Ge 6:19 to keep them **a** with you;
6:20 in to you, to keep them **a**.
7: 3 to keep their kind **a** on the face of all the earth.
16:13 "Have I really seen God and remained **a**
43: 7 saying, 'Is your father still **a**?
43:27 of whom you spoke? Is he still **a**?"
43:28 "Your servant our father is well; he is still **a**."
45: 3 Is my father still **a**?"
45: 7 and to keep **a** for you many survivors.
45:26 And they told him, "Joseph is still **a**!
45:28 My son Joseph is still **a**.
46:30 having seen for myself that you are still **a**."
Ex 22: 4 is found **a** in the thief's possession,
Lev 16:10 for Azazel shall be presented **a** before the LORD
18:18 while her sister is still **a**.
Nu 14:38 and Caleb son of Jephunneh alone remained **a**,
16:30 and they go down **a** into Sheol,
16:33 that belonged to them went down **a** into Sheol;
31:18 not known a man by sleeping with him, keep **a**
Dt 4: 4 to the LORD your God are all **a** today.
5: 3 but with us, who are all of us here **a** today.
5:26 as we have, and remained **a**?
6:24 for our lasting good, so as to keep us **a**,
20:16 you must not let anything that breathes remain **a**.
31:27 so rebellious toward the LORD while I am still **a**
32:39 I kill and I make **a**; I wound and I heal;
Jos 8:23 the king of Ai was taken **a** and brought to Joshua.
14:10 And now, as you see, the LORD has kept me **a**,
Jdg 8:19 as the LORD lives, if you had saved them **a**,
21:14 the women whom they had saved **a** of the women
1Sa 15: 8 He took King Agag of the Amalekites **a**,
20:14 If I am still **a**, show me the faithful love of
27: 9 leaving neither man nor woman **a**,
27:11 nor woman **a** to be brought back to Gath,
2Sa 12:18 for they said, "While the child was still **a**,
12:21 You fasted and wept for the child while it was **a**;
12:22 He said, "While the child was still **a**,
18:14 while he was still **a** in the oak.
19: 6 if Absalom were **a** and all of us were dead today,
1Ki 3:23 king said, "The one says, 'This is my son that is **a**,
3:26 the woman whose son was **a** said to the king—
12: 6 while he was still **a**, saying,
17:23 then Elijah said, "See, your son is **a**."
18: 5 to keep the horses and mules **a**,
20:18 "If they have come out for peace, take them **a**;
20:18 if they have come out for war, take them **a**."
20:32 And he said, "Is he still **a**?
21:15 for Naboth is not **a**, but dead."
2Ki 7:12 we shall take them **a** and get into the city.' "
10:14 He said, "Take them **a**."
10:14 They took them **a**, and slaughtered them at the pit
2Ch 10: 6 while he was still **a**, saying,
14:13 and the Ethiopians fell until no one remained **a**;
25:12 people of Judah captured another ten thousand **a**,
Ne 5: 2 we must get grain, so that we may eat and stay **a**."
Job 36: 6 He does not keep the wicked **a**,
Ps 33:19 and to keep them **a** in famine.
41: 2 The LORD protects them and keeps them **a**;
55:15 let them go down **a** to Sheol;
124: 3 up **a**, when their anger was kindled against us;
Pr 1:12 like Sheol let us swallow them **a** and whole,
Ecc 4: 2 more fortunate than the living, who are still **a**;
Isa 7:21 On that day one will keep **a** a young cow
Jer 49:11 Leave your orphans, I will keep them **a**;
La 3:53 they flung me **a** into a pit and hurled stones
Eze 7:13 to what has been sold as long as they remain **a**.
13:19 and keeping **a** persons who should not live,
Da 5:19 kept **a** those he wanted to keep **a**,
Zec 13: 8 and one-third shall be left **a**.
Mt 6:30 which is **a** today and tomorrow is thrown into
27:63 that impostor said while he was still **a**,
Mk 16:11 ⟦they heard that he was **a** and had been seen⟧
Lk 12:28 which is **a** today and tomorrow is thrown into
15:24 for this son of mine was dead and is **a** again;
20:38 for to him all of them are **a**."
24:23 a vision of angels who said that he was **a**.
Jn 4:51 and told him that his child was **a**.
Ac 1: 3 After his suffering he presented himself **a** to them
9:41 he showed her to be **a**.
20:12 the boy away **a** and were not a little comforted.
25:19 who had died, but whom Paul asserted to be **a**.
Ro 6:11 also must consider yourselves dead to sin and **a**
7: 3 with another man while her husband is **a**.
7: 9 I was once **a** apart from the law,
1Co 15: 6 most of whom are still **a**, though some have died.
15:22 so all will be made **a** in Christ.
2Co 6: 9 as dying, and see—we are **a**;
Gal 3:21 For if a law had been given that could make **a**,
Eph 2: 5 made us **a** together with Christ—
Col 2:13 God made you **a** together with him,
1Th 4:15 to you by the word of the Lord, that we who are **a**,
4:17 Then we who are **a**, who are left,
Heb 9:17 not in force as long as the one who made it is **a**.
1Pe 3:18 but made **a** in the spirit,
Rev 1:18 I was dead, and see, I am **a** forever and ever;
3: 1 you have a name of being **a**, but you are dead.
19:20 These two were thrown **a** into the lake of fire
Tob 5:10 Although still **a**, I am among the dead.
7: 5 They replied, "He is **a** and in good health."
8:12 of the maids and have her go in to see if he is **a**.
8:14 that he was **a** and that nothing was wrong.
14:10 while still **a**, brought down into the earth?
Jdt 10:19 It is not wise to leave one of their men **a**,
AdE 4:13 that you alone among all the Jews will escape **a**.
Sir 17:28 those who are **a** and well sing the Lord's praises.
33:21 While you are still **a** and have breath in you,
44:17 in the time of wrath he kept the race **a**;
1Mc 1: 6 among them while he was still **a**.
8: 7 they took him **a** and decreed that he
10:85 with those burned **a**, came to eight thousand.
14: 2 he sent one of his generals to take him **a**.
2Mc 5:27 and kept himself and his companions **a** in
7:24 The youngest brother being still **a**,
10:36 they kindled fires and burned the blasphemers **a**.
12:35 wishing to take the accursed man **a**,
14:45 Still **a** and aflame with anger, he rose,
3Mc 5:18 the Jews had been allowed to remain **a** through
2Es 3: 5 and he was made **a** in your presence.
4:26 He answered me and said, "If you are **a**,
4:51 Or who will be **a** in those days?"
5:41 you have charge of those who are **a** at the end,
7:45 Blessed are those who are **a**
7:67 What does it profit us that we shall be preserved **a**
7:87 in whose presence they sinned while they were **a**,
7:129 [59] the way of which Moses, while he was **a**,
12:33 first he will bring them **a** before his judgment seat,
14:34 and discipline your hearts, you shall be kept **a**,
4Mc 18:19 'I kill and I make **a**: this is your life and the length

ALL‡ (6485)

A. ALL ... PEOPLE (383)
B. ALL ISRAEL (166)
C. ALL THINGS (146)
D. ALL ... NATIONS (118)
E. ALL THE EARTH (65)
F. ALL THE DAYS (64)
G. ALL ... PEOPLES (61)
H. ALL THESE THINGS (55)
I. ALL THE LAND (53)
J. ALL ... HEART (44)
K. ALL THE WORDS (39)
L. ALL THE INHABITANTS (38)
M. ALL FLESH (37)
N. ALL THE ISRAELITES (37)
O. ALL ... GENERATIONS (36)
P. ALL THE KINGS (32)
Q. ALL ... SERVANTS (32)
R. ALL THE ... KINGDOMS (27)
S. ALL THE TRIBES (27)
T. ALL JUDAH (26)
U. ALL THE CONGREGATION (25)
V. ALL THE WORK (25)
W. ALL THE FIRSTBORN (22)
X. ALL [THE] JEWS (22)
Y. AT ALL TIMES (22)
Z. ALL THE MEN (21)
ALL THE ASSEMBLY (20) See ASSEMBLY
FOR ALL TIME (20) See TIME
ALL THE WORLD (10) See WORLD

Ge 1:26 and over **a** the wild animals of the earth,
1:29 upon the face of **a** the earth, E
2: 1 and the earth were finished, and **a** their multitude.
2: 2 seventh day from **a** the work that he had done. V
2: 3 God rested from **a** the work that he had done V
2:20 The man gave names to **a** cattle,
3:14 among **a** animals and among **a** wild creatures;
3:14 and dust you shall eat **a** the days of your life. F
3:17 in toil you shall eat of it **a** the days of your life; F
3:20 because she was the mother of **a** living.
4:21 the ancestor of **a** those who play the lyre and pipe.
4:22 who made **a** kinds of bronze and iron tools.
5: 5 Thus **a** the days that Adam lived were F
5: 8 Thus **a** the days of Seth were nine hundred F
5:11 Thus **a** the days of Enosh were nine hundred F
5:14 Thus **a** the days of Kenan were nine hundred F
5:17 Thus **a** the days of Mahalalel F
5:20 Thus **a** the days of Jared were nine hundred F
5:23 Thus **a** the days of Enoch F
5:27 Thus **a** the days of Methuselah F
5:31 Thus **a** the days of Lamech F
6: 2 and they took wives for themselves of **a**
6:12 **a** flesh had corrupted its ways upon the earth. M
6:13 "I have determined to make an end of **a** flesh, M
6:17 **a** flesh in which is the breath of life; M
6:19 And of every living thing, of **a** flesh, M
6:22 Noah did this; he did **a** that God commanded him.
7: 1 "Go into the ark, you and **a** your household,
7: 2 Take with you seven pairs of **a** clean animals,
7: 3 keep their kind alive on the face of **a** the earth. E
7: 5 Noah did **a** that the LORD had commanded him.
7:11 on that day **a** the fountains of
7:14 and **a** domestic animals of every kind,
7:15 and two of **a** flesh in which there was the breath M
7:16 those that entered, male and female of **a** flesh, M
7:19 that **a** the high mountains under the whole heaven
7:21 And **a** flesh died that moved on the earth, birds, M
7:21 **a** swarming creatures that swarm on the earth,
and **a** human beings;
8: 1 But God remembered Noah and **a**
8: 1 and **a** the domestic animals that were with him in
8:17 that is with you of **a** flesh— M
9: 2 and on **a** the fish of the sea;
9:11 that never again shall **a** flesh be cut off by M
9:12 that is with you, for **a** future generations:
9:15 and you and every living creature of **a** flesh; M
9:15 never again become a flood to destroy **a** flesh. M
9:16 God and every living creature of **a** flesh M
9:17 that I have established between me and **a** flesh M
9:29 **A** the days of Noah were nine hundred fifty F
10:10 Erech, and Accad, **a** of them in the land of Shinar.
10:21 To Shem also, the father of **a** the children of Eber,
10:29 **a** these were the descendants of Joktan.
11: 6 and they have **a** one language;
11: 8 from there over the face of **a** the earth, E
11: 9 the LORD confused the language of **a** the earth; E
11: 9 over the face of **a** the earth. E
12: 3 in you **a** the families of the earth shall be blessed."
12: 5 and **a** the possessions that they had gathered,
12:20 with his wife and **a** that he had.
13: 1 and **a** that he had, and Lot with him,
13:11 So Lot chose for himself **a** the plain of the Jordan,
13:15 for **a** the land that you see I will give to you and I
14: 3 **A** these joined forces in the Valley of Siddim
14: 7 and subdued **a** the country of the Amalekites,
14:11 enemy took **a** the goods of Sodom and Gomorrah,
14:11 and **a** their provisions, and went their way;
14:16 Then he brought back **a** the goods,
15:10 He brought him **a** these and cut them in two,
16:12 and he shall live at odds with **a** his kin."
17: 8 **a** the land of Canaan, for a perpetual holding; I
17:23 and **a** the slaves born in his house or bought
17:27 and **a** the men of his house, Z

Ge 18:18 a the nations of the earth shall be blessed in him? D
18:25 Shall not the Judge of a the earth do what is just? E
19: 4 both young and old, a the people to the last man, A
19:25 and he overthrew those cities, and a the Plain,
19:25 and a the inhabitants of the cities, L
19:28 Sodom and Gomorrah and toward a the land of I
19:31 to come in to us after the manner of a the world.
20: 7 you and a that are yours."
20: 8 in the morning, and called a his servants Q
20: 8 and told them a these things; H
20:11 There is no fear of God at a in this place,
20:16 it is your exoneration before a who are with you;
20:18 For the LORD had closed fast a the wombs of
21:22 "God is with you in a that you do;
22:18 and by your offspring shall a the nations of D
23:10 of a who went in at the gate of his city,
23:17 that was in it and a the trees that were in the field,
23:18 in the presence of a who went in at the gate
24: 1 and the LORD had blessed Abraham in a things. C
24: 2 who had charge of a that he had,
24:10 taking a kinds of choice gifts from his master;
24:20 and she drew for a his camels.
24:36 and he has given him a that he has.
24:66 servant told Isaac a the things that he had done.
25: 4 A these were the children of Keturah.
25: 5 Abraham gave a he had to Isaac.
25:18 he settled down alongside of a his people. A
25:25 first came out red, a his body like a hairy mantle;
26: 3 and to your descendants I will give a these lands,
26: 4 and will give to your offspring a these lands;
26: 4 and a the nations of the earth shall gain blessing D
26:11 So Abimelech warned a the people, saying, A
26:15 up and filled with earth a the wells
27:33 and I ate it a before you came,
27:37 and I have given him a his brothers as servants,
28:14 and a the families of the earth shall be blessed
28:22 of a that you give me I will surely give one tenth
29: 3 and when a the flocks were gathered there,
29: 8 until a the flocks are gathered together,
29:13 Jacob told Laban a these things, H
29:22 gathered together a the people of the place, A
30:32 let me pass through a your flock today, removing
30:35 a the female goats that were speckled and spotted,
31: 1 "Jacob has taken a that was our father's;
31: 1 he has gained a this wealth from what belonged
31: 6 that I have served your father with a my strength;
31: 8 then a the flock bore speckled;
31: 8 then a the flock bore striped.
31:12 that a the goats that leap on the flock are striped,
31:12 for I have seen a that Laban is doing to you.
31:16 A the property that God has taken away
31:18 and he drove away a his livestock,
31:18 a the property that he had gained,
31:21 So he fled with a that he had;
31:34 Laban felt a about in the tent,
31:37 Although you have felt about through a my goods,
31:37 what have you found of a your household goods?
31:43 and a that you see is mine.
31:54 and they ate bread and tarried a night in
32:10 least of a the steadfast love and a the faithfulness
32:11 he may come and kill us a,
32:19 and the third and a who followed the droves,
33: 2 and Rachel and Joseph last of a.
33: 8 "What do you mean by a this company
33:13 and if they are overdriven for one day, a
34:19 Now he was the most honored of a his family.
34:23 their property, and a their animals be ours?
34:24 And a who went out of
34:24 a who went out of the gate of his city.
34:25 against the city unawares, and killed a the males.
34:29 A their wealth, a their little ones and their wives,
34:29 a that was in the houses,
35: 2 So Jacob said to his household and to a who were
35: 4 to Jacob a the foreign gods that they had,
35: 5 from God fell upon the cities a around them,
35: 6 he and a the people who were with him, A
36: 6 and a the members of his household, his cattle, a his livestock, and a the property he had acquired
37: 4 their father loved him more than a his brothers,
37:35 A his sons and a his daughters sought to comfort
39: 3 that the LORD caused a that he did to prosper
39: 4 of his house and put him in charge of a
39: 5 that he made him overseer in his house and over a
39: 5 the blessing of the LORD was on a that he had,
39: 6 So he left a that he had in Joseph's charge;
39:22 The chief jailer committed to Joseph's care a
40:17 and in the uppermost basket there were a sorts
40:20 he made a feast for a his servants, Q
41: 8 for a the magicians of Egypt and a its wise men.
41:19 Never had I seen such ugly ones in a the land I
41:29 of great plenty throughout a the land of Egypt. I
41:30 a the plenty will be forgotten in the land of Egypt;
41:35 Let them gather a the food of these good years
41:37 The proposal pleased Pharaoh and a his servants. Q
41:39 "Since God has shown you a this,
41:40 and a my people shall order themselves A
41:41 "See, I have set you over a the land of Egypt." I
41:43 Thus he set him over a the land of Egypt. I
41:44 up hand or foot in a the land of Egypt." I
41:46 and went through a the land of Egypt. I
41:48 He gathered up a the food of the seven years
41:51 "God has made me forget a my hardship
41:51 and a my father's house."
41:55 When a the land of Egypt was famished, I
41:55 Pharaoh said to a the Egyptians, "Go to Joseph;
41:56 And since the famine had spread over a the land, I
41:56 Joseph opened a the storehouses,

Ge 41:57 a the world came to Joseph in Egypt to buy grain,
42: 6 it was he who sold to a the people of the land. A
42:11 We are a sons of one man;
42:17 he put them a together in prison for three days.
42:29 they told him a that had happened to them, saying,
42:36 A this has happened to me!"
44:32 the blame in the sight of my father a my life.'
45: 1 before a those who stood by him,
45: 8 a father to Pharaoh, and lord of a his house
45: 8 his house and ruler over a the land of Egypt. I
45: 9 God has made me lord of a Egypt;
45:10 your herds, and a that you have.
45:11 that you and your household, and a that you have,
45:13 and a that you have seen.
45:15 And he kissed a his brothers and wept upon them;
45:20 for the best of a the land of Egypt is yours.' " I
45:26 He is even ruler over a the land of Egypt." I
45:27 But when they told him a the words of Joseph K
46: 1 with a that he had and came to Beer-sheba,
46: 6 Jacob and a his offspring with him,
46: 7 a his offspring he brought with him into Egypt.
46:15 a his sons and his daughters numbered
46:22 to Jacob—fourteen persons in a).
46:25 to Jacob—seven persons in a).
46:26 A the persons belonging to Jacob who came
46:26 were sixty-six persons in a.
46:27 a the persons of the house of Jacob who came
46:32 and their herds, and a that they have.'
46:34 a shepherds are abhorrent to the Egyptians."
47: 1 and herds and a that they possess, have come from
47:12 and a his father's household with food,
47:13 Now there was no food in a the land, I
47:14 Joseph collected a the money to be found in
47:15 a the Egyptians came to Joseph, and said,
47:17 with food in exchange for a their livestock.
47:18 not hide from my lord that our money is a spent;
47:20 Joseph bought a the land of Egypt for Pharaoh. I
47:20 A the Egyptians sold their fields,
48:15 the God who has been my shepherd a my life
48:16 the angel who has redeemed me from a harm,
49:28 A these are the twelve tribes of Israel,
50: 7 With him went up a the servants of Pharaoh, Q
50: 7 and a the elders of the land of Egypt,
50: 8 as well as a the household of Joseph,
50:14 with his brothers and a who had gone up with him
50:15 against us and pays us back in full for a the wrong
Ex 1: 6 Then Joseph died, and a his brothers,
1:14 in a the tasks that they imposed on them.
1:22 Then Pharaoh commanded a his people, A
3:15 and this my title for a generations. O
3:20 with a my wonders that I will perform in it;
4:19 for a those who were seeking your life are dead."
4:21 that you perform before Pharaoh a the wonders
4:28 Moses told Aaron a the words of the LORD K
4:28 and a the signs with which he had charged him.
4:29 and Aaron went and assembled a the elders of
4:30 Aaron spoke a the words that the LORD K
5:23 and you have done nothing at a
6:29 tell Pharaoh king of Egypt a that I am speaking
7: 2 You shall speak a that I command you,
7:19 and its ponds, and a its pools of water—
7:20 and a the water in the river was turned into blood,
7:24 And a the Egyptians had to dig along the Nile
8: 4 and on your people and on a your officials.' "
8:17 a the dust of the earth turned into gnats throughout
8:24 in a of Egypt the land was ruined because of
9: 4 so that nothing shall die of a that belongs to
9: 6 a the livestock of the Egyptians died,
9: 9 It shall become fine dust a over the land of Egypt,
9:11 boils afflicted the magicians as well as a the
9:14 For this time I will send a my plagues
9:14 that there is no one like me in a the earth. E
9:16 to make my name resound through a the earth. E
9:22 and a the plants of the field in the land of Egypt."
9:24 such heavy hail as had never fallen in a the land I
9:25 in the open field throughout a the land of Egypt, I
9:25 the hail also struck down a the plants of the field,
10: 6 of a your officials and of a the Egyptians—
10:12 a that the hail has left."
10:13 east wind upon the land a that day and a that night
10:14 The locusts came upon a the land of Egypt I
10:15 they ate a the plants in the land and a the fruit of
10:15 no plant in the field, in a the land of Egypt. I
10:19 a single locust was left in a the country of Egypt.
10:22 and there was dense darkness in a the land I
10:23 but a the Israelites had light where they lived. N
11: 5 and a the firstborn of the livestock. W
11: 8 a these officials of yours shall come down to me,
11: 8 Leave us, you and a the people who follow you. A
11:10 Moses and Aaron performed a these wonders
12:12 on a the gods of Egypt I will execute judgments:
12:20 in a your settlements you shall eat unleavened
12:21 Then Moses called a the elders of Israel and said
12:29 the LORD struck down a the firstborn in the land W
12:29 and a the firstborn of the livestock. W
12:30 he and a his officials and a the Egyptians;
12:33 for they said, "We shall a be dead."
12:41 a the companies of the LORD went out from
12:42 a vigil to be kept for the LORD by a the Israelites N
12:48 a his males shall be circumcised;
12:50 A the Israelites did just as N
13: 2 Consecrate to me a the firstborn; W
13: 7 be seen among you in a your territory.
13:12 you shall set apart to the LORD a that first opens
13:12 A the firstborn of your livestock W
13:15 LORD killed a the firstborn in the land of Egypt, W
14: 4 for myself over Pharaoh and a his army;

Ex 14: 7 a the other chariots of Egypt with officers over a
14: 9 a Pharaoh's horses and chariots,
14:17 for myself over Pharaoh and a his army,
14:20 one did not come near the other a night.
14:21 by a strong east wind a night, and turned the sea
14:23 a of Pharaoh's horses, chariots,
15:15 a the inhabitants of Canaan melted away. L
15:20 and a the women went out after her
15:26 to his commandments and keep a his statutes,
16: 6 So Moses and Aaron said to a the Israelites, N
16:16 a providing for those in their own tents.' "
16:22 When a the leaders of the congregation came
16:23 to boil, and a that is left over put aside to be kept
18: 1 heard of a that God had done for Moses and
18: 8 Then Moses told his father-in-law a that
18: 8 a the hardship that had beset them on the way,
18: 9 for a the good that the LORD had done to Israel,
18:11 I know that the LORD is greater than a gods,
18:12 and Aaron came with a the elders of Israel
18:14 When Moses' father-in-law saw a that he was
18:14 while a the people stand around you A
18:21 also look for able men among a the people, A
18:22 Let them sit as judges for the people at a times; Y
18:23 a these people will go to their home in peace." A
18:24 So Moses listened to his father-in-law and did a
18:25 from a Israel and appointed them as heads over B
18:26 And they judged the people at a times; Y
19: 5 be my treasured possession out of a the peoples. G
19: 7 and set before them a these words that
19: 8 The people a answered as one:
19:11 upon Mount Sinai in the sight of a the people. A
19:12 You shall set limits for the people a around,
19:16 a blast of a trumpet so loud that a the people A
20: 1 Then God spoke a these words:
20: 9 Six days you shall labor and do a your work.
20:11 and a that is in them, but rested the seventh day;
20:18 a the people witnessed the thunder and lightning, A
23:13 Be attentive to a that I have said to you.
23:17 Three times in the year a your males shall appear
23:22 But if you listen attentively to his voice and do a
23:27 and will throw into confusion a the people A
23:27 and I will make a your enemies turn their backs
24: 3 Moses came and told the people a the words of K
24: 3 the words of the LORD and a the ordinances;
24: 3 and a the people answered with one voice, A
24: 3 and said, "A the words that the LORD K
24: 4 Moses wrote down a the words of the LORD. K
24: 7 "A that the LORD has spoken we will do,
24: 8 with you in accordance with a these words."
25: 2 from a whose hearts prompt them
25: 9 In accordance with a that I show you concerning
25: 9 the pattern of the tabernacle and of a its furniture,
25:11 a molding of gold upon it a around.
25:22 to you a my commands for the Israelites.
25:39 and a these utensils, shall be made from a talent
26: 2 a the curtains shall be of the same size.
26:17 shall make these for a the frames of the tabernacle.
27: 3 you shall make a its utensils of bronze.
27:17 A the pillars around the court shall be banded
27:19 A the utensils of the tabernacle for every use,
27:19 and a its pegs and a the pegs of the court,
28: 3 And you shall speak to a who have ability,
28:31 You shall make the robe of the ephod a of blue.
28:33 and crimson yarns, a around the lower hem,
28:33 with bells of gold between them a around—
28:34 a pomegranate alternating a around the lower hem
29:12 and a the rest of the blood you shall pour out at
29:13 You shall take a the fat that covers the entrails,
29:16 and shall take its blood and dash it against a sides
29:20 and dash the rest of the blood against a sides of
29:24 and you shall place a these on the palms of Aaron
30: 3 its top, and its sides a around and its horns;
30: 3 you shall make for it a molding of gold a around.
30:12 at registration a of them shall give a ransom
30:27 and the table and a its utensils,
30:28 of burnt offering with a its utensils, and the basin
31: 6 and I have given skill to a the skillful,
31: 6 that they may make a that I have commanded you:
31: 7 and a the furnishings of the tent,
31: 8 and the pure lampstand with a its utensils,
31: 9 and the altar of burnt offering with a its utensils,
32: 3 So a the people took off the gold rings A
32:13 and a this land that I have promised I will give
32:26 And a the sons of Levi gathered around him.
33: 8 a the people would rise and stand, each of them, A
33:10 When a the people saw the pillar A
33:10 a the people would rise and bow down, A
33:10 a of them, at the entrance of their tent.
33:19 "I will make a my goodness pass before you,
34: 3 not let anyone be seen throughout a the mountain;
34:10 Before a your people I will perform marvels, A
34:10 such as have not been performed in a the earth E
34:10 and a the people among whom you live shall see A
34:19 A that first opens the womb is mine,
34:19 a your male livestock, the firstborn of cow
34:20 A the firstborn of your sons you shall redeem. W
34:23 Three times in the year a your males shall appear
34:30 When Aaron and a the Israelites saw Moses, N
34:31 and a the leaders of the congregation returned
34:32 Afterward a the Israelites came near, N
34:32 in commandment a that the LORD had spoken
35: 1 Moses assembled a the congregation of the U
35: 3 You shall kindle no fire in a your dwellings on
35: 4 said to a the congregation of the Israelites: U
35:10 A who are skillful among you shall come
35:10 and make a that the LORD has commanded:
35:13 with its poles and a its utensils, and the bread of

Ex 35:16 and **a** its utensils, the basin with its stand;
35:20 Then **a** the congregation of the Israelites U
35:21 and for **a** its service, and for the sacred vestments.
35:22 **a** who were of a willing heart brought brooches
35:22 and earrings and signet rings and pendants, **a** sorts
35:25 **A** the skillful women spun with their hands,
35:26 **a** the women whose hearts moved them
35:29 **A** the Israelite men and women whose hearts made
36: 1 the sanctuary shall work in accordance with **a** that
36: 3 from Moses **a** the freewill offerings that
36: 4 so that **a** the artisans who were doing every sort
36: 7 was more than enough to do **a** the work. V
36: 8 **A** those with skill among the workers made
36: 9 **a** the curtains were of the same size.
36:22 he did this for **a** the frames of the tabernacle.
37:24 and **a** its utensils of a talent of pure gold.
37:26 its top, and its sides **a** around, and its horns;
37:26 and he made for it a molding of gold **a** around,
38: 3 He made **a** the utensils of the altar, the pots,
38: 3 **a** its utensils he made of bronze.
38:16 **A** the hangings around the court were
38:17 **a** the pillars of the court were banded with silver.
38:20 **A** the pegs for the tabernacle and for the court **a**
38:22 made **a** that the LORD commanded Moses;
38:24 **A** the gold that was used for the work,
38:24 in **a** the construction of the sanctuary,
38:30 the bronze altar and the bronze grating for it and **a**
38:31 the bases **a** around the court,
38:31 **a** the pegs of the tabernacle,
38:31 and **a** the pegs around the court.
39:22 He also made the robe of the ephod woven **a**
39:25 the pomegranates on the lower hem of the robe **a**
39:26 and a pomegranate **a** around on the lower hem of
39:32 In this way **a** the work of the tabernacle V
39:33 the tent and **a** its utensils, its hooks, its frames,
39:36 with **a** its utensils, and the bread of the Presence;
39:37 on it and **a** its utensils, and the oil for the light;
39:39 its poles, and **a** its utensils;
39:40 and **a** the utensils for the service of the tabernacle,
39:42 The Israelites had done **a** of the work just as
39:43 When Moses saw that they had done **a** the work V
40: 8 You shall set up the court **a** around,
40: 9 and anoint the tabernacle and **a** that is in it,
40: 9 and consecrate it and **a** its furniture,
40:10 the altar of burnt offering and **a** its utensils,
40:15 a perpetual priesthood throughout **a** generations O
40:38 the eyes of **a** the house of Israel at each stage
Lev 1: 5 against **a** sides of the altar that is at the entrance of
1:11 the priests shall dash its blood against **a** sides of
2: 2 of the choice flour and oil, with **a** its frankincense,
2:13 with **a** your offerings you shall offer salt.
2:16 of the coarse grain and oil with **a** its frankincense;
3: 2 the priests shall dash the blood against **a** sides of
3: 3 the entrails and **a** the fat that is around the entrails;
3: 8 against **a** sides of the altar.
3: 9 and **a** the fat that is around the entrails;
3:13 of Aaron shall dash its blood against **a** sides of
3:14 and **a** the fat that is around the entrails;
3:16 **A** fat is the LORD's.
3:17 throughout your generations, in **a** your settlements:
4: 8 He shall remove **a** the fat from the bull
4: 8 the entrails and **a** the fat that is around the entrails;
4:11 But the skin of the bull and **a** its flesh,
4:12 **a** the rest of the bull—
4:19 He shall remove **a** its fat and turn it into smoke on
4:22 doing unintentionally any one of **a** the things that
4:26 **A** its fat he shall turn into smoke on the altar,
4:31 He shall remove **a** its fat,
4:35 You shall remove **a** its fat,
6: 9 the hearth upon the altar **a** night until the morning,
6:15 with **a** the frankincense that is on the offering,
7: 2 and its blood shall be dashed against **a** sides of
7: 3 **A** its fat shall be offered:
7: 9 and **a** that is prepared in a pan or on a griddle,
7:10 shall belong to **a** the sons of Aaron equally.
7:19 other flesh, **a** who are clean may eat such flesh.
8:10 the anointing oil and anointed the tabernacle and **a**
8:11 and anointed the altar and **a** its utensils,
8:16 Moses took **a** the fat that was around the entrails,
8:19 Moses dashed the blood against **a** sides of
8:24 the rest of the blood against **a** sides of the altar.
8:25 broad tail, **a** the fat that was around the entrails,
8:27 He placed **a** these on the palms of Aaron and on
8:36 Aaron and his sons did **a** the things that
9:12 and he dashed it against **a** sides of the altar.
9:18 which he dashed against **a** sides of the altar,
9:23 the glory of the LORD appeared to **a** the people. A
9:24 and when **a** the people saw it, A
10: 3 and before **a** the people I will be glorified.' " A
10: 6 and wrath will strike **a** the congregation; U
10:11 of Israel **a** the statutes that the LORD has spoken
11: 2 From among **a** the land animals,
11: 9 These you may eat, of **a** that are in the waters.
11:10 the swarming creatures in the waters and among **a**
11:20 **A** winged insects that walk upon **a** fours are
11:21 that walk on **a** fours you may eat those
11:23 But **a** other winged insects
11:27 **A** that walk on their paws,
11:27 among the animals that walk on **a** fours,
11:31 These are unclean for you among **a** that swarm;
11:33 **a** that is in it shall be unclean,
11:41 **A** creatures that swarm upon
11:42 and whatever moves on **a** fours,
11:42 **a** the creatures that swarm upon the earth,
13:12 so that it covers **a** the skin of the diseased person
13:13 and if the disease has covered **a** his body,
13:13 since it has **a** turned white, he is clean.
Lev 14: 8 and shave off **a** his hair,
14: 9 On the seventh day he shall shave **a** his hair:
14: 9 he shall shave **a** his hair.
14:36 or **a** that is in the house will become unclean;
14:45 and timber and **a** the plaster of the house,
14:46 **A** who enter the house while it is shut up shall
14:47 **a** who sleep in the house shall wash their clothes;
14:47 **a** who eat in the house shall wash their clothes.
15: 6 **A** who sit on anything on which the one with
15: 7 **A** who touch the body of the one with
15:10 **A** who touch anything that was under him shall
15:10 **a** who carry such a thing shall wash their clothes,
15:11 **A** those whom the one with the discharge touches
15:25 **a** the days of the discharge she shall continue F
15:26 she lies during **a** the days of her discharge F
16:16 and because of their transgressions, **a** their sins;
16:17 and for his house and for **a** the assembly of Israel.
16:21 and confess over it **a** the iniquities of the people
16:21 and **a** their transgressions, **a** their sins,
16:22 The goat shall bear on itself **a** their iniquities to
16:30 from **a** your sins you shall be clean before
16:33 the priests and for **a** the people of the assembly. A
16:34 of Israel once in the year for **a** their sins.
17: 2 Aaron and his sons and to **a** the people of Israel A
17:15 **A** persons, citizens or aliens,
18:24 by **a** these practices the nations I am casting out
18:27 committed **a** of these abominations,
19: 2 Speak to **a** the congregation of the people U
19: 7 If it is eaten at **a** on the third day,
19: 8 **A** who eat it shall be subject to punishment,
19:23 into the land and plant **a** kinds of trees for food,
19:24 In the fourth year **a** their fruit shall be set apart
19:37 You shall keep **a** my statutes
19:37 and **a** my ordinances, and observe them:
20: 5 and **a** who follow them in prostituting themselves
20: 9 **A** who curse father or mother shall be put
20:22 You shall keep **a** my statutes
20:22 and **a** my ordinances, and observe them,
20:23 they did **a** these things, I abhorred them. H
21:24 and to his sons and to **a** the people of Israel. A
22: 3 If anyone among **a** your offspring
22:18 to Aaron and his sons and **a** the people of Israel A
23:14 throughout your generations in **a** your settlements.
23:21 in **a** your settlements throughout your generations.
23:31 throughout your generations in **a** your settlements.
23:38 and apart from **a** your votive offerings,
23:38 and apart from **a** your freewill offerings,
23:42 **a** that are citizens in Israel shall live in booths,
24:14 and let **a** who were within hearing lay their hands
25: 7 for the wild animals in your land **a** its yield shall
25: 9 the trumpet sounded throughout **a** your land.
25:10 throughout the land to **a** its inhabitants.
25:34 for that is their possession for **a** time.
26:14 and do not observe **a** these commandments,
26:15 so that you will not observe **a** my commandments,
26:44 Yet for **a** that, when they are in the land
27:25 **A** assessments shall be by the sanctuary shekel:
27:30 **A** tithes from the land, whether the seed from
27:32 **A** tithes of herd and flock,
Nu 1:50 over **a** its equipment, and over **a** that belongs to it;
1:50 to carry the tabernacle and **a** its equipment,
3: 8 they shall be in charge of **a** the furnishings of
3:12 for **a** the firstborn that open the womb among W
3:13 for **a** the firstborn are mine; W
3:13 I killed **a** the firstborn in the land of Egypt, W
3:13 consecrated for my own **a** the firstborn in Israel, W
3:22 counting **a** the males from a month old
3:26 **a** the service pertaining to these.
3:28 Counting **a** the males, from a month old
3:31 **a** the service pertaining to these.
3:34 counting **a** the males from a month old
3:36 the pillars, the bases, and **a** their accessories—
3:36 **a** the service pertaining to these;
3:37 also the pillars of the court **a** around,
3:39 **a** the males from a month old and upward,
3:40 Enroll **a** the firstborn males of the Israelites, W
3:41 for **a** the firstborn among the Israelites, W
3:41 Levites as substitutes for **a** the firstborn among W
3:42 So Moses enrolled **a** the firstborn among W
3:43 **a** the firstborn males from a month old W
3:45 Levites as substitutes for **a** the firstborn among W
4: 3 **a** who qualify to do work relating to the tent
4: 6 and spread over that a cloth **a** of blue,
4: 9 and **a** the vessels for oil with which it is supplied;
4:10 with **a** its utensils in a covering of fine leather,
4:12 and they shall take **a** the utensils of the service
4:14 on it **a** the utensils of the altar, which are used for
4:14 and the basins, **a** the utensils of the altar;
4:15 and **a** the furnishings of the sanctuary,
4:16 oversight of **a** the tabernacle and **a** that is in it,
4:23 **a** who qualify to do work in the tent of meeting.
4:26 and **a** the equipment for their service;
4:26 and they shall do **a** that needs to be done
4:27 **A** the service of the Gershonites shall be at
4:27 in **a** that they are to carry,
4:27 and in **a** that they have to do;
4:27 and you shall assign to their charge **a** that they are
4:32 the pillars of the court **a** around with their bases,
4:32 and cords, with **a** their equipment
4:32 and **a** their related service;
4:37 **a** who served at the tent of meeting,
4:41 **a** who served at the tent of meeting,
4:46 **A** those who were enrolled of the Levites,
5: 9 Among **a** the sacred donations of the Israelites,
5:10 The sacred donations of **a** are their own;
6: 4 **A** their days as nazirites they shall eat nothing
6: 5 **A** the days of their nazirite vow no razor shall F
Nu 6: 6 **A** the days that they separate themselves to F
6: 8 **A** their days as nazirites they are holy to
7: 1 and consecrated it with **a** its furnishings,
7: 1 and consecrated the altar with **a** its utensils,
7:85 and each basin seventy, **a** the silver of
7:86 to the shekel of the sanctuary, **a** the gold of
7:87 **a** the livestock for the burnt offering twelve bulls,
7:88 and **a** the livestock for the sacrifice
8:16 in place of **a** that open the womb,
8:16 the firstborn of **a** the Israelites. N
8:17 **a** the firstborn among the Israelites are mine, W
8:17 On the day that I struck down **a** the firstborn in W
8:18 in place of **a** the firstborn among the Israelites. W
9: 3 according to **a** its statutes
9: 3 and **a** its regulations you shall keep it.
9:12 to **a** the statute for the passover they shall keep it.
10:25 acting as the rear guard of **a** the camps, set out,
11: 6 there is nothing at **a** but this manna to look at."
11:10 **a** at the entrances of their tents.
11:11 that you lay the burden of **a** this people on me? A
11:12 Did I conceive **a** this people? A
11:13 Where am I to get meat to give to **a** this people? A
11:14 I am not able to carry **a** this people alone, A
11:17 with you so that you will not bear it **a** by yourself.
11:24 and placed them **a** around the tent.
11:29 Would that **a** the LORD's people were prophets,
11:31 and a day's journey on the other side, **a** around
11:32 So the people worked **a** that day and night and **a**
the next day, gathering the quails;
11:32 and they spread them out for themselves **a** around
12: 7 he is entrusted with **a** my house.
13: 3 **a** of them leading men among the Israelites.
13:26 to Moses and Aaron and to **a** the congregation of U
13:26 back word to them and to **a** the congregation, U
13:32 **a** the people that we saw in it are of great size. A
14: 1 Then **a** the congregation raised a loud cry, U
14: 2 And **a** the Israelites complained against Moses N
14: 5 Then Moses and Aaron fell on their faces before **a**
14: 7 and said to **a** the congregation of the Israelites, U
14:10 at the tent of meeting to **a** the Israelites. N
14:11 of **a** the signs that I have done among them?
14:15 Now if you kill this people **a** at one time,
14:21 and as **a** the earth shall be filled with the glory E
14:29 and of **a** your number, included in the census,
14:35 to **a** this wicked congregation gathered together
14:36 and made **a** the congregation complain U
14:39 When Moses told these words to **a** the Israelites, N
15:22 to observe **a** these commandments that
15:25 for **a** the congregation of the Israelites, U
15:26 **A** the congregation of the Israelites shall U
15:35 **a** the congregation shall stone him outside U
15:39 you will remember **a** the commandments of
15:40 you shall remember and do **a** my commandments,
16: 3 **A** the congregation are holy, everyone of them, U
16: 5 Then he said to Korah and **a** his company,
16: 6 Do this: take censers, Korah and **a** your company,
16:10 and **a** your brother Levites with you;
16:11 and **a** your company have gathered together
16:16 "As for you and **a** your company,
16:22 said, "O God, the God of the spirits of **a** flesh, M
16:26 or you will be swept away for **a** their sins."
16:28 that the LORD has sent me to do **a** these works;
16:30 with **a** that belongs to them,
16:31 As soon as he finished speaking **a** these words,
16:32 to Korah and **a** their goods.
16:33 with **a** that belonged to them went down alive
16:34 **A** Israel around them fled at their outcry, B
17: 2 from **a** the leaders of their ancestral houses.
17: 6 and **a** their leaders gave him staffs,
17: 9 Then Moses brought out **a** the staffs from before
17: 9 from before the LORD to **a** the Israelites; N
17:12 we are lost, **a** of us are lost!
17:13 Are we **a** to perish?"
18: 4 for **a** the service of the tent;
18: 7 in **a** that concerns the altar and the area behind
18: 8 **a** the holy gifts of the Israelites;
18:11 from the gifts of **a** the elevation offerings of
18:12 **A** the best of the oil and **a** the best of the wine
18:13 The first fruits of **a** that is in their land,
18:15 The first issue of the womb of **a** creatures,
18:19 **A** the holy offerings that the Israelites present to
18:28 the LORD from **a** the tithes that you receive from
18:29 Out of **a** the gifts to you,
18:29 the best of **a** of them is the part to be consecrated.
19:13 **A** who touch a corpse, the body of
19:18 and sprinkle it on the tent, on **a** the furnishings,
20:14 You know **a** the adversity that has befallen us:
20:29 **a** the congregation saw that Aaron had died, U
20:29 **a** the house of Israel mourned
21:23 Sihon gathered **a** his people together, A
21:25 Israel took **a** these towns,
21:25 and Israel settled in **a** the towns of the Amorites,
21:25 in Heshbon, and in **a** its villages.
21:26 the former king of Moab and captured **a** his land
21:33 he and **a** his people, to battle at Edrei. A
21:34 with **a** his people, and all his land. A
21:34 with all his people, and **a** his land.
21:35 So they killed him, his sons, and **a** his people, A
22: 2 of Zippor saw **a** that Israel had done to
22: 4 "This horde will now lick up **a** that is around us,
22:30 which you have ridden **a** your life to this day?
23: 6 beside his burnt offerings with **a** the officials
23:13 and shall not see them **a;**
23:25 Balak said to Balaam, "Do not curse them at **a,**
23:25 and do not bless them at **a."**
24:17 and the territory of **a** the Shethites.
25: 4 "Take **a** the chiefs of the people,

Nu 26:43 A the clans of the Shuhamites:
27: 2 the leaders, and a the congregation, U
27:16 the God of the spirits of a flesh, M
27:19 before Eleazar the priest and a the congregation, U
27:20 a the congregation of the Israelites may obey. U
27:21 both he and a the Israelites with him, N
30: 2 according to a that proceeds out of his mouth.
30: 4 then a her vows shall stand,
30:11 then a her vows shall stand,
30:14 then he validates a her vows, or a her pledges,
31: 9 they took a their cattle, their flocks, and a their
31:10 A their towns where they had settled,
31:10 and a their encampments, they burned,
31:11 but they took a the spoil and a the booty,
31:13 and a the leaders of the congregation went
31:15 "Have you allowed a the women to live?
31:18 But a the young girls who have not known a man
31:27 who went out to battle and a the congregation. U
31:30 donkeys, sheep, or goats—a the animals—
31:35 and thirty-two thousand persons in a,
31:51 a in the form of crafted articles.
31:52 And a the gold of the offering that they offered to
31:53 (The troops had a taken plunder for themselves.)
32:13 until a the generation that had done evil in
32:15 and you will destroy a this people." A
32:18 not return to our homes until a the Israelites N
32:21 and a those of you who bear arms cross the Jordan
32:26 and a our livestock shall remain there in the towns
33: 3 the Israelites went out boldly in the sight of a
33: 4 while the Egyptians were burying a their firstborn,
33:52 you shall drive out a the inhabitants of the land L
33:52 destroy a their figured stones, destroy a their cast images, and demolish a their high places.
34:12 be your land with its boundaries a around.
35: 3 for their livestock, and for a their animals.
35: 4 of the town outward a thousand cubits a around.
36: 7 for a Israelites shall retain the inheritance
36: 8 so that a Israelites may continue
Dt 1: 1 Moses spoke to a Israel beyond the Jordan— B
1:12 the heavy burden of your disputes a by myself?
1:18 at that time with a the things that you should do.
1:19 through a that great and terrible wilderness
1:22 A of you came to me and said,
1:31 a the way that you traveled
1:41 So a of you strapped on your battle gear,
2: 7 your God has blessed you in a your undertakings;
2:15 from the camp, until a had perished.
2:16 as soon as a the warriors had died off from among
2:32 he and a his people for battle at Jahaz, A
2:33 along with his offspring and a his people. A
2:34 At that time we captured a his towns,
3: 1 he and a his people, for battle at Edrei. A
3: 3 over to us King Og of Bashan and a his people. A
3: 4 At that time we captured a his towns;
3: 5 A these were fortress towns with high walls,
3: 7 But a the livestock and the plunder of
3:10 a the towns of the tableland,
3:10 and a of Bashan, as far as Salecah and Edrei,
3:13 the rest of Gilead and a of Bashan,
3:13 a that portion of Bashan used to be called a land
3:18 to occupy, a your troops shall cross over armed as
3:21 to a the kingdoms into which you are about R
4: 4 to the LORD your God are a alive today.
4: 6 who, when they hear a these statutes, will say,
4: 9 nor to let them slip from your mind a the days F
4:19 the moon, and the stars, a the host of heaven,
4:19 the LORD your God has allotted to a the peoples G
4:29 you search after him with a your heart and soul. J
4:30 when a these things have happened to you H
4:40 that the LORD your God is giving you for a time.
4:49 with a the Arabah on the east side of the Jordan
5: 1 Moses convened a Israel, and said to them: B
5: 3 but with us, who are a of us here alive today.
5:13 Six days you shall labor and do a your work.
5:23 a the heads of your tribes and your elders;
5:26 For who is there of a flesh that has heard M
5:27 and hear a that the LORD our God will say.
5:28 they are right in a that they have spoken.
5:29 and to keep a my commandments always,
5:31 and I will tell you a the commandments,
6: 2 the LORD your God a the days of your life, F
6: 2 and keep a his decrees and his commandments
6: 5 the LORD your God with a your heart, J
6: 5 and with a your soul, and with a your might.
6:11 houses filled with a sorts of goods that you did
6:14 of the gods of the peoples who are a around you,
6:19 thrusting out a your enemies from before you,
6:22 against Pharaoh and a his household.
6:24 LORD commanded us to observe a these statutes,
7: 6 God has chosen you out of a the peoples G
7: 7 for you were the fewest of a peoples. G
7:15 a the dread diseases of Egypt
7:15 but he will lay them on a who hate you.
7:16 You shall devour a the peoples that G
7:18 to Pharaoh and to a Egypt,
7:19 same to a the peoples of whom you are afraid. G
8:13 and a that you have is multiplied,
9:10 on them were a the words that the LORD K
9:18 because of a the sin you had committed,
10:12 to walk in a his ways, to love him,
10:12 to serve the LORD your God with a your heart J
10:12 with all your heart and with a your soul,
10:14 the earth with a that is in it,
10:15 descendants after them, out of a the peoples, G
11: 3 the king of Egypt, and to a his land;
11: 6 the midst of a Israel the earth opened its mouth B
11:13 and serving him with a your heart J
Dt 11:13 with all your heart and with a your soul—
11:22 walking in a his ways, and holding fast to him,
11:23 LORD will drive out a these nations before you, D
11:25 of you on a the land on which you set foot, I
11:32 you must diligently observe a the statutes
12: 1 has given you to occupy a the days that you live F
12: 2 You must demolish completely a the places where
12: 5 of a your tribes as his habitation
12: 7 rejoicing in a the undertakings in which
12: 8 a of us according to our own desires,
12:10 and when he gives you rest from your enemies a
12:11 and your donations, and a your choice votive gifts
12:18 of the LORD your God in a your undertakings.
12:25 so that a may go well with you and your children
12:28 to obey a these words that I command you today,
13: 3 the LORD your God with a your heart and soul. J
13: 9 and afterwards the hand of a the people. A
13:11 Then a Israel shall hear and be afraid, B
13:16 A of its spoil you shall gather
13:16 then burn the town and a its spoil with fire,
13:18 by keeping a his commandments
14: 2 the LORD has chosen out of a the peoples G
14: 9 Of a that live in water you may eat these:
14:19 And a winged insects are unclean for you;
14:22 of a the yield of your seed that is brought in yearly
14:29 the LORD your God may bless you in a the work V
15:10 in a your work and in a that you undertake.
15:18 LORD your God will bless you in a that you do.
16: 3 that a the days of your life you may remember F
16: 4 with you in a your territory for seven days;
16:15 in a your produce and in a your undertakings,
16:16 Three times a year a your males shall appear
16:17 a shall give as they are able,
16:18 throughout your tribes, in a your towns that
17: 7 and afterward the hands of a the people. A
17:13 A the people will hear and be afraid, A
17:14 like a the nations that are around me," D
17:19 with him and he shall read in it a the days of F
17:19 diligently observing a the words of this law K
18: 5 of a your tribes, to stand and minister in the name
18: 5 him and his sons for a time.
18: 7 like a his fellow-Levites who stand
19: 8 and he will give you a the land I
20:11 a the people in it shall serve you at forced labor. A
20:13 you shall put a its males to the sword.
20:14 and everything else in the town, a its spoil.
20:15 Thus you shall treat a the towns that are very far
20:18 not teach you to do a the abhorrent things
21: 5 and by their decision a cases of dispute
21: 6 A the elders of that town nearest
21:17 giving him a double portion of a that he has;
21:21 a the men of the town shall stone him to death. Z
21:21 and a Israel will hear, and be afraid. B
21:23 his corpse must not remain a night upon the tree;
23:20 in a your undertakings in the land that you are
24:19 your God may bless you in a your undertakings.
25:16 For a who do such things, a who act dishonestly,
25:18 and struck down a who lagged behind you;
25:19 from a your enemies on every hand, in the land
26: 2 you shall take some of the first of a the fruit of
26:11 shall celebrate with a the bounty that
26:12 When you have finished paying a the tithe
26:16 so observe them diligently with a your heart and J
26:16 with all your heart and with a your soul.
26:19 set you high above a nations that he has made, D
27: 1 and the elders of Israel charged a the people A
27: 3 You shall write on them a the words of this law K
27: 8 write on the stones a the words of this law K
27: 9 Moses and the levitical priests spoke to a Israel, B
27:14 declare in a loud voice to a the Israelites: N
27:15 A the people shall respond, saying, "Amen!" A
27:16 A the people shall say, "Amen!" A
27:17 A the people shall say, "Amen!" A
27:18 A the people shall say, "Amen!" A
27:19 A the people shall say, "Amen!" A
27:20 A the people shall say, "Amen!" A
27:21 A the people shall say, "Amen!" A
27:22 A the people shall say, "Amen!" A
27:23 A the people shall say, "Amen!" A
27:24 A the people shall say, "Amen!" A
27:25 A the people shall say, "Amen!" A
27:26 A the people shall say, "Amen!" A
28: 1 by diligently observing a his commandments
28: 1 your God will set you high above a the nations D
28: 2 a these blessings shall come upon you
28: 8 and in a that you undertake;
28:10 A the peoples of the earth shall see G
28:12 in its season and to bless a your undertakings.
28:15 by diligently observing a his commandments
28:15 then a these curses shall come upon you
28:25 object of horror to a the kingdoms of the earth. R
28:32 you will strain your eyes looking for them a day
28:33 up the fruit of your ground and of a your labors;
28:37 and a byword among a the peoples where G
28:40 throughout a your territory,
28:42 A your trees and the fruit of your ground
28:45 A these curses shall come upon you,
28:52 in a your towns until your high and fortified walls,
28:52 it shall besiege you in a your towns throughout
28:55 the enemy siege will reduce you in a your towns.
28:58 not diligently observe a the words of this law K
28:60 He will bring back upon you a the diseases
28:64 The LORD will scatter you among a peoples, G
29: 2 Moses summoned a Israel and said to them: B
29: 2 You have seen a that the LORD did
29: 2 land of Egypt, to Pharaoh and to a his servants Q
29: 2 and to all his servants and to a his land,
Dt 29:10 You stand assembled today, a of you,
29:10 elders, and your officials, a the men of Israel, Z
29:19 A who hear the words of this oath
29:20 A the curses written in this book will descend
29:21 The LORD will single them out from a the tribes S
29:21 with a the curses of the covenant written
29:23 a its soil burned out by sulfur and salt,
29:24 they and indeed a the nations will wonder, D
29:29 to observe a the words of this law. K
30: 1 When a these things have happened to you, H
30: 1 if you call them to mind among a the nations D
30: 2 and your children obey him with a your heart J
30: 2 with all your heart and with a your soul,
30: 3 gathering you again from a the peoples G
30: 6 love the LORD your God with a your heart J
30: 6 with all your heart and with a your soul,
30: 7 The LORD your God will put a these curses
30: 8 observing a his commandments
30: 9 in a your undertakings, in the fruit of your body,
30:10 to the LORD your God with a your heart and J
30:10 with all your heart and with a your soul.
31: 1 When Moses had finished speaking a these words
31: 1 finished speaking all these words to a Israel, B
31: 7 and said to him in the sight of a Israel: B
31: 9 and to a the elders of Israel.
31:11 when a Israel comes to appear before B
31:11 you shall read this law before a Israel B
31:12 and to observe diligently a the words of this law, K
31:18 that day I will surely hide my face on account of a
31:28 to me a the elders of your tribes and your officials,
32: 4 Rock, his work is perfect, and a his ways are just.
32:27 it was not the LORD who did a this."
32:43 O heavens, his people, worship him, a you gods!
32:44 recited a the words of this song in the hearing K
32:45 When Moses had finished reciting a these words
32:45 finished reciting all these words to a Israel, B
32:46 to hear[r] a the words that I am giving in witness K
32:46 so that they may diligently observe a the words K
33: 3 a his holy ones were in your charge;
33:12 the High God surrounds him a day long—
34: 2 a Naphtali, the land of Ephraim and Manasseh, all
34: 2 a the land of Judah as far as the Western Sea, I
34:11 He was unequaled for a the signs and wonders
34:11 and a his servants and his entire land, Q
34:12 for a the mighty deeds and a the terrifying displays
34:12 that Moses performed in the sight of a Israel. B
Jos 1: 2 to cross the Jordan, you and a this people, A
1: 4 the river Euphrates, a the land of the Hittites, I
1: 5 to stand against you a the days of your life. F
1: 7 being careful to act in accordance with a the law
1: 8 to act in accordance with a that is written in it.
1:14 But a the warriors among you shall cross
1:16 "A that you have commanded us we will do,
1:17 Just as we obeyed Moses in a things, C
2: 9 has fallen on us, and that a the inhabitants L
2:13 and a who belong to them,
2:18 your brothers, and a your family.
2:22 The pursuers had searched a along the way
2:23 and told him a that had happened to them.
2:24 the LORD has given a the land into our hands; I
2:24 a the inhabitants of the land melt in fear L
3: 1 and set out from Shittim with a the Israelites, N
3: 7 to exalt you in the sight of a Israel, B
3:11 Lord of a the earth is going to pass before you E
3:13 of a the earth, rest in the waters of the Jordan, E
3:15 Now the Jordan overflows a its banks throughout
3:17 While a Israel were crossing over on dry ground, B
4:10 to a that Moses had commanded Joshua.
4:11 soon as a the people had finished crossing over, A
4:14 the LORD exalted Joshua in the sight of a Israel; B
4:14 as they had stood in awe of Moses, a the days F
4:18 to their place and overflowed a its banks,
4:24 so that a the peoples of the earth may know that G
5: 1 When a the kings of the Amorites beyond P
5: 1 and a the kings of the Canaanites by the sea, P
5: 4 a the males of the people who came out of Egypt,
5: 4 the people who came out of Egypt, a the warriors,
5: 5 Although a the people who came out A
5: 5 yet a the people born on the journey A
5: 6 until a the nation, the warriors who came out
5: 8 When the circumcising of a the nation was done,
6: 3 a the warriors circling the city once.
6: 5 then a the people shall shout with a great shout; A
6: 5 and a the people shall charge straight ahead." A
6:17 and a that is in it shall be devoted to the LORD
6:17 Only Rahab the prostitute and a who are with her
6:19 But a silver and gold, and vessels of bronze
6:21 to destruction by the edge of the sword a in
6:22 and bring the woman out of it and a who belong
6:23 her brothers, and a who belonged to her—
6:23 they brought a her kindred out—
6:25 with her family and a who belonged to her,
6:27 and his fame was in a the land. I
7: 3 "Not a the people need go up; A
7: 7 the Jordan at a, to hand us over to the Amorites so
7: 9 and a the inhabitants of the land will hear of it, L
7:15 together with a that he has,
7:23 and brought them to Joshua and a the Israelites; N
7:24 Then Joshua and a Israel with him took Achan B
7:24 and sheep, and his tent and a that he had;
7:25 And a Israel stoned him to death; B
8: 1 take a the fighting men with you,
8: 3 and a the fighting men set out to go up against Ai.
8: 4 do not go very far from the city, but a
8: 5 and a the people who are with me will approach A
8:11 A the fighting men who were with him went up,
8:14 the king of Ai saw this, he and a his people, A

Jos 8:15 and a Israel made a pretense of being beaten B
8:16 So a the people who were in A
8:21 and a Israel saw that the ambush had taken B
8:24 finished slaughtering a the inhabitants of Ai L
8:24 and when a of them to the very last had fallen by
8:24 the sword, a Israel returned to Ai, and attacked it B
8:25 was twelve thousand—a the people of Ai. A
8:26 until he had utterly destroyed a the inhabitants L
8:33 A Israel, alien as well as citizen, B
8:34 And afterward he read a the words of the law, K
8:34 according to a that is written in the book of
8:35 There was not a word of a that Moses commanded
8:35 that Joshua did not read before a the assembly
9: 1 when a the kings who were beyond the Jordan P
9: 1 and in the lowland a along the coast
9: 5 and a their provisions were dry and moldy.
9: 9 of a that he did in Egypt,
9:10 and of a that he did to the two kings of
9:11 and a the inhabitants of our country said to us, L
9:18 a the congregation murmured against the leaders. U
9:19 But a the leaders said to all the congregation,
9:19 But all the leaders said to a the congregation, U
9:21 and drawers of water for a the congregation, U
9:24 to give you a the land, and to destroy all I
9:24 destroy a the inhabitants of the land before you; L
10: 2 and a its men were warriors.
10: 5 with a their armies and camped against Gibeon,
10: 6 for a the kings of the Amorites who live in P
10: 7 he and a the fighting force with him, a the mighty
10: 9 having marched up a night from Gilgal.
10:15 Then Joshua returned, and a Israel with him, B
10:21 a the people returned safe to Joshua in the camp A
10:24 Joshua summoned a the Israelites, N
10:25 for thus the LORD will do to a the enemies
10:29 and a Israel with him, to Libnah, B
10:31 and a Israel with him, to Lachish, B
10:34 From Lachish Joshua passed on with a Israel B
10:36 Then Joshua went up with a Israel from Eglon B
10:38 Then Joshua, with a Israel, B
10:39 and he took it with its king and a its towns;
10:40 and the lowland and the slopes, and a their kings;
10:40 but utterly destroyed a that breathed,
10:41 and a the country of Goshen, as far as Gibeon.
10:42 Joshua took a these kings and their land
10:43 Then Joshua returned, and a Israel with him, B
11: 4 They came out, with a their troops, a great army,
11: 5 A these kings joined their forces,
11: 6 tomorrow at this time I will hand over a of them,
11: 7 upon them with a his fighting force,
11:10 that time Hazor was the head of a those kingdoms.
11:11 And they put to the sword a who were in it,
11:12 And a the towns of those kings, and a their kings,
11:14 A the spoil of these towns, and the livestock,
11:14 but a the people they struck down with the edge A
11:15 of a that the LORD had commanded Moses.
11:16 So Joshua took a that land:
11:16 the hill country and a the Negeb and all the land
11:16 and a the land of Goshen and the lowland I
11:17 He took a their kings, struck them down,
11:18 Joshua made war a long time with a those kings.
11:19 of Gibeon; a were taken in battle.
11:21 from Anab, and from a the hill country of Judah,
11:21 and from a the hill country of Israel;
11:23 according to a that the LORD had spoken
12: 1 with a the Arabah eastward:
12: 5 over Mount Hermon and Salecah and a Bashan to
12:24 the king of Tirzah one thirty-one kings in a.
13: 2 a the regions of the Philistines, and a those of the
13: 4 a the land of the Canaanites, I
13: 5 and a Lebanon, toward the east,
13: 6 a the inhabitants of the hill country L
13: 6 from Lebanon to Misrephoth-maim, even a
13: 9 and a the tableland from Medeba as far as Dibon;
13:10 and a the cities of King Sihon of the Amorites,
13:11 and a Mount Hermon, and a Bashan to Salecah;
13:12 a the kingdom of Og in Bashan, who reigned
13:16 and a the tableland by Medeba;
13:17 and a its towns that are in the tableland;
13:21 a the towns of the tableland,
13:21 and a the kingdom of King Sihon of the Amorites,
13:25 and a the towns of Gilead,
13:30 through a Bashan, the whole kingdom of King Og
13:30 and a the settlements of Jair, which are in Bashan,
15:32 in a, twenty-nine towns, with their villages.
15:46 a that were near Ashdod, with their villages.
16: 9 a those towns with their villages.
17:14 whom a along the LORD has blessed?"
17:16 yet a the Canaanites who live in
18:20 boundary by boundary a around.
19: 8 together with a the villages a around these towns
20: 9 the cities designated for a the Israelites, N
21:19 were thirteen in a, with their pasture lands.
21:26 of the rest of the Kohathites were ten in a,
21:33 of the Gershonites were in a thirteen,
21:39 with its pasture lands—four towns in a.
21:40 those allotted to them were twelve in a.
21:41 in a forty-eight towns with their pasture lands.
21:42 so it was with a these towns.
21:43 Israel a the land that he swore to their ancestors I
21:44 not one of a their enemies had withstood them,
21:44 for the LORD had given a their enemies
21:45 of a the good promises that the LORD had made
21:45 of Israel had failed; a came to pass.
22: 2 "You have observed a that Moses the servant of
22: 2 have obeyed me in a that I have commanded you;
22: 5 to walk in a his ways, to keep his commandments,
22: 5 with a your heart and with all your soul." J

Jos 22: 5 with all your heart and with a your soul."
22:20 and wrath fell upon a the congregation of Israel? U
23: 1 to Israel from a their enemies a around,
23: 2 Joshua summoned a Israel, their elders B
23: 3 and you have seen a that the LORD your God
23: 3 the LORD your God has done to a these nations D
23: 4 with a the nations that I have already cut off, D
23: 6 to observe and do a that is written in the book of
23:14 now I am about to go the way of a the earth, E
23:14 and you know in your hearts and souls, a of you,
23:14 that not one thing has failed of a the good things
23:14 a have come to pass for you,
23:15 But just as a the good things that
23:15 the LORD will bring upon you a the bad things,
24: 1 gathered a the tribes of Israel to Shechem, S
24: 2 And Joshua said to a the people, A
24: 3 beyond the River and led him through a the land I
24:17 He protected us along a the way that we went,
24:17 among a the peoples through whom we passed; G
24:18 and the LORD drove out before us a the peoples, G
24:27 Joshua said to a the people, "See, A
24:27 for it has heard a the words of the LORD K
24:31 Israel served the LORD a the days of Joshua, F
24:31 and a the days of the elders who outlived Joshua F
24:31 and had known a the work that the LORD V
Jdg 1:25 but they let the man and a his family go.
2: 4 the LORD spoke these words to a the Israelites, N
2: 6 the Israelites a went to their own inheritances
2: 7 The people worshiped the LORD a the days F
2: 7 and a the days of the elders who outlived Joshua, F
2: 7 who had seen a the great work that the LORD V
2:12 the gods of the peoples who were a around them,
2:14 sold them into the power of their enemies a around
2:18 the hand of their enemies a the days of the judge; F
3: 1 to test a those in Israel who had no experience
3: 3 and a the Canaanites, and the Sidonians,
3:19 and a his attendants went out from his presence.
3:29 a strong, able-bodied men; no one escaped.
4:13 Sisera called out a his chariots,
4:13 and a the troops who were with him,
4:15 And the LORD threw Sisera and a his chariots
4:15 and all his chariots and a his army into a panic
4:16 A the army of Sisera fell by the sword;
5:31 "So perish a your enemies, O LORD!
6: 9 and from the hand of a who oppressed you,
6:13 why then has a this happened to us?
6:13 And where are a his wonderful deeds
6:31 But Joash said to a who were arrayed against him,
6:33 Then a the Midianites and the Amalekites and
6:35 He sent messengers throughout a Manasseh,
6:37 and it is dry on a the ground,
6:39 and on a the ground let there be dew."
6:40 and on a the ground there was dew.
7: 1 and a the troops that were with him rose early
7: 5 "A those who lap the water with their tongues,
7: 5 a those who kneel down to drink,
7: 6 a the rest of the troops knelt down to drink water.
7: 7 Let a the others go to their homes."
7: 8 he sent a the rest of Israel back to their own tents,
7:12 and a the people of the east lay along the valley A
7:14 into his hand God has given Midian and a
7:16 and put trumpets into the hands of a of them,
7:18 I blow the trumpet, I and a who are with me,
7:21 Every man stood in his place a around the camp,
7:21 and a the men in camp ran; Z
7:22 against his fellow and against a the army;
7:23 and from Asher and from a Manasseh,
7:24 Then Gideon sent messengers throughout a
7:24 So a the men of Ephraim were called out, Z
8:10 a who were left of a the army of the people of
8:12 and threw a the army into a panic.
8:27 and a Israel prostituted themselves to it there, B
8:34 from the hand of a their enemies on every side;
8:35 in return for a the good that he had done to Israel.
9: 2 "Say in the hearing of a the lords of Shechem,
9: 2 a seventy of the sons of Jerubbaal rule over you,
9: 3 So his mother's kinsfolk spoke a these words
9: 3 on his behalf in the hearing of a the lords
9: 6 Then a the lords of Shechem and a Beth-millo
9:14 So a the trees said to the bramble,
9:25 They robbed a who passed by them along
9:34 and a the troops with him got up by night and lay
9:44 while the two companies rushed on a who were in
9:45 Abimelech fought against the city a that day;
9:46 a the lords of the Tower of Shechem heard of it,
9:47 Abimelech was told that a the lords of the Tower
9:48 he and a the troops that were with him.
9:49 a the people of the Tower of Shechem also died, A
9:51 and a the men and women and all the lords of Z
9:51 and women and a the lords of the city fled to it
9:55 that Abimelech was dead, they a went home.
9:57 and God also made a the wickedness of the people
10: 8 eighteen years they oppressed a the Israelites N
10:18 shall be head over a the inhabitants of Gilead." L
11: 8 over a the inhabitants of Gilead." L
11:11 and Jephthah spoke a his words before the LORD
11:20 so Sihon gathered a his people together, A
11:21 gave Sihon and a his people into the hand A
11:21 so Israel occupied a the land of the Amorites, I
11:22 They occupied a the territory of the Amorites
11:26 and in a the towns that are along the Arnon,
12: 4 Then Jephthah gathered a the men of Gilead Z
13:13 "Let the woman give heed to a that I said to her.
13:23 or shown us a these things, H
14: 3 woman among your kin, or among a our people, A
16: 2 and lay in wait for him a night at the city gate.
16: 2 They kept quiet a night, thinking,

Jdg 16: 3 bar and a, put them on his shoulders,
16:27 a the lords of the Philistines were there,
16:30 He strained with a his might;
16:30 on the lords and a the people who were in it. A
16:31 Then his brothers and a his family came down
17: 6 a the people did what was right in their own A
19:20 I will care for a your wants;
19:25 abused her a through the night until the morning.
19:29 and sent her throughout a the territory of Israel.
19:30 saying, "Thus shall you say to a the Israelites, N
20: 1 Then a the Israelites came out, N
20: 2 The chiefs of a the people, A
20: 2 of a the tribes of Israel, presented themselves S
20: 7 So now, you Israelites, a of you,
20: 8 A the people got up as one, saying, A
20:10 ten men of a hundred throughout a the tribes of S
20:10 of Benjamin for a the disgrace that they have done
20:11 So a the men of Israel gathered against the city, Z
20:12 of Israel sent men through a the tribe of Benjamin,
20:16 Of a this force, there were seven hundred picked
20:17 armed men, a of them warriors.
20:25 down eighteen thousand of the Israelites, a
20:26 Then a the Israelites, the whole army, N
20:34 ten thousand picked men out of a Israel, B
20:35 of Benjamin that day, a of them armed.
20:44 a of them courageous fighters.
20:46 So a who fell that day of Benjamin
20:46 a of them courageous fighters.
20:48 city, the people, the animals, and a that remained.
21: 5 "Which of a the tribes of Israel did not come up S
21:25 a the people did what was right in their own A
Ru 2:11 "A that you have done for your mother-in-law
2:21 until they have finished a my harvest.' "
3: 5 She said to her, "A that you tell me I will do."
3:11 do not be afraid, I will do for you a that you ask,
3:11 for a the assembly of my people know
3:16 Then she told her a that the man had done for her,
4: 9 Then Boaz said to the elders and a the people, A
4: 9 the hand of Naomi a that belonged to Elimelech
4: 9 and a that belonged to Chilion
4:11 Then a the people who were at the gate, A
1Sa 1: 4 to his wife Peninnah and to a her sons
1:16 of my great anxiety and vexation a this time."
1:21 The man Elkanah and a his household went up
1:22 I will offer him as a nazirite for a time."
2:14 a that the fork brought up the priest would take
2:14 at Shiloh to a the Israelites who came there. N
2:22 He heard a that his sons were doing to all Israel,
2:22 He heard all that his sons were doing to a Israel, B
2:23 I hear of your evil dealings from a these people. A
2:28 of a the tribes of Israel to be my priest, to go up S
2:28 the family of your ancestor a my offerings by fire
2:32 in distress you will look with greedy eye on a
2:33 a the members of your household shall die by
3:12 On that day I will fulfill against Eli a
3:17 you hide anything from me of a that he told you."
3:20 And a Israel from Dan to Beer-sheba knew B
4: 1 And the word of Samuel came to a Israel. B
4: 5 a Israel gave a mighty shout, B
4:13 into the city and told the news, a the city cried out.
5: 5 of Dagon and a who enter the house of Dagon do
5: 8 So they sent and gathered together a the lords of
5:11 and gathered together a the lords of the Philistines,
6: 3 but by a means return him a guilt offering.
6: 4 for the same plague was upon a of you and
6:18 of a the cities of the Philistines belonging to
7: 2 a the house of Israel lamented after the LORD.
7: 3 Then Samuel said to a the house of Israel,
7: 3 you are returning to the LORD with a your heart, J
7: 5 Then Samuel said, "Gather a Israel at Mizpah, B
7:13 the LORD was against the Philistines a the days F
7:15 Samuel judged Israel a the days of his life. F
7:16 and he judged Israel in a these places.
8: 4 Then a the elders of Israel gathered together
8: 7 to the voice of the people in a that they say to you;
8:10 So Samuel reported a the words of the LORD to K
8:21 Samuel had heard a the words of the people, K
9:19 in the morning I will let you go and will tell you a
9:20 And on whom is a Israel's desire fixed,
9:20 if not on you and on a your ancestral house?"
9:21 and my family is the humblest of a the families of
10: 1 from the hand of their enemies a around.
10: 9 and a these signs were fulfilled that day.
10:11 When a who knew him before saw
10:18 and from the hand of a the kingdoms R
10:19 from a your calamities and your distresses;
10:20 Then Samuel brought a the tribes of Israel near, S
10:24 Samuel said to a the people, A
10:24 There is no one like him among a the people." A
10:24 And a the people shouted, "Long live the king!" A
10:25 Samuel sent a the people back to their homes. A
11: 1 and a the men of Jabesh said to Nahash, Z
11: 2 and thus put disgrace upon a Israel." B
11: 3 that we may send messengers through a
11: 4 and a the people wept aloud. A
11: 7 and cut them in pieces and sent them throughout a
11:15 So a the people went to Gilgal, A
11:15 there Saul and a the Israelites rejoiced greatly. N
12: 1 Samuel said to a Israel, "I have listened to you B
12: 1 "I have listened to you in a that you have said
12: 7 and I will declare to you a the saving deeds of
12:18 and a the people greatly feared the LORD A
12:19 A the people said to Samuel, A
12:19 to a our sins the evil of demanding a king
12:20 you have done a this evil,
12:20 but serve the LORD with a your heart; J
12:24 and serve him faithfully with a your heart; J

1Sa 13: 3 And Saul blew the trumpet throughout a the land, I
13: 4 When a Israel heard that Saul had defeated B
13: 7 and a the people followed him trembling. A
13:19 no smith to be found throughout a the land of I
13:20 so a the Israelites went down to the Philistines N
14: 7 "Do a that your mind inclines to.
14:15 in the field, and among a the people; A
14:20 and a the people who were with him rallied A
14:22 when a the Israelites who had gone into hiding N
14:25 A the troops came upon a honeycomb;
14:34 'Let a bring their oxen or their sheep,
14:34 So a of the troops brought their oxen with them
14:38 "Come here, a you leaders of the people;
14:39 among a the people who answered him. A
14:40 He said to a Israel, "You shall be on one side, B
14:47 he fought against a his enemies on every side—
14:52 hard fighting against the Philistines a the days F
15: 3 and utterly destroy a that they have;
15: 6 you showed kindness to a the people of Israel A
15: 8 but utterly destroyed a the people with the edge A
15: 9 and the lambs, and a that was valuable,
15: 9 a that was despised and worthless they utterly
15:11 and he cried out to the LORD a night.
16:11 Samuel said to Jesse, "Are a your sons here?"
17:11 and a Israel heard these words of the Philistine, B
17:19 Now Saul, and they, and a the men of Israel, Z
17:24 A the Israelites, when they saw the man, N
17:46 so that a the earth may know that there is a God E
17:47 and that a this assembly may know that
18: 5 a the people, even the servants of Saul, A
18: 6 the women came out of a the towns of Israel,
18:14 David had success in a his undertakings;
18:16 But a Israel and Judah loved David; B
18:22 and a his servants love you; Q
18:30 David had more success than a the servants of Q
19: 1 with his son Jonathan and with a his servants Q
19: 5 LORD brought about a great victory for a Israel. B
19: 7 and related a these things to him. H
19:18 and told him a that Saul had done to him.
19:24 He lay naked a that day and a that night.
20: 6 If your father misses me at a, then say,
20: 6 there is a yearly sacrifice there for a the family.'
22: 1 his brothers and a his father's house heard of it,
22: 4 with him a the time that David was in
22: 6 and a his servants were standing around him. Q
22: 7 and vineyards, will he make you a commanders
22: 8 Is that why a of you have conspired against me?
22:11 and for a his father's house, the priests who were
22:11 and a of them came to the king.
22:14 among a your servants is so faithful as David? Q
22:15 for your servant has known nothing of a this,
22:16 Ahimelech, you and a your father's house."
22:22 for the lives of a your father's house.
23: 8 Saul summoned a the people to war, A
23:23 and learn a the hiding places where he lurks,
23:23 if he is in the land, I will search him out among a
24: 2 men out of a Israel, and went to look for David B
25: 1 and a Israel assembled and mourned for him. B
25: 6 and peace be to a that you have.
25: 7 a the time they were in Carmel.
25: 9 they said a this to Nabal in the name of David;
25:12 and came back and told him a this.
25:16 a the while we were with them keeping the sheep.
25:17 against our master and against a his house;
25:21 in vain that I protected a that this fellow has in
25:21 that nothing was missed of a that belonged to him;
25:22 so much as one male of a who belong to him."
25:30 to a the good that he has spoken concerning you,
25:36 she told him nothing at a until the morning light.
26:12 for they were a asleep, because a deep sleep from
26:24 and may he rescue me from a tribulation."
27:11 Such was his practice a the time he lived in
28: 3 a Israel had mourned for him and buried him B
28: 4 Saul gathered a Israel, and they encamped B
28:20 for he had eaten nothing a day and a night.
29: 1 the Philistines gathered a their forces at Aphek,
30: 2 and taken captive the women and a who were
30: 6 of stoning him, because a the people were bitter A
30:16 they were spread out a over the ground,
30:18 David recovered a that the Amalekites had taken;
30:20 David also captured a the flocks and herds,
30:22 Then a the corrupt and worthless fellows among
30:31 in Hebron, a the places where David
31: 6 and his armor-bearer and a his men died together
31:12 a the valiant men set out,
31:12 traveled a night long, and took the body of Saul
2Sa 1:11 and a the men who were with him did the same. Z
2: 9 Jezreel, Ephraim, Benjamin, and over a Israel. B
2:23 And a those who came to the place
2:28 the trumpet and a the people stopped; A
2:29 Abner and his men traveled a that night through
2:30 and when he had gathered a the people together, A
2:32 Joab and his men marched a night,
3:12 and I will give you my support to bring a Israel B
3:16 as he walked behind her a the way to Bahurim.
3:18 and from a their enemies."
3:19 at Hebron a that Israel and the whole house
3:21 Let me go and rally a Israel to my lord the king, B
3:21 that you may reign over a that your heart desires."
3:23 Joab and a the army that was with him came,
3:25 to learn your comings and goings and to learn a
3:29 and on a his father's house;
3:31 to Joab and to a the people who were with him, A
3:32 at the grave of Abner, and a the people wept. A
3:34 And a the people wept over him again. A
3:35 Then a the people came to persuade David A
3:36 A the people took notice of it, and it pleased A

2Sa 3:36 as everything the king did pleased a the people. A
3:37 So a the people and all Israel understood that A
3:37 So all the people and a Israel understood that B
4: 1 his courage failed, and a Israel was dismayed. B
4: 7 and traveled by way of the Arabah a night long.
5: 1 a the tribes of Israel came to David at Hebron, S
5: 3 a the elders of Israel came to the king at Hebron;
5: 5 over a Israel and Judah thirty-three years. B
5: 9 the city a around from the Millo inward.
5:17 a the Philistines went up in search of David;
5:25 struck down the Philistines from Geba a the way
6: 1 David again gathered a the chosen men of Israel,
6: 2 David and a the people with him set out and A
6: 5 and a the house of Israel were dancing before the
LORD with a their might,
6:11 LORD blessed Obed-edom and a his household.
6:12 the household of Obed-edom and a that belongs
6:14 David danced before the LORD with a his might;
6:15 and a the house of Israel brought up the ark of
6:19 and distributed food among a the people, A
6:19 Then a the people went back to their homes. A
6:21 in place of your father and a his household,
7: 1 the LORD had given him rest from a his enemies
7: 3 "Go, do a that you have in mind;
7: 7 I have moved about among a the people A
7: 9 and have cut off a your enemies from before you;
7:11 and I will give you rest from a your enemies.
7:17 with a these words and with a this vision,
7:21 you have wrought a this greatness,
7:22 according to a that we have heard with our ears.
8: 4 David hamstrung a the chariot horses,
8:11 and gold that he dedicated from a the nations D
8:14 throughout a Edom he put garrisons,
8:14 and a the Edomites became David's servants.
8:15 So David reigned over a Israel; B
8:15 and equity to a his people. A
9: 7 to you a the land of your grandfather Saul, I
9: 9 "A that belonged to Saul and to a his house
9:11 to a that my lord the king commands his servant,
9:12 And a who lived in Ziba's house
10: 7 he sent Joab and a the army with the warriors.
10:17 it was told David, he gathered a Israel together, B
10:19 When a the kings who were servants P
11: 1 David sent Joab with his officers and a Israel B
11: 9 the king's house with a the servants of his lord, Q
11:18 Then Joab sent and told David a the news about
11:19 "When you have finished telling the king a
11:22 and came and told David a that Joab had sent him
12:12 but I will do this thing before a Israel, B
12:16 and went in and lay a night on the ground.
12:29 So David gathered a the people together A
12:31 Thus he did to a the cities of the Ammonites.
12:31 David and a the people returned to Jerusalem. A
13:21 When King David heard of a these things, H
13:23 and Absalom invited a the king's sons.
13:25 "No, my son, let us not a go,
13:27 until he let Amnon and a the king's sons go
13:29 Then a the king's sons rose,
13:30 that Absalom had killed a the king's sons,
13:31 and a his servants who were standing Q
13:32 "Let not my lord suppose that they have killed a
13:33 as if a the king's sons were dead;
13:36 king and a his servants also wept very bitterly. Q
14:14 We must a die; we are like water
14:19 king said, "Is the hand of Joab with you in a this?"
14:19 it was he who put a these words into the mouth
14:20 the wisdom of the angel of God to know a things C
14:25 in a Israel there was no one to be praised so B
15: 4 Then a who had a suit or cause might come to me,
15:10 secret messengers throughout a the tribes S
15:14 to a his officials who were with him at Jerusalem,
15:16 So the king left, followed by a his household,
15:17 The king left, followed by a the people; A
15:18 A his officials passed by him;
15:18 and a the Cherethites, and a the Pelethites,
15:18 and a the six hundred Gittites who had followed
15:22 with a his men and a the little ones who were
15:23 The whole country wept aloud as a the people A
15:23 a the people moved on toward the wilderness. A
15:24 and Zadok also, with a the Levites,
15:24 until the people had a passed out of the city.
15:30 and a the people who were with him A
16: 4 "A that belonged to Mephibosheth is now yours."
16: 6 He threw stones at David and at a the servants Q
16: 6 now a the people and all the warriors were A
16: 6 and a the warriors were on his right and on his left.
16: 8 The LORD has avenged on a of you the blood of
16:11 David said to Abishai and to a his servants, Q
16:14 The king and a the people who were A
16:15 Absalom and a the Israelites came to Jerusalem; N
16:18 and this people and a the Israelites have chosen, N
16:21 after the house; and a Israel will hear B
16:21 of a who are with you will be strengthened."
16:22 to his father's concubines in the sight of a Israel. B
16:23 so a the counsel of Ahithophel was esteemed,
17: 2 and a the people who are with him will flee. A
17: 3 and I will bring a the people back to you as A
17: 3 and a the people will be at peace." A
17: 4 advice pleased Absalom and a the elders of Israel.
17:10 for a Israel knows that your father is a warrior, B
17:11 my counsel is that a Israel be gathered to you, B
17:13 then a Israel will bring ropes to that city, B
17:14 Absalom and a the men of Israel said, Z
17:16 but by a means cross over;
17:16 the king and a the people who are with him will A
17:22 and a the people who were with him set out A
17:24 Absalom crossed the Jordan with a the men Z

2Sa 18: 4 while a the army marched out by hundreds and
18: 5 a the people heard when the king gave orders A
18: 5 the people heard when the king gave orders to a
18: 8 The battle spread over the face of a the country;
18:17 Meanwhile a the Israelites fled to their homes. N
18:28 Then Ahimaaz cried out to the king, "A is well!"
18:31 delivering you from the power of a who rose up
18:32 and a who rise up to do you harm,
19: 2 that day was turned into mourning for a
19: 5 of a your officers who have saved your life today,
19: 6 for I perceive that if Absalom were alive and a
19: 8 The troops were a told, "See,
19: 8 and a the troops came before the king.
19: 8 a the Israelites had fled to their homes. N
19: 9 A the people were disputing throughout A
19: 9 disputing throughout a the tribes of Israel, S
19:11 The talk of a Israel has come to the king. B
19:14 Amasa swayed the hearts of a the people of A
19:14 "Return, both you and a your servants." Q
19:20 therefore, see, I have come this day, the first of a
19:28 For a my father's house were doomed to death
19:30 Mephibosheth said to the king, "Let him take it a,
19:38 and a that you desire of me I will do for you."
19:39 Then a the people crossed over the Jordan, A
19:40 a the people of Judah, and also half the people A
19:41 Then a the people of Israel came to the king, A
19:41 and a David's men with him?"
19:42 A the people of Judah answered the people A
19:42 Have we eaten at a at the king's expense?
20: 2 So a the people of Israel withdrew from David A
20: 7 the Pelethites, and a the warriors;
20:12 the man saw that a the people were stopping. A
20:12 he saw that a who came by him were stopping,
20:13 a the people went on after Joab A
20:14 Sheba passed through a the tribes of Israel S
20:14 and a the Bichrites assembled,
20:22 woman went to a the people with her wise plan. A
20:22 and a went to their homes,
20:23 Joab was in command of a the army of Israel;
21: 5 so that we should have no place in a the territory
21:14 they did a that the king commanded.
22: 1 from the hand of a his enemies,
22:23 For a his ordinances were before me,
22:31 he is a shield for a who take refuge in him.
23: 5 ordered in a things and secure. C
23: 5 not cause to prosper a my help and my desire?
23: 6 the godless are a like thorns that are thrown away;
23:39 Uriah the Hittite—thirty-seven in a.
24: 2 "Go through a the tribes of Israel, S
24: 7 and came to the fortress of Tyre and to a the cities
24: 8 So when they had gone through a the land, I
24:23 A this, O king, Araunah gives to the king."
1Ki 1: 3 a beautiful girl throughout a the territory of Israel,
1: 9 and he invited a his brothers, the king's sons,
1: 9 the king's sons, and a the royal officials of Judah,
1:19 and has invited a the children of the king,
1:20 of a Israel are on you to tell them who shall sit B
1:25 and has invited a the king's children,
1:39 they blew the trumpet, and a the people said, A
1:40 And a the people went up following him, A
1:41 and a the guests who were with him heard it
1:49 Then a the guests of Adonijah got up trembling
2: 2 "I am about to go the way of a the earth. E
2: 3 so that you may prosper in a that you do
2: 4 walk before me in faithfulness with a their heart J
2: 4 with all their heart and with a their soul,
2:15 and that a Israel expected me to reign; B
2:26 you shared in a the hardships my father endured."
2:44 in your own heart a the evil that you did
3:13 both riches and honor a your life;
3:15 and provided a feast for a his servants. Q
3:28 A Israel heard of the judgment that B
4: 1 King Solomon was king over a Israel, B
4: 7 Solomon had twelve officials over a Israel, B
4:10 (to him belonged Socoh and a the land of Hepher) I
4:11 in a Naphath-dor (he had Taphath,
4:12 in Taanach, Megiddo, and a Beth-shean,
4:21 Solomon was sovereign over a the kingdoms R
4:21 brought tribute and served Solomon a the days F
4:24 For he had dominion over a the region west of
4:24 over a the kings west of the Euphrates; P
4:24 and he had peace on a sides.
4:25 a of them under their vines and fig trees.
4:27 and for a who came to King Solomon's table,
4:30 the wisdom of a the people of the east, A
4:30 and a the wisdom of Egypt.
4:31 throughout a the surrounding nations.
4:34 People came from a the nations to hear D
4:34 from a the kings of the earth who had heard P
5: 8 I will fulfill a your needs in the matter of cedar
5:13 Solomon conscripted forced labor out of a Israel; B
6: 5 and he made side chambers a around.
6:12 keep a my commandments by walking in them,
6:18 a was cedar, no stone was seen.
6:29 the house a around about with carved engravings
6:38 the house was finished in a its parts,
6:38 and according to a its specifications.
7: 5 A the doorways and doorposts had four-sided
7: 9 A these were made of costly stones,
7:12 to one layer of cedar beams a around;
7:14 He came to King Solomon, and did a his work.
7:20 two hundred pomegranates in rows a around;
7:24 Under its brim were panels a around it,
7:33 their spokes, and their hubs were a cast.
7:36 where each had space, with wreaths a around.
7:37 a of them were cast alike,
7:40 So Hiram finished a the work that he did V

1Ki 7:45 a these vessels that Hiram made
7:47 Solomon left a the vessels unweighed,
7:48 So Solomon made a the vessels that were in
7:51 Thus a the work that King Solomon did on V
8: 1 the elders of Israel and a the heads of the tribes,
8: 2 A the people of Israel assembled to King A
8: 3 And a the elders of Israel came,
8: 4 and a the holy vessels that were in the tent;
8: 5 King Solomon and a the congregation of Israel, U
8:14 the king turned around and blessed a the assembly
8:14 while a the assembly of Israel stood.
8:22 before the altar of the LORD in the presence of a
8:23 before you with a their heart, J
8:38 any individual or from a your people Israel, A
8:38 a knowing the afflictions of their own hearts so
8:39 and render to a whose hearts you know—
8:39 according to a their ways,
8:40 that they may fear you a the days that they live F
8:43 do according to a that the foreigner calls to you,
8:43 so that a the peoples of the earth may know G
8:48 if they repent with a their heart and soul in J
8:50 and a their transgressions
8:53 separated them from among a the peoples of G
8:54 when Solomon finished offering a this prayer
8:55 he stood and blessed a the assembly of Israel with
8:56 to his people Israel according to a
8:56 not one word has failed of a his good promise,
8:58 to walk in a his ways,
8:60 so that a the peoples of the earth may know that G
8:62 Then the king, and a Israel with him, B
8:63 and a the people of Israel dedicated the house of A
8:65 the festival at that time, and a Israel with him— B
8:66 and in good spirits because of a the goodness that
9: 1 and the king's house and a that Solomon desired
9: 3 my eyes and my heart will be there for a time.
9: 4 doing according to a that I have commanded you,
9: 7 a proverb and a taunt among a peoples. G
9:19 as well as a of Solomon's storage cities,
9:19 in Lebanon, and in a the land of his dominion. I
9:20 A the people who were left of the Amorites, A
10: 2 she told him a that was on her mind.
10: 3 Solomon answered a her questions;
10: 4 of Sheba had observed a the wisdom of Solomon,
10:15 and from a the kings of Arabia and the governors P
10:21 A King Solomon's drinking vessels were of gold,
10:21 and a the vessels of the House of the Forest
10:23 King Solomon excelled a the kings of the earth P
10:29 they were exported to a the kings of the Hittites P
11: 8 He did the same for a his foreign wives,
11:16 (for Joab and a Israel remained there six months, B
11:25 of Israel a the days of Solomon, making trouble F
11:28 over a the forced labor of the house of Joseph.
11:32 that I have chosen out of a the tribes of Israel. S
11:34 but will make him ruler a the days of his life, F
11:37 and you shall reign over a that your soul desires;
11:38 If you will listen to a that I command you,
11:41 a that he did as well as his wisdom,
11:42 in Jerusalem over a Israel was forty years. B
12: 1 a Israel had come to Shechem to make him king. B
12: 3 and Jeroboam and a the assembly of Israel came
12:12 a the people came to Rehoboam the third day, A
12:16 a Israel saw that the king would not listen B
12:18 a Israel stoned him to death. B
12:20 When a Israel heard that Jeroboam had returned, B
12:20 the assembly and made him king over a Israel. B
12:21 he assembled a the house of Judah and the tribe
12:23 and to a the house of Judah and Benjamin,
12:31 and appointed priests from among a the people, A
13:11 One of his sons came and told him a that the man
13:32 and against a the houses of the high places that are
13:33 the high places again from among a the people; A
14: 8 and followed me with a his heart, J
14: 9 above a those who were before you and have gone
14:10 just as one burns up dung until it is a gone.
14:13 A Israel shall mourn for him and bury him; B
14:18 A Israel buried him and mourned for him, B
14:21 that the LORD had chosen out of a the tribes S
14:22 more than a that their ancestors had done.
14:24 They committed a the abominations of the nations
14:26 He also took away a the shields of gold
14:29 rest of the acts of Rehoboam, and a that he did,
15: 3 He committed a the sins that his father did
15: 5 anything that he commanded him a the days F
15: 6 Rehoboam and Jeroboam continued a the days F
15: 7 The rest of the acts of Abijam, and a that he did,
15:12 removed a the idols that his ancestors had made.
15:14 the heart of Asa was true to the LORD a his days.
15:16 and King Baasha of Israel a their days.
15:18 Then Asa took a the silver and the gold
15:20 Dan, Abel-beth-maacah, and a Chinneroth,
15:20 and all Chinneroth, with a the land of Naphtali. I
15:22 Then King Asa made a proclamation to a Judah, T
15:23 Now the rest of a the acts of Asa, a his power,
15:23 a that he did, and the cities that he built,
15:27 and a Israel were laying siege to Gibbethon. B
15:29 he killed a the house of Jeroboam;
15:31 the rest of the acts of Nadab, and a that he did,
15:32 and King Baasha of Israel a their days.
15:33 son of Ahijah began to reign over a Israel B
16: 7 of a the evil that he did in the sight of the LORD,
16:11 he killed a the house of Baasha;
16:12 Thus Zimri destroyed a the house of Baasha,
16:13 of a the sins of Baasha and the sins of his son Elah
16:14 Now the rest of the acts of Elah, and a that he did,
16:16 therefore a Israel made Omri, B
16:17 and a Israel with him, and they besieged Tirzah. B
16:25 he did more evil than a who were before him.

1Ki 16:26 he walked in a the way of Jeroboam son of Nebat,
16:30 of the LORD more than a who were before him.
16:33 than had a the kings of Israel who were P
18: 5 to a the springs of water and to a the wadis;
18:19 have a Israel assemble for me at Mount Carmel, B
18:20 So Ahab sent to a the Israelites, N
18:21 Elijah then came near to a the people, and said, A
18:24 A the people answered, "Well spoken!" A
18:30 Elijah said to a the people, "Come closer to me"; A
18:30 and a the people came closer to him. A
18:35 so that the water ran a around the altar,
18:36 that I have done a these things at your bidding. H
18:39 When a the people saw it, A
19: 1 Ahab told Jezebel a that Elijah had done,
19: 1 how he had killed a the prophets with the sword.
19:18 a the knees that have not bowed to Baal,
20: 1 of Aram gathered a his army together;
20: 4 my lord, O king, I am yours, and a that I have."
20: 7 the king of Israel called a the elders of the land,
20: 8 Then a the elders and all the people said to him,
20: 8 Then all the elders and a the people said to him, A
20: 9 A that you first demanded of your servant
20:13 Have you seen a this great multitude?
20:15 after them he mustered a the people of Israel, A
20:28 I will give a this great multitude into your hand,
22:10 and a the prophets were prophesying before them.
22:12 A the prophets were prophesying the same
22:17 "I saw a Israel scattered on the mountains, B
22:19 on his throne, with a the host of heaven standing
22:22 be a lying spirit in the mouth of a his prophets.'
22:23 in the mouth of a these your prophets;
22:28 And he said, "Hear, you peoples, a of you!"
22:39 the rest of the acts of Ahab, and a that he did,
22:39 and a the cities that he built,
22:43 He walked in a the way of his father Asa;
2Ki 3: 6 of Samaria at that time and mustered a Israel. B
3:19 a springs of water you shall stop up,
3:21 When a the Moabites heard that
3:21 a who were able to put on armor,
4: 3 borrow vessels from a your neighbors,
4: 4 and start pouring into a these vessels;
4:13 Since you have taken a this trouble for us,
4:23 She said, "It will be a right."
4:26 and say to her, Are you a right?
4:26 Is your husband a right?
4:26 Is the child a right?"
4:26 She answered, "It is a right."
5:12 better than a the waters of Israel?
5:13 How much more, when a he said to you was,
5:15 to the man of God, he and a his company;
5:15 there is no God in a the earth except in Israel; E
5:21 to meet him and said, "Is everything a right?"
5:25 "Your servant has not gone anywhere at a."
6:15 an army with horses and chariots was a around
6:17 of horses and chariots of fire a around Elisha.
7: 5 there was no one there at a.
8: 4 "Tell me a the great things that Elisha has done."
8: 6 saying, "Restore a that was hers,
8: 6 together with a the revenue of the fields from
8: 9 a kinds of goods of Damascus, forty camel loads.
8:21 Joram crossed over to Zair with a his chariots.
8:23 the rest of the acts of Joram, and a that he did,
9: 7 and the blood of a the servants of the LORD. Q
9:11 they said to him, "Is everything a right?
9:13 Then hurriedly they a took their cloaks
9:14 a Israel had been on guard at Ramoth-gilead B
9:24 Jehu drew his bow with a his strength,
10: 9 he stood and said to a the people, A
10: 9 but who struck down a these?
10:11 So Jehu killed a who were left of the house
10:11 a his leaders, close friends, and priests,
10:14 forty-two in a; he spared none of them.
10:17 he killed a who were left to Ahab in Samaria,
10:18 Jehu assembled a the people and said to them, A
10:19 therefore summon to me a the prophets of Baal,
10:19 a his worshipers, and a his priests;
10:21 Jehu sent word throughout a Israel; B
10:21 a the worshipers of Baal came,
10:22 "Bring out the vestments for a the worshipers
10:30 with a that was in my heart have dealt with
10:31 of the LORD the God of Israel with a his heart; J
10:33 a the land of Gilead, the Gadites, the Reubenites, I
10:34 the acts of Jehu, a that he did, and a his power,
11: 1 she set about to destroy a the royal family.
11: 9 to a that the priest Jehoiada commanded;
11:14 and a the people of the land rejoicing A
11:18 a the people of the land went to the house of A
11:19 the guards, and a the people of the land; A
11:20 So a the people of the land rejoiced; A
12: 2 in the sight of the LORD a his days,
12: 4 "A the money offered as sacred donations
12: 9 in it a the money that was brought into the house
12:18 of Judah took a the votive gifts that Jehoshaphat,
12:18 a the gold that was found in the treasuries of
12:19 the rest of the acts of Joash, and a that he did,
13: 8 the rest of the acts of Jehoahaz and a that he did,
13:11 he did not depart from a the sins of Jeroboam son
13:12 the rest of the acts of Joash, and a that he did,
13:22 of Aram oppressed Israel a the days of Jehoahaz. F
14: 3 in a things he did as his father Joash had done. C
14: 6 but a shall be put to death for their own sins."
14:14 He seized a the gold and silver,
14:14 and a the vessels that were found in the house of
14:21 A the people of Judah took Azariah, A
14:24 he did not depart from a the sins of Jeroboam son
14:28 the rest of the acts of Jeroboam, and a that he did,
15: 6 the rest of the acts of Azariah, and a that he did,

2Ki 15:16 a who were in it and its territory from Tirzah on;
15:16 He ripped open a the pregnant women in it.
15:18 he did not depart a his days from any of the sins
15:20 that is, from a the wealthy,
15:21 rest of the deeds of Menahem, and a that he did,
15:26 rest of the deeds of Pekahiah, and a that he did,
15:29 Gilead, and Galilee, a the land of Naphtali; I
15:31 the rest of the acts of Pekah, and a that he did,
15:36 the rest of the acts of Jotham, and a that he did,
16:10 and its pattern, exact in a its details.
16:11 with a that King Ahaz had sent from Damascus,
16:15 the burnt offering of a the people of the land, A
16:15 dash against it a the blood of the burnt offering,
16:15 and a the blood of the sacrifice;
17: 5 the king of Assyria invaded a the land and came I
17: 9 at a their towns, from watchtower to fortified city;
17:11 there they made offerings on a the high places,
17:13 with a the law that I commanded your ancestors
17:16 They rejected a the commandments of
17:16 worshiped a the host of heaven, and served Baal.
17:20 The LORD rejected a the descendants of Israel;
17:22 The people of Israel continued in a the sins
17:23 as he had foretold through a his servants Q
17:32 among themselves a sorts of people as priests A
17:39 of the hand of a your enemies."
18: 5 that there was no one like him among a the kings P
18:12 a that Moses the servant of
18:13 King Sennacherib of Assyria came up against a
18:15 Hezekiah gave him a the silver that was found in
18:21 Such is Pharaoh king of Egypt to a who rely
18:35 Who among a the gods of
19: 4 be that the LORD your God heard a the words of K
19:11 the kings of Assyria have done to a lands,
19:15 you alone, of a the kingdoms of the earth; R
19:19 a the kingdoms of the earth may know that you, R
19:24 with the sole of my foot a the streams of Egypt.'
19:35 when morning dawned, they were a dead bodies.
20:13 he showed them a his treasure house, the silver,
20:13 his armory, a that was found in his storehouses;
20:13 or in a his realm that Hezekiah did not show them.
20:15 "They have seen a that is in my house;
20:17 Days are coming when a that is in your house,
20:20 The rest of the deeds of Hezekiah, a his power,
21: 3 worshiped a the host of heaven, and served them.
21: 5 for a the host of heaven in the two courts of
21: 7 which I have chosen out of a the tribes of Israel, S
21: 8 to do according to a that I have commanded them,
21: 8 and according to a the law
21:11 has done things more wicked than a that
21:14 a prey and a spoil to a their enemies,
21:17 the rest of the acts of Manasseh, a that he did,
21:21 in a the way in which his father walked, served
21:24 of the land killed a those who had conspired
22: 2 and walked in a the way of his father David;
22:13 for the people, and for a Judah, T
22:13 to do according to a that is written concerning us."
22:16 a the words of the book that the king K
22:17 they have provoked me to anger with a the work V
22:20 not see a the disaster that I will bring
23: 1 Then the king directed that a the elders of Judah
23: 2 and with him went a the people of Judah, A
23: 2 a the inhabitants of Jerusalem, the priests, L
23: 2 the priests, the prophets, and a the people, A
23: 2 he read in their hearing a the words of the book K
23: 3 and his statutes, with a his heart and all his soul, J
23: 3 and his statutes, with all his heart and a his soul,
23: 3 A the people joined in the covenant. A
23: 4 of the temple of the LORD a the vessels made
23: 4 for Asherah, and for a the host of heaven;
23: 5 the constellations, and a the host of the heavens.
23: 8 He brought a the priests out of the towns of Judah,
23:19 Josiah removed a the shrines of the high places
23:20 He slaughtered on the altars a the priests of
23:21 The king commanded a the people, A
23:22 or during a the days of the kings of Israel or of F
23:24 and a the abominations that were seen in the land
23:25 who turned to the LORD with a his heart, J
23:25 with a his soul, and with all his might,
23:25 with all his soul, and with a his might,
23:25 according to a the law of Moses;
23:26 because of a the provocations
23:28 the rest of the acts of Josiah, and a that he did,
23:35 from a according to their assessment,
23:37 just as a his ancestors had done.
24: 3 for a that he had committed,
24: 5 rest of the deeds of Jehoiakim, and a that he did,
24: 7 over a that belonged to the king of Egypt from
24:13 He carried off a the treasures of the house of
24:13 he cut in pieces a the vessels of gold in the temple
24:13 a this as the LORD had foretold.
24:14 He carried away a Jerusalem, a the officials, a the warriors, ten thousand captives, a the artisans and
24:16 brought captive to Babylon a the men of valor, Z
24:16 one thousand, a of them strong and fit for war.
25: 1 with a his army against Jerusalem, and laid siege
25: 1 they built siegeworks against it a around.
25: 4 with a the soldiers fled by night by the way of
25: 4 though the Chaldeans were a around the city.
25: 5 a his army was scattered, deserting him.
25: 9 the king's house, and a the houses of Jerusalem;
25:10 A the army of the Chaldeans who were with
25:11 a the rest of the population.
25:14 a the bronze vessels used in the temple service,
25:16 bronze of a these vessels was beyond weighing.
25:17 a of bronze, were on the capital a around.
25:23 Now when a the captains of the forces
25:26 Then a the people, high and low and the A

1Ch 1:23 a these were the descendants of Joktan.
1:33 A these were the descendants of Keturah.
2:4 Judah had five sons in a.
2:6 Zimri, Ethan, Heman, Calcol, and Dara, five in a.
2:23 A these were descendants of Machir,
3:9 A these were David's sons,
4:27 nor did a their family multiply like the Judeans.
4:33 with a their villages that were around these towns
5:10 in their tents throughout a the region east
5:16 and in a the pasture lands of Sharon to their limits.
5:17 A of these were enrolled by genealogies in
5:20 and a who were with them were given
6:48 and their kindred the Levites were appointed for a
6:49 doing a the work of the most holy place, V
6:49 according to a that Moses the servant
6:60 A their towns throughout their families
7:3 Obadiah, Joel, and Isshiah, five, a of them chiefs;
7:5 Their kindred belonging to a the families
7:5 in a eighty-seven thousand mighty warriors,
7:8 A these were the sons of Becher;
7:11 A these were the sons of Jediael according to
7:40 A of these were men of Asher,
8:38 a these were the sons of Azel.
8:40 A these were Benjaminites.
9:1 So a Israel was enrolled by genealogies; B
9:9 A these were heads of families according
9:22 A these, who were chosen as gatekeepers at
9:29 and over a the holy utensils,
10:6 and his three sons and a his house died together.
10:7 When a the men of Israel who were in Z
10:11 But when a Jabesh-gilead heard everything that
10:12 a the valiant warriors got up and took away
11:1 Then a Israel gathered together to David B
11:3 a the elders of Israel came to the king at Hebron,
11:4 David and a Israel marched to Jerusalem, B
11:8 He built the city a around,
11:10 together with a Israel, to make him king, B
12:15 when it was overflowing a its banks,
12:15 and put to flight a those in the valleys,
12:21 for they were a warriors and commanders in
12:32 and a their kindred under their command.
12:33 equipped for battle with a the weapons of war,
12:37 one hundred twenty thousand armed with a
12:38 A these, warriors arrayed in battle order,
12:38 with full intent to make David king over a Israel; B
12:38 likewise a the rest of Israel were of a single mind
13:2 to our kindred who remain in a the land of Israel, I
13:4 for the thing pleased a the people. A
13:5 So David assembled a Israel from the Shihor B
13:6 And David and a Israel went up to Baalah, B
13:8 David and a Israel were dancing before God B
13:8 dancing before God with a their might,
13:14 the household of Obed-edom and a that he had.
14:8 David had been anointed king over a Israel, B
14:8 a the Philistines went up in search of David;
14:17 The fame of David went out into a lands,
14:17 the LORD brought the fear of him on a nations. D
15:3 David assembled a Israel in Jerusalem to bring B
15:27 also were a the Levites who were carrying the ark,
15:28 So a Israel brought up the ark of the covenant of B
16:9 sing praises to him, tell of a his wonderful works.
16:14 his judgments are in a the earth. E
16:23 Sing to the LORD, a the earth. E
16:24 his marvelous works among a the peoples. G
16:25 he is to be revered above a gods.
16:26 For a the gods of the peoples are idols,
16:30 tremble before him, a the earth. E
16:32 Let the sea roar, and a that fills it;
16:36 Then a the people said "Amen!" A
16:40 to a that is written in the law of the LORD
16:43 Then a the people departed to their homes, A
17:2 "Do a that you have in mind,
17:6 Wherever I have moved about among a Israel, B
17:8 and have cut off a your enemies before you;
17:10 and I will subdue a your enemies.
17:15 with a these words and a this vision,
17:19 you have done a these great deeds,
17:19 making known a these great things.
17:20 according to a that we have heard with our ears.
18:4 David hamstrung a the chariot horses,
18:10 He sent a sorts of articles of gold, of silver,
18:11 gold that he had carried off from a the nations, D
18:13 and a the Edomites became subject to David.
18:14 So David reigned over a Israel; B
18:14 administered justice and equity to a his people. A
19:8 he sent Joab and a the army of the warriors.
19:17 David was informed, he gathered a Israel B
20:3 Thus David did to a the cities of the Ammonites.
20:3 David and a the people returned to Jerusalem. A
21:3 my lord the king, a of them my lord's servants?
21:4 So Joab departed and went throughout a Israel, B
21:5 In a Israel there were one million one hundred thousand men B
21:12 the LORD destroying throughout a the territory
21:23 for a grain offering. I give it a."
22:5 famous and glorified throughout a lands;
22:9 I will give him peace from a his enemies
22:15 and a kinds of artisans without number,
22:17 David also commanded a the leaders of Israel
23:2 David assembled a the leaders of Israel and
23:28 the cleansing of a that is holy,
23:29 and a measures of quantity or size.
24:5 They organized them by lot, a alike,
25:5 A these were the sons of Heman the king's seer,
25:6 They were a under the direction of their father for
25:7 in singing to the LORD, a of whom were skillful,
26:8 A these, sons of Obed-edom with their sons
1Ch 26:11 a the sons and brothers of Hosah totaled thirteen.
26:26 and his brothers were in charge of a the treasuries
26:28 Also a that Samuel the seer, and Saul son of Kish,
26:28 a dedicated gifts were in the care of Shelomoth
26:30 west of the Jordan for a the work of the LORD V
27:1 and their officers who served the king in a matters
27:3 and was chief of a the commanders of the army
27:31 A these were stewards of King David's property.
28:1 David assembled at Jerusalem a the officials
28:1 the stewards of a the property and cattle of
28:1 the mighty warriors, and a the warriors.
28:4 of Israel chose me from a my ancestral house to
28:4 in making me king over a Israel. B
28:5 of a my sons, for the LORD has given me many,
28:8 Now therefore in the sight of a Israel, B
28:8 observe and search out a the commandments of
28:12 and the plan of a that he had in mind:
28:12 a the surrounding chambers,
28:13 and a the work of the service in the house of V
28:13 for a the vessels for the service in the house of
28:14 of gold for a golden vessels for each service,
28:19 "A this, in writing at the LORD's direction,
28:19 the plan of a the works."
28:20 until a the work for the service of the house of V
28:21 the Levites for a the service of the house of God;
28:21 and with you in a the work will be every V
28:21 also the officers and a the people will be wholly A
29:2 colored stones, a sorts of precious stones,
29:3 to a that I have provided for the holy house,
29:5 and for a the work to be done by artisans, V
29:10 the LORD in the presence of a the assembly;
29:11 a that is in the heavens and on the earth is yours;
29:11 O LORD, and you are exalted as head above a.
29:12 and honor come from you, and you rule over a.
29:12 to make great and to give strength to a.
29:14 For a things come from you, C
29:15 and transients before you, as were a our ancestors;
29:16 a this abundance that we have provided
29:16 from your hand and is a your own.
29:17 of my heart I have freely offered a these things, H
29:19 and your statutes, performing a of them,
29:20 And a the assembly blessed the LORD,
29:21 and sacrifices in abundance for a Israel; B
29:23 he prospered, and a Israel obeyed him. B
29:24 A the leaders and the mighty warriors,
29:24 and also a the sons of King David,
29:25 highly exalted Solomon in the sight of a Israel, B
29:26 Thus David son of Jesse reigned over a Israel. B
29:30 with accounts of a his rule and his might and
29:30 him and Israel and a the kingdoms of the earth. R
2Ch 1:2 Solomon summoned a Israel, B
1:2 the judges, and a the leaders of all Israel,
1:2 the judges, and all the leaders of a Israel, B
1:17 through them these were exported to a the kings P
2:14 to do a sorts of engraving and execute any design
2:17 a census of a the aliens who were residing in
4:3 Under it were panels a around, each of ten cubits,
4:16 and a the equipment for these Huram-abi made
4:18 Solomon made a these things in great quantities, H
4:19 So Solomon made a the things that were in
5:1 Thus a the work that Solomon did for the house V
5:1 a the vessels in the treasuries of the house of God.
5:2 the elders of Israel and a the heads of the tribes,
5:3 And a the Israelites assembled before the king N
5:4 And a the elders of Israel came,
5:5 and a the holy vessels that were in the tent;
5:6 King Solomon and a the congregation of Israel, U
5:11 (for a the priests who were present had sanctified
5:12 and a the levitical singers,
6:3 the king turned around and blessed a the assembly
6:3 while a the assembly of Israel stood.
6:14 before you with a their heart— J
6:29 any individual or from a your people Israel, A
6:29 a knowing their own suffering
6:30 forgive, and render to a whose heart you know, J
6:30 according to a their ways,
6:31 walk in your ways a the days that they live in F
6:33 in order that a the peoples of G
6:38 if they repent with a their heart and soul in J
7:3 When a the people of Israel saw the fire come A
7:4 the king and a the people offered sacrifice A
7:5 and a the people dedicated the house of God. A
7:6 the priests sounded trumpets; and a Israel stood. B
7:8 and a Israel with him, a very great congregation, B
7:11 a that Solomon had planned to do in the house of
7:16 my eyes and my heart will be there for a time.
7:17 doing according to a that I have commanded you
7:20 a proverb and a byword among a peoples. G
7:22 he has brought a this calamity upon them.'"
8:4 and a the storage towns that he built in Hamath.
8:6 as well as a Solomon's storage towns,
8:6 and a the towns for his chariots,
8:6 in Lebanon, and in a the land of his dominion. I
8:7 A the people who were left of the Hittites, A
8:15 the priests and Levites regarding anything at a,
8:16 Thus a the work of Solomon was accomplished V
9:1 she discussed with him a that was on her mind.
9:2 Solomon answered a her questions;
9:14 and a the kings of Arabia and the governors of P
9:20 A King Solomon's drinking vessels were of gold,
9:20 and a the vessels of the House of the Forest
9:22 Thus King Solomon excelled a the kings of P
9:23 A the kings of the earth sought the presence P
9:26 over a the kings from the Euphrates to the land P
9:28 for Solomon from Egypt and from a lands.
9:30 in Jerusalem over a Israel forty years. B
10:1 a Israel had come to Shechem to make him king. B
1Ch 10:3 and a Israel came and said to Rehoboam, B
10:12 a the people came to Rehoboam the third day, A
10:16 a Israel saw that the king would not listen B
10:16 So a Israel departed to their tents. B
11:3 and to a Israel in Judah and Benjamin, B
11:12 He also put large shields and spears in a the cities,
11:13 in a Israel presented themselves to him B
11:13 to him from a their territories.
11:16 a the tribes of Israel to Jerusalem to sacrifice S
11:21 of Absalom more than a his other wives
11:23 through a the districts of Judah and Benjamin,
11:23 of Judah and Benjamin, in a the fortified cities;
12:1 he and a Israel with him. B
12:13 the LORD had chosen out of a the tribes of Israel S
13:4 and said, "Listen to me, Jeroboam and a Israel! B
13:15 defeated Jeroboam and a Israel before Abijah B
14:5 from a the cities of Judah the high places and
14:8 a these were mighty warriors.
14:14 They defeated a the cities around Gerar,
14:14 They plundered a the cities;
15:2 "Hear me, Asa, and a Judah and Benjamin: T
15:5 for great disturbances afflicted a the inhabitants L
15:8 put away the abominable idols from a the land I
15:9 He gathered a Judah and Benjamin, T
15:12 with a their heart and with all their soul. J
15:12 with all their heart and with a their soul.
15:15 A Judah rejoiced over the oath; T
15:15 for they had sworn with a their heart, J
15:15 and the LORD gave them rest a around.
15:17 Nevertheless the heart of Asa was true a his days.
16:4 Abel-maim, and a the store-cities of Naphtali.
16:6 Then King Asa brought a Judah, T
17:2 He placed forces in a the fortified cities of Judah,
17:5 A Judah brought tribute to Jehoshaphat, T
17:9 around through a the cities of Judah and taught
17:10 of the LORD fell on a the kingdoms of the lands R
17:19 in the fortified cities throughout a Judah. T
18:9 and a the prophets were prophesying before them.
18:11 A the prophets were prophesying the same
18:16 "I saw a Israel scattered on the mountains, B
18:18 with a the host of heaven standing to the right and
18:21 be a lying spirit in the mouth of a his prophets.'
18:27 And he said, "Hear, you peoples, a of you!"
19:5 in the land in a the fortified cities of Judah,
19:11 Amariah the chief priest is over you in a matters
19:11 of the house of Judah, in a the king's matters;
20:3 and proclaimed a fast throughout a Judah. T
20:4 from a the towns of Judah they came to seek
20:6 not rule over a the kingdoms of the nations? R
20:13 Meanwhile a Judah stood before the LORD, T
20:15 "Listen, a Judah and inhabitants of Jerusalem, T
20:18 and a Judah and the inhabitants of Jerusalem fell T
20:23 they a helped to destroy one another.
20:27 Then a the people of Judah and Jerusalem, A
20:29 of God came on a the kingdoms of the countries R
20:30 for his God gave him rest a around.
21:2 a these were the sons of King Jehoshaphat
21:4 he put a his brothers to the sword,
21:9 over with his commanders and a his chariots.
21:14 your children, your wives, and a your possessions,
21:17 and carried away a the possessions they found
21:18 After a this the LORD struck him in his bowels
22:1 the Arabs to the camp had killed a the older sons.
22:9 who sought the LORD with a his heart." J
22:10 about to destroy a the royal family of the house
23:2 through Judah and gathered the Levites from a
23:5 a the people shall be in the courts of the house A
23:6 for they are holy, but a the other people A
23:8 The Levites and a Judah did according to all that T
23:8 did according to a that the priest Jehoiada
23:10 and he set a the people as a guard for the king, A
23:13 and a the people of the land rejoicing A
23:16 a covenant between himself and a the people A
23:17 Then a the people went to the house of Baal, A
23:20 and a the people of the land, A
23:21 So a the people of the land rejoiced, A
24:2 of the LORD a the days of the priest Jehoiada. F
24:5 gather money from a Israel to repair the house B
24:7 even used a the dedicated things of the house of
24:10 A the leaders and all the people rejoiced
24:10 and a the people rejoiced and brought their tax A
24:14 in the house of the LORD regularly a the days F
24:23 and destroyed a the officials of the people from
24:23 and sent a the booty they took to the king
25:4 but a shall be put to death for their own sins."
25:5 of the thousands and of the hundreds for a Judah T
25:7 with Israel—a these Ephraimites.
25:12 so that a of them were dashed to pieces.
25:24 He seized a the gold and silver,
25:24 a the vessels that were found in the house of God,
26:1 Then a the people of Judah took Uzziah, A
26:14 Uzziah provided for a the army the shields,
26:20 When the chief priest Azariah, and a the priests,
27:7 and a his wars and his ways,
28:6 a of them valiant warriors,
28:14 the booty before the officials and a the assembly.
28:15 and with the booty they clothed a that were naked
28:15 and carrying a the feeble among them on donkeys,
28:23 But they were the ruin of him, and of a Israel. B
28:26 Now the rest of his acts and a his ways,
29:16 and they brought out a the unclean things
29:18 "We have cleansed a the house of the LORD,
29:18 the altar of burnt offering and a its utensils,
29:18 the table for the rows of bread and a its utensils.
29:19 A the utensils that King Ahaz repudiated
29:24 to make atonement for a Israel. B
29:24 and the sin offering should be made for a Israel. B

2Ch 29:28 **a** this continued until the burnt offering
29:29 the king and **a** who were present with him bowed
29:31 and thank offerings; and **a** who were of
29:32 **a** these were for a burnt offering to the LORD.
29:34 But the priests were too few and could not skin **a**
29:36 And Hezekiah and **a** the people rejoiced because A
30: 1 Hezekiah sent word to **a** Israel and Judah, B
30: 2 For the king and his officials and **a** the assembly
30: 4 plan seemed right to the king and **a** the assembly.
30: 5 throughout **a** Israel, from Beer-sheba to Dan, B
30: 6 So couriers went throughout **a** Israel and Judah B
30:14 the altars that were in Jerusalem, and **a** the altars
30:18 "The good LORD pardon **a**
30:22 to **a** the Levites who showed good skill in
31: 1 Now when **a** this was finished,
31: 1 **a** Israel who were present went out to the cities B
31: 1 the high places and the altars throughout **a** Judah T
31: 1 until they had destroyed them **a.**
31: 1 **a** the people of Israel returned to their cities, A
31: 1 **a** to their individual properties.
31: 5 wine, oil, honey, and of **a** the produce of the field;
31:16 **a** who entered the house of the LORD as the duty
31:18 priests were enrolled with **a** their little children,
31:20 Hezekiah did this throughout **a** Judah; T
31:21 he did with **a** his heart; and he prospered. J
32: 4 and they stopped **a** the springs and the wadi
32: 7 before the king of Assyria and **a** the horde that is
32: 9 of Assyria was at Lachish with **a** his forces,
32: 9 to King Hezekiah of Judah and to **a** the people A
32:13 I and my ancestors have done to **a** the peoples G
32:13 the gods of the nations of those lands at **a** able
32:14 Who among **a** the gods of those nations
32:21 And the LORD sent an angel who cut off **a**
32:22 of Assyria and from the hand of **a** his enemies;
32:23 that he was exalted in the sight of **a** nations from D
32:27 for shields, and for **a** kinds of costly objects;
32:28 and stalls for **a** kinds of cattle, and sheepfolds.
32:30 Hezekiah prospered in **a** his works.
32:31 to test him and to know **a** that was in his heart.
32:33 and **a** Judah and the inhabitants T
33: 3 worshiped **a** the host of heaven, and served them.
33: 5 for **a** the host of heaven in the two courts of
33: 7 which I have chosen out of **a** the tribes of Israel, S
33: 8 to do **a** that I have commanded them, **a** the law,
33:14 of the army in **a** the fortified cities in Judah.
33:15 and **a** the altars that he had built on the mountain
33:19 **a** his sin and his faithlessness,
33:22 Amon sacrificed to **a** the images
33:25 of the land killed **a** those who had conspired
34: 6 and as far as Naphtali, in their ruins **a** around,
34: 7 and demolished **a** the incense altars throughout
34: 7 the incense altars throughout **a** the land of Israel, I
34: 9 Ephraim and from **a** the remnant of Israel and
34: 9 of Israel and from **a** Judah and Benjamin and T
34:12 **a** skillful with instruments of music,
34:13 the burden bearers and directed **a** who did work
34:16 reported to the king, "**A** that was committed
34:21 in accordance with **a** that is written in this book."
34:24 upon its inhabitants, **a** the curses that are written
34:25 so that they have provoked me to anger with **a**
34:28 not see **a** the disaster that I will bring on this place
34:29 Then the king sent word and gathered together **a**
34:30 with **a** the people of Judah, A
34:30 **a** the people both great and small; A
34:30 he read in their hearing **a** the words of the book K
34:31 and his statutes, with **a** his heart and all his soul, J
34:31 and his statutes, with all his heart and **a** his soul,
34:32 Then he made **a** who were present in Jerusalem
34:33 Josiah took away **a** the abominations from **a** the
34:33 and made **a** who were in Israel worship
34:33 **A** his days they did not turn away from following
35: 3 He said to the Levites who taught **a** Israel B
35: 7 as passover offerings for **a** that were present,
35:13 and carried them quickly to **a** the people. A
35:16 **a** the service of the LORD was prepared that day,
35:18 by **a** Judah and Israel who were present, T
35:20 After **a** this, when Josiah had set the temple
35:24 **A** Judah and Jerusalem mourned for Josiah. T
35:25 a lament for Josiah, and **a** the singing men
36:14 **A** the leading priests and the people
36:14 following **a** the abominations of the nations;
36:17 he gave them **a** into his hand.
36:18 **A** the vessels of the house of God, large and small,
36:18 **a** these he brought to Babylon.
36:19 burned **a** its palaces with fire,
36:19 and destroyed **a** its precious vessels.
36:21 **A** the days that it lay desolate it kept sabbath, F
36:22 that he sent a herald throughout **a** his kingdom
36:23 has given me **a** the kingdoms of the earth, R
36:23 Whoever is among you of **a** his people, A
Ezr 1: 1 so that he sent a herald throughout **a** his kingdom,
1: 2 has given me **a** the kingdoms of the earth, R
1: 4 and let **a** survivors, in whatever place they reside,
1: 6 **A** their neighbors aided them with silver vessels,
1: 6 besides **a** that was freely offered.
1:11 **A** these Sheshbazzar brought up,
2: 1 to Jerusalem and Judah, **a** to their own towns.
2:42 and of Shobai, in **a** one hundred thirty-nine.
2:58 **A** the temple servants and the descendants
2:70 and **a** Israel in their towns. B
3: 5 at the new moon and at **a** the sacred festivals of
3: 8 and the Levites and **a** who had come to Jerusalem
3:11 And **a** the people responded with a great shout A
5: 7 "To Darius the king, **a** peace!
6:12 let it be done with **a** diligence."
6:13 with **a** diligence what King Darius had ordered.
6:17 and as a sin offering for **a** Israel, B

Ezr 6:20 had purified themselves; **a** of them were clean.
6:20 the passover lamb for **a** the returned exiles,
6:21 and also by **a** who had joined them
7: 6 and the king granted him **a** that he asked,
7:16 with **a** the silver and gold that you shall find in
7:17 then, you shall with **a** diligence buy bulls, rams,
7:21 decree to **a** the treasurers in the province Beyond
7:21 requires of you, let it be done with **a** diligence,
7:25 and judges who may judge **a** the people A
7:26 **A** who will not obey the law of your God and
7:28 and before **a** the king's mighty officers.
8:20 These were **a** mentioned by name.
8:21 our children, and **a** our possessions.
8:22 of our God is gracious to **a** who seek him,
8:22 and his wrath are against **a** who forsake him.
8:25 his lords, and **a** Israel there present had offered; B
8:35 twelve bulls for **a** Israel, ninety-six rams, B
8:35 **a** this was a burnt offering to the LORD.
9: 4 **a** who trembled at the words of the God of Israel,
9:13 After **a** that has come upon us for our evil deeds
10: 3 to send away **a** these wives and their children,
10: 5 and **a** Israel swear that they would do as B
10: 7 to **a** the returned exiles that they should assemble
10: 8 and the elders **a** their property should be forfeited,
10: 9 Then **a** the people of Judah and Benjamin A
10: 9 **A** the people sat in the open square before A
10:12 Then **a** the assembly answered with a loud voice,
10:14 the whole assembly, and let **a** in our towns
10:17 they had come to the end of **a** the men Z
10:44 **A** these had married foreign women,
Ne 4: 6 **a** the wall was joined together to half its height;
4: 8 and **a** plotted together to come and fight
4:12 "From **a** the places where they live they will come
4:15 we **a** returned to the wall, each to his work.
5: 7 "You are **a** taking interest from your own people."
5:13 And **a** the assembly said, "Amen,"
5:16 **a** my servants were gathered there for the work. Q
5:18 with **a** this I did not demand the food allowance
5:19 O my God, **a** that I have done for this people.
6: 9 —for they **a** wanted to frighten us,
6:12 and saw that God had not sent him at **a,**
6:16 And when **a** our enemies heard of it,
6:16 **a** the nations around us were afraid D
7:60 **A** the temple servants and the descendants
7:73 and **a** Israel settled in their towns. B
8: 1 **a** the people gathered together into the square A
8: 2 both men and women and **a** who could hear
8: 3 ears of **a** the people were attentive to the book A
8: 5 opened the book in the sight of **a** the people, A
8: 5 for he was standing above **a** the people; A
8: 5 and when he opened it, **a** the people stood up. A
8: 6 great God, and **a** the people answered, "Amen, A
8: 9 people said to **a** the people, "This day is holy A
8: 9 **a** the people wept when they heard the words A
8:11 So the Levites stilled **a** the people, saying, A
8:12 And **a** the people went their way to eat and A
8:13 heads of ancestral houses of **a** the people, A
8:15 and proclaim in **a** their towns and in Jerusalem
8:17 And **a** the assembly of those who had returned
9: 2 from **a** foreigners, and stood
9: 5 which is exalted above **a** blessing and praise."
9: 6 heavens, with **a** their host, the earth and **a** that is
on it, the seas and **a** that is in them.
9: 6 To **a** of them you give life,
9:10 and **a** his servants and all the people of his land, Q
9:10 and all his servants and **a** the people of his land, A
9:25 and took possession of houses filled with **a** sorts
9:32 do not treat lightly **a** the hardship that has come
9:32 our prophets, our ancestors, and **a** your people, A
9:33 You have been just in **a** that has come upon us,
9:38 of **a** this we make a firm agreement in writing,
10:28 and **a** who have separated themselves from
10:28 **a** who have knowledge and understanding,
10:29 and to observe and do **a** the commandments of
10:33 and for **a** the work of the house of our God. V
10:35 the first fruits of **a** fruit of every tree, year by year,
10:37 the tithes in **a** our rural towns.
11: 2 the people blessed **a** those who willingly offered
11: 3 but in the towns of Judah **a** lived on their property
11: 6 **A** the descendants of Perez who lived
11:18 **A** the Levites in the holy city were two hundred
11:20 were in **a** the towns of Judah,
11:20 **a** of them in their inheritance.
11:24 was at the king's hand in **a** matters concerning
12:27 the Levites in **a** their places,
12:47 of Nehemiah **a** Israel gave the daily portions for B
13: 3 from Israel **a** those of foreign descent.
13: 8 and I threw **a** the household furniture
13:12 Then **a** Judah brought the tithe of the grain, T
13:15 also wine, grapes, figs, and **a** kinds of burdens,
13:16 in fish and **a** kinds of merchandise and sold them
13:18 and did not our God bring **a** this disaster on us and
13:20 and sellers of **a** kinds of merchandise spent
13:26 and God made him king over **a** Israel; B
13:27 Shall we then listen to you and do **a** this great evil
Est 1: 3 he gave a banquet for **a** his officials and ministers.
1: 4 one hundred eighty days in **a.**
1: 5 for **a** the people present in the citadel of Susa, A
1: 8 for the king had given orders to **a** the officials
1:13 the king's procedure toward **a** who were versed
1:16 to **a** the officials and all the peoples who are in
1:16 to all the officials and **a** the peoples who are in G
1:16 and all the peoples who are in **a** the provinces
1:17 of the queen will be made known to **a** women,
1:20 the king is proclaimed throughout **a** his kingdom,
1:20 **a** women will give honor to their husbands,
1:22 he sent letters to **a** the royal provinces,

Est 2: 3 the king appoint commissioners in **a** the provinces
2: 3 to gather **a** the beautiful young virgins
2:15 Now Esther was admired by **a** who saw her.
2:17 king loved Esther more than **a** the other women;
2:17 of **a** the virgins she won his favor and devotion,
2:18 a great banquet to **a** his officials and ministers—
3: 1 and set his seat above **a** the officials who were
3: 2 And **a** the king's servants who were at
3: 6 Haman plotted to destroy **a** the Jews, X
3: 8 the peoples in **a** the provinces of your kingdom;
3:12 according to **a** that Haman commanded,
3:12 and to the governors over **a** the provinces and
3:12 provinces and to the officials of **a** the peoples, G
3:13 by couriers to **a** the king's provinces,
3:13 to kill, and to annihilate **a** Jews, young and old, X
3:14 calling on **a** the peoples to be ready for that day. G
4: 1 When Mordecai learned **a** that had been done,
4: 7 Mordecai told him **a** that had happened to him,
4:11 "**A** the king's servants and the people of
4:11 **a** alike are to be put to death.
4:13 you will escape any more than **a** the other Jews.
4:16 gather **a** the Jews to be found in Susa, X
5:11 **a** the promotions with which the king honored him,
5:13 Yet **a** this does me no good so long as I see
5:14 Then his wife Zeresh and **a** his friends said to him,
6:13 and **a** his friends everything that had happened
8: 5 to destroy the Jews who are in **a** the provinces of
8: 9 according to **a** that Mordecai commanded,
8:12 throughout **a** the provinces of King Ahasuerus,
8:13 in every province and published to **a** peoples, G
9: 2 throughout **a** the provinces of King Ahasuerus
9: 2 the fear of them had fallen upon **a** peoples. G
9: 3 **A** the officials of the provinces,
9: 4 and his fame spread throughout **a** the provinces as
9: 5 Jews struck down **a** their enemies with the sword,
9:20 and sent letters to **a** the Jews who were in X
9:20 the Jews who were in **a** the provinces of King
9:24 the enemy of **a** the Jews, had plotted against X
9:26 Thus because of **a** that was written in this letter,
9:27 and their descendants and **a** who joined them,
9:30 wishing peace and security to **a** the Jews, X
10: 2 **A** the acts of his power and might,
10: 3 for the welfare of **a** his descendants.
Job 1: 3 so that this man was the greatest of **a** the people A
1: 5 according to the number of them **a;**
1:10 a fence around him and his house and **a** that he has,
1:11 and touch **a** that he has, and he will curse you
1:12 "Very well, **a** that he has is in your power;
1:22 In **a** this Job did not sin or charge God
2: 4 **A** that people have they will give
2:10 In **a** this Job did not sin with his lips.
2:11 when Job's three friends heard of **a** these troubles
4:14 and trembling, which made **a** my bones shake.
6: 2 and **a** my calamity laid in the balances!
8:13 Such are the paths of **a** who forget God;
9:22 It is **a** one; therefore I say,
9:28 I become afraid of **a** my suffering,
11:20 **a** way of escape will be lost to them,
12: 9 Who among **a** these does not know that the hand
13: 1 "Look, my eye has seen **a** this,
13: 4 **a** of you are worthless physicians.
13:27 in the stocks, and watch **a** my paths;
14:14 **A** the days of my service I would wait F
15:20 The wicked writhe in pain **a** their days,
15:20 **a** the years that are laid up for the ruthless.
16: 2 miserable comforters are you **a.**
16: 7 he has made desolate **a** my company.
17: 7 and **a** my members are like a shadow.
17:10 But you, come back now, **a** of you,
19:19 **A** my intimate friends abhor me,
20:22 **a** the force of misery will come upon them.
24: 4 the poor of the earth **a** hide themselves.
24: 7 They lie **a** night naked, without clothing,
24:17 For deep darkness is morning to **a** of them;
27:10 Will they call upon God at **a** times? Y
27:12 **A** of you have seen it yourselves;
28:21 It is hidden from the eyes of **a** living,
29:19 with the dew **a** night on my branches;
30: 2 **A** their vigor is gone
30:23 and to the house appointed for **a** living.
31: 4 not see my ways, and number **a** my steps?
31:12 and it would burn to the root **a** my harvest.
31:37 I would give him an account of **a** my steps;
33: 1 hear my speech, O Job, and listen to **a** my words.
33:11 in the stocks, and watches **a** my paths.'
33:29 "God indeed does **a** these things, twice, H
34:15 **a** flesh would perish together, M
34:15 and **a** mortals return to dust.
34:19 for they are **a** the work of his hands? V
34:21 and he sees **a** their steps.
36:19 or will **a** the force of your strength?
36:25 **A** people have looked on it; A
37: 7 so that **a** whom he has made may know it.
37:12 to accomplish **a** that he commands them on
38: 7 when the morning stars sang together and **a**
38:18 Declare, if you know **a** this.
40:11 and look on **a** who are proud, and abase them.
40:12 Look on **a** who are proud, and bring them low;
40:13 Hide them **a** in the dust together;
40:20 For the mountains yield food for it where **a**
41:14 There is terror **a** around its teeth.
41:34 it is king over **a** that are proud."
42: 2 "I know that you can do **a** things, C
42:11 Then there came to him **a** his brothers and sisters
and **a** who had known him before,
42:11 for **a** the evil that the LORD had brought upon him;
42:15 In **a** the land there were no women so beautiful I

Ps 1: 3 In a that they do, they prosper.
2:12 Happy are a who take refuge in him.
3: 6 who have set themselves against me a around.
3: 7 For you strike a my enemies on the cheek;
5: 5 before your eyes; you hate a evildoers.
5:11 But let a who take refuge in you rejoice;
6: 7 they grow weak because of a my foes.
6: 8 Depart from me, a you workers of evil,
6:10 A my enemies shall be ashamed and struck
7: 1 save me from a my pursuers, and deliver me,
8: 1 how majestic is your name in a the earth! E
8: 6 you have put a things under their feet, C
8: 7 a sheep and oxen, and also the beasts of the field,
8: 9 how majestic is your name in a the earth! E
9: 1 I will tell of a your wonderful deeds.
9:14 so that I may recount a your praises,
9:17 a the nations that forget God. D
10: 4 a their thoughts are, "There is no God."
10: 5 Their ways prosper at a times; Y
10: 6 throughout a generations we shall O
12: 3 May the LORD cut off a flattering lips,
13: 2 and have sorrow in my heart a day long?
14: 3 They have a gone astray, they are a alike perverse;
14: 4 a the evildoers who eat up my people
16: 3 they are the noble, in whom is a my delight.
18: T *delivered him from the hand of a his enemies,*
18:22 For a his ordinances were before me,
18:30 he is a shield for a who take refuge in him.
19: 4 yet their voice goes out through a the earth, E
20: 3 May he remember a your offerings,
20: 4 your heart's desire, and fulfill a your plans.
20: 5 May the LORD fulfill a your petitions.
21: 8 Your hand will find out a your enemies;
22: 7 A who see me mock at me;
22:14 and a my bones are out of joint;
22:16 For dogs are a around me;
22:17 I can count a my bones.
22:23 A you offspring of Jacob, glorify him;
22:23 stand in awe of him, a you offspring of Israel!
22:27 A the ends of the earth shall remember and turn to
22:27 and a the families of the nations shall worship
22:29 indeed, shall a who sleep in the earth bow down;
22:29 before him shall bow a who go down to the dust,
23: 6 and mercy shall follow me a the days of my life, F
24: 1 and a that is in it, the world, and those who live
25: 5 for you I wait a day long.
25:10 A the paths of the LORD are steadfast love
25:18 and my trouble, and forgive a my sins.
25:22 Redeem Israel, O God, out of a its troubles.
26: 7 and telling a your wondrous deeds.
27: 4 in the house of the LORD a the days of my life, F
27: 6 above my enemies a around me, and I will offer
29: 9 and in his temple a say, "Glory!"
31:11 I am the scorn of a my adversaries,
31:13 the whispering of many—terror a around!—
31:23 Love the LORD, a you his saints.
31:24 a you who wait for the LORD.
32: 3 through my groaning a day long.
32: 6 let a who are faithful offer prayer to you;
32:11 and shout for joy, a you upright in heart.
33: 4 and a his work is done in faithfulness.
33: 6 and a their host by the breath of his mouth.
33: 8 Let a the earth fear the LORD; E
33: 8 let a the inhabitants of the world stand in awe L
33:11 the thoughts of his heart to a generations. O
33:13 from heaven; he sees a humankind.
33:14 he watches a the inhabitants of the earth— L
33:15 he who fashions the hearts of them a,
33:15 and observes a their deeds.
34: 1 I will bless the LORD at a times; Y
34: 4 and delivered me from a my fears.
34:17 and rescues them from a their troubles.
34:19 but the LORD rescues them from them a.
34:20 He keeps a their bones;
35:10 A my bones shall say, "O LORD,
35:26 Let a those who rejoice at my calamity be put
35:28 and of your praise a day long.
36: 7 A people may take refuge in the shadow A
38: 6 a day long I go around mourning.
38: 9 O Lord, a my longing is known to you;
38:12 and meditate treachery a day long.
39: 8 Deliver me from a my transgressions.
39:12 an alien, like a my forebears.
40:14 Let a those be put to shame
40:16 may a who seek you rejoice and be glad in you;
41: 3 in their illness you heal a their infirmities.
41: 7 A who hate me whisper together about me;
42: 7 a your waves and your billows have gone over me.
44:15 A day long my disgrace is before me,
44:17 A this has come upon us,
44:22 Because of you we are being killed a day long,
45: 8 your robes are a fragrant with myrrh and aloes
45:13 with a kinds of wealth.
45:16 you will make them princes in a the earth. E
45:17 to be celebrated in a generations; O
47: 1 Clap your hands, a you peoples; G
47: 2 is awesome, a great king over a the earth. E
47: 7 For God is the king of a the earth; E
48: 2 is the joy of a the earth, Mount Zion, E
48:12 Walk about Zion, go a around it, count its towers,
49: 1 Hear this, a you peoples; give ear, G
49: 1 give ear, a inhabitants of the world,
49:11 their dwelling places to a generations, O
50: 3 and a mighty tempest a around him.
50:11 I know a the birds of the air,
50:11 and a that moves in the field is mine.
50:12 for the world and a that is in it is mine.

Ps 51: 9 and blot out a my iniquities.
52: 1 mischief done against the godly? A day long
52: 4 You love a words that devour, O deceitful tongue.
53: 3 They have a fallen away, they are a alike perverse;
56: 1 a day long foes oppress me;
56: 2 my enemies trample on me a day long,
56: 5 A day long they seek to injure my cause;
56: 5 a their thoughts are against me for evil.
57: 5 Let your glory be over a the earth. E
57:11 Let your glory be over a the earth. E
59: 5 Awake to punish a the nations; D
59: 8 you hold a the nations in derision. D
61: 6 may his years endure to a generations! O
62: 3 a of you, as you would a leaning wall,
62: 8 Trust in him at a times, O people; Y
62:12 For you repay to a according to their work.
63:11 a who swear by him shall exult,
64: 8 a who see them will shake with horror.
64:10 Let a the upright in heart glory.
65: 2 To you a flesh shall come. M
65: 5 you are the hope of a the ends of the earth
66: 1 Make a joyful noise to God, a the earth; E
66: 4 A the earth worships you; E
66:16 and hear, a you who fear God,
67: 2 your saving power among a nations. D
67: 3 let a the peoples praise you. G
67: 5 let a the peoples praise you. G
67: 7 let a the ends of the earth revere him.
69:19 my foes are a known to you.
70: 4 Let a who seek you rejoice and be glad in you.
71: 8 and with your glory a day long.
71:15 of your deeds of salvation a day long,
71:18 until I proclaim your might to a the generations O
71:24 A day long my tongue will talk
72: 5 throughout a generations. O
72:11 May a kings fall down before him,
72:11 a nations give him service. D
72:15 and blessings invoked for him a day long.
72:17 May a nations be blessed in him; D
73:13 A in vain I have kept my heart clean
73:14 For a day long I have been plagued,
73:28 to tell of a your works.
74: 6 they smashed a its carved work.
74: 8 they burned a the meeting places of God in
74:17 You have fixed a the bounds of the earth;
74:22 how the impious scoff at you a day long.
75: 3 When the earth totters, with a its inhabitants,
75: 8 he will pour a draught from it, and a the wicked of
75:10 A the horns of the wicked I will cut off,
76: 9 to save a the oppressed of the earth.
76:11 let a who are around him bring gifts to
77: 8 Are his promises at an end for a time?
77:12 I will meditate on a your work,
78:14 and a night long with a fiery light.
78:28 within their camp, a around their dwellings.
78:32 In spite of a this they still sinned;
78:38 and did not stir up a his wrath.
78:51 He struck a the firstborn in Egypt, W
79: 3 They have poured out their blood like water a
80:12 so that a who pass along the way pluck its fruit?
80:13 and a that move in the field feed on it.
82: 5 a the foundations of the earth are shaken.
82: 6 children of the Most High, a of you;
82: 8 for a the nations belong to you! D
83:11 a their princes like Zebah and Zalmunna,
83:18 are the Most High over a the earth. E
85: 2 of your people; you pardoned a their sin.
85: 3 You withdrew a your wrath;
85: 5 Will you prolong your anger to a generations? O
86: 3 O Lord, for to you do I cry a day long.
86: 5 abounding in steadfast love to a who call on you.
86: 9 A the nations you have made shall come and D
87: 2 the LORD loves the gates of Zion more than a
87: 7 "A my springs are in you."
88: 7 and you overwhelm me with a your waves.
88:17 They surround me like a flood a day long;
88:17 from a sides they close in on me.
89: 1 will proclaim your faithfulness to a generations. O
89: 4 and build your throne for a generations.' " O
89: 7 great and awesome above a that are around him?
89:11 the world and a that is in it—
89:16 they exult in your name a day long,
89:35 Once and for a I have sworn by my holiness;
89:40 You have broken through a his walls;
89:41 A who pass by plunder him;
89:42 you have made a his enemies rejoice.
89:47 for what vanity you have created a mortals!
90: 1 our dwelling place in a generations. O
90: 9 For a our days pass away under your wrath;
90:14 so that we may rejoice and be glad a our days.
91:11 concerning you to guard you in a your ways.
92: 7 wicked sprout like grass and a evildoers flourish,
92: 9 a evildoers shall be scattered.
94: 4 their arrogant words; a the evildoers boast.
94:15 and a the upright in heart will follow it.
95: 3 and a great King above a gods.
96: 1 sing to the LORD, a the earth. E
96: 3 his marvelous works among a the peoples. G
96: 4 he is to be revered above a gods.
96: 5 For a the gods of the peoples are idols,
96: 9 tremble before him, a the earth. E
96:11 let the sea roar, and a that fills it;
96:12 Then shall a the trees of the forest sing for joy
97: 2 Clouds and thick darkness are a around him;
97: 5 before the Lord of a the earth. E
97: 6 and a the peoples behold his glory. G
97: 7 A worshipers of images are put to shame,

Ps 97: 7 a gods bow down before him.
97: 9 you, O LORD, are most high over a the earth; E
97: 9 you are exalted far above a gods.
98: 3 A the ends of the earth have seen the victory
98: 4 Make a joyful noise to the LORD, a the earth; E
98: 7 Let the sea roar, and a that fills it;
99: 2 he is exalted over a the peoples. G
100: 1 Make a joyful noise to the LORD, a the earth. E
100: 5 and his faithfulness to a generations. O
101: 8 by morning I will destroy a the wicked in the land,
101: 8 cutting off a evildoers from the city of the LORD.
102: 8 A day long my enemies taunt me;
102:12 your name endures to a generations. O
102:15 and a the kings of the earth your glory. P
102:24 throughout a generations." O
102:26 they will a wear out like a garment.
103: 1 and a that is within me, bless his holy name.
103: 2 O my soul, and do not forget a his benefits—
103: 3 who forgives a your iniquity,
103: 3 who heals a your diseases,
103: 6 and justice for a who are oppressed.
103:19 and his kingdom rules over a.
103:21 Bless the LORD, a his hosts,
103:22 Bless the LORD, a his works,
103:22 in a places of his dominion.
104:20 a the animals of the forest come creeping out.
104:24 In wisdom you have made them a;
104:27 These a look to you to give them their food
105: 2 tell of a his wonderful works.
105: 7 his judgments are in a the earth. E
105:21 and ruler of a his possessions,
105:35 they devoured a the vegetation in their land,
105:36 He struck down a the firstborn in their land, W
105:36 the first issue of a their strength.
106: 2 of the LORD, or declare a his praise?
106: 3 who do righteousness at a times. Y
106:46 to be pitied by a who held them captive.
106:48 And let a the people say, "Amen." A
107:42 and a wickedness stops its mouth.
108: 5 and let your glory be over a the earth. E
109:11 May the creditor seize a that he has;
111: 2 studied by a who delight in them.
111: 7 a his precepts are trustworthy.
111:10 a those who practice it have a good understanding.
113: 4 The LORD is high above a nations, D
115: 8 so are a who trust in them.
116:12 What shall I return to the LORD for a his bounty
116:14 to the LORD in the presence of a his people. A
116:18 to the LORD in the presence of a his people, A
117: 1 Praise the LORD, a you nations! D
117: 1 Extol him, a you peoples! G
118:10 A nations surrounded me; D
119: 6 having my eyes fixed on a your commandments.
119:13 With my lips I declare a the ordinances
119:14 in the way of your decrees as much as in a riches.
119:20 with longing for your ordinances at a times. Y
119:58 I implore your favor with a my heart; J
119:63 I am a companion of a who fear you,
119:86 A your commandments are enduring;
119:90 Your faithfulness endures to a generations; O
119:91 for a things are your servants. C
119:96 I have seen a limit to a perfection,
119:97 It is my meditation a day long.
119:99 I have more understanding than a my teachers,
119:118 You spurn a who go astray from your statutes;
119:119 A the wicked of the earth you count as dross;
119:128 Truly I direct my steps by a your precepts;
119:138 in righteousness and in a faithfulness.
119:151 O LORD, and a your commandments are true.
119:168 for a my ways are before you.
119:172 for a your commandments are right.
121: 7 The LORD will keep you from a evil;
128: 5 prosperity of Jerusalem a the days of your life. F
129: 5 May a who hate Zion be put to shame
130: 8 It is he who will redeem Israel from a its iniquities.
132: 1 in David's favor a the hardships he endured;
134: 1 bless the LORD, a you servants of the LORD, Q
135: 5 our Lord is above a gods.
135: 6 in heaven and on earth, in the seas and a deeps.
135: 9 O Egypt, against Pharaoh and a his servants. Q
135:11 king of Bashan, and a the kingdoms of Canaan R
135:13 your renown, O LORD, throughout a ages.
135:18 and a who trust them shall become like them.
136:25 who gives food to a flesh, M
138: 4 A the kings of the earth shall praise you, P
139: 3 and are acquainted with a my ways.
139:16 In your book were written a the days F
143: 5 I think about a your deeds,
143:12 and destroy a my adversaries,
145: 9 The LORD is good to a,
145: 9 and his compassion is over a that he has made.
145:10 A your works shall give thanks to you, O LORD,
145:10 O LORD, and a your faithful shall bless you.
145:12 to make known to a people your mighty deeds, A
145:13 dominion endures throughout a generations. O
145:13 The LORD is faithful in a his words,
145:13 and gracious in a his deeds.
145:14 The LORD upholds a who are falling,
145:14 and raises up a who are bowed down.
145:15 The eyes of a look to you,
145:17 The LORD is just in a his ways,
145:17 and kind in a his doings.
145:18 The LORD is near to a who call on him,
145:18 to a who call on him in truth.
145:19 He fulfills the desire of a who fear him;
145:20 The LORD watches over a who love him,
145:20 but a the wicked he will destroy.

Ps 145:21 a flesh will bless his holy name forever M
146: 2 I will sing praises to my God a my life long.
146: 6 the sea, and a that is in them;
146:10 your God, O Zion, for a generations. O
147: 4 he gives to a of them their names.
148: 2 Praise him, a his angels; praise him, a his host!
148: 3 praise him, a you shining stars!
148: 7 you sea monsters and a deeps,
148: 9 Mountains and a hills, fruit trees and a cedars!
148:10 Wild animals and a cattle,
148:11 Kings of the earth and a peoples, G
148:11 princes and a rulers of the earth!
148:14 a horn for his people, praise for a his faithful,
149: 9 This is glory for a his faithful ones.
Pr 1:13 We shall find a kinds of costly things;
1:14 we will a have one purse"—
1:19 Such is the end of a who are greedy for gain;
1:25 and because you have ignored a my counsel
1:30 and despised a my reproof,
3: 5 Trust in the LORD with a your heart, J
3: 6 In a your ways acknowledge him,
3: 9 and with the first fruits of a your produce;
3:17 and a her paths are peace.
4:22 and healing to a their flesh.
4:23 Keep your heart with a vigilance,
4:26 and a your ways will be sure.
5:19 May her breasts satisfy you at a times; Y
5:21 and he examines a their paths.
6:31 they will forfeit a the goods of their house.
8: 4 O people, I call, and my cry is to a that live.
8: 8 A the words of my mouth are righteous; K
8: 9 They are a straight to one who understands
8:11 a that you may desire cannot compare with her.
8:16 and nobles, a who govern rightly.
8:36 a who hate me love death."
10:12 Hatred stirs up strife, but love covers a offenses.
11:24 Some give freely, yet grow a the richer;
13:16 The clever do a things intelligently, C
14:23 In a toil there is profit,
15:15 A the days of the poor are hard, F
16: 2 A one's ways may be pure in one's own eyes,
16: 5 A those who are arrogant are an abomination to
16:11 a the weights in the bag are his work.
17:17 A friend loves at a times, Y
18: 1 for a who have sound judgment.
20: 8 of judgment winnows a evil with his eyes.
20:24 A our steps are ordered by the LORD;
21: 2 A deeds are right in the sight of the doer,
21:26 A day long the wicked covet,
22: 2 the LORD is the maker of them a.
22:18 if a of them are ready on your lips.
24: 4 by knowledge the rooms are filled with a precious
24: 9 and the scoffer is an abomination to a.
24:12 And will he not repay a according to their deeds?
24:31 it was a overgrown with thorns;
27:24 nor a crown for a generations. O
29:12 a his officials will be wicked.
30: 4 Who has established a the ends of the earth?
30:27 yet a of them march in rank;
31: 5 and will pervert the rights of a the afflicted.
31: 8 for the rights of a the destitute.
31:12 good, and not harm, a the days of her life. F
31:21 for a her household are clothed in crimson.
31:29 have done excellently, but you surpass them a."
Ecc 1: 2 vanity of vanities! A is vanity.
1: 3 from a the toil at which they toil under the sun?
1: 7 A streams run to the sea, but the sea is not full;
1: 8 A things are wearisome; more than one can C
1:13 to seek and to search out by wisdom a that is done
1:14 I saw a the deeds that are done under the sun;
1:14 and see, a is vanity and a chasing after wind.
1:16 surpassing a who were over Jerusalem before me;
2: 5 and planted in them a kinds of fruit trees.
2: 9 So I became great and surpassed a who were
2:10 for my heart found pleasure in a my toil,
2:10 and this was my reward for a my toil.
2:11 Then I considered a that my hands had done
2:11 and again, a was vanity and a chasing after wind,
2:14 I perceived that the same fate befalls a of them.
2:16 the days to come a will have been long forgotten.
2:17 for a is vanity and a chasing after wind.
2:18 I hated a my toil in which I had toiled under
2:19 of a for which I toiled and used my wisdom under
2:20 to despair concerning a the toil of my labors under
2:21 and knowledge and skill must leave a to
2:22 What do mortals get from a the toil and strain
2:23 For a their days are full of pain,
3:13 that a should eat and drink and take pleasure in a their toil.
3:14 so that a should stand in awe before him.
3:19 They a have the same breath,
3:19 no advantage over the animals; for a is vanity.
3:20 A go to one place; a are from the dust, and a turn to dust again.
3:22 that a should enjoy their work, for that is their lot;
4: 1 Again I saw a the oppressions that are practiced
4: 4 Then I saw that a toil and a skill in work come
4: 8 yet there is no end to a their toil,
4:15 I saw a the living who, moving about under
4:16 there was no end to a those people whom he led. A
5: 9 But a things considered, this is an advantage for C
5:17 Besides, a their days they eat in darkness,
5:18 to eat and drink and find enjoyment in a the toil
5:19 Likewise a to whom God gives wealth
6: 2 so that they lack nothing of a that they desire,
6: 6 do not a go to one place?
6: 7 A human toil is for the mouth,
Ecc 7:23 A this I have tested by wisdom;
7:28 but a woman among a these I have not found.
8: 9 A this I observed, applying my mind to a that is
8:17 then I saw a the work of God, V
9: 1 A this I laid to heart, examining it a,
9: 2 since the same fate comes to a,
9: 3 This is an evil in a that happens under the sun,
9: 3 Moreover, the hearts of a are full of evil;
9: 4 But whoever is joined with a the living has hope,
9: 6 never again will they have any share in a
9: 9 a the days of your vain life that are given you F
9:11 but time and chance happen to them a.
11: 8 who live many years should rejoice in them a;
11: 8 A that comes is vanity.
11: 9 that for a these things God will bring you H
12: 4 and a the daughters of song are brought low;
12: 5 because a must go to their eternal home,
12: 8 Vanity of vanities, says the Teacher; a is vanity.
12:13 The end of the matter; a has been heard.
SS 3: 6 with a the fragrant powders of the merchant?
3: 8 a equipped with swords and expert in war,
4: 2 a of which bear twins, and not one among them
4: 4 a of them shields of warriors.
4:13 an orchard of pomegranates with a choicest fruits,
4:14 with a trees of frankincense, myrrh and aloes, with a chief spices—
5:10 My beloved is a radiant and ruddy,
6: 6 a of them bear twins, and not one among them
7:13 and over our doors are a choice fruits,
8: 7 If one offered for love a the wealth of his house,
Isa 1:25 as with lye and remove a your alloy.
2: 2 a the nations shall stream to it. D
2:12 LORD of hosts has a day against a that is proud
2:12 against a that is lifted up and high;
2:13 against a the cedars of Lebanon, lofty and lifted up
2:13 and against a the oaks of Bashan;
2:14 against a the high mountains,
2:14 and against a the lofty hills;
2:16 against a the ships of Tarshish,
2:16 and against a the beautiful craft.
3: 1 a support of bread, and a support of water—
4: 5 Indeed over a the glory there will be a canopy.
5:14 her throng and a who exult in her.
5:25 For a this his anger has not turned away,
5:28 a their bows bent, their horses' hoofs seem
7: 9 you shall not stand at a.
7:19 they will a come and settle in the steep ravines,
7:19 and on a the thornbushes, and on a the pastures.
7:24 for a the land will be briers and thorns; I
7:25 as for a the hills that used to be hoed with a hoe,
8: 7 the king of Assyria and a his glory;
8: 7 above a its channels and overflow a its banks;
8: 9 listen, a you far countries;
8:12 Do not call conspiracy a that this people calls
9: 5 For a the boots of the tramping warriors and
9: 5 and a the garments rolled in blood
9: 9 and a the people knew it— A
9:12 For a this his anger has not turned away;
9:17 For a this his anger has not turned away,
9:21 For a this his anger has not turned away;
10: 4 For a this his anger has not turned away;
10: 8 For he says: "Are not my commanders a kings?
10:12 the Lord has finished a his work on Mount Zion
10:14 so I have gathered a the earth; E
10:23 as decreed, in a the earth. E
11: 9 not hurt or destroy on a my holy mountain;
12: 5 let this be known in a the earth. E
13: 7 Therefore a hands will be feeble,
13:14 a will turn to their own people,
13:14 and a will flee to their own lands.
13:20 be inhabited or lived in for a generations; O
14: 9 a who were leaders of the earth;
14: 9 it raises from their thrones a who were kings of
14:10 A of them will speak and say to you:
14:18 A the kings of the nations lie in glory, P
14:26 the hand that is stretched out over a the nations. D
14:29 not rejoice, a you Philistines, that the rod
14:31 melt in fear, O Philistia, a of you!
16:14 in spite of a its great multitude;
18: 3 A you inhabitants of the world,
18: 6 They shall a be left to the birds of prey
18: 6 and a the animals of the earth will winter on them.
19: 7 and a that is sown by the Nile will dry up,
19: 8 a who cast hooks in the Nile will lament,
19:10 and a who work for wages will be grieved.
19:14 and they have made Egypt stagger in a its doings
21: 2 a the sighing she has caused I bring to an end.
21: 9 and a the images of her gods lie shattered on
21:16 a the glory of Kedar will come to an end;
22: 1 a of you, to the housetops,
22: 3 Your rulers have a fled together;
22: 3 A of you who were found were captured,
22:24 every small vessel, from the cups to a the flagons.
23: 9 to defile the pride of a glory,
23: 9 to shame a the honored of the earth.
23:17 and will prostitute herself with a the kingdoms R
24: 7 the vine languishes, a the merry-hearted sigh.
24:11 a joy has reached its eventide;
25: 6 the LORD of hosts will make for a peoples G
25: 7 the shroud that is cast over a peoples, G
25: 7 the sheet that is spread over a nations; D
25: 8 Lord GOD will wipe away the tears from a faces,
25: 8 of his people he will take away from a the earth, E
26:12 a that we have done, you have done for us.
26:14 and wiped out a memory of them.
26:15 you have enlarged a the borders of the land.
27: 9 when he makes a the stones of the altars
Isa 28: 8 A tables are covered with filthy vomit;
29: 7 of a the nations that fight against Ariel, D
29: 7 a that fight against her and her stronghold,
29: 8 shall the multitude of a the nations be that fight D
29:11 of a this has become for you like the words of
29:20 a those alert to do evil shall be cut off—
30:18 blessed are a those who wait for him.
31: 3 and they will a perish together.
31: 7 on that day a of you shall throw away your idols
32:13 yes, for a the joyous houses in the jubilant city.
34: 1 Let the earth hear, and a that fills it;
34: 1 the world, and a that comes from it.
34: 2 For the LORD is enraged against a the nations, D
34: 2 and furious against a their hoards;
34: 4 A the host of heaven shall rot away,
34: 4 A their host shall wither like a leaf withering
34:12 and a its princes shall be nothing.
36: 1 King Sennacherib of Assyria came up against a
36: 6 Such is Pharaoh king of Egypt to a who rely
36:20 Who among a the gods of these
37:11 the kings of Assyria have done to a lands,
37:16 you alone, of a the kingdoms of the earth; R
37:17 hear a the words of Sennacherib, K
37:18 kings of Assyria have laid waste a the nations D
37:20 so that a the kingdoms of the earth may know R
37:25 with the sole of my foot a the streams of Egypt.'
37:36 when morning dawned, they were a dead bodies.
38:13 like a lion he breaks a my bones;
38:15 A my sleep has fled because of the bitterness
38:16 and in a these is the life of my spirit.
38:17 for you have cast a my sins behind your back.
38:20 a the days of our lives, at the house of the LORD. F
39: 2 a that was found in his storehouses.
39: 2 or in a his realm that Hezekiah did not show them.
39: 4 "They have seen a that is in my house;
39: 6 Days are coming when a that is in your house,
40: 2 from the LORD's hand double for a her sins.
40: 5 and a people shall see it together, A
40: 6 A people are grass, their constancy is like the A
40:17 A the nations are as nothing before him; D
40:26 and numbers them, calling them a by name;
41:11 a who are incensed against you shall be ashamed
41:12 against you shall be as nothing at a.
41:20 so that a may see and know,
41:20 a may consider and understand,
41:24 indeed, are nothing and your work is nothing at a;
41:29 No, they are a a delusion;
42:10 Let the sea roar and a that fills it,
42:15 and dry up a their herbage;
42:22 a of them are trapped in holes and hidden
42:25 it set him on fire a around,
43: 9 Let a the nations gather together, D
43:14 to Babylon and break down a the bars,
44: 9 A who make idols are nothing,
44:11 Look, a its devotees shall be put to shame;
44:11 Let them a assemble, let them stand up;
44:11 they shall a be put to shame.
44:24 I am the LORD, who made a things, C
44:28 and he shall carry out a my purpose";
45: 7 I the LORD do a these things. H
45:12 and I commanded a their host.
45:13 and I will make a his paths straight;
45:16 A of them are put to shame and confounded,
45:17 not be put to shame or confounded to a eternity.
45:22 Turn to me and be saved, a the ends of the earth!
45:24 a who were incensed against him shall come
45:25 the LORD a the offspring of Israel shall triumph
46: 3 a the remnant of the house of Israel,
47:15 they a wander about in their own paths;
48: 6 now see a this; and will you not declare it?
48:14 Assemble, a of you, and hear!
49: 9 on a the bare heights shall be their pasture;
49:11 And I will turn a my mountains into a road,
49:18 Lift up your eyes a around and see;
49:18 they a gather, they come to you.
49:18 you shall put a of them on like an ornament,
49:21 I was left a alone—where then have these come
49:26 Then a flesh shall know that I am the LORD M
50: 9 A of them will wear out like a garment;
50:11 a of you are kindlers of fire, lighters of firebrands.
51: 3 he will comfort a her waste places,
51: 8 and my salvation to a generations. O
51:13 You fear continually a day long because of
51:18 to guide her among a the children she has borne;
51:18 the hand among a the children she has brought up.
52: 5 and continually, a day long, my name is despised.
52:10 before the eyes of a the nations; D
52:10 and a the ends of the earth shall see the salvation
53: 6 A we like sheep have gone astray;
53: 6 we have a turned to our own way,
53: 6 the LORD has laid on him the iniquity of us a.
54:12 and a your wall of precious stones.
54:13 A your children shall be taught by the LORD,
55:12 and a the trees of the field shall clap their hands.
56: 6 and to be his servants, a who keep the sabbath,
56: 7 be called a house of prayer for a peoples. G
56: 9 A you wild animals, a you wild animals in the
56:10 they are a without knowledge;
56:10 they are a silent dogs that cannot bark;
56:11 they have a turned to their own way,
56:11 to their own gain, one and a.
58: 3 and oppress a your workers.
59:11 We a growl like bears; like doves
60: 4 they a gather together, they come to you;
60: 6 a those from Sheba shall come.
60: 7 A the flocks of Kedar shall be gathered to you,
60:14 a who despised you shall bow down at your feet;

Isa 60:21 Your people shall a be righteous;
61: 2 of our God; to comfort a who mourn;
61: 9 a who see them shall acknowledge that they are
61:11 and praise to spring up before a the nations. D
62: 2 and a the kings your glory; P
62: 6 a day and a night they shall never be silent.
63: 3 on my garments, and stained a my robes.
63: 7 because of a that the LORD has done for us,
63: 9 in a their distress. It was no messenger
63: 9 he lifted them up and carried them a the days F
64: 6 We have a become like one who is unclean,
64: 6 and a our righteous deeds are like a filthy cloth.
64: 6 We a fade like a leaf, and our iniquities,
64: 8 we are a the work of your hand. V
64: 9 Now consider, we are a your people. A
64:11 and a our pleasant places have become ruins.
64:12 After a this, will you restrain yourself, O LORD?
65: 2 I held out my hands a day long to
65: 5 a fire that burns a day long.
65: 8 for my servants' sake, and not destroy them a.
65:12 and a of you shall bow down to the slaughter;
65:25 not hurt or destroy on a my holy mountain,
66: 2 A these things my hand has made, H
66: 2 and so a these things are mine, says the LORD. H
66:10 and be glad for her, a you who love her;
66:10 a you who mourn over her—
66:16 and by his sword, on a flesh; M
66:18 I am coming to gather a nations and tongues; D
66:20 They shall bring a your kindred from
66:20 from a the nations as an offering to the LORD, D
66:23 a flesh shall come to worship before me, M
66:24 and they shall be an abhorrence to a flesh. M
Jer 1: 7 for you shall go to a to whom I send you,
1:14 disaster shall break out on a the inhabitants of L
1:15 now I am calling a the tribes of the kingdoms S
1:15 and a of them shall set their thrones at
1:15 against a its surrounding walls and against a the
1:16 for a their wickedness in forsaking me;
2: 3 A who ate of it were held guilty;
2: 4 and a the families of the house of Israel.
2:29 You have a rebelled against me, says the LORD.
2:34 Yet in spite of a these things H
3: 5 but you have done a the evil that you could.
3: 7 "After she has done a this she will return to me";
3: 8 that for a the adulteries of that faithless one,
3:10 Yet for a this her false sister Judah did not return
3:17 and a nations shall gather to it, D
3:19 the most beautiful heritage of a the nations. D
3:24 from our youth the shameful thing has devoured a
4:24 and a the hills moved to and fro.
4:25 I looked, and lo, there was no one at a,
4:25 and a the birds of the air had fled.
4:26 a its cities were laid in ruins before the LORD,
4:29 a the towns are forsaken, and no one lives
5: 5 But they a alike had broken the yoke,
5:16 a of them are mighty warriors.
5:19 "Why has the LORD our God done a these things H
6: 3 they shall pasture, a in their places.
6:28 They are a stubbornly rebellious,
6:28 they are bronze and iron, a of them act corruptly.
7: 2 a you people of Judah, you that enter these gates A
7:10 only to go on doing a these abominations?
7:13 And now, because you have done a these things, H
7:15 just as I cast out a your kinsfolk,
7:15 a the offspring of Ephraim.
7:25 have persistently sent a my servants the prophets Q
7:27 So you shall speak a these words to them,
8: 2 and a the host of heaven, which they have loved
8: 3 be preferred to life by a the remnant that remains
of this evil family in a the places
8: 6 A of them turn to their own course,
8:12 yet they were not at a ashamed,
8:16 They come and devour the land and a that fills it,
9: 2 For they are a adulterers, a band of traitors.
9: 4 for a your kin are supplanters,
9: 5 They a deceive their neighbors,
9: 8 They a speak friendly words to their neighbors,
9:25 to a those who are circumcised only in
9:26 and a those with shaven temples who live in
9:26 For a these nations are uncircumcised, D
9:26 a the house of Israel is uncircumcised in heart.
10: 7 among a the wise ones of the nations and in a their
10: 9 they are a the product of skilled workers.
10:14 goldsmiths are a put to shame by their idols;
10:16 for he is the one who formed a things, C
10:20 My tent is destroyed, and a my cords are broken;
10:21 and a their flock is scattered.
11: 4 Listen to my voice, and do a that I command you.
11: 6 Proclaim a these words in the cities of Judah,
11: 8 brought upon them a the words of this covenant, K
12: 1 Why do a who are treacherous thrive?
12: 9 Are the birds of prey a around her?
12: 9 Go, assemble a the wild animals;
12:12 Upon a the bare heights in
12:14 concerning a my evil neighbors who touch
13:13 I am about to fill a the inhabitants of this land— L
13:13 and a the inhabitants of Jerusalem— L
13:19 a Judah is taken into exile, T
14:22 for it is you who do a this.
15: 4 a horror to a the kingdoms of the earth because R
15:10 nor have I borrowed, yet a of them curse me.
15:13 for a your sins, throughout a your territory.
16:10 And when you tell this people a these words,
16:10 "Why has the LORD pronounced a this great evil
16:15 and out of a the lands where he had driven them."
16:17 For my eyes are on a their ways;
17: 3 Your wealth and a your treasures I will give

Jer 17: 3 the price of your sin throughout a your territory.
17: 9 The heart is devious above a else;
17:10 to give to a according to their ways,
17:11 so are a who amass wealth unjustly;
17:13 A who forsake you shall be put to shame;
17:19 and in a the gates of Jerusalem,
17:20 and a Judah, and all the inhabitants of Jerusalem, T
17:20 and all Judah, and a the inhabitants of Jerusalem, L
18:11 Turn now, a of you from your evil way,
18:16 A who pass by it are horrified
18:23 you, O LORD, know a their plotting to kill me.
19: 8 and will hiss because of a its disasters.
19: 9 a shall eat the flesh of their neighbors in the siege,
19:13 a the houses upon whose roofs offerings have
19:14 the LORD's house and said to a the people: A
19:15 upon this city and upon a its towns a the disaster
20: 4 a terror to yourself and to a your friends;
20: 4 And I will give a Judah into the hand of the king T
20: 5 I will give a the wealth of this city, a its gains,
20: 5 a its prized belongings, and a the treasures
20: 6 And you, Pashhur, and a who live in your house,
20: 6 you shall be buried, you and a your friends,
20: 7 I have become a laughingstock a day long;
20: 8 for me a reproach and derision a day long.
20:10 For I hear many whispering: "Terror is a around!
20:10 A my close friends are watching for me
21:14 and it shall devour a that is around it.
22: 7 against you, a with their weapons;
22: 8 and a of them will say one to another,
22:20 for a your lovers are crushed.
22:22 The wind shall shepherd a your shepherds,
22:22 and dismayed because of a your wickedness.
23: 3 the remnant of my flock out of a the lands
23: 8 and out of a the lands where he had driven them."
23: 9 My heart is crushed within me, a my bones shake;
23:14 a of them have become like Sodom to me,
23:17 a who stubbornly follow their own stubborn hearts,
23:32 so they do not profit this people at a,
24: 9 an evil thing, to a the kingdoms of the earth— R
24: 9 a curse in a the places where I shall drive them.
25: 1 that came to Jeremiah concerning a the people A
25: 2 the prophet Jeremiah spoke to a the people A
25: 2 to all the people of Judah and a the inhabitants L
25: 4 the LORD persistently sent you a his servants Q
25: 9 for a the tribes of the north, says the LORD, S
25: 9 and against a these nations around; D
25:13 land a the words that I have uttered against it, K
25:13 which Jeremiah prophesied against a the nations. D
25:15 make a the nations to whom I send you drink it. D
25:17 and made a the nations to whom D
25:19 his servants, his officials, and a his people; A
25:20 a the mixed people; all the kings of the A
25:20 a the kings of the land of Uz; P
25:20 a the kings of the land of the Philistines— P
25:22 a the kings of Tyre, all the kings of Sidon, P
25:22 a the kings of Sidon, and the kings of P
25:23 Tema, Buz, and a who have shaven temples;
25:24 a the kings of Arabia and all the kings of P
25:24 and a the kings of the mixed peoples that live in P
25:25 a the kings of Zimri, all the kings of Elam, P
25:25 a the kings of Elam, and all the kings of Media; P
25:25 all the kings of Elam, and a the kings of Media; P
25:26 a the kings of the north, P
25:26 and a the kingdoms of the world that are on R
25:29 a sword against a the inhabitants of the earth, L
25:30 shall prophesy against them a these words,
25:30 against a the inhabitants of the earth. L
25:31 he is entering into judgment with a flesh, M
26: 2 in the court of the LORD's house, and speak to a
26: 2 speak to them a the words that I command you; K
26: 3 It may be that they will listen, a of them,
26: 6 and I will make this city a curse for a the nations D
26: 7 The priests and the prophets and a the people A
26: 8 And when Jeremiah had finished speaking a that
26: 8 commanded him to speak to a the people, A
26: 8 the prophets and a the people laid hold of him, A
26: 9 And a the people gathered around Jeremiah in A
26:11 said to the officials and to a the people, A
26:12 Then Jeremiah spoke to a the officials and
26:12 spoke to all the officials and a the people, A
26:12 against this house and this city a the words K
26:15 the LORD sent me to you to speak a these words
26:16 the officials and a the people said to the priests A
26:17 arose and said to a the assembled people, A
26:18 said to a the people of Judah: A
26:19 of Judah and a Judah actually put him to death? T
26:21 with a his warriors and a the officials,
27: 6 Now I have given a these lands into the hand
27: 7 A the nations shall serve him and his son D
27:16 Then I spoke to the priests and to a this people, A
27:20 and a the nobles of Judah and Jerusalem—
28: 1 in the presence of the priests and a the people, A
28: 3 to this place a the vessels of the LORD's house,
28: 4 and a the exiles from Judah who went to Babylon,
28: 5 the priests and a the people who were standing A
28: 6 the vessels of the house of the LORD, and a
28: 7 and in the hearing of a the people. A
28:11 Hananiah spoke in the presence of a the people, A
28:11 from the neck of a the nations within two years." D
28:14 an iron yoke on the neck of a these nations so D
29: 1 and to the priests, the prophets, and a the people, A
29: 4 to a the exiles whom I have sent into exile
29:13 if you seek me with a your heart, J
29:14 and gather you from a the nations and D
29:14 and a the places where I have driven you,
29:16 concerning a the people who live in this city, A
29:18 and will make them a horror to a the kingdoms R

Jer 29:18 among a the nations where I have driven them, D
29:20 a you exiles whom I sent away from Jerusalem
29:22 on account of them this curse shall be used by a
29:25 a letter to a the people who are in Jerusalem, A
29:25 and to a the priests, saying,
29:31 Send to a the exiles, saying, Thus says the LORD
30: 2 in a book a the words that I have spoken to you. K
30:11 of a the nations among which I scattered you, D
30:14 A your lovers have forgotten you;
30:16 Therefore a who devour you shall be devoured,
30:16 and a your foes, everyone of them,
30:16 and a who prey on you I will make a prey.
30:20 and I will punish a who oppress them.
31: 1 I will be the God of a the families of Israel,
31:24 Judah and a its towns shall live there together,
31:25 and a who are faint I will replenish.
31:30 But a shall die for their own sins;
31:34 "Know the LORD," for they shall a know me,
31:37 then I will reject a the offspring of Israel because
31:37 of Israel because of a they have done,
31:40 and a the fields as far as the Wadi Kidron,
32:12 the presence of a the Judeans who were sitting in
32:19 whose eyes are open to a the ways of mortals,
32:19 rewarding a according to their ways and according
32:20 and to this day in Israel and among a humankind,
32:23 of a you commanded them to do, they did nothing.
32:23 you have made a these disasters come upon them.
32:27 the God of a flesh; is anything too hard for me? M
32:32 of a the evil of the people of Israel and the people
32:37 I am going to gather them from a the lands
32:39 that they may fear me for a time,
32:41 with a my heart and all my soul. J
32:41 with all my heart and a my soul.
32:42 Just as I have brought a this great disaster
32:42 so I will bring upon them a the good fortune that I
33: 5 from this city because of a their wickedness.
33: 8 I will cleanse them from a the guilt of their sin
33: 8 and I will forgive a the guilt of their sin
33: 9 before a the nations of the earth who shall hear D
33: 9 of the earth who shall hear of a the good that I do
33: 9 a the good and a the prosperity I provide for it.
33:12 or animals, and in a its towns there shall again
33:18 and to make sacrifices for a time.
34: 1 and a his army and all the kingdoms of the earth
34: 1 and all his army and a the kingdoms of the earth R
34: 1 the kingdoms of the earth and a the peoples G
34: 1 against Jerusalem and a its cities:
34: 6 Then the prophet Jeremiah spoke a these words
34: 7 against a the cities of Judah that were left, Lachish
34: 8 a covenant with a the people in Jerusalem A
34: 9 that a should set free their Hebrew slaves,
34:10 a the officials and all the people who had entered
34:10 the officials and a the people who had entered A
34:10 that a would set free their slaves, male or female,
34:17 I will make you a horror to a the kingdoms R
34:19 a the people of the land who passed between A
35: 3 and his brothers, and a his sons,
35: 7 but you shall live in tents a your days,
35: 8 of our ancestor Jonadab son of Rechab in a
35: 8 to drink no wine a our days, ourselves, our wives,
35:10 and have obeyed and done a that our ancestor
35:15 I have sent to you a my servants the prophets, Q
35:17 on a the inhabitants of Jerusalem every disaster L
35:18 of your ancestor Jonadab, and kept a his precepts,
35:18 and done a that he commanded you,
35:19 a descendant to stand before me for a time.
36: 2 and write on it a the words that I have spoken K
36: 2 against Israel and Judah and a the nations, D
36: 3 of Judah hears of a the disasters that I intend to do
36: 3 a of them may turn from their evil ways,
36: 4 at Jeremiah's dictation a the words of the LORD K
36: 6 the hearing of a the people of Judah who come A
36: 7 and that a of them will turn from their evil ways,
36: 8 And Baruch son of Neriah did a that
36: 9 in the ninth month, a the people in Jerusalem A
36: 9 and a the people who came from the towns A
36:10 Then, in the hearing of a the people, A
36:11 son of Shaphan heard a the words of the LORD K
36:12 and a the officials were sitting there:
36:12 Zedekiah son of Hananiah, and a the officials.
36:13 Micaiah told them a the words that he had heard, K
36:14 Then a the officials sent Jehudi son
36:16 When they heard a the words, K
36:16 "We certainly must report a these words to
36:17 "Tell us now, how did you write a these words?
36:18 "He dictated a these words to me,
36:20 and they reported a the words to the king. K
36:21 to the king and a the officials who stood beside
36:24 nor any of his servants who heard a these words,
36:28 and write on it a the former words that were in
36:31 of Jerusalem, and on the people of Judah, a
36:32 at Jeremiah's dictation a the words of the scroll K
37:21 until a the bread of the city was gone.
38: 1 that Jeremiah was saying to a the people, A
38: 4 a the people, by speaking such words to them. A
38: 9 these men have acted wickedly in a they did to
38:22 of a the women remaining in the house of the king
38:23 A your wives and your children shall be led out to
38:27 A the officials did come to Jeremiah
39: 1 and a his army came against Jerusalem
39: 3 a the officials of the king of Babylon came and sat
39: 3 Nergal-sharezer the Rabmag, with a the rest
39: 4 and a the soldiers saw them, they fled, going out
39: 6 also the king of Babylon slaughtered a the nobles
39:13 a the chief officers of the king of Babylon sent
40: 1 in fetters along with a the captives of Jerusalem
40: 3 because a of you sinned against the LORD

Jer 40: 7 When **a** the leaders of the forces in
40:11 when **a** the Judeans who were in Moab and among
40:12 then **a** the Judeans returned from **a** the places
40:13 Now Johanan son of Kareah and **a** the leaders of
40:14 "Are you at **a** aware that Baalis king of
40:15 so that **a** the Judeans who are gathered
41: 3 also killed **a** the Judeans who were with Gedaliah
41: 9 Now the cistern into which Ishmael had thrown **a**
41:10 Then Ishmael took captive **a** the rest of
41:10 and **a** the people who were left at Mizpah, A
41:11 But when Johanan son of Kareah and **a** the leaders
41:11 with him heard of **a** the crimes that Ishmael son
41:12 they took **a** their men and went to fight
41:13 And when **a** the people who were with Ishmael A
41:13 of Kareah and **a** the leaders of the forces with him,
41:14 So **a** the people whom Ishmael had carried away A
41:16 Then Johanan son of Kareah and **a** the leaders of
41:16 the leaders of the forces with him took **a** the rest
42: 1 Then **a** the commanders of the forces,
42: 1 and **a** the people from the least to the greatest, A
42: 2 for us—for **a** this remnant.
42: 8 Then he summoned Johanan son of Kareah and **a**
42: 8 and **a** the people from the least to the greatest, A
42:17 **A** the people who have determined to go A
43: 1 Jeremiah finished speaking to **a** the people A
43: 1 the people **a** these words of the LORD their God,
43: 2 and Johanan son of Kareah and **a** the other
43: 4 So Johanan son of Kareah and **a** the commanders
43: 4 and **a** the people did not obey the voice A
43: 5 But Johanan son of Kareah and **a** the commanders
43: 5 the commanders of the forces took **a** the remnant
43: 5 to settle in the land of Judah from **a** the nations D
44: 1 that came to Jeremiah for **a** the Judeans living in
44: 2 You yourselves have seen **a** the disaster
44: 2 on Jerusalem and on **a** the towns of Judah.
44: 4 Yet I persistently sent to you **a** my servants Q
44: 8 of cursing and ridicule among **a** the nations of D
44:11 to bring **a** Judah to an end. T
44:15 Then **a** the men who were aware Z
44:15 and **a** the women who stood by, a great assembly,
44:15 **a** the people who lived in Pathros in the land A
44:20 Then Jeremiah said to **a** the people, A
44:20 **a** the people who were giving him this answer: A
44:24 Jeremiah said to **a** the people and all the women, A
44:24 Jeremiah said to all the people and **a** the women,
44:24 **a** you Judeans who are in the land of Egypt,
44:25 By **a** means, keep your vows
44:26 **a** you Judeans who live in the land of Egypt:
44:26 lips of any of the people of Judah in **a** the land I
44:27 **a** the people of Judah who are in the land A
44:28 and **a** the remnant of Judah,
45: 5 for I am going to bring disaster upon **a** flesh, M
46: 5 They do not look back—terror is **a** around!
46:28 I will make an end of **a** the nations D
47: 2 they shall overflow the land and **a** that fills it,
47: 2 and **a** the inhabitants of the land shall wail. L
47: 4 the day that is coming to destroy **a** the Philistines,
48:17 Mourn over him, **a** you his neighbors,
48:17 all you his neighbors, and **a** who know his name;
48:24 and **a** the towns of the land of Moab, far and near.
48:31 Therefore I wail for Moab; I cry out for **a** Moab;
48:37 on **a** the hands there are gashes,
48:38 On **a** the housetops of Moab and in
48:39 a derision and a horror to **a** his neighbors.
49: 5 from **a** your neighbors, and you will be scattered,
49:13 and **a** her towns shall be perpetual wastes.
49:17 and will hiss because of **a** its disasters.
49:26 and **a** her soldiers shall be destroyed in that day,
49:29 their curtains and **a** their goods;
49:29 and a cry shall go up: "Terror is **a** around!"
49:36 and I will scatter them to **a** these winds,
50: 7 **A** who found them have devoured them,
50:10 **a** who plunder her shall be sated, says the LORD.
50:13 be appalled and hiss because of **a** her wounds.
50:14 **a** you that bend the bow;
50:15 Raise a shout against her from **a** sides,
50:16 of the destroying sword **a** of them shall return
50:16 and **a** of them shall flee to their own land
50:21 do **a** that I have commanded you.
50:27 Kill **a** her bulls, let them go down to the slaughter.
50:29 against Babylon, **a** who bend the bow.
50:29 Encamp **a** around her; let no one escape.
50:30 and **a** her soldiers shall be destroyed on that day,
50:33 **a** their captors have held them fast and refuse
50:37 and against **a** the foreign troops in her midst,
50:37 A sword against **a** her treasures,
50:39 or inhabited for **a** generations. O
51: 7 making **a** the earth drunken; E
51:17 goldsmiths are **a** put to shame by their idols;
51:19 for he is the one who formed **a** things, C
51:24 I will repay Babylon and **a** the inhabitants L
51:24 of Chaldea before your very eyes for **a** the wrong
51:47 and **a** her slain shall fall in her midst.
51:48 the heavens and the earth, and **a** that is in them,
51:49 of **a** the earth have fallen because of Babylon. E
51:52 and through **a** her land the wounded shall groan.
51:60 in a scroll **a** the disasters that would come
51:60 **a** these words that are written
51:61 see that you read **a** these words,
52: 4 with **a** his army against Jerusalem,
52: 4 they built siegeworks against it **a** around.
52: 7 and **a** the soldiers fled and went out from the city
52: 7 though the Chaldeans were **a** around the city.
52: 8 and **a** his army was scattered, deserting him.
52:10 and also killed **a** the officers of Judah at Riblah.
52:13 the king's house, and **a** the houses of Jerusalem;
52:14 **A** the army of the Chaldeans,

Jer 52:14 broke down **a** the walls around Jerusalem.
52:17 and carried **a** the bronze to Babylon.
52:18 **a** the vessels of bronze used in the temple service.
52:20 bronze of **a** these vessels was beyond weighing.
52:22 latticework and pomegranates, **a** of bronze,
52:23 **a** the pomegranates encircling
52:30 **a** the persons were four thousand six hundred.
La 1: 2 among **a** her lovers she has no one to comfort her;
1: 2 **a** her friends have dealt treacherously with her,
1: 3 her pursuers have **a** overtaken her in the midst
1: 4 **a** her gates are desolate, her priests groan;
1: 6 From daughter Zion has departed **a** her majesty.
1: 7 **a** the precious things that were hers in days of old.
1: 8 **a** who honored her despise her,
1:10 over **a** her precious things;
1:11 **A** her people groan as they search for bread; A
1:12 Is it nothing to you, **a** you who pass by?
1:13 he has left me stunned, faint **a** day long.
1:15 The LORD has rejected **a** my warriors in
1:18 hear, **a** you peoples, and behold my suffering; G
1:21 **A** my enemies heard of my trouble;
1:22 Let **a** their evil doing come before you;
1:22 with me because of **a** my transgressions;
2: 2 The Lord has destroyed without mercy **a**
2: 3 He has cut down in fierce anger **a** the might
2: 3 like a flaming fire in Jacob, consuming **a** around.
2: 4 he has killed **a** in whom we took pride in the tent
2: 5 He has destroyed **a** its palaces,
2:15 **A** who pass along the way clap their hands at you;
2:15 the perfection of beauty, the joy of **a** the earth?" E
2:16 **A** your enemies open their mouths against you;
2:22 You invited my enemies from **a** around as if for
3: 3 again and again, **a** day long.
3:14 have become the laughingstock of **a** my people, A
3:14 the object of their taunt-songs **a** day long.
3:18 and **a** that I had hoped for from the LORD."
3:34 **a** the prisoners of the land are crushed under foot,
3:46 **A** our enemies have opened their mouths
3:51 at the fate of **a** the young women in my city.
3:60 have seen **a** their malice, **a** their plots against me.
3:61 O LORD, **a** their plots against me.
3:62 of my assailants are against me **a** day long.
5:19 your throne endures to **a** generations. O
Eze 1:18 for the rims of **a** four were full of eyes **a** around.
1:27 something that looked like fire enclosed **a** around;
1:27 and there was a splendor **a** around.
1:28 such was the appearance of the splendor **a** around.
3: 7 because **a** the house of Israel have a hard forehead
3:10 **a** my words that I shall speak to you receive
4: 2 and plant battering rams against it **a** around.
5: 2 and strike with the sword **a** around the city;
5: 4 from there a fire will come out against **a** the house
5: 5 with countries **a** around her.
5: 6 the nations and the countries **a** around her,
5: 7 the nations that are **a** around you, and have
5: 7 to the ordinances of the nations that are **a** around
5: 9 And because of **a** your abominations,
5:11 with **a** your detestable things and with **a** your abominations—
5:14 in the sight of **a** that pass by.
6: 9 that they have committed, for **a** their abominations.
6:11 for **a** the vile abominations of the house of Israel!
6:13 on **a** the mountain tops, under every green tree,
6:13 they offered pleasing odor to **a** their idols.
6:14 throughout **a** their settlements,
7: 3 I will punish you for **a** your abominations.
7: 8 and punish you for **a** your abominations.
7:12 for wrath is upon **a** their multitude.
7:13 For the vision concerns **a** their multitude;
7:14 for my wrath is upon **a** their multitude.
7:16 **a** of them moaning over their iniquity.
7:17 **A** hands shall grow feeble, **a** knees turn to water.
7:18 Shame shall be on **a** faces, baldness on **a** their heads.
8:10 there, portrayed on the wall **a** around,
8:10 were **a** kinds of creeping things,
8:10 and **a** the idols of the house of Israel
9: 4 over **a** the abominations that are committed in it."
9: 8 will you destroy **a** who remain of Israel
10:12 the four of them—were full of eyes **a** around.
11:15 the whole house of Israel, **a** of them,
11:18 **a** its detestable things and **a** its abominations.
11:25 And I told the exiles **a** the things that
12:10 This oracle concerns the prince in Jerusalem and **a**
12:14 I will scatter to every wind **a** who are around him,
12:14 his helpers and **a** his troops;
12:16 that they may tell of **a** their abominations among
12:19 their land shall be stripped of **a** it contains,
12:19 on account of the violence of **a** those who live
13:18 Woe to the women who sew bands on **a** wrists,
14: 5 **a** of whom are estranged from me
14: 6 turn away your faces from **a** your abominations.
14:11 with **a** their transgressions.
14:22 for **a** that I have brought upon it.
14:23 without cause that I did **a** that I have done in it,
15: 2 does the wood of the vine surpass **a** other wood—
16:22 in **a** your abominations and your whorings you did
16:23 After **a** your wickedness (woe, woe to you!
16:30 says the Lord GOD, that you did **a** these things, H
16:33 Gifts are given to **a** whores;
16:33 but you gave your gifts to **a** your lovers,
16:33 to come to you from **a** around for your whorings.
16:36 and because of **a** your abominable idols,
16:37 I will gather **a** your lovers,
16:37 **a** those you loved and **a** those you hated;
16:37 I will gather them against you from **a** around,
16:37 so that they may see **a** your nakedness.

Eze 16:43 but have enraged me with **a** these things; H
16:43 beyond **a** your abominations?
16:47 you were more corrupt than they in **a** your ways.
16:51 and have made your sisters appear righteous by **a**
16:54 and be ashamed of **a** that you have done,
16:57 to the daughters of Aram and **a** her neighbors,
16:57 those **a** around who despise you.
16:63 when I forgive you **a** that you have done,
17:18 he gave his hand and yet did **a** these things, H
17:21 **A** the pick of his troops shall fall by the sword,
17:24 **A** the trees of the field shall know that I am
18: 4 Know that **a** lives are mine;
18:13 He has done **a** these abominable things;
18:14 a son who sees **a** the sins that his father has done,
18:19 and has been careful to observe **a** my statutes,
18:21 But if the wicked turn away from **a** their sins
18:21 that they have committed and keep **a** my statutes
18:28 from **a** the transgressions that they had committed,
18:30 **a** of you according to your ways,
18:30 Repent and turn from **a** your transgressions;
18:31 Cast away from you **a** the transgressions
19: 7 the land was appalled, and **a** in it,
19: 8 nations set upon him from the provinces **a** around;
20: 6 the most glorious of **a** lands.
20:15 the most glorious of **a** lands,
20:26 in their offering up **a** their firstborn,
20:31 you defile yourselves with **a** your idols to this day.
20:40 there **a** the house of Israel, **a** of them,
20:40 with **a** your sacred things.
20:43 There you shall remember your ways and **a**
20:43 and you shall loathe yourselves for **a** the evils
20:47 **a** faces from south to north shall be scorched by it.
20:48 **A** flesh shall see that I the LORD have kindled it; M
21: 4 of its sheath against **a** flesh from south to north; M
21: 5 and **a** flesh shall know that I the LORD have M
21: 7 Every heart will melt and **a** hands will be feeble,
21: 7 spirit will faint and **a** knees will turn to water.
21:10 You have despised the rod, and **a** discipline.
21:12 it is against **a** Israel's princes;
21:15 At **a** their gates I have set the point of the sword.
21:24 so that in **a** your deeds your sins appear—
22: 2 Then declare to it **a** its abominable deeds.
22: 4 and a mockery to **a** the countries.
22:18 **a** of them, silver, bronze, tin, iron, and lead.
22:19 Because you have **a** become dross,
23: 6 **a** of them handsome young men,
23: 7 the choicest men of Assyria **a** of them;
23: 7 with **a** the idols of everyone for whom she lusted.
23:12 **a** of them handsome young men.
23:15 **a** of them looking like officers—
23:23 the Babylonians and **a** the Chaldeans,
23:23 and **a** the Assyrians with them,
23:23 governors and commanders **a** of them,
23:23 officers and warriors, **a** of them riding on horses.
23:29 and take away **a** the fruit of your labor,
23:48 so that **a** women may take warning and
24: 4 **a** the good pieces, the thigh and the shoulder;
24: 6 Empty it piece by piece, making no choice at **a**.
25: 6 and rejoiced with **a** the malice within you against
25: 8 The house of Judah is like **a** the other nations, D
26:11 of his horses he shall trample **a** your streets.
26:16 Then **a** the princes of the sea shall step down
26:17 who imposed your terror on **a** the mainland!
27: 5 They made **a** your planks of fir trees from Senir;
27: 9 **a** the ships of the sea with their mariners were
27:11 of Arvad and Helech were on your walls **a** around;
27:11 They hung their quivers **a** around your walls;
27:21 Arabia and **a** the princes of Kedar
27:22 they exchanged for your wares the best of **a** kinds
27:22 and **a** precious stones, and gold.
27:27 and **a** your warriors within you,
27:27 with **a** the company that is with you,
27:29 down from their ships come **a** that handle the oar.
27:29 The mariners and **a** the pilots of the sea stand on
27:34 your merchandise and **a** your crew have sunk
27:35 **A** the inhabitants of the coastlands are appalled L
28:18 on the earth in the sight of **a** who saw you.
28:19 **A** who know you among the peoples are appalled
28:24 among **a** their neighbors who have treated them
28:26 upon **a** their neighbors who have treated them
29: 2 and prophesy against him and against **a** Egypt;
29: 4 with **a** the fish of your channels sticking
29: 5 you and **a** the fish of your channels;
29: 6 Then **a** the inhabitants of Egypt shall know L
29: 7 you broke, and tore **a** their shoulders;
29: 7 you broke, and made **a** their legs unsteady.
30: 5 Ethiopia, and Put, and Lud, and **a** Arabia,
30: 8 and **a** who help it are broken.
31: 4 sending forth its streams to **a** the trees of the field.
31: 5 So it towered high above **a** the trees of the field;
31: 6 **A** the birds of the air made their nests in its boughs
31: 6 under its branches **a** the animals of the field
31: 6 and in its shade **a** great nations lived. D
31: 9 of **a** the trees of Eden that were in the garden
31:12 and in **a** the valleys its branches have fallen,
31:12 and its boughs lie broken in **a** the watercourses of
31:12 and **a** the peoples of the earth went away G
31:13 On its fallen trunk settle **a** the birds of the air,
31:13 and among its boughs lodge **a** the wild animals.
31:14 **A** this is in order that no trees by
31:14 For **a** of them are handed over to death,
31:14 along with **a** mortals, with those who go down
31:15 and **a** the trees of the field fainted because of it.
31:16 and **a** the trees of Eden,
31:16 and best of Lebanon, **a** that were well watered,
31:18 This is Pharaoh and **a** his horde,
32: 4 will cause **a** the birds of the air to settle on you,

Eze 32: 8 A the shining lights of the heavens I will darken
32:12 a of them most terrible among the nations.
32:12 and a its hordes shall perish.
32:13 I will destroy a its livestock from
32:15 and when the land is stripped of a that fills it,
32:15 when I strike down a who live in it,
32:16 Over Egypt and a its hordes they shall chant it,
32:22 Assyria is there, and a its company, their graves a around it, a of them killed,
32:23 Its company is a around its grave, a of them killed,
32:24 and a its hordes around its grave; a of them killed,
32:25 the slain with a its hordes, their graves a around it,
32:25 a of them uncircumcised, killed by the sword;
32:26 and a their multitude, their graves a around them,
32:26 a of them uncircumcised, killed by the sword;
32:29 Edom is there, its kings and a its princes,
32:29 for a their might are laid with those who are killed
32:30 a of them, and a the Sidonians,
32:30 for a the terror that they caused by their might;
32:31 he will be consoled for a his hordes—
32:31 Pharaoh and a his army, killed by the sword,
32:32 Pharaoh and a his multitude, says the Lord GOD.
33:20 I will judge a of you according to your ways!
33:29 of a their abominations that they have committed.
34: 5 they became food for a the wild animals.
34: 6 over a the mountains and on every high hill;
34: 6 my sheep were scattered over a the face of the
34: 8 and my sheep have become food for a
34:12 I will rescue them from a the places
34:13 and in a the inhabited parts of the land.
34:21 and butted at a the weak animals with your horns
35: 7 and I will cut off from it a who come and go.
35: 8 and in a your watercourses those killed with
35:12 have heard a the abusive speech that you uttered
35:15 be desolate, Mount Seir, and a Edom, a of it.
36: 3 and crushed you from a sides,
36: 4 of derision to the rest of the nations a around;
36: 5 and against a Edom, who,
36: 7 I swear that the nations that are a
36:10 the whole house of Israel, a of it;
36:24 and gather you from a the countries,
36:25 and you shall be clean from a your uncleannesses,
36:25 and from a your idols I will cleanse you.
36:29 I will save you from a your uncleannesses,
36:33 the day that I cleanse you from a your iniquities,
36:34 that it was in the sight of a who passed by.
36:36 the nations that are left a around you shall know
37: 2 He led me a around them;
37:16 of Ephraim) and a the house of Israel associated
37:22 and one king shall be king over them a.
37:23 from a the apostasies into which they have fallen,
37:24 and they shall a have one shepherd.
38: 4 and I will lead you out with a your army,
38: 4 a of them clothed in full armor, a great company,
38: 4 a of them with shield and buckler,
38: 5 a of them with buckler and helmet;
38: 6 Gomer and a its troops; Beth-togarmah from the
38: 6 the remotest parts of the north with a its troops—
38: 7 you and a the companies that are assembled
38: 8 from the nations and now are living in safety, a
38: 9 a cloud covering the land, you and a your troops,
38:11 a of them living without walls,
38:13 of Tarshish and a its young warriors will say
38:15 a of them riding on horses, a great horde,
38:20 and a creeping things that creep on the ground,
38:20 a human beings that are on the face of the earth,
38:21 the sword against Gog in a my mountains,
38:21 the swords of a will be against their comrades.
39: 4 you and a your troops and the peoples that are
39:11 for there Gog and a his horde will be buried;
39:13 A the people of the land shall bury them; A
39:17 the birds of every kind and to a the wild animals:
39:17 Assemble and come, gather from a around to
39:18 of bulls, a of them fatlings of Bashan.
39:20 with warriors and a kinds of soldiers,
39:21 and a the nations shall see my judgment D
39:23 and they a fell by the sword.
39:26 a the treachery they have practiced against me,
40: 4 and set your mind upon a that I shall show you,
40: 4 declare a that you see to the house of Israel."
40: 5 a wall a around the outside of the temple area.
40:16 inside of the gateway a around, and the vestibules
40:16 also had windows on the inside a around;
40:17 and a pavement, a around the court;
40:25 There were windows a around in it and
40:29 and there were windows a around in it and
40:30 There were vestibules a around,
40:33 and there were windows a around in it
40:36 and it had windows a around.
40:43 fastened a around the inside.
41: 5 four cubits, a around the temple.
41: 6 There were offsets a around the wall of the temple
41: 7 the structure was supplied with a stairway a around
41: 8 that the temple had a raised platform a around;
41:10 of the court was a width of twenty cubits a around
41:11 the part that was left free was five cubits a around.
41:12 and the wall of the building was five cubits thick a
41:16 and, a around, all three had windows
41:16 a three had windows with recessed frames.
41:16 the threshold the temple was paneled with wood a
41:17 And on a the walls a around in the inner room
41:19 They were carved on the whole temple a around;
42:15 and measured the temple area a around.
43:11 When they are ashamed of a that they have done,
43:11 a its ordinances and its entire plan and a its laws;
43:11 and follow the entire plan and a its ordinances.
43:12 the whole territory on the top of the mountain a
Eze 43:20 and upon the rim a around;
44: 5 and listen attentively to a that I shall tell you
44: 5 concerning a the ordinances of the temple of the LORD and a its laws;
44: 5 to the temple and a those who are to be excluded
44: 6 let there be an end to a your abominations
44: 7 with a your abominations.
44: 9 in heart and flesh, of a the foreigners who are
44:14 to do a its chores, a that is to be done in it.
44:24 my statutes regarding a my appointed festivals,
44:30 The first of a the first fruits of a kinds,
44:30 every offering of a kinds from a your offerings,
45:16 A the people of the land shall join with the A
45:17 a the appointed festivals of the house of Israel:
45:22 prince shall provide for himself and a the people A
46:14 this is the ordinance for a time.
46:23 at the bottom of the rows a around.
47:12 there will grow a kinds of trees for food.
48:19 workers of the city, from a the tribes of Israel, S
Da 1:15 that they appeared better and fatter than a
1:17 Daniel also had insight into a visions and dreams.
1:19 And among them a, no one was found to compare
1:20 he found them ten times better than a
2:12 a violent rage and commanded that a the wise men
2:35 were a broken in pieces and became like the chaff
2:38 whom he has established as ruler over them a—
2:40 it shall crush and shatter a these.
2:44 It shall crush a these kingdoms and bring them to
2:48 and chief prefect over a the wise men of Babylon.
3: 2 and a the officials of the provinces to assemble
3: 3 and a the officials of the provinces,
3: 7 as a the peoples heard the sound of the horn, G
3: 7 and entire musical ensemble, a the peoples, G
4: 1 King Nebuchadnezzar to a peoples, nations, G
4: 6 that a the wise men of Babylon should be brought
4:12 its fruit abundant, and it provided food for a.
4:12 and from it a living beings were fed.
4:17 in order that a who live may know that
4:18 since a the wise men of my kingdom are unable
4:21 and which provided food for a,
4:28 A this came upon King Nebuchadnezzar.
4:35 A the inhabitants of the earth are accounted L
4:37 for a his works are truth, and his ways are justice;
5: 8 Then a the king's wise men came in,
5:19 of the greatness that he gave him, a peoples, G
5:22 even though you knew a this!
5:23 and to whom belong a your ways,
6: 3 above a the other presidents and satraps because
6: 7 A the presidents of the kingdom,
6:24 and broke a their bones in pieces.
6:25 King Darius wrote to a peoples and nations G
6:26 in a my royal dominion people should tremble
7: 7 It was different from a the beasts that preceded it,
7:14 and glory and kingship, that a peoples, nations, G
7:16 to ask him the truth concerning a this.
7:19 which was different from a the rest,
7:23 that shall be different from a the other kingdoms; R
7:27 and a dominions shall serve and obey them."
8: 4 A beasts were powerless to withstand it,
9: 6 our ancestors, and to a the people of the land. A
9: 7 the inhabitants of Jerusalem, and a Israel, B
9: 7 in a the lands to which you have driven them,
9:11 "A Israel has transgressed your law B
9:13 a this calamity has come upon us.
9:14 the LORD our God is right in a that he has done;
9:16 O Lord, in view of a your righteous acts,
9:16 a disgrace among a our neighbors.
10: 3 and I had not anointed myself at a,
11: 2 The fourth shall be far richer than a of them,
11: 2 he shall stir up a against the kingdom of Greece.
11:16 and a of it shall be in his power.
11:37 for he shall consider himself greater than a.
11:43 and a the riches of Egypt;
12: 7 a these things would be accomplished. H
Hos 2:11 I will put an end to a her mirth, her festivals,
2:11 her sabbaths, and a her appointed festivals.
4: 3 the land mourns, and a who live in it languish;
5: 2 but I will punish a of them.
7: 2 not consider that I remember a their wickedness.
7: 4 They are a adulterers; they are like a heated oven,
7: 6 a night their anger smolders;
7: 7 A of them are hot as an oven,
7: 7 A their kings have fallen; none of them calls upon
7:10 to the LORD their God, or seek him, for a this.
9: 1 a prostitute's pay on a threshing floors.
9: 4 a who eat of it shall be defiled;
9: 8 yet a fowler's snare is on a his ways,
9:15 a their officials are rebels.
10:14 and a your fortresses shall be destroyed,
11: 7 but he does not raise them up at a.
12: 1 and pursues the east wind a day long;
12: 8 in a of my gain no offense has been found in me
13: 2 a of them the work of artisans.
13:10 Where in a your cities are your rulers,
14: 2 say to him, "Take away a guilt;
Joel 1: 2 O elders, give ear, a inhabitants of the land!
1: 5 and wail, a you wine-drinkers,
1:12 a the trees of the field are dried up;
1:14 Gather the elders and a the inhabitants of the L
1:19 and flames have burned a the trees of the field.
2: 1 Let a the inhabitants of the land tremble, L
2: 6 them peoples are in anguish, a faces grow pale.
2:12 says the LORD, return to me with a your heart, J
2:28 afterward I will pour out my spirit on a flesh; M
3: 2 I will gather a the nations and bring them down D
3: 4 O Tyre and Sidon, and a the regions of Philistia?
3: 9 Let a the soldiers draw near, let them come up.
Joel 3:11 Come quickly, a you nations all around, D
3:11 Come quickly, all you nations a around,
3:12 I will sit to judge a the neighboring nations. D
3:18 a the stream beds of Judah shall flow with water;
3:20 and Jerusalem to a generations. O
Am 1:11 with the sword and cast off a pity;
2: 3 and will kill a its officials with him,
3: 2 You only have I known of a the families of
3: 2 therefore I will punish you for a your iniquities.
4: 6 I gave you cleanness of teeth in a your cities,
4: 6 and lack of bread in a your places,
5:16 In a the squares there shall be wailing;
5:16 and in a the streets they shall say, "Alas!
5:17 in a the vineyards there shall be wailing,
6: 8 and I will deliver up the city and a that is in it.
7:10 the land is not able to bear a his words.
8: 8 and a of it rise like the Nile,
8:10 and a your songs into lamentation;
8:10 I will bring sackcloth on a loins,
9: 1 and shatter them on the heads of a the people; A
9: 5 and a who live in it mourn,
9: 5 and a of it rises like the Nile, and sinks again,
9: 9 shake the house of Israel among a the nations D
9:10 A the sinners of my people shall die by the sword,
9:12 and a the nations who are called by my name, D
9:13 and a the hills shall flow with it.
Ob 1: 7 A your allies have deceived you,
1:15 day of the LORD is near against a the nations. D
1:16 a the nations around you shall drink; D
Jnh 2: 3 a your waves and your billows passed over me.
3: 8 A shall turn from their evil ways and from
Mic 1: 2 Hear, you peoples, a of you;
1: 2 listen, O earth, and a that is in it;
1: 5 A this is for the transgression of Jacob and for
1: 7 A her images shall be beaten to pieces,
1: 7 a her wages shall be burned with fire,
1: 7 and a her idols I will lay waste;
1:10 Tell it not in Gath, weep not at a;
2:12 I will surely gather a of you, O Jacob,
3: 7 they shall a cover their lips,
3: 9 who abhor justice and pervert a equity,
4: 4 but they shall a sit under their own vines and
4: 5 For a the peoples walk, each in the name G
5: 9 and a your enemies shall be cut off.
5:11 of your land and throw down a your strongholds;
6:16 the statutes of Omri and a the works of the house
7: 2 they a lie in wait for blood,
7:16 nations shall see and be ashamed of a their might;
7:19 You will cast a our sins into the depths of the sea.
Na 1: 4 and he dries up a the rivers;
1: 5 the world and a who live in it.
2: 1 gird your loins; collect a your strength.
2:10 a loins quake, a faces grow pale!
3: 7 Then a who see you will shrink from you and say,
3:10 a her dignitaries were bound in fetters.
3:12 A your fortresses are like fig trees
3:19 A who hear the news about you clap their hands
Hab 1: 9 They a come for violence,
1:15 The enemy brings a of them up with a hook;
2: 5 They gather a nations for themselves, D
2: 5 and collect a peoples as their own. G
2: 8 a that survive of the peoples shall plunder you—
2: 8 to cities and a who live in them.
2:17 to cities and a who live in them.
2:19 and there is no breath in it at a.
2:20 let a the earth keep silence before him! E
Zep 1: 4 and against a the inhabitants of Jerusalem; L
1: 8 and the king's sons and a who dress themselves
1: 9 On that day I will punish a who leap over
1:11 for a the traders have perished;
1:11 a who weigh out silver are cut off.
1:18 a terrible end he will make of a the inhabitants of L
2: 3 Seek the LORD, a you humble of the land,
2:11 he will shrivel a the gods of the earth,
2:11 a the coasts and islands of the nations.
3: 7 not lose sight of a that I have brought upon it."
3: 7 the more eager to make a their deeds corrupt.
3: 8 a the heat of my anger;
3: 8 of my passion a the earth shall be consumed. E
3: 9 that a of them may call on the name of the LORD
3:11 because of a the deeds by which you have rebelled
3:14 Rejoice and exult with a your heart, J
3:19 I will deal with a your oppressors at that time.
3:19 into praise and renown in a the earth. E
3:20 and praised among a the peoples of the earth, G
Hag 1: 9 while a of you hurry off to your own houses.
1:11 and animals, and on a their labors.
1:12 the high priest, with a the remnant of the people,
1:14 and the spirit of a the remnant of the people;
2: 4 take courage, a you people of the land, A
2: 7 and I will shake a the nations, D
2: 7 so that the treasure of a nations shall come, D
2:17 I struck you and a the products of your toil
Zec 2: 5 For I will be a wall of fire a around it,
2:13 Be silent, a people, before the LORD; A
4: 2 And I said, "I see a lampstand a of gold,
5: 6 And he said, "This is their iniquity in a the land." I
6: 5 before the LORD of a the earth. E
7: 5 Say to a the people of the land and the priests: A
7:14 with a whirlwind among a the nations D
8:10 and I set them a against one other.
8:12 of this people to possess a these things. H
8:17 for a these are things that I hate, says the LORD.
9: 1 as do a the tribes of Israel; S
10:11 and a the depths of the Nile dried up.
11:10 the covenant that I had made with a the peoples. G
12: 2 a cup of reeling for a the surrounding peoples; G

Zec 12: 3 Jerusalem a heavy stone for a the people; G
12: 3 a who lift it shall grievously hurt themselves.
12: 3 And a the nations of the earth shall come D
12: 6 right and to the left a the surrounding peoples, G
12: 9 on that day I will seek to destroy a the nations D
12:14 and a the families that are left,
14: 2 For I will gather a the nations against Jerusalem D
14: 5 and a the holy ones with him.
14: 9 the LORD will become king over a the earth; E
14:12 the LORD will strike a the peoples that wage war G
14:14 And the wealth of a the surrounding nations D
14:16 Then a who survive of the nations that have come
14:19 the punishment of a the nations that do not go D
14:21 so that a who sacrifice may come and use them
Mal 2: 9 despised and abased before a the people, A
2:10 Have we not a one father?
2:17 "A who do evil are good in the sight of the LORD,
3:12 Then a nations will count you happy, D
4: 1 a the arrogant and a evildoers will be stubble;
4: 4 that I commanded him at Horeb for a Israel. B
Mt 1:17 So a the generations from Abraham O
1:22 A this took place to fulfill what had been spoken
2: 3 he was frightened, and a Jerusalem with him;
2: 4 and calling together a the chief priests and scribes
2:16 and he sent and killed a the children in and
3: 5 of Jerusalem and a Judea were going out to him,
3: 5 and a the region along the Jordan,
3:15 for us in this way to fulfill a righteousness."
4: 8 and showed him a the kingdoms of the world R
4: 9 "A these I will give you,
4:24 So his fame spread throughout a Syria,
4:24 and they brought to him a the sick,
5:11 and utter a kinds of evil against you falsely
5:15 and it gives light to a in the house.
5:18 will pass from the law until a is accomplished.
5:34 But I say to you, Do not swear at a,
6:29 in a his glory was not clothed like one of these.
6:32 it is the Gentiles who strive for a these things; H
6:32 that you need a these things. H
6:33 and a these things will be given to you as well. H
8:16 and cured a who were sick.
9:35 Then Jesus went about a the cities and villages,
10:22 and you will be hated by a because of my name.
10:23 not have gone through a the towns of Israel before
10:30 And even the hairs of your head are a counted.
11:13 For a the prophets and the law prophesied
11:27 A things have been handed over to me C
11:28 "Come to me, a you that are weary
12:15 and he cured a of them,
12:23 A the crowds were amazed and said,
13:32 it is the smallest of a the seeds,
13:33 and mixed in with three measures of flour until a
13:34 Jesus told the crowds a these things in parables; H
13:41 out of his kingdom a causes of sin and a evildoers,
13:44 in his joy he goes and sells a that he has and buys
13:46 he went and sold a that he had and bought it.
13:51 "Have you understood a this?"
13:56 And are not a his sisters with us?
13:56 Where then did this man get a this?"
14:20 And a ate and were filled;
14:35 the region and brought a who were sick to him,
14:36 and a who touched it were healed.
15:23 But he did not answer her at a.
15:37 And a of them ate and were filled;
17:11 Elijah is indeed coming and will restore a things; C
18:25 with his wife and children and a his possessions,
18:31 and reported to their lord a that had taken place.
18:32 I forgave you a that debt because you pleaded
19:20 The young man said to him, "I have kept a these;
19:26 but for God a things are possible." C
19:28 "Truly I tell you, at the renewal of a things, C
20: 6 'Why are you standing here idle a day?'
21:12 and drove out a who were selling and buying in
21:19 to it and found nothing at a on it but leaves.
21:26 for a regard John as a prophet."
22:10 into the streets and gathered a whom they found,
22:27 Last of a, the woman herself died.
22:28 For a of them had married her."
22:37 love the Lord your God with a your heart, J
22:37 and with a your soul, and with a your mind.'
22:40 On these two commandments hang a the law and
23: 5 They do a their deeds to be seen by others;
23: 8 for you have one teacher, and you are a students.
23:12 A who exalt themselves will be humbled,
23:12 and a who humble themselves will be exalted.
23:27 of the bones of the dead and of a kinds of filth.
23:35 upon you may come a the righteous blood shed
23:36 a this will come upon this generation.
24: 2 he asked them, "You see a these, do you not?
24: 2 upon another; a will be thrown down."
24: 8 a this is but the beginning of the birth pangs.
24: 9 be hated by a nations because of my name. D
24:14 as a testimony to a the nations; D
24:30 and then a the tribes of the earth will mourn, S
24:33 So also, when you see a these things, H
24:34 until a these things have taken place. H
24:39 until the flood came and swept them a away,
24:47 he will put that one in charge of a his possessions.
25: 5 a of them became drowsy and slept.
25: 7 Then a those bridesmaids got up
25:29 For to a those who have, more will be given,
25:31 and a the angels with him,
25:32 A the nations will be gathered before him, D
26: 1 When Jesus had finished saying a these things, H
26:27 saying, "Drink from it, a of you;
26:31 "You will a become deserters because
26:33 "Though a become deserters because of you,
Mt 26:35 And so said a the disciples.
26:52 for a who take the sword will perish by the sword.
26:56 But a this has taken place,
26:56 Then a the disciples deserted him and fled.
26:70 But he denied it before a of them, saying,
27: 1 a the chief priests and the elders of
27:22 A of them said, "Let him be crucified!"
27:23 they shouted a the more, "Let him be crucified!"
28:18 "A authority in heaven and
28:19 Go therefore and make disciples of a nations, D
Mk 1: 5 the whole Judean countryside and a the people A
1:27 They were a amazed, and they kept
1:32 to him a who were sick or possessed with demons.
2:12 the mat and went out before a of them;
2:12 so that they were a amazed and glorified God,
3: 8 hearing a that he was doing,
3:10 so that a who had diseases pressed upon him
4:13 Then how will you understand a the parables?
4:31 is the smallest of a the seeds on earth;
4:32 up and becomes the greatest of a shrubs,
5:26 and had spent a that she had;
5:32 He looked a around to see who had done it.
5:40 Then he put them a outside,
6: 2 They said, "Where did this man get a this?
6:12 they went out and proclaimed that a should repent.
6:30 and told him a that they had done and taught.
6:31 a deserted place a by yourselves and rest a while."
6:33 and they hurried there on foot from a the towns
6:39 Then he ordered them to get a the people to sit A
6:41 and he divided the two fish among them a.
6:42 And a ate and were filled;
6:50 for they a saw him and were terrified.
6:56 and a who touched it were healed.
7: 3 (For the Pharisees, and a the Jews, X
7:14 "Listen to me, a of you, and understand:
7:19 (Thus he declared a foods clean.)
7:23 A these evil things come from within,
8:32 He said a this quite openly.
9:12 "Elijah is indeed coming first to restore a things. C
9:23 A things can be done for the one who believes." C
9:35 to be first must be last of a and servant of a."
10:20 "Teacher, I have kept a these since my youth."
10:27 for God a things are possible." C
10:44 to be first among you must be slave of a.
11:17 called a house of prayer for a the nations'? D
11:32 for a regarded John as truly a prophet.
12:22 Last of a the woman herself died.
12:28 "Which commandment is the first of a?"
12:30 love the Lord your God with a your heart, J
12:30 and with a your soul, and with a your mind, and with a your strength.'
12:33 and 'to love him with a the heart, J
12:33 and with a the understanding, with a the strength,'
12:33 much more important than a whole burnt offerings
12:43 in more than a those who are contributing to
12:44 a of them have contributed out of their abundance;
12:44 in everything she had, a she had to live on."
13: 2 upon another; a will be thrown down."
13: 4 a these things are about to be accomplished?" H
13:10 good news must first be proclaimed to a nations. D
13:13 and you will be hated by a because of my name.
13:30 until a these things have taken place. H
13:37 And what I say to you I say to a: Keep awake."
14:23 and a of them drank from it.
14:27 Jesus said to them, "You will a become deserters;
14:29 "Even though a become deserters, I will not."
14:31 And a of them said the same.
14:36 "Abba, Father, for you a things are possible; C
14:50 A of them deserted him and fled.
14:53 and a the chief priests, the elders,
14:64 A of them condemned him as deserving death.
15:14 But they shouted a the more, "Crucify him!"
16:15 ⟦Go into a the world and proclaim the good news⟧
16: S ⟦And a that had been commanded them they told⟧
Lk 1: 6 according to a the commandments and regulations
1:48 from now on a generations will call me blessed; O
1:63 And a of them were amazed.
1:65 Fear came over a their neighbors,
1:65 and a these things were talked about throughout H
1:66 A who heard them pondered them and said,
1:71 and from the hand of a who hate us.
1:75 and righteousness before him a our days.
2: 1 a decree went out from Emperor Augustus that a
2: 3 A went to their own towns to be registered.
2:10 good news of great joy for a the people: A
2:18 and a who heard it were amazed at what
2:19 But Mary treasured a these words
2:20 glorifying and praising God for a they had heard
2:31 prepared in the presence of a peoples, G
2:38 to speak about the child to a who were looking for
2:47 And a who heard him were amazed
2:51 His mother treasured a these things in her heart. H
3: 3 He went into a the region around the Jordan,
3: 6 and a flesh shall see the salvation of God.'" M
3:15 and a were questioning in their hearts
3:16 John answered a of them by saying, "I baptize you
3:19 because of a the evil things that Herod had done,
3:20 added to them a by shutting up John in prison.
3:21 Now when a the people were baptized, A
4: 2 He ate nothing at a during those days,
4: 5 up and showed him in an instant a the kingdoms R
4: 6 "To you I will give their glory and a this authority;
4: 7 If you, then, will worship me, it will a be yours."
4:14 and a report about him spread through a
4:20 The eyes of a in the synagogue were fixed on him.
4:22 A spoke well of him and were amazed at
4:25 and there was a severe famine over a the land; I
Lk 4:28 a in the synagogue were filled with rage.
4:36 They were a amazed and kept saying
4:40 a those who had any who were sick
5: 5 we have worked a night long
5: 9 For he and a who were with him were amazed at
5:26 Amazement seized a of them,
6:10 After looking around at a of them, he said to him,
6:17 and a great multitude of people from a Judea,
6:19 And a in the crowd were trying to touch him,
6:19 power came out from him and healed a of them.
6:26 "Woe to you when a speak well of you,
7: 1 After Jesus had finished a his sayings in
7:16 Fear seized a of them;
7:17 throughout Judea and a the surrounding country.
7:18 disciples of John reported a these things to him. H
7:29 (And a the people who heard this, A
7:35 wisdom is vindicated by a her children."
8:37 Then a the people of the surrounding country A
8:40 for they were a waiting for him.
8:43 and though she had spent a she had on physicians,
8:45 When a denied it, Peter said, "Master,
8:47 she declared in the presence of a the people A
8:52 They were a weeping and wailing for her;
9: 1 and gave them power and authority over a demons
9: 7 Herod the ruler heard about a that had taken place,
9:10 the apostles told Jesus a they had done.
9:13 we are to go and buy food for a these people." A
9:15 They did so and made them a sit down.
9:17 And a ate and were filled.
9:23 Then he said to them a,
9:39 and a at once he shrieks.
9:43 And a were astounded at the greatness of God.
9:43 everyone was amazed at a that he was doing,
9:48 for the least among a of you is the greatest."
10:19 and over a the power of the enemy;
10:22 A things have been handed over to me C
10:27 love the Lord your God with a your heart, J
10:27 and with a your soul, and with a your strength, and with a your mind;
10:40 care that my sister has left me to do a the work V
11:42 For you tithe mint and rue and herbs of a kinds,
11:50 be charged with the blood of a the prophets shed
12: 7 But even the hairs of your head are a counted.
12:15 Be on your guard against a kinds of greed;
12:18 and there I will store a my grain and my goods.
12:27 in a his glory was not clothed like one of these.
12:30 of the world that strive after a these things, H
12:44 he will put that one in charge of a his possessions.
13: 2 they were worse sinners than a other Galileans?
13: 3 unless you repent, you will a perish as they did.
13: 4 that they were worse offenders than a
13: 5 you repent, you will a perish just as they did."
13:17 he said this, a his opponents were put to shame;
13:17 at a the wonderful things that he was doing.
13:21 and mixed in with three measures of flour until a
13:27 go away from me, a you evildoers!'
13:28 when you see Abraham and Isaac and Jacob and a
14:10 in the presence of a who sit at the table with you.
14:11 For a who exalt themselves will be humbled,
14:18 But they a alike began to make excuses.
14:29 a who see it will begin to ridicule him,
14:33 if you do not give up a your possessions.
15: 1 Now a the tax collectors and sinners were coming
15:13 the younger son gathered a he had and traveled to
15:29 For a these years I have been working like a slave
15:31 and a that is mine is yours.
16:14 who were lovers of money, heard a this,
16:26 Besides a this, between you and us
17:10 you have done a that you were ordered to do,
17:27 and the flood came and destroyed a of them.
17:29 and sulfur from heaven and destroyed a of them
18:12 I give a tenth of a my income.'
18:14 for a who exalt themselves will be humbled,
18:14 but a who humble themselves will be exalted."
18:21 He replied, "I have kept a these since my youth."
18:22 Sell a that you own and distribute the money to
18:34 they understood nothing about a these things; H
18:43 and a the people, when they saw it, praised God. A
19: 7 A who saw it began to grumble and said,
19:26 'I tell you, to a those who have,
19:37 to praise God joyfully with a loud voice for a
19:48 a the people were spellbound by what they A
20: 6 'Of human origin,' a the people will stone us; A
20:31 and so in the same way a seven died childless.
20:38 for to him a of them are alive."
20:45 hearing of a the people he said to the disciples, A
21: 3 this poor widow has put in more than a of them;
21: 4 a of them have contributed out of their abundance,
21: 4 of her poverty has put in a she had to live on."
21: 6 upon another; a will be thrown down."
21:12 "But before a this occurs,
21:17 You will be hated by a because of my name.
21:22 as a fulfillment of a that is written.
21:24 and be taken away as captives among a nations; D
21:29 "Look at the fig tree and a the trees;
21:32 not pass away until a things have taken place. C
21:35 For it will come upon a who live on the face of
21:36 Be alert at a times, praying that you may Y
21:36 to escape a these things that will take place, H
21:38 And a the people would get up early in A
22:31 Satan has demanded to sift a of you like wheat,
22:70 A of them asked, "Are you, then,
23: 5 up the people by teaching throughout a Judea,
23:18 Then they a shouted out together,
23:48 And when a the crowds who had gathered there
23:49 But a his acquaintances, including
24: 9 they told a this to the eleven and to a the rest.

Lk 24:14 and talking with each other about a these things H
24:19 in deed and word before God and a the people, A
24:21 and besides a this, it is now the third day
24:25 to believe a that the prophets have declared!
24:27 Then beginning with Moses and a the prophets,
24:27 the things about himself in a the scriptures.
24:47 to be proclaimed in his name to a nations, D
Jn 1: 3 A things came into being through him, C
1: 4 and the life was the light of a people. A
1: 7 so that a might believe through him.
1:12 But to a who received him,
1:16 From his fullness we have a received,
2:15 he drove a of them out of the temple,
2:24 because he knew a people A
3:20 For a who do evil hate the light and do not come
3:26 here he is baptizing, and a are going to him."
3:31 The one who comes from above is above a;
3:31 The one who comes from heaven is above a.
3:35 Father loves the Son and has placed a things C
4:25 When he comes, he will proclaim a things to us." C
4:45 since they had seen a that he had done
5:18 For this reason the Jews were seeking a the more
5:20 the Son and shows him a that he himself is doing;
5:22 but has given a judgment to the Son,
5:23 a may honor the Son just as they honor the Father.
5:28 when a who are in their graves will hear his voice
6:10 so they sat down, about five thousand in a.
6:39 I should lose nothing of a that he has given me,
6:40 that a who see the Son and believe
6:45 'And they shall a be taught by God.'
7:21 and a of you are astonished.
8: 2 ⟦A the people came to him and he sat down⟧ A
8: 3 ⟦and making her stand before a of them,⟧
8:25 Jesus said to them, "Why do I speak to you at a?
10: 4 When he has brought out a his own,
10: 8 A who came before me are thieves and bandits;
10:29 What my Father has given me is greater than a else
11:12 "Lord, if he has fallen asleep, he will be a right."
11:49 said to them, "You know nothing at a!
12:32 up from the earth, will draw a people to myself." A
13: 3 that the Father had given a things into his hands, C
13:10 And you are clean, though not a of you."
13:11 for this reason he said, "Not a of you are clean."
13:18 I am not speaking of a of you;
14: 9 "Have I been with you a this time, Philip,
14:26 and remind you of a that I have said to you.
15:21 they will do a these things to you on account of H
16:13 he will guide you into a the truth;
16:15 A that the Father has is mine.
16:30 Now we know that you know a things, C
17: 2 you have given him authority over a people, A
17: 2 to give eternal life to a whom you have given him.
17:10 A mine are yours, and yours are mine;
17:21 that they may a be one.
18: 4 Then Jesus, knowing a that was to happen to him,
18:20 where a the Jews come together. X
19:28 this, when Jesus knew that a was now finished,
Ac 1: 1 I wrote about a that Jesus did and taught from
1: 8 be my witnesses in Jerusalem, in a Judea
1:14 A these were constantly devoting themselves
1:18 in the middle and a his bowels gushed out.
1:19 This became known to a the residents
1:21 of the men who have accompanied us during a
2: 1 they were a together in one place.
2: 4 A of them were filled with the Holy Spirit
2: 7 "Are not a these who are speaking Galileans?
2:12 A were amazed and perplexed,
2:14 "Men of Judea and a who live in Jerusalem,
2:17 that I will pour out my Spirit upon a flesh, M
2:32 and of that a of us are witnesses.
2:39 for your children, and for a who are far away,
2:44 A who believed were together and had all things
2:44 were together and had a things in common; C
2:45 and goods and distribute the proceeds to a,
2:47 and having the goodwill of a the people. A
3: 9 A the people saw him walking and praising God, A
3:11 a the people ran together to them in A
3:16 in the presence of a of you.
3:18 what he had foretold through a the prophets,
3:24 And a the prophets, as many as have spoken,
3:25 'And in your descendants a the families of
4: 6 and a who were of the high-priestly family.
4:10 let it be known to a of you,
4:10 and to a the people of Israel, A
4:16 For it is obvious to a who live in Jerusalem that
4:18 not to speak or teach at a in the name of Jesus.
4:21 for a of them praised God for what had happened.
4:29 to speak your word with a boldness,
4:31 and they were a filled with the Holy Spirit
4:33 and great grace was upon them a.
5: 5 And great fear seized a who heard of it.
5:11 the whole church and a who heard of these things.
5:12 And they were a together in Solomon's Portico.
5:16 by unclean spirits, and they were a cured.
5:17 he and a who were with him (that is,
5:34 a teacher of the law, respected by a the people, A
5:36 and a who followed him were dispersed
5:37 and a who followed him were scattered.
6:15 a who sat in the council looked intently at him,
7:10 and rescued him from a his afflictions,
7:10 over Egypt and over a his household.
7:14 a his relatives to come to him, seventy-five in a;
7:22 So Moses was instructed in a the wisdom of
7:50 Did not my hand make a these things?' H
7:57 with a loud shout a rushed together against him.
8: 1 and a except the apostles were scattered
8:10 A of them, from the least to the greatest,
Ac 8:40 he proclaimed the good news to a the towns
9:14 the chief priests to bind a who invoke your name."
9:21 A who heard him were amazed and said,
9:26 and they were a afraid of him,
9:32 Peter went here and there among a the believers,
9:35 And a the residents of Lydda and Sharon saw him
9:39 A the widows stood beside him,
9:40 Peter put a of them outside,
10: 2 devout man who feared God with a his household;
10:12 In it were a kinds of four-footed creatures
10:33 So now a of us are here in the presence of God to listen to a that the Lord has commanded you
10:36 by Jesus Christ—he is Lord of a.
10:38 and healing a who were oppressed by the devil,
10:39 to a that he did both in Judea and in Jerusalem.
10:41 a the people but to us who were chosen by God A
10:43 A the prophets testify about him
10:44 the Holy Spirit fell upon a who heard the word
11:23 and he exhorted them a to remain faithful to
11:28 that there would be a severe famine over a
12:11 from a that the Jewish people were expecting."
13:10 you enemy of a righteousness,
13:10 full of a deceit and villainy,
13:22 who will carry out a my wishes.'
13:24 a baptism of repentance to a the people of Israel. A
13:39 from a those sins from which you could not
14:15 the heaven and the earth and the sea and a that is
14:16 In past generations he allowed a the nations D
14:27 they called the church together and related a
15: 3 and brought great joy to a the believers.
15: 4 and they reported a that God had done with them.
15:12 and listened to Barnabas and Paul as they told of a
15:17 so that a other peoples may seek the Lord— G
15:17 peoples may seek the Lord—even a the Gentiles
16: 3 for they a knew that his father was a Greek.
16:26 and immediately a the doors were opened
16:28 "Do not harm yourself, for we are a here."
16:32 of the Lord to him and to a who were in his house.
17: 7 They are a acting contrary to the decrees of
17:21 Now a the Athenians and the foreigners
17:25 since he himself gives to a mortals life and breath
17:25 to all mortals life and breath and a things. C
17:26 From one ancestor he made a nations to inhabit D
17:30 he commands a people everywhere to repent, A
17:31 of this he has given assurance to a by raising him
18: 2 Claudius had ordered a Jews to leave Rome. X
18: 8 together with a his household;
18:17 Then a of them seized Sosthenes,
18:23 strengthening a the disciples.
19:10 so that a the residents of Asia,
19:16 the evil spirit leaped on them, mastered them a,
19:17 this became known to a residents of Ephesus,
19:27 be deprived of her majesty that brought a Asia and
19:34 for about two hours a of them shouted in unison,
20:19 serving the Lord with a humility and with tears,
20:28 Keep watch over yourselves and over a the flock,
20:32 the inheritance among a who are sanctified.
20:35 In a this I have given you an example that
20:36 he knelt down with them a and prayed.
20:37 There was much weeping among them a;
21: 5 and a of them, with wives and children,
21:18 and a the elders were present.
21:20 and they are a zealous for the law.
21:21 you teach a the Jews living among the Gentiles X
21:24 Thus a will know that there is nothing
21:30 Then a the city was aroused,
21:31 to the tribune of the cohort that a Jerusalem was in
22: 3 being zealous for God, just as a of you are today.
22:12 and well spoken of by a the Jews living there, X
22:15 to a the world of what you have seen and heard.
23: 8 but the Pharisees acknowledge a three.)
24: 5 agitator among a the Jews throughout the world, X
24: 9 in the charge by asserting that a this was true.
24:16 a clear conscience toward God and a people. A
25:24 "King Agrippa and a here present with us,
25:26 Therefore I have brought him before a of you,
26: 2 I am to make my defense today against a
26: 3 with a the customs and controversies of the Jews;
26: 4 A the Jews know my way of life from my youth, X
26:11 in a the synagogues I tried to force them
26:14 When we had a fallen to the ground,
26:29 that not only you but also a who are listening
27:20 a hope of our being saved was at last abandoned.
27:24 God has granted safety to a those who are sailing
27:33 Paul urged a of them to take some food, saying,
27:35 and giving thanks to God in the presence of a,
27:36 Then a of them were encouraged and took food
27:37 (We were in a two hundred seventy-six persons
27:44 And so it was that a were brought safely to land.
28: 2 they kindled a fire and welcomed a of us
28:10 they put on board a the provisions we needed.
28:30 at his own expense and welcomed a who came
28:31 about the Lord Jesus Christ with a boldness and
Ro 1: 5 about the obedience of faith among a the Gentiles
1: 7 To a God's beloved in Rome, who are called to
1: 8 I thank my God through Jesus Christ for a of you,
1:18 against a ungodliness and wickedness
2:12 A who have sinned apart from the law will
2:12 and a who have sinned under the law will
2:16 will judge the secret thoughts of a.
3: 9 No, not at a; for we have already charged that a,
3:12 A have turned aside, together they have become
3:22 through faith in Jesus Christ for a who believe.
3:23 a have sinned and fall short of the glory of God;
4:11 of a who believe without being circumcised
4:16 on grace and be guaranteed to a his descendants,
4:16 the faith of Abraham (for he is the father of a
Ro 5:12 and so death spread to a because a have sinned—
5:18 as one man's trespass led to condemnation for a,
5:18 to justification and life for a.
5:20 where sin increased, grace abounded a the more,
6: 3 not know that a of us who have been baptized
6:10 The death he died, he died to sin, once for a;
7: 8 produced in me a kinds of covetousness.
8:14 For a who are led by the Spirit of God are children
8:28 We know that a things work together for good C
8:32 but gave him up for a of us,
8:36 "For your sake we are being killed a day long;
8:37 in a these things we are more than conquerors H
8:39 nor depth, nor anything else in a creation,
9: 5 who is over a, God blessed forever.
9: 6 For not a Israelites truly belong to Israel,
9: 7 a of Abraham's children are his true descendants;
9:10 Nor is that a; something similar happened to
9:17 that my name may be proclaimed in a the earth." E
10:12 Lord of a and is generous to a who call on him.
10:16 But not a have obeyed the good news;
10:18 for "Their voice has gone out to a the earth, E
10:21 "A day long I have held out my hands to
11:26 And so a Israel will be saved; B
11:32 For God has imprisoned a in disobedience so that he may be merciful to a.
11:36 and through him and to him are a things. C
12: 4 and not a the members have the same function,
12:17 but take thought for what is noble in the sight of a.
12:18 so far as it depends on you, live peaceably with a.
13: 7 Pay to a what is due them—
14: 5 while others judge a days to be alike.
14: 5 Let a be fully convinced in their own minds.
14:10 we will a stand before the judgment seat of God.
15:11 a you Gentiles, and let all the peoples praise him";
15:11 you Gentiles, and let a the peoples praise him"; G
15:13 May the God of hope fill you with a joy and peace
15:14 of goodness, filled with a knowledge, and able
15:33 The God of peace be with a of you. Amen.
16: 4 but also a the churches of the Gentiles.
16:15 and Olympas, and a the saints who are with them.
16:16 A the churches of Christ greet you.
16:19 For while your obedience is known to a,
16:26 through the prophetic writings is made known to a
1Co 1: 2 with a those who in every place call on the name
1:10 that a of you be in agreement and that there
2:15 Those who are spiritual discern a things, C
3:21 about human leaders. For a things are yours, C
3:22 or the future—a belong to you,
4: 6 I have applied a this to Apollos and myself
4: 8 Already you have a you want!
4: 9 that God has exhibited us apostles as last of a,
4:13 the dregs of a things, to this very day. C
5:10 not at a meaning the immoral of this world,
6: 7 at a with one another is already a defeat for you.
6:12 "A things are lawful for me," C
6:12 but not a things are beneficial. C
6:12 "A things are lawful for me," C
7: 7 I wish that a were as I myself am.
7:16 for a you know, you might save your husband.
7:16 Husband, for a you know, you might save your
7:17 This is my rule in a the churches.
8: 1 we know that "a of us possess knowledge."
8: 6 from whom are a things and for whom we exist, C
8: 6 whom are a things and through whom we exist. C
9:19 For though I am free with respect to a,
9:19 I have made myself a slave to a,
9:22 I have become a things to all people, C
9:22 I have become all things to a people, A
9:22 that I might by a means save some.
9:23 I do it a for the sake of the gospel,
9:24 not know that in a race the runners a compete,
9:25 Athletes exercise self-control in a things; C
10: 1 that our ancestors were a under the cloud,
10: 1 and a passed through the sea,
10: 2 and a were baptized into Moses in the cloud and
10: 3 and a ate the same spiritual food,
10: 4 and a drank the same spiritual drink.
10:17 for we a partake of the one bread.
10:23 "A things are lawful," C
10:23 but not a things are beneficial. C
10:23 "A things are lawful," but not all things build up. C
10:23 "All things are lawful," but not a things build up. C
11:12 but a things come from God. C
11:29 a who eat and drink without discerning the body,
12: 6 but it is the same God who activates a of them
12:11 A these are activated by one and the same Spirit,
12:12 and a the members of the body, though many,
12:13 the one Spirit we were a baptized into one body—
12:13 and we were a made to drink of one Spirit.
12:19 If a were a single member,
12:26 If one member suffers, a suffer together with it;
12:26 one member is honored, a rejoice together with it.
12:29 Are a apostles? Are a prophets?
12:29 Are a teachers? Do a work miracles?
12:30 Do a possess gifts of healing?
12:30 Do a speak in tongues? Do a interpret?
13: 2 a mysteries and a knowledge, and if I have a faith,
13: 3 If I give away a my possessions,
13: 7 It bears a things, believes all things, C
13: 7 It bears all things, believes a things, C
13: 7 believes all things, hopes a things, C
13: 7 hopes all things, endures a things. C
14: 5 Now I would like a of you to speak in tongues,
14:18 I thank God that I speak in tongues more than a
14:23 the whole church comes together and a speak
14:24 But if a prophesy, an unbeliever or outsider who enters is reproved by a and called to account by a.

1Co 14:26 Let **a** things be done for building up. C
14:31 For you can **a** prophesy one by one, so that **a** may learn and **a** be encouraged.
14:33 (As in **a** the churches of the saints,
14:40 **a** things should be done decently and in order. C
15: 7 Then he appeared to James, then to **a** the apostles.
15: 8 Last of **a**, as to one untimely born,
15:19 we are of **a** people most to be pitied. A
15:22 for as **a** die in Adam,
15:22 so **a** will be made alive in Christ.
15:25 For he must reign until he has put **a** his enemies
15:27 For "God has put **a** things in subjection C
15:27 when it says, "**A** things are put in subjection," C
15:27 this does not include the one who put **a** things C
15:28 When **a** things are subjected to him, C
15:28 one who put **a** things in subjection under him, C
15:28 so that God may be **a** in **a**.
15:29 If the dead are not raised at **a**,
15:39 Not **a** flesh is alike, but there is one flesh M
15:51 We will not **a** die, but we will **a** be changed,
16:12 but he was not at **a** willing to come now.
16:14 Let **a** that you do be done in love.
16:20 **A** the brothers and sisters send greetings.
16:24 My love be with **a** of you in Christ Jesus.
2Co 1: 1 including **a** the saints throughout Achaia:
1: 3 Father of mercies and the God of **a** consolation,
1: 4 who consoles us in **a** our affliction,
1:12 and **a** the more toward you.
2: 3 for I am confident about **a** of you,
2: 3 that my joy would be the joy of **a** of you.
2: 5 not to exaggerate it—to **a** of you.
3: 2 written on our hearts, to be known and read by **a**;
3:18 And **a** of us, with unveiled faces,
4:17 for an eternal weight of glory beyond **a** measure,
5:10 For **a** of us must appear before the judgment seat
5:14 because we are convinced that one has died for **a**; therefore **a** have died.
5:15 for **a**, so that those who live might live no longer
5:18 **A** this is from God, who reconciled us to himself
7: 4 I am overjoyed in **a** our affliction.
7:13 because his mind has been set at rest by **a** of you.
7:15 And his heart goes out **a** the more to you,
7:15 as he remembers the obedience of **a** of you,
8:18 the brother who is famous among **a** the churches
9:13 of your sharing with them and with **a** others,
10:14 we were the first to come **a** the way to you with
11: 6 and in **a** things we have made this evident to you. C
11:28 under daily pressure because of my anxiety for **a**
12: 9 I will boast **a** the more gladly of my weaknesses,
12:11 for I am not at **a** inferior to these super-apostles,
12:19 Have you been thinking **a** along
13: 2 I warned those who sinned previously and **a**
13:12 **A** the saints greet you.
13:13 communion of the Holy Spirit be with **a** of you.
Gal 1: 2 and **a** the members of God's family who are
2:14 I said to Cephas before them **a**, "If you,
3: 8 saying, "**A** the Gentiles shall be blessed in you."
3:10 For **a** who rely on the works of the law are under
3:10 not observe and obey **a** the things written in
3:22 But the scripture has imprisoned **a** things under C
3:26 for in Christ Jesus you are **a** children of God
3:28 for **a** of you are one in Christ Jesus.
4: 1 though they are the owners of **a** the property;
4:18 be made much of for a good purpose at **a** times, Y
6: 4 **A** must test their own work;
6: 5 For **a** must carry their own loads.
6: 6 the word must share in **a** good things
6:10 let us work for the good of **a**,
Eph 1: 8 that he lavished on us. With **a** wisdom and insight
1:10 to gather up **a** things in him, C
1:11 to the purpose of him who accomplishes **a** things C
1:15 the Lord Jesus and your love toward **a** the saints,
1:21 far above **a** rule and authority and power
1:22 And he has put **a** things under his feet C
1:22 and has made him the head over **a** things for C
1:23 the fullness of him who fills **a** in **a**.
2: 3 **A** of us once lived among them in the passions
3: 8 Although I am the very least of **a** the saints,
3: 9 for ages in God who created **a** things; C
3:18 with **a** the saints, what is the breadth and length
3:19 that you may be filled with **a** the fullness of God.
3:20 accomplish abundantly far more than **a** we can ask
3:21 the church and in Christ Jesus to **a** generations, O
4: 2 with **a** humility and gentleness,
4: 6 one God and Father of **a**, who is above **a** and through **a** and in **a**.
4:10 same one who ascended far above **a** the heavens,
4:10 so that he might fill **a** things.) C
4:13 until **a** of us come to the unity of the faith and of
4:19 They have lost **a** sensitivity
4:25 let **a** of us speak the truth to our neighbors,
4:31 from you **a** bitterness and wrath and anger
4:31 and wrangling and slander, together with **a** malice,
5: 9 for the fruit of the light is found in **a** that is good
5:20 to God the Father at **a** times and for everything Y
6:16 With **a** of these, take the shield of faith,
6:16 to quench **a** the flaming arrows of the evil one.
6:18 at **a** times in every prayer and supplication. Y
6:18 always persevere in supplication for **a** the saints.
6:24 Grace be with **a** who have an undying love
Php 1: 1 To **a** the saints in Christ Jesus who are in Philippi,
1: 4 with joy in every one of my prayers for **a** of you,
1: 7 It is right for me to think this way about **a** of you,
1: 7 for **a** of you share in God's grace with me,
1: 8 for **a** of you with the compassion of Christ Jesus.
1:20 but that by my speaking with **a** boldness,
1:25 with **a** of you for your progress and joy in faith,
Php 2:14 Do **a** things without murmuring and arguing, C
2:17 I am glad and rejoice with **a** of you—
2:21 **A** of them are seeking their own interests,
2:26 for he has been longing for **a** of you,
2:29 Welcome him then in the Lord with **a** joy,
3: 8 For his sake I have suffered the loss of **a** things, C
3:21 that also enables him to make **a** things subject C
4: 7 peace of God, which surpasses **a** understanding,
4:12 and **a** circumstances I have learned the secret
4:13 I can do **a** things through him who strengthens C
4:22 **A** the saints greet you, especially those of
Col 1: 4 in Christ Jesus and of the love that you have for **a**
1: 9 the knowledge of God's will in **a** spiritual wisdom
1:11 be made strong with **a** the strength that comes
1:15 the firstborn of **a** creation;
1:16 for in him **a** things in heaven and C
1:16 **a** things have been created through him and C
1:17 He himself is before **a** things, C
1:17 and in him **a** things hold together. C
1:19 in him **a** the fullness of God was pleased to dwell,
1:20 to reconcile to himself **a** things, C
1:28 and teaching everyone in **a** wisdom,
1:29 with **a** the energy that he powerfully inspires
2: 1 and for **a** who have not seen me face to face.
2: 2 so that they may have **a** the riches
2: 3 in whom are hidden **a** the treasures of wisdom
2:13 when he forgave us **a** our trespasses,
2:22 **A** these regulations refer to things that perish
3: 8 But now you must get rid of **a** such things—
3:11 but Christ is **a** and in **a**!
3:14 Above **a**, clothe yourselves with love,
3:16 teach and admonish one another in **a** wisdom;
4: 7 Tychicus will tell you **a** the news about me;
1Th 1: 2 for **a** of you and mention you in our prayers,
1: 7 so that you became an example to **a** the believers
3: 7 and sisters, during **a** our distress
3: 9 in return for **a** the joy that we feel before our God
3:12 and abound in love for one another and for **a**,
3:13 at the coming of our Lord Jesus with **a** his saints.
4: 6 because the Lord is an avenger in **a** these things, H
4:10 and indeed you do love **a** the brothers and sisters
5: 5 you are **a** children of light and children of the day;
5:14 help the weak, be patient with **a** of them.
5:15 always seek to do good to one another and to **a**.
5:18 give thanks in **a** circumstances;
5:26 Greet **a** the brothers and sisters with a holy kiss.
5:27 by the Lord that this letter be read to **a** of them.
2Th 1: 4 during **a** your persecutions and the afflictions
1:10 at on that day among **a** who have believed,
2: 9 who uses **a** power, signs, lying wonders,
2:12 so that **a** who have not believed the truth
3: 2 and evil people; for not **a** have faith.
3:16 of peace himself give you peace at **a** times Y
3:16 give you peace at all times in **a** ways.
3:16 The Lord be with **a** of you.
3:18 grace of our Lord Jesus Christ be with **a** of you.
1Ti 2: 1 First of **a**, then, I urge that supplications, prayers,
2: 2 for kings and **a** who are in high positions,
2: 2 and peaceable life in **a** godliness and dignity.
2: 6 who gave himself a ransom for **a**—
3:11 not slanderers, but temperate, faithful in **a** things. C
4:10 who is the Savior of **a** people, A
4:15 so that **a** may see your progress.
5:20 rebuke them in the presence of **a**,
6: 1 Let **a** who are under the yoke
6: 1 as worthy of **a** honor, so that the name of God and
6: 2 rather they must serve them **a** the more,
6:10 For the love of money is a root of **a** kinds of evil,
6:11 But as for you, man of God, shun **a** this;
6:13 the presence of God, who gives life to **a** things, C
2Ti 1:15 that **a** who are in Asia have turned away from me,
2: 7 the Lord will give you understanding in **a** things. C
2:21 **A** who cleanse themselves of the things
3: 6 overwhelmed by their sins and swayed by **a** kinds
3:11 Yet the Lord rescued me from **a** of them.
3:12 **a** who want to live a godly life in Christ Jesus will
3:16 **A** scripture is inspired by God and is useful
4: 8 and not only to me but also to **a** who have longed
4:13 also the books, and above **a** the parchments.
4:16 to my support, but **a** deserted me.
4:17 the message might be fully proclaimed and **a** the
4:21 as do Pudens and Linus and Claudia and **a** the
Tit 1:15 To the pure **a** things are pure, C
2: 7 in **a** respects a model of good works,
2:11 of God has appeared, bringing salvation to **a**,
2:14 that he might redeem us from **a** iniquity and purify
2:15 exhort and reprove with **a** authority.
3:15 **A** who are with me send greetings to you.
3:15 Grace be with **a** of you.
Phm 1: 5 of your love for **a** the saints and your faith toward
1: 6 when you perceive **a** the good that we may do
Heb 1: 2 whom he appointed heir of **a** things, C
1: 3 and he sustains **a** things by his powerful word. C
1: 6 he says, "Let **a** God's angels worship him."
1:11 they will **a** wear out like clothing;
1:14 Are not **a** angels spirits in the divine service,
2: 8 subjecting **a** things under their feet." C
2: 8 Now in subjecting **a** things to them, C
2:10 for whom and through whom **a** things exist, C
2:11 and those who are sanctified **a** have one Father.
2:15 and free those who **a** their lives were held
3: 2 as Moses also "was faithful in **a** God's house."
3: 4 but the builder of **a** things is God.) C
3: 5 Moses was faithful in **a** God's house as a servant,
3:16 not **a** those who left Egypt under the leadership
4: 4 God rested on the seventh day from **a** his works."
4:13 but **a** are naked and laid bare to the eyes of
Heb 5: 9 of eternal salvation for **a** who obey him,
6:16 as confirmation puts an end to **a** dispute.
7:25 for **a** time to save those who approach God
7:27 this he did once for **a** when he offered himself.
8: 4 if he were on earth, he would not be a priest at **a**,
8:11 'Know the Lord,' for they shall **a** know me,
9: 4 and the ark of the covenant overlaid on **a** sides
9:12 he entered once for **a** into the Holy Place,
9:19 commandment had been told to **a** the people, A
9:19 sprinkled both the scroll itself and **a** the people, A
9:21 with the blood both the tent and **a** the vessels used
9:26 he has appeared once for **a** at the end of the age
10: 2 since the worshipers, cleansed once for **a**,
10:10 the offering of the body of Jesus Christ once for **a**.
10:12 But when Christ had offered for **a** time
10:14 for **a** time those who are sanctified.
10:25 and **a** the more as you see the Day approaching.
11:13 **A** of these died in faith without having received
11:39 Yet **a** these, though they were commended
12: 8 not have that discipline in which **a** children share,
12:23 and to God the judge of **a**,
13: 4 Let marriage be held in honor by **a**,
13: 9 be carried away by **a** kinds of strange teachings;
13:18 desiring to act honorably in **a** things. C
13:19 I urge you **a** the more to do this,
13:24 Greet **a** your leaders and **a** the saints.
13:25 Grace be with **a** of you.
Jas 1: 5 who gives to **a** generously and ungrudgingly,
1:21 of **a** sordidness and rank growth of wickedness,
2:10 in one point has become accountable for **a** of it.
3: 2 For **a** of us make many mistakes.
4: 6 But he gives **a** the more grace;
4:16 in your arrogance; **a** such boasting is evil.
5:12 Above **a**, my beloved, do not swear,
1Pe 1:13 set **a** your hope on the grace
1:15 be holy yourselves in **a** your conduct;
1:17 the one who judges **a** people impartially A
1:24 "**A** flesh is like grass and all its glory like the M
1:24 like grass and **a** its glory like the flower of grass.
2: 1 Rid yourselves, therefore, of **a** malice, and **a** guile, insincerity, envy, and **a** slander.
2:18 the authority of your masters with **a** deference,
3: 8 Finally, **a** of you, have unity of spirit, sympathy,
3:18 For Christ also suffered for sins once for **a**,
4: 7 The end of **a** things is near; C
4: 8 Above **a**, maintain constant love for one another,
4:11 be glorified in **a** things through Jesus Christ. C
5: 5 And **a** of you must clothe yourselves
5: 7 Cast **a** your anxiety on him,
5: 9 for you know that your brothers and sisters in **a**
5:10 of **a** grace, who has called you to his eternal glory
5:14 Peace to **a** of you who are in Christ.
2Pe 1:10 be **a** the more eager to confirm your call
1:20 First of **a** you must understand this,
3: 3 First of **a** you must understand this,
3: 4 ancestors died, **a** things continue as they were C
3: 9 but **a** to come to repentance.
3:11 **a** these things are to be dissolved in this way, H
3:16 speaking of this as he does in **a** his letters.
1Jn 1: 5 God is light and in him there is no darkness at **a**.
1: 7 the blood of Jesus his Son cleanses us from **a** sin.
1: 9 and cleanse us from **a** unrighteousness.
2:16 for **a** that is in the world—
2:20 and **a** of you have knowledge.
2:27 But as his anointing teaches you about **a** things, C
3: 3 **a** who have this hope in him purify themselves,
3:10 **a** who do not do what is right are not from God,
3:15 **A** who hate a brother or sister are murderers,
3:24 **A** who obey his commandments abide in him,
5:17 **A** wrongdoing is sin, but there is sin that is
2Jn 1: 1 and not only I but also **a** who know the truth,
3Jn 1: 2 that **a** may go well with you and that you may be
Jude 1: 3 for the faith that was once for **a** entrusted to
1: 5 who once for **a** saved a people out of the land
1:15 to execute judgment on **a**,
1:15 to convict everyone of **a** the deeds of ungodliness
1:15 and of **a** the harsh things
1:25 and authority, before **a** time and now and forever.
Rev 1: 2 even to **a** that he saw.
1: 7 on his account **a** the tribes of the earth will wail. S
2:23 And **a** the churches will know that I am
4: 8 are full of eyes **a** around and inside.
4:11 for you created **a** things, and by your will C
5: 6 seven spirits of God sent out into **a** the earth. E
5:13 and **a** that is in them, singing,
7: 9 from **a** tribes and peoples and languages,
7:11 And **a** the angels stood around the throne and
8: 3 with the prayers of **a** the saints on the golden altar
8: 7 and **a** green grass was burned up.
11:18 the prophets and saints and **a** who fear your name,
12: 5 who is to rule **a** the nations with a rod of iron. D
13: 8 and **a** the inhabitants of the earth will worship it, L
13:12 It exercises **a** the authority of the first beast
13:13 down from heaven to earth in the sight of **a**;
13:16 Also it causes **a**, both small and great,
14: 8 She has made **a** nations drink of the wine of D
15: 4 **A** nations will come and worship before you, D
18: 3 For **a** the nations have drunk of the wine of D
18:12 purple, silk and scarlet, **a** kinds of scented wood,
18:12 **a** articles of ivory, **a** articles of costly wood,
18:14 **a** your dainties and your splendor are lost to you,
18:17 in one hour **a** this wealth has been laid waste!"
18:17 And **a** shipmasters and seafarers, sailors and **a** whose trade is on the sea,
18:19 **a** who had ships at sea grew rich by her wealth!
18:23 and **a** nations were deceived by your sorcery. D
18:24 and of **a** who have been slaughtered on earth."

Rev 19: 5 a you his servants, and all who fear him, Q
19: 5 and a who fear him, small and great."
19:17 with a loud voice he called to a the birds that fly
19:18 flesh of a, both free and slave,
19:21 and a the birds were gorged with their flesh.
20:13 a were judged according to what they had done.
21: 5 "See, I am making a things new." C
21: 8 the sorcerers, the idolaters, and a liars,
22:21 The grace of the Lord Jesus be with a the saints.
Tob 1: 3 in the ways of truth and righteousness a the days F
1: 4 city had been chosen from among a the tribes S
1: 4 where a the tribes of Israel should offer sacrifice S
1: 4 and established for a generations forever. O
1: 5 A my kindred and our ancestral house
1: 5 in Dan and on a the mountains of Galilee.
1: 6 for a Israel by an everlasting decree. B
1:12 Because I was mindful of God with a my heart, J
1:20 Then a my property was confiscated;
1:21 the son of my brother Hanael over a the accounts
2: 6 and a your songs into lamentation."
2:10 A my kindred were sorry for me,
3: 2 O Lord, and a your deeds are just;
3: 2 a your ways are mercy and truth;
3: 4 and an object of reproach among a the nations D
3:11 let a your works praise you forever.
3:17 before a others who had desired to marry her.
4: 3 and do not abandon her a the days of her life. F
4: 5 "Revere the Lord a your days, my son,
4: 5 Live uprightly a the days of your life, F
4: 6 with truth will prosper in a their activities.
4: 6 To a those who practice righteousness
4:11 Indeed, almsgiving, for a who practice it,
4:12 of a, marry a woman from among the descendants
4:12 a took wives from among their kindred.
4:14 and discipline yourself in a your conduct.
4:16 Give a your surplus as alms,
4:19 At a times bless the Lord God, Y
4:19 and that a your paths and plans may prosper.
5: 6 I am acquainted with it and know a the roads.
5: 8 He replied, "A right, I will wait;
5:10 "I can go with him and I know a the roads,
5:10 to Media and have crossed a its plains,
5:10 and I am familiar with its mountains and a
6:12 have before a other men a hereditary claim on her.
7:11 and a died on the night when they went in to her.
8: 5 blessed is your name in a generations forever. O
8:15 let a your chosen ones bless you.
10: 6 and stop worrying, my dear; he is a right.
10: 7 mourn and weep a night long, getting no sleep at a.
10:10 as well as half of a his property:
10:12 do nothing to grieve her a the days of your life. F
10:12 May we a prosper together all the days
10:12 May we all prosper together a the days F
10:13 King over a, because he had made his journey
10:13 by the Lord to honor you a the days of my life." F
11:14 and blessed be a his holy angels.
11:14 his holy name be blessed throughout a the ages.
11:17 Before them a, Tobit acknowledged
11:17 that day there was rejoicing among a the Jews X
12: 4 to receive half of a that he brought back."
12: 5 for your wages half of a that you brought back,
12: 6 of a the living for the good things he has done
12: 6 With fitting honor declare to a people the deeds A
12:20 down a these things that have happened to you." H
13: 1 because his kingdom lasts throughout a ages.
13: 5 but he will again show mercy on a of you.
13: 5 He will gather you from a the nations D
13: 6 If you turn to him with a your heart J
13: 6 to him with all your heart and with a your soul,
13: 8 Let a people speak of his majesty, A
13:10 he cheer a those within you who are captives,
13:10 and love a those within you who are distressed,
13:10 who are distressed, to a generations forever. O
13:11 A bright light will shine to a the ends of the earth;
13:12 Cursed are a who speak a harsh word against you;
13:12 cursed are a who conquer you and pull
13:12 a who overthrow your towers and set your homes
13:12 But blessed forever will be a who revere you.
13:14 also are a people who grieve with you because A
13:14 with you and witness a your glory forever.
13:16 For Jerusalem will be built as his house for a ages.
13:16 and a your walls with precious stones.
13:17 and a her houses will cry, 'Hallelujah!
14: 4 that a these things will take place H
14: 4 None of a their words will fail,
14: 4 but a will come true at their appointed times.
14: 4 A of our kindred, inhabitants of the land of Israel,
14: 5 After this they a will return from their exile
14: 6 the nations in the whole world will a be converted
14: 6 They will a abandon their idols,
14: 7 A the Israelites who are saved in those days N
14: 7 and injustice will vanish from a the earth. E
14:8,9 and to bless his name at a times with sincerity Y
14:8,9 with sincerity and with a their strength.
14:15 for a he had done to the people of Nineveh
Jdt 1: 6 to him a the people of the hill country A
1: 6 of the hill country and a those who lived along
1: 7 to a who lived in Persia and to a who lived in
1: 7 and a who lived along the seacoast,
1: 9 and a who were in Samaria and its towns,
1:10 and a who lived in Egypt as far as the borders
1:11 But a who lived in the whole region disregarded
1:12 with his sword also a the inhabitants of the land L
1:12 and the people of Ammon, and a Judea,
1:13 of Arphaxad and a his cavalry and a his chariots.
1:15 thus destroying him once and for a.
1:16 he and a his combined forces,

Jdt 2: 2 He summoned a his ministers and a his nobles
2: 2 with his own lips, a the wickedness of the region.
2: 6 March out against a the land to the west, I
2:10 You shall go and seize a their territory for me
2:14 and summoned a the commanders, generals,
2:23 and plundered a the Rassisites and the Ishmaelites
2:24 and passed through Mesopotamia and destroyed a
2:26 He surrounded a the Midianites,
2:27 during the wheat harvest, and burned a their fields
2:27 and ravaged their lands and put a their young men
2:28 dread of him fell upon a the people who lived A
2:28 in Sur and Ocina and a who lived in Jamnia.
3: 3 and a our land and a our wheat fields
3: 3 and herds and a our encampments lie before you;
3: 5 The men came to Holofernes and told him a this.
3: 7 and a in the countryside welcomed him
3: 8 Yet he demolished a their shrines and cut
3: 8 for he had been commissioned to destroy a
3: 8 a nations should worship Nebuchadnezzar alone, D
3: 8 and that a their dialects and tribes should call
3:10 a whole month in order to collect a the supplies
4: 1 he had plundered and destroyed a their temples,
4: 3 and a the people of Judea had just A
4: 5 They immediately seized a the high hilltops
4:10 they a put sackcloth around their waists.
4:11 And a the Israelite men, women,
4:14 and a the priests who stood before the Lord
4:15 the Lord with a their might to look with favor on
5: 1 and fortified a the high hilltops
5: 2 In great anger he called together a the princes
5: 2 of Ammon and a the governors of the coastland,
5: 4 why have they alone, of a who live in the west,
5: 5 Then Achior, the leader of a the Ammonites,
5:14 They drove out a the people of the desert, A
5:15 and by their might destroyed a the inhabitants L
5:15 over the Jordan they took possession of a
5:16 and a the Gergesites, and lived there a long time.
5:22 a the people standing around the tent began A
5:22 Holofernes' officers and a the inhabitants of L
6: 1 in the presence of a the foreign contingents:
6:12 and a the slingers kept them from coming up
6:16 They called together a the elders of the town,
6:16 and a their young men and women ran to
6:16 They set Achior in the midst of a their people, A
6:17 and a that he had said in the presence of
6:17 and a that Holofernes had boasted he would do
6:21 and a that night they called on the God of Israel
7: 1 and a the allies who had joined him,
7: 2 So a their warriors marched off that day;
7: 5 Yet they a seized their weapons,
7: 5 they remained on guard a that night.
7: 6 the second day Holofernes led out a his cavalry
7: 8 Then a the chieftains of the Edomites and all
7: 8 the chieftains of the Edomites and a the leaders of
7:12 and keep a the men in your forces with you; Z
7:13 where a the people of Bethulia get their water. A
7:16 and a his attendants, and he gave orders to do
7:19 because a their enemies had surrounded them,
7:20 until a the water containers of every inhabitant
7:23 Then a the people, the young men, the women, A
7:23 and said before a the elders,
7:26 to the army of Holofernes and to a his forces.
8: 6 She fasted a the days of her widowhood, F
8: 9 and when she heard a that Uzziah said to them,
8:10 who was in charge of a she possessed,
8:14 to search out God, who made a these things, H
8:21 a Judea will be captured and our sanctuary will
8:22 a this he will bring on our heads among
8:28 "A that you have said was spoken out of
8:29 but from the beginning of your life a the people A
8:32 down through a generations of our descendants. O
9: 4 and a their booty to be divided
9: 6 For a your ways are prepared in advance,
9:12 Creator of the waters, King of a your creation,
9:14 the God of a power and might,
10: 1 and had ended a these words,
10: 4 bracelets, rings, earrings, and a her other jewelry.
10: 4 entice the eyes of a the men who might see her. Z
10: 5 then she wrapped up a her dishes and gave them
10:13 by which he can go and capture a the hill country
10:20 and a his servants came out and led her into Q
10:23 they a marveled at the beauty of her face.
11: 1 to serve Nebuchadnezzar, king of a the earth. E
11: 4 Rather, a will treat you well,
11: 7 under Nebuchadnezzar and a his house.
11: 9 and he told them a he had said to you.
11:12 and have determined to use a that God by his laws
11:16 I, your slave, learned a this, I fled from them.
11:20 Her words pleased Holofernes and a his servants. Q
12:15 to dress herself in a her woman's finery.
13: 1 for they a were weary because
13: 4 said in her heart, "O Lord God of a might,
13: 8 Then she struck his neck twice with a her might,
13:13 They a ran together, both small and great,
13:17 A the people were greatly astonished. A
13:18 by the Most High God above a other women
13:20 And a the people said, "Amen. A
14: 4 Then you and a who live within the borders
14: 5 But before you do a this,
14: 8 So Judith told him in the presence of the people a
14:10 Achior saw a that the God of Israel had done,
14:11 Then they a took their weapons,
14:12 and the captains and to a their other officers.
14:13 to the steward in charge of a his personal affairs,
15: 2 but with one impulse a rushed out and fled
15: 4 and to a the frontiers of Israel,
15: 4 to tell what had taken place and to urge a to rush

Jdt 15: 5 in Jerusalem and a the hill country also came,
15: 9 they a blessed her with one accord and said to her,
15:10 You have done a this with your own hand;
15:10 And a the people said, "Amen." A
15:11 A the people plundered the camp for thirty days. A
15:11 the tent of Holofernes and a his silver dinnerware,
15:11 his beds, his bowls, and a his furniture.
15:12 A the women of Israel gathered to see her,
15:13 She went before a the people in the dance, A
15:13 in the dance, leading a the women,
15:13 while a the men of Israel followed, Z
15:14 Judith began this thanksgiving before a Israel, B
15:14 and a the people loudly sang this song of praise. A
16:14 Let a your creatures serve you, for you spoke,
16:16 and the fat of a whole burnt offerings to you
16:19 to God a the possessions of Holofernes, which
16:21 After this they a returned home
16:22 but she gave herself to no man a the days F
16:24 to a those who were next of kin
AdE 1:11 to have her display her beauty to a the governors
1:16 not only the king but also a the king's governors
1:20 thus a women will give honor to their husbands,
1:22 The king sent the decree into a his kingdom,
2: 3 The king shall appoint officers in a the provinces
2:15 Esther found favor in the eyes of a who saw her.
2:17 and she found favor beyond a the other virgins,
2:18 a banquet lasting seven days for a his Friends and
3: 1 and granting him precedence over a
3: 2 So a who were at court used to do obeisance
3: 6 to destroy a the Jews under Artaxerxes' rule. X
3: 8 among the other nations in a your kingdom;
3:12 in a, and the governors were addressed each
3:13 by couriers throughout a the empire of Artaxerxes
3:14 and a the nations were ordered to be prepared D
4: 1 When Mordecai learned of a that had been done,
4: 9 in and told Esther a these things. H
4:11 'A nations of the empire know that if any man D
4:13 you alone among a the Jews will escape alive. X
4:16 and gather a the Jews who are in Susa and fast X
8: 1 that very day King Artaxerxes granted to Esther a
8: 3 to avert a the evil that Haman had planned against
8: 7 that I have granted a of Haman's property to you
8: 9 and a that he commanded with respect to
8:12 throughout a the kingdom of Artaxerxes.
8:13 be posted conspicuously in a the kingdom,
8:13 and let a the Jews be ready on that day to fight X
8:14 on horseback set out with a speed to perform what
9:27 and upon a who would join them,
9:28 of Purim were to be observed for a time,
10: 9 the Lord has rescued us from a these evils;
10:10 for the people of God and one for a the nations, D
10:11 of decision before God and among a the nations. D
11:12 seeking a day to understand it in every detail.
13: 2 and open to travel throughout a its extent,
13: 2 to restore the peace desired by a people. A
13: 4 among a the nations in the world there is D
13: 5 doing a the harm they can so
13: 6 of affairs and is our second father, shall a—
13: 8 calling to remembrance a the works of the Lord.
13: 9 "O Lord, Lord, you rule as King over a things, C
13:11 of a, and there is no one who can resist you,
13:12 You know a things; you know, C
13:18 And a Israel cried out mightily, B
14: 5 O Lord, took Israel out of a the nations, D
14: 5 and our ancestors from among a their forebears,
14: 5 and that you did for them a that you promised.
14:12 O King of the gods and Master of a dominion!
14:15 You have knowledge of a things, C
14:19 O God, whose might is over a,
15: 6 When she had gone through a the doors,
15: 6 a covered with gold and precious stones.
15:16 and a his servants tried to comfort her. Q
16: 8 to render our kingdom quiet and peaceable for a,
16:11 to by a as the person second to the royal throne.
16:18 at the gate of Susa with a his household—
16:18 for God, who rules over a things, C
16:21 For God, who rules over a things, C
16:22 with a good cheer as a notable day
16:24 most hateful to wild animals and birds for a time.
Wis 1: 7 holds a things together knows what is said, C
1:10 because a jealous ear hears a things, C
1:14 For he created a things so that they might exist; C
4: 2 throughout a time it marches, crowned in triumph,
5: 9 "A those things have vanished like a shadow,
5:17 and will arm a creation to repel his enemies;
6: 7 For the Lord of a will not stand in awe of anyone,
6: 7 and he takes thought for a alike.
7: 3 my first sound was a cry, as is true of a.
7: 6 there is for a one entrance into life,
7: 9 because a gold is but a little sand in her sight,
7:11 A good things came to me along with her,
7:12 I rejoiced in them a, because wisdom leads them;
7:16 as are a understanding and skill in crafts.
7:22 the fashioner of a things, taught me. C
7:23 free from anxiety, all-powerful, overseeing a,
7:23 penetrating through a spirits that are intelligent,
7:24 she pervades and penetrates a things. C
7:27 Although she is but one, she can do a things, C
7:27 while remaining in herself, she renews a things; C
8: 1 and she orders a things well. C
8: 3 and the Lord of a loves her.
8: 5 the active cause of a things? C
9: 1 who have made a things by your word, C
9:11 For she knows and understands a things, C
10: 2 and gave him strength to rule a things. C
11:20 But you have arranged a things by measure C
11:23 But you are merciful to a,

Wis 11:23 you are merciful to all, for you can do **a** things, C
11:24 For you love **a** things that exist, C
11:26 You spare **a** things, for they are yours, O Lord, C
12: 1 For your immortal spirit is in **a** things. C
12: 7 the land most precious of **a** to you might receive
12:13 whose care is for **a** people, A
12:15 and you rule **a** things righteously, C
12:16 your sovereignty over **a** causes you to spare **a.**
13: 1 For **a** people who were ignorant A
13:11 to handle and skillfully strip off **a** its bark,
14:25 and **a** is a raging riot of blood and murder,
15: 1 patient, and ruling **a** things in mercy. C
15: 7 and those for contrary uses, making **a** alike;
15: 8 to the earth from which **a** mortals are taken,
15:13 For these persons, more than **a** others,
15:14 are **a** the enemies who oppressed your people.
15:15 they thought that **a** their heathen idols were gods,
15:18 which are worse than **a** others when judged
16: 7 but by you, the Savior of **a.**
16:12 it was your word, O Lord, that heals **a** people. A
16:17 For—most incredible of **a**—
16:17 in water, which quenches **a** things, C
16:25 Therefore at that time also, changed into **a** forms,
17:14 they **a** slept the same sleep,
17:17 for with one chain of darkness they **a** were bound.
18: 5 you destroyed them **a** together by a mighty flood.
18:12 and they **a** together, by the one form
18:14 For while gentle silence enveloped **a** things, C
18:16 and stood and filled **a** things with death, C
19:17 by yawning darkness, **a** of them tried to find
19:22 not neglected to help them at **a** times and Y
19:22 to help them at all times and in **a** places.
Sir 1: 1 **A** wisdom is from the Lord,
1: 4 Wisdom was created before **a** other things,
1: 9 he poured her out upon **a** his works,
1:10 upon **a** the living according to his gift;
3:13 you have **a** your faculties do not despise him.
4:15 and **a** who listen to her will live secure.
6:26 Come to her with **a** your soul,
6:26 and keep her ways with **a** your might.
6:37 and meditate at **a** times on his commandments. Y
7:27 With **a** your heart honor your father, J
7:29 With **a** your soul fear the Lord,
7:30 With **a** your might love your Maker,
7:33 Give graciously to **a** the living;
7:36 In **a** you do, remember the end of your life,
8: 5 remember that we **a** deserve punishment.
8: 7 remember that we must **a** die.
9:12 that they will not be held guiltless **a** their lives.
9:15 and let **a** your discussion be about the law of
10: 2 as the ruler of the city is, so are **a** its inhabitants.
12: 5 then you will receive twice as much evil for **a**
12:13 or **a** those who go near wild animals?
13:16 **A** living beings associate with their own kind,
13:23 The rich person speaks and **a** are silent;
14:17 **A** living beings become old like a garment,
15:13 The Lord hates **a** abominations;
16:27 and their dominion for **a** generations. O
16:30 With **a** kinds of living beings he covered its surface
17: 4 He put the fear of them in **a** living beings,
17:14 He said to them, "Beware of **a** evil."
17:19 **A** their works are as clear as the sun before him,
17:20 and **a** their sins are before the Lord.
17:32 but **a** human beings are dust and ashes.
18:12 therefore he grants them forgiveness **a** the more.
18:26 **a** things move swiftly before the Lord. C
18:27 sin is **a** around, one guards against wrongdoing.
19: 7 and you will lose nothing at **a.**
19:20 and in **a** wisdom there is the fulfillment of the law.
21: 3 **A** lawlessness is like a two-edged sword;
22: 6 a thrashing and discipline are at **a** times wisdom. Y
22:12 for the foolish or the ungodly it lasts **a** the days F
23:17 To a fornicator **a** bread is sweet;
23:23 of **a,** she has disobeyed the law of the Most High;
24: 6 Over waves of the sea, over **a** the earth, E
24: 7 Among **a** these I sought a resting place;
24: 8 the Creator of **a** things gave me a command, C
24: 9 and for **a** the ages I shall not cease to be,
24:23 **A** this is the book of the covenant of
24:33 and leave it to **a** future generations.
24:34 but for **a** who seek wisdom.
25:24 and because of her we **a** die.
26: 4 and at **a** times his face is cheerful. Y
26: 5 **a** these are worse than death.
26: 6 and a tongue-lashing makes it known to **a.**
26:26 *A wife honoring her husband will seem wise to* **a,**
26:26 *in her pride she will be known to* **a** *as ungodly.*
27:23 In your presence his mouth is **a** sweetness,
27:24 I have hated many things, but him above **a;**
29:14 one who has lost **a** sense of shame will fail him.
32: 2 when you have fulfilled **a** your duties,
32:13 But above **a** bless your Maker,
33: 7 when **a** the daylight in the year is from the sun?
33:10 **A** human beings come from the ground,
33:13 so **a** are in the hand of their Maker,
33:15 Look at **a** the works of the Most High;
33:18 but for **a** who seek instruction.
33:23 Excel in **a** that you do;
35: 7 for **a** that you offer is in fulfillment of
35:24 and the works of **a** according to their thoughts;
36: 1 Have mercy upon us, O God of **a,**
36: 2 and put **a** the nations in fear of you. D
36:13 Gather **a** the tribes of Jacob, S
36:22 and **a** who are on the earth will know that you are
37: 7 **A** counselors praise the counsel they give,
37:15 But above **a** pray to the Most High
37:17 The mind is the root of **a** conduct;
Sir 37:20 he will be destitute of **a** food,
37:21 since he is lacking in **a** wisdom.
37:24 and **a** who see him will call him happy.
38: 8 and from him health spreads over **a** the earth. E
38:10 and cleanse your heart from **a** sin.
38:31 **A** these rely on their hands,
38:31 and **a** are skillful in their own work.
39: 1 He seeks out the wisdom of **a** the ancients,
39: 9 and his name will live through **a** generations. O
39:14 bless the Lord for **a** his works.
39:16 "**A** the works of the Lord are very good,
39:17 for at the appointed time **a** such questions will
39:19 The works of **a** are before him,
39:27 **A** these are good for the godly,
39:29 **a** these have been created for vengeance;
39:32 the beginning I have been convinced of **a** this
39:33 **A** the works of the Lord are good,
39:35 So now sing praise with **a** your heart and voice, J
40: 1 the day they return to the mother of **a** the living.
40: 8 To **a** creatures, human and animal,
40:10 **A** these were created for the wicked,
40:11 **A** that is of earth returns to earth,
40:12 **A** bribery and injustice will be blotted out,
41: 2 to one who is contrary, and has lost **a** patience!
41: 4 This is the Lord's decree for **a** flesh; M
42: 7 and when you give or receive, put it **a** in writing.
42: 8 and will be approved by **a.**
42:15 and **a** his creatures do his will.
42:17 to recount **a** his marvelous works,
42:18 For the Most High knows **a** that may be known;
42:21 he is from **a** eternity one and the same.
42:22 How desirable are **a** his works,
42:23 **A** these things live and remain forever; H
42:24 **A** things come in pairs, one opposite the other, C
43:22 **A** mist quickly heals **a** things; C
43:25 **a** kinds of living things, and huge sea-monsters.
43:26 and by his word **a** things hold together. C
43:27 let the final word be: "He is the **a.**"
43:28 For he is greater than **a** his works.
43:30 When you exalt him, summon **a** your strength,
43:33 For the Lord has made **a** things, C
44: 7 **a** these were honored in their generations,
44:16 an example of repentance to **a** generations. O
44:18 that **a** flesh should never again be blotted out by M
44:22 The blessing of **a** people and the covenant A
44:23 who found favor in the sight of **a**
45: 4 choosing him out of **a** humankind.
45: 9 with many golden bells **a** around,
45:16 He chose him out of **a** the living to offer sacrifice
45:26 through **a** their generations. O
46:10 so that **a** the Israelites might see how good it is N
46:18 of the enemy and **a** the rulers of the Philistines.
47: 8 In **a** that he did he gave thanks to the Holy One,
47: 8 he sang praise with **a** his heart, J
47:13 because God made **a** his borders tranquil,
48:12 nor could anyone intimidate him at **a.**
48:15 Despite **a** this the people did not repent,
48:15 and were scattered over **a** the earth. E
49: 4 **a** of them were great sinners,
49: 9 also mentioned Job who held fast to **a** the ways
50: 9 a vessel of hammered gold studded with **a** kinds
50:13 **A** the sons of Aaron in their splendor held
50:15 a pleasing odor to the Most High, the king of **a.**
50:17 Then **a** the people together quickly fell to A
50:22 And now bless the God of **a,**
51:12 *Give thanks to him who formed* **a** *things,* C
51:12 *praise for* **a** *his loyal ones.*
Bar 1: 3 and to **a** the people who came to hear the book, A
1: 4 and to the elders, and to **a** the people, A
1: 4 **a** who lived in Babylon by the river Sud.
1: 7 and to **a** the people who were present with him A
1:21 in **a** the words of the prophets whom he sent K
1:22 but **a** of us followed the intent
2: 4 He made them subject to **a** the kingdoms R
2: 4 to be an object of scorn and a desolation among **a**
2: 7 **A** those calamities with which
2: 9 in **a** the works that he has commanded us to do
2:12 O Lord our God, against **a** your ordinances.
2:15 that **a** the earth may know that you are the Lord E
2:27 with us, O Lord our God, in **a** your kindness and
2:27 and in **a** your great compassion,
3: 7 for we have put away from our hearts **a**
3: 8 and punished for **a** the iniquities of our ancestors,
3:32 But the one who knows **a** things knows her, C
3:32 The one who prepared the earth for **a** time filled it
4: 1 **A** who hold her fast will live,
4:20 I will cry to the Everlasting **a** my days.
LtJ 6: 5 So beware of becoming at **a** like the foreigners or
6:51 to **a** the nations and kings that they are not gods D
Aza 1: 4 For you are just in **a** you have done;
1: 4 **a** your works are true and your ways right,
1: 4 and **a** your judgments are true.
1: 5 in **a** you have brought upon us and
1: 5 a true judgment you have brought **a** this upon us
1: 6 in **a** matters we have sinned grievously.
1: 8 So **a** that you have brought upon us,
1: 8 and **a** that you have done to us,
1: 9 the most wicked in **a** the world.
1:14 and are brought low this day in **a** the world
1:18 And now with **a** our heart we follow you; J
1:21 Let **a** who do harm to your servants be put
1:21 let them be disgraced and deprived of **a** power,
1:27 not touch them at **a** and caused them no pain
1:35 "Bless the Lord, **a** you works of the Lord;
1:38 Bless the Lord, **a** you waters above the heavens;
1:39 Bless the Lord, **a** you powers of the Lord;
1:42 "Bless the Lord, **a** rain and dew;
Aza 1:43 Bless the Lord, **a** you winds;
1:54 Bless the Lord, **a** that grows in the ground;
1:57 you whales and **a** that swim in the waters;
1:58 Bless the Lord, **a** birds of the air;
1:59 Bless the Lord, **a** wild animals and cattle;
1:60 "Bless the Lord, **a** people on earth; A
1:68 **A** who worship the Lord, bless the God of gods,
Sus 1: 4 because he was the most honored of them **a.**
1: 6 **a** who had a case to be tried came to them there.
1:30 her children, and **a** her relatives.
1:33 with her and **a** who saw her were weeping.
1:42 know what is secret and are aware of **a** things C
1:47 **A** the people turned to him and asked, A
1:50 So **a** the people hurried back. A
1:63 and so did her husband Joakim and **a** her relatives,
Bel 1: 2 and was the most honored of **a** his friends.
1: 5 and has dominion over **a** living creatures."
1:12 if you do not find that Bel has eaten it **a,**
1:18 O Bel, and in you there is no deceit at **a!"**
1Mc 1: 9 They **a** put on crowns after his death,
1:21 the lampstand for the light, and **a** its utensils.
1:22 of the temple; he stripped it **a** off.
1:24 Taking them **a,** he went into his own land.
1:28 and **a** the house of Jacob was clothed with shame.
1:36 an evil adversary of Israel at **a** times. Y
1:41 to his whole kingdom that **a** should be one people,
1:42 and that **a** should give up their particular customs.
1:43 **A** the Gentiles accepted the command of the king.
1:49 so that they would forget the law and change **a**
1:51 over **a** the people and commanded the towns A
2:11 **A** her adornment has been taken away;
2:18 as **a** the Gentiles and the people of Judah
2:19 "Even if **a** the nations that live under the rule of D
2:23 in the sight of **a** to offer sacrifice on the altar
2:28 Then he and his sons fled to the hills and left **a**
2:37 "Let us **a** die in our innocence;
2:40 And **a** said to their neighbors:
2:40 "If we **a** do as our kindred have done and refuse
2:41 let us not **a** die as our kindred died
2:42 **a** who offered themselves willingly for the law.
2:43 And **a** who became fugitives
2:46 they forcibly circumcised **a** the uncircumcised
2:67 You shall rally around you **a** who observe the law,
2:70 **a** Israel mourned for him with great lamentation. B
3: 2 **A** his brothers and **a** who had joined his father
3: 6 **a** the evildoers were confounded;
3:25 and terror fell on the Gentiles **a** around them.
3:27 he sent and gathered **a** the forces of his kingdom,
3:34 and gave him orders about **a** that he wanted done.
3:36 settle aliens in **a** their territory,
4: 7 strong and fortified, with cavalry **a** around it;
4:11 Then **a** the Gentiles will know
4:15 and **a** those in the rear fell by the sword.
4:22 they **a** fled into the land of the Philistines.
4:26 and reported to Lysias **a** that had happened.
4:33 and let **a** who know your name praise you
4:37 **a** the army assembled and went up to Mount Zion.
4:51 they finished **a** the work they had undertaken. V
4:55 **A** the people fell on their faces and worshiped A
4:59 Then Judas and his brothers and **a** the assembly
4:60 with high walls and strong towers **a** around,
5: 1 When the Gentiles **a** around heard that
5: 5 and burned with fire their towers and **a** who were
5:13 and **a** our kindred who were in the land
5:15 and **a** Galilee of the Gentiles,
5:23 and children, and **a** they possessed, and led them
5:25 and told them **a** that had happened to their kindred
5:26 **a** these towns were strong and large—
5:27 and destroy **a** these people in a single day." A
5:28 then he seized **a** its spoils and burned it with fire.
5:29 they went **a** the way to the stronghold of Dathema.
5:38 "**A** the Gentiles around us have gathered to him;
5:42 but make them **a** enter the battle."
5:43 **A** the Gentiles were defeated before him,
5:44 together with **a** who were in them.
5:45 Judas gathered together **a** the Israelites in Gilead, N
5:49 the army that **a** should encamp where they were.
5:50 fought against the town **a** that day and **a** the night,
5:53 the laggards and encouraging the people **a** the way
5:63 and his brothers were greatly honored in **a** Israel B
5:63 in all Israel and among **a** the Gentiles,
5:65 and burned its towers on **a** sides.
6:10 So he called **a** his Friends and said to them,
6:12 I seized **a** its vessels of silver and gold,
6:14 and made him ruler over **a** his kingdom.
6:19 and assembled **a** the people to besiege them. A
6:25 also attacked **a** the lands on their borders.
6:28 He assembled **a** his Friends,
6:41 **A** who heard the noise made by their multitude,
6:43 It was taller than **a** the others,
6:58 and make peace with them and with **a** their nation.
6:59 that they became angry and did **a** these things." H
6:62 and gave orders to tear down the wall **a** around.
7: 5 to him **a** the renegade and godless men of Israel;
7: 6 and his brothers have destroyed **a** your Friends,
7: 7 and see **a** the ruin that Judas has brought on us and
7: 7 and let him punish them and **a** who help them."
7:17 and their blood they poured out **a**
7:18 the fear and dread of them fell on **a** the people, A
7:22 and **a** who were troubling their people joined him.
7:23 And Judas saw **a** the wrongs that Alcimus
7:24 So Judas went out into **a** the surrounding parts
7:46 People came out of **a** the surrounding villages
7:46 so that they **a** fell by the sword;
8: 1 and were well-disposed toward **a** who made
8:14 Yet for **a** this not one of them has put on a crown
8:16 to rule over them and to control **a** their land;

1Mc 8:16 they **a** heed the one man,
8:23 "May **a** go well with the Romans and with
8:24 or to any of their allies in **a** their dominion,
9:11 as did **a** the chief warriors.
9:14 then **a** the stouthearted men went with him,
9:20 **A** Israel made great lamentation for him; B
9:23 the renegades emerged in **a** parts of Israel;
9:23 **a** the wrongdoers reappeared.
9:28 Then **a** the friends of Judas assembled and said
9:33 and his brother Simon and **a** who were
9:34 and he with **a** his army crossed the Jordan.
9:36 from Medeba came out and seized John and **a**
9:40 and the Jews took **a** their goods.
9:58 Then **a** the lawless plotted and said, "See!
9:58 and he will capture them **a** in one night."
9:60 and secretly sent letters to **a** his allies in Judea,
9:63 he assembled **a** his forces,
10: 5 for he will remember **a** the wrongs that we did
10: 7 read the letter in the hearing of **a** the people A
10:13 **a** of them left their places and went back
10:15 Now King Alexander heard of **a** the promises
10:29 and exempt **a** the Jews from payment of tribute X
10:30 from this day and for **a** time.
10:33 and let **a** officials cancel also the taxes
10:34 "**A** the festivals and sabbaths and new moons
10:34 let them **a** be days of immunity and release for all
10:34 days of immunity and release for **a** the Jews X
10:36 the maintenance be given them that is due to **a**
10:41 And **a** the additional funds that
10:43 And **a** who take refuge at the temple in Jerusalem,
10:43 and receive back **a** their property in my kingdom.
10:45 the walls of Jerusalem and fortifying it **a** around,
10:47 and they remained his allies **a** his days.
10:64 and saw him clothed in purple, they **a** fled.
10:89 He also gave him Ekron and **a** its environs
11:26 he exalted him in the presence of **a** his Friends.
11:29 wrote a letter to Jonathan about **a** these things; H
11:34 the latter, with **a** the region bordering them,
11:34 To **a** those who offer sacrifice
11:35 from **a** these we shall grant them release.
11:38 he dismissed **a** his troops,
11:38 **a** of them to their own homes,
11:38 So **a** the troops who had served
11:39 he saw that **a** the troops were grumbling
11:43 for **a** my troops have revolted."
11:47 and they **a** rallied around him and then spread out
11:51 of the king and of **a** the people in his kingdom, A
11:53 he broke his word about **a** that he had promised;
11:55 **A** the troops that Demetrius had discharged
11:60 and **a** the army of Syria gathered to him as allies.
11:70 **A** the men with Jonathan fled; Z
12:27 at hand so as to be ready **a** night for battle,
12:32 and marched through **a** that region.
12:43 with honor and commended him to **a** his Friends,
12:44 "Why have you put **a** these people to A
12:45 and the remaining troops and **a** the officials,
12:48 and they killed with the sword **a** who had entered
12:49 the Great Plain to destroy **a** Jonathan's soldiers.
12:52 So they **a** reached the land of Judah safely,
12:52 and **a** Israel mourned deeply. B
12:53 **A** the nations around them tried to destroy them, D
13: 4 By reason of this **a** my brothers have perished for
13: 6 for **a** the nations have gathered together out D
13: 9 and **a** that you say to us we will do."
13:10 So he assembled **a** the warriors and hurried
13:22 So Trypho got **a** his cavalry ready to go,
13:26 **A** Israel bewailed him with great lamentation, B
13:29 so that they could be seen by **a** who sail the sea.
13:33 up the strongholds of Judea and walled them **a**
13:34 for **a** that Trypho did was to plunder.
13:38 **A** the grants that we have made
13:48 He removed **a** uncleanness from it,
13:53 and so he made him commander of **a** the forces;
14: 4 The land had rest **a** the days of Simon. F
14: 4 as was the honor shown him, **a** his days.
14: 5 To crown **a** his honors he took Joppa for a harbor,
14: 9 they **a** talked together of good things,
14:12 **A** the people sat under their own vines A
14:14 He gave help to **a** the humble among his people;
14:14 and did away with **a** the renegades and outlaws.
14:35 because he had done **a** these things and because H
14:43 and that he should be obeyed by **a**,
14:43 that **a** contracts in the country should be written
14:46 **A** the people agreed to grant Simon the right A
14:47 and to be protector of them **a**.
15: 1 and ethnarch of the Jews, and to **a** the nation;
15: 5 therefore I confirm to you **a** the tax remissions
15: 5 and a release from **a** the other payments
15: 7 **A** the weapons that you have prepared and
15: 8 for you from henceforth and for **a** time.
15: 9 your glory will become manifest in **a** the earth." E
15:10 **A** the troops rallied to him,
15:23 and to **a** the countries, and to Sampsames,
15:27 and broke **a** the agreements he formerly had made
15:36 also the splendor of Simon and **a** that he had seen.
2Mc 1: 3 May he give you **a** a heart to worship him and
1:22 a great fire blazed up, so that **a** marveled.
1:24 "O Lord, Lord God, Creator of **a** things, C
1:26 sacrifice on behalf of **a** your people Israel A
2:14 In the same way Judas also collected **a** the books
2:17 It is God who has saved **a** his people, A
2:17 and has returned the inheritance to **a**,
2:23 **a** this, which has been set forth by Jason
2:25 to memorize, and to profit **a** readers.
3: 3 from his own revenues **a** the expenses connected
3:11 that it totaled in **a** four hundred talents of silver
3:20 they **a** made supplication.

2Mc 3:24 and of **a** authority caused so great a manifestation
that **a** who had been so bold as
3:28 with a great retinue and **a** his bodyguard but was
3:34 report to **a** people the majestic power of God." A
3:36 He bore testimony to **a** concerning the deeds of
3:38 thoroughly flogged, if he survives at **a**;
4: 5 both public and private, of **a** the people. A
4:42 and killed some, and put **a** the rest to flight;
4:47 Menelaus, the cause of **a** the trouble,
5: 2 over **a** the city golden-clad cavalry charging
5: 3 of golden trappings, and armor of **a** kinds.
5:15 Antiochus dared to enter the most holy temple in **a**
5:20 of the Almighty was restored again in **a** its glory
5:24 and commanded him to kill **a** the grown men and
5:26 to the sword **a** those who came out to see them,
6:11 to Philip and were **a** burned together,
6:20 as **a** ought to go who have the courage
7:23 of humankind and devised the origin of **a** things, C
7:25 Since the young man would not listen to him at **a**,
7:31 who have contrived **a** sorts of evil against
7:34 you, unholy wretch, you most defiled of **a** mortals,
7:41 Last of **a**, the mother died, after her sons.
8: 2 upon the people who were oppressed by **a**;
8: 9 of **a** nations, to wipe out the whole race D
8:14 Others sold **a** their remaining property,
8:24 and forced them **a** to flee.
8:31 and carefully stored **a** of them in strategic places;
9: 8 making the power of God manifest to **a**.
9:15 **a** of them, equal to citizens of Athens;
9:16 and **a** the holy vessels he would give back,
9:17 in addition to **a** this he also would become a Jew
9:18 up **a** hope for himself and wrote to the Jews
9:21 to take thought for the general security of **a**.
10:17 and beat off **a** who fought upon the wall,
11: 2 about eighty thousand infantry and **a** his cavalry
11: 6 and **a** the people, with lamentations and tears, A
11: 9 And together they **a** praised the merciful God,
11:11 and forced **a** the rest to flee.
11:15 agreed to **a** that Lysias urged.
12:11 and to help his people in **a** other ways.
12:13 and inhabited by **a** sorts of Gentiles.
12:21 because of the narrowness of **a** the approaches.
12:22 to them of him who sees **a** things. C
12:27 with multitudes of people of **a** nationalities.
12:40 to **a** that this was the reason these men had fallen.
12:41 So they **a** blessed the ways of the Lord,
13: 4 that this man was to blame for **a** the trouble,
13: 5 around it that on **a** sides inclines precipitously into
13: 6 There they **a** push to destruction anyone guilty
13:12 When they had **a** joined in the same petition
13:23 yielded and swore to observe **a** their rights,
14: 9 with the gracious kindness that you show to **a**.
14:35 "O Lord of **a**, though you have need
14:36 O holy One, Lord of **a** holiness,
15: 2 for the day that he who sees **a** things has honored C
15: 7 to trust with **a** confidence that he would get help
15:11 and he cheered them **a** by relating a dream,
15:12 from childhood in **a** that belongs to excellence,
15:17 by fighting hand to hand with **a** courage,
15:20 **a** were now looking forward to the coming issue,
15:34 And they **a**, looking to heaven,
15:36 And they **a** decreed by public vote never
1Es 1:13 and carried them to **a** the people. A
1:21 and **a** of Israel who were living in Jerusalem.
1:25 After **a** these acts of Josiah,
1:32 In **a** Judea they mourned for Josiah.
1:49 and lawlessness beyond **a** the unclean deeds of
1:49 all the unclean deeds of **a** the nations, D
1:53 for he gave them **a** into their hands.
1:54 They took **a** the holy vessels of the Lord,
1:56 and utterly destroyed **a** its glorious things.
1:58 it shall keep sabbath **a** the time of its desolation
2: 2 a proclamation throughout **a** his kingdom and
2: 8 and **a** whose spirit the Lord had stirred to go up
2:14 **A** the vessels were handed over, gold and silver,
3: 1 Now King Darius gave a great banquet for **a**
3: 1 **a** that were born in his house,
3: 1 and **a** the nobles of Media and Persia,
3: 2 and **a** the satraps and generals and governors
3:12 but above **a** things truth is victor." C
3:14 Then he sent and summoned **a** the nobles of Persia
3:18 It leads astray the minds of **a** who drink it.
3:20 and forgets **a** sorrow and debt.
3:21 It makes **a** hearts feel rich,
4: 2 who rule over land and sea and **a** that is in them?
4:10 **A** his people and his armies obey him. A
4:19 they let **a** those things go,
4:19 and **a** prefer her to gold or silver
4:28 Do not **a** lands fear to touch him?
4:35 But truth is great, and stronger than **a** things. C
4:36 **A** God's works quake and tremble,
4:37 **a** human beings are unrighteous,
4:37 **a** their works are unrighteous, and **a** such things.
4:40 the kingship and the power and the majesty of **a**
4:41 **a** the people shouted and said, "Great is truth, A
4:41 "Great is truth, and strongest of **a**!"
4:44 and to send back **a** the vessels that were taken
4:47 to **a** the treasurers and governors and generals
4:47 to him and to **a** who were going up with him
4:48 to **a** the governors in Coelesyria and Phoenicia
4:49 He wrote in behalf of **a** the Jews X
4:50 that **a** the country that they would occupy should
4:53 and that **a** who came from Babylonia to build
4:53 and their children and **a** the priests who came.
4:56 and wages should be provided for **a** who guarded
4:57 And he sent back from Babylon **a** the vessels
4:61 and went to Babylon and told this to **a** his kindred.

1Es 5: 3 **a** their kindred were making merry.
5:28 in **a** one hundred thirty-nine.
5:35 **A** the temple servants and the descendants
5:41 **A** those of Israel, twelve or more years of age,
5:46 the gatekeepers, and **a** Israel in their towns. B
5:47 and the Israelites were **a** in their own homes,
5:50 for **a** the peoples of the land were hostile to them G
5:52 and at new moons and at **a** the consecrated feasts.
5:53 And **a** who had made any vow to God began
5:56 and the levitical priests and **a** who had come back
5:58 with their sons and kindred, **a** the Levites,
5:61 and his glory are forever upon **a** Israel." B
5:62 And **a** the people sounded trumpets and shouted A
6: 4 and this roof and finishing **a** the other things?
6:10 and being completed with **a** splendor and care.
6:19 that he should take **a** these vessels back
6:32 and **a** property forfeited to the king.
6:34 be done with **a** diligence as here prescribed."
7: 8 for the sin of **a** Israel, according to the number B
7:11 Not **a** of the returned captives were purified,
7:11 but the Levites were **a** purified together,
7:12 the passover lamb for **a** the returned captives and
7:13 **a** those who had separated themselves from
8: 4 he found favor before the king in **a** his requests.
8: 7 taught **a** Israel all the ordinances and judgments. B
8: 7 taught all Israel **a** the ordinances and judgments.
8:13 and to collect for the Lord in Jerusalem **a** the gold
8:21 Let **a** things prescribed in the law of God C
8:23 to judge **a** those who know the law of your God,
8:23 throughout **a** Syria and Phoenicia;
8:24 **A** who transgress the law of your God or the law
8:26 and his counselors and **a** his Friends and nobles.
8:49 the list of **a** their names was reported.
8:55 and the nobles and **a** Israel had given. B
8:65 the God of Israel, twelve bulls for **a** Israel, B
8:66 **a** as a sacrifice to the Lord.
8:72 And **a** who were ever moved at the word of
8:86 And **a** that has happened to us has come about
8:93 that we will put away **a** our foreign wives,
8:94 as seems good to you and to **a** who obey the law
8:96 of the priests and Levites of **a** Israel swear B
9: 3 and Jerusalem to **a** who had returned from exile
9: 6 **A** the multitude sat in the open square before
9:10 Then **a** the multitude shouted and said with
9:12 the leaders of the multitude stay, and let **a** those
9:15 from exile acted in accordance with **a** this.
9:16 of their ancestral houses, **a** of them by name;
9:36 **A** these had married foreign women,
9:40 **a** the multitude, men and women, and **a** the priests
9:41 and **a** the multitude gave attention to the law.
9:45 for he had the place of honor in the presence of **a**.
9:46 When he opened the law, they **a** stood erect.
9:49 who were teaching the multitude, and to **a**,
9:50 now they were **a** weeping as they heard the law—
9:53 The Levites commanded **a** the people, saying, A
9:54 Then they **a** went their way,
Man 1: 2 and earth with **a** their order;
1: 4 at whom **a** things shudder, C
1:15 will praise you continually **a** the days of my life. F
1:15 For **a** the host of heaven sings your praise,
3Mc 1: 1 he gave orders to **a** his forces,
1: 4 with wailing and tears, her locks **a** disheveled,
1: 8 he was **a** the more eager to visit them as soon
1:11 not even **a** of the priests, but only
1:11 only the high priest who was pre-eminent over **a**—
1:16 in **a** their vestments prostrated themselves
1:27 to call upon him who has **a** power to defend them
1:29 because indeed **a** at that time preferred death to
2: 2 king of the heavens, and sovereign of **a** creation,
2: 3 the creator of **a** things and the governor of all, C
2: 3 the creator of all things and the governor of **a**,
2:21 Thereupon God, who oversees **a** things, C
2:21 the first Father of **a**, holy among the holy ones,
2:28 and **a** Jews shall be subjected to X
2:30 that he might not appear to be an enemy of **a**,
3: 1 and he ordered that **a** should promptly be gathered
3: 6 which was common talk among **a**;
3:12 and soldiers in Egypt and **a** its districts, greetings
3:18 of the benevolence that we have toward **a**.
3:19 among **a** nations who hold their heads high D
3:20 since we treat **a** nations with benevolence. D
3:21 to **a** our amnesty toward their compatriots here,
3:26 For when **a** of these have been punished,
3:29 and shall become useless for **a** time
4: 3 What district or city, or what habitable place at **a**,
4: 4 **a** together, by the generals in the several cities,
4: 6 **a** together raising a lament instead of
4:11 to **a** coming back into the city and to those from
4:16 organizing feasts in honor of **a** his idols,
4:18 task was impossible for **a** the generals in Egypt.
5: 2 and ordered him on the following day to drug **a**
5: 7 with tears and a voice hard to silence they **a** called
5: 7 upon the Almighty Lord and Ruler of **a** power,
5:17 of the banquet joyful by celebrating **a** the more.
5:21 **a** those present readily and joyfully
5:21 and **a** went to their own homes.
5:22 in devising **a** sorts of insults for those they thought
5:28 This was the act of God who rules over **a** things, C
5:29 Then Hermon and **a** the king's Friends pointed out
6: 2 governing **a** creation with mercy,
6: 6 and turning the flame against **a** their enemies.
6: 8 over and restored unharmed to **a** his family.
6: 9 all-merciful and protector of **a**,
6:12 O Eternal One, who have **a** might and **a** power,
6:15 be shown to **a** the Gentiles that you are with us,
6:16 with the animals and **a** the arrogance of his forces.
6:18 visible to **a** but the Jews.

3Mc 6:23 and saw them **a** fallen headlong to destruction,
6:26 from the beginning differed from **a** nations D
6:30 with **a** joyfulness in that same place
6:32 Putting an end to **a** mourning and wailing,
6:39 the Lord of **a** most gloriously revealed his mercy
6:39 and rescued them **a** together and unharmed.
7: 1 and **a** in authority in his government, greetings
7: 4 ill-will that these people had toward **a** nations. D
7: 6 toward **a** people we barely spared their lives. A
7: 8 We also have ordered **a** people to return A
7: 8 at **a** or reproaching them for the irrational things
7: 9 against them or cause them any grief at **a,**
7:16 crowned with **a** sorts of very fragrant flowers,
7:16 of praise and **a** kinds of melodious songs.
7:18 king had generously provided **a** things to them C
7:18 to them for their journey until **a** of them arrived
7:19 And when they had **a** landed in peace
7:20 since at the king's command they had **a**
7:21 not subject at **a** to confiscation of their belongings
7:22 Besides, they **a** recovered **a** of their property,
7:23 Blessed be the Deliverer of Israel through **a** times!
2Es 1: 8 the hair of your head and hurl **a** evils upon them,
1:10 down Pharaoh with his servants and **a** his army.
1:11 I destroyed **a** nations before them, D
1:11 Tyre and Sidon; I killed **a** their enemies.
2:42 and they **a** were praising the Lord with songs.
3:10 And the same fate befell **a** of them:
3:11 **a** the righteous who have descended from him.
3:21 as were also **a** who were descended from him.
3:26 as Adam and **a** his descendants had done,
4:38 **a** of us also are full of ungodliness.
5: 7 and **a** shall hear his voice.
5: 9 and **a** friends shall conquer one another;
5:23 and from **a** its trees you have chosen one vine,
5:24 and from **a** the lands of the world you have chosen
5:24 from **a** the flowers of the world you have chosen
5:25 and from **a** the depths of the sea you have filled
5:25 for yourself one river, and from **a** the cities
5:26 and from **a** the birds that have been created
5:26 for yourself one dove, and from **a** the flocks
5:27 from **a** the multitude of peoples you have gotten
5:27 you have given the law that is approved by **a.**
5:45 If therefore **a** creatures will live at one time and
5:45 be able to support **a** of them present at one time."
6:20 and **a** shall see my judgment together.
6:23 the trumpet shall sound aloud, and when **a** hear it,
6:25 that whoever remains after **a** that I have foretold
6:33 Therefore he sent me to show you **a** these things, H
6:54 as ruler over **a** the works that you had made;
6:54 and from him we have **a** come,
6:55 "**A** this I have spoken before you, O Lord,
7: 6 and it is full of **a** good things;
7:29 and **a** who draw human breath.
7:42 by which **a** shall see what has been destined.
7:48 for a few but for almost **a** who have been created."
7:65 let **a** who have been born lament,
7:68 **a** who have been born are entangled in iniquities,
7:70 and Adam and **a** who have come from him,
7:78 first of **a** it adores the glory of the Most High.
7:87 which is worse than **a** the ways
7:91 First of **a,** they shall see with great joy the glory
7:98 which is greater than **a** that have been mentioned,
7:104 The day of judgment is decisive and displays to **a**
7:105 for then **a** shall bear their own righteousness
7:117 [47] what good is it to **a** that they live in sorrow
7:127 [57] that **a** who are born on earth shall wage:
8:15 About **a** humankind you know best;
8:41 **a** that have been sown will come up in due season,
8:41 and not **a** that were planted will take root;
8:41 in the world will not **a** be saved."
8:44 and for whose sake you have formed **a** things— C
8:62 I have not shown this to **a** people, A
9: 7 that **a** who will be saved and will be able to escape
9:45 I and my husband and **a** my neighbors;
10: 2 So **a** of us put out our lamps,
10: 2 and **a** my neighbors attempted to console me;
10: 3 But when **a** of them had stopped consoling me,
10: 7 For Zion, the mother of us **a,**
10: 8 to mourn now, because we are **a** mourning,
10: 8 and to be sorrowful, because we are **a** sorrowing;
10:10 From the beginning **a** have been born of her,
10:10 and, lo, almost **a** go to perdition,
10:23 worst of **a,** the seal of Zion has been deprived
11: 2 and **a** the winds of heaven blew upon it,
11: 6 how **a** things under heaven were subjected to it, C
11: 8 "Do not **a** watch at the same time;
11:12 and it reigned over **a** the earth. E
11:16 you who have ruled the earth **a** this time;
11:19 And so it went with **a** the wings;
11:32 the world than **a** the wings that had gone before.
11:40 have conquered **a** the beasts
11:40 and over **a** the earth with grievous oppression; E
12:13 it shall be more terrifying than **a** the kingdoms R
12:24 its inhabitants more oppressively than **a** who were
12:31 and as for **a** his words that you have heard,
12:37 write **a** these things that you have seen in a book, H
12:40 When **a** the people heard that the seven days A
12:40 they **a** gathered together, from the least to
12:42 For of **a** the prophets you alone are left to us,
13: 2 wind arose from the sea and stirred up **a** its waves.
13: 4 **a** who heard his voice melted as wax melts
13: 8 that **a** who had gathered together against him,
13:11 **A** these were mingled together,
13:11 and burned up **a** of them,
13:33 "Then, when **a** the nations hear his voice, D
13:33 **a** the nations shall leave their own lands and D
13:36 and be made manifest to **a** people, A
2Es 14:27 and I gathered **a** the people together, and said, A
15: 4 For **a** unbelievers shall die in their unbelief.
15: 9 to myself **a** the innocent blood from among them.
15:11 as before, and will destroy **a** its land.
15:20 how I am calling together **a** the kings of the earth P
15:26 For God knows **a** who sin against him;
15:29 so that **a** who hear them will fear and tremble.
15:40 and destroy **a** the earth and its inhabitants, E
15:41 that **a** the fields and **a** the streams shall be filled
15:44 they shall pour out on it the tempest and **a** its fury;
15:44 and **a** who are around it shall mourn for it.
15:48 You have imitated that hateful one in **a** her deeds
15:57 be wiped out, and **a** your people who are in A
15:59 Unhappy above **a** others, you shall come
15:62 with fire **a** your forests and your fruitful trees.
16:18 the beginning of calamities, when **a** shall tremble.
16:20 for **a** this they will not turn from their iniquities,
16:26 For in **a** places there shall be great solitude;
16:32 its roads and **a** its paths shall bring forth thorns,
16:62 who surely made **a** things C
16:64 The Lord will strictly examine **a** their works,
16:64 and will make a public spectacle of **a** of you.
16:67 and deliver you from **a** tribulation.
4Mc 1: 9 **A** of these, by despising sufferings
1:11 **A** people, even their torturers, A
1:14 and whether reason rules over **a** these.
1:19 Rational judgment is supreme over **a** of these,
1:25 which is the most complex of **a** the emotions.
1:30 now, first of **a,** that rational judgment is sovereign
1:34 and animals and **a** sorts of foods that are forbidden
1:35 **a** the impulses of the body are bridled by reason.
2: 6 I could prove to you **a** the more that reason is able
2: 9 In **a** other matters we can recognize
2:16 temperate mind repels **a** these malicious emotions,
2:22 the senses as a sacred governor over them **a.**
3: 7 the Philistines **a** day long,
3: 9 Now **a** the rest were at supper,
3:18 and by nobility of reason spurn **a** domination by
4: 1 When despite **a** manner of slander he was unable
4: 7 and did **a** that they could to prevent it.
4:11 in the temple area that was open to **a,**
4:12 the blessedness of the holy place before **a** people. A
4:14 having been saved beyond **a** expectations,
4:24 but saw that **a** his threats
5:23 so that we master **a** pleasures and desires,
5:24 so that in **a** our dealings we act impartially,
6:20 while and during that time be a laughingstock to **a**
7:17 "Not **a** have full command of their emotions,
7:17 because not **a** have prudent reason."
8:29 **a** with one voice together, as from one mind, said:
9:18 through **a** these tortures I will convince you
9:26 While **a** were marveling at his courageous spirit,
9:28 flayed **a** his flesh up to his chin,
10: 8 he saw his own flesh torn **a** around and drops
11: 5 of **a** things and live according to his virtuous law?C
11:10 and **a** his members were disjointed.
12: 1 the seventh and youngest of **a** came forward.
12: 8 to the king and to **a** his friends that are with him."
12:11 most impious of **a** the wicked,
12:12 and these throughout **a** time will never let you go.
13:13 and **a** of them together looking at one another,
13:13 with **a** our hearts consecrate ourselves to God,
13:17 and **a** the fathers will praise us."
13:24 they loved one another **a** the more.
14: 5 but **a** of them, as though running the course
15:12 But each child separately and **a** of them together
15:24 this noble mother disregarded **a** these because
16: 7 O seven childbirths **a** in vain,
16:25 as do Abraham and Isaac and Jacob and **a**
17:17 and **a** his council marveled at their endurance,
17:19 "**A** who are consecrated are under your hands."
17:24 and he ravaged and conquered **a** his enemies.
18: 2 that devout reason is master of **a** emotions,

ALL-MERCIFUL (1) [MERCY]
3Mc 6: 9 you who hate insolence, **a** and protector of all,

ALL-NOURISHING (1) [NOURISH]
Wis 16:25 changed into all forms, it served your **a** bounty,

ALL-POWERFUL (4) [POWER]
Wis 7:23 humane, steadfast, sure, free from anxiety, **a,**
11:17 For your **a** hand, which created the world out
18:15 your **a** word leaped from heaven,
3Mc 5:13 the might of his **a** hand to the arrogant Gentiles.

ALL-SEEING (3) [SEE]
AdE 15: 2 after invoking the aid of the **a** God and Savior,
2Mc 7:35 yet escaped the judgment of the almighty, **a** God.
9: 5 But the **a** Lord, the God of Israel,

ALL-WISE (2) [WISE]
4Mc 1:12 giving glory to the **a** God.
13:19 which the divine and **a** Providence has bequeathed

ALLAMMELECH (1)
Jos 19:26 **A,** Amad, and Mishal;

ALLEGIANCE (3) [ALLY]
1Ch 12:29 the majority had continued to keep their **a** to
29:24 pledged their **a** to King Solomon.
Isa 19:18 the language of Canaan and swear **a** to the LORD

ALLEGING (1)
3Mc 3: 7 **a** that these people were loyal neither to the king

ALLEGING (KJV) See also PROVING

ALLEGORICALLY See Index to Footnotes

ALLEGORIES (1) [ALLEGORY]
Eze 20:49 they are saying of me, 'Is he not a maker of **a?**' "

ALLEGORY (3) [ALLEGORIES]
Eze 17: 2 and speak an **a** to the house of Israel.
24: 3 utter an **a** to the rebellious house and say to them,
Gal 4:24 Now this is an **a:** these women are two covenants.

ALLELUIA (KJV) See HALLELUJAH

ALLIANCE (24) [ALLY]
Jdg 3:13 In **a** with the Ammonites and the Amalekites,
1Ki 3: 1 Solomon made a marriage **a** with Pharaoh king
15:19 "Let there be an **a** between me and you,
15:19 go, break your **a** with King Baasha of Israel,
2Ch 16: 3 "Let there be an **a** between me and you,
16: 3 go, break your **a** with King Baasha of Israel,
18: 1 and he made a marriage **a** with Ahab.
Isa 30: 1 who make an **a,** but against my will,
Da 11: 6 After some years they shall make an **a,**
11:23 And after an **a** is made with him,
1Mc 8: 1 and were well-disposed toward all who made an **a**
8:17 sent them to Rome to establish friendship and **a,**
8:20 of the Jews have sent us to you to establish **a**
8:22 with them there as a memorial of peace and **a:**
12: 3 to renew the former friendship and **a** with them."
12: 8 which contained a clear declaration of **a**
12:16 to renew our former friendship and **a** with them.
14:18 the friendship and **a** that they had established
14:24 to confirm the **a** with the Romans.
15:17 and allies to renew our ancient friendship and **a.**
15:19 or make **a** with those who war against them.
2Mc 4:11 on the mission to establish friendship and **a** with
3Mc 3:14 by the gods' deliberate **a** with us in battle,
3:21 both because of their **a** with us and

ALLIED (5) [ALLY]
1Ki 20:16 he and the thirty-two kings **a** with him.
Ps 94:20 Can wicked rulers be **a** with you,
Isa 7: 2 the house of David heard that Aram had **a** itself
Eze 30: 5 and the people of the **a** land shall fall with them
2Es 11:30 And I saw how it **a** the two heads with itself,

ALLIES (17) [ALLY]
Ge 14:13 of Aner; these were **a** of Abram.
Ps 69:22 be a trap for them, a snare for their **a.**
Jer 13:21 those whom you have trained to be your **a?**
Eze 31:17 to those killed by the sword, along with its **a,**
Ob 1: 7 All your **a** have deceived you,
Jdt 7: 1 and all the **a** who had joined him,
1Mc 8:20 so that we may be enrolled as your **a** and friends."
8:24 to Rome or to any of their **a** in all their dominion,
8:25 of the Jews shall act as their **a** wholeheartedly,
8:27 the Romans shall willingly act as their **a,**
8:31 on our friends and **a** the Jews?
9:60 and secretly sent letters to all his **a** in Judea,
10:47 and they remained his **a** all his days.
11:60 and all the army of Syria gathered to him as **a.**
12:14 We were unwilling to annoy you and our other **a**
14:40 by the Romans as friends and **a** and brothers,
15:17 and **a** to renew our ancient friendship and alliance.

ALLON (2)
1Ch 4:37 Ziza son of Shiphi son of **A** son of Jedaiah son
1Es 5:31 the descendants of Shaphat, the descendants of **A.**

ALLON-BACUTH (1)
Ge 35: 8 So it was called **A.**

ALLOT (5) [ALLOTMENT, ALLOTMENTS, ALLOTS, ALLOTTED, ALLOTTING]
Jos 13: 6 only **a** the land to Israel for an inheritance,
Isa 53:12 Therefore I will **a** him a portion with the great,
Eze 45: 1 When you **a** the land as an inheritance,
47:22 You shall **a** it as an inheritance for yourselves and
48:29 that you shall **a** as an inheritance among the tribes

ALLOTMENT (14) [ALLOT]
Nu 18:20 You shall have no **a** in their land,
18:23 But among the Israelites they shall have no **a,**
18:24 that they shall have no **a** among the Israelites.
26:62 the Israelites because there was no **a** given to them
Dt 10: 9 Levi has no **a** or inheritance with his kindred;
12:12 in your towns (since they have no **a** or inheritance
14:27 because they have no **a** or inheritance with you.
14:29 because they have no **a** or inheritance with you,
18: 1 shall have no **a** or inheritance within Israel.
33:21 for there a commander's **a** was reserved;
Jos 16: 1 The **a** of the Josephites went from the Jordan
17: 1 Then **a** was made to the tribe of Manasseh,
Eze 48:10 an **a** measuring twenty-five thousand cubits on
48:13 an **a** twenty-five thousand cubits in length

ALLOTMENTS (4) [ALLOT]

Jos 11:23 an inheritance to Israel according to their tribal **a.**
12: 7 of Israel as a possession according to their **a,**
17: 2 **a** were made to the rest of the tribe of Manasseh,
Eze 48:10 These shall be the **a** of the holy portion:

ALLOTS (1) [ALLOT]

1Co 12:11 who **a** to each one individually just as

ALLOTTED (32) [ALLOT]

Lev 7:35 This is the portion **a** to Aaron and to his sons from
Nu 36: 3 so it will be taken away from the **a** portion
Dt 4:19 things that the LORD your God has **a** to all
19:14 the property that will be **a** to you in the land that
29:26 not known and whom he had not **a** to them;
32: 9 own portion was his people, Jacob his **a** share.
Jos 13:29 it was **a** to the half-tribe of the Manassites
13:31 these were **a** to the people of Machir son
14: 5 as the LORD commanded Moses; they **a** the land.
17: 1 the father of Gilead, were **a** Gilead and Bashan,
17: 6 land of Gilead was **a** to the rest of the Manassites.
18:11 the territory **a** to it fell between the tribe of Judah
21:20 towns **a** to them were out of the tribe of Ephraim.
21:40 those **a** to them were twelve in all.
23: 4 I have **a** to you as an inheritance
Jdg 1: 3 "Come up with me into the territory **a** to me,
1: 3 I too will go with you into the territory **a** to you."
18: 1 among the tribes of Israel had been **a** to them.
1Ch 6:62 to their families were **a** thirteen towns out of
6:63 to their families were **a** twelve towns out of
26:15 and to his sons was **a** the storehouse.
Ne 9:22 and **a** to them every corner,
Job 7: 3 so I am **a** months of emptiness,
Ps 125: 3 of wickedness shall not rest on the land **a** to
Eze 47:22 with you they shall be **a** an inheritance among
Ac 1:17 among us and was **a** his share in this ministry."
17:26 and he **a** the times of their existence and
Wis 2: 5 For our **a** time is the passing of a shadow,
Sir 11:18 and the reward **a** to him is this:
17:11 and **a** to them the law of life.
45:20 he **a** to him the best of the first fruits,
2Mc 8:27 for that day and **a** it to them as the beginning

ALLOTTING‡ (1) [ALLOT]

Dt 12:10 and live in the land that the LORD your God is **a**

ALLOW‡ (24) [ALLOWANCE, ALLOWED, ALLOWS]

Ge 30:27 But Laban said to him, "If you will **a** me to say so,
Ex 12:23 the LORD will pass over that door and will not **a**
Nu 16: 5 the one whom he will choose he will **a**
16: 9 to **a** you to approach him in order to perform
21:23 not **a** Israel to pass through his territory.
30:13 her husband may **a** to stand,
Dt 2:28 Only **a** me to pass through on foot—
Jdg 1:34 they did not **a** them to come down to the plain.
13:15 "**A** us to detain you, and prepare a kid for you."
15: 1 But her father would not **a** him to go in.
21:22 'Be generous and **a** us to have them;
2Sa 21:10 not **a** the birds of the air to come on the bodies
Da 1: 8 the palace master to **a** him not to defile himself.
Mk 11:16 not **a** anyone to carry anything through the temple.
Lk 4:41 he rebuked them and would not **a** them to speak,
8:51 he did not **a** anyone to enter with him,
Ac 16: 7 but the Spirit of Jesus did not **a** them;
Jdt 1: 4 and forty cubits wide to **a** his armies to march out
4:12 to **a** their infants to be carried off and their wives
12: 6 "Let my lord now give orders to **a** your servant
Sir 18:31 If you **a** your soul to take pleasure in base desire,
25:25 **A** no outlet to water, and no boldness of speech to
27:19 And as you **a** a bird to escape from your hand,
2Es 15:10 not **a** them to live any longer in the land of Egypt,

ALLOWANCE (12) [ALLOW]

Ge 47:22 for the priests had a fixed **a** from Pharaoh,
47:22 and lived on the **a** that Pharaoh gave them;
1Ki 11:18 who gave him a house, assigned him an **a** of food,
2Ki 25:30 For his **a,** a regular **a** was given him by the king,
Ne 5:14 nor my brothers ate the food **a** of the governor.
5:18 yet with all this I did not demand the food **a** of
Jer 40: 5 the captain of the guard gave him an **a** of food and
52:34 For his **a,** a regular daily **a** was given him
Mt 24:45 the other slaves their **a** of food at the proper time?
Lk 12:42 to give them their **a** of food at the proper time?

ALLOWED‡ (34) [ALLOW]

Ex 1:18 "Why have you done this, and **a** the boys to live?"
Nu 16: 5 and who will be **a** to approach him;
16:10 He has **a** you to approach him,
31:15 "Have you **a** all the women to live?
Jdg 3:28 and **a** no one to cross over.
1Ch 16:21 he **a** no one to oppress them;
Est 8:11 By these letters the king **a** the Jews who were
9:13 the Jews who are in Susa be **a** tomorrow also to do
Ps 105:14 he **a** no one to oppress them;
Da 1: 9 Now God **a** Daniel to receive favor
Mt 19: 8 that Moses **a** you to divorce your wives,
20:15 Am I not **a** to do what I choose with what belongs
Mk 5:37 He **a** no one to follow him except Peter, James,
10: 4 "Moses **a** a man to write a certificate of dismissal
11: 6 and they **a** them to take it.
Ac 10:40 but God raised him on the third day and **a** him
14:16 In past generations he **a** all the nations
22:22 For he should not be **a** to live."
27: 3 and **a** him to go to his friends to be cared for.
28: 4 justice has not **a** him to live."
28:16 Paul was **a** to live by himself,
Rev 9: 5 They were **a** to torture them for five months,
13: 5 and it was **a** to exercise authority
13: 7 Also it was **a** to make war on the saints and
13:14 and by the signs that it is **a** to perform on behalf of
13:15 and it was **a** to give breath to the image of
16: 8 and it was **a** to scorch them with fire;
AdE 4: 2 because no one was **a** to enter
9:13 "Let the Jews be **a** to do the same tomorrow.
Sir 45: 5 He **a** him to hear his voice,
2Mc 2:31 but the one who recasts the narrative should be **a**
11:24 and ask that their own customs be **a** them.
3Mc 1:11 even members of their own nation were **a** to enter,
5:18 to know why the Jews had been **a** to remain alive

ALLOWS (1) [ALLOW]

2Ki 10:24 "Whoever **a** any of those to escape whom I deliver

ALLOY (1)

Isa 1:25 as with lye and remove all your **a.**

ALLURE (1) [ALLURED, ALLURING]

Hos 2:14 Therefore, I will now **a** her,

ALLURED (1) [ALLURE]

Job 36:16 He also **a** you out of distress into a broad place

ALLURING (1) [ALLURE]

Na 3: 4 gracefully **a,** mistress of sorcery,

ALLY (7) [ALLEGIANCE, ALLIANCE, ALLIED, ALLIES]

Ps 7: 4 if I have repaid my **a** with harm
Pr 18:19 An **a** offended is stronger than a city;
1Mc 10: 6 to equip them with arms, and to become his **a;**
10:16 Come now, we will make him our friend and **a."**
2Mc 8:24 With the Almighty as their **a,**
11:10 having their heavenly **a,** for the Lord had mercy
12:36 Judas called upon the Lord to show himself their **a**

ALMIGHTY‡ (97) [MIGHT]

A. *LORD ALMIGHTY (14)
B. *GOD ALMIGHTY (8)

Ge 17: 1 "I am God **A;** walk before me, and be blameless. B
28: 3 May God **A** bless you and make you fruitful B
35:11 God said to him, "I am God **A:** B
43:14 may God **A** grant you mercy before the man, B
48: 3 "God **A** appeared to me at Luz in the land B
49:25 the **A** who will bless you with blessings of heaven
Ex 6: 3 to Abraham, Isaac, and Jacob as God **A,** B
Nu 24: 4 who sees the vision of the **A,** who falls down,
24:16 who sees the vision of the **A,** who falls down,
Ru 1:20 call me Mara, for the **A** has dealt bitterly with me.
1:21 and the **A** has brought calamity upon me?"
Job 5:17 therefore do not despise the discipline of the **A.**
6: 4 For the arrows of the **A** are in me;
6:14 from a friend forsake the fear of the **A.**
8: 3 Or does the **A** pervert the right?
8: 5 you will seek God and make supplication to the **A,**
11: 7 Can you find out the limit of the **A?**
13: 3 But I would speak to the **A,**
15:25 and bid defiance to the **A,**
21:15 What is the **A,** that we should serve him?
21:20 and let them drink of the wrath of the **A.**
22: 3 Is it any pleasure to the **A** if you are righteous,
22:17 'Leave us alone,' and 'What can the **A** do to us?'
22:23 If you return to the **A,** you will be restored,
22:25 and if the **A** is your gold and your precious silver,
22:26 then you will delight yourself in the **A,**
23:16 has made my heart faint; the **A** has terrified me;
24: 1 "Why are times not kept by the **A,**
27: 2 who has taken away my right, and the **A,**
27:10 Will they take delight in the **A?**
27:11 that which is with the **A** I will not conceal.
27:13 the heritage that oppressors receive from the **A:**
29: 5 the **A** was still with me, when my children were
31: 2 and my heritage from the **A** on high?
31:35 let the **A** answer me!)
32: 8 truly it is the spirit in a mortal, the breath of the **A,**
33: 4 and the breath of the **A** gives me life.
34:10 and from the **A** that he should do wrong.
34:12 and the **A** will not pervert justice.
35:13 nor does the **A** regard it.
37:23 The **A**—we cannot find him;
40: 2 "Shall a faultfinder contend with the **A?**
Ps 68:14 the **A** scattered kings there, snow fell on Zalmon.
91: 1 who abide in the shadow of the **A,**
Isa 13: 6 it will come like destruction from the **A!**
Eze 1:24 like the thunder of the **A,** a sound of tumult like
10: 5 like the voice of God **A** when he speaks. B
Joel 1:15 and as destruction from the **A** it comes.
2Co 6:18 be my sons and daughters, says the Lord **A."** A
Rev 1: 8 who is and who was and who is to come, the **A.**
4: 8 Lord God the **A,** who was and is and is to come."
11:17 Lord God **A,** who are and who were, B
15: 3 and amazing are your deeds, Lord God the **A!**
16: 7 the **A,** your judgments are true and just!"
16:14 for battle on the great day of God the **A.**
19: 6 For the Lord our God the **A** reigns.
Rev 19:15 of the fury of the wrath of God the **A.**
21:22 for its temple is the Lord God the **A** and the Lamb.
Jdt 4:13 in Jerusalem before the sanctuary of the Lord **A.** A
8:13 You are putting the Lord **A** to the test, A
15:10 May the **A** Lord bless you forever!"
16: 5 Lord **A** has foiled them by the hand of a woman. A
16:17 The Lord **A** will take vengeance on them in A
Wis 7:25 and a pure emanation of the glory of the **A;**
Sir 42:17 which the Lord the **A** has established so that
50:14 the offering to the Most High, the **A,**
50:17 on their faces to worship their Lord, the **A,**
Bar 3: 1 O Lord **A,** God of Israel, the soul in anguish A
3: 4 O Lord **A,** God of Israel, hear now the prayer A
2Mc 1:25 you alone are just and **a** and eternal.
3:22 While they were calling upon the **A** Lord
3:30 now that the **A** Lord had appeared.
5:20 of the **A** was restored again in all its glory when
6:26 or die I shall not escape the hands of the **A.**
7:35 You have not yet escaped the judgment of the **a,**
7:38 to an end the wrath of the **A** that has justly fallen
8:11 not expecting the judgment from the **A** that was
8:18 he said, "but we trust in the **A** God,
8:24 With the **A** as their ally,
15: 8 to look for the victory that the **A** would give them.
15:32 against the holy house of the **A.**
1Es 9:46 the Lord God Most High, the God of hosts, the **A,**
Man 1: 1 O Lord **A,** God of our ancestors, A
3Mc 2: 2 holy among the holy ones, the only ruler, **a,**
2: 8 of your hands, they praised you, the **A.**
5: 7 to silence they all called upon the **A** Lord
6: 2 **A** God Most High, governing all creation
6:18 Then the most glorious, **a,**
6:28 the children of the **a** and living God of heaven,
2Es 1:15 "Thus says the Lord **A:** The quails were a sign A
1:22 Thus says the Lord **A:** When you were A
1:28 "Thus says the Lord **A:** Have I not entreated A
1:33 "Thus says the Lord **A:** Your house is desolate; A
2: 9 not listened to me, says the Lord **A."** A
2:31 for I am merciful, says the Lord **A.** A
13:23 who have works and faith toward the **A.**
16:62 and the spirit of **A** God,

ALMODAD (2)

Ge 10:26 Joktan became the father of **A,** Sheleph,
1Ch 1:20 Joktan became the father of **A,** Sheleph,

ALMON (1)

Jos 21:18 and **A** with its pasture lands—four towns.

ALMON-DIBLATHAIM (2) [BETH-DIBLATHAIM]

Nu 33:46 They set out from Dibon-gad and camped at **A.**
33:47 They set out from **A** and camped in the mountains

ALMOND (9) [ALMONDS]

Ge 30:37 Jacob took fresh rods of poplar and **a** and plane,
Ex 25:33 like **a** blossoms, each with calyx and petals,
25:33 and three cups shaped like **a** blossoms,
25:34 be four cups shaped like **a** blossoms,
37:19 like **a** blossoms, each with calyx and petals,
37:19 and three cups shaped like **a** blossoms,
37:20 like **a** blossoms, each with its calyxes
Ecc 12: 5 the **a** tree blossoms, the grasshopper drags itself
Jer 1:11 And I said, "I see a branch of an **a** tree."

ALMONDS (2) [ALMOND]

Ge 43:11 gum, resin, pistachio nuts, and **a.**
Nu 17: 8 produced blossoms, and bore ripe **a.**

ALMOST (14)

Ex 17: 4 They are **a** ready to stone me."
Jdg 19: 9 "Look, the day has worn on until it is **a** evening.
Ps 73: 2 But as for me, my feet had **a** stumbled;
119:87 They have **a** made an end of me on earth;
Lk 24:29 it is **a** evening and the day is now nearly over."
Ac 13:44 The next sabbath **a** the whole city gathered to hear
19:26 also see and hear that not only in Ephesus but in **a**
21:27 When the seven days were **a** completed,
Heb 9:22 under the law **a** everything is purified with blood,
Jdt 11:12 and their water has **a** given out,
2Mc 5: 2 And it happened that, for **a** forty days,
2Es 7:*48* for a few but for **a** all who have been created."
10:10 and, lo, **a** all go to perdition,
10:22 name by which we are called has been **a** profaned;

ALMS (24) [ALMSGIVING]

Mt 6: 2 "So whenever you give **a,**
6: 3 when you give **a,** do not let your left hand know
6: 4 so that your **a** may be done in secret;
Lk 11:41 So give for **a** those things that are within;
12:33 Sell your possessions, and give **a.**
Ac 3: 2 so that he could ask for **a** from those entering
3: 3 about to go into the temple, he asked them for **a.**
3:10 and ask for **a** at the Beautiful Gate of the temple;
10: 2 he gave **a** generously to the people
10: 4 "Your prayers and your **a** have ascended as
10:31 and your **a** have been remembered before God.
24:17 after some years I came to bring **a** to my nation
Tob 4: 7 give **a** from your possessions,
4:16 Give all your surplus as **a,**
4:16 and do not let your eye begrudge your giving of **a.**
12: 8 It is better to give **a** than to lay up gold.
12: 9 Those who give **a** will enjoy a full life,

Tob 14: 2 giving **a** and continually blessing God
14:8,9 be commanded to do what is right and to give **a,**
14:10 Because he gave **a,** Ahikar escaped the fatal trap
Sir 7:10 do not neglect to give **a.**
12: 3 in evil or to one who does not give **a.**
29: 8 and do not keep him waiting for your **a.**
35: 4 and one who gives **a** sacrifices a thank offering.

ALMSDEEDS (KJV) See ACTS OF CHARITY

ALMSGIVING (10) [ALMS]

Tob 4:10 For **a** delivers from death and keeps you
4:11 Indeed, **a,** for all who practice it,
12: 8 but better than both is **a** with righteousness.
12: 9 For **a** saves from death and purges away every sin.
14:11 So now, my children, see what **a** accomplishes,
Sir 3:30 As water extinguishes a blazing fire, so **a** atones
17:22 One's **a** is like a signet ring with the Lord,
29:12 Store up **a** in your treasury,
40:17 like a garden of blessings, and **a** endures forever.
40:24 but **a** rescues better than either.

ALMUG (3) [ALGUM]

1Ki 10:11 a great quantity of **a** wood and precious stones.
10:12 the **a** wood the king made supports for the house
10:12 no such **a** wood has come or been seen to this day.

ALOES (5)

Nu 24: 6 like **a** that the LORD has planted,
Ps 45: 8 your robes are all fragrant with myrrh and **a**
Pr 7:17 I have perfumed my bed with myrrh, **a,**
SS 4:14 myrrh and **a,** with all chief spices—
Jn 19:39 also came, bringing a mixture of myrrh and **a,**

ALOFT (5)

Dt 32:11 takes them up, and bears them **a** on its pinions,
Job 39:18 When it spreads its plumes **a,**
Eze 19:11 it towered **a** among the thick boughs;
Ob 1: 4 Though you soar **a** like the eagle,
Zec 14:10 But Jerusalem shall remain **a** on its site from

ALONE‡ (201) [LONELY]

Ge 2:18 "It is not good that the man should be **a;**
7: 1 for I have seen that you **a** are righteous before me
32:24 Jacob was left **a;** and a man wrestled with him
42:38 for his brother is dead, and he **a** is left.
44:20 he **a** is left of his mother's children,
47:26 land of the priests **a** did not become Pharaoh's.
Ex 4:26 So he let him **a.**
12:16 that **a** may be prepared by you.
14:12 'Let us **a** and let us serve the Egyptians'?
18:14 Why do you sit **a,** while all the people stand
18:18 the task is too heavy for you; you cannot do it **a.**
21: 4 be her master's and he shall go out **a.**
22:20 to any god, other than the LORD **a,** shall
24: 2 Moses **a** shall come near the LORD;
32:10 Now let me **a,** so that my wrath may burn hot
Lev 13:46 he is unclean. He shall live **a;**
Nu 11:14 I am not able to carry all this people **a,**
14:38 and Caleb son of Jephunneh **a** remained alive,
18: 1 and your sons **a** shall bear responsibility
23: 9 Here is a people living **a,** and not reckoning itself
Dt 6: 4 The LORD is our God, the LORD **a.**
6:13 and by his name **a** you shall swear.
8: 3 that one does not live by bread **a,**
9:14 Let me **a** that I may destroy them
10:15 in love on your ancestors **a** and chose you,
10:20 fear the LORD your God; him **a** you shall worship;
13: 4 your God you shall follow, him **a** you shall fear,
32:12 the LORD **a** guided him;
Jos 13:12 and in Edrei (he **a** was left of the survivors of
13:14 To the tribe of Levi **a** Moses gave no inheritance;
22:20 And he did not perish **a** for his iniquity!' "
Jdg 3:20 While he was sitting **a** in his cool roof chamber,
6:37 if there is dew on the fleece **a,**
1Sa 21: 1 "Why are you **a,** and no one with you?"
25:24 She fell at his feet and said, "Upon me **a,** my lord,
2Sa 13:32 the young men the king's sons; Amnon **a** is dead.
13:33 the king's sons were dead; for Amnon **a** is dead."
16:11 Let him **a,** and let him curse;
18:24 and when he looked up, he saw a man running **a.**
18:25 The king said, "If he is **a,**
18:26 "See, another man running **a!"**
20:21 give him up **a,** and I will withdraw from the city."
24:17 "I **a** have sinned, and I **a** have done wickedly;
1Ki 11:29 The two of them were **a** in the open country
12:20 except the tribe of Judah **a.**
12:33 in the month that he **a** had devised;
14:13 he **a** of Jeroboam's family shall come to the grave,
19:10 I **a** am left, and they are seeking my life,
19:14 I **a** am left, and they are seeking my life,
2Ki 4:27 But the man of God said, "Let her **a,**
17:18 none was left but the tribe of Judah **a.**
19:15 you **a,** of all the kingdoms of the earth;
19:19 that you, O LORD, are God **a."**
23:18 So they let his bones **a,**
1Ch 29: 1 "My son Solomon, whom **a** God has chosen,
Ezr 4: 3 but we **a** will build to the LORD,
6: 7 let the work on this house of God **a;**
Ne 9: 6 And Ezra said: "You are the LORD, you **a;**
Est 3: 6 to lay hands on Mordecai **a.**
Job 1:15 I **a** have escaped to tell you."
Job 1:16 I **a** have escaped to tell you."
1:17 I **a** have escaped to tell you."
1:19 I **a** have escaped to tell you."
7:16 Let me **a,** for my days are a breath.
7:19 let me **a** until I swallow my spittle?
9: 8 who **a** stretched out the heavens and trampled
10:20 Let me **a,** that I may find
15:19 to whom **a** the land was given,
21:14 They say to God, 'Leave us **a!**
22:17 They said to God, 'Leave us **a,'**
23:13 But he stands **a** and who can dissuade him?
31:17 or have eaten my morsel **a,** and the orphan has
Ps 4: 8 for you **a,** O LORD, make me lie down in safety.
51: 4 Against you, you **a,** have I sinned,
62: 1 For God **a** my soul waits in silence;
62: 2 He **a** is my rock and my salvation, my fortress;
62: 5 For God **a** my soul waits in silence,
62: 6 He **a** is my rock and my salvation, my fortress;
71:16 I will praise your righteousness, yours **a.**
72:18 the God of Israel, who **a** does wondrous things.
83:18 Let them know that you **a,**
86:10 and do wondrous things; you **a** are God.
136: 4 who **a** does great wonders,
141:10 into their own nets, while I **a** escape.
148:13 for his name **a** is exalted;
Pr 5:17 Let them be for yourself **a,**
9:12 if you scoff, you **a** will bear it.
16:33 but the decision is the LORD's **a.**
18: 1 The one who lives **a** is self-indulgent,
Ecc 4:10 but woe to one who is **a** and falls and does
4:11 but how can one keep warm **a?**
7:29 this **a** I found, that God made human beings
Isa 2:11 and the LORD **a** will be exalted in that day.
2:17 and the LORD **a** will be exalted on that day.
5: 8 and you are left to live **a** in the midst of the land!
26:13 but we acknowledge your name **a.**
37:16 you **a,** of all the kingdoms of the earth;
37:20 of the earth may know that you **a** are the LORD."
44:24 who **a** stretched out the heavens,
45:14 saying, "God is with you **a,** and there is no other;
49:21 I was left all **a**—where then have these come from?
63: 3 "I have trodden the wine press **a,**
Jer 15:17 under the weight of your hand I sat **a,**
49:31 that has no gates or bars, that lives **a.**
La 3: 3 against me **a** he turns his hand,
3:28 to sit **a** in silence when the Lord has imposed it,
Eze 9: 8 While they were killing, and I was left **a,**
14:16 they **a** would be saved, but the land would
14:18 but they **a** would be saved.
40:46 these are the descendants of Zadok, who **a** among
Da 10: 7 I, Daniel, **a** saw the vision;
10: 8 So I was left **a** to see this great vision.
Hos 4:17 Ephraim is joined to idols—let him **a.**
8: 9 up to Assyria, a wild ass wandering **a;**
Mic 7:14 lives **a** in a forest in the midst of a garden land;
Mt 4: 4 "It is written, 'One does not live by bread **a,**
14:23 When evening came, he was there **a,**
15:14 Let them **a;** they are blind guides of the blind.
17: 8 they saw no one except Jesus himself **a.**
18:15 and point out the fault when the two of you are **a.**
Mk 2: 7 Who can forgive sins but God **a?"**
4:10 When he was **a,** those who were around him along
6:47 and he was **a** on the land.
10:18 No one is good but God **a.**
14: 6 Jesus said, "Let her **a;** why do you trouble her?
Lk 4: 4 "It is written, 'One does not live by bread **a.'** "
4:34 "Let us **a!** What have you to do
5:21 Who can forgive sins but God **a?"**
9:18 Once when Jesus was praying **a,**
9:36 When the voice had spoken, Jesus was found **a.**
13: 8 He replied, 'Sir, let it **a** for one more year,
18:19 No one is good but God **a.**
Jn 5:44 the glory that comes from the one who **a** is God?
6:22 but that his disciples had gone away **a.**
8: 9 ⟦and Jesus was left **a** with the woman standing⟧
8:16 for it is not I **a** who judge,
8:29 he has not left me **a,**
12: 7 Jesus said, "Leave her **a.**
16:32 each one to his home, and you will leave me **a.**
16:32 Yet I am not **a** because the Father is with me.
Ac 5:38 keep away from these men and let them **a;**
Ro 4:23 were written not for his sake **a,**
11: 3 I **a** am left, and they are seeking my life."
Php 4:15 the matter of giving and receiving, except you **a.**
1Th 3: 1 we decided to be left **a** in Athens;
1Ti 5: 5 left **a,** has set her hope on God and continues
6:16 It is he **a** who has immortality and dwells
Jas 2:24 a person is justified by works and not by faith **a.**
Rev 15: 4 For you **a** are holy. All nations will come
Tob 1: 6 But I **a** went often to Jerusalem for the festivals,
8: 6 'It is not good that the man should be **a;**
Jdt 3: 8 that all nations should worship Nebuchadnezzar **a,**
5: 4 And why have they **a,** of all who live in the west,
9:14 the people of Israel but you **a!"**
11: 8 throughout the whole world that you **a** are the best
13: 2 But Judith was left **a** in the tent,
AdE 4:13 that you **a** among all the Jews will escape alive.
13: 5 We understand that this people, and it **a,**
14: 3 help me, who am **a** and have no helper but you,
14:14 who am **a** and have no helper but you, O Lord.
Wis 10: 1 when he **a** had been created;
17:21 while over those people a heavy night was spread,
Sir 11: 2 or loathe anyone because of appearance **a.**
18: 2 the Lord **a** is just.
24: 5 **A** I compassed the vault of heaven and traversed
24:34 Observe that I have not labored for myself **a,**
33:18 Consider that I have not labored for myself **a,**
Sir 45:25 so the heritage of Aaron is for his descendants **a.**
46: 8 And these two **a** were spared out
Aza 1:22 Let them know that you **a** are the Lord God,
Sus 1:14 for a time when they could find her **a.**
1:36 "While we were walking in the garden **a,**
Bel 1:14 the whole temple in the presence of the king **a.**
1Mc 6:25 It is not against us **a**
13: 4 for the sake of Israel, and I **a** am left.
2Mc 1:24 you **a** are king and are kind,
1:25 you **a** are bountiful, you **a** are just and almighty
6:13 of great kindness not to let the impious **a** for long,
7:37 and plagues to make you confess that he **a** is God,
8:35 took off his splendid uniform and made his way **a**
15:39 harmful to drink wine **a,** or, again, to drink water **a,**
1Es 5:71 for we **a** will build it for the Lord of Israel,
8:25 Then Ezra the scribe said, "Blessed be the Lord **a,**
2Es 3:14 and to him **a** you revealed the end of the times,
6: 6 and they were made through me **a** and not
6: 6 just as the end shall come through me **a** and not
7:*44* and to you **a** I have shown these things."
7:*118* [48] you who sinned, the fall was not yours **a,**
8: 7 For you **a** exist, and we are a work of your hands,
9:41 She said to me, "Let me **a,** my lord,
10:11 or you who are grieving for one **a?**
12:36 And you **a** were worthy to learn this secret of
12:42 For of all the prophets you **a** are left to us,
13:53 And you **a** have been enlightened about this,
4Mc 7:18 these **a** are able to control the passions of
9:18 that children of the Hebrews **a** are invincible
15:17 who **a** gave birth to such complete devotion!
16:10 so many and beautiful children am a widow and **a,**

ALONG‡ (194) [ALONGSIDE]

Ge 6:13 now I am going to destroy them **a** with the earth.
21:10 for the son of this slave woman shall not inherit **a**
21:14 putting it on her shoulder, **a** with the child,
24:59 and her nurse **a** with Abraham's servant
45:24 "Do not quarrel **a** the way."
49:17 a viper **a** the path, that bites the horse's heels so
Ex 7:24 the Egyptians had to dig **a** the Nile for water
13:21 to lead them **a** the way,
18: 3 **a** with her two sons. The name of the one
38:18 It was twenty cubits long and, **a** the width of it,
Lev 14:11 **a** with these things, before the LORD,
14:12 **a** with the log of oil,
14:31 other for a burnt offering, **a** with a grain offering;
14:51 **a** with the living bird, and dip them in the blood of
23:18 they shall be a burnt offering to the LORD, **a**
Nu 1:47 not numbered by their ancestral tribe **a** with them.
11:17 and they shall bear the burden of the people **a**
13:29 the Canaanites live by the sea, and **a** the Jordan."
16: 1 **a** with Dathan and Abiram sons of Eliab,
16:32 **a** with their households—
20:17 we will go **a** the King's Highway,
21:15 and lie **a** the border of Moab."
26:10 up **a** with Korah, when that company died,
31: 6 **a** with Phinehas son of Eleazar the priest,
34: 3 from the wilderness of Zin **a** the side of Edom.
Dt 2: 8 When we had headed out **a** the route of
2:27 I will travel only **a** the road;
2:33 **a** with his offspring and all his people.
3: 2 **a** with his people and his land.
11: 6 **a** with their households, their tents,
23:14 the LORD your God travels **a** with your camp,
Jos 2:22 The pursuers had searched all **a** the way
6: 2 **a** with its king and soldiers.
6:23 **a** with her father, her mother, her brothers,
9: 1 and in the lowland all **a** the coast of the Great Sea
13:22 **A** with the rest of those they put to death,
15: 3 the ascent of Akrabbim, passes **a** to Zin, and goes
15: 3 and goes up south of Kadesh-barnea, **a** by Hezron,
15: 4 passes **a** to Azmon, goes out by the Wadi
15: 6 and passes **a** north of Beth-arabah;
15: 7 boundary passes **a** to the waters of En-shemesh,
15:10 passes **a** to the northern slope of Mount Jearim
15:10 down to Beth-shemesh, and passes **a** by Timnah;
15:11 and passes **a** to Mount Baalah,
16: 2 it passes **a** to Ataroth, the territory of the Archites;
16: 6 and passes **a** beyond it on the east to Janoah,
17: 4 to give us an inheritance **a** with our male kin."
17: 6 of Manasseh received an inheritance **a**
17: 7 the boundary goes **a** southward to the inhabitants
17: 9 the boundary of Manasseh goes **a** the north side of
17:14 whom all **a** the LORD has blessed?"
18:13 the boundary passes **a** southward in the direction
19:13 from there it passes **a** on the east toward
21: 2 **a** with their pasture lands for our livestock."
21:11 **a** with the pasture lands around it.
23: 4 **a** with all the nations that I have already cut off,
24:17 He protected us **a** all the way that we went,
Jdg 7:12 the Amalekites and all the people of the east lay **a**
9:25 They robbed all who passed by them **a** that way;
11:26 and in all the towns that are **a** the Arnon,
15: 1 Samson went to visit his wife, bringing **a** a kid.
18:20 and the idol, and went **a** with the people.
19:19 and the woman and the young man **a** with us.
20:31 the troops, **a** the main roads, one of which goes up
Ru 4:11 **a** with the elders, said, "We are witnesses.
1Sa 1:24 **a** with a three-year-old bull, an ephah of flour,
6:12 in the direction of Beth-shemesh **a** one highway,
10: 6 be in a prophetic frenzy **a** with them and be turned
10:10 and he fell into a prophetic frenzy **a** with them.
14: 3 **a** with Ahijah son of Ahitub,
18:27 **a** with his men, and killed one hundred of
28:19 Moreover the LORD will give Israel **a** with you
2Sa 2: 2 So David went up there, **a** with his two wives,

2Sa 5:11 to David, **a** with cedar trees, and carpenters
16:13 while Shimei went **a** on the hillside opposite him
20: 7 **a** with the Cherethites, the Pelethites,
1Ki 11: 1 King Solomon loved many foreign women **a** with
20: 1 **a** with horses and chariots.
20:38 and waited for the king **a** the road,
2Ki 5: 5 and I will send **a** a letter to the king of Israel."
10: 5 **a** with the elders and the guardians,
15:25 the citadel of the palace **a** with Argob and Arieh;
23:15 he pulled down that altar **a** with the high place.
25:25 down Gedaliah so that he died, **a** with the Judeans
1Ch 4:33 **a** with all their villages that were
7: 4 and **a** with them, by their generations,
7:29 also **a** the borders of the Manassites,
14: 1 **a** with cedar logs, and masons and carpenters
24: 3 **A** with Zadok of the sons of Eleazar,
2Ch 12:11 the guard would come **a** bearing them,
21:17 **a** with his sons and his wives,
34:12 **a** with Zechariah and Meshullam,
36:10 **a** with the precious vessels of the house of
Ezr 3: 9 Binnui and Hodaviah **a** with the sons of Henadad,
8:31 from the hand of the enemy and from ambushes **a**
Ne 7: 2 **a** with Hananiah the commander of the citadel—
Est 9:29 of Abihail, **a** with the Jew Mordecai,
Job 42:15 and their father gave them an inheritance **a**
Ps 8: 8 whatever passes **a** the paths of the seas.
45:15 With joy and gladness they are led **a** as they enter
80:12 so that all who pass **a** the way pluck its fruit?
140: 5 **a** the road they have set snares for me.
Pr 7: 8 passing **a** the street near her corner,
8:20 in the way of righteousness, **a** the paths of justice,
27:22 in a mortar with a pestle **a** with crushed grain,
Ecc 12: 5 the grasshopper drags itself **a** and desire fails;
Isa 3:16 mincing **a** as they go, tinkling with their feet;
5:18 you who drag iniquity **a** with cords of falsehood,
5:18 who drag sin **a** as with cart ropes,
49: 9 They shall feed **a** the ways,
59:10 We grope like the blind **a** a wall,
Jer 40: 1 in fetters **a** with all the captives of Jerusalem
41: 8 and did not kill them **a** with their companions.
La 2:15 All who pass **a** the way clap their hands at you;
Eze 1:20 they went, and the wheels rose **a** with them;
1:21 the wheels rose **a** with them;
16:53 and I will restore your own fortunes **a** with theirs,
25:10 I will give it **a** with Ammon to the people of
31:14 **a** with all mortals, with those who go down
31:17 to those killed by the sword, **a** with its allies,
40:18 The pavement ran **a** the side of the gates,
42:12 from the east, **a** the matching wall.
47: 6 Then he led me back **a** the bank of the river.
47:18 **a** the Jordan between Gilead and the land
47:19 from there **a** the Wadi of Egypt to the Great Sea.
48:28 from there **a** the Wadi of Egypt to the Great Sea.
Hos 5: 7 new moon shall devour them **a** with their fields.
Hab 3: 6 **a** his ancient pathways the everlasting hills sank
Zec 7: 7 **a** with the towns around it,
Mt 3: 5 and all the region **a** the Jordan,
9: 9 As Jesus was walking **a**, he saw
12:45 Then it goes and brings **a**
13:29 the weeds you would uproot the wheat **a**
15:29 he passed **a** the Sea of Galilee,
18:16 take one or two others **a** with you,
22:16 **a** with the Herodians, saying, "Teacher,
27:41 **a** with the scribes and elders, were mocking him,
Mk 1:16 As Jesus passed **a** the Sea of Galilee,
2:14 As he was walking **a**, he saw Levi son
4:10 around him **a** with the twelve asked him about
15:31 **a** with the scribes, were also mocking him
Lk 9:57 As they were going **a** the road,
19:36 As he rode **a**, people kept spreading their cloaks
24:17 with each other while you walk **a**?"
Jn 4:53 he himself believed, **a** with his whole household.
9: 1 As he walked **a**, he saw a man blind from birth.
Ac 7:43 No; you took **a** the tent of Moloch,
8:36 As they were going **a** the road,
9: 3 as he was going **a** and approaching Damascus,
12:10 and they went outside and walked **a** a lane,
15:25 **a** with our beloved Barnabas and Paul,
21:16 Some of the disciples from Caesarea also came **a**
25: 3 in fact, planning an ambush to kill him **a** the way.
26:13 when at midday **a** the road,
27: 2 that was about to set sail to the ports **a** the coast
1Co 11:32 that we may not be condemned **a** with the world.
2Co 12:19 Have you been thinking all **a**
Gal 2: 1 to Jerusalem with Barnabas, taking Titus **a**
2Ti 2:22 **a** with those who call on the Lord from
Jas 2:22 You see that faith was active **a** with his works,
Jude 1:12 They are waterless clouds carried **a** by the winds;
Tob 6: 2 the dog came out with him and went **a** with them.
6: 2 So they both journeyed **a**,
11: 4 And the dog went **a** behind them.
11:16 walking **a** in full vigor and
Jdt 1: 6 of the hill country and all those who lived **a**
1: 7 and all who lived **a** the seacoast,
2:17 He took **a** a vast number of camels and donkeys
2:20 **A** with them went a mixed crowd like a swarm
2:24 the fortified towns **a** the brook Abron,
2:28 upon all the people who lived **a** the seacoast,
6: 8 You will not die until you perish **a** with them.
9: 3 and you struck down slaves **a** with princes,
AdE 9:29 of Aminadab **a** with Mordecai the Jew wrote
Wis 7:11 All good things came to me **a** with her,
10:17 she guided them **a** a marvelous way,
Sir 32: 2 so that you may be merry **a** with them and receive
LtJ 6:42 sit **a** the passageways, burning bran for incense.
1Mc 6:33 by a forced march **a** the road to Beth-zechariah,
11: 4 for they had piled them in heaps **a** his route.
1Mc 12:50 that Jonathan had been seized and had perished **a**
13:20 and his army kept marching **a** opposite him
15:41 so that they might go out and make raids **a**
2Mc 7:29 so that in God's mercy I may get you back again **a**
8:20 when eight thousand Jews fought **a**
9: 7 that he fell out of his chariot as it was rushing **a**,
9:25 how the princes **a** the borders and the neighbors
3Mc 4: 7 and in public view they were violently dragged **a**
5:23 began to move them **a** in the great colonnade.
5:47 rushed out in full force **a** with the animals,
2Es 3:22 in the hearts of the people **a** with the evil root;
16:32 because no sheep will go **a** them.
4Mc 4:25 were thrown headlong from heights **a**
8: 3 were brought before him **a** with their aged mother.

ALONGSIDE (10) [ALONG]

Ge 25:18 he settled down **a** of all his people.
33:12 "Let us journey on our way, and I will go **a** you."
Ex 20:23 You shall not make gods of silver **a** me,
2Ch 8:14 for their offices of praise and ministry **a** the priests
Eze 45: 6 **A** the portion set apart as
45: 7 **a** the holy district and the holding of the city,
48:13 **A** the territory of the priests,
48:18 The remainder of the length **a** the holy portion
48:18 and it shall be **a** the holy portion.
1Mc 13:52 the fortifications of the temple hill **a** the citadel,

ALOOF (4)

2Sa 18:13 then you yourself would have stood **a.**"
Job 30:10 They abhor me, they keep **a** from me;
Ps 38:11 and companions stand **a** from my affliction,
Sir 13:10 do not stand **a**, or you will be forgotten.

ALOUD‡ (55) [LOUD]

Ge 29:11 Then Jacob kissed Rachel, and wept **a.**
Lev 5: 4 Or when any of you utter **a** a rash oath for a bad or
Jdg 9: 7 and cried **a** and said to them, "Listen to me,
Ru 1: 9 Then she kissed them, and they wept **a.**
1:14 Then they wept **a** again.
1Sa 11: 4 and all the people wept **a.**
2Sa 13:19 and went away, crying **a** as she went.
15:23 whole country wept **a** as all the people passed by;
1Ki 18:27 At noon Elijah mocked them, saying, "Cry **a!**
18:28 Then they cried **a** and, as was their custom,
2Ki 22:10 Shaphan then read it **a** to the king.
2Ch 34:18 Shaphan then read it **a** to the king.
Ezr 3:12 though many shouted **a** for joy,
Job 2:12 and they raised their voices and wept **a;**
19: 7 I am not answered; I call **a**, but there is no justice.
Ps 3: 4 I cry **a** to the LORD,
26: 7 singing **a** a song of thanksgiving,
27: 7 Hear, O LORD, when I cry **a**,
51:14 and my tongue will sing **a** of your deliverance.
59:16 I will sing **a** of your steadfast love in the morning.
66:17 I cried **a** to him, and he was extolled
77: 1 I cry **a** to God, **a** to God, that he may hear me.
81: 1 Sing **a** to God our strength;
145: 7 and shall sing **a** of your righteousness.
Isa 10:30 Cry **a**, O daughter Gallim!
12: 6 Shout **a** and sing for joy, O royal Zion,
13: 2 On a bare hill raise a signal, cry **a** to them;
42:13 he cries out, he shouts **a**, he shows himself mighty
Jer 4: 5 shout **a** and say, "Gather together,
31: 7 Sing **a** with gladness for Jacob,
31:12 They shall come and sing **a** on the height of Zion,
La 2:18 Cry **a** to the Lord!
Eze 24:17 Sigh, but not **a;** make no mourning for the dead.
27:30 and wail **a** over you, and cry bitterly.
Da 3: 4 the herald proclaimed **a**, "You are commanded,
4:14 He cried **a** and said: 'Cut down the
5: 7 The king cried **a** to bring in the enchanters,
Mic 4: 9 Now why do you cry **a?**
Zep 1:14 of the LORD is bitter, the warrior cries **a** there.
3:14 Sing **a**, O daughter Zion; shout, O Israel!
Zec 9: 9 Shout **a**, O daughter Jerusalem!
Mt 12:19 He will not wrangle or cry **a**,
Jn 12:44 Then Jesus cried **a:** "Whoever believes in me
Ac 15:21 for he has been read **a** every sabbath in
Rev 1: 3 the one who reads **a** the words of the prophecy,
18:15 in fear of her torment, weeping and mourning **a**,
Bar 1:14 And you shall read **a** this scroll
Aza 1: 2 Then Azariah stood still in the fire and prayed **a:**
1Mc 3:50 and they cried **a** to Heaven,
5:33 who sounded their trumpets and cried **a** in prayer.
2Mc 6:30 to die under the blows, he groaned **a** and said:
8:23 to read **a** from the holy book, and gave
1Es 9:41 He read **a** in the open square before the gate of
2Es 6:23 the trumpet shall sound **a**,

ALPHA (3)

Rev 1: 8 "I am the **A** and the Omega," says the Lord God,
21: 6 I am the **A** and the Omega,
22:13 I am the **A** and the Omega, the first and the last,

ALPHAEUS (5)

Mt 10: 3 James son of **A**, and Thaddaeus;
Mk 2:14 he saw Levi son of **A** sitting at the tax booth,
3:18 and Thomas, and James son of **A**, and Thaddaeus,
Lk 6:15 and Thomas, and James son of **A**, and Simon,
Ac 1:13 Bartholomew and Matthew, James son of **A**,

ALREADY‡ (105)

Ge 27:37 "I have **a** made him your lord,
Ex 1: 5 Joseph was **a** in Egypt.
Ex 36: 7 what they had **a** brought was more than enough
Lev 10:16 and—it had **a** been burned!
Nu 16:47 where the plague had **a** begun among the people.
Dt 22:23 a virgin **a** engaged to be married,
29:18 whose heart is **a** turning away from
31:27 If you **a** have been so rebellious toward
Jos 23: 4 along with all the nations that I have **a** cut off,
Jdg 8: 6 "Do you **a** have in your possession the hands
8:15 'Do you **a** have in your possession the hands
1Sa 17:12 of Saul the man was **a** old and advanced in years.
1Ki 20:19 But these had **a** come out of the city:
2Ki 7:13 of Israel that have perished **a;**
2Ch 20: 2 **a** they are at Hazazon-tamar" (that is, En-gedi).
28:13 For our guilt is **a** great,
Ecc 1:10 It has **a** been, in the ages before us.
2:12 Only what has **a** been done.
3:15 That which is, **a** has been; that which is to be, **a** is;
4: 2 And I thought the dead, who have **a** died,
6:10 Whatever has come to be has **a** been named,
9: 6 and their hate and their envy have **a** perished;
Isa 48: 7 so that you could not say, "I **a** knew them."
56: 8 to them besides those **a** gathered.
Mal 2: 2 indeed I have **a** cursed them,
Mt 5:28 at a woman with lust has **a** committed adultery
17:12 but I tell you that Elijah has **a** come,
Mk 4:37 so that the boat was **a** being swamped.
11:11 around at everything, as it was **a** late,
13:23 But be alert; I have **a** told you everything.
15:44 Then Pilate wondered if he were **a** dead;
16: 4 which was very large, had **a** been rolled back.
Lk 11: 7 the door has **a** been locked,
12:49 and how I wish it were **a** kindled!
21:30 for yourselves and know that summer is **a** near.
22:12 a large room upstairs, **a** furnished.
Jn 3:18 but those who do not believe are condemned **a**,
4:36 The reaper is **a** receiving wages
9:22 for the Jews had **a** agreed
9:27 He answered them, "I have told you **a**,
11:17 that Lazarus had **a** been in the tomb four days.
11:39 of the dead man, said to him, "Lord, **a** there is
13: 2 The devil had **a** put it into the heart of Judas son
15: 3 You have **a** been cleansed by the word
19:33 they came to Jesus and saw that he was **a** dead,
Ac 4: 3 in custody until the next day, for it was **a** evening.
13:24 before his coming John had **a** proclaimed
27: 9 because even the Fast had **a** gone by,
Ro 3: 9 No, not at all; for we have **a** charged that all,
4:19 which was **a** as good as dead (for he was about
15:20 not where Christ has **a** been named,
1Co 4: 8 **A** you have all you want!
4: 8 **A** you have become rich!
5: 3 and as if present I have **a** pronounced judgment
6: 7 at all with one another is **a** a defeat for you.
7:18 Was anyone at the time of his call **a** circumcised?
2Co 1:14 as you have **a** understood us in part—
8: 6 as he had **a** made a beginning,
10:16 of work **a** done in someone else's sphere
Gal 1:17 up to Jerusalem to those who were **a** apostles
Eph 3: 2 for surely you have **a** heard of the commission
Php 3:12 that I have **a** obtained this or have **a** reached
1Th 2: 2 but though we had **a** suffered
4: 6 just as we have **a** told you beforehand
2Th 2: 2 to the effect that the day of the Lord is **a** here.
2: 7 For the mystery of lawlessness is **a** at work,
1Ti 5:15 For some have **a** turned away to follow Satan.
2Ti 2:18 that the resurrection has **a** taken place.
4: 6 As for me, I am **a** being poured out as a libation,
Heb 4: 7 in the words **a** quoted, "Today,
1Pe 4: 3 You have **a** spent enough time in doing what
2Pe 1:12 though you know them **a** and are established in
1Jn 2: 8 and the true light is **a** shining.
4: 3 and now it is **a** in the world.
Tob 2: 8 He has **a** been hunted down to be put to death
3: 8 you have **a** been married to seven husbands
3:15 **A** seven husbands of mine have died.
6:10 and **a** was approaching Ecbatana,
6:14 that she **a** has been married to seven husbands and
10: 7 I have **a** explained to you how I left him."
12:11 **A** I have declared it to you when I said,
Wis 18: 9 **a** they were singing the praises of the ancestors.
18:23 the dead had **a** fallen on one another in heaps,
19:16 with terrible sufferings those who had **a** shared
1Mc 12: 7 **A** in time past a letter was sent to
2Mc 2:32 without adding any more to what has **a** been said;
4:39 many of the gold vessels had **a** been stolen.
4:45 But Menelaus, **a** as good as beaten,
15:20 and the enemy was **a** close at hand
3Mc 3:10 And **a** some of their neighbors and friends
4:20 and the pens they used for writing had **a** given out.
5:15 that the hour of the banquet was **a** slipping by,
6: 5 who had **a** gained control of the whole world by
2Es 2:13 kingdom is **a** prepared for you; be on the watch!
4:11 And how can one who is **a** worn out by
5:55 that **a** is aging and passing the strength of youth."
8:63 you have **a** shown me a great number of the signs
12: 3 When I looked again, they were **a** vanishing.
14:11 and nine of its parts have **a** passed,
14:18 that you saw in the vision is **a** hurrying to come."
15:27 **A** calamities have come upon the whole earth,
4Mc 9:21 the ligaments joining his bones were **a** severed,
12: 2 for this child when he saw that he was **a** in fetters.

ALSO (1224) See Index of Articles Etc.

ALTAR‡ (432) [ALTARS]

Ge 8:20 Then Noah built an **a** to the LORD,

Ge 8:20 and offered burnt offerings on the **a**.
12: 7 So he built there an **a** to the LORD,
12: 8 and there he built an **a** to the LORD and invoked
13: 4 to the place where he had made an **a** at the first;
13:18 and there he built an **a** to the LORD.
22: 9 Abraham built an **a** there and laid the wood
22: 9 He bound his son Isaac, and laid him on the **a**,
26:25 So he built an **a** there,
33:20 an **a** and called it El-Elohe-Israel.
35: 1 Make an **a** there to the God who appeared to you
35: 3 an **a** there to the God who answered me in the day
35: 7 there he built an **a** and called the place El-bethel,
Ex 17:15 And Moses built an **a** and called it,
20:24 You need make for me only an **a** of earth
20:25 But if you make for me an **a** of stone,
20:26 You shall not go up by steps to my **a**,
21:14 you shall take the killer from my **a** for execution.
24: 4 and built an **a** at the foot of the mountain,
24: 6 and half of the blood he dashed against the **a**.
27: 1 You shall make the **a** of acacia wood,
27: 1 **a** shall be square, and it shall be three cubits high.
27: 5 of the **a** so that the net shall extend halfway down
27: 5 so that the net shall extend halfway down the **a**.
27: 6 You shall make poles for the **a**,
27: 7 so that the poles shall be on the two sides of the **a**
28:43 they come near the **a** to minister in the holy place;
29:12 and put it on the horns of the **a** with your finger,
29:12 the blood you shall pour out at the base of the **a**.
29:13 and turn them into smoke on the **a**.
29:16 and dash it against all sides of the **a**.
29:18 and turn the whole ram into smoke on the **a**;
29:20 dash the rest of the blood against all sides of the **a**.
29:21 you shall take some of the blood that is on the **a**,
29:25 the **a** on top of the burnt offering of pleasing odor
29:36 Also you shall offer a sin offering for the **a**,
29:37 Seven days you shall make atonement for the **a**,
29:37 and consecrate it, and the **a** shall be most holy;
29:37 whatever touches the **a** shall become holy.
29:38 Now this is what you shall offer on the **a**:
29:44 I will consecrate the tent of meeting and the **a**;
30: 1 You shall make an **a** on which to offer incense;
30:18 of meeting and the **a**, and you shall put water in it;
30:20 or when they come near the **a** to minister,
30:27 and the lampstand and its utensils, and the **a**
30:28 and the **a** of burnt offering with all its utensils,
31: 8 the pure lampstand with all its utensils, and the **a**
31: 9 and the **a** of burnt offering with all its utensils,
32: 5 When Aaron saw this, he built an **a** before it;
35:15 and the **a** of incense, with its poles,
35:16 the **a** of burnt offering, with its grating
37:25 He made the **a** of incense of acacia wood,
38: 1 the **a** of burnt offering also of acacia wood;
38: 3 He made all the utensils of the **a**, the pots,
38: 4 He made for the **a** a grating, a network of bronze,
38: 7 through the rings on the sides of the **a**, to carry it
38:30 the bronze **a** and the bronze grating for it and all
the utensils of the **a**,
39:38 the golden **a**, the anointing oil and
39:39 the bronze **a**, and its grating of bronze, its poles,
40: 5 You shall put the golden **a** for incense before
40: 6 the **a** of burnt offering before the entrance of
40: 7 the basin between the tent of meeting and the **a**,
40:10 You shall also anoint the **a** of burnt offering
40:10 and all its utensils, and consecrate the **a**, so that
40:10 so that the **a** shall be most holy.
40:26 He put the golden **a** in the tent of meeting before
40:29 He set the **a** of burnt offering at the entrance of
40:30 the basin between the tent of meeting and the **a**,
40:32 and when they approached the **a**, they washed;
40:33 up the court around the tabernacle and the **a**,
Lev 1: 5 the **a** that is at the entrance of the tent of meeting.
1: 7 The sons of the priest Aaron shall put fire on the **a**
1: 8 on the wood that is on the fire on the **a**;
1: 9 the priest shall turn the whole into smoke on the **a**
1:11 It shall be slaughtered on the north side of the **a**
1:11 against all sides of the **a**.
1:12 on the wood that is on the fire on the **a**;
1:13 the whole and turn it into smoke on the **a**;
1:15 priest shall bring it to the **a** and wring off its head,
1:15 and turn it into smoke on the **a**;
1:15 be drained out against the side of the **a**.
1:16 and throw it at the east side of the **a**,
1:17 Then the priest shall turn it into smoke on the **a**,
2: 2 on the **a**, an offering by fire of pleasing odor to
2: 8 he shall take it to the **a**.
2: 9 and turn this into smoke on the **a**,
2:12 not be offered on the **a** for a pleasing odor.
3: 2 the blood against all sides of the **a**.
3: 5 Aaron's sons shall turn these into smoke on the **a**,
3: 8 against all sides of the **a**.
3:11 on the **a** as a food offering by fire to the LORD.
3:13 against all sides of the **a**.
3:16 the **a** as a food offering by fire for a pleasing odor.
4: 7 the blood on the horns of the **a** of fragrant incense
4: 7 of the bull he shall pour out at the base of the **a**
4:10 The priest shall turn them into smoke upon the **a**
4:18 on the horns of the **a** that is before the LORD in
4:18 of the **a** of burnt offering that is at the entrance of
4:19 and turn it into smoke on the **a**.
4:25 and put it on the horns of the **a** of burnt offering,
4:25 of its blood at the base of the **a** of burnt offering.
4:26 All its fat he shall turn into smoke on the **a**,
4:30 and put it on the horns of the **a** of burnt offering,
4:30 the rest of its blood at the base of the **a**.
4:31 and the priest shall turn it into smoke on the **a** for
4:34 and put it on the horns of the **a** of burnt offering,
4:34 pour out the rest of its blood at the base of the **a**.
Lev 4:35 and the priest shall turn it into smoke on the **a**,
5: 9 the sin offering on the side of the **a**, while the rest
5: 9 the blood shall be drained out at the base of the **a**;
5:12 and turn this into smoke on the **a**,
6: 9 the hearth upon the **a** all night until the morning,
6: 9 while the fire on the **a** shall be kept burning.
6:10 the fire has reduced the burnt offering on the **a**,
6:10 and place them beside the **a**.
6:12 The fire on the **a** shall be kept burning;
6:13 A perpetual fire shall be kept burning on the **a**;
6:14 before the LORD, in front of the **a**.
6:15 on the **a** as a pleasing odor to the LORD.
7: 2 its blood shall be dashed against all sides of the **a**.
7: 5 The priest shall turn them into smoke on the **a** as
7:31 The priest shall turn the fat into smoke on the **a**,
8:11 He sprinkled some of it on the **a** seven times,
8:11 and anointed the **a** and all its utensils,
8:15 on each of the horns of the **a**, purifying the **a**;
8:15 then he poured out the blood at the base of the **a**.
8:16 and turned them into smoke on the **a**.
8:19 Moses dashed the blood against all sides of the **a**.
8:21 Moses turned into smoke the whole ram on the **a**;
8:24 the rest of the blood against all sides of the **a**.
8:28 into smoke on the **a** with the burnt offering.
8:30 of the blood that was on the **a** and sprinkled them
9: 7 "Draw near to the **a** and sacrifice your sin offering
9: 8 Aaron drew near to the **a**,
9: 9 in the blood and put it on the horns of the **a**;
9: 9 of the blood he poured out at the base of the **a**.
9:10 the sin offering he turned into smoke on the **a**, as
9:12 and he dashed it against all sides of the **a**.
9:13 which he turned into smoke on the **a**.
9:14 turned them into smoke on the **a**.
9:17 he turned it into smoke on the **a**,
9:18 which he dashed against all sides of the **a**,
9:20 and the fat was turned into smoke on the **a**;
9:24 the burnt offering and the fat on the **a**;
10:12 and eat it unleavened beside the **a**,
14:20 the burnt offering and the grain offering on the **a**.
16:12 a censer full of coals of fire from the **a** before
16:18 Then he shall go out to the **a** that is before
16:18 and put it on each of the horns of the **a**.
16:20 the holy place and the tent of meeting and the **a**,
16:25 the sin offering he shall turn into smoke on the **a**.
16:33 for the tent of meeting and for the **a**,
17: 6 The priest shall dash the blood against the **a** of
17:11 for making atonement for your lives on the **a**;
21:23 near the curtain or approach the **a**, because he has
22:22 or put any of them on the **a** as offerings by fire to
Nu 3:26 the court that is around the tabernacle and the **a**,
4:11 Over the golden **a** they shall spread a blue cloth,
4:13 They shall take away the ashes from the **a**,
4:14 on it all the utensils of the **a**, which are used for
4:14 and the basins, all the utensils of the **a**;
4:26 and the **a**, and their cords, and all the equipment
5:25 before the LORD and bring it to the **a**;
5:26 and turn it into smoke on the **a**,
7: 1 and consecrated the **a** with all its utensils,
7:10 also presented offerings for the dedication of the **a**
7:10 the leaders presented their offering before the **a**.
7:11 one leader each day, for the dedication of the **a**.
7:84 This was the dedication offering for the **a**,
7:88 This was the dedication offering for the **a**,
16:38 into hammered plates as a covering for the **a**,
16:39 they were hammered out as a covering for the **a**—
16:46 put fire on it from the **a** and lay incense on it,
18: 3 either the utensils of the sanctuary or the **a**,
18: 5 the duties of the sanctuary and the duties of the **a**,
18: 7 in all that concerns the **a** and the area behind
18:17 You shall dash their blood on the **a**,
23: 2 and Balaam offered a bull and a ram on each **a**.
23: 4 and have offered a bull and a ram on each **a**."
23:14 and offered a bull and a ram on each **a**.
23:30 and offered a bull and a ram on each **a**.
Dt 12:27 on the **a** of the LORD your God;
12:27 beside the **a** of the LORD your God,
16:21 as a sacred pole beside the **a** that you make for
26: 4 from your hand and sets it down before the **a** of
27: 5 you shall build an **a** there to the LORD your God,
27: 5 an **a** of stones on which you have not used
27: 6 the **a** of the LORD your God of unhewn stones.
33:10 and whole burnt offerings on your **a**.
Jos 8:30 Joshua built on Mount Ebal an **a** to the LORD,
8:31 of the law of Moses, "an **a** of unhewn stones,
9:27 for the congregation and for the **a** of the LORD,
22:10 built there an **a** by the Jordan, an **a** of great size.
22:11 and the half-tribe of Manasseh had built an **a** at
22:16 by building yourselves an **a** today in rebellion
22:19 by building yourselves an **a** other than the **a** of
22:23 an **a** to turn away from following the LORD;
22:26 Therefore we said, 'Let us now build an **a**,
22:28 'Look at this copy of the **a** of the LORD,
22:29 by building an **a** for burnt offering,
22:29 other than the **a** of the LORD our God that stands
22:34 Reubenites and the Gadites called the **a** Witness;
Jdg 6:24 Then Gideon built an **a** there to the LORD,
6:25 the **a** of Baal that belongs to your father, and cut
6:26 and build an **a** to the LORD your God on the top
6:28 the **a** of Baal was broken down,
6:28 and the second bull was offered on the **a**
6:30 for he has pulled down the **a** of Baal and cut down
6:31 because his **a** has been pulled down."
6:32 because he pulled down his **a**.
13:20 the flame went up toward heaven from the **a**,
13:20 of the **a** while Manoah and his wife looked on;
21: 4 the people got up early, and built an **a** there,
1Sa 2:28 to go up to my **a**, to offer incense,
1Sa 2:33 of you whom I shall not cut off from my **a** shall
7:17 and built there an **a** to the LORD.
14:35 And Saul built an **a** to the LORD;
14:35 it was the first **a** that he built to the LORD.
2Sa 24:18 and erect an **a** to the LORD on the threshing floor
24:21 the threshing floor from you in order to build an **a**
24:25 David built there an **a** to the LORD,
1Ki 1:50 got up and went to grasp the horns of the **a**.
1:51 see, he has laid hold of the horns of the **a**, saying,
1:53 to have him brought down from the **a**.
2:28 of the LORD and grasped the horns of the **a**.
2:29 to the tent of the LORD and now is beside the **a**,"
3: 4 to offer a thousand burnt offerings on that **a**.
6:20 He also overlaid the **a** with cedar.
6:22 even the whole **a** that belonged to
7:48 the golden **a**, the golden table for the bread of
8:22 Then Solomon stood before the **a** of the LORD in
8:31 and comes and swears before your **a** in this house,
8:54 he arose from facing the **a** of the LORD,
8:64 the sacrifices of well-being, because the bronze **a**
9:25 and sacrifices of well-being on the **a** that he built
12:32 and he offered sacrifices on the **a**;
12:33 He went up to the **a** that he had made in Bethel on
12:33 and he went up to the **a** to offer incense.
13: 1 Jeroboam was standing by the **a** to offer incense,
13: 2 and proclaimed against the **a** by the word of the
LORD, and said, "O **a**, **a**, thus says the LORD:
13: 3 'The **a** shall be torn down,
13: 4 the man of God cried out against the **a** at Bethel,
13: 4 Jeroboam stretched out his hand from the **a**,
13: 5 The **a** also was torn down,
13: 5 and the ashes poured out from the **a**,
13:32 by the word of the LORD against the **a** in Bethel,
16:32 He erected an **a** for Baal in the house of Baal,
18:26 They limped about the **a** that they had made.
18:30 the **a** of the LORD that had been thrown down;
18:32 the stones he built an **a** in the name of the LORD.
18:32 Then he made a trench around the **a**,
18:35 so that the water ran all around the **a**,
2Ki 11:11 around the **a** and the house,
12: 9 the **a** on the right side as one entered the house of
16:10 he saw the **a** that was at Damascus.
16:10 to the priest Uriah a model of the **a**,
16:11 The priest Uriah built the **a**;
16:12 king came from Damascus, the king viewed the **a**.
16:12 Then the king drew near to the **a**, went up on it,
16:13 of his offerings of well-being against the **a**.
16:14 The bronze **a** that was before
16:14 from the place between his **a** and the house of
16:14 and put it on the north side of his **a**.
16:15 the great **a** offer the morning burnt offering,
16:15 but the bronze **a** shall be for me to inquire by."
18:22 'You shall worship before this **a** in Jerusalem'?
23: 9 not come up to the **a** of the LORD in Jerusalem,
23:15 Moreover, the **a** at Bethel,
23:15 he pulled down that **a** along with the high place.
23:16 and burned them on the **a**, and defiled it,
23:16 when Jeroboam stood by the **a** at the festival;
23:17 that you have done against the **a** at Bethel."
1Ch 6:49 the **a** of burnt offering and on the **a** of incense,
16:40 to the LORD on the **a** of burnt offering regularly,
21:18 and erect an **a** to the LORD on the threshing floor
21:22 of the threshing floor that I may build on it an **a** to
21:26 an **a** to the LORD and presented burnt offerings
21:26 with fire from heaven on the **a** of burnt offering.
21:29 and the **a** of burnt offering were at that time in
22: 1 the LORD God and here the **a** of burnt offering
28:18 **a** of incense made of refined gold, and its weight;
2Ch 1: 5 Moreover the bronze **a** that Bezalel son of Uri,
1: 6 Solomon went up there to the bronze **a** before
4: 1 He made an **a** of bronze, twenty cubits long,
4:19 the golden **a**, the tables for the bread of
5:12 with cymbals, harps, and lyres, stood east of the **a**
6:12 Then Solomon stood before the **a** of the LORD in
6:22 and comes and swears before your **a** in this house,
7: 7 the bronze **a** Solomon had made could not hold
7: 9 of the **a** seven days and the festival seven days,
8:12 on the **a** of the LORD that he had built in front of
15: 8 He repaired the **a** of the LORD that was in front
23:10 around the **a** and the house.
26:16 the LORD to make offering on the **a** of incense.
26:19 of the priests in the house of the LORD, by the **a**
29:18 the **a** of burnt offering and all its utensils,
29:19 see, they are in front of the **a** of the LORD."
29:21 the descendants of Aaron to offer them on the **a** of
29:22 the blood and dashed it against the **a**;
29:22 and their blood was dashed against the **a**;
29:22 and their blood was dashed against the **a**.
29:24 and made a sin offering with their blood at the **a**,
29:27 that the burnt offering be offered on the **a**.
32:12 saying, 'Before one **a** you shall worship,
33:16 He also restored the **a** of the LORD and offered
35:16 the passover and to offer burnt offerings on the **a**
Ezr 3: 2 of Shealtiel with his kin set out to build the **a** of
3: 3 They set up the **a** on its foundation,
7:17 on the **a** of the house of your God in Jerusalem.
Ne 10:34 to burn on the **a** of the LORD our God,
Ps 26: 6 and go around your **a**, O LORD,
43: 4 Then I will go to the **a** of God,
51:19 then bulls will be offered on your **a**.
118:27 up to the horns of the **a**.
Isa 6: 6 holding a live coal that had been taken from the **a**
19:19 On that day there will be an **a** to the LORD in
36: 7 'You shall worship before this **a**'?
56: 7 and their sacrifices will be accepted on my **a**;
60: 7 they shall be acceptable on my **a**,
La 2: 7 Lord has scorned his **a**, disowned his sanctuary;

Eze 8: 5 and there, north of the **a** gate, in the entrance,
8:16 between the porch and the **a**,
9: 2 They went in and stood beside the bronze **a**.
40:46 for the priests who have charge of the **a**;
40:47 and the **a** was in front of the temple.
41:22 an **a** of wood, three cubits high, two cubits long,
43:13 of the **a** by cubits (the cubit being one cubit and
43:13 This shall be the height of the **a**:
43:15 and the **a** hearth, four cubits;
43:15 from the **a** hearth projecting upward, four horns.
43:16 The **a** hearth shall be square,
43:18 These are the ordinances for the **a**:
43:20 and put it on the four horns of the **a**,
43:22 **a** shall be purified, as it was purified with the bull.
43:26 Seven days shall they make atonement for the **a**
43:27 upon the **a** your burnt offerings and your offerings
45:19 the four corners of the ledge of the **a**,
47: 1 of the threshold of the temple, south of the **a**.
Joel 1:13 wail, you ministers of the **a**.
2:17 Between the vestibule and the **a** let the priests,
Am 2: 8 down beside every **a** on garments taken in pledge;
3:14 and the horns of the **a** shall be cut off and fall to
9: 1 I saw the LORD standing beside the **a**,
Zec 9:15 drenched like the corners of the **a**.
14:20 be as holy as the bowls in front of the **a**;
Mal 1: 7 By offering polluted food on my **a**.
1:10 so that you would not kindle fire on my **a** in vain!
2:13 You cover the LORD's **a** with tears,
Mt 5:23 So when you are offering your gift at the **a**,
5:24 leave your gift there before the **a** and go;
23:18 'Whoever swears by the **a** is bound by nothing,
23:18 by the gift that is on the **a** is bound by the oath.'
23:19 the gift or the **a** that makes the gift sacred?
23:20 So whoever swears by the **a**,
23:35 between the sanctuary and the **a**.
Lk 1:11 standing at the right side of the **a** of incense.
11:51 who perished between the **a** and the sanctuary.
Ac 17:23 I found among them an **a** with the inscription,
1Co 9:13 serve at the **a** share in what is sacrificed on the **a**?
10:18 not those who eat the sacrifices partners in the **a**?
Heb 7:13 from which no one has ever served at the **a**.
9: 4 In it stood the golden **a** of incense and the ark of
13:10 We have an **a** from which those who officiate in
Jas 2:21 by works when he offered his son Isaac on the **a**?
Rev 6: 9 the **a** the souls of those who had been slaughtered
8: 3 with a golden censer came and stood at the **a**;
8: 3 the saints on the golden **a** that is before the throne.
8: 5 and filled it with fire from the **a** and threw it on
9:13 from the four horns of the golden **a** before God,
11: 1 "Come and measure the temple of God and the **a**
14:18 Then another angel came out from the **a**,
16: 7 And I heard the **a** respond, "Yes, O Lord God,
Tob 1: 7 the sons of Aaron, at the **a**;
Jdt 4: 3 and the **a** and the temple had been consecrated
4:12 even draped the **a** with sackcloth and cried out
8:24 both the temple and the **a**— rests upon us.
9: 8 to break off the horns of your **a** with the sword.
AdE 14: 9 and to quench your **a** and the glory of your house,
Wis 9: 8 and an **a** in the city of your habitation,
Sir 35: 8 The offering of the righteous enriches the **a**,
47: 9 He placed singers before the **a**,
50:11 when he went up to the holy **a**,
50:12 as he stood by the hearth of the **a** with a garland
50:15 he poured it out at the foot of the **a**,
Bar 1:10 and offer them on the **a** of the Lord our God;
1Mc 1:21 the sanctuary and took the golden **a**,
1:54 a desolating sacrilege on the **a** of burnt offering.
1:59 the **a** that was on top of the **a** of burnt offering.
2:23 in the sight of all to offer sacrifice on the **a**
2:24 he ran and killed him on the **a**.
2:25 and he tore down the **a**.
4:38 the **a** profaned, and the gates burned.
4:44 They deliberated what to do about the **a**
4:45 So they tore down the **a**,
4:47 and built a new **a** like the former one.
4:49 the **a** of incense, and the table into the temple.
4:50 on the **a** and lit the lamps on the lampstand,
4:53 on the new **a** of burnt offering that they had built.
4:56 So they celebrated the dedication of the **a**
4:59 of dedication of the **a** should be observed with joy
5: 1 the **a** had been rebuilt and the sanctuary dedicated
6: 7 down the abomination that he had erected on the **a**
7:36 At this the priests went in and stood before the **a**
2Mc 1:18 who built the temple and the **a**, offered sacrifices.
1:19 the fire of the **a** and secretly hid it in the hollow of
1:32 when the light from the **a** shone back, it went out.
2: 5 and he brought there the tent and the ark and the **a**
2:19 and the dedication of the **a**,
3:15 before the **a** in their priestly vestments and called
4:14 upon their service at the **a**.
6: 5 The **a** was covered with abominable offerings
10: 3 and made another **a** of sacrifice;
10:26 Falling upon the steps before the **a**,
13: 8 against the **a** whose fire and ashes were holy,
14: 3 to be safe or to have access again to the holy **a**,
14:33 of God to the ground and tear down the **a**,
15:31 and stationed the priests before the **a**,
1Es 1:18 the sacrifices were offered on the **a** of the Lord,
4:52 be offered on the **a** every day, in accordance with
5:48 took their places and prepared the **a** of the God
5:50 And they erected the **a** in its place,
8:15 as to offer sacrifices on the **a** of their Lord that is
2Es 10:21 our **a** thrown down, our temple destroyed;

ALTARS (68) [ALTAR]

Ex 34:13 You shall tear down their **a**, break their pillars,
Lev 26:30 and cut down your incense **a**;
Nu 3:31 the table, the lampstand, the **a**,
23: 1 Balaam said to Balak, "Build me seven **a** here,
23: 4 Balaam said to him, "I have arranged the seven **a**,
23:14 He built seven **a**, and offered a bull and a ram
23:29 Balaam said to Balak, "Build me seven **a** here,
Dt 7: 5 break down their **a**, smash their pillars,
12: 3 Break down their **a**, smash their pillars,
Jdg 2: 2 of this land; tear down their **a**.'
1Ki 19:10 thrown down your **a**, and killed your prophets
19:14 thrown down your **a**, and killed your prophets
2Ki 11:18 his **a** and his images they broke in pieces,
11:18 the priest of Baal, before the **a**.
18:22 and **a** Hezekiah has removed,
21: 3 he erected **a** for Baal, made a sacred pole,
21: 4 He built **a** in the house of the LORD,
21: 5 He built **a** for all the host of heaven in
23:12 The **a** on the roof of the upper chamber of Ahaz,
23:12 the **a** that Manasseh had made in the two courts of
23:20 He slaughtered on the **a** all the priests of
2Ch 14: 3 He took away the foreign **a** and the high places,
14: 5 of Judah the high places and the incense **a**.
23:17 his **a** and his images they broke in pieces,
23:17 the priest of Baal, in front of the **a**.
28:24 of the LORD and made himself **a** in every corner
30:14 to work and removed the **a** that were in Jerusalem,
30:14 and all the **a** for offering incense they took away
31: 1 the high places and the **a** throughout all Judah
32:12 and his **a** and commanded Judah and Jerusalem,
33: 3 and erected **a** to the Baals, made sacred poles,
33: 4 He built **a** in the house of the LORD,
33: 5 He built **a** for all the host of heaven in
33:15 and all the **a** that he had built on the mountain of
34: 4 In his presence they pulled down the **a** of
34: 4 he demolished the incense **a** that stood
34: 5 He also burned the bones of the priests on their **a**,
34: 7 down the **a**, beat the sacred poles and the images
34: 7 and demolished all the incense **a** throughout all
Ps 84: 3 where she may lay her young, at your **a**,
Isa 17: 8 they will not have regard for the **a**,
17: 8 either the sacred poles or the **a** of incense.
27: 9 the stones of the **a** like chalkstones crushed
27: 9 no sacred poles or incense **a** will remain standing.
36: 7 and **a** Hezekiah has removed,
Jer 11:13 the streets of Jerusalem are the **a** you have set up
11:13 **a** to make offerings to Baal.
17: 1 and on the horns of their **a**,
17: 2 while their children remember their **a**
Eze 6: 4 Your **a** shall become desolate,
6: 5 and I will scatter your bones around your **a**.
6: 6 so that your **a** will be waste and ruined,
6:13 their slain lie among their idols around their **a**,
Hos 4:19 and they shall be ashamed because of their **a**.
8:11 When Ephraim multiplied **a** to expiate sin,
8:11 they became to him **a** for sinning.
10: 1 The more his fruit increased the more **a** he built;
10: 2 The LORD will break down their **a**,
10: 8 Thorn and thistle shall grow up on their **a**.
12:11 so their **a** shall be like stone heaps on the furrows
Am 3:14 I will punish the **a** of Bethel,
Ro 11: 3 they have demolished your **a**;
Sir 50:14 Finishing the service at the **a**,
1Mc 1:47 to build **a** and sacred precincts and shrines
1:54 also built **a** in the surrounding towns of Judah,
2:45 and his friends went around and tore down the **a**;
5:68 he tore down their **a**, and the carved images
2Mc 10: 2 down the **a** that had been built in the public square

ALTER (3) [ALTERED, ALTERS]

Ezr 6:12 or people that shall put forth a hand to **a** this,
Ps 89:34 or **a** the word that went forth from my lips.
3Mc 3:23 that we may soon **a** our policy.

ALTERED (3) [ALTER]

Est 1:19 so that it may not be **a**, that Vashti is never again
AdE 1:19 of the Medes and Persians so that it may not be **a**,
4Mc 4:19 the nation's way of life and **a** its form

ALTERNATING (1) [ALTERNATIONS]

Ex 28:34 and a pomegranate **a** all around the lower hem of

ALTERNATIONS (1) [ALTERNATING]

Wis 7:18 **a** of the solstices and the changes of the seasons,

ALTERS (2) [ALTER]

Ezr 6:11 Furthermore I decree that if anyone **a** this edict,
Mic 2: 4 the LORD **a** the inheritance of my people;

ALTHOUGH (65) [THOUGH]

Ge 31:37 **A** you have felt about through all my goods,
39:10 And **a** she spoke to Joseph day after day,
42: 8 **A** Joseph had recognized his brothers,
Ex 13:17 of the land of the Philistines, **a** that was nearer;
34: 9 **A** this is a stiff-necked people,
Nu 9: 7 "**A** we are unclean through touching a corpse,
22:18 "**A** Balak were to give me his house full of silver
Dt 1:43 **A** I told you, you would not listen.
3:18 "**A** the LORD your God has given you this land
10:14 **A** heaven and the heaven of heavens belong to
18:14 **A** these nations that you are about
19: 6 **a** a death sentence was not deserved,
20:19 **A** you may take food from them,
28:62 **A** once you were as numerous as the stars
32:52 **A** you may view the land from a distance,
Jos 5: 5 **A** all the people who came out had been
circumcised,
Jdg 13: 3 "**A** you are barren, having borne no children,
2Sa 21: 2 **a** the people of Israel had sworn to spare them,
1Ki 1: 1 and **a** they covered him with clothes,
3: 7 **a** I am only a little child;
18:12 **a** I your servant have revered the LORD
2Ch 24:24 **A** the army of Aram had come with few men,
Job 2: 3 **a** you incited me against him,
10: 7 **a** you know that I am not guilty,
Ecc 8: 6 **a** the troubles of mortals lie heavy upon them.
Isa 53: 9 **a** he had done no violence,
Jer 5: 2 **A** they say, "As the LORD lives,"
14: 7 **A** our iniquities testify against us, act, O LORD,
14:12 **A** they fast, I do not hear their cry,
14:12 and **a** they offer burnt offering and grain offering,
44:14 **A** they long to go back to live there,
49:16 **A** you make your nest as high as the eagle's,
La 3:32 **A** he causes grief, he will have compassion
Eze 13:22 **a** I have not disheartened them,
15: 7 **a** they escape from the fire,
35:10 **a** the LORD was there—
Da 6:10 **A** Daniel knew that the document had been signed,
Hos 13:15 **A** he may flourish among rushes,
Jn 4: 2 —**a** it was not Jesus himself but his disciples
12:37 **A** he had performed so many signs
20:26 **A** the doors were shut, Jesus came and stood
Ro 3: 4 **A** everyone is a liar, let God be proved true,
2Co 7:12 So **a** I wrote to you,
Eph 3: 8 **A** I am the very least of all the saints,
Heb 5: 8 **A** he was a Son, he learned obedience
1Pe 1: 8 **A** you have not seen him, you love him;
2Jn 1:12 **A** I have much to write to you,
Tob 5:10 **A** still alive, I am among the dead.
12:19 **A** you were watching me,
Wis 7:27 **A** she is but one, she can do all things,
12:18 **A** you are sovereign in strength,
Sus 1:39 **A** we saw them embracing,
1Mc 11:25 **A** certain renegades of his
2Mc 4:27 **A** Menelaus continued to hold the office,
6:16 **A** he disciplines us with calamities,
7:20 **A** she saw her seven sons perish within
1Es 1:48 **A** King Nebuchadnezzar had made him swear by
6:20 **A** it has been in process of construction from
4Mc 4:13 **a** otherwise he had scruples about doing so,
5: 7 **A** you have had them for so long a time,
6: 7 **A** he fell to the ground because his body could
7: 4 **A** his sacred life was consumed by tortures
9:21 **A** the ligaments joining his bones were already
13:27 But **a** nature and companionship
15:24 **A** she witnessed the destruction of seven children

ALTOGETHER (10) [TOGETHER]

Ge 18:21 down and see whether they have done **a** according
1Sa 14:23 with Saul numbered **a** about ten thousand men.
Job 27:12 why then have you become **a** vain?
Ps 19: 9 ordinances of the LORD are true and righteous **a**.
37:38 But transgressors shall be **a** destroyed;
SS 4: 7 You are **a** beautiful, my love;
5:16 His speech is most sweet, and he is **a** desirable.
Ac 19: 7 **a** there were about twelve of them.
Wis 7:23 that are intelligent, pure, and **a** subtle.
4Mc 3:15 considered it an **a** fearful danger to his soul

ALUSH (2)

Nu 33:13 They set out from Dophkah and camped at **A**.
33:14 They set out from **A** and camped at Rephidim,

ALVAH‡ (1) [=ALIAH]

Ge 36:40 the clans Timna, **A**, Jetheth,

ALVAN (1) [=ALIAN]

Ge 36:23 **A**, Manahath, Ebal, Shepho, and Onam.

ALWAYS‡ (105)

Ex 25:30 the bread of the Presence on the table before me **a**.
28:38 it shall **a** be on his forehead,
Nu 9:16 It was **a** so: the cloud covered it by day
Dt 5:29 to fear me and to keep all my commandments **a**,
11: 1 his ordinances, and his commandments **a**.
11:12 The eyes of the LORD your God are **a** on it,
14:23 that you may learn to fear the LORD your God **a**.
19: 9 the LORD your God and walking **a** in his ways—
Jos 9:23 you are cursed, and some of you shall **a** be slaves,
1Sa 9: 6 Whatever he says **a** comes true.
21: 5 "Indeed women have been kept from us as **a**
27:12 therefore he shall **a** be my servant."
2Sa 9: 7 and you yourself shall eat at my table **a**."
9:10 your master's grandson Mephibosheth shall **a** eat
9:13 for he **a** ate at the king's table.
1Ki 5: 1 for Hiram had been **a** friend to David.
11:36 so that my servant David may **a** have a lamp
2Ki 17:37 you shall **a** be careful to observe.
Job 1: 5 This is what Job **a** did.
Ps 9:18 For the needy shall not **a** be forgotten,
16: 8 I keep the LORD **a** before me;
61: 8 So I will **a** sing praises to your name,
73:12 **a** at ease, they increase in riches.
89:21 my hand shall **a** remain with him;
92:14 they are **a** green and full of sap,
103: 9 He will not **a** accuse, nor will he keep his anger
119:98 for it is **a** with me.
Pr 5:19 may you be intoxicated **a** by her love.
6:21 Bind them upon your heart **a**;

Pr 8:30 and I was daily his delight, rejoicing before him a,
23:17 but a continue in the fear of the LORD.
Ecc 9: 8 Let your garments a be white;
Isa 57:16 I will not continually accuse, nor will I a be angry;
60:11 Your gates shall a be open;
Mt 26:11 For you a have the poor with you,
26:11 but you will not a have me.
28:20 remember, I am with you a, to the end of the age."
Mk 5: 5 the tombs and on the mountains he was a howling
14: 7 For you a have the poor with you,
14: 7 but you will not a have me.
Lk 15:31 the father said to him, 'Son, you are a with me,
18: 1 about their need to pray a and not to lose heart.
Jn 6:34 They said to him, "Sir, give us this bread a."
7: 6 but your time is a here.
8:29 for I a do what is pleasing to him."
11:42 I knew that you a hear me,
12: 8 You a have the poor with you, but you do not a have me."
18:20 I have a taught in synagogues and in the temple,
Ac 2:25 'I saw the Lord a before me,
24:16 Therefore I do my best a to have
Ro 1: 9 without ceasing I remember you a in my prayers,
1Co 1: 4 to my God a for you because of the grace of God
15:58 immovable, a excelling in the work of the Lord,
2Co 1:19 but in him it is a "Yes."
2:14 who in Christ a leads us in triumphal procession,
4:10 a carrying in the body the death of Jesus,
4:11 we are a being given up to death for Jesus' sake,
5: 6 So we are a confident;
6:10 as sorrowful, yet a rejoicing;
9: 8 so that by a having enough of everything,
Gal 2: 5 the truth of the gospel might a remain with you.
Eph 6:18 that end keep alert and a persevere in supplication
Php 1:20 Christ will be exalted now as a in my body,
2:12 my beloved, just as you have a obeyed me,
4: 4 Rejoice in the Lord a; again I will say, Rejoice.
Col 1: 3 In our prayers for you we a thank God,
4: 6 Let your speech a be gracious, seasoned with salt,
4:12 He is a wrestling in his prayers on your behalf,
1Th 1: 2 We a give thanks to God for all of you
3: 6 He has told us also that you a remember us kindly
5:15 but a seek to do good to one another and to all.
5:16 Rejoice a,
2Th 1: 3 We must a give thanks to God for you,
1:11 To this end we a pray for you,
2:13 But we must a give thanks to God for you,
2Ti 3: 7 who are a being instructed and can never arrive at
4: 5 As for you, a be sober, endure suffering,
Tit 1:12 "Cretans are a liars, vicious brutes, lazy gluttons."
Phm 1: 4 in my prayers, I a thank my God
Heb 3:10 and I said, 'They a go astray in their hearts,
7:25 since he a lives to make intercession for them.
12:11 discipline a seems painful rather than pleasant at
1Pe 3:15 A be ready to make your defense
AdE 13: 2 but a acting reasonably and with kindness),
16: 4 of God, who a sees everything.
16: 9 and a judging what comes before our eyes
Wis 11:21 For it is a in your power to show great strength,
14:31 a pursues the transgression of the unrighteous.
17:11 it has a exaggerated the difficulties.
Sir 17:15 Their ways are a known to him;
23:10 so also the person who a swears and utters
27:11 The conversation of the godly is a wise,
38:29 he is a deeply concerned over his products,
39:31 a ready for his service on earth;
40:23 A friend or companion is a welcome,
1Mc 2:65 a listen to him; he shall be your father.
2Mc 14:15 and a upholds his own heritage
14:24 And he kept Judas a in his presence;
1Es 1:32 it was ordained that this should a be done
3Mc 7: 6 a taking their part as a father does for his children,
7: 9 we a shall have not a mortal but the Ruler
2Es 7:*80* a grieving and sad, in seven ways.
8:30 love those who have a put their trust in your glory.
15:47 who have a lusted after you.

AM (1265) [BE] See Index of Articles Etc.— See also selected listing under I AM

AMAD (1)
Jos 19:26 A, and Mishal; on the west it touches Carmel

AMAL (1)
1Ch 7:35 Zophah, Imna, Shelesh, and A.

AMALEK‡ (20) [AMALEKITE, AMALEKITES]
Ge 36:12 Esau's son; she bore A to Eliphaz.)
36:16 Gatam, and A; these are the clans of Eliphaz
Ex 17: 8 Then A came and fought with Israel at Rephidim.
17: 9 for us and go out, fight with A.
17:10 Joshua did as Moses told him, and fought with A,
17:11 and whenever he lowered his hand, A prevailed.
17:13 Joshua defeated A and his people with the sword.
17:14 I will utterly blot out the remembrance of A from
17:16 The LORD will have war with A from generation
Nu 24:20 he looked on A, and uttered his oracle, saying:
24:20 "First among the nations was A,
Dt 25:17 Remember what A did to you on your journey out
25:19 you shall blot out the remembrance of A from
1Sa 15: 3 Now go and attack A, and utterly destroy all
15:20 I have brought Agag the king of A,
28:18 and did not carry out his fierce wrath against A,
2Sa 8:12 Moab, the Ammonites, the Philistines, A,
1Ch 1:36 Omar, Zephi, Gatam, Kenaz, Timna, and A.
18:11 Moab, the Ammonites, the Philistines, and A.
Ps 83: 7 and Ammon and A, Philistia with the inhabitants

AMALEKITE (3) [AMALEK]
1Sa 30:13 "I am a young man of Egypt, servant to an A.
2Sa 1: 8 I answered him, 'I am an A.'
1:13 "I am the son of a resident alien, an A."

AMALEKITES (28) [AMALEK]
Ge 14: 7 Kadesh), and subdued all the country of the A,
Nu 13:29 The A live in the land of the Negeb;
14:25 since the A and the Canaanites live in the valleys,
14:43 the A and the Canaanites will confront you there,
14:45 Then the A and the Canaanites who lived in
Jdg 1:16 Then they went and settled with the A.
3:13 In alliance with the Ammonites and the A,
6: 3 and the A and the people of the east would come
6:33 Then all the Midianites and the A and the people
7:12 and the A and all the people of the east lay along
10:12 The Sidonians also, and the A, and the Maonites,
12:15 in the hill country of the A.
1Sa 14:48 He did valiantly, and struck down the A,
15: 2 'I will punish the A for what they did in opposing
15: 5 to the city of the A and lay in wait in the valley.
15: 6 Withdraw from among the A,
15: 6 So the Kenites withdrew from the A.
15: 7 Saul defeated the A, from Havilah as far as Shur,
15: 8 He took King Agag of the A alive,
15:15 Saul said, "They have brought them from the A;
15:18 and said, 'Go, utterly destroy the sinners, the A,
15:20 and I have utterly destroyed the A.
15:32 "Bring Agag king of the A here to me."
27: 8 on the Geshurites, the Girzites, and the A;
30: 1 A had made a raid on the Negeb and on Ziklag.
30:18 David recovered all that the A had taken;
2Sa 1: 1 when David had returned from defeating the A,
1Ch 4:43 the remnant of the A that had escaped,

AMAM (1)
Jos 15:26 A, Shema, Moladah,

AMANA‡ (1)
SS 4: 8 Depart from the peak of A,

AMARIAH (18)
1Ch 6: 7 Meraioth of A, A of Ahitub,
6:11 Azariah became the father of A, A of Ahitub,
6:52 Meraioth his son, A his son, Ahitub his son,
23:19 Jeriah the chief, A the second, Jahaziel the third,
24:23 Jeriah the chief, A the second, Jahaziel the third,
2Ch 19:11 A the chief priest is over you in all matters of
31:15 Eden, Miniamin, Jeshua, Shemaiah, A,
Ezr 7: 3 son of A, son of Azariah, son of Meraioth,
10:42 Shallum, A, and Joseph.
Ne 10: 3 Pashhur, A, Malchijah,
11: 4 of Zechariah son of A son of Shephatiah son
12: 2 A, Malluch, Hattush,
12:13 of Ezra, Meshullam; of A, Jehohanan;
Zep 1: 1 of Gedaliah son of A son of Hezekiah,
1Es 8: 2 of A son of Uzzi son of Bukki son of Abishua son
2Es 1: 2 of Phinehas son of Eli son of A son of Azariah son

AMASA (18)
2Sa 17:25 Now Absalom had set A over the army in
17:25 A was the son of a man named Ithra
19:13 say to A, 'Are you not my bone and my flesh?
19:14 A swayed the hearts of all the people of Judah
20: 4 Then the king said to A,
20: 5 So A went to summon Judah;
20: 8 at the large stone that is in Gibeon, A came
20: 9 Joab said to A, "Is it well with you, my brother?"
20: 9 And Joab took A by the beard with his right hand
20:10 But A did not notice the sword in Joab's hand;
20:11 And one of Joab's men took his stand by A,
20:12 A lay wallowing in his blood on the highway,
20:12 he carried A from the highway into a field,
1Ki 2: 5 and A son of Jether, whom he murdered,
2:32 of Israel, and A son of Jether, commander of
1Ch 2:17 Abigail bore A, and the father of A was Jether the
2Ch 28:12 Jehizkiah son of Shallum, and A son of Hadlai,

AMASAI (5)
1Ch 6:25 The sons of Elkanah: A and Ahimoth,
6:35 son of Elkanah, son of Mahath, son of A,
12:18 Then the spirit came upon A, chief of the Thirty,
15:24 Shebaniah, Joshaphat, Nethanel, A, Zechariah,
2Ch 29:12 Then the Levites arose, Mahath son of A,

AMASHSAI (1)
Ne 11:13 and A son of Azarel son of Ahzai son

AMASIAH (1)
2Ch 17:16 and next to him A son of Zichri,

AMASS (2) [AMASSED]
Jer 17:11 so are all who a wealth unjustly;
Sir 31: 3 The rich person toils to a a fortune,

AMASSED (2) [AMASS]
Eze 28: 4 and your understanding you have a wealth
Sir 47:18 you gathered gold like tin and a silver like lead.

AMAW (1)
Nu 22: 5 which is on the Euphrates, in the land of A,

AMAZED (53) [AMAZING]
Ecc 5: 8 do not be a at the matter;
Mt 8:10 he was a and said to those who followed him,
8:27 They were a, saying, "What sort of man is this,
9:33 and the crowds were a and said,
12:23 All the crowds were a and said,
15:31 crowd was a when they saw the mute speaking,
21:20 When the disciples saw it, they were a, saying,
22:22 When they heard this, they were a;
27:14 so that the governor was greatly a.
Mk 1:27 They were all a, and they kept
2:12 so that they were all a and glorified God, saying,
5:20 for him; and everyone was a.
6: 6 And he was a at their unbelief.
10:32 they were a, and those who followed were afraid.
12:17 And they were utterly a at him.
15: 5 Jesus made no further reply, so that Pilate was a.
Lk 1:63 And all of them were a.
2:18 and all who heard it were a at what
2:33 and mother were a at what was being said
2:47 And all who heard him were a
4:22 of him and were a at the gracious words that came
4:36 They were all a and kept saying to one another,
5: 9 and all who were with him were a at the catch
7: 9 When Jesus heard this he was a at him,
8:25 They were afraid and a, and said to one another,
9:43 While everyone was a at all that he was doing,
11:14 who had been mute spoke, and the crowds were a.
11:38 The Pharisee was a to see that he did
20:26 and being a by his answer, they became silent.
24:12 then he went home, a at what had happened.
Ac 2: 7 A and astonished, they asked,
2:12 All were a and perplexed, saying to one another,
4:13 they were a and recognized them as companions
7:31 When Moses saw it, he was a at the sight;
8: 9 in the city and a the people of Samaria,
8:11 for a long time he had a them with his magic.
8:13 with Philip and was a when he saw the signs
9:21 All who heard him were a and said,
12:16 they opened the gate, they saw him and were a.
13:41 Be a and perish, for in your days I am doing
Rev 17: 6 When I saw her, I was greatly a.
17: 7 But the angel said to me, "Why are you so a?
17: 8 will be a when they see the beast,
Tob 11:16 and with no one leading him, they were a.
Jdt 15: 1 they were a at what had happened.
Wis 5: 2 be a at the unexpected salvation of the righteous.
13: 4 And if people were a at their power and working,
Sir 43:18 and the mind is a as it falls.
1Mc 15:32 and his great magnificence, he was a.
2Es 9: 9 those who have now abused my ways shall be a,
13:11 When I saw it, I was a.
4Mc 6:11 he a even his torturers by his courageous spirit.
17:16 of the divine legislation? Who were not a?

AMAZEMENT (7) [AMAZING]
Ge 43:33 the men looked at one another in a.
Mk 5:42 At this they were overcome with a.
16: 8 for terror and a had seized them;
Lk 5:26 A seized all of them, and they glorified God
Ac 3:10 with wonder and a at what had happened to him.
Rev 13: 3 In a the whole earth followed the beast.
Sir 11:13 and raises up their heads to the a of the many.

AMAZIAH (41)
2Ki 12:21 then his son A succeeded him.
13:12 as the might with which he fought against King A
14: 1 King A son of Joash of Judah, began to reign.
14: 8 Then A sent messengers to King Jehoash son
14: 9 King Jehoash of Israel sent word to King A
14:11 But A would not listen.
14:11 and King A of Judah faced one another in battle
14:13 of Israel captured King A of Judah son of Jehoash,
14:15 and how he fought with King A of Judah,
14:17 King A son of Joash of Judah lived fifteen years
14:18 Now the rest of the deeds of A,
14:21 and made him king to succeed his father A.
14:22 after King A slept with his ancestors.
14:23 the fifteenth year of King A son of Joash of Judah,
15: 1 of King Jeroboam of Israel King Azariah son of A
15: 3 just as his father A had done.
1Ch 3:12 A his son, Azariah his son, Jotham his son,
4:34 Meshobab, Jamlech, Joshah son of A,
6:45 son of Hashabiah, son of A, son of Hilkiah,
2Ch 24:27 And his son A succeeded him.
25: 1 A was twenty-five years old when he began
25: 5 A assembled the people of Judah,
25: 9 A said to the man of God,
25:10 Then A discharged the army that had come to him
25:11 A took courage, and led out his people;
25:13 But the men of the army whom A sent back,
25:14 after A came from the slaughter of the Edomites,
25:15 The LORD was angry with A and sent to him
25:17 Then King A of Judah took counsel and sent
25:18 King Joash of Israel sent word to King A of Judah,
25:20 But A would not listen—it was God's doing,
25:21 and King A of Judah faced one another in battle
25:23 King Joash of Israel captured King A of Judah,
25:25 King A son of Joash of Judah,
25:26 Now the rest of the deeds of A, from first to last,
25:27 that A turned away from the LORD they made
26: 1 and made him king to succeed his father A.

2Ch 26: 4 just as his father A had done.
Am 7:10 Then A, the priest of Bethel,
7:12 And A said to Amos, "O seer, go,
7:14 Then Amos answered A, "I am no prophet,

AMAZING (10) [AMAZED, AMAZEMENT]

Isa 29:14 so I will again do a things with this people, shocking and a.
Mt 21:15 the chief priests and the scribes saw the a things
21:42 this was the Lord's doing, and it is a in our eyes'?
Mk 12:11 this was the Lord's doing, and it is a in our eyes'?"
Rev 15: 1 Then I saw another portent in heaven, great and a:
15: 3 "Great and a are your deeds,
4Mc 2: 1 And why is it a that the desires of the mind for
7:13 Most a, indeed, though he was an old man,
14:11 Do not consider it a that reason had full command

AMBASSAGE (KJV) See DELEGATION

AMBASSADOR‡ (1) [AMBASSADORS]

Eph 6:20 for which I am an a in chains.

AMBASSADORS (5) [AMBASSADOR]

Isa 18: 2 sending a by the Nile in vessels of papyrus on
Eze 17:15 But he rebelled against him by sending a to Egypt,
2Co 5:20 So we are a for Christ,
1Mc 9:70 he sent a to him to make peace with him
10:51 Then Alexander sent a to Ptolemy king of Egypt

AMBER (3)

Eze 1: 4 something like gleaming a.
1:27 like the loins I saw something like gleaming a,
8: 2 like the appearance of brightness, like gleaming a.

AMBITION (6)

Ro 15:20 Thus I make it my a to proclaim the good news,
Php 1:17 the others proclaim Christ out of selfish a,
2: 3 Do nothing from selfish a or conceit,
Jas 3:14 you have bitter envy and selfish a in your hearts,
3:16 For where there is envy and selfish a,
Wis 14:18 the a of the artisan impelled even those who did

AMBUSH (34) [AMBUSHED, AMBUSHES]

Jos 8: 2 Set an a against the city, behind it."
8: 4 "You shall lie in a against the city, behind it;
8: 7 you shall rise up from the a and seize the city;
8: 9 and they went to the place of a,
8:12 he set them in a between Bethel and Ai,
8:14 not know that there was an a against him behind
8:19 the troops in a rose quickly out of their place
8:21 and all Israel saw that the a had taken the city and
Jdg 9:35 and the troops with him rose from the a.
20:29 So Israel stationed men in a around Gibeah.
20:33 while those Israelites who were in a rushed out
20:36 in a that they had stationed against Gibeah.
20:37 The troops in a rushed quickly upon Gibeah.
20:38 of Israel and the men in a was that when they sent
2Ch 13:13 Jeroboam had sent an a around to come on them
13:13 and the a was behind them.
20:22 the LORD set an a against the Ammonites,
Ps 10: 8 They sit in a in the villages;
17:12 like a young lion lurking in a.
64: 4 shooting from a at the blameless;
Pr 1:11 let us wantonly a the innocent;
1:18 and set an a— for their own lives!
12: 6 The words of the wicked are a deadly a,
Jer 9: 8 but inwardly are planning to lay an a.
Ac 23:16 Now the son of Paul's sister heard about the a;
23:21 for more than forty of their men are lying in a
25: 3 in fact, planning an a to kill him along the way.
Sir 8:11 or they may lie in a against your words.
1Mc 1:36 for the citadel became an a against the sanctuary,
9:40 on them from the a and began killing them.
10:80 Jonathan learned that there was an a behind him,
11:68 they had set an a against him in the mountains,
11:69 in a emerged from their places and joined battle.
2Es 15:33 of the Assyrians an enemy in a shall attack them

AMBUSHED (1) [AMBUSH]

1Mc 5: 4 a snare to the people and a them on the highways.

AMBUSHES (3) [AMBUSH]

Jdg 9:25 the lords of Shechem set a on the mountain tops.
Ezr 8:31 the hand of the enemy and from a along the way.
Jer 51:12 post sentinels; prepare the a;

AMEN‡ (65)

Nu 5:22 And the woman shall say, "A. A."
Dt 27:15 All the people shall respond, saying, "A!"
27:16 All the people shall say, "A!"
27:17 All the people shall say, "A!"
27:18 All the people shall say, "A!"
27:19 All the people shall say, "A!"
27:20 All the people shall say, "A!"
27:21 All the people shall say, "A!"
27:22 All the people shall say, "A!"
27:23 All the people shall say, "A!"
27:24 All the people shall say, "A!"
27:25 All the people shall say, "A!"
27:26 All the people shall say, "A!"
1Ki 1:36 Benaiah son of Jehoiada answered the king, "A!
1Ch 16:36 Then all the people said "A!"
Ne 5:13 all the assembly said, "A," and praised the LORD.
8: 6 great God, and all the people answered, "A, A,"
Ps 41:13 from everlasting to everlasting. A and A.
72:19 may his glory fill the whole earth. A and A.
89:52 Blessed be the LORD forever. A and A.
106:48 And let all the people say, "A."
Jer 28: 6 and the prophet Jeremiah said, "A!
Ro 1:25 who is blessed forever! A.
9: 5 over all, God blessed forever. A.
11:36 To him be the glory forever. A.
15:33 The God of peace be with all of you. A.
16:27 to whom be the glory forever! A.
1Co 14:16 of an outsider say the "A" to your thanksgiving,
2Co 1:20 this reason it is through him that we say the "A,"
Gal 1: 5 to whom be the glory forever and ever. A.
6:18 with your spirit, brothers and sisters. A.
Eph 3:21 to all generations, forever and ever. A.
Php 4:20 be glory forever and ever. A.
1Ti 1:17 and glory forever and ever. A.
6:16 be honor and eternal dominion. A.
2Ti 4:18 be the glory forever and ever. A.
Heb 13:21 be the glory forever and ever. A.
1Pe 4:11 and the power forever and ever. A.
5:11 To him be the power forever and ever. A.
2Pe 3:18 now and to the day of eternity. A.
Jude 1:25 before all time and now and forever. A.
Rev 1: 6 and dominion forever and ever. A.
1: 7 of the earth will wail. So it is to be. A.
3:14 The words of the A, the faithful and true witness,
5:14 And the four living creatures said, "A!"
7:12 "A! Blessing and glory and wisdom
7:12 to our God forever and ever! A."
19: 4 on the throne, saying, "A.
22:20 "Surely I am coming soon." A.
22:21 of the Lord Jesus be with all the saints. A.
Tob 8: 8 And they both said, "A, A."
14:15 and he blessed the Lord God forever and ever. A.
Jdt 13:20 And all the people said, "A. A."
15:10 And all the people said, "A."
1Es 9:47 and the multitude answered, "A."
Man 1:15 and yours is the glory forever. A.
3Mc 7:23 of Israel through all times! A.
4Mc 18:24 to whom be glory forever and ever. A.

AMEND (5) [AMENDS]

Jer 7: 3 A your ways and your doings,
7: 5 For if you truly a your ways and your doings,
18:11 and a your ways and your doings.
26:13 Now therefore a your ways and your doings,
35:15 and a your doings, and do not go after other gods

AMENDS (2) [AMEND]

Lev 26:41 and they make a for their iniquity,
26:43 while they shall make a for their iniquity,

AMERCE (KJV) See FINE

AMETHYST (3)

Ex 28:19 and the third row a jacinth, an agate, and an a;
39:12 and the third row, a jacinth, an agate, and an a;
Rev 21:20 the eleventh jacinth, the twelfth a.

AMI (1)

Ezr 2:57 Shephatiah, Hattil, Pochereth-hazzebaim, and A.

AMIABLE (KJV) See LOVELY

AMID (7) [MIDDLE]

Job 4:13 A thoughts from visions of the night,
30:14 a wide breach they come; a the crash they roll on.
Am 2: 2 and Moab shall die a uproar,
2: 2 a shouting and the sound of the trumpet;
Zec 4: 7 he shall bring out the top stone a shouts of 'Grace,
2Es 8: 8 what you have created is preserved a fire
8:27 those who have kept your covenants a afflictions.

AMINADAB (5) [=AMMINADAB]

Mt 1: 4 Aram the father of A, and A the father of Nahshon,
AdE 2: 7 the daughter of his father's brother, A,
2:15 the time was fulfilled for Esther daughter of A,
9:29 of A along with Mordecai the Jew wrote

AMINADAB (KJV) See also AMMINADAB

AMISS (KJV) See BLASPHEMY, WRONG

AMITTAI (2)

2Ki 14:25 which he spoke by his servant Jonah son of A,
Jnh 1: 1 the word of the LORD came to Jonah son of A,

AMMAH (1)

2Sa 2:24 sun was going down they came to the hill of A,

AMMI (1) [LO-AMMI]

Hos 2: 1 Say to your brother, A, and to your sister,

AMMIDIANS (1)

1Es 5:20 The Chadiasans and A, four hundred twenty-two.

AMMIEL (6)

Nu 13:12 from the tribe of Dan, A son of Gemalli;
2Sa 9: 4 "He is in the house of Machir son of A,
9: 5 from the house of Machir son of A,
17:27 and Machir son of A from Lo-debar,
1Ch 3: 5 and Solomon, four by Bath-shua, daughter of A;
26: 5 A the sixth, Issachar the seventh, Peullethai

AMMIHUD (10)

Nu 1:10 from Ephraim, Elishama son of A;
2:18 the people of Ephraim shall be Elishama son of A,
7:48 On the seventh day Elishama son of A,
7:53 This was the offering of Elishama son of A.
10:22 over the whole company was Elishama son of A.
34:20 Of the tribe of the Simeonites, Shemuel son of A.
34:28 of the Naphtalites a leader, Pedahel son of A.
2Sa 13:37 But Absalom fled, and went to Talmai son of A,
1Ch 7:26 Ladan his son, A his son, Elishama his son,
9: 4 of A, son of Omri, son of Imri, son of Bani,

AMMINADAB (14) [=AMINADAB]

Ex 6:23 daughter of A and sister of Nahshon,
Nu 1: 7 From Judah, Nahshon son of A.
2: 3 of the people of Judah shall be Nahshon son of A,
7:12 the first day was Nahshon son of A, of the tribe
7:17 This was the offering of Nahshon son of A.
10:14 over the whole company was Nahshon son of A.
Ru 4:19 Hezron of Ram, Ram of A,
4:20 A of Nahshon, Nahshon of Salmon,
1Ch 2:10 Ram became the father of A, and A became the
6:22 The sons of Kohath: A his son, Korah his son,
15:10 of Uzziel, A the chief, with one hundred twelve
15:11 Asaiah, Joel, Shemaiah, Eliel, and A.
Lk 3:33 son of A, son of Admin, son of Arni, son

AMMINADAB (KJV) See also AMINADAB

AMMINADIB (KJV) See PRINCE

AMMISHADDAI (5)

Nu 1:12 From Dan, Ahiezer son of A.
2:25 leader of the Danites shall be Ahiezer son of A,
7:66 On the tenth day Ahiezer son of A,
7:71 This was the offering of Ahiezer son of A.
10:25 over the whole company was Ahiezer son of A.

AMMIZABAD (1)

1Ch 27: 6 his son A was in charge of his division.

AMMON (9) [AMMONITE, AMMONITES, BEN-AMMI]

2Ch 20:10 See now, the people of A, Moab, and Mount Seir,
Ne 13:23 of Ashdod, A, and Moab;
Ps 83: 7 and A and Amalek, Philistia with the inhabitants
Eze 25: 5 I will make Rabbah a pasture for camels and A
25:10 I will give it along with A to the people of the east
25:10 Thus A shall be remembered no more among
Jdt 1:12 and the people of A, and all Judea,
5: 2 and the commanders of A and all the governors of
2Mc 4:26 was driven as a fugitive into the land of A.

AMMONITE (16) [AMMON]

Dt 23: 3 No A or Moabite shall be admitted to
1Sa 11: 1 Nahash the A went up and besieged Jabesh-gilead;
11: 2 But Nahash the A said to them,
2Sa 23:37 Zelek the A; Naharai of Beeroth,
1Ki 11: 1 Moabite, A, Edomite, Sidonian,
14:21 His mother's name was Naamah the A.
14:31 His mother's name was Naamah the A.
1Ch 11:39 Zelek the A, Naharai of Beeroth, the armor-bearer
2Ch 12:13 His mother's name was Naamah the A.
24:26 against him were Zabad son of Shimeath the A,
Ne 2:10 the Horonite and Tobiah the A official heard this,
2:19 Sanballat the Horonite and Tobiah the A official,
4: 3 Tobiah the A was beside him, and he said,
13: 1 that no A or Moabite should ever enter
Jdt 6: 5 "As for you, Achior, you A mercenary,
14: 5 the A to me so that he may see and recognize

AMMONITES‡ (115) [AMMON]

Ge 19:38 he is the ancestor of the A to this day.
Nu 21:24 as far as to the A;
21:24 for the boundary of the A was strong.
Dt 2:19 When you approach the frontier of the A,
2:19 not give the land of the A to you as a possession,
2:20 though the A call them Zamzummim,
2:21 the A so that they could dispossess them and settle
2:37 however, on the land of the A,
3:11 an iron bed, can still be seen in Rabbah of the A.
3:16 the wadi being boundary of the A;
Jos 12: 2 the boundary of the A, that is, half of Gilead,
13:10 as far as the boundary of the A;
13:25 and half the land of the A, to Aroer,
Jdg 3:13 In alliance with the A and the Amalekites,
10: 6 the gods of the A, and the gods of the Philistines.
10: 7 of the Philistines and into the hand of the A,
10: 9 The A also crossed the Jordan to fight
10:11 from the A and from the Philistines?
10:17 Then the A were called to arms,
10:18 "Who will begin the fight against the A?
11: 4 After a time the A made war against Israel.
11: 5 And when the A made war against Israel,

Jdg 11: 6 so that we may fight with the **A**."
11: 8 so that you may go with us and fight with the **A**,
11: 9 "If you bring me home again to fight with the **A**,
11:12 to the king of the **A** and said,
11:13 of the **A** answered the messengers of Jephthah,
11:14 Jephthah sent messengers to the king of the **A**
11:15 the land of Moab or the land of the **A**,
11:27 decide today for the Israelites or for the **A**."
11:28 But the king of the **A** did not heed the message
11:29 and from Mizpah of Gilead he passed on to the **A**.
11:30 and said, "If you will give the **A** into my hand,
11:31 when I return victorious from the **A**,
11:32 So Jephthah crossed over to the **A** to fight
11:33 So the **A** were subdued before the people of Israel.
11:36 against your enemies, the **A**."
12: 1 "Why did you cross over to fight against the **A**,
12: 2 in conflict with the **A** who oppressed us severely.
12: 3 and crossed over against the **A**,
1Sa 10:27 Now Nahash, king of the **A**,
10:27 king of the **A**, had not gouged out.
10:27 from the **A** and had entered Jabesh-gilead.
11:11 into the camp and cut down the **A** until the heat of
12:12 when you saw that King Nahash of the **A** came
14:47 against Moab, against the **A**, against Edom,
2Sa 8:12 Moab, the **A**, the Philistines, Amalek,
10: 1 Some time afterward, the king of the **A** died,
10: 2 When David's envoys came into the land of the **A**,
10: 3 the princes of the **A** said to their lord Hanun,
10: 6 the **A** saw that they had become odious to David,
10: 6 the **A** sent and hired the Arameans of Beth-rehob
10: 8 The **A** came out and drew up in battle array at
10:10 and he arrayed them against the **A**.
10:11 but if the **A** are too strong for you,
10:14 When the **A** saw that the Arameans fled,
10:14 Then Joab returned from fighting against the **A**,
10:19 the Arameans were afraid to help the **A** any more.
11: 1 they ravaged the **A**, and besieged Rabbah.
12: 9 and have killed him with the sword of the **A**.
12:26 Now Joab fought against Rabbah of the **A**,
12:31 Thus he did to all the cities of the **A**.
17:27 Shobi son of Nahash from Rabbah of the **A**,
1Ki 11: 5 and Milcom the abomination of the **A**.
11: 7 and for Molech the abomination of the **A**,
11:33 and Milcom the god of the **A**,
2Ki 23:13 and for Milcom the abomination of the **A**.
24: 2 bands of the Moabites, and bands of the **A**;
1Ch 18:11 Moab, the **A**, the Philistines, and Amalek.
19: 1 Some time afterward, King Nahash of the **A** died,
19: 2 to Hanun in the land of the **A**,
19: 3 the officials of the **A** said to Hanun,
19: 6 the **A** saw that they had made themselves odious
19: 6 Hanun and the **A** sent a thousand talents of silver
19: 7 the **A** were mustered from their cities and came
19: 9 The **A** came out and drew up in battle array at
19:11 and they were arrayed against the **A**.
19:12 the **A** are too strong for you, then I will help you.
19:15 When the **A** saw that the Arameans fled,
19:19 not willing to help the **A** any more.
20: 1 ravaged the country of the **A**,
20: 3 Thus David did to all the cities of the **A**.
2Ch 20: 1 After this the Moabites and **A**,
20:22 the LORD set an ambush against the **A**, Moab,
20:23 For the **A** and Moab attacked the inhabitants
26: 8 The **A** paid tribute to Uzziah,
27: 5 with the king of the **A** and prevailed against them.
27: 5 **A** gave him that year one hundred talents of silver,
27: 5 The **A** paid him the same amount in the second
Ezr 9: 1 the Jebusites, the **A**, the Moabites, the Egyptians,
Ne 4: 7 the Arabs and the **A** and the Ashdodites heard that
Isa 11:14 and the **A** shall obey them.
Jer 9:26 Judah, Edom, the **A**, Moab,
25:21 Edom, Moab, and the **A**;
27: 3 the king of Moab, the king of the **A**,
40:11 the Judeans who were in Moab and among the **A**
40:14 that Baalis king of the **A** has sent Ishmael son
41:10 and set out to cross over to the **A**.
41:15 from Johanan with eight men, and went to the **A**.
49: 1 Concerning the **A**. Thus says the LORD:
49: 2 the battle alarm against Rabbah of the **A**;
49: 6 But afterward I will restore the fortunes of the **A**,
Eze 21:20 of the **A** or to Judah and to Jerusalem the fortified.
21:28 Thus says the Lord GOD concerning the **A**,
25: 2 toward the **A** and prophesy against them.
25: 3 Say to the **A**, Hear the word of the Lord GOD:
Da 11:41 and Moab and the main part of the **A** shall escape
Am 1:13 For three transgressions of the **A**, and for four,
Zep 2: 8 the taunts of Moab and the revilings of the **A**,
2: 9 Moab shall become like Sodom and the **A**
Jdt 5: 5 Then Achior, the leader of all the **A**, said to him,
7:17 So the army of the **A** moved forward,
7:18 And the Edomites and **A** went up and encamped in
1Mc 5: 6 Then he crossed over to attack the **A**,
2Mc 5: 7 and fled again into the country of the **A**.

AMNESTY‡ (1)

3Mc 3:21 to all our **a** toward their compatriots here,

AMNON (27) [AMNON'S]

2Sa 3: 2 his firstborn was **A**, of Ahinoam of Jezreel;
13: 1 and David's son **A** fell in love with her.
13: 2 **A** was so tormented that he made himself ill
13: 2 for she was a virgin and it seemed impossible to **A**
13: 3 But **A** had a friend whose name was Jonadab,
13: 4 **A** said to him, "I love Tamar,
13: 6 So **A** lay down, and pretended to be ill;
13: 6 when the king came to see him, **A** said to the king,
2Sa 13: 9 **A** said, "Send out everyone from me."
13:10 Then **A** said to Tamar, "Bring the food into
13:10 brought them into the chamber to **A** her brother.
13:15 **A** was seized with a very great loathing for her;
13:15 **A** said to her, "Get out!"
13:20 "Has **A** your brother been with you?
13:21 but he would not punish his son **A**,
13:22 But Absalom spoke to **A** neither good nor bad; for Absalom hated **A**,
13:26 "If not, please let my brother **A** go with us."
13:27 until he let **A** and all the king's sons go with him.
13:28 and when I say to you, 'Strike **A**,' then kill him.
13:29 of Absalom did to **A** as Absalom had commanded.
13:32 all the young men the king's sons; **A** alone is dead.
13:32 from the day **A** raped his sister Tamar.
13:33 all the king's sons were dead; for **A** alone is dead."
13:39 for he was now consoled over the death of **A**.
1Ch 3: 1 the firstborn **A**, by Ahinoam the Jezreelite;
4:20 **A**, Rinnah, Ben-hanan, and Tilon.

AMNON'S (3) [AMNON]

2Sa 13: 7 saying, "Go to your brother **A** house,
13: 8 So Tamar went to her brother **A** house,
13:28 "Watch when **A** heart is merry with wine,

AMOK (2)

Ne 12: 7 **A**, Hilkiah, Jedaiah. These were the leaders of the
12:20 of Sallai, Kallai; of **A**, Eber;

AMON‡ (18)

1Ki 22:26 and return him to **A** the governor of the city and
2Ki 21:18 His son **A** succeeded him.
21:19 **A** was twenty-two years old when he began
21:23 The servants of **A** conspired against him,
21:24 against King **A**, and the people of
21:25 Now the rest of the acts of **A** that he did,
1Ch 3:14 **A** his son, Josiah his son.
2Ch 18:25 and return him to **A** the governor of the city and
33:20 His son **A** succeeded him.
33:21 **A** was twenty-two years old when he began
33:22 **A** sacrificed to all the images
33:23 but this **A** incurred more and more guilt.
33:25 killed all those who had conspired against King **A**;
Ne 7:59 of Hattil, of Pochereth-hazzebaim, of **A**.
Jer 1: 2 in the days of King Josiah son of **A** of Judah,
25: 3 from the thirteenth year of King Josiah son of **A**
46:25 See, I am bringing punishment upon **A** of Thebes,
Zep 1: 1 in the days of King Josiah son of **A** of Judah.

AMONG‡ (1054)

Ge 3: 8 from the presence of the LORD God **a** the trees
3:14 cursed are you **a** all animals and
3:14 among all animals and **a** all wild creatures;
13:12 while Lot settled **a** the cities of the Plain
17:10 Every male **a** you shall be circumcised.
17:12 Throughout your generations every male **a**
17:23 every male **a** the men of Abraham's house,
23: 4 "I am a stranger and an alien residing **a** you;
23: 4 give me property **a** you for a burying place,
23: 6 you are a mighty prince **a** us.
23:10 Now Ephron was sitting **a** the Hittites;
23:16 according to the weights current **a** the merchants.
24: 3 the daughters of the Canaanites, **a** whom I live,
30:32 and the spotted and speckled **a** the goats;
30:33 not speckled and spotted **a** the goats and black
30:33 spotted among the goats and black **a**
30:41 that they might breed **a** the rods,
33: 1 the children **a** Leah and Rachel and the two maids.
34:15 that you will become as we are and every male **a**
34:16 and we will live **a** you and become one people.
34:22 Only on this condition will they agree to live **a** us,
34:22 that every male **a** us be circumcised
34:23 and they will live **a** us."
35: 2 "Put away the foreign gods that are **a** you,
39:14 my husband has brought **a** us a Hebrew
39:17 whom you have brought **a** us,
40:20 and the head of the chief baker **a** his servants.
42: 5 of Israel were **a** the other people who came
47: 2 From **a** his brothers he took five men
47: 6 if you know that there are capable men **a** them,
Ex 2: 3 the child in it and placed it **a** the reeds on the bank
2: 5 She saw the basket **a** the reeds and sent her maid
7: 5 against Egypt and bring the Israelites out from **a**
10: 1 in order that I may show these signs of mine **a**
10: 2 of the Egyptians and what signs I have done **a**
12:49 for the native and for the alien who resides **a** you.
13: 2 the first to open the womb **a** the Israelites,
13: 7 no leaven shall be seen **a** you in all your territory.
13:13 firstborn male **a** your children you shall redeem.
15:11 "Who is like you, O LORD, **a** the gods?
17: 7 saying, "Is the LORD **a** us or not?"
18:21 You should also look for able men **a** all
22:25 you lend money to my people, to the poor **a** you,
23:25 and I will take sickness away from **a** you.
25: 8 so that I may dwell **a** them.
28: 1 from **a** the Israelites, to serve me as priests—
29:45 I will dwell **a** the Israelites,
29:46 of the land of Egypt that I might dwell **a** them;
31:14 on it shall be cut off from **a** the people.
33: 3 but I will not go up **a** you,
33: 5 if for a single moment I should go up **a** you,
34:10 the people **a** whom you live shall see the work of
34:12 or it will become a snare **a** you.
34:15 someone **a** them will invite you,
34:16 And you will take wives from **a** their daughters
Ex 35: 5 Take from **a** you an offering to the LORD;
35:10 All who are skillful **a** you shall come and make all
36: 8 with skill **a** the workers made the tabernacle
Lev 4:27 of the ordinary people **a** you sins unintentionally
6:18 Every male **a** the descendants of Aaron shall eat
6:22 from **a** Aaron's descendants as a successor,
6:29 Every male **a** the priests shall eat of it;
7: 6 Every male **a** the priests shall eat of it;
7:33 the one **a** the sons of Aaron who offers the blood
11: 2 From **a** all the land animals,
11: 4 **a** those that chew the cud or have divided hoofs,
11:10 of the swarming creatures in the waters and **a** all
11:13 These you shall regard as detestable **a** the birds.
11:21 But **a** the winged insects that walk
11:27 **a** the animals that walk on all fours,
11:29 for you **a** the creatures that swarm upon the earth:
11:31 These are unclean for you **a** all that swarm;
16:29 neither the citizen nor the alien who resides **a** you.
17: 8 of the house of Israel or of the aliens who reside **a**
17:10 of the house of Israel or of the aliens who reside **a**
17:12 No person **a** you shall eat blood,
17:12 nor shall any alien who resides **a** you eat blood.
17:13 or of the aliens who reside **a** them,
18:26 either the citizen or the alien who resides **a** you
19:16 around as a slanderer **a** your people, and you shall
19:34 with you shall be to you as the citizen **a** you;
20: 5 and will cut them off from **a** their people,
20:14 that there may be no depravity **a** you.
21: 1 No one shall defile himself for a dead person **a**
21: 4 as a husband **a** his people and so profane himself.
21:15 that he may not profane his offspring **a** his kin;
22: 3 If anyone **a** all your offspring
22:32 that I may be sanctified **a** the people of Israel:
24:10 and whose father was an Egyptian came out **a**
25:33 in the cities of the Levites are their possession **a**
25:45 also acquire them from **a** the aliens residing
25:47 If resident aliens **a** you prosper,
26:12 And I will walk **a** you, and will be your God,
26:25 I will send pestilence **a** you,
26:33 And you I will scatter **a** the nations,
26:38 You shall perish **a** the nations,
Nu 2:33 the Levites were not enrolled **a** the other Israelites.
3: 9 they are unreservedly given to him from **a**
3:12 I hereby accept the Levites from **a** the Israelites
3:12 the firstborn that open the womb **a** the Israelites.
3:41 as substitutes for all the firstborn **a** the Israelites,
3:41 as substitutes for all the firstborn **a** the livestock of
3:42 So Moses enrolled all the firstborn **a** the Israelites,
3:45 as substitutes for all the firstborn **a** the Israelites,
4:18 of the Kohathites be destroyed from **a** the Levites.
5: 3 they must not defile their camp, where I dwell **a**
5: 9 **A** all the sacred donations of the Israelites,
5:21 an execration and an oath **a** your people,
5:27 woman shall become an execration **a** her people.
8: 6 the Levites from **a** the Israelites and cleanse them.
8:14 Thus you shall separate the Levites from **a**
8:16 For they are unreservedly given to me from **a**
8:17 For all the firstborn **a** the Israelites are mine,
8:18 in place of all the firstborn **a** the Israelites.
8:19 the Levites as a gift to Aaron and his sons from **a**
8:19 be no plague **a** the Israelites for coming too close
9: 7 the LORD's offering at its appointed time **a**
9:14 Any alien residing **a** you who wishes to keep
11: 4 The rabble **a** them had a strong craving;
11:20 you have rejected the LORD who is **a** you,
11:26 they were **a** those registered,
12: 6 When there are prophets **a** you,
13: 2 every one a leader **a** them."
13: 3 all of them leading men **a** the Israelites.
14: 6 who were **a** those who had spied out the land,
14:11 in spite of all the signs that I have done **a** them?
14:13 in your might you brought up this people from **a**
15:14 or who takes up permanent residence **a** you,
15:26 as well as the aliens residing **a** them,
15:29 the native **a** the Israelites and the alien residing
15:29 the Israelites and the alien residing **a** them—
15:30 and shall be cut off from **a** the people.
16: 3 everyone of them, and the LORD is **a** them.
16:47 where the plague had already begun **a** the people.
17: 6 and the staff of Aaron was **a** theirs.
18: 6 It is I who now take your brother Levites from **a**
18:20 nor shall you have any share **a** them;
18:20 I am your share and your possession **a**
18:23 But **a** the Israelites they shall have no allotment,
18:24 that they shall have no allotment **a** the Israelites.
19:10 for the Israelites and for the alien residing **a** them.
21: 6 the LORD sent poisonous serpents **a** the people,
23: 9 and not reckoning itself **a** the nations!
23:21 acclaimed as a king **a** them.
24:20 "First **a** the nations was Amalek,
25: 8 So the plague was stopped **a** the people of Israel.
25:11 by manifesting such zeal **a** them on my behalf that
26:62 for they were not enrolled **a** the Israelites
26:62 because there was no allotment given to them **a**
26:64 **A** these there was not one of those enrolled
27: 3 he was not **a** the company
27: 4 Give to us a possession **a** our father's brothers."
27: 7 you shall indeed let them possess an inheritance **a**
31:16 plague came **a** the congregation of the LORD.
31:17 Now therefore, kill every male **a** the little ones,
32:30 they shall have possessions **a** you in the land
33: 4 whom the LORD had struck down **a** them.
35:15 for the resident or transient alien **a** them,
35:34 for I the LORD dwell **a** the Israelites.
Dt 2:16 Just as soon as all the warriors had died off from **a**
4: 3 from **a** you everyone who followed the Baal
4:27 The LORD will scatter you **a** the peoples;

Dt 4:27 only a few of you will be left **a** the nations where
7:14 with neither sterility nor barrenness **a** you
13:1 by dreams appear **a** you and promise you omens
13:13 that scoundrels from **a** you have gone out and led
13:14 that such an abhorrent thing has been done **a** you,
14:6 and chews the cud, **a** the animals, you may eat.
15:4 There will, however, be no one in need **a** you,
15:7 If there is **a** you anyone in need,
16:11 the orphans, and the widows who are **a** you—
17:2 If there is found **a** you,
18:2 but they shall have no inheritance **a**
18:10 be found **a** you who makes a son or daughter pass
18:15 a prophet like me from **a** your own people;
18:18 I will raise up for them a prophet like you from **a**
19:20 as this shall never again be committed **a** you.
21:11 suppose you see **a** the captives
23:14 so that he may not see anything indecent **a** you
26:11 with the Levites and the aliens who reside **a** you,
28:37 and a byword **a** all the peoples where
28:43 Aliens residing **a** you shall ascend
28:46 They shall be **a** you and your descendants as
28:54 and gentle of men **a** you will begrudge food
28:56 She who is the most refined and gentle **a** you,
28:64 The LORD will scatter you **a** all peoples,
28:65 **A** those nations you shall find no ease,
29:17 of silver and gold, that were **a** them.
29:18 It may be that there is **a** you a man or woman,
29:18 be that there is **a** you a root sprouting poisonous
30:1 if you call them to mind **a** all the nations where
30:3 gathering you again from all the peoples **a** whom
31:27 toward the LORD while I am still alive **a** you,
32:51 both of you broke faith with me **a** the Israelites at
32:51 by failing to maintain my holiness **a** the Israelites.
33:3 Indeed, O favorite **a** peoples,
33:16 on the brow of the prince **a** his brothers.
Jos 1:14 But all the warriors **a** you shall cross over armed
3:5 for tomorrow the LORD will do wonders **a** you."
3:10 "By this you shall know that **a** you is
4:6 so that this may be a sign **a** you.
7:11 and they have put them **a** their own belongings.
7:12 unless you destroy the devoted things from **a** you.
7:13 "There are devoted things **a** you, O Israel;
7:13 until you take away the devoted things from **a**
7:21 I saw **a** the spoil a beautiful mantle from Shinar,
8:35 and the aliens who resided **a** them.
9:7 to the Hivites, "Perhaps you live **a** us;
9:16 that they were their neighbors and were living **a**
9:22 while in fact you are living **a** us?
10:1 of Gibeon had made peace with Israel and were **a**
14:3 but to the Levites he gave no inheritance **a** them.
14:15 this Arba was the greatest man **a** the Anakim.
15:13 to Caleb son of Jephunneh a portion **a** the people
17:4 of the LORD he gave them an inheritance **a**
17:9 to the south of the wadi, **a** the towns of Manasseh,
18:2 There remained **a** the Israelites seven tribes whose
18:7 The Levites have no portion **a** you,
19:49 an inheritance **a** them to Joshua son of Nun.
20:9 and for the aliens residing **a** them,
22:14 every one of them the head of a family **a** the clans
22:19 and take for yourselves a possession **a** us;
22:31 "Today we know that the LORD is **a** us,
23:7 not be mixed with these nations left here **a** you,
23:12 join the survivors of these nations left here **a** you,
24:17 and **a** all the peoples through whom we passed;
24:23 "Then put away the foreign gods that are **a** you,
Jdg 1:21 in Jerusalem **a** the Benjaminites to this day.
1:29 but the Canaanites lived **a** them in Gezer.
1:30 but the Canaanites lived **a** them,
1:32 but the Asherites lived **a** the Canaanites,
1:33 but lived **a** the Canaanites,
2:12 they followed other gods, from **a** the gods of
3:5 So the Israelites lived **a** the Canaanites,
5:8 Was shield or spear to be seen **a** forty thousand
5:9 of Israel who offered themselves willingly **a**
5:15 **A** the clans of Reuben there were great searchings
5:16 Why did you tarry **a** the sheepfolds,
5:16 **A** the clans of Reuben there were great searchings
10:16 So they put away the foreign gods from **a** them
14:3 "Is there not a woman **a** your kin,
14:3 or **a** all our people, that you must go to take a wife
18:1 for until then no territory **a** the tribes
18:25 "You had better not let your voice be heard **a** us
20:12 "What crime is this that has been committed **a**
21:9 For when the roll was called **a** the people,
21:12 And they found **a** the inhabitants
Ru 2:2 "Let me go to the field and glean **a** the ears
2:7 and gather **a** the sheaves behind the reapers.'
2:15 "Let her glean even **a** the standing sheaves,
1Sa 4:3 that he may come **a** us and save us from the power
4:17 there has also been a great slaughter **a** the troops;
6:19 because the LORD had made a great slaughter **a**
7:3 the foreign gods and the Astartes from **a** you.
9:2 There was not a man **a** the people
10:11 Is Saul also **a** the prophets?"
10:12 it became a proverb, "Is Saul also **a** the prophets?"
10:22 "See, he has hidden himself **a** the baggage."
10:23 When he took his stand **a** the people,
10:24 There is no one like him **a** all the people."
14:15 in the field, and **a** all the people;
14:30 the slaughter **a** the Philistines has not been great."
14:34 Saul said, "Disperse yourselves **a** the troops,
14:39 But there was no one **a** all
15:6 Withdraw from **a** the Amalekites,
15:33 so your mother shall be childless **a** women."
16:1 for I have provided for myself a king **a** his sons."
19:24 Therefore it is said, "Is Saul also **a** the prophets?"
22:14 "Who **a** all your servants is so faithful as David?
1Sa 23:19 "David is hiding **a** us in the strongholds
23:23 the land, I will search him out **a** all the thousands
30:22 and worthless fellows **a** the men who had gone
2Sa 6:19 and distributed food **a** all the people,
7:7 Wherever I have moved about **a** all the people
8:6 David put garrisons **a** the Arameans of Damascus;
11:17 some of the servants of David **a** the people fell.
15:31 that Ahithophel was **a** the conspirators
17:9 a slaughter **a** the troops who follow Absalom.'
19:28 you set your servant **a** those who eat at your table.
22:50 For this I will extol you, O LORD, **a** the nations,
23:9 Next to him **a** the three warriors was Eleazar son
23:23 He was renowned **a** the Thirty,
23:24 **A** the Thirty were Asahel brother of Joab;
24:16 to the angel who was bringing destruction **a**
1Ki 2:7 and let them be **a** those who eat at your table;
5:6 for you know that there is no one **a** us who knows
6:13 I will dwell **a** the children of Israel,
8:53 For you have separated them from **a** all
9:7 and Israel will become a proverb and a taunt **a**
11:3 **A** his wives were seven hundred princesses
11:20 Genubath was in Pharaoh's house **a** the children
12:31 and appointed priests from **a** all the people,
13:33 but made priests for the high places again from **a**
14:7 Because I exalted you from **a** the people,
2Ki 2:16 we have fifty strong men **a** your servants;
4:13 She answered, "I live **a** my own people."
4:18 he went out one day to his father **a** the reapers.
6:11 tell me who **a** us sides with the king of Israel?"
10:23 that there is no worshiper of the LORD here **a**
11:2 from **a** the king's children who were about to
17:25 therefore the LORD sent lions **a** them,
17:26 therefore he has sent lions **a** them;
17:32 from **a** themselves all sorts of people as priests of
17:33 from **a** whom they had been carried away.
18:5 so that there was no one like him **a** all the kings
18:5 or **a** those who were before him.
18:24 then can you repulse a single captain **a** the least
18:35 Who **a** all the gods of the countries have delivered
23:9 but ate unleavened bread **a** their kindred.
1Ch 5:2 though Judah became prominent **a** his brothers
11:12 to him **a** the three warriors was Eleazar son
11:25 He was renowned **a** the Thirty,
12:1 they were **a** the mighty warriors who helped him
12:4 a warrior **a** the Thirty and a leader over the Thirty;
16:8 make known his deeds **a** the peoples.
16:24 Declare his glory **a** the nations,
16:24 his marvelous works **a** all the peoples.
16:31 and let them say **a** the nations,
16:35 and gather and rescue us from **a** the nations,
17:6 Wherever I have moved about **a** all Israel,
23:14 his sons were to be reckoned **a** the tribe of Levi.
24:4 were found **a** the sons of Eleazar than **a** the sons of
24:5 and officers of God **a** both the sons of Eleazar and
26:19 the divisions of the gatekeepers **a** the Korahites
26:31 and men of great ability **a** them were found
28:4 and in the house of Judah my father's house, and **a**
2Ch 7:13 or send pestilence **a** my people,
7:20 will make it a proverb and a byword **a** all peoples.
11:22 of Maacah as chief prince **a** his brothers,
17:9 around through all the cities of Judah and taught **a**
19:4 then he went out again **a** the people,
22:11 from **a** the king's children who were about to
24:16 they buried him in the city of David **a** the kings,
24:19 Yet he sent prophets **a** them to bring them back to
24:23 and destroyed all the officials of the people from **a**
26:6 of Ashdod and elsewhere **a** the Philistines.
28:15 the booty they clothed all that were naked **a** them;
28:15 and carrying all the feeble **a** them on donkeys,
31:19 to every male **a** the priests and to everyone **a** the
32:14 Who **a** all the gods of those nations
36:23 Whoever is **a** you of all his people,
Ezr 1:3 Any of those **a** you who are of his people—
Ne 1:8 I will scatter you **a** the peoples;
6:6 In it was written, "It is reported **a** the nations—
7:3 Appoint guards from **a** the inhabitants
7:64 These sought their registration **a** those enrolled in
9:17 not mindful of the wonders that you performed **a**
10:34 We have also cast lots **a** the priests, the Levites,
11:17 and Bakbukiah, the second **a** his associates;
13:26 **A** the many nations there was no king like him,
Est 1:19 and let it be written **a** the laws of the Persians and
2:6 Kish had been carried away from Jerusalem **a**
3:8 and separated **a** the peoples in all the provinces
4:3 there was great mourning **a** the Jews,
8:17 there was gladness and joy **a** the Jews,
9:28 of Purim should never fall into disuse **a** the Jews,
9:28 the commemoration of these days cease **a**
10:3 and he was powerful **a** the Jews and popular
Job 1:6 and Satan also came **a** them.
2:1 and Satan also came **a** them to present himself
2:8 a potsherd with which to scrape himself, and sat **a**
3:6 let it not rejoice **a** the days of the year;
8:17 around the stoneheap; they live **a** the rocks.
12:9 Who **a** all these does not know that the hand of
15:19 and no stranger passed **a** them.
17:10 and I shall not find a sensible person **a** you.
18:19 They have no offspring or descendant **a**
29:25 and I lived like a king **a** his troops,
30:7 **A** the bushes they bray;
32:12 no one **a** you that answered his words.
34:4 let us determine **a** ourselves what is good.
34:37 he claps his hands **a** us,
41:6 Will they divide it up **a** the merchants?
Ps 9:11 Declare his deeds **a** the peoples.
12:8 as vileness is exalted **a** humankind.
18:49 For this I will extol you, O LORD, **a** the nations,
Ps 21:10 and their children from **a** humankind.
22:18 they divide my clothes **a** themselves,
30:3 restored me to life from **a** those gone down to
44:11 and have scattered us **a** the nations.
44:14 You have made us a byword **a** the nations,
44:14 a laughingstock **a** the peoples.
45:9 daughters of kings are **a** your ladies of honor;
46:10 I am exalted **a** the nations,
54:T *and told Saul, "David is in hiding a us."*
57:4 down **a** lions that greedily devour human prey;
57:9 I will give thanks to you, O Lord, **a** the peoples;
57:9 I will sing praises to you **a** the nations.
66:5 he is awesome in his deeds **a** mortals.
66:9 who has kept us **a** the living,
67:2 your saving power **a** all nations.
68:13 though they stay **a** the sheepfolds—
68:30 Rebuke the wild animals that live **a** the reeds,
69:28 let them not be enrolled **a** the righteous.
74:9 and there is no one **a** us who knows how long.
77:14 you have displayed your might **a** the peoples.
78:45 He sent **a** them swarms of flies,
78:60 the tent where he dwelt **a** mortals,
79:10 the outpoured blood of your servants be known **a**
80:6 our enemies laugh **a** themselves.
81:9 There shall be no strange god **a** you;
86:8 There is none like you **a** the gods, O Lord,
87:4 **A** those who know me I mention Rahab
88:4 I am counted **a** those who go down to the Pit;
88:5 like those forsaken **a** the dead,
89:6 Who **a** the heavenly beings is like the LORD,
96:3 Declare his glory **a** the nations,
96:3 his marvelous works **a** all the peoples.
96:10 Say **a** the nations, "The LORD is king!
99:6 Moses and Aaron were **a** his priests,
99:6 Samuel also was **a** those who called on his name.
104:12 have their habitation; they sing **a** the branches.
105:1 make known his deeds **a** the peoples.
105:27 They performed his signs **a** them,
105:37 and there was no one **a** their tribes who stumbled.
106:15 but sent a wasting disease **a** them.
106:27 would disperse their descendants **a** the nations,
106:29 and a plague broke out **a** them.
106:47 and gather us from **a** the nations,
108:3 I will give thanks to you, O LORD, **a** the peoples,
108:3 and I will sing praises to you **a** the nations.
110:6 He will execute judgment **a** the nations,
120:5 that I must live **a** the tents of Kedar.
120:6 Too long have I had my dwelling **a**
126:2 then it was said **a** the nations,
136:11 and brought Israel out from **a** them,
Pr 1:14 Throw in your lot **a** us;
7:7 I saw **a** the simple ones, I observed **a** the youths,
15:31 that heeds wholesome admonition will lodge **a**
16:19 of a lowly spirit **a** the poor than to divide the spoil
23:20 not be **a** winebibbers, or **a** gluttonous eaters
30:14 the needy from **a** mortals.
30:30 which is mightiest **a** wild animals and does
31:23 taking his seat **a** the elders of the land.
Ecc 7:28 One man **a** a thousand I found,
7:28 but a woman **a** all these I have not found.
9:17 to be heeded than the shouting of a ruler **a** fools.
SS 1:8 If you do not know, O fairest **a** women,
1:9 my love, to a mare **a** Pharaoh's chariots.
2:2 a lily **a** brambles, so is my love **a** maidens.
2:3 As an apple tree **a** the trees of the wood,
2:3 so is my beloved **a** young men.
2:16 he pastures his flock **a** the lilies.
4:2 and not one **a** them is bereaved.
4:5 twins of a gazelle, that feed **a** the lilies.
5:9 more than another beloved, O fairest **a** women?
5:10 distinguished **a** ten thousand.
6:1 Where has your beloved gone, O fairest **a** women?
6:3 he pastures his flock **a** the lilies.
6:6 and not one **a** them is bereaved.
Isa 5:17 fatlings and kids shall feed **a** the ruins.
6:5 and I live **a** a people of unclean lips;
8:15 And many **a** them shall stumble;
8:16 seal the teaching **a** my disciples.
10:4 to crouch **a** the prisoners or fall **a** the slain?
10:16 will send wasting sickness **a** his stout warriors,
12:4 make known his deeds **a** the nations;
14:32 the needy **a** his people will find refuge in her."
16:4 let the outcasts of Moab settle **a** you;
24:13 For thus it shall be on the earth and **a** the nations,
30:14 that is smashed so ruthlessly that **a** its fragments
33:14 "Who **a** us can live with the devouring fire?
33:14 Who **a** us can live with everlasting flames?"
36:9 then can you repulse a single captain **a** the least
36:20 Who **a** all the gods of these
38:11 upon mortals no more **a** the inhabitants of
41:28 **a** these there is no counselor who, when I ask,
42:23 Who **a** you will give heed to this,
43:9 Who **a** them declared this,
43:12 when there was no strange god **a** you;
44:14 and lets it grow strong **a** the trees of the forest.
48:14 Who **a** them has declared these things?
50:10 Who **a** you fears the LORD and obeys the voice
50:11 and **a** the brands that you have kindled!
51:18 to guide her **a** all the children she has borne;
51:18 by the hand **a** all the children she has brought up.
57:5 with lust **a** the oaks, under every green tree;
57:6 **A** the smooth stones of the valley is your portion;
58:9 If you remove the yoke from **a** you,
59:10 **a** the vigorous as though we were dead.
61:9 Their descendants shall be known **a** the nations,
61:9 and their offspring **a** the peoples;
66:19 and I will set a sign **a** them.

Isa 66:19 and they shall declare my glory **a** the nations.
Jer 3:13 and scattered your favors **a** strangers
3:19 I thought how I would set you **a** my children,
4: 3 up your fallow ground, and do not sow **a** thorns.
4:29 they enter thickets; they climb **a** rocks;
5:26 For scoundrels are found **a** my people;
6:15 Therefore they shall fall **a** those who fall;
6:27 I have made you a tester and a refiner **a** my people
8:12 Therefore they shall fall **a** those who fall;
8:17 See, I am letting snakes loose **a** you,
9:16 I will scatter them **a** nations that neither they
10: 7 **a** all the wise ones of the nations and
11: 9 Conspiracy exists **a** the people of Judah and
12:14 I will pluck up the house of Judah from **a** them.
18:13 Ask **a** the nations: Who has heard the like of this?
22:23 O inhabitant of Lebanon, nested **a** the cedars,
23:35 Thus shall you say to one another, **a** yourselves,
25:16 because of the sword that I am sending **a** them.
25:27 because of the sword that I am sending **a** you.
29: 1 from Jerusalem to the remaining elders **a**
29: 8 Do not let the prophets and the diviners who are **a**
29:18 and a derision **a** all the nations
29:32 he shall not have anyone living **a** this people
30:11 an end of all the nations **a** which I scattered you,
31: 8 **a** them the blind and the lame,
32:20 and to this day in Israel and **a** all humankind,
37: 4 Jeremiah was still going in and out **a** the people,
37:12 to receive his share of property **a** the people there.
40: 5 and stay with him **a** the people;
40: 6 and stayed with him **a** the people who were left in
40:11 in Moab and **a** the Ammonites and in Edom and
41: 8 there were ten men **a** them who said to Ishmael,
44: 8 and become an object of cursing and ridicule **a** all
46:18 one is coming like Tabor **a** the mountains,
46:28 of all the nations **a** which I have banished you,
48:27 though he was not caught **a** thieves;
49:14 and a messenger has been sent **a** the nations:
49:15 For I will make you least **a** the nations,
50: 2 Declare **a** the nations and proclaim, set up
50:23 How Babylon has become a horror **a** the nations!
50:46 and her cry shall be heard **a** the nations.
51:27 blow the trumpet **a** the nations;
51:41 How Babylon has become an object of horror **a**
La 1: 1 she that was great **a** the nations!
1: 1 a princess **a** the provinces has become a vassal.
1: 2 **a** all her lovers she has no one to comfort her;
1: 3 she lives now **a** the nations,
1:17 Jerusalem has become a filthy thing **a** them.
2: 9 her king and princes are **a** the nations;
3:45 You have made us filth and rubbish **a** the peoples.
4:15 it was said **a** the nations,
4:20 "Under his shadow we shall live **a** the nations."
Eze 1: 1 as I was **a** the exiles by the river Chebar,
1:13 like torches moving to and fro **a**
2: 5 they shall know that there has been a prophet **a**
2: 6 and thorns surround you and you live **a** scorpions;
3:15 And I sat there **a** them, stunned, for seven days.
3:25 so that you cannot go out **a** the people;
4:13 unclean, **a** the nations to which I will drive them."
5: 8 I will execute judgments **a** you in the sight of
5:12 of pestilence or be consumed by famine **a** you;
5:14 an object of mocking **a** the nations around you,
6: 8 Some of you shall escape the sword **a** the nations
6: 9 Those of you who escape shall remember me **a**
6:13 their slain lie **a** their idols around their altars,
7: 4 while your abominations are **a** you.
7: 9 while your abominations are **a** you.
7:11 not their wealth; no pre-eminence **a** them.
8:11 with Jaazaniah son of Shaphan standing **a** them.
9: 2 **a** them was a man clothed in linen,
10: 2 fill your hands with burning coals from **a**
10: 6 from within the wheelwork, from **a** the cherubim,"
10: 7 from **a** the cherubim to the fire that was **a** the
11: 1 **a** them I saw Jaazaniah son of Azzur,
11:16 Though I removed them far away **a** the nations,
11:16 and though I scattered them **a** the countries,
12:12 the prince who is **a** them shall lift his baggage
12:15 when I disperse them **a** the nations
12:16 so that they may tell of all their abominations **a**
13: 4 Your prophets have been like jackals **a** ruins,
13:18 Will you hunt down lives **a** my people,
13:19 You have profaned me **a** my people for handfuls
15: 2 the vine branch that is **a** the trees of the forest?
15: 6 Like the wood of the vine **a** the trees of the forest,
16:14 Your fame spread **a** the nations on account
18:18 and did what is not good **a** his people,
19: 2 What a lioness was your mother **a** lions!
19: 2 She lay down **a** young lions, rearing her cubs.
19: 6 He prowled **a** the lions; he became a young lion,
19:11 it towered aloft **a** the thick boughs;
20: 9 in the sight of the nations **a** whom they lived,
20:23 in the wilderness that I would scatter them **a**
20:38 I will purge out the rebels **a** you,
20:41 and I will manifest my holiness **a** you in the sight
22:15 I will scatter you **a** the nations and disperse you
22:26 so that I am profaned **a** them.
22:30 And I sought for anyone **a** them who would repair
23:10 and she became a byword **a** women.
25: 4 They shall set their encampments **a** you
25:10 Thus Ammon shall be remembered no more **a**
26:20 and I will make you live in the world below, **a**
27:36 The merchants **a** the peoples hiss at you;
28:14 you walked **a** the stones of fire.
28:16 and the guardian cherub drove you out from **a**
28:19 All who know you **a** the peoples are appalled
28:24 a pricking brier or a piercing thorn **a**
28:25 from the peoples **a** whom they are scattered,
Eze 29:12 I will make the land of Egypt a desolation **a**
29:12 a desolation forty years **a** cities that are laid waste.
29:12 I will scatter the Egyptians **a** the nations,
29:12 and disperse them **a** the countries.
29:13 from the peoples **a** whom they were scattered;
29:21 and I will open your lips **a** them.
30: 7 be desolated **a** other desolated countries,
30: 7 and their cities shall lie **a** cities laid waste.
30:23 I will scatter the Egyptians **a** the nations,
30:26 the Egyptians **a** the nations and disperse them
31: 3 and of great height, its top **a** the clouds.
31:10 it towered high and set its top **a** the clouds,
31:13 and **a** its boughs lodge all the wild animals.
31:14 to lofty height or set their tops **a** the clouds,
31:17 those who lived in its shade **a** the nations.
31:18 Which **a** the trees of Eden was like you in glory
31:18 you shall lie **a** the uncircumcised,
32: 2 You consider yourself a lion **a** the nations,
32: 9 as I carry you captive **a** the nations,
32:12 all of them most terrible **a** the nations.
32:20 They shall fall **a** those who are killed by
32:25 They have made Elam a bed **a** the slain
32:25 they are placed **a** the slain.
32:28 you shall be broken and lie **a** the uncircumcised,
32:32 he shall be laid to rest **a** the uncircumcised,
33:33 they shall know that a prophet has been **a** them.
34:12 As shepherds seek out their flocks when they are **a**
34:24 and my servant David shall be prince **a** them;
35:11 and I will make myself known **a** you,
36: 3 and you became an object of gossip and slander **a**
36:19 I scattered them **a** the nations,
36:21 the house of Israel had profaned **a** the nations
36:22 of my holy name, which you have profaned **a**
36:23 which has been profaned **a** the nations,
36:23 and which you have profaned **a** them;
36:30 the disgrace of famine **a** the nations.
37:21 of Israel from the nations **a** which they have gone,
37:26 and will set my sanctuary **a** them forevermore.
37:28 when my sanctuary is **a** them forevermore.
39: 7 My holy name I will make known **a**
39:21 I will display my glory **a** the nations;
39:28 because I sent them into exile **a** the nations,
40:46 these are the descendants of Zadok, who alone **a**
43: 7 where I will reside **a** the people of Israel forever.
43: 9 and I will reside **a** them forever.
44: 9 of all the foreigners who are **a** the people of Israel,
47:13 for inheritance **a** the twelve tribes of Israel.
47:21 So you shall divide this land **a** you according to
47:22 for the aliens who reside **a** you and have begotten children **a** you.
47:22 with you they shall be allotted an inheritance **a**
48:29 that you shall allot as an inheritance **a** the tribes
Da 1: 6 **A** them were Daniel, Hananiah, Mishael,
1:19 And **a** them all, no one was found to compare
2:25 "I have found **a** the exiles from Judah
7: 5 had three tusks in its mouth **a** its teeth
7: 8 a little one coming up **a** them;
9:16 and your people have become a disgrace **a**
11:14 lawless **a** your own people shall lift themselves up
11:33 The wise **a** the people shall give understanding
Hos 5: 9 **a** the tribes of Israel I declare what is sure.
8: 8 now they are **a** the nations as a useless vessel.
9:17 they shall become wanderers **a** the nations.
13:15 Although he may flourish **a** rushes,
Joel 1:12 surely, joy withers away **a** the people.
2:17 not make your heritage a mockery, a byword **a**
2:17 Why should it be said **a** the peoples,
2:19 I will no more make you a mockery **a** the nations.
2:32 as the LORD has said, and **a** the survivors shall
3: 2 because they have scattered them **a** the nations.
3: 9 Proclaim this **a** the nations:
Am 1: 1 who was **a** the shepherds of Tekoa,
2:16 of heart **a** the mighty shall flee away naked in
4:10 I sent **a** you a pestilence after the manner
9: 9 the house of Israel **a** all the nations as one shakes
Ob 1: 1 and a messenger has been sent **a** the nations:
1: 2 I will surely make you least **a** the nations;
1: 4 though your nest is set **a** the stars,
Mic 2: 4 **A** our captors he parcels out our fields."
5: 8 And **a** the nations the remnant of Jacob,
5: 8 shall be like a lion **a** the animals of the forest,
5: 8 like a young lion **a** the flocks of sheep, which,
5:10 from **a** you and will destroy your chariots;
5:13 from **a** you, and you shall bow down no more to
5:14 and I will uproot your sacred poles from **a** you
Zep 3:20 for I will make you renowned and praised **a** all
Hag 2: 3 Who is left **a** you that saw this house
2: 5 My spirit abides **a** you; do not fear.
Zec 1: 8 He was standing **a** the myrtle trees in the glen;
1:10 So the man who was standing **a**
1:11 the LORD who was standing **a** the myrtle trees,
3: 7 the right of access **a** those who are standing here.
7:14 with a whirlwind **a** all the nations that they had
8:13 Just as you have been a cursing **a** the nations,
10: 9 Though I scattered them **a** the nations,
12: 6 like a flaming torch **a** sheaves;
12: 8 the feeblest **a** them on that day shall be like David,
Mal 1:10 that someone **a** you would shut the temple doors,
1:11 to its setting my name is great **a** the nations,
1:11 for my name is great **a** the nations,
1:14 and my name is reverenced **a** the nations.
Mt 2: 6 are by no means least **a** the rulers of Judah;
4:23 and curing every disease and every sickness **a**
7: 9 Is there anyone **a** you who,
10: 5 "Go nowhere **a** the Gentiles,
11:11 Truly I tell you, **a** those born
13: 7 Other seeds fell **a** thorns, and the thorns grew up
Mt 13:22 As for what was sown **a** thorns,
13:25 an enemy came and sowed weeds **a** the wheat,
18: 2 He called a child, whom he put **a** them,
18:20 or three are gathered in my name, I am there **a**
20:26 It will not be so **a** you;
20:26 but whoever wishes to be great **a** you must
20:27 and whoever wishes to be first **a** you must
22:25 Now there were seven brothers **a** us;
23:11 The greatest **a** you will be your servant.
26: 5 or there may be a riot **a** the people."
27:35 they divided his clothes **a** themselves
27:56 **A** them were Mary Magdalene,
28:15 And this story is still told **a** the Jews to this day.
Mk 2: 8 that they were discussing these questions **a**
4: 7 Other seed fell **a** thorns, and the thorns grew up
4:18 And others are those sown **a** the thorns:
5: 3 He lived **a** the tombs;
5: 5 Night and day **a** the tombs and on
6: 4 except in their hometown, and **a** their own kin,
6: 6 Then he went about **a** the villages teaching.
6:41 and he divided the two fish **a** them all.
9:19 how much longer must I be **a** you?
9:36 Then he took a little child and put it **a** them;
10:42 that **a** the Gentiles those whom they recognize
10:43 But it is not so **a** you;
10:43 but whoever wishes to become great **a** you must
10:44 and whoever wishes to be first **a** you must
14: 2 or there may be a riot **a** the people."
15:24 they crucified him, and divided his clothes **a** them,
15:31 were also mocking him **a** themselves and saying,
15:40 **a** them were Mary Magdalene,
Lk 1: 1 of the events that have been fulfilled **a** us,
1:25 and took away the disgrace I have endured **a**
1:42 "Blessed are you **a** women,
2:14 and on earth peace **a** those whom he favors!"
2:44 Then they started to look for him **a** their relatives
2:46 the temple, sitting **a** the teachers, listening to them
7:16 saying, "A great prophet has risen **a** us!"
7:28 I tell you, **a** those born of women
7:49 at the table with him began to say **a** themselves,
8: 7 Some fell **a** thorns, and the thorns grew with it
8:14 what fell **a** the thorns, these are the ones who hear;
9:46 An argument arose **a** them as to which one
9:48 for the least **a** all of you is the greatest."
11:11 Is there anyone **a** you who,
17: 7 "Who **a** you would say to your
17:21 For, in fact, the kingdom of God is **a** you."
20:14 they discussed it **a** themselves and said,
21:24 of the sword and be taken away as captives **a**
21:25 and on the earth distress **a** nations confused by
22:17 "Take this and divide it **a** yourselves;
22:24 also arose **a** them as to which one of them was to
22:26 the greatest **a** you must become like the youngest,
22:27 But I am **a** you as one who serves.
22:37 'And he was counted **a** the lawless';
22:55 of the courtyard and sat down together, Peter sat **a**
23:27 A great number of the people followed him, and **a**
24: 5 "Why do you look for the living **a** the dead?
24:36 Jesus himself stood **a** them and said to them,
Jn 1:14 And the Word became flesh and lived **a** us,
1:26 **A** you stands one whom you do not know,
6: 9 But what are they **a** so many people?"
6:43 "Do not complain **a** yourselves.
6:52 The Jews then disputed **a** themselves, saying,
6:64 But **a** you there are some who do not believe."
7:12 considerable complaining about him **a** the crowds.
7:35 the Dispersion **a** the Greeks and teach the Greeks?
8: 7 ⟦"Let anyone **a** you who is without sin be the first⟧
11:54 Jesus therefore no longer walked about openly **a**
12:20 Now **a** those who went up to worship at
15:24 not done **a** them the works that no one else did,
16:19 "Are you discussing **a** yourselves what I meant
19:24 "They divided my clothes **a** themselves,
20:19 Jesus came and stood **a** them and said,
20:26 Jesus came and stood **a** them and said,
Ac 1:15 In those days Peter stood up **a** the believers
1:17 for he was numbered **a** us and was allotted his
1:21 the time that the Lord Jesus went in and out **a** us,
2: 3 Divided tongues, as of fire, appeared **a** them,
2:22 and signs that God did through him **a** you,
4:12 under heaven given **a** mortals by which we must
4:17 But to keep it from spreading further **a** the people,
4:34 There was not a needy person **a** them,
5:12 and wonders were done **a** the people through
6: 3 from **a** yourselves seven men of good standing,
6: 8 did great wonders and signs **a** the people.
9:21 not this the man who made havoc in Jerusalem **a**
9:28 So he went in and out **a** them in Jerusalem,
9:32 as Peter went here and there **a** all the believers,
11:20 But **a** them were some men of Cyprus
12:18 there was no small commotion **a** the soldiers
15: 7 that in the early days God made a choice **a** you,
15:12 and wonders that God had done through them **a**
15:14 to take from **a** them a people for his name.
15:22 from **a** their members and to send them to Antioch
15:22 Barsabbas, and Silas, leaders **a** the brothers,
17:23 I found **a** them an altar with the inscription,
18:11 teaching the word of God **a** them.
20:18 how I lived **a** you the entire time from the first day
20:25 **a** whom I have gone about proclaiming
20:29 savage wolves will come in **a** you,
20:32 to build you up and to give you the inheritance **a**
20:37 There was much weeping **a** them all;
21:19 by one the things that God had done **a** the Gentiles
21:20 many thousands of believers there are **a** the Jews,
21:21 the Jews living **a** the Gentiles to forsake Moses,
24: 5 an agitator **a** all the Jews throughout the world,

Ac 25: 6 After he had stayed a them not more than eight
26: 4 the beginning a my own people and in Jerusalem.
26:18 a place a those who are sanctified by faith in me.'
27:21 Paul then stood up a them and said, "Men,
27:22 for there will be no loss of life a you,
Ro 1: 5 of faith a all the Gentiles for the sake of his name,
1:13 that I may reap some harvest a you as I have
1:13 among you as I have a the rest of the Gentiles.
1:24 to the degrading of their bodies a themselves,
2:24 "The name of God is blasphemed a the Gentiles
12: 3 the grace given to me I say to everyone a you not
15: 9 "Therefore I will confess you a the Gentiles,
15:26 to share their resources with the poor a the saints
16: 6 Greet Mary, who has worked very hard a you.
16: 7 they are prominent a the apostles,
1Co 1: 6 as the testimony of Christ has been strengthened a
1:10 in agreement and that there be no divisions a you,
1:11 to me by Chloe's people that there are quarrels a
2: 2 to know nothing a you except Jesus Christ,
2: 6 Yet a the mature we do speak wisdom,
3: 3 as long as there is jealousy and quarreling a you,
5: 1 that there is sexual immorality a you,
5: 1 and of a kind that is not found even a pagans;
5: 2 would have been removed from a you?
5:13 "Drive out the wicked person from a you."
6: 5 that there is no one a you wise enough to decide
9:11 If we have sown spiritual good a you,
11:18 I hear that there are divisions a you;
11:19 Indeed, there have to be factions a you,
11:19 so will it become clear who a you are genuine.
14:25 declaring, "God is really a you."
16:10 see that he has nothing to fear a you,
2Co 1:19 Jesus Christ, whom we proclaimed a you,
2:15 aroma of Christ to God a those who are being saved and a those who are perishing;
6:16 as God said, "I will live in them and walk a them,
8: 6 also complete this generous undertaking a you.
8:18 the brother who is famous a all the churches
10:15 that, as your faith increases, our sphere of action a
12:12 The signs of a true apostle were performed a you
Gal 1:14 I advanced in Judaism beyond many a my people
1:16 so that I might proclaim him a the Gentiles,
2: 2 the gospel that I proclaim a the Gentiles,
3: 5 and work miracles a you by your doing the works
Eph 1:18 the riches of his glorious inheritance a the saints,
2: 2 that is now at work a those who are disobedient.
2: 3 All of us once lived a them in the passions
5: 3 or greed, must not even be mentioned a you,
5: 3 not even be mentioned among you, as is proper a
5:19 and hymns and spiritual songs a yourselves,
Php 1: 6 the one who began a good work a you will bring it
Col 1: 6 so it has been bearing fruit a yourselves from
1:27 how great a the Gentiles are the riches of the glory
4:11 These are the only ones of the circumcision a
4:16 And when this letter has been read a you,
1Th 1: 5 of persons we proved to be a you for your sake.
1: 9 about us what kind of welcome we had a you,
2: 7 But we were gentle a you,
5:12 to respect those who labor a you,
5:13 Be at peace a yourselves.
2Th 1: 4 Therefore we ourselves boast of you a
1:10 by his saints and to be marveled at on that day a
3: 1 just as it is a you,
1Ti 1:20 a them are Hymenaeus and Alexander,
3:16 proclaimed a Gentiles, believed in throughout
6: 5 and wrangling a those who are depraved in mind
2Ti 2:17 A them are Hymenaeus and Philetus,
3: 6 For a them are those who make their way
Heb 5: 1 Every high priest chosen from a mortals is put
10:39 But we are not a those who shrink back and
10:39 but a those who have faith and so are saved.
13:21 working a us that which is pleasing in his sight,
Jas 2: 4 have you not made distinctions a yourselves,
3: 6 The tongue is placed a our members as a world
3:13 Who is wise and understanding a you?
4: 1 Those conflicts and disputes a you,
5:13 Are any a you suffering?
5:14 Are any a you sick?
5:19 if anyone a you wanders from the truth
1Pe 2:12 Conduct yourselves honorably a the Gentiles,
4:12 at the fiery ordeal that is taking place a you
5: 1 I exhort the elders a you
2Pe 1: 8 if these things are yours and are increasing a you,
2: 1 But false prophets also arose a the people,
2: 1 just as there will be false teachers a you,
2: 8 living a them day after day,
1Jn 4: 9 God's love was revealed a us in this way:
4:17 Love has been perfected a us in this:
Jude 1: 4 For certain intruders have stolen in a you,
Rev 2: 1 who walks a the seven golden lampstands:
2:13 who was killed a you, where Satan lives.
5: 6 the throne and the four living creatures and a
6:15 hid in the caves and a the rocks of the mountains,
21: 3 "See, the home of God is a mortals.
Tob 1: 4 This city had been chosen from a all the tribes
2: 2 of our people a the exiles in Nineveh,
3: 4 an object of reproach a all the nations a whom you
4:12 from a the descendants of your ancestors;
4:12 all took wives from a their kindred.
4:13 by refusing to take a wife for yourself from a
5:10 Although still alive, I am a the dead.
10: 4 "My child has perished and is no longer a
11:17 So on that day there was rejoicing a all
13: 3 for he has scattered you a them.
13: 5 the nations a whom you have been scattered.
Jdt 1: 8 and those a the nations of Carmel and Gilead,
6: 2 to prophesy a us as you have done today
Jdt 6: 6 and you shall fall a their wounded.
8:22 all this he will bring on our heads a the Gentiles,
9: 4 to be divided a your beloved children who burned
10:19 who have women like this a them?
16: 2 he sets up his camp a his people;
16:25 No one ever again spread terror a the Israelites
AdE 2: 6 he had been taken captive from Jerusalem a
3: 8 a certain nation scattered a the other nations
4: 3 a loud cry of mourning and lamentation a
4:13 that you alone a all the Jews will escape alive.
9:28 the commemoration of them was never to cease a
10: 9 wonders that have never happened a the nations.
10:11 and moment and day of decision before God and a
10:13 to generation forever a his people Israel."
13: 3 who excels a us in sound judgment,
13: 4 that a all the nations in the world there is scattered
14: 5 and our ancestors from a all their forebears,
16:22 as a notable day a your commemorative festivals,
Wis 4:10 and while living a sinners were taken up.
4:18 and an outrage a the dead forever;
5: 5 Why have they been numbered a the children
5: 5 And why is their lot a the saints?
8:10 Because of her I shall have glory a the multitudes
8:15 a the people I shall show myself capable,
9: 4 and do not reject me from a your servants.
9: 6 for even one who is perfect a human beings will
12:17 you rebuke any insolence a those who know it.
13: 7 For while they live a his works,
13:13 But a cast-off piece from a them,
19:21 the flesh of perishable creatures that walked a
Sir 1:15 She made a human beings an eternal foundation,
1:15 and a their descendants she will abide faithfully.
7: 7 and do not disgrace yourself a the people.
9:13 Know that you are stepping a snares,
10:20 A family members their leader is worthy of honor,
11: 1 and seats them a the great.
11: 3 The bee is small a flying creatures,
16:17 A so many people I am unknown,
18:10 so are a few years a the days of eternity.
23:14 Remember your father and mother when you sit a
24: 7 A all these I sought a resting place;
25: 1 agreement a brothers and sisters, friendship a
25:18 Her husband sits a the neighbors,
26: 3 be granted a the blessings of the man who fears
27:12 A stupid people limit your time,
27:12 but a thoughtful people linger on.
28: 9 the sinner disrupts friendships and sows discord a
28:23 it will burn a them and will not be put out.
29:18 and they have wandered a foreign nations.
30: 2 and will boast of him a acquaintances.
30: 3 and will glory in him a his friends.
31: 9 For he has done wonders a his people.
31:18 If you are seated a many persons,
32: 1 be a them as one of their number.
32: 9 A the great do not act as their equal;
33:19 Hear me, you who are great a the people,
37:26 One who is wise a his people will inherit honor,
38:33 and they are not found a the rulers.
39: 4 He serves a the great and appears before rulers;
41: 1 of you to the one at peace a possessions,
42:12 or spend her time a married women;
44:23 and distributed them a twelve tribes.
45:22 and he has no portion a the people;
50: 6 Like the morning star a the clouds,
Bar 2: 4 and a desolation a all the surrounding peoples,
2:13 a the nations where you have scattered us.
2:29 surely turn into a small number a the nations,
3:11 that you are counted a those in Hades?
Sus 1:48 Taking his stand a them he said,
1:50 "Come, sit a us and inform us,
1:64 that day onward Daniel had a great reputation a
1Mc 1: 6 and divided his kingdom a them
2:18 and your sons will be numbered a the Friends of
3:38 able men a the Friends of the king,
4:58 There was very great joy a the people,
5: 2 to destroy the descendants of Jacob who lived a
5: 2 So they began to kill and destroy a the people.
5:63 in all Israel and a all the Gentiles,
6:35 They distributed the animals a the phalanxes;
7:13 The Hasideans were first a the Israelites
7:23 and those with him had done a the Israelites;
8: 2 the brave deeds that they were doing a the Gauls,
8:16 and there is no envy or jealousy a them.
9:27 the time that prophets ceased to appear a them.
10:65 Thus the king honored him and enrolled him a
11:27 and caused him to be reckoned a his chief Friends.
11:60 and traveled beyond the river and a the towns,
12: 7 the high priest Onias from Arius, who was king a
13:17 he would not arouse great hostility a the people,
14:14 He gave help to all the humble a his people;
15:35 they were causing great damage a the people and
2Mc 1:27 set free those who are slaves a the Gentiles,
7:16 and said, "Because you have authority a mortals,
8:28 the rest a themselves and their children.
9:28 a the mountains in a strange land.
12: 3 they invited the Jews who lived a them to embark,
12: 8 to wipe out the Jews who were living a them,
14:35 that there should be a temple for your habitation a
1Es 8:91 for there was great weeping a the multitude.
Pm 151: 1 I was small a my brothers, and the youngest
3Mc 2: 2 and sovereign of all creation, holy a the holy ones,
2: 4 a whom were even giants who trusted
2:21 the first Father of all, holy a the holy ones,
3: 6 which was common talk a all;
3:19 they become the only people a
3:21 A other things, we made known to all our amnesty
3:23 and by silence they abominate those few a
3Mc 3:25 you are to send to us those who live a you,
4: 2 But a the Jews there was incessant mourning,
6: 1 famous a the priests of the country,
7:21 also possessed greater prestige a their enemies,
2Es 1:14 and did great wonders a you.
1:21 I divided fertile lands a you;
2: 7 Let them be scattered a the nations;
2:26 for I will require them from a your number.
3:33 For I have traveled widely a the nations
5:28 and scattered your only one a the many?
7:*46* For who a the living is there that has not sinned,
7:*46* or who is there a mortals that has not transgressed
7:*76* or number yourself a those who are tormented.
8:35 For in truth there is no one a
8:35 a those who have existed there is no one who has
8:49 have not considered yourself to be a the righteous.
9:26 there I sat a the flowers and ate of the plants of
9:29 you showed yourself a us,
10:16 and will be praised a women.
12:38 you shall teach them to the wise a your people,
14: 9 for you shall be taken up from a humankind,
14:13 comfort the lowly a them,
14:46 in order to give them to the wise a your people.
15: 9 to myself all the innocent blood from a them.
15:16 For there shall be unrest a people;
4Mc 2:22 the same time he enthroned the mind a the senses
14:15 a birds, the ones that are tame protect their young

AMORITE (8) [AMORITES]

Ge 14:13 who was living by the oaks of Mamre the A,
Nu 21:29 and his daughters captives, to an A king, Sihon.
Dt 2:24 I have handed over to you King Sihon the A
Ne 9: 8 the Hittite, the A, the Perizzite, the Jebusite,
Eze 16: 3 your father was an A, and your mother a Hittite.
16:45 Your mother was a Hittite and your father an A.
Am 2: 9 Yet I destroyed the A before them,
2:10 to possess the land of the A.

AMORITES (81) [AMORITE]

Ge 10:16 and the Jebusites, the A, the Girgashites,
14: 7 and also the A who lived in Hazazon-tamar.
15:16 for the iniquity of the A is not yet complete."
15:21 the A, the Canaanites, the Girgashites,
48:22 that I took from the hand of the A with my sword
Ex 3: 8 the Hittites, the A, the Perizzites, the Hivites,
3:17 to the land of the Canaanites, the Hittites, the A,
13: 5 the Hittites, the A, the Hivites, and the Jebusites,
23:23 and brings you to the A, the Hittites,
33: 2 the A, the Hittites, the Perizzites, the Hivites,
34:11 See, I will drive out before you the A,
Nu 13:29 the Jebusites, and the A live in the hill country;
21:13 that extends from the boundary of the A;
21:13 between Moab and the A.
21:21 Israel sent messengers to King Sihon of the A,
21:25 and Israel settled in all the towns of the A,
21:26 For Heshbon was the city of King Sihon of the A,
21:31 Thus Israel settled in the land of the A.
21:32 and dispossessed the A who were there.
21:34 to him as you did to King Sihon of the A,
22: 2 of Zippor saw all that Israel had done to the A.
32:33 of the A and the kingdom of King Og of Bashan,
32:39 and dispossessed the A who were there;
Dt 1: 4 after he had defeated King Sihon of the A,
1: 7 and go into the hill country of the A as well as into
1:19 on the way to the hill country of the A,
1:20 "You have reached the hill country of the A,
1:27 to hand us over to the A to destroy us.
1:44 The A who lived in that hill country then came out
3: 2 Do to him as you did to King Sihon of the A,
3: 8 the two kings of the A the land beyond the Jordan,
3: 9 while the A call it Senir),
4:46 in the land of King Sihon of the A,
4:47 the two kings of the A on the eastern side of
7: 1 the Hittites, the Girgashites, the A, the Canaanites,
20:17 and the A, the Canaanites and the Perizzites,
31: 4 the kings of the A, and to their land,
Jos 2:10 and what you did to the two kings of the A
3:10 Hivites, Perizzites, Girgashites, A, and Jebusites:
5: 1 When all the kings of the A beyond the Jordan to
7: 7 to hand us over to the A so as to destroy us?
9: 1 the Hittites, the A, the Canaanites, the Perizzites,
9:10 that he did to the two kings of the A who were
10: 5 Then the five kings of the A—
10: 6 of the A who live in the hill country are gathered
10:12 when the LORD gave the A over to the Israelites,
11: 3 the A, the Hittites, the Perizzites,
12: 2 King Sihon of the A who lived at Heshbon,
12: 8 A, Canaanites, Perizzites, Hivites, and Jebusites):
13: 4 to Aphek, to the boundary of the A,
13:10 of King Sihon of the A, who reigned in Heshbon,
13:21 and all the kingdom of King Sihon of the A,
24: 8 Then I brought you to the land of the A,
24:11 and also the A, the Perizzites, the Canaanites,
24:12 before you the two kings of the A;
24:15 or the gods of the A in whose land you are living;
24:18 the A who lived in the land.
Jdg 1:34 A pressed the Danites back into the hill country;
1:35 The A continued to live in Har-heres, in Aijalon,
1:36 border of the A ran from the ascent of Akrabbim,
3: 5 the Hittites, the A, the Perizzites, the Hivites,
6:10 you shall not pay reverence to the gods of the A,
10: 8 that were beyond the Jordan in the land of the A,
10:11 from the Egyptians and from the A,
11:19 then sent messengers to King Sihon of the A, king
11:21 so Israel occupied all the land of the A,
11:22 the territory of the A from the Arnon to the Jabbok

Jdg 11:23 the **A** for the benefit of his people Israel.
1Sa 7:14 There was peace also between Israel and the **A**.
2Sa 21: 2 but of the remnant of the **A**;
1Ki 4:19 of King Sihon of the **A** and of King Og of Bashan.
9:20 All the people who were left of the **A**, the Hittites,
21:26 as the **A** had done, whom the LORD drove out
2Ki 21:11 that the **A** did, who were before him,
1Ch 1:14 and the Jebusites, the **A**, the Girgashites,
2Ch 8: 7 All the people who were left of the Hittites, the **A**,
Ezr 9: 1 the Moabites, the Egyptians, and the **A**.
Ps 135:11 king of the **A**, and Og, king of Bashan,
136:19 of the **A**, for his steadfast love endures forever;
Isa 17: 9 like the deserted places of the Hivites and the **A**,
Jdt 5:15 the land of the **A**, and by their might destroyed all

AMOS (12)

Am 1: 1 The words of **A**, who was among the shepherds
7: 8 the LORD said to me, "**A**, what do you see?"
7:10 "**A** has conspired against you in the very center of
7:11 For thus **A** has said, 'Jeroboam shall die by
7:12 And Amaziah said to **A**, "O seer, go,
7:14 Then **A** answered Amaziah, "I am no prophet,
8: 2 He said, "**A**, what do you see?"
Mt 1:10 Manasseh the father of **A**, and **A** the father of
Lk 3:25 son of **A**, son of Nahum, son of Esli,
Tob 2: 6 Then I remembered the prophecy of **A**,
2Es 1:39 and Hosea and **A** and Micah and Joel and Obadiah

AMOUNT (25) [AMOUNTS]

Ex 22:17 he shall pay an **a** equal to the bride-price
Lev 6: 5 the principal **a** and shall add one-fifth to it.
1Sa 30:16 the great **a** of spoil they had taken from the land of
2Sa 8: 8 King David took a great **a** of bronze.
12:30 the spoil of the city, a very great **a**.
1Ch 20: 2 the booty of the city, a very great **a**.
2Ch 24:11 they saw that there was a large **a** of money in it,
27: 5 The Ammonites paid him the same **a** in the second
Eze 38:13 to seize a great **a** of booty?"
Lk 3:13 "Collect no more than the **a** prescribed for you."
Jdt 2:18 a huge **a** of gold and silver from the royal palace.
15: 7 in the hill country and in the plain got a great **a**
Sir 6:15 no **a** can balance their worth.
1Mc 4:23 and they seized a great **a** of gold and silver,
9:35 with them the great **a** of baggage that they had.
9:39 and saw a tumultuous procession with a great **a**
10:87 then returned to Jerusalem with a large **a** of booty.
11:48 the city and seized a large **a** of spoil on that day,
11:51 they returned to Jerusalem with a large **a** of spoil.
15:26 and gold and a large **a** of military equipment.
2Mc 3: 6 so that the **a** of the funds could not be reckoned,
8:20 and took a great **a** of booty.
8:30 and they divided a very large **a** of plunder,
12:43 to the **a** of two thousand drachmas of silver,
2Es 8: 2 a large **a** of clay from which earthenware is made,

AMOUNTS (1) [AMOUNT]

1Mc 3:41 they took silver and gold in immense **a**,

AMOZ (13)

2Ki 19: 2 to the prophet Isaiah son of **A**.
19:20 Then Isaiah son of **A** sent to Hezekiah, saying,
20: 1 The prophet Isaiah son of **A** came to him,
2Ch 26:22 the prophet Isaiah son of **A** wrote.
32:20 the prophet Isaiah son of **A** prayed because of this
32:32 of **A** in the Book of the Kings of Judah and Israel.
Isa 1: 1 The vision of Isaiah son of **A**,
2: 1 of **A** saw concerning Judah and Jerusalem.
13: 1 concerning Babylon that Isaiah son of **A** saw.
20: 2 the LORD had spoken to Isaiah son of **A**,
37: 2 to the prophet Isaiah son of **A**.
37:21 Then Isaiah son of **A** sent to Hezekiah, saying:
38: 1 The prophet Isaiah son of **A** came to him,

AMPHIPOLIS (1)

Ac 17: 1 and Silas had passed through **A** and Apollonia,

AMPLE (3)

Lk 12:19 'Soul, you have **a** goods laid up for many years;
Jdt 2:18 also **a** rations for everyone,
Sir 31:19 How **a** a little is for a well-disciplined person!

AMPLIAS (KJV) See AMPLIATUS

AMPLIATUS (1)

Ro 16: 8 Greet **A**, my beloved in the Lord.

AMRAM (12) [AMRAM'S, AMRAMITES]

Ex 6:18 The sons of Kohath: **A**, Izhar, Hebron, and Uzziel,
6:20 **A** married Jochebed his father's sister
Nu 3:19 **A**, Izhar, Hebron, and Uzziel.
26:58 Now Kohath was the father of **A**.
26:59 in Egypt; and she bore to **A**:
1Ch 6: 2 The sons of Kohath: **A**, Izhar, Hebron, and Uzziel.
6: 3 The children of **A**: Aaron, Moses, and Miriam.
6:18 The sons of Kohath: **A**, Izhar, Hebron, and Uzziel.
23:12 **A**, Izhar, Hebron, and Uzziel, four.
23:13 The sons of **A**: Aaron and Moses.
24:20 of the sons of **A**, Shubael;
Ezr 10:34 Of the descendants of Bani: Maadai, **A**, Uel,

AMRAM'S (2) [AMRAM]

Ex 6:20 of **A** life was one hundred thirty-seven years.
Nu 26:59 name of **A** wife was Jochebed daughter of Levi,

AMRAMITES (2) [AMRAM]

Nu 3:27 To Kohath belonged the clan of the **A**,
1Ch 26:23 Of the **A**, the Izharites, the Hebronites,

AMRAPHEL (2)

Ge 14: 1 In the days of King **A** of Shinar,
14: 9 King **A** of Shinar, and King Arioch of Ellasar,

AMULETS (1)

Isa 3:20 the sashes, the perfume boxes, and the **a**;

AMUSE (1)

Sir 32:12 **A** yourself there to your heart's content,

AMZI (2)

1Ch 6:46 son of **A**, son of Bani, son of Shemer,
Ne 11:12 of **A** son of Zechariah son of Pashhur son

AN (1495) [A] See Index of Articles Etc.

ANAB (2)

Jos 11:21 from **A**, and from all the hill country of Judah,
15:50 **A**, Eshtemoh, Anim,

ANAH (12)

Ge 36: 2 of Elon the Hittite, Oholibamah daughter of **A** son
36:14 daughter of **A** son of Zibeon:
36:18 of Esau's wife Oholibamah, the daughter of **A**.
36:20 Lotan, Shobal, Zibeon, **A**,
36:24 These are the sons of Zibeon: Aiah and **A**;
36:24 the **A** who found the springs in the wilderness,
36:25 These are the children of **A**:
36:25 Dishon and Oholibamah daughter of **A**.
36:29 the clans Lotan, Shobal, Zibeon, **A**,
1Ch 1:38 The sons of Seir: Lotan, Shobal, Zibeon, **A**,
1:40 The sons of Zibeon: Aiah and **A**.
1:41 The sons of **A**: Dishon.

ANAHARATH (1)

Jos 19:19 Hapharaim, Shion, **A**,

ANAIAH (2)

Ne 8: 4 and beside him stood Mattithiah, Shema, **A**,
10:22 Pelatiah, Hanan, **A**,

ANAK (6) [ANAKIM, ANAKITES]

Nu 13:28 and besides, we saw the descendants of **A** there.
Jos 15:13 that is, Hebron (Arba was the father of **A**).
15:14 Caleb drove out from there the three sons of **A**:
15:14 Ahiman, and Talmai, the descendants of **A**.
21:11 the father of **A**), that is Hebron, in the hill country
Jdg 1:20 and he drove out from it the three sons of **A**.

ANAKIM (10) [ANAK]

Dt 1:28 We actually saw there the offspring of the **A**!' "
2:10 a large and numerous people, as tall as the **A**—
2:11 Like the **A**, they are usually reckoned as Rephaim,
2:21 a strong and numerous people, as tall as the **A**.
9: 2 the offspring of the **A**, whom you know.
9: 2 "Who can stand up to the **A**?"
Jos 11:21 that time Joshua came and wiped out the **A** from
11:22 None of the **A** was left in the land of the Israelites;
14:12 for you heard on that day how the **A** were there,
14:15 this Arba was the greatest man among the **A**.

ANAKIMS (KJV) See ANAKIM

ANAKITES (2) [ANAK]

Nu 13:22 Ahiman, Sheshai, and Talmai, the **A**, were there.
13:33 the Nephilim (the **A** come from the Nephilim);

ANAMIM (2)

Ge 10:13 Egypt became the father of Ludim, **A**, Lehabim,
1Ch 1:11 Egypt became the father of Ludim, **A**, Lehabim,

ANAMMELECH (1)

2Ki 17:31 in the fire to Adrammelech and **A**,

ANAN (1)

Ne 10:26 Ahiah, Hanan, **A**,

ANANI (1)

1Ch 3:24 Pelaiah, Akkub, Johanan, Delaiah, and **A**, seven.

ANANIAH (2)

Ne 3:23 of **A** made repairs beside his own house.
11:32 Anathoth, Nob, **A**,

ANANIAS (13)

Ac 5: 1 But a man named **A**, with the consent
5: 3 "**A**," Peter asked, "why has Satan filled your heart
5: 5 when **A** heard these words, he fell down and died.
9:10 Now there was a disciple in Damascus named **A**.
9:10 The Lord said to him in a vision, "**A**."
9:12 a vision a man named **A** come in and lay his hands
9:13 But **A** answered, "Lord, I have heard from many
9:17 So **A** went and entered the house.
22:12 "A certain **A**, who was a devout man according to
23: 2 the high priest **A** ordered those standing near him
24: 1 the high priest **A** came down with some elders and
Jdt 8: 1 of Oziel son of Elkiah son of **A** son of Gideon son
1Es 9:43 Shema, **A**, Azariah, Uriah, Hezekiah,

ANARCHY (1)

Sir 26:27 *and every person like this lives in the **a** of war.*

ANASIB (1)

1Es 5:24 of Jedaiah son of Jeshua, of the descendants of **A**,

ANATH (2)

Jdg 3:31 After him came Shamgar son of **A**,
5: 6 "In the days of Shamgar son of **A**,

ANATHEMA (KJV) See ACCURSED

ANATHOTH (21)

Jos 21:18 **A** with its pasture lands, and Almon
2Sa 23:27 Abiezer of **A**; Mebunnai the Hushathite;
1Ki 2:26 The king said to the priest Abiathar, "Go to **A**,
1Ch 6:60 and **A** with its pasture lands.
7: 8 Eliezer, Elioenai, Omri, Jeremoth, Abijah, **A**,
11:28 Ira son of Ikkesh of Tekoa, Abiezer of **A**,
12: 3 of Azmaveth; Beracah, Jehu of **A**,
27:12 Ninth, for the ninth month, was Abiezer of **A**,
Ezr 2:23 Of **A**, one hundred twenty-eight.
Ne 7:27 Of **A**, one hundred twenty-eight.
10:19 Hariph, **A**, Nebai,
11:32 **A**, Nob, Ananiah,
Isa 10:30 O Laishah! Answer her, O **A**!
Jer 1: 1 the priests who were in **A** in the land of Benjamin,
11:21 thus says the LORD concerning the people of **A**,
11:23 For I will bring disaster upon the people of **A**,
29:27 not rebuked Jeremiah of **A** who plays the prophet
32: 7 "Buy my field that is at **A**,
32: 8 "Buy my field that is at **A** in the land of Benjamin,
32: 9 I bought the field at **A** from my cousin Hanamel,
1Es 5:18 Those from **A**, one hundred fifty-eight.

ANCESTOR‡ (56) [ANCESTOR'S, ANCESTORS, ANCESTORS', ANCESTRAL, ANCESTRY]

Ge 4:20 the **a** of those who live in tents and have livestock.
4:21 the **a** of all those who play the lyre and pipe.
17: 4 You shall be the **a** of a multitude of nations.
17: 5 I have made you the **a** of a multitude of nations.
19:37 he is the **a** of the Moabites to this day.
19:38 he is the **a** of the Ammonites to this day.
36: 9 **a** of the Edomites, in the hill country of Seir.
Dt 26: 5 "A wandering Aramean was my **a**;
Jos 19:47 calling Leshem, Dan, after their **a** Dan.
Jdg 18:29 They named the city Dan, after their **a** Dan,
1Sa 2:27 'I revealed myself to the family of your **a** in Egypt
2:28 and I gave to the family of your **a** all my offerings
2:30 of your **a** should go in and out before me forever';
1Ki 15:26 of his **a** and in the sin that he caused Israel
2Ki 14: 3 yet not like his **a** David;
15:38 his **a**; his son Ahaz succeeded him.
16: 2 as his **a** David had done,
18: 3 of the LORD just as his **a** David had done.
20: 5 Thus says the LORD, the God of your **a** David:
1Ch 24:19 for them by their **a** Aaron,
29:10 the God of our **a** Israel, forever and ever.
2Ch 28: 1 as his **a** David had done,
29: 2 just as his **a** David had done.
34: 2 and walked in the ways of his **a** David;
34: 3 he began to seek the God of his **a** David,
Isa 38: 5 Thus says the LORD, the God of your **a** David:
43:27 Your first **a** sinned, and your interpreters transgressed against me.
58:14 I will feed you with the heritage of your **a** Jacob,
Jer 35: 6 for our **a** Jonadab son of Rechab commanded us,
35: 8 We have obeyed the charge of our **a** Jonadab son
35:10 and done all that our **a** Jonadab commanded us.
35:16 the command that their **a** gave them,
35:18 you have obeyed the command of your **a** Jonadab,
Mt 3: 9 'We have Abraham as our **a**';
Mk 11:10 Blessed is the coming kingdom of our **a** David!
Lk 1:32 to him the throne of his **a** David.
1:73 the oath that he swore to our **a** Abraham,
3: 8 'We have Abraham as our **a**';
Jn 4:12 Are you greater than our **a** Jacob,
8:56 Your **a** Abraham rejoiced
Ac 2:29 of our **a** David that he both died and was buried,
4:25 the Holy Spirit through our **a** David, your servant:
7: 2 of glory appeared to our **a** Abraham when he was
17:26 From one **a** he made all nations to inhabit
Ro 4: 1 our **a** according to the flesh?
4:11 the **a** of all who believe without being circumcised
4:12 and likewise the **a** of the circumcised who are
4:12 the example of the faith that our **a** Abraham had
9:10 by one husband, our **a** Isaac.
Heb 7:10 in the loins of his **a** when Melchizedek met him.
Jas 2:21 Was not our **a** Abraham justified by works
Tob 1: 4 of my **a** Naphtali deserted the house of David
Jdt 9: 2 "O Lord God of my **a** Simeon, to whom you gave
Sir 48:22 and he kept firmly to the ways of his **a** David,
1Mc 2:54 Phinehas our **a**, because he was deeply zealous,
4Mc 16:20 to sacrifice his son Isaac, the **a** of our nation;

ANCESTOR'S (2) [ANCESTOR]

1Sa 2:31 and the strength of your **a** family,
Jer 35:14 for they have obeyed their **a** command.

ANCESTORS‡ (475) [ANCESTOR]

A. GOD OF ... ANCESTORS (61)

Ge 15:15 As for yourself, you shall go to your **a** in peace;
31: 3 "Return to the land of your **a** and to your kindred,
46:34 from our youth even until now, both we and our **a**'
47: 3 "Your servants are shepherds, as our **a** were."
47: 9 not compare with the years of the life of my **a**
47:30 When I lie down with my **a**,
48:15 before whom my **a** Abraham and Isaac walked,
48:16 and the name of my **a** Abraham and Isaac;
48:21 and will bring you again to the land of your **a**.
49:29 to my people. Bury me with my **a**—
Ex 3:13 'The God of your **a** has sent me to you,' A
3:15 the God of your **a**, the God of Abraham, A
3:16 and say to them, 'The LORD, the God of your **a**, A
4: 5 the God of their **a**, the God of Abraham, A
13: 5 which he swore to your **a** to give you,
13:11 as he swore to you and your **a**,
Lev 26:39 because of the iniquities of their **a**.
26:40 of their **a**, in that they committed treachery
26:45 the covenant with their **a** whom I brought out of
Nu 11:12 to the land that you promised on oath to their **a**?
14:23 shall see the land that I swore to give to their **a**;
20:15 how our **a** went down to Egypt, and we lived
20:15 and the Egyptians oppressed us and our **a**;
36: 3 be taken from the inheritance of our **a** and added
Dt 1: 8 of the land that I swore to your **a**,
1:11 May the LORD, the God of your **a**, A
1:21 take possession, as the LORD, the God of your **a**, A
1:35 the good land that I swore to give to your **a**,
4: 1 the God of your **a**, is giving you. A
4:31 not forget the covenant with your **a** that he swore
4:37 And because he loved your **a**,
5: 3 with our **a** did the LORD make this covenant,
6: 3 the God of your **a**, has promised you. A
6:10 that he swore to your **a**, to Abraham, to Isaac,
6:18 the good land that the LORD swore to your **a**
6:23 the land that he promised on oath to our **a**.
7: 8 and kept the oath that he swore to your **a**,
7:12 the covenant loyalty that he swore to your **a**;
7:13 in the land that he swore to your **a** to give you.
8: 1 that the LORD promised on oath to your **a**.
8: 3 nor your **a** were acquainted,
8:16 in the wilderness with manna that your **a** did
8:18 that he swore to your **a**,
9: 5 that the LORD made on oath to your **a**,
10:11 the land that I swore to their **a** to give them."
10:15 the LORD set his heart in love on your **a** alone
10:22 Your **a** went down to Egypt seventy persons;
11: 9 that the LORD swore to your **a** to give them and
11:21 that the LORD swore to your **a** to give them,
12: 1 that the LORD, the God of your **a**, has given you A
13: 6 whom neither you nor your **a** have known,
13:17 as he swore to your **a**,
19: 8 as he swore to your **a**—
19: 8 the land that he promised your **a** to give you,
26: 3 into the land that the LORD swore to our **a**
26: 7 to the LORD, the God of our **a**; A
26:15 as you swore to our **a**—
27: 3 as the LORD, the God of your **a**, promised you. A
28:11 that the LORD swore to your **a** to give you.
28:36 a nation that neither you nor your **a** have known,
28:64 which neither you nor your **a** have known.
29:13 as he promised you and as he swore to your **a**,
29:25 of the LORD, the God of their **a**, which he made A
30: 5 that your **a** possessed, and you will possess it;
30: 5 and numerous than your **a**.
30: 9 just as he delighted in prospering your **a**,
30:20 the land that the LORD swore to give to your **a**,
31: 7 that the LORD has sworn to their **a** to give them;
31:16 "Soon you will lie down with your **a**.
31:20 which I promised on oath to their **a**,
32:17 whom your **a** had not feared.
Jos 1: 6 in possession of the land that I swore to their **a**
5: 6 the land that he had sworn to their **a** to give us,
18: 3 the God of your **a**, has given you? A
21:43 that he swore to their **a** that he would give them;
21:44 on every side just as he had sworn to their **a**;
22:28 which our **a** made, not for burnt offerings,
24: 2 Long ago your **a**—Terah and his sons Abraham
24: 6 When I brought your **a** out of Egypt,
24: 6 and the Egyptians pursued your **a** with chariots
24:14 that your **a** served beyond the River and in Egypt,
24:15 whether the gods your **a** served in the region
24:17 the LORD our God who brought us and our **a** up
Jdg 2: 1 into the land that I had promised to your **a**.
2:10 that whole generation was gathered to their **a**,
2:12 the God of their **a**, who had brought them out A
2:17 in which their **a** had walked, who had obeyed
2:19 they would relapse and behave worse than their **a**,
2:20 that I commanded their **a**,
2:22 to walk in the way of the LORD as their **a** did,
3: 4 which he commanded their **a** by Moses.
6:13 that our **a** recounted to us,
1Sa 12: 6 and Aaron and brought your **a** up out of the land
12: 7 that he performed for you and for your **a**.
12: 8 then your **a** cried to the LORD and
12: 8 who brought forth your **a** out of Egypt,
2Sa 7:12 and you lie down with your **a**,
1Ki 1:21 when my lord the king sleeps with his **a**,
2:10 Then David slept with his **a**,
1Ki 8:21 that he made with our **a** when he brought them out
8:34 to the land that you gave to their **a**.
8:40 that they live in the land that you gave to our **a**.
8:48 which you gave to their **a**,
8:53 when you brought our **a** out of Egypt,
8:57 LORD our God be with us, as he was with our **a**;
8:58 and his ordinances, which he commanded our **a**.
9: 9 who brought their **a** out of the land of Egypt,
11:21 in Egypt that David slept with his **a** and that Joab
11:43 Solomon slept with his **a** and was buried in
14:15 of this good land that he gave to their **a**,
14:20 then he slept with his **a**,
14:22 more than all that their **a** had done.
14:31 slept with his **a** and was buried with his **a**
15: 8 Abijam slept with his **a**, and they buried him in
15:12 and removed all the idols that his **a** had made.
15:24 Then Asa slept with his **a**,
15:24 with his **a** in the city of his father David;
16: 6 Baasha slept with his **a**, and was buried at Tirzah;
16:28 Omri slept with his **a**, and was buried in Samaria;
19: 4 take away my life, for I am no better than my **a**."
22:40 So Ahab slept with his **a**;
22:50 slept with his **a** and was buried with his **a**
2Ki 8:24 So Joram slept with his **a**,
9:28 and buried him in his tomb with his **a** in the city
10:35 So Jehu slept with his **a**,
12:18 Jehoram, and Ahaziah, his **a**, the kings of Judah,
12:21 He was buried with his **a** in the city of David;
13: 9 So Jehoahaz slept with his **a**,
13:13 So Joash slept with his **a**,
14:16 with his **a**, and was buried in Samaria with
14:20 he was buried in Jerusalem with his **a** in the city
14:22 after King Amaziah slept with his **a**.
14:29 Jeroboam slept with his **a**, the kings of Israel;
15: 7 Azariah slept with his **a**; they buried him with his **a** in the city of David;
15: 9 in the sight of the LORD, as his **a** had done.
15:22 Menahem slept with his **a**,
15:38 Jotham slept with his **a**, and was buried with his **a**
16:20 Azariah slept with his **a**, and was buried with his **a**
17:13 the law that I commanded your **a** and that I sent
17:14 not listen but were stubborn, as their **a** had been,
17:15 and his covenant that he made with their **a**,
17:41 to do as their **a** did.
20:17 that which your **a** have stored up until this day,
20:21 Hezekiah slept with his **a**;
21: 8 of the land that I gave to their **a**,
21:15 since the day their **a** came out of Egypt,
21:18 Manasseh slept with his **a**,
21:22 the LORD, the God of his **a**, and did not walk in A
22:13 because our **a** did not obey the words of this book,
22:20 Therefore, I will gather you to your **a**,
23:32 just as his **a** had done.
23:37 just as all his **a** had done.
24: 6 So Jehoiakim slept with his **a**;
1Ch 5:25 But they transgressed against the God of their **a**, A
9:19 as their **a** had been in charge of the camp of
12:17 may the God of our **a** see and give judgment." A
17:11 your days are fulfilled to go to be with your **a**,
29:15 and transients before you, as were all our **a**;
29:18 the God of Abraham, Isaac, and Israel, our **a**,
29:20 the God of their **a**, and bowed their heads A
2Ch 6:25 to the land that you gave to them and to their **a**.
6:31 that they live in the land that you gave to our **a**.
6:38 which you gave to their **a**,
7:22 God of their **a** who brought them out of the land A
9:31 Solomon slept with his **a** and was buried in
11:16 to sacrifice to the LORD, the God of their **a**. A
12:16 with his **a** and was buried in the city of David;
13:12 the God of your **a**; for you cannot succeed." A
13:18 on the LORD, the God of their **a**. A
14: 1 So Abijah slept with his **a**,
14: 4 the LORD, the God of their **a**, and to keep A
15:12 the LORD, the God of their **a**, with all their heart A
16:13 Then Asa slept with his **a**,
19: 4 to the LORD, the God of their **a**. A
20: 6 God of our **a**, are you not God in heaven? A
20:33 not yet set their hearts upon the God of their **a**. A
21: 1 slept with his **a** and was buried with his **a**
21:10 the LORD, the God of his **a**. A
21:19 like the fires made for his **a**.
24:18 the God of their **a**, and served the sacred poles A
24:24 the LORD, the God of their **a**. A
25:28 he was buried with his **a** in the city of David.
26: 2 after the king slept with his **a**.
26:23 Uzziah slept with his **a**; they buried him near his **a**
27: 9 Jotham slept with his **a**, and they buried him in
28: 6 the LORD, the God of their **a**. A
28: 9 the God of your **a**, was angry with Judah, A
28:25 provoking to anger the LORD, the God of his **a**. A
28:27 Ahaz slept with his **a**, and they buried him in
29: 5 of the LORD, the God of your **a**, and carry out A
29: 6 For our **a** have been unfaithful
30: 7 Do not be like your **a** and your kindred,
30: 7 who were faithless to the LORD God of their **a**, A
30: 8 Do not now be stiff-necked as your **a** were,
30:19 the LORD the God of their **a**, A
30:22 to the LORD the God of their **a**. A
32:13 Do you not know what I and my **a** have done
32:14 that my **a** utterly destroyed was able
32:15 from my hand or from the hand of my **a**.
32:33 Hezekiah slept with his **a**,
33: 8 of Israel from the land that I appointed for your **a**,
33:12 before the God of his **a**. A
33:20 So Manasseh slept with his **a**,
34:21 our **a** did not keep the word of the LORD,
34:28 to your **a** and you shall be gathered to your grave
2Ch 34:32 to the covenant of God, the God of their **a**. A
34:33 from following the LORD the God of their **a**. A
35:24 and was buried in the tombs of his **a**.
36:15 The LORD, the God of their **a**, A
Ezr 4:15 that a search may be made in the annals of your **a**.
5:12 But because our **a** had angered the God of heaven,
7:27 Blessed be the LORD, the God of our **a**, A
8:28 to the LORD, the God of your **a**. A
9: 7 the days of our **a** to this day we have been deep
10:11 make confession to the LORD the God of your **a**, A
Ne 9: 2 and the iniquities of their **a**.
9: 9 the distress of our **a** in Egypt and heard their cry at
9:10 you knew that they acted insolently against our **a**.
9:16 "But they and our **a** acted presumptuously
9:23 into the land that you had told their **a** to enter
9:32 our officials, our priests, our prophets, our **a**,
9:34 and our **a** have not kept your law or heeded
9:36 in the land that you gave to our **a** to enjoy its fruit
13:18 Did not your **a** act in this way,
Job 8: 8 and consider what their **a** have found;
15:18 what sages have told, and their **a** have not hidden,
Ps 22: 4 In you our **a** trusted; they trusted,
44: 1 O God, our **a** have told us,
45:16 In the place of **a** you, O king, shall have sons;
49:19 they will go to the company of their **a**,
78: 3 that our **a** have told us.
78: 5 which he commanded our **a** to teach
78: 8 and that they should not be like their **a**,
78:12 of their **a** he worked marvels in the land of Egypt,
78:57 but turned away and were faithless like their **a**;
79: 8 not remember against us the iniquities of our **a**;
95: 9 when your **a** tested me, and put me to the proof,
106: 6 Both we and our **a** have sinned;
106: 7 Our **a**, when they were in Egypt,
Pr 22:28 the ancient landmark that your **a** set up.
Isa 39: 6 that which your **a** have stored up until this day,
64:11 where our **a** praised you, has been burned by fire,
Jer 2: 5 What wrong did your **a** find in me
3:18 the land of the north to the land that I gave your **a**
3:24 for which our **a** had labored,
3:25 we and our **a**, from our youth even to this day;
7: 7 in the land that I gave of old to your **a** forever
7:14 and to the place that I gave to you and to your **a**,
7:22 For in the day that I brought your **a** out of the land
7:25 the day that your **a** came out of the land of Egypt
7:26 They did worse than their **a** did.
9:14 after the Baals, as their **a** taught them.
9:16 that neither they nor their **a** have known;
11: 4 which I commanded your **a**
11: 5 that I may perform the oath that I swore to your **a**,
11: 7 For I solemnly warned your **a**
11:10 They have turned back to the iniquities of their **a**
11:10 the covenant that I made with their **a**.
14:20 O LORD, the iniquity of our **a**,
16:11 It is because your **a** have forsaken me,
16:12 and because you have behaved worse than your **a**,
16:13 a land that neither you nor your **a** have known,
16:15 to their own land that I gave to their **a**.
16:19 Our **a** have inherited nothing but lies,
17:22 the sabbath day holy, as I commanded your **a**.
19: 4 in it to other gods whom neither they nor their **a**
23:27 just as their **a** forgot my name for Baal.
23:39 you and the city that I gave to you and your **a**.
24:10 from the land that I gave to them and their **a**.
25: 5 that the LORD has given to you and your **a** from
30: 3 to their **a** and they shall take possession of it.
31:32 not be like the covenant that I made with their **a**
32:22 which you swore to their **a** to give them,
34: 5 And as spices were burned for your **a**,
34:13 a covenant with your **a** when I brought them out
34:14 But your **a** did not listen to me or incline their ears
35:15 in the land that I gave to you and your **a**.'
44: 3 neither they, nor you, nor your **a**.
44: 9 Have you forgotten the crimes of your **a**,
44:10 that I set before you and before your **a**.
44:17 just as we and our **a**, our kings and our officials,
44:21 you and your **a**, your kings and your officials,
50: 7 the true pasture, the LORD, the hope of their **a**."
La 5: 7 Our **a** sinned; they are no more,
Eze 2: 3 they and their **a** have transgressed against me
20: 4 Then let them know the abominations of their **a**,
20:27 In this again your **a** blasphemed me,
20:30 after the manner of your **a** and go astray
20:36 with your **a** in the wilderness of the land of Egypt,
20:42 the country that I swore to give to your **a**.
36:28 you shall live in the land that I gave to your **a**;
37:25 to my servant Jacob, in which your **a** lived;
47:14 I swore to give it to your **a**,
Da 2:23 To you, O God of my **a**, I give thanks and praise, A
9: 6 and our **a**, and to all the people of the land.
9: 8 and our **a**, because we have sinned against you.
9:16 because of our sins and the iniquities of our **a**,
11:37 He shall pay no respect to the gods of his **a**,
11:38 a god whom his **a** did not know he shall honor
Hos 9:10 in its first season, I saw your **a**.
Joel 1: 2 or in the days of your **a**?
Am 2: 4 by the same lies after which their **a** walked.
Mic 7:20 as you have sworn to our **a** from the days of old.
Zec 1: 2 The LORD was very angry with your **a**.
1: 4 Do not be like your **a**,
1: 5 Your **a**, where are they?
1: 6 did they not overtake your **a**?
8:14 when your **a** provoked me to wrath,
Mal 2:10 profaning the covenant of our **a**?
3: 7 of your **a** you have turned aside from my statutes
Mt 23:30 'If we had lived in the days of our **a**,
23:32 Fill up, then, the measure of your **a**.

Lk 1:55 according to the promise he made to our a,
1:72 Thus he has shown the mercy promised to our a,
6:23 for that is what their a did to the prophets.
6:26 for that is what their a did to the false prophets.
11:47 the tombs of the prophets whom your a killed.
11:48 and approve of the deeds of your a;
Jn 4:20 Our a worshiped on this mountain,
6:31 Our a ate the manna in the wilderness;
6:49 Your a ate the manna in the wilderness,
6:58 not like that which your a ate, and they died.
Ac 3:13 the God of our a has glorified his servant Jesus, A
3:25 and of the covenant that God gave to your a,
5:30 The God of our a raised up Jesus, A
7:11 and great suffering, and our a could find no food.
7:12 he sent our a there on their first visit.
7:15 He himself died there as well as our a,
7:19 He dealt craftily with our race and forced our a
7:32 'I am the God of your a, A
7:38 to him at Mount Sinai, and with our a;
7:39 Our a were unwilling to obey him;
7:44 "Our a had the tent of testimony in the wilderness,
7:45 Our a in turn brought it in with Joshua
7:45 the nations that God drove out before our a.
7:51 just as your a used to do.
7:52 Which of the prophets did your a not persecute?
13:17 of this people Israel chose our a and made
13:32 the good news that what God promised to our a
13:36 was laid beside his a, and experienced corruption;
15:10 the neck of the disciples a yoke that neither our a
22:14 God of our a has chosen you to know his will, A
24:14 they call a sect, I worship the God of our a, A
26:6 of my hope in the promise made by God to our a,
28:17 against our people or the customs of our a,
28:25 in saying to your a through the prophet Isaiah,
Ro 11:28 for the sake of their a;
1Co 10:1 that our a were all under the cloud,
Gal 1:14 I was far more zealous for the traditions of my a.
2Ti 1:3 with a clear conscience, as my a did—
Heb 1:1 Long ago God spoke to our a in many
3:9 where your a put me to the test,
8:9 not like the covenant that I made with their a, on
11:2 Indeed, by faith our a received approval.
1Pe 1:18 from the futile ways inherited from your a,
2Pe 3:4 For ever since our a died,
Tob 3:3 and those that my a committed before you.
4:12 a woman from among the descendants of your a;
4:12 Abraham, Isaac, and Jacob, our a of old,
8:5 "Blessed are you, O God of our a, A
Jdt 5:7 to follow the gods of their a who were in Chaldea.
5:8 Since they had abandoned the ways of their a,
5:8 their a drove them out from the presence
7:28 the Lord of our a, who punishes us for our sins
and the sins of our a;
8:3 So they buried him with his a in the field
8:19 That was why our a were handed over to
8:25 who is putting us to the test as he did our a.
10:8 "May the God of our a grant you favor and A
AdE 14:5 and our a from among all their forebears,
16:16 for us and for our a in the most excellent order.
Wis 9:1 "O God of my a and Lord of mercy, A
12:6 you willed to destroy by the hands of our a,
12:21 to whose a you gave oaths and covenants full
18:6 That night was made known beforehand to our a,
18:9 and already they were singing the praises of the a.
18:22 to the oaths and covenants given to our a.
18:24 of the a were engraved on the four rows of stones,
Sir Pr:1 and the Prophets and the other books of our a,
8:4 or your a may be insulted.
44:1 HYMN IN HONOR OF OUR A
44:1 our a in their generations.
47:23 Solomon rested with his a,
Bar 1:16 our rulers, our priests, our prophets, and our a,
1:19 From the time when the Lord brought our a out of
1:20 at the time when he brought our a out of the land
2:6 there is open shame on us and our a this very day.
2:19 of any righteous deeds of our a or our kings
2:21 you will remain in the land that I gave to your a.
2:24 and the bones of our a would be brought out
2:33 for they will remember the ways of their a,
2:34 that I swore to give to their a, to Abraham, Isaac,
3:5 Do not remember the iniquities of our a,
3:7 the iniquity of our a who sinned against you.
3:8 and punished for all the iniquities of our a,
Aza 1:3 O Lord, God of our a, and worthy of praise; A
1:5 and upon Jerusalem, the holy city of our a;
1:29 God of our a, and to be praised A
Bel 1:1 When King Astyages was laid to rest with his a,
1Mc 2:19 of them abandoning the religion of their a,
2:20 to live by the covenant of our a.
2:50 and give your lives for the covenant of our a.
2:51 "Remember the deeds of the a,
2:69 Then he blessed them, and was gathered to his a.
2:70 and was buried in the tomb of his a at Modein.
4:9 Remember how our a were saved at the Red Sea,
4:10 with our a and crush this army before us today.
7:2 As he was entering the royal palace of his a,
9:19 and buried him in the tomb of their a at Modein.
10:52 on the throne of my a, and established my rule—
10:55 the land of your a and took your seat on the throne
10:67 of Demetrius came from Crete to the land of his a.
10:72 your a were twice put to flight in their own land.
13:25 and buried him in Modein, the city of his a.
15:3 gained control of the kingdom of our a,
15:10 and invaded the land of his a.
15:33 but only the inheritance of our a,
15:34 we are firmly holding the inheritance of our a.
2Mc 1:19 For when our a were being led captive to Persia,
2Mc 1:25 you chose the a and consecrated them.
4:15 disdaining the honors prized by their a and putting
5:10 of any sort and no place in the tomb of his a.
6:1 to forsake the laws of their a and no longer to live
6:6 nor observe the festivals of their a,
7:2 to die rather than transgress the laws of our a."
7:8 He replied in the language of his a and said
7:21 of them in the language of their a.
7:24 if he would turn from the ways of his a,
7:30 of the law that was given to our a through Moses.
7:37 give up body and life for the laws of our a,
8:15 for the sake of the covenants made with their a,
8:19 of the occasions when help came to their a;
8:33 of their a, they burned those who had set fire to
11:25 according to the customs of their a.
12:37 In the language of their a he raised the battle cry,
12:39 with their kindred in the sepulchres of their a.
15:29 the Sovereign Lord in the language of their a.
1Es 1:31 and was buried in the tomb of his a.
1:50 of their a sent his messenger to call them back, A
2:21 search may be made in the records of your a.
4:60 I give you thanks, O Lord of our a."
4:62 And they praised the God of their a, A
6:15 But when our a sinned against the Lord
8:58 the gold are vowed to the Lord, the Lord of our a.
8:76 from the times of our a,
8:77 Because of our sins and the sins of our a,
9:8 and give glory to the Lord the God of our a, A
Man 1:1 O Lord Almighty, God of our a, A
3Mc 5:31 a full and firm loyalty to my a.
6:28 who from the time of our a until now has granted
6:32 of dirges and took up the song of their a,
7:7 that they had toward us and our a,
7:16 to the one God of their a, A
2Es 3:12 to be more ungodly than were their a.
4:23 the law of our a has been brought to destruction
7:*106* [36] and Moses for our a who sinned in the desert,
8:31 For we and our a have passed our lives in ways
9:29 to our a in the wilderness when they came out
9:32 But though our a received the law,
14:29 At first our a lived as aliens in Egypt,
14:31 and your a committed iniquity and did not keep
4Mc 3:8 the whole army of our a had encamped.
3:20 when our a were enjoying profound peace because
5:29 the sacred oaths of my a concerning the keeping
5:37 My a will receive me as pure,
9:24 the just Providence of our a may become merciful
9:29 of death for the religion of our a!"
12:17 on the God of our a to be merciful to our nation; A

ANCESTORS' (4) [ANCESTOR]

Ne 2:3 when the city, the place of my a graves,
2:5 to the city of my a graves,
Isa 65:7 and their a iniquities together, says the LORD;
Eze 20:24 and their eyes were set on their a idols.

ANCESTRAL (137) [ANCESTOR]

Ex 6:14 The following are the heads of their a houses:
6:25 These are the heads of the a houses of the Levites
Lev 25:41 to their own family and return to their a property.
Nu 1:2 by a houses, according to the number of names,
1:4 each man the head of his a house.
1:16 the leaders of their a tribes,
1:18 in their clans, by their a houses,
1:20 their lineage, in their clans, by their a houses,
1:22 their lineage, in their clans, by their a houses,
1:24 their lineage, in their clans, by their a houses,
1:26 their lineage, in their clans, by their a houses,
1:28 their lineage, in their clans, by their a houses,
1:30 their lineage, in their clans, by their a houses,
1:32 their lineage, in their clans, by their a houses,
1:34 their lineage, in their clans, by their a houses,
1:36 their lineage, in their clans, by their a houses,
1:38 their lineage, in their clans, by their a houses,
1:40 their lineage, in their clans, by their a houses,
1:42 their lineage, in their clans, by their a houses,
1:44 twelve men, each representing his a house.
1:45 whole number of the Israelites, by their a houses,
1:47 not numbered by their a tribe along with them.
2:2 under ensigns by their a houses;
2:32 the enrollment of the Israelites by their a houses;
2:34 everyone by clans, according to a houses.
3:15 Enroll the Levites by a houses and by clans.
3:20 the clans of the Levites, by their a houses.
3:24 of Lael as head of the a house of the Gershonites.
3:30 of Uzziel as head of the a house of the clans of
3:35 the a house of the clans of Merari was Zuriel son
4:2 by their clans and their a houses,
4:22 by their a houses and by their clans;
4:29 by their clans and their a houses;
4:34 by their clans and their a houses,
4:38 by their clans and their a houses,
4:40 their a houses was two thousand six hundred thirty.
4:42 by their clans and their a houses,
4:46 by their clans and their a houses,
7:2 heads of their a houses, the leaders of the tribes,
13:2 from each of their a tribes you shall send a man,
17:2 each a house, from all the leaders of their a houses.
17:3 be one staff for the head of each a house.
17:6 one for each leader, according to their a houses,
18:1 You and your sons and your a house
18:2 your a tribe, in order that they may be joined
25:14 head of an a house belonging to the Simeonites.
25:15 who was the head of a clan, an a house in Midian.
26:2 by their a houses, everyone in Israel able to go
26:55 to the names of their a tribes they shall inherit.
Nu 31:26 the priest and the heads of the a houses of
32:28 to the heads of the a houses of the Israelite tribes.
33:54 according to your a tribes you shall inherit.
34:14 the Reubenites by their a houses and the tribe of
34:14 by their a houses have taken their inheritance,
36:1 of the a houses of the clans of the descendants
36:1 the heads of the a houses of the Israelites;
36:4 be taken from the inheritance of our a tribe."
36:7 the inheritance of their a tribes.
36:8 to possess their a inheritance.
1Sa 9:20 if not on you and on all your a house?"
1Ki 8:1 the leaders of the a houses of the Israelites,
13:22 your body shall not come to your a tomb."
21:3 that I should give you my a inheritance."
21:4 "I will not give you my a inheritance."
1Ch 7:2 Ibsam, and Shemuel, heads of their a houses,
7:4 by their generations, according to their a houses,
7:7 Uzziel, Jerimoth, and Iri, five, heads of a houses,
7:9 as heads of their a houses, mighty warriors,
7:11 of Jediael according to the heads of their a houses,
7:40 heads of a houses, select mighty warriors,
8:6 the sons of Ehud (they were heads of a houses of
8:10 These were his sons, heads of a houses.
8:13 of a houses of the inhabitants of Aijalon, who put
8:28 These were the heads of a houses,
9:9 of families according to their a houses.
9:13 besides their kindred, heads of their a houses,
9:19 and his kindred of his a house, the Korahites,
9:33 the heads of a houses of the Levites,
9:34 These were heads of a houses of the Levites,
12:28 twenty-two commanders from his own a house.
12:30 mighty warriors, notables in their a houses.
23:24 These were the sons of Levi by their a houses,
24:4 under sixteen heads of a houses of the sons
24:6 heads of a houses of the priests and of the Levites;
24:6 one a house being chosen for Eleazar
24:30 the sons of the Levites according to their a houses.
24:31 heads of a houses of the priests and of the Levites,
26:6 in their a houses, for they were men
26:13 and they cast lots by a houses,
28:4 from all my a house to be king over Israel forever;
29:6 leaders of a houses made their freewill offerings,
2Ch 5:2 the leaders of the a houses of the people of Israel,
17:14 This was the muster of them by a houses:
25:5 by a houses under commanders of the thousands
26:12 The whole number of the heads of a houses
31:17 of the priests was according to their a houses;
35:4 Make preparations by your a houses
35:5 to the groupings of the a houses of your kindred
35:5 be Levites for each division of an a house.
35:12 to the groupings of the a houses of the people,
Ne 7:61 not prove their a houses or their descent,
7:70 Now some of the heads of a houses contributed to
7:71 And some of the heads of a houses gave into
8:13 On the second day the heads of a houses of all
10:34 to bring it into the house of our God, by a houses,
11:13 heads of a houses, two hundred forty-two;
12:12 the days of Joiakim the priests, heads of a houses,
12:22 there were recorded the heads of a houses;
12:23 The Levites, heads of a houses,
Isa 7:17 and on your people and on your a house such days
22:23 he will become a throne of honor to his a house.
22:24 on him the whole weight of his a house,
Ac 22:3 educated strictly according to our a law,
Tob 1:5 and our a house of Naphtali sacrificed to the calf
AdE 8:6 How can I be safe if my a nation is destroyed?"
2Mc 8:17 and besides, the overthrow of their a way of life.
14:7 Therefore I have laid aside my a glory—
1Es 1:5 to the groupings of the a houses of you Levites,
1:11 the grouping of the a houses, before the people,
5:1 this the heads of a houses were chosen to go up,
5:4 according to their a houses in the tribes,
5:37 by their a houses or lineage that they belonged
5:63 of the levitical priests and heads of a houses,
5:68 and Jeshua and the heads of the a houses and said
5:70 the heads of the a houses in Israel said to them,
8:28 according to their a houses and their groups,
8:59 and to the heads of the a houses of Israel,
9:16 for himself the leading men of their a houses, all
3Mc 1:3 and apostatized from the a traditions, had led
1:23 the a law, and created a considerable disturbance
4Mc 4:23 the a law they should die.
5:33 I do not so pity my old age as to break the a law
8:7 the a tradition of your national life.
9:1 to die rather than transgress our a commandments;
16:16 Fight zealously for our a law.
18:5 to become pagans and to abandon their a customs,

ANCESTRY (3) [ANCESTOR]

1Ch 6:19 the clans of the Levites according to their a.
Heb 7:6 But this man, who does not belong to their a,
Tob 5:14 brother, because I wanted to be sure about your a.

ANCHOR (4) [ANCHORS]

Ac 27:13 so they weighed a and began to sail past Crete,
27:17 they lowered the sea a and so were driven.
28:13 then we weighed a and came to Rhegium.
Heb 6:19 a sure and steadfast a of the soul,

ANCHORS (3) [ANCHOR]

Ac 27:29 they let down four a from the stern and prayed
27:30 on the pretext of putting out a from the bow,
27:40 So they cast off the a and left them in the sea.

ANCIENT‡ (36) [ANCIENTS]
Dt 33:15 with the finest produce of the a mountains,
33:27 He subdues the a gods, shatters the forces of old;
1Sa 24:13 As the a proverb says, 'Out of
1Ch 4:22 but returned to Lehem (now the records are a).
Ps 24: 7 and be lifted up, O a doors!
24: 9 and be lifted up, O a doors!
68:33 in the heavens, the a heavens;
Pr 22:28 the a landmark that your ancestors set up.
23:10 Do not remove an a landmark or encroach on
Isa 19:11 "I am one of the sages, a descendant of a kings"?
46:10 from the beginning and from a times things not
58:12 Your a ruins shall be rebuilt;
61: 4 They shall build up the a ruins,
Jer 5:15 It is an enduring nation, it is an a nation,
6:16 and ask for the a paths, where the good way lies;
18:15 they have stumbled in their ways, in the a roads,
28: 8 and me from a times prophesied war,
Eze 35: 5 Because you cherished an a enmity,
36: 2 and, "The a heights have become our possession,"
Da 7: 9 and an A One took his throne,
7:13 And he came to the A One and was presented
7:22 until the A One came;
Mic 5: 2 whose origin is from of old, from a days.
Hab 3: 6 his a pathways the everlasting hills sank low.
Mt 5:21 that it was said to those of a times, 'You shall
5:33 you have heard that it was said to those of a times,
Lk 9: 8 by others that one of the a prophets had arisen.
9:19 still others, that one of the a prophets has arisen."
2Pe 2: 5 not spare the a world, even though he saved Noah,
Rev 12: 9 great dragon was thrown down, that a serpent,
20: 2 He seized the dragon, that a serpent,
AdE 16: 7 so much from the more a records that we hand on,
Wis 13:10 or a useless stone, the work of an a hand.
Sir 16: 7 He did not forgive the a giants who revolted
1Mc 15:17 as our friends and allies to renew our a friendship
1Es 1:24 In a times the events of his

ANCIENTS (1) [ANCIENT]
Sir 39: 1 He seeks out the wisdom of all the a,

ANCLE, ANCLES (KJV) See ANKLE, ANKLES

AND (41295) See Index of Articles Etc.

ANDREW (13)
Mt 4:18 Simon, who is called Peter, and A his brother,
10: 2 Simon, also known as Peter, and his brother A;
Mk 1:16 he saw Simon and his brother A casting a net into
1:29 they entered the house of Simon and A,
3:18 and A, and Philip, and Bartholomew,
13: 3 Peter, James, John, and A asked him privately,
Lk 6:14 whom he named Peter, and his brother A,
Jn 1:40 who heard John speak and followed him was A,
1:44 Philip was from Bethsaida, the city of A and Peter.
6: 8 One of his disciples, A, Simon Peter's brother,
12:22 Philip went and told A; then A and Philip went
Ac 1:13 and John, and James, and A, Philip and Thomas,

ANDRONICUS (7)
Ro 16: 7 Greet A and Junia, my relatives who were
2Mc 4:31 leaving A, a man of high rank,
4:32 of the temple and gave them to A;
4:34 Menelaus, taking A aside, urged him to kill Onias.
4:34 A came to Onias, and resorting to treachery,
4:38 the purple robe from A, tore off his purple robe,
5:23 and at Gerizim, A; and besides these Menelaus,

ANEM (1)
1Ch 6:73 and A with its pasture lands;

ANER (3)
Ge 14:13 brother of Eshcol and of A;
14:24 of the men who went with me—A, Eshcol,
1Ch 6:70 of Manasseh, A with its pasture lands, and Bileam

ANETHOTHITE, ANETOTHITE (KJV) See ANATHOTH

ANEW‡ (2) [NEW]
1Pe 1:23 You have been born a, not of perishable but
Wis 19: 6 the whole creation in its nature was fashioned a,

ANGEL‡ (237) [ANGEL'S, ANGELS, ARCHANGEL, ARCHANGEL'S]
A. ANGEL OF THE †LORD (56)
B. ANGEL OF *GOD (19)
C. ANGEL OF THE *LORD (14)

Ge 16: 7 The a of the LORD found her by a spring A
16: 9 The a of the LORD said to her, A
16:10 The a of the LORD also said to her, A
16:11 And the a of the LORD said to her, A
21:17 and the a of God called to Hagar from heaven, B
22:11 the a of the LORD called to him from heaven, A
22:15 The a of the LORD called to Abraham A
24: 7 he will send his a before you,
24:40 will send his a with you
31:11 Then the a of God said to me in the dream, B
48:16 the a who has redeemed me from all harm, bless
Ex 3: 2 the a of the LORD appeared to him in a flame A
14:19 The a of God who was going before B
23:20 I am going to send an a in front of you,
23:23 When my a goes in front of you,
32:34 see, my a shall go in front of you.
33: 2 I will send an a before you,
Nu 20:16 and sent an a and brought us out of Egypt;
22:22 and the a of the LORD took his stand in the road A
22:23 The donkey saw the a of the LORD standing in A
22:24 Then the a of the LORD stood in a narrow path A
22:25 When the donkey saw the a of the LORD, A
22:26 Then the a of the LORD went ahead, A
22:27 When the donkey saw the a of the LORD, A
22:31 he saw the a of the LORD standing in the road, A
22:32 The a of the LORD said to him, A
22:34 Then Balaam said to the a of the LORD, A
22:35 The a of the LORD said to Balaam, A
Jdg 2: 1 a of the LORD went up from Gilgal to Bochim, A
2: 4 When the a of the LORD spoke these words A
5:23 "Curse Meroz, says the a of the LORD, A
6:11 the a of the LORD came and sat under the oak A
6:12 a of the LORD appeared to him and said to him, A
6:20 The a of God said to him, B
6:21 the a of the LORD reached out the tip of the staff A
6:21 and the a of the LORD vanished from his sight. A
6:22 Gideon perceived that it was the a of the LORD; A
6:22 For I have seen the a of the LORD face to face." A
13: 3 And the a of the LORD appeared to the woman A
13: 6 and his appearance was like that of an a of God, B
13: 9 the a of God came again to the woman as she B
13:13 The a of the LORD said to Manoah, A
13:15 Manoah said to the a of the LORD, A
13:16 The a of the LORD said to Manoah, A
13:16 did not know that he was the a of the LORD A
13:17 Then Manoah said to the a of the LORD, A
13:18 But the a of the LORD said to him, A
13:20 the a of the LORD ascended in the flame of A
13:21 The a of the LORD did not appear again A
13:21 Manoah realized that it was the a of the LORD. A
1Sa 29: 9 as blameless in my sight as an a of God; B
2Sa 14:17 for my lord the king is like the a of God, B
14:20 like the wisdom of the a of God to know all B
19:27 But my lord the king is like the a of God; B
24:16 the a stretched out his hand toward Jerusalem
24:16 and said to the a who was bringing destruction
24:16 The a of the LORD was then by the threshing A
24:17 David saw the a who was destroying the people,
1Ki 13:18 and an a spoke to me by the word of the LORD:
19: 5 Suddenly an a touched him and said to him,
19: 7 The a of the LORD came a second time, A
2Ki 1: 3 the a of the LORD said to Elijah the Tishbite, A
1:15 Then the a of the LORD said to Elijah, A
19:35 That very night the a of the LORD set out A
1Ch 21:12 pestilence on the land, and the a of the LORD A
21:15 And God sent an a to Jerusalem to destroy it;
21:15 he said to the destroying a, "Enough!
21:15 The a of the LORD was then standing by A
21:16 the a of the LORD standing between earth A
21:18 the a of the LORD commanded Gad to tell David A
21:20 Ornan turned and saw the a;
21:27 Then the LORD commanded the a,
21:30 he was afraid of the sword of the a of the LORD. A
2Ch 32:21 And the LORD sent an a who cut off all
Job 33:23 Then, if there should be for one of them an a,
Ps 34: 7 The a of the LORD encamps A
35: 5 with the a of the LORD driving them on. A
35: 6 with the a of the LORD pursuing them. A
Isa 37:36 Then the a of the LORD set out and struck A
63: 9 no messenger or a but his presence that saved them
Da 3:28 and Abednego, who has sent his a and delivered
6:22 My God sent his a and shut the lions' mouths so
Hos 12: 4 He strove with the a and prevailed,
Zec 1: 9 The a who talked with me said to me,
1:11 to the a of the LORD who was standing among A
1:12 Then the a of the LORD said, A
1:13 and comforting words to the a who talked
1:14 So the a who talked with me said to me,
1:19 I asked the a who talked with me,
2: 3 Then the a who talked with me came forward,
2: 3 and another a came forward to meet him,
3: 1 priest Joshua standing before the a of the LORD, A
3: 3 with filthy clothes as he stood before the a.
3: 4 The a said to those who were standing before him,
3: 5 and the a of the LORD was standing by. A
3: 6 Then the a of the LORD assured Joshua, saying A
4: 1 The a who talked with me came again,
4: 4 I said to the a who talked with me,
4: 5 Then the a who talked with me answered me,
5: 5 the a who talked with me came forward and said
5:10 Then I said to the a who talked with me,
6: 4 Then I said to the a who talked with me,
6: 5 The a answered me, "These are the four winds
12: 8 like the a of the LORD, at their head. A
Mt 1:20 an a of the Lord appeared to him in a dream C
1:24 he did as the a of the Lord commanded him; C
2:13 an a of the Lord appeared to Joseph in a dream C
2:19 an a of the Lord suddenly appeared in a dream C
28: 2 for an a of the Lord, descending from heaven, C
28: 5 But the a said to the women, "Do not be afraid;
Lk 1:11 Then there appeared to him an a of the Lord, C
1:13 But the a said to him, "Do not be afraid,
1:18 Zechariah said to the a, "How will I know
1:19 The a replied, "I am Gabriel.
1:26 In the sixth month the a Gabriel was sent by God
1:30 The a said to her, "Do not be afraid, Mary,
1:34 Mary said to the a, "How can this be,
Lk 1:35 The a said to her, "The Holy Spirit will come
1:38 Then the a departed from her.
2: 9 Then an a of the Lord stood before them, C
2:10 But the a said to them, "Do not be afraid;
2:13 And suddenly there was with the a a multitude of
2:21 the name given by the a before he was conceived
22:43 ⟦Then an a from heaven appeared to him⟧
Jn 12:29 Others said, "An a has spoken to him."
Ac 5:19 an a of the Lord opened the prison doors, C
6:15 they saw that his face was like the face of an a.
7:30 an a appeared to him in the wilderness
7:35 and liberator through the a who appeared to him
7:38 with the a who spoke to him at Mount Sinai,
8:26 Then an a of the Lord said to Philip, C
10: 3 in which he clearly saw an a of God coming in B
10: 7 When the a who spoke to him had left,
10:22 a holy a to send for you to come to his house and
11:13 the a standing in his house and saying, 'Send
12: 7 an a of the Lord appeared and a light shone in C
12: 8 The a said to him, "Fasten your belt and put
12:10 when suddenly the a left him.
12:11 that the Lord has sent his a and rescued me from
12:15 They said, "It is his a."
12:23 an a of the Lord struck him down, C
23: 8 Sadducees say that there is no resurrection, or a,
23: 9 What if a spirit or an a has spoken to him?"
27:23 For last night there stood by me an a of the God B
2Co 11:14 Even Satan disguises himself as an a of light.
Gal 1: 8 an a from heaven should proclaim to you a gospel
4:14 welcomed me as an a of God, as Christ Jesus. B
Rev 1: 1 by sending his a to his servant John,
2: 1 "To the a of the church in Ephesus write:
2: 8 "And to the a of the church in Smyrna write:
2:12 "And to the a of the church in Pergamum write:
2:18 "And to the a of the church in Thyatira write:
3: 1 "And to the a of the church in Sardis write:
3: 7 "And to the a of the church in Philadelphia write:
3:14 "And to the a of the church in Laodicea write:
5: 2 I saw a mighty a proclaiming with a loud voice,
7: 2 I saw another a ascending from the rising of
8: 3 Another a with a golden censer came and stood at
8: 4 rose before God from the hand of the a.
8: 5 Then the a took the censer and filled it with fire
8: 7 The first a blew his trumpet,
8: 8 The second a blew his trumpet,
8:10 The third a blew his trumpet,
8:12 The fourth a blew his trumpet,
9: 1 And the fifth a blew his trumpet,
9:11 as king over them the a of the bottomless pit;
9:13 Then the sixth a blew his trumpet,
9:14 saying to the sixth a who had the trumpet,
10: 1 And I saw another mighty a coming down
10: 5 Then the a whom I saw standing on the sea and
10: 7 when the seventh a is to blow his trumpet,
10: 8 in the hand of the a who is standing on the sea and
10: 9 to the a and told him to give me the little scroll;
10:10 the little scroll from the hand of the a and ate it;
11:15 Then the seventh a blew his trumpet,
14: 6 Then I saw another a flying in midheaven,
14: 8 Then another a, a second, followed, saying,
14: 9 Then another a, a third, followed them,
14:15 Another a came out of the temple,
14:17 Then another a came out of the temple in heaven,
14:18 Then another a came out from the altar,
14:18 the a who has authority over fire,
14:19 the a swung his sickle over the earth and gathered
16: 2 the first a went and poured his bowl on the earth,
16: 3 The second a poured his bowl into the sea,
16: 4 The third a poured his bowl into the rivers and
16: 5 And I heard the a of the waters say, "You are just,
16: 8 The fourth a poured his bowl on the sun,
16:10 fifth a poured his bowl on the throne of the beast,
16:12 The sixth a poured his bowl on
16:17 The seventh a poured his bowl into the air,
17: 7 But the a said to me, "Why are you so amazed?
18: 1 this I saw another a coming down from heaven,
18:21 a mighty a took up a stone like a great millstone
19: 9 And the a said to me, "Write this:
19:17 Then I saw an a standing in the sun,
20: 1 Then I saw an a coming down from heaven,
21:15 The a who talked to me had a measuring rod
21:17 by human measurement, which the a was using.
22: 1 the a showed me the river of the water of life,
22: 6 of the spirits of the prophets, has sent his a
22: 8 to worship at the feet of the a who showed them
22:16 who sent my a to you with this testimony for
Tob 5: 4 and found the a Raphael standing in front of him;
5: 4 but he did not perceive that he was an a of God. B
5:17 and may his a, my son, accompany you both
5:22 For a good a will accompany him;
6: 1 The young man went out and the a went with him;
6: 4 But the a said to the young man,
6: 5 Then the a said to him,
6: 7 the young man questioned the a and said to him,
12:22 when an a of God had appeared to them. B
AdE 15:13 "I saw you, my lord, like an a of God, B
Sir 48:21 and his a wiped them out.
LtJ 6: 7 For my a is with you,
Aza 1:26 the a of the Lord came down into the furnace C
Sus 1:55 the a of God has received the sentence from God B
1:59 the a of God is waiting with his sword to split B
Bel 1:34 But the a of the Lord said to Habakkuk, C
1:36 Then the a of the Lord took him by the crown C
1:39 the a of God immediately returned Habakkuk B
1Mc 7:41 your a went out and struck
2Mc 11: 6 prayed the Lord to send a good a to save Israel.
15:22 you sent your a in the time of King Hezekiah

2Mc 15:23 a good **a** to spread terror and trembling before us.
2Es 2:44 Then I asked an **a**, "Who are these, my lord?"
2:46 Then I said to the **a**, "Who is that young man
2:48 Then the **a** said to me, "Go,
4: 1 Then the **a** that had been sent to me,
5:15 the **a** who had come and talked with me held me
5:20 as the **a** Uriel had commanded me.
5:31 the **a** who had come to me on
7: 1 the **a** who had been sent to me on
10:28 "Where is the **a** Uriel, who came to me
10:29 the **a** who had come to me at first came to me,
12:51 as the **a** had commanded me;
4Mc 7:11 of the people and conquered the fiery **a**,

ANGEL'S (1) [ANGEL]

Ac 12: 9 that what was happening with the **a** help was real;

ANGELS‡ (103) [ANGEL]

Ge 19: 1 The two **a** came to Sodom in the evening,
19:15 When morning dawned, the **a** urged Lot, saying,
28:12 the **a** of God were ascending and descending on it.
32: 1 Jacob went on his way and the **a** of God met him;
Job 4:18 and his **a** he charges with error;
Ps 78:25 Mortals ate of the bread of **a**;
78:49 and distress, a company of destroying **a**.
91:11 For he will command his **a** concerning you
103:20 Bless the LORD, O you his **a**,
148: 2 Praise him, all his **a**; praise him, all his host!
Mt 4: 6 'He will command his **a** concerning you,'
4:11 and suddenly **a** came and waited on him.
13:39 harvest is the end of the age, and the reapers are **a**.
13:41 The Son of Man will send his **a**,
13:49 The **a** will come out and separate the evil from
16:27 the Son of Man is to come with his **a** in the glory
18:10 for, I tell you, in heaven their **a** continually see
22:30 but are like **a** in heaven.
24:31 he will send out his **a** with a loud trumpet call,
24:36 neither the **a** of heaven, nor the Son,
25:31 and all the **a** with him,
25:41 the eternal fire prepared for the devil and his **a**;
26:53 at once send me more than twelve legions of **a**?
Mk 1:13 and the **a** waited on him.
8:38 in the glory of his Father with the holy **a**."
12:25 but are like **a** in heaven.
13:27 Then he will send out the **a**,
13:32 neither the **a** in heaven, nor the Son,
Lk 2:15 When the **a** had left them and gone into heaven,
4:10 'He will command his **a** concerning you,
9:26 and the glory of the Father and of the holy **a**.
12: 8 also will acknowledge before the **a** of God;
12: 9 before others will be denied before the **a** of God.
15:10 of the **a** of God over one sinner who repents."
16:22 The poor man died and was carried away by the **a**
20:36 because they are like **a** and are children of God,
24:23 that they had indeed seen a vision of **a** who said
Jn 1:51 and the **a** of God ascending and descending upon
20:12 and she saw two **a** in white,
Ac 7:53 the ones that received the law as ordained by **a**,
Ro 8:38 I am convinced that neither death, nor life, nor **a**,
1Co 4: 9 a spectacle to the world, to **a** and to mortals.
6: 3 Do you not know that we are to judge **a**—
11:10 of authority on her head, because of the **a**.
13: 1 If I speak in the tongues of mortals and of **a**,
Gal 3:19 and it was ordained through **a** by a mediator.
Col 2:18 insisting on self-abasement and worship of **a**,
2Th 1: 7 Jesus is revealed from heaven with his mighty **a**
1Ti 3:16 seen by **a**, proclaimed among Gentiles,
5:21 of God and of Christ Jesus and of the elect **a**,
Heb 1: 4 having become as much superior to **a** as
1: 5 For to which of the **a** did God ever say,
1: 6 he says, "Let all God's **a** worship him."
1: 7 Of the **a** he says, "He makes his **a** winds,
1:13 But to which of the **a** has he ever said,
1:14 Are not all **a** spirits in the divine service,
2: 2 For if the message declared through **a** was valid,
2: 5 about which we are speaking, to **a**.
2: 7 for a little while lower than the **a**;
2: 9 who for a little while was made lower than the **a**,
2:16 For it is clear that he did not come to help **a**,
12:22 and to innumerable **a** in festal gathering,
13: 2 that some have entertained **a** without knowing it.
1Pe 1:12 things into which **a** long to look!
3:22 and is at the right hand of God, with **a**, authorities,
2Pe 2: 4 For if God did not spare the **a** when they sinned,
2:11 whereas **a**, though greater in might and power, do
Jude 1: 6 And the **a** who did not keep their own position,
Rev 1:20 the seven stars are the **a** of the seven churches,
3: 5 before my Father and before his **a**.
5:11 the voice of many **a** surrounding the throne and
7: 1 After this I saw four **a** standing at the four corners
7: 2 to the four **a** who had been given power
7:11 And all the **a** stood around the throne and around
8: 2 And I saw the seven **a** who stand before God,
8: 6 Now the seven **a** who had the seven trumpets
8:13 the blasts of the other trumpets that the three **a** are
9:14 "Release the four **a** who are bound at
9:15 So the four **a** were released,
12: 7 Michael and his **a** fought against the dragon.
12: 7 The dragon and his **a** fought back,
12: 9 and his **a** were thrown down with him.
14:10 the presence of the holy **a** and in the presence of
15: 1 seven **a** with seven plagues, which are the last,
15: 6 and out of the temple came the seven **a** with
15: 7 the seven **a** seven golden bowls full of the wrath
15: 8 until the seven plagues of the seven **a** were ended.
16: 1 a loud voice from the temple telling the seven **a**,
Rev 17: 1 of the seven **a** who had the seven bowls came
21: 9 of the seven **a** who had the seven bowls full of
21:12 and at the gates twelve **a**,
Tob 11:14 and blessed be all his holy **a**.
12:15 of the seven **a** who stand ready and enter before
Wis 16:20 of these things you gave your people food of **a**,
Aza 1:37 Bless the Lord, you **a** of the Lord;
3Mc 6:18 from which two glorious **a** of fearful aspect
2Es 1:19 you ate the bread of **a**.
6: 3 the innumerable hosts of **a** were gathered together,
7:*85* how the habitations of the others are guarded by **a**
7:*95* into their chambers and guarded by **a**
8:21 before whom the hosts of **a** stand trembling
4Mc 4:10 **a** on horseback with lightning flashing

ANGER‡ (319) [ANGERED, ANGERS, ANGRILY, ANGRY]

Ge 27:45 until your brother's **a** against you turns away,
49: 6 for in their **a** they killed men,
49: 7 Cursed be their **a**, for it is fierce, and their wrath,
Ex 4:14 the **a** of the LORD was kindled against Moses
11: 8 And in hot **a** he left Pharaoh.
32:19 the dancing, Moses' **a** burned hot, and he threw
32:22 Aaron said, "Do not let the **a** of my lord burn hot;
34: 6 a God merciful and gracious, slow to **a**,
Nu 11: 1 the LORD heard it and his **a** was kindled.
11:33 **a** of the LORD was kindled against the people,
12: 9 the **a** of the LORD was kindled against them,
14:18 'The LORD is slow to **a**,
22:22 God's **a** was kindled because he was going,
22:27 and Balaam's **a** was kindled,
24:10 Then Balak's **a** was kindled against Balaam,
25: 3 and the LORD's **a** was kindled against Israel.
25: 4 that the fierce **a** of the LORD may turn away
32:10 LORD's **a** was kindled on that day and he swore,
32:13 And the LORD's **a** was kindled against Israel,
32:14 to increase the LORD's fierce **a** against Israel!
Dt 4:25 of the LORD your God, and provoking him to **a**,
6:15 The **a** of the LORD your God would be kindled
7: 4 the **a** of the LORD would be kindled against you,
9:19 that the **a** that the LORD bore against you was
11:17 the **a** of the LORD will be kindled against you
13:17 so that the LORD may turn from his fierce **a**
19: 6 of blood in hot **a** might pursue and overtake
29:20 LORD's **a** and passion will smoke against them.
29:23 which the LORD destroyed in his fierce **a**—
29:24 What caused this great display of **a**?"
29:27 the **a** of the LORD was kindled against that land,
29:28 The LORD uprooted them from their land in **a**,
31:17 My **a** will be kindled against them in that day.
31:29 to **a** through the work of your hands."
32:22 For a fire is kindled by my **a**,
Jos 7: 1 the **a** of the LORD burned against the Israelites.
7:26 Then the LORD turned from his burning **a**.
23:16 the **a** of the LORD will be kindled against you,
Jdg 2:12 and they provoked the LORD to **a**.
2:14 So the **a** of the LORD was kindled against Israel,
2:20 So the **a** of the LORD was kindled against Israel;
3: 8 the **a** of the LORD was kindled against Israel,
6:39 "Do not let your **a** burn against me,
8: 3 When he said this, their **a** against him subsided.
9:30 the words of Gaal son of Ebed, his **a** was kindled.
10: 7 So the **a** of the LORD was kindled against Israel,
14:19 In hot **a** he went back to his father's house.
1Sa 11: 6 and his **a** was greatly kindled.
17:28 and Eliab's **a** was kindled against David.
20:30 Then Saul's **a** was kindled against Jonathan.
20:34 in fierce **a** and ate no food on the second day of
2Sa 6: 7 The **a** of the LORD was kindled against Uzzah;
11:20 if the king's **a** rises, and if he says to you,
12: 5 David's **a** was greatly kindled against the man.
24: 1 the **a** of the LORD was kindled against Israel,
1Ki 14: 9 and cast images, provoking me to **a**,
14:15 provoking the LORD to **a**.
15:30 of the **a** to which he provoked the LORD,
16: 2 provoking me to **a** with their sins,
16: 7 provoking him to **a** with the work of his hands,
16:13 the LORD God of Israel to **a** with their idols.
16:26 the God of Israel, to **a** by their idols.
16:33 Ahab did more to provoke the **a** of the LORD,
21:22 because you have provoked me to **a**
22:53 he provoked the LORD, the God of Israel, to **a**,
2Ki 13: 3 The **a** of the LORD was kindled against Israel,
17:11 provoking the LORD to **a**;
17:17 in the sight of the LORD, provoking him to **a**.
21: 6 in the sight of the LORD, provoking him to **a**.
21:15 in my sight and have provoked me to **a**,
22:17 that they have provoked me to **a** with all the work
23:19 provoking the LORD to **a**;
23:26 by which his **a** was kindled against Judah,
1Ch 13:10 The **a** of the LORD was kindled against Uzzah;
2Ch 21:16 the **a** of the Philistines and of the Arabs who are
25:10 and returned home in fierce **a**.
28:25 provoking to **a** the LORD,
29:10 so that his fierce **a** may turn away from us.
30: 8 so that his fierce **a** may turn away from you.
33: 6 in the sight of the LORD, provoking him to **a**.
34:25 so that they have provoked me to **a** with all
Ne 9:17 slow to **a** and abounding in steadfast love,
Est 1:12 and his **a** burned within him.
2: 1 when the **a** of King Ahasuerus had abated,
7:10 Then the **a** of the king abated.
Job 4: 9 and by the blast of his **a** they are consumed.
9: 5 when he overturns them in his **a**;
9:13 "God will not turn back his **a**;
18: 4 You who tear yourself in your **a**—
Job 20:23 to the full God will send his fierce **a** into them,
21:17 How often does God distribute pains in his **a**?
35:15 And now, because his **a** does not punish,
36:13 "The godless in heart cherish **a**;
36:33 he is jealous with **a** against iniquity.
40:11 Pour out the overflowings of your **a**,
Ps 6: 1 do not rebuke me in your **a**,
7: 6 up, O LORD, in your **a**;
27: 9 Do not turn your servant away in **a**,
30: 5 For his **a** is but for a moment;
37: 8 Refrain from **a**, and forsake wrath.
38: 1 do not rebuke me in your **a**,
55: 3 and in **a** they cherish enmity against me.
69:24 and let your burning **a** overtake them.
74: 1 Why does your **a** smoke against the sheep
76: 7 before you when once your **a** is roused?
77: 9 Has he in **a** shut up his compassion?"
78:21 his **a** mounted against Israel,
78:31 the **a** of God rose against them and he killed
78:38 he restrained his **a**, and did not stir up all his wrath.
78:49 He let loose on them his fierce **a**, wrath,
78:50 He made a path for his **a**;
78:58 For they provoked him to **a** with their high places;
79: 6 Pour out your **a** on the nations that do
85: 3 you turned from your hot **a**.
85: 5 Will you prolong your **a** to all generations?
86:15 slow to **a** and abounding in steadfast love
90: 7 For we are consumed by your **a**;
90:11 Who considers the power of your **a**?
95:11 in my **a** I swore, "They shall not enter my rest."
102:10 because of your indignation and **a**;
103: 8 slow to **a** and abounding in steadfast love.
103: 9 nor will he keep his **a** forever.
106:29 they provoked the LORD to **a** with their deeds,
106:40 **a** of the LORD was kindled against his people,
124: 3 when their **a** was kindled against us;
145: 8 slow to **a** and abounding in steadfast love.
Pr 12:16 Fools show their **a** at once,
14:29 Whoever is slow to **a** has great understanding,
15: 1 but a harsh word stirs up **a**.
15:18 but those who are slow to **a** calm contention.
16:32 One who is slow to **a** is better than the mighty,
19:11 Those with good sense are slow to **a**,
19:12 A king's **a** is like the growling of a lion,
20: 2 dread **a** of a king is like the growling of a lion;
20: 2 anyone who provokes him to **a** forfeits life itself.
21:14 A gift in secret averts **a**;
22: 8 and the rod of **a** will fail.
22:24 Make no friends with those given to **a**,
24:18 and turn away his **a** from them.
27: 4 Wrath is cruel, **a** is overwhelming,
29:11 A fool gives full vent to **a**,
29:22 One given to **a** stirs up strife,
30:33 so pressing **a** produces strife.
Ecc 7: 9 Do not be quick to **a**, for **a** lodges in the bosom of fools.
10: 4 If the **a** of the ruler rises against you,
Isa 5:25 **a** of the LORD was kindled against his people,
5:25 For all this his **a** has not turned away,
7: 4 because of the fierce **a** of Rezin and Aram and
9:12 For all this his **a** has not turned away;
9:17 For all this his **a** has not turned away,
9:21 For all this his **a** has not turned away;
10: 4 For all this his **a** has not turned away;
10: 5 Ah, Assyria, the rod of my **a**—
10:25 and my **a** will be directed to their destruction.
12: 1 your **a** turned away, and you comforted me.
13: 3 my proudly exulting ones, to execute my **a**.
13: 9 cruel, with wrath and fierce **a**,
13:13 of the LORD of hosts in the day of his fierce **a**.
14: 6 the nations in **a** with unrelenting persecution.
30:27 burning with his **a**, and in thick rising smoke;
30:30 in furious **a** and a flame of devouring fire,
42:25 upon him the heat of his **a** and the fury of war;
48: 9 For my name's sake I defer my **a**,
63: 3 I trod them in my **a** and trampled them in my wrath
63: 6 I trampled down peoples in my **a**,
66:15 to pay back his **a** in fury, and his rebuke in flames
Jer 2:35 surely his **a** has turned from me."
3:12 I will not look on you in **a**, for I am merciful,
4: 8 "The fierce **a** of the LORD has not turned away
4:26 in ruins before the LORD, before his fierce **a**.
7:18 to other gods, to provoke me to **a**.
7:20 My **a** and my wrath shall be poured out
8:19 ("Why have they provoked me to **a**
10:24 not in your **a**, or you will bring me to nothing.
11:17 provoking me to **a** by making offerings to Baal.
12:13 of their harvests because of the fierce **a** of
15:14 in my **a** a fire is kindled that shall burn forever.
17: 4 in my **a** a fire is kindled that shall burn forever.
21: 5 in **a**, in fury, and in great wrath.
23:20 The **a** of the LORD will not turn back
25: 6 not provoke me to **a** with the work of your hands.
25: 7 and so you have provoked me to **a** with the work
25:37 because of the fierce **a** of the LORD.
25:38 and because of his fierce **a**.
30:24 The fierce **a** of the LORD will not turn back
32:29 to other gods, to provoke me to **a**.
32:30 of Israel have done nothing but provoke me to **a**
32:31 This city has aroused my **a** and wrath,
32:32 of Judah that they did to provoke me to **a**—
32:37 to which I drove them in my **a** and my wrath and
33: 5 of those whom I shall strike down in my **a**
36: 7 the **a** and wrath that the LORD has pronounced
42:18 Just as my **a** and my wrath were poured out on
44: 3 that they committed, provoking me to **a**, in
44: 6 and my **a** were poured out and kindled in

Jer 44: 8 Why do you provoke me to **a** with the works
49:37 I will bring disaster upon them, my fierce **a**,
51:45 each of you, from the fierce **a** of the LORD!
La 1:12 the LORD inflicted on the day of his fierce **a**.
2: 1 the Lord in his **a** has humiliated daughter Zion!
2: 1 not remembered his footstool in the day of his **a**.
2: 3 He has cut down in fierce **a** all the might of Israel;
2:21 in the day of your **a** you have killed them,
2:22 on the day of the **a** of the LORD no one escaped
3:43 with **a** and pursued us, killing without pity;
3:66 Pursue them in **a** and destroy them from under
4:11 he poured out his hot **a**,
Eze 5:13 My **a** shall spend itself, and I will vent my fury
5:15 when I execute judgments on you in **a** and fury,
7: 3 end is upon you, I will let loose my **a** upon you;
7: 8 I will spend my **a** against you.
8:17 and provoke my **a** still further?
13:13 and in my **a** there shall be a deluge of rain,
16:26 multiplying your whoring, to provoke me to **a**.
20: 8 and spend my **a** against them in the midst of
20:21 and spend my **a** against them in the wilderness.
22:20 so I will gather you in my **a** and in my wrath,
25:14 and they shall act in Edom according to my **a** and
35:11 I will deal with you according to the **a** and envy
43: 8 therefore I have consumed them in my **a**.
Da 9:16 let your **a** and wrath, we pray,
11:20 though not in **a** or in battle.
Hos 7: 6 all night their **a** smolders;
8: 5 My **a** burns against them.
11: 9 I will not execute my fierce **a**;
13:11 I gave you a king in my **a**,
14: 4 for my **a** has turned from them.
Joel 2:13 slow to **a**, and abounding in steadfast love,
Am 1:11 he maintained his **a** perpetually,
Jnh 3: 9 he may turn from his fierce **a**,
4: 2 slow to **a**, and abounding in steadfast love,
Mic 5:15 And in **a** and wrath I will execute vengeance on
7:18 He does not retain his **a** forever,
Na 1: 3 The LORD is slow to **a** but great in power,
1: 6 Who can endure the heat of his **a**?
Hab 3: 8 Or your **a** against the rivers,
3:12 in **a** you trampled nations.
Zep 2: 2 there comes upon you the fierce **a** of the LORD,
3: 8 all the heat of my **a**;
Zec 10: 3 My **a** is hot against the shepherds,
Mt 18:34 And in **a** his lord handed him over to be tortured
Mk 3: 5 He looked around at them with **a**;
14: 4 But some were there who said to one another in **a**,
2Co 12:20 jealousy, **a**, selfishness, slander, gossip, conceit,
Gal 5:20 enmities, strife, jealousy, **a**, quarrels, dissensions,
Eph 4:26 do not let the sun go down on your **a**,
4:31 Put away from you all bitterness and wrath and **a**
6: 4 And, fathers, do not provoke your children to **a**,
Col 3: 8 But now you must get rid of all such things—**a**,
1Ti 2: 8 lifting up holy hands without **a** or argument;
Heb 3:11 in my **a** I swore, 'They will not enter my rest.' "
4: 3 just as God has said, "As in my **a** I swore,
11:27 By faith he left Egypt, unafraid of the king's **a**;
Jas 1:19 slow to speak, slow to **a**;
1:20 for your **a** does not produce God's righteousness.
Rev 14:10 poured unmixed into the cup of his **a**,
Tob 1:18 For in his **a** he put to death many Israelites;
2:14 I became flushed with **a** against her over this.
Jdt 2: 7 for I am coming against them in my **a**,
5: 2 In great **a** he called together all the princes
8:14 No, my brothers, do not **a** the Lord our God.
9: 8 and bring down their power in your **a**;
11:11 by which they are about to provoke their God to **a**
AdE 2: 1 After these things, the king's **a** abated,
5: 9 the Jew in the courtyard, he was filled with **a**.
7:10 With that the **a** of the king abated.
15: 7 flushed with splendor, he looked at her in fierce **a**.
Wis 10: 3 an unrighteous man departed from her in his **a**,
18:21 he withstood the **a** and put an end to the disaster,
19: 1 the ungodly were assailed to the end by pitiless **a**,
Sir 1:22 Unjust **a** cannot be justified,
1:22 for **a** tips the scale to one's ruin.
4: 2 Do not grieve the hungry, or **a** one in need.
5: 4 for the Lord is slow to **a**.
5: 6 and his **a** will rest on sinners.
10:18 or violent **a** for those born of women.
25:15 and no **a** worse than a woman's wrath.
26: 8 A drunken wife arouses great **a**;
26:28 and because of a third **a** comes over me:
27:30 **A** and wrath, these also are abominations,
28: 3 Does anyone harbor **a** against another,
28:10 in proportion to a person's strength will be his **a**,
28:19 who has not been exposed to its **a**,
30:24 Jealousy and **a** shorten life,
31:30 Drunkenness increases the **a** of a fool
36: 8 Rouse your **a** and pour out your wrath;
39:28 and in their **a** they can dislodge mountains;
39:28 and calm the **a** of their Maker.
40: 5 there is **a** and envy and trouble and unrest,
45:18 and the company of Korah, in wrath and **a**.
45:19 and in the heat of his **a** they were destroyed;
Bar 1:13 to this day the **a** of the Lord and his wrath have
2:13 Let your **a** turn away from us, for we are left,
2:20 For you have sent your **a** and your wrath upon us,
1Mc 2:24 He gave vent to righteous **a**;
2:44 and struck down sinners in their **a** and renegades
2:49 it is a time of ruin and furious **a**.
7:35 and in **a** he swore this oath,
7:35 And he went out in great **a**.
2Mc 4:38 Inflamed with **a**, he immediately stripped off
4:40 crowds were becoming aroused and filled with **a**,
10:35 fired with **a** because of the blasphemies,
2Mc 13: 4 But the King of kings aroused the **a** of Antiochus
14:45 Still alive and aflame with **a**, he rose,
1Es 1:52 until in his **a** against his people because
3Mc 5: 1 was filled with overpowering **a** and wrath;
6:22 the king's **a** was turned to pity and tears because
2Es 10: 5 and answered her in **a** and said,
4Mc 1: 4 that stand in the way of courage, namely **a**, fear,
1:24 **A**, as a person will see by reflecting
2:16 as it repels **a**—for it is sovereign over even this.
2:17 he did nothing against them in **a**,
2:17 but controlled his **a** by reason.
2:19 saying, "Cursed be their **a**"?
2:20 For if reason could not control **a**,
3: 3 No one of us can eradicate **a** from the mind,
3: 3 but reason can help to deal with **a**.
8: 9 But if by disobedience you rouse my **a**,

ANGERED (9) [ANGER]

2Ki 24:20 and Judah so **a** the LORD that he expelled them
Ezr 5:12 because our ancestors had **a** the God of heaven,
Ps 106:32 They **a** the LORD at the waters of Meribah,
Jer 52: 3 and Judah so **a** the LORD that he expelled them
Bar 4: 6 over to your enemies because you **a** God.
1Mc 3:27 Antiochus heard these reports, he was greatly **a**;
2Mc 5:17 and did not perceive that the Lord was **a** for a little
2Es 1: 7 But they have **a** me and despised my counsels.
4Mc 4:21 The divine justice was **a** by these acts

ANGERS‡ (1) [ANGER]

Sir 3:16 and whoever **a** a mother is cursed by the Lord.

ANGLE (5)

2Ch 26: 9 at the Valley Gate, and at the A,
Ne 3:19 the ascent to the armory at the **A**.
3:20 of Zabbai repaired another section from the **A** to
3:24 the house of Azariah to the **A** and to the corner.
3:25 Palal son of Uzai repaired opposite the **A** and

ANGRILY (1) [ANGER]

3Mc 6:23 he wept and **a** threatened his Friends, saying,

ANGRY‡ (123) [ANGER]

Ge 4: 5 So Cain was very **a**, and his countenance fell.
4: 6 The LORD said to Cain, "Why are you **a**,
18:30 he said, "Oh do not let the Lord be **a** if I speak.
18:32 not let the Lord be **a** if I speak just once more.
30: 2 Jacob became very **a** with Rachel and said,
31:35 not my lord be **a** that I cannot rise before you,
31:36 Then Jacob became **a**, and upbraided Laban.
34: 7 the men were indignant and very **a**,
40: 2 Pharaoh was **a** with his two officers,
41:10 Once Pharaoh was **a** with his servants,
44:18 and do not be **a** with your servant;
45: 5 now do not be distressed, or **a** with yourselves,
Ex 16:20 And Moses was **a** with them.
Lev 10:16 He was **a** with Eleazar and Ithamar,
Nu 11:10 Then the LORD became very **a**,
16:15 Moses was very **a** and said to the LORD,
16:22 and you become **a** with the whole congregation?"
31:14 Moses became **a** with the officers of the army,
Dt 1:37 Even with me the LORD was **a** on your account,
3:26 But the LORD was **a** with me on your account
4:21 The LORD was **a** with me because of you,
9: 8 the LORD was so **a** with you that he was ready
9:20 so **a** with Aaron that he was ready to destroy him,
Jos 22:18 he will be **a** with the whole congregation
Jdg 19: 2 But his concubine became **a** with him,
1Sa 15:11 not carried out my commands." Samuel was **a**;
18: 8 Saul was very **a**, for this saying displeased him.
20: 7 it will be well with your servant; but if he is **a**,
29: 4 commanders of the Philistines were **a** with him;
2Sa 3: 8 The words of Ishbaal made Abner very **a**;
6: 8 David was **a** because the LORD had burst forth
13:21 of all these things, he became very **a**,
19:42 Why then are you **a** over this matter?
22: 8 and quaked, because he was **a**.
1Ki 8:46 you are **a** with them and give them to an enemy,
11: 9 Then the LORD was **a** with Solomon,
2Ki 5:11 But Naaman became **a** and went away, saying,
13:19 Then the man of God was **a** with him, and said,
17:18 Therefore the LORD was very **a** with Israel
1Ch 13:11 David was **a** because the LORD had burst out
2Ch 6:36 you are **a** with them and give them to an enemy,
16:10 Then Asa was **a** with the seer,
25:10 But they became very **a** with Judah,
25:15 The LORD was **a** with Amaziah and sent to him
26:19 Then Uzziah was **a**.
26:19 and when he became **a** with the priests
28: 9 was **a** with Judah, he gave them into your hand,
Ezr 9:14 be **a** with us until you destroy us without remnant
Ne 4: 1 he was **a** and greatly enraged,
4: 7 to be closed, they were very **a**,
5: 6 I was very **a** when I heard their outcry
13: 8 And I was very **a**, and I threw all
Est 2:21 the threshold, became **a** and conspired
Job 32: 2 the Buzite, of the family of Ram, became **a**.
32: 2 He was **a** at Job because he justified himself
32: 3 he was **a** also at Job's three friends
32: 5 in the mouths of these three men, he became **a**.
Ps 2:12 or he will be **a**, and you will perish in the way;
18: 7 and quaked, because he was **a**.
60: 1 you have been **a**; now restore us!
79: 5 Will you be **a** forever?
80: 4 long will you be **a** with your people's prayers?
Ps 85: 5 Will you be **a** with us forever?
112:10 The wicked see it and are **a**;
Pr 22:14 he with whom the LORD is **a** falls into it.
25:23 and a backbiting tongue, **a** looks.
Ecc 5: 6 why should God be **a** at your words,
SS 1: 6 My mother's sons were **a** with me;
Isa 12: 1 O LORD, for though you were **a** with me,
47: 6 I was **a** with my people, I profaned my heritage;
54: 9 over the earth, so I have sworn that I will not be **a**
57:16 nor will I always be **a**;
57:17 Because of their wicked covetousness I was **a**;
57:17 I struck them, I hid and was **a**;
64: 5 But you were **a**, and we sinned;
64: 9 Do not be exceedingly **a**, O LORD,
Jer 3: 5 will he be **a** forever, will he be indignant to
3:12 I will not be **a** forever.
18:23 deal with them while you are **a**.
La 5:22 and are **a** with us beyond measure.
Eze 16:42 I will be calm, and will be **a** no longer.
Jnh 4: 1 to Jonah, and he became **a**.
4: 4 And the LORD said, "Is it right for you to be **a**?"
4: 9 "Is it right for you to be **a** about the bush?"
4: 9 And he said, "Yes, **a** enough to die."
Zec 1: 2 The LORD was very **a** with your ancestors.
1:12 with which you have been **a** these seventy years?"
1:15 I am extremely **a** with the nations that are at ease;
1:15 I was only a little **a**, they made the disaster worse.
Mal 1: 4 the people with whom the LORD is **a** forever.
Mt 5:22 that if you are **a** with a brother or sister, you will
20:24 the ten heard it, they were **a** with the two brothers.
21:15 to the Son of David," they became **a**
26: 8 when the disciples saw it, they were **a** and said,
Mk 10:41 they began to be **a** with James and John.
Lk 14:21 owner of the house became **a** and said to his slave,
15:28 Then he became **a** and refused to go in.
Jn 7:23 are you **a** with me because I healed
Ac 12:20 Herod was **a** with the people of Tyre and Sidon.
Ro 10:19 with a foolish nation I will make you **a**."
Eph 4:26 Be **a** but do not sin; do not let the sun go down
Heb 3:10 Therefore I was **a** with that generation, and I said,
3:17 But with whom was he **a** forty years?
Rev 12:17 Then the dragon was **a** with the woman,
Jdt 1:12 Then Nebuchadnezzar became very **a**
AdE 2:21 were **a** because of Mordecai's advancement,
3: 5 to him, he became furiously **a**,
Sir 10: 6 Do not get **a** with your neighbor for every injury,
28: 7 and do not be **a** with your neighbor;
Bel 1: 8 Then the king was **a** and called the priests of Bel
1Mc 5: 1 as it was before, they became very **a**,
6:59 of their laws that we abolished that they became **a**
9:69 So he was very **a** at the renegades
11:22 When he heard this he was **a**,
15:36 And the king was very **a**.
2Mc 7:33 And if our living Lord is **a** for a little while,
13:25 so **a** that they wanted to annul its terms.
1Es 8:88 not **a** enough with us to destroy us without leaving
Man 1:13 not be **a** with me forever or store up evil for me;
2Es 8:30 Do not be **a** with those who are deemed worse
8:34 But what are mortals, that you are **a** with them;
16:48 the more **a** I will be with them for their sins,
4Mc 2:17 When Moses was **a** with Dathan and Abiram,

ANGUISH‡ (50)

Ge 42:21 we saw his **a** when he pleaded with us,
42:21 That is why this **a** has come upon us."
Dt 2:25 they will tremble and be in **a** because of you."
Job 7:11 I will speak in the **a** of my spirit;
15:24 distress and **a** terrify them;
Ps 55: 4 My heart is in **a** within me,
116: 3 on me; I suffered distress and **a**.
119:143 Trouble and **a** have come upon me,
Pr 1:27 when distress and **a** come upon you.
Isa 8:22 and darkness, the gloom of **a**;
9: 1 there will be no gloom for those who were in **a**.
13: 8 they will be in **a** like a woman in labor.
21: 3 Therefore my loins are filled with **a**;
23: 5 they will be in **a** over the report about Tyre.
53:11 Out of his **a** he shall see light;
65:14 and shall wail for **a** of spirit.
Jer 4:19 My **a**, my **a**! I writhe in pain!
4:31 **a** as of one bringing forth her first child,
5: 3 You have struck them, but they felt no **a**;
6:24 **a** has taken hold of us, pain as of a woman in labor.
15: 8 I have made **a** and terror fall upon her suddenly.
48: 5 Horonaim they have heard the distressing cry of **a**.
49:24 **a** and sorrows have taken hold of her,
50:43 **a** seized him, pain like that of a woman in labor.
La 3:65 Give them **a** of heart; your curse be on them!
Eze 7:25 When **a** comes, they will seek peace,
30: 4 and **a** shall be in Ethiopia,
30: 9 and **a** shall come upon them on the day
Da 12: 1 There shall be a time of **a**,
Joel 2: 6 Before them peoples are in **a**, all faces grow pale.
Zep 1:15 day will be a day of wrath, a day of distress and **a**,
Zec 9: 5 Gaza too, and shall writhe in **a**;
Lk 22:44 ⟦In his **a** he prayed more earnestly,⟧
Jn 16:21 she no longer remembers the **a** because of the joy
Ro 2: 9 be **a** and distress for everyone who does evil,
9: 2 I have great sorrow and unceasing **a** in my heart.
2Co 2: 4 For I wrote you out of much distress and **a**
Tob 3: 1 Then with much grief and **a** of heart I wept,
Wis 4:19 and barren, and they will suffer **a**,
5: 3 and in **a** of spirit they will groan, and say,
Sir 48:19 and they were in **a**, like women in labor.
Bar 3: 1 the soul in **a** and the wearied spirit cry out to you.
2Mc 3:16 the change in his color disclosed the **a** of his soul.

2Mc 3:21 and the anxiety of the high priest in his great **a.**
9: 9 and while he was still living in **a** and pain,
2Es 2:27 for when the day of tribulation and **a** comes,
16:19 and **a** are sent as scourges for the correction
4Mc 11:11 gasping for breath and in **a** of body,
14:17 by flying in circles around them in the **a** of love,

ANIAM (1)

1Ch 7:19 of Shemida were Ahian, Shechem, Likhi, and **A.**

ANIM (1)

Jos 15:50 Anab, Eshtemoh, **A,**

ANIMAL‡ (84) [ANIMALS]

Ge 2:19 of the ground the LORD God formed every **a** of
2:20 and to every **a** of the field;
3: 1 the serpent was more crafty than any other wild **a**
7:14 they and every wild **a** of every kind,
8:19 And every **a,** every creeping thing, and every bird,
8:20 and took of every clean **a** and of every clean bird,
9: 2 and dread of you shall rest on every **a** of the earth,
9: 5 from every **a** I will require it and
9:10 and every **a** of the earth with you,
37:20 then we shall say that a wild **a** has devoured him,
37:33 A wild **a** has devoured him;
43:16 and slaughter an **a** and make ready,
Ex 9:19 every human or **a** that is in the open field and is
9:25 the land of Egypt, both human and **a;**
12:46 you shall not take any of the **a** outside the house,
19:13 whether **a** or human being, they shall not live.'
21:34 to its owner, but keeping the dead **a.**
21:35 and the dead **a** they shall also divide.
21:36 for ox, but keep the dead **a.**
22: 4 When the **a,** whether ox or donkey or sheep,
22:10 ox, sheep, or any other **a** for safekeeping,
22:14 When someone borrows an **a** from another
22:19 Whoever lies with an **a** shall be put to death.
Lev 3: 1 if you offer an **a** of the herd,
7:21 or an unclean **a** or any unclean creature—
7:24 of an **a** that died or was torn by wild animals may
7:25 the fat from an **a** of which an offering by fire may
7:26 either of bird or of **a,** in any of your settlements.
11: 3 Any **a** that has divided hoofs and is cleft-footed
11:26 Every **a** that has divided hoofs but is
11:39 If an **a** of which you may eat dies,
11:46 This is the law pertaining to land **a** and bird
17:13 who hunts down an **a** or bird that may
18:23 You shall not have sexual relations with any **a**
18:23 nor shall any woman give herself to an **a**
20:15 If a man has sexual relations with an **a,**
20:15 and you shall kill the **a.**
20:16 If a woman approaches any **a** and has sexual
20:16 you shall kill the woman and the **a;**
20:25 between the clean **a** and the unclean,
20:25 on yourselves by **a** or by bird or by anything
22:24 Any **a** that has its testicles bruised or crushed
22:28 an **a** with its young on the same day.
24:18 Anyone who kills an **a** shall make restitution
24:21 One who kills an **a** shall make restitution for it;
27: 9 an **a** that may be brought as an offering to
27:10 and if one **a** is substituted for another,
27:11 If it concerns any unclean **a** that may not
27:11 the **a** shall be presented before the priest.
27:27 If it is an unclean **a,** it shall be ransomed
27:28 be it human or **a,** or inherited landholding,
Nu 3:13 both human and **a;** they shall be mine.
8:17 among the Israelites are mine, both human and **a.**
18:15 human and **a,** which is offered to the LORD,
31:26 of the booty captured, both human and **a.**
Dt 4:17 the likeness of any **a** that is on the earth,
14: 6 Any **a** that divides the hoof and has the hoof cleft
27:21 "Cursed be anyone who lies with any **a.**"
28:26 be food for every bird of the air and **a** of the earth,
2Ki 4:24 and said to her servant, "Urge the **a** on;
14: 9 a wild **a** of Lebanon passed by and trampled down
2Ch 25:18 a wild **a** of Lebanon passed by and trampled down
Ne 2:12 The only **a** I took was the **a** I rode.
2:14 but there was no place for the **a** I was riding
Job 39:15 and that a wild **a** may trample them.
Ps 50:10 For every wild **a** of the forest is mine,
104:11 giving drink to every wild **a;**
Jer 33:10 without inhabitants, human or **a,**
Eze 29: 8 and will cut off from you human being and **a;**
29:11 and no **a** foot shall pass through it;
44:31 priests shall not eat of anything, whether bird or **a,**
Da 4:16 and let the mind of an **a** be given to him.
5:21 and his mind was made like that of an **a.**
Hos 13: 8 as a wild **a** would mangle them.
Jnh 3: 7 No human being or **a,** no herd or flock,
Zep 2:14 Herds shall lie down in it, every wild **a;**
Lk 10:34 Then he put him on his own **a,**
Heb 12:20 "If even an **a** touches the mountain,
Wis 13:14 like some worthless **a,** giving it a coat of red paint
Sir 40: 8 To all creatures, human and **a,**
1Mc 6:36 took their position beforehand wherever the **a** was;
6:37 they were fastened on each **a** by special harness,
4Mc 5: 8 the very excellent meat of this **a?**

ANIMALS‡ (222) [ANIMAL]

Ge 1:24 cattle and creeping things and wild **a** of the earth
1:25 God made the wild **a** of the earth of every kind,
1:26 and over all the wild **a** of the earth,
3:14 among all **a** and among all wild creatures;
6: 7 with **a** and creeping things and birds of the air,
6:20 and of the **a** according to their kinds,
7: 2 Take with you seven pairs of all clean **a,**
7: 2 and a pair of the **a** that are not clean,
7: 8 Of clean **a,** and of **a** that are not clean,
7:14 and all domestic **a** of every kind,
7:21 birds, domestic **a,** wild **a,** all swarming creatures
7:23 human beings and **a** and creeping things and birds
8: 1 the wild **a** and all the domestic **a** that were
8:17 birds and **a** and every creeping thing that creeps
9:10 the birds, the domestic **a,** and every animal of
29: 7 it is not time for the **a** to be gathered together.
30:40 the striped and the completely black **a** in the flock
34:23 their property, and all their **a** be ours?
45:17 load your **a** and go back to the land of Canaan.
Ex 8:17 and gnats came on humans and **a** alike;
8:18 There were gnats on both humans and **a.**
9: 9 and shall cause festering boils on humans and **a**
9:10 and it caused festering boils on humans and **a.**
9:22 on humans and **a** and all the plants of the field in
11: 7 not at people, not at **a**—
12:12 both human beings and **a;**
13: 2 of human beings and **a,** is mine.
13:15 from human firstborn to the firstborn of **a.**
23:11 and what they leave the wild **a** may eat.
23:29 and the wild **a** would multiply against you.
Lev 7:24 of an animal that died or was torn by wild **a** may
11: 2 From among all the land **a,**
11:27 among the **a** that walk on all fours,
17:15 of itself or what has been torn by wild **a,**
19:19 not let your **a** breed with a different kind;
22: 8 which died or was torn by wild **a** he shall not eat,
22:25 nor shall you accept any such **a** from a foreigner
25: 7 wild **a** in your land all its yield shall be for food.
26: 6 I will remove dangerous **a** from the land,
26:22 I will let loose wild **a** against you,
27:26 A firstling of **a,** however,
Nu 18:15 and the firstborn of unclean **a** you shall redeem.
31:11 the spoil and all the booty, both people and **a.**
31:30 sheep, or goats—all the **a**—
31:47 of **a,** and gave them to the Levites who had charge
35: 3 for their livestock, and for all their **a.**
Dt 7:22 otherwise the wild **a** would become too numerous
14: 4 These are the **a** you may eat:
14: 6 and chews the cud, among the **a,** you may eat.
Jdg 20:48 the city, the people, the **a,** and all that remained.
1Sa 17:44 the birds of the air and to the wild **a** of the field."
17:46 the birds of the air and to the wild **a** of the earth,
2Sa 21:10 the air to come on the bodies by day, or the wild **a**
1Ki 4:33 he would speak of **a,** and birds, and reptiles,
18: 5 and not lose some of the **a.**"
2Ki 3: 9 for the army or for the **a** that were with them.
3:17 you, your cattle, and your **a.**'
Ezr 1: 4 with goods and with **a,** besides freewill offerings
1: 6 with goods, with **a,** and with valuable gifts,
Job 5:22 and shall not fear the wild **a** of the earth.
5:23 and the wild **a** shall be at peace with you.
12: 7 "But ask the **a,** and they will teach you;
28: 8 The proud wild **a** have not trodden it;
35:11 who teaches us more than the **a** of the earth,
37: 8 the **a** go into their lairs and remain in their dens.
40:20 for it where all the wild **a** play.
Ps 36: 6 you save humans and **a** alike, O LORD.
49:12 they are like the **a** that perish.
49:20 they are like the **a** that perish.
68:30 Rebuke the wild **a** that live among the reeds,
74:19 not deliver the soul of your dove to the wild **a;**
79: 2 the flesh of your faithful to the wild **a** of the earth.
104:20 when all the **a** of the forest come creeping out.
135: 8 both human beings and **a;**
147: 9 He gives to the **a** their food,
148:10 Wild **a** and all cattle, creeping things
Pr 9: 2 She has slaughtered her **a,**
12:10 The righteous know the needs of their **a,**
30:30 among wild **a** and does not turn back before any;
Ecc 3:18 to show that they are but **a.**
3:19 the fate of humans and the fate of **a** is the same;
3:19 and humans have no advantage over the **a;**
3:21 and the spirit of **a** goes downward to the earth?
Isa 13:21 But wild **a** will lie down there,
18: 6 of prey of the mountains and to the **a** of the earth.
18: 6 and all the **a** of the earth will winter on them.
23:13 They destined Tyre for wild **a.**
30: 6 An oracle concerning the **a** of the Negeb.
40:16 nor are its **a** enough for a burnt offering.
43:20 The wild **a** will honor me,
46: 1 things you carry are loaded as burdens on weary **a.**
56: 9 All you wild **a,** all you wild **a** in the forest,
Jer 7:20 on this place, on human beings and **a,** on the trees
7:33 and for the **a** of the earth;
9:10 birds of the air and the **a** have fled and are gone.
12: 4 the wickedness of those who live in it the **a** and
12: 9 Go, assemble all the wild **a;**
15: 3 and the birds of the air and the wild **a** of the earth
16: 4 the birds of the air and for the wild **a** of the earth.
19: 7 for food to the birds of the air and to the wild **a** of
21: 6 both human beings and **a;**
27: 5 with the people and **a** that are on the earth,
27: 6 and I have given him even the wild **a** of the field
28:14 I have even given him the wild **a.**
31:27 with the seed of humans and the seed of **a.**
32:43 It is a desolation, without human beings or **a;**
33:10 "It is a waste without human beings or **a,**"
33:12 without human beings or **a,**
34:20 for the birds of the air and the wild **a** of the earth.
36:29 and will cut off from it human beings and **a?**
50: 3 both human beings and **a** shall flee away.
50:39 wild **a** shall live with hyenas in Babylon,
51:62 so that neither human beings nor **a** shall live in it,
Eze 4:14 of itself or was torn by **a,**
5:17 I will send famine and wild **a** against you,
8:10 of creeping things, and loathsome **a,**
14:13 and cut off from it human beings and **a,**
14:15 If I send wild **a** through the land to ravage it,
14:15 and no one may pass through because of the **a;**
14:17 and I cut off human beings and **a** from it;
14:19 to cut off humans and **a** from it;
14:21 wild **a,** and pestilence, to cut off humans and **a** from it!
25:13 and cut off from it humans and **a,**
29: 5 To the **a** of the earth and to the birds of
31: 6 under its branches all the **a** of the field gave birth
31:13 and among its boughs lodge all the wild **a.**
32: 4 the wild **a** of the whole earth gorge themselves
33:27 in the open field I will give to the wild **a** to
34: 5 and scattered, they became food for all the wild **a.**
34: 8 my sheep have become food for all the wild **a,**
34:21 and butted at all the weak **a** with your horns
34:25 with them a covenant of peace and banish wild **a**
34:28 nor shall the **a** of the land devour them;
36:11 and I will multiply human beings and **a** upon you.
38:20 and the birds of the air, and the **a** of the field,
39: 4 to birds of prey of every kind and to the wild **a** to
39:17 to the birds of every kind and to all the wild **a:**
44:31 that died of itself or was torn by **a.**
Da 2:38 the wild **a** of the field, and the birds of the air,
4:12 The **a** of the field found shade under it,
4:14 Let the **a** flee from beneath it and the birds
4:15 and let his lot be with the **a** of the field in the grass
4:21 under which **a** of the field lived,
4:23 and let his lot be with the **a** of the field,
4:25 and your dwelling shall be with the wild **a.**
4:32 and your dwelling shall be with the **a** of the field.
Hos 2:12 and the wild **a** shall devour them.
2:18 a covenant on that day with the wild **a,** the birds
4: 3 together with the wild **a** and the birds of the air,
Joel 1:18 How the **a** groan! The herds of cattle
1:20 Even the wild **a** cry to you because
2:22 Do not fear, you **a** of the field,
Am 5:22 of well-being of your fatted **a** I will not look upon.
Jnh 3: 8 and **a** shall be covered with sackcloth,
4:11 from their left, and also many **a?**"
Mic 5: 8 shall be like a lion among the **a** of the forest,
Hab 2:17 the destruction of the **a** will terrify you—
Zep 1: 3 I will sweep away humans and **a;**
2:15 What a desolation it has become, a lair for wild **a!**
Hag 1:11 on human beings and **a,** and on all their labors.
Zec 2: 4 because of the multitude of people and **a** in it.
8:10 for people or for **a,** nor was there any safety from
14:15 and whatever **a** may be in those camps.
Mal 1: 8 you offer blind **a** in sacrifice, is that not wrong?
Ac 11: 6 As I looked at it closely I saw four-footed **a,**
Ro 1:23 a mortal human being or birds or four-footed **a**
1Co 15:32 If with merely human hopes I fought with wild **a**
15:39 another for **a,** another for birds,
Heb 13:11 the bodies of those **a** whose blood is brought into
2Pe 2:12 These people, however, are like irrational **a,**
Jude 1:10 like irrational **a,** they know by instinct.
Rev 6: 8 and pestilence, and by the wild **a** of the earth.
Jdt 11: 7 also the **a** of the field and the cattle and the birds
AdE 16:24 also most hateful to wild **a** and birds for all time.
Wis 7:20 the natures of **a** and the tempers of wild **a,**
11:15 to worship irrational serpents and worthless **a,**
12: 9 at one blow by dread wild **a** or your stern word.
12:24 as gods those **a** that even their enemies despised;
13:10 and likenesses of **a,** or a useless stone,
15:18 Moreover, they worship even the most hateful **a,**
15:19 even as **a** they are not so beautiful in appearance
16: 1 and were tormented by a multitude of **a.**
16: 5 the terrible rage of wild **a** came upon your people
17: 9 by the passing of wild **a** and the hissing of snakes
17:19 or the unseen running of leaping **a,**
19:10 of producing **a** the earth brought forth gnats,
19:19 For land **a** were transformed into water creatures,
Sir 12:13 or all those who go near wild **a?**
39:30 the fangs of wild **a** and scorpions and vipers,
Bar 3:16 and those who lorded it over the **a** on earth;
LtJ 6:68 The wild **a** are better than they are,
Aza 1:59 Bless the Lord, all wild **a** and cattle;
1Mc 1:47 to sacrifice swine and other unclean **a,**
6:35 They distributed the **a** among the phalanxes;
6:43 that one of the **a** was equipped with royal armor.
2Mc 5:27 in the mountains as wild **a** do;
9:15 to throw out with their children for the wild **a** and
10: 6 in the mountains and caves like wild **a.**
11: 9 not only humans but the wildest **a** or walls of iron.
3Mc 4: 9 They were brought on board like wild **a,**
5:23 Hermon, having equipped the **a,**
5:29 and all the king's Friends pointed out that the **a**
5:31 be a rich feast for the savage **a** instead of the Jews,
5:42 mangled by the knees and feet of the **a,**
5:45 **a** had been brought virtually to a state of madness,
5:47 rushed out in full force along with the **a,**
6: 7 down into the ground to lions as food for wild **a,**
6:16 at the hippodrome with the **a** and all the arrogance
6:21 The **a** turned back upon the armed forces following
2Es 5: 8 the wild **a** shall roam beyond their haunts,
6:53 wild **a,** and creeping things;
7:65 but let the wild **a** of the field be glad;
8:30 with those who are deemed worse than wild **a,**
4Mc 1:34 Therefore when we crave seafood and fowl and **a**
14:14 Even unreasoning **a,** as well as human beings,
14:18 for children by the example of unreasoning **a,**

ANISE (KJV) See DILL

ANKLE-DEEP (1) [ANKLES, DEEP]

Eze 47: 3 through the water; and it was **a.**

ANKLES (1) [ANKLE-DEEP, ANKLETS]

Ac 3: 7 and immediately his feet and **a** were made strong.

ANKLETS (2) [ANKLES]

Isa 3:18 the Lord will take away the finery of the **a,**
Jdt 10: 4 She put sandals on her feet, and put on her **a,**

ANNA‡ (7)

Lk 2:36 **A** the daughter of Phanuel, of the tribe of Asher.
Tob 1:20 not taken into the royal treasury except my wife **A**
2: 1 and my wife **A** and my son Tobias were restored
2:11 also, my wife **A** earned money at women's work.
10: 4 His wife **A** said, "My child has perished
11: 5 Meanwhile **A** sat looking intently down the road
11: 9 Then **A** ran up to her son and threw her arms

ANNALS (46)

A. BOOK OF THE ANNALS (35)

1Ki 14:19 are written in the Book of the **A** of the Kings A
14:29 not written in the Book of the **A** of the Kings A
15: 7 not written in the Book of the **A** of the Kings A
15:23 not written in the Book of the **A** of the Kings A
15:31 not written in the Book of the **A** of the Kings A
16: 5 not written in the Book of the **A** of the Kings A
16:14 not written in the Book of the **A** of the Kings A
16:20 not written in the Book of the **A** of the Kings A
16:27 not written in the Book of the **A** of the Kings A
22:39 not written in the Book of the **A** of the Kings A
22:45 not written in the Book of the **A** of the Kings A
2Ki 1:18 not written in the Book of the **A** of the Kings A
8:23 not written in the Book of the **A** of the Kings A
10:34 not written in the Book of the **A** of the Kings A
12:19 not written in the Book of the **A** of the Kings A
13: 8 not written in the Book of the **A** of the Kings A
13:12 not written in the Book of the **A** of the Kings A
14:15 not written in the Book of the **A** of the Kings A
14:18 not written in the Book of the **A** of the Kings A
14:28 not written in the Book of the **A** of the Kings A
15: 6 not written in the Book of the **A** of the Kings A
15:11 are written in the Book of the **A** of the Kings A
15:15 are written in the Book of the **A** of the Kings A
15:21 not written in the Book of the **A** of the Kings A
15:26 are written in the Book of the **A** of the Kings A
15:31 are written in the Book of the **A** of the Kings A
15:36 not written in the Book of the **A** of the Kings A
16:19 not written in the Book of the **A** of the Kings A
20:20 not written in the Book of the **A** of the Kings A
21:17 not written in the Book of the **A** of the Kings A
21:25 not written in the Book of the **A** of the Kings A
23:28 not written in the Book of the **A** of the Kings A
24: 5 not written in the Book of the **A** of the Kings A
1Ch 27:24 into the account of the **A** of King David.
2Ch 20:34 are written in the **A** of Jehu son of Hanani,
33:18 these are in the **A** of the Kings of Israel.
Ezr 4:15 a search may be made in the **a** of your ancestors.
4:15 You will discover in the **a** that this is
Ne 12:23 in the Book of the **A** until the days of Johanan A
Est 2:23 in the book of the **a** in the presence of the king. A
6: 1 the **a,** and they were read to the king.
10: 2 are they not written in the **a** of the kings of Media
AdE 10: 2 the **a** of the kings of the Persians and the Medes.
1Mc 16:24 are written in the **a** of his high priesthood,
1Es 1:42 are written in the **a** of the kings.
2:22 You will find in the **a** what has been written

ANNAN (1)

1Es 9:32 Of the descendants of **A,** Elionas and Asaias

ANNAS (4)

Lk 3: 2 during the high priesthood of **A** and Caiaphas,
Jn 18:13 First they took him to **A,**
18:24 **A** sent him bound to Caiaphas the high priest.
Ac 4: 6 with **A** the high priest, Caiaphas, John,

ANNEXED (1)

1Mc 10:38 be **a** to Judea so that they may be considered to be

ANNIAS (1)

1Es 5:16 The descendants of **A,** one hundred one.

ANNIHILATE (5) [ANNIHILATED, ANNIHILATING, ANNIHILATION]

Dt 20:17 You shall **a** them—the Hittites
Est 3:13 giving orders to destroy, to kill, and to **a** all Jews,
8:11 to **a** any armed force of any people or province
AdE 13:15 for the eyes of our foes are upon us to **a** us,
1Mc 5:15 had gathered together against them "to **a** us."

ANNIHILATED (2) [ANNIHILATE]

Est 7: 4 to be destroyed, to be killed, and to be **a.**
Sir 47: 7 and **a** his adversaries the Philistines;

ANNIHILATING (1) [ANNIHILATE]

2Th 2: 8 **a** him by the manifestation of his coming.

ANNIHILATION (1) [ANNIHILATE]

AdE 16:15 to **a** by this thrice-accursed man,

ANNIUTH (1)

1Es 9:48 Jeshua and **A** and Sherebiah, Jadinus, Akkub,

ANNIVERSARY (1)

4Mc 1:10 On this **a** it is fitting for me to praise

ANNOUNCE (10) [ANNOUNCED, ANNOUNCES, ANNOUNCING]

Dt 17: 9 they shall **a** to you the decision in the case.
17:10 the decision that they **a** to you from the place that
17:11 that they interpret for you or the ruling that they **a**
17:11 not turn aside from the decision that they **a** to you,
Isa 21: 6 "Go, post a lookout, let him **a** what he sees.
21:10 the God of Israel, I **a** to you.
58: 1 **A** to my people their rebellion,
Da 11: 2 "Now I will **a** the truth to you.
Sir 16:22 Who is to **a** his acts of justice?
2Es 11:16 I **a** this to you before you disappear.

ANNOUNCED (16) [ANNOUNCE]

Jdg 13:23 or now **a** to us such things as these."
2Ki 9: 5 and he **a,** "I have a message for you, commander."
Isa 44: 7 Who has **a** from of old the things to come?
48: 5 before they came to pass I **a** them to you,
La 1:21 Bring on the day you have **a,**
Jn 20:18 Mary Magdalene went and **a** to the disciples,
Ac 3:21 that God **a** long ago through his holy prophets.
5:25 Then someone arrived and **a,** "Look,
10:37 beginning in Galilee after the baptism that John **a:**
12:14 in and **a** that Peter was standing at the gate.
Gal 4:13 a physical infirmity that I first **a** the gospel to you;
1Pe 1:12 in regard to the things that have now been **a** to you
1:25 That word is the good news that was **a** to you.
Rev 10: 7 as he **a** to his servants the prophets."
Jdt 11:19 it was **a** to me, and I was sent to tell you."
2Es 7:99 of the souls of the righteous, as henceforth is **a;**

ANNOUNCES (2) [ANNOUNCE]

Isa 52: 7 the feet of the messenger who **a** peace,
52: 7 who brings good news, who **a** salvation,

ANNOUNCING (2) [ANNOUNCE]

Isa 63: 1 "It is I, **a** vindication, mighty to save."
Ro 1: 9 whom I serve with my spirit by **a** the gospel

ANNOY (3) [ANNOYANCE, ANNOYED, ANNOYING]

1Mc 10:35 from them or **a** any of them about any matter.
10:63 and let no one **a** him for any reason."
12:14 We were unwilling to **a** you and our other allies

ANNOYANCE (1) [ANNOY]

1Es 2:29 wicked proceedings go no further to the **a** of kings.

ANNOYED (2) [ANNOY]

Ac 4: 2 much **a** because they were teaching the people
16:18 very much **a,** turned and said to the spirit,

ANNOYING (1) [ANNOY]

2Mc 9:21 from the region of Persia I suffered an **a** illness,

ANNUAL (1) [ANNUALLY]

2Ch 8:13 the new moons, and the three **a** festivals—

ANNUALLY (1) [ANNUAL]

4Mc 4:17 king three thousand six hundred sixty talents **a.**

ANNUL (5) [ANNULLED, ANNULLING, ANNULS]

Isa 14:27 LORD of hosts has planned, and who will **a** it?
Gal 3:17 does not **a** a covenant previously ratified by God,
Aza 1:11 and do not **a** your covenant.
2Mc 13:25 so angry that they wanted to **a** its terms.
14:28 and grieved that he had to **a** their agreement when

ANNULLED (3) [ANNUL]

Isa 28:18 Then your covenant with death will be **a,**
Zec 11:11 So it was **a** on that day, and the sheep merchants,
Jn 10:35 and the scripture cannot be **a—**

ANNULLING (2) [ANNUL]

Zec 11:10 **a** the covenant that I had made with all
11:14 **a** the family ties between Judah and Israel.

ANNULS‡ (1) [ANNUL]

Gal 3:15 no one adds to it or **a** it.

ANNUNUS (1)

1Es 8:48 and **A** and his brother Jeshaiah, of the descendants

ANOINT (34) [ANOINTED, ANOINTING]

Ex 28:41 shall **a** them and ordain them and consecrate them,
29: 7 and pour it on his head and **a** him.
29:36 when you make atonement for it, and shall **a** it,
30:26 With it you shall **a** the tent of meeting and the ark
30:30 You shall **a** Aaron and his sons,
40: 9 and **a** the tabernacle and all that is in it,
40:10 You shall also **a** the altar of burnt offering
40:11 You shall also **a** the basin with its stand,
40:13 and you shall **a** him and consecrate him,
40:15 and **a** them, as you anointed their father,
Dt 28:40 but you shall not **a** yourself with the oil,
Jdg 9: 8 trees once went out to **a** a king over themselves.
Ru 3: 3 Now wash and **a** yourself,
1Sa 9:16 you shall **a** him to be ruler over my people Israel.
15: 1 to **a** you king over his people Israel;
16: 3 you shall **a** for me the one whom I name to you."
16:12 LORD said, "Rise and **a** him; for this is the one."
2Sa 14: 2 do not **a** yourself with oil,
1Ki 1:34 and the prophet Nathan **a** him king over Israel;
19:15 you arrive, you shall **a** Hazael as king over Aram.
19:16 you shall **a** Jehu son of Nimshi as king over Israel;
19:16 and you shall **a** Elisha son of Shaphat
2Ki 9: 3 I **a** you king over Israel.'
9: 6 I **a** you king over the people of the LORD,
9:12 'Thus says the LORD, I **a** you king over Israel.' "
Ps 23: 5 you **a** my head with oil; my cup overflows.
141: 5 Never let the oil of the wicked **a** my head,
Da 9:24 and to **a** a most holy place.
Am 6: 6 and **a** themselves with the finest oils,
Mic 6:15 but not **a** yourselves with oil;
Mk 16: 1 so that they might go and **a** him.
Lk 7:46 You did not **a** my head with oil,
Rev 3:18 and salve to **a** your eyes so that you may see.
Tob 6: 9 And as for the gall, **a** a person's eyes

ANOINTED‡ (105) [ANOINT]

A. †LORD'S ANOINTED (12)

Ge 31:13 where you **a** a pillar and made a vow to me.
Ex 29:29 they shall be **a** in them and ordained in them.
40:15 as you **a** their father, that they may serve me
Lev 4: 3 If it is the **a** priest who sins,
4: 5 The **a** priest shall take some of the blood of
4:16 The **a** priest shall bring some of the blood of
6:20 to the LORD on the day when he is **a:**
6:22 **a** from among Aaron's descendants as
7:36 be given them, when he **a** them, as a perpetual due
8:10 the anointing oil and **a** the tabernacle and all
8:11 and **a** the altar and all its utensils,
8:12 of the anointing oil on Aaron's head and **a** him,
16:32 The priest who is **a** and consecrated as priest
Nu 3: 3 the names of the sons of Aaron, the **a** priests,
7: 1 had **a** and consecrated it with all its furnishings,
7: 1 and had **a** and consecrated the altar
7:10 of the altar at the time when it was **a;**
7:84 at the time when it was **a,**
7:88 the dedication offering for the altar, after it was **a.**
35:25 until the death of the high priest who was **a** with
1Sa 2:10 and exalt the power of his **a."**
2:35 he shall go in and out before my **a** one forever.
10: 1 LORD has **a** you ruler over his people Israel.
10: 1 be the sign to you that the LORD has **a** you ruler
12: 3 against me before the LORD and before his **a.**
12: 5 and his **a** is witness this day,
15:17 The LORD **a** you king over Israel.
16: 6 the LORD's **a** is now before the LORD." A
16:13 and **a** him in the presence of his brothers;
24: 6 the LORD's **a,** to raise my hand against him; A
24: 6 for he is the LORD's **a."** A
24:10 for he is the LORD's **a.'** A
26: 9 who can raise his hand against the LORD's **a,** A
26:11 that I should raise my hand against the LORD's **a;** A
26:16 not kept watch over your lord, the LORD's **a.** A
26:23 I would not raise my hand against the LORD's **a.** A
2Sa 1:14 to lift your hand to destroy the LORD's **a?"** A
1:16 saying, 'I have killed the LORD's **a.'** " A
1:21 the shield of Saul, **a** with oil no more.
2: 4 there they **a** David king over the house of Judah.
2: 7 and the house of Judah has **a** me king over them."
3:39 Today I am powerless, even though **a** king;
5: 3 and they **a** David king over Israel.
5:17 the Philistines heard that David had been **a** king
12: 7 I **a** you king over Israel, and I rescued you from
12:20 David rose from the ground, washed, **a** himself,
19:10 Absalom, whom we **a** over us, is dead in battle.
19:21 because he cursed the LORD's **a?"** A
22:51 and shows steadfast love to his **a,**
23: 1 the **a** of the God of Jacob,
1Ki 1:39 the horn of oil from the tent and **a** Solomon.
1:45 and the prophet Nathan have **a** him king at Gihon;
5: 1 when he heard that they had **a** him king in place
2Ki 11:12 they proclaimed him king, and **a** him;
23:30 **a** him, and made him king in place of his father.
1Ch 11: 3 And they **a** David king over Israel,
14: 8 the Philistines heard that David had been **a** king
16:22 "Do not touch my **a** ones;
29:22 they **a** him as the LORD's prince,
2Ch 6:42 O LORD God, do not reject your **a** one.
22: 7 the LORD had **a** to destroy the house of Ahab.
23:11 and Jehoiada and his sons **a** him;
28:15 provided them with food and drink, and **a** them;
Ps 2: 2 against the LORD and his **a,** saying,
18:50 and shows steadfast love to his **a,**
20: 6 Now I know that the LORD will help his **a;**
28: 8 he is the saving refuge of his **a.**
45: 7 has **a** you with the oil of gladness
84: 9 look on the face of your **a.**
89:20 with my holy oil I have **a** him;
89:38 you are full of wrath against your **a.**

Ps 89:51 with which they taunted the footsteps of your **a.**
105:15 "Do not touch my **a** ones;
132:10 not turn away the face of your **a** one.
132:17 I have prepared a lamp for my **a** one.
Isa 45: 1 Thus says the LORD to his **a,** to Cyrus,
61: 1 because the LORD has **a** me;
La 4:20 The LORD's **a,** the breath of our life, A
Eze 16: 9 and washed off the blood from you, and **a** you
28:14 With an **a** cherub as guardian I placed you;
Da 9:25 of an **a** prince, there shall be seven weeks;
9:26 an **a** one shall be cut off and shall have nothing,
10: 3 and I had not **a** myself at all,
Hab 3:13 to save your people, to save your **a.**
Zec 4:14 "These are the two **a** ones who stand by the Lord
Mk 6:13 **a** with oil many who were sick and cured them.
14: 8 she has **a** my body beforehand for its burial.
Lk 4:18 he has **a** me to bring good news to the poor.
7:46 but she has **a** my feet with ointment.
Jn 1:41 found the Messiah" (which is translated **A**).
11: 2 Mary was the one who **a** the Lord with perfume
12: 3 **a** Jesus' feet, and wiped them with her hair.
Ac 4:27 against your holy servant Jesus, whom you **a,**
10:38 how God **a** Jesus of Nazareth with the Holy Spirit
2Co 1:21 with you in Christ and has **a** us,
Heb 1: 9 therefore God, your God, has **a** you with the oil
1Jn 2:20 But you have been **a** by the Holy One,
Jdt 10: 3 and **a** herself with precious ointment.
16: 7 She **a** her face with perfume;
Sir 45:15 Moses ordained him, and **a** him with holy oil;
46:13 the Lord, he established the kingdom and **a** rulers
46:19 Samuel bore witness before the Lord and his **a:**
48: 8 You **a** kings to inflict retribution,
2Mc 1:10 who is of the family of the **a** priests,
Pm 151: 4 and **a** me with his anointing oil.

ANOINTING (31) [ANOINT]

Ex 25: 6 spices for the **a** oil and for the fragrant incense,
29: 7 You shall take the **a** oil,
29:21 and some of the **a** oil, and sprinkle it on Aaron
30:25 and you shall make of these a sacred **a** oil blended
30:25 it shall be a holy **a** oil.
30:31 be my holy **a** oil throughout your generations.
30:32 It shall not be used in any ordinary **a** of the body,
31:11 **a** oil and the fragrant incense for the holy place.
35: 8 spices for the **a** oil and for the fragrant incense,
35:15 and the **a** oil and the fragrant incense,
35:28 and for the **a** oil, and for the fragrant incense.
37:29 He made the holy **a** oil also,
39:38 the **a** oil and the fragrant incense,
40: 9 Then you shall take the **a** oil,
40:15 and their **a** shall admit them to
Lev 8: 2 the vestments, the **a** oil, the bull of sin offering,
8:10 the **a** oil and anointed the tabernacle and all
8:12 of the **a** oil on Aaron's head and anointed him,
8:30 Then Moses took some of the **a** oil and some of
10: 7 for the **a** oil of the LORD is on you."
21:10 on whose head the **a** oil has been poured
21:12 consecration of the **a** oil of his God is upon him:
Nu 4:16 the regular grain offering, and the **a** oil,
Jdg 9:15 'If in good faith you are **a** me king over you,
SS 1: 3 your **a** oils are fragrant, your name is perfume
Lk 7:38 Then she continued kissing his feet and **a** them
Jas 5:14 **a** them with oil in the name of the Lord.
1Jn 2:27 the **a** that you received from him abides in you,
2:27 But as his **a** teaches you about all things,
AdE 2:12 six months while they are **a** themselves with oil
Pm 151: 4 and anointed me with his **a** oil.

ANON (KJV) See AT ONCE, IMMEDIATELY

ANOTHER‡ (593) [ANOTHER'S]

A. ONE ANOTHER (207)
B. LOVE ONE ANOTHER (15)

Ge 4:25 "God has appointed for me **a** child instead
8:10 He waited **a** seven days, and again he sent out
8:12 he waited **a** seven days, and sent out the dove;
9: 5 each one for the blood of **a,**
11: 3 And they said to one **a,** "Come, A
25: 1 Abraham took **a** wife, whose name was Keturah.
26:21 Then they dug **a** well, and they quarreled over
26:22 He moved from there and dug **a** well,
29:27 also in return for serving me **a** seven years."
29:30 He served Laban for **a** seven years.
30:24 saying, "May the LORD add to me **a** son!"
35:17 for now you will have **a** son."
37: 9 He had **a** dream, and told it to his brothers, saying,
"Look, I have had **a** dream:
37:19 They said to one **a,** "Here comes this dreamer. A
42: 1 "Why do you keep looking at one **a?** A
42:21 They said to one **a,** "Alas, A
42:28 and turned trembling to one **a,** A
43: 6 as to tell the man that you had **a** brother?"
43: 7 'Is your father still alive? Have you **a** brother?'
43:33 the men looked at one **a** in amazement. A
Ex 10:23 People could not see one **a,** A
16:15 Israelites saw it, they said to one **a,** "What is it?" A
18:16 to me and I decide between one person and **a,**
21:10 If he takes **a** wife to himself,
21:14 someone willfully attacks and kills **a** by treachery,
21:35 If someone's ox hurts the ox of **a,** so that it dies,
22:10 When someone delivers to **a** a donkey, ox, sheep,
22:14 When someone borrows an animal from **a**
25:20 They shall face one to **a;**
26: 3 Five curtains shall be joined to one **a;** A
Ex 26: 3 the other five curtains shall be joined to one **a.** A
26: 5 the loops shall be opposite one **a.** A
26: 6 and join the curtains to one **a** with the clasps, A
36:10 He joined five curtains to one **a,** A
36:10 and the other five curtains he joined to one **a.** A
36:12 the loops were opposite one **a.** A
37: 9 with their wings. They faced one **a;** A
Lev 19:11 and you shall not lie to one **a.** A
19:20 for **a** man but not ransomed or given her freedom,
24:19 Anyone who maims **a** shall suffer the same injury
25:14 you shall not cheat one **a.** A
25:17 You shall not cheat one **a,** A
26:37 They shall stumble over one **a,** A
27:10 A shall not be exchanged or substituted for it,
27:10 and if one animal is substituted for **a,**
Nu 5: 6 When a man or a woman wrongs **a,**
8: 8 and you shall take **a** young bull for a sin offering.
14: 4 So they said to one **a,** "Let us choose a captain, A
23:13 with me to **a** place from which you may see them;
23:27 "Come now, I will take you to **a** place;
35:16 But anyone who strikes **a** with an iron object,
35:17 Or anyone who strikes **a** with a stone in hand
35:18 Or anyone who strikes **a** with a weapon of wood
35:20 Likewise, if someone pushes **a** from hatred,
35:20 or hurls something at **a,** lying in wait,
35:21 or in enmity strikes **a** with the hand,
35:22 But if someone pushes **a** suddenly without enmity,
35:23 unintentionally drops it on **a** and death ensues,
35:30 If anyone kills **a,** the murderer shall be put
36: 3 But if they are married into **a** Israelite tribe,
36: 7 be transferred from one tribe to **a;**
36: 9 be transferred from one tribe to **a;**
Dt 1:16 and judge rightly between one person and **a,**
4:34 a nation for himself from the midst of **a** nation,
4:42 someone who unintentionally kills **a** person,
17: 8 between one kind of bloodshed and **a,** one kind
17: 8 one kind of legal right and **a,**
17: 8 or one kind of assault and **a—**
19: 4 someone who has killed **a** person unintentionally
19: 5 with **a** to cut wood, and when one of them swings
19:11 with **a** lies in wait and attacks and takes the life of
19:18 having testified falsely against **a,**
20: 5 or he might die in the battle and **a** dedicate it.
20: 6 in the battle and **a** be first to enjoy its fruit.
20: 7 or he might die in the battle and **a** marry her."
22:22 If a man is caught lying with the wife of **a** man,
23:19 not charge interest on loans to **a** Israelite,
23:20 on loans to **a** Israelite you may not charge interest,
24: 2 and goes off to become **a** man's wife.
24: 7 If someone is caught kidnaping **a** Israelite,
25:11 If men get into a fight with one **a,** A
28:30 but **a** man shall lie with her.
28:32 and daughters shall be given to **a** people,
29:28 fury, and great wrath, and cast them into **a** land,
Jos 18:14 Then the boundary goes in **a** direction,
Jdg 2:10 and **a** generation grew up after them,
6:29 So they said to one **a,** "Who has done this?" A
10:18 of the people of Gilead said to one **a,** A
11: 2 for you are the son of **a** woman."
Ru 2: 8 do not go to glean in **a** field or leave this one,
2:22 otherwise you might be bothered in **a** field."
3:12 there is **a** kinsman more closely related than I.
3:14 but got up before one person could recognize **a;**
1Sa 2:25 If one person sins against **a,**
10: 3 **a** carrying three loaves of bread,
10: 3 and **a** carrying a skin of wine.
10: 9 to leave Samuel, God gave him **a** heart;
10:11 the people said to one **a,** A
13:18 **a** company turned toward Beth-horon,
13:18 and **a** company turned toward the mountain
17:30 He turned away from him toward **a** and spoke in
18: 7 the women sang to one **a** as they made merry, A
21:11 Did they not sing to one **a** of him in dances, A
29: 5 of whom they sing to one **a** in dances, A
2Sa 3:11 And Ishbaal could not answer Abner **a** word,
7:23 Is there **a** nation on earth whose God went
11:25 for the sword devours now one and now **a;**
14: 6 and they fought with one **a** in the field; A
18:20 you may carry tidings **a** day,
18:26 Then the sentinel saw **a** man running;
18:26 "See, **a** man running alone!"
21:19 there was **a** battle with the Philistines at Gob;
1Ki 11:23 God raised up **a** adversary against Solomon,
13:10 So he went **a** way, and did not return by the way
14: 5 When she came, she pretended to be **a** woman.
14: 6 why do you pretend to be **a?**
18: 6 and Obadiah went in **a** direction by himself.
20:29 They encamped opposite one **a** seven days. A
20:35 of a company of prophets said to **a,**
20:37 Then he found **a** man and said, "Strike me!"
21: 6 if you prefer, I will give you **a** vineyard for it';
22:20 Then one said one thing, and **a** said **a,**
2Ki 1:11 Again the king sent to him **a** captain of fifty
3:23 must have fought together, and killed one **a.** A
4: 6 she said to her son, "Bring me **a** vessel."
7: 3 who said to one **a,** "Why should we sit here A
7: 6 so that they said to one **a,** A
7: 8 Then they came back, entered **a** tent,
7: 9 they said to one **a,** "What we are doing is wrong. A
11: 6 (**a** third being at the gate Sur and a third at
14: 8 saying, "Come, let us look one **a** in the face." A
14:11 King Amaziah of Judah faced one **a** in battle A
21:16 until he had filled Jerusalem from one end to **a,**
1Ch 2:26 Jerahmeel also had **a** wife,
16:20 from one kingdom to **a** people,
2Ch 6:22 "If someone sins against **a** and is required to take
18:19 Then one said one thing, and **a** said **a,**
2Ch 20:23 they all helped to destroy one **a.** A
25:12 people of Judah captured **a** ten thousand alive,
25:17 saying, "Come, let us look one **a** in the face." A
25:21 King Amaziah of Judah faced one **a** in battle A
30:23 to keep the festival for **a** seven days;
30:23 so they kept it for **a** seven days with gladness.
32: 5 and outside it he built **a** wall;
Ne 3:11 of Pahath-moab repaired **a** section and the Tower
3:19 repaired **a** section opposite the ascent to
3:20 After him Baruch son of Zabbai repaired **a** section
3:21 of Uriah son of Hakkoz repaired **a** section from
3:24 him Binnui son of Henadad repaired **a** section,
3:27 After him the Tekoites repaired **a** section opposite
3:30 and Hanun sixth son of Zalaph repaired **a** section.
4:19 and we are separated far from one **a** on the wall. A
9: 3 for **a** fourth they made confession and worshiped
Est 1:19 to **a** who is better than she.
4:14 for the Jews from **a** quarter,
9:19 on which they send gifts of food to one **a.** A
9:22 for sending gifts of food to one **a** and presents A
Job 1:16 While he was still speaking, **a** came and said,
1:17 While he was still speaking, **a** came and said,
1:18 While he was still speaking, **a** came and said,
13: 9 can you deceive him, as one person deceives **a?**
19:27 and my eyes shall behold, and not **a.**
21:25 **A** dies in bitterness of soul,
31: 8 then let me sow, and **a** eat;
31:10 then let my wife grind for **a,**
41:16 so near to **a** that no air can come between them.
41:17 They are joined one to **a;**
Ps 16: 4 Those who choose **a** god multiply their sorrows;
75: 7 putting down one and lifting up **a.**
105:13 from one kingdom to **a** people,
109: 8 May his days be few; may **a** seize his position.
145: 4 One generation shall laud your works to **a,**
Pr 5:20 by **a** woman and embrace the bosom of
6: 1 if you have bound yourself to **a,**
6:24 to preserve you from the wife of **a,**
6:26 but the wife of **a** stalks a man's very life.
11:12 Whoever belittles **a** lacks sense,
23:35 I will seek **a** drink."
26:17 by the ears is one who meddles in the quarrel of **a.**
27: 2 Let **a** praise you, and not your own mouth—
27:17 and one person sharpens the wits of **a.**
27:19 so one human heart reflects **a.**
28: 8 by exorbitant interest gathers it for **a** who is kind
28:17 If someone is burdened with the blood of **a,**
Ecc 2:21 to be enjoyed by **a** who did not toil for it.
4: 4 in work come from one person's envy of **a.**
4:10 to one who is alone and falls and does not have **a**
4:12 And though one might prevail against **a,**
7:27 adding one thing to **a** to find the sum,
8: 9 while one person exercises authority over **a** to
SS 5: 9 What is your beloved more than **a** beloved,
5: 9 What is your beloved more than **a** beloved,
Isa 3: 5 everyone by **a** and everyone by a neighbor;
6: 3 And one called to **a** and said:
9:19 for the fire; no one spared **a.**
13: 8 They will look aghast at one **a;** A
41: 6 Each one helps the other, saying to one **a,** A
44: 5 **a** will be called by the name of Jacob,
44: 5 yet **a** will write on the hand, "The LORD's,"
48:11 My glory I will not give to **a.**
65:22 They shall not build and **a** inhabit;
65:22 they shall not plant and **a** eat;
Jer 3: 1 and she goes from him and becomes **a** man's wife,
3:16 nor shall **a** one be made.
7: 5 if you truly act justly one with **a,**
13:14 And I will dash them one against **a,**
18: 4 and he reworked it into **a** vessel,
18: 9 at a moment I may declare concerning a nation or
22: 8 and all of them will say one to **a,**
22:26 and the mother who bore you into **a** country,
23:27 by their dreams that they tell one **a,** A
23:30 says the LORD, who steal my words from one **a.** A
23:35 Thus shall you say to one **a,** among yourselves, A
25:26 after **a,** and all the kingdoms of the world that are
26:20 There was **a** man prophesying in the name of
31:34 No longer shall they teach one **a,** A
34: 9 so that no one should hold **a** Judean in slavery.
34:15 to one **a,** and you made a covenant before me in A
36:16 turned to one **a** in alarm, and said to Baruch, A
36:28 Take **a** scroll and write on it all the former words
36:32 Then Jeremiah took **a** scroll and gave it to
46:16 and one said to **a,** "Come,
51:31 One runner runs to meet **a,**
51:31 and one messenger to meet **a,**
51:46 one year one rumor comes, the next year **a,**
Eze 1: 9 their wings touched one **a;** A
1:11 each of which touched the wing of **a,**
1:23 wings were stretched out straight, one toward **a;**
3:13 of the living creatures brushing against one **a,** A
4:17 they will look at one **a** in dismay, A
12: 3 an exile from your place to **a** place in their sight.
17: 7 There was **a** great eagle, with great wings
19: 5 she took **a** of her cubs and made him a young lion.
22:11 **a** lewdly defiles his daughter-in-law;
22:11 **a** in you defiles his sister, his father's daughter.
24:23 in your iniquities and groan to one **a.** A
33:30 and at the doors of the houses, say to one **a,** A
37:16 then take **a** stick and write on it,
41: 6 side chambers were in three stories, one over **a,**
41:11 and **a** door toward the south;
45: 5 **A** section, twenty-five thousand cubits long
Da 2:39 After you shall arise **a** kingdom inferior to yours,
2:43 so will they mix with one **a** in marriage, A
2:44 nor shall this kingdom be left to **a** people.

Da 7: 3 up out of the sea, different from one **a**. A
7: 5 **A** beast appeared, a second one,
7: 6 this, as I watched, **a** appeared, like a leopard.
7: 8 when **a** horn appeared, a little one coming up
7: 24 and **a** shall arise after them.
8: 9 Out of one of them came **a** horn, a little one,
8: 13 and **a** holy one said to the one that spoke,
Joel 1: 3 and their children **a** generation.
2: 8 not jostle one **a**, each keeps to its own track; A
Am 4: 7 and send no rain on **a** city;
Jnh 1: 7 The sailors said to one **a**, "Come, let us cast lots, A
Zec 2: 3 and **a** angel came forward to meet him,
7: 9 show kindness and mercy to one **a**; A
7: 10 do not devise evil in your hearts against one **a**. A
8: 16 Speak the truth to one **a**, A
8: 17 do not devise evil in your hearts against one **a**, A
8: 21 of one city shall go to **a**, saying, "Come, let us go
11: 9 let those that are left devour the flesh of one **a**!" A
Mal 2: 10 Why then are we faithless to one **a**, A
3: 16 those who revered the LORD spoke with one **a**. A
Mt 2: 12 they left for their own country by **a** road.
8: 9 and I say to one, 'Go,' and he goes, and to **a**,
8: 21 **A** of his disciples said to him, "Lord,
11: 3 or are we to wait for **a**?"
11: 16 in the marketplaces and calling to one **a**, A
13: 23 one case a hundredfold, in **a** sixty, and in **a** thirty."
13: 24 He put before them **a** parable:
13: 31 He put before them **a** parable:
13: 33 He told them **a** parable: "The kingdom of heaven
15: 14 And if one blind person guides **a**,
16: 7 They said to one **a**, "It is A
18: 15 "If **a** member of the church sins against you,
18: 21 "Lord, if **a** member of the church sins against me,
19: 9 and marries **a** commits adultery."
21: 25 And they argued with one **a**, "If we say, A
21: 33 "Listen to **a** parable. There was a landowner
21: 33 Then he leased it to tenants and went to **a** country.
21: 35 his slaves and beat one, killed **a**, and stoned **a**.
22: 5 one to his farm, **a** to his business,
24: 2 not one stone will be left here upon **a**;
24: 10 and they will betray one **a** and hate one another. A
24: 10 and they will betray one another and hate one **a**. A
25: 15 to **a** two, to **a** one, to each according to his ability.
25: 32 from **a** as a shepherd separates the sheep from
26: 22 and began to say to him one after **a**,
26: 71 he went out to the porch, **a** servant-girl saw him,
Mk 1: 27 and they kept on asking one **a**, "What is this? A
4: 41 were filled with great awe and said to one **a**, A
8: 16 They said to one **a**, "It is A
9: 34 on the way they had argued with one **a** who was A
9: 50 and be at peace with one **a**." A
10: 11 and marries **a** commits adultery against her;
10: 12 and if she divorces her husband and marries **a**,
10: 26 They were greatly astounded and said to one **a**, A
11: 31 They argued with one **a**, "If we say, A
12: 1 then he leased it to tenants and went to **a** country.
12: 4 And again he sent **a** slave to them;
12: 5 Then he sent **a**, and that one they killed.
12: 7 But those tenants said to one **a**, 'This is the heir; A
12: 28 near and heard them disputing with one **a**, A
13: 2 Not one stone will be left here upon **a**;
14: 4 But some were there who said to one **a** in anger, A
14: 19 to be distressed and to say to him one after **a**,
14: 58 and in three days I will build **a**,
16: 3 They had been saying to one **a**, A
16: 12 ⟦After this he appeared in **a** form to two of them,⟧
Lk 2: 15 the shepherds said to one **a**, A
4: 36 They were all amazed and kept saying to one **a**, A
6: 6 On **a** sabbath he entered the synagogue
6: 11 and discussed with one **a** what they might do A
7: 8 and I say to one, 'Go,' and he goes, and to **a**,
7: 19 or are we to wait for **a**?"
7: 20 or are we to wait for **a**?' "
7: 32 calling to one **a**, 'We played the flute for you, A
8: 25 They were afraid and amazed, and said to one **a**, A
9: 56 Then they went on to **a** village.
9: 59 To **a** he said, "Follow me."
9: 61 **A** said, "I will follow you, Lord;
12: 1 so that they trampled on one **a**, A
13: 22 Jesus went through one town and village after **a**,
14: 19 **A** said, 'I have bought five yoke of oxen,
14: 20 **A** said, 'I have just been married,
14: 31 what king, going out to wage war against **a** king,
16: 7 Then he asked **a**, 'And how much do you owe?'
16: 12 you have not been faithful with what belongs to **a**,
16: 18 and marries **a** commits adultery,
17: 3 If **a** disciple sins, you must rebuke the offender,
19: 44 they will not leave within you one stone upon **a**;
20: 5 They discussed it with one **a**, saying, "If we say, A
20: 9 and went to **a** country for a long time.
20: 11 Next he sent **a** slave; that one
20: 40 For they no longer dared to ask him **a** question.
21: 6 when not one stone will be left upon **a**;
22: 23 Then they began to ask one **a**, A
22: 59 Then about an hour later still **a** kept insisting,
Jn 4: 33 So the disciples said to one **a**, A
4: 37 the saying holds true, 'One sows and **a** reaps.'
5: 32 There is **a** who testifies on my behalf,
5: 43 if **a** comes in his own name, you will accept him.
5: 44 you accept glory from one **a** and do not seek A
7: 35 The Jews said to one **a**, A
10: 1 the sheepfold by the gate but climbs in by **a** way is
11: 56 were asking one **a** as they stood in the temple, A
12: 19 The Pharisees then said to one **a**, "You see, A
13: 22 The disciples looked at one **a**, A
13: 34 a new commandment, that you love one **a**. AB
13: 34 you also should love one **a**. AB

Jn 13: 35 if you have love for one **a**." A
14: 16 and he will give you **a** Advocate,
15: 12 that you love one **a** as I have loved you. AB
15: 17 so that you may love one **a**. AB
16: 17 Then some of his disciples said to one **a**, A
18: 15 Simon Peter and **a** disciple followed Jesus.
19: 24 So they said to one **a**, "Let us not tear it, A
19: 37 And again **a** passage of scripture says,
Ac 1: 20 and 'Let **a** take his position of overseer.'
2: 12 All were amazed and perplexed, saying to one **a**, A
4: 15 while they discussed the matter with one **a**. A
7: 18 until **a** king who had not known Joseph ruled
12: 17 Then he left and went to **a** place.
13: 35 Therefore he has also said in **a** psalm,
17: 7 saying that there is **a** king named Jesus."
19: 32 some were shouting one thing, some **a**;
19: 38 let them bring charges there against one **a**. A
21: 6 and said farewell to one **a**. A
21: 34 Some in the crowd shouted one thing, some **a**;
26: 31 they said to one **a**, "This man is doing nothing A
28: 4 said to one **a**, "This man must be a murderer; A
Ro 1: 27 were consumed with passion for one **a**. A
2: 1 in passing judgment on **a** you condemn yourself,
7: 3 if she lives with **a** man while her husband is alive.
7: 3 she is free from that law, and if she marries **a** man,
7: 4 so that you may belong to **a**,
7: 23 but I see in my members **a** law at war with the law
9: 21 of the same lump one object for special use and **a**
12: 5 and individually we are members one of **a**.
12: 10 love one **a** with mutual affection; AB
12: 10 outdo one **a** in showing honor. A
12: 16 Live in harmony with one **a**; A
13: 8 Owe no one anything, except to love one **a**; AB
13: 8 for the one who loves **a** has fulfilled the law.
14: 4 Who are you to pass judgment on servants of **a**?
14: 5 Some judge one day to be better than **a**,
14: 13 therefore no longer pass judgment on one **a**, A
14: 13 a stumbling block or hindrance in the way of **a**.
15: 5 to live in harmony with one **a**, A
15: 7 Welcome one **a**, therefore, A
15: 14 and able to instruct one **a**. A
16: 16 Greet one **a** with a holy kiss. A
1Co 3: 4 For when one says, "I belong to Paul," and **a**,
4: 6 of you will be puffed up in favor of one against **a**.
6: 1 When any of you has a grievance against **a**,
6: 5 to decide between one believer and **a**,
6: 7 at all with one **a** is already a defeat for you. A
7: 5 not deprive one **a** except perhaps by agreement A
7: 7 one having one kind and **a** a different kind.
11: 21 and one goes hungry and **a** becomes drunk.
11: 33 when you come together to eat, wait for one **a**. A
12: 8 and to **a** the utterance of knowledge according to
12: 9 to **a** faith by the same Spirit, to **a** gifts of healing
by the one Spirit,
12: 10 to **a** the working of miracles, to **a** prophecy, to **a**
the discernment of spirits, to **a** various kinds of
tongues, to **a** the interpretation of tongues.
12: 25 the members may have the same care for one **a**. A
15: 39 **a** for animals, **a** for birds, and **a** for fish.
15: 40 and that of the earthly is **a**.
15: 41 and **a** glory of the moon, and **a** glory of the stars;
16: 20 Greet one **a** with a holy kiss. A
2Co 2: 1 up my mind not to make you **a** painful visit.
3: 18 the same image from one degree of glory to **a**;
10: 12 But when they measure themselves by one **a**, A
10: 12 and compare themselves with one **a**, A
11: 4 and proclaims **a** Jesus than the one we proclaimed,
13: 11 listen to my appeal, agree with one **a**, A
13: 12 Greet one **a** with a holy kiss. A
Gal 1: 7 not that there is **a** gospel,
5: 13 but through love become slaves to one **a**. A
5: 15 If, however, you bite and devour one **a**, A
5: 15 take care that you are not consumed by one **a**. A
5: 26 competing against one **a**, envying one another. A
5: 26 competing against one another, envying one **a**. A
Eph 4: 2 with patience, bearing with one **a** in love, A
4: 25 for we are members of one **a**. A
4: 32 and be kind to one **a**, A
4: 32 tenderhearted, forgiving one **a**, A
5: 21 Be subject to one **a** out of reverence for Christ. A
Php 2: 27 so that I would not have one sorrow after **a**.
Col 3: 9 Do not lie to one **a**, A
3: 13 Bear with one **a** and, if anyone has a complaint A
3: 13 if anyone has a complaint against **a**,
3: 16 teach and admonish one **a** in all wisdom; A
1Th 3: 12 and abound in love for one **a** and for all, A
4: 9 by God to love one **a**; AB
4: 18 Therefore encourage one **a** with these words. A
5: 11 encourage one **a** and build up each other, A
5: 15 but always seek to do good to one **a** and to all. A
2Th 1: 3 love of everyone of you for one **a** is increasing. A
Tit 3: 3 in malice and envy, despicable, hating one **a**. A
Heb 3: 13 But exhort one **a** every day, A
4: 8 God would not speak later about **a** day.
5: 6 as he says also in **a** place,
7: 11 to speak of **a** priest arising according to the order
7: 13 to **a** tribe, from which no one has ever served at
7: 15 It is even more obvious when **a** priest arises,
8: 11 they shall not teach one **a** or say to each other, A
10: 24 let us consider how to provoke one **a** to love A
10: 25 as is the habit of some, but encouraging one **a**, A
12: 19 the hearers beg that not **a** word be spoken to them.
Jas 2: 25 the messengers and sent them out by **a** road?
4: 11 Do not speak evil against one **a**, A
4: 11 Whoever speaks evil against **a** or judges **a**,
5: 9 Beloved, do not grumble against one **a**, A
5: 16 Therefore confess your sins to one **a**, A

Jas 5: 16 and pray for one **a**, so that you may be healed. A
5: 19 from the truth and is brought back by **a**,
1Pe 1: 22 love one **a** deeply from the heart. AB
3: 8 love for one **a**, a tender heart, and a humble A
4: 8 Above all, maintain constant love for one **a**, A
4: 9 Be hospitable to one **a** without complaining. A
4: 10 serve one **a** with whatever gift each A
5: 5 with humility in your dealings with one **a**, A
5: 14 Greet one **a** with a kiss of love. A
1Jn 1: 7 we have fellowship with one **a**, A
2: 11 But whoever hates **a** believer is in the darkness,
3: 11 that we should love one **a**. AB
3: 14 from death to life because we love one **a**. AB
3: 16 and we ought to lay down our lives for one **a**. A
3: 23 name of his Son Jesus Christ and love one **a**, AB
4: 7 Beloved, let us love one **a**, AB
4: 11 we also ought to love one **a**. AB
4: 12 No one has ever seen God; if we love one **a**, AB
2Jn 1: 5 from the beginning, let us love one **a**. AB
Rev 6: 4 And out came **a** horse, bright red;
6: 4 so that people would slaughter one **a**; A
7: 2 I saw **a** angel ascending from the rising of the sun,
8: 3 **A** angel with a golden censer came and stood at
10: 1 I saw **a** mighty angel coming down from heaven,
12: 3 Then **a** portent appeared in heaven:
13: 11 Then I saw **a** beast that rose out of the earth;
14: 6 Then I saw **a** angel flying in midheaven,
14: 8 Then **a** angel, a second, followed, saying, "Fallen,
14: 9 Then **a** angel, a third, followed them,
14: 15 **A** angel came out of the temple,
14: 17 Then **a** angel came out of the temple in heaven,
14: 18 Then **a** angel came out from the altar,
15: 1 I saw **a** portent in heaven, great and amazing:
18: 1 this I saw **a** angel coming down from heaven,
18: 4 Then I heard **a** voice from heaven saying,
20: 12 Also **a** book was opened, the book of life.
Tob 6: 13 to **a** man without incurring the penalty of death
Jdt 7: 4 they were greatly terrified and said to one **a**, A
10: 19 They said to one **a**, A
15: 2 they did not wait for one **a**, A
AdE 4: 14 to the Jews from **a** quarter,
9: 19 and send presents of food to one **a**, A
9: 19 also sending presents to one **a**. A
Wis 5: 3 They will speak to one **a** in repentance, A
14: 24 but they either treacherously kill one **a**, A
14: 24 or grieve one **a** by adultery, A
16: 14 A person in wickedness kills **a**,
16: 19 and at **a** time even in the midst
18: 18 and one here and **a** there, hurled
18: 23 the dead had already fallen on one **a** in heaps, A
19: 3 they reached **a** foolish decision,
19: 18 For the elements changed places with one **a**, A
Sir Pr: 2 the same sense when translated into **a** language.
9: 8 and do not gaze at beauty belonging to **a**;
9: 9 Never dine with **a** man's wife,
11: 8 and do not interrupt when **a** is speaking.
14: 15 Will you not leave the fruit of your labors to **a**,
14: 18 one dies and **a** is born.
16: 28 They do not crowd one **a**, A
20: 23 **A** out of shame makes promises to a friend,
23: 22 and presents him with an heir by **a** man.
23: 23 and brought forth children by **a** man.
28: 3 Does anyone harbor anger against **a**,
28: 4 If one has no mercy toward **a** like himself,
32: 9 and when **a** is speaking, do not babble.
33: 7 Why is one day more important than **a**,
33: 20 and do not give your property to **a**,
34: 28 When one builds and **a** tears down,
34: 29 When one prays and **a** curses,
36: 23 yet one food is better than **a**.
36: 26 but one girl is preferable to **a**.
40: 29 When one looks to the table of **a**,
40: 29 One loses self-respect with **a** person's food,
41: 21 and of gazing at **a** man's wife;
Bar 4: 3 Do not give your glory to **a**,
LtJ 6: 15 **A** has a dagger in its right hand, and an ax,
1Mc 3: 43 But they said to one **a**, A
5: 37 After these things Timothy gathered **a** army
7: 29 and they greeted one **a** peaceably; A
10: 16 So he said, "Shall we find **a** such man?
10: 54 therefore let us establish friendship with one **a**; A
10: 56 so that we may see one **a**, A
11: 6 and they greeted one **a** and spent the night there. A
12: 50 and they encouraged one **a** and kept marching A
13: 28 He also erected seven pyramids, opposite one **a**, A
2Mc 3: 37 of person would be suitable to send on **a** mission
4: 8 and from **a** source of revenue eighty talents.
4: 19 but to expend it for **a** purpose.
4: 26 by **a** man, was driven as a fugitive into the land
7: 5 and their mother encouraged one **a** to die nobly, A
10: 3 and made **a** altar of sacrifice;
14: 26 when Alcimus noticed their goodwill for one **a**, A
15: 13 Then in the same fashion **a** appeared,
1Es 3: 4 over the person of the king, said to one **a**, A
4: 4 If he tells them to make war on one **a**, they do it; A
4: 6 and they compel one **a** to pay taxes to the king. A
4: 33 Then the king and the nobles looked at one **a**; A
2Es 3: 32 Or has **a** nation known you besides Israel?
5: 9 and all friends shall conquer one **a**; A
5: 46 'If you bear ten children, why one after **a**?'
6: 6 through me alone and not through **a**;
6: 6 through me alone and not through **a**."
7: 6 **A** example: There is a city built
7: *105* so no one shall ever pray for **a** on that day,
7: *105* neither shall anyone lay a burden on **a**;
11: 19 after **a** and then were never seen again.
12: 14 And twelve kings shall reign in it, one after **a**.

2Es 13:12 and call to himself **a** multitude that was peaceable.
13:31 They shall plan to make war against one **a**, A
13:33 and the warfare that they have against one **a**; A
13:39 for your seeing him gather to himself **a** multitude
13:40 and they were taken into **a** land.
15:16 growing strong against one **a**, A
15:35 They shall clash against one **a** and shall pour A
15:38 and from the north, and **a** part from the west.
16:27 a person will long to see **a** human being,
4Mc 13: 8 a holy chorus of religion and encouraged one **a**, A
13:11 While one said, "Courage, brother," **a** said,
13:12 **a** reminded them, "Remember whence you came,
13:13 and all of them together looking at one **a**, A
13:23 brothers were the more sympathetic to one **a**. A
13:24 they loved one **a** all the more. A
13:25 strengthened their goodwill toward one **a**, A

ANOTHER'S (7) [ANOTHER]

Ge 11: 7 so that they will not understand one **a** speech."
Job 1: 4 to go and hold feasts in one **a** houses in turn;
Pr 25: 9 and do not disclose **a** secret;
Jn 13:14 you also ought to wash one **a** feet.
Gal 6: 2 Bear one **a** burdens, and in this
Sir 29: 5 One kisses **a** hands until he gets a loan,
3Mc 5:49 embracing relatives and falling into one **a** arms—

ANSWER‡ (177) [ANSWERABLE, ANSWERED, ANSWERING, ANSWERS]

Ge 30:33 So my honesty will **a** for me later,
41:16 God will give Pharaoh a favorable **a**."
43: 7 What we told him was in **a** to these questions.
45: 3 But his brothers could not **a** him,
Ex 13:14 you shall **a**, 'By strength of hand
19:19 Moses would speak and God would **a** him
Jos 22:21 the half-tribe of Manasseh said in **a** to the heads of
Jdg 5:29 Her wisest ladies make **a**, indeed,
19:28 But there was no **a**.
1Sa 4:20 But she did not **a** or give heed.
8:18 but the LORD will not **a** you in that day."
14:37 But he did not **a** him that day.
26:14 "Abner! Will you not **a**?"
28: 6 the LORD did not **a** him, not by dreams,
2Sa 3:11 And Ishbaal could not **a** Abner another word,
22:42 they cried to the LORD, but he did not **a** them.
24:13 and decide what **a** I shall return to
1Ki 12: 6 saying, "How do you advise me to **a** this people?"
12: 7 and speak good words to them when you **a** them,
12: 9 that we **a** this people who have said to me,
18:21 The people did not **a** him a word.
18:26 from morning until noon, crying, "O Baal, **a** us!"
18:26 But there was no voice, and no **a**.
18:29 but there was no voice, no **a**, and no response.
18:37 **A** me, O LORD, **a** me,
2Ki 4:29 and if anyone greets you, do not **a**;
18:36 for the king's command was, "Do not **a** him."
1Ch 21:12 Now decide what **a** I shall return to
2Ch 10: 6 saying, "How do you advise me to **a** this people?"
10: 9 that we **a** this people who have said to me,
Ezr 4:17 The king sent an **a**: "To Rehum
5: 5 a report reached Darius and then **a** was returned
Job 5: 1 "Call now; is there anyone who will **a** you?
9: 3 one could not **a** him once in a thousand.
9:14 then can I **a** him, choosing my words with him?
9:15 Though I am innocent, I cannot **a** him;
9:32 For he is not a mortal, as I am, that I might **a** him,
13:22 and I will **a**; or let me speak, and you reply to me.
14:15 You would call, and I would **a** you;
15: 2 "Should the wise **a** with windy knowledge,
19:16 I call to my servant, but he gives me no **a**;
20: 2 My thoughts urge me to **a**,
23: 5 I would learn what he would **a** me,
30:20 I cry to you and you do not **a** me;
31:14 When he makes inquiry, what shall I **a** him?
31:35 let the Almighty **a** me!)
32: 1 So these three men ceased to **a** Job,
32: 3 because they had found no **a**,
32: 5 when Elihu saw that there was no **a** in the mouths
32:14 and I will not **a** him with your speeches.
32:15 "They are dismayed, they **a** no more;
32:16 because they stand there, and **a** no more?
32:17 I also will give my **a**;
32:20 I must open my lips and **a**.
33: 5 **A** me, if you can; set your words in order
33:12 I will **a** you: God is greater than any mortal.
33:13 saying, 'He will **a** none of my words'?
33:32 If you have anything to say, **a** me;
35: 4 I will **a** you and your friends with you.
35:12 There they cry out, but he does not **a**,
40: 4 of small account; what shall I **a** you?
40: 5 I have spoken once, and I will not **a**;
Ps 4: 1 **A** me when I call, O God
13: 3 Consider and **a** me, O LORD my God!
17: 6 I call upon you, for you will **a** me, O God;
18:41 they cried to the LORD, but he did not **a** them.
20: 1 The LORD **a** you in the day of trouble!
20: 6 he will **a** him from his holy heaven
20: 9 O LORD; **a** us when we call.
22: 2 O my God, I cry by day, but you do not **a**;
27: 7 when I cry aloud, be gracious to me and **a** me!
38:15 it is you, O LORD my God, who will **a**.
55: 2 and **a** me; I am troubled in my complaint.
60: 5 and **a** us, so that those whom you love may
65: 2 O you who **a** prayer! To you all flesh shall come.
65: 5 By awesome deeds you **a** us with deliverance,
69:13 in the abundance of your steadfast love, **a** me.
Ps 69:16 **A** me, O LORD, for your steadfast love is good;
69:17 in distress—make haste to **a** me.
86: 1 O LORD, and **a** me, for I am poor and needy.
86: 7 of my trouble I call on you, for you will **a** me.
91:15 When they call to me, I will **a** them;
102: 2 **a** me speedily in the day when I call.
108: 6 Give victory with your right hand, and **a** me,
119:42 Then I shall have an **a** for those who taunt me,
119:145 With my whole heart I cry; **a** me, O LORD.
120: 1 to the LORD, that he may **a** me:
143: 1 **a** me in your righteousness.
143: 7 **A** me quickly, O LORD;
Pr 1:28 Then they will call upon me, but I will not **a**;
15: 1 A soft **a** turns away wrath,
15:23 To make an apt **a** is a joy to anyone,
15:28 The mind of the righteous ponders how to **a**,
16: 1 but the **a** of the tongue is from the LORD.
18:13 one gives **a** before hearing, it is folly and shame.
18:23 The poor use entreaties, but the rich **a** roughly.
22:21 that you may give a true **a** to those who sent you?
24:26 One who gives an honest **a** gives a kiss on
26: 4 Do not **a** fools according to their folly,
26: 5 **A** fools according to their folly,
26:16 in self-esteem than seven who can **a** discreetly.
27:11 so that I may **a** whoever reproaches me.
SS 3: 1 I called him, but he gave no **a**.
5: 6 I called him, but he gave no **a**.
Isa 10:30 Listen, O Laishah! **A** her,
14:32 What will one **a** the messengers of the nation?
30:19 when he hears it, he will **a** you.
36:21 for the king's command was, "Do not **a** him."
41:17 I the LORD will **a** them,
41:28 when I ask, gives an **a**.
46: 7 it does not **a** or save anyone from trouble.
50: 2 Why did no one **a** when I called?
58: 9 Then you shall call, and the LORD will **a**;
65:12 because, when I called, you did not **a**,
65:24 Before they call I will **a**,
Jer 7:13 and when I called you, you did not **a**,
7:27 You shall call to them, but they will not **a** you.
22: 9 And they will **a**, "Because they abandoned
33: 3 Call to me and I will **a** you,
44:20 all the people who were giving him this **a**:
Eze 14: 4 I the LORD will **a** those who come with
14: 7 I the LORD will **a** them myself.
Da 9: 3 an **a** by prayer and supplication with fasting
Hos 2:21 On that day I will **a**, says the LORD, I will **a** the
heavens and they shall **a** the earth;
2:22 the earth shall **a** the grain, the wine, and the oil,
and they shall **a** Jezreel;
14: 8 It is I who **a** and look after you.
Am 6:10 the **a** will come, "No."
Mic 3: 4 but he will not **a** them;
3: 7 for there is no **a** from God.
6: 3 In what have I wearied you? **A** me!
Hab 2: 1 and what he will **a** concerning my complaint.
Zec 10: 6 for I am the LORD their God and I will **a** them.
13: 6 the **a** will be "The wounds I received in the house
13: 9 They will call on my name, and I will **a** them.
Mal 2:12 any to witness or **a**, or to bring an offering to
Mt 15:23 But he did not **a** her at all.
21:24 if you tell me the **a**,
22:46 No one was able to give him an **a**,
25:37 Then the righteous will **a** him, 'Lord,
25:40 And the king will **a** them, 'Truly I tell you,
25:44 Then they also will **a**, 'Lord,
25:45 Then he will **a** them, 'Truly I tell you,
26:62 high priest stood up and said, "Have you no **a**?
27:12 by the chief priests and elders, he did not **a**.
27:14 But he gave him no **a**, not even to a single charge,
Mk 11:29 **a** me, and I will tell you
11:30 or was it of human origin? **A** me."
14:60 before them and asked Jesus, "Have you no **a**?
14:61 But he was silent and did not **a**.
15: 4 Pilate asked him again, "Have you no **a**?
Lk 10:28 And he said to him, "You have given the right **a**;
20:26 and being amazed by his **a**, they became silent,
22:68 and if I question you, you will not **a**.
23: 9 but Jesus gave him no **a**.
Jn 1:22 Let us have an **a** for those who sent us.
18:22 saying, "Is that how you **a** the high priest?"
19: 9 But Jesus gave him no **a**.
Ac 12:13 a maid named Rhoda came to **a**.
2Co 5:12 to **a** those who boast in outward appearance and
Col 4: 6 that you may know how you ought to **a** everyone.
Tob 6:14 Then Tobias said in **a** to Raphael,
AdE 4:15 the messenger this **a** to take back to Mordecai:
Sir 5:12 If you know what to say, **a** your neighbor;
8: 9 how to understand and to give an **a** when
11: 8 Do not **a** before you listen,
33: 4 draw upon your training, and give your **a**.
1Mc 2:36 But they did not **a** them or hurl a stone at them
15:35 Athenobius did not **a** him a word,
2Es 4: 9 and you have given me no **a** about them."
5:11 And it will **a**, 'No.'
5:53 And she herself will **a** you,
7:73 or how will they **a** in the last times?
8:25 and as long as I have understanding I will **a**.

ANSWERABLE (1) [ANSWER]

1Co 11:27 of the Lord in an unworthy manner will be **a** for

ANSWERED‡ (490) [ANSWER]

Ge 18:27 Abraham **a**, "Let me take it upon myself to speak
18:29 He **a**, "For the sake of forty I will not do it."
18:30 He **a**, "I will not do it, if I find thirty there."
Ge 18:31 He **a**, "For the sake of twenty I will
18:32 He **a**, "For the sake of ten I will not destroy it."
23: 5 The Hittites **a** Abraham,
23:10 and Ephron the Hittite **a** Abraham in the hearing
23:14 Ephron **a** Abraham,
24:50 Then Laban and Bethuel **a**,
27: 1 to him, "My son"; and he **a**,
27:20 He **a**, "Because the LORD your God granted me
27:24 "Are you really my son Esau?" He **a**,
27:32 He **a**, "I am your firstborn son, Esau."
27:37 Isaac **a** Esau, "I have already made him your lord,
27:39 Then his father Isaac **a** him:
31:14 Then Rachel and Leah **a** him,
31:31 Jacob **a** Laban, "Because I was afraid,
31:43 Then Laban **a** and said to Jacob,
33: 8 Jacob **a**, "To find favor with my lord."
34:13 The sons of Jacob **a** Shechem
35: 3 to the God who **a** me in the day of my distress
37:13 He **a**, "Here I am."
38:17 He **a**, "I will send you a kid from the flock."
40:18 And Joseph **a**, "This is its interpretation:
41:16 Joseph **a** Pharaoh, "It is not I;
42:22 Then Reuben **a** them, "Did I not tell you not
47:16 And Joseph **a**, "Give me your livestock,
47:30 He **a**, "I will do as you have said."
50: 6 Pharaoh **a**, "Go up, and bury your father,
Ex 2:14 He **a**, "Who made you a ruler and judge over us?
4: 1 Then Moses **a**, "But suppose they do
19: 8 The people all **a** as one:
24: 3 and all the people **a** with one voice, and said,
Nu 23:12 He **a**, "Must I not take care to say what
23:26 But Balaam **a** Balak, "Did I not tell you,
32:31 The Gadites and the Reubenites **a**,
Dt 1:14 You **a** me, "The plan you have proposed is
1:41 You **a** me, "We have sinned against the LORD!
Jos 1:16 They **a** Joshua: "All that you have commanded us
7:20 And Achan **a** Joshua, "It is true;
9:24 They **a** Joshua, "Because it was told
24:16 Then the people **a**, "Far be it from us
Jdg 6:13 Gideon **a** him, "But sir, if the LORD is with us,
7:14 And his comrade **a**, "This is no other than
8: 8 of Penuel **a** him as the people of Succoth had **a**.
8:18 They **a**, "As you are, so were they,
8:25 "We will willingly give them," they **a**.
9: 9 The olive tree **a** them, 'Shall I stop producing
9:11 But the fig tree **a** them,
11:13 of the Ammonites **a** the messengers of Jephthah,
15:12 Samson **a** them, "Swear to me
19:18 He **a** him, "We are passing from Bethlehem
20: 4 the husband of the woman who was murdered, **a**,
20:18 And the LORD **a**, "Judah shall go up first."
20:28 or shall we desist?" The LORD **a**, "Go up,
Ru 2: 4 They **a**, "The LORD bless you."
2: 6 The servant who was in charge of the reapers **a**,
2:11 But Boaz **a** her, "All that you have done
3: 9 And she **a**, "I am Ruth, your servant;
1Sa 1:15 But Hannah **a**, "No, my lord,
1:17 Then Eli **a**, "Go in peace;
6: 4 They **a**, "Five gold tumors and five gold mice,
7: 9 to the LORD for Israel, and the LORD **a** him.
9: 8 The boy **a** Saul again, "Here,
9:12 They **a**, "Yes, there he is just ahead of you.
9:19 Samuel **a** Saul, "I am the seer;
9:21 Saul **a**, "I am only a Benjaminite,
10:12 A man of the place **a**, "And who is their father?"
14:39 there was no one among all the people who **a** him.
14:41 why have you not **a** your servant today?
16:18 of the young men **a**, "I have seen a son of Jesse
17:27 The people **a** him in the same way,
17:30 and the people **a** him again as before.
17:58 And David **a**, "I am the son of your servant Jesse
19:17 Michal **a** Saul, "He said to me, 'Let me go;
20:28 Jonathan **a** Saul, "David earnestly asked leave
20:32 Then Jonathan **a** his father Saul,
21: 4 The priest **a** David, "I have no ordinary bread
21: 5 David **a** the priest, "Indeed women have been kept
22: 9 **a**, "I saw the son of Jesse coming to Nob,
22:12 He **a**, "Here I am, my lord."
22:14 Then Ahimelech **a** the king,
23: 4 The LORD **a** him, "Yes, go down to Keilah;
25:10 But Nabal **a** David's servants, "Who is David?
28:11 He **a**, "Bring up Samuel for me."
28:15 Saul **a**, "I am in great distress,
30: 8 Shall I overtake them?" He **a** him, "Pursue;
2Sa 1: 4 He **a**, "The army fled from the battle,
1: 7 I **a**, 'Here sir.'
1: 8 I **a** him, 'I am an Amalekite.'
1:13 He **a**, "I am the son of a resident alien,
2:20 He **a**, "Yes, it is."
4: 9 David **a** Rechab and his brother Baanah,
9: 6 He **a**, "I am your servant."
13:12 She **a** him, "No, my brother, do not force me;
14: 5 She **a**, "Alas, I am a widow; my husband is dead.
14:18 Then the king **a** the woman,
14:19 The woman **a** and said, "As surely as you live,
14:32 Absalom **a** Joab, "Look, I sent word to you:
15:21 But Ittai **a** the king, "As the LORD lives,
16: 2 Ziba **a**, "The donkeys are for the king's household
18:29 Ahimaaz **a**, "When Joab sent your servant,
18:32 The Cushite **a**, "May the enemies of my lord
19:21 Abishai son of Zeruiah **a**,
19:26 He **a**, "My lord, O king, my servant deceived me;
19:38 The king **a**, "Chimham shall go over with me,
19:42 All the people of Judah **a** the people of Israel,
19:43 But the people of Israel **a** the people of Judah,
20:17 the woman said, "Are you Joab?" He **a**, "I am."
20:17 He **a**, "I am listening."

2Sa 20:20 Joab **a**, "Far be it from me, far be it,
24:25 So the LORD **a** his supplication for the land,
1Ki 1:28 King David **a**, "Summon Bathsheba to me."
1:36 Benaiah son of Jehoiada **a** the king, "Amen!
1:43 Jonathan **a** Adonijah, "No,
2:22 King Solomon **a** his mother,
2:30 saying, "Thus said Joab, and thus he **a** me."
10: 3 Solomon **a** all her questions;
12: 7 They **a** him, "If you will be a servant
12:13 The king **a** the people harshly.
12:16 the people **a** the king, "What share do we have
13:14 of God who came from Judah?" He **a**,
18: 8 He **a** him, "It is I.
18:18 He **a**, "I have not troubled Israel;
18:24 All the people **a**, "Well spoken!"
19:10 He **a**, "I have been very zealous for the LORD,
19:14 He **a**, "I have been very zealous for the LORD,
20: 4 The king of Israel **a**, "As you say, my lord,
20:11 The king of Israel **a**, "Tell him:
20:14 "Who shall begin the battle?" He **a**,
21: 6 but he **a**, 'I will not give you my vineyard.' "
21:20 He **a**, "I have found you.
22:15 He **a** him, "Go up and triumph;
2Ki 1: 6 They **a** him, "There came a man to meet us,
1: 8 They **a** him, "A hairy man,
1:10 But Elijah **a** the captain of fifty,
1:12 But Elijah **a** them, "If I am a man of God,
2: 5 And he **a**, "Yes, I know; be silent."
3: 7 against Moab?" He **a**, "I will;
3: 8 Jehoram **a**, "By the way of the wilderness
3:11 Then one of the servants of the king of Israel **a**,
4: 2 She **a**, "Your servant has nothing in the house,
4:13 She **a**, "I live among my own people."
4:14 Gehazi **a**, "Well, she has no son,
4:26 She **a**, "It is all right."
5:25 He **a**, "Your servant has not gone anywhere
6: 2 and build a place there for us to live." He **a**,
6: 3 And he **a**, "I will."
6:22 He **a**, "No! Did you capture with your
6:28 She **a**, "This woman said to me,
7:19 the captain had **a** the man of God,
7:19 And he had **a**, "You shall see it
8:12 He **a**, "Because I know the evil that you will do to
8:13 Elisha **a**, "The LORD has shown me that you are
8:14 to you?" And he **a**, "He told me
9:11 He **a** them, "You know the sort and
9:19 Jehu **a**, "What have you to do with peace?
9:22 He **a**, "What peace can there be,
10:13 They **a**, "We are kin of Ahaziah;
10:15 as mine is to yours?" Jehonadab **a**,
18:36 But the people were silent and **a** him not a word,
20:10 Hezekiah **a**, "It is normal for the shadow
20:14 Hezekiah **a**, "They have come from a far country,
20:15 Hezekiah **a**, "They have seen all that is
1Ch 21:26 and he **a** him with fire from heaven on the altar
21:28 that the LORD had **a** him at the threshing floor
2Ch 1:11 God **a** Solomon, "Because this was in your heart,
2:11 Then King Huram of Tyre **a** in a letter that he sent
9: 2 Solomon **a** all her questions;
10: 7 They **a** him, "If you will be kind to this people
10:13 The king **a** them harshly.
10:16 the people **a** the king, "What share do we have
18: 3 He **a** him, "I am with you,
18:14 He **a**, "Go up and triumph;
25: 9 The man of God **a**, "The LORD is able
31:10 who was of the house of Zadok, **a** him,
32:24 and he **a** him and gave him a sign.
Ezr 10:12 all the assembly **a** with a loud voice, "It is so;
Ne 6: 4 and I **a** them in the same manner.
8: 6 the great God, and all the people **a**, "Amen,
Est 7: 3 Then Queen Esther **a**, "If I have won your favor,
Job 1: 7 Satan **a** the LORD, "From going to and fro on
1: 9 Then Satan **a** the LORD, "Does Job fear God
2: 2 Satan **a** the LORD, "From going to and fro on
2: 4 Then Satan **a** the LORD, "Skin for skin!
4: 1 Then Eliphaz the Temanite **a**:
6: 1 Then Job **a**:
8: 1 Then Bildad the Shuhite **a**:
9: 1 Then Job **a**:
9:16 If I summoned him and he **a** me,
11: 1 Then Zophar the Naamathite **a**:
12: 1 Then Job **a**:
12: 4 I, who called upon God and he **a** me,
15: 1 Then Eliphaz the Temanite **a**:
16: 1 Then Job **a**:
18: 1 Then Bildad the Shuhite **a**:
19: 1 Then Job **a**:
19: 7 I am not **a**; I call aloud, but there is no justice.
20: 1 Then Zophar the Naamathite **a**:
21: 1 Then Job **a**:
22: 1 Then Eliphaz the Temanite **a**:
23: 1 Then Job **a**:
25: 1 Then Bildad the Shuhite **a**:
26: 1 Then Job **a**:
32: 6 Elihu son of Barachel the Buzite **a**:
32:12 no one among you that **a** his words.
38: 1 Then the LORD **a** Job out of the whirlwind:
40: 3 Then Job **a** the LORD:
40: 6 Then the LORD **a** Job out of the whirlwind:
42: 1 Then Job **a** the LORD:
Ps 34: 4 I sought the LORD, and he **a** me,
81: 7 I **a** you in the secret place of thunder;
99: 6 They cried to the LORD, and he **a** them.
99: 8 O LORD our God, you **a** them;
118: 5 the LORD **a** me and set me in a broad place.
118:21 I thank you that you have **a** me
119:26 When I told of my ways, you **a** me;
Ps 138: 3 On the day I called, you **a** me,
Isa 36:21 But they were silent and **a** him not a word,
39: 3 Hezekiah **a**, "They have come to me from
39: 4 Hezekiah **a**, "They have seen all that is
49: 8 In a time of favor I have **a** you,
66: 4 because, when I called, no one **a**, when I spoke,
Jer 11: 5 Then I **a**, "So be it, LORD."
23:35 among yourselves, "What has the LORD **a**?"
23:37 "What has the LORD **a** you?"
35: 6 But they **a**, "We will drink no wine,
35:17 I have called to them and they have not **a**.
36:18 Baruch **a** them, "He dictated all these words
38:27 and he **a** them in the very words
44:15 in Pathros in the land of Egypt, **a** Jeremiah:
Eze 37: 3 I **a**, "O Lord GOD, you know."
Da 2: 5 king **a** the Chaldeans, "This is a public decree:
2: 7 They **a** a second time, "Let
2: 8 The king **a**, "I know with certainty
2:10 The Chaldeans **a** the king,
2:27 Daniel **a** the king, "No wise men, enchanters,
3:16 Shadrach, Meshach, and Abednego **a** the king,
3:24 They **a** the king, "True, O king."
4:19 Belteshazzar **a**, "My lord,
5:17 Then Daniel **a** in the presence of the king,
6:12 The king **a**, "The thing stands fast,
8:14 And he **a** him, "For two thousand three hundred
Am 7:14 Then Amos **a** Amaziah, "I am no prophet,
Jnh 2: 2 to the LORD out of my distress, and he **a** me;
Mic 6: 5 what Balaam son of Beor **a** him,
Hab 2: 2 Then the LORD **a** me and said:
Hag 2:12 does it become holy? The priests **a**,
2:13 The priests **a**, "Yes, it becomes unclean."
Zec 1:10 man who was standing among the myrtle trees **a**,
1:19 And he **a** me, "These are the horns
1:21 He **a**, "These are the horns that scattered Judah,
2: 2 He **a** me, "To measure Jerusalem,
4: 5 Then the angel who talked with me **a** me,
5: 2 I **a**, "I see a flying scroll;
6: 5 The angel **a** me, "These are the four winds
Mt 3:15 But Jesus **a** him, "Let it be so now;
4: 4 But he **a**, "It is written, 'One does not live
8: 8 The centurion **a**, "Lord, I am not worthy
11: 4 Jesus **a** them, "Go and tell John what you hear
12:39 But he **a** them, "An evil
13:11 He **a**, "To you it has been given to know
13:28 He **a**, 'An enemy has done this.'
13:37 He **a**, "The one who sows the good seed is
13:51 "Have you understood all this?" They **a**, "Yes."
14:28 Peter **a** him, "Lord, if it is you,
15: 3 He **a** them, "And why do you break
15:13 He **a**, "Every plant that my heavenly Father has
15:24 He **a**, "I was sent only to the lost sheep of
15:26 He **a**, "It is not fair to take the children's food
15:28 Then Jesus **a** her, "Woman, great is your faith!
16: 2 He **a** them, "When it is evening, you say,
16:16 Simon Peter **a**, "You are the Messiah,
16:17 And Jesus **a** him, "Blessed are you,
17:17 Jesus **a**, "You faithless and perverse generation,
19: 4 He **a**, "Have you not read that
20:22 Jesus **a**, "You do not know what you are asking.
21:21 Jesus **a** them, "Truly I tell you,
21:27 So they **a** Jesus, "We do not know."
21:29 He **a**, 'I will not'; but later he changed his mind
21:30 and he **a**, 'I go, sir'; but he did not go.
22:21 They **a**, "The emperor's."
22:29 Jesus **a** them, "You are wrong,
24: 4 Jesus **a** them, "Beware
26:23 He **a**, "The one who has dipped his hand into
26:66 They **a**, "He deserves death."
27:25 Then the people as a whole **a**,
Mk 1:38 He **a**, "Let us go on to the neighboring towns,
6:37 But he **a** them, "You give them something to eat."
7:28 But she **a** him, "Sir, even the dogs under
8:28 And they **a** him, "John the Baptist;
8:29 Peter **a** him, "You are the Messiah."
9:17 Someone from the crowd **a** him, "Teacher,
9:19 He **a** them, "You faithless generation,
10: 3 He **a** them, "What did Moses command you?"
11:22 Jesus **a** them, "Have faith in God.
11:33 So they **a** Jesus, "We do not know."
12:16 They **a**, "The emperor's."
12:28 and seeing that he **a** them well, he asked him,
12:29 Jesus **a**, "The first is, 'Hear, O Israel:
12:34 When Jesus saw that he **a** wisely, he said to him,
15: 2 He **a** him, "You say so."
15: 9 Then he **a** them, "Do you want me to release
Lk 3:16 John **a** all of them by saying, "I baptize you
4: 4 Jesus **a** him, "It is written,
4: 8 Jesus **a** him, "It is written,
4:12 Jesus **a** him, "It is said, 'Do not put
5: 5 Simon **a**, "Master, we have worked all night long
5:22 Jesus perceived their questionings, he **a** them,
5:31 Jesus **a**, "Those who are well have no need of
6: 3 Jesus **a**, "Have you not read what David did
7:22 he **a** them, "Go and tell John what you have seen
7:43 Simon **a**, "I suppose the one
9:19 They **a**, "John the Baptist;
9:20 Peter **a**, "The Messiah of God."
9:41 Jesus **a**, "You faithless and perverse generation,
9:49 John **a**, "Master, we saw someone casting out
10:27 He **a**, "You shall love the Lord your God
10:41 But the Lord **a** her, "Martha, Martha,
11:45 One of the lawyers **a** him, "Teacher,
13:15 But the Lord **a** him and said, "You hypocrites!
15:29 But he **a** his father, 'Listen!
16: 6 He **a**, 'A hundred jugs of olive oil.'
17:20 and he **a**, "The kingdom of God is not coming
Lk 19:40 He **a**, "I tell you, if these were silent,
20: 3 He **a** them, "I will also ask you a question,
20: 7 they **a** that they did not know where it came from.
20:39 Then some of the scribes **a**, "Teacher,
23: 3 He **a**, "You say so."
24:18 one of them, whose name was Cleopas, **a** him,
Jn 1:21 "Are you the prophet?" He **a**,
1:26 John **a** them, "I baptize with water.
1:48 Jesus **a**, "I saw you under the fig tree
1:50 Jesus **a**, "Do you believe because I told you
2:19 Jesus **a** them, "Destroy this temple,
3: 3 Jesus **a** him, "Very truly, I tell you,
3: 5 Jesus **a**, "Very truly, I tell you,
3:10 Jesus **a** him, "Are you a teacher of Israel,
3:27 John **a**, "No one can receive anything except what
4:10 Jesus **a** her, "If you knew the gift of God,
4:17 The woman **a** him, "I have no husband."
5: 7 The sick man **a** him, "Sir,
5:11 But he **a** them, "The man who made me well said
5:17 But Jesus **a** them, "My Father is still working,
6: 7 Philip **a** him, "Six months' wages would
6:26 Jesus **a** them, "Very truly, I tell you,
6:29 Jesus **a** them, "This is the work of God,
6:43 Jesus **a** them, "Do not complain
6:68 Simon Peter **a** him, "Lord, to whom can we go?
6:70 Jesus **a** them, "Did I not choose you, the twelve?
7:16 Then Jesus **a** them, "My teaching is not mine
7:20 The crowd **a**, "You have a demon!
7:21 Jesus **a** them, "I performed one work,
7:46 police **a**, "Never has anyone spoken like this!"
8:14 Jesus **a**, "Even if I testify on my own behalf,
8:19 Jesus **a**, "You know neither me nor my Father.
8:33 They **a** him, "We are descendants of Abraham
8:34 Jesus **a** them, "Very truly, I tell you,
8:39 They **a** him, "Abraham is our father."
8:48 The Jews **a** him, "Are we not right in saying
8:49 Jesus **a**, "I do not have a demon;
8:54 Jesus **a**, "If I glorify myself, my glory is nothing.
9: 3 Jesus **a**, "Neither this man nor his parents sinned;
9:11 He **a**, "The man called Jesus made mud,
9:20 His parents **a**, "We know that this is our son,
9:25 He **a**, "I do not know whether he is a sinner.
9:27 He **a** them, "I have told you already,
9:30 The man **a**, "Here is an astonishing thing!
9:34 They **a** him, "You were born entirely in sins,
9:36 He **a**, "And who is he, sir?
10:25 Jesus **a**, "I have told you, and you do not believe.
10:33 The Jews **a**, "It is not for a good work
10:34 Jesus **a**, "Is it not written in your law, 'I said,
11: 9 Jesus **a**, "Are there not twelve hours of daylight?
12:23 Jesus **a** them, "The hour has come for the Son
12:30 Jesus **a**, "This voice has come for your sake,
12:34 The crowd **a** him, "We have heard from the law
13: 7 Jesus **a**, "You do not know now what I am doing,
13: 8 Jesus **a**, "Unless I wash you,
13:26 Jesus **a**, "It is the one to whom I give this piece
13:36 Jesus **a**, "Where I am going,
13:38 Jesus **a**, "Will you lay down your life for me?
14:23 Jesus **a** him, "Those who love me will keep my word,
16:31 Jesus **a** them, "Do you now believe?
18: 5 They **a**, "Jesus of Nazareth."
18: 8 Jesus **a**, "I told you that I am he.
18:20 Jesus **a**, "I have spoken openly to the world;
18:23 Jesus **a**, "If I have spoken wrongly,
18:30 They **a**, "If this man were not a criminal,
18:34 Jesus **a**, "Do you ask this on your own,
18:36 Jesus **a**, "My kingdom is not from this world.
18:37 Jesus **a**, "You say that I am a king.
19: 7 The Jews **a** him, "We have a law,
19:11 Jesus **a** him, "You would have no power over me
19:15 The chief priests **a**, "We have no king but
19:22 Pilate **a**, "What I have written I have written."
20:28 Thomas **a** him, "My Lord and my God!"
21: 5 They **a** him, "No."
Ac 4:19 But Peter and John **a** them,
5:29 But Peter and the apostles **a**,
8:24 Simon **a**, "Pray for me to the Lord,
9:10 He **a**, "Here I am, Lord."
9:13 But Ananias **a**, "Lord, I have heard from many
10: 4 He **a**, "Your prayers and your alms have ascended
10:22 They **a**, "Cornelius, a centurion,
11: 9 But a second time the voice **a** from heaven,
16:31 They **a**, "Believe on the Lord Jesus,
19: 3 They **a**, "Into John's baptism."
21:13 Then Paul **a**, "What are you doing,
22: 8 I **a**, 'Who are you, Lord?'
22:28 The tribune **a**, "It cost me a large sum of money
23:20 He **a**, "The Jews have agreed to ask you
26:15 Lord **a**, 'I am Jesus whom you are persecuting.
Tob 5: 1 Then Tobias **a** his father Tobit,
5: 3 Then Tobit **a** his son Tobias,
5:10 He **a**, "I can go with him and I know all the roads,
5:16 Raphael **a**, "I will go with him; so do not fear.
6:11 "Here I am," he **a**.
7: 3 They **a**, "We belong to the descendants
10: 7 She **a** him, "Be quiet yourself!
Jdt 6:17 He **a** and told them what had taken place at
11: 5 Judith **a** him, "Accept the words of your slave,
14:15 But when no one **a**, he opened it and went into
AdE 1:13 "This is how Vashti has **a** me.
6: 5 The servants of the king **a**,
7: 3 She **a** and said, "If I have found favor with
Sir 39:17 at the appointed time all such questions will be **a**.
46: 5 great Lord **a** him with hailstones of mighty power.
Sus 1:54 He **a**, "Under a mastic tree."
1:58 He **a**, "Under an evergreen oak."

Bel 1: 5 He a, "Because I do not revere idols made
1: 17 He a, "They are unbroken, O king."
1Mc 2: 19 But Mattathias a and said in a loud voice:
13: 8 and they a in a loud voice,
2Mc 14: 5 and intentions of the Jews. He a:
1Es 6: 13 They a us, 'We are the servants of
9: 47 and the multitude a, "Amen."
3Mc 1: 14 And someone a thoughtlessly that it was wrong
2Es 2: 45 He a and said to me, "These are they who have put
2: 47 He a and said to me, "He is the Son of God,
4: 1 that had been sent to me, whose name was Uriel, a
4: 6 I a and said, "Who of those
4: 13 He a me and said, "I went into a forest of trees of
4: 19 I a and said, "Each made a foolish plan,
4: 20 He a me and said, "You have judged rightly,
4: 22 Then I a and said, "I implore you, my lord,
4: 26 He a me and said, "If you are alive, you will see,
4: 33 Then I a and said, "How long?
4: 34 He a me and said, "Do not be in
4: 36 And the archangel Jeremiel a and said,
4: 38 Then I a and said, "But, O sovereign Lord,
4: 40 He a me and said, "Go and ask
4: 44 I a and said, "If I have found favor in your sight,
4: 52 He a me and said, "Concerning the signs
5: 43 Then I a and said, "Could you not have created
6: 7 I a and said, "What will be the dividing of
6: 11 I a and said, "O sovereign Lord,
6: 13 He a and said to me,
7: 17 Then I a and said, "O sovereign Lord,
7: *45* I a and said, "O sovereign Lord,
7: *49* He a me and said, "Listen to me, Ezra,
7: *59* He a me and said, "Consider
7: *70* He a me and said, "When the Most High made
7: *75* I a and said, "If I have found favor in your sight,
7: *76* He a me and said, "I will show you that also,
7: *100* Then I a and said, "Will time therefore be given to
7: *102* I a and said, "If I have found favor in your sight,
7: *104* He a me and said, "Since you have found favor
7: *106* [36] I a and said, "How then do we find
7: *112* [42] He a me and said, "This present world is not
7: *116* [46] I a and said, "This is my first and last
7: *127* [57] He a and said, "This is the significance of
7: *132* [62] I a and said, "I know, O Lord,
8: 1 He a me and said, "The Most High made this
8: 4 I a and said, "Then drink your fill
8: 37 He a me and said, "Some things you have spoken
8: 42 I a and said, "If I have found favor in your sight,
8: 46 He a me and said, "Things that are present are
8: 62 Then I a and said,
9: 1 He a me and said, "Measure carefully
9: 14 I a and said,
9: 17 He a me and said, "As is the field, so is the seed;
10: 5 and a her in anger and said,
10: 38 He a me and said, "Listen to me,
12: 45 Then I a them and said,
13: 20 in the last days." He a me and said,
14: 2 And I a, "Here I am, Lord," and I rose to my feet.
14: 19 Then I a and said, "Let me speak
14: 23 He a me and said, "Go and gather the people,

ANSWERING‡ (1) [ANSWER]
Sir 5: 11 Be quick to hear, but deliberate in a.

ANSWERS (12) [ANSWER]
Jdg 5: 29 indeed, she a the question herself:
1Sa 20: 10 "Who will tell me if your father a you harshly?"
28: 15 God has turned away from me and a me no more,
1Ki 18: 24 the god who a by fire is indeed God."
Job 20: 3 and a spirit beyond my understanding a me.
21: 34 There is nothing left of your a but falsehood."
34: 36 because his a are those of the wicked.
Ps 3: 4 and he a me from his holy hill.
Jer 42: 4 and whatever the LORD a you I will tell you;
Lk 2: 47 at his understanding and his a.
11: 7 And he a from within, 'Do not bother me;
Sir 47: 17 and the a you gave astounded the nations.

ANT (1) [ANTS]
Pr 6: 6 Go to the a, you lazybones;

ANTAGONIST (4)
AdE 7: 4 Our a brings shame on the king's court."
3Mc 7: 9 and inescapably as an a to avenge such acts.
4Mc 3: 5 reason does not uproot the emotions but is their a.
17: 14 the a, and the world and the human race were

ANTELOPE (2)
Dt 14: 5 the roebuck, the wild goat, the ibex, the a,
Isa 51: 20 they lie at the head of every street like an a in

ANTHOTHIJAH (1)
1Ch 8: 24 Hananiah, Elam, A,

ANTICHRIST (4) [ANTICHRISTS]
1Jn 2: 18 As you have heard that a is coming,
2: 22 This is the a, the one who denies the Father and
4: 3 And this is the spirit of the a,
2Jn 1: 7 any such person is the deceiver and the a!

ANTICHRISTS (1) [ANTICHRIST]
1Jn 2: 18 so now many a have come.

ANTICIPATE (1)
Ecc 9: 12 For no one can a the time of disaster.

ANTICIPATED See Index to Footnotes

ANTILEBANON (1)
Jdt 1: 7 and Damascus, Lebanon and A, and all who lived

ANTIMONY (2)
1Ch 29: 2 a, colored stones, all sorts of precious stones,
Isa 54: 11 I am about to set your stones in a,

ANTIOCH (34) [ANTIOCHIAN]
Ac 6: 5 Timon, Parmenas, and Nicolaus, a proselyte of A.
11: 19 as far as Phoenicia, Cyprus, and A, and they spoke
11: 20 on coming to A, spoke to the Hellenists also,
11: 22 and they sent Barnabas to A.
11: 26 and when he had found him, he brought him to A.
11: 26 and it was in A that the disciples were first called
11: 27 prophets came down from Jerusalem to A.
13: 1 the church at A there were prophets and teachers:
13: 14 they went on from Perga and came to A in Pisidia.
14: 19 But Jews came there from A and Iconium and won
14: 21 they returned to Lystra, then on to Iconium and A.
14: 26 From there they sailed back to A,
15: 22 from among their members and to send them to A
15: 23 the elders, to the believers of Gentile origin in A
15: 30 So they were sent off and went down to A.
15: 35 But Paul and Barnabas remained in A, and there,
18: 22 and then went down to A.
Gal 2: 11 But when Cephas came to A,
2Ti 3: 11 and suffering the things that happened to me in A,
1Mc 3: 37 and left A his capital in the one hundred
4: 35 he withdrew to A and enlisted mercenaries
6: 63 Then he set off in haste and returned to A.
10: 68 he was greatly distressed and returned to A.
11: 13 Ptolemy entered A and put on the crown of Asia.
11: 44 to him at A, and when they came to the king,
11: 56 the elephants and gained control of A.
2Mc 4: 9 to enroll the people of Jerusalem as citizens of A.
4: 33 to a place of sanctuary at Daphne near A.
5: 21 from the temple, and hurried away to A, thinking
8: 35 across the country until he reached A,
11: 36 For we are on our way to A.
13: 23 in charge of the government, had revolted in A;
13: 26 gained their goodwill, and set out for A.
14: 27 and commanding him to send Maccabeus to A as

ANTIOCHIAN‡ (1) [ANTIOCH]
2Mc 4: 19 chosen as being A citizens from Jerusalem,

ANTIOCHIS (1)
2Mc 4: 30 their cities had been given as a present to A,

ANTIOCHUS (70)
1Mc 1: 10 From them came forth a sinful root, A Epiphanes,
son of King A; he had been a hostage in Rome.
1: 16 When A saw that his kingdom was established,
1: 20 A returned in the one hundred forty-third year.
3: 27 When King A heard these reports,
3: 33 also to take care of his son A until he returned.
6: 1 King A was going through the upper provinces
6: 15 so that he might guide his son A and bring him up
6: 16 Thus King A died there in
6: 17 he set up A the king's son to reign.
6: 55 whom King A while still living had appointed to
bring up his son A to be king,
7: 2 army seized A and Lysias to bring them to him.
8: 6 They also had defeated A the Great, king of Asia,
10: 1 son of A, landed and occupied Ptolemais.
11: 39 the Arab, who was bringing up A, the young son
11: 40 and insistently urged him to hand A over to him,
11: 54 and with him the young boy A who began to reign
11: 57 Then the young A wrote to Jonathan, saying,
12: 16 We therefore have chosen Numenius son of A
12: 39 and to raise his hand against King A.
13: 31 Trypho dealt treacherously with the young King A;
14: 22 'Numenius son of A and Antipater son of Jason,
15: 1 A, son of King Demetrius,
15: 2 "King A to Simon the high priest and ethnarch and
15: 10 In the one hundred seventy-fourth year A set out
15: 11 A pursued him, and Trypho came in his flight
15: 13 So A encamped against Dor,
15: 25 King A besieged Dor for the second time,
15: 26 And Simon sent to A two thousand picked troops,
2Mc 1: 14 A came to the place together with his Friends,
1: 15 of Nanea had set out the treasures and A had come
2: 20 the wars against A Epiphanes and his son Eupator,
4: 7 When Seleucus died and A,
4: 21 A learned that Philometor had become hostile
4: 37 A was grieved at heart and filled with pity,
5: 1 About this time A made his second invasion
5: 5 When a false rumor arose that A was dead,
5: 15 A dared to enter the most holy temple in all
5: 17 A was elated in spirit, and did not perceive that
5: 21 So A carried off eighteen hundred talents from
5: 24 A sent Apollonius, the captain of the Mysians,
7: 24 A felt that he was being treated with contempt,
7: 24 A not only appealed to him in words,
9: 1 A had retreated in disorder from the region
9: 2 and A and his army were defeated,
9: 2 that A was put to flight by the inhabitants and beat
9: 19 A their king and general sends hearty greetings
2Mc 9: 25 So I have appointed my son A to be king,
9: 29 then, fearing the son of A,
10: 9 Such then was the end of A,
10: 10 we will tell what took place under A Eupator,
10: 13 and had gone over to A Epiphanes.
11: 22 "King A to his brother Lysias, greetings.
11: 27 "King A to the senate of the Jews and to
13: 1 to Judas and his men that A Eupator was coming
13: 3 also joined them and with utter hypocrisy urged A
13: 4 the King of kings aroused the anger of A against
14: 2 with A and his guardian Lysias.
3Mc 1: 1 that he had controlled had been seized by A,
1: 1 where the army of A was encamped.
1: 4 and matters were turning out rather in favor of A,
4Mc 4: 15 his son A Epiphanes succeeded to the throne,
4: 21 by these acts and caused A himself to make war
5: 1 The tyrant A, sitting in state with his counselors
5: 5 When A saw him he said,
5: 16 O A, who have been persuaded to govern our lives
10: 17 and utterly abominable A gave orders
17: 23 For the tyrant A, when he saw the courage
18: 5 The tyrant A was both punished on earth

ANTIPAS (1)
Rev 2: 13 in me even in the days of A my witness,

ANTIPATER (2)
1Mc 12: 16 Numenius son of Antiochus and A son of Jason,
14: 22 'Numenius son of Antiochus and A son of Jason,

ANTIPATRIS (1)
Ac 23: 31 took Paul and brought him during the night to A.

ANTIQUITY (KJV) See OLD

ANTOTHIJAH (KJV) See ANTHOTHIJAH

ANTOTHITE (KJV) See ANATHOTH

ANTS (1) [ANT]
Pr 30: 25 the a are a people without strength,

ANUB (1)
1Ch 4: 8 Koz became the father of A, Zobebah,

ANVIL (2)
Isa 41: 7 the hammer encourages the one who strikes the a,
Sir 38: 28 So too is the smith, sitting by the a,

ANXIETIES (2) [ANXIETY]
1Co 7: 32 I want you to be free from a.
4Mc 16: 8 and the more grievous a of your upbringing.

ANXIETY (14) [ANXIETIES, ANXIOUS, ANXIOUSLY]
1Sa 1: 16 for I have been speaking out of my great a
Pr 12: 25 A weighs down the human heart,
Ecc 11: 10 Banish a from your mind,
Lk 2: 48 and I have been searching for you in great a."
2Co 11: 28 I am under daily pressure because of my a for all
1Pe 5: 7 Cast all your a on him, because he cares for you.
AdE 14: 1 Then Queen Esther, seized with deadly a,
Wis 7: 23 humane, steadfast, sure, free from a, all-powerful,
Sir 30: 24 and a brings on premature old age.
31: 1 and a about it drives away sleep.
31: 2 Wakeful a prevents slumber,
42: 9 A daughter is a secret a to her father,
2Mc 3: 21 the prostration of the whole populace and the a of
1Es 8: 71 and sat down in a and grief.

ANXIOUS‡ (10) [ANXIETY]
Ps 127: 2 eating the bread of a toil; for he gives sleep
Jer 17: 8 in the year of drought it is not a,
1Co 7: 32 unmarried man is a about the affairs of the Lord,
7: 33 married man is a about the affairs of the world,
7: 34 and the virgin are a about the affairs of the Lord,
7: 34 married woman is a about the affairs of the world,
Php 2: 28 and that I may be less a.
Sir 40: 2 and a thought of the day of their death.
41: 2 worn down by age and a about everything;
Bar 3: 18 and were a, but there is no trace of their works?
2Mc 15: 19 being a over the encounter in the open country.
2Es 2: 27 Do not be a, for when the day of tribulation
3: 3 and I began to speak a words to the Most High,

ANXIOUSLY (2) [ANXIETY]
Da 6: 20 he cried out a to Daniel, "O Daniel,
Mic 1: 12 For the inhabitants of Maroth wait a for good,

ANY‡ (697) [ANYBODY, ANYMORE, ANYONE, ANYONE'S, ANYTHING, ANYWHERE]
Ge 3: 1 serpent was more crafty than a other wild animal
3: 1 'You shall not eat from a tree in the garden'?"
8: 12 and it did not return to him a more.
17: 12 from a foreigner who is not of your offspring.
17: 14 A uncircumcised male who is not circumcised in
23: 6 none of us will withhold from you a burial ground
29: 19 to you than that I should give her to a other man;

Ge 31:14 "Is there **a** portion or inheritance left to us
36:31 before **a** king reigned over the Israelites.
37: 3 Now Israel loved Joseph more than **a** other
43: 7 Could we in **a** way know that he would say,
43:34 as much as **a** of theirs.
44: 9 Should it be found with **a** one of your servants,
Ex 3:22 and **a** woman living in the neighbor's house
11: 7 But not **a** dog shall growl at **a** of the Israelites—
12: 9 Do not eat **a** of it raw or boiled in water,
12:39 nor had they prepared **a** provisions for themselves.
12:44 but **a** slave who has been purchased may eat of it
12:46 not take **a** of the animal outside the house,
12:46 and you shall not break **a** of its bones.
15:26 not bring upon you **a** of the diseases that I brought
16:19 "Let no one leave **a** of it over until morning."
18:26 but **a** minor case they decided themselves.
19:12 **A** who touch the mountain shall be put to death.
20:10 you shall not do **a** work—
21:23 If **a** harm follows, then you shall give life for life,
22: 9 In **a** case of disputed ownership involving ox,
22: 9 clothing, or **a** other loss, of which one party says,
22:10 ox, sheep, or **a** other animal for safekeeping,
22:20 Whoever sacrifices to **a** god,
22:22 You shall not abuse **a** widow or orphan.
22:31 therefore you shall not eat **a** meat that is mangled
28:38 and Aaron shall take on himself **a** guilt incurred in
29:34 If **a** of the flesh for the ordination, or of the bread,
30:32 not be used in **a** ordinary anointing of the body,
30:33 Whoever compounds **a** like it or whoever puts **a**
30:38 Whoever makes **a** like it to use as perfume shall
31:14 whoever does **a** work on it shall be cut off from
31:15 whoever does **a** work on the sabbath day shall
34:10 not been performed in all the earth or in **a** nation;
35: 2 whoever does **a** work on it shall be put to death.
35:24 and everyone who possessed acacia wood of **a** use
35:35 by **a** sort of artisan or skilled designer.
36: 1 to know how to do **a** work in the construction of
Lev 1: 2 When **a** of you bring an offering of livestock to
2: 8 the LORD the grain offering that is prepared in **a**
2:11 not turn **a** leaven or honey into smoke as
3:17 you must not eat **a** fat or **a** blood.
4: 2 in **a** of the LORD's commandments about things not to be done, and does **a** one
4:13 and they do **a** one of the things that by
4:22 doing unintentionally **a** one of all the things that
4:27 among you sins unintentionally in doing **a** one of
5: 1 When **a** of you sin in that you have heard
5: 2 Or when **a** of you touch **a** unclean thing—
5: 3 **a** uncleanness by which one can become unclean—
5: 4 Or when **a** of you utter aloud a rash oath for a bad
5: 4 you shall in **a** of these be guilty.
5: 5 When you realize your guilt in **a** of these,
5:15 When **a** of you commit a trespass
5:15 and sins unintentionally in **a** of the holy things of
5:17 If **a** of you sin without knowing it,
5:17 doing **a** of the things that by
6: 2 When **a** of you sin and commit a trespass against
6: 3 if you swear falsely regarding **a** of
6: 7 be forgiven for **a** of the things that one may do
6:27 and when **a** of its blood is spattered on a garment,
6:30 be eaten from which **a** blood is brought into
7:15 you shall not leave **a** of it until morning.
7:18 If **a** of the flesh of your sacrifice
7:19 that touches **a** unclean thing shall not be eaten;
7:21 When **a** one of you touches **a** unclean thing—
7:21 or an unclean animal or **a** unclean creature—
7:24 or was torn by wild animals may be put to **a** use,
7:25 If **a** one of you eats the fat from an animal
7:26 You must not eat **a** blood whatever,
7:26 of bird or of animal, in **a** of your settlements.
7:27 **A** one of you who eats **a** blood shall be cut off
7:29 **A** one of you who would offer to
10:14 and daughters as well may eat in **a** clean place;
11: 3 **A** animal that has divided hoofs and is cleft-footed
11:14 the buzzard, the kite of **a** kind;
11:15 every raven of **a** kind;
11:16 the nighthawk, the sea gull, the hawk of **a** kind;
11:19 the heron of **a** kind, the hoopoe, and the bat.
11:24 of **a** of them shall be unclean until the evening,
11:25 whoever carries a part of the carcass of **a** of them
11:27 of **a** of them shall be unclean until the evening,
11:32 And anything upon which **a** of them falls
11:32 **a** article that is used for a purpose;
11:33 And if **a** of them falls into **a** earthen vessel,
11:34 **A** food that could be eaten shall be unclean if water from **a** such vessel comes upon it; and **a** liquid that could be drunk shall be unclean if it was in **a** such vessel.
11:35 on which **a** part of the carcass falls shall
11:37 If **a** part of their carcass falls upon **a** seed set aside
11:38 on the seed and **a** part of their carcass falls on it,
11:43 not make yourselves detestable with **a** creature
11:44 with **a** swarming creature that moves on the earth.
12: 4 she shall not touch **a** holy thing,
14:54 This is the ritual for **a** leprous disease: for an itch,
15: 2 When **a** man has a discharge from his member,
15: 9 **A** saddle on which the one with
15:12 **A** earthen vessel that the one with
15:24 If **a** man lies with her, and her impurity falls
16: 2 not to come just at **a** time into the sanctuary inside
17:10 of the aliens who reside among them eats **a** blood,
17:12 shall **a** alien who resides among you eat blood.
17:14 You shall not eat the blood of **a** creature,
18:21 not give **a** of your offspring to sacrifice them
18:23 You shall not have sexual relations with **a** animal
18:23 nor shall **a** woman give herself to an animal
18:24 Do not defile yourselves in **a** of these ways,
Lev 18:29 For whoever commits **a** of these
18:30 to commit **a** of these abominations that were done
19: 8 and **a** such person shall be cut off from the people.
19:18 not take vengeance or bear a grudge against **a**
19:28 You shall not make **a** gashes in your flesh for the dead or tattoo **a** marks
20: 2 **A** of the people of Israel,
20: 2 or of the aliens who reside in Israel, who give **a**
20: 6 If **a** turn to mediums and wizards,
20:16 If a woman approaches **a** animal
21: 5 or make **a** gashes in their flesh.
22: 5 and whoever touches **a** swarming thing
22: 5 or **a** human being by whom he may
22: 6 the person who touches **a** such shall be unclean
22:22 or put **a** of them on the altar as offerings by fire to
22:24 **A** animal that has its testicles bruised or crushed
22:25 nor shall you accept **a** such animals from
22:30 you shall not leave **a** of it until morning:
23:30 anyone who does **a** work during that entire day,
25:35 If **a** of your kin fall into difficulty
25:39 If **a** who are dependent on you become
25:47 and if **a** of your kin fall into difficulty with one
25:54 if they have not been redeemed in **a** of these ways,
27: 8 If **a** cannot afford the equivalent,
27: 9 **a** such that may be given to the LORD shall
27:11 If it concerns **a** unclean animal that may not
27:16 to the LORD **a** inherited landholding,
27:31 If persons wish to redeem **a** of their tithes,
Nu 1:51 **a** outsider who comes near shall be put to death.
3:10 **a** outsider who comes near shall be put to death.
3:38 **a** outsider who came near was to be put to death.
5:12 **a** man's wife goes astray and is unfaithful to him,
6: 3 and shall not drink **a** grape juice or eat grapes,
9:14 **A** alien residing among you who wishes to keep
16:15 and I have not harmed **a** one of them."
18: 7 **a** outsider who approaches shall be put to death.
18:20 nor shall you have **a** share among them;
18:31 You may eat it in **a** place,
19:11 of **a** human being shall be unclean seven days.
19:20 **A** who are unclean but do not purify themselves,
20:17 or drink water from **a** well;
21:22 we will not drink the water of **a** well;
24:11 but the LORD has denied you **a** reward."
25: 5 "Each of you shall kill **a**
30: 4 then all her vows shall stand, and **a** pledge
30: 6 by her vows or **a** thoughtless utterance of her lips
30:11 **a** pledge by which she bound herself shall stand.
30:13 **A** vow or **a** binding oath to deny herself,
31:19 of you has killed **a** person or touched a corpse,
35:22 or hurls **a** object without lying in wait,
35:23 while handling **a** stone that could cause death,
35:26 at **a** time go outside the bounds of the original city
36: 8 in **a** tribe of the Israelites shall marry one from
Dt 1:17 **A** case that is too hard for you, bring to me,
1:45 neither heed your voice nor pay you **a** attention.
2: 9 I will not give you **a** of its land as a possession,
4:16 in the form of **a** figure—
4:17 the likeness of **a** animal that is on the earth,
4:17 the likeness of **a** winged bird that flies in the air,
4:18 the likeness of **a** fish that is in the water under
4:33 Has **a** people ever heard the voice of
4:34 Or has **a** god ever attempted to go and take
5:14 you shall not do **a** work—
5:14 or your ox or your donkey, or **a** of your livestock,
5:25 we hear the voice of the LORD our God **a** longer,
6:14 **a** of the gods of the peoples who are all
7: 7 you were more numerous than **a** other people
10:16 and do not be stubborn **a** longer.
12:13 at **a** place you happen to see.
12:15 and eat meat within **a** of your towns,
12:17 **a** of your votive gifts that you vow,
12:21 as I have commanded you **a** of your herd or flock
13: 7 **a** of the gods of the peoples that are around you,
13: 8 you must not yield to or heed **a** such persons.
13:11 and never again do **a** such wickedness.
14: 3 You shall not eat **a** abhorrent thing.
14: 6 **A** animal that divides the hoof and has
14:11 You may eat **a** clean birds.
14:13 the buzzard, the kite, of **a** kind;
14:14 every raven of **a** kind;
14:15 the nighthawk, the sea gull, the hawk, of **a** kind;
14:18 the heron, of **a** kind; the hoopoe and the bat.
14:20 You may eat **a** clean winged creature.
15: 3 you must remit your claim on whatever **a** member
15: 7 **a** member of your community in **a** of your towns
15:21 But if it has **a** defect—
15:21 **a** serious defect, such as lameness or blindness—
16: 5 the passover sacrifice within **a** of your towns that
16:21 You shall not plant **a** tree as a sacred pole beside
17: 3 the sun or the moon or **a** of the host of heaven,
17: 8 **a** such matters of dispute in your towns—
18: 6 If a Levite leaves **a** of your towns,
18:16 "If I hear the voice of the LORD my God **a** more,
18:20 **a** prophet who speaks in the name of other gods,
19: 3 so that **a** homicide can flee to one of them.
19:15 **a** person of **a** crime or wrongdoing in connection
19:15 or wrongdoing in connection with **a** offense
22: 6 in **a** tree or on the ground, with fledglings or eggs,
23: 7 You shall not abhor **a** of the Edomites,
23: 7 You shall not abhor **a** of the Egyptians,
23: 9 you shall guard against **a** impropriety.
23:16 in **a** place they choose in **a** one of your towns,
23:18 of the LORD your God in payment for **a** vow,
23:24 but you shall not put **a** in a container.
24: 5 with the army or be charged with **a** related duty.
24:10 When you make your neighbor a loan of **a** kind,
26:13 I have neither transgressed nor forgotten **a**
Dt 26:14 I have not removed **a** of it while I was unclean;
26:14 and I have not offered **a** of it to the dead.
27:21 "Cursed be anyone who lies with **a** animal."
28:14 and if you do not turn aside from **a** of the words
28:55 giving to none of them **a** of the flesh
29:23 nothing sprouting, unable to support **a** vegetation,
Jos 2:11 and there was no courage left in **a** of us because
2:19 If **a** of you go out of the doors of your house into
2:19 hand is laid upon **a** who are with you in the house,
3: 4 do not come **a** nearer to it."
5: 1 and there was no longer **a** spirit in them,
6:18 so as not to covet and take **a** of the devoted things
10:21 no one dared to speak against **a** of the Israelites.
11:14 and they did not leave **a** who breathed.
Jdg 2:19 They would not drop **a** of their practices
2:21 before them **a** of the nations that Joshua left
3: 1 in Israel who had no experience of **a** war
11:25 Now are you **a** better than King Balak son
13:14 or strong drink, or eat **a** unclean thing.
20: 8 saying, "We will not **a** of us go to our tents,
20: 8 nor will **a** of us return to our houses.
21: 7 that we will not give them **a** of our daughters
21:18 Yet we cannot give **a** of our daughters to them
1Sa 10:23 he was head and shoulders taller than **a** of them.
13:22 nor spear was to be found in the possession of **a** of
14:52 and when Saul saw **a** strong or valiant warrior,
16:10 "The LORD has not chosen **a** of these."
22:15 or to **a** member of my father's house;
27: 1 then Saul will despair of seeking me **a** longer
30:22 we will not give them **a** of the spoil
2Sa 2: 1 "Shall I go up into **a** of the cities of Judah?"
2:28 or engaged in battle **a** further.
6:20 as **a** vulgar fellow might shamelessly uncover
7: 7 did I ever speak a word with **a** of the tribal leaders
10:19 to help the Ammonites **a** more.
17:12 he will not survive, nor will **a** of those with him.
19: 7 for you than **a** disaster that has come upon you
19:29 "Why speak **a** more of your affairs?
19:42 Or has he given us **a** gift?"
21:17 "You shall not go out with us to battle **a** longer,
1Ki 1: 6 His father had never at **a** time displeased him
2:36 and do not go out from there to **a** place whatever.
2:42 on the day you go out and go to **a** place whatever,
6: 7 nor ax nor **a** tool of iron was heard in the temple
8:16 from **a** of the tribes of Israel in which to build
8:37 if their enemy besieges them in **a** of their cities;
8:38 from **a** individual or from all your people Israel,
10:20 Nothing like it was ever made in **a** kingdom.
13:33 **a** who wanted to be priests he consecrated for
2Ki 5:17 or sacrifice to **a** god except the LORD.
6:33 Why should I hope in the LORD **a** longer?"
10:24 "Whoever allows **a** of those
12: 5 and let them repair the house wherever **a** need
12: 7 Now therefore do not accept **a** more money
12:12 as well as for **a** outlay for repairs of the house.
12:13 bowls, trumpets, or **a** vessels of gold, or of silver,
15:18 he did not depart all his days from **a** of the sins
18:33 Has **a** of the gods of the nations ever delivered
21: 8 the feet of Israel to wander **a** more out of the land
23:25 nor did **a** like him arise after him.
1Ch 1:43 of Edom before **a** king reigned over the Israelites:
17: 6 did I ever speak a word with **a** of the judges
19:19 not willing to help the Ammonites **a** more.
23:26 the tabernacle or **a** of the things for its service"—
23:28 and **a** work for the service of the house of God;
28:21 be every volunteer who has skill for **a** kind
29:25 as had not been on **a** king before him in Israel.
2Ch 2:14 to do all sorts of engraving and execute **a** design
6: 5 from **a** of the tribes of Israel in which to build
6:28 if their enemies besiege them in **a** of
6:29 from **a** individual or from all your people Israel,
9:19 The like of it was never made in **a** kingdom.
23:19 no one should enter who was in **a** way unclean.
32:15 for no god of **a** nation or kingdom has been able
Ezr 1: 3 **A** of those among you who are of his people—
6:12 has established his name there overthrow **a** king
7:13 that **a** of the people of Israel or their priests
7:24 or toll on **a** of the priests, the Levites, the singers,
10: 8 and that if **a** did not come within three days,
Ne 4: 3 **a** fox going up on it would break it down!"
10:31 of the land bring in merchandise or **a** grain on
13:19 to prevent **a** burden from being brought in on
Est 4:11 that if **a** man or woman goes to the king inside
4:13 the king's palace you will escape **a** more than all
8:11 and to annihilate **a** armed force of a people
Job 2:10 "You speak as **a** foolish woman would speak.
4:20 they perish forever without **a** regarding it.
6: 6 or is there **a** flavor in the juice of mallows?
6:13 and **a** resource is driven from me.
6:30 Is there **a** wrong on my tongue?
7:10 nor do their places know them **a** more.
8:12 they wither before **a** other plant.
10:18 Would that I had died before **a** eye had seen me,
20: 9 nor will their place behold them **a** longer.
21:22 Will **a** teach God knowledge,
22: 3 Is it **a** pleasure to the Almighty
25: 3 Is there **a** number to his armies?
27: 6 my heart does not reproach me for **a** of my days.
31: 7 and if **a** spot has clung to my hands;
32:21 not show partiality to **a** person or use flattery
33:12 I will answer you: God is greater than **a** mortal.
34:27 and had no regard for **a** of his ways,
34:31 I will not offend **a** more;
36: 5 "Surely God is mighty and does not despise **a**;
37:24 not regard **a** who are wise in their own conceit."
41: 9 **A** hope of capturing it will be disappointed;
Ps 14: 2 on humankind to see if there are **a** who are wise,

Ps 53: 2 on humankind to see if there are a who are wise,
74: 9 there is no longer a prophet,
82: 7 you shall die like mortals, and fall like a prince."
86: 8 O Lord, nor are there a works like yours.
107:18 they loathed a kind of food,
115:17 nor do a that go down into silence.
139:24 See if there is a wicked way in me,
141: 4 Do not turn my heart to a evil,
147:20 He has not dealt thus with a other nation;
Pr 3:31 the violent and do not choose a of their ways;
6: 7 Without having a chief or officer or ruler,
14:34 but sin is a reproach to a people.
30:30 and does not turn back before a;
Ecc 1:11 nor will there be a remembrance of people yet
2: 7 and flocks, more than a who had been before me
9: 6 never again will they have a share in all
SS 4:10 and the fragrance of your oils than a spice!
Isa 2: 4 neither shall they learn war a more.
30:20 yet your Teacher will not hide himself a more,
35: 9 nor shall a ravenous beast come up on it;
36:18 Has a of the gods of the nations saved their land
43:10 nor shall there be a after me.
44: 8 Is there a god besides me?
56: 2 not profaning it, and refrains from doing a evil.
64: 4 no eye has seen a God besides you,
Jer 9: 4 and put no trust in a of your kin;
12:17 But if a nation will not listen,
14:22 Can a idols of the nations bring rain?
17:22 of your houses on the sabbath or do a work,
18:18 and let us not heed a of his words."
20: 9 or speak a more in his name,"
23: 4 and they shall not fear a longer, or be dismayed,
23: 4 nor shall a be missing, says the LORD.
27: 8 if a nation or kingdom will not serve this king,
27:11 But a nation that will bring its neck under
27:13 concerning a nation that will not serve the king
29:26 of the LORD to control a madman who plays
33:20 If a of you could break my covenant with the day
33:26 and not choose a of his descendants as rulers over
34:14 you must set free a Hebrews who have been sold
36:24 nor a of his servants who heard all these words,
37:17 and said, "Is there a word from the LORD?"
44:26 the lips of a of the people of Judah in all the land
La 1:12 Look and see if there is a sorrow like my sorrow,
3: 2 and brought me into darkness without a light;
3:39 Why should a who draw breath complain about
4:12 nor did a of the inhabitants of the world,
Eze 1:17 in a of the four directions without veering
5:10 a of you who survive I will scatter to every wind.
6:12 a who are left and are spared shall die of famine.
7:16 If a survivors escape, they shall be found on
10:11 in a of the four directions without veering
12:24 be a false vision or flattering divination within
12:28 None of my words will be delayed a longer,
14: 4 A of those of the house
14: 7 For a of those of the house of Israel,
14:11 nor defile themselves a more
15: 3 a peg from it on which to hang a object?
16: 5 to do a of these things for you out of compassion
16:15 and lavished your whorings on a passer-by.
18:11 who does a of these things
18:23 Have I a pleasure in the death of the wicked,
20:28 wherever they saw a high hill or a leafy tree,
23:27 or remember Egypt a more.
32:13 and no human foot shall trouble them a more,
33: 4 then if a who hear the sound of the trumpet do
33: 6 and the sword comes and takes a of them,
37:23 or with a of their transgressions.
39: 7 I will not let my holy name be profaned a more;
39:10 to take wood out of the field or cut down a trees in
39:14 the land regularly and bury a invaders who remain
44:13 nor come near a of my sacred offerings,
46:16 If the prince makes a gift to a of his sons out
46:18 The prince shall not take a of the inheritance of
48:14 They shall not sell or exchange a of it;
Da 2:10 a thing of a magician or enchanter or Chaldean.
2:30 not been revealed to me because of a wisdom
2:30 that I have more than a other living being,
3:27 that the fire had not had a power over the bodies
3:28 and worship a god except their own God.
3:29 Therefore I make a decree: A people, nation,
6: 4 for complaint or a corruption,
6: 5 "We shall not find a ground for complaint
11:36 and consider himself greater than a god,
11:37 he shall pay no respect to a other god,
Am 8: 7 Surely I will never forget a of their deeds.
Mic 4: 3 neither shall they learn war a more;
5: 7 not depend upon people or wait for a mortal.
Hag 2:12 or oil, or a kind of food, does it become holy?
2:13 by contact with a dead body touches a of these,
2:19 Is there a seed left in the barn?
Zec 8:10 nor was there a safety from the foe
13: 3 And if a prophets appear again,
14:17 If a of the families of the earth do not go up
Mal 1: 9 Will he show favor to a of you?
2:12 a to witness or answer, or to bring an offering to
Mt 6:27 And can a of you by worrying add a single hour
16: 5 they had forgotten to bring a bread.
16:24 "If a want to become my followers,
18: 6 "If a of you put a stumbling block before one
19: 3 for a man to divorce his wife for a cause?"
22:46 to ask him a more questions.
Mk 2:26 which it is not lawful for a but the priests to eat,
5: 3 and no one could restrain him a more,
5:35 Why trouble the teacher a further?"
6:11 If a place will not welcome you and they refuse
8:14 Now the disciples had forgotten to bring a bread;
Mk 8:34 "If a want to become my followers,
9: 8 they saw no one with them a more, but only Jesus.
9:42 "If a of you put a stumbling block before one
12:34 After that no one dared to ask him a question.
16:18 ⟦and if they drink a deadly thing,⟧
Lk 4:35 of him without having done him a harm.
4:40 all those who had a who were sick
6: 4 which it is not lawful for a but the priests to eat,
8:49 do not trouble the teacher a longer."
9:23 "If a want to become my followers,
9:36 and in those days told no one a of
11:24 not finding a, it says, 'I will return to my house
12:25 And can a of you by worrying add a single hour
16: 2 because you cannot be my manager a longer.'
23:14 not found this man guilty of a of your charges
Jn 5:14 Do not sin a more, so that nothing worse happens
7:48 Has a one of the authorities or of the Pharisees
15:15 I do not call you servants a longer,
16:29 not in a figure of speech!
20:23 you forgive the sins of a, they are forgiven them;
20:23 if you retain the sins of a, they are retained."
Ac 2:45 and distribute the proceeds to all, as a had need.
4:32 no one claimed private ownership of a possessions,
4:35 and it was distributed to each as a had need.
5:29 "We must obey God rather than a human authority.
7: 5 He did not give him a of it as a heritage,
8:16 (for as yet the Spirit had not come upon a of them;
9: 2 so that if he found a who belonged to the Way,
13:15 if you have a word of exhortation for the people,
18:17 But Gallio paid no attention to a of these things.
20:24 But I do not count my life of a value to myself,
20:26 that I am not responsible for the blood of a of you,
24:18 without a crowd or disturbance.
24:23 to let him have some liberty and not to prevent a
25:18 they did not charge him with a of the crimes
25:24 shouting that he ought not to live a longer.
26: 8 Why is it thought incredible by a of you
Ro 3: 9 Are we a better off?
8:33 Who will bring a charge against God's elect?
13: 9 and a other commandment, are summed up in this
1Co 1: 7 in a spiritual gift as you wait for the revealing
3:11 For no one can lay a foundation other than the one
4: 3 be judged by you or by a human court.
6: 1 When a of you has a grievance against another,
7:12 that if a believer has a wife who is an unbeliever,
7:13 if a woman has a husband who is an unbeliever,
7:35 not to put a restraint upon you,
9: 7 Who at a time pays the expenses
9: 7 Who plants a vineyard and does not eat a
9: 7 who tends a flock and does not get a of its milk?
9:15 But I have made no use of a of these rights,
10:25 in the meat market without raising a question on
10:27 without raising a question on the ground
11: 4 A man who prays or prophesies with something
11: 5 but a woman who prays or prophesies
12:15 that would not make it a less a part of the body.
12:16 that would not make it a less a part of the body.
15:10 On the contrary, I worked harder than a of them—
16: 3 I will send a whom you approve with letters
2Co 1: 4 be able to console those who are in a affliction
7: 9 so that you were not harmed in a way by us.
11: 9 to refrain from burdening you in a way.
12:17 of you through a of those whom I sent to you?
13: 1 "A charge must be sustained by the evidence
Gal 1:16 I did not confer with a human being,
1:19 but I did not see a other apostle except James
Eph 5: 3 But fornication and impurity of a kind, or greed,
5: 5 has a inheritance in the kingdom of Christ and
Php 1:20 and hope that I will not be put to shame in a way,
2: 1 If then there is a encouragement in Christ, a
consolation from love, a sharing in the Spirit, a
compassion and sympathy,
4: 8 whatever is commendable, if there is a excellence
4:12 In a and all circumstances I have learned
4:14 In a case, it was kind of you to share my distress.
1Th 2: 9 not burden a of you while we proclaimed to you
2Th 2: 3 Let no one deceive you in a way;
3: 8 so that we might not burden a of you.
3:11 mere busybodies, not doing a work.
1Ti 1: 3 not to teach a different doctrine,
3:16 Without a doubt, the mystery
5:16 a believing woman has relatives who are really
widows,
5:19 Never accept a accusation against an elder except
Tit 1:16 disobedient, unfit for a good work.
2: 8 then a opponent will be put to shame,
3: 5 of a works of righteousness that we had done,
Phm 1:18 If he has wronged you in a way,
Heb 4:12 sharper than a two-edged sword,
8: 2 and not a mortal, has set up.
10: 2 would no longer have a consciousness of sin?
10:18 there is no longer a offering for sin.
Jas 1: 2 whenever you face trials of a kind,
1: 5 If a of you is lacking in wisdom, ask God,
1:23 For if a are hearers of the word and not doers,
1:26 If a think they are religious,
5:12 either by heaven or by earth or by a other oath,
5:13 Are a among you suffering? They should pray.
5:13 Are a cheerful? They should sing songs of praise.
5:14 Are a among you sick?
1Pe 4:16 Yet if a of you suffers as a Christian,
2Pe 1:15 that after my departure you may be able at a time
3: 9 but is patient with you, not wanting a to perish,
2Jn 1: 7 a such person is the deceiver and the antichrist!
Rev 2:24 to you I say, I do not lay on you a other burden;
7: 1 on earth or sea or against a tree.
7:16 the sun will not strike them, nor a scorching heat;
Rev 9: 4 grass of the earth or a green growth or a tree,
12: 8 there was no longer a place for them in heaven.
18:22 an artisan of a trade will be found in you no more;
22: 3 Nothing accursed will be found there a more.
Tob 1:17 of a of my people thrown out behind the wall
1:18 I also buried a whom King Sennacherib put
3:13 the earth and not listen to such reproaches a more.
3:14 that I am innocent of a defilement with a man,
4:18 and do not despise a useful counsel.
5:10 Tobit retorted, "What joy is left for me a more?
6: 8 and never remain with that person a longer.
6:13 that you, rather than a other man, are entitled
6:18 and will never be seen near her a more.
7:10 at liberty to give her to a other man than yourself,
Jdt 2:13 not to transgress a of your lord's commands,
4: 7 and it would be easy to stop a who tried to enter,
5:20 if there is a oversight in this people and they sin
7:22 they no longer had a strength.
8:15 to protect us within a time he pleases,
8:18 has there been a tribe or family or people or town
8:20 and so we hope that he will not disdain us or a
11: 3 In a event, you have come to safety.
11:13 for a of the people even to touch with their hands.
12:10 and did not invite a of his officers.
12:20 much more than he had ever drunk in a one day
AdE 4:11 of the empire know that if a man or woman goes
13:12 that it was not in insolence or pride or for a love
14:15 the bed of the uncircumcised and of a alien.
Wis 6:24 and a sensible king is the stability of a people.
7: 9 Neither did I liken to her a priceless gem,
7:24 For wisdom is more mobile than a motion;
12:13 For neither is there a god besides you,
12:14 nor can a king or monarch confront you
12:17 you rebuke a insolence among those who know it.
Sir 7:13 Refuse to utter a lie, for it is a habit that results
8: 7 Do not rejoice over a one's death;
22:18 a fool's resolve will not stand firm against a fear.
22:22 in these cases a friend will take to flight.
25:13 A wound, but not a wound of the heart!
25:13 A wickedness, but not the wickedness of a woman!
25:14 A suffering, but not suffering from those who hate!
25:14 a vengeance, but not the vengeance of enemies!
25:19 A iniquity is small compared to
26:12 and drinks from a water near him,
30:15 Health and fitness are better than a gold,
31:13 Therefore it sheds tears for a reason.
36:23 The stomach will take a food,
36:26 A woman will accept a man as a husband,
37:11 an idler about a work or with a seasonal laborer
37:11 pay no attention to a advice they give.
40:16 The reeds by a water or river bank are plucked up
40:16 or river bank are plucked up before a grass;
40:27 and covers a person better than a glory.
42:12 Do not let her parade her beauty before a man,
47:22 or cause a of his works to perish;
48:12 Never in his lifetime did he tremble before a ruler,
Bar 2:19 of a righteous deeds of our ancestors or our kings
LtJ 6:27 if a of these gods falls to the ground,
Aza 1:14 O Lord, have become fewer than a other nation,
1Mc 2:13 Why should we live a longer?"
3:28 and ordered them to be ready for a need.
8:24 If war comes first to Rome or to a of their allies
8:26 without receiving a return.
8:30 and a addition or deletion
10:33 from the land of Judah into a part of my kingdom,
10:35 from them or annoy a of them about a matter.
10:43 in Jerusalem, or in a of its precincts,
10:63 to bring charges against him about a matter,
10:63 and let no one annoy him for a reason."
13: 5 be it from me to spare my life in a time of distress,
13:39 We pardon a errors and offenses committed
13:40 And if a of you are qualified to be enrolled
14:44 the people or priests shall be permitted to nullify a
14:45 or rejects a of them shall be liable to punishment."
15: 8 to the royal treasury and a such future debts shall
15:21 a scoundrels have fled to you from their country,
2Mc 2:32 let us begin our narrative, without adding a more
3:13 said that this money must in a case be confiscated
3:29 of the divine intervention and deprived of a hope
3:38 "If you have a enemy or plotter
4:27 he did not pay regularly a of the money promised
5:10 of a sort and no place in the tomb of his ancestors.
9: 7 Yet he did not in a way stop his insolence,
9:18 But when his sufferings did not in a way abate,
9:24 or a unwelcome news came,
11:31 and none of them shall be molested in a way
1Es 1:24 the Lord beyond a other people or kingdom,
2: 5 If a of you, therefore, are of his people,
4:18 and silver or a other beautiful thing,
4:19 to gold or silver or a other beautiful thing.
5:53 And all who had made a vow to God began
6:32 that if anyone should transgress or nullify a of
8:22 no tribute or a other tax is to be laid on a of the
8:22 that no one has authority to impose a tax on them.
9: 4 if a did not meet there within two or three days,
3Mc 2:30 "But if a of them prefer to join those
3:19 and are unwilling to regard a action as sincere.
3:27 But those who shelter a of the Jews,
3:28 A who are willing to give information will receive
3:29 for all time to a mortal creature."
4:11 in a way claim to be inside the circuit of the city.
4:13 not omitting a detail of their punishment.
5: 6 that the Jews were left without a aid,
7: 5 without a inquiry or examination to put them
7: 8 with no one in a place doing them harm at all
7: 9 For you should know that if we devise a evil
7: 9 against them or cause them a grief at all,

3Mc 7:14 to a public and shameful death a whom they met
7:21 at all to confiscation of their belongings by a one.
7:22 so that those who held a of it restored it to them
2Es 2:23 When you find a who are dead,
2:43 taller than a of the others,
3:28 the deeds of those who inhabit Babylon a better?
4:40 her womb can keep the fetus within her a longer."
5:49 not bring forth a longer, so I have made
7:66 for a judgment, and they do not know of a torment
8:55 not ask a more questions about the great number
9:34 or the sea a ship, or a dish food or drink,
10:45 in the world before a offering was offered in it.
10:53 where there was no foundation of a building,
12:15 for a longer time than a other one of the twelve.
13:9 nor held a spear or a weapon of war;
15:10 I will not allow them to live a longer in the land
4Mc 4:23 a decree that if a of them were found observing
4:24 in a way to put an end to the people's observance
5:3 If a were not willing to eat defiling food,
5:13 of yours, it will excuse you from a transgression
5:17 that we should not transgress it in a respect.
5:23 so that we endure a suffering willingly;
7:22 that it is blessed to endure a suffering for the sake
8:2 and that a who ate defiling food would be freed
8:2 but if a were to refuse,
8:27 neither said a of these things nor
9:29 "How sweet is a kind of death for the religion
10:7 they were not able in a way to break his spirit,
15:6 more than a other mother, loved her children.
16:12 not wail with such a lament for a of them,
16:12 nor did she dissuade a of them from dying,
16:19 and therefore you ought to endure a suffering for

ANYBODY (1) [ANY]

Jdg 4:20 and if a comes and asks you, 'Is anyone here?'

ANYMORE (3) [ANY]

Lk 20:36 Indeed they cannot die a,
Rev 18:11 since no one buys their cargo a,
Tob 3:10 that I may die and not listen to these reproaches a."

ANYONE‡ (367) [ANY, ONE]

Ge 4:14 and a who meets me may kill me."
19:12 Then the men said to Lot, "Have you a else here?
19:12 sons, daughters, or a you have in the city—
31:32 a with whom you find your gods shall not live.
41:38 "Can we find a else like this—
Ex 20:7 LORD will not acquit a who misuses his name.
22:10 or is injured or is carried off, without a seeing it,
34:3 do not let a be seen throughout all the mountain;
Lev 2:1 When a presents a grain offering to the LORD,
4:2 When a sins unintentionally in any of
4:27 If a of the ordinary people
11:39 a who touches its carcass shall be unclean until
13:40 If a loses the hair from his head,
15:5 A who touches his bed shall wash his clothes,
15:33 for a, male or female, who has a discharge,
17:3 If a of the house of Israel slaughters an ox or
17:8 A of the house of Israel or of the aliens who reside
17:10 If a of the house of Israel or of
17:13 And a of the people of Israel,
18:6 None of you shall approach a near of kin
19:17 You shall not hate in your heart a of your kin;
22:3 If a among all your offspring
22:11 but if a priest acquires a by purchase,
22:18 When a of the house of Israel or of
22:21 a offers a sacrifice of well-being to the LORD,
23:29 For a who does not practice self-denial during
23:30 And a who does any work during that entire day,
24:15 A who curses God shall bear the sin.
24:17 A who kills a human being shall be put to death.
24:18 A who kills an animal shall make restitution for it,
24:19 A who maims another shall suffer the same injury
25:25 If a of your kin falls into difficulty and sells
25:29 If a sells a dwelling house in a walled city,
25:49 or a of their family who is of their own flesh
27:26 cannot be consecrated by a;
Nu 5:10 whatever a gives to the priest shall be his.
9:10 A of you or your descendants who is unclean
9:13 But a who is clean and is not on a journey,
11:32 the least a gathered was ten homers;
12:3 more so than a else on the face of the earth.
15:29 you shall have the same law for a who acts
19:22 a who touches it shall be unclean until evening.
35:15 a who kills a person without intent may flee there.
35:16 But a who strikes another with an iron object,
35:17 Or a who strikes another with a stone in hand
35:18 Or a who strikes another with a weapon of wood
35:30 If a kills another, the murderer shall be put
Dt 1:17 you shall not be intimidated by a,
5:11 LORD will not acquit a who misuses his name.
13:6 If a secretly entices you—
15:7 If there is among you a in need,
17:12 As for a who presumes to disobey
18:19 A who does not heed the words that
20:5 "Has a built a new house but not dedicated it?
20:6 Has a planted a vineyard but not
20:7 Has a become engaged to a woman but not
20:8 saying, "Is a afraid or disheartened?
21:23 for a hung on a tree is under God's curse.
22:8 on your house, if a should fall from it.
27:15 be a who makes an idol or casts an image,
27:16 "Cursed be a who dishonors father or mother."
27:17 be a who moves a neighbor's boundary marker."
27:18 be a who misleads a blind person on the road."
Dt 27:19 "Cursed be a who deprives the alien, the orphan,
27:20 "Cursed be a who lies with his father's wife,
27:21 "Cursed be a who lies with any animal."
27:22 "Cursed be a who lies with his sister,
27:23 "Cursed be a who lies with his mother-in-law."
27:24 be a who strikes down a neighbor in secret."
27:25 be a who takes a bribe to shed innocent blood."
27:26 be a who does not uphold the words of this law
28:29 be continually abused and robbed, without a
28:31 be given to your enemies, without a to help you.
Jos 6:26 the LORD be a who tries to build this city—
20:3 so that a who kills a person without intent or
20:9 that a who killed a person without intent
Jdg 4:20 and if anybody comes and asks you, 'Is a here?'
16:7 then I shall become weak, and be like a else."
16:11 then I shall become weak, and be like a else."
16:13 then I shall become weak, and be like a else."
16:17 I would become weak, and be like a else."
21:8 "Is there a from the tribes of Israel who did
21:18 "Cursed be a who gives a wife to Benjamin."
1Sa 2:13 to the people. When a offered sacrifice,
3:11 in Israel that will make both ears of a who hears
9:9 a who went to inquire of God would say, "Come,
12:4 or taken anything from the hand of a."
14:24 "Cursed be a who eats food before it is evening
14:28 saying, 'Cursed be a who eats food this day.'
25:29 If a should rise up to pursue you and
26:12 No one saw it, or knew it, nor did a awake;
2Sa 9:1 "Is there still a left of the house of Saul
9:3 "Is there a remaining of the house of Saul
14:10 The king said, "If a says anything to you,
15:2 a brought a suit before the king for judgment,
19:22 Shall a be put to death in Israel this day?
21:4 neither is it for us to put a to death in Israel."
1Ki 4:31 He was wiser than a else,
14:11 A belonging to Jeroboam who dies in the city,
14:11 and a who dies in the open country,
15:17 to prevent a from going out or coming in
16:4 A belonging to Baasha who dies in the city
16:4 and a of his who dies in the field the birds of
21:24 A belonging to Ahab who dies in the city
21:24 and a of his who dies in the open country the birds
2Ki 4:29 If you meet a, give no greeting, and if a greets you,
10:5 We will not make a king;
11:15 and kill with the sword a who follows her."
18:21 which will pierce the hand of a who leans on it.
2Ch 15:5 In those times it was not safe for a to go or come,
16:1 to prevent a from going out or coming into
23:6 Do not let a enter the house of the LORD except
23:14 a who follows her is to be put to the sword."
Ezr 6:11 Furthermore I decree that if a alters this edict,
Job 5:1 "Call now; is there a who will answer you?
31:19 if I have seen a perish for lack of clothing,
32:21 to any person or use flattery toward a.
34:23 nor appointed a time for a to go before God
34:31 has a said to God, 'I have endured punishment;
36:29 Can a understand the spreading of the clouds,
37:20 Did a ever wish to be swallowed up?
40:2 A who argues with God must respond."
Ps 12:1 O LORD, for there is no longer a who is godly;
109:12 nor a to pity his orphaned children.
Pr 3:30 Do not quarrel with a without cause,
15:23 To make an apt answer is a joy to a,
20:2 a who provokes him to anger forfeits life itself.
27:18 A who tends a fig tree will eat its fruit,
27:18 and a who takes care of a master will be honored.
28:19 A who tills the land will have plenty of bread,
28:24 A who robs father or mother and says,
29:20 There is more hope for a fool than for a like that.
Ecc 10:14 and who can tell a what the future holds?
Isa 36:6 which will pierce the hand of a who leans on it.
45:10 Woe to a who says to a father,
46:7 it does not answer or save a from trouble.
54:15 If a stirs up strife, it is not from me;
Jer 11:3 Cursed be a who does not heed the words
16:7 nor shall a give them the cup of consolation
21:12 the hand of the oppressor a who has been robbed,
22:3 the hand of the oppressor a who has been robbed.
29:32 he shall not have a living among this people to see
38:24 "Do not let a else know of this conversation,
41:4 after the murder of Gedaliah, before a knew of it,
49:18 no one shall live there, nor shall a settle in it.
49:33 no one shall live there, nor shall a settle in it.
50:40 so no one shall live there, nor shall a settle in her.
La 3:33 for he does not willingly afflict or grieve a.
Eze 18:7 does not oppress a, but restores to
18:16 does not wrong a, exacts no pledge,
18:32 For I have no pleasure in the death of a,
22:30 And I sought for a among them who would repair
39:15 a who sees a human bone shall set up a sign by it,
45:20 the seventh day of the month for a who has sinned
Da 6:7 that whoever prays to a, divine or human,
6:12 that a who prays to a, divine or human,
Am 6:10 in the innermost parts of the house, "Is a else
Zec 5:4 the house of a who swears falsely by my name;
13:6 And if a asks them, "What are these wounds
Mal 2:12 from the tents of Jacob a who does this—
2:15 do not let a be faithless to the wife of his youth.
3:8 Will a rob God? Yet you are robbing me!
Mt 5:32 But I say to you that a who divorces his wife,
5:39 But if a strikes you on the right cheek,
5:40 and if a wants to sue you and take your coat,
5:41 and if a forces you to go one mile,
5:42 do not refuse a who wants to borrow from you.
7:9 Is there a among you who,
8:4 Jesus said to him, "See that you say nothing to a;
10:14 If a will not welcome you or listen to your words,
Mt 11:6 And blessed is a who takes no offense at me."
11:15 Let a with ears listen!
11:27 and no one knows the Father except the Son and a
12:19 nor will a hear his voice in the streets.
13:9 Let a with ears listen!"
13:19 When a hears the word of the kingdom and does
13:43 Let a with ears listen!
16:20 the disciples not to tell a that he was the Messiah.
19:12 Let a accept this who can."
21:3 If a says anything to you, just say this,
21:44 and it will crush a on whom it falls."
22:46 that day did a dare to ask him any more questions.
24:23 Then if a says to you, 'Look!
27:15 a prisoner for the crowd, a whom they wanted.
Mk 1:44 "See that you say nothing to a;
4:9 And he said, "Let a with ears to hear listen!"
4:23 Let a with ears to hear listen!"
7:11 But you say that if a tells father or mother,
7:24 a house and did not want a to know he was there.
8:30 he sternly ordered them not to tell a about him.
9:30 He did not want a to know it;
11:3 If a says to you, 'Why are you doing this?'
11:16 not allow a to carry anything through the temple.
11:25 forgive, if you have anything against a;
13:21 And if a says to you at that time, 'Look!
15:6 a prisoner for them, a for whom they asked.
16:8 and they said nothing to a, for they were afraid.
Lk 3:11 has two coats must share with a who has none;
3:14 "Do not extort money from a by threats
4:6 and I give it to a I please.
6:29 If a strikes you on the cheek, offer the other also;
6:29 from a who takes away your coat do not withhold
6:30 and if a takes away your goods,
7:23 And blessed is a who takes no offense at me."
8:8 he called out, "Let a with ears to hear listen!"
8:51 he did not allow a to enter with him, except Peter,
9:21 and commanded them not to tell a,
10:6 And if a is there who shares in peace,
10:22 and a to whom the Son chooses to reveal him."
11:11 Is there a among you who,
14:15 "Blessed is a who will eat bread in the kingdom
14:35 Let a with ears to hear listen!"
16:18 "A who divorces his wife and marries another
17:1 but woe to a by whom they come!
17:31 a on the housetop who has belongings in
17:31 and likewise a in the field must not turn back.
18:4 I have no fear of God and no respect for a,
19:8 and if I have defrauded a of anything,
19:31 If a asks you, 'Why are you untying it?'
20:18 and it will crush a on whom it falls."
Jn 2:25 and needed no one to testify about a;
3:4 "How can a be born after having grown old?
5:23 A who does not honor the Son does not honor
5:24 I tell you, a who hears my word
6:37 and a who comes to me I will never drive away;
6:46 that a has seen the Father except the one who is
7:17 A who resolves to do the will of God
7:37 he cried out, "Let a who is thirsty come to me,
7:46 police answered, "Never has a spoken like this!"
8:7 ⟦"Let a among you who is without sin be the first⟧
8:33 of Abraham and have never been slaves to a.
9:22 that a who confessed Jesus to be
9:32 the world began has it been heard that a opened
10:1 a who does not enter the sheepfold by the gate
11:57 the Pharisees had given orders that a who knew
12:47 I do not judge a who hears my words and does
16:30 and do not need to have a question you;
18:31 "We are not permitted to put a to death."
Ac 4:17 let us warn them to speak no more to a
8:19 so that a on whom I lay my hands may receive
10:28 that I should not call a profane or unclean.
10:35 but in every nation a who fears him
10:47 "Can a withhold the water for baptizing these
19:38 the artisans with him have a complaint against a,
24:12 with a in the temple or stirring up a crowd either
25:16 the custom of the Romans to hand over a before
Ro 5:7 Indeed, rarely will a die for a righteous person—
6:16 if you present yourselves to a as obedient slaves,
8:9 A who does not have the Spirit of Christ does
12:17 Do not repay a evil for evil,
14:14 but it is unclean for a who thinks it unclean.
1Co 1:16 I do not know whether I baptized a else.)
3:12 Now if a builds on the foundation with gold,
3:17 If a destroys God's temple,
5:11 to you not to associate with a who bears the name
6:17 a united to the Lord becomes one spirit with him.
7:18 Was a at the time of his call already circumcised?
7:18 Was a at the time of his call uncircumcised?
7:36 If a thinks that he is not behaving properly
7:39 husband dies, she is free to marry a she wishes,
8:2 A who claims to know something does not
8:3 but a who loves God is known by him.
11:16 But if a is disposed to be contentious—
14:7 how will a know what is being played?
14:9 how will a know what is being said?
14:16 how can a in the position of an outsider say
14:27 If a speaks in a tongue, let there be only two or
14:37 A who claims to be a prophet,
14:38 A who does not recognize this is not to
16:22 Let a be accursed who has no love for the Lord.
2Co 2:5 if a has caused pain, he has caused it not to me,
2:10 A whom you forgive, I also forgive.
5:17 So if a is in Christ, there is a new creation:
11:9 I did not burden a, for my needs were supplied by
11:21 But whatever a dares to boast of—
Gal 1:9 if a proclaims to you a gospel contrary
6:1 My friends, if a is detected in a transgression,

Php 3: 4 If a else has reason to be confident in the flesh,
Col 2:16 Therefore do not let a condemn you in matters
2:18 Do not let a disqualify you,
3:13 if a has a complaint against another,
1Th 4: 9 you do not need to have a write to you,
2Th 3:10 A unwilling to work should not eat.
1Ti 5:22 Do not ordain a hastily, and do not participate in
Tit 3:10 to do with a who causes divisions,
Heb 10:28 A who has violated the law of Moses dies
10:38 My soul takes no pleasure in a who shrinks back."
13: 6 What can a do to me?"
Jas 1:12 Blessed is a who endures temptation.
2:13 be without mercy to a who has shown no mercy;
3: 2 A who makes no mistakes in speaking is perfect,
4:17 A, then, who knows the right thing to do and fails
5:15 and a who has committed sins will be forgiven.
5:19 if a among you wanders from the truth
1Pe 3:15 to make your defense to a who demands from you
2Pe 1: 9 a who lacks these things is nearsighted and blind,
1Jn 2: 1 But if a does sin, we have an advocate with
2:27 and so you do not need a to teach you.
3:17 in a who has the world's goods and sees a brother
2Jn 1:10 into the house or welcome a who comes to you
Rev 2: 7 Let a who has an ear listen to what the Spirit
2:11 Let a who has an ear listen to what the Spirit
2:17 Let a who has an ear listen to what the Spirit
2:29 Let a who has an ear listen to what the Spirit
3: 6 Let a who has an ear listen to what the Spirit
3:13 Let a who has an ear listen to what the Spirit
3:22 Let a who has an ear listen to what the Spirit
11: 5 And if a wants to harm them,
11: 5 a who wants to harm them must be killed
13: 9 Let a who has an ear listen:
13:18 let a with understanding calculate the number of
14:11 and its image and for a who receives the mark
20:15 and a whose name was not found written in
21:27 nor a who practices abomination or falsehood,
22:17 Let a who wishes take the water of life as a gift.
22:18 if a adds to them, God will add to that person
22:19 if a takes away from the words of the book
Tob 4: 7 Do not turn your face away from a who is poor,
4:15 And what you hate, do not do to a.
6:15 but it kills a who desires to approach her.
8:12 he is dead, let us bury him without a knowing it."
Jdt 11: 1 for I have never hurt a who chose
AdE 5:12 not invite a to the dinner with the king except me;
13:14 and I will not bow down to a but you,
Wis 4: 9 but understanding is gray hair for a,
6: 7 For the Lord of all will not stand in awe of a,
8: 7 if a loves righteousness, her labors are virtues;
8: 8 And if a longs for wide experience,
12:11 of a that you left them unpunished for their sins.
12:15 to your power to condemn a who does not deserve
Sir 2:10 has a trusted in the Lord and been disappointed?
2:10 Or has a persevered in the fear of the Lord
2:10 Or has a called upon him and been neglected?
8:19 Do not reveal your thoughts to a,
11: 2 or loathe a because of appearance alone.
15:20 He has not commanded a to be wicked,
15:20 and he has not given a permission to sin.
22: 2 a that picks it up will shake it off his hand.
27: 7 Do not praise a before he speaks,
28: 3 Does a harbor anger against another,
33:21 do not let a take your place.
33:30 Do not be overbearing toward a,
34: 2 so is a who believes in dreams.
46:19 so much as a pair of shoes, have I taken from a!"
48:12 nor could a intimidate him at all.
49:15 Nor was a ever born like Joseph;
LtJ 6:14 but is unable to destroy a who offends it.
6:18 on every side against a who has offended a king,
6:27 If a sets it upright, it cannot move itself;
6:36 They cannot save a from death or rescue the weak
6:40 Why then must a think that they are gods,
6:44 Why then must a think that they are gods,
6:56 then must a admit or think that they are gods?
6:58 A who can will strip them of their gold and silver
6:64 not able either to decide a case or to do good to a.
1Mc 1:57 A found possessing the book of the covenant,
1:57 or a who adhered to the law,
2:41 "Let us fight against a who comes to attack us on
2Mc 1:19 that the place was unknown to a.
13: 6 to destruction a guilty of sacrilege or notorious
1Es 6:32 that if a should transgress or nullify any of
2Es 3:31 and have not shown to a how your way may
5:11 or a who does right, passed through you?'
7:*105* neither shall a lay a burden on another;
8:59 For the Most High did not intend that a should

ANYONE'S (3) [ANY, ONE]

Lev 7: 8 the priest who offers a burnt offering shall keep
2Co 6: 3 We are putting no obstacle in a way,
2Th 3: 8 and we did not eat a bread without paying for it;

ANYTHING‡ (196) [ANY, THING]

Ge 14:23 a thread or a sandal-thong or a that is yours,
18:14 Is a too wonderful for the LORD?
22:12 "Do not lay your hand on the boy or do a to him;
24:50 we cannot speak to you a bad or good.
30:31 Jacob said, "You shall not give me a;
39: 6 he had no concern for a but the food that he ate.
39: 8 my master has no concern about a in the house,
39: 9 nor has he kept back a from me except yourself,
39:23 The chief jailer paid no heed to a that was
Ex 12:10 a that remains until the morning you shall burn.
20: 4 whether in the form of a that is in heaven above,
Ex 20:17 or donkey, or a that belongs to your neighbor.
23:18 the blood of my sacrifice with a leavened,
35:29 to bring a for the work that
36: 6 to make a else as an offering for the sanctuary."
Lev 6: 5 or a else about which you have sworn falsely,
6:18 a that touches them shall become holy.
11:10 But a in the seas or the streams that does
11:32 And a upon which any of them falls
13:48 or in a skin or in a made of skin,
13:49 whether in warp or woof or in skin or in a made
13:52 or a of skin, for it is a spreading leprous disease;
13:53 in warp or woof or in a of skin,
13:57 in warp or woof, or in a of skin, it is spreading;
13:58 or a of skin from which the disease disappears
13:59 either in warp or woof, or in a of skin,
15: 6 All who sit on a on which the one with
15:10 All who touch a that was under him shall
15:22 Whoever touches a upon which
15:23 whether it is the bed or a upon which she sits,
19: 6 and a left over until the third day shall
19:26 You shall not eat a with its blood.
20:25 or by bird or by a with which the ground teems,
22: 4 Whoever touches a made unclean by a corpse or
22:20 You shall not offer a that has a blemish,
22:22 A blind, or injured, or maimed,
Nu 22:16 'Do not let a hinder you from coming to me;
22:38 but do I have power to say just a?
Dt 4: 2 You must neither add a to what I command you
nor take away a from it,
4:18 the likeness of a that creeps on the ground,
4:23 not to make for yourselves an idol in the form of a
4:25 by making an idol in the form of a,
4:32 has a so great as this ever happened or has its
5: 8 whether in the form of a that is in heaven above,
5:21 or donkey, or a that belongs to your neighbor.
12:32 do not add to it or take a from it.
13:17 not let a devoted to destruction stick to your hand,
14:21 You shall not eat a that dies of itself;
16: 3 You must not eat with it a leavened.
17: 1 or a sheep that has a defect, a seriously wrong;
20:16 you must not let a that breathes remain alive.
22: 3 with a else that your neighbor loses and you find.
23:14 so that he may not see a indecent among you
23:19 interest on provisions, interest on a that is lent.
27:15 a abhorrent to the LORD, the work of an artisan,
28:32 for them all day but be powerless to do a.
28:57 she is eating them in secret for lack of a else,
Jdg 11: 2 "You shall not inherit a in our father's house;
13: 4 to drink wine or strong drink, or to eat a unclean,
13:14 She may not eat of a that comes from the vine.
18:10 a place where there is no lack of a on earth."
1Sa 3:17 if you hide a from me of all that he told you."
10:16 he did not tell him a.
12: 4 not defrauded us or oppressed us or taken a from
12: 5 that you have not found a in my hand."
19: 3 if I learn a I will tell you."
20:26 Saul did not say a that day;
21: 2 'No one must know a of the matter
22:15 the king impute a to his servant or to any member
25:15 we never missed a when we were in the fields,
30:19 sons or daughters, spoil or a that had been taken;
2Sa 3:35 I taste bread or a else before the sun goes down!"
13: 2 and it seemed impossible to Amnon to do a to her.
13:12 do not do a so vile!
14:10 The king said, "If anyone says a to you,
14:18 "Do not withhold from me a I ask you."
14:19 one cannot turn right or left from a that my lord
1Ki 10:21 it was not considered as a in the days of Solomon.
15: 5 not turn aside from a that he commanded him all
22: 8 for he never prophesies a favorable about me,
22:18 that he would not prophesy a favorable about me,
2Ki 10: 5 we will do a you say.
2Ch 8:15 the priests and Levites regarding a at all,
9:20 not considered as a in the days of Solomon.
18: 7 for he never prophesies a favorable about me,
18:17 that he would not prophesy a favorable about me,
Ne 4:11 or see a before we come upon them and kill them
Job 31:16 "If I have withheld a that the poor desired,
33:32 If you have a to say, answer me;
Ps 101: 3 I will not set before my eyes a that is base.
Ecc 3:14 nothing can be added to it, nor a taken from it;
6: 5 moreover it has not seen the sun or known a;
7:14 so that mortals may not find out a that will come
12:12 Of a beyond these, my child, beware.
Isa 19:15 will be able to do a for Egypt.
Jer 32:27 is a too hard for me?
38:14 do not hide a from me."
42:21 not obeyed the voice of the LORD your God in a
La 4: 4 the children beg for food, but no one gives them a.
Eze 15: 3 Is wood taken from it to make a?
15: 4 and the middle of it is charred, is it useful for a?
15: 5 can it ever be used for a!
29:18 yet neither he nor his army got a from Tyre to pay
44:18 not bind themselves with a that causes sweat.
44:31 The priests shall not eat of a,
Jnh 3: 7 no herd or flock, shall taste a.
Mt 5:13 It is no longer good for a,
5:37 a more than this comes from the evil one.
9:33 "Never has a like this been seen in Israel."
18:19 if two of you agree on earth about a you ask,
21: 3 If anyone says a to you, just say this,
Mk 2:12 saying, "We have never seen a like this!"
4:22 nor is a secret, except to come to light.
7: 4 not eat a from the market unless they wash it;
7:12 then you no longer permit doing a for a father
8: 1 when there was again a great crowd without a
8:23 he asked him, "Can you see a?"
Mk 9:22 you are able to do a, have pity on us and help us."
11:13 he went to see whether perhaps he would find a
11:16 and he would not allow anyone to carry a through
11:25 forgive, if you have a against anyone;
13:15 not go down or enter the house to take a away;
Lk 8:17 nor is a secret that will not become known
11: 7 I cannot get up and give you a.'
11: 8 not get up and give him a because he is his friend,
15:16 and no one gave him a.
19: 8 and if I have defrauded anyone of a,
19:48 but they did not find a they could do,
22:35 bag, or sandals, did you lack a?"
24:41 he said to them, "Have you a here to eat?"
Jn 1:46 "Can a good come out of Nazareth?"
3:27 "No one can receive a except what has been given
14:14 If in my name you ask me for a, I will do it.
16:23 I tell you, if you ask a of the Father in my name,
16:24 Until now you have not asked for a in my name.
Ac 10:14 I have never eaten a that is profane or unclean."
17:25 as though he needed a, since he himself gives
19:39 If there is a further you want to know,
20:20 I did not shrink from doing a helpful,
24:19 if they have a against me.
25: 5 and if there is a wrong about the man,
28:21 or spoken a evil about you.
Ro 8:39 nor depth, nor a else in all creation,
9:11 or had done a good or bad (so that God's purpose
13: 8 Owe no one a, except to love one another;
14: 2 Some believe in eating a,
14:21 or do a that makes your brother or sister stumble.
15:18 to speak of a except what Christ has accomplished
1Co 3: 7 the one who plants nor the one who waters is a,
4: 4 I am not aware of a against myself,
4: 7 For who sees a different in you?
6:12 but I will not be dominated by a.
9:12 but we endure a rather than put an obstacle in
10:19 food sacrificed to idols is a, or that an idol is a?
14:35 If there is a they desire to know,
2Co 2:10 What I have forgiven, if I have forgiven a,
3: 5 Not that we are competent of ourselves to claim a
13: 7 we pray to God that you may not do a wrong—
13: 8 For we cannot do a against the truth,
Gal 5: 6 nor uncircumcision counts for a;
6:14 of a except the cross of our Lord Jesus Christ,
6:15 For neither circumcision nor uncircumcision is a;
Eph 5:27 without a spot or wrinkle or a of the kind—
Php 3:15 and if you think differently about a,
4: 6 Do not worry about a, but in everything by prayer
4: 8 if there is any excellence and if there is a worthy
1Th 5: 1 you do not need to have a written to you.
Phm 1:18 If he has wronged you in any way, or owes you a,
Jas 1:7,8 must not expect to receive a from the Lord.
1Jn 5:14 that if we ask a according to his will, he hears us.
Tob 2:13 for we have no right to eat a stolen."
4: 3 and do not grieve her in a.
7:11 nor drink a until you settle the things that pertain
12:19 I really did not eat or drink a—
Jdt 8:13 but you will never learn a!
AdE 6: 3 "You have not done a for him."
Wis 10:12 that godliness is more powerful than a else.
11:24 for you would not have made a if you had hated it.
11:25 would a have endured if you had not willed it?
11:25 Or how would a not called forth
Sir 8:12 but if you do lend a, count it as a loss.
25: 3 how can you find a in your old age?
50:29 they will be equal to a,
Bel 1: 7 and it never ate or drank a."
1Mc 8:30 both parties shall determine to add or delete a,
10:35 No one shall have authority to exact a from them
2Mc 9:24 if a unexpected happened
12:18 he had by then left there without accomplishing a,
1Es 4:39 but it does what is righteous instead of a
3Mc 2: 3 and you judge those who have done a in insolence
2: 9 though you have no need of a;
2Es 2:28 but they shall not be able to do a against you,
4Mc 2: 5 "You shall not covet your neighbor's wife or a
9:12 without accomplishing a,

ANYWHERE (2) [ANY, WHERE]

Ge 19:17 do not look back or stop a in the Plain;
2Ki 5:25 He answered, "Your servant has not gone a at all."

APACE (KJV) See HASTE, KEPT

APAME (1)

1Es 4:29 Yet I have seen him with A, the king's concubine,

APART‡ (79) [PART]

Ge 21:28 Abraham set a seven ewe lambs of the flock.
21:29 of these seven ewe lambs that you have set a?"
30:40 and he put his own droves a,
49:26 the brow of him who was set a from his brothers.
Ex 8:22 But on that day I will set a the land of Goshen,
13:12 you shall set a to the LORD all that first opens
Lev 19:24 In the fourth year all their fruit shall be set a
20:25 which I have set a for you to hold unclean.
23:38 a from the sabbaths of the LORD, and a from your
gifts, and a from all your votive offerings, and a
from all your freewill offerings,
Nu 6:21 a from what else they can afford.
16:31 the ground under them was split a.
18:24 which they set a as an offering to the LORD.
18:26 you shall set a an offering from it to the LORD,
18:28 also shall set a an offering to the LORD from all
18:29 you shall set a every offering due to the LORD;

Nu 18:30 When you have set **a** the best of it,
Dt 4:41 Then Moses set **a** on the east side of
7:26 or you will be set **a** for destruction like it.
7:26 for it is set **a** for destruction.
10: 8 the LORD set **a** the tribe of Levi to carry the ark
14:22 Set **a** a tithe of all the yield of your seed
19: 2 you shall set **a** three cities in the land that
19: 7 I command you: You shall set **a** three cities.
Jos 16: 9 with the towns that were set **a** for the Ephraimites
20: 7 So they set **a** Kedesh in Galilee in the hill country
Jdg 8:26 of gold (**a** from the crescents and the pendants and
14: 6 tore the lion **a** barehanded as one might tear **a**
20:17 And the Israelites, **a** from Benjamin,
1Ch 23:13 Aaron was set **a** to consecrate
25: 1 the officers of the army also set **a** for the service
Ezr 8:20 whom David and his officials had set **a** to attend
8:24 Then I set **a** twelve of the leading priests:
Ne 12:47 They set **a** that which was for the Levites;
12:47 and the Levites set **a** that which was for
Ps 4: 3 that the LORD has set **a** the faithful for himself;
7: 2 or like a lion they will tear me **a**;
16: 2 I have no good **a** from you."
50:22 then, you who forget God, or I will tear you **a**,
141: 7 a rock that one breaks **a** and shatters on the land,
Ecc 2:25 for **a** from him who can eat
Jer 12: 3 and set them **a** for the day of slaughter.
Eze 39:14 They will set **a** men to pass through
45: 6 Alongside the portion set **a** as
48: 8 shall be the portion that you shall set **a**,
48: 9 that you shall set **a** for the LORD shall
48:20 The whole portion that you shall set **a** shall
Mt 10:29 of them will fall to the ground **a** from your Father.
Mk 1:10 the heavens torn **a** and the Spirit descending like
5: 4 but the chains he wrenched **a**,
9: 2 and led them up a high mountain **a**,
Jn 3: 2 for no one can do these signs that you do **a** from
15: 5 because **a** from me you can do nothing.
Ac 13: 2 "Set **a** for me Barnabas and Saul for the work
Ro 1: 1 called to be an apostle, set **a** for the gospel of God,
2:12 All who have sinned **a** from the law will also
perish **a** from the law,
3:21 But now, **a** from law, the righteousness
3:28 For we hold that a person is justified by faith **a**
4: 6 of those to whom God reckons righteousness **a**
7: 8 **A** from the law sin lies dead.
7: 9 I was once alive **a** from the law,
1Co 4: 8 Quite **a** from us you have become kings!
Gal 1:15 who had set me **a** before I was born and called me
Heb 11:40 **a** from us, be made perfect.
Jas 2:18 Show me your faith **a** from your works,
2:20 that faith **a** from works is barren?
Tob 6:18 she was set **a** for you before the world was made.
Wis 11:20 Even **a** from these, people could fall at
Sir 6: 2 or you may be torn **a** as by a bull.
47: 2 As the fat is set **a** from the offering of well-being,
47: 2 so David was set **a** from the Israelites.
1Es 4:44 which Cyrus set **a** when he began
4:57 from Babylon all the vessels that Cyrus had set **a**;
8:54 Then I set **a** twelve of the leaders of the priests,
2Es 3:16 You set **a** Jacob for yourself,

APARTMENT (1)

Jer 36:22 Now the king was sitting in his winter **a** (it was

APELLES (1)

Ro 16:10 Greet **A**, who is approved in Christ.

APES (2)

1Ki 10:22 silver, ivory, **a**, and peacocks.
2Ch 9:21 silver, ivory, **a**, and peacocks.

APHAIREMA (1)

1Mc 11:34 the three districts of **A** and Lydda and Rathamin;

APHARSACHITES, APHARSATHCHITES (KJV) See ENVOYS

APHARSITES (KJV) See PERSIANS

APHEK (8)

Jos 12:18 the king of **A** one the king of Lasharon one
13: 4 and Mearah that belongs to the Sidonians, to **A**,
19:30 **A**, and Rehob—twenty-two towns with their
1Sa 4: 1 and the Philistines encamped at **A**.
29: 1 Now the Philistines gathered all their forces at **A**,
1Ki 20:26 and went up to **A** to fight against Israel.
20:30 The rest fled into the city of **A**;
2Ki 13:17 the Arameans in **A** until you have made an end

APHEKAH (1)

Jos 15:53 Janim, Beth-tappuah, **A**,

APHERRA (1)

1Es 5:34 the descendants of **A**, the descendants of Barodis,

APHIAH (1)

1Sa 9: 1 of Abiel son of Zeror son of Becorath son of **A**,

APHIK (1)

Jdg 1:31 or of Achzib, or of Helbah, or of **A**, or of Rehob;

APHRAH (KJV) See BETH-LEAPHRAH

APHSES (KJV) See HAPPIZZEZ

APIECE (4) [PIECE]

Ex 16:22 as much food, two omers **a**.
Nu 3:47 you shall accept five shekels **a**,
7:86 weighing ten shekels **a** according to the shekel of
Eze 41:24 The doors had two leaves **a**,

APIS (1)

Jer 46:15 Why has **A** fled? Why did your bull

APOLLONIA (1)

Ac 17: 1 and Silas had passed through Amphipolis and **A**,

APOLLONIUS (20)

1Mc 3:10 **A** now gathered together Gentiles and
3:12 and Judas took the sword of **A**,
10:69 And Demetrius appointed **A** the governor
10:74 When Jonathan heard the words of **A**,
10:75 for **A** had a garrison in Joppa.
10:77 **A** heard of it, he mustered three thousand cavalry
10:79 Now **A** had secretly left a thousand cavalry
2Mc 3: 5 he went to **A** of Tarsus,
3: 7 When **A** met the king, he told him of the money
4: 4 that the rivalry was serious and that **A** son
4:21 When **A** son of Menestheus was sent to Egypt for
5:24 Antiochus sent **A**, the captain of the Mysians,
12: 2 Timothy and **A** son of Gennaeus,
4Mc 4: 2 So he came to **A**, governor of Syria, Phoenicia,
4: 4 When **A** learned the details of these things,
4: 8 But, uttering threats, **A** went on to the temple.
4:10 and while **A** was going up with his armed forces
4:11 Then **A** fell down half dead in the temple area
4:13 that **A** had been overcome by human treachery
4:14 So **A**, having been saved beyond all expectations,

APOLLOPHANES (1)

2Mc 10:37 and his brother Chaereas, and **A**.

APOLLOS (10)

Ac 18:24 Now there came to Ephesus a Jew named **A**,
19: 1 While **A** was in Corinth, Paul passed through
1Co 1:12 or "I belong to **A**," or "I belong to Cephas,"
3: 4 "I belong to Paul," and another, "I belong to **A**,"
3: 5 What then is **A**? What is Paul?
3: 6 I planted, **A** watered, but God gave the growth.
3:22 whether Paul or **A** or Cephas or the world or life
4: 6 I have applied all this to **A** and myself
16:12 Now concerning our brother **A**,
Tit 3:13 Make every effort to send Zenas the lawyer and **A**

APOLLYON (1) [=ABADDON]

Rev 9:11 and in Greek he is called **A**.

APOLOGIES (1) [APOLOGIZED]

Sir 13: 3 a poor person suffers wrong, and must add **a**.

APOLOGIZED (1) [APOLOGIES]

Ac 16:39 so they came and **a** to them.

APOSTASIES (4) [APOSTASY]

Jer 2:19 and your **a** will convict you.
5: 6 their transgressions are many, their **a** are great.
14: 7 our **a** indeed are many, and we have sinned
Eze 37:23 from all the **a** into which they have fallen,

APOSTASY (1) [APOSTASIES, APOSTATIZED]

1Mc 2:15 the **a** came to the town of Modein

APOSTATIZED (1) [APOSTASY]

3Mc 1: 3 by birth who later changed his religion and **a** from

APOSTLE‡ (21) [APOSTLES, APOSTLES', APOSTLESHIP, SUPER-APOSTLES]

Ro 1: 1 Paul, a servant of Jesus Christ, called to be an **a**,
11:13 Inasmuch then as I am an **a** to the Gentiles,
1Co 1: 1 to be an **a** of Christ Jesus by the will of God,
9: 1 Am I not an **a**?
9: 2 If I am not an **a** to others, at least I am to you;
15: 9 the least of all the apostles, unfit to be called an **a**,
2Co 1: 1 Paul, an **a** of Christ Jesus by the will of God,
12:12 The signs of a true **a** were performed among you
Gal 1: 1 Paul an **a**—sent neither by human
1:19 but I did not see any other **a** except James
2: 8 through Peter making him an **a** to the circumcised
Eph 1: 1 Paul, an **a** of Christ Jesus by the will of God,
Col 1: 1 Paul, an **a** of Christ Jesus by the will of God,
1Ti 1: 1 Paul, an **a** of Christ Jesus by the command of God
2: 7 appointed a herald and an **a** (I am telling the truth,
2Ti 1: 1 Paul, an **a** of Christ Jesus by the will of God,
1:11 For this gospel I was appointed a herald and an **a**
Tit 1: 1 Paul, a servant of God and an **a** of Jesus Christ,
Heb 3: 1 Jesus, the **a** and high priest of our confession,
1Pe 1: 1 Peter, an **a** of Jesus Christ,
2Pe 1: 1 Simeon Peter, a servant and **a** of Jesus Christ,

APOSTLES‡ (52) [APOSTLE]

Mt 10: 2 These are the names of the twelve **a**:
Mk 3:14 And he appointed twelve, whom he also named **a**,
6:30 The **a** gathered around Jesus,
Lk 6:13 and chose twelve of them, whom he also named **a**:
9:10 On their return the **a** told Jesus all they had done.
11:49 'I will send them prophets and **a**,
17: 5 The **a** said to the Lord, "Increase our faith!"
22:14 he took his place at the table, and the **a** with him.
24:10 the other women with them who told this to the **a**.
Ac 1: 2 the Holy Spirit to the **a** whom he had chosen.
1:26 and he was added to the eleven **a**.
2:37 to the heart and said to Peter and to the other **a**,
2:43 and signs were being done by the **a**.
4:33 the **a** gave their testimony to the resurrection of
4:36 Joseph, to whom the **a** gave the name Barnabas
5:12 among the people through the **a**.
5:18 arrested the **a** and put them in the public prison.
5:29 But Peter and the **a** answered,
5:40 and when they had called in the **a**,
6: 6 They had these men stand before the **a**,
8: 1 the **a** were scattered throughout the countryside
8:14 Now when the **a** at Jerusalem heard
9:27 But Barnabas took him, brought him to the **a**,
11: 1 the **a** and the believers who were in Judea heard
14: 4 some sided with the Jews, and some with the **a**.
14: 6 the **a** learned of it and fled to Lystra and Derbe,
14:14 When the **a** Barnabas and Paul heard of it,
15: 2 up to Jerusalem to discuss this question with the **a**
15: 4 they were welcomed by the church and the **a** and
15: 6 The **a** and the elders met together
15:22 Then the **a** and the elders,
15:23 "The brothers, both the **a** and the elders,
16: 4 the decisions that had been reached by the **a**
Ro 16: 7 they are prominent among the **a**,
1Co 4: 9 I think that God has exhibited us **a** as last of all,
9: 5 as do the other **a** and the brothers of the Lord
12:28 And God has appointed in the church first **a**,
12:29 Are all **a**? Are all prophets?
15: 7 Then he appeared to James, then to all the **a**.
15: 9 For I am the least of the **a**,
2Co 11:13 For such boasters are false **a**, deceitful workers,
disguising themselves as **a** of Christ.
Gal 1:17 up to Jerusalem to those who were already **a**
Eph 2:20 built upon the foundation of the **a** and prophets,
3: 5 now been revealed to his holy **a** and prophets by
4:11 The gifts he gave were that some would be **a**,
1Th 2: 7 we might have made demands as **a** of Christ.
2Pe 3: 2 of the Lord and Savior spoken through your **a**.
Jude 1:17 the predictions of the **a** of our Lord Jesus Christ;
Rev 2: 2 you have tested those who claim to be **a** but are
18:20 O heaven, you saints and **a** and prophets!
21:14 and on them are the twelve names of the twelve **a**

APOSTLES' (5) [APOSTLE]

Ac 2:42 They devoted themselves to the **a** teaching
4:35 They laid it at the **a** feet,
4:37 then brought the money, and laid it at the **a** feet.
5: 2 and brought only a part and laid it at the **a** feet.
8:18 through the laying on of the **a** hands,

APOSTLESHIP (3) [APOSTLE]

Ac 1:25 and **a** from which Judas turned aside to go
Ro 1: 5 through whom we have received grace and **a**
1Co 9: 2 for you are the seal of my **a** in the Lord.

APOTHECARIES, APOTHECARY (KJV) See PERFUMER

APOTHECARIES' (KJV) See PERFUMERS'

APPAIM (2)

1Ch 2:30 Seled and **A**; and Seled died childless.
2:31 The son of **A**: Ishi.

APPALLED (21) [APPALLING]

Lev 26:32 to settle in it shall be **a** at it.
Ezr 9: 3 from my head and beard, and sat **a**.
9: 4 around me while I sat **a** until the evening sacrifice.
Job 17: 8 The upright are **a** at this,
18:20 They of the west are **a** at their fate,
21: 5 and be **a**, and lay your hand upon your mouth.
Ps 40:15 Let those be **a** because of their shame who say
143: 4 my heart within me is **a**.
Isa 21: 4 My mind reels, horror has **a** me;
59:16 and was **a** that there was no one to intervene;
Jer 2:12 Be **a**, O heavens, at this, be shocked,
4: 9 the priests shall be **a** and the prophets astounded.
49:20 surely their fold shall be **a** at their fate.
50:13 everyone who passes by Babylon shall be **a**
50:45 surely their fold shall be **a** at their fate.
Eze 19: 7 the land was **a**, and all in it,
26:16 they shall tremble every moment, and be **a** at you.
27:35 All the inhabitants of the coastlands are **a** at you;
28:19 All who know you among the peoples are **a**
32:10 I will make many peoples **a** at you;
Wis 17: 3 terribly alarmed, and **a** by specters.

APPALLING (2) [APPALLED]

Jer 5:30 An **a** and horrible thing has happened in the land:
La 1: 9 her downfall was **a**, with none to comfort her.

APPAREL (5)
Dt 22: 5 A woman shall not wear a man's **a,**
2Sa 1:24 in luxury, who put ornaments of gold on your **a.**
Zec 3: 4 and I will clothe you with festal **a.**"
3: 5 on his head and clothed him with the **a;**
AdE 14: 2 She took off her splendid **a** and put on

APPAREL (KJV) See also CLOTHES, GARMENTS, ROBES, VESTMENTS

APPARENT (1)
2Th 2: 9 The coming of the lawless one is **a** in the working

APPARENTLY (KJV) See CLEARLY

APPARITION (1) [APPARITIONS]
2Mc 5: 4 Therefore everyone prayed that the **a** might prove

APPARITIONS (1) [APPARITION]
Wis 18:17 Then at once **a** in dreadful

APPEAL (23) [APPEALED, APPEALING, APPEALS]
2Sa 19:28 What further right have I, then, to **a** to the king?"
2Ki 8: 3 to **a** to the king for her house and her land.
Job 9:15 I must **a** for mercy to my accuser.
Mt 26:53 Do you think that I cannot **a** to my Father,
Ac 25:11 I **a** to the emperor."
28:19 I was compelled to **a** to the emperor—
Ro 12: 1 I **a** to you therefore, brothers and sisters,
15:30 I **a** to you, brothers and sisters,
1Co 1:10 Now I **a** to you, brothers and sisters,
4:16 I **a** to you, then, be imitators of me.
2Co 5:20 since God is making his **a** through us;
8:17 For he not only accepted our **a,**
10: 1 **a** to you by the meekness and gentleness
13:11 Put things in order, listen to my **a,**
1Th 2: 3 For our **a** does not spring from deceit
5:12 But we **a** to you, brothers and sisters,
Phm 1: 9 yet I would rather **a** to you on the basis of love—
Heb 13:22 I **a** to you, brothers and sisters,
1Pe 3:21 but as an **a** to God for a good conscience,
Jude 1: 3 I find it necessary to write and **a** to you to contend
Sir 41:21 and of rejecting the **a** of a relative;
1Mc 8:32 If now they **a** again for help against you,
2Es 6:44 in endless abundance and of varied **a** to the taste,

APPEALED (13) [APPEAL]
2Ki 8: 5 the woman whose son he had restored to life **a** to
Lk 7: 4 When they came to Jesus, they **a** to him earnestly,
Ac 25: 2 a report against Paul. They **a** to him
25:12 replied, "You have **a** to the emperor;
25:21 But when Paul had **a** to be kept in custody for
25:25 and when he **a** to his Imperial Majesty,
26:32 "This man could have been set free if he had not **a**
2Co 12: 8 Three times I **a** to the Lord about this,
Wis 8:21 so I **a** to the Lord and implored him,
2Mc 4: 5 So he **a** to the king,
4:36 the Jews in the city **a** to him with regard to
7:24 Antiochus not only **a** to him in words,
4Mc 12: 6 When he had thus **a** to him,

APPEALING (5) [APPEAL]
Mt 8: 5 a centurion came to him, **a** to him
Ac 25:10 Paul said, "I am **a** to the emperor's tribunal;
Phm 1:10 I am **a** to you for my child, Onesimus,
Wis 18:22 **a** to the oaths and covenants given
2Mc 7:37 **a** to God to show mercy soon to our nation and

APPEALS (1) [APPEAL]
Wis 13:18 For health he **a** to a thing that is weak;

APPEAR‡ (53) [APPEARANCE, APPEARANCES, APPEARED, APPEARING, APPEARS, REAPPEARED]
Ge 1: 9 and let the dry land **a.**"
Ex 4: 1 but say, 'The LORD did not **a** to you.' "
8:23 This sign shall **a** tomorrow.' "
23:15 No one shall **a** before me empty-handed.
23:17 Three times in the year all your males shall **a**
34:20 No one shall **a** before me empty-handed.
34:23 Three times in the year all your males shall **a**
34:24 up to **a** before the LORD your God three times in
Lev 9: 4 For today the LORD will **a** to you.' "
9: 6 so that the glory of the LORD may **a** to you."
13: 7 he shall **a** again before the priest.
16: 2 for I **a** in the cloud upon the mercy seat.
Dt 13: 1 by dreams **a** among you and promise you omens
16:16 Three times a year all your males shall **a** before
16:16 not **a** before the LORD empty-handed;
19:17 parties to the dispute shall **a** before the LORD,
31:11 to **a** before the LORD your God at the place
Jdg 13:21 The angel of the LORD did not **a** again to Manoah
1Sa 1:22 that he may **a** in the presence of the LORD,
3:21 The LORD continued to **a** at Shiloh,
2Sa 3:13 you shall never **a** in my presence
Ps 21: 9 like a fiery furnace when you **a.**
102:16 LORD will build up Zion; he will **a** in his glory.
SS 2:12 The flowers **a** on the earth;
Isa 1:12 When you come to **a** before me,
Isa 60: 2 and his glory will **a** over you.
Eze 16:51 and have made your sisters **a** righteous by all
16:52 for you have made your sisters **a** righteous.
21:24 so that in all your deeds your sins **a—**
Zec 9:14 Then the LORD will **a** over them,
13: 3 And if any prophets **a** again,
Mt 24:24 and false prophets will **a** and produce great signs
24:30 Then the sign of the Son of Man will **a** in heaven,
Mk 13:22 and false prophets will **a** and produce signs
Lk 19:11 that the kingdom of God was to **a** immediately.
Ac 10:40 on the third day and allowed him to **a,**
26:16 and to those in which I will **a** to you.
2Co 5:10 all of us must **a** before the judgment seat of Christ,
13: 7 not that we may **a** to have met the test,
Heb 9:24 now to **a** in the presence of God on our behalf.
9:28 will **a** a second time, not to deal with sin,
Tob 10: 1 when the days had passed and his son did not **a,**
AdE 14:16 upon my head on days when I **a** in public.
Sir 35: 6 Do not **a** before the Lord empty-handed,
1Mc 9:27 not been since the time that prophets ceased to **a**
2Mc 2: 8 and the glory of the Lord and the cloud will **a,**
1Es 5:40 until a high priest should **a** wearing Urim
3Mc 2:30 In order that he might not **a** to be an enemy of all,
2Es 6:22 Sown places shall suddenly **a** unsown,
7:26 that the city that now is not seen shall **a,**
7:*36* The pit of torment shall **a,**
9: 3 So when there shall **a** in the world earthquakes,
4Mc 7:20 therefore arises when some persons **a** to

APPEARANCE‡ (60) [APPEAR]
Ge 12:11 "I know well that you are a woman beautiful in **a;**
26: 7 because she is attractive in **a.**"
Ex 24:17 Now the **a** of the glory of the LORD was like
Nu 9:15 over the tabernacle, having the **a** of fire.
9:16 cloud covered it by day and the **a** of fire by night.
Jdg 13: 6 and his **a** was like that of an angel of God,
1Sa 16: 7 not look on his **a** or on the height of his stature,
16: 7 they look on the outward **a,**
17:42 for he was only a youth, ruddy and handsome in **a.**
28:14 He said to her, "What is his **a?"**
Job 4:16 It stood still, but I could not discern its **a.**
SS 5:15 His **a** is like Lebanon, choice as the cedars.
Isa 52:14 —so marred was his **a,** beyond human semblance,
53: 2 nothing in his **a** that we should desire him.
Eze 1: 5 This was their **a:** they were of human form.
1:10 As for the **a** of their faces:
1:16 As for the **a** of the wheels and their construction:
1:16 their **a** was like the gleaming of beryl;
1:26 like a throne, in **a** like sapphire;
1:28 such was the **a** of the splendor all around.
1:28 the **a** of the likeness of the glory of the LORD.
8: 2 and above the loins it was like the **a** of brightness,
10: 9 and the **a** of the wheels was like gleaming beryl.
10:10 And as for their **a,** the four looked alike,
10:22 they were the same faces whose **a** I had seen by
40: 3 a man was there, whose **a** shone like bronze,
Da 1:13 You can then compare our **a** with the **a** of the young men who eat the royal rations,
2:31 before you, and its **a** was frightening.
3:25 and the fourth has the **a** of a god."
8:15 having the **a** of a man,
Joel 2: 4 They have the **a** of horses,
Na 2: 4 their **a** is like torches, they dart like lightning.
Mt 16: 3 You know how to interpret the **a** of the sky,
28: 3 His **a** was like lightning, and his clothing white
Mk 12:40 and for the sake of **a** say long prayers.
Lk 9:29 while he was praying, the **a** of his face changed,
12:56 You know how to interpret the **a** of earth and sky,
20:47 and for the sake of **a** say long prayers.
2Co 5:12 to answer those who boast in outward **a** and not in
Col 2:23 an **a** of wisdom in promoting self-imposed piety,
Rev 9: 7 In **a** the locusts were like horses equipped
Jdt 8: 7 She was beautiful in **a,** and was very lovely
10: 7 When they saw her transformed in **a**
11:23 You are not only beautiful in **a,**
AdE 2: 7 The girl was beautiful in **a.**
Wis 14:17 they imagined their **a** far away,
15: 5 whose **a** arouses yearning in fools,
15:19 and even as animals they are not so beautiful in **a**
17: 6 that they saw to be worse than that unseen **a.**
Sir 11: 2 or loathe anyone because of a mere **a.**
19:29 A person is known by his **a,**
25:17 A woman's wickedness changes her **a,**
LtJ 6:63 not to be compared with them in **a** or power.
Sus 1:31 a woman of great refinement and beautiful in **a.**
2Mc 3:16 To see the **a** of the high priest was to be wounded
1Es 4:18 and then see a woman lovely in **a** and beauty,
2Es 15:34 Their **a** is exceedingly threatening,
4Mc 8: 4 And struck by their **a** and nobility,
8:10 have compassion for your youth and handsome **a.**

APPEARANCES (2) [APPEAR]
Jn 7:24 Do not judge by **a,** but judge with right judgment."
2Mc 2:21 and the **a** that came from heaven

APPEARED (116) [APPEAR]
A. THE †LORD ... APPEARED (21)
B. *GOD ... APPEARED (8)

Ge 8: 5 the tops of the mountains **a.**
12: 7 Then the LORD **a** to Abram, and said, A
12: 7 So he built there an altar to the LORD, who had **a** A
17: 1 the LORD **a** to Abram, and said to him, A
18: 1 The LORD **a** to Abraham by the oaks of Mamre, A
26: 2 The LORD **a** to Isaac and said, A
Ge 26:24 And that very night the LORD **a** to him and said, A
35: 1 Make an altar there to the God who **a** to you B
35: 9 God **a** to Jacob again when he came B
48: 3 "God Almighty **a** to me at Luz in the land B
Ex 3: 2 There the angel of the LORD **a** to him in a flame A
3:16 of Isaac, and of Jacob, has **a** to me, saying:
4: 5 and the God of Jacob, has **a** to you." B
6: 3 I **a** to Abraham, Isaac, and Jacob
16:10 and the glory of the LORD **a** in the cloud. A
Lev 9:23 and the glory of the LORD **a** to all the people. A
Nu 14:10 the glory of the LORD **a** at the tent of meeting A
16:19 glory of the LORD **a** to the whole congregation. A
16:42 and the glory of the LORD **a.** A
20: 6 and the glory of the LORD **a** to them. A
Dt 31:15 and the LORD **a** at the tent in a pillar of cloud; A
Jdg 6:12 The angel of the LORD **a** to him and said to him, A
13: 3 the angel of the LORD **a** to the woman and said A
13:10 man who came to me the other day has **a** to me."
19:26 As morning **a,** the woman came and fell down at
1Ki 3: 5 At Gibeon the LORD **a** to Solomon in a dream A
9: 2 the LORD **a** to Solomon a second time, A
9: 2 as he had **a** to him at Gibeon.
11: 9 the God of Israel, who had **a** to him twice, B
2Ch 1: 7 That night God **a** to Solomon, and said to him, B
3: 1 where the LORD had **a** to his father David, A
7:12 LORD **a** to Solomon in the night and said to him: A
Jer 31: 3 the LORD **a** to him from far away. A
Eze 1:27 from what **a** like the loins I saw something
8: 2 below what **a** to be its loins it was fire,
10: 1 the cherubim there **a** above them something like
10: 8 The cherubim **a** to have the form of a human hand
Da 1:15 of ten days it was observed that they **a** better
5: 5 a human hand **a** and began writing on the plaster
7: 5 Another beast **a,** a second one,
7: 6 After this, as I watched, another **a,** like a leopard.
7: 8 I was considering the horns, when another horn **a,**
8: 1 of the reign of King Belshazzar a vision **a** to me,
8: 1 Daniel, after the one that had **a** to me at first.
8: 5 As I was watching, a male goat **a** from the west,
8:15 Then someone **a** standing before me,
12: 5 Then I, Daniel, looked, and two others **a,**
Mt 1:20 an angel of the Lord **a** to him in a dream and said,
2: 7 from them the exact time when the star had **a.**
2:13 angel of the Lord **a** to Joseph in a dream and said,
2:19 the Lord suddenly **a** in a dream to Joseph in Egypt
3: 1 In those days John the Baptist **a** in the wilderness
13:26 then the weeds **a** as well.
17: 3 Suddenly there **a** to them Moses and Elijah,
27:53 the tombs and entered the holy city and **a** to many.
Mk 1: 4 John the baptizer **a** in the wilderness,
9: 4 And there **a** to them Elijah with Moses,
16: 9 ⟦he **a** first to Mary Magdalene,⟧
16:12 ⟦After this he **a** in another form to two of them,⟧
16:14 ⟦Later he **a** to the eleven themselves⟧
Lk 1:11 Then there **a** to him an angel of the Lord,
1:80 the wilderness until the day he **a** publicly to Israel.
9: 8 by some that Elijah had **a,**
9:31 They **a** in glory and were speaking
13:11 And just then there **a** a woman with a spirit
22:43 ⟦from heaven **a** to him and gave him strength.⟧
24:34 and he has **a** to Simon!"
Jn 21:14 that Jesus **a** to the disciples after he was raised
Ac 2: 3 Divided tongues, as of fire, **a** among them,
7: 2 The God of glory **a** to our ancestor Abraham B
7:30 angel **a** to him in the wilderness of Mount Sinai,
7:35 as both ruler and liberator through the angel who **a**
9:17 the Lord Jesus, who **a** to you on your way here,
10:17 suddenly the men sent by Cornelius **a.**
12: 7 Suddenly an angel of the Lord **a** and a light shone
13:31 and for many days he **a** to those who came up
26:16 for I have **a** to you for this purpose,
27:20 When neither sun nor stars **a** for many days,
1Co 15: 5 and that he **a** to Cephas, then to the twelve.
15: 6 Then he **a** to more than five hundred brothers
15: 7 Then he **a** to James, then to all the apostles.
15: 8 as to one untimely born, he **a** also to me.
Tit 2:11 For the grace of God has **a,**
3: 4 and loving kindness of God our Savior **a,**
Heb 9:26 he has **a** once for all at the end of the age
Rev 12: 1 A great portent **a** in heaven:
12: 3 Then another portent **a** in heaven:
15: 2 I saw what **a** to be a sea of glass mixed with fire,
Tob 6: 9 a person's eyes where white films have **a** on them;
12:22 when an angel of God had **a** to them. B
Wis 17: 4 and dismal phantoms with gloomy faces **a.**
Bar 3:37 Afterward she **a** on earth and lived
1Mc 4: 6 At daybreak Judas **a** in the plain
4:19 a detachment **a,** coming out of the hills.
7:12 a group of scribes **a** in a body before Alcimus
2Mc 1:33 the liquid had **a** with which Nehemiah
3:25 there **a** to them a magnificently caparisoned horse,
3:26 Two young men also **a** to him, remarkably strong,
3:30 now that the Almighty Lord had **a.**
3:33 the same young men **a** again
5: 2 that, for almost forty days, there **a** over all
10:29 the battle became fierce, there **a** to the enemy
11: 8 a horseman **a** at their head,
12:16 **a** to be running over with blood.
12:22 But when Judas's first division **a,**
14:20 and it had **a** that they were of one mind,
15:13 Then in the same fashion another **a,**
3Mc 3: 4 For this reason they **a** hateful to some;
5: 6 For to the Gentiles it **a** that the Jews were left
2Es 3: 6 that your right hand had planted before the earth **a.**
3:33 not **a** and their labor has borne no fruit.
7:*114* [44] righteousness has increased and truth has **a.**
10:41 The woman who **a** to you a little while ago,

2Es 10:42 but there **a** to you a city being built)
12:11 up from the sea is the fourth kingdom that **a** in
4Mc 4:10 with lightning flashing from their weapons **a**

APPEARING‡ (6) [APPEAR]

Hos 6: 3 his **a** is as sure as the dawn;
Ac 1: 3 **a** to them during forty days and speaking about
2Ti 1:10 but it has now been revealed through the **a**
4: 1 and in view of his **a** and his kingdom,
4: 8 to me but also to all who have longed for his **a.**
2Es 15:28 What a terrifying sight, **a** from the east!

APPEARS‡ (25) [APPEAR]

Lev 13: 3 and the disease **a** to be deeper than the skin
13: 4 and **a** no deeper than the skin,
13:14 if raw flesh ever **a** on him, he shall be unclean;
13:19 in the place of the boil there **a** a white swelling or
13:20 and if it **a** deeper than the skin
13:25 in the spot has turned white and it **a** deeper than
13:30 If it **a** deeper than the skin and the hair
13:31 and it **a** no deeper than the skin
13:32 and the itch **a** to be no deeper than the skin,
13:34 not spread in the skin and it **a** to be no deeper than
13:47 when a leprous disease **a** in it,
13:54 to wash the article in which the disease **a,**
13:57 If it **a** again in the garment, in warp or woof,
13:57 with fire that in which the disease **a.**
14:37 and if it **a** to be deeper than the surface,
14:40 that the stones in which the disease **a** be taken out
Pr 27:25 When the grass is gone, and new growth **a,**
Mal 3: 2 and who can stand when he **a?**
Jas 4:14 a mist that **a** for a little while and then vanishes.
1Pe 5: 4 And when the chief shepherd **a,**
Wis 6:16 and she graciously **a** to them in their paths,
Sir 27: 4 When a sieve is shaken, the refuse **a;**
39: 4 He serves among the great and **a** before rulers;
43: 2 The sun, when it **a,** proclaims as it rises what
43:16 when he **a,** the mountains shake.

APPEASE (2) [APPEASED]

Ge 32:20 "I may **a** him with the present that goes ahead
Pr 16:14 and whoever is wise will **a** it.

APPEASED‡ (2) [APPEASE]

Isa 57: 6 Shall I be **a** for these things?
2Mc 13:26 convinced them, **a** them, gained their goodwill,

APPENDAGE (11)

Ex 29:13 and the **a** of the liver,
29:22 the fat that covers the entrails, the **a** of the liver,
Lev 3: 4 and the **a** of the liver,
3:10 and the **a** of the liver,
3:15 and the **a** of the liver,
4: 9 and the **a** of the liver,
7: 4 and the **a** of the liver,
8:16 and the **a** of the liver,
8:25 the entrails, the **a** of the liver, and the two kidneys
9:10 the **a** of the liver from the sin offering he turned
9:19 and the fat on them, and the **a** of the liver.

APPENDED (1)

1Mc 12: 7 that you are our brothers, as the **a** copy shows.

APPERTAIN (KJV) See DUE

APPETITE (15) [APPETITES]

Job 6: 7 My **a** refuses to touch them;
38:39 or satisfy the **a** of the young lions,
Pr 6:30 not despised who steal only to satisfy their **a**
13: 4 The **a** of the lazy craves, and gets nothing,
13: 4 while the **a** of the diligent is richly supplied.
13:25 The righteous have enough to satisfy their **a,**
16:26 The **a** of workers works for them;
23: 2 and put a knife to your throat if you have a big **a.**
27: 7 The sated **a** spurns honey,
27: 7 but to a ravenous **a** even the bitter is sweet.
Ecc 6: 7 yet the **a** is not satisfied.
Isa 5:14 Therefore Sheol has enlarged its **a**
56:11 dogs have a mighty **a;** they never have enough.
Wis 16: 2 a delicacy to satisfy the desire of **a;**
16: 3 of **a** because of the odious creatures sent to them,

APPETITES (5) [APPETITE]

Job 33:20 their lives loathe bread, and their **a** dainty food.
Ro 16:18 not serve our Lord Christ, but their own **a,** and
Sir 18:30 not follow your base desires, but restrain your **a.**
4Mc 1:33 Is it not because reason is able to rule over **a?**
1:35 For the emotions of the **a** are restrained,

APPHIA (1)

Phm 1: 2 to **A** our sister, to Archippus our fellow soldier,

APPHUS (1) [=JONATHAN]

1Mc 2: 5 Eleazar called Avaran, and Jonathan called **A.**

APPII (KJV) See APPIUS

APPIUS (1)

Ac 28:15 came as far as the Forum of **A** and Three Taverns

APPLAUD (1) [APPLAUDED]

Ro 1:32 but even **a** others who practice them.

APPLAUDED (1) [APPLAUD]

3Mc 7:13 When they had **a** him in fitting manner,

APPLE (8) [APPLES]

Dt 32:10 cared for him, guarded him as the **a** of his eye.
Ps 17: 8 Guard me as the **a** of the eye;
Pr 7: 2 keep my teachings as the **a** of your eye;
SS 2: 3 As an **a** tree among the trees of the wood,
8: 5 Under the **a** tree I awakened you.
Joel 1:12 Pomegranate, palm, and **a**—
Zec 2: 8 one who touches you touches the **a** of my eye.
Sir 17:22 and he will keep a person's kindness like the **a**

APPLES (3) [APPLE]

Pr 25:11 A word fitly spoken is like **a** of gold in a setting
SS 2: 5 Sustain me with raisins, refresh me with **a;**
7: 8 and the scent of your breath like **a,**

APPLIED (12) [APPLY]

Lev 25:50 price of the sale shall be **a** to the number of years:
1Ki 6:35 with gold evenly **a** upon the carved work.
Ecc 1:13 **a** my mind to seek and to search out
1:17 And I **a** my mind to know wisdom and
8:16 When I **a** my mind to know wisdom,
1Co 4: 6 I have **a** all this to Apollos and myself
9:15 am I writing this so that they may be **a** in my case.
Tob 11:11 With this he **a** the medicine on his eyes,
Sir Pr: 3 During that time I have **a** my skill day and night
2Mc 4:20 but by the decision of its carriers it was **a** to
2Es 13:54 and have **a** yourself to mine,
4Mc 11:19 To his back they **a** sharp spits

APPLIES (2) [APPLY]

Nu 8:24 This **a** to the Levites: from twenty-five
AdE 15:10 for our law **a** only to our subjects.

APPLY‡ (6) [APPLIED, APPLIES, APPLYING]

Nu 5:30 and the priest shall **a** this entire law to her.
2Ki 20: 7 Let them take it and **a** it to the boil,
Pr 22:17 and **a** your mind to my teaching;
23:12 **A** your mind to instruction and your ear to words
Isa 38:21 "Let them take a lump of figs, and **a** it to the boil,
Sir 6:32 and if you **a** yourself you will become clever.

APPLYING (2) [APPLY]

Ecc 8: 9 **a** my mind to all that is done under the sun,
Eph 5:32 and I am **a** it to Christ and the church.

APPOINT (38) [APPOINTED, APPOINTMENT, APPOINTS, REAPPOINTED]

Ge 41:34 Let Pharaoh proceed to **a** overseers over the land,
Ex 21:13 then I will **a** for you a place to which
Nu 1:50 Rather you shall **a** the Levites over the tabernacle
27:16 **a** someone over the congregation
Dt 16:18 You shall **a** judges and officials
Jos 20: 2 '**A** the cities of refuge, of which I spoke to you
1Sa 8: 5 **a** for us, then, a king to govern us,
8:11 and **a** them to his chariots and to be his horsemen,
8:12 and he will **a** for himself commanders
2Sa 6:21 to **a** me as prince over Israel,
7:10 And I will **a** a place for my people Israel
1Ch 15:16 the Levites to **a** their kindred as the singers to play
17: 9 I will **a** a place for my people Israel,
Ezr 7:25 **a** magistrates and judges who may judge all
Ne 7: 3 **A** guards from among the inhabitants
Est 2: 3 the king **a** commissioners in all the provinces
Job 14:13 that you would **a** me a set time,
Ps 61: 7 **a** steadfast love and faithfulness to watch
75: 2 At the set time that I **a** I will judge with equity.
109: 6 They say, "**A** a wicked man against him;
Isa 60:17 I will **a** Peace as your overseer and Righteousness
Jer 1:10 today I **a** you over nations and over kingdoms,
15: 3 And I will **a** over them four kinds of destroyers,
23:32 when I did not send them or **a** them;
49:19 and I will **a** over it whomever I choose.
50:44 and I will **a** over her whomever I choose.
51:27 **a** a marshal against her, bring up horses like
Eze 44:14 Yet I will **a** them to keep charge of the temple,
Da 6: 3 king planned to **a** him over the whole kingdom.
11:39 and shall **a** them as rulers over many,
Hos 1:11 and they shall **a** for themselves one head;
Ac 6: 3 whom we may **a** to this task,
26:16 for this purpose, to **a** you to serve and testify to
1Co 6: 4 do you **a** as judges those who have no standing in
Tit 1: 5 and should **a** elders in every town,
AdE 2: 3 The king shall **a** officers in all the provinces
1Mc 14:42 and **a** officials over its tasks and over the country
1Es 8:23 **a** judges and justices to judge all those who know

APPOINTED‡ (193) [APPOINT]

A. APPOINTED FESTIVALS (19)
B. APPOINTED TIME (19)
C. TIME APPOINTED (8)
D. APPOINTED TIMES (5)

Ge 4:25 "God has **a** for me another child instead of Abel,
24:14 the one whom you have **a** for your servant Isaac.
24:44 let her be the woman whom the LORD has **a**
Ex 18:25 Moses chose able men from all Israel and **a** them
23:15 seven days at the **a** time in the month of Abib, B
31: 6 I have **a** with him Oholiab son of Ahisamach,
34:18 at the time **a** in the month of Abib; C
Lev 23: 2 These are the **a** festivals of the LORD A
23: 2 as holy convocations, my **a** festivals. A
23: 4 These are the **a** festivals of the LORD, A
23: 4 which you shall celebrate at the time **a** for them. C
23:37 These are the **a** festivals of the LORD, A
23:44 the people of Israel the **a** festivals of the LORD. A
Nu 4:49 through Moses they were **a** to their several tasks
9: 2 Let the Israelites keep the passover at its **a** time. B
9: 3 at twilight, you shall keep it at its **a** time; B
9: 7 the LORD's offering at its **a** time among B
9:13 not presenting the LORD's offering at its **a** time; B
10:10 on your days of rejoicing, at your **a** festivals, A
15: 3 or as a freewill offering or at your **a** festivals— A
28: 2 you shall take care to offer to me at its **a** time. B
29:39 to the LORD at your **a** festivals, A
Dt 17:12 for anyone who presumes to disobey the priest **a**
Jos 4: 4 whom he had **a,** one from each tribe.
20: 8 they **a** Bezer in the wilderness on the tableland,
1Sa 9:24 Eat; for it is set before you at the **a** time, B
12: 6 the people, "The LORD is witness, who **a** Moses
13: 8 He waited seven days, the time **a** by Samuel; C
13:11 and that you did not come within the days **a,**
13:14 the LORD has **a** him to be ruler over his people,
25:30 and has **a** you prince over Israel,
29:10 and go to the place that I **a** for you.
2Sa 7:11 the time that I **a** judges over my people Israel;
20: 5 beyond the set time that had been **a** him.
24:15 on Israel from that morning until the **a** time; B
1Ki 1:35 for I have **a** him to be ruler over Israel and
12:31 and **a** priests from among all the people,
12:32 Jeroboam **a** a festival on the fifteenth day of
12:33 he **a** a festival for the people of Israel,
2Ki 7:17 Now the king had **a** the captain
8: 6 So the king **a** an official for her, saying,
17:32 the LORD and **a** from among themselves all sorts
25:22 He **a** Gedaliah son of Ahikam son of Shaphan
25:23 the king of Babylon had **a** Gedaliah as governor,
1Ch 6:48 and their kindred the Levites were **a** for all
9:29 Others of them were **a** over the furniture,
15:17 So the Levites **a** Heman son of Joel;
16: 4 He **a** certain of the Levites as ministers before
16: 7 on that day David first **a** the singing of praises to
16:42 The sons of Jeduthun were **a** to the gate.
17:10 the time that I **a** judges over my people Israel;
23:31 new moons, and **a** festivals, A
24: 3 David organized them according to the **a** duties
24:19 as their **a** duty in their service to enter the house of
26:29 Chenaniah and his sons were **a** to outside duties
26:32 King David **a** him and his brothers,
2Ch 2: 4 and the **a** festivals of the LORD our God, A
8:14 he **a** the divisions of the priests for their service,
11:15 and had **a** his own priests for the high places,
11:22 Rehoboam **a** Abijah son of Maacah as chief prince
19: 5 He **a** judges in the land in all the fortified cities
19: 8 in Jerusalem Jehoshaphat **a** certain Levites
20:21 he **a** those who were to sing to the LORD
31: 2 Hezekiah **a** the divisions of the priests and of
31: 3 the new moons, and the **a** festivals, A
32: 6 He **a** combat commanders over the people,
33: 8 of Israel from the land that I **a** for your ancestors,
34:12 Over them were **a** the Levites Jahath and Obadiah,
35: 2 He **a** the priests to their offices
Ezr 3: 8 They **a** the Levites, from twenty years old
10:14 at **a** times, and with them the elders and judges D
Ne 5:14 from the time that I was **a** to be their governor in
7: 1 the singers, and the Levites had been **a,**
10:33 the sabbaths, the new moons, the **a** festivals, A
10:34 by ancestral houses, at **a** times, year by year, D
12:31 and **a** two great companies that gave thanks
12:44 On that day men were **a** over the chambers for
13: 4 who was **a** over the chambers of the house
13:13 And I **a** as treasurers over the storehouses
13:31 at **a** times, and for the first fruits. D
Est 4: 5 who had been **a** to attend her,
9:27 as it was written and at the time **a.** C
9:31 of Purim should be observed at their **a** seasons,
Job 14: 5 and you have **a** the bounds that they cannot pass,
30:23 and to the house **a** for all living.
34:23 not **a** a time for anyone to go before God
Ps 7: 6 O my God; you have **a** a judgment.
49:14 Like sheep they are **a** for Sheol;
78: 5 and **a** a law in Israel,
102:13 to favor it; the **a** time has come. B
104: 8 ran down to the valleys to the place that you **a**
119:138 You have **a** your decrees in righteousness and
Ecc 3:17 for he has **a** a time for every matter,
Isa 1:14 and your **a** festivals my soul hates; A
33:20 Look on Zion, the city of our **a** festivals! A
Jer 1: 5 I **a** you a prophet to the nations."
5:24 and keeps for us the weeks **a** for the harvest."
33:20 day and night would not come at their **a** time, B
40: 5 of Babylon **a** governor of the towns of Judah,
40: 7 that the king of Babylon had **a** Gedaliah son
40:11 in Judah and had **a** Gedaliah son of Ahikam son
41: 2 king of Babylon had **a** him governor in the land.
47: 7 against the seashore—there he has **a** it.
Eze 22: 4 the **a** time of your years has come. B
36:38 like the flock at Jerusalem during her **a** festivals, A
43:21 be burnt in the **a** place belonging to the temple,
44: 8 but you have **a** foreigners to act for you
44:24 and my statutes regarding all my **a** festivals, A

Eze 45:17 all the **a** festivals of the house of Israel: A
46: 9 the land come before the LORD at the **a** festivals, A
46:11 the festivals and the **a** seasons the grain offering
Da 1:10 he has **a** your food and your drink.
1:11 the guard whom the palace master had **a**
2:24 whom the king had **a** to destroy the wise men
2:49 and he **a** Shadrach, Meshach,
3:12 There are certain Jews whom you have **a** over
8:19 for it refers to the **a** time of the end. B
11:27 for there remains an end at the time **a**. C
11:29 time **a** he shall return and come into the south, C
11:35 for there is still an interval until the time **a**. C
Hos 2:11 her sabbaths, and all her **a** festivals. A
6:11 For you also, O Judah, a harvest is **a**.
9: 5 What will you do on the day of **a** festival,
12: 9 as in the days of the **a** festival.
Jnh 4: 6 The LORD God **a** a bush,
4: 7 God **a** a worm that attacked the bush,
Hab 2: 3 For there is still a vision for the **a** time; B
Mk 3:14 And he **a** twelve, whom he also named apostles,
3:16 So he **a** the twelve: Simon (to whom
Lk 10: 1 After this the Lord **a** seventy others and sent them
Jn 15:16 And I **a** you to go and bear fruit,
Ac 3:20 and that he may send the Messiah **a** for you,
7:10 who **a** him ruler over Egypt and
12:21 On an **a** day Herod put on his royal robes,
14:23 after they had **a** elders for them in each church,
15: 2 and Barnabas and some of the others were **a** to go
17:31 in righteousness by a man whom he has **a**,
Ro 13: 2 whoever resists authority resists what God has **a**,
1Co 7:29 brothers and sisters, the **a** time has grown short; B
12:28 And God has **a** in the church first apostles,
2Co 8:19 but he has also been **a** by the churches to travel
1Ti 1:12 he judged me faithful and **a** me to his service,
2: 7 For this I was **a** a herald and an apostle
2Ti 1:11 For this gospel I was **a** a herald and an apostle and
Heb 1: 2 whom he **a** heir of all things,
3: 2 was faithful to the one who **a** him,
5: 5 but was **a** by the one who said to him,
8: 3 every high priest is **a** to offer gifts and sacrifices;
9:27 And just as it is **a** for mortals to die once,
Tob 1:21 He **a** Ahikar, the son of my brother Hanael
14: 4 but all will come true at their **a** times. D
AdE 2:13 she is handed to the person **a**,
Sir 17:17 He **a** a ruler for every nation,
33: 8 and he **a** the different seasons and festivals.
33:11 and **a** their different ways.
36:10 Hasten the day, and remember the **a** time, B
39:16 he commands will be done at the **a** time. B
39:17 the **a** time all such questions will be answered. B
39:34 for everything proves good in its **a** time. B
43:10 of the Holy One they stand in their **a** places;
48:10 At the **a** time, it is written, B
Bar 1:14 on the days of the festivals and at **a** seasons.
Sus 1: 5 year two elders from the people were **a** as judges.
1Mc 1:51 He **a** inspectors over all the people
3:55 After this Judas **a** leaders of the people,
6:55 whom King Antiochus while still living had **a**
10:20 And so we have **a** you today to be the high priest
10:34 and **a** days, and the three days before a festival
10:69 And Demetrius **a** Apollonius the governor
11:59 He **a** Jonathan's brother Simon governor from
16:11 Now Ptolemy son of Abubus had been **a** governor
2Mc 5:22 character more barbarous than the man who **a** him;
8: 9 Ptolemy promptly **a** Nicanor son of Patroclus,
8:22 He **a** his brothers also, Simon and Joseph
8:23 he **a** Eleazar to read aloud from the holy book,
9:23 into the upper country, **a** his successor,
9:25 So I have **a** my son Antiochus to be king,
10:11 **a** one Lysias to have charge of the government
14:12 in command of the elephants, **a** him governor
14:26 he had **a** that conspirator against the kingdom,
1Es 5:58 They **a** the Levites who were twenty
6:27 and those who were **a** as local rulers in Syria
9:12 who have foreign wives come at the time **a**, C
Man 1: 7 of your mercies you have **a** repentance for sinners,
1: 8 have not **a** repentance for the righteous,
1: 8 but you have **a** repentance for me,
3Mc 5:13 Then the Jews, since they had escaped the **a** hour,
2Es 3: 7 and immediately you **a** death for him and
4:27 to the righteous in their **a** times, D
7: 9 unless by passing through the **a** danger?"
8:52 plenty is provided, a city is built, rest is **a**,
4Mc 4:16 from the priesthood and **a** Onias's brother Jason
4:18 the king **a** him high priest and ruler of the nation.

APPOINTMENT (5) [APPOINT]

1Sa 20:35 into the field to the **a** with David,
21: 2 I have made an **a** with the young men for such
2Ch 31:13 by the **a** of King Hezekiah and of Azariah
Ps 119:91 By your **a** they stand today,
Am 3: 3 unless they have made an **a**?

APPOINTS (3) [APPOINT]

Job 23:14 For he will complete what he **a** for me;
Heb 7:28 For the law **a** as high priests those who are subject
7:28 **a** a Son who has been made perfect forever.

APPORTION (6) [PORTION]

Nu 33:54 You shall **a** the land by lot according
34:17 the names of the men who shall **a** the land to you
34:18 You shall take one leader of every tribe to **a**
34:29 the LORD commanded to **a** the inheritance for
2Ch 31:14 to **a** the contribution reserved for the LORD and
Isa 49: 8 to establish the land, to **a** the desolate heritages;

APPORTIONED (12) [PORTION]

Nu 26:53 the land shall be **a** for inheritance according to
26:55 But the land shall be **a** by lot;
26:56 be **a** according to lot between the larger and
Dt 32: 8 When the Most High **a** the nations,
Jos 18: 2 seven tribes whose inheritance had not yet been **a**.
18:10 and there Joshua **a** the land to the Israelites,
Job 7: 3 and nights of misery are **a** to me.
28:25 and **a** out the waters by measure;
Ps 78:55 he **a** them for a possession and settled the tribes
Heb 7: 2 and to him Abraham **a** "one-tenth of everything."
Sir 44: 2 The Lord **a** to them great glory,
3Mc 6:31 and full of joy they **a** to celebrants the place

APPORTIONING, APPORTIONS See Index to Footnotes

APPRECIATE (1) [APPRECIATES]

Sir 31:22 and in the end you will **a** my words.

APPRECIATES (1) [APPRECIATE]

Sir 3:29 The mind of the intelligent **a** proverbs,

APPREHEND (KJV) See OBTAIN, SEIZE

APPROACH (45) [APPROACHED, APPROACHES, APPROACHING]

Ex 19:22 Even the priests who **a** the LORD must consecrate
Lev 18: 6 None of you shall **a** anyone near of kin
18:14 that is, you shall not **a** his wife; she is your aunt.
18:19 not **a** a woman to uncover her nakedness
21:17 a blemish may **a** to offer the food of his God.
21:23 he shall not come near the curtain or **a** the altar,
Nu 16: 5 and who will be allowed to **a** him;
16: 5 one whom he will choose he will allow to **a** him.
16: 9 to allow you to **a** him in order to perform
16:10 He has allowed you to **a** him,
16:40 shall **a** to offer incense before the LORD,
18: 3 not **a** either the utensils of the sanctuary or
18: 4 of the tent; no outsider shall **a** you.
18:22 the Israelites shall no longer **a** the tent of meeting,
Dt 2:19 When you **a** the frontier of the Ammonites,
Jos 8: 5 and all the people who are with me will **a** the city.
Job 31:37 like a prince I would **a** him.
40:19 only its Maker can **a** it with the sword.
Isa 41: 1 let them **a**, then let them speak;
Jer 30:21 I will bring him near, and he shall **a** me,
30:21 for who would otherwise dare to **a** me?
37:11 from Jerusalem at the **a** of Pharaoh's army,
Eze 18: 6 does not defile his neighbor's wife or **a** a woman
42:13 where the priests who **a** the LORD shall eat
44:16 it is they who shall **a** my table, to minister to me,
45: 4 for the priests, who minister in the sanctuary and **a**
Heb 4:16 therefore **a** the throne of grace with boldness,
7:19 through which we **a** God.
7:25 for all time to save those who **a** God through him,
10: 1 make perfect those who **a**.
10:22 let us **a** with a true heart in full assurance of faith,
11: 6 for whoever would **a** him must believe
Tob 6:15 but it kills anyone who desires to **a** her.
Jdt 4: 2 they were therefore greatly terrified at his **a**;
4: 7 to enter, for the **a** was narrow,
Wis 1: 5 and will be ashamed at the **a** of unrighteousness.
Sir 1:28 do not **a** him with a divided mind.
9:13 But if you **a** them, make no misstep,
21: 2 for if you **a** sin, it will bite you.
41:22 and do not **a** her bed;
2Mc 12:21 When Timothy learned of the **a** of Judas,
3Mc 1:26 took heed of nothing, and began now to **a**,
2Es 10:25 so that I was too frightened to **a** her,
4Mc 14:19 sting those who **a** their hive and defend it even to
15:19 saw in their nostrils the signs of the **a** of death.

APPROACHED (36) [APPROACH]

Ge 20: 4 Now Abimelech had not **a** her;
50:16 So they **a** Joseph, saying, "Your father gave this
Ex 40:32 and when they **a** the altar, they washed;
Nu 31:48 and the commanders of hundreds, **a** Moses,
Dt 4:11 you **a** and stood at the foot of the mountain while
5:23 you **a** me, all the heads of your tribes
1Sa 9:18 Then Saul **a** Samuel inside the gate, and said,
1Ki 20:22 the prophet **a** the king of Israel and said to him,
20:28 A man of God **a** and said to the king of Israel,
2Ki 4:27 Gehazi **a** to push her away.
5:13 But his servants **a** and said to him, "Father,
Ezr 4: 2 they **a** Zerubbabel and the heads of families
9: 1 the officials **a** me and said, "The people of Israel,
Est 5: 2 Then Esther **a** and touched the top of the scepter.
Jer 42: 1 and all the people from the least to the greatest, **a**
Da 3:26 Nebuchadnezzar then **a** the door of the furnace
6:12 they **a** the king and said concerning the interdict,
7:16 I **a** one of the attendants to ask him the truth
Mt 8:19 A scribe then **a** and said, "Teacher,
13:36 And his disciples **a** him, saying,
15:12 Then the disciples **a** and said to him,
Lk 7:12 As he **a** the gate of the town,
15:25 and when he came and **a** the house,
17:12 As he entered a village, ten lepers **a** him.
18:35 As he **a** Jericho, a blind man was sitting by
22:47 He **a** Jesus to kiss him;
Ac 7:31 as he **a** to look, there came the voice of the Lord:
Tob 11: 7 Raphael said to Tobias, before he had **a** his father,
Jdt 12:13 and **a** her and said, "Let this pretty girl not hesitate
1Mc 3:16 When he **a** the ascent of Beth-horon,
5:42 When Judas **a** the stream of water,
11: 4 When he **a** Azotus, they showed him
13:23 When he **a** Baskama, he killed Jonathan,
2Mc 11: 5 Invading Judea, he **a** Beth-zur,
1Es 5:68 So they **a** Zerubbabel and Jeshua and the heads of
3Mc 5:14 **a** the king and nudged him.

APPROACHES (9) [APPROACH]

Lev 20:16 If a woman **a** any animal and has sexual relations
Nu 17:13 Everyone who **a** the tabernacle of
18: 7 any outsider who **a** shall be put to death.
2Ki 11: 8 and whoever **a** the ranks is to be killed.
Jer 48:16 of Moab is near at hand and his doom **a** swiftly.
Jdt 7: 7 He reconnoitered the **a** to their town,
Sir 42:11 no spot that overlooks the **a** to the house.
2Mc 12:21 of access because of the narrowness of all the **a**.
2Es 12:21 and four shall be kept for the time when its end **a**,

APPROACHING‡ (11) [APPROACH]

Ge 27:41 "The days of mourning for my father are **a**;
Da 8: 7 I saw it **a** the ram.
Mk 11: 1 When they were **a** Jerusalem,
Lk 19:37 As he was now **a** the path down from the Mount
Ac 9: 3 Now as he was going along and **a** Damascus,
10: 9 as they were on their journey and **a** the city,
22: 6 "While I was on my way and **a** Damascus,
Heb 10:25 and all the more as you see the Day **a**.
Tob 6:10 he entered Media and already was **a** Ecbatana,
2Es 5:50 Or is she now **a** old age?"
13: 9 When he saw the onrush of the **a** multitude,

APPROPRIATE (8) [APPROPRIATED]

Est 3: 8 so that it is not **a** for the king to tolerate them.
2Co 8:10 it is **a** for you who began last year not only
1Mc 10:40 of the king's revenues from **a** places.
12:11 both at our festivals and on other **a** days,
2Mc 11:36 so that we may make proposals **a** for you.
3Mc 7:19 they had all landed in peace with **a** thanksgiving,
2Es 10: 8 It is most **a** to mourn now,
4Mc 5:11 adopt a mind **a** to your years,

APPROPRIATED (1) [APPROPRIATE]

4Mc 3:20 had both **a** money to them for the temple service

APPROVAL (11) [APPROVE]

Est 8: 5 and I have his **a**, let an order be written to revoke
Ro 13: 3 Then do what is good, and you will receive its **a**;
14:18 to God and has human **a**.
Gal 1:10 Am I now seeking human **a**, or God's **a**?
Heb 11: 2 Indeed, by faith our ancestors received **a**.
11: 4 Through this he received **a** as righteous,
11: 4 God himself giving **a** to his gifts;
1Pe 2:20 and suffer for it, you have God's **a**.
Sir 32:10 and **a** goes before one who is modest.
3Mc 5:21 and joyfully with one accord gave their **a**,

APPROVE (5) [APPROVAL, APPROVED, APPROVES, APPROVING]

1Sa 29: 6 Nevertheless the lords do not **a** of you.
Lk 11:48 So you are witnesses and **a** of the deeds
Ro 14:22 to condemn themselves because of what they **a**.
1Co 16: 3 I will send any whom you **a** with letters
4Mc 15:27 She did not **a** the deliverance that would preserve

APPROVED (13) [APPROVE]

1Sa 18: 5 And all the people, even the servants of Saul, **a**.
Job 29:11 it commended me, and when the eye saw, it **a**;
Ecc 9: 7 for God has long ago **a** what you do.
Ac 8: 1 And Saul **a** of their killing him.
Ro 16:10 Greet Apelles, who is **a** in Christ
2Co 10:18 not those who commend themselves that are **a**,
1Th 2: 4 but just as we have been **a** by God to be entrusted
2Ti 2:15 Do your best to present yourself to God as one **a**
Sir 41:16 nor is every kind of abashment to be **a**.
42: 8 and will be **a** by all.
2Mc 4: 3 by one of Simon's **a** agents,
1Es 6:22 and if it is **a** by our lord the king,
2Es 5:27 you have given the law that is **a** by all.

APPROVES (1) [APPROVE]

1Es 4:39 unrighteous or wicked. Everyone **a** its deeds,

APPROVING (2) [APPROVE]

Ac 22:20 **a** and keeping the coats of those who killed him.'
3Mc 7:12 admitting and **a** the truth of what they said,

APRON (1) [APRONS]

Lk 17: 8 put on your **a** and serve me while I eat and drink;

APRONS (1) [APRON]

Ac 19:12 or **a** that had touched his skin were brought to

APT (4)

Pr 15:23 To make an **a** answer is a joy to anyone,
1Ti 3: 2 sensible, respectable, hospitable, an **a** teacher,
2Ti 2:24 but kindly to everyone, an **a** teacher,
Sir 18:29 and pour forth **a** proverbs.

AQUILA (6)
Ac 18: 2 There he found a Jew named **A**,
18:18 accompanied by Priscilla and **A**.
18:26 but when Priscilla and **A** heard him,
Ro 16: 3 Greet Prisca and **A**, who work with me
1Co 16:19 **A** and Prisca, together with the church
2Ti 4:19 Greet Prisca and **A**, and the household

AR (6)
Nu 21:15 slopes of the wadis that extend to the seat of **A**,
21:28 It devoured **A** of Moab, and swallowed up
Dt 2: 9 of its land as a possession, since I have given **A** as
2:18 to cross the boundary of Moab at **A**.
2:29 for me and likewise the Moabites who live in **A**—
Isa 15: 1 **A** is laid waste in a night, Moab is undone;

ARA (1)
1Ch 7:38 The sons of Jether: Jephunneh, Pispa, and **A**.

ARAB (5) [ARABIA, ARABS]
Jos 15:52 **A**, Dumah, Eshan,
Ne 2:19 and Geshem the **A** heard of it,
6: 1 to Sanballat and Tobiah and to Geshem the **A** and
1Mc 11:17 the **A** cut off the head of Alexander and sent it
11:39 So he went to Imalkue the **A**,

ARABAH[‡] (25) [BETH-ARABAH]
Dt 1: 7 the **A**, the hill country, the Shephelah, the Negeb,
2: 8 leaving behind the route of the **A**,
3:17 the **A** also, with the Jordan and its banks, from
Chinnereth down to the sea of the **A**,
4:49 with all the **A** on the east side of the Jordan as far
as the Sea of the **A**,
11:30 in the land of the Canaanites who live in the **A**,
Jos 3:16 while those flowing toward the sea of the **A**,
8:14 in the morning to the meeting place facing the **A**
11: 2 and in the **A** south of Chinneroth,
11:16 the land of Goshen and the lowland and the **A** and
12: 1 to Mount Hermon, with all the **A** eastward:
12: 3 and the **A** to the Sea of Chinneroth eastward,
12: 3 to the sea of the **A**, the Dead Sea,
12: 8 in the **A**, in the slopes, in the wilderness,
18:18 of the slope of Beth-arabah it goes down to the **A**;
1Sa 23:24 in the **A** to the south of Jeshimon.
2Sa 2:29 and his men traveled all that night through the **A**;
4: 7 and traveled by way of the **A** all night long.
2Ki 14:25 from Lebo-hamath as far as the Sea of the **A**,
25: 4 They went in the direction of the **A**.
Jer 39: 4 and they went toward the **A**.
52: 7 They went in the direction of the **A**.
Eze 47: 8 the eastern region and goes down into the **A**;
Am 6:14 from Lebo-hamath to the Wadi **A**.

ARABIA (10) [ARAB]
1Ki 10:15 and from all the kings of **A** and the governors of
2Ch 9:14 of **A** and the governors of the land brought gold
Jer 25:24 of **A** and all the kings of the mixed peoples
Eze 27:21 **A** and all the princes of Kedar
30: 5 Ethiopia, and Put, and Lud, and all **A**, and Libya,
Gal 1:17 but I went away at once into **A**,
4:25 Now Hagar is Mount Sinai in **A** and corresponds
Jdt 2:25 to the southern borders of Japheth, facing **A**.
1Mc 11:16 So Alexander fled into **A** to find protection there,
2Es 15:29 The nations of the dragons of **A** shall come out

ARABS (11) [ARAB]
2Ch 17:11 and silver for tribute; and the **A** also brought him
21:16 the anger of the Philistines and of the **A** who are
22: 1 the **A** to the camp had killed all the older sons.
26: 7 against the **A** who lived in Gur-baal,
Ne 4: 7 and Tobiah and the **A** and the Ammonites and
Isa 13:20 **A** will not pitch their tents there,
Ac 2:11 Cretans and **A**—in our own languages we hear
1Mc 5:39 They also have hired **A** to help them,
12:31 against the **A** who are called Zabadeans,
2Mc 5: 8 Accused before Aretas the ruler of the **A**,
12:10 against Timothy, at least five thousand **A**

ARAD (5)
Nu 21: 1 When the Canaanite, the king of **A**,
33:40 The Canaanite, the king of **A**,
Jos 12:14 the king of Hormah one the king of **A** one
Jdg 1:16 which lies in the Negeb near **A**.
1Ch 8:15 Zebadiah, **A**, Eder,

ARADUS (1)
1Mc 15:23 and to **A** and Gortyna and Cnidus and Cyprus

ARAH (5)
1Ch 7:39 The sons of Ulla: **A**, Hanniel, and Rizia.
Ezr 2: 5 Of **A**, seven hundred seventy-five.
Ne 6:18 he was the son-in-law of Shecaniah son of **A**:
7:10 Of **A**, six hundred fifty-two.
1Es 5:10 The descendants of **A**, seven hundred fifty-six.

ARAM[‡] (73) [ARAMAIC, ARAMEAN, ARAMEANS, PADDAN-ARAM]
Ge 10:22 Elam, Asshur, Arpachshad, Lud, and **A**.
10:23 The descendants of **A**: Uz, Hul, Gether, and Mash.
22:21 Buz his brother, Kemuel the father of **A**,
Nu 23: 7 "Balak has brought me from **A**,
Jdg 3:10 the LORD gave King Cushan-rishathaim of **A**
10: 6 the gods of **A**, the gods of Sidon,
18: 7 from the Sidonians and had no dealings with **A**.
18:28 from Sidon and they had no dealings with **A**.
2Sa 15: 8 a vow while I lived at Geshur in **A**:
1Ki 10:29 to all the kings of the Hittites and the kings of **A**.
11:25 he despised Israel and reigned over **A**.
15:18 of Tabrimmon son of Hezion of **A**,
19:15 you shall anoint Hazael as king over **A**.
20: 1 of **A** gathered all his army together;
20:20 but King Ben-hadad of **A** escaped on a horse with
20:22 for in the spring the king of **A** will come up
20:23 The servants of the king of **A** said to him,
22: 1 three years **A** and Israel continued without war.
22: 3 to take it out of the hand of the king of **A**?"
22:31 of **A** had commanded the thirty-two captains
2Ki 5: 1 commander of the army of the king of **A**,
5: 1 by him the LORD had given victory to **A**.
5: 5 And the king of **A** said, "Go then,
6: 8 Once when the king of **A** was at war with Israel,
6:11 The mind of the king of **A** was greatly perturbed
6:24 of **A** mustered his entire army;
8: 7 to Damascus while King Ben-hadad of **A** was ill.
8: 9 "Your son King Ben-hadad of **A** has sent me
8:13 that you are to be king over **A**."
8:28 of Ahab to wage war against King Hazael of **A**
8:29 when he fought against King Hazael of **A**.
9:14 at Ramoth-gilead against King Hazael of **A**;
9:15 when he fought against King Hazael of **A**.
12:17 At that time King Hazael of **A** went up,
12:18 and sent these to King Hazael of **A**.
13: 3 into the hand of King Hazael of **A**,
13: 4 how the king of **A** oppressed them.
13: 7 the king of **A** had destroyed them and made them
13:17 the arrow of victory over **A**!
13:19 down **A** until you had made an end of it,
13:19 but now you will strike down **A** only three times."
13:22 of **A** oppressed Israel all the days of Jehoahaz.
13:24 When King Hazael of **A** died,
15:37 of **A** and Pekah son of Remaliah against Judah.
16: 5 Then King Rezin of **A** and King Pekah son
16: 7 and rescue me from the hand of the king of **A** and
1Ch 1:17 Elam, Asshur, Arpachshad, Lud, **A**, Uz, Hul,
2:23 But Geshur and **A** took from them Havvoth-jair,
7:34 sons of Shemer: Ahi, Rohgah, Hubbah, and **A**.
18: 6 Then David put garrisons in **A** of Damascus;
2Ch 1:17 to all the kings of the Hittites and the kings of **A**.
16: 2 and sent them to King Ben-hadad of **A**,
16: 7 "Because you relied on the king of **A**,
16: 7 the army of the king of **A** has escaped you.
18:30 of **A** had commanded the captains of his chariots,
22: 5 of Israel to make war against King Hazael of **A**
22: 6 when he fought King Hazael of **A**.
24:23 of the year the army of **A** came up against Joash.
24:24 Although the army of **A** had come with few men,
28: 5 into the hand of the king of **A**,
28:23 "Because the gods of the kings of **A** helped them,
Isa 7: 1 King Rezin of **A** and King Pekah son of Remaliah
7: 2 the house of David heard that **A** had allied itself
7: 4 because of the fierce anger of Rezin and **A** and
7: 5 Because **A**—with Ephraim and the son of
7: 8 For the head of **A** is Damascus,
17: 3 of **A** will be like the glory of the children of Israel,
Eze 16:57 Now you are a mockery to the daughters of **A**
Hos 12:12 Jacob fled to the land of **A**,
Am 1: 5 and the people of **A** shall go into exile to Kir,
Zec 9: 1 For to the LORD belongs the capital of **A**,
Mt 1: 3 and Hezron the father of **A**,
1: 4 and **A** the father of Aminadab,

ARAM-MAACAH (1) [MAACAH]
1Ch 19: 6 from Mesopotamia, from **A** and from Zobah.

ARAM-NAHARAIM (3)
Ge 24:10 and he set out and went to **A**, to the city of Nahor.
Jdg 3: 8 into the hand of King Cushan-rishathaim of **A**;
Ps 60: T *when he struggled with **A** and with Aram-zobah,*

ARAM-ZOBAH (1)
Ps 60: T *he struggled with Aram-naharaim and with **A**,*

ARAMAIC[‡] (5) [ARAM]
2Ki 18:26 "Please speak to your servants in the **A** language,
Ezr 4: 7 the letter was written in **A** and translated.
Isa 36:11 "Please speak to your servants in **A**,
Da 2: 4 The Chaldeans said to the king (in **A**), "O king,
2Mc 15:36 which is called Adar in the **A** language—

ARAMEAN (16) [ARAM]
Ge 25:20 the **A** of Paddan-aram, sister of Laban the **A**.
28: 5 to Laban son of Bethuel the **A**,
31:20 And Jacob deceived Laban the **A**,
31:24 But God came to Laban the **A** in a dream by night,
Dt 26: 5 "A wandering **A** was my ancestor;
1Ki 20:29 killed one hundred thousand **A** foot soldiers
2Ki 5:20 "My master has let that **A** Naaman off too lightly
7: 4 Therefore, let us desert to the **A** camp;
7: 5 So they arose at twilight to go to the **A** camp;
7: 5 but when they came to the edge of the **A** camp,
7: 6 the Lord had caused the **A** army to hear the sound
7:10 and told them, "We went to the **A** camp,
7:14 and the king sent them after the **A** army, saying,
1Ch 7:14 Asriel, whom his **A** concubine bore;
19:18 and David killed seven thousand **A** charioteers

ARAMEANS[‡] (55) [ARAM]
2Sa 8: 5 the **A** of Damascus came to help King Hadadezer
8: 5 David killed twenty-two thousand men of the **A**.
8: 6 David put garrisons among the **A** of Damascus;
8: 6 **A** became servants to David and brought tribute.
10: 6 hired the **A** of Beth-rehob and the **A** of Zobah,
10: 8 but the **A** of Zobah and of Rehob,
10: 9 and arrayed them against the **A**;
10:11 He said, "If the **A** are too strong for me,
10:13 with him moved forward into battle against the **A**;
10:14 When the Ammonites saw that the **A** fled,
10:15 the **A** saw that they had been defeated by Israel,
10:16 Hadadezer sent and brought out the **A** who were
10:17 The **A** arrayed themselves against David
10:18 The **A** fled before Israel;
10:18 of the **A** seven hundred chariot teams,
10:19 **A** were afraid to help the Ammonites any more.
1Ki 20:20 the **A** fled and Israel pursued them,
20:21 and defeated the **A** with a great slaughter.
20:26 the **A** and went up to Aphek to fight against Israel.
20:27 while the **A** filled the country.
20:28 Because the **A** have said, 'The LORD is a god of
22:11 With these you shall gore the **A**
22:35 king was propped up in his chariot facing the **A**,
2Ki 5: 2 Now the **A** on one of their raids had taken
6: 9 because the **A** are going down there."
6:18 When the **A** came down against him,
6:23 **A** no longer came raiding into the land of Israel.
7:12 "I will tell you what the **A** have prepared
7:15 and equipment that the **A** had thrown away
7:16 people went out, and plundered the camp of the **A**.
8:28 where the **A** wounded Joram.
8:29 in Jezreel of the wounds that the **A** had inflicted
9:15 in Jezreel of the wounds that the **A** had inflicted
13: 5 so that they escaped from the hand of the **A**;
13:17 the **A** in Aphek until you have made an end
24: 2 bands of the **A**, bands of the Moabites,
1Ch 18: 5 the **A** of Damascus came to help King Hadadezer
18: 5 David killed twenty-two thousand **A**.
18: 6 **A** became subject to David, and brought tribute.
19:10 of Israel and arrayed them against the **A**;
19:12 He said, "If the **A** are too strong for me,
19:14 with him advanced toward the **A** for battle;
19:15 When the Ammonites saw that the **A** fled,
19:16 the **A** saw that they had been defeated by Israel,
19:16 and brought out the **A** who were beyond
19:17 When David set the battle in array against the **A**,
19:18 The **A** fled before Israel;
19:19 So the **A** were not willing to help
2Ch 18:10 With these you shall gore the **A**
18:34 up in his chariot facing the **A** until evening;
22: 5 at Ramoth-gilead. The **A** wounded Joram,
Isa 9:12 the **A** on the east and the Philistines on the west,
Jer 35:11 the army of the Chaldeans and the army of the **A**.'
Am 9: 7 the Philistines from Caphtor and the **A** from Kir?

ARAMITESS (KJV) See ARAMEAN

ARAN (2)
Ge 36:28 These are the sons of Dishan: Uz and **A**.
1Ch 1:42 The sons of Dishan: Uz and **A**.

ARARAT (5)
Ge 8: 4 the ark came to rest on the mountains of **A**.
2Ki 19:37 and they escaped into the land of **A**.
Isa 37:38 and they escaped into the land of **A**.
Jer 51:27 summon against her the kingdoms, **A**, Minni,
Tob 1:21 and they fled to the mountains of **A**,

ARAUNAH (9) [=ORNAN]
2Sa 24:16 of the LORD was then by the threshing floor of **A**
24:18 an altar to the LORD on the threshing floor of **A**
24:20 When **A** looked down, he saw the king
24:20 and **A** went out and prostrated himself before
24:21 **A** said, "Why has my lord the king come
24:22 Then **A** said to David, "Let my lord the king take
24:23 All this, O king, **A** gives to the king."
24:23 And **A** said to the king, "May the LORD your God
24:24 But the king said to **A**, "No,

ARBA[‡] (3)
Jos 14:15 this **A** was the greatest man among the Anakim.
15:13 that is, Hebron (**A** was the father of Anak).
21:11 They gave them Kiriath-arba (**A** being the father

ARBAH (KJV) See KIRIATH-ARBA

ARBATHITE (2)
2Sa 23:31 Abi-albon the **A**; Azmaveth of Bahurim;
1Ch 11:32 Hurai of the wadis of Gaash, Abiel the **A**,

ARBATTA (1)
1Mc 5:23 Then he took the Jews of Galilee and **A**,

ARBELA (1)
1Mc 9: 2 to Gilgal and encamped against Mesaloth in **A**,

ARBITE (1)
2Sa 23:35 Hezro of Carmel; Paarai the **A**;

ARBITER (1) [ARBITRATE]
Isa 29:21 who set a trap for the a in the gate,

ARBITRARILY (1)
4Mc 8:25 the law itself would a put us to death for fearing

ARBITRATE (2) [ARBITER, ARBITRATOR]
Isa 2: 4 and shall a for many peoples;
Mic 4: 3 and shall a between strong nations far away;

ARBITRATOR (1) [ARBITRATE]
Lk 12:14 "Friend, who set me to be a judge or a over you?"

ARC (1)
Sir 43:12 It encircles the sky with its glorious a;

ARCHANGEL (2) [ANGEL]
Jude 1: 9 But when the a Michael contended with the devil
2Es 4:36 And the a Jeremiel answered and said,

ARCHANGEL'S (1) [ANGEL]
1Th 4:16 the a call and with the sound of God's trumpet,

ARCHELAUS (1)
Mt 2:22 But when he heard that A was ruling over Judea

ARCHER (5) [ARCHERS]
Pr 26:10 an a who wounds everybody is one who hires
Jer 4:29 At the noise of horseman and a every town takes
51: 3 Let not the a bend his bow,
2Es 16: 7 Can one turn back an arrow shot by a strong a?
16:16 as an arrow shot by a mighty a does not return,

ARCHERS (12) [ARCHER]
Ge 49:23 The a fiercely attacked him;
1Sa 31: 3 a found him, and he was badly wounded by them.
2Sa 11:24 Then the a shot at your servants from the wall;
1Ch 8:40 The sons of Ulam were mighty warriors, a,
10: 3 a found him, and he was wounded by the a.
12: 2 They were a, and could shoot arrows
2Ch 35:23 The a shot King Josiah;
Job 16:13 his a surround me. He slashes open my kidneys,
Jer 50:29 Summon a against Babylon,
Jdt 2:15 together with twelve thousand a on horseback,
1Mc 9:11 and the slingers and the a went ahead of the army,

ARCHES (KJV) See VESTIBULE

ARCHEVITES (KJV) See ERECH

ARCHIPPUS (2)
Col 4:17 And say to A, "See that you complete the task
Phm 1: 2 to A our fellow soldier, and to the church

ARCHITE (5) [ARCHITES, ARKITES?]
2Sa 15:32 Hushai the A came to meet him with his coat torn
16:16 When Hushai the A, David's friend,
17: 5 Then Absalom said, "Call Hushai the A also,
17:14 the A is better than the counsel of Ahithophel."
1Ch 27:33 and Hushai the A was the king's friend.

ARCHITECT (1)
Heb 11:10 whose a and builder is God.

ARCHITES (1) [ARCHITE]
Jos 16: 2 it passes along to Ataroth, the territory of the A;

ARCHIVES (5)
Ezr 5:17 a search made in the royal a there in Babylon,
6: 1 the a where the documents were stored
1Mc 14:23 and to put a copy of their words in the public a,
1Es 6:21 be made in the royal a of our lord the king that are
6:23 in the royal a that were deposited in Babylon.

ARCTURUS (KJV) See BEAR

ARD (3) [ARDITES]
Ge 46:21 Rosh, Muppim, Huppim, and A
Nu 26:40 And the sons of Bela were A and Naaman:
26:40 of A, the clan of the Ardites;

ARDAB See Index to Footnotes

ARDAT (1)
2Es 9:26 as he directed me, into the field that is called A;

ARDENT (1)
Ro 12:11 Do not lag in zeal, be a in spirit, serve the Lord.

ARDITES (1) [ARD]
Nu 26:40 of Ard, the clan of the A;

ARDON (1)
1Ch 2:18 these were her sons: Jesher, Shobab, and A.

ARDUOUS (1)
Wis 10:12 in his a contest she gave him the victory,

ARE (4738) [BE] See Index of Articles Etc.

AREA (19)
Ge 23:17 that were in the field, throughout its whole a,
Lev 10:17 not eat the sin offering in the sacred a?
13: 3 and if the hair in the diseased a has turned white
Nu 18: 7 in all that concerns the altar and the a behind
Dt 23:12 You shall have a designated a outside the camp
1Sa 14:14 an a about half a furrow long in an acre of land.
Ne 3:22 him the priests, the men of the surrounding a,
Eze 40: 5 a wall all around the outside of the temple a.
41:11 The side chambers opened onto the a left free,
41:20 from the floor to the a above the door,
42:10 opposite the vacant a and opposite the building,
42:13 and the south chambers opposite the vacant a are
42:14 before they go near to the a open to the people."
42:15 the interior of the temple a,
42:15 and measured the temple a all around.
43:21 to the temple, outside the sacred a.
45: 6 for the city an a five thousand cubits wide,
Tob 5: 6 for it lies in a mountainous a,
4Mc 4:11 down half dead in the temple a that was open

ARELI (2) [ARELITES]
Ge 46:16 Ziphion, Haggi, Shuni, Ezbon, Eri, Arodi, and A.
Nu 26:17 of A, the clan of the Arelites.

ARELITES (1) [ARELI]
Nu 26:17 of Areli, the clan of the A.

ARENA (2)
2Mc 4:14 the unlawful proceedings in the wrestling a after
4Mc 11:20 of us brothers have been summoned to an a

AREOPAGITE (1) [AREOPAGUS]
Ac 17:34 Dionysius the A and a woman named Damaris,

AREOPAGUS (2) [AREOPAGITE]
Ac 17:19 So they took him and brought him to the A
17:22 Then Paul stood in front of the A and said,

ARETAS (2)
2Co 11:32 under King A guarded the city of Damascus
2Mc 5: 8 Accused before A the ruler of the Arabs,

ARGOB (5)
Dt 3: 4 sixty towns, the whole region of A,
3:13 Og's kingdom. (The whole region of A:
3:14 Jair the Manassite acquired the whole region of A
1Ki 4:13 which are in Gilead, and he had the region of A,
2Ki 15:25 the citadel of the palace along with A and Arieh;

ARGUE (10) [ARGUED, ARGUES, ARGUING, ARGUMENT, ARGUMENTS]
Job 13: 3 and I desire to a my case with God.
15: 3 Should they a in unprofitable talk,
Pr 25: 9 A your case with your neighbor directly,
Isa 1:18 Come now, let us a it out, says the LORD:
3:13 The LORD rises to a his case;
Mk 8:11 The Pharisees came and began to a with him,
Ac 18: 4 Every sabbath he would a in the synagogue
Ro 9:20 a human being, to a with God?
Sir 8: 3 Do not a with the loud of mouth,
11: 9 Do not a about a matter that does not concern you,

ARGUED (10) [ARGUE]
1Ki 3:22 So they a before the king.
Mt 21:25 And they a with one another, "If we say,
Mk 9:34 on the way they had a with one another who was
11:31 They a with one another, "If we say,
Ac 6: 9 stood up and a with Stephen.
9:29 He spoke and a with the Hellenists;
17: 2 and on three sabbath days a with them from
17:17 So he a in the synagogue with the Jews and
19: 8 and a persuasively about the kingdom of God.
19: 9 and a daily in the lecture hall of Tyrannus.

ARGUES (1) [ARGUE]
Job 40: 2 Anyone who a with God must respond."

ARGUING‡ (4) [ARGUE]
Mk 9:14 and some scribes a with them.
9:16 "What are you a about with them?"
9:33 "What were you a about on the way?"
Php 2:14 Do all things without murmuring and a,

ARGUMENT (5) [ARGUE]
Job 19: 5 and make my humiliation an a against me,
Lk 9:46 An a arose among them as to which one
1Ti 2: 8 lifting up holy hands without anger or a;
4Mc 1: 5 Their attempt at a is ridiculous!
3: 1 But this a is entirely ridiculous;

ARGUMENTS (5) [ARGUE]
Job 23: 4 and fill my mouth with a.
Ac 2:40 he testified with many other a and exhorted them,
2Co 10: 4 to destroy strongholds. We destroy a
Col 2: 4 so that no one may deceive you with plausible a.
4Mc 8:16 what a might have been used if some

ARIARATHES (1)
1Mc 15:22 to King Demetrius and to Attalus and A

ARID (1)
Dt 8:15 a wasteland with poisonous snakes and scorpions.

ARIDAI (1)
Est 9: 9 Parmashta, Arisai, A, Vaizatha,

ARIDATHA (1)
Est 9: 8 Poratha, Adalia, A,

ARIEH (1)
2Ki 15:25 the citadel of the palace along with Argob and A;

ARIEL (8)
2Sa 23:20 he struck down two sons of A of Moab.
1Ch 11:22 he struck down two sons of A of Moab.
Ezr 8:16 Then I sent for Eliezer, A, Shemaiah, Elnathan,
Isa 29: 1 Ah, A, A, the city where David encamped!
29: 2 Yet I will distress A, and there shall be moaning
29: 2 and Jerusalem shall be to me like an A.
29: 7 multitude of all the nations that fight against A,

ARIGHT (1) [RIGHT]
Sir 6:17 Those who fear the Lord direct their friendship a,

ARIMATHAEA (KJV) See ARIMATHEA

ARIMATHEA (4)
Mt 27:57 it was evening, there came a rich man from A,
Mk 15:43 Joseph of A, a respected member of the council,
Lk 23:51 He came from the Jewish town of A,
Jn 19:38 After these things, Joseph of A,

ARIOCH (8)
Ge 14: 1 King A of Ellasar, King Chedorlaomer of Elam,
14: 9 King Amraphel of Shinar, and King A of Ellasar,
Da 2:14 with prudence and discretion to A,
2:15 he asked A, the royal official, "Why is the decree
2:15 A then explained the matter to Daniel.
2:24 Therefore Daniel went to A,
2:25 Then A quickly brought Daniel before the king
Jdt 1: 6 the Tigris, and the Hydaspes, and, on the plain, A,

ARISAI (1)
Est 9: 9 Parmashta, A, Aridai, Vaizatha,

ARISE‡ (37) [RISE]
Ge 35: 1 God said to Jacob, "A, go up to Bethel,
41:30 After them there will a seven years of famine,
Nu 10:35 Whenever the ark set out, Moses would say, "A,
Jdg 5:12 A, Barak, lead away your captives,
1Ki 3:12 before you and no one like you shall a after you.
2Ki 23:25 nor did any like him a after him.
Job 25: 3 Upon whom does his light not a?
SS 2:10 "A, my love, my fair one, and come away;
2:13 A, my love, my fair one, and come away.
Isa 33:10 "Now I will a," says the LORD,
60: 1 A, shine; for your light has come,
60: 2 but the LORD will a upon you,
La 2:19 A, cry out in the night, at the beginning of
Da 2:39 you shall a another kingdom inferior to yours,
7: 5 "A, devour many bodies!"
7:17 four kings shall a out of the earth.
7:24 ten horns, out of this kingdom ten kings shall a,
7:24 and another shall a after them.
8:22 four kingdoms shall a from his nation,
8:23 a king of bold countenance shall a,
11: 2 Three more kings shall a in Persia.
11: 3 Then a warrior king shall a,
11:20 "Then shall a in his place one who shall send
11:21 In his place shall a a contemptible person
12: 1 the protector of your people, shall a.
Mic 2:10 A and go; for this is no place to rest,
4:13 A and thresh, O daughter Zion,
Hab 1: 3 before me; strife and contention a.
Zep 3: 8 for the day when I a as a witness.
Mt 24:11 many false prophets will a and lead many astray.
Lk 24:38 and why do doubts a in your hearts?
Jn 7:52 Search and you will see that no prophet is to a
Bar 5: 5 A, O Jerusalem, stand upon the height;
1Mc 14:41 until a trustworthy prophet should a,
2Es 12:18 of the time of that kingdom great struggles shall a,
12:20 Eight kings shall a in it, whose times shall
12:32 who will a from the offspring of David,

ARISEN (6) [RISE]
Dt 34:10 since has there a a prophet in Israel like Moses,
1Sa 14:38 and let us find out how this sin has a today.
Mt 11:11 of women no one has a greater than John
Lk 9: 8 by others that one of the ancient prophets had a.
9:19 still others, that one of the ancient prophets has a."
Bar 3:19 and others have a in their place.

ARISES (7) [RISE]

Mt 13:21 trouble or persecution a on account of the word,
Mk 4:17 trouble or persecution a on account of the word,
Heb 7:15 It is even more obvious when another priest a,
Sir 8: 9 and to give an answer when the need a.
3Mc 3:24 if a sudden disorder later a against us,
4Mc 5:13 from any transgression that a out of compulsion."
7:20 therefore a when some persons appear to

ARISING (2) [RISE]

Heb 7:11 to speak of another priest a according to the order
3Mc 5:32 not for an affection a from our nurture in common

ARISTARCHUS (5)

Ac 19:29 dragging with them Gaius and A,
20: 4 by A and Secundus from Thessalonica,
27: 2 we put to sea, accompanied by A,
Col 4:10 A my fellow prisoner greets you,
Phm 1:24 A, Demas, and Luke, my fellow workers.

ARISTOBULUS (2)

Ro 16:10 Greet those who belong to the family of A.
2Mc 1:10 To A, who is of the family of the anointed priests,

ARIUS (2)

1Mc 12: 7 a letter was sent to the high priest Onias from A,
12:20 "King A of the Spartans,

ARK (232)

A. ARK OF THE/HIS COVENANT (58)
B. ARK OF [THE] *GOD (44)
C. ARK OF THE †LORD (38)

Ge 6:14 Make yourself an a of cypress wood;
6:14 make rooms in the a, and cover it inside and out
6:15 the length of the a three hundred cubits,
6:16 a roof for the a, and finish it to a cubit above;
6:16 and put the door of the a in its side;
6:18 and you shall come into the a, you, your sons,
6:19 you shall bring two of every kind into the a,
7: 1 Then the LORD said to Noah, "Go into the a,
7: 7 and his wife and his sons' wives went into the a
7: 9 male and female, went into the a with Noah,
7:13 and the three wives of his sons entered the a,
7:15 They went into the a with Noah,
7:17 and the waters increased, and bore up the a,
7:18 and the a floated on the face of the waters.
7:23 and those that were with him in the a.
8: 1 the domestic animals that were with him in the a.
8: 4 the a came to rest on the mountains of Ararat.
8: 6 of forty days Noah opened the window of the a
8: 9 and it returned to him to the a,
8: 9 and took it and brought it into the a with him.
8:10 and again he sent out the dove from the a;
8:13 and Noah removed the covering of the a,
8:16 of the a, you and your wife, and your sons
8:19 went out of the a by families.
9:10 as many as came out of the a.
9:18 sons of Noah who went out of the a were Shem,
Ex 25:10 They shall make an a of acacia wood;
25:14 the poles into the rings on the sides of the a,
25:14 by which to carry the a.
25:15 The poles shall remain in the rings of the a;
25:16 into the a the covenant that I shall give you.
25:21 You shall put the mercy seat on the top of the a;
25:21 and in the a you shall put the covenant
25:22 two cherubim that are on the a of the covenant, A
26:33 and bring the a of the covenant in there, A
26:34 on the a of the covenant in the most holy place. A
30: 6 the curtain that is above the a of the covenant, A
30:26 the tent of meeting and the a of the covenant, A
31: 7 and the a of the covenant, A
35:12 the a with its poles, the mercy seat, and the curtain
37: 1 Bezalel made the a of acacia wood;
37: 5 put the poles into the rings on the sides of the a,
37: 5 the rings on the sides of the ark, to carry the a.
39:35 the a of the covenant with its poles and A
40: 3 You shall put in it the a of the covenant, A
40: 3 and you shall screen the a with the curtain.
40: 5 altar for incense before the a of the covenant, A
40:20 He took the covenant and put it into the a,
40:20 and put the poles on the a,
40:20 and set the mercy seat above the a;
40:21 and he brought the a into the tabernacle, and set
40:21 and screened the a of the covenant; A
Lev 16: 2 the mercy seat that is upon the a, or he will die;
Nu 3:31 Their responsibility was to be the a, the table,
4: 5 and cover the a of the covenant with it; A
7:89 the mercy seat that was on the a of the covenant A
10:33 three days' journey with the a of the covenant A
10:35 Whenever the a set out, Moses would say, "Arise,
14:44 even though the a of the covenant of the LORD, A
Dt 10: 1 and make an a of wood.
10: 2 and you shall put them in the a."
10: 3 So I made an a of acacia wood,
10: 5 and put the tablets in the a that I had made;
10: 8 the tribe of Levi to carry the a of the covenant A
31: 9 who carried the a of the covenant of the LORD, A
31:25 the Levites who carried the a of the covenant A
31:26 the law and put it beside the a of the covenant A
Jos 3: 3 "When you see the a of the covenant of A
3: 6 "Take up the a of the covenant, A
3: 6 So they took up the a of the covenant and went A
3: 8 the priests who bear the a of the covenant, A
Jos 3:11 the a of the covenant of the Lord of all A
3:13 the priests who bear the a of the LORD, the Lord C
3:14 a of the covenant were in front of the people. A
3:15 those who bore the a had come to the Jordan,
3:15 the feet of the priests bearing the a were dipped in
3:17 the priests who bore the a of the covenant of A
4: 5 "Pass on before the a of the LORD your God C
4: 7 in front of the a of the covenant of the LORD. A
4: 9 feet of the priests bearing the a of the covenant A
4:10 The priests who bore the a remained standing in
4:11 the a of the LORD, and the priests, C
4:16 the priests who bear the a of the covenant, A
4:18 the a of the covenant of the LORD came up from A
6: 4 of rams' horns before the a.
6: 6 "Take up the a of the covenant, A
6: 6 of rams' horns in front of the a of the LORD." C
6: 7 armed men pass on before the a of the LORD. C
6: 8 with the a of the covenant of the LORD A
6: 9 the rear guard came after the a,
6:11 So the a of the LORD went around the city, C
6:12 and the priests took up the a of the LORD. C
6:13 trumpets of rams' horns before the a of the LORD C
6:13 and the rear guard came after the a of the LORD, C
7: 6 the ground on his face before the a of the LORD C
8:33 of the a in front of the levitical priests who carried
8:33 priests who carried the a of the covenant A
Jdg 20:27 inquired of the LORD (for the a of the covenant A
1Sa 3: 3 where the a of God was. B
4: 3 the a of the covenant of the LORD here A
4: 4 and brought from there the a of the covenant of A
4: 4 were there with the a of the covenant of God. A
4: 5 When the a of the covenant of the LORD came A
4: 6 that the a of the LORD had come to the camp, C
4:11 The a of God was captured; B
4:13 for his heart trembled for the a of God. B
4:17 are dead, and the a of God has been captured." B
4:18 When he mentioned the a of God, B
4:19 the news that the a of God was captured, B
4:21 because the a of God had been captured and B
4:22 for the a of God has been captured." B
5: 1 When the Philistines captured the a of God, B
5: 2 the Philistines took the a of God and brought it B
5: 3 his face to the ground before the a of the LORD. C
5: 4 before the a of the LORD, and the head of Dagon C
5: 7 a of the God of Israel must not remain with us; B
5: 8 "What shall we do with the a of the God B
5: 8 "Let the a of God be moved on to us." B
5: 8 they moved the a of the God of Israel to Gath. B
5:10 So they sent the a of the God of Israel to Ekron. B
5:10 But when the a of God came to Ekron, B
5:10 around to us the a of the God of Israel to kill us B
5:11 and said, "Send away the a of the God of Israel, B
6: 1 The a of the LORD was in the country of C
6: 2 "What shall we do with the a of the LORD? C
6: 3 "If you send away the a of the God of Israel, B
6: 8 Take the a of the LORD and place it on the cart, C
6:11 They put the a of the LORD on the cart, C
6:13 When they looked up and saw the a,
6:15 the a of the LORD and the box that was beside it, C
6:18 beside which they set down the a of the LORD, C
6:19 when they greeted the a of the LORD; C
6:21 Philistines have returned the a of the LORD. C
7: 1 came and took up the a of the LORD, C
7: 1 Eleazar, to have charge of the a of the LORD. C
7: 2 the day that the a was lodged at Kiriath-jearim,
14:18 Saul said to Ahijah, "Bring the a of God here." B
14:18 at that time the a of God went with the Israelites. B
2Sa 6: 2 to bring up from there the a of God, B
6: 3 They carried the a of God on a new cart, B
6: 4 with the a of God; and Ahio went in front B
6: 4 and Ahio went in front of the a.
6: 6 Uzzah reached out his hand to the a of God B
6: 7 because he reached out his hand to the a;
6: 7 and he died there beside the a of God. B
6: 9 can the a of the LORD come into my care?" C
6:10 to take the a of the LORD into his care in the city C
6:11 The a of the LORD remained in the house C
6:12 because of the a of God." B
6:12 So David went and brought up the a of God B
6:13 the a of the LORD had gone six paces, C
6:15 the house of Israel brought up the a of the LORD C
6:16 the a of the LORD came into the city of David, C
6:17 They brought in the a of the LORD, C
7: 2 but the a of God stays in a tent." B
11:11 "The a and Israel and Judah remain in booths;
15:24 carrying the a of the covenant of God. A
15:24 They set down the a of God, B
15:25 "Carry the a of God back into the city. B
15:29 So Zadok and Abiathar carried the a of God B
1Ki 2:26 the a of the Lord GOD before my father David,
3:15 where he stood before the a of the covenant A
6:19 to set there the a of the covenant of the LORD. A
8: 1 the a of the covenant of the LORD out of the city A
8: 3 and the priests carried the a.
8: 4 So they brought up the a of the LORD, C
8: 5 were with him before the a,
8: 6 Then the priests brought the a of the covenant A
8: 7 over the place of the a,
8: 7 so that the cherubim made a covering above the a
8: 9 There was nothing in the a except the two tablets
8:21 There I have provided a place for the a,
1Ch 6:31 after the a came to rest there.
13: 3 Then let us bring again the a of our God to us; B
13: 5 to bring the a of God from Kiriath-jearim. B
13: 6 to bring up from there the a of God, the LORD, BC
13: 7 They carried the a of God on a new cart, B
13: 9 Uzzah put out his hand to hold the a,
1Ch 13:10 down because he put out his hand to the a;
13:12 "How can I bring the a of God into my care?" B
13:13 not take the a into his care into the city of David;
13:14 The a of God remained with the household B
15: 1 a place for the a of God and pitched a tent for it. B
15: 2 but the Levites were to carry the a of God, B
15: 2 had chosen them to carry the a of the LORD C
15: 3 in Jerusalem to bring up the a of the LORD C
15:12 so that you may bring up the a of the LORD, C
15:14 themselves to bring up the a of the LORD, C
15:15 Levites carried the a of God on their shoulders B
15:23 and Elkanah were to be gatekeepers for the a.
15:24 were to blow the trumpets before the a of God. B
15:24 and Jehiah also were to be gatekeepers for the a.
15:25 to bring up the a of the covenant of the LORD A
15:26 Levites who were carrying the a of the covenant A
15:27 also were all the Levites who were carrying the a,
15:28 the a of the covenant of the LORD with shouting, A
15:29 As the a of the covenant of the LORD came to A
16: 1 They brought in the a of God, B
16: 4 Levites as ministers before the a of the LORD, C
16: 6 before the a of the covenant of God. A
16:37 his kinsfolk there before the a of the covenant A
16:37 to minister regularly before the a as each day
17: 1 a of the covenant of the LORD is under a tent." A
22:19 so that the a of the covenant of the LORD A
28: 2 to build a house of rest for the a of the covenant A
28:18 and covered the a of the covenant of the LORD. A
2Ch 1: 4 the a of God up from Kiriath-jearim to the place B
5: 2 the a of the covenant of the LORD out of the city A
5: 4 and the Levites carried the a.
5: 5 So they brought up the a, the tent of meeting,
5: 6 who had assembled before him, were before the a,
5: 7 Then the priests brought the a of the covenant A
5: 8 over the place of the a,
5: 8 so that the cherubim made a covering above the a
5:10 There was nothing in the a except the two tablets
6:11 There I have set the a,
6:41 you and the a of your might.
8:11 to which the a of the LORD has come are holy." C
35: 3 "Put the holy a in the house that Solomon son
Ps 132: 8 you and the a of your might.
Jer 3:16 "The a of the covenant of the LORD." A
Mt 24:38 until the day Noah entered the a,
Lk 17:27 until the day Noah entered the a,
Heb 9: 4 altar of incense and the a of the covenant A
11: 7 the warning and built an a to save his household;
1Pe 3:20 during the building of the a, in which a few,
Rev 11:19 a of his covenant was seen within his temple; A
2Mc 2: 4 that the tent and the a should follow with him,
2: 5 and he brought there the tent and the a and
1Es 1: 3 to the Lord and put the holy a of the Lord in
2Es 10:22 the a of our covenant has been plundered, A
4Mc 15:31 Just as Noah's a, carrying the world in

ARKESAEUS (2)

AdE 1:14 A, Sarsathaeus, and Malesear,
1:14 A, Sarsathaeus, and Malesear,

ARKITES (2) [ARCHITE?]

Ge 10:17 the Hivites, the A, the Sinites,
1Ch 1:15 the Hivites, the A, the Sinites,

ARM‡ (85) [ARMAMENT, ARMED, ARMIES, ARMLET, ARMLETS, ARMOR, ARMOR-BEARER, ARMOR-BEARERS, ARMORY, ARMPITS, ARMS, ARMS-BEARING, ARMY, BODY-ARMOR]

Ex 6: 6 I will redeem you with an outstretched a and
15:16 by the might of your a,
Nu 31: 3 "A some of your number for the war,
Dt 4:34 by war, by a mighty hand and an outstretched a,
5:15 with a mighty hand and an outstretched a;
7:19 the mighty hand and the outstretched a by which
9:29 by your great power and by your outstretched a."
11: 2 his mighty hand and his outstretched a,
26: 8 with a mighty hand and an outstretched a, with
33:20 Gad lives like a lion; he tears at a and scalp.
2Sa 1:10 on his head and the armlet that was on his a,
23:10 down the Philistines until his a grew weary,
1Ki 8:42 your mighty hand, and your outstretched a—
10:19 a rests and two lions standing beside the a rests,
2Ki 5:18 of Rimmon to worship there, leaning on my a,
17:36 with great power and with an outstretched a;
2Ch 6:32 and your mighty hand, and your outstretched a,
9:18 a rests and two lions standing beside the a rests,
32: 8 With him is an a of flesh;
Job 26: 2 How you have assisted the a that has no strength!
31:22 and let my a be broken from its socket.
35: 9 they call for help because of the a of the mighty.
38:15 and their uplifted a is broken.
40: 9 Have you an a like God,
Ps 10:15 Break the a of the wicked and evildoers;
44: 3 nor did their own a give them victory;
44: 3 but your right hand, and your a,
77:15 With your strong a you redeemed your people,
83: 8 they are the strong a of the children of Lot.
89:10 you scattered your enemies with your mighty a.
89:13 You have a mighty a; strong is your hand,
89:21 my a also shall strengthen him.
98: 1 and his holy a have gotten him victory.
136:12 with a strong hand and an outstretched a,
SS 8: 6 as a seal upon your a;
Isa 30:30 to be heard and the descending blow of his a to

Isa 30:32 battling with brandished **a** he will fight with him.
33: 2 Be our **a** every morning, our salvation in the time
40:10 and his **a** rules for him;
44:12 and forging it with his strong **a**;
45: 5 I **a** you, though you do not know me,
48:14 and his **a** shall be against the Chaldeans.
51: 5 coastlands wait for me, and for my **a** they hope.
51: 9 awake, put on strength, O **a** of the LORD!
52:10 The LORD has bared his holy **a** before the eyes
53: 1 to whom has the **a** of the LORD been revealed?
59:16 so his own **a** brought him victory,
62: 8 by his right hand and by his mighty **a**:
63: 5 so my own **a** brought me victory,
63:12 who caused his glorious **a** to march at
66:12 and you shall nurse and be carried on her **a**,
Jer 21: 5 against you with outstretched hand and mighty **a**,
27: 5 and my outstretched **a** have made the earth,
32:17 by your great power and by your outstretched **a**!
32:21 with a strong hand and outstretched **a**,
48:25 The horn of Moab is cut off, and his **a** is broken,
Eze 4: 7 with your **a** bared you shall prophesy against it.
17: 9 No strong **a** or mighty army will be needed
20:33 surely with a mighty hand and an outstretched **a**,
20:34 with a mighty hand and an outstretched **a**,
30:21 I have broken the **a** of Pharaoh king of Egypt;
30:22 both the strong **a** and the one that was broken;
Zec 11:17 May the sword strike his **a** and his right eye!
11:17 Let his **a** be completely withered,
Lk 1:51 He has shown strength with his **a**;
Jn 12:38 to whom has the **a** of the Lord been revealed?"
Ac 13:17 and with uplifted **a** he led them out of it.
1Pe 4: 1 **a** yourselves also with the same intention
Wis 5:16 and with his **a** he will shield them.
5:17 and will **a** all creation to repel his enemies;
11:21 and who can withstand the might of your **a**?
16:16 were flogged by the strength of your **a**,
Sir 21:21 and like a bracelet on the right **a**.
36: 7 make your hand and right **a** glorious.
38:30 He molds the clay with his **a** and makes it pliable
47: 5 and he gave strength to his right **a** to strike down
Bar 2:11 and with great power and outstretched **a**,
1Mc 3:58 And Judas said, "**A** yourselves and be courageous.
2Mc 12:35 down on him and cut off his **a**;
15:24 of your **a** may these blasphemers who come
15:30 to cut off Nicanor's head and **a** and carry them
15:32 the vile Nicanor's head and that profane man's **a**,
2Es 15:11 with a mighty hand and with an uplifted **a**,

ARMAMENT (1) [ARM]

Sir 46: 6 so that the nations might know his **a**,

ARMED‡ (52) [ARM]

Nu 20:20 against them with a large force, heavily **a**.
31: 5 twelve thousand **a** for battle.
32:27 everyone **a** for war, to do battle for the LORD,
32:29 everyone **a** for battle before the LORD,
32:30 but if they will not cross over with you **a**,
32:32 over **a** before the LORD into the land of Canaan,
Dt 3:18 all your troops shall cross over **a** as the vanguard
Jos 1:14 among you shall cross over **a** before your kindred
4:12 of Manasseh crossed over **a** before the Israelites,
4:13 About forty thousand **a** for war crossed over
6: 7 the **a** men pass on before the ark of the LORD."
6: 9 And the **a** men went before the priests who blew
6:13 The **a** men went before them,
Jdg 7:11 with his servant Purah to the outposts of the **a** men
18:11 of the Danite clan, **a** with weapons of war, set out
18:16 **a** with their weapons of war,
18:17 the gate with the six hundred men **a** with weapons
20:15 Benjaminites mustered twenty-six thousand **a** men
20:17 mustered four hundred thousand **a** men,
20:25 of the Israelites, all of them **a** men.
20:35 of Benjamin that day, all of them **a**.
1Sa 17: 5 and he was **a** with a coat of mail;
1Ch 12:23 of the divisions of the **a** troops who came to David
12:24 numbered six thousand eight hundred **a** troops.
12:34 with whom there were thirty-seven thousand **a**
12:37 one hundred twenty thousand **a** with all
2Ch 14: 8 **a** with large shields and spears,
17:17 with two hundred thousand **a** with bow and shield,
17:18 with one hundred eighty thousand **a** for war.
Est 8:11 to annihilate any **a** force of any people or province
Ps 78: 9 The Ephraimites, **a** with the bow,
Pr 6:11 and want, like an **a** warrior.
24:34 and want, like an **a** warrior.
Lk 11:21 When a strong man, fully **a**, guards his castle,
1Mc 6:35 a thousand men **a** with coats of mail,
6:37 on each were four **a** men who fought from there,
14:32 he **a** the soldiers of his nation
2Mc 4:40 Lysimachus **a** about three thousand men
5: 2 in companies fully **a** with lances
5:26 with his **a** warriors and killed great numbers
13: 2 and three hundred chariots **a** with scythes.
14:22 Judas posted **a** men in readiness at key places
15:11 He **a** each of them not so much with confidence
1Es 2:30 with cavalry and a large number of **a** troops,
3Mc 5:29 that the animals and the **a** forces were ready,
5:44 and they confidently posted the **a** forces at
5:48 at the gate and by the following **a** forces,
6:21 the **a** forces following them and began trampling
4Mc 3:12 respecting the king's desire, **a** themselves fully,
4:10 while Apollonius was going up with his **a** forces
5: 1 and with his **a** soldiers standing around him,
7:11 For just as our father Aaron, **a** with the censer,

ARMENIA (KJV) See ARARAT

ARMIES (29) [ARM]

Jos 10: 5 gathered their forces, and went up with all their **a**
1Sa 17: 1 Now the Philistines gathered their **a** for battle;
17:26 that he should defy the **a** of the living God?"
17:36 since he has defied the **a** of the living God."
17:45 the God of the **a** of Israel, whom you have defied.
23: 3 to Keilah against the **a** of the Philistines?"
1Ki 2: 5 how he dealt with the two commanders of the **a**
15:20 and sent the commanders of his **a** against the cities
1Ch 11:26 The warriors of the **a** were Asahel brother of Joab,
2Ch 16: 4 and sent the commanders of his **a** against the cities
Job 25: 3 Is there any number to his **a**?
Ps 44: 9 and have not gone out with our **a**.
60:10 You do not go out, O God, with our **a**.
68:12 "The kings of the **a**, they flee,
108:11 You do not go out, O God, with our **a**.
SS 6:13 as upon a dance before two **a**?
Da 11:22 **A** shall be utterly swept away and broken
Lk 21:20 "When you see Jerusalem surrounded by **a**,
Heb 11:34 became mighty in war, put foreign **a** to flight.
Rev 19:14 And the **a** of heaven, wearing fine linen,
19:19 the earth with their **a** gathered to make war against
Jdt 1: 4 and forty cubits wide to allow his **a** to march out
1Mc 6: 5 in Persia and reported that the **a** that had gone into
6: 6 that they had taken from the **a** they had cut down;
7:43 So the **a** met in battle on the thirteenth day of
9:13 The earth was shaken by the noise of the **a**,
10:78 and the **a** engaged in battle.
2Mc 10:28 Just as dawn was breaking, the two **a** joined battle,
1Es 4:10 All his people and his **a** obey him.

ARMLET (1) [ARM]

2Sa 1:10 that was on his head and the **a** that was on his arm,

ARMLETS (2) [ARM]

Nu 31:50 articles of gold, **a** and bracelets, signet rings,
Isa 3:20 the **a**, the sashes, the perfume boxes,

ARMONI (1)

2Sa 21: 8 whom she bore to Saul, **A** and Mephibosheth;

ARMOR (33) [ARM]

Jdg 9:54 the young man who carried his **a** and said to him,
1Sa 14: 1 of Saul said to the young man who carried his **a**,
14: 6 Jonathan said to the young man who carried his **a**,
17:38 Saul clothed David with his **a**;
17:39 David strapped Saul's sword over the **a**,
17:54 but he put his **a** in his tent.
18: 4 and gave it to David, and his **a**,
31: 9 They cut off his head, stripped off his **a**,
31:10 They put his **a** in the temple of Astarte;
1Ki 20:11 on **a** should not brag like one who takes it off."
22:34 of Israel between the scale **a** and the breastplate;
2Ki 3:21 all who were able to put on **a**,
1Ch 10: 9 They stripped him and took his head and his **a**,
10:10 They put his **a** in the temple of their gods,
2Ch 18:33 of Israel between the scale **a** and the breastplate;
Eze 23:12 warriors clothed in full **a**, mounted horsemen,
38: 4 horses and horsemen, all of them clothed in full **a**,
Lk 11:22 he takes away his **a** in which he trusted
Ro 13:12 the works of darkness and put on the **a** of light;
Eph 6:11 Put on the whole **a** of God,
6:13 Therefore take up the whole **a** of God,
Wis 5:17 The Lord will take his zeal as his whole **a**,
1Mc 3: 3 he bound on his **a** of war and waged battles,
4: 6 not have **a** and swords such as they desired.
4:30 and of the man who carried his **a**.
6:43 that one of the animals was equipped with royal **a**.
13:29 and on the columns he put suits of **a** for
13:29 and beside the suits of **a** he carved ships,
2Mc 3:25 Its rider was seen to have **a** and weapons of gold.
5: 3 the flash of golden trappings, and **a** of all kinds.
10:30 and shielding him with their own **a** and weapons,
15:28 they recognized Nicanor, lying dead, in full **a**.
4Mc 13:16 Therefore let us put on the full **a** of self-control,

ARMOR-BEARER (17) [ARM, BEAR]

1Sa 14: 7 His **a** said to him, "Do all that your mind
14:12 The men of the garrison hailed Jonathan and his **a**,
14:12 Jonathan said to his **a**, "Come up after me;
14:13 with his **a** following after him.
14:13 The Philistines fell before Jonathan, and his **a**,
14:14 and his **a** killed about twenty men within an area
14:17 Jonathan and his **a** were not there.
16:21 Saul loved him greatly, and he became his **a**.
31: 4 Then Saul said to his **a**, "Draw your sword
31: 4 But his **a** was unwilling; for he was terrified.
31: 5 When his **a** saw that Saul was dead,
31: 6 and his **a** and all his men died together on
2Sa 23:37 Naharai of Beeroth, the **a** of Joab son of Zeruiah;
1Ch 10: 4 Then Saul said to his **a**, "Draw your sword,
10: 4 But his **a** was unwilling, for he was terrified.
10: 5 When his **a** saw that Saul was dead,
11:39 Naharai of Beeroth, the **a** of Joab son of Zeruiah,

ARMOR-BEARERS (1) [ARM, BEAR]

2Sa 18:15 And ten young men, Joab's **a**,

ARMORY (4) [ARM]

2Ki 20:13 his **a**, all that was found in his storehouses;
Ne 3:19 the ascent to the **a** at the Angle.
Isa 39: 2 his whole **a**, all that was found in his storehouses.
Jer 50:25 The LORD has opened his **a**,

ARMOURBEARER (KJV) See ARMOR-BEARER

ARMOURY (KJV) See ARMORY

ARMPITS (1) [ARM]

Jer 38:12 "Just put the rags and clothes between your **a** and

ARMS‡ (76) [ARM]

Ge 24:22 two bracelets for her **a** weighing ten gold shekels,
24:30 and the bracelets on his sister's **a**,
24:47 and the bracelets on her **a**.
49:24 and his **a** were made agile by the hands of
Nu 32:17 but we will take up **a** as a vanguard before
32:20 you take up **a** to go before the LORD for the war,
32:21 and all those of you who bear **a** cross the Jordan
Jdg 8:10 hundred twenty thousand men bearing **a** had fallen.
10:17 Then the Ammonites were called to **a**,
12: 1 The men of Ephraim were called to **a**,
15:14 and the ropes that were on his **a** became like flax
16:12 But he snapped the ropes off his **a** like a thread.
20: 2 four hundred thousand foot-soldiers bearing **a**.
2Sa 22:35 so that my **a** can bend a bow of bronze.
Job 22: 9 and the **a** of the orphans you have crushed.
Ps 18:34 so that my **a** can bend a bow of bronze.
37:17 For the **a** of the wicked shall be broken,
129: 7 not fill their hands or binders of sheaves their **a**,
Pr 31:17 with strength, and makes her **a** strong.
SS 5:14 His **a** are rounded gold, set with jewels.
Isa 17: 5 and their **a** harvest the ears,
40:11 he will gather the lambs in his **a**,
51: 5 my salvation has gone out and my **a** will rule
60: 4 your daughters shall be carried on their nurses' **a**.
Eze 13:20 I will tear them from your **a**,
16:11 I put bracelets on your **a**, a chain on your neck,
23:42 and they put bracelets on the **a** of the women,
30:22 of Egypt, and will break his **a**, both the strong arm
30:24 I will strengthen the **a** of the king of Babylon,
30:24 but I will break the **a** of Pharaoh,
30:25 I will strengthen the **a** of the king of Babylon,
30:25 but the **a** of Pharaoh shall fall.
Da 2:32 its chest and **a** of silver,
10: 6 his **a** and legs like the gleam of burnished bronze,
Hos 7:15 It was I who trained and strengthened their **a**,
11: 3 I took them up in my **a**;
Mk 9:36 and taking it in his **a**, he said to them,
10:16 And he took them up in his **a**,
Lk 2:28 Simeon took him in his **a** and praised God, saying,
15:20 he ran and put his **a** around him and kissed him.
Ac 20:10 and bending over him took him in his **a**, and said,
Tob 11: 9 Then Anna ran up to her son and threw her **a**
11:13 Tobit saw his son and threw his **a** around him,
Jdt 14: 3 Then they will seize their **a** and go into the camp
15:13 bearing their **a** and wearing garlands
AdE 15: 8 and took her in his **a** until she came to herself.
Wis 18:22 not by strength of body, not by force of **a**, but
1Mc 1:35 they stored up **a** and food,
5:43 and they threw away their **a** and fled into
6: 6 that the Jews had grown strong from the **a**,
6:41 of the multitude and the clanking of their **a**,
7:44 they threw down their **a** and fled.
8:26 **a**, money, or ships, just as Rome has decided;
8:28 to their enemies there shall not be given grain, **a**,
10: 6 to equip them with **a**, and to become his ally;
10:21 and he recruited troops and equipped them with **a**
11:51 And they threw down their **a** and made peace.
12:27 to keep their **a** at hand so as to be ready all night
14:33 formerly the **a** of the enemy had been stored,
2Mc 5:25 he ordered his troops to parade under **a**.
8:18 "For they trust to **a** and acts of daring," he said,
8:27 When they had collected the **a** of the enemy
8:31 They collected the **a** of the enemy,
9: 2 Therefore the people rushed to the rescue with **a**,
10:23 Having success at **a** in everything he undertook,
10:27 And rising from their prayer they took up their **a**
11: 7 Maccabeus himself was the first to take up **a**,
15: 5 to take up **a** and finish the king's business."
15:21 of him and the varied supply of **a** and the savagery
15:21 for he knew that it is not by **a**,
3Mc 1: 2 of the Ptolemaic **a** that had been previously issued
1:23 to their compatriots to take **a** and die courageously
5:49 and falling into one another's **a**—
4Mc 6: 3 they had tied his **a** on each side they flogged him,
9:11 they bound his hands and **a** with thongs
10: 6 breaking his fingers and **a** and legs and elbows.

ARMS-BEARING (1) [ARM, BEAR]

Jdg 20:46 of Benjamin were twenty-five thousand **a** men,

ARMY‡ (339) [ARM]

Ge 21:22 with Phicol the commander of his **a**,
21:32 Abimelech, with Phicol the commander of his **a**,
26:26 and Phicol the commander of his **a**.
Ex 14: 4 for myself over Pharaoh and all his **a**;
14: 6 and took his **a** with him;
14: 9 his chariot drivers and his **a**;
14:17 for myself over Pharaoh and all his **a**,
14:19 the Israelite **a** moved and went behind them;
14:20 between the **a** of Egypt and the **a** of Israel.

Ex 14:24 and cloud looked down upon the Egyptian **a**,
14:24 and threw the Egyptian **a** into panic.
14:28 the entire **a** of Pharaoh that had followed them
15: 4 "Pharaoh's chariots and his **a** he cast into the sea;
Nu 31:14 Moses became angry with the officers of the **a**,
31:48 the officers who were over the thousands of the **a**,
Dt 11: 4 to the Egyptian **a**, to their horses and chariots,
20: 1 an **a** larger than your own,
24: 5 with the **a** or be charged with any related duty.
Jos 5:14 but as commander of the **a** of the LORD I have
5:15 commander of the **a** of the LORD said to Joshua,
11: 4 They came out, with all their troops, a great **a**,
Jdg 4: 2 the commander of his **a** was Sisera,
4: 7 I will draw out Sisera, the general of Jabin's **a**,
4:15 and all his chariots and all his **a** into a panic
4:16 the chariots and the **a** to Harosheth-ha-goiim.
4:16 All the **a** of Sisera fell by the sword;
7:14 into his hand God has given Midian and all the **a**."
7:15 for the LORD has given the **a** of Midian
7:22 against his fellow and against all the **a**;
7:22 the **a** fled as far as Beth-shittah toward Zererah,
8: 6 that we should give bread to your **a**?"
8:10 Zebah and Zalmunna were in Karkor with their **a**,
8:10 all who were left of all the **a** of the people of
8:11 and attacked the **a**; for the **a** was off its guard.
8:12 and threw all the **a** into a panic.
9:29 I would say to him, 'Increase your **a**,
20:26 Then all the Israelites, the whole **a**,
20:31 When the Benjaminites went out against the **a**,
1Sa 12: 9 commander of the **a** of King Jabin of Hazor,
13:15 The rest of the people followed Saul to join the **a**;
14:50 of the commander of his **a** was Abner son of Ner,
17:20 to the encampment as the **a** was going forth to
17:21 the Philistines drew up for battle, **a** against **a**.
17:46 the Philistine **a** this very day to the birds of the air
17:55 he said to Abner, the commander of the **a**,
18: 5 as a result, Saul set him over the **a**.
18:13 David marched out and came in, leading the **a**.
26: 5 with Abner son of Ner, the commander of his **a**.
26: 5 while the **a** was encamped around him.
26: 7 So David and Abishai went to the **a** by night;
26: 7 and Abner and the **a** lay around him.
26:14 David called to the **a** and to Abner son of Ner,
28: 1 you and your men are to go out with me in the **a**."
28: 5 When Saul saw the **a** of the Philistines,
28:19 the **a** of Israel into the hands of the Philistines."
2Sa 1: 4 He answered, "The **a** fled from the battle,
1: 4 but also many of the **a** fell and died;
1:12 for the **a** of the LORD and for the house of Israel,
2: 8 But Abner son of Ner, commander of Saul's **a**,
3:23 When Joab and all the **a** that was with him came,
5:24 before you to strike down the **a** of the Philistines."
8: 9 that David had defeated the whole **a** of Hadadezer,
8:16 Joab son of Zeruiah was over the **a**;
10: 7 he sent Joab and all the **a** with the warriors.
10:16 to Helam, with Shobach the commander of the **a**
10:18 and wounded Shobach the commander of their **a**,
17:25 Now Absalom had set Amasa over the **a** in
18: 2 And David divided the **a** into three groups:
18: 4 the **a** marched out by hundreds and by thousands.
18: 6 So the **a** went out into the field against Israel;
19:13 you are not the commander of my **a** from now on,
20:23 Now Joab was in command of all the **a** of Israel;
23:11 and the **a** fled from the Philistines.
24: 2 king said to Joab and the commanders of the **a**,
24: 4 against Joab and the commanders of the **a**.
24: 4 of the **a** went out from the presence of the king
1Ki 1:19 and Joab the commander of the **a**;
1:25 Joab the commander of the **a**,
2:32 Abner son of Ner, commander of the **a** of Israel,
2:32 commander of the **a** of Judah.
2:35 The king put Benaiah son of Jehoiada over the **a**
4: 4 of Jehoiada was in command of the **a**;
11:15 the commander of the **a** went up to bury the dead,
11:21 and that Joab the commander of the **a** was dead,
16:16 all Israel made Omri, the commander of the **a**,
20: 1 of Aram gathered all his **a** together;
20:19 and the **a** that followed them.
20:25 and muster an **a** like the **a** that you have lost,
22:36 Then about sunset a shout went through the **a**,
2Ki 3: 9 of seven days, there was no water for the **a** or for
4:13 to the king or to the commander of the **a**?"
5: 1 Naaman, commander of the **a** of the king of Aram,
6:14 So he sent horses and chariots there and a great **a**;
6:15 **a** with horses and chariots was all around the city.
6:24 of Aram mustered his entire **a**;
7: 6 For the Lord had caused the Aramean **a** to hear
7: 6 and of horses, the sound of a great **a**,
7:14 and the king sent them after the Aramean **a**,
8:21 who had surrounded him; but his **a** fled home.
9: 5 He arrived while the commanders of the **a** were
11:15 the captains who were set over the **a**,
13: 7 an **a** of not more than fifty horsemen, ten chariots
18:17 and the Rabshakeh with a great **a** from Lachish
25: 1 of Babylon came with all his **a** against Jerusalem,
25: 5 But the **a** of the Chaldeans pursued the king,
25: 5 all his **a** was scattered, deserting him.
25:10 the **a** of the Chaldeans who were with the captain
25:19 the commander of the **a** who mustered the people
1Ch 10: 7 in the valley saw that the **a** had fled and that Saul
11: 2 it was you who commanded the **a** of Israel.
11:15 the **a** of Philistines was encamped in the valley
12:14 These Gadites were officers of the **a**,
12:21 they were all warriors and commanders in the **a**.
12:22 until there was a great **a**, like an **a** of God.
14:15 before you to strike down the **a** of the Philistines."
14:16 and they struck down the Philistine **a** from Gibeon

1Ch 18: 9 the whole **a** of King Hadadezer of Zobah,
18:15 Joab son of Zeruiah was over the **a**;
19: 7 and the king of Maacah with his **a**,
19: 8 he sent Joab and all the **a** of the warriors.
19:16 with Shophach the commander of the **a**
19:18 also killed Shophach the commander of their **a**.
20: 1 to battle, Joab led out the **a**, ravaged the country
21: 2 David said to Joab and the commanders of the **a**,
25: 1 the officers of the **a** also set apart for the service
26:26 and the commanders of the **a**, had dedicated.
27: 3 of all the commanders of the **a** for the first month.
27:34 Joab was commander of the king's **a**.
2Ch 12: 3 A countless **a** came with him from Egypt—
13: 3 having an **a** of valiant warriors,
13:17 and his **a** defeated them with great slaughter;
14: 8 an **a** of three hundred thousand from Judah, armed
14: 9 an **a** of a million men and three hundred chariots,
14:13 the **a** with him pursued them as far as Gerar,
14:13 for they were broken before the LORD and his **a**.
16: 7 the **a** of the king of Aram has escaped you.
16: 8 Were not the Ethiopians and the Libyans a huge **a**
20:21 as they went before the **a**, saying,
23:14 the **a**, saying to them, "Bring her out between
24:23 of the year the **a** of Aram came up against Joash.
24:24 Although the **a** of Aram had come with few men,
24:24 LORD delivered into their hand a very great **a**,
25: 7 "O king, do not let the **a** of Israel go with you,
25: 9 about the hundred talents that I have given to the **a**
25:10 Then Amaziah discharged the **a** that had come
25:13 But the men of the **a** whom Amaziah sent back,
26:11 Moreover Uzziah had an **a** of soldiers, fit for war,
26:13 Under their command was an **a**
26:14 Uzziah provided for all the **a** the shields, spears,
28: 9 he went out to meet the **a** that came to Samaria,
33:11 against them the commanders of the **a** of the king
33:14 of the **a** in all the fortified cities in Judah.
Ne 2: 9 the king had sent officers of the **a** and cavalry
4: 2 in the presence of his associates and of the **a**
Est 1: 3 The **a** of Persia and Media and the nobles
Ps 27: 3 an **a** encamp against me, my heart shall not fear;
33:16 A king is not saved by his great **a**;
136:15 but overthrew Pharaoh and his **a** in the Red Sea,
SS 6: 4 terrible as an **a** with banners.
6:10 bright as the sun, terrible as an **a** with banners?"
Isa 13: 4 The LORD of hosts is mustering an **a** for battle.
36: 2 to King Hezekiah at Jerusalem, with a great **a**.
43:17 who brings out chariot and horse, **a** and warrior;
Jer 32: 2 At that time the **a** of the king of Babylon
34: 1 of Babylon and all his **a** and all the kingdoms of
34: 7 when the **a** of the king of Babylon was fighting
34:21 to the **a** of the king of Babylon,
35:11 for fear of the **a** of the Chaldeans and the **a** of the
37: 5 the **a** of Pharaoh had come out of Egypt;
37: 7 who sent you to me to inquire of me, Pharaoh's **a**,
37:10 the whole **a** of Chaldeans who are fighting
37:11 the Chaldean **a** had withdrawn from Jerusalem at
the approach of Pharaoh's **a**,
38: 3 over to the **a** of the king of Babylon and be taken.
39: 1 of Babylon and all his **a** came against Jerusalem
39: 5 But the **a** of the Chaldeans pursued them,
46: 2 Concerning Egypt, about the **a** of Pharaoh Neco,
51: 3 utterly destroy her entire **a**.
52: 4 of Babylon came with all his **a** against Jerusalem,
52: 8 But the **a** of the Chaldeans pursued the king,
52: 8 and all his **a** was scattered, deserting him.
52:14 All the **a** of the Chaldeans,
52:25 the commander of the **a** who mustered the people
Eze 1:24 a sound of tumult like the sound of an **a**;
17: 9 or mighty **a** will be needed to pull it from its roots.
17:15 that they might give him horses and a large **a**.
17:17 Pharaoh with his mighty **a** and great company will
26: 7 chariots, cavalry, and a great and powerful **a**.
27:10 Paras and Lud and Put were in your **a**,
29:18 of Babylon made his **a** labor hard against Tyre;
29:18 yet neither he nor his **a** got anything from Tyre
29:19 and it shall be the wages for his **a**.
32:31 Pharaoh and all his **a**, killed by the sword,
38: 4 and I will lead you out with all your **a**,
38:15 a great horde, a mighty **a**;
Da 3:20 and ordered some of the strongest guards in his **a**
11: 7 He shall come against the **a** and enter the fortress
11:13 after some years he shall advance with a great **a**
11:25 against the king of the south with a great **a**,
11:25 with a much greater and stronger **a**.
11:26 They shall break him, his **a** shall be swept away,
Joel 2: 2 upon the mountains a great and powerful **a** comes;
2: 5 like a powerful **a** drawn up for battle.
2:11 The LORD utters his voice at the head of his **a**;
2:20 I will remove the northern **a** far from you,
2:25 the destroyer, and the cutter, my great **a**,
2Ti 2: 4 in the **a** gets entangled in everyday affairs;
Rev 19:19 against the rider on the horse and against his **a**.
Jdt 1:13 the whole **a** of Arphaxad and all his cavalry
2: 4 the chief general of his **a**, second only to himself,
2:14 generals, and officers of the Assyrian **a**.
2:16 and he organized them as a great **a** is marshaled
2:19 Then he set out with his whole **a**,
2:22 From there Holofernes took his whole **a**,
3: 6 the seacoast with his **a** and stationed garrisons in
3:10 in order to collect all the supplies for his **a**.
5: 1 the general of the Assyrian **a**,
5: 3 How large is their **a**, and in what does their power
5: 3 Who rules over them as king and leads their **a**?
5:24 and your vast **a** will swallow them up."
6: 1 Holofernes, the commander of the Assyrian **a**,
6: 6 Then at my return the sword of my **a** and the spear
7: 1 The next day Holofernes ordered his whole **a**,

Jdt 7: 7 and then returned to his **a**.
7: 9 my lord, and your **a** will suffer no losses.
7:11 and not a man of your **a** will fall.
7:17 So the **a** of the Ammonites moved forward,
7:18 The rest of the Assyrian **a** encamped in the plain,
7:20 The whole Assyrian **a**, their infantry, chariots,
7:26 the whole town as booty to the **a** of Holofernes
10:13 to see Holofernes the commander of your **a**,
11:18 so that you may go out with your whole **a**,
13:15 the commander of the Assyrian **a**,
14: 3 the camp and rouse the officers of the Assyrian **a**.
14:19 When the leaders of the Assyrian **a** heard this,
16:12 they perished before the **a** of my Lord.
Wis 12: 8 as forerunners of your **a** to destroy them little
1Mc 1: 4 a very strong **a** and ruled over countries,
2:44 They organized an **a**, and struck down sinners
2:66 he shall command the **a** for you and fight
3:13 When Seron, the commander of the Syrian **a**,
3:15 Once again a strong **a** of godless men went up
3:17 But when they saw the **a** coming to meet them,
3:19 on the size of the **a** that victory in battle depends,
3:23 he rushed suddenly against Seron and his **a**,
3:27 the forces of his kingdom, a very strong **a**.
3:57 the **a** marched out and encamped to the south
4:10 with our ancestors and crush this **a**
4:20 They saw that their **a** had been put to flight,
4:21 and when they also saw the **a** of Judas drawn up in
4:30 When he saw that their **a** was strong, he prayed,
4:31 Hem in this **a** by the hand of your people Israel,
4:34 there fell of the **a** of Lysias five thousand men;
4:35 to invade Judea again with an even larger **a**.
4:37 all the **a** assembled and went up to Mount Zion.
5:28 Then Judas and his **a** quickly turned back by
5:34 the **a** of Timothy realized that it was Maccabeus,
5:37 After these things Timothy gathered another **a**
5:40 Judas and his **a** drew near to the stream of water,
5:42 the **a** at the stream and gave them this command,
5:43 and the whole **a** followed him.
5:49 to the **a** that all should encamp where they were.
6:33 the king set out and took his **a** by a forced march
6:38 on the two flanks of the **a**,
6:40 of the king's **a** was spread out on the high hills,
6:41 trembled, for the **a** was very large and strong.
6:42 But Judas and his **a** advanced to the battle,
6:42 and six hundred of the king's **a** fell.
6:48 of the king's **a** went up to Jerusalem against them,
7: 2 the **a** seized Antiochus and Lysias to bring them
7: 4 So the **a** killed them, and Demetrius took his seat
7:14 priest of the line of Aaron has come with the **a**,
7:32 About five hundred of the **a** of Nicanor fell,
7:35 and his **a** are delivered into my hands this time,
7:38 Take vengeance on this man and on his **a**,
7:39 and the Syrian **a** joined him.
7:42 So also crush this **a** before us today;
7:43 The **a** of Nicanor was crushed,
7:44 When his **a** saw that Nicanor had fallen,
8: 6 and with cavalry and chariots and a very large **a**.
9: 1 that Nicanor and his **a** had fallen in battle,
9: 1 and with them the right wing of the **a**.
9: 7 When Judas saw that his **a** had slipped away and
9:11 the **a** of Bacchides marched out from the camp
9:11 the slingers and the archers went ahead of the **a**,
9:14 that Bacchides and the strength of his **a** were on
9:34 and he with all his **a** crossed the Jordan.
10: 2 he assembled a very large **a** and marched out
10:49 and the **a** of Demetrius fled,
10:53 and he and his **a** were crushed by us,
10:73 not be able to withstand my cavalry and such an **a**
10:77 he mustered three thousand cavalry and a large **a**,
10:80 for they surrounded his **a** and shot arrows
11:60 and all the **a** of Syria gathered to him as allies.
11:63 to Kadesh in Galilee with a large **a**,
11:67 and his **a** encamped by the waters of Gennesaret.
11:68 there in the plain the **a** of the foreigners met him;
11:70 commanders of the forces of the **a**.
12:42 Trypho saw that he had come with a large **a**,
13: 1 Simon heard that Trypho had assembled a large **a**
13:11 and with him a considerable **a**;
13:12 with a large **a** to invade the land of Judah,
13:20 and his **a** kept marching along opposite him
14: 3 The general went and defeated the **a** of Demetrius,
16: 6 Then he and his **a** lined up against them.
16: 7 Then he divided the **a** and placed the cavalry in
16: 8 and Cendebeus and his **a** were put to flight;
2Mc 4:22 Then he marched his **a** into Phoenicia.
5:24 with an **a** of twenty-two thousand,
8: 5 As soon as Maccabeus got his **a** organized,
8:12 he told his companions of the arrival of the **a**,
8:21 then he divided his **a** into four parts.
8:24 and wounded and disabled most of Nicanor's **a**,
8:35 in the destruction of his own **a**!
9: 2 and Antiochus and his **a** were defeated,
9: 9 the stench the whole **a** felt revulsion at his decay.
10:35 twenty young men in the **a** of Maccabeus,
12:20 But Maccabeus arranged his **a** in divisions,
12:38 Then Judas assembled his **a** and went to the city
13: 1 that Antiochus Eupator was coming with a great **a**
13:13 the king's **a** could enter Judea and get possession
14: 1 the harbor of Tripolis with a strong **a** and a fleet,
14:21 A chariot came forward from each **a**;
15:20 at hand with their **a** drawn up for battle,
1Es 4: 6 not serve in the **a** or make war but till the soil;
3Mc 1: 1 where the **a** of Antiochus was encamped.
5: 3 the **a** who were especially hostile toward the Jews.
6: 4 with his arrogant **a** by drowning them in the sea,
6:17 and brought an uncontrollable terror upon the **a**.
2Es 1:10 down Pharaoh with his servants and all his **a**.

2Es 15:33 and fear and trembling shall come upon their **a**,
4Mc 3: 8 the whole **a** of our ancestors had encamped.
4:11 for him and propitiate the wrath of the heavenly **a**.

ARNA (1)
2Es 1: 2 of **A** son of Uzzi son of Borith son of Abishua son

ARNAN (1)
1Ch 3:21 his son **A**, his son Obadiah, his son Shecaniah.

ARNI (1)
Lk 3:33 son of Admin, son of **A**, son of Hezron,

ARNON (25)
Nu 21:13 and camped on the other side of the **A**,
21:13 for the **A** is the boundary of Moab,
21:14 "Waheb in Suphah and the wadis. The **A**
21:24 the **A** to the Jabbok, as far as to the Ammonites;
21:26 of Moab and captured all his land as far as the **A**.
21:28 and swallowed up the heights of the **A**.
22:36 on the boundary formed by the **A**,
Dt 2:24 "Proceed on your journey and cross the Wadi **A**.
2:36 the edge of the Wadi **A** (including the town that is
3: 8 from the Wadi **A** to Mount Hermon
3:12 that is on the edge of the Wadi **A**,
3:16 from Gilead as far as the Wadi **A**, with the middle
4:48 which is on the edge of the Wadi **A**,
Jos 12: 1 from the Wadi **A** to Mount Hermon,
12: 2 which is on the edge of the Wadi **A**,
13: 9 which is on the edge of the Wadi **A**,
13:16 which is on the edge of the Wadi **A**,
Jdg 11:13 took away my land from the **A** to the Jabbok and
11:18 and camped on the other side of the **A**.
11:18 for the **A** was the boundary of Moab.
11:22 from the **A** to the Jabbok and from the wilderness
11:26 and in all the towns that are along the **A**,
2Ki 10:33 from Aroer, which is by the Wadi **A**, that is,
Isa 16: 2 so are the daughters of Moab at the fords of the **A**.
Jer 48:20 Tell it by the **A**, that Moab is laid waste.

AROD (1) [ARODI]
Nu 26:17 of **A**, the clan of the Arodites;

ARODI (1) [AROD, ARODITES]
Ge 46:16 Ziphion, Haggi, Shuni, Ezbon, Eri, **A**, and Areli.

ARODITES (1) [ARODI]
Nu 26:17 of Arod, the clan of the **A**;

AROER‡ (15) [AROERITE]
Nu 32:34 And the Gadites rebuilt Dibon, Ataroth, **A**,
Dt 2:36 From **A** on the edge of the Wadi Arnon (including
3:12 and Gadites the territory north of **A**,
4:48 from **A**, which is on the edge of the Wadi Arnon,
Jos 12: 2 from **A**, which is on the edge of the Wadi Arnon,
13: 9 from **A**, which is on the edge of the Wadi Arnon,
13:16 Their territory was from **A**,
13:25 and half the land of the Ammonites, to **A**,
Jdg 11:26 and in **A** and its villages,
11:33 on them from **A** to the neighborhood of Minnith,
1Sa 30:28 in **A**, in Siphmoth, in Eshtemoa,
2Sa 24: 5 from **A** and from the city that is in the middle of
2Ki 10:33 from **A**, which is by the Wadi Arnon, that is,
1Ch 5: 8 who lived in **A**, as far as Nebo and Baal-meon.
Jer 48:19 Stand by the road and watch, you inhabitant of **A**!

AROERITE (1) [AROER]
1Ch 11:44 Shama and Jeiel sons of Hotham the **A**,

AROM (1)
1Es 5:16 one hundred one. The descendants of **A**.

AROMA (2) [AROMATIC]
Jer 48:11 his flavor has remained and his **a** is unspoiled.
2Co 2:15 For we are the **a** of Christ to God

AROMATIC (1) [AROMA]
Ex 30:23 and two hundred fifty of **a** cane,

AROSE‡ (35) [RISE]
Ge 22:19 and they **a** and went together to Beer-sheba;
31:17 So Jacob **a**, and set his children and his wives
Ex 1: 8 new king **a** over Egypt, who did not know Joseph.
12:30 Pharaoh **a** in the night, he and all his officials
Dt 33: 5 There **a** a king in Jeshurun,
Jdg 5: 7 because you **a**, Deborah, **a** as a mother in Israel.
11:39 So there **a** an Israelite custom that
1Ki 2:40 Shimei **a** and saddled a donkey, and went
8:54 he **a** from facing the altar of the LORD,
2Ki 7: 5 So they **a** at twilight to go to the Aramean camp;
12:20 His servants **a**, devised a conspiracy,
2Ch 29:12 Then the Levites **a**, Mahath son of Amasai,
Job 1:20 Then Job **a**, tore his robe, shaved his head,
SS 5: 5 I **a** to open to my beloved,
Jer 26:17 of the land **a** and said to all the assembled people,
Da 8:22 in place of which four others **a**,
8:27 then I **a** and went about the king's business.
Mt 8:24 A windstorm **a** on the sea,
Mk 4:37 A great windstorm **a**, and the waves beat into
Lk 6:48 when a flood **a**, the river burst against that house
9:46 An argument **a** among them as to which one
22:24 also **a** among them as to which one of them was to
Jn 3:25 about purification **a** between John's disciples and
Ac 23: 9 Then a great clamor **a**, and certain scribes of
2Pe 2: 1 But false prophets also **a** among the people,
Tob 8: 9 But Raguel **a** and called his servants to him,
Jdt 7:29 Then great and general lamentation **a** throughout
Sir 47:21 and a rebel kingdom **a** out of Ephraim.
48: 1 Then Elijah **a**, a prophet like fire,
1Mc 13:44 and a great tumult **a** in the city.
2Mc 5: 5 When a false rumor **a** that Antiochus was dead,
1Es 2: 8 Then **a** the heads of families of the tribes of Judah
5:58 And Jeshua **a**, and his sons and kindred
2Es 13: 2 a wind **a** from the sea and stirred up all its waves.

AROUND‡ (456) [TERROR-ALL-AROUND]
Ge 2:11 the one that flows **a** the whole land of Havilah,
2:13 it is the one that flows **a** the whole land of Cush.
35: 5 a terror from God fell upon the cities all **a** them,
37: 7 then your sheaves gathered **a** it,
41:42 and put a gold chain **a** his neck.
41:48 up in every city the food from the fields **a** it.
49: 1 Then Jacob called his sons, and said: "Gather **a**,
Ex 16:13 the morning there was a layer of dew **a** the camp.
18:13 people stood **a** him from morning until evening.
18:14 while all the people stand **a** you from morning
19:12 You shall set limits for the people all **a**, saying,
19:23 'Set limits **a** the mountain and keep it holy.' "
21:19 but recovers and walks **a** outside with the help of
25:11 you shall make a molding of gold upon it all **a**.
25:24 and make a molding of gold **a** it.
25:25 You shall make **a** it a rim a handbreadth wide,
25:25 and a molding of gold **a** the rim.
27:17 the pillars **a** the court shall be banded with silver;
28:32 with a woven binding **a** the opening,
28:33 purple, and crimson yarns, all **a** the lower hem,
28:33 with bells of gold between them all **a**—
28:34 and a pomegranate alternating all **a** the lower hem
30: 3 its top, and its sides all **a** and its horns;
30: 3 and you shall make for it a molding of gold all **a**.
32: 1 the people gathered **a** Aaron, and said to him,
32:26 And all the sons of Levi gathered **a** him.
37: 2 and made a molding of gold **a** it.
37:11 and made a molding of gold **a** it.
37:12 He made **a** it a rim a handbreadth wide,
37:12 and made a molding of gold **a** the rim.
37:26 its top, and its sides all **a**, and its horns;
37:26 and he made for it a molding of gold all **a**,
38:16 All the hangings **a** the court were
38:20 the pegs for the tabernacle and for the court all **a**
38:31 the bases all **a** the court,
38:31 and all the pegs **a** the court.
39:23 with a binding **a** the opening,
39:25 of the robe all **a**, between the pomegranates;
39:26 a bell and a pomegranate all **a** on the lower hem of
40: 8 You shall set up the court all **a**,
40:33 He set up the court **a** the tabernacle and the altar,
Lev 3: 3 the entrails and all the fat that is **a** the entrails;
3: 9 and all the fat that is **a** the entrails;
3:14 and all the fat that is **a** the entrails;
4: 8 the entrails and all the fat that is **a** the entrails;
8: 7 He put the tunic on him, fastened the sash **a** him,
8: 7 then put the decorated band of the ephod **a** him,
8:13 and fastened sashes **a** them,
8:16 Moses took all the fat that was **a** the entrails,
8:25 the broad tail, all the fat that was **a** the entrails,
19:16 not go **a** as a slanderer among your people,
25:31 But houses in villages that have no walls **a**
25:34 But the open land **a** their cities may not be sold;
25:44 from the nations **a** you that you may acquire male
Nu 1:50 and shall camp **a** the tabernacle.
1:53 but the Levites shall camp **a** the tabernacle of
3:26 of the court that is **a** the tabernacle and the altar,
3:37 also the pillars of the court all **a**,
4:26 of the gate of the court that is **a** the tabernacle and
4:32 of the court all **a** with their bases, pegs, and cords,
11: 8 The people went **a** and gathered it,
11:24 and placed them all **a** the tent.
11:31 a day's journey on the other side, all **a** the camp,
11:32 and they spread them out for themselves all **a**
16:34 All Israel **a** them fled at their outcry, for they said,
21: 4 to go **a** the land of Edom;
22: 4 "This horde will now lick up all that is **a** us,
34:12 This shall be your land with its boundaries all **a**.
35: 4 of the town outward a thousand cubits all **a**.
Dt 3:27 up to the top of Pisgah and look **a** you to the west,
6:14 any of the gods of the peoples who are all **a** you,
12:10 when he gives you rest from your enemies all **a** so
13: 7 any of the gods of the peoples that are **a** you,
17:14 like all the nations that are **a** me,"
Jos 6: 3 You shall march **a** the city,
6: 4 On the seventh day you shall march **a**
6: 7 "Go forward and march **a** the city;
6:11 ark of the LORD went **a** the city, circling it once;
6:14 the second day they marched **a** the city once and
6:15 and marched **a** the city in the same manner seven
6:15 that day that they marched **a** the city seven times.
15: 9 then the boundary bends **a** to Baalah (that is,
15:11 then the boundary bends **a** to Shikkeron,
18:20 boundary by boundary all **a**.
19: 8 together with all the villages all **a** these towns
21:11 along with the pasture lands **a** it.
21:42 Each of these towns had its pasture lands **a** it;
23: 1 to Israel from all their enemies all **a**,
Jdg 2:12 the peoples who were all **a** them, and bowed down
2:14 he sold them into the power of their enemies all **a**,
7:18 you also blow the trumpets **a** the whole camp,
7:21 Every man stood in his place all **a** the camp,
11: 3 Outlaws collected **a** Jephthah and went raiding
11:18 went **a** the land of Edom and the land of Moab,
16: 2 So they circled **a** and lay in wait for him all night
18:23 who turned **a** and said to Micah,
20:29 So Israel stationed men in ambush **a** Gibeah.
1Sa 5:10 "Why have they brought **a** to us the ark of the God
10: 1 from the hand of their enemies all **a**.
22: 6 and all his servants were standing **a** him.
22: 7 Saul said to his servants who stood **a** him,
22:17 The king said to the guard who stood **a** him,
23:23 Look **a** and learn all the hiding places
26: 5 while the army was encamped **a** him.
26: 7 and Abner and the army lay **a** him.
2Sa 2:25 The Benjaminites rallied **a** Abner and formed
5: 9 David built the city all **a** from the Millo inward.
5:23 go **a** to their rear, and come upon them opposite
7: 1 from all his enemies **a** him,
22:12 He made darkness **a** him a canopy, thick clouds,
24: 6 and from Dan they went **a** to Sidon,
1Ki 2: 5 putting the blood of war on the belt **a** his waist,
3: 1 the house of the LORD and the wall **a** Jerusalem.
6: 5 running **a** the walls of the house,
6: 5 and he made side chambers all **a**.
6: 6 for **a** the outside of the house he made offsets on
6:29 of the house all **a** about with carved engravings
7:12 of dressed stone to one layer of cedar beams all **a**;
7:18 the columns with two rows **a** each latticework
7:20 two hundred pomegranates in rows all **a**;
7:24 Under its brim were panels all **a** it,
7:36 where each had space, with wreaths all **a**.
8:14 the king turned **a** and blessed all the assembly
11:24 He gathered followers **a** him and became leader of
18:32 Then he made a trench **a** the altar,
18:35 so that the water ran all **a** the altar,
20:31 let us put sackcloth **a** our waists and ropes
20:32 So they tied sackcloth **a** their waists,
22:34 so he said to the driver of his chariot, "Turn **a**,
2Ki 1: 8 "A hairy man, with a leather belt **a** his waist."
2:24 When he turned **a** and saw them,
6:15 army with horses and chariots was all **a** the city.
6:17 of horses and chariots of fire all **a** Elisha.
11:11 **a** the altar and the house,
17:15 they followed the nations that were **a** them,
23: 5 in the high places at the cities of Judah and **a**
25: 1 they built siegeworks against it all **a**.
25: 4 though the Chaldeans were all **a** the city.
25:10 the captain of the guard broke down the walls **a**
25:17 all of bronze, were on the capital all **a**.
1Ch 4:33 with all their villages that were **a** these towns
11: 8 the city all **a**, from the Millo in complete circuit;
14:14 go **a** and come on them opposite the balsam trees.
2Ch 4: 3 Under it were panels all **a**, each of ten cubits,
6: 3 the king turned **a** and blessed all the assembly
13: 7 and certain worthless scoundrels gathered **a** him
13:13 Jeroboam had sent an ambush **a** to come on them
14:14 They defeated all the cities **a** Gerar,
15:15 and the LORD gave them rest all **a**.
17: 9 they went **a** through all the cities of Judah
17:10 the LORD fell on all the kingdoms of the lands **a**
18:33 so he said to the driver of his chariot, "Turn **a**,
20:30 for his God gave him rest all **a**.
23: 2 They went **a** through Judah and gathered
23:10 **a** the altar and the house.
33:14 he carried it **a** Ophel, and raised it to
34: 6 and as far as Naphtali, in their ruins all **a**,
Ezr 9: 4 gathered **a** me while I sat appalled until
Ne 5:17 besides those who came to us from the nations **a**
6:16 all the nations **a** us were afraid and fell greatly
12:28 from the circuit **a** Jerusalem and from the villages
12:29 for the singers had built for themselves villages **a**
Est 2:11 Every day Mordecai would walk **a** in front of
Job 1:10 a fence **a** him and his house and all that he has,
8:17 Their roots twine **a** the stoneheap;
17: 2 Surely there are mockers **a** me,
19: 6 and closed his net **a** me.
19:12 up siegeworks against me, and encamp **a** my tent.
21:11 and their children dance **a**.
22:10 Therefore snares are **a** you,
29: 5 when my children were **a** me;
36:30 he scatters his lightning **a** him and covers the roots
37:22 **a** God is awesome majesty.
41:14 There is terror all **a** its teeth.
Ps 3: 3 O LORD, are a shield **a** me, my glory,
3: 6 people who have set themselves against me all **a**.
7: 7 Let the assembly of the peoples be gathered **a** you,
18:11 He made darkness his covering **a** him,
22:16 For dogs are all **a** me;
26: 6 and go **a** your altar, O LORD,
27: 6 my head is lifted up above my enemies all **a** me,
31:13 For I hear the whispering of many—terror all **a**!—
34: 7 of the LORD encamps **a** those who fear him,
38: 6 all day long I go **a** mourning.
44:13 the derision and scorn of those **a** us.
48:12 Walk about Zion, go all **a** it, count its towers,
50: 3 and a mighty tempest all **a** him.
55:10 Day and night they go **a** it on its walls,
76:10 when you bind the last bit of your wrath **a** you.
76:11 let all who are **a** him bring gifts to
78:28 within their camp, all **a** their dwellings.
79: 3 They have poured out their blood like water all **a**
79: 4 mocked and derided by those **a** us.
82: 5 nor understanding, they walk **a** in darkness;
89: 7 great and awesome above all that are **a** him?
97: 2 Clouds and thick darkness are all **a** him;
109:19 May it be like a garment that he wraps **a** himself,
128: 3 your children will be like olive shoots **a**

Ps 139:11 and the light a me become night,"
Pr 3: 3 bind them a your neck, write them on the tablet
6:12 and a villain goes a with crooked speech,
6:21 upon your heart always; tie them a your neck.
Ecc 1: 6 wind blows to the south, and goes a to the north;
SS 3: 7 A it are sixty mighty men of the mighty men
Isa 11: 5 Righteousness shall be the belt a his waist,
11: 5 and faithfulness the belt a his loins.
15: 8 For a cry has gone a the land of Moab;
19:14 in all its doings as a drunkard staggers a in vomit.
42:25 it set him on fire all a, but he did not understand;
49:18 Lift up your eyes all a and see;
60: 4 Lift up your eyes and look a;
Jer 4:17 They have closed in a her like watchers of a field,
5: 1 to and fro through the streets of Jerusalem, look a
6: 3 They shall pitch their tents a her;
9: 4 and every neighbor goes a like a slanderer.
12: 9 Are the birds of prey all a her?
17:26 the towns of Judah and the places a Jerusalem,
20:10 For I hear many whispering: "Terror is all a!
21:14 and it shall devour all that is a it.
25: 9 and against all these nations a;
26: 9 the people gathered a Jeremiah in the house of
32:44 in the land of Benjamin, in the places a Jerusalem,
33:13 the places a Jerusalem, and in the towns of Judah,
34:11 But afterward they turned a and took back
34:16 but then you turned a and profaned my name
40:15 that all the Judeans who are gathered a you would
41:14 from Mizpah turned a and came back,
46: 5 They do not look back—terror is all a!
46:14 for the sword shall devour those a you."
49:29 and a cry shall go up: "Terror is all a!"
50:14 Take up your positions a Babylon,
50:29 Encamp all a her; let no one escape.
50:32 and it will devour everything a him.
52: 4 they built siegeworks against it all a.
52: 7 though the Chaldeans were all a the city.
52:14 broke down all the walls a Jerusalem.
La 2: 3 like a flaming fire in Jacob, consuming all a.
2:22 You invited my enemies from all a as if for a day
Eze 1: 4 a great cloud with brightness a it
1:18 for the rims of all four were full of eyes all a.
1:27 something that looked like fire enclosed all a;
1:27 and there was a splendor all a.
1:28 such was the appearance of the splendor all a.
4: 2 and plant battering rams against it all a.
5: 2 and strike with the sword all a the city;
5: 5 the center of the nations, with countries all a her.
5: 6 the nations and the countries all a her,
5: 7 the nations that are all a you, and have
5: 7 to the ordinances of the nations that are all a you;
5:12 one third shall fall by the sword a you;
5:14 an object of mocking among the nations a you,
5:15 a warning and a horror, to the nations a you,
6: 5 and I will scatter your bones a your altars.
6:13 their slain lie among their idols a their altars,
8:10 there, portrayed on the wall all a,
10:12 were full of eyes all a.
11:12 to the ordinances of the nations that are a you."
12:14 I will scatter to every wind all who are a him,
16:33 to come to you from all a for your whorings.
16:37 I will gather them against you from all a,
16:57 those all a who despise you.
19: 8 nations set upon him from the provinces all a;
23:15 with belts a their waists, with flowing turbans
23:42 The sound of a raucous multitude was a her,
27:11 of Arvad and Helech were on your walls all a;
27:11 They hung their quivers all a your walls;
31: 4 making its rivers flow a the place it was planted,
32:22 and all its company, their graves all a it,
32:23 Its company is all a its grave, all of them killed,
32:24 Elam is there, and all its hordes a its grave;
32:25 their graves all a it, all of them uncircumcised,
32:26 their graves all a them, all of them uncircumcised,
34:26 I will make them and the region a my hill
36: 4 of derision to the rest of the nations all a;
36: 7 that are all a you shall themselves suffer insults.
36:36 the nations that are left all a you shall know that I,
37: 2 He led me all a them;
38: 4 I will turn you a and put hooks into your jaws,
38: 7 and all the companies that are assembled a you,
39: 2 I will turn you a and drive you forward,
39:17 and come, gather from all a to the sacrificial feast
40: 5 a wall all a the outside of the temple area.
40:16 with shutters on the inside of the gateway all a,
40:16 vestibules also had windows on the inside all a;
40:17 and a pavement, all a the court;
40:25 There were windows all a in it and in its vestibule,
40:29 there were windows all a in it and in its vestibule;
40:30 There were vestibules all a,
40:33 there were windows all a in it and in its vestibule;
40:36 and it had windows all a.
40:43 one handbreadth long, fastened all a the inside.
41: 5 four cubits, all a the temple.
41: 6 There were offsets all a the wall of the temple
41: 7 for the structure was supplied with a stairway all a
41: 8 also that the temple had a raised platform all a;
41:10 of twenty cubits all a the temple on every side.
41:11 of the part that was left free was five cubits all a.
41:12 the wall of the building was five cubits thick all a,
41:16 all a, all three had windows with recessed frames.
41:16 the temple was paneled with wood all a,
41:17 And on all the walls all a in the inner room and
41:19 They were carved on the whole temple all a;
42:15 and measured the temple area all a.
42:20 It had a wall a it,
43:12 the whole territory on the top of the mountain all a
Eze 43:13 with a rim of one span a its edge.
43:17 with a rim a it half a cubit wide,
43:20 and upon the rim all a;
45: 2 with fifty cubits for an open space a it.
46:23 a each of the four courts was a row of masonry,
46:23 with hearths made at the bottom of the rows all a.
47: 2 and led me a on the outside to the outer gate
Da 5: 7 have a chain of gold a his neck,
5:16 have a chain of gold a your neck,
5:29 a chain of gold was put a his neck,
10: 5 with a belt of gold from Uphaz a his waist.
Joel 3:11 Come quickly, all you nations all a,
Ob 1:16 all the nations a you shall drink;
Jnh 2: 5 weeds were wrapped a my head
Mic 5: 1 Now you are walled a with a wall;
Na 3: 8 with water a her, her rampart a sea,
Hab 2:16 The cup in the LORD's right hand will come a
Zec 2: 5 For I will be a wall of fire all a it,
7: 7 along with the towns a it,
Mt 2:16 in and a Bethlehem who were two years old or
3: 4 of camel's hair with a leather belt a his waist,
8:18 Now when Jesus saw great crowds a him,
13: 2 Such great crowds gathered a him that he got into
18: 6 if a great millstone were fastened a your neck
20: 6 and found others standing a;
21:33 put a fence a it, dug a wine press in it,
27:27 and they gathered the whole cohort a him.
Mk 1: 6 with a leather belt a his waist,
1:33 And the whole city was gathered a the door.
2: 2 So many gathered a that there was no longer room
2:13 whole crowd gathered a him, and he taught them.
3: 5 He looked a at them with anger;
3: 8 and the region a Tyre and Sidon.
3:32 A crowd was sitting a him;
3:34 And looking at those who sat a him, he said,
4: 1 a very large crowd gathered a him that he got into
4:10 those who were a him along with
5:21 a great crowd gathered a him;
5:32 He looked all a to see who had done it.
6:30 The apostles gathered a Jesus,
7: 1 who had come from Jerusalem gathered a him,
9: 8 Suddenly when they looked a,
9:14 they saw a great crowd a them,
9:42 for you if a great millstone were hung a your neck
10: 1 And crowds again gathered a him;
10:23 Then Jesus looked a and said to his disciples,
11:11 and when he had looked a at everything,
12: 1 "A man planted a vineyard, put a fence a it,
12:38 who like to walk a in long robes,
16: S ⟦they told briefly to those a Peter.⟧
Lk 2: 9 and the glory of the Lord shone a them,
3: 3 He went into all the region a the Jordan,
6:10 After looking a at all of them, he said to him,
13: 8 until I dig a it and put manure on it.
15:20 he ran and put his arms a him and kissed him.
17: 2 for you if a millstone were hung a your neck
19:43 when your enemies will set up ramparts a you
20:46 who like to walk a in long robes,
22:49 those who were a him saw what was coming,
Jn 4:35 But I tell you, look a you,
10:24 So the Jews gathered a him and said to him,
13: 4 took off his outer robe, and tied a towel a himself.
13: 5 to wipe them with the towel that was tied a him.
18:18 they were standing a it and warming themselves.
20:14 she turned a and saw Jesus standing there,
21:18 a belt a you and take you where you do not wish
Ac 5:16 of people would also gather from the towns a
9: 3 suddenly a light from heaven flashed a him.
12: 8 "Wrap your cloak a you and follow me."
26:13 shining a me and my companions.
28: 2 they kindled a fire and welcomed all of us a it.
Ro 15:19 and as far a as Illyricum I have fully proclaimed
Eph 6:14 and fasten the belt of truth a your waist,
1Pe 5: 8 a roaring lion your adversary the devil prowls a,
Rev 4: 3 and a the throne is a rainbow that looks like
4: 4 A the throne are twenty-four thrones,
4: 6 A the throne, and on each side of the throne,
4: 8 are full of eyes all a and inside.
7:11 the angels stood a the throne and a the elders
Tob 11: 9 Anna ran up to her son and threw her arms a him,
11:13 Then Tobit saw his son and threw his arms a him,
Jdt 1: 2 He built walls a Ecbatana
4:10 they all put sackcloth a their waists.
4:14 with sackcloth a their loins,
5:22 the people standing a the tent began to complain;
7:23 gathered a Uzziah and the rulers of the town
8: 5 She put sackcloth a her waist and dressed
10:18 They came and gathered a her as she stood outside
13:10 through the camp, circled a the valley, and went
13:13 they lit a fire to give light, and gathered a them.
15: 3 Those who had camped in the hills a Bethulia
AdE 1: 6 with roses arranged a them.
9:19 On this account then the Jews who are scattered a
Wis 17: 4 but terrifying sounds rang out a them,
Sir 9: 7 Do not look a in the streets of a city,
18:27 when sin is all a, one guards against wrongdoing.
45: 9 with many golden bells all a,
50:12 the hearth of the altar with a garland of brothers a
Bar 2: 4 He made them subject to all the kingdoms a us,
2:23 from the region a Jerusalem the voice of mirth and
LtJ 6:42 And the women, with cords a them,
Aza 1: 1 They walked a in the midst of the flames,
1Mc 1:11 and make a covenant with the Gentiles a us,
2:45 and his friends went a and tore down the altars;
2:67 You shall rally a you all who observe the law,
3:25 and terror fell on the Gentiles all a them.
4: 7 strong and fortified, with cavalry all a it;
1Mc 4:60 with high walls and strong towers all a,
5: 1 When the Gentiles all a heard that
5:10 Gentiles a us have gathered together to destroy us.
5:38 "All the Gentiles a us have gathered to him;
5:46 and they could not go a it to the right or to the left;
5:57 let us go and make war on the Gentiles a us."
6:18 the citadel kept hemming Israel in a the sanctuary.
6:62 and gave orders to tear down the wall all a.
7:17 and their blood they poured out all a Jerusalem,
10:45 the walls of Jerusalem and fortifying it all a,
11:47 and they all rallied a him and then spread out
11:55 that Demetrius had discharged gathered a him;
12:13 the kings a us have waged war against us.
12:27 and he stationed outposts a the camp.
12:45 and will turn a and go home.
12:53 All the nations a them tried to destroy them,
13:20 and he circled a by the way to Adora.
13:33 up the strongholds of Judea and walled them all a,
2Mc 4:38 and led him a the whole city to that very place
4:41 of the ashes that were lying a,
6:10 They publicly paraded them a the city,
10:36 in the same way wheeled a against the defenders
13: 5 and it has a rim running a it that
1Es 1:53 These killed their young men with the sword a
3: 6 and a necklace a his neck;
4:11 but they keep watch a him,
8:72 at the word of the Lord of Israel gathered a me,
8:91 there gathered a him a very great crowd of men
3Mc 1:27 When those who were a him observed this,
1:29 the people but also the walls and the whole earth a
3: 8 an unexpected tumult a these people and
6: 1 the elders a him to stop calling upon the holy God,
2Es 9:38 When I said these things in my heart, I looked a,
11: 2 and the clouds were gathered a it.
15:44 and all who are a it shall mourn for it.
16:38 has great pains a her womb for two
4Mc 3: 8 and quite exhausted, to the royal tent, a which
5: 1 and with his armed soldiers standing a him,
9:13 When the noble youth was stretched out a this,
10: 8 he saw his own flesh torn all a and drops
11:10 they twisted his back a the wedge on the wheel,
14: 7 the seven days of creation move in choral dance a
14:17 by flying in circles a them in the anguish of love,

AROUSE‡ (5) [ROUSE]

Zec 9:13 I will a your sons, O Zion, against your sons,
2Pe 3: 1 in them I am trying to a your sincere intention
1Mc 6:34 of grapes and mulberries, to a them for battle.
13:17 he would not a great hostility among the people,
2Es 4:37 or a them until that measure is fulfilled.' "

AROUSED (12) [ROUSE]

2Ch 21:16 The LORD a against Jehoram the anger of
Isa 45:13 I have a Cyrus in righteousness,
Jer 32:31 This city has a my anger and wrath,
Eze 38:18 says the Lord GOD, my wrath shall be a.
Ac 21:30 all the city was a, and the people rushed together.
Ro 7: 5 our sinful passions, a by the law,
Jdt 12:16 with her and his passion was a,
1Mc 10:74 the words of Apollonius, his spirit was a.
2Mc 4:40 the crowds were becoming a and filled with anger,
13: 4 the King of kings a the anger of Antiochus against
15:10 When he had a their courage, he issued his orders,
2Es 6:37 My spirit was greatly a, and my soul was

AROUSES (3) [ROUSE]

Pr 6:34 For jealousy a a husband's fury,
Wis 15: 5 whose appearance a yearning in fools,
Sir 26: 8 A drunken wife a great anger;

AROUSING (1) [ROUSE]

2Mc 15:17 and so effective in a valor and awaking courage in

ARPACHSHAD (9) [=ARPHAXAD]

Ge 10:22 Elam, Asshur, A, Lud, and Aram.
10:24 A became the father of Shelah;
11:10 he became the father of A two years after
11:11 Shem lived after the birth of A five hundred years,
11:12 When A had lived thirty-five years,
11:13 and A lived after the birth of Shelah
1Ch 1:17 The descendants of Shem: Elam, Asshur, A, Lud,
1:18 A became the father of Shelah;
1:24 Shem, A, Shelah;

ARPAD‡ (6)

2Ki 18:34 Where are the gods of Hamath and A?
19:13 Where is the king of Hamath, the king of A,
Isa 10: 9 Is not Hamath like A?
36:19 Where are the gods of Hamath and A?
37:13 Where is the king of Hamath, the king of A,
Jer 49:23 Hamath and A are confounded,

ARPHAD (KJV) See ARPAD

ARPHAXAD (6) [=ARPACHSHAD]

Lk 3:36 son of A, son of Shem, son of Noah,
Jdt 1: 1 In those days A ruled over the Medes in Ecbatana.
1: 5 against King A in the great plain that is on
1:13 against King A and defeated him in battle,
1:13 of A and all his cavalry and all his chariots.
1:15 He captured A in the mountains of Ragau

ARRANGE (7) [ARRANGED, ARRANGEMENT, ARRANGEMENTS, ARRANGING]
Ex 21:19 and to a for full recovery.
40: 4 You shall bring in the table, and a its setting;
Lev 1: 7 on the altar and a wood on the fire.
1: 8 Aaron's sons the priests shall a the parts,
1:12 and the priest shall a them on the wood that is on
2Co 9: 5 and a in advance for this bountiful gift
Tob 6:13 concerning the girl and a her engagement to you.

ARRANGED (15) [ARRANGE]
Nu 23: 4 and Balaam said to him, "I have a the seven altars,
1Co 12:18 But as it is, God a the members in the body,
12:24 But God has so a the body,
AdE 1: 6 with roses a around them.
Wis 11:20 But you have a all things by measure and number
Sir 16:27 he a his works in an eternal order,
47:10 and a their times throughout the year,
Sus 1:14 Then together they a for a time
2Mc 12:20 But Maccabeus a his army in divisions,
3Mc 1: 3 and a that a certain insignificant man should sleep
3: 2 While these matters were being a,
4: 1 a feast at public expense was a for the Gentiles
5: 5 and bound the hands of the wretched people and a
6:31 a for a banquet of deliverance instead of a bitter
6:35 a the aforementioned choral group and passed

ARRANGEMENT (5) [ARRANGE]
1Sa 20:39 only Jonathan and David knew the a.
Eze 43:11 make known to them the plan of the temple, its a,
Ac 20:13 for he had made this a,
1Es 1:15 in their place according to the a made by David,
2Es 6:45 and the a of the stars to come into being;

ARRANGEMENTS (1) [ARRANGE]
Eze 42:11 with the same exits and a and doors.

ARRANGING (2) [ARRANGE]
Ecc 12: 9 weighing and studying and a many proverbs.
Sir 50:14 and a the offering to the Most High, the Almighty,

ARRAY‡ (9) [ARRAYED]
Jdg 20:30 and set themselves in a against Gibeah, as before.
2Sa 10: 8 and drew up in battle a at the entrance of the gate;
1Ch 19: 9 and drew up in battle a at the entrance of the city,
19:17 David set the battle in a against the Arameans,
Jer 50: 9 and they shall a themselves against her;
50:42 set in a as a warrior for battle, against you,
51: 3 and let him not a himself in his coat of mail.
AdE 15: 6 clothed in the full a of his majesty,
Sir 43: 9 a glittering a in the heights of the Lord.

ARRAYED (18) [ARRAY]
Ge 41:42 he a him in garments of fine linen,
Jdg 6:31 But Joash said to all who were a against him,
2Sa 10: 9 and a them against the Arameans;
10:10 and he a them against the Ammonites.
10:17 The Arameans a themselves against David
1Ki 22:10 a in their robes, at the threshing floor at
1Ch 12:38 All these, warriors a in battle order,
19:10 of the picked men of Israel and a them against
19:11 and they were a against the Ammonites.
2Ch 5:12 a in fine linen, with cymbals, harps, and lyres,
18: 9 were sitting on their thrones, a in their robes;
Job 6: 4 the terrors of God are a against me.
Ps 55:18 for many are a against me.
AdE 15: 1 and a herself in splendid attire.
1Es 1: 2 a in their vestments, in the temple of the Lord.
5:59 And the priests stood a in their vestments,
7: 9 the Levites stood a in their vestments,
3Mc 1:19 women who had recently been a for marriage

ARREST (20) [ARRESTED, ARRESTING]
Jer 36:26 of Azriel and Shelemiah son of Abdeel to a
Mt 21:46 They wanted to a him, but they feared the crowds,
26: 4 they conspired to a Jesus by stealth and kill him.
26:48 "The one I will kiss is the man; a him."
26:55 with swords and clubs to a me as though I were
26:55 and you did not a me.
Mk 12:12 they wanted to a him, but they feared the crowd.
14: 1 and the scribes were looking for a way to a Jesus
14:44 a him and lead him away under guard."
14:48 with swords and clubs to a me as though I were
14:49 and you did not a me.
Lk 21:12 all this occurs, they will a you and persecute you;
Jn 7:30 Then they tried to a him,
7:32 and Pharisees sent temple police to a him.
7:44 Some of them wanted to a him,
7:45 who asked them, "Why did you not a him?"
10:39 Then they tried to a him again,
11:57 so that they might a him.
Ac 12: 3 he proceeded to a Peter also.
2Mc 14:39 sent more than five hundred soldiers to a him;

ARRESTED (19) [ARREST]
Jer 37:13 of Hananiah a the prophet Jeremiah saying,
37:14 and a Jeremiah and brought him to the officials.
Mt 4:12 Now when Jesus heard that John had been a,
14: 3 For Herod had a John, bound him,
26:50 they came and laid hands on Jesus and a him.
26:57 Those who had a Jesus took him to Caiaphas
Mk 1:14 Now after John was a, Jesus came to Galilee,
6:17 For Herod himself had sent men who a John,
14:46 Then they laid hands on him and a him.
Jn 8:20 in the treasury of the temple, but no one a him,
18:12 and the Jewish police a Jesus and bound him.
Ac 1:16 who became a guide for those who a Jesus—
4: 3 So they a them and put them in custody until
5:18 a the apostles and put them in the public prison.
21:33 Then the tribune came, a him,
28:17 yet I was a in Jerusalem and handed over to
Bel 1:21 and he a the priests and their wives and children.
2Mc 7: 1 also that seven brothers and their mother were a
4Mc 16:15 For when you and your sons were a together,

ARRESTING (1) [ARREST]
2Mc 14:40 for he thought that by a him he would do them

ARRIVAL (8) [ARRIVE]
Nu 10:21 and the tabernacle was set up before their a.
Ezr 3: 8 In the second year after their a at the house of God
Ac 10:25 On Peter's a Cornelius met him,
18:27 On his a he greatly helped those who
2Co 7: 6 consoled us by the a of Titus,
Jdt 10:18 for her a was reported from tent to tent.
1Mc 11:44 the king rejoiced at their a.
2Mc 8:12 when he told his companions of the a of the army,

ARRIVE (9) [ARRIVAL, ARRIVED, ARRIVES, ARRIVING]
Ge 19:22 for I can do nothing until you a there."
Ex 10:26 to use to worship the LORD until we a there."
1Ki 19:15 you a, you shall anoint Hazael as king over Aram.
2Ki 9: 2 When you a, look there for Jehu son
Ne 2: 7 that they may grant me passage until I a in Judah;
Ac 23:35 "I will give you a hearing when your accusers a."
1Co 16: 3 And when I a, I will send any whom you approve
1Ti 4:13 Until I a, give attention to the public reading
2Ti 3: 7 who are always being instructed and can never a

ARRIVED (66) [ARRIVE]
Dt 32:17 to new ones recently a, whom your ancestors
Jdg 3:27 When he a, he sounded the trumpet in the hill
7:13 When Gideon a, there was a man telling a dream
11:18 a on the east side of the land of Moab,
19:10 and a opposite Jebus (that is, Jerusalem).
1Sa 4:13 When he a, Eli was sitting upon his seat by
13:10 the burnt offering, Samuel a;
26: 4 and learned that Saul had indeed a.
2Sa 3:22 then the servants of David a with Joab from a raid,
13:36 king's sons a, and raised their voices and wept;
16:14 and all the people who were with him a weary at
19:30 since my lord the king has a home safely."
1Ki 1:42 Jonathan son of the priest Abiathar a.
2Ki 6:32 Before the messenger a, Elisha said to the elders,
9: 5 He a while the commanders of the army were
16:11 before King Ahaz a from Damascus.
18:17 When they a, they came and stood by the conduit
Est 6:14 the king's eunuchs a and hurried Haman off to
Jer 41: 5 eighty men a from Shechem and Shiloh
43: 7 And they a at Tahpanhes.
Eze 16: 7 up and became tall and a at full womanhood;
Da 7:22 for the holy ones of the Most High, and the time a
Zec 6:10 who have a from Babylon;
Mt 26:47 he was still speaking, Judas, one of the twelve, a;
Mk 6:33 on foot from all the towns and a ahead of them.
14:43 Judas, one of the twelve, a;
Lk 8:26 Then they a at the country of the Gerasenes,
11: 6 for a friend of mine has a,
Jn 11:17 When Jesus a, he found
Ac 5:21 When the high priest and those with him a,
5:25 Then someone a and announced, "Look,
9:39 when he a, they took him to the room upstairs.
11:11 a at the house where we were.
13: 5 When they a at Salamis, they proclaimed the word
14:27 When they a, they called the church together
17:10 when they a, they went to the Jewish synagogue.
18: 5 When Silas and Timothy a from Macedonia,
20:15 and on the following day we a opposite Chios.
21: 7 the voyage from Tyre, we a at Ptolemais;
21:17 When we a in Jerusalem, the brothers welcomed
25: 1 Three days after Festus had a in the province,
25: 7 When he a, the Jews who had gone down
25:13 and Bernice a at Caesarea to welcome Festus.
27: 7 a number of days and a with difficulty off Cnidus,
2Ti 1:17 when he a in Rome, he eagerly searched for me
3Jn 1: 3 of the friends a and testified to your faithfulness to
Jdt 16:18 When they a at Jerusalem, they worshiped God.
AdE 6:14 the eunuchs a and hurriedly brought Haman to
9: 1 which is Adar, the decree written by the king a.
Sir 33:17 by the blessing of the Lord I a first,
1Mc 3:40 they a they encamped near Emmaus in the plain.
15:15 Numenius and his companions a from Rome,
2Mc 3: 9 When he had a at Jerusalem
3:24 But when he a at the treasury with his bodyguard,
5:25 When this man a in Jerusalem,
15:31 When he a there and had called his compatriots
1Es 8: 6 on the new moon of the first month and a
8:61 we a in Jerusalem by the mighty hand of our Lord,
3Mc 1: 9 After he had a in Jerusalem,
2:25 When he a in Egypt, he increased in his deeds
3:20 "But we, when we a in Egypt victorious,
4: 1 In every place, then, where this decree a,
5:26 Hermon a and invited him to come out,
6:16 the king a at the hippodrome with the animals
3Mc 7:17 When they had a at Ptolemais,
7:18 to them for their journey until all of them a

ARRIVES (5) [ARRIVE]
Mt 24:46 whom his master will find at work when he a.
Lk 12:43 whom his master will find at work when he a.
Ac 23:15 we are ready to do away with him before he a."
3Mc 3:25 we have given orders that, as soon as this letter a,
4Mc 2: 8 and to cancel the debt when the seventh year a.

ARRIVING (3) [ARRIVE]
2Ki 9:17 on the tower spied the company of Jehu a,
2Mc 2:28 while devoting our effort to a at the outlines of
4:21 upon a at Joppa he proceeded to Jerusalem.

ARROGANCE (36) [ARROGANT, ARROGANTLY]
1Sa 2: 3 let not a come from your mouth;
2Ki 19:28 against me and your a has come to my ears,
Ps 10: 2 In a the wicked persecute the poor—
Pr 8:13 Pride and a and the way of evil
Isa 9: 9 but in pride and a of heart they said:
16: 6 of his a, his pride, and his insolence;
37:29 against me and your a has come to my ears,
Jer 48:29 of his loftiness, his pride, and his a,
Eze 7:24 I will put an end to the a of the strong,
Jas 4:16 it is, you boast in your a; all such boasting is evil.
Jdt 6:19 of heaven, see their a, and have pity on our people
9:10 crush their a by the hand of a woman.
AdE 16:12 But, unable to restrain his a,
Wis 5: 8 What has our a profited us?
Sir 10: 7 A is hateful to the Lord and to mortals,
15: 8 She is far from a, and liars will never think of her.
16: 8 whom he loathed on account of their a.
22:22 But as for reviling, a, disclosure of secrets,
48:18 and made great boasts in his a.
1Mc 1:24 He shed much blood, and spoke with great a.
2:49 "A and scorn have now become strong;
2Mc 5:21 in his a that he could sail on the land and walk on
7:36 will receive just punishment for your a.
9: 4 For in his a he said,
9: 7 but was even more filled with a,
9: 8 while before had thought in his superhuman a
9:11 to lose much of his a and to come to his senses
13: 9 The king with barbarous a was coming to show
15: 6 and a had determined to erect a public monument
3Mc 1:26 But he, in his a, took heed of nothing,
2: 3 those who have done anything in insolence and a.
2:17 in their wrath and exult in the a of their tongue,
3:18 they were carried away by their traditional a,
6:16 at the hippodrome with the animals and all the a
4Mc 2:15 lust for power, vainglory, boasting, a, and malice.
8:19 up this vain opinion and this a that threatens

ARROGANT‡ (33) [ARROGANCE]
Ps 36:11 Do not let the foot of the a tread on me,
73: 3 For I was envious of the a;
94: 4 They pour out their a words;
101: 5 A haughty look and an a heart I will not tolerate.
119:51 The a utterly deride me, but I do not turn away
119:69 The a smear me with lies,
119:78 Let the a be put to shame,
119:85 a have dug pitfalls for me; they flout your law.
140: 5 The a have hidden a trap for me,
Pr 16: 5 All those who are a are an abomination to
21:24 named "Scoffer," acts with a pride.
Isa 10:12 he will punish the a boasting of the king
13:11 I will put an end to the pride of the a,
Jer 50:31 I am against you, O a one,
50:32 The a one shall stumble and fall,
Da 7:11 I watched then because of the noise of the a words
Hab 2: 5 wealth is treacherous; the a do not endure.
Mal 3:15 Now we count the a happy,
4: 1 when all the a and all evildoers will be stubble;
1Co 4:18 that I am not coming to you, have become a.
4:19 and I will find out not the talk of these a people
5: 2 And you are a! Should you not rather have
13: 4 love is not envious or boastful or a
2Ti 3: 2 boasters, a, abusive, disobedient to their parents,
Tit 1: 7 he must not be a or quick-tempered or addicted
Wis 14: 6 in the beginning, when a giants were perishing,
Sir 23: 8 by them the reviler and the a are tripped up.
1Mc 2:47 They hunted down the a, and the work prospered
3Mc 1:25 in various ways to change his a mind from
5:13 of his all-powerful hand to the a Gentiles.
6: 4 with his a army by drowning them in the sea,
4Mc 4:15 to the throne, an a and terrible man,
9:30 the a design of your tyranny being defeated

ARROGANTLY (11) [ARROGANCE]
Ex 18:11 when they dealt a with them."
Job 36: 9 and their transgressions, that they are behaving a.
Ps 17:10 with their mouths they speak a.
Jer 50:29 for she has a defied the LORD,
Da 7: 8 in this horn, and a mouth speaking a.
7:20 the horn that had eyes and a mouth that spoke a,
8:11 Even against the prince of the host it acted a;
1Mc 1:21 He a entered the sanctuary and took
7:34 and derided them and defiled them and spoke a,
7:47 and the right hand that he had so a stretched out,
3Mc 2: 5 and sulfur the people of Sodom who acted a,

ARROW (25) [ARROWS]

1Sa 20:36 As the boy ran, he shot an a beyond him.
20:37 to the place where Jonathan's a had fallen,
20:37 "Is the a not beyond you?"
2Ki 9:24 so that the a pierced his heart;
13:17 Then he said, "The LORD's a of victory, the a of victory over Aram!
19:32 He shall not come into this city, shoot an a there,
Job 20:24 a bronze a will strike them through.
41:28 The a cannot make it flee;
Ps 11:2 they have fitted their a to the string,
64:7 But God will shoot his a at them;
91:5 or the a that flies by day,
Pr 7:23 until an a pierces its entrails.
25:18 or a sharp a is one who bears false witness against
Isa 37:33 He shall not come into this city, shoot an a there,
49:2 he made me a polished a,
Jer 9:8 Their tongue is a deadly a;
La 3:12 he bent his bow and set me as a mark for his a.
Zec 9:13 I have made Ephraim its a.
9:14 and his a go forth like lightning;
Wis 5:12 when an a is shot at a target, the air, thus divided,
Sir 19:12 Like an a stuck in a person's thigh,
26:12 of every tent peg and open her quiver to the a.
2Es 16:7 Can one turn back an a shot by a strong archer?
16:16 as an a shot by a mighty archer does not return,

ARROWS‡ (49) [ARROW]

Ex 19:13 but they shall be stoned or shot with a;
Nu 24:8 He shall strike with his a.
Dt 32:23 spend my a against them:
32:42 I will make my a drunk with blood,
1Sa 20:20 I will shoot three a to the side of it,
20:21 Then I will send the boy, saying, 'Go, find the a.'
20:21 'Look, the a are on this side of you, collect them,'
20:22 'Look, the a are beyond you,' then go;
20:36 "Run and find the a that I shoot."
20:38 So Jonathan's boy gathered up the a and came
2Sa 22:15 He sent out a, and scattered them—lightning,
2Ki 13:15 Elisha said to him, "Take a bow and a";
13:15 so he took a bow and a.
13:18 He continued, "Take the a"; and he took them.
1Ch 12:2 and could shoot a and sling stones with either
2Ch 26:15 and the corners for shooting a and large stones.
Job 6:4 For the a of the Almighty are in me;
Ps 7:13 his deadly weapons, making his a fiery shafts.
18:14 And he sent out his a, and scattered them;
38:2 For your a have sunk into me,
45:5 Your a are sharp in the heart of the king's enemies
57:4 their teeth are spears and a,
64:3 who aim bitter words like a,
76:3 There he broke the flashing a, the shield,
77:17 your a flashed on every side.
120:4 A warrior's sharp a, with glowing coals of the
127:4 Like a in the hand of a warrior are the sons
144:6 send out your a and rout them.
Pr 26:18 a maniac who shoots deadly firebrands and a,
Isa 5:28 their a are sharp, all their bows bent,
7:24 With bow and a one will go there,
Jer 50:9 Their a are like the a of a skilled warrior who does
50:14 spare no a, for she has sinned against the LORD.
51:11 Sharpen the a! Fill the quivers!
La 3:13 He shot into my vitals the a of his quiver;
Eze 5:16 my deadly a of famine, a for destruction,
21:21 he shakes the a, he consults the teraphim,
39:3 and will make your a drop out of your right hand.
39:9 bucklers and shields, bows and a,
Hab 3:9 sated were the a at your command.
3:11 at the light of your a speeding by,
3:14 with his own a the head of his warriors,
Eph 6:16 be able to quench all the flaming a of the evil one.
1Mc 6:51 machines to shoot a, and catapults.
10:80 and shot a at his men from early morning
2Mc 10:30 They showered a and thunderbolts on the enemy,
2Es 16:13 and his a that he shoots are sharp and

ARSACES (3)

1Mc 14:2 When King A of Persia and Media heard
14:3 and seized him and took him to A,
15:22 and to Attalus and Ariarathes and A,

ARSAEUS (1)

AdE 9:9 Marmasima, Aruphaeus, A, Zabutheus,

ARSINOË (2)

3Mc 1:1 took with him his sister A,
1:4 A went to the troops with wailing and tears,

ARSIPHURITH (1)

1Es 5:16 The descendants of A, one hundred twelve.

ART (4) [ARTISAN, ARTISANS, ARTIST, ARTISTIC, ARTS]

2Ch 16:14 of spices prepared by the perfumer's a;
Ac 17:29 an image formed by the a and imagination
Wis 15:4 neither has the evil intent of human a misled us,
17:7 The delusions of their magic a lay humbled,

ARTAXERXES (47) [ARTAXERXES']

Ezr 4:7 the days of A, Bishlam and Mithredath and Tabeel
4:7 and the rest of their associates wrote to King A
4:8 a letter against Jerusalem to King A as follows
4:11 that they sent): "To King A:
6:14 Darius, and King A of Persia;
7:1 After this, in the reign of King A of Persia,
7:7 in the seventh year of King A.
7:11 of the letter that King A gave to the priest Ezra,
7:12 "A, king of kings, to the priest Ezra, the scribe of
7:21 King A, decree to all the treasurers in the province
8:1 in the reign of King A:
Ne 2:1 in the twentieth year of King A,
5:14 to the thirty-second year of King A,
13:6 of King A of Babylon I went to the king.
AdE 1:1 in the days of A, the same A who ruled over
1:2 when King A was enthroned in the city of Susa,
1:9 for the women in the palace where King A was.
1:10 the seven eunuchs who served King A,
1:17 "And just as she defied King A,
2:16 So Esther went in to King A in the twelfth month,
2:21 and they plotted to kill King A.
3:1 After these events King A promoted Haman son
3:7 In the twelfth year of King A Haman came to
3:8 Then Haman said to King A,
3:12 of King A to the magistrates and the governors
3:13 of A to destroy the Jewish people on a given day
6:2 on guard and sought to lay hands on King A.
8:1 On that very day King A granted to Esther all
8:12 which is Adar, throughout all the kingdom of A.
9:20 to the Jews in the kingdom of A both near and far,
10:3 on behalf of King A and was great in the kingdom,
11:2 In the second year of the reign of A the Great,
12:2 that they were preparing to lay hands on King A;
13:1 This is a copy of the letter: "The Great King, A,
16:1 A, to the governors of the provinces from India
1Es 2:16 In the time of King A of the Persians, Bishlam,
2:17 "To King A our lord, your servants
2:30 Then, when the letter from King A was read,
7:4 So with the consent of Cyrus and Darius and A,
8:1 After these things, when A,
8:6 of the reign of A, in the fifth month (this was
8:8 from King A that was delivered to Ezra the priest
8:9 "King A to Ezra the priest and reader of the law of
8:19 King A, have commanded the treasurers of Syria
8:28 in the reign of King A:
2Es 1:3 in the country of the Medes in the reign of A,

ARTAXERXES' (2) [ARTAXERXES]

Ezr 4:23 the copy of King A letter was read before Rehum
AdE 3:6 and plotted to destroy all the Jews under A rule.

ARTEMAS (1)

Tit 3:12 When I send A to you, or Tychicus,

ARTEMIS (5)

Ac 19:24 a silversmith who made silver shrines of A,
19:27 the temple of the great goddess A will be scorned,
19:28 "Great is A of the Ephesians!"
19:34 "Great is A of the Ephesians!"
19:35 the great A and of the statue that fell from heaven?

ARTICLE (7) [ARTICLES]

Lev 11:32 whether an a of wood or cloth or skin or sacking,
11:32 any a that is used for any purpose;
13:50 and put the diseased a aside for seven days.
13:54 the priest shall command them to wash the a
13:55 the diseased a after it has been washed.
Nu 31:20 You shall purify every garment, every a of skin,
31:20 of goats' hair, and every a of wood."

ARTICLES (6) [ARTICLE]

Nu 31:50 a of gold, armlets and bracelets, signet rings,
31:51 all in the form of crafted a.
2Sa 8:10 Joram brought with him a of silver, gold,
1Ch 18:10 He sent all sorts of a of gold, of silver,
Rev 18:12 all a of ivory, all a of costly wood, bronze,

ARTIFICIAL (1)

Ne 3:16 as far as the a pool and the house of the warriors.

ARTIFICER[S] (KJV) See ARTISAN[S]

ARTILLERY (KJV) See WEAPONS

ARTISAN (19) [ART]

Ex 35:35 an a or by a designer or by an embroiderer in blue,
35:35 by any sort of a or skilled designer.
Dt 27:15 the work of an a, and sets it up in secret."
1Ki 7:14 a man of Tyre, had been an a in bronze;
2Ch 2:7 So now send me an a skilled to work in gold,
2:13 "I have dispatched Huram-abi, a skilled a,
Isa 40:20 then seeks out a skilled a to set up an image
41:7 The a encourages the goldsmith,
Jer 10:3 and worked with an ax by the hands of an a;
10:9 They are the work of the a and of the hands of
Hos 8:6 an a made it; it is not God.
Rev 18:22 and an a of any trade will be found in you no more;
Wis 13:1 the one who exists, nor did they recognize the a
14:2 and wisdom was the a who built it;
14:18 the ambition of the a impelled even those who did
Sir 9:17 A work is praised for the skill of the a;
38:27 So too is every a and master a who labors
45:11 with twisted crimson, the work of an a;

ARTISANS‡ (18) [ART]

Ex 36:4 that all the a who were doing every sort of task on
2Ki 24:14 ten thousand captives, all the a and the smiths;
24:16 seven thousand, the a and the smiths,
1Ch 4:14 so-called because they were a.
22:15 carpenters, and all kinds of a without number,
29:5 and for all the work to be done by a,
2Ch 2:14 with your a, the a of my lord,
Ne 11:35 Lod, and Ono, the valley of a.
Isa 44:11 the a too are merely human.
Jer 24:1 together with the officials of Judah, the a,
29:2 the leaders of Judah and Jerusalem, the a,
52:15 together with the rest of the a.
Eze 27:9 The elders of Gebal and its a were within you,
Hos 13:2 all of them the work of a.
Ac 19:24 brought no little business to the a.
19:38 the a with him have a complaint against anyone,
LtJ 6:45 they can be nothing but what the a wish them

ARTIST (1) [ART]

4Mc 17:7 to paint the history of your religion as an a might,

ARTISTIC (2) [ART]

Ex 31:4 to devise a designs, to work in gold, silver,
35:32 to devise a designs, to work in gold, silver,

ARTS (5) [ART]

Ex 7:11 did the same by their secret a.
7:22 magicians of Egypt did the same by their secret a;
8:7 But the magicians did the same by their secret a,
8:18 magicians tried to produce gnats by their secret a,
Wis 18:13 because of their magic a, yet,

ARUBBOTH (1)

1Ki 4:10 in A (to him belonged Socoh and all the land

ARUMAH (2)

Jdg 9:31 He sent messengers to Abimelech at A, saying,
9:41 So Abimelech resided at A;

ARUPHAEUS (1)

AdE 9:9 Marmasima, A, Arsaeus, Zabutheus,

ARVAD (2) [ARVADITES]

Eze 27:8 The inhabitants of Sidon and A were your rowers;
27:11 of A and Helech were on your walls all around;

ARVADITES (2) [ARVAD]

Ge 10:18 the A, the Zemarites, and the Hamathites.
1Ch 1:16 the A, the Zemarites, and the Hamathites.

ARZA (1)

1Ki 16:9 drinking himself drunk in the house of A,

ARZARETH (1)

2Es 13:45 and that country is called A.

AS (4664) See Index of Articles Etc.

ASA‡ (58)

1Ki 15:8 Then his son A succeeded him.
15:9 A began to reign over Judah;
15:11 A did what was right in the sight of the LORD,
15:13 A cut down her image and burned it at
15:14 the heart of A was true to the LORD all his days.
15:16 There was war between A and King Baasha
15:17 from going out or coming in to King A of Judah.
15:18 Then A took all the silver and the gold
15:18 King A sent them to King Ben-hadad son
15:20 Ben-hadad listened to King A,
15:22 Then King A made a proclamation to all Judah,
15:22 with them King A built Geba of Benjamin
15:23 Now the rest of all the acts of A, all his power,
15:24 Then A slept with his ancestors,
15:25 over Israel in the second year of King A of Judah;
15:28 in the third year of King A of Judah,
15:32 There was war between A and King Baasha
15:33 In the third year of King A of Judah,
16:8 In the twenty-sixth year of King A of Judah,
16:10 in the twenty-seventh year of King A of Judah,
16:15 In the twenty-seventh year of King A of Judah,
16:23 In the thirty-first year of King A of Judah,
16:29 In the thirty-eighth year of King A of Judah,
22:41 Jehoshaphat son of A began to reign over Judah in
22:43 He walked in all the way of his father A;
22:46 in the land in the days of his father A,
1Ch 3:10 Rehoboam, Abijah his son, A his son,
9:16 son of Jeduthun, and Berechiah son of A,
2Ch 14:1 His son A succeeded him.
14:2 A did what was good and right in the sight of
14:8 A had an army of three hundred thousand
14:10 A went out to meet him,
14:11 A cried to the LORD his God, "O LORD,
14:12 the LORD defeated the Ethiopians before A and
14:13 A and the army with him pursued them as far
15:2 to meet A and said to him, "Hear me, A, and all
15:8 When A heard these words,
15:10 of the fifteenth year of the reign of A.
15:16 King A even removed his mother Maacah
15:16 A cut down her image, crushed it,
15:17 Nevertheless the heart of A was true all his days.

2Ch 15:19 until the thirty-fifth year of the reign of **A.**
16: 1 In the thirty-sixth year of the reign of **A,**
16: 1 or coming into the territory of King **A** of Judah.
16: 2 Then **A** took silver and gold from the treasures of
16: 4 Ben-hadad listened to King **A,**
16: 6 Then King **A** brought all Judah,
16: 7 At that time the seer Hanani came to King **A**
16:10 Then **A** was angry with the seer,
16:10 And **A** inflicted cruelties on some of the people at
16:11 The acts of **A,** from first to last,
16:12 In the thirty-ninth year of his reign **A** was diseased
16:13 Then **A** slept with his ancestors,
17: 2 the cities of Ephraim that his father **A** had taken.
20:32 in the way of his father **A** and did not turn aside
21:12 or in the ways of King **A** of Judah,
Jer 41: 9 the large cistern that King **A** had made for defense

ASAHEL (19)

2Sa 2:18 sons of Zeruiah were there, Joab, Abishai, and **A.**
2:18 Now **A** was as swift of foot as a wild gazelle.
2:19 **A** pursued Abner, turning neither to the right nor
2:20 Then Abner looked back and said, "Is it you, **A?**"
2:21 But **A** would not turn away from following him.
2:22 to **A,** "Turn away from following me;
2:23 to the place where **A** had fallen and died,
2:30 of David's servants nineteen men besides **A.**
2:32 up **A** and buried him in the tomb of his father,
3:27 So he died for shedding the blood of **A,**
3:30 because he had killed their brother **A** in the battle
23:24 Among the Thirty were **A** brother of Joab;
1Ch 2:16 The sons of Zeruiah: Abishai, Joab, and **A,** three.
11:26 The warriors of the armies were **A** brother of Joab,
27: 7 **A** brother of Joab was fourth,
2Ch 17: 8 Shemaiah, Nethaniah, Zebadiah, **A,** Shemiramoth,
31:13 **A,** Jerimoth, Jozabad, Eliel, Ismachiah, Mahath,
Ezr 10:15 of **A** and Jahzeiah son of Tikvah opposed this,
1Es 9:14 of **A** and Jahzeiah son of Tikvah undertook

ASAHIAH (KJV) See ASAIAH

ASAIAH (8)

2Ki 22:12 Shaphan the secretary, and the king's servant **A,**
22:14 and **A** went to the prophetess Huldah the wife
1Ch 4:36 Jaakobah, Jeshohaiah, **A,** Adiel, Jesimiel,
6:30 Shimea his son, Haggiah his son, and **A** his son.
9: 5 of the Shilonites: **A** the firstborn, and his sons.
15: 6 **A** the chief, with two hundred twenty
15:11 and the Levites Uriel, **A,** Joel, Shemaiah, Eliel,
2Ch 34:20 the secretary Shaphan, and the king's servant **A:**

ASAIAS (1)

1Es 9:32 Elionas and **A** and Melchias and Sabbaias

ASAPH (52)

2Ki 18:18 and Shebnah the secretary, and Joah son of **A,**
18:37 and Shebna the secretary, and Joah son of **A,**
1Ch 6:39 and his brother **A,** who stood
6:39 namely, **A** son of Berechiah, son of Shimea,
9:15 of Mica, son of Zichri, son of **A;**
15:17 and of his kindred **A** son of Berechiah;
15:19 **A,** and Ethan were to sound bronze cymbals;
16: 5 **A** was the chief, and second to him Zechariah,
16: 5 **A** was to sound the cymbals,
16: 7 of praises to the LORD by **A** and his kindred.
16:37 David left **A** and his kinsfolk there before the ark
25: 1 also set apart for the service the sons of **A,**
25: 2 Of the sons of **A:** Zaccur, Joseph, Nethaniah, and
Asarelah, sons of **A,** under the direction of **A,**
25: 6 **A,** Jeduthun, and Heman were under the order of
25: 9 The first lot fell for **A** to Joseph;
26: 1 Meshelemiah son of Kore, of the sons of **A.**
2Ch 5:12 **A,** Heman, and Jeduthun, their sons and kindred,
20:14 son of Mattaniah, a Levite of the sons of **A,**
29:13 and of the sons of **A,** Zechariah and Mattaniah;
29:30 with the words of David and of the seer **A.**
35:15 The singers, the descendants of **A,**
35:15 and **A,** and Heman, and the king's seer Jeduthun.
Ezr 2:41 the descendants of **A,** one hundred twenty-eight.
3:10 and the Levites, the sons of **A,** with cymbals,
Ne 2: 8 to **A,** the keeper of the king's forest, directing him
7:44 the descendants of **A,** one hundred forty-eight.
11:17 and Mattaniah son of Mica son of Zabdi son of **A,**
11:22 of the descendants of **A,** the singers,
12:35 of Micaiah son of Zaccur son of **A;**
12:46 For in the days of David and **A** long ago there was
Ps 50: T *A Psalm of* **A.**
73: T *A Psalm of* **A.**
74: T *A Maskil of* **A.**
75: T *To the leader: Do Not Destroy. A Psalm of* **A.**
76: T *with stringed instruments. A Psalm of* **A.**
77: T *To the leader: according to Jeduthun. Of* **A.**
78: T *A Maskil of* **A.**
79: T *A Psalm of* **A.**
80: T *To the leader: on Lilies, a Covenant. Of* **A.**
81: T *To the leader: according to The Gittith. Of* **A.**
82: T *A Psalm of* **A.**
83: T *A Song. A Psalm of* **A.**
Isa 36: 3 and Shebna the secretary, and Joah son of **A,**
36:22 and Shebna the secretary, and Joah son of **A,**
Mt 1: 7 and Abijah the father of **A,**
1: 8 and **A** the father of Jehoshaphat,
1Es 1:15 The temple singers, the sons of **A,**
1:15 and also **A,** Zechariah, and Eddinus,
5:27 the descendants of **A,** one hundred twenty-eight.
1Es 5:59 and the Levites, the sons of **A,** with cymbals,

ASARAMEL (1)

1Mc 14:28 in **A,** in the great assembly of the priests and

ASAREL (1)

1Ch 4:16 The sons of Jehallelel: Ziph, Ziphah, Tiria, and **A.**

ASARELAH‡ (1)

1Ch 25: 2 Zaccur, Joseph, Nethaniah, and **A,** sons of Asaph,

ASBASARETH See Index to Footnotes

ASBEBIAS See Index to Footnotes

ASCALON (1) [=ASHKELON]

Jdt 2:28 in Azotus and **A** feared him greatly.

ASCEND (11) [ASCENDED, ASCENDING, ASCENT, ASCENTS]

Dt 28:43 among you shall **a** above you higher and higher,
32:49 "**A** this mountain of the Abarim,
32:50 on the mountain that you **a** and shall be gathered
Ps 24: 3 Who shall **a** the hill of the LORD?
139: 8 If I **a** to heaven, you are there;
Isa 14:13 You said in your heart, "I will **a** to heaven;
14:14 I will **a** to the tops of the clouds,
Ac 2:34 For David did not **a** into the heavens,
Ro 10: 6 'Who will **a** into heaven?' "
Rev 17: 8 to **a** from the bottomless pit and go to destruction.
2Es 4: 8 neither did I ever **a** into heaven.'

ASCENDED (15) [ASCEND]

Jdg 13:20 the angel of the LORD **a** in the flame of the altar
2Ki 2:11 and Elijah **a** in a whirlwind into heaven.
2Ch 21: 4 When Jehoram had **a** the throne of his father
Ps 68:18 You **a** the high mount, leading captives
Pr 30: 4 Who has **a** to heaven and come down?
Eze 11:23 glory of the LORD **a** from the middle of the city,
41: 7 One **a** from the bottom story to
Jn 3:13 No one has **a** into heaven except
20:17 because I have not yet **a** to the Father.
Ac 10: 4 and your alms have **a** as a memorial before God.
Eph 4: 8 he **a** on high he made captivity itself a captive;
4: 9 (When it says, "He **a,**" what does it mean but
4:10 the same one who **a** far above all the heavens,
Tob 12:20 that have happened to you." And he **a.**
3Mc 5: 9 So their entreaty **a** fervently to heaven.

ASCENDING (8) [ASCEND]

Ge 28:12 the angels of God were **a** and descending on it.
1Ch 26:16 at the gate of Shallecheth on the **a** road.
Eze 8:11 and the fragrant cloud of incense was **a.**
Jn 1:51 the angels of God **a** and descending upon the Son
6:62 Then what if you were to see the Son of Man **a** to
20:17 'I am **a** to my Father and your Father,
Rev 7: 2 I saw another angel **a** from the rising of the sun,
Tob 12:20 See, I am **a** to him who sent me.

ASCENT‡ (17) [ASCEND]

Nu 34: 4 of the **a** of Akrabbim, and cross to Zin,
Jos 10:10 chased them by the way of the **a** of Beth-horon,
15: 3 it goes out southward of the **a** of Akrabbim,
15: 7 which is opposite the **a** of Adummim,
18:17 which is opposite the **a** of Adummim;
Jdg 1:36 of the Amorites ran from the **a** of Akrabbim,
8:13 of Joash returned from the battle by the **a**
2Sa 15:30 But David went up the **a** of the Mount of Olives,
2Ki 9:27 And they shot him in the chariot at the **a** to Gur,
2Ch 20:16 they will come up by the **a** of Ziz;
32:33 on the **a** to the tombs of the descendants of David;
Ne 3:19 repaired another section opposite the **a** to
12:37 at the **a** of the wall, above the house of David,
Isa 15: 5 For at the **a** of Luhith they go up weeping;
Jer 48: 5 For at the **a** of Luhith they go up weeping bitterly;
Sir 25:20 A sandy **a** for the feet of the aged—
1Mc 3:16 When he approached the **a** of Beth-horon,

ASCENTS (15) [ASCEND]

Ps 120: T *A Song of* **A.**
121: T *A Song of* **A.**
122: T *A Song of* **A.** *Of David.*
123: T *A Song of* **A.**
124: T *A Song of* **A.** *Of David.*
125: T *A Song of* **A.**
126: T *A Song of* **A.**
127: T *A Song of* **A.** *Of Solomon.*
128: T *A Song of* **A.**
129: T *A Song of* **A.**
130: T *A Song of* **A.**
131: T *A Song of* **A.** *Of David.*
132: T *A Song of* **A.**
133: T *A Song of* **A.**
134: T *A Song of* **A.**

ASCRIBE (14) [ASCRIBED]

Dt 32: 3 of the LORD; **a** greatness to our God!
1Ch 16:28 **A** to the LORD, O families of the peoples,
16:28 **a** to the LORD glory and strength.
16:29 **A** to the LORD the glory due his name;
Job 36: 3 and **a** righteousness to my Maker.
Ps 29: 1 **A** to the LORD, O heavenly beings,
29: 1 **a** to the LORD glory and strength.
29: 2 **A** to the LORD the glory of his name;
68:34 **A** power to God, whose majesty is over Israel;
96: 7 **A** to the LORD, O families of the peoples,
96: 7 **a** to the LORD glory and strength.
96: 8 **A** to the LORD the glory due his name;
Sir 39:15 **A** majesty to his name and give thanks to him
Bar 2:17 will not **a** glory or justice to the Lord;

ASCRIBED (3) [ASCRIBE]

1Sa 18: 8 He said, "They have **a** to David ten thousands, and
to me they have **a** thousands;
Pm 151: T *This psalm is* **a** *to David as his own composition*

ASENATH (3)

Ge 41:45 and he gave him **A** daughter of Potiphera,
41:50 whom **A** daughter of Potiphera, priest of On,
46:20 whom **A** daughter of Potiphera, priest of On,

ASER (KJV) See ASHER

ASH (5) [ASHES]

Lev 4:12 to the **a** heap, and shall burn it on a wood fire;
4:12 at the **a** heap it shall be burned.
1Sa 2: 8 he lifts the needy from the **a** heap,
Ps 113: 7 and lifts the needy from the **a** heap,
La 4: 5 up in purple cling to **a** heaps.

ASHAMED (77) [SHAME]

Ge 2:25 and his wife were both naked, and were not **a.**
2Sa 10: 5 he sent to meet them, for the men were greatly **a.**
19: 3 into the city that day as soldiers steal in who are **a**
2Ki 2:17 But when they urged him until he was **a,** he said,
8:11 and stared at him, until he was **a.**
2Ch 30:15 The priests and the Levites were **a,**
Ezr 8:22 For I was **a** to ask the king for a band of soldiers
9: 6 I am too **a** and embarrassed to lift my face to you,
Job 19: 3 are you not **a** to wrong me?
Ps 6:10 All my enemies shall be **a** and struck with terror;
25: 3 let them be **a** who are wantonly treacherous.
34: 5 so your faces shall never be **a.**
Isa 1:29 you shall be **a** of the oaks in which you delighted;
23: 4 Be **a,** O Sidon, for the sea has spoken,
24:23 Then the moon will be abashed, and the sun **a;**
26:11 Let them see your zeal for your people, and be **a.**
29:22 No longer shall Jacob be **a,**
41:11 all who are incensed against you shall be **a**
45:24 against him shall come to him and be **a.**
54: 4 Do not fear, for you will not be **a;**
Jer 3: 3 the forehead of a whore, you refuse to be **a.**
6:15 they were not **a,** they did not know how to blush.
8:12 yet they were not at all **a,**
12:13 be **a** of their harvests because of the fierce anger
14: 3 They are **a** and dismayed and cover their heads,
22:22 then you will be **a** and dismayed because
31:19 I was **a,** and I was dismayed because I bore
48:13 Then Moab shall be **a** of Chemosh,
48:13 as the house of Israel was **a** of Bethel,
Eze 16:27 who were **a** of your lewd behavior.
16:52 So be **a,** you also, and bear your disgrace,
16:54 in order that you may bear your disgrace and be **a**
16:61 and be **a** when I take your sisters,
36:32 Be **a** and dismayed for your ways,
43:10 and let them be **a** of their iniquities.
43:11 When they are **a** of all that they have done,
Hos 4:19 and they shall be **a** because of their altars.
10: 6 and Israel shall be **a** of his idol.
Mic 7:16 The nations shall see and be **a** of all their might;
Zec 13: 4 On that day the prophets will be **a,** every one,
Mk 8:38 Those who are **a** of me and of my words
8:38 be **a** when he comes in the glory of his Father with
Lk 9:26 Those who are **a** of me and of my words,
9:26 of them the Son of Man will be **a** when he comes
16: 3 I am not strong enough to dig, and I am **a** to beg.
Ro 1:16 For I am not **a** of the gospel;
6:21 then get from the things of which you now are **a?**
1Co 4:14 I am not writing this to make you **a,**
2Co 10: 8 I will not be **a** of it.
2Th 3:14 to do with them, so that they may be **a.**
2Ti 1: 8 Do not be **a,** then, of the testimony about our Lord
1:12 But I am not **a,** for I know the one
1:16 he often refreshed me and was not **a** of my chain;
2:15 a worker who has no need to be **a,**
Heb 2:11 For this reason Jesus is not **a** to call them brothers
11:16 Therefore God is not **a** to be called their God;
Jdt 9: 3 which was **a** of the deceit they had practiced,
Wis 1: 5 and will be **a** at the approach of unrighteousness.
13:17 he is not **a** to address a lifeless thing.
Sir 4:20 and beware of evil, and do not be **a** to be yourself.
4:25 but be **a** of your ignorance.
4:26 Do not be **a** to confess your sins,
22:25 I am not **a** to shelter a friend,
41:17 Be **a** of sexual immorality,
41:19 Be **a** of breaking an oath or agreement,
42: 1 Be **a** of repeating what you hear,
42: 1 Of the following things do not be **a,**
42: 2 be **a** of the law of the Most High and his covenant,
42: 8 Do not be **a** to correct the stupid or foolish or
51:29 and may you never be **a** to praise him.
Sus 1:11 for they were **a** to disclose their lustful desire
1:27 the servants felt very much **a,**
1Mc 4:31 and let them be **a** of their troops and their cavalry.
1Es 8:51 For I was **a** to ask the king for foot soldiers

1Es 8:74 "O Lord, I am **a** and confused before your face.
4Mc 12:11 were you not **a** to murder his servants and torture
12:13 As a man, were you not **a**, you most savage beast,

ASHAN (4)
Jos 15:42 Libnah, Ether, **A**,
19: 7 Rimmon, Ether, and **A**—four towns with their
1Ch 4:32 Ain, Rimmon, Tochen, and **A**, five towns,
6:59 **A** with its pasture lands, and Beth-shemesh

ASHBEL (3) [ASHBELITES]
Ge 46:21 The children of Benjamin: Bela, Becher, **A**, Gera,
Nu 26:38 of **A**, the clan of the Ashbelites;
1Ch 8: 1 **A** the second, Aharah the third,

ASHBELITES (1) [ASHBEL]
Nu 26:38 of Ashbel, the clan of the **A**;

ASHCHENAZ (KJV) See ASHKENAZ

ASHDOD (20) [ASHDOD'S, ASHDODITES]
Jos 11:22 some remained only in Gaza, in Gath, and in **A**.
13: 3 those of Gaza, **A**, Ashkelon, Gath, and Ekron),
15:46 all that were near **A**, with their villages.
15:47 **A**, its towns and its villages;
1Sa 5: 1 they brought it from Ebenezer to **A**;
5: 3 When the people of **A** rose early the next day,
5: 5 on the threshold of Dagon in **A** to this day.
5: 6 of the LORD was heavy upon the people of **A**,
5: 6 both in **A** and in its territory.
5: 7 when the inhabitants of **A** saw how things were,
6:17 one for **A**, one for Gaza, one for Ashkelon,
2Ch 26: 6 of Gath and the wall of Jabneh and the wall of **A**;
26: 6 he built cities in the territory of **A** and elsewhere
Ne 13:23 also I saw Jews who had married women of **A**,
13:24 and half of their children spoke the language of **A**,
Isa 20: 1 came to **A** and fought against it and took it—
Jer 25:20 Ashkelon, Gaza, Ekron, and the remnant of **A**;
Am 1: 8 I will cut off the inhabitants from **A**,
3: 9 Proclaim to the strongholds in **A**,
Zec 9: 6 a mongrel people shall settle in **A**,

ASHDOD'S (1) [ASHDOD]
Zep 2: 4 **A** people shall be driven out at noon,

ASHDODITES (1) [ASHDOD]
Ne 4: 7 the Arabs and the Ammonites and the **A** heard that

ASHDOTHPISGAH (KJV) See PISGAH

ASHER (41) [ASHER'S, ASHERITES]
Ge 30:13 women will call me happy"; so she named him **A**.
35:26 The sons of Zilpah, Leah's maid: Gad and **A**.
46:17 The children of **A**: Imnah,
Ex 1: 4 Dan and Naphtali, Gad and **A**.
Nu 1:13 From **A**, Pagiel son of Ochran.
1:40 The descendants of **A**, their lineage, in their clans,
1:41 of **A** were forty-one thousand five hundred.
2:27 Those to camp next to him shall be the tribe of **A**.
10:26 Over the company of the tribe of **A** was Pagiel son
13:13 from the tribe of **A**, Sethur son of Michael;
26:44 The descendants of **A** by their families:
26:46 And the name of the daughter of **A** was Serah.
Dt 27:13 Reuben, Gad, **A**, Zebulun, Dan, and Naphtali.
33:24 And of **A** he said: Most blessed of sons be **A**;
Jos 17: 7 of Manasseh reached from **A** to Michmethath,
17:10 on the north **A** is reached, and on the east Issachar.
17:11 Within Issachar and **A**, Manasseh had Beth-shean
19:24 The fifth lot came out for the tribe of **A** according
19:31 This is the inheritance of the tribe of **A** according
19:34 touching Zebulun at the south, and **A** on the west,
21: 6 from the tribe of **A**, from the tribe of Naphtali,
21:30 Out of the tribe of **A**:
Jdg 1:31 **A** did not drive out the inhabitants of Acco,
5:17 **A** sat still at the coast of the sea,
6:35 He also sent messengers to **A**, Zebulun,
7:23 from Naphtali and from **A** and from all Manasseh,
1Ki 4:16 Baana son of Hushai, in **A** and Bealoth;
1Ch 2: 2 Dan, Joseph, Benjamin, Naphtali, Gad, and **A**.
6:62 **A**, Naphtali, and Manasseh in Bashan.
6:74 out of the tribe of **A**:
7:30 The sons of **A**: Imnah, Ishvah,
7:40 All of these were men of **A**,
12:36 Of **A**, forty thousand seasoned troops ready
2Ch 30:11 Only a few from **A**, Manasseh,
Eze 48: 2 from the east side to the west, **A**, one portion.
48: 3 Adjoining the territory of **A**,
48:34 three gates, the gate of Gad, the gate of **A**,
Lk 2:36 Anna the daughter of Phanuel, of the tribe of **A**.
Rev 7: 6 from the tribe of **A** twelve thousand,
Tob 1: 2 above **A** toward the west, and north of Phogor.

ASHER'S‡ (1) [ASHER]
Ge 49:20 **A** food shall be rich, and he shall provide royal delicacies.

ASHERAH‡ (7) [ASHERAHS, ASTARTE]
1Ki 15:13 she had made an abominable image for **A**;
18:19 of Baal and the four hundred prophets of **A**,
2Ki 21: 7 of **A** that he had made he set in the house of which
23: 4 for **A**, and for all the host of heaven;
23: 6 He brought out the image of **A** from the house of
2Ki 23: 7 where the women did weaving for **A**.
2Ch 15:16 because she had made an abominable image for **A**.

ASHERAHS (1) [ASHERAH, ASTARTES]
Jdg 3: 7 and worshiping the Baals and the **A**.

ASHERIM See Index to Footnotes

ASHERITES (5) [ASHER]
Nu 2:27 The leader of the **A** shall be Pagiel son of Ochran,
7:72 of Ochran, the leader of the **A**:
26:47 These are the clans of the **A**:
34:27 And of the tribe of the **A** a leader,
Jdg 1:32 the **A** lived among the Canaanites, the inhabitants

ASHEROTH See Index to Footnotes

ASHES‡ (61) [ASH]
Ge 18:27 I who am but dust and **a**.
Ex 27: 3 You shall make pots for it to receive its **a**,
Lev 1:16 at the east side of the altar, in the place for **a**.
6:10 up the **a** to which the fire has reduced
6:11 carry the **a** out to a clean place outside the camp.
Nu 4:13 They shall take away the **a** from the altar,
19: 9 Then someone who is clean shall gather up the **a**
19:10 the **a** of the heifer shall wash his clothes and
19:17 For the unclean they shall take some **a** of
2Sa 13:19 But Tamar put **a** on her head,
1Ki 13: 3 and the **a** that are on it shall be poured out.' "
13: 5 and the **a** poured out from the altar,
2Ki 23: 4 and carried their **a** to Bethel.
Est 4: 1 and **a**, and went through the city, wailing with
4: 3 and most of them lay in sackcloth and **a**.
Job 2: 8 to scrape himself, and sat among the **a**.
13:12 Your maxims are proverbs of **a**,
30:19 and I have become like dust and **a**.
42: 6 and repent in dust and **a**."
Ps 102: 9 For I eat **a** like bread,
147:16 He gives snow like wool; he scatters frost like **a**.
Isa 44:20 He feeds on **a**; a deluded mind has led him astray,
58: 5 and to lie in sackcloth and **a**?
61: 3 to give them a garland instead of **a**,
Jer 6:26 O my poor people, put on sackcloth, and roll in **a**;
25:34 Wail, you shepherds, and cry out; roll in **a**,
31:40 The whole valley of the dead bodies and the **a**,
La 3:16 and made me cower in **a**;
Eze 27:30 They throw dust on their heads and wallow in **a**;
28:18 to **a** on the earth in the sight of all who saw you.
Da 9: 3 and supplication with fasting and sackcloth and **a**.
Jnh 3: 6 covered himself with sackcloth, and sat in **a**.
Mal 4: 3 for they will be **a** under the soles of your feet,
Mt 11:21 would have repented long ago in sackcloth and **a**.
Lk 10:13 sitting in sackcloth and **a**.
Heb 9:13 with the sprinkling of the **a** of a heifer,
2Pe 2: 6 of Sodom and Gomorrah to **a** he condemned them
Jdt 4:11 before the temple and put **a** on their heads
4:15 With **a** on their turbans, they cried out to the Lord
9: 1 Then Judith prostrated herself, put **a** on her head,
AdE 4: 1 put on sackcloth, and sprinkled himself with **a**;
4: 2 to enter the courtyard clothed in sackcloth and **a**.
4: 3 and they put on sackcloth and **a**.
14: 2 of costly perfumes she covered her head with **a**
Wis 2: 3 the body will turn to **a**,
15:10 Their heart is **a**, their hope is cheaper than dirt,
Sir 10: 9 How can dust and **a** be proud?
17:32 but all human beings are dust and **a**.
40: 3 to the one who grovels in dust and **a**,
Bel 1:14 Then Daniel ordered his servants to bring **a**,
1Mc 3:47 put on sackcloth and sprinkled **a** on their heads,
4:39 they sprinkled themselves with **a**
2Mc 4:41 and others took handfuls of the **a** that were lying
13: 5 there is a tower there, fifty cubits high, full of **a**,
13: 5 that on all sides inclines precipitously into the **a**.
13: 8 whose fire and **a** were holy, he met his death in **a**.
3Mc 4: 6 their myrrh-perfumed hair sprinkled with **a**,
2Es 2: 9 whose land lies in lumps of pitch and heaps of **a**.
9:38 and there were **a** on her head.
13:11 the innumerable multitude but only the dust of **a**

ASHHUR (2)
1Ch 2:24 Abijah wife of Hezron bore him **A**,
4: 5 **A** father of Tekoa had two wives,

ASHIMA (1) [=ASHIMAH]
2Ki 17:30 the people of Hamath made **A**;

ASHIMAH (1) [=ASHIMA]
Am 8:14 Those who swear by **A** of Samaria, and say,

ASHKELON (13) [=ASCALON, =ASKALON]
Jos 13: 3 **A**, Gath, and Ekron), and those of the Avvim,
Jdg 1:18 **A** with its territory, and Ekron with its territory.
14:19 and he went down to **A**.
1Sa 6:17 one for Ashdod, one for Gaza, one for **A**,
2Sa 1:20 proclaim it not in the streets of **A**;
Jer 25:20 **A**, Gaza, Ekron, and the remnant of Ashdod;
47: 5 Baldness has come upon Gaza, **A** is silenced.
47: 7 Against **A** and against the seashore—
Am 1: 8 and the one who holds the scepter from **A**;
Zep 2: 4 and **A** shall become a desolation;
2: 7 in the houses of **A** they shall lie down at evening.
Zec 9: 5 **A** shall see it and be afraid;
Zec 9: 5 from Gaza; **A** shall be uninhabited;

ASHKENAZ (3)
Ge 10: 3 **A**, Riphath, and Togarmah.
1Ch 1: 6 **A**, Diphath, and Togarmah.
Jer 51:27 against her the kingdoms, Ararat, Minni, and **A**;

ASHNAH (2)
Jos 15:33 And in the Lowland, Eshtaol, Zorah, **A**,
15:43 Iphtah, **A**, Nezib,

ASHORE (7) [SHORE]
Mt 13:48 when it was full, they drew it **a**, sat down, and put
14:14 When he went **a**, he saw a great crowd;
Mk 6:34 As he went **a**, he saw a great crowd;
Jn 21: 9 When they had gone **a**, they saw
21:11 So Simon Peter went aboard and hauled the net **a**,
Ac 27:39 on which they planned to run the ship **a**,
2Mc 5: 8 he was cast **a** in Egypt.

ASHPENAZ (1)
Da 1: 3 Then the king commanded his palace master **A**

ASHRIEL (KJV) See ASRIEL

ASHTAROTH (6)
Dt 1: 4 who reigned in **A** and in Edrei.
Jos 9:10 and King Og of Bashan who lived in **A**.
12: 4 who lived at **A** and at Edrei
13:12 who reigned in **A** and in Edrei (he alone was left
13:31 and **A**, and Edrei, the towns of the kingdom of Og
1Ch 6:71 with its pasture lands and **A** with its pasture lands;

ASHTERATHITE (1)
1Ch 11:44 Uzzia the **A**, Shama and Jeiel sons of Hotham

ASHTEROTH-KARNAIM (1)
Ge 14: 5 with him came and subdued the Rephaim in **A**,

ASHUR (KJV) See ASHHUR

ASHURITES (1)
2Sa 2: 9 He made him king over Gilead, the **A**, Jezreel,

ASHVATH (1)
1Ch 7:33 The sons of Japhlet: Pasach, Bimhal, and **A**.

ASIA (31)
Ac 2: 9 Judea and Cappadocia, Pontus and **A**,
6: 9 and others of those from Cilicia and **A**,
16: 6 by the Holy Spirit to speak the word in **A**.
19:10 so that all the residents of **A**,
19:22 while he himself stayed for some time longer in **A**.
19:26 in almost the whole of **A** this Paul has persuaded
19:27 be deprived of her majesty that brought all **A** and
19:31 even some officials of the province of **A**,
20: 4 as well as by Tychicus and Trophimus from **A**.
20:16 so that he might not have to spend time in **A**;
20:18 from the first day that I set foot in **A**,
21:27 the Jews from **A**, who had seen him in the temple,
24:19 But there were some Jews from **A**—
27: 2 about to set sail to the ports along the coast of **A**,
Ro 16: 5 who was the first convert in **A** for Christ.
1Co 16:19 The churches of **A** send greetings.
2Co 1: 8 of the affliction we experienced in **A**;
2Ti 1:15 that all who are in **A** have turned away from me,
1Pe 1: 1 Galatia, Cappadocia, **A**, and Bithynia,
Rev 1: 4 John to the seven churches that are in **A**:
1Mc 8: 6 also had defeated Antiochus the Great, king of **A**,
11:13 and put on the crown of **A**,
11:13 the crown of Egypt and that of **A**.
12:39 Then Trypho attempted to become king in **A**
13:32 putting on the crown of **A**;
2Mc 3: 3 to the extent that King Seleucus of **A** defrayed
10:24 of mercenaries and collected the cavalry from **A**
3Mc 3:14 When our expedition took place in **A**,
2Es 15:46 **A**, who share in the splendor of Babylon and
16: 1 Woe to you, Babylon and **A**!
4Mc 3:20 so that even Seleucus Nicanor, king of **A**,

ASIARCHS See Index to Footnotes

ASIBIAS (1)
1Es 9:26 Izziah, Malchijah, Mijamin, and Eleazar, and **A**,

ASIDE‡ (115) [SIDE]
Ge 19: 2 turn **a** to your servant's house and spend the night,
19: 3 so they turned **a** to him and entered his house;
Ex 3: 3 "I must turn **a** and look at this great sight,
3: 4 When the LORD saw that he had turned **a** to see,
16:23 that is left over put **a** to be kept until morning.' "
16:24 So they put it **a** until morning,
32: 8 to turn **a** from the way that I commanded them;
Lev 11:37 upon any seed set **a** for sowing, it is clean;
13:50 and put the diseased article **a** for seven days.
13:54 and he shall put it **a** seven days more.
Nu 5:19 if you have not turned **a** to uncleanness while
18:11 as a perpetual due, whatever is set **a** from the gifts
20:17 along the King's Highway, not turning **a** to
21:22 we will not turn **a** into field or vineyard;

Nu 23: 3 beside your burnt offerings while I go **a.**
31:28 set **a** as tribute for the LORD,
Dt 2:27 I will turn **a** neither to the right nor to the left.
17:11 do not turn **a** from the decision that they announce
17:20 nor turning **a** from the commandment,
28:14 and if you do not turn **a** from any of the words
31:29 surely act corruptly, turning **a** from the way
Jos 23: 6 turning **a** from it neither to the right nor to the left,
Jdg 2:17 They soon turned **a** from the way
4:18 "Turn **a,** my lord, turn **a** to me; have no fear."
4:18 So he turned **a** to her into the tent,
14: 8 and he turned **a** to see the carcass of the lion,
19:11 let us turn **a** to this city of the Jebusites,
19:12 "We will not turn **a** into a city of foreigners,
19:15 They turned **a** there, to go in and spend the night
1Sa 8: 3 not follow in his ways, but turned **a** after gain;
9:23 the one I asked you to put **a."**
12:20 yet do not turn **a** from following the LORD,
12:21 not turn **a** after useless things that cannot profit
2Sa 3:27 Joab took him **a** in the gateway to speak
18:30 The king said, "Turn **a,** and stand here."
18:30 So he turned **a,** and stood still.
22:23 and from his statutes I did not turn **a.**
1Ki 9: 6 "If you turn **a** from following me,
15: 5 and did not turn **a** from anything
22:43 he did not turn **a** from it,
2Ki 4: 4 when each is full, set it **a."**
10:29 not turn **a** from the sins of Jeroboam son of Nebat,
22: 2 he did not turn **a** to the right or to the left.
25:29 So Jehoiachin put **a** his prison clothes.
2Ch 7:19 "But if you turn **a** and forsake my statutes
20:32 in the way of his father Asa and did not turn **a**
34: 2 he did not turn **a** to the right or to the left.
35:12 They set **a** the burnt offerings so
Job 6:18 The caravans turn **a** from their course;
23:11 I have kept his way and have not turned **a.**
31: 7 if my step has turned **a** from the way,
33:17 that he may turn them **a** from their deeds,
34:27 because they turned **a** from following him,
36:18 do not let the greatness of the ransom turn you **a.**
Ps 102:10 for you have lifted me up and thrown me **a.**
125: 5 But those who turn **a** to their own crooked ways
Pr 7:25 Do not let your hearts turn **a** to her ways;
9: 6 Lay **a** immaturity, and live,
Isa 10: 2 to turn **a** the needy from justice and to rob
30:11 the way, turn **a** from the path, let us hear no more
Jer 5:23 they have turned **a** and gone away.
14: 8 like a traveler turning **a** for the night?
15: 5 Who will turn **a** to ask about your welfare?
48: 9 Set **a** salt for Moab, for she will surely fall;
52:33 So Jehoiachin put **a** his prison clothes,
Eze 45: 1 you shall set **a** for the LORD a portion of
Da 9: 5 turning **a** from your commandments
9:11 "All Israel has transgressed your law and turned **a,**
Hos 4:14 for the men themselves go **a** with whores,
Am 5:12 who take a bribe, and push **a** the needy in the gate.
Ob 1:11 On the day that you stood **a,**
Mal 2: 8 But you have turned **a** from the way;
3: 5 against those who thrust **a** the alien,
3: 7 since the days of your ancestors you have turned **a**
Mt 16:22 And Peter took him **a** and began to rebuke him,
20:17 he took the twelve disciples **a** by themselves,
Mk 7:33 He took him **a** in private, away from the crowd,
8:32 And Peter took him **a** and began to rebuke him.
10:32 He took the twelve **a** again and began
Lk 18:31 Then he took the twelve **a** and said to them, "See,
Ac 1:25 and apostleship from which Judas turned **a** to go
7:27 who was wronging his neighbor pushed Moses **a,**
7:39 instead, they pushed him **a,**
18:26 they took him **a** and explained the Way of God
23:19 drew him **a** privately, and asked,
Ro 3:12 All have turned **a,** together they have become worthless;
13:12 Let us then lay **a** the works of darkness and put on
1Co 16: 2 to put **a** and save whatever extra you earn,
2Co 3: 7 because of the glory of his face, a glory now set **a,**
3:11 for if what was set **a** came through glory,
3:13 at the end of the glory that was being set **a.**
3:14 since only in Christ is it set **a.**
Col 2:14 He set this **a,** nailing it to the cross.
Heb 12: 1 also lay **a** every weight and the sin that clings
Jdt 11:13 which they had consecrated and set **a** for the priests
Sir 6:21 and they will not delay in casting her **a.**
9: 9 or your heart may turn **a** to her,
28: 6 Remember the end of your life, and set enmity **a;**
37: 9 and then stand **a** to see what happens to you.
1Mc 2:22 the king's words by turning **a** from our religion to
5:35 Next he turned **a** to Maapha,
5:68 But Judas turned **a** to Azotus in the land of
12:31 So Jonathan turned **a** against
12:33 He turned **a** to Joppa and took it by surprise,
2Mc 4:11 He set **a** the existing royal concessions to
4:34 Therefore Menelaus, taking Andronicus **a,**
4:46 the king **a** into a colonnade as if for refreshment,
6:21 in charge of that unlawful sacrifice took the man **a**
14: 7 Therefore I have laid **a** my ancestral glory—
1Es 1:27 Stand **a,** and do not oppose the Lord."
3Mc 3:10 of them **a** privately and were pledging
2Es 2:14 I set **a** evil and created good;
10:24 and lay **a** your many sorrows,
4Mc 15:18 firstborn breathed his last, it did not turn you **a,**

ASIEL (3)

1Ch 4:35 Jehu son of Joshibiah son of Seraiah son of **A,**
Tob 1: 1 of Gabael son of Raphael of the descendants of **A,**
2Es 14:24 Dabria, Selemia, Ethanus, and **A—**

ASK‡ (183) [ASKED, ASKING, ASKS]

Ge 24:57 They said, "We will call the girl, and **a** her."
32:29 But he said, "Why is it that you **a** my name?"
34:12 and I will give whatever you **a** me;
47: 4 Now, we **a** you, let your servants settle in the land
Ex 3:13 and they **a** me, 'What is his name?'
3:22 each woman shall **a** her neighbor
11: 2 Tell the people that every man is to **a** his neighbor
11: 2 and every woman is to **a** her neighbor for objects
12:26 And when your children **a** you,
Lev 25:20 Should you **a,** What shall we eat in
Dt 4:32 For **a** now about former ages,
4:32 **a** from one end of heaven to the other:
6:20 When your children **a** you in time to come,
32: 7 **a** your father, and he will inform you;
Jos 4: 6 When your children **a** in time to come,
4:21 your children **a** their parents in time to come,
9:14 and did not **a** direction from the LORD.
15:18 she urged him to **a** her father for a field.
Jdg 1:14 she urged him to **a** her father for a field.
13: 6 I did not **a** him where he came from,
13:18 "Why do you **a** my name?
14:13 So they said to him, "**A** your riddle; let us hear it."
18:24 How then can you **a** me, 'What is the matter?' "
Ru 3:11 do not be afraid, I will do for you all that you **a,**
1Sa 25: 8 **A** your young men, and they will tell you.
28:16 Samuel said, "Why then do you **a** me,
2Sa 14:18 "Do not withhold from me anything I **a** you."
1Ki 2:17 He said, "Please **a** King Solomon—
2:22 "And why do you **a** Abishag the Shunammite
2:22 **A** for him the kingdom as well!
2:22 **a** not only for him but also for the priest Abiathar
3: 5 and God said, "**A** what I should give you."
2Ki 4:28 Then she said, "Did I **a** my lord for a son?
12:15 They did not **a** an accounting from those
2Ch 1: 7 and said to him, "**A** what I should give you."
6:33 and do whatever the foreigners **a** of you,
Ezr 8:22 to **a** the king for a band of soldiers and cavalry
Ne 2: 5 I **a** that you send me to Judah,
Job 12: 7 "But **a** the animals, and they will teach you;
12: 8 **a** the plants of the earth, and they will teach you;
35: 3 If you **a,** 'What advantage have I?
Ps 2: 8 **A** of me, and I will make the nations your heritage,
35:11 they **a** me about things I do not know.
119:82 I **a,** "When will you comfort me?"
Pr 30: 7 Two things I **a** of you;
Ecc 4: 8 "For whom am I toiling," they **a,**
7:10 For it is not from wisdom that you **a** this.
Isa 7:11 **A** a sign of the LORD your God;
7:12 But Ahaz said, I will not **a,**
41:28 among these there is no counselor who, when I **a,**
58: 2 they **a** of me righteous judgments,
65: 1 to be sought out by those who did not **a,**
Jer 6:16 and look, and **a** for the ancient paths,
15: 5 Who will turn aside to **a** about your welfare?
18:13 **A** among the nations: Who has heard the like of
23:37 Thus you shall **a** the prophet,
30: 6 **A** now, and see, can a man bear a child?
38:14 king said to Jeremiah, "I have something to **a** you;
39:12 but deal with him as he may **a** you."
48:19 **A** the man fleeing and the woman escaping;
50: 5 They shall **a** the way to Zion,
Eze 36:37 I will also let the house of Israel **a** me to do this
Da 7:16 I approached one of the attendants to **a** him
Mic 7: 3 the official and the judge **a** for a bribe,
Hag 2:11 **A** the priests for a ruling:
Zec 7: 3 to **a** the priests of the house of the LORD of hosts
10: 1 **A** rain from the LORD in the season of
Mal 2:14 You **a,** "Why does he not?"
Mt 6: 8 Father knows what you need before you **a** him.
7: 7 "**A,** and it will be given you;
7:11 in heaven give good things to those who **a** him!
9:38 therefore **a** the Lord of the harvest
14: 7 on oath to grant her whatever she might **a.**
18:19 if two of you agree on earth about anything you **a,**
19:17 "Why do you **a** me about what is good?
21:22 Whatever you **a** for in prayer with faith,
21:24 Jesus said to them, "I will also **a** you one question;
22:46 to **a** him any more questions.
27:20 the elders persuaded the crowds to **a** for Barabbas
Mk 6:22 "**A** me for whatever you wish, and I will give it."
6:23 he solemnly swore to her, "Whatever you **a** me,
6:24 and said to her mother, "What should I **a** for?"
8:12 "Why does this generation **a** for a sign?
9:32 and were afraid to **a** him.
10:35 we want you to do for us whatever we **a** of you."
11:24 So I tell you, whatever you **a** for in prayer,
11:29 Jesus said to them, "I will **a** you one question;
12:34 After that no one dared to **a** him any question.
15: 8 to **a** Pilate to do for them according to his custom.
Lk 6: 9 Then Jesus said to them, "I **a** you,
6:30 and if anyone takes away your goods, do not **a**
7:19 and sent them to the Lord to **a,**
7:20 "John the Baptist has sent us to you to **a,**
9:45 And they were afraid to **a** him about this saying.
10: 2 therefore **a** the Lord of the harvest
11: 9 "So I say to you, **A,** and it will be given you;
11:13 the Holy Spirit to those who **a** him!"
20: 3 He answered them, "I will also **a** you a question,
20:40 they no longer dared to **a** him another question.
22:23 Then they began to **a** one another,
Jn 1:19 and Levites from Jerusalem to **a** him,
4: 9 a Jew, **a** a drink of me, a woman of Samaria?"
9: 8 before as a beggar began to **a,**
9:15 also began to **a** him how he had received his sight.
9:21 **A** him; he is of age.
Jn 9:23 Therefore his parents said, "He is of age; **a** him."
11:22 that God will give you whatever you **a** of him."
13:24 Simon Peter therefore motioned to him to **a** Jesus
14:13 I will do whatever you **a** in my name,
14:14 If in my name you **a** me for anything, I will do it.
14:16 And I will **a** the Father,
15: 7 If you abide in me, and my words abide in you, **a**
15:16 that the Father will give you whatever you **a** him
16:19 Jesus knew that they wanted to **a** him,
16:23 On that day you will **a** nothing of me.
16:23 if you **a** anything of the Father in my name,
16:24 **A** and you will receive, so that your joy may
16:26 On that day you will **a** in my name.
16:26 to you that I will **a** the Father on your behalf;
17:15 but I **a** you to protect them from the evil one.
17:20 "I **a** not only on behalf of these,
18:21 Why do you **a** me?
18:21 **A** those who heard what I said to them;
18:34 Jesus answered, "Do you **a** this on your own,
21:12 Now none of the disciples dared to **a** him,
Ac 3: 2 so that he could **a** for alms from those entering
3:10 and **a** for alms at the Beautiful Gate of the temple;
8:34 eunuch asked Philip, "About whom, may I **a** you,
10:18 They called out to **a** whether Simon,
10:29 Now may I **a** why you sent for me?"
10:32 Send therefore to Joppa and **a** for Simon,
23:20 "The Jews have agreed to **a** you to bring Paul
Ro 10:18 But I **a,** have they not heard?
10:19 Again I **a,** did Israel not understand?
10:20 I have shown myself to those who did not **a**
11: 1 I **a,** then, has God rejected his people?
11:11 So I **a,** have they stumbled so as to fall?
1Co 14:35 let them **a** their husbands at home.
15:35 But someone will **a,** "How are the dead raised?
2Co 10: 2 I **a** that when I am present I need
Eph 3:20 accomplish abundantly far more than all we can **a**
Php 4: 3 Yes, and I **a** you also, my loyal companion,
1Th 4: 1 we **a** and urge you in the Lord Jesus that,
Jas 1: 5 If any of you is lacking in wisdom, **a** God,
1: 6 But **a** in faith, never doubting,
4: 2 You do not have, because you do not **a.**
4: 3 You **a** and do not receive, because you **a** wrongly,
1Jn 3:22 and we receive from him whatever we **a,**
5:14 that if we **a** anything according to his will,
5:15 if we know that he hears us in whatever we **a,**
5:16 you will **a,** and God will give life to such a one—
2Jn 1: 5 But now, dear lady, I **a** you,
Tob 4:19 and **a** him that your ways may be made straight
7: 9 **a** Raguel to give me my kinswoman Sarah."
AdE 9:12 Whatever more you **a** will be done for you."
Wis 19:11 when desire led them to **a** for luxurious food;
Sir 21: 1 but **a** forgiveness for your past sins.
33:20 in case you change your mind and must **a** for it.
33:22 that your children should **a** from you than
1Mc 3:44 and to pray and **a** for mercy and compassion.
7:12 before Alcimus and Bacchides to **a** for just terms.
10:72 **A** and learn who I am and who the others are
2Mc 7: 2 said, "What do you intend to **a** and learn from us?
11:24 and **a** that their own customs be allowed them.
1Es 4:42 Then the king said to him, "**A** what you wish,
4:46 this is what I **a** and request of you,
8:51 For I was ashamed to **a** the king for foot soldiers
2Es 2: 4 Go, my children, and **a** for mercy from the Lord.'
4: 6 that you should **a** me about such things?"
4:28 For the evil about which you **a** me has been sown,
4:35 not the souls of the righteous in their chambers **a**
4:40 "Go and **a** a pregnant woman whether,
4:52 "Concerning the signs about which you **a** me,
5:11 One country shall **a** its neighbor,
5:37 and then I will explain to you the travail that you **a**
5:46 He said to me, "**A** a woman's womb, and say to it,
5:51 He replied to me, "**A** a woman who bears children,
7:54 but **a** the earth and she will tell you;
8: 2 Just as, when you **a** the earth,
8:55 not **a** any more questions about the great number
10: 9 Now **a** the earth, and she will tell you
4Mc 1: 5 Some might perhaps **a,** "If reason rules

ASKALON (3) [=ASHKELON]

1Mc 10:86 Then Jonathan left there and encamped against **A,**
11:60 to **A,** the people of the city met him
12:33 and marched through the country as far as **A** and

ASKED‡ (245) [ASK]

Ge 24:47 Then I **a** her, 'Whose daughter are you?'
26: 7 When the men of the place **a** him about his wife,
32:29 Then Jacob **a** him, "Please tell me your name."
37:15 the man **a** him, "What are you seeking?"
38:21 He **a** the townspeople, "Where is
40: 7 So he **a** Pharaoh's officers,
44:19 My lord **a** his servants, saying,
Ex 5:14 and were **a,** "Why did you not finish
8:31 And the LORD did as Moses **a:**
12:35 they had **a** the Egyptians for jewelry of silver
12:36 so that they let them have what they **a.**
18: 7 each **a** after the other's welfare,
33:17 "I will do the very thing that you have **a;**
Nu 14:20 LORD said, "I do forgive, just as you have **a;**
Jos 19:50 the LORD they gave him the town that he **a** for,
Jdg 5:25 He **a** water and she gave him milk,
14:16 You have **a** a riddle of my people,
15: 6 Then the Philistines **a,** "Who has done this?"
18: 3 so they went over and **a** him,
1Sa 1:20 for she said, "I have **a** him of the LORD."
9:23 the one I **a** you to put aside."
12:13 whom you have chosen, for whom you have **a;**

1Sa 19:22 he **a**, "Where are Samuel and David?"
20: 6 'David earnestly **a** leave of me to run
20:28 "David earnestly **a** leave of me to go
27:10 When Achish **a**, "Against whom have you made
2Sa 1: 5 David **a** the young man who was reporting to him,
9: 1 David **a**, "Is there still anyone left of the house
11: 7 David **a** how Joab and the people fared,
12:20 when he **a**, they set food before him and he ate.
14: 5 The king **a** her, "What is your trouble?"
24:13 So Gad came to David and told him; he **a** him,
1Ki 2:13 She **a**, "Do you come peaceably?"
3:10 It pleased the Lord that Solomon had **a** this.
3:11 God said to him, "Because you have **a** this,
3:11 and have not **a** for yourself long life or riches,
3:11 but have **a** for yourself understanding
3:13 I give you also what you have not **a**,
19: 4 He **a** that he might die:
22:22 the LORD **a** him. He replied,
2Ki 2:10 He responded, "You have **a** a hard thing;
3: 8 Then he **a**, "By which way shall we march?"
6:18 So he struck them with blindness as Elisha had **a**.
6:28 then the king **a** her, "What is your complaint?"
8:12 Hazael **a**, "Why does my lord weep?"
9: 5 "For which one of us?" **a** Jehu.
22: 7 be **a** from them for the money that is delivered
1Ch 4:10 And God granted what he **a**.
2Ch 1:11 and you have not **a** for possessions, wealth, honor,
1:11 and have not even **a** for long life,
1:11 but have **a** for wisdom and knowledge for yourself
18:20 The LORD **a** him, 'How?'
Ezr 5: 4 They also **a** them this, "What are the names of
5: 9 Then we spoke to those elders and **a** them,
5:10 We also **a** them their names, for your information,
7: 6 and the king granted him all that he **a**,
Ne 1: 2 and I **a** them about the Jews that survived,
2: 8 And the king granted me what I **a**,
13: 6 After some time I **a** leave of the king
Est 2:13 the king she was given whatever she **a** for to take
2:15 she **a** for nothing except what Hegai
Job 21:29 Have you not **a** those who travel the roads,
Ps 21: 4 He **a** you for life; you gave it to him—
27: 4 One thing I **a** of the LORD, that will I seek after:
105:40 They **a**, and he brought quails,
106:15 he gave them what they **a**,
137: 3 For there our captors **a** us for songs,
137: 3 and our tormentors **a** for mirth, saying,
Isa 1:12 who **a** this from your hand?
Da 1: 8 so he **a** the palace master to allow him not
1:11 Then Daniel **a** the guard whom
2:10 has ever **a** such a thing of any magician
2:15 he **a** Arioch, the royal official, "Why is the decree
2:23 and have now revealed to me what we **a** of you,
Jnh 4: 8 on the head of Jonah so that he was faint and **a**
Zec 1:19 I **a** the angel who talked with me,
1:21 And I **a**, "What are they coming to do?"
2: 2 Then I **a**, "Where are you going?"
Mt 12:10 with a withered hand, and they **a** him, "Is it lawful
13:10 Then the disciples came and **a** him,
15:34 Jesus **a** them, "How many loaves have you?"
16: 1 and to test Jesus they **a** him to show them a sign
16:13 the district of Caesarea Philippi, he **a** his disciples,
17:10 And the disciples **a** him, "Why, then,
18: 1 At that time the disciples came to Jesus and **a**,
19: 3 and to test him they **a**,
20:20 and kneeling before him, she **a** a favor of him.
22:23 and they **a** him a question, saying,
22:35 a lawyer, **a** him a question to test him.
22:41 Jesus **a** them this question:
24: 2 Then he **a** them, "You see all these, do you not?
27:11 governor **a** him, "Are you the King of the Jews?"
27:23 Then he **a**, "Why, what evil has he done?"
27:58 He went to Pilate and **a** for the body of Jesus;
Mk 4:10 along with the twelve **a** him about the parables.
5: 9 Then Jesus **a** him, "What is your name?"
7: 5 So the Pharisees and the scribes **a** him,
7:17 his disciples **a** him about the parable.
8: 5 He **a** them, "How many loaves do you have?"
8:23 he **a** him, "Can you see anything?"
8:27 and on the way he **a** his disciples,
8:29 He **a** them, "But who do you say that I am?"
9:11 Then they **a** him, "Why do the scribes say
9:16 He **a** them, "What are you arguing about
9:18 and I **a** your disciples to cast it out,
9:21 Jesus **a** the father, "How long has this been
9:28 his disciples **a** him privately,
9:33 and when he was in the house he **a** them,
10: 2 Some Pharisees came, and to test him they **a**,
10:10 Then in the house the disciples **a** him again
10:17 a man ran up and knelt before him, and **a** him,
12:18 came to him and **a** him a question, saying,
12:28 and seeing that he answered them well, he **a** him,
13: 2 Jesus **a** him, "Do you see these great buildings?
13: 3 Peter, James, John, and Andrew **a** him privately,
14:60 the high priest stood up before them and **a** Jesus,
14:61 Again the high priest **a** him,
15: 2 Pilate **a** him, "Are you the King of the Jews?"
15: 4 Pilate **a** him again, "Have you no answer?
15: 6 a prisoner for them, anyone for whom they **a**.
15:14 Pilate **a** them, "Why, what evil has he done?"
15:43 went boldly to Pilate and **a** for the body of Jesus.
15:44 he **a** him whether he had been dead for some time.
Lk 1:63 He **a** for a writing tablet and wrote,
3:10 the crowds **a** him, "What then should we do?"
3:12 tax collectors came to be baptized, and they **a** him,
3:14 Soldiers also **a** him, "And we,
4:38 and they **a** him about her.
5: 3 and **a** him to put out a little way from the shore.
Lk 7:36 One of the Pharisees **a** Jesus to eat with him,
8: 9 Then his disciples **a** him what this parable meant.
8:30 Jesus then **a** him, "What is your name?"
8:37 the surrounding country of the Gerasenes **a** Jesus
8:45 Then Jesus **a**, "Who touched me?"
9:18 he **a** them, "Who do the crowds say that I am?"
10:29 But wanting to justify himself, he **a** Jesus,
10:40 so she came to him and **a**, "Lord,
13: 2 He **a** them, "Do you think that
13:23 Someone **a** him, "Lord, will only a few be saved?"
14: 3 And Jesus **a** the lawyers and Pharisees,
15:26 of the slaves and **a** what was going on.
16: 5 his master's debtors one by one, he **a** the first,
16: 7 Then he **a** another, 'And how much do you owe?'
17:17 Then Jesus **a**, "Were not ten made clean?
17:20 Once Jesus was **a** by the Pharisees when
17:37 Then they **a** him, "Where, Lord?"
18:18 A certain ruler **a** him, "Good Teacher,
18:36 he **a** what was happening.
18:40 and when he came near, he **a** him,
19:33 As they were untying the colt, its owners **a** them,
20:21 So they **a** him, "Teacher, we know
20:28 and **a** him a question, "Teacher, Moses wrote
21: 7 They **a** him, "Teacher, when will this be,
22: 9 They **a** him, "Where do you want us
22:49 they **a**, "Lord, should we strike with the sword?"
22:70 All of them **a**, "Are you, then, the Son of God?"
23: 3 Pilate **a** him, "Are you the King of the Jews?"
23: 6 he **a** whether the man was a Galilean.
23:25 He released the man they **a** for,
23:52 This man went to Pilate and **a** for the body
24:19 He **a** them, "What things?"
Jn 1:21 And they **a** him, "What then?"
1:25 They **a** him, "Why then are you baptizing
1:48 Nathanael **a** him, "Where did you get
4:10 'Give me a drink,' you would have **a** him,
4:40 they **a** him to stay with them;
4:52 So he **a** them the hour when he began to recover,
5:12 They **a** him, "Who is the man who said to you,
6:67 So Jesus **a** the twelve, "Do you also wish
7:41 But some **a**, "Surely the Messiah does not come
7:45 who **a** them, "Why did you not arrest him?"
7:50 and who was one of them, **a**,
9: 2 His disciples **a** him, "Rabbi, who sinned,
9:19 and **a** them, "Is this your son,
13:25 So while reclining next to Jesus, he **a** him, "Lord,
16:24 now you have not **a** for anything in my name.
18: 4 came forward and **a** them,
18: 7 Again he **a** them, "Whom are you looking for?"
18:25 They **a** him, "You are not also one
18:26 **a**, "Did I not see you in the garden with him?"
18:33 and **a** him, "Are you the King of the Jews?"
18:37 Pilate **a** him, "So you are a king?"
18:38 Pilate **a** him, "What is truth?"
19: 9 He entered his headquarters again and **a** Jesus,
19:15 Pilate **a** them, "Shall I crucify your King?"
19:31 So they **a** Pilate to have the legs of
19:38 **a** Pilate to let him take away the body of Jesus.
Ac 1: 6 So when they had come together, they **a** him,
2: 7 Amazed and astonished, they **a**,
3: 3 and John about to go into the temple, he **a** them
3:14 the Holy and Righteous One and **a** to have
4: 9 and are **a** how this man has been healed,
5: 3 Peter **a**, "why has Satan filled your heart to lie to
7: 1 Then the high priest **a** him, "Are these things so?"
7:46 and **a** that he might find a dwelling place for
8:30 He **a**, "Do you understand what you are reading?"
8:34 The eunuch **a** Philip, "About whom,
9: 2 **a** him for letters to the synagogues at Damascus,
9: 5 He **a**, "Who are you, Lord?"
12:20 the king's chamberlain, they **a** for a reconciliation,
13:21 Then they **a** for a king;
13:28 they **a** Pilate to have him killed.
16:39 they took them out and **a** them to leave the city.
17:19 and brought him to the Areopagus and **a** him,
18:20 When they **a** him to stay longer, he declined;
22:10 I **a**, 'What am I to do, Lord?'
22:27 The tribune came and **a** Paul, "Tell me,
23:18 and **a** me to bring this young man to you;
23:19 and **a**, "What is it that you have to report to me?"
23:34 he **a** what province he belonged to,
25: 9 But Festus, wishing to do the Jews a favor, **a** Paul,
25:15 of the Jews informed me about him and **a** for
25:20 I **a** whether he wished to go to Jerusalem and
26:15 I **a**, 'Who are you, Lord?'
28:20 therefore I have **a** to see you and speak with you,
Gal 2:10 They **a** only one thing, that we remember
Tob 4: 2 "Now I have **a** for death.
7: 4 Then she **a** them, "Is he in good health?"
8:19 this he **a** his wife to bake many loaves of bread;
Jdt 10:12 They **a** her, "To what people do you belong,
AdE 6: 4 The king **a**, "Who is in the courtyard?"
8: 3 she **a** him to avert all the evil
13: 3 "When I **a** my counselors how this might
16:13 with intricate craft and deceit **a** for the destruction
Sir 32: 7 but no more than twice, and only if **a**.
41: 4 there are no questions **a** in Hades.
51:14 Before the temple I **a** for her,
Sus 1:50 seize this woman and **a** who the young man was,
1:47 All the people turned to him and **a**,
1Mc 11:28 Then Jonathan **a** the king to free Judea and
11:66 Then they **a** him to grant them terms of peace,
2Mc 2: 8 and as Solomon **a** that the place should
3:37 the king **a** Heliodorus what sort of person would
7: 7 the skin of his head with the hair, and **a** him,
11:17 and have **a** about the matters indicated in it.
14: 5 and was **a** about the attitude and intentions of
2Mc 15: 3 the thrice-accursed wretch **a** if there were
1Es 6:11 Then we **a** these elders, 'At whose
6:12 and **a** them for a list of the names of those who are
2Es 2:44 Then I **a** an angel, "Who are these, my lord?"
4: 7 And he said to me, "If I had **a** you,
4: 9 But now I have **a** you only about fire and wind
4:25 It is about these things that I have **a**."
5:39 concerning the things that you have **a** me?"
4Mc 5:14 Eleazar **a** to have a word.

ASKELON (KJV) See ASHKELON

ASKING (34) [ASK]

Ex 10:11 for that is what you are **a**."
1Sa 8:10 of the LORD to the people who were **a** him for
1Ki 1: 6 at any time displeased him by **a**,
Job 31:30 I have not let my mouth sin by **a** for their lives
Isa 30: 2 to Egypt without **a** for my counsel, to take refuge
Da 2:11 The thing that the king is **a** is too difficult,
2:27 to the king the mystery that the king is **a**,
Mal 2:17 Or by **a**, "Where is the God of justice?"
Mt 2: 2 **a**, "Where is the child who has been born king of
17:25 when he came home, Jesus spoke of it first, **a**,
20:22 "You do not know what you are **a**.
21:10 the whole city was in turmoil, **a**, "Who is this?"
Mk 1:27 and they kept on **a** one another, "What is this?
3:32 and your brothers and sisters are outside, **a**
8:11 **a** him for a sign from heaven, to test him.
10:38 "You do not know what you are **a**.
Lk 2:46 listening to them and **a** them questions.
7: 3 **a** him to come and heal his slave.
22:64 they also blindfolded him and kept **a** him,
Jn 9:10 But they kept **a** him,
11:56 for Jesus and were **a** one another as they stood in
17: 9 I am **a** on their behalf; I am not **a** on behalf of the
17:15 I am not **a** you to take them out of the world,
Ac 10:17 They were **a** for Simon's house and were standing
20:17 **a** the elders of the church to meet him.
Ro 1:10 **a** that by God's will I may somehow
Col 1: 9 and **a** that you may be filled with the knowledge
2Th 1:11 **a** that our God will make you worthy of his call
1Mc 12: 4 **a** them to provide for the envoys safe conduct to
13:45 **a** Simon to make peace with them;
16:18 **a** him to send troops to aid him and to turn over
16:19 he sent letters to the captains **a** them to come
3Mc 6:37 **a** for dismissal to their homes.

ASKS‡ (22) [ASK]

Ge 32:17 "When Esau my brother meets you, and **a** you,
Ex 13:14 When in the future your child **a** you,
Jdg 4:20 and if anybody comes and **a** you,
Jer 23:33 When this people, or a prophet, or a priest **a** you,
Zec 13: 6 And if anyone **a** them, "What are these wounds
Mt 7: 8 For everyone who **a** receives,
7: 9 if your child **a** for bread, will give a stone?
7:10 Or if the child **a** for a fish, will give a snake?
12:39 "An evil and adulterous generation **a** for a sign,
16: 4 An evil and adulterous generation **a** for a sign,
Mk 14:14 say to the owner of the house, 'The Teacher **a**,
Lk 11:10 For everyone who **a** receives,
11:11 if your child **a** for a fish,
11:12 Or if the child **a** for an egg, will give a scorpion?
11:29 it **a** for a sign, but no sign will be given
14:32 he sends a delegation and **a** for the terms of peace.
19:31 If anyone **a** you, 'Why are you untying it?'
22:11 'The teacher **a** you, "Where is the guest room,
Jn 16: 5 yet none of you **a** me, 'Where are you going?'
Wis 13:19 and work and success with his hands he **a** strength
Sir 20:15 Today he lends and tomorrow he **a** it back;
39: 5 he opens his mouth in prayer and **a** a pardon

ASLEEP‡ (28) [SLEEP]

Ge 41: 5 Then he fell **a** and dreamed a second time;
41:22 I fell **a** a second time and I saw
Jdg 4:21 he was lying fast **a** from weariness—and he died.
16:19 She let him fall **a** on her lap;
1Sa 26:12 for they were all **a**, because a deep sleep from
1Ki 18:27 or perhaps he is **a** and must be awakened."
19: 5 Then he lay down under the broom tree and fell **a**.
Job 3:13 be lying down and quiet; I would be **a**;
Jnh 1: 5 of the ship and had lain down, and was fast **a**.
1: 6 "What are you doing sound **a**?
Na 3:18 Your shepherds are **a**, O king of Assyria;
Mt 8:24 by the waves; but he was **a**.
13:25 but while everybody was **a**,
27:52 of the saints who had fallen **a** were raised.
28:13 by night and stole him away while we were **a**.'
Mk 4:38 But he was in the stern, **a** on the cushion;
13:36 else he may find you **a** when he comes suddenly.
14:37 and he said to Peter, "Simon, are you **a**?
Lk 8:23 and while they were sailing he fell **a**.
Jn 11:11 he told them, "Our friend Lazarus has fallen **a**,
11:12 disciples said to him, "Lord, if he has fallen **a**,
1Th 5: 6 So then let us not fall **a** as others do,
5:10 whether we are awake or **a** we may live with him.
2Pe 2: 3 has not been idle, and their destruction is not **a**.
Tob 8:13 and she went in and found them sound **a** together.
Sir 46:20 Even after he had fallen **a**,
2Mc 12:45 that is laid up for those who fall **a** in godliness,
2Es 7:*32* The earth shall give up those who are **a** in it,

ASMODEUS (2)

Tob 3: 8 and the wicked demon **A** had killed each of them
3:17 and by setting her free from the wicked demon **A**.

ASNAH (2)
Ezr 2:50 A, Meunim, Nephisim,
1Es 5:31 the descendants of Basthai, the descendants of A,

ASNAPPER (KJV) See OSNAPPER

ASP (1) [ASPS]
Isa 11: 8 The nursing child shall play over the hole of the a,

ASP, ASPS (KJV) See VIPERS

ASPATHA (1)
Est 9: 7 They killed Parshandatha, Dalphon, A,

ASPECT (3)
Da 1:17 and skill in every a of literature and wisdom;
Sir 23:19 they look upon every a of human behavior and see
3Mc 6:18 of fearful a descended, visible to all but

ASPHAR (1)
1Mc 9:33 and camped by the water of the pool of A.

ASPHARASUS (1)
1Es 5: 8 A, Reeliah, Rehum, and Baanah, their leaders.

ASPIRE (1) [ASPIRES]
1Th 4:11 to a to live quietly, to mind your own affairs,

ASPIRES (1) [ASPIRE]
1Ti 3: 1 whoever a to the office of bishop desires

ASPS (3) [ASP]
Dt 32:33 the poison of serpents, the cruel venom of a.
Job 20:14 it is the venom of a within them.
20:16 They will suck the poison of a;

ASRIEL (3) [ASRIELITES]
Nu 26:31 and of A, the clan of the Asrielites;
Jos 17: 2 by their families, Abiezer, Helek, A, Shechem,
1Ch 7:14 A, whom his Aramean concubine bore;

ASRIELITES (1) [ASRIEL]
Nu 26:31 and of Asriel, the clan of the A;

ASS‡ (9) [ASSES]
Ge 16:12 He shall be a wild a of a man,
Job 6: 5 Does the wild a bray over its grass,
11:12 when a wild a is born human.
39: 5 "Who has let the wild a go free?
39: 5 Who has loosed the bonds of the swift a,
Jer 2:24 a wild a at home in the wilderness,
48: 6 Be like a wild a in the desert!
Hos 8: 9 a wild a wandering alone;
Sir 25: 8 the one who does not plow with ox and a together.

ASS, ASS'S, ASSES (KJV) See also DONKEY

ASSAIL (5) [ASSAILANT, ASSAILANTS, ASSAILED]
Ps 27: 2 When evildoers a me to devour my flesh—
62: 3 How long will you a a person,
Eze 38:12 to a the waste places that are now inhabited,
2Mc 11: 9 to a not only humans but the wildest animals
4Mc 15:32 and withstood the wintry storms that a religion.

ASSAILANT (1) [ASSAIL]
Ex 21:19 then the a shall be free of liability,

ASSAILANTS (6) [ASSAIL]
2Sa 22:40 you made my a sink under me.
Ps 18:39 you made my a sink under me.
44: 5 through your name we tread down our a.
92:11 my ears have heard the doom of my evil a.
109:28 Let my a be put to shame;
La 3:62 and murmurs of my a are against me all day long.

ASSAILED (4) [ASSAIL]
2Sa 22: 5 the torrents of perdition a me;
Ps 18: 4 the torrents of perdition a me;
Wis 18:17 and unexpected fears a them;
19: 1 the ungodly were a to the end by pitiless anger,

ASSAPHIOTH (1)
1Es 5:33 the descendants of A, the descendants of Peruda,

ASSASSINATE (2) [ASSASSINS]
Est 2:21 became angry and conspired to a King Ahasuerus.
6: 2 and who had conspired to a King Ahasuerus.

ASSASSINS (1) [ASSASSINATE]
Ac 21:38 up a revolt and led the four thousand a out into

ASSAULT (6) [ASSAULTED, ASSAULTS]
Dt 17: 8 or one kind of a and another—
21: 5 by their decision all cases of dispute and a shall
Est 7: 8 "Will he even a the queen in my presence,
AdE 7: 8 "Will he dare even a my wife in my own house?"
2Mc 5: 5 a thousand men and suddenly made an a on
2Es 15:19 shall make an a upon their houses with the sword,

ASSAULTED (4) [ASSAULT]
Jos 10:31 to Lachish, and laid siege to it, and a it.
10:34 and they laid siege to it, and a it;
10:36 from Eglon to Hebron; they a it,
10:38 with all Israel, turned back to Debir and a it,

ASSAULTED (KJV) See also ATTACKED

ASSAULTS (1) [ASSAULT]
Ps 88:16 over me; your dread a destroy me.

ASSAY (KJV) See VENTURES

ASSEMBLE (31) [ASSEMBLED, ASSEMBLES, ASSEMBLIES, ASSEMBLY]
Ge 49: 2 A and hear, O sons of Jacob;
Ex 3:16 Go and a the elders of Israel, and say to them,
Lev 8: 3 and a the whole congregation at the entrance of
Nu 8: 9 and a the whole congregation of the Israelites.
10: 3 the whole congregation shall a before you at
10: 4 the heads of the tribes of Israel, shall a before you.
20: 8 the staff, and a the congregation, you
Dt 4:10 the LORD said to me, "A the people for me,
31:12 A the people—men, women,
31:28 A to me all the elders of your tribes
1Ki 18:19 have all Israel a for me at Mount Carmel,
Ezr 10: 7 the returned exiles that they should a at Jerusalem,
Ne 7: 5 into my mind to a the nobles and the officials and
Est 8:11 in every city to a and defend their lives,
Isa 11:12 and will a the outcasts of Israel,
43: 9 the nations gather together, and let the peoples a.
44:11 Let them all a, let them stand up;
45:20 A yourselves and come together, draw near,
48:14 A, all of you, and hear!
Jer 12: 9 Go, a all the wild animals;
Eze 11:17 I will gather you from the peoples, and a you out
39:17 A and come, gather from all around to
Da 3: 2 and all the officials of the provinces to a and come
11:10 "His sons shall wage war and a a multitude
Joel 2:16 Sanctify the congregation; a the aged;
Am 3: 9 and say, "A yourselves on Mount Samaria,
Mic 4: 6 In that day, says the LORD, I will a the lame
Zep 3: 8 my decision is to gather nations, to a kingdoms,
Rev 16:14 to a them for battle on the great day of God
1Mc 9: 7 for he had no time to a them.
1Es 9: 3 from exile that they should a at Jerusalem,

ASSEMBLED‡ (78) [ASSEMBLE]
Ex 4:29 Then Moses and Aaron went and a all the elders
12: 6 then the whole a congregation
35: 1 Moses a all the congregation of the Israelites
Lev 8: 4 the congregation was a at the entrance of the tent
Nu 1:18 and on the first day of the second month they a
16: 3 They a against Moses and against Aaron,
16:19 Then Korah a the whole congregation
16:42 And when the congregation had a against them,
Dt 29:10 You stand a today, all of you,
33: 5 when the leaders of the people a—
Jos 18: 1 whole congregation of the Israelites a at Shiloh,
Jdg 20: 1 the congregation a in one body before the LORD
1Sa 25: 1 and all Israel a and mourned for him.
28: 4 Philistines a, and came and encamped at Shunem.
2Sa 20:14 and all the Bichrites a, and followed him inside.
1Ki 8: 1 Then Solomon a the elders of Israel and all
8: 2 All the people of Israel a to King Solomon at
8: 5 the congregation of Israel, who had a before him,
12:21 he a all the house of Judah and the tribe
18:20 and a the prophets at Mount Carmel.
2Ki 10:18 Then Jehu a all the people and said to them,
1Ch 13: 5 So David a all Israel from the Shihor of Egypt
15: 3 David a all Israel in Jerusalem to bring up the ark
23: 2 David a all the leaders of Israel and the priests and
28: 1 David a at Jerusalem all the officials of Israel,
2Ch 5: 2 Then Solomon a the elders of Israel and all
5: 3 the Israelites a before the king at the festival
5: 6 who had a before him, were before the ark,
11: 1 he a one hundred eighty thousand chosen troops
20: 4 Judah a to seek help from the LORD;
20:26 On the fourth day they a in the Valley of Beracah,
24: 5 He a the priests and the Levites and said to them,
25: 5 Amaziah a the people of Judah,
29: 4 the Levites and a them in the square on the east.
29:20 a the officials of the city,
30: 3 nor had the people a in Jerusalem).
Ezr 10: 9 the people of Judah and Benjamin a at Jerusalem
Ne 9: 1 of Israel were a with fasting and in sackcloth,
Ps 48: 4 Then the kings a, they came on together.
Jer 26:17 of the land arose and said to all the a people,
Eze 38: 7 you and all the companies that are a around you,
38:13 Have you a your horde to carry off plunder,
Da 3: 3 a for the dedication of the statue
Mic 4:11 Now many nations are a against you, saying,
Mt 28:12 After the priests had a with the elders,
Mk 14:53 the elders, and the scribes were a.
Ac 4: 5 elders, and scribes a in Jerusalem,
10:27 he went in and found that many had a;
28:17 When they had a, he said to them, "Brothers,
1Co 5: 4 When you are a, and my spirit is present with
Rev 16:16 And they a them at the place that
Sir 16:10 or on the six hundred thousand foot soldiers who a
1Mc 2:16 and Mattathias and his sons were a.
3:44 So the congregation a to be ready for battle,
3:52 Here the Gentiles are a against us to destroy us;
3:58 to fight with these Gentiles who have a against us
4:37 So all the army a and went up to Mount Zion.
6:19 and a all the people to besiege them.
6:28 He a all his Friends, the commanders of his forces
9:28 all the friends of Judas a and said to Jonathan,
9:63 Bacchides learned of this, he a all his forces,
10: 2 he a a very large army and marched out
10:48 Now King Alexander a large forces
10:69 he a a large force and encamped against Jamnia.
11:20 In those days Jonathan a the Judeans to attack
11:45 Then the people of the city a within the city,
13: 1 that Trypho had a a large army to invade the land
13:10 So he a all the warriors and hurried to complete
14: 1 King Demetrius a his forces and marched into
2Mc 6:11 Others who had a in the caves nearby,
12:38 Judas a his army and went to the city of Adullam.
1Es 8:41 I a them at the river called Theras,
9: 5 of the tribe of Judah and Benjamin a at Jerusalem
3Mc 5:14 seeing that the guests were a,
5:24 the city had been a for this most pitiful spectacle
5:34 the a people to their own occupations.
2Es 6: 1 and before the a winds blew,
13:37 will reprove the a nations

ASSEMBLES (1) [ASSEMBLE]
Job 11:10 and a for judgment, who can hinder him?

ASSEMBLIES (2) [ASSEMBLE]
Isa 1:13 I cannot endure solemn a with iniquity.
Am 5:21 and I take no delight in your solemn a.

ASSEMBLY (148) [ASSEMBLE]
A. WHOLE ASSEMBLY (22)
B. ALL THE ASSEMBLY (20)
C. ASSEMBLY OF ISRAEL (14)
D. ASSEMBLY OF THE †LORD (10)
E. SOLEMN ASSEMBLY (10)

Ex 12:16 On the first day you shall hold a solemn a, E
12:16 and on the seventh day a solemn a; E
16: 3 into this wilderness to kill this whole a A
Lev 4:13 of the a, and they do any one of the things that by
4:14 the a shall offer a bull of the herd for
4:21 it is the sin offering for the a.
16:17 for his house and for all the a of Israel. BC
16:33 for the priests and for all the people of the a.
23:36 by fire; it is a solemn a; E
Nu 10: 7 But when the a is to be gathered, you shall blow,
14: 5 their faces before all the a of the congregation B
15:15 As for the a, there shall be for both you and
16: 2 leaders of the congregation, chosen from the a,
16: 3 you exalt yourselves above the a of the LORD?" D
16:33 and they perished from the midst of the a.
16:47 and ran into the middle of the a,
19:20 those persons shall be cut off from the a,
20: 4 the a of the LORD into this wilderness for us D
20: 6 from the a to the entrance of the tent of meeting;
20:10 and Aaron gathered the a together before the rock,
20:12 therefore you shall not bring this a into the land
29:35 On the eighth day you shall have a solemn a; E
Dt 5:22 a loud voice to your whole a at the mountain, A
9:10 at the mountain out of the fire on the day of the a.
10: 4 the mountain out of the fire on the day of the a;
16: 8 and on the seventh day there shall be a solemn a E
18:16 the LORD your God at Horeb on the day of the a
23: 1 shall be admitted to the a of the LORD. D
23: 2 shall not be admitted to the a of the LORD. D
23: 2 shall be admitted to the a of the LORD. D
23: 3 Moabite shall be admitted to the a of the LORD. D
23: 3 shall be admitted to the a of the LORD, D
23: 8 may be admitted to the a of the LORD. D
31:30 in the hearing of the whole a of Israel: AC
33: 4 as a possession for the a of Jacob.
Jos 8:35 Joshua did not read before all the a of Israel, BC
22:12 the whole a of the Israelites gathered at Shiloh, A
Jdg 20: 2 presented themselves in the a of the people
21: 5 of Israel did not come up in the a to the LORD?"
21: 8 from Jabesh-gilead had come to the camp, to the a.
Ru 3:11 for all the a of my people know that you are B
1Sa 17:47 and that all this a may know that the LORD does
1Ki 8:14 turned around and blessed all the a of Israel, BC
8:14 while all the a of Israel stood. BC
8:22 the LORD in the presence of all the a of Israel, BC
8:55 blessed all the a of Israel with a loud voice: BC
8:65 a great a, people from Lebo-hamath to the Wadi
12: 3 all the a of Israel came and said to Rehoboam, BC
12:20 and called him to the a and made him king
21: 9 and seat Naboth at the head of the a;
21:12 a fast and seated Naboth at the head of the a.
2Ki 10:20 Jehu decreed, "Sanctify a solemn a for Baal." E
1Ch 13: 2 David said to the whole a of Israel, AC
13: 4 The whole a agreed to do so, A
28: 8 in the sight of all Israel, the a of the LORD, D
29: 1 King David said to the whole a, A
29:10 the LORD in the presence of all the a; B
29:20 Then David said to the whole a, A
29:20 And all the a blessed the LORD, B
2Ch 1: 3 Then Solomon, and the whole a with him, A
1: 5 And Solomon and the a inquired at it.

2Ch 6: 3 turned around and blessed all the **a** of Israel, BC
6: 3 while all the **a** of Israel stood. BC
6: 12 LORD in the presence of the whole **a** of Israel, AC
6: 13 knees in the presence of the whole **a** of Israel, AC
7: 9 On the eighth day they held a solemn **a;** E
20: 5 Jehoshaphat stood in the **a** of Judah
20: 14 in the middle of the **a.**
23: 3 Then the whole **a** made a covenant with the king A
28: 14 and the booty before the officials and all the **a.** B
29: 23 to the king and the **a;**
29: 28 The whole **a** worshiped, the singers sang, A
29: 31 The **a** brought sacrifices and thank offerings;
29: 32 that the **a** brought was seventy bulls,
30: 2 all the **a** in Jerusalem had taken counsel to keep B
30: 4 The plan seemed right to the king and all the **a.** B
30: 13 in the second month, a very large **a.**
30: 17 in the **a** who had not sanctified themselves;
30: 23 the whole **a** agreed together to keep the festival A
30: 24 the **a** a thousand bulls and seven thousand sheep
30: 24 the **a** a thousand bulls and ten thousand sheep.
30: 25 whole **a** of Judah, the priests and the Levites, A
30: 25 and the whole **a** that came out of Israel, A
Ezr 2: 64 whole **a** together was forty-two thousand A
10: 1 a very great **a** of men, women,
10: 12 all the **a** answered with a loud voice, "It is so; B
10: 14 Let our officials represent the whole **a,** A
Ne 5: 7 And I called a great **a** to deal with them,
5: 13 all the **a** said, "Amen," and praised the LORD. B
7: 66 whole **a** together was forty-two thousand A
8: 2 the priest Ezra brought the law before the **a,**
8: 17 And all the **a** of those who had returned from B
8: 18 and on the eighth day there was a solemn **a,** E
13: 1 or Moabite should ever enter the **a** of God,
Job 30: 28 I stand up in the **a** and cry for help.
Ps 7: 7 Let the **a** of the peoples be gathered around you,
89: 5 your faithfulness in the **a** of the holy ones.
107: 32 and praise him in the **a** of the elders.
149: 1 his praise in the **a** of the faithful.
Pr 5: 14 Now I am at the point of utter ruin in the public **a."**
21: 16 from the way of understanding will rest in the **a** of
26: 26 the enemy's wickedness will be exposed in the **a.**
Isa 4: 5 over its places of **a** a cloud by day and smoke and
14: 13 on the mount of **a** on the heights of Zaphon;
Jer 44: 15 and all the women who stood by, a great **a,**
Eze 23: 46 Bring up an **a** against them,
23: 47 The **a** shall stone them and
32: 3 In an **a** of many peoples I will throw my net
Hos 7: 12 according to the report made to their **a.**
Joel 1: 14 Sanctify a fast, call a solemn **a.** E
2: 15 sanctify a fast; call a solemn **a;** E
Mic 2: 5 to cast the line by lot in the **a** of the LORD. D
6: 9 Hear, O tribe and **a** of the city!
Lk 1: 10 the whole **a** of the people was praying outside. A
22: 66 When day came, the **a** of the elders of the people,
23: 1 **a** rose as a body and brought Jesus before Pilate.
Ac 15: 12 The whole **a** kept silence, A
17: 5 for Paul and Silas to bring them out to the **a,**
19: 32 for the **a** was in confusion,
19: 39 it must be settled in the regular **a.**
19: 41 When he had said this, he dismissed the **a.**
23: 7 and the Sadducees, and the **a** was divided.
Heb 12: 23 the **a** of the firstborn who are enrolled in heaven,
Jas 2: 2 and in fine clothes comes into your **a,**
Jdt 6: 16 and all their young men and women ran to the **a.**
6: 21 from the **a** to his own house and gave a banquet
7: 29 and general lamentation arose throughout the **a,**
14: 6 the hand of one of the men in the **a** of the people,
AdE 10: 13 with an **a** and joy and gladness before God,
Sir 7: 14 Do not babble in the **a** of the elders,
15: 5 and will open his mouth in the midst of the **a.**
16: 6 In an **a** of sinners a fire is kindled,
21: 9 An **a** of the wicked is like a bundle of tow,
21: 17 utterance of a sensible person is sought in the **a,**
23: 24 She herself will be brought before the **a,**
24: 2 In the **a** of the Most High she opens her mouth,
31: 11 and the **a** will proclaim his acts of charity.
38: 33 nor do they attain eminence in the public **a.**
42: 11 a byword in the city and the **a** of the people,
44: 15 The **a** declares their wisdom,
Sus 1: 41 the **a** believed them and condemned her to death.
1: 60 whole **a** raised a great shout and blessed God, A
1Mc 2: 56 Caleb, because he testified in the **a,**
4: 59 his brothers and all the **a** of Israel determined BC
5: 16 people heard these messages, a great **a** was called
14: 19 And these were read before the **a** in Jerusalem.
14: 28 in the great **a** of the priests and the people and
14: 44 an **a** in the country without his permission,

ASSENTED (1)
2Mc 4: 10 When the king **a** and Jason came to office,

ASSERT (1) [ASSERTED, ASSERTING, ASSERTIONS]
Sir 7: 5 Do not **a** your righteousness before the Lord,

ASSERTED (1) [ASSERT]
Ac 25: 19 who had died, but whom Paul **a** to be alive.

ASSERTING (1) [ASSERT]
Ac 24: 9 The Jews also joined in the charge by **a**

ASSERTIONS (1) [ASSERT]
1Ti 1: 7 or the things about which they make **a.**

ASSES (6) [ASS]
Job 24: 5 Like wild **a** in the desert they go out to their toil,
Ps 104: 11 the wild **a** quench their thirst.
Isa 32: 14 the joy of wild **a,** a pasture for flocks;
Jer 14: 6 The wild **a** stand on the bare heights,
Da 5: 21 His dwelling was with the wild **a,**
Sir 13: 19 Wild **a** in the wilderness are the prey of lions;

ASSESS (4) [ASSESSED, ASSESSES, ASSESSMENT, ASSESSMENTS]
Lev 27: 8 before the priest and the priest shall **a** them;
27: 8 the priest shall **a** them according
27: 12 The priest shall **a** it: whether good
27: 14 a house to the LORD, the priest shall **a** it:

ASSESSED (3) [ASSESS]
Lev 27: 15 one-fifth shall be added to its **a** value,
27: 19 then one-fifth shall be added to its **a** value,
2Ki 12: 4 the money for which each person is **a—**

ASSESSES (1) [ASSESS]
Lev 27: 14 whether good or bad, as the priest **a** it,

ASSESSMENT (11) [ASSESS]
Lev 27: 12 according to the **a** of the priest, so it shall be.
27: 13 one-fifth must be added to the **a.**
27: 16 its **a** shall be in accordance
27: 17 as of the year of jubilee, that **a** shall stand;
27: 18 and the **a** shall be reduced.
27: 23 for it the proportionate **a** up to the year of jubilee,
27: 23 and the **a** shall be paid as of that day,
27: 27 it shall be ransomed at its **a,** with one-fifth added;
27: 27 if it is not redeemed, it shall be sold at its **a.**
2Ki 12: 4 the money from the **a** of persons—
23: 35 from all according to their **a,**

ASSESSMENTS (1) [ASSESS]
Lev 27: 25 All **a** shall be by the sanctuary shekel:

ASSHUR (5)
Ge 10: 22 Elam, **A,** Arpachshad, Lud, and Aram.
Nu 24: 22 How long shall **A** take you away captive?"
24: 24 from Kittim and shall afflict **A** and Eber;
1Ch 1: 17 The descendants of Shem: Elam, **A,** Arpachshad,
Eze 27: 23 Haran, Canneh, Eden, the merchants of Sheba, **A,**

ASSHURIM (1)
Ge 25: 3 sons of Dedan were **A,** Letushim, and Leummim.

ASSIGN (7) [ASSIGNED, ASSIGNING, ASSIGNMENT]
Nu 4: 19 Aaron and his sons shall go in and **a** each to
4: 27 and you shall **a** to their charge all that they are
4: 32 and you shall **a** by name the objects
Eze 4: 5 For I **a** to you a number of days,
4: 6 forty days I **a** you, one day for each year.
45: 6 the portion set apart as the holy district you shall **a**
47: 23 there you shall **a** them their inheritance,

ASSIGNED‡ (19) [ASSIGN]
Lev 10: 14 for they have been **a** to you and your children
Nu 3: 36 The responsibility **a** to the sons of Merari was to
1Sa 29: 4 he may return to the place that you have **a** to him;
2Sa 11: 16 he **a** Uriah to the place
1Ki 11: 18 **a** him an allowance of food, and gave him land.
2Ch 2: 14 and execute any design that may be **a** him,
2: 18 Seventy thousand of them he **a** as laborers,
23: 18 Jehoiada **a** the care of the house of the LORD to
Pr 8: 29 when he **a** to the sea its limit,
Da 1: 5 The king **a** them a daily portion of
Ac 22: 10 there you will be told everything that has been **a**
Ro 12: 3 according to the measure of faith that God has **a.**
1Co 3: 5 as the Lord **a** to each.
7: 17 let each of you lead the life that the Lord has **a,**
2Co 10: 13 but will keep within the field that God has **a** to us,
1Mc 5: 20 Then three thousand men were **a** to Simon to go
6: 35 and five hundred picked horsemen were **a**
2Es 4: 19 for the land has been **a** to the forest,
4: 21 For as the land has been **a** to the forest and the sea

ASSIGNING (1) [ASSIGN]
Nu 8: 26 with the Levites in **a** their duties.

ASSIGNMENT (1) [ASSIGN]
Ex 5: 13 the same daily **a** as when you were given straw."

ASSIR (4)
Ex 6: 24 The sons of Korah: **A,** Elkanah, and Abiasaph;
1Ch 6: 22 Amminadab his son, Korah his son, **A** his son,
6: 23 Elkanah his son, Ebiasaph his son, **A** his son,
6: 37 son of **A,** son of Ebiasaph, son of Korah,

ASSIST (9) [ASSISTANCE, ASSISTANT, ASSISTED, ASSISTING]
Nu 1: 5 These are the names of the men who shall **a** you:
3: 6 so that they may **a** him.
8: 26 They may **a** their brothers in the tent of meeting
1Ch 23: 28 be to **a** the descendants of Aaron for the service of
23: 29 to **a** also with the rows of bread,
Ac 13: 5 And they had John also to **a** them.
1Ti 5: 16 relatives who are really widows, let her **a** them;
5: 16 so that it can **a** those who are real widows.
Sir 29: 20 **A** your neighbor to the best of your ability,

ASSISTANCE (4) [ASSIST]
Pr 28: 17 until death; let no one offer **a.**
1Co 12: 28 deeds of power, then gifts of healing, forms of **a,**
Sir 51: 7 I looked for human **a,** and there was none.
3Mc 3: 10 and to exert more earnest efforts for their **a.**

ASSISTANT (6) [ASSIST]
Ex 24: 13 So Moses set out with his **a** Joshua,
33: 11 but his young **a,** Joshua son of Nun,
Nu 11: 28 And Joshua son of Nun, the **a** of Moses,
Dt 1: 38 Joshua son of Nun, your **a,** shall enter there;
Jos 1: 1 to Joshua son of Nun, Moses' **a,**
Ne 13: 13 as their **a** Hanan son of Zaccur son of Mattaniah,

ASSISTED (2) [ASSIST]
Ezr 1: 4 be **a** by the people of their place with silver
Job 26: 2 How you have **a** the arm that has no strength!

ASSISTING (3) [ASSIST]
2Ch 31: 13 and Benaiah were overseers **a** Conaniah
31: 15 and Shecaniah were faithfully **a** him in the cities
1Es 7: 2 **a** the elders of the Jews and the chief officers of

ASSOCIATE‡ (13) [ASSOCIATED, ASSOCIATES, ASSOCIATION]
Pr 20: 19 therefore do not **a** with a babbler.
22: 24 and do not **a** with hotheads,
Zec 13: 7 against the man who is my **a,"**
Ac 10: 28 that it is unlawful for a Jew to **a** with or to visit
Ro 12: 16 do not be haughty, but **a** with the lowly;
1Co 5: 9 not to **a** with sexually immoral persons—
5: 11 to you not to **a** with anyone who bears the name
Wis 6: 23 for envy does not **a** with wisdom.
8: 4 and an **a** in his works.
Sir 13: 2 or **a** with one mightier and richer than you.
13: 2 How can the clay pot **a** with the iron kettle?
13: 16 All living beings **a** with their own kind,
37: 12 But **a** with a godly person whom you know to be

ASSOCIATED (6) [ASSOCIATE]
Eze 37: 16 "For Judah, and the Israelites **a** with it";
37: 16 (the stick of Ephraim) and all the house of Israel **a**
37: 19 in the hand of Ephraim) and the tribes of Israel **a**
Eph 5: 7 Therefore do not be **a** with them.
2Mc 8: 9 He **a** with him Gorgias, a general and a man
1Es 2: 25 and the others **a** with them and living in Samaria

ASSOCIATES (31) [ASSOCIATE]
Ezr 4: 7 and the rest of their **a** wrote to King Artaxerxes
4: 9 and the rest of their **a,** the judges, the envoys,
4: 17 and the rest of their **a** who live in Samaria and in
4: 23 and the scribe Shimshai and their **a,**
5: 3 and their **a** came to them and spoke to them thus,
5: 6 Beyond the River and Shethar-bozenai and his **a**
6: 6 Shethar-bozenai, and you, their **a,**
6: 13 the River, Shethar-bozenai, and their **a** did
Ne 4: 2 the presence of his **a** and of the army of Samaria,
10: 10 and their **a,** Shebaniah, Hodiah,
11: 12 and their **a** who did the work of the house,
11: 13 and his **a,** heads of ancestral
11: 14 and their **a,** valiant warriors,
11: 17 and Bakbukiah, the second among his **a;**
11: 19 The gatekeepers, Akkub, Talmon and their **a,**
12: 7 These were the leaders of the priests and of their **a**
12: 8 and Mattaniah, who with his **a** was in charge of
12: 9 and Unno their **a** stood opposite them in
12: 24 with their **a** over against them,
13: 13 and their duty was to distribute to their **a.**
Sir 12: 14 So no one pities a person who **a** with a sinner
13: 1 whoever **a** with a proud person becomes like him.
2Mc 1: 33 and his **a** had burned the materials of the sacrifice,
1: 36 Nehemiah and his **a** called this "nephthar,"
1Es 2: 16 the scribe Shimshai, and the rest of their **a,**
2: 30 and the scribe Shimshai and their **a** went quickly
6: 3 and Phoenicia and Sathrabuzanes and their **a** came
6: 7 and their **a** the local rulers in Syria and Phoenicia,
6: 27 and Sathrabuzanes, and their **a,**
7: 1 and their **a,** following the orders of King Darius,
3Mc 3: 10 and friends and business **a** had taken some

ASSOCIATION (1) [ASSOCIATE]
3Mc 2: 31 to enhance their reputation by their future **a** with

ASSOS (2)
Ac 20: 13 We went ahead to the ship and set sail for **A,**
20: 14 When he met us in **A,**

ASSUAGE (1) [ASSUAGED, ASSUAGING]
Job 16: 5 and the solace of my lips would **a** your pain.

ASSUAGED (1) [ASSUAGE]
Job 16: 6 "If I speak, my pain is not **a,** and if I forbear,

ASSUAGING (1) [ASSUAGE]
Na 3: 19 There is no **a** your hurt, your wound is mortal.

ASSUME (2) [ASSUMED, ASSUMING]
AdE 16: 4 even **a** that they will escape the evil-hating justice
1Mc 10:70 Why do you **a** authority against us in

ASSUMED (3) [ASSUME]
2Co 12:16 Let it be **a** that I did not burden you.
Wis 13: 3 in the beauty of these things people **a** them to
1Es 5:38 Of the priests the following had **a** the priesthood

ASSUMING (2) [ASSUME]
Lk 2:44 **A** that he was in the group of travelers,
3Mc 3:11 but **a** that he would persevere constantly

ASSUR (KJV) See ASSYRIA

ASSURANCE (7) [ASSURE, ASSURED, ASSUREDLY, REASSURE, REASSURED]
Dt 28:66 night and day you shall be in dread, with no **a**
Ac 17:31 of this he has given **a** to all by raising him from
Heb 6:11 so as to realize the full **a** of hope to the very end,
10:22 let us approach with a true heart in full **a** of faith,
11: 1 Now faith is the **a** of things hoped for,
Wis 6:18 and giving heed to her laws is **a** of immortality,
Sir 44:22 the same **a** for the sake of his father Abraham.

ASSURE (1) [ASSURANCE]
Sir 29:21 bread, and clothing, and also a house to **a** privacy.

ASSURED (10) [ASSURANCE]
Ge 43:23 He replied, "Rest **a**, do not be afraid;
Pr 11:21 Be **a**, the wicked will not go unpunished,
16: 5 be **a**, they will not go unpunished.
Isa 33:16 their food will be supplied, their water **a**.
Zec 3: 6 Then the angel of the LORD **a** Joshua, saying
Col 2: 2 of **a** understanding and have the knowledge
4:12 so that you may stand mature and fully **a**
Sir 44:21 the Lord **a** him with an oath that the nations would
2Es 7:*131* [61] as joy over those to whom salvation is **a**."
16:21 upon earth that people will imagine that peace is **a**

ASSUREDLY (3) [ASSURANCE]
Jos 23:13 know **a** that the LORD your God will
Jer 11:11 **a** I am going to bring disaster upon them
51:47 **A**, the days are coming when I will punish

ASSWAGE (KJV) See ASSUAGE

ASSYRIA (136) [ASSYRIAN, ASSYRIANS]
Ge 2:14 of the third river is Tigris, which flows east of **A**.
10:11 From that land he went into **A**, and built Nineveh,
25:18 which is opposite Egypt in the direction of **A**;
2Ki 15:19 King Pul of **A** came against the land;
15:20 to give to the king of **A**.
15:20 So the king of **A** turned back,
15:29 King Tiglath-pileser of **A** came and captured Ijon,
15:29 and he carried the people captive to **A**.
16: 7 to King Tiglath-pileser of **A**,
16: 8 and sent a present to the king of **A**.
16: 9 The king of **A** listened to him;
16: 9 the king of **A** marched up against Damascus,
16:10 to Damascus to meet King Tiglath-pileser of **A**,
16:18 He did this because of the king of **A**.
17: 3 King Shalmaneser of **A** came up against him;
17: 4 But the king of **A** found treachery in Hoshea;
17: 4 and offered no tribute to the king of **A**,
17: 4 the king of **A** confined him and imprisoned him.
17: 5 Then the king of **A** invaded all the land and came
17: 6 year of Hoshea the king of **A** captured Samaria;
17: 6 he carried the Israelites away to **A**.
17:23 So Israel was exiled from their own land to **A**
17:24 The king of **A** brought people from Babylon,
17:26 So the king of **A** was told,
17:27 Then the king of **A** commanded,
18: 7 against the king of **A** and would not serve him.
18: 9 King Shalmaneser of **A** came up against Samaria,
18:11 king of **A** carried the Israelites away to **A**,
18:13 King Sennacherib of **A** came up against all
18:14 King Hezekiah of Judah sent to the king of **A**
18:14 The king of **A** demanded of King Hezekiah
18:16 of Judah had overlaid and gave it to the king of **A**.
18:17 The king of **A** sent the Tartan, the Rabsaris,
18:19 Thus says the great king, the king of **A**:
18:23 make a wager with my master the king of **A**:
18:28 "Hear the word of the great king, the king of **A**!
18:30 not be given into the hand of the king of **A**.'
18:31 for thus says the king of **A**:
18:33 of the hand of the king of **A**?
19: 4 whom his master the king of **A** has sent to mock
19: 6 the servants of the king of **A** have reviled me.
19: 8 and found the king of **A** fighting against Libnah;
19:10 not be given into the hand of the king of **A**.
19:11 you have heard what the kings of **A** have done
19:17 of **A** have laid waste the nations and their lands,
19:20 to me about King Sennacherib of **A**.
19:32 thus says the LORD concerning the king of **A**:
19:36 Then King Sennacherib of **A** left, went home,
20: 6 and this city out of the hand of the king of **A**;
23:29 up to the king of **A** to the river Euphrates.
1Ch 5: 6 whom King Tilgath-pilneser of **A** carried away
5:26 of Israel stirred up the spirit of King Pul of **A**,
5:26 the spirit of King Tilgath-pilneser of **A**,
2Ch 28:16 that time King Ahaz sent to the king of **A** for help.
2Ch 28:20 So King Tilgath-pilneser of **A** came against him,
28:21 and gave tribute to the king of **A**;
30: 6 from the hand of the kings of **A**.
32: 1 King Sennacherib of **A** came and invaded Judah
32: 7 or dismayed before the king of **A** and all the horde
32: 9 while King Sennacherib of **A** was at Lachish
32:10 "Thus says King Sennacherib of **A**:
32:11 from the hand of the king of **A**'?
32:21 and officers in the camp of the king of **A**.
32:22 from the hand of King Sennacherib of **A** and from
33:11 the commanders of the army of the king of **A**,
Ezr 4: 2 of King Esar-haddon of **A** who brought us here."
6:22 and had turned the heart of the king of **A** to them,
Ne 9:32 since the time of the kings of **A** until today.
Ps 83: 8 **A** also has joined them; they are the strong arm
Isa 7:17 from Judah—the king of **A**."
7:18 and for the bee that is in the land of **A**.
7:20 beyond the River—with the king of **A**—
8: 4 of Samaria will be carried away by the king of **A**.
8: 7 the king of **A** and all his glory;
10: 5 Ah, **A**, the rod of my anger—
10:12 of the king of **A** and his haughty pride.
11:11 from **A**, from Egypt, from Pathros, from Ethiopia,
11:16 from **A** for the remnant that is left of his people,
19:23 that day there will be a highway from Egypt to **A**,
19:23 into **A**, and the Egyptians will worship with
19:24 that day Israel will be the third with Egypt and **A**,
19:25 and **A** the work of my hands,
20: 1 who was sent by King Sargon of **A**,
20: 4 the king of **A** lead away the Egyptians as captives
20: 6 for help and deliverance from the king of **A**!
23:13 This is the people; it was not **A**.
27:13 in the land of **A** and those who were driven out to
36: 1 King Sennacherib of **A** came up against all
36: 2 The king of **A** sent the Rabshakeh from Lachish
36: 4 Thus says the great king, the king of **A**:
36: 8 make a wager with my master the king of **A**:
36:13 "Hear the words of the great king, the king of **A**!
36:15 not be given into the hand of the king of **A**.'
36:16 for thus says the king of **A**:
36:18 of the hand of the king of **A**?
37: 4 whom his master the king of **A** has sent to mock
37: 6 the servants of the king of **A** have reviled me.
37: 8 and found the king of **A** fighting against Libnah;
37:10 not be given into the hand of the king of **A**.
37:11 you have heard what the kings of **A** have done
37:18 the kings of **A** have laid waste all the nations
37:21 to me concerning King Sennacherib of **A**,
37:33 thus says the LORD concerning the king of **A**:
37:37 Then King Sennacherib of **A** left, went home,
38: 6 and this city out of the hand of the king of **A**,
Jer 2:18 Or what do you gain by going to **A**,
2:36 to shame by Egypt as you were put to shame by **A**.
50:17 First the king of **A** devoured it,
50:18 as I punished the king of **A**.
La 5: 6 We have made a pact with Egypt and **A**,
Eze 23: 7 the choicest men of **A** all of them;
31: 3 Consider **A**, a cedar of Lebanon,
32:22 **A** is there, and all its company,
Hos 5:13 then Ephraim went to **A**, and sent to the great king.
7:11 they call upon Egypt, they go to **A**.
8: 9 For they have gone up to **A**,
9: 3 and in **A** they shall eat unclean food.
10: 6 The thing itself shall be carried to **A** as tribute to
11: 5 and **A** shall be their king,
11:11 and like doves from the land of **A**;
12: 1 they make a treaty with **A**,
14: 3 **A** shall not save us; we will
Mic 5: 6 They shall rule the land of **A** with the sword,
7:12 In that day they will come to you from **A** to Egypt,
Na 3:18 Your shepherds are asleep, O king of **A**;
Zep 2:13 against the north, and destroy **A**;
Zec 10:10 from the land of Egypt, and gather them from **A**;
10:11 The pride of **A** shall be laid low,
Tob 1:10 After I was carried away captive to **A** and came as
1:22 of the accounts under King Sennacherib of **A**;
14: 4 that all these things will take place and overtake **A**
14: 4 it will be safer in Media than in **A** and Babylon.
14:15 to the people of Nineveh and **A**;
2Es 2: 8 **A**, who conceal the unrighteous within you!
4Mc 13: 9 in **A** who despised the same ordeal of the furnace.

ASSYRIAN (20) [ASSYRIA]
2Ch 32: 4 the **A** kings come and find water in abundance?"
Isa 14:25 I will break the **A** in my land,
19:23 and the **A** will come into Egypt,
30:31 The **A** will be terror-stricken at the voice of
31: 8 "Then the **A** shall fall by a sword, not of mortals;
52: 4 the **A**, too, has oppressed them without cause.
Jdt 2:14 generals, and officers of the **A** army.
5: 1 the general of the **A** army,
6: 1 Holofernes, the commander of the **A** army,
6:17 that he had said in the presence of the **A** leaders,
7:18 The rest of the **A** army encamped in the plain,
7:20 The whole **A** army, their infantry, chariots,
10:11 on through the valley, an **A** patrol met her
12:13 like one of the **A** women who serve in the palace
13:15 the commander of the **A** army,
14: 2 down to the plain against the **A** outpost;
14: 3 the camp and rouse the officers of the **A** army.
14:19 When the leaders of the **A** army heard this,
15: 6 of Bethulia fell upon the **A** camp and plundered it,
16: 3 **A** came down from the mountains of the north;

ASSYRIANS (32) [ASSYRIA]
2Ki 19:35 in the camp of the **A**;
Isa 10:24 do not be afraid of the **A** when they beat you with
19:23 and the Egyptians will worship with the **A**.
37:36 in the camp of the **A**;
Eze 16:28 You played the whore with the **A**,
23: 5 she lusted after her lovers the **A**,
23: 9 into the hands of the **A**, for whom she lusted.
23:12 She lusted after the **A**, governors
23:23 Pekod and Shoa and Koa, and all the **A** with them,
Mic 5: 5 the **A** come into our land and tread upon our soil,
5: 6 from the **A** if they come into our land or tread
Tob 1: 2 the days of King Shalmaneser of the **A** was taken
1: 3 with me in exile to Nineveh in the land of the **A**.
Jdt 1: 1 who ruled over the **A** in the great city of Nineveh.
1: 7 Then Nebuchadnezzar, king of the **A**,
1:11 king of the **A**, and refused to join him in the war;
2: 1 king of the **A**, about carrying out his revenge on
2: 4 king of the **A**, called Holofernes,
4: 1 the general of Nebuchadnezzar, the king of the **A**,
7:17 together with five thousand **A**,
7:24 a great injury in not making peace with the **A**.
8: 9 to surrender the town to the **A** after five days,
9: 7 "Here now are the **A**, a greatly increased force,
14:12 **A** saw them they sent word to their commanders,
Sir 48:21 The Lord struck down the camp of the **A**,
1Mc 7:41 down one hundred eighty-five thousand of the **A**.
1Es 5:69 since the days of King Esar-haddon of the **A**,
7:15 the will of the king of the **A** concerning them,
3Mc 6: 5 in his countless forces, oppressive king of the **A**,
2Es 13:40 whom Shalmaneser, king of the **A**, made captives;
15:30 a portion of the land of the **A** with their teeth.
15:33 of the **A** an enemy in ambush shall attack them

ASTAROTH (KJV) See ASHTAROTH

ASTARTE (4) [ASHERAH, ASTARTES]
1Sa 31:10 They put his armor in the temple of **A**;
1Ki 11: 5 Solomon followed **A** the goddess of the Sidonians,
11:33 worshiped **A** the goddess of the Sidonians,
2Ki 23:13 which King Solomon of Israel had built for **A**

ASTARTES (5) [ASHERAHS, ASTARTE]
Jdg 2:13 and worshiped Baal and the **A**.
10: 6 worshiping the Baals and the **A**,
1Sa 7: 3 then put away the foreign gods and the **A** from
7: 4 So Israel put away the Baals and the **A**,
12:10 and have served the Baals and the **A**;

ASTIN See Index to Footnotes

ASTONISH (1) [ASTONISHED, ASTONISHING, ASTONISHMENT]
Jdt 11:16 to accomplish with you things that will **a**

ASTONISHED (20) [ASTONISH]
1Ki 9: 8 everyone passing by it will be **a**, and will hiss;
2Ch 7:21 now exalted, everyone passing by will be **a**,
Isa 52:14 Just as there were many who were **a** at him
Da 3:24 King Nebuchadnezzar was **a** and rose up quickly.
Hab 1: 5 at the nations, and see! Be **a**!
Lk 2:48 When his parents saw him they were **a**;
Jn 3: 7 Do not be **a** that I said to you,
4:27 They were **a** that he was speaking with a woman,
5:20 so that you will be **a**.
5:28 Do not be **a** at this; for the hour is coming
7:15 The Jews were **a** at it, saying,
7:21 "I performed one work, and all of you are **a**.
Ac 2: 7 Amazed and **a**, they asked,
3:11 in the portico called Solomon's Portico, utterly **a**.
13:12 for he was **a** at the teaching about the Lord.
Gal 1: 6 I am **a** that you are so quickly deserting
1Jn 3:13 Do not be **a**, brothers and sisters,
Jdt 13:17 All the people were greatly **a**.
Sir 40: 7 **a** that his fears were groundless.
2Mc 7:12 the king himself and those with him were **a** at

ASTONISHING (1) [ASTONISH]
Jn 9:30 The man answered, "Here is an **a** thing!

ASTONISHMENT (1) [ASTONISH]
2Ch 29: 8 and he has made them an object of horror, of **a**,

ASTOUNDED (22) [ASTOUNDING]
Job 26:11 pillars of heaven tremble, and are **a** at his rebuke.
Ps 48: 5 As soon as they saw it, they were **a**;
Jer 4: 9 the priests shall be appalled and the prophets **a**.
Hab 1: 5 and see! Be astonished! Be **a**!
Mt 7:28 the crowds were **a** at his teaching,
13:54 so that they were **a** and said,
19:25 disciples heard this, they were greatly **a** and said,
22:33 the crowd heard it, they were **a** at his teaching.
Mk 1:22 They were **a** at his teaching,
6: 2 and many who heard him were **a**.
6:51 and the wind ceased. And they were utterly **a**,
7:37 They were **a** beyond measure, saying,
10:26 They were greatly **a** and said to one another,
Lk 4:32 They were **a** at his teaching,
8:56 Her parents were **a**; but he ordered them to tell
9:43 And all were **a** at the greatness of God.
24:22 Moreover, some women of our group **a** us.
Ac 10:45 with Peter were **a** that the gift of
Jdt 10: 7 they were very greatly **a** at her beauty and said
Sir 47:17 and the answers you gave **a** the nations.

1Mc 6: 8 king heard this news, he was **a** and badly shaken.
2Mc 3:24 as to accompany him were **a** by the power of God,

ASTOUNDING (2) [ASTOUNDED]

Jdt 11: 8 most informed and the most **a** in military strategy.
2Mc 7:18 Therefore **a** things have happened.

ASTRAY (75) [STRAY]

Ex 23: 4 upon your enemy's ox or donkey going **a**,
Nu 5:12 If any man's wife goes **a** and is unfaithful to him,
5:20 But if you have gone **a** while
5:29 goes **a** and defiles herself,
Dt 4:19 be led **a** and bow down to them and serve them,
13:13 and led the inhabitants of the town **a**,
30:17 but are led **a** to bow down to other gods
2Ch 21:11 into unfaithfulness, and made Judah go **a**.
Ps 14: 3 They have all gone **a**, they are all alike perverse;
40: 4 to those who go **a** after false gods.
58: 3 The wicked go **a** from the womb;
95:10 "They are a people whose hearts go **a**,
119:67 Before I was humbled I went **a**,
119:118 You spurn all who go **a** from your statutes;
119:176 I have gone **a** like a lost sheep;
Pr 10:17 but one who rejects a rebuke goes **a**.
12:26 but the way of the wicked leads **a**.
20: 1 and whoever is led **a** by it is not wise.
Isa 9:16 for those who led this people led them **a**,
19:13 the cornerstones of its tribes have led Egypt **a**.
30:28 the jaws of the peoples a bridle that leads them **a**.
35: 8 no traveler, not even fools, shall go **a**.
44:20 He feeds on ashes; a deluded mind has led him **a**,
47:10 Your wisdom and your knowledge led you **a**,
53: 6 All we like sheep have gone **a**;
Jer 8: 4 If they go **a**, do they not turn back?
23:13 by Baal and led my people Israel **a**.
23:32 and who lead my people **a** by their lies
50: 6 their shepherds have led them **a**,
Eze 14:11 the house of Israel may no longer go **a** from me,
20:30 after the manner of your ancestors and go **a**
44:10 **a** from me after their idols when Israel went **a**,
44:15 of my sanctuary when the people of Israel went **a**
48:11 not go **a** when the people of Israel went **a**,
Hos 4:12 For a spirit of whoredom has led them **a**,
Am 2: 4 not kept his statutes, but they have been led **a** by
Mic 3: 5 concerning the prophets who lead my people **a**,
Mt 18:12 and one of them has gone **a**,
18:12 and go in search of the one that went **a**?
18:13 over the ninety-nine that never went **a**.
24: 4 "Beware that no one leads you **a**.
24: 5 and they will lead many **a**.
24:11 many false prophets will arise and lead many **a**.
24:24 to lead **a**, if possible, even the elect.
Mk 13: 5 "Beware that no one leads you **a**.
13: 6 and they will lead many **a**.
13:22 to lead **a**, if possible, the elect.
Lk 21: 8 And he said, "Beware that you are not led **a**;
1Co 12: 2 you were enticed and led **a** to idols that could
2Co 11: 3 your thoughts will be led **a** from a sincere
Gal 2:13 that even Barnabas was led **a** by their hypocrisy.
Tit 3: 3 led **a**, slaves to various passions and pleasures,
Heb 3:10 and I said, 'They always go **a** in their hearts,
1Pe 2:25 For you were going **a** like sheep,
2Pe 2:15 They have left the straight road and have gone **a**,
Tob 5:14 and worshiped with me there, and were not led **a**.
Wis 2:21 Thus they reasoned, but they were led **a**,
11:15 which led them **a** to worship irrational serpents
12:24 For they went far **a** on the paths of error,
13: 6 for perhaps they go **a** while seeking God
17: 1 therefore uninstructed souls have gone **a**.
Sir 3:24 For their conceit has led many **a**,
4:19 If they go **a** she will forsake them,
13: 8 Take care not to be led **a** and humiliated
15:12 Do not say, "It was he who led me **a**";
19: 2 Wine and women lead intelligent men **a**,
31: 5 one who pursues money will be led **a** by it.
42:10 or having a husband, for fear she may go **a**, or,
Bar 4:28 For just as you were disposed to go **a** from God,
2Mc 2: 2 or to be led **a** in their thoughts on seeing the gold
6:25 they would be led **a** because of me,
1Es 3:18 It leads **a** the minds of all who drink it.
2Es 7:92 that it might not lead them **a** from life into death.

ASTROLOGERS See Index to Footnotes

ASTYAGES (1)

Bel 1: 1 When King **A** was laid to rest with his ancestors,

ASUNDER (3)

Ps 2: 3 "Let us burst their bonds **a**,
107:14 of darkness and gloom, and broke their bonds **a**.
Isa 24:19 The earth is utterly broken, the earth is torn **a**,

ASUPPIM (KJV) See STOREHOUSE

ASUR (1)

1Es 5:31 the descendants of **A**, the descendants

ASYNCRITUS (1)

Ro 16:14 Greet **A**, Phlegon, Hermes, Patrobas, Hermas,

AT (2631) See Index of Articles Etc.

ATAD (2)

Ge 50:10 When they came to the threshing floor of **A**,
50:11 the mourning on the threshing floor of **A**,

ATARAH (1)

1Ch 2:26 whose name was **A**; she was the mother of Onam.

ATARGATIS (1)

2Mc 12:26 against Carnaim and the temple of **A**,

ATAROTH (4)

Nu 32: 3 "**A**, Dibon, Jazer, Nimrah,
32:34 And the Gadites rebuilt Dibon, **A**, Aroer,
Jos 16: 2 it passes along to **A**, the territory of the Archites;
16: 7 it goes down from Janoah to **A** and to Naarah,

ATAROTH-ADDAR (2)

Jos 16: 5 on the east was **A** as far as Upper Beth-horon,
18:13 Bethel), then the boundary goes down to **A**,

ATE‡ (121) [EAT]

Ge 3: 6 she took of its fruit and **a**;
3: 6 to her husband who was with her, and he **a**.
3:12 she gave me fruit from the tree, and I **a**."
3:13 woman said, "The serpent tricked me, and I **a**."
18: 8 and he stood by them under the tree while they **a**.
19: 3 and baked unleavened bread, and they **a**.
24:54 he and the men who were with him **a** and drank,
25:34 and he **a** and drank, and rose and went his way.
26:30 So he made them a feast, and they **a** and drank.
27:25 So he brought it to him, and he **a**;
27:33 and I **a** it all before you came,
31:46 and they **a** there by the heap.
31:54 and they **a** bread and tarried all night in
39: 6 for anything but the food that he **a**.
41: 4 and thin cows **a** up the seven sleek and fat cows.
41:20 thin and ugly cows **a** up the first seven fat cows,
43:32 and the Egyptians who **a** with him by themselves,
Ex 10:15 and they **a** all the plants in the land and all
16: 3 we sat by the fleshpots and **a** our fill of bread;
16:35 The Israelites **a** manna forty years,
16:35 they **a** manna, until they came to the border of
24:11 also they beheld God, and they **a** and drank.
34:28 he neither **a** bread nor drank water.
Nu 25: 2 and the people **a** and bowed down to their gods.
Dt 9: 9 I neither **a** bread nor drank water.
9:18 I neither **a** bread nor drank water,
32:15 Jacob **a** his fill; Jeshurun grew fat, and kicked.
32:38 who **a** the fat of their sacrifices,
Jos 5:11 on that very day, they **a** the produce of the land,
5:12 The manna ceased on the day they **a** the produce
5:12 they **a** the crops of the land of Canaan that year.
Jdg 9:27 **a** and drank, and ridiculed Abimelech.
14: 9 he gave some to them, and they **a** it.
19: 4 so they **a** and drank, and he stayed there.
19: 6 So the two men sat and **a** and drank together;
19: 8 and the two of them **a** and drank.
19:21 they washed their feet, and **a** and drank.
Ru 2:14 She **a** until she was satisfied,
1Sa 1:18 **a** and drank with her husband,
9:24 So Saul **a** with Samuel that day.
14:32 and the troops **a** them with the blood.
20:34 in fierce anger and **a** no food on the second day of
28:25 before Saul and his servants, and they **a**.
30:11 They gave him bread and he **a**,
2Sa 9:11 Mephibosheth **a** at David's table,
9:13 for he always **a** at the king's table.
12:20 when he asked, they set food before him and he **a**.
12:21 but when the child died, you rose and **a** food."
1Ki 4:20 they **a** and drank and were happy.
13:19 and **a** food and drank water in his house.
17:15 as well as he and her household **a** for many days.
19: 6 He **a** and drank, and lay down again.
19: 8 He got up, and **a** and drank;
19:21 and gave it to the people, and they **a**.
2Ki 4:44 He set it before them, they **a**, and had some left,
6:23 after they **a** and drank, he sent them on their way,
6:29 So we cooked my son and **a** him.
7: 8 **a** and drank, carried off silver, gold, and clothing,
9:34 Then he went in and **a** and drank;
23: 9 but **a** unleavened bread among their kindred.
1Ch 29:22 and they **a** and drank before the LORD on
2Ch 30:18 they **a** the passover otherwise than as prescribed.
30:22 people **a** the food of the festival for seven days,
Ne 5:14 neither I nor my brothers **a** the food allowance of
9:25 so they **a**, and were filled and became fat,
Job 42:11 and they **a** bread with him in his house;
Ps 41: 9 who **a** of my bread, has lifted the heel against me.
78:25 Mortals **a** of the bread of angels;
78:29 And they **a** and were well filled,
105:35 and **a** up the fruit of their ground.
106:28 and **a** sacrifices offered to the dead;
Jer 2: 3 All who **a** of it were held guilty;
15:16 Your words were found, and I **a** them,
41: 1 As they **a** bread together there at Mizpah,
Eze 3: 3 I **a** it; and in my mouth it was as sweet as honey.
Da 4:33 **a** grass like oxen, and his body was bathed with
Ob 1: 7 those who **a** your bread have set a trap for you—
Mt 12: 4 the house of God and **a** the bread of the Presence,
13: 4 and the birds came and **a** them up.
14:20 And all **a** and were filled;
14:21 And those who **a** were about five thousand men,
15:37 And all of them **a** and were filled;
Mk 1: 6 and he **a** locusts and wild honey.
Mk 2:26 and **a** the bread of the Presence,
4: 4 and the birds came and **a** it up.
6:42 And all **a** and were filled;
8: 8 They **a** and were filled;
Lk 4: 2 He **a** nothing at all during those days,
6: 1 rubbed them in their hands, and **a** them.
6: 4 of God and took and **a** the bread of the Presence,
8: 5 and the birds of the air **a** it up.
9:17 And all **a** and were filled.
13:26 you will begin to say, 'We **a** and drank with you,
24:43 and he took it and **a** in their presence.
Jn 6:26 but because you **a** your fill of the loaves.
6:31 Our ancestors **a** the manna in the wilderness;
6:49 Your ancestors **a** the manna in the wilderness,
6:58 not like that which your ancestors **a**,
13:18 'The one who **a** my bread has lifted his heel
Ac 2:46 and **a** their food with glad and generous hearts,
9: 9 For three days he was without sight, and neither **a**
10:41 and who **a** and drank with him after he rose from
1Co 10: 3 and all **a** the same spiritual food,
Rev 10:10 the little scroll from the hand of the angel and **a** it;
Tob 1:10 everyone of my kindred and my people **a** the food
2: 5 I washed myself and **a** my food in sorrow.
6: 6 then he roasted and **a** some of the fish,
Jdt 12: 9 in the tent until she **a** her food toward evening.
12:19 Then she took what her maid had prepared and **a**
Bar 2: 3 of us **a** the flesh of their sons and others the flesh
Bel 1: 7 and it never **a** or drank anything."
1:15 and they **a** and drank everything.
1:27 The dragon **a** them, and burst open.
1:39 So Daniel got up and **a**.
1Es 3: 3 They **a** and drank,
7:13 people of Israel who had returned from exile **a** it,
2Es 1:19 you **a** the bread of angels.
9:26 among the flowers and **a** of the plants of the field,
12:51 and I **a** only of the flowers of the field,
14:42 and **a** their bread at night.
4Mc 8: 2 and that any who **a** defiling food would be freed

ATER (7)

Ezr 2:16 Of **A**, namely of Hezekiah, ninety-eight.
2:42 of Shallum, of **A**, of Talmon, of Akkub, of Hatita,
Ne 7:21 Of **A**, namely of Hezekiah, ninety-eight.
7:45 the descendants of Shallum, of **A**, of Talmon,
10:17 **A**, Hezekiah, Azzur,
1Es 5:15 The descendants of **A**, namely of Hezekiah,
5:28 the descendants of Shallum, the descendants of **A**,

ATHA See Index to Footnotes

ATHACH (1)

1Sa 30:30 in Hormah, in Bor-ashan, in **A**,

ATHAIAH (1)

Ne 11: 4 **A** son of Uzziah son of Zechariah son

ATHALIAH (17)

2Ki 8:26 His mother's name was **A**,
11: 1 Now when **A**, Ahaziah's mother,
11: 2 Thus she hid him from **A**,
11: 3 while **A** reigned over the land.
11:13 **A** heard the noise of the guard and of the people,
11:14 **A** tore her clothes and cried, "Treason!
11:20 and the city was quiet after **A** had been killed with
1Ch 8:26 Shamsherai, Shehariah, **A**,
2Ch 22: 2 His mother's name was **A**,
22:10 Now when **A**, Ahaziah's mother,
22:11 hid him from **A**, so that she did not kill him;
22:12 while **A** reigned over the land.
23:12 When **A** heard the noise of the people running
23:13 **A** tore her clothes, and cried, "Treason!
23:21 and the city was quiet after **A** had been killed with
24: 7 For the children of **A**, that wicked woman,
Ezr 8: 7 Of the descendants of Elam, Jeshaiah son of **A**,

ATHARIM (1)

Nu 21: 1 heard that Israel was coming by the way of **A**,

ATHENIAN (1) [ATHENS]

2Mc 6: 1 the king sent an **A** senator to compel the Jews

ATHENIANS (2) [ATHENS]

Ac 17:21 Now all the **A** and the foreigners living there
17:22 Paul stood in front of the Areopagus and said, "**A**,

ATHENOBIUS (3)

1Mc 15:28 He sent to him **A**, one of his Friends,
15:32 So **A**, the king's Friend, came to Jerusalem,
15:35 **A** did not answer him a word,

ATHENS (5) [ATHENIAN, ATHENIANS]

Ac 17:15 who conducted Paul brought him as far as **A**;
17:16 While Paul was waiting for them in **A**,
18: 1 After this Paul left **A** and went to Corinth.
1Th 3: 1 we decided to be left alone in **A**;
2Mc 9:15 all of them, equal to citizens of **A**;

ATHLAI (1)

Ezr 10:28 Jehohanan, Hananiah, Zabbai, and **A**.

ATHLETE (2) [ATHLETES]

2Ti 2: 5 And in the case of an a,
4Mc 6:10 Like a noble a the old man, while being beaten,

ATHLETES (3) [ATHLETE]

1Co 9:25 A exercise self-control in all things;
4Mc 17:15 and gave the crown to its own a.
17:16 not admire the a of the divine legislation?

ATONE‡ (4) [ATONEMENT]

Da 4:27 a for your sins with righteousness,
9:24 to put an end to sin, and to a for iniquity,
Sir 3: 3 Those who honor their father a for sins,
20:28 and those who please the great a for injustice.

ATONED (1) [ATONEMENT]

Pr 16: 6 By loyalty and faithfulness iniquity is a for,

ATONEMENT‡ (92) [ATONE, ATONED, ATONES, ATONING]

Ex 29:33 the food by which a is made,
29:36 a bull as a sin offering for a.
29:36 when you make a for it, and shall anoint it,
29:37 Seven days you shall make a for the altar,
30:10 Once a year Aaron shall perform the rite of a
30:10 the a for it once a year with the blood of
30:15 to the LORD to make a for your lives.
30:16 You shall take the a money from the Israelites
32:30 perhaps I can make a for your sin."
Lev 1: 4 it shall be acceptable in your behalf as a for you.
4:20 The priest shall make a for them,
4:26 the priest shall make a on his behalf for his sin,
4:31 Thus the priest shall make a on your behalf,
4:35 the priest shall make a on your behalf for the sin
5: 6 the priest shall make a on your behalf for your sin.
5:10 the priest shall make a on your behalf for the sin
5:13 Thus the priest shall make a on your behalf
5:16 The priest shall make a on your behalf with
5:18 the priest shall make a on your behalf for the error
6: 7 The priest shall make a on your behalf before
6:30 into the tent of meeting for a in the holy place;
7: 7 the priest who makes a with it shall have it.
8:15 Thus he consecrated it, to make a for it.
8:34 the LORD has commanded to be done to make a
9: 7 and make a for yourself and for the people;
9: 7 the offering of the people, and make a for them;
10:17 to make a on their behalf before the LORD.
12: 7 and make a on her behalf;
12: 8 and the priest shall make a on her behalf,
14:18 Then the priest shall make a on his behalf before
14:19 to make a for the one to be cleansed
14:20 the priest shall make a on his behalf and he shall
14:21 to make a on his behalf, and one-tenth of an ephah
14:29 to make a on his behalf before the LORD.
14:31 and the priest shall make a before the LORD
14:53 so he shall make a for the house,
15:15 and the priest shall make a on his behalf before
15:30 and the priest shall make a on her behalf before
16: 6 and shall make a for himself and for his house.
16:10 be presented alive before the LORD to make a
16:11 and shall make a for himself and for his house;
16:16 Thus he shall make a for the sanctuary,
16:17 from the time he enters to make a in the sanctuary
16:17 until he comes out and has made a for himself and
16:18 to the altar that is before the LORD and make a
16:24 making a for himself and for the people.
16:27 to make a in the holy place, shall be taken outside
16:30 For on this day a shall be made for you,
16:32 as priest in his father's place shall make a,
16:33 He shall make a for the sanctuary,
16:33 and he shall make a for the tent of meeting and for
16:33 and he shall make a for the priests and for all
16:34 to make a for the people of Israel once in the year
17:11 to you for making a for your lives on the altar;
17:11 for, as life, it is the blood that makes a.
19:22 And the priest shall make a for him with the ram
23:27 tenth day of this seventh month is the day of a;
23:28 for it is a day of a, to make a on your behalf before
25: 9 of the seventh month—on the day of a—
Nu 5: 8 to the ram of a with which atonement is made for
5: 8 to the ram of atonement with which a is made for
6:11 the other as a burnt offering, and make a for them,
8:12 to make a for the Levites.
8:19 and to make a for the Israelites,
8:21 and Aaron made a for them to cleanse them.
15:25 The priest shall make a for all the congregation of
15:28 And the priest shall make a before the LORD for
15:28 when it is unintentional, to make a for the person,
16:46 to the congregation and make a for them.
16:47 He put on the incense, and made a for the people.
25:13 and made a for the Israelites.' "
28:22 also one male goat for a sin offering, to make a
28:30 with one male goat, to make a for you.
29: 5 with one male goat for a sin offering, to make a
29:11 in addition to the sin offering of a,
31:50 to make a for ourselves before the LORD."
1Ch 6:49 to make a for Israel, according to all that Moses
2Ch 29:24 to make a for all Israel.
Ne 10:33 and the sin offerings to make a for Israel,
Eze 43:20 thus you shall purify it and make a for it.
43:26 Seven days shall they make a for the altar
45:15 and offerings of well-being, to make a for them,
45:17 to make a for the house of Israel.
45:20 so you shall make a for the temple.
Ro 3:25 whom God put forward as a sacrifice of a
Heb 2:17 to make a sacrifice of a for the sins of the people.
Sir 35: 5 and to forsake unrighteousness is an a.
45:16 to make a for the people.
45:23 and he made a for Israel.
2Mc 3:33 While the high priest was making an a,
12:45 Therefore he made a for the dead,

ATONES (1) [ATONEMENT]

Sir 3:30 a blazing fire, so almsgiving a for sin.

ATONING (6) [ATONEMENT]

Ex 30:10 a year with the blood of the a sin offering.
Lev 16:20 When he has finished a for the holy place and
1Jn 2: 2 and he is the a sacrifice for our sins,
4:10 and sent his Son to be the a sacrifice for our sins.
Sir 28: 5 who will make an a sacrifice for his sins?
4Mc 17:22 and their death as an a sacrifice,

ATOP (1) [TOP]

Dt 32:13 He set him a the heights of the land,

ATROTH-BETH-JOAB (1)

1Ch 2:54 Bethlehem, the Netophathites, A,

ATROTH-SHOPHAN (1)

Nu 32:35 A, Jazer, Jogbehah,

ATTACH (7) [ATTACHED]

Ex 28:14 and you shall a the corded chains to the settings.
28:25 of the two cords you shall a to the two settings,
28:25 so a it in front to the shoulder-pieces of the ephod.
28:27 and a them in front to the lower part of
Isa 14: 1 and aliens will join them and a themselves to
Sir 6:34 A yourself to such a one.
11:31 and to worthy actions they a blame.

ATTACHED (11) [ATTACH]

Ex 28: 7 It shall have two shoulder-pieces a
39:18 of the two cords they had a to the two settings
39:18 in this way they a it in front to the shoulder-pieces
39:20 and a them in front to the lower part of
Nu 18: 4 They are a to you in order to perform the duties of
2Ch 9:18 which were a to the throne,
Ps 106:28 Then they a themselves to the Baal of Peor,
Tob 1: 8 to the converts who had a themselves to Israel.
AdE 1: 6 of purple linen a to gold and silver blocks
2Mc 14:24 he was warmly a to the man.
3Mc 3: 7 So they a no ordinary reproach to them.

ATTACK (59) [ATTACKED, ATTACKING, ATTACKS, COUNTERATTACKS]

Ge 34:30 if they gather themselves against me and a me,
Jos 7: 3 or three thousand men should go up and a Ai.
9:18 But the Israelites did not a them,
10: 4 up and help me, and let us a Gibeon;
10:19 pursue your enemies, and a them from the rear.
Jdg 7: 9 a the camp; for I have given it into your hand.
7:10 But if you fear to a, go down to the camp
7:11 be strengthened to a the camp."
15:12 "Swear to me that you yourselves will not a me."
18:25 among us or else hot-tempered fellows will a you,
1Sa 7:10 the Philistines drew near to a Israel;
15: 3 Now go and a Amalek, and utterly destroy all
19: 8 He launched a heavy a on them,
22:17 the king would not raise their hand to a the priests
22:18 "You, Doeg, turn and a the priests."
23: 2 "Shall I go and a these Philistines?"
23: 2 "Go and a the Philistines and save Keilah."
24: 7 and did not permit them to a Saul.
2Sa 5: 8 let him get up the water shaft to a the lame and
11:25 press your a on the city, and overthrow it.'
15:14 and a the city with the edge of the sword."
17: 9 And when some of our troops fall at the first a,
2Ki 3:24 as they entered Moab they continued the a.
Est 8:11 of any people or province that might a them,
Ps 69:26 those whom you have wounded, they a still more.
109: 3 with words of hate, and a me without cause.
Isa 7: 1 of Remaliah of Israel went up to a Jerusalem,
7: 1 but could not mount an a against it.
Jer 6: 4 up, and let us a at noon!"
6: 5 "Up, and let us a by night,
46:13 of King Nebuchadrezzar of Babylon to a the land
49: 4 saying, "Who will a me?"
50:21 and a the inhabitants of Pekod and utterly destroy
Eze 21:16 A to the right! Engage to the
Da 11:40 of the end the king of the south shall a him.
Hab 3:16 of calamity to come upon the people who a us.
Ac 18:12 the Jews made a united a on Paul and brought him
2Ti 4:18 The Lord will rescue me from every evil a
Jdt 6: 4 Not even their footprints will survive our a;
AdE 16:20 against those who a them at the time
1Mc 2:41 "Let us fight against anyone who comes to a us on
4: 2 upon the camp of the Jews and a them suddenly.
4: 3 and his warriors moved out to a the king's force
4:30 who crushed the a of the mighty warrior by
5: 6 Then he crossed over to a the Ammonites,
5:27 to a the strongholds tomorrow and capture
6:47 the Jews saw the royal might and the fierce a of
9:48 and the enemy did not cross the Jordan to a them.
9:67 he began to a and went into battle with his forces;
11:20 In those days Jonathan assembled the Judeans to a
12:26 the enemy were being drawn up in formation to a
2Mc 4:40 and launched an unjust a,
13:26 how the king's a and withdrawal turned out.
15: 1 to a them with complete safety on the day of rest.
15: 8 He exhorted his troops not to fear the a of
15:17 not to carry on a campaign but to a bravely,
1Es 4: 8 if he tells them to a, they a;
2Es 15:33 of the Assyrians an enemy in ambush shall a them

ATTACKED (48) [ATTACK]

Ge 49:23 The archers fiercely a him;
Dt 25:18 how he a you on the way, when you were faint
Jos 8:24 and a it with the edge of the sword.
11: 8 who a them and chased them as far as Great Sidon
Jdg 8:11 and a the army; for the army was off its guard.
1Sa 19: 5 for he took his life in his hand when he a
22:18 Doeg the Edomite turned and a the priests;
30: 1 They had a Ziklag, burned it down,
30:17 David a them from twilight until the evening of
30:23 and handed over to us the raiding party that a us.
2Sa 4: 7 they a him, killed him, and beheaded him.
8: 1 David a the Philistines and subdued them;
21:17 and a the Philistine and killed him.
1Ki 2:32 the knowledge of my father David, he a and killed
13:28 The lion had not eaten the body or a the donkey.
20: 1 laid siege to it, and a it.
20:21 king of Israel went out, a the horses and chariots,
2Ki 3:24 the Israelites rose up and a the Moabites,
3:25 until the slingers surrounded and a it.
8:21 He set out by night and a the Edomites
15:25 and a him in Samaria, in the citadel of the palace
15:30 against Pekah son of Remaliah, a him,
18: 8 He a the Philistines as far as Gaza and its territory,
1Ch 4:41 of King Hezekiah of Judah, and a their tents and
18: 1 David a the Philistines and subdued them;
20: 1 Joab a Rabbah, and overthrew it.
2Ch 14:15 They also a the tents of those who had livestock,
20:23 For the Ammonites and Moab a the inhabitants
21: 9 He set out by night and a the Edomites,
Ps 124: 2 on our side, when our enemies a us,
129: 1 "Often have they a me from my
129: 2 "often have they a me from my youth,
Jer 47: 1 concerning the Philistines, before Pharaoh a Gaza:
Jnh 4: 7 God appointed a worm that a the bush,
Ac 17: 5 to the assembly, they a Jason's house.
1Mc 2:35 Then the enemy quickly a them.
2:38 So they a them on the sabbath, and they died,
4:34 Then both sides a, and there fell of the army
5:16 in distress and were being a by enemies.
6:25 they have also a all the lands on their borders.
8:10 they sent a general against the Greeks and a them.
2Mc 12: 6 a the murderers of his kindred.
12: 9 he a the Jamnites by night and set fire to
12:10 with five hundred cavalry a them.
12:13 He also a a certain town that was strongly fortified
13:15 he a the king's pavilion at night and killed
13:19 was turned back, a again, and was defeated.
13:22 received theirs, withdrew, a Judas and his men,

ATTACKING (9) [ATTACK]

2Ki 16: 7 the hand of the king of Israel, who are a me."
Da 11: 8 For some years he shall refrain from a the king of
Ac 16:22 The crowd joined in a them,
1Mc 5:30 to capture the stronghold, and a the Jews within.
2Mc 4:41 Jews became aware that Lysimachus was a them,
10:14 and at every turn kept a the Jews.
10:17 A them vigorously, they gained possession of
13:18 tried strategy in a their positions.
4Mc 3: 7 David had been a the Philistines all day long,

ATTACKS (9) [ATTACK]

Ex 21:14 But if someone willfully a and kills another
Dt 19:11 with another lies in wait and a and takes the life of
22:26 that of someone who a and murders a neighbor.
Jos 15:16 "Whoever a Kiriath-sepher and takes it,
Jdg 1:12 "Whoever a Kiriath-sepher and takes it,
1Ch 11: 6 "Whoever a the Jebusites first shall be chief
Lk 11:22 one stronger than he a him and overpowers him,
2Mc 5: 3 a and counterattacks made on this side and on
8: 7 the nights most advantageous for such a.

ATTAI (4)

1Ch 2:35 to his slave Jarha; and she bore him A.
2:36 A became the father of Nathan,
12:11 A sixth, Eliel seventh,
2Ch 11:20 who bore him Abijah, A, Ziza, and Shelomith.

ATTAIN (15) [ATTAINABLE, ATTAINED]

2Sa 23:19 but he did not a to the Three.
23:23 but he did not a to the Three.
1Ch 11:21 but he did not a to the Three.
11:25 but he did not a to the Three.
Ps 101: 2 When shall I a it?
139: 6 it is so high that I cannot a it.
Pr 8:12 and I a knowledge and discretion.
Da 12:12 and a the thousand three hundred thirty-five days.
Ac 26: 7 a promise that our twelve tribes hope to a,
Php 3:11 somehow I may a the resurrection from the dead.
AdE 13: 5 so that our kingdom may not a stability.
Sir 27: 8 you will a it and wear it like a glorious robe.
38:33 nor do they a eminence in the public assembly.
2Mc 14: 6 and will not let the kingdom a tranquility.
2Es 13:18 for the last days, but cannot a them.

ATTAINABLE (1) [ATTAIN]
Heb 7:11 Now if perfection had been **a** through

ATTAINED (4) [ATTAIN]
Ro 9:30 who did not strive for righteousness, have **a** it,
Php 3:16 Only let us hold fast to what we have **a.**
AdE 13: 3 and has **a** the second place in the kingdom—
3Mc 6: 1 who had **a** a ripe old age and

ATTALIA (1)
Ac 14:25 the word in Perga, they went down to **A.**

ATTALUS (1)
1Mc 15:22 to King Demetrius and to **A** and Ariarathes

ATTEMPT (6) [ATTEMPTED, ATTEMPTING, ATTEMPTS]
Dt 28:20 panic, and frustration in everything you **a** to do,
Da 7:25 shall **a** to change the sacred seasons and the law;
Ac 14: 5 when an **a** was made by both Gentiles and Jews,
2Mc 2:23 we shall **a** to condense into a single book.
4Mc 1: 5 Their **a** at argument is ridiculous!
8: 2 tyrant was conspicuously defeated in his first **a,**

ATTEMPTED (11) [ATTEMPT]
Dt 4:34 Or has any god ever **a** to go and take a nation
Ac 9:26 he **a** to join the disciples;
16: 7 they **a** to go into Bithynia,
Heb 11:29 when the Egyptians **a** to do so they were drowned.
Bel 1:42 into the den those who had **a** his destruction,
1Mc 12:39 Then Trypho **a** to become king in Asia and put on
2Mc 9: 2 the city called Persepolis and **a** to rob the temples
10:12 and **a** to maintain peaceful relations with them.
3Mc 2:32 for life they confidently **a** to save themselves from
2Es 10: 2 and all my neighbors **a** to console me;
4Mc 3:21 at that time certain persons **a** a revolution against

ATTEMPTING‡ (2) [ATTEMPT]
Ac 9:29 but they were **a** to kill him.
3Mc 6:24 you are now **a** to deprive of dominion and life

ATTEMPTS (1) [ATTEMPT]
Isa 64: 7 or **a** to take hold of you;

ATTEND (20) [ATTENDANCE, ATTENDANT, ATTENDANTS, ATTENDED, ATTENDING]
Nu 3: 8 and **a** to the duties for the Israelites
3:10 it is they who shall **a** to the priesthood,
1Sa 16:16 now command the servants who **a** you to look
1Ki 10: 8 who continually **a** you and hear your wisdom!
1Ch 23:32 and shall **a** the descendants of Aaron,
2Ch 9: 7 who continually **a** you and hear your wisdom!
Ezr 8:20 whom David and his officials had set apart to **a**
Est 4: 5 who had been appointed to **a** her,
Ps 17: 1 Hear a just cause, O LORD; **a** to my cry;
55: 2 **A** to me, and answer me;
Isa 42:23 who will **a** and listen for the time to come?
Jer 9:25 surely coming, says the LORD, when I will **a**
23: 2 So I will **a** to you for your evil doings,
32: 5 and there he shall remain until I **a** to him,
Eze 44:11 and they shall **a** on them and serve them.
44:15 they shall **a** me to offer me the fat and the blood,
Sir 11:20 Stand by your agreement and **a** to it,
1Es 4:11 and no one may go away to **a** to his own affairs,
2Es 8:24 of your creature; **a** to my words.
4Mc 7:18 But as many as **a** to religion with a whole heart,

ATTENDANCE (5) [ATTEND]
Nu 8:22 in the tent of meeting in **a** on Aaron and his sons.
1Ki 10: 5 and the **a** of his servants, their clothing, his valets,
2Ch 9: 4 and the **a** of his servants, and their clothing,
Est 7: 9 Harbona, one of the eunuchs in **a** on the king,
Isa 6: 2 Seraphs were in **a** above him;

ATTENDANT (5) [ATTEND]
Jdg 16:26 Samson said to the **a** who held him by the hand,
1Ki 1: 2 and let her wait on the king, and be his **a;**
1: 4 She became the king's **a** and served him,
2Ki 6:15 an **a** of the man of God rose early in the morning
Lk 4:20 And he rolled up the scroll, gave it back to the **a,**

ATTENDANTS (10) [ATTEND]
Ex 2: 5 while her **a** walked beside the river.
Jdg 3:19 and all his **a** went out from his presence.
Jer 48: 7 with his priests and his **a.**
49: 3 with his priests and his **a.**
Da 7:16 of the **a** to ask him the truth concerning all this.
11: 6 she and her **a** and her child and
Mt 22:13 Then the king said to the **a,**
Jdt 7:16 These words pleased Holofernes and all his **a,**
12:10 a banquet for his personal **a** only,
13: 1 and shut out the **a** from his master's presence.

ATTENDED (13) [ATTEND]
Ge 39: 4 So Joseph found favor in his sight and **a** him;
1Sa 25:42 on a donkey; her five maids **a** her.
1Ki 12: 6 with the older men who had **a** his father Solomon
12: 8 up with him and now **a** him.
1Ch 27:32 Jehiel son of Hachmoni **a** the king's sons.
2Ch 10: 6 with the older men who had **a** his father Solomon
10: 8 up with him and now **a** him.
22: 8 who **a** Ahaziah, and he killed them.
Est 1:10 Zethar and Carkas, the seven eunuchs who **a** him,
2: 2 Then the king's servants who **a** him said,
6: 3 The king's servants who **a** him said,
Jer 23: 2 and you have not **a** to them.
AdE 4: 5 the eunuch who **a** her, and ordered him

ATTENDING (5) [ATTEND]
Nu 3:28 **a** to the duties of the sanctuary.
1Sa 4:20 she was about to die, the women **a** her said to her,
1Ki 1:15 Abishag the Shunammite was **a** the king.
Da 7:10 and ten thousand times ten thousand stood **a** him.
1Mc 16:14 the towns of the country and **a** to their needs,

ATTENTION (40) [ATTENTIVE, ATTENTIVELY]
Ex 5: 9 at it and pay no **a** to deceptive words."
Nu 16:15 "Pay no **a** to their offering.
Dt 1:45 would neither heed your voice nor pay you any **a.**
9:27 pay no **a** to the stubbornness of this people,
Job 20: 2 "Pay **a!** My thoughts urge me to answer,
24:12 yet God pays no **a** to their prayer.
32:12 I gave you my **a,** but there was in fact no one
Pr 27:23 and give **a** to your herds;
Isa 28:23 Pay **a,** and hear my speech.
48:13 when I summon them, they stand at **a.**
48:18 O that you had paid **a** to my commandments!
49: 1 Listen to me, O coastlands, pay **a,**
Jer 7:26 or pay **a,** but they stiffened their necks.
27:22 until the day when I give **a** to them,
Da 6:13 one of the exiles from Judah, pays no **a** to you,
10:11 pay **a** to the words that I am going to speak to you.
Mk 4:24 And he said to them, "Pay **a** to what you hear;
Lk 8:18 Then pay **a** to how you listen;
Ac 3: 5 And he fixed his **a** on them,
18:17 But Gallio paid no **a** to any of these things.
27:11 But the centurion paid more **a** to the pilot and to
1Ti 4: 1 by paying **a** to deceitful spirits and teachings
4:13 give **a** to the public reading of scripture,
4:16 Pay close **a** to yourself and to your teaching;
Tit 1:14 not paying **a** to Jewish myths or
Heb 2: 1 we must pay greater **a** to what we have heard,
3Jn 1:10 I will call **a** to what he is doing
Sir Pr: 2 therefore to read it with goodwill and **a,**
6:33 and if you pay **a** you will become wise.
16:24 and pay close **a** to my words.
34: 6 by intervention from the Most High, pay no **a**
37:11 pay no **a** to any advice they give.
1Mc 7:11 But they paid no **a** to their words,
10:61 but the king paid no **a** to them.
2Mc 4: 6 the king's **a** public affairs could not again reach
1Es 9:41 and all the multitude gave **a** to the law.
3Mc 2: 2 give **a** to us who are suffering grievously from
2Es 5:32 pay **a** to me, and I will tell you more."
4Mc 1: 1 So it is right for me to advise you to pay earnest **a**
15:21 the songs of swans attract the **a** of their hearers

ATTENTIVE (17) [ATTENTION]
Ex 23:13 Be **a** to all that I have said to you.
23:21 Be **a** to him and listen to his voice;
2Ch 6:40 be open and your ears **a** to prayer from this place.
7:15 be open and my ears **a** to the prayer that is made
Ne 1: 6 let your ear be **a** and your eyes open to hear
1:11 let your ear be **a** to the prayer of your servant,
8: 3 and the ears of all the people were **a** to the book of
Ps 130: 2 Let your ears be **a** to the voice of my supplications!
Pr 2: 2 making your ear **a** to wisdom
4: 1 Listen, children, to a father's instruction, and be **a,**
4:20 My child, be **a** to my words;
5: 1 My child, be **a** to my wisdom;
7:24 listen to me, and be **a** to the words of my mouth.
16:20 Those who are **a** to a matter will prosper,
2Pe 1:19 to be **a** to this as to a lamp shining in a dark place,
Sir 3:29 and an **a** ear is the desire of the wise.
25: 9 and the one who speaks to **a** listeners.

ATTENTIVELY (3) [ATTENTION]
Ex 23:22 if you listen **a** to his voice and do all that I say,
Eze 40: 4 man said to me, "Mortal, look closely and listen **a,**
44: 5 Mortal, mark well, look closely, and listen **a** to all

ATTESTED (8) [ATTESTING]
Isa 8: 2 and have it **a** for me by reliable witnesses,
Ac 2:22 a man **a** to you by God with deeds of power,
Ro 3:21 and is **a** by the law and the prophets,
1Ti 2: 6 who gave himself a ransom for all—this was **a** at
5:10 she must be well **a** for her good works,
Heb 2: 3 and it was **a** to us by those who heard him,
7:17 For it is **a** of him, "You are a priest forever,
11: 5 For it was **a** before he was taken away

ATTESTING (1) [ATTESTED]
Ru 4: 7 this was the manner of **a** in Israel.

ATTHARATES (1)
1Es 9:49 Then **A** said to Ezra the chief priest and reader,

ATTHARIAS (1)
1Es 5:40 And Nehemiah and **A** told them not to share in

ATTIRE (6)
Jer 2:32 Can a girl forget her ornaments, or a bride her **a?**
Zep 1: 8 and all who dress themselves in foreign **a.**
Jdt 10: 3 and dressed herself in the festive **a** that she used
AdE 15: 1 and arrayed herself in splendid **a.**
Sir 19:30 A person's **a** and hearty laughter,
1Mc 14: 9 and the youths put on splendid military **a.**

ATTIRE (KJV) See also DECKED, TURBAN

ATTITUDE (2)
2Mc 14: 5 and was asked about the **a** and intentions of
4Mc 15:14 because of religion did not change her **a.**

ATTORNEY (1)
Ac 24: 1 down with some elders and an **a,**

ATTRACT (1) [ATTRACTED, ATTRACTIVE]
4Mc 15:21 the songs of swans **a** the attention of their hearers

ATTRACTED (2) [ATTRACT]
Wis 14:20 **a** by the charm of his work,
4Mc 1:33 when we are **a** to forbidden foods we abstain from

ATTRACTIVE (4) [ATTRACT]
Ge 26: 7 because she is **a** in appearance."
Sir 25: 4 How **a** is sound judgment in the gray-haired,
25: 5 How **a** is wisdom in the aged,
LtJ 6:43 not as **a** as herself and her cord was not broken.

ATTRIBUTE (1)
4Mc 6:33 we properly **a** to it the power to govern.

AUDACIOUS (2) [AUDACITY]
3Mc 2: 6 **a** Pharaoh who had enslaved your holy people
2:14 In our downfall this **a** and profane man undertakes

AUDACITY (3) [AUDACIOUS]
3Mc 2: 2 puffed up in his **a** and power.
2:21 who had exalted himself in insolence and **a.**
2:26 with such **a** that he framed evil reports in

AUDIENCE (1)
Ac 25:23 the **a** hall with the military tribunes and

AUGMENT (KJV) See INCREASE

AUGMENTED (1) [AUGMENTS]
4Mc 13:27 and companionship and virtuous habits had **a**

AUGMENTS (1) [AUGMENTED]
Pr 28: 8 One who **a** wealth by exorbitant interest gathers it

AUGUR (1) [AUGURY]
Dt 18:10 or is a soothsayer, or an **a,** or a sorcerer,

AUGURY (4) [AUGUR]
Lev 19:26 You shall not practice **a** or witchcraft.
2Ki 17:17 they used divination and **a;**
21: 6 he practiced soothsaying and **a,**
2Ch 33: 6 practiced soothsaying and **a** and sorcery,

AUGUST (1)
4Mc 17: 5 with the stars, does not stand so **a** as you, who,

AUGUSTAN (1) [AUGUSTUS]
Ac 27: 1 to a centurion of the **A** Cohort,

AUGUSTUS (1) [AUGUSTAN]
Lk 2: 1 In those days a decree went out from Emperor **A**

AUL (KJV) See AWL

AUNT (1)
Lev 18:14 you shall not approach his wife; she is your **a.**

AURANUS (1)
2Mc 4:40 under the leadership of a certain **A,**

AUSTERE (1) [AUSTERITY]
2Mc 14:30 that Nicanor was more **a** in his dealings with him

AUSTERE (KJV) See also HARSH

AUSTERITY (1) [AUSTERE]
2Mc 14:30 that this **a** did not spring from the best motives.

AUTHENTIC (2)
AdE 11: 1 which they said was **a** and had been translated
Wis 18:16 carrying the sharp sword of your **a** command,

AUTHOR (2)
Ac 3:15 and you killed the **A** of life,
Wis 13: 3 for the **a** of beauty created them.

AUTHORITIES (16) [AUTHORITY]

Lk 12:11 and the a, do not worry about how you are
Jn 7:26 be that the a really know that this is the Messiah?
7:48 Has any one of the a or of the Pharisees believed
12:42 many, even of the a, believed in him.
Ac 16:19 into the marketplace before the a.
17: 6 and some believers before the city a,
Ro 13: 1 Let every person be subject to the governing a;
13: 1 and those a that exist have been instituted by God.
13: 6 for the a are God's servants,
Gal 1: 1 from human a, but through Jesus Christ and God
Eph 3:10 now be made known to the rulers and a in
6:12 but against the rulers, against the a,
Col 2:15 the rulers and a and made a public example
Tit 3: 1 Remind them to be subject to rulers and a,
1Pe 3:22 with angels, a, and powers made subject to him.
3Mc 3: 7 to the king nor to his a,

AUTHORITY‡ (135) [AUTHORITIES, AUTHORIZED]

Ge 41:35 and lay up grain under the a of Pharaoh for food
41:45 Thus Joseph gained a over the land of Egypt.
Lev 25:41 with them shall be free from your a;
25:53 by the year they shall be under the alien's a,
Nu 5:19 to uncleanness while under your husband's a,
5:20 while under your husband's a,
5:29 when a wife, while under her husband's a,
27:20 You shall give him some of your a,
1Ch 26: 6 his son Shemaiah sons were born who exercised a
2Ch 8:10 who exercised a over the people.
28: 7 and Elkanah the next in a to the king.
Est 9:29 along with the Jew Mordecai, gave full written a,
Pr 29: 2 When the righteous are in a, the people rejoice;
29:16 When the wicked are in a, transgression increases,
Ecc 8: 9 while one person exercises a over another to
Isa 9: 6 a rests upon his shoulders;
9: 7 His a shall grow continually,
22:21 I will commit your a to his hand,
Mt 7:29 for he taught them as one having a,
8: 9 I also am a man under a, with soldiers under me;
9: 6 the Son of Man has a on earth to forgive sins"—
9: 8 who had given such a to human beings.
10: 1 and gave them a over unclean spirits,
21:23 and said, "By what a are you doing these things,
21:23 and who gave you this a?"
21:24 I will also tell you by what a I do these things.
21:27 by what a I am doing these things.
28:18 "All a in heaven and on earth has been given
Mk 1:22 for he taught them as one having a,
1:27 A new teaching—with a!
2:10 the Son of Man has a on earth to forgive sins"—
3:15 and to have a to cast out demons.
6: 7 and gave them a over the unclean spirits.
11:28 "By what a are you doing these things?
11:28 Who gave you this a to do them?"
11:29 and I will tell you by what a I do these things.
11:33 by what a I am doing these things."
Lk 4: 6 "To you I will give their glory and all this a;
4:32 at his teaching, because he spoke with a.
4:36 For with a and power he commands
5:24 the Son of Man has a on earth to forgive sins"—
7: 8 For I also am a man set under a,
9: 1 and gave them power and a over all demons and
10:19 I have given you a to tread on snakes
12: 5 after he has killed, has a to cast into hell.
20: 2 "Tell us, by what a are you doing these things?
20: 2 Who is it who gave you this a?"
20: 8 by what a I am doing these things."
20:20 so as to hand him over to the jurisdiction and a of
22:25 and those in a over them are called benefactors.
Jn 5:27 and he has given him a to execute judgment,
17: 2 since you have given him a over all people,
Ac 1: 7 or periods that the Father has set by his own a.
5:29 "We must obey God rather than any human a.
9:14 and here he has a from the chief priests
25: 5 "let those of you who have the a come down
26:10 with a received from the chief priests,
26:12 with the a and commission of the chief priests,
Ro 13: 1 for there is no a except from God,
13: 2 whoever resists a resists what God has appointed,
13: 3 Do you wish to have no fear of the a?
13: 4 for the a does not bear the sword in vain!
1Co 7: 4 For the wife does not have a over her own body,
7: 4 the husband does not have a over his own body,
9: 8 Do I say this on human a?
11:10 a woman ought to have a symbol of a on her head,
15:24 after he has destroyed every ruler and every a
2Co 10: 8 Now, even if I boast a little too much of our a,
11:17 I am saying not with the Lord's a, but as a fool;
13:10 the a that the Lord has given me for building up
Eph 1:21 far above all rule and a and power and dominion,
Col 2:10 who is the head of every ruler and a.
1Th 4: 8 whoever rejects this rejects not human a but God,
1Ti 2:12 I permit no woman to teach or to have a over
Tit 2:15 exhort and reprove with all a.
1Pe 2:13 the a of every human institution,
2:18 accept the a of your masters with all deference,
3: 1 in the same way, accept the a of your husbands,
3: 5 to adorn themselves by accepting the a
5: 5 you who are younger must accept the a of
2Pe 2:10 in depraved lust, and who despise a.
3Jn 1: 9 does not acknowledge our a.
Jude 1: 8 reject a, and slander the glorious ones.
1:25 and a, before all time and now and forever.
Rev 2:26 I will give a over the nations;
Rev 2:28 even as I also received a from my Father.
6: 8 they were given a over a fourth of the earth,
9: 3 and they were given a like the a of scorpions
11: 3 And I will grant my two witnesses a to prophesy
11: 6 They have a to shut the sky,
11: 6 and they have a over the waters to turn them
12:10 the kingdom of our God and the a of his Messiah,
13: 2 and his throne and great a.
13: 4 for he had given his a to the beast,
13: 5 it was allowed to exercise a for forty-two months.
13: 7 It was given a over every tribe and people
13:12 It exercises all the a of the first beast on its behalf,
14:18 the angel who has a over fire,
16: 9 who had a over these plagues,
17:12 but they are to receive a as kings for one hour,
17:13 These are united in yielding their power and a to
18: 1 down from heaven, having great a;
20: 4 and those seated on them were given a to judge.
Tob 1:21 and he had a over the entire administration.
AdE 8:10 The edict was written with the king's a and sealed
9:29 and gave full a to the letter about Purim.
10: 3 with a on behalf of King Artaxerxes and was great
13: 2 the whole world (not elated with presumption of a
16: 5 of those who are set in places of a have been made
16: 7 of those who exercise a unworthily can be seen,
Wis 10:14 the scepter of a kingdom and a over his masters.
14:21 in bondage to misfortune or to royal a,
Sir 17: 2 but granted them a over everything on the earth.
20: 8 and whoever pretends to a is hated.
45: 8 and strengthened him with the symbols of a,
45:17 In his commandments he gave him a and statutes
1Mc 6:28 the commanders of his forces and those in a.
10: 6 So Demetrius gave him a to recruit troops,
10: 8 that the king had given him a to recruit troops.
10:35 No one shall have a to exact anything from them
10:38 to be under one ruler and obey no other a than
10:70 Why do you assume a against us in
2Mc 3:24 and of all a caused so great a manifestation
4: 9 by his a a gymnasium and a body of youth for it,
4:24 extolled him with an air of a,
7:16 and said, "Because you have a among mortals,
15:13 and of marvelous majesty and a.
1Es 8:22 and that no one has a to impose any tax on them.
3Mc 7: 1 in a in his government, greetings and good health:
7:12 and without royal a or supervision,
2Es 2:41 implore the Lord's a that your people,
4Mc 4: 5 On receiving a to deal with this matter,
4: 6 with the king's a to seize the private funds in
8: 7 have positions of a in my government if you will renounce

AUTHORIZED (1) [AUTHORITY]

1Mc 1:13 who a them to observe the ordinances of

AUTUMN (2)

Jer 5:24 the a rain and the spring rain,
Jude 1:12 a trees without fruit, twice dead, uprooted;

AUXILIARIES (1)

Jdt 3: 6 and took picked men from them as a.

AVA (KJV) See AVVA

AVAIL‡ (7) [AVAILS]

Est 3: 4 to see whether Mordecai's words would a;
Job 36:19 Will your cry a to keep you from distress,
41:26 Though the sword reaches it, it does not a,
Ps 39: 2 I was silent and still; I held my peace to no a;
Pr 21:30 no counsel, can a against the LORD.
Jer 7: 8 Here you are, trusting in deceptive words to no a.
Wis 17: 5 the brilliant flames of the stars a to illumine

AVAILS (1) [AVAIL]

Ps 49: 7 Truly, no ransom a for one's life,

AVARAN (2) [=ELEAZAR]

1Mc 2: 5 Eleazar called A, and Jonathan called Apphus.
6:43 Now Eleazar, called A, saw that one of

AVARICE (1)

Mk 7:22 a, wickedness, deceit, licentiousness, envy,

AVEN (2) [BETH-AVEN]

Hos 10: 8 The high places of A, the sin of Israel,
Am 1: 5 and cut off the inhabitants from the Valley of A,

AVENGE (14) [VENGEANCE]

Nu 31: 2 "A the Israelites on the Midianites;
Dt 32:43 For he will a the blood of his children,
1Sa 24:12 May the LORD a me on you;
2Ki 9: 7 that I may a on Jezebel the blood of my servants
2Ch 24:22 he said, "May the LORD see and a!"
Isa 1:24 and a myself on my foes!
Joel 3:21 I will a their blood, and I will not clear the guilty,
Ro 12:19 Beloved, never a yourselves,
Rev 6:10 and a our blood on the inhabitants of the earth?"
1Mc 2:67 and a the wrong done to your people.
6:22 to do justice and to a our kindred?
13: 6 But I will a my nation and the sanctuary
3Mc 7: 9 and inescapably as an antagonist to a such acts.
2Es 15: 9 I will surely a them, says the Lord,

AVENGED‡ (11) [VENGEANCE]

Ge 4:24 If Cain is a sevenfold, truly Lamech seventy-sevenfold."
Jdg 9:24 of Jerubbaal might be a and their blood be laid
1Sa 14:24 before it is evening and I have been a
18:25 that he may be a on the king's enemies.' "
2Sa 4: 8 the LORD has a my lord the king this day
16: 8 The LORD has a on all of you the blood of
Jer 51:35 May my torn flesh be a on Babylon,"
51:35 "May my blood be a on the inhabitants
Ac 7:24 the oppressed man and a him by striking down
Rev 19: 2 and he has a on her the blood of his servants."
1Mc 9:42 After they had fully a the blood of their brother,

AVENGER (21) [VENGEANCE]

Nu 35:12 The cities shall be for you a refuge from the a,
35:19 The a of blood is the one who shall put
35:19 the a of blood shall execute the sentence.
35:21 the a of blood shall put the murderer to death,
35:24 the slayer and the a of blood, in accordance
35:25 the congregation shall rescue the slayer from the a
35:27 and is found by the a of blood outside the bounds
35:27 and is killed by the a,
Dt 19: 6 the a of blood in hot anger might pursue
19:12 from there and handed over to the a of blood to
Jos 20: 3 they shall be for you a refuge from the a of blood.
20: 5 And if the a of blood is in pursuit,
20: 9 so as not to die by the hand of the a of blood,
2Sa 14:11 so that the a of blood may kill no more,
Ps 8: 2 to silence the enemy and the a.
44:16 at the sight of the enemy and the a.
99: 8 but an a of their wrongdoings.
1Th 4: 6 because the Lord is an a in all these things,
Wis 18:22 but by his word he subdued the a,
Sir 30: 6 He has left behind him an a against his enemies,
4Mc 11:23 and I myself will bring a great a upon you,

AVENGES (1) [VENGEANCE]

Ps 9:12 For he who a blood is mindful of them;

AVENGING (4) [VENGEANCE]

1Sa 25:33 and from a myself by my own hand!
Ps 79:10 Let the a of the outpoured blood of your servants
Na 1: 2 A jealous and a God is the LORD,
1: 2 the LORD is a and wrathful;

AVERT (8) [AVERTED, AVERTS]

Est 8: 3 at his feet, weeping and pleading with him to a
Jer 11:15 Can vows and sacrificial flesh a your doom?
Eze 7:22 I will a my face from them,
AdE 8: 3 to a all the evil that Haman had planned against
Sir 4: 5 Do not a your eye from the needy,
27: 1 and those who seek to get rich will a their eyes.
3Mc 1:16 to a the violence of this evil design, and they filled
5: 8 that he a with vengeance the evil plot against them

AVERTED (5) [AVERT]

2Sa 24:21 so that the plague may be a from the people."
24:25 and the plague was a from Israel.
1Ch 21:22 so that the plague may be a from the people."
Ezr 10:14 the fierce wrath of our God on this account is a
Jdt 13:20 and you a our ruin, walking in the straight path

AVERTS (1) [AVERT]

Pr 21:14 A gift in secret a anger;

AVID (1)

Sir 31: 7 It is a stumbling block to those who are a for it,

AVIM, AVIMS (KJV) See AVVIM

AVITES (KJV) See AVVIM, AVVITES

AVITH (2)

Ge 36:35 the name of his city being A.
1Ch 1:46 and the name of his city was A.

AVOID (18) [AVOIDED, AVOIDING, AVOIDS]

Pr 4:15 A it; do not go on it;
13:14 so that one may a the snares of death.
14:27 so that one may a the snares of death.
15:24 in order to a Sheol below.
Jer 25:29 and how can you possibly a punishment?
Jn 18:28 so as to a ritual defilement and to be able to eat
Ro 16:17 that you have learned; a them.
1Ti 6:20 A the profane chatter and contradictions
2Ti 2:14 that they are to a wrangling over words,
2:16 A profane chatter, for it will lead people into more
3: 5 but denying its power. A them!
Tit 3: 2 to a quarreling, to be gentle,
3: 9 But a stupid controversies, genealogies,
Sir 7:34 Do not a those who weep,
22:13 A him and you will find rest,
38:17 to a criticism; then be comforted for your grief.
2Mc 6:26 the present I would a the punishment of mortals,
2Es 7:21 and what they should observe to a punishment.

AVOIDED (4) [AVOID]

2Ch 20:10 and whom they a and did not destroy—
Ps 17: 4 by the word of your lips I have a the ways of
Ac 27:21 from Crete and thereby a this damage and loss.

Wis 17:10 though it nowhere could be a.

AVOIDING (1) [AVOID]
Dt 2:37 a the whole upper region of the Wadi Jabbok

AVOIDS (3) [AVOID]
Pr 16: 6 and by the fear of the LORD one a evil.
16:17 The highway of the upright a evil;
Wis 2:16 and he a our ways as unclean;

AVVA (1)
2Ki 17:24 Cuthah, A, Hamath, and Sepharvaim,

AVVIM (3)
Dt 2:23 the A, who had lived in settlements in the vicinity
Jos 13: 3 Ashkelon, Gath, and Ekron), and those of the A,
18:23 A, Parah, Ophrah,

AVVITES (1)
2Ki 17:31 the A made Nibhaz and Tartak;

AWAIT (3) [WAIT]
Sir 16:22 Or who can a them?
2Es 8:59 For just as the things that I have predicted a you,
8:59 so the thirst and torment that are prepared a them.

AWAITS‡ (1) [WAIT]
2Es 7:*93* and the punishment that a them.

AWAKE‡ (48) [WAKE]
Jdg 5:12 "A, a, Deborah! A, a, utter a song!
1Sa 26:12 No one saw it, or knew it, nor did anyone a;
Job 14:12 they will not a or be roused out of their sleep.
Ps 7: 6 a, O my God; you have appointed a judgment.
17:15 I a I shall be satisfied, beholding your likeness.
44:23 A, do not cast us off forever!
57: 8 A, my soul! A, O harp and lyre! I will a the dawn.
59: 5 A to punish all the nations;
102: 7 I lie a; I am like a lonely bird on the housetop.
108: 1 I will sing and make melody. A, my soul!
108: 2 A, O harp and lyre! I will a the dawn.
119:148 My eyes are a before each watch of the night,
Pr 6:22 and when you a, they will talk with you.
23:35 When shall I a? I will seek another drink."
SS 4:16 A, O north wind, and come, O south wind!
5: 2 I slept, but my heart was a.
Isa 26:19 O dwellers in the dust, a and sing for joy!
51: 9 A, a, put on strength, O arm of the LORD!
51: 9 A, as in days of old, the generations of long ago!
52: 1 A, a, put on your strength, O Zion!
Da 12: 2 of those who sleep in the dust of the earth shall a,
Zec 13: 7 "A, O sword, against my shepherd,
Mt 24:42 Keep a therefore, for you do not know
24:43 the thief was coming, he would have stayed a
25:13 Keep a therefore, for you know neither the day
26:38 remain here, and stay a with me."
26:40 "So, could you not stay a with me one hour?
26:41 Stay a and pray that you may not come into
Mk 13:35 keep a—for you do not know
13:37 And what I say to you I say to all: Keep a."
14:34 to death; remain here, and keep a."
14:37 Could you not keep a one hour?
14:38 Keep a and pray that you may not come into
Lk 9:32 but since they had stayed a,
Eph 5:14 "Sleeper, a! Rise from the dead,
1Th 5: 6 but let us keep a and be sober;
5:10 whether we are a or asleep we may live with him.
Rev 16:15 Blessed is the one who stays a and is clothed,
2Es 7:31 After seven days the world that is not yet a shall
7:*35* be manifested; righteous deeds shall a,

AWAKEN (5) [WAKE]
SS 2: 7 do not stir up or a love until it is ready!
3: 5 do not stir up or a love until it is ready!
8: 4 do not stir up or a love until it is ready!
Jn 11:11 but I am going there to a him."
4Mc 5:11 Will you not a from your foolish philosophy,

AWAKENED (4) [WAKE]
1Ki 18:27 or perhaps he is asleep and must be a."
2Ki 4:31 to meet him and told him, "The child has not a."
SS 8: 5 Under the apple tree I a you.
Eze 7: 6 It has a against you; see, it comes!

AWAKES (1) [WAKE]
Ps 73:20 They are like a dream when one a;

AWAKING (2) [WAKE]
Ps 73:20 on a you despise their phantoms.
2Mc 15:17 and so effective in arousing valor and a courage in

AWARDED (1) [AWARDS]
3Mc 3:28 and will be a their freedom.

AWARDS (1) [AWARDED]
4Mc 17:12 for on that day virtue gave the a and tested them

AWARE (23)
2Ki 6:32 "Are you a that this murderer has sent someone
SS 6:12 Before I was a, my fancy set me in a chariot
Jer 40:14 "Are you at all a that Baalis king of
42:19 Be well a that I have warned you today
42:22 Be well a, then, that you shall die by the sword,
44:15 Then all the men who were a
Mt 12:15 When Jesus became a of this, he departed.
16: 8 And becoming a of it, Jesus said,
22:18 But Jesus, a of their malice, said,
26:10 But Jesus, a of this, said to them,
Mk 5:30 Immediately a that power had gone forth
8:17 And becoming a of it, Jesus said to them,
Lk 9:47 But Jesus, a of their inner thoughts,
Jn 6:61 being a that his disciples were complaining
15:18 be a that it hated me before it hated you.
1Co 4: 4 I am not a of anything against myself,
2Ti 1:15 You are a that all who are
1Pe 2:19 For it is a credit to you if, being a of God,
Tob 11: 2 "You are a of how we left your father.
Sus 1:42 you know what is secret and are a of all things
2Mc 4:33 When Onias became fully a of these acts,
4:41 But when the Jews became a
14:31 When the latter became a

AWAY‡ (1007)
Ge 4:14 Today you have driven me a from the soil,
4:16 Cain went a from the presence of the LORD,
9:23 their faces were turned a,
15:11 down on the carcasses, Abram drove them a.
16: 6 and she ran a from her.
16: 8 "I am running a from my mistress Sarai."
18:23 "Will you indeed sweep a the righteous with
18:24 will you then sweep a the place and not forgive it
21:14 along with the child, and sent her a.
22: 4 up and saw the place far a.
24:59 So they sent a their sister Rebekah and her nurse
25: 6 and he sent them a from his son Isaac,
26:16 And Abimelech said to Isaac, "Go a from us;
26:27 that you hate me and have sent me a from you?"
26:29 to you nothing but good and have sent you a
27:35 and he has taken a your blessing."
27:36 He took a my birthright;
27:36 and look, now he has taken a my blessing."
27:39 a from the fatness of the earth shall your home be,
27:39 and a from the dew of heaven on high.
27:44 until your brother's fury turns a—
27:45 until your brother's anger against you turns a,
28: 5 Thus Isaac sent Jacob a;
28: 6 and sent him a to Paddan-aram to take a wife
30:15 a small matter that you have taken a my husband?
30:15 Would you take a my son's mandrakes also?"
30:23 and said, "God has taken a my reproach";
30:25 Jacob said to Laban, "Send me a,
31: 9 Thus God has taken a the livestock of your father,
31:16 that God has taken a from our father belongs to us
31:18 and he drove a all his livestock,
31:26 carried a my daughters like captives of the sword.
31:27 I would have sent you a with mirth and songs,
31:42 now you would have sent me a empty-handed.
34:26 of Shechem's house, and went a.
35: 2 "Put a the foreign gods that are among you,
37:17 The man said, "They have gone a,
38:19 Then she got up and went a,
42:24 He turned a from them and wept;
44: 3 the men were sent a with their donkeys.
45: 1 and he cried out, "Send everyone a from me."
Ex 2:17 But some shepherds came and drove them a.
5: 4 why are you taking the people a from their work?
8: 8 "Pray to the LORD to take a the frogs from me
8:28 provided you do not go very far a.
10:28 Then Pharaoh said to him, "Get a from me!
11: 1 indeed, when he lets you go, he will drive you a.
12:31 go a from my people, both you and the Israelites!
14:11 that you have taken us a to die in the wilderness?
15:15 all the inhabitants of Canaan melted a.
18: 2 After Moses had sent a his wife Zipporah,
23:25 and I will take sickness a from among you.
33:23 I will take a my hand, and you shall see my back;
Lev 10: 4 and carry your kinsmen a from the front of
16:10 that it may be sent a into the wilderness to Azazel.
16:21 and sending it a into the wilderness by means
26:16 that waste the eyes and cause life to pine a.
Nu 4:13 They shall take a the ashes from the altar,
9:10 through touching a corpse, or is on a journey,
12:10 When the cloud went a from over the tent,
16:24 Get a from the dwellings of Korah, Dathan,
16:26 "Turn a from the tents of these wicked men,
16:26 or you will be swept a for all their sins."
16:27 So they got a from the dwellings of Korah,
16:45 "Get a from this congregation,
20: 6 Then Moses and Aaron went a from the assembly
20:21 so Israel turned a from them.
21: 7 to the LORD to take a the serpents from us."
22:33 and turned a from me these three times.
22:33 If it had not turned a from me,
24: 6 Like palm groves that stretch far a,
24:22 How long shall Asshur take you a captive?"
25: 4 that the fierce anger of the LORD may turn a
27: 4 be taken a from his clan because he had no son?
32:15 If you turn a from following him,
36: 3 so it will be taken a from the allotted portion
Dt 4: 2 to what I command you nor take a anything
6: 7 when you are at home and when you are a,
7: 1 and he clears a many nations before you—
7: 4 would turn a your children from following me,
7:15 The LORD will turn a from you every illness;
7:22 The LORD your God will clear a these nations
11:16 Take care, or you will be seduced into turning a,
Dt 11:19 when you are at home and when you are a,
13: 7 whether near you or far a from you,
13:10 Stone them to death for trying to turn you a from
14:24 to set his name is too far a from you,
17:17 or else his heart will turn a;
22: 1 not watch your neighbor's ox or sheep straying a
23:14 not see anything indecent among you and turn a
24: 4 who sent her a, is not permitted to take her again
28:26 and there shall be no one to frighten them a.
28:49 The LORD will bring a nation from far a,
29:18 whose heart is already turning a from
30:11 not too hard for you, nor is it too far a.
30:17 But if your heart turns a and you do not hear,
Jos 2:21 She sent them a and they departed.
5: 9 "Today I have rolled a from you the disgrace
6:18 keep a from the things devoted to destruction,
7:13 to stand before your enemies until you take a
8: 6 after us until we have drawn them a from the city;
8:16 as they pursued Joshua they were drawn a from
22: 6 So Joshua blessed them and sent them a,
22: 7 Joshua sent them a to their tents and blessed them,
22:16 in turning a today from following the LORD,
22:18 you must turn a today from following the LORD!
22:23 an altar to turn a from following the LORD;
22:29 and turn a this day from following the LORD
24:14 put a the gods that your ancestors served beyond
24:23 "Then put a the foreign gods that are among you,
24:28 So Joshua sent the people a to their inheritances.
Jdg 4:11 and had encamped as far a as Elon-bezaanannim,
4:15 Sisera got down from his chariot and fled a
4:17 Now Sisera had fled a on foot to the tent
5:12 Arise, Barak, lead a your captives,
5:21 The torrent Kishon swept them a,
7: 2 Israel would only take the credit a from me,
9:21 Then Jotham ran a and fled, going to Beer,
10:16 So they put a the foreign gods from among them
11: 2 his wife's sons grew up, they drove Jephthah a,
11:13 took a my land from the Arnon to the Jabbok and
11:15 Israel did not take a the land of Moab or the land
11:38 "Go," he said and sent her a for two months.
15:17 he had finished speaking, he threw a the jawbone;
16:14 But he awoke from his sleep, and pulled a the pin,
18:24 and the priest, and go a, and what have I left?
19: 2 and she went a from him to her father's house
20:31 they were drawn a from the city.
20:32 and draw them a from the city toward the roads."
20:42 Therefore they turned a from the Israelites in
Ru 1:21 I went a full, but the LORD has brought me back
1Sa 1:14 Put a your wine."
5:11 and said, "Send a the ark of the God of Israel,
6: 3 "If you send a the ark of the God of Israel,
6: 7 but take their calves home, a from them.
7: 3 then put a the foreign gods and the Astartes from
7: 4 So Israel put a the Baals and the Astartes,
10: 9 As he turned a to leave Samuel,
12:22 For the LORD will not cast a his people,
12:25 But if you still do wickedly, you shall be swept a,
13: 8 and the people began to slip a from Saul.
13:11 I saw that the people were slipping a from me,
15:27 As Samuel turned to go a,
17:26 and takes a the reproach from Israel?
17:30 He turned a from him toward another and spoke in
19:12 through the window; he fled a and escaped.
20:13 and send you a, so that you may go in safety.
20:22 for the LORD has sent you a.
20:29 if I have found favor in your sight, let me get a,
21: 6 be replaced by hot bread on the day it is taken a.
23: 5 with the Philistines, brought a their livestock,
23:26 David was hurrying to get a from Saul,
24:19 and sent the enemy safely a?
25:10 There are many servants today who are breaking a
25:12 So David's young men turned a,
25:42 Abigail got up hurriedly and rode a on a donkey;
26:12 at Saul's head and the water jar, and they went a.
26:13 and stood on top of a hill far a,
26:20 a from the presence of the LORD;
27: 9 but took a the sheep, the oxen, the donkeys,
28:15 and God has turned a from me
28:25 Then they rose and went a that night.
2Sa 2:21 But Asahel would not turn a from following him.
2:22 "Turn a from following me;
2:23 But he refused to turn a.
3:21 David dismissed Abner, and he went a in peace.
3:22 and he had gone a in peace.
3:23 and he has gone a in peace."
3:24 why did you dismiss him, so that he got a?
5:21 and David and his men carried them a.
7:15 whom I put a from before you.
10: 4 in the middle at their hips, and sent them a.
12:13 "Now the LORD has put a your sin;
13:16 for this wrong in sending me a is greater than
13:19 she put her hand on her head, and went a,
14:14 But God will not take a a life;
17:18 so both of them went a quickly,
19:41 the people of Judah stolen you a,
23: 6 the godless are all like thorns that are thrown a;
24:10 I pray you, take a the guilt of your servant;
1Ki 2:31 and thus take a from me and
2:39 of three years that two of Shimei's slaves ran a
5: 9 I will have them broken up there for you to take a.
8:46 they are carried a captive to the land of the enemy,
8:66 On the eighth day he sent the people a;
11: 3 and his wives turned a his heart.
11: 4 his wives turned a his heart after other gods;
11: 9 because his heart had turned a from the LORD,
11:13 I will not, however, tear a the entire kingdom;
11:34 Nevertheless I will not take the whole kingdom a

1Ki 11:35 the kingdom **a** from his son and give it to you—
12: 5 He said to them, "Go **a** for three days,
12: 5 So the people went **a**.
12:16 So Israel went **a** to their tents.
13:24 Then as he went **a**, a lion met him on the road
14: 8 the kingdom **a** from the house of David to give it
14:17 Then Jeroboam's wife got up and went **a**,
14:26 he took **a** the treasures of the house of the LORD
14:26 He also took **a** all the shields of gold
15:12 He put **a** the male temple prostitutes out of
15:14 But the high places were not taken **a**.
15:22 they carried **a** the stones of Ramah and its timber,
18:27 either he is meditating, or he has wandered **a**,
19: 4 now, O LORD, take **a** my life,
19:10 and they are seeking my life, to take it **a**."
19:14 and they are seeking my life, to take it **a**."
20: 6 on whatever pleases them, and take it **a**."
20:41 Then he quickly took the bandage **a** from his eyes.
21: 4 He lay down on his bed, turned **a** his face,
22:43 yet the high places were not taken **a**,
2Ki 2: 3 the LORD will take your master **a** from you?"
2: 5 the LORD will take your master **a** from you?"
2:23 and jeered at him, saying, "Go **a**, baldhead! Go **a**,
4:27 Gehazi approached to push her **a**.
5:11 But Naaman became angry and went **a**, saying,
5:12 He turned and went **a** in a rage.
7: 7 So they fled **a** in the twilight
7:15 and equipment that the Arameans had thrown **a**
11: 2 and stole him **a** from among
12: 3 Nevertheless the high places were not taken **a**;
15: 4 Nevertheless the high places were not taken **a**;
15:24 not turn **a** from the sins of Jeroboam son of Nebat,
17: 6 he carried the Israelites **a** to Assyria.
17:11 as the nations did whom the LORD carried **a**
17:26 "The nations that you have carried **a** and placed in
17:27 "Send there one of the priests whom you carried **a**
17:28 So one of the priests whom they had carried **a**
17:33 from among whom they had been carried **a**.
18:11 king of Assyria carried the Israelites **a** to Assyria,
18:32 and take you **a** to a land like your own land,
20:18 to you shall be taken **a**;
23:24 Moreover Josiah put **a** the mediums, wizards,
23:34 to Jehoiakim. But he took Jehoahaz **a**;
24:14 He carried **a** all Jerusalem, all the officials,
24:15 He carried **a** Jehoiachin to Babylon;
25:14 They took **a** the pots, the shovels, the snuffers,
25:15 the captain of the guard took **a** for the gold,
1Ch 5: 6 whom King Tilgath-pilneser of Assyria carried **a**
5:26 and he carried them **a**, namely, the Reubenites,
8: 8 after he had sent **a** his wives Hushim and Baara.
10:12 all the valiant warriors got up and took **a** the body
12:19 of the Philistines took counsel and sent him **a**,
12:40 as far **a** as Issachar and Zebulun and Naphtali,
19: 4 in the middle at their hips, and sent them **a**;
21: 8 now, I pray you, take **a** the guilt of your servant;
2Ch 6:36 that they are carried **a** captive to a land far or near;
7:10 of the seventh month he sent the people **a**
8:15 not turn **a** from what the king had commanded
10: 5 So the people went **a**.
12: 9 he took **a** the treasures of the house of the LORD
12: 9 He also took **a** the shields of gold
14: 3 He took **a** the foreign altars and the high places,
14:13 The people of Judah carried **a** a great quantity
14:15 and carried **a** sheep and goats in abundance,
15: 8 and put **a** the abominable idols from all the land
16: 6 they carried **a** the stones of Ramah and its timber,
18:31 God drew them **a** from him,
21:17 and carried **a** all the possessions they found
22:11 and stole him **a** from among
25:27 that Amaziah turned **a** from the LORD they made
28:17 and defeated Judah, and carried **a** captives.
29: 6 and have turned **a** their faces from the dwelling of
29:10 so that his fierce anger may turn **a** from us.
30: 8 so that his fierce anger may turn **a** from you.
30: 9 and will not turn **a** his face from you,
30:14 and all the altars for offering incense they took **a**
32:12 not this same Hezekiah who took **a** his high places
33:15 He took **a** the foreign gods and the idol from
34:33 Josiah took **a** all the abominations from all
34:33 All his days they did not turn **a** from following
35:22 But Josiah would not turn **a** from him,
35:23 and the king said to his servants, "Take me **a**,
Ezr 1: 7 that Nebuchadnezzar had carried **a** from Jerusalem
3:13 so loudly that the sound was heard far **a**.
5:12 who destroyed this house and carried **a** the people
6: 6 in the province Beyond the River, keep **a**;
10: 3 a covenant with our God to send **a** all these wives
10:19 They pledged themselves to send **a** their wives,
10:44 and they sent them **a** with their children.
Ne 6:11 But I said, "Should a man like me run **a**?
12:43 The joy of Jerusalem was heard far **a**.
13:28 I chased him **a** from me.
Est 2: 6 Kish had been carried **a** from Jerusalem among the captives carried **a** with King Jeconiah
2: 6 of Babylon had carried **a**.
4:17 Mordecai then went **a** and did everything
Job 1: 1 one who feared God and turned **a** from evil.
1: 8 and upright man who fears God and turns **a**
1:21 the LORD gave, and the LORD has taken **a**;
2: 3 and upright man who fears God and turns **a**
6:15 like a torrent-bed, like freshets that pass **a**,
7:19 Will you not look **a** from me for a while,
7:21 pardon my transgression and take **a** my iniquity?
9:12 He snatches **a**; who can stop him?
9:25 they flee **a**, they see no good.
9:34 If he would take his rod **a** from me,
11:14 If iniquity is in your hand, put it far **a**,
Job 11:16 you will remember it as waters that have passed **a**.
12:17 He leads counselors **a** stripped,
12:19 He leads priests **a** stripped,
12:20 and takes **a** the discernment of the elders.
12:23 he enlarges nations, then leads them **a**.
13:28 One wastes **a** like a rotten thing,
14: 6 look **a** from them, and desist, that they may enjoy,
14:11 and a river wastes **a** and dries up,
14:18 "But the mountain falls and crumbles **a**,
14:19 the waters wear **a** the stones;
14:19 the torrents wash **a** the soil of the earth;
14:20 against them, and they pass **a**;
14:20 you change their countenance, and send them **a**.
15: 4 But you are doing **a** with the fear of God,
15:12 Why does your heart carry you **a**,
15:30 and their blossom will be swept **a** by the wind.
20: 8 They will fly **a** like a dream, and not be found;
20: 8 they will be chased **a** like a vision of the night.
20:28 The possessions of their house will be carried **a**,
21:18 and like chaff that the storm carries **a**?
22: 9 You have sent widows **a** empty-handed,
22:16 They were snatched **a** before their time;
22:16 their foundation was washed **a** by a flood.
24: 3 They drive **a** the donkey of the orphan;
24:19 Drought and heat snatch **a** the snow waters;
27: 2 who has taken **a** my right, and the Almighty,
27: 5 until I die I will not put **a** my integrity from me.
27: 8 when God takes **a** their lives?
28: 4 in a valley **a** from human habitation;
30:15 and my prosperity has passed **a** like a cloud.
33:21 Their flesh is so wasted **a** that it cannot be seen;
34: 5 'I am innocent, and God has taken **a** my right;
34:20 at midnight the people are shaken and pass **a**,
34:20 and the mighty are taken **a** by no human hand.
36: 3 I will bring my knowledge from far **a**,
36:25 everyone watches it from far **a**.
39:29 its eyes see it from far **a**.
Ps 1: 4 but are like chaff that the wind drives **a**.
6: 7 My eyes waste **a** because of grief;
7: 2 they will drag me **a**, with no one to rescue.
18:22 and his statutes I did not put **a** from me.
22:19 But you, O LORD, do not be far **a**!
26: 9 Do not sweep me **a** with sinners,
27: 9 Do not turn your servant **a** in anger,
28: 3 Do not drag me **a** with the wicked,
31: 9 my eye wastes **a** from grief,
31:10 because of my misery, and my bones waste **a**.
32: 3 While I kept silence, my body wasted **a**
34: T *so that he drove him out, and he went* ***a****.*
36:11 or the hand of the wicked drive me **a**.
37:20 like smoke they vanish **a**.
39:13 Turn your gaze **a** from me, that I may smile again,
40:14 and confusion who seek to snatch **a** my life;
49:14 and their form shall waste **a**;
49:17 For when they die they will carry nothing **a**;
51:11 Do not cast me **a** from your presence,
53: 3 They have all fallen **a**, they are all alike perverse;
55: 6 I would fly **a** and be at rest;
55: 7 I would flee far **a**; I would lodge in the
58: 7 Let them vanish like water that runs **a**;
58: 9 whether green or ablaze, may he sweep them **a**!
68: 2 As smoke is driven **a**, so drive them **a**;
73:19 swept **a** utterly by terrors!
78:57 turned **a** and were faithless like their ancestors;
85: 4 and put **a** your indignation toward us.
90: 5 You sweep them **a**; they are like a
90: 9 For all our days pass **a** under your wrath;
90:10 they are soon gone, and we fly **a**.
101: 3 I hate the work of those who fall **a**;
102: 3 For my days pass **a** like smoke,
102:11 like an evening shadow; I wither **a** like grass.
102:24 "do not take me **a** at the mid-point of my life,
102:26 You change them like clothing, and they pass **a**;
104:29 when you take **a** their breath,
106:23 to turn **a** his wrath from destroying them.
107:26 their courage melted **a** in their calamity;
112:10 they gnash their teeth and melt **a**;
119:22 take **a** from me their scorn and contempt
119:28 My soul melts **a** for sorrow;
119:39 Turn **a** the disgrace that I dread,
119:51 but I do not turn **a** from your law.
119:102 I do not turn **a** from your ordinances,
119:115 Go **a** from me, you evildoers,
124: 4 then the flood would have swept us **a**,
125: 5 to their own crooked ways the LORD will lead **a**
132:10 For your servant David's sake do not turn **a**
138: 6 but the haughty he perceives from far **a**.
139: 2 you discern my thoughts from far **a**.
Pr 1:19 it takes **a** the life of its possessors.
3: 7 fear the LORD, and turn **a** from evil.
4: 5 nor turn **a** from the words of my mouth.
4:15 turn **a** from it and pass on.
4:24 Put **a** from you crooked speech,
4:27 turn your foot **a** from evil.
6:33 and his disgrace will not be wiped **a**.
7:22 Right **a** he follows her, and goes like an ox to
11:30 but violence takes lives **a**.
13:19 but to turn **a** from evil is an abomination to fools.
13:23 but it is swept **a** through injustice.
14:16 The wise are cautious and turn **a** from evil,
15: 1 A soft answer turns **a** wrath,
19:26 chase **a** their mother are children who cause shame
20:14 bad," says the buyer, then goes **a** and boasts.
20:30 Blows that wound cleanse **a** evil;
21: 7 The violence of the wicked will sweep them **a**,
22:15 but the rod of discipline drives it far **a**.
24:11 if you hold back from rescuing those taken **a**
Pr 24:18 and turn **a** his anger from them.
25: 4 Take **a** the dross from the silver,
25: 5 take **a** the wicked from the presence of the king,
27:10 neighbor who is nearby than kindred who are far **a**.
29: 8 but the wise turn **a** wrath.
31:14 she brings her food from far **a**.
Ecc 3: 5 a time to throw **a** stones, and a time
3: 6 a time to keep, and a time to throw **a**;
5:15 which they may carry **a** with their hands.
11:10 and put **a** pain from your body;
SS 2:10 "Arise, my love, my fair one, and come **a**;
2:13 Arise, my love, my fair one, and come **a**.
5: 7 they wounded me, they took **a** my mantle,
6: 5 Turn **a** your eyes from me,
Isa 1:25 I will smelt **a** your dross as with lye
2:18 The idols shall utterly pass **a**.
2:20 On that day people will throw **a** to the moles and
2:22 Turn **a** from mortals, who have only breath
3: 1 is taking **a** from Jerusalem and
3:18 the Lord will take **a** the finery of the anklets,
4: 1 by your name; take **a** our disgrace."
4: 4 the Lord has washed **a** the filth of the daughters
5:25 For all this his anger has not turned **a**,
5:26 He will raise a signal for a nation far **a**,
6:12 until the LORD sends everyone far **a**,
8: 4 the spoil of Samaria will be carried **a** by the king
9:12 For all this his anger has not turned **a**;
9:17 For all this his anger has not turned **a**,
9:21 For all this his anger has not turned **a**;
10: 3 in the calamity that will come from far **a**?
10: 4 For all this his anger has not turned **a**;
10:18 and it will be as when an invalid wastes **a**.
12: 1 your anger turned **a**, and you comforted me.
14:19 **a** from your grave, like loathsome carrion,
15: 7 they carry **a** over the Wadi of the Willows.
16:10 and gladness are taken **a** from the fruitful field;
17:11 yet the harvest will flee **a** in a day of grief
17:13 but he will rebuke them, and they will flee far **a**,
18: 5 and the spreading branches he will hew **a**.
19: 6 reeds and rushes will rot **a**.
19: 7 be driven **a**, and be no more.
20: 4 so shall the king of Assyria lead **a** the Egyptians
22: 3 though they had fled far **a**.
22: 4 Look **a** from me, let me weep bitter tears;
22: 8 He has taken **a** the covering of Judah.
22:17 The LORD is about to hurl you **a** violently,
23: 7 whose feet carried her to settle far **a**?
24:16 But I say, I pine **a**, I pine **a**.
25: 8 Lord GOD will wipe **a** the tears from all faces,
25: 8 the disgrace of his people he will take **a** from all
28:17 hail will sweep **a** the refuge of lies,
30:22 you will say to them, "**A** with you!"
30:27 See, the name of the LORD comes from far **a**,
31: 7 For on that day all of you shall throw **a** your idols
31: 9 His rock shall pass **a** in terror,
33: 9 Lebanon is confounded and withers **a**;
33:13 Hear, you who are far **a**, what I have done;
33:15 who wave **a** a bribe instead of accepting it,
33:17 they will behold a land that stretches far **a**.
34: 4 All the host of heaven shall rot **a**,
35:10 and sorrow and sighing shall flee **a**.
36:17 and take you **a** to a land like your own land,
39: 7 to you shall be taken **a**;
41:16 and the wind shall carry them **a**,
43: 6 bring my sons from far **a** and my daughters from
44:22 I have swept **a** your transgressions like a cloud,
47:11 which you cannot charm **a**;
49: 1 pay attention, you peoples from far **a**!
49: 2 in his quiver he hid me **a**.
49:12 Lo, these shall come from far **a**, and lo,
49:17 and those who laid you waste go **a** from you.
49:19 and those who swallowed you up will be far **a**.
49:21 I was bereaved and barren, exiled and put **a**—
50: 1 bill of divorce with which I put her **a**?
50: 1 for your transgressions your mother was put **a**.
51:11 and sorrow and sighing shall flee **a**.
52: 5 seeing that my people are taken **a** without cause?
53: 8 By a perversion of justice he was taken **a**.
57: 1 the devout are taken **a**, while no one understands.
57: 1 For the righteous are taken **a** from calamity,
57: 9 you sent your envoys far **a**,
57:13 a breath will take them **a**.
59:13 and turning **a** from following our God,
60: 4 your sons shall come from far **a**,
60: 9 to bring your children from far **a**,
64: 6 and our iniquities, like the wind, take us **a**.
66:19 and Javan, to the coastlands far **a** that have
Jer 1:13 "I see a boiling pot, tilted **a** from the north."
2:37 From there also you will come **a** with your hands
3: 8 Israel, I had sent her **a** with a decree of divorce;
4: 8 "The fierce anger of the LORD has not turned **a**
5:10 strip **a** her branches, for they are not the LORD's.
5:15 I am going to bring upon you a nation from far **a**,
5:23 they have turned aside and gone **a**.
5:25 Your iniquities have turned these **a**,
7:29 Cut off your hair and throw it **a**;
7:33 and no one will frighten them **a**.
8: 5 Why then has this people turned **a**
8:13 and what I gave them has passed **a** from them.
9: 2 that I might leave my people and go **a** from them!
12: 4 in it the animals and the birds are swept **a**,
15: 3 the sword to kill, the dogs to drag **a**,
15: 9 bore seven has languished; she has swooned **a**;
15:15 In your forbearance do not take me **a**;
16: 5 for I have taken **a** my peace from this people,
17: 5 whose hearts turn **a** from the LORD.
17:13 those who turn **a** from you shall be recorded in

Jer 17:16 not run **a** from being a shepherd in your service,
18:20 to turn **a** your wrath from them.
22:10 weep rather for him who goes **a,**
22:11 and who went **a** from this place:
22:28 Why are he and his offspring hurled out and cast **a**
23: 2 and have driven them **a,** and you have
23:39 I will surely lift you up and cast you **a**
24: 5 as good the exiles from Judah, whom I have sent **a**
27:20 not take **a** when he took into exile from Jerusalem
28: 3 which King Nebuchadnezzar of Babylon took **a**
29:20 all you exiles whom I sent **a** from Jerusalem
30:10 for I am going to save you from far **a,**
31: 3 the LORD appeared to him from far **a.**
31:10 O nations, and declare it in the coastlands far **a;**
31:19 For after I had turned **a** I repented;
37: 9 saying, "The Chaldeans will surely go **a** from us," for they will not go **a.**
41:14 the people whom Ishmael had carried **a** captive
41:16 of Nethaniah had carried **a** captive from Mizpah
43:12 and he shall burn them and carry them **a** captive;
46: 6 swift cannot flee **a,** nor can the warrior escape;
46:22 She makes a sound like a snake gliding **a;**
46:27 for I am going to save you from far **a,**
48:33 and joy have been taken **a** from the fruitful land
49:19 I will suddenly chase Edom **a** from it;
49:20 the little ones of the flock shall be dragged **a;**
49:30 Flee, wander far **a,** hide in deep places,
50: 3 both human beings and animals shall flee **a.**
50: 6 turning them **a** on the mountains;
50:17 Israel is a hunted sheep driven **a** by lions.
50:44 I will suddenly chase them **a** from her;
50:45 the little ones of the flock shall be dragged **a;**
52:18 They took **a** the pots, the shovels, the snuffers,
52:19 captain of the guard took **a** the small bowls also,
La 1: 5 her children have gone **a,** captives before the foe.
1: 8 she herself groans, and turns her face **a.**
3: 4 He has made my flesh and my skin waste **a,**
4: 9 whose life drains **a,** deprived of the produce of
4:15 "**A!** Unclean!" people shouted at them; "**A! A!**
Eze 3:14 The spirit lifted me up and bore me **a;**
4:17 and waste **a** under their punishment.
6: 9 by their wanton heart that turned **a** from me,
11:16 Though I removed them far **a** among the nations,
14: 6 Repent and turn **a** from your idols;
14: 6 and turn **a** your faces from all your abominations.
16:42 and my jealousy shall turn **a** from you;
17:13 under oath (he had taken **a** the chief men of
18:21 But if the wicked turn **a** from all their sins
18:24 when the righteous turn **a** from their righteousness
18:26 the righteous turn **a** from their righteousness
18:27 when the wicked turn **a** from
18:28 Because they considered and turned **a** from all
18:31 Cast **a** from you all the transgressions
20: 7 Cast **a** the detestable things your eyes feast on,
20: 8 not one of them cast **a** the detestable things
23:26 of your clothes and take **a** your fine jewels.
23:29 and take **a** all the fruit of your labor,
23:40 They even sent for men to come from far **a,**
24:16 about to take **a** from you the delight of your eyes;
24:23 you shall not mourn or weep, but you shall pine **a**
30: 4 and its wealth is carried **a,**
31:12 the peoples of the earth went **a** from its shade
32:20 carry **a** both it and its hordes.
33: 4 and the sword comes and takes them **a,**
33: 6 they are taken **a** in their iniquity,
33:10 and we waste **a** because of them;
38:13 carry **a** silver and gold, to take **a** cattle and goods,
42: 5 for the galleries took more **a** from them than from
43: 9 Now let them put **a** their idolatry and the corpses
45: 9 Put **a** violence and oppression,
Da 2:35 and the wind carried them **a,**
4:25 You shall be driven **a** from human society,
4:32 You shall be driven **a** from human society,
4:33 He was driven **a** from human society,
7:12 the rest of the beasts, their dominion was taken **a,**
7:14 an everlasting dominion that shall not pass **a,**
7:26 and his dominion shall be taken **a,**
8:11 it took the regular burnt offering **a** from him
9: 7 those who are near and those who are far **a,**
9:16 we pray, turn **a** from your city Jerusalem,
11:22 Armies shall be utterly swept **a** and broken
11:26 They shall break him, his army shall be swept **a,**
12:11 the time that the regular burnt offering is taken **a**
Hos 2: 2 that she put **a** her whoring from her face,
2: 9 and I will take **a** my wool and my flax,
4:11 Wine and new wine take **a** the understanding.
5:14 I myself will tear and go **a;**
6: 4 like the dew that goes **a** early.
9:11 Ephraim's glory shall fly **a** like a bird—
11: 7 My people are bent on turning **a** from me.
13: 3 the morning mist or like the dew that goes **a** early,
13:11 and I took him **a** in my wrath.
14: 2 say to him, "Take **a** all guilt;
Joel 1:12 surely, joy withers **a** among the people.
3: 8 to a nation far **a;** for the LORD has spoken.
Am 2:16 among the mighty shall flee **a** naked in that day,
4: 2 when they shall take you **a** with hooks,
4:10 I carried **a** your horses; and I made the stench
5:23 Take **a** from me the noise of your songs;
6: 3 O you that put far **a** the evil day,
6: 7 and the revelry of the loungers shall pass **a.**
7:11 and Israel must go into exile **a** from his land.' "
7:12 flee **a** to the land of Judah, earn your bread there,
7:17 Israel shall surely go into exile **a** from its land.' "
9: 1 not one of them shall flee **a,**
Jnh 1: 3 **a** from the presence of the LORD.
2: 4 Then I said, 'I am driven **a** from your sight;
Jnh 2: 7 my life was ebbing **a,** I remembered the LORD;
Mic 2: 2 and seize them; houses, and take them **a;**
2: 9 from their young children you take **a** my glory
4: 3 and shall arbitrate between strong nations far **a;**
4: 6 and gather those who have been driven **a,**
6:14 you shall put **a,** but not save, and what you save,
Na 1:12 they will be cut off and pass **a.**
2: 7 the city be exiled, its slave women led **a,** moaning
2: 8 Nineveh is like a pool whose waters run **a.**
3:16 The locust sheds its skin and flies **a.**
3:17 when the sun rises, they fly **a;**
Hab 1: 8 Their horsemen come from far **a;**
Zep 1: 2 I will utterly sweep **a** everything from the face of
1: 3 I will sweep **a** humans and animals;
1: 3 I will sweep **a** the birds of the air and the fish of
2: 2 before you are driven **a** like the drifting chaff,
3:15 LORD has taken **a** the judgments against you,
3:15 he has turned **a** your enemies.
Hag 1: 9 and when you brought it home, I blew it **a.**
Zec 3: 4 "See, I have taken your guilt **a** from you,
9: 7 I will take **a** its blood from its mouth,
Mt 2:22 he went **a** to the district of Galilee.
4:10 Jesus said to him, "**A** with you, Satan!
5:18 For truly I tell you, until heaven and earth pass **a,**
5:29 tear it out and throw it **a;**
5:30 cut it off and throw it **a;**
7:23 go **a** from me, you evildoers.'
9:15 when the bridegroom is taken **a** from them,
9:16 for the patch pulls **a** from the cloak,
9:24 "Go **a;** for the girl is not dead but sleeping."
9:31 But they went **a** and spread the news about him
9:32 After they had gone **a,** a demoniac who was mute
11: 7 As they went **a,** Jesus began to speak to
13: 6 and since they had no root, they withered **a.**
13:12 even what they have will be taken **a.**
13:19 the evil one comes and snatches **a** what is sown in
13:21 that person immediately falls **a.**
13:25 among the wheat, and then went **a.**
14:15 the crowds **a** so that they may go into the villages
14:16 Jesus said to them, "They need not go **a;**
15:21 Jesus left that place and went **a** to the district
15:23 "Send her **a,** for she keeps shouting after us."
15:32 and I do not want to send them **a** hungry,
15:39 After sending **a** the crowds,
16: 4 Then he left them and went **a.**
18: 8 cut it off and throw it **a;**
18: 9 tear it out and throw it **a;**
19:22 young man heard this word, he went **a** grieving,
21:43 the kingdom of God will be taken **a** from you
22: 5 But they made light of it and went **a,**
22:22 and they left him and went **a.**
24: 1 As Jesus came out of the temple and was going **a,**
24:10 Then many will fall **a,**
24:34 not pass **a** until all these things have taken place.
24:35 Heaven and earth will pass **a,**
24:35 but my words will not pass **a.**
24:39 until the flood came and swept them all **a,**
25:15 to his ability. Then he went **a.**
25:29 even what they have will be taken **a.**
25:46 And these will go **a** into eternal punishment,
26:42 Again he went **a** for the second time and prayed,
26:44 he went **a** and prayed for the third time,
27: 2 They bound him, led him **a,**
27:31 Then they led him **a** to crucify him.
27:60 a great stone to the door of the tomb and went **a.**
27:64 otherwise his disciples may go and steal him **a,**
28:13 by night and stole him **a** while we were asleep.'
Mk 1:43 After sternly warning him he sent him **a** at once,
2:20 when the bridegroom is taken **a** from them,
2:21 otherwise, the patch pulls **a** from it,
4: 6 and since it had no root, it withered **a.**
4:15 Satan immediately comes and takes **a** the word
4:17 on account of the word, immediately they fall **a.**
4:25 even what they have will be taken **a.**"
5:20 And he went **a** and began to proclaim in
6:31 "Come **a** to a deserted place all by yourselves
6:32 And they went **a** in the boat to a deserted place
6:36 send them **a** so that they may go into
7:24 From there he set out and went **a** to the region
7:33 He took him aside in private, **a** from the crowd,
8: 3 If I send them **a** hungry to their homes,
8: 9 And he sent them **a.**
8:26 Then he sent him **a** to his home, saying,
10:22 he was shocked and went **a** grieving,
11: 4 They went **a** and found a colt tied near a door,
11:20 they saw the fig tree withered **a** to its roots.
12: 3 and beat him, and sent him **a** empty-handed.
12:12 So they left him and went **a.**
13:15 down or enter the house to take anything **a;**
13:30 not pass **a** until all these things have taken place.
13:31 Heaven and earth will pass **a,** but my words will not pass **a.**
14:39 And again he went **a** and prayed,
14:44 arrest him and lead him **a** under guard."
15: 1 They bound Jesus, led him **a,**
16: 3 "Who will roll **a** the stone for us from the entrance
Lk 1:25 on me and took **a** the disgrace I have endured
1:53 and sent the rich **a** empty.
5: 8 "Go **a** from me, Lord, for I am a sinful man!"
5:35 when the bridegroom will be taken **a** from them,
6:29 and from anyone who takes **a** your coat do
6:30 and if anyone takes **a** your goods,
8:12 then the devil comes and takes **a** the word
8:13 for a while and in a time of testing fall **a.**
8:18 even what they seem to have will be taken **a.**"
8:38 but Jesus sent him **a,** saying,
8:39 So he went **a,** proclaiming throughout the city
Lk 9:12 "Send the crowd **a,** so that they may go into
10:30 beat him, and went **a,** leaving him half dead.
10:42 which will not be taken **a** from her."
11:22 he takes **a** his armor in which he trusted
11:52 For you have taken **a** the key of knowledge;
13:15 and lead it **a** to give it water?
13:27 go **a** from me, all you evildoers!'
13:31 "Get **a** from here, for Herod wants to kill you."
14: 4 So Jesus took him and healed him, and sent him **a.**
14:32 If he cannot, then, while the other is still far **a,**
14:35 for the manure pile; they throw it **a.**
16: 3 that my master is taking the position **a** from me?
16:17 But it is easier for heaven and earth to pass **a,**
16:22 The poor man died and was carried **a** by
16:23 he looked up and saw Abraham far **a** with Lazarus
17:31 in the house must not come down to take them **a;**
19:26 even what they have will be taken **a.**
20:10 tenants beat him and sent him **a** empty-handed.
20:11 and insulted and sent **a** empty-handed.
21:24 the edge of the sword and be taken **a** as captives
21:32 not pass **a** until all things have taken place.
21:33 Heaven and earth will pass **a,** but my words will not pass **a.**
22: 4 he went **a** and conferred with the chief priests
22:54 Then they seized him and led him **a,**
23:18 they all shouted out together, "**A** with this fellow!
23:26 As they led him **a,** they seized a man,
23:32 were led **a** to be put to death with him.
24: 2 They found the stone rolled **a** from the tomb,
Jn 1:29 the Lamb of God who takes **a** the sin of the world!
5:15 The man went **a** and told the Jews
6:22 but that his disciples had gone **a** alone.
6:37 anyone who comes to me I will never drive **a;**
6:67 "Do you also wish to go **a?**"
8: 9 ⟦When they heard it, they went **a,** one by one,⟧
8:21 Again he said to them, "I am going **a,**
10:12 the wolf coming and leaves the sheep and runs **a**—
10:13 The hired hand runs **a** because a hired hand does
10:40 He went **a** again across the Jordan to the place
11:18 Bethany was near Jerusalem, some two miles **a,**
11:39 Jesus said, "Take **a** the stone."
11:41 So they took **a** the stone.
14:28 You heard me say to you, 'I am going **a,**
15: 6 Whoever does not abide in me is thrown **a** like
16: 7 to your advantage that I go **a,** for if I do not go **a,**
19:15 They cried out, "**A** with him! **A** with him!
19:38 asked Pilate to let him take **a** the body of Jesus.
20:13 She said to them, "They have taken **a** my Lord,
20:15 she said to him, "Sir, if you have carried him **a,**
20:15 and I will take him **a.**"
Ac 1:12 a sabbath day's journey **a.**
2:39 for your children, and for all who are far **a,**
5:38 keep **a** from these men and let them alone;
7:42 But God turned **a** from them and handed them
8:33 For his life is taken **a** from the earth."
8:39 the Spirit of the Lord snatched Philip **a;**
13: 8 and tried to turn the proconsul **a** from the faith.
15:39 Barnabas took Mark with him and sailed **a**
17:14 the believers immediately sent Paul **a** to the coast,
19:26 and drawn **a** a considerable number of people
20:12 the boy **a** alive and were not a little comforted.
21:36 crowd that followed kept shouting, "**A** with him!"
22:16 Get up, be baptized, and have your sins washed **a,**
22:21 'Go, for I will send you far **a** to the Gentiles.' "
22:22 "**A** with such a fellow from the earth!
23:15 we are ready to do **a** with him before he arrives."
24:25 and said, "Go **a** for the present;
27:32 soldiers cut **a** the ropes of the boat and set it adrift.
27:42 so that none might swim **a** and escape;
Ro 11:27 when I take **a** their sins."
1Co 7:31 For the present form of this world is passing **a.**
13: 3 If I give **a** all my possessions,
2Co 4:16 Even though our outer nature is wasting **a,**
5: 6 while we are at home in the body we are **a** from
5: 8 be **a** from the body and at home with the Lord.
5: 9 So whether we are at home or **a,**
5:17 everything old has passed **a;**
10: 1 but bold toward you when I am **a!**—
13:10 So I write these things while I am **a** from you,
Gal 1:17 but I went **a** at once into Arabia,
5: 4 you have fallen **a** from grace.
Eph 4:22 You were taught to put **a** your former way of life,
4:25 So then, putting **a** falsehood,
4:31 Put **a** from you all bitterness and wrath and anger
2Th 3: 6 to keep **a** from believers who are living in idleness
1Ti 5:15 For some have already turned **a** to follow Satan.
6:10 to be rich some have wandered **a** from the faith
2Ti 1:15 that all who are in Asia have turned **a** from me,
2:19 on the name of the Lord turn **a** from wickedness."
4: 4 and will turn **a** from listening to the truth and wander **a** to myths.
Heb 2: 1 so that we do not drift **a** from it.
3:12 unbelieving heart that turns **a** from the living God.
6: 6 and then have fallen **a,** since
10: 4 for the blood of bulls and goats to take **a** sins.
10:11 the same sacrifices that can never take **a** sins.
11: 5 before he was taken **a** that "he had pleased God."
13: 9 not be carried **a** by all kinds of strange teachings;
Jas 1:11 in the midst of a busy life, they will wither **a.**
1:24 for they look at themselves and, on going **a,**
1Pe 3:11 let them turn **a** from evil and do good;
5: 4 the crown of glory that never fades **a.**
2Pe 3:10 and then the heavens will pass **a** with a loud noise,
3:17 beware that you are not carried **a** with the error of
1Jn 2: 8 because the darkness is passing **a** and
2:17 And the world and its desire are passing **a,**
3: 5 You know that he was revealed to take **a** sins,

Rev 7:17 and God will wipe **a** every tear from their eyes."
12: 5 But her child was snatched **a** and taken to God
12:15 to sweep her **a** with the flood.
16:20 And every island fled **a,** and no mountains were to
17: 3 So he carried me **a** in the spirit into a wilderness,
21: 1 the first heaven and the first earth had passed **a,**
21: 4 for the first things have passed **a.**"
21:10 And in the spirit he carried me **a** to a great,
22:19 if anyone takes **a** from the words of the book
22:19 God will take **a** that person's share in the tree
Tob 1:10 After I was carried **a** captive to Assyria and came
1:19 I was afraid and ran **a.**
2: 8 to be put to death for doing this, and he ran **a;**
3: 6 and do not, O Lord, turn your face **a** from me.
4: 7 Do not turn your face **a** from anyone who is poor,
4: 7 and the face of God will not be turned **a** from you.
5:18 "Why is it that you have sent my child **a?**
6: 5 Keep them with you, but throw **a** the intestines.
6: 8 and every affliction will flee **a** and never remain
7:16 Then, wiping **a** the tears, she said to her,
12: 9 from death and purges **a** every sin.
13:11 many nations will come to you from far **a,**
Jdt 2: 9 I will lead them **a** captive to the ends of
5:18 in many battles and were led **a** captive to
6:10 and take him **a** to Bethulia and hand him over to
7:14 They and their wives and children will waste **a**
16: 7 For she put **a** her widow's clothing to exalt
AdE 4:17 Mordecai went **a** and did what Esther had told him
7: 8 Haman, when he heard, turned **a** his face.
12: 3 they were led **a** to execution.
16: 4 They not only take **a** thankfulness from others,
16: 4 carried **a** by the boasts of those who know nothing
Wis 1:16 they pined **a** and made a covenant with him,
2: 4 our life will pass **a** like the traces of a cloud,
5:14 and like a light frost driven **a** by a storm;
5:23 and like a tempest it will winnow them **a.**
14:17 they imagined their appearance far **a,**
16:29 and flow **a** like waste water.
18: 5 in punishment took **a** a multitude of their children;
Sir 3:15 like frost in fair weather, your sins will melt **a.**
4: 4 or turn your face **a** from the poor.
6:13 Keep **a** from your enemies,
7: 2 Stay **a** from wrong, and it will turn **a** from you.
8: 5 Do not reproach one who is turning **a** from sin;
8:19 or you may drive **a** your happiness.
9: 8 Turn **a** your eyes from a shapely woman,
13:21 he is pushed **a** even by friends.
14: 8 he turns **a** and disregards people.
14:19 and the one who made it will pass **a** with it.
15:11 Do not say, "It was the Lord's doing that I fell **a**";
17:26 Return to the Most High and turn **a** from iniquity,
18:24 of vengeance when he turns **a** his face.
19: 3 and the reckless person will be snatched **a.**
21: 4 Panic and insolence will waste **a** riches;
22:20 One who throws a stone at birds scares them **a,**
24:32 and I will make it clear from far **a.**
26: 9 an unchaste wife; her eyelids give her **a.**
29: 9 in their need do not send them **a** empty-handed.
31: 1 Wakefulness over wealth wastes **a** one's flesh,
31: 1 and anxiety about it drives **a** sleep.
33:32 If you ill-treat him, and he leaves you and runs **a,**
34:26 To take **a** a neighbor's living is to commit murder;
38: 7 By them the physician heals and takes **a** pain;
38:19 When a person is taken **a,** sorrow is over;
38:20 drive it **a,** and remember your own end.
41:21 of taking **a** someone's portion or gift,
42:21 Nothing can be added or taken **a,**
45:23 and standing firm, when the people turned **a,**
46:11 not fall into idolatry and who did not turn **a** from
47: 4 and take **a** the people's disgrace,
47:11 The Lord took **a** his sins,
Bar 1: 8 which had been carried **a** from the temple,
1: 9 of Babylon had carried **a** from Jerusalem Jeconiah
1:13 the Lord and his wrath have not turned **a** from us.
2: 8 not entreated the favor of the Lord by turning **a,**
2:13 Let your anger turn **a** from us, for we are left,
3: 7 in our exile, for we have put **a** from our hearts all
4:11 but I sent them **a** with weeping and sorrow.
4:12 because they turned **a** from the law of God.
4:16 They led **a** the widow's beloved sons,
4:26 they were taken **a** like a flock carried off by
4:34 I will take **a** her pride in her great population,
4:37 your children are coming, whom you sent **a;**
5: 6 For they went out from you on foot, led **a**
LtJ 6: 3 after that I will bring you **a** from there in peace.
6:20 are eaten **a** when crawling creatures from
Aza 1: 6 and broken your law in turning **a** from you;
Sus 1: 9 and turned **a** their eyes from looking to Heaven
1:21 and this was why you sent your maids **a.**"
1:39 and he opened the doors and got **a.**
1Mc 2:11 All her adornment has been taken **a;**
3: 8 thus he turned **a** wrath from Israel.
4: 5 "These men are running **a** from us."
5:43 and they threw **a** their arms and fled into
6:32 Then Judas marched **a** from the citadel
6:47 and the fierce attack of the forces, they turned **a**
7:10 So they marched **a** and came with a large force
9: 6 and many slipped **a** from the camp,
9: 7 When Judas saw that his army had slipped **a** and
11:12 So he took his daughter **a** from him and gave her
12:25 So he marched **a** from Jerusalem and met them in
12:46 he sent **a** the troops, and they returned to the land
14:14 and did **a** with all the renegades and outlaws.
14:16 It was heard in Rome, and as far **a** as Sparta,
16:13 against Simon and his sons, to do **a** with them.
16:19 He sent other troops to Gazara to do **a** with John;
2Mc 3:28 and carried him **a**—this man who had just entered
5:16 and swept **a** with profane hands
5:21 and hurried **a** to Antioch, thinking in his arrogance
5:27 with about nine others, got **a** to the wilderness,
8:13 and distrustful of God's justice ran off and got **a.**
9: 9 his flesh rotted **a,** and because of the stench
10:20 let some of them slip **a.**
11:12 Most of them got **a** stripped and wounded,
14: 2 having made **a** with Antiochus
14:34 Having said this, he went **a.**
1Es 1:30 "Take me **a** from the battle, for I am very weak."
1:40 with a chain of bronze and took him **a** to Babylon.
1:41 and carried them **a,** and stored them in his temple
1:54 and carried them **a** to Babylon.
1:56 The survivors he led **a** to Babylon with the sword,
2:10 that Nebuchadnezzar had carried **a** from Jerusalem
3: 3 and when they were satisfied they went **a,**
4:11 and no one may go **a** to attend to his own affairs,
5: 7 of Babylon had carried **a** to Babylon
5:65 so that the sound was heard far **a;**
6:16 and carried the people **a** captive to Babylon.
6:26 the house in Jerusalem and carried **a** to Babylon,
6:27 to keep **a** from the place,
8:69 and the Levites have not put **a** from themselves
8:93 that we will put **a** all our foreign wives,
9:20 They pledged themselves to put **a** their wives,
9:36 and they put them **a** together with their children.
Pm 151: 7 and took **a** disgrace from the people of Israel.
3Mc 1: 3 had led the king **a** and arranged that
2:19 Wipe **a** our sins and disperse our errors,
2:24 but went **a** uttering bitter threats.
3:18 they were carried **a** by their traditional arrogance,
4: 5 sluggish and bent with age, was being led **a,**
4: 6 and were carried **a** unveiled,
5:34 The king's Friends one by one sullenly slipped **a**
6: 8 And Jonah, wasting **a** in the belly of a huge,
2Es 3:20 "Yet you did not take **a** their evil heart from them,
4:29 where the evil has been sown does not pass **a,**
5: 6 and the birds shall fly **a** together;
5:19 "Go **a** from me and do not come near me
6:20 seal is placed upon the age that is about to pass **a,**
7:33 and compassion shall pass **a,**
7:87 because they shall utterly waste **a** in confusion
7:113 [43] in which corruption has passed **a,**
7:135 [65] because he would rather give than take **a;**
8:23 whose indignation makes the mountains melt **a,**
8:54 sorrows have passed **a,** and in the end the treasure
13:40 that were taken **a** from their own land into exile in
14:14 and put **a** from you mortal thoughts;
14:14 cast **a** from you the burdens of humankind,
14:18 Truth shall go farther **a,**
15:63 They shall carry your children **a** captive,
16: 5 and who is there to drive them **a?**
16: 8 and who will drive them **a?**
16:68 of you **a** and force you to eat what was sacrificed
4Mc 4:14 went **a** to report to the king what had happened
9:28 up to his chin, and tore **a** his scalp.
13:18 to each of the brothers who were being dragged **a,**
14:17 If they are not able to keep the intruder **a,**
15:29 who carried **a** the prize of the contest

AWE (22) [AWE-INSPIRING, AWED, AWESOME, AWESTRUCK]

Jos 4:14 stood in **a** of him, as they had stood in **a** of Moses,
1Sa 18:15 he stood in **a** of him.
1Ki 3:28 and they stood in **a** of the king,
Ps 5: 7 I will bow down toward your holy temple in **a**
22:23 stand in **a** of him, all you offspring of Israel!
33: 8 the inhabitants of the world stand in **a** of him.
119:161 but my heart stands in **a** of your words.
Ecc 3:14 so that all should stand in **a** before him.
Isa 29:23 and will stand in **a** of the God of Israel.
Hos 3: 5 in **a** to the LORD and to his goodness in
Hab 3: 2 I have heard of your renown, and I stand in **a,**
Mal 2: 5 and he revered me and stood in **a** of my name.
Mt 9: 8 When the crowds saw it, they were filled with **a,**
Mk 4:41 And they were filled with great **a** and said
9:15 they were immediately overcome with **a,**
Lk 5:26 and they glorified God and were filled with **a,**
Ac 2:43 **A** came upon everyone, because many wonders
Ro 11:20 So do not become proud, but stand in **a.**
Heb 12:28 an acceptable worship with reverence and **a;**
Wis 6: 7 For the Lord of all will not stand in **a** of anyone,
3Mc 7:21 being held in honor and **a;**

AWE-INSPIRING (2) [AWE, INSPIRE]

Jdg 13: 6 like that of an angel of God, most **a;**
2Mc 1:24 you are **a** and strong and just and merciful,

AWED (1) [AWE]

Ps 65: 8 Those who live at earth's farthest bounds are **a**

AWESOME‡ (29) [AWE]

Ge 28:17 And he was afraid, and said, "How **a** is this place!
Ex 15:11 majestic in holiness, **a** in splendor,
34:10 for it is an **a** thing that I will do with you.
Dt 6:22 before our eyes great and **a** signs and wonders
7:21 who is present with you, is a great and **a** God.
10:17 the great God, mighty and **a,**
10:21 who has done for you these great and **a** things
28:58 fearing this glorious and **a** name,
2Sa 7:23 doing great and **a** things for them,
Ne 1: 5 and **a** God who keeps covenant and steadfast love
4:14 Remember the LORD, who is great and **a,**
9:32 the great and mighty and **a** God,
Job 37:22 comes golden splendor; around God is **a** majesty.
Ps 47: 2 For the LORD, the Most High, is **a,**
65: 5 By **a** deeds you answer us with deliverance,
66: 3 Say to God, "How **a** are your deeds!
66: 5 he is **a** in his deeds among mortals.
68:35 **A** is God in his sanctuary, the God of Israel;
76: 7 But you indeed are **a!**
76:11 around him bring gifts to the one who is **a,**
89: 7 great and **a** above all that are around him?
99: 3 Let them praise your great and **a** name.
106:22 and **a** deeds by the Red Sea.
111: 9 Holy and **a** is his name.
145: 6 The might of your **a** deeds shall be proclaimed,
Isa 64: 3 When you did **a** deeds that we did not expect,
Eze 1:18 Their rims were tall and **a,**
Da 9: 4 saying, "Ah, Lord, great and **a** God,
Sir 43:29 **A** is the Lord and very great,

AWESTRUCK (1) [AWE]

Ac 19:17 both Jews and Greeks, everyone was **a;**

AWL (2)

Ex 21: 6 and his master shall pierce his ear with an **a;**
Dt 15:17 an **a** and thrust it through his earlobe into the door,

AWNING (1)

Eze 27: 7 and purple from the coasts of Elishah was your **a.**

AWOKE (13) [WAKE]

Ge 9:24 When Noah **a** from his wine
41: 4 and fat cows. And Pharaoh **a.**
41: 7 Pharaoh **a,** and it was a dream.
41:21 as ugly as before. Then I **a.**
Jdg 16:14 But he **a** from his sleep, and pulled away the pin,
16:20 When he **a** from his sleep, he thought,
1Ki 3:15 Then Solomon **a;** it had been a dream.
Ps 78:65 Then the Lord **a** as from sleep,
Jer 31:26 Thereupon I **a** and looked,
Mt 1:24 When Joseph **a** from sleep,
AdE 11:12 and after he **a** he had it on his mind,
1Es 3:13 When the king **a,** they took the writing and gave it
2Es 11:29 (the one that was in the middle) suddenly **a;**

AX‡ (11) [AXES]

Dt 19: 5 when one of them swings the **a** to cut down a tree,
20:19 you must not destroy its trees by wielding an **a**
Jdg 9:48 Abimelech took an **a** in his hand,
1Ki 6: 7 nor **a** nor any tool of iron was heard in the temple
2Ki 6: 5 his **a** head fell into the water;
Isa 10:15 Shall the **a** vaunt itself over the one who wields it,
10:34 down the thickets of the forest with an **a,**
Jer 10: 3 and worked with an **a** by the hands of an artisan;
Mt 3:10 Even now the **a** is lying at the root of the trees;
Lk 3: 9 Even now the **a** is lying at the root of the trees;
LtJ 6:15 Another has a dagger in its right hand, and an **a,**

AXES (7) [AX]

1Sa 13:20 to sharpen their plowshare, mattocks, **a,**
13:21 and one-third of a shekel for sharpening the **a** and
2Sa 12:31 to work with saws and iron picks and iron **a,**
1Ch 20: 3 set them to work with saws and iron picks and **a.**
Ps 74: 5 the wooden trellis with **a.**
Jer 46:22 and come against her with **a,**
Eze 26: 9 and break down your towers with his **a.**

AXLE (1) [AXLES]

Sir 33: 5 and his thoughts like a turning **a.**

AXLES (4) [AXLE]

1Ki 7:30 Each stand had four bronze wheels and **a**
7:32 the **a** of the wheels were in the stands;
7:33 their **a,** their rims, their spokes
4Mc 9:20 of flesh were falling off the **a** of the machine.

AXLETREES (KJV) See AXLE

AYYAH (1)

1Ch 7:28 Shechem and its towns, as far as **A** and its towns;

AZAEL (1)

1Es 9:34 Shashai, Azarel, **A,** Samatus, Zambris, Joseph.

AZAL (1)

Zec 14: 5 valley between the mountains shall reach to **A;**

AZALIAH (2)

2Ki 22: 3 the king sent Shaphan son of **A,**
2Ch 34: 8 he sent Shaphan son of **A,**

AZANIAH (1)

Ne 10: 9 Jeshua son of **A,** Binnui of the sons of Henadad,

AZARAEL, AZAREEL (KJV) See AZAREL

AZAREL (7)

1Ch 12: 6 Isshiah, **A,** Joezer, and Jashobeam, the Korahites;
25:18 eleventh to **A,** his sons and his brothers, twelve;

2Ch 27:22 for Dan, A son of Jeroham.
Ezr 10:41 A, Shelemiah, Shemariah,
Ne 11:13 of A son of Ahzai son of Meshillemoth son
12:36 Shemaiah, A, Milalai, Gilalai, Maai, Nethanel,
1Es 9:34 Shashai, A, Azael, Samatus, Zambris, Joseph.

AZARIAH (71) [=ABEDNEGO, =UZZIAH]

1Ki 4: 2 A son of Zadok was the priest;
4: 5 A son of Nathan was over the officials;
2Ki 14:21 All the people of Judah took A,
15: 1 of Israel King A son of Amaziah of Judah began
15: 6 Now the rest of the acts of A, and all that he did,
15: 7 A slept with his ancestors;
15: 8 In the thirty-eighth year of King A of Judah,
15:17 In the thirty-ninth year of King A of Judah,
15:23 In the fiftieth year of King A of Judah,
15:27 In the fifty-second year of King A of Judah,
1Ch 2: 8 and Ethan's son was A.
2:38 Obed became the father of Jehu, and Jehu of A.
2:39 A became the father of Helez,
3:12 Amaziah his son, A his son, Jotham his son,
6: 9 Ahimaaz of A, A of Johanan,
6:10 and Johanan of A (it was he who served as priest
6:11 A became the father of Amariah,
6:13 Shallum of Hilkiah, Hilkiah of A,
6:14 A of Seraiah, Seraiah of Jehozadak;
6:36 son of Joel, son of A, son of Zephaniah,
9:11 and A son of Hilkiah, son of Meshullam, son
2Ch 15: 1 The spirit of God came upon A son of Oded.
15: 8 the prophecy of A son of Oded, he took courage,
21: 2 sons of Jehoshaphat: A, Jehiel, Zechariah, A,
23: 1 A son of Jeroham, Ishmael son of Jehohanan, A
26:17 But the priest A went in after him,
26:20 When the chief priest A, and all the priests,
28:12 A son of Johanan, Berechiah son of Meshillemoth,
29:12 and Joel son of A, of the sons of the Kohathites;
29:12 Kish son of Abdi, and A son of Jehallelel;
31:10 The chief priest A, who was of the house
31:13 by the appointment of King Hezekiah and of A
Ezr 7: 1 Ezra son of Seraiah, son of A, son of Hilkiah,
7: 3 son of Amariah, son of A, son of Meraioth,
Ne 3:23 After them A son of Maaseiah son
3:24 the house of A to the Angle and to the corner.
7: 7 Nehemiah, A, Raamiah, Nahamani, Mordecai,
8: 7 Akkub, Shabbethai, Hodiah, Maaseiah, Kelita, A,
10: 2 Seraiah, A, Jeremiah,
12:33 and A, Ezra, Meshullam,
Jer 42: 1 Johanan son of Kareah and A son of Hoshaiah,
43: 2 A son of Hoshaiah and Johanan son of Kareah
Da 1: 6 Mishael, and A, from the tribe of Judah.
1: 7 and A he called Abednego.
1:11 Hananiah, Mishael, and A:
1:19 Hananiah, Mishael, and A;
2:17 Hananiah, Mishael, and A,
Tob 5:13 "I am A, the son of the great Hananiah,
6: 7 to him, "Brother A, what medicinal value is there
6:14 Tobias said in answer to Raphael, "Brother A,
7: 1 Tobias said to him, "Brother A,
7: 9 Tobias said to Raphael, "Brother A,
9: 2 "Brother A, take four servants and two camels
Aza 1: 2 Then A stood still in the fire and prayed aloud:
1:26 the Lord came down into the furnace to be with A
1:66 "Bless the Lord, Hananiah, A, and Mishael;
1Mc 2:59 A, and Mishael believed and were saved from
5:18 But he left Joseph, son of Zechariah, and A,
5:56 and A, the commanders of the forces,
5:60 Then Joseph and A were routed,
1Es 8: 1 of Seraiah son of A son of Hilkiah son of Shallum
9:21 and Maaseiah and Shemaiah and Jehiel and A.
9:43 A, Uriah, Hezekiah, and Baalsamus on his right,
9:48 Hodiah, Maiannas and Kelita, A and Jozabad,
2Es 1: 1 of the prophet Ezra son of Seraiah son of A son
1: 2 of Amariah son of A son of Meraimoth son
4Mc 16:21 A, and Mishael were hurled into the fiery furnace
18:12 and he taught you about Hananiah, A,

AZARU (1)

1Es 5:15 The descendants of A, four hundred thirty-two.

AZAZ (1)

1Ch 5: 8 of A, son of Shema, son of Joel, who lived

AZAZEL (4)

Lev 16: 8 one lot for the LORD and the other lot for A.
16:10 on which the lot fell for A shall be presented alive
16:10 that it may be sent away into the wilderness to A.
16:26 for A shall wash his clothes and bathe his body

AZAZIAH (3)

1Ch 15:21 and A were to lead with lyres according to
27:20 for the Ephraimites, Hoshea son of A;
2Ch 31:13 A, Nahath, Asahel, Jerimoth, Jozabad, Eliel,

AZBUK (1)

Ne 3:16 After him Nehemiah son of A,

AZEKAH (7)

Jos 10:10 and struck them down as far as A and Makkedah.
10:11 from heaven on them as far as A, and they died;
15:35 Jarmuth, Adullam, Socoh, A,
1Sa 17: 1 and encamped between Socoh and A,
2Ch 11: 9 Adoraim, Lachish, A,
Ne 11:30 Lachish and its fields, and A and its villages.
Jer 34: 7 the cities of Judah that were left, Lachish and A;

AZEL (6)

1Ch 8:37 Raphah was his son, Eleasah his son, A his son.
8:38 A had six sons, and these are their names:
8:38 all these were the sons of A.
9:43 Rephaiah was his son, Eleasah his son, A his son.
9:44 A had six sons, and these are their names:
9:44 these were the sons of A.

AZEM (KJV) See EZEM

AZETAS (1)

1Es 5:15 The descendants of Kilan and A, sixty-seven.

AZGAD (6)

Ezr 2:12 Of A, one thousand two hundred twenty-two.
8:12 the descendants of A, Johanan son of Hakkatan,
Ne 7:17 Of A, two thousand three hundred twenty-two.
10:15 Bunni, A, Bebai,
1Es 5:13 six hundred twenty-three. The descendants of A,
8:38 the descendants of A, Johanan son of Hakkatan,

AZIEL (1)

1Ch 15:20 A, Shemiramoth, Jehiel, Unni, Eliab, Maaseiah,

AZIZA (1)

Ezr 10:27 Eliashib, Mattaniah, Jeremoth, Zabad, and A.

AZMAVETH (8) [BETH-AZMAVETH]

2Sa 23:31 Abi-albon the Arbathite; A of Bahurim;
1Ch 8:36 and Jehoaddah became the father of Alemeth, A,
9:42 and Jarah of Alemeth, A, and Zimri;
11:33 A of Baharum, Eliahba of Shaalbon,
12: 3 also Jeziel and Pelet sons of A;
27:25 Over the king's treasuries was A son of Adiel.
Ezr 2:24 The descendants of A, forty-two.
Ne 12:29 and from the region of Geba and A;

AZMON (3)

Nu 34: 4 then it shall go on to Hazar-addar, and cross to A;
34: 5 boundary shall turn from A to the Wadi of Egypt,
Jos 15: 4 passes along to A, goes out by the Wadi of Egypt,

AZNOTH-TABOR (1) [TABOR]

Jos 19:34 then the boundary turns westward to A,

AZOR (2)

Mt 1:13 and Eliakim the father of A,
1:14 and A the father of Zadok,

AZOTUS (13)

Ac 8:40 But Philip found himself at A,
Jdt 2:28 in A and Ascalon feared him greatly.
1Mc 4:15 and to the plains of Idumea, and to A and Jamnia;
5:68 But Judas turned aside to A in the land of
9:15 and he pursued them as far as Mount A.
10:77 and went to A as though he were going farther.
10:78 Jonathan pursued him to A,
10:83 They fled to A and entered Beth-dagon,
10:84 But Jonathan burned A and the surrounding towns
11: 4 When he approached A, they showed him
11: 4 and A and its suburbs destroyed,
14:34 and Gazara, which is on the borders of A,
16:10 into the towers that were in the fields of A,

AZRIEL (3)

1Ch 5:24 Epher, Ishi, Eliel, A, Jeremiah, Hodaviah,
27:19 for Naphtali, Jerimoth son of A;
Jer 36:26 of A and Shelemiah son of Abdeel to arrest

AZRIKAM (6)

1Ch 3:23 sons of Neariah: Elioenai, Hizkiah, and A, three.
8:38 Azel had six sons, and these are their names: A,
9:14 Shemaiah son of Hasshub, son of A,
9:44 Azel had six sons, and these are their names: A,
2Ch 28: 7 A the commander of the palace,
Ne 11:15 of Hasshub son of A son of Hashabiah son

AZUBAH‡ (4)

1Ki 22:42 His mother's name was A daughter of Shilhi.
1Ch 2:18 Caleb son of Hezron had children by his wife A,
2:19 When A died, Caleb married Ephrath,
2Ch 20:31 His mother's name was A daughter of Shilhi.

AZUR (KJV) See AZZUR

AZZAH (KJV) See GAZA

AZZAN (1)

Nu 34:26 of the Issacharites a leader, Paltiel son of A.

AZZUR (3)

Ne 10:17 Ater, Hezekiah, A,
Jer 28: 1 the prophet Hananiah son of A, from Gibeon,
Eze 11: 1 among them I saw Jaazaniah son of A,

B

BAAL (68) [BAAL'S, BAALS, BAMOTH-BAAL, GUR-BAAL, KIRIATH-BAAL]

Nu 25: 3 Thus Israel yoked itself to the B of Peor,
25: 5 who have yoked themselves to the B of Peor."
Dt 4: 3 the LORD did with regard to the B of Peor—
4: 3 among you everyone who followed the B of Peor,
Jdg 2:13 and worshiped B and the Astartes.
6:25 the altar of B that belongs to your father, and cut
6:28 the altar of B was broken down,
6:30 for he has pulled down the altar of B and cut down
6:31 "Will you contend for B?
6:32 that is to say, "Let B contend against him,"
1Ki 16:31 and went and served B, and worshiped him.
16:32 He erected an altar for B in the house of B,
18:19 of B and the four hundred prophets of Asherah,
18:21 but if B, then follow him."
18:25 Then Elijah said to the prophets of B,
18:26 called on the name of B from morning until noon,
18:26 crying, "O B, answer us!"
18:40 Elijah said to them, "Seize the prophets of B;
19:18 all the knees that have not bowed to B,
22:53 He served B and worshiped him;
2Ki 3: 2 the pillar of B that his father had made.
10:18 "Ahab offered B small service;
10:19 therefore summon to me all the prophets of B,
10:19 for I have a great sacrifice to offer to B;
10:19 in order to destroy the worshipers of B.
10:20 Jehu decreed, "Sanctify a solemn assembly for B."
10:21 all the worshipers of B came,
10:21 They entered the temple of B,
10:21 until the temple of B was filled from wall to wall.
10:22 the vestments for all the worshipers of B."
10:23 the temple of B with Jehonadab son of Rechab;
10:23 he said to the worshipers of B,
10:23 but only worshipers of B."
10:25 and then went into the citadel of the temple of B.
10:26 the pillar that was in the temple of B,
10:27 Then they demolished the pillar of B,
10:27 and destroyed the temple of B,
10:28 Thus Jehu wiped out B from Israel.
11:18 all the people of the land went to the house of B,
11:18 and they killed Mattan, the priest of B,
17:16 worshiped all the host of heaven, and served B.
21: 3 he erected altars for B, made a sacred pole,
23: 4 for B, for Asherah, and for all the host of heaven;
23: 5 those also who made offerings to B, to the sun,
1Ch 4:33 that were around these towns as far as B.
5: 5 Micah his son, Reaiah his son, B his son,
8:30 His firstborn son: Abdon, then Zur, Kish, B,
9:36 His firstborn son was Abdon, then Zur, Kish, B,
2Ch 23:17 Then all the people went to the house of B,
23:17 and they killed Mattan, the priest of B,
Ps 106:28 Then they attached themselves to the B of Peor,
Jer 2: 8 the prophets prophesied by B,
7: 9 swear falsely, make offerings to B,
11:13 altars to make offerings to B.
11:17 provoking me to anger by making offerings to B.
12:16 as they taught my people to swear by B,
19: 5 building the high places of B to burn their children
in the fire as burnt offerings to B,
23:13 prophesied by B and led my people Israel astray.
23:27 just as their ancestors forgot my name for B.
32:29 on whose roofs offerings have been made to B
32:35 They built the high places of B in the valley of
Hos 2: 8 upon her silver and gold that they used for B.
2:16 and no longer will you call me, "My B."
13: 1 but he incurred guilt through B and died.
Zep 1: 4 from this place every remnant of B and the name
Ro 11: 4 not bowed the knee to B."

BAAL'S (1) [BAAL]

1Ki 18:22 but B prophets number four hundred fifty.

BAAL-BERITH (2)

Jdg 8:33 with the Baals, making B their god.
9: 4 of B with which Abimelech hired worthless

BAAL-GAD (3) [GAD]

Jos 11:17 as far as B in the valley
12: 7 from B in the valley of Lebanon to Mount Halak,
13: 5 from B below Mount Hermon to Lebo-hamath,

BAAL-HAMON (1) [HAMON-GOG]

SS 8:11 Solomon had a vineyard at B;

BAAL-HANAN (5)

Ge 36:38 and B son of Achbor succeeded him as king.
36:39 B son of Achbor died, and Hadar succeeded him
1Ch 1:49 Shaul died, B son of Achbor succeeded him.
1:50 When B died, Hadad succeeded him;
27:28 and sycamore trees in the Shephelah was B

BAAL-HAZOR (1) [HAZOR]
2Sa 13:23 two full years Absalom had sheepshearers at B,

BAAL-HERMON (2) [HERMON]
Jdg 3: 3 from Mount B as far as Lebo-hamath.
1Ch 5:23 they were very numerous from Bashan to B,

BAAL-MEON (3) [BETH-BAAL-MEON, BETH-MEON]
Nu 32:38 and B (some names being changed), and Sibmah;
1Ch 5: 8 who lived in Aroer, as far as Nebo and B.
Eze 25: 9 the glory of the country, Beth-jeshimoth, B,

BAAL-PEOR (1) [PEOR]
Hos 9:10 But they came to B, and consecrated themselves to

BAAL-PERAZIM (4) [PERAZIM]
2Sa 5:20 David came to B, and David defeated them there.
5:20 Therefore that place is called B.
1Ch 14:11 he went up to B, and David defeated them there.
14:11 Therefore that place is called B.

BAAL-SHALISHAH (1) [SHALISHAH]
2Ki 4:42 from B, bringing food from the first fruits to

BAAL-TAMAR (1)
Jdg 20:33 of the Israelites drew back its battle line to B,

BAAL-ZEBUB (4)
2Ki 1: 2 telling them, "Go, inquire of B, the god of Ekron,
1: 3 in Israel that you are going to inquire of B,
1: 6 in Israel that you are sending to inquire of B,
1:16 you have sent messengers to inquire of B,

BAAL-ZEPHON (3)
Ex 14: 2 between Migdol and the sea, in front of B;
14: 9 by Pi-hahiroth, in front of B.
Nu 33: 7 which faces B; and they camped before Migdol.

BAALAH (5) [=KIRIATH-JEARIM]
Jos 15: 9 then the boundary bends around to B (that is,
15:10 and the boundary circles west of B to Mount Seir,
15:11 and passes along to Mount B,
15:29 B, Iim, Ezem,
1Ch 13: 6 And David and all Israel went up to B, that is,

BAALATH (3)
Jos 19:44 Eltekeh, Gibbethon, B,
1Ki 9:18 B, Tamar in the wilderness, within the land,
2Ch 8: 6 and B, as well as all Solomon's storage towns,

BAALATH-BEER (1)
Jos 19: 8 the villages all around these towns as far as B,

BAALE-JUDAH (1)
2Sa 6: 2 the people with him set out and went from B,

BAALI (KJV) See BAAL

BAALIM (KJV) See BAALS

BAALIS (1)
Jer 40:14 "Are you at all aware that B king of

BAALS (18) [BAAL]
Jdg 2:11 in the sight of the LORD and worshiped the B;
3: 7 and worshiping the B and the Asherahs.
8:33 and prostituted themselves with the B,
10: 6 worshiping the B and the Astartes,
10:10 and have worshiped the B."
1Sa 7: 4 So Israel put away the B and the Astartes,
12:10 and have served the B and the Astartes;
1Ki 18:18 of the LORD and followed the B.
2Ch 17: 3 he did not seek the B,
24: 7 of the house of the LORD for the B.
28: 2 He even made cast images for the B;
33: 3 and erected altars to the B, made sacred poles,
34: 4 down the altars of the B;
Jer 2:23 "I am not defiled, I have not gone after the B"?
9:14 and have gone after the B,
Hos 2:13 I will punish her for the festival days of the B,
2:17 I will remove the names of the B from her mouth,
11: 2 they kept sacrificing to the B,

BAALSAMUS (1)
1Es 9:43 Azariah, Uriah, Hezekiah, and B on his right,

BAANA (3)
1Ki 4:12 B son of Ahilud, in Taanach, Megiddo,
4:16 B son of Hushai, in Asher and Bealoth;
Ne 3: 4 Next to them Zadok son of B made repairs.

BAANAH (10)
2Sa 4: 2 the name of the one was B,
4: 5 sons of Rimmon the Beerothite, Rechab and B,
4: 6 then Rechab and his brother B escaped.
4: 9 David answered Rechab and his brother B,
2Sa 23:29 Heleb son of B of Netophah;
1Ch 11:30 Heled son of B of Netophah,
Ezr 2: 2 Bilshan, Mispar, Bigvai, Rehum, and B.
Ne 7: 7 Mordecai, Bilshan, Mispereth, Bigvai, Nehum, B.
10:27 Malluch, Harim, and B.
1Es 5: 8 Aspharasus, Reeliah, Rehum, and B, their leaders.

BAARA (1)
1Ch 8: 8 after he had sent away his wives Hushim and B.

BAASEIAH (1)
1Ch 6:40 son of Michael, son of B, son of Malchijah,

BAASHA (28)
1Ki 15:16 between Asa and King B of Israel all their days.
15:17 King B of Israel went up against Judah,
15:19 go, break your alliance with King B of Israel,
15:21 When B heard of it, he stopped building Ramah
15:22 with which B had been building;
15:27 B son of Ahijah, of the house of Issachar,
15:27 and B struck him down at Gibbethon,
15:28 So B killed Nadab in the third year of King Asa
15:32 between Asa and King B of Israel all their days.
15:33 B son of Ahijah began to reign over all Israel
16: 1 the LORD came to Jehu son of Hanani against B,
16: 3 I will consume B and his house,
16: 4 Anyone belonging to B who dies in the city
16: 5 Now the rest of the acts of B, what he did,
16: 6 B slept with his ancestors,
16: 7 by the prophet Jehu son of Hanani against B
16: 8 Elah son of B began to reign over Israel in Tirzah;
16:11 he killed all the house of B;
16:12 Thus Zimri destroyed all the house of B,
16:12 which he spoke against B by the prophet Jehu—
16:13 of all the sins of B and the sins of his son Elah
21:22 and like the house of B son of Ahijah,
2Ki 9: 9 and like the house of B son of Ahijah.
2Ch 16: 1 King B of Israel went up against Judah,
16: 3 go, break your alliance with King B of Israel,
16: 5 When B heard of it, he stopped building Ramah,
16: 6 with which B had been building,
Jer 41: 9 for defense against King B of Israel;

BABBLE (4) [BABBLER, BABBLERS, BABBLING]
2Ki 9:11 "You know the sort and how they b."
Job 11: 3 Should your b put others to silence,
Sir 7:14 Do not b in the assembly of the elders,
32: 9 and when another is speaking, do not b.

BABBLER (2) [BABBLE]
Pr 20:19 therefore do not associate with a b.
Ac 17:18 Some said, "What does this b want to say?"

BABBLERS (1) [BABBLE]
Sir 21:25 The lips of b speak of what is not their concern.

BABBLING‡ (3) [BABBLE]
Pr 10: 8 but a b fool will come to ruin.
10:14 but the b of a fool brings ruin near.
Hos 7:16 So much for their b in the land of Egypt.

BABBLINGS (KJV) See CHATTER

BABEL‡ (2) [BABYLON]
Ge 10:10 The beginning of his kingdom was B, Erech,
11: 9 Therefore it was called B,

BABE, BABES (KJV) See also CHILD, CHILDREN, INFANTS

BABES (3) [BABY]
Ps 8: 2 of the mouths of b and infants you have founded
Isa 3: 4 and b shall rule over them.
La 2:11 infants and b faint in the streets of the city.

BABIES (5) [BABY]
Mt 21:16 of infants and nursing b you have prepared praise
2Mc 6:10 with their b hanging at their breasts,
8: 4 also the lawless destruction of the innocent b and
3Mc 5:49 and daughters, and others with b
5:50 removing the b from their breasts,

BABOONS See Index to Footnotes

BABY (1) [BABES, BABIES]
Ex 2: 2 and when she saw that he was a fine b,

BABYLON‡ (340) [BABEL, BABYLON'S, BABYLONIA, BABYLONIANS]
A. KING OF BABYLON (85)
B. DAUGHTER BABYLON (5)

2Ki 17:24 The king of Assyria brought people from B,
17:30 the people of B made Succoth-benoth, the people
20:12 of Baladan of B sent envoys with letters and
20:14 "They have come from a far country, from B."
20:17 up until this day, shall be carried to B;
20:18 be eunuchs in the palace of the king of B." A
24: 1 In his days King Nebuchadnezzar of B came up;
24: 7 the king of B had taken over all that belonged A
24:10 the servants of King Nebuchadnezzar of B came
24:11 King Nebuchadnezzar of B came to the city,
24:12 of Judah gave himself up to the king of B, A
24:12 king of B took him prisoner in the eighth year A
24:15 He carried away Jehoiachin to B;
24:15 he took into captivity from Jerusalem to B.
24:16 The king of B brought captive to Babylon all A
24:16 The king of Babylon brought captive to B all
24:17 The king of B made Mattaniah, A
24:20 Zedekiah rebelled against the king of B. A
25: 1 King Nebuchadnezzar of B came with all his army
25: 6 and brought him up to the king of B at Riblah, A
25: 7 they bound him in fetters and took him to B.
25: 8 of King Nebuchadnezzar, king of B— A
25: 8 a servant of the king of B, came to Jerusalem. A
25:11 the deserters who had defected to the king of B A
25:13 and carried the bronze to B.
25:20 and brought them to the king of B at Riblah. A
25:21 The king of B struck them down and put them A
25:22 whom King Nebuchadnezzar of B had left.
25:23 king of B had appointed Gedaliah as governor, A
25:24 live in the land, serve the king of B, A
25:27 King Evil-merodach of B,
25:28 of the kings who were with him in B.
1Ch 9: 1 into exile in B because of their unfaithfulness.
2Ch 32:31 in the matter of the envoys of the officials of B,
33:11 bound him with fetters, and brought him to B.
36: 6 Against him King Nebuchadnezzar of B came up,
36: 6 and bound him with fetters to take him to B.
36: 7 of the LORD to B and put them in his palace in B.
36:10 to B, along with the precious vessels of the house
36:18 all these he brought to B.
36:20 He took into exile in B those who had escaped
Ezr 2: 1 of B had carried captive to Babylonia;
5:12 into the hand of King Nebuchadnezzar of B,
5:13 However, King Cyrus of B,
5:14 and had brought into the temple of B,
5:14 these King Cyrus took out of the temple of B,
5:17 a search made in the royal archives there in B,
6: 1 where the documents were stored in B.
6: 5 and brought to B, be restored and brought back to
7: 9 the first month the journey up from B was begun,
Ne 7: 6 of B had carried into exile;
13: 6 of King Artaxerxes of B I went to the king.
Est 2: 6 King Nebuchadnezzar of B had carried away.
Ps 87: 4 those who know me I mention Rahab and B;
137: 1 By the rivers of B—there we sat down and
137: 8 O daughter B, you devastator! B
Isa 13: 1 oracle concerning B that Isaiah son of Amoz saw.
13:19 And B, the glory of kingdoms,
14: 4 you will take up this taunt against the king of B: A
14:22 and will cut off from B name and remnant,
21: 9 Then he responded, "Fallen, fallen is B;
39: 1 of Baladan of B sent envoys with letters and
39: 3 to me from a far country, from B."
39: 6 up until this day, shall be carried to B;
39: 7 be eunuchs in the palace of the king of B." A
43:14 For your sake I will send to B and break down all
47: 1 and sit in the dust, virgin daughter B! B
48:14 he shall perform his purpose on B,
48:20 Go out from B, flee from Chaldea,
Jer 20: 4 into the hand of the king of B; A
20: 4 he shall carry them captive to B,
20: 5 and seize them, and carry them to B.
20: 6 shall go into captivity, and to B you shall go;
21: 2 for King Nebuchadrezzar of B is making war
21: 4 which you are fighting against the king of B A
21: 7 into the hands of King Nebuchadrezzar of B,
21:10 it shall be given into the hands of the king of B, A
22:25 even into the hands of King Nebuchadrezzar of B
24: 1 after King Nebuchadrezzar of B had taken
24: 1 and the smiths, and had brought them to B.
25: 1 the first year of King Nebuchadrezzar of B),
25: 9 even for King Nebuchadrezzar of B, my servant,
25:11 the king of B seventy years. A
25:12 I will punish the king of B and that nation, A
27: 6 into the hand of King Nebuchadnezzar of B,
27: 8 of B, and put its neck under the yoke of the king
27: 8 and put its neck under the yoke of the king of B, A
27: 9 'You shall not serve the king of B.' A
27:11 under the yoke of the king of B and serve him, A
27:12 your necks under the yoke of the king of B, A
27:13 that will not serve the king of B? A
27:14 not to serve the king of B, A
27:16 be brought back from B," for they are prophesying
27:17 Do not listen to them; serve the king of B and A
27:18 and in Jerusalem may not go to B.
27:20 of B did not take away when he took into exile
27:20 into exile from Jerusalem to B King Jeconiah son
27:22 They shall be carried to B,
28: 2 I have broken the yoke of the king of B. A
28: 3 which King Nebuchadnezzar of B took away
28: 3 from this place and carried to B.
28: 4 and all the exiles from Judah who went to B,
28: 4 for I will break the yoke of the king of B." A
28: 6 and bring back to this place from B the vessels of
28:11 of King Nebuchadnezzar of B from the neck of all
28:14 that they may serve King Nebuchadnezzar of B,
29: 1 into exile from Jerusalem to B.
29: 3 of Judah sent to B to King Nebuchadnezzar of B.
29: 4 into exile from Jerusalem to B:
29:15 "The LORD has raised up prophets for us in B,"—
29:20 from Jerusalem to B, hear the word of
29:21 into the hand of King Nebuchadrezzar of B,
29:22 be used by all the exiles from Judah in B:

Jer 29:22 whom the king of **B** roasted in the fire," A
29:28 For he has actually sent to us in **B**, saying,
32: 2 of the king of **B** was besieging Jerusalem, A
32: 3 the hand of the king of **B**, and he shall take it; A
32: 4 into the hands of the king of **B**, and shall speak A
32: 5 to **B**, and there he shall remain until I attend
32:28 and into the hand of King Nebuchadrezzar of **B**,
32:36 "It is being given into the hand of the king of **B** A
34: 1 when King Nebuchadrezzar of **B** and all his army
34: 2 to give this city into the hand of the king of **B**, A
34: 3 king of **B** eye to eye and speak with him face A
34: 3 and you shall go to **B**.
34: 7 the king of **B** was fighting against Jerusalem A
34:21 to the army of the king of **B**, A
35:11 when King Nebuchadrezzar of **B** came up against
36:29 the king of **B** will certainly come and destroy A
37: 1 whom King Nebuchadrezzar of **B** made king in
37:17 "You shall be handed over to the king of **B**." A
37:19 'The king of **B** will not come against you and A
38: 3 be handed over to the army of the king of **B** A
38:17 to the officials of the king of **B**, A
38:18 not surrender to the officials of the king of **B**, A
38:22 to the officials of the king of **B** and saying, A
38:23 but shall be seized by the king of **B**; A
39: 1 King Nebuchadrezzar of **B** and all his army came
39: 3 of the king of **B** came and sat in the middle gate: A
39: 3 with all the rest of the officials of the king of **B**. A
39: 5 up to King Nebuchadrezzar of **B**, at Riblah,
39: 6 The king of **B** slaughtered the sons of Zedekiah A
39: 6 king of **B** slaughtered all the nobles of Judah. A
39: 7 and bound him in fetters to take him to **B**.
39: 9 the captain of the guard exiled to **B** the rest of
39:11 King Nebuchadrezzar of **B** gave command
39:13 and all the chief officers of the king of **B** sent A
40: 1 and Judah who were being exiled to **B**.
40: 4 If you wish to come with me to **B**, come,
40: 4 but if you do not wish to come with me to **B**,
40: 5 king of **B** appointed governor of the towns of A
40: 7 that the king of **B** had appointed Gedaliah son A
40: 7 of the land who had not been taken into exile to **B**,
40: 9 Stay in the land and serve the king of **B**, A
40:11 in other lands heard that the king of **B** had left A
41: 2 king of **B** had appointed him governor in the A
41:18 the king of **B** had made governor over the land. A
42:11 Do not be afraid of the king of **B**, A
43: 3 that they may kill us or take us into exile in **B**."
43:10 and take my servant King Nebuchadrezzar of **B**,
44:30 into the hand of King Nebuchadrezzar of **B**,
46: 2 and which King Nebuchadrezzar of **B** defeated in
46:13 the coming of King Nebuchadrezzar of **B** to attack
46:26 to King Nebuchadrezzar of **B** and his officers.
49:28 of Hazor that King Nebuchadrezzar of **B** defeated.
49:30 For King Nebuchadrezzar of **B** has made a plan
50: 1 The word that the LORD spoke concerning **B**,
50: 2 **B** is taken, Bel is put to shame,
50: 8 from **B**, and go out of the land of the Chaldeans,
50: 9 up and bring against **B** a company of great nations
50:13 everyone who passes by **B** shall be appalled
50:14 Take up your positions around **B**,
50:16 Cut off from **B** the sower,
50:17 of **B** has gnawed its bones.
50:18 I am going to punish the king of **B** and his land, A
50:23 How **B** has become a horror among the nations!
50:24 O **B**, but you did not know it;
50:28 of **B** are coming to declare in Zion the vengeance
50:29 Summon archers against **B**, all who bend the bow.
50:34 but unrest to the inhabitants of **B**.
50:35 says the LORD, and against the inhabitants of **B**,
50:39 wild animals shall live with hyenas in **B**,
50:42 against you, O daughter **B**! B
50:43 The king of **B** heard news of them, A
50:45 hear the plan that the LORD has made against **B**,
50:46 of the capture of **B** the earth shall tremble,
51: 1 to stir up a destructive wind against **B** and against
51: 2 and I will send winnowers to **B**,
51: 6 Flee from the midst of **B**, save your lives,
51: 7 **B** was a golden cup in the LORD's hand,
51: 8 Suddenly **B** has fallen and is shattered;
51: 9 We tried to heal **B**, but she could not be healed.
51:11 because his purpose concerning **B** is to destroy it,
51:12 Raise a standard against the walls of **B**;
51:12 concerning the inhabitants of **B**.
51:24 I will repay **B** and all the inhabitants of Chaldea
51:29 for the LORD's purposes against **B** stand,
51:29 to make the land of **B** a desolation,
51:30 The warriors of **B** have given up fighting,
51:31 to tell the king of **B** that his city is taken from A
51:33 Daughter **B** is like a threshing floor at the time B
51:34 "King Nebuchadrezzar of **B** has devoured me,
51:35 May my torn flesh be avenged on **B**,"
51:37 and **B** shall become a heap of ruins,
51:41 How **B** has become an object of horror among the
51:42 The sea has risen over **B**;
51:44 I will punish Bel in **B**,
51:44 the wall of **B** has fallen.
51:47 when I will punish the images of **B**;
51:48 and all that is in them, shall shout for joy over **B**;
51:49 **B** must fall for the slain of Israel,
51:49 the slain of all the earth have fallen because of **B**.
51:53 Though **B** should mount up to heaven,
51:54 Listen!—a cry from **B**!
51:55 For the LORD is laying **B** waste,
51:56 for a destroyer has come against her, against **B**;
51:58 The broad wall of **B** shall be leveled to the ground,
51:59 when he went with King Zedekiah of Judah to **B**,
51:60 in a scroll all the disasters that would come on **B**,
51:60 all these words that are written concerning **B**.
Jer 51:61 "When you come to **B**, see
51:64 'Thus shall **B** sink, to rise no more,
52: 3 Zedekiah rebelled against the king of **B**. A
52: 4 King Nebuchadrezzar of **B** came with all his army A
52: 9 to the king of **B** at Riblah in the land of Hamath, A
52:10 king of **B** killed the sons of Zedekiah before A
52:11 and the king of **B** took him to Babylon, A
52:11 and the king of Babylon took him to **B**,
52:12 of King Nebuchadrezzar, king of **B**— A
52:12 of the bodyguard who served the king of **B**, A
52:15 the deserters who had defected to the king of **B**, A
52:17 and carried all the bronze to **B**.
52:26 and brought them to the king of **B** at Riblah. A
52:27 And the king of **B** struck them down, A
52:31 King Evil-merodach of **B**,
52:32 of the other kings who were with him in **B**.
52:34 the king of **B**, as long as he lived, up to the day A
Eze 12:13 and I will bring him to **B**,
17:12 Tell them: The king of **B** came to Jerusalem, A
17:12 and brought them back with him to **B**.
17:16 with him he broke—in **B** he shall die.
17:20 to **B** and enter into judgment with him there for
19: 9 and brought him to the king of **B**; A
21:19 out two roads for the sword of the king of **B** A
21:21 the king of **B** stands at the parting of the way, A
24: 2 king of **B** has laid siege to Jerusalem this very A
26: 7 from the north King Nebuchadrezzar of **B**,
29:18 of **B** made his army labor hard against Tyre;
29:19 the land of Egypt to King Nebuchadrezzar of **B**;
30:10 by the hand of King Nebuchadrezzar of **B**.
30:24 I will strengthen the arms of the king of **B**, A
30:25 I will strengthen the arms of the king of **B**, A
30:25 I put my sword into the hand of the king of **B**. A
32:11 sword of the king of **B** shall come against you. A
Da 1: 1 King Nebuchadnezzar of **B** came to Jerusalem
2:12 and commanded that all the wise men of **B**
2:14 who had gone out to execute the wise men of **B**;
2:18 the rest of the wise men of **B** might not perish.
2:24 the wise men of **B**, and said to him, "Do not
destroy the wise men of **B**;
2:48 of **B** and chief prefect over all the wise men of **B**.
2:49 Abednego over the affairs of the province of **B**.
3: 1 up on the plain of Dura in the province of **B**.
3:12 over the affairs of the province of **B**:
3:30 Meshach, and Abednego in the province of **B**.
4: 6 the wise men of **B** should be brought before me,
4:29 on the roof of the royal palace of **B**,
4:30 "Is this not magnificent **B**,
5: 7 and the king said to the wise men of **B**,
7: 1 In the first year of King Belshazzar of **B**,
Mic 4:10 in the open country; you shall go to **B**.
Zec 2: 7 Escape to Zion, you that live with daughter **B**. B
6:10 who have arrived from **B**;
Mt 1:11 at the time of the deportation to **B**.
1:12 And after the deportation to **B**:
1:17 and from David to the deportation to **B**,
1:17 and from the deportation to **B** to the Messiah,
Ac 7:43 so I will remove you beyond **B**.'
1Pe 5:13 Your sister church in **B**, chosen together with you,
Rev 14: 8 followed, saying, "Fallen, fallen is **B** the great!
16:19 God remembered great **B** and gave her
17: 5 "**B** the great, mother of whores and
18: 2 "Fallen, fallen is **B** the great!
18:10 "Alas, alas, the great city, **B**, the mighty city!
18:21 "With such violence **B** the great city will
Tob 14: 4 So it will be safer in Media than in Assyria and **B**.
AdE 2: 6 whom King Nebuchadnezzar of **B** had captured.
11: 4 of **B** had brought from Jerusalem
Bar 1: 1 of Hasadiah son of Hilkiah wrote in **B**,
1: 4 all who lived in **B** by the river Sud.
1: 9 after King Nebuchadnezzar of **B** had carried away
1: 9 and the people of the land, and brought them to **B**.
1:11 pray for the life of King Nebuchadnezzar of **B**,
1:12 the protection of King Nebuchadnezzar of **B**,
2:21 Bend your shoulders and serve the king of **B**, A
2:22 of the Lord and will not serve the king of **B**, A
2:24 to serve the king of **B**; A
LtJ 6: 1 to those who were to be taken to **B** as exiles by
6: 2 be taken to **B** as exiles by Nebuchadnezzar,
6: 3 when you have come to **B** you will remain there
6: 4 in **B** you will see gods made of silver and gold
Sus 1: 1 a man living in **B** whose name was Joakim.
1: 5 "Wickedness came forth from **B**,
Bel 1:34 "Take the food that you have to **B**, to Daniel,
1:35 Habakkuk said, "Sir, I have never seen **B**,
1:36 with the speed of the wind he set him down in **B**,
1Mc 6: 4 in great disappointment left there to return to **B**.
1Es 1:40 King Nebuchadnezzar of **B** came up against him;
1:40 with a chain of bronze and took him away to **B**.
1:41 and stored them in his temple in **B**.
1:45 and removed him to **B**, with the holy vessels of
1:54 and the royal stores, and carried them away to **B**.
1:56 The survivors he led away to **B** with the sword,
2:15 by Sheshbazzar with the returning exiles from **B**
4:44 when he began to destroy **B**,
4:57 from **B** all the vessels that Cyrus had set apart;
4:61 and went to **B** and told this to all his kindred.
5: 7 Nebuchadnezzar of **B** had carried away to **B**
6:15 into the hands of King Nebuchadnezzar of **B**, king
6:16 and carried the people away captive to **B**.
6:18 from the temple in **B**, and they were delivered
6:21 of our lord the king that are in **B**;
6:23 in the royal archives that were deposited in **B**.
6:26 of the house in Jerusalem and carried away to **B**,
8: 3 up from **B** as a scribe skilled in the law of Moses,
8: 6 for they left **B** on the new moon of the first month
8:28 who went up with me from **B**,
3Mc 6: 6 in **B** who had voluntarily surrendered their lives to
2Es 3: 1 I was in **B**—I, Salathiel, who am also called Ezra.
3: 2 of Zion and the wealth of those who lived in **B**.
3:28 Are the deeds of those who inhabit **B** any better?
3:31 Are the deeds of **B** better than those of Zion?
15:43 They shall go on steadily to **B** and blot it out.
15:46 in the splendor of **B** and the glory of her person—
15:60 when they return from devastated **B**.
16: 1 Woe to you, **B** and Asia!

BABYLON'S (1) [BABYLON]

Jer 29:10 **B** seventy years are completed will I visit you,

BABYLONIA (10) [BABYLON]

Ezr 1:11 the exiles were brought up from **B** to Jerusalem.
2: 1 of Babylon had carried captive to **B**;
5:12 and carried away the people to **B**.
7: 6 this Ezra went up from **B**.
7:16 that you shall find in the whole province of **B**,
8: 1 with me from **B**, in the reign of King Artaxerxes:
2Mc 8:20 in **B**, when eight thousand Jews fought along
1Es 4:53 and that all who came from **B** to build
6:17 that Cyrus reigned over the country of **B**,
8:13 and silver that may be found in the country of **B**,

BABYLONIANS (9) [BABYLON]

Ezr 4: 9 the **B**, the people of Susa, that is, the Elamites,
Eze 23:15 a picture of **B** whose native land was Chaldea.
23:17 And the **B** came to her into the bed of love,
23:23 the **B** and all the Chaldeans,
LtJ 6: 1 be taken to Babylon as exiles by the king of the **B**,
6: 2 as exiles by Nebuchadnezzar, king of the **B**.
Bel 1: 3 Now the **B** had an idol called Bel,
1:23 a great dragon, which the **B** revered.
1:28 When the **B** heard about it,

BABYLONISH (KJV) See SHINAR

BACA (1)

Ps 84: 6 As they go through the valley of **B** they make it

BACCHIDES (22) [BACCHIDES']

1Mc 7: 8 So the king chose **B**, one of the king's Friends,
7:12 a body before Alcimus and **B** to ask for just terms.
7:19 Then **B** withdrew from Jerusalem and encamped
7:20 then **B** went back to the king.
9: 1 he sent **B** and Alcimus into the land of Judah
9:11 Then the army of **B** marched out from the camp
9:12 **B** was on the right wing.
9:14 that **B** and the strength of his army were on
9:25 **B** chose the godless and put them in charge of
9:26 for the friends of Judas, and brought them to **B**,
9:29 like him to go against our enemies and **B**,
9:32 When **B** learned of this, he tried to kill him.
9:34 **B** found this out on the sabbath day,
9:43 When **B** heard of this, he came with a large force
9:47 and Jonathan stretched out his hand to strike **B**,
9:50 Then **B** returned to Jerusalem
9:57 When **B** saw that Alcimus was dead,
9:58 So now let us bring **B** back,
9:63 **B** learned of this, he assembled all his forces,
9:68 They fought with **B**, and he was crushed by them.
10:12 in the strongholds that **B** had built fled;
2Mc 8:30 and **B** they killed more than twenty thousand

BACCHIDES' (1) [BACCHIDES]

1Mc 9:49 And about one thousand of **B** men fell that day.

BACCHURUS See Index to Footnotes

BACHRITES (KJV) See BECHERITES

BACENOR'S (1)

2Mc 12:35 But a certain Dositheus, one of **B** men,

BACK‡ (575) [BACKBITING, BACKBONE, BACKS, BACKSLIDING, BACKWARD]

Ge 8:11 the dove came **b** to him in the evening, and there
14: 7 they turned **b** and came to En-mishpat (that is,
14:16 Then he brought **b** all the goods,
14:16 and also brought **b** his nephew Lot with his goods,
15:16 they shall come **b** here in the fourth generation;
19: 9 But they replied, "Stand **b**!"
19:17 do not look **b** or stop anywhere in the Plain;
19:26 But Lot's wife, behind him, looked **b**,
22: 5 we will worship, and then we will come **b** to you."
24: 5 must I then take your son **b** to the land
24: 6 "See to it that you do not take my son **b** there.
24: 8 only you must not take my son **b** there."
24:54 he said, "Send me **b** to my master."
27:45 then I will send, and bring you **b** from there.
28:15 and will bring you **b** to this land;
29: 3 the stone **b** in its place on the mouth of the well.
37:14 and bring word **b** to me."
38:29 But just then he drew **b** his hand,
39: 9 has he kept **b** anything from me except yourself,
42:28 "My money has been put **b**;
42:37 "You may kill my two sons if I do not bring him **b**
42:37 and I will bring him **b** to you."
43: 9 not bring him **b** to you and set him before you,
43:12 Carry **b** with you the money that was returned in

Ge 43:14 he may send **b** your other brother and Benjamin.
43:21 So we have brought it **b** with us.
44: 8 we brought **b** to you from the land of Canaan;
44:24 When we went **b** to your servant my father we told
44:32 saying, 'If I do not bring him **b** to you,
44:33 and let the boy go **b** with his brothers.
44:34 can I go **b** to my father if the boy is not with me?
45:17 load your animals and go **b** to the land of Canaan.
50:15 and pays us **b** in full for all the wrong that we did
Ex 2:18 "How is it that you have come **b** so soon today?"
4: 3 and Moses drew **b** from it.
4: 7 God said, "Put your hand **b** into your cloak"—
4: 7 so he put his hand **b** into his cloak,
4:18 Moses went **b** to his father-in-law Jethro and said
4:18 "Please let me go **b** to my kindred in Egypt
4:19 LORD said to Moses in Midian, "Go **b** to Egypt;
4:20 on a donkey and went **b** to the land of Egypt;
4:21 LORD said to Moses, "When you go **b** to Egypt,
10: 8 So Moses and Aaron were brought **b** to Pharaoh,
14: 2 Tell the Israelites to turn **b** and camp in front
14:10 As Pharaoh drew near, the Israelites looked **b,**
14:21 the sea **b** by a strong east wind all night,
14:26 so that the water may come **b** upon the Egyptians,
15:19 the LORD brought **b** the waters of the sea
18: 2 his father-in-law Jethro took her **b,**
23: 4 or donkey going astray, you shall bring it **b.**
23: 5 and you would hold **b** from setting it free,
26:12 shall hang over the **b** of the tabernacle.
32:15 written on the front and on the **b.**
32:27 Go **b** and forth from gate to gate throughout
33:23 and you shall see my **b;**
Lev 25:41 they shall go **b** to their own family and return
26:23 of these punishments you have not turned **b** to me,
Nu 10:30 I will go **b** to my own land and to my kindred."
13:26 they brought **b** word to them and to all
14: 3 would it not be better for us to go **b** to Egypt?"
14: 4 "Let us choose a captain, and go **b** to Egypt."
14:43 you have turned **b** from following the LORD,
17:10 "Put **b** the staff of Aaron before the covenant,
22: 8 "Stay here tonight, and I will bring **b** word to you,
22:23 to turn it **b** onto the road.
24:25 Then Balaam got up and went **b** to his place,
25:11 has turned **b** my wrath from the Israelites
33: 7 and turned **b** to Pi-hahiroth,
35:25 Then the congregation shall send the slayer **b** to
Dt 1:22 the land for us and bring **b** a report to us regarding
1:25 They brought **b** a report to us, and said,
1:40 But as for you, journey **b** into the wilderness,
2: 1 we journeyed **b** into the wilderness,
8: 4 on your **b** did not wear out and your feet did
16: 7 the next morning you may go **b** to your tents.
20: 5 He should go **b** to his house,
20: 6 He should go **b** to his house,
20: 7 He should go **b** to his house,
20: 8 He should go **b** to his house,
22: 1 you shall take them **b** to their owner.
23:11 he may come **b** into the camp.
23:15 from their owners shall not be given **b** to them.
24:13 You shall give the pledge **b** by sunset,
24:19 you shall not go **b** to get it;
28:60 He will bring **b** upon you all the diseases of Egypt,
28:68 The LORD will bring you **b** in ships to Egypt,
29: 5 The clothes on your **b** have not worn out,
30: 4 and from there he will bring you **b.**
Jos 8:20 So when the men of Ai looked **b,**
8:20 for the people who fled to the wilderness turned **b**
8:21 then they turned **b** and struck down the men of Ai.
8:26 For Joshua did not draw **b** his hand,
10:38 with all Israel, turned **b** to Debir and assaulted it,
11:10 Joshua turned **b** at that time, and took Hazor,
18: 4 Then come **b** to me.
18: 8 the land and write a description of it, and come **b**
18: 9 then they came **b** to Joshua in the camp at Shiloh,
22: 8 "Go **b** to your tents with much wealth,
22:32 to the Israelites, and brought **b** word to them.
23: 5 LORD your God will push them **b** before you,
23:12 For if you turn **b,** and join the survivors
Jdg 1: 7 as I have done, so God has paid me **b.**"
1:34 The Amorites pressed the Danites **b** into
3:19 But he himself turned **b** at the sculptured stones
7: 8 he sent all the rest of Israel **b** to their own tents,
8: 9 "When I come **b** victorious,
9:57 the wickedness of the people of Shechem fall **b**
11: 8 "Nevertheless, we have now turned **b** to you,
11:35 and I cannot take **b** my vow."
14:19 In hot anger he went **b** to his father's house.
16:28 so that with this one act of revenge I may pay **b**
18:26 he turned and went **b** to his home.
19: 3 to speak tenderly to her and bring her **b.**
20:26 the whole army, went **b** to Bethel and wept,
20:33 the Israelites drew **b** its battle line to Baal-tamar,
20:48 the Israelites turned **b** against the Benjaminites,
Ru 1: 7 and they went on their way to go **b** to the land
1: 8 "Go **b** each of you to your mother's house.
1:11 But Naomi said, "Turn **b,** my daughters,
1:12 Turn **b,** my daughters, go your way,
1:15 your sister-in-law has gone **b** to her people and
1:16 to leave you or to turn **b** from following you!
1:21 but the LORD has brought me **b** empty;
1:22 who came **b** with her from the country of Moab.
2: 6 "She is the Moabite who came **b** with Naomi from
3:15 and put it on her **b;** then he went into the city.
3:17 not go **b** to your mother-in-law empty-handed.' "
4: 3 who has come **b** from the country of Moab,
1Sa 1:19 then they went **b** to their house at Ramah.
5: 3 So they took Dagon and put him **b** in his place.
7:17 Then he would come **b** to Ramah,
1Sa 9: 5 "Let us turn **b,** or my father will stop worrying
10:25 Then Samuel sent all the people **b** to their homes.
14:16 as the multitude was surging **b** and forth.
15:11 for he has turned **b** from following me,
15:31 So Samuel turned **b** after Saul;
17:15 but David went **b** and forth from Saul
17:53 The Israelites came **b** from chasing the Philistines,
23:23 and come **b** to me with sure information.
25:12 and came **b** and told him all this.
25:39 and has kept **b** his servant from evil;
26:21 Then Saul said, "I have done wrong; come **b,**
27: 9 and the clothing, and came **b** to Achish.
27:11 nor woman alive to be brought **b** to Gath,
29: 4 of the Philistines said to him, "Send the man **b,**
29: 7 So go **b** now; and go peaceably;
30:19 David brought **b** everything.
2Sa 1:22 the bow of Jonathan did not turn **b,**
2:20 Abner looked **b** and said, "Is it you, Asahel?"
2:23 so that the spear came out at his **b.**
3:16 Abner said to him, "Go **b** home!" So he went **b.**
3:26 and they brought him **b** from the cistern of Sirah;
3:39 The LORD pay **b** the one who does wickedly
5: 6 even the blind and the lame will turn you **b**"—
6:19 Then all the people went **b** to their homes.
11:12 and tomorrow I will send you **b.**"
11:15 and then draw **b** from him,
11:23 but we drove them **b** to the entrance of the gate.
12:23 Can I bring him **b** again?
14:21 go, bring **b** the young man Absalom."
15: 8 If the LORD will indeed bring me **b** to Jerusalem,
15:19 Go **b,** and stay with the king;
15:20 Go **b,** and take your kinsfolk with you;
15:25 "Carry the ark of God **b** into the city.
15:25 he will bring me **b** and let me see both it and
15:27 "Look, go **b** to the city in peace, you and Abiathar,
15:29 So Zadok and Abiathar carried the ark of God **b**
16: 3 Israel will give me **b** my grandfather's kingdom.' "
17: 3 the people **b** to you as a bride comes home
18:16 and the troops came **b** from pursuing Israel,
19:10 about bringing the king **b?**"
19:11 'Why should you be the last to bring the king **b**
19:12 then should you be the last to bring **b** the king?'
19:15 So the king came **b** to the Jordan;
19:24 from the day the king left until the day he came **b**
19:43 not the first to speak of bringing **b** our king?"
22:38 and did not turn **b** until they were consumed.
23:10 people came **b** to him—but only to strip the dead.
24: 8 they came **b** to Jerusalem at the end
1Ki 2:32 The LORD will bring **b** his bloody deeds
2:33 So shall their blood come **b** on the head of Joab
2:44 LORD will bring **b** your evil on your own head.
7: 8 in the other court **b** of the hall,
7: 9 **b** and front, from the foundation to the coping,
10:19 The top of the throne was rounded in the **b,**
13: 4 against him withered so that he could not draw it **b**
13:18 Bring him **b** with you into your house so
13:19 Then the man of God went **b** with him,
13:20 to the prophet who had brought him **b;**
13:22 but have come **b** and have eaten food
13:23 to the prophet who had brought him **b.**
13:26 When the prophet who had brought him **b** from
13:29 laid it on the donkey, and brought it **b** to the city,
14: 9 and have thrust me behind your **b;**
14:28 the guard carried them and brought them **b** to
18:37 are God, and that you have turned their hearts **b.**"
19:20 Then Elijah said to him, "Go **b** again;
22:33 they turned **b** from pursuing him.
2Ki 1: 6 'Go **b** to the king who sent you, and say to him:
2:13 and went **b** and stood on the bank of the Jordan.
2:18 they came **b** to him (he had remained at Jericho),
4:22 to the man of God and come **b** again."
4:24 do not hold **b** for me unless I tell you."
4:31 He came **b** to meet him and told him,
7: 8 Then they came **b,** entered another tent,
9:11 When Jehu came **b** to his master's officers,
9:18 but he is not coming **b.**"
9:20 "He reached them, but he is not coming **b.**
9:30 When they came **b** and told him, he said,
15:20 So the king of Assyria turned **b,**
19:21 behind your **b,** daughter Jerusalem.
19:28 I will turn you **b** on the way by which you came.
20: 5 "Turn **b,** and say to Hezekiah prince
20:11 and he brought the shadow **b** the ten intervals,
22:20 They took the message **b** to the king.
1Ch 19: 4 throughout all Israel, and came **b** to Jerusalem.
21:27 and he put his sword **b** into its sheath.
2Ch 11: 4 of the LORD and turned **b** from the expedition
12:11 and would then bring them **b** to the guardroom.
18:32 they turned **b** from pursuing him.
19: 4 and brought them **b** to the LORD,
24:19 Yet he sent prophets among them to bring them **b**
25:13 But the men of the army whom Amaziah sent **b,**
25:28 They brought him **b** on horses;
28:11 and send **b** the captives whom you have taken
34:28 They took the message **b** to the king.
Ezr 6: 5 and brought **b** to the temple in Jerusalem, each
Ne 2:15 Then I turned **b** and entered by the Valley Gate,
4: 4 turn their taunt **b** on their own heads,
5: 8 bought **b** our Jewish kindred who had been sold
5: 8 who must then be bought **b** by us!"
7: 5 of those who were the first to come **b,** and I found
9:26 who had warned them in order to turn them **b**
9:29 And you warned them in order to turn them **b**
13: 9 and I brought **b** the vessels of the house of God,
13:10 had gone **b** to their fields.
Est 2:14 in the morning she came **b** to the second harem
Job 9:13 "God will not turn **b** his anger;
Job 17:10 But you, come **b** now, all of you,
20:10 and their hands will give **b** their wealth.
20:18 They will give **b** the fruit of their toil,
21:19 Let it be paid **b** to them, so that they may know it.
33:27 and it was not paid **b** to me.
33:30 to bring **b** their souls from the Pit,
34:14 If he should take **b** his spirit to himself,
34:33 Will he then pay **b** to suit you,
39:22 it does not turn **b** from the sword.
41:15 Its **b** is made of shields in rows,
Ps 6:10 they shall turn **b,** and in a moment be put
9: 3 When my enemies turned **b,**
18:37 and did not turn **b** until they were consumed.
19:13 Keep **b** your servant also from the insolent;
35: 4 be turned **b** and confounded who devise evil
37:21 The wicked borrow, and do not pay **b,**
40:14 let those be turned **b** and brought
44:10 You made us turn **b** from the foe,
44:18 Our heart has not turned **b,**
59: 6 Each evening they come **b,**
59:14 Each evening they come **b,**
68:22 The Lord said, "I will bring them **b** from Bashan,
68:22 I will bring them **b** from the depths of the sea,
70: 2 be turned **b** and brought to dishonor who desire
70: 3 turn **b** because of their shame.
74:11 Why do you hold **b** your hand;
78: 9 armed with the bow, turned **b** on the day of battle.
80:18 Then we will never turn **b** from you;
89:43 you have turned **b** the edge of his sword,
90: 3 You turn us **b** to dust, and say, "Turn **b,**
114: 3 The sea looked and fled; Jordan turned **b.**
114: 5 O Jordan, that you turn **b?**
119:101 I hold **b** my feet from every evil way,
129: 3 The plowers plowed on my **b;**
132:11 to David a sure oath from which he will not turn **b:**
137: 8 be who pay you **b** what you have done to us!
Pr 2:19 those who go to her never come **b,**
10:13 but a rod is for the **b** of one who lacks sense.
11:26 The people curse those who hold **b** grain,
19:24 and will not even bring it **b** to the mouth.
21:26 but the righteous give and do not hold **b.**
24:11 if you hold **b** from rescuing those taken away
24:29 I will pay them **b** for what they have done."
26: 3 and a rod for the **b** of fools.
26:15 and is too tired to bring it **b** to the mouth.
26:27 stone will come **b** on the one who starts it rolling.
29:11 but the wise quietly holds it **b.**
30:30 among wild animals and does not turn **b**
Ecc 11: 1 for after many days you will get it **b.**
SS 3:10 He made its posts of silver, its **b** of gold,
Isa 14:27 His hand is stretched out, and who will turn it **b?**
21:12 If you will inquire, inquire; come **b** again."
28: 6 strength to those who turn **b** the battle at the gate.
31: 2 he does not call **b** his words,
31: 6 Turn **b** to him whom you have deeply betrayed,
37:22 behind your **b,** daughter Jerusalem.
37:29 I will turn you **b** on the way by which you came.
38: 8 on the dial of Ahaz turn **b** ten steps."
38: 8 So the sun turned **b** on the dial the ten steps
38:17 but you have held **b** my life from the pit
38:17 for you have cast all my sins behind your **b.**
42:17 They shall be turned **b** and utterly put to shame—
44:25 who turns **b** the wise, and makes their knowledge
49: 5 to bring Jacob **b** to him, and that Israel might be
50: 6 I gave my **b** to those who struck me,
51:23 and you have made your **b** like the ground and like
54: 2 be stretched out; do not hold **b;**
55:12 For you shall go out in joy, and be led **b** in peace;
57:17 but they kept turning **b** to their own ways.
58: 1 Shout out, do not hold **b!**
59:14 Justice is turned **b,** and righteousness stands at
63:17 Turn **b** for the sake of your servants,
66:15 to pay **b** his anger in fury,
Jer 4:28 I have not relented nor will I turn **b.**
5: 3 they have refused to turn **b.**
8: 4 If they go astray, do they not turn **b?**
11:10 They have turned **b** to the iniquities
15:19 says the LORD: If you turn **b,** I will take you **b,**
16:15 For I will bring them **b** to their own land
18:17 I will show them my **b,** not my face,
21: 4 to turn **b** the weapons of war that are in your hands
23: 3 and I will bring them **b** to their fold,
23:20 of the LORD will not turn **b** until he has executed
23:26 Will the hearts of the prophets ever turn **b**—
24: 6 and I will bring them **b** to this land.
26: 2 do not hold **b** a word.
27:16 of the LORD's house will soon be brought **b**
28: 3 Within two years I will bring **b** to this place all
28: 4 I will also bring **b** to this place King Jeconiah son
28: 6 that you have prophesied, and bring **b** to this place
29:10 to you my promise and bring you **b** to this place.
29:14 and I will bring you **b** to the place
30: 3 and I will bring them **b** to the land that I gave
30:24 of the LORD will not turn **b** until he has executed
31: 9 and with consolations I will lead them **b,**
31:16 they shall come **b** from the land of the enemy;
31:17 your children shall come **b** to their own country.
31:18 Bring me **b,** let me come **b,**
32:37 I will bring them **b** to this place,
32:40 never to draw **b** from doing good to them;
34:11 But afterward they turned around and took **b**
34:16 of you took **b** your male and female slaves,
34:22 and will bring them **b** to this city;
37:20 to my plea, and do not send me **b** to the house of
38:26 the king not to send me **b** to the house of Jonathan
41:14 from Mizpah turned around and came **b,**
41:16 whom Johanan brought **b** from Gibeon.

Jer 42: 4 I will keep nothing **b** from you.”
44:14 Although they long to go **b** to live there,
44:14 they shall not go **b**, except some fugitives.
46: 5 Why do I see them terrified? They have fallen **b**;
46: 5 They do not look **b**—terror is all around!
46:16 let us go **b** to our own people and to the land
47: 3 parents do not turn **b** for children,
48:10 the one who keeps **b** the sword from bloodshed.
48:39 How Moab has turned his **b** in shame!
49: 8 Flee, turn **b**, get down low, inhabitants of Dedan!
La 1:13 for my feet; he turned me **b**;
3:64 Pay them **b** for their deeds, O LORD,
Eze 2:10 it had writing on the front and on the **b**,
9:11 with the writing case at his side, brought **b** word,
17:12 and brought them **b** with him to Babylon.
23:35 you have forgotten me and cast me behind your **b**,
29:14 and bring them **b** to the land of Pathros,
33:11 turn **b**, turn **b** from your evil ways;
33:15 give **b** what they have taken by robbery,
34: 4 you have not brought **b** the strayed,
34:16 I will seek the lost, and I will bring **b** the strayed,
37:12 and I will bring you **b** to the land of Israel.
39:27 when I have brought them **b** from the peoples
40:13 the gate from the **b** of the one recess to the **b** of
42: 6 for this reason the upper chambers were set **b** from
44: 1 he brought me **b** to the outer gate of the sanctuary,
47: 1 he brought me **b** to the entrance of the temple;
47: 6 Then he led me **b** along the bank of the river.
47: 7 As I came **b**, I saw on the bank of the river
Da 7: 6 The beast had four wings of a bird on its **b**
11:18 indeed, he shall turn his insolence **b** upon him.
11:19 Then he shall turn **b** toward the fortresses
11:30 He shall turn **b** and pay heed to those who forsake
12: 4 Many shall be running **b** and forth,
Hos 2: 9 Therefore I will take **b** my grain in its time,
12:14 down on him and pay him **b** for his insults.
Joel 3: 4 Are you paying me **b** for something?
3: 4 If you are paying me **b**,
3: 4 I will turn your deeds **b**
3: 7 and I will turn your deeds **b** upon your own heads.
Jnh 1:13 the men rowed hard to bring the ship **b** to land,
Na 2: 8 Halt!”—but no one turns **b**.
Zep 1: 6 those who have turned **b** from following
Zec 5: 8 So he thrust her **b** into the basket,
10: 6 I will bring them **b** because I have compassion
Mt 24:18 the one in the field must not turn **b** to get a coat.
26:52 Jesus said to him, “Put your sword **b** into its place;
27: 3 he repented and brought **b** the thirty pieces
28: 2 came and rolled **b** the stone and sat on it.
Mk 6:25 Immediately she rushed **b** to the king
11: 3 and will send it **b** here immediately.’ ”
13:16 the one in the field must not turn **b** to get a coat.
15:13 They shouted **b**, “Crucify him!”
16: 4 which was very large, had already been rolled **b**.
16:13 ⟦And they went **b** and told the rest,⟧
Lk 4:20 he rolled up the scroll, gave it **b** to the attendant,
6:38 measure you give will be the measure you get **b**.”
8:31 They begged him not to order them to go **b** into
9:42 healed the boy, and gave him **b** to his father.
9:62 to the plow and looks **b** is fit for the kingdom
10:35 of him; and when I come **b**,
15:27 because he has got him **b** safe and sound.’
15:30 But when this son of yours came **b**,
17: 4 and turns **b** to you seven times and says, ‘I repent,’
17:15 when he saw that he was healed, turned **b**,
17:31 and likewise anyone in the field must not turn **b**.
18:30 who will not get **b** very much more in this age,
19: 8 I will pay **b** four times as much.”
19:13 ‘Do business with these until I come **b**.’
22:32 and you, when once you have turned **b**,
23:11 then he put an elegant robe on him, and sent him **b**
23:15 Neither has Herod, for he sent him **b** to us.
24:23 they came **b** and told us that they had indeed seen
Jn 4: 3 he left Judea and started **b** to Galilee.
4:16 “Go, call your husband, and come **b**.”
4:28 woman left her water jar and went **b** to the city.
6:66 of his disciples turned **b** and no longer went about
7:45 Then the temple police went **b** to the chief priests
9: 7 Then he went and washed and came **b** able to see.
11:28 she went **b** and called her sister Mary,
18: 6 “I am he,” they stepped **b** and fell to the ground.
18:11 “Put your sword **b** into its sheath.
Ac 5: 2 he kept **b** some of the proceeds,
5: 3 the Holy Spirit and to keep **b** part of the proceeds
7:16 and their bodies were brought **b** to Shechem
7:39 and in their hearts they turned **b** to Egypt,
14:26 From there they sailed **b** to Antioch,
22: 5 and to bring them **b** to Jerusalem for punishment.
22:29 about to examine him drew **b** from him;
Ro 8:15 For you did not receive a spirit of slavery to fall **b**
11:24 be grafted **b** into their own olive tree.
2Co 1:16 and to come **b** to you from Macedonia
Gal 2:12 he drew **b** and kept himself separate for fear of
4: 9 how can you turn **b** again to the weak
Col 3:25 be paid **b** for whatever wrong has been done,
2Ti 4:14 the Lord will pay him **b** for his deeds.
Tit 2: 9 they are not to talk **b**,
Phm 1:12 I am sending him, that is, my own heart, **b** to you.
1:15 so that you might have him **b** forever,
Heb 10:38 soul takes no pleasure in anyone who shrinks **b**.”
10:39 But we are not among those who shrink **b** and
11:19 and figuratively speaking, he did receive him **b**.
13:20 who brought **b** from the dead our Lord Jesus,
Jas 5: 4 which you kept **b** by fraud, cry out,
5:19 from the truth and is brought **b** by another,
5:20 you should know that whoever brings **b** a sinner
2Pe 2:21 to turn **b** from the holy commandment
2Pe 2:22 “The dog turns **b** to its own vomit,” and,
Rev 5: 1 a scroll written on the inside and on the **b**, sealed
7: 1 holding **b** the four winds of the earth so
12: 7 The dragon and his angels fought **b**,
Tob 2: 2 I will wait for you, until you come **b**.”
5: 3 But get **b** the money from Gabael.”
5:22 and he will come **b** in good health.”
6:13 from Rages we will take her and bring her **b**
10: 7 Tobias came to him and said, “Send me **b**,
10: 9 I beg you to send me **b** to my father.”
10:12 the Lord of heaven bring you **b** safely,
12: 2 to give him half of the possessions brought **b**
12: 3 For he has led me **b** to you safely,
12: 3 he brought the money **b** with me,
12: 4 my child, to receive half of all that he brought **b**.”
12: 5 for your wages half of all that you brought **b**,
13: 6 ‘Turn **b**, you sinners, and do what is right
14: 5 and God will bring them **b** into the land of Israel;
Jdt 1:11 So they sent **b** his messengers empty-handed and
5:19 and have come **b** from the places
6: 7 to take you **b** into the hill country and put you
7:15 Thus you will pay them **b** with evil,
11:14 in order to bring **b** permission from the council of
16:11 and the enemy were turned **b**.
AdE 4:13 Mordecai told him to go **b** and say to her,
4:15 the messenger this answer to take **b** to Mordecai:
6:12 and Haman hurried **b** to his house,
9:25 against the Jews came **b** upon himself,
Wis 2: 5 because it is sealed up and no one turns **b**.
16:13 down to the gates of Hades and **b** again.
16:14 but cannot bring **b** the departed spirit,
17:19 an echo thrown **b** from a hollow of the mountains,
18:10 But the discordant cry of their enemies echoed **b**,
18:23 he intervened and held **b** the wrath,
Sir 1:23 and then cheerfulness comes **b** to them.
1:24 They hold **b** their words until the right moment;
4:18 Then she will come straight **b** to them again
5: 7 Do not delay to turn **b** to the Lord,
12: 5 hold **b** their bread, and do not give it to them,
17:25 Turn **b** to the Lord and forsake your sins;
18:13 and turns them **b**, as a shepherd his flock.
20:10 and the gift to be paid **b** double.
20:15 Today he lends and tomorrow he asks it **b**;
21:15 he laughs at it and throws it behind his **b**.
22:21 do not despair, for there is a way **b**.
26:28 a man who turns **b** from righteousness to sin—
27:27 If a person does evil, it will roll **b** upon him,
29: 5 and pays **b** with empty promises,
29: 6 If he can pay, his creditor will hardly get **b** half,
36:25 but a person with experience will pay him **b**.
38:21 Do not forget, there is no coming **b**;
42: 5 of drawing blood from the **b** of a wicked slave.
Bar 4:23 but God will give you **b** to me with joy
5: 6 but God will bring them **b** to you, carried in glory,
Sus 1:14 But turning **b**, they met again;
1:50 So all the people hurried **b**.
1Mc 2:68 Pay **b** the Gentiles in full,
3: 6 Lawbreakers shrank **b** for fear of him;
4:16 Judas and his force turned **b** from pursuing them,
5:28 Then Judas and his army quickly turned **b** by
7:20 then Bacchides went **b** to the king.
7:46 and they outflanked the enemy and drove them **b**
9: 9 and let us come **b** with our kindred and fight them;
9:58 So now let us bring Bacchides **b**,
9:69 Then he decided to go **b** to his own land.
9:72 then he turned and went **b** to his own land,
10:13 all of them left their places and went **b**
10:43 and receive **b** all their property in my kingdom.
11:42 And Demetrius sent this message **b** to Jonathan:
11:72 Then he turned **b** to the battle against the enemy
12:51 that they would fight for their lives, they turned **b**.
13:24 Then Trypho turned and went **b** to his own land.
13:27 with polished stone at the front and **b**.
2Mc 1:32 when the light from the altar shone **b**, it went out.
3:38 for you will get him **b** thoroughly flogged,
5: 5 the troops on the wall had been forced **b** and at last
5:18 this man would have been flogged and turned **b**
7:11 and from him I hope to get them **b** again.”
7:23 in his mercy give life and breath **b** to you again,
7:29 that in God's mercy I may get you **b** again along
9:16 and all the holy vessels he would give **b**,
9:21 On my way **b** from the region of Persia I suffered
12:12 receiving his pledges they went **b** to their tents.
12:39 the bodies of the fallen and to bring them **b** to lie
13:19 was turned **b**, attacked again, and was defeated.
14:44 But as they quickly drew **b**,
14:46 upon the Lord of life and spirit to give them **b**
1Es 1:28 Josiah, however, did not turn **b** to his chariot,
1:31 and after he was brought **b** to Jerusalem he died,
1:38 and seized his brother Zarius and brought him **b**
1:50 their ancestors sent his messenger to call them **b**,
2:15 and they were carried **b** by Sheshbazzar with
4:24 he brings it **b** to the woman he loves.
4:44 and to send **b** all the vessels that were taken
4:44 and vowed to send them **b** there.
4:57 And he sent **b** from Babylon all the vessels
5: 2 a thousand cavalry to take them **b** to Jerusalem
5:56 and all who had come **b** to Jerusalem from exile;
6:19 that he should take all these vessels **b**
8:87 but we turned **b** again to transgress your law
3Mc 4:11 to make them an obvious spectacle to all coming **b**
6:21 The animals turned **b** upon
6:27 Send them **b** to their homes in peace,
2Es 2:11 Moreover, I will take **b** to myself their glory,
4: 5 or call **b** for me the day that is past.”
4:42 to give **b** those things that were committed to them
7:30 be turned **b** to primeval silence for seven days,
2Es 10:16 you will receive your son **b** in due time,
16: 3 and who is there to turn it **b**?
16: 7 Can one turn **b** an arrow shot by a strong archer?
4Mc 11:10 they twisted his **b** around the wedge on the wheel,
11:10 so that he was completely curled **b** like a scorpion,
11:18 upon it, his **b** was broken, and he was roasted
11:19 To his **b** they applied sharp spits
13: 5 in those who were not turned **b** by fiery agonies?
13: 6 For just as towers jutting out over harbors hold **b**
18:20 to the catapult and **b** again to more tortures,

BACKBITING (1) [BACK, BITE]

Pr 25:23 The north wind produces rain, and a **b** tongue,

BACKBITING, BACKBITINGS (KJV) See also SLANDER

BACKBONE (1) [BACK, BONE]

Lev 3: 9 which shall be removed close to the **b**,

BACKS (18) [BACK]

Ex 23:27 I will make all your enemies turn their **b** to you.
Dt 33:29 and you shall tread on their **b**.
Jos 7: 8 now that Israel has turned their **b** to their enemies!
7:12 they turn their **b** to their enemies,
2Sa 22:41 You made my enemies turn their **b** to me,
2Ch 29: 6 the dwelling of the LORD, and turned their **b**.
Ne 9:26 against you and cast your law behind their **b**
Ps 18:40 You made my enemies turn their **b** to me,
66:11 you laid burdens on our **b**;
Pr 14: 3 The talk of fools is a rod for their **b**,
19:29 and flogging for the **b** of fools.
Isa 11:14 down on the **b** of the Philistines in the west,
30: 6 they carry their riches on the **b** of donkeys,
Jer 2:27 they have turned their **b** to me, and not their faces.
32:33 They have turned their **b** to me, not their faces;
Eze 8:16 with their **b** to the temple of the LORD,
Ro 11:10 and keep their **b** forever bent.”
3Mc 3:24 behind our **b** as traitors and barbarous enemies.

BACKSLIDERS, BACKSLIDING (KJV) See also APOSTASIES, DISLOYALTY, FAITHLESS, PERVERSE, STUBBORN, UNFAITHFUL, WAYWARDNESS

BACKSLIDING (1) [BACK]

Jer 8: 5 then has this people turned away in perpetual **b**?

BACKWARD (11) [BACK]

Ge 9:23 and walked **b** and covered the nakedness
49:17 that bites the horse's heels so that its rider falls **b**.
1Sa 4:18 Eli fell over **b** from his seat by the side of the gate;
Job 23: 8 or **b**, I cannot perceive him;
Ps 129: 5 be put to shame and turned **b**.
Isa 28:13 in order that they may go, and fall **b**,
50: 5 and I was not rebellious, I did not turn **b**.
Jer 7:24 and looked **b** rather than forward.
15: 6 says the LORD, you are going **b**;
Sir 48:23 In Isaiah's days the sun went **b**,
3Mc 1:20 and without a **b** look they crowded together at

BAD‡ (59) [BADLY, WORSE, WORST]

Ge 24:50 we cannot speak to you anything **b** or good.
31:24 that you say not a word to Jacob, either good or **b**.”
31:29 that you speak to Jacob neither good nor **b**.’
37: 2 Joseph brought a **b** report of them to their father.
Ex 5:21 You have brought us into **b** odor with Pharaoh
Lev 5: 4 Or when any of you utter aloud a rash oath for a **b**
27:10 either good for **b** or **b** for good;
27:12 The priest shall assess it: whether good or **b**,
27:14 whether good or **b**, as the priest assesses it,
27:33 Let no one inquire whether it is good or **b**,
Nu 13:19 and whether the land they live in is good or **b**,
14:36 against him by bringing a **b** report about
24:13 to do either good or **b** of my own will;
Jos 23:15 so the LORD will bring upon you all the **b** things,
2Sa 13:22 But Absalom spoke to Amnon neither good nor **b**;
2Ki 2:19 but the water is **b**, and the land is unfruitful.”
Ne 6:13 and so they could give me a **b** name,
Job 2:10 at the hand of God, and not receive the **b**?”
Pr 13:17 A **b** messenger brings trouble,
20:14 **“B, b,”** says the buyer, then goes away and boasts.
25:19 Like a **b** tooth or a lame foot is trust in
29:21 from childhood will come to a **b** end.
Ecc 5:14 and those riches were lost in a **b** venture;
Jer 24: 2 but the other basket had very **b** figs, so **b** that they
24: 3 the **b** figs very **b**, so **b** that they cannot be eaten.”
24: 8 the **b** figs that are so **b** they cannot be eaten,
29:17 like rotten figs that are so **b** they cannot be eaten.
42: 6 Whether it is good or **b**,
49:23 for they have heard **b** news;
La 3:38 of the Most High that good and **b** come?
Eze 8:17 Is it not **b** enough that the house of Judah commits
Mt 7:17 but the **b** tree bears **b** fruit.
7:18 A good tree cannot bear **b** fruit, nor can a **b** tree bear good fruit.
12:33 or make the tree **b**, and its fruit **b**;
13:48 and put the good into baskets but threw out the **b**.
22:10 gathered all whom they found, both good and **b**;
Lk 6:43 “No good tree bears **b** fruit, nor again does a **b** tree bear good fruit;

Ro 9:11 or had done anything good or **b**
13: 3 rulers are not a terror to good conduct, but to **b.**
1Co 15:33 "**B** company ruins good morals."
2Ti 3:13 But wicked people and impostors will go from **b**
Sir 6: 1 for a **b** name incurs shame and reproach;
11:14 Good things and **b,** life and death,
23:14 and behave like a fool through **b** habit;
26: 7 A **b** wife is a chafing yoke;
31:13 Remember that a greedy eye is a **b** thing.
37:27 see what is **b** for you and do not give in to it.
39:25 but for sinners good things and **b.**
1Es 9: 6 shivering because of the **b** weather that prevailed.

BADE (1) [BID]
Tob 10:12 Then he **b** them farewell and let them go.

BADGER (2) [BADGERS]
Lev 11: 5 The rock **b,** for even though it chews the cud,
Dt 14: 7 the camel, the hare, and the rock **b,**

BADGERS (1) [BADGER]
Pr 30:26 the **b** are a people without power,

BADGERS' SKINS (KJV) See FINE LEATHER

BADLY (6) [BAD]
Ge 43: 6 "Why did you treat me so **b** as to tell the man
Nu 11:11 "Why have you treated your servant so **b?**
1Sa 31: 3 and he was **b** wounded by them.
2Ch 35:23 "Take me away, for I am **b** wounded."
Sir 3:26 A stubborn mind will fare **b** at the end,
1Mc 6: 8 he was astounded and **b** shaken.

BAEAN (1)
1Mc 5: 4 also remembered the wickedness of the sons of **B,**

BAFFLES (1)
Sir 10:10 A long illness **b** the physician;

BAG (20) [BAGGAGE, BAGS, HANDBAGS]
Ge 42:35 there in each one's sack was his **b** of money.
Dt 25:13 You shall not have in your **b** two kinds of weights,
1Sa 17:40 and put them in his shepherd's **b,** in the pouch;
17:49 David put his hand in his **b,** took out a stone,
Job 14:17 my transgression would be sealed up in a **b,**
Pr 7:20 He took a **b** of money with him;
16:11 all the weights in the **b** are his work.
SS 1:13 to me a **b** of myrrh that lies between my breasts.
Mic 6:11 Can I tolerate wicked scales and a **b**
Hag 1: 6 that earn wages earn wages to put them into a **b**
Mt 10:10 no **b** for your journey, or two tunics, or sandals,
Mk 6: 8 no bread, no **b,** no money in their belts;
Lk 9: 3 "Take nothing for your journey, no staff, nor **b,**
10: 4 Carry no purse, no **b,** no sandals;
22:35 "When I sent you out without a purse, **b,**
22:36 a purse must take it, and likewise a **b.**
Tob 8: 2 and he took the fish's liver and heart out of the **b**
Jdt 10: 5 and filled a **b** with roasted grain, dried fig cakes,
13:10 who placed it in her food **b.**
13:15 the head out of the **b** and showed it to them,

BAGGAGE (17) [BAG]
1Sa 10:22 "See, he has hidden himself among the **b.**"
17:22 the things in charge of the keeper of the **b,**
25:13 while two hundred remained with the **b.**
30:24 as the share of the one who stays by the **b;**
Isa 10:28 at Michmash he stores his **b;**
Eze 12: 3 mortal, prepare for yourself an exile's **b,**
12: 4 your **b** by day in their sight, as **b** for exile;
12: 5 and carry the **b** through it.
12: 6 In their sight you shall lift the **b** on your shoulder,
12: 7 I brought out my **b** by day, as **b** for exile,
12:12 And the prince who is among them shall lift his **b**
Jdt 7: 2 counting the **b** and the foot soldiers handling it,
1Mc 9:35 with them the great amount of **b** that they had.
9:39 a tumultuous procession with a great amount of **b;**
2Mc 12:21 the women and the children and also the **b** to

BAGOAS (6)
Jdt 12:11 He said to **B,** the eunuch who had charge
12:13 So **B** left the presence of Holofernes,
12:15 the lambskins she had received from **B**
13: 1 **B** closed the tent from outside and shut out
13: 3 She had said the same thing to **B.**
14:14 So **B** went in and knocked at the entry of the tent,

BAGS‡ (8) [BAG]
Ge 42:25 Joseph then gave orders to fill their **b** with grain,
43:11 in your **b,** and carry them down as a present to
2Ki 5:23 and tied up two talents of silver in two **b,**
5:24 he came to the citadel, he took the **b** from them,
12:10 and tied it up in **b.**
Jer 46:19 Pack your **b** for exile, sheltered daughter Egypt!
Tob 1:14 of Media I left **b** of silver worth ten talents in trust
9: 5 to him the money **b,** with their seals intact;

BAHARUM (1)
1Ch 11:33 Azmaveth of **B,** Eliahba of Shaalbon,

BAHURIM (6)
2Sa 3:16 weeping as he walked behind her all the way to **B.**
16: 5 When King David came to **B,**
17:18 and came to the house of a man at **B,**
19:16 Shimei son of Gera, the Benjaminite, from **B,**
23:31 Abi-albon the Arbathite; Azmaveth of **B;**
1Ki 2: 8 from **B,** who cursed me with a terrible curse on

BAIL (1)
Ac 17: 9 after they had taken **b** from Jason and the others,

BAITED (1)
Pr 1:17 in vain is the net **b** while the bird is looking on;

BAITERUS (1)
1Es 5:17 The descendants of **B,** three thousand five.

BAJITH (KJV) See TEMPLE

BAKBAKKAR (1)
1Ch 9:15 and **B,** Heresh, Galal, and Mattaniah son

BAKBUK (2)
Ezr 2:51 **B,** Hakupha, Harhur,
Ne 7:53 of **B,** of Hakupha, of Harhur,

BAKBUKIAH (3)
Ne 11:17 and **B,** the second among his associates;
12: 9 And **B** and Unno their associates stood opposite
12:25 Mattaniah, **B,** Obadiah, Meshullam, Talmon,

BAKE (6) [BAKED, BAKER, BAKERS, BAKERS', BAKES, BAKING]
Ex 16:23 **b** what you want to **b** and boil what you want to
Lev 24: 5 and **b** twelve loaves of it;
26:26 ten women shall **b** your bread in a single oven,
Eze 46:20 and where they shall **b** the grain offering,
Tob 8:19 this he asked his wife to **b** many loaves of bread;

BAKED (15) [BAKE]
Ge 19: 3 and he made them a feast, and **b** unleavened bread,
40:17 the uppermost basket there were all sorts of **b** food
Ex 12:39 They **b** unleavened cakes of the dough
Lev 2: 4 When you present a grain offering **b** in the oven,
6:17 It shall not be **b** with leaven.
6:21 as a grain offering of **b** pieces,
7: 9 And every grain offering **b** in the oven,
23:17 they shall be of choice flour, **b** with leaven,
Nu 11: 8 the taste of it was like the taste of cakes **b** with oil.
1Sa 28:24 kneaded it, and **b** unleavened cakes.
2Sa 13: 8 made cakes in his sight, and **b** the cakes.
1Ki 17:12 "As the LORD your God lives, I have nothing **b,**
19: 6 and there at his head was a cake **b** on hot stones,
1Ch 23:29 the wafers of unleavened bread, the **b** offering,
Isa 44:19 I also **b** bread on its coals,

BAKEMEATS (KJV) See BAKED FOOD

BAKER (9) [BAKE]
Ge 40: 1 of the king of Egypt and his **b** offended their lord
40: 2 the chief cupbearer and the chief **b,**
40: 5 the cupbearer and the **b** of the king of Egypt,
40:16 chief **b** saw that the interpretation was favorable,
40:20 of the chief cupbearer and the head of the chief **b**
40:22 but the chief **b** he hanged,
41:10 and put me and the chief **b** in custody in the house
41:13 to my office, and the **b** was hanged."
Hos 7: 4 whose **b** does not need to stir the fire,

BAKERS (1) [BAKE]
1Sa 8:13 to be perfumers and cooks and **b.**

BAKERS' (1) [BAKE]
Jer 37:21 of bread was given him daily from the **b** street,

BAKES (1) [BAKE]
Isa 44:15 he kindles a fire and **b** bread.

BAKING (1) [BAKE]
Eze 4:12 **b** it in their sight on human dung.

BALAAM (62) [BALAAM'S]
Nu 22: 5 He sent messengers to **B** son of Beor at Pethor,
22: 7 they came to **B,** and gave him Balak's message.
22: 8 so the officials of Moab stayed with **B.**
22: 9 God came to **B** and said,
22:10 **B** said to God, "King Balak son of Zippor
22:12 God said to **B,** "You shall not go with them;
22:13 So **B** rose in the morning,
22:14 and said, "**B** refuses to come with us."
22:16 They came to **B** and said to him,
22:18 But **B** replied to the servants of Balak,
22:20 That night God came to **B** and said to him,
22:21 So **B** got up in the morning, saddled his donkey,
22:23 **B** struck the donkey, to turn it back onto the road.
22:27 the angel of the LORD, it lay down under **B;**
22:28 and it said to **B,** "What have I done to you,
22:29 **B** said to the donkey, "Because you have made
Nu 22:30 But the donkey said to **B,** "Am I not your donkey,
22:31 Then the LORD opened the eyes of **B,**
22:34 Then **B** said to the angel of the LORD,
22:35 angel of the LORD said to **B,** "Go with the men;
22:35 So **B** went on with the officials of Balak.
22:36 When Balak heard that **B** had come,
22:37 Balak said to **B,** "Did I not send to summon you?
22:38 **B** said to Balak, "I have come to you now,
22:39 Then **B** went with Balak, and they came
22:40 and sent them to **B** and to the officials who were
22:41 On the next day Balak took **B** and brought him up
23: 1 Then **B** said to Balak, "Build me seven altars here,
23: 2 Balak did as **B** had said; and Balak and **B** offered
23: 3 Then **B** said to Balak, "Stay here
23: 4 Then God met **B;** and **B** said to him,
23: 7 Then **B** uttered his oracle, saying:
23:11 Balak said to **B,** "What have you done to me?
23:15 **B** said to Balak, "Stand here
23:16 The LORD met **B,** put a word into his mouth,
23:18 Then **B** uttered his oracle, saying:
23:25 Then Balak said to **B,** "Do not curse them at all,
23:26 But **B** answered Balak, "Did I not tell you,
23:27 So Balak said to **B,** "Come now,
23:28 So Balak took **B** to the top of Peor,
23:29 **B** said to Balak, "Build me seven altars here,
23:30 So Balak did as **B** had said,
24: 1 **B** saw that it pleased the LORD to bless Israel,
24: 2 **B** looked up and saw Israel camping tribe by tribe.
24: 3 "The oracle of **B** son of Beor,
24:10 Then Balak's anger was kindled against **B,**
24:10 to **B,** "I summoned you to curse my enemies,
24:12 And **B** said to Balak, "Did I
24:15 "The oracle of **B** son of Beor,
24:25 Then **B** got up and went back to his place,
31: 8 and they also killed **B** son of Beor with the sword.
Dt 23: 4 and because they hired against you **B** son of Beor,
23: 5 (Yet the LORD your God refused to heed **B;**
Jos 13:22 the Israelites also put to the sword **B** son of Beor,
24: 9 He sent and invited **B** son of Beor to curse you,
24:10 but I would not listen to **B;**
Ne 13: 2 but hired **B** against them to curse them—
Mic 6: 5 what **B** son of Beor answered him,
2Pe 2:15 following the road of **B** son of Bosor,
Rev 2:14 of **B,** who taught Balak to put a stumbling block

BALAAM'S (5) [BALAAM]
Nu 22:25 and scraped **B** foot against the wall;
22:27 and **B** anger was kindled, and he struck
23: 5 The LORD put a word in **B** mouth, and said,
31:16 These women here, on **B** advice,
Jude 1:11 and abandon themselves to **B** error for the sake

BALAC (KJV) See BALAK

BALADAN (2) [MERODACH-BALADAN]
2Ki 20:12 At that time King Merodach-baladan son of **B**
Isa 39: 1 At that time King Merodach-baladan son of **B**

BALAH (1)
Jos 19: 3 Hazar-shual, **B,** Ezem,

BALAK (43) [BALAK'S]
Nu 22: 2 Now **B** son of Zippor saw all that Israel had done
22: 4 **B** son of Zippor was king of Moab at that time.
22:10 "King **B** son of Zippor of Moab,
22:13 and said to the officials of **B,**
22:14 So the officials of Moab rose and went to **B,**
22:15 Once again **B** sent officials,
22:16 "Thus says **B** son of Zippor:
22:18 But Balaam replied to the servants of **B,**
"Although **B** were to give me his house full
22:35 So Balaam went on with the officials of **B.**
22:36 When **B** heard that Balaam had come,
22:37 **B** said to Balaam, "Did I not send
22:38 Balaam said to **B,** "I have come to you now,
22:39 Then Balaam went with **B,**
22:40 **B** sacrificed oxen and sheep,
22:41 On the next day **B** took Balaam and brought him
23: 1 to **B,** "Build me seven altars here,
23: 2 **B** did as Balaam had said; and **B** and Balaam
23: 3 to **B,** "Stay here beside your burnt offerings
23: 5 "Return to **B,** and this is what you must say."
23: 6 to **B,** who was standing beside his burnt offerings
23: 7 "**B** has brought me from Aram,
23:11 **B** said to Balaam, "What have you done to me?
23:13 So **B** said to him, "Come with me to another place
23:15 to **B,** "Stand here beside your burnt offerings,
23:16 put a word into his mouth, and said, "Return to **B,**
23:17 **B** said to him, "What has the LORD said?"
23:18 "Rise, **B,** and hear; listen to me, O son of Zippor:
23:25 Then **B** said to Balaam, "Do not curse them at all,
23:26 But Balaam answered **B,** "Did I not tell you,
23:27 So **B** said to Balaam, "Come now,
23:28 So **B** took Balaam to the top of Peor,
23:29 Balaam said to **B,** "Build me seven altars here,
23:30 So **B** did as Balaam had said,
24:10 **B** said to Balaam, "I summoned you
24:12 And Balaam said to **B,** "Did I
24:13 'If **B** should give me his house full of silver
24:25 and **B** also went his way.
Jos 24: 9 Then King **B** son of Zippor of Moab,
Jdg 11:25 Now are you any better than King **B** son of Zippor
Mic 6: 5 remember now what King **B** of Moab devised,
Rev 2:14 of Balaam, who taught **B** to put a stumbling block

BALAK'S (2) [BALAK]
Nu 22: 7 they came to Balaam, and gave him **B** message.
24:10 Then **B** anger was kindled against Balaam,

BALAL See Index to Footnotes

BALAMON (1)
Jdt 8: 3 in the field between Dothan and **B.**

BALANCE‡ (10) [BALANCES, BALANCINGS]
Job 31: 6 in a just **b**, and let God know my integrity!—
Pr 11: 1 A false **b** is an abomination to the LORD,
Isa 40:12 the mountains in scales and the hills in a **b?**
2Co 8:13 but it is a question of a fair **b** between
8:14 in order that there may be a fair **b.**
Sir 6:15 no amount can **b** their worth.
21:25 but the words of the prudent are weighed in the **b.**
2Mc 9: 8 that he could weigh the high mountains in a **b,**
2Es 3:34 in a **b** our iniquities and those of the inhabitants of
4:36 for he has weighed the age in the **b,**

BALANCES (9) [BALANCE]
Lev 19:36 You shall have honest **b**, honest weights,
Job 6: 2 and all my calamity laid in the **b!**
Ps 62: 9 in the **b** they go up; they are together lighter than
Pr 16:11 Honest **b** and scales are the LORD's;
Eze 5: 1 then take **b** for weighing, and divide the hair.
45:10 You shall have honest **b**, an honest ephah,
Hos 12: 7 A trader, in whose hands are false **b,**
Am 8: 5 and practice deceit with false **b,**
Sir 28:25 so make **b** and scales for your words.

BALANCINGS (1) [BALANCE]
Job 37:16 Do you know the **b** of the clouds,

BALBAIM (1)
Jdt 7: 3 in breadth over Dothan as far as **B** and in length

BALD (13) [BALDHEAD, BALDNESS]
Lev 11:22 the **b** locust according to its kind,
13:40 he is **b** but he is clean.
13:42 But if there is on the **b** head or the **b** forehead
13:42 breaking out on his **b** head or his **b** forehead.
13:43 on his **b** head or on his **b** forehead,
21: 5 They shall not make **b** spots upon their heads,
Eze 27:31 they make themselves **b** for you,
29:18 head was made **b** and every shoulder was rubbed
Mic 1:16 Make yourselves **b** and cut off your hair
1:16 make yourselves as **b** as the eagle,

BALDHEAD (2) [BALD, HEAD]
2Ki 2:23 saying, "Go away, **b!** Go away, **b!**"

BALDNESS (7) [BALD]
Lev 13:41 he has **b** of the forehead but he is clean.
Isa 3:24 and instead of well-set hair, **b;**
15: 2 On every head is **b**, every beard is shorn;
22:12 to **b** and putting on sackcloth;
Jer 47: 5 **B** has come upon Gaza, Ashkelon is silenced.
Eze 7:18 Shame shall be on all faces, **b** on all their heads.
Am 8:10 I will bring sackcloth on all loins, and **b**

BALL (1)
Isa 22:18 and throw you like a **b** into a wide land;

BALLAD (1)
Nu 21:27 **b** singers say, "Come to Heshbon, let it be built;

BALLOTS (1)
4Mc 15:26 this mother held two **b**, one bearing death and

BALM (6)
Ge 37:25 with their camels carrying gum, **b**, and resin,
43:11 a little **b** and a little honey, gum, resin,
Jer 8:22 Is there no **b** in Gilead?
46:11 Go up to Gilead, and take **b,**
51: 8 Bring **b** for her wound; perhaps she may be healed.
Eze 27:17 from Minnith, millet, honey, oil, and **b.**

BALSAM (4)
2Sa 5:23 and come upon them opposite the **b** trees.
5:24 of marching in the tops of the **b** trees,
1Ch 14:14 go around and come on them opposite the **b** trees.
14:15 of marching in the tops of the **b** trees, then go out

BAMAH (1)
Eze 20:29 So it is called **B** to this day.)

BAMOTH (2) [BAMOTH-BAAL]
Nu 21:19 from Mattanah to Nahaliel, from Nahaliel to **B,**
21:20 from **B** to the valley lying in the region of Moab

BAMOTH-BAAL (2) [BAAL, BAMOTH]
Nu 22:41 and brought him up to **B;**
Jos 13:17 Dibon, and **B**, and Beth-baal-meon,

BAN See Index to Footnotes

BAND (29) [BANDED, BANDS]
Ex 28: 8 The decorated **b** on it shall be of
28:27 at its joining above the decorated **b** of the ephod.
28:28 so that it may lie on the decorated **b** of the ephod,
29: 5 and gird him with the decorated **b** of the ephod;
39: 5 The decorated **b** on it was of the same materials
39:20 at its joining above the decorated **b** of the ephod.
39:21 that it should lie on the decorated **b** of the ephod,
Lev 8: 7 then put the decorated **b** of the ephod around him,
1Sa 10: 5 to the town, you will meet a **b** of prophets coming
10:10 a **b** of prophets met him;
30: 8 of the LORD, "Shall I pursue this **b?**
2Sa 2:25 around Abner and formed a single **b;**
23:13 a **b** of Philistines was encamped in the valley
1Ki 7:35 of the stand there was a round **b** half a cubit high;
11:24 around him and became leader of a marauding **b,**
2Ki 13:21 a marauding **b** was seen and the man was thrown
19:31 and from Mount Zion a **b** of survivors.
1Ch 12:21 They helped David against the **b** of raiders,
Ezr 8:22 for a **b** of soldiers and cavalry to protect us against
Job 38: 9 and thick darkness its swaddling **b,**
Ps 86:14 a **b** of ruffians seeks my life,
94:21 They **b** together against the life of the righteous,
Isa 8: 9 **B** together, you peoples, and be dismayed;
31: 4 when a **b** of shepherds is called out against it—
37:32 and from Mount Zion a **b** of survivors.
Jer 9: 2 For they are all adulterers, a **b** of traitors.
Da 4:15 with a **b** of iron and bronze,
4:23 with a **b** of iron and bronze,
1Mc 5: 6 where he found a strong **b** and many people,

BANDAGE (3) [BANDAGED]
1Ki 20:38 disguising himself with a **b** over his eyes.
20:41 Then he quickly took the **b** away from his eyes.
Eze 30:21 up for healing or wrapped with a **b,**

BANDAGED (2) [BANDAGE]
Lk 10:34 He went to him and **b** his wounds,
Sir 27:21 For a wound may be **b,**

BANDED (3) [BAND]
Ex 27:17 the pillars around the court shall be **b** with silver;
38:17 and all the pillars of the court were **b** with silver.
Hos 6: 9 so the priests are **b** together;

BANDIT (5) [BANDITS]
Mt 26:55 and clubs to arrest me as though I were a **b?**
Mk 14:48 and clubs to arrest me as though I were a **b?**
Lk 22:52 with swords and clubs as if I were a **b?**
Jn 10: 1 but climbs in by another way is a thief and a **b.**
18:40 Now Barabbas was a **b.**

BANDITS (6) [BANDIT]
Hos 7: 1 the thief breaks in, and the **b** raid outside.
Mt 27:38 Then two **b** were crucified with him,
27:44 The **b** who were crucified with him
Mk 15:27 And with him they crucified two **b,**
Jn 10: 8 All who came before me are thieves and **b;**
2Co 11:26 danger from **b**, danger from my own people,

BANDS (19) [BAND]
Ex 27:10 hooks of the pillars and their **b** shall be of silver.
27:11 hooks of the pillars and their **b** shall be of silver.
38:10 the hooks of the pillars and their **b** were of silver.
38:11 the hooks of the pillars and their **b** were of silver.
38:12 the hooks of the pillars and their **b** were of silver.
38:17 the hooks of the pillars and their **b** were of silver;
38:19 overlaying of their capitals and their **b** of silver.
38:28 and overlaid their capitals and made **b** for them.
2Sa 4: 2 Saul's son had two captains of raiding **b;**
2Ki 13:20 Now **b** of Moabites used to invade the land in
24: 2 The LORD sent against him **b** of the Chaldeans,
24: 2 **b** of the Arameans, **b** of the Moabites, and **b** of the Ammonites;
Eze 13:18 Woe to the women who sew **b** on all wrists,
13:20 I am against your **b** with which you hunt lives;
Hos 11: 4 with cords of human kindness, with **b** of love.
Lk 2: 7 to her firstborn son and wrapped him in **b** of cloth,
2:12 you will find a child wrapped in **b** of cloth

BANI‡ (18)
2Sa 23:36 Igal son of Nathan of Zobah; **B** the Gadite;
1Ch 6:46 son of Amzi, son of **B**, son of Shemer,
9: 4 son of **B**, from the sons of Perez son of Judah.
Ezr 2:10 Of **B**, six hundred forty-two.
8:10 the descendants of **B**, Shelomith son of Josiphiah,
10:29 Of the descendants of **B:** Meshullam,
10:34 Of the descendants of **B:** Maadai, Amram, Uel,
Ne 3:17 the Levites made repairs: Rehum son of **B;**
8: 7 Also Jeshua, **B**, Sherebiah, Jamin, Akkub,
9: 4 Then Jeshua, **B**, Kadmiel, Shebaniah, Bunni,
9: 4 Bani, Kadmiel, Shebaniah, Bunni, Sherebiah, **B,**
9: 5 Then the Levites, Jeshua, Kadmiel, **B,**
10:13 Hodiah, **B**, Beninu.
10:14 Parosh, Pahath-moab, Elam, Zattu, **B,**
11:22 of the Levites in Jerusalem was Uzzi son of **B** son
1Es 5:12 The descendants of **B**, six hundred forty-eight.
8:36 the descendants of **B**, Shelomith son of Josiphiah,
9:34 Of the descendants of **B:** Jeremai,

BANISH (7) [BANISHED, BANISHMENT]
Ecc 11:10 **B** anxiety from your mind,
Jer 16: 9 I am going to **b** from this place,
25:10 And I will **b** from them the sound of mirth and
Eze 34:25 with them a covenant of peace and **b** wild animals
Ro 11:26 he will **b** ungodliness from Jacob."
1Mc 3:35 he was to **b** the memory of them from the place,
4Mc 8:23 Why do we **b** ourselves from this

BANISHED (9) [BANISH]
2Sa 14:13 as the king does not bring his **b** one home again.
14:14 not to keep an outcast **b** forever from his presence.
1Ki 2:27 So Solomon **b** Abiathar from being priest to
2Ki 13:23 nor has he **b** them from his presence until now.
17:20 until he had **b** them from his presence.
Isa 24:11 the gladness of the earth is **b.**
Jer 46:28 of all the nations among which I have **b** you,
2Mc 10:15 they received those who were **b** from Jerusalem,
2Es 8:53 illness is **b** from you, and death is hidden;

BANISHMENT (1) [BANISH]
Ezr 7:26 for death or for **b** or for confiscation of their goods

BANK (13) [BANKERS, BANKS]
Ge 41: 3 and stood by the other cows on the **b** of the Nile.
Ex 2: 3 and placed it among the reeds on the **b** of the river.
7:15 stand by the river **b** to meet him,
2Ki 2:13 and went back and stood on the **b** of the Jordan.
Eze 47: 6 Then he led me back along the **b** of the river.
47: 7 I saw on the **b** of the river a great many trees on
Da 10: 4 I was standing on the **b** of the great river (that is,
12: 5 one standing on this **b** of the stream and one on
Mt 8:32 the steep **b** into the sea and perished in the water.
Mk 5:13 rushed down the steep **b** into the sea,
Lk 8:33 and the herd rushed down the steep **b** into the lake
19:23 Why then did you not put my money into the **b?**
Sir 40:16 The reeds by any water or river **b** are plucked up

BANKERS (1) [BANK]
Mt 25:27 you ought to have invested my money with the **b,**

BANKS (10) [BANK]
Ge 41:17 "In my dream I was standing on the **b** of the Nile;
Dt 3:17 with the Jordan and its **b,**
Jos 3:15 the Jordan overflows all its **b** throughout the time
4:18 to their place and overflowed all its **b,**
13:23 border of the Reubenites was the Jordan and its **b.**
13:27 of King Sihon of Heshbon, the Jordan and its **b,**
1Ch 12:15 when it was overflowing all its **b,**
Isa 8: 7 above all its channels and overflow all its **b;**
Eze 47:12 On the **b**, on both sides of the river,
1Mc 9:43 with a large force on the sabbath day to the **b** of

BANNAS (1)
1Es 5:26 the descendants of Jeshua and Kadmiel and **B**

BANNED (1)
Ezr 10: 8 and they themselves **b** from the congregation of

BANNER (4) [BANNERS]
Ex 17:15 an altar and called it, The LORD is my **b.**
17:16 He said, "A hand upon the **b** of the LORD!
Ps 60: 4 You have set up a **b** for those who fear you,
Jer 50: 2 set up a **b** and proclaim, do not conceal it, say:

BANNERS (3) [BANNER]
Ps 20: 5 and in the name of our God set up our **b.**
SS 6: 4 comely as Jerusalem, terrible as an army with **b.**
6:10 bright as the sun, terrible as an army with **b?"**

BANQUET (43) [BANQUETING, BANQUETS]
Est 1: 3 he gave a **b** for all his officials and ministers.
1: 5 both great and small, a **b** lasting for seven days,
1: 9 Queen Vashti gave a **b** for the women in
2:18 Then the king gave a great **b** to all his officials and ministers—"Esther's **b.**"
5: 4 and Haman come today to a **b** that I have prepared
5: 5 So the king and Haman came to the **b**
5: 8 let the king and Haman come tomorrow to the **b**
5:12 with the king to the **b** that she prepared.
5:14 then go with the king to the **b** in good spirits."
6:14 to the **b** that Esther had prepared.
7: 8 king returned from the palace garden to the **b** hall,
Mt 22: 2 be compared to a king who gave a wedding **b**
22: 3 to the wedding **b**, but they would
22: 4 and everything is ready; come to the wedding **b.'**
22: 9 and invite everyone you find to the wedding **b.'**
25:10 with him into the wedding **b;**
Mk 6:21 on his birthday gave a **b** for his courtiers
Lk 5:29 Then Levi gave a great **b** for him in his house;
12:36 for their master to return from the wedding **b,**
14: 8 you are invited by someone to a wedding **b,**
14:13 But when you give a **b**, invite the poor,
Jdt 6:21 from the assembly to his own house and gave a **b**
12:10 On the fourth day Holofernes held a **b**
13: 1 for they all were weary because the **b** had lasted
AdE 1: 3 he gave a **b** for his Friends and other persons
2:18 a **b** lasting seven days for all his Friends and
6:14 and hurriedly brought Haman to the **b**
7: 7 The king rose from the **b** and went into the garden,

AdE 8:17 the Jews had joy and gladness, a **b** and a holiday.
Sir 31:31 Do not reprove your neighbor at a **b** of wine,
32: 5 in a setting of gold is a concert of music at a **b**
49: 1 and like music at a **b** of wine.
LtJ 6:32 before their gods as some do at a funeral **b**.
1Mc 16:15 he gave them a great **b**, and hid men there.
16:16 in the **b** hall and killed him and his two sons,
2Mc 2:27 for one who prepares a **b** and seeks the benefit
1Es 3: 1 Now King Darius gave a great **b** for all that were
3Mc 5:15 that the hour of the **b** was already slipping by,
5:16 and ordered those present for the **b**
5:17 and to make the present portion of the **b** joyful
6:31 arranged for a **b** of deliverance instead of a bitter
6:33 after convening a great **b** to celebrate these events,

BANQUETING (2) [BANQUET]

SS 2: 4 He brought me to the **b** house,
Da 5:10 of the king and his lords, came into the **b** hall.

BANQUETS (3) [BANQUET]

Mt 23: 6 of honor at **b** and the best seats in the synagogues,
Mk 12:39 in the synagogues and places of honor at **b**!
Lk 20:46 in the synagogues and places of honor at **b**.

BAPTISM‡ (21) [BAPTIZE]

Mt 3: 7 and Sadducees coming for **b**,
21:25 Did the **b** of John come from heaven,
Mk 1: 4 proclaiming a **b** of repentance for the forgiveness
10:38 or be baptized with the **b** that I am baptized with?"
10:39 and with the **b** with which I am baptized,
11:30 Did the **b** of John come from heaven,
Lk 3: 3 proclaiming a **b** of repentance for the forgiveness
7:29 because they had been baptized with John's **b**.
12:50 I have a **b** with which to be baptized,
20: 4 Did the **b** of John come from heaven,
Ac 1:22 the **b** of John until the day when he was taken up
10:37 in Galilee after the **b** that John announced:
13:24 a **b** of repentance to all the people of Israel.
18:25 though he knew only the **b** of John.
19: 3 They answered, "Into John's **b**."
19: 4 Paul said, "John baptized with the **b** of repentance,
Ro 6: 4 we have been buried with him by **b** into death,
1Co 15:29 what will those people do who receive **b** on behalf
Eph 4: 5 one Lord, one faith, one **b**,
Col 2:12 when you were buried with him in **b**,
1Pe 3:21 And **b**, which this prefigured, now saves you—

BAPTISMS (2) [BAPTIZE]

Heb 6: 2 about **b**, laying on of hands, resurrection of
9:10 but deal only with food and drink and various **b**,

BAPTIST (12) [BAPTIZE]

Mt 3: 1 John the **B** appeared in the wilderness of Judea,
11:11 no one has arisen greater than John the **B**;
11:12 the days of John the **B** until now the kingdom
14: 2 and he said to his servants, "This is John the **B**;
14: 8 the head of John the **B** here on a platter."
16:14 And they said, "Some say John the **B**,
17:13 that he was speaking to them about John the **B**.
Mk 6:25 to give me at once the head of John the **B** on
8:28 And they answered him, "John the **B**;
Lk 7:20 they said, "John the **B** has sent us to you to ask,
7:33 For John the **B** has come eating no bread
9:19 They answered, "John the **B**;

BAPTIZE (9) [BAPTISM, BAPTISMS, BAPTIST, BAPTIZED, BAPTIZER, BAPTIZES, BAPTIZING]

Mt 3:11 "I **b** you with water for repentance,
3:11 He will **b** you with the Holy Spirit and fire.
Mk 1: 8 but he will **b** you with the Holy Spirit."
Lk 3:16 of them by saying, "I **b** you with water;
3:16 He will **b** you with the Holy Spirit and fire.
Jn 1:26 John answered them, "I **b** with water.
1:33 the one who sent me to **b** with water said to me,
1Co 1:16 (I did **b** also the household of Stephanas;
1:17 For Christ did not send me to **b** but to proclaim

BAPTIZED‡ (52) [BAPTIZE]

Mt 3: 6 and they were **b** by him in the river Jordan,
3:13 from Galilee to John at the Jordan, to be **b** by him.
3:14 "I need to be **b** by you, and do you come to me?"
3:16 And when Jesus had been **b**,
Mk 1: 5 and were **b** by him in the river Jordan,
1: 8 I have **b** you with water;
1: 9 from Nazareth of Galilee and was **b** by John in
10:38 or be **b** with the baptism that I am **b** with?"
10:39 with the baptism with which I am **b**, you will be **b**;
16:16 ⟦The one who believes and is **b** will be saved;⟧
Lk 3: 7 John said to the crowds that came out to be **b**
3:12 Even tax collectors came to be **b**,
3:21 Now when all the people were **b**,
3:21 and when Jesus also had been **b** and was praying,
7:29 because they had been **b** with John's baptism.
7:30 But by refusing to be **b** by him,
12:50 I have a baptism with which to be **b**,
Jn 3:22 and he spent some time there with them and **b**.
3:23 and people kept coming and were being **b**
4: 2 it was not Jesus himself but his disciples who **b**—
Ac 1: 5 for John **b** with water, but you will be **b** with the Holy Spirit not many days
2:38 be **b** every one of you in the name of Jesus Christ
2:41 So those who welcomed his message were **b**,
8:12 they were **b**, both men and women.
8:13 After being **b**, he stayed constantly with Philip
8:16 they had only been **b** in the name of
8:36 What is to prevent me from being **b**?"
8:38 went down into the water, and Philip **b** him.
9:18 Then he got up and was **b**,
10:48 So he ordered them to be **b** in the name
11:16 how he had said, 'John **b** with water, but you will be **b** with the Holy Spirit.'
16:15 When she and her household were **b**, she urged us,
16:33 then he and his entire family were **b** without delay.
18: 8 who heard Paul became believers and were **b**.
19: 3 Then he said, "Into what then were you **b**?"
19: 4 Paul said, "John **b** with the baptism of repentance,
19: 5 they were **b** in the name of the Lord Jesus.
22:16 Get up, be **b**, and have your sins washed away,
Ro 6: 3 Do you not know that all of us who have been **b** into Christ Jesus were **b** into his death?
1Co 1:13 Or were you **b** in the name of Paul?
1:14 I thank God that I **b** none of you except Crispus
1:15 that no one can say that you were **b** in my name.
1:16 I do not know whether I **b** anyone else.)
10: 2 all were **b** into Moses in the cloud and in the sea,
12:13 in the one Spirit we were all **b** into one body—
15:29 why are people **b** on their behalf?
Gal 3:27 as were **b** into Christ have clothed yourselves

BAPTIZER (3) [BAPTIZE]

Mk 1: 4 John the **b** appeared in the wilderness,
6:14 "John the **b** has been raised from the dead;
6:24 She replied, "The head of John the **b**."

BAPTIZES (1) [BAPTIZE]

Jn 1:33 and remain is the one who **b** with the Holy Spirit.'

BAPTIZING‡ (9) [BAPTIZE]

Mt 28:19 **b** them in the name of the Father and of the Son
Jn 1:25 then are you **b** if you are neither the Messiah,
1:28 in Bethany across the Jordan where John was **b**.
1:31 but I came **b** with water for this reason,
3:23 John also was **b** at Aenon near Salim
3:26 here he is **b**, and all are going to him."
4: 1 "Jesus is making and **b** more disciples than John"
10:40 to the place where John had been **b** earlier,
Ac 10:47 the water for **b** these people who have received

BAR (8) [BARS]

Ex 26:28 The middle **b**, halfway up the frames,
36:33 He made the middle **b** to pass through from end
Jos 7:21 and a **b** of gold weighing fifty shekels,
7:24 and the **b** of gold, with his sons and daughters,
Jdg 16: 3 **b** and all, put them on his shoulders,
2Sa 23: 7 to touch them one uses an iron **b** or the shaft of
Ne 7: 3 let them shut and **b** the doors.
Isa 9: 4 and the **b** across their shoulders,

BAR-JESUS (1) [=ELYMAS]

Ac 13: 6 a Jewish false prophet, named **B**.

BARABBAS (11)

Mt 27:16 a notorious prisoner, called Jesus **B**.
27:17 Jesus **B** or Jesus who is called the Messiah?"
27:20 the elders persuaded the crowds to ask for **B** and
27:21 to release for you?" And they said, "**B**."
27:26 So he released **B** for them;
Mk 15: 7 Now a man called **B** was in prison with
15:11 the crowd to have him release **B** for them instead.
15:15 wishing to satisfy the crowd, released **B** for them;
Lk 23:18 with this fellow! Release **B** for us!"
Jn 18:40 They shouted in reply, "Not this man, but **B**!"
18:40 Now **B** was a bandit.

BARACHEL (2)

Job 32: 2 Then Elihu son of **B** the Buzite,
32: 6 Elihu son of **B** the Buzite answered:

BARACHIAH (1)

Mt 23:35 to the blood of Zechariah son of **B**,

BARACHIAS (KJV) See BARACHIAH

BARAK (15)

Jdg 4: 6 and summoned **B** son of Abinoam from Kedesh
4: 8 **B** said to her, "If you will go with me, I will go;
4: 9 Then Deborah got up and went with **B** to Kedesh.
4:10 **B** summoned Zebulun and Naphtali to Kedesh;
4:12 that **B** son of Abinoam had gone up
4:14 Then Deborah said to **B**, "Up!
4:14 So **B** went down from Mount Tabor
4:15 and all his army into a panic before **B**;
4:16 while **B** pursued the chariots and the army
4:22 Then, as **B** came in pursuit of Sisera,
5: 1 Deborah and **B** son of Abinoam sang on that day,
5:12 Arise, **B**, lead away your captives,
5:15 and Issachar faithful to **B**;
1Sa 12:11 And the LORD sent Jerubbaal and **B**,
Heb 11:32 For time would fail me to tell of Gideon, **B**,

BARBARIAN (2) [BARBARIANS]

Col 3:11 circumcised and uncircumcised, **b**, Scythian,
2Mc 2:21 the whole land and pursued the **b** hordes,

BARBARIANS (1) [BARBARIAN]

Ro 1:14 I am a debtor both to Greeks and to **b**,

BARBARIANS, BARBAROUS (KJV) See also NATIVES

BARBAROUS (5) [BARBAROUSLY]

2Mc 5:22 by birth a Phrygian and in character more **b** than
10: 4 not be handed over to blasphemous and **b** nations.
13: 9 The king with **b** arrogance was coming to show
3Mc 3:24 behind our backs as traitors and **b** enemies.
7: 3 and to punish them with **b** penalties as traitors;

BARBAROUSLY (1) [BARBAROUS]

2Mc 15: 2 "Do not destroy so savagely and **b**,

BARBER'S (1)

Eze 5: 1 a **b** razor and run it over your head and your beard;

BARBS (1)

Nu 33:55 then those whom you let remain shall be as **b**

BARE‡ (38) [BARED, BAREFOOT, BAREHANDED]

Lev 19:10 You shall not strip your vineyard **b**,
20:18 he has laid **b** her flow
20:18 and she has laid **b** her flow of blood;
20:19 for that is to lay **b** one's own flesh;
Nu 23: 3 And he went to a **b** height.
2Sa 22:16 the world were laid **b** at the rebuke of the LORD,
1Ki 21:27 and put sackcloth over his **b** flesh;
2Ki 9:13 and spread them for him on the **b** steps;
Ps 18:15 and the foundations of the world were laid **b**
29: 9 the oaks to whirl, and strips the forest **b**;
Isa 3:17 and the LORD will lay **b** their secret parts.
13: 2 On a **b** hill raise a signal, cry aloud to them;
19: 7 There will be **b** places by the Nile,
32:11 strip, and make yourselves **b**,
41:18 I will open rivers on the **b** heights,
49: 9 on all the **b** heights shall be their pasture;
Jer 3: 2 Look up to the **b** heights, and see!
3:21 A voice on the **b** heights is heard,
4:11 the **b** heights in the desert toward my poor people,
7:29 raise a lamentation on the **b** heights,
12:12 the **b** heights in the desert spoilers have come;
14: 6 The wild asses stand on the **b** heights,
49:10 But as for me, I have stripped Esau **b**,
La 4:21 you shall become drunk and strip yourself **b**.
Eze 13:14 so that its foundation will be laid **b**;
16: 7 yet you were naked and **b**.
16:22 when you were naked and **b**,
16:39 and leave you naked and **b**.
23:29 and leave you naked and **b**,
24: 7 she placed it on a **b** rock;
24: 8 I have placed the blood she shed on a **b** rock,
26: 4 I will scrape its soil from it and make it a **b** rock.
26:14 I will make you a **b** rock;
29:18 and every shoulder was rubbed **b**;
Hab 3:13 laying it **b** from foundation to roof.
Zep 2:14 for its cedar work will be laid **b**.
1Co 15:37 you do not sow the body that is to be, but a **b** seed,
Heb 4:13 but all are naked and laid **b** to the eyes of the one

BAREA (1)

AdE 9: 8 Pharadatha, **B**, Sarbacha,

BARED (2) [BARE]

Isa 52:10 The LORD has **b** his holy arm before the eyes
Eze 4: 7 and with your arm **b** you shall prophesy against it.

BAREFOOT (5) [BARE, FOOT]

2Sa 15:30 with his head covered and walking **b**;
Isa 20: 2 and he had done so, walking naked and **b**.
20: 3 "Just as my servant Isaiah has walked naked and **b**
20: 4 both the young and the old, naked and **b**,
Mic 1: 8 I will go **b** and naked;

BAREHANDED (1) [BARE, HAND]

Jdg 14: 6 and he tore the lion apart **b** as one might tear apart

BARELY (2)

3Mc 1:23 being **b** restrained by the old men and the elders,
7: 6 toward all people we **b** spared their lives.

BARGAIN (4) [BARGAINED]

Job 6:27 over the orphan, and **b** over your friend.
41: 6 Will traders **b** over it?
Isa 57: 8 and you have made a **b** for yourself with them,
Hos 8:10 they **b** with the nations, I will now gather them up.

BARGAINED (1) [BARGAIN]

Hos 8: 9 wandering alone; Ephraim has **b** for lovers.

BARIAH (1)

1Ch 3:22 Hattush, Igal, **B**, Neariah, and Shaphat, six.

BARK (3)

Isa 56:10 they are all silent dogs that cannot **b**;

Joel 1: 7 it has stripped off their **b** and thrown it down;
Wis 13:11 to handle and skillfully strip off all its **b**,

BARKOS (3)

Ezr 2:53 **B**, Sisera, Temah,
Ne 7:55 of **B**, of Sisera, of Temah,
1Es 5:32 the descendants of Charea, the descendants of **B**,

BARLEY‡ (36) [BARLEY-CAKE]

Ex 9:31 (Now the flax and the **b** were ruined,
9:31 for the **b** was in the ear and the flax was in bud.
Lev 27:16 fifty shekels of silver to a homer of **b** seed.
Nu 5:15 one-tenth of an ephah of **b** flour.
Dt 8: 8 a land of wheat and **b**,
Jdg 7:13 and in it a cake of **b** bread tumbled into the camp
Ru 1:22 to Bethlehem at the beginning of the **b** harvest.
2:17 and it was about an ephah of **b**.
2:23 gleaning until the end of the **b** and wheat harvests;
3: 2 he is winnowing **b** tonight at the threshing floor.
3:15 and he measured out six measures of **b**,
3:17 "He gave me these six measures of **b**, for he said,
2Sa 14:30 Joab's field is next to mine, and he has **b** there;
17:28 and earthen vessels, wheat, **b**, meal, parched grain,
21: 9 at the beginning of **b** harvest.
1Ki 4:28 also brought to the required place **b** and straw for
2Ki 4:42 twenty loaves of **b** and fresh ears of grain
7: 1 and two measures of **b** for a shekel,
7:16 and two measures of **b** for a shekel,
7:18 "Two measures of **b** shall be sold for a shekel,
1Ch 11:13 There was a plot of ground full of **b**.
2Ch 2:10 twenty thousand cors of **b**,
2:15 Now, as for the wheat, **b**, oil, and wine,
27: 5 ten thousand cors of wheat and ten thousand of **b**.
Job 31:40 and foul weeds instead of **b**."
Isa 28:25 and plant wheat in rows and **b** in its proper place,
Jer 41: 8 "Do not kill us, for we have stores of wheat, **b**, oil,
Eze 4: 9 And you, take wheat and **b**, beans and lentils,
13:19 among my people for handfuls of **b** and for pieces
45:13 and one-sixth of an ephah from each homer of **b**,
Hos 3: 2 of silver and a homer of **b** and a measure of wine.
Joel 1:11 wail, you vinedressers, over the wheat and the **b**;
Jn 6: 9 a boy here who has five **b** loaves and two fish.
6:13 and from the fragments of the five **b** loaves,
Rev 6: 6 and three quarts of **b** for a day's pay,
Jdt 8: 2 had died during the **b** harvest.

BARLEY-CAKE (1) [BARLEY, CAKE]

Eze 4:12 You shall eat it as a **b**,

BARN (3) [BARNS]

Hag 2:19 Is there any seed left in the **b**?
Mt 13:30 but gather the wheat into my **b**.' "
Lk 12:24 they have neither storehouse nor **b**,

BARNABAS (31) [=JOSEPH]

Ac 4:36 the apostles gave the name **B** (which means "son
9:27 But **B** took him, brought him to the apostles,
11:22 and they sent **B** to Antioch.
11:25 Then **B** went to Tarsus to look for Saul,
11:30 sending it to the elders by **B** and Saul.
12:25 after completing their mission **B** and Saul returned
13: 1 **B**, Simeon who was called Niger,
13: 2 "Set apart for me **B** and Saul for the work
13: 7 who summoned **B** and Saul and wanted to hear
13:42 As Paul and **B** were going out,
13:43 to Judaism followed Paul and **B**,
13:46 Then both Paul and **B** spoke out boldly, saying,
13:50 and stirred up persecution against Paul and **B**,
14: 1 where Paul and **B** went into the Jewish synagogue
14:12 **B** they called Zeus, and Paul they called Hermes,
14:14 When the apostles **B** and Paul heard of it,
14:20 The next day he went on with **B** to Derbe.
15: 2 And after Paul and **B** had no small dissension
15: 2 Paul and **B** and some of the others were appointed
15:12 and listened to **B** and Paul as they told of all
15:22 and to send them to Antioch with Paul and **B**.
15:25 along with our beloved **B** and Paul,
15:35 But Paul and **B** remained in Antioch, and there,
15:36 After some days Paul said to **B**, "Come,
15:37 **B** wanted to take with them John called Mark.
15:39 **B** took Mark with him and sailed away to Cyprus.
1Co 9: 6 Or is it only **B** and I who have no right to refrain
Gal 2: 1 up again to Jerusalem with **B**,
2: 9 to **B** and me the right hand of fellowship,
2:13 so that even **B** was led astray by their hypocrisy.
Col 4:10 as does Mark the cousin of **B**,

BARNS (5) [BARN]

Dt 28: 8 upon you in your **b**, and in all that you undertake;
Ps 144:13 May our **b** be filled, with produce of every kind;
Pr 3:10 then your **b** will be filled with plenty,
Mt 6:26 they neither sow nor reap nor gather into **b**,
Lk 12:18 I will pull down my **b** and build larger ones,

BARODIS (1)

1Es 5:34 the descendants of Apherra, the descendants of **B**,

BARRACKS (6)

Ac 21:34 he ordered him to be brought into the **b**.
21:37 Just as Paul was about to be brought into the **b**,
22:24 that he was to be brought into the **b**,
23:10 take him by force, and bring him into the **b**.
23:16 and gained entrance to the **b** and told Paul.
23:32 while they returned to the **b**.

BARREL[S] (KJV) See JAR[S]

BARREN (27) [BARRENNESS]

Ge 11:30 Now Sarai was **b**; she had no child.
25:21 to the LORD for his wife, because she was **b**;
29:31 he opened her womb; but Rachel was **b**.
Ex 23:26 No one shall miscarry or be **b** in your land;
Lev 16:22 on itself all their iniquities to a **b** region;
Jdg 13: 2 His wife was **b**, having borne no children.
13: 3 "Although you are **b**, having borne no children,
1Sa 2: 5 The **b** has borne seven, but she who has many
Job 3: 7 let that night be **b**; let no joyful cry be heard in it.
15:34 For the company of the godless is **b**,
Ps 113: 9 He gives the **b** woman a home,
Pr 30:16 the **b** womb, the earth ever thirsty for water,
Isa 49:21 I was bereaved and **b**, exiled and put away—
54: 1 Sing, O **b** one who did not bear;
Mal 3:11 and your vine in the field shall not be **b**,
Lk 1: 7 they had no children, because Elizabeth was **b**,
1:36 the sixth month for her who was said to be **b**.
23:29 'Blessed are the **b**, and the wombs that never bore,
Heb 11:11 though he was too old—and Sarah herself was **b**—
Jas 2:20 that faith apart from works is **b**?
Wis 3:13 For blessed is the **b** woman who is undefiled,
4:19 they will be left utterly dry and **b**,
Sir 42:10 or, though married, for fear she may be **b**.
2Es 5: 1 and the land shall be **b** of faith.
9:43 "Your servant was **b** and had no child,
10:45 for her telling you that she was **b** for thirty years,
10:46 then it was that the **b** woman bore a son.

BARRENNESS (2) [BARREN]

Dt 7:14 with neither sterility nor **b** among you
Ro 4:19 or when he considered the **b** of Sarah's womb.

BARRICADES (1)

Jdt 5: 1 and fortified all the high hilltops and set up **b** in

BARRIER (3) [BARRIERS]

Jer 5:22 a perpetual **b** that it cannot pass;
Eze 40:12 There was a **b** before the recesses,
1Mc 12:36 to erect a high **b** between the citadel and the city

BARRIERS (1) [BARRIER]

Isa 59: 2 your iniquities have been **b** between you

BARS (48) [BAR]

Ex 26:26 You shall make **b** of acacia wood,
26:27 and five **b** for the frames of the other side of
26:27 and five **b** for the frames of the side of
26:29 and shall make their rings of gold to hold the **b**;
26:29 and you shall overlay the **b** with gold.
35:11 its clasps and its frames, its **b**, its pillars,
36:31 He made **b** of acacia wood,
36:32 and five **b** for the frames of the other side of
36:32 and five **b** for the frames of the tabernacle at
36:34 and made rings of gold for them to hold the **b**,
36:34 and overlaid the **b** with gold.
39:33 its hooks, its frames, its **b**, its pillars, and its bases;
Lev 26:13 the **b** of your yoke and made you walk erect.
Nu 3:36 the **b**, the pillars, the bases,
4:31 the frames of the tabernacle, with its **b**, pillars,
Dt 3: 5 double gates, and **b**, besides a great many villages.
33:25 Your **b** are iron and bronze;
1Sa 23: 7 in by entering a town that has gates and **b**."
1Ki 4:13 sixty great cities with walls and bronze **b**);
2Ch 8: 5 fortified cities, with walls, gates, and **b**,
14: 7 with walls and towers, gates and **b**;
Ne 3: 3 and set up its doors, its bolts, and its **b**.
3: 6 and set up its doors, its bolts, and its **b**.
3:13 and set up its doors, its bolts, and its **b**,
3:14 and set up its doors, its bolts, and its **b**.
3:15 and set up its doors, its bolts, and its **b**;
Job 17:16 Will it go down to the **b** of Sheol?
38:10 and prescribed bounds for it, and set **b** and doors,
40:18 its limbs like **b** of iron.
Ps 107:16 and cuts in two the **b** of iron.
147:13 For he strengthens the **b** of your gates;
Pr 18:19 such quarreling is like the **b** of a castle.
Isa 43:14 to Babylon and break down all the **b**,
45: 2 in pieces the doors of bronze and cut through the **b**
Jer 27: 2 Make yourself a yoke of straps and **b**,
28:13 You have broken wooden **b** only to forge iron **b**
49:31 that has no gates or **b**, that lives alone.
51:30 her buildings are set on fire, her **b** are broken.
La 2: 9 he has ruined and broken her **b**;
Eze 34:27 when I break the **b** of their yoke,
38:11 and having no **b** or gates";
Am 1: 5 I will break the gate **b** of Damascus,
Jnh 2: 6 down to the land whose **b** closed upon me forever;
Na 3:13 fire has devoured the **b** of your gates.
Sir 49:13 set up gates and **b**, and rebuilt our ruined houses.
LtJ 6:18 with doors and locks and **b**,
1Mc 9:50 and Tephon, with high walls and gates and **b**.

BARSABBAS (2) [=JOSEPH, =JUDAS, =JUSTUS]

Ac 1:23 So they proposed two, Joseph called **B**,
15:22 They sent Judas called **B**, and Silas,

BARTACUS (1)

1Es 4:29 the daughter of the illustrious **B**;

BARTER (1) [BARTERED]

Eze 27: 9 the sea with their mariners were within you, to **b**

BARTERED (1) [BARTER]

Eze 27:19 and sweet cane were **b** for your merchandise.

BARTHOLOMEW (4) [=NATHANAEL?]

Mt 10: 3 Philip and **B**; Thomas
Mk 3:18 and Philip, and **B**, and Matthew, and Thomas,
Lk 6:14 and James, and John, and Philip, and **B**,
Ac 1:13 and Andrew, Philip and Thomas, **B** and Matthew,

BARTIMAEUS (1)

Mk 10:46 **B** son of Timaeus, a blind beggar,

BARUCH (29)

Ne 3:20 After him **B** son of Zabbai
10: 6 Daniel, Ginnethon, **B**,
11: 5 and Maaseiah son of **B** son of Col-hozeh son
Jer 32:12 of purchase to **B** son of Neriah son of Mahseiah,
32:13 In their presence I charged **B**, saying,
32:16 the deed of purchase to **B** son of Neriah, I prayed
36: 4 Then Jeremiah called **B** son of Neriah,
36: 4 and **B** wrote on a scroll at Jeremiah's dictation all
36: 5 And Jeremiah ordered **B**, saying,
36: 8 And **B** son of Neriah did all that
36:10 **B** read the words of Jeremiah from the scroll,
36:13 **B** read the scroll in the hearing of the people.
36:14 of Shelemiah son of Cushi to say to **B**,
36:14 So **B** son of Neriah took the scroll in his hand
36:15 So **B** read it to them.
36:16 they turned to one another in alarm, and said to **B**,
36:17 Then they questioned **B**, "Tell us now,
36:18 **B** answered them, "He dictated all these words
36:19 Then the officials said to **B**, "Go and hide,
36:26 to arrest the secretary **B** and the prophet Jeremiah.
36:27 that **B** wrote at Jeremiah's dictation, the word of
36:32 to the secretary **B** son of Neriah, who wrote on it
43: 3 but **B** son of Neriah is inciting you against us,
43: 6 also the prophet Jeremiah and **B** son of Neriah.
45: 1 to **B** son of Neriah, when he wrote these words in
45: 2 the God of Israel, to you, O **B**:
Bar 1: 1 the words of the book that **B** son of Neriah son
1: 3 **B** read the words of this book to Jeconiah son
1: 8 **B** took the vessels of the house of the Lord,

BARZILLAI (13)

2Sa 17:27 and **B** the Gileadite from Rogelim,
19:31 **B** the Gileadite had come down from Rogelim;
19:32 **B** was a very aged man, eighty years old.
19:33 The king said to **B**, "Come over with me,
19:34 But **B** said to the king,
19:39 the king kissed **B** and blessed him,
21: 8 of Saul, whom she bore to Adriel son of **B**
1Ki 2: 7 however, with the sons of **B** the Gileadite,
Ezr 2:61 of Habaiah, Hakkoz, and **B** (who had married one
2:61 of the daughters of **B** the Gileadite,
Ne 7:63 of **B** (who had married one of the daughters
7:63 of the daughters of **B** the Gileadite and was called
1Es 5:38 one of the daughters of **B**,

BASE (28) [BASED, BASELY, BASES, BASIS]

Ex 25:31 The **b** and the shaft of the lampstand shall be made
29:12 of the blood you shall pour out at the **b** of the altar.
37:17 The **b** and the shaft of the lampstand were made
38:27 for the hundred talents, a talent for a **b**.
Lev 4: 7 the blood of the bull he shall pour out at the **b** of
4:18 and the rest of the blood he shall pour out at the **b**
4:25 of its blood at the **b** of the altar of burnt offering.
4:30 and he shall pour out the rest of its blood at the **b**
4:34 pour out the rest of its blood at the **b** of the altar.
5: 9 the blood shall be drained out at the **b** of the altar;
8:11 and the basin and its **b**, to consecrate them.
8:15 then he poured out the blood at the **b** of the altar.
9: 9 rest of the blood he poured out at the **b** of the altar.
Nu 8: 4 From its **b** to its flowers, it was hammered work;
2Ki 18:19 On what do you **b** this confidence of yours?
Ps 101: 3 I will not set before my eyes anything that is **b**.
Isa 3: 5 and the **b** to the honorable.
36: 4 On what do you **b** this confidence of yours?
Eze 41:22 its corners, its **b**, and its walls were of wood.
43:13 its **b** shall be one cubit high, and one cubit wide,
43:14 the **b** on the ground to the lower ledge, two cubits,
43:17 and its surrounding **b**, one cubit.
Zec 5:11 they will set the basket down there on its **b**."
1Ti 6: 4 dissension, slander, **b** suspicions,
Wis 2:16 We are considered by him as something **b**,
15:12 however one can, even by **b** means.
Sir 18:30 not follow your **b** desires,
18:31 If you allow your soul to take pleasure in **b** desire,

BASED (3) [BASE]

Ro 9:31 who did strive for the righteousness that is **b** on
9:32 but as if it were **b** on works.
Php 3: 9 the righteousness from God **b** on faith.

BASELY (1) [BASE]

4Mc 6:17 think so **b** that out of cowardice we feign

BASEMATH (7)
Ge 26:34 and **B** daughter of Elon the Hittite;
36:3 and **B**, Ishmael's daughter, sister of Nebaioth.
36:4 Adah bore Eliphaz to Esau; **B** bore Reuel;
36:10 Reuel, the son of Esau's wife **B**.
36:13 These were the sons of Esau's wife, **B**.
36:17 they are the sons of Esau's wife **B**.
1Ki 4:15 in Naphtali (he had taken **B**, Solomon's daughter,

BASER (KJV) See RUFFIANS

BASES (57) [BASE]
Ex 26:19 and you shall make forty **b** of silver under
26:19 two **b** under the first frame for its two pegs,
26:19 and two **b** under the next frame for its two pegs;
26:21 their forty **b** of silver, two **b** under the first frame,
26:21 and two **b** under the next frame;
26:25 with their **b** of silver, sixteen **b**;
26:25 two **b** under the first frame, and two **b** under the
26:32 which have hooks of gold and rest on four **b**
26:37 and you shall cast five **b** of bronze for them.
27:10 its twenty pillars and their twenty **b** shall be
27:11 their pillars twenty and their **b** twenty, of bronze,
27:12 with ten pillars and ten **b**.
27:14 with three pillars and three **b**.
27:15 with three pillars and three **b**.
27:16 it shall have four pillars and with them four **b**.
27:17 their hooks shall be of silver, and their **b**
27:18 with hangings of fine twisted linen and **b**
35:11 its bars, its pillars, and its **b**;
35:17 and its **b**, and the screen for the gate of the court;
36:24 he made forty **b** of silver under the twenty frames,
36:24 two **b** under the first frame for its two pegs,
36:24 and two **b** under the next frame for its two pegs.
36:26 and their forty **b** of silver,
36:26 two **b** under the first frame and two **b** under the
36:30 There were eight frames with their **b** of silver:
36:30 sixteen **b**, under every frame two **b**.
36:36 and he cast for them four **b** of silver.
36:38 He overlaid their capitals and their **b** with gold,
36:38 but their five **b** were of bronze.
38:10 its twenty pillars and their twenty **b** were
38:11 its twenty pillars and their twenty **b** were
38:12 with ten pillars and ten **b**;
38:14 with three pillars and three **b**.
38:15 with three pillars and three **b**.
38:17 The **b** for the pillars were of bronze,
38:19 their four **b** were of bronze, their hooks of silver,
38:27 the **b** of the sanctuary, and the **b** of the curtain;
38:27 one hundred **b** for the hundred talents,
38:30 with it he made the **b** for the entrance of the tent
38:31 the **b** all around the court,
38:31 and the **b** of the gate of the court,
39:33 its hooks, its frames, its bars, its pillars, and its **b**;
39:40 and its **b**, and the screen for the gate of the court,
40:18 Moses set up the tabernacle; he laid its **b**,
Nu 3:36 the pillars, the **b**, and all their accessories—
3:37 with their **b** and pegs and cords.
4:31 with its bars, pillars, and **b**,
4:32 and the pillars of the court all around with their **b**,
Job 38:6 On what were its **b** sunk,
SS 5:15 His legs are alabaster columns, set upon **b** of gold.
Sir 26:18 Like golden pillars on silver **b**,

BASEST (KJV) See LOWLY

BASHAN (60)
Nu 21:33 Then they turned and went up the road to **B**;
21:33 and King Og of **B** came out against them,
32:33 the Amorites and the kingdom of King Og of **B**,
Dt 1:4 who reigned in Heshbon, and King Og of **B**,
3:1 When we headed up the road to **B**,
3:1 King Og of **B** came out against us,
3:3 over to us King Og of **B** and all his people.
3:4 of Argob, the kingdom of Og in **B**.
3:10 and all of **B**, as far as Salecah and Edrei,
3:10 towns of Og's kingdom in **B**.
3:11 (Now only King Og of **B** was left of the remnant
3:13 of Manasseh the rest of Gilead and all of **B**,
3:13 all that portion of **B** used to be called a land
3:14 **B**—after himself, Havvoth-jair, as it is to this day.)
4:43 and Golan in **B** belonging to the Manassites.
4:47 of King Og of **B**, the two kings of the Amorites on
29:7 of Heshbon and King Og of **B** came out against us
32:14 **B** bulls and goats, together with the choicest wheat
33:22 Dan is a lion's whelp that leaps forth from **B**.
Jos 9:10 and King Og of **B** who lived in Ashtaroth.
12:4 of **B**, one of the last of the Rephaim, who lived
12:5 and all **B** to the boundary of the Geshurites and
13:11 and all Mount Hermon, and all **B** to Salecah;
13:12 the kingdom of Og in **B**, who reigned in Ashtaroth
13:30 through all **B**, the whole kingdom of King Og of
B, and all the settlements of Jair, which are in **B**,
13:31 and Edrei, the towns of the kingdom of Og in **B**;
17:1 the father of Gilead, were allotted Gilead and **B**,
17:5 besides the land of Gilead and **B**,
20:8 and Golan in **B**, from the tribe of Manasseh.
21:6 and from the half-tribe of Manasseh in **B**.
21:27 Golan in **B** with its pasture lands,
22:7 of Manasseh Moses had given a possession in **B**;
1Ki 4:13 and he had the region of Argob, which is in **B**,
4:19 of the Amorites and of King Og of **B**.
2Ki 10:33 which is by the Wadi Arnon, that is, Gilead and **B**.
1Ch 5:11 of Gad lived beside them in the land of **B** as far
1Ch 5:12 Shapham the second, Janai, and Shaphat in **B**.
5:16 in **B** and in its towns,
5:23 they were very numerous from **B** to Baal-hermon,
6:62 Asher, Naphtali, and Manasseh in **B**.
6:71 Golan in **B** with its pasture lands and Ashtaroth
Ne 9:22 of Heshbon and the land of King Og of **B**.
Ps 22:12 strong bulls of **B** surround me;
68:15 O mighty mountain, mountain of **B**;
68:15 O many-peaked mountain, mountain of **B**!
68:22 The Lord said, "I will bring them back from **B**,
135:11 king of **B**, and all the kingdoms of Canaan—
136:20 king of **B**, for his steadfast love endures forever;
Isa 2:13 and against all the oaks of **B**;
33:9 and **B** and Carmel shake off their leaves.
Jer 22:20 and cry out, and lift up your voice in **B**;
50:19 and it shall feed on Carmel and in **B**,
Eze 27:6 From oaks of **B** they made your oars;
39:18 and of goats, of bulls, all of them fatlings of **B**.
Am 4:1 you cows of **B** who are on Mount Samaria,
Mic 7:14 let them feed in **B** and Gilead as in the days of old.
Na 1:4 **B** and Carmel wither, and the bloom of Lebanon
Zec 11:2 Wail, oaks of **B**, for the thick forest

BASHANHAVOTHJAIR (KJV) See HAVVOTH-JAIR

BASHEMATH (KJV) See BASEMATH

BASIC (3)
Heb 5:12 to teach you again the **b** elements of the oracles
6:1 leaving behind the **b** teaching about Christ,
Sir 39:26 The **b** necessities of human life are water and fire

BASIN (31) [BASINS, WASHBASIN]
Ex 12:22 dip it in the blood that is in the **b**,
12:22 and the two doorposts with the blood in the **b**.
30:18 You shall make a bronze **b** with a bronze stand
30:28 and the **b** with its stand;
31:9 and the **b** with its stand,
35:16 its poles, and all its utensils, the **b** with its stand;
38:8 He made the **b** of bronze with its stand of bronze,
39:39 and all its utensils; the **b** with its stand;
40:7 and place the **b** between the tent of meeting and
40:11 You shall also anoint the **b** with its stand,
40:30 the **b** between the tent of meeting and the altar,
Lev 8:11 and the **b** and its base, to consecrate them.
Nu 7:13 one silver **b** weighing seventy shekels,
7:19 one silver **b** weighing seventy shekels,
7:25 one silver **b** weighing seventy shekels,
7:31 one silver **b** weighing seventy shekels,
7:37 one silver **b** weighing seventy shekels,
7:43 one silver **b** weighing seventy shekels,
7:49 one silver **b** weighing seventy shekels,
7:55 one silver **b** weighing seventy shekels,
7:61 one silver **b** weighing seventy shekels,
7:67 one silver **b** weighing seventy shekels,
7:73 one silver **b** weighing seventy shekels,
7:79 one silver **b** weighing seventy shekels,
7:85 and each **b** seventy, all the silver of
1Ki 7:30 at the four corners were supports for a **b**.
7:38 of bronze; each **b** held forty baths,
7:38 each **b** measured four cubits;
7:38 there was a **b** for each of the ten stands.
Jn 13:5 into a **b** and began to wash the disciples' feet and
4Mc 13:6 for those who sail into the inner **b**,

BASINS‡ (24) [BASIN]
Ex 24:6 Moses took half of the blood and put it in **b**,
27:3 and shovels and **b** and forks and firepans;
38:3 the shovels, the **b**, the forks, and the firepans:
Nu 4:14 the shovels, and the **b**, all the utensils of the altar:
7:84 twelve silver plates, twelve silver **b**,
2Sa 17:28 **b**, and earthen vessels, wheat, barley, meal,
1Ki 7:38 He made ten **b** of bronze;
7:40 Hiram also made the pots, the shovels, and the **b**.
7:43 the ten stands, the ten **b** on the stands;
7:45 The pots, the shovels, and the **b**,
7:50 **b**, dishes for incense, and firepans, of pure gold;
2Ki 12:13 But for the house of the LORD no **b** of silver,
25:15 as well as the firepans and the **b**.
1Ch 28:17 and pure gold for the forks, the **b**, and the cups;
2Ch 4:6 He also made ten **b** in which to wash,
4:8 And he made one hundred **b** of gold.
4:11 And Huram made the pots, the shovels, and the **b**.
4:14 He made the stands, the **b** on the stands,
4:22 **b**, ladles, and firepans, of pure gold.
Ezr 1:9 inventory: gold **b**, thirty; silver **b**, one thousand;
Ne 7:70 fifty **b**, and five hundred thirty priestly robes.
Jer 52:18 the shovels, the snuffers, the **b**, the ladles,
52:19 the firepans, the **b**, the pots, the lampstands,

BASIS‡ (5) [BASE]
Lk 23:4 "I find no **b** for an accusation against this man."
Ro 9:32 Because they did not strive for it on the **b** of faith,
11:6 if it is by grace, it is no longer on the **b** of works,
1Ti 5:21 doing nothing on the **b** of partiality.
Phm 1:9 yet I would rather appeal to you on the **b** of love—

BASKAMA (1)
1Mc 13:23 When he approached **B**, he killed Jonathan,

BASKET‡ (34) [BASKETS]
Ge 40:17 the uppermost **b** there were all sorts of baked food
Ge 40:17 the birds were eating it out of the **b** on my head."
Ex 2:3 a papyrus **b** for him, and plastered it with bitumen
2:5 She saw the **b** among the reeds and sent her maid
29:3 You shall put them in one **b** and bring them in
29:3 in one basket and bring them in the **b**,
29:23 out of the **b** of unleavened bread that is before
29:32 the flesh of the ram and the bread that is in the **b**,
Lev 8:2 the two rams, and the **b** of unleavened bread;
8:26 From the **b** of unleavened bread that was before
8:31 the bread that is in the **b** of ordination offerings,
Nu 6:15 and a **b** of unleavened bread,
6:17 with the **b** of unleavened bread;
6:19 and one unleavened cake out of the **b**,
Dt 26:2 and you shall put it in a **b** and go to the place that
26:4 the priest takes the **b** from your hand and sets it
28:5 Blessed shall be your **b** and your kneading bowl.
28:17 Cursed shall be your **b** and your kneading bowl.
Jdg 6:19 the meat he put in a **b**,
Ps 81:6 your hands were freed from the **b**.
Jer 24:2 One **b** had very good figs, like first-ripe figs, but
the other **b** had very bad figs,
Am 8:1 the Lord GOD showed me—a **b** of summer fruit.
8:2 And I said, "A **b** of summer fruit."
Zec 5:6 He said, "This is a **b** coming out."
5:7 and there was a woman sitting in the **b**!
5:8 So he thrust her back into the **b**,
5:9 and they lifted up the **b** between earth and sky.
5:10 "Where are they taking the **b**?"
5:11 they will set the **b** down there on its base."
Mt 5:15 after lighting a lamp puts it under the bushel **b**,
Mk 4:21 "Is a lamp brought in to be put under the bushel **b**,
Ac 9:25 an opening in the wall, lowering him in a **b**.
2Co 11:33 but I was let down in a **b** through a window in

BASKETS (15) [BASKET]
Ge 40:16 there were three cake **b** on my head,
40:18 the three **b** are three days;
2Ki 10:7 they put their heads in **b** and sent them to him
Jer 24:1 The LORD showed me two **b** of figs placed
Mt 13:48 and put the good into **b** but threw out the bad.
14:20 over of the broken pieces, twelve **b** full.
15:37 up the broken pieces left over, seven **b** full.
16:9 and how many **b** you gathered?
16:10 and how many **b** you gathered?
Mk 6:43 up twelve **b** full of broken pieces and of the fish.
8:8 up the broken pieces left over, seven **b** full.
8:19 many **b** full of broken pieces did you collect?"
8:20 many **b** full of broken pieces did you collect?"
Lk 9:17 twelve **b** of broken pieces.
Jn 6:13 left by those who had eaten, they filled twelve **b**.

BASMATH (KJV) See BASEMATH

BASON[S] (KJV) See BASIN[S]

BASTARD[S] (KJV) See BORN OF AN ILLICIT UNION, ILLEGITIMATE, MONGREL

BASTHAI (1)
1Es 5:31 the descendants of Hasrah, the descendants of **B**,

BAT (2) [BATS]
Lev 11:19 the heron of any kind, the hoopoe, and the **b**.
Dt 14:18 of any kind; the hoopoe and the **b**.

BATCH (6)
Nu 15:20 From your first **b** of dough you shall present a loaf
15:21 to the LORD a donation from the first of your **b**
Ro 11:16 then the whole **b** is holy;
1Co 5:6 that a little yeast leavens the whole **b** of dough?
5:7 the old yeast so that you may be a new **b**,
Gal 5:9 A little yeast leavens the whole **b** of dough.

BATH (5) [BATHS]
Isa 5:10 For ten acres of vineyard shall yield but one **b**,
Eze 45:10 an honest ephah, and an honest **b**.
45:11 The ephah and the **b** shall be of the same measure,
45:11 the **b** containing one-tenth of a homer,
45:14 one-tenth of a **b** from each cor (the cor,

BATH-RABBIM (1)
SS 7:4 Your eyes are pools in Heshbon, by the gate of **B**.

BATH-SHUA (2)
1Ch 2:3 these three the Canaanite woman **B** bore to him.
3:5 and Solomon, four by **B**, daughter of Ammiel;

BATHE (29) [BATHED, BATHING]
Ex 2:5 daughter of Pharaoh came down to **b** at the river,
Lev 14:8 and shave off all his hair, and **b** himself in water,
14:9 he shall wash his clothes, and **b** his body in water,
15:5 and **b** in water, and be unclean until the evening.
15:6 and **b** in water, and be unclean until the evening.
15:7 and **b** in water, and be unclean until the evening.
15:8 then they shall wash their clothes, and **b** in water,
15:10 and **b** in water, and be unclean until the evening.
15:11 and **b** in water, and be unclean until the evening.
15:13 he shall wash his clothes and **b** his body
15:16 he shall **b** his whole body in water,
15:18 both of them shall **b** in water,
15:21 and **b** in water, and be unclean until the evening.

Lev 15:22 and **b** in water, and be unclean until the evening;
15:27 and **b** in water, and be unclean until the evening.
16: 4 He shall **b** his body in water,
16:24 He shall **b** his body in water in a holy place,
16:26 for Azazel shall wash his clothes and **b** his body
16:28 and **b** his body in water,
17:15 and **b** themselves in water,
17:16 if they do not wash themselves or **b** their body,
Nu 19: 7 the priest shall wash his clothes and **b** his body
19: 8 in water and **b** his body in water;
19:19 and **b** themselves in water,
Ps 58:10 they will **b** their feet in the blood of the wicked.
68:23 so that you may **b** your feet in blood,
Lk 7:38 to **b** his feet with her tears and to dry them
Sus 1:15 and wished to **b** in the garden, for it was a hot day.
1:17 and shut the garden doors so that I can **b.**"

BATHED (15) [BATHE]

SS 5: 3 I had **b** my feet; how could I soil them?
5:12 **b** in milk, fitly set.
Eze 16: 9 Then I **b** you with water and washed off the blood
23:40 For them you **b** yourself, painted your eyes,
Da 4:15 Let him be **b** with the dew of heaven.
4:23 and let him be **b** with the dew of heaven,
4:25 you shall be **b** with the dew of heaven,
4:33 and his body was **b** with the dew of heaven,
5:21 and his body was **b** with the dew of heaven,
Lk 7:44 for my feet, but she has **b** my feet with her tears
Jn 13:10 "One who has **b** does not need to wash,
Tob 7: 9 When they had **b** and washed themselves
Jdt 10: 3 **b** her body with water, and anointed herself
12: 7 and **b** at the spring in the camp.
4Mc 6:11 with his face **b** in sweat,

BATHING (2) [BATHE]

2Sa 11: 2 that he saw from the roof a woman **b;**
Jdt 12: 8 After **b,** she prayed the Lord God of Israel

BATHS (9) [BATH]

1Ki 7:26 like the flower of a lily; it held two thousand **b.**
7:38 of bronze; each basin held forty **b,**
2Ch 2:10 twenty thousand **b** of wine, and twenty thousand **b** of oil."
4: 5 like the flower of a lily; it held three thousand **b.**
Ezr 7:22 one hundred **b** of wine, one hundred **b** of oil,
Eze 45:14 like the homer, contains ten **b);**
1Es 8:20 a hundred **b** of wine, and salt in abundance.

BATHSHEBA (11)

2Sa 11: 3 It was reported, "This is **B** daughter of Eliam,
12:24 Then David consoled his wife **B,** and went to her,
1Ki 1:11 Then Nathan said to **B,** Solomon's mother,
1:15 So **B** went to the king in his room.
1:16 **B** bowed and did obeisance to the king,
1:28 King David answered, "Summon **B** to me."
1:31 Then **B** bowed with her face to the ground,
2:13 Then Adonijah son of Haggith came to **B,**
2:18 **B** said, "Very well; I will speak to the
2:19 So **B** went to King Solomon,
Ps 51: T *Nathan came to him, after he had gone in to* **B.**

BATS (2) [BAT]

Isa 2:20 to the **b** their idols of silver and their idols of gold,
LtJ 6:22 **B,** swallows, and birds alight on their bodies

BATTER (1) [BATTERED, BATTERING, BATTERING-RAMS]

Ps 62: 3 will you **b** your victim, all of you,

BATTERED (3) [BATTER]

Isa 24:12 the gates are **b** into ruins.
Mt 14:24 **b** by the waves, was far from the land,
1Mc 13:43 and **b** and captured one tower.

BATTERING (6) [BATTER]

2Sa 20:15 Joab's forces were **b** the wall to break it down.
Isa 22: 5 a **b** down of walls and a cry for help
Eze 4: 2 and plant **b** rams against it all around.
21:22 to set **b** rams, to call out for slaughter,
21:22 to set **b** rams against the gates, to cast up ramps,
26: 9 of his **b** rams against your walls and break

BATTERING-RAMS (1) [BATTER]

2Mc 12:15 without **b** or engines of war overthrew Jericho in

BATTLE (263) [BATTLEFIELD, BATTLEMENT, BATTLEMENTS, BATTLES, BATTLING]

Ge 14: 8 and they joined **b** in the Valley of Siddim
Ex 13:18 up out of the land of Egypt prepared for **b.**
Nu 21:33 he and all his people, to **b** at Edrei.
31: 5 twelve thousand armed for **b.**
31: 7 They did **b** against Midian,
31:21 the priest said to the troops who had gone to **b:**
31:27 between the warriors who went out to **b** and all
31:28 From the share of the warriors who went out to **b,**
32:27 everyone armed for war, to do **b** for the LORD,
32:29 everyone armed for **b** before the LORD,
Dt 1:41 So all of you strapped on your **b** gear,
2: 5 not to engage in **b** with them,
2: 9 "Do not harass Moab or engage them in **b,**
Dt 2:19 do not harass them or engage them in **b,**
2:24 Begin to take possession by engaging him in **b.**
2:32 he and all his people for **b** at Jahaz,
3: 1 he and all his people, for **b** at Edrei.
20: 2 in **b,** the priest shall come forward and speak to
20: 3 Today you are drawing near to do **b**
20: 5 or he might die in the **b** and another dedicate it.
20: 6 in the **b** and another be first to enjoy its fruit.
20: 7 or he might die in the **b** and another marry her."
29: 7 and King Og of Bashan came out against us for **b,**
Jos 4:13 before the LORD to the plains of Jericho for **b.**
8:14 the Arabah to meet Israel in **b;**
11:19 of Gibeon; all were taken in **b.**
11:20 so that they would come against Israel in **b,**
Jdg 8:13 When Gideon son of Joash returned from the **b** by
20:14 to go out to **b** against the Israelites.
20:18 "Which of us shall go up first to **b** against
20:20 The Israelites went out to **b** against Benjamin;
20:20 and the Israelites drew up the **b** line against them
20:22 and again formed the **b** line in the same place
20:23 near to **b** against our kinsfolk the Benjaminites?"
20:28 to **b** against our kinsfolk the Benjaminites,
20:33 of the Israelites drew back its **b** line to Baal-tamar,
20:34 of all Israel, and the **b** was fierce.
20:39 the main body of Israel should turn in **b.**
20:39 before us, as in the first **b.**"
20:42 but the **b** overtook them, and those who came out
21:22 we did not capture in **b** a wife for each man.
1Sa 4: 1 and Israel went out to **b** against them;
4: 2 and when the **b** was joined,
4: 2 about four thousand men on the field of **b.**
4:12 A man of Benjamin ran from the **b** line,
4:16 The man said to Eli, "I have just come from the **b;**
4:16 I fled from the **b** today."
13:22 of the **b** neither sword nor spear was to be found in
14:20 with him rallied and went into the **b;**
14:22 they too followed closely after them in the **b.**
14:23 The **b** passed beyond Beth-aven,
14:23 The **b** spread out over the hill country of Ephraim.
17: 1 Now the Philistines gathered their armies for **b;**
17: 8 "Why have you come out to draw up for **b?**
17:13 of Jesse had followed Saul to the **b;**
17:13 of his three sons who went to the **b** were Eliab
17:20 as the army was going forth to the **b** line,
17:21 Israel and the Philistines drew up for **b,**
17:28 for you have come down just to see the **b.**"
17:47 for the **b** is the LORD's and he will give you
17:48 David ran quickly toward the **b** line to meet
18:30 the commanders of the Philistines came out to **b;**
26:10 or he will go down into **b** and perish.
29: 4 he shall not go down with us to **b,**
29: 4 or else he may become an adversary to us in the **b.**
29: 9 'He shall not go up with us to the **b.**'
30:24 down into the **b** shall be the same as the share of
31: 3 The **b** pressed hard upon Saul;
2Sa 1: 4 He answered, "The army fled from the **b,**
1:25 How the mighty have fallen in the midst of the **b!**
2:17 The **b** was very fierce that day;
2:28 or engaged in **b** any further.
3:30 because he had killed their brother Asahel in the **b**
10: 8 and drew up in **b** array at the entrance of the gate;
10: 9 When Joab saw that the **b** was set against him both
10:13 with him moved forward into **b** against
11: 1 the time when kings go out to **b,**
17:11 and that you go to **b** in person.
18: 6 and the **b** was fought in the forest of Ephraim.
18: 8 The **b** spread over the face of all the country;
19: 3 in who are ashamed when they flee in **b.**
19:10 Absalom, whom we anointed over us, is dead in **b.**
21:17 "You shall not go out with us to **b** any longer,
21:18 this a **b** took place with the Philistines, at Gob;
21:19 there was another **b** with the Philistines at Gob;
22:40 For you girded me with strength for the **b;**
23: 9 the Philistines who were gathered there for **b.**
1Ki 8:44 "If your people go out to **b** against their enemy,
20:14 Then he said, "Who shall begin the **b?**"
20:29 Then on the seventh day the **b** began;
20:39 "Your servant went out into the thick of the **b;**
22: 4 "Will you go with me to **b** at Ramoth-gilead?"
22: 6 "Shall I go to **b** against Ramoth-gilead,
22:15 "Micaiah, shall we go to Ramoth-gilead to **b,**
22:30 "I will disguise myself and go into **b,**
22:30 king of Israel disguised himself and went into **b.**
22:34 and carry me out of the **b,** for I am wounded."
22:35 The **b** grew hot that day, and the king was propped
2Ki 3: 7 will you go with me to **b** against Moab?"
3:26 When the king of Moab saw that the **b** was going
14:11 and King Amaziah of Judah faced one another in **b**
1Ch 5:20 for they cried to God in the **b,**
10: 3 The **b** pressed hard on Saul;
11:13 when the Philistines were gathered there for **b.**
12:19 when he came with the Philistines for the **b**
12:33 equipped for **b** with all the weapons of war,
12:35 twenty-eight thousand six hundred equipped for **b.**
12:36 forty thousand seasoned troops ready for **b.**
12:38 All these, warriors arrayed in **b** order,
14:15 in the tops of the balsam trees, then go out to **b;**
19: 7 from their cities and came to **b.**
19: 9 and drew up in **b** array at the entrance of the city,
19:10 that the line of **b** was set against him both in front
19:14 with him advanced toward the Arameans for **b;**
19:17 David set the **b** in array against the Arameans,
20: 1 the time when kings go out to **b,**
2Ch 6:34 "If your people go out to **b** against their enemies,
13: 3 Abijah engaged in **b,** having an army
13: 3 and Jeroboam drew up his line of **b** against him
13:12 and his priests have their **b** trumpets to sound
2Ch 13:12 to sound the call to **b** against you.
13:14 the **b** was in front of them and behind them.
13:15 Then the people of Judah raised the **b** shout.
14:10 and they drew up their lines of **b** in the valley
18: 5 "Shall we go to **b** against Ramoth-gilead,
18:14 "Micaiah, shall we go to Ramoth-gilead to **b,**
18:29 "I will disguise myself and go into **b,**
18:29 of Israel disguised himself, and they went into **b.**
18:33 and carry me out of the **b,** for I am wounded."
18:34 The **b** grew hot that day, and the king
20: 1 came against Jehoshaphat for **b.**
20:15 for the **b** is not yours but God's.
20:17 This **b** is not for you to fight;
25: 8 Rather, go by yourself and act; be strong in **b,**
25:13 not letting them go with him to **b,**
25:21 and King Amaziah of Judah faced one another in **b**
35:22 but joined **b** in the plain of Megiddo.
Job 15:24 like a king prepared for **b.**
38:23 for the day of **b** and war?
39:25 From a distance it smells the **b,**
41: 8 think of the **b;** you will not do it again!
Ps 18:39 For you girded me with strength for the **b;**
24: 8 strong and mighty, the LORD, mighty in **b.**
55:18 He will redeem me unharmed from the **b**
78: 9 armed with the bow, turned back on the day of **b.**
89:43 and you have not supported him in **b.**
140: 7 you have covered my head in the day of **b.**
144: 1 for war, and my fingers for **b;**
Pr 21:31 The horse is made ready for the day of **b,**
Ecc 8: 8 there is no discharge from the **b,**
9:11 nor the **b** to the strong, nor bread to the wise,
Isa 3:25 by the sword and your warriors in **b.**
13: 4 The LORD of hosts is mustering an army for **b.**
21:15 from the bent bow, and from the stress of **b.**
22: 2 nor are they dead in **b.**
27: 4 I will march to **b** against it.
28: 6 strength to those who turn back the **b** at the gate.
Jer 6:23 they ride on horses, equipped like a warrior for **b,**
8: 6 like a horse plunging headlong into **b.**
18:21 their youths be slain by the sword in **b.**
46: 3 Prepare buckler and shield, and advance for **b!**
49: 2 when I will sound the **b** alarm against Rabbah of
49:14 and come against her, and rise up for **b!**"
50:22 The noise of **b** is in the land, and great destruction!
50:42 set in array as a warrior for **b,** against you,
51:20 You are my war club, my weapon of **b:**
Eze 7:14 but no one goes to **b,**
13: 5 that it might stand in **b** on the day of the LORD.
21:22 to call out for slaughter, for raising the **b** cry,
Da 11:11 the king of the south shall go out and do **b** against
11:20 though not in anger or in **b.**
Hos 10:14 the day of **b** when mothers were dashed in pieces
Joel 2: 5 like a powerful army drawn up for **b.**
Am 1:14 with shouting on the day of **b,**
Ob 1: 1 Let us rise against it for **b!**"
Zep 1:16 and **b** cry against the fortified cities and against
Zec 9:10 and the **b** bow shall be cut off,
10: 4 of them the **b** bow, out of them every commander.
10: 5 Together they shall be like warriors in **b,**
14: 2 I will gather all the nations against Jerusalem to **b,**
14: 3 as when he fights on a day of **b.**
1Co 14: 8 who will get ready for **b?**
Rev 9: 7 the locusts were like horses equipped for **b.**
9: 9 of many chariots with horses rushing into **b.**
16:14 to assemble them for **b** on the great day of God
20: 8 Gog and Magog, in order to gather them for **b;**
Jdt 1:13 against King Arphaxad and defeated him in **b,**
14:13 so bold as to come down against us to give **b,**
Wis 12: 9 the ungodly into the hands of the righteous in **b,**
Sir 37: 5 yet in **b** they will carry his shield.
37: 6 Do not forget a friend during the **b,**
46: 6 He overwhelmed that nation in **b,**
1Mc 1:18 He engaged King Ptolemy of Egypt in **b,**
2:32 they encamped opposite them and prepared for **b**
2:66 he shall command the army for you and fight the **b**
3:12 and used it in the rest of his life.
3:13 with him and went out to **b,**
3:19 on the size of the army that victory in **b** depends,
3:44 So the congregation assembled to be ready for **b,**
3:59 in **b** than to see the misfortunes of our nation and
4:13 they went out from their camp to **b,**
4:14 and engaged in **b.** The Gentiles were crushed,
4:17 for there is a **b** before us;
4:21 the army of Judas drawn up in the plain for **b,**
5:19 not engage in **b** with the Gentiles until we return."
5:31 So Judas saw that the **b** had begun and that the cry
5:42 but make them all enter the **b.**"
5:59 of the town to meet them in **b.**
5:67 fell in **b,** for they went out to **b** unwisely.
6: 4 and they withstood him in **b.**
6:33 for **b** and sounded their trumpets.
6:34 of grapes and mulberries, to arouse them for **b.**
6:42 But Judas and his army advanced to the **b,**
7:31 to meet Judas in **b** near Caphar-salama.
7:43 in **b** on the thirteenth day of the month of Adar.
7:43 and he himself was the first to fall in the **b.**
7:45 and as they followed they kept sounding the **b** call
8: 5 They had crushed in **b** and conquered Philip,
9: 1 that Nicanor and his army had fallen in **b,**
9: 7 and the **b** was imminent, he was crushed in spirit,
9:13 and the **b** raged from morning until evening.
9:17 The **b** became desperate, and many on
9:30 as our ruler and leader, to fight our **b.**"
9:45 the **b** is in front of us and behind us;
9:47 the **b** began, and Jonathan stretched out his hand
9:67 he began to attack and went into **b** with his forces;
10: 2 and marched out to meet him in **b.**

1Mc 10:49 The two kings met in **b**,
10:50 He pressed the **b** strongly until the sun set,
10:53 I met him in **b**, and he and his army were crushed
10:78 and the armies engaged in **b**.
10:82 the phalanx in **b** (for the cavalry was exhausted);
11:15 Alexander heard of it, he came against him in **b**.
11:69 in ambush emerged from their places and joined **b**.
11:72 Then he turned back to the **b** against the enemy
12:27 at hand so as to be ready all night for **b**,
12:28 for **b**, they were afraid and were terrified at heart;
12:50 and kept marching in close formation, ready for **b**.
13:14 and that he was about to join **b** with him,
15:14 and the ships joined **b** from the sea;
2Mc 8:20 of the **b** against the Galatians that took place
8:23 then, leading the first division himself, he joined **b**
10:28 the two armies joined **b**, the one having as pledge
10:29 When the **b** became fierce,
11:10 They advanced in **b** order,
12:34 When they joined **b**, it happened that a few of
12:36 to show himself their ally and leader in the **b**.
12:37 the language of their ancestors he raised the **b** cry,
14:16 from there immediately and engaged them in **b** at
14:18 of Judas and his troops and their courage in **b**
15:20 at hand with their army drawn up for **b**,
15:25 with trumpets and **b** songs,
15:26 but Judas and his troops met the enemy in **b**
1Es 1:29 He joined **b** with him in the plain of Megiddo,
1:30 "Take me away from the **b**, for I am very weak."
1:30 his servants took him out of the line of **b**.
3Mc 1: 4 of gold if they won the **b**.
3:14 by the gods' deliberate alliance with us in **b**,
2Es 15:30 in **b**, and with their tusks they shall devastate
16:40 Hear my words, O my people; prepare for **b**,
4Mc 9:24 Fight the sacred and noble **b** for religion.
17:24 and courageous for infantry **b** and siege,

BATTLEFIELD (1) [BATTLE, FIELD]
Sir 40: 6 of his mind like one who has escaped from the **b**.

BATTLEMENT (1) [BATTLE]
SS 8: 9 she is a wall, we will build upon her a **b** of silver;

BATTLEMENT (KJV) See also PARAPET

BATTLEMENTS (4) [BATTLE]
Zep 1:16 against the fortified cities and against the lofty **b**.
3: 6 I have cut off nations; their **b** are in ruins;
Tob 13:16 and their **b** with pure gold.
Sir 9:13 and that you are walking on the city **b**.

BATTLES (13) [BATTLE]
1Sa 8:20 and go out before us and fight our **b**."
18:17 only be valiant for me and fight the LORD's **b**."
25:28 because my lord is fighting the **b** of the LORD;
1Ch 26:27 in **b** they dedicated gifts for the maintenance of
2Ch 32: 8 to help us and to fight our **b**."
Jdt 5:18 in many **b** and were led away captive to
1Mc 1: 2 He fought many **b**, conquered strongholds,
3: 3 he bound on his armor of war and waged **b**,
3:26 and the Gentiles talked of the **b** of Judas.
5: 7 He engaged in many **b** with them,
5:21 to Galilee and fought many **b** against the Gentiles,
10:15 of the **b** that Jonathan and his brothers had fought,
13: 9 Fight our **b**, and all that you say to us we will do."

BATTLING (1) [BATTLE]
Isa 30:32 **b** with brandished arm he will fight with him.

BAVAI (KJV) See BINNUI

BAVVAI See Index to Footnotes

BAY (4)
Jos 15: 2 from the **b** that faces southward;
15: 5 on the north side runs from the **b** of the sea
18:19 boundary ends at the northern **b** of the Dead Sea,
Ac 27:39 but they noticed a **b** with a beach,

BAZAARS (1)
1Ki 20:34 and you may establish **b** for yourself in Damascus,

BAZAN (1)
AdE 1:10 he told Haman, **B**, Tharra, Boraze, Zatholtha,

BAZLITH (1) [=BAZLUTH]
Ne 7:54 of **B**, of Mehida, of Harsha,

BAZLUTH (2) [=BAZLITH]
Ezr 2:52 **B**, Mehida, Harsha,
1Es 5:31 of Pharakim, the descendants of **B**,

BDELLIUM (1)
Ge 2:12 **b** and onyx stone are there.

BDELLIUM (KJV) See also RESIN

BE (6394) [AM, ARE, BEEN, BEING, BEINGS, IS, WAS, WELL-BEING, WERE] See Index of Articles Etc.

BEACH (5)
Mt 13: 2 while the whole crowd stood on the **b**.
Jn 21: 4 Just after daybreak, Jesus stood on the **b**;
Ac 21: 5 There we knelt down on the **b** and prayed
27:39 but they noticed a bay with a **b**,
27:40 the foresail to the wind, they made for the **b**.

BEACHES See Index to Footnotes

BEACON (1)
Sir 43: 8 a **b** to the hosts on high, shining in the vault of the heavens!

BEACON (KJV) See also FLAGSTAFF

BEAK (1)
Ge 8:11 and there in its **b** was a freshly plucked olive leaf;

BEALIAH (1)
1Ch 12: 5 **B**, Shemariah, Shephatiah the Haruphite;

BEALOTH (2)
Jos 15:24 Ziph, Telem, **B**,
1Ki 4:16 Baana son of Hushai, in Asher and **B**;

BEAM‡ (8) [BEAMS]
1Sa 17: 7 The shaft of his spear was like a weaver's **b**,
2Sa 21:19 the shaft of whose spear was like a weaver's **b**.
1Ch 11:23 in his hand a spear like a weaver's **b**;
20: 5 the shaft of whose spear was like a weaver's **b**.
Ezr 6:11 a **b** shall be pulled out of the house of
Sir 22:16 A wooden **b** firmly bonded into a building is
LtJ 6:20 They are just like a **b** of the temple,
1Es 6:32 a **b** should be taken out of the house of

BEAMS (12) [BEAM]
1Ki 6: 6 the wall in order that the supporting **b** should not
6: 9 he roofed the house with **b** and planks of cedar.
6:36 of dressed stone to one course of cedar **b**.
7: 2 with cedar **b** on the pillars.
7:12 of dressed stone to one layer of cedar **b** all around;
2Ch 3: 7 its **b**, its thresholds, its walls, and its doors;
34:11 and **b** for the buildings that the kings
Ne 2: 8 directing him to give me timber to make **b** for
3: 3 they laid its **b** and set up its doors, its bolts,
3: 6 they laid its **b** and set up its doors, its bolts,
Ps 104: 3 you set the **b** of your chambers on the waters,
SS 1:17 the **b** of our house are cedar, our rafters are pine.

BEAN See Index to Footnotes

BEANS (2)
2Sa 17:28 wheat, barley, meal, parched grain, **b** and lentils,
Eze 4: 9 And you, take wheat and barley, **b** and lentils,

BEAR‡ (182) [AFTERBIRTH, ARMOR-BEARER, ARMOR-BEARERS, ARMS-BEARING, BEAR'S, BEARERS, BEARING, BEARS, BIRTH, BIRTHDAY, BIRTHRIGHT, BIRTHSTOOL, BORE, BORN, BORNE, CHILDBEARING, CHILDBIRTH, CHILDBIRTHS, CUPBEARER, CUPBEARING, FIRSTBORN, HOMEBORN, INBORN, NEWBORN, REBIRTH, ROSE-BEARING, SEA-BORN, SHE-BEAR, SHE-BEARS, SHIELD-BEARER, STILLBORN]
Ge 1:11 and fruit trees of every kind on earth that **b** fruit
4:13 "My punishment is greater than I can **b**!
16:11 "Now you have conceived and shall **b** a son;
17:17 Can Sarah, who is ninety years old, **b** a child?"
17:19 "No, but your wife Sarah shall **b** you a son,
17:21 whom Sarah shall **b** to you
18:13 'Shall I indeed **b** a child, now that I am old?'
30: 3 go in to her, that she may **b** upon my knees and
43: 9 then let me **b** the blame forever.
44:32 then I will **b** the blame in the sight
Ex 18:22 and they will **b** the burden with you.
20:16 not **b** false witness against your neighbor.
23: 2 when you **b** witness in a lawsuit,
28:12 and Aaron shall **b** their names before the LORD
28:29 So Aaron shall **b** the names of the sons of Israel in
28:30 thus Aaron shall **b** the judgment of the Israelites
Lev 16:22 The goat shall **b** on itself all their iniquities to
17:16 or bathe their body, they shall **b** their guilt.
19:18 not take vengeance or **b** a grudge against any
22:16 causing them to **b** guilt requiring a guilt offering,
24:15 Anyone who curses God shall **b** the sin.
Nu 5:31 but the woman shall **b** her iniquity.
9:13 such a one shall **b** the consequences for the sin.
11:17 and they shall **b** the burden of the people along
11:17 with you so that you will not **b** it all by yourself.
12:14 would she not **b** her shame for seven days?
14:34 for every day a year, you shall **b** your iniquity,
15:31 a person shall be utterly cut off and **b** the guilt.
18: 1 with you shall **b** responsibility
18: 1 and your sons alone shall **b** responsibility
Nu 18:23 they shall **b** responsibility for their own offenses;
30:15 then he shall **b** her guilt.
32:21 and all those of you who **b** arms cross the Jordan
Dt 1: 9 "I am unable by myself to **b** you.
1:12 how can I **b** the heavy burden of your disputes all
5:20 Neither shall you **b** false witness
Jos 2:19 we shall **b** the responsibility for their death.
3: 8 the one who shall command the priests who **b**
3:13 the feet of the priests who **b** the ark of the LORD,
4:16 the priests who **b** the ark of the covenant,
Jdg 5:14 and from Zebulun those who **b** the marshal's staff;
10:16 and he could no longer **b** to see Israel suffer.
13: 3 you shall conceive and **b** a son.
13: 5 for you shall conceive and **b** a son.
13: 7 'You shall conceive and **b** a son.
Ru 1:12 if I should have a husband tonight and **b** sons,
1Sa 17:34 and whenever a lion or a **b** came,
17:37 the paw of the lion and from the paw of the **b**,
2Sa 17: 8 like a **b** robbed of her cubs in the field.
19:19 may the king not **b** it in mind.
2Ki 18:14 whatever you impose on me I will **b**."
19:30 take root downward, and **b** fruit upward;
Est 8: 6 For how can I **b** to see the calamity that is coming
8: 6 how can I **b** to see the destruction of my kindred?"
Job 9: 9 the **B** and Orion, the Pleiades and the chambers of
21: 3 **B** with me, and I will speak;
36: 2 "**B** with me a little, and I will show you, for I have
38:32 or can you guide the **B** with its children?
Ps 5:10 Make them **b** their guilt, O God;
13: 2 How long must I **b** pain in my soul,
55:12 It is not enemies who taunt me—I could **b** that;
68:29 of your temple at Jerusalem kings **b** gifts to you.
89:50 how I **b** in my bosom the insults of the peoples,
91:12 On their hands they will **b** you up,
Pr 9:12 if you scoff, you alone will **b** it.
18:14 but a broken spirit—who can **b**?
28:15 a charging **b** is a wicked ruler over a poor people.
30:21 under four it cannot **b** up:
SS 4: 2 all of which **b** twins, and not one among them is bereaved.
6: 6 all of them **b** twins, and not one among them is bereaved.
Isa 7:14 the young woman is with child and shall **b** a son,
11: 7 The cow and the **b** shall graze,
37:31 again take root downward, and **b** fruit upward;
46: 4 I have made, and I will **b**;
53:11 and he shall **b** their iniquities.
54: 1 Sing, O barren one who did not **b**;
65:23 or **b** children for calamity;
Jer 10:19 "Truly this is my punishment, and I must **b** it."
16: 3 and concerning the mothers who **b** them and
17: 8 and it does not cease to **b** fruit.
17:21 not **b** a burden on the sabbath day or bring it in by
29: 6 that they may **b** sons and daughters;
30: 6 Ask now, and see, can a man **b** a child?
44:22 The LORD could no longer **b** the sight
La 3:10 He is a **b** lying in wait for me, a lion in hiding;
3:27 It is good for one to **b** the yoke in youth,
5: 7 they are no more, and we **b** their iniquities.
Eze 4: 4 you shall **b** their punishment for the number of
4: 5 you shall **b** the punishment of the house of Israel.
4: 6 and **b** the punishment of the house of Judah;
14:10 And they shall **b** their punishment—
16:52 **B** your disgrace, you also,
16:52 So be ashamed, you also, and **b** your disgrace,
16:54 that you may **b** your disgrace and be ashamed
16:58 You must **b** the penalty of your lewdness
17: 8 so that it might produce branches and **b** fruit
17:23 in order that it may produce boughs and **b** fruit,
23:35 behind your back, therefore **b** the consequences
23:49 you shall **b** the penalty for your sinful idolatry;
32:24 They **b** their shame with those who go down to
32:25 and they **b** their shame with those who go down to
32:30 **b** their shame with those who go down to the Pit.
36:15 no longer shall you **b** the disgrace of the peoples;
44:10 when Israel went astray, shall **b** their punishment.
44:12 that they shall **b** their punishment.
44:13 but they shall **b** their shame,
47:12 but they will **b** fresh fruit every month,
Da 7: 5 a second one, that looked like a **b**.
9:19 because your city and your people **b** your name!"
Hos 9:16 their root is dried up, they shall **b** no fruit.
10: 2 Their heart is false; now they must **b** their guilt.
13: 8 I will fall upon them like a **b** robbed of her cubs,
13:16 Samaria shall **b** her guilt, because she has rebelled
Am 5:19 and was met by a **b**;
7:10 the land is not able to **b** all his words.
Mic 6:16 so you shall **b** the scorn of my people.
7: 9 I must **b** the indignation of the LORD,
Zep 3:18 so that you will not **b** reproach for it.
Zec 6:13 he shall **b** royal honor, and shall sit and rule
Mal 3: 5 I will be swift to **b** witness against the sorcerers,
Mt 1:21 She will **b** a son, and you are to name him Jesus,
1:23 the virgin shall conceive and **b** a son,
3: 8 **B** fruit worthy of repentance.
3:10 that does not **b** good fruit is cut down and thrown
4: 6 and 'On their hands they will **b** you up,
7:18 A good tree cannot **b** bad fruit, nor can a bad tree **b** good fruit.
7:19 that does not **b** good fruit is cut down and thrown
19:18 You shall not **b** false witness;
23: 4 They tie up heavy burdens, hard to **b**,
Mk 4:20 they hear the word and accept it and **b** fruit,
9:41 a cup of water to drink because you **b** the name
10:19 You shall not **b** false witness;
Lk 1:13 Your wife Elizabeth will **b** you a son,
1:31 now, you will conceive in your womb and **b** a son,

Lk 3: 8 **B** fruits worthy of repentance.
3: 9 that does not **b** good fruit is cut down and thrown
4:11 and 'On their hands they will **b** you up,
6:43 nor again does a bad tree **b** good fruit;
8:15 and **b** fruit with patient endurance.
9:41 much longer must I be with you and **b** with you?
11:46 For you load people with burdens hard to **b**,
18:20 You shall not **b** false witness;
20:24 Whose head and whose title does it **b**?"
Jn 15: 2 that bears fruit he prunes to make it **b** more fruit.
15: 4 the branch cannot **b** fruit by itself unless it abides
15: 5 Those who abide in me and I in them **b** much fruit,
15: 8 that you **b** much fruit and become my disciples.
15:16 And I appointed you to go and **b** fruit,
16:12 but you cannot **b** them now.
Ac 15:10 nor we have been able to **b**?
23:11 so you must **b** witness also in Rome."
Ro 7: 4 the dead in order that we may **b** fruit for God.
7: 5 were at work in our members to **b** fruit for death.
13: 4 for the authority does not **b** the sword in vain!
1Co 15:49 we will also **b** the image of the man of heaven.
2Co 11: 1 I wish you would **b** with me in a little foolishness. Do **b** with me!
Gal 4:27 you who **b** no children, burst into song and shout,
6: 2 **B** one another's burdens,
Col 1:10 as you **b** fruit in every good work and as you grow
3:13 **B** with one another and, if anyone has a complaint
1Th 3: 1 Therefore when we could **b** it no longer,
3: 5 For this reason, when I could **b** it no longer,
1Ti 5:14 I would have younger widows marry, **b** children,
Heb 9:28 having been offered once to **b** the sins of many,
13:13 Let us then go to him outside the camp and **b**
13:22 **b** with my word of exhortation,
1Pe 4:16 but glorify God because you **b** this name.
Rev 12: 4 before the woman who was about to **b** a child,
Jdt 7: 4 nor the valleys nor the hills will **b** their weight."
Sir 22:15 a piece of iron are easier to **b** than a stupid person.
23:25 and her branches will not **b** fruit.
25:17 and darkens her face like that of a **b**.
29:28 a sensible person to **b** scolding about lodging and
36:20 **B** witness to those whom you created in
2Es 5:46 'If you **b** ten children, why one after another?'
7:*105* for then all shall **b** their own righteousness
10:15 **b** bravely the troubles that have come upon you.
16:25 The trees shall **b** fruit, but who will gather it?
4Mc 13:11 "Courage, brother," another said, "**B** up nobly,"
16:16 the contest to which you are called to **b** witness for

BEAR'S (1) [BEAR]

Rev 13: 2 its feet were like a **b**,

BEARD (17) [BEARDS]

Lev 13:29 or woman has a disease on the head or in the **b**,
13:30 it is an itch, a leprous disease of the head or the **b**.
14: 9 of head, **b**, eyebrows; he shall shave all his hair.
19:27 on your temples or mar the edges of your **b**.
1Sa 21:13 and let his spittle run down his **b**.
2Sa 10: 4 shaved off half the **b** of each,
19:24 he had not taken care of his feet, or trimmed his **b**,
20: 9 And Joab took Amasa by the **b** with his right hand
Ezr 9: 3 and pulled hair from my head and **b**,
Ps 133: 2 running down upon the **b**, on the **b** of Aaron,
Isa 7:20 and it will take off the **b** as well.
15: 2 On every head is baldness, every **b** is shorn;
50: 6 and my cheeks to those who pulled out the **b**;
Jer 48:37 For every head is shaved and every **b** cut off;
Eze 5: 1 and run it over your head and your **b**;
1Es 8:71 and pulled out hair from my head and **b**,

BEARDS (5) [BEARD]

Lev 21: 5 or shave off the edges of their **b**,
2Sa 10: 5 "Remain at Jericho until your **b** have grown,
1Ch 19: 5 "Remain at Jericho until your **b** have grown,
Jer 41: 5 with their **b** shaved and their clothes torn,
LtJ 6:31 with their clothes torn, their heads and **b** shaved,

BEARERS (4) [BEAR]

2Ch 34:13 over the burden **b** and directed all who did work
Ne 4:10 "The strength of the burden **b** is failing,
4:17 The burden **b** carried their loads in such a way
Lk 7:14 and touched the bier, and the **b** stood still.

BEARING (33) [BEAR]

Ge 1:12 and trees of every kind **b** fruit with the seed in it.
16: 2 that the LORD has prevented me from **b** children;
29:35 therefore she named him Judah; then she ceased **b**.
30: 9 When Leah saw that she had ceased **b** children,
Nu 4:24 of the Gershonites, in serving and **b** burdens:
4:47 of service and the work of **b** burdens relating to
Jos 3:14 the priests **b** the ark of the covenant were in front
3:15 and the feet of the priests **b** the ark were dipped in
4: 9 the place where the feet of the priests **b** the ark of
4:18 When the priests **b** the ark of the covenant of
6: 4 with seven priests **b** seven trumpets of rams' horns
Jdg 8:10 hundred twenty thousand men **b** arms had fallen.
20: 2 four hundred thousand foot-soldiers **b** arms.
1Ki 10: 2 with camels **b** spices, and very much gold,
1Ch 12:24 The people of Judah **b** shield
2Ch 9: 1 having a very great retinue and camels **b** spices
12:11 the guard would come along **b** them,
Ps 126: 6 Those who go out weeping, **b** the seed for sowing,
Isa 1:14 a burden to me, I am weary of **b** them.
Ro 8:16 it is that very Spirit **b** witness with our spirit
Gal 4:24 is Hagar, from Mount Sinai, **b** children for slavery.
Eph 4: 2 with patience, **b** with one another in love,
Col 1: 6 as it is **b** fruit and growing in the whole world,
1: 6 so it has been **b** fruit among yourselves from
2Ti 2:19 God's firm foundation stands, **b** this inscription:
Rev 2: 3 also know that you are enduring patiently and **b** up
Tob 13:11 **b** gifts in their hands for the King of heaven.
Jdt 15:13 **b** their arms and wearing garlands
Wis 10: 7 plants **b** fruit that does not ripen,
Sus 1:61 Daniel had convicted them of **b** false witness;
2Mc 15:12 of modest **b** and gentle manner,
4Mc 15:26 one **b** death and the other deliverance
16: 6 **b** seven children, I am now the mother of none!

BEARS‡ (35) [BEAR]

Ge 49:21 Naphtali is a doe let loose that **b** lovely fawns.
50:15 "What if Joseph still **b** a grudge against us
Ex 21: 4 If his master gives him a wife and she **b** him sons
Lev 12: 2 If a woman conceives and **b** a male child,
12: 5 If she **b** a female child, she shall
12: 7 This is the law for her who **b** a child,
Dt 25: 6 and the firstborn whom she **b** shall succeed to
28:57 and the children that she **b**,
32:11 takes them up, and **b** them aloft on its pinions,
1Sa 17:36 Your servant has killed both lions and **b**;
Ps 68:19 Blessed be the Lord, who daily **b** us up;
Pr 12:12 but the root of the righteous **b** fruit.
25:18 or a sharp arrow is one who **b** false witness against
Isa 3: 9 The look on their faces **b** witness against them;
59:11 We all growl like **b**; like doves we moan
Jer 29:23 I am the one who knows and **b** witness,
32:34 in the house that **b** my name,
Da 9:18 at our desolation and the city that **b** your name.
Joel 2:22 the tree **b** its fruit, the fig tree and vine give
Mt 7:17 In the same way, every good tree **b** good fruit, but the bad tree **b** bad fruit.
13:23 who indeed **b** fruit and yields,
Lk 6:43 "No good tree **b** bad fruit,
13: 9 If it **b** fruit next year, well and good;
Jn 12:24 but if it dies, it **b** much fruit.
15: 2 He removes every branch in me that **b** no fruit.
15: 2 that **b** fruit he prunes to make it bear more fruit.
Ro 2:15 to which their own conscience also **b** witness;
1Co 5:11 not to associate with anyone who **b** the name
13: 7 It **b** all things, believes all things, hopes all things,
Wis 11:17 the means to send upon them a multitude of **b**,
Sir 47: 3 and with **b** as though they were lambs of the flock.
2Es 5:51 He replied to me, "Ask a woman who **b** children,
7:*94* they see the witness that he who formed them **b**
8: 6 by which every mortal who **b** the likeness of

BEAST‡ (53) [BEASTS]

Ge 1:30 And to every **b** of the earth,
Lev 5: 2 an unclean **b** or the carcass of unclean livestock or
Ps 73:22 I was like a brute **b** toward you.
Isa 35: 9 nor shall any ravenous **b** come up on it;
Da 7: 5 Another **b** appeared, a second one,
7: 6 The **b** had four wings of a bird on its back
7: 7 After this I saw in the visions by night a fourth **b**,
7:11 And as I watched, the **b** was put to death,
7:19 concerning the fourth **b**, which was different
7:23 This is what he said: "As for the fourth **b**,
Jas 3: 7 For every species of **b** and bird,
Rev 11: 7 the **b** that comes up from
13: 1 a **b** rising out of the sea having ten horns
13: 2 And the **b** that I saw was like a leopard,
13: 3 In amazement the whole earth followed the **b**.
13: 4 for he had given his authority to the **b**,
13: 4 and they worshiped the **b**, saying,
13: 4 "Who is like the **b**, and who can fight against it?"
13: 5 The **b** was given a mouth uttering haughty
13:11 Then I saw another **b** that rose out of the earth;
13:12 It exercises all the authority of the first **b**
13:12 the earth and its inhabitants worship the first **b**,
13:14 that it is allowed to perform on behalf of the **b**,
13:14 to make an image for the **b** that had been wounded
13:15 to give breath to the image of the **b** so that
13:15 that the image of the **b** could even speak
13:15 not worship the image of the **b** to be killed.
13:17 the name of the **b** or the number of its name.
13:18 with understanding calculate the number of the **b**,
14: 9 "Those who worship the **b** and its image,
14:11 or night for those who worship the **b** and its image
15: 2 and those who had conquered the **b** and its image
16: 2 the mark of the **b** and who worshiped its image.
16:10 fifth angel poured his bowl on the throne of the **b**,
16:13 from the mouth of the **b**,
17: 3 on a scarlet **b** that was full of blasphemous names,
17: 7 and of the **b** with seven heads and ten horns
17: 8 The **b** that you saw was, and is not,
17: 8 will be amazed when they see the **b**,
17:11 As for the **b** that was and is not,
17:12 as kings for one hour, together with the **b**.
17:13 in yielding their power and authority to the **b**;
17:16 they and the **b** will hate the whore;
17:17 by agreeing to give their kingdom to the **b**,
18: 2 a haunt of every foul and hateful **b**.
19:19 Then I saw the **b** and the kings of the earth
19:20 And the **b** was captured, and with it
19:20 of the **b** and those who worshiped its image.
20: 4 They had not worshiped the **b** or its image and had
20:10 where the **b** and the false prophet were,
1Mc 6:35 picked horsemen were assigned to each **b**.
2Mc 4:25 of a cruel tyrant and the rage of a savage wild **b**.
4Mc 12:13 a man, were you not ashamed, you most savage **b**,

BEASTS‡ (20) [BEAST]

Ge 31:39 which was torn by wild **b** I did not bring to you;
Ex 22:13 it was mangled by **b**, let it be brought as evidence;
22:31 not eat any meat that is mangled by **b** in the field;
Dt 32:24 The teeth of **b** I will send against them,
Ps 8: 7 all sheep and oxen, and also the **b** of the field,
Isa 1:11 of burnt offerings of rams and the fat of fed **b**;
46: 1 Nebo stoops, their idols are on **b** and cattle;
Da 7: 3 and four great **b** came up out of the sea,
7: 7 It was different from all the **b** that preceded it,
7:12 As for the rest of the **b**,
7:17 "As for these four great **b**,
8: 4 All **b** were powerless to withstand it,
Mk 1:13 and he was with the wild **b**;
Ac 11: 6 **b** of prey, reptiles, and birds of the air.
Wis 11:18 or newly-created unknown **b** full of rage, or such
17:19 or the sound of the most savage roaring **b**,
Sir 17: 4 and gave them dominion over **b** and birds.
2Es 11:39 of the four **b** that I had made to reign in my world,
11:40 have conquered all the **b** that have gone before;
4Mc 9:28 These leopard-like **b** tore out his sinews with

BEAT (44) [BEATEN, BEATING, BEATINGS]

Ex 30:36 and you shall **b** some of it into powder,
Nu 11: 8 ground it in mills or **b** it in mortars,
Dt 1:44 They **b** you down in Seir as far as Hormah.
24:20 you **b** your olive trees, do not strip what is left;
Jdg 5:22 "Then loud **b** the horses' hoofs with the galloping,
Ru 2:17 Then she **b** out what she had gleaned,
2Sa 22:43 I **b** them fine like the dust of the earth,
2Ki 23: 6 **b** it to dust and threw the dust of it upon the graves
2Ch 34: 7 **b** the sacred poles and the images into powder,
Ne 13:25 with them and cursed them and **b** some of them
Ps 18:42 I **b** them fine, like dust before the wind;
Pr 23:13 if you **b** them with a rod, they will not die.
23:14 If you **b** them with the rod,
23:35 they **b** me, but I did not feel it.
SS 5: 7 they **b** me, they wounded me,
Isa 2: 4 they shall **b** their swords into plowshares,
10:24 do not be afraid of the Assyrians when they **b** you
32:12 **B** your breasts for the pleasant fields,
Jer 37:15 and they **b** him and imprisoned him in the house
Joel 3:10 **B** your plowshares into swords,
Jnh 4: 8 and the sun **b** down on the head of Jonah so
Mic 4: 3 they shall **b** their swords into plowshares,
4:13 you shall **b** in pieces many peoples,
Mt 7:25 and the winds blew and **b** on that house,
7:27 and the winds blew and **b** against that house,
21:35 But the tenants seized his slaves and **b** one,
24:49 and he begins to **b** his fellow slaves,
Mk 4:37 and the waves **b** into the boat,
12: 3 But they seized him, and **b** him,
12: 4 this one they **b** over the head and insulted.
12: 5 some they **b**, and others they killed.
14:65 The guards also took him over and **b** him.
Lk 10:30 **b** him, and went away, leaving him half dead.
12:45 and if he begins to **b** the other slaves,
20:10 tenants **b** him and sent him away empty-handed.
20:11 that one also they **b** and insulted
22:63 were holding Jesus began to mock him and **b** him;
Ac 18:17 and **b** him in front of the tribunal.
22:19 and **b** those who believed in you.
Tob 3: 9 Why do you **b** us?
Wis 5:11 by the **b** of its pinions and pierced by the force
Sir 30:12 and **b** his sides while he is young,
2Mc 9: 2 by the inhabitants and **b** a shameful retreat.
10:17 and **b** off all who fought upon the wall,

BEATEN (31) [BEAT]

Ex 5:14 over them, were **b**, and were asked, "Why did you
5:16 Look how your servants are **b**!
22: 2 If a thief is found breaking in, and is **b** to death,
27:20 the Israelites to bring you pure oil of **b** olives for
29:40 with one-fourth of a hin of **b** oil,
Lev 24: 2 to bring you pure oil of **b** olives for the lamp,
Nu 28: 5 mixed with one-fourth of a hin of **b** oil.
Dt 25: 2 the judge shall make that person lie down and be **b**
Jos 8:15 and all Israel made a pretense of being **b**
2Sa 2:17 the men of Israel were **b** by the servants of David.
1Ki 10:16 Solomon made two hundred large shields of **b** gold
10:17 He made three hundred shields of **b** gold;
2Ch 9:15 Solomon made two hundred large shields of **b** gold
9:15 shekels of **b** gold went into each large shield.
9:16 He made three hundred shields of **b** gold;
Isa 17: 6 as when an olive tree is **b**—
24:13 as when an olive tree is **b**,
28:18 through you will be **b** down by it.
28:27 dill is **b** out with a stick, and cummin with a rod.
Jer 10: 9 **B** silver is brought from Tarshish,
46: 5 their warriors are **b** down, and have fled in haste.
Mic 1: 7 All her images shall be **b** to pieces,
Mk 13: 9 and you will be **b** in synagogues;
Ac 16:22 of their clothing and ordered them to be **b**
16:37 But Paul replied, "They have **b** us in public,
1Co 4:11 we are poorly clothed and **b** and homeless,
2Co 11:25 Three times I was **b** with rods.
1Pe 2:20 If you endure when you are **b** for doing wrong,
2Mc 4:45 But Menelaus, already as good as **b**,
2Es 15:51 like a wretched woman who is **b** and wounded,
4Mc 6:10 Like a noble athlete the old man, while being **b**,

BEATING (16) [BEAT]

Ex 2:11 He saw an Egyptian **b** a Hebrew,
Jdg 6:11 his son Gideon was **b** out wheat in the wine press,
Pr 28: 3 A ruler who oppresses the poor is a **b** rain

Jer 4:19 My heart is **b** wildly; I cannot keep silent;
Na 2: 7 moaning like doves and **b** their breasts.
Lk 12:47 or do what was wanted, will receive a severe **b.**
12:48 did what deserved a **b** will receive a light **b.**
18:13 but was **b** his breast and saying, 'God,
23:27 among them were women who were **b** their breasts
23:48 they returned home, **b** their breasts.
Ac 21:32 the tribune and the soldiers, they stopped **b** Paul.
1Co 9:26 nor do I box as though **b** the air;
Wis 2: 2 reason is a spark kindled by the **b** of our hearts;
2Mc 6:30 in my body under this **b,**
4Mc 9:12 When they had worn themselves out **b** him

BEATINGS (3) [BEAT]

Pr 20:30 **b** make clean the innermost parts.
Isa 1: 5 Why do you seek further **b?**
2Co 6: 5 **b,** imprisonments, riots, labors,

BEAUTIFICATION (1) [BEAUTY]

AdE 2:12 During this time the days of **b** are completed—

BEAUTIFUL‡ (88) [BEAUTY]

Ge 12:11 that you are a woman **b** in appearance;
12:14 the Egyptians saw that the woman was very **b.**
29:17 and Rachel was graceful and **b.**
Dt 21:11 among the captives a **b** woman whom you desire
Jos 7:21 I saw among the spoil a **b** mantle from Shinar,
1Sa 16:12 he was ruddy, and had **b** eyes, and was handsome.
25: 3 The woman was clever and **b,**
2Sa 11: 2 a woman bathing; the woman was very **b.**
13: 1 a **b** sister whose name was Tamar;
14:27 whose name was Tamar; she was a **b** woman.
1Ki 1: 3 for a **b** girl throughout all the territory of Israel,
1: 4 The girl was very **b.**
Est 2: 2 "Let **b** young virgins be sought out for the king.
2: 3 of his kingdom to gather all the **b** young virgins to
2: 7 the girl was fair and **b,**
Job 42:15 In all the land there were no women so **b**
Ps 48: 2 **b** in elevation, is the joy of all
Pr 4: 9 she will bestow on you a **b** crown."
11:22 in a pig's snout is a **b** woman without good sense.
SS 1: 5 I am black and **b,** O daughters of Jerusalem,
1:15 Ah, you are **b,** my love; ah, you are **b;**
1:16 Ah, you are **b,** my beloved, truly lovely.
4: 1 How **b** you are, my love, how very **b!**
4: 7 You are altogether **b,** my love;
6: 4 You are **b** as Tirzah, my love,
Isa 2:16 and against all the **b** craft.
4: 2 the branch of the LORD shall be **b** and glorious,
5: 9 many houses shall be desolate, large and **b** houses,
52: 1 Put on your **b** garments, O Jerusalem, the holy city;
52: 7 How **b** upon the mountains are the feet of
64:11 Our holy and **b** house,
Jer 3:19 the most **b** heritage of all the nations.
13:18 for your **b** crown has come down from your head."
13:20 is the flock that was given you, your **b** flock?
46:20 A **b** heifer is Egypt—a gadfly from the
Eze 7:20 From their **b** ornament, in which they took pride,
16:12 and a **b** crown upon your head.
16:13 You grew exceedingly **b,** fit to be a queen.
16:17 also took your **b** jewels of my gold and my silver
16:39 and take your **b** objects and leave you naked
23:42 and **b** crowns upon their heads.
31: 7 It was **b** in its greatness, in the length
31: 9 I made it **b** with its mass of branches,
33:32 a **b** voice and plays well on an instrument;
Da 4:12 Its foliage was **b,** its fruit abundant,
4:21 whose foliage was **b** and its fruit abundant,
8: 9 toward the east, and toward the **b** land.
11:16 He shall take a position in the **b** land,
11:41 He shall come into the **b** land,
11:45 between the sea and the **b** holy mountain.
Am 8:13 the **b** young women and the young men shall faint
Mt 23:27 which on the outside look **b,**
Lk 21: 5 with **b** stones and gifts dedicated to God,
Ac 3: 2 the temple called the **B** Gate so that he could ask
3:10 to sit and ask for alms at the **B** Gate of the temple;
7:20 and he was **b** before God.
Ro 10:15 **b** are the feet of those who bring good news!"
Heb 11:23 because they saw that the child was **b;**
Tob 6:12 Moreover, the girl is sensible, brave, and very **b,**
Jdt 8: 7 She was **b** in appearance, and was very lovely
10: 4 Thus she made herself very **b,**
10:14 she was in their eyes marvelously **b—**
11:21 from one end of the earth to the other looks so **b**
11:23 You are not only **b** in appearance,
AdE 1:11 for she was indeed a **b** woman.
2: 2 "Let **b** and virtuous girls be sought out for
2: 3 and they shall select **b** young virgins to be brought
2: 7 The girl was **b** in appearance.
Wis 5:16 a glorious crown and a **b** diadem from the hand of
7:29 She is more **b** than the sun,
13: 7 because the things that are seen are **b.**
14:19 skillfully forced the likeness to take more **b** form,
15:19 not so **b** in appearance that one would desire them,
Sir 25: 1 and they are **b** in the sight of God and of mortals:
26:17 so is a **b** face on a stately figure.
43:11 it is exceedingly **b** in its brightness.
45:13 Before him such **b** things did not exist.
Sus 1: 2 a very **b** woman and one who feared the Lord.
1:31 a woman of great refinement and **b** in appearance.
2Mc 3:26 gloriously **b** and splendidly dressed,
10: 7 carrying ivy-wreathed wands and **b** branches and
1Es 4:18 If men gather gold and silver or any other **b** thing,
4:19 all prefer her to gold or silver or any other **b** thing.
3Mc 3:17 with magnificent and most **b** offerings,
2Es 6: 3 and before the **b** flowers were seen,
4Mc 16:10 so many and **b** children am a widow and alone,

BEAUTIFY (3) [BEAUTY]

Isa 60:13 and the pine, to **b** the place of my sanctuary;
Jer 4:30 In vain you **b** yourself. Your lovers despise you;
2Es 15:54 **B** your face!

BEAUTY‡ (65) [BEAUTIFICATION, BEAUTIFUL, BEAUTIFY]

2Sa 14:25 to be praised so much for his **b** as Absalom;
Est 1:11 to show the peoples and the officials her **b;**
Ps 27: 4 to behold the **b** of the LORD,
45:11 and the king will desire your **b.**
50: 2 Out of Zion, the perfection of **b,** God shines forth.
96: 6 strength and **b** are in his sanctuary.
Pr 6:25 Do not desire her **b** in your heart,
20:29 but the **b** of the aged is their gray hair.
31:30 Charm is deceitful, and **b** is vain,
Isa 3:24 of sackcloth; instead of **b,**
28: 1 and the fading flower of its glorious **b,**
28: 4 And the fading flower of its glorious **b,**
28: 5 and a diadem of **b,** to the remnant of his people;
33:17 Your eyes will see the king in his **b;**
44:13 he makes it in human form, with human **b,**
62: 3 be a crown of **b** in the hand of the LORD,
La 2:15 "Is this the city that was called the perfection of **b,**
Eze 16:14 among the nations on account of your **b,**
16:15 But you trusted in your **b,**
16:25 and prostituted your **b,** offering yourself
27: 3 O Tyre, you have said, "I am perfect in **b."**
27: 4 your builders made perfect your **b.**
27:11 they made perfect your **b.**
28: 7 the **b** of your wisdom and defile your splendor.
28:12 full of wisdom and perfect in **b.**
28:17 Your heart was proud because of your **b;**
31: 8 no tree in the garden of God was like it in **b.**
32:19 "Whom do you surpass in **b?**
Hos 14: 6 his **b** shall be like the olive tree,
Zec 9:17 For what goodness and **b** are his!
Jas 1:11 its flower falls, and its **b** perishes.
1Pe 3: 4 be the inner self with the lasting **b** of a gentle
Jdt 10: 7 they were very greatly astounded at her **b** and said
10:19 They marveled at her **b** and admired the Israelites,
10:23 they all marveled at the **b** of her face.
16: 6 with the **b** of her countenance undid him.
16: 9 her **b** captivated his mind,
AdE 1:11 and to have her display her **b** to all the governors
15: 5 She was radiant with perfect **b,**
Wis 7:10 I loved her more than health and **b,**
8: 2 and became enamored of her **b.**
13: 3 in the **b** of these things people assumed them to
13: 3 for the author of **b** created them.
13: 5 from the greatness and **b** of created things comes
Sir 9: 8 and do not gaze at **b** belonging to another;
9: 8 many have been seduced by a woman's **b,**
25:21 Do not be ensnared by a woman's **b,**
26:16 is the **b** of a good wife in her well-ordered home.
36:27 A woman's **b** lights up a man's face,
40:22 The eye desires grace and **b,**
42:12 Do not let her parade her **b** before any man,
43: 9 The glory of the stars is the **b** of heaven,
43:18 The eye is dazzled by the **b** of its whiteness,
47:10 He gave **b** to the festivals,
Bar 5: 1 and put on forever the **b** of the glory from God.
LtJ 6:24 As for the gold that they wear for **b—**
Sus 1:32 so that they might feast their eyes on her **b.**
1:56 of Canaan and not of Judah, **b** has beguiled you
1Mc 1:26 the **b** of the women faded.
2:12 And see, our holy place, our **b,**
1Es 4:18 and then see a woman lovely in appearance and **b,**
3Mc 1: 9 and being impressed by its excellence and its **b,**
2Es 10:50 and the loveliness of her **b.**
4Mc 2: 1 for the enjoyment of **b** are rendered powerless?
8: 5 and greatly respect the **b** and the number

BEBAI‡ (10)

Ezr 2:11 Of **B,** six hundred twenty-three.
8:11 Of the descendants of **B,** Zechariah son of **B,**
10:28 Of the descendants of **B:** Jehohanan,
Ne 7:16 Of **B,** six hundred twenty-eight.
10:15 Bunni, Azgad, **B,**
1Es 5:13 The descendants of **B,** six hundred twenty-three.
8:37 Of the descendants of **B,** Zechariah son of **B,**
9:29 Of the descendants of **B:** Jehohanan

BECAME (399) [BECOME]

Ge 2: 7 and the man **b** a living being.
5: 3 he **b** the father of a son in his likeness,
5: 4 The days of Adam after he **b** the father
5: 6 he **b** the father of Enosh.
5: 9 he **b** the father of Kenan.
5:12 he **b** the father of Mahalalel.
5:15 he **b** the father of Jared.
5:18 Jared had lived one hundred sixty-two years he **b**
5:21 he **b** the father of Methuselah.
5:25 he **b** the father of Lamech.
5:28 he **b** the father of a son;
5:32 Noah **b** the father of Shem, Ham, and Japheth.
9:21 He drank some of the wine and **b** drunk,
10: 8 Cush **b** the father of Nimrod;
10:13 Egypt **b** the father of Ludim, Anamim, Lehabim,
10:15 Canaan **b** the father of Sidon his firstborn,
Ge 10:24 Arpachshad **b** the father of Shelah;
10:24 and Shelah **b** the father of Eber.
10:26 Joktan **b** the father of Almodad, Sheleph,
11:10 he **b** the father of Arpachshad two years after
11:12 he **b** the father of Shelah;
11:14 he **b** the father of Eber;
11:16 he **b** the father of Peleg;
11:18 he **b** the father of Reu;
11:20 he **b** the father of Serug;
11:22 he **b** the father of Nahor;
11:24 he **b** the father of Terah;
11:26 he **b** the father of Abram, Nahor, and Haran.
19:26 behind him, looked back, and she **b** a pillar of salt.
19:36 the daughters of Lot **b** pregnant by their father.
20:12 of my mother; and she **b** my wife.
21:20 and **b** an expert with the bow.
22:23 Bethuel **b** the father of Rebekah.
24:67 He took Rebekah, and she **b** his wife;
26:13 and the man **b** rich; he prospered more and more until he **b** very wealthy.
30: 2 Jacob **b** very angry with Rachel and said,
31:36 Then Jacob **b** angry, and upbraided Laban.
39: 2 and he **b** a successful man;
39:19 the way your servant treated me," he **b** enraged.
41:57 because the famine **b** severe throughout the world.
44:32 For your servant **b** surety for the boy to my father,
47:20 upon them; and the land **b** Pharaoh's.
49:15 and **b** a slave at forced labor.
Ex 1:13 The Egyptians **b** ruthless in imposing tasks on
1:20 and the people multiplied and **b** very strong.
4: 3 he threw the staff on the ground, and it **b** a snake;
4: 4 and it **b** a staff in his hand—
7:10 before Pharaoh and his officials, and it **b** a snake.
7:12 Each one threw down his staff, and they **b** snakes;
9:24 in all the land of Egypt since it **b** a nation.
15:16 they **b** still as a stone until your people, O LORD,
15:25 he threw it into the water, and the water **b** sweet.
16:20 and it bred worms and **b** foul.
Lev 18:25 Thus the land **b** defiled;
18:27 of these abominations, and the land **b** defiled);
Nu 11:10 LORD **b** very angry, and Moses was displeased.
16:38 before the LORD and they **b** holy.
21: 4 but the people **b** impatient on the way.
26:10 two hundred fifty men; and they **b** a warning.
31:14 Moses **b** angry with the officers of the army,
Dt 26: 5 few in number, and there he **b** a great nation,
Jos 9:21 So they **b** hewers of wood and drawers of water
10: 2 he **b** greatly frightened, because Gibeon was
14:14 So Hebron **b** the inheritance of Caleb son
24:32 it **b** an inheritance of the descendants of Joseph.
Jdg 1:30 and **b** subject to forced labor.
1:33 of Beth-anath **b** subject to forced labor for them.
1:35 and they **b** subject to forced labor.
8:27 and it **b** a snare to Gideon and to his family.
15:14 and the ropes that were on his arms **b** like flax
17: 5 and installed one of his sons, who **b** his priest.
17:11 and the young man **b** to him like one of his sons.
17:12 and the young man **b** his priest,
19: 2 But his concubine **b** angry with him,
Ru 4:13 So Boaz took Ruth and she **b** his wife.
4:16 and laid him in her bosom, and **b** his nurse.
4:17 he **b** the father of Jesse, the father of David.
4:18 Perez **b** the father of Hezron,
1Sa 8: 1 Samuel **b** old, he made his sons judges over Israel.
10:12 it **b** a proverb, "Is Saul also among the prophets?"
14:15 and it **b** a very great panic.
16:21 Saul loved him greatly, and he **b** his armor-bearer.
18:30 so that his fame **b** very great.
22: 2 and he **b** captain over them.
25:37 within him; he **b** like a stone.
25:42 after the messengers of David and **b** his wife.
25:43 both of them **b** his wives.
2Sa 3: 1 while the house of Saul **b** weaker and weaker.
3:14 to whom I **b** engaged at the price
4: 4 it happened that he fell and **b** lame.
5:10 And David **b** greater and greater, for the LORD
7:24 and you, O LORD, **b** their God.
8: 2 Moabites **b** servants to David and brought tribute.
8: 6 Arameans **b** servants to David and brought tribute.
8:14 and all the Edomites **b** David's servants.
9:12 in Ziba's house **b** Mephibosheth's servants.
10:19 with Israel, and **b** subject to them.
11:27 and she **b** his wife, and bore him a son.
12:15 that Uriah's wife bore to David, and it **b** very ill.
13:21 of all these things, he **b** very angry, but he would
23:19 of the Thirty, and **b** their commander;
1Ki 1: 4 She **b** the king's attendant and served him,
11:24 He gathered followers around him and **b** leader of
12:30 And this thing **b** a sin,
13: 6 and the king's hand was restored to him, and **b**
13:34 This matter **b** sin to the house of Jeroboam,
16:22 so Tibni died, and Omri **b** king.
17:17 the mistress of the house, **b** ill;
19:21 he set out and followed Elijah, and **b** his servant.
2Ki 3: 1 Jehoram son of Ahab **b** king over Israel
4:34 the flesh of the child **b** warm.
5:11 But Naaman **b** angry and went away, saying,
6:25 famine in Samaria **b** so great that
8:17 He was thirty-two years old when he **b** king,
17: 3 Hoshea **b** his vassal, and paid him tribute.
17:15 They went after false idols and **b** false;
20: 1 In those days Hezekiah **b** sick and was at the point
24: 1 Jehoiakim **b** his servant for three years;
25: 3 the fourth month the famine **b** so severe in the city
1Ch 1:10 Cush **b** the father of Nimrod;
1:11 Egypt **b** the father of Ludim, Anamim, Lehabim,
1:13 Canaan **b** the father of Sidon his firstborn,

1Ch 1:18 Arpachshad **b** the father of Shelah;
1:18 and Shelah **b** the father of Eber.
1:20 Joktan **b** the father of Almodad, Sheleph,
1:34 Abraham **b** the father of Isaac.
2:10 Ram **b** the father of Amminadab,
2:10 and Amminadab **b** the father of Nahshon,
2:11 Nahshon **b** the father of Salma, Salma of Boaz,
2:13 Jesse **b** the father of Eliab his firstborn,
2:20 Hur **b** the father of Uri,
2:20 and Uri **b** the father of Bezalel.
2:22 and Segub **b** the father of Jair,
2:36 Attai **b** the father of Nathan, and Nathan of Zabad.
2:37 Zabad **b** the father of Ephlal, and Ephlal of Obed.
2:38 Obed **b** the father of Jehu, and Jehu of Azariah.
2:39 Azariah **b** the father of Helez,
2:40 Eleasah **b** the father of Sismai,
2:41 Shallum **b** the father of Jekamiah,
2:44 Shema **b** father of Raham, father of Jorkeam;
2:44 and Rekem **b** the father of Shammai.
2:46 and Haran **b** the father of Gazez.
4:2 Reaiah son of Shobal **b** the father of Jahath,
4:2 and Jahath **b** the father of Ahumai and Lahad.
4:8 Koz **b** the father of Anub, Zobebah,
4:11 the brother of Shuhah **b** the father of Mehir,
4:12 Eshton **b** the father of Beth-rapha, Paseah,
4:14 Meonothai **b** the father of Ophrah;
4:14 Seraiah **b** the father of Joab father of Ge-harashim,
4:31 These were their towns until David **b** king.
5:2 though Judah **b** prominent among his brothers and
6:4 Eleazar **b** the father of Phinehas,
6:11 Azariah **b** the father of Amariah,
7:32 Heber **b** the father of Japhlet, Shomer, Hotham,
8:1 Benjamin **b** the father of Bela his firstborn,
8:7 Heglam, who **b** the father of Uzza and Ahihud.
8:32 who **b** the father of Shimeah.
8:33 Ner **b** the father of Kish, Kish of Saul,
8:34 and Merib-baal **b** the father of Micah.
8:36 Ahaz **b** the father of Jehoaddah;
8:36 and Jehoaddah **b** the father of Alemeth, Azmaveth,
8:36 Zimri **b** the father of Moza.
8:37 Moza **b** the father of Binea;
9:38 and Mikloth **b** the father of Shimeam;
9:39 Ner **b** the father of Kish, Kish of Saul,
9:40 and Merib-baal **b** the father of Micah.
9:42 and Ahaz **b** the father of Jarah, and Jarah
9:42 and Zimri **b** the father of Moza.
9:43 Moza **b** the father of Binea;
11:6 Joab son of Zeruiah went up first, so he **b** chief.
11:9 And David **b** greater and greater,
11:21 of the Thirty, and **b** their commander;
14:3 David **b** the father of more sons and daughters.
17:22 and you, O LORD, **b** their God.
18:2 Moabites **b** subject to David and brought tribute.
18:6 Arameans **b** subject to David, and brought tribute.
18:13 and all the Edomites **b** subject to David.
19:19 they made peace with David, and **b** subject to him.
24:2 so Eleazar and Ithamar **b** the priests.
2Ch 11:21 and **b** the father of twenty-eight sons
13:21 and **b** the father of twenty-two sons
16:12 in his feet, and his disease **b** severe;
24:3 and he **b** the father of sons and daughters.
25:10 But they **b** very angry with Judah,
26:8 even to the border of Egypt, for he **b** very strong.
26:15 for he was marvelously helped until he **b** strong.
26:19 and when he **b** angry with the priests
27:6 So Jotham **b** strong because he ordered his ways
28:22 In the time of his distress he **b** yet more faithless
32:24 In those days Hezekiah **b** sick and was at the point
36:16 until the wrath of the LORD against his people **b**
36:20 and they **b** servants to him and to his sons until
Ne 9:25 so they ate, and were filled and **b** fat,
Est 2:21 the threshold, **b** angry and conspired
Job 32:2 of the family of Ram, **b** angry.
32:5 in the mouths of these three men, he **b** angry.
Ps 39:3 my heart **b** hot within me.
69:11 I **b** a byword to them.
83:10 who **b** dung for the ground.
106:9 He rebuked the Red Sea, and it **b** dry;
106:36 They served their idols, which **b** a snare to them.
106:39 Thus they **b** unclean by their acts,
114:2 Judah **b** God's sanctuary, Israel his dominion.
Ecc 2:9 So I **b** great and surpassed all who were before me
Isa 9:19 and the people **b** like fuel for the fire;
38:1 In those days Hezekiah **b** sick and was at the point
63:8 not deal falsely"; and he **b** their savior
63:10 therefore he **b** their enemy;
Jer 2:5 and **b** worthless themselves?
15:8 Their widows **b** more numerous than the sand of
15:16 and your words **b** to me a joy and the delight
44:6 and they **b** a waste and a desolation,
44:22 your land **b** a desolation and a waste and a curse,
52:6 the fourth month the famine **b** so severe in the city
La 4:10 they **b** their food in the destruction of my people.
4:15 So they **b** fugitives and wanderers;
Eze 16:7 up and **b** tall and arrived at full womanhood;
16:8 says the Lord GOD, and you **b** mine.
17:6 It sprouted and **b** a vine spreading out, but low;
17:6 So it **b** a vine; it brought forth branches,
19:3 he **b** a young lion, and he learned to catch prey;
19:6 he **b** a young lion, and he learned to catch prey;
19:11 Its strongest stem **b** a ruler's scepter;
23:4 They **b** mine, and they bore sons and daughters.
23:10 and she **b** a byword among women.
34:5 and scattered, they **b** food for all the wild animals.
36:3 that you **b** the possession of the rest of the nations,
36:3 the possession of the rest of the nations, and you **b**
41:7 For this reason the structure **b** wider from story
Da 2:35 were all broken in pieces and **b** like the chaff of
2:35 that struck the statue **b** a great mountain and filled
4:33 as long as eagles' feathers and his nails **b**
5:9 Then King Belshazzar **b** greatly terrified
8:4 it did as it pleased and **b** strong.
8:17 when he came, I **b** frightened and fell prostrate.
9:1 who **b** king over the realm of the Chaldeans—
Hos 7:5 On the day of our king the officials **b** sick with
8:11 they **b** to him altars for sinning.
9:10 and **b** detestable like the thing they loved.
Joel 2:18 Then the LORD **b** jealous for his land,
Jnh 4:1 this was very displeasing to Jonah, and he **b** angry.
Na 2:11 What **b** of the lions' den,
3:10 Yet she **b** an exile, she went into captivity;
Zec 11:7 I **b** the shepherd of the flock doomed to slaughter.
Mt 12:15 When Jesus **b** aware of this, he departed.
14:30 when he noticed the strong wind, he **b** frightened,
17:2 and his clothes **b** dazzling white.
21:15 to the Son of David," they **b** angry
25:5 all of them **b** drowsy and slept.
26:22 And they **b** greatly distressed and began to say
28:4 fear of him the guards shook and **b** like dead men.
Mk 9:3 and his clothes **b** dazzling white,
Lk 1:80 The child grew and **b** strong in spirit,
2:40 The child grew and **b** strong, filled with wisdom;
6:16 and Judas Iscariot, who **b** a traitor.
9:29 and his clothes **b** dazzling white.
11:30 just as Jonah **b** a sign to the people of Nineveh,
13:19 it grew and **b** a tree,
14:21 owner of the house **b** angry and said to his slave,
15:28 Then he **b** angry and refused to go in.
18:23 when he heard this, he **b** sad; for he was very rich.
20:26 and being amazed by his answer, they **b** silent.
22:44 ⟦and his sweat **b** like great drops of blood falling⟧
23:12 That same day Herod and Pilate **b** friends
Jn 1:14 And the Word **b** flesh and lived among us,
6:18 sea **b** rough because a strong wind was blowing.
Ac 1:16 who **b** a guide for those who arrested Jesus—
1:19 This **b** known to all the residents of Jerusalem,
6:7 a great many of the priests **b** obedient to the faith.
7:8 And so Abraham **b** the father of Isaac
7:8 and Isaac **b** the father of Jacob,
7:13 and Joseph's family **b** known to Pharaoh.
7:29 Moses fled and **b** a resident alien in the land
7:29 There he **b** the father of two sons.
7:54 they **b** enraged and ground their teeth at Stephen.
9:22 Saul **b** increasingly more powerful
9:24 but their plot **b** known to Saul.
9:37 At that time she **b** ill and died.
9:42 This **b** known throughout Joppa,
10:10 He **b** hungry and wanted something to eat;
11:21 a great number **b** believers and turned to the Lord.
13:48 as had been destined for eternal life **b** believers.
14:1 of both Jews and Greeks **b** believers.
15:39 disagreement **b** so sharp that they parted company;
17:5 But the Jews **b** jealous, and with the help
17:34 But some of them joined him and **b** believers,
18:8 **b** a believer in the Lord, together
18:8 of the Corinthians who heard Paul **b** believers
19:2 the Holy Spirit when you **b** believers?"
19:17 When this **b** known to all residents of Ephesus,
19:18 Also many of those who **b** believers confessed
22:2 in Hebrew, they **b** even more quiet.
23:10 When the dissension **b** violent, the tribune,
24:25 Felix **b** frightened and said,
Ro 1:21 but they **b** futile in their thinking,
1:22 Claiming to be wise, they **b** fools;
13:11 to us now than when we **b** believers;
1Co 1:30 who **b** for us wisdom from God,
4:15 in Christ Jesus I **b** your father through the gospel.
9:20 To the Jews I **b** as a Jew, in order to win Jews.
9:20 To those under the law I **b** as one under the law
9:21 To those outside the law I **b** as one outside the law
9:22 To the weak I **b** weak,
13:11 when I **b** an adult, I put an end to childish ways.
15:45 "The first man, Adam, **b** a living being";
15:45 the last Adam **b** a life-giving spirit.
2Co 8:9 yet for your sakes he **b** poor,
Php 2:8 he humbled himself and **b** obedient to the point
Col 1:23 I, Paul, **b** a servant of this gospel.
1:25 I **b** its servant according to God's commission
1Th 1:6 And you **b** imitators of us and of the Lord,
1:7 so that you **b** an example to all the believers
2:14 **b** imitators of the churches of God in Christ Jesus
1Ti 2:14 but the woman was deceived and **b** a transgressor.
Heb 5:9 he **b** the source of eternal salvation
7:20 for others who **b** priests took their office without
7:21 but this one **b** a priest with an oath,
11:7 the world and **b** an heir to the righteousness that is
11:34 won strength out of weakness, **b** mighty in war,
Rev 6:12 the sun **b** black as sackcloth,
6:12 the full moon **b** like blood,
8:9 A third of the sea **b** blood,
8:11 A third of the waters **b** wormwood,
16:3 and it **b** like the blood of a corpse,
16:4 and the springs of water, and they **b** blood.
Tob 1:9 When I **b** a man I married a woman,
1:9 and by her I **b** the father of
1:15 the highways into Media **b** unsafe
2:10 until I **b** completely blind.
2:14 I **b** flushed with anger against her over this.
Jdt 1:12 Then Nebuchadnezzar **b** very angry
5:10 There they **b** so great a multitude
5:11 So the king of Egypt **b** hostile to them;
16:23 She **b** more and more famous,
AdE 1:12 This offended the king and he **b** furious.
2:22 The matter **b** known to Mordecai,
AdE 3:5 not doing obeisance to him, he **b** furiously angry,
8:17 of the Gentiles were circumcised and **b** Jews out
10:6 There was the little spring that **b** a river,
Wis 2:14 He **b** to us a reproof of our thoughts;
8:2 and **b** enamored of her beauty.
10:17 and **b** a shelter to them by day,
12:27 For when in their suffering they **b** incensed
14:11 they **b** an abomination, snares for human souls and
14:21 And this **b** a hidden trap for humankind,
Sir 24:31 And lo, my canal **b** a river, and my river a sea.
46:1 He **b**, as his name implies,
46:15 by his words he **b** known as a trustworthy seer.
1Mc 1:3 When the earth **b** quiet before him, he was exalted,
1:4 nations, and princes, and they **b** tributary to him.
1:26 young women and young men **b** faint,
1:33 and strong towers, and it **b** their citadel.
1:35 of Jerusalem they stored them there, and **b**
1:36 for the citadel **b** an ambush against the sanctuary,
1:38 she **b** a dwelling of strangers;
1:38 she **b** strange to her offspring,
1:39 Her sanctuary **b** desolate like a desert;
2:43 And all who **b** fugitives to escape
2:53 of his distress kept the commandment, and **b** lord
2:55 because he fulfilled the command, **b** a judge
5:1 as it was before, they **b** very angry,
6:8 to his bed and **b** sick from disappointment,
6:24 of our people besieged the citadel and **b** hostile
6:59 of their laws that we abolished that they **b** angry
7:3 But when this act **b** known to him, he said,
7:30 It **b** known to Judas that Nicanor had come to him
8:10 but this **b** known to them,
9:8 He **b** faint, but he said to those who were left,
9:17 The battle **b** desperate, and many on
9:60 because their plan **b** known.
10:76 people of the city **b** afraid and opened the gates,
11:12 and their enmity **b** manifest.
11:19 So Demetrius **b** king in the one hundred
11:53 he **b** estranged from Jonathan and did not repay
13:32 **b** king in his place, putting on the crown of Asia;
14:30 Jonathan rallied the nation, **b** their high priest,
15:27 and **b** estranged from him.
16:24 from the time that he **b** high priest after his father.
2Mc 1:33 When this matter **b** known,
2:22 the Lord with great kindness **b** gracious to them—
3:24 by the power of God, and **b** faint with terror.
4:16 and wished to imitate completely **b** their enemies
4:33 When Onias **b** fully aware of these acts,
4:41 But when the Jews **b** aware
5:20 in all its glory when the great Lord **b** reconciled.
10:14 When Gorgias **b** governor of the region,
10:29 the battle **b** fierce, there appeared to the enemy
12:40 And it **b** clear to all that this was
14:27 The king **b** excited and, provoked by
14:31 When the latter **b** aware
1Es 1:43 His son Jehoiachin **b** king in his place;
4:43 that you made on the day when you **b** king,
3Mc 3:1 he **b** so infuriated that not only was he enraged
2Es 3:16 and Jacob **b** a great multitude.
3:22 Thus the disease **b** permanent;
11:3 but they **b** little, puny wings.
4Mc 1:11 and they **b** the cause of the downfall of tyranny
7:13 his sinews feeble, he **b** young again

BECAUSE‡ (1672)

Ge 2:3 **b** on it God rested from all the work
3:10 and I was afraid, **b** I was naked; and I hid myself."
3:14 "**B** you have done this, cursed are you among all
3:17 "**B** you have listened to the voice of your wife,
3:17 cursed is the ground **b** of you;
3:20 **b** she was the mother of all living.
4:25 for me another child instead of Abel, **b**
5:24 then he was no more, **b** God took him.
6:13 for the earth is filled with violence **b** of them;
8:21 the ground **b** of humankind, for the inclination of
11:9 **b** there the LORD confused the language of all
12:13 so that it may go well with me **b** of you,
12:17 and his house with great plagues **b** of Sarai,
19:13 **b** the outcry against its people has become great
20:3 to die **b** of the woman whom you have taken;
20:11 Abraham said, "I did it **b** I thought,
20:11 and they will kill me **b** of my wife.
20:18 the wombs of the house of Abimelech **b** of Sarah,
21:12 "Do not be distressed **b** of the boy and **b** of your
21:13 a nation of him also, **b** he is your offspring."
21:31 **b** there both of them swore an oath.
22:16 **B** you have done this, and have
22:18 **b** you have obeyed my voice."
25:21 to the LORD for his wife, **b** she was barren;
25:28 Isaac loved Esau, **b** he was fond of game;
26:5 **b** Abraham obeyed my voice and kept my charge,
26:7 **b** she is attractive in appearance."
26:9 "**B** I thought I might die **b** of her."
26:20 **b** they contended with him.
27:20 "**B** the LORD your God granted me success."
27:23 not recognize him, **b** his hands were hairy
27:41 Now Esau hated Jacob **b** of the blessing
27:46 "I am weary of my life **b** of the Hittite women.
28:11 and stayed there for the night, **b** the sun had set.
29:15 Laban said to Jacob, "**B** you are my kinsman,
29:20 to him but a few days **b** of the love he had for her.
29:32 "**B** the LORD has looked on my affliction;
29:33 and said, "**B** the LORD has heard that I am hated,
29:34 **b** I have borne him three sons";
30:18 "God has given me my hire **b** I gave my maid
30:20 **b** I have borne him six sons";
30:27 by divination that the LORD has blessed me **b**

Ge 31:30 to go **b** you longed greatly for your father's house,
31:31 Jacob answered Laban, "**B** I was afraid,
32:12 which cannot be counted **b** of their number.' "
32:31 as he passed Penuel, limping **b** of his hip.
32:32 **b** he struck Jacob on the hip socket at
33:11 **b** God has dealt graciously with me,
33:11 and **b** I have everything I want."
34:7 **b** he had committed an outrage in Israel by lying
34:13 **b** he had defiled their sister Dinah.
34:19 **b** he was delighted with Jacob's daughter.
34:27 **b** their sister had been defiled.
35:7 **b** it was there that God had revealed himself
36:7 where they were staying could not support them **b**
37:3 **b** he was the son of his old age;
37:8 So they hated him even more **b** of his dreams
39:9 from me except yourself, **b** you are his wife.
39:23 **b** the LORD was with him;
41:31 The plenty will no longer be known in the land **b**
41:57 **b** the famine became severe throughout the world.
43:18 Now the men were afraid **b** they were brought
43:18 and they said, "It is **b** of the money,
43:30 **b** he was overcome with affection for his brother,
43:32 **b** the Egyptians could not eat with the Hebrews,
45:5 or angry with yourselves, **b** you sold me here;
46:34 **b** all shepherds are abhorrent to the Egyptians."
47:4 for your servants' flocks **b** the famine is severe in
47:13 of Egypt and the land of Canaan languished **b** of
47:20 **b** the famine was severe upon them;
49:4 you shall no longer excel **b** you went
Ex 1:19 "**B** the Hebrew women are not like
1:21 And **b** the midwives feared God,
2:10 She named him Moses, "**b**," she said,
6:9 **b** of their broken spirit and their cruel slavery.
8:24 in all of Egypt the land was ruined **b** of the flies.
9:11 The magicians could not stand before Moses **b** of
10:9 **b** we have the LORD's festival to celebrate."
12:39 not leavened, **b** they were driven out of Egypt
13:3 **b** the LORD brought you out from there
13:8 'It is **b** of what the LORD did for me
14:11 "Was it **b** there were no graves in Egypt
15:23 not drink the water of Marah **b** it was bitter.
16:7 **b** he has heard your complaining against
16:8 **b** the LORD has heard the complaining
17:7 **b** the Israelites quarreled and tested the LORD,
18:11 **b** he delivered the people from the Egyptians,
18:15 "**B** the people come to me to inquire of God.
19:11 **b** on the third day the LORD will come down
19:18 **b** the LORD had descended upon it in fire;
29:33 but no one else shall eat of them, **b** they are holy.
29:34 it shall not be eaten, **b** it is holy.
31:14 You shall keep the sabbath, **b** it is holy for you;
32:35 **b** they made the calf—the one that Aaron made.
34:14 **b** the LORD, whose name is Jealous,
34:29 of his face shone **b** he had been talking with God.
40:35 Moses was not able to enter the tent of meeting **b**
Lev 10:13 **b** it is your due and your sons' due,
16:16 **b** of the uncleannesses of the people of Israel,
16:16 and **b** of their transgressions, all their sins;
19:8 **b** they have profaned what is holy to the LORD;
20:3 **b** they have given of their offspring to Molech,
20:23 **B** they did all these things, I abhorred them.
21:3 close to him **b** she has had no husband,
21:23 **b** he has a blemish, that he may
25:33 **b** the houses in the cities of
26:39 in the land of your enemies **b** of their iniquities;
26:39 also they shall languish **b** of the iniquities
26:43 **b** they dared to spurn my ordinances,
Nu 6:7 **b** their consecration to God is upon the head.
6:11 **b** they incurred guilt by reason of the corpse.
6:12 **b** the consecrated head was defiled.
7:9 **b** they were charged with the care of
11:3 **b** the fire of the LORD burned against them.
11:20 **b** you have rejected the LORD who is
11:34 **b** there they buried the people who had
12:1 Miriam and Aaron spoke against Moses **b** of
13:24 **b** of the cluster that the Israelites cut down
14:16 'It is **b** the LORD was not able
14:24 **b** he has a different spirit
14:43 **b** you have turned back from following
15:26 **b** the whole people was involved in the error.
15:31 **B** of having despised the word of the LORD
15:34 **b** it was not clear what should be done to him.
18:24 **b** I have given to the Levites as their portion
20:12 "**B** you did not trust in me,
20:24 **b** you rebelled against my command at the waters
22:3 **b** they were so numerous;
22:22 God's anger was kindled **b** he was going,
22:29 "**B** you have made a fool of me!
22:32 **b** your way is perverse before me.
25:13 **b** he was zealous for his God,
26:62 for they were not enrolled among the Israelites **b**
27:4 be taken away from his clan **b** he had no son?
27:14 **b** you rebelled against my word in the wilderness
30:5 **b** her father had expressed to her his disapproval.
30:14 he has validated them, **b** he said nothing to her at
32:11 **b** they have not unreservedly followed me—
32:17 the fortified towns **b** of the inhabitants of the land.
32:19 **b** our inheritance has come to us on this side of
Dt 1:27 "It is **b** the LORD hates us
1:36 **b** of his complete fidelity to the LORD."
2:19 **b** I have given it to the descendants of Lot."
2:25 they will tremble and be in anguish **b** of you."
3:28 **b** it is he who shall cross over at the head
4:21 The LORD was angry with me **b** of you,
4:31 **B** the LORD your God is a merciful God,
4:37 And **b** he loved your ancestors,
5:5 for you were afraid **b** of the fire and did not go up
Dt 6:15 **b** the LORD your God, who is present
7:7 It was not **b** you were more numerous than any
7:8 It was **b** the LORD loved you and kept the oath
7:25 **b** you could be ensnared by it;
8:20 **b** you would not obey the voice of
9:4 "It is **b** of my righteousness that
9:4 it is rather **b** of the wickedness of these nations
9:5 It is not **b** of your righteousness or the uprightness
9:5 but **b** of the wickedness of these nations
9:6 not giving you this good land to occupy **b**
9:18 **b** of all the sin you had committed,
9:28 '**B** the LORD was not able to bring them into
9:28 and **b** he hated them, he has brought them out
12:20 **b** you wish to eat meat,
12:25 **b** you do what is right in the sight of the LORD.
12:28 **b** you will be doing what is good and right in
12:31 **b** every abhorrent thing that
14:7 **b** they chew the cud but do not divide the hoof;
14:8 **b** it divides the hoof but does not chew the cud,
14:24 that you are unable to transport it, **b** the place
14:27 **b** they have no allotment or inheritance with you.
14:29 **b** they have no allotment or inheritance with you,
15:2 **b** the LORD's remission has been proclaimed.
15:4 **b** the LORD is sure to bless you in the land that
15:16 **b** he loves you and your household,
15:18 **b** for six years they have given you services worth
16:3 **b** you came out of the land of Egypt in great haste,
18:12 it is **b** of such abhorrent practices that
21:9 **b** you must do what is right in the sight of
22:19 to the young woman's father) **b** he has slandered
22:21 **b** she committed a disgraceful act in Israel
22:24 the young woman **b** she did not cry for help in
22:24 and the man **b** he violated his neighbor's wife.
22:26 an offense punishable by death, **b** this case is like
22:29 **B** he violated her he shall not be permitted
23:4 **b** they did not meet you with food and water
23:4 and **b** they hired against you Balaam son of Beor,
23:5 **b** the LORD your God loved you.)
23:7 **b** you were an alien residing in their land.
23:10 of you becomes unclean **b** of a nocturnal emission,
23:14 **B** the LORD your God travels along
24:1 not please him **b** he finds something objectionable
24:15 **b** they are poor and their livelihood depends
27:20 **b** he has violated his father's rights."
28:20 of the evil of your deeds, **b** you have forsaken me.
28:45 **b** you did not obey the LORD your God,
28:47 **B** you did not serve the LORD your God joyfully
28:55 **b** nothing else remains to him,
28:57 **b** she is eating them in secret for lack
28:62 **b** you did not obey the LORD your God.
28:67 **b** of the dread that your heart shall feel and
29:25 "It is **b** they abandoned the covenant of
30:10 **b** you turn to the LORD your God
31:6 **b** it is the LORD your God who goes with you;
31:17 not these troubles come upon us **b** our God is not
31:21 **b** it will not be lost from the mouths
31:29 **b** you will do what is evil in the sight of
32:35 **b** the day of their calamity is at hand,
32:51 **b** both of you broke faith with me among
34:9 **b** Moses had laid his hands on him;
Jos 2:11 there was no courage left in any of us **b** of you.
5:1 and there was no longer any spirit in them, **b** of
5:7 **b** they had not been circumcised on the way.
6:1 Now Jericho was shut up inside and out **b** of
6:17 and all who are with her in her house shall live **b**
7:12 they turn their backs to their enemies, **b**
9:9 **b** of the name of the LORD your God;
9:18 **b** the leaders of the congregation had sworn
9:20 **b** of the oath that we swore to them."
9:24 "**B** it was told to your servants for a certainty that
9:24 so we were in great fear for our lives **b** of you,
10:2 **b** Gibeon was a large city,
10:11 there were more who died **b** of the hailstones than
10:42 **b** the LORD God of Israel fought for Israel.
14:9 **b** you have wholeheartedly followed
14:14 **b** he wholeheartedly followed the LORD,
17:1 of Gilead, were allotted Gilead and Bashan, **b**
17:6 **b** the daughters of Manasseh received
19:9 **b** the portion of the tribe of Judah was too large
20:5 **b** the neighbor was killed by mistake,
22:31 **b** you have not committed this treachery against
Jdg 1:19 **b** they had chariots of iron.
2:18 by their groaning **b** of those who persecuted
2:20 "**B** this people have transgressed my covenant
3:12 against Israel, **b** they had done what was evil in
5:7 **b** you arose, Deborah, arose as a mother in Israel.
5:23 **b** they did not come to the help of the LORD,
6:2 and **b** of Midian the Israelites provided
6:6 Thus Israel was greatly impoverished **b** of Midian;
6:27 but **b** he was too afraid of his family and
6:31 **b** his altar has been pulled down."
6:32 **b** he pulled down his altar.
8:20 for he was afraid, **b** he was still a boy.
8:24 (For the enemy had golden earrings, **b**
9:18 over the lords of Shechem, **b** he is your kinsman—
10:10 **b** we have abandoned our God
11:13 "**B** Israel, on coming from Egypt,
12:4 the men of Gilead defeated Ephraim, **b** they said,
14:3 "Get her for me, **b** she pleases me."
14:17 **b** she nagged him, on the seventh day he told her.
15:6 **b** he has taken Samson's wife and given her
17:13 **b** the Levite has become my priest."
18:28 **b** it was far from Sidon and they had no dealings
20:36 **b** they trusted to the troops in ambush
21:15 on Benjamin **b** the LORD had made a breach in
21:22 **b** we did not capture in battle a wife for each man.
Ru 1:13 **b** the hand of the LORD has turned against me."
Ru 1:19 the whole town was stirred **b** of them;
1Sa 1:5 but to Hannah he gave a double portion, **b**
1:6 to irritate her, **b** the LORD had closed her womb.
2:1 **b** I rejoice in my victory.
3:13 **b** his sons were blaspheming God,
4:21 **b** the ark of God had been captured and **b** of her
6:19 The people mourned **b** the LORD had made
8:18 And in that day you will cry out **b** of your king,
9:12 **b** the people have a sacrifice today at the shrine.
9:16 **b** their outcry has come to me."
12:10 'We have sinned, **b** we have forsaken the LORD,
12:22 **b** it has pleased the LORD to make you a people
13:14 be ruler over his people, **b** you have not kept what
14:29 see how my eyes have brightened **b** I tasted a little
15:23 **B** you have rejected the word of the LORD,
15:24 **b** I feared the people and obeyed their voice.
16:7 on the height of his stature, **b** I have rejected him;
17:32 "Let no one's heart fail **b** of him;
18:3 **b** he loved him as his own soul.
18:12 **b** the LORD was with him but had departed
19:4 **b** he has not sinned against you,
19:4 and **b** his deeds have been of good service to you;
20:18 you will be missed, **b** your place will be empty.
20:34 and **b** his father had disgraced him.
21:8 **b** the king's business required haste."
22:17 **b** their hand also is with David;
24:5 the heart **b** he had cut off a corner of Saul's cloak.
25:28 **b** my lord is fighting the battles of the LORD;
26:12 for they were all asleep, **b** a deep sleep from
26:16 **b** you have not kept watch over your lord,
26:21 **b** my life was precious in your sight today;
28:18 **B** you did not obey the voice of the LORD,
28:20 filled with fear **b** of the words of Samuel;
30:6 of stoning him, **b** all the people were bitter in spirit
30:13 behind **b** I fell sick three days ago.
30:16 **b** of the great amount of spoil they had taken from
30:22 "**B** they did not go with us,
2Sa 1:12 **b** they had fallen by the sword.
2:5 **b** you showed this loyalty to Saul your lord,
2:6 I too will reward you **b** you have done this thing.
3:11 not answer Abner another word, **b** he feared him.
3:30 So Joab and his brother Abishai murdered Abner **b**
6:7 and God struck him there **b**
6:8 David was angry **b** the LORD had burst forth
6:12 **b** of the ark of God."
7:21 **B** of your promise,
8:10 and to congratulate him **b** he had fought
10:3 that David is honoring your father just **b**
12:6 **b** he did this thing, and **b** he had no pity."
12:14 **b** by this deed you have utterly scorned
12:25 so he named him Jedidiah, **b** of the LORD.
13:2 that he made himself ill **b** of his sister Tamar,
13:21 **b** he loved him, for he was his firstborn.
13:22 **b** he had raped his sister Tamar.
14:15 Now I have come to say this to my lord the king **b**
16:10 If he is cursing **b** the LORD has said to him,
18:20 not do so, **b** the king's son is dead."
19:9 and now he has fled out of the land **b** of Absalom.
19:21 **b** he cursed the LORD's anointed?"
19:42 "**B** the king is near of kin to us.
21:1 **b** he put the Gibeonites to death."
21:7 **b** of the oath of the LORD that was
22:8 the heavens trembled and quaked, **b** he was angry.
22:20 he delivered me, **b** he delighted in me.
24:10 David was stricken to the heart **b** he had numbered
1Ki 2:26 **b** you carried the ark of the Lord GOD
2:26 and **b** you shared in all the hardships
2:32 **b**, without the knowledge of my father David,
3:2 **b** no house had yet been built for the name of
3:6 **b** he walked before you in faithfulness,
3:11 God said to him, "**B** you have asked this,
3:19 Then this woman's son died in the night, **b** she lay
3:26 **b** compassion for her son burned within her—
3:28 **b** they perceived that the wisdom of God was
5:3 the name of the LORD his God **b** of the warfare
7:47 **b** there were so many of them;
8:11 priests could not stand to minister **b** of the cloud;
8:35 "When heaven is shut up and there is no rain **b**
8:35 and turn from their sin, **b** you punish them,
8:41 comes from a distant land **b** of your name
8:64 and the fat pieces of the sacrifices of well-being, **b**
8:66 joyful and in good spirits **b** of all the goodness that
9:9 '**B** they have forsaken the LORD their God,
10:9 **B** the LORD loved Israel forever,
11:9 **b** his heart had turned away from the LORD,
11:33 This is **b** he has forsaken me,
12:15 **b** it was a turn of affairs brought about by
13:21 **B** you have disobeyed the word of the LORD,
14:4 for his eyes were dim **b** of his age.
14:7 **B** I exalted you from among the people,
14:13 of Jeroboam's family shall come to the grave, **b**
14:15 **b** they have made their sacred poles,
14:16 He will give Israel up **b** of the sins of Jeroboam,
15:5 **b** David did what was right in the sight of
15:13 **b** she had made an abominable image for Asherah;
15:30 **b** of the sins of Jeroboam that he committed and
15:30 **b** of the anger to which he provoked the LORD,
16:7 both **b** of all the evil that he did in the sight of
16:7 and also **b** he destroyed it.
16:13 **b** of all the sins of Baasha and the sins
16:19 **b** of the sins that he committed,
17:7 the wadi dried up, **b** there was no rain in the land.
18:18 and your father's house, **b** you have forsaken
20:28 **B** the Arameans have said,
20:36 "**B** you have not obeyed the voice of the LORD,
20:42 '**B** you have let the man go whom I had devoted
21:2 **b** it is near my house;

1Ki 21: 4 and sullen **b** of what Naboth the Jezreelite had said
21: 6 "**B** I spoke to Naboth the Jezreelite and said
21:20 **B** you have sold yourself to do what is evil in
21:22 **b** you have provoked me to anger
21:29 **B** he has humbled himself before me,
2Ki 1: 3 'Is it **b** there is no God in Israel that you are going
1: 6 Is it **b** there is no God in Israel
1:16 **B** you have sent messengers to inquire
1:16 is it **b** there is no God in Israel to inquire
1:17 of King Jehoram son of Jehoshaphat of Judah, **b**
5: 1 **b** by him the LORD had given victory to Aram.
6: 9 **b** the Arameans are going down there."
6:11 the king of Aram was greatly perturbed **b** of this;
8:12 "**B** I know the evil that you will do to the people
8:29 down to see Joram son of Ahab in Jezreel, **b**
10:30 The LORD said to Jehu, "**B** you have done well
12: 2 **b** the priest Jehoiada instructed him.
13:23 **b** of his covenant with Abraham, Isaac, and Jacob,
15:16 **b** they did not open it to him, he sacked it.
16:18 He did this **b** of the king of Assyria.
17: 7 This occurred **b** the people of Israel had sinned
17:26 they are killing them, **b** they do not know the law
18:12 **b** they did not obey the voice of
19: 6 not be afraid **b** of the words that you have heard,
19:28 **B** you have raged against me
21:11 "**B** King Manasseh of Judah
21:15 **b** they have done what is evil in my sight
22:13 against us, **b** our ancestors did not obey the words
22:17 **B** they have abandoned me
22:19 **b** your heart was penitent,
22:19 **b** you have torn your clothes and wept before me,
23:26 by which his anger was kindled against Judah, **b**
25:24 "Do not be afraid **b** of the Chaldean officials;
1Ch 4: 9 saying, "**B** I bore him in pain."
4:14 so-called **b** they were artisans.
4:41 **b** there was pasture there for their flocks.
5: 1 (He was the firstborn, but **b**
5: 9 **b** their cattle had multiplied in the land of Gilead.
5:20 and he granted their entreaty **b** they trusted in him.
5:22 Many fell slain, **b** the war was of God.
7:21 killed them, **b** they came down to raid their cattle.
7:23 **b** disaster had befallen his house.
9: 1 into exile in Babylon **b** of their unfaithfulness.
12: 1 not move about freely **b** of Saul son of Kish;
13:10 he struck him down **b** he put out his hand to
13:11 David was angry **b** the LORD had burst out
15:13 **B** you did not carry it the first time,
15:13 **b** we did not give it proper care."
15:26 And **b** God helped the Levites who were carrying
18:10 **b** he had fought against Hadadezer
19: 3 "Do you think, **b** David has sent consolers to you,
22: 8 not build a house to my name, **b** you have shed
29: 3 and **b** of my devotion to the house
29: 9 the people rejoiced **b** these had given willingly,
2Ch 1:11 "**B** this was in your heart,
2:11 in a letter that he sent to Solomon, "**B**
5:14 priests could not stand to minister **b** of the cloud;
6:26 "When heaven is shut up and there is no rain **b**
6:26 and turn from their sin, **b** you punish them,
6:32 come from a distant land **b** of your great name,
7: 2 **b** the glory of the LORD filled
7: 7 and the fat of the offerings of well-being **b**
7:10 joyful and in good spirits **b** of the goodness that
7:22 '**B** they abandoned the LORD the God
9: 8 **B** your God loved Israel and would establish them
10:15 **b** it was a turn of affairs brought about by God so
11:14 **b** Jeroboam and his sons had prevented them
12: 2 **b** they had been unfaithful to the LORD,
12: 5 who had gathered at Jerusalem **b** of Shishak,
12:12 **B** he humbled himself the wrath of
13: 8 **b** you are a great multitude and have with you
13:18 **b** they relied on the LORD,
14: 7 the land is still ours **b** we have sought
15:16 from being queen mother **b** she had made
16: 7 "**B** you relied on the king of Aram,
16: 8 Yet **b** you relied on the LORD,
16:10 in prison, for he was in a rage with him **b** of this.
17: 3 **b** he walked in the earlier ways of his father;
19: 2 **B** of this, wrath has gone out against you from
20:25 the booty, **b** of its abundance.
20:37 saying, "**B** you have joined with Ahaziah,
21: 3 the kingdom to Jehoram, **b** he was the firstborn.
21: 7 not destroy the house of David **b** of the covenant
21:10 **b** he had forsaken the LORD,
21:12 **B** you have not walked in the ways
21:13 and **b** you also have killed your brothers,
21:15 day after day, **b** of the disease."
21:19 his bowels came out **b** of the disease,
22: 6 to see Joram son of Ahab in Jezreel, **b** he was sick.
22:11 **b** she was a sister of Ahaziah—
24:16 **b** he had done good in Israel,
24:20 **B** you have forsaken the LORD,
24:24 **b** they had abandoned the LORD,
24:25 his servants conspired against him **b** of the blood
25:16 **b** you have done this and have not listened
25:20 **b** they had sought the gods of Edom.
26:20 **b** the LORD had struck him.
27: 6 So Jotham became strong **b** he ordered his ways
28: 6 **b** they had abandoned the LORD,
28: 9 "**B** the LORD, the God of your ancestors,
28:19 For the LORD brought Judah low **b** of King Ahaz
28:23 "**B** the gods of the kings of Aram helped them,
29:36 the people rejoiced **b** of what God had done for
30: 3 (for they could not keep it at its proper time **b**
32:20 the prophet Isaiah son of Amoz prayed **b** of this
34:21 of the LORD that is poured out on us is great, **b**
34:25 **B** they have forsaken me and have made offerings
2Ch 34:27 **b** your heart was penitent
35:14 **b** the priests the descendants
36:15 **b** he had compassion on his people and
Ezr 3: 3 **b** they were in dread of the neighboring peoples,
3:11 **b** the foundation of the house of
4:14 Now **b** we share the salt of the palace and it is
5:12 **b** our ancestors had angered the God of heaven,
9: 4 **b** of the faithlessness of the returned exiles,
9:15 though no one can face you **b** of this."
10: 9 trembling **b** of this matter and **b** of the heavy rain.
Ne 5:15 But I did not do so, **b** of the fear of God.
5:18 **b** of the heavy burden of labor on the people.
6:12 but he had pronounced the prophecy against me **b**
6:18 **b** he was the son-in-law of Shecaniah son of Arah:
8:12 **b** they had understood the words
9:37 the kings whom you have set over us **b** of our sins;
9:38 **B** of all this we make a firm agreement in writing,
13: 2 **b** they did not meet the Israelites with bread
13:29 O my God, **b** they have defiled the priesthood,
Est 1:15 be done to Queen Vashti **b** she has not performed
8: 7 **b** he plotted to lay hands on the Jews.
8:17 **b** the fear of the Jews had fallen upon them.
9: 2 **b** the fear of them had fallen upon all peoples.
9: 3 **b** the fear of Mordecai had fallen upon them.
9:26 Thus **b** of all that was written in this letter,
Job 3:10 **b** it did not shut the doors of my mother's womb,
6:20 They are disappointed **b** they were confident;
11:18 And you will have confidence, **b** there is hope;
15:25 **B** they stretched out their hands against God,
15:27 **b** they have covered their faces with their fat,
18: 4 shall the earth be forsaken **b** of you,
20: 2 **b** of the agitation within me.
22:30 they will escape **b** of the cleanness of your hands."
29:12 **b** I delivered the poor who cried,
30:11 **B** God has loosed my bowstring and humbled me,
31:21 **b** I saw I had supporters at the gate;
31:25 if I have rejoiced **b** my wealth was great,
31:25 or **b** my hand had gotten much;
31:34 **b** I stood in great fear of the multitude,
32: 1 **b** he was righteous in his own eyes.
32: 2 at Job **b** he justified himself rather than God;
32: 3 at Job's three friends **b** they had found no answer,
32: 4 **b** they were older than he.
32:16 to wait, **b** they do not speak, **b** they stand there,
34:27 **b** they turned aside from following him,
34:33 Will he then pay back to suit you, **b** you reject it?
34:36 **b** his answers are those of the wicked.
35: 9 "**B** of the multitude of oppressions people cry out;
35: 9 they call for help **b** of the arm of the mighty.
35:12 but he does not answer, **b** of the pride of evildoers.
35:15 And now, **b** his anger does not punish,
36:21 **b** of that you have been tried by affliction.
37:17 when the earth is still **b** of the south wind?
37:19 we cannot draw up our case **b** of darkness.
39:11 Will you depend on it **b** its strength is great,
39:17 **b** God has made it forget wisdom,
Ps 5: 8 O LORD, in your righteousness **b** of my enemies;
5:10 **b** of their many transgressions cast them out,
6: 7 My eyes waste away **b** of grief;
6: 7 they grow weak **b** of all my foes.
8: 2 and infants you have founded a bulwark **b**
12: 5 "**B** the poor are despoiled, **b** the needy groan,
13: 4 my foes will rejoice **b** I am shaken.
13: 6 **b** he has dealt bountifully with me.
16: 8 **b** he is at my right hand, I shall not be moved.
18: 7 also of the mountains trembled and quaked, **b**
18:19 he delivered me, **b** he delighted in me.
27:11 and lead me on a level path **b** of my enemies.
28: 5 **B** they do not regard the works of the LORD,
31: 7 **b** you have seen my affliction;
31:10 my strength fails **b** of my misery,
33:21 **b** we trust in his holy name.
37: 1 Do not fret **b** of the wicked;
37:40 and saves them, **b** they take refuge in him.
38: 3 There is no soundness in my flesh **b**
38: 3 there is no health in my bones **b** of my sin.
38: 5 My wounds grow foul and fester **b**
38: 8 I groan **b** of the tumult of my heart.
38:20 for good are my adversaries **b** I follow after good.
40:15 Let those be appalled **b** of their shame who say
41:11 **b** my enemy has not triumphed over me.
41:12 But you have upheld me **b** of my integrity,
42: 9 about mournfully **b** the enemy oppresses me?"
43: 2 Why must I walk about mournfully **b** of
44:22 **B** of you we are being killed all day long,
48:11 let the towns of Judah rejoice **b** of your judgments.
52: 9 I will thank you forever, **b** of what you have done.
55: 3 **b** of the clamor of the wicked.
55:19 **b** they do not change, and do not fear God.
63: 3 **B** your steadfast love is better than life,
64: 8 **B** of their tongue he will bring them to ruin;
66: 3 **B** of your great power, your enemies cringe
66:20 **b** he has not rejected my prayer
68:29 **B** of your temple at Jerusalem kings bear gifts
69: 6 be put to shame **b** of me, O Lord GOD of hosts;
69: 6 not let those who seek you be dishonored **b** of me,
69:18 redeem me, set me free **b** of my enemies.
70: 3 turn back **b** of their shame.
78:22 **b** they had no faith in God,
78:65 like a warrior shouting **b** of wine.
86:17 be put to shame, **b** you, LORD, have helped me
91: 9 **B** you have made the LORD your refuge,
97: 8 **b** of your judgments, O God.
102: 5 **B** of my loud groaning my bones cling to my skin.
102:10 **b** of your indignation and anger;
107:17 and **b** of their iniquities endured affliction;
107:30 Then they were glad **b** they had quiet,
Ps 107:34 **b** of the wickedness of its inhabitants.
109:21 **b** your steadfast love is good, deliver me.
116: 1 **b** he has heard my voice and my supplications.
116: 2 **B** he inclined his ear to me,
119:47 in your commandments, **b** I love them.
119:53 Hot indignation seizes me **b** of the wicked,
119:62 **b** of your righteous ordinances.
119:74 **b** I have hoped in your word.
119:78 **b** they have subverted me with guile;
119:131 **b** I long for your commandments.
119:136 My eyes shed streams of tears **b** your law is
119:139 zeal consumes me **b** my foes forget your words.
119:158 **b** they do not keep your commands.
119:171 **b** you teach me your statutes.
Pr 1:24 **B** I have called and you refused,
1:25 and **b** you have ignored all my counsel
1:29 **B** they hated knowledge and did not choose
5:23 and **b** of their great folly they are lost.
21: 7 **b** they refuse to do what is just.
22:22 Do not rob the poor **b** they are poor,
24:19 Do not fret **b** of evildoers.
Ecc 2:17 **b** what is done under the sun was grievous to me;
2:21 **b** sometimes one who has toiled with wisdom
4: 9 **b** they have a good reward for their toil.
5:20 **b** God keeps them occupied with the joy
8: 2 Keep the king's command **b** of your sacred oath.
8:11 **B** sentence against an evil deed is
8:12 **b** they stand in fear before him,
8:13 **b** they do not stand in fear before God.
9: 9 **b** that is your portion in life and in your toil
12: 3 women who grind cease working **b** they are few,
12: 5 **b** all must go to their eternal home,
SS 1: 6 Do not gaze at me **b** I am dark,
1: 6 **b** the sun has gazed on me.
3: 8 with his sword at his thigh **b** of alarms by night.
Isa 3: 8 **b** their speech and their deeds are against
3:16 **B** the daughters of Zion are haughty and walk
7: 4 be faint **b** of these two smoldering stumps
7: 4 **b** of the fierce anger of Rezin and Aram and
7: 5 **B** Aram—with Ephraim
7:22 and will eat curds **b** of the abundance of milk
8: 6 **B** this people has refused the waters of Shiloah
14:20 **b** you have destroyed your land,
14:21 Prepare slaughter for his sons **b** of the guilt
15: 1 **B** Ar is laid waste in a night, Moab is undone;
15: 1 **b** Kir is laid waste in a night, Moab is undone.
17: 9 which they deserted **b** of the children of Israel,
19:17 to whom it is mentioned will fear **b** of the plan that
19:20 when they cry to the LORD **b** of oppressors,
20: 5 And they shall be dismayed and confounded **b**
26: 3 in peace **b** they trust in you.
26:14 **b** you have punished and destroyed them,
26:17 so were we **b** of you, O LORD;
28:15 **B** you have said, "We have made a covenant
29:13 **B** these people draw near with their mouths
30:12 **B** you reject this word, and put your trust in
31: 1 in chariots **b** they are many and in horsemen **b**
37: 6 not be afraid **b** of the words that you have heard,
37:21 **B** you have prayed to me
37:29 **B** you have raged against me
38:15 All my sleep has fled **b** of the bitterness
40:26 **b** he is great in strength, mighty in power,
43: 4 **B** you are precious in my sight, and honored,
48: 4 **B** I know that you are obstinate,
49: 7 **b** of the LORD, who is faithful,
50: 1 No, **b** of your sins you were sold,
51:13 You fear continually all day long **b** of the fury of
52:15 kings shall shut their mouths **b** of him;
53:12 **b** he poured out himself to death,
54:15 whoever stirs up strife with you shall fall **b** of you.
55: 5 **b** of the LORD your God, the Holy One of Israel,
57:17 **B** of their wicked covetousness I was angry;
60: 5 **b** the abundance of the sea shall be brought to you,
60: 9 for the Holy One of Israel, **b** he has glorified you.
61: 1 **b** the LORD has anointed me;
61: 7 **B** their shame was double,
63: 7 **b** of all that the LORD has done for us,
64: 5 **b** you hid yourself we transgressed.
65: 7 **b** they offered incense on the mountains
65:12 **b**, when I called, you did not answer,
65:16 **b** the former troubles are forgotten and are hidden
66: 4 **b**, when I called, no one answered, when I spoke,
Jer 3: 9 **B** she took her whoredom so lightly,
3:21 **b** they have perverted their way,
4: 4 **b** of the evil of your doings.
4: 8 **B** of this put on sackcloth, lament and wail:
4:17 **b** she has rebelled against me, says the LORD.
4:28 **B** of this the earth shall mourn,
5: 6 **b** their transgressions are many,
5:14 **B** they have spoken this word,
6:19 **b** they have not given heed to my words;
7:13 And now, **b** you have done all these things,
8:10 **b** from the least to the greatest everyone is greedy
8:14 **b** we have sinned against the LORD.
9:10 **b** they are laid waste so that no one passes
9:13 **B** they have forsaken my law that I set
9:19 **b** we have left the land, **b** they have cast down our
10:19 Woe is me **b** of my hurt!
11:17 **b** of the evil that the house of Israel and the house
12: 4 and **b** people said, "He is blind to our ways."
12:13 be ashamed of their harvests **b** of the fierce anger
13:17 **b** the LORD's flock has been taken captive.
13:25 **b** you have forgotten me and trusted in lies.
14: 4 **b** the ground is cracked.
14: 4 **B** there has been no rain on the land
14: 5 the doe in the field forsakes her newborn fawn **b**
14: 6 their eyes fail **b** there is no herbage.

Jer 15: 4 of the earth **b** of what King Manasseh son
16:11 It is **b** your ancestors have forsaken me,
16:12 **b** you have behaved worse than your ancestors,
16:18 **b** they have polluted my land with the carcasses
19: 4 **B** the people have forsaken me,
19: 4 and **b** they have filled this place with the blood of
19: 8 be horrified and will hiss **b** of all its disasters.
19:15 **b** they have stiffened their necks,
20:17 **b** he did not kill me in the womb;
21:12 with no one to quench it, **b** of your evil doings.
22: 9 "**B** they abandoned the covenant of
22:15 Are you a king **b** you compete in cedar?
22:22 then you will be ashamed and dismayed **b**
23: 9 **b** of the LORD and **b** of his holy words.
23:10 **b** of the curse the land mourns,
23:38 **B** you have said these words,
25: 8 **B** you have not obeyed my words,
25:16 of their minds **b** of the sword that I am sending
25:27 **b** of the sword that I am sending among you.
25:37 **b** of the fierce anger of the LORD.
25:38 **b** of the cruel sword, and **b** of his fierce anger.
26: 3 about the disaster that I intend to bring on them **b**
26:11 of death **b** he has prophesied against this city,
28:16 **b** you have spoken rebellion against the LORD."
29:15 **B** you have said, "The LORD has raised
29:19 **b** they did not heed my words,
29:23 **b** they have perpetrated outrage in Israel
29:31 **B** Shemaiah has prophesied to you,
30:14 **b** your guilt is great, **b** your sins are so numerous.
30:15 **B** your guilt is great, **b** your sins are so numerous,
30:17 **b** they have called you an outcast:
31:15 be comforted for her children, **b** they are no more.
31:19 I was ashamed, and I was dismayed **b** I bore
31:37 the offspring of Israel **b** of all they have done,
32:32 **b** of all the evil of the people of Israel and
33: 5 for I have hidden my face from this city **b**
33: 9 they shall fear and tremble **b** of all the good
35:17 **b** I have spoken to them and they have
35:18 **B** you have obeyed the command
38: 4 **b** he is discouraging the soldiers who are left
39:18 **b** you have trusted in me, says the LORD.
40: 3 **b** all of you sinned against the LORD and did
41: 2 **b** the king of Babylon had appointed him governor
41:18 **b** of the Chaldeans; for they were afraid of them,
41:18 for they were afraid of them, **b** Ishmael son
44: 3 **b** of the wickedness that they committed,
44:23 It is **b** you burned offerings,
44:23 and **b** you sinned against the LORD and did
46:15 —**b** the LORD thrust him down.
46:16 **b** of the destroying sword."
46:23 **b** they are more numerous than locusts;
47: 4 **b** of the day that is coming to destroy all
48: 7 **b** you trusted in your strongholds
48:26 **b** he magnified himself against the LORD;
48:42 **b** he magnified himself against the LORD.
49:17 be horrified and will hiss **b** of all its disasters.
50: 7 **b** they have sinned against the LORD,
50:13 **B** of the wrath of the LORD she shall not
50:13 be appalled and hiss **b** of all her wounds.
50:16 **b** of the destroying sword all of them shall return
50:24 **b** you challenged the LORD.
51: 6 Do not perish **b** of her guilt,
51:11 **b** his purpose concerning Babylon is to destroy it,
51:49 the slain of all the earth have fallen **b** of Babylon.
51:64 **b** of the disasters that I am bringing on her.' "
La 1: 5 **b** the LORD has made her suffer for
1:20 **b** I have been very rebellious.
1:22 and deal with them as you have dealt with me **b**
2:11 on the ground **b** of the destruction of my people,
2:11 **b** infants and babes faint in the streets of the city.
3:48 of tears **b** of the destruction of my people.
5: 9 **b** of the sword in the wilderness.
5:17 **B** of this our hearts are sick,
5:17 **b** of these things our eyes have grown dim:
5:18 **b** of Mount Zion, which lies desolate;
Eze 3: 7 **b** all the house of Israel have a hard forehead and
3:20 **b** you have not warned them,
3:21 they shall surely live, **b** they took warning;
5: 7 **B** you are more turbulent than the nations
5: 9 And **b** of all your abominations,
5:11 **b** you have defiled my sanctuary
7:13 **B** of their iniquity, they cannot maintain their lives.
12:19 **b** their land shall be stripped of all it contains,
13: 8 **B** you have uttered falsehood and envisioned lies,
13:10 **B**, in truth, **b** they have misled my people,
13:10 and **b**, when the people build a wall,
13:22 **B** you have disheartened the righteous falsely,
14:15 and no one may pass through **b** of the animals;
15: 8 **b** they have acted faithlessly,
16:14 for it was perfect **b** of my splendor
16:15 and played the whore **b** of your fame,
16:28 with the Assyrians, **b** you were insatiable;
16:31 not like a whore, **b** you scorned payment.
16:36 **B** your lust was poured out
16:36 and **b** of all your abominable idols,
16:36 and **b** of the blood of your children that you gave
16:43 **B** you have not remembered the days
16:52 **b** of your sins in which you acted more abominably
16:63 never open your mouth again **b** of your shame,
17:18 **B** he despised the oath and broke the covenant,
17:18 **b** he gave his hand and yet did all these things,
18:18 As for his father, **b** he practiced extortion,
18:28 **B** they considered and turned away from all
20:16 **b** they rejected my ordinances and did
20:24 **b** they had not executed my ordinances,
21: 4 **B** I will cut off from you both righteous
21: 7 you shall say, "**B** of the news that has come.

Eze 21:24 **B** you have brought your guilt to remembrance,
21:24 **b** you have come to remembrance,
22:19 **B** you have all become dross,
23:30 **b** you played the whore with the nations,
23:35 **B** you have forgotten me and cast me
23:45 **b** they are adulteresses and blood is on their hands.
25: 3 Thus says the Lord GOD, **B** you said, "Aha!"
25: 6 **B** you have clapped your hands
25: 8 Thus says the Lord GOD: **B** Moab said,
25:12 **B** Edom acted revengefully against the house
25:15 **B** with unending hostilities the Philistines acted
26: 2 **b** Tyre said concerning Jerusalem, "Aha,
27:16 with you **b** of your abundant goods;
27:18 **b** of your great wealth of every kind—
28: 2 **B** your heart is proud and you have said,
28: 6 **B** you compare your mind with the mind of a god,
28:17 Your heart was proud **b** of your beauty;
29: 6 **b** you were a staff of reed to the house of Israel;
29: 9 **B** you said, "The Nile is mine, and I made it,"
29:20 **b** they worked for me, says the Lord GOD.
31:10 **B** it towered high and set its top among the clouds,
31:15 and all the trees of the field fainted **b** of it.
32:10 their kings shall shudder **b** of you.
33:10 and we waste away **b** of them;
33:29 and a waste **b** of all their abominations
34: 5 So they were scattered, **b** there was no shepherd;
34: 8 **b** my sheep have become a prey,
34: 8 **b** my shepherds have not searched for my sheep,
34:21 **B** you pushed with flank and shoulder,
35: 5 **B** you cherished an ancient enmity,
35:10 **B** you said, "These two nations
35:11 according to the anger and envy that you showed **b**
35:15 **b** it was desolate, so I will deal with you;
36: 2 **B** the enemy said of you, "Aha!"
36: 3 **B** they made you desolate indeed,
36: 5 took my land as their possession, **b** of its pasture,
36: 6 **b** you have suffered the insults of the nations;
36:13 Thus says the Lord GOD: **B** they say to you,
39:23 **b** they dealt treacherously with me.
39:28 the LORD their God **b** I sent them into exile
44: 3 Only the prince, **b** he is a prince,
44:12 **B** they ministered to them before their idols
47:12 **b** the water for them flows from the sanctuary.
Da 2: 8 **b** you see I have firmly decreed:
2:12 **B** of this the king flew into a violent rage
2:30 this mystery has not been revealed to me **b**
3:22 **B** the king's command was urgent and
5:12 **b** an excellent spirit, knowledge,
5:19 And **b** of the greatness that he gave him,
6: 3 and satraps **b** an excellent spirit was in him,
6: 4 for complaint or any corruption, **b** he was faithful,
6:22 **b** I was found blameless before him;
6:23 **b** he had trusted in his God.
7:11 then **b** of the noise of the arrogant words that
8:12 **B** of wickedness, the host was given over
9: 7 **b** of the treachery that they have committed
9: 8 and our ancestors, **b** we have sinned against you.
9:11 **b** we have sinned against you.
9:16 **b** of our sins and the iniquities of our ancestors,
9:19 **b** your city and your people bear your name!"
10:12 and I have come **b** of your words.
10:16 **b** of the vision such pains have come upon me
Hos 2: 4 **b** they are children of whoredom.
4: 6 **b** you have rejected knowledge,
4:10 **b** they have forsaken the LORD
4:13 poplar, and terebinth, **b** their shade is good.
4:19 and they shall be ashamed **b** of their altars.
5:11 **b** he was determined to go after vanity.
7:16 their officials shall fall by the sword **b** of the rage
8: 1 **b** they have broken my covenant,
9: 7 **B** of your great iniquity, your hostility is great.
9:15 **B** of the wickedness of their deeds I will drive
9:17 **B** they have not listened to him,
10:13 **B** you have trusted in your power and in
10:15 O Bethel, **b** of your great wickedness.
11: 5 **b** they have refused to return to me.
11: 6 and devours **b** of their schemes.
13:16 **b** she has rebelled against her God,
14: 1 for you have stumbled **b** of your iniquity.
Joel 1:17 the granaries are ruined **b** the grain has failed.
1:18 of cattle wander about **b** there is no pasture
1:20 to you **b** the watercourses are dried up,
3: 2 **b** they have scattered them among the nations.
3:19 **b** of the violence done to the people of Judah,
Am 1: 3 **b** they have threshed Gilead with threshing sledges
1: 6 **b** they carried into exile entire communities,
1: 9 **b** they delivered entire communities over to Edom,
1:11 **b** he pursued his brother with the sword
1:13 **b** they have ripped open pregnant women
2: 1 **b** he burned to lime the bones of the king of Edom.
2: 4 **b** they have rejected the law of the LORD,
2: 6 **b** they sell the righteous for silver,
4:12 **b** I will do this to you, prepare to meet your God,
5:11 Therefore **b** you trample on the poor and take
Jnh 1:10 **b** he had told them so.
1:12 for I know it is **b** of me
Mic 2: 1 they perform it, **b** it is in their power.
2:10 for this is no place to rest, **b** of uncleanness
3: 4 **b** they have acted wickedly.
3:12 Therefore **b** of you Zion shall be plowed as a field;
6:13 making you desolate **b** of your sins.
7: 9 **b** I have sinned against him,
7:13 But the earth will be desolate **b** of its inhabitants,
7:18 **b** he delights in showing clemency.
Na 3: 4 **B** of the countless debaucheries of the prostitute,
Hab 2: 8 **B** you have plundered many nations,
2: 8 **b** of human bloodshed, and violence to the earth,

Hab 2:17 **b** of human bloodshed and violence to the earth,
Zep 1:17 **b** they have sinned against the LORD,
2:10 **b** they scoffed and boasted against the people of
3:11 On that day you shall not be put to shame **b** of all
Hag 1: 9 **B** my house lies in ruins,
Zec 2: 4 **b** of the multitude of people and animals in it.
8: 4 each with staff in hand **b** of their great age.
9: 5 Ekron also, **b** its hopes are withered.
9:11 you also, **b** of the blood of my covenant with you,
10: 6 I will bring them back **b** I have compassion
Mal 2: 2 **b** you do not lay it to heart.
2:13 with weeping and groaning **b** he no longer regards
2:14 **B** the LORD was a witness between you and
Mt 2:18 she refused to be consoled, **b** they are no more."
6: 7 that they will be heard **b** of their many words.
7:25 but it did not fall, **b** it had been founded on rock.
9:36 **b** they were harassed and helpless,
10:18 be dragged before governors and kings **b** of me,
10:22 and you will be hated by all **b** of my name.
11:20 of his deeds of power had been done, **b** they did
11:25 **b** you have hidden these things from the wise and
12:41 **b** they repented at the proclamation of Jonah,
12:42 **b** she came from the ends of the earth to listen to
13:58 And he did not do many deeds of power there, **b**
14: 4 **b** John had been telling him,
14: 5 **b** they regarded him as a prophet.
15:32 **b** they have been with me now for three days
16: 7 "It is **b** we have brought no bread."
17:20 He said to them, "**B** of your little faith.
18: 7 Woe to the world **b** of stumbling blocks!
18:32 I forgave you all that debt **b** you pleaded with me.
19: 8 "It was **b** you were so hard-hearted
20: 7 They said to him, '**B** no one has hired us.'
20:15 Or are you envious **b** I am generous?'
21:46 **b** they regarded him as a prophet.
22:29 **b** you know neither the scriptures nor the power
24: 9 and you will be hated by all nations **b** of my name.
24:12 And **b** of the increase of lawlessness,
26:31 "You will all become deserters **b** of me this night;
26:33 "Though all become deserters **b** of you,
27:19 for today I have suffered a great deal **b** of a dream
Mk 1:34 not permit the demons to speak, **b** they knew him.
2: 4 they could not bring him to Jesus **b** of the crowd,
3: 9 to have a boat ready for him **b** of the crowd,
4:29 in with his sickle, **b** the harvest has come."
6:17 his brother Philip's wife, **b** Herod had married her.
6:34 **b** they were like sheep without a shepherd;
8: 2 **b** they have been with me now for three days
8:16 "It is **b** we have no bread."
9:38 **b** he was not following us."
9:41 whoever gives you a cup of water to drink **b**
10: 5 But Jesus said to them, "**B** of your hardness
11:18 of him, **b** the whole crowd was spellbound
13: 9 and you will stand before governors and kings **b**
13:13 and you will be hated by all **b** of my name.
16:14 ⟦**b** they had not believed those who saw him⟧
Lk 1: 7 But they had no children, **b** Elizabeth was barren,
1:20 But now, **b** you did not believe my words,
2: 4 **b** he was descended from the house and family
2: 7 **b** there was no place for them in the inn.
3:19 who had been rebuked by him **b** of Herodias,
3:19 and **b** of all the evil things that Herod had done,
4:18 **b** he has anointed me to bring good news to
4:32 **b** he spoke with authority.
4:41 **b** they knew that he was the Messiah.
5:19 but finding no way to bring him in **b** of the crowd,
6:48 but could not shake it, **b** it had been well built.
7:29 **b** they had been baptized with John's baptism.
8:19 but they could not reach him **b** of the crowd.
9: 7 **b** it was said by some that John had been raised
9:49 **b** he does not follow with us."
9:53 **b** his face was set toward Jerusalem.
10:21 **b** you have hidden these things from the wise and
11: 8 though he will not get up and give him anything **b**
11: 8 at least **b** of his persistence he will get up
11:31 **b** she came from the ends of the earth to listen to
11:32 **b** they repented at the proclamation of Jonah,
13: 2 "Do you think that **b** these Galileans suffered
13:14 indignant **b** Jesus had cured on the sabbath,
13:33 **b** it is impossible for a prophet to be killed outside
14:14 And you will be blessed, **b** they cannot repay you,
15:27 **b** he has got him back safe and sound.'
15:32 **b** this brother of yours was dead and has come
16: 2 **b** you cannot be my manager any longer.'
16: 8 the dishonest manager **b** he had acted shrewdly;
18: 5 yet **b** this widow keeps bothering me,
19: 3 **b** he was short in stature.
19: 4 **b** he was going to pass that way.
19: 9 **b** he too is a son of Abraham.
19:11 on to tell a parable, **b** he was near Jerusalem,
19:11 and **b** they supposed that the kingdom of God was
19:17 **B** you have been trustworthy in a very small thing,
19:21 **b** you are a harsh man;
19:44 **b** you did not recognize the time of your visitation
20:36 **b** they are like angels and are children of God,
21:12 before kings and governors **b** of my name.
21:17 You will be hated by all **b** of my name.
21:28 **b** your redemption is drawing near."
22:45 to the disciples and found them sleeping **b** of grief,
23: 8 **b** he had heard about him and was hoping
24:29 **b** it is almost evening and the day is
Jn 1:15 'He who comes after me ranks ahead of me **b**
1:30 'After me comes a man who ranks ahead of me **b**
1:50 "Do you believe **b** I told you that I saw you under
2:23 many believed in his name **b** they saw the signs
2:24 not entrust himself to them, **b** he knew all people
3:18 not believe are condemned already, **b** they have

Jn 3:19 and people loved darkness rather than light **b**
3:23 at Aenon near Salim **b** water was abundant there;
4:39 Many Samaritans from that city believed in him **b**
4:41 And many more believed **b** of his word.
4:42 "It is no longer **b** of what you said that we believe,
5:16 **b** he was doing such things on the sabbath.
5:18 **b** he was not only breaking the sabbath,
5:27 **b** he is the Son of Man.
5:30 **b** I seek to do not my own will but the will
5:38 **b** you do not believe him whom he has sent.
5:39 "You search the scriptures **b** you think that
6: 2 **b** they saw the signs that he was doing for the sick.
6:18 sea became rough **b** a strong wind was blowing.
6:26 you are looking for me, not **b** you saw signs,
6:26 but **b** you ate your fill of the loaves.
6:41 the Jews began to complain about him **b** he said,
6:57 and I live **b** of the Father,
6:57 so whoever eats me will live **b** of me.
6:66 **B** of this many of his disciples turned back
7: 1 to go about in Judea **b** the Jews were looking for
7: 7 but it hates me **b** I testify against it
7:23 with me **b** I healed a man's whole body on
7:29 I know him, **b** I am from him, and he sent me."
7:30 **b** his hour had not yet come.
7:39 there was no Spirit, **b** Jesus was not yet glorified.
7:43 So there was a division in the crowd **b** of him.
8:14 my testimony is valid **b** I know where I have come
8:20 **b** his hour had not yet come.
8:37 **b** there is no place in you for my word.
8:43 It is **b** you cannot accept my word.
8:44 **b** there is no truth in him.
8:45 But **b** I tell the truth, you do not believe me.
9:22 His parents said this **b** they were afraid of
10: 4 and the sheep follow him **b** they know his voice.
10: 5 but they will run from him **b** they do not know
10:13 The hired hand runs away **b** a hired hand does
10:17 **b** I lay down my life in order to take it up again.
10:19 Again the Jews were divided **b** of these words.
10:26 **b** you do not belong to my sheep.
10:33 **b** you, though only a human being,
10:36 and sent into the world is blaspheming **b** I said,
11: 9 **b** they see the light of this world.
11:10 **b** the light is not in them."
11:31 They followed her **b** they thought
11:39 a stench **b** he has been dead four days."
12: 6 (He said this not **b** he cared about the poor,
12: 6 but **b** he was a thief;
12: 9 not only **b** of Jesus but also to see Lazarus,
12:18 also **b** they heard that he had performed this sign
12:39 And so they could not believe, **b** Isaiah also said,
12:41 Isaiah said this **b** he saw his glory and spoke
12:42 But **b** of the Pharisees they did not confess it,
13:29 **b** Judas had the common purse,
14:11 then believe me **b** of the works themselves.
14:12 **b** I am going to the Father.
14:17 **b** it neither sees him nor knows him.
14:17 You know him, **b** he abides with you,
14:19 **b** I live, you also will live.
14:28 **b** the Father is greater than I.
15: 5 **b** apart from me you can do nothing.
15:15 **b** the servant does not know what
15:15 **b** I have made known to you everything
15:19 **B** you do not belong to the world,
15:21 **b** they do not know him who sent me.
15:27 also are to testify **b** you have been with me from
16: 3 And they will do this **b** they have not known
16: 4 not say these things to you from the beginning, **b**
16: 6 But **b** I have said these things to you,
16: 9 about sin, **b** they do not believe in me;
16:10 **b** I am going to the Father
16:11 **b** the ruler of this world has been condemned.
16:14 **b** he will take what is mine and declare it to you.
16:17 and '**B** I am going to the Father'?"
16:21 she has pain, **b** her hour has come.
16:21 she no longer remembers the anguish **b** of the joy
16:27 **b** you have loved me and have believed
16:32 Yet I am not alone **b** the Father is with me.
17: 9 of those whom you gave me, **b** they are yours.
17:14 and the world has hated them **b** they do not belong
17:24 which you have given me **b** you loved me before
18: 2 **b** Jesus often met there with his disciples.
18:18 the police had made a charcoal fire **b** it was cold,
19: 7 to that law he ought to die **b** he has claimed to be
19:20 **b** the place where Jesus was crucified was near
19:31 especially **b** that sabbath was a day
19:38 though a secret one **b** of his fear of the Jews,
19:42 And so, **b** it was the Jewish day of Preparation,
20:17 **b** I have not yet ascended to the Father.
20:29 "Have you believed **b** you have seen me?
21: 6 now they were not able to haul it in **b** there were
21:12 **b** they knew it was the Lord.
21:17 Peter felt hurt **b** he said to him the third time,
Ac 2: 6 **b** each one heard them speaking in
2:24 **b** it was impossible for him to be held in its power.
2:43 **b** many wonders and signs were being done by
4: 2 much annoyed **b** they were teaching the people
4: 9 if we are questioned today **b** of a good deed done
4:21 finding no way to punish them **b** of the people,
5:38 **b** if this plan or this undertaking is
6: 1 the Hebrews **b** their widows were being neglected
8:11 to him **b** for a long time he had amazed them
8:20 **b** you thought you could obtain God's gift
9: 7 with him stood speechless **b** they heard the voice
11:19 Now those who were scattered **b** of
12:20 for a reconciliation, **b** their country depended on
12:23 immediately, **b** he had not given the glory to God,
13:27 **B** the residents of Jerusalem and their leaders did
Ac 14:12 **b** he was the chief speaker.
16: 3 and had him circumcised **b** of the Jews who were
17:18 (This was **b** he was telling the good news
17:31 **b** he has fixed a day on which he will have
18: 2 **b** Claudius had ordered all Jews to leave Rome.
18: 3 **b** he was of the same trade, he stayed with them,
20:38 grieving especially **b** of what he had said,
21: 3 **b** the ship was to unload its cargo there.
21:34 and as he could not learn the facts **b** of the uproar,
22:11 I could not see **b** of the brightness of that light,
22:18 **b** they will not accept your testimony about me.'
24: 2 **b** of you we have long enjoyed peace,
24: 2 and reforms have been made for this people **b**
26: 3 **b** you are especially familiar with all the customs
27: 4 **b** the winds were against us.
27: 9 **b** even the Fast had already gone by,
28:18 **b** there was no reason for the death penalty
Ro 1: 8 **b** your faith is proclaimed throughout the world.
1:19 **b** God has shown it to them.
1:25 **b** they exchanged the truth about God for a lie
2: 1 **b** you, the judge, are doing the very same things.
2:18 and determine what is best **b** you are instructed in
2:24 of God is blasphemed among the Gentiles **b**
3:25 **b** in his divine forbearance he had passed over
5: 5 **b** God's love has been poured into our hearts
5:12 and so death spread to all **b** all have sinned—
5:17 If, **b** of the one man's trespass,
6:15 Should we sin **b** we are not under law but
6:19 in human terms **b** of your natural limitations.
8:10 Christ is in you, though the body is dead **b** of sin,
8:10 the Spirit is life **b** of righteousness.
8:27 **b** the Spirit intercedes for the saints according to
9:32 **B** they did not strive for it on the basis of faith,
10: 9 **b** if you confess with your lips that Jesus is Lord
11:20 They were broken off **b** of their unbelief,
11:30 now received mercy **b** of their disobedience,
13: 5 only **b** of wrath but also **b** of conscience.
14:22 to condemn themselves **b** of what they approve.
14:23 **b** they do not act from faith;
15:15 **b** of the grace given me by God
1Co 1: 4 to my God always for you **b** of the grace of God
2:14 and they are unable to understand them **b**
3:13 **b** it will be revealed with fire,
4: 9 **b** we have become a spectacle to the world,
7: 2 But **b** of cases of sexual immorality,
7: 5 so that Satan may not tempt you **b** of your lack
10:17 **B** there is one bread, we who are many are one
10:30 be denounced **b** of that for which I give thanks?
11: 2 I commend you **b** you remember me in everything
11:10 a symbol of authority on her head, **b** of the angels.
11:17 **b** when you come together it is not for the better
12:15 If the foot would say, "**B** I am not a hand,
12:16 And if the ear would say, "**B** I am not an eye,
15: 9 **b** I persecuted the church of God.
15:15 **b** we testified of God that he raised Christ—
15:58 **b** you know that in the Lord your labor is not
16:17 **b** they have made up for your absence;
2Co 1:24 **b** you stand firm in the faith.
2:13 not rest **b** I did not find my brother Titus there.
3: 7 not gaze at Moses' face **b** of the glory of his face,
3:10 what once had glory has lost its glory **b** of
4:14 **b** we know that the one who raised
4:18 **b** we look not at what can be seen but
5: 4 **b** we wish not to be unclothed but to
5:14 **b** we are convinced that one has died for all;
7: 9 Now I rejoice, not **b** you were grieved,
7: 9 but **b** your grief led to repentance;
7:13 **b** his mind has been set at rest by all of you.
7:16 I rejoice, **b** I have complete confidence in you.
8:22 but who is now more eager than ever **b**
9:14 for you and pray for you **b** of the surpassing grace
11: 7 **b** I proclaimed God's good news to you free
11:11 And why? **B** I do not love you? God knows I do!
11:28 I am under daily pressure **b** of my anxiety for all
12:14 **b** I do not want what is yours but you;
Gal 1:24 And they glorified God **b** of me.
2: 4 But **b** of false believers secretly brought in,
2:11 **b** he stood self-condemned;
2:16 **b** no one will be justified by the works of the law.
3:19 It was added **b** of transgressions,
4: 6 And **b** you are children, God has sent the Spirit
4:13 You know that it was **b** of a physical infirmity
Eph 4:18 alienated from the life of God **b** of their ignorance
5: 6 for **b** of these things the wrath of God comes
5:16 making the most of the time, **b** the days are evil.
5:30 **b** we are members of his body.
Php 1: 5 **b** of your sharing in the gospel from the first day
1: 7 **b** you hold me in your heart,
2:26 has been distressed **b** you heard that he was ill.
2:30 **b** he came close to death for the work of Christ,
3: 7 these I have come to regard as loss **b** of Christ.
3: 8 as loss **b** of the surpassing value
3:12 **b** Christ Jesus has made me his own.
Col 1: 5 **b** of the hope laid up for you in heaven.
1Th 1: 5 **b** our message of the gospel came to you not
2: 8 **b** you have become very dear to us.
3: 9 the joy that we feel before our God **b** of you?
4: 6 **b** the Lord is an avenger in all these things,
5:13 esteem them very highly in love **b** of their work.
2Th 1: 3 as is right, **b** your faith is growing abundantly,
1:10 **b** our testimony to you was believed.
2:10 **b** they refused to love the truth and so be saved.
2:13 **b** God chose you as the first fruits for salvation
3: 9 This was not **b** we do not have that right,
1Ti 1:12 **b** he judged me faithful and appointed me
1:13 But I received mercy **b** I had acted ignorantly
4:10 **b** we have our hope set on the living God,
2Ti 1:16 **b** he often refreshed me and was not ashamed
3: 9 But they will not make much progress, **b**,
Tit 3: 5 **b** of any works of righteousness that we had done,
Phm 1: 5 **b** I hear of your love for all the saints
1: 7 **b** the hearts of the saints have been refreshed
Heb 2: 9 with glory and honor **b** of the suffering of death,
2:18 **B** he himself was tested by what he suffered,
3:19 that they were unable to enter **b** of unbelief.
4: 2 but the message they heard did not benefit them, **b**
4: 6 the good news failed to enter **b** of disobedience,
5: 3 and **b** of this he must offer sacrifice
5: 7 and he was heard **b** of his reverent submission.
6:13 **b** he had no one greater by whom to swear,
7:18 the abrogation of an earlier commandment **b**
7:21 **b** of the one who said to him,
7:23 **b** they were prevented by death from continuing
7:24 but he holds his priesthood permanently, **b**
9:15 **b** a death has occurred that redeems them from
11: 5 and "he was not found, **b** God had taken him."
11:11 **b** he considered him faithful who had promised.
11:23 **b** they saw that the child was beautiful;
11:31 **b** she had received the spies in peace.
Jas 1: 3 **b** you know that the testing
1:10 **b** the rich will disappear like a flower in the field.
4: 2 You do not have, **b** you do not ask.
4: 3 You ask and do not receive, **b** you ask wrongly,
1Pe 2: 8 They stumble **b** they disobey the word,
2:21 **b** Christ also suffered for you,
4:14 **b** the spirit of glory, which is the Spirit of God,
4:16 but glorify God **b** you bear this name.
5: 7 Cast all your anxiety on him, **b** he cares for you.
2Pe 1: 4 from the corruption that is in the world **b** of lust,
1:21 **b** no prophecy ever came by human will,
2: 2 and **b** of these teachers the way of truth will
3:12 **b** of which the heavens will be set ablaze
1Jn 2: 8 **b** the darkness is passing away and
2:11 **b** the darkness has brought on blindness.
2:12 **b** your sins are forgiven on account of his name.
2:13 **b** you know him who is from the beginning.
2:13 young people, **b** you have conquered the evil one.
2:14 I write to you, children, **b** you know the Father.
2:14 **b** you know him who is from the beginning.
2:14 **b** you are strong and the word of God abides
2:21 I write to you, not **b** you do not know the truth,
2:21 but **b** you know it, and you know that no lie comes
3: 9 **b** God's seed abides in them;
3: 9 they cannot sin, **b** they have been born of God.
3:12 **B** his own deeds were evil
3:14 We know that we have passed from death to life **b**
3:22 **b** we obey his commandments
4: 7 let us love one another, **b** love is from God;
4:13 **b** he has given us of his Spirit.
4:17 **b** as he is, so are we in this world.
4:19 We love **b** he first loved us.
2Jn 1: 2 **b** of the truth that abides in us and will be
Rev 1: 9 the island called Patmos **b** of the word of God and
3:10 **B** you have kept my word of patient endurance,
3:16 So, **b** you are lukewarm, and neither cold nor hot,
5: 4 to weep bitterly **b** no one was found worthy
8:11 from the water, **b** it was made bitter.
11:10 **b** these two prophets had been a torment to
12:12 **b** he knows that his time is short!"
14:15 **b** the harvest of the earth is fully ripe."
16: 6 **b** they shed the blood of saints and prophets,
16:11 and cursed the God of heaven **b** of their pains
17: 8 **b** it was and is not and is to come.
Tob 1:12 **B** I was mindful of God with all my heart,
1:18 that the king of heaven executed upon him **b**
2: 9 and my face was uncovered **b** of the heat.
3: 6 **b** I have had to listen to undeserved insults,
3: 9 **B** your husbands are dead?
3:10 but she hanged herself **b** of her distress.'
4: 4 **b** she faced many dangers for you while you were
4:13 **b** idleness is the mother of famine.
4:21 Do not be afraid, my son, **b** we have become poor.
5:14 brother, **b** I wanted to be sure about your ancestry.
5:16 in good health and return to you in good health, **b**
7:10 **b** you are my nearest relative.
8: 7 not **b** of lust, but with sincerity.
8:16 Blessed are you **b** you have made me glad.
8:17 Blessed are you **b** you had compassion
10:13 **b** he had made his journey a success.
13: 1 **b** his kingdom lasts throughout all ages.
13: 4 **b** he is our Lord and he is our God;
13:14 Happy also are all people who grieve with you **b**
14:10 **b** he tried to kill Ahikar.
14:10 **B** he gave alms, Ahikar escaped the fatal trap
Jdt 2: 6 **b** they disobeyed my orders.
5: 7 **b** they did not wish to follow the gods
5:19 in the hill country, **b** it was uninhabited.
6: 2 the people of Israel **b** their God will defend them?
7:15 with evil, **b** they rebelled and did
7:19 **b** all their enemies had surrounded them,
8: 9 **b** they were faint for lack of water,
11: 7 Not only do human beings serve him **b** of you,
11: 7 and the birds of the air will live, **b** of your power,
12:18 **b** today is the greatest day in my whole life."
13: 1 for they all were weary **b** the banquet had lasted
13:20 **b** you risked your own life
AdE 2:21 were angry **b** of Mordecai's advancement,
4: 2 **b** no one was allowed to enter
6:13 **b** the living God is with him."
8: 7 and have hanged him on a tree **b** he acted against
9: 2 no one resisted, **b** they feared them.
9: 3 **b** fear of Mordecai weighed upon them.
9:26 **b** of the lots (for in their language this is the word
9:26 And so, **b** of what was written in this letter,

AdE 9:26 and **b** of what they had experienced in this affair
12: 6 determined to injure Mordecai and his people **b** of
14: 7 **b** we glorified their gods. You are righteous,
Wis 1: 2 **b** he is found by those who do not put him to
1: 4 **b** wisdom will not enter a deceitful soul,
1: 6 **b** God is witness of their inmost feelings,
1: 7 **B** the spirit of the Lord has filled the world,
1:10 **b** a jealous ear hears all things,
1:11 **b** no secret word is without result,
1:13 **b** God did not make death,
1:16 **b** they are fit to belong to his company.
2: 5 **b** it is sealed up and no one turns back.
2: 9 **b** this is our portion, and this our lot.
2:12 **b** he is inconvenient to us and opposes our actions;
2:15 **b** his manner of life is unlike that of others,
3: 5 **b** God tested them and found them worthy
3: 9 **b** grace and mercy are upon his holy ones,
4: 1 **b** it is known both by God and by mortals.
4:19 **b** he will dash them speechless to the ground,
5:14 **B** the hope of the ungodly is
5:16 **b** with his right hand he will cover them,
6: 4 **B** as servants of his kingdom you did
6: 5 **b** severe judgment falls on those in high places.
6: 7 **b** he himself made both small and great,
6:16 **b** she goes about seeking those worthy of her,
7: 9 **b** all gold is but a little sand in her sight,
7:10 **b** her radiance never ceases.
7:12 I rejoiced in them all, **b** wisdom leads them;
7:24 **b** of her pureness she pervades
8:10 **B** of her I shall have glory among the multitudes
8:13 **B** of her I shall have immortality,
10: 3 he perished **b** in rage he killed his brother.
10: 4 When the earth was flooded **b** of him,
10: 8 For **b** they passed wisdom by,
11:22 **B** the whole world before you is like a speck
12:19 **b** you give repentance for sins.
13: 7 **b** the things that are seen are beautiful.
13:16 **b** he knows that it cannot help itself,
14: 3 **b** you have given it a path in the sea,
14: 8 and the perishable thing **b** it was named a god.
14:11 **b**, though part of what God created,
14:21 for humankind, **b** people, in bondage to misfortune
14:29 for **b** they trust in lifeless idols they swear wicked
14:30 **b** they thought wrongly about God
14:30 to idols, and **b** in deceit they swore unrighteously
15: 2 **b** we know that you acknowledge us as yours.
15:11 **b** they failed to know the one who formed them
16: 3 of appetite **b** of the odious creatures sent to them,
16: 9 **b** they deserved to be punished by such things.
18:13 For though they had disbelieved everything **b**
19:13 for they justly suffered **b** of their wicked acts;
Sir 1:30 **b** you did not come in the fear of the Lord,
3:13 **b** you have all your faculties do not despise him.
7:35 **b** for such deeds you will be loved.
8: 8 **b** from them you will learn discipline and how
8:14 for the decision will favor him **b** of his standing.
8:16 **b** bloodshed means nothing to them,
11: 2 or loathe anyone **b** of appearance alone.
14:16 **b** in Hades one cannot look for luxury.
16: 9 on those dispossessed **b** of their sins;
20: 6 Some people keep silent **b** they have nothing
20: 6 others keep silent **b** they know when to speak.
20:22 or lose it **b** of human respect.
22:26 But if harm should come to me **b** of him,
22:27 so that I may not fall **b** of them,
23: 1 and do not let me fall **b** of them!
25:24 and **b** of her we all die.
26:28 and **b** of a third anger comes over me:
28:18 but not as many as have fallen **b** of the tongue.
29: 7 Many refuse to lend, not **b** of meanness,
31: 6 Many have come to ruin **b** of gold,
33:31 **b** you have bought him with blood.
34:13 but have escaped **b** of these experiences.
41: 7 for they suffer disgrace **b** of him.
43:26 **B** of him each of his messengers succeeds,
44: 3 those who gave counsel **b** they were intelligent;
47:12 a wise son rose up who **b** of him lived in security:
47:13 **b** God made all his borders tranquil,
47:21 **b** the sovereignty was divided and
Bar 1:17 **b** we have sinned before the Lord.
2: 5 **b** our nation sinned against the Lord our God,
2:19 not **b** of any righteous deeds of our ancestors
2:26 **b** of the wickedness of the house of Israel and
3:28 so they perished **b** they had no wisdom,
4: 6 but you were handed over to your enemies **b**
4:12 I was left desolate **b** of the sins of my children,
4:12 **b** they turned away from the law of God.
4:27 **b** of the mercy that will soon come to you
LtJ 6: 2 **B** of the sins that you have committed before God,
6:13 their faces are wiped **b** of the dust from
6:27 **b**, if any of these gods falls to
6:43 **b** she was not as attractive as herself
Aza 1: 5 upon us **b** of our sins.
1:14 and are brought low this day in all the world **b**
Sus 1: 4 to him **b** he was the most honored of them all.
1:18 they did not see the elders, **b** they were hiding.
1:39 **b** he was stronger than we,
1:41 **B** they were elders of the people and judges,
1:61 And they took action against the two elders, **b** out
1:63 **b** she was found innocent of a shameful deed.
Bel 1: 5 "**B** I do not revere idols made with hands,
1: 9 **b** he has spoken blasphemy against Bel."
1Mc 1:38 **B** of them the residents of Jerusalem fled;
2:30 **b** troubles pressed heavily upon them.
2:54 Phinehas our ancestor, **b** he was deeply zealous,
2:55 Joshua, **b** he fulfilled the command,
2:56 Caleb, **b** he testified in the assembly,
1Mc 2:57 David, **b** he was merciful,
2:58 Elijah, **b** of great zeal for the law,
2:60 Daniel, **b** of his innocence,
2:63 **b** they will have returned to the dust,
3:29 that the revenues from the country were small **b** of
3:46 **b** Israel formerly had a place of prayer in Mizpah.
4: 5 **b** he said, "These men are running away from us."
5: 3 at Akrabattene, **b** they kept lying in wait for Israel.
5:54 **b** they had returned in safety;
5:61 Thus the people suffered a great rout **b**,
6: 3 but he could not **b** his plan had become known to
6: 8 **b** things had not turned out for him
6: 9 **b** deep disappointment continually gripped him,
6:13 that it is **b** of this that these misfortunes have come
6:49 the town **b** they had no provisions there
6:53 **b** it was the seventh year;
9:60 **b** their plan became known.
10:42 **b** it belongs to the priests who minister there.
10:43 **b** they owe money to the king or are in debt,
10:46 **b** they remembered the great wrongs
10:47 **b** he had been the first to speak peaceable words
10:70 I have fallen into ridicule and disgrace **b** of you.
11:11 on Alexander **b** he coveted his kingdom.
11:14 **b** the people of that region were in revolt.
11:33 **b** of the goodwill they show toward us.
13:18 "It was **b** Simon did not send him the money and
13:22 and he did not go **b** of the snow.
13:51 **b** a great enemy had been crushed and removed
14:35 **b** he had done all these things and **b** of the justice
2Mc 2:11 "They were consumed **b** the sin offering had
2:24 the narratives of history **b** of the mass of material,
3: 1 and the laws were strictly observed **b** of the piety
3:13 Heliodorus, **b** of the orders he had from the king,
3:18 a general supplication **b** the holy place was about
3:29 speechless **b** of the divine intervention
4:13 and increase in the adoption of foreign ways **b** of
4:19 to use it for sacrifice, **b** that was inappropriate,
4:30 of Mallus revolted **b** their cities had been given as
4:37 and wept **b** of the moderation and good conduct of
4:39 the populace gathered against Lysimachus, **b**
4:50 But Menelaus, **b** of the greed of those in power,
5: 9 in hope of finding protection **b** of their kinship.
5:17 for a little while **b** of the sins of those who lived in
5:21 and walk on the sea, **b** his mind was elated.
6:11 to Philip and were all burned together, **b**
6:21 of that unlawful sacrifice took the man aside **b**
6:25 they would be led astray **b** of me,
6:29 **b** the words he had uttered were
6:30 but in my soul I am glad to suffer these things **b**
7: 9 **b** we have died for his laws."
7:11 and **b** of his laws I disdain them,
7:16 and said, "**B** you have authority among mortals,
7:18 **b** of our sins against our own God.
7:20 she bore it with good courage **b** of her hope in
7:32 For we are suffering **b** of our own sins.
8:15 and **b** he had called them by his holy
8:25 they were obliged to return **b** the hour was late.
8:36 **b** they followed the laws ordained by him.
9: 9 and **b** of the stench the whole army felt revulsion
9:10 **B** of his intolerable stench no one was able
10:12 took the lead in showing justice to the Jews **b** of
10:13 **b** he had abandoned Cyprus,
10:35 fired with anger **b** of the blasphemies,
11:13 and realized that the Hebrews were invincible **b**
12: 4 **b** they wished to live peaceably
12: 7 Then, **b** the city's gates were closed, he withdrew,
12:21 and difficult of access **b** of the narrowness of all
12:24 **b** he held the parents of most of them,
13: 3 but **b** he thought that he would be established
13: 8 **b** he had committed many sins against
13:17 **b** the Lord's help protected him.
14: 8 first **b** I am genuinely concerned for the interests
14: 8 second **b** I have regard also for my compatriots.
14:17 but had been temporarily checked **b** of
15:17 **b** the city and the sanctuary and the temple were
1Es 1:14 **b** the priests were offering the fat until nightfall;
1:50 **b** he would have spared them
1:52 until in his anger against his people **b**
3: 7 and **b** of his wisdom he shall sit next to Darius
4:26 Many men have lost their minds **b** of women,
4:26 and have become slaves **b** of them.
4:27 or stumbled, or sinned **b** of women.
4:62 **b** he had given them release and permission
5:65 so that the people could not hear the trumpets **b** of
7:15 **b** he had changed the will of the king of
8:77 **B** of our sins and the sins of our ancestors,
8:86 And all that has happened to us has come about **b**
8:90 for we can no longer stand in your presence **b**
9: 6 shivering **b** of the bad weather that prevailed.
9:55 **b** they were inspired by the words
Man 1: 9 up and see the height of heaven **b** of the multitude
1:10 so that I am rejected **b** of my sins,
3Mc 1:11 When they said that this was not permitted, **b** not
1:21 the supplications of those gathered there **b** of what
1:29 **b** indeed all at that time preferred death to
2:10 And **b** you love the house of Israel,
2:12 And **b** oftentimes when our fathers were oppressed
2:13 that **b** of our many and great sins we are crushed
2:16 But **b** you graciously bestowed your glory
3: 4 but **b** they worshiped God
3:17 **b** when we proposed to enter their inner temple
3:18 but they were spared the exercise of our power **b**
3:21 both **b** of their alliance with us and
4: 2 and they groaned **b** of the unexpected destruction
4:17 the census of the Jews **b** of their immense number,
5: 7 **b** in their bonds they were forcibly confined
5:30 with an overpowering wrath, **b** by the providence
3Mc 5:41 a result the city is in a tumult **b** of its expectation;
6:22 the king's anger was turned to pity and tears **b** of
6:36 but **b** of the deliverance that had come to them
7: 4 **b** of the ill-will that these people had
7:17 called "rose-bearing" **b** of a characteristic of
2Es 1:20 **B** of the heat I clothed you with the leaves
1:25 **B** you have forsaken me, I also will forsake you.
1:34 **b** with you they have neglected my commandment
2: 2 'Go, my children, **b** I am a widow and forsaken.
2: 3 but with mourning and sorrow I have lost you, **b**
2: 5 **b** they would not keep my covenant,
2: 7 **b** they have despised my covenant.
2:15 strengthen their feet, **b** I have chosen you,
2:16 **b** I recognize my name in them.
2:24 my people, **b** your rest will come.
2:30 O mother, with your children, **b** I will deliver you,
2:31 **b** I will bring them out of the hiding places of
2:32 **b** my springs run over, and my grace will not fail."
2:34 **b** he who will come at the end of the age is close
2:35 **b** perpetual light will shine on you forevermore.
3: 2 **b** I saw the desolation of Zion and the wealth
3:30 **b** I have seen how you endure those who sin,
4:26 **b** the age is hurrying swiftly to its end.
4:27 **b** this age is full of sadness and infirmities.
5:34 "No, my lord, but **b** of my grief I have spoken;
6: 8 **b** from him were born Jacob and Esau,
6:15 **b** the word concerns the end,
6:32 **b** your voice has surely been heard by
6:55 **b** you have said that it was for us
7:*60* **b** it is they who have made my glory to prevail
7:*64* **b** we perish and we know it.
7:*72* **b** though they had understanding,
7:*74* but **b** of the times that he has foreordained."
7:*81* **b** they have scorned the law of the Most High.
7:*82* **b** they cannot now make a good repentance so
7:*87* **b** they shall utterly waste away in confusion and
7:*92* **b** they have striven with great effort to overcome
7:*93* **b** they see the perplexity in which the souls of
7:*98* **b** they shall rejoice with boldness,
7:*124* [54] **b** we have lived in perverse ways?
7:*132* [62] **b** he has mercy on those who have not yet
7:*133* [63] **b** he is gracious to those who turn
7:*134* [64] and patient, **b** he shows patience
7:*135* [65] **b** he would rather give than take away;
7:*136* [66] **b** he makes his compassions abound more
7:*138* [68] **b** if he did not give out of his goodness so
7:*139* [69] **b** if he did not pardon those who were created
8: 8 And **b** you give life to the body that is
8:31 it is **b** of us sinners that you are called merciful.
8:43 **b** it has not received your rain in due season,
8:44 by your hands and are called your own image **b**
8:49 **b** you have humbled yourself,
8:50 **b** they have walked in great pride.
8:52 **b** it is for you that paradise is opened,
9:20 I saw that my earth was in peril **b** of the devices
9:22 **b** with much labor I have perfected them.
9:32 for it could not, **b** it was yours.
9:33 **b** they did not keep what had been sown in them.
10: 8 **b** we are all mourning, and to be sorrowful, **b** we
are all sorrowing;
10:20 and be consoled **b** of the sorrow of Jerusalem.
10:32 I said, "It was **b** you abandoned me.
10:54 **b** no work of human construction could endure in
12: 4 **b** you search out the ways of the Most High.
12: 5 a little strength is left in me, **b** of the great fear
12:25 **b** it is they who shall sum up his wickedness
13:18 **b** they understand the things that are reserved for
13:54 **b** you have forsaken your own ways
13:58 and **b** he governs the times
15: 6 **b** iniquity has spread throughout every land,
15:12 **b** of the plague of chastisement and castigation
15:13 **b** their seed shall fail to grow and their trees shall
15:18 **B** of their pride the cities shall be in confusion,
15:19 **b** of hunger for bread and **b** of great tribulation.
15:27 **b** you have sinned against him.
16:32 **b** no sheep will go along them.
16:33 Virgins shall mourn **b** they have no bridegrooms,
16:33 women shall mourn **b** they have no husbands;
16:33 their daughters shall mourn, **b** they have no help.
16:45 **B** of this those who labor, labor in vain;
4Mc 1:33 Is it not **b** reason is able to rule over appetites?
1:34 we abstain **b** of domination by reason.
2: 2 **b** by mental effort he overcame sexual desire.
3:12 When his guards complained bitterly **b** of
3:20 our ancestors were enjoying profound peace **b**
4: 3 "I have come here **b** I am loyal to
4:25 **b** they had circumcised their sons,
5: 4 to many in the tyrant's court **b** of his philosophy.
6: 7 Although he fell to the ground **b** his body could
7:16 **b** of piety an aged man despised tortures even
7:17 **b** not all have prudent reason."
7:20 be dominated by their emotions **b** of the weakness
9: 6 of the Hebrews **b** of their religion lived piously
9: 7 and if you take our lives **b** of our religion,
9: 9 **b** of your bloodthirstiness toward us,
9:15 not **b** I am a murderer,
9:15 but **b** I protect the divine law."
10:10 are suffering **b** of our godly training and virtue,
10:11 **b** of your impiety and bloodthirstiness,
11: 5 Is it **b** we revere the Creator of all things and live
11:12 **b** through these noble sufferings you give us
12: 3 for they died in torments **b** of their disobedience.
12:12 **B** of this, justice has laid up for you intense
12:15 Then **b** he too was about to die, he said,
13:26 **b** they could make their brotherly love more
15: 4 who **b** of their birth pangs have a deeper sympathy
15: 7 and **b** of the many pains she suffered with each

4Mc 15: 8 yet **b** of the fear of God she disdained
15: 9 but also **b** of the nobility of her sons
15:14 **b** of religion did not change her attitude.
15:24 this noble mother disregarded all these **b** of faith
17: 9 **b** of the violence of the tyrant who wished
17:18 **b** of which they now stand before
17:20 but also by the fact that **b** of them our enemies did
18: 4 **B** of them the nation gained peace,

BECHER (5) [BECHERITES]

Ge 46:21 The children of Benjamin: Bela, **B,** Ashbel, Gera,
Nu 26:35 of **B,** the clan of the Becherites;
1Ch 7: 6 The sons of Benjamin: Bela, **B,** and Jediael, three.
7: 8 The sons of **B:** Zemirah, Joash,
7: 8 All these were the sons of **B;**

BECHERITES (1) [BECHER]

Nu 26:35 of Becher, the clan of the **B;**

BECHORATH (KJV) See BECORATH

BECOME‡ (477) [BECAME, BECOMES, BECOMING]

Ge 2:24 and clings to his wife, and they **b** one flesh.
3:22 "See, the man has **b** like one of us,
9:15 and the waters shall never again **b** a flood
10: 8 he was the first on earth to **b** a mighty warrior.
18:18 that Abraham shall **b** a great and mighty nation,
19:13 against its people has **b** great before the LORD,
24:35 greatly blessed my master, and he has **b** wealthy;
24:60 "May you, our sister, **b** thousands of myriads;
26:16 you have **b** too powerful for us."
28: 3 that you may **b** a company of peoples.
32:10 and now I have **b** two companies.
34:15 that you will **b** as we are and every male
34:16 and we will live among you and **b** one people.
34:22 to live among us, to **b** one people:
37:20 and we shall see what will **b** of his dreams."
44: 9 moreover the rest of us will **b** my lord's slaves."
44:10 he with whom it is found shall **b** my slave,
47:19 We with our land will **b** slaves to Pharaoh;
47:19 and that the land may not **b** desolate."
47:26 The land of the priests alone did not **b** Pharaoh's.
48:19 he also shall **b** a people, and he also shall be great.
48:19 and his offspring shall **b** a multitude of nations."
Ex 4: 9 that you shall take from the Nile will **b** blood on
7: 9 and it will **b** a snake.' "
7:19 so that they may **b** blood;
8:16 so that it may **b** gnats throughout the whole land
9: 9 It shall **b** fine dust all over the land of Egypt,
15: 2 and he has **b** my salvation;
16:24 it did not **b** foul, and there were no worms in it.
22:24 and your wives shall **b** widows
23:29 or the land would **b** desolate and
29:37 whatever touches the altar shall **b** holy.
30:29 whatever touches them will **b** holy.
32: 1 we do not know what has **b** of him."
32:23 we do not know what has **b** of him.'
34:12 or it will **b** a snare among you.
40: 9 so that it shall **b** holy.
Lev 5: 2 and are unaware of it, you have **b** unclean,
5: 3 any uncleanness by which one can **b** unclean—
6:18 anything that touches them shall **b** holy.
6:27 Whatever touches its flesh shall **b** holy;
11:24 By these you shall **b** unclean;
11:43 not defile yourselves with them, and so **b** unclean.
14:36 or all that is in the house will **b** unclean;
19:29 the land not **b** prostituted and full of depravity.
25:35 and **b** dependent on you, you shall support them;
25:39 If any who are dependent on you **b**
Nu 5:27 woman shall **b** an execration among her people.
12:10 Miriam had **b** leprous, as white as snow.
14: 3 Our wives and our little ones will **b** booty;
14:31 But your little ones, who you said would **b** booty,
16:22 and you **b** angry with the whole congregation?"
16:38 the censers of these sinners have **b** holy at the cost
16:40 so as not to **b** like Korah and his company—
19:12 and on the seventh day, they will not **b** clean.
24:18 Edom will **b** a possession,
Dt 1:39 your little ones, who you thought would **b** booty,
4:20 to **b** a people of his very own possession,
4:25 and **b** complacent in the land,
7:22 otherwise the wild animals would **b** too numerous
20: 7 Has anyone **b** engaged to a woman but not
22:29 and she shall **b** his wife.
24: 2 and goes off to **b** another man's wife.
27: 9 This very day you have **b** the people of
28:25 You shall **b** an object of horror to all the kingdoms
28:30 You shall **b** engaged to a woman,
28:37 You shall **b** an object of horror, a proverb,
30:16 then you shall live and **b** numerous,
31:17 from them; they will **b** easy prey,
Jos 7:12 to their enemies, because they have **b**
Jdg 2: 3 but they shall **b** adversaries to you,
11: 8 and fight with the Ammonites, and **b** head over us,
11:35 you have **b** the cause of great trouble to me.
16: 7 then I shall **b** weak, and be like anyone else."
16:11 then I shall **b** weak, and be like anyone else."
16:13 then I shall **b** weak, and be like anyone else."
16:17 I would **b** weak, and be like anyone else."
17:13 because the Levite has **b** my priest."
18: 4 and he hired me, and I have **b** his priest."
Ru 1:11 in my womb that they may **b** your husbands?
1Sa 4: 9 not to **b** slaves to the Hebrews as they have been
1Sa 13: 4 and also that Israel had **b** odious to the Philistines,
18:22 now then, **b** the king's son-in-law.' "
18:23 to you a little thing to **b** the king's son-in-law,
18:27 that he might **b** the king's son-in-law.
28:16 LORD has turned from you and **b** your enemy?
29: 4 or else he may **b** an adversary to us in the battle.
2Sa 10: 6 Ammonites saw that they had **b** odious to David,
15:10 Absalom has **b** king at Hebron!"
19:22 that you should today **b** an adversary to me?
1Ki 1:11 not heard that Adonijah son of Haggith has **b** king
1:18 But now suddenly Adonijah has **b** king,
2:15 the kingdom has turned about and **b** my brother's,
9: 7 and Israel will **b** a proverb and a taunt
9: 8 This house will **b** a heap of ruins;
2Ki 19:26 they have **b** like plants of the field and
21:14 they shall **b** a prey and a spoil to all their enemies,
22:19 that they should **b** a desolation and a curse,
2Ch 26:16 he had **b** strong he grew proud, to his destruction.
Ne 6: 6 according to this report you wish to **b** their king.
Job 6:21 Such you have now **b** to me;
7:20 Why have I **b** a burden to you?
9:28 I **b** afraid of all my suffering,
15:28 houses destined to **b** heaps of ruins;
19:15 I have **b** an alien in their eyes.
27:12 why then have you **b** altogether vain?
30:19 and I have **b** like dust and ashes.
33:25 let his flesh **b** fresh with youth;
38:30 The waters **b** hard like stone,
39: 4 Their young ones **b** strong,
Ps 31:12 I have **b** like a broken vessel.
37:26 and their children **b** a blessing.
49:16 Do not be afraid when some **b** rich,
69: 8 I have **b** a stranger to my kindred,
79: 4 We have **b** a taunt to our neighbors,
89:41 he has **b** the scorn of his neighbors.
94:22 But the LORD has **b** my stronghold,
109:24 through fasting; my body has **b** gaunt.
118:14 and my might; he has **b** my salvation.
118:21 you have answered me and have **b** my salvation.
118:22 the builders rejected has **b** the chief cornerstone.
119:76 Let your steadfast love **b** my comfort according
119:83 For I have **b** like a wineskin in the smoke,
135:18 and all who trust them shall **b** like them.
139:11 and the light around me **b** night,"
Pr 9: 9 and they will **b** wiser still;
11:16 timid **b** destitute, but the aggressive gain riches.
17:18 to **b** surety for a neighbor.
21:11 When a scoffer is punished, the simple **b** wiser;
22:26 of those who give pledges, who **b** surety for debts.
25:17 the neighbor will **b** weary of you and hate you.
Isa 1: 9 like Sodom, and **b** like Gomorrah.
1:14 they have **b** a burden to me,
1:18 they are red like crimson, they shall **b** like wool.
1:21 How the faithful city has **b** a whore!
1:22 Your silver has **b** dross, your wine is mixed
1:31 The strong shall **b** like tinder,
5:24 so their root will **b** rotten,
7:23 a thousand shekels of silver, will **b** briers
7:25 but they will **b** a place where cattle are let loose
8:14 He will **b** a sanctuary, a stone one strikes against;
8:14 of Israel he will **b** a rock one stumbles over—
10:17 The light of Israel will **b** a fire,
12: 2 and my might; he has **b** my salvation.
14:10 "You too have **b** as weak as we!
14:10 You have **b** like us!"
17: 1 and will **b** a heap of ruins.
19: 6 its canals will **b** foul, and the branches
19:13 The princes of Zoan have **b** fools,
19:17 the land of Judah will **b** a terror to the Egyptians;
22:23 he will **b** a throne of honor to his ancestral house.
29:11 The vision of all this has **b** for you like the words
29:17 not Lebanon in a very little while **b** a fruitful field,
30: 3 the protection of Pharaoh shall **b** your shame,
30:13 therefore this iniquity shall **b** for you like a break
32:14 the hill and the watchtower will **b** dens forever,
34: 9 her land shall **b** burning pitch.
35: 7 the burning sand shall **b** a pool,
35: 7 the haunt of jackals shall **b** a swamp,
35: 7 the grass shall **b** reeds and rushes.
37:27 they have **b** like plants of the field and
40: 4 the uneven ground shall **b** level,
42:22 they have **b** a prey with no one to rescue,
49: 5 and my God has **b** my strength—
60:22 The least of them shall **b** a clan,
64: 6 We have all **b** like one who is unclean,
64:10 Your holy cities have **b** a wilderness,
64:10 Zion has **b** a wilderness, Jerusalem a desolation.
64:11 and all our pleasant places have **b** ruins.
65:10 Sharon shall **b** a pasture for flocks,
Jer 2:14 Why then has he **b** plunder?
2:21 then did you turn degenerate and **b** a wild vine?
5:27 therefore they have **b** great and rich,
7:11 **b** a den of robbers in your sight?
7:34 for the land shall **b** a waste.
11:13 your gods have **b** as many as your towns, O Judah;
12: 8 My heritage has **b** to me like a lion in the forest;
16: 4 they shall **b** like dung on the surface of the ground.
16: 4 and their dead bodies shall **b** food for the birds of
17:17 Do not **b** a terror to me;
18:21 let their wives **b** childless and widowed.
20: 7 I have **b** a laughingstock all day long;
20: 8 the word of the LORD has **b** for me a reproach
22: 5 that this house shall **b** a desolation.
23: 9 I have **b** like a drunkard, like one overcome by
23:14 all of them have **b** like Sodom to me,
25:11 This whole land shall **b** a ruin and a waste,
25:33 they shall **b** dung on the surface of the ground.
Jer 25:38 for their land has **b** a waste because of
26:18 Jerusalem shall **b** a heap of ruins,
27:17 Why should this city **b** a desolation?
31: 9 for I have **b** a father to Israel,
31:12 their life shall **b** like a watered garden,
34:20 Their corpses shall **b** food for the birds of the air
42:18 You shall **b** an object of execration and horror,
44: 8 and **b** an object of cursing and ridicule among all
44:12 they shall **b** an object of execration and horror,
46:19 For Memphis shall **b** a waste, a ruin,
47: 2 See, waters are rising out of the north and shall **b**
48: 9 her towns shall **b** a desolation,
48:26 he too shall **b** a laughingstock.
48:34 For even the waters of Nimrim have **b** desolate.
48:39 So Moab has **b** a derision and a horror
49: 2 it shall **b** a desolate mound,
49:13 Bozrah shall **b** an object of horror and ridicule,
49:17 Edom shall **b** an object of horror;
49:24 Damascus has **b** feeble, she turned to flee,
49:32 Their camels shall **b** booty,
49:33 Hazor shall **b** a lair of jackals,
50:23 How Babylon has **b** a horror among the nations!
50:36 so that they may **b** fools!
50:37 so that they may **b** women!
51:30 their strength has failed, they have **b** women;
51:37 and Babylon shall **b** a heap of ruins,
51:39 until they **b** merry and then sleep a perpetual sleep
51:41 How Babylon has **b** an object of horror among the
51:43 Her cities have **b** an object of horror,
La 1: 1 How like a widow she has **b,**
1: 1 She that was a princess among the provinces has **b**
1: 2 with her, they have **b** her enemies.
1: 5 Her foes have **b** the masters, her enemies prosper,
1: 6 Her princes have **b** like stags that find no pasture;
1: 8 so she has **b** a mockery;
1:11 Look, O LORD, and see how worthless I have **b.**
1:17 against Jacob that his neighbors should **b** his foes;
1:17 Jerusalem has **b** a filthy thing among them.
2: 5 The Lord has **b** like an enemy;
3:14 I have **b** the laughingstock of all my people,
4: 3 but my people has **b** cruel,
4: 8 it has **b** as dry as wood.
4:21 you shall **b** drunk and strip yourself bare.
5: 3 We have **b** orphans, fatherless;
Eze 6: 4 Your altars shall **b** desolate,
12:20 and the land shall **b** a desolation;
17: 8 that it might produce branches and bear fruit and **b**
17:23 that it may produce boughs and bear fruit, and **b**
22: 4 You have **b** guilty by the blood
22:18 the house of Israel has **b** dross to me;
22:18 In the smelter they have **b** dross.
22:19 Because you have all **b** dross,
24:11 Stand it empty upon the coals, so that it may **b** hot,
24:13 you did not **b** clean from your filth;
26: 5 It shall **b,** in the midst of the sea,
26: 5 It shall **b** plunder for the nations,
28: 5 and your heart has **b** proud in your wealth.
30:21 so that it may **b** strong to wield the sword.
34: 8 because my sheep have **b** a prey,
34: 8 and my sheep have **b** food for all the wild animals,
35: 4 I lay your towns in ruins; you shall **b** a desolation,
36: 2 and, "The ancient heights have **b** our possession,"
36: 4 which have **b** a source of plunder and an object
36:35 "This land that was desolate has **b** like the garden
37:17 so that they may **b** one in your hand.
44:26 After he has **b** clean, they shall count seven days
47: 8 the sea of stagnant waters, the water will **b** fresh.
47: 9 once these waters reach there. It will **b** fresh;
47:11 But its swamps and marshes will not **b** fresh;
Da 9:16 Jerusalem and your people have **b** a disgrace
11: 2 and when he has **b** strong through his riches,
11:23 he shall act deceitfully and **b** strong with
11:43 He shall **b** ruler of the treasures of gold and
Hos 4:15 O Israel, do not let Judah **b** guilty.
5: 9 Ephraim shall **b** a desolation in the day
5:10 of Judah have **b** like those who remove
7:11 Ephraim has **b** like a dove, silly and without sense;
7:16 they have **b** like a defective bow;
9:17 they shall **b** wanderers among the nations.
13: 7 So I will **b** like a lion to them,
Joel 3:19 Egypt shall **b** a desolation and Edom
Am 7:17 'Your wife shall **b** a prostitute in the city,
8: 3 songs of the temple shall **b** wailings in that day,"
Jnh 4: 5 waiting to see what would **b** of the city.
Mic 3:12 Jerusalem shall **b** a heap of ruins,
7: 1 For I have **b** like one who,
Hab 1:11 they transgress and **b** guilty;
Zep 2: 4 and Ashkelon shall **b** a desolation;
2: 7 The seacoast shall **b** the possession of the remnant
2: 9 Moab shall **b** like Sodom and the Ammonites like
2:15 What a desolation it has **b,** a lair for wild animals!
Hag 2:12 or wine, or oil, or any kind of food, does it **b** holy?
2:13 of these, does it **b** unclean?"
Zec 2: 9 and they shall **b** plunder for their own slaves.
4: 7 Before Zerubbabel you shall **b** a plain;
10: 7 Then the people of Ephraim shall **b** like warriors,
11: 5 "Blessed be the LORD, for I have **b** rich";
11: 8 for I had **b** impatient with them,
14: 9 And the LORD will **b** king over all the earth;
Mt 4: 3 command these stones to **b** loaves of bread."
10:26 and nothing secret that will not **b** known.
16:24 "If any want to **b** my followers,
18: 3 unless you change and **b** like children,
19: 5 and the two shall **b** one flesh'?
21:42 that the builders rejected has **b** the cornerstone;
23:26 so that the outside also may **b** clean.
26:31 "You will all **b** deserters because of me this night;

Mt 26:33 “Though all **b** deserters because of you,
Mk 6:14 for Jesus’ name had **b** known.
8:34 and said to them, “If any want to **b** my followers,
10: 8 and the two shall **b** one flesh.’
10:43 but whoever wishes to **b** great among you must
12:10 that the builders rejected has **b** the cornerstone;
14:27 And Jesus said to them, “You will all **b** deserters;
14:29 Peter said to him, “Even though all **b** deserters,
Lk 1:20 you will **b** mute, unable to speak,
1:66 “What then will this child **b**?”
4: 3 command this stone to **b** a loaf of bread.”
8:17 nor is anything secret that will not **b** known
9:23 “If any want to **b** my followers,
12: 2 and nothing secret that will not **b** known.
14:33 none of you can **b** my disciple if you do not give
20:17 that the builders rejected has **b** the cornerstone’?
22:26 the greatest among you must **b** like the youngest,
Jn 1:12 he gave power to **b** children of God,
2: 9 the steward tasted the water that had **b** wine,
2:10 the inferior wine after the guests have **b** drunk.
4:14 The water that I will give will **b** in them a spring
9:27 Do you also want to **b** his disciples?”
9:39 and those who do see may **b** blind.”
12:36 so that you may **b** children of light.”
15: 8 that you bear much fruit and **b** my disciples.
17:23 that they may **b** completely one,
Ac 1:20 ‘Let his homestead **b** desolate,
1:22 one of these must **b** a witness with us
4:11 the builders; it has **b** the cornerstone.’
7:52 and now you have **b** his betrayers and murderers.
12:18 among the soldiers over what had **b** of Peter.
15: 7 the message of the good news and **b** believers.
16:34 and his entire household rejoiced that he had **b**
18:27 through grace had **b** believers,
21:25 But as for the Gentiles who have **b** believers,
26:28 so quickly persuading me to **b** a Christian?”
26:29 to me today might **b** such as I am—
Ro 2:25 your circumcision has **b** uncircumcision.
3:12 together they have **b** worthless;
4:18 that he would **b** “the father of many nations,”
6:17 have **b** obedient from the heart to the form
6:18 have **b** slaves of righteousness.
7:13 the commandment might **b** sinful beyond measure.
11: 9 David says, “Let their table **b** a snare and a trap,
11:20 So do not **b** proud, but stand in awe.
15: 8 that Christ has **b** a servant of the circumcised
1Co 3:13 the work of each builder will **b** visible,
3:18 you should **b** fools so that you may **b** wise.
4: 8 Already you have **b** rich!
4: 8 Quite apart from us you have **b** kings!
4: 8 Indeed, I wish that you had **b** kings,
4: 9 because we have **b** a spectacle to the world,
4:13 We have **b** like the rubbish of the world,
4:18 that I am not coming to you, have **b** arrogant.
7:23 do not **b** slaves of human masters.
8: 7 some have **b** so accustomed to idols until now,
8: 9 of yours does not somehow **b** a stumbling block to
9:22 I have **b** all things to all people,
10: 7 Do not **b** idolaters as some of them did;
11:19 only so will it **b** clear who among you are genuine.
2Co 5:17 see, everything has **b** new!
5:21 that in him we might **b** the righteousness of God.
8: 9 so that by his poverty you might **b** rich.
13: 9 This is what we pray for, that you may **b** perfect.
Gal 4:12 I beg you, **b** as I am, for I also have **b** as you are.
4:15 What has **b** of the goodwill you felt?
4:16 Have I now **b** your enemy by telling you the truth?
5:13 but through love **b** slaves to one another.
5:26 Let us not **b** conceited, competing
6: 4 that work, rather than their neighbor’s work, will **b**
Eph 3: 6 the Gentiles have **b** fellow heirs,
3: 7 Of this gospel I have **b** a servant according to
5:31 and the two will **b** one flesh.”
Php 1:13 so that it has **b** known throughout
1Th 1: 8 but in every place your faith in God has **b** known,
2: 8 because you have **b** very dear to us.
2Ti 2:21 the things I have mentioned will **b** special utensils,
3: 9 their folly will **b** plain to everyone.
Tit 1:13 so that they may **b** sound in the faith,
3: 7 we might **b** heirs according to the hope
Phm 1: 6 that the sharing of your faith may **b** effective
1:10 whose father I have **b** during my imprisonment.
Heb 1: 4 having **b** as much superior to angels as
2:17 Therefore he had to **b** like his brothers and sisters
3:14 For we have **b** partners of Christ,
5:11 since you have **b** dull in understanding.
6:12 so that you may not **b** sluggish,
6:20 having **b** a high priest forever according to
7:16 one who has **b** a priest,
7:22 Jesus has also **b** the guarantee of a better covenant.
12:15 and through it many **b** defiled.
Jas 1:18 we would **b** a kind of first fruits of his creatures.
2: 4 and **b** judges with evil thoughts?
2:10 but fails in one point has **b** accountable for all
2:11 you have **b** a transgressor of the law.
3: 1 Not many of you should **b** teachers,
1Pe 2: 7 that the builders rejected has **b** the very head of
3: 6 You have **b** her daughters as long
4:18 what will **b** of the ungodly and the sinners?”
2Pe 1: 4 and may **b** participants of the divine nature.
2:20 the last state has **b** worse for them than the first.
3Jn 1: 8 so that we may **b** co-workers with the truth.
Rev 11:15 of the world has **b** the kingdom of our Lord and
17: 2 the inhabitants of the earth have **b** drunk.”
18: 2 It has **b** a dwelling place of demons,
Tob 3: 4 exile, and death, to **b** the talk, the byword,
3: 6 be released from the face of the earth and **b** dust.
Tob 4:21 Do not be afraid, my son, because we have **b** poor.
7: 7 an upright and beneficent man has **b** blind!”
8:10 that he will die and we will **b** an object of ridicule
Jdt 5:21 we shall **b** the laughingstock of the whole world.”
7:27 We shall indeed **b** slaves, but our lives will
12:13 and to **b** today like one of
AdE 13: 2 “Having **b** ruler of many nations and master of
16: 2 the more proud do they **b**,
16:10 of our kindliness), having **b** our guest,
Wis 4:18 After this they will **b** dishonored corpses,
16:11 not fall into deep forgetfulness and **b** unresponsive
Sir 6: 1 and do not **b** an enemy instead of a friend;
6:11 When you are prosperous, they **b** your second self,
6:27 Search out and seek, and she will **b** known to you;
6:29 Then her fetters will **b** for you a strong defense,
6:32 and if you apply yourself you will **b** clever.
6:33 and if you pay attention you will **b** wise.
7: 6 Do not seek to **b** a judge,
12:11 to be sure it does not **b** completely tarnished.
14:17 All living beings **b** old like a garment,
18:29 Those who are skilled in words **b** wise themselves,
18:32 or you may **b** impoverished by its expense.
18:33 not **b** a beggar by feasting with borrowed money,
19: 1 The one who does this will not **b** rich;
23:15 to using abusive language will never **b** disciplined
24:17 and my blossoms **b** glorious and abundant fruit.
30:12 or else he will **b** stubborn and disobey you,
36:30 a man will **b** a fugitive and a wanderer.
38:24 only the one who has little business can **b** wise.
38:25 How can one **b** wise who handles the plow,
42:10 be seduced and **b** pregnant in her father’s house;
44: 9 they have **b** as though they had never been born,
46: 4 through him that the sun stood still and one day **b**
50:28 and those who lay them to heart will **b** wise.
Aza 1:10 have **b** a shame and a reproach.
1:14 we, O Lord, have **b** fewer than any other nation,
Bel 1:28 saying, “The king has **b** a Jew;
1Mc 1: 1 (He had previously **b** king of Greece.)
1:16 he determined to **b** king of the land of Egypt,
2: 8 Her temple has **b** like a person without honor;
2:11 no longer free, she has **b** a slave.
2:49 “Arrogance and scorn have now **b** strong;
6: 3 but he could not because his plan had **b** known to
10: 6 to equip them with arms, and to **b** his ally;
10:54 and I will **b** your son-in-law,
10:56 and I will **b** your father-in-law, as you have said.”
11:40 to **b** king in place of his father.
12:10 so that we may not **b** estranged from you,
12:39 Then Trypho attempted to **b** king in Asia and put
14:17 that his brother Simon had **b** high priest
15: 9 so that your glory will **b** manifest in all the earth.”
2Mc 4:21 that Philometor had **b** hostile to his government,
4:50 having **b** the chief plotter against his compatriots.
5:15 who had **b** a traitor both to the laws and
9:17 and in addition to all this he also would **b** a Jew
12:39 On the next day, as had now **b** necessary,
1Es 4:26 and have **b** slaves because of them.
3Mc 3:19 toward us, they **b** the only people
3:29 shall **b** useless for all time to any mortal creature.”
6:10 “Even if our lives have **b** entangled in impieties
6:34 the Jews would be destroyed and **b** food for birds,
7:14 of their compatriots who had **b** defiled.
2Es 2:12 and they shall neither toil nor **b** weary.
5:35 Or why did not my mother’s womb **b** my grave,
5:49 and a woman who has **b** old does
9:19 have **b** corrupt in their ways.
10:28 my end has **b** corruption, and my prayer
14:35 then the names of the righteous shall **b** manifest,
15:31 remembering their origin, shall **b** still stronger;
4Mc 6:19 and ourselves **b** a pattern of impiety to the young
9:24 of our ancestors may **b** merciful to our nation
17:21 they having **b**, as it were, a ransom for the sin
18: 5 to compel the Israelites to **b** pagans and

BECOMES (39) [BECOME]

Ge 2:10 and from there it divides and **b** four branches.
Lev 4:14 when the sin that they have committed **b** known,
13:24 on the skin and the raw flesh of the burn **b** a spot,
27:21 as a devoted field; it **b** the priest’s holding.
Nu 11:20 until it comes out of your nostrils and **b** loathsome
Dt 23:10 of you **b** unclean because of a nocturnal emission,
2Ch 13: 9 be consecrated with a young bull or seven rams **b**
Pr 13:20 Whoever walks with the wise **b** wise,
30:22 a slave when he **b** king, and a fool when glutted
Isa 18: 5 blossom is over and the flower **b** a ripening grape,
32:15 and the wilderness **b** a fruitful field,
44:12 he **b** hungry and his strength fails,
Jer 3: 1 and she goes from him and **b** another man’s wife,
Hab 1: 4 So the law **b** slack and justice never prevails.
Hag 2:13 The priests answered, “Yes, it **b** unclean.”
Mt 13:32 when it has grown it is the greatest of shrubs and **b**
18: 4 Whoever **b** humble like this child is the greatest in
24:32 as its branch **b** tender and puts forth its leaves,
Mk 4:32 yet when it is sown it grows up and **b** the greatest
9:18 and he foams and grinds his teeth and **b** rigid;
13:28 as its branch **b** tender and puts forth its leaves,
Lk 11:17 “Every kingdom divided against itself **b** a desert,
Ro 3:27 Then what **b** of boasting?
1Co 6:16 that whoever is united to a prostitute **b** one body
6:17 anyone united to the Lord **b** one spirit with him.
11:21 and one goes hungry and another **b** drunk.
Eph 5:13 but everything exposed by the light **b** visible,
5:14 for everything that **b** visible is light.
Heb 12:16 See to it that no one **b** like Esau,
Jas 4: 4 to be a friend of the world **b** an enemy of God.
Sir 4:24 For wisdom **b** known through speech,
Sir 10: 3 but a city **b** fit to live in through the understanding
11:18 One **b** rich through diligence and self-denial,
11:28 by how he ends, a person **b** known.
12:14 with a sinner and **b** involved in the other’s sins.
13: 1 and whoever associates with a proud person **b**
16: 4 but through a clan of outlaws it **b** desolate.
31: 4 and if ever he rests he **b** needy.
2Es 14:17 For the weaker the world **b** through old age,

BECOMING (14) [BECOME]

Lev 15:32 an emission of semen, **b** unclean thereby,
22: 8 by wild animals he shall not eat, **b** unclean by it:
Pr 17: 7 Fine speech is not **b** to a fool;
Eze 5: 6 **b** more wicked than the nations and
16:54 of all that you have done, **b** a consolation to them.
Mt 16: 8 And **b** aware of it, Jesus said, “You of little faith,
Mk 8:17 And **b** aware of it, Jesus said to them,
Gal 3:13 Christ redeemed us from the curse of the law by **b**
Php 3:10 and the sharing of his sufferings by **b** like him
Heb 5: 5 Christ did not glorify himself in **b** a high priest,
Sir Pr: 1 so that by **b** familiar also with his book
LtJ 6: 5 of **b** at all like the foreigners or of letting fear
2Mc 4:40 the crowds were **b** aroused and filled with anger,
2Es 8:49 as is **b** for you, and have not considered yourself

BECORATH (1)

1Sa 9: 1 of Abiel son of Zeror son of **B** son of Aphiah,

BECTILETH (2)

Jdt 2:21 for three days from Nineveh to the plain of **B**,
2:21 and camped opposite **B** near the mountain that is

BED‡ (99) [BED-COVER, BEDCHAMBER, BEDPOST, BEDRIDDEN, BEDROOM, BEDS, SICKBED, SICKBEDS]

Ge 47:31 Then Israel bowed himself on the head of his **b**.
48: 2 he summoned his strength and sat up in **b**.
49: 4 because you went up onto your father’s **b**;
49:33 he drew up his feet into the **b**, breathed his last,
Ex 8: 3 into your bedchamber and your **b**,
21:18 though not dead, is confined to **b**,
Lev 15: 4 Every **b** on which the one with the discharge lies
15: 5 Anyone who touches his **b** shall wash his clothes,
15:21 Whoever touches her **b** shall wash his clothes,
15:23 whether it is the **b** or anything upon which she sits,
15:24 and every **b** on which he lies shall be unclean.
15:26 Every **b** on which she lies during all the days of
her discharge shall be treated as the **b** of her
Dt 3:11 In fact his **b**, an iron **b**, can still be seen
1Sa 9:25 a **b** was spread for Saul on the roof,
19:13 Michal took an idol and laid it on the **b**;
19:15 He said, “Bring him up to me in the **b**,
19:16 the messengers came in, the idol was in the **b**,
28:23 So he got up from the ground and sat on the **b**.
2Sa 4:11 a righteous man on his **b** in his own house!
13: 5 Jonadab said to him, “Lie down on your **b**,
1Ki 1:47 The king bowed in worship on the **b**
17:19 and laid him on his own **b**.
21: 4 He lay down on his **b**, turned away his face,
2Ki 1: 4 ‘You shall not leave the **b** to which you have gone,
1: 6 you shall not leave the **b** to which you have gone,
1:16 you shall not leave the **b** to which you have gone,
4:10 and put there for him a **b**, a table, a chair,
4:21 She went up and laid him on the **b** of the man
4:32 he saw the child lying dead on his **b**.
4:34 Then he got up on the **b** and lay upon the child,
1Ch 5: 1 he defiled his father’s **b** his birthright was given
2Ch 24:25 and they killed him on his **b**.
Job 7:13 When I say, ‘My **b** will comfort me,
27:19 They go to **b** with wealth, but will do so no more;
Ps 6: 6 every night I flood my **b** with tears;
63: 6 when I think of you on my **b**, and meditate on you
132: 3 “I will not enter my house or get into my **b**;
139: 8 if I make my **b** in Sheol, you are there.
Pr 7:17 I have perfumed my **b** with myrrh,
22:27 why should your **b** be taken from under you?
26:14 so does a lazy person in **b**.
SS 3: 1 my **b** at night I sought him whom my soul loves;
Isa 14:11 maggots are the **b** beneath you,
28:20 For the **b** is too short to stretch oneself on it,
57: 7 a high and lofty mountain you have set your **b**,
57: 8 for, in deserting me, you have uncovered your **b**,
57: 8 for yourself with them, you have loved their **b**,
Eze 17: 7 From the **b** where it was planted
17:10 wither on the **b** where it grew?
23:17 the Babylonians came to her into the **b** of love,
32:25 They have made Elam a **b** among the slain
Da 2:28 of your head as you lay in **b** were these:
2:29 O king, as you lay in **b**,
4: 5 in **b** and the visions of my head terrified me.
4:10 Upon my **b** this is what I saw;
4:13 in the visions of my head as I lay in **b**,
7: 1 a dream and visions of his head as he lay in **b**.
Am 3:12 with the corner of a couch and part of a **b**.
Mt 8:14 he saw his mother-in-law lying in **b** with a fever;
9: 2 a paralyzed man lying on a **b**.
9: 6 “Stand up, take your **b** and go to your home.”
Mk 1:30 Now Simon’s mother-in-law was in **b** with a fever,
4:21 or under the **b**, and not on the lampstand?
7:30 So she went home, found the child lying on the **b**,
Lk 5:18 carrying a paralyzed man on a **b**.
5:19 and let him down with his **b** through the tiles into
5:24 stand up and take your **b** and go to your home.”
8:16 or puts it under a **b**, but puts it on a lampstand,

Lk 11: 7 and my children are with me in **b**;
17:34 I tell you, on that night there will be two in one **b**;
Ac 9:34 get up and make your **b**!"
28: 8 so happened that the father of Publius lay sick in **b**
Heb 13: 4 and let the marriage **b** be kept undefiled;
Rev 2:22 Beware, I am throwing her on a **b**,
Tob 6:18 Now when you are about to go to **b** with her,
7:16 and made the **b** in the room as he had told her,
8: 4 Tobias got out of **b** and said to Sarah, "Sister,
14:11 Then they laid him on his **b**, and he died;
Jdt 8: 3 and took to his **b** and died in his town Bethulia.
9: 3 you gave up their rulers to be killed, and their **b**,
10:21 Holofernes was resting on his **b** under a canopy
13: 1 They went to **b**, for they all were weary because
13: 2 with Holofernes stretched out on his **b**,
13: 4 Then Judith, standing beside his **b**,
13: 7 She came close to his **b**,
13: 9 Next she rolled his body off the **b** and pulled down
AdE 14:15 the wicked and abhor the **b** of the uncircumcised
Sir 23:18 The one who sins against his marriage **b** says
31:19 He does not breathe heavily when in **b**.
40: 5 And when one rests upon his **b**,
41:22 and do not approach her **b**;
LtJ 6:43 by one of the passers-by and is taken to **b** by him,
6:70 Like a scarecrow in a cucumber **b**,
1Mc 6: 8 to his **b** and became sick from disappointment,
1Es 3: 6 and drink from gold cups, and sleep on a gold **b**,
2Es 3: 1 I was troubled as I lay on my **b**,
12:26 one of the kings shall die in his **b**, but in agonies.

BED-COVER (1) [BED, COVER]
2Ki 8:15 the next day he took the **b** and dipped it in water

BEDAD (2)
Ge 36:35 Husham died, and Hadad son of **B**,
1Ch 1:46 When Husham died, Hadad son of **B**,

BEDAN‡ (1)
1Ch 7:17 The son of Ulam: **B**.

BEDCHAMBER (7) [BED, CHAMBER]
Ex 8: 3 they shall come up into your palace, into your **b**
2Sa 4: 7 while he was lying on his couch in his **b**;
2Ki 6:12 of Israel the words that you speak in your **b**."
Jdt 13: 3 the **b** and to wait for her to come out, as she did on
13: 4 and no one, either small or great, was left in the **b**.
14:15 the **b** and found him sprawled on the floor dead,
16:19 that she had taken for herself from his **b** she gave

BEDCHAMBER (KJV) See also BEDROOM

BEDEIAH (2)
Ezr 10:35 Benaiah, **B**, Cheluhi,
1Es 9:34 Maerus, Joel, Mamdai and **B** and Vaniah,

BEDPOST (1) [BED, POST]
Jdt 13: 6 She went up to the **b** near Holofernes' head,

BEDRIDDEN (1) [BED]
Ac 9:33 who had been **b** for eight years,

BEDROOM (5) [BED, ROOM]
2Ki 11: 2 she put him and his nurse in a **b**.
2Ch 22:11 she put him and his nurse in a **b**.
Ecc 10:20 or curse the rich, even in your **b**;
Tob 8: 1 the young man and brought him into the **b**.
1Es 3: 3 and King Darius went to his **b**;

BEDS‡ (12) [BED]
2Sa 17:28 brought **b**, basins, and earthen vessels,
Job 33:15 while they slumber on their **b**,
33:19 They are also chastened with pain upon their **b**,
Ps 4: 4 ponder it on your **b**, and be silent.
36: 4 They plot mischief while on their **b**;
SS 5:13 His cheeks are like **b** of spices, yielding fragrance.
6: 2 the **b** of spices, to pasture his flock in the gardens,
Hos 7:14 but they wail upon their **b**;
Joel 3:18 all the stream **b** of Judah shall flow with water;
Am 6: 4 Alas for those who lie on **b** of ivory,
Mic 2: 1 and evil deeds on their **b**!
Jdt 15:11 his **b**, his bowls, and all his furniture.

BEE (2) [BEES]
Isa 7:18 and for the **b** that is in the land of Assyria.
Sir 11: 3 The **b** is small among flying creatures,

BEELIADA (1)
1Ch 14: 7 Elishama, **B**, and Eliphelet.

BEELSARUS (1)
1Es 5: 8 **B**, Aspharasus, Reeliah, Rehum, and Baanah,

BEELZEBUL (7)
Mt 10:25 If they have called the master of the house **B**,
12:24 the Pharisees heard it, they said, "It is only by **B**,
12:27 If I cast out demons by **B**,
Mk 3:22 from Jerusalem said, "He has **B**, and by the ruler
Lk 11:15 some of them said, "He casts out demons by **B**,
11:18 —for you say that I cast out the demons by **B**.
11:19 Now if I cast out the demons by **B**,

BEEN (1259) [BE] See Index of Articles Etc.

BEER (2)
Nu 21:16 From there they continued to **B**;
Jdg 9:21 Then Jotham ran away and fled, going to **B**,

BEER-ELIM (1)
Isa 15: 8 to Eglaim, the wailing reaches to **B**.

BEER-LAHAI-ROI (3)
Ge 16:14 Therefore the well was called **B**;
24:62 Now Isaac had come from **B**,
25:11 And Isaac settled at **B**.

BEER-SHEBA (34)
Ge 21:14 and wandered about in the wilderness of **B**.
21:31 Therefore that place was called **B**;
21:32 When they had made a covenant at **B**, Abimelech,
21:33 Abraham planted a tamarisk tree in **B**,
22:19 and they arose and went together to **B**; and Abraham lived at **B**.
26:23 From there he went up to **B**.
26:33 therefore the name of the city is **B** to this day.
28:10 Jacob left **B** and went toward Haran.
46: 1 on his journey with all that he had and came to **B**,
46: 5 Then Jacob set out from **B**;
Jos 15:28 Hazar-shual, **B**, Biziothiah,
19: 2 It had for its inheritance **B**, Sheba, Moladah,
Jdg 20: 1 Then all the Israelites came out, from Dan to **B**,
1Sa 3:20 to **B** knew that Samuel was a trustworthy prophet
8: 2 Abijah; they were judges in **B**.
2Sa 3:10 over Israel and over Judah, from Dan to **B**."
17:11 that all Israel be gathered to you, from Dan to **B**,
24: 2 from Dan to **B**, and take a census of the people,
24: 7 and they went out to the Negeb of Judah at **B**.
24:15 of the people died, from Dan to **B**.
1Ki 4:25 and Israel lived in safety, from Dan even to **B**, all
19: 3 he got up and fled for his life, and came to **B**,
2Ki 12: 1 His mother's name was Zibiah of **B**.
23: 8 the priests had made offerings, from Geba to **B**;
1Ch 4:28 They lived in **B**, Moladah, Hazar-shual,
21: 2 from **B** to Dan, and bring me a report,
2Ch 19: 4 from **B** to the hill country of Ephraim,
24: 1 his mother's name was Zibiah of **B**.
30: 5 from **B** to Dan, that the people should come
Ne 11:27 in Hazar-shual, in **B** and its villages,
11:30 So they camped from **B** to the valley of Hinnom.
Am 5: 5 and do not enter into Gilgal or cross over to **B**;
8:14 O Dan," and, "As the way of **B** lives"—

BEERA (1)
1Ch 7:37 Bezer, Hod, Shamma, Shilshah, Ithran, and **B**.

BEERAH (1)
1Ch 5: 6 **B** his son, whom King Tilgath-pilneser

BEERI (2)
Ge 26:34 he married Judith daughter of **B** the Hittite,
Hos 1: 1 word of the LORD that came to Hosea son of **B**,

BEEROTH (10) [BEEROTHITE, BEEROTH-BENE-JAAKAN]
Jos 9:17 Now their cities were Gibeon, Chephirah, **B**,
18:25 Gibeon, Ramah, **B**,
2Sa 4: 2 They were sons of Rimmon a Benjaminite from **B**
4: 2 for **B** is considered to belong to Benjamin.
4: 3 the people of **B** had fled to Gittaim and are there
23:37 of **B**, the armor-bearer of Joab son of Zeruiah;
1Ch 11:39 the Ammonite, Naharai of **B**, the armor-bearer
Ezr 2:25 Of Kiriatharim, Chephirah, and **B**,
Ne 7:29 Of Kiriath-jearim, Chephirah, and **B**,
1Es 5:19 Those from Chephirah and **B**,

BEEROTH-BENE-JAAKAN (1) [BEEROTH, BENE-JAAKAN]
Dt 10: 6 (The Israelites journeyed from **B** to Moserah.

BEEROTHITE (2) [BEEROTH]
2Sa 4: 5 Now the sons of Rimmon the **B**,
4: 9 the sons of Rimmon the **B**, "As the LORD lives,

BEES (4) [BEE]
Dt 1:44 then came out against you and chased you as **b** do.
Jdg 14: 8 and there was a swarm of **b** in the body of the lion,
Ps 118:12 They surrounded me like **b**;
4Mc 14:19 since even **b** at the time

BEESHTERAH (1)
Jos 21:27 and **B** with its pasture lands—two towns.

BEETLE (KJV) See CRICKET

BEEVES (KJV) See CATTLE, HERD, OXEN

BEFALL (9) [BEFALLEN, BEFALLS, BEFELL]
Ge 41:36 the seven years of famine that are to **b** the land
Dt 31:29 In time to come trouble will **b** you,
Job 31: 3 Does not calamity **b** the unrighteous,
34:11 according to their ways he will make it **b** them.
Ps 91:10 no evil shall **b** you, no scourge come
Isa 47:13 and at each new moon predict what shall **b** you.
Am 3: 6 Does disaster **b** a city, unless the LORD has done it?
Sir 25:19 may a sinner's lot **b** her!
33: 1 No evil will **b** the one who fears the Lord,

BEFALLEN (11) [BEFALL]
Lev 10:19 and yet such things as these have **b** me!
Nu 20:14 You know all the adversity that has **b** us:
1Sa 20:26 for he thought, "Something has **b** him;
1Ch 7:23 because disaster had **b** his house.
Isa 51:19 These two things have **b** you—who will grieve
Jer 44:23 that this disaster has **b** you,
La 5: 1 Remember, O LORD, what has **b** us;
AdE 6:13 and his friends what had **b** him.
9:26 in this affair and what had **b** them,
2Mc 11:13 he pondered over the defeat that had **b** him,
2Es 12:43 Are not the disasters that have **b** us enough?

BEFALLS (5) [BEFALL]
Job 3:25 and what I dread **b** me.
Pr 15: 6 but trouble **b** the income of the wicked.
Ecc 2:14 Yet I perceived that the same fate **b** all of them.
Sir 2: 4 Accept whatever **b** you, and in times
3:28 When calamity **b** the proud, there is no healing,

BEFELL (4) [BEFALL]
1Ch 29:30 and of the events that **b** him and Israel and all
2Mc 5:20 the place itself shared in the misfortunes that **b**
2Es 3:10 And the same fate **b** all of them:
10:48 this was the destruction that **b** Jerusalem.

BEFITS (5) [BEFITTING]
Ps 33: 1 O you righteous. Praise **b** the upright.
93: 5 holiness **b** your house, O LORD, forevermore.
Sir 31:17 Be the first to stop, as **b** good manners,
1Es 4:46 and request of you, and this **b** your greatness.
3Mc 3:25 the sure and shameful death that **b** enemies.

BEFITTING (2) [BEFITS]
3Mc 4:10 they would undergo treatment **b** traitors during
4Mc 11:20 being tortured he said, "O contest **b** holiness,

BEFORE‡ (1748) [BEFOREHAND]
Ge 7: 1 for I have seen that you alone are righteous **b** me
10: 9 He was a mighty hunter **b** the LORD;
10: 9 "Like Nimrod a mighty hunter **b** the LORD."
11:28 Haran died **b** his father Terah in the land
13: 9 Is not the whole land **b** you?
13:10 this was **b** the LORD had destroyed Sodom
17: 1 walk **b** me, and be blameless.
18: 8 the calf that he had prepared, and set it **b** them;
18:22 while Abraham remained standing **b** the LORD.
19: 4 But **b** they lay down, the men of the city,
19:13 against its people has become great **b** the LORD,
19:27 in the morning to the place where he had stood **b**
20:15 Abimelech said, "My land is **b** you;
20:16 it is your exoneration **b** all who are with you;
23:12 Abraham bowed down **b** the people of the land.
24: 7 he will send his angel **b** you,
24:15 **B** he had finished speaking, there was Rebekah,
24:33 Then food was set **b** him to eat;
24:40 But he said to me, 'The LORD, **b** whom I walk,
24:45 "**B** I had finished speaking in my heart,
24:51 Look, Rebekah is **b** you, take her and go,
24:52 he bowed himself to the ground **b** the LORD.
27: 4 so that I may bless you **b** I die."
27: 7 that I may bless you **b** the LORD **b** I die.'
27:10 so that he may bless you **b** he dies."
27:33 and I ate it all **b** you came,
29:26 giving the younger **b** the firstborn.
30:30 For you had little **b** I came,
30:41 Jacob laid the rods in the troughs **b** the eyes of
31: 2 not regard him as favorably as he did **b**.
31: 5 not regard me as favorably as he did **b**.
31:35 "Let not my lord be angry that I cannot rise **b** you,
31:37 Set it here **b** my kinsfolk and your kinsfolk,
32: 3 Jacob sent messengers **b** him to his brother Esau in
33:14 the pace of the cattle that are **b** me and according
33:18 and he camped **b** the city.
36:31 **b** any king reigned over the Israelites.
37:10 and bow to the ground **b** you?"
37:18 and **b** he came near to them,
40: 9 "In my dream there was a vine **b** me,
41:14 and changed his clothes, he came in **b** Pharaoh.
41:21 for they were still as ugly as **b**.
41:50 **B** the years of famine came, Joseph had two sons,
42: 6 and bowed themselves **b** him with their faces to
42:24 And he picked out Simeon and had him bound **b**
43: 9 I do not bring him back to you and set him **b** you,
43:14 may God Almighty grant you mercy **b** the man,
43:15 on their way down to Egypt, and stood **b** Joseph.
43:26 and bowed to the ground **b** him.
43:33 When they were seated **b** him,
44:14 and they fell to the ground **b** him.
45: 1 Then Joseph could no longer control himself **b**
45: 5 for God sent me **b** you to preserve life.
45: 7 God sent me **b** you to preserve for you a remnant
45:28 I must go and see him **b** I die."
46:28 Israel sent Judah ahead to Joseph to lead the way **b**
47: 6 The land of Egypt is **b** you;
47: 7 and presented him **b** Pharaoh,

Ge 47:15 Why should we die **b** your eyes?
47:19 Shall we die **b** your eyes, both we and our land?
48: 5 of Egypt **b** I came to you in Egypt, are now mine;
48:15 "The God **b** whom my ancestors Abraham
49: 8 your father's sons shall bow down **b** you.
50:16 "Your father gave this instruction **b** he died,
50:18 Then his brothers also wept, fell down **b** him,
Ex 1:19 and give birth **b** the midwife comes to them."
4:21 see that you perform **b** Pharaoh all the wonders
5: 7 as **b;** let them go and gather straw for themselves.
5:14 of bricks yesterday and today, as you did **b?"**
7: 9 'Take your staff and throw it down **b** Pharaoh,
7:10 down his staff **b** Pharaoh and his officials,
8:20 "Rise early in the morning and present yourself **b**
9:10 they took soot from the kiln, and stood **b** Pharaoh,
9:11 The magicians could not stand **b** Moses because of
9:13 in the morning and present yourself **b** Pharaoh,
10: 3 long will you refuse to humble yourself **b** me?
10:14 a dense swarm of locusts as had never been **b,**
11:10 and Aaron performed all these wonders **b** Pharaoh;
12:34 So the people took their dough **b** it was leavened,
14:19 of God who was going **b** the Israelite army moved
14:27 As the Egyptians fled **b** it,
16:33 and place it **b** the LORD,
16:34 so Aaron placed it **b** the covenant, for safekeeping.
18:19 You should represent the people **b** God,
18:19 and you should bring their cases **b** God;
19: 7 and set **b** them all these words that
20: 3 you shall have no other gods **b** me.
21: 1 These are the ordinances that you shall set **b** them:
21: 6 then his master shall bring him **b** God.
22: 8 the owner of the house shall be brought **b** God,
22: 9 the case of both parties shall come **b** God;
22:11 an oath **b** the LORD shall decide between the two
22:26 you shall restore it **b** the sun goes down;
23:15 No one shall appear **b** me empty-handed.
23:17 in the year all your males shall appear **b**
23:28 the Canaanites, and the Hittites from **b** you.
23:29 I will not drive them out from **b** you in one year,
23:30 Little by little I will drive them out from **b** you,
23:31 and you shall drive them out **b** you.
25:30 of the Presence on the table **b** me always.
27:21 outside the curtain that is **b** the covenant,
27:21 from evening to morning **b** the LORD.
28:12 and Aaron shall bear their names **b** the LORD
28:29 for a continual remembrance **b** the LORD.
28:30 on Aaron's heart when he goes in **b** the LORD;
28:30 the judgment of the Israelites on his heart **b**
28:35 when he goes into the holy place **b** the LORD,
28:38 in order that they may find favor **b** the LORD.
29:11 and you shall slaughter the bull **b** the LORD,
29:23 out of the basket of unleavened bread that is **b**
29:24 raise them as an elevation offering **b** the LORD.
29:25 the burnt offering of pleasing odor **b** the LORD;
29:26 and raise it as an elevation offering **b** the LORD;
29:42 the entrance of the tent of meeting **b** the LORD,
30: 8 a regular incense offering **b** the LORD
30:16 **b** the LORD it will be a reminder to the Israelites
30:36 and put part of it **b** the covenant in the tent
32: 1 "Come, make gods for us, who shall go **b** us;
32: 5 When Aaron saw this, he built an altar **b** it;
32:23 'Make us gods, who shall go **b** us;
33: 2 I will send an angel **b** you,
33:19 he said, "I will make all my goodness pass **b** you,
33:19 and will proclaim **b** you the name, 'The LORD';
34: 6 The LORD passed **b** him, and proclaimed,
34:10 **B** all your people I will perform marvels,
34:11 See, I will drive out **b** you the Amorites,
34:20 No one shall appear **b** me empty-handed.
34:23 in the year all your males shall appear **b**
34:24 For I will cast out nations **b** you,
34:24 up to appear **b** the LORD your God three times in
34:34 in **b** the LORD to speak with him, he would take
40: 5 You shall put the golden altar for incense **b** the ark
40: 6 of burnt offering **b** the entrance of the tabernacle
40:23 and set the bread in order on it **b** the LORD;
40:25 and set up the lamps **b** the LORD;
40:26 He put the golden altar in the tent of meeting **b**
40:38 **b** the eyes of all the house of Israel at each stage
Lev 1: 3 for acceptance in your behalf **b** the LORD.
1: 5 The bull shall be slaughtered **b** the LORD;
1:11 be slaughtered on the north side of the altar **b**
3: 1 you shall offer one without blemish **b** the LORD.
3: 7 you shall bring it **b** the LORD
3: 8 It shall be slaughtered **b** the tent of meeting,
3:12 you shall bring it **b** the LORD
3:13 it shall be slaughtered **b** the tent of meeting;
4: 4 to the entrance of the tent of meeting **b** the LORD
4: 4 the bull shall be slaughtered **b** the LORD.
4: 6 of the blood seven times **b** the LORD in front of
4: 7 of fragrant incense that is in the tent of meeting **b**
4:14 of the herd for a sin offering and bring it **b** the tent
4:15 on the head of the bull **b** the LORD,
4:15 and the bull shall be slaughtered **b** the LORD.
4:17 and sprinkle it seven times **b** the LORD,
4:18 on the horns of the altar that is **b** the LORD in
4:24 the spot where the burnt offering is slaughtered **b**
5:19 you have incurred guilt **b** the LORD.
6: 7 The priest shall make atonement on your behalf **b**
6:14 The sons of Aaron shall offer it **b** the LORD,
6:25 The sin offering shall be slaughtered **b** the LORD
7:30 the breast may be raised as an elevation offering **b**
8:26 From the basket of unleavened bread that was **b**
8:27 raised them as an elevation offering **b** the LORD.
8:29 the breast and raised it as an elevation offering **b**
9: 2 without blemish, and offer them **b** the LORD.
9: 4 a ram for an offering of well-being to sacrifice **b**
Lev 9: 5 and the whole congregation drew near and stood **b**
9:21 as an elevation offering **b** the LORD,
10: 1 and they offered unholy fire **b** the LORD,
10: 2 and they died **b** the LORD.
10: 3 and **b** all the people I will be glorified.' "
10:15 to raise for an elevation offering **b** the LORD;
10:17 to make atonement on their behalf **b** the LORD.
10:19 and their burnt offering **b** the LORD;
12: 7 He shall offer it **b** the LORD,
13: 7 he shall appear again **b** the priest.
14:11 along with these things, **b** the LORD,
14:12 raise them as an elevation offering **b** the LORD.
14:16 and sprinkle some oil with his finger seven times **b**
14:18 the priest shall make atonement on his behalf **b**
14:23 the priest, to the entrance of the tent of meeting, **b**
14:24 as an elevation offering **b** the LORD.
14:27 that is in his left hand seven times **b** the LORD.
14:29 to make atonement on his behalf **b** the LORD.
14:31 and the priest shall make atonement **b** the LORD
14:36 the house **b** the priest goes to examine the disease,
15:14 and come **b** the LORD to the entrance of the tent
15:15 the priest shall make atonement on his behalf **b**
15:30 the priest shall make atonement on her behalf **b**
16: 1 when they drew near **b** the LORD and died.
16: 2 at any time into the sanctuary inside the curtain **b**
16: 7 and set them **b** the LORD at the entrance of
16:10 for Azazel shall be presented alive **b** the LORD
16:12 a censer full of coals of fire from the altar **b**
16:13 and put the incense on the fire **b** the LORD,
16:14 and **b** the mercy seat he shall sprinkle the blood
16:15 upon the mercy seat and **b** the mercy seat.
16:18 the altar that is **b** the LORD and make atonement
16:30 from all your sins you shall be clean **b** the LORD.
17: 4 as an offering to the LORD **b** the tabernacle of
18:24 the nations I am casting out **b**
18:27 who were **b** you, committed all
18:28 as it vomited out the nation that was **b** you.
18:30 that were done **b** you, and not to defile yourselves
19:14 the deaf or put a stumbling block **b** the blind;
19:22 the ram of guilt offering **b** the LORD for his sin
19:32 You shall rise **b** the aged, and defer to the old;
20:23 the practices of the nation that I am driving out **b**
23:11 He shall raise the sheaf **b** the LORD,
23:20 an elevation offering **b** the LORD, together with
23:28 of atonement, to make atonement on your behalf **b**
23:40 and you shall rejoice **b** the LORD your God
24: 3 from evening to morning **b** the LORD regularly;
24: 4 up the lamps on the lampstand of pure gold **b**
24: 8 Every sabbath day Aaron shall set them in order **b**
25:30 If it is not redeemed **b** a full year has elapsed,
26: 7 and they shall fall **b** you by the sword.
26: 8 your enemies shall fall **b** you by the sword.
27: 8 they shall be brought **b** the priest and
27:11 the animal shall be presented **b** the priest.
Nu 3: 4 Nadab and Abihu died **b** the LORD
3: 4 before the LORD when they offered illicit fire **b**
3: 6 and set them **b** Aaron the priest,
5:16 and set her **b** the LORD;
5:18 The priest shall set the woman **b** the LORD,
5:25 and shall elevate the grain offering **b** the LORD
5:30 then he shall set the woman **b** the LORD,
6:16 The priest shall present them **b** the LORD
6:20 as an elevation offering **b** the LORD;
7: 3 They brought their offerings **b** the LORD,
7: 3 they presented them **b** the tabernacle.
7:10 the leaders presented their offering **b** the altar.
8: 9 You shall bring the Levites **b** the tent of meeting,
8:10 When you bring the Levites **b** the LORD,
8:11 and Aaron shall present the Levites **b** the LORD
8:13 Then you shall have the Levites stand **b** Aaron
8:21 as an elevation offering **b** the LORD,
9: 6 They came **b** Moses and Aaron on that day,
10: 3 the whole congregation shall assemble **b** you at
10: 4 the heads of the tribes of Israel, shall assemble **b**
10: 9 be remembered **b** the LORD your God and
10:10 a reminder on your behalf **b** the LORD your God:
10:21 and the tabernacle was set up **b** their arrival.
10:33 with the ark of the covenant of the LORD going **b**
10:35 and your foes flee **b** you."
11:20 and have wailed **b** him, saying,
11:33 But while the meat was still between their teeth, **b**
13:22 (Hebron was built seven years **b** Zoan in Egypt.)
13:30 But Caleb quieted the people **b** Moses, and said,
14: 5 and Aaron fell on their faces **b** all the assembly of
14:37 about the land died by a plague **b** the LORD.
14:42 not let yourselves be struck down **b** your enemies.
15:15 you and the alien shall be alike **b** the LORD.
15:25 and their sin offering **b** the LORD, for their error.
15:28 And the priest shall make atonement **b** the LORD
16: 7 and lay incense on them **b** the LORD;
16: 9 and to stand **b** the congregation and serve them?
16:16 be present tomorrow **b** the LORD,
16:17 each one of you present his censer **b** the LORD,
16:38 for they presented them **b** the LORD
16:40 shall approach to offer incense **b** the LORD,
17: 4 Place them in the tent of meeting **b** the covenant,
17: 7 the staffs **b** the LORD in the tent of the covenant.
17: 9 the staffs from **b** the LORD to all the Israelites;
17:10 "Put back the staff of Aaron **b** the covenant,
18:19 a covenant of salt forever **b** the LORD for you
20: 3 "Would that we had died when our kindred died **b**
20: 8 command the rock **b** their eyes to yield its water.
20: 9 So Moses took the staff from **b** the LORD,
20:10 and Aaron gathered the assembly together **b**
20:12 to show my holiness **b** the eyes of the Israelites,
22:32 because your way is perverse **b** me.
25: 4 and impale them in the sun **b** the LORD,
Nu 26:61 and Abihu died when they offered illicit fire **b**
27: 2 They stood **b** Moses, Eleazar the priest,
27: 5 Moses brought their case **b** the LORD.
27:14 not show my holiness **b** their eyes at the waters."
27:17 who shall go out **b** them and come in **b** them,
27:19 have him stand **b** Eleazar the priest and all
27:21 But he shall stand **b** Eleazar the priest,
27:21 for him by the decision of the Urim **b** the LORD;
27:22 He took Joshua and had him stand **b** Eleazar
31:50 to make atonement for ourselves **b** the LORD."
31:54 as a memorial for the Israelites **b** the LORD.
32: 4 that the LORD subdued **b** the congregation
32:17 but we will take up arms as a vanguard **b**
32:20 you take up arms to go **b** the LORD for the war,
32:21 of you who bear arms cross the Jordan **b**
32:21 until he has driven out his enemies from **b** him
32:22 and the land is subdued **b** the LORD—
32:22 this land shall be your possession **b** the LORD.
32:29 everyone armed for battle **b** the LORD,
32:29 with you and the land shall be subdued **b** you,
32:32 over armed **b** the LORD into the land of Canaan,
33: 7 and they camped **b** Migdol.
33:47 and camped in the mountains of Abarim, **b** Nebo.
33:52 the inhabitants of the land from **b** you,
33:55 from **b** you, then those whom you let remain shall
35:12 so that the slayer may not die until there is a trial **b**
35:32 the fugitive to return to live in the land **b** the death
Dt 1: 8 See, I have set the land **b** you;
1:30 The LORD your God, who goes **b** you,
1:30 just as he did for you in Egypt **b** your very eyes,
1:33 who goes **b** you on the way to seek out a place
1:45 When you returned and wept **b** the LORD,
2:21 the LORD destroyed them from **b** the Ammonites
2:22 by destroying the Horim **b** them so
4: 8 as this entire law that I am setting **b** you today?
4:10 how you once stood **b** the LORD your God
4:32 For ask now about former ages, long **b** your own,
4:34 as the LORD your God did for you in Egypt **b**
4:38 driving out **b** you nations greater
4:42 the two not having been at enmity **b;**
4:44 This is the law that Moses set **b** the Israelites.
5: 7 you shall have no other gods **b** me.
6:19 thrusting out all your enemies from **b** you,
6:22 The LORD displayed **b** our eyes great
6:25 we diligently observe this entire commandment **b**
7: 1 and he clears away many nations **b** you—
7:22 LORD your God will clear away these nations **b**
8:20 Like the nations that the LORD is destroying **b**
9: 3 the one who crosses over **b** you as
9: 3 he will defeat them and subdue them **b** you,
9: 4 the LORD your God thrusts them out **b** you,
9: 4 that the LORD is dispossessing them **b** you.
9: 5 the LORD your God is dispossessing them **b** you,
9:17 smashing them **b** your eyes.
9:18 Then I lay prostrate **b** the LORD as **b,**
9:25 and forty nights that I lay prostrate **b** the LORD
10: 4 Then he wrote on the tablets the same words as **b,**
10: 8 to stand **b** the LORD to minister to him,
11:23 the LORD will drive out all these nations **b** you,
11:26 I am setting **b** you today a blessing and a curse:
11:32 the statutes and ordinances that I am setting **b**
12:12 And you shall rejoice **b** the LORD your God,
12:29 When the LORD your God has cut off **b** you
12:30 after they have been destroyed **b** you:
16:11 Rejoice **b** the LORD your God—
16:16 Three times a year all your males shall appear **b**
16:16 not appear **b** the LORD empty-handed;
18: 7 to minister there **b** the LORD.
18:12 the LORD your God is driving them out **b** you.
19: 4 when the two had not been at enmity **b:**
19: 6 since the two had not been at enmity **b.**
19:17 parties to the dispute shall appear **b** the LORD,
19:17 **b** the priests and the judges who are in office
20: 2 **B** you engage in battle, the priest shall come
22:17 Then they shall spread out the cloth **b** the elders of
24:13 it will be to your credit **b** the LORD your God.
24:15 You shall pay them their wages daily **b** sunset,
26: 4 from your hand and sets it down **b** the altar of
26: 5 you shall make this response **b**
26:10 You shall set it down **b** the LORD your God
26:10 before the LORD your God and bow down **b**
26:13 then you shall say **b** the LORD your God:
27: 7 rejoicing **b** the LORD your God.
28: 7 against you to be defeated **b** you;
28: 7 and flee **b** you seven ways.
28:25 The LORD will cause you to be defeated **b**
28:25 against them one way and flee **b** them seven ways.
28:31 Your ox shall be butchered **b** your eyes,
28:66 Your life shall hang in doubt **b** you;
29: 2 You have seen all that the LORD did **b** your eyes
29:10 all of you, **b** the LORD your God—
29:14 not only with you who stand here with us today **b**
30: 1 the blessings and the curses that I have set **b** you,
30:15 See, I have set **b** you today life and prosperity,
30:19 to witness against you today that I have set **b**
31: 3 LORD your God himself will cross over **b** you.
31: 3 He will destroy these nations **b** you,
31: 3 Joshua also will cross over **b** you,
31: 8 It is the LORD who goes **b** you.
31:11 to appear **b** the LORD your God at the place
31:11 you shall read this law **b** all Israel in their hearing.
31:21 **b** I have brought them into the land
33: 1 the man of God, blessed the Israelites **b** his death.
33:10 place incense **b** you, and whole burnt offerings
33:27 he drove out the enemy **b** you, and said,
Jos 1:14 among you shall cross over armed **b** your kindred
2: 8 **B** they went to sleep, she came up to them on

Jos 2: 9 all the inhabitants of the land melt in fear **b** you.
2:10 the water of the Red Sea **b** you when you came out
2:24 all the inhabitants of the land melt in fear **b** us."
3: 1 They camped there **b** crossing over.
3: 4 for you have not passed this way **b.**
3:10 without fail will drive out from **b** you
3:11 the Lord of all the earth is going to pass **b** you into
4: 5 "Pass on **b** the ark of the LORD your God into
4:12 of Manasseh crossed over armed **b** the Israelites,
4:13 for war crossed over **b** the LORD to the plains
4:18 to their place and overflowed all its banks, as **b.**
5:13 and saw a man standing **b** him with a drawn sword
6: 4 of rams' horns **b** the ark.
6: 7 the armed men pass on **b** the ark of the LORD."
6: 8 of rams' horns **b** the LORD went forward,
6: 9 And the armed men went **b** the priests who blew
6:13 of rams' horns **b** the ark of the LORD passed on,
6:13 The armed men went **b** them,
6:26 "Cursed **b** the LORD be anyone who tries
7: 4 and they fled **b** the men of Ai.
7: 6 to the ground on his face **b** the ark of the LORD
7:12 the Israelites are unable to stand **b** their enemies;
7:13 to stand **b** your enemies until you take away
7:23 and they spread them out **b** the LORD.
8: 5 When they come out against us, as **b,**
8: 6 for they will say, 'They are fleeing from us, as **b.'**
8:10 with the elders of Israel, **b** the people to Ai.
8:11 and drew near **b** the city,
8:15 and all Israel made a pretense of being beaten **b**
8:35 that Moses commanded that Joshua did not read **b**
9:24 and to destroy all the inhabitants of the land **b** you;
10: 8 not one of them shall stand **b** you."
10:10 And the LORD threw them into a panic **b** Israel,
10:11 As they fled **b** Israel, while they were going down
10:14 There has been no day like it **b** or since,
11:10 **B** that time Hazor was the head
13: 6 I will myself drive them out from **b** the Israelites;
17: 4 They came **b** the priest Eleazar and Joshua son
18: 1 The land lay subdued **b** them.
18: 6 I will cast lots for you here **b** the LORD our God.
18: 8 and I will cast lots for you here **b** the LORD
18:10 Joshua cast lots for them in Shiloh **b** the LORD;
19:51 of the Israelites distributed by lot at Shiloh **b**
20: 5 there having been no enmity between them **b.**
20: 6 in that city until there is a trial **b** the congregation,
20: 9 until there was a trial **b** the congregation.
22:29 the LORD our God that stands **b** his tabernacle!"
23: 5 The LORD your God will push them back **b** you,
23: 9 For the LORD has driven out **b** you great
23:13 not continue to drive out these nations **b** you;
24: 1 and they presented themselves **b** God.
24: 8 and I destroyed them **b** you.
24:12 which drove out **b** you the two kings of
24:18 and the LORD drove out **b** us all the peoples,
Jdg 2: 3 So now I say, I will not drive them out **b** you;
2:21 I will no longer drive out **b** them any of
3: 2 to teach those who had no experience of it **b):**
4:14 The LORD is indeed going out **b** you."
4:15 and all his chariots and all his army into a panic **b**
4:23 on that day God subdued King Jabin of Canaan **b**
5: 5 The mountains quaked **b** the LORD,
5: 5 the One of Sinai, **b** the LORD, the God of Israel.
6: 9 and drove them out **b** you,
6:18 and bring out my present, and set it **b** you."
8:28 So Midian was subdued **b** the Israelites,
9:40 Abimelech chased him, and he fled **b** him.
11:11 and Jephthah spoke all his words **b** the LORD
11:33 Ammonites were subdued **b** the people of Israel.
14:16 Samson's wife wept **b** him, saying, "You hate me;
14:17 She wept **b** him the seven days
14:18 to him on the seventh day **b** the sun went down,
20: 1 and the congregation assembled in one body **b**
20:23 The Israelites went up and wept **b** the LORD
20:26 sitting there **b** the LORD;
20:26 and sacrifices of well-being **b** the LORD.
20:28 son of Aaron, ministered **b** it in those days),
20:30 and set themselves in array against Gibeah, as **b.**
20:31 As **b** they began to inflict casualties on the troops,
20:32 "They are being routed **b** us, as previously."
20:35 The LORD defeated Benjamin **b** Israel;
20:39 so they thought, "Surely they are defeated **b** us,
21: 2 and sat there until evening **b** God,
Ru 2:11 and came to a people that you did not know **b.**
3:14 but got up **b** one person could recognize another;
1Sa 1: 9 Hannah rose and presented herself **b** the LORD.
1:11 a male child, then I will set him **b** you as a nazirite
1:12 As she continued praying **b** the LORD,
1:15 but I have been pouring out my soul **b** the LORD.
1:19 They rose early in the morning and worshiped **b**
2:15 Moreover, **b** the fat was burned,
2:18 Samuel was ministering **b** the LORD,
2:28 to offer incense, to wear an ephod **b** me;
2:30 the family of your ancestor should go in and out **b**
2:35 he shall go in and out **b** my anointed one forever.
3:10 the LORD came and stood there, calling as **b,**
4: 3 the LORD put us to rout today **b** the Philistines?
4: 7 For nothing like this has happened **b.**
4:17 "Israel has fled **b** the Philistines,
5: 3 on his face to the ground **b** the ark of the LORD.
5: 4 on his face to the ground **b** the ark of the LORD,
6:20 "Who is able to stand **b** the LORD,
7: 6 and drew water and poured it out **b** the LORD.
7:10 and they were routed **b** Israel.
8:11 and to be his horsemen, and to run **b** his chariots;
8:20 and that our king may govern us and go out **b** us
9:13 **b** he goes up to the shrine to eat.
9:15 Now the day **b** Saul came,
1Sa 9:19 go up **b** me to the shrine,
9:24 up the thigh and what went with it and set them **b**
9:24 Samuel said, "See, what was kept is set **b** you.
9:24 Eat; for it is set **b** you at the appointed time,
9:27 Samuel said to Saul, "Tell the boy to go on **b** us,
10:11 When all who knew him **b** saw how he prophesied
10:19 Now therefore present yourselves **b** the LORD
10:25 and he wrote them in a book and laid it up **b**
11:15 there they made Saul king **b** the LORD in Gilgal.
11:15 There they sacrificed offerings of well-being **b**
12: 3 against me **b** the LORD and **b** his anointed.
12: 7 I may enter into judgment with you **b** the LORD,
12:16 and see this great thing that the LORD will do **b**
14:13 The Philistines fell **b** Jonathan,
14:24 "Cursed be anyone who eats food **b** it is evening
14:33 roll a large stone **b** me here."
15:30 now **b** the elders of my people and **b** Israel,
15:33 And Samuel hewed Agag in pieces **b** the LORD
16: 6 the LORD's anointed is now **b** the LORD."
16: 8 and made him pass **b** Samuel.
16:10 Jesse made seven of his sons pass **b** Samuel,
17: 7 and his shield-bearer went **b** him.
17:23 and spoke the same words as **b.**
17:30 and the people answered him again as **b.**
17:31 they repeated them **b** Saul; and he sent for him.
17:57 Abner took him and brought him **b** Saul,
18:26 be the king's son-in-law. **B** the time had expired,
19: 7 and he was in his presence as **b.**
19: 8 so that they fled **b** him.
19:24 and he too fell into a frenzy **b** Samuel.
20: 1 He came **b** Jonathan and said, "What have I done?
21: 6 which is removed from **b** the LORD,
21: 7 of Saul was there that day, detained **b** the LORD;
21:13 So he changed his behavior **b** them;
23:18 the two of them made a covenant **b** the LORD;
25:23 fell **b** David on her face, bowing to the ground.
26:19 if it is mortals, may they be cursed **b** the LORD,
28:22 let me set a morsel of bread **b** you.
28:25 She put them **b** Saul and his servants, and they ate.
29:10 for you have done well **b** me.
31: 1 and the men of Israel fled **b** the Philistines,
2Sa 2:14 the young men come forward and have a contest **b**
2:24 which lies **b** Giah on the way to the wilderness
2:26 How long will it be **b** you order your people
3:28 "I and my kingdom are forever guiltless **b**
3:34 as one falls **b** the wicked you have fallen."
3:35 to me, and more, if I taste bread or anything else **b**
5: 3 a covenant with them at Hebron **b** the LORD,
5:20 LORD has burst forth against my enemies **b** me,
5:24 then the LORD has gone out **b** you to strike down
6: 5 David and all the house of Israel were dancing **b**
6:14 David danced **b** the LORD with all his might;
6:16 and saw King David leaping and dancing **b**
6:17 and offerings of well-being **b** the LORD.
6:20 uncovering himself today **b** the eyes
6:21 David said to Michal, "It was **b** the LORD,
6:21 that I have danced **b** the LORD.
7: 9 and have cut off all your enemies from **b** you;
7:15 whom I put away from **b** you.
7:16 and your kingdom shall be made sure forever **b**
7:18 Then King David went in and sat **b** the LORD,
7:23 by driving out **b** his people nations and their gods?
7:26 of your servant David will be established **b** you.
7:29 so that it may continue forever **b** you;
10:13 against the Arameans; and they fled **b** him.
10:14 they likewise fled **b** Abishai, and entered the city.
10:18 The Arameans fled **b** Israel;
12:11 and I will take your wives **b** your eyes,
12:12 but I will do this thing **b** all Israel, and **b** the sun."
12:20 and when he asked, they set food **b** him and he ate.
13: 9 Then she took the pan and set them out **b** him,
14:33 with his face to the ground **b** the king;
15: 2 anyone brought a suit **b** the king for judgment,
15:18 from Gath, passed on **b** the king.
18:21 The Cushite bowed **b** Joab, and ran.
18:28 He prostrated himself **b** the king with his face to
19: 8 and all the troops came **b** the king.
19:18 Shimei son of Gera fell down **b** the king,
19:28 For all my father's house were doomed to death **b**
21: 6 and we will impale them **b** the LORD at Gibeon
21: 9 they impaled them on the mountain **b** the LORD.
22:13 of the brightness **b** him coals of fire flamed forth.
22:23 For all his ordinances were **b** me,
22:24 I was blameless **b** him, and I kept myself
24:13 Or will you flee three months **b** your foes
24:20 and prostrated himself **b** the king with his face to
1Ki 1: 5 and fifty men to run **b** him.
1:23 When he came in **b** the king,
1:25 who are now eating and drinking **b** him,
1:28 So she came into the king's presence, and stood **b**
1:32 When they came **b** the king,
2: 4 'If your heirs take heed to their way, to walk **b** me
2:26 because you carried the ark of the Lord GOD **b**
2:45 and the throne of David shall be established **b**
3: 6 because he walked **b** you in faithfulness,
3:12 no one like you has been **b** you and no one
3:15 He came to Jerusalem where he stood **b** the ark of
3:16 to the king and stood **b** him.
3:22 So they argued **b** the king.
3:24 and they brought a sword **b** the king.
8: 1 **b** King Solomon in Jerusalem,
8: 5 who had assembled **b** him,
8: 5 were with him **b** the ark,
8:22 Then Solomon stood **b** the altar of the LORD in
8:23 and steadfast love for your servants who walk **b**
8:25 'There shall never fail you a successor **b** me to sit
8:25 to walk **b** me as you have walked **b** me.'
1Ki 8:31 and comes and swears **b** your altar in this house,
8:33 are defeated **b** an enemy but turn again to you,
8:59 with which I pleaded **b** the LORD,
8:62 offered sacrifice **b** the LORD.
8:64 of well-being, because the bronze altar that was **b**
8:65 **b** the LORD our God, seven days.
9: 3 and your plea, which you made **b** me;
9: 4 As for you, if you will walk **b** me,
9: 6 and my statutes that I have set **b** you,
9:25 offering incense **b** the LORD.
11:36 that my servant David may always have a lamp **b**
12:30 the people went to worship **b** the one at Bethel and **b** the other as far as Dan.
13: 6 to him, and became as it was **b.**
14: 9 but you have done evil above all those who were **b**
14:24 the nations that the LORD drove out **b** the people
15: 3 He committed all the sins that his father did **b** him;
16:25 he did more evil than all who were **b** him.
16:30 the sight of the LORD more than all who were **b**
16:33 than had all the kings of Israel who were **b** him.
17: 1 the God of Israel lives, **b** whom I stand, there shall
18:15 "As the LORD of hosts lives, **b** whom I stand,
18:44 'Harness your chariot and go down **b**
19:11 "Go out and stand on the mountain **b** the LORD,
19:11 in pieces **b** the LORD, but the LORD was not in
21:26 whom the LORD drove out **b** the Israelites.)
21:29 "Have you seen how Ahab has humbled himself **b**
21:29 Because he has humbled himself **b** me,
22:10 and all the prophets were prophesying **b** them.
22:21 a spirit came forward and stood **b** the LORD,
2Ki 1:13 and came and fell on his knees **b** Elijah,
2: 9 **b** I am taken from you."
2:15 to meet him and bowed to the ground **b** him.
3:24 up and attacked the Moabites, who fled **b** them;
4:12 When he had called her, she stood **b** him.
4:38 As the company of prophets was sitting **b** him,
4:43 "How can I set this **b** a hundred people?"
4:44 He set it **b** them, they ate, and had some left,
5:15 he came and stood **b** him and said,
5:25 He went in and stood **b** his master;
6:22 and water **b** them so that they may eat and drink;
6:32 **B** the messenger arrived, Elisha said to the elders,
8: 9 When he entered and stood **b** him, he said,
11:18 the priest of Baal, **b** the altars.
13:14 and wept **b** him, crying, "My father, my father!
16: 3 of the nations whom the LORD drove out **b**
16:11 **b** King Ahaz arrived from Damascus.
16:14 that was **b** the LORD he removed from the front
17: 2 yet not like the kings of Israel who were **b** him.
17: 8 of the nations whom the LORD drove out **b**
17:11 the nations did whom the LORD carried away **b**
18: 5 or among those who were **b** him.
18:22 'You shall worship **b** this altar in Jerusalem'?
19:14 up to the house of the LORD and spread it **b**
19:15 And Hezekiah prayed **b** the LORD, and said:
19:26 like grass on the housetops, blighted **b** it is grown.
19:32 shoot an arrow there, come **b** it with a shield,
20: 3 how I have walked **b** you in faithfulness with
20: 4 **B** Isaiah had gone out of the middle court,
21: 2 the nations that the LORD drove out **b** the people
21: 9 the nations had done that the LORD destroyed **b**
21:11 who were **b** him, and has caused Judah also to sin
22:19 and you humbled yourself **b** the LORD,
22:19 you have torn your clothes and wept **b** me,
23: 3 by the pillar and made a covenant **b** the LORD,
23:25 **B** him there was no king like him,
25: 7 They slaughtered the sons of Zedekiah **b** his eyes,
1Ch 1:43 of Edom **b** any king reigned over the Israelites:
5:25 whom God had destroyed **b** them.
6:32 with song **b** the tabernacle of the tent of meeting,
10: 1 and the men of Israel fled **b** the Philistines,
11: 3 and David made a covenant with them at Hebron **b**
13: 8 David and all Israel were dancing **b** God
13:10 and he died there **b** God.
14:15 for God has gone out **b** you to strike down
15:24 were to blow the trumpets **b** the ark of God.
16: 1 and offerings of well-being **b** God.
16: 4 He appointed certain of the Levites as ministers **b**
16: 6 **b** the ark of the covenant of God.
16:27 Honor and majesty are **b** him;
16:29 bring an offering, and come **b** him.
16:30 tremble **b** him, all the earth.
16:33 the trees of the forest sing for joy **b** the LORD,
16:37 and his kinsfolk there **b** the ark of the covenant of
16:37 the covenant of the LORD to minister regularly **b**
16:39 and his kindred the priests **b** the tabernacle of
17: 8 and have cut off all your enemies **b** you;
17:13 as I took it from him who was **b** you,
17:16 Then King David went in and sat **b** the LORD,
17:21 and terrible things, in driving out nations **b**
17:25 your servant has found it possible to pray **b** you.
17:27 that it may continue forever **b** you.
19: 7 who came and camped **b** Medeba.
19:14 for battle; and they fled **b** him.
19:15 they likewise fled **b** Abishai, Joab's brother,
19:18 The Arameans fled **b** Israel;
21:30 but David could not go **b** it to inquire of God,
22: 5 So David provided materials in great quantity **b**
22:18 the land is subdued **b** the LORD and his people.
23:13 and his sons forever should make offerings **b**
23:31 to the number required of them, regularly **b**
24: 2 But Nadab and Abihu died **b** their father,
29:15 For we are aliens and transients **b** you,
29:20 and bowed their heads and prostrated themselves **b**
29:22 and drank **b** the LORD on that day with great joy.
29:25 as had not been on any king **b** him in Israel.
2Ch 1: 6 Solomon went up there to the bronze altar **b**

2Ch 1:10 and knowledge to go out and come in **b**
1:12 such as none of the kings had who were **b** you,
2: 4 to him for offering fragrant incense **b** him,
2: 6 except as a place to make offerings **b** him?
4:20 to burn **b** the inner sanctuary, as prescribed;
5: 3 the Israelites assembled **b** the king at the festival
5: 6 who had assembled **b** him, were **b** the ark,
6:12 Then Solomon stood **b** the altar of the LORD in
6:14 in steadfast love with your servants who walk **b**
6:16 'There shall never fail you a successor **b** me to sit
6:16 to walk in my law as you have walked **b** me.'
6:22 to take an oath and comes and swears **b** your altar
6:24 are defeated **b** an enemy but turn again to you,
7: 4 and all the people offered sacrifice **b** the LORD.
7:17 As for you, if you walk **b** me,
7:19 and my commandments that I have set **b** you,
9:11 there never was seen the like of them **b** in the land
13:15 God defeated Jeroboam and all Israel **b** Abijah
13:16 The Israelites fled **b** Judah,
14:12 LORD defeated the Ethiopians **b** Asa and **b** Judah,
14:13 for they were broken **b** the LORD and his army.
18: 9 and all the prophets were prophesying **b** them.
18:20 a spirit came forward and stood **b** the LORD,
19:10 so that they may not incur guilt **b** the LORD
20: 5 in the house of the LORD, **b** the new court,
20: 7 the inhabitants of this land **b** your people Israel,
20: 9 we will stand **b** this house, and **b** you,
20:13 Meanwhile all Judah stood **b** the LORD,
20:16 **b** the wilderness of Jeruel.
20:18 and the inhabitants of Jerusalem fell down **b**
20:21 as they went **b** the army, saying,
25: 8 or God will fling you down **b** the enemy;
27: 6 because he ordered his ways **b**
28: 3 of the nations whom the LORD drove out **b**
28:14 and the booty **b** the officials and all the assembly.
31:20 he did what was good and right and faithful **b**
32: 7 Do not be afraid or dismayed **b** the king of Assyria
32:12 saying, '**B** one altar you shall worship,
33: 2 of the nations whom the LORD drove out **b**
33: 9 the LORD had destroyed **b** the people of Israel.
33:12 and humbled himself greatly **b** the God
33:19 and set up the sacred poles and the images, **b**
33:23 He did not humble himself **b** the LORD,
34:24 in the book that was read **b** the king of Judah.
34:27 and you humbled yourself **b** God
34:27 and you have humbled yourself **b** me,
34:27 and have torn your clothes and wept **b** me,
34:31 The king stood in his place and made a covenant **b**
36:12 He did not humble himself **b**
Ezr 4:18 that you sent to us has been read in translation **b**
4:23 of King Artaxerxes' letter was read **b** Rehum and
7:19 you shall deliver **b** the God of Jerusalem.
7:28 to me steadfast love **b** the king and his counselors,
7:28 and **b** all the king's mighty officers.
8:21 that we might deny ourselves **b** our God,
8:29 Guard them and keep them until you weigh them **b**
9: 9 to us his steadfast love **b** the kings of Persia,
9:15 Here we are **b** you in our guilt,
10: 1 weeping and throwing himself down **b** the house
10: 6 Then Ezra withdrew from **b** the house of God,
10: 9 All the people sat in the open square **b** the house
Ne 1: 4 fasting and praying **b** the God of heaven.
1: 6 now pray **b** you day and night for your servants,
2: 1 Now, I had never been sad in his presence **b**.
4:11 "They will not know or see anything **b** we come
5:15 The former governors who were **b**
7: 3 and others **b** their own houses."
8: 1 all the people gathered together into the square **b**
8: 2 the priest Ezra brought the law **b** the assembly,
8: 3 He read from it facing the square **b** the Water Gate
9: 8 and you found his heart faithful **b** you, and made
9:11 And you divided the sea **b** them,
9:24 you subdued **b** them the inhabitants of the land,
9:28 But after they had rest, they again did evil **b** you,
9:35 and in the large and rich land that you set **b** them,
13: 4 Now **b** this, the priest Eliashib,
13:19 to be dark at the gates of Jerusalem **b** the sabbath,
Est 1:11 to bring Queen Vashti **b** the king, wearing
1:17 to be brought **b** him, and she did
1:19 Vashti is never again to come **b** King Ahasuerus;
3: 7 **b** Haman for the day and for the month,
5: 9 observed that he neither rose nor trembled **b** him,
6: 9 through the open square of the city, proclaiming **b**
6:13 "If Mordecai, **b** whom your downfall has begun,
6:13 but will surely fall **b** him."
7: 6 Haman was terrified **b** the king and the queen.
8: 1 and Mordecai came **b** the king,
8: 5 and Esther rose and stood **b** the king.
8: 5 and if the thing seems right **b** the king,
9:25 but when Esther came **b** the king,
Job 1: 6 the heavenly beings came to present themselves **b**
2: 1 the heavenly beings came to present themselves **b**
2: 1 among them to present himself **b** the LORD.
4:16 A form was **b** my eyes; there was silence,
4:17 'Can mortals be righteous **b** God?
4:17 Can human beings be pure **b** their Maker?
8:12 they wither **b** any other plant.
8:16 The wicked thrive **b** the sun,
9: 2 but how can a mortal be just **b** God?
10:18 Would that I had died **b** any eye had seen me,
10:21 **b** I go, never to return, to the land of gloom
13:16 that the godless shall not come **b** him.
15: 4 and hindering meditation **b** God.
15: 7 Were you brought forth **b** the hills?
15:32 It will be paid in full **b** their time,
17: 6 and I am one **b** whom people spit.
21: 8 and their offspring **b** their eyes.

Job 21:18 How often are they like straw **b** the wind,
21:33 and those who went **b** are innumerable.
22:16 They were snatched away **b** their time;
23: 4 I would lay my case **b** him,
25: 4 How then can a mortal be righteous **b** God?
26: 6 Sheol is naked **b** God,
33: 5 set your words in order **b** me; take your stand.
33: 6 See, **b** God I am as you are;
34:23 For he has not appointed a time for anyone to go **b**
35: 2 You say, 'I am in the right **b** God.'
35:14 that the case is **b** him,
41:10 Who can stand **b** it?
41:22 In its neck abides strength, and terror dances **b** it.
42:10 the LORD gave Job twice as much as he had **b**.
42:11 and all who had known him **b**, and they ate bread
Ps 5: 5 The boastful will not stand **b** your eyes;
5: 8 make your way straight **b** me.
9: 3 they stumbled and perished **b** you.
9:19 let the nations be judged **b** you.
16: 8 I keep the LORD always **b** me;
18:12 Out of the brightness **b** him there broke
18:22 For all his ordinances were **b** me,
18:23 I was blameless **b** him, and I kept myself
18:42 I beat them fine, like dust **b** the wind;
22:25 my vows I will pay **b** those who fear him.
22:27 all the families of the nations shall worship **b** him.
22:29 **b** him shall bow all who go down to the dust,
23: 5 a table **b** me in the presence of my enemies;
26: 3 For your steadfast love is **b** my eyes,
34: T *Of David, he feigned madness **b** Abimelech,*
35: 5 Let them be like chaff **b** the wind,
36: 1 there is no fear of God **b** their eyes.
37: 7 Be still **b** the LORD, and wait patiently for him;
39:13 **b** I depart and am no more."
44:15 All day long my disgrace is **b** me,
50: 3 **b** him is a devouring fire,
50: 8 your burnt offerings are continually **b** me.
50:21 But now I rebuke you, and lay the charge **b** you.
51: 3 and my sin is ever **b** me.
54: 3 they do not set God **b** them.
56:13 so that I may walk **b** God in the light of life.
61: 7 May he be enthroned forever **b** God;
62: 8 pour out your heart **b** him; God is a refuge for us.
66: 3 of your great power, your enemies cringe **b** you.
68: 1 let those who hate him flee **b** him.
68: 2 as wax melts **b** the fire,
68: 2 let the wicked perish **b** God.
68: 3 let them exult **b** God; let them be jubilant with joy.
68: 4 his name is the LORD—be exultant **b** him.
68: 7 O God, when you went out **b** your people,
68:28 O God, as you have done for us **b**.
72: 9 May his foes bow down **b** him,
72:11 May all kings fall down **b** him,
76: 7 can stand **b** you when once your anger is
78:30 But **b** they had satisfied their craving,
78:55 He drove out nations **b** them;
79:10 of your servants be known among the nations **b**
79:11 Let the groans of the prisoners come **b** you;
80: 2 **b** Ephraim and Benjamin and Manasseh.
81:15 Those who hate the LORD would cringe **b** him,
83:13 like whirling dust, like chaff **b** the wind.
85:13 Righteousness will go **b** him,
86: 9 and bow down **b** you, O Lord,
86:14 and they do not set you **b** them.
88: 2 let my prayer come **b** you;
88:13 in the morning my prayer comes **b** you.
89:14 steadfast love and faithfulness go **b** you.
89:23 I will crush his foes **b** him and strike
89:36 and his throne endure **b** me like the sun.
90: 2 **B** the mountains were brought forth,
90: 8 You have set our iniquities **b** you,
95: 6 let us kneel **b** the LORD, our Maker!
96: 6 Honor and majesty are **b** him;
96: 9 tremble **b** him, all the earth.
96:13 **b** the LORD; for he is coming,
97: 3 Fire goes **b** him, and consumes his adversaries
97: 5 The mountains melt like wax **b** the LORD,
97: 5 **b** the Lord of all the earth.
97: 7 all gods bow down **b** him.
98: 6 and the sound of the horn make a joyful noise **b**
101: 3 I will not set **b** my eyes anything that is base.
102: T *when faint and pleading **b** the LORD.*
106:23 his chosen one, stood in the breach **b** him,
109:14 May the iniquity of his father be remembered **b**
109:15 Let them be **b** the LORD continually,
116: 9 I walk **b** the LORD in the land of the living.
119:30 I set your ordinances **b** me.
119:46 I will also speak of your decrees **b** kings,
119:67 **B** I was humbled I went astray,
119:147 I rise **b** dawn and cry for help;
119:148 My eyes are awake **b** each watch of the night,
119:168 for all my ways are **b** you.
119:169 Let my cry come **b** you, O LORD;
119:170 Let my supplication come **b** you;
129: 6 the grass on the housetops that withers **b** it grows
138: 1 **b** the gods I sing your praise;
139: 4 Even **b** a word is on my tongue, O LORD,
139: 5 You hem me in, behind and **b**,
141: 2 Let my prayer be counted as incense **b** you,
142: 2 I pour out my complaint **b** him;
142: 2 I tell my trouble **b** him.
143: 2 for no one living is righteous **b** you.
147:17 who can stand **b** his cold?
Pr 4:25 and your gaze be straight **b** you.
8:23 at the first, **b** the beginning of the earth.
8:25 **B** the mountains had been shaped, **b** the hills,
8:30 I was daily his delight, rejoicing **b** him always,

Pr 14:19 The evil bow down **b** the good,
15:11 Sheol and Abaddon lie open **b** the LORD,
15:33 and humility goes **b** honor.
16:18 Pride goes **b** destruction, and a haughty spirit **b** a fall.
17:14 so stop **b** the quarrel breaks out.
18:12 **B** destruction one's heart is haughty, but humility goes **b** honor.
18:13 one gives answer **b** hearing, it is folly and shame.
23: 1 observe carefully what is **b** you,
25:26 the righteous who give way **b** the wicked.
27: 4 but who is able to stand **b** jealousy?
30: 7 do not deny them to me **b** I die:
30:30 among wild animals and does not turn back **b** any;
30:31 the he-goat, and a king striding **b** his people.
Ecc 1:10 It has already been, in the ages **b** us.
1:16 surpassing all who were over Jerusalem **b** me;
2: 7 more than any who had been **b** me in Jerusalem.
2: 9 So I became great and surpassed all who were **b**
3:14 so that all should stand in awe **b** him.
5: 2 nor let your heart be quick to utter a word **b** God,
5: 6 do not say **b** the messenger that it was a mistake;
6: 8 how to conduct themselves **b** the living?
7:17 why should you die **b** your time?
8:12 because they stand in fear **b** him,
8:13 because they do not stand in fear **b** God.
10:11 If the snake bites **b** it is charmed,
12: 1 **b** the days of trouble come,
12: 2 **b** the sun and the light and the moon and
12: 6 **b** the silver cord is snapped,
SS 6:12 **B** I was aware, my fancy set me in a chariot
6:13 as upon a dance **b** two armies?
Isa 1:12 When you come to appear **b** me,
1:16 remove the evil of your doings from **b** my eyes;
1:23 and the widow's cause does not come **b** them.
7: 2 as the trees of the forest shake **b** the wind.
7:16 For **b** the child knows how to refuse the evil
7:16 the land **b** whose two kings you are in dread will
8: 4 for **b** the child knows how to call "My father"
8: 6 and melt in fear **b** Rezin and the son of Remaliah;
9: 3 they rejoice **b** you as with joy at the harvest,
13:16 Their infants will be dashed to pieces **b** their eyes;
17:13 the mountains **b** the wind and whirling dust **b** the
17:14 **B** morning, they are no more.
18: 5 For **b** the harvest, when the blossom is over and
19:16 and tremble with fear **b** the hand that the LORD
24:23 and **b** his elders he will manifest his glory.
28: 4 will be like a first-ripe fig **b** the summer;
30: 8 Go now, write it **b** them on a tablet,
33: 3 **b** your majesty, nations scattered.
36: 7 'You shall worship **b** this altar'?
37:14 up to the house of the LORD and spread it **b**
37:27 like grass on the housetops, blighted **b** it is grown.
37:33 shoot an arrow there, come **b** it with a shield,
38: 3 how I have walked **b** you in faithfulness with
40:10 his reward is with him, and his recompense **b** him.
40:17 All the nations are as nothing **b** him;
42: 9 **b** they spring forth, I tell you of them.
42:16 I will turn the darkness **b** them into light,
43:10 **B** me no god was formed,
44: 7 let them declare and set it forth **b** me.
44:15 makes it a carved image and bows down **b** it.
44:19 Shall I fall down **b** a block of wood?"
45: 1 subdue nations **b** him and strip kings of their robes,
45: 1 open doors **b** him—and the gates shall not be
45: 2 I will go **b** you and level the mountains,
47:14 for warming oneself is this, no fire to sit **b**!
48: 5 **b** they came to pass I announced them to you,
48: 7 **b** today you have never heard of them,
48:19 be cut off or destroyed from **b** me.
49: 1 The LORD called me **b** I was born,
49:16 your walls are continually **b** me.
52:10 The LORD has bared his holy arm **b** the eyes
52:12 for the LORD will go **b** you,
53: 2 For he grew up **b** him like a young plant,
53: 7 and like a sheep that **b** its shearers is silent,
55:12 the mountains and the hills **b** you shall burst
57:16 for then the spirits would grow faint **b** me,
58: 8 your vindicator shall go **b** you,
59:12 For our transgressions **b** you are many,
61:11 and praise to spring up **b** all the nations.
62:11 and his recompense **b** him."
63:12 who divided the waters **b** them to make
65: 6 it is written **b** me: I will
65:24 **B** they call I will answer,
66: 7 **B** she was in labor she gave birth;
66: 7 **b** her pain came upon her she delivered a son.
66:22 which I will make, shall remain **b** me,
66:23 all flesh shall come to worship **b** me,
Jer 1: 5 "**B** I formed you in the womb I knew you,
1: 5 and **b** you were born I consecrated you;
1:17 Do not break down **b** them,
1:17 or I will break you **b** them.
2:22 the stain of your guilt is still **b** me,
4:26 and all its cities were laid in ruins **b** the LORD,
4:26 in ruins before the LORD, **b** his fierce anger.
4:31 I am fainting **b** killers!"
5:22 says the LORD; Do you not tremble **b** me?
6: 7 sickness and wounds are ever **b** me.
6:21 See, I am laying **b** this people stumbling blocks
7:10 and stand **b** me in this house, which is called
8: 2 be spread **b** the sun and the moon and all the host
9:13 they have forsaken my law that I set **b** them,
13:16 to the LORD your God **b** he brings darkness,
13:16 **b** your feet stumble on the mountains at twilight;
13:27 How long will it be **b** you are made clean?
15: 1 Though Moses and Samuel stood **b** me,

Jer 15: 9 of them I will give to the sword **b** their enemies,
15:19 I will take you back, and you shall stand **b** me.
16: 9 in your days and **b** your eyes,
17:16 from my lips; it was **b** your face.
18:17 I will scatter them **b** the enemy.
18:20 Remember how I stood **b** you to speak good
18:23 Let them be tripped up **b** you;
19: 7 will make them fall by the sword **b** their enemies,
21: 8 See, I am setting **b** you the way of life and the way
24: 1 of figs placed **b** the temple of the LORD.
26: 4 to walk in my law that I have set **b** you,
29:21 and he shall kill them **b** your eyes.
30:20 their congregation shall be established **b** me;
31:36 the offspring of Israel would cease to be a nation **b**
33: 4 a defense against the siege ramps and **b** the sword:
33: 9 a glory **b** all the nations of the earth who shall hear
34:15 and you made a covenant **b** me in the house
34:18 the covenant that they made **b** me, I will make like
35: 5 Then I set **b** the Rechabites pitchers full of wine,
35:19 of Rechab shall not lack a descendant to stand **b**
36: 7 It may be that their plea will come **b** the LORD,
36: 9 to Jerusalem proclaimed a fast **b** the LORD.
36:22 and there was a fire burning in the brazier **b** him.
38:10 the prophet Jeremiah up from the cistern **b**
39: 6 the sons of Zedekiah at Riblah **b** his eyes;
40: 4 See, the whole land is **b** you;
40:10 to represent you **b** the Chaldeans who come to us;
41: 4 after the murder of Gedaliah, **b** anyone knew of it,
42: 9 to whom you sent me to present your plea **b** him:
44:10 law and my statutes that I set **b** you and **b** your
47: 1 the prophet Jeremiah concerning the Philistines, **b**
48:43 Terror, pit, and trap are **b** you,
49:19 Who is the shepherd who can stand **b** me?
49:37 I will terrify Elam **b** their enemies,
49:37 and **b** those who seek their life;
50:44 Who is the shepherd who can stand **b** me?
51: 5 their land is full of guilt **b** the Holy One of Israel.
51:24 and all the inhabitants of Chaldea **b** your very eyes
52:10 The king of Babylon killed the sons of Zedekiah **b**
La 1: 5 her children have gone away, captives **b** the foe.
1: 6 they fled without strength **b** the pursuer.
1:22 Let all their evil doing come **b** you;
2:19 Pour out your heart like water **b** the presence of
Eze 2:10 He spread it **b** me; it had writing on the
3:20 and I lay a stumbling block **b** them, they shall die;
4: 1 And you, O mortal, take a brick and set it **b** you.
8: 1 with the elders of Judah sitting **b** me,
8:11 **B** them stood seventy of the elders of the house
14: 1 Certain elders of Israel came to me and sat down **b**
14: 3 placed their iniquity as a stumbling block **b** them;
14: 4 and place their iniquity as a stumbling block **b**
14: 7 and placing their iniquity as a stumbling block **b**
16:18 and set my oil and my incense **b** them.
16:19 you set it **b** them as a pleasing odor;
16:50 and did abominable things **b** me;
16:57 **b** your wickedness was uncovered?
20: 1 to consult the LORD, and sat down **b** me.
21: 6 with breaking heart and bitter grief **b** their eyes.
22: 4 I have made you a disgrace **b** the nations,
22:30 and stand in the breach **b** me on behalf of the land,
23:41 with a table spread **b** it
28:17 I exposed you **b** kings, to feast their eyes on you.
30:24 the arms of Pharaoh, and he will groan **b** him with
32:10 When I brandish my sword **b** them,
33:22 of the LORD had been upon me the evening **b**
33:31 and they sit **b** you as my people,
36:11 and will do more good to you than ever **b**.
36:23 through you I display my holiness **b** their eyes.
37:20 on which you write are in your hand **b** their eyes,
38:16 O Gog, I display my holiness **b** their eyes.
40:12 There was a barrier **b** the recesses,
41:22 "This is the table that stands **b** the LORD."
42:14 they shall put on other garments **b** they go near to
43:24 You shall present them **b** the LORD,
44: 3 may sit in it to eat food **b** the LORD;
44:12 Because they ministered to them **b** their idols
46: 3 down at the entrance of that gate **b** the LORD on
46: 9 When the people of the land come **b** the LORD at
Da 2: 2 When they came in and stood **b** the king,
2:24 bring me in **b** the king,
2:25 Then Arioch quickly brought Daniel **b** the king
2:31 its brilliance extraordinary; it was standing **b** you,
3: 3 When they were standing **b** the statue
3:13 so they brought those men **b** the king.
4: 6 the wise men of Babylon should be brought **b** me,
4: 8 At last Daniel came in **b** me—
5:13 Then Daniel was brought in **b** the king.
5:15 have been brought in **b** me to read this writing
5:19 nations, and languages trembled and feared **b** him.
5:23 vessels of his temple have been brought in **b** you,
6:11 and found Daniel praying and seeking mercy **b**
6:22 because I was found blameless **b** him;
6:22 and also **b** you, O king, I have done no wrong."
6:24 **B** they reached the bottom of the den
6:26 and fear **b** the God of Daniel:
7:13 to the Ancient One and was presented **b** him.
8:15 Then someone appeared standing **b** me,
9:10 which he set **b** us by his servants the prophets.
9:12 against Jerusalem has never **b** been done under
9:18 not present our supplication **b** you on the ground
9:20 and presenting my supplication **b**
9:21 the man Gabriel, whom I had seen **b** in a vision,
10:12 to gain understanding and to humble yourself **b**
10:16 and said to the one who stood **b** me, "My lord,
11:22 Armies shall be utterly swept away and broken **b**
11:29 but this time it shall not be as it was **b**.
Hos 6: 2 up, that we may live **b** him.
Hos 7: 2 their deeds surround them, they are **b** my face.
Joel 1:16 Is not the food cut off **b** our eyes,
2: 3 **B** them the land is like the garden of Eden,
2: 6 **B** them peoples are in anguish,
2:10 The earth quakes **b** them, the heavens tremble.
2:23 the early and the later rain, as **b**.
2:31 **b** the great and terrible day of the LORD comes.
Am 1: 1 two years **b** the earthquake.
2: 9 Yet I destroyed the Amorite **b** them,
Jnh 1: 2 for their wickedness has come up **b** me."
Mic 2:13 The one who breaks out will go up **b** them;
2:13 Their king will pass on **b** them,
6: 1 Rise, plead your case **b** the mountains,
6: 4 and I sent **b** you Moses, Aaron, and Miriam.
6: 6 "With what shall I come **b** the LORD,
6: 6 and bow myself **b** God on high?
6: 6 Shall I come **b** him with burnt offerings,
Na 1: 5 The mountains quake **b** him, and the hills melt;
1: 5 the earth heaves **b** him, the world and all who live
1: 6 Who can stand **b** his indignation?
Hab 1: 3 Destruction and violence are **b** me;
2:20 let all the earth keep silence **b** him!
3: 5 **B** him went pestilence,
Zep 1: 7 Be silent **b** the Lord GOD!
2: 2 **b** you are driven away like the drifting chaff,
2: 2 **b** there comes upon you the fierce anger
2: 2 **b** there comes upon you the day of the LORD's
3:20 when I restore your fortunes **b** your eyes,
Hag 2:14 So is it with this people, and with this nation **b** me,
2:15 **B** a stone was placed upon a stone in
Zec 2:13 Be silent, all people, **b** the LORD;
3: 1 the high priest Joshua standing **b** the angel of
3: 3 with filthy clothes as he stood **b** the angel.
3: 4 The angel said to those who were standing **b** him,
3: 8 you and your colleagues who sit **b** you!
3: 9 For on the stone that I have set **b** Joshua,
4: 7 **B** Zerubbabel you shall become a plain;
6: 5 after presenting themselves **b** the LORD of all
8:10 For **b** those days there were no wages for people
10: 8 and they shall be as numerous as they were **b**.
14: 4 which lies **b** Jerusalem on the east;
Mal 2: 9 I make you despised and abased **b** all the people,
3: 1 I am sending my messenger to prepare the way **b**
3:14 or by going about as mourners **b** the LORD
3:16 and a book of remembrance was written **b** him
4: 5 the prophet Elijah **b** the great and terrible day of
Mt 1:18 to Joseph, but **b** they lived together, she was found
5:12 the prophets who were **b** you.
5:16 In the same way, let your light shine **b** others,
5:24 leave your gift there **b** the altar and go;
6: 1 "Beware of practicing your piety **b** others in order
6: 2 do not sound a trumpet **b** you,
6: 8 your Father knows what you need **b** you ask him.
7: 6 and do not throw your pearls **b** swine,
8: 2 and there was a leper who came to him and knelt **b**
8:29 Have you come here to torment us **b** the time?"
9:18 a leader of the synagogue came in and knelt **b** him,
10:18 be dragged **b** governors and kings because of me,
10:23 not have gone through all the towns of Israel **b**
10:32 "Everyone therefore who acknowledges me **b**
10:32 I also will acknowledge **b** my Father in heaven;
10:33 but whoever denies me **b** others,
10:33 I also will deny **b** my Father in heaven.
11:10 who will prepare your way **b** you.'
13:24 He put **b** them another parable:
13:31 He put **b** them another parable:
14: 6 the daughter of Herodias danced **b** the company,
15: 2 For they do not wash their hands **b** they eat."
15:25 But she came and knelt **b** him, saying, "Lord,
16:28 not taste death **b** they see the Son of Man coming
17: 2 And he was transfigured **b** them,
17:14 a man came to him, knelt **b** him,
18: 6 "If any of you put a stumbling block **b** one
18:26 So the slave fell on his knees **b** him, saying,
20:20 and kneeling **b** him, she asked a favor of him.
24:38 For as in those days **b** the flood they were eating
25:32 All the nations will be gathered **b** him,
26:34 "Truly I tell you, this very night, **b** the cock crows,
26:63 "I put you under oath **b** the living God,
26:70 But he denied it **b** all of them, saying,
26:75 "**B** the cock crows, you will deny me three times."
27:11 Now Jesus stood **b** the governor;
27:24 he took some water and washed his hands **b**
27:29 in his right hand and knelt **b** him and mocked him,
27:62 chief priests and the Pharisees gathered **b** Pilate
Mk 2:12 and immediately took the mat and went out **b** all
3:11 they fell down **b** him and shouted,
5: 6 he ran and bowed down **b** him;
5:33 fell down **b** him, and told him the whole truth.
6:41 and gave them to his disciples to set **b** the people;
9: 2 And he was transfigured **b** them,
9:42 "If any of you put a stumbling block **b** one
10:17 a man ran up and knelt **b** him, and asked him,
13: 9 and you will stand **b** governors and kings because
14: 1 It was two days **b** the Passover and the festival
14:28 after I am raised up, I will go **b** you to Galilee."
14:30 this day, this very night, **b** the cock crows twice,
14:60 the high priest stood up **b** them and asked Jesus,
14:72 to him, "**B** the cock crows twice,
15:42 that is, the day **b** the sabbath,
Lk 1: 6 Both of them were righteous **b** God,
1: 8 as priest **b** God and his section was on duty,
1:15 **b** his birth he will be filled with the Holy Spirit.
1:17 With the spirit and power of Elijah he will go **b**
1:75 in holiness and righteousness **b** him all our days.
1:76 for you will go **b** the Lord to prepare his ways,
2: 9 Then an angel of the Lord stood **b** them,
Lk 2:21 the name given by the angel **b** he was conceived in
2:26 by the Holy Spirit that he would not see death **b**
4:35 When the demon had thrown him down **b** them,
5:18 They were trying to bring him in and lay him **b**
5:25 Immediately he stood up **b** them,
7:27 who will prepare your way **b** you.'
8:28 down **b** him and shouted at the top of his voice,
8:47 down **b** him, she declared in the presence of all
9:16 and gave them to the disciples to set **b** the crowd.
9:27 not taste death **b** they see the kingdom of God."
10: 8 eat what is set **b** you;
11: 6 and I have nothing to set **b** him.'
11:38 to see that he did not first wash **b** dinner.
12: 8 everyone who acknowledges me **b** others,
12: 8 also will acknowledge **b** the angels of God;
12: 9 but whoever denies me **b** others will be denied **b** the angels of God.
12:11 When they bring you **b** the synagogues, the rulers,
12:58 when you go with your accuser **b** a magistrate,
12:58 or you may be dragged **b** the judge,
15:18 "Father, I have sinned against heaven and **b** you;
15:21 'Father, I have sinned against heaven and **b** you;
21:12 "But **b** all this occurs, they will arrest you
21:12 and you will be brought **b** kings and governors
21:36 and to stand **b** the Son of Man."
22:15 to eat this Passover with you **b** I suffer;
22:61 how he had said to him, "**B** the cock crows today,
23: 1 the assembly rose as a body and brought Jesus **b**
23:12 **b** this they had been enemies.
24:19 a prophet mighty in deed and word **b** God and all
Jn 1:15 after me ranks ahead of me because he was **b**
1:30 a man who ranks ahead of me because he was **b**
1:48 "I saw you under the fig tree **b** Philip called you."
4:49 "Sir, come down **b** my little boy dies."
5:45 Do not think that I will accuse you **b** the Father;
6:62 the Son of Man ascending to where he was **b?**
7:50 Nicodemus, who had gone to Jesus **b**,
8: 3 ⟦and making her stand **b** all of them,⟧
8: 9 ⟦with the woman standing **b** him.⟧
8:58 "Very truly, I tell you, **b** Abraham was, I am."
9: 8 and those who had seen him **b** as a beggar began
10: 8 All who came **b** me are thieves and bandits;
11:55 and many went up from the country to Jerusalem **b**
12: 1 Six days **b** the Passover Jesus came to Bethany,
13: 1 Now **b** the festival of the Passover,
13:19 I tell you this now, **b** it occurs,
13:38 Very truly, I tell you, **b** the cock crows,
14:29 And now I have told you this **b** it occurs,
15:18 be aware that it hated me **b** it hated you.
17: 5 that I had in your presence **b** the world existed.
17:24 which you have given me because you loved me **b**
Ac 2:20 **b** the coming of the Lord's great and glorious day.
2:25 'I saw the Lord always **b** me,
4:10 that this man is standing **b** you in good health by
5:27 they had them stand **b** the council.
6: 6 They had these men stand **b** the apostles,
6:12 seized him, and brought him **b** the council.
7: 2 when he was in Mesopotamia, **b** he lived in Haran,
7:10 to win favor and to show wisdom when he stood **b**
7:20 and he was beautiful **b** God.
7:45 the nations that God drove out **b** our ancestors.
8:21 for your heart is not right **b** God.
8:32 and like a lamb silent **b** its shearer,
9:15 to bring my name **b** Gentiles and kings and **b**
9:21 of bringing them bound **b** the chief priests?"
10: 4 and your alms have ascended as a memorial **b**
10:30 when suddenly a man in dazzling clothes stood **b**
10:31 and your alms have been remembered **b** God.
12: 6 very night **b** Herod was going to bring him out,
12:10 they came **b** the iron gate leading into the city.
13:24 **b** his coming John had already proclaimed
16:19 and Silas and dragged them into the marketplace **b**
16:20 When they had brought them **b** the magistrates,
16:29 he fell down trembling **b** Paul and Silas.
16:34 He brought them up into the house and set food **b**
17: 6 and some believers **b** the city authorities,
18:12 a united attack on Paul and brought him **b**
19: 9 and spoke evil of the Way **b** the congregation,
19:33 and tried to make a defense **b** the people.
22: 1 listen to the defense that I now make **b** you."
22:30 He brought Paul down and had him stand **b** them.
23: 1 with a clear conscience **b** God."
23:15 we are ready to do away with him **b** he arrives."
23:30 also to state **b** you what they have against him."
23:33 they presented Paul also **b** him.
24:19 they ought to be here **b** you to make an accusation,
24:20 when I stood **b** the council,
24:21 that I called out while standing **b** them,
24:21 the resurrection of the dead that I am on trial **b**
25: 9 to go up to Jerusalem and be tried there **b** me
25:14 Festus laid Paul's case **b** the king, saying,
25:16 the custom of the Romans to hand over anyone **b**
25:26 Therefore I have brought him **b** all of you,
25:26 and especially **b** you, King Agrippa, so that,
26: 2 "I consider myself fortunate that it is **b** you,
27:24 you must stand **b** the emperor;
27:33 Just **b** daybreak, Paul urged all of them
Ro 3:18 "There is no fear of God **b** their eyes."
4: 2 he has something to boast about, but not **b** God.
4:10 Was it **b** or after he had been circumcised?
4:10 It was not after, but **b** he was circumcised.
4:12 of the faith that our ancestor Abraham had **b**
5:13 sin was indeed in the world **b** the law,
9:11 Even **b** they had been born
14: 4 It is **b** their own lord that they stand or fall.
14:10 For we will all stand **b** the judgment seat of God.
14:22 have as your own conviction **b** God.

Ro 16: 7 and they were in Christ **b** I was.
1Co 2: 7 which God decreed **b** the ages for our glory.
4: 5 Therefore do not pronounce judgment **b** the time,
4: 5 the time, **b** the Lord comes, who will bring to light
6: 1 do you dare to take it to court **b** the unrighteous,
6: 1 instead of taking it **b** the saints?
6: 6 and **b** unbelievers at that?
10:27 eat whatever is set **b** you
14:25 person will bow down **b** God and worship him,
2Co 5:10 of us must appear **b** the judgment seat of Christ,
7: 3 for I said **b** that you are in our hearts,
7:12 for us might be made known to you **b** God.
8:24 Therefore openly **b** the churches,
10: 7 Look at what is **b** your eyes.
12:19 along that we have been defending ourselves **b**
12:19 We are speaking in Christ **b** God.
12:21 my God may humble me **b** you,
Gal 1: 9 As we have said **b,** so now I repeat,
1:15 who had set me apart **b** I was born and called me
1:17 to Jerusalem to those who were already apostles **b**
1:20 In what I am writing to you, **b** God, I do not lie!
2: 2 Then I laid **b** them (though only in
2:14 I said to Cephas **b** them all, "If you, though a Jew,
3: 1 **b** your eyes that Jesus Christ was publicly
3:11 Now it is evident that no one is justified **b** God by
3:23 Now **b** faith came, we were imprisoned
5:21 I am warning you, as I warned you **b:**
Eph 1: 4 in Christ **b** the foundation of the world to be holy
and blameless **b** him in love.
3:14 For this reason I bow my knees **b** the Father,
Col 1: 5 You have heard of this hope **b** in the word of
1:17 He himself is **b** all things,
1:22 and blameless and irreproachable **b** him—
1Th 1: 3 remembering **b** our God and Father your work
2:19 For what is our hope or joy or crown of boasting **b**
3: 9 the joy that we feel **b** our God because of you?
3:13 be blameless **b** our God and Father at the coming
1Ti 4: 6 If you put these instructions **b** the brothers
6:13 who in his testimony **b** Pontius Pilate made
2Ti 1: 9 This grace was given to us in Christ Jesus **b**
2:14 and warn them **b** God that they are
4:21 Do your best to come **b** winter.
Tit 1: 2 who never lies, promised **b** the ages began—
Heb 4:13 And **b** him no creature is hidden,
6:18 be strongly encouraged to seize the hope set **b** us.
11: 5 For it was attested **b** he was taken away
12: 1 with perseverance the race that is set **b** us,
12: 2 for the sake of the joy that was set **b** him endured
Jas 1:27 Religion that is pure and undefiled **b** God,
4:10 Humble yourselves **b** the Lord,
1Pe 1:20 He was destined **b** the foundation of the world,
1Jn 2:28 and not be put to shame **b** him at his coming.
3:19 from the truth and will reassure our hearts **b** him
3:21 not condemn us, we have boldness **b** God;
3Jn 1: 6 they have testified to your love **b** the church.
Jude 1:25 and authority, **b** all time and now and forever.
Rev 1: 4 and from the seven spirits who are **b** his throne,
2:14 to put a stumbling block **b** the people of Israel,
3: 5 I will confess your name **b** my Father and **b**
3: 8 Look, I have set **b** you an open door,
3: 9 I will make them come and bow down **b** your feet,
4:10 the twenty-four elders fall **b** the one who is seated
4:10 they cast their crowns **b** the throne, singing,
5: 8 and the twenty-four elders fell **b** the Lamb,
6:10 be **b** you judge and avenge our blood on
7: 9 standing **b** the throne and **b** the Lamb,
7:11 on their faces **b** the throne and worshiped God,
7:15 For this reason they are **b** the throne of God,
8: 2 And I saw the seven angels who stand **b** God,
8: 3 the saints on the golden altar that is **b** the throne.
8: 4 rose **b** God from the hand of the angel.
9:13 a voice from the four horns of the golden altar **b**
11: 4 and the two lampstands that stand **b** the Lord of
11:16 the twenty-four elders who sit on their thrones **b**
12: 4 the dragon stood **b** the woman who was about
12:10 who accuses them day and night **b** our God.
14: 3 and they sing a new song **b** the throne
14: 3 **b** the four living creatures and **b** the elders.
15: 4 All nations will come and worship **b** you,
20:12 standing **b** the throne, and books were opened.
Tob 1:21 But not forty days passed **b** two
2: 2 for me and an abundance of food placed **b** me,
2: 4 Then I sprang up, left the dinner **b** even tasting it,
2:10 and Ahikar took care of me for two years **b**
3: 3 and those that my ancestors committed **b** you.
3: 5 and have not walked in accordance with truth **b**
3: 8 of them **b** they had been with her as is customary
3:17 to have her **b** all others who had desired
4: 2 and explain to him about the money **b** I die?"
5:17 **B** he went out to start his journey,
5:18 the staff of our hand as he goes in and out **b** us?
6:12 have **b** all other men a hereditary claim on her.
6:18 she was set apart for you **b** the world was made.
8:18 Then he ordered his servants to fill in the grave **b**
10:11 and may I see children of yours **b** I die."
10:12 to see children of you and of my daughter Sarah **b**
11: 7 **b** he had approached his father,
11:17 **B** them all, Tobit acknowledged
12:12 the record of your prayer **b** the glory of the Lord,
12:15 of the seven angels who stand ready and enter **b**
13: 3 Acknowledge him **b** the nations,
13: 6 to do what is true **b** him,
13: 6 you sinners, and do what is right **b** him;
14:15 **B** he died he heard of the destruction of Nineveh,
14:15 **b** he died he rejoiced over Nineveh,
Jdt 2: 2 and set **b** them his secret plan and recounted fully,
3: 2 the Great King, lie prostrate **b** you.
Jdt 3: 3 and herds and all our encampments lie **b** you;
4:11 at Jerusalem prostrated themselves **b** the temple
4:11 on their heads and spread out their sackcloth **b**
4:13 throughout Judea and in Jerusalem **b** the sanctuary
4:14 the priests who stood **b** the Lord and ministered to
5:13 Then God dried up the Red Sea **b** them,
5:16 They drove out **b** them the Canaanites,
6:14 and brought him into Bethulia and placed him **b**
7:14 and **b** the sword reaches them they will be strewn
7:23 and said **b** all the elders,
7:25 to be strewn **b** them in thirst and exhaustion.
7:27 and we shall not witness our little ones dying **b**
8: 6 except the day **b** the sabbath and the sabbath itself,
8: 6 day **b** the new moon and the day of the new moon,
8:19 so they suffered a great catastrophe **b** our enemies.
8:35 "Go in peace, and may the Lord God go **b** you,
9: 5 and those that went **b** and those that followed.
10:16 When you stand **b** him, have no fear in your heart,
10:22 with silver lamps carried **b** him.
12: 4 the supplies I have with me **b** the Lord carries out
12:15 and spread for her on the ground **b** Holofernes
12:19 and ate and drank **b** him.
13:20 walking in the straight path **b** our God."
14: 3 and they will flee **b** you.
14: 5 But **b** you do all this,
15:13 She went **b** all the people in the dance,
15:14 Judith began this thanksgiving **b** all Israel,
16:12 they perished **b** the army of my Lord.
16:15 **b** your glance the rocks shall melt like wax.
16:20 the people continued feasting in Jerusalem **b**
16:24 **B** she died she distributed her property
AdE 6:13 and you have begun to be humiliated **b** him,
8: 4 and she rose and stood **b** the king.
10:11 to the hour and moment and day of decision **b** God
10:13 with an assembly and joy and gladness **b** God,
13:18 for their death was **b** their eyes.
14: 6 And now we have sinned **b** you,
14:13 Put eloquent speech in my mouth **b** the lion,
15: 6 through all the doors, she stood **b** the king.
16: 9 and always judging what comes **b** our eyes
Wis 2: 8 Let us crown ourselves with rosebuds **b**
4: 5 The branches will be broken off **b** they come
5:14 it is dispersed like smoke **b** the wind,
7: 9 and silver will be accounted as clay **b** her.
10: 5 the righteous man and preserved him blameless **b**
11:14 they had mockingly rejected him who long **b**
11:22 Because the whole world **b** you is like a speck
12:12 Or who will come **b** you to plead as an advocate
12:27 as the true God the one whom they had **b** refused
14:20 as an object of worship the one whom shortly **b**
15: 8 of earth a short time **b** and after a little while go to
16:28 that one must rise **b** the sun to give you thanks,
19: 7 and dry land emerging where water had stood **b,**
Sir 1: 4 Wisdom was created **b** all other things,
1:29 Do not be a hypocrite **b** others,
1:30 and overthrow you **b** the whole congregation,
2:17 and humble themselves **b** him.
7: 5 Do not assert your righteousness **b** the Lord,
7: 5 or display your wisdom **b** the king.
11: 7 Do not find fault **b** you investigate;
11: 8 Do not answer **b** you listen,
11:28 Call no one happy **b** his death;
14:13 Do good to friends **b** you die,
15:16 He has placed **b** you fire and water;
15:17 **B** each person are life and death,
17:19 All their works are as clear as the sun **b** him,
17:20 and all their sins are **b** the Lord.
18:19 **B** you speak, learn;
18:19 and **b** you fall ill, take care of your health.
18:20 **B** judgment comes, examine yourself;
18:21 **B** falling ill, humble yourself;
18:23 **B** making a vow, prepare yourself;
18:26 all things move swiftly **b** the Lord.
19:17 Question your neighbor **b** you threaten him;
23: 3 and I may fall **b** my adversaries,
23:20 **B** the universe was created, it was known to him,
23:24 She herself will be brought **b** the assembly,
24: 9 **B** the ages, in the beginning, he created me,
24:10 In the holy tent I ministered **b** him,
26:24 *will even be embarrassed* ***b*** *her husband.*
27: 7 Do not praise anyone **b** he speaks,
27:29 and pain will consume them **b** their death.
31:16 Eat what is set **b** you like
31:18 do not help yourself **b** they do.
32:10 and approval goes **b** one who is modest.
34:24 a son **b** his father's eyes is the person who offers
35: 6 Do not appear **b** the Lord empty-handed,
35: 8 and its pleasing odor rises **b** the Most High.
39: 4 He serves among the great and appears **b** rulers;
39:19 The works of all are **b** him,
40:16 by any water or river bank are plucked up **b**
41: 3 remember those who went **b** you
41:17 Be ashamed of sexual immorality, **b** your father
41:17 and of a lie, **b** a prince or a ruler;
41:18 of a crime, **b** a judge or magistrate;
41:18 **b** the congregation and the people;
41:18 of unjust dealing, **b** your partner or your friend;
41:20 and of silence, **b** those who greet you;
41:22 of abusive words, **b** friends—
42:12 Do not let her parade her beauty **b** any man,
45:13 **B** him such beautiful things did not exist.
46: 3 Who **b** him ever stood so firm?
46:19 **B** the time of his eternal sleep,
46:19 Samuel bore witness **b** the Lord and his anointed:
47: 9 He placed singers **b** the altar,
48:10 to calm the wrath of God **b** it breaks out in fury,
48:12 Never in his lifetime did he tremble **b** any ruler,
Sir 48:25 and the hidden things **b** they happened.
50:13 in their hands **b** the whole congregation of Israel.
50:16 a mighty fanfare as a reminder **b** the Most High.
50:19 of the Lord Most High offered their prayers **b**
51:13 **b** I went on my travels,
51:14 **B** the temple I asked for her,
Bar 1: 5 they wept, and fasted, and prayed **b** the Lord;
1:17 because we have sinned **b** the Lord.
1:18 to walk in the statutes of the Lord that he set **b** us.
2:10 to walk in the statutes of the Lord that he set **b** us.
2:19 of our ancestors or our kings that we bring **b**
2:33 of their ancestors, who sinned **b** the Lord.
3: 2 and have mercy, for we have sinned **b** you.
3: 4 the children of those who sinned **b** you,
LtJ 6: 2 of the sins that you have committed **b** God,
6: 6 the multitude **b** and behind them worshiping them.
6:27 Gifts are placed **b** them just as **b** the dead.
6:32 They howl and shout **b** their gods as some do at
Aza 1:15 to make an offering **b** you and to find mercy.
Sus 1:15 she went in as **b** with only two maids,
1:34 up **b** the people and laid their hands on her head.
1:42 and are aware of all things **b** they come to be;
Bel 1:42 and they were instantly eaten **b** his eyes.
1Mc 1: 3 When the earth became quiet **b** him,
1:18 and Ptolemy turned and fled **b** him,
3:22 He himself will crush them **b** us;
3:23 and they were crushed **b** him.
3:30 not have such funds as he had **b** for his expenses
4:10 with our ancestors and crush this army **b** us today.
4:17 for there is a battle **b** us;
4:60 and trampling them down as they had done **b.**
5: 1 and the sanctuary dedicated as it was **b,**
5: 7 and they were crushed **b** him;
5:21 and the Gentiles were crushed **b** him.
5:34 they fled **b** him, and he dealt them a heavy blow.
5:43 All the Gentiles were defeated **b** him,
5:44 they could stand **b** Judas no longer.
5:52 Then they crossed the Jordan into the large plain **b**
5:55 in Gilead and their brother Simon was in Galilee **b**
6: 6 but had turned and fled **b** the Jews;
6: 7 the sanctuary with high walls as **b,**
6:45 and they parted **b** him on both sides.
6:51 Then he encamped **b** the sanctuary for many days.
6:59 to let them live by their laws as they did **b;**
7:12 a group of scribes appeared in a body **b** Alcimus
7:36 At this the priests went in and stood **b** the altar and
7:42 So also crush this army **b** us today;
9:44 for today things are not as they were **b.**
10: 4 with him **b** he makes peace with Alexander
10:34 and the three days **b** a festival and the three after
10:72 People will tell you that you cannot stand **b** us,
10:75 He encamped **b** Joppa, but the people of
11:38 that the land was quiet **b** him and
11:52 and the land was quiet **b** him.
11:65 Simon encamped **b** Beth-zur and fought against it
12:24 with a larger force than **b,**
14:19 And these were read **b** the assembly in Jerusalem.
15: 5 to you all the tax remissions that the kings **b**
2Mc 3:15 The priests prostrated themselves **b** the altar
3:30 a little while **b** was full of fear and disturbance,
4:44 three men sent by the senate presented the case **b**
4:47 if they had pleaded even **b** Scythians.
5: 8 Accused **b** Aretas the ruler of the Arabs,
6:29 a little **b** had acted toward him with goodwill
8:14 by the ungodly Nicanor **b** he ever met them,
8:17 keeping **b** their eyes the lawless outrage that
8:26 It was the day **b** the sabbath,
9: 8 while **b** had thought in his superhuman arrogance
9:10 to carry the man who a little while **b** had thought
10: 6 remembering how not long **b,**
10:13 As a result he was accused **b** Eupator by
10:24 Timothy, who had been defeated by the Jews **b,**
10:26 Falling upon the steps **b** the altar,
11:18 the king of everything that needed to be brought **b**
12:27 Stalwart young men took their stand **b** the walls
13:13 of God **b** the king's army could enter Judea
14:14 Gentiles throughout Judea, who had fled **b** Judas,
15:23 send a good angel to spread terror and trembling **b**
15:31 and stationed the priests **b** the altar,
15:36 the day **b** Mordecai's day.
1Es 1: 5 who minister **b** your kindred the people of Israel,
1:11 **b** the people, to make the offering to the Lord
1:33 and the things that he had done **b,**
3:22 and **b** long they draw their swords.
5: 6 who spoke wise words **b** King Darius of
5:47 they gathered with a single purpose in the square **b**
7:14 of unleavened bread seven days, rejoicing **b**
8: 4 for he found favor **b** the king in all his requests.
8:50 There I proclaimed a fast for the young men **b**
8:74 "O Lord, I am ashamed and confused **b** your face.
8:90 See, we are now **b** you in our iniquities;
8:91 weeping and lying on the ground **b** the temple,
9: 6 the multitude sat in the open square **b** the temple,
9:38 with one accord in the open square **b** the east gate
9:41 He read aloud in the open square **b** the gate of
Man 1: 4 and tremble **b** your power,
3Mc 1:24 Meanwhile the crowd, as **b,**
4: 4 perceiving the common object of pity **b** their eyes,
4: 8 seeing death immediately **b** them.
4:14 the hard labor that has been briefly mentioned **b,**
5:50 the help that they had received **b** from heaven,
6:35 The Jews, as we have said **b,**
2Es 1:11 I destroyed all nations **b** them,
1:21 the Perizzites, and the Philistines **b** you.
2: 3 because you have sinned **b** the Lord God
3: 6 into the garden that your right hand had planted **b**
4: 3 and to put **b** you three problems.

2Es 4:14 that it may recede **b** us and so that we may make
4:48 and lo, a flaming furnace passed by **b** me,
4:49 And after this a cloud full of water passed **b** me
5:41 but what will those do who lived **b** me, or we,
5:50 now given me the opportunity, let me speak **b** you.
5:52 not like those whom you bore **b**,
5:54 in stature than those who were **b** you,
6: 1 **b** the portals of the world were in place,
6: 1 and **b** the assembled winds blew,
6: 2 and **b** the rumblings of thunder sounded,
6: 2 and **b** the flashes of lightning shone,
6: 2 and **b** the foundations of paradise were laid,
6: 3 and **b** the beautiful flowers were seen,
6: 3 and **b** the powers of movements were established,
6: 3 and **b** the innumerable hosts
6: 4 and **b** the heights of the air were lifted up,
6: 4 and **b** the measures of the firmaments were named,
6: 4 and **b** the footstool of Zion was established,
6: 5 and **b** the present years were reckoned
6: 5 and **b** the imaginations of those who now sin
6: 5 and **b** those who stored up treasures
6:20 books shall be opened **b** the face of the firmament,
6:35 and fasted seven days in the same way as **b**,
6:42 be planted and cultivated and be of service **b** you.
6:53 the earth to bring forth **b** you cattle, wild animals,
6:55 "All this I have spoken **b** you, O Lord,
7:20 the law of God that is set **b** them be disregarded!
8: 6 grant to your servant that we may pray **b** you,
8:17 I will pray **b** you for myself and for them,
8:19 and I will speak **b** you."
8:19 of the words of Ezra's prayer, **b** he was taken up.
8:21 **b** whom the hosts of angels stand trembling
8:48 But even in this respect you will be praiseworthy **b**
9:15 "I said **b**, and I say now, and will say it again:
9:18 **b** the world was made for them to live in,
9:27 my heart was troubled again as it was **b**.
9:28 and I began to speak **b** the Most High, and said,
10:34 so that I may not die **b** my time.
10:45 that there were three thousand years in the world **b**
11:16 I announce this to you **b** you disappear.
11:32 over the world than all the wings that had gone **b**.
11:40 have conquered all the beasts that have gone **b**;
11:43 Your insolence has come up **b** the Most High,
12: 7 and if I have been accounted righteous **b** you
12: 7 and if my prayer has indeed come up **b** your face,
12:13 the kingdoms that have been **b** it.
12:24 more oppressively than all who were **b**
12:32 will display **b** them their contemptuous dealings.
12:33 first he will bring them alive **b** his judgment seat,
13:32 and the signs occur that I showed you **b**,
15:11 and will strike Egypt with plagues, as **b**,
16:53 "I have not sinned **b** God and his glory."
16:65 be put to shame when your sins come out **b** others,
16:66 will you hide your sins **b** the Lord and his glory?
4Mc 4:12 the blessedness of the holy place **b** all people.
5: 4 leader of the flock, was brought **b** the king.
5: 6 "**B** I begin to torture you,
6:15 We will set **b** you some cooked meat;
8: 3 were brought **b** him along with their aged mother.
8:13 When the guards had placed **b** them wheels
9:27 **B** torturing him, they inquired if he were willing
12: 4 will be miserably tortured and die **b** your time,
13: 3 Instead, by reason, which is praised **b** God,
13:15 the soul and the danger of eternal torment lying **b**
13:18 or betray the brothers who have died **b** us."
17: 5 stand in honor **b** God and are firmly set in heaven
17:18 now stand **b** the divine throne and live the life

BEFOREHAND (16) [BEFORE]

Isa 41:26 and **b**, so that we might say, "He is right"?
Mt 24:25 Take note, I have told you **b**.
Mk 13:11 do not worry **b** about what you are to say;
14: 8 she has anointed my body **b** for its burial.
Ro 1: 2 which he promised **b** through his prophets in
9:23 which he has prepared **b** for glory—
Gal 3: 8 declared the gospel **b** to Abraham, saying,
Eph 2:10 which God prepared **b** to be our way of life.
1Th 3: 4 we told you **b** that we were to suffer persecution;
4: 6 just as we have already told you **b**
Wis 18: 6 That night was made known **b** to our ancestors,
1Mc 6:36 These took their position **b** wherever
3Mc 6:22 because of the things that he had devised **b**.
2Es 8:52 goodness is established and wisdom perfected **b**.
16:38 around her womb for two or three hours **b**,
4Mc 4:25 they had known **b** that they would suffer this—

BEG (31) [BEGGAR, BEGGARLY, BEGGED, BEGGING, BEGS]

Ge 19: 7 "I **b** you, my brothers, do not act so wickedly.
50:17 I **b** you, forgive the crime of your brothers and
2Sa 13:13 Now therefore, I **b** you, speak to the king;
Est 7: 7 but Haman stayed to **b** his life from Queen Esther,
Ps 109:10 May his children wander about and **b**;
Jer 44: 4 "I **b** you not to do this abominable thing
La 4: 4 the children **b** for food, but no one gives them
Hos 5:15 In their distress they will **b** my favor:
Am 7: 2 I said, "O Lord GOD, forgive, I **b** you!
7: 5 Then I said, "O Lord GOD, cease, I **b** you!
Mk 5:17 they began to **b** Jesus to leave their neighborhood.
Lk 8:28 I **b** you, do not torment me"—
9:38 I **b** you to look at my son; he is my only child.
16: 3 and I am ashamed to **b**.
16:27 father, I **b** you to send him to my father's house—
Jn 9: 8 "Is this not the man who used to sit and **b**?"
Ac 21:39 I **b** you, let me speak to the people."
Ac 24: 4 I **b** you to hear us briefly
26: 3 therefore I **b** of you to listen to me patiently.
Gal 4:12 Friends, I **b** you, become as I am,
Eph 4: 1 **b** you to lead a life worthy of the calling
2Th 2: 1 we **b** you, brothers and sisters,
Heb 12:19 and a voice whose words made the hearers **b** that
Tob 10: 7 So I **b** of you, father, to let me go so
10: 9 I **b** you to send me back to my father."
AdE 7: 7 and Haman began to **b** for his life from the queen,
Sir 40:28 it is better to die than to **b**.
2Mc 7:28 I **b** you, my child, to look at the heaven and
9:26 I therefore urge and **b** you to remember the public
2Es 1:25 you **b** mercy of me, I will show you no mercy.
10:37 Now therefore I **b** you to give your servant

BEGAN‡ (285) [BEGIN]

Ge 4:26 At that time people **b** to invoke the name of
6: 1 people **b** to multiply on the face of the ground,
41:54 and the seven years of famine **b** to come,
Lev 24:10 and a certain Israelite **b** fighting in the camp.
Nu 25: 1 the people **b** to have sexual relations with
Jos 18:12 On the north side their boundary **b** at the Jordan;
Jdg 13:25 spirit of the LORD **b** to stir him in Mahaneh-dan,
16:19 He **b** to weaken, and his strength left him.
16:22 But the hair of his head **b** to grow again
19:25 And as the dawn **b** to break, they let her go.
20:31 As before they **b** to inflict casualties on the troops,
20:40 cloud, a column of smoke, **b** to rise out of the city,
1Sa 13: 1 Saul was . . . years old when he **b** to reign;
13: 8 and the people **b** to slip away from Saul.
2Sa 2:10 was forty years old when he **b** to reign over Israel,
5: 4 David was thirty years old when he **b** to reign,
24: 5 and **b** from Aroer and from the city that is in
1Ki 6: 1 he **b** to build the house of the LORD.
14:21 Rehoboam was forty-one years old when he **b**
15: 1 Abijam **b** to reign over Judah.
15: 9 Asa **b** to reign over Judah;
15:25 Nadab son of Jeroboam **b** to reign over Israel in
15:33 Baasha son of Ahijah **b** to reign over all Israel
16: 8 of Baasha **b** to reign over Israel in Tirzah;
16:11 When he **b** to reign, as soon
16:23 Omri **b** to reign over Israel;
16:29 Ahab son of Omri **b** to reign over Israel;
20:29 Then on the seventh day the battle **b**;
22:41 Jehoshaphat son of Asa **b** to reign over Judah in
22:42 Jehoshaphat was thirty-five years old when he **b**
22:51 of Ahab **b** to reign over Israel in Samaria in
2Ki 3:20 suddenly water **b** to flow from the direction
8:16 Jehoram son of King Jehoshaphat of Judah **b**
8:25 Ahaziah son of King Jehoram of Judah **b** to reign.
8:26 Ahaziah was twenty-two years old when he **b**
9:29 Ahaziah **b** to reign over Judah.
10:32 In those days the LORD **b** to trim off parts
11:21 Jehoash was seven years old when he **b** to reign.
12: 1 In the seventh year of Jehu, Jehoash **b** to reign;
13: 1 Jehoahaz son of Jehu **b** to reign over Israel
13:10 Jehoash son of Jehoahaz **b** to reign over Israel
14: 1 King Amaziah son of Joash of Judah, **b** to reign.
14: 2 He was twenty-five years old when he **b** to reign,
14:23 King Jeroboam son of Joash of Israel **b** to reign
15: 1 of Israel King Azariah son of Amaziah of Judah **b**
15: 2 He was sixteen years old when he **b** to reign,
15:13 of Jabesh **b** to reign in the thirty-ninth year
15:17 Menahem son of Gadi **b** to reign over Israel;
15:23 Pekahiah son of Menahem **b** to reign over Israel
15:27 of Remaliah **b** to reign over Israel in Samaria;
15:32 King Jotham son of Uzziah of Judah **b** to reign.
15:33 He was twenty-five years old when he **b** to reign
15:37 In those days the LORD **b** to send King Rezin
16: 1 King Ahaz son of Jotham of Judah **b** to reign.
16: 2 Ahaz was twenty years old when he **b** to reign;
17: 1 Hoshea son of Elah **b** to reign in Samaria
18: 1 Hezekiah son of King Ahaz of Judah **b** to reign.
18: 2 He was twenty-five years old when he **b** to reign;
21: 1 Manasseh was twelve years old when he **b**
21:19 Amon was twenty-two years old when he **b**
22: 1 Josiah was eight years old when he **b** to reign;
23:31 Jehoahaz was twenty-three years old when he **b**
23:36 Jehoiakim was twenty-five years old when he **b**
24: 8 Jehoiachin was eighteen years old when he **b**
24:18 Zedekiah was twenty-one years old when he **b**
25:27 in the year that he **b** to reign,
1Ch 27:24 Joab son of Zeruiah **b** to count them,
2Ch 3: 1 Solomon **b** to build the house of the LORD
3: 2 He **b** to build on the second day of
12:13 Rehoboam was forty-one years old when he **b**
13: 1 Abijah **b** to reign over Judah.
20:22 As they **b** to sing and praise,
20:31 He was thirty-five years old when he **b** to reign;
21: 5 Jehoram was thirty-two years old when he **b**
21:20 He was thirty-two years old when he **b** to reign;
22: 2 Ahaziah was forty-two years old when he **b**
24: 1 Joash was seven years old when he **b** to reign;
25: 1 Amaziah was twenty-five years old when he **b**
26: 3 Uzziah was sixteen years old when he **b** to reign,
27: 1 Jotham was twenty-five years old when he **b**
27: 8 He was twenty-five years old when he **b** to reign;
28: 1 Ahaz was twenty years old when he **b** to reign;
29: 1 Hezekiah **b** to reign when he was twenty-five
29:17 They **b** to sanctify on the first day of
29:27 When the burnt offering **b**,
29:27 the song to the LORD **b** also, and the trumpets,
31: 7 In the third month they **b** to pile up the heaps,
31:10 "Since they **b** to bring the contributions into
33: 1 Manasseh was twelve years old when he **b**
33:21 Amon was twenty-two years old when he **b**
2Ch 34: 1 Josiah was eight years old when he **b** to reign;
34: 3 he **b** to seek the God of his ancestor David,
34: 3 the twelfth year he **b** to purge Judah and Jerusalem
36: 2 Jehoahaz was twenty-three years old when he **b**
36: 5 Jehoiakim was twenty-five years old when he **b**
36: 9 Jehoiachin was eight years old when he **b** to reign;
36:11 Zedekiah was twenty-one years old when he **b**
Ezr 3: 6 the seventh month they **b** to offer burnt offerings
Ne 13:19 When it **b** to be dark at the gates of Jerusalem
Job 38:12 the morning since your days **b**,
Jer 52: 1 Zedekiah was twenty-one years old when he **b**
52:31 in the year he **b** to reign,
Eze 9: 6 So they **b** with the elders who were in front of
Da 5: 5 of a human hand appeared and **b** writing on
Hos 9:15 Every evil of theirs **b** at Gilgal;
Am 7: 1 at the time the latter growth **b** to sprout (it was
Jnh 3: 4 Jonah **b** to go into the city, going a day's walk.
Mt 4:17 From that time Jesus **b** to proclaim, "Repent,
5: 2 Then he **b** to speak, and taught them, saying:
8:15 and she got up and **b** to serve him.
11: 7 Jesus **b** to speak to the crowds about John:
11:20 Then he **b** to reproach the cities in which most
12: 1 and they **b** to pluck heads of grain and to eat.
13:54 and **b** to teach the people in their synagogue,
16:21 Jesus **b** to show his disciples that he must go
16:22 And Peter took him aside and **b** to rebuke him,
18:24 When he **b** the reckoning,
26:16 from that moment he **b** to look for an opportunity
26:22 And they became greatly distressed and **b** to say
26:37 and **b** to be grieved and agitated.
26:74 Then he **b** to curse, and he swore an oath,
Mk 1:28 At once his fame **b** to spread throughout
1:31 Then the fever left her, and she **b** to serve them.
1:45 But he went out and **b** to proclaim it freely,
2:23 and as they made their way his disciples **b**
4: 1 Again he **b** to teach beside the sea.
4: 2 He **b** to teach them many things in parables,
5:17 they **b** to beg Jesus to leave their neighborhood.
5:20 And he went away and **b** to proclaim in
5:42 and **b** to walk about (she was twelve years of age).
6: 2 On the sabbath he **b** to teach in the synagogue,
6: 7 He called the twelve and **b** to send them out two
6:34 and he **b** to teach them many things.
6:55 and rushed about that whole region and **b** to bring
8:11 The Pharisees came and **b** to argue with him,
8:31 Then he **b** to teach them that the Son
8:32 And Peter took him aside and **b** to rebuke him.
10:28 Peter **b** to say to him, "Look,
10:32 the twelve aside again and **b** to tell them what was
10:41 they **b** to be angry with James and John.
10:47 he **b** to shout out and say, "Jesus, Son of David,
11:15 and **b** to drive out those who were selling
12: 1 Then he **b** to speak to them in parables.
13: 5 Then Jesus **b** to say to them,
14:11 So he **b** to look for an opportunity to betray him.
14:19 They **b** to be distressed and to say to him one
14:33 and **b** to be distressed and agitated.
14:65 Some **b** to spit on him, to blindfold him,
14:69 on seeing him, **b** again to say to the bystanders,
14:71 But he **b** to curse, and he swore an oath,
15: 8 the crowd came and **b** to ask Pilate to do for them
15:18 And they **b** saluting him, "Hail, King of the Jews!"
Lk 1:62 Then they **b** motioning to his father
1:64 and he **b** to speak, praising God.
2:38 and **b** to praise God and to speak about the child
3:23 about thirty years old when he **b** his work.
4:15 He **b** to teach in their synagogues and was praised
4:21 Then he **b** to say to them,
4:37 And a report about him **b** to reach every place in
4:39 Immediately she got up and **b** to serve them.
5: 7 so that they **b** to sink.
5:21 Then the scribes and the Pharisees **b** to question,
7:15 The dead man sat up and **b** to speak,
7:24 Jesus **b** to speak to the crowds about John:
7:38 and **b** to bathe his feet with her tears and
7:49 But those who were at the table with him **b** to say
11:29 When the crowds were increasing, he **b** to say,
11:53 the Pharisees **b** to be very hostile toward him and
12: 1 he **b** to speak first to his disciples,
13:13 she stood up straight and **b** praising God.
14:18 But they all alike **b** to make excuses.
14:30 'This fellow **b** to build and was not able to finish.'
15:14 and he **b** to be in need.
15:24 And they **b** to celebrate.
15:28 His father came out and **b** to plead with him.
19: 7 All who saw it **b** to grumble and said,
19:37 of the disciples **b** to praise God joyfully with
19:45 Then he entered the temple and **b**
20: 9 He **b** to tell the people this parable:
22: 6 So he consented and **b** to look for an opportunity
22:23 Then they **b** to ask one another,
22:63 the men who were holding Jesus **b** to mock him
23: 2 They **b** to accuse him, saying,
23: 5 from Galilee where he **b** even to this place."
Jn 4:52 So he asked them the hour when he **b** to recover,
5: 9 and he took up his mat and **b** to walk.
6:14 they **b** to say, "This is indeed the prophet who is
6:41 the Jews **b** to complain about him because he said,
7:14 of the festival Jesus went up into the temple and **b**
8: 2 ⟦and he sat down and **b** to teach them.⟧
9: 8 and those who had seen him before as a beggar **b**
9:15 also **b** to ask him how he had received his sight.
9:32 the world **b** has it been heard that anyone opened
11:35 Jesus **b** to weep.
13: 5 and **b** to wash the disciples' feet and to wipe them
Ac 2: 4 All of them were filled with the Holy Spirit and **b**
3: 8 Jumping up, he stood and **b** to walk,

Ac 7:32 Moses **b** to tremble and did not dare to look.
7:58 Then they dragged him out of the city and **b**
8: 1 That day a severe persecution **b** against the church
8:35 Then Philip **b** to speak, and starting
9:20 and immediately he **b** to proclaim Jesus in
10:34 Then Peter **b** to speak to them:
11: 4 Then Peter **b** to explain it to them, step by step,
11:15 And as I **b** to speak,
13:16 So Paul stood up and with a gesture **b** to speak:
14:10 And the man sprang up and **b** to walk.
18:26 He **b** to speak boldly in the synagogue;
20: 9 **b** to sink off into a deep sleep
23: 7 a dissension **b** between the Pharisees and
24: 2 Tertullus **b** to accuse him, saying:
26: 1 Then Paul stretched out his hand and **b**
27:13 When a moderate south wind **b** to blow,
27:13 so they weighed anchor and **b** to sail past Crete,
27:18 the next day they **b** to throw the cargo overboard,
27:35 he broke it and **b** to eat.
28: 6 they changed their minds and **b** to say that he was
2Co 8:10 for you who **b** last year not only to do something
Php 1: 6 that the one who **b** a good work
2Ti 1: 9 to us in Christ Jesus before the ages **b,**
Tit 1: 2 who never lies, promised before the ages **b—**
3Jn 1: 7 for they **b** their journey for the sake of Christ,
Rev 5: 4 And I **b** to weep bitterly
Tob 2:13 When she returned to me, the goat **b** to bleat.
3: 1 and with groaning **b** to pray:
5:18 But his mother **b** to weep, and said to Tobit,
7:14 Then they **b** to eat and drink.
8: 5 and they **b** to pray and implore that they might
8: 5 Tobias **b** by saying, "Blessed are you,
8:19 So they **b** to make preparations.
10: 3 And he **b** to worry.
10: 4 And she **b** to weep and mourn for her son, saying,
Jdt 5:22 the people standing around the tent **b** to complain;
14: 8 the day she left until the moment she **b** speaking
15:14 Judith **b** this thanksgiving before all Israel,
AdE 7: 7 and Haman **b** to beg for his life from the queen,
14:11 make an example of him who **b** this against us.
Wis 7: 3 when I was born, I **b** to breathe the common air,
Sus 1: 8 and they **b** to lust for her.
1Mc 1: 8 Then his officers **b** to rule, each in his own place.
1:10 **b** to reign in the one hundred thirty-seventh year
3:25 Then Judas and his brothers **b** to be feared,
5: 2 So they **b** to kill and destroy among the people.
7: 1 with a few men to a town by the sea, and there **b**
9:40 on them from the ambush and **b** killing them.
9:47 the battle **b,** and Jonathan stretched out his hand
9:55 But he only **b** to tear it down,
9:67 he **b** to attack and went into battle with his forces;
9:73 Jonathan settled in Michmash and **b** to judge
10: 1 They welcomed him, and there he **b** to reign.
10:10 in Jerusalem and **b** to rebuild and restore the city.
11:46 of the city seized the main streets of the city and **b**
11:54 with him the young boy Antiochus who **b** to reign
13:42 people **b** to write in their documents and contracts,
15:40 So Cendebeus came to Jamnia and **b** to provoke
2Mc 9:11 he **b** to lose much of his arrogance and to come
1Es 1:39 Jehoiakim was twenty-five years old when he **b**
1:57 to him and to his sons until the Persians **b** to reign,
2:30 and **b** to hinder the builders.
3:17 of the strength of wine, **b** and said:
4: 1 of the strength of the king, **b** to speak:
4:13 of women and truth (this was Zerubbabel), **b**
4:33 and he **b** to speak about truth:
4:44 which Cyrus set apart when he **b**
5:53 And all who had made any vow to God **b**
6: 2 of Jozadak **b** to build the house of the Lord that is
9:16 the tenth month they **b** their sessions to investigate
3Mc 1:26 took heed of nothing, and **b** now to approach,
5:23 **b** to move them along in the great colonnade.
6:20 Even the king **b** to shudder bodily,
6:21 the armed forces following them and **b** trampling
7:16 the full enjoyment of deliverance **b** their departure
2Es 2:47 So I **b** to praise those who had stood valiantly for
3: 3 and I **b** to speak anxious words to the Most High,
3:12 "When those who lived on earth **b** to multiply,
3:12 and peoples and many nations, and again they **b** to
5:22 and I **b** once more to speak words in the presence
6:29 by little the place where I was standing **b** to rock
6:36 and I **b** to speak in the presence of the Most High.
9:28 and I **b** to speak before the Most High, and said,
10:25 her face suddenly **b** to shine exceedingly;
10:41 whom you saw mourning and whom you **b**
10:49 and you **b** to console her for what had happened.
4Mc 5:15 he **b** to address the people as follows:
6: 8 the cruel guards rushed at him and **b** to kick him in

BEGAT See Index to Footnotes

BEGAT, BEGET, BEGETTEST, BEGETTETH (KJV) See also FATHER

BEGET (3) [BEGETS, BEGETTING, BEGOT, BEGOTTEN]

Ecc 6: 3 A man may **b** a hundred children,
Jer 16: 3 and the fathers who **b** them in this land:
Sir 41: 9 you will **b** them only for groaning.

BEGETS (2) [BEGET]

Pr 17:21 The one who **b** a fool gets trouble;
23:24 he who **b** a wise son will be glad in him.

BEGETTING (2) [BEGET]

Isa 45:10 to anyone who says to a father, "What are you **b?"**
59: 4 conceiving mischief and **b** iniquity.

BEGGAR (4) [BEG]

Mk 10:46 Bartimaeus son of Timaeus, a blind **b,**
Jn 9: 8 and those who had seen him before as a **b** began
Sir 18:33 not become a **b** by feasting with borrowed money,
40:28 My child, do not lead the life of a **b;**

BEGGARLY (1) [BEG]

Gal 4: 9 to the weak and **b** elemental spirits?

BEGGED (26) [BEG]

Mt 8:31 The demons **b** him, "If you cast us out,
8:34 they **b** him to leave their neighborhood.
14:36 and **b** him that they might touch even the fringe
Mk 5:10 He **b** him earnestly not to send them out of
5:12 the unclean spirits **b** him, "Send us into the swine;
5:18 the man who had been possessed by demons **b** him
5:23 and **b** him repeatedly, "My little daughter is at
6:56 and **b** him that they might touch even the fringe
7:26 She **b** him to cast the demon out of her daughter.
7:32 and they **b** him to lay his hand on him.
8:22 a blind man to him and **b** him to touch him.
Lk 5:12 he bowed with his face to the ground and **b** him,
8:31 They **b** him not to order them to go back into
8:32 and the demons **b** Jesus to let them enter these.
8:38 the demons had gone **b** that he might be with him;
8:41 at Jesus' feet and **b** him to come to his house,
9:40 I **b** your disciples to cast it out,
Jn 4:47 he went and **b** him to come down and heal his son,
Wis 18: 2 and they **b** their pardon for having been
19: 3 as fugitives those whom they had **b** and compelled
Sir 51: 9 and **b** for rescue from death.
1Mc 9:35 as leader of the multitude and **b** the Nabateans,
2Mc 3:31 of Heliodorus's friends quickly **b** Onias to call
12:11 The defeated nomads **b** Judas
12:24 With great guile he **b** them to let him go in safety,
4Mc 4:11 and with tears **b** the Hebrews to pray for him

BEGGING (6) [BEG]

Ps 37:25 the righteous forsaken or their children **b** bread.
Mk 1:40 A leper came to him **b** him,
Lk 18:35 a blind man was sitting by the roadside **b.**
2Co 8: 4 **b** us earnestly for the privilege of sharing
Sir 40:30 In the mouth of the shameless **b** is sweet,
3Mc 6:27 **b** pardon for your former actions!

BEGIN (33) [BEGAN, BEGINNING, BEGINNINGS, BEGINS, BEGUN]

Nu 8:24 and upward they shall **b** to do duty in the service
34: 3 Your southern boundary shall **b** from the end of
Dt 2:24 **B** to take possession by engaging him in battle.
2:25 This day I will **b** to put the dread and fear of you
2:31 **B** now to take possession of his land."
16: 9 **b** to count the seven weeks from the time
31:16 Then this people will **b** to prostitute themselves to
Jos 3: 7 "This day I will **b** to exalt you in the sight
18: 4 and I will send them out that they may **b** to go
Jdg 10:18 "Who will **b** the fight against the Ammonites?
13: 5 It is he who shall **b** to deliver Israel from the hand
1Ki 20:14 Then he said, "Who shall **b** the battle?"
1Ch 22:16 Now **b** the work, and the LORD be with you."
Ne 11:17 to **b** the thanksgiving in prayer, and Bakbukiah,
Pr 20:25 and **b** to reflect only after making a vow.
Ecc 10:13 The words of their mouths **b** in foolishness,
Eze 9: 6 And **b** at my sanctuary."
Lk 3: 8 Do not **b** to say to yourselves,
13:25 you **b** to stand outside and to knock at the door,
13:26 Then you will **b** to say,
14:29 all who see it will **b** to ridicule him,
21:28 Now when these things **b** to take place,
23:30 they will **b** to say to the mountains, 'Fall on us';
1Co 11:18 to **b** with, when you come together as a church,
1Pe 4:17 for judgment to **b** with the household of God;
Jdt 16: 1 Judith said, **B** a song to my God with tambourines,
Sir 38:16 and as one in great pain **b** the lament.
2Mc 2:32 At this point therefore let us **b** our narrative,
2Es 5: 4 and the sun shall suddenly **b** to shine at night,
14:10 age has lost its youth, and the times **b** to grow old.
14:26 tomorrow at this hour you shall **b** to write."
4Mc 1:12 I shall **b** by stating my main principle,
5: 6 "Before I **b** to torture you,

BEGINNING‡ (150) [BEGIN]

Ge 1: 1 the **b** when God created the heavens and the earth,
10:10 The **b** of his kingdom was Babel, Erech,
11: 6 and this is only the **b** of what they will do;
13: 3 to the place where his tent had been at the **b,**
44:12 **b** with the eldest and ending with the youngest;
Ex 12: 2 This month shall mark for you the **b** of months;
Dt 11:12 from the **b** of the year to the end of the year.
Jdg 7:19 with him came to the outskirts of the camp at the **b**
Ru 1:22 to Bethlehem at the **b** of the barley harvest.
1Sa 3:12 that I have spoken concerning his house, from **b**
2Sa 21: 9 at the **b** of barley harvest.
21:10 from the **b** of harvest until rain fell on them from
23:13 the **b** of harvest three of the thirty chiefs went
1Ch 5: 9 to the east as far as the **b** of the desert this side of
Ezr 3: 8 of Shealtiel and Jeshua son of Jozadak made a **b,**
Ne 4: 7 and the gaps were **b** to be closed,
Job 8: 7 Though your **b** was small,
Job 42:12 the latter days of Job more than his **b;**
Ps 111:10 The fear of the LORD is the **b** of wisdom;
Pr 1: 7 The fear of the LORD is the **b** of knowledge;
4: 7 The **b** of wisdom is this:
8:22 The LORD created me at the **b** of his work,
8:23 at the first, before the **b** of the earth.
9:10 The fear of the LORD is the **b** of wisdom,
17:14 The **b** of strife is like letting out water;
20:21 An estate quickly acquired in the **b** will not
Ecc 3:11 from the **b** to the end.
7: 8 Better is the end of a thing than its **b;**
Isa 1:26 and your counselors as at the **b.**
40:21 Has it not been told you from the **b?**
41: 4 calling the generations from the **b?**
41:26 Who declared it from the **b,**
46:10 the **b** and from ancient times things not yet done,
48:16 From the **b** I have not spoken in secret,
Jer 17:12 O glorious throne, exalted from the **b,**
25:29 I am **b** to bring disaster on the city that is called
26: 1 the **b** of the reign of King Jehoiakim son of Josiah
27: 1 the **b** of the reign of King Zedekiah son of Josiah
28: 1 at the **b** of the reign of King Zedekiah of Judah,
49:34 at the **b** of the reign of King Zedekiah of Judah.
La 2:19 Arise, cry out in the night, at the **b** of the watches!
Eze 40: 1 at the **b** of the year, on the tenth day of the month,
48: 1 **B** at the northern border, on the Hethlon road,
Da 9:23 At the **b** of your supplications a word went out,
Jnh 4: 2 That is why I fled to Tarshish at the **b;**
Mic 1:13 it was the **b** of sin to daughter Zion,
Mt 14:30 he became frightened, and **b** to sink, he cried out,
19: 4 the one who made them at the **b** 'made them male
19: 8 but from the **b** it was not so.
20: 8 **b** with the last and then going to the first.'
24: 8 all this is but the **b** of the birth pangs.
24:21 as has not been from the **b** of the world until now,
27:24 but rather that a riot was **b,**
Mk 1: 1 The **b** of the good news of Jesus Christ,
10: 6 But from the **b** of creation,
13: 8 This is but the **b** of the birth pangs.
13:19 the **b** of the creation that God created until now,
Lk 1: 2 the **b** were eyewitnesses and servants of the word,
5: 6 they caught so many fish that their nets were **b**
23:54 the day of Preparation, and the sabbath was **b.**
24:27 Then **b** with Moses and all the prophets,
24:47 to be proclaimed in his name to all nations, **b**
Jn 1: 1 In the **b** was the Word,
1: 2 He was in the **b** with God.
8: 9 ⟦they went away, one by one, **b** with the elders;⟧
8:44 He was a murderer from the **b** and does not stand
15:27 because you have been with me from the **b.**
16: 4 "I did not say these things to you from the **b,**
Ac 1: 1 about all that Jesus did and taught from the **b**
1:22 **b** from the baptism of John until the day
10:37 **b** in Galilee after the baptism
11:15 upon them just as it had upon us at the **b.**
26: 4 a life spent from the **b** among my own people and
2Co 3: 1 Are we **b** to commend ourselves again?
8: 6 as he had already made a **b,**
Col 1:18 He is the head of the body, the church; he is the **b,**
Heb 1:10 And, "In the **b,** Lord, you founded the earth,
7: 3 having neither **b** of days nor end of life,
2Pe 3: 4 all things continue as they were from the **b**
1Jn 1: 1 We declare to you what was from the **b,**
2: 7 old commandment that you have had from the **b;**
2:13 fathers, because you know him who is from the **b.**
2:14 fathers, because you know him who is from the **b.**
2:24 Let what you heard from the **b** abide in you.
2:24 If what you heard from the **b** abides in you,
3: 8 for the devil has been sinning from the **b.**
3:11 For this is the message you have heard from the **b,**
2Jn 1: 5 but one we have had from the **b,**
1: 6 as you have heard it from the **b—**
Rev 21: 6 I am the Alpha and the Omega, the **b** and the end.
22:13 the first and the last, the **b** and the end."
Jdt 8:29 but from the **b** of your life all
AdE 13:15 the inheritance that has been yours from the **b.**
Wis 6:17 The **b** of wisdom is the most sincere desire
6:22 but I will trace her course from the **b** of creation,
7: 5 For no king has had a different **b** of existence;
7:18 the **b** and end and middle of times,
9: 8 copy of the holy tent that you prepared from the **b.**
12:11 For they were an accursed race from the **b,**
14: 6 in the **b,** when arrogant giants were perishing,
14:12 the idea of making idols was the **b** of fornication,
14:13 for they did not exist from the **b,**
14:27 be named is the **b** and cause and end of every evil.
Sir 1:14 To fear the Lord is the **b** of wisdom;
10:12 The **b** of human pride is to forsake the Lord;
10:13 For the **b** of pride is sin,
15:14 It was he who created humankind in the **b,**
16:26 When the Lord created his works from the **b,** and,
18: 7 When human beings have finished, they are just **b,**
24: 9 Before the ages, in the **b,** he created me,
25:24 From a woman sin had its **b,**
36:16 and give them their inheritance, as at the **b.**
36:20 Bear witness to those whom you created in the **b,**
37:16 Discussion is the **b** of every work,
39:20 the **b** to the end of time he can see everything,
39:25 From the **b** good things were created for the good,
39:32 So from the **b** I have been convinced of all this
44: 2 to them great glory, his majesty from the **b.**
1Mc 4:59 **b** with the twenty-fifth day of the month
2Mc 7:23 who shaped the **b** of humankind and devised
8:27 that day and allotted it to them as the **b** of mercy.
1Es 5:56 of Shealtiel and Jeshua son of Jozadak made a **b,**
8:70 and from the **b** of this matter the leaders and
3Mc 3:21 affairs liberally entrusted to them from the **b;**

3Mc 5:11 that beneficence that from the **b**, night and day,
6:26 the **b** differed from all nations in their goodwill
2Es 2:41 who have been called from the **b**,
3: 4 not speak at the **b** when you planted the earth—
4:30 of evil seed was sown in Adam's heart from the **b**,
4:42 that were committed to them from the **b**.
6: 1 He said to me, "At the **b** of the circle of the earth,
6: 7 of the first age and the **b** of the age that follows?"
6: 8 for Jacob's hand held Esau's heel from the **b**.
6: 9 and Jacob is the **b** of the age that follows.
6:10 The **b** of a person is the hand,
6:38 I said, "O Lord, you spoke at the **b** of creation,
7:*113* [43] and the **b** of the immortal age to come,
8:19 The **b** of the words of Ezra's prayer,
9: 4 from the days that were of old, from the **b**.
9: 5 the **b** is evident, and the end manifest;
9: 8 which I have sanctified for myself from the **b**.
10:10 From the **b** all have been born of her,
10:14 so the earth also has from the **b** given her fruit,
12:34 of which I spoke to you at the **b**.
13:14 the **b** you have shown your servant these wonders,
14:22 that has happened in the world from the **b**,
16:18 The **b** of sorrows, when there shall
16:18 the **b** of famine, when many shall perish;
16:18 the **b** of wars, when the powers shall be terrified;
16:18 the **b** of calamities, when all shall tremble.

BEGINNINGS (4) [BEGIN]

Nu 10:10 and at the **b** of your months,
28:11 At the **b** of your months you shall offer
2Es 7:30 as it was at the first **b**, so that no one shall be left.
9: 6 the **b** are manifest in wonders and mighty works,

BEGINS (4) [BEGIN]

Jos 18:15 southern side **b** at the outskirts of Kiriath-jearim;
Mt 24:49 and he **b** to beat his fellow slaves,
Lk 12:45 and if he **b** to beat the other slaves,
1Pe 4:17 if it **b** with us, what will be the end

BEGOT‡ (2) [BEGET]

Pr 23:22 Listen to your father who **b** you,
4Mc 10: 2 the same father **b** me as well as those who died,

BEGOTTEN‡ (8) [BEGET]

Lev 18:11 **b** by your father, since she is your sister.
Job 38:28 or who has **b** the drops of dew?
Ps 2: 7 "You are my son; today I have **b** you.
Eze 47:22 among you and have **b** children among you.
Ac 13:33 'You are my Son; today I have **b** you.'
Heb 1: 5 "You are my Son; today I have **b** you"?
5: 5 "You are my Son, today I have **b** you";
2Es 6:58 whom you have called your firstborn, only **b**,

BEGRUDGE (4) [BEGRUDGES, BEGRUDGING]

Dt 28:54 of men among you will **b** food to his own brother,
28:56 will **b** food to the husband whom she embraces,
Tob 4: 7 do not let your eye **b** the gift when you make it.
4:16 and do not let your eye **b** your giving of alms.

BEGRUDGES (1) [BEGRUDGE]

Sir 14:10 A miser **b** bread, and it is lacking at his table.

BEGRUDGING (1) [BEGRUDGE]

Dt 28:57 **b** even the afterbirth that comes out from

BEGS (2) [BEG]

Mt 5:42 Give to everyone who **b** from you,
Lk 6:30 Give to everyone who **b** from you;

BEGUILE‡ (3) [BEGUILED, BEGUILING]

Jdt 10:19 for if we let them go they will be able to **b**
16: 8 with a tiara and put on a linen gown to **b** him.
AdE 16: 6 of their evil natures **b** the sincere goodwill

BEGUILE, BEGUILED, BEGUILING

(KJV) See also DECEIVE, DISQUALIFY, ENTICE, TRICK

BEGUILED (1) [BEGUILE]

Sus 1:56 beauty has **b** you and lust has perverted your heart.

BEGUILING (1) [BEGUILE]

Rev 2:20 and **b** my servants to practice fornication and

BEGUN (16) [BEGIN]

Nu 16:46 from the LORD; the plague has **b**."
16:47 where the plague had already **b** among the people.
Dt 2:31 I have **b** to give Sihon and his land over to you.
3:24 "O Lord GOD, you have only **b**
Jdg 20:39 But Benjamin had **b** to inflict casualties on
1Sa 3: 2 whose eyesight had **b** to grow dim so that he could
1Ki 15: 6 The war **b** between Rehoboam
Ezr 7: 9 the journey up from Babylon was **b**,
Est 6:13 "If Mordecai, before whom your downfall has **b**,
9:23 Jews adopted as a custom what they had **b** to do,
Mic 6:13 Therefore I have **b** to strike you down,
Ac 28: 2 Since it had **b** to rain and was cold,
Rev 11:17 you have taken your great power and **b** to reign.
AdE 6:13 and you have **b** to be humiliated before him,
1Mc 5:31 So Judas saw that the battle had **b** and that the cry
2Mc 13:11 to let the people who had just **b** to revive fall into

BEHALF (94)

Lev 1: 3 for acceptance in your **b** before the LORD.
1: 4 and it shall be acceptable in your **b** as atonement
4:26 Thus the priest shall make atonement on his **b**
4:31 Thus the priest shall make atonement on your **b**,
4:35 Thus the priest shall make atonement on your **b**
5: 6 and the priest shall make atonement on your **b**
5:10 Thus the priest shall make atonement on your **b**
5:13 Thus the priest shall make atonement on your **b**
5:16 The priest shall make atonement on your **b** with
5:18 and the priest shall make atonement on your **b** for
6: 7 The priest shall make atonement on your **b** before
10:17 to make atonement on their **b** before the LORD.
12: 7 and make atonement on her **b**;
12: 8 and the priest shall make atonement on her **b**,
14:18 the priest shall make atonement on his **b** before
14:20 Thus the priest shall make atonement on his **b**
14:21 to make atonement on his **b**,
14:29 to make atonement on his **b** before the LORD.
14:31 before the LORD on **b** of the one being cleansed.
15:15 the priest shall make atonement on his **b** before
15:30 the priest shall make atonement on her **b** before
16:18 before the LORD and make atonement on its **b**,
19: 5 in such a way that it is acceptable on your **b**.
22:19 in your **b** it shall be a male without blemish,
22:20 for it will not be acceptable in your **b**.
22:25 they shall not be accepted in your **b**.
22:29 so that it may be acceptable in your **b**.
23:28 of atonement, to make atonement on your **b** before
Nu 10:10 a reminder on your **b** before the LORD your God:
25:11 by manifesting such zeal among them on my **b**
Dt 9:20 I interceded also on **b** of Aaron at that same time.
Jdg 9: 3 on his **b** in the hearing of all the lords of Shechem;
1Ki 2:18 I will speak to the king on your **b**."
2:19 to speak to him on **b** of Adonijah.
2Ki 4:13 on your **b** to the king or to the commander of
2Ch 19: 6 not on **b** of human beings but on the LORD's **b**;
20:17 and see the victory of the LORD on your **b**,
35: 6 and on **b** of your kindred make preparations,
Ne 13: 7 the wrong that Eliashib had done on **b** of Tobiah,
Est 4:16 and hold a fast on my **b**,
Job 36: 2 for I have yet something to say on God's **b**.
Ps 109:21 act on my **b** for your name's sake;
Isa 8:19 the dead on **b** of the living,
Jer 7:16 do not raise a cry or prayer on their **b**,
11:14 or lift up a cry or prayer on their **b**,
21: 2 of the LORD on our **b**, for King Nebuchadrezzar
29: 7 and pray to the LORD on its **b**,
Eze 22:28 Its prophets have smeared whitewash on their **b**,
22:30 and stand in the breach before me on **b** of the land,
Da 9:20 the LORD my God on **b** of the holy mountain
Zec 11: 7 So, on **b** of the sheep merchants,
Jn 5:32 There is another who testifies on my **b**,
5:36 testify on my **b** that the Father has sent me.
5:37 Father who sent me has himself testified on my **b**.
5:39 and it is they that testify on my **b**.
8:13 "You are testifying on your own **b**;
8:14 Jesus answered, "Even if I testify on my own **b**,
8:18 I testify on my own **b**,
8:18 and the Father who sent me testifies on my **b**."
15:26 he will testify on my **b**.
16:26 not say to you that I will ask the Father on your **b**;
17: 9 I am asking on their **b**;
17: 9 I am not asking on **b** of the world,
17: 9 but on **b** of those whom you gave me,
17:20 "I ask not only on **b** of these,
17:20 but also on **b** of those who will believe in me
Ro 15: 8 the circumcised on **b** of the truth of God in order
15:30 to join me in earnest prayer to God on my **b**,
1Co 15:29 people do who receive baptism on **b** of the dead?
15:29 why are people baptized on their **b**?
2Co 1:11 on our **b** for the blessing granted us through
5:20 we entreat you on **b** of Christ,
12: 5 On **b** of such a one I will boast,
12: 5 but on my own **b** I will not boast,
Col 1: 7 He is a faithful minister of Christ on your **b**,
4:12 He is always wrestling in his prayers on your **b**,
Heb 5: 1 in charge of things pertaining to God on their **b**,
6:20 a forerunner on our **b**, has entered,
9:24 now to appear in the presence of God on our **b**.
Rev 13:12 the authority of the first beast on its **b**,
13:14 and by the signs that it is allowed to perform on **b**
Tob 7:11 and the Lord will act on **b** of you both."
AdE 4: 8 the king and plead for his favor in **b** of the people.
4: 8 then speak to the king in our **b**,
4:16 the Jews who are in Susa and fast on my **b**;
10: 3 on **b** of King Artaxerxes and was great in
Wis 16:24 in kindness relaxes on **b** of those who trust in you.
2Mc 1:26 Accept this sacrifice on **b** of all your people Israel
11:15 in **b** of the Jews which Maccabeus delivered
1Es 4:49 He wrote in **b** of all the Jews who were going up
2Es 4:34 but the Highest is in a hurry on **b** of many.
4Mc 5:31 and cowardly as not to be young in reason on **b**
14: 3 of the seven brothers on **b** of religion!

BEHAVE (5) [BEHAVED, BEHAVING, BEHAVIOR]

Jdg 2:19 and **b** worse than their ancestors,
2Sa 14: 2 not anoint yourself with oil, but **b** like
1Th 4:12 so that you may **b** properly toward outsiders and
1Ti 3:15 how one ought to **b** in the household of God,
Sir 23:14 and **b** like a fool through bad habit;

BEHAVED (5) [BEHAVE]

2Ch 28:19 for he had **b** without restraint in Judah
Jer 16:12 because you have **b** worse than your ancestors,
2Co 1:12 we have **b** in the world with frankness
2Mc 1:17 on those who have **b** impiously.
12:14 **b** most insolently toward Judas and his men,

BEHAVING (3) [BEHAVE]

Job 36: 9 that they are **b** arrogantly.
1Co 3: 3 and **b** according to human inclinations?
7:36 that he is not **b** properly toward his fiancée,

BEHAVIOR (7) [BEHAVE]

1Sa 21:13 So he changed his **b** before them;
2Ch 13:22 The rest of the acts of Abijah, his **b** and his deeds,
Est 1:18 of the queen's **b** will rebel against
Eze 16:27 who were ashamed of your lewd **b**.
Tit 2: 3 Likewise, tell the older women to be reverent in **b**,
AdE 16: 7 wickedly accomplished through the pestilent **b**
Sir 23:19 they look upon every aspect of human **b** and see

BEHEADED (7) [HEAD]

2Sa 4: 7 they attacked him, killed him, and **b** him.
Mt 14:10 he sent and had John **b** in the prison.
Mk 6:16 when Herod heard of it, he said, "John, whom I **b**,
6:27 He went and **b** him in the prison,
Lk 9: 9 Herod said, "John I **b**;
Rev 20: 4 I also saw the souls of those who had been **b**
Pm 151: 7 But I drew his own sword; I **b** him,

BEHELD (5) [BEHOLD]

Ex 24:11 also they **b** God, and they ate and drank.
Nu 23:21 He has not **b** misfortune in Jacob;
Ps 139:16 Your eyes **b** my unformed substance.
Wis 16: 7 not by the thing that was **b**, but by you,
4Mc 17: 7 would not those who first **b** it have shuddered

BEHEMOTH (3)

Job 40:15 "Look at **B**, which I made just as I made you;
2Es 6:49 the one you called **B** and the name of the other
6:51 And you gave **B** one of the parts that had been

BEHIND‡ (112)

Ge 18:10 Sarah was listening at the tent entrance **b** him.
19:26 But Lot's wife, **b** him, looked back,
32:18 and moreover he is **b** us.' "
32:20 'Moreover your servant Jacob is **b** us.' "
Ex 10:24 Only your flocks and your herds shall remain **b**.
10:26 not a hoof shall be left **b**,
11: 5 to the firstborn of the female slave who is **b**
14:19 before the Israelite army moved and went **b** them;
14:19 from in front of them and took its place **b** them.
Nu 3:23 the Gershonites were to camp **b** the tabernacle on
18: 7 that concerns the altar and the area **b** the curtain.
Dt 2: 8 leaving **b** the route of the Arabah,
2: 8 and leaving **b** Elath and Ezion-geber.
3:19 shall stay **b** in the towns that I have given to you.
25:18 and struck down all who lagged **b** you;
Jos 8: 2 Set an ambush against the city, **b** it."
8: 4 "You shall lie in ambush against the city, **b** it;
8:14 not know that there was an ambush against him **b**
Jdg 4:10 and ten thousand warriors went up **b** him;
20:40 the Benjaminites looked **b** them—
Ru 2: 2 **b** someone in whose sight I may find favor."
2: 3 She came and gleaned in the field **b** the reapers.
2: 7 and gather among the sheaves **b** the reapers.'
2: 9 the field that is being reaped, and follow **b** them.
1Sa 11: 5 Now Saul was coming from the field **b** the oxen;
21: 9 is here wrapped in a cloth **b** the ephod;
24: 8 When Saul looked **b** him, David bowed
30: 9 where those stayed who were left **b**.
30:10 two hundred stayed **b**, too exhausted to cross
30:13 master left me **b** because I fell sick three days
2Sa 1: 7 he looked **b** him, he saw me, and called to me.
3:16 as he walked **b** her all the way to Bahurim.
15:16 except ten concubines whom he left **b** to look after
1Ki 14: 9 and have thrust me **b** your back;
2Ki 4: 4 go in, and shut the door **b** you and your children,
4: 5 and shut the door **b** her and her children;
6:32 Is not the sound of his master's feet **b** him?"
9:18 have you to do with peace? Fall in **b** me."
9:19 have you to do with peace? Fall in **b** me."
9:25 when you and I rode side by side **b** his father Ahab
11: 6 at the gate Sur and a third at the gate **b** the guards),
19:21 **b** your back, daughter Jerusalem.
2Ch 13:13 an ambush around to come on them from **b**;
13:13 and the ambush was **b** them.
13:14 the battle was in front of them and **b** them.
Ne 4:13 So in the lowest parts of the space **b** the wall,
4:16 the leaders posted themselves **b** the whole house
9:26 and rebelled against you and cast your law **b**
Job 41:32 It leaves a shining wake **b** it;
Ps 45:14 **b** her the virgins, her companions, follow.
50:17 you hate discipline, and you cast my words **b** you.
139: 5 You hem me in, **b** and before,
SS 2: 9 Look, there he stands **b** our wall,
4: 1 Your eyes are doves **b** your veil.
4: 3 Your cheeks are like halves of a pomegranate **b**
6: 7 Your cheeks are like halves of a pomegranate **b**
Isa 26:20 enter your chambers, and shut your doors **b** you;
30:21 your ears shall hear a word **b** you, saying,
37:22 **b** your back, daughter Jerusalem.
38:17 for you have cast all my sins **b** your back.

Isa 57: 8 **B** the door and the doorpost you have set
Jer 9:22 like sheaves **b** the reaper, and no one shall gather
Eze 3:12 I heard **b** me the sound of loud rumbling;
12:14 and I will unsheathe the sword **b** them.
23:35 you have forgotten me and cast me **b** your back,
24:21 and your sons and your daughters whom you left **b**
39:28 I will leave none of them **b**;
Hos 5: 8 Sound the alarm at Beth-aven; look **b** you,
Joel 2: 3 and **b** them a flame burns.
2:14 and leave a blessing **b** him,
Hab 3: 5 him went pestilence, and plague followed close **b**.
Zec 1: 8 and **b** him were red, sorrel, and white horses.
Mt 9:20 from hemorrhages for twelve years came up **b** him
16:23 But he turned and said to Peter, "Get **b** me, Satan!
Mk 4:36 And leaving the crowd **b**,
5:27 came up **b** him in the crowd and touched his cloak,
8:33 he rebuked Peter and said, "Get **b** me, Satan!
Lk 2:43 the boy Jesus stayed **b** in Jerusalem,
7:38 She stood **b** him at his feet, weeping,
8:44 up **b** him and touched the fringe of his clothes,
12: 3 and what you have whispered **b** closed doors will
23:26 and made him carry it **b** Jesus.
Ac 17:14 but Silas and Timothy remained **b**.
Php 3:13 forgetting what lies **b** and straining forward
Tit 1: 5 I left you **b** in Crete for this reason,
Heb 6: 1 leaving **b** the basic teaching about Christ,
6:19 a hope that enters the inner shrine **b** the curtain,
9: 3 **B** the second curtain was a tent called the Holy
11:15 of the land that they had left **b**,
Rev 1:10 and I heard **b** me a loud voice like a trumpet
4: 6 full of eyes in front and **b**:
Tob 1:17 the dead body of any of my people thrown out **b**
11: 4 And the dog went along **b** them.
Wis 1: 5 and will leave foolish thoughts **b**,
17: 3 that in their secret sins they were unobserved **b**
Sir 21:15 he laughs at it and throws it **b** his back.
22:11 Weep for the dead, for he has left the light **b**;
22:11 weep for the fool, for he has left intelligence **b**.
23:26 She will leave **b** an accursed memory
30: 4 for he has left **b** him one like himself,
30: 6 He has left **b** him an avenger against his enemies,
44: 8 Some of them have left **b** a name,
47:23 and left **b** him one of his sons,
LtJ 6: 6 the multitude before and **b** them worshiping them.
1Mc 5:33 Then he came up **b** them in three companies,
9:16 and followed close **b** Judas and his men.
9:45 the battle is in front of us and **b** us;
10:79 a thousand cavalry **b** them.
10:80 Jonathan learned that there was an ambush **b** him,
3Mc 1:17 those who remained **b** in the city were agitated
3:24 not have these impious people **b** our backs
4Mc 13:18 Those who were left **b** said to each of

BEHOLD‡ (24) [BEHELD, BEHOLDING, BEHOLDS]

Nu 23: 9 from the hills I **b** him;
24:17 I **b** him, but not near—
Est 1:11 for she was fair to **b**.
Job 19:27 and my eyes shall **b**, and not another.
20: 9 nor will their place **b** them any longer.
23: 9 on the left he hides, and I cannot **b** him;
34:29 When he hides his face, who can **b** him,
Ps 11: 4 His eyes **b**, his gaze examines humankind.
11: 7 the upright shall **b** his face.
17:15 As for me, I shall **b** your face in righteousness;
27: 4 to **b** the beauty of the LORD,
37:37 Mark the blameless, and **b** the upright,
42: 2 When shall I come and **b** the face of God?
46: 8 **b** the works of the LORD;
84: 9 **B** our shield, O God; look on the
97: 6 and all the peoples **b** his glory.
119:18 so that I may **b** wondrous things out of your law.
Isa 33:17 they will **b** a land that stretches far away.
Jer 2:31 And you, O generation, **b** the word of the LORD!
La 1:18 but hear, all you peoples, and **b** my suffering;
Hab 1:13 Your eyes are too pure to **b** evil,
Jdt 8: 7 and was very lovely to **b**.
Sir 43: 1 as glorious to **b** as the sight of the heavens.
2Es 10:44 which you now **b** as a city being built.

BEHOLDING (2) [BEHOLD]

Ps 17:15 when I awake I shall be satisfied, **b** your likeness.
63: 2 in the sanctuary, **b** your power and glory.

BEHOLDS (2) [BEHOLD]

Nu 12: 8 and he **b** the form of the LORD.
Job 7: 8 The eye that **b** me will see me no more;

BEHOVED (KJV) See HAD TO

BEING‡ (351) [BE]

A. HUMAN BEING (37)
B. LIVING BEING (7)

Ge 2: 7 and the man became a living **b**. B
19:16 the LORD **b** merciful to him,
36:32 the name of his city **b** Dinhabah.
36:35 the name of his city **b** Avith.
36:39 the name of his city **b** Pau;
37: 2 Joseph, **b** seventeen years old,
38:25 As she was **b** brought out,
50:26 And Joseph died, **b** one hundred ten years old;
Ex 19:13 whether animal or human **b**, they shall not live.' A
22:14 and it is injured or dies, the owner not **b** present,
Ex 25:40 which is **b** shown you on the mountain.
30:12 no plague may come upon them for **b** registered.
36: 4 each from the task **b** performed,
38:21 the Levites **b** under the direction of Ithamar son of
Lev 14:31 before the LORD on behalf of the one **b** cleansed.
22: 5 which he may be made unclean or any human **b** A
24:17 who kills a human **b** shall be put to death. A
24:21 one who kills a human **b** shall be put to death. A
25:16 it is a certain number of harvests that are **b** sold
27: 2 concerning the equivalent for a human **b**, A
Nu 7:86 of the dishes **b** one hundred twenty shekels;
10:34 the LORD **b** over them by day when they set out
19:11 of any human **b** shall be unclean seven days. A
19:13 the body of a human **b** who has died, A
23:19 God is not a human **b**, A
32:38 and Baal-meon (some names **b** changed),
Dt 3:16 the wadi **b** boundary of the Ammonites;
11: 6 their tents, and every living **b** in the company; B
21:15 the firstborn **b** the son of the one who is disliked,
24: 8 of a leprous skin disease by **b** very careful;
Jos 1: 7 **b** careful to act in accordance with all the law
3: 3 the covenant of the LORD your God **b** carried by
8:15 and all Israel made a pretense of **b** beaten
21:11 They gave them Kiriath-arba (Arba **b** the father
24:29 died, **b** one hundred ten years old.
Jdg 20:32 "They are **b** routed before us, as previously."
Ru 2: 9 Keep your eyes on the field that is **b** reaped,
1Sa 8: 7 but they have rejected me from **b** king over them.
15:23 he has also rejected you from **b** king."
15:26 LORD has rejected you from **b** king over Israel."
16: 1 I have rejected him from **b** king over Israel.
28:13 "I see a divine **b** coming up out of the ground."
2Sa 13:14 **b** stronger than she, he forced her and lay with her.
17:17 for they could not risk **b** seen entering the city.
1Ki 2:27 So Solomon banished Abiathar from **b** priest to
6: 7 in the temple while it was **b** built.
15:13 from **b** queen mother, because she had made
16: 7 in **b** like the house of Jeroboam,
2Ki 2:10 yet, if you see me as I am **b** taken from you,
11: 6 (another third **b** at the gate Sur and a third at
13:21 a man was **b** buried, a marauding band was seen
1Ch 7: 2 of David **b** twenty-two thousand six hundred.
24: 6 one ancestral house **b** chosen for Eleazar
27:32 **b** a man of understanding and a scribe;
2Ch 15:16 from **b** queen mother because she had made
26:21 and **b** leprous lived in a separate house,
Ezr 5: 8 It is **b** built of hewn stone,
5: 8 this work is **b** done diligently and prospers
8:13 those who came later, their names **b** Eliphelet,
Ne 7:73 the people of Israel **b** settled in their towns—
13:19 to prevent any burden from **b** brought in on
Est 2:12 after **b** twelve months under the regulations for
2:19 When the virgins were **b** gathered together,
4:11 to the king inside the inner court without **b** called,
Job 12:10 and the breath of every human **b**. A
21:23 **b** wholly at ease and secure,
25: 6 a maggot, and a human **b**, who is a worm!" A
34: 6 in spite of **b** right I am counted a liar;
Ps 44:22 Because of you we are **b** killed all day long,
51: 6 You desire truth in the inward **b**;
78:38 Yet he, **b** compassionate, forgave their iniquity,
104:33 I will sing praise to my God while I have **b**.
139:15 when I was **b** made in secret,
Pr 1:22 O simple ones, will you love **b** simple?
3:26 and will keep your foot from **b** caught.
24:10 in the day of adversity, your strength **b** small;
27:21 so a person is tested by **b** praised.
Ecc 12: 9 Besides **b** wise, the Teacher also taught
SS 5: 4 and my inmost **b** yearned for him.
Isa 51:12 a human **b** who fades like grass? A
61:10 my whole **b** shall exult in my God;
66: 3 an ox is like one who kills a human **b**; A
Jer 17:16 not run away from **b** a shepherd in your service,
32:36 "It is **b** given into the hand of the king of Babylon
38:22 of the king of Judah **b** led out to the officials of
40: 1 of Jerusalem and Judah who were **b** exiled
44:19 to her without our husbands' **b** involved?"
48: 2 "Come, let us cut her off from **b** a nation!"
Eze 1:10 the four had the face of a human **b**, A
1:16 the same form, their construction **b** something like
3:14 the hand of the LORD **b** strong upon me.
8: 2 there was a figure that looked like a human **b**; A
10:14 the second face was that of a human **b**, A
29: 8 and will cut off from you human **b** and animal; A
36:34 instead of **b** the desolation that it was in the sight
40: 5 each **b** a cubit and a handbreadth in length;
43:13 of the altar by cubits (the cubit **b** one cubit and
48:31 gates of the city **b** named after the tribes of Israel.
Da 2:30 that I have more than any other living **b**, B
5:31 **b** about sixty-two years old.
7: 4 and made to stand on two feet like a human **b**; A
7:13 I saw one like a human **b** coming with the clouds
of heaven. A
Hos 4: 6 I reject you from **b** a priest to me.
Jnh 3: 7 No human **b** or animal, no herd or flock, A
4:10 it came into **b** in a night and perished in a night.
Hab 1: 5 For a work is **b** done in your days that you would
Mt 1:19 **b** a righteous man and unwilling to expose her
2:22 And after **b** warned in a dream,
8:24 great that the boat was **b** swamped by the waves;
12:12 much more valuable is a human **b** than a sheep! A
19:13 Then little children were **b** brought to him in order
23:33 How can you escape **b** sentenced to hell?
Mk 4:37 so that the boat was already **b** swamped.
6: 2 What deeds of power are **b** done by his hands!
9:31 and three days after **b** killed, he will rise again."
12:26 And as for the dead **b** raised,
Lk 1:74 **b** rescued from the hands of our enemies,
2:33 and mother were amazed at what was **b** said
7:12 a man who had died was **b** carried out.
12:20 This very night your life is **b** demanded of you.
16:23 In Hades, where he was **b** tormented,
17:27 and marrying and **b** given in marriage,
20:26 and **b** amazed by his answer, they became silent.
20:36 **b** children of the resurrection.
22:37 and indeed what is written about me is **b** fulfilled."
Jn 1: 3 All things came into **b** through him, and without
him not one thing came into **b**. What has come
into **b**
1:10 and the world came into **b** through him;
3: 3 no one can see the kingdom of God without **b** born
3: 5 the kingdom of God without **b** born of water
3:23 and people kept coming and were **b** baptized
6:61 **b** aware that his disciples were complaining
10:33 because you, though only a human **b**, A
11:51 but **b** high priest that year he prophesied
16:21 because of the joy of having brought a human **b** A
18:36 be fighting to keep me from **b** handed over to
Ac 2:33 **B** therefore exalted at the right hand of God,
2:43 because many wonders and signs were **b** done by
2:47 to their number those who were **b** saved.
3: 2 And a man lame from birth was **b** carried in.
5:17 the sect of the Sadducees), **b** filled with jealousy,
5:26 for they were afraid of **b** stoned by the people.
6: 1 because their widows were **b** neglected in
7:24 When he saw one of them **b** wronged,
8:13 After **b** baptized, he stayed constantly with Philip
8:36 What is to prevent me from **b** baptized?"
10:10 and while it was **b** prepared, he fell into a trance.
10:11 **b** lowered to the ground by its four corners.
11: 5 **b** lowered by its four corners;
13: 4 So, **b** sent out by the Holy Spirit,
16:10 **b** convinced that God had called us to proclaim
17:28 For 'In him we live and move and have our **b**';
19:40 we are in danger of **b** charged with rioting today,
22: 3 **b** zealous for God, just as all of you are today.
22:30 to find out what Paul was **b** accused of by
25: 4 Festus replied that Paul was **b** kept at Caesarea,
26:10 against them when they were **b** condemned
26:23 and that, by **b** the first to rise from the dead,
27:18 We were **b** pounded by the storm so violently that
27:20 all hope of our **b** saved was at last abandoned.
27:41 stern was **b** broken up by the force of the waves.
Ro 1:23 mortal human **b** or birds or four-footed animals A
3: 7 why am I still **b** condemned as a sinner?
3:20 For "no human **b** will be justified in his sight" A
4:11 of all who believe without **b** circumcised
4:21 **b** fully convinced that God was able
6: 9 We know that Christ, **b** raised from the dead,
8:36 "For your sake we are **b** killed all day long;
9:20 But who indeed are you, a human **b**, A
10: 3 **b** ignorant of the righteousness that comes
14:15 your brother or sister is **b** injured by what you eat,
1Co 1:18 but to us who are **b** saved it is the power of God.
2:11 what human **b** knows what is truly human A
7:37 **b** under no necessity but having his own desire
8: 7 and their conscience, **b** weak, is defiled.
14: 7 how will anyone know what is **b** played?
14: 9 how will anyone know what is **b** said?
15: 2 also you are **b** saved, if you hold firmly to
15:21 For since death came through a human **b**, A
15:21 of the dead has also come through a human **b**; A
15:45 "The first man, Adam, became a living **b**"; B
2Co 1: 6 If we are **b** afflicted, it is for your consolation
1: 6 if we are **b** consoled, it is for your consolation,
2:15 of Christ to God among those who are **b** saved and
3:13 at the end of the glory that was **b** set aside.
3:18 are **b** transformed into the same image
4:11 we are always **b** given up to death for Jesus' sake,
4:16 our inner nature is **b** renewed day by day.
11:19 you gladly put up with fools, **b** wise yourselves!
12: 7 Therefore, to keep me from **b** too elated,
12: 7 to keep me from **b** too elated.
Gal 1:16 I did not confer with any human **b**, A
3:11 why am I still **b** persecuted
Eph 2:12 **b** aliens from the commonwealth of Israel,
3:16 in your inner **b** with power through his Spirit,
3:17 as you are **b** rooted and grounded in love.
6: 6 not only while **b** watched,
Php 2: 2 **b** in full accord and of one mind.
2: 7 **b** born in human likeness.
2: 7 And **b** found in human form,
2:17 if I am **b** poured out as a libation over the sacrifice
4:11 Not that I am referring to **b** in need;
4:12 the secret of **b** well-fed and of going hungry,
4:12 of having plenty and of **b** in need.
Col 3:10 which is **b** renewed in knowledge according to
3:22 only while **b** watched and in order to please them,
1Th 2:17 we were made orphans by **b** separated from you—
2Th 2: 1 and our **b** gathered together to him,
2Ti 2: 9 even to the point of **b** chained like a criminal.
3: 7 who are always **b** instructed and can never arrive
3:13 deceiving others and **b** deceived.
4: 6 As for me, I am already **b** poured out as a libation,
Tit 2: 5 kind, **b** submissive to their husbands,
3:11 and sinful, **b** self-condemned.
Heb 1: 3 and the exact imprint of God's very **b**,
2:18 he is able to help those who are **b** tested.
5:13 on milk, **b** still an infant, is unskilled in the word
6: 8 it is worthless and on the verge of **b** cursed;
10: 2 Otherwise, would they not have ceased **b** offered,
10:33 sometimes **b** publicly exposed to abuse
10:33 and sometimes **b** partners with those so treated.
13: 3 those who are **b** tortured,

Heb 13: 3 as though you yourselves were **b** tortured.
Jas 1:7,8 **b** double-minded and unstable in every way,
1: 9 Let the believer who is lowly boast in **b** raised up,
1:10 and the rich in **b** brought low,
1:13 should say, "I am **b** tempted by God";
1:14 **b** lured and enticed by it;
1:25 **b** not hearers who forget but doers who act—
5: 7 **b** patient with it until it receives the early and
5:17 Elijah was a human **b** like us, A
1Pe 1: 5 who are **b** protected by the power of God
1: 7 **b** more precious than gold that, though perishable,
2:19 For it is a credit to you if, **b** aware of God,
2Pe 1: 8 from **b** ineffective and unfruitful in the knowledge
3: 7 **b** kept until the day of judgment and destruction of
Rev 3: 1 you have a name of **b** alive, but you are dead.
3:18 to keep the shame of your nakedness from **b** seen;
Tob 1:19 the king knew about me and that I was **b** searched
13: 4 Exalt him in the presence of every living **b**, B
14:15 and he saw its prisoners **b** led into Media,
Jdt 8:16 for God is not like a human **b**, to be threatened, A
9: 1 the evening incense was **b** offered in the house
11: 7 him who has sent you to direct every living **b**! B
AdE 4: 1 "An innocent nation is **b** destroyed!"
4: 8 **b** brought up under my care—
4:11 to the king inside the inner court without **b** called,
14:11 do not surrender your scepter to what has no **b**;
Wis 4:13 **B** perfected in a short time,
8:20 or rather, **b** good, I entered an undefiled body.
11: 9 though they were **b** disciplined in mercy,
12:27 **b** punished by means of them,
13:13 he forms it in the likeness of a human **b**, A
14:15 as a god what was once a dead human **b**, A
14:20 before they had honored as a human **b**. A
15:16 For a human **b** made them, A
16: 4 how their enemies were **b** tormented.
16: 5 upon your people and they were **b** destroyed by
16:18 that they were **b** pursued by the judgment of God;
16:22 that the crops of their enemies were **b** destroyed
Sir 20: 5 while others are detested for **b** talkative.
29: 7 but from fear of **b** defrauded needlessly.
29:18 **B** surety has ruined many who were prosperous,
29:23 and you will hear no reproach for **b** a guest.
29:25 the host and provide drink without **b** thanked,
45:23 of Eleazar ranks third in glory for **b** zealous in
49:16 above every other created living **b** was Adam. B
LtJ 6:24 even when they were **b** cast, they did not feel it.
Sus 1:45 Just as she was **b** led off to execution,
1:54 Under what tree did you see them **b** intimate
1:58 Under what tree did you catch them **b** intimate
1Mc 2: 6 He saw the blasphemies **b** committed in Judah
5:14 While the letter was still **b** read, other messengers,
5:16 in distress and were **b** attacked by enemies.
6:38 to harass the enemy while **b** themselves protected
7:33 to show him the burnt offering that was **b** offered
12:26 the enemy were **b** drawn up in formation to attack
2Mc 1:19 when our ancestors were **b** led captive to Persia,
1:23 And while the sacrifice was **b** consumed,
2: 1 Jeremiah ordered those who were **b** deported
2: 2 instructed those who were **b** deported not to forget
2: 9 It was also made clear that **b** possessed
4:18 When the quadrennial games were **b** held at Tyre
4:19 chosen as **b** Antiochian citizens from Jerusalem,
5: 5 and at last the city was **b** taken,
6:18 was **b** forced to open his mouth
7: 1 and were **b** compelled by the king,
7:14 to cherish the hope God gives of **b** raised again
7:22 "I do not know how you came into **b** in my womb.
7:24 that he was **b** treated with contempt,
7:24 The youngest brother **b** still alive,
7:28 And in the same way the human race came into **b**.
7:39 **b** exasperated at his scorn.
8: 3 to have mercy on the city that was **b** destroyed and
10:30 they kept him from **b** wounded.
11: 1 **b** vexed at what had happened,
13:10 to help those who were on the point of **b** deprived
14:41 **B** surrounded, Razis fell upon his own sword,
15:19 **b** anxious over the encounter in the open country.
1Es 6:10 in their hands and **b** completed with all splendor
8:39 their names **b** Eliphelet, Jeuel, and Shemaiah,
3Mc 1: 9 and **b** impressed by its excellence and its beauty,
1:23 **b** barely restrained by the old men and the elders,
2:22 besides **b** paralyzed in his limbs,
3: 2 While these matters were **b** arranged,
3: 2 a pretext **b** given by a report
3: 8 **b** grieved at the situation, and expected
4: 4 a harsh and ruthless spirit were they **b** sent off,
4: 5 sluggish and bent with age, was **b** led away,
5:27 the report and **b** struck by the unusual invitation
5:41 and also in constant danger of **b** plundered."
5:46 the city now **b** filled with countless masses
6: 9 who are **b** outrageously treated by the abominable
6:12 of the lawless are **b** deprived of life in the manner
6:40 **b** provided with everything by the king,
7:21 **b** held in honor and awe;
2Es 2:45 Now they are **b** crowned, and receive palms."
6:45 and the arrangement of the stars to come into **b**;
7:95 **b** gathered into their chambers and guarded
7:97 **b** incorruptible from then on.
8: 6 the likeness of a human **b** may be able to live. A
8:47 of **b** able to love my creation more than I love it.
10: 9 over so many who have come into **b** upon her.
10:27 but a city was **b** built,
10:42 but there appeared to you a city **b** built)
10:44 which you now behold as a city **b** built.
15:10 my people are **b** led like a flock to the slaughter;
16:27 a person will long to see another human **b**, A
4Mc 4: 9 to shield the holy place that was **b** treated
4Mc 4:24 and punishments were **b** disregarded
6: 5 was unmoved, as though **b** tortured in a dream;
6: 6 his flesh was **b** torn by scourges,
6: 6 and his sides were **b** cut to pieces.
6:10 Like a noble athlete the old man, while **b** beaten,
7:12 Eleazar, though **b** consumed by the fire,
8: 2 **b** unable to compel an aged man
8:24 against compulsion or take hollow pride in **b** put
9:20 the heap of coals was **b** quenched by the drippings
9:30 that you are **b** tortured more than I,
9:30 of your tyranny **b** defeated by our endurance for
10: 8 and while his vertebrae were **b** dislocated by this,
11: 1 When he too died, after **b** cruelly tortured,
11:20 While **b** tortured he said, "O contest befitting
13:12 to **b** slain for the sake of religion."
13:18 to each of the brothers who were **b** dragged away,
13:27 while watching their brothers **b** maltreated
15:15 She watched the flesh of her children **b** consumed
16: 9 or have the happiness of **b** called grandmother.
16:15 you stood and watched Eleazar **b** tortured,
18: 5 on earth and is **b** chastised after his death.

BEINGS‡ (84) [BE]

A. HUMAN BEINGS (73)

Ge 6: 7 from the earth the human **b** I have created— A
7:21 that swarm on the earth, and all human **b**; A
7:23 human **b** and animals and creeping things A
9: 5 and from human **b**, each one for the blood A
Ex 12:12 both human **b** and animals; A
13: 2 of human **b** and animals, is mine. A
Lev 27:29 No human **b** who have been devoted A
Nu 18:15 but the firstborn of human **b** you shall redeem, A
Dt 4:32 ever since the day that God created human **b** on A
20:19 in the field human **b** that they should come A
2Sa 7:14 with blows inflicted by human **b**. A
2Ch 19: 6 on behalf of human **b** but on the LORD's behalf; A
Job 1: 6 the heavenly **b** came to present themselves before
2: 1 the heavenly **b** came to present themselves before
4:17 Can human **b** be pure before their Maker? A
5: 7 but human **b** are born to trouble just A
7: 1 "Do not human **b** have a hard service on earth, A
7:17 What are human **b**, that you make so much A
35: 8 and your righteousness, other human **b**. A
38: 7 and all the heavenly **b** shouted for joy?
Ps 8: 4 what are human **b** that you are mindful of them, A
29: 1 O heavenly **b**, ascribe to the LORD glory
89: 6 Who among the heavenly **b** is like the LORD,
115:16 but the earth he has given to human **b**. A
135: 8 both human **b** and animals; A
144: 3 what are human **b** that you regard them, A
Ecc 1:13 that God has given to human **b** to be busy with. A
3:18 with regard to human **b** that God is testing them A
6:10 and it is known what human **b** are, A
7:29 that God made human **b** straightforward, A
Jer 5:26 Like fowlers they set a trap; they catch human **b**. A
7:20 human **b** and animals, on the trees of the field A
10:23 that the way of human **b** is not in their control, A
21: 6 both human **b** and animals; A
32:43 It is a desolation, without human **b** or animals; A
33:10 "It is a waste without human **b** or animals," A
33:12 without human **b** or animals, A
36:29 and will cut off from it human **b** and animals? A
50: 3 both human **b** and animals shall flee away. A
51:62 that neither human **b** nor animals shall live in it, A
Eze 14:13 and cut off from it human **b** and animals, A
14:17 and I cut off human **b** and animals from it; A
27:13 they exchanged human **b** and vessels of bronze A
36:11 I will multiply human **b** and animals upon you. A
38:20 and all human **b** that are on the face of the earth, A
Da 2:38 into whose hand he has given human **b**, A
4:12 and from it all living **b** were fed.
4:17 and sets over it the lowliest of human **b**.' A
Jnh 3: 8 Human **b** and animals shall be covered A
Hag 1:11 on human **b** and animals, and on all their labors. A
Mt 9: 8 who had given such authority to human **b**. A
Lk 16:15 human **b** is an abomination in the sight of God. A
Jn 5:41 I do not accept glory from human **b**. A
1Co 15:39 but there is one flesh for human **b**, A
2Co 10: 3 Indeed, we live as human **b**, A
Gal 4: 8 you were enslaved to **b** that by nature are not gods.
Heb 2: 6 What are human **b** that you are mindful of them, A
6:16 Human **b**, of course, swear A
Jdt 11: 7 Not only do human **b** serve him because of you, A
AdE 16:24 shall be made not only impassable for human **b**, A
Wis 7:20 powers of spirits and the thoughts of human **b**, A
9: 6 even one who is perfect among human **b** will A
Sir 1:15 She made among human **b** an eternal foundation, A
10:18 Pride was not created for human **b**, A
13:16 All living **b** associate with their own kind,
14:17 All living **b** become old like a garment,
16:30 With all kinds of living **b** he covered its surface,
17: 1 The Lord created human **b** out of earth, A
17: 4 He put the fear of them in all living **b**,
17:30 since human **b** are not immortal. A
17:32 but all human **b** are dust and ashes. A
18: 7 When human **b** have finished, A
18: 8 What are human **b**, and of what use are they? A
18:13 compassion of human **b** is for their neighbors, A
31:27 Wine is very life to human **b** if taken A
33:10 All human **b** come from the ground, A
38: 6 And he gave skill to human **b** that he might A
LtJ 6:11 with garments like human **b**— A
1Es 4:37 all human **b** are unrighteous, A
3Mc 2:15 unapproachable by human **b**. A
2Es 13:41 where no human **b** had ever lived, A
2Es 16:61 He formed human **b** and put a heart in the midst A
4Mc 2:21 Now when God fashioned human **b**, A
14:14 Even unreasoning animals, as well as human **b**, A

BEKA (1)

Ex 38:26 a **b** a head (that is, half a shekel, measured by

BEL (19)

Isa 46: 1 **B** bows down, Nebo stoops,
Jer 50: 2 Babylon is taken, **B** is put to shame,
51:44 I will punish **B** in Babylon,
LtJ 6:40 they bring **B** and pray that the mute may speak,
6:40 as though **B** were able to understand!
Bel 1: 3 Now the Babylonians had an idol called **B**,
1: 4 king said to him, "Why do you not worship **B**?"
1: 6 "Do you not think that **B** is a living god?
1: 8 the king was angry and called the priests of **B**
1: 9 But if you prove that **B** is eating them,
1: 9 because he has spoken blasphemy against **B**."
1:10 Now there were seventy priests of **B**,
1:10 So the king went with Daniel into the temple of **B**.
1:11 priests of **B** said, "See, we are now going outside;
1:12 if you do not find that **B** has eaten it all,
1:14 they had gone out, the king set out the food for **B**.
1:18 and shouted in a loud voice, "You are great, O **B**,
1:22 king put them to death, and gave **B** over to Daniel,
1:28 he has destroyed **B**, and killed the dragon,

BELA (14) [BELAITES]

Ge 14: 2 and the king of **B** (that is, Zoar).
14: 8 the king of Zeboiim, and the king of **B** (that is,
36:32 **B** son of Beor reigned in Edom,
36:33 **B** died, and Jobab son of Zerah
46:21 The children of Benjamin: **B**, Becher, Ashbel,
Nu 26:38 of **B**, the clan of the Belaites;
26:40 And the sons of **B** were Ard and Naaman:
1Ch 1:43 **B** son of Beor, whose city was called Dinhabah.
1:44 When **B** died, Jobab son of Zerah
5: 8 and **B** son of Azaz, son of Shema, son
7: 6 sons of Benjamin: **B**, Becher, and Jediael, three.
7: 7 The sons of **B**: Ezbon, Uzzi,
8: 1 Benjamin became the father of **B** his firstborn,
8: 3 And **B** had sons: Addar, Gera, Abihud,

BELAITES (1) [BELA]

Nu 26:38 of Bela, the clan of the **B**;

BELCH (1)

Wis 11:18 or **b** forth a thick pall of smoke,

BELCH (KJV) See also BELLOWING

BELIAR (1)

2Co 6:15 What agreement does Christ have with **B**?

BELIEF (2) [BELIEVE]

2Th 2:13 through sanctification by the Spirit and through **b**
2Mc 15:11 a sort of vision, which was worthy of **b**.

BELIEVE‡ (173) [BELIEF, BELIEVED, BELIEVER, BELIEVER'S, BELIEVERS, BELIEVES, BELIEVING]

Ge 45:26 He was stunned; he could not **b** them.
Ex 4: 1 "But suppose they do not **b** me or listen to me,
4: 5 "so that they may **b** that the LORD,
4: 8 "If they will not **b** you or heed the first sign,
4: 8 they may **b** the second sign.
4: 9 they will not **b** even these two signs or heed you,
Nu 14:11 And how long will they refuse to **b** in me,
1Ki 10: 7 but I did not **b** the reports until I came
2Ki 17:14 who did not **b** in the LORD their God.
2Ch 9: 6 but I did not **b** the reports until I came
20:20 **B** in the LORD your God and you will be
established; **b** his prophets."
32:15 or mislead you in this fashion, and do not **b** him,
Job 9:16 I do not **b** that he would listen to my voice.
Ps 27:13 I **b** that I shall see the goodness of the LORD in
78:32 they did not **b** in his wonders.
119:66 for I **b** in your commandments.
Pr 14:15 The simple **b** everything,
26:25 when an enemy speaks graciously, do not **b** it,
Isa 43:10 so that you may know and **b** me and understand
Jer 12: 6 do not **b** them, though they speak friendly words
40:14 But Gedaliah son of Ahikam would not **b** them.
La 4:12 The kings of the earth did not **b**,
Hab 1: 5 in your days that you would not **b** if you were told.
Mt 9:28 "Do you **b** that I am able to do this?"
18: 6 before one of these little ones who **b** in me,
21:25 he will say to us, 'Why then did you not **b** him?'
21:32 in the way of righteousness and you did not **b** him,
21:32 you did not change your minds and **b** him.
24:23 or 'There he is!'—do not **b** it.
24:26 He is in the inner rooms,' do not **b** it.
27:42 down from the cross now, and we will **b** in him.
Mk 1:15 repent, and **b** in the good news."
5:36 the leader of the synagogue, "Do not fear, only **b**."
9:24 Immediately the father of the child cried out, "I **b**;
9:42 before one of these little ones who **b** in me,
11:23 but **b** that what you say will come to pass,
11:24 **b** that you have received it, and it will be yours.
11:31 he will say, 'Why then did you not **b** him?'
13:21 There he is!'—do not **b** it.

Mk 15:32 so that we may see and **b.**"
16:11 ⟦and had been seen by her, they would not **b** it.⟧
16:13 ⟦but they did not **b** them.⟧
16:16 ⟦but the one who does not **b** will be condemned.⟧
16:17 ⟦And these signs will accompany those who **b:**⟧
Lk 1:20 But now, because you did not **b** my words,
8:12 so that they may not **b** and be saved.
8:13 they **b** only for a while and in a time
8:50 Only **b,** and she will be saved."
20: 5 he will say, 'Why did you not **b** him?'
22:67 He replied, "If I tell you, you will not **b;**
24:11 and they did not **b** them.
24:25 of heart to **b** all that the prophets have declared!
Jn 1: 7 so that all might **b** through him.
1:50 "Do you **b** because I told you that I saw you under
3:12 about earthly things and you do not **b,**
3:12 how can you **b** if I tell you about heavenly things?
3:18 Those who **b** in him are not condemned;
3:18 but those who do not **b** are condemned already,
4:21 Jesus said to her, "Woman, **b** me,
4:42 because of what you said that we **b,**
4:48 Unless you see signs and wonders you will not **b.**"
5:38 because you do not **b** him whom he has sent.
5:44 How can you **b** when you accept glory
5:46 If you believed Moses, you would **b** me,
5:47 But if you do not **b** what he wrote,
5:47 how will you **b** what I say?"
6:29 that you **b** in him whom he has sent."
6:30 so that we may see it and **b** you?
6:36 to you that you have seen me and yet do not **b.**
6:40 the Son and **b** in him may have eternal life;
6:64 But among you there are some who do not **b.**"
6:64 from the first who were the ones that did not **b,**
6:69 to **b** and know that you are the Holy One of God."
8:24 for you will die in your sins unless you **b**
8:45 But because I tell the truth, you do not **b** me.
8:46 If I tell the truth, why do you not **b** me?
9:18 The Jews did not **b** that he had been blind
9:35 he said, "Do you **b** in the Son of Man?"
9:36 Tell me, so that I may **b** in him."
9:38 He said, "Lord, I **b.**" And he worshiped him.
10:25 "I have told you, and you do not **b.**
10:26 but you do not **b,** because you do not belong
10:37 the works of my Father, then do not **b** me.
10:38 even though you do not **b** me, **b** the works,
11:15 not there, so that you may **b.**
11:25 Those who **b** in me, even though they die,
11:26 in me will never die. Do you **b** this?"
11:27 I **b** that you are the Messiah, the Son of God,
11:42 so that they may **b** that you sent me."
11:48 we let him go on like this, everyone will **b** in him,
12:36 While you have the light, **b** in the light,
12:37 they did not **b** in him.
12:39 And so they could not **b,** because Isaiah also said,
13:19 you may **b** that I am he.
14: 1 **B** in God, **b** also in me.
14:10 not **b** that I am in the Father and the Father is
14:11 **B** me that I am in the Father and the Father is
14:11 then **b** me because of the works themselves.
14:29 so that when it does occur, you may **b.**
16: 9 about sin, because they do not **b** in me;
16:30 by this we **b** that you came from God."
16:31 Jesus answered them, "Do you now **b?**
17:20 of those who will **b** in me through their word,
17:21 so that the world may **b** that you have sent me.
19:35 so that you also may **b.**
20:25 of the nails and my hand in his side, I will not **b.**"
20:27 Do not doubt but **b.**"
20:29 not seen and yet have come to **b.**"
20:31 that you may come to **b** that Jesus is the Messiah,
Ac 9:26 for they did not **b** that he was a disciple.
13:41 a work that you will never **b,**
14:23 to the Lord in whom they had come to **b.**
15:11 we **b** that we will be saved through the grace of
16:31 They answered, "**B** on the Lord Jesus,
19: 4 telling the people to **b** in the one who was to come
19: 9 When some stubbornly refused to **b** and spoke evil
26:27 King Agrippa, do you **b** the prophets?
26:27 I know that you **b.**"
28:24 by what he had said, while others refused to **b.**
Ro 3:22 of God through faith in Jesus Christ for all who **b.**
4:11 of all who **b** without being circumcised
4:24 to us who **b** in him who raised Jesus our Lord
6: 8 we **b** that we will also live with him.
10: 9 and **b** in your heart that God raised him from
10:14 to **b** in one of whom they have never heard?
14: 2 Some **b** in eating anything,
1Co 1:21 of our proclamation, to save those who **b.**
3: 5 Servants through whom you came to **b,**
11:18 and to some extent I **b** it.
15: 2 unless you have come to **b** in vain.
15:11 so we proclaim and so you have come to **b.**
2Co 4:13 we also **b,** and so we speak,
Gal 2:16 And we have come to **b** in Christ Jesus,
3: 7 those who **b** are the descendants of Abraham.
3: 9 For this reason, those who **b** are blessed
3:22 in Jesus Christ might be given to those who **b.**
Eph 1:19 of his power for us who **b,**
1Th 4:14 For since we **b** that Jesus died and rose again,
2Th 2:11 leading them to **b** what is false,
1Ti 1:16 an example to those who would come to **b** in him
4: 3 to be received with thanksgiving by those who **b**
4:10 especially of those who **b.**
Tit 3: 8 to **b** in God may be careful to devote themselves
Heb 11: 6 for whoever would approach him must **b**
Jas 2: 1 do you with your acts of favoritism really **b**
2:19 You **b** that God is one; you do well.
Jas 2:19 Even the demons **b**—and shudder.
1Pe 1: 8 even though you do not see him now, you **b** in him
2: 7 To you then who **b,** he is precious;
2: 7 but for those who do not **b,**
1Jn 3:23 that we should **b** in the name
4: 1 Beloved, do not **b** every spirit,
4:16 we have known and **b** the love that God has for us.
5:10 Those who **b** in the Son of God have the testimony
5:10 Those who do not **b** in God have made him a liar
5:13 I write these things to you who **b** in the name of
Jude 1: 5 afterward destroyed those who did not **b.**
Tob 2:14 But I did not **b** her,
10: 7 and mother do not **b** that they will see me again.
14: 4 for I **b** the word of God that Nahum spoke
14: 4 For I know and **b** that whatever God has said will
Sir 19:15 so do not **b** everything you hear.
1Mc 10:46 they did not **b** or accept them,
1Es 4:28 And now do you not **b** me?
2Es 1:35 who without having heard me will **b.**
1:37 with the spirit they will **b** the things I have said.
6:33 '**B** and do not be afraid!
7:*130* [60] But they did not **b** him or the prophets after
4Mc 5:25 since we **b** that the law was established by God,
7:19 since they **b** that they, like our patriarchs Abraham

BELIEVED (67) [BELIEVE]

Ge 15: 6 And he **b** the LORD;
Ex 4:31 The people **b;** and when they heard
14:31 the people feared the LORD and **b** in the LORD
Ps 106:12 Then they **b** his words; they sang his praise.
Isa 53: 1 Who has **b** what we have heard?
Jnh 3: 5 And the people of Nineveh **b** God;
Mt 21:32 but the tax collectors and the prostitutes **b** him;
Mk 16:14 ⟦not **b** those who saw him after he had risen.⟧
Lk 1:45 And blessed is she who **b** that there would be
Jn 1:12 But to all who received him, who **b** in his name,
2:11 and his disciples **b** in him.
2:22 and they **b** the scripture and the word
2:23 many **b** in his name because they saw the signs
3:18 not **b** in the name of the only Son of God.
4:39 Many Samaritans from that city **b** in him because
4:41 And many more **b** because of his word.
4:50 The man **b** the word that Jesus spoke to him
4:53 So he himself **b,** along with his whole household.
5:46 If you **b** Moses, you would believe me,
7: 5 (For not even his brothers **b** in him.)
7:31 Yet many in the crowd **b** in him and were saying,
7:48 of the authorities or of the Pharisees **b** in him?
8:30 As he was saying these things, many **b** in him.
8:31 Then Jesus said to the Jews who had **b** in him,
10:42 And many **b** in him there.
11:40 Jesus said to her, "Did I not tell you that if you **b,**
11:45 with Mary and had seen what Jesus did, **b** in him.
12:38 "Lord, who has **b** our message,
12:42 many, even of the authorities, **b** in him.
16:27 because you have loved me and have **b** that I came
17: 8 and they have **b** that you sent me.
20: 8 also went in, and he saw and **b;**
20:29 "Have you **b** because you have seen me?
Ac 2:44 All who **b** were together and had all things
4: 4 But many of those who heard the word **b;**
4:32 the whole group of those who **b** were of one heart
8:12 But when they **b** Philip, who was proclaiming
8:13 Even Simon himself **b.**
9:42 and many **b** in the Lord.
11:17 the same gift that he gave us when we **b** in
13:12 When the proconsul saw what had happened, he **b,**
17:12 Many of them therefore **b,**
22:19 and beat those who **b** in you.
Ro 4: 3 "Abraham **b** God, and it was reckoned to him
4:17 in the presence of the God in whom he **b,**
4:18 he **b** that he would become "the father
10:14 are they to call on one in whom they have not **b?**
10:16 for Isaiah says, "Lord, who has **b** our message?"
2Co 4:13 "I **b,** and so I spoke"—
Gal 3: 6 as Abraham "**b** God, and it was reckoned to him
3: 9 who believe are blessed with Abraham who **b.**
Eph 1:13 the gospel of your salvation, and had **b** in him,
2Th 1:10 be marveled at on that day among all who have **b,**
1:10 because our testimony to you was **b.**
2:12 that all who have not **b** the truth but took pleasure
1Ti 3:16 **b** in throughout the world, taken up in glory.
2Ti 3:14 continue in what you have learned and firmly **b,**
Heb 4: 3 For we who have **b** enter that rest,
Jas 2:23 that says, "Abraham **b** God, and it was reckoned
Jdt 14:10 the God of Israel had done, he **b** firmly in God.
Sus 1:41 the assembly **b** them and condemned her to death.
1Mc 1:30 he spoke peaceable words to them, and they **b** him;
2:59 and Mishael **b** and were saved from the flame.
3Mc 6:34 Those who had previously **b** that the Jews would
2Es 3:32 so **b** the covenants as these tribes of Jacob?
5:29 on those who **b** your covenants.
9: 7 or on account of the faith by which they have **b,**

BELIEVER (10) [BELIEVE]

Ac 16: 1 the son of a Jewish woman who was a **b;**
16:34 that he had become a **b** in God.
18: 8 a **b** in the Lord, together with all his household;
1Co 6: 5 among you wise enough to decide between one **b**
6: 6 but a **b** goes to court against a **b**—
7:12 that if any **b** has a wife who is an unbeliever,
2Co 6:15 Or what does a **b** share with an unbeliever?
Jas 1: 9 Let the **b** who is lowly boast in being raised up,
1Jn 2:11 But whoever hates another **b** is in the darkness,

BELIEVER'S (1) [BELIEVE]

Jn 7:38 of the **b** heart shall flow rivers of living water.' "

BELIEVERS‡ (54) [BELIEVE]

Jn 7:39 which **b** in him were to receive;
Ac 1:15 In those days Peter stood up among the **b**
5:14 Yet more than ever **b** were added to the Lord,
9:30 When the **b** learned of it,
9:32 Now as Peter went here and there among all the **b,**
10:23 and some of the **b** from Joppa accompanied him.
10:45 The circumcised **b** who had come
11: 1 the apostles and the **b** who were in Judea heard
11: 2 the circumcised **b** criticized him,
11:21 a great number became **b** and turned to the Lord.
11:29 each would send relief to the **b** living in Judea;
12:17 And he added, "Tell this to James and to the **b.**"
13:48 as had been destined for eternal life became **b.**
14: 1 of both Jews and Greeks became **b.**
15: 3 and brought great joy to all the **b.**
15: 5 But some **b** who belonged to the sect of
15: 7 the message of the good news and become **b.**
15:23 the elders, to the **b** of Gentile origin in Antioch
15:32 said much to encourage and strengthen the **b.**
15:33 in peace by the **b** to those who had sent them.
15:36 the **b** in every city where we proclaimed the word
15:40 the **b** commending him to the grace of the Lord.
16: 2 He was well spoken of by the **b** in Lystra
17: 6 and some **b** before the city authorities,
17:10 very night the **b** sent Paul and Silas off to Beroea;
17:14 the **b** immediately sent Paul away to the coast,
17:34 But some of them joined him and became **b,**
18: 8 of the Corinthians who heard Paul became **b**
18:18 Paul said farewell to the **b** and sailed for Syria,
18:27 the **b** encouraged him and wrote to the disciples
18:27 through grace had become **b,**
19: 2 the Holy Spirit when you became **b?**"
19:18 Also many of those who became **b** confessed
20: 2 and had given the **b** much encouragement,
21: 7 and we greeted the **b** and stayed with them
21:20 many thousands of **b** there are among the Jews,
21:25 But as for the Gentiles who have become **b,**
28:14 There we found **b** and were invited to stay
28:15 The **b** from there, when they heard of us,
Ro 13:11 to us now than when we became **b;**
1Co 6: 8 you yourselves wrong and defraud—and **b** at that.
8:11 So by your knowledge those weak **b**
14:22 then, are a sign not for **b** but for unbelievers,
14:22 while prophecy is not for unbelievers but for **b.**
Gal 2: 4 But because of false **b** secretly brought in,
1Th 1: 7 so that you became an example to all the **b**
2:10 and blameless our conduct was toward you **b.**
2:13 God's word, which is also at work in you **b.**
2Th 3: 6 to keep away from **b** who are living in idleness
3:15 not regard them as enemies, but warn them as **b.**
1Ti 4:12 but set the **b** an example in speech and conduct,
6: 2 since those who benefit by their service are **b**
Tit 1: 6 married only once, whose children are **b,**
1Pe 2:17 Love the family of **b.**

BELIEVES‡ (25) [BELIEVE]

Mk 9:23 All things can be done for the one who **b.**"
16:16 ⟦The one who **b** and is baptized will be saved;⟧
Jn 3:15 that whoever **b** in him may have eternal life.
3:16 so that everyone who **b** in him may not perish
3:36 Whoever **b** in the Son has eternal life;
5:24 and **b** him who sent me has eternal life,
6:35 and whoever **b** in me will never be thirsty.
6:47 Very truly, I tell you, whoever **b** has eternal life.
7:38 and let the one who **b** in me drink.
11:26 everyone who lives and **b** in me will never die.
12:44 "Whoever **b** in me **b** not in me but in him who sent me.
12:46 so that everyone who **b** in me should not remain in
14:12 the one who **b** in me will also do the works
Ac 10:43 the prophets testify about him that everyone who **b**
13:39 by this Jesus everyone who **b** is set free
Ro 9:33 and whoever **b** in him will not be put to shame."
10: 4 be righteousness for everyone who **b.**
10:10 For one **b** with the heart and so is justified,
10:11 "No one who **b** in him will be put to shame."
1Co 13: 7 It bears all things, **b** all things, hopes all things,
1Pe 2: 6 and whoever **b** in him will not be put to shame."
1Jn 5: 1 Everyone who **b** that Jesus is
5: 5 the world but the one who **b** that Jesus is the Son
Sir 34: 2 so is anyone who **b** in dreams.

BELIEVING (11) [BELIEVE]

Jn 12:11 that many of the Jews were deserting and were **b**
20:31 and that through **b** you may have life in his name.
Ac 24:14 **b** everything laid down according to the law
Ro 15:13 of hope fill you with all joy and peace in **b,**
1Co 9: 5 not have the right to be accompanied by a **b** wife,
Gal 3: 2 the works of the law or by **b** what you heard?
3: 5 or by your **b** what you heard?
Php 1:29 of **b** in Christ, but of suffering for him as well—
1Ti 5:16 any **b** woman has relatives who are really widows,
6: 2 Those who have **b** masters must not
1Jn 5:10 a liar by not **b** in the testimony that God has given

BELITTLES (1)

Pr 11:12 Whoever **b** another lacks sense,

BELL (3) [BELLS]

Ex 28:34 a golden **b** and a pomegranate alternating all

Ex 39:26 a **b** and a pomegranate, a **b** and a pomegranate all

BELLIES (3) [BELLY]

Job 20:15 God casts them out of their **b.**
20:20 "They knew no quiet in their **b;**
Ps 17:14 May their **b** be filled with what you have stored up

BELLOWING (1)

Ps 59: 7 There they are, **b** with their mouths,

BELLOWS (2)

Jer 6:29 **b** blow fiercely, the lead is consumed by the fire;
4Mc 8:13 and wedges and **b,** the tyrant resumed speaking:

BELLS (5) [BELL]

Ex 28:33 with **b** of gold between them all around—
39:25 They also made **b** of pure gold,
39:25 the **b** between the pomegranates on the lower hem
Zec 14:20 On that day there shall be inscribed on the **b** of
Sir 45: 9 with many golden **b** all around,

BELLY‡ (19) [BELLIES, BELLY'S]

Ge 3:14 upon your **b** you shall go,
Lev 11:42 Whatever moves on its **b,**
Nu 25: 8 the Israelite and the woman, through the **b.**
Jdg 3:21 and thrust it into Eglon's **b;**
3:22 for he did not draw the sword out of his **b;**
2Sa 20:10 the **b** so that his entrails poured out on the ground,
Job 20:23 To fill their **b** to the full God will send his fierce
40:16 and its power in the muscles of its **b.**
Pr 13:25 but the **b** of the wicked is empty.
SS 7: 2 Your **b** is a heap of wheat, encircled with lilies.
Jer 51:34 he has filled his **b** with my delicacies,
Jnh 1:17 in the **b** of the fish three days and three nights.
2: 1 to the LORD his God from the **b** of the fish,
2: 2 out of the **b** of Sheol I cried,
Mt 12:40 as Jonah was three days and three nights in the **b**
Php 3:19 Their end is destruction; their god is the **b;**
Sir 51: 5 from the deep **b** of Hades, from an unclean tongue
3Mc 6: 8 And Jonah, wasting away in the **b** of a huge,
2Es 15:35 be blood from the sword as high as a horse's **b**

BELLY'S (1) [BELLY]

3Mc 7:11 that those who for the **b** sake had transgressed

BELMAIN (1)

Jdt 4: 4 **B,** and Jericho, and to Choba and Aesora,

BELNUUS (1)

1Es 9:31 and Naidus, and Bescaspasmys and Sesthel, and **B**

BELONG (84) [BELONGED, BELONGING, BELONGINGS, BELONGS]

Ge 32:17 and asks you, 'To whom do you **b?**
32:18 then you shall say, 'They **b** to your servant Jacob;
40: 8 "Do not interpretations **b** to God?
Lev 7: 9 shall **b** to the priest who offers it.
7:10 shall **b** to all the sons of Aaron equally.
7:14 it shall **b** to the priest who dashes the blood of
7:31 but the breast shall **b** to Aaron and his sons.
Nu 18: 9 or guilt offering, shall **b** to you and your sons.
33:54 the inheritance shall **b** to the person on whom
35: 5 this shall **b** to them as pasture land for their towns.
Dt 10:14 the heaven of heavens **b** to the LORD your God,
29:29 The secret things **b** to the LORD our God,
29:29 revealed things **b** to us and to our children forever,
Jos 2:13 my brothers and sisters, and all who **b** to them,
6:22 and bring the woman out of it and all who **b** to her,
17: 9 among the towns of Manasseh, **b** to Ephraim.
Jdg 19:12 who do not **b** to the people of Israel;
Ru 2: 5 "To whom does this young woman **b?"**
1Sa 25:22 so much as one male of all who **b** to him."
30:13 Then David said to him, "To whom do you **b?**
2Sa 3:12 saying, "To whom does the land **b?**
4: 2 for Beeroth is considered to **b** to Benjamin.
Ne 5: 5 and our fields and vineyards now **b** to others."
Ps 47: 9 shields of the earth **b** to God; he is highly exalted.
82: 8 for all the nations **b** to you!
Pr 16: 1 The plans of the mind **b** to mortals,
Eze 44:30 of all kinds from all your offerings, shall **b** to
45: 6 it shall **b** to the whole house of Israel.
45: 7 And to the prince shall **b** the land on both sides of
46:16 to any of his sons out of his inheritance, it shall **b**
48:12 It shall **b** to them as a special portion from
48:21 and of the property of the city shall **b** to the prince.
48:21 it shall **b** to the prince.
Da 5:23 and to whom **b** all your ways,
9: 9 To the Lord our God **b** mercy and forgiveness,
Lk 15:12 give me the share of the property that will **b**
20:34 "Those who **b** to this age marry and are given
Jn 10:16 I have other sheep that do not **b** to this fold.
10:26 because you do not **b** to my sheep.
15:19 Because you do not **b** to the world,
17:14 because they do not **b** to the world, just as I do not **b** to the world.
17:16 They do not **b** to the world, just as I do not **b** to the world.
Ac 27:23 of the God to whom I **b** and whom I worship,
Ro 1: 6 including yourselves who are called to **b**
7: 4 so that you may **b** to another,
8: 9 not have the Spirit of Christ does not **b** to him.
9: 4 They are Israelites, and to them **b** the adoption,
Ro 9: 5 to them **b** the patriarchs, and from them,
9: 6 For not all Israelites truly **b** to Israel,
16:10 Greet those who **b** to the family of Aristobulus.
16:11 in the Lord who **b** to the family of Narcissus.
1Co 1:12 "I **b** to Paul," or "I **b** to Apollos," or "I **b** to Cephas," or "I **b** to Christ."
3: 4 says, "I **b** to Paul," and another, "I **b** to Apollos,"
3:22 or the future—all **b** to you,
3:23 and you **b** to Christ, and Christ belongs to God.
12:15 "Because I am not a hand, I do not **b** to the body,"
12:16 "Because I am not an eye, I do not **b** to the body,"
15:23 then at his coming those who **b** to Christ.
2Co 10: 7 If you are confident that you **b** to Christ,
10: 7 that just as you **b** to Christ, so also do we.
Gal 3:29 And if you **b** to Christ,
5:24 And those who **b** to Christ Jesus have crucified
1Th 5: 8 But since we **b** to the day, let us be sober,
Heb 3: 6 if we hold firm the confidence and the pride that **b**
6: 9 of better things in your case, things that **b**
7: 6 But this man, who does not **b** to their ancestry,
1Pe 4:11 To him **b** the glory and the power forever
1Jn 2:19 They went out from us, but they did not **b** to us;
Tob 7: 3 They answered, "We **b** to the descendants
8:21 and we **b** to you as well as to your wife now
Jdt 10:12 They asked her, "To what people do you **b,**
Wis 1:16 because they are fit to **b** to his company.
2:24 and those who **b** to his company experience it.
1Mc 5:62 But they did not **b** to the family of those men
12:23 and your property **b** to us, and ours **b** to you.
2Mc 3: 6 that they did not **b** to the account of the sacrifices,
4Mc 4: 3 which are not the property of the temple but **b**

BELONGED (51) [BELONG]

Ge 31: 1 he has gained all this wealth from what **b**
Ex 29:27 from that which **b** to Aaron and his sons.
Nu 3:21 To Gershon **b** the clan of the Libnites and the clan
3:27 To Kohath **b** the clan of the Amramites,
3:33 To Merari **b** the clan of the Mahlites and the clan
16:32 everyone who **b** to Korah and all their goods.
16:33 with all that **b** to them went down alive into Sheol;
Jos 6:23 her mother, her brothers, and all who **b** to her—
6:25 with her family and all who **b** to her,
17: 8 The land of Tappuah **b** to Manasseh,
17: 8 the boundary of Manasseh **b** to the Ephraimites.
21:10 one of the families of the Kohathites who **b** to
Jdg 6:11 which **b** to Joash the Abiezrite,
18:27 and the priest who **b** to him, came to Laish,
Ru 4: 3 the parcel of land that **b** to our kinsman Elimelech.
4: 9 all that **b** to Elimelech and all that **b** to Chilion
1Sa 25:21 so that nothing was missed of all that **b** to him;
27: 6 Ziklag has **b** to the kings of Judah to this day.
2Sa 9: 9 that **b** to Saul and to all his house I have given
16: 4 "All that **b** to Mephibosheth is now yours."
1Ki 4:10 in Arubboth (to him **b** Socoh and all the land
6:22 that **b** to the inner sanctuary he overlaid with gold.
15:27 which **b** to the Philistines;
16:15 which **b** to the Philistines,
2Ki 12:16 of the LORD; it **b** to the priests.
14:28 for Israel Damascus and Hamath, which had **b**
24: 7 that **b** to the king of Egypt from the Wadi of Egypt
1Ch 4:40 for the former inhabitants there **b** to Ham.
5: 2 yet the birthright **b** to Joseph.)
2Ch 21:17 the possessions they found that **b** to
26:23 near his ancestors in the burial field that **b** to
34:33 from all the territory that **b** to the people of Israel,
Ezr 2:59 or their descent, whether they **b** to Israel:
Ne 7:61 or their descent, whether they **b** to Israel:
Eze 42: 3 Across the twenty cubits that **b** to the inner court,
42: 3 and facing the pavement that **b** to the outer court,
Lk 1: 5 who **b** to the priestly order of Abijah.
Jn 15:19 If you **b** to the world,
Ac 4:37 He sold a field that **b** to him,
6: 9 of those who **b** to the synagogue of the Freedmen
9: 2 so that if he found any who **b** to the Way,
12: 1 upon some who **b** to the church.
15: 5 But some believers who **b** to the sect of
23:34 he asked what province he **b** to,
26: 5 that I have **b** to the strictest sect of our religion
Col 2:20 why do you live as if you still **b** to the world?
Heb 7:13 Now the one of whom these things are spoken **b**
1Jn 2:19 for if they had **b** to us,
Jdt 8: 2 who **b** to her tribe and family,
1Es 5:37 by their ancestral houses or lineage that they **b**

BELONGING (31) [BELONG]

Ge 46:26 All the persons **b** to Jacob who came into Egypt,
Lev 25:32 of redemption of the houses in the cities **b** to them.
25:33 houses sold in a city **b** to them—
Nu 25:14 head of an ancestral house **b** to the Simeonites.
Dt 4:43 Bezer in the wilderness on the tableland **b** to
4:43 Ramoth in Gilead **b** to the Gadites,
4:43 and Golan in Bashan **b** to the Manassites.
Jos 15:21 The towns **b** to the tribe of the people of Judah in
18:14 Kiriath-jearim), a town **b** to the tribe of Judah.
21:20 of the Kohathites **b** to the Kohathite families of
Ru 2: 3 she came to the part of the field **b** to Boaz,
1Sa 6:18 the number of all the cities of the Philistines **b** to
1Ki 13:23 they saddled for him a donkey **b** to
14:11 Anyone **b** to Jeroboam who dies in the city,
16: 4 Anyone **b** to Baasha who dies in the city
21:24 Anyone **b** to Ahab who dies in the city
2Ki 9:25 and throw him on the plot of ground **b** to Naboth
1Ch 7: 5 Their kindred **b** to all the families of Issachar were
26:21 the sons of the Gershonites **b** to Ladan,
26:21 the heads of families **b** to Ladan the Gershonite:
2Ch 31:19 in the fields of common land **b** to their towns,
Ne 12:44 for the priests and for the Levites from the fields **b**
Isa 8: 1 **"B** to Maher-shalal-hash-baz,"
Eze 43:21 be burnt in the appointed place **b** to the temple,
Lk 5: 3 He got into one of the boats, the one **b** to Simon,
Ac 2:10 Egypt and the parts of Libya **b** to Cyrene,
7: 6 be resident aliens in a country **b** to others,
28: 7 in the neighborhood of that place were lands **b** to
1Co 7:22 the Lord as a slave is a freed person **b** to the Lord,
Sir 9: 8 and do not gaze at beauty **b** to another;
2Mc 3:10 that there were some deposits **b** to widows

BELONGINGS (4) [BELONG]

Jos 7:11 and they have put them among their own **b.**
Jer 20: 5 all its gains, all its prized **b,**
Lk 17:31 on the housetop who has **b** in the house must
3Mc 7:21 at all to confiscation of their **b** by any one.

BELONGS‡ (56) [BELONG]

Ge 31:16 that God has taken away from our father **b** to us
Ex 9: 4 nothing shall die of all that **b** to the Israelites.' "
20:17 or donkey, or anything that **b** to your neighbor.
Lev 14:13 guilt offering, like the sin offering, **b** to the priest:
27:26 however, which as a firstling **b** to the LORD,
Nu 1:50 and over all its equipment, and over all that **b** to it;
16:30 with all that **b** to them,
28:23 which **b** to the regular burnt offering.
Dt 5:21 or donkey, or anything that **b** to your neighbor.
Jos 13: 4 and Mearah that **b** to the Sidonians, to Aphek,
22:11 on the side that **b** to the Israelites.
Jdg 6:24 which **b** to the Abiezrites.
6:25 pull down the altar of Baal that **b** to your father,
18:28 It was in the valley that **b** to Beth-rehob.
19:14 down on them near Gibeah, which **b** to Benjamin.
20: 4 answered, "I came to Gibeah that **b** to Benjamin,
1Sa 17: 1 they were gathered at Socoh, which **b** to Judah,
30:14 that which **b** to Judah and on the Negeb of Caleb;
2Sa 6:12 the household of Obed-edom and all that **b** to him,
1Ki 17: 9 which **b** to Sidon, and live there;
19: 3 and came to Beer-sheba, which **b** to Judah;
22: 3 "Do you know that Ramoth-gilead **b** to us,
2Ki 14:11 in battle at Beth-shemesh, which **b** to Judah.
1Ch 13: 6 that is, to Kiriath-jearim, which **b** to Judah,
2Ch 25:21 in battle at Beth-shemesh, which **b** to Judah.
Ps 3: 8 Deliverance **b** to the LORD;
22:28 For dominion **b** to the LORD,
62:11 twice have I heard this: that power **b** to God,
62:12 and steadfast love **b** to you,
68:20 and to GOD, the Lord, **b** escape from death.
89:18 For our shield **b** to the LORD,
Pr 21:31 but the victory **b** to the LORD.
Eze 48:22 be in the middle of that which **b** to the prince.
Jnh 2: 9 Deliverance **b** to the LORD!"
Mic 7:14 that **b** to you, which lives alone in a forest in
Zec 9: 1 For to the LORD **b** the capital of Aram,
Mt 19:14 to such as these that the kingdom of heaven **b."**
20:14 Take what **b** to you and go;
20:15 Am I not allowed to do what I choose with what **b**
Mk 10:14 it is to such as these that the kingdom of God **b.**
Lk 16:12 you have not been faithful with what **b** to another,
18:16 it is to such as these that the kingdom of God **b.**
Jn 3:31 the one who is of the earth **b** to the earth
18:37 Everyone who **b** to the truth listens to my voice."
1Co 3:23 and you belong to Christ, and Christ **b** to God.
2Co 4: 7 that this extraordinary power **b** to God
Col 2:17 but the substance **b** to Christ.
2Ti 3:17 so that everyone who **b** to God may be proficient,
1Jn 2:19 that none of them **b** to us.
Rev 7:10 "Salvation **b** to our God who is seated on
17:11 it is an eighth but it **b** to the seven,
Tob 5: 9 about his family and to what tribe he **b,**
1Mc 10:42 because it **b** to the priests who minister there.
2Mc 15:12 and had been trained from childhood in all that **b**
1Es 4:40 To it **b** the strength and the kingship and
2Es 9:13 the age **b** and for whose sake the age was made."

BELOVED‡ (136) [LOVE]

A. MY BELOVED (43)
B. BELOVED SON; SON, THE BELOVED (9)
C. YOUR BELOVED (8)

Dt 33:12 The **b** of the LORD rests in safety—
33:12 the **b** rests between his shoulders.
2Sa 1:23 Saul and Jonathan, **b** and lovely!
1:26 greatly **b** were you to me;
Ne 13:26 and he was **b** by his God,
Ps 127: 2 for he gives sleep to his **b.**
SS 1:13 My **b** is to me a bag of myrrh that lies A
1:14 My **b** is to me a cluster of henna blossoms in A
1:16 Ah, you are beautiful, my **b,** truly lovely. A
2: 3 so is my **b** among young men. A
2: 8 The voice of my **b!** A
2: 9 My **b** is like a gazelle or a young stag. A
2:10 My **b** speaks and says to me: A
2:16 My **b** is mine and I am his; A
2:17 day breathes and the shadows flee, turn, my **b,** A
4:16 Let my **b** come to his garden, A
5: 2 Listen! my **b** is knocking. A
5: 4 My **b** thrust his hand into the opening, A
5: 5 I arose to open to my **b,** A
5: 6 I opened to my **b,** but my beloved had turned A
5: 6 but my **b** had turned and was gone. A
5: 8 O daughters of Jerusalem, if you find my **b,** A
5: 9 What is your **b** more than another beloved, C
5: 9 What is your beloved more than another **b,**
5: 9 What is your **b** more than another beloved, C

SS 5: 9 What is your beloved more than another **b**,
5:10 My **b** is all radiant and ruddy, A
5:16 This is my **b** and this is my friend, A
6: 1 has your **b** gone, O fairest among women? C
6: 1 Which way has your **b** turned, C
6: 2 My **b** has gone down to his garden, A
6: 3 I am my beloved's and my **b** is mine; A
7:11 Come, my **b**, let us go forth into the fields, A
7:13 which I have laid up for you, O my **b**. A
8: 5 up from the wilderness, leaning upon her **b**?
8:14 my **b**, and be like a gazelle or a young stag A
Isa 5: 1 for my **b** my love-song concerning his vineyard: A
5: 1 My **b** had a vineyard on a very fertile hill. A
22: 4 comfort me for the destruction of my **b** people. A
Jer 11:15 What right has my **b** in my house, A
12: 7 the **b** of my heart into the hands of her enemies.
Da 9:23 to declare it, for you are greatly **b**.
10:11 He said to me, "Daniel, greatly **b**,
10:19 He said, "Do not fear, greatly **b**, you are safe.
11:37 or to the one **b** by women;
Mt 3:17 voice from heaven said, "This is my Son, the **B**, B
12:18 my **b**, with whom my soul is well pleased. A
17: 5 my Son, the **B**; with him I am well pleased; B
Mk 1:11 my Son, the **B**; with you I am well pleased." B
9: 7 "This is my Son, the **B**; listen to him!" B
12: 6 He had still one other, a **b** son. B
Lk 3:22 my Son, the **B**; with you I am well pleased." B
20:13 I will send my **b** son; AB
Ac 15:25 along with our **b** Barnabas and Paul,
Ro 1: 7 To all God's **b** in Rome, who are called to
9:25 and her who was not **b** I will call '**b**.' "
11:28 but as regards election they are **b**,
12:19 **B**, never avenge yourselves,
16: 5 Greet my **b** Epaenetus, who was the first convert A
16: 8 Greet Ampliatus, my **b** in the Lord. A
16: 9 our co-worker in Christ, and my **b** Stachys. A
16:12 Greet the **b** Persis, who has worked hard in
1Co 4:14 but to admonish you as my **b** children. A
4:17 who is my **b** and faithful child in the Lord, A
15:58 Therefore, my **b**, be steadfast, immovable, A
2Co 7: 1 Since we have these promises, **b**,
12:19 **b**, is for the sake of building you up.
Eph 1: 6 that he freely bestowed on us in the **B**.
5: 1 Therefore be imitators of God, as **b** children,
Php 1:12 to know, **b**, that what has happened
2:12 my **b**, just as you have always obeyed me, A
3:13 **B**, I do not consider that I have made it my own;
4: 1 stand firm in the Lord in this way, my **b**. A
4: 8 Finally, **b**, whatever is true,
Col 1: 7 from Epaphras, our **b** fellow servant.
1:13 transferred us into the kingdom of his **b** Son, B
3:12 As God's chosen ones, holy and **b**,
4: 7 he is a **b** brother, a faithful minister,
4: 9 the faithful and **b** brother, who is one of you.
4:14 Luke, the **b** physician, and Demas greet you.
1Th 1: 4 For we know, brothers and sisters **b** by God,
4:10 But we urge you, **b**, to do so more and more,
5: 4 But you, **b**, are not in darkness,
5:14 And we urge you, **b**, to admonish the idlers,
5:25 **B**, pray for us.
2Th 2:13 brothers and sisters **b** by the Lord,
3: 6 Now we command you, **b**,
1Ti 6: 2 by their service are believers and **b**.
2Ti 1: 2 To Timothy, my **b** child: Grace, A
Phm 1:16 as a slave but more than a slave, a **b** brother—
Heb 6: 9 Even though we speak in this way, **b**,
Jas 1:16 Do not be deceived, my **b**. A
1:19 You must understand this, my **b**: A
2: 5 Listen, my **b** brothers and sisters. A
5: 7 therefore, **b**, until the coming of the Lord.
5: 9 **B**, do not grumble against one another,
5:10 As an example of suffering and patience, **b**,
5:12 Above all, my **b**, do not swear, A
1Pe 2:11 **B**, I urge you as aliens and exiles to abstain from
4:12 **B**, do not be surprised at the fiery ordeal
2Pe 1:17 my Son, my **B**, with whom I am well pleased." AB
3: 1 **b**, the second letter I am writing to you;
3: 8 But do not ignore this one fact, **b**,
3:14 **b**, while you are waiting for these things,
3:15 So also our **b** brother Paul wrote to you according
3:17 You therefore, **b**, since you are forewarned,
1Jn 2: 7 **B**, I am writing you no new commandment,
3: 2 **B**, we are God's children now;
3:21 **B**, if our hearts do not condemn us,
4: 1 **B**, do not believe every spirit,
4: 7 **B**, let us love one another,
4:11 **B**, since God loved us so much,
3Jn 1: 1 The elder to the **b** Gaius, whom I love in truth.
1: 2 **B**, I pray that all may go well with you and
1: 5 **B**, you do faithfully whatever you do for
1:11 **B**, do not imitate what is evil
Jude 1: 1 who are **b** in God the Father and kept safe
1: 3 **B**, while eagerly preparing to write to you about
1:17 **b**, must remember the predictions of the apostles
1:20 **b**, build yourselves up on your most holy faith;
Rev 20: 9 the camp of the saints and the **b** city.
Tob 3:10 'You had only one **b** daughter
10:12 on I am your mother and Sarah is your **b** wife. C
Jdt 9: 4 be divided among your **b** children who burned C
AdE 10: 3 His way of life was such as to make him **b**
15: 5 as if **b**, but her heart was frozen with fear.
Sir 20:13 The wise make themselves **b** by only few words,
24:11 Thus in the **b** city he gave me a resting place,
45: 1 and was **b** by God and people,
46:13 Samuel was **b** by his Lord;
Bar 4:16 They led away the widow's **b** sons,
Aza 1:12 for the sake of Abraham your **b** and for the sake C
1Mc 6:11 For I was kind and **b** in my power.'
3Mc 6:11 at the destruction of your **b** people, C
4Mc 5:34 nor will I renounce you, **b** self-control.

BELOVED'S (2) [LOVE]

SS 6: 3 I am my **b** and my beloved is mine;
7:10 I am my **b**, and his desire is for me.

BELOW (30)

Ge 35: 8 died, and she was buried under an oak **b** Bethel.
Jos 2:11 in heaven above and on earth **b**.
11:17 in the valley of Lebanon **b** Mount Hermon.
13: 5 from Baal-gad **b** Mount Hermon to Lebo-hamath,
Jdg 7: 1 **b** the hill of Moreh, in the valley.
7: 8 The camp of Midian was **b** him in the valley.
1Ki 4:12 which is beside Zarethan **b** Jezreel,
7:29 both above and **b** the lions and oxen,
1Ch 27:23 David did not count those **b** twenty years of age,
Job 26: 5 shades **b** tremble, the waters and their inhabitants.
40:13 bind their faces in the world **b**.
Pr 15:24 in order to avoid Sheol **b**.
Jer 31:37 and the foundations of the earth **b** can be explored,
Eze 8: 2 **b** what appeared to be its loins it was fire,
26:20 and I will make you live in the world **b**,
31:14 of them are handed over to death, to the world **b**;
31:16 were consoled in the world **b**.
31:18 down with the trees of Eden to the world **b**;
32:18 to the world **b**, with those who go down to the Pit.
32:24 who went down uncircumcised into the world **b**,
47: 1 from **b** the threshold of the temple toward the east
47: 1 the water was flowing down from **b** the south end
Mk 14:66 While Peter was **b** in the courtyard,
Jn 8:23 He said to them, "You are from **b**,
Ac 2:19 in the heaven above and signs on the earth **b**,
20: 9 he fell to the ground three floors **b** and was picked
Jdt 6:11 and came to the springs **b** Bethulia.
6:13 So having taken shelter **b** the hill,
Sir 51: 6 and my life was on the brink of Hades **b**.
3Mc 2:30 not appear to be an enemy of all, he inscribed **b**:

BELSHAZZAR (10)

Da 5: 1 King **B** made a great festival for a thousand
5: 2 **B** commanded that they bring in the vessels
5: 9 Then King **B** became greatly terrified
5:22 And you, **B** his son, have not humbled your heart,
5:29 Then **B** gave the command,
5:30 That very night **B**, the Chaldean king, was killed.
7: 1 In the first year of King **B** of Babylon,
8: 1 of the reign of King **B** a vision appeared to me,
Bar 1:11 and for the life of his son **B**,
1:12 and under the protection of his son **B**,

BELT (19) [BELTS]

1Sa 18: 4 and even his sword and his bow and his **b**.
2Sa 18:11 to give you ten pieces of silver and a **b**."
20: 8 a **b** with a sword in its sheath fastened at his waist;
1Ki 2: 5 putting the blood of war on the **b** around his waist,
2Ki 1: 8 "A hairy man, with a leather **b** around his waist."
Job 12:21 and looses the **b** of the strong.
Ps 109:19 like a **b** that he wears every day."
Isa 11: 5 Righteousness shall be the **b** around his waist,
11: 5 and faithfulness the **b** around his loins.
Da 10: 5 with a **b** of gold from Uphaz around his waist.
Mt 3: 4 of camel's hair with a leather **b** around his waist,
Mk 1: 6 with a leather **b** around his waist,
Lk 12:37 he will fasten his **b** and have them sit down to eat,
Jn 21:18 you used to fasten your own **b** and
21:18 and someone else will fasten a **b** around you
Ac 12: 8 "Fasten your **b** and put on your sandals."
21:11 He came to us and took Paul's **b**,
21:11 the man who owns this **b** and will hand him over
Eph 6:14 and fasten the **b** of truth around your waist,

BELTED See Index to Footnotes

BELTESHAZZAR (10) [=DANIEL]

Da 1: 7 Daniel he called **B**, Hananiah he called Shadrach,
2:26 The king said to Daniel, whose name was **B**,
4: 8 he who was named **B** after the name of my god,
4: 9 "O **B**, chief of the magicians, I know
4:18 Now you, **B**, declare the interpretation,
4:19 Then Daniel, who was called **B**,
4:19 The king said, "**B**, do not let the dream or
4:19 **B** answered, "My lord, may the dream be
5:12 in this Daniel, whom the king named **B**.
10: 1 a word was revealed to Daniel, who was named **B**.

BELTETHMUS (2)

1Es 2:16 Bishlam, Mithridates, Tabeel, Rehum, **B**,
2:25 Then the king, in reply to the recorder Rehum, **B**,

BELTS (3) [BELT]

Eze 23:15 with **b** around their waists, with flowing turbans
Mt 10: 9 Take no gold, or silver, or copper in your **b**,
Mk 6: 8 no bread, no bag, no money in their **b**;

BEMOAN (4) [MOAN]

Jer 15: 5 O Jerusalem, or who will **b** you?
16: 5 or go to lament, or **b** them;
22:10 Do not weep for him who is dead, nor **b** him;
Na 3: 7 "Nineveh is devastated; who will **b** her?"

BEMOAN, BEMOANED, BEMOANING

(KJV) See also MOURN, PLEADING, SYMPATHY

BEN See Index to Footnotes

BEN-ABINADAB (1)

1Ki 4:11 **B**, in all Naphath-dor (he had Taphath,

BEN-AMMI (1) [AMMON]

Ge 19:38 The younger also bore a son and named him **B**;

BEN-DEKER (1)

1Ki 4: 9 **B**, in Makaz, Shaalbim, Beth-shemesh,

BEN-GEBER (1)

1Ki 4:13 **B**, in Ramoth-gilead (he had the villages

BEN-HADAD‡ (28)

1Ki 15:18 to King **B** son of Tabrimmon son of Hezion
15:20 **B** listened to King Asa, and sent the commanders
20: 1 King **B** of Aram gathered all his army together;
20: 2 and said to him: "Thus says **B**:
20: 5 messengers came again and said: "Thus says **B**:
20: 9 So he said to the messengers of **B**,
20:10 **B** sent to him and said, "The gods do so to me,
20:12 When **B** heard this message—
20:16 while **B** was drinking himself drunk in the booths,
20:17 **B** had sent out scouts, and they reported to him,
20:20 but King **B** of Aram escaped on a horse with
20:26 the spring **B** mustered the Arameans and went up
20:30 **B** also fled, and entered the city to hide.
20:32 "Your servant **B** says, 'Please let me live.' "
20:33 up from him and said, "Yes, **B** is your brother."
20:33 So **B** came out to him;
20:34 **B** said to him, "I will restore the towns
2Ki 6:24 Some time later King **B** of Aram
8: 7 to Damascus while King **B** of Aram was ill.
8: 9 "Your son King **B** of Aram has sent me to you,
8:14 Then he left Elisha, and went to his master **B**,
13: 3 then into the hand of **B** son of Hazael.
13:24 of Aram died, his son **B** succeeded him.
13:25 from **B** son of Hazael the towns that he had taken
2Ch 16: 2 and sent them to King **B** of Aram,
16: 4 **B** listened to King Asa, and sent the commanders
Jer 49:27 and it shall devour the strongholds of **B**.
Am 1: 4 and it shall devour the strongholds of **B**.

BEN-HAIL (1)

2Ch 17: 7 **B**, Obadiah, Zechariah, Nethanel, and Micaiah,

BEN-HANAN (1)

1Ch 4:20 sons of Shimon: Amnon, Rinnah, **B**, and Tilon.

BEN-HESED (1)

1Ki 4:10 **B**, in Arubboth (to him belonged Socoh and all

BEN-HINNOM (1) [HINNOM]

2Ki 23:10 He defiled Topheth, which is in the valley of **B**,

BEN-HUR (1)

1Ki 4: 8 **B**, in the hill country of Ephraim;

BEN-ONI (1) [=BENJAMIN]

Ge 35:18 (for she died), she named him **B**;

BEN-ZOHETH (1)

1Ch 4:20 The sons of Ishi: Zoheth and **B**.

BENAIAH (46)

2Sa 8:18 **B** son of Jehoiada was over the Cherethites and
20:23 **B** son of Jehoiada was in command of
23:20 **B** son of Jehoiada was a valiant warrior
23:21 but **B** went against him with a staff,
23:22 Such were the things **B** son of Jehoiada did,
23:30 **B** of Pirathon; Hiddai of the torrents of Gaash;
1Ki 1: 8 But the priest Zadok, and **B** son of Jehoiada,
1:10 not invite the prophet Nathan or **B** or the warriors
1:26 and **B** son of Jehoiada, and your servant Solomon.
1:32 the prophet Nathan, and **B** son of Jehoiada."
1:36 **B** son of Jehoiada answered the king, "Amen!
1:38 the prophet Nathan, and **B** son of Jehoiada,
1:44 the prophet Nathan, and **B** son of Jehoiada,
2:25 So King Solomon sent **B** son of Jehoiada;
2:29 Solomon sent **B** son of Jehoiada, saying, "Go,
2:30 **B** came to the tent of the LORD and said to him,
2:30 Then **B** brought the king word again, saying,
2:34 Then **B** son of Jehoiada went up and struck him
2:35 The king put **B** son of Jehoiada over the army
2:46 Then the king commanded **B** son of Jehoiada;
4: 4 **B** son of Jehoiada was in command of the army;
1Ch 4:36 Jaakobah, Jeshohaiah, Asaiah, Adiel, Jesimiel, **B**,
11:22 **B** son of Jehoiada was a valiant man of Kabzeel,
11:23 but **B** went against him with a staff,
11:24 Such were the things **B** son of Jehoiada did,
11:31 of Gibeah of the Benjaminites, **B** of Pirathon,
15:18 Unni, Eliab, **B**, Maaseiah, Mattithiah, Eliphelehu,
15:20 and **B** were to play harps according to Alamoth;
15:24 Amasai, Zechariah, **B**, and Eliezer, the priests,

1Ch 16: 5 Jeiel, Shemiramoth, Jehiel, Mattithiah, Eliab, **B**,
16: 6 and the priests **B** and Jahaziel were
18:17 **B** son of Jehoiada was over the Cherethites and
27: 5 was **B** son of the priest Jehoiada, as chief;
27: 6 This is the **B** who was a mighty man of the Thirty
27:14 for the eleventh month, was **B** of Pirathon,
27:34 Ahithophel came Jehoiada son of **B**, and Abiathar.
2Ch 20:14 son of **B**, son of Jeiel, son of Mattaniah,
31:13 and **B** were overseers assisting Conaniah
Ezr 10:25 Malchijah, Mijamin, Eleazar, Hashabiah, and **B**.
10:30 Adna, Chelal, **B**, Maaseiah, Mattaniah, Bezalel,
10:35 **B**, Bedeiah, Cheluhi,
10:43 Mattithiah, Zabad, Zebina, Jaddai, Joel, and **B**.
Eze 11: 1 and Pelatiah son of **B**, officials of the people.
11:13 while I was prophesying, Pelatiah son of **B** died.
1Es 9:26 Mijamin, and Eleazar, and Asibias, and **B**.
9:35 Mazitias, Zabad, Iddo, Joel, **B**.

BENCH (1) [BENCHES]

Jn 19:13 he brought Jesus outside and sat on the judge's **b**

BENCHES (1) [BENCH]

3Mc 4: 9 some were fastened by the neck to the **b** of

BEND‡ (12) [BENDING, BENDS, BENT]

2Sa 22:35 so that my arms can **b** a bow of bronze.
Ps 11: 2 the wicked **b** the bow, they have fitted their arrow
18:34 so that my arms can **b** a bow of bronze.
37:14 the sword and **b** their bows to bring down the poor
Jer 9: 3 They **b** their tongues like bows;
50:14 all you that **b** the bow;
50:29 against Babylon, all who **b** the bow.
51: 3 Let not the archer **b** his bow,
Php 2:10 so that at the name of Jesus every knee should **b**,
Sir 6:25 **B** your shoulders and carry her,
Bar 2:21 **B** your shoulders and serve the king of Babylon,
Man 1:11 And now I **b** the knee of my heart,

BENDING (3) [BEND]

Isa 60:14 of those who oppressed you shall come **b** low
Ac 20:10 and **b** over him took him in his arms, and said,
3Mc 2: 1 **b** his knees and extending his hands

BENDS (5) [BEND]

Jos 15: 9 then the boundary **b** around to Baalah (that is,
15:11 then the boundary **b** around to Shikkeron,
18:17 then it **b** in a northerly direction going on
19:13 and going on to Rimmon it **b** toward Neah;
2Es 16:13 For his right hand that **b** the bow is strong,

BENE-BERAK (1)

Jos 19:45 Jehud, **B**, Gath-rimmon,

BENE-JAAKAN (2) [BEEROTH-BENE-JAAKAN]

Nu 33:31 They set out from Moseroth and camped at **B**.
33:32 from **B** and camped at Hor-haggidgad.

BENEATH (22)

Ge 49:25 blessings of the deep that lies **b**,
Ex 20: 4 or that is on the earth **b**,
26:24 they shall be separate **b**, but joined at the top,
36:29 They were separate **b**, but joined at the top,
Dt 4:39 in heaven above and on the earth **b**;
5: 8 or that is on the earth **b**,
33:13 and of the deep that lies **b**;
1Ki 8:23 like you in heaven above or on earth **b**,
Est 3: 6 But he thought it **b** him to lay hands
Job 9:13 the helpers of Rahab bowed **b** him.
18:16 roots dry up **b**, and their branches wither above.
Isa 14: 9 Sheol **b** is stirred up to meet you when you come;
14:11 maggots are the bed **b** you,
51: 6 and look at the earth **b**;
Da 4:14 Let the animals flee from **b** it and the birds
Hos 14: 7 They shall again live **b** my shadow,
Am 2: 9 I destroyed his fruit above, and his roots **b**.
Hab 3:16 and my steps tremble **b** me.
Jdt 13:15 the canopy **b** which he lay in his drunken stupor.
Bel 1:13 for **b** the table they had made a hidden entrance,
1Mc 6:46 He got under the elephant, stabbed it from **b**,
2Es 6:41 and the other part remain **b**.

BENEFACTOR (5) [BENEFACTORS]

Ro 16: 2 she has been a **b** of many and of myself as well.
AdE 16:13 our savior and perpetual **b**, and of Esther,
2Mc 4: 2 the government the man who was the **b** of the city,
3Mc 6:24 and even me, your **b**, you are now attempting
4Mc 8: 6 so I can be a **b** to those who obey me.

BENEFACTORS (5) [BENEFACTOR]

Lk 22:25 and those in authority over them are called **b**.
AdE 16: 2 with the most generous kindness of their **b**,
16: 3 even undertake to scheme against their own **b**.
Wis 19:14 but these made slaves of guests who were their **b**.
3Mc 3:19 in defiance of kings and their own **b**,

BENEFICENCE (1) [BENEFIT]

3Mc 5:11 that **b** that from the beginning, night and day,

BENEFICENT (2) [BENEFIT]

Tob 7: 7 that such an upright and **b** man has become blind!"
Wis 7:23 **b**, humane, steadfast, sure, free

BENEFICIAL‡ (3) [BENEFIT]

1Co 6:12 but not all things are **b**.
10:23 "All things are lawful," but not all things are **b**.
4Mc 5:11 philosophize according to the truth of what is **b**,

BENEFIT‡ (16) [BENEFICENCE, BENEFICENT, BENEFICIAL, BENEFITED, BENEFITS]

Jdg 11:23 the Amorites for the **b** of his people Israel.
11:24 the LORD our God has conquered for our **b**?
2Ch 32:25 not respond according to the **b** done to him,
1Co 4: 6 to Apollos and myself for your **b**,
7:35 I say this for your own **b**,
14: 6 how will I **b** you unless I speak to you
Gal 5: 2 Christ will be of no **b** to you.
1Ti 6: 2 since those who **b** by their service are believers
Phm 1:20 brother, let me have this **b** from you in the Lord!
Heb 4: 2 but the message they heard did not **b** them,
Wis 11: 5 they themselves received **b** in their need.
11:13 the righteous had received **b**,
Sir 5: 8 for it will not **b** you on the day of calamity.
11:23 and what further **b** can be mine?"
30:25 Those who are cheerful and merry at table will **b**
2Mc 2:27 for one who prepares a banquet and seeks the **b**

BENEFITED (2) [BENEFIT]

Heb 13: 9 which have not **b** those who observe them.
3Mc 5:20 said that the Jews were **b** by today's sleep, "but,"

BENEFITS (6) [BENEFIT]

Ps 103: 2 O my soul, and do not forget all his **b**—
1Co 9:11 is it too much if we reap your material **b**?
2Mc 5:20 the nation and afterward participated in its **b**;
2Es 1: 9 on whom I have bestowed such great **b**?
1:17 Where are the **b** that I bestowed on you?
9:10 though they received my **b**,

BENEVOLENCE‡ (3)

3Mc 3:15 should cherish them with clemency and great **b**,
3:18 of our power because of the **b** that we have
3:20 since we treat all nations with **b**.

BENINU (1)

Ne 10:13 Hodiah, Bani, **B**.

BENJAMIN‡ (137) [=BEN-ONI, BENJAMIN'S, BENJAMINITE, BENJAMINITES]

A. TRIBE OF BENJAMIN (23)
B. JUDAH AND BENJAMIN (17)

Ge 35:18 but his father called him **B**.
35:24 The sons of Rachel: Joseph and **B**.
42: 4 not send Joseph's brother **B** with his brothers,
42:36 and now you would take **B**.
43:14 that he may send back your other brother and **B**.
43:15 the money with them, as well as **B**.
43:16 When Joseph saw **B** with them,
43:29 Then he looked up and saw his brother **B**,
45:12 now your eyes and the eyes of my brother **B** see
45:14 while **B** wept upon his neck.
45:22 but to **B** he gave three hundred pieces of silver
46:19 children of Jacob's wife Rachel: Joseph and **B**.
46:21 The children of **B**: Bela, Becher,
49:27 **B** is a ravenous wolf, in the morning devouring
Ex 1: 3 Issachar, Zebulun, and **B**,
Nu 1:11 From **B**, Abidan son of Gideoni.
1:36 The descendants of **B**, their lineage, in their clans,
1:37 tribe of **B** were thirty-five thousand four A
2:22 Then the tribe of **B**: The leader of the A
10:24 the company of the tribe of **B** was Abidan son A
13: 9 from the tribe of **B**, Palti son of Raphu; A
26:38 The descendants of **B** by their clans:
26:41 These are the descendants of **B** by their clans;
34:21 Of the tribe of **B**, Elidad son of Chislon. A
Dt 27:12 Simeon, Levi, Judah, Issachar, Joseph, and **B**.
33:12 Of **B** he said: The beloved of the
Jos 18:11 the tribe of **B** according to its families came up, A
18:20 This is the inheritance of the tribe of **B**, A
18:21 the tribe of **B** according to their families were A
18:28 This is the inheritance of the tribe of **B** A
21: 4 from the tribes of Judah, Simeon, and **B**.
21:17 Out of the tribe of **B**: A
Jdg 5:14 following you, **B**, with your kin;
10: 9 against Judah and against **B** and against the house
19:14 down on them near Gibeah, which belongs to **B**.
20: 4 answered, "I came to Gibeah that belongs to **B**,
20:10 of **B** for all the disgrace that they have done
20:12 of Israel sent men through all the tribe of **B**, A
20:17 And the Israelites, apart from **B**,
20:20 The Israelites went out to battle against **B**;
20:25 **B** moved out against them from Gibeah
20:35 The LORD defeated **B** before Israel;
20:35 twenty-five thousand one hundred men of **B** that
20:36 The Israelites gave ground to **B**,
20:39 **B** had begun to inflict casualties on the Israelites,
20:46 of **B** were twenty-five thousand arms-bearing men,
21: 1 of us shall give his daughter in marriage to **B**."
21: 6 But the Israelites had compassion for **B** their kin,
21:14 **B** returned at that time;
21:15 on **B** because the LORD had made a breach in
21:16 since there are no women left in **B**?"
21:17 "There must be heirs for the survivors of **B**,
21:18 "Cursed be anyone who gives a wife to **B**."
21:21 and go to the land of **B**.
1Sa 4:12 A man of **B** ran from the battle line,
9: 1 There was a man of **B** whose name was Kish son
9: 4 Then he passed through the land of **B**,
9:16 to you a man from the land of **B**,
9:21 the humblest of all the families of the tribe of **B**. A
10: 2 by Rachel's tomb in the territory of **B** at Zelzah;
10:20 and the tribe of **B** was taken by lot. A
10:21 He brought the tribe of **B** near by its families, A
13: 2 a thousand were with Jonathan in Gibeah of **B**;
13:15 they went up from Gilgal toward Gibeah of **B**.
13:16 with them stayed in Geba of **B**;
14:16 Saul's lookouts in Gibeah of **B** were watching as
2Sa 2: 9 Jezreel, Ephraim, **B**, and over all Israel.
2:15 twelve for **B** and Ishbaal son of Saul,
2:31 of David had killed of **B** three hundred sixty
3:19 that Israel and the whole house of **B** were ready
4: 2 for Beeroth is considered to belong to **B**.
19:17 with him were a thousand people from **B**.
21:14 and of his son Jonathan in the land of **B** in Zela,
1Ki 4:18 Shimei son of Ela, in **B**;
12:21 the house of Judah and the tribe of **B**, A
12:23 and to all the house of Judah and **B**, B
15:22 with them King Asa built Geba of **B** and Mizpah.
1Ch 2: 2 Dan, Joseph, **B**, Naphtali, Gad, and Asher.
6:60 From the tribe of **B**, Geba with its pasture lands, A
6:65 and **B** these towns that are mentioned by name.
7: 6 The sons of **B**: Bela, Becher, and Jediael, three.
7:10 Jeush, **B**, Ehud, Chenaanah, Zethan, Tarshish,
8: 1 **B** became the father of Bela his firstborn,
9: 3 And some of the people of Judah, **B**, Ephraim,
21: 6 he did not include Levi and **B** in the numbering,
27:21 for **B**, Jaasiel son of Abner;
2Ch 11: 1 the house of Judah and **B** to fight against Israel, B
11: 3 son of Solomon, and to all Israel in Judah and **B**, B
11:10 fortified cities that are in Judah and in **B**.
11:12 So he held Judah and **B**. B
11:23 through all the districts of Judah and **B**, in all B
14: 8 from **B** who carried shields and drew bows; B
15: 2 "Hear me, Asa, and all Judah and **B**: B
15: 8 of Judah and **B** and from the towns that he had B
15: 9 He gathered all Judah and **B**, B
17:17 Of **B**: Eliada, a mighty warrior,
25: 5 and of the hundreds for all Judah and **B**. B
31: 1 and the altars throughout all Judah and **B**, B
34: 9 from all Judah and **B** and from the inhabitants B
34:32 in Jerusalem and in **B** pledge themselves to it.
Ezr 1: 5 The heads of the families of Judah and **B**, B
4: 1 of Judah and **B** heard that the returned exiles B
10: 9 people of Judah and **B** assembled at Jerusalem B
10:32 **B**, Malluch, and Shemariah.
Ne 3:23 **B** and Hasshub made repairs opposite their house.
11:31 The people of **B** also lived from Geba onward,
11:36 of the Levites in Judah were joined to **B**.
12:34 Judah, **B**, Shemaiah, and Jeremiah,
Ps 68:27 There is **B**, the least of them, in the lead,
80: 2 before Ephraim and **B** and Manasseh.
Jer 1: 1 the priests who were in Anathoth in the land of **B**,
6: 1 Flee for safety, O children of **B**,
17:26 from the land of **B**, from the Shephelah,
20: 2 in the upper **B** Gate of the house of the LORD.
32: 8 "Buy my field that is at Anathoth in the land of **B**,
32:44 in the land of **B**, in the places around Jerusalem,
33:13 in the land of **B**, the places around Jerusalem,
37:12 to the land of **B** to receive his share of property
37:13 When he reached the **B** Gate,
38: 7 The king happened to be sitting at the **B** Gate,
Eze 48:22 the territory of Judah and the territory of **B**.
48:23 from the east side to the west, **B**, one portion.
48:24 Adjoining the territory of **B**,
48:32 three gates, the gate of Joseph, the gate of **B**,
Hos 5: 8 at Beth-aven; look behind you, **B**!
Ob 1:19 and **B** shall possess Gilead.
Zec 14:10 from the Gate of **B** to the place of the former gate,
Ac 13:21 a man of the tribe of **B**, A
Ro 11: 1 a member of the tribe of **B**. A
Php 3: 5 member of the people of Israel, of the tribe of **B**, A
Rev 7: 8 from the tribe of **B** twelve thousand sealed. A
AdE 2: 5 of Shimei son of Kish, of the tribe of **B**; A
11: 2 of the tribe of **B**, had a dream. A
2Mc 3: 4 But a man named Simon, of the tribe of **B**, A
1Es 2: 8 heads of families of the tribes of Judah and **B**, B
5:66 the enemies of the tribe of Judah and **B** heard it, B
9: 5 the tribe of Judah and **B** assembled at Jerusalem B

BENJAMIN'S (3) [BENJAMIN]

Ge 43:34 **B** portion was five times as much as any of theirs.
44:12 and the cup was found in **B** sack.
45:14 Then he fell upon his brother **B** neck and wept,

BENJAMINITE (11) [BENJAMIN]

Jdg 3:15 Ehud son of Gera, the **B**, a left-handed man.
1Sa 9: 1 of Zeror son of Becorath son of Aphiah, a **B**,
9:21 Saul answered, "I am only a **B**,
2Sa 4: 2 They were sons of Rimmon a **B** from Beeroth—
16:11 how much more now may this **B**!
19:16 Shimei son of Gera, the **B**, from Bahurim,
20: 1 Now a scoundrel named Sheba son of Bichri, a **B**,
1Ki 2: 8 the **B** from Bahurim, who cursed me with
1Ch 27:12 a **B**; in his division were twenty-four thousand.
Est 2: 5 of Jair son of Shimei son of Kish, a **B**.
Ps 7: T *he sang to the LORD concerning Cush, a **B**.*

BENJAMINITES (39) [BENJAMIN]
Nu 2:22 leader of the **B** shall be Abidan son of Gideoni,
7:60 of Gideoni, the leader of the **B:**
Jdg 1:21 But the **B** did not drive out the Jebusites who lived
1:21 the Jebusites have lived in Jerusalem among the **B**
19:16 (The people of the place were **B.**)
20: 3 the **B** heard that the people of Israel had gone up
20:13 **B** would not listen to their kinsfolk, the Israelites.
20:14 The **B** came together out of the towns to Gibeah,
20:15 the **B** mustered twenty-six thousand armed men
20:18 of us shall go up first to battle against the **B?"**
20:21 The **B** came out of Gibeah,
20:23 near to battle against our kinsfolk the **B?"**
20:24 Israelites advanced against the **B** the second day.
20:28 to battle against our kinsfolk the **B,**
20:30 Israelites went up against the **B** on the third day,
20:31 When the **B** went out against the army,
20:32 The **B** thought, "They are being routed before us,
20:34 But the **B** did not realize that disaster was close
20:36 Then the **B** saw that they were defeated.
20:40 the **B** looked behind them—
20:41 and the **B** were dismayed,
20:43 down the **B,** they pursued them from Nohah
20:44 Eighteen thousand **B** fell,
20:48 the Israelites turned back against the **B,**
21:13 to the **B** who were at the rock of Rimmon,
21:20 And they instructed the **B,** saying,
21:23 The **B** did so; they took wives
1Sa 22: 7 around him, "Hear now, you **B;**
2Sa 2:25 **B** rallied around Abner and formed a single band;
3:19 Abner also spoke directly to the **B;**
23:29 Ittai son of Ribai of Gibeah of the **B;**
1Ch 8:40 one hundred fifty. All these were **B.**
9: 7 Of the **B:** Sallu son of Meshullam,
11:31 Ithai son of Ribai of Gibeah of the **B,**
12: 2 they were **B,** Saul's kindred.
12:16 Some **B** and Judahites came to the stronghold
12:29 Of the **B,** the kindred of Saul, three thousand,
Ne 11: 4 of the Judahites and of the **B.**
11: 7 And these are the **B:** Sallu son of Meshullam

BENO (2)
1Ch 24:26 The sons of Jaaziah: **B.**
24:27 of Jaaziah, **B,** Shoham, Zaccur, and Ibri.

BENT (23) [BEND]
Ex 32:22 you know the people, that they are **b** on evil.
2Ki 4:34 and while he lay **b** over him,
4:35 then got up again and **b** over him;
Ps 7:12 he has **b** and strung his bow;
Ecc 12: 3 and the strong men are **b,** and
Isa 5:28 all their bows **b,** their horses' hoofs seem
21:15 from the **b** bow, and from the stress of battle.
51:13 the fury of the oppressor, who is **b** on destruction.
La 2: 4 He has **b** his bow like an enemy,
3:12 he **b** his bow and set me as a mark for his arrow.
Eze 22: 6 have been **b** on shedding blood.
Da 11:27 The two kings, their minds **b** on evil,
Hos 11: 4 I **b** down to them and fed them.
11: 7 My people are **b** on turning away from me.
Zec 9:13 For I have **b** Judah as my bow;
Lk 13:11 She was **b** over and was quite unable to stand
Jn 8: 6 ⟦Jesus **b** down and wrote with his finger on⟧
8: 8 ⟦once again he **b** down and wrote on the ground.⟧
20: 5 He **b** down to look in and saw
20:11 As she wept, she **b** over to look into the tomb;
Ro 11:10 and keep their backs forever **b."**
3Mc 4: 5 sluggish and **b** with age, was being led away,
2Es 3:18 You **b** down the heavens and shook the earth,

BEON (1)
Nu 32: 3 Nimrah, Heshbon, Elealeh, Sebam, Nebo, and **B—**

BEOR‡ (10) [BOSOR]
Ge 36:32 Bela son of **B** reigned in Edom,
Nu 22: 5 He sent messengers to Balaam son of **B** at Pethor,
24: 3 "The oracle of Balaam son of **B,**
24:15 "The oracle of Balaam son of **B,**
31: 8 they also killed Balaam son of **B** with the sword.
Dt 23: 4 because they hired against you Balaam son of **B,**
Jos 13:22 Israelites also put to the sword Balaam son of **B,**
24: 9 He sent and invited Balaam son of **B** to curse you,
1Ch 1:43 Bela son of **B,** whose city was called Dinhabah.
Mic 6: 5 what Balaam son of **B** answered him,

BEQUEATHED (1)
4Mc 13:19 and all-wise Providence has **b** through the fathers

BERA (1)
Ge 14: 2 these kings made war with King **B** of Sodom,

BERAAH See Index to Footnotes

BERACAH (3)
1Ch 12: 3 and Pelet sons of Azmaveth; **B,** Jehu of Anathoth,
2Ch 20:26 the fourth day they assembled in the Valley of **B,**
20:26 place has been called the Valley of **B** to this day.

BERACHAH (KJV) See BERACAH

BERACHIAH (KJV) See BERECHIAH

BERAIAH (1)
1Ch 8:21 Adaiah, **B,** and Shimrath were the sons of Shimei.

BEREA (1) [=BEROEA]
1Mc 9: 4 and went to **B** with twenty thousand foot soldiers

BEREAVE (6) [BEREAVED, BEREAVEMENT, BEREAVES, BEREFT]
Lev 26:22 and they shall **b** you of your children
Dt 32:25 In the street the sword shall **b,**
Eze 36:12 No longer shall you **b** them of children.
36:13 and you **b** your nation of children,"
36:14 and no longer **b** your nation of children, says
Hos 9:12 I will **b** them until no one is left.

BEREAVED (10) [BEREAVE]
Ge 42:36 "I am the one you have **b** of children:
43:14 for me, if I am **b** of my children, I am **b."**
SS 4: 2 and not one among them is **b.**
6: 6 and not one among them is **b.**
Isa 49:21 I was **b** and barren, exiled and put away—
Jer 15: 7 I have **b** them, I have destroyed my people;
Bar 4:12 a widow and **b** of many;
4:16 and **b** the lonely woman of her daughters.
4Mc 12: 6 to show compassion on her who had been **b** of

BEREAVEMENT (3) [BEREAVE]
Isa 49:20 in the time of your **b** will yet say in your hearing:
Wis 14:15 a father, consumed with grief at an untimely **b,**
4Mc 18: 9 and did not have the grief of **b.**

BEREAVES (1) [BEREAVE]
La 1:20 In the street the sword **b;** in the house it is like death.

BERECHIAH (11)
1Ch 3:20 Ohel, **B,** Hasadiah, and Jushab-hesed, five.
6:39 who stood on his right, namely, Asaph son of **B,**
9:16 son of Galal, son of Jeduthun, and **B** son of Asa,
15:17 and of his kindred Asaph son of **B;**
15:23 **B** and Elkanah were to be gatekeepers for the ark.
2Ch 28:12 **B** son of Meshillemoth, Jehizkiah son of Shallum,
Ne 3: 4 Next to them Meshullam son of **B** son
3:30 of **B** made repairs opposite his living quarters.
6:18 the daughter of Meshullam son of **B.**
Zec 1: 1 to the prophet Zechariah son of **B** son of Iddo,
1: 7 to the prophet Zechariah son of **B** son of Iddo;

BERED (2)
Ge 16:14 it lies between Kadesh and **B.**
1Ch 7:20 The sons of Ephraim: Shuthelah, and **B** his son,

BEREFT (2) [BEREAVE]
La 3:17 my soul is **b** of peace;
1Ti 6: 5 among those who are depraved in mind and **b** of

BERI (1)
1Ch 7:36 The sons of Zophah: Suah, Harnepher, Shual, **B,**

BERIAH (11) [BERIITES]
Ge 46:17 Ishvi, **B,** and their sister Serah. The children of **B:**
Nu 26:44 of **B,** the clan of the Beriites.
26:45 Of the descendants of **B:** of Heber,
1Ch 7:23 and bore a son; and he named him **B,**
7:30 Imnah, Ishvah, Ishvi, **B,** and their sister Serah.
7:31 The sons of **B:** Heber
8:13 and **B** and Shema (they were heads
8:16 Michael, Ishpah, and Joha were sons of **B.**
23:10 the sons of Shimei: Jahath, Zina, Jeush, and **B.**
23:11 but Jeush and **B** did not have many sons,

BERIITES (1) [BERIAH]
Nu 26:44 of Beriah, the clan of the **B.**

BERITES See Index to Footnotes

BERITH (KJV) See EL-BERITH

BERNICE (3)
Ac 25:13 and **B** arrived at Caesarea to welcome Festus.
25:23 So on the next day Agrippa and **B** came
26:30 the governor and **B** and those who had been seated

BERODACHBALADAN (KJV) See MERODACH-BALADAN

BEROEA (4) [=BEREA]
Ac 17:10 the believers sent Paul and Silas off to **B;**
17:13 of God had been proclaimed by Paul in **B** as well,
20: 4 by Sopater son of Pyrrhus from **B,**
2Mc 13: 4 the trouble, he ordered them to take him to **B** and

BEROTHAH (1)
Eze 47:16 **B,** Sibraim (which lies between the border

BEROTHAI (1)
2Sa 8: 8 From Betah and from **B,** towns of Hadadezer,

BERRIES (1)
Isa 17: 6 two or three **b** in the top of the highest bough,

BERRIES (KJV) See also OLIVES

BERYL (7)
Ex 28:20 and the fourth row a **b,** an onyx, and a jasper;
39:13 a **b,** an onyx, and a jasper;
Eze 1:16 their appearance was like the gleaming of **b;**
10: 9 the appearance of the wheels was like gleaming **b.**
28:13 chrysolite, and moonstone, **b,** onyx, and jasper,
Da 10: 6 His body was like **b,** his face like lightning,
Rev 21:20 the seventh chrysolite, the eighth **b,**

BESAI (2)
Ezr 2:49 Uzza, Paseah, **B,**
Ne 7:52 of **B,** of Meunim, of Nephushesim,

BESCASPASMYS (1)
1Es 9:31 and **B** and Sesthel, and Belnuus and Manasseas.

BESEECH (3)
1Sa 23:11 O LORD, the God of Israel, I **b** you,
Ps 118:25 Save us, we **b** you, O LORD!
118:25 O LORD, we **b** you, give us success!

BESEECH, BESEECHING, BESOUGHT (KJV) See also APPEAL, ASKING, BEG, ENTREATED, IMPLORE, PLEAD, PLEASE, PRAY, URGE

BESET (3)
Ex 18: 8 all the hardship that had **b** them on the way,
Ps 31:21 to me when I was **b** as a city under siege.
109: 3 They **b** me with words of hate,

BESIDE‡ (130)
Ge 23: 3 Abraham rose up from **b** his dead,
28:13 And the LORD stood **b** him and said,
29: 2 the field and three flocks of sheep lying there **b** it;
39:10 he would not consent to lie **b** her or to be with her.
39:15 he left his garment **b** me, and fled outside."
39:18 he left his garment **b** me, and fled outside."
Ex 2: 5 while her attendants walked **b** the river.
Lev 6:10 and place them **b** the altar.
10:12 and eat it unleavened **b** the altar,
Nu 11:31 from the sea and let them fall **b** the camp,
23: 3 "Stay here **b** your burnt offerings while I go aside.
23: 6 who was standing **b** his burnt offerings with all
23:15 "Stand here **b** your burnt offerings,
23:17 he was standing **b** his burnt offerings with
24: 6 that stretch far away, like gardens **b** a river,
24: 6 like cedar trees **b** the waters.
Dt 11:30 opposite Gilgal, **b** the oak of Moreh.
12:27 be poured out **b** the altar of the LORD your God,
16:21 You shall not plant any tree as a sacred pole **b**
31:26 "Take this book of the law and put it **b** the ark of
Jos 3:16 the city that is **b** Zarethan,
22: 7 to the other half Joshua had given a possession **b**
Jdg 6:25 and cut down the sacred pole that is **b** it;
6:28 and the sacred pole **b** it was cut down,
6:30 the altar of Baal and cut down the sacred pole **b**
7: 1 with him rose early and encamped **b** the spring
Ru 2:14 So she sat **b** the reapers,
1Sa 1: 9 the priest was sitting on the seat **b** the doorpost of
5: 2 into the house of Dagon and placed it **b** Dagon.
6:15 down the ark of the LORD and the box that was **b**
6:18 **b** which they set down the ark of the LORD,
19: 3 and stand **b** my father in the field where you are,
20:19 and remain **b** the stone there.
20:41 from **b** the stone heap and prostrated himself
24: 3 He came to the sheepfolds **b** the road,
26: 3 which is opposite Jeshimon **b** the road.
2Sa 4:12 and hung their bodies **b** the pool at Hebron.
6: 7 and he died there **b** the ark of God.
12:17 The elders of his house stood **b** him,
15: 2 Absalom used to rise early and stand **b** the road
23:18 and won a name **b** the Three.
23:22 and won a name **b** the three warriors.
1Ki 1: 9 and fatted cattle by the stone Zoheleth, which is **b**
2:29 to the tent of the LORD and now is **b** the altar,"
3:20 in the middle of the night and took my son from **b**
4:12 which is **b** Zarethan below Jezreel,
7:20 the rounded projection that was **b** the latticework;
10:19 of the seat were arm rests and two lions standing **b**
13:24 donkey stood **b** it; the lion also stood **b** the body.
13:28 with the donkey and the lion standing **b** the body.
13:31 lay my bones **b** his bones.
21: 1 **b** the palace of King Ahab of Samaria.
22:19 the host of heaven standing **b** him to the right and
2Ki 11:14 with the captains and the trumpeters **b** the king,
12: 9 and set it **b** the altar on the right side
1Ch 5:11 of Gad lived **b** them in the land of Bashan as far
11:20 and won a name **b** the Three.
11:24 and he won a name **b** the three warriors.
2Ch 9:18 of the seat were arm rests and two lions standing **b**
23:13 and the captains and the trumpeters **b** the king,
Ne 2: 6 king said to me (the queen also was sitting **b** him),
3:23 of Maaseiah son of Ananiah made repairs **b**
4: 3 Tobiah the Ammonite was **b** him, and he said,
4:18 The man who sounded the trumpet was **b** me.

Ne 8: 4 and **b** him stood Mattithiah, Shema, Anaiah,
Job 1:14 and the donkeys were feeding **b** them,
41:25 at the crashing they are **b** themselves.
Ps 23: 2 he leads me **b** still waters;
Pr 3:29 against your neighbor who lives trustingly **b** you.
8: 2 On the heights, **b** the way,
8: 3 **b** the gates in front of the town, at the entrance of
8:30 then I was **b** him, like a master worker;
8:34 watching daily at my gates, waiting **b** my doors.
SS 1: 7 for why should I be like one who is veiled **b**
1: 8 and pasture your kids **b** the shepherds' tents.
5:12 His eyes are like doves **b** springs of water,
6:12 my fancy set me in a chariot **b** my prince.
Isa 32:20 Happy will you be who sow **b** every stream,
Jer 17: 2 **b** every green tree, and on the high hills,
36:21 the king and all the officials who stood **b** the king.
Eze 1:15 I saw a wheel on the earth **b** the living creatures,
1:19 living creatures moved, the wheels moved **b** them;
3:13 and the sound of the wheels **b** them,
9: 2 They went in and stood **b** the bronze altar.
10: 6 he went in and stood **b** a wheel.
10: 9 four wheels **b** the cherubim, one **b** each cherub;
10:16 the cherubim moved, the wheels moved **b** them;
10:19 in my sight as they went out with the wheels **b**
11:22 up their wings, with the wheels **b** them;
32:13 I will destroy all its livestock from **b**
40:49 and there were pillars **b** the pilasters on either side.
43: 6 While the man was standing **b** me,
43: 8 and their doorposts **b** my doorposts, with only
47:10 People will stand fishing **b** the sea from En-gedi
Da 8: 3 I looked up and saw a ram standing **b** the river.
8: 6 the two horns that I had seen standing **b** the river,
Hos 13: 7 like a leopard I will lurk **b** the way.
Am 2: 8 down **b** every altar on garments taken in pledge;
7: 7 the Lord was standing **b** a wall built with
9: 1 I saw the LORD standing **b** the altar, and he said:
Mt 13: 1 of the house and sat **b** the sea.
Mk 2:13 Jesus went out again **b** the sea;
4: 1 Again he began to teach **b** the sea.
4: 1 while the whole crowd was **b** the sea on the land.
Lk 5: 1 while Jesus was standing **b** the lake of Gennesaret,
24: 4 suddenly two men in dazzling clothes stood **b**
Jn 19:26 and the disciple whom he loved standing **b** her,
Ac 4:14 the man who had been cured standing **b** them,
5:10 they carried her out and buried her **b** her husband.
8:31 And he invited Philip to get in and sit **b** him.
9:39 All the widows stood **b** him,
13:36 died, was laid **b** his ancestors,
22:13 and standing **b** me, he said, 'Brother Saul,
2Co 5:13 For if we are **b** ourselves, it is for God;
Php 4: 3 for they have struggled **b** me in the work of
Rev 15: 2 standing **b** the sea of glass with harps of God
Tob 4: 4 when she dies, bury her **b** me in the same grave.
7: 1 where they found him sitting **b** the courtyard door.
14:10 On whatever day you bury your mother **b** me,
14:12 Tobias's mother died, he buried her **b** his father.
Jdt 6: 7 the hill country and put you in one of the towns **b**
7: 3 near Bethulia, **b** the spring, and they spread out
7:18 which is near Chusi **b** the Wadi Mochmur.
13: 4 Then Judith, standing **b** his bed, said in her heart,
AdE 1:14 and Malesear, who sat **b** him in the chief seats—
Sir 24:14 and like a plane tree **b** water I grew tall.
1Mc 13:29 and **b** the suits of armor he carved ships,
1Es 9:43 and **b** him stood Mattithiah,

BESIDES‡ (79)

Ge 20:12 **B,** she is indeed my sister,
26: 1 **b** the former famine that had occurred in the days
Ex 12:37 six hundred thousand men on foot, **b** children.
Nu 13:28 and **b,** we saw the descendants of Anak there.
16:49 **b** those who died in the affair of Korah.
29:34 **b** the regular burnt offering, its grain offering,
Dt 3: 5 double gates, and bars, **b** a great many villages.
4:35 there is no other **b** him.
32:39 there is no god **b** me.
Jos 17: 5 **b** the land of Gilead and Bashan,
Jdg 20:15 **b** the inhabitants of Gibeah.
1Sa 2: 2 no one **b** you; there is no Rock like our God.
2Sa 2:30 of David's servants nineteen men **b** Asahel.
7:22 and there is no God **b** you,
17: 8 **B,** your father is expert in war;
1Ki 4:23 one hundred sheep, **b** deer, gazelles, roebucks,
5:16 **b** Solomon's three thousand three hundred
10:15 **b** that which came from the traders and from
2Ki 21:16 **b** the sin that he caused Judah to sin so
1Ch 3: 9 **b** the sons of the concubines;
9:13 **b** their kindred, heads of their
17:20 O LORD, and there is no God **b** you,
29: 2 **b** great quantities of onyx and stones for setting,
2Ch 9:14 **b** that which the traders and merchants brought;
17:19 **b** those whom the king had placed in
29:35 **B** the great number of burnt offerings there was
Ezr 1: 4 **b** freewill offerings for the house of God
1: 6 **b** all that was freely offered.
2:65 **b** their male and female servants,
8:20 **b** two hundred twenty of the temple servants,
Ne 5:15 and took food and wine from them, **b** forty shekels
5:17 **b** those who came to us from the nations
7:67 **b** their male and female slaves,
Ps 18:31 And who is a rock **b** our God?—
Ecc 5:17 **B,** all their days they eat in darkness,
12: 9 **B** being wise, the Teacher also taught
Isa 26:13 other lords **b** you have ruled over us,
43:11 I, I am the LORD, and **b** me there is no savior.
44: 6 **b** me there is no god.
44: 8 Is there any god **b** me?
Isa 45: 5 **b** me there is no god.
45: 6 that there is no one **b** me;
45:14 there is no god **b** him."
45:21 There is no other god **b** me,
45:21 there is no one **b** me.
47: 8 "I am, and there is no one **b** me;
47:10 "I am, and there is no one **b** me."
56: 8 to them **b** those already gathered.
64: 4 no eye has seen any God **b** you,
Da 11: 4 be uprooted and go to others **b** these.
Hos 13: 4 and **b** me there is no savior.
Mt 14:21 about five thousand men, **b** women and children.
15:38 four thousand men, **b** women and children.
Mk 12:32 and **b** him there is no other';
Lk 16:26 **B** all this, between you and us
24:21 and **b** all this, it is now the third day
Ro 13:11 **B** this, you know what time it is,
2Co 11:28 **b** other things, I am under daily pressure because
1Ti 5:13 **B** that, they learn to be idle,
Wis 12:13 For neither is there any god **b** you,
Sir 29:25 and **b** this you will hear rude words like these:
LtJ 6:40 **B,** even the Chaldeans themselves dishonor them;
6:56 **B,** they can offer no resistance to king or enemy.
Bel 1:10 **b** their wives and children.
1:41 the God of Daniel, and there is no other **b** you!"
2Mc 5:23 and **b** these Menelaus, who lorded it
6: 4 **b** brought in things for sacrifice that were unfit.
8:17 and **b,** the overthrow of their ancestral way of life.
8:23 **B,** he appointed Eleazar to read aloud from
10:15 **B** this, the Idumeans, who had control
10:31 were slaughtered, **b** six hundred cavalry.
14: 4 and **b** these some of the customary olive branches
1Es 2: 7 **b** the other things added as votive offerings for
5:41 **b** male and female servants,
3Mc 2:22 **b** being paralyzed in his limbs,
7:22 **B,** they all recovered all of their property,
2Es 3:32 Or has another nation known you **b** Israel?
7:96 and **b** they see the straits and toil
14:12 so two of its parts remain, **b** half of the tenth part.

BESIEGE (10) [SIEGE]

Dt 20:12 but makes war against you, then you shall **b** it;
20:19 If you **b** a town for a long time,
28:52 It shall **b** you in all your towns until your high
28:52 it shall **b** you in all your towns throughout the land
1Sa 23: 8 to go down to Keilah, to **b** David and his men.
2Ch 6:28 if their enemies **b** them in any of the settlements of
Isa 29: 3 I will **b** you with towers and raise siegeworks
1Mc 6:19 and assembled all the people to **b** them.
2Mc 10:19 a force sufficient to **b** them;
12:21 for that place was hard to **b** and difficult of access

BESIEGED (22) [SIEGE]

1Sa 11: 1 the Ammonite went up and **b** Jabesh-gilead;
2Sa 11: 1 they ravaged the Ammonites, and **b** Rabbah.
20:15 Joab's forces came and **b** him in Abel
1Ki 16:17 and all Israel with him, and they **b** Tirzah.
2Ki 16: 5 they **b** Ahaz but could not conquer him.
17: 5 for three years he **b** it.
18: 9 of Assyria came up against Samaria, **b** it,
24:10 up to Jerusalem, and the city was **b.**
25: 2 So the city was **b** until the eleventh year
1Ch 20: 1 of the Ammonites, and came and **b** Rabbah.
Ecc 9:14 A great king came against it and **b** it,
Isa 1: 8 like a shelter in a cucumber field, like a **b** city.
Jer 39: 1 and all his army came against Jerusalem and **b** it;
52: 5 So the city was **b** until the eleventh year
La 3: 5 he has **b** and enveloped me with bitterness
Da 1: 1 of Babylon came to Jerusalem and **b** it.
1Mc 6:20 and **b** the citadel in the one hundred fiftieth year;
6:24 For this reason the sons of our people **b** the citadel
11:61 So he **b** it and burned its suburbs with fire
15:25 King Antiochus **b** Dor for the second time,
2Mc 10:33 and they **b** the fort for four days.
4Mc 7: 4 No city **b** with many ingenious war machines

BESIEGERS (2) [SIEGE]

Jer 4:16 "**B** come from a distant land;
4Mc 7: 4 the **b** with the shield of his devout reason.

BESIEGES (1) [SIEGE]

1Ki 8:37 if their enemy **b** them in any of their cities;

BESIEGING‡ (8) [SIEGE]

2Sa 11:16 As Joab was **b** the city,
2Ki 24:11 while his servants were **b** it;
Jer 21: 4 and against the Chaldeans who are **b** you outside
21: 9 to the Chaldeans who are **b** you shall live
32: 2 the army of the king of Babylon was **b** Jerusalem,
37: 5 the Chaldeans who were **b** Jerusalem heard news
1Mc 11:21 the king and reported to him that Jonathan was **b**
2Mc 11: 6 and his men got word that Lysias was **b**

BESODEIAH (1)

Ne 3: 6 and Meshullam son of **B** repaired the Old Gate;

BESOM (KJV) See BROOM

BESOR (3)

1Sa 30: 9 They came to the Wadi **B,**
30:10 too exhausted to cross the Wadi **B.**
30:21 and who had been left at the Wadi **B.**

BESPATTERED (1) [SPATTERED]

Lev 6:27 you shall wash the **b** part in a holy place.

BEST (60) [GOOD]

Ge 27:15 the **b** garments of her elder son Esau, which were
45:18 so that I may give you the **b** of the land of Egypt,
45:20 for the **b** of all the land of Egypt is yours.' "
47: 6 settle your father and your brothers in the **b** part of
47:11 in the **b** part of the land, in the land of Rameses,
Ex 22: 5 from the **b** in the owner's field or vineyard.
34:26 The **b** of the first fruits
Nu 18:12 All the **b** of the oil and all the **b** of the wine and
18:29 the **b** of all of them is the part to be consecrated.
18:30 When you have set apart the **b** of it,
18:32 when you have offered the **b** of it.
36: 6 'Let them marry whom they think **b;**
Dt 33:21 He chose the **b** for himself,
Jdg 9:33 you may deal with them as **b** you can."
14:20 who had been his **b** man.
Ru 3: 3 and put on your **b** clothes and go down to
1Sa 1:23 "Do what seems **b** to you,
8:14 He will take the **b** of your fields and vineyards
8:16 and the **b** of your cattle and donkeys,
15: 9 **b** of the sheep and of the cattle and of the fatlings,
15:15 the people spared the **b** of the sheep and the cattle,
15:21 the **b** of the things devoted to destruction,
2Sa 18: 4 "Whatever seems **b** to you I will do."
2Ki 10: 3 the son of your master who is the **b** qualified,
Est 2: 9 and advanced her and her maids to the **b** place in
SS 7: 9 like the **b** wine that goes down smoothly,
Eze 27:22 they exchanged for your wares the **b** of all kinds
31:16 all the trees of Eden, the choice and **b** of Lebanon,
Mic 7: 4 The **b** of them is like a brier,
Mt 23: 6 the place of honor at banquets and the **b** seats in
Mk 12:39 the **b** seats in the synagogues and places of honor
Lk 15:22 bring out a robe—the **b** one—
20:46 the **b** seats in the synagogues and places of honor
Ac 24:16 Therefore I do my **b** always to have
Ro 2:18 and know his will and determine what is **b**
Php 1:10 to help you to determine what is **b,**
2Ti 2:15 Do your **b** to present yourself to God
4: 9 Do your **b** to come to me soon,
4:21 Do your **b** to come before winter.
Tit 3:12 do your **b** to come to me at Nicopolis,
Heb 12:10 for a short time as seemed **b** to them,
Jdt 11: 8 that you alone are the **b** in the whole kingdom,
AdE 8: 8 Write in my name what you think **b** and seal it
Sir 11: 3 but what it produces is the **b** of sweet things.
29:20 Assist your neighbor to the **b** of your ability,
36:29 He who acquires a wife gets his **b** possession,
45:20 he allotted to him the **b** of the first fruits,
1Mc 4:45 And they thought it **b** to tear it down,
8: 7 and surrender some of their **b** provinces,
2Mc 4:19 however, thought **b** not to use it for sacrifice,
13:26 made the **b** possible defense, convinced them,
14:30 not spring from the **b** motives.
15:38 that was the **b** I could do.
1Es 2:20 we think it **b** not to neglect such a matter,
5:44 vowed that, to the **b** of their ability,
3Mc 1: 2 took with him the **b** of the Ptolemaic arms
3:26 for ourselves in good order and in the **b** state.
2Es 8:15 About all humankind you know **b;**
4Mc 1: 8 but I can demonstrate it **b** from the noble bravery

BESTIR (1) [STIR]

Ps 35:23 **B** yourself for my defense, for my cause,

BESTOW (6) [BESTOWED, BESTOWER, BESTOWS]

Ru 4:11 May you produce children in Ephrathah and **b**
Ps 21: 5 splendor and majesty you **b** on him.
21: 6 You **b** on him blessings forever;
Pr 4: 9 she will **b** on you a beautiful crown."
AdE 6: 3 "What honor or dignity did we **b**
1Mc 15: 9 we will **b** great honor on you and your nation and

BESTOWED (17) [BESTOW]

1Sa 2:32 on all the prosperity that shall be **b** upon Israel;
1Ch 29:25 and **b** upon him such royal majesty as had
Ne 9:35 and in the great goodness you **b** on them,
Est 6: 3 or distinction has been **b** on Mordecai for this?"
Eze 16:14 because of my splendor that I had **b** on you,
23: 7 She **b** her favors upon them,
Ac 28:10 They **b** many honors on us,
1Co 2:12 that we may understand the gifts **b** on us by God.
Eph 1: 6 to the praise of his glorious grace that he freely **b**
AdE 5:11 about his riches and the honor that the king had **b**
Wis 14:21 **b** on objects of stone or wood the name that ought
Sir 17:11 He **b** knowledge upon them,
47: 6 and praised him for the blessings **b** by the Lord,
3Mc 2:16 you graciously **b** your glory on your people Israel,
5:11 is **b** by him who grants it to whomever he wishes.
2Es 1: 9 on whom I have **b** such great benefits?
1:17 Where are the benefits that I **b** on you?

BESTOWER (1) [BESTOW]

Isa 23: 8 the **b** of crowns, whose merchants were princes,

BESTOWS (1) [BESTOW]

Ps 84:11 a sun and shield; he **b** favor and honor.

BETAH (1)
2Sa 8: 8 From **B** and from Berothai, towns of Hadadezer,

BETEN (1)
Jos 19:25 Its boundary included Helkath, Hali, **B**,

BETH-ANATH (3)
Jos 19:38 Migdal-el, Horem, **B**, and Beth-shemesh—
Jdg 1:33 or the inhabitants of **B**, but lived among
1:33 and of **B** became subject to forced labor for them.

BETH-ANOTH (1)
Jos 15:59 **B**, and Eltekon: six towns with their villages.

BETH-ARABAH (4) [ARABAH]
Jos 15: 6 and passes along north of **B**;
15:61 In the wilderness, **B**, Middin, Secacah,
18:18 on to the north of the slope of **B** it goes down to
18:22 **B**, Zemaraim, Bethel,

BETH-ARBEL (1)
Hos 10:14 as Shalman destroyed **B** on the day of battle

BETH-ASHBEA (1)
1Ch 4:21 the families of the guild of linen workers at **B**;

BETH-AVEN (7) [AVEN]
Jos 7: 2 which is near **B**, east of Bethel, and said to them,
18:12 and it ends at the wilderness of **B**.
1Sa 13: 5 up and encamped at Michmash, to the east of **B**.
14:23 The battle passed beyond **B**,
Hos 4:15 Do not enter into Gilgal, or go up to **B**,
5: 8 Sound the alarm at **B**; look behind you, Benjamin!
10: 5 inhabitants of Samaria tremble for the calf of **B**.

BETH-AZMAVETH (1) [AZMAVETH]
Ne 7:28 Of **B**, forty-two.

BETH-BAAL-MEON (1) [BAAL-MEON]
Jos 13:17 Dibon, and Bamoth-baal, and **B**,

BETH-BARAH (2)
Jdg 7:24 as far as **B**, and also the Jordan."
7:24 and they seized the waters as far as **B**,

BETH-BIRI (1)
1Ch 4:31 Hazar-susim, **B**, and Shaaraim.

BETH-CAR (1)
1Sa 7:11 and struck them down as far as beyond **B**.

BETH-DAGON (3) [DAGON]
Jos 15:41 **B**, Naamah, and Makkedah:
19:27 goes to **B**, and touches Zebulun and the valley
1Mc 10:83 They fled to Azotus and entered **B**,

BETH-DIBLATHAIM (1) [ALMON-DIBLATHAIM]
Jer 48:22 and Dibon, and Nebo, and **B**,

BETH-EDEN (1) [EDEN]
Am 1: 5 and the one who holds the scepter from **B**;

BETH-EKED (2)
2Ki 10:12 On the way, when he was at **B** of the Shepherds,
10:14 and slaughtered them at the pit of **B**,

BETH-EMEK (1)
Jos 19:27 the valley of Iphtah-el northward to **B** and Neiel;

BETH-EZEL (1)
Mic 1:11 **B** is wailing and shall remove its support from you.

BETH-GADER (1)
1Ch 2:51 of Bethlehem, and Hareph father of **B**.

BETH-GAMUL (1)
Jer 48:23 and Kiriathaim, and **B**, and Beth-meon,

BETH-GILGAL (1) [GILGAL]
Ne 12:29 also from **B** and from the region of Geba

BETH-HACCHEREM (2)
Ne 3:14 ruler of the district of **B**, repaired the Dung Gate;
Jer 6: 1 and raise a signal on **B**;

BETH-HAGGAN (1)
2Ki 9:27 he fled in the direction of **B**.

BETH-HARAM (1)
Jos 13:27 the valley **B**, Beth-nimrah, Succoth, and Zaphon,

BETH-HARAN (1) [HARAN]
Nu 32:36 and **B**, fortified cities, and folds for sheep.

BETH-HOGLAH (3)
Jos 15: 6 the boundary goes up to **B**, and passes along north
18:19 boundary passes on to the north of the slope of **B**;
18:21 according to their families were Jericho, **B**,

BETH-HORON (19) [HORONITE]
Jos 10:10 chased them by the way of the ascent of **B**,
10:11 while they were going down the slope of **B**,
16: 3 as far as the territory of Lower **B**, then to Gezer,
16: 5 on the east was Ataroth-addar as far as Upper **B**,
18:13 on the mountain that lies south of Lower **B**.
18:14 opposite **B**, and it ends at Kiriath-baal (that is,
21:22 and **B** with its pasture lands—four towns.
1Sa 13:18 another company turned toward **B**,
1Ki 9:17 so Solomon rebuilt Gezer), Lower **B**,
1Ch 6:68 with its pasture lands, **B** with its pasture lands,
7:24 who built both Lower and Upper **B**,
2Ch 8: 5 He also built Upper **B** and Lower **B**,
25:13 fell on the cities of Judah from Samaria to **B**;
Jdt 4: 4 and to Kona, **B**, Belmain, and Jericho,
1Mc 3:16 When he approached the ascent of **B**,
3:24 They pursued them down the descent of **B** to
7:39 from Jerusalem and encamped in **B**,
9:50 the fortress in Jericho, and Emmaus, and **B**,

BETH-JESHIMOTH (4)
Nu 33:49 by the Jordan from **B** as far as Abel-shittim in
Jos 12: 3 and in the direction of **B**, to the sea of the Arabah,
13:20 and Beth-peor, and the slopes of Pisgah, and **B**,
Eze 25: 9 the glory of the country, **B**, Baal-meon,

BETH-LEAPHRAH (1)
Mic 1:10 in **B** roll yourselves in the dust.

BETH-LEBAOTH (1) [LEBAOTH]
Jos 19: 6 **B**, and Sharuhen—thirteen towns with their

BETH-LEHEM-JUDAH (KJV) See BETHLEHEM IN JUDAH

BETH-MAACAH (2) [MAACAH]
2Sa 20:14 through all the tribes of Israel to Abel of **B**;
20:15 and besieged him in Abel of **B**;

BETH-MARCABOTH (2)
Jos 19: 5 Ziklag, **B**, Hazar-susah,
1Ch 4:31 **B**, Hazar-susim, Beth-biri,

BETH-MEON (1) [BAAL-MEON]
Jer 48:23 and Kiriathaim, and Beth-gamul, and **B**,

BETH-MILLO (3)
Jdg 9: 6 all the lords of Shechem and all **B** came together,
9:20 and devour the lords of Shechem, and **B**;
9:20 and from **B**, and devour Abimelech."

BETH-NIMRAH (2) [NIMRAH]
Nu 32:36 **B**, and Beth-haran, fortified cities, and folds
Jos 13:27 **B**, Succoth, and Zaphon, the rest of the kingdom

BETH-PALET (KJV) See BETH-PELET

BETH-PAZZEZ (1)
Jos 19:21 Remeth, En-gannim, En-haddah, **B**;

BETH-PELET (2)
Jos 15:27 Hazar-gaddah, Heshmon, **B**,
Ne 11:26 and in Jeshua and in Moladah and **B**,

BETH-PEOR (4) [PEOR]
Dt 3:29 So we remained in the valley opposite **B**.
4:46 beyond the Jordan in the valley opposite **B**,
34: 6 opposite **B**, but no one knows his burial place
Jos 13:20 and **B**, and the slopes of Pisgah,

BETH-RAPHA (1) [RAPHA]
1Ch 4:12 Eshton became the father of **B**, Paseah,

BETH-REHOB (2) [REHOB]
Jdg 18:28 It was in the valley that belongs to **B**.
2Sa 10: 6 the Ammonites sent and hired the Arameans of **B**

BETH-SHAN (6) [=BETH-SHEAN]
1Sa 31:10 and they fastened his body to the wall of **B**.
31:12 and the bodies of his sons from the wall of **B**.
2Sa 21:12 who had stolen them from the public square of **B**,
1Mc 5:52 the Jordan into the large plain before **B**.
12:40 and he marched out and came to **B**.
12:41 forty thousand picked warriors, and he came to **B**.

BETH-SHEAN (6) [=BETH-SHAN]
Jos 17:11 Manasseh had **B** and its villages,
17:16 of iron, both those in **B** and its villages and those
Jdg 1:27 not drive out the inhabitants of **B** and its villages,
1Ki 4:12 and all **B**, which is beside Zarethan below Jezreel,
4:12 and from **B** to Abel-meholah,
1Ch 7:29 **B** and its towns, Taanach and its towns,

BETH-SHEMESH (22) [=IR-SHEMESH]
Jos 15:10 and goes down to **B**, and passes along by Timnah;
19:22 and **B**, and its boundary ends at the Jordan—
19:38 and **B**—nineteen towns with their villages.
21:16 and **B** with its pasture lands—
Jdg 1:33 Naphtali did not drive out the inhabitants of **B**,
1:33 of **B** and of Beth-anath became subject
1Sa 6: 9 if it goes up on the way to its own land, to **B**,
6:12 in the direction of **B** along one highway, lowing
6:12 after them as far as the border of **B**.
6:13 the people of **B** were reaping their wheat harvest
6:14 The cart came into the field of Joshua of **B**,
6:15 Then the people of **B** offered burnt offerings
6:18 is a witness to this day in the field of Joshua of **B**.
6:19 not rejoice with the people of **B** when they greeted
6:20 Then the people of **B** said,
1Ki 4: 9 in Makaz, Shaalbim, **B**, and Elon-beth-hanan;
2Ki 14:11 of Judah faced one another in battle at **B**,
14:13 of Judah son of Jehoash, son of Ahaziah, at **B**;
1Ch 6:59 and **B** with its pasture lands.
2Ch 25:21 of Judah faced one another in battle at **B**,
25:23 son of Joash, son of Ahaziah, at **B**;
28:18 and had taken **B**, Aijalon, Gederoth,

BETH-SHEMITE (KJV) See OF BETH-SHEMESH

BETH-SHITTAH (1)
Jdg 7:22 and the army fled as far as **B** toward Zererah,

BETH-TAPPUAH (1) [TAPPUAH]
Jos 15:53 Janim, **B**, Aphekah,

BETH-TOGARMAH (2)
Eze 27:14 **B** exchanged for your wares horses, war horses,
38: 6 **B** from the remotest parts of the north

BETH-ZAITH (1)
1Mc 7:19 withdrew from Jerusalem and encamped in **B**.

BETH-ZATHA (1)
Jn 5: 2 called in Hebrew **B**, which has five porticoes.

BETH-ZECHARIAH (2) [ZECHARIAH]
1Mc 6:32 from the citadel and encamped at **B**,
6:33 by a forced march along the road to **B**,

BETH-ZUR (19)
Jos 15:58 Halhul, **B**, Gedor,
1Ch 2:45 and Maon was the father of **B**.
2Ch 11: 7 **B**, Soco, Adullam,
Ne 3:16 ruler of half the district of **B**,
1Mc 4:29 They came into Idumea and encamped at **B**,
4:61 he also fortified **B** to guard it,
6: 7 with high walls as before, and also **B**,
6:26 they have fortified both the sanctuary and **B**;
6:31 through Idumea and encamped against **B**, and
6:49 He made peace with the people of **B**,
6:50 king took **B** and stationed a guard there to hold it.
9:52 He also fortified the town of **B**, and Gazara,
10:14 in **B** did some remain who had forsaken the law
11:65 Simon encamped before **B** and fought against it
14: 7 he ruled over Gazara and **B** and the citadel,
14:33 and **B** on the borders of Judea,
2Mc 11: 5 Invading Judea, he approached **B**,
13:19 He advanced against **B**, a strong fortress of
13:22 a second time with the people in **B**,

BETHABARA (KJV) See BETHANY

BETHARAM (KJV) See BETH-HARAM

BETHANY (13)
Mt 21:17 He left them, went out of the city to **B**,
26: 6 Jesus was at **B** in the house of Simon the leper,
Mk 11: 1 at Bethphage and **B**, near the Mount of Olives,
11:11 he went out to **B** with the twelve.
11:12 On the following day, when they came from **B**,
14: 3 he was at **B** in the house of Simon the leper,
Lk 19:29 When he had come near Bethphage and **B**,
24:50 Then he led them out as far as **B**, and,
Jn 1:28 in **B** across the Jordan where John was baptizing.
11: 1 Now a certain man was ill, Lazarus of **B**,
11:18 Now **B** was near Jerusalem, some two miles away,
12: 1 Six days before the Passover Jesus came to **B**,
Jdt 1: 9 as far as Jerusalem and **B** and Chelous and Kadesh

BETHASMOTH (1)
1Es 5:18 Those from **B**, forty-two.

BETHBASI (2)
1Mc 9:62 and Simon, withdrew to **B** in the wilderness;
9:64 Then he came and encamped against **B**;

BETHBIREI (KJV) See BETH-BIRI

BETHEL‡ (75) [EL-BETHEL, =LUZ]
Ge 12: 8 east of **B**, and pitched his tent, with **B** on the west
13: 3 on by stages from the Negeb as far as **B**,

Ge 13: 3 at the beginning, between **B** and Ai,
28:19 He called that place **B;**
31:13 I am the God of **B,**
35: 1 God said to Jacob, "Arise, go up to **B,**
35: 3 let us go up to **B,**
35: 6 Jacob came to Luz (that is, **B**),
35: 8 died, and she was buried under an oak below **B.**
35:15 the place where God had spoken with him **B.**
35:16 Then they journeyed from **B;**
Jos 7: 2 which is near Beth-aven, east of **B,**
8: 9 and lay between **B** and Ai, to the west of Ai;
8:12 he set them in ambush between **B** and Ai,
8:17 There was not a man left in Ai or **B** who did
12: 9 the king of Ai, which is next to **B** one
12:16 the king of Makkedah one the king of **B** one
16: 1 going up from Jericho into the hill country to **B;**
16: 2 from **B** to Luz, it passes along to Ataroth,
18:13 to the slope of Luz (that is, **B**),
18:22 Beth-arabah, Zemaraim, **B,**
Jdg 1:22 The house of Joseph also went up against **B;**
1:23 The house of Joseph sent out spies to **B** (the name
4: 5 under the palm of Deborah between Ramah and **B**
20:18 The Israelites proceeded to go up to **B,**
20:26 the whole army, went back to **B** and wept,
20:31 of which goes up to **B** and the other to Gibeah,
21: 2 And the people came to **B,**
21:19 which is north of **B,** on the east of the highway
21:19 of the highway that goes up from **B** to Shechem,
1Sa 7:16 He went on a circuit year by year to **B,** Gilgal,
10: 3 up to God at **B** will meet you there,
13: 2 with Saul in Michmash and the hill country of **B,**
30:27 it was for those in **B,**
1Ki 12:29 He set one in **B,** and the other he put in Dan.
12:30 for the people went to worship before the one at **B**
12:32 so he did in **B,** sacrificing to the calves
12:32 And he placed in **B** the priests of the high places
12:33 the altar that he had made in **B** on the fifteenth day
13: 1 of Judah by the word of the LORD to **B**
13: 4 the man of God cried out against the altar at **B,**
13:10 did not return by the way that he had come to **B.**
13:11 Now there lived an old prophet in **B.**
13:11 that the man of God had done that day in **B;**
13:32 by the word of the LORD against the altar in **B,**
16:34 In his days Hiel of **B** built Jericho;
2Ki 2: 2 for the LORD has sent me as far as **B."**
2: 2 So they went down to **B.**
2: 3 The company of prophets who were in **B** came out
2:23 He went up from there to **B;**
10:29 the golden calves that were in **B** and in Dan.
17:28 from Samaria came and lived in **B;**
23: 4 and carried their ashes to **B.**
23:15 at **B,** the high place erected by Jeroboam son
23:17 that you have done against the altar at **B."**
23:19 he did to them just as he had done at **B.**
1Ch 7:28 Their possessions and settlements were **B**
2Ch 13:19 **B** with its villages and Jeshanah with its villages
Ezr 2:28 Of **B** and Ai, two hundred twenty-three.
Ne 7:32 Of **B** and Ai, one hundred twenty-three.
11:31 at Michmash, Aija, **B** and its villages,
Jer 48:13 as the house of Israel was ashamed of **B,**
Hos 10:15 Thus it shall be done to you, O **B,**
12: 4 he met him at **B,** and there he spoke with him.
Am 3:14 I will punish the altars of **B,**
4: 4 Come to **B**— and transgress;
5: 5 not seek **B,** and do not enter into Gilgal or cross
5: 5 and **B** shall come to nothing.
5: 6 and it will devour **B,** with no one to quench it.
7:10 Then Amaziah, the priest of **B,**
7:13 but never again prophesy at **B,**
Zec 7: 2 of **B** had sent Sharezer and Regem-melech
Tob 2: 6 the prophecy of Amos, how he said against **B,**
1Mc 9:50 and **B,** and Timnath, and Pharathon, and Tephon,

BETHELITE (KJV) See BETHEL

BETHER See Index to Footnotes

BETHESDA See Index to Footnotes

BETHLEHEM‡ (49) [BETHLEHEMITE, EPHRATH]

Ge 35:19 on the way to Ephrath (that is, **B**),
48: 7 on the way to Ephrath" (that is, **B**).
Jos 19:15 Idalah, and **B**—twelve towns with their villages.
Jdg 12: 8 After him Ibzan of **B** judged Israel.
12:10 Then Ibzan died, and was buried at **B.**
17: 7 Now there was a young man of **B** in Judah,
17: 8 This man left the town of **B** in Judah,
17: 9 He replied, "I am a Levite of **B** in Judah,
19: 1 took to himself a concubine from **B** in Judah.
19: 2 from him to her father's house at **B** in Judah,
19:18 from **B** in Judah to the remote parts of
19:18 I went to **B** in Judah; and I am going to my home.
Ru 1: 1 of **B** in Judah went to live in the country of Moab,
1: 2 they were Ephrathites from **B** in Judah.
1:19 So the two of them went on until they came to **B.**
1:19 to **B,** the whole town was stirred because of them;
1:22 to **B** at the beginning of the barley harvest.
2: 4 Just then Boaz came from **B.**
4:11 in Ephrathah and bestow a name in **B;**
1Sa 16: 4 the LORD commanded, and came to **B.**
17:12 David was the son of an Ephrathite of **B** in Judah,
17:15 and forth from Saul to feed his father's sheep at **B.**
20: 6 of me to run to **B** his city;
1Sa 20:28 "David earnestly asked leave of me to go to **B;**
2Sa 2:32 in the tomb of his father, which was at **B.**
23:14 and the garrison of the Philistines was then at **B.**
23:15 to drink from the well of **B** that is by the gate!"
23:16 drew water from the well of **B** that was by
23:24 Elhanan son of Dodo of **B;**
1Ch 2:51 Salma father of **B,** and Hareph father
2:54 The sons of Salma: **B,** the Netophathites,
4: 4 the firstborn of Ephrathah, the father of **B.**
11:16 and the garrison of the Philistines was then at **B.**
11:17 to drink from the well of **B** that is by the gate!"
11:18 and drew water from the well of **B** that was by
11:26 Elhanan son of Dodo of **B,**
2Ch 11: 6 He built up **B,** Etam, Tekoa,
Ezr 2:21 Of **B,** one hundred twenty-three.
Ne 7:26 The people of **B** and Netophah,
Jer 41:17 and stopped at Geruth Chimham near **B,**
Mic 5: 2 But you, O **B** of Ephrathah,
Mt 2: 1 after Jesus was born in **B** of Judea,
2: 5 They told him, "In **B** of Judea;
2: 6 **B,** in the land of Judah, are by no means least
2: 8 Then he sent them to **B,** saying,
2:16 in and around **B** who were two years old or under,
Lk 2: 4 to the city of David called **B,**
2:15 now to **B** and see this thing that has taken place,
Jn 7:42 from David and comes from **B,**

BETHLEHEMITE (4) [BETHLEHEM]

1Sa 16: 1 I will send you to Jesse the **B,**
16:18 "I have seen a son of Jesse the **B** who is skillful
17:58 "I am the son of your servant Jesse the **B."**
2Sa 21:19 and Elhanan son of Jaare-oregim, the **B,**

BETHLOMON (1)

1Es 5:17 The descendants of **B,** one hundred twenty-three.

BETHPHAGE (3)

Mt 21: 1 they had come near Jerusalem and had reached **B,**
Mk 11: 1 at **B** and Bethany, near the Mount of Olives,
Lk 19:29 When he had come near **B** and Bethany,

BETHPHELET (KJV) See BETH-PELET

BETHSAIDA‡ (7)

Mt 11:21 Chorazin! Woe to you, **B!**
Mk 6:45 to **B,** while he dismissed the crowd.
8:22 They came to **B.** Some people brought a blind man
Lk 9:10 and withdrew privately to a city called **B.**
10:13 "Woe to you, Chorazin! Woe to you, **B!**
Jn 1:44 Philip was from **B,** the city of Andrew and Peter.
12:21 They came to Philip, who was from **B** in Galilee,

BETHUEL (10)

Ge 22:22 Chesed, Hazo, Pildash, Jidlaph, and **B."**
22:23 **B** became the father of Rebekah.
24:15 who was born to **B** son of Milcah,
24:24 "I am the daughter of **B** son of Milcah,
24:47 She said, 'The daughter of **B,** Nahor's son,
24:50 Then Laban and **B** answered,
25:20 daughter of **B** the Aramean of Paddan-aram,
28: 2 Go at once to Paddan-aram to the house of **B,**
28: 5 to Laban son of **B** the Aramean,
1Ch 4:30 **B,** Hormah, Ziklag,

BETHUL (1)

Jos 19: 4 Eltolad, **B,** Hormah,

BETHULIA (20)

Jdt 4: 6 wrote to the people of **B** and Betomesthaim,
6:10 and take him away to **B** and hand him over to
6:11 the hill country and came to the springs below **B.**
6:14 and brought him into **B** and placed him before
7: 1 to break camp and move against **B,**
7: 3 They encamped in the valley near **B,**
7: 3 as Balbaim and in length from **B** to Cyamon,
7: 6 in full view of the Israelites in **B.**
7:13 this is where all the people of **B** get their water.
7:20 of every inhabitant of **B** were empty;
8: 3 and took to his bed and died in his town **B.**
8:11 "Listen to me, rulers of the people of **B!**
10: 6 of **B** and found Uzziah standing there with
11: 9 of **B** spared him and he told them all he had said
12: 7 She went out each night to the valley of **B,**
13:10 and went up the mountain to **B,**
15: 3 Those who had camped in the hills around **B**
15: 6 of **B** fell upon the Assyrian camp and plundered it,
16:21 Judith went to **B,** and remained on her estate.
16:23 She died in **B,** and they buried her in the cave

BETIMES (KJV) See EARLY, PERSISTENTLY, SCAVENGING, SEEK

BETOLIO (1)

1Es 5:21 one hundred twenty-two. Those from **B,**

BETOMASTHAIM (1) [=BETOMESTHAIM?]

Jdt 15: 4 Uzziah sent men to **B** and Choba and Kola,

BETOMESTHAIM (1) [=BETOMASTHAIM?]

Jdt 4: 6 wrote to the people of Bethulia and **B,**

BETONIM (1)

Jos 13:26 and from Heshbon to Ramath-mizpeh and **B,**

BETRAY (23) [BETRAYED, BETRAYER, BETRAYERS, BETRAYING, BETRAYS]

1Ch 12:17 but if you have come to **b** me to my adversaries,
Isa 16: 3 hide the outcasts, do not **b** the fugitive;
Mt 10:21 Brother will **b** brother to death,
24:10 and they will **b** one another and hate one another.
26:15 "What will you give me if I **b** him to you?"
26:16 to look for an opportunity to **b** him.
26:21 he said, "Truly I tell you, one of you will **b** me."
26:23 into the bowl with me will **b** me.
Mk 13:12 Brother will **b** brother to death,
14:10 went to the chief priests in order to **b** him to them.
14:11 So he began to look for an opportunity to **b** him.
14:18 Jesus said, "Truly I tell you, one of you will **b** me,
Lk 22: 4 of the temple police about how he might **b** him
22: 6 and began to look for an opportunity to **b** him
Jn 6:64 and who was the one that would **b** him.
6:71 though one of the twelve, was going to **b** him.
12: 4 of his disciples (the one who was about to **b** him),
13: 2 the heart of Judas son of Simon Iscariot to **b** him.
13:11 For he knew who was to **b** him;
13:21 "Very truly, I tell you, one of you will **b** me."
21:20 "Lord, who is it that is going to **b** you?"
Sir 27:17 but if you **b** his secrets, do not follow after him.
4Mc 13:18 or **b** the brothers who have died before us."

BETRAYED (18) [BETRAY]

Isa 31: 6 Turn back to him whom you have deeply **b,**
Mt 10: 4 and Judas Iscariot, the one who **b** him.
17:22 Son of Man is going to be **b** into human hands,
26:24 but woe to that one by whom the Son of Man is **b!**
26:25 Judas, who **b** him, said, "Surely not I, Rabbi?"
26:45 and the Son of Man is **b** into the hands of sinners.
Mk 3:19 and Judas Iscariot, who **b** him.
9:31 "The Son of Man is to be **b** into human hands,
14:21 but woe to that one by whom the Son of Man is **b!**
14:41 the Son of Man is **b** into the hands of sinners.
Lk 9:44 Son of Man is going to be **b** into human hands."
21:16 You will be **b** even by parents and brothers,
22:22 but woe to that one by whom he is **b!"**
Jn 18: 2 Now Judas, who **b** him, also knew the place,
18: 5 Judas, who **b** him, was standing with them.
1Co 11:23 on the night when he was **b** took a loaf of bread,
Sir 27:21 but whoever has **b** secrets is without hope.
2Mc 6:11 were **b** to Philip and were all burned together,

BETRAYER (7) [BETRAY]

Pr 14:25 but one who utters lies is a **b.**
Isa 21: 2 the **b** betrays, and the destroyer destroys.
Mt 26:46 Get up, let us be going. See, my **b** is at hand."
26:48 Now the **b** had given them a sign, saying,
27: 3 his **b,** saw that Jesus was condemned,
Mk 14:42 Get up, let us be going. See, my **b** is at hand."
14:44 Now the **b** had given them a sign, saying,

BETRAYERS (1) [BETRAY]

Ac 7:52 and now you have become his **b** and murderers.

BETRAYING (4) [BETRAY]

Mt 27: 4 He said, "I have sinned by **b** innocent blood."
Lk 22:48 is it with a kiss that you are **b** the Son of Man?"
Sir 42: 1 of repeating what you hear, and of **b** secrets.
4Mc 4: 1 he fled the country with the purpose of **b** it.

BETRAYS (5) [BETRAY]

Isa 21: 2 the betrayer **b,** and the destroyer destroys.
Mt 26:73 also one of them, for your accent **b** you."
Lk 22:21 But see, the one who **b** me is with me,
Sir 26: 9 The haughty stare **b** an unchaste wife;
27:16 Whoever **b** secrets destroys confidence,

BETTER‡ (195) [GOOD]

Ge 29:19 "It is **b** that I give her to you than
Ex 14:12 For it would have been **b** for us to serve
Nu 11:18 Surely it was **b** for us in Egypt.'
14: 3 would it not be **b** for us to go back to Egypt?"
Jdg 8: 2 Is not the gleaning of the grapes of Ephraim **b** than
9: 2 of Shechem, 'Which is **b** for you, that all seventy
11:25 Now are you any **b** than King Balak son of Zippor
18:19 Is it **b** for you to be priest to the house
18:25 "You had **b** not let your voice be heard among us
Ru 2:22 Naomi said to Ruth, her daughter-in-law, "It is **b,**
3:10 this last instance of your loyalty is **b** than the first;
1Sa 14:30 How much **b** if today the troops had eaten freely
15:22 Surely, to obey is **b** than sacrifice,
15:28 to a neighbor of yours, who is **b** than you.
16:16 he will play it, and you will feel **b."**
16:23 and Saul would be relieved and feel **b,**
27: 1 there is nothing **b** for me than to escape to the land
2Sa 14:32 It would be **b** for me to be there still.'
17:14 the Archite is **b** than the counsel of Ahithophel."
18: 3 it is **b** that you send us help from the city."
1Ki 2:32 and **b** than himself, Abner son of Ner, commander
19: 4 for I am no **b** than my ancestors."
21: 2 I will give you a **b** vineyard for it;
2Ki 5:12 **b** than all the waters of Israel?
2Ch 21:13 who were **b** than yourself,
Est 1:19 to another who is **b** than she.
Job 35: 3 How am I **b** off than if I had sinned?'

Ps 37:16 **B** is a little that the righteous person has than
63: 3 Because your steadfast love is **b** than life,
84:10 day in your courts is **b** than a thousand elsewhere.
118: 8 It is **b** to take refuge in the LORD than
118: 9 It is **b** to take refuge in the LORD than
119:72 The law of your mouth is **b** to me than thousands
Pr 3:14 for her income is **b** than silver,
3:14 and her revenue **b** than gold.
8:11 for wisdom is **b** than jewels,
8:19 My fruit is **b** than gold, even fine gold,
12: 9 **B** to be despised and have a servant,
15:16 **B** is a little with the fear of the LORD
15:17 **B** is a dinner of vegetables where love is than
16: 8 **B** is a little with righteousness than large income
16:16 How much **b** to get wisdom than gold!
16:19 It is **b** to be of a lowly spirit among the poor than
16:32 One who is slow to anger is **b** than the mighty,
17: 1 **B** is a dry morsel with quiet than a house full
17:12 **B** to meet a she-bear robbed of its cubs than
19: 1 **B** the poor walking in integrity than one perverse
19:22 and it is **b** to be poor than a liar.
21: 9 It is **b** to live in a corner of the housetop than in
21:19 It is **b** to live in a desert land than with
22: 1 and favor is **b** than silver or gold.
25: 7 for it is **b** to be told, "Come up here,"
25:24 It is **b** to live in a corner of the housetop than in
27: 5 **B** is open rebuke than hidden love.
27:10 **B** is a neighbor who is nearby than kindred who
28: 6 **B** to be poor and walk in integrity than to
Ecc 2:24 There is nothing **b** for mortals than to eat
3:12 that there is nothing **b** for them than to be happy
3:22 So I saw that there is nothing **b** than
4: 3 but **b** than both is the one who has not yet been,
4: 6 **B** is a handful with quiet than two handfuls
4: 9 Two are **b** than one, because they have
4:13 **B** is a poor but wise youth than an old
5: 1 to draw near to listen is **b** than the sacrifice offered
5: 5 It is **b** that you should not vow than
6: 3 I say that a stillborn child is **b** off than he.
6: 9 **B** is the sight of the eyes than the wandering
6:11 the more vanity, so how is one the **b?**
7: 1 A good name is **b** than precious ointment,
7: 2 It is **b** to go to the house of mourning than to go to
7: 3 Sorrow is **b** than laughter,
7: 5 It is **b** to hear the rebuke of the wise than to hear
7: 8 **B** is the end of a thing than its beginning;
7: 8 the patient in spirit are **b** than the proud in spirit.
7:10 "Why were the former days **b** than these?"
8:15 for there is nothing **b** for people under the sun than
9: 4 for a living dog is **b** than a dead lion.
9:16 So I said, "Wisdom is **b** than might;
9:18 Wisdom is **b** than weapons of war,
SS 1: 2 For your love is **b** than wine,
4:10 how much **b** is your love than wine,
Isa 56: 5 monument and a name **b** than sons and daughters;
Jer 10: 8 the instruction given by idols is no **b** than wood!
Da 1:15 of ten days it was observed that they appeared **b**
1:20 he found them ten times **b** than all the magicians
Hos 2: 7 for it was **b** with me then than now."
Am 6: 2 Are you **b** than these kingdoms?
Jnh 4: 3 for it is **b** for me to die than to live."
4: 8 He said, "It is **b** for me to die than to live."
Na 3: 8 Are you **b** than Thebes that sat by the Nile,
Mt 5:29 it is **b** for you to lose one of your members than
5:30 it is **b** for you to lose one of your members than
18: 6 be **b** for you if a great millstone were fastened
18: 8 it is **b** for you to enter life maimed or lame than
18: 9 it is **b** for you to enter life with one eye than
19:10 it is **b** not to marry."
25: 9 you had **b** go to the dealers and buy some
26:24 It would have been **b** for that one not
Mk 5:26 and she was no **b,** but rather grew worse.
9:42 be **b** for you if a great millstone were hung
9:43 it is **b** for you to enter life maimed than
9:45 it is **b** for you to enter life lame than
9:47 it is **b** for you to enter the kingdom of God
14:21 It would have been **b** for that one not
Lk 10:42 Mary has chosen the **b** part,
17: 2 It would be **b** for you if a millstone were hung
Jn 11:50 that it is **b** for you to have one man die for
18:14 that it was **b** to have one person die for the people.
Ro 3: 9 Are we any **b** off?
14: 5 Some judge one day to be **b** than another,
1Co 7: 9 For it is **b** to marry than to be aflame with passion.
7:38 and he who refrains from marriage will do **b.**
8: 8 and no **b** off if we do.
11:17 because when you come together it is not for the **b**
2Co 11:23 I am talking like a madman—I am a **b** one:
12: 6 so that no one may think **b** of me than what is seen
Gal 4: 1 as long as they are minors, are no **b** than slaves,
Php 1:23 to depart and be with Christ, for that is far **b;**
2: 3 but in humility regard others as **b** than yourselves.
Heb 6: 9 beloved, we are confident of **b** things in your case,
7:19 on the other hand, the introduction of a **b** hope,
7:22 also become the guarantee of a **b** covenant.
8: 6 to that degree he is the mediator of a **b** covenant,
8: 6 which has been enacted through **b** promises.
9:23 heavenly things themselves need **b** sacrifices than
10:34 that you yourselves possessed something **b**
11:16 But as it is, they desire a **b** country, that is,
11:35 in order to obtain a **b** resurrection.
11:40 since God had provided something **b** so
12:24 to the sprinkled blood that speaks a **b** word than
1Pe 3:17 For it is **b** to suffer for doing good,
2Pe 2:21 For it would have been **b** for them never
Tob 3: 6 For it is **b** for me to die than to live,
3: 6 it is **b** for me to die than to see so much distress in
Tob 3:10 It is **b** for me not to hang myself,
12: 8 but **b** than both is almsgiving with righteousness.
12: 8 A little with righteousness is **b** than wealth
12: 8 It is **b** to give alms than to lay up gold.
Jdt 7:27 For it would be **b** for us to be captured by them.
AdE 1:19 to a woman **b** than she.
Wis 4: 1 **B** than this is childlessness with virtue,
13: 3 how much **b** than these is their Lord,
15:17 for they are **b** than the objects they worship,
Sir 10:27 **B** is the worker who has goods in plenty than
16: 3 for one can be **b** than a thousand,
16: 3 to die childless **b** than to have ungodly children.
18:16 So a word is **b** than a gift.
19:24 **B** are the God-fearing who lack understanding
20: 2 How much **b** it is to rebuke than to fume!
20:18 slip on the pavement is **b** than a slip of the tongue;
20:31 **B** are those who hide their folly than those who
23:27 that nothing is **b** than the fear of the Lord,
29:13 **b** than a stout shield and a sturdy spear,
29:22 **B** is the life of the poor under their own crude roof
30:14 **B** off poor, healthy, and fit than rich and afflicted
30:15 Health and fitness are **b** than any gold,
30:16 There is no wealth **b** than health of body,
30:17 Death is **b** than a life of misery,
33:22 For it is **b** that your children should ask
36:23 yet one food is **b** than another.
37:14 our own mind sometimes keeps us **b** informed than
40:18 but **b** than either is finding a treasure.
40:19 but **b** than either is the one who finds wisdom.
40:19 but a blameless wife is accounted **b** than either.
40:20 but the love of friends is **b** than either.
40:21 but a pleasant voice is **b** than either.
40:23 but a sensible wife is **b** than either.
40:24 but almsgiving rescues **b** than either.
40:26 but the fear of the Lord is **b** than either.
40:27 and covers a person **b** than any glory.
40:28 it is **b** to die than to beg.
41:15 **B** are those who hide their folly than those who
42:14 **B** is the wickedness of a man than
LtJ 6:59 So it is **b** to be a king who shows his courage,
6:59 **b** even the door of a house
6:59 **b** also a wooden pillar in a palace,
6:68 The wild animals are **b** than they are,
6:73 **B,** therefore, is someone upright who has no idols;
1Mc 3:59 It is **b** for us to die in battle than to see
10:11 for **b** fortification; and they did so.
13: 5 for I am not **b** than my brothers.
2Es 1:18 It would have been **b** for us to serve
3:28 the deeds of those who inhabit Babylon any **b?**
3:31 Are the deeds of Babylon **b** than those of Zion?
4:12 "It would have been **b** for us not to be here than
7:19 "You are not a **b** judge than the Lord,
7:*63* For it would have been **b** if the dust itself had
7:*66* It is much **b** with them than with us;
7:*69* perhaps it would have been **b** for us."
7:*116* [46] it would have been **b** if the earth had
12:44 how much **b** it would have been for us if we
12:45 For we are no **b** than those who died there."
13:20 Yet it is **b** to come into these things,
4Mc 2: 7 a glutton, or even a drunkard can learn a **b** way,
2:18 the temperate mind is able to get the **b** of

BETWEEN‡ (244)

Ge 3:15 I will put enmity **b** you and the woman,
3:15 and **b** your offspring and hers;
9:12 the sign of the covenant that I make **b** me and you
9:13 and it shall be a sign of the covenant **b** me and
9:15 I will remember my covenant that is **b** me and you
9:16 and remember the everlasting covenant **b** God
9:17 that I have established **b** me and all flesh that is on
10:12 Resen **b** Nineveh and Calah; that is the great city.
13: 3 where his tent had been at the beginning, **b** Bethel
13: 7 and there was strife **b** the herders
13: 8 "Let there be no strife **b** you and me,
13: 8 and **b** your herders and my herders;
15:17 a smoking fire pot and a flaming torch passed **b**
16: 5 May the LORD judge **b** you and me!"
16:14 it lies **b** Kadesh and Bered.
17: 2 And I will make my covenant **b** me and you,
17: 7 I will establish my covenant **b** me and you,
17:10 **b** me and you and your offspring after you:
17:11 it shall be a sign of the covenant **b** me and you.
20: 1 and settled **b** Kadesh and Shur.
23:15 what is that **b** you and me?
26:28 so we say, let there be an oath **b** you and us,
30:36 and he set a distance of three days' journey **b**
31:37 so that they may decide **b** us two.
31:44 and let it be a witness **b** you and me."
31:48 "This heap is a witness **b** you and me today."
31:49 for he said, "The LORD watch **b** you and me,
31:50 remember that God is witness **b** you and me."
31:51 which I have set **b** you and me.
31:53 of their father—"judge **b** us."
32:16 and put a space **b** drove and drove."
49:10 nor the ruler's staff from **b** his feet,
49:14 lying down **b** the sheepfolds;
Ex 8:23 Thus I will make a distinction **b** my people
9: 4 the LORD will make a distinction **b** the livestock
11: 7 the LORD makes a distinction **b** Egypt and Israel.
14: 2 **b** Migdol and the sea, in front of Baal-zephon;
14:20 It came **b** the army of Egypt and the army
16: 1 which is **b** Elim and Sinai,
18:16 to me and I decide **b** one person and another,
22:11 before the LORD shall decide **b** the two of them
25:22 from **b** the two cherubim that are on the ark of
28:33 with bells of gold **b** them all around—
Ex 30:18 You shall put it **b** the tent of meeting and the altar,
31:13 a sign **b** me and you throughout your generations,
31:17 It is a sign forever **b** me and the people of Israel
39:25 the bells **b** the pomegranates on the lower hem of
39:25 of the robe all around, **b** the pomegranates;
40: 7 place the basin **b** the tent of meeting and the altar,
40:30 He set the basin **b** the tent of meeting and the altar,
Lev 10:10 You are to distinguish **b** the holy and the common,
10:10 and **b** the unclean and the clean;
11:47 to make a distinction **b** the unclean and the clean,
11:47 and **b** the living creature that may be eaten and
20:25 a distinction **b** the clean animal and the unclean,
20:25 and **b** the unclean bird and the clean;
26:46 the LORD established **b** himself and the people
Nu 7:89 the ark of the covenant from **b** the two cherubim;
11:33 But while the meat was still **b** their teeth,
13:23 and they carried it on a pole **b** two of them.
16:48 He stood **b** the dead and the living;
21:13 **b** Moab and the Amorites.
22:24 the LORD stood in a narrow path **b** the vineyards,
26:56 be apportioned according to lot **b** the larger and
31:27 **b** the warriors who went out to battle and all
35:24 then the congregation shall judge **b** the slayer and
Dt 1: 1 on the plain opposite Suph, **b** Paran and Tophel,
1:16 and judge rightly **b** one person and another,
5: 5 (At that time I was standing **b** the LORD and you
17: 8 to make **b** one kind of bloodshed and another,
25: 1 and the judges decide **b** them,
28:57 the afterbirth that comes out from **b** her thighs,
33:12 the beloved rests **b** his shoulders.
Jos 3: 4 Yet there shall be a space **b** you and it,
8: 9 and lay **b** Bethel and Ai, to the west of Ai;
8:11 with a ravine **b** them and Ai.
8:12 he set them in ambush **b** Bethel and Ai,
18:11 the territory allotted to it fell **b** the tribe of Judah
20: 5 there having been no enmity **b** them before.
22:25 For the LORD has made the Jordan a boundary **b**
22:27 but to be a witness **b** us and you,
22:27 and **b** the generations after us,
22:28 nor for sacrifice, but to be a witness **b** us and you.'
22:34 "it is a witness **b** us that the LORD is God."
24: 7 he put darkness **b** you and the Egyptians,
Jdg 4: 5 of Deborah **b** Ramah and Bethel in the hill country
4:17 for there was peace **b** King Jabin of Hazor and
9:23 But God sent an evil spirit **b** Abimelech and
11:10 "The LORD will be witness **b** us;
11:12 "What is there **b** you and me,
13:25 to stir him in Mahaneh-dan, **b** Zorah and Eshtaol.
15: 4 and put a torch **b** each pair of tails.
16:25 They made him stand **b** the pillars;
16:31 and buried him **b** Zorah and Eshtaol in the tomb
20:38 Now the agreement **b** the main body of Israel and
20:42 of the city were slaughtering them in **b.**
1Sa 7:12 Then Samuel took a stone and set it up **b** Mizpah
7:14 There was peace also **b** Israel and the Amorites.
14:42 "Cast the lot **b** me and my son Jonathan."
17: 1 and encamped **b** Socoh and Azekah,
17: 3 on the mountain on the other side, with a valley **b**
17: 6 and a javelin of bronze slung **b** his shoulders.
20: 3 there is but a step **b** me and death."
20:23 the LORD is witness **b** you and me forever."
20:42 saying, 'The LORD shall be **b** me and you,
20:42 and **b** my descendants and your descendants,
24:12 May the LORD judge **b** me and you!
24:15 and give sentence **b** me and you.
26:13 with a great distance **b** them.
2Sa 3: 1 There was a long war **b** the house of Saul and
3: 6 While there was war **b** the house of Saul and
18: 9 and he was left hanging **b** heaven and earth,
18:24 Now David was sitting **b** the two gates.
21: 4 "It is not a matter of silver or gold **b** us and Saul
21: 7 of the oath of the LORD that was **b** them,
21: 7 **b** David and Jonathan son of Saul.
1Ki 3: 9 able to discern **b** good and evil;
5:12 There was peace **b** Hiram and Solomon;
7:46 in the clay ground **b** Succoth and Zarethan.
14:30 There was war **b** Rehoboam
15: 6 The war begun **b** Rehoboam
15: 7 There was war **b** Abijam and Jeroboam.
15:16 There was war **b** Asa and King Baasha
15:19 "Let there be an alliance **b** me and you,
15:19 like that **b** my father and your father:
15:32 There was war **b** Asa and King Baasha
18: 6 So they divided the land **b** them to pass through it;
18:42 down upon the earth and put his face **b** his knees.
22:34 of Israel **b** the scale armor and the breastplate;
2Ki 9:24 and shot Joram **b** the shoulders,
11:15 "Bring her out **b** the ranks,
11:17 a covenant **b** the LORD and the king and people,
11:17 also **b** the king and the people.
16:14 the place **b** his altar and the house of the LORD,
25: 4 the soldiers fled by night by the way of the gate **b**
1Ch 21:16 and saw the angel of the LORD standing **b** earth
2Ch 4:17 in the clay ground **b** Succoth and Zeredah.
12: 8 so that they may know the difference **b** serving me
12:15 There were continual wars **b** Rehoboam
13: 2 Now there was war **b** Abijah and Jeroboam.
14:11 there is no difference for you **b** helping the mighty
16: 3 "Let there be an alliance **b** me and you,
16: 3 like that **b** my father and your father;
18:33 of Israel **b** the scale armor and the breastplate;
23:14 saying to them, "Bring her out **b** the ranks;
23:16 Jehoiada made a covenant **b** himself and all
Ne 3:32 And **b** the upper room of the corner and
Job 4:20 **B** morning and evening they are destroyed;
9:33 There is no umpire **b** us,
24:11 **b** their terraces they press out oil;

Job 26:10 at the boundary b light and darkness.
41:16 One is so near to another that no air can come b
Ps 68:25 b them girls playing tambourines:
104:10 in the valleys; they flow b the hills,
Pr 18:18 to disputes and decides b powerful contenders.
SS 1:13 My beloved is to me a bag of myrrh that lies b
Isa 2: 4 He shall judge b the nations,
5: 3 judge b me and my vineyard.
22:11 You made a reservoir b the two walls for the water
59: 2 your iniquities have been barriers b you
Jer 34:18 like the calf when they cut it in two and passed b
34:19 the people of the land who passed b the parts of
38:12 the rags and clothes b your armpits and the ropes."
39: 4 the king's garden through the gate b the two walls;
52: 7 by night by the way of the gate b the two walls,
Eze 4: 3 an iron plate and place it as an iron wall b you and
8: 3 and the spirit lifted me up b earth and heaven,
8:16 at the entrance of the temple of the LORD, b
18: 8 executes true justice b contending parties,
20:12 I gave them my sabbaths, as a sign b me and them,
20:20 and hallow my sabbaths that they may be a sign b
22:26 they have made no distinction b the holy and
22:26 the difference b the unclean and the clean,
34:17 I shall judge b sheep and sheep, b rams and goats:
34:20 I myself will judge b the fat sheep and
34:22 and I will judge b sheep and sheep.
40: 7 and the space b the recesses, five cubits;
41: 9 the free space b the side chambers of the temple
41:18 a palm tree b cherub and cherub.
42:20 to make a separation b the holy and the common.
43: 8 with only a wall b me and them,
44:23 They shall teach my people the difference b
44:23 and show them how to distinguish b the unclean
47:16 Sibraim (which lies b the border of Damascus and
47:18 On the east side, b Hauran and Damascus;
47:18 along the Jordan b Gilead and the land of Israel;
48:22 of the prince shall lie b the territory of Judah and
Da 8: 5 The goat had a horn b its eyes.
8:21 and the great horn b its eyes is the first king.
11:45 He shall pitch his palatial tents b the sea and
Hos 2: 2 and her adultery from b her breasts,
Joel 2:17 B the vestibule and the altar let the priests,
Mic 4: 3 He shall judge b many peoples,
4: 3 and shall arbitrate b strong nations far away;
Zec 5: 9 and they lifted up the basket b earth and sky.
6: 1 up and saw four chariots coming out from b
6:13 with peaceful understanding b the two of them.
9: 7 and its abominations from b its teeth;
11:14 annulling the family ties b Judah and Israel.
14: 5 for the valley b the mountains shall reach to Azal;
Mal 2:14 Because the LORD was a witness b you and
3:18 Then once more you shall see the difference b
3:18 b one who serves God and one who does
Mt 23:35 whom you murdered b the sanctuary and the altar.
Lk 11:51 who perished b the altar and the sanctuary.
15:12 So he divided his property b them.
16:26 b you and us a great chasm has been fixed,
17:11 to Jerusalem Jesus was going through the region b
Jn 3:25 about purification arose b John's disciples and
19:18 one on either side, with Jesus b them.
Ac 11:12 to go with them and not to make a distinction b
12: 6 was sleeping b two soldiers,
15: 9 by faith he has made no distinction b them and us.
23: 7 a dissension began b the Pharisees and
Ro 10:12 For there is no distinction b Jew and Greek;
1Co 6: 5 among you wise enough to decide b one believer
2Co 6:14 For what partnership is there b righteousness
6:14 Or what fellowship is there b light and darkness?
8:13 but it is a question of a fair balance b
Eph 2:14 down the dividing wall, that is, the hostility b us.
Php 1:23 I am hard pressed b the two:
1Ti 2: 5 there is also one mediator b God and humankind,
Rev 5: 6 Then I saw b the throne and
Jdt 3:10 he camped b Geba and Scythopolis,
7:24 "Let God judge b you and us!
8: 3 with his ancestors in the field b Dothan
8:11 you have even sworn and pronounced this oath b
Sir 13:18 What peace is there b a hyena and a dog?
13:18 And what peace b the rich and the poor?
27: 2 As a stake is driven firmly into a fissure b stones,
27: 2 so sin is wedged in b selling and buying.
LtJ 6:55 they are like crows b heaven and earth.
1Mc 3:18 of Heaven there is no difference b saving by many
7:28 "Let there be no fighting b you and me;
12:36 and to erect a high barrier b the citadel and the city
13:40 let them be enrolled, and let there be peace b us."
16: 5 and a stream lay b them.
2Mc 10:30 Two of them took Maccabeus b them,
2Es 4:18 If now you were a judge b them,
6:10 Ezra, b the heel and the hand, Ezra!"
7: 8 There is only one path lying b them, that is,
7: 8 that is, b the fire and the water,
11:28 the two that remained were planning b themselves

BEULAH See Index to Footnotes

BEVELED (1)

1Ki 7:29 there were wreaths of b work.

BEWAIL (1) [WAIL]

Jdg 11:37 and b my virginity, my companions and I."

BEWAIL, BEWAILED (KJV) See also MOURN, WAILING, WEEP

BEWAILED (3) [WAIL]

Ge 37:35 Thus his father b him.
Jdg 11:38 and b her virginity on the mountains.
1Mc 13:26 All Israel b him with great lamentation,

BEWARE‡ (35)

Job 36:18 B that wrath does not entice you into scoffing,
36:21 B! Do not turn to iniquity;
Ecc 12:12 Of anything beyond these, my child, b.
Jer 9: 4 B of your neighbors, and put no trust in any
Mt 6: 1 "B of practicing your piety before others in order
7:15 "B of false prophets, who come to you
10:17 B of them, for they will hand you over to councils
16: 6 b of the yeast of the Pharisees and Sadducees."
16:11 B of the yeast of the Pharisees and Sadducees!"
16:12 that he had not told them to b of the yeast
24: 4 "B that no one leads you astray.
Mk 8:15 b of the yeast of the Pharisees and the yeast
12:38 As he taught, he said, "B of the scribes,
13: 5 "B that no one leads you astray.
13: 9 for yourselves, b; for they will hand you over to
13:33 B, keep alert; for you do not know when the time
Lk 12: 1 "B of the yeast of the Pharisees, that is,
20:46 "B of the scribes, who like to walk around
21: 8 And he said, "B that you are not led astray;
Ac 13:40 B, therefore, that what the prophets said does
Php 3: 2 B of the dogs, b of the evil workers, b of those who mutilate the flesh!
2Ti 4:15 You also must b of him,
2Pe 3:17 b that you are not carried away with the error of
Rev 2:10 B, the devil is about to throw some of you
2:22 B, I am throwing her on a bed,
Tob 4:12 "B, my son, of every kind of fornication.
Wis 1:11 B then of useless grumbling,
Sir 4:20 Watch for the opportune time, and b of evil,
11:33 B of scoundrels, for they devise evil,
17:14 He said to them, "B of all evil."
22:26 whoever hears of it will b of him.
LtJ 6: 5 So b of becoming at all like the foreigners or
2Es 15: 5 B, says the Lord, I am bringing evils upon

BEWILDERED (1) [BEWILDERMENT]

Ac 2: 6 And at this sound the crowd gathered and was b,

BEWILDERING (1) [BEWILDERMENT]

2Es 10:37 an explanation of this b vision."

BEWILDERMENT (2) [BEWILDERED, BEWILDERING]

2Es 10:28 into this overpowering b;
13:30 And b of mind shall come over those who inhabit

BEWITCHED (1)

Gal 3: 1 You foolish Galatians! Who has b you?

BEWRAY, BEWRAYETH (KJV) See BETRAY

BEYOND‡ (141)

Ge 31:52 that I will not pass b this heap to you,
31:52 you will not pass b this heap and this pillar to me,
35:21 and pitched his tent b the tower of Eder.
41:49 that he stopped measuring it; it was b measure.
50:10 which is b the Jordan, they held there a very great
50:11 place was named Abel-mizraim; it is b the Jordan.
Ex 3: 1 he led his flock b the wilderness,
Lev 15:25 if she has a discharge b the time of her impurity,
Nu 22:18 not go b the command of the LORD my God,
24:13 to go b the word of the LORD, to do either good
32:19 with them on the other side of the Jordan and b,
34:15 and the half-tribe have taken their inheritance b
35:14 you shall designate three cities b the Jordan,
Dt 1: 1 that Moses spoke to all Israel b the Jordan—
1: 5 B the Jordan in the land of Moab,
3: 8 from the two kings of the Amorites the land b
3:20 the LORD your God is giving them b the Jordan,
3:25 Let me cross over to see the good land b
4:46 b the Jordan in the valley opposite Beth-peor,
11:30 As you know, they are b the Jordan,
30:13 Neither is it b the sea, that you should say,
Jos 1:14 in the land that Moses gave you b the Jordan.
1:15 the servant of the LORD gave you b the Jordan to
2:10 to the two kings of the Amorites that were b
5: 1 When all the kings of the Amorites b the Jordan to
7: 7 that we had been content to settle b the Jordan!
9: 1 the kings who were b the Jordan in the hill country
9:10 to the two kings of the Amorites who were b
12: 1 whose land they occupied b the Jordan toward
13: 8 which Moses gave them, b the Jordan eastward,
13:27 the lower end of the Sea of Chinnereth, eastward b
13:32 b the Jordan east of Jericho.
14: 3 an inheritance to the two and one-half tribes b
16: 6 and passes along b it on the east to Janoah,
18: 7 of Manasseh have received their inheritance b
20: 8 And b the Jordan east of Jericho,
24: 2 lived b the Euphrates and served other gods.
24: 3 Then I took your father Abraham from b the River
24:14 the gods that your ancestors served b the River
24:15 the region b the River or the gods of the Amorites
Jdg 3:26 and passed b the sculptured stones,
5:17 Gilead stayed b the Jordan;
Jdg 7:25 of Oreb and Zeeb to Gideon b the Jordan.
10: 8 that were b the Jordan in the land of the Amorites,
1Sa 7:11 and struck them down as far as b Beth-car.
14:23 The battle passed b Beth-aven,
20:22 'Look, the arrows are b you,' then go;
20:36 As the boy ran, he shot an arrow b him.
20:37 "Is the arrow not b you?"
31: 7 the valley and those b the Jordan saw that the men
2Sa 10:16 and brought out the Arameans who were b
16: 1 When David had passed a little b the summit,
20: 5 but he delayed b the set time
1Ki 14:15 and scatter them b the Euphrates,
2Ki 25:16 the bronze of all these vessels was b weighing.
1Ch 12:37 and Gadites and the half-tribe of Manasseh from b
19:16 and brought out the Arameans who were b
22: 3 as well as bronze in quantities b weighing,
22:14 and bronze and iron b weighing,
2Ch 9:12 well b what she had brought to the king.
20: 2 against you from Edom, from b the sea;
Ezr 4:10 in the rest of the province B the River wrote—
4:11 the people of the province B the River,
4:16 then have no possession in the province B
4:17 in Samaria and in the rest of the province B
4:20 over the whole province B the River,
5: 3 of the province B the River and Shethar-bozenai
5: 6 of the province B the River and Shethar-bozenai
5: 6 in the province B the River sent to King Darius;
6: 6 Tattenai, governor of the province B the River,
6: 6 the envoys in the province B the River,
6: 8 the tribute of the province B the River.
6:13 Tattenai, the governor of the province B the River,
7:21 to all the treasurers in the province B the River:
7:25 the people in the province B the River who know
8:36 and to the governors of the province B the River;
Ne 2: 7 be given me to the governors of the province B
2: 9 Then I came to the governors of the province B
3: 7 the jurisdiction of the governor of the province B
Job 9:10 who does great things b understanding,
20: 3 and a spirit b my understanding answers me.
Ps 45: 7 with the oil of gladness b your companions;
147: 5 his understanding is b measure.
Pr 6:15 in a moment, damage b repair.
29: 1 will suddenly be broken b healing.
Ecc 12:12 Of anything b these, my child, beware.
Isa 5:14 and opened its mouth b measure;
7:20 that day the Lord will shave with a razor hired b
9: 1 the land b the Jordan, Galilee of the nations.
18: 1 land of whirring wings b the rivers of Ethiopia,
52:14 marred was his appearance, b human semblance,
52:14 and his form b that of mortals—
56:12 tomorrow will be like today, great b measure."
Jer 22:19 and thrown out b the gates of Jerusalem.
52:20 the bronze of all these vessels was b weighing.
La 5:22 and are angry with us b measure.
Eze 16:43 not committed lewdness b all your abominations?
41: 4 and its width, twenty cubits, b the nave.
Am 5:27 therefore I will take you into exile b Damascus,
Zep 3:10 From b the rivers of Ethiopia my suppliants,
Mal 1: 5 "Great is the LORD b the borders of Israel!"
Mt 4:25 Jerusalem, Judea, and from b the Jordan.
19: 1 he left Galilee and went to the region of Judea b
Mk 3: 8 Jerusalem, Idumea, b the Jordan,
7:37 They were astounded b measure, saying,
10: 1 and went to the region of Judea and b the Jordan.
Ac 7:43 so I will remove you b Babylon.'
Ro 7:13 commandment might become sinful b measure.
1Co 1:16 b that, I do not know whether I baptized anyone
4: 6 "Nothing b what is written,"
10:13 and he will not let you be tested b your strength,
2Co 4:17 for an eternal weight of glory b all measure,
8: 3 according to their means, and even b their means,
10:13 We, however, will not boast b limits,
10:15 We do not boast b limits, that is,
10:16 we may proclaim the good news in lands b you,
Gal 1:14 I advanced in Judaism b many among my people
Heb 1: 9 with the oil of gladness b your companions."
7: 7 It is b dispute that the inferior is blessed by
2Jn 1: 9 but goes b it, does not have God;
Jdt 1: 9 and b the Jordan as far as Jerusalem and Bethany
1:10 even b Tanis and Memphis,
15: 5 even b Damascus and its borders.
AdE 2:17 And the king loved Esther and she found favor b
Sir 3:21 nor investigate what is b your power.
3:23 Do not meddle in matters that are b you,
6:15 Faithful friends are b price;
8:13 Do not give surety b your means;
1Mc 7: 8 governor of the province B the River;
11:60 Then Jonathan set out and traveled b the river and
1Es 1:24 toward the Lord b any other people or kingdom,
1:49 and lawlessness b all the unclean deeds of all
4:42 even b what is written, and we will give it to you,
2Es 5: 2 be increased b what you yourself see,
5: 2 and b what you heard of formerly.
5: 8 the wild animals shall roam b their haunts,
5:28 and dishonored the one root b the others,
8:21 whose throne is b measure and whose glory is b
12: 7 if I have been accounted righteous before you b
4Mc 4:14 Apollonius, having been saved b all expectations,

BEZAI (4)

Ezr 2:17 Of B, three hundred twenty-three.
Ne 7:23 Of B, three hundred twenty-four.
10:18 Hodiah, Hashum, B,
1Es 5:16 The descendants of B, three hundred twenty-three.

BEZALEL (9)
Ex 31: 2 I have called by name **B** son of Uri son of Hur,
35:30 the LORD has called by name **B** son of Uri son
36: 1 **B** and Oholiab and every skillful one to whom
36: 2 then called **B** and Oholiab and every skillful one
37: 1 **B** made the ark of acacia wood;
38:22 **B** son of Uri son of Hur, of the tribe of Judah,
1Ch 2:20 and Uri became the father of **B**.
2Ch 1: 5 Moreover the bronze altar that **B** son of Uri,
Ezr 10:30 Adna, Chelal, Benaiah, Maaseiah, Mattaniah, **B**,

BEZEK (3)
Jdg 1: 4 and they defeated ten thousand of them at **B**.
1: 5 They came upon Adoni-bezek at **B**,
1Sa 11: 8 When he mustered them at **B**,

BEZER (5)
Dt 4:43 **B** in the wilderness on the tableland belonging to
Jos 20: 8 they appointed **B** in the wilderness on
21:36 **B** with its pasture lands, Jahzah
1Ch 6:78 **B** in the steppe with its pasture lands,
7:37 **B**, Hod, Shamma, Shilshah, Ithran, and Beera.

BICHRI (8) [BICHRITES]
2Sa 20: 1 Now a scoundrel named Sheba son of **B**,
20: 2 from David and followed Sheba son of **B**;
20: 6 of **B** will do us more harm than Absalom;
20: 7 from Jerusalem to pursue Sheba son of **B**.
20:10 and his brother Abishai pursued Sheba son of **B**.
20:13 on after Joab to pursue Sheba son of **B**.
20:21 of **B**, has lifted up his hand against King David;
20:22 And they cut off the head of Sheba son of **B**,

BICHRITES (1) [BICHRI]
2Sa 20:14 and all the **B** assembled, and followed him inside.

BID (1) [BADE, BIDDEN, BIDDING]
Job 15:25 and **b** defiance to the Almighty,

BID, BIDDEN, BIDDETH (KJV) See also CALLED, INVITE, PROCLAIM, SAID, SAY, SAYING, TEACH, WELCOME

BIDDEN‡ (2) [BID]
2Sa 16:11 and let him curse; for the LORD has **b** him.
2Mc 3:35 and having **b** Onias farewell,

BIDDING (4) [BID]
1Sa 22:14 and is quick to do your **b**,
1Ki 18:36 and that I have done all these things at your **b**.
Ps 103:20 O you his angels, you mighty ones who do his **b**,
Sir 39:31 They take delight in doing his **b**,

BIDKAR (1)
2Ki 9:25 Jehu said to his aide **B**, "Lift him out,

BIER (3)
2Sa 3:31 And King David followed the **b**.
2Ch 16:14 on a **b** that had been filled with various kinds
Lk 7:14 Then he came forward and touched the **b**,

BIG (11) [BIGGER]
Ex 29:20 and on the **b** toes of their right feet,
Lev 8:23 of his right hand and on the **b** toe of his right foot.
8:24 the thumbs of their right hands and on the **b** toes
14:14 and on the **b** toe of the right foot.
14:17 and on the **b** toe of the right foot,
14:25 and on the **b** toe of the right foot
14:28 and the **b** toe of the right foot,
Jdg 1: 6 and caught him, and cut off his thumbs and **b** toes.
1: 7 with their thumbs and **b** toes cut off used to pick
Pr 23: 2 put a knife to your throat if you have a **b** appetite.
Sir 37:11 with a lazy servant about a **b** task—

BIGGER (1) [BIG]
1Ki 18:44 a little cloud no **b** than

BIGTHA (1) [=BIGTHAN?, =BIGTHANA?]
Est 1:10 Harbona, **B** and Abagtha, Zethar and Carkas,

BIGTHAN (1) [=BIGTHA?]
Est 2:21 **B** and Teresh, two of the king's eunuchs,

BIGTHANA (1) [=BIGTHA?]
Est 6: 2 how Mordecai had told about **B** and Teresh,

BIGVAI (8)
Ezr 2: 2 Seraiah, Reelaiah, Mordecai, Bilshan, Mispar, **B**,
2:14 Of **B**, two thousand fifty-six.
8:14 Of the descendants of **B**, Uthai and Zaccur,
Ne 7: 7 Nahamani, Mordecai, Bilshan, Mispereth, **B**,
7:19 Of **B**, two thousand sixty-seven.
10:16 Adonijah, **B**, Adin,
1Es 5:14 The descendants of **B**, two thousand sixty-six.
8:40 Of the descendants of **B**, Uthai son of Istalcurus,

BILDAD (5)
Job 2:11 Eliphaz the Temanite, **B** the Shuhite,
8: 1 Then **B** the Shuhite answered:
18: 1 Then **B** the Shuhite answered:
25: 1 Then **B** the Shuhite answered:
42: 9 So Eliphaz the Temanite and **B** the Shuhite and

BILE (1)
La 2:11 my **b** is poured out on the ground because of

BILEAM (1)
1Ch 6:70 and **B** with its pasture lands,

BILGAH (3)
1Ch 24:14 the fifteenth to **B**, the sixteenth to Immer,
Ne 12: 5 Mijamin, Maadiah, **B**,
12:18 of **B**, Shammua; of Shemaiah, Jehonathan;

BILGAI (1)
Ne 10: 8 Maaziah, **B**, Shemaiah; these are the priests.

BILHAH (11)
Ge 29:29 (Laban gave his maid **B** to his daughter Rachel to
30: 3 Then she said, "Here is my maid **B**;
30: 4 So she gave him her maid **B** as a wife;
30: 5 And **B** conceived and bore Jacob a son.
30: 7 Rachel's maid **B** conceived again and bore Jacob
35:22 and lay with **B** his father's concubine;
35:25 The sons of **B**, Rachel's maid: Dan and Naphtali.
37: 2 he was a helper to the sons of **B** and Zilpah,
46:25 of **B**, whom Laban gave to his daughter Rachel,
1Ch 4:29 **B**, Ezem, Tolad,
7:13 Guni, Jezer, and Shallum, the descendants of **B**.

BILHAN (4)
Ge 36:27 These are the sons of Ezer: **B**, Zaavan, and Akan.
1Ch 1:42 The sons of Ezer: **B**, Zaavan, and Jaakan.
7:10 The sons of Jediael: **B**. And the sons of **B**:

BILL (4)
Dt 24: 3 writes her a **b** of divorce, puts it in her hand,
Isa 50: 1 Where is your mother's **b** of divorce
Lk 16: 6 He said to him, 'Take your **b**, sit down quickly,
16: 7 He said to him, 'Take your **b** and make it eighty.'

BILLOWS (3) [BILLOWY]
Ps 42: 7 all your waves and your **b** have gone over me.
Jnh 2: 3 all your waves and your **b** passed over me.
Wis 14: 5 through the **b** on a raft they come safely to land.

BILLOWY (1) [BILLOWS]
Wis 5:10 the **b** water, and when it has passed no trace can

BILSHAN (2)
Ezr 2: 2 Seraiah, Reelaiah, Mordecai, **B**, Mispar, Bigvai,
Ne 7: 7 Mordecai, **B**, Mispereth, Bigvai, Nehum, Baanah.

BIMHAL (1)
1Ch 7:33 The sons of Japhlet: Pasach, **B**, and Ashvath.

BIND‡ (40) [BINDERS, BINDING, BINDS, BOUND]
Nu 30: 2 or swears an oath to **b** himself by a pledge,
Dt 6: 8 **B** them as a sign on your hand,
11:18 and you shall **b** them as a sign on your hand,
Jdg 15:10 They said, "We have come up to **b** Samson,
15:12 They said to him, "We have come down to **b** you
15:13 We will only **b** you and give you into their hands;
16: 5 so that we may **b** him in order to subdue him;
16: 7 "If they **b** me with seven fresh bowstrings that are
16:11 they **b** me with new ropes that have not been used,
Job 31:36 I would **b** it on me like a crown;
38:31 "Can you **b** the chains of the Pleiades,
40:13 **b** their faces in the world below.
Ps 76:10 when you **b** the last bit of your wrath around you.
118:27 **B** the festal procession with branches,
149: 8 to **b** their kings with fetters and their nobles
Pr 3: 3 **b** them around your neck,
6:21 **B** them upon your heart always;
7: 3 **b** them on your fingers, write them on the tablet
Isa 8:16 **B** up the testimony, seal the teaching
15: 3 in the streets they **b** on sackcloth;
22:21 with your robe and **b** your sash on him.
49:18 and like a bride you shall **b** them on.
61: 1 to **b** up the brokenhearted,
Eze 5: 3 and **b** them in the skirts of your robe.
24:17 **B** on your turban, and put your sandals
34:16 and I will **b** up the injured,
44:18 not **b** themselves with anything that causes sweat.
Da 3:20 of the strongest guards in his army to **b** Shadrach,
Hos 6: 1 he has struck down, and he will **b** us up.
Na 1:13 from you and snap the bonds that **b** you."
Mt 13:30 Collect the weeds first and **b** them in bundles to
16:19 whatever you **b** on earth will be bound in heaven,
18:18 whatever you **b** on earth will be bound in heaven,
22:13 king said to the attendants, '**B** him hand and foot,
Ac 9:14 the chief priests to **b** all who invoke your name."
21:11 in Jerusalem will **b** the man who owns this belt
22: 5 to **b** those who were there and to bring them back
Jdt 8:16 Do not try to **b** the purposes of the Lord our God;
Sir 30: 7 Whoever spoils his son will **b** up his wounds,
2Es 16: 2 **B** on sackcloth and cloth of goats' hair,

BINDERS (2) [BIND]
2Ch 34:11 to buy quarried stone, and timber for **b**, and beams
Ps 129: 7 with which reapers do not fill their hands or **b**

BINDING (12) [BIND]
Ge 37: 7 There we were, **b** sheaves in the field.
49:11 **B** his foal to the vine and his donkey's colt to
Ex 28:32 with a woven **b** around the opening,
39:23 with a **b** around the opening,
Nu 30: 9 by which she has bound herself, shall be **b**
30:13 Any vow or any **b** oath to deny herself,
Pr 26: 8 like **b** a stone in a sling to give honor to a fool.
Isa 3:24 and instead of a rich robe, a **b** of sackcloth;
Ac 22: 4 I persecuted this Way up to the point of death by **b**
Ro 7: 1 that the law is **b** on a person only during
Jdt 8: 3 as he stood overseeing those who were **b** sheaves
3Mc 6:19 **b** them with immovable shackles.

BINDS (9) [BIND]
Nu 30: 3 or **b** herself by a pledge,
Job 5:18 For he wounds, but he **b** up;
12:18 and **b** a waistcloth on their loins.
26: 8 He **b** up the waters in his thick clouds,
36:13 they do not cry for help when he **b** them.
Ps 147: 3 the brokenhearted, and **b** up their wounds.
Isa 30:26 when the LORD **b** up the injuries of his people,
Col 3:14 which **b** everything together in perfect harmony.
4Mc 10: 3 I do not renounce the noble kinship that **b** me

BINEA (2)
1Ch 8:37 Moza became the father of **B**;
9:43 Moza became the father of **B**;

BINNUI (11)
Ezr 3: 9 **B** and Hodaviah along with the sons of Henadad,
8:33 Jozabad son of Jeshua and Noadiah son of **B**.
10:30 Chelal, Benaiah, Maaseiah, Mattaniah, Bezalel, **B**,
10:38 Of the descendants of **B**: Shimei,
Ne 3:18 After him their kin made repairs: **B**,
3:24 him **B** son of Henadad repaired another section,
7:15 Of **B**, six hundred forty-eight.
10: 9 Jeshua son of Azaniah, **B** of the sons of Henadad,
12: 8 And the Levites: Jeshua, **B**, Kadmiel, Sherebiah,
1Es 8:63 of Jeshua and Moeth son of **B**,
9:34 Eliasis, **B**, Elialis, Shimei, Shelemiah, Nethaniah.

BIRD‡ (47) [BIRD'S, BIRDS, BIRDS']
Ge 1:21 and every winged **b** of every kind.
1:30 and to every **b** of the air,
2:19 the field and every **b** of the air, and brought them
7:14 and every **b** of every kind—
7:14 every **b**, every winged creature.
8:19 every animal, every creeping thing, and every **b**,
8:20 took of every clean animal and of every clean **b**,
9: 2 and on every **b** of the air,
Lev 7:26 either of **b** or of animal,
11:46 This is the law pertaining to land animal and **b**
14: 6 He shall take the living **b** with the cedarwood and
14: 6 and dip them and the living **b** in the blood of the **b** that was slaughtered over the fresh water.
14: 7 and he shall let the living **b** go into the open field.
14:51 along with the living **b**, and dip them in the blood of the slaughtered **b** and
14:52 with the blood of the **b**, and with the fresh water, and with the living **b**,
14:53 and he shall let the living **b** go out of the city into
17:13 or **b** that may be eaten shall pour out its blood
20:25 and between the unclean **b** and the clean;
20:25 by **b** or by anything with which the ground teems,
Dt 4:17 the likeness of any winged **b** that flies in the air,
28:26 Your corpses shall be food for every **b** of the air
Job 28: 7 "That path no **b** of prey knows,
41: 5 Will you play with it as with a **b**,
Ps 11: 1 can you say to me, "Flee like a **b** to the mountains;
102: 7 I lie awake; I am like a lonely **b** on the housetop.
124: 7 We have escaped like a **b** from the snare of
Pr 1:17 in vain is the net baited while the **b** is looking on;
6: 5 like a **b** from the hand of the fowler.
7:23 He is like a **b** rushing into a snare,
27: 8 Like a **b** that strays from its nest is one who strays
Ecc 10:20 for a **b** of the air may carry your voice,
12: 4 and one rises up at the sound of a **b**,
Isa 46:11 calling a **b** of prey from the east,
La 3:52 without cause have hunted me like a **b**;
Eze 17:23 Under it every kind of **b** will live;
44:31 whether **b** or animal, that died of itself or was torn
Da 7: 6 The beast had four wings of a **b** on its back
Hos 9:11 Ephraim's glory shall fly away like a **b**—
Am 3: 5 Does a **b** fall into a snare on the earth,
Jas 3: 7 For every species of beast and **b**,
Rev 18: 2 a haunt of every foul **b**,
Wis 5:11 when a **b** flies through the air,
Sir 27:19 And as you allow a **b** to escape from your hand,
LtJ 6:71 a thornbush in a garden on which every **b** perches;

BIRD'S (1) [BIRD]
Dt 22: 6 If you come on a **b** nest, in any tree

BIRDS‡ (108) [BIRD]

Ge 1:20 and let **b** fly above the earth across the dome of
1:22 and let **b** multiply on the earth."
1:26 and over the **b** of the air, and over the cattle,
1:28 over the **b** of the air and over every living thing
2:20 and to the **b** of the air,
6: 7 with animals and creeping things and **b** of the air,
6:20 Of the **b** according to their kinds,
7: 3 and seven pairs of the **b** of the air also,
7: 8 and of animals that are not clean, and of **b**,
7:21 And all flesh died that moved on the earth, **b**,
7:23 and animals and creeping things and **b** of the air;
8:17 **b** and animals and every creeping thing that creeps
9:10 the **b**, the domestic animals,
15:10 but he did not cut the **b** in two.
15:11 And when **b** of prey came down on the carcasses,
40:17 the **b** were eating it out of the basket on my head."
40:19 and the **b** will eat the flesh from you."
Lev 1:14 to the LORD is a burnt offering of **b**,
11:13 These you shall regard as detestable among the **b**.
14: 4 the priest shall command that two living clean **b**
14: 5 that one of the **b** be slaughtered over fresh water in
14:49 For the cleansing of the house he shall take two **b**,
14:50 and shall slaughter one of the **b** over fresh water in
Dt 14:11 You may eat any clean **b**.
1Sa 17:44 and I will give your flesh to the **b** of the air and to
17:46 the Philistine army this very day to the **b** of the air
2Sa 21:10 not allow the **b** of the air to come on the bodies
1Ki 4:33 he would speak of animals, and **b**, and reptiles,
14:11 the **b** of the air shall eat;
16: 4 and anyone of his who dies in the field the **b** of
21:24 in the open country the **b** of the air shall eat."
Job 12: 7 the **b** of the air, and they will tell you;
28:21 and concealed from the **b** of the air.
35:11 and makes us wiser than the **b** of the air?'
Ps 8: 8 the **b** of the air, and the fish of
50:11 I know all the **b** of the air,
78:27 winged **b** like the sand of the seas;
79: 2 the bodies of your servants to the **b** of the air
104:12 the streams the **b** of the air have their habitation;
104:17 In them the **b** build their nests;
148:10 creeping things and flying **b**!
Ecc 9:12 and like **b** caught in a snare,
Isa 16: 2 Like fluttering **b**, like scattered nestlings,
18: 6 the **b** of prey of the mountains and to the animals
18: 6 And the **b** of prey will summer on them,
31: 5 Like **b** hovering overhead,
Jer 4:25 and all the **b** of the air had fled.
5:27 a cage full of **b**, their houses are full of treachery;
7:33 The corpses of this people will be food for the **b** of
9:10 both the **b** of the air and the animals have fled
12: 4 in it the animals and the **b** are swept away,
12: 9 Are the **b** of prey all around her?
15: 3 the sword to kill, the dogs to drag away, and the **b**
16: 4 and their dead bodies shall become food for the **b**
19: 7 for food to the **b** of the air and to the wild animals
34:20 the **b** of the air and the wild animals of the earth.
Eze 13:20 the lives that you hunt down like **b**.
29: 5 of the earth and to the **b** of the air I have given you
31: 6 All the **b** of the air made their nests in its boughs;
31:13 On its fallen trunk settle all the **b** of the air,
32: 4 and will cause all the **b** of the air to settle on you,
38:20 and the **b** of the air, and the animals of the field,
39: 4 to **b** of prey of every kind and to the wild animals
39:17 to the **b** of every kind and to all the wild animals:
Da 2:38 the wild animals of the field, and the **b** of the air,
4:12 the **b** of the air nested in its branches,
4:14 Let the animals flee from beneath it and the **b**
4:21 and in whose branches the **b** of the air had nests—
Hos 2:18 **b** of the air, and the creeping things of the ground;
4: 3 together with the wild animals and the **b** of the air,
7:12 I will bring them down like **b** of the air;
11:11 They shall come trembling like **b** from Egypt,
Zep 1: 3 I will sweep away the **b** of the air and the fish of
Mt 6:26 Look at the **b** of the air;
8:20 "Foxes have holes, and **b** of the air have nests;
13: 4 and the **b** came and ate them up.
13:32 **b** of the air come and make nests in its branches."
Mk 4: 4 and the **b** came and ate it up.
4:32 that the **b** of the air can make nests in its shade."
Lk 8: 5 and the **b** of the air ate it up.
9:58 "Foxes have holes, and **b** of the air have nests;
12:24 Of how much more value are you than the **b**!
13:19 and the **b** of the air made nests in its branches."
Ac 10:12 of four-footed creatures and reptiles and **b** of
11: 6 beasts of prey, reptiles, and **b** of the air.
Ro 1:23 a mortal human being or **b** or four-footed animals
1Co 15:39 another for **b**, and another for fish.
Rev 19:17 and with a loud voice he called to all the **b** that fly
19:21 and all the **b** were gorged with their flesh.
Jdt 11: 7 the animals of the field and the cattle and the **b** of
AdE 16:24 most hateful to wild animals and **b** for all time.
Wis 17:18 melodious sound of **b** in wide-spreading branches,
19:11 Afterward they saw also a new kind of **b**,
Sir 17: 4 and gave them dominion over beasts and **b**.
22:20 One who throws a stone at **b** scares them away,
27: 9 **B** roost with their own kind,
43:14 and the clouds fly out like **b**.
43:17 He scatters the snow like **b** flying down,
Bar 3:17 of the **b** of the air, and who hoarded up silver
LtJ 6:22 swallows, and **b** alight on their bodies and heads;
Aza 1:58 Bless the Lord, all **b** of the air;
2Mc 9:15 for the **b** to eat, he would make, all of them, equal
15:33 and said that he would feed it piecemeal to the **b**
3Mc 6:34 be destroyed and become food for **b**,
2Es 5: 6 and the **b** shall fly away together;
2Es 5:26 the **b** that have been created you have named
6:47 to bring forth living creatures, **b**, and fishes;
4Mc 14:15 For example, among **b**, the ones

BIRDS' (1) [BIRD]

Da 4:33 and his nails became like **b** claws.

BIRSHA (1)

Ge 14: 2 King **B** of Gomorrah, King Shinab of Admah,

BIRTH‡ (103) [BEAR]

Ge 5: 7 after the **b** of Enosh eight hundred seven years,
5:10 after the **b** of Kenan eight hundred fifteen years,
5:13 Kenan lived after the **b** of Mahalalel eight hundred
5:16 after the **b** of Jared eight hundred thirty years,
5:19 after the **b** of Enoch eight hundred years,
5:22 after the **b** of Methuselah three hundred years,
5:26 the **b** of Lamech seven hundred eighty-two years,
5:30 after the **b** of Noah five hundred ninety-five years,
11:11 after the **b** of Arpachshad five hundred years,
11:13 after the **b** of Shelah four hundred three years,
11:15 after the **b** of Eber four hundred three years,
11:17 after the **b** of Peleg four hundred thirty years,
11:19 after the **b** of Reu two hundred nine years,
11:21 after the **b** of Serug two hundred seven years,
11:23 after the **b** of Nahor two hundred years,
11:25 after the **b** of Terah one hundred nineteen years,
11:28 before his father Terah in the land of his **b**,
24: 7 and from the land of my **b**,
25:13 named in the order of their **b**:
25:24 When her time to give **b** was at hand,
31:13 at once and return to the land of your **b**.' "
Ex 1:19 and give **b** before the midwife comes to them."
28:10 in the order of their **b**.
Nu 11:12 Did I give **b** to them, that you should say to me,
Dt 32:18 you forgot the God who gave you **b**.
Jdg 13: 5 for the boy shall be a nazirite to God from **b**.
13: 7 a nazirite to God from **b** to the day of his death.' "
1Sa 4:19 was pregnant, about to give **b**.
4:19 and her husband were dead, she bowed and gave **b**;
1Ki 3:17 and I gave **b** while she was in the house.
3:18 third day after I gave **b**, this woman also gave **b**.
11:20 of Tahpenes gave **b** by him to his son Genubath,
2Ki 19: 3 children have come to the **b**,
Job 3: 1 and cursed the day of his **b**.
3:11 "Why did I not die at **b**,
38:29 and who has given **b** to the hoarfrost of heaven?
39: 1 "Do you know when the mountain goats give **b**?
39: 2 and do you know the time when they give **b**,
39: 3 when they crouch to give **b** to their offspring,
Ps 22:10 On you I was cast from my **b**,
58: 3 they err from their **b**, speaking lies.
58: 8 like the untimely **b** that never sees the sun.
71: 6 Upon you I have leaned from my **b**;
Ecc 7: 1 and the day of death, than the day of **b**.
Isa 23: 4 "I have neither labored nor given **b**,
26:18 we writhed, but we gave **b** only to wind.
26:19 and the earth will give **b** to those long dead.
37: 3 children have come to the **b**,
46: 3 who have been borne by me from your **b**,
48: 8 and that from **b** you were called a rebel.
66: 7 Before she was in labor she gave **b**;
Jer 2:27 and to a stone, "You gave me **b**."
46:16 to our own people and to the land of our **b**,
Eze 16: 3 and your **b** were in the land of the Canaanites;
16: 4 As for your **b**, on the day you were born
31: 6 the animals of the field gave **b** to their young;
Da 9: 1 by **b** a Mede, who became king over the realm of
Hos 9:11 no **b**, no pregnancy, no conception!
9:16 Even though they give **b**, I will kill the cherished
Mt 1:18 the **b** of Jesus the Messiah took place in this way.
19:12 For there are eunuchs who have been so from **b**,
24: 8 all this is but the beginning of the **b** pangs.
Mk 13: 8 This is but the beginning of the **b** pangs.
Lk 1:14 and many will rejoice at his **b**,
1:15 before his **b** he will be filled with the Holy Spirit.
1:57 Now the time came for Elizabeth to give **b**,
2: 7 And she gave **b** to her firstborn son
Jn 9: 1 As he walked along, he saw a man blind from **b**.
Ac 3: 2 And a man lame from **b** was being carried in.
14: 8 for he had been crippled from **b**.
1Co 1:26 not many were of noble **b**.
Gal 2:15 We ourselves are Jews by **b** and
4:27 you who endure no **b** pangs;
Eph 2:11 remember that at one time you Gentiles by **b**,
Heb 11:23 for three months after his **b**, because they saw that
Jas 1:15 when that desire has conceived, it gives **b** to sin,
1:15 when it is fully grown, gives **b** to death.
1:18 In fulfillment of his own purpose he gave us **b** by
1Pe 1: 3 a new **b** into a living hope through the resurrection
Rev 12: 2 She was pregnant and was crying out in **b** pangs,
12: 2 in the agony of giving **b**.
12: 5 And she gave **b** to a son, a male child,
12:13 the woman who had given **b** to the male child.
Tob 10:12 as much your parents as those who gave you **b**.
Wis 8: 3 She glorifies her noble **b** by living with God,
Sir 7:27 and do not forget the **b** pangs of your mother.
19:11 the fool suffers **b** pangs like a woman in labor
22: 3 and the **b** of a daughter is a loss.
23:14 and you will curse the day of your **b**.
50:22 who fosters our growth from **b**,
2Mc 5:22 at Jerusalem, Philip, by **b** a Phrygian and
14:42 and suffer outrages unworthy of his noble **b**.
1Es 4:15 Women gave **b** to the king and to every people
3Mc 1: 3 a Jew by **b** who later changed his religion
2Es 4:42 in labor makes haste to escape the pangs of **b**,
6:21 and pregnant women shall give **b**
6:26 who from their **b** have not tasted death;
4Mc 15: 4 because of their **b** pangs have a deeper sympathy
15: 5 that mothers are the weaker sex and give **b**
15:16 even the **b** pangs you suffered for them!
15:17 who alone gave **b** to such complete devotion!
16: 8 In vain, my sons, I endured many **b** pangs for you,

BIRTH-PANGS, BIRTHPANGS See BIRTH, PANGS

BIRTHDAY (4) [BEAR, DAY]

Ge 40:20 On the third day, which was Pharaoh's **b**,
Mt 14: 6 But when Herod's **b** came,
Mk 6:21 an opportunity came when Herod on his **b** gave
2Mc 6: 7 On the monthly celebration of the king's **b**,

BIRTHRIGHT (10) [BEAR, RIGHT]

Ge 25:31 Jacob said, "First sell me your **b**."
25:32 of what use is a **b** to me?"
25:33 So he swore to him, and sold his **b** to Jacob.
25:34 Thus Esau despised his **b**.
27:36 He took away my **b**;
43:33 to his **b** and the youngest according to his youth,
1Ch 5: 1 because he defiled his father's bed his **b** was given
5: 1 not enrolled in the genealogy according to the **b**;
5: 2 yet the **b** belonged to Joseph.)
Heb 12:16 who sold his **b** for a single meal.

BIRTHSTOOL (1) [BEAR]

Ex 1:16 and see them on the **b**, if it is a boy, kill him;

BIRZAITH (1)

1Ch 7:31 Heber and Malchiel, who was the father of **B**.

BISHLAM (2)

Ezr 4: 7 **B** and Mithredath and Tabeel and the rest
1Es 2:16 In the time of King Artaxerxes of the Persians, **B**,

BISHOP (3) [BISHOPS]

1Ti 3: 1 whoever aspires to the office of **b** desires
3: 2 Now a **b** must be above reproach,
Tit 1: 7 For a **b**, as God's steward, must be blameless;

BISHOPRICK (KJV) See OVERSEER

BISHOPS (1) [BISHOP]

Php 1: 1 in Christ Jesus who are in Philippi, with the **b**

BIT (7) [BITE, BITS]

Nu 21: 6 and they **b** the people, so that many Israelites died.
21: 9 and whenever a serpent **b** someone,
Jdg 19: 5 "Fortify yourself with a **b** of food,
2Ki 19:28 I will put my hook in your nose and my **b**
Ps 32: 9 whose temper must be curbed with **b** and bridle,
76:10 you bind the last **b** of your wrath around you.
Isa 37:29 I will put my hook in your nose and my **b**

BITE (4) [BACKBITING, BIT, BITES, BITTEN]

Jer 8:17 and they shall **b** you, says the LORD.
Am 9: 3 the sea-serpent, and it shall **b** them.
Gal 5:15 If, however, you **b** and devour one another,
Sir 21: 2 for if you approach sin, it will **b** you.

BITES (5) [BITE]

Ge 49:17 that **b** the horse's heels so that its rider falls
Pr 23:32 At the last it **b** like a serpent,
Ecc 10:11 If the snake **b** before it is charmed,
Wis 16: 5 by the **b** of writhing serpents, your wrath did
16: 9 For they were killed by the **b** of locusts and flies,

BITHIAH (1)

1Ch 4:17 These are the sons of **B**, daughter of Pharaoh,

BITHYNIA (2)

Ac 16: 7 they attempted to go into **B**,
1Pe 1: 1 Galatia, Cappadocia, Asia, and **B**,

BITS (3) [BIT]

Pr 8:26 or the world's first **b** of soil.
Am 6:11 and the great house shall be shattered to **b**,
Jas 3: 3 If we put **b** into the mouths of horses

BITTEN (5) [BITE]

Nu 21: 8 and everyone who is **b** shall look at it and live."
Ecc 10: 8 and whoever breaks through a wall will be **b** by
Am 5:19 and rested a hand against the wall, and was **b** by
Wis 16:11 To remind them of your oracles they were **b**,
Sir 12:13 Who pities a snake charmer when he is **b**,

BITTER‡ (63) [BITTERLY, BITTERNESS, EMBITTERED]

Ge 26:35 and they made life **b** for Isaac and Rebekah.
27:34 he cried out with an exceedingly great and **b** cry,

Ex 1:14 and made their lives **b** with hard service in mortar
12: 8 over the fire with unleavened bread and **b** herbs.
15:23 not drink the water of Marah because it was **b.**
Nu 5:24 the curse shall enter her and cause **b** pain.
5:27 the curse shall enter into her and cause **b** pain,
9:11 with unleavened bread and **b** herbs.
Dt 29:18 a root sprouting poisonous and **b** growth.
32:24 burning consumption, **b** pestilence.
32:32 of poison, their clusters are **b;**
Ru 1:13 it has been far more **b** for me than for you,
1Sa 30: 6 of stoning him, because all the people were **b**
2Sa 2:26 Do you not know that the end will be **b?**
2Ki 4:27 "Let her alone, for she is in **b** distress;
14:26 LORD saw that the distress of Israel was very **b;**
Est 4: 1 wailing with a loud and **b** cry;
Job 3:20 and life to the **b** in soul,
13:26 For you write **b** things against me,
23: 2 "Today also my complaint is **b;**
27: 2 and the Almighty, who has made my soul **b,**
Ps 64: 3 who aim **b** words like arrows,
106:33 for they made his spirit **b,**
Pr 5: 4 but in the end she is **b** as wormwood,
27: 7 but to a ravenous appetite even the **b** is sweet.
31: 6 and wine to those in **b** distress;
Ecc 7:26 I found more **b** than death the woman who is
Isa 5:20 who put **b** for sweet and sweet for **b!**
22: 4 Look away from me, let me weep **b** tears;
24: 9 strong drink is **b** to those who drink it.
Jer 2:19 and **b** for you to forsake the LORD your God;
4:18 This is your doom; how **b** it is!
6:26 as for an only child, most **b** lamentation:
31:15 lamentation and **b** weeping.
La 1: 4 her young girls grieve, and her lot is **b.**
Eze 21: 6 with breaking heart and **b** grief before their eyes.
27:31 over you in bitterness of soul, with **b** mourning.
Hos 12:14 Ephraim has given **b** offense,
Am 8:10 and the end of it like a **b** day.
Mic 2: 4 and wail with **b** lamentation, and say,
Zep 1:14 the sound of the day of the LORD is **b,**
Jas 3:14 But if you have **b** envy and selfish ambition
Rev 8:11 from the water, because it was made **b.**
10: 9 it will be **b** to your stomach,
10:10 but when I had eaten it, my stomach was made **b.**
Tob 5:14 Do not feel **b** toward me, brother,
AdE 14: 8 now they are not satisfied that we are in **b** slavery,
Wis 19:13 for they practiced a more **b** hatred of strangers.
Sir 38:17 Let your weeping be **b** and your wailing fervent;
41: 1 how **b** is the thought of you to the one at peace
1Mc 6:13 perishing of **b** disappointment in a strange land."
2Mc 6: 7 under **b** constraint, to partake of the sacrifices;
3Mc 1: 4 When a **b** fight resulted,
2:24 but went away uttering **b** threats.
4:15 with **b** haste and zealous intensity from the rising
6:31 of deliverance instead of a **b** and lamentable death,
2Es 1:22 When you were in the wilderness, at the **b** stream,
8:34 that you are so **b** against it?
4Mc 15:16 tried now by more **b** pains than even
18:20 O **b** was that day—and yet not **b—**
18:20 that **b** tyrant of the Greeks quenched fire with fire

BITTERLY (24) [BITTER]

Jdg 5:23 curse **b** its inhabitants, because they did not come
21: 2 and they lifted up their voices and wept **b.**
Ru 1:20 for the Almighty has dealt **b** with me.
1Sa 1:10 and prayed to the LORD, and wept **b.**
2Sa 13:36 and the king and all his servants also wept very **b.**
2Ki 20: 3 in your sight." Hezekiah wept **b.**
Ezr 10: 1 of Israel; the people also wept **b.**
Isa 33: 7 the envoys of peace weep **b.**
38: 3 in your sight." And Hezekiah wept **b.**
Jer 13:17 my eyes will weep **b** and run down with tears,
48: 5 For at the ascent of Luhith they go up weeping **b;**
La 1: 2 She weeps **b** in the night, with tears on her cheeks;
Eze 27:30 and wail aloud over you, and cry **b.**
Zec 12:10 an only child, and weep **b** over him, as one weeps
Mt 26:75 And he went out and wept **b.**
Lk 22:62 And he went out and wept **b.**
Rev 5: 4 to weep **b** because no one was found worthy
Sir 22:11 Weep less **b** for the dead, for he is at rest;
25:18 and he cannot help sighing **b.**
3Mc 3: 1 but was still more **b** hostile toward those in
4:12 the city frequently went out in secret to lament **b**
4Mc 3:12 When his guards complained **b** because of
6:16 as though more **b** tormented by this counsel,
12:14 but you will wail **b** for having killed without cause

BITTERN (KJV) See HEDGEHOG, OWL

BITTERNESS‡ (25) [BITTER]

Nu 5:18 the priest shall have the water of **b** that brings
5:19 be immune to this water of **b** that brings the curse.
5:23 and wash them off into the water of **b.**
5:24 He shall make the woman drink the water of **b**
1Sa 15:32 Agag said, "Surely this is the **b** of death."
Job 7:11 I will complain in the **b** of my soul.
9:18 not let me get my breath, but fills me with **b.**
10: 1 I will speak in the **b** of my soul.
21:25 Another dies in **b** of soul,
Pr 14:10 The heart knows its own **b,**
17:25 a grief to their father and **b** to her who bore them.
Isa 38:15 All my sleep has fled because of the **b** of my soul.
38:17 Surely it was for my welfare that I had great **b;**
La 3: 5 he has besieged and enveloped me with **b**
3:15 He has filled me with **b,**
Eze 3:14 I went in **b** in the heat of my spirit,
27:31 and they weep over you in **b** of soul,
Ac 8:23 in the gall of **b** and the chains of wickedness."
Ro 3:14 "Their mouths are full of cursing and **b.**"
Eph 4:31 from you all **b** and wrath and anger and wrangling
Heb 12:15 that no root of **b** springs up and causes trouble,
Wis 8:16 for companionship with her has no **b,**
Sir 4: 6 for if in **b** of soul some should curse you,
21:12 but there is a cleverness that increases **b.**
31:29 Wine drunk to excess leads to **b** of spirit,

BITUMEN (3)

Ge 11: 3 And they had brick for stone, and **b** for mortar.
14:10 Now the Valley of Siddim was full of **b** pits;
Ex 2: 3 and plastered it with **b** and pitch;

BIZIOTHIAH (1)

Jos 15:28 Hazar-shual, Beer-sheba, **B,**

BIZJOTHJAH (KJV) See BIZIOTHIAH

BIZTHA (1)

Est 1:10 he commanded Mehuman, **B,** Harbona,

BLACK (19) [BLACKENED, BLACKER, BLACKNESS]

Ge 30:32 and every **b** lamb, and the spotted and speckled
30:33 not speckled and spotted among the goats and **b**
30:35 and every lamb that was **b,**
30:40 toward the striped and the completely **b** animals in
Ex 10:15 so that the land was **b;**
Lev 13:31 the skin and there is no **b** hair in it,
13:37 and **b** hair has grown in it, the itch is healed,
1Ki 18:45 while the heavens grew **b** with clouds and wind;
Job 30:30 My skin turns **b** and falls from me,
SS 1: 5 I am **b** and beautiful, O daughters of Jerusalem,
5:11 his locks are wavy, **b** as a raven.
Jer 4:28 and the heavens above grow **b;**
La 5:10 Our skin is **b** as an oven from the scorching heat
Mic 3: 6 and the day shall be **b** over them;
Zec 6: 2 the second chariot **b** horses,
6: 6 with the **b** horses goes toward the north country,
Mt 5:36 for you cannot make one hair white or **b.**
Rev 6: 5 I looked, and there was a **b** horse!
6:12 the sun became **b** as sackcloth,

BLACKENED (1) [BLACK]

LtJ 6:21 when their faces have been **b** by the smoke of

BLACKER (2) [BLACK]

La 4: 8 Now their visage is **b** than soot;
2Es 7:*125* [55] but our faces shall be **b** than darkness?

BLACKNESS (3) [BLACK]

Job 3: 5 let the **b** of the day terrify it.
Isa 50: 3 I clothe the heavens with **b,**
Joel 2: 2 Like **b** spread upon the mountains a great

BLACKSMITHS (1) [SMITH]

Zec 1:20 Then the LORD showed me four **b.**

BLADE (3)

Jdg 3:22 went in after the **b,** and the fat closed over the **b,**
Job 31:22 then let my shoulder **b** fall from my shoulder,

BLAINS (KJV) See BOILS

BLAME (10) [BLAMED, BLAMELESS, BLAMELESSLY]

Ge 43: 9 then let me bear the **b** forever.
44:32 the **b** in the sight of my father all my life.'
Jdg 15: 3 to the Philistines, I will be without **b.**"
2Co 8:20 that no one should **b** us about this generous gift
1Ti 6:14 to keep the commandment without spot or **b** until
Sir 11:31 and to worthy actions they attach **b.**
41: 7 Children will **b** an ungodly father,
1Mc 11: 5 to throw **b** on him; but the king kept silent.
11:11 He threw **b** on Alexander
2Mc 13: 4 when Lysias informed him that this man was to **b**

BLAMED (1) [BLAME]

Wis 13: 6 Yet these people are little to be **b,**

BLAMELESS (57) [BLAME]

Ge 6: 9 Noah was a righteous man, **b** in his generation;
17: 1 walk before me, and be **b.**
1Sa 29: 9 "I know that you are as **b** in my sight as an angel
2Sa 22:24 I was **b** before him, and I kept myself from guilt.
22:26 with the **b** you show yourself **b;**
Job 1: 1 That man was **b** and upright,
1: 8 a **b** and upright man who fears God
2: 3 a **b** and upright man who fears God
8:20 "See, God will not reject a **b** person,
9:20 though I am **b,** he would prove me perverse.
9:21 I am **b;** I do not know myself; I loathe my life.
9:22 I say, he destroys both the **b** and the wicked.
12: 4 a just and **b** man, I am a laughingstock.
22: 3 or is it gain to him if you make your ways **b?**
Ps 18:23 I was **b** before him, and I kept myself from guilt.
18:25 with the **b** you show yourself **b;**
19:13 I shall be **b,** and innocent of great transgression.
37:18 The LORD knows the days of the **b,**
37:37 Mark the **b,** and behold the upright,
51: 4 in your sentence and **b** when you pass judgment.
64: 4 shooting from ambush at the **b;**
101: 2 I will study the way that is **b.**
101: 6 whoever walks in the way that is **b** shall minister
119: 1 Happy are those whose way is **b,**
119:80 May my heart be **b** in your statutes,
Pr 11: 5 righteousness of the **b** keeps their ways straight,
11:20 but those of **b** ways are his delight.
28:10 but the **b** will have a goodly inheritance.
29:10 The bloodthirsty hate the **b,**
Eze 28:15 You were **b** in your ways from the day
Da 6:22 because I was found **b** before him;
1Co 1: 8 you may be **b** on the day of our Lord Jesus Christ.
Eph 1: 4 of the world to be holy and **b** before him in love.
Php 1:10 so that in the day of Christ you may be pure and **b,**
2:15 so that you may be **b** and innocent,
3: 6 as to righteousness under the law, **b.**
Col 1:22 so as to present you holy and **b** and irreproachable
1Th 2:10 and **b** our conduct was toward you believers.
3:13 that you may be **b** before our God and Father at
5:23 and **b** at the coming of our Lord Jesus Christ.
1Ti 3:10 then, if they prove themselves **b,**
Tit 1: 6 someone who is **b,** married only once,
1: 7 For a bishop, as God's steward, must be **b;**
Heb 7:26 holy, **b,** undefiled, separated from sinners,
Rev 14: 5 and in their mouth no lie was found; they are **b.**
AdE 16:13 and of Esther, the **b** partner of our kingdom,
Wis 2:22 nor discerned the prize for **b** souls;
4: 9 and a **b** life is ripe old age.
10: 5 recognized the righteous man and preserved him **b**
10:15 A holy people and **b** race wisdom delivered from
18:21 For a **b** man was quick to act as their champion;
Sir 11:10 if you multiply activities, you will not be held **b.**
31: 8 Blessed is the rich person who is found **b,**
40:19 but a **b** wife is accounted better than either.
1Mc 4:42 He chose **b** priests devoted to the law,

BLAMELESSLY (3) [BLAME]

Ps 15: 2 Those who walk **b,** and do what is right,
Pr 2: 7 he is a shield to those who walk **b,**
Lk 1: 6 living **b** according to all the commandments

BLASPHEME (5) [BLASPHEMED, BLASPHEMER, BLASPHEMERS, BLASPHEMES, BLASPHEMIES, BLASPHEMING, BLASPHEMOUS, BLASPHEMY]

Lev 24:16 Aliens as well as citizens, when they **b** the Name,
Ac 26:11 in all the synagogues I tried to force them to **b;**
1Ti 1:20 so that they may learn not to **b.**
Jas 2: 7 Is it not they who **b** the excellent name
1Pe 4: 4 in the same excesses of dissipation, and so they **b.**

BLASPHEMED‡ (5) [BLASPHEME]

Lev 24:11 The Israelite woman's son **b** the Name in a curse.
Eze 20:27 In this again your ancestors **b** me,
Mt 26:65 high priest tore his clothes and said, "He has **b!**
Ro 2:24 of God is **b** among the Gentiles because of you."
1Ti 6: 1 the name of God and the teaching may not be **b.**

BLASPHEMER (6) [BLASPHEME]

Lev 24:14 Take the **b** outside the camp;
24:16 the whole congregation shall stone the **b.**
24:23 and they took the **b** outside the camp,
1Ti 1:13 even though I was formerly a **b,**
Sir 3:16 Whoever forsakes a father is like a **b,**
2Mc 9:28 So the murderer and **b,** having endured

BLASPHEMERS (4) [BLASPHEME]

Ac 19:37 are neither temple robbers nor **b** of our goddess.
Wis 1: 6 but will not free **b** from the guilt of their words;
2Mc 10:36 they kindled fires and burned the **b** alive.
15:24 By the might of your arm may these **b** who come

BLASPHEMES (3) [BLASPHEME]

Lev 24:16 who **b** the name of the LORD shall be put to death;
Mk 3:29 but whoever **b** against the Holy Spirit can never have forgiveness,
Lk 12:10 **b** against the Holy Spirit will not be forgiven.

BLASPHEMIES (11) [BLASPHEME]

Ne 9:18 and had committed great **b,**
9:26 and they committed great **b.**
Mk 3:28 for their sins and whatever **b** they utter;
Lk 5:21 "Who is this who is speaking **b?**
Rev 13: 6 It opened its mouth to utter **b** against God,
Tob 1:18 of heaven executed upon him because of his **b.**
1Mc 2: 6 the **b** being committed in Judah and Jerusalem,
7:38 remember their **b,** and let them live no longer."
2Mc 8: 4 of the innocent babies and the **b** committed
10:35 fired with anger because of the **b,**
2Es 1:23 I did not send fire on you for your **b,**

BLASPHEMING‡ (8) [BLASPHEME]

1Sa 3:13 because his sons were **b** God,

Mt 9: 3 of the scribes said to themselves, "This man is **b**."
Jn 10:36 and sent into the world is **b** because I said,
Ac 13:45 and **b**, they contradicted what was spoken by Paul.
Rev 13: 6 **b** his name and his dwelling, that is,
2Mc 10:34 kept **b** terribly and uttering wicked words.
12:14 at them and even **b** and saying unholy things.
2Es 1:22 at the bitter stream, thirsty and **b** my name,

BLASPHEMOUS (6) [BLASPHEME]
Ac 6:11 "We have heard him speak **b** words against Moses
Rev 13: 1 and on its heads were **b** names.
13: 5 a mouth uttering haughty and **b** words,
17: 3 on a scarlet beast that was full of **b** names,
2Mc 10: 4 not be handed over to **b** and barbarous nations.
13:11 to revive fall into the hands of the **b** Gentiles.

BLASPHEMY‡ (9) [BLASPHEME]
Da 3:29 Any people, nation, or language that utters **b**
Mt 12:31 people will be forgiven for every sin and **b**,
12:31 but **b** against the Spirit will not be forgiven.
26:65 You have now heard his **b**.
Mk 2: 7 "Why does this fellow speak in this way? It is **b**!
14:64 You have heard his **b**!
Jn 10:33 to stone you, but for **b**, because you, though only
Bel 1: 9 because he has spoken **b** against Bel."
1Mc 7:41 "When the messengers from the king spoke **b**,

BLAST (13) [BLASTS]
Ex 15: 8 At the **b** of your nostrils the waters piled up,
19:13 When the trumpet sounds a long **b**,
19:16 and a **b** of a trumpet so loud that all
19:19 As the **b** of the trumpet grew louder and louder,
Jos 6: 5 When they make a long **b** with the ram's horn,
2Sa 22:16 at the **b** of the breath of his nostrils.
Job 4: 9 and by the **b** of his anger they are consumed.
Ps 18:15 O LORD, at the **b** of the breath of your nostrils.
Isa 25: 4 the **b** of the ruthless was like a winter rainstorm,
27: 8 with his fierce **b** he removed them in the day of
Hos 13:15 a **b** from the LORD, rising from the wilderness;
Zep 1:16 a day of trumpet **b** and battle cry against
2Es 4: 5 or measure for me a **b** of wind,

BLASTS (2) [BLAST]
Lev 23:24 holy convocation commemorated with trumpet **b**.
Rev 8:13 the **b** of the other trumpets that the three angels are

BLASTUS (1)
Ac 12:20 and after winning over **B**, the king's chamberlain,

BLAZE (2) [ABLAZE, BLAZED, BLAZES, BLAZING]
Nu 16:37 the priest to take the censers out of the **b**;
2Mc 4:22 and ushered in with a **b** of torches and with shouts.

BLAZED (4) [BLAZE]
Ps 118:12 they **b** like a fire of thorns;
Wis 16:22 that **b** in the hail and flashed in the showers
2Mc 1:22 shone out, a great fire **b** up, so that all marveled.
1:32 When this was done, a flame **b** up;

BLAZES (3) [BLAZE]
Hos 7: 6 in the morning it **b** like a flaming fire.
Sir 16: 6 and in a disobedient nation wrath **b** up.
23:16 Hot passion that **b** like a fire will not be quenched

BLAZING (17) [BLAZE]
Ex 3: 2 he looked, and the bush was **b**,
Dt 4:11 the foot of the mountain while the mountain was **b**
Eze 20:47 the **b** flame shall not be quenched,
38:19 For in my jealousy and in my **b** wrath I declare:
Da 3: 6 be thrown into a furnace of **b** fire."
3:11 be thrown into a furnace of **b** fire.
3:15 be thrown into a furnace of **b** fire,
3:17 from the furnace of **b** fire and out of your hand,
3:20 and to throw them into the furnace of **b** fire.
3:21 and they were thrown into the furnace of **b** fire.
3:23 fell down, bound, into the furnace of **b** fire.
3:26 then approached the door of the furnace of **b** fire
Zec 12: 6 that day I will make the clans of Judah like a **b** pot
Heb 12:18 a **b** fire, and darkness, and gloom, and a tempest,
Rev 8:10 and a great star fell from heaven, **b** like a torch,
Sir 3:30 As water extinguishes a **b** fire,
21: 9 and their end is a **b** fire.

BLEACH (1)
Mk 9: 3 such as no one on earth could **b** them.

BLEAT (1) [BLEATING]
Tob 2:13 When she returned to me, the goat began to **b**.

BLEATING (1) [BLEAT]
1Sa 15:14 "What then is this **b** of sheep in my ears,

BLEEDING (1) [BLOOD]
Isa 1: 6 but bruises and sores and **b** wounds;

BLEMISH (68) [BLEMISHED, BLEMISHES]
Ex 12: 5 Your lamb shall be without **b**, a year-old male;
29: 1 Take one young bull and two rams without **b**,
Lev 1: 3 you shall offer a male without **b**;
1:10 your offering shall be a male without **b**.
3: 1 you shall offer one without **b** before the LORD.
3: 6 male or female, you shall offer one without **b**.
4: 3 the herd without **b** as a sin offering to the LORD.
4:23 as his offering a male goat without **b**.
4:28 a female goat without **b** as your offering,
4:32 you shall bring a female without **b**.
5:15 a ram without **b** from the flock,
5:18 You shall bring to the priest a ram without **b** from
6: 6 a ram without **b** from the flock, or its equivalent,
9: 2 without **b**, and offer them before the LORD.
9: 3 a calf and a lamb, yearlings without **b**,
14:10 without **b**, and one ewe lamb in its first year without **b**,
21:17 a **b** may approach to offer the food of his God.
21:18 For no one who has a **b** shall draw near,
21:20 or a man with a **b** in his eyes or an itching disease
21:21 of Aaron the priest who has a **b** shall come near
21:21 since he has a **b**, he shall not come near to offer
21:23 a **b**, that he may not profane my sanctuaries;
22:19 in your behalf it shall be a male without **b**,
22:20 You shall not offer anything that has a **b**,
22:21 there shall be no **b** in it.
22:25 since they are mutilated, with a **b** in them,
23:12 without **b**, as a burnt offering to the LORD.
23:18 with the bread seven lambs a year old without **b**,
Nu 6:14 a year old without **b** as a burnt offering,
6:14 a year old without **b** as a sin offering,
6:14 one ram without **b** as an offering of well-being,
19: 2 a red heifer without defect, in which there is no **b**
28: 3 two male lambs a year old without **b**, daily,
28: 9 two male lambs a year old without **b**,
28:11 one ram, seven male lambs a year old without **b**;
28:19 see that they are without **b**.
28:31 They shall be without **b**.
29: 2 one ram, seven male lambs a year old without **b**.
29: 8 They shall be without **b**.
29:13 They shall be without **b**.
29:17 fourteen male lambs a year old without **b**,
29:20 fourteen male lambs a year old without **b**,
29:23 fourteen male lambs a year old without **b**,
29:26 fourteen male lambs a year old without **b**,
29:29 fourteen male lambs a year old without **b**,
29:32 fourteen male lambs a year old without **b**,
29:36 one ram, seven male lambs a year old without **b**,
2Sa 14:25 of his foot to the crown of his head there was no **b**
Job 11:15 Surely then you will lift up your face without **b**;
Eze 43:22 a male goat without **b** for a sin offering;
43:23 you shall offer a bull without **b** and a ram from the flock without **b**.
43:25 also a bull and a ram from the flock, without **b**,
45:18 you shall take a young bull without **b**,
45:23 and seven rams without **b**, on each of
46: 4 be six lambs without **b** and a ram without **b**;
46: 6 a young bull without **b**, and six lambs and a ram,
46: 6 which shall be without **b**;
46:13 He shall provide a lamb, a yearling, without **b**,
Eph 5:27 yes, so that she may be holy and without **b**.
Php 2:15 of God without **b** in the midst of a crooked
Heb 9:14 the eternal Spirit offered himself without **b** to God,
1Pe 1:19 like that of a lamb without defect or **b**.
2Pe 3:14 to be found by him at peace, without spot or **b**;
Jude 1:24 and to make you stand without **b** in the presence
Wis 13:14 and coloring its surface red and covering every **b**

BLEMISHED (2) [BLEMISH]
Mal 1:14 and yet sacrifices to the Lord what is **b**;
Sir 34:21 If one sacrifices ill-gotten goods, the offering is **b**;

BLEMISHES (2) [BLEMISH]
2Pe 2:13 and **b**, reveling in their dissipation while they feast
Jude 1:12 These are **b** on your love-feasts,

BLENDED (4)
Ex 30:25 a sacred anointing oil **b** as by the perfumer;
30:35 and make an incense **b** as by the perfumer,
37:29 the pure fragrant incense, **b** as by the perfumer.
Sir 49: 1 of Josiah is like **b** incense prepared by the skill of

BLESS‡ (177) [BLESSED, BLESSEDNESS, BLESSES, BLESSING, BLESSINGS]
A. BLESS YOU (41)
B. BLESS THE *LORD (37)
C. BLESS THE †LORD (23)

Ge 12: 2 make of you a great nation, and I will **b** you, A
12: 3 I will **b** those who bless you,
12: 3 I will bless those who **b** you, A
17:16 I will **b** her, and moreover I will give you a son
17:16 I will **b** her, and she shall give rise to nations;
17:20 I will **b** him and make him fruitful
22:17 indeed **b** you, and I will make your offspring A
26: 3 and I will be with you, and will **b** you; A
26:24 will **b** you and make your offspring numerous A
27: 4 so that I may **b** you before I die." A
27: 7 that I may **b** you before the LORD before I die.' A
27:10 so that he may **b** you before he dies." A
27:19 sit up and eat of my game, so that you may **b** me."
27:25 that I may eat of my son's game and **b** you." A
27:31 so that you may **b** me."
27:34 and said to his father, "**B** me, me also, father!"
27:38 **B** me, me also, father!"
28: 3 May God Almighty **b** you and make you fruitful A
32:26 "I will not let you go, unless you **b** me."
48: 9 "Bring them to me, please, that I may **b** them."
48:16 the angel who has redeemed me from all harm, **b**
49:25 by the Almighty who will **b** you with blessings A
Ex 20:24 to be remembered I will come to you and **b** you. A
23:25 and I will **b** your bread and your water;
Nu 6:23 saying, Thus you shall **b** the Israelites:
6:24 The LORD **b** you and keep you; A
6:27 on the Israelites, and I will **b** them.
22: 6 for I know that whomever you **b** is blessed,
23:11 but now you have done nothing but **b** them."
23:20 See, I received a command to **b**;
23:25 and do not **b** them at all."
24: 1 Balaam saw that it pleased the LORD to **b** Israel,
Dt 1:11 increase you a thousand times more and **b** you, A
7:13 he will love you, **b** you, and multiply you; A
7:13 he will **b** the fruit of your womb and the fruit
8:10 You shall eat your fill and **b** the LORD your God C
10: 8 and to **b** in his name, to this day.
14:29 the LORD your God may **b** you in all the work A
15: 4 because the LORD is sure to **b** you in the land A
15:10 the LORD your God will **b** you in all your work A
15:18 the LORD your God will **b** you in all that you do. A
16:15 for the LORD your God will **b** you A
23:20 so that the LORD your God may **b** you A
24:13 your neighbor may sleep in the cloak and **b** you; A
24:19 so that the LORD your God may **b** you A
26:15 and **b** your people Israel and the ground
28: 8 he will **b** you in the land that A
28:12 in its season and to **b** all your undertakings.
29:19 the words of this oath and **b** themselves, thinking
30:16 and the LORD your God will **b** you in the land A
33:11 **B**, O LORD, his substance,
Jos 8:33 that they should **b** the people of Israel.
Jdg 5: 2 people offer themselves willingly—**b** the LORD! C
5: 9 among the people. **B** the LORD. C
Ru 2: 4 They answered, "The LORD **b** you." A
1Sa 2:20 Then Eli would **b** Elkanah and his wife, and say,
9:13 since he must **b** the sacrifice;
2Sa 6:20 David returned to **b** his household.
7:29 now therefore may it please you to **b** the house
21: 3 that you may **b** the heritage of the LORD?"
1Ch 4:10 "Oh that you would **b** me and enlarge my border,
16:43 and David went home to **b** his household.
17:27 may it please you to **b** the house of your servant,
29:20 "**B** the LORD your God." C
Ne 9: 5 up and **b** the LORD your God from everlasting C
Ps 5:12 For you **b** the righteous, O LORD;
16: 7 I **b** the LORD who gives me counsel; C
26:12 in the great congregation I will **b** the LORD. C
28: 9 O save your people, and **b** your heritage;
29:11 May the LORD **b** his people with peace!
34: 1 I will **b** the LORD at all times; C
62: 4 they **b** with their mouths,
63: 4 So I will **b** you as long as I live; A
66: 8 **B** our God, O peoples, let the sound of his praise
67: 1 to us and **b** us and make his face to shine upon us,
67: 7 May God continue to **b** us;
68:26 "**B** God in the great congregation,
96: 2 Sing to the LORD, **b** his name;
100: 4 Give thanks to him, **b** his name.
103: 1 **B** the LORD, O my soul, and all that is C
103: 1 and all that is within me, **b** his holy name.
103: 2 **B** the LORD, O my soul, C
103:20 **B** the LORD, O you his angels, C
103:21 **B** the LORD, all his hosts, C
103:22 **B** the LORD, all his works, C
103:22 **B** the LORD, O my soul. C
104: 1 **B** the LORD, O my soul. C
104:35 **B** the LORD, O my soul. C
109:28 Let them curse, but you will **b**.
115:12 The LORD has been mindful of us; he will **b** us;
115:12 he will **b** the house of Israel;
115:12 he will **b** the house of Aaron;
115:13 he will **b** those who fear the LORD,
115:18 But we will **b** the LORD from this time on C
118:26 We **b** you from the house of the LORD. A
128: 5 The LORD **b** you from Zion. A
129: 8 We **b** you in the name of the LORD!" A
132:15 I will abundantly **b** its provisions;
134: 1 **b** the LORD, all you servants of the LORD, C
134: 2 up your hands to the holy place, and **b** the LORD. C
134: 3 maker of heaven and earth, **b** you from Zion. A
135:19 O house of Israel, **b** the LORD! C
135:19 O house of Aaron, **b** the LORD! C
135:20 O house of Levi, **b** the LORD! C
135:20 You that fear the LORD, **b** the LORD! C
145: 1 and **b** your name forever and ever.
145: 2 Every day I will **b** you, A
145:10 O LORD, and all your faithful shall **b** you. A
145:21 all flesh will **b** his holy name forever and ever.
Pr 30:11 and do not **b** their mothers.
Isa 65:16 in the land shall **b** by the God of faithfulness,
Jer 31:23 "The LORD **b** you, O abode of righteousness, A
Eze 37:26 and I will **b** them and multiply them,
Hag 2:19 From this day on I will **b** you. A
Lk 6:28 **b** those who curse you, pray for those who abuse
Ac 3:26 to **b** you by turning each of you A
Ro 12:14 **B** those who persecute you; **b** and do not curse
1Co 4:12 of our own hands. When reviled, we **b**;
10:16 The cup of blessing that we **b**,
Heb 6:14 saying, "I will surely **b** you and multiply you." A
Jas 3: 9 With it we **b** the Lord and Father, B
Tob 4:19 At all times **b** the Lord God, B
8: 5 heavens and the whole creation **b** you forever. A
8:15 let all your chosen ones **b** you. A

Tob 8:15 Let them **b** you forever. A
12:6 **"B** God and acknowledge him in the presence
12:6 **B** and sing praise to his name.
12:17 **B** God forevermore.
12:18 **B** him each and every day; sing his praises.
13:6 **B** the Lord of righteousness, B
13:10 for he is good, and **b** the King of the ages,
13:17 blessed will **b** the holy name forever and ever."
14:8,9 be mindful of God and to **b** his name at all times
Jdt 15:10 May the Almighty Lord **b** you forever!" A
Sir 31:23 People **b** the one who is liberal with food,
32:13 But above all **b** your Maker,
39:14 **b** the Lord for all his works. B
39:35 and **b** the name of the Lord.
45:15 and serve as priest and **b** his people in his name.
45:26 **b** the Lord who has crowned you with glory. B
50:22 And now **b** the God of all,
51:12 and I **b** the name of the Lord.
LtJ 6:66 They can neither curse nor **b** kings;
Aza 1:35 **"B** the Lord, all you works of the Lord; B
1:36 **B** the Lord, you heavens; sing praise to him B
1:37 **B** the Lord, you angels of the Lord; B
1:38 **B** the Lord, all you waters above the heavens; B
1:39 **B** the Lord, all you powers of the Lord; B
1:40 **B** the Lord, sun and moon; B
1:41 **B** the Lord, stars of heaven; B
1:42 **"B** the Lord, all rain and dew; B
1:43 **B** the Lord, all you winds; B
1:44 **B** the Lord, fire and heat; B
1:45 **B** the Lord, winter cold and summer heat; B
1:46 **B** the Lord, dews and falling snow; B
1:47 **B** the Lord, nights and days; B
1:48 **B** the Lord, light and darkness; B
1:49 **B** the Lord, ice and cold; B
1:50 **B** the Lord, frosts and snows; B
1:51 **B** the Lord, lightnings and clouds; B
1:52 "Let the earth **b** the Lord; B
1:53 **B** the Lord, mountains and hills; B
1:54 **B** the Lord, all that grows in the ground; B
1:55 **B** the Lord, seas and rivers; B
1:56 **B** the Lord, you springs; sing praise to him B
1:57 **B** the Lord, you whales and all that swim in B
1:58 **B** the Lord, all birds of the air; B
1:59 **B** the Lord, all wild animals and cattle; B
1:60 **"B** the Lord, all people on earth; B
1:61 **B** the Lord, O Israel; sing praise to him B
1:62 **B** the Lord, you priests of the Lord; B
1:63 **B** the Lord, you servants of the Lord; B
1:64 **B** the Lord, spirits and souls of the righteous; B
1:65 **B** the Lord, you who are holy and humble B
1:66 **"B** the Lord, Hananiah, Azariah, and Mishael; B
1:68 All who worship the Lord, **b** the God of gods,

BLESSED‡ (335) [BLESS]

A. BLESSED BE THE †LORD (26)
B. BLESSED [BE] ... *GOD (15)
C. *GOD BLESSED (7)
D. †LORD BLESSED (7)
E. BLESSED BE THE *LORD (4)

Ge 1:22 God **b** them, saying, "Be fruitful and multiply C
1:28 God **b** them, and God said to them, C
2:3 So God **b** the seventh day and hallowed it, C
5:2 and he **b** them and named them "Humankind"
9:1 God **b** Noah and his sons, and said to them, C
9:26 He also said, **"B** by the LORD my God be Shem;
12:3 and in you all the families of the earth shall be **b."**
14:19 **b** him and said, **"B** be Abram by God Most High,
14:20 and **b** be God Most High, B
18:18 and all the nations of the earth shall be **b** in him?
24:1 and the LORD had **b** Abraham in all things.
24:27 and said, **"B** be the LORD, the God A
24:31 He said, "Come in, O **b** of the LORD.
24:35 The LORD has greatly **b** my master,
24:48 and worshiped the LORD, and **b** the LORD,
24:60 And they **b** Rebekah and said to her, "May you,
25:11 After the death of Abraham God **b** his son Isaac. C
26:12 reaped a hundredfold. The LORD **b** him, D
26:29 You are now the **b** of the LORD."
27:23 like his brother Esau's hands; so he **b** him.
27:27 he smelled the smell of his garments, and **b** him,
27:27 like the smell of a field that the LORD has **b.**
27:29 and **b** be everyone who blesses you!"
27:33 and I have **b** him?—yes, and **b** he shall be!"
27:41 of the blessing with which his father had **b** him,
28:1 Then Isaac called Jacob and **b** him,
28:6 that Isaac had **b** Jacob and sent him away
28:6 and that as he **b** him he charged him,
28:14 the earth shall be **b** in you and in your offspring.
30:27 by divination that the LORD has **b** me because
30:30 and the LORD has **b** you wherever I turned.
31:55 and his daughters and **b** them;
32:29 And there he **b** him.
35:9 when he came from Paddan-aram, and he **b** him.
39:5 LORD **b** the Egyptian's house for Joseph's sake; D
47:7 before Pharaoh, and Jacob **b** Pharaoh.
47:10 Then Jacob **b** Pharaoh, and went out from
48:3 to me at Luz in the land of Canaan, and he **b** me,
48:15 He **b** Joseph, and said, "The God
48:20 So he **b** them that day, saying,
49:28 what their father said to them when he **b** them,
Ex 18:10 Jethro said, **"B** be the LORD, A
20:11 the LORD **b** the sabbath day and consecrated it. D
39:43 as the LORD had commanded, he **b** them.
Lev 9:22 toward the people and **b** them;
9:23 and then came out and **b** the people;

Nu 22:6 for I know that whomever you bless is **b,**
22:12 you shall not curse the people, for they are **b."**
23:20 he has **b,** and I cannot revoke it.
24:9 **B** is everyone who blesses you,
24:10 but instead you have **b** them these three times.
Dt 2:7 Surely the LORD your God has **b** you
7:14 You shall be the most **b** of peoples,
12:7 in which the LORD your God has **b** you.
14:24 But if, when the LORD your God has **b** you,
15:6 When the LORD your God has **b** you,
15:14 with which the LORD your God has **b** you.
28:3 **B** shall you be in the city,
28:3 and **b** shall you be in the field.
28:4 **B** shall be the fruit of your womb,
28:5 **B** shall be your basket and your kneading bowl.
28:6 **B** shall you be when you come in,
28:6 and **b** shall you be when you go out.
33:1 the man of God, **b** the Israelites before his death.
33:13 **B** by the LORD be his land,
33:20 And of Gad he said: **B** be the enlargement of Gad!
33:24 Most **b** of sons be Asher; may he be the favorite
Jos 14:13 Then Joshua **b** him, and gave Hebron to Caleb son
17:14 whom all along the LORD has **b?"**
22:6 So Joshua **b** them and sent them away,
22:7 Joshua sent them away to their tents and **b** them,
22:33 and the Israelites **b** God and spoke no more
24:10 to Balaam; therefore he **b** you;
Jdg 5:24 "Most **b** of women be Jael,
5:24 of tent-dwelling women most **b.**
13:24 The boy grew, and the LORD **b** him. D
17:2 "May my son be **b** by the LORD!"
Ru 2:19 **B** be the man who took notice of you."
2:20 **"B** be he by the LORD,
3:10 He said, "May you be **b** by the LORD,
4:14 the women said to Naomi, **"B** be the LORD, A
1Sa 15:13 Saul said to him, "May you be **b** by the LORD;
23:21 be **b** by the LORD for showing me compassion!
25:32 David said to Abigail, **"B** be the LORD, A
25:33 **B** be your good sense, and **b** be you,
25:39 **"B** be the LORD who has judged the case A
26:25 Saul said to David, **"B** be you, my son David!
2Sa 2:5 and said to them, "May you be **b** by the LORD,
6:11 the LORD **b** Obed-edom and all his household. D
6:12 "The LORD has **b** the household of Obed-edom
6:18 he **b** the people in the name of the LORD
7:29 the house of your servant be **b** forever."
14:22 to the ground and did obeisance, and **b** the king;
18:28 and said, **"B** be the LORD your God, A
19:39 the king kissed Barzillai and **b** him,
22:47 **B** be my rock, and exalted be my God,
1Ki 1:48 **'B** be the LORD, the God of Israel, A
2:45 But King Solomon shall be **b,**
5:7 and said, **"B** be the LORD today, A
8:14 the king turned around and **b** all the assembly
8:15 He said, **"B** be the LORD, the God of Israel, A
8:55 and **b** all the assembly of Israel with a loud voice:
8:56 **"B** be the LORD, who has given rest A
8:66 and they **b** the king, and went to their tents,
10:9 **B** be the LORD your God, A
1Ch 13:14 the LORD **b** the household of Obed-edom and D
16:2 he **b** the people in the name of the LORD;
16:36 **B** be the LORD, the God of Israel, A
17:27 you, O LORD, have **b** and are **b** forever."
26:5 Peullethai the eighth; for God **b** him. C
29:10 Then David **b** the LORD in the presence of all
29:10 **"B** are you, O LORD, the God
29:20 And all the assembly **b** the LORD,
2Ch 2:12 Huram also said, **"B** be the LORD God of Israel, A
6:3 the king turned around and **b** all the assembly
6:4 And he said, **"B** be the LORD, the God of Israel, A
9:8 **B** be the LORD your God, A
20:26 for there they **b** the LORD;
30:27 priests and the Levites stood up and **b** the people,
31:8 they **b** the LORD and his people Israel.
31:10 for the LORD has **b** his people,
Ezr 7:27 **B** be the LORD, the God of our ancestors, A
Ne 8:6 Then Ezra **b** the LORD, the great God,
9:5 **B** be your glorious name, which is exalted
11:2 the people **b** all those who willingly offered to live
Job 1:10 You have **b** the work of his hands,
1:21 **b** be the name of the LORD."
31:20 not **b** me, and who was not warmed with the fleece
42:12 The LORD **b** the latter days D
Ps 18:46 **B** be my rock, and exalted be the God
28:6 **B** be the LORD, for he has heard the sound A
31:21 **B** be the LORD, for he has wondrously shown A
37:22 for those **b** by the LORD shall inherit the land,
41:13 **B** be the LORD, the God of Israel, A
45:2 therefore God has **b** you forever.
66:20 **B** be God, because he has not rejected my prayer B
67:6 God, our God, has **b** us.
68:19 **B** be the Lord, who daily bears us up; E
68:35 and strength to his people. **B** be God! B
72:17 May all nations be **b** in him;
72:18 **B** be the LORD, the God of Israel, A
72:19 **B** be his glorious name forever;
89:52 **B** be the LORD forever. Amen and Amen. A
106:48 **B** be the LORD, the God of Israel, A
112:2 the generation of the upright will be **b.**
113:2 **B** be the name of the LORD from this time on
115:15 May you be **b** by the LORD,
118:26 **B** is the one who comes in the name of
119:12 **B** are you, O LORD; teach me your statutes.
124:6 **B** be the LORD, who has not given us as prey A
128:4 Thus shall the man be **b** who fears the LORD.
135:21 **B** be the LORD from Zion, A
144:1 **B** be the LORD, my rock, who trains my hands A

Pr 5:18 Let your fountain be **b,** and rejoice in the wife
20:21 in the beginning will not be **b** in the end.
22:9 Those who are generous are **b,**
Isa 19:25 whom the LORD of hosts has **b,**
19:25 saying, **"B** be Egypt my people,
30:18 **b** are all those who wait for him.
51:2 but I **b** him and made him many.
61:9 that they are a people whom the LORD has **b.**
65:23 for they shall be offspring **b** by the LORD—
Jer 4:2 and in uprightness, then nations shall be **b** by him,
17:7 **B** are those who trust in the LORD,
20:14 The day when my mother bore me, let it not be **b!**
Da 2:19 and Daniel **b** the God of heaven. B
2:20 **"B** be the name of God from age to age,
3:28 Nebuchadnezzar said, **"B** be the God of B
4:34 I **b** the Most High, and praised and honored
Zec 11:5 and those who sell them say, **"B** be the LORD, A
Mt 5:3 **"B** are the poor in spirit,
5:4 **"B** are those who mourn, for they will
5:5 **"B** are the meek, for they will inherit the earth.
5:6 **"B** are those who hunger and thirst
5:7 **"B** are the merciful, for they will receive mercy.
5:8 **"B** are the pure in heart, for they will see God.
5:9 **"B** are the peacemakers, for they will
5:10 **"B** are those who are persecuted
5:11 **"B** are you when people revile you
11:6 And **b** is anyone who takes no offense at me."
13:16 But **b** are your eyes, for they see, and your ears,
14:19 and **b** and broke the loaves,
16:17 And Jesus answered him, **"B** are you,
21:9 **B** is the one who comes in the name of the Lord!
23:39 **'B** is the one who comes in the name of
24:46 **B** is that slave whom his master will find at work
25:34 'Come, you that are **b** by my Father,
Mk 6:41 and **b** and broke the loaves,
10:16 laid his hands on them, and **b** them.
11:9 **B** is the one who comes in the name of the Lord!
11:10 **B** is the coming kingdom of our ancestor David!
14:61 "Are you the Messiah, the Son of the **B** One?"
Lk 1:42 **"B** are you among women, and **b** is the fruit of
your womb.
1:45 And **b** is she who believed that there would be
1:48 from now on all generations will call me **b;**
1:68 **"B** be the Lord God of Israel, E
2:34 Then Simeon **b** them and said to his mother Mary,
6:20 **"B** are you who are poor, for yours is the kingdom
6:21 **"B** are you who are hungry now,
6:21 **"B** are you who weep now, for you will laugh.
6:22 **"B** are you when people hate you,
7:23 And **b** is anyone who takes no offense at me."
9:16 he looked up to heaven, and **b** and broke them,
10:23 **"B** are the eyes that see what you see!
11:27 **"B** is the womb that bore you and the breasts
11:28 **"B** rather are those who hear the word of God
12:37 **B** are those slaves whom the master finds alert
12:38 and finds them so, **b** are those slaves.
12:43 **B** is that slave whom his master will find at work
13:35 **'B** is the one who comes in the name of
14:14 And you will be **b,** because they cannot repay you,
14:15 **"B** is anyone who will eat bread in the kingdom
19:38 **"B** is the king who comes in the name of the Lord!
23:29 **'B** are the barren, and the wombs that never bore,
24:30 he took bread, **b** and broke it, and gave it to them.
24:50 and, lifting up his hands, he **b** them.
Jn 12:13 **B** is the one who comes in the name of the Lord—
13:17 you know these things, you are **b** if you do them.
20:29 **B** are those who have not seen and yet have come
Ac 3:25 the families of the earth shall be **b.'**
20:35 'It is more **b** to give than to receive.' "
Ro 1:25 the Creator, who is **b** forever!
4:7 **"B** are those whose iniquities are forgiven,
4:8 **b** is the one against whom the Lord will
9:5 who is over all, God **b** forever. C
14:22 **B** are those who have no reason
1Co 7:40 But in my judgment she is more **b** if she remains
2Co 1:3 **B** be the God and Father of our Lord Jesus D
11:31 and Father of the Lord Jesus (**b** be he forever!)
Gal 3:8 saying, "All the Gentiles shall be **b** in you."
3:9 For this reason, those who believe are **b**
Eph 1:3 **B** be the God and Father of our Lord Jesus B
1:3 has **b** us in Christ with every spiritual blessing
1Ti 1:11 that conforms to the glorious gospel of the **b** God,
6:15 he who is the **b** and only Sovereign,
Tit 2:13 while we wait for the **b** hope and the manifestation
Heb 7:1 from defeating the kings and **b** him";
7:6 from Abraham and **b** him who had received
7:7 It is beyond dispute that the inferior is **b** by
11:21 when dying, **b** each of the sons of Joseph,
Jas 1:12 **B** is anyone who endures temptation.
1:25 they will be **b** in their doing.
5:11 Indeed we call **b** those who showed endurance.
1Pe 1:3 **B** be the God and Father of our Lord Jesus B
3:14 if you do suffer for doing what is right, you are **b.**
4:14 you are reviled for the name of Christ, you are **b,**
Rev 1:3 **B** is the one who reads aloud the words of
1:3 and **b** are those who hear
14:13 **B** are the dead who from now on die in the Lord."
16:15 **B** is the one who stays awake and is clothed,
19:9 **B** are those who are invited to the marriage supper
20:6 **B** and holy are those who share in
22:7 **B** is the one who keeps the words of the prophecy
22:14 **B** are those who wash their robes,
Tob 3:11 **"B** are you, merciful God! **B** is your name forever;
4:12 They were **b** in their children,
8:5 Tobias began by saying, **"B** are you,
8:5 and **b** is your name in all generations forever.
8:15 So they **b** the God of heaven, and Raguel said, B

Tob 8:15 "**B** are you, O God, with every pure blessing;
8:16 **B** are you because you have made me glad.
8:17 **B** are you because you had compassion
9: 6 who wept and **b** him with the words,
9: 6 **B** be God, for I see in Tobias the very image B
10:13 Finally, he **b** Raguel and his wife Edna, and said,
11:14 "**B** be God, and blessed be his great name, B
11:14 he said, "Blessed be God, and **b** be his great name,
11:14 and **b** be all his holy angels.
11:14 May his holy name be **b** throughout all the ages.
11:17 he **b** her saying, "Come in, my daughter,
11:17 **B** be your God who has brought you to us, B
11:17 **B** be your father and your mother,
11:17 **b** be my son Tobias, and blessed be you,
11:17 blessed be my son Tobias, and **b** be you,
13: 1 Then Tobit said: "**B** be God who lives forever, B
13:12 But **b** forever will be all who revere you.
13:17 **B** be the God of Israel!" B
13:17 the **b** will bless the holy name forever and ever."
14:15 and he **b** the Lord God forever and ever.
Jdt 13:17 and said with one accord, "**B** are you our God,
13:18 you are **b** by the Most High God
13:18 and **b** be the Lord God, E
14: 7 and said, "**B** are you in every tent of Judah!
15: 9 they all **b** her with one accord and said to her,
15:12 the women of Israel gathered to see her, and **b** her,
Wis 3:13 For **b** is the barren woman who is undefiled,
3:14 **B** also is the eunuch whose hands have done no
14: 7 For **b** is the wood by which righteousness comes.
Sir 1:13 on the day of their death they will be **b**.
25: 7 I can think of nine whom I would call **b**,
31: 8 **B** is the rich person who is found blameless,
33:12 Some he **b** and exalted, and some he made holy
44:21 that the nations would be **b** through his offspring;
45: 1 Moses, whose memory is **b**.
45: 7 He **b** him with stateliness,
46:11 from the Lord—may their memory be **b**!
Aza 1: 3 "**B** are you, O Lord, God of our ancestors,
1:28 with one voice praised and glorified and **b** God in
1:29 "**B** are you, O Lord, God of our ancestors,
1:30 And **b** is your glorious, holy name,
1:31 **B** are you in the temple of your holy glory,
1:32 **B** are you who look into the depths
1:33 **B** are you on the throne of your kingdom,
1:34 **B** are you in the firmament of heaven,
Sus 1:60 whole assembly raised a great shout and **b** God,
1Mc 2:69 Then he **b** them, and was gathered to his ancestors.
3: 7 and his memory is **b** forever.
4:30 he prayed, saying, "**B** are you, O Savior of Israel,
4:55 on their faces and worshiped and **b** Heaven,
2Mc 1:17 **B** in every way be our God,
10:38 with hymns and thanksgivings they **b**
12:41 So they all **b** the ways of the Lord,
15:29 and they **b** the Sovereign Lord in the language
15:34 **b** the Lord who had manifested himself, saying,
15:34 "**B** is he who has kept his own place undefiled!"
1Es 4:40 **B** be the God of truth!" B
4:60 **B** are you, who have given me wisdom;
8:25 Then Ezra the scribe said, "**B** be the Lord alone, E
9:46 And Ezra **b** the Lord God Most High,
3Mc 7:23 **B** be the Deliverer of Israel through all times!
2Es 7:*45* **B** are those who are alive
10:57 For you are more **b** than many,
13:24 who are left are more **b** than those who have died.
4Mc 1:10 but I would also call them **b** for the honor
7:15 O man of **b** age and of venerable gray hair and
7:22 and knows that it is **b** to endure any suffering for
10:15 No—by the **b** death of my brothers,
12: 1 he too, thrown into the caldron, had died a **b** death,
18:13 in the den of the lions and **b** him.

BLESSEDNESS (4) [BLESS]

Ro 4: 6 So also David speaks of the **b** of those
4: 9 Is this **b**, then, pronounced only on
4Mc 4:12 and that if he were spared he would praise the **b** of
17:18 the divine throne and live the life of eternal **b**.

BLESSES‡ (9) [BLESS]

Ge 27:29 and blessed be everyone who **b** you!"
Nu 24: 9 Blessed is everyone who **b** you,
Ps 147:13 he **b** your children within you.
Pr 3:33 but he **b** the abode of the righteous.
27:14 Whoever **b** a neighbor with a loud voice,
Isa 66: 3 of frankincense, like one who **b** an idol.
Tob 13:15 My soul **b** the Lord, the great King!
Sir 4:13 and the Lord **b** the place she enters.
1Es 4:36 whole earth calls upon truth, and heaven **b** her.

BLESSING‡ (99) [BLESS]

Ge 12: 2 and make your name great, so that you will be a **b**.
22:18 the nations of the earth gain **b** for themselves,
26: 4 the nations of the earth shall gain **b** for themselves
27:12 and bring a curse on myself and not a **b**."
27:30 As soon as Isaac had finished **b** Jacob,
27:35 and he has taken away your **b**."
27:36 and look, now he has taken away my **b**."
27:36 Then he said, "Have you not reserved a **b** for me?"
27:38 Esau said to his father, "Have you only one **b**,
27:41 of the **b** with which his father had blessed him,
28: 4 May he give to you the **b** of Abraham,
39: 5 the **b** of the LORD was on all that he had,
49:28 **b** each one of them with a suitable **b**.
Ex 12:32 And bring a **b** on me too!"
32:29 and so have brought a **b** on yourselves this day."
Lev 25:21 I will order my **b** for you in the sixth year,
Dt 11:26 See, I am setting before you today a **b** and a curse:
11:27 the **b**, if you obey the commandments of
11:29 you shall set the **b** on Mount Gerizim and
12:15 to the **b** that the LORD your God has given you;
16:10 in proportion to the **b** that you have received from
16:17 according to the **b** of the LORD your God
23: 5 the LORD your God turned the curse into a **b**
27:12 these shall stand on Mount Gerizim for the **b** of
28: 8 The LORD will command the **b** upon you
33: 1 This is the **b** with which Moses, the man of God,
33:23 sated with favor, full of the **b** of the LORD,
2Sa 7:29 and with your **b** shall the house of your servant
13:25 but he would not go but gave him his **b**.
Ne 9: 5 which is exalted above all **b** and praise."
13: 2 yet our God turned the curse into a **b**.
Job 29:13 The **b** of the wretched came upon me,
Ps 3: 8 may your **b** be on your people!
24: 5 They will receive **b** from the LORD,
37:26 and their children become a **b**.
65:10 softening it with showers, and **b** its growth.
107:38 By his **b** they multiply greatly,
109:17 He did not like **b**; may it be far from him.
119:56 This **b** has fallen to me,
129: 8 "The **b** of the LORD be upon you!
133: 3 there the LORD ordained his **b**, life forevermore.
Pr 10: 7 The memory of the righteous is a **b**,
10:22 The **b** of the LORD makes rich,
11:11 By the **b** of the upright a city is exalted,
11:26 but a **b** is on the head of those who sell it.
24:25 and a good **b** will come upon them.
Isa 19:24 a **b** in the midst of the earth,
44: 3 and my **b** on your offspring.
65: 8 "Do not destroy it, for there is a **b** in it,"
65:16 Then whoever invokes a **b** in the land shall bless
Eze 34:26 and the region around my hill a **b**;
34:26 they shall be showers of **b**.
44:30 in order that a **b** may rest on your house.
Joel 2:14 and leave a **b** behind him,
Zec 8:13 so I will save you and you shall be a **b**.
Mal 3:10 for you and pour down for you an overflowing **b**.
Mt 26:26 and after **b** it he broke it, gave it to the disciples,
Mk 8: 7 They had also a few small fish; and after **b** them,
14:22 and after **b** it he broke it, gave it to them, and said,
Lk 24:51 While he was **b** them, he withdrew from them
24:53 and they were continually in the temple **b** God.
Ro 15:29 I will come in the fullness of the **b** of Christ.
1Co 10:16 The cup of **b** that we bless,
14:16 Otherwise, if you say a **b** with the spirit,
2Co 1:11 for the **b** granted us through the prayers of many.
9: 8 And God is able to provide you with every **b**
Gal 3:14 that in Christ Jesus the **b** of Abraham might come
Eph 1: 3 who has blessed us in Christ with every spiritual **b**
Heb 6: 7 for whom it is cultivated, receives a **b** from God.
12:17 when he wanted to inherit the **b**, he was rejected,
12:17 even though he sought the **b** with tears.
Jas 3:10 From the same mouth come **b** and cursing.
1Pe 3: 9 but, on the contrary, repay with a **b**.
3: 9 that you might inherit a **b**.
Rev 5:12 wisdom and might and honor and glory and **b**!"
5:13 the one seated on the throne and to the Lamb be **b**
7:12 **B** and glory and wisdom and thanksgiving
Tob 8:15 "Blessed are you, O God, with every pure **b**;
9: 6 May the Lord grant the **b** of heaven to you
11:17 and welcome, with **b** and joy.
12:22 They kept **b** God and singing his praises,
14: 2 giving alms and continually **b** God
Wis 15:19 both the praise of God and his **b**.
Sir 3: 8 that his **b** may come upon you.
3: 9 a father's **b** strengthens the houses of the children,
7:32 so that your **b** may be complete.
11:22 The **b** of the Lord is the reward of the pious,
11:22 and quickly God causes his **b** to flourish.
26: 3 A good wife is a great **b**;
33:17 by the **b** of the Lord I arrived first,
34:20 he gives health and life and **b**.
39:22 "His **b** covers the dry land like a river,
40:27 The fear of the Lord is like a garden of **b**,
44:22 The **b** of all people and the covenant
50:20 to pronounce the **b** of the Lord with his lips,
50:21 to receive the **b** from the Most High.
Aza 1: 1 singing hymns to God and **b** the Lord.
1Es 5:60 the Lord and **b** him, according to the directions

BLESSINGS (30) [BLESS]

Ge 48:20 saying, "By you Israel will invoke **b**, saying,
49:25 the Almighty who will bless you with **b** of heaven
49:25 **b** of the deep that lies beneath,
49:25 **b** of the breasts and of the womb.
49:26 The **b** of your father are stronger than
49:26 the **b** of the eternal mountains, the bounties of
Dt 21: 5 to minister to him and to pronounce **b** in the name
28: 2 all these **b** shall come upon you and overtake you,
30: 1 the **b** and the curses that I have set before you,
30:19 that I have set before you life and death, **b**
Jos 8:34 the words of the law, **b** and curses, according to all
1Ch 23:13 to him and pronounce **b** in his name forever;
Ps 21: 3 For you meet him with rich **b**;
21: 6 You bestow on him **b** forever;
72:15 and **b** invoked for him all day long.
144:15 Happy are the people to whom such **b** fall;
Pr 10: 6 **B** are on the head of the righteous,
28:20 The faithful will abound with **b**,
Mal 2: 2 the curse on you and I will curse your **b**;
Ro 15:27 Gentiles have come to share in their spiritual **b**,
1Co 9:23 so that I may share in its **b**.
Heb 11:20 By faith Isaac invoked **b** for the future on Jacob
Tob 5:17 So Tobit said to him, "**B** be upon you, brother."
7: 7 He also spoke to him as follows, "**B** on you,
Jdt 13:20 and may he reward you with **b**,
Wis 18: 9 the same things, both **b** and dangers;
Sir 26: 3 be granted among the **b** of the man who fears
40:17 but kindness is like a garden of **b**,
44:23 he acknowledged him with his **b**,
47: 6 and praised him for the **b** bestowed by the Lord,

BLEW (28) [BLOW]

Ex 15:10 You **b** with your wind, the sea covered them;
Jos 6: 9 And the armed men went before the priests who **b**
6: 9 while the trumpets **b** continually.
6:13 while the trumpets **b** continually.
Jdg 7:19 and they **b** the trumpets and smashed the jars
7:20 three companies **b** the trumpets and broke the jars,
7:22 When they **b** the three hundred trumpets,
1Sa 13: 3 And Saul **b** the trumpet throughout all the land,
2Sa 20:22 So he **b** the trumpet, and they dispersed from
1Ki 1:39 Then they **b** the trumpet, and all the people said,
2Ki 9:13 and they **b** the trumpet, and proclaimed,
2Ch 13:14 and the priests **b** the trumpets.
Hag 1: 9 and when you brought it home, I **b** it away.
Mt 7:25 and the winds **b** and beat on that house,
7:27 and the winds **b** and beat against that house,
Rev 8: 7 The first angel **b** his trumpet,
8: 8 The second angel **b** his trumpet,
8:10 The third angel **b** his trumpet,
8:12 The fourth angel **b** his trumpet,
9: 1 And the fifth angel **b** his trumpet,
9:13 Then the sixth angel **b** his trumpet,
11:15 Then the seventh angel **b** his trumpet,
Tob 11:11 and holding him firmly, he **b** into his eyes, saying,
Sir 50:16 they **b** their trumpets of hammered metal;
1Mc 4:13 Then the men with Judas **b** their trumpets
9:12 and the men with Judas also **b** their trumpets.
2Es 6: 1 and before the assembled winds **b**,
11: 2 and all the winds of heaven **b** upon it,

BLIGHT (6) [BLIGHTED]

Dt 28:22 with fiery heat and drought, and with **b**
1Ki 8:37 "If there is famine in the land, if there is plague, **b**,
2Ch 6:28 "If there is famine in the land, if there is plague, **b**,
Am 4: 9 I struck you with **b** and mildew;
Hag 2:17 and all the products of your toil with **b** and mildew
2Es 15:13 and their trees shall be ruined by **b** and hail and by

BLIGHTED (5) [BLIGHT]

Ge 41: 6 Then seven ears, thin and **b** by the east wind,
41:23 thin, and **b** by the east wind, sprouting after them;
41:27 as are the seven empty ears **b** by the east wind.
2Ki 19:26 like grass on the housetops, **b** before it is grown.
Isa 37:27 like grass on the housetops, **b** before it is grown.

BLIND‡ (86) [BLINDED, BLINDFOLD, BLINDFOLDED, BLINDLY, BLINDNESS, BLINDS]

Ex 4:11 Who makes them mute or deaf, seeing or **b**?
Lev 19:14 the deaf or put a stumbling block before the **b**;
21:18 one who is **b** or lame,
22:22 Anything **b**, or injured, or maimed,
Dt 27:18 be anyone who misleads a **b** person on the road."
28:29 you shall grope about at noon as **b** people grope
1Sa 12: 3 a bribe to **b** my eyes with it?
2Sa 5: 6 even the **b** and the lame will turn you back"—
5: 8 up the water shaft to attack the lame and the **b**,
5: 8 **b** and the lame shall not come into the house."
Job 29:15 I was eyes to the **b**, and feet to the lame.
Ps 146: 8 the LORD opens the eyes of the **b**.
Pr 28:27 but one who turns a **b** eye will get many a curse.
Isa 29: 9 **b** yourselves and be **b**!
29:18 and darkness the eyes of the **b** shall see.
35: 5 Then the eyes of the **b** shall be opened,
42: 7 to open the eyes that are **b**,
42:16 I will lead the **b** by a road they do not know,
42:18 and you that are **b**, look up and see!
42:19 Who is **b** but my servant,
42:19 Who is **b** like my dedicated one,
42:19 or **b** like the servant of the LORD?
43: 8 Bring forth the people who are **b**, yet have eyes,
56:10 Israel's sentinels are **b**, they are all
59:10 We grope like the **b** along a wall,
Jer 12: 4 and because people said, "He is **b** to our ways."
31: 8 among them the **b** and the lame,
Zep 1:17 upon people that they shall walk like the **b**;
Mal 1: 8 you offer **b** animals in sacrifice, is that not wrong?
Mt 9:27 two **b** men followed him, crying loudly,
9:28 he entered the house, the **b** men came to him;
11: 5 the **b** receive their sight, the lame walk,
12:22 Then they brought to him a demoniac who was **b**
15:14 Let them alone; they are **b** guides of the **b**.
15:14 And if one **b** person guides another,
15:30 bringing with them the lame, the maimed, the **b**,
15:31 the lame walking, and the **b** seeing.
20:30 There were two **b** men sitting by the roadside.
21:14 The **b** and the lame came to him in the temple,
23:16 "Woe to you, **b** guides, who say,
23:17 You **b** fools! For which is greater,
23:19 How **b** you are! For which is greater,
23:24 You **b** guides! You strain out a gnat
23:26 You **b** Pharisee! First clean the inside of
Mk 8:22 a **b** man to him and begged him to touch him.
8:23 He took the **b** man by the hand and led him out of

Mk 10:46 Bartimaeus son of Timaeus, a **b** beggar,
10:49 they called the **b** man, saying to him, "Take heart;
10:51 **b** man said to him, "My teacher, let me see again."
Lk 4:18 to the captives and recovery of sight to the **b**,
6:39 "Can a **b** person guide a **b** person?
7:21 and had given sight to many who were **b**.
7:22 the **b** receive their sight, the lame walk,
14:13 invite the poor, the crippled, the lame, and the **b**.
14:21 the crippled, the **b**, and the lame.'
18:35 a **b** man was sitting by the roadside begging.
Jn 5: 3 In these lay many invalids—**b**, lame,
9: 1 As he walked along, he saw a man **b** from birth.
9: 2 this man or his parents, that he was born **b**?"
9: 3 he was born **b** so that God's works might
9:13 to the Pharisees the man who had formerly been **b**.
9:17 So they said again to the **b** man,
9:18 that he had been **b** and had received his sight
9:19 "Is this your son, who you say was born **b**?
9:20 and that he was born **b**;
9:24 second time they called the man who had been **b**,
9:25 One thing I do know, that though I was **b**,
9:32 that anyone opened the eyes of a person born **b**.
9:39 and those who do see may become **b**."
9:40 "Surely we are not **b**, are we?"
9:41 Jesus said to them, "If you were **b**,
10:21 Can a demon open the eyes of the **b**?"
11:37 of the **b** man have kept this man from dying?"
Ac 13:11 and you will be **b** for a while,
Ro 2:19 and if you are sure that you are a guide to the **b**,
2Pe 1: 9 and **b**, and is forgetful of the cleansing of
Rev 3:17 pitiable, poor, **b**, and naked.
Tob 2:10 until I became completely **b**.
7: 7 an upright and beneficent man has become **b**!"
Sir 20:29 Favors and gifts **b** the eyes of the wise;
43: 4 and its bright rays **b** the eyes.
LtJ 6:37 They cannot restore sight to the **b**;
2Es 2:21 and let the **b** have a vision of my splendor.

BLINDED (5) [BLIND]

Zec 11:17 be completely withered, his right eye utterly **b**!
Jn 12:40 "He has **b** their eyes and hardened their heart,
2Co 4: 4 In their case the god of this world has **b** the minds
Wis 2:21 for their wickedness **b** them,
2Mc 10:30 confused and **b**, they were thrown into disorder

BLINDFOLD (1) [BLIND]

Mk 14:65 Some began to spit on him, to **b** him,

BLINDFOLDED (1) [BLIND]

Lk 22:64 they also **b** him and kept asking him,

BLINDLY (1) [BLIND]

La 4:14 **B** they wandered through the streets,

BLINDNESS (7) [BLIND]

Ge 19:11 with **b** the men who were at the door of the house,
Dt 15:21 any serious defect, such as lameness or **b**—
28:28 The LORD will afflict you with madness, **b**,
2Ki 6:18 and said, "Strike this people, please, with **b**."
6:18 So he struck them with **b** as Elisha had asked.
Zec 12: 4 when I strike every horse of the peoples with **b**.
1Jn 2:11 because the darkness has brought on **b**.

BLINDS (2) [BLIND]

Ex 23: 8 You shall take no bribe, for a bribe **b** the officials,
Dt 16:19 not accept bribes, for a bribe **b** the eyes of the wise

BLOATED (3)

Dt 32:15 You grew fat, **b**, and gorged!
Isa 28: 1 which is on the head of those **b** with rich food,
28: 4 which is on the head of those **b** with rich food,

BLOCK‡ (10) [BLOCKADES, BLOCKED, BLOCKS]

Lev 19:14 You shall not revile the deaf or put a stumbling **b**
Isa 44:19 Shall I fall down before a **b** of wood?"
Eze 3:20 and I lay a stumbling **b** before them, they shall die;
7:19 For it was the stumbling **b** of their iniquity.
14: 3 placed their iniquity as a stumbling **b** before them;
14: 4 as a stumbling **b** before them, and yet come to
14: 7 and placing their iniquity as a stumbling **b**
39:11 it shall **b** the path of the travelers,
Mt 16:23 You are a stumbling **b** to me;
18: 6 "If any of you put a stumbling **b** before one
18: 7 woe to the one by whom the stumbling **b** comes!
Mk 9:42 "If any of you put a stumbling **b** before one
Ro 11: 9 a stumbling **b** and a retribution for them;
14:13 a stumbling **b** or hindrance in the way of another.
1Co 1:23 a stumbling **b** to Jews and foolishness to Gentiles,
8: 9 of yours does not somehow become a stumbling **b**
Rev 2:14 of Balaam, who taught Balak to put a stumbling **b**
Sir 31: 7 It is a stumbling **b** to those who are avid for it,
1Mc 2:36 or hurl a stone at them or **b** up their hiding places,

BLOCKADES (1) [BLOCK]

1Es 2:23 and that the Jews were rebels and kept setting up **b**

BLOCKED (5) [BLOCK]

La 3: 9 he has **b** my ways with hewn stones,
1Th 2:18 and again—but Satan **b** our way.
Jdt 16: 3 their numbers **b** up the wadis,
1Mc 5:47 But the people of the town shut them out and **b** up
2Es 4:17 for the sand stood firm and **b** it.

BLOCKS (4) [BLOCK]

Jer 6:21 See, I am laying before this people stumbling **b**
Mt 18: 7 Woe to the world because of stumbling **b**!
AdE 1: 6 and silver **b** on pillars of marble and other stones.
2Mc 4:41 some picked up stones, some **b** of wood,

BLOOD‡ (449) [BLEEDING, BLOODGUILT, BLOODSHED, BLOODSTAINS, BLOODTHIRSTINESS, BLOODTHIRSTY, BLOODY, LIFEBLOOD]

Ge 4:10 your brother's **b** is crying out to me from
4:11 to receive your brother's **b** from your hand.
9: 4 you shall not eat flesh with its life, that is, its **b**.
9: 5 each one for the **b** of another,
9: 6 Whoever sheds the **b** of a human,
9: 6 by a human shall that person's **b** be shed;
37:22 Reuben said to them, "Shed no **b**;
37:26 if we kill our brother and conceal his **b**?
37:31 slaughtered a goat, and dipped the robe in the **b**.
42:22 So now there comes a reckoning for his **b**."
49:11 in wine and his robe in the **b** of grapes;
Ex 4: 9 that you shall take from the Nile will become **b** on
4:25 "Truly you are a bridegroom of **b** to me!"
4:26 "A bridegroom of **b** by circumcision."
7:17 and it shall be turned to **b**.
7:18 so that they may become **b**;
7:19 and there shall be **b** throughout the whole land
7:20 and all the water in the river was turned into **b**,
7:21 there was **b** throughout the whole land of Egypt.
12: 7 the **b** and put it on the two doorposts and the lintel
12:13 The **b** shall be a sign for you on the houses
12:13 when I see the **b**, I will pass over you,
12:22 dip it in the **b** that is in the basin,
12:22 and the two doorposts with the **b** in the basin.
12:23 the **b** on the lintel and on the two doorposts,
23:18 the **b** of my sacrifice with anything leavened,
24: 6 Moses took half of the **b** and put it in basins,
24: 6 and half of the **b** he dashed against the altar.
24: 8 Moses took the **b** and dashed it on the people,
24: 8 the **b** of the covenant that the LORD has made
29:12 the **b** of the bull and put it on the horns of the altar
29:12 of the **b** you shall pour out at the base of the altar.
29:16 and shall take its **b** and dash it against all sides of
29:20 of its **b** and put it on the lobe of Aaron's right ear
29:20 dash the rest of the **b** against all sides of the altar.
29:21 you shall take some of the **b** that is on the altar,
30:10 the atonement for it once a year with the **b** of
34:25 not offer the **b** of my sacrifice with leaven,
Lev 1: 5 and Aaron's sons the priests shall offer the **b**,
1: 5 dashing the **b** against all sides of the altar that is at
1:11 the priests shall dash its **b** against all sides of
1:15 and its **b** shall be drained out against the side of
3: 2 the priests shall dash the **b** against all sides of
3: 8 and Aaron's sons shall dash its **b** against all sides
3:13 the sons of Aaron shall dash its **b** against all sides
3:17 you must not eat any fat or any **b**.
4: 5 The anointed priest shall take some of the **b** of
4: 6 dip his finger in the **b** and sprinkle some
4: 6 of the **b** seven times before the LORD in front of
4: 7 The priest shall put some of the **b** on the horns of
4: 7 and the rest of the **b** of the bull he shall pour out at
4:16 The anointed priest shall bring some of the **b** of
4:17 in the **b** and sprinkle it seven times before
4:18 He shall put some of the **b** on the horns of the altar
4:18 and the rest of the **b** he shall pour out at the base
4:25 the **b** of the sin offering with his finger and put it
4:25 and pour out the rest of its **b** at the base of the altar
4:30 The priest shall take some of its **b** with his finger
4:30 and he shall pour out the rest of its **b** at the base of
4:34 the **b** of the sin offering with his finger and put it
4:34 pour out the rest of its **b** at the base of the altar.
5: 9 of the **b** of the sin offering on the side of the altar,
5: 9 the rest of the **b** shall be drained out at the base of
6:27 and when any of its **b** is spattered on a garment,
6:30 be eaten from which any **b** is brought into the tent
7: 2 its **b** shall be dashed against all sides of the altar.
7:14 it shall belong to the priest who dashes the **b** of
7:26 You must not eat any **b** whatever,
7:27 Any one of you who eats any **b** shall be cut off
7:33 the one among the sons of Aaron who offers the **b**
8:15 Moses took the **b** and with his finger put some
8:15 then he poured out the **b** at the base of the altar.
8:19 Moses dashed the **b** against all sides of the altar.
8:23 of its **b** and put it on the lobe of Aaron's right ear
8:24 of the **b** on the lobes of their right ears and on
8:24 the rest of the **b** against all sides of the altar.
8:30 of the anointing oil and some of the **b** that was on
9: 9 The sons of Aaron presented the **b** to him,
9: 9 and he dipped his finger in the **b** and put it on
9: 9 rest of the **b** he poured out at the base of the altar.
9:12 Aaron's sons brought him the **b**,
9:18 Aaron's sons brought him the **b**,
10:18 Its **b** was not brought into the inner part of
12: 4 of **b** purification shall be thirty-three days;
12: 5 her time of **b** purification shall be sixty-six days.
12: 7 then she shall be clean from her flow of **b**.
14: 6 in the **b** of the bird that was slaughtered over
14:14 the **b** of the guilt offering and put it on the lobe of
14:17 on top of the **b** of the guilt offering.
14:25 of the guilt offering and shall take some of the **b** of
Lev 14:28 where the **b** of the guilt offering was placed.
14:51 and dip them in the **b** of the slaughtered bird and
14:52 with the **b** of the bird, and with the fresh water,
15:19 of **b** that is her regular discharge from her body,
15:25 If a woman has a discharge of **b** for many days,
16:14 He shall take some of the **b** of the bull,
16:14 and before the mercy seat he shall sprinkle the **b**
16:15 for the people and bring its **b** inside the curtain,
16:15 do with its **b** as he did with the **b** of the bull,
16:18 of the **b** of the bull and of the **b** of the goat,
16:19 of the **b** on it with his finger seven times,
16:27 whose **b** was brought in to make atonement in
17: 4 he has shed **b**, and he shall be cut off from
17: 6 The priest shall dash the **b** against the altar of
17:10 of the aliens who reside among them eats any **b**,
17:10 I will set my face against that person who eats **b**,
17:11 For the life of the flesh is in the **b**;
17:11 for, as life, it is the **b** that makes atonement.
17:12 No person among you shall eat **b**,
17:12 nor shall any alien who resides among you eat **b**.
17:13 that may be eaten shall pour out its **b** and cover it
17:14 For the life of every creature—its **b** is its life;
17:14 You shall not eat the **b** of any creature,
17:14 for the life of every creature is its **b**;
19:16 and you shall not profit by the **b** of your neighbor:
19:26 You shall not eat anything with its **b**.
20: 9 having cursed father or mother, their **b** is
20:11 to death; their **b** is upon them.
20:12 they have committed perversion, their **b** is
20:13 to death; their **b** is upon them.
20:16 they shall be put to death, their **b** is upon them.
20:18 and she has laid bare her flow of **b**;
20:27 they shall be stoned to death, their **b** is upon them.
Nu 18:17 You shall dash their **b** on the altar,
19: 4 The priest Eleazar shall take some of its **b**
19: 5 its skin, its flesh, and its **b**, with its dung,
23:24 down until it has eaten the prey and drunk the **b** of
35:19 of **b** is the one who shall put the murderer
35:19 the avenger of **b** shall execute the sentence.
35:21 the avenger of **b** shall put the murderer to death,
35:24 the slayer and the avenger of **b**, in accordance
35:25 the slayer from the avenger of **b**.
35:27 by the avenger of **b** outside the bounds of the city
35:33 for **b** pollutes the land, and no expiation can
35:33 for the **b** that is shed in it,
35:33 except by the **b** of the one who shed it.
Dt 12:16 The **b**, however, you must not eat;
12:23 Only be sure that you do not eat the **b**;
12:23 for the **b** is the life,
12:27 and the **b**, on the altar of the LORD your God;
12:27 the **b** of your other sacrifices shall be poured out
15:23 Its **b**, however, you must not eat;
19: 6 of **b** in hot anger might pursue and overtake
19:10 that the **b** of an innocent person may not be shed
19:12 from there and handed over to the avenger of **b** to
19:13 you shall purge the guilt of innocent **b** from Israel,
21: 7 "Our hands did not shed this **b**,
21: 8 not let the guilt of innocent **b** remain in the midst
21: 9 So you shall purge the guilt of innocent **b**
27:25 be anyone who takes a bribe to shed innocent **b**."
32:14 you drank fine wine from the **b** of grapes.
32:42 I will make my arrows drunk with **b**,
32:42 with the **b** of the slain and the captives,
32:43 For he will avenge the **b** of his children,
Jos 20: 3 be for you a refuge from the avenger of **b**.
20: 5 And if the avenger of **b** is in pursuit,
20: 9 so as not to die by the hand of the avenger of **b**,
Jdg 9:24 of Jerubbaal might be avenged and their **b** be laid
1Sa 14:32 and the troops ate them with the **b**.
14:33 against the LORD by eating with the **b**."
14:34 not sin against the LORD by eating with the **b**.' "
25:31 for having shed **b** without cause or
26:20 Now therefore, do not let my **b** fall to the ground,
2Sa 1:16 David said to him, "Your **b** be on your head;
1:22 From the **b** of the slain, from the fat of the mighty,
3:27 So he died for shedding the **b** of Asahel,
3:28 before the LORD for the **b** of Abner son of Ner.
4:11 And now shall I not require his **b** at your hand,
14:11 so that the avenger of **b** may kill no more,
16: 8 The LORD has avenged on all of you the **b** of
16: 8 for you are a man of **b**."
20:12 Amasa lay wallowing in his **b** on the highway,
23:17 Can I drink the **b** of the men who went at the risk
1Ki 2: 5 in time of peace for **b** that had been shed in war,
2: 5 putting the **b** of war on the belt around his waist,
2: 9 and you must bring his gray head down with **b**
2:31 the guilt for the **b** that Joab shed without cause.
2:33 So shall their **b** come back on the head of Joab and
2:37 your **b** shall be on your own head."
18:28 with swords and lances until the **b** gushed out
21:19 In the place where dogs licked up the **b** of Naboth,
21:19 dogs will also lick up your **b**."
22:35 the **b** from the wound had flowed into the bottom
22:38 the dogs licked up his **b**,
2Ki 3:22 Moabites saw the water opposite them as red as **b**.
3:23 "This is **b**; the kings must have fought together,
9: 7 that I may avenge on Jezebel the **b** of my servants
9: 7 and the **b** of all the servants of the LORD.
9:26 the **b** of Naboth and for the **b** of his children
9:33 of her **b** spattered on the wall and on the horses,
16:13 and dashed the **b** of his offerings of well-being
16:15 then dash against it all the **b** of the burnt offering,
16:15 and all the **b** of the sacrifice;
21:16 Moreover Manasseh shed very much innocent **b**,
24: 4 and also for the innocent **b** that he had shed;
24: 4 for he filled Jerusalem with innocent **b**,
1Ch 11:19 Can I drink the **b** of these men?

1Ch 22: 8 to me, saying, 'You have shed much **b**
22: 8 you have shed so much **b** in my sight on the earth.
28: 3 for you are a warrior and have shed **b.'**
2Ch 24:25 because of the **b** of the son of the priest Jehoiada,
29:22 and the priests received the **b** and dashed it against
29:22 the rams and their **b** was dashed against the altar;
29:22 the lambs and their **b** was dashed against the altar.
29:24 and made a sin offering with their **b** at the altar,
30:16 the priests dashed the **b** that they received from
35:11 priests dashed the **b** that they received from them,
Job 16:18 "O earth, do not cover my **b;**
39:30 Its young ones suck up **b;**
Ps 9:12 For he who avenges **b** is mindful of them;
16: 4 their drink offerings of **b** I will not pour out
50:13 Do I eat the flesh of bulls, or drink the **b** of goats?
58:10 they will bathe their feet in the **b** of the wicked.
68:23 so that you may bathe your feet in **b,**
72:14 and precious is their **b** in his sight.
78:44 He turned their rivers to **b,**
79: 3 They have poured out their **b** like water all
79:10 the outpoured **b** of your servants be known among
105:29 He turned their waters into **b,**
106:38 they poured out innocent **b,** the **b** of their sons and
106:38 and the land was polluted with **b.**
Pr 1:11 If they say, "Come with us, let us lie in wait for **b;**
1:16 for their feet run to evil, and they hurry to shed **b.**
6:17 a lying tongue, and hands that shed innocent **b,**
28:17 If someone is burdened with the **b** of another,
30:33 and pressing the nose produces **b,**
Isa 1:11 I do not delight in the **b** of bulls, or of lambs,
1:15 your hands are full of **b.**
9: 5 the garments rolled in **b** shall be burned as fuel for
15: 9 For the waters of Dibon are full of **b;**
26:21 the earth will disclose the **b** shed on it,
34: 3 the mountains shall flow with their **b.**
34: 6 The LORD has a sword; it is sated with **b,**
34: 6 it is gorged with fat, with the **b** of lambs and goats,
34: 7 Their land shall be soaked with **b,**
49:26 they shall be drunk with their own **b** as with wine.
59: 3 For your hands are defiled with **b,**
59: 7 and they rush to shed innocent **b;**
66: 3 like one who offers swine's **b;**
Jer 7: 6 and the widow, or shed innocent **b** in this place,
19: 4 and because they have filled this place with the **b**
22: 3 and the widow, or shed innocent **b** in this place.
22:17 for shedding innocent **b,** and for practicing
26:15 you will be bringing innocent **b** upon yourselves
46:10 and drink its fill of their **b.**
51:35 "May my **b** be avenged on the inhabitants
La 4:13 who shed the **b** of the righteous in the midst
4:14 so defiled with **b** that no one was able
Eze 3:18 but their **b** I will require at your hand.
3:20 but their **b** I will require at your hand.
14:19 and pour out my wrath upon it with **b,**
16: 6 and saw you flailing about in your **b.**
16: 6 As you lay in your **b,** I said to you, "Live!
16: 9 with water and washed off the **b** from you,
16:22 and bare, flailing about in your **b.**
16:36 of the **b** of your children that you gave to them,
16:38 and shed **b** are judged, and bring **b** upon you
18:10 If he has a son who is violent, a shedder of **b,**
18:13 his **b** shall be upon himself.
21:32 your **b** shall enter the earth;
22: 3 A city! Shedding **b** within itself;
22: 4 the **b** that you have shed, and defiled by the idols
22: 6 have been bent on shedding **b.**
22: 9 In you are those who slander to shed **b,**
22:12 In you, they take bribes to shed **b;**
22:13 and at the **b** that has been shed within you.
22:27 shedding **b,** destroying lives to get dishonest gain.
23:37 and **b** is on their hands;
23:45 they are adulteresses and **b** is on their hands.
24: 7 For the **b** she shed is inside it;
24: 8 I have placed the **b** she shed on a bare rock,
32: 6 the land with your flowing **b** up to the mountains,
33: 4 their **b** shall be upon their own heads.
33: 5 their **b** shall be upon themselves.
33: 6 but their **b** I will require at the sentinel's hand.
33: 8 but their **b** I will require at your hand.
33:25 You eat flesh with the **b,** and lift up your eyes
33:25 and lift up your eyes to your idols, and shed **b;**
35: 6 says the Lord GOD, I will prepare you for **b,**
35: 6 for blood, and **b** shall pursue you;
36:18 So I poured out my wrath upon them for the **b**
39:17 and you shall eat flesh and drink **b.**
39:18 and drink the **b** of the princes of the earth—
39:19 and drink **b** until you are drunk,
43:18 upon it and for dashing **b** against it,
43:20 And you shall take some of its **b,**
44: 7 when you offer to me my food, the fat and the **b.**
44:15 they shall attend me to offer me the fat and the **b,**
45:19 the **b** of the sin offering and put it on the doorposts
Hos 1: 4 while I will punish the house of Jehu for the **b**
6: 8 Gilead is a city of evildoers, tracked with **b.**
Joel 2:30 **b** and fire and columns of smoke.
2:31 sun shall be turned to darkness, and the moon to **b,**
3:19 in whose land they have shed innocent **b.**
3:21 I will avenge their **b,** and I will not clear
Jnh 1:14 Do not make us guilty of innocent **b;**
Mic 3:10 who build Zion with **b** and Jerusalem with wrong!
7: 2 they all lie in wait for **b,** and they hunt each other
Zep 1:17 their **b** shall be poured out like dust,
Zec 9: 7 I will take away its **b** from its mouth,
9:11 because of the **b** of my covenant with you,
9:15 they shall drink their **b** like wine,
Mt 16:17 For flesh and **b** has not revealed this to you,
23:30 not have taken part with them in shedding the **b** of
Mt 23:35 that upon you may come all the righteous **b** shed
23:35 from the **b** of righteous Abel to the **b** of Zechariah
26:28 for this is my **b** of the covenant,
27: 4 He said, "I have sinned by betraying innocent **b."**
27: 6 into the treasury, since they are **b** money."
27: 8 that field has been called the Field of **B**
27:24 saying, "I am innocent of this man's **b;**
27:25 "His **b** be on us and on our children!"
Mk 14:24 He said to them, "This is my **b** of the covenant,
Lk 11:50 the **b** of all the prophets shed since the foundation
11:51 from the **b** of Abel to the **b** of Zechariah,
13: 1 about the Galileans whose **b** Pilate had mingled
22:20 for you is the new covenant in my **b.**
22:44 ⟦like great drops of **b** falling down on the ground.⟧
Jn 1:13 not of **b** or of the will of the flesh or of the will
6:53 the flesh of the Son of Man and drink his **b,**
6:54 and drink my **b** have eternal life,
6:55 for my flesh is true food and my **b** is true drink.
6:56 Those who eat my flesh and drink my **b** abide
19:34 and at once **b** and water came out.
Ac 1:19 in their language Hakeldama, that is, Field of **B.)**
2:19 **b,** and fire, and smoky mist.
2:20 sun shall be turned to darkness and the moon to **b,**
5:28 and you are determined to bring this man's **b**
15:20 and from whatever has been strangled and from **b.**
15:29 to idols and from **b** and from what is strangled and
18: 6 "Your **b** be on your own heads!
20:26 to you this day that I am not responsible for the **b**
20:28 of God that he obtained with the **b** of his own Son.
21:25 to idols and from **b** and from what is strangled and
22:20 while the **b** of your witness Stephen was shed,
Ro 3:15 "Their feet are swift to shed **b;**
3:25 as a sacrifice of atonement by his **b,**
5: 9 now that we have been justified by his **b,**
1Co 10:16 is it not a sharing in the **b** of Christ?
11:25 saying, "This cup is the new covenant in my **b.**
11:27 be answerable for the body and **b** of the Lord.
15:50 flesh and **b** cannot inherit the kingdom of God,
Eph 1: 7 In him we have redemption through his **b,**
2:13 near by the **b** of Christ.
6:12 our struggle is not against enemies of **b** and flesh,
Col 1:20 by making peace through the **b** of his cross.
Heb 2:14 Since, therefore, the children share flesh and **b,**
9: 7 without taking the **b** that he offers for himself and
9:12 the **b** of goats and calves, but with his own **b,**
9:13 For if the **b** of goats and bulls,
9:14 how much more will the **b** of Christ,
9:18 even the first covenant was inaugurated without **b.**
9:19 he took the **b** of calves and goats,
9:20 the **b** of the covenant that God has ordained
9:21 the same way he sprinkled with the **b** both the tent
9:22 under the law almost everything is purified with **b,**
9:22 without the shedding of **b** there is no forgiveness
9:25 the Holy Place year after year with **b** that is
10: 4 For it is impossible for the **b** of bulls and goats
10:19 to enter the sanctuary by the **b** of Jesus,
10:29 profaned the **b** of the covenant
11:28 the Passover and the sprinkling of **b,**
12: 4 not yet resisted to the point of shedding your **b.**
12:24 to the sprinkled **b** that speaks a better word than
the **b** of Abel.
13:11 For the bodies of those animals whose **b** is brought
13:12 in order to sanctify the people by his own **b.**
13:20 by the **b** of the eternal covenant,
1Pe 1: 2 to Jesus Christ and to be sprinkled with his **b:**
1:19 but with the precious **b** of Christ,
1Jn 1: 7 and the **b** of Jesus his Son cleanses us from all sin.
5: 6 This is the one who came by water and **b,**
5: 6 with the water only but with the water and the **b.**
5: 8 the Spirit and the water and the **b,**
Rev 1: 5 and freed us from our sins by his **b,**
5: 9 and by your **b** you ransomed for God saints
6:10 and avenge our **b** on the inhabitants of the earth?"
6:12 the full moon became like **b,**
7:14 and made them white in the **b** of the Lamb.
8: 7 mixed with **b,** and they were hurled to the earth;
8: 9 A third of the sea became **b,**
11: 6 over the waters to turn them into **b,**
12:11 But they have conquered him by the **b** of
14:20 and **b** flowed from the wine press,
16: 3 and it became like the **b** of a corpse,
16: 4 and the springs of water, and they became **b.**
16: 6 because they shed the **b** of saints and prophets,
16: 6 you have given them **b** to drink.
17: 6 And I saw that the woman was drunk with the **b** of
the saints and the **b** of the witnesses
18:24 in you was found the **b** of prophets and of saints,
19: 2 and he has avenged on her the **b** of his servants."
19:13 He is clothed in a robe dipped in **b,**
Jdt 6: 4 their mountains will be drunk with their **b,**
8:21 he will make us pay for its desecration with our **b.**
9: 3 the deceit they had practiced, was stained with **b,**
9: 4 and abhorred the pollution of their **b** and called
AdE 16: 5 in part responsible for the shedding of innocent **b,**
16:10 a Macedonian (really an alien to the Persian **b,**
Wis 7: 2 of ten months, compacted with **b,** from the seed of
11: 6 stirred up and defiled with **b**
12: 5 and their sacrificial feasting on human flesh and **b.**
14:25 and all is a raging riot of **b** and murder,
Sir 9: 9 and in **b** you may be plunged into destruction.
11:32 and a sinner lies in wait to shed **b.**
12:16 opportunity he will never have enough of your **b.**
14:18 so are the generations of flesh and **b:**
17:31 So flesh and **b** devise evil.
28:11 and a hasty dispute sheds **b.**
33:31 because you have bought him with **b.**
34:27 to deprive an employee of wages is to shed **b.**
Sir 39:26 the **b** of the grape and oil and clothing.
42: 5 and of drawing **b** from the back of a wicked slave.
50:15 for the cup and poured a drink offering of the **b** of
Sus 1:46 "I want no part in shedding this woman's **b!"**
1:62 Thus innocent **b** was spared that day.
1Mc 1:24 He shed much **b,** and spoke with great arrogance.
1:37 of the sanctuary they shed innocent **b;**
7:17 and their **b** they poured out all around Jerusalem,
9:42 After they had fully avenged the **b** of their brother,
2Mc 1: 8 and burned the gate and shed innocent **b.**
8: 3 to hearken to the **b** that cried out to him;
12:16 appeared to be running over with **b.**
14:45 and though his **b** gushed forth
14:46 with his **b** now completely drained from him,
2Es 1:26 for you have defiled your hands with **b,**
1:32 I will require their **b** of you, says the Lord.
5: 5 **B** shall drip from wood,
15: 8 Innocent and righteous **b** cries out to me,
15: 9 and will receive to myself all the innocent **b** from
15:22 not cease from those who shed innocent **b**
15:35 and there shall be **b** from the sword as high as
15:58 for bread and drink their own **b** in thirst for water.
4Mc 3:15 to drink what was regarded as equivalent to **b.**
6: 6 his **b** flowing, and his sides were being cut
6:29 Make my **b** their purification,
7: 8 with their own **b** and noble sweat in sufferings
9:20 The wheel was completely smeared with **b,**
10: 8 around and drops of **b** flowing from his entrails.
13:20 from the same **b** and through the same life,
17:22 through the **b** of those devout ones and their death

BLOODGUILT (9) [BLOOD, GUILT]

Ex 22: 2 and is beaten to death, no **b** is incurred;
22: 3 but if it happens after sunrise, **b** is incurred.
Nu 35:27 of refuge, and is killed by the avenger, no **b** shall
Dt 19:10 thereby bringing **b** upon you.
21: 8 Then they will be absolved of **b.**
22: 8 otherwise you might have **b** on your house,
1Sa 25:26 since the LORD has restrained you from **b** and
25:33 who have kept me today from **b** and
2Sa 21: 1 LORD said, "There is **b** on Saul and on his house,

BLOODGUILTINESS (KJV) See BLOODSHED

BLOODSHED (25) [BLOOD, SHED]

Lev 17: 4 he shall be held guilty of **b;**
Dt 17: 8 between one kind of **b** and another, one kind
2Ch 19:10 concerning **b,** law or commandment,
Ps 51:14 Deliver me from **b,** O God,
Isa 5: 7 he expected justice, but saw **b;**
33:15 from hearing of **b** and shut their eyes from looking
Jer 48:10 the one who keeps back the sword from **b.**
Eze 5:17 pestilence and **b** shall pass through you;
9: 9 the land is full of **b** and the city full of perversity;
23:45 shall declare them guilty of adultery and of **b;**
28:23 for I will send pestilence into it, and **b**
35: 6 you did not hate **b,** **b** shall pursue you.
38:22 With pestilence and **b** I will enter into judgment
Hos 4: 2 and adultery break out; **b** follows **b.**
Na 3: 1 City of **b,** utterly deceitful, full of booty—
Hab 2: 8 because of human **b,** and violence to the earth,
2:12 "Alas for you who build a town by **b,**
2:17 because of human **b** and violence to the earth,
Sir 8:16 because **b** means nothing to them,
22:24 the furnace precede the fire; so insults precede **b.**
27:15 The strife of the proud leads to **b,**
40: 9 come death and **b** and strife and sword,
2Mc 14:18 shrank from deciding the issue by **b.**

BLOODSTAINS (1) [BLOOD, STAIN]

Isa 4: 4 and cleansed the **b** of Jerusalem from its midst by

BLOODTHIRSTINESS (2) [BLOOD]

4Mc 9: 9 because of your **b** toward us,
10:11 because of your impiety and **b,**

BLOODTHIRSTY (8) [BLOOD]

Ps 5: 6 the LORD abhors the **b** and deceitful.
26: 9 nor my life with the **b,**
55:23 **b** and treacherous shall not live out half their days.
59: 2 from those who work evil; from the **b** save me.
139:19 O God, and that the **b** would depart from me—
Pr 29:10 The **b** hate the blameless, and they seek the life of
2Mc 4:38 and there he dispatched the **b** fellow.
4Mc 10:17 When he heard this, the **b,** murderous,

BLOODY (5) [BLOOD]

1Ki 2:32 The LORD will bring back his **b** deeds
Eze 7:23 land is full of **b** crimes; the city is full of violence.
22: 2 mortal, will you judge, will you judge the **b** city?
24: 6 Woe to the **b** city, the pot whose rust is in it,
24: 9 Woe to the **b** city! I will even make the pile great.

BLOOM (5)

SS 6:11 whether the pomegranates were in **b.**
7:12 and the pomegranates are in **b.**
Na 1: 4 and the **b** of Lebanon fades.
Sir 26:19 *My child, keep sound the **b** of your youth,*
2Es 5:36 and make the withered flowers **b** again for me;

BLOSSOM (15) [BLOSSOMED, BLOSSOMS]

Job 15:30 and their **b** will be swept away by the wind.
Ps 72:16 and may people **b** in the cities like the grass of
SS 2:13 fig tree puts forth its figs, and the vines are in **b;**
2:15 for our vineyards are in **b.**"
Isa 5:24 and their **b** go up like dust;
17:11 and make them **b** in the morning that you sow;
18: 5 **b** is over and the flower becomes a ripening grape,
27: 6 Israel shall **b** and put forth shoots,
35: 1 the desert shall rejoice and **b;**
35: 2 it shall **b** abundantly, and rejoice with joy
Hos 14: 5 he shall **b** like the lily,
14: 7 they shall **b** like the vine, their fragrance shall be
Hab 3:17 the fig tree does not **b,** and no fruit is on the vines;
Sir 39:13 and **b** like a rose growing by a stream of water.
51:15 the first **b** to the ripening grape my heart delighted

BLOSSOMED (1) [BLOSSOM]

Eze 7:10 The rod has **b,** pride has budded.

BLOSSOMS (15) [BLOSSOM]

Ge 40:10 its **b** came out and the clusters ripened into grapes.
Ex 25:33 three cups shaped like almond **b,** each with calyx
25:33 and three cups shaped like almond **b,**
25:34 be four cups shaped like almond **b,**
37:19 three cups shaped like almond **b,** each with calyx
37:19 and three cups shaped like almond **b,**
37:20 like almond **b,** each with its calyxes
Nu 17: 8 It put forth buds, produced **b,**
Job 15:33 and cast off their **b,** like the olive tree.
Ecc 12: 5 the almond tree **b,** the grasshopper drags itself
SS 1:14 a cluster of henna **b** in the vineyards of En-gedi.
6:11 to look at the **b** of the valley,
7:12 the grape **b** have opened and the pomegranates are
Sir 24:17 and my **b** become glorious and abundant fruit.
39:14 and put forth **b** like a lily.

BLOT (24) [BLOTS, BLOTTED]

Ge 6: 7 "I will **b** out from the earth
7: 4 and every living thing that I have made I will **b** out
Ex 17:14 I will utterly **b** out the remembrance of Amalek
23:23 the Hivites, and the Jebusites, and I **b** them out,
32:32 if not, **b** me out of the book that you have written."
32:33 "Whoever has sinned against me I will **b** out
Dt 7:24 and you shall **b** out their name from under heaven;
9:14 that I may destroy them and **b** out their name from
12: 3 and thus **b** out their name from their places.
25:19 you shall **b** out the remembrance of Amalek from
29:20 LORD will **b** out their names from under heaven.
32:26 and **b** out the memory of them from humankind;
2Ki 14:27 But the LORD had not said that he would **b** out
Ps 51: 1 to your abundant mercy **b** out my transgressions.
51: 9 and **b** out all my iniquities.
Jer 18:23 do not **b** out their sin from your sight.
Eze 32: 7 When I **b** you out, I will cover the heavens,
Rev 3: 5 and I will not **b** your name out of the book of life;
Sir 20:24 A lie is an ugly **b** on a person;
46:20 to **b** out the wickedness of the people.
47:22 he will never **b** out the descendants
1Mc 12:53 Now therefore let us make war on them and **b** out
2Es 7:*139* [69] his word and **b** out the multitude of their sins,
15:43 They shall go on steadily to Babylon and **b** it out.

BLOTS (2) [BLOT]

Isa 43:25 I am He who **b** out your transgressions
2Pe 2:13 They are **b** and blemishes,

BLOTTED (19) [BLOT]

Ge 7:23 He **b** out every living thing that was on the face of
7:23 they were **b** out from the earth.
Dt 25: 6 so that his name may not be **b** out of Israel.
Jdg 21:17 in order that a tribe may not be **b** out from Israel.
Ne 4: 5 and do not let their sin be **b** out from your sight;
Ps 9: 5 you have **b** out their name forever and ever.
69:28 Let them be **b** out of the book of the living;
109:13 may his name be **b** out in the second generation.
109:14 and do not let the sin of his mother be **b** out.
Isa 6: 7 your guilt has departed and your sin is **b** out."
Sir 23:26 and her disgrace will never be **b** out.
39: 9 it will never be **b** out.
40:12 All bribery and injustice will be **b** out,
41:11 but a virtuous name will never be **b** out.
44:13 and their glory will never be **b** out.
44:18 with him that all flesh should never again be **b** out
2Mc 12:42 that had been committed might be wholly **b** out.
2Es 2: 7 let their names be **b** out from the earth,
6:27 evil shall be **b** out, and deceit shall be quenched;

BLOW (52) [BLEW, BLOWING, BLOWN, BLOWS, DEATH-BLOW]

Ge 8: 1 And God made a wind **b** over the earth,
Nu 10: 5 When you **b** an alarm, the camps on
10: 6 when you **b** a second alarm,
10: 7 when the assembly is to be gathered, you shall **b,**
10: 8 sons of Aaron, the priests, shall **b** the trumpets;
10:10 you shall **b** the trumpets over your burnt offerings
29: 1 It is a day for you to **b** the trumpets,
35:21 then the one who struck the **b** shall be put to death;
Jdg 5:26 she struck Sisera a **b,** she crushed his head,
7:18 When I **b** the trumpet, I and all who are with me,
7:18 you also **b** the trumpets around the whole camp,
Jdg 7:20 and in their right hands the trumpets to **b;**
2Sa 20:10 He did not strike a second **b.**
1Ki 1:34 **b** the trumpet, and say, 'Long live King Solomon!'
1Ch 15:24 were to **b** the trumpets before the ark of God.
16: 6 and Jahaziel were to **b** trumpets regularly,
Ps 78:26 He caused the east wind to **b** in the heavens,
81: 3 **B** the trumpet at the new moon, at the full moon,
147:18 he makes his wind **b,** and the waters flow.
SS 4:16 **B** upon my garden that its fragrance may be wafted
Isa 30:26 and heals the wounds inflicted by his **b.**
30:30 to be heard and the descending **b** of his arm to
Jer 4: 5 **B** the trumpet through the land;
6: 1 **B** the trumpet in Tekoa, and raise a signal
6:29 The bellows **b** fiercely, the lead is consumed by
14:17 is struck down with a crushing **b,**
30:14 for I have dealt you the **b** of an enemy,
51:27 **b** the trumpet among the nations;
Eze 21:31 with the fire of my wrath I will **b** upon you.
22:20 to **b** the fire upon them in order to melt them;
22:21 I will gather you and **b** upon you with the fire
24:16 with one **b** I am about to take away from you
33: 6 the sentinel sees the sword coming and does not **b**
Hos 5: 8 **B** the horn in Gibeah, the trumpet in Ramah.
Joel 2: 1 **B** the trumpet in Zion; sound the alarm on my
2:15 **B** the trumpet in Zion; sanctify a fast;
Ac 27:13 When a moderate south wind began to **b,**
Rev 7: 1 the earth so that no wind could **b** on earth or sea or
8: 6 the seven trumpets made ready to **b** them.
8:13 that the three angels are about to **b!**"
10: 7 when the seventh angel is to **b** his trumpet,
Tob 6: 9 **b** upon them, upon the white films,
Wis 12: 9 at one **b** by dread wild animals or your stern word.
Sir 22:22 disclosure of secrets, or a treacherous **b—**
27:25 and a treacherous **b** opens up many wounds.
28:12 If you **b** on a spark, it will glow;
28:17 The **b** of a whip raises a welt,
28:17 but a **b** of the tongue crushes the bones.
1Mc 1:30 he suddenly fell upon the city, dealt it a severe **b,**
5: 3 a heavy **b** and humbled them and despoiled them.
5:34 they fled before him, and he dealt them a heavy **b.**
2Mc 9: 5 struck him with an incurable and invisible **b.**

BLOWING‡ (8) [BLOW]

Jos 6: 4 the priests **b** the trumpets.
6: 8 of rams' horns before the LORD went forward, **b**
6:13 **b** the trumpets continually.
2Ki 11:14 all the people of the land rejoicing and **b** trumpets.
2Ch 23:13 all the people of the land rejoicing and **b** trumpets,
Lk 12:55 And when you see the south wind **b,** you say,
Jn 6:18 sea became rough because a strong wind was **b.**
2Es 6:39 Then the spirit was **b,** and darkness

BLOWN (10) [BLOW]

Nu 10: 3 both are **b,** the whole congregation shall assemble
10: 4 But if only one is **b,** then the leaders,
10: 6 An alarm is to be **b** whenever they are to set out.
Jos 6:16 when the priests had **b** the trumpets,
6:20 So the people shouted, and the trumpets were **b.**
Isa 18: 3 When a trumpet is **b,** listen!
27:13 And on that day a great trumpet will be **b,**
Eze 7:14 They have **b** the horn and made everything ready;
Am 3: 6 Is a trumpet **b** in a city,
Eph 4:14 to and fro and **b** about by every wind of doctrine,

BLOWS (16) [BLOW]

2Sa 7:14 with **b** inflicted by human beings.
Ps 39:10 I am worn down by the **b** of your hand.
Pr 17:10 a discerning person than a hundred **b** into a fool.
20:30 **B** that wound cleanse away evil;
Ecc 1: 6 wind **b** to the south, and goes around to the north;
Isa 14: 6 down the peoples in wrath with unceasing **b,**
40: 7 when the breath of the LORD **b** upon it;
40:24 when he **b** upon them, and they wither,
54:16 the smith who **b** the fire of coals, and produces
Eze 33: 3 the sword coming upon the land and **b** the trumpet
Jn 3: 8 The wind **b** where it chooses,
Sir 43:16 At his will the south wind **b;**
43:20 cold north wind **b,** and ice freezes on the water;
LtJ 6:61 and the wind likewise **b** in every land.
2Mc 3:26 and flogged him continuously, inflicting many **b**
6:30 When he was about to die under the **b,**

BLUE (50)

Ex 25: 4 **b,** purple, and crimson yarns
26: 1 and **b,** purple, and crimson yarns;
26: 4 of **b** on the edge of the outermost curtain in
26:31 You shall make a curtain of **b,** purple,
26:36 of **b,** purple, and crimson yarns,
27:16 of **b,** purple, and crimson yarns,
28: 5 **b,** purple, and crimson yarns, and fine linen.
28: 6 They shall make the ephod of gold, of **b,** purple,
28: 8 of gold, of **b,** purple, and crimson yarns,
28:15 of gold, of **b** and purple and crimson yarns,
28:28 by its rings to the rings of the ephod with a **b** cord,
28:31 You shall make the robe of the ephod all of **b.**
28:33 of **b,** purple, and crimson yarns, all around
28:37 You shall fasten it on the turban with a **b** cord;
35: 6 **b,** purple, and crimson yarns, and fine linen;
35:23 And everyone who possessed **b** or purple
35:25 in **b** and purple and crimson yarns and fine linen;
35:35 by an embroiderer in **b,** purple, and crimson yarns,
36: 8 they were made of fine twisted linen, and **b,**
36:11 of **b** on the edge of the outermost curtain of
36:35 He made the curtain of **b,** purple,
Ex 36:37 of **b,** purple, and crimson yarns,
38:18 the court was embroidered with needlework in **b,**
38:23 engraver, designer, and embroiderer in **b,** purple,
39: 1 Of the **b,** purple, and crimson yarns they made
39: 2 He made the ephod of gold, of **b,** purple,
39: 3 and cut into threads to work into the **b,**
39: 5 of gold, of **b,** purple, and crimson yarns,
39: 8 like the work of the ephod, of gold, of **b,** purple,
39:21 by its rings to the rings of the ephod with a **b** cord,
39:22 the robe of the ephod woven all of **b** yarn;
39:24 of the robe they made pomegranates of **b,**
39:29 and of **b,** purple, and crimson yarns,
39:31 They tied to it a **b** cord,
Nu 4: 6 and spread over that a cloth all of **b,**
4: 7 of the Presence they shall spread a **b** cloth, and put
4: 9 They shall take a **b** cloth, and cover the lampstand
4:11 Over the golden altar they shall spread a **b** cloth,
4:12 and put them in a **b** cloth,
15:38 throughout their generations and to put a **b** cord on
2Ch 2: 7 crimson, and **b** fabrics, trained also in engraving,
2:14 bronze, iron, stone, and wood, and in purple, **b,**
3:14 of **b** and purple and crimson fabrics and fine linen,
Est 1: 6 and **b** hangings tied with cords of fine linen
8:15 wearing royal robes of **b** and white,
Jer 10: 9 their clothing is **b** and purple;
Eze 23: 6 clothed in **b,** governors and commanders, all
27: 7 **b** and purple from the coasts
27:24 in clothes of **b** and embroidered work,
1Mc 4:23 and cloth dyed **b** and sea purple, and great riches.

BLUNDER (1)

Sir 14: 1 Happy are those who do not **b** with their lips,

BLUNT (1)

Ecc 10:10 If the iron is **b,** and one does not whet the edge,

BLUSH (3)

Isa 1:29 you shall **b** for the gardens that you have chosen.
Jer 6:15 they did not know how to **b.**
8:12 they did not know how to **b.**

BOANERGES (1)

Mk 3:17 (to whom he gave the name **B,** that is, Sons

BOAR (1) [BOARS]

Ps 80:13 The **b** from the forest ravages it,

BOARD (8) [BOARDS, SIDEBOARD]

Jnh 1: 3 so he paid his fare and went on **b,**
Ac 20:13 intending to take Paul on **b** there;
20:14 we took him on **b** and went to Mitylene.
21: 2 we went on **b** and set sail.
21: 6 we went on **b** the ship, and they returned home.
27: 6 for Italy and put us on **b.**
28:10 they put on **b** all the provisions we needed.
3Mc 4: 9 They were brought on **b** like wild animals,

BOARDS (6) [BOARD]

Ex 27: 8 You shall make it hollow, with **b.**
38: 7 he made it hollow, with **b.**
1Ki 6:15 the walls of the house on the inside with **b**
6:15 and he covered the floor of the house with **b**
6:16 the rear of the house with **b** of cedar from the floor
SS 8: 9 she is a door, we will enclose her with **b** of cedar.

BOARS‡ (1) [BOAR]

2Es 15:30 shall go forth like wild **b** from the forest,

BOAST‡ (72) [BOASTED, BOASTER, BOASTERS, BOASTFUL, BOASTFULLY, BOASTFULNESS, BOASTING, BOASTS]

Jdg 9:38 Then Zebul said to him, "Where is your **b** now,
Ps 10: 3 For the wicked **b** of the desires of their heart,
34: 2 My soul makes its **b** in the LORD;
38:16 those who **b** against me when my foot slips."
49: 6 those who trust in their wealth and **b** of
52: 1 Why do you **b,** O mighty one, of mischief done
75: 4 I say to the boastful, "Do not **b,**"
94: 4 their arrogant words; all the evildoers **b.**
97: 7 those who make their **b** in worthless idols;
Pr 27: 1 Do not **b** about tomorrow,
Isa 20: 5 of Ethiopia their hope and of Egypt their **b.**
Jer 4: 2 and by him they shall **b.**
9:23 Do not let the wise **b** in their wisdom,
9:23 do not let the mighty **b** in their might,
9:23 do not let the wealthy **b** in their wealth;
9:24 but let those who **b** **b** in this,
49: 4 Why do you **b** in your strength?
Ro 2:17 and rely on the law and **b** of your relation to God
2:23 You that **b** in the law,
4: 2 he has something to **b** about, but not before God.
5: 2 and we **b** in our hope of sharing the glory of God.
5: 3 And not only that, but we also **b** in our sufferings,
5:11 we even **b** in God through our Lord Jesus Christ,
11:18 do not **b** over the branches.
11:18 If you do **b,** remember that it is not you
15:17 then, I have reason to **b** of my work for God.
1Co 1:29 so that no one might **b** in the presence of God.
1:31 "Let the one who boasts, **b** in the Lord."
3:21 So let no one **b** about human leaders.

1Co 4: 7 why do you **b** as if it were not a gift?
13: 3 and if I hand over my body so that I may **b,**
15:31 a **b** that I make in Christ Jesus our Lord.
2Co 1:12 this is our **b,** the testimony of our conscience:
1:14 we are your **b** even as you are our **b.**
5:12 but giving you an opportunity to **b** about us,
5:12 to answer those who **b** in outward appearance and
7: 4 I often **b** about you; I have great pride in you;
10: 8 Now, even if I **b** a little too much of our authority,
10:13 We, however, will not **b** beyond limits,
10:15 We do not **b** beyond limits, that is,
10:17 "Let the one who boasts, **b** in the Lord."
11:10 this **b** of mine will not be silenced in the regions
11:12 be recognized as our equals in what they **b** about.
11:16 so that I too may **b** a little.
11:18 since many **b** according to human standards, I will also **b.**
11:21 But whatever anyone dares to **b** of—
11:21 I also dare to **b** of that.
11:30 If I must **b,** I will **b** of the things that show my weakness.
12: 1 It is necessary to **b;** nothing is to be
12: 5 On behalf of such a one I will **b,**
12: 5 but on my own behalf I will not **b,**
12: 6 But if I wish to **b,** I will not be a fool,
12: 9 So, I will **b** all the more gladly of my weaknesses,
Gal 6:13 to be circumcised so that they may **b**
6:14 May I never **b** of anything except the cross
Eph 2: 9 not the result of works, so that no one may **b.**
Php 2:16 by your holding fast to the word of life that I can **b**
3: 3 and **b** in Christ Jesus and have no confidence in
2Th 1: 4 Therefore we ourselves **b** of you among
Jas 1: 9 Let the believer who is lowly **b** in being raised up,
4:16 As it is, you **b** in your arrogance;
Jdt 15: 9 you are the great **b** of Israel,
Wis 6: 2 that rule over multitudes, and **b** of many nations.
Sir 10:26 and do not **b** when you are in need.
11: 4 Do not **b** about wearing fine clothes,
25: 6 and their **b** is the fear of the Lord.
30: 2 and will **b** of him among acquaintances.
3Mc 2:17 the transgressors will **b** in their wrath and exult in

BOASTED (7) [BOAST]
Ps 44: 8 In God we have **b** continually,
Ob 1:12 you should not have **b** on the day of distress.
Zep 2:10 because they scoffed and **b** against the people of
Jdt 6:17 and all that Holofernes had **b** he would do against
16: 4 He **b** that he would burn up my territory,
Wis 5: 8 And what good has our **b** wealth brought us?
17: 7 and their **b** wisdom was scornfully rebuked.

BOASTER (1) [BOAST]
Sir 10:27 has goods in plenty than the **b** who lacks bread.

BOASTERS (2) [BOAST]
2Co 11:13 For such **b** are false apostles, deceitful workers,
2Ti 3: 2 **b,** arrogant, abusive, disobedient to their parents,

BOASTFUL (9) [BOAST]
Ps 5: 5 The **b** will not stand before your eyes;
75: 4 I say to the **b,** "Do not boast," and to the wicked,
Ro 1:30 God-haters, insolent, haughty, **b,** inventors of evil,
1Co 13: 4 love is not envious or **b** or arrogant
2Co 7:14 For if I have been somewhat **b** about you to him,
11:17 What I am saying in regard to this **b** confidence,
Jas 3:14 do not be **b** and false to the truth.
3Mc 3:11 Then the king, **b** of his present good fortune,
6: 4 exalted with lawless insolence and **b** tongue,

BOASTFULLY (1) [BOAST]
2Mc 15:32 which had been **b** stretched out against

BOASTFULNESS (3) [BOAST]
2Ch 25:19 and your heart has lifted you up in **b.**
2Mc 15: 6 in his utter **b** and arrogance had determined
4Mc 1:26 In the soul it is **b,** covetousness, thirst for honor,

BOASTING‡ (20) [BOAST]
Isa 10:12 he will punish the arrogant **b** of the king
Ro 3:27 Then what becomes of **b?**
1Co 5: 6 Your **b** is not a good thing.
9:15 no one will deprive me of my ground for **b!**
9:16 this gives me no ground for **b,**
15:31 brothers and sisters, as my **b** of you—
2Co 7:14 so our **b** to Titus has proved true as well.
8:24 of your love and of our reason for **b** about you.
9: 2 of my **b** about you to the people of Macedonia,
9: 3 But I am sending the brothers in order that our **b**
10:16 without **b** of work already done
Php 1:26 so that I may share abundantly in your **b**
1Th 2:19 or joy or crown of **b** before our Lord Jesus
Jas 4:16 in your arrogance; all such **b** is evil.
Jdt 9: 7 **b** in the strength of their foot soldiers,
Sir 20: 7 but a **b** fool misses the right moment.
31:10 Let it be for him a ground for **b.**
47: 4 in the sling and struck down the **b** Goliath?
3Mc 6: 5 speaking grievous words with **b** and insolence,
4Mc 2:15 lust for power, vainglory, **b,** arrogance,

BOASTS (13) [BOAST]
Ps 12: 3 the tongue that makes great **b,**
Pr 20:14 "Bad, bad," says the buyer, then goes away and **b.**
Pr 25:14 Like clouds and wind without rain is one who **b** of
Isa 16: 6 and his insolence; his **b** are false.
Jer 48:30 his **b** are false, his deeds are false.
Zep 2: 8 how they have taunted my people and made **b**
1Co 1:31 "Let the one who **b,** boast in the Lord."
2Co 10:17 "Let the one who **b,** boast in the Lord."
Jas 3: 5 yet it **b** of great exploits.
AdE 16: 4 carried away by the **b** of those who know nothing
Wis 2:16 and **b** that God is his father.
Sir 25: 2 a pauper who **b,** a rich person who lies,
48:18 and made great **b** in his arrogance.

BOAT‡ (50) [BOATS]
Mt 4:21 in the **b** with their father Zebedee,
4:22 Immediately they left the **b** and their father,
8:23 when he got into the **b,** his disciples followed him.
8:24 great that the **b** was being swamped by the waves;
9: 1 a **b** he crossed the sea and came to his own town.
13: 2 around him that he got into a **b** and sat there,
14:13 he withdrew from there in a **b** to a deserted place
14:22 Immediately he made the disciples get into the **b**
14:24 but by this time the **b,** battered by the waves,
14:29 So Peter got out of the **b,**
14:32 When they got into the **b,** the wind ceased.
14:33 And those in the **b** worshiped him, saying,
15:39 into the **b** and went to the region of Magadan.
Mk 1:19 who were in their **b** mending the nets.
1:20 and they left their father Zebedee in the **b** with
3: 9 to have a **b** ready for him because of the crowd,
4: 1 that he got into a **b** on the sea and sat there,
4:36 they took him with them in the **b,** just as he was.
4:37 and the waves beat into the **b,**
4:37 so that the **b** was already being swamped.
5: 2 And when he had stepped out of the **b,**
5:18 As he was getting into the **b,**
5:21 Jesus had crossed again in the **b** to the other side,
6:32 And they went away in the **b** to a deserted place
6:45 Immediately he made his disciples get into the **b**
6:47 When evening came, the **b** was out on the sea,
6:51 he got into the **b** with them and the wind ceased.
6:53 they came to land at Gennesaret and moored the **b.**
6:54 When they got out of the **b,**
8:10 the **b** with his disciples and went to the district
8:13 And he left them, and getting into the **b** again,
8:14 and they had only one loaf with them in the **b.**
Lk 5: 3 he sat down and taught the crowds from the **b.**
5: 7 So they signaled their partners in the other **b**
8:22 One day he got into a **b** with his disciples,
8:23 and the **b** was filling with water,
8:37 So he got into the **b** and returned.
Jn 6:17 got into a **b,** and started across the sea
6:19 on the sea and coming near the **b,**
6:21 Then they wanted to take him into the **b,**
6:21 and immediately the **b** reached the land
6:22 the sea saw that there had been only one **b** there.
6:22 that Jesus had not got into the **b** with his disciples,
21: 3 They went out and got into the **b,**
21: 6 "Cast the net to the right side of the **b,**
21: 8 But the other disciples came in the **b,**
Ac 27:16 to get the ship's **b** under control.
27:30 to escape from the ship and had lowered the **b** into
27:32 Then the soldiers cut away the ropes of the **b**
Sir 33: 2 but the one who is hypocritical about it is like a **b**

BOATS (10) [BOAT]
Mk 4:36 Other **b** were with him.
Lk 5: 2 he saw two **b** there at the shore of the lake;
5: 3 He got into one of the **b,**
5: 7 And they came and filled both **b,**
5:11 When they had brought their **b** to shore,
Jn 6:23 Then some **b** from Tiberias came near the place
6:24 the **b** and went to Capernaum looking for Jesus.
2Mc 12: 3 on **b** that they had provided,
12: 6 He set fire to the harbor by night, burned the **b,**
3Mc 4: 9 by the neck to the benches of the **b,**

BOAZ (29)
Ru 2: 1 of the family of Elimelech, whose name was **B.**
2: 3 she came to the part of the field belonging to **B,**
2: 4 Just then **B** came from Bethlehem.
2: 5 Then **B** said to his servant who was in charge of
2: 8 Then **B** said to Ruth, "Now listen, my daughter,
2:11 But **B** answered her, "All that you have done
2:14 At mealtime **B** said to her, "Come here,
2:15 she got up to glean, **B** instructed his young men,
2:19 name of the man with whom I worked today is **B."**
2:23 So she stayed close to the young women of **B,**
3: 2 Now here is our kinsman **B,**
3: 7 When **B** had eaten and drunk,
4: 1 No sooner had **B** gone up to the gate and sat
4: 1 of whom **B** had spoken, came passing by.
4: 1 So **B** said, "Come over, friend; sit down here."
4: 2 Then **B** took ten men of the elders of the city,
4: 5 Then **B** said, "The day you acquire the field from
4: 8 So when the next-of-kin said to **B,**
4: 9 Then **B** said to the elders and all the people,
4:13 So **B** took Ruth and she became his wife.
4:21 Salmon of **B, B** of Obed,
1Ki 7:21 he set up the pillar on the north and called it **B.**
1Ch 2:11 Nahshon became the father of Salma, Salma of **B,**
2:12 **B** of Obed, Obed of Jesse.
2Ch 3:17 and the one on the left, **B.**
Mt 1: 5 and Salmon the father of **B** by Rahab, and **B** the father of Obed by Ruth,
Lk 3:32 son of **B,** son of Sala, son of Nahshon,

BOCHERU (2)
1Ch 8:38 Azrikam, **B,** Ishmael, Sheariah, Obadiah,
9:44 Azrikam, **B,** Ishmael, Sheariah, Obadiah,

BOCHIM (2)
Jdg 2: 1 the angel of the LORD went up from Gilgal to **B,**
2: 5 So they named that place **B,**

BODIES‡ (71) [BODY]
Ge 47:18 in the sight of my lord but our **b** and our lands.
Nu 14:29 your dead **b** shall fall in this very wilderness;
14:32 for you, your dead **b** shall fall in this wilderness.
14:33 until the last of your dead **b** lies in the wilderness.
1Sa 17:46 the dead **b** of the Philistine army this very day to
31:12 and the **b** of his sons from the wall of Beth-shan.
2Sa 4:12 and hung their **b** beside the pool at Hebron.
21:10 not allow the birds of the air to come on the **b**
2Ki 19:35 when morning dawned, they were all dead **b.**
1Ch 10:12 up and took away the body of Saul and the **b**
Ne 9:37 over our **b** and over our livestock at their pleasure,
Job 14:22 They feel only the pain of their own **b,**
20:11 Their **b,** once full of youth,
Ps 44:25 our **b** cling to the ground.
73: 4 For they have no pain; their **b** are sound and sleek.
79: 2 They have given the **b** of your servants to the birds
Isa 37:36 when morning dawned, they were all dead **b.**
66:14 your **b** shall flourish like the grass;
66:24 And they shall go out and look at the dead **b** of
Jer 16: 4 and their dead **b** shall become food for the birds of
19: 7 I will give their dead **b** for food to the birds of
31:40 The whole valley of the dead **b** and the ashes,
33: 5 with the dead **b** of those whom I shall strike down
41: 5 and their **b** gashed, bringing grain offerings
41: 9 the cistern into which Ishmael had thrown all the **b**
La 4: 7 their **b** were more ruddy than coral,
Eze 1:11 while two covered their **b.**
Da 3:27 that the fire had not had any power over the **b**
3:28 and yielded up their **b** rather than serve
7: 5 and was told, "Arise, devour many **b!"**
Am 8: 3 "the dead **b** shall be many, cast out in every place.
Na 3: 3 dead **b** without end—they stumble over the **b!**
Mt 27:52 The tombs also were opened, and many **b** of
Jn 19:31 the Jews did not want the **b** left on the cross during
19:31 of the crucified men broken and the **b** removed.
Ac 7:16 and their **b** were brought back to Shechem and laid
Ro 1:24 to the degrading of their **b** among themselves,
6:12 do not let sin exercise dominion in your mortal **b,**
8:11 to your mortal **b** also through his Spirit that dwells
8:23 for adoption, the redemption of our **b.**
12: 1 to present your **b** as a living sacrifice,
1Co 6:15 not know that your **b** are members of Christ?
15:40 There are both heavenly **b** and earthly **b,**
2Co 4:10 the life of Jesus may also be made visible in our **b.**
7: 5 when we came into Macedonia, our **b** had no rest,
Eph 5:28 as they do their own **b.**
Heb 3:17 whose **b** fell in the wilderness?
10:22 from an evil conscience and our **b** washed
13:11 the **b** of those animals whose blood is brought into
Jas 3: 3 to make them obey us, we guide their whole **b.**
Jude 1:23 hating even the tunic defiled by their **b.**
Rev 11: 8 and their dead **b** will lie in the street of
11: 9 and languages and nations will gaze at their dead **b**
Tob 1:18 but I would secretly remove the **b** and bury them.
AdE 9:13 Also, hang up the **b** of Haman's ten sons."
9:14 over to the Jews of the city the **b** of Haman's sons
Sir 44:14 Their **b** are buried in peace,
Bar 2:17 whose spirit has been taken from their **b,**
LtJ 6:22 swallows, and birds alight on their **b** and heads;
Bel 1:32 and every day they had been given two human **b**
1Mc 5:51 he passed through the town over the **b** of the dead.
11: 4 the charred **b** of those whom Jonathan had burned
2Mc 12:39 and his men went to take up the **b** of the fallen and
3Mc 2:29 on their **b** by fire with the ivy-leaf symbol
2Es 1:32 and killed them and torn their **b** in pieces;
7:*100* after they have been separated from the **b,**
4Mc 13:13 and let us use our **b** as a bulwark for the law.
14:10 and it consumed their **b** quickly.
18: 3 Therefore those who gave over their **b** in suffering

BODILY (9) [BODY]
Lk 3:22 the Holy Spirit descended upon him in **b** form like
2Co 10:10 but his **b** presence is weak,
Col 2: 9 For in him the whole fullness of deity dwells **b,**
Jas 2:16 and yet you do not supply their **b** needs,
2Mc 3:17 For terror and **b** trembling had come over the man,
3Mc 6:20 Even the king began to shudder **b,**
2Es 1:37 though they do not see me with **b** eyes,
4Mc 3:18 it can overthrow **b** agonies even when they are
10:20 we let our **b** members be mutilated.

BODY‡ (290) [ABLE-BODIED, BODIES, BODILY, BODY'S, BODY-ARMOR, BODYGUARD, BODYGUARDS]
A. WHOLE BODY (18)
B. ONE BODY (11)

Ge 25:25 first came out red, all his **b** like a hairy mantle;
Ex 4: 7 it was restored like the rest of his **b—**
30:32 not be used in any ordinary anointing of the **b,**
Lev 6:10 on his linen undergarments next to his **b;**
13: 2 When a person has on the skin of his **b** a swelling
13: 2 it turns into a leprous disease on the skin of his **b,**
13: 3 the disease on the skin of his **b,** and if the hair in

Lev 13: 3 the skin of his **b**, it is a leprous disease;
13: 4 But if the spot is white in the skin of his **b**,
13:11 it is a chronic leprous disease in the skin of his **b**.
13:13 and if the disease has covered all his **b**,
13:18 on the skin of one's **b** a boil that has healed,
13:24 the **b** has a burn on the skin and the raw flesh of
13:38 a man or a woman has spots on the skin of the **b**,
13:39 if the spots on the skin of the **b** are of a dull white,
13:43 a leprous disease in the skin of the **b**,
14: 9 he shall wash his clothes, and bathe his **b** in water,
15: 7 All who touch the **b** of the one with
15:13 he shall wash his clothes and bathe his **b**
15:16 he shall bathe his whole **b** in water, A
15:19 of blood that is her regular discharge from her **b**,
16: 4 shall have the linen undergarments next to his **b**,
16: 4 He shall bathe his **b** in water,
16:24 He shall bathe his **b** in water in a holy place,
16:26 for Azazel shall wash his clothes and bathe his **b**
16:28 and bathe his **b** in water,
17:16 if they do not wash themselves or bathe their **b**,
21:11 He shall not go where there is a dead **b**;
22: 6 of the sacred donations unless he has washed his **b**
Nu 8: 7 on them, have them shave their whole **b** with A
19: 7 the priest shall wash his clothes and bathe his **b**
19: 8 in water and bathe his **b** in water;
19:11 the dead **b** of any human being shall
19:13 the **b** of a human being who has died,
Dt 21: 1 a **b** is found lying in open country,
21: 2 the distances to the towns that are near the **b**.
21: 3 The elders of the town nearest the **b** shall take
21: 6 that town nearest the **b** shall wash their hands over
30: 9 in the fruit of your **b**, in the fruit of your livestock,
Jos 8:29 and they took his **b** down from the tree,
Jdg 14: 8 and there was a swarm of bees in the **b** of the lion,
20: 1 and the congregation assembled in one **b** before B
20:33 The main **b** of the Israelites drew back its battle
20:38 Now the agreement between the main **b** of Israel
20:39 the main **b** of Israel should turn in battle.
20:41 Then the main **b** of Israel turned,
1Sa 31:10 and they fastened his **b** to the wall of Beth-shan.
31:12 and took the **b** of Saul and the bodies of his sons
2Sa 7:12 who shall come forth from your **b**,
1Ki 13:22 your **b** shall not come to your ancestral tomb."
13:24 His **b** was thrown in the road,
13:24 the lion also stood beside the **b**.
13:25 People passed by and saw the **b** thrown in
13:25 with the lion standing by the **b**.
13:28 and he went and found the **b** thrown in the road,
13:28 with the donkey and the lion standing beside the **b**.
13:28 lion had not eaten the **b** or attacked the donkey.
13:29 The prophet took up the **b** of the man of God,
13:30 He laid the **b** in his own grave;
2Ki 6:30 that he had sackcloth on his **b** underneath—
1Ch 10:12 all the valiant warriors got up and took away the **b**
Job 7:15 and death rather than this **b**.
20:25 It is drawn forth and comes out of their **b**,
Ps 16: 9 and my soul rejoices; my **b** also rests secure.
31: 9 from grief, my soul and my **b** also.
32: 3 While I kept silence, my **b** wasted away
42:10 As with a deadly wound in my **b**,
68:27 the princes of Judah in a **b**, the princes of Zebulun,
109:18 may it soak into his **b** like water,
109:24 through fasting; my **b** has become gaunt.
132:11 of the sons of your **b** I will set on your throne.
Pr 3: 8 for your flesh and a refreshment for your **b**.
5:11 when your flesh and **b** are consumed,
15:30 and good news refreshes the **b**.
16:24 sweetness to the soul and health to the **b**.
18: 8 they go down into the inner parts of the **b**.
26:22 they go down into the inner parts of the **b**.
Ecc 2: 3 with my mind how to cheer my **b** with wine—
11:10 and put away pain from your **b**;
SS 5:14 His **b** is ivory work, encrusted with sapphires.
Isa 10:18 the LORD will destroy, both soul and **b**,
Jer 26:23 down with the sword and threw his dead **b** into
36:30 and his dead **b** shall be cast out to the heat by day
Eze 1:23 each of the creatures had two wings covering its **b**.
10:12 Their entire **b**, their rims, their spokes,
36:26 from your **b** the heart of stone and give you a heart
Da 4:33 and his **b** was bathed with the dew of heaven,
5:21 and his **b** was bathed with the dew of heaven,
7:11 and its **b** destroyed and given over to be burned
10: 6 His **b** was like beryl, his face like lightning,
Am 6:10 shall take up the **b** to bring it out of the house,
Mic 6: 7 the fruit of my **b** for the sin of my soul?"
Hag 2:13 by contact with a dead **b** touches any of these,
Mt 5:29 lose one of your members than for your whole **b** A
5:30 lose one of your members than for your whole **b** A
6:22 "The eye is the lamp of the **b**.
6:22 your whole **b** will be full of light; A
6:23 your whole **b** will be full of darkness. A
6:25 or about your **b**, what you will wear.
6:25 and the **b** more than clothing?
10:28 Do not fear those who kill the **b** but cannot kill
10:28 rather fear him who can destroy both soul and **b**
14:12 His disciples came and took the **b** and buried it;
26:12 on my **b** she has prepared me for burial.
26:26 and said, "Take, eat; this is my **b**."
27:58 He went to Pilate and asked for the **b** of Jesus;
27:59 the **b** and wrapped it in a clean linen cloth
Mk 5:29 she felt in her **b** that she was healed of her disease.
6:29 they came and took his **b**, and laid it in a tomb.
14: 8 she has anointed my **b** beforehand for its burial.
14:22 and said, "Take; this is my **b**."
15:43 went boldly to Pilate and asked for the **b** of Jesus.
15:45 he granted the **b** to Joseph.
15:46 a linen cloth, and taking down the **b**, wrapped it in
Mk 15:47 the mother of Joses saw where the **b** was laid.
Lk 11:34 Your eye is the lamp of your **b**.
11:34 your eye is healthy, your whole **b** is full of light; A
11:34 but if it is not healthy, your **b** is full of darkness.
11:36 If then your whole **b** is full of light, A
12: 4 my friends, do not fear those who kill the **b**,
12:22 or about your **b**, what you will wear.
12:23 and the **b** more than clothing.
22:19 saying, "This is my **b**, which is given for you.
23: 1 Then the assembly rose as a **b** and brought Jesus
23:52 This man went to Pilate and asked for the **b**
23:55 and they saw the tomb and how his **b** was laid.
24: 3 but when they went in, they did not find the **b**.
24:23 and when they did not find his **b** there,
Jn 2:21 But he was speaking of the temple of his **b**.
7:23 I healed a man's whole **b** on the sabbath? A
19:38 asked Pilate to let him take away the **b** of Jesus.
19:38 so he came and removed his **b**.
19:40 They took the **b** of Jesus and wrapped it with
20:12 sitting where the **b** of Jesus had been lying,
Ac 5: 6 The young men came and wrapped up his **b**,
5:21 they called together the council and the whole **b** A
9:40 He turned to the **b** and said, "Tabitha, get up."
12:20 So they came to him in a **b**;
Ro 4:19 not weaken in faith when he considered his own **b**,
6: 6 with him so that the **b** of sin might be destroyed,
7: 4 you have died to the law through the **b** of Christ,
7:24 Who will rescue me from this **b** of death?
8:10 though the **b** is dead because of sin,
8:13 if by the Spirit you put to death the deeds of the **b**,
12: 4 For as in one **b** we have many members, B
12: 5 who are many, are one **b** in Christ, B
1Co 5: 3 For though absent in **b**, I am present in spirit;
6:13 The **b** is meant not for fornication but for the Lord,
6:13 and the Lord for the **b**.
6:16 to a prostitute becomes one **b** with her? B
6:18 Every sin that a person commits is outside the **b**;
6:18 but the fornicator sins against the **b** itself.
6:19 not know that your **b** is a temple of the Holy Spirit
6:20 therefore glorify God in your **b**.
7: 4 the wife does not have authority over her own **b**,
7: 4 husband not have authority over his own **b**,
7:34 so that they may be holy in **b** and spirit;
9:27 but I punish my **b** and enslave it,
10:16 is it not a sharing in the **b** of Christ?
10:17 there is one bread, we who are many are one **b**, B
11:24 he broke it and said, "This is my **b** that is for you.
11:27 an unworthy manner will be answerable for the **b**
11:29 For all who eat and drink without discerning the **b**,
12:12 For just as the **b** is one and has many members,
12:12 and all the members of the **b**, though many,
12:12 though many, are one **b**, so it is with Christ. B
12:13 in the one Spirit we were all baptized into one **b** B
12:14 the **b** does not consist of one member but of many.
12:15 I do not belong to the **b**,"
12:15 that would not make it any less a part of the **b**.
12:16 "Because I am not an eye, I do not belong to the **b**,
12:16 that would not make it any less a part of the **b**.
12:17 whole **b** were an eye, where would the hearing A
12:17 If the whole **b** were hearing, A
12:18 But as it is, God arranged the members in the **b**,
12:19 all were a single member, where would the **b** be?
12:20 As it is, there are many members, yet one **b**. B
12:22 of the **b** that seem to be weaker are indispensable,
12:23 of the **b** that we think less honorable we clothe
12:24 But God has so arranged the **b**,
12:25 that there may be no dissension within the **b**,
12:27 the **b** of Christ and individually members of it.
13: 3 and if I hand over my **b** so that I may boast,
15:35 With what kind of **b** do they come?"
15:37 what you sow, you do not sow the **b** that is to be,
15:38 But God gives it a **b** as he has chosen,
15:38 and to each kind of seed its own **b**.
15:44 It is sown a physical **b**, it is raised a spiritual **b**.
15:44 there is a physical **b**, there is also a spiritual **b**.
15:53 For this perishable **b** must put on imperishability,
15:53 and this mortal **b** must put on immortality.
15:54 When this perishable **b** puts on imperishability,
15:54 and this mortal **b** puts on immortality,
2Co 4:10 always carrying in the **b** the death of Jesus,
5: 6 while we are at home in the **b** we are away from
5: 8 be away from the **b** and at home with the Lord.
5:10 for what has been done in the **b**,
7: 1 from every defilement of **b** and of spirit,
12: 2 whether in the **b** or out of the **b** I do not know;
12: 3 whether in the **b** or out of the **b** I do not know;
Gal 6:17 for I carry the marks of Jesus branded on my **b**.
Eph 1:23 which is his **b**, the fullness of him who fills all
2:16 might reconcile both groups to God in one **b** B
3: 6 members of the same **b**, and sharers in the promise
4: 4 There is one **b** and one Spirit, B
4:12 for building up the **b** of Christ,
4:16 whom the whole **b**, joined and knit together A
5:23 the **b** of which he is the Savior.
5:29 For no one ever hates his own **b**,
5:30 because we are members of his **b**.
Php 1:20 Christ will be exalted now as always in my **b**,
3:21 He will transform the **b** of our humiliation that it
may be conformed to the **b** of his glory,
Col 1:18 He is the head of the **b**, the church;
1:22 now reconciled in his fleshly **b** through death,
1:24 in Christ's afflictions for the sake of his **b**,
2: 5 For though I am absent in **b**,
2:11 the **b** of the flesh in the circumcision of Christ;
2:19 to the head, from whom the whole **b**, nourished A
2:23 humility, and severe treatment of the **b**,
3:15 to which indeed you were called in the one **b**. B
1Th 4: 4 how to control your own **b** in holiness and honor,
5:23 and may your spirit and soul and **b** be kept sound
Heb 9:10 regulations for the **b** imposed until the time comes
10: 5 but a **b** you have prepared for me;
10:10 through the offering of the **b** of Jesus Christ once
Jas 2:26 For just as the **b** without the spirit is dead,
3: 2 able to keep the whole **b** in check with a bridle. A
3: 6 the whole **b**, sets on fire the cycle of nature, A
1Pe 2:24 He himself bore our sins in his **b** on the cross,
3:21 not as a removal of dirt from the **b**,
2Pe 1:13 I think it right, as long as I am in this **b**,
Jude 1: 9 with the devil and disputed about the **b** of Moses,
Tob 1:17 if I saw the dead **b** of any of my people thrown out
2: 4 and removed the **b** from the square and laid it
Jdt 1:16 he and all his combined forces, a vast **b** of troops;
10: 3 bathed her **b** with water, and anointed herself
13: 9 Next she rolled his **b** off the bed and pulled down
AdE 14: 2 and she utterly humbled her **b**;
Wis 1: 4 or dwell in a **b** enslaved to sin.
2: 3 the **b** will turn to ashes,
8:20 or rather, being good, I entered an undefiled **b**.
9:15 for a perishable **b** weighs down the soul,
18:22 He conquered the wrath not by strength of **b**,
Sir 10: 9 Even in life the human **b** decays.
30:14 healthy, and fit than rich and afflicted in **b**.
30:15 and a robust **b** than countless riches.
30:16 There is no wealth better than health of **b**,
38:16 Lay out the **b** with due ceremony,
41:11 The human **b** is a fleeting thing,
47:19 through your **b** you were brought into subjection.
48:13 and when he was dead, his **b** prophesied.
1Mc 3:13 including a **b** of faithful soldiers who stayed
7:12 a group of scribes appeared in a **b** before Alcimus
2Mc 4: 9 to establish by his authority a gymnasium and a **b**
6:30 I am enduring terrible sufferings in my **b**
6:31 only to the young but to the great **b** of his nation.
7: 7 "Will you eat rather than have your **b** punished
7:37 give up **b** and life for the laws of our ancestors,
9: 7 fall was so hard as to torture every limb of his **b**.
9: 9 so the ungodly man's **b** swarmed with worms,
9:29 And Philip, one of his courtiers, took his **b** home;
14:38 and he had most zealously risked **b** and life
15:12 with outstretched hands for the whole **b** of A
15:30 the man who was ever in **b** and soul the defender
3Mc 7: 3 the Jews of the kingdom in a **b** and to punish them
2Es 3: 5 and it gave you Adam, a lifeless **b**?
5:14 Then I woke up, and my **b** shuddered violently,
7:*78* that a person shall die, as the spirit leaves the **b**
7:*88* when they shall be separated from their mortal **b**.
8: 8 to the **b** that is now fashioned in the womb,
11:10 but from the middle of its **b**.
11:23 on the eagle's **b** except the three heads that were
11:45 your most evil talons, and your whole worthless **b**,
12: 3 The whole **b** of the eagle was burned, A
12:17 from the eagle's heads but from the midst of its **b**,
16:61 and put a heart in the midst of each **b**,
4Mc 1:20 of these is by nature concerned with both **b**
1:27 in the **b**, indiscriminate eating, gluttony,
1:28 and pain are two plants growing from the **b** and
1:35 and all the impulses of the **b** are bridled by reason.
3: 1 not over its own emotions, but over those of the **b**.
6: 7 Although he fell to the ground because his **b** could
7:13 his **b** no longer tense and firm, his muscles flabby,
11:11 gasping for breath and in anguish of **b**,
17: 1 into the flames so that no one might touch her **b**.

BODY'S (1) [BODY]

Eph 4:16 promotes the **b** growth in building itself up

BODY-ARMOR (1) [ARM, BODY]

Ne 4:16 and half held the spears, shields, bows, and **b**;

BODYGUARD (9) [BODY, GUARD]

1Sa 28: 2 "Very well, I will make you my **b** for life."
2Sa 23:23 And David put him in charge of his **b**.
2Ki 25: 8 Nebuzaradan, the captain of the **b**,
1Ch 11:25 And David put him in charge of his **b**.
Jer 52:12 Nebuzaradan the captain of the **b** who served
1Mc 13:40 if any of you are qualified to be enrolled in our **b**,
2Mc 3:24 But when he arrived at the treasury with his **b**,
3:28 and all his **b** but was now unable to help himself.
1Es 3: 4 Then the three young men of the **b**,

BODYGUARDS (2) [BODY, GUARD]

AdE 2:21 Now the king's eunuchs, who were chief **b**,
3Mc 2:23 both friends and **b**, seeing the severe punishment

BOG (1)

Ps 40: 2 out of the miry **b**, and set my feet upon a rock,

BOHAN (2)

Jos 15: 6 and the boundary goes up to the Stone of **B**,
18:17 it goes down to the Stone of **B**, Reuben's son;

BOIL (20) [BOILED, BOILING, BOILS]

Ex 16:23 what you want to bake and **b** what you want to **b**,
23:19 You shall not **b** a kid in its mother's milk.
29:31 and **b** its flesh in a holy place;
34:26 You shall not **b** a kid in its mother's milk.
Lev 8:31 "**B** the flesh at the entrance of the tent of meeting,
13:18 on the skin of one's body a **b** that has healed,
13:19 the place of the **b** there appears a white swelling or

Lev 13:20 this is a leprous disease, broken out in the **b**.
13:23 it is the scar of the **b**;
Dt 14:21 You shall not **b** a kid in its mother's milk.
2Ki 20: 7 Let them take it and apply it to the **b**,
Job 41:31 It makes the deep **b** like a pot;
Isa 38:21 and apply it to the **b**, so that he may recover."
64: 2 and the fire causes water to **b**—
Eze 24: 5 **b** its pieces, seethe also its bones in it.
24:10 Heap up the logs, kindle the fire; **b** the meat well,
46:20 where the priests shall **b** the guilt offering and
46:24 at the temple shall **b** the sacrifices of the people."
Zec 14:21 that all who sacrifice may come and use them to **b**

BOILED (11) [BOIL]

Ex 12: 9 Do not eat any of it raw or **b** in water,
Lev 6:28 earthen vessel in which it was **b** shall be broken;
6:28 but if it is **b** in a bronze vessel,
Nu 6:19 the ram, when it is **b**, and one unleavened cake out
11: 8 then **b** it in pots and made cakes of it;
1Sa 2:15 he will not accept **b** meat from you, but only raw."
1Ki 19:21 he **b** their flesh, and gave it to the people,
2Ch 35:13 and they **b** the holy offerings in pots, in caldrons,
La 4:10 compassionate women have **b** their own children;
Bel 1:27 fat, and hair, and **b** them together and made cakes,
1Es 1:12 they **b** the sacrifices in bronze pots and caldrons,

BOILING (3) [BOIL]

1Sa 2:13 while the meat was **b**, with a three-pronged fork
Job 41:20 as from a **b** pot and burning rushes.
Jer 1:13 I said, "I see a **b** pot, tilted away from the north."

BOILINGS See Index to Footnotes

BOILS (6) [BOIL]

Ex 9: 9 and shall cause festering **b** on humans and animals
9:10 and it caused festering **b** on humans and animals.
9:11 not stand before Moses because of the **b**,
9:11 for the **b** afflicted the magicians as well as all
Dt 28:27 The LORD will afflict you with the **b** of Egypt,
28:35 on the legs with grievous **b** of which you cannot

BOLD‡ (15) [BOLDER, BOLDLY, BOLDNESS]

Nu 13:20 Be **b**, and bring some of the fruit of the land."
Dt 31: 6 Be strong and **b**; have no fear
31: 7 "Be strong and **b**, for you are the one who will go
31:23 "Be strong and **b**, for you shall bring the Israelites
Job 10:16 **B** as a lion you hunt me;
Pr 21:29 The wicked put on a **b** face,
28: 1 but the righteous are as **b** as a lion.
Da 8:23 a king of **b** countenance shall arise,
Ro 10:20 Then Isaiah is so **b** as to say,
2Co 10: 1 but **b** toward you when I am away!—
Phm 1: 8 though I am **b** enough in Christ to command you
2Pe 2:10 **B** and willful, they are not afraid to slander
Jdt 14:13 so **b** as to come down against us to give battle,
Wis 11:17 to send upon them a multitude of bears, or **b** lions,
2Mc 3:24 so great a manifestation that all who had been so **b**

BOLDER (1) [BOLD]

3Mc 1:22 the **b** of the citizens would not tolerate

BOLDLY (15) [BOLD]

Ex 14: 8 the Israelites, who were going out **b**.
Nu 33: 3 the day after the passover the Israelites went out **b**
Pr 10:10 but the one who rebukes **b** makes peace.
Mk 15:43 went **b** to Pilate and asked for the body of Jesus.
Ac 9:27 how in Damascus he had spoken **b** in the name
9:28 speaking **b** in the name of the Lord.
13:46 Then both Paul and Barnabas spoke out **b**, saying,
14: 3 a long time, speaking **b** for the Lord, who testified
18:26 He began to speak **b** in the synagogue;
19: 8 the synagogue and for three months spoke out **b**,
Ro 15:15 on some points I have written to you rather **b**
Eph 6:20 Pray that I may declare it **b**, as I must speak.
1Mc 4:18 and afterward seize the plunder **b**."
4Mc 3:14 and from it **b** brought the king a drink.
15:19 at the eyes of each one in his tortures gazing **b** at

BOLDNESS (23) [BOLD]

Ac 4:13 Now when they saw the **b** of Peter and John
4:29 to your servants to speak your word with all **b**,
4:31 the Holy Spirit and spoke the word of God with **b**.
28:31 and teaching about the Lord Jesus Christ with all **b**
2Co 3:12 then, we have such a hope, we act with great **b**,
10: 2 when I am present I need not show **b** by daring
Eph 3:12 to God in **b** and confidence through faith in him.
6:19 be given to me to make known with **b** the mystery
Php 1:14 to speak the word with greater **b** and without fear.
1:20 but that by my speaking with all **b**,
1Ti 3:13 a good standing for themselves and great **b** in
Heb 4:16 therefore approach the throne of grace with **b**,
1Jn 3:21 if our hearts do not condemn us, we have **b**
4:17 that we may have **b** on the day of judgment,
5:14 And this is the **b** we have in him,
Jdt 16:10 The Persians trembled at her **b**,
Sir 25:25 and no **b** of speech to an evil wife.
1Mc 4:32 melt the **b** of their strength;
4:35 of his troops and observed the **b** that inspired those
3Mc 2: 4 even giants who trusted in their strength and **b**,
6:34 their fire-breathing **b** was ignominiously quenched.
2Es 7:*98* because they shall rejoice with **b**,
4Mc 10: 5 Enraged by the man's **b**, they disjointed his hands

BOLSTER (KJV) See HEAD

BOLT (3) [BOLTED, BOLTS]

2Sa 13:17 and **b** the door after her."
SS 5: 5 upon the handles of the **b**.
Sir 28:25 so make a door and a **b** for your mouth.

BOLTED (1) [BOLT]

2Sa 13:18 So his servant put her out, and **b** the door after her.

BOLTS (7) [BOLT]

Ne 3: 3 they laid its beams and set up its doors, its **b**,
3: 6 they laid its beams and set up its doors, its **b**,
3:13 they rebuilt it and set up its doors, its **b**,
3:14 he rebuilt it and set up its doors, its **b**, and its bars.
3:15 and covered it and set up its doors, its **b**,
1Mc 12:38 he fortified it and installed gates with **b**.
13:33 with high towers and great walls and gates and **b**,

BOMBASTIC (2)

2Pe 2:18 For they speak **b** nonsense,
Jude 1:16 they are **b** in speech, flattering people

BOND (11) [BONDAGE, BONDED, BONDS]

Dt 32:36 neither **b** nor free remaining.
1Ki 14:10 both **b** and free in Israel,
21:21 and will cut off from Ahab every male, **b** or free,
2Ki 9: 8 I will cut off from Ahab every male, **b** or free,
14:26 there was no one left, **b** or free,
Eze 20:37 and will bring you within the **b** of the covenant.
Eph 4: 3 to maintain the unity of the Spirit in the **b**
Tob 5: 3 "He gave me his **b** and I gave him my **b**.
9: 2 Go to the home of Gabael, give him the **b**,
9: 5 Raphael gave him the **b** and informed him

BONDAGE (7) [BOND]

Lk 13:16 be set free from this **b** on the sabbath day?"
Ro 8:21 from its **b** to decay and will obtain the freedom of
Wis 14:21 in **b** to misfortune or to royal authority,
1Es 8:80 Even in our **b** we were not forsaken by our Lord,
2Es 1: 7 out of the house of **b**?
2: 1 I brought this people out of **b**,
14: 3 and spoke to Moses when my people were in **b**

BONDED (1) [BOND]

Sir 22:16 A wooden beam firmly **b** into a building is

BONDMAID, BONDMAIDS (KJV) See FEMALE SLAVE, SLAVE, SLAVE WOMAN

BONDMAN See Index to Footnotes

BONDMAN, BONDMEN (KJV) See SLAVE

BONDS (20) [BOND]

Jdg 15:14 and his **b** melted off his hands.
Job 39: 5 Who has loosed the **b** of the swift ass,
Ps 2: 3 "Let us burst their **b** asunder,
69:33 and does not despise his own that are in **b**.
107:14 and broke their **b** asunder.
116:16 You have loosed my **b**.
Isa 28:22 do not scoff, or your **b** will be made stronger;
52: 2 loose the **b** from your neck,
58: 6 to loose the **b** of injustice,
Jer 2:20 long ago you broke your yoke and burst your **b**,
5: 5 the yoke, they had burst the **b**.
30: 8 and I will burst his **b**,
Na 1:13 from you and snap the **b** that bind you."
Lk 8:29 with chains and shackles, but he would break the **b**
Sir 6:25 and do not fret under her **b**.
6:30 and her **b** a purple cord.
3Mc 4: 7 In **b** and in public view they were violently
4: 9 driven under the constraint of iron **b**;
5: 7 because in their **b** they were forcibly confined
6:27 Loose and untie their unjust **b**!

BONDSERVANT (KJV) See SLAVE

BONDWOMAN See Index to Footnotes

BONDWOMAN, BONDWOMEN (KJV) See SLAVE, SLAVE WOMAN

BONE (14) [BACKBONE, BONES, JAWBONE]

Ge 2:23 at last is **b** of my bones and flesh of my flesh;
29:14 "Surely you are my **b** and my flesh!"
Nu 9:12 nor break a **b** of it;
19:16 or who has died naturally, or a human **b**,
19:18 and on whoever touched the **b**, the slain,
Jdg 9: 2 Remember also that I am your **b** and your flesh."
2Sa 5: 1 and said, "Look, we are your **b** and flesh.
19:12 You are my kin, you are my **b** and my flesh;
2Sa 19:13 say to Amasa, 'Are you not my **b** and my flesh?
1Ch 11: 1 "See, we are your **b** and flesh.
Job 2: 5 But stretch out your hand now and touch his **b**
Eze 37: 7 and the bones came together, **b** to its **b**.
39:15 anyone who sees a human **b** shall set up a sign

BONES‡ (99) [BONE]

Ge 2:23 "This at last is bone of my **b** and flesh of my flesh;
50:25 you shall carry up my **b** from here."
Ex 12:46 and you shall not break any of its **b**.
13:19 the **b** of Joseph who had required a solemn oath of
13:19 then you must carry my **b** with you from here."
Nu 24: 8 the nations that are his foes and break their **b**.
Jos 24:32 The **b** of Joseph, which the Israelites had brought
1Sa 31:13 Then they took their **b** and buried them under
2Sa 21:12 David went and took the **b** of Saul and the **b** of
21:13 the **b** of Saul and the **b** of his son Jonathan;
21:13 the **b** of those who had been impaled.
21:14 They buried the **b** of Saul and of his son Jonathan
1Ki 13: 2 and human **b** shall be burned on you.' "
13:31 lay my **b** beside his **b**.
2Ki 13:21 as soon as the man touched the **b** of Elisha,
23:14 and covered the sites with human **b**.
23:16 and he sent and took the **b** out of the tombs,
23:18 He said, "Let him rest; let no one move his **b**."
23:18 So they let his **b** alone,
23:18 the **b** of the prophet who came out of Samaria.
23:20 and burned human **b** on them.
1Ch 10:12 Then they buried their **b** under the oak in Jabesh,
2Ch 34: 5 He also burned the **b** of the priests on their altars,
Job 4:14 and trembling, which made all my **b** shake.
10:11 and knit me together with **b** and sinews.
19:20 My **b** cling to my skin and to my flesh,
21:24 of milk and the marrow of his **b** moist.
30:17 The night racks my **b**, and the pain
30:30 and my **b** burn with heat.
33:19 and with continual strife in their **b**,
33:21 and their **b**, once invisible, now stick out.
40:18 Its **b** are tubes of bronze,
Ps 6: 2 heal me, for my **b** are shaking with terror.
22:14 and all my **b** are out of joint;
22:17 I can count all my **b**.
31:10 because of my misery, and my **b** waste away.
34:20 He keeps all their **b**; not one of them
35:10 All my **b** shall say, "O LORD, who is like you?
38: 3 there is no health in my **b** because of my sin.
51: 8 let the **b** that you have crushed rejoice.
53: 5 For God will scatter the **b** of the ungodly;
102: 3 and my **b** burn like a furnace.
102: 5 of my loud groaning my **b** cling to my skin.
109:18 into his body like water, like oil into his **b**.
141: 7 so shall their **b** be strewn at the mouth of Sheol.
Pr 12: 4 she who brings shame is like rottenness in his **b**.
14:30 but passion makes the **b** rot.
17:19 one who builds a high threshold invites broken **b**.
17:22 but a downcast spirit dries up the **b**.
25:15 and a soft tongue can break **b**.
Ecc 11: 5 as you do not know how the breath comes to the **b**
Isa 38:13 like a lion he breaks all my **b**;
58:11 in parched places, and make your **b** strong;
Jer 8: 1 says the LORD, the **b** of the kings of Judah, the **b**
of its officials, the **b** of the priests, the **b** of the
prophets, and the **b** of the inhabitants of Jerusalem
20: 9 like a burning fire shut up in my **b**;
23: 9 My heart is crushed within me, all my **b** shake;
50:17 of Babylon has gnawed its **b**.
La 1:13 From on high he sent fire; it went deep into my **b**;
3: 4 and my skin waste away, and broken my **b**;
4: 8 Their skin has shriveled on their **b**;
Eze 6: 5 and I will scatter your **b** around your altars.
24: 4 and the shoulder; fill it with choice **b**.
24: 5 boil its pieces, seethe also its **b** in it.
24:10 mix in the spices, let the **b** be burned.
32:27 and whose shields are upon their **b**;
37: 1 of a valley; it was full of **b**.
37: 3 He said to me, "Mortal, can these **b** live?"
37: 4 Then he said to me, "Prophesy to these **b**,
37: 4 O dry **b**, hear the word of the LORD.
37: 5 Thus says the Lord GOD to these **b**:
37: 7 and the **b** came together, bone to its bone.
37:11 "Mortal, these **b** are the whole house of Israel.
37:11 They say, 'Our **b** are dried up,
Da 6:24 the lions overpowered them and broke all their **b**
Am 2: 1 he burned to lime the **b** of the king of Edom.
Mic 3: 2 and the flesh off their **b**;
3: 3 break their **b** in pieces, and chop them up like meat
Hab 3:16 Rottenness enters into my **b**,
Mt 23:27 but inside they are full of the **b** of the dead and
Lk 24:39 for a ghost does not have flesh and **b** as you see
Jn 19:36 "None of his **b** shall be broken."
Sir 26:13 and her skill puts flesh on his **b**.
28:17 but a blow of the tongue crushes the **b**.
46:12 May their **b** send forth new life from
49:10 the **b** of the Twelve Prophets send forth new life
49:15 even his **b** were cared for.
Bar 2:24 the prophets, that the **b** of our kings and the **b** of
our ancestors
1Mc 13:25 Simon sent and took the **b** of his brother Jonathan,
4Mc 6:26 When he was now burned to his very **b** and about
9:21 the ligaments joining his **b** were already severed,
18:17 the query of Ezekiel, 'Shall these dry **b** live?'

BONNETS (KJV) See HEADDRESSES, TURBANS

BONUS (2)

Tob 12: 1 and give him a **b** as well.”
12: 3 How much extra shall I give him as a **b?”**

BOOK (171) [BOOKS]

A. BOOK OF THE ANNALS (35)
B. BOOK OF THE/THIS LAW (22)
C. BOOK OF MOSES (12)
D. BOOK OF THE KINGS (11)
E. BOOK OF LIFE (7)
F. BOOK OF THE COVENANT (6)

Ex 17: 14 as a reminder in a **b** and recite it in the hearing
24: 7 Then he took the **b** of the covenant, F
32: 32 if not, blot me out of the **b** that you have written.”
32: 33 against me I will blot out of my **b.**
Nu 21: 14 Wherefore it is said in the **B** of the Wars of
Dt 28: 58 the words of this law that are written in this **b,**
28: 61 even though not recorded in the **b** of this law, B
29: 20 the curses written in this **b** will descend on them,
29: 21 of the covenant written in this **b** of the law. B
29: 27 bringing on it every curse written in this **b.**
30: 10 and decrees that are written in this **b** of the law, B
31: 24 down in a **b** the words of this law to the very end,
31: 26 “Take this **b** of the law and put it beside the ark B
Jos 1: 8 This **b** of the law shall not depart out B
8: 31 as it is written in the **b** of the law of Moses, B
8: 34 to all that is written in the **b** of the law. B
10: 13 Is this not written in the **B** of Jashar?
18: 9 a **b** a description of it by towns in seven divisions;
23: 6 do all that is written in the **b** of the law of Moses, B
24: 26 Joshua wrote these words in the **b** of the law B
1Sa 10: 25 and he wrote them in a **b** and laid it up before
2Sa 1: 18 it is written in the **B** of Jashar.)
1Ki 11: 41 not written in the **B** of the Acts of Solomon?
14: 19 are written in the **B** of the Annals of the Kings A
14: 29 not written in the **B** of the Annals of the Kings A
15: 7 not written in the **B** of the Annals of the Kings A
15: 23 not written in the **B** of the Annals of the Kings A
15: 31 not written in the **B** of the Annals of the Kings A
16: 5 not written in the **B** of the Annals of the Kings A
16: 14 not written in the **B** of the Annals of the Kings A
16: 20 not written in the **B** of the Annals of the Kings A
16: 27 not written in the **B** of the Annals of the Kings A
22: 39 not written in the **B** of the Annals of the Kings A
22: 45 not written in the **B** of the Annals of the Kings A
2Ki 1: 18 not written in the **B** of the Annals of the Kings A
8: 23 not written in the **B** of the Annals of the Kings A
10: 34 not written in the **B** of the Annals of the Kings A
12: 19 not written in the **B** of the Annals of the Kings A
13: 8 not written in the **B** of the Annals of the Kings A
13: 12 not written in the **B** of the Annals of the Kings A
14: 6 to what is written in the **b** of the law of Moses, B
14: 15 not written in the **B** of the Annals of the Kings A
14: 18 not written in the **B** of the Annals of the Kings A
14: 28 not written in the **B** of the Annals of the Kings A
15: 6 not written in the **B** of the Annals of the Kings A
15: 11 are written in the **B** of the Annals of the Kings A
15: 15 are written in the **B** of the Annals of the Kings A
15: 21 not written in the **B** of the Annals of the Kings A
15: 26 are written in the **B** of the Annals of the Kings A
15: 31 are written in the **B** of the Annals of the Kings A
15: 36 not written in the **B** of the Annals of the Kings A
16: 19 not written in the **B** of the Annals of the Kings A
20: 20 not written in the **B** of the Annals of the Kings A
21: 17 not written in the **B** of the Annals of the Kings A
21: 25 not written in the **B** of the Annals of the Kings A
22: 8 “I have found the **b** of the law in the house of B
22: 8 When Hilkiah gave the **b** to Shaphan, he read it.
22: 10 “The priest Hilkiah has given me a **b.”**
22: 11 the king heard the words of the **b** of the law, B
22: 13 the words of this **b** that has been found;
22: 13 our ancestors did not obey the words of this **b,**
22: 16 the words of the **b** that the king of Judah has read.
23: 2 hearing all the words of the **b** of the covenant F
23: 3 of this covenant that were written in this **b.**
23: 21 God as prescribed in this **b** of the covenant.” F
23: 24 the **b** that the priest Hilkiah had found in the house
23: 28 not written in the **B** of the Annals of the Kings A
24: 5 not written in the **B** of the Annals of the Kings A
1Ch 9: 1 these are written in the **B** of the Kings of Israel. D
2Ch 16: 11 are written in the **B** of the Kings of Judah D
17: 9 having the **b** of the law of the LORD with them; B
20: 34 are recorded in the **B** of the Kings of Israel. D
24: 27 in the Commentary on the **B** of the Kings. D
25: 4 in the **b** of Moses, where the LORD commanded, C
25: 26 they not written in the **B** of the Kings of Judah D
27: 7 are written in the **B** of the Kings of Israel D
28: 26 are written in the **B** of the Kings of Judah D
32: 32 Amoz in the **B** of the Kings of Judah and Israel. D
34: 14 the priest Hilkiah found the **b** of the law of B
34: 15 “I have found the **b** of the law in the house of B
34: 15 and Hilkiah gave the **b** to Shaphan.
34: 16 Shaphan brought the **b** to the king,
34: 18 “The priest Hilkiah has given me a **b.”**
34: 21 concerning the words of the **b** that has been found;
34: 21 in accordance with all that is written in this **b.”**
34: 24 all the curses that are written in the **b** that was read
34: 30 hearing all the words of the **b** of the covenant F
34: 31 of the covenant that were written in this **b.**
35: 12 as it is written in the **b** of Moses. C
35: 27 are written in the **B** of the Kings of Israel D
36: 8 in the **B** of the Kings of Israel and Judah; D
Ezr 6: 18 as it is written in the **b** of Moses. C
Ne 7: 5 the **b** of the genealogy of those who were the first
Ne 8: 1 scribe Ezra to bring the **b** of the law of Moses, B
8: 3 all the people were attentive to the **b** of the law. B
8: 5 Ezra opened the **b** in the sight of all the people,
8: 8 So they read from the **b,** from the law of God,
8: 18 he read from the **b** of the law of God. B
9: 3 in their place and read from the **b** of the law B
12: 23 the **B** of the Annals until the days of Johanan A
13: 1 from the **b** of Moses in the hearing of the people; C
Est 2: 23 the **b** of the annals in the presence of the king. A
6: 1 and he gave orders to bring the **b** of records,
Job 19: 23 O that they were inscribed in a **b!**
Ps 40: 7 in the scroll of the **b** it is written of me.
69: 28 Let them be blotted out of the **b** of the living;
139: 16 In your **b** were written all the days that were
Isa 30: 8 and inscribe it in a **b,**
34: 16 Seek and read from the **b** of the LORD:
Jer 25: 13 everything written in this **b,**
30: 2 in a **b** all the words that I have spoken to you.
Da 10: 21 I am to tell you what is inscribed in the **b** of truth.
12: 1 everyone who is found written in the **b.**
12: 4 the words secret and the **b** sealed until the time of
Na 1: 1 The **b** of the vision of Nahum of Elkosh.
Mal 3: 16 and a **b** of remembrance was written before him
Mk 12: 26 have you not read in the **b** of Moses, C
Lk 3: 4 in the **b** of the words of the prophet Isaiah,
20: 42 For David himself says in the **b** of Psalms,
Jn 20: 30 which are not written in this **b.**
Ac 1: 1 In the first **b,** Theophilus,
1: 20 “For it is written in the **b** of Psalms,
7: 42 as it is written in the **b** of the prophets:
Gal 3: 10 obey all the things written in the **b** of the law.” B
Php 4: 3 whose names are in the **b** of life. E
Heb 10: 7 O God’ (in the scroll of the **b** it is written of me).”
Rev 1: 11 a **b** what you see and send it to the seven churches,
3: 5 and I will not blot your name out of the **b** of life; E
13: 8 from the foundation of the world in the **b** of life E
17: 8 names have not been written in the **b** of life E
20: 12 Also another **b** was opened, the book of life.
20: 12 Also another book was opened, the **b** of life. E
20: 15 not found written in the **b** of life was thrown into E
21: 27 those who are written in the Lamb’s **b** of life. E
22: 7 the words of the prophecy of this **b.”**
22: 9 and with those who keep the words of this **b.**
22: 10 not seal up the words of the prophecy of this **b,**
22: 18 the words of the prophecy of this **b:**
22: 18 to that person the plagues described in this **b;**
22: 19 if anyone takes away from the words of the **b**
22: 19 which are described in this **b.**
Tob 1: 1 This **b** tells the story of Tobit son of Tobiel son
6: 13 death according to the decree of the **b** of Moses. C
7: 11 in accordance with the decree in the **b** of Moses, C
7: 12 the law and decree written in the **b** of Moses. C
AdE 6: 1 so he gave orders to his secretary to bring the **b**
9: 20 Mordecai recorded these things in a **b,**
Sir Pr: 1 with his **b** those who love learning might make
Pr: 2 Not only this **b,** but even the Law itself,
Pr: 3 and labor to the translation of this **b.**
Pr: 3 the **b** for those living abroad who wished
24: 23 the **b** of the covenant of the Most High God, F
50: 27 and knowledge I have written in this **b,**
Bar 1: 1 the words of the **b** that Baruch son of Neriah son
1: 3 the words of this **b** to Jeconiah son of Jehoiakim,
1: 3 and to all the people who came to hear the **b,**
4: 1 She is the **b** of the commandments of God,
1Mc 1: 57 Anyone found possessing the **b** of the covenant, F
3: 48 the **b** of the law to inquire into those matters B
2Mc 2: 23 we shall attempt to condense into a single **b.**
6: 12 Now I urge those who read this **b** not to
8: 23 the holy **b,** and gave the watchword, “The help
1Es 1: 11 to the Lord as it is written in the **b** of Moses; C
1: 33 These things are written in the **b** of the histories
1: 33 are recorded in the **b** of the kings of Israel and D
5: 49 the directions in the **b** of Moses the man of God. C
7: 6 according to what was written in the **b** of Moses. C
7: 9 in accordance with the **b** of Moses; C
9: 43 Then Ezra took up the **b** of the law in the sight B
2Es 1: 1 The **b** of the prophet Ezra son of Seraiah son
12: 37 write all these things that you have seen in a **b,**

BOOKS‡ (18) [BOOK]

Ecc 12: 12 Of making many **b** there is no end,
Da 7: 10 The court sat in judgment, and the **b** were opened.
9: 2 perceived in the **b** the number of years that,
Jn 21: 25 the world itself could not contain the **b** that would
Ac 19: 19 of those who practiced magic collected their **b**
19: 19 when the value of these **b** was calculated,
2Ti 4: 13 also the **b,** and above all the parchments.
Rev 20: 12 standing before the throne, and **b** were opened.
20: 12 according to their works, as recorded in the **b.**
Sir Pr: 1 and the Prophets and the other **b** of our ancestors,
Pr: 2 of the **b** differ not a little when read in the original.
1Mc 1: 56 The **b** of the law that they found they tore
12: 9 as encouragement the holy **b** that are in our hands,
2Mc 2: 13 that he founded a library and collected the **b** about
2: 14 In the same way Judas also collected all the **b**
2Es 6: 20 the **b** shall be opened before the face of
14: 44 during the forty days, ninety-four **b** were written.
14: 45 the twenty-four **b** that you wrote first,

BOOR (1)

Sir 21: 23 A **b** peers into the house from the door,

BOORISHLY See Index to Footnotes

BOOTH (7) [BOOTHS]

Isa 1: 8 And daughter Zion is left like a **b** in a vineyard,
La 2: 6 He has broken down his **b** like a garden,
Am 9: 11 On that day I will raise up the **b** of David
Jnh 4: 5 and made a **b** for himself there.
Mt 9: 9 he saw a man called Matthew sitting at the tax **b;**
Mk 2: 14 he saw Levi son of Alphaeus sitting at the tax **b,**
Lk 5: 27 a tax collector named Levi, sitting at the tax **b;**

BOOTHS‡ (28) [BOOTH]

A. FESTIVAL OF BOOTHS (16)

Ge 33: 17 and made **b** for his cattle;
Lev 23: 34 there shall be the festival of **b** to the LORD. A
23: 42 You shall live in **b** for seven days;
23: 42 all that are citizens in Israel shall live in **b,**
23: 43 in **b** when I brought them out of the land of Egypt:
Dt 16: 13 You shall keep the festival of **b** for seven days, A
16: 16 at the festival of weeks, and at the festival of **b.** A
31: 10 of remission, during the festival of **b,** A
2Sa 11: 11 “The ark and Israel and Judah remain in **b;**
1Ki 20: 12 now he had been drinking with the kings in the **b**—
20: 16 Ben-hadad was drinking himself drunk in the **b,**
2Ch 8: 13 the festival of weeks, and the festival of **b.** A
Ezr 3: 4 And they kept the festival of **b,** as prescribed, A
Ne 8: 14 that the people of Israel should live in **b** during
8: 15 and other leafy trees to make **b,** as it is written.”
8: 16 and made **b** for themselves,
8: 17 from the captivity made **b** and lived in them;
Job 27: 18 like **b** made by sentinels of the vineyard.
Zec 14: 16 the LORD of hosts, and to keep the festival of **b.** A
14: 18 that do not go up to keep the festival of **b.** A
14: 19 that do not go up to keep the festival of **b.** A
Jn 7: 2 Now the Jewish festival of **B** was near. A
1Mc 10: 21 one hundred sixtieth year, at the festival of **b,** A
2Mc 1: 9 And now see that you keep the festival of **b** in A
1: 18 also may celebrate the festival of **b** and A
10: 6 in the manner of the festival of **b,** A
10: 6 not long before, during the festival of **b,** A
1Es 5: 51 They kept the festival of **b,** A

BOOTS (1)

Isa 9: 5 For all the **b** of the tramping warriors and all

BOOTY (42)

Nu 14: 3 Our wives and our little ones will become **b;**
14: 31 your little ones, who you said would become **b,**
31: 9 their flocks, and all their goods as **b.**
31: 11 but they took all the spoil and all the **b,**
31: 12 the captives and the **b** and the spoil to Moses,
31: 26 an inventory of the **b** captured,
31: 27 Divide the **b** into two parts,
31: 32 The **b** remaining from the spoil that
Dt 1: 39 who you thought would become **b,** your children,
20: 14 You may, however, take as your **b** the women,
Jos 8: 2 and its livestock you may take as **b** for yourselves.
8: 27 and the spoil of that city Israel took as their **b,**
11: 14 and the livestock, the Israelites took for their **b;**
Jdg 8: 24 each of you give me an earring he has taken as **b.”**
8: 25 and each threw into it an earring he had taken as **b.**
1Ch 20: 2 He also brought out the **b** of the city,
26: 27 From **b** won in battles they dedicated gifts for
2Ch 14: 13 people of Judah carried away a great quantity of **b.**
15: 11 from the **b** that they had brought,
20: 25 and his people came to take the **b** from them,
20: 25 They spent three days taking the **b,**
24: 23 sent all the **b** they took to the king of Damascus.
25: 13 in them, and took much **b.**
28: 8 also took much **b** from them and brought the **b**
28: 14 and the **b** before the officials and all the assembly.
28: 15 and with the **b** they clothed all that were naked
Pr 1: 13 we shall fill our houses with **b.**
Jer 49: 32 Their camels shall become **b,**
Eze 7: 21 I will hand it over to strangers as **b,**
38: 13 to seize a great amount of **b?”**
Na 3: 1 City of bloodshed, utterly deceitful, full of **b**—
Hab 2: 7 Then you will be **b** for them.
Jdt 4: 12 to be carried off and their wives to be taken as **b,**
7: 26 the whole town as **b** to the army of Holofernes and
9: 4 You gave up their wives for **b** and their daughters
9: 4 and all their **b** to be divided
15: 7 and in the plain got a great amount of **b,**
16: 4 and seize my children as **b,**
LtJ 6: 58 and go off with this **b,**
1Mc 10: 87 to Jerusalem with a large amount of **b.**
2Mc 8: 20 and took a great amount of **b.**

BOOZ (KJV) See BOAZ

BOR-ASHAN (1)

1Sa 30: 30 in Hormah, in **B,** in Athach,

BORAZE (1)

AdE 1: 10 he told Haman, Bazan, Tharra, **B,** Zatholtha,

BORDER‡ (36) [BORDERING, BORDERLANDS, BORDERS]

Ge 49: 13 and his **b** shall be at Sidon.
Ex 16: 35 until they came to the **b** of the land of Canaan.
Nu 20: 23 on the **b** of the land of Edom,
21: 15 and lie along the **b** of Moab.”

Dt 3:14 as the **b** of the Geshurites and the Maacathites,
Jos 4:19 and they camped in Gilgal on the east **b** of Jericho.
13:23 **b** of the Reubenites was the Jordan and its banks.
18:16 the **b** of the mountain that overlooks the valley of
18:19 of the Jordan: this is the southern **b**.
19:46 Me-jarkon, and Rakkon at the **b** opposite Joppa.
Jdg 1:36 The **b** of the Amorites ran from the ascent
7:22 as far as the **b** of Abel-meholah, by Tabbath.
1Sa 6:12 of the Philistines went after them as far as the **b**
1Ki 4:21 even to the **b** of Egypt;
2Ki 14:25 the **b** of Israel from Lebo-hamath as far as the Sea
1Ch 4:10 "Oh that you would bless me and enlarge my **b**,
2Ch 9:26 and to the **b** of Egypt.
26:8 and his fame spread even to the **b** of Egypt,
Isa 19:19 and a pillar to the LORD at its **b**.
28:25 and barley in its proper place, and spelt as the **b?**
Eze 11:10 I will judge you at the **b** of Israel.
11:11 I will judge you at the **b** of Israel.
29:10 from Migdol to Syene, as far as the **b** of Ethiopia.
47:16 Sibraim (which lies between the **b** of Damascus and the **b** of Hamath),
47:16 which is on the **b** of Hauran.
47:17 which is north of the **b** of Damascus,
47:17 with the **b** of Hamath to the north.
48:1 Beginning at the northern **b**, on the Hethlon road,
48:1 far as Hazar-enon (which is on the **b** of Damascus,
48:21 of the holy portion to the east **b**,
48:21 the twenty-five thousand cubits to the west **b**,
Joel 3:6 removing them far from their own **b**.
Ob 1:7 they have driven you to the **b**;
Mic 5:6 if they come into our land or tread within our **b**.
Jdt 2:23 the Rassisites and the Ishmaelites on the **b** of

BORDERING (2) [BORDER]

Nu 21:11 in the wilderness **b** Moab toward the sunrise.
1Mc 11:34 the latter, with all the region **b** them,

BORDERLANDS (1) [BORDER, LAND]

Nu 24:17 it shall crush the **b** of Moab,

BORDERS‡ (38) [BORDER]

Ex 23:31 I will set your **b** from the Red Sea to the sea of
34:24 before you, and enlarge your **b**;
Jos 17:18 you shall clear it and possess it to its farthest **b**;
1Sa 27:1 of seeking me any longer within the **b** of Israel,
1Ki 7:28 of the stands: they had **b**;
7:28 the **b** were within the frames;
7:29 on the **b** that were set in the frames were lions,
7:31 its **b** were four-sided, not round.
7:32 The four wheels were underneath the **b**;
7:35 its stays and its **b** were of one piece with it.
7:36 of its stays and on its **b** he carved cherubim,
1Ch 6:54 according to their settlements within their **b**:
7:29 also along the **b** of the Manassites,
Ps 147:14 He grants peace within your **b**;
Isa 26:15 you have enlarged all the **b** of the land.
60:18 devastation or destruction within your **b**;
Eze 27:4 Your **b** are in the heart of the seas;
Zec 9:2 which **b** on it, Tyre and Sidon,
Mal 1:5 "Great is the LORD beyond the **b** of Israel!"
Jdt 1:5 in the great plain that is on the **b** of Ragau.
1:10 all who lived in Egypt as far as the **b** of Ethiopia.
2:25 Then he came to the southern **b** of Japheth,
14:4 the **b** of Israel will pursue them and cut them
15:5 even beyond Damascus and its **b**.
Sir 47:13 because God made all his **b** tranquil,
1Mc 2:46 that they found within the **b** of Israel.
3:32 the king's affairs from the river Euphrates to the **b**
5:60 and were pursued to the **b** of Judea;
6:25 they have also attacked all the lands on their **b**.
11:59 from the Ladder of Tyre to the **b** of Egypt.
14:6 He extended the **b** of his nation,
14:33 and Beth-zur on the **b** of Judea,
14:34 and Gazara, which is on the **b** of Azotus,
15:30 the places that you have conquered outside the **b**
2Mc 9:25 how the princes along the **b** and the neighbors
2Es 9:8 will see my salvation in my land and within my **b**,
12:34 those who have been saved throughout my **b**,
13:48 who are found within my holy **b**, shall be saved.

BORE‡ (152) [BEAR]

Ge 4:1 and she conceived and **b** Cain, saying,
4:2 Next she **b** his brother Abel.
4:17 and she conceived and **b** Enoch;
4:20 Adah **b** Jabal; he was the ancestor of those
4:22 Zillah **b** Tubal-cain, who made all kinds of bronze
4:25 and she **b** a son and named him Seth, for she said,
6:4 the daughters of humans, who **b** children to them.
7:17 and the waters increased, and **b** up the ark,
16:1 Now Sarai, Abram's wife, **b** him no children.
16:15 Hagar **b** Abram a son;
16:15 Abram named his son, whom Hagar **b**, Ishmael.
16:16 when Hagar **b** him Ishmael.
19:37 The firstborn **b** a son, and named him Moab;
19:38 younger also **b** a son and named him Ben-ammi;
20:17 and female slaves so that they **b** children.
21:2 Sarah conceived and **b** Abraham a son
21:3 the name Isaac to his son whom Sarah **b** him.
22:23 These eight Milcah **b** to Nahor,
22:24 whose name was Reumah, **b** Tebah, Gaham,
24:24 of Bethuel son of Milcah, whom she **b** to Nahor."
24:36 And Sarah my master's wife **b** a son to my master
24:47 Nahor's son, whom Milcah **b** to him.'
25:2 She **b** him Zimran, Jokshan, Medan, Midian,
Ge 25:12 Sarah's slave-girl, **b** to Abraham.
25:26 Isaac was sixty years old when she **b** them.
29:32 Leah conceived and **b** a son,
29:33 She conceived again and **b** a son, and said,
29:34 Again she conceived and **b** a son, and said,
29:35 She conceived again and **b** a son, and said,
30:1 When Rachel saw that she **b** Jacob no children,
30:5 And Bilhah conceived and **b** Jacob a son.
30:7 Rachel's maid Bilhah conceived again and **b** Jacob
30:10 Then Leah's maid Zilpah **b** Jacob a son.
30:12 Leah's maid Zilpah **b** Jacob a second son.
30:17 and she conceived and **b** Jacob a fifth son.
30:19 Leah conceived again, and she **b** Jacob a sixth son.
30:21 Afterwards she **b** a daughter,
30:23 She conceived and **b** a son, and said,
31:8 then all the flock **b** speckled;
31:8 then all the flock **b** striped.
31:39 I **b** the loss of it myself;
36:4 Adah **b** Eliphaz to Esau; Basemath **b** Reuel;
36:5 and Oholibamah **b** Jeush, Jalam,
36:12 she **b** Amalek to Eliphaz.)
36:14 she **b** to Esau Jeush, Jalam, and Korah.
38:3 She conceived and **b** a son; and he named him Er.
38:4 and **b** a son whom she named Onan.
38:5 Yet again she **b** a son, and she named him Shelah.
38:5 She was in Chezib when she **b** him.
41:50 of Potiphera, priest of On, **b** to him.
44:27 'You know that my wife **b** me two sons;
46:15 whom she **b** to Jacob in Paddan-aram,
46:18 and these she **b** to Jacob—sixteen persons).
46:20 of Potiphera, priest of On, **b** to him.
46:25 and these she **b** to Jacob—seven persons in all).
Ex 2:2 The woman conceived and **b** a son;
2:22 She **b** a son, and he named him Gershom;
6:20 and she **b** him Aaron and Moses,
6:23 and she **b** him Nadab, Abihu, Eleazar,
6:25 of the daughters of Putiel, and she **b** him Phinehas.
19:4 and how I **b** you on eagles' wings and brought you
Nu 17:8 produced blossoms, and **b** ripe almonds.
26:59 in Egypt; and she **b** to Amram:
Dt 9:19 that the anger that the LORD **b** against you was
32:18 You were unmindful of the Rock that **b** you;
Jos 3:15 when those who **b** the ark had come to the Jordan,
3:17 the priests who **b** the ark of the covenant of
4:10 The priests who **b** the ark remained standing in
Jdg 4:24 Then the hand of the Israelites **b** harder and harder
8:31 His concubine who was in Shechem also **b** him
11:2 Gilead's wife also **b** him sons;
13:24 The woman **b** a son, and named him Samson.
Ru 4:12 whom Tamar **b** to Judah."
4:13 the LORD made her conceive, and she **b** a son.
1Sa 1:20 In due time Hannah conceived and **b** a son.
2:21 she conceived and **b** three sons and two daughters.
2Sa 6:13 and when those who **b** the ark of
11:27 and she became his wife, and **b** him a son.
12:15 The LORD struck the child that Uriah's wife **b**
12:24 and she **b** a son, and he named him Solomon.
21:8 whom she **b** to Saul, Armoni and Mephibosheth;
21:8 of Saul, whom she **b** to Adriel son of Barzillai
2Ki 4:17 The woman conceived and **b** a son at that season,
1Ch 1:32 she **b** Zimran, Jokshan, Medan, Midian, Ishbak,
2:3 these three the Canaanite woman Bath-shua **b**
2:4 His daughter-in-law Tamar also **b** him Perez
2:17 Abigail **b** Amasa, and the father
2:19 Caleb married Ephrath, who **b** him Hur.
2:21 when he was sixty years old; and she **b** him Segub;
2:24 Abijah wife of Hezron **b** him Ashhur,
2:29 and she **b** him Ahban and Molid.
2:35 to his slave Jarha; and she **b** him Attai.
2:46 Ephah also, Caleb's concubine, **b** Haran, Moza,
2:48 Caleb's concubine, **b** Sheber and Tirhanah.
2:49 She also **b** Shaaph father of Madmannah,
4:6 Naarah **b** him Ahuzzam, Hepher, Temeni,
4:9 saying, "Because I **b** him in pain."
4:17 and she conceived and **b** Miriam, Shammai,
4:18 And his Judean wife **b** Jered father of Gedor,
7:14 Asriel, whom his Aramean concubine **b**;
7:14 she **b** Machir the father of Gilead.
7:16 Maacah the wife of Machir **b** a son,
7:18 And his sister Hammolecheth **b** Ishhod, Abiezer,
7:23 and she conceived and **b** a son;
2Ch 11:19 She **b** him sons: Jeush, Shemariah, and Zaham.
11:20 who **b** him Abijah, Attai, Ziza, and Shelomith.
Ps 22:10 and since my mother **b** me you have been my God.
68:11 great is the company of those who **b** the tidings:
Pr 17:25 to their father and bitterness to her who **b** them.
23:25 let her who **b** you rejoice.
SS 6:9 flawless to her that **b** her.
8:2 and into the chamber of the one who **b** me.
8:5 there she who **b** you was in labor.
Isa 8:3 and she conceived and **b** a son.
22:6 Elam **b** the quiver with chariots and cavalry,
51:2 to Abraham your father and to Sarah who **b** you;
53:12 yet he **b** the sin of many, and made intercession
Jer 15:9 She who **b** seven has languished;
15:10 Woe is me, my mother, that you ever **b** me,
20:14 day when my mother **b** me, let it not be blessed!
22:26 and the mother who **b** you into another country,
31:19 I was ashamed, and I was dismayed because I **b**
50:12 and she who **b** you shall be disgraced.
La 2:22 whom I **b** and reared my enemy has
Eze 3:14 The spirit lifted me up and **b** me away;
23:4 and they **b** sons and daughters.
Hos 1:3 and she conceived and **b** him a son.
1:6 She conceived again and **b** a daughter.
1:8 she conceived and **b** a son.
Zec 13:3 their fathers and mothers who **b** them will say
Zec 13:3 and their mothers who **b** them shall pierce them
Mt 8:17 "He took our infirmities and **b** our diseases."
13:26 So when the plants came up and **b** grain,
Lk 1:57 for Elizabeth to give birth, and she **b** a son.
11:27 "Blessed is the womb that **b** you and the breasts
23:29 and the wombs that never **b**,
1Pe 2:24 He himself **b** our sins in his body on the cross,
Sir 46:19 Samuel **b** witness before the Lord
2Mc 3:36 He **b** testimony to all concerning the deeds of
7:6 that **b** witness against the people to their faces,
7:20 she **b** it with good courage because of her hope in
12:30 the Jews who lived there **b** witness to the goodwill
12:35 when one of the Thracian cavalry **b** down on him
2Es 2:2 The mother who **b** them says to them, 'Go,
5:52 not like those whom you **b** before,
10:12 which I brought forth in pain and **b** in sorrow;
10:46 then it was that the barren woman **b** a son.
4Mc 6:9 But he **b** the pains and scorned the punishment
10:2 and the same mother **b** me,
14:9 but also **b** the sufferings patiently,
14:12 for the mother of the seven young men **b** up under

BORITH (1)

2Es 1:2 of Arna son of Uzzi son of **B** son of Abishua son

BORN‡ (175) [BEAR]

Ge 4:18 To Enoch was **b** Irad;
4:26 To Seth also a son was **b**,
6:1 and daughters were **b** to them,
10:1 children were **b** to them after the flood.
10:21 the elder brother of Japheth, children were **b**.
10:25 To Eber were **b** two sons:
14:14 **b** in his house, three hundred eighteen of them,
15:3 and so a slave **b** in my house is to be my heir."
17:12 the slave **b** in your house and the one bought
17:13 Both the slave **b** in your house and the one bought
17:17 a child be **b** to a man who is a hundred years old?
17:23 and all the slaves **b** in his house or bought
17:27 slaves **b** in the house and those bought with money
21:5 a hundred years old when his son Isaac was **b**
24:15 who was **b** to Bethuel son of Milcah,
25:23 and two peoples **b** of you shall be divided;
35:26 These were the sons of Jacob who were **b** to him
36:5 of Esau who were **b** to him in the land of Canaan.
36:18 these are the clans **b** of Esau's wife Oholibamah,
46:20 the land of Egypt were **b** Manasseh and Ephraim,
46:22 who were **b** to Jacob—fourteen persons in all).
46:27 children of Joseph, who were **b** to him in Egypt,
48:5 who were **b** to you in the land of Egypt
48:6 offspring **b** to you after them, they shall be yours.
50:23 of Manasseh were also **b** on Joseph's knees.
Ex 1:5 total number of people **b** to Jacob was seventy.
1:22 that is **b** to the Hebrews you shall throw into
Lev 18:9 whether **b** at home or **b** abroad.
22:11 those that are **b** in his house may eat of his food.
22:27 When an ox or a sheep or a goat is **b**,
25:45 who have been **b** in your land;
Nu 26:59 who was **b** to Levi in Egypt;
26:60 To Aaron were **b** Nadab, Abihu, Eleazar,
Dt 15:19 Every firstling male **b** of your herd
23:2 Those **b** of an illicit union shall not be admitted to
23:8 The children of the third generation that are **b**
Jos 5:5 the people **b** on the journey through the wilderness
Jdg 13:8 to do concerning the boy who will be **b**."
18:29 after their ancestor Dan, who was **b** to Israel;
Ru 4:17 saying, "A son has been **b** to Naomi."
2Sa 3:2 Sons were **b** to David at Hebron:
3:5 These were **b** to David in Hebron.
5:13 and more sons and daughters were **b** to David.
5:14 These are the names of those who were **b** to him
12:14 the child that is **b** to you shall die."
14:27 There were **b** to Absalom three sons,
1Ki 1:6 and he was **b** next after Absalom.
8:19 be **b** to you shall build the house for my name.'
13:2 'A son shall be **b** to the house of David,
2Ki 20:18 Some of your own sons who are **b** to you shall
1Ch 1:19 To Eber were **b** two sons:
2:9 The sons of Hezron, who were **b** to him:
3:1 the sons of David who were **b** to him in Hebron:
3:4 six were **b** to him in Hebron,
3:5 These were **b** to him in Jerusalem:
7:21 Now the people of Gath, who were **b** in the land,
22:9 See, a son shall be **b** to you;
26:6 Shemaiah sons were **b** who exercised authority
2Ch 6:9 be **b** to you shall build the house for my name.'
Job 1:2 There were **b** to him seven sons
3:3 "Let the day perish in which I was **b**,
5:7 but human beings are **b** to trouble just
11:12 when a wild ass is **b** human.
14:1 **b** of woman, few of days and full of trouble,
15:14 Or those **b** of woman, that they can be righteous?
25:4 How can one **b** of woman be pure?
38:21 Surely you know, for you were **b** then,
Ps 51:5 I was **b** guilty, a sinner
87:4 "This one was **b** there," they say.
87:5 "This one and that one were **b** in it";
87:6 as he registers the peoples, "This one was **b** there."
Pr 17:17 and kinsfolk are **b** to share adversity.
Ecc 2:7 and had slaves who were **b** in my house;
3:2 a time to be **b**, and a time to die;
4:14 even though **b** poor in the kingdom.
Isa 9:6 For a child has been **b** for us, a son given to us;
26:18 and no one is **b** to inhabit the world.
39:7 Some of your own sons who are **b** to you shall
49:1 The LORD called me before I was **b**,

Isa 49:20 The children **b** in the time
66: 8 Shall a land be **b** in one day?
Jer 1: 5 and before you were **b** I consecrated you;
16: 3 the sons and daughters who are **b** in this place,
20:14 Cursed be the day on which I was **b!**
20:15 saying, "A child is **b** to you, a son,"
22:26 where you were not **b,** and there you shall die.
Eze 16: 4 the day you were **b** your navel cord was not cut,
16: 5 for you were abhorred on the day you were **b.**
Hos 2: 3 and expose her as in the day she was **b,**
Mt 1:16 of whom Jesus was **b,** who is called the Messiah.
2: 1 after Jesus was **b** in Bethlehem of Judea,
2: 2 is the child who has been **b** king of the Jews?
2: 4 of them where the Messiah was to be **b.**
11:11 Truly I tell you, among those **b**
26:24 for that one not to have been **b."**
Mk 14:21 for that one not to have been **b."**
Lk 1:35 therefore the child to be **b** will be holy;
2:11 to you is **b** this day in the city of David a Savior,
7:28 I tell you, among those **b** of women
Jn 1:13 who were **b,** not of blood or of the will of the flesh
3: 3 the kingdom of God without being **b** from above."
3: 4 "How can anyone be **b** after having grown old?
3: 4 a second time into the mother's womb and be **b?"**
3: 5 the kingdom of God without being **b** of water
3: 6 What is **b** of the flesh is flesh,
3: 6 and what is **b** of the Spirit is spirit.
3: 7 'You must be **b** from above.'
3: 8 So it is with everyone who is **b** of the Spirit."
9: 2 this man or his parents, that he was **b** blind?"
9: 3 he was **b** blind so that God's works might
9:19 "Is this your son, who you say was **b** blind?
9:20 and that he was **b** blind;
9:32 that anyone opened the eyes of a person **b** blind.
9:34 They answered him, "You were **b** entirely in sins,
16:21 But when her child is **b,**
18:37 For this I was **b,** and for this I came into
Ac 7:20 At this time Moses was **b,**
22: 3 **b** in Tarsus in Cilicia, but brought up in this city at
22:28 Paul said, "But I was **b** a citizen."
Ro 9:11 before they had been **b** or had done anything good
1Co 15: 8 Last of all, as to one untimely **b,**
Gal 1:15 who had set me apart before I was **b** and called me
4: 4 **b** of a woman, **b** under the law,
4:23 the child of the slave, was **b** according to the flesh;
4:23 was **b** through the promise.
4:29 as at that time the child who was **b** according to
4:29 the child who was **b** according to the Spirit,
Php 2: 7 being **b** in human likeness.
3: 5 of the tribe of Benjamin, a Hebrew **b** of Hebrews;
Heb 11:12 and this one as good as dead, descendants were **b,**
Jas 3:13 that your works are done with gentleness **b**
1Pe 1:23 You have been **b** anew, not of perishable but
2Pe 2:12 **b** to be caught and killed.
1Jn 2:29 that everyone who does right has been **b** of him.
3: 9 Those who have been **b** of God do not sin,
3: 9 they cannot sin, because they have been **b** of God.
4: 7 everyone who loves is **b** of God and knows God.
5: 1 that Jesus is the Christ has been **b** of God,
5: 4 for whatever is **b** of God conquers the world.
5:18 We know that those who are **b** of God do not sin,
5:18 but the one who was **b** of God protects them,
Rev 12: 4 that he might devour her child as soon as it was **b.**
Jdt 12:20 in any one day since he was **b.**
AdE 14: 5 Ever since I was **b** I have heard in the tribe
Wis 2: 2 For we were **b** by mere chance,
4: 6 For children **b** of unlawful unions are witnesses
5:13 So we also, as soon as we were **b,** ceased to be,
7: 3 when I was **b,** I began to breathe the common air,
Sir 7:28 Remember that it was of your parents you were **b;**
10:18 or violent anger for those **b** of women.
14:18 one dies and another is **b.**
23:14 then you will wish that you had never been **b,**
44: 9 as though they had never been **b,**
49:15 Nor was anyone ever **b** like Joseph;
Bar 3:26 The giants were **b** there, who were famous of old,
1Mc 2: 7 Why was I **b** to see this, the ruin of my people,
1Es 3: 1 all that were **b** in his house,
2Es 4: 6 "Who of those that have been **b** can do that,
5:35 Why then was I **b?**
5:53 'Those **b** in the strength of youth are different
from those **b** during the time of old age,
5:55 as **b** of a creation that already is aging and passing
6: 8 because from him were **b** Jacob and Esau,
7:63 if the dust itself had not been **b,**
7:65 let all who have been **b** lament,
7:68 all who have been **b** are entangled in iniquities,
7:*127* [57] contest that all who are **b** on earth shall wage:
8:35 among those who have been **b** who has
9:22 So let the multitude perish that has been **b** in vain,
10:10 From the beginning all have been **b** of her,
14:20 but who will warn those who will be **b** hereafter?
4Mc 11:15 Since to this end we were **b** and bred,
13:21 When they were **b** after an equal time of gestation,

BORNE‡ (33) [BEAR]

Ge 21: 7 Yet I have **b** him a son in his old age."
21: 9 whom she had **b** to Abraham,
22:20 "Milcah also has **b** children,
29:34 because I have **b** him three sons";
30:20 because I have **b** him six sons";
30:25 When Rachel had **b** Joseph, Jacob said to Laban,
31:43 or about their children whom they have **b?**
34: 1 whom she had **b** to Jacob,
Dt 21:15 if both the loved and the disliked have **b** him sons,
Jdg 13: 2 His wife was barren, having **b** no children.
Jdg 13: 3 "Although you are barren, having **b** no children,
Ru 4:15 who is more to you than seven sons, has **b** him."
1Sa 2: 5 The barren has **b** seven, but she who has many
4:20 "Do not be afraid, for you have **b** a son."
6: 7 a new cart and two milch cows that have never **b**
1Ki 3:21 clearly it was not the son I had **b."**
Ps 69: 7 It is for your sake that I have **b** reproach,
Isa 46: 3 who have been **b** by me from your birth,
49:21 you will say in your heart, "Who has **b** me these?
51:18 to guide her among all the children she has **b;**
53: 4 he has **b** our infirmities and carried our diseases;
La 2:20 the children they have **b?**
Eze 16:20 whom you had **b** to me,
23:37 up to them for food the children whom they had **b**
Hos 5: 7 for they have **b** illegitimate children.
Mt 1:25 with her until she had **b** a son;
20:12 and you have made them equal to us who have **b**
1Co 15:49 Just as we have **b** the image of the man of dust,
Tob 3: 8 and have not **b** the name of a single one of them.
Sir 28:19 who has not **b** its yoke, and has not been bound
Man 1: 5 for your glorious splendor cannot be **b,** and
2Es 3:33 not appeared and their labor has **b** no fruit.
5:52 'Why are those whom you have **b** recently not

BORROW (6) [BORROWED, BORROWER, BORROWS]

Dt 15: 6 you will lend to many nations, but you will not **b;**
28:12 You will lend to many nations, but you will not **b.**
2Ki 4: 3 "Go outside, **b** vessels from all your neighbors,
Ne 5: 4 to **b** money on our fields and vineyards to pay
Ps 37:21 The wicked **b,** and do not pay back,
Mt 5:42 do not refuse anyone who wants to **b** from you.

BORROWED (5) [BORROW]

2Ki 6: 5 he cried out, "Alas, master! It was **b."**
Jer 15:10 I have not lent, nor have I **b,**
Wis 15: 8 the time comes to return the souls that were **b.**
15:16 and one whose spirit is **b** formed them;
Sir 18:33 not become a beggar by feasting with **b** money,

BORROWER (3) [BORROW]

Pr 22: 7 and the **b** is the slave of the lender.
Isa 24: 2 as with the lender, so with the **b;**
Sir 29: 6 the **b** has robbed the other of his money,

BORROWS (1) [BORROW]

Ex 22:14 When someone **b** an animal from another

BOSCATH (KJV) See BOZKATH

BOSOM‡ (25) [BOSOMS]

Nu 11:12 that you should say to me, 'Carry them in your **b,**
Ru 4:16 Then Naomi took the child and laid him in her **b,**
2Sa 12: 3 and lie in his **b,** and it was like a daughter to him.
12: 8 and your master's wives into your **b,**
1Ki 1: 2 let her lie in your **b,**
17:19 He took him from her **b,**
Job 23:12 I have treasured in my **b** the words of his mouth.
31:33 by hiding my iniquity in my **b,**
Ps 35:13 I prayed with head bowed on my **b,**
41: 9 Even my **b** friend in whom I trusted,
74:11 why do you keep your hand in your **b?**
79:12 Return sevenfold into the **b** of our neighbors
89:50 how I bear in my **b** the insults of the peoples,
Pr 5:20 by another woman and embrace the **b** of
6:27 be carried in the **b** without burning one's clothes?
21:14 and a concealed bribe in the **b,** strong wrath.
Ecc 7: 9 for anger lodges in the **b** of fools.
Isa 40:11 and carry them in his **b,** and gently lead the
49:22 and they shall bring your sons in their **b,**
66:11 with delight from her glorious **b.**
La 2:12 as their life is poured out on their mothers' **b.**
Eze 23: 8 and fondled her virgin **b** and poured out their lust
23:21 when the Egyptians fondled your **b**
Sir 9: 1 Do not be jealous of the wife of your **b,**
2Es 15:21 so I will do, and will repay into their **b.**

BOSOMS (1) [BOSOM]

Eze 23: 3 and their virgin **b** were fondled.

BOSOR (3) [BEOR]

2Pe 2:15 following the road of Balaam son of **B,**
1Mc 5:26 in Bozrah and **B,** in Alema and Chaspho, Maked
5:36 Maked, and **B,** and the other towns of Gilead.

BOTH‡ (327)

Ge 2:25 And the man and his wife were **b** naked,
3: 7 Then the eyes of **b** were opened,
9:23 laid it on **b** their shoulders,
13: 6 land could not support **b** of them living together;
17:13 **B** the slave born in your house and the one bought
19: 4 **b** young and old, all the people to the last man,
19:11 **b** small and great, so that they were unable to find
19:36 Thus **b** the daughters of Lot became pregnant
21:31 because there **b** of them swore an oath.
27:45 Why should I lose **b** of you in one day?"
34:30 I shall be destroyed, **b** I and my household."
40: 5 One night they **b** dreamed—
44:16 here we are then, my lord's slaves, **b** we and also
46:34 **b** we and our ancestors'—
47:19 Shall we die before your eyes, **b** we and our land?
Ge 48:13 Joseph took them **b,** Ephraim in his right hand
50: 9 **B** chariots and charioteers went up with him.
Ex 8:18 There were gnats on **b** humans and animals.
9:25 all the land of Egypt, **b** human and animal;
12:12 **b** human beings and animals;
12:31 go away from my people, **b** you and the Israelites!
12:38 and livestock in great numbers, **b** flocks and herds.
18:18 **b** you and these people with you.
22: 9 the case of **b** parties shall come before God;
26:24 it shall be the same with **b** of them;
32:15 tablets that were written on **b** sides,
35:22 So they came, **b** men and women;
35:34 **b** him and Oholiab son of Ahisamach,
Lev 15:18 **b** of them shall bathe in water,
16:21 Then Aaron shall lay **b** his hands on the head of
20:10 **b** the adulterer and the adulteress shall be put
20:11 **b** of them shall be put to death;
20:12 **b** of them shall be put to death;
20:13 **b** of them have committed an abomination;
20:14 they shall be burned to death, **b** he and they,
20:18 **b** of them shall be cut off from their people.
27:10 **b** that one and its substitute shall be holy.
27:33 for it, then **b** it and the substitute shall be holy
Nu 3:13 **b** human and animal; they shall be mine.
5: 3 you shall put out **b** male and female,
7:13 **b** of them full of choice flour mixed with oil for
7:19 **b** of them full of choice flour mixed with oil for
7:25 **b** of them full of choice flour mixed with oil for
7:31 **b** of them full of choice flour mixed with oil for
7:37 **b** of them full of choice flour mixed with oil for
7:43 **b** of them full of choice flour mixed with oil for
7:49 **b** of them full of choice flour mixed with oil for
7:55 **b** of them full of choice flour mixed with oil for
7:61 **b** of them full of choice flour mixed with oil for
7:67 **b** of them full of choice flour mixed with oil for
7:73 **b** of them full of choice flour mixed with oil for
7:79 **b** of them full of choice flour mixed with oil for
8:17 the firstborn among the Israelites are mine, **b**
9:14 you shall have one statute for **b** the resident alien
10: 3 When **b** are blown, the whole congregation shall
12: 5 Aaron and Miriam; and they **b** came forward.
15:15 be for **b** you and the resident alien a single statute,
15:29 For **b** the native among the Israelites and
18: 3 otherwise **b** they and you will die.
27:21 **b** he and all the Israelites with him,
31:11 the spoil and all the booty, **b** people and animals.
31:26 an inventory of the booty captured, **b** human
31:47 **b** of persons and of animals,
Dt 12:27 **b** the meat and the blood, on the altar of
19:17 then **b** parties to the dispute shall appear before
21:15 **b** the loved and the disliked have borne him sons,
22: 9 **b** the crop that you have sown and the yield of
22:22 with the wife of another man, **b** of them shall die,
22:24 you shall bring **b** of them to the gate of that town
23:18 **b** of these are abhorrent to the LORD your God.
28: 4 **b** the increase of your cattle and the issue
28:59 then the LORD will overwhelm **b** you
29:11 **b** those who cut your wood
32:51 because **b** of you broke faith with me among
Jos 6:21 **b** men and women, young and old, oxen, sheep,
8:25 total of those who fell that day, **b** men and women,
17:16 **b** those in Beth-shean and its villages and those in
Ru 1: 5 **b** Mahlon and Chilion also died,
1Sa 2:26 the boy Samuel continued to grow **b** in stature and
2:34 **b** of them shall die on the same day.
3:11 about to do something in Israel that will make **b**
5: 4 of Dagon and **b** his hands were lying cut off upon
5: 6 **b** in Ashdod and in its territory.
5: 9 he struck the inhabitants of the city, **b** young
6:18 **b** fortified cities and unwalled villages.
9:26 and **b** he and Samuel went out into the street.
12:14 and if **b** you and the king who reigns
12:25 you shall be swept away, **b** you and your king."
14:11 So **b** of them showed themselves to the garrison of
15: 3 do not spare them, but kill **b** man and woman,
17:36 Your servant has killed **b** lions and bears;
20:11 So they **b** went out into the field.
20:42 **b** of us have sworn in the name of the LORD,
25:16 they were a wall to us **b** by night and by day,
25:43 **b** of them became his wives.
30: 2 the women and all who were in it, **b** small
2Sa 6:19 the whole multitude of Israel, **b** men and women,
9:13 Now he was lame in **b** his feet.
10: 9 that the battle was set against him **b** in front and in
14:16 the man who would cut **b** me and my son off from
15:25 and let me see **b** it and the place where it stays.
16:23 **b** by David and by Absalom.
17:18 so **b** of them went away quickly,
19:14 "Return, **b** you and all your servants."
1Ki 3:13 **b** riches and honor all your life;
6: 5 **b** the nave and the inner sanctuary;
6:25 **b** cherubim had the same measure and
7:29 **b** above and below the lions and oxen,
14:10 **b** bond and free in Israel,
16: 7 **b** because of all the evil that he did in the sight of
2Ki 2: 7 as they **b** were standing by the Jordan.
23: 2 the prophets, and all the people, **b** small and great;
1Ch 7:24 who built **b** Lower and Upper Beth-horon,
12: 3 then Joash, **b** sons of Shemaah of Gibeah;
19:10 that the line of battle was set against him **b** in front
24: 5 of God among **b** the sons of Eleazar and the sons
2Ch 26:10 **b** in the Shephelah and in the plain,
32:26 **b** he and the inhabitants of Jerusalem,
34:30 all the people **b** great and small;
Ezr 6:20 For **b** the priests and the Levites had purified
Ne 1: 6 **B** I and my family have sinned.
8: 2 **b** men and women and all who could hear

Ne 12:40 So **b** companies of those who gave thanks stood in
Est 1: 5 for all the people present in the citadel of Susa, **b**
2:23 **b** the men were hanged on the gallows.
9:20 the provinces of King Ahasuerus, **b** near and far,
Job 9:22 I say, he destroys **b** the blameless and the wicked.
9:33 who might lay his hand on us **b.**
Ps 4: 8 I will **b** lie down and sleep in peace;
49: 2 **b** low and high, rich and poor together.
76: 6 O God of Jacob, **b** rider and horse lay stunned.
104:25 living things **b** small and great.
106: 6 **B** we and our ancestors have sinned;
115:13 the LORD, **b** small and great.
115:14 the LORD give you increase, **b** you
135: 8 **b** human beings and animals;
Pr 17:15 and one who condemns the righteous are **b** alike
20:10 Diverse weights and diverse measures are **b** alike
20:12 the LORD has made them **b.**
24:22 and who knows the ruin that **b** can bring?
27: 3 but a fool's provocation is heavier than **b.**
29:13 the LORD gives light to the eyes of **b.**
Ecc 2: 8 I got singers, **b** men and women,
4: 3 but better than **b** is the one who has not yet been,
7:18 for the one who fears God shall succeed with **b.**
11: 6 this or that, or whether **b** alike will be good.
Isa 8:14 for **b** houses of Israel he will become
10:18 and his fruitful land the LORD will destroy, **b**
20: 4 **b** the young and the old, naked and barefoot,
47: 9 **b** these things shall come upon you in a moment,
Jer 6:11 **b** husband and wife shall be taken,
9:10 **b** the birds of the air and the animals have fled
10: 8 They are **b** stupid and foolish;
14:18 For **b** prophet and priest ply their trade throughout
16: 6 **B** great and small shall die in this land;
21: 6 **b** human beings and animals;
23:11 **B** prophet and priest are ungodly;
32:14 **b** this sealed deed of purchase and this open deed,
46:12 against warrior; **b** have fallen together.
50: 3 **b** human beings and animals shall flee away.
51:12 the LORD has **b** planned and done what he spoke
52:19 **b** those of gold and those of silver.
Eze 15: 4 the fire has consumed **b** ends of it and the middle
16:61 **b** your elder and your younger,
21: 3 and will cut off from you **b** righteous and wicked.
21: 4 I will cut off from you **b** righteous and wicked,
21:19 **b** of them shall issue from the same land.
22:12 you take **b** advance interest and accrued interest,
23:13 they **b** took the same way.
30:22 **b** the strong arm and the one that was broken;
32:20 carry away **b** it and its hordes.
45: 4 be **b** a place for their houses and a holy place for
45: 7 And to the prince shall belong the land on **b** sides
47:12 On the banks, on **b** sides of the river,
48:21 What remains on **b** sides of the holy portion and of
Da 2: 5 not tell me **b** the dream and its interpretation,
8: 3 **B** horns were long, but one was longer than
9:24 to seal **b** vision and prophet,
Zec 5: 4 and it shall abide in that house and consume it, **b**
Mal 2:15 **B** flesh and spirit are his.
Mt 9:17 but new wine is put into fresh wineskins, and so **b**
10:28 rather fear him who can destroy **b** soul and body
13:30 Let **b** of them grow together until the harvest;
15:14 **b** will fall into a pit."
22:10 the streets and gathered all whom they found, **b**
Lk 1: 6 **B** of them were righteous before God,
1: 7 and **b** were getting on in years.
5: 7 And they came and filled **b** boats,
6:39 Will not **b** fall into a pit?
7:42 he canceled the debts for **b** of them.
14: 9 the host who invited **b** of you may come and say
22:66 **b** chief priests and scribes, gathered together,
Jn 2:15 **b** the sheep and the cattle.
11:48 and destroy **b** our holy place and our nation."
15:24 they have seen and hated **b** me and my Father.
Ac 2:10 and visitors from Rome, **b** Jews and proselytes,
2:18 Even upon my slaves, **b** men and women,
2:29 to you confidently of our ancestor David that he **b**
2:33 he has poured out this that you **b** see and hear.
2:36 with certainty that God has made him **b** Lord
4:27 For in this city, in fact, **b** Herod and Pontius Pilate,
5:14 great numbers of **b** men and women,
7:35 and whom God now sent as **b** ruler and liberator
8: 3 dragging off **b** men and women,
8:12 they were baptized, **b** men and women.
8:38 He commanded the chariot to stop, and **b** of them,
10:39 We are witnesses to all that he did **b** in Judea and
13:46 Then **b** Paul and Barnabas spoke out boldly,
14: 1 and spoke in such a way that a great number of **b**
14: 5 an attempt was made by **b** Gentiles and Jews,
15: 3 as they passed through **b** Phoenicia and Samaria,
15:23 "The brothers, **b** the apostles and the elders,
19:10 **b** Jews and Greeks, heard the word of the Lord.
19:17 **b** Jews and Greeks, everyone was awestruck;
20:21 to **b** Jews and Greeks about repentance
22: 4 to the point of death by binding **b** men and women
24:15 that there will be a resurrection of **b** the righteous
25:24 **b** in Jerusalem and here, shouting that he ought
26:22 and so I stand here, testifying to **b** small and great,
26:23 he would proclaim light **b** to our people and to
28:23 of God and trying to convince them about Jesus **b**
Ro 1:12 be mutually encouraged by each other's faith, **b**
1:14 I am a debtor **b** to Greeks and to barbarians,
1:14 **b** to the wise and to the foolish
3: 9 **b** Jews and Greeks, are under the power of sin,
14: 9 that he might be Lord of **b** the dead and the living.
1Co 1: 2 on the name of our Lord Jesus Christ, **b** their Lord
1:24 **b** Jews and Greeks, Christ the power of God and
6:13 and God will destroy **b** one and the other.
1Co 15:40 There are **b** heavenly bodies and earthly bodies,
Eph 2:14 in his flesh he has made **b** groups into one
2:16 and might reconcile **b** groups to God in one body
2:18 him **b** of us have access in one Spirit to the Father.
6: 9 for you know that **b** of you have the same Master
Php 1: 7 **b** in my imprisonment and in the defense
2:13 enabling you **b** to will and to work
1Th 2:15 who killed **b** the Lord Jesus and the prophets,
1Ti 4: 8 holding promise for **b** the present life and the life
4:16 in these things, for in doing this you will save **b**
Tit 1: 9 be able **b** to preach with sound doctrine and
Phm 1:11 but now he is indeed useful **b** to you and to me.
1:16 **b** in the flesh and in the Lord.
Heb 9:19 and sprinkled **b** the scroll itself and all the people,
9:21 with the blood **b** the tent and all the vessels used
Jas 3:11 Does a spring pour forth from the same opening **b**
2Pe 3:18 be the glory **b** now and to the day of eternity.
2Jn 1: 9 whoever abides in the teaching has **b** the Father
Rev 6:11 be complete **b** of their fellow servants and
11:18 and all who fear your name, **b** small and great,
13:16 **b** small and great, **b** rich and poor, **b** free and slave
19:18 flesh of all, **b** free and slave, **b** small and great."
Tob 3:16 of **b** of them were heard in the glorious presence
3:17 So Raphael was sent to heal **b** of them:
5:17 my son, accompany you **b** for your safety."
6: 2 So they **b** journeyed along,
6:18 **b** of you must first stand up and pray,
7:11 and the Lord will act on behalf of you **b."**
7:11 and prosper you **b** this night and grant you mercy
8: 8 And they **b** said, "Amen, Amen."
9: 6 In the morning they **b** got up early and went to
10:12 Then she kissed them **b** and saw them safely off.
11:13 with **b** his hands he peeled off the white films
12: 8 but better than **b** is almsgiving with righteousness.
14:13 He inherited **b** the property of Raguel and that
Jdt 4: 2 they were alarmed **b** for Jerusalem and for
8:24 **b** the temple and the altar—rests upon us.
13:13 They all ran together, **b** small and great,
AdE 5: 5 So they **b** came to the dinner
6: 9 and let **b** be given to one of
9:20 to the Jews in the kingdom of Artaxerxes **b** near
10: 1 The king levied a tax upon his kingdom **b** by land
11: 6 two great dragons came forward, **b** ready to fight,
16:16 the kingdom **b** for us and for our ancestors in
16:23 **b** now and hereafter it may represent deliverance
Wis 4: 1 because it is known **b** by God and by mortals.
6: 7 because he himself made **b** small and great,
7:16 For **b** we and our words are in his hand,
7:21 I learned **b** what is secret and what is manifest,
15: 7 of the same clay **b** the vessels that serve clean uses
15:19 but they have escaped **b** the praise of God
18: 9 that the saints would share alike the same things, **b**
Sir 5: 6 for **b** mercy and wrath are with him,
10: 7 and injustice is outrageous to **b.**
18:17 **B** are to be found in a gracious person.
20:25 but the lot of **b** is ruin.
22: 5 and husband, and is despised by **b.**
28:12 yet **b** come out of your mouth.
Sus 1:10 **B** were overwhelmed with passion for her,
1:13 So they **b** left and parted from each other.
1:59 so as to destroy you **b."**
1Mc 1:16 in order that he might reign over **b** kingdoms.
4:34 Then **b** sides attacked, and there fell of the army
6:26 they have fortified **b** the sanctuary and Beth-zur;
6:45 and they parted before him on **b** sides.
8:30 in effect **b** parties shall determine to add
9:17 and many on **b** sides were wounded and fell.
11:34 as their possession **b** the territory of Judea and
12:11 **b** at our festivals and on other appropriate days,
2Mc 4: 5 **b** public and private, of all the people.
5:15 who had become a traitor **b** to the laws and
14:46 in **b** hands and hurled them at the crowd,
1Es 2:22 troubling **b** kings and other cities,
6:26 **b** of gold and of silver,
8:14 **b** gold and silver for bulls and rams and lambs
9:41 in the presence of **b** men and women;
3Mc 1: 1 by Antiochus, he gave orders to all his forces, **b**
2:23 Then **b** friends and bodyguards,
3:21 **b** because of their alliance with us and
3:21 and we ventured to make a change, by deciding **b**
3:23 but also **b** by speech and
4:20 and proved that **b** the paper and the pens they used
6:30 to the Jews **b** wines and everything else needed for
2Es 6:50 had been gathered together could not hold them **b.**
8: 9 But that which keeps and that which is kept shall **b**
9:19 which is supplied **b** with an unfailing table and
4Mc 1:20 and each of these is by nature concerned with **b**
1:21 of **b** pleasure and pain have many consequences.
1:32 and reason obviously rules over **b.**
3:20 had **b** appropriated money to them for
12:18 on you he will take vengeance **b** in this present life
13: 4 for the brothers mastered **b** emotions and pains.
13:22 and from **b** general education and our discipline in
15: 4 a small child a wondrous likeness **b** of mind and
18: 5 The tyrant Antiochus was **b** punished on earth

BOTHER (2) [BOTHERED, BOTHERING]

Ru 2: 9 I have ordered the young men not to **b** you.
Lk 11: 7 And he answers from within, 'Do not **b** me;

BOTHERED (1) [BOTHER]

Ru 2:22 otherwise you might be **b** in another field."

BOTHERING (1) [BOTHER]

Lk 18: 5 yet because this widow keeps **b** me,

BOTTLE (2)

Ps 33: 7 He gathered the waters of the sea as in a **b;**
56: 8 put my tears in your **b.**

BOTTOM (8)

Dt 28:13 you shall be only at the top, and not at the **b—**
1Ki 22:35 the blood from the wound had flowed into the **b** of
Eze 41: 7 from the **b** story to the uppermost story by way of
46:23 with hearths made at the **b** of the rows all around.
Da 6:24 the **b** of the den the lions overpowered them
Am 9: 3 though they hide from my sight at the **b** of the sea,
Mt 27:51 of the temple was torn in two, from top to **b.**
Mk 15:38 of the temple was torn in two, from top to **b.**

BOTTOMLESS (6)

Rev 9: 1 and he was given the key to the shaft of the **b** pit;
9: 2 he opened the shaft of the **b** pit,
9:11 They have as king over them the angel of the **b** pit;
11: 7 the **b** pit will make war on them and conquer them
17: 8 to ascend from the **b** pit and go to destruction.
20: 1 in his hand the key to the **b** pit and a great chain.

BOUGEAN‡ (3)

AdE 3: 1 a **B,** advancing him and granting him precedence
9:10 the **B,** the enemy of the Jews—
12: 6 But Haman son of Hammedatha, a **B,**

BOUGH‡ (3) [BOUGHS]

Ge 49:22 Joseph is a fruitful **b,** a fruitful **b** by a spring;
Isa 17: 6 two or three berries in the top of the highest **b,**

BOUGHS‡ (12) [BOUGH]

Lev 23:40 **b** of leafy trees, and willows of the brook;
Isa 10:33 will lop the **b** with terrifying power;
27:11 When its **b** are dry, they are broken;
Eze 17:23 in order that it may produce **b** and bear fruit,
19:11 it towered aloft among the thick **b;**
31: 5 its **b** grew large and its branches long,
31: 6 All the birds of the air made their nests in its **b;**
31: 8 nor the fir trees equal its **b;**
31:12 its **b** lie broken in all the watercourses of the land;
31:13 and among its **b** lodge all the wild animals.
Wis 4: 4 For even if they put forth **b** for a while,
Sir 14:26 under her shelter, and lodges under her **b;**

BOUGHT‡ (41) [BUY]

Ge 17:12 in your house and the one **b** with your money
17:13 in your house and the one **b** with your money must
17:23 the slaves born in his house or **b** with his money,
17:27 slaves born in the house and those **b** with money
33:19 he **b** for one hundred pieces of money the plot
39: 1 **b** him from the Ishmaelites who had brought him
47:14 in exchange for the grain that they **b;**
47:20 So Joseph **b** all the land of Egypt for Pharaoh.
47:23 I have this day **b** you and your land for Pharaoh,
49:30 the field that Abraham **b** from Ephron the Hittite
50:13 which Abraham **b** as a burial site from Ephron
Lev 27:24 to the one from whom it was **b,**
Jos 24:32 in the portion of ground that Jacob had **b** from
2Sa 12: 3 but one little ewe lamb, which he had **b.**
24:24 So David **b** the threshing floor and the oxen
1Ki 16:24 He **b** the hill of Samaria from Shemer
Ne 5: 8 have **b** back our Jewish kindred who had been sold
5: 8 who must then be **b** back by us!"
Ecc 2: 7 I **b** male and female slaves,
Isa 43:24 You have not **b** me sweet cane with money,
Jer 13: 2 So I **b** a loincloth according to the word of
13: 4 "Take the loincloth that you **b** and are wearing,
32: 9 I **b** the field at Anathoth from my cousin Hanamel,
32:15 Houses and fields and vineyards shall again be **b**
32:43 be **b** in this land of which you are saying, It is
32:44 Fields shall be **b** for money,
La 5: 4 the wood we get must be **b.**
Hos 3: 2 So I **b** her for fifteen shekels of silver and a homer
Am 2: 8 and in the house of their God they drink wine **b**
Mt 13:46 he went and sold all that he had and **b** it.
Mk 15:46 Then Joseph **b** a linen cloth,
16: 1 the mother of James, and Salome **b** spices,
Lk 14:18 The first said to him, 'I have **b** a piece of land,
14:19 Another said, 'I have **b** five yoke of oxen,
Jn 12: 7 She **b** it so that she might keep it for the day
Ac 7:16 in the tomb that Abraham had **b** for a sum of silver
1Co 6:20 For you were **b** with a price;
7:23 You were **b** with a price;
2Pe 2: 1 They will even deny the Master who **b** them—
Sir 33:31 because you have **b** him with blood.
LtJ 6:25 They are **b** without regard to cost,

BOUND‡ (102) [BIND, BOUNDARY]

Ge 22: 9 He **b** his son Isaac, and laid him on the altar,
38:28 midwife took and **b** on his hand a crimson thread,
42:24 And he picked out Simeon and had him **b**
44:30 then, as his life is **b** up in the boy's life,
Ex 12:45 no **b** or hired servant may eat of it.
28:28 The breastpiece shall be **b** by its rings to the rings
39:21 They **b** the breastpiece by its rings to the rings of
Lev 22:10 No **b** or hired servant of the priest shall eat of
25: 6 your hired and your **b** laborers who live with you;
25:40 They shall remain with you as hired or **b** laborers.
Nu 30: 4 by which she has **b** herself, and says nothing
30: 4 any pledge by which she has **b** herself shall stand.
30: 5 and no pledge by which she has **b** herself,

Nu 30: 6 of her lips by which she has **b** herself,
30: 7 her pledges by which she has **b** herself shall stand.
30: 8 of her lips, by which she has **b** herself;
30: 9 by which she has **b** herself,
30:10 or **b** herself by a pledge with an oath,
30:11 and any pledge by which she **b** herself shall stand.
Jdg 15:13 So they **b** him with two new ropes,
16: 6 and how you could be **b,**
16: 8 and she **b** him with them.
16:10 please tell me how you could be **b."**
16:12 So Delilah took new ropes and **b** him with them,
16:13 tell me how you could be **b."**
16:21 down to Gaza and **b** him with bronze shackles;
1Sa 18: 1 the soul of Jonathan was **b** to the soul of David,
25:29 be **b** in the bundle of the living under the care of
2Sa 3:34 Your hands were not **b,** your feet were
2Ki 25: 7 they **b** him in fetters and took him to Babylon.
2Ch 33:11 **b** him with fetters, and brought him to Babylon.
36: 6 and **b** him with fetters to take him to Babylon.
Ne 6:18 For many in Judah were **b** by oath to him,
Job 13:27 you set a **b** to the soles of my feet.
28: 3 the farthest **b** the ore in gloom and deep darkness.
36: 8 And if they are **b** in fetters and caught in the cords
Ps 122: 3 built as a city that is **b** firmly together.
Pr 6: 1 if you have **b** yourself to another,
22:15 Folly is **b** up in the heart of a boy,
Isa 1: 6 they have not been drained, or **b** up,
Jer 39: 7 and **b** him in fetters to take him to Babylon.
40: 1 when he took him **b** in fetters along with all
52:11 of Zedekiah, and **b** him in fetters, and the king
La 1:14 My transgressions were **b** into a yoke;
Eze 3:25 and you shall be **b** with them,
16:10 I **b** you in fine linen and covered you
27:24 **b** with cords and made secure;
30:21 it has not been **b** up for healing or wrapped with
34: 4 you have not **b** up the injured,
Da 3:21 So the men were **b,** still wearing their tunics,
3:23 Shadrach, Meshach, and Abednego, fell down, **b,**
3:24 not three men that we threw **b** into the fire?"
Hos 13:12 Ephraim's iniquity is **b** up; his sin is kept in store.
Na 3:10 all her dignitaries were **b** in fetters.
Mt 14: 3 For Herod had arrested John, **b** him,
16:19 whatever you bind on earth will be **b** in heaven,
18: 7 Occasions for stumbling are **b** to come,
18:18 whatever you bind on earth will be **b** in heaven,
23:16 'Whoever swears by the sanctuary is **b** by nothing,
23:16 by the gold of the sanctuary is **b** by the oath.'
23:18 'Whoever swears by the altar is **b** by nothing,
23:18 by the gift that is on the altar is **b** by the oath.'
27: 2 They **b** him, led him away,
Mk 6:17 **b** him, and put him in prison on account
15: 1 They **b** Jesus, led him away,
Lk 8:29 under guard and **b** with chains and shackles,
13:16 a daughter of Abraham whom Satan **b**
17: 1 "Occasions for stumbling are **b** to come,
Jn 11:44 his hands and feet **b** with strips of cloth,
18:12 and the Jewish police arrested Jesus and **b** him.
18:24 Annas sent him **b** to Caiaphas the high priest.
Ac 9: 2 he might bring them **b** to Jerusalem.
9:21 not come here for the purpose of bringing them **b**
12: 6 before Herod was going to bring him out, Peter, **b**
21: 2 When we found a ship **b** for Phoenicia,
21:11 **b** his own feet and hands with it, and said,
21:13 be **b** but even to die in Jerusalem for the name of
21:33 and ordered him to be **b** with two chains;
22:29 a Roman citizen and that he had **b** him.
23:12 the Jews joined in a conspiracy and **b** themselves
23:14 "We have strictly **b** ourselves by an oath
23:21 They have **b** themselves by an oath neither to eat
27: 6 There the centurion found an Alexandrian ship **b**
28:20 of the hope of Israel that I am **b** with this chain."
Ro 7: 2 a married woman is **b** by the law to her husband
1Co 7:15 in such a case the brother or sister is not **b.**
7:27 Are you **b** to a wife?
7:39 A wife is **b** as long as her husband lives.
Rev 9:14 "Release the four angels who are **b** at
20: 2 and **b** him for a thousand years,
Tob 8: 3 and at once **b** him there hand and foot.
Jdt 6:13 they **b** Achior and left him lying at the foot of
Wis 17:17 for with one chain of darkness they all were **b.**
Sir 28:19 and has not been **b** with its fetters.
1Mc 3: 3 he **b** on his armor of war and waged battles,
1Es 1:40 he **b** him with a chain of bronze
3Mc 3:25 and **b** securely with iron fetters,
5: 5 the Jews went out in the evening and **b** the hands
2Es 13:13 of them were **b,** and some were bringing others
4Mc 9:11 they **b** his hands and arms with thongs
9:26 they **b** him to the torture machine and catapult.
11: 9 the guards **b** him and dragged him to the catapult;

BOUNDARIES‡ (8) [BOUNDARY]

Nu 34: 2 the land of Canaan, defined by its **b),**
34:12 This shall be your land with its **b** all around.
Dt 32: 8 the **b** of the peoples according to the number of
Pr 15:25 but maintains the widow's **b.**
Isa 10:13 I have removed the **b** of peoples,
Eze 47:13 These are the **b** by which you shall divide the land
Ac 17:26 the times of their existence and the **b** of the places
Sir 16:26 and, in making them, determined their **b,**

BOUNDARY‡ (93) [BOUND, BOUNDARIES, BOUNDING, BOUNDLESS, BOUNDS]

Nu 21:13 in the wilderness that extends from the **b** of
21:13 for the Arnon is the **b** of Moab,
21:24 for the **b** of the Ammonites was strong.
22:36 on the **b** formed by the Arnon,
22:36 at the farthest point of the **b.**
34: 3 Your southern **b** shall begin from the end of
34: 4 your **b** shall turn south of the ascent of Akrabbim,
34: 5 the **b** shall turn from Azmon to the Wadi of Egypt,
34: 6 For the western **b,** you shall have the Great Sea
34: 6 this shall be your western **b.**
34: 7 This shall be your northern **b:**
34: 8 and the outer limit of the **b** shall be at Zedad;
34: 9 the **b** shall extend to Ziphron, and its end shall be
34: 9 this shall be your northern **b.**
34:10 You shall mark out your eastern **b**
34:11 and the **b** shall continue down from Shepham
34:11 the **b** shall go down, and reach the eastern slope of
34:12 and the **b** shall go down to the Jordan,
Dt 2:18 "Today you are going to cross the **b** of Moab
3:16 with the middle of the wadi as a **b,**
3:16 the wadi being **b** of the Ammonites;
19:14 You must not move your neighbor's **b** marker,
27:17 be anyone who moves a neighbor's **b** marker."
Jos 12: 2 the **b** of the Ammonites, that is, half of Gilead,
12: 5 to the **b** of the Geshurites and the Maacathites,
12: 5 and over half of Gilead to the **b** of King Sihon
13: 3 northward to the **b** of Ekron,
13: 4 to Aphek, to the **b** of the Amorites,
13:10 as far as the **b** of the Ammonites;
15: 1 to their families reached southward to the **b**
15: 2 their south **b** ran from the end of the Dead Sea,
15: 4 This shall be your south **b.**
15: 5 east **b** is the Dead Sea, to the mouth of the Jordan.
15: 5 the **b** on the north side runs from the bay of the sea
15: 6 and the **b** goes up to Beth-hoglah, and passes
15: 6 **b** goes up to the Stone of Bohan, Reuben's son;
15: 7 the **b** goes up to Debir from the Valley of Achor,
15: 7 the **b** passes along to the waters of En-shemesh,
15: 8 the **b** goes up by the valley of the son of Hinnom
15: 8 the **b** goes up to the top of the mountain that lies
15: 9 then the **b** extends from the top of the mountain to
15: 9 **b** bends around to Baalah (that is, Kiriath-jearim);
15:10 the **b** circles west of Baalah to Mount Seir, passes
15:11 the **b** goes out to the slope of the hill north
15:11 then the **b** bends around to Shikkeron,
15:11 then the **b** comes to an end at the sea.
15:12 the west **b** was the Mediterranean with its coast.
15:12 the **b** surrounding the people of Judah according
15:21 toward the **b** of Edom, were Kabzeel, Eder, Jagur,
16: 5 the **b** of their inheritance on
16: 6 and the **b** goes from there to the sea;
16: 6 the east the **b** makes a turn toward Taanath-shiloh,
16: 8 the **b** goes westward to the Wadi Kanah,
17: 7 then the **b** goes along southward to the inhabitants
17: 8 on the **b** of Manasseh belonged to the Ephraimites.
17: 9 Then the **b** went down to the Wadi Kanah.
17: 9 Then the **b** of Manasseh goes along the north side
17:10 with the sea forming its **b;**
18:12 On the north side their **b** began at the Jordan;
18:12 the **b** goes up to the slope of Jericho on the north,
18:13 the **b** passes along southward in the direction
18:13 Bethel), then the **b** goes down to Ataroth-addar,
18:14 Then the **b** goes in another direction,
18:15 and the **b** goes from there to Ephron,
18:16 the **b** goes down to the border of the mountain
18:19 then the **b** passes on to the north of the slope
18:19 the **b** ends at the northern bay of the Dead Sea,
18:20 The Jordan forms its **b** on the eastern side.
18:20 according to its families, **b** by **b** all around.
19:10 The **b** of its inheritance reached as far as Sarid;
19:11 then its **b** goes up westward, and on to Maralah,
19:12 toward the sunrise to the **b** of Chisloth-tabor;
19:14 then on the north the **b** makes a turn to Hannathon,
19:22 the **b** also touches Tabor, Shahazumah,
19:22 and Beth-shemesh, and its **b** ends at the Jordan—
19:25 Its **b** included Helkath, Hali, Beten, Achshaph,
19:29 the **b** turns to Ramah, reaching to the fortified city
19:29 then the **b** turns to Hosah, and it ends at the sea;
19:33 And its **b** ran from Heleph,
19:34 then the **b** turns westward to Aznoth-tabor,
22:25 the LORD has made the Jordan a **b** between us
Jdg 11:18 for the Arnon was the **b** of Moab.
Job 26:10 at the **b** between light and darkness.
Ps 16: 6 The **b** lines have fallen for me in pleasant places;
104: 9 You set a **b** that they may not pass,
Jer 5:22 I placed the sand as a **b** for the sea,
Eze 45: 7 and extending from the western to the eastern **b**
47:15 This shall be the **b** of the land:
47:17 So the **b** shall run from the sea to Hazar-enon,
47:20 be the **b** to a point opposite Lebo-hamath.
48:28 the **b** shall run from Tamar to the waters
Mic 7:11 In that day the **b** shall be far extended.

BOUNDING (2) [BOUNDARY]

SS 2: 8 leaping upon the mountains, **b** over the hills.
Na 3: 2 galloping horse and **b** chariot!

BOUNDLESS (4) [BOUNDARY]

Eph 3: 8 to the Gentiles the news of the **b** riches of Christ,
Sir 16:17 for what am I in a **b** creation?
3Mc 2: 4 by bringing on them a **b** flood.
2: 9 you had created the **b** and immeasurable earth,

BOUNDS (11) [BOUNDARY]

Nu 35:26 But if the slayer shall at any time go outside the **b**
35:27 and is found by the avenger of blood outside the **b**
Jdg 2: 9 So they buried him within the **b** of his inheritance
1Ki 21:23 dogs shall eat Jezebel within the **b** of Jezreel.'
Job 14: 5 you have appointed the **b** that they cannot pass,
38:10 and prescribed **b** for it, and set bars and doors,
Ps 65: 8 Those who live at earth's farthest **b** are awed
74:17 You have fixed all the **b** of the earth;
148: 6 he fixed their **b,** which cannot be passed.
Pr 7:22 or **b** like a stag toward the trap
Bar 3:25 It is great and has no **b;**

BOUNTEOUS (1) [BOUNTY]

2Sa 1:21 let there be no dew or rain upon you, nor **b** fields!

BOUNTIES (1) [BOUNTY]

Ge 49:26 the **b** of the everlasting hills;

BOUNTIFUL (4) [BOUNTY]

2Co 9: 5 in advance for this **b** gift that you have promised,
AdE 1: 4 the splendor of his **b** celebration during the course
2Mc 1:25 you alone are **b,** you alone are just and almighty
2Es 7:*135* [65] **b,** because he would rather give than take

BOUNTIFULLY (6) [BOUNTY]

Ps 13: 6 because he has dealt **b** with me.
116: 7 to your rest, for the LORD has dealt **b** with you.
119:17 Deal **b** with your servant, so that I may live
142: 7 for you will deal **b** with me.
2Co 9: 6 and the one who sows **b** will also reap **b.**

BOUNTY (8) [BOUNTEOUS, BOUNTIES, BOUNTIFUL, BOUNTIFULLY]

Dt 15:14 thus giving to him some of the **b** with which
26:11 with all the **b** that the LORD your God has given
1Ki 10:13 as what he gave her out of Solomon's royal **b.**
Est 1: 7 and the royal wine was lavished according to the **b**
Ps 65:11 You crown the year with your **b;**
116:12 What shall I return to the LORD for all his **b**
Jer 31:14 and my people shall be satisfied with my **b,**
Wis 16:25 it served your all-nourishing **b,**

BOW (118) [BOWED, BOWING, BOWS, BOWSHOT, BOWSTRING, BOWSTRINGS]

Ge 9:13 I have set my **b** in the clouds,
9:14 over the earth and the **b** is seen in the clouds,
9:16 When the **b** is in the clouds,
21:20 and became an expert with the **b.**
27: 3 then, take your weapons, your quiver and your **b,**
27:29 Let peoples serve you, and nations **b** down to you.
27:29 and may your mother's sons **b** down to you.
37:10 and **b** to the ground before you?"
41:43 and they cried out in front of him, **"B** the knee!"
48:22 of the Amorites with my sword and with my **b."**
49: 8 your father's sons shall **b** down before you.
49:24 Yet his **b** remained taut,
Ex 11: 8 and **b** low to me, saying, 'Leave us,
20: 5 You shall not **b** down to them or worship them;
23:24 you shall not **b** down to their gods,
33:10 all the people would rise and **b** down, all of them,
Dt 4:19 be led astray and **b** down to them and serve them,
5: 9 You shall not **b** down to them or worship them;
26:10 before the LORD your God and **b** down before
30:17 but are led astray to **b** down to other gods
Jos 23: 7 or serve them, or **b** yourselves down to them,
23:16 and go and serve other gods and **b** down to them,
24:12 it was not by your sword or by your **b.**
1Sa 18: 4 and even his sword and his **b** and his belt.
2Sa 1:18 (He ordered that The Song of the **B** be taught to
1:22 the **b** of Jonathan did not turn back,
22:35 so that my arms can bend a **b** of bronze.
1Ki 22:34 a certain man drew his **b** and unknowingly struck
2Ki 5:18 and I **b** down in the house of Rimmon,
5:18 when I do **b** down in the house of Rimmon,
6:22 with your sword and your **b** those whom you want
9:24 Jehu drew his **b** with all his strength,
13:15 Elisha said to him, "Take a **b** and arrows";
13:15 so he took a **b** and arrows.
13:16 Then he said to the king of Israel, "Draw the **b";**
17:35 "You shall not worship other gods or **b** yourselves
17:36 you shall **b** yourselves to him,
1Ch 5:18 who carried shield and sword, and drew the **b,**
2Ch 17:17 with two hundred thousand armed with **b**
18:33 a certain man drew his **b** and unknowingly struck
Est 3: 2 But Mordecai did not **b** down or do obeisance.
3: 5 When Haman saw that Mordecai did not **b** down
Job 29:20 and my **b** ever new in my hand.'
Ps 5: 7 I will **b** down toward your holy temple in awe
7:12 he has bent and strung his **b;**
11: 2 the wicked bend the **b,** they have fitted their arrow
18:34 so that my arms can bend a **b** of bronze.
22:29 indeed, shall all who sleep in the earth **b** down;
22:29 before him shall **b** all who go down to the dust,
44: 6 not in my **b** do I trust, nor can my sword save me.
45:11 Since he is your lord, **b** to him;
46: 9 he breaks the **b,** and shatters the spear;
72: 9 May his foes **b** down before him,
78: 9 The Ephraimites, armed with the **b,**
78:57 they twisted like a treacherous **b.**
81: 9 you shall not **b** down to a foreign god.
86: 9 the nations you have made shall come and **b** down
95: 6 O come, let us worship and **b** down,
97: 7 all gods **b** down before him.
138: 2 I **b** down toward your holy temple and give thanks
144: 5 **B** your heavens, O LORD, and come down;
Pr 14:19 The evil **b** down before the good,

Isa 2: 8 they **b** down to the work of their hands,
7:24 With **b** and arrows one will go there,
21:15 from the bent **b**, and from the stress of battle.
22: 3 they were captured without the use of a **b**.
41: 2 like driven stubble with his **b**.
45:14 they shall come over in chains and **b** down to you.
45:23 "To me every knee shall **b**,
46: 2 They stoop, they **b** down together;
49:23 With their faces to the ground they shall **b** down
51:23 "**B** down, that we may walk on you";
58: 5 Is it to **b** down the head like a bulrush,
60:14 all who despised you shall **b** down at your feet;
65:12 and all of you shall **b** down to the slaughter;
66:19 and Lud—which draw the **b**—
Jer 6:23 They grasp the **b** and the javelin,
46: 9 the Ludim, who draw the **b**.
49:35 I am going to break the **b** of Elam,
50:14 all you that bend the **b**;
50:29 against Babylon, all who bend the **b**.
50:42 They wield **b** and spear, they are cruel
51: 3 Let not the archer bend his **b**,
La 2: 4 He has bent his **b** like an enemy,
3:12 he bent his **b** and set me as a mark for his arrow.
Eze 1:28 Like the **b** in a cloud on a rainy day,
39: 3 I will strike your **b** from your left hand,
46: 2 and he shall **b** down at the threshold of the gate.
46: 3 the land shall **b** down at the entrance of that gate
Hos 1: 5 that day I will break the **b** of Israel in the valley
1: 7 I will not save them by **b**, or by sword, or by war,
2:18 and I will abolish the **b**, the sword,
7:16 they have become like a defective **b**;
Am 2:15 the **b** shall not stand, and those who are swift
Mic 5:13 and you shall **b** down no more to the work
6: 6 and **b** myself before God on high?
Hab 3: 9 You brandished your naked **b**,
Zep 1: 5 those who **b** down on the roofs to the host of
1: 5 those who **b** down and swear to the LORD,
2:11 and to him shall **b** down, each in its place,
Zec 9:10 and the battle **b** shall be cut off,
9:13 For I have bent Judah as my **b**;
10: 4 of them the battle **b**, out of them every commander.
Ac 27:30 on the pretext of putting out anchors from the **b**,
27:41 the **b** stuck and remained immovable,
Ro 14:11 "As I live, says the Lord, every knee shall **b** to me,
1Co 14:25 person will **b** down before God and worship him,
Eph 3:14 For this reason I **b** my knees before the Father,
Rev 3: 9 I will make them come and **b** down
6: 2 and there was a white horse! Its rider had a **b**;
Jdt 9: 7 and trusting in shield and spear, in **b** and sling.
AdE 13:12 and refused to **b** down to this proud Haman;
13:14 and I will not **b** down to anyone but you,
Wis 5:21 the clouds to the target, as from a well-drawn **b**,
Sir 4: 7 **b** your head low to the great.
30:12 **B** down his neck in his youth,
33:27 Yoke and thong will **b** the neck,
2Es 16:13 For his right hand that bends the **b** is strong,

BOWED (72) [BOW]

Ge 18: 2 and **b** down to the ground.
19: 1 and **b** down with his face to the ground.
23: 7 Abraham rose and **b** to the Hittites,
23:12 Abraham **b** down before the people of the land.
24:26 The man **b** his head and worshiped the LORD
24:48 Then I **b** my head and worshiped the LORD,
24:52 he **b** himself to the ground before the LORD.
33: 6 they and their children, and **b** down;
33: 7 and her children drew near and **b** down;
33: 7 and Rachel drew near, and they **b** down.
37: 7 and **b** down to my sheaf."
42: 6 and **b** themselves before him with their faces to
43:26 and **b** to the ground before him.
43:28 And they **b** their heads and did obeisance.
47:31 Then Israel **b** himself on the head of his bed.
48:12 and he **b** himself with his face to the earth.
49:15 so he **b** his shoulder to the burden,
Ex 4:31 they **b** down and worshiped.
12:27 And the people **b** down and worshiped.
18: 7 he **b** down and kissed him;
34: 8 And Moses quickly **b** his head toward the earth,
Nu 22:31 and he **b** down, falling on his face.
25: 2 and the people ate and **b** down to their gods.
Jdg 2:12 of the peoples who were all around them, and **b**
2:17 they lusted after other gods and **b** down to them.
1Sa 4:19 and her husband were dead, she **b** and gave birth;
20:41 He **b** three times, and they kissed each other,
24: 8 David **b** with his face to the ground,
25:41 She rose and **b** down, with her face to the ground,
28:14 and he **b** with his face to the ground,
2Sa 18:21 The Cushite **b** before Joab, and ran.
22:10 He **b** the heavens, and came down;
1Ki 1:16 Bathsheba **b** and did obeisance to the king,
1:31 Then Bathsheba **b** with her face to the ground,
1:47 The king **b** in worship on the bed
2:19 The king rose to meet her, and **b** down to her;
18:42 there he **b** himself down upon the earth
19:18 all the knees that have not **b** to Baal,
2Ki 2:15 to meet him and **b** to the ground before him.
1Ch 29:20 and **b** their heads and prostrated themselves before
2Ch 7: 3 they **b** down on the pavement with their faces to
20:18 Jehoshaphat **b** down with his face to the ground,
29:29 the king and all who were present with him **b**
29:30 and they **b** down and worshiped.
Ne 8: 6 Then they **b** their heads and worshiped the LORD
Est 3: 2 the king's servants who were at the king's gate **b**
Job 9:13 the helpers of Rahab **b** beneath him.
Ps 18: 9 He **b** the heavens, and came down;
Ps 35:13 I prayed with head **b** on my bosom,
35:14 I went about as one who laments for a mother, **b**
38: 6 I am utterly **b** down and prostrate;
57: 6 They set a net for my steps; my soul was **b** down.
107:12 Their hearts were **b** down with hard labor;
145:14 and raises up all who are **b** down.
146: 8 The LORD lifts up those who are **b** down;
Isa 5:15 People are **b** down, everyone is brought low,
21: 3 I am **b** down so that I cannot hear,
La 2:10 the young girls of Jerusalem have **b** their heads to
3:20 My soul continually thinks of it and is **b** down
Mk 5: 6 he ran and **b** down before him;
7:25 and she came and **b** down at his feet.
Lk 5:12 he **b** with his face to the ground and begged him,
24: 5 The women were terrified and **b** their faces to
Jn 19:30 Then he **b** his head and gave up his spirit.
Ro 11: 4 for myself seven thousand who have not **b**
Jdt 10: 8 She **b** down to God.
13:17 They **b** down and worshiped God,
AdE 16:11 that he was called our father and was continually **b**
Sir 12:11 Even if he humbles himself and walks **b** down,
19:26 There is the villain **b** down in mourning,
50:21 and they **b** down in worship a second time,
Bar 2:18 but the person who is deeply grieved, who walks **b**

BOWELS (8)

Nu 5:22 that brings the curse enter your **b**
2Ch 21:15 a severe sickness with a disease of your **b**,
21:15 until your **b** come out, day after day,
21:18 After all this the LORD struck him in his **b** with
21:19 his **b** came out because of the disease,
Ac 1:18 in the middle and all his **b** gushed out.
2Mc 9: 5 with a pain in his **b**, for which there was no relief,
9: 6 the **b** of others with many and strange inflictions.

BOWING (6) [BOW]

Ge 33: 3 **b** himself to the ground seven times,
37: 9 the moon, and eleven stars were **b** down to me."
Jdg 2:19 worshiping them and **b** down to them.
1Sa 25:23 fell before David on her face, **b** to the ground.
2Ki 4:37 She came and fell at his feet, **b** to the ground;
Heb 11:21 "**b** in worship over the top of his staff."

BOWL (22) [BOWLS]

Dt 28: 5 Blessed shall be your basket and your kneading **b**.
28:17 Cursed shall be your basket and your kneading **b**.
Jdg 5:25 she brought him curds in a lordly **b**.
6:38 he wrung enough dew from the fleece to fill a **b**
2Ki 2:20 He said, "Bring me a new **b**, and put salt in it."
Ecc 12: 6 and the golden **b** is broken,
SS 7: 2 a rounded **b** that never lacks mixed wine.
Isa 51:17 who have drunk to the dregs the **b** of staggering.
51:22 you shall drink no more from the **b** of my wrath.
Zec 4: 2 with a **b** on the top of it;
4: 3 one on the right of the **b** and the other on its left."
9:15 like wine, and be full like a **b**,
Mt 26:23 "The one who has dipped his hand into the **b**
Mk 14:20 one who is dipping bread into the **b** with me.
Rev 16: 2 the first angel went and poured his **b** on the earth,
16: 3 The second angel poured his **b** into the sea,
16: 4 The third angel poured his **b** into the rivers and
16: 8 The fourth angel poured his **b** on the sun,
16:10 fifth angel poured his **b** on the throne of the beast,
16:12 The sixth angel poured his **b** on the great river
16:17 The seventh angel poured his **b** into the air,
Bel 1:33 he had made a stew and had broken bread into a **b**,

BOWLS (31) [BOWL]

Ex 8: 3 and into your ovens and your kneading **b**.
12:34 with their kneading **b** wrapped up in their cloaks
25:29 and **b** with which to pour drink offerings;
37:16 and its **b** and flagons with which
Nu 4: 7 the **b**, and the flagons for the drink offering;
1Ki 7:41 the two **b** of the capitals that were on the tops of
7:41 the two **b** of the capitals that were on the tops of
7:42 the two **b** of the capitals that were on the pillars;
2Ki 12:13 **b**, trumpets, or any vessels of gold, or of silver,
1Ch 28:17 for the golden **b** and the weight of each;
28:17 for the silver **b** and the weight of each;
2Ch 4:12 the **b**, and the two capitals on the top of the pillars;
4:12 the two **b** of the capitals that were on the top of
4:13 the two **b** of the capitals that were on the pillars.
Ezr 1:10 gold **b**, thirty; other silver bowls,
1:10 other silver **b**, four hundred ten;
8:27 twenty gold **b** worth a thousand darics,
Jer 52:19 captain of the guard took away the small **b** also,
52:19 the lampstands, the ladles, and the **b** for libation,
Am 6: 6 from **b**, and anoint themselves with the finest oils,
Zec 14:20 of the LORD shall be as holy as the **b** in front of
Rev 5: 8 each holding a harp and golden **b** full of incense,
15: 7 the seven angels seven golden **b** full of the wrath
16: 1 and pour out on the earth the seven **b** of the wrath
17: 1 of the seven angels who had the seven **b** came
21: 9 of the seven angels who had the seven **b** full of
Jdt 15:11 his beds, his **b**, and all his furniture.
1Mc 1:22 the **b**, the golden censers, the curtain, the crowns,
1Es 2:13 twenty-nine silver censers, thirty gold **b**,
2:13 two thousand four hundred ten silver **b**,
8:57 and twenty golden **b**, and twelve bronze vessels

BOWS‡ (17) [BOW]

1Sa 2: 4 The **b** of the mighty are broken,
2Ch 14: 8 from Benjamin who carried shields and drew **b**;
26:14 helmets, coats of mail, **b**, and stones for slinging.
Ne 4:13 with their swords, their spears, and their **b**.
4:16 and half held the spears, shields, **b**,
Ps 21:12 you will aim at their faces with your **b**.
37:14 the sword and bend their **b** to bring down the poor
37:15 and their **b** shall be broken.
Isa 5:28 all their **b** bent, their horses' hoofs seem like flint,
13:18 Their **b** will slaughter the young men;
21:17 the remaining **b** of Kedar's warriors will be few;
44:15 makes it a carved image and **b** down before it.
44:17 his idol, **b** down to it and worships it;
46: 1 Bel **b** down, Nebo stoops,
Jer 9: 3 They bend their tongues like **b**;
51:56 her warriors are taken, their **b** are broken;
Eze 39: 9 bucklers and shields, **b** and arrows,

BOWSHOT (2) [BOW, SHOOT]

Ge 21:16 about the distance of a **b**;
Ps 60: 4 to rally to it out of **b**.

BOWSTRING (1) [BOW, STRING]

Job 30:11 Because God has loosed my **b** and humbled me,

BOWSTRINGS (3) [BOW, STRING]

Jdg 16: 7 "If they bind me with seven fresh **b** that are
16: 8 the Philistines brought her seven fresh **b** that had
16: 9 the **b**, as a strand of fiber snaps when it touches

BOX (4) [BOXES]

1Sa 6: 8 and put in a **b** at its side the figures of gold,
6:11 and the **b** with the gold mice and the images
6:15 the ark of the LORD and the **b** that was beside it,
1Co 9:26 nor do I **b** as though beating the air;

BOXES (1) [BOX]

Isa 3:20 the sashes, the perfume **b**, and the amulets;

BOX (KJV) See FLASK, JAR

BOXWOOD See Index to Footnotes

BOY (75) [BOY'S, BOYHOOD, BOYS, SERVANT-BOY]

Ge 21:12 not be distressed because of the **b** and because
21:17 And God heard the voice of the **b**;
21:17 for God has heard the voice of the **b** where he is.
21:18 lift up the **b** and hold him fast with your hand,
21:19 and gave the **b** a drink.
21:20 God was with the **b**, and he grew up;
22: 5 the **b** and I will go over there;
22:12 not lay your hand on the **b** or do anything to him;
37:30 and said, "The **b** is gone; and I, where can I turn?"
42:22 "Did I not tell you not to wrong the **b**?
43: 8 "Send the **b** with me, and let us be on our way,
44:22 We said to my lord, 'The **b** cannot leave his father,
44:30 when I come to your servant my father and the **b** is
44:31 when he sees that the **b** is not with us, he will die;
44:32 your servant became surety for the **b** to my father,
44:33 as a slave to my lord in place of the **b**;
44:33 and let the **b** go back with his brothers.
44:34 can I go back to my father if the **b** is not with me?
Ex 1:16 and see them on the birthstool, if it is a **b**, kill him;
1:22 "Every **b** that is born to
21:31 If it gores a **b** or a girl,
Jdg 8:20 But the **b** did not draw his sword,
8:20 for he was afraid, because he was still a **b**.
13: 5 for the **b** shall be a nazirite to God from birth.
13: 7 for the **b** shall be a nazirite to God from birth to
13: 8 to do concerning the **b** who will be born."
13:24 The **b** grew, and the LORD blessed him.
1Sa 2:11 while the **b** remained to minister to the LORD,
2:18 a **b** wearing a linen ephod.
2:21 **b** Samuel grew up in the presence of the LORD.
2:26 the **b** Samuel continued to grow both in stature
3: 1 Now the **b** Samuel was ministering to the LORD
3: 8 Eli perceived that the LORD was calling the **b**.
9: 5 Saul said to the **b** who was with him,
9: 7 Then Saul replied to the **b**, "But if we go,
9: 8 The **b** answered Saul again, "Here,
9:10 Saul said to the **b**, "Good; come, let us go."
9:27 "Tell the **b** to go on before us,
10:14 Saul's uncle said to him and to the **b**,
17:33 for you are just a **b**,
20:21 I will send the **b**, saying, 'Go, find the arrows.'
20:21 If I say to the **b**, 'Look,
20:35 and with him was a little **b**.
20:36 He said to the **b**, "Run and find the arrows
20:36 As the **b** ran, he shot an arrow beyond him.
20:37 When the **b** came to the place
20:37 Jonathan called after the **b** and said,
20:38 Jonathan called after the **b**, "Hurry, be quick,
20:38 So Jonathan's **b** gathered up the arrows and came
20:39 But the **b** knew nothing; only Jonathan
20:40 Jonathan gave his weapons to the **b** and said
20:41 As soon as the **b** had gone,
2Sa 17:18 But a **b** saw them, and told Absalom;
1Ki 3:25 The king said, "Divide the living **b** in two;
3:26 "Please, my lord, give her the living **b**;
3:27 "Give the first woman the living **b**;
11:17 He was a young **b** at that time.
2Ki 5:14 his flesh was restored like the flesh of a young **b**,
2Ch 34: 3 while he was still a **b**,

Pr 22:15 Folly is bound up in the heart of a **b**,
Jer 1: 6 for I am only a **b**."
1: 7 LORD said to me, "Do not say, 'I am only a **b**';
51:22 with you I smash the old man and the **b**;
Mt 17:18 and the **b** was cured instantly.
Mk 9:20 And they brought the **b** to him.
9:20 the spirit saw him, immediately it convulsed the **b**,
9:25 that keeps this **b** from speaking and hearing,
9:26 it came out, and the **b** was like a corpse,
Lk 2:43 the **b** Jesus stayed behind in Jerusalem,
9:42 But Jesus rebuked the unclean spirit, healed the **b**,
Jn 4:49 "Sir, come down before my little **b** dies."
6: 9 a **b** here who has five barley loaves and two fish.
Ac 20:12 the **b** away alive and were not a little comforted.
1Mc 11:54 the young **b** Antiochus who began to reign and put
4Mc 11:13 he too had died, the sixth, a mere **b**, was led in.

BOY'S (4) [BOY]
Ge 44:30 then, as his life is bound up in the **b** life,
Jdg 13:12 what is to be the **b** rule of life; what is he to do?"
4Mc 12: 6 he sent for the **b** mother to show compassion
12: 9 Extremely pleased by the **b** declaration,

BOYHOOD (1) [BOY]
1Mc 6:17 Lysias had brought him up from **b**;

BOYS (16) [BOY]
Ge 25:27 When the **b** grew up, Esau was a skillful hunter,
48:16 from all harm, bless the **b**;
Ex 1:17 of Egypt commanded them, but they let the **b** live.
1:18 and allowed the **b** to live?"
1Sa 9: 3 "Take one of the **b** with you;
2Ki 2:23 up on the way, some small **b** came out of the city
2:24 of the woods and mauled forty-two of the **b**.
Isa 3: 4 And I will make **b** their princes,
La 5:13 and **b** stagger under loads of wood.
Joel 3: 3 and traded **b** for prostitutes,
Zec 8: 5 of the city shall be full of **b** and girls playing
1Mc 2:46 they forcibly circumcised all the uncircumcised **b**
2Mc 5:13 destruction of **b**, women, and children,
5:24 the grown men and to sell the women and **b**
4Mc 11:24 We six **b** have paralyzed your tyranny.
15: 6 The mother of the seven **b**,

BOZEZ (1)
1Sa 14: 4 the name of the one was **B**,

BOZKATH (2)
Jos 15:39 Lachish, **B**, Eglon,
2Ki 22: 1 name was Jedidah daughter of Adaiah of **B**.

BOZRAH (10)
Ge 36:33 Jobab son of Zerah of **B** succeeded him as king.
1Ch 1:44 Jobab son of Zerah of **B** succeeded him.
Isa 34: 6 For the LORD has a sacrifice in **B**,
63: 1 from **B** in garments stained crimson?
Jer 48:24 and **B**, and all the towns of the land of Moab,
49:13 **B** shall become an object of horror and ridicule,
49:22 and spread his wings against **B**,
Am 1:12 and it shall devour the strongholds of **B**.
1Mc 5:26 up in **B** and Bosor, in Alema and Chaspho, Maked
5:28 by the wilderness road to **B**;

BRACELET (1) [BRACELETS]
Sir 21:21 and like a **b** on the right arm.

BRACELETS (8) [BRACELET]
Ge 24:22 and two **b** for her arms weighing ten gold shekels,
24:30 and the **b** on his sister's arms,
24:47 I put the ring on her nose, and the **b** on her arms.
Nu 31:50 armlets and **b**, signet rings, earrings, and pendants,
Isa 3:19 the pendants, the **b**, and the scarfs;
Eze 16:11 I put **b** on your arms, a chain on your neck,
23:42 and they put **b** on the arms of the women,
Jdt 10: 4 **b**, rings, earrings, and all her other jewelry.

BRACKISH (1)
Jas 3:11 from the same opening both fresh and **b** water?

BRAG (1) [BRAGGART]
1Ki 20:11 on armor should not **b** like one who takes it off."

BRAGGART (1) [BRAG]
Jer 46:17 the name "**B** who missed his chance."

BRAIDED (1) [BRAIDING]
1Ti 2: 9 not with their hair **b**, or with gold, pearls,

BRAIDING (1) [BRAIDED]
1Pe 3: 3 Do not adorn yourselves outwardly by **b** your hair,

BRAMBLE (4) [BRAMBLES]
Jdg 9:14 So all the trees said to the **b**,
9:15 And the **b** said to the trees,
9:15 let fire come out of the **b** and devour the cedars
Lk 6:44 nor are grapes picked from a **b** bush.

BRAMBLE (KJV) See also THORNBUSH

BRAMBLES (1) [BRAMBLE]
SS 2: 2 As a lily among **b**, so is my love among maidens.

BRAN (1)
LtJ 6:42 sit along the passageways, burning **b** for incense.

BRANCH‡ (30) [BRANCHES]
Ex 25:33 each with calyx and petals, on one **b**,
25:33 each with calyx and petals, on the other **b**—
37:19 each with calyx and petals, on one **b**,
37:19 each with calyx and petals, on the other **b**—
Lev 25:47 or to a **b** of the alien's family,
Nu 13:23 and cut down from there a **b** with a single cluster
Job 15:32 and their **b** will not be green.
Isa 4: 2 On that day the **b** of the LORD shall be beautiful
9:14 palm **b** and reed in one day—
11: 1 and a **b** shall grow out of his roots.
19:15 Neither head nor tail, palm **b** or reed,
Jer 1:11 And I said, "I see a **b** of an almond tree."
23: 5 when I will raise up for David a righteous **B**,
33:15 at that time I will cause a righteous **B** to spring up
Eze 8:17 See, they are putting the **b** to their nose!
15: 2 the vine **b** that is among the trees of the forest?
Da 1: 4 versed in every **b** of wisdom,
11: 7 a **b** from her roots shall rise up in his place.
Zec 3: 8 I am going to bring my servant the **B**.
6:12 Here is a man whose name is **B**:
6:12 for he shall **b** out in his place,
Mal 4: 1 so that it will leave them neither root nor **b**.
Mt 24:32 as its **b** becomes tender and puts forth its leaves,
Mk 13:28 as its **b** becomes tender and puts forth its leaves,
Jn 15: 2 He removes every **b** in me that bears no fruit.
15: 2 Every **b** that bears fruit he prunes
15: 4 as the **b** cannot bear fruit by itself unless it abides
15: 6 in me is thrown away like a **b** and withers;
19:29 the wine on a **b** of hyssop and held it to his mouth.
1Mc 13:37 We have received the gold crown and the palm **b**

BRANCHES (89) [BRANCH]
Ge 2:10 and from there it divides and becomes four **b**.
40:10 and on the vine there were three **b**.
40:12 the three **b** are three days;
49:22 his **b** run over the wall.
Ex 25:32 six **b** going out of its sides, three **b** of the
25:32 and three **b** of the lampstand out of the other side
25:33 so for the six **b** going out of the lampstand.
25:35 the first pair of **b**, a calyx of one piece with it
25:35 calyx of one piece with it under the next pair of **b**,
25:35 a calyx of one piece with it under the last pair of **b**
25:35 so for the six **b** that go out of the lampstand.
25:36 Their calyxes and their **b** shall be of one piece
37:18 There were six **b** going out of its sides,
37:18 three **b** of the lampstand out of one side of it
37:18 and three **b** of the lampstand out of the other side
37:19 so for the six **b** going out of the lampstand.
37:21 of one piece with it under the first pair of **b**,
37:21 calyx of one piece with it under the next pair of **b**,
37:21 calyx of one piece with it under the last pair of **b**.
37:22 Their calyxes and their **b** were of one piece with it,
Lev 23:40 **b** of palm trees, boughs of leafy trees,
2Sa 18: 9 and the mule went under the thick **b** of a great oak.
Ne 8:15 "Go out to the hills and bring **b** of olive,
Job 14: 9 at the scent of water it will bud and put forth **b** like
18:16 up beneath, and their **b** wither above.
29:19 with the dew all night on my **b**;
Ps 80:10 the mighty cedars with its **b**;
80:11 it sent out its **b** to the sea,
104:12 have their habitation; they sing among the **b**.
118:27 Bind the festal procession with **b**,
SS 7: 8 the palm tree and lay hold of its **b**.
Isa 17: 6 four or five on the **b** of a fruit tree,
18: 5 and the spreading **b** he will hew away.
19: 6 the **b** of Egypt's Nile will diminish and dry up,
27:10 there they lie down, and strip its **b**.
Jer 5:10 strip away her **b**, for they are not the LORD's.
6: 9 pass your hand again over its **b**.
11:16 and its **b** will be consumed.
48:32 Your **b** crossed over the sea,
Eze 17: 6 Its **b** turned toward him, its roots remained
17: 6 it brought forth **b**, put forth foliage.
17: 7 It shot out its **b** toward him,
17: 8 that it might produce **b** and bear fruit and become
17:23 of its **b** will nest winged creatures of every kind.
19:10 fruitful and full of **b** from abundant water.
19:11 it stood out in its height with its mass of **b**.
19:14 has consumed its **b** and fruit,
31: 3 a cedar of Lebanon, with fair **b** and forest shade,
31: 5 its boughs grew large and its **b** long,
31: 6 under its **b** all the animals of the field gave birth
31: 7 in the length of its **b**;
31: 8 plane trees were as nothing compared with its **b**;
31: 9 I made it beautiful with its mass of **b**,
31:12 and in all the valleys its **b** have fallen,
36: 8 you, O mountains of Israel, shall shoot out your **b**,
Da 4:12 the birds of the air nested in its **b**,
4:14 'Cut down the tree and chop off its **b**,
4:14 from beneath it and the birds from its **b**.
4:21 and in whose **b** the birds of the air had nests—
Joel 1: 7 their **b** have turned white.
Na 2: 2 ravagers have ravaged them and ruined their **b**.)
Zec 4:12 "What are these two **b** of the olive trees,
Mt 13:32 the birds of the air come and make nests in its **b**."
21: 8 and others cut **b** from the trees and spread them on
Mk 4:32 the greatest of all shrubs, and puts forth large **b**, so
11: 8 and others spread leafy **b** that they had cut in
Lk 13:19 and the birds of the air made nests in its **b**."
Jn 12:13 So they took **b** of palm trees and went out
15: 5 I am the vine, you are the **b**.
15: 6 such **b** are gathered, thrown into the fire,
Ro 11:16 and if the root is holy, then the **b** also are holy.
11:17 But if some of the **b** were broken off, and you,
11:18 do not boast over the **b**.
11:19 "**B** were broken off so that I might be grafted in."
11:21 For if God did not spare the natural **b**,
11:24 how much more will these natural **b**
Rev 7: 9 robed in white, with palm **b** in their hands.
Wis 4: 5 **b** will be broken off before they come to maturity,
17:18 a melodious sound of birds in wide-spreading **b**,
Sir 1:20 and her **b** are long life.
23:25 and her **b** will not bear fruit.
24:16 Like a terebinth I spread out my **b**,
24:16 and my **b** are glorious and graceful.
37:18 it sprouts four **b**, good and evil, life and death;
40:15 The children of the ungodly put out few **b**;
1Mc 13:51 the Jews entered it with praise and palm **b**,
2Mc 10: 7 carrying ivy-wreathed wands and beautiful **b** and
14: 4 and besides these some of the customary olive **b**

BRAND (2) [BRANDS, FIREBRANDS]
Am 4:11 and you were like a **b** snatched from the fire;
Zec 3: 2 Is not this man a **b** plucked from the fire?"

BRANDED (2)
Gal 6:17 for I carry the marks of Jesus **b** on my body.
3Mc 2:29 those who are registered are also to be **b**

BRANDISH (1) [BRANDISHED, BRANDISHING]
Eze 32:10 When I **b** my sword before them,

BRANDISHED (4) [BRANDISH]
Pr 26: 9 Like a thornbush **b** by the hand of a drunkard is
Isa 30:32 battling with **b** arm he will fight with him.
Hab 3: 9 You **b** your naked bow, sated were the arrows
Sir 46: 2 when he lifted his hands and **b** his sword against

BRANDISHING (2) [BRANDISH]
2Mc 5: 3 **b** of shields, massing of spears,
11: 8 clothed in white and **b** weapons of gold.

BRANDS (1) [BRAND]
Isa 50:11 and among the **b** that you have kindled!

BRASEN (KJV) See BRONZE

BRASS (3)
Isa 48: 4 your neck is an iron sinew and your forehead **b**,
1Mc 6:35 and with **b** helmets on their heads;
6:39 When the sun shone on the shields of gold and **b**,

BRASS (KJV) See also BRONZE

BRAVE (12) [BRAVELY, BRAVERY, BRAVEST]
Tob 6:12 Moreover, the girl is sensible, **b**,
Sir 19:10 Be **b**, it will not make you burst!
1Mc 5:56 heard of their **b** deeds and of
5:61 thinking to do a **b** deed,
5:67 who wished to do a **b** deed, fell in battle,
8: 2 the **b** deeds that they were doing among the Gauls,
9:22 and his wars and the **b** deeds that he did,
10:15 of the **b** deeds that they had done,
16:23 of John and his wars and the **b** deeds that he did,
2Mc 15:11 and spears as with the inspiration of **b** words,
4Mc 15:10 For they were righteous and self-controlled and **b**
17:24 and this made them **b** and courageous

BRAVELY (9) [BRAVE]
1Mc 9:10 If our time has come, let us die **b** for our kindred,
2Mc 2:21 from heaven to those who fought **b** for Judaism,
6:27 Therefore, by **b** giving up my life now,
10:35 **b** stormed the wall and with savage fury cut
13:14 and exhorting his troops to fight **b** to the death for
14:43 and **b** threw himself down into the crowd.
15:17 not to carry on a campaign but to attack **b**,
3Mc 1: 4 and their children and wives **b**,
2Es 10:15 and bear **b** the troubles that have come upon you.

BRAVERY (2) [BRAVE]
AdE 10: 2 And as for his power and **b**,
4Mc 1: 8 from the noble **b** of those who died for the sake

BRAVERY (KJV) See also FINERY

BRAVEST (1) [BRAVE]
2Mc 13:15 and with a picked force of the **b** young men,

BRAWLER (1)
Pr 20: 1 Wine is a mocker, strong drink a **b**,

BRAY (2)
Job 6: 5 Does the wild ass **b** over its grass,
30: 7 Among the bushes they **b**;

BRAZEN (1)
Eze 16:30 the deeds of a **b** whore;

BRAZIER (3) [BRAZIERS]
Jer 36:22 and there was a fire burning in the **b** before him.
36:23 a penknife and throw them into the fire in the **b**,
36:23 in the fire that was in the **b**.

BRAZIERS (3) [BRAZIER]
4Mc 8:13 **b** and thumbscrews and iron claws and wedges
12:10 Running to the nearest of the **b**,
12:19 he flung himself into the **b** and so ended his life.

BREACH‡ (12) [BREACHED, BREACHES]
Ge 38:29 she said, "What a **b** you have made for yourself!"
Jos 22:22 in rebellion or in **b** of faith toward the LORD,
Jdg 21:15 on Benjamin because the LORD had made a **b** in
2Ki 25: 4 Then a **b** was made in the city wall;
Job 30:14 a wide **b** they come; amid the crash they roll on.
Ps 106:23 his chosen one, stood in the **b** before him,
144:14 May there be no **b** in the walls, no exile,
Isa 58:12 you shall be called the repairer of the **b**,
Jer 39: 2 a **b** was made in the city.
52: 7 Then a **b** was made in the city wall;
Eze 22:30 and stand in the **b** before me on behalf of the land,
Sir 41:18 and of a **b** of the law,

BREACHED (3) [BREACH]
Pr 25:28 Like a city **b**, without walls,
Eze 26:10 he enters your gates like those entering a **b** city.
30:16 Thebes shall be **b**, and Memphis face adversaries

BREACHES (4) [BREACH]
Isa 22: 9 and you saw that there were many **b** in the city
Eze 13: 5 You have not gone up into the **b**,
Am 4: 3 Through **b** in the wall you shall leave,
9:11 and repair its **b**, and raise up its ruins,

BREAD‡ (330)
A. UNLEAVENED BREAD (45)
B. FESTIVAL OF UNLEAVENED BREAD (15)

Ge 3:19 of your face you shall eat **b** until you return to
14:18 And King Melchizedek of Salem brought out **b**
18: 5 a little **b**, that you may refresh yourselves,
19: 3 he made them a feast, and baked unleavened **b**, A
21:14 and took **b** and a skin of water,
25:34 Then Jacob gave Esau **b** and lentil stew,
27:17 and the **b** that she had prepared, to her son Jacob.
28:20 and will give me **b** to eat and clothing to wear,
31:54 on the height and called his kinsfolk to eat **b**;
31:54 they ate **b** and tarried all night in the hill country.
41:54 but throughout the land of Egypt there was **b**.
41:55 the people cried to Pharaoh for **b**.
45:23 **b**, and provision for his father on the journey.
Ex 2:20 Invite him to break **b**."
12: 8 over the fire with unleavened **b** and bitter herbs. A
12:15 Seven days you shall eat unleavened **b**; A
12:15 from your houses, for whoever eats leavened **b**
12:17 You shall observe the festival of unleavened **b**, AB
12:18 you shall eat unleavened **b**. A
12:20 all your settlements you shall eat unleavened **b**. A
13: 3 no leavened **b** shall be eaten.
13: 6 Seven days you shall eat unleavened **b**, A
13: 7 Unleavened **b** shall be eaten for seven days; A
13: 7 no leavened **b** shall be seen in your possession,
16: 3 when we sat by the fleshpots and ate our fill of **b**;
16: 4 "I am going to rain **b** from heaven for you,
16: 8 of **b** in the morning, because the LORD has heard
16:12 and in the morning you shall have your fill of **b**;
16:15 "It is the **b** that the LORD has given you to eat.
18:12 to eat **b** with Moses' father-in-law in the presence
23:15 You shall observe the festival of unleavened **b**; AB
23:15 I commanded you, you shall eat unleavened **b** A
23:25 and I will bless your **b** and your water;
25:30 And you shall set the **b** of the Presence on
29: 2 and unleavened **b**, unleavened cakes mixed A
29:23 and one loaf of **b**, one cake of bread made
29:23 one cake of **b** made with oil, and one wafer,
29:23 out of the basket of unleavened **b** that is before A
29:32 the flesh of the ram and the **b** that is in the basket,
29:34 If any of the flesh for the ordination, or of the **b**,
34:18 You shall keep the festival of unleavened **b**. AB
34:18 Seven days you shall eat unleavened **b**, A
34:28 he neither ate **b** nor drank water.
35:13 and the **b** of the Presence;
39:36 and the **b** of the Presence;
40:23 and set the **b** in order on it before the LORD;
Lev 7:13 shall bring your offering with cakes of leavened **b**.
8: 2 the two rams, and the basket of unleavened **b**; A
8:26 From the basket of unleavened **b** that was A
8:26 he took one cake of unleavened **b**, A
8:26 one cake of **b** with oil, and one wafer,
8:31 the **b** that is in the basket of ordination offerings,
8:32 of the flesh and the **b** you shall burn with fire.
23: 6 the same month is the festival of unleavened **b** AB
23: 6 seven days you shall eat unleavened **b**. A
23:14 You shall eat no **b** or parched grain or fresh ears

Lev 23:17 from your settlements two loaves of **b** as
23:18 with the **b** seven lambs a year old without blemish,
23:20 the **b** of the first fruits as an elevation offering
24: 7 to be a token offering for the **b**,
26: 5 you shall eat your **b** to the full,
26:26 When I break your staff of **b**,
26:26 ten women shall bake your **b** in a single oven,
26:26 and they shall dole out your **b** by weight;
Nu 4: 7 the table of the **b** of the Presence they shall spread
4: 7 the regular **b** also shall be on it;
6:15 and a basket of unleavened **b**, A
6:17 with the basket of unleavened **b**; A
9:11 with unleavened **b** and bitter herbs. A
14: 9 for they are no more than **b** for us;
15:19 whenever you eat of the **b** of the land,
28:17 seven days shall unleavened **b** be eaten. A
Dt 8: 3 that one does not live by **b** alone,
8: 9 a land where you may eat **b** without scarcity,
9: 9 I neither ate **b** nor drank water.
9:18 I neither ate **b** nor drank water,
16: 3 seven days you shall eat unleavened **b** with it— A
16: 3 the **b** of affliction—because you came out of
16: 8 six days you shall continue to eat unleavened **b**, A
16:16 at the festival of unleavened **b**, AB
29: 6 not eaten **b**, and you have not drunk wine
Jos 9:12 Here is our **b**; it was still warm
Jdg 7:13 and in it a cake of barley **b** tumbled into the camp
8: 5 "Please give some loaves of **b** to my followers,
8: 6 that we should give **b** to your army?"
8:15 of Zebah and Zalmunna, that we should give **b**
19:19 with **b** and wine for me and the woman and
Ru 2:14 "Come here, and eat some of this **b**,
1Sa 2: 5 for **b**, but those who were hungry are fat
2:36 to implore him for a piece of silver or a loaf of **b**,
2:36 that I may eat a morsel of **b**.' "
9: 7 For the **b** in our sacks is gone,
10: 3 another carrying three loaves of **b**,
10: 4 They will greet you and give you two loaves of **b**,
16:20 Jesse took a donkey loaded with **b**, a skin of wine,
21: 3 Give me five loaves of **b**, or whatever is here."
21: 4 "I have no ordinary **b** at hand, only holy **b**—
21: 6 So the priest gave him the holy **b**;
21: 6 for there was no **b** there except the **b** of
21: 6 to be replaced by hot **b** on the day it is taken away.
22:13 by giving him **b** and a sword,
25:11 Shall I take my **b** and my water and the meat
28:22 let me set a morsel of **b** before you.
30:11 They gave him **b** and he ate,
30:12 not eaten **b** or drunk water for three days
2Sa 3:35 "So may God do to me, and more, if I taste **b**
6:19 both men and women, to each a cake of **b**,
16: 1 carrying two hundred loaves of **b**,
16: 2 the **b** and summer fruit for the young men to eat,
1Ki 7:48 the golden table for the **b** of the Presence,
17: 6 ravens brought him **b** and meat in the morning,
17: 6 and **b** and meat in the evening;
17:11 "Bring me a morsel of **b** in your hand."
18: 4 and provided them with **b** and water.)
18:13 and provided them with **b** and water?
22:27 and feed him on reduced rations of **b** and water
2Ki 18:32 a land of **b** and vineyards,
23: 9 but ate unleavened **b** among their kindred. A
1Ch 9:32 of the Kohathites had charge of the rows of **b**,
16: 3 to each a loaf of **b**, a portion of meat,
23:29 to assist also with the rows of **b**,
23:29 the wafers of unleavened **b**, the baked offering, A
28:16 the weight of gold for each table for the rows of **b**,
2Ch 2: 4 and for the regular offering of the rows of **b**,
4:19 golden altar, the tables for the **b** of the Presence,
8:13 festival of unleavened **b**, the festival of weeks, AB
13:11 set out the rows of **b** on the table of pure gold,
18:26 and feed him on reduced rations of **b** and water
29:18 and the table for the rows of **b** and all its utensils.
30:13 festival of unleavened **b** in the second month, AB
30:21 the festival of unleavened **b** seven days AB
35:17 and the festival of unleavened **b** seven days. AB
Ezr 6:22 the festival of unleavened **b** seven days; AB
10: 6 He did not eat **b** or drink water,
Ne 9:15 For their hunger you gave them **b** from heaven,
10:33 for the rows of **b**, the regular grain offering,
13: 2 with **b** and water, but hired Balaam against them
Job 3:24 For my sighing comes like my **b**,
15:23 They wander abroad for **b**, saying, 'Where is it?'
22: 7 and you have withheld **b** from the hungry.
28: 5 As for the earth, out of it comes **b**;
33:20 so that their lives loathe **b**,
42:11 and they ate **b** with him in his house;
Ps 14: 4 the evildoers who eat up my people as they eat **b**,
37:25 the righteous forsaken or their children begging **b**.
41: 9 who ate of my **b**, has lifted the heel against me.
53: 4 who eat up my people as they eat **b**,
78:20 can he also give **b**, or provide meat for his people?
78:25 Mortals ate of the **b** of angels;
80: 5 You have fed them with the **b** of tears,
102: 4 I am too wasted to eat my **b**.
102: 9 For I eat ashes like **b**,
104:15 and **b** to strengthen the human heart.
105:16 and broke every staff of **b**,
127: 2 eating the **b** of anxious toil;
132:15 I will satisfy its poor with **b**.
Pr 4:17 For they eat the **b** of wickedness and drink
6:26 for a prostitute's fee is only a loaf of **b**,
9: 5 eat of my **b** and drink of the wine I have mixed.
9:17 and **b** eaten in secret is pleasant."
20:13 open your eyes, and you will have plenty of **b**.
20:17 **B** gained by deceit is sweet,
22: 9 for they share their **b** with the poor.

Pr 23: 6 Do not eat the **b** of the stingy;
25:21 If your enemies are hungry, give them **b** to eat;
28:19 Anyone who tills the land will have plenty of **b**,
28:21 yet for a piece of **b** a person may do wrong.
31:27 and does not eat the **b** of idleness.
Ecc 9: 7 Go, eat your **b** with enjoyment,
9:11 nor **b** to the wise, nor riches to the intelligent,
11: 1 Send out your **b** upon the waters,
Isa 3: 1 all support of **b**, and all support of water—
3: 7 in my house there is neither **b** nor cloak;
4: 1 "We will eat our own **b** and wear our own clothes;
21:14 the thirsty, meet the fugitive with **b**, O inhabitants
28:28 for **b**, but one does not thresh it forever;
30:20 Though the Lord may give you the **b** of adversity
36:17 a land of **b** and vineyards.
44:15 he kindles a fire and bakes **b**.
44:19 I also baked **b** on its coals,
51:14 and go down to the Pit, nor shall they lack **b**.
55: 2 for that which is not **b**,
55:10 giving seed to the sower and **b** to the eater,
58: 7 Is it not to share your **b** with the hungry,
Jer 16: 7 No one shall break **b** for the mourner,
37:21 of **b** was given him daily from the bakers' street,
37:21 until all the **b** of the city was gone.
38: 9 for there is no **b** left in the city."
41: 1 As they ate **b** together there at Mizpah,
42:14 or be hungry for **b**, and there we will stay,'
La 1:11 All her people groan as they search for **b**;
2:12 They cry to their mothers, "Where is **b** and wine?"
5: 6 a pact with Egypt and Assyria, to get enough **b**.
5: 9 We get our **b** at the peril of our lives,
Eze 4: 9 put them into one vessel, and make **b** for yourself.
4:13 "Thus shall the people of Israel eat their **b**,
4:15 on which you may prepare your **b**."
4:16 I am going to break the staff of **b** in Jerusalem;
4:16 they shall eat **b** by weight and with fearfulness;
4:17 Lacking **b** and water, they will look at one another
5:16 and break your staff of **b**.
12:18 eat your **b** with quaking, and drink your water
12:19 They shall eat their **b** with fearfulness,
13:19 for handfuls of barley and for pieces of **b**,
14:13 and break its staff of **b** and send famine upon it,
16:19 Also my **b** that I gave you—
18: 7 gives his **b** to the hungry and covers the naked
18:16 but gives his **b** to the hungry and covers the naked
24:17 not cover your upper lip or eat the **b** of mourners.
24:22 not cover your upper lip or eat the **b** of mourners.
45:21 and for seven days unleavened **b** shall be eaten. A
Hos 2: 5 they give me my **b** and my water,
9: 4 Such sacrifices shall be like mourners' **b**;
9: 4 for their **b** shall be for their hunger only;
Am 4: 5 bring a thank offering of leavened **b**,
4: 6 and lack of **b** in all your places,
7:12 flee away to the land of Judah, earn your **b** there,
8:11 not a famine of **b**, or a thirst for water,
Ob 1: 7 those who ate your **b** have set a trap for you—
Hag 2:12 and with the fold touches **b**, or stew, or wine,
Mt 4: 3 command these stones to become loaves of **b**."
4: 4 "It is written, 'One does not live by **b** alone,
6:11 Give us this day our daily **b**.
7: 9 if your child asks for **b**, will give a stone?
12: 4 the house of God and ate the **b** of the Presence,
15:33 to get enough **b** in the desert to feed so great
16: 5 they had forgotten to bring any **b**.
16: 7 "It is because we have brought no **b**."
16: 8 why are you talking about having no **b**?
16:11 to perceive that I was not speaking about **b**?
16:12 not told them to beware of the yeast of **b**,
26:17 first day of Unleavened **B** the disciples came A
26:26 While they were eating, Jesus took a loaf of **b**,
Mk 2:26 and ate the **b** of the Presence,
6: 8 no **b**, no bag, no money in their belts;
6:37 to go and buy two hundred denarii worth of **b**,
8: 4 "How can one feed these people with **b** here in
8:14 Now the disciples had forgotten to bring any **b**;
8:16 "It is because we have no **b**."
8:17 "Why are you talking about having no **b**?
14: 1 the Passover and the festival of Unleavened **B**. AB
14:12 On the first day of Unleavened **B**, A
14:20 one who is dipping **b** into the bowl with me.
14:22 While they were eating, he took a loaf of **b**,
Lk 4: 3 command this stone to become a loaf of **b**."
4: 4 "It is written, 'One does not live by **b** alone.' "
6: 4 of God and took and ate the **b** of the Presence,
7:33 For John the Baptist has come eating no **b**
9: 3 nor **b**, nor money—not even an extra tunic.
11: 3 Give us each day our daily **b**.
11: 5 'Friend, lend me three loaves of **b**;
14:15 "Blessed is anyone who will eat **b** in the kingdom
15:17 of my father's hired hands have **b** enough and
22: 1 Now the festival of Unleavened **B**, AB
22: 7 Then came the day of Unleavened **B**, A
22:19 Then he took a loaf of **b**,
24:30 When he was at the table with them, he took **b**,
24:35 to them in the breaking of the **b**.
Jn 6: 5 "Where are we to buy **b** for these people to eat?"
6: 7 not buy enough **b** for each of them to get a little."
6:23 near the place where they had eaten the **b** after
6:31 'He gave them **b** from heaven to eat.' "
6:32 it was not Moses who gave you the **b** from heaven,
6:32 but it is my Father who gives you the true **b**
6:33 For the **b** of God is that which comes down
6:34 They said to him, "Sir, give us this **b** always."
6:35 Jesus said to them, "I am the **b** of life.
6:41 "I am the **b** that came down from heaven."
6:48 I am the **b** of life.
6:50 This is the **b** that comes down from heaven,

Jn 6:51 I am the living **b** that came down from heaven.
6:51 Whoever eats of this **b** will live forever;
6:51 and the **b** that I will give for the life of the world
6:58 This is the **b** that came down from heaven,
6:58 But the one who eats this **b** will live forever."
13:18 one who ate my **b** has lifted his heel against me.'
13:26 "It is the one to whom I give this piece of **b**
13:26 So when he had dipped the piece of **b**,
13:27 he received the piece of **b**, Satan entered into him.
13:30 receiving the piece of **b**, he immediately went out.
21: 9 a charcoal fire there, with fish on it, and **b**.
21:13 Jesus came and took the **b** and gave it to them,
Ac 2:42 to the breaking of **b** and the prayers.
2:46 they broke **b** at home and ate their food with glad
12: 3 (This was during the festival of Unleavened **B**.) AB
20: 6 from Philippi after the days of Unleavened **B**, A
20: 7 when we met to break **b**, Paul was holding
20:11 and after he had broken **b** and eaten,
27:35 After he had said this, he took **b**;
1Co 5: 8 but with the unleavened **b** of sincerity and truth. A
10:16 The **b** that we break, is it not a sharing in the body
10:17 there is one **b**, we who are many are one body,
10:17 for we all partake of the one **b**.
11:23 the night when he was betrayed took a loaf of **b**,
11:26 For as often as you eat this **b** and drink the cup,
11:27 eats the **b** or drinks the cup of the Lord in
11:28 and only then eat of the **b** and drink of the cup.
2Co 9:10 and **b** for food will supply and multiply your seed
2Th 3: 8 we did not eat anyone's **b** without paying for it;
Heb 9: 2 the table, and the **b** of the Presence;
Tob 4:17 Place your **b** on the grave of the righteous,
8:19 this he asked his wife to bake many loaves of **b**;
Jdt 10: 5 dried fig cakes, and fine **b**;
Wis 16:20 from heaven with **b** ready to eat,
16:21 and the **b**, ministering to the desire of
Sir 10:27 in plenty than the boaster who lacks **b**.
12: 5 hold back their **b**, and do not give it to them,
14:10 A miser begrudges **b**, and it is lacking at his table.
15: 3 She will feed him with the **b** of learning,
20:16 Those who eat my **b** are evil-tongued."
23:17 To a fornicator all **b** is sweet;
29:21 The necessities of life are water, **b**, and clothing,
33:25 **B** and discipline and work for a slave.
34:25 The **b** of the needy is the life of the poor;
45:20 and prepared **b** of first fruits in abundance;
Bel 1:33 he had made a stew and had broken **b** into a bowl,
1Mc 1:22 He took also the table for the **b** of the Presence,
4:51 They placed the **b** on the table and hung up
2Mc 10: 3 and lighted lamps and set out the **b** of
1Es 1:10 and the Levites, having the unleavened **b**, A
1:19 and the festival of unleavened **b** seven days. AB
7:14 kept the festival of unleavened **b** seven days, AB
9: 2 and he did not eat **b** or drink water,
2Es 1:19 you ate the **b** of angels.
5:18 Rise therefore and eat some **b**,
14:42 they wrote during the daytime, and ate their **b**
15:19 of hunger for **b** and because of great tribulation.
15:58 for **b** and drink their own blood in thirst for water.

BREADTH (8) [BROAD]

Ge 13:17 walk through the length and the **b** of the land,
1Ki 4:29 and **b** of understanding as vast as the sand on
Isa 8: 8 and its outspread wings will fill the **b** of your land,
Hab 1: 6 the **b** of the earth to seize dwellings not their own.
Eph 3:18 what is the **b** and length and height and depth,
Rev 20: 9 over the **b** of the earth and surrounded the camp of
Jdt 7: 3 in **b** over Dothan as far as Balbaim and in length
Sir 1: 3 The height of heaven, the **b** of the earth, the abyss,

BREAK‡ (133) [BREAKING, BREAKS, BROKE, BROKEN, BROKENHEARTED, DAYBREAK, LAWBREAKER, LAWBREAKERS, OUTBREAK]

Ge 19: 9 and came near the door to **b** it down.
27:40 but when you **b** loose, you shall **b** his yoke from
Ex 2:20 Invite him to **b** bread."
12:46 and you shall not **b** any of its bones.
13:13 if you do not redeem it, you must **b** its neck.
19:21 "Go down and warn the people not to **b** through to
19:22 or the LORD will **b** out against them."
19:24 or the people **b** through to come up to the LORD;
19:24 otherwise he will **b** out against them."
23:24 and **b** their pillars in pieces.
34:13 You shall tear down their altars, **b** their pillars,
34:20 or if you will not redeem it you shall **b** its neck.
Lev 2: 6 **b** it in pieces, and pour oil on it;
11:33 and you shall **b** the vessel.
26:15 all my commandments, and you **b** my covenant,
26:19 I will **b** your proud glory,
26:26 When I **b** your staff of bread,
26:44 so as to destroy them utterly and **b** my covenant
Nu 9:12 nor **b** a bone of it;
24: 8 the nations that are his foes and **b** their bones.
30: 2 he shall not **b** his word;
Dt 7: 5 **b** down their altars, smash their pillars,
12: 3 **B** down their altars, smash their pillars,
21: 4 and shall **b** the heifer's neck there in the wadi.
Jos 22:20 Did not Achan son of Zerah **b** faith in the matter
Jdg 2: 1 I said, 'I will never **b** my covenant with you.
8: 9 I will **b** down this tower."
19:25 And as the dawn began to **b**, they let her go.
1Sa 9:26 the **b** of dawn Samuel called to Saul upon the roof,
2Sa 20:15 Joab's forces were battering the wall to **b** it down.
1Ki 15:19 go, **b** your alliance with King Baasha of Israel,
2Ki 3:26 with him seven hundred swordsmen to **b** through,
2Ch 16: 3 go, **b** your alliance with King Baasha of Israel,
Ezr 9:14 shall we **b** your commandments again
Ne 4: 3 any fox going up on it would **b** it down!"
4:21 the spears from **b** of dawn until the stars came out.
Job 19: 2 and **b** me in pieces with words?
30:13 They **b** up my path, they promote my calamity;
Ps 2: 9 You shall **b** them with a rod of iron,
3: 7 you **b** the teeth of the wicked.
10:15 **B** the arm of the wicked and evildoers;
28: 5 he will **b** them down and build them up no more.
52: 5 But God will **b** you down forever;
58: 6 O God, **b** the teeth in their mouths;
98: 4 **b** forth into joyous song and sing praises.
Pr 25:15 and a soft tongue can **b** bones.
Ecc 3: 3 a time to **b** down, and a time to build up;
Isa 5: 5 I will **b** down its wall, and it shall be trampled
14: 7 and quiet; they **b** forth into singing.
14:25 I will **b** the Assyrian in my land,
30:13 for you like a **b** in a high wall, bulging out,
35: 6 For waters shall **b** forth in the wilderness,
42: 3 not **b**, and a dimly burning wick he will
43:14 For your sake I will send to Babylon and **b**
44:23 **b** forth into singing, O mountains, O forest,
45: 2 I will **b** in pieces the doors of bronze and cut
49:13 **b** forth, O mountains, into singing!
52: 9 **B** forth together into singing,
58: 6 to let the oppressed go free, and to **b** every yoke?
58: 8 Then your light shall **b** forth like the dawn,
Jer 1:14 the north disaster shall **b** out on all the inhabitants
1:17 Do not **b** down before them, or I will **b** you before them.
4: 3 **B** up your fallow ground, and do not sow among
14:21 remember and do not **b** your covenant with us.
15:12 Can iron and bronze **b** iron from the north?
16: 7 No one shall **b** bread for the mourner,
18: 7 that I will pluck up and **b** down and destroy it,
19:10 Then you shall **b** the jug in the sight
19:11 So will I **b** this people and this city,
28: 4 for I will **b** the yoke of the king of Babylon."
28:11 how I will **b** the yoke of King Nebuchadnezzar
30: 8 I will **b** the yoke from off his neck,
31:28 as I have watched over them to pluck up and **b**
33:20 If any of you could **b** my covenant with the day
43:13 He shall **b** the obelisks of Heliopolis,
45: 4 I am going to **b** down what I have built,
48:12 and empty his vessels, and **b** his jars in pieces.
49:35 I am going to **b** the bow of Elam,
Eze 4:16 I am going to **b** the staff of bread in Jerusalem;
5:16 and **b** your staff of bread.
13:11 and a stormy wind will **b** out.
13:13 In my wrath I will make a stormy wind **b** out,
13:14 I will **b** down the wall that you have smeared
14:13 and **b** its staff of bread and send famine upon it,
16:39 down your platform and **b** down your lofty places;
17:15 Can he **b** the covenant and yet escape?
17:22 I will **b** off a tender one from the topmost of its young twigs;
26: 4 They shall destroy the walls of Tyre and **b**
26: 9 of his battering rams against your walls and **b**
26:12 they shall **b** down your walls
30:18 when I **b** there the dominion of Egypt,
30:22 of Egypt, and will **b** his arms, both the strong arm
30:24 but I will **b** the arms of Pharaoh,
34:27 when I **b** the bars of their yoke,
Da 6:19 at **b** of day, the king got up and hurried to the den
7:23 and trample it down, and **b** it to pieces.
11:26 They shall **b** him, his army shall be swept away,
Hos 1: 5 On that day I will **b** the bow of Israel in the valley
4: 2 lying, and murder, and stealing and adultery **b** out;
10: 2 The LORD will **b** down their altars,
10:11 but I will make Ephraim **b** the ground;
10:12 reap steadfast love; **b** up your fallow ground;
Am 1: 5 I will **b** the gate bars of Damascus,
5: 6 he will **b** out against the house of Joseph like fire,
Jnh 1: 4 upon the sea that the ship threatened to **b** up.
Mic 2:13 they will **b** through and pass the gate,
3: 3 **b** their bones in pieces, and chop them up like meat
Na 1:13 And now I will **b** off his yoke from you and snap
Mt 6:19 and rust consume and where thieves **b** in and steal;
6:20 nor rust consumes and where thieves do not **b** in
12: 5 the sabbath the priests in the temple **b** the sabbath
12:20 not **b** a bruised reed or quench a smoldering wick
15: 2 "Why do your disciples **b** the tradition of
15: 3 "And why do you **b** the commandment of God for
Lk 1:78 the dawn from on high will **b** upon us,
5: 6 so many fish that their nets were beginning to **b**.
8:29 and shackles, but he would **b** the bonds and
Jn 19:33 they did not **b** his legs.
Ac 20: 7 when we met to **b** bread, Paul was holding
Ro 2:25 but if you **b** the law,
2:27 that have the written code and circumcision but **b**
1Co 10:16 The bread that we **b**, is it not a sharing in the body
Rev 5: 2 "Who is worthy to open the scroll and **b** its seals?"
Jdt 7: 1 to **b** camp and move against Bethulia,
8:30 and made us take an oath that we cannot **b**.
9: 8 **B** their strength by your might,
9: 8 and to **b** off the horns of your altar with the sword.
Sir 10:19 Those who **b** the commandments.
2Es 5: 8 fire shall often **b** out, the wild animals shall roam
4Mc 5:33 not so pity my old age as to **b** the ancestral law
10: 7 Since they were not able in any way to **b** his spirit,

BREAKFAST (2)

Jn 21:12 Jesus said to them, "Come and have **b**."
21:15 When they had finished **b**,

BREAKING (23) [BREAK]

Ge 32:26 Then he said, "Let me go, for the day is **b**."
Ex 22: 2 If a thief is found **b** in, and is beaten to death,
Lev 13:42 it is a leprous disease **b** out on his bald head
Nu 5: 6 a woman wrongs another, **b** faith with the LORD,
10: 2 for summoning the congregation, and for **b** camp.
Dt 31:16 **b** my covenant that I have made with them.
31:20 despising me and **b** my covenant.
1Sa 25:10 There are many servants today who are **b** away
1Ki 19:11 and **b** rocks in pieces before the LORD,
Isa 30:14 its **b** is like that of a potter's vessel that is smashed
Jer 2:34 though you did not catch them **b** in.
Eze 16:59 you who have despised the oath, **b** the covenant;
21: 6 with **b** heart and bitter grief before their eyes.
Da 7: 7 **b** in pieces, and stamping what was left
8: 7 against it and struck the ram, **b** its two horns.
Lk 24:35 and how he had been made known to them in the **b**
Jn 5:18 because he was not only **b** the sabbath,
Ac 2:42 to the **b** of bread and the prayers.
21:13 "What are you doing, weeping and **b** my heart?
Ro 2:23 do you dishonor God by **b** the law?
Sir 41:19 Be ashamed of **b** an oath or agreement,
2Mc 10:28 Just as dawn was **b**, the two armies joined battle,
4Mc 10: 6 and **b** his fingers and arms and legs and elbows.

BREAKS (24) [BREAK]

Ex 22: 6 When fire **b** out and catches in thorns so that
Lev 13:12 But if the disease **b** out in the skin,
14:43 If the disease **b** out again in the house,
Job 7: 5 my skin hardens, then **b** out again.
19:10 He **b** me down on every side, and I am gone,
Ps 29: 5 The voice of the LORD **b** the cedars;
29: 5 the LORD **b** the cedars of Lebanon.
46: 9 he **b** the bow, and shatters the spear;
141: 7 a rock that one **b** apart and shatters on the land,
Pr 15: 4 but perverseness in it **b** the spirit.
17:14 so stop before the quarrel **b** out.
Ecc 10: 8 and whoever **b** through a wall will be bitten by
Isa 38:13 like a lion he **b** all my bones;
66: 3 like one who **b** a dog's neck;
Jer 19:11 as one **b** a potter's vessel,
23:29 and like a hammer that **b** a rock in pieces?
Hos 7: 1 for they deal falsely, the thief **b** in,
Mic 2:13 The one who **b** out will go up before them;
Mt 5:19 whoever **b** one of the least
Jdt 14: 2 As soon as day **b** and the sun rises on the earth,
Sir 35:23 and **b** the scepters of the unrighteous;
48:10 to calm the wrath of God before it **b** out in fury,
LtJ 6:55 When fire **b** out in a temple
4Mc 2:11 so that one rebukes her when she **b** the law.

BREAST (23) [BREASTPIECE, BREASTPLATE, BREASTPLATES, BREASTS]

Ex 29:26 the **b** of the ram of Aaron's ordination and raise it
29:27 the **b** that was raised as an elevation offering and
Lev 7:30 you shall bring the fat with the **b**,
7:30 so that the **b** may be raised as an elevation offering
7:31 but the **b** shall belong to Aaron and his sons.
7:34 For I have taken the **b** of the elevation offering,
8:29 the **b** and raised it as an elevation offering before
10:14 the **b** that is elevated and the thigh that is raised,
10:15 and the **b** that is elevated they shall bring, together
Nu 6:20 the **b** that is elevated and the thigh that is offered.
18:18 just as the **b** that is elevated and as
1Ki 3:20 laid him at her **b**, and laid her dead son at my **b**.
Job 24: 9 the orphan child from the **b**,
Ps 22: 9 you kept me safe on my mother's **b**.
22:14 it is melted within my **b**;
SS 8: 1 who nursed at my mother's **b**!
Isa 28: 9 from milk, those taken from the **b**?
66:11 and be satisfied from her consoling **b**;
La 4: 3 Even the jackals offer the **b** and nurse their young,
Joel 2:16 gather the children, even infants at the **b**.
Lk 18:13 but was beating his **b** and saying, 'God,
2Es 14:40 and wisdom increased in my **b**,

BREASTPIECE (25) [BREAST, PIECE]

Ex 25: 7 and gems to be set in the ephod and for the **b**.
28: 4 These are the vestments that they shall make: a **b**,
28:15 You shall make a **b** of judgment, in skilled work;
28:22 You shall make for the **b** chains of pure gold,
28:23 and you shall make for the **b** two rings of gold,
28:23 and put the two rings on the two edges of the **b**.
28:24 of gold in the two rings at the edges of the **b**;
28:26 and put them at the two ends of the **b**,
28:28 The **b** shall be bound by its rings to the rings of
28:28 so that the **b** shall not come loose from the ephod.
28:29 the sons of Israel in the **b** of judgment on his heart
28:30 In the **b** of judgment you shall put the Urim and
29: 5 and the **b**, and gird him with the decorated band of
35: 9 and gems to be set in the ephod and the **b**.
35:27 and gems to be set in the ephod and the **b**,
39: 8 He made the **b**, in skilled work,
39: 9 It was square; the **b** was made double,
39:15 They made on the **b** chains of pure gold,
39:16 and put the two rings on the two edges of the **b**;
39:17 of gold in the two rings at the edges of the **b**.
39:19 and put them at the two ends of the **b**,
39:21 the **b** by its rings to the rings of the ephod with
39:21 that the **b** should not come loose from the ephod;
Lev 8: 8 He placed the **b** on him,
8: 8 and in the **b** he put the Urim and the Thummim.

BREASTPLATE (8) [BREAST, PLATE]
1Ki 22:34 of Israel between the scale armor and the **b**;
2Ch 18:33 of Israel between the scale armor and the **b**;
Isa 59:17 He put on righteousness like a **b**,
Eph 6:14 and put on the **b** of righteousness.
1Th 5:8 let us be sober, and put on the **b** of faith and love,
Wis 5:18 on righteousness as a **b**, and wear impartial justice
Sir 43:20 and the water puts it on like a **b**.
1Mc 3:3 Like a giant he put on his **b**;

BREASTPLATES (3) [BREAST, PLATE]
Rev 9:9 they had scales like iron **b**,
9:17 the riders wore **b** the color of fire and of sapphire
1Mc 6:2 containing golden shields, **b**,

BREASTS (31) [BREAST]
Ge 49:25 blessings of the **b** and of the womb.
Lev 9:20 They first laid the fat on the **b**,
9:21 and the **b** and the right thigh Aaron raised as
Job 3:12 or **b** for me to suck?
Pr 5:19 May her **b** satisfy you at all times;
SS 1:13 to me a bag of myrrh that lies between my **b**.
4:5 Your two **b** are like two fawns, twins of a gazelle,
7:3 Your two **b** are like two fawns, twins of a gazelle.
7:7 and your **b** are like its clusters.
7:8 Oh, may your **b** be like clusters of the vine,
8:8 We have a little sister, and she has no **b**.
8:10 I was a wall, and my **b** were like towers;
Isa 32:12 Beat your **b** for the pleasant fields,
60:16 you shall suck the **b** of kings;
Eze 16:7 your **b** were formed, and your hair had grown;
23:3 their **b** were caressed there,
23:21 and caressed your young **b**.
23:34 and gnaw its sherds, and tear out your **b**;
Hos 2:2 and her adultery from between her **b**,
9:14 Give them a miscarrying womb and dry **b**.
Na 2:7 moaning like doves and beating their **b**.
Lk 11:27 "Blessed is the womb that bore you and the **b**
23:27 among them were women who were beating their **b**
23:29 and the **b** that never nursed.'
23:48 they returned home, beating their **b**.
2Mc 3:19 Women, girded with sackcloth under their **b**,
6:10 with their babies hanging at their **b**,
3Mc 5:49 at their **b** who were drawing their last milk.
5:50 removing the babies from their **b**,
2Es 8:10 (that is, from the **b**) milk, the fruit of the **b**,

BREATH‡ (84) [BREATHE, BREATHED, BREATHES, BREATHING, FIRE-BREATHING]
A. BREATH OF ... LIFE (8)

Ge 1:30 everything that has the **b** of life, A
2:7 and breathed into his nostrils the **b** of life; A
6:17 under heaven all flesh in which is the **b** of life; A
7:15 of all flesh in which there was the **b** of life; A
7:22 on dry land in whose nostrils was the **b** of life. A
2Sa 22:16 at the blast of the **b** of his nostrils.
1Ki 17:17 his illness was so severe that there was no **b** left
Job 4:9 By the **b** of God they perish,
7:7 "Remember that my life is a **b**;
7:16 Let me alone, for my days are a **b**.
9:18 he will not let me get my **b**,
12:10 the life of every living thing and the **b**
19:17 My **b** is repulsive to my wife;
27:3 as long as my **b** is in me and the spirit of God is
32:8 in a mortal, the **b** of the Almighty, that makes
33:4 and the **b** of the Almighty gives me life.
34:14 and gather to himself his **b**,
37:10 By the **b** of God ice is given,
41:21 Its **b** kindles coals, and a flame comes out
Ps 18:15 O LORD, at the blast of the **b** of your nostrils.
33:6 and all their host by the **b** of his mouth.
39:5 Surely everyone stands as a mere **b**.
39:11 surely everyone is a mere **b**.
62:9 of low estate are but a **b**, those of high estate are
62:9 they are together lighter than a **b**.
78:33 So he made their days vanish like a **b**,
94:11 that they are but an empty **b**.
104:29 when you take away their **b**,
135:17 and there is no **b** in their mouths.
144:4 They are like a **b**; their days are like a
146:4 When their **b** departs, they return to the earth;
Ecc 3:19 They all have the same **b**,
11:5 as you do not know how the **b** comes to the bones
12:7 and the **b** returns to God who gave it.
SS 7:8 and the scent of your **b** like apples,
Isa 2:22 who have only **b** in their nostrils,
11:4 and with the **b** of his lips he shall kill the wicked.
30:28 his **b** is like an overflowing stream that reaches up
30:33 **b** of the LORD, like a stream of sulfur, kindles it.
33:11 your **b** is a fire that will consume you.
40:7 when the **b** of the LORD blows upon it;
42:5 who gives **b** to the people upon it and spirit
57:13 wind will carry them off, a **b** will take them away.
Jer 4:31 the cry of daughter Zion gasping for **b**,
10:14 their images are false, and there is no **b** in them.
51:17 their images are false, and there is no **b** in them.
La 3:39 Why should any who draw **b** complain about
4:20 The LORD's anointed, the **b** of our life, A
Eze 37:5 I will cause **b** to enter you, and you shall live.
37:6 and cover you with skin, and put **b** in you,
37:8 but there was no **b** in them.
Eze 37:9 Then he said to me, "Prophesy to the **b**, prophesy, mortal, and say to the **b**:
37:9 Come from the four winds, O **b**,
37:10 and the **b** came into them, and they lived,
Da 5:23 but the God in whose power is your very **b**,
10:17 no strength remains in me, and no **b** is left in me."
Hab 2:19 and there is no **b** in it at all.
Ac 17:25 since he himself gives to all mortals life and **b**
2Th 2:8 whom the Lord Jesus will destroy with the **b**
Rev 11:11 the **b** of life from God entered them, A
13:15 and it was allowed to give **b** to the image of
Tob 14:11 But now my **b** fails me."
Jdt 7:27 and our wives and children drawing their last **b**.
Wis 2:2 for the **b** in our nostrils is smoke,
7:25 For she is a **b** of the power of God,
11:18 or such as breathe out fiery **b**,
11:20 at a single **b** when pursued by justice and scattered
11:20 by justice and scattered by the **b** of your power.
15:15 nor nostrils with which to draw **b**,
Sir 33:21 While you are still alive and have **b** in you,
38:28 the **b** of the fire melts his flesh,
LtJ 6:25 but there is no **b** in them.
2Mc 3:31 to one who was lying quite at his last **b**.
7:9 And when he was at his last **b**, he said,
7:22 It was not I who gave you life and **b**,
7:23 will in his mercy give life and **b** back to you again,
2Es 3:5 and you breathed into him the **b** of life, A
7:29 and all who draw human **b**.
13:10 and from his lips a flaming **b**,
13:11 of fire and the flaming **b** and the great storm,
16:61 and gave each person **b** and life and understanding
4Mc 6:11 and gasping heavily for **b**,
11:11 gasping for **b** and in anguish of body,

BREATHE (5) [BREATH]
Job 11:20 and their hope is to **b** their last."
Eze 37:9 and **b** upon these slain, that they may live."
Wis 7:3 when I was born, I began to **b** the common air,
11:18 or such as **b** out fiery breath,
Sir 31:19 He does not **b** heavily when in bed.

BREATHED (17) [BREATH]
Ge 2:7 and **b** into his nostrils the breath of life;
25:8 Abraham **b** his last and died in a good old age,
25:17 he **b** his last and died,
35:29 And Isaac **b** his last; he died
49:33 he drew up his feet into the bed, **b** his last,
Jos 10:40 but utterly destroyed all that **b**,
11:11 there was no one left who **b**,
11:14 and they did not leave any who **b**.
1Ki 15:29 he left to the house of Jeroboam not one that **b**,
Mt 27:50 Jesus cried again with a loud voice and **b** his last.
Mk 15:37 Then Jesus gave a loud cry and **b** his last.
15:39 saw that in this way he **b** his last, he said,
Lk 23:46 Having said this, he **b** his last.
Jn 20:22 he had said this, he **b** on them and said to them,
Wis 15:11 with active souls and **b** a living spirit into them.
2Es 3:5 and you **b** into him the breath of life,
4Mc 15:18 When the firstborn **b** his last,

BREATHES (6) [BREATH]
Dt 20:16 you must not let anything that **b** remain alive.
Ps 150:6 Let everything that **b** praise the LORD!
Pr 14:5 but a false witness **b** out lies.
SS 2:17 Until the day **b** and the shadows flee,
4:6 Until the day **b** and the shadows flee,
Sir 43:4 it **b** out fiery vapors, and its bright rays blind

BREATHING (4) [BREATH]
Ps 27:12 and they are **b** out violence.
Ac 9:1 still **b** threats and murder against the disciples of
2Mc 7:5 still **b**, and to fry him in a pan.
9:7 **b** fire in his rage against the Jews,

BRED (5) [BREED]
Ge 30:38 And since they **b** when they came to drink,
30:39 the flocks **b** in front of the rods,
Ex 16:20 and it **b** worms and became foul.
Est 8:10 by mounted couriers riding on fast steeds **b** from
4Mc 11:15 Since to this end we were born and **b**,

BREECHES (KJV) See UNDERGARMENT

BREED (3) [BRED, BREEDER, BREEDING, BREEDS, ILL-BRED]
Ge 30:41 that they might **b** among the rods,
Lev 19:19 not let your animals **b** with a different kind;
2Ti 2:23 you know that they **b** quarrels.

BREEDER (1) [BREED]
2Ki 3:4 Now King Mesha of Moab was a sheep **b**,

BREEDING (1) [BREED]
Ge 30:41 Whenever the stronger of the flock were **b**,

BREEDS (1) [BREED]
Job 21:10 Their bull **b** without fail; their cow calves

BREEZE (1)
Ge 3:8 in the garden at the time of the evening **b**,

BRETHREN (KJV) See BROTHERS, SISTERS

BREVITY (1) [BRIEF]
2Mc 2:31 the narrative should be allowed to strive for **b**

BRIBE (21) [BRIBED, BRIBERY, BRIBES, BRIBING]
Ex 23:8 You shall take no **b**, for a **b** blinds the officials,
Dt 10:17 who is not partial and takes no **b**,
16:19 for a **b** blinds the eyes of the wise and subverts
27:25 be anyone who takes a **b** to shed innocent blood."
1Sa 12:3 Or from whose hand have I taken a **b**
Job 6:22 Or, 'From your wealth offer a **b** for me'?
Ps 15:5 and do not take a **b** against the innocent.
Pr 6:35 and refuses a **b** no matter how great.
17:8 A **b** is like a magic stone in the eyes
17:23 a concealed **b** to pervert the ways of justice.
21:14 and a concealed **b** in the bosom, strong wrath.
Ecc 7:7 and a **b** corrupts the heart.
Isa 1:23 Everyone loves a **b** and runs after gifts.
5:23 who acquit the guilty for a **b**,
33:15 who wave away a **b** instead of accepting it,
Am 5:12 you who afflict the righteous, who take a **b**,
Mic 3:11 Its rulers give judgment for a **b**,
7:3 the official and the judge ask for a **b**,
Sir 35:14 Do not offer him a **b**, for he will not accept it;
2Mc 4:45 a substantial **b** to Ptolemy son of Dorymenes

BRIBED (3) [BRIBE]
Ezr 4:5 and they **b** officials to frustrate their plan
2Mc 10:20 were **b** by some of those who were in the towers,
3Mc 4:19 that they had been **b** to contrive a means of escape,

BRIBERY (2) [BRIBE]
Job 15:34 and fire consumes the tents of **b**.
Sir 40:12 All **b** and injustice will be blotted out,

BRIBES (6) [BRIBE]
Dt 16:19 and you must not accept **b**,
1Sa 8:3 they took **b** and perverted justice.
2Ch 19:7 or partiality, or taking of **b**."
Ps 26:10 and whose right hands are full of **b**.
Pr 15:27 but those who hate **b** will live.
Eze 22:12 In you, they take **b** to shed blood;

BRIBING (1) [BRIBE]
Eze 16:33 to all your lovers, **b** them to come to you from all

BRICK (4) [BRICKS, BRICKWORKS]
Ge 11:3 And they had **b** for stone, and bitumen for mortar.
Ex 1:14 in mortar and **b** and in every kind of field labor.
Eze 4:1 And you, O mortal, take a **b** and set it before you.
Na 3:14 tread the mortar, take hold of the **b** mold!

BRICKKILN (KJV) See BRICK MOLD, BRICKWORKS, CLAY PAVEMENT

BRICKS (10) [BRICK]
Ge 11:3 they said to one another, "Come, let us make **b**,
Ex 5:7 the people straw to make **b**, as before;
5:8 of **b** as they have made previously;
5:14 the required quantity of **b** yesterday and today,
5:16 yet they say to us, 'Make **b**!'
5:18 but you shall still deliver the same number of **b**."
5:19 "You shall not lessen your daily number of **b**."
Isa 9:10 "The **b** have fallen, but we will build
65:3 sacrificing in gardens and offering incense on **b**;
Jdt 5:11 he exploited them and forced them to make **b**.

BRICKWORKS (1) [BRICK]
2Sa 12:31 or sent them to the **b**.

BRIDAL (5) [BRIDE]
Tob 6:14 and that they died in the **b** chamber.
6:17 When you enter the **b** chamber,
1Mc 1:27 she who sat in the **b** chamber was mourning.
3Mc 1:19 for marriage abandoned the **b** chambers prepared
4:6 the **b** chamber to share married life exchanged joy

BRIDE‡ (28) [BRIDAL, BRIDE-PRICE, BRIDEGROOM, BRIDEGROOM'S, BRIDEGROOMS, BRIDESMAIDS]
2Sa 17:3 the people back to you as a **b** comes home
SS 4:8 Come with me from Lebanon, my **b**;
4:9 You have ravished my heart, my sister, my **b**,
4:10 How sweet is your love, my sister, my **b**!
4:11 Your lips distill nectar, my **b**;
4:12 A garden locked is my sister, my **b**,
5:1 I come to my garden, my sister, my **b**;
Isa 49:18 and like a **b** you shall bind them on.
61:10 and as a **b** adorns herself with her jewels.
62:5 and as the bridegroom rejoices over the **b**,

Jer 2: 2 the devotion of your youth, your love as a **b**,
2:32 Can a girl forget her ornaments, or a **b** her attire?
7:34 of the **b** and bridegroom in the cities of Judah and
16: 9 the voice of the bridegroom and the voice of the **b**.
25:10 the voice of the bridegroom and the voice of the **b**,
33:11 the voice of the bridegroom and the voice of the **b**,
Joel 2:16 bridegroom leave his room, and the **b** her canopy.
Jn 3:29 He who has the **b** is the bridegroom.
Rev 18:23 of bridegroom and **b** will be heard in you no more;
19: 7 and his **b** has made herself ready;
21: 2 prepared as a **b** adorned for her husband.
21: 9 I will show you the **b**, the wife of the Lamb."
22:17 The Spirit and the **b** say, "Come."
Tob 6:13 so that we may take her to be your **b**.
Wis 8: 2 I desired to take her for my **b**,
Sir 15: 2 and like a young **b** she will welcome him.
Bar 2:23 the voice of the bridegroom and the voice of the **b**,
1Mc 9:37 and are conducting the **b**, a daughter of one of

BRIDE-PRICE (2) [BRIDE, PRICE]
Ex 22:16 he shall give the **b** for her and make her his wife.
22:17 he shall pay an amount equal to the **b** for virgins.

BRIDECHAMBER (KJV) See BRIDEGROOM

BRIDEGROOM (28) [BRIDE]
Ex 4:25 and said, "Truly you are a **b** of blood to me!"
4:26 "A **b** of blood by circumcision."
Ps 19: 5 like a **b** from his wedding canopy,
Isa 61:10 as a **b** decks himself with a garland,
62: 5 and as the **b** rejoices over the bride,
Jer 7:34 the voice of the bride and **b** in the cities of Judah
16: 9 the voice of the **b** and the voice of the bride.
25:10 the voice of the **b** and the voice of the bride,
33:11 the voice of the **b** and the voice of the bride,
Joel 2:16 Let the **b** leave his room, and the bride her canopy.
Mt 9:15 as long as the **b** is with them,
9:15 The days will come when the **b** is taken away
25: 1 and went to meet the **b**.
25: 5 As the **b** was delayed, all of them became drowsy
25: 6 midnight there was a shout, 'Look! Here is the **b**!
25:10 And while they went to buy it, the **b** came,
Mk 2:19 "The wedding guests cannot fast while the **b** is
2:19 As long as they have the **b** with them,
2:20 The days will come when the **b** is taken away
Lk 5:34 while the **b** is with them,
5:35 The days will come when the **b** will be taken away
Jn 2: 9 drawn the water knew), the steward called the **b**
3:29 He who has the bride is the **b**.
3:29 The friend of the **b**, who stands and hears him,
Rev 18:23 voice of **b** and bride will be heard in you no more;
Bar 2:23 the voice of the **b** and the voice of the bride,
1Mc 1:27 Every **b** took up the lament;
9:39 the **b** came out with his friends and his brothers

BRIDEGROOM'S (1) [BRIDE]
Jn 3:29 rejoices greatly at the **b** voice.

BRIDEGROOMS (2) [BRIDE]
2Es 16:33 Virgins shall mourn because they have no **b**;
16:34 Their **b** shall be killed in war,

BRIDESMAIDS (3) [BRIDE]
Mt 25: 1 Ten **b** took their lamps and went to meet
25: 7 Then all those **b** got up and trimmed their lamps.
25:11 Later the other **b** came also, saying, 'Lord, lord,

BRIDLE‡ (6) [BRIDLED, BRIDLES]
Ps 32: 9 whose temper must be curbed with bit and **b**,
Pr 26: 3 A whip for the horse, a **b** for the donkey,
Isa 30:28 the jaws of the peoples a **b** that leads them astray.
Jas 1:26 and do not **b** their tongues but deceive their hearts,
3: 2 able to keep the whole body in check with a **b**.
Rev 14:20 as high as a horse's **b**,

BRIDLED (1) [BRIDLE]
4Mc 1:35 and all the impulses of the body are **b** by reason.

BRIDLES (2) [BRIDLE]
2Mc 10:29 on horses with golden **b**, and they were leading
1Es 3: 6 and have a chariot with gold **b**,

BRIEF (9) [BREVITY, BRIEFLY]
Ezr 9: 8 But now for a **b** moment favor has been shown by
Isa 54: 7 For a **b** moment I abandoned you,
Wis 15: 9 that their life is **b**, but they compete with workers
Sir 32: 8 Be **b**; say much in few words;
2Mc 6:25 for the sake of living a **b** moment longer,
7:36 a **b** suffering have drunk of ever-flowing life,
10:10 a **b** summary of the principal calamities of
2Es 12: 2 and their reign was **b** and full of tumult.
12:30 this was the reign which was **b** and full of tumult,

BRIEFLY (6) [BRIEF]
Mk 16: S ⟦all that had been commanded them they told **b**⟧
Ac 24: 4 to hear us **b** with your customary graciousness.
2Co 7: 8 that I grieved you with that letter, though only **b**).
Heb 13:22 for I have written to you **b**.

2Mc 6:17 we must go on **b** with the story.
3Mc 4:14 the hard labor that has been **b** mentioned before,

BRIER (3) [BRIERS]
Isa 55:13 instead of the **b** shall come up the myrtle;
Eze 28:24 of Israel shall no longer find a pricking **b** or
Mic 7: 4 The best of them is like a **b**,

BRIERS‡ (11) [BRIER]
Jdg 8: 7 on the thorns of the wilderness and on **b**."
8:16 of the wilderness and **b** and with them he trampled
Isa 5: 6 and it shall be overgrown with **b** and thorns;
7:23 will become **b** and thorns.
7:24 for all the land will be **b** and thorns;
7:25 you will not go there for fear of **b** and thorns;
9:18 For wickedness burned like a fire, consuming **b**
10:17 and it will burn and devour his thorns and **b**
27: 4 If it gives me thorns and **b**,
32:13 the soil of my people growing up in thorns and **b**;
Eze 2: 6 though **b** and thorns surround you and you live

BRIGANDINE (KJV) See COAT OF MAIL

BRIGHT (15) [BRIGHTEN, BRIGHTENED, BRIGHTER, BRIGHTNESS]
Job 25: 5 If even the moon is not **b** and the stars are not pure
37:21 no one can look on the light when it is **b** in
Ps 139:12 the night is as **b** as the day,
SS 6:10 **b** as the sun, terrible as an army with banners?"
Eze 1:13 the fire was **b**, and lightning issued from the fire.
Mt 17: 5 suddenly a **b** cloud overshadowed them,
Rev 6: 4 And out came another horse, **b** red;
15: 6 with the seven plagues, robed in pure **b** linen,
18: 1 and the earth was made **b** with his splendor.
19: 8 to be clothed with fine linen, **b** and pure"—
22: 1 the river of the water of life, **b** as crystal, flowing
22:16 and the descendant of David, the **b** morning star."
Tob 13:11 A **b** light will shine to all the ends of the earth;
Sir 43: 4 and its **b** rays blind the eyes.
LtJ 6:60 For sun and moon and stars are **b**,

BRIGHTEN‡ (1) [BRIGHT]
Ezr 9: 8 in order that he may **b** our eyes and grant us

BRIGHTENED (2) [BRIGHT]
1Sa 14:27 to his mouth; and his eyes **b**.
14:29 see how my eyes have **b** because I tasted a little

BRIGHTER (6) [BRIGHT]
Job 11:17 And your life will be **b** than the noonday;
Pr 4:18 which shines **b** and **b** until full day.
Ac 26:13 I saw a light from heaven, **b** than the sun,
Sir 17:31 What is **b** than the sun?
23:19 the eyes of the Lord are ten thousand times **b** than

BRIGHTNESS‡ (15) [BRIGHT]
2Sa 22:13 Out of the **b** before him coals of fire flamed forth.
Ps 18:12 Out of the **b** before him there broke
Isa 59: 9 there is darkness; and for **b**, but we walk in gloom.
60: 3 and kings to the **b** of your dawn.
60:19 nor for **b** shall the moon give light to you by night;
Eze 1: 4 with **b** around it and fire flashing forth continually,
8: 2 above the loins it was like the appearance of **b**,
10: 4 court was full of the **b** of the glory of the LORD.
Da 12: 3 Those who are wise shall shine like the **b** of
Am 5:20 not light, and gloom with no **b** in it?
Hab 3: 4 The **b** was like the sun;
Ac 22:11 Since I could not see because of the **b** of that light,
Sir 43:11 it is exceedingly beautiful in its **b**.
2Es 6:45 the fourth day you commanded the **b** of the sun,
7:*42* or dawn or shining or **b** or light,

BRILLIANCE (2) [BRILLIANT]
Da 2:31 This statue was huge, its **b** extraordinary;
2Es 10:50 has shown you the **b** of her glory,

BRILLIANT (2) [BRILLIANCE]
Wis 17: 5 nor did the **b** flames of the stars avail to illumine
17:20 For the whole world was illumined with **b** light,

BRIM (6)
1Ki 7:23 it was round, ten cubits from **b** to **b**,
7:24 Under its **b** were panels all around it,
7:26 its **b** was made like the **b** of a cup,
Jn 2: 7 And they filled them up to the **b**.

BRIMSTONE (KJV) See SULFUR

BRING‡ (765) [BRINGING, BRINGS, BROUGHT, BROUGHT-UP]
Ge 1:20 "Let the waters **b** forth swarms of living creatures,
1:24 the earth **b** forth living creatures of every kind:
3:16 in pain you shall **b** forth children,
3:18 thorns and thistles it shall **b** forth for you;
5:29 the LORD has cursed this one shall **b** us relief
6:17 I am going to **b** a flood of waters on the earth,
6:19 you shall **b** two of every kind into the ark,
8:17 **B** out with you every living thing that is with you

Ge 9:14 When I **b** clouds over the earth and
15: 9 He said to him, "**B** me a heifer three years old,
15:14 but I will **b** judgment on the nation that they serve,
18: 5 Let me **b** a little bread,
18:19 so that the LORD may **b** about
19: 5 **B** them out to us, so that we may know them."
19: 8 let me **b** them out to you,
19:12 **b** them out of the place.
27: 4 such as I like, and **b** it to me to eat,
27: 5 Esau went to the field to hunt for game and **b** it,
27: 7 '**B** me game, and prepare for me savory food
27:12 and **b** a curse on myself and not a blessing."
27:25 Then he said, "**B** it to me,
27:45 then I will send, and **b** you back from there.
28:15 and will **b** you back to this land;
31:39 which was torn by wild beasts I did not **b** to you;
37:14 and **b** word back to me."
38:24 Judah said, "**B** her out, and let her be burned."
41:32 and God will shortly **b** it about.
42:16 Let one of you go and **b** your brother,
42:20 and **b** your youngest brother to me.
42:34 **B** your youngest brother to me,
42:37 "You may kill my two sons if I do not **b** him back
42:37 and I will **b** him back to you."
42:38 you would **b** down my gray hairs with sorrow
43: 7 that he would say, '**B** your brother down'?"
43: 9 I do not **b** him back to you and set him before you,
43:16 "**B** the men into the house,
44:21 you said to your servants, '**B** him down to me,
44:29 you will **b** down my gray hairs in sorrow
44:31 and your servants will **b** down the gray hairs
44:32 saying, 'If I do not **b** him back to you,
45:13 Hurry and **b** my father down here."
45:19 and **b** your father, and come.
46: 4 and I will also **b** you up again;
48: 9 And he said, "**B** them to me, please,
48:21 and will **b** you again to the land of your ancestors.
50:24 but God will surely come to you, and **b** you up out
Ex 2: 5 among the reeds and sent her maid to **b** it.
3: 8 and to **b** them up out of that land to a good
3:10 come, I will send you to Pharaoh to **b** my people,
3:11 and **b** the Israelites out of Egypt?"
3:17 that I will **b** you up out of the misery of Egypt,
3:21 I will **b** this people into such favor with
6: 8 I will **b** you into the land that I swore to give
6:26 "**B** the Israelites out of the land of Egypt,
6:27 to Pharaoh king of Egypt to **b** the Israelites out
7: 4 I will lay my hand upon Egypt and **b** my people
7: 5 when I stretch out my hand against Egypt and **b**
10: 4 tomorrow I will **b** locusts into your country.
11: 1 "I will **b** one more plague upon Pharaoh and
12:32 And **b** a blessing on me too!"
12:42 to **b** them out of the land of Egypt.
15:26 not **b** upon you any of the diseases that I brought
16: 5 when they prepare what they **b** in,
17: 3 "Why did you **b** us out of Egypt,
18:19 and you should **b** their cases before God;
18:22 let them **b** every important case to you,
21: 6 then his master shall **b** him before God.
23: 4 or donkey going astray, you shall **b** it back.
23:19 of the first fruits of your ground you shall **b** into
23:20 to guard you on the way and to **b** you to the place
26:33 and **b** the ark of the covenant in there,
27:20 the Israelites to **b** you pure oil of beaten olives for
28: 1 Then **b** near to you your brother Aaron,
28:43 or they will **b** guilt on themselves and die.
29: 3 You shall put them in one basket and **b** them in
29: 3 and **b** the bull and the two rams.
29: 4 You shall **b** Aaron and his sons to the entrance of
29: 8 Then you shall **b** his sons, and put tunics on them,
29:10 You shall **b** the bull in front of the tent of meeting.
30:15 when you **b** this offering to the LORD
32: 2 your sons, and your daughters, and **b** them to me."
32:12 change your mind and do not **b** disaster
32:14 the disaster that he planned to **b** on his people.
33:12 "See, you have said to me, '**B** up this people';
34:26 of the first fruits of your ground you shall **b** to
35: 5 of a generous heart **b** the LORD's offering:
35:29 to **b** anything for the work that
40: 4 You shall **b** in the table, and arrange its setting;
40: 4 you shall **b** in the lampstand, and set up its lamps.
40:12 Then you shall **b** Aaron and his sons to
40:14 You shall **b** his sons also and put tunics on them,
Lev 1: 2 of you **b** an offering of livestock to the LORD,
1: 2 you shall **b** your offering from the herd or from
1: 3 you shall **b** it to the entrance of the tent
1:15 priest shall **b** it to the altar and wring off its head,
2: 2 and **b** it to Aaron's sons the priests.
2: 8 You shall **b** to the LORD the grain offering
2:11 No grain offering that you **b** to the LORD shall
2:12 You may **b** them to the LORD as an offering
2:14 you **b** a grain offering of first fruits to the LORD,
2:14 you shall **b** as the grain offering
3: 7 you shall **b** it before the LORD
3:12 you shall **b** it before the LORD
4: 4 He shall **b** the bull to the entrance of the tent
4: 5 of the blood of the bull and **b** it into the tent
4:14 a bull of the herd for a sin offering and **b** it before
4:16 The anointed priest shall **b** some of the blood of
4:23 he shall **b** as his offering a male goat
4:28 you shall **b** a female goat without blemish
4:32 If the offering you **b** as a sin offering is a sheep,
4:32 you shall **b** a female without blemish.
5: 6 And you shall **b** to the LORD,
5: 7 you shall **b** to the LORD,
5: 8 You shall **b** them to the priest,
5:11 you shall **b** as your offering for the sin

Lev 5:12 You shall **b** it to the priest,
5:15 you shall **b,** as your guilt offering to the LORD,
5:18 You shall **b** to the priest a ram without blemish
6: 6 And you shall **b** to the priest,
6:21 you shall **b** it well soaked,
7:13 of well-being you shall **b** your offering with cakes
7:29 of well-being must yourself **b** to
7:30 Your own hands shall **b** the LORD's offering
7:30 you shall **b** the fat with the breast,
7:38 of Israel to **b** their offerings to the LORD,
10:15 the breast that is elevated they shall **b,** together
12: 6 she shall **b** to the priest at the entrance of the tent
14:23 On the eighth day he shall **b** them for his cleansing
15:29 and **b** them to the priest to the entrance of the tent
16:12 and he shall **b** it inside the curtain
16:15 for the people and **b** its blood inside the curtain,
17: 4 not **b** it to the entrance of the tent of meeting,
17: 5 of Israel may **b** their sacrifices that they offer in
17: 5 that they may **b** them to the LORD,
17: 9 does not **b** it to the entrance of the tent of meeting,
19:21 but he shall **b** a guilt offering for himself to
20:22 so that the land to which I **b** you to settle in may
20:25 not **b** abomination on yourselves by animal or
23:10 and you reap its harvest, you shall **b** the sheaf of
23:15 on which you **b** the sheaf of the elevation offering,
23:17 You shall **b** from your settlements two loaves
24: 2 Command the people of Israel to **b** you pure oil
26:16 I will **b** terror on you;
26:25 I will **b** the sword against you,
Nu 3: 6 **B** the tribe of Levi near,
5: 9 every gift that they **b** to the priest shall be his.
5:15 then the man shall **b** his wife to the priest.
5:15 And he shall **b** the offering required for her,
5:16 Then the priest shall **b** her near,
5:25 the grain offering before the LORD and **b** it to
6:10 On the eighth day they shall **b** two turtledoves
6:12 and **b** a male lamb a year old as a guilt offering.
8: 9 You shall **b** the Levites before the tent of meeting,
8:10 When you **b** the Levites before the LORD,
11:16 **b** them to the tent of meeting,
13:20 Be bold, and **b** some of the fruit of the land."
14: 8 he will **b** us into this land and give it to us,
14:16 because the LORD was not able to **b** this people
14:24 I will **b** into the land into which he went,
14:31 who you said would become booty, I will **b** in,
18: 2 **b** with you also your brothers of the tribe of Levi,
18:13 which they **b** to the LORD, shall be yours;
19: 2 the Israelites to **b** you a red heifer without defect,
20: 5 to **b** us to this wretched place?
20: 8 Thus you shall **b** water out of the rock for them;
20:10 shall we **b** water for you out of this rock?"
20:12 therefore you shall not **b** this assembly into
20:25 and **b** them up Mount Hor;
22: 8 "Stay here tonight, and I will **b** back word to you,
27:17 who shall lead them out and **b** them in,
Dt 1:17 Any case that is too hard for you, **b** to me,
1:22 for us and **b** back a report to us regarding the route
4:38 to **b** you in, giving you their land for a possession,
6:23 He brought us out from there in order to **b** us in,
7:26 Do not **b** an abhorrent thing into your house,
9:28 'Because the LORD was not able to **b** them into
12:11 then you shall **b** everything that I command you to
12:26 you shall **b** to the place that
14:28 Every third year you shall **b** out the full tithe
17: 5 then you shall **b** out to your gates that man or
21: 4 the elders of that town shall **b** the heifer down to
21:12 and so you **b** her home to your house:
21:19 and **b** him out to the elders of his town at the gate
22: 2 you shall **b** it to your own house,
22:21 then they shall **b** the young woman out to
22:24 you shall **b** both of them to the gate of that town
23:18 You shall not **b** the fee of a prostitute or the wages
24: 4 the LORD, and you shall not **b** guilt on the land
26:10 now I **b** the first of the fruit of the ground that you,
28:36 The LORD will **b** you,
28:49 The LORD will **b** a nation from far away,
28:60 He will **b** back upon you all the diseases of Egypt,
28:68 The LORD will **b** you back in ships to Egypt,
30: 4 and from there he will **b** you back.
30: 5 The LORD your God will **b** you into the land
31:23 for you shall **b** the Israelites into the land
33: 7 give heed to Judah, and **b** him to his people;
Jos 2: 3 "**B** out the men who have come to you,
6:22 **b** the woman out of it and all who belong to her,
7:25 Joshua said, "Why did you **b** trouble on us?
10:22 and **b** those five kings out to me from the cave."
18: 6 in seven divisions and **b** the description here
23:15 so the LORD will **b** upon you all the bad things,
Jdg 2:15 the LORD was against them to **b** misfortune,
6: 5 and they would even **b** their tents,
6:13 saying, 'Did not the LORD **b** us up from Egypt?'
6:18 and **b** out my present, and set it before you."
6:30 the townspeople said to Joash, "**B** out your son,
11: 5 of Gilead went to **b** Jephthah from the land of Tob.
11: 9 "If you **b** me home again to fight with
19: 3 to speak tenderly to her and **b** her back.
19:22 "**B** out the man who came into your house,
19:24 let me **b** them out now.
20:10 to **b** provisions for the troops,
Ru 3:15 "**B** the cloak you are wearing and hold it out."
1Sa 1:22 "As soon as the child is weaned, I will **b** him,
4: 3 Let us **b** the ark of the covenant of
9: 7 "But if we go, what can we **b** the man?
9: 7 and there is no present to **b** to the man of God.
9:23 "**B** the portion I gave you,
13: 9 So Saul said, "**B** the burnt offering here to me,
14:18 Saul said to Ahijah, "**B** the ark of God here."
1Sa 14:34 'Let all **b** their oxen or their sheep,
15:32 "**B** Agag king of the Amalekites here to me."
16:11 And Samuel said to Jesse, "Send and **b** him;
16:17 for me someone who can play well, and **b** him
17:18 and **b** some token from them."
19:15 He said, "**B** him up to me in the bed,
20: 8 why should you **b** me to your father?"
20:31 send and **b** him to me, for he shall surely die."
21: 8 I did not **b** my sword or my weapons with me,
23: 9 he said to the priest Abiathar, "**B** the ephod here."
28: 8 and **b** up for me the one whom I name to you."
28: 9 Why then are you laying a snare for my life to **b**
28:11 the woman said, "Whom shall I **b** up for you?"
28:11 He answered, "**B** up Samuel for me."
30: 7 to the priest Abiathar son of Ahimelech, "**B** me
2Sa 3:12 and I will give you my support to **b** all Israel over
3:13 unless you **b** Saul's daughter Michal
3:18 then **b** it about; for the LORD has promised David:
6: 2 to **b** up from there the ark of God,
9:10 and shall **b** in the produce,
12:23 Can I **b** him back again?
13:10 "**B** the food into the chamber,
14:10 **b** him to me, and he shall never touch you again."
14:13 the king does not **b** his banished one home again.
14:21 go, **b** back the young man Absalom."
15: 8 If the LORD will indeed **b** me back to Jerusalem,
15:14 and **b** disaster down upon us,
15:25 he will **b** me back and let me see both it and
17: 3 and I will **b** all the people back to you as
17:13 then all Israel will **b** ropes to that city,
17:14 so that the LORD might **b** ruin on Absalom.
19:11 'Why should you be the last to **b** the king back
19:12 then should you be the last to **b** back the king?'
19:15 to meet the king and to **b** him over the Jordan.
19:18 to **b** over the king's household,
22:28 your eyes are upon the haughty to **b** them down.
1Ki 1:33 and **b** him down to Gihon.
1:42 a worthy man and surely you **b** good news."
2: 9 to do to him, and you must **b** his gray head down
2:32 The LORD will **b** back his bloody deeds
2:44 LORD will **b** back your evil on your own head.
3:24 So the king said, "**B** me a sword,"
5: 9 My servants shall **b** it down to the sea from
8: 1 to **b** up the ark of the covenant of the LORD out
8:34 and **b** them again to the land that you gave
13:18 **B** him back with you into your house so
14:10 I will **b** evil upon the house of Jeroboam.
17:10 "**B** me a little water in a vessel,
17:11 As she was going to **b** it, he called to her and said,
17:11 "**B** me a morsel of bread in your hand."
17:13 but first make me a little cake of it and **b** it to me,
17:18 to me to **b** my sin to remembrance,
20:33 Then he said, "Go and **b** him."
21:10 and have them **b** a charge against him, saying,
21:21 I will **b** disaster on you;
21:29 I will not **b** the disaster in his days;
21:29 but in his son's days I will **b** the disaster
22: 9 "**B** quickly Micaiah son of Imlah."
2Ki 2:20 He said, "**B** me a new bowl, and put salt in it."
4: 6 she said to her son, "**B** me another vessel."
4:41 He said, "Then **b** some flour."
6:19 and I will **b** you to the man whom you seek."
10:22 "**B** out the vestments for all the worshipers
11:15 "**B** her out between the ranks,
19: 3 and there is no strength to **b** them forth.
19:25 I planned from days of old what now I **b** to pass,
20: 7 Then Isaiah said, "**B** a lump of figs.
22:16 I will indeed **b** disaster on this place and
22:20 your eyes shall not see all the disaster that I will **b**
23: 4 to **b** out of the temple of the LORD all
1Ch 13: 3 Then let us **b** again the ark of our God to us;
13: 5 to **b** the ark of God from Kiriath-jearim.
13: 6 to **b** up from there the ark of God, the LORD,
13:12 "How can I **b** the ark of God into my care?"
15: 3 David assembled all Israel in Jerusalem to **b** up
15:12 so that you may **b** up the ark of the LORD,
15:14 the Levites sanctified themselves to **b** up the ark of
15:25 went to **b** up the ark of the covenant of the LORD
16:29 **b** an offering, and come before him.
21: 2 from Beer-sheba to Dan, and **b** me a report,
21: 3 Why should he **b** guilt on Israel?"
2Ch 2:16 and **b** it to you as rafts by sea to Joppa;
5: 2 to **b** up the ark of the covenant of the LORD out
6:25 and **b** them again to the land that you gave to them
12:11 and would then **b** them back to the guardroom.
18: 8 "**B** quickly Micaiah son of Imlah."
21:14 the LORD will **b** a great plague on your people,
23:14 saying to them, "**B** her out between the ranks;
24: 6 to **b** in from Judah and Jerusalem the tax levied
24: 9 and Jerusalem to **b** in for the LORD the tax
24:19 Yet he sent prophets among them to **b** them back
26:18 and it will **b** you no honor from the LORD God."
28:13 "You shall not **b** the captives in here,
28:13 to **b** on us guilt against the LORD in addition
28:27 but they did not **b** him into the tombs of the kings
29:31 near, **b** sacrifices and thank offerings to the house
31:10 "Since they began to **b** the contributions into
34:24 I will indeed **b** disaster upon this place and
34:28 your eyes shall not see all the disaster that I will **b**
Ezr 3: 7 and the Tyrians to **b** cedar trees from Lebanon to
8:30 to **b** them to Jerusalem, to the house of our God.
Ne 1: 9 and **b** them to the place at which I have chosen
8: 1 the scribe Ezra to **b** the book of the law of Moses,
8:15 "Go out to the hills and **b** branches of olive,
10:31 and if the peoples of the land **b** in merchandise
10:34 to **b** it into the house of our God,
10:35 to **b** the first fruits of our soil and the first fruits
Ne 10:36 also to **b** to the house of our God,
10:37 to **b** the first of our dough, and our contributions,
10:37 and to **b** to the Levites the tithes from our soil,
10:38 and the Levites shall **b** up a tithe of the tithes to
10:39 the sons of Levi shall **b** the contribution of grain,
11: 1 of the people cast lots to **b** one out of ten to live in
12:27 to **b** them to Jerusalem to celebrate the dedication
13:18 and did not our God **b** all this disaster on us and
13:18 Yet you **b** more wrath on Israel by profaning
Est 1:11 to **b** Queen Vashti before the king, wearing
5: 5 Then the king said, "**B** Haman quickly,
6: 1 and he gave orders to **b** the book of records,
Job 10:17 you **b** fresh troops against me.
10:18 "Why did you **b** me forth from the womb?
12: 6 who **b** their god in their hands.
14: 3 Do you **b** me into judgment with you?
14: 4 Who can **b** a clean thing out of an unclean?
15:35 and **b** forth evil and their heart prepares deceit."
28:11 hidden things they **b** to light.
30:23 I know that you will **b** me to death,
33:22 and their lives to those who **b** death.
33:30 to **b** back their souls from the Pit,
36: 3 I will **b** my knowledge from far away,
38:26 to **b** rain on a land where no one lives,
39:12 and **b** your grain to your threshing floor?
40:12 Look on all who are proud, and **b** them low;
Ps 7:14 and are pregnant with mischief, and **b** forth lies.
18:27 but the haughty eyes you **b** down.
25:17 and **b** me out of my distress.
37:14 the sword and bend their bows to **b** down the poor
43: 3 let them **b** me to your holy hill and
50:23 Those who **b** thanksgiving
55: 3 For they **b** trouble upon me,
59:11 and **b** them down, O Lord, our shield.
60: 9 Who will **b** me to the fortified city?
62: 4 Their only plan is to **b** down a person
64: 8 Because of their tongue he will **b** them to ruin;
65: 4 Happy are those whom you choose and **b** near
68:22 The Lord said, "I will **b** them back from Bashan,
68:22 I will **b** them back from the depths of the sea,
71:20 the depths of the earth you will **b** me up again.
72:10 may the kings of Sheba and Seba **b** gifts.
76:11 around him **b** gifts to the one who is awesome,
96: 8 **b** an offering, and come into his courts.
104:14 to **b** forth food from the earth,
108:10 Who will **b** me to the fortified city?
142: 7 **B** me out of prison, so that I may give thanks
143:11 In your righteousness **b** me out of trouble.
Pr 13:13 Those who despise the word **b** destruction
16:15 his favor is like the clouds that **b** the spring rain.
18: 6 A fool's lips **b** strife, and a fool's mouth invites
19:24 and will not even **b** it back to the mouth.
19:26 children who cause shame and **b** reproach.
24:22 and who knows the ruin that both can **b?**
25: 8 do not hastily **b** into court;
25:10 or else someone who hears you will **b** shame
26:15 and is too tired to **b** it back to the mouth.
27: 1 for you do not know what a day may **b.**
29:23 A person's pride will **b** humiliation,
Ecc 3:22 who can **b** them to see what will be after them?
10:12 Words spoken by the wise **b** them favor,
11: 9 for all these things God will **b** you into judgment.
12:14 For God will **b** every deed into judgment,
SS 8: 2 I would lead you and **b** you into the house
8:11 each one was to **b** for its fruit a thousand pieces
Isa 7:17 The LORD will **b** on you and on your people and
14: 2 nations will take them and **b** them to their place,
15: 9 yet I will **b** upon Dibon even more—
21: 2 all the sighing she has caused I **b** to an end.
21:14 **B** water to the thirsty, meet the fugitive
33:11 You conceive chaff, you **b** forth stubble;
37: 3 and there is no strength to **b** them forth.
37:26 I planned from days of old what now I **b** to pass,
38:12 from day to night you **b** me to an end;
38:13 from day to night you **b** me to an end.
41:21 **b** your proofs, says the King of Jacob.
41:22 Let them **b** them, and tell us what is to happen.
42: 1 he will **b** forth justice to the nations.
42: 3 he will faithfully **b** forth justice.
42: 7 to **b** out the prisoners from the dungeon,
43: 5 I will **b** your offspring from the east,
43: 6 **b** my sons from far away and my daughters from
43: 8 **B** forth the people who are blind, yet have eyes,
43: 9 Let them **b** their witnesses to justify them,
46:11 I have spoken, and I will **b** it to pass;
46:13 I **b** near my deliverance, it is not far off,
49: 5 to **b** Jacob back to him, and that Israel might be
49:22 and they shall **b** your sons in their bosom,
51: 5 I will **b** near my deliverance swiftly,
55:10 making it **b** forth and sprout,
56: 7 these I will **b** to my holy mountain,
58: 7 and **b** the homeless poor into your house;
60: 6 They shall **b** gold and frankincense,
60: 9 to **b** your children from far away,
60:11 so that nations shall **b** you their wealth,
60:17 Instead of bronze I will **b** gold,
60:17 instead of iron I will **b** silver;
61: 1 he has sent me to **b** good news to the oppressed,
65: 9 I will **b** forth descendants from Jacob,
66: 4 and **b** upon them what they fear;
66:20 They shall **b** all your kindred from all the nations
66:20 as the Israelites **b** a grain offering in a clean vessel
Jer 3:14 and I will **b** you to Zion.
5: 9 shall I not **b** retribution on a nation such as this?
5:15 I am going to **b** upon you a nation from far away,
5:29 shall I not **b** retribution on a nation such as this?
6:19 I am going to **b** disaster on this people,

Jer 7:34 I will **b** to an end the sound of mirth and gladness,
9: 9 shall I not **b** retribution on a nation such as this?
10:18 and I will **b** distress on them,
10:24 not in your anger, or you will **b** me to nothing.
11:11 to **b** disaster upon them that they cannot escape;
11:23 For I will **b** disaster upon the people of Anathoth,
12: 2 they grow and **b** forth fruit;
12: 9 all the wild animals; **b** them to devour her.
12:15 and I will **b** them again to their heritage and
14:22 Can any idols of the nations **b** rain?
15:15 and **b** down retribution for me on my persecutors.
16:15 For I will **b** them back to their own land
17:18 **b** on them the day of disaster;
17:21 a burden on the sabbath day or **b** it in by the gates
17:24 and **b** in no burden by the gates of this city on
18: 8 about the disaster that I intended to **b** on it.
18:18 Come, let us **b** charges against him,
18:22 when you **b** the marauder suddenly upon them!
19: 3 I am going to **b** such disaster upon this place that
21: 4 I will **b** them together into the center of this city.
23: 3 and I will **b** them back to their fold,
23:12 for I will **b** disaster upon them in the year
23:40 And I will **b** upon you everlasting disgrace
24: 6 and I will **b** them back to this land.
25: 9 I will **b** them against this land and its inhabitants,
25:13 I will **b** upon that land all the words
25:29 to **b** disaster on the city that is called by my name,
26: 3 the disaster that I intend to **b** on them because
26:19 But we are about to **b** great disaster on ourselves!"
27:11 But any nation that will **b** its neck under the yoke
27:12 **B** your necks under the yoke of the king
27:22 I will **b** them up and restore them to this place.
28: 3 Within two years I will **b** back to this place all
28: 4 I will also **b** back to this place King Jeconiah son
28: 6 that you have prophesied, and **b** back to this place
29:10 to you my promise and **b** you back to this place.
29:14 and I will **b** you back to the place
30: 3 and I will **b** them back to the land that I gave
30:21 I will **b** him near, and he shall approach me,
31: 8 I am going to **b** them from the land of the north,
31:18 **B** me back, let me come back,
31:28 to overthrow, destroy, and **b** evil,
31:32 by the hand to **b** them out of the land of Egypt—
32:37 I will **b** them back to this place,
32:42 so I will **b** upon them all the good fortune that I
33: 6 I am going to **b** it recovery and healing;
33:11 they **b** thank offerings to the house of the LORD:
34:22 says the LORD, and will **b** them back to this city;
35: 2 and **b** them to the house of the LORD,
35:17 I am going to **b** on Judah and on all the inhabitants
36:14 "**B** the scroll that you read in the hearing of
36:31 I will **b** on them, and on the inhabitants
44:11 I am determined to **b** disaster on you,
44:11 to **b** all Judah to an end.
45: 5 for I am going to **b** disaster upon all flesh,
48:35 And I will **b** to an end in Moab, says the LORD,
48:44 For I will **b** these things upon Moab in the year
49: 5 I am going to **b** terror upon you,
49: 8 For I will **b** the calamity of Esau upon him,
49:16 from there I will **b** you down, says the LORD.
49:32 and I will **b** calamity against them from every side,
49:36 and I will **b** upon Elam the four winds from
49:37 I will **b** disaster upon them, my fierce anger,
50: 9 and **b** against Babylon a company of great nations
51: 8 **B** balm for her wound; perhaps she may be healed.
51:27 **b** up horses like bristling locusts.
51:40 I will **b** them down like lambs to the slaughter,
La 1:21 **B** on the day you have announced,
Eze 5:16 and when I **b** more and more famine upon you,
5:17 and I will **b** the sword upon you.
6: 3 I, I myself will **b** a sword upon you,
6:10 not threaten in vain to **b** this disaster upon them.
7:24 I will **b** the worst of the nations to take possession
9:10 but I will **b** down their deeds upon their heads."
11: 8 I will **b** the sword upon you, says the Lord GOD.
11:21 I will **b** their deeds upon their own heads,
12: 4 You shall **b** out your baggage by day in their sight,
12:13 and I will **b** him to Babylon,
13:14 and **b** it to the ground, so that its foundation will
14:17 Or if I **b** a sword upon that land and say,
16:38 and **b** blood upon you in wrath and jealousy.
16:40 They shall **b** up a mob against you,
17:20 I will **b** him to Babylon and enter into judgment
17:24 I **b** low the high tree, I make high the low tree;
20: 6 that I would **b** them out of the land of Egypt into
20:15 to them in the wilderness that I would not **b** them
20:34 I will **b** you out from the peoples
20:35 and I will **b** you into the wilderness of the peoples,
20:37 and will **b** you within the bond of the covenant.
20:38 I will **b** them out of the land where they reside
20:41 when I **b** you out from the peoples,
20:42 when I **b** you into the land of Israel,
23:22 and I will **b** them against you from every side:
23:46 **B** up an assembly against them,
26: 7 I will **b** against Tyre from
26:19 when I **b** up the deep over you,
26:21 I will **b** you to a dreadful end,
28: 7 I will **b** strangers against you,
29: 8 I will **b** a sword upon you,
29:14 and **b** them back to the land of Pathros,
30:12 I will **b** desolation upon the land and everything
32:12 They shall **b** to ruin the pride of Egypt,
33: 2 If I **b** the sword upon a land,
34:13 I will **b** them out from the peoples and gather them
34:13 and will **b** them into their own land;
34:16 I will seek the lost, and I will **b** back the strayed,
36:24 and **b** you into your own land.
Eze 37:12 and **b** you up from your graves, O my people;
37:12 and I will **b** you back to the land of Israel.
37:13 and **b** you up from your graves, O my people.
37:21 and **b** them to their own land.
38:16 In the latter days I will **b** you against my land,
38:17 for years that I would **b** you against them?
39: 2 and **b** you up from the remotest parts of the north,
39:13 and it will **b** them honor on the day
46:20 in order not to **b** them out into the outer court and
Da 1: 3 to **b** some of the Israelites of the royal family and
2:24 **b** me in before the king,
2:44 and **b** them to an end, and it shall stand forever;
4:37 and he is able to **b** low those who walk in pride.
5: 2 Belshazzar commanded that they **b** in the vessels
5: 7 The king cried aloud to **b** in the enchanters,
9:24 to **b** in everlasting righteousness,
11:17 and he shall **b** terms of peace and perform them.
11:44 with great fury to **b** ruin and complete destruction
Hos 2:14 and **b** her into the wilderness,
7:12 I will **b** them down like birds of the air;
9:12 Even if they **b** up children,
12:10 and through the prophets I will **b** destruction.
12:14 so his Lord will **b** his crimes down on him
Joel 3: 2 I will gather all the nations and **b** them down to
3:11 **B** down your warriors, O LORD.
Am 4: 1 to their husbands, "**B** something to drink!"
4: 4 **b** your sacrifices every morning,
4: 5 **b** a thank offering of leavened bread,
5: 7 and **b** righteousness to the ground!
5:25 Did you **b** to me sacrifices and offerings
6: 3 and **b** near a reign of violence?
6:10 shall take up the body to **b** it out of the house,
8: 4 and **b** to ruin the poor of the land,
8:10 I will **b** sackcloth on all loins,
9: 2 from there I will **b** them down.
9: 7 Did I not **b** Israel up from the land of Egypt,
Ob 1: 3 "Who will **b** me down to the ground?"
1: 4 from there I will **b** you down, says the LORD.
Jnh 1:13 the men rowed hard to **b** the ship back to land,
3:10 about the calamity that he had said he would **b**
Mic 1:15 I will again **b** a conqueror upon you,
7: 9 He will **b** me out to the light;
Zep 1:17 I will **b** such distress upon people
3:10 my scattered ones, shall **b** my offering.
3:20 At that time I will **b** you home,
Hag 1: 8 Go up to the hills and **b** wood and build the house,
Zec 3: 8 I am going to **b** my servant the Branch.
4: 7 he shall **b** out the top stone amid shouts of 'Grace,
8: 8 and I will **b** them to live in Jerusalem.
8:14 Just as I purposed to **b** disaster upon you,
10: 6 I will **b** them back because I have compassion
10:10 I will **b** them home from the land of Egypt,
10:10 I will **b** them to the land of Gilead and to Lebanon,
Mal 1:13 You **b** what has been taken by violence or is lame
1:13 and this you **b** as your offering!
2:12 or to **b** an offering to the LORD of hosts.
3:10 **B** the full tithe into the storehouse,
Mt 2: 8 and when you have found him, **b** me word so
6:13 And do not **b** us to the time of trial,
6:34 for tomorrow will **b** worries of its own.
10:34 not think that I have come to **b** peace to the earth;
10:34 I have not come to **b** peace, but a sword.
14:18 And he said, "**B** them here to me."
16: 5 they had forgotten to **b** any bread.
17:17 **B** him here to me."
21: 2 untie them and **b** them to me.
27: 1 against Jesus in order to **b** about his death.
Mk 2: 4 And when they could not **b** him to Jesus because
6:27 a soldier of the guard with orders to **b** John's head.
6:55 and rushed about that whole region and began to **b**
8:14 Now the disciples had forgotten to **b** any bread;
9:19 longer must I put up with you? **B** him to me."
11: 2 that has never been ridden; untie it and **b** it.
12:15 **B** me a denarius and let me see it."
13:11 When they **b** you to trial and hand you over,
15: 4 See how many charges they **b** against you."
Lk 1:19 to speak to you and to **b** you this good news.
4:18 he has anointed me to **b** good news to the poor.
5:18 They were trying to **b** him in and lay him
5:19 finding no way to **b** him in because of the crowd,
9:41 with you? **B** your son here."
11: 4 And do not **b** us to the time of trial."
12:11 When they **b** you before the synagogues,
12:49 "I came to **b** fire to the earth,
12:51 Do you think that I have come to **b** peace to
14:21 at once into the streets and lanes of the town and **b**
15:22 father said to his slaves, 'Quickly, **b** out a robe—
19:27 **b** them here and slaughter them in my presence.' "
19:30 Untie it and **b** it here.
Jn 8: 6 ⟦they might have some charge to **b** against him.⟧
10:16 I must **b** them also, and they will listen
18:29 "What accusation do you **b** against this man?"
21:10 "**B** some of the fish that you have just caught."
Ac 5:28 and you are determined to **b** this man's blood
9: 2 he might **b** them bound to Jerusalem.
9:15 an instrument whom I have chosen to **b** my name
11:13 'Send to Joppa and **b** Simon, who is called Peter;
12: 4 to **b** him out to the people after the Passover.
12: 6 very night before Herod was going to **b** him out,
13:32 And we **b** you the good news
13:47 you may **b** salvation to the ends of the earth.' "
14:15 and we **b** you good news,
17: 5 for Paul and Silas to **b** them out to the assembly,
19:38 let them **b** charges there against one another.
22: 5 and to **b** them back to Jerusalem for punishment.
23:10 take him by force, and **b** him into the barracks.
23:15 the council must notify the tribune to **b** him down
Ac 23:18 and asked me to **b** this young man to you;
23:20 "The Jews have agreed to ask you to **b** Paul down
24:13 to you the charge that they now **b** against me.
24:17 after some years I came to **b** alms to my nation
28:19 though I had no charge to **b** against my nation.
Ro 1: 5 and apostleship to **b** about the obedience of faith
7:13 Did what is good, then, **b** death to me?
8:33 Who will **b** any charge against God's elect?
10: 6 (that is, to **b** Christ down)
10: 7 (that is, to **b** Christ up from the dead).
10:15 beautiful are the feet of those who **b** good news!"
16:26 to **b** about the obedience of faith—
1Co 4: 5 who will **b** to light the things now hidden
8: 8 "Food will not **b** us close to God."
2Co 4:14 and will **b** us with you into his presence.
Eph 3: 8 this grace was given to me to **b** to the Gentiles
6: 4 but **b** them up in the discipline and instruction of
Php 1: 6 a good work among you will **b** it to completion by
1Th 4:14 God will **b** with him those who have died.
1Ti 6:15 which he will **b** about at the right time—
2Ti 4:11 Get Mark and **b** him with you,
4:13 **b** the cloak that I left with Carpus at Troas,
Jas 4:14 Yet you do not even know what tomorrow will **b**.
1Pe 1:13 that Jesus Christ will **b** you when he is revealed.
3:18 in order to **b** you to God.
2Pe 2: 1 who will secretly **b** in destructive opinions.
2:11 do not **b** against them a slanderous judgment from
2Jn 1:10 to you and does not **b** this teaching;
Jude 1: 9 he did not dare to **b** a condemnation of slander
Rev 21:24 and the kings of the earth will **b** their glory into it.
21:26 People will **b** into it the glory and the honor of
Tob 1: 8 I would **b** it and give it to them in the third year,
2: 2 and **b** whatever poor person you may find
3:10 And I shall **b** my father in his old age down
5:17 in heaven **b** you safely there and return you
6:13 from Rages we will take her and **b** her back
6:15 that I may die and **b** my father's and mother's life
7:12 Take her and **b** her safely to your father.
7:13 and told her to **b** writing material;
8:17 **b** their lives to fulfillment in happiness
9: 2 then **b** him with you to the wedding celebration.
10:12 the Lord of heaven **b** you back safely,
14: 5 and God will **b** them back into the land of Israel;
Jdt 8:22 all this he will **b** on our heads among the Gentiles,
8:23 For our slavery will not **b** us into favor,
9: 8 and **b** down their power in your anger;
9:13 Make my deceitful words **b** wound and bruise
11:14 in order to **b** back permission from the council of
11:22 to strengthen our hands and **b** destruction
12: 1 to **b** her in where his silver dinnerware was kept,
14: 5 **b** Achior the Ammonite to me so that he may see
AdE 4: 7 into the royal treasury to **b** about the destruction of
5: 5 Then the king said, "**B** Haman quickly,
6: 1 so he gave orders to his secretary to **b** the book
6: 8 let the king's servants **b** out the fine linen robe that
Wis 1:12 or **b** on destruction by the works of your hands;
16:14 but cannot **b** back the departed spirit,
Sir 1:30 or you may fall and **b** dishonor upon yourself.
4:17 she will **b** fear and dread upon them,
8:11 Do not let the insolent **b** you to your feet,
17:23 and he will **b** their recompense on their heads.
33:23 **b** no stain upon your honor.
Bar 2:19 or our kings that we **b** before you our prayer
2:34 I will **b** them again into the land that I swore
4:29 upon you will **b** you everlasting joy
5: 6 but God will **b** them back to you, carried in glory,
LtJ 6: 3 after that I will **b** you away from there in peace.
6:40 they **b** Bel and pray that the mute may speak,
Aza 1:20 and **b** glory to your name, O Lord.
Sus 1:17 "**B** me olive oil and ointments,
1:18 to **b** what they had been commanded;
1:56 he ordered them to **b** the other.
Bel 1:14 Then Daniel ordered his servants to **b** ashes,
1Mc 6:15 that he might guide his son Antiochus and **b** him
6:55 to **b** up his son Antiochus to be king,
7: 2 the army seized Antiochus and Lysias to **b** them
9:58 So now let us **b** Bacchides back,
10:63 of the city and proclaim that no one is to **b** charges
2Mc 1: 4 and his commandments, and may he **b** peace.
1:20 he ordered them to dip it out and **b** it.
6:21 and privately urged him to **b** meat
7:38 and through me and my brothers to **b** to an end
12:39 the bodies of the fallen and to **b** them back to lie
1Es 1:52 to **b** against them the kings of the Chaldeans.
4: 5 they **b** everything to the king—
4: 6 whenever they sow and reap, and **b** some to
4:17 Women make men's clothes; they **b** men glory;
4:22 and **b** everything and give it to women?
4:48 to **b** cedar timber from Lebanon to Jerusalem,
5:55 to **b** cedar logs from Lebanon and convey them
9:39 the chief priest and reader to **b** the law of Moses
3Mc 1: 8 to **b** him gifts of welcome,
1:26 determined to **b** the aforesaid plan to a conclusion.
2Es 2: 6 so that you may **b** confusion on them
2: 6 on them and **b** their mother to ruin,
2:15 **b** them up with gladness, as does a dove;
2:16 and **b** them out from their tombs,
2:31 I will **b** them out of the hiding places of the earth,
4:27 not be able to **b** the things that have been promised
5: 8 and menstruous women shall **b** forth monsters.
5:37 and **b** out for me the winds shut up in them,
5:49 For as an infant does not **b** forth,
5:49 who has become old does not **b** forth any longer,
6:47 to **b** forth living creatures, birds, and fishes;
6:53 the earth to **b** forth before you cattle, wild animals,
7:47 I see that the world to come will **b** delight to few,
7:*119* [49] but we have done deeds that **b** death?

2Es 8:31 have passed our lives in ways that **b** death;
9:31 and it shall **b** forth fruit in you,
12:33 first he will **b** them alive before his judgment seat,
15:11 but I will **b** them out with a mighty hand and with
15:12 and castigation that the Lord will **b** upon it.
16:32 and its roads and all its paths shall **b** forth thorns,
4Mc 1:9 All of these, by despising sufferings that **b** death,
11:23 and I myself will **b** a great avenger upon you,

BRINGING‡ (80) [BRING]

Ex 14:11 What have you done to us, **b** us out of Egypt?
18:5 **b** Moses' sons and wife to him.
19:24 "Go down, and come up **b** Aaron with you;
35:22 everyone **b** an offering of gold to the LORD.
36:3 still kept **b** him freewill offerings every morning,
36:5 "The people are **b** much more than enough
36:6 So the people were restrained from **b**;
Lev 4:3 thus **b** guilt on the people,
18:3 in the land of Canaan, to which I am **b** you.
Nu 5:15 **b** iniquity to remembrance.
14:3 Why is the LORD **b** us into this land to fall by
14:36 against him by **b** a bad report about the land—
15:18 After you come into the land to which I am **b** you,
Dt 8:7 the LORD your God is **b** you into a good land,
12:6 **b** there your burnt offerings and your sacrifices,
19:10 thereby **b** bloodguilt upon you.
28:63 so the LORD will take delight in **b** you to ruin
29:19 we go our own stubborn ways" (thus **b** disaster
29:27 **b** on it every curse written in this book.
Jos 6:18 of Israel an object for destruction, **b** trouble
7:25 The LORD is **b** trouble on you today."
Jdg 4:6 **b** ten thousand from the tribe of Naphtali and
15:1 Samson went to visit his wife, **b** along a kid.
1Sa 28:15 "Why have you disturbed me by **b** me up?"
2Sa 3:22 with Joab from a raid, **b** much spoil with them.
4:10 'See, Saul is dead,' thought he was **b** good news,
18:26 The king said, "He also is **b** tidings."
19:10 why do you say nothing about **b** the king back?"
19:43 not the first to speak of **b** back our king?"
24:16 and said to the angel who was **b** destruction
1Ki 8:32 the guilty by **b** their conduct on their own head,
10:22 the fleet of ships of Tarshish used to come **b** gold,
2Ki 4:5 they kept **b** vessels to her, and she kept pouring.
4:42 **b** food from the first fruits to the man of God:
21:12 I am **b** upon Jerusalem and Judah such evil that
1Ch 12:40 came **b** food on donkeys, camels, mules,
2Ch 6:23 the guilty by **b** their conduct on their own head,
9:21 the ships of Tarshish used to come **b** gold,
34:14 While they were **b** out the money
Ne 13:15 **b** in heaps of grain and loading them on donkeys;
Ps 74:7 the dwelling place of your name, **b** it to
Isa 1:13 **b** offerings is futile; incense is an abomination
8:7 the Lord is **b** up against it the mighty flood waters
Jer 2:35 Now I am **b** you to judgment for saying,
4:6 do not delay, for I am **b** evil from the north,
4:31 anguish as of one **b** forth her first child,
17:26 **b** burnt offerings and sacrifices,
17:26 and **b** thank offerings to the house of the LORD.
19:15 now **b** upon this city and upon all its towns all
26:15 you will be **b** innocent blood upon yourselves and
41:5 **b** grain offerings and incense to present at
42:17 from the disaster that I am **b** upon them.
46:25 See, I am **b** punishment upon Amon of Thebes,
51:64 because of the disasters that I am **b** on her.' "
Eze 20:9 to them in **b** them out of the land of Egypt.
21:23 but he brings their guilt to remembrance, **b**
Da 9:12 by **b** upon us a calamity so great
Mt 15:30 Great crowds came to him, **b** with them the lame,
25:20 **b** five more talents, saying, 'Master,
Mk 2:3 some people came, **b** to him a paralyzed man,
10:13 People were **b** little children to him in order
Lk 2:10 I am **b** you good news of great joy for all
8:1 proclaiming and **b** the good news of the kingdom
9:6 **b** the good news and curing diseases everywhere.
18:15 People were **b** even infants to him
22:54 **b** him into the high priest's house.
Jn 19:4 I am **b** him out to you to let you know
19:39 also came, **b** a mixture of myrrh and aloes,
Ac 5:16 **b** the sick and those tormented by unclean spirits,
9:21 not come here for the purpose of **b** them bound
25:7 **b** many serious charges against him,
Tit 2:11 the grace of God has appeared, **b** salvation to all,
Heb 2:10 in **b** many children to glory,
2Pe 2:1 **b** swift destruction on themselves.
1Mc 11:39 the Arab, who was **b** up Antiochus, the young son
3Mc 2:4 whom you destroyed by **b** on them
2Es 13:13 and some were **b** others as offerings.
15:5 says the Lord, I am **b** evils upon the world,
15:49 **b** ruin to your houses, **b** destruction and death.

BRINGS‡ (76) [BRING]

Ex 13:5 the LORD **b** you into the land of the Canaanites,
23:23 and **b** you to the Amorites, the Hittites,
Nu 5:18 the priest shall have the water of bitterness that **b**
5:19 be immune to this water of bitterness that **b**
5:22 that **b** the curse enter your bowels
5:24 the woman drink the water of bitterness that **b**
5:24 and the water that **b** the curse shall enter her
5:27 the water that **b** the curse shall enter into her
23:22 God, who **b** them out of Egypt,
24:8 God who **b** him out of Egypt,
Dt 7:1 When the LORD your God **b** you into the land
24:11 to whom you are making the loan **b** the pledge out
1Sa 2:6 The LORD kills and **b** to life;
2:6 he **b** down to Sheol and raises up.
1Sa 2:7 The LORD makes poor and makes rich; he **b** low,
Job 9:23 When disaster **b** sudden death,
12:22 and **b** deep darkness to light.
19:29 for wrath **b** the punishment of the sword,
Ps 33:10 LORD **b** the counsel of the nations to nothing;
34:21 Evil **b** death to the wicked,
135:7 the rain and **b** out the wind from his storehouses.
146:9 but the way of the wicked he **b** to ruin.
Pr 10:5 but a child who sleeps in harvest **b** shame.
10:14 but the babbling of a fool **b** ruin near.
10:31 The mouth of the righteous **b** forth wisdom,
11:15 To guarantee loans for a stranger **b** trouble,
12:4 she who **b** shame is like rottenness in his bones.
12:18 but the tongue of the wise **b** healing.
13:17 A bad messenger **b** trouble, but a faithful envoy,
16:30 one who compresses the lips **b** evil to pass.
18:20 the yield of the lips **b** satisfaction.
19:4 Wealth **b** many friends,
19:15 Laziness **b** on deep sleep;
31:14 she **b** her food from far away.
SS 8:10 then I was in his eyes as one who **b** peace.
Isa 30:5 that **b** neither help nor profit,
31:2 Yet he too is wise and **b** disaster;
40:23 who **b** princes to naught, and makes the rulers of
40:26 He who **b** out their host and numbers them,
43:17 who **b** out chariot and horse, army and warrior;
52:7 who **b** good news, who announces salvation,
59:4 No one **b** suit justly, no one goes to law honestly;
61:11 For as the earth **b** forth its shoots,
Jer 10:13 and he **b** out the wind from his storehouses.
13:16 before he **b** darkness, and before your feet stumble
51:16 and he **b** out the wind from his storehouses.
Eze 21:23 but he **b** their guilt to remembrance,
Na 1:15 the mountains the feet of one who **b** good tidings,
Hab 1:15 The enemy **b** all of them up with a hook;
Mt 12:20 a smoldering wick until he **b** justice to victory.
12:35 good person **b** good things out of a good treasure,
12:35 the evil person **b** evil things out of an evil treasure.
12:45 Then it goes and **b** along seven
13:52 a household who **b** out of his treasure what is new
Lk 11:26 and **b** seven other spirits more evil than itself,
Ro 4:15 For the law **b** wrath;
5:16 free gift following many trespasses **b** justification.
2Co 7:10 that leads to salvation and **b** no regret,
Heb 1:6 And again, when he **b** the firstborn into the world,
10:35 of yours; it **b** a great reward.
Jas 5:20 you should know that whoever **b** back a sinner
Tob 13:2 and he **b** up from the great abyss,
14:11 and what injustice does—it **b** death!
AdE 7:4 Our antagonist **b** shame on the king's court."
Wis 6:19 and immortality **b** one near to God;
Sir 10:13 the Lord **b** upon them unheard-of calamities,
11:17 and his favor **b** lasting success.
22:19 One who pricks the eye **b** tears,
26:2 A loyal wife **b** joy to her husband,
30:24 and anxiety **b** on premature old age.
37:30 for overeating **b** sickness,
42:14 it is woman who **b** shame and disgrace.
2Mc 3:39 over that place himself and **b** it aid,
1Es 4:24 he **b** it back to the woman he loves.
2Es 13:23 The one who **b** the peril at
4Mc 8:18 and venture upon a disobedience that **b** death?

BRINK (2)

Isa 19:7 bare places by the Nile, on the **b** of the Nile;
Sir 51:6 and my life was on the **b** of Hades below.

BRISTLED (1) [BRISTLING]

Job 4:15 spirit glided past my face; the hair of my flesh **b**.

BRISTLING (1) [BRISTLED]

Jer 51:27 bring up horses like **b** locusts.

BRITTLE (1)

Da 2:42 so the kingdom shall be partly strong and partly **b**.

BROAD‡ (26) [BREADTH, BROADER]

Ge 29:7 He said, "Look, it is still **b** daylight;
Ex 3:8 up out of that land to a good and **b** land,
Lev 3:9 the whole **b** tail, which shall be removed close to
7:3 the **b** tail, the fat that covers the entrails,
8:25 the **b** tail, all the fat that was around the entrails,
9:19 the **b** tail, the fat that covers the entrails,
Jdg 18:10 to an unsuspecting people. The land is **b**—
2Sa 22:20 He brought me out into a **b** place;
1Ch 4:40 good pasture, and the land was very **b**, quiet,
Ne 3:8 and they restored Jerusalem as far as the **B** Wall.
12:38 above the Tower of the Ovens, to the **B** Wall,
Job 36:16 He also allured you out of distress into a **b** place
37:10 and the **b** waters are frozen fast.
Ps 18:19 He brought me out into a **b** place;
31:8 you have set my feet in a **b** place.
118:5 the LORD answered me and set me in a **b** place.
119:96 but your commandment is exceedingly **b**.
Isa 30:23 On that day your cattle will graze in **b** pastures;
33:21 in majesty will be for us a place of **b** rivers
Jer 51:58 **b** wall of Babylon shall be leveled to the ground,
Hos 4:16 now feed them like a lamb in a **b** pasture?
Am 8:9 and darken the earth in **b** daylight.
Mt 23:5 for they make their phylacteries **b**
Sir 47:23 **b** in folly and lacking in sense, Rehoboam,
2Es 7:5 how can they come to the **b** part unless they pass
7:13 the entrances of the greater world are **b** and safe,

BROADCASTS (1)

Pr 12:23 but the mind of a fool **b** folly.

BROADER (1) [BROAD]

Job 11:9 the earth, and **b** than the sea.

BROIDED (KJV) See BRAIDED

BROILED (1)

Lk 24:42 They gave him a piece of **b** fish,

BROKE (91) [BREAK]

Ex 32:19 the tablets from his hands and **b** them at the foot of
34:1 that were on the former tablets, which you **b**.
Dt 32:51 both of you **b** faith with me among the Israelites at
Jos 7:1 Israelites **b** faith in regard to the devoted things:
Jdg 7:20 three companies blew the trumpets and **b** the jars,
8:17 He also **b** down the tower of Penuel,
1Sa 5:9 both young and old, so that tumors **b** out on them.
2Sa 2:32 and the day **b** upon them at Hebron.
23:16 Then the three warriors **b** through the camp of
2Ki 11:18 his altars and his images they **b** in pieces,
14:13 to Jerusalem, and **b** down the wall of Jerusalem
18:4 He removed the high places, **b** down the pillars,
18:4 He **b** in pieces the bronze serpent
23:7 He **b** down the houses of the male temple
23:8 he **b** down the high places of the gates that were at
23:12 he pulled down from there and **b** in pieces,
23:14 He **b** the pillars in pieces,
25:10 of the guard **b** down the walls around Jerusalem.
25:13 the Chaldeans **b** in pieces,
1Ch 11:18 The Three **b** through the camp of the Philistines,
20:4 After this, war **b** out with the Philistines at Gezer;
2Ch 14:3 **b** down the pillars, hewed down the sacred poles,
23:17 his altars and his images they **b** in pieces,
25:23 he brought him to Jerusalem, and **b** down the wall
26:6 and **b** down the wall of Gath and the wall
26:19 the priests a leprous disease **b** out on his forehead,
31:1 to the cities of Judah and **b** down the pillars,
34:4 He **b** down the sacred poles and the carved and
34:7 he **b** down the altars, beat the sacred poles and
36:19 **b** down the wall of Jerusalem,
Job 16:12 I was at ease, and he **b** me in two;
29:17 I **b** the fangs of the unrighteous,
Ps 18:12 before him there **b** through his clouds hailstones
74:13 you **b** the heads of the dragons in the waters.
76:3 There he **b** the flashing arrows, the shield,
105:16 and **b** every staff of bread,
106:18 Fire also **b** out in their company;
106:29 and a plague **b** out among them.
107:14 and **b** their bonds asunder.
Pr 3:20 by his knowledge the deeps **b** open,
Isa 22:10 and you **b** down the houses to fortify the wall.
Jer 2:20 long ago you **b** your yoke and burst your bonds,
28:10 from the neck of the prophet Jeremiah, and **b** it.
31:32 that they **b**, though I was their husband, says
39:8 and **b** down the walls of Jerusalem.
52:14 **b** down all the walls around Jerusalem.
52:17 the Chaldeans **b** in pieces,
Eze 17:4 **b** off its topmost shoot; He carried it to a
17:16 and whose covenant with him he **b**—
17:18 Because he despised the oath and **b** the covenant,
17:19 and my covenant that he **b**.
29:7 you **b**, and tore all their shoulders;
29:7 and when they leaned on you, you **b**,
Da 2:34 the statue on its feet of iron and clay and **b** them
6:24 the lions overpowered them and **b** all their bones
7:19 and which devoured and **b** in pieces,
Zec 11:10 I took my staff Favor and **b** it,
11:14 Then I **b** my second staff Unity,
Mt 14:19 and blessed and **b** the loaves,
15:36 and after giving thanks he **b** them and gave them
26:26 and after blessing it he **b** it, gave it to the disciples,
Mk 5:4 and the shackles he **b** in pieces;
6:41 and blessed and **b** the loaves,
8:6 and after giving thanks he **b** them and gave them
8:19 When I **b** the five loaves for the five thousand,
14:3 and she **b** open the jar and poured the ointment
14:22 and after blessing it he **b** it, gave it to them,
14:72 And he **b** down and wept.
Lk 9:16 he looked up to heaven, and blessed and **b** them,
22:19 he **b** it and gave it to them, saying,
24:30 blessed and **b** it, and gave it to them.
Jn 19:32 the soldiers came and **b** the legs of the first and of
Ac 2:46 they **b** bread at home and ate their food with glad
13:43 When the meeting of the synagogue **b** up,
19:23 that time no little disturbance **b** out concerning
27:35 he **b** it and began to eat.
1Co 11:24 he **b** it and said, "This is my body that is for you.
Rev 12:7 And war **b** out in heaven;
1Mc 3:5 He searched out and pursued those who **b** the law;
6:62 he **b** the oath he had sworn and gave orders to tear
11:53 But he **b** his word about all that he had promised;
12:32 Then he **b** camp and went to Damascus,
13:19 Trypho **b** his word and did not release Jonathan.
15:27 and **b** all the agreements he formerly had made
2Mc 10:36 Others **b** open the gates and let in the rest of
1Es 1:48 he **b** his oath and rebelled;
1:55 **b** down the walls of Jerusalem,
3Mc 6:5 **b** in pieces, showing your power to many nations.
2Es 10:5 Then I **b** off the reflections
4Mc 7:5 our father Eleazar **b** the maddening waves of
9:25 the saintly youth **b** the thread of life.

BROKEN‡ (142) [BREAK]

Ge 17:14 from his people; he has **b** my covenant."
Ex 6:9 because of their **b** spirit and their cruel slavery.
Lev 6:28 earthen vessel in which it was boiled shall be **b**;
11:35 whether an oven or stove, it shall be **b** in pieces;
13:20 this is a leprous disease, **b** out in the boil.
13:25 it has **b** out in the burn,
13:39 it is a rash that has **b** out on the skin; he is clean.
15:12 that the one with the discharge touches shall be **b**;
21:19 or one who has a **b** foot or a **b** hand,
26:13 I have **b** the bars of your yoke
Nu 15:31 the word of the LORD and **b** his commandment,
Dt 21:6 over the heifer whose neck was **b** in the wadi,
Jdg 6:28 the altar of Baal was **b** down,
1Sa 2:4 The bows of the mighty are **b**,
4:18 and his neck was **b** and he died,
1Ki 5:9 I will have them **b** up there for you to take away.
2Ki 18:21 that **b** reed of a staff,
2Ch 14:13 for they were **b** before the LORD and his army.
15:6 They were **b** in pieces, nation against nation
24:7 that wicked woman, had **b** into the house of God,
32:5 the entire wall that was **b** down, and raised towers
Ezr 10:2 "We have **b** faith with our God
Ne 1:3 the wall of Jerusalem is **b** down,
2:13 of Jerusalem that had been **b** down and its gates
Job 4:10 and the teeth of the young lions are **b**.
17:1 My spirit is **b**, my days are extinct,
17:11 My days are past, my plans are **b** off,
24:20 so wickedness is **b** like a tree.
31:22 and let my arm be **b** from its socket.
38:15 and their uplifted arm is **b**.
Ps 31:12 I have become like a **b** vessel.
34:20 not one of them will be **b**.
37:15 and their bows shall be **b**.
37:17 For the arms of the wicked shall be **b**,
44:19 yet you have **b** us in the haunt of jackals,
51:17 The sacrifice acceptable to God is a **b** spirit;
51:17 **b** and contrite heart, O God, you will not despise.
60:1 you have rejected us, **b** our defenses;
69:20 Insults have **b** my heart, so that I am in despair.
80:12 Why then have you **b** down its walls,
89:40 You have **b** through all his walls;
102:23 He has **b** my strength in midcourse;
119:126 for your law has been **b**.
124:7 the snare is **b**, and we have escaped.
Pr 15:13 but by sorrow of heart the spirit is **b**.
17:19 one who builds a high threshold invites **b** bones.
18:14 but a **b** spirit—who can bear?
24:31 and its stone wall was **b** down.
29:1 will suddenly be **b** beyond healing.
Ecc 4:12 A threefold cord is not quickly **b**.
12:6 and the golden bowl is **b**,
12:6 and the pitcher is **b** at the fountain,
12:6 and the wheel **b** at the cistern,
Isa 5:27 not a loincloth is loose, not a sandal-thong **b**;
8:15 they shall fall and be **b**;
9:4 you have **b** as on the day of Midian.
14:5 The LORD has **b** the staff of the wicked,
14:29 that the rod that struck you is **b**,
24:5 violated the statutes, **b** the everlasting covenant.
24:10 The city of chaos is **b** down,
24:19 The earth is utterly **b**, the earth is torn asunder,
27:11 When its boughs are dry, they are **b**;
28:13 and fall backward, and be **b**, and snared,
33:8 The treaty is **b**, its oaths are despised,
33:20 and none of whose ropes will be **b**.
36:6 you are relying on Egypt, that **b** reed of a staff,
Jer 2:16 and Tahpanhes have **b** the crown of your head.
5:5 But they all alike had **b** the yoke,
10:20 My tent is destroyed, and all my cords are **b**;
11:10 the house of Israel and the house of Judah have **b**
22:28 Is this man Coniah a despised **b** pot,
28:2 I have **b** the yoke of the king of Babylon.
28:12 after the prophet Hananiah had **b** the yoke from
28:13 You have **b** wooden bars only to forge iron bars
33:21 with my servant David be **b**,
48:1 the fortress is put to shame and **b** down;
48:17 say, "How the mighty scepter is **b**,
48:20 Moab is put to shame, for it is **b** down;
48:25 The horn of Moab is cut off, and his arm is **b**,
48:38 for I have **b** Moab like a vessel that no one wants,
48:39 How it is **b**! How they wail!
50:23 the hammer of the whole earth is cut down and **b**!
51:30 her buildings are set on fire, her bars are **b**.
51:56 her warriors are taken, their bows are **b**;
La 2:2 in his wrath he has **b** down the strongholds
2:6 He has **b** down his booth like a garden,
2:9 he has ruined and **b** her bars;
3:4 and my skin waste away, and **b** my bones;
Eze 6:4 and your incense stands shall be **b**;
6:6 your idols **b** and destroyed,
26:2 "Aha, **b** is the gateway of the peoples;
30:8 and all who help it are **b**.
30:21 I have **b** the arm of Pharaoh king of Egypt;
30:22 both the strong arm and the one that was **b**;
31:12 its boughs lie **b** in all the watercourses of the land;
32:28 you shall be **b** and lie among the uncircumcised,
44:7 have **b** my covenant with all your abominations.
Da 2:35 were all **b** in pieces and became like the chaff of
8:8 at the height of its power, the great horn was **b**,
8:22 As for the horn that was **b**,
8:25 But he shall be **b**, and not by human hands.
11:4 be **b** and divided toward the four winds of heaven,
11:20 but within a few days he shall be **b**,
11:22 Armies shall be utterly swept away and **b**
Hos 8:1 because they have **b** my covenant,
Hos 8:6 The calf of Samaria shall be **b** to pieces.
Na 1:6 and by him the rocks are **b** in pieces.
Mt 14:20 they took up what was left over of the **b** pieces,
15:37 and they took up the **b** pieces left over,
21:44 The one who falls on this stone will be **b** to pieces;
24:43 and would not have let his house be **b** into.
Mk 6:43 up twelve baskets full of **b** pieces and of the fish.
8:8 and they took up the **b** pieces left over,
8:19 many baskets full of **b** pieces did you collect?"
8:20 many baskets full of **b** pieces did you collect?"
Lk 9:17 twelve baskets of **b** pieces.
12:39 he would not have let his house be **b** into.
20:18 Everyone who falls on that stone will be **b**
Jn 7:23 in order that the law of Moses may not be **b**,
19:31 of the crucified men **b** and the bodies removed.
19:36 "None of his bones shall be **b**."
Ac 20:11 and after he had **b** bread and eaten,
27:41 the stern was being **b** up by the force of the waves.
Ro 11:17 But if some of the branches were **b** off, and you,
11:19 "Branches were **b** off so that I might
11:20 They were **b** off because of their unbelief,
Eph 2:14 into one and has **b** down the dividing wall,
Wis 4:5 The branches will be **b** off before they come
Sir 21:14 The mind of a fool is like a **b** jar;
43:15 and the hailstones are **b** in pieces.
LtJ 6:17 For just as someone's dish is useless when it is **b**,
6:43 not as attractive as herself and her cord was not **b**.
Aza 1:6 and **b** your law in turning away from you;
1:21 and let their strength be **b**.
Bel 1:33 he had made a stew and had **b** bread into a bowl,
2Mc 9:11 Then it was that, **b** in spirit,
1Es 9:7 "You have **b** the law and married foreign women,
3Mc 2:20 in the mouth of those who are downcast and **b**
2Es 15:61 You shall be **b** down by them like stubble,
4Mc 5:3 they were to be **b** on the wheel and killed.
11:18 upon it, his back was **b**, and he was roasted

BROKENHEARTED (4) [BREAK, HEART]

Ps 34:18 The LORD is near to the **b**,
109:16 the poor and needy and the **b** to their death.
147:3 He heals the **b**, and binds up their wounds.
Isa 61:1 the oppressed, to bind up the **b**, to proclaim liberty

BRONZE (166)

Ge 4:22 who made all kinds of **b** and iron tools.
Ex 25:3 from them: gold, silver, and **b**,
26:11 You shall make fifty clasps of **b**,
26:37 and you shall cast five bases of **b** for them.
27:2 and you shall overlay it with **b**.
27:3 you shall make all its utensils of **b**.
27:4 also make for it a grating, a network of **b**;
27:4 and on the net you shall make four **b** rings
27:6 poles of acacia wood, and overlay them with **b**;
27:10 and their twenty bases shall be of **b**,
27:11 their pillars twenty and their bases twenty, of **b**,
27:17 their hooks shall be of silver, and their bases of **b**.
27:18 with hangings of fine twisted linen and bases of **b**.
27:19 and all the pegs of the court, shall be of **b**.
30:18 You shall make a **b** basin with a **b** stand
31:4 to work in gold, silver, and **b**,
35:5 bring the LORD's offering: gold, silver, and **b**;
35:16 with its grating of **b**, its poles, and all its utensils,
35:24 of silver or **b** brought it as the LORD's offering;
35:32 to work in gold, silver, and **b**,
36:18 He made fifty clasps of **b** to join the tent together
36:38 but their five bases were of **b**.
38:2 of one piece with it, and he overlaid it with **b**.
38:3 all its utensils he made of **b**.
38:4 He made for the altar a grating, a network of **b**,
38:5 the four corners of the **b** grating to hold the poles;
38:6 and overlaid them with **b**.
38:8 He made the basin of **b** with its stand of **b**,
38:10 its twenty pillars and their twenty bases were of **b**,
38:11 its twenty pillars and their twenty bases were of **b**,
38:17 The bases for the pillars were of **b**,
38:19 There were four pillars; their four bases were of **b**,
38:20 and for the court all around were of **b**.
38:29 The **b** that was contributed was seventy talents,
38:30 **b** altar and the **b** grating for it and all the utensils
39:39 the **b** altar, and its grating of **b**, its poles,
Lev 6:28 but if it is boiled in a **b** vessel,
Nu 16:39 So Eleazar the priest took the **b** censers
21:9 Moses made a serpent of **b**, and put it upon a pole;
21:9 that person would look at the serpent of **b** and live.
31:22 gold, silver, **b**, iron, tin, and lead—
Dt 28:23 The sky over your head shall be **b**,
33:25 Your bars are iron and **b**;
Jos 6:19 But all silver and gold, and vessels of **b** and iron,
6:24 and the vessels of **b** and iron,
22:8 and with very much livestock, with silver, gold, **b**,
Jdg 16:21 down to Gaza and bound him with **b** shackles;
1Sa 17:5 He had a helmet of **b** on his head,
17:5 weight of the coat was five thousand shekels of **b**.
17:6 greaves of **b** on his legs and a javelin of **b** slung
17:38 a **b** helmet on his head and clothed him with a coat
2Sa 8:8 King David took a great amount of **b**.
8:10 with him articles of silver, gold, and **b**;
21:16 whose spear weighed three hundred shekels of **b**,
22:35 so that my arms can bend a bow of **b**.
1Ki 4:13 sixty great cities with walls and **b** bars);
7:14 a man of Tyre, had been an artisan in **b**;
7:14 intelligence, and knowledge in working **b**.
7:15 He cast two pillars of **b**.
7:16 He also made two capitals of molten **b**,
7:27 He also made the ten stands of **b**;
1Ki 7:30 Each stand had four **b** wheels and axles of **b**;
7:38 He made ten basins of **b**;
7:45 for the house of the LORD were of burnished **b**.
7:47 the weight of the **b** was not determined.
8:64 of the sacrifices of well-being, because the **b** altar
14:27 so King Rehoboam made shields of **b** instead,
2Ki 16:14 The **b** altar that was before
16:15 but the **b** altar shall be for me to inquire by."
16:17 he removed the sea from the **b** oxen that were
18:4 in pieces the **b** serpent that Moses had made,
25:13 The **b** pillars that were in the house of the LORD,
25:13 and the **b** sea that were in the house of the LORD,
25:13 and carried the **b** to Babylon.
25:14 and all the **b** vessels used in the temple service,
25:16 the **b** of all these vessels was beyond weighing.
25:17 and on it was a **b** capital;
25:17 latticework and pomegranates, all of **b**,
1Ch 15:19 Asaph, and Ethan were to sound **b** cymbals;
18:8 David took a vast quantity of **b**;
18:8 the **b** sea and the pillars and the vessels of **b**.
18:10 of articles of gold, of silver, and of **b**;
22:3 as well as **b** in quantities beyond weighing,
22:14 and **b** and iron beyond weighing,
22:16 silver, **b**, and iron. Now begin the work,
29:2 and the **b** for the things of **b**,
29:7 eighteen thousand talents of **b**,
2Ch 1:5 Moreover the **b** altar that Bezalel son of Uri,
1:6 Solomon went up there to the **b** altar before
2:7 silver, **b**, and iron, and in purple, crimson,
2:14 He is trained to work in gold, silver, **b**, iron, stone,
4:1 He made an altar of **b**, twenty cubits long,
4:9 he overlaid their doors with **b**.
4:16 of burnished **b** for King Solomon for the house of
4:18 so that the weight of the **b** was not determined.
6:13 Solomon had made a **b** platform five cubits long,
7:7 the **b** altar Solomon had made could not hold
12:10 in place of them shields of **b**,
24:12 and also workers in iron and **b** to repair the house
Ezr 8:27 two vessels of fine polished **b** as precious as gold.
Job 6:12 the strength of stones, or is my flesh **b**?
20:24 a **b** arrow will strike them through.
40:18 Its bones are tubes of **b**, its limbs like bars of iron.
41:27 It counts iron as straw, and **b** as rotten wood.
Ps 18:34 so that my arms can bend a bow of **b**.
68:31 Let **b** be brought from Egypt;
107:16 For he shatters the doors of **b**,
Isa 45:2 in pieces the doors of **b** and cut through the bars
60:17 Instead of **b** I will bring gold,
60:17 instead of wood, **b**, instead of stones, iron.
Jer 1:18 and a **b** wall, against the whole land—
6:28 they are **b** and iron, all of them act corruptly.
15:12 Can iron and **b** break iron from the north?
15:20 to this people a fortified wall of **b**;
52:17 pillars of **b** that were in the house of the LORD,
52:17 and the **b** sea that were in the house of the LORD,
52:17 and carried all the **b** to Babylon.
52:18 and all the vessels of **b** used in the temple service.
52:20 the twelve **b** bulls that were under the sea,
52:20 the **b** of all these vessels was beyond weighing.
52:22 Upon it was a capital of **b**;
52:22 latticework and pomegranates, all of **b**,
Eze 1:7 and they sparkled like burnished **b**.
9:2 They went in and stood beside the **b** altar.
22:18 all of them, silver, **b**, tin, iron, and lead.
22:20 As one gathers silver, **b**, iron, lead,
27:13 they exchanged human beings and vessels of **b**
40:3 a man was there, whose appearance shone like **b**,
Da 2:32 its middle and thighs of **b**,
2:35 Then the iron, the clay, the **b**, the silver,
2:39 and yet a third kingdom of **b**,
2:45 and that it crushed the iron, the **b**, the clay,
4:15 with a band of iron and **b**,
4:23 with a band of iron and **b**, in the grass of the field;
5:4 the gods of gold and silver, **b**, iron, wood,
5:23 You have praised the gods of silver and gold, of **b**,
7:19 with its teeth of iron and claws of **b**,
10:6 his arms and legs like the gleam of burnished **b**,
Mic 4:13 for I will make your horn iron and your hoofs **b**;
Zec 6:1 between two mountains—mountains of **b**.
Mk 7:4 the washing of cups, pots, and **b** kettles.)
Rev 1:15 his feet were like burnished **b**,
2:18 and whose feet are like burnished **b**:
9:20 of gold and silver and **b** and stone and wood,
18:12 all articles of ivory, all articles of costly wood, **b**,
Sir 28:20 and its fetters are fetters of **b**;
Bel 1:7 for this thing is only clay inside and **b** outside,
1Mc 8:22 on **b** tablets, and sent to Jerusalem to remain
14:18 they wrote to him on **b** tablets to renew with him
14:27 on **b** tablets and put it on pillars on Mount Zion.
14:48 to inscribe this decree on **b** tablets,
1Es 1:12 they boiled the sacrifices in **b** pots and caldrons,
1:40 he bound him with a chain of **b** and took him away
8:57 and twelve **b** vessels of fine **b** that glittered
2Es 7:55 Say to her, 'You produce gold and silver and **b**,
7:56 and **b** than silver, and iron than **b**,

BROOCHES (1)

Ex 35:22 all who were of a willing heart brought **b** and

BROOD (11)

Nu 32:14 And now you, a **b** of sinners,
Job 30:8 A senseless, disreputable **b**,
Ecc 5:20 they will scarcely **b** over the days of their lives,
Isa 34:15 the owl nest and lay and hatch and **b** in its shadow;
Mt 3:7 he said to them, "You **b** of vipers!

Mt 12:34 You **b** of vipers! How can you speak good things,
23:33 You snakes, you **b** of vipers!
23:37 as a hen gathers her **b** under her wings,
Lk 3: 7 to be baptized by him, "You **b** of vipers!
13:34 as a hen gathers her **b** under her wings,
Wis 4: 3 But the prolific **b** of the ungodly will be of no use,

BROOK (4) [BROOKS]

Lev 23:40 boughs of leafy trees, and willows of the **b**;
2Sa 17:20 "They have crossed over the **b** of water."
Jer 15:18 Truly, you are to me like a deceitful **b**,
Jdt 2:24 the fortified towns along the **b** Abron,

BROOKS (2) [BROOK]

Isa 30:25 and every high hill there will be **b** running
Jer 31: 9 I will let them walk by **b** of water,

BROOKS (KJV) See also NILE, STREAMS, TORRENT-BED, TORRENTS, WADI

BROOM (5)

1Ki 19: 4 and came and sat down under a solitary **b** tree.
19: 5 Then he lay down under the **b** tree and fell asleep.
Job 30: 4 and to warm themselves the roots of **b**.
Ps 120: 4 with glowing coals of the **b** tree!
Isa 14:23 and I will sweep it with the **b** of destruction,

BROTH (3)

Jdg 6:19 meat he put in a basket, and the **b** he put in a pot,
6:20 and put them on this rock, and pour out the **b**."
Isa 65: 4 with **b** of abominable things in their vessels;

BROTHER‡ (357) [BROTHER'S, BROTHER-IN-LAW, BROTHERLY, BROTHERLY-LOVING, BROTHERS, BROTHERS']

A. BROTHER ... SISTER (22)

Ge 4: 2 Next she bore his **b** Abel.
4: 8 Cain said to his **b** Abel,
4: 8 Cain rose up against his **b** Abel, and killed him.
4: 9 the LORD said to Cain, "Where is your **b** Abel?"
10:21 the elder **b** of Japheth, children were born.
14:12 the son of Abram's **b**, who lived in Sodom,
14:13 **b** of Eshcol and of Aner;
20: 5 And she herself said, 'He is my **b**.'
20:13 say of me, He is my **b**.' "
20:16 I have given your **b** a thousand pieces of silver;
22:20 "Milcah also has borne children, to your **b** Nahor:
22:21 Buz his **b**, Kemuel the father of Aram,
22:23 These eight Milcah bore to Nahor, Abraham's **b**.
24:15 the wife of Nahor, Abraham's **b**,
24:29 Rebekah had a **b** whose name was Laban;
24:53 to her **b** and to her mother costly ornaments.
24:55 Her **b** and her mother said,
25:26 Afterward his **b** came out,
27: 6 "I heard your father say to your **b** Esau,
27:11 "Look, my **b** Esau is a hairy man,
27:23 his hands were hairy like his **b** Esau's hands;
27:30 his **b** Esau came in from his hunting.
27:35 But he said, "Your **b** came deceitfully,
27:40 and you shall serve your **b**;
27:41 then I will kill my **b** Jacob."
27:42 "Your **b** Esau is consoling himself by planning
27:43 flee at once to my **b** Laban in Haran,
28: 2 of the daughters of Laban, your mother's **b**.
28: 5 the **b** of Rebekah, Jacob's and Esau's mother.
29:10 the daughter of his mother's **b** Laban,
29:10 and the sheep of his mother's **b** Laban,
29:10 and watered the flock of his mother's **b** Laban.
32: 3 Jacob sent messengers before him to his **b** Esau in
32: 6 saying, "We came to your **b** Esau,
32:11 Deliver me, please, from the hand of my **b**,
32:13 with him he took a present for his **b** Esau,
32:17 "When Esau my **b** meets you, and asks you,
33: 3 until he came near his **b**.
33: 9 But Esau said, "I have enough, my **b**;
35: 1 to you when you fled from your **b** Esau."
35: 7 to him when he fled from his **b**.
36: 6 to a land some distance from his **b** Jacob.
37:26 if we kill our **b** and conceal his blood?
37:27 and not lay our hands on him, for he is our **b**,
38: 8 raise up offspring for your **b**."
38: 9 so that he would not give offspring to his **b**.
38:29 then he drew back his hand, and out came his **b**;
38:30 Afterward his **b** came out with the crimson thread
42: 4 not send Joseph's **b** Benjamin with his brothers,
42:15 unless your youngest **b** comes here!
42:16 Let one of you go and bring your **b**,
42:20 and bring your youngest **b** to me.
42:21 the penalty for what we did to our **b**;
42:34 Bring your youngest **b** to me,
42:34 Then I will release your **b** to you,
42:38 for his **b** is dead, and he alone is left.
43: 3 'You shall not see my face unless your **b** is
43: 4 If you will send our **b** with us,
43: 5 unless your **b** is with you.' "
43: 6 as to tell the man that you had another **b**?"
43: 7 'Is your father still alive? Have you another **b**?'
43: 7 that he would say, 'Bring your **b** down'?"
43:13 Take your **b** also, and be on your way again to
Ge 43:14 that he may send back your other **b** and Benjamin.
43:29 Then he looked up and saw his **b** Benjamin,
43:29 and said, "Is this your youngest **b**,
43:30 because he was overcome with affection for his **b**,
44:19 saying, 'Have you a father or a **b**?'
44:20 'We have a father, an old man, and a young **b**,
44:20 of his old age. His **b** is dead;
44:23 'Unless your youngest **b** comes down with you,
44:26 Only if our youngest **b** goes with us,
44:26 the man's face unless our youngest **b** is with us.'
45: 4 He said, "I am your **b**, Joseph,
45:12 now your eyes and the eyes of my **b** Benjamin see
45:14 he fell upon his **b** Benjamin's neck and wept,
48:19 his younger **b** shall be greater than he,
Ex 4:14 "What of your **b** Aaron, the Levite?
7: 1 and your **b** Aaron shall be your prophet.
7: 2 and your **b** Aaron shall tell Pharaoh to let
28: 1 Then bring near to you your **b** Aaron,
28: 2 for the glorious adornment of your **b** Aaron.
28: 4 for your **b** Aaron and his sons to serve me
28:41 You shall put them on your **b** Aaron,
32:27 and each of you kill your **b**, your friend,
32:29 each one at the cost of a son or a **b**,
Lev 16: 2 Tell your **b** Aaron not to come just at any time into
18:14 the nakedness of your father's **b**, that is, you shall
21: 2 his mother, his father, his son, his daughter, his **b**;
Nu 6: 7 Even if their father or mother, **b** or sister, A
16:10 and all your **b** Levites with you;
18: 6 It is I who now take your **b** Levites from among
20: 8 you and your **b** Aaron, and command the rock
20:14 to the king of Edom, "Thus says your **b** Israel:
27:13 be gathered to your people, as your **b** Aaron was,
36: 2 to give the inheritance of our **b** Zelophehad
Dt 13: 6 even if it is your **b**, your father's son
25: 5 Her husband's **b** shall go in to her,
25: 5 and performing the duty of a husband's **b** to her,
25: 6 to the name of the deceased **b**,
25: 7 at the gate and say, "My husband's **b** refuses
25: 7 not perform the duty of a husband's **b** to me."
28:54 among you will begrudge food to his own **b**,
32:50 as your **b** Aaron died on Mount Hor
Jos 15:17 Othniel son of Kenaz, the **b** of Caleb, took it;
Jdg 1: 3 Judah said to his **b** Simeon,
1:13 Othniel son of Kenaz, Caleb's younger **b**, took it;
1:17 Judah went with his **b** Simeon,
3: 9 Othniel son of Kenaz, Caleb's younger **b**.
9: 3 for they said, "He is our **b**."
9:21 where he remained for fear of his **b** Abimelech.
9:24 and their blood be laid on their **b** Abimelech,
1Sa 14: 3 Ichabod's **b**, son of Phinehas son of Eli,
17:28 His eldest **b** Eliab heard him talking to the men;
20:29 and my **b** has commanded me to be there.
26: 6 and to Joab's **b** Abishai son of Zeruiah,
2Sa 1:26 I am distressed for you, my **b** Jonathan;
2:22 How then could I show my face to your **b** Joab?"
3:27 for shedding the blood of Asahel, Joab's **b**.
3:30 So Joab and his **b** Abishai murdered Abner
3:30 because he had killed their **b** Asahel in the battle
4: 6 then Rechab and his **b** Baanah escaped.
4: 9 David answered Rechab and his **b** Baanah,
10:10 of his men he put in the charge of his **b** Abishai,
13: 3 the son of David's **b** Shimeah;
13: 4 "I love Tamar, my **b** Absalom's sister."
13: 7 saying, "Go to your **b** Amnon's house,
13: 8 So Tamar went to her **b** Amnon's house,
13:10 brought them into the chamber to Amnon her **b**.
13:12 She answered him, "No, my **b**, do not force me;
13:16 But she said to him, "No, my **b**;
13:20 Her **b** Absalom said to her,
13:20 "Has Amnon your **b** been with you?
13:20 Be quiet for now, my sister; he is your **b**;
13:20 a desolate woman, in her **b** Absalom's house.
13:26 "If not, please let my **b** Amnon go with us."
13:32 But Jonadab, the son of David's **b** Shimeah, said,
14: 7 They say, 'Give up the man who struck his **b**,
14: 7 for the life of his **b** whom he murdered,
18: 2 the command of Abishai son of Zeruiah, Joab's **b**,
20: 9 Joab said to Amasa, "Is it well with you, my **b**?"
20:10 Then Joab and his **b** Abishai pursued Sheba son
21:21 Jonathan son of David's **b** Shimei, killed him.
23:18 Now Abishai son of Zeruiah, the **b** of Joab,
23:24 Among the Thirty were Asahel **b** of Joab;
1Ki 1:10 or Benaiah or the warriors or his **b** Solomon.
2: 7 when I fled from your **b** Absalom.
2:21 the Shunammite be given to your **b** Adonijah
2:22 For he is my elder **b**;
9:13 of cities are these that you have given me, my **b**?"
13:30 and they mourned over him, saying, "Alas, my **b**!"
20:32 "Is he still alive? He is my **b**."
20:33 "Yes, Ben-hadad is your **b**."
2Ki 1:17 His **b**, Jehoram succeeded him as king in
1Ch 1:19 and the name of his **b** Joktan.
2:32 The sons of Jada, Shammai's **b**:
2:42 The sons of Caleb **b** of Jerahmeel:
4:11 the **b** of Shuhah became the father of Mehir,
6:39 and his **b** Asaph, who stood
7:16 the name of his **b** was Sheresh;
7:35 The sons of Helem his **b**:
8:39 The sons of his **b** Eshek:
11:20 Abishai, the **b** of Joab, was chief of the Thirty.
11:26 The warriors of the armies were Asahel **b** of Joab,
11:38 Joel the **b** of Nathan, Mibhar son of Hagri,
11:45 Jediael son of Shimri, and his **b** Joha the Tizite,
19:11 of his troops he put in the charge of his **b** Abishai,
19:15 they likewise fled before Abishai, Joab's **b**,
20: 5 of Jair killed Lahmi the **b** of Goliath the Gittite,
20: 7 Jonathan son of Shimea, David's **b**, killed him.
1Ch 24:25 The **b** of Micah, Isshiah;
24:31 the chief as well as the youngest **b**.
26:22 The sons of Jehieli, Zetham and his **b** Joel,
27: 7 Asahel **b** of Joab was fourth, for the fourth month,
2Ch 31:12 with his **b** Shimei as second;
31:13 and his **b** Shimei, by the appointment
36: 4 of Egypt made his **b** Eliakim king over Judah
36: 4 but Neco took his **b** Jehoahaz and carried him
36:10 and made his **b** Zedekiah king over Judah
Ne 7: 2 I gave my **b** Hanani charge over Jerusalem,
Job 30:29 I am a **b** of jackals, and a companion of ostriches.
Ps 35:14 as though I grieved for a friend or a **b**;
SS 8: 1 O that you were like a **b** to me,
Jer 22:18 not lament for him, saying, "Alas, my **b**!"
Eze 18:18 because he practiced extortion, robbed his **b**,
44:25 **b** or unmarried sister they may defile themselves.
Hos 2: 1 Say to your **b**, Ammi, and to your sister,
12: 3 In the womb he tried to supplant his **b**,
Am 1:11 because he pursued his **b** with the sword
Ob 1:10 the slaughter and violence done to your **b** Jacob,
1:12 But you should not have gloated over your **b** on
Mal 1: 2 Is not Esau Jacob's **b**?
Mt 4:18 Simon, who is called Peter, and Andrew his **b**,
4:21 James son of Zebedee and his **b** John,
5:22 to you that if you are angry with a **b** or sister, A
5:22 and if you insult a **b** or sister, A
5:23 that your **b** or sister has something against you, A
5:24 first be reconciled to your **b** or sister, A
10: 2 Simon, also known as Peter, and his **b** Andrew;
10: 2 James son of Zebedee, and his **b** John;
10:21 **B** will betray **b** to death,
12:50 will of my Father in heaven is my **b** and sister A
14: 3 on account of Herodias, his **b** Philip's wife,
17: 1 and his **b** John and led them up a high mountain,
18:35 not forgive your **b** or sister from your heart." A
22:24 his **b** shall marry the widow,
22:24 and raise up children for his **b**.'
22:25 and died childless, leaving the widow to his **b**.
Mk 1:16 he saw Simon and his **b** Andrew casting a net into
1:19 he saw James son of Zebedee and his **b** John,
3:17 James son of Zebedee and John the **b** of James
3:35 Whoever does the will of God is my **b** and sister A
5:37 James, and John, the **b** of James.
6: 3 and **b** of James and Joses and Judas and Simon,
6:17 on account of Herodias, his **b** Philip's wife,
12:19 Moses wrote for us that 'if a man's **b** dies,
12:19 the widow and raise up children for his **b**.'
13:12 **B** will betray **b** to death,
Lk 3: 1 and his **b** Philip ruler of the region of Ituraea
6:14 whom he named Peter, and his **b** Andrew,
12:13 tell my **b** to divide the family inheritance
15:27 He replied, 'Your **b** has come,
15:32 this **b** of yours was dead and has come to life;
20:28 Moses wrote for us that if a man's **b** dies,
20:28 the widow and raise up children for his **b**.
Jn 1:40 and followed him was Andrew, Simon Peter's **b**.
1:41 He first found his **b** Simon and said to him,
6: 8 One of his disciples, Andrew, Simon Peter's **b**,
11: 2 with her hair; her **b** Lazarus was ill.
11:19 to Martha and Mary to console them about their **b**.
11:21 if you had been here, my **b** would not have died.
11:23 Jesus said to her, "Your **b** will rise again."
11:32 if you had been here, my **b** would not have died."
Ac 9:17 He laid his hands on Saul and said, "**B** Saul,
12: 2 He had James, the **b** of John,
21:20 Then they said to him, "You see, **b**,
22:13 and standing beside me, he said, '**B** Saul,
Ro 14:10 Why do you pass judgment on your **b** or sister? A
14:10 Or you, why do you despise your **b** or sister? A
14:15 your **b** or sister is being injured by what you eat, A
14:21 do anything that makes your **b** or sister stumble. A
16:23 Erastus, the city treasurer, and our **b** Quartus,
1Co 1: 1 by the will of God, and our **b** Sosthenes,
5:11 anyone who bears the name of **b** or sister A
7:15 in such a case the **b** or sister is not bound. A
16:12 Now concerning our **b** Apollos,
2Co 1: 1 and Timothy our **b**, To the church of God that is
2:13 not rest because I did not find my **b** Titus there.
8:18 With him we are sending the **b** who is famous
8:22 we are sending our **b** whom we have often tested
12:18 I urged Titus to go, and sent the **b** with him.
Gal 1:19 see any other apostle except James the Lord's **b**.
Eph 6:21 He is a dear **b** and a faithful minister in the Lord.
Php 2:25 my **b** and co-worker and fellow soldier,
Col 1: 1 by the will of God, and Timothy our **b**,
4: 7 he is a beloved **b**, a faithful minister,
4: 9 the faithful and beloved **b**, who is one of you.
1Th 3: 2 our **b** and co-worker for God in proclaiming
4: 6 wrong or exploit a **b** or sister in this matter, A
Phm 1: 1 a prisoner of Christ Jesus, and Timothy our **b**,
1: 7 the saints have been refreshed through you, my **b**.
1:16 as a slave but more than a slave, a beloved **b**—
1:20 **b**, let me have this benefit from you in the Lord!
Heb 13:23 to know that our **b** Timothy has been set free;
Jas 2:15 If a **b** or sister is naked and lacks daily food, A
1Pe 5:12 Through Silvanus, whom I consider a faithful **b**,
2Pe 3:15 So also our beloved **b** Paul wrote to you according
1Jn 2: 9 while hating a **b** or sister, is still in the darkness. A
2:10 Whoever loves a **b** or sister lives in the light, A
3:12 from the evil one and murdered his **b**.
3:15 All who hate a **b** or sister are murderers, A
3:17 sees a **b** or sister in need and yet refuses help? A
4:20 not love a **b** or sister whom they have seen, A
5:16 If you see your **b** or sister committing what is A
Jude 1: 1 Jude, a servant of Jesus Christ and **b** of James,
Rev 1: 9 your **b** who share with you in Jesus
Tob 1:14 in trust with Gabael, the **b** of Gabri.

Tob 1:21 the son of my **b** Hanael over all the accounts
5:10 I will pay your wages, **b."**
5:11 Then Tobit said to him, **"B,**
5:11 from what tribe? Tell me, **b."**
5:12 But Tobit said, "I want to be sure, **b,**
5:14 "Welcome! God save you, **b.**
5:14 Do not feel bitter toward me, **b,**
5:17 So Tobit said to him, "Blessings be upon you, **b."**
5:17 for the journey and set out with your **b.**
6:7 to him, **"B** Azariah, what medicinal value is there
6:11 to the young man, **"B** Tobias."
6:13 So listen to me, **b;** tonight I will speak to her
6:13 So now listen to me, **b,** and tonight we shall speak
6:14 Tobias said in answer to Raphael, **"B** Azariah,
6:16 listen to me, **b,** and say no more about this demon.
7:1 Tobias said to him, **"B** Azariah,
7:1 take me straight to our **b** Raguel."
7:9 Tobias said to Raphael, **"B** Azariah,
7:10 For no one except you, **b,**
7:11 from now on you are her **b** and she is your sister.
9:2 **"B** Azariah, take four servants and two camels
10:12 Then Edna said to Tobias, "My child and dear **b,**
Jdt 8:26 the sheep of Laban, his mother's **b.**
AdE 2:7 the daughter of his father's **b,** Aminadab,
2:15 the **b** of Mordecai's father, to go in to the king,
Wis 10:3 he perished because in rage he killed his **b.**
Sir 7:12 Do not devise a lie against your **b,**
7:18 or a real **b** for the gold of Ophir.
29:10 Lose your silver for the sake of a **b** or a friend,
29:27 my **b** has come for a visit,
33:20 To son or wife, to **b** or friend,
33:31 If you have but one slave, treat him like a **b,**
45:6 a holy man like Moses who was his **b,**
1Mc 2:65 "Here is your **b** Simeon who, I know,
5:17 Then Judas said to his **b** Simon,
5:17 Jonathan my **b** and I will go to Gilead."
5:24 Judas Maccabeus and his **b** Jonathan crossed
5:55 and their **b** Simon was in Galilee before Ptolemais,
9:19 and Simon took their **b** Judas and buried him in
9:29 the death of your **b** Judas there has been no one
9:31 the leadership at that time in place of his **b** Judas.
9:33 and his **b** Simon and all who were with him heard
9:35 So Jonathan sent his **b** as leader of the multitude
9:37 to Jonathan and his **b** Simon,
9:38 Remembering how their **b** John had been killed,
9:42 After they had fully avenged the blood of their **b,**
9:65 But Jonathan left his **b** Simon in the town,
10:18 "King Alexander to his **b** Jonathan, greetings.
10:74 and his **b** Simon met him to help him.
11:30 to his **b** Jonathan and to the nation of the Jews,
11:59 He appointed Jonathan's **b** Simon governor from
11:64 but left his **b** Simon in the country.
13:8 in place of Judas and your **b** Jonathan.
13:14 that Simon had risen up in place of his **b** Jonathan,
13:15 "It is for the money that your **b** Jonathan owed
13:25 Simon sent and took the bones of his **b** Jonathan,
14:17 that his **b** Simon had become high priest
16:9 At that time Judas the **b** of John was wounded,
2Mc 4:7 Jason the **b** of Onias obtained the high priesthood
4:23 the **b** of the previously mentioned Simon,
4:26 who after supplanting his own **b** was supplanted
4:29 Menelaus left his own **b** Lysimachus as deputy in
7:7 After the first **b** had died in this way,
7:8 in turn underwent tortures as the first **b** had done.
7:24 The youngest **b** being still alive,
10:37 who was hiding in a cistern, and his **b** Chaereas,
11:22 "King Antiochus to his **b** Lysias, greetings.
14:17 Simon, the **b** of Judas, had encountered Nicanor,
1Es 1:9 And Jeconiah and Shemaiah and his **b** Nethanel,
1:37 The king of Egypt made his **b** Jehoiakim king
1:38 and seized his **b** Zarius and brought him back
5:58 and his sons and kindred and his **b** Kadmiel and
8:48 also Hashabiah and Annunus and his **b** Jeshaiah,
2Es 12:11 that appeared in a vision to your **b** Daniel.
4Mc 4:16 from the priesthood and appointed Onias's **b** Jason
10:16 from them that I am a **b** to those who have just
13:11 While one said, "Courage, **b,"** another said,
13:18 "Do not put us to shame, **b,**

BROTHER'S‡ (27) [BROTHER]

Ge 4:9 He said, "I do not know; am I my **b** keeper?"
4:10 your **b** blood is crying out to me from the ground!
4:11 to receive your **b** blood from your hand.
4:21 His **b** name was Jubal; he was the ancestor of all
10:25 and his **b** name was Joktan.
12:5 Abram took his wife Sarai and his **b** son Lot,
27:44 until your **b** fury turns away—
27:45 until your **b** anger against you turns away,
38:8 "Go in to your **b** wife and perform the duty of
38:9 on the ground whenever he went in to his **b** wife,
Lev 18:16 not uncover the nakedness of your **b** wife;
18:16 of your brother's wife; it is your **b** nakedness.
20:21 If a man takes his **b** wife, it is impurity;
20:21 he has uncovered his **b** nakedness;
Dt 25:7 But if the man has no desire to marry his **b** widow,
25:7 then his **b** widow shall go up to the elders at
25:7 to perpetuate his **b** name in Israel;
25:9 then his **b** wife shall go up to him in the presence
25:9 to the man who does not build up his **b** house."
1Ki 2:15 the kingdom has turned about and become my **b,**
Job 1:13 and drinking wine in the eldest **b** house,
1:18 and drinking wine in their eldest **b** house,
Mk 6:18 "It is not lawful for you to have your **b** wife."
Lk 3:19 because of Herodias, his **b** wife, and because of all
1Jn 3:12 his own deeds were evil and his **b** righteous.
Wis 10:10 When a righteous man fled from his **b** wrath,
1Mc 16:3 Take my place and my **b,**

BROTHER-IN-LAW (1) [BROTHER]

Ge 38:8 to your brother's wife and perform the duty of a **b**

BROTHERHOOD See Index to Footnotes

BROTHERLY‡ (3) [BROTHER]

4Mc 13:23 sympathy and **b** affection had been so established,
13:26 because they could make their **b** love more fervent
14:1 but also mastered the emotions of **b** love.

BROTHERLY-LOVING (1) [BROTHER, LOVE]

4Mc 13:21 From such embraces **b** souls are nourished;

BROTHERS‡ (402) [BROTHER]

A. BROTHERS ... SISTERS (99)

Ge 9:22 and told his two **b** outside.
9:25 lowest of slaves shall he be to his **b."**
19:7 "I beg you, my **b,** do not act so wickedly.
27:29 Be lord over your **b,** and may your mother's sons
27:37 and I have given him all his **b** as servants,
29:4 Jacob said to them, "My **b,**
34:11 Shechem also said to her father and to her **b,**
34:25 Simeon and Levi, Dinah's **b,**
37:2 was shepherding the flock with his **b;**
37:4 when his **b** saw that their father loved him more than all his **b,**
37:5 and when he told it to his **b,**
37:8 His **b** said to him, "Are you indeed to reign
37:9 He had another dream, and told it to his **b,** saying,
37:10 But when he told it to his father and to his **b,**
37:10 I and your mother and your **b,**
37:11 So his **b** were jealous of him,
37:12 Now his **b** went to pasture their father's flock
37:13 "Are not your **b** pasturing the flock at Shechem?
37:14 see if it is well with your **b** and with the flock;
37:16 "I am seeking my **b,"** he said;
37:17 So Joseph went after his **b,**
37:23 So when Joseph came to his **b,**
37:26 Then Judah said to his **b,**
37:27 our own flesh." And his **b** agreed.
37:30 He returned to his **b,** and said, "The boy is gone;
38:1 that Judah went down from his **b** and settled near
38:11 for he feared that he too would die, like his **b.**
42:3 of Joseph's **b** went down to buy grain in Egypt.
42:4 not send Joseph's brother Benjamin with his **b,**
42:6 And Joseph's **b** came and bowed themselves
42:7 When Joseph saw his **b,** he recognized them,
42:8 Although Joseph had recognized his **b,**
42:13 They said, "We, your servants, are twelve **b,**
42:19 of your **b** stay here where you are imprisoned.
42:28 He said to his **b,** "My money has been put back;
42:32 We are twelve **b,** sons of our father;
42:33 leave one of your **b** with me,
44:14 Judah and his **b** came to Joseph's house
44:33 and let the boy go back with his **b.**
45:1 when Joseph made himself known to his **b.**
45:3 Joseph said to his **b,** "I am Joseph.
45:3 But his **b** could not answer him,
45:4 Then Joseph said to his **b,** "Come closer to me."
45:15 And he kissed all his **b** and wept upon them;
45:15 and after that his **b** talked with him.
45:16 in Pharaoh's house, "Joseph's **b** have come,"
45:17 Pharaoh said to Joseph, "Say to your **b,** 'Do this:
45:24 Then he sent his **b** on their way,
46:31 Joseph said to his **b** and to his father's household,
46:31 'My **b** and my father's household,
47:1 "My father and my **b,** with their flocks and herds
47:2 among his **b** he took five men and presented them
47:3 Pharaoh said to his **b,** "What is your occupation?"
47:5 "Your father and your **b** have come to you.
47:6 settle your father and your **b** in the best part of
47:11 Joseph settled his father and his **b,**
47:12 And Joseph provided his father, his **b,**
48:6 be recorded under the names of their **b** with regard
48:22 I now give to you one portion more than to your **b,**
49:5 Simeon and Levi are **b;** weapons of violence
49:8 Judah, your **b** shall praise you;
49:26 on the brow of him who was set apart from his **b.**
50:8 his **b,** and his father's household.
50:14 with his **b** and all who had gone up with him
50:15 that their father was dead, Joseph's **b** said, "What
50:17 forgive the crime of your **b** and the wrong they did
50:18 Then his **b** also wept, fell down before him,
50:24 Then Joseph said to his **b,** "I am about to die;
Ex 1:6 Then Joseph died, and all his **b,**
Lev 25:48 one of their **b** may redeem them,
Nu 8:26 They may assist their **b** in the tent of meeting
18:2 So bring with you also your **b** of the tribe of Levi,
27:4 Give to us a possession among our father's **b."**
27:7 among their father's **b** and pass the inheritance
27:9 then you shall give his inheritance to his **b.**
27:10 If he has no **b,** then you shall give his inheritance to his father's **b.**
27:11 And if his father has no **b,**
32:6 "Shall your **b** go to war while you sit here?
36:11 married sons of their father's **b.**
Dt 25:5 When **b** reside together, and one of them dies
33:16 on the brow of the prince among his **b.**
33:24 may he be the favorite of his **b,**
Jos 2:13 my **b** and sisters, and all who belong to them, A
2:18 your **b,** and all your family.
6:23 her mother, her **b,** and all who belonged to her—
Jdg 8:19 And he replied, "They were my **b,**
9:5 and killed his **b** the sons of Jerubbaal,
9:24 who strengthened his hands to kill his **b.**
9:56 against his father in killing his seventy **b;**
11:3 Then Jephthah fled from his **b** and lived in
16:31 Then his **b** and all his family came down
19:23 went out to them and said to them, "No, my **b,**
21:22 if their fathers or their **b** come to complain to us,
1Sa 16:13 and anointed him in the presence of his **b;**
17:17 "Take for your **b** an ephah of this parched grain
17:17 and carry them quickly to the camp to your **b;**
17:18 See how your **b** fare, and bring some token
17:22 ran to the ranks, and went and greeted his **b.**
20:29 let me get away, and see my **b.'**
22:1 when his **b** and all his father's house heard of it,
30:23 But David said, "You shall not do so, my **b,**
2Sa 3:8 to his **b,** and to his friends,
1Ki 1:9 which is beside En-rogel, and he invited all his **b,**
1Ch 4:9 Jabez was honored more than his **b;**
4:27 but his **b** did not have many children,
5:2 though Judah became prominent among his **b** and
7:22 and his **b** came to comfort him.
25:9 second to Gedaliah, to him and his **b** and his sons,
25:10 the third to Zaccur, his sons and his **b,** twelve;
25:11 the fourth to Izri, his sons and his **b,** twelve;
25:12 the fifth to Nethaniah, his sons and his **b,** twelve;
25:13 the sixth to Bukkiah, his sons and his **b,** twelve;
25:14 his sons and his **b,** twelve;
25:15 the eighth to Jeshaiah, his sons and his **b,** twelve;
25:16 the ninth to Mattaniah, his sons and his **b,** twelve;
25:17 the tenth to Shimei, his sons and his **b,** twelve;
25:18 the eleventh to Azarel, his sons and his **b,** twelve;
25:19 his sons and his **b,** twelve;
25:20 Shubael, his sons and his **b,** twelve;
25:21 Mattithiah, his sons and his **b,** twelve;
25:22 to Jeremoth, his sons and his **b,** twelve;
25:23 to Hananiah, his sons and his **b,** twelve;
25:24 to Joshbekashah, his sons and his **b,** twelve;
25:25 to Hanani, his sons and his **b,** twelve;
25:26 to Mallothi, his sons and his **b,** twelve;
25:27 to Eliathah, his sons and his **b,** twelve;
25:28 to Hothir, his sons and his **b,** twelve;
25:29 to Giddalti, his sons and his **b,** twelve;
25:30 to Mahazioth, his sons and his **b,** twelve;
25:31 to Romamti-ezer, his sons and his **b,** twelve.
26:7 whose **b** were able men, Elihu and Semachiah.
26:8 sons of Obed-edom with their sons and **b,**
26:9 Meshelemiah had sons and **b,** able men, eighteen.
26:11 all the sons and **b** of Hosah totaled thirteen.
26:25 His **b:** from Eliezer were his son Rehabiah,
26:26 and his **b** were in charge of all the treasuries of
26:28 in the care of Shelomoth and his **b.**
26:30 Of the Hebronites, Hashabiah and his **b,**
26:32 King David appointed him and his **b,**
27:18 for Judah, Elihu, one of David's **b;**
28:2 "Hear me, my **b** and my people.
2Ch 11:22 of Maacah as chief prince among his **b,**
21:2 He had **b,** the sons of Jehoshaphat:
21:4 he put all his **b** to the sword,
21:13 and because you also have killed your **b,**
22:8 the officials of Judah and the sons of Ahaziah's **b,**
29:15 They gathered their **b,** sanctified themselves,
35:9 Conaniah also, and his **b** Shemaiah and Nethanel,
Ezr 10:18 of Jeshua son of Jozadak and his **b:**
Ne 1:2 one of my **b,** Hanani, came with certain men
4:23 So neither I nor my **b** nor my servants nor the men
5:10 and my **b** and my servants are lending them money
5:14 nor my **b** ate the food allowance of the governor.
11:8 his **b** Gabbai, Sallai: nine hundred twenty-eight.
Job 42:11 Then there came to him all his **b** and sisters A
42:15 an inheritance along with their **b.**
Ps 22:22 I will tell of your name to my **b** and sisters; A
Ecc 4:8 the case of solitary individuals, without sons or **b;**
Jer 35:3 and his **b,** and all his sons,
Mt 1:2 and Jacob the father of Judah and his **b,**
1:11 and Josiah the father of Jechoniah and his **b,**
4:18 As he walked by the Sea of Galilee, he saw two **b,**
4:21 As he went from there, he saw two other **b,**
5:47 And if you greet only your **b** and sisters, A
12:46 his mother and his **b** were standing outside,
12:47 your mother and your **b** are standing outside,
12:48 "Who is my mother, and who are my **b?"**
12:49 he said, "Here are my mother and my **b!**
13:55 not his **b** James and Joseph and Simon and Judas?
19:29 And everyone who has left houses or **b** or sisters A
20:24 the ten heard it, they were angry with the two **b.**
22:25 Now there were seven **b** among us;
28:10 go and tell my **b** to go to Galilee;
Mk 3:31 Then his mother and his **b** came;
3:32 "Your mother and your **b** and sisters are outside, A
3:33 And he replied, "Who are my mother and my **b?"**
3:34 he said, "Here are my mother and my **b!**
10:29 there is no one who has left house or **b** or sisters A
10:30 houses, **b** and sisters, mothers and children, A
12:20 There were seven **b;** the first married and,
Lk 8:19 Then his mother and his **b** came to him,
8:20 "Your mother and your **b** are standing outside,
8:21 and my **b** are those who hear the word of God
14:12 not invite your friends or your **b** or your relatives
14:26 **b** and sisters, yes, and even life itself, A
16:28 for I have five **b**—that he may warn them,
18:29 there is no one who has left house or wife or **b**
20:29 Now there were seven **b;**
21:16 You will be betrayed even by parents and **b,**

Lk 22:32 once you have turned back, strengthen your **b**."
Jn 2:12 down to Capernaum with his mother, his **b**,
7: 3 So his **b** said to him, "Leave here and go to Judea
7: 5 (For not even his **b** believed in him.)
7:10 But after his **b** had gone to the festival,
20:17 But go to my **b** and say to them,
Ac 1:14 the mother of Jesus, as well as his **b**.
2:37 and said to Peter and to the other apostles, "**B**,
7: 2 And Stephen replied: "**B** and fathers, listen to me.
7:13 to his **b**, and Joseph's family became known
7:26 'Men, you are **b**; why do you wrong each other?'
11:12 These six **b** also accompanied me,
13:15 the synagogue sent them a message, saying, "**B**,
13:26 "My **b**, you descendants of Abraham's family,
13:38 Let it be known to you therefore, my **b**,
14: 2 and poisoned their minds against the **b**.
15: 1 down from Judea and were teaching the **b**,
15: 7 Peter stood up and said to them, "My **b**,
15:13 they finished speaking, James replied, "My **b**,
15:22 and Silas, leaders among the **b**,
15:23 "The **b**, both the apostles and the elders,
16:40 and encouraged the **b** and sisters there, A
21:17 the **b** welcomed us warmly.
22: 1 "**B** and fathers, listen to the defense that I
22: 5 also received letters to the **b** in Damascus,
23: 1 "**B**, up to this day I have lived my life with
23: 5 And Paul said, "I did not realize, **b**,
23: 6 he called out in the council, "**B**, I am a Pharisee,
28:11 an Alexandrian ship with the Twin **B**
28:17 When they had assembled, he said to them, "**B**,
28:21 and none of the **b** coming here has reported
Ro 1:13 I want you to know, **b** and sisters, A
7: 1 Do you not know, **b** and sisters— A
8:12 So then, **b** and sisters, we are debtors, A
10: 1 **B** and sisters, my heart's desire and prayer to A
11:25 **b** and sisters, I want you to understand this A
12: 1 I appeal to you therefore, **b** and sisters, A
15:14 my **b** and sisters, that you yourselves are full A
15:30 I appeal to you, **b** and sisters, A
16:14 and the **b** and sisters who are with them. A
16:17 **b** and sisters, to keep an eye on those who A
1Co 1:10 Now I appeal to you, **b** and sisters, A
1:11 are quarrels among you, my **b** and sisters. A
1:26 Consider your own call, **b** and sisters: A
2: 1 When I came to you, **b** and sisters, A
3: 1 And so, **b** and sisters, I could not speak to you A
4: 6 **b** and sisters, so that you may learn through us A
7:24 **b** and sisters, there remain with God. A
7:29 **b** and sisters, the appointed time has grown A
9: 5 as do the other apostles and the **b** of the Lord
10: 1 I do not want you to be unaware, **b** and sisters, A
11:33 So then, my **b** and sisters, A
12: 1 Now concerning spiritual gifts, **b** and sisters, A
14: 6 **b** and sisters, if I come to you speaking in A
14:20 **B** and sisters, do not be children in your A
15: 1 Now I would remind you, **b** and sisters, A
15: 6 to more than five hundred **b** and sisters at one A
15:31 That is as certain, **b** and sisters, A
15:50 What I am saying, **b** and sisters, is this: A
16:11 for I am expecting him with the **b**.
16:12 I strongly urged him to visit you with the other **b**,
16:15 **b** and sisters, you know that members of A
16:20 All the **b** and sisters send greetings. A
2Co 1: 8 do not want you to be unaware, **b** and sisters, A
8: 1 We want you to know, **b** and sisters, A
8:23 as for our **b**, they are messengers of the churches,
9: 3 But I am sending the **b** in order that our boasting
9: 5 So I thought it necessary to urge the **b** to go on
11:26 danger at sea, danger from false **b** and sisters; A
13:11 Finally, **b** and sisters, farewell. A
Gal 1:11 For I want you to know, **b** and sisters, A
3:15 **B** and sisters, I give an example from daily life: A
5:13 For you were called to freedom, **b** and sisters; A
6:18 Jesus Christ be with your spirit, **b** and sisters. A
Php 1:14 and most of the **b** and sisters, A
3: 1 Finally, my **b** and sisters, rejoice in the Lord. A
3:17 **B** and sisters, join in imitating me, A
4: 1 Therefore, my **b** and sisters, A
Col 1: 2 To the saints and faithful **b** and sisters in Christ A
4:15 my greetings to the **b** and sisters in Laodicea, A
1Th 1: 4 For we know, **b** and sisters beloved by God, A
2: 1 You yourselves know, **b** and sisters, A
2: 9 You remember our labor and toil, **b** and sisters; A
2:14 **b** and sisters, became imitators of the churches A
2:17 As for us, **b** and sisters, when, for a short time, A
3: 7 For this reason, **b** and sisters, A
4: 1 **b** and sisters, we ask and urge you in A
4: 9 Now concerning love of the **b** and sisters, A
4:10 and indeed you do love all the **b** and sisters A
4:13 **b** and sisters, about those who have died, A
5: 1 the times and the seasons, **b** and sisters, you do A
5:12 But we appeal to you, **b** and sisters, A
5:26 Greet all the **b** and sisters with a holy kiss. A
2Th 1: 3 to God for you, **b** and sisters, as is right, A
2: 1 we beg you, **b** and sisters, A
2:13 **b** and sisters beloved by the Lord, A
2:15 So then, **b** and sisters, stand firm and hold fast A
3: 1 Finally, **b** and sisters, pray for us, A
3:13 **B** and sisters, do not be weary A
1Ti 4: 6 put these instructions before the **b** and sisters, A
5: 1 to him as to a father, to younger men as **b**,
2Ti 4:21 Linus and Claudia and all the **b** and sisters. A
Heb 2:11 Jesus is not ashamed to call them **b** and sisters, A
2:12 "I will proclaim your name to my **b** and sisters, A
2:17 Therefore he had to become like his **b** and sisters A
3: 1 **b** and sisters, holy partners in a heavenly calling, A
3:12 **b** and sisters, that none of you may have an evil, A
Heb 13:22 I appeal to you, **b** and sisters, A
Jas 1: 2 My **b** and sisters, whenever you face trials A
2: 1 My **b** and sisters, do you with your acts A
2: 5 Listen, my beloved **b** and sisters. A
2:14 What good is it, my **b** and sisters, A
3: 1 should become teachers, my **b** and sisters, A
3:10 My **b** and sisters, this ought not to be so. A
3:12 Can a fig tree, my **b** and sisters, yield olives, A
4:11 not speak evil against one another, **b** and sisters. A
5:19 My **b** and sisters, if anyone among you wanders A
1Pe 5: 9 for you know that your **b** and sisters in all A
2Pe 1:10 Therefore, **b** and sisters, be all the more eager A
1Jn 3:10 nor are those who do not love their **b** and sisters. A
3:13 Do not be astonished, **b** and sisters, A
4:20 "I love God," and hate their **b** or sisters, are liars; A
4:21 who love God must love their **b** and sisters also. A
Rev 6:11 their fellow servants and of their **b** and sisters, A
Tob 6:18 and they will be as **b** to you.
7: 1 "Joyous greetings, **b**; welcome and good health!"
7: 3 saying, "Where are you from, **b**?"
Jdt 7:30 Uzziah said to them, "Courage, my **b** and sisters! A
8:14 No, my **b**, do not anger the Lord our God.
8:24 my **b**, let us set an example for our kindred,
Sir 25: 1 agreement among **b** and sisters, friendship A
50: 1 The leader of his **b** and the pride of his people was
50:12 by the hearth of the altar with a garland of **b**
1Mc 2:17 and supported by sons and **b**.
2:20 I and my sons and my **b** will continue to live by
3: 2 All his **b** and all who had joined his father helped
3:25 Then Judas and his **b** began to be feared,
3:42 and his **b** saw that misfortunes had increased and
4:36 Then Judas and his **b** said, "See,
4:59 and his **b** and all the assembly of Israel determined
5:10 and sent to Judas and his **b** a letter that said,
5:61 they did not listen to Judas and his **b**.
5:63 and his **b** were greatly honored in all Israel and
5:65 and his **b** went out and fought the descendants
7: 6 "Judas and his **b** have destroyed all your Friends,
7:10 and his **b** with peaceable but treacherous words.
7:27 to Judas and his **b** this peaceable message,
8:20 and his **b** and the people of the Jews have sent us
9:39 the bridegroom came out with his friends and his **b**
10: 5 that we did to him and to his **b** and his nation."
10:15 of the battles that Jonathan and his **b** had fought,
12: 6 rest of the Jewish people to their **b** the Spartans,
12: 7 stating that you are our **b**,
12:11 as it is right and proper to remember **b**.
12:21 and the Jews that they are **b** and are of the family
13: 3 "You yourselves know what great things my **b**
13: 3 and the difficulties that my **b** and I have seen.
13: 4 By reason of this all my **b** have perished for
13: 5 for I am not better than my **b**.
13:27 a monument over the tomb of his father and his **b**;
13:28 for his father and mother and four **b**.
14:18 that they had established with his **b** Judas
14:20 the priests and the rest of the Jewish people, our **b**,
14:26 For he and his **b** and the house
14:29 a priest of the sons of Joarib, and his **b**,
14:40 by the Romans as friends and allies and **b**,
16: 2 "My **b** and I and my father's house have fought
16:21 at Gazara that his father and **b** had perished,
2Mc 2:19 The story of Judas Maccabeus and his **b**,
7: 1 also that seven **b** and their mother were arrested
7: 4 while the rest of the **b** and the mother looked on.
7: 5 but the **b** and their mother encouraged one another
7:29 but prove worthy of your **b**.
7:29 I may get you back again along with your **b**."
7:36 For our **b** after enduring a brief suffering have
7:37 like my **b**, give up body and life for the laws
7:38 through me and my **b** to bring to an end the wrath
8:22 He appointed his **b** also, Simon and Joseph
12:24 the **b** of some, to whom no consideration would
15:18 and also for **b** and sisters and relatives, A
Pm 151: 1 I was small among my **b**, and the youngest
151: 5 My **b** were handsome and tall,
2Es 7:*103* **b** for **b**, relatives for their kindred,
4Mc 1: 8 Eleazar and the seven **b** and their mother.
8: 3 When the tyrant had given these orders, seven **b**—
8: 5 the beauty and the number of such **b**.
8:19 O men and **b**, should we not fear the instruments
9:23 "Imitate me, **b**," he said.
10: 3 the noble kinship that binds me to my **b**."
10:12 he too had died in a manner worthy of his **b**,
10:13 do not give way to the same insanity as your **b**,
10:15 No—by the blessed death of my **b**,
11:14 "I am younger in age than my **b**,
11:20 in which so many of us **b** have been summoned to
11:22 I also, equipped with nobility, will die with my **b**,
12: 2 tyrant had been vehemently reproached by the **b**,
12:16 "I do not desert the excellent example of my **b**,
13: 1 the seven **b** despised sufferings even unto death,
13: 4 for the **b** mastered both emotions and pains.
13: 9 "**B**, let us die like brothers for the sake of the law;
13: 9 let us die like **b** for the sake of the law;
13:18 to each of the **b** who were being dragged away,
13:18 brother, or betray the **b** who have died before us."
13:20 There each of the **b** spent the same length of time
13:23 the **b** were the more sympathetic to one another.
13:27 while watching their **b** being maltreated
14: 3 and harmonious concord of the seven **b** on behalf
14: 7 O most holy seven, **b** in harmony!
15:10 and loved their **b** and their mother,
17:13 the competition, and the **b** contended.

BROTHERS' (1) [BROTHER]

4Mc 12: 3 "You see the result of your **b** stupidity,

BROUGHT‡ (949) [BRING]

Ge 1:12 The earth **b** forth vegetation:
2:19 **b** them to the man to see what he would call them;
2:22 from the man he made into a woman and **b** her to
4: 3 of time Cain **b** to the LORD an offering of
4: 4 Abel for his part **b** of the firstlings of his flock,
8: 9 So he put out his hand and took it and **b** it into
14:16 Then he **b** back all the goods,
14:16 and also **b** back his nephew Lot with his goods,
14:18 King Melchizedek of Salem **b** out bread and wine;
15: 5 He **b** him outside and said,
15: 7 the LORD who **b** you from Ur of the Chaldeans,
15:10 He **b** him all these and cut them in two,
18: 4 Let a little water be **b**, and wash your feet,
19:10 the men inside reached out their hands and **b** Lot
19:16 and they **b** him out and left him outside the city.
19:17 When they had **b** them outside, they said,
20: 9 that you have **b** such great guilt on me
21: 6 Now Sarah said, "God has **b** laughter for me;
24:53 the servant **b** out jewelry of silver and of gold,
24:67 Then Isaac **b** her into his mother Sarah's tent.
26:10 and you would have **b** guilt upon us."
27:14 he went and got them and **b** them to his mother;
27:25 So he **b** it to him, and he ate;
27:25 and he **b** him wine, and he drank.
27:31 and **b** it to his father.
27:33 "Who was it then that hunted game and **b** it to me,
29:13 he embraced him and kissed him, and **b** him
29:23 in the evening he took his daughter Leah and **b** her
30:14 and **b** them to his mother Leah.
33:11 Please accept my gift that is **b** to you,
34:30 "You have **b** trouble on me by making me odious
37: 2 and Joseph **b** a bad report of them to their father.
38:25 As she was being **b** out,
39: 1 from the Ishmaelites who had **b** him down there.
39:14 my husband has **b** among us a Hebrew
39:17 whom you have **b** among us,
41:14 and he was hurriedly **b** out of the dungeon.
43: 2 when they had eaten up the grain that they had **b**
43:17 and **b** the men to Joseph's house.
43:18 Now the men were afraid because they were **b**
43:18 that we have been **b** in,
43:21 So we have **b** it back with us.
43:22 Moreover we have **b** down
43:23 Then he **b** Simeon out to them.
43:24 the steward had **b** the men into Joseph's house,
43:26 they **b** him the present that they had carried into
44: 8 we **b** back to you from the land of Canaan;
46: 7 all his offspring he **b** with him into Egypt.
46:32 and they have **b** their flocks, and their herds,
47: 7 Then Joseph **b** in his father Jacob,
47:14 and Joseph **b** the money into Pharaoh's house.
47:17 So they **b** their livestock to Joseph;
48:10 So Joseph **b** them near him;
48:13 in his left hand toward Israel's right, and **b** them
Ex 2:10 child grew up, she **b** him to Pharaoh's daughter,
3:12 when you have **b** the people out of Egypt,
5:21 You have **b** us into bad odor with Pharaoh
8: 7 and **b** frogs up on the land of Egypt.
8:12 concerning the frogs that he had **b** upon Pharaoh.
9:19 and everything that you have in the open field **b** to
9:19 in the open field and is not **b** under shelter will die
10: 8 So Moses and Aaron were **b** back to Pharaoh,
10:13 and the LORD **b** an east wind upon the land all
10:13 morning came, the east wind had **b** the locusts.
12:17 for on this very day I **b** your companies out of
12:39 of the dough that they had **b** out of Egypt;
12:51 That very day the LORD **b** the Israelites out of
13: 3 LORD **b** you out from there by strength of hand;
13: 9 with a strong hand the LORD **b** you out of Egypt.
13:11 LORD has **b** you into the land of the Canaanites,
13:14 'By strength of hand the LORD **b** us out
13:16 that by strength of hand the LORD **b** us out
15:17 You **b** them in and planted them on the mountain
15:19 LORD **b** back the waters of the sea upon them;
15:26 not bring upon you any of the diseases that I **b**
16: 3 for you have **b** us out into this wilderness
16: 6 that it was the LORD who **b** you out of the land
16:32 when I **b** you out of the land of Egypt.' "
18: 1 how the LORD had **b** Israel out of Egypt.
18:12 **b** a burnt offering and sacrifices to God;
18:26 hard cases they **b** to Moses,
19: 4 I bore you on eagles' wings and **b** you to myself.
19:17 Moses **b** the people out of the camp to meet God.
20: 2 who **b** you out of the land of Egypt,
21: 6 He shall be **b** to the door or the doorpost;
22: 8 the owner of the house shall be **b** before God,
22:13 If it was mangled by beasts, let it be **b** as evidence;
29:46 who **b** them out of the land of Egypt
32: 1 the man who **b** us up out of the land of Egypt,
32: 3 the gold rings from their ears, and **b** them
32: 4 O Israel, who **b** you up out of the land of Egypt!"
32: 6 and offered burnt offerings and **b** sacrifices
32: 7 whom you **b** up out of the land of Egypt,
32: 8 O Israel, who **b** you up out of the land of Egypt!' "
32:11 whom you **b** out of the land of Egypt
32:12 with evil intent that he **b** them out to kill them in
32:21 to you that you have **b** so great a sin upon them?"
32:23 the man who **b** us up out of the land of Egypt,
32:29 and so have **b** a blessing on yourselves this day."
33: 1 you and the people whom you have **b** up out of
35:21 and **b** the LORD's offering to be used for the tent
35:22 all who were of a willing heart **b** brooches
35:23 or tanned rams' skins or fine leather, **b** them.
35:24 of silver or bronze **b** it as the LORD's offering;
35:24 of any use in the work, **b** it.

Ex 35:25 and **b** what they had spun in blue and purple
35:27 And the leaders **b** onyx stones and gems to be set
35:29 **b** it as a freewill offering to the LORD.
36: 3 that the Israelites had **b** for doing the work on
36: 7 for what they had already **b** was more than enough
39:33 Then they **b** the tabernacle to Moses,
40:21 and he **b** the ark into the tabernacle, and set up
Lev 6:30 from which any blood is **b** into the tent of meeting
7:35 once they have been **b** forward to serve
8: 6 Then Moses **b** Aaron and his sons forward,
8:13 And Moses **b** forward Aaron's sons,
8:18 Then he **b** forward the ram of burnt offering.
8:22 Then he **b** forward the second ram,
8:24 After Aaron's sons were **b** forward,
9: 5 They **b** what Moses commanded to the front of
9:12 Aaron's sons **b** him the blood,
9:13 And they **b** him the burnt offering piece by piece,
9:18 Aaron's sons **b** him the blood,
10:18 not **b** into the inner part of the sanctuary.
11:45 the LORD who **b** you up from the land of Egypt,
13: 2 be **b** to Aaron the priest or to one of his sons
13: 9 he shall be **b** to the priest.
14: 2 He shall be **b** to the priest;
14: 4 and hyssop be **b** for the one who is to be cleansed.
16:27 whose blood was **b** in to make atonement in
19:36 who **b** you out of the land of Egypt.
22:33 I who **b** you out of the land of Egypt to
23:14 until you have **b** the offering of your God:
23:43 in booths when I **b** them out of the land of Egypt:
24:11 And they **b** him to Moses—
25:38 who **b** you out of the land of Egypt,
25:42 whom I **b** out of the land of Egypt;
25:55 they are my servants whom I **b** out from the land
26:13 the LORD your God who **b** you out of the land
26:41 continued hostile to them and **b** them into the land
26:45 the covenant with their ancestors whom I **b** out of
27: 8 they shall be **b** before the priest and
27: 9 that may be **b** as an offering to the LORD,
27:11 that may not be **b** as an offering to the LORD,
Nu 6:13 be **b** to the entrance of the tent of meeting,
7: 3 They **b** their offerings before the LORD,
11:31 and it **b** quails from the sea and let them fall
12:14 and after that she may be **b** in again."
12:15 not set out on the march until Miriam had been **b**
13:23 They also **b** some pomegranates and figs.
13:26 they **b** back word to them and to all
13:32 So they **b** to the Israelites an unfavorable report of
14:13 for in your might you **b** up this people from
14:37 the men who **b** an unfavorable report about
15:25 and they have **b** their offering,
15:33 Those who found him gathering sticks **b** him
15:36 The whole congregation **b** him outside the camp
15:41 who **b** you out of the land of Egypt,
16:13 that you have **b** us up out of a land flowing
16:14 not **b** us into a land flowing with milk and honey,
17: 9 Then Moses **b** out all the staffs from before
20: 4 Why have you **b** the assembly of the LORD
20: 5 Why have you **b** us up out of Egypt,
20:16 and sent an angel and **b** us out of Egypt;
21: 5 "Why have you **b** us up out of Egypt to die in
22:41 On the next day Balak took Balaam and **b** him up
23: 7 "Balak has **b** me from Aram,
23:11 I **b** you to curse my enemies,
25: 6 of the Israelites came and **b** a Midianite woman
27: 5 Moses **b** their case before the LORD.
31:12 Then they **b** the captives and the booty and
31:50 And we have **b** the LORD's offering,
31:54 and **b** it into the tent of meeting as a memorial for
32:17 until we have **b** them to their place.
Dt 1:25 which they **b** down to us.
1:25 They **b** back a report to us, and said,
1:27 because the LORD hates us that he has **b** us out
4:20 But the LORD has taken you and **b** you out of
4:37 He **b** you out of Egypt with his own presence,
5: 6 who **b** you out of the land of Egypt,
5:15 the LORD your God **b** you out from there with
6:10 the LORD your God has **b** you into the land
6:12 who **b** you out of the land of Egypt,
6:21 the LORD **b** us out of Egypt with a mighty hand.
6:23 He **b** us out from there in order to bring us in,
7: 8 that the LORD has **b** you out with a mighty hand,
7:19 by which the LORD your God **b** you out.
8:14 who **b** you out of the land of Egypt,
9: 4 that the LORD has **b** me in to occupy this land";
9:12 for your people whom you have **b**
9:26 whom you **b** out of Egypt with a mighty hand.
9:28 the land from which you have **b** us might say,
9:28 he has **b** them out to let them die in
9:29 whom you **b** out by your great power and
11:29 the LORD your God has **b** you into the land
13: 5 who **b** you out of the land of Egypt
13:10 who **b** you out of the land of Egypt,
14:22 of all the yield of your seed that is **b** in yearly
16: 1 the month of Abib the LORD your God **b** you out
20: 1 who **b** you up from the land of Egypt.
26: 8 The LORD **b** us out of Egypt with a mighty hand
26: 9 and he **b** us into this place and gave us this land,
29:25 which he made with them when he **b** them out of
31:20 For when I have **b** them into the land flowing
31:21 before I have **b** them into the land
Jos 2: 6 **b** them up to the roof and hidden them with
6:23 spies went in and **b** Rahab out,
6:23 they **b** all her kindred out—
7: 7 Why have you **b** this people across the Jordan
7:16 and **b** Israel near tribe by tribe,
7:17 He **b** near the clans of Judah,
7:17 and he **b** near the clan of the Zerahites,
Jos 7:18 And he **b** near his household one by one,
7:23 the tent and **b** them to Joshua and all the Israelites;
7:24 and they **b** them up to the Valley of Achor.
8:23 the king of Ai was taken alive and **b** to Joshua.
10:23 and **b** the five kings out to him from the cave,
10:24 When they **b** the kings out to Joshua,
14: 7 and I **b** him an honest report.
22:32 to the Israelites, and **b** back word to them.
24: 5 and afterwards I **b** you out.
24: 6 When I **b** your ancestors out of Egypt,
24: 8 Then I **b** you to the land of the Amorites,
24:17 the LORD our God who **b** us and our ancestors
24:32 which the Israelites had **b** up from Egypt,
Jdg 1: 7 They **b** him to Jerusalem, and he died there.
2: 1 and said, "I **b** you up from Egypt,
2: 1 and **b** you into the land that I had promised
2:12 who had **b** them out of the land of Egypt;
5:25 she **b** him curds in a lordly bowl.
6: 8 and **b** you out of the house of slavery;
6:19 **b** them to him under the oak and presented them.
7: 5 So he **b** the troops down to the water;
7:25 They **b** the heads of Oreb and Zeeb to Gideon
11:35 You have **b** me very low;
12: 9 and **b** in thirty young women from outside
14:11 they **b** thirty companions to be with him.
15:13 and **b** him up from the rock.
16: 8 of the Philistines **b** her seven fresh bowstrings
16:18 and **b** the money in their hands.
16:21 They **b** him down to Gaza and bound him
16:31 down and took him and **b** him up and buried him
18: 3 they went over and asked him, "Who **b** you here?
19:21 So he **b** him into his house, and fed the donkeys;
21:12 with a man and **b** them to the camp at Shiloh,
Ru 1:21 but the LORD has **b** me back empty;
1:21 and the Almighty has **b** calamity upon me?"
1Sa 1:24 She **b** him to the house of the LORD at Shiloh;
1:25 and they **b** the child to Eli.
2:14 the fork **b** up the priest would take for himself.
4: 4 and **b** from there the ark of the covenant of
5: 1 they **b** it from Ebenezer to Ashdod;
5: 2 then the Philistines took the ark of God and **b** it
5: 9 But after they had **b** it to Gath,
5:10 "Why have they **b** around to us the ark of the God
7: 1 and **b** it to the house of Abinadab on the hill.
8: 8 from the day I **b** them up out of Egypt to this day,
9:22 and his servant-boy and **b** them into the hall,
10:18 the God of Israel, 'I **b** up Israel out of Egypt,
10:20 Then Samuel **b** all the tribes of Israel near,
10:21 He **b** the tribe of Benjamin near by its families,
10:21 Finally he **b** the family of the Matrites near man
10:23 Then they ran and **b** him from there.
10:27 They despised him and **b** him no present.
11:13 for today the LORD has **b** deliverance to Israel."
12: 6 and Aaron and **b** your ancestors up out of the land
12: 8 who **b** forth your ancestors out of Egypt,
14:34 all of the troops **b** their oxen with them that night,
15:15 "They have **b** them from the Amalekites;
15:20 I have **b** Agag the king of Amalek,
16:12 He sent and **b** him in.
17:54 the head of the Philistine and **b** it to Jerusalem;
17:57 Abner took him and **b** him before Saul,
18:27 and David **b** their foreskins,
19: 5 the LORD **b** about a great victory for all Israel.
19: 7 Jonathan then **b** David to Saul,
20: 8 for you have **b** your servant into a sacred covenant
21:14 why then have you **b** him to me?
21:15 that you have **b** this fellow to play the madman
23: 5 fought with the Philistines, **b** away their livestock,
25:27 And now let this present that your servant has **b**
25:35 David received from her hand what she had **b** him;
27:11 nor woman alive to be **b** back to Gath,
30: 7 So Abiathar **b** the ephod to David.
30:11 an Egyptian, and **b** him to David.
30:19 that had been taken; David **b** back everything.
2Sa 1:10 and I have **b** them here to my lord."
2: 3 David **b** up the men who were with him,
2: 8 and **b** him over to Mahanaim.
3:26 and they **b** him back from the cistern of Sirah;
4: 8 They **b** the head of Ishbaal to David at Hebron
5: 2 it was you who led out Israel and **b** it in.
6: 3 and **b** it out of the house of Abinadab,
6:12 So David went and **b** up the ark of God from
6:15 of Israel **b** up the ark of the LORD with shouting,
6:17 They **b** in the ark of the LORD,
7: 6 not lived in a house since the day I **b** up the people
7:18 that you have **b** me thus far?
8: 2 Moabites became servants to David and **b** tribute.
8: 6 Arameans became servants to David and **b** tribute.
8: 7 by the servants of Hadadezer, and **b** them
8:10 Joram **b** with him articles of silver, gold,
9: 5 Then King David sent and **b** him from the house
10:16 Hadadezer sent and **b** out the Arameans who were
11:27 David sent and **b** her to his house,
12: 3 He **b** it up, and it grew up with him and
12:30 He also **b** forth the spoil of the city,
12:31 He **b** out the people who were in it,
13:10 **b** them into the chamber to Amnon her brother.
13:11 But when she **b** them near him to eat,
14: 2 to Tekoa and **b** from there a wise woman.
14:23 went to Geshur, and **b** Absalom to Jerusalem.
15: 2 anyone **b** a suit before the king for judgment,
16: 2 The king said to Ziba, "Why have you **b** these?"
17:28 **b** beds, basins, and earthen vessels,
19:40 of Judah, and also half the people of Israel, **b**
19:41 and **b** the king and his household over the Jordan,
21:13 He **b** up from there the bones of Saul and
22:20 He **b** me out into a broad place;
2Sa 22:48 the God who gave me vengeance and **b**
22:49 who **b** me out from my enemies;
23:10 The LORD **b** about a great victory that day.
23:12 and the LORD **b** about a great victory.
23:16 of Bethlehem that was by the gate, and **b** it
1Ki 1: 3 and **b** her to the king.
1:27 Has this thing been **b** about by my lord the king
1:53 Then King Solomon sent to have him **b** down
2:19 and had a throne **b** for the king's mother,
2:30 Then Benaiah **b** the king word again, saying,
2:40 Shimei went and **b** his slaves from Gath.
3: 1 he took Pharaoh's daughter and **b** her into the city
3:24 and they **b** a sword before the king.
4:21 they **b** tribute and served Solomon all the days
4:28 They also **b** to the required place barley and straw
7:51 **b** in the things that his father David had
8: 4 So they **b** up the ark of the LORD,
8: 4 the priests and the Levites **b** them up.
8: 6 the priests **b** the ark of the covenant of the LORD
8:16 the day that I **b** my people Israel out of Egypt,
8:21 with our ancestors when he **b** them out of the land
8:51 which you **b** out of Egypt,
8:53 when you **b** our ancestors out of Egypt,
9: 9 who **b** their ancestors out of the land of Egypt,
9: 9 the LORD has **b** this disaster upon them.' "
10:11 **b** from Ophir a great quantity of almug wood
10:25 Every one of them **b** a present,
12:15 because it was a turn of affairs **b** about by
12:28 O Israel, who **b** you up out of the land of Egypt."
13:20 to the prophet who had **b** him back;
13:23 to the prophet who had **b** him back.
13:26 When the prophet who had **b** him back from
13:29 laid it on the donkey, and **b** it back to the city,
14:28 the guard carried them and **b** them back to
15:15 He **b** into the house of the LORD the votive gifts
17: 6 The ravens **b** him bread and meat in the morning,
17:20 have you **b** calamity even upon the widow
17:23 **b** him down from the upper chamber into
18:40 and Elijah **b** them down to the Wadi Kishon,
20: 9 The messengers left and **b** him word again.
20:39 then a soldier turned and **b** a man to me, and said,
21:13 and the scoundrels **b** a charge against Naboth,
22:37 So the king died, and was **b** to Samaria;
2Ki 2:20 So they **b** it to him.
4:20 He carried him and **b** him to his mother;
5: 6 He **b** the letter to the king of Israel, which read,
10: 8 "They have **b** the heads of the king's sons,"
10:22 So he **b** out the vestments for them.
10:26 They **b** out the pillar that was in the temple
11: 9 each **b** his men who were to go off duty on
11:12 Then he **b** out the king's son,
11:19 then they **b** the king down from the house of
12: 4 that is **b** into the house of the LORD, the money
12: 4 and the money from the voluntary offerings **b** into
12: 9 the threshold put in it all the money that was **b** into
12:13 from the money that was **b** into the house of
12:16 from the sin offerings was not **b** into the house of
14:20 They **b** him on horses; he was buried in Jerusalem
17: 7 who had **b** them up out of the land of Egypt from
17:24 The king of Assyria **b** people from Babylon,
17:36 who **b** you out of the land of Egypt
20:11 and he **b** the shadow back the ten intervals,
20:20 how he made the pool and the conduit and **b** water
22: 4 the entire sum of the money that has been **b** into
23: 6 He **b** out the image of Asherah from the house of
23: 8 He **b** all the priests out of the towns of Judah,
23:30 in a chariot from Megiddo, **b** him to Jerusalem,
24:16 The king of Babylon **b** captive to Babylon all
25: 6 and **b** him up to the king of Babylon at Riblah,
25:20 and **b** them to the king of Babylon at Riblah.
1Ch 5:26 and **b** them to Halah, Habor, Hara,
9:28 to count them when they were **b** in and taken out.
10:12 and the bodies of his sons, and **b** them to Jabesh.
11:18 and they **b** it to David.
11:19 For at the risk of their lives they **b** it."
14:17 and the LORD **b** the fear of him on all nations.
15:28 So all Israel **b** up the ark of the covenant of
16: 1 They **b** in the ark of God,
17: 5 not lived in a house since the day I **b** out Israel
17:16 that you have **b** me thus far?
18: 2 Moabites became subject to David and **b** tribute.
18: 6 Arameans became subject to David, and **b** tribute.
18: 7 by the servants of Hadadezer, and **b** them
19:16 and **b** out the Arameans who were beyond
20: 2 He also **b** out the booty of the city,
20: 3 He **b** out the people who were in it,
22: 4 and Tyrians **b** great quantities of cedar to David.
22:19 of God may be **b** into a house built for the name of
2Ch 1: 4 (But David had **b** the ark of God up
5: 1 **b** in the things that his father David had
5: 5 So they **b** up the ark, the tent of meeting,
5: 5 the priests and the Levites **b** them up.
5: 7 the priests **b** the ark of the covenant of the LORD
6: 5 that I **b** my people out of the land of Egypt, I have
7:22 of their ancestors who **b** them out of the land
7:22 therefore he has **b** all this calamity upon them.' "
8:11 Solomon **b** Pharaoh's daughter from the city
8:18 of gold and **b** it to King Solomon.
9:10 of Huram and the servants of Solomon who **b** gold
9:10 from Ophir **b** algum wood and precious stones.
9:12 well beyond what she had **b** to the king.
9:14 besides that which the traders and merchants **b**;
9:14 and the governors of the land **b** gold and silver
9:24 Every one of them **b** a present,
10:15 because it was a turn of affairs **b** about by God so
15:11 from the booty that they had **b**,
15:18 He **b** into the house of God the votive gifts

2Ch 16: 6 Then King Asa **b** all Judah,
17: 5 All Judah **b** tribute to Jehoshaphat,
17:11 Some of the Philistines **b** Jehoshaphat presents,
17:11 also **b** him seven thousand seven hundred rams
19: 4 and **b** them back to the LORD,
22: 9 while hiding in Samaria and was **b** to Jehu,
23: 8 each **b** his men, who were to come on duty on
23:11 Then he **b** out the king's son,
23:14 the priest Jehoiada **b** out the captains who were set
23:20 and they **b** the king down from the house of
24:10 the people rejoiced and **b** their tax and dropped it
24:11 Whenever the chest was **b** to the king's officers by
24:14 they **b** the rest of the money to the king
25:14 he **b** the gods of the people of Seir,
25:23 he **b** him to Jerusalem, and broke down the wall
25:28 They **b** him back on horses;
28: 5 a great number of his people and **b** them
28: 8 also took much booty from them and **b** the booty
28:15 they **b** them to their kindred at Jericho,
28:19 the LORD **b** Judah low because of King Ahaz
29: 4 He **b** in the priests and the Levites
29:16 and they **b** out all the unclean things
29:21 They **b** seven bulls, seven rams, seven lambs,
29:23 Then the male goats for the sin offering were **b** to
29:31 The assembly **b** sacrifices and thank offerings;
29:31 all who were of a willing heart **b** burnt offerings.
29:32 that the assembly **b** was seventy bulls,
30:15 and **b** burnt offerings into the house of
31: 5 and they **b** in abundantly the tithe of everything.
31: 6 and Judah who lived in the cities of Judah also **b**
31:12 Faithfully they **b** in the contributions,
32:23 Many **b** gifts to the LORD in Jerusalem
33:11 the LORD **b** against them the commanders of
33:11 bound him with fetters, and **b** him to Babylon.
34: 9 the money that had been **b** into the house of God,
34:14 that had been **b** into the house of the LORD,
34:16 Shaphan **b** the book to the king,
35:24 and carried him in his second chariot and **b** him
36:10 of the year King Nebuchadnezzar sent and **b** him
36:17 he **b** up against them the king of the Chaldeans,
36:18 all these he **b** to Babylon.
Ezr 1: 7 King Cyrus himself **b** out the vessels of the house
1:11 All these Sheshbazzar **b** up,
1:11 the exiles were **b** up from Babylonia to Jerusalem.
4: 2 of King Esar-haddon of Assyria who **b** us here."
5:14 the temple in Jerusalem and had **b** into the temple
6: 3 sacrifices are offered and burnt offerings are **b**;
6: 5 and **b** to Babylon, be restored and **b** back to the
8:18 they **b** us a man of discretion,
Ne 5: 7 I **b** charges against the nobles and the officials;
8: 2 the priest Ezra **b** the law before the assembly,
8:16 So the people went out and **b** them,
9: 7 the God who chose Abram and **b** him out of Ur of
9:15 their thirst you **b** water for them out of the rock,
9:18 'This is your God who **b** you up out of Egypt,'
9:23 and **b** them into the land
12:31 Then I **b** the leaders of Judah up onto the wall,
13: 9 and I **b** back the vessels of the house of God,
13:12 Then all Judah **b** the tithe of the grain, wine,
13:15 which they **b** into Jerusalem on the sabbath day;
13:16 **b** in fish and all kinds of merchandise
13:19 to prevent any burden from being **b** in on
Est 1:17 to be **b** before him, and she did
2: 7 Mordecai had **b** up Hadassah, that is Esther,
2:20 as when she was **b** up by him.
6: 8 let royal robes be **b**, which the king has worn,
Job 5:13 and the schemes of the wily are **b** to a quick end.
14:21 they are **b** low, and it goes unnoticed.
15: 7 Were you **b** forth before the hills?
18:14 and are **b** to the king of terrors.
31:13 when they **b** a complaint against me;
42:11 for all the evil that the LORD had **b** upon him;
Ps 18:19 He **b** me out into a broad place;
30: 3 O LORD, you **b** up my soul from Sheol,
37:33 or let them be condemned when they are **b** to trial.
40:14 and **b** to dishonor who desire my hurt.
46: 8 see what desolations he has **b** on the earth.
64: 9 they will tell what God has **b** about,
66:11 You **b** us into the net;
66:12 yet you have **b** us out to a spacious place.
68:31 Let bronze be **b** from Egypt;
70: 2 be turned back and **b** to dishonor who desire
78:54 And he **b** them to his holy hill,
78:71 from tending the nursing ewes he **b** him to be
79: 8 to meet us, for we are **b** very low.
80: 8 You **b** a vine out of Egypt;
81:10 who **b** you up out of the land of Egypt.
90: 2 Before the mountains were **b** forth,
105:37 Then he **b** Israel out with silver and gold,
105:40 They asked, and he **b** quails,
105:43 So he **b** his people out with joy,
106:42 and they were **b** into subjection under their power.
106:43 and were **b** low through their iniquity.
107:14 he **b** them out of darkness and gloom,
107:28 and he **b** them out from their distress;
107:30 and he **b** them to their desired haven.
107:39 they are diminished and **b** low through oppression,
116: 6 when I was **b** low, he saved me.
136:11 and **b** Israel out from among them,
142: 6 Give heed to my cry, for I am **b** very low.
Pr 8:24 When there were no depths I was **b** forth,
8:25 before the hills, I was **b** forth—
21:22 and **b** down the stronghold in which they trusted.
21:27 how much more when **b** with evil intent.
Ecc 12: 4 and all the daughters of song are **b** low;
SS 1: 4 The king has **b** me into his chambers.
2: 4 He **b** me to the banqueting house,

SS 3: 4 and would not let him go until I **b** him
Isa 1: 2 I reared children and **b** them up,
2: 9 so people are humbled, and everyone is **b** low—
2:11 The haughty eyes of people shall be **b** low,
2:17 and the pride of everyone shall be **b** low;
3: 9 For they have **b** evil on themselves.
5:15 People are bowed down, everyone is **b** low,
8:10 Take counsel together, but it shall be **b** to naught;
9: 1 In the former time he **b** into contempt the land
10:13 like a bull I have **b** down those who sat on thrones.
10:33 and the lofty will be **b** low.
14:11 Your pomp is **b** down to Sheol,
14:15 you are **b** down to Sheol, to the depths of the Pit.
16:14 the glory of Moab will be **b** into contempt,
17: 4 On that day the glory of Jacob will be **b** low,
18: 7 At that time gifts will be **b** to the LORD of hosts
23: 4 I have neither reared young men nor **b**
25:12 The high fortifications of his walls will be **b** down,
26: 5 For he has **b** low the inhabitants of the height;
43:23 You have not **b** me your sheep for burnt offerings,
48:15 even I, have spoken and called him, I have **b** him,
51:18 by the hand among all the children she has **b** up.
57: 6 you have **b** a grain offering.
59:16 so his own arm **b** him victory,
60: 5 because the abundance of the sea shall be **b** to you,
63: 5 so my own arm **b** me victory,
63:11 Where is the one who **b** them up out of the sea
Jer 2: 6 is the LORD who **b** us up from the land of Egypt,
2: 7 I **b** you into a plentiful land to eat its fruits
2:17 Have you not **b** this upon yourself by forsaking
4:18 Your ways and your doings have **b** this upon you.
7:22 in the day that I **b** your ancestors out of the land
8: 1 of the inhabitants of Jerusalem shall be **b** out
10: 9 Beaten silver is **b** from Tarshish,
11: 4 when I **b** them out of the land of Egypt,
11: 7 when I **b** them up out of the land of Egypt,
11: 8 So I **b** upon them all the words of this covenant,
15: 8 I have **b** against the mothers of youths a destroyer
16:14 the LORD lives who **b** the people of Israel up out
16:15 the LORD lives who **b** the people of Israel up out
20:15 Cursed be the man who **b** the news to my father,
23: 7 the LORD lives who **b** the people of Israel up out
23: 8 the LORD lives who **b** out and led the offspring
24: 1 and the smiths, and had **b** them to Babylon.
26:23 and they took Uriah from Egypt and **b** him
27:16 of the LORD's house will soon be **b** back
32:21 You **b** your people Israel out of the land of Egypt
32:42 as I have **b** all this great disaster upon this people,
34:11 and **b** them again into subjection as slaves.
34:13 a covenant with your ancestors when I **b** them out
34:16 you **b** them again into subjection to be your slaves.
35: 4 I **b** them to the house of the LORD into
37:14 and arrested Jeremiah and **b** him to the officials.
39: 5 and when they had taken him, they **b** him up
39:14 of Ahikam son of Shaphan to be **b** home.
40: 3 and now the LORD has **b** it about,
41:16 and eunuchs, whom Johanan **b** back from Gibeon.
42:10 I am sorry for the disaster that I have **b** upon you.
44: 2 the disaster that I have **b** on Jerusalem and on all
48: 2 You also, O Madmen, shall be **b** to silence;
50:25 and **b** out the weapons of his wrath,
51:10 The LORD has **b** forth our vindication;
52: 9 and **b** him up to the king of Babylon at Riblah in
52:26 and **b** them to the king of Babylon at Riblah.
52:31 to King Jehoiachin of Judah and **b** him out
La 1:12 if there is any sorrow like my sorrow, which was **b**
2: 2 he has **b** down to the ground in dishonor
3: 2 and **b** me into darkness without any light;
4: 5 those who were **b** up in purple cling to ash heaps.
Eze 8: 3 and **b** me in visions of God to Jerusalem,
8: 7 And he **b** me to the entrance of the court;
8:14 Then he **b** me to the entrance of the north gate of
8:16 And he **b** me into the inner court of the house of
9:11 with the writing case at his side, **b** back word,
11: 1 The spirit lifted me up and **b** me to the east gate of
11:24 The spirit lifted me up and **b** me in a vision by
12: 7 I **b** out my baggage by day, as baggage for exile,
12: 7 I **b** it out in the dark,
14:22 sons and daughters who will be **b** out;
14:22 you will be consoled for the evil that I have **b**
14:22 for all that I have **b** upon it.
16:52 for you have **b** about for your sisters
17: 6 it **b** forth branches, put forth foliage.
17:12 and **b** them back with him to Babylon.
19: 4 and they **b** him with hooks to the land of Egypt.
19: 9 and **b** him to the king of Babylon;
19: 9 they **b** him into custody, so that his voice should
20:10 So I led them out of the land of Egypt and **b** them
20:14 in whose sight I had **b** them out.
20:22 in whose sight I had **b** them out.
20:28 For when I had **b** them into the land that I swore
21:24 Because you have **b** your guilt to remembrance,
22: 4 you have **b** your day near,
23:27 an end to your lewdness and your whoring **b** from
23:30 have **b** this upon you, because you played
23:42 of the rabble **b** in drunken from the wilderness;
27:15 they **b** you in payment ivory tusks and ebony.
27:26 Your rowers have **b** you into the high seas.
28:18 So I **b** out fire from within you;
30:11 shall be **b** in to destroy the land;
31:18 Now you shall be **b** down with the trees of Eden to
34: 4 you have not **b** back the strayed,
37: 1 and he **b** me out by the spirit of the LORD
38: 8 its people were **b** out from the nations and
39:27 when I have **b** them back from the peoples
40: 1 of the LORD was upon me, and he **b** me there.
40: 2 He **b** me, in visions of God, to the land of Israel,

Eze 40: 3 When he **b** me there, a man was there,
40: 4 for you were **b** here in order that I might show it
40:17 Then he **b** me into the outer court;
40:28 Then he **b** me to the inner court by the south gate,
40:32 Then he **b** me to the inner court on the east side,
40:35 he **b** me to the north gate, and he measured it;
40:48 Then he **b** me to the vestibule of the temple
41: 1 he **b** me to the nave, and measured the pilasters;
42: 1 and he **b** me to the chambers that were opposite
43: 1 Then he **b** me to the gate, the gate facing east.
43: 5 and **b** me into the inner court;
44: 1 he **b** me back to the outer gate of the sanctuary,
44: 4 Then he **b** me by way of the north gate to the front
46:19 Then he **b** me through the entrance,
46:21 Then he **b** me out to the outer court,
47: 1 Then he **b** me back to the entrance of the temple;
47: 2 Then he **b** me out by way of the north gate,
Da 1: 2 These he **b** to the land of Shinar,
1:18 the time that the king had set for them to be **b** in,
1:18 the palace master **b** them into the presence
2:25 Then Arioch quickly **b** Daniel before the king
3:13 Meshach, and Abednego be **b** in;
3:13 so they **b** those men before the king.
4: 6 the wise men of Babylon should be **b** before me,
5: 3 So they **b** in the vessels of gold and silver
5:13 Then Daniel was **b** in before the king.
5:13 whom my father the king **b** from Judah?
5:15 have been **b** in before me to read this writing
5:23 vessels of his temple have been **b** in before you,
5:26 the days of your kingdom and **b** it to an end;
6:16 and Daniel was **b** and thrown into the den of lions.
6:17 A stone was **b** and laid on the mouth of the den,
6:18 no food was **b** to him, and sleep fled from him.
6:24 and those who had accused Daniel were **b**
9:14 over this calamity until he **b** it upon us.
9:15 who **b** your people out of the land of Egypt with
Hos 12:13 By a prophet the LORD **b** Israel up from Egypt,
Am 2:10 Also I **b** you up out of the land of Egypt,
3: 1 against the whole family that I **b** up out of the land
Jnh 2: 6 you **b** up my life from the Pit, O LORD my God.
Mic 5: 3 until the time when she who is in labor has **b** forth;
6: 4 For I **b** you up from the land of Egypt,
Zep 3: 7 it will not lose sight of all that I have **b** upon it."
Hag 1: 9 and when you **b** it home, I blew it away.
Mt 4:24 and they **b** to him all the sick,
8:16 That evening they **b** to him many who were
9:32 a demoniac who was mute was **b** to him.
11: 5 and the poor have good news **b** to them.
11:23 No, you will be **b** down to Hades.
12:22 Then they **b** to him a demoniac who was blind
13: 8 Other seeds fell on good soil and **b** forth grain,
14:11 The head was **b** on a platter and given to the girl,
14:11 who **b** it to her mother.
14:35 throughout the region and **b** all who were sick
16: 7 "It is because we have **b** no bread."
17:16 And I **b** him to your disciples,
18:24 one who owed him ten thousand talents was **b**
19:13 Then little children were being **b** to him in order
19:13 The disciples spoke sternly to those who **b** them;
21: 7 they **b** the donkey and the colt,
22:19 And they **b** him a denarius.
27: 3 he repented and **b** back the thirty pieces of silver
Mk 1:32 they **b** to him all who were sick or possessed
4: 8 Other seed fell into good soil and **b** forth grain,
4:21 "Is a lamp **b** in to be put under the bushel basket,
6:28 **b** his head on a platter,
7:32 They **b** to him a deaf man who had an impediment
8:22 Some people **b** a blind man to him
9:17 "Teacher, I **b** you my son;
9:20 And they **b** the boy to him.
11: 7 Then they **b** the colt to Jesus
12:16 And they **b** one. Then he said to them,
15:22 Then they **b** Jesus to the place called Golgotha
Lk 1:52 He has **b** down the powerful from their thrones,
2:22 they **b** him up to Jerusalem to present him to
2:27 and when the parents **b** in the child Jesus,
4:16 he came to Nazareth, where he had been **b** up,
4:40 with various kinds of diseases **b** them to him;
5:11 When they had **b** their boats to shore,
7:22 the poor have good news **b** to them.
7:37 **b** an alabaster jar of ointment.
10:15 No, you will be **b** down to Hades.
10:34 he put him on his own animal, **b** him to an inn,
16: 1 and charges were **b** to him
18:40 Jesus stood still and ordered the man to be **b**
19:35 Then they **b** it to Jesus;
21:12 over to synagogues and prisons, and you will be **b**
22:66 gathered together, and they **b** him to their council.
23: 1 assembly rose as a body and **b** Jesus before Pilate.
23:14 "You **b** me this man as one who was perverting
Jn 1:42 He **b** Simon to Jesus, who looked at him and said,
4:33 "Surely no one has **b** him something to eat?"
8: 3 ⟦the Pharisees **b** a woman who had been caught⟧
9:13 They **b** to the Pharisees the man who had formerly
10: 4 When he has **b** out all his own,
16:21 because of the joy of having **b** a human being into
18: 3 So Judas **b** a detachment of soldiers together
18:16 the woman who guarded the gate, and **b** Peter in.
19:13 he **b** Jesus outside and sat on the judge's bench at
Ac 4:34 as many as owned lands or houses sold them and **b**
4:37 then **b** the money, and laid it at the apostles' feet.
5: 2 and **b** only a part and laid it at the apostles' feet.
5:19 of the Lord opened the prison doors, **b** them out,
5:21 and sent to the prison to have them **b**.
5:26 captain went with the temple police and **b** them,
5:27 When they had **b** them, they had them stand
6:12 seized him, and **b** him before the council.

Ac 7:16 and their bodies were **b** back to Shechem and laid
7:20 three months he was **b** up in his father's house;
7:21 Pharaoh's daughter adopted him and **b** him up
7:45 in turn **b** it in with Joshua when they dispossessed
9: 8 by the hand and **b** him into Damascus.
9:27 But Barnabas took him, **b** him to the apostles,
9:30 they **b** him down to Caesarea and sent him off
11:24 And a great many people were **b** to the Lord.
11:26 and when he had found him, he **b** him to Antioch.
12:17 how the Lord had **b** him out of the prison.
12:25 and Saul returned to Jerusalem and **b**
13:23 Of this man's posterity God has **b** to Israel
14:13 **b** oxen and garlands to the gates;
15: 3 and **b** great joy to all the believers.
16:16 a spirit of divination and **b** her owners a great deal
16:20 When they had **b** them before the magistrates,
16:30 Then he **b** them outside and said, "Sirs,
16:34 He **b** them up into the house and set food
17:15 Those who conducted Paul **b** him as far as Athens;
17:19 So they took him and **b** him to the Areopagus
18:12 the Jews made a united attack on Paul and **b** him
19:12 or aprons that had touched his skin were **b** to
19:24 **b** no little business to the artisans.
19:27 be deprived of her majesty that **b** all Asia and
19:37 You have **b** these men here who are neither
20:38 Then they **b** him to the ship.
21:16 along and **b** us to the house of Mnason of Cyprus,
21:28 that, he has actually **b** Greeks into the temple
21:29 they supposed that Paul had **b** him into the temple.
21:34 he ordered him to be **b** into the barracks.
21:37 Just as Paul was about to be **b** into the barracks,
22: 3 but **b** up in this city at the feet of Gamaliel,
22:24 the tribune directed that he was to be **b** into
22:30 He **b** Paul down and had him stand before them.
23:18 So he took him, **b** him to the tribune, and said,
23:28 I had him **b** to their council.
23:31 took Paul and **b** him during the night to Antipatris.
25: 6 on the tribunal and ordered Paul to be **b.**
25:17 on the tribunal and ordered the man to be **b.**
25:23 Then Festus gave the order and Paul was **b** in.
25:26 Therefore I have **b** him before all of you,
27:44 And so it was that all were **b** safely to land.
Ro 5:16 judgment following one trespass **b** condemnation,
6:13 to God as those who have been **b** from death
Gal 2: 4 But because of false believers secretly **b** in,
Eph 2:13 you who once were far off have been **b** near
1Th 3: 6 and has **b** us the good news of your faith and love.
1Ti 5:10 as one who has **b** up children, shown hospitality,
6: 7 for we **b** nothing into the world,
2Ti 1:10 who abolished death and **b** life and immortality
Heb 13:11 the bodies of those animals whose blood is **b** into
13:20 who **b** back from the dead our Lord Jesus,
Jas 1:10 and the rich in being **b** low,
2:22 and faith was **b** to completion by the works.
5:19 among you wanders from the truth and is **b** back
1Pe 1:12 to you through those who **b** you good news by
2Pe 2: 5 when he **b** a flood on a world of the ungodly;
1Jn 2:11 because the darkness has **b** on blindness.
Tob 7: 1 Then he **b** them into his house.
7:16 in the room as he had told her, and **b** Sarah there.
8: 1 the young man and **b** him into the bedroom.
8:19 and **b** two steers and four rams and ordered them
11:15 that he had **b** the money,
11:17 Blessed be your God who has **b** you to us,
12: 2 to give him half of the possessions **b** back
12: 3 he **b** the money back with me, and he healed you.
12: 4 my child, to receive half of all that he **b** back."
12: 5 "Take for your wages half of all that you **b** back,
12:12 it was I who **b** and read the record of your prayer
14:10 while still alive, **b** down into the earth?
Jdt 6:14 and **b** him into Bethulia and placed him before
10:17 and they **b** them to the tent of Holofernes.
11: 2 They have **b** this on themselves.
12: 2 I will have enough with the things I **b** with me."
12: 5 the servants of Holofernes **b** her into the tent,
13:20 when our nation was **b** low,
14:18 One Hebrew woman has **b** disgrace on the house
AdE 2: 3 to be **b** to the harem in Susa,
2: 7 he **b** her up to womanhood as his own.
2: 8 Esther also was **b** to Gai,
4: 8 being **b** up under my care—
6:14 the eunuchs arrived and hurriedly **b** Haman to
11: 1 and his son Ptolemy **b** to Egypt
11: 4 of Babylon had **b** from Jerusalem
13: 4 that we honorably intend cannot be **b** about.
14:18 since the day that I was **b** here until now,
Wis 5: 8 And what good has our boasted wealth **b** us?
10:14 until she **b** him the scepter of a kingdom
10:18 She **b** them over the Red Sea,
18:21 he **b** forward the shield of his ministry,
19:10 of producing animals the earth **b** forth gnats,
Sir 6:12 but if you are **b** low,
23:23 and **b** forth children by another man.
23:24 She herself will be **b** before the assembly,
33:12 and some he made holy and **b** near to himself;
33:12 but some he cursed and **b** low,
44:23 From his descendants the Lord **b** forth
47:19 But you **b** in women to lie at your side,
47:19 and through your body you were **b** into subjection.
47:20 so that you **b** wrath upon your children,
48: 2 He **b** a famine upon them,
48: 3 and also three times **b** down fire.
48:17 and **b** water into its midst;
Bar 1: 9 and the people of the land, and **b** them to Babylon.
1:19 From the time when the Lord **b** our ancestors out
1:20 at the time when he **b** our ancestors out of the land
2: 5 They were **b** down and not raised up,
Bar 2: 9 and the Lord has **b** them upon us,
2:11 who **b** your people out of the land of Egypt with
2:24 and the bones of our ancestors would be **b** out
3:29 and taken her, and **b** her down from the clouds?
4: 8 You forgot the everlasting God, who **b** you up,
4: 9 God has **b** great sorrow upon me;
4:10 which the Everlasting **b** upon them.
4:14 which the Everlasting **b** upon them.
4:15 For he **b** a distant nation against them,
4:18 For he who **b** these calamities
4:27 for you will be remembered by the one who **b** this
4:29 For the one who **b** these calamities
Aza 1: 5 in all you have **b** upon us and upon Jerusalem,
1: 5 by a true judgment you have **b** all this upon us
1: 8 So all that you have **b** upon us,
1:14 and are **b** low this day in all the world because
1Mc 1: 6 who had been **b** up with him from youth,
3:49 They also **b** the vestments of the priesthood and
4:49 They made new holy vessels, and **b** the lampstand,
4:58 and the disgrace **b** by the Gentiles was removed.
6:17 Lysias had **b** him up from boyhood;
7: 6 They **b** to the king this accusation against
7: 7 that Judas has **b** on us and on the land of the king,
7:25 to the king and **b** malicious charges against them.
7:47 **b** them and displayed them just outside Jerusalem.
9:26 for the friends of Judas, and **b** them to Bacchides,
10:82 Then Simon **b** forward his force and engaged
13:32 and he **b** great calamity on the land.
13:43 He made a siege engine, **b** it up to the city,
14:29 and they **b** great glory to their nation.
15:18 have **b** a gold shield weighing one thousand minas.
2Mc 1:17 in every way be our God, who has **b** judgment
2: 5 and he **b** there the tent and the ark and the altar
3:18 the holy place was about to be **b** into dishonor.
4:43 Charges were **b** against Menelaus
6: 4 besides **b** in things for sacrifice that were unfit.
6:10 For example, two women were **b** in
7: 7 they **b** forward the second for their sport.
7:15 Next they **b** forward the fifth and maltreated him.
7:18 After him they **b** forward the sixth.
7:27 and have reared you and **b** you up to this point
8:34 who had **b** the thousand merchants to buy
9: 8 was **b** down to earth and carried in a litter,
11:18 of everything that needed to be **b** before him,
14:41 they ordered that fire be **b** and the doors burned.
1Es 1:31 and after he was **b** back to Jerusalem he died,
1:38 and seized his brother Zarius and **b** him back
2:10 King Cyrus also **b** out the holy vessels of the Lord
2:11 When King Cyrus of the Persians **b** these out,
4:16 and women **b** up the very men who plant
4:20 A man leaves his own father, who **b** him up,
5:69 of the Assyrians, who **b** us here."
8:47 of our Lord they **b** us competent men of
8:80 he **b** us into favor with the kings of the Persians,
9:17 the men who had foreign wives were **b** to an end
9:18 those who were **b** in and found
9:40 So Ezra the chief priest **b** the law,
3Mc 3:14 as you yourselves know, it was **b** to conclusion,
4: 9 They were **b** on board like wild animals,
4:11 When these people had been **b** to
5:45 animals had been **b** virtually to a state of madness,
6: 7 you **b** up to the light unharmed.
6:17 with them and **b** an uncontrollable terror upon
7:20 of them been **b** safely by land and sea and river
2Es 1: 7 Was it not I who **b** them out of the land of Egypt,
1:13 Surely it was I who **b** you through the sea,
2: 1 I **b** this people out of bondage,
2: 3 I **b** you up with gladness;
3: 9 in its time you **b** the flood upon the inhabitants of
3:17 you **b** them to Mount Sinai.
4:23 the law of our ancestors has been **b** to destruction
6:40 Then you commanded a ray of light to be **b** out
7:*48* and has **b** us into corruption and the ways of death,
7:*62* I replied and said, "O earth, what have you **b** forth,
9:46 And I **b** him up with much care.
10:12 which I **b** forth in pain and bore in sorrow,
10:14 'Just as you **b** forth in sorrow,
10:28 For it was he who **b** me
10:47 her telling you that she **b** him up with much care,
11:42 the homes of those who **b** forth fruit,
12: 4 "You have **b** this upon me,
4Mc 3:14 and from it boldly **b** the king a drink.
5: 4 leader of the flock, was **b** before the king.
6:24 the guards **b** him to the fire.
8: 2 that others of the Hebrew captives be **b,**
8: 3 were **b** before him along with their aged mother.
8:12 to be **b** forward so as to persuade them out of fear
9:11 at his command the guards **b** forward the eldest,
9:26 the guards **b** in the next eldest,
10: 2 and that I was **b** up on the same teachings?
10: 8 They immediately **b** him to the wheel,
13:20 they were **b** to the light of day.
13:24 trained in the same virtues and **b** up in right living,
18:20 and in his burning rage **b** those seven sons of

BROUGHT-UP (1) [BRING]

Sir 31:16 Eat what is set before you like a well **b** person,

BROW (3) [EYEBROWS]

Ge 49:26 the **b** of him who was set apart from his brothers.
Dt 33:16 on the **b** of the prince among his brothers.
Lk 4:29 to the **b** of the hill on which their town was built,

BRUISE‡ (1) [BRUISED, BRUISES, BRUISING, BRUSHING]

Jdt 9:13 and **b** on those who have planned cruel things

BRUISED (3) [BRUISE]

Lev 22:24 that has its testicles **b** or crushed or torn or cut,
Isa 42: 3 a **b** reed he will not break,
Mt 12:20 not break a **b** reed or quench a smoldering wick

BRUISES (3) [BRUISE]

Isa 1: 6 but **b** and sores and bleeding wounds;
53: 5 and by his **b** we are healed.
Sir 23:10 under scrutiny will not lack **b,**

BRUISING (1) [BRUISE]

Mk 5: 5 and **b** himself with stones.

BRUIT (KJV) See NEWS, NOISE

BRUSHING (1) [BRUISE]

Eze 3:13 the sound of the wings of the living creatures **b**

BRUSHWOOD (4) [WOOD]

Jdg 9:48 cut down a bundle of **b,**
Isa 64: 2 fire kindles **b** and the fire causes water to boil—
Ac 28: 3 Paul had gathered a bundle of **b** and was putting it
Aza 1:23 the furnace with naphtha, pitch, tow, and **b.**

BRUTE (1) [BRUTES, BRUTISH]

Ps 73:22 I was like a **b** beast toward you.

BRUTES (2) [BRUTE]

2Ti 3: 3 slanderers, profligates, **b,** haters of good,
Tit 1:12 who said, "Cretans are always liars, vicious **b,**

BRUTISH (1) [BRUTE]

Eze 21:31 I will deliver you into **b** hands,

BUCKET (3) [BUCKETS]

Isa 40:15 Even the nations are like a drop from a **b,**
Jn 4:11 The woman said to him, "Sir, you have no **b,**
2Es 6:56 to a drop from a **b.**

BUCKETS (1) [BUCKET]

Nu 24: 7 Water shall flow from his **b,**

BUCKLE (3)

1Mc 10:89 and he sent to him a golden **b,**
11:58 and dress in purple and wear a gold **b.**
14:44 or to be clothed in purple or put on a gold **b.**

BUCKLER (6) [BUCKLERS]

Ps 35: 2 Take hold of shield and **b,** and rise up to help me!
91: 4 his faithfulness is a shield and **b.**
Jer 46: 3 Prepare **b** and shield, and advance for battle!
Eze 23:24 against you on every side with **b,**
38: 4 a great company, all of them with shield and **b,**
38: 5 all of them with **b** and helmet;

BUCKLERS (2) [BUCKLER]

SS 4: 4 hang a thousand **b,** all of them shields of warriors.
Eze 39: 9 **b** and shields, bows and arrows,

BUCKLERS (KJV) See also SHIELDS

BUD (3) [BUDDED, BUDS, ROSEBUDS]

Ex 9:31 for the barley was in the ear and the flax was in **b.**
Job 14: 9 the scent of water it will **b** and put forth branches
Sir 24:17 Like the vine I **b** forth delights,

BUDDED (5) [BUD]

Ge 40:10 As soon as it **b,** its blossoms came out and
SS 6:11 to see whether the vines had **b,**
7:12 and see whether the vines have **b,**
Eze 7:10 The rod has blossomed, pride has **b.**
Heb 9: 4 Aaron's rod that **b,** and the tablets of the covenant;

BUDS (1) [BUD]

Nu 17: 8 It put forth **b,** produced blossoms,

BUFFET (KJV) See STRIKE, TORMENT

BUFFETED (1)

4Mc 7: 2 and though **b** by the stormings of the tyrant

BUGATHAN (1)

AdE 7: 9 Then **B,** one of the eunuchs, said to the king,

BUGLE (1)

1Co 14: 8 And if the **b** gives an indistinct sound,

BUILD‡ (171) [BUILDER, BUILDERS, BUILDING, BUILDINGS, BUILDS, BUILT, REBUILD, REBUILDING, REBUILT, UPBUILDING]

Ge 11: 4 Then they said, "Come, let us **b** ourselves a city,
Ex 20:25 do not **b** it of hewn stones;
Nu 23: 1 Balaam said to Balak, **"B** me seven altars here,
23:29 Balaam said to Balak, **"B** me seven altars here,
32:16 "We will **b** sheepfolds here for our flocks,
32:24 **B** towns for your little ones,
Dt 6:10 a land with fine, large cities that you did not **b,**
22: 8 When you **b** a new house,
25: 9 to the man who does not **b** up his brother's house."
27: 5 you shall **b** an altar there to the LORD your God,
27: 6 You must **b** the altar of the LORD your God
28:30 You shall **b** a house, but not live in it.
Jos 6:26 the LORD be anyone who tries to **b** this city—
22:26 Therefore we said, 'Let us now **b** an altar,
Jdg 6:26 and **b** an altar to the LORD your God on the top
1Sa 2:35 I will **b** him a sure house,
2Sa 7: 5 Are you the one to **b** me a house to live in?
7:13 He shall **b** a house for my name,
7:27 saying, 'I will **b** you a house';
24:21 "To buy the threshing floor from you in order to **b**
1Ki 2:36 and said to him, **"B** yourself a house in Jerusalem,
5: 3 not **b** a house for the name of the LORD his God
5: 5 to **b** a house for the name of the LORD my God,
5: 5 shall **b** the house for my name.'
5:18 and prepared the timber and the stone to **b**
6: 1 he began to **b** the house of the LORD.
8:16 a city from any of the tribes of Israel in which to **b**
8:17 in mind to **b** a house for the name of the LORD,
8:19 nevertheless you shall not **b** the house,
8:19 be born to you shall **b** the house for my name.'
9: 1 the king's house and all that Solomon desired to **b,**
9:15 to **b** the house of the LORD and his own house,
9:19 and whatever Solomon desired to **b,** in Jerusalem,
11:38 and will **b** you an enduring house,
2Ki 6: 2 and **b** a place there for us to live."
16:11 just so did the priest Uriah **b** it,
1Ch 14: 1 and masons and carpenters to **b** a house for him.
17: 4 You shall not **b** me a house to live in.
17:10 to you that the LORD will **b** you a house.
17:12 He shall **b** a house for me,
17:25 to your servant that you will **b** a house for him;
21:22 of the threshing floor that I may **b** on it an altar to
22: 6 for his son Solomon and charged him to **b** a house
22: 7 to **b** a house to the name of the LORD my God.
22: 8 you shall not **b** a house to my name,
22:10 He shall **b** a house for my name.
22:19 Go and **b** the sanctuary of the LORD God so that
28: 2 to **b** a house of rest for the ark of the covenant of
28: 3 'You shall not **b** a house for my name,
28: 6 'It is your son Solomon who shall **b** my house
28:10 for the LORD has chosen you to **b** a house as
29:19 and that he may **b** the temple
2Ch 2: 1 Solomon decided to **b** a temple for the name of
2: 3 and sent him cedar to **b** himself a house to live in.
2: 4 to **b** a house for the name of the LORD my God
2: 5 The house that I am about to **b** will be great,
2: 6 But who is able to **b** him a house, since heaven,
2: 6 Who am I to **b** a house for him,
2: 9 house I am about to **b** will be great and wonderful.
2:12 who will **b** a temple for the LORD,
3: 1 Solomon began to **b** the house of the LORD
3: 2 to **b** on the second day of the second month of
6: 5 a city from any of the tribes of Israel in which to **b**
6: 7 in mind to **b** a house for the name of the LORD,
6: 9 nevertheless you shall not **b** the house,
6: 9 be born to you shall **b** the house for my name.'
8: 6 and whatever Solomon desired to **b,** in Jerusalem,
14: 7 He said to Judah, "Let us **b** these cities,
36:23 he has charged me to **b** him a house at Jerusalem,
Ezr 1: 2 the earth, and he has charged me to **b** him a house
3: 2 of Shealtiel with his kin set out to **b** the altar of
4: 2 of families and said to them, "Let us **b** with you,
4: 3 but we alone will **b** to the LORD,
4: 4 and made them afraid to **b,**
5: 3 "Who gave you a decree to **b** this house and
5: 9 'Who gave you a decree to **b** this house and
Job 20:19 they have seized a house that they did not **b.**
27:18 They **b** their houses like nests,
30:12 they send me sprawling, and **b** roads for my ruin.
Ps 28: 5 he will break them down and **b** them up no more.
89: 4 and **b** your throne for all generations.' "
102:16 LORD will **b** up Zion; he will appear in his glory.
104:17 In them the birds **b** their nests;
127: 1 those who **b** it labor in vain.
Pr 24:27 and after that **b** your house.
Ecc 3: 3 a time to break down, and a time to **b** up;
SS 8: 9 we will **b** upon her a battlement of silver;
Isa 9:10 but we will **b** with dressed stones;
45:13 he shall **b** my city and set my exiles free,
57:14 It shall be said, **"B** up, **b** up, prepare the way,
60:10 Foreigners shall **b** up your walls,
61: 4 They shall **b** up the ancient ruins,
62:10 **b** up, **b** up the highway, clear it of stones,
65:21 They shall **b** houses and inhabit them;
65:22 They shall not **b** and another inhabit;
66: 1 what is the house that you would **b** for me,
Jer 1:10 to destroy and to overthrow, to **b** and to plant."
18: 9 a nation or a kingdom that I will **b** and plant it,
22:14 "I will **b** myself a spacious house
24: 6 I will **b** them up, and not tear them down;
29: 5 **B** houses and live in them;
Jer 29:28 **b** houses and live in them,
31: 4 Again I will **b** you, and you shall be built,
31:28 so I will watch over them to **b** and to plant,
35: 7 nor shall you ever **b** a house, or sow seed;
35: 9 and not to **b** houses to live in.
42:10 then I will **b** you up and not pull you down;
Eze 4: 2 and **b** a siege wall against it,
11: 3 'The time is not near to **b** houses;
13:10 and because, when the people **b** a wall,
21:22 to cast up ramps, to **b** siege towers.
28:26 and shall **b** houses and plant vineyards.
Hos 2: 6 and I will **b** a wall against her,
Mic 3:10 who **b** Zion with blood and Jerusalem with wrong!
Hab 2:12 "Alas for you who **b** a town by bloodshed,
Zep 1:13 Though they **b** houses, they shall not inhabit them;
Hag 1: 8 Go up to the hills and bring wood and **b** the house,
Zec 5:11 "To the land of Shinar, to **b** a house for it;
6:12 and he shall **b** the temple of the LORD.
6:13 It is he that shall **b** the temple of the LORD;
6:15 Those who are far off shall come and help to **b**
Mal 1: 4 They may **b,** but I will tear down,
Mt 16:18 you are Peter, and on this rock I will **b** my church,
23:29 For you **b** the tombs of the prophets and decorate
26:61 'I am able to destroy the temple of God and to **b** it
27:40 "You who would destroy the temple and **b** it
Mk 14:58 and in three days I will **b** another,
15:29 You who would destroy the temple and **b** it
Lk 11:47 For you **b** the tombs of
11:48 for they killed them, and you **b** their tombs.
12:18 I will pull down my barns and **b** larger ones,
14:28 For which of you, intending to **b** a tower,
14:30 'This fellow began to **b** and was not able
Ac 7:49 What kind of house will you **b** for me,
20:32 a message that is able to **b** you up and to give you
Ro 15:20 so that I do not **b** on someone else's foundation,
1Co 3:10 Each builder must choose with care how to **b** on it.
10:23 "All things are lawful," but not all things **b** up.
14: 4 Those who speak in a tongue **b** up themselves,
14: 4 but those who prophesy **b** up the church.
Gal 2:18 I **b** up again the very things that I once tore down,
1Th 5:11 encourage one another and **b** up each other,
Jude 1:20 beloved, **b** yourselves up on your most holy faith;
Wis 9: 8 You have given command to **b** a temple
Sir 40:26 Riches and strength **b** up confidence,
47:13 so that he might **b** a house in his name and provide
49: 7 and likewise to **b** and to plant.
1Mc 1:47 to **b** altars and sacred precincts and shrines
10:11 the work to **b** the walls and encircle Mount Zion
12:35 the people and planned with them to **b** strongholds
12:36 to **b** the walls of Jerusalem still higher,
15:39 to **b** up Kedron and fortify its gates,
2Mc 14:33 and **b** here a splendid temple to Dionysus."
1Es 2: 4 and he has commanded me to **b** him a house
2: 5 and **b** the house of the Lord of Israel—
2: 8 to go up to **b** the house in Jerusalem for the Lord;
4: 8 if he tells them to **b,** they **b;**
4:43 on the day when you became king, to **b** Jerusalem,
4:45 You also vowed to **b** the temple,
4:47 to all who were going up with him to **b** Jerusalem.
4:48 and to help him **b** the city.
4:53 and that all who came from Babylonia to **b**
4:63 up and **b** Jerusalem and the temple that is called
5:68 the ancestral houses and said to them, "We will **b**
5:71 for we alone will **b** it for the Lord of Israel,
6: 2 of Jozadak began to **b** the house of the Lord that is
6:27 of the Jews to **b** this house of the Lord on its site.
2Es 3:24 You commanded him to **b** a city for your name,

BUILDER (11) [BUILD]

Isa 62: 5 so shall your **b** marry you,
1Co 3:10 like a skilled master **b** I laid a foundation,
3:10 Each **b** must choose with care how to build on it.
3:13 the work of each **b** will become visible,
3:14 the **b** will receive a reward.
3:15 If the work is burned up, the **b** will suffer loss;
3:15 the **b** will be saved, but only as through fire.
Heb 3: 3 just as the **b** of a house has more honor than
3: 4 but the **b** of all things is God.)
11:10 whose architect and **b** is God.
2Mc 2:29 as the master **b** of a new house must be concerned

BUILDERS (19) [BUILD]

1Ki 5:18 So Solomon's **b** and Hiram's **b** and
2Ki 12:11 and the **b** who worked on the house of the LORD,
22: 6 to the carpenters, to the **b,** to the masons;
2Ch 34:11 to the carpenters and the **b** to buy quarried stone,
Ezr 3:10 **b** laid the foundation of the temple of the LORD,
Ne 4: 5 for they have hurled insults in the face of the **b.**
4:18 of the **b** had his sword strapped at his side
Ps 118:22 the **b** rejected has become the chief cornerstone.
Isa 49:17 Your **b** outdo your destroyers,
Eze 27: 4 your **b** made perfect your beauty.
Mt 21:42 that the **b** rejected has become the cornerstone;
Mk 12:10 that the **b** rejected has become the cornerstone;
Lk 20:17 that the **b** rejected has become the cornerstone'?
Ac 4:11 the **b;** it has become the cornerstone.'
1Pe 2: 7 that the **b** rejected has become the very head of
1Es 2:30 and began to hinder the **b.**
5:58 So the **b** built the temple of the Lord.
6: 4 And who are the **b** that are finishing these things?"

BUILDING (91) [BUILD]

Ge 11: 8 and they left off **b** the city.
Dt 20:20 in **b** siegeworks against the town that makes war
Jos 22:16 by **b** yourselves an altar today in rebellion against
Jos 22:19 the LORD, or rebel against us by **b** yourselves
22:23 for **b** an altar to turn away from following
22:29 the LORD by **b** an altar for burnt offering,
1Ki 3: 1 of David, until he had finished **b** his own house
6:12 "Concerning this house that you are **b,**
6:38 He was seven years in **b** it.
7: 1 Solomon was **b** his own house thirteen years,
8:18 'You did well to consider **b** a house for my name;
9: 1 When Solomon had finished **b** the house of
15:21 he stopped **b** Ramah and lived in Tirzah.
15:22 with which Baasha had been **b;**
1Ch 22: 2 to prepare dressed stones for **b** the house of God.
22:11 so that you may succeed in **b** the house of
28: 2 and I made preparations for **b.**
29:16 all this abundance that we have provided for **b** you
2Ch 3: 3 These are Solomon's measurements for **b**
6: 8 'You did well to consider **b** a house for my name;
16: 5 When Baasha heard of it, he stopped **b** Ramah,
16: 6 with which Baasha had been **b,**
20:36 He joined him in **b** ships to go to Tarshish;
27: 3 and did extensive **b** on the wall of Ophel.
Ezr 2:69 to the **b** fund sixty-one thousand darics of gold,
4: 1 the returned exiles were **b** a temple to the LORD,
4: 3 "You shall have no part with us in **b** a house
5: 4 the names of the men who are **b** this **b?"**
6:14 They finished their **b** by command of the God
Ne 2:18 Then they said, "Let us start **b!"**
2:20 and we his servants are going to start **b;**
4: 1 when Sanballat heard that we were **b** the wall,
4: 3 and he said, "That stone wall they are **b—**
4:17 who were **b** the wall.
6: 6 that is why you are **b** the wall;
7:71 into the **b** fund twenty thousand darics of gold
Ps 144:12 cut for the **b** of a palace.
Ecc 9:14 **b** great siegeworks against it.
Jer 7:31 And they go on **b** the high place of Topheth,
19: 5 on **b** the high places of Baal to burn their children
Eze 16:31 **b** your platform at the head of every street,
41:12 The **b** that was facing the temple yard on
41:12 the wall of the **b** was five cubits thick all around,
41:13 and the yard and the **b** with its walls,
41:15 the depth of the **b** facing the yard at the west,
42: 1 the temple yard and opposite the **b** on the north.
42: 2 The length of the **b** that was on
42: 5 from the lower and middle chambers in the **b.**
42:10 opposite the vacant area and opposite the **b,**
Mic 7:11 A day for the **b** of your walls!
Lk 6:48 That one is like a man **b** a house,
17:28 buying and selling, planting and **b,**
Ro 15: 2 for the good purpose of **b** up the neighbor.
1Co 3: 9 you are God's field, God's **b.**
3:10 and someone else is **b** on it.
14:12 strive to excel in them for **b** up the church.
14:26 Let all things be done for **b** up.
2Co 5: 1 we have a **b** from God, a house not made with
10: 8 the Lord gave for **b** you up and not for tearing you
12:19 beloved, is for the sake of **b** you up.
13:10 the authority that the Lord has given me for **b** up
Eph 4:12 for **b** up the body of Christ,
4:16 promotes the body's growth in **b** itself up in love.
4:29 but only what is useful for **b** up, as there is need,
1Pe 3:20 during the **b** of the ark, in which a few, that is,
Sir 22:16 A wooden beam firmly bonded into a **b** is
40:19 Children and the **b** of a city establish one's name,
1Mc 3:56 Those who were **b** houses,
16:23 and the **b** of the walls that he completed,
1Es 2:18 from you to us have gone to Jerusalem and are **b**
2:20 Since the **b** of the temple is now going on,
2:28 from **b** the city and to take care that nothing more
2:30 And the **b** of the temple in Jerusalem stopped until
4:51 that twenty talents a year should be given for the **b**
5:63 the **b** of this one with outcries and loud weeping,
5:67 from exile were **b** the temple for the Lord God
5:70 "You have nothing to do with us in **b** the house for
5:72 cut off their supplies, and hindered their **b;**
5:73 of the **b** as long as King Cyrus lived.
5:73 They were kept from **b** for two years,
6: 4 "By whose order are you **b** this house and this roof
6: 6 they were not prevented from **b** until word could
6: 9 **b** in the city of Jerusalem a great new house for
6:11 'At whose command are you **b** this house
6:22 if it is found that the **b** of the house of the Lord
6:24 the **b** of the house of the Lord in Jerusalem,
2Es 10:53 the field where there was no foundation of any **b,**
10:55 go in and see the splendor or the vastness of the **b,**
4Mc 14:15 the ones that are tame protect their young by **b** on
14:16 by **b** in precipitous chasms and in holes and tops

BUILDINGS (7) [BUILD]

Jdg 18:14 "Do you know that in these **b** there are an ephod,
2Ch 34:11 for the **b** that the kings of Judah had let go to ruin.
Jer 51:30 her **b** are set on fire, her bars are broken.
Mt 24: 1 his disciples came to point out to him the **b** of
Mk 13: 1 Teacher, what large stones and what large **b!"**
13: 2 Jesus asked him, "Do you see these great **b?**
Jdt 3: 3 our **b** and all our land and all our wheat fields

BUILDS (11) [BUILD]

Ps 127: 1 Unless the LORD **b** the house,
147: 2 The LORD **b** up Jerusalem;
Pr 14: 1 The wise woman **b** her house,
17:19 one who **b** a high threshold invites broken bones.
Jer 22:13 Woe to him who **b** his house by unrighteousness,
Am 9: 6 who **b** his upper chambers in the heavens,
1Co 3:12 Now if anyone **b** on the foundation with gold,

1Co 8: 1 Knowledge puffs up, but love **b** up.
Sir 21: 8 Whoever **b** his house with other people's money is
34:28 When one **b** and another tears down,
2Es 16:42 and let the one who **b** a house be like one who will

BUILT‡ (238) [BUILD]

Ge 4:17 and he **b** a city, and named it Enoch
8:20 Then Noah **b** an altar to the LORD,
10:11 and **b** Nineveh, Rehoboth-ir, Calah,
11: 5 to see the city and the tower, which mortals had **b**.
12: 7 So he **b** there an altar to the LORD,
12: 8 and there he **b** an altar to the LORD and invoked
13:18 and there he **b** an altar to the LORD.
22: 9 Abraham **b** an altar there and laid the wood
26:25 So he **b** an altar there,
33:17 **b** himself a house, and made booths for his cattle;
35: 7 there he **b** an altar and called the place El-bethel,
Ex 1:11 They **b** supply cities, Pithom and Rameses,
17:15 And Moses **b** an altar and called it,
24: 4 and **b** an altar at the foot of the mountain,
32: 5 When Aaron saw this, he **b** an altar before it;
Nu 13:22 (Hebron was **b** seven years before Zoan in Egypt.)
21:27 ballad singers say, "Come to Heshbon, let it be **b**;
23:14 He **b** seven altars, and offered a bull and a ram
Dt 8:12 and have **b** fine houses and live in them,
20: 5 "Has anyone **b** a new house but not dedicated it?
Jos 8:30 Joshua **b** on Mount Ebal an altar to the LORD,
22:10 the Gadites and the half-tribe of Manasseh **b** there
22:11 the Gadites and the half-tribe of Manasseh had **b**
24:13 and towns that you had not **b**,
Jdg 1:26 man went to the land of the Hittites and **b** a city,
6:24 Then Gideon **b** an altar there to the LORD,
6:28 on the altar that had been **b**.
21: 4 the people got up early, and **b** an altar there,
Ru 4:11 who together **b** up the house of Israel.
1Sa 7:17 and **b** there an altar to the LORD.
14:35 And Saul **b** an altar to the LORD;
14:35 it was the first altar that he **b** to the LORD.
2Sa 5: 9 David **b** the city all around from the Millo inward.
5:11 and carpenters and masons who **b** David a house.
7: 7 "Why have you not **b** me a house of cedar?"
24:25 David **b** there an altar to the LORD,
1Ki 3: 2 because no house had yet been **b** for the name of
6: 2 The house that King Solomon **b** for the LORD
6: 5 He also **b** a structure against the wall of the house,
6: 7 The house was **b** with stone finished at the quarry,
6: 7 in the temple while it was being **b**.
6: 9 So he **b** the house, and finished it;
6:10 He **b** the structure against the whole house,
6:14 So Solomon **b** the house, and finished it.
6:16 He **b** twenty cubits of the rear of the house
6:16 and he **b** this within as an inner sanctuary,
6:36 He **b** the inner court with three courses
7: 2 He **b** the House of the Forest of the Lebanon
7: 2 **b** on four rows of cedar pillars,
8:13 I have **b** you an exalted house,
8:20 and have **b** the house for the name of the LORD,
8:27 much less this house that I have **b**!
8:43 on this house that I have **b**.
8:44 that you have chosen and the house that I have **b**
8:48 and the house that I have **b** for your name;
9: 3 I have consecrated this house that you have **b**,
9:10 in which Solomon had **b** the two houses,
9:24 that Solomon had **b** for her; then he **b** the Millo.
9:25 of well-being on the altar that he **b** for the LORD,
9:26 King Solomon **b** a fleet of ships at Ezion-geber,
10: 4 the house that he had **b**,
11: 7 Then Solomon **b** a high place for Chemosh
11:27 Solomon **b** the Millo, and closed up the gap in
11:38 as I **b** for David, and I will give Israel to you.
12:25 Then Jeroboam **b** Shechem in the hill country
12:25 he went out from there and **b** Penuel.
14:23 For they also **b** for themselves high places, pillars,
15:17 up against Judah, and **b** Ramah, to prevent anyone
15:22 with them King Asa **b** Geba of Benjamin
15:23 all that he did, and the cities that he **b**,
16:24 he fortified the hill, and called the city that he **b**,
16:32 an altar for Baal in the house of Baal, which he **b**
16:34 In his days Hiel of Bethel **b** Jericho;
18:32 the stones he **b** an altar in the name of the LORD.
22:39 ivory house that he **b**, and all the cities that he **b**,
2Ki 15:35 He **b** the upper gate of the house of the LORD.
16:11 The priest Uriah **b** the altar;
16:18 on the sabbath that had been **b** inside the palace,
17: 9 They **b** for themselves high places
21: 4 He **b** altars in the house of the LORD,
21: 5 He **b** altars for all the host of heaven in
23:13 which King Solomon of Israel had **b** for Astarte
25: 1 they **b** siegeworks against it all around.
1Ch 6:10 in the house that Solomon **b** in Jerusalem).
6:32 until Solomon had **b** the house of the LORD
7:24 who **b** both Lower and Upper Beth-horon,
8:12 and Shemed, who **b** Ono and Lod with its towns,
11: 8 He **b** the city all around, from the Millo
15: 1 David **b** houses for himself in the city of David,
17: 6 saying, Why have you not **b** me a house of cedar?
21:26 David **b** there an altar to the LORD
22: 5 and the house that is to be **b** for the LORD must
22:19 into a house **b** for the name of the LORD."
2Ch 6: 2 I have **b** you an exalted house,
6:10 and have **b** the house for the name of the LORD,
6:18 how much less this house that I have **b**!
6:33 on this house that I have **b**.
6:34 that you have chosen and the house that I have **b**
6:38 and the house that I have **b** for your name,
8: 1 during which Solomon had **b** the house of
2Ch 8: 4 He **b** Tadmor in the wilderness and all the storage
towns that he **b**
8: 5 also **b** Upper Beth-horon and Lower Beth-horon,
8:11 from the city of David to the house that he had **b**
8:12 on the altar of the LORD that he had **b** in front of
9: 3 the house that he had **b**,
11: 5 and he **b** cities for defense in Judah.
11: 6 He **b** up Bethlehem, Etam, Tekoa,
14: 6 He **b** fortified cities in Judah while
14: 7 So they **b** and prospered.
16: 1 up against Judah, and **b** Ramah, to prevent anyone
16: 6 and with them he **b** up Geba and Mizpah.
17:12 He **b** fortresses and storage cities in Judah.
20: 8 and in it have **b** you a sanctuary for your name,
20:36 they **b** the ships in Ezion-geber.
26: 6 he **b** cities in the territory of Ashdod
26: 9 Uzziah **b** towers in Jerusalem at the Corner Gate,
26:10 He **b** towers in the wilderness
27: 3 He **b** the upper gate of the house of the LORD,
27: 4 Moreover he **b** cities in the hill country of Judah,
32: 5 and **b** up the entire wall that was broken down,
32: 5 and outside it he **b** another wall;
33: 4 He **b** altars in the house of the LORD,
33: 5 He **b** altars for all the host of heaven in
33:14 Afterward he **b** an outer wall for the city
33:15 and all the altars that he had **b** on the mountain of
33:19 the sites on which he **b** high places and set up
35: 3 **b**; you need no longer carry it on your shoulders.
Ezr 5: 8 It is being **b** of hewn stone,
5:11 the house that was **b** many years ago,
5:11 which a great king of Israel **b** and finished.
6:14 So the elders of the Jews **b** and prospered,
Ne 3: 2 And the men of Jericho **b** next to him.
3: 2 And next to them Zaccur son of Imri **b**.
3: 3 The sons of Hassenaah **b** the Fish Gate;
3:15 and he **b** the wall of the Pool of Shelah of
4:18 at his side while he **b**.
6: 1 the Arab and to the rest of our enemies that I had **b**
7: 1 the wall had been **b** and I had set up the doors,
7: 4 within it were few and no houses had been **b**.
12:29 for the singers had **b** for themselves villages
Ps 78:69 He **b** his sanctuary like the high heavens,
122: 3 **b** as a city that is bound firmly together.
Pr 9: 1 Wisdom has **b** her house, she has hewn her seven
24: 3 By wisdom a house is **b**, and
Ecc 2: 4 I **b** houses and planted vineyards for myself;
SS 4: 4 Your neck is like the tower of David, **b** in courses;
Isa 5: 2 he **b** a watchtower in the midst of it,
Jer 12:16 then they shall be **b** up in the midst of my people.
31: 4 Again I will build you, and you shall be **b**,
32:31 from the day it was **b** until this day,
32:35 They **b** the high places of Baal in the valley of
45: 4 I am going to break down what I have **b**,
52: 4 they **b** siegeworks against it all around.
Eze 16:24 you **b** yourself a platform and made yourself
16:25 at the head of every street you **b** your lofty place
17:17 up and siege walls **b** to cut off many lives.
Da 4:30 which I have **b** as a royal capital
9:25 for sixty-two weeks it shall be **b** again with streets
Hos 8:14 Israel has forgotten his Maker, and **b** palaces;
10: 1 The more his fruit increased the more altars he **b**;
Am 5:11 you have **b** houses of hewn stone,
7: 7 the Lord was standing beside a wall **b** with
Zec 1:16 my house shall be **b** in it,
9: 3 Tyre has **b** itself a rampart,
Mt 5:14 A city **b** on a hill cannot be hid.
7:24 on them will be like a wise man who **b** his house
7:26 be like a foolish man who **b** his house on sand.
21:33 dug a wine press in it, and **b** a watchtower.
Mk 12: 1 dug a pit for the wine press, and **b** a watchtower;
Lk 4:29 to the brow of the hill on which their town was **b**,
6:48 could not shake it, because it had been well **b**.
6:49 not act is like a man who **b** a house on the ground
7: 5 and it is he who **b** our synagogue for us."
Ac 7:47 But it was Solomon who **b** a house for him.
9:31 Galilee, and Samaria had peace and was **b** up.
1Co 3:14 If what has been **b** on the foundation survives,
14: 5 so that the church may be **b** up.
14:17 but the other person is not **b** up.
Eph 2:20 **b** upon the foundation of the apostles
2:22 also are **b** together spiritually into a dwelling place
Col 2: 7 rooted and **b** up in him and established in the faith,
Heb 3: 4 (For every house is **b** by someone,
11: 7 the warning and **b** an ark to save his household;
1Pe 2: 5 let yourselves be **b** into a spiritual house,
Rev 21:18 The wall is **b** of jasper, while the city is pure gold,
Tob 13:16 For Jerusalem will be **b** as his house for all ages.
13:16 of Jerusalem will be **b** with sapphire and emerald,
13:16 The towers of Jerusalem will be **b** with gold,
Jdt 1: 2 He **b** walls around Ecbatana
Wis 14: 2 and wisdom was the artisan who **b** it;
Sir 48:17 and **b** cisterns for the water.
49:12 in their days they **b** the house and raised
1Mc 1:14 So they **b** a gymnasium in Jerusalem,
1:54 also **b** altars in the surrounding towns of Judah,
4:47 and **b** a new altar like the former one.
4:53 on the new altar of burnt offering that they had **b**.
6:20 and he **b** siege towers and other engines of war.
6:31 for many days they fought and **b** engines of war;
8:15 but they have **b** for themselves a senate chamber,
9:50 to Jerusalem and **b** strong cities in Judea:
10:12 in the strongholds that Bacchides had **b** fled;
11:20 and he **b** many engines of war to use against it.
12:38 Simon also **b** Adida in the Shephelah;
13:27 And Simon **b** a monument over the tomb
13:30 This is the tomb that he **b** in Modein;
13:33 But Simon **b** up the strongholds of Judea
1Mc 13:38 and let the strongholds that you have **b**
13:48 He also strengthened its fortifications and **b** in it
14:36 who had **b** themselves a citadel
14:37 and **b** the walls of Jerusalem higher.
15: 7 that you have **b** and now hold shall remain yours.
15:41 He **b** up Kedron and stationed horsemen
16: 9 until Cendebeus reached Kedron, which he had **b**.
16:15 the little stronghold called Dok, which he had **b**;
2Mc 1:18 who **b** the temple and the altar, offered sacrifices.
10: 2 the altars that had been **b** in the public square by
1Es 1: 3 that King Solomon, son of David, had **b**;
2:19 Now if this city is **b** and the walls finished,
2:24 that if this city is **b** and its walls finished,
4:55 the temple would be finished and Jerusalem **b**.
5:53 though the temple of God was not yet **b**.
5:58 So the builders **b** the temple of the Lord.
6:14 The house was **b** many years ago by a king
6:28 "And I command that it be **b** completely,
3Mc 4:11 that had been **b** with a monstrous perimeter wall
2Es 5:25 that have been **b** you have consecrated Zion
7: 6 There is a city **b** and set on a plain,
8:52 plenty is provided, a city is **b**, rest is appointed,
9:24 into a field of flowers where no house has been **b**,
10:27 but a city was being **b**,
10:42 but there appeared to you a city being **b**)
10:44 which you now behold as a city being **b**.
10:46 And after three thousand years Solomon **b** the city,
10:51 to remain in the field where no house had been **b**,
13:36 be made manifest to all people, prepared and **b**,

BUKKI (6)

Nu 34:22 Of the tribe of the Danites a leader, **B** son of Jogli.
1Ch 6: 5 Abishua of **B**, **B** of Uzzi,
6:51 **B** his son, Uzzi his son, Zerahiah his son,
Ezr 7: 4 son of Zerahiah, son of Uzzi, son of **B**,
1Es 8: 2 of **B** son of Abishua son of Phineas son

BUKKIAH (2)

1Ch 25: 4 Of Heman, the sons of Heman: **B**, Mattaniah,
25:13 the sixth to **B**, his sons and his brothers, twelve;

BUL (1)

1Ki 6:38 In the eleventh year, in the month of **B**,

BULGING (1)

Isa 30:13 **b** out, and about to collapse,

BULL (101) [BULLS]

Ex 29: 1 Take one young **b** and two rams without blemish,
29: 3 and bring the **b** and the two rams.
29:10 You shall bring the **b** in front of the tent
29:10 on the head of the **b**,
29:11 and you shall slaughter the **b** before the LORD,
29:12 and shall take some of the blood of the **b** and put it
29:14 But the flesh of the **b**, and its skin, and its dung,
29:36 Also every day you shall offer a **b** as a sin offering
Lev 1: 5 The **b** shall be slaughtered before the LORD;
4: 3 a **b** of the herd without blemish as a sin offering to
4: 4 the **b** to the entrance of the tent of meeting before
the LORD and lay his hand on the head of the **b**;
the **b** shall be slaughtered before the LORD.
4: 5 of the blood of the **b** and bring it into the tent
4: 7 and the rest of the blood of the **b** he shall pour out
4: 8 He shall remove all the fat from the **b**
4:11 But the skin of the **b** and all its flesh,
4:12 all the rest of the **b**—
4:14 a **b** of the herd for a sin offering and bring it
4:15 on the head of the **b** before the LORD,
4:15 and the **b** shall be slaughtered before the LORD.
4:16 of the blood of the **b** into the tent of meeting,
4:20 He shall do with the **b** just as is done with the **b**
4:21 He shall carry the **b** outside the camp,
4:21 and burn it as he burned the first **b**;
8: 2 the anointing oil, the **b** of sin offering,
8:14 He led forward the **b** of sin offering;
8:14 upon the head of the **b** of sin offering,
8:17 But the **b** itself, its skin and flesh and its dung,
9: 2 "Take a **b** calf for a sin offering and a ram for
16: 3 with a young **b** for a sin offering and a ram for
16: 6 Aaron shall offer the **b** as a sin offering
16:11 Aaron shall present the **b** as a sin offering
16:11 he shall slaughter the **b** as a sin offering
16:14 He shall take some of the blood of the **b**,
16:15 do with its blood as he did with the blood of the **b**,
16:18 of the blood of the **b** and of the blood of the goat,
16:27 The **b** of the sin offering and the goat of
23:18 one young **b**, and two rams;
Nu 7:15 one young **b**, one ram, one male lamb a year old,
7:21 one young **b**, one ram, one male lamb a year old,
7:27 one young **b**, one ram, one male lamb a year old,
7:33 one young **b**, one ram, one male lamb a year old,
7:39 one young **b**, one ram, one male lamb a year old,
7:45 one young **b**, one ram, one male lamb a year old,
7:51 one young **b**, one ram, one male lamb a year old,
7:57 one young **b**, one ram, one male lamb a year old,
7:63 one young **b**, one ram, one male lamb a year old,
7:69 one young **b**, one ram, one male lamb a year old,
7:75 one young **b**, one ram, one male lamb a year old,
7:81 one young **b**, one ram, one male lamb a year old,
8: 8 Then let them take a young **b** and its grain offering
8: 8 you shall take another young **b** for a sin offering.
15: 8 you offer a **b** as a burnt offering or a sacrifice,
15: 9 then you shall present with the **b** a grain offering,
15:24 the whole congregation shall offer one young **b** for

Nu 23: 2 and Balaam offered a **b** and a ram on each altar.
23: 4 and have offered a **b** and a ram on each altar."
23:14 and offered a **b** and a ram on each altar.
23:30 and offered a **b** and a ram on each altar.
28:12 mixed with oil, for each **b;**
28:14 be half a hin of wine for a **b,**
28:20 three-tenths of an ephah shall you offer for a **b,**
28:28 three-tenths of an ephah for each **b,**
29: 2 one young **b,** one ram, seven male lambs
29: 3 three-tenths of one ephah for the **b,**
29: 8 one young **b,** one ram, seven male lambs
29: 9 three-tenths of an ephah for the **b,**
29:36 one **b,** one ram, seven male lambs a year old
29:37 the grain offering and the drink offerings for the **b,**
Dt 33:17 A firstborn **b**— majesty is his!
Jdg 6:25 the LORD said to him, "Take your father's **b,**
6:25 the second **b** seven years old,
6:26 the second **b,** and offer it as a burnt offering with
6:28 and the second **b** was offered on the altar
1Sa 1:24 along with a three-year-old **b,** an ephah of flour,
1:25 Then they slaughtered the **b,**
1Ki 18:23 let them choose one **b** for themselves,
18:23 I will prepare the other **b** and lay it on the wood,
18:25 "Choose for yourselves one **b** and prepare it first,
18:26 So they took the **b** that was given them,
18:33 Next he put the wood in order, cut the **b** in pieces,
2Ch 13: 9 Whoever comes to be consecrated with a young **b**
Job 21:10 Their **b** breeds without fail;
Ps 50: 9 I will not accept a **b** from your house,
69:31 the LORD more than an ox or a **b** with horns
Isa 10:13 a **b** I have brought down those who sat on thrones.
Jer 46:15 Why did your **b** not stand?
Eze 43:19 says the Lord GOD, a **b** for a sin offering.
43:21 You shall also take the **b** of the sin offering,
43:22 as it was purified with the **b.**
43:23 you shall offer a **b** without blemish and a ram
43:25 also a **b** and a ram from the flock,
45:18 you shall take a young **b** without blemish,
45:22 the people of the land a young **b** for a sin offering.
45:24 as a grain offering an ephah for each **b,**
46: 6 the day of the new moon he shall offer a young **b**
46: 7 an ephah with the **b** and an ephah with the ram,
46:11 the grain offering with a young **b** shall be
Sir 6: 2 or you may be torn apart as by a **b.**

BULLOCK (KJV) See BULL, CALF, OX

BULLS‡ (63) [BULL]

Ge 32:15 forty cows and ten **b,** twenty female donkeys
Nu 7:87 all the livestock for the burnt offering twelve **b,**
7:88 for the sacrifice of well-being twenty-four **b,**
8:12 Levites shall lay their hands on the heads of the **b,**
23: 1 and prepare seven **b** and seven rams for me."
23:29 and prepare seven **b** and seven rams for me."
28:11 two young **b,** one ram, seven male lambs
28:19 two young **b,** one ram, and seven male lambs
28:27 two young **b,** one ram, seven male lambs
29:13 thirteen young **b,** two rams,
29:14 three-tenths of an ephah for each of the thirteen **b,**
29:17 On the second day: twelve young **b,** two rams,
29:18 the grain offering and the drink offerings for the **b,**
29:20 On the third day: eleven **b,** two rams,
29:21 the grain offering and the drink offerings for the **b,**
29:23 On the fourth day: ten **b,** two rams,
29:24 the grain offering and the drink offerings for the **b,**
29:26 On the fifth day: nine **b,** two rams,
29:27 the grain offering and the drink offerings for the **b,**
29:29 On the sixth day: eight **b,** two rams,
29:30 the grain offering and the drink offerings for the **b,**
29:32 On the seventh day: seven **b,** two rams,
29:33 the grain offering and the drink offerings for the **b,**
Dt 32:14 **b** and goats, together with the choicest wheat—
1Ki 18:23 Let two **b** be given to us;
1Ch 15:26 they sacrificed seven **b** and seven rams.
29:21 a thousand **b,** a thousand rams,
2Ch 29:21 They brought seven **b,** seven rams, seven lambs,
29:22 So they slaughtered the **b,**
29:32 that the assembly brought was seventy **b,**
29:33 The consecrated offerings were six hundred **b**
30:24 of Judah gave the assembly a thousand **b**
30:24 the assembly a thousand **b** and ten thousand sheep.
35: 7 of thirty thousand, and three thousand **b;**
35: 8 and kids and three hundred **b.**
35: 9 and kids and five hundred **b.**
35:12 And they did the same with the **b.**
Ezr 6: 9 Whatever is needed—young **b,** rams,
6:17 the dedication of this house of God one hundred **b,**
7:17 then, you shall with all diligence buy **b,** rams,
8:35 twelve **b** for all Israel, ninety-six rams,
Job 42: 8 Now therefore take seven **b** and seven rams,
Ps 22:12 Many **b** encircle me, strong **b** of Bashan surround
50:13 Do I eat the flesh of **b,**
51:19 then **b** will be offered on your altar.
66:15 I will make an offering of **b** and goats.
68:30 the herd of **b** with the calves of the peoples.
Isa 1:11 I do not delight in the blood of **b,** or of lambs,
34: 7 and young steers with the mighty **b.**
Jer 50:27 Kill all her **b,** let them go down to the slaughter.
52:20 the twelve bronze **b** that were under the sea,
Eze 39:18 of rams, of lambs, and of goats, of **b,**
45:23 as a burnt offering to the LORD seven young **b**
Hos 12:11 In Gilgal they sacrifice **b,**
Heb 9:13 For if the blood of goats and **b,**
10: 4 For it is impossible for the blood of **b** and goats
Sir 38:25 and whose talk is about **b?**
Aza 1:17 though it were with burnt offerings of rams and **b,**
1Es 6:29 for **b** and rams and lambs,
7: 7 of the temple of the Lord one hundred **b,**
8:14 and silver for **b** and rams and lambs and what goes
8:65 the God of Israel, twelve **b** for all Israel,

BULRUSH (1) [RUSHES]

Isa 58: 5 Is it to bow down the head like a **b,**

BULWARK (3) [BULWARKS]

Ps 8: 2 of babes and infants you have founded a **b** because
1Ti 3:15 the pillar and **b** of the truth.
4Mc 13:13 and let us use our bodies as a **b** for the law.

BULWARKS (2) [BULWARK]

Isa 26: 1 he sets up victory like walls and **b.**
Jer 50:15 her **b** have fallen, her walls are thrown down."

BUNAH (1)

1Ch 2:25 Ram his firstborn, **B,** Oren, Ozem, and Ahijah.

BUNCH (1) [BUNCHES]

Ex 12:22 Take a **b** of hyssop, dip it in the blood that is in

BUNCHES (1) [BUNCH]

2Sa 16: 1 of bread, one hundred **b** of raisins, one hundred

BUNDLE (6) [BUNDLES]

Jdg 9:48 cut down a **b** of brushwood,
9:49 down a **b** and following Abimelech put it against
1Sa 25:29 be bound in the **b** of the living under the care of
Jer 10:17 Gather up your **b** from the ground,
Ac 28: 3 a **b** of brushwood and was putting it on the fire,
Sir 21: 9 An assembly of the wicked is like a **b** of tow,

BUNDLES (3) [BUNDLE]

Ge 42:35 When they and their father saw their **b** of money,
Ru 2:16 also pull out some handfuls for her from the **b,**
Mt 13:30 the weeds first and bind them in **b** to be burned,

BUNGLER (1)

Ecc 9:18 but one **b** destroys much good.

BUNNI (3)

Ne 9: 4 Then Jeshua, Bani, Kadmiel, Shebaniah, **B,**
10:15 **B,** Azgad, Bebai,
11:15 of Azrikam son of Hashabiah son of **B;**

BURDEN‡ (51) [BURDENED, BURDENING, BURDENS, BURDENSOME]

Ge 49:15 so he bowed his shoulder to the **b,**
Ex 18:22 and they will bear the **b** with you.
23: 5 the donkey of one who hates you lying under its **b**
Nu 4:19 in and assign each to a particular task or **b.**
11:11 that you lay the **b** of all this people on me?
11:17 the **b** of the people along with you so that you will
Dt 1:12 how can I bear the heavy **b** of your disputes all
2Sa 15:33 "If you go on with me, you will be a **b** to me.
19:35 then should your servant be an added **b** to my lord
2Ch 34:13 over the **b** bearers and directed all who did work
Ne 4:10 "The strength of the **b** bearers is failing,
4:17 The **b** bearers carried their loads in such a way
5:18 because of the heavy **b** of labor on the people.
13:19 to prevent any **b** from being brought in on
Job 7:20 Why have I become a **b** to you?
Ps 38: 4 they weigh like a **b** too heavy for me.
55:22 Cast your **b** on the LORD,
81: 6 "I relieved your shoulder of the **b;**
Isa 1:14 they have become a **b** to me,
9: 4 For the yoke of their **b,**
10:27 that day his **b** will be removed from your shoulder,
14:25 and his **b** from their shoulders.
46: 2 they cannot save the **b,** but themselves go
Jer 17:21 of your lives, take care that you do not bear a **b** on
17:22 not carry a **b** out of your houses on the sabbath
17:24 in no **b** by the gates of this city on the sabbath day,
17:27 and to carry in no **b** through the gates of Jerusalem
23:33 "What is the **b** of the LORD?"
23:33 you shall say to them, "You are the **b,**
23:34 or the people who say, "The **b** of the LORD,"
23:36 "the **b** of the LORD" you shall mention no more,
23:36 for the **b** is everyone's own word,
23:38 But if you say, "the **b** of the LORD,"
23:38 you have said these words, "the **b** of the LORD,"
23:38 saying, You shall not say, "the **b** of the LORD,"
Hos 8:10 They shall soon writhe under the **b** of kings
Mt 11:30 For my yoke is easy, and my **b** is light."
20:12 to us who have borne the **b** of the day and
Ac 15:28 on you no further **b** than these essentials:
2Co 5: 4 we are still in this tent, we groan under our **b,**
11: 9 I did not **b** anyone, for my needs were supplied by
12:13 except that I myself did not **b** you?
12:14 And I will not be a **b,**
12:16 Let it be assumed that I did not **b** you.
1Th 2: 9 not **b** any of you while we proclaimed to you
2Th 3: 8 so that we might not **b** any of you.
Rev 2:24 to you I say, I do not lay on you any other **b;**
Wis 2:15 the very sight of him is a **b** to us,
Sir 21:16 A fool's chatter is like a **b** on a journey,
1Es 8:86 For you, O Lord, lifted the **b** of our sins
2Es 7:*105* neither shall anyone lay a **b** on another;

BURDENED (7) [BURDEN]

Pr 28:17 If someone is **b** with the blood of another,
Isa 43:23 I have not **b** you with offerings,
43:24 But you have **b** me with your sins;
1Ti 5:16 let the church not be **b,**
Sir 3:27 A stubborn mind will be **b** by troubles,
2Es 3:21 For the first Adam, **b** with an evil heart,
7:*68* and are full of sins and **b** with transgressions.

BURDENING (1) [BURDEN]

2Co 11: 9 and will continue to refrain from **b** you

BURDENS (15) [BURDEN]

Ex 6: 6 and I will free you from the **b** of the Egyptians
6: 7 who has freed you from the **b** of the Egyptians.
Nu 4:24 of the Gershonites, in serving and bearing **b:**
4:47 of service and the work of bearing **b** relating to
Ne 5:15 before me laid heavy **b** on the people,
13:15 and also wine, grapes, figs, and all kinds of **b,**
Ps 66:11 you laid **b** on our backs;
Isa 46: 1 these things you carry are loaded as **b**
Mt 11:28 all you that are weary and are carrying heavy **b,**
23: 4 They tie up heavy **b,** hard to bear,
Lk 11:46 For you load people with **b** hard to bear,
Gal 6: 2 Bear one another's **b,** and
Wis 9:15 and this earthy tent **b** the thoughtful mind.
Sir 33:25 Fodder and a stick and **b** for a donkey;
2Es 14:14 cast away from you the **b** of humankind,

BURDENSOME (3) [BURDEN]

2Sa 13:25 let us not all go, or else we will be **b** to you."
1Jn 5: 3 And his commandments are not **b,**
Sir 8:15 or they will be **b** to you;

BURIAL (22) [BURY]

Ge 23: 6 Bury your dead in the choicest of our **b** places;
23: 6 none of us will withhold from you any **b** ground
47:30 of Egypt and bury me in their **b** place."
49:30 from Ephron the Hittite as a **b** site.
50:13 which Abraham bought as a **b** site from Ephron
Dt 34: 6 but no one knows his **b** place to this day.
2Ch 26:23 near his ancestors in the **b** field that belonged to
Ecc 6: 3 not enjoy life's good things, or has no **b,**
Isa 14:20 You will not be joined with them in **b,**
Jer 22:19 With the **b** of a donkey he shall be buried—
26:23 the sword and threw his dead body into the **b** place
Eze 39:11 that day I will give to Gog a place for **b** in Israel,
Mt 26:12 on my body she has prepared me for **b.**
Mk 14: 8 she has anointed my body beforehand for its **b.**
Jn 12: 7 so that she might keep it for the day of my **b.**
19:40 according to the **b** custom of the Jews.
Heb 11:22 of the Israelites and gave instructions about his **b.**
Tob 4: 3 "My son, when I die, give me a proper **b.**
Sir 21: 8 like one who gathers stones for his **b** mound.
38:16 and do not neglect the **b.**
2Mc 13: 7 without even **b** in the earth.
3Mc 6:31 that had been prepared for their destruction and **b.**

BURIED‡ (122) [BURY]

Ge 15:15 you shall be **b** in a good old age.
23:19 Abraham **b** Sarah his wife in the cave of the field
25: 9 and Ishmael **b** him in the cave of Machpelah,
25:10 There Abraham was **b,** with his wife Sarah.
35: 8 died, and she was **b** under an oak below Bethel.
35:19 and she was **b** on the way to Ephrath (that is,
35:29 and his sons Esau and Jacob **b** him.
48: 7 and I **b** her there on the way to Ephrath" (that is,
49:31 Abraham and his wife Sarah were **b;** there Isaac
and his wife Rebekah were **b;** and there I **b** Leah—
50:13 They carried him to the land of Canaan and **b** him
50:14 After he had **b** his father,
Nu 11:34 there they **b** the people who had the craving.
20: 1 Miriam died there, and was **b** there.
Dt 10: 6 There Aaron died, and there he was **b;**
34: 6 He was **b** in a valley in the land of Moab,
Jos 24:30 They **b** him in his own inheritance
24:32 were **b** at Shechem, in the portion of ground
24:33 and they **b** him at Gibeah,
Jdg 2: 9 So they **b** him within the bounds of his inheritance
8:32 and was **b** in the tomb of his father Joash
10: 2 Then he died, and was **b** at Shamir.
10: 5 Jair died, and was **b** in Kamon.
12: 7 and was **b** in his town in Gilead.
12:10 Then Ibzan died, and was **b** at Bethlehem.
12:12 and was **b** at Aijalon in the land of Zebulun.
12:15 and was **b** at Pirathon in the land of Ephraim,
16:31 down and took him and brought him up and **b** him
Ru 1:17 Where you die, I will die—there will I be **b.**
1Sa 25: 1 They **b** him at his home in Ramah.
28: 3 and all Israel had mourned for him and **b** him
31:13 and **b** them under the tamarisk tree in Jabesh,
2Sa 2: 4 "It was the people of Jabesh-gilead who **b** Saul,"
2: 5 to Saul your lord, and **b** him!
2:32 up Asahel and **b** him in the tomb of his father,
3:32 They **b** Abner at Hebron.
4:12 of Ishbaal they took and **b** in the tomb of Abner
17:23 he died and was **b** in the tomb of his father.
21:14 They **b** the bones of Saul and of his son Jonathan
1Ki 2:10 and was **b** in the city of David.
2:34 and he was **b** at his own house near the wilderness.

1Ki 11:43 Solomon slept with his ancestors and was **b** in
13:31 After he had **b** him, he said to his sons,
13:31 in the grave in which the man of God is **b;**
14:18 All Israel **b** him and mourned for him,
14:31 with his ancestors and was **b** with his ancestors in
15: 8 and they **b** him in the city of David.
15:24 and was **b** with his ancestors in the city
16: 6 with his ancestors, and was **b** at Tirzah;
16:28 with his ancestors, and was **b** in Samaria;
22:37 they **b** the king in Samaria.
22:50 with his ancestors and was **b** with his ancestors in
2Ki 8:24 and was **b** with them in the city of David;
9:28 and **b** him in his tomb with his ancestors in
10:35 and they **b** him in Samaria.
12:21 He was **b** with his ancestors in the city of David;
13: 9 and they **b** him in Samaria;
13:13 Joash was **b** in Samaria with the kings of Israel.
13:20 So Elisha died, and they **b** him.
13:21 a man was being **b,** a marauding band was seen
14:16 and was **b** in Samaria with the kings of Israel;
14:20 he was **b** in Jerusalem with his ancestors in
15: 7 they **b** him with his ancestors in the city of David;
15:38 and was **b** with his ancestors in the city of David,
16:20 and was **b** with his ancestors in the city of David;
21:18 and was **b** in the garden of his house,
21:26 He was **b** in his tomb in the garden of Uzza;
23:30 and **b** him in his own tomb.
1Ch 10:12 Then they **b** their bones under the oak in Jabesh,
2Ch 9:31 Solomon slept with his ancestors and was **b** in
12:16 with his ancestors and was **b** in the city of David;
14: 1 and they **b** him in the city of David.
16:14 They **b** him in the tomb that he had hewn out
21: 1 with his ancestors and was **b** with his ancestors in
21:20 They **b** him in the city of David,
22: 9 They **b** him, for they said,
24:16 they **b** him in the city of David among the kings,
24:25 So he died; and they **b** him in the city of David,
25:28 he was **b** with his ancestors in the city of David.
26:23 they **b** him near his ancestors in the burial field
27: 9 and they **b** him in the city of David;
28:27 and they **b** him in the city, in Jerusalem;
32:33 and they **b** him on the ascent to the tombs of
33:20 and they **b** him in his house.
35:24 and was **b** in the tombs of his ancestors.
Job 3:16 Or why was I not **b** like a stillborn child,
Ecc 8:10 Then I saw the wicked **b;**
Jer 8: 2 and they shall not be gathered or **b;**
16: 4 They shall not be lamented, nor shall they be **b;**
16: 6 they shall not be **b,** and no one shall lament
20: 6 there you shall die, and there you shall be **b,**
22:19 With the burial of a donkey he shall be **b—**
25:33 They shall not be lamented, or gathered, or **b;**
43:10 above these stones that I have **b,**
Eze 29: 5 and not be gathered and **b.**
39:11 for there Gog and all his horde will be **b;**
39:15 the buriers have **b** it in the Valley of Hamon-gog.
Mt 14:12 His disciples came and took the body and **b** it;
Lk 16:22 The rich man also died and was **b.**
Ac 2:29 of our ancestor David that he both died and was **b,**
5: 6 then carried him out and **b** him.
5: 9 of those who have **b** your husband are at the door,
5:10 they carried her out and **b** her beside her husband.
8: 2 Devout men **b** Stephen and made loud lamentation
Ro 6: 4 we have been **b** with him by baptism into death,
1Co 15: 4 and that he was **b,** and that he was raised on
Col 2:12 when you were **b** with him in baptism,
Tob 1:18 I also **b** any whom King Sennacherib put to death
2: 7 the sun had set, I went and dug a grave and **b** him.
14: 2 and was **b** with great honor in Nineveh.
14:12 Tobias's mother died, he **b** her beside his father.
14:13 and **b** them in Ecbatana of Media.
Jdt 8: 3 So they **b** him with his ancestors in the field
16:23 they **b** her in the cave of her husband Manasseh;
Sir 44:14 Their bodies are **b** in peace.
1Mc 2:70 and was **b** in the tomb of his ancestors at Modein.
9:19 and Simon took their brother Judas and **b** him in
13:23 he killed Jonathan, and he was **b** there.
13:25 and **b** him in Modein, the city of his ancestors.
1Es 1:31 and was **b** in the tomb of his ancestors.
4Mc 17: 9 "Here lie **b** an aged priest and an aged woman

BURIERS (1) [BURY]

Eze 39:15 the **b** have buried it in the Valley of Hamon-gog.

BURIES (3) [BURY]

Job 27:15 Those who survive them the pestilence **b,**
Pr 19:24 The lazy person **b** a hand in the dish,
26:15 The lazy person **b** a hand in the dish,

BURLAP (1)

Sir 40: 4 and a crown to the one who is clothed in **b,**

BURN‡ (91) [BURNED, BURNED-OUT, BURNING, BURNS, BURNT, BURNT-OUT]

Ge 11: 3 let us make bricks, and **b** them thoroughly."
Ex 12:10 that remains until the morning you shall **b.**
21:25 **b** for **b,** wound for wound, stripe for stripe.
22:24 my wrath will **b,** and I will kill you with
27:20 so that a lamp may be set up to **b** regularly.
29:14 you shall **b** with fire outside the camp;
29:34 then you shall **b** the remainder with fire;
32:10 so that my wrath may **b** hot against them
32:11 why does your wrath **b** hot against your people,
32:22 Aaron said, "Do not let the anger of my lord **b** hot;
Lev 4:12 to the ash heap, and shall **b** it on a wood fire;
4:21 and **b** it as he burned the first bull;
8:32 of the flesh and the bread you shall **b** with fire.
13:24 the body has a **b** on the skin and the raw flesh of
the **b** becomes a spot,
13:25 it has broken out in the **b,**
13:28 it is a swelling from the **b,**
13:28 for it is the scar of the **b.**
13:52 He shall **b** the clothing, whether diseased in warp
13:55 you shall **b** it in fire,
13:57 you shall **b** with fire that in which
24: 3 to **b** from evening to morning before
Dt 7: 5 and **b** their idols with fire.
7:25 The images of their gods you shall **b** with fire.
12: 3 smash their pillars, **b** their sacred poles with fire,
12:31 They would even **b** their sons and their daughters
13:16 then **b** the town and all its spoil with fire,
Jos 11: 6 and **b** their chariots with fire."
11:13 on mounds except Hazor, which Joshua did **b.**
Jdg 6:39 "Do not let your anger **b** against me,
9:52 and came near to the entrance of the tower to **b** it
12: 1 We will **b** your house down over you!"
14:15 or we will **b** you and your father's house with fire.
1Sa 2:16 if the man said to him, "Let them **b** the fat first,
2Ch 4:20 the lampstands and their lamps of pure gold to **b**
13:11 so that its lamps may **b** every evening;
Ne 10:34 to **b** on the altar of the LORD our God,
Job 30:30 and my bones **b** with heat.
31:12 and it would **b** to the root all my harvest.
Ps 79: 5 Will your jealous wrath **b** like fire?
89:46 How long will your wrath **b** like fire?
102: 3 and my bones **b** like a furnace.
Isa 1:31 they and their work shall **b** together,
10:17 and it will **b** and devour his thorns and briers
27: 4 I will **b** it up.
57: 5 you that **b** with lust among the oaks,
Jer 4: 4 and **b** with no one to quench it,
7:20 it will **b** and not be quenched.
7:31 to **b** their sons and their daughters in the fire—
15:14 in my anger a fire is kindled that shall **b** forever.
17: 4 in my anger a fire is kindled that shall **b** forever.
18:15 they **b** offerings to a delusion;
19: 5 to **b** their children in the fire as burnt offerings
21:10 and he shall **b** it with fire.
21:12 or else my wrath will go forth like fire, and **b,**
32:29 set it on fire, and **b** it,
34: 2 and he shall **b** it with fire.
34: 5 so they shall **b** spices for you and lament for you,
34:22 and take it, and **b** it with fire.
36:25 and Delaiah and Gemariah urged the king not to **b**
36:29 You have dared to **b** this scroll, saying,
37: 8 they shall take it and **b** it with fire.
37:10 they would rise up and **b** this city with fire.
38:18 and they shall **b** it with fire,
43:12 and he shall **b** them and carry them away captive;
43:13 temples of the gods of Egypt he shall **b** with fire.
Eze 5: 2 the hair you shall **b** in the fire inside the city,
5: 4 throw them into the fire and **b** them up;
16:41 They shall **b** your houses and execute judgments
23:47 they shall kill their sons and their daughters, and **b**
39: 9 and make fires of the weapons and **b** them—
Ob 1:18 they shall **b** them and consume them,
Na 2:13 and I will **b** your chariots in smoke,
Mal 4: 1 the day that comes shall **b** them up,
Mt 3:12 but the chaff he will **b** with unquenchable fire."
Lk 3:17 but the chaff he will **b** with unquenchable fire."
Rev 4: 5 and in front of the throne **b** seven flaming torches,
17:16 they will devour her flesh and **b** her up with fire.
Tob 6: 8 you must **b** them to make a smoke in the presence
Jdt 16: 4 He boasted that he would **b** up my territory,
Wis 13:12 and **b** the cast-off pieces of his work
Sir 28:10 In proportion to the fuel, so will the fire **b,**
28:23 it will **b** among them and will not be put out.
1Mc 7:35 then if I return safely I will **b** up this house."
2Es 7:61 they are set on fire and **b** hotly,
15:62 they shall **b** with fire all your forests
16: 6 a fire in the stubble once it has started to **b?**
16:53 for God will **b** coals of fire on the head
4Mc 5:30 even if you gouge out my eyes and **b** my entrails.
9:17 Cut my limbs, **b** my flesh, and twist my joints;

BURNED‡ (163) [BURN]

Ge 38:24 And Judah said, "Bring her out, and let her be **b.**"
Ex 3: 3 and see why the bush is not **b** up."
32:19 and the dancing, Moses' anger **b** hot, and he threw
32:20 He took the calf that they had made, **b** it with fire,
Lev 4:12 at the ash heap it shall be **b.**
4:21 and burn it as he **b** the first bull;
6:23 Every grain offering of a priest shall be wholly **b;**
6:30 it shall be **b** with fire.
7:17 of the sacrifice shall be **b** up on the third day.
7:19 be eaten; it shall be **b** up.
8:17 he **b** with fire outside the camp,
9:11 flesh and the skin he **b** with fire outside the camp.
10:16 and—it had already been **b!**
13:52 it shall be **b** in fire.
20:14 they shall be **b** to death, both he and they,
21: 9 she shall be **b** to death.
Nu 11: 1 Then the fire of the LORD **b** against them,
11: 3 because the fire of the LORD **b** against them.
16:39 that had been presented by those who were **b;**
19: 5 Then the heifer shall be **b** in his sight;
19: 5 its flesh, and its blood, with its dung, shall be **b.**
31:10 and all their encampments, they **b,**
Dt 9:21 the calf, and **b** it with fire and crushed it,
29:23 all its soil **b** out by sulfur and salt,
Jos 6:24 They **b** down the city, and everything in it;
7: 1 the anger of the LORD **b** against the Israelites.
7:15 as having the devoted things shall be **b** with fire,
7:25 they **b** them with fire, cast stones on them,
8:28 So Joshua **b** Ai, and made it forever a heap
11: 9 and **b** their chariots with fire.
11:11 and he **b** Hazor with fire.
11:13 But Israel **b** none of the towns that stood
Jdg 15: 5 and **b** up the shocks and the standing grain,
15: 6 the Philistines came up, and **b** her and her father.
18:27 put them to the sword, and **b** down the city.
1Sa 2:15 Moreover, before the fat was **b,**
30: 1 They had attacked Ziklag, **b** it down,
30: 3 to the city, they found it **b** down, and their wives
30:14 of Caleb; and we **b** Ziklag down."
31:12 They came to Jabesh and **b** them there.
1Ki 3:26 because compassion for her son **b** within her—
9:16 and **b** it down, had killed the Canaanites who lived
13: 2 and human bones shall be **b** on you.' "
15:13 down her image and **b** it at the Wadi Kidron.
16:18 he **b** down the king's house over himself with fire,
2Ki 10:26 the pillar that was in the temple of Baal, and **b** it.
17:31 the Sepharvites **b** their children in the fire
23: 4 he **b** them outside Jerusalem in the fields of
23: 6 to the Wadi Kidron, **b** it at the Wadi Kidron,
23:11 then he **b** the chariots of the sun with fire.
23:15 He **b** the high place, crushing it to dust;
23:15 he also **b** the sacred pole.
23:16 and **b** them on the altar, and defiled it,
23:20 and **b** human bones on them.
25: 9 He **b** the house of the LORD, the king's house,
25: 9 every great house he **b** down.
1Ch 14:12 and at David's command they were **b.**
2Ch 15:16 crushed it, and **b** it at the Wadi Kidron.
34: 5 He also **b** the bones of the priests on their altars,
36:19 They **b** the house of God,
36:19 **b** all its palaces with fire,
Ne 2:17 how Jerusalem lies in ruins with its gates **b.**
4: 2 of rubbish—and **b** ones at that?"
Est 1:12 and his anger **b** within him.
Job 1:16 from heaven and **b** up the sheep and the servants,
Ps 39: 3 While I mused, the fire **b;**
74: 8 they **b** all the meeting places of God in the land.
80:16 They have **b** it with fire, they have cut it down;
106:18 the flame **b** up the wicked.
Isa 1: 7 your cities are **b** with fire;
6:13 Even if a tenth part remain in it, it will be **b** again,
9: 5 the garments rolled in blood shall be **b** as fuel for
9:18 For wickedness **b** like a fire,
9:19 the wrath of the LORD of hosts the land was **b,**
33:12 And the peoples will be as if **b** to lime,
33:12 like thorns cut down, that are **b** in the fire."
42:25 it **b** him, but he did not take it to heart.
43: 2 when you walk through fire you shall not be **b,**
44:19 "Half of it I **b** in the fire;
64:11 has been **b** by fire, and all our pleasant places
Jer 34: 5 And as spices were **b** for your ancestors,
36:27 after the king had **b** the scroll with the words
36:28 which King Jehoiakim of Judah has **b.**
36:32 of the scroll that King Jehoiakim of Judah had **b** in
38:17 and this city shall not be **b** with fire,
38:23 and this city shall be **b** with fire."
39: 8 The Chaldeans **b** the king's house and the houses
44:23 It is because you **b** offerings,
49: 2 and its villages shall be **b** with fire;
51:32 the marshes have been **b** with fire,
51:58 and her high gates shall be **b** with fire.
52:13 He **b** the house of the LORD, the king's house,
52:13 every great house he **b** down.
La 2: 3 he has **b** like a flaming fire in Jacob,
Eze 24:10 mix in the spices, let the bones be **b.**
Da 7:11 and its body destroyed and given over to be **b**
Joel 1:19 and flames have **b** all the trees of the field.
Am 2: 1 because he **b** to lime the bones of the king of Edom
Mic 1: 7 all her wages shall be **b** with fire,
Mt 13:30 the weeds first and bind them in bundles to be **b,**
13:40 Just as the weeds are collected and **b** up with fire,
22: 7 destroyed those murderers, and **b** their city.
Jn 15: 6 thrown into the fire, and **b.**
Ac 19:19 collected their books and **b** them publicly;
1Co 3:15 If the work is **b** up, the builder will suffer loss;
Heb 6: 8 its end is to be **b** over.
13:11 the high priest as a sacrifice for sin are **b** outside
Rev 8: 7 and a third of the earth was **b** up,
8: 7 and a third of the trees were **b** up,
8: 7 and all green grass was **b** up.
18: 8 and she will be **b** with fire;
Tob 14: 4 the temple of God in it will be **b** to the ground,
Jdt 2:26 and **b** their tents and plundered their sheepfolds.
2:27 and **b** all their fields and destroyed their flocks
9: 4 to be divided among your beloved children who **b**
Wis 16:19 in the midst of water it **b** more intensely than fire,
Sir 8:10 or you may be **b** in their flaming fire.
28:22 they will not be **b** in its flame.
45:14 be wholly **b** twice every day continually.
48: 1 a prophet like fire, and his word **b** like a torch.
Bar 1: 2 the Chaldeans took Jerusalem and **b** it with fire.
LtJ 6:55 but the gods will be **b** up like timbers.
Aza 1:25 and **b** those Chaldeans who were caught near
1Mc 1:31 He plundered the city, **b** it with fire,
1:56 of the law that they found they tore to pieces and **b**
2:24 he **b** with zeal and his heart was stirred.
2:26 Thus he **b** with zeal for the law,
3: 5 he **b** those who troubled his people.
4:38 the altar profaned, and the gates **b.**
5: 5 **b** with fire their towers and all who were in them.
5:28 then he seized all its spoils and **b** it with fire.

1Mc 5:35 plundered it, and **b** it with fire.
5:44 But he took the town and **b** the sacred precincts
5:65 down its strongholds and **b** its towers on all sides.
5:68 and the carved images of their gods he **b** with fire;
6:31 but the Jews sallied out and **b** these with fire,
10:84 But Jonathan **b** Azotus and the surrounding towns
10:84 and those who had taken refuge in it, he **b**
10:85 with those **b** alive, came to eight thousand.
11: 4 the charred bodies of those whom Jonathan had **b**
11:61 and **b** its suburbs with fire and plundered them.
16:10 and John **b** it with fire,
2Mc 1: 8 and **b** the gate and shed innocent blood.
1:33 with which Nehemiah and his associates had **b**
6:11 were betrayed to Philip and were all **b** together,
8:33 they **b** those who had set fire to the sacred gates,
10:36 they kindled fires and **b** the blasphemers alive.
12: 6 He set fire to the harbor by night, **b** the boats,
14:41 they ordered that fire be brought and the doors **b**.
1Es 1:55 They **b** the house of the Lord,
1:55 the walls of Jerusalem, **b** their towers with fire,
4:45 which the Edomites **b** when Judea was laid waste
6:16 and **b** it, and carried the people away captive
3Mc 3:29 to be made unapproachable and **b** with fire,
2Es 10:22 our priests have been **b** to death,
12: 3 The whole body of the eagle was **b**,
13:11 and **b** up all of them,
14:21 For your law has been **b**,
4Mc 6:25 There they **b** him with maliciously
6:26 When he was now **b** to his very bones and about
11:19 pierced his ribs so that his entrails were **b** through.
15:14 who saw them tortured and **b** one by one,
15:20 of children **b** upon the flesh of other children,

BURNED-OUT (1) [BURN]

Jer 51:25 and make you a **b** mountain.

BURNING‡ (53) [BURN]

Lev 6: 9 while the fire on the altar shall be kept **b**.
6:12 fire on the altar shall be kept **b; it shall not go out.
6:13 A perpetual fire shall be kept **b** on the altar;
10: 6 may mourn the **b** that the LORD has sent.
24: 2 that a light may be kept **b** regularly.
Nu 19: 6 throw them into the fire in which the heifer is **b**.
24:22 yet Kain is destined for **b**.
Dt 5:23 while the mountain was **b** with fire,
32:24 **b** consumption, bitter pestilence.
Jos 7:26 Then the LORD turned from his **b** anger.
Job 41:20 as from a boiling pot and **b** rushes.
Ps 38: 7 For my loins are filled with **b**,
69:24 and let your **b** anger overtake them.
140:10 Let **b** coals fall on them!
Pr 6:27 be carried in the bosom without **b** one's clothes?
Isa 4: 4 by a spirit of judgment and by a spirit of **b**.
10:16 and under his glory a **b** will be kindled, like the **b** of fire.
30:27 **b** with his anger, and in thick rising smoke;
30:33 For his **b** place has long been prepared;
34: 9 her land shall become **b** pitch.
35: 7 the **b** sand shall become a pool,
42: 3 and a dimly **b** wick he will not quench;
62: 1 and her salvation like a **b** torch.
Jer 20: 9 then within me there is something like a **b** fire shut
36:22 and there was a fire **b** in the brazier before him.
Eze 1:13 like **b** coals of fire, like torches moving to and fro
10: 2 fill your hands with **b** coals from among
Da 7: 9 and its wheels were **b** fire.
Mal 4: 1 See, the day is coming, **b** like an oven,
Lk 24:32 not our hearts **b** within us while he was talking
Jn 5:35 He was a **b** and shining lamp,
Ac 7:30 in the flame of a **b** bush.
18:25 with **b** enthusiasm and taught accurately the things
Ro 12:20 for by doing this you will heap **b** coals
Rev 8: 8 and something like a great mountain, **b** with fire,
18: 9 over her when they see the smoke of her **b**;
18:18 and cried out as they saw the smoke of her **b**,
Jdt 8: 3 he was overcome by the **b** heat,
Sir 43: 3 and who can withstand its **b** heat?
43: 4 A man tending a furnace works in **b** heat,
LtJ 6:42 sit along the passageways, **b** bran for incense.
Aza 1:66 delivered us from the midst of the **b** fiery furnace;
Sus 1:20 We are **b** with desire for you;
1Mc 4:20 and that the Jews were **b** the camp,
12:29 for they saw the fires **b**.
3Mc 4: 2 everywhere their hearts were **b**,
5:43 and by **b** to the ground the temple inaccessible
2Es 12:44 if we also had been consumed in the **b** of Zion.
16:68 **b** wrath of a great multitude is kindled over you;
4Mc 3:15 But David, though he was **b** with thirst,
6:27 I am dying in **b** torments for the sake of the law.
18:20 and in his **b** rage brought those seven sons of

BURNISHED (6)

1Ki 7:45 for the house of the LORD were of **b** bronze.
2Ch 4:16 of **b** bronze for King Solomon for the house of
Eze 1: 7 and they sparkled like **b** bronze.
Da 10: 6 his arms and legs like the gleam of **b** bronze,
Rev 1:15 his feet were like **b** bronze,
2:18 and whose feet are like **b** bronze:

BURNS (16) [BURN]

Lev 16:28 The one who **b** them shall wash his clothes
Nu 19: 8 The one who **b** the heifer shall wash his clothes
Dt 32:22 and **b** to the depths of Sheol;
1Ki 14:10 just as one **b** up dung until it is all gone.
Ps 46: 9 he **b** the shields with fire.
Isa 44:16 Half of it he **b** in the fire;
65: 5 a fire that **b** all day long.
Hos 7: 6 For they are kindled like an oven, their heart **b**
8: 5 My anger **b** against them.
Joel 2: 3 and behind them a flame **b**.
Am 6:10 And if a relative, one who **b** the dead,
Rev 19:20 into the lake of fire that **b** with sulfur.
21: 8 their place will be in the lake that **b** with fire
Sir 23:16 like a fire will not be quenched until it **b** itself out;
23:16 near of kin will never cease until the fire **b** him up.
43:21 the mountains and **b** up the wilderness,

BURNT‡ (323) [BURN]

A. BURNT OFFERING (201)
B. BURNT OFFERINGS (118)

Ge 8:20 and offered **b** offerings on the altar. B
22: 2 and offer him there as a **b** offering on one of A
22: 3 he cut the wood for the **b** offering, A
22: 6 of the **b** offering and laid it on his son Isaac, A
22: 7 but where is the lamb for a **b** offering?" A
22: 8 the lamb for a **b** offering, A
22:13 offered it up as a **b** offering instead of his son. A
Ex 10:25 and **b** offerings to sacrifice to the LORD our God. B
18:12 brought a **b** offering and sacrifices to God; A
20:24 of earth and sacrifice on it your **b** offerings B
24: 5 who offered **b** offerings and sacrificed oxen B
29:18 it is a **b** offering to the LORD; A
29:25 the **b** offering of pleasing odor before the LORD; A
29:42 a regular **b** offering throughout your generations A
30: 9 or a **b** offering, or a grain offering; A
30:28 and the altar of **b** offering with all its utensils, A
31: 9 and the altar of **b** offering with all its utensils, A
32: 6 and offered **b** offerings and brought sacrifices B
35:16 altar of **b** offering, with its grating of bronze, A
38: 1 the altar of **b** offering also of acacia wood; A
40: 6 **b** offering before the entrance of the tabernacle A
40:10 You shall also anoint the altar of **b** offering A
40:29 of **b** offering at the entrance of the tabernacle A
40:29 on it the **b** offering and the grain offering as A
Lev 1: 3 If the offering is a **b** offering from the herd, A
1: 4 on the head of the **b** offering, A
1: 6 **b** offering shall be flayed and cut up into A
1: 9 whole into smoke on the altar as a **b** offering, A
1:10 If your gift for a **b** offering is from the flock, A
1:13 a **b** offering, an offering by fire of pleasing odor A
1:14 If your offering to the LORD is a **b** offering A
1:17 a **b** offering, an offering by fire of pleasing odor A
3: 5 the **b** offering that is on the wood on the fire, A
4: 7 at the base of the altar of **b** offering, A
4:10 into smoke upon the altar of **b** offering. A
4:18 the altar of **b** offering that is at the entrance of A
4:24 the spot where the **b** offering is slaughtered A
4:25 and put it on the horns of the altar of **b** offering, A
4:25 of its blood at the base of the altar of **b** offering. A
4:29 be slaughtered at the place of the **b** offering. A
4:30 and put it on the horns of the altar of **b** offering, A
4:33 at the spot where the **b** offering is slaughtered. A
4:34 and put it on the horns of the altar of **b** offering, A
5: 7 for a sin offering and the other for a **b** offering. A
5:10 second he shall offer for a **b** offering according A
6: 9 This is the ritual of the **b** offering. A
6: 9 The **b** offering itself shall remain on the hearth A
6:10 the fire has reduced the **b** offering on the altar, A
6:12 lay out the **b** offering on it, A
6:25 at the spot where the **b** offering is slaughtered; A
7: 2 at the spot where the **b** offering is slaughtered, A
7: 8 priest who offers anyone's **b** offering shall keep A
7: 8 the skin of the **b** offering that he has offered. A
7:37 This is the ritual of the **b** offering, A
8:18 Then he brought forward the ram of **b** offering. A
8:21 it was a **b** offering for a pleasing odor, A
8:28 into smoke on the altar with the **b** offering. A
9: 2 for a sin offering and a ram for a **b** offering, A
9: 3 yearlings without blemish, for a **b** offering; A
9: 7 sacrifice your sin offering and your **b** offering, A
9:12 Then he slaughtered the **b** offering. A
9:13 they brought him the **b** offering piece by piece, A
9:14 the legs and, with the **b** offering, turned them A
9:16 He presented the **b** offering, A
9:17 in addition to the **b** offering of the morning. A
9:22 the **b** offering, and the offering of well-being. A
9:24 from the LORD and consumed the **b** offering A
10:19 and their **b** offering before the LORD; A
12: 6 a lamb in its first year for a **b** offering, A
12: 8 for a **b** offering and the other for a sin offering; A
14:13 sin offering and the **b** offering are slaughtered A
14:19 Afterward he shall slaughter the **b** offering; A
14:20 the **b** offering and the grain offering on the altar. A
14:22 for a sin offering and the other for a **b** offering. A
14:31 a sin offering and the other for a **b** offering, A
15:15 for a sin offering and the other for a **b** offering; A
15:30 for a sin offering and the other for a **b** offering; A
16: 3 for a sin offering and a ram for a **b** offering. A
16: 5 and one ram for a **b** offering. A
16:24 then he shall come out and offer his **b** offering A
16:24 and offer his burnt offering and the **b** offering A
17: 8 among them who offers a **b** offering or sacrifice, A
22:18 that is offered to the LORD as a **b** offering, A
23:12 without blemish, as a **b** offering to the LORD. A
23:18 they shall be a **b** offering to the LORD, A
23:37 **b** offerings and grain offerings, B
Nu 6:11 as a sin offering and the other as a **b** offering, A
6:14 a year old without blemish as a **b** offering, A
6:16 and offer their sin offering and **b** offering, A
7:15 one male lamb a year old, for a **b** offering; A
7:21 one male lamb a year old, as a **b** offering; A
7:27 one male lamb a year old, for a **b** offering; A
7:33 one male lamb a year old, for a **b** offering; A
7:39 one male lamb a year old, for a **b** offering; A
7:45 one male lamb a year old, for a **b** offering; A
7:51 one male lamb a year old, for a **b** offering; A
7:57 one male lamb a year old, for a **b** offering; A
7:63 one male lamb a year old, for a **b** offering; A
7:69 one male lamb a year old, for a **b** offering; A
7:75 one male lamb a year old, for a **b** offering; A
7:81 one male lamb a year old, for a **b** offering; A
7:87 all the livestock for the **b** offering twelve bulls, A
8:12 for a sin offering and the other for a **b** offering A
10:10 shall blow the trumpets over your **b** offerings B
15: 3 whether a **b** offering or a sacrifice, A
15: 5 of wine as a drink offering with the **b** offering A
15: 8 you offer a bull as a **b** offering or a sacrifice, A
15:24 for a **b** offering, a pleasing odor to A
19:17 the **b** purification offering, and running water
23: 3 beside your **b** offerings while I go aside. B
23: 6 who was standing beside his **b** offerings with all B
23:15 "Stand here beside your **b** offerings, B
23:17 beside his **b** offerings with the officials of Moab. B
28: 6 It is a regular **b** offering, A
28:10 this is the **b** offering for every sabbath, A
28:10 to the regular **b** offering and its drink offering. A
28:11 of your months you shall offer a **b** offering to A
28:13 a **b** offering of pleasing odor, A
28:14 This is the **b** offering of every month throughout A
28:15 to the regular **b** offering and its drink offering. A
28:19 a **b** offering to the LORD: A
28:23 shall offer these in addition to the **b** offering A
28:23 which belongs to the regular **b** offering. A
28:24 to the regular **b** offering and its drink offering. A
28:27 You shall offer a **b** offering, A
28:31 to the regular **b** offering with its grain offering, A
29: 2 and you shall offer a **b** offering, a pleasing odor A
29: 6 in addition to the **b** offering of the new moon A
29: 6 and the regular **b** offering and its grain offering, A
29: 8 You shall offer a **b** offering to the LORD, A
29:11 and the regular **b** offering and its grain offering, A
29:13 You shall offer a **b** offering, an offering by fire, A
29:16 in addition to the regular **b** offering, A
29:19 to the regular **b** offering and its grain offering, A
29:22 to the regular **b** offering and its grain offering A
29:25 in addition to the regular **b** offering, A
29:28 to the regular **b** offering and its grain offering A
29:31 in addition to the regular **b** offering, A
29:34 besides the regular **b** offering, its grain offering, A
29:36 You shall offer a **b** offering, an offering by fire, A
29:38 to the regular **b** offering and its grain offering A
29:39 as your **b** offerings, your grain offerings, B
Dt 12: 6 bringing there your **b** offerings B
12:11 your **b** offerings and your sacrifices, B
12:13 not offer your **b** offerings at any place you B
12:14 there you shall offer your **b** offerings B
12:27 You shall present your **b** offerings, B
13:16 as a whole **b** offering to the LORD your God. A
27: 6 offer up **b** offerings on it to the LORD your God, B
33:10 and whole **b** offerings on your altar. B
Jos 8:31 and they offered on it **b** offerings to the LORD, B
22:23 if we did so to offer **b** offerings or grain B
22:26 'Let us now build an altar, not for **b** offering, A
22:27 of the LORD in his presence with our **b** offerings B
22:28 which our ancestors made, not for **b** offerings, B
22:29 the LORD by building an altar for **b** offering, A
Jdg 6:26 as a **b** offering with the wood of the sacred pole A
11:31 to be offered up by me as a **b** offering." A
13:16 but if you want to prepare a **b** offering, A
13:23 have accepted a **b** offering and a grain offering A
20:26 Then they offered **b** offerings and sacrifices B
21: 4 offered **b** offerings and sacrifices of well-being. B
1Sa 6:14 of the cart and offered the cows as a **b** offering A
6:15 the people of Beth-shemesh offered **b** offerings B
7: 9 and offered it as a whole **b** offering to the LORD; A
7:10 As Samuel was offering up the **b** offering, A
10: 8 to you to present **b** offerings and offer sacrifices B
13: 9 So Saul said, "Bring the **b** offering here to me, A
13: 9 And he offered the **b** offering. A
13:10 soon as he had finished offering the **b** offering, A
13:12 so I forced myself, and offered the **b** offering." A
15:22 "Has the LORD as great delight in **b** offerings B
2Sa 6:17 and David offered **b** offerings and offerings B
6:18 David had finished offering the **b** offerings B
24:22 here are the oxen for the **b** offering, A
24:24 I will not offer **b** offerings to the LORD my God B
24:25 offered **b** offerings and offerings of well-being. B
1Ki 3: 4 Solomon used to offer a thousand **b** offerings B
3:15 up **b** offerings and offerings of well-being, B
8:64 the **b** offerings and the grain offerings and B
8:64 to receive the **b** offerings and the grain offerings B
9:25 offer up **b** offerings and sacrifices of well-being B
10: 5 and his **b** offerings that he offered at the house B
18:33 and pour it on the **b** offering and on the wood." A
18:38 of the LORD fell and consumed the **b** offering, A
2Ki 3:27 and offered him as a **b** offering on the wall. A
5:17 for your servant will no longer offer **b** offering A
10:24 proceeded to offer sacrifices and **b** offerings. B
10:25 as he had finished presenting the **b** offering, A
16:13 and offered his **b** offering and his grain offering, A
16:15 the great altar offer the morning **b** offering, A
16:15 and the king's **b** offering, and his grain offering, A
16:15 with the **b** offering of all the people of the land, A
16:15 dash against it all the blood of the **b** offering, A
1Ch 6:49 altar of **b** offering and on the altar of incense, A
16: 1 and they offered **b** offerings and offerings B

1Ch 16: 2 David had finished offering the **b** offerings B
16:40 to offer **b** offerings to the LORD on the altar B
16:40 to the LORD on the altar of **b** offering regularly, A
21:23 see, I present the oxen for **b** offerings, B
21:24 nor offer **b** offerings that cost me nothing." B
21:26 an altar to the LORD and presented **b** offerings B
21:26 with fire from heaven on the altar of **b** offering. A
21:29 of **b** offering were at that time in the high place A
22: 1 of the LORD God and here the altar of **b** offering A
23:31 and whenever **b** offerings are offered to B
29:21 next day they offered sacrifices and **b** offerings B
2Ch 1: 6 and offered a thousand **b** offerings on it. B
2: 4 and for **b** offerings morning and evening, B
4: 6 to rinse what was used for the **b** offering. A
7: 1 down from heaven and consumed the **b** offering A
7: 7 for there he offered the **b** offerings and the fat B
7: 7 not hold the **b** offering and the grain offering A
8:12 up **b** offerings to the LORD on the altar of B
9: 4 and his **b** offerings that he offered at the house B
13:11 and every evening **b** offerings B
23:18 to offer **b** offerings to the LORD, B
24:14 utensils for the service and for the **b** offerings, B
24:14 They offered **b** offerings in the house of B
29: 7 have not offered incense or made **b** offerings B
29:18 the altar of **b** offering and all its utensils, A
29:24 the **b** offering and the sin offering should be A
29:27 Then Hezekiah commanded that the **b** offering A
29:27 When the **b** offering began, A
29:28 this continued until the **b** offering was finished. A
29:31 of a willing heart brought **b** offerings. B
29:32 The number of the **b** offerings that B
29:32 all these were for a **b** offering to the LORD. A
29:34 and could not skin all the **b** offerings, so, B
29:35 Besides the great number of **b** offerings there B
29:35 were the drink offerings for the **b** offerings. B
30:15 and brought **b** offerings into the house of B
31: 2 for **b** offerings and offerings of well-being, B
31: 3 his own possessions was for the **b** offerings: B
31: 3 the **b** offerings of morning and evening, B
31: 3 and the **b** offerings for the sabbaths, B
35:12 the **b** offerings so that they might distribute B
35:14 were occupied in offering the **b** offerings B
35:16 the passover and to offer **b** offerings on the altar B
Ezr 3: 2 to offer **b** offerings on it, B
3: 3 and they offered **b** offerings upon it to the LORD, B
3: 4 the daily **b** offerings by number according to B
3: 5 and after that the regular **b** offerings, B
3: 6 seventh month they began to offer **b** offerings B
6: 3 and **b** offerings are brought; B
6: 9 or sheep for **b** offerings to the God of heaven, B
8:35 offered **b** offerings to the God of Israel, B
8:35 all this was a **b** offering to the LORD. A
Ne 10:33 the regular grain offering, the regular **b** offering, A
Job 1: 5 and offer **b** offerings according to the number B
42: 8 and offer up for yourselves a **b** offering; A
Ps 20: 3 and regard with favor your **b** sacrifices.
40: 6 **B** offering and sin offering you have not A
50: 8 your **b** offerings are continually before me. B
51:16 if I were to give a **b** offering, A
51:19 in **b** offerings and whole burnt offerings; B
51:19 in burnt offerings and whole **b** offerings; B
66:13 I will come into your house with **b** offerings; B
66:15 I will offer to you **b** offerings of fatlings, B
Isa 1:11 of **b** offerings of rams and the fat of fed beasts; B
19:21 and will worship with sacrifice and **b** offering, A
40:16 nor are its animals enough for a **b** offering. A
43:23 not brought me your sheep for **b** offerings, B
56: 7 their **b** offerings and their sacrifices will B
Jer 6:20 Your **b** offerings are not acceptable, B
7:21 Add your **b** offerings to your sacrifices, B
7:22 or command them concerning **b** offerings B
14:12 although they offer **b** offering and grain offering, A
17:26 bringing **b** offerings and sacrifices, B
19: 5 to burn their children in the fire as **b** offerings B
33:18 a man in my presence to offer **b** offerings, B
Eze 40:38 where the **b** offering was to be washed. A
40:39 on which the **b** offering and the sin offering and A
40:42 also four tables of hewn stone for the **b** offering, A
40:42 **b** offerings and the sacrifices were slaughtered. B
43:18 day when it is erected for offering **b** offerings B
43:21 and it shall be **b** in the appointed place belonging
43:24 and offer them up as a **b** offering to the LORD. A
43:27 the altar your **b** offerings and your offerings B
44:11 shall slaughter the **b** offering and the sacrifice A
45:15 is the offering for grain offerings, **b** offerings, B
45:17 of the prince regarding the **b** offerings, B
45:17 the **b** offerings, and the offerings of well-being, B
45:23 of the festival he shall provide as a **b** offering to A
45:25 **b** offerings, and grain offerings, and for the oil. B
46: 2 The priests shall offer his **b** offering A
46: 4 The **b** offering that the prince offers to the LORD A
46:12 either a **b** offering or offerings of well-being as A
46:12 and he shall offer his **b** offering or his offerings A
46:13 for a **b** offering to the LORD daily; A
46:15 morning by morning, as a regular **b** offering. A
Da 8:11 it took the regular **b** offering away from him A
8:12 over to it together with the regular **b** offering; A
8:13 concerning the regular **b** offering, A
11:31 They shall abolish the regular **b** offering A
12:11 time that the regular **b** offering is taken away A
Hos 6: 6 the knowledge of God rather than **b** offerings. B
Am 5:22 offer me your **b** offerings and grain offerings, B
Mic 6: 6 Shall I come before him with **b** offerings, B
Mk 12:33 much more important than all whole **b** offerings B
Heb 10: 6 in **b** offerings and sin offerings you have taken no pleasure. B
10: 8 in sacrifices and offerings and **b** offerings B
Jdt 4:14 the daily **b** offerings, the votive offerings, B
16:16 and the fat of all whole **b** offerings to you is B
16:18 they offered their **b** offerings, B
Wis 3: 6 like a sacrificial **b** offering he accepted them. A
Bar 1:10 with the money **b** offerings and sin offerings B
Aza 1:15 no **b** offering, or sacrifice, or oblation, A
1:17 though it were with **b** offerings of rams and B
1Mc 1:45 to forbid **b** offerings and sacrifices B
1:54 a desolating sacrilege on the altar of **b** offering. A
1:59 altar that was on top of the altar of **b** offering. A
4:44 to do about the altar of **b** offering, A
4:53 the new altar of **b** offering that they had built. A
4:56 and joyfully offered **b** offerings; B
5:54 offered **b** offerings, because they had returned B
7:33 show him the **b** offering that was being offered A
2Mc 2:10 down and consumed the whole **b** offerings. B
1Es 4:52 **b** offerings to be offered on the altar every day, B
5:49 to offer **b** offerings upon it, B
5:50 **b** offerings to the Lord morning and evening. B
2Es 15:23 of the earth and the sinners, like **b** straw.
4Mc 18:11 and Isaac who was offered as a **b** offering, A

BURNT-OUT (1) [BURN]

1Mc 11: 4 they showed him the **b** temple of Dagon,

BURST (28) [BURSTING, BURSTS, OUTBURST]

Ge 7:11 that day all the fountains of the great deep **b** forth,
Jos 9:13 when we filled them, and see, they are **b**;
2Sa 5:20 LORD has **b** forth against my enemies before me,
6: 8 David was angry because the LORD had **b** forth
1Ch 13:11 David was angry because the LORD had **b** out
14:11 "God has **b** out against my enemies by my hand,
15:13 the LORD our God **b** out against us,
Job 32:19 like new wineskins, it is ready to **b**.
38: 8 "Or who shut in the sea with doors when it **b** out
Ps 2: 3 "Let us **b** their bonds asunder,
Isa 54: 1 **b** into song and shout, you who have not been
55:12 the mountains and the hills before you shall **b**
Jer 2:20 long ago you broke your yoke and **b** your bonds,
5: 5 But they all alike had broken the yoke, they had **b**
23:19 it will **b** upon the head of the wicked.
30: 8 and I will **b** his bonds,
30:23 it will **b** upon the head of the wicked.
Joel 2: 8 they **b** through the weapons and are not halted.
Mic 1: 4 under him and the valleys will **b** open,
Mt 9:17 otherwise, the skins **b**, and the wine is spilled,
Mk 2:22 otherwise, the wine will **b** the skins,
Lk 5:37 the new wine will **b** the skins and will be spilled,
6:48 river **b** against that house but could not shake it,
6:49 When the river **b** against it, immediately it fell,
Ac 1:18 and falling headlong, he **b** open in the middle
Gal 4:27 you who bear no children, **b** into song and shout,
Sir 19:10 Be brave, it will not make you **b**!
Bel 1:27 The dragon ate them, and **b** open.

BURSTING‡ (3) [BURST]

2Sa 5:20 against my enemies before me, like a **b** flood."
1Ch 14:11 against my enemies by my hand, like a **b** flood."
Pr 3:10 and your vats will be **b** with wine.

BURSTS (1) [BURST]

Job 16:14 He **b** upon me again and again;

BURY (50) [BURIAL, BURIED, BURIERS, BURIES, BURYING]

Ge 23: 4 so that I may **b** my dead out of my sight."
23: 6 **B** your dead in the choicest of our burial places;
23: 8 "If you are willing that I should **b** my dead out
23:11 of my people I give it to you; **b** your dead."
23:13 accept it from me, so that I may **b** my dead there."
23:15 between you and me? **B** your dead."
47:29 Do not **b** me in Egypt.
47:30 of Egypt and **b** me in their burial place."
49:29 **B** me with my ancestors—
50: 5 in the land of Canaan, there you shall **b** me.'
50: 5 therefore let me go up, so that I may **b** my father;
50: 6 Pharaoh answered, "Go up, and **b** your father,
50: 7 So Joseph went up to **b** his father.
50:14 and all who had gone up with him to **b** his father.
Dt 21:23 you shall **b** him that same day,
1Ki 2:31 "Do as he has said, strike him down and **b** him;
11:15 the commander of the army went up to **b** the dead,
13:29 to mourn and to **b** him.
13:31 **b** me in the grave in which the man
14:13 All Israel shall mourn for him and **b** him;
2Ki 9:10 and no one shall **b** her."
9:34 he said, "See to that cursed woman and **b** her;
9:35 But when they went to **b** her,
2Ch 24:25 but they did not **b** him in the tombs of the kings.
Ps 79: 3 and there was no one to **b** them.
Jer 7:32 they will **b** in Topheth until there is no more room.
14:16 There shall be no one to **b** them—
19:11 Topheth they shall **b** until there is no more room to **b**.
43: 9 and **b** them in the clay pavement that is at
Eze 39:13 All the people of the land shall **b** them;
39:14 the land regularly and **b** any invaders who remain
Hos 9: 6 Egypt shall gather them, Memphis shall **b** them.
Mt 8:21 "Lord, first let me go and **b** my father."
8:22 "Follow me, and let the dead **b** their own dead."
27: 7 to buy the potter's field as a place to **b** foreigners.
Lk 9:59 he said, "Lord, first let me go and **b** my father."
9:60 Jesus said to him, "Let the dead **b** their own dead;
Tob 1:17 behind the wall of Nineveh, I would **b** it.
1:18 I would secretly remove the bodies and **b** them.
2: 4 in one of the rooms until sunset when I might **b** it.
4: 4 when she dies, **b** her beside me in the same grave.
6:15 and they have no other son to **b** them."
8:12 let us **b** him without anyone knowing it."
12:12 and likewise whenever you would **b** the dead.
12:13 up and leave your dinner to go and **b** the dead,
14:10 On whatever day you **b** your mother beside me,
Wis 18:12 For the living were not sufficient even to **b** them,
1Mc 7:17 and there was no one to **b** them."
4Mc 16:11 when I die, I shall have none of my sons to **b** me."

BURYING (9) [BURY]

Ge 23: 4 give me property among you for a **b** place,
23: 6 from you any burial ground for **b** your dead."
23: 9 in your presence as a possession for a **b** place."
23:20 into Abraham's possession as a **b** place.
Nu 33: 4 while the Egyptians were **b** all their firstborn,
Eze 39:12 the house of Israel shall spend **b** them,
Tob 1:19 that I was **b** them; so I hid myself.
2: 8 yet here he is again **b** the dead!"
2Mc 9:15 not considered worth **b** but had planned

BUSH‡ (16) [BUSHES, ROSEBUSHES, THORNBUSH, THORNBUSHES]

Ex 3: 2 to him in a flame of fire out of a **b**;
3: 2 he looked, and the **b** was blazing,
3: 3 and see why the **b** is not burned up."
3: 4 God called to him out of the **b**, "Moses, Moses!"
Jnh 4: 6 The LORD God appointed a **b**,
4: 6 so Jonah was very happy about the **b**.
4: 7 God appointed a worm that attacked the **b**,
4: 9 "Is it right for you to be angry about the **b**?"
4:10 the LORD said, "You are concerned about the **b**,
Mk 12:26 in the story about the **b**, how God said to him,
Lk 6:44 nor are grapes picked from a bramble **b**.
20:37 in the story about the **b**,
Ac 7:30 in the flame of a burning **b**.
7:35 through the angel who appeared to him in the **b**.
2Es 14: 1 suddenly a voice came out of a **b** opposite me
14: 3 "I revealed myself in a **b** and spoke to Moses

BUSHEL‡ (2) [BUSHELS]

Mt 5:15 after lighting a lamp puts it under the **b** basket,
Mk 4:21 "Is a lamp brought in to be put under the **b** basket,

BUSHELS (1) [BUSHEL]

Bel 1: 3 for it twelve **b** of choice flour and forty sheep

BUSHES (4) [BUSH]

Ge 21:15 she cast the child under one of the **b**.
Job 30: 4 they pick mallow and the leaves of **b**,
30: 7 Among the **b** they bray;
1Mc 4:38 In the courts they saw **b** sprung up as in a thicket,

BUSHY (KJV) See WAVY

BUSIEST (1) [BUSY]

Pr 1:21 At the **b** corner she cries out;

BUSINESS (27) [BUSY]

Jos 2:14 If you do not tell this **b** of ours,
2:20 But if you tell this **b** of ours,
Jdg 18: 3 What is your **b** here?"
1Sa 21: 8 because the king's **b** required haste."
1Ki 10:15 from the traders and from the **b** of the merchants,
Est 3: 9 of those who have charge of the king's **b**,
Ps 107:23 doing **b** on the mighty waters;
Ecc 1:13 an unhappy **b** that God has given to human beings
3:10 I have seen the **b** that God has given to everyone
4: 8 This also is vanity and an unhappy **b**.
8:16 and to see the **b** that is done on earth,
Eze 27:12 Tarshish did **b** with you out of the abundance
27:16 Edom did **b** with you because
27:21 in these they did **b** with you.
Da 8:27 then I arose and went about the king's **b**.
Mt 22: 5 one to his farm, another to his **b**,
Lk 19:13 'Do **b** with these until I come back.'
Ac 19:24 brought no little **b** to the artisans.
19:25 you know that we get our wealth from this **b**.
Jas 4:13 doing **b** and making money."
Sir 37:11 a merchant about **b** or with a buyer about selling,
38:24 only the one who has little **b** can become wise.
2Mc 4:23 the king and to complete the records of essential **b**.
15: 5 to take up arms and finish the king's **b**."
3Mc 3:10 and friends and **b** associates had taken some
2Es 16:42 the one who does **b** be like one who will not make
16:47 Those who conduct **b**, do so only

BUSY (8) [BUSIEST, BUSINESS, BUSYBODIES]

1Ki 20:40 your servant was **b** here and there, he was gone."
Ps 141: 4 to **b** myself with wicked deeds in company
Ecc 1:13 that God has given to human beings to be **b** with.
3:10 that God has given to everyone to be **b** with.
Ro 13: 6 for the authorities are God's servants, **b** with this
Jas 1:11 in the midst of a **b** life, they will wither away.
Sir 8: 8 but **b** yourself with their maxims;

Sir 11:10 My child, do not **b** yourself with many matters;

BUSYBODIES (2) [BUSY]
2Th 3:11 mere **b,** not doing any work.
1Ti 5:13 they are not merely idle, but also gossips and **b,**

BUSYBODY (KJV) See MISCHIEF MAKER

BUT (5047) See Index of Articles Etc.

BUTCHER (1) [BUTCHERED]
2Mc 7:29 Do not fear this **b,** but prove worthy

BUTCHERED (2) [BUTCHER]
Dt 28:31 Your ox shall be **b** before your eyes,
1Sa 25:11 and the meat that I have **b** for my shearers,

BUTLER (KJV) See CUPBEARER

BUTT (1)
2Sa 2:23 Abner struck him in the stomach with the **b** of his

BUTTED (1)
Eze 34:21 and **b** at all the weak animals with your horns

BUTTER (1)
Ps 55:21 with speech smoother than **b,** but with a heart set

BUTTOCKS (1)
Isa 20:4 with **b** uncovered, to the shame of Egypt.

BUY (63) [BOUGHT, BUYER, BUYING, BUYS]
Ge 41:57 all the world came to Joseph in Egypt to **b** grain,
42:2 go down and **b** grain for us there,
42:3 So ten of Joseph's brothers went down to **b** grain
42:5 among the other people who came to **b** grain,
42:7 They said, "From the land of Canaan, to **b** food."
42:10 your servants have come to **b** food.
43:2 "Go again, **b** us a little more food."
43:4 we will go down and **b** you food;
43:20 my lord, we came down the first time to **b** food;
43:22 down with us additional money to **b** food.
44:25 when our father said, 'Go again, **b** us a little food,'
47:19 **B** us and our land in exchange for food.
47:22 Only the land of the priests he did not **b;**
Ex 21:2 When you **b** a male Hebrew slave,
Lev 25:14 a sale to your neighbor or **b** from your neighbor,
25:15 When you **b** from your neighbor,
Dt 2:6 and you shall also **b** water from them for money,
Ru 4:4 **B** it in the presence of those sitting here,
2Sa 24:21 "To **b** the threshing floor from you in order
24:24 "No, but I will **b** them from you for a price;
2Ki 12:12 to **b** timber and quarried stone for making repairs
22:6 to **b** timber and quarried stone to repair the house.
1Ch 21:24 I will **b** them for the full price.
2Ch 34:11 the carpenters and the builders to **b** quarried stone,
Ezr 7:17 then, you shall with all diligence **b** bulls, rams,
Ne 10:31 not **b** it from them on the sabbath or on a holy day;
Pr 17:16 a price in hand to **b** wisdom,
23:23 **B** truth, and do not sell it;
23:23 **b** wisdom, instruction, and understanding.
Isa 55:1 and you that have no money, come, **b** and eat!
55:1 Come, **b** wine and milk without money
Jer 13:1 "Go and **b** yourself a linen loincloth,
19:1 Go and **b** a potter's earthenware jug.
32:7 "**B** my field that is at Anathoth,
32:8 "**B** my field that is at Anathoth in the land
32:8 and redemption is yours; **b** it for yourself."
32:25 "**B** the field for money and get witnesses"—
Zec 11:5 Those who **b** them kill them and go unpunished;
Mt 14:15 so that they may go into the villages and **b** food
25:9 you had better go to the dealers and **b** some
25:10 And while they went to **b** it, the bridegroom came,
27:7 to **b** the potter's field as a place to bury foreigners.
Mk 6:36 and villages and **b** something for themselves
6:37 to go and **b** two hundred denarii worth of bread,
Lk 9:13 we are to go and **b** food for all these people."
22:36 who has no sword must sell his cloak and **b** one.
Jn 4:8 (His disciples had gone to the city to **b** food.)
6:5 "Where are we to **b** bread for these people to eat?"
6:7 "Six months' wages would not **b** enough bread
13:29 "**B** what we need for the festival";
1Co 7:30 those who **b** as though they had no possessions,
Rev 3:18 Therefore I counsel you to **b** from me gold refined
13:17 no one can **b** or sell who does not have the mark,
Tob 1:13 and I used to **b** everything he needed.
1:14 Until his death I used to go into Media, and **b**
Sir 20:12 Some **b** much for little, but pay for it seven times
Bar 1:10 so **b** with the money burnt offerings
3:30 and found her, and will **b** her for pure gold?
1Mc 12:36 to isolate it so that its garrison could neither **b**
13:49 from going in and out to **b** and sell in the country.
2Mc 8:11 inviting them to **b** Jewish slaves and promising
8:25 the money of those who had come to **b** them
8:34 who had brought the thousand merchants to **b**

BUYER (5) [BUY]
Dt 28:68 as male and female slaves, but there will be no **b.**
Pr 20:14 "Bad, bad," says the **b,** then goes away and boasts.
Isa 24:2 as with the **b,** so with the seller;
Eze 7:12 let not the **b** rejoice, nor the seller mourn,
Sir 37:11 a **b** about selling, with a miser about generosity

BUYING (5) [BUY]
Am 8:6 **b** the poor for silver and the needy for a pair
Mt 21:12 and drove out all who were selling and **b** in
Mk 11:15 and those who were **b** in the temple,
Lk 17:28 they were eating and drinking, **b** and selling,
Sir 27:2 so sin is wedged in between selling and **b.**

BUYS (4) [BUY]
Pr 31:16 She considers a field and **b** it;
Mt 13:44 in his joy he goes and sells all that he has and **b**
Rev 18:11 since no one **b** their cargo anymore,
2Es 16:41 let the one who **b** be like one who will lose;

BUZ (3) [BUZITE]
Ge 22:21 **B** his brother, Kemuel the father of Aram,
1Ch 5:14 son of Jeshishai, son of Jahdo, son of **B;**
Jer 25:23 Tema, **B,** and all who have shaven temples;

BUZI (1)
Eze 1:3 of the LORD came to the priest Ezekiel son of **B,**

BUZITE (2) [BUZ]
Job 32:2 Then Elihu son of Barachel the **B,**
32:6 Elihu son of Barachel the **B** answered:

BUZZARD (2) [BUZZARDS]
Lev 11:14 the **b,** the kite of any kind;
Dt 14:13 the **b,** the kite, of any kind;

BUZZARDS (1) [BUZZARD]
Isa 34:15 there too the **b** shall gather, each one with its mate.

BY (3455) See Index of Articles Etc.

BYGONE (1)
Job 8:8 "For inquire now of **b** generations,

BYPATHS (1) [PATH]
Jer 18:15 and have gone into **b,** not the highway,

BYSTANDERS (8) [STAND]
Mt 26:71 and she said to the **b,**
26:73 After a little while the **b** came up and said to Peter,
27:47 When some of the **b** heard it, they said,
Mk 11:5 some of the **b** said to them,
14:69 on seeing him, began again to say to the **b,**
14:70 Then after a little while the **b** again said to Peter,
15:35 When some of the **b** heard it, they said, "Listen,
Lk 19:24 to the **b,** 'Take the pound from him and give it to

BYWAYS (1) [WAY]
Jdg 5:6 caravans ceased and travelers kept to the **b.**

BYWORD (14) [WORD]
Dt 28:37 and a **b** among all the peoples where
2Ch 7:20 will make it a proverb and a **b** among all peoples.
Job 17:6 "He has made me a **b** of the peoples,
30:9 now they mock me in song; I am a **b** to them.
Ps 44:14 You have made us a **b** among the nations,
69:11 I became a **b** to them.
Jer 24:9 a disgrace, a **b,** a taunt, and a curse in all
Eze 14:8 a **b** and cut them off from the midst of my people;
16:56 not your sister Sodom a **b** in your mouth in the day
23:10 and she became a **b** among women.
Joel 2:17 not make your heritage a mockery, a **b** among
Tob 3:4 exile, and death, to become the talk, the **b,**
Wis 5:4 in derision and made a **b** of reproach—
Sir 42:11 a **b** in the city and the assembly of the people,

C

CABBON (1)
Jos 15:40 **C,** Lahmam, Chitlish,

CABINS (KJV) See CELLS

CABUL (2)
Jos 19:27 then it continues in the north to **C,**
1Ki 9:13 So they are called the land of **C** to this day.

CAESAREA (17)
Mt 16:13 when Jesus came into the district of **C** Philippi,
Mk 8:27 on with his disciples to the villages of **C** Philippi;
Ac 8:40 the good news to all the towns until he came to **C.**
9:30 they brought him down to **C** and sent him off
10:1 In **C** there was a man named Cornelius,
Ac 10:24 The following day they came to **C.**
11:11 that very moment three men, sent to me from **C,**
12:19 down from Judea to **C** and stayed there.
18:22 When he had landed at **C,**
21:8 The next day we left and came to **C;**
21:16 Some of the disciples from **C** also came along
23:23 "Get ready to leave by nine o'clock tonight for **C**
23:33 When they came to **C** and delivered the letter to
25:1 he went up from **C** to Jerusalem
25:4 Festus replied that Paul was being kept at **C,**
25:6 or ten days, he went down to **C;**
25:13 and Bernice arrived at **C** to welcome Festus.

CAGE (3)
Jer 5:27 a **c** full of birds, their houses are full of treachery;
Eze 19:9 With hooks they put him in a **c,**
Sir 11:30 Like a decoy partridge in a **c,**

CAIAPHAS (9)
Mt 26:3 in the palace of the high priest, who was called **C,**
26:57 Those who had arrested Jesus took him to **C**
Lk 3:2 during the high priesthood of Annas and **C,**
Jn 11:49 But one of them, **C,** who was high priest that year,
18:13 who was the father-in-law of **C,**
18:14 **C** was the one who had advised the Jews
18:24 Then Annas sent him bound to **C** the high priest.
18:28 they took Jesus from **C** to Pilate's headquarters.
Ac 4:6 **C,** John, and Alexander, and all who were of

CAIN‡ (19) [CAIN'S]
Ge 4:1 and she conceived and bore **C,** saying,
4:2 and **C** a tiller of the ground.
4:3 of time **C** brought to the LORD an offering of
4:5 but for **C** and his offering he had no regard.
4:5 So **C** was very angry, and his countenance fell.
4:6 The LORD said to **C,** "Why are you angry,
4:8 **C** said to his brother Abel,
4:8 **C** rose up against his brother Abel, and killed him.
4:9 LORD said to **C,** "Where is your brother Abel?"
4:13 **C** said to the LORD, "My punishment is greater
4:15 Whoever kills **C** will suffer a sevenfold vengeance.
4:15 And the LORD put a mark on **C,**
4:16 **C** went away from the presence of the LORD,
4:17 **C** knew his wife, and she conceived
4:24 If **C** is avenged sevenfold,
4:25 child instead of Abel, because **C** killed him."
1Jn 3:12 We must not be like **C** who was from the evil one
Jude 1:11 For they go the way of **C,**
4Mc 18:11 He read to you about Abel slain by **C,**

CAIN'S (1) [CAIN]
Heb 11:4 to God a more acceptable sacrifice than **C.**

CAINAN (2) [=KENAN]
Lk 3:36 son of **C,** son of Arphaxad, son of Shem,
3:37 son of Jared, son of Mahalaleel, son of **C,**

CAKE‡ (14) [BARLEY-CAKE, CAKES]
Ge 40:16 there were three **c** baskets on my head,
Ex 29:23 one **c** of bread made with oil, and one wafer,
Lev 7:14 From this you shall offer one **c**
8:26 he took one **c** of unleavened bread,
8:26 one **c** of bread with oil, and one wafer,
Nu 6:19 and one unleavened **c** out of the basket,
Jdg 7:13 and in it a **c** of barley bread tumbled into the camp
1Sa 30:12 also gave him a piece of fig **c** and two clusters
2Sa 6:19 both men and women, to each a **c** of bread,
6:19 a portion of meat, and a **c** of raisins.
1Ki 17:13 but first make me a little **c** of it and bring it to me,
19:6 and there at his head was a **c** baked on hot stones,
1Ch 16:3 a portion of meat, and a **c** of raisins.
Hos 7:8 Ephraim is a **c** not turned.

CAKES (31) [CAKE]
Ge 18:6 of choice flour, knead it, and make **c."**
Ex 12:39 They baked unleavened **c** of the dough
29:2 unleavened **c** mixed with oil,
Lev 2:4 unleavened **c** mixed with oil,
6:16 it shall be eaten as unleavened **c** in a holy place;
7:12 the thank offering unleavened **c** mixed with oil,
7:12 and **c** of choice flour well soaked in oil.
7:13 of well-being you shall bring your offering with **c**
Nu 6:15 **c** of choice flour mixed with oil
11:8 then boiled it in pots and made **c** of it;
11:8 taste of it was like the taste of **c** baked with oil.
Jos 5:11 unleavened **c** and parched grain.
Jdg 6:19 and unleavened **c** from an ephah of flour;
6:20 "Take the meat and the unleavened **c,**
6:21 and touched the meat and the unleavened **c;**
6:21 and consumed the meat and the unleavened **c;**
1Sa 25:18 and two hundred **c** of figs.
28:24 kneaded it, and baked unleavened **c.**
2Sa 13:6 and make a couple of **c** in my sight,
13:8 made **c** in his sight, and baked the **c.**
13:10 So Tamar took the **c** she had made,
1Ki 14:3 Take with you ten loaves, some **c,**
1Ch 9:31 was in charge of making the flat **c.**
12:40 abundant provisions of meal, **c** of figs,
Isa 16:7 utterly stricken, for the raisin **c** of Kir-hareseth.
Jer 7:18 to make **c** for the queen of heaven;
44:19 do you think that we made **c** for her,
Hos 3:1 though they turn to other gods and love raisin **c."**
Jdt 10:5 and filled a bag with roasted grain, dried fig **c,**

Bel 1:27 and hair, and boiled them together and made **c**,

CALAH (2)

Ge 10:11 and built Nineveh, Rehoboth-ir, **C**,
10:12 Resen between Nineveh and **C**;

CALAMITIES (30) [CALAMITY]

1Sa 10:19 who saves you from all your **c** and your distresses;
Ps 71:20 and **c** will revive me again;
2Co 6: 4 great endurance, in afflictions, hardships, **c**,
12:10 persecutions, and **c** for the sake of Christ;
Tob 7: 7 "O most miserable of **c** that such an upright
AdE 16: 5 and have been involved in irremediable **c**,
Sir 10:13 the Lord brings upon them unheard-of **c**,
23:11 for his house will be filled with **c**.
40: 9 **c** and famine and ruin and plague.
Bar 1:20 to us the **c** and the curse that the Lord declared
2: 7 All those **c** with which the Lord threatened us
2: 9 And the Lord has kept the **c** ready,
3: 4 so that **c** have clung to us.
4:18 For he who brought these **c**
4:29 For the one who brought these **c**
2Mc 6:12 not to be depressed by such **c**,
6:16 Although he disciplines us with **c**,
10:10 and will give a brief summary of the principal **c** of
14:14 and **c** of the Jews would mean prosperity
2Es 15:27 Already **c** have come upon the whole earth,
16: 5 **C** have been sent upon you,
16: 8 Lord God sends **c**, and who will drive them away?
16:14 **C** are sent forth and shall not return
16:16 the **c** that are sent upon the earth shall not return.
16:18 the beginning of **c**, when all shall tremble.
16:18 What shall they do, when the **c** come?
16:21 and then **c** shall spring up on the earth—
16:37 The **c** draw near, and are not delayed.
16:39 so the **c** will not delay in coming upon the earth,
16:40 in the midst of the **c** be like strangers on the earth.

CALAMITY (58) [CALAMITIES]

A. DAY OF ... CALAMITY (12)

Dt 29:21 from all the tribes of Israel for **c**,
32:35 because the day of their **c** is at hand, A
Ru 1:21 and the Almighty has brought **c** upon me?"
2Sa 22:19 They came upon me in the day of my **c**, A
1Ki 17:20 have you brought **c** even upon the widow
1Ch 21:15 LORD took note and relented concerning the **c**;
2Ch 7:22 therefore he has brought all this **c** upon them.' "
Est 8: 6 For how can I bear to see the **c** that is coming
Job 6: 2 and all my **c** laid in the balances!
6:21 you see my **c**, and are afraid.
6:30 Cannot my taste discern **c**?
9:23 he mocks at the **c** of the innocent.
18:12 and **c** is ready for their stumbling.
21:17 How often does **c** come upon them?
21:30 that the wicked are spared in the day of **c**, A
30:13 They break up my path, they promote my **c**;
31: 3 Does not **c** befall the unrighteous,
31:23 For I was in terror of **c** from God,
Ps 18:18 They confronted me in the day of my **c**; A
35:26 Let all those who rejoice at my **c** be put to shame
107:26 their courage melted away in their **c**;
Pr 1:26 I also will laugh at your **c**;
1:27 and your **c** comes like a whirlwind,
6:15 on such a one **c** will descend suddenly;
17: 5 those who are glad at **c** will not go unpunished.
17:20 and the perverse of tongue fall into **c**.
22: 8 Whoever sows injustice will reap **c**,
24:16 but the wicked are overthrown by **c**.
27:10 to the house of your kindred in the day of your **c**. A
28:14 but one who is hard-hearted will fall into **c**.
Ecc 9:12 so mortals are snared at a time of **c**,
Isa 10: 3 in the **c** that will come from far away?
57: 1 For the righteous are taken away from **c**,
65:23 not labor in vain, or bear children for **c**;
Jer 18:17 not my face, in the day of their **c**. A
23:17 they say, "No **c** shall come upon you."
46:21 for the day of their **c** has come upon them, A
48:16 The **c** of Moab is near at hand
49: 8 For I will bring the **c** of Esau upon him,
49:32 and I will bring **c** against them from every side,
Eze 35: 5 to the power of the sword at the time of their **c**, at
Da 9:12 upon us a **c** so great that what has been done
9:13 all this **c** has come upon us.
9:14 over this **c** until he brought it upon us.
Ob 1:13 the gate of my people on the day of their **c**; A
1:13 over Judah's disaster on the day of his **c**; A
1:13 not have looted his goods on the day of his **c**. A
Jnh 1: 7 on whose account this **c** has come upon us."
1: 8 "Tell us why this **c** has come upon us.
3:10 the **c** that he had said he would bring upon them;
Hab 3:16 day of **c** to come upon the people who attack us. A
Sir 2: 2 and do not be impetuous in time of **c**.
3:28 When **c** befalls the proud, there is no healing,
5: 8 for it will not benefit you on the day of **c**. A
41: 9 If you have children, **c** will be theirs;
LtJ 6:48 For when war or **c** comes upon them,
6:49 for they cannot save themselves from war or **c**?
1Mc 13:32 and he brought great **c** on the land.

CALAMOLALUS (1)

1Es 5:22 The descendants of the other **C** and Ono,

CALAMUS (1)

SS 4:14 **c** and cinnamon, with all trees of frankincense,

CALCOL (2)

1Ki 4:31 and Heman, **C**, and Darda, children of Mahol;
1Ch 2: 6 Zimri, Ethan, Heman, **C**, and Dara, five in all.

CALCULATE (2) [CALCULATED]

Dt 19: 3 You shall **c** the distances and divide
Rev 13:18 let anyone with understanding **c** the number of

CALCULATED (1) [CALCULATE]

Ac 19:19 when the value of these books was **c**,

CALCULATION See Index to Footnotes

CALDRON (3) [CALDRONS]

1Sa 2:14 and he would thrust it into the pan, or kettle, or **c**,
Mic 3: 3 up like meat in a kettle, like flesh in a **c**.
4Mc 12: 1 When he too, thrown into the **c**,

CALDRONS (5) [CALDRON]

2Ch 35:13 and they boiled the holy offerings in pots, in **c**,
2Mc 7: 3 and gave orders to have pans and **c** heated.
1Es 1:12 they boiled the sacrifices in bronze pots and **c**,
4Mc 8:13 rack and hooks and catapults and **c**,
18:20 the Greeks quenched fire with fire in his cruel **c**,

CALEB (35) [CALEB'S, CALEB-EPHRATHAH, CALEBITE]

Nu 13: 6 from the tribe of Judah, **C** son of Jephunneh;
13:30 But **C** quieted the people before Moses, and said,
14: 6 And Joshua son of Nun and **C** son of Jephunneh,
14:24 But my servant **C**, because he has a different spirit
14:30 except **C** son of Jephunneh and Joshua son
14:38 and **C** son of Jephunneh alone remained alive,
26:65 except **C** son of Jephunneh and Joshua son
32:12 none except **C** son of Jephunneh the Kenizzite
34:19 Of the tribe of Judah, **C** son of Jephunneh.
Dt 1:36 except **C** son of Jephunneh.
Jos 14: 6 and **C** son of Jephunneh the Kenizzite said to him,
14:13 and gave Hebron to **C** son of Jephunneh for
14:14 of **C** son of Jephunneh the Kenizzite to this day,
15:13 to **C** son of Jephunneh a portion among the people
15:14 **C** drove out from there the three sons of Anak:
15:16 And **C** said, "Whoever attacks Kiriath-sepher
15:17 Othniel son of Kenaz, the brother of **C**, took it;
15:18 she dismounted from her donkey, **C** said to her,
15:19 So **C** gave her the upper springs and
21:12 the town and its villages had been given to **C** son
Jdg 1:12 Then **C** said, "Whoever attacks Kiriath-sepher
1:14 she dismounted from her donkey, **C** said to her,
1:15 So **C** gave her Upper Gulloth and Lower Gulloth.
1:20 Hebron was given to **C**, as Moses had said;
1Sa 30:14 to Judah and on the Negeb of **C**;
1Ch 2:18 **C** son of Hezron had children by his wife Azubah,
2:19 When Azubah died, **C** married Ephrath,
2:42 The sons of **C** brother of Jerahmeel:
2:49 and the daughter of **C** was Achsah.
2:50 These were the descendants of **C**.
4:15 The sons of **C** son of Jephunneh:
6:56 and its villages they gave to **C** son of Jephunneh.
Sir 46: 7 he and **C** son of Jephunneh:
46: 9 The Lord gave **C** strength,
1Mc 2:56 **C**, because he testified in the assembly,

CALEB'S (4) [CALEB]

Jdg 1:13 Othniel son of Kenaz, **C** younger brother, took it;
3: 9 Othniel son of Kenaz, **C** younger brother.
1Ch 2:46 Ephah also, **C** concubine, bore Haran, Moza,
2:48 Maacah, **C** concubine, bore Sheber and Tirhanah.

CALEB-EPHRATHAH (1) [CALEB, EPHRATH]

1Ch 2:24 After the death of Hezron, in **C**,

CALEBITE (1) [CALEB]

1Sa 25: 3 but the man was surly and mean; he was a **C**.

CALF (29) [CALF'S, CALVES, CALVING]

Ge 18: 7 Abraham ran to the herd, and took a **c**,
18: 8 and milk and the **c** that he had prepared, and set it
Ex 32: 4 formed it in a mold, and cast an image of a **c**;
32: 8 they have cast for themselves an image of a **c**,
32:19 As soon as he came near the camp and saw the **c**
32:20 He took the **c** that they had made,
32:24 and I threw it into the fire, and out came this **c**!"
32:35 they made the **c**—the one that Aaron made.
Lev 9: 2 "Take a bull **c** for a sin offering and a ram for
9: 3 a **c** and a lamb, yearlings without blemish,
9: 8 and slaughtered the **c** of the sin offering,
Dt 9:16 by casting for yourselves an image of a **c**;
9:21 Then I took the sinful thing you had made, the **c**,
1Sa 28:24 Now the woman had a fatted **c** in the house.
Ne 9:18 when they had cast an image of a **c** for themselves
Ps 29: 6 He makes Lebanon skip like a **c**,
106:19 a **c** at Horeb and worshiped a cast image.
Isa 11: 6 the **c** and the lion and the fatling together,
Jer 31:18 I was like a **c** untrained.
34:18 I will make like the **c** when they cut it in two
Jer 34:19 of the land who passed between the parts of the **c**
Hos 8: 5 Your **c** is rejected, O Samaria.
8: 6 The **c** of Samaria shall be broken to pieces.
10: 5 The inhabitants of Samaria tremble for the **c**
Lk 15:23 And get the fatted **c** and kill it,
15:27 and your father has killed the fatted **c**,
15:30 you killed the fatted **c** for him!'
Ac 7:41 At that time they made a **c**,
Tob 1: 5 of Naphtali sacrificed to the **c** that King Jeroboam

CALF'S (1) [CALF]

Eze 1: 7 soles of their feet were like the sole of a **c** foot;

CALL‡ (210) [CALLED, CALLING, CALLS, SO-CALLED]

Ge 2:19 to the man to see what he would **c** them;
16:11 you shall **c** him Ishmael,
17:15 "As for Sarai your wife, you shall not **c** her Sarai,
24:57 They said, "We will **c** the girl, and ask her."
30:13 For the women will **c** me happy";
Dt 2:11 though the Moabites **c** them Emim.
2:20 though the Ammonites **c** them Zamzummim,
3: 9 (the Sidonians **c** Hermon Sirion, while the Amorites **c** it Senir),
4: 7 near to it as the LORD our God is whenever we **c**
4:26 I **c** heaven and earth to witness against you today
30: 1 if you **c** them to mind among all the nations where
30:19 I **c** heaven and earth to witness against you today
31:14 **c** Joshua and present yourselves in the tent
31:28 in their hearing and **c** heaven and earth to witness
33:19 They **c** peoples to the mountain;
Jdg 8: 1 not to **c** us when you went to fight against
12: 1 and did not **c** us to go with you?
16:25 their hearts were merry, they said, "**C** Samson,
Ru 1:20 "**C** me no longer Naomi, **c** me Mara,
1:21 why **c** me Naomi when the LORD has dealt harshly
1Sa 3: 5 But he said, "I did not **c**; lie down again."
3: 6 But he said, "I did not **c**, my son; lie down again."
12:17 I will **c** upon the LORD,
14:17 "**C** the roll and see who has gone from us."
2Sa 15: 2 Absalom would **c** out and say,
17: 5 Then Absalom said, "**C** Hushai the Archite also,
20: 4 "**C** the men of Judah together to me
22: 4 I **c** upon the LORD, who is worthy to be praised,
1Ki 8:52 listening to them whenever they **c** to you.
18:24 Then you **c** on the name of your god and I will **c** on the name of the LORD;
18:25 **c** on the name of your god, but put no fire to it."
2Ki 4:12 "**C** the Shunammite woman."
4:15 He said, "**C** her." When he had called her,
4:36 "**C** the Shunammite woman."
5:11 stand and **c** on the name of the LORD his God,
1Ch 16: 8 O give thanks to the LORD, **c** on his name,
2Ch 13:12 to sound the **c** to battle against you.
Job 5: 1 "**C** now; is there anyone who will answer you?
13:22 Then **c**, and I will answer;
14:15 You would **c**, and I would answer you;
19: 7 I **c** aloud, but there is no justice.
19:16 I **c** to my servant, but he gives me no answer;
27:10 Will they **c** upon God at all times?
35: 9 they **c** for help because of the arm of the mighty.
Ps 4: 1 Answer me when I **c**, O God
4: 3 the LORD hears when I **c** to him.
10:13 "You will not **c** us to account"?
14: 4 and do not **c** upon the LORD?
17: 6 I **c** upon you, for you will answer me, O God;
18: 3 I **c** upon the LORD, who is worthy to be praised,
20: 9 O LORD; answer us when we **c**.
28: 1 To you, O LORD, I **c**; my rock,
31:17 O LORD, for I **c** on you;
50:15 **C** on me in the day of trouble;
53: 4 and do not **c** upon God?
55:16 But I **c** upon God, and the LORD will save me.
56: 9 Then my enemies will retreat in the day when I **c**.
61: 2 From the end of the earth I **c** to you,
63: 4 I will lift up my hands and **c** on your name.
72:12 For he delivers the needy when they **c**,
77:11 I will **c** to mind the deeds of the LORD;
79: 6 and on the kingdoms that do not **c** on your name.
80:18 give us life, and we will **c** on your name.
86: 5 abounding in steadfast love to all who **c** on you.
86: 7 In the day of my trouble I **c** on you,
88: 9 Every day I **c** on you, O LORD;
91:15 When they **c** to me, I will answer them;
102: 2 answer me speedily in the day when I **c**.
105: 1 O give thanks to the LORD, **c** on his name,
116: 2 therefore I will **c** on him as long as I live.
116:13 of salvation and **c** on the name of the LORD,
116:17 to you a thanksgiving sacrifice and **c** on the name
141: 1 I **c** upon you, O LORD;
141: 1 give ear to my voice when I **c** to you.
145:18 The LORD is near to all who **c** on him,
145:18 to all who **c** on him in truth.
Pr 1:28 Then they will **c** upon me, but I will not answer;
7: 4 and **c** insight your intimate friend,
8: 1 Does not wisdom **c**, and does
8: 4 O people, I **c**, and my cry is to all that live.
19: 7 When they **c** after them, they are not there.
31:28 Her children rise up and **c** her happy;
Isa 5:20 Ah, you who **c** evil good and good evil,
8: 4 for before the child knows how to **c** "My father"
8:12 Do not **c** conspiracy all
12: 4 Give thanks to the LORD, **c** on his name;
22:20 On that day I will **c** my servant Eliakim son
31: 2 he does not **c** back his words,

Isa 34:14 goat-demons shall c to each other;
43:22 Yet you did not c upon me, O Jacob;
45: 3 the God of Israel, who c you by your name.
45: 4 I c you by your name, I surname you,
48: 2 For they c themselves after the holy city,
55: 5 See, you shall c nations that you do not know,
55: 6 c upon him while he is near;
58: 5 you c this a fast, a day acceptable to the LORD?
58: 9 Then you shall c, and the LORD will answer;
58:13 if you c the sabbath a delight and the holy day of
60:14 they shall c you the City of the LORD,
60:18 you shall c your walls Salvation,
65: 1 here I am," to a nation that did not c on my name.
65:24 Before they c I will answer,
Jer 3:19 And I thought you would c me, My Father,
7:27 You shall c to them, but they will not answer you.
9:17 Consider, and c for the mourning women to come;
10:25 and on the peoples that do not c on your name;
11:14 for I will not listen when they c to me in the time
29:12 when you c upon me and come and pray to me,
31: 6 be a day when sentinels will c in the hill country
33: 3 C to me and I will answer you,
La 3: 8 I c and cry for help, he shuts out my prayer;
3:21 But this I c to mind, and therefore I have hope:
Eze 21:22 to c out for slaughter, for raising the battle cry,
Hos 2:16 On that day, says the LORD, you will c me, "My husband," and no longer will you c me, "My Baal."
7:11 they c upon Egypt, they go to Assyria.
11: 7 To the Most High they c,
Joel 1:14 Sanctify a fast, c a solemn assembly.
2:15 sanctify a fast; c a solemn assembly;
Am 5:16 They shall c the farmers to mourning,
Jnh 1: 6 Get up, c on your god!
Zep 3: 9 that all of them may c on the name of the LORD
Zec 13: 9 They will c on my name, and I will answer them.
Mt 9:13 I have come to c not the righteous but sinners."
20: 8 'C the laborers and give them their pay,
22: 3 He sent his slaves to c those who had been invited
23: 7 and to have people c them rabbi.
23: 9 And c no one your father on earth,
24:31 he will send out his angels with a loud trumpet c,
Mk 2:17 I have come to c not the righteous but sinners."
10:18 Jesus said to him, "Why do you c me good?
10:49 Jesus stood still and said, "C him here."
15:12 to do with the man you c the King of the Jews?"
Lk 1:48 from now on all generations will c me blessed;
5:32 to c not the righteous but sinners to repentance."
6:46 "Why do you c me 'Lord, Lord,'
18:19 Jesus said to him, "Why do you c me good?
Jn 4:16 Jesus said to her, "Go, c your husband,
13:13 You c me Teacher and Lord—
15:15 I do not c you servants any longer,
Ac 10:15 What God has made clean, you must not c profane.
10:28 that I should not c anyone profane or unclean.
11: 9 What God has made clean, you must not c profane.
24:14 that according to the Way, which they c a sect,
Ro 2:17 But if you c yourself a Jew and rely on the law
9:12 not by works but by his c) she was told,
9:25 not my people I will c 'my people,'
9:25 and her who was not beloved I will c 'beloved.' "
10:12 of all and is generous to all who c on him.
10:14 But how are they to c on one in whom they have
1Co 1: 2 with all those who in every place c on the name
1:26 Consider your own c, brothers and sisters:
7:18 at the time of his c already circumcised?
7:18 Was anyone at the time of his c uncircumcised?
2Co 1:23 But I c on God as witness against me:
Php 3:14 the prize of the heavenly c of God in Christ Jesus.
1Th 4: 7 For God did not c us to impurity but in holiness.
4:16 with the archangel's c and with the sound
2Th 1:11 asking that our God will make you worthy of his c
2Ti 2:22 with those who c on the Lord from a pure heart.
Heb 2:11 not ashamed to c them brothers and sisters,
Jas 5:11 Indeed we c blessed those who showed endurance.
5:14 They should c for the elders of the church
2Pe 1:10 the more eager to confirm your c and election,
3Jn 1:10 I will c attention to what he is doing
Rev 2:24 not learned what some c 'the deep things
6: 1 and I heard one of the four living creatures c out,
6: 3 I heard the second living creature c out, "Come!"
6: 5 I heard the third living creature c out, "Come!"
6: 7 the voice of the fourth living creature c out,
13:10 a c for the endurance and faith of the saints.
14:12 Here is a c for the endurance of the saints,
Tob 4: 2 Why do I not c my son Tobias and explain to him
5: 9 He replied, "C the man in, my son,
Jdt 3: 8 that all their dialects and tribes should c upon him
7:28 We c to witness against you heaven and earth
8:17 let us c upon him to help us,
16: 1 exalt him, and c upon his name.
AdE 4: 8 and demands our death. C upon the Lord;
Wis 14:22 they c such great evils peace.
Sir 11:28 C no one happy before his death;
25: 7 I can think of nine whom I would c blessed,
37:24 and all who see him will c him happy.
42:15 I will now c to mind the works of the Lord,
Bar 3: 7 in our hearts so that we would c upon your name;
LtJ 6:40 that they are gods, or c them gods?
6:44 that they are gods, or c them gods?
6:64 that they are gods, nor c them gods, for they are
1Mc 7:45 as they followed they kept sounding the battle c
2Mc 3:31 of Heliodorus's friends quickly begged Onias to c
6: 2 also to pollute the temple in Jerusalem and to c it
6: 2 and to c the one in Gerizim the temple
13:10 he ordered the people to c upon the Lord day
1Es 1:50 their ancestors sent his messenger to c them back,
3:16 He said, "C the young men,
3Mc 1:27 to c upon him who has all power to defend them
2:17 or c us to account for this profanation,
2Es 1:26 When you c to me, I will not listen to you;
1:37 I c to witness the gratitude of the people that is
2: 5 Now I c upon you, father,
2:14 C, O c heaven and earth to witness:
2:36 I publicly c on my savior to witness.
4: 5 or c back for me the day that is past."
13:12 the mountain and c to himself another multitude
4Mc 1:10 but I would also c them blessed for the honor
12:17 and I c on the God of our ancestors to be merciful

CALLED‡ (612) [CALL]

Ge 1: 5 God c the light Day, and the darkness he c Night.
1: 8 God c the dome Sky.
1:10 God c the dry land Earth,
1:10 the waters that were gathered together he c Seas.
2:19 and whatever the man c every living creature,
2:23 this one shall be c Woman,
3: 9 But the LORD God c to the man,
11: 9 Therefore it was c Babel, because there
12:18 So Pharaoh c Abram, and said,
13: 4 and there Abram c on the name of the LORD.
16:14 Therefore the well was c Beer-lahai-roi;
19: 5 and they c to Lot, "Where are the men who came
19:22 Therefore the city was c Zoar.
20: 8 c all his servants and told them all these things;
20: 9 Then Abimelech c Abraham, and said to him,
21:17 and the angel of God c to Hagar from heaven,
21:31 Therefore that place was c Beer-sheba;
21:33 and c there on the name of the LORD,
22:11 the angel of the LORD c to him from heaven,
22:14 Abraham c that place "The LORD will provide";
22:15 of the LORD c to Abraham a second time
24:58 And they c Rebekah, and said to her,
25:30 (Therefore he was c Edom.)
26: 9 So Abimelech c for Isaac, and said,
26:20 So he c the well Esek,
26:21 that one also; so he c it Sitnah.
26:22 so he c it Rehoboth, saying,
26:25 c on the name of the LORD,
26:33 He c it Shibah; therefore the name of the
27: 1 he c his elder son Esau and said to him, "My son";
27:42 so she sent and c her younger son Jacob and said
28: 1 Then Isaac c Jacob and blessed him,
28:19 He c that place Bethel;
31: 4 So Jacob sent and c Rachel and Leah into the field
31:47 Laban c it Jegar-sahadutha: but Jacob c it Galeed.
31:48 and me today." Therefore he c it Galeed,
31:54 on the height and c his kinsfolk to eat bread;
32: 2 So he c that place Mahanaim.
32:28 the man said, "You shall no longer be c Jacob,
32:30 So Jacob c the place Peniel, saying,
33:17 therefore the place is c Succoth.
33:20 There he erected an altar and c it El-Elohe-Israel.
35: 7 there he built an altar and c the place El-bethel,
35: 8 So it was c Allon-bacuth.
35:10 no longer shall you be c Jacob,
35:10 So he was c Israel.
35:15 So Jacob c the place where God had spoken
35:18 but his father c him Benjamin.
39:14 she c out to the members of her household
41: 8 so he sent and c for all the magicians of Egypt
47:29 he c his son Joseph and said to him,
49: 1 Then Jacob c his sons, and said:
Ex 2: 8 So the girl went and c the child's mother.
3: 4 God c to him out of the bush, "Moses, Moses!"
8: 8 Then Pharaoh c Moses and Aaron, and said,
12:21 Moses c all the elders of Israel and said to them,
15:23 That is why it was c Marah.
16:31 The house of Israel c it manna;
17: 7 He c the place Massah and Meribah,
17:15 And Moses built an altar and c it,
19: 3 the LORD c to him from the mountain, saying,
24:16 on the seventh day he c to Moses out of the cloud.
31: 2 I have c by name Bezalel son of Uri son of Hur,
33: 7 he c it the tent of meeting.
34:31 But Moses c to them;
35:30 the LORD has c by name Bezalel son of Uri son
36: 2 then c Bezalel and Oholiab and every skillful one
Nu 11: 3 So that place was c Taberah,
11:34 So that place was c Kibroth-hattaavah,
12: 5 and c Aaron and Miriam;
13:24 That place was c the Wadi Eshcol,
21: 3 so the place was c Hormah.
Dt 3:13 all that portion of Bashan used to be c a land
28:10 All the peoples of the earth shall see that you are c
Jos 5: 9 And so that place is c Gilgal to this day.
7:26 that place to this day is c the Valley of Achor.
8:16 the people who were in the city were c together
22:34 Reubenites and the Gadites c the altar Witness;
Jdg 1:17 So the city was c Hormah.
4:13 Sisera c out all his chariots,
6:24 Gideon built an altar there to the LORD, and c it,
6:32 Therefore on that day Gideon was c Jerubbaal,
6:34 and the Abiezrites were c out to follow him.
6:35 and they too were c out to follow him.
7:23 of Israel were c out from Naphtali and from Asher
7:24 So all the men of Ephraim were c out,
9:54 he c to the young man who carried his armor
10: 4 and are c Havvoth-jair to this day.
10:17 Then the Ammonites were c to arms,
12: 1 The men of Ephraim were c to arms,
12: 2 I c you, you did not deliver me from their hand.
15:17 and that place was c Ramath-lehi.
15:18 and he c on the LORD, saying,
Jdg 16:18 she sent and c the lords of the Philistines, saying,
16:19 and she c a man, and had him shave off
16:25 So they c Samson out of the prison,
16:28 Then Samson c to the LORD and said,
18:12 On this account that place is c Mahaneh-dan
18:22 in the houses near Micah's house were c out,
21: 9 For when the roll was c among the people,
1Sa 3: 4 Then the LORD c, "Samuel!
3: 5 ran to Eli, and said, "Here I am, for you c me."
3: 6 The LORD c again, "Samuel!"
3: 6 and said, "Here I am, for you c me."
3: 8 The LORD c Samuel again, a third time.
3: 8 and said, "Here I am, for you c me."
3:16 But Eli c Samuel and said, "Samuel, my son."
6: 2 the Philistines c for the priests and the diviners
9: 9 now c a prophet was formerly c a seer.)
9:26 the break of dawn Samuel c to Saul upon the roof,
12:18 So Samuel c upon the LORD,
13: 4 the people were c out to join Saul at Gilgal.
14:17 When they had c the roll,
16: 8 Then Jesse c Abinadab, and made him pass
19: 7 So Jonathan c David and related all these things
20:37 Jonathan c after the boy and said,
20:38 Jonathan c after the boy, "Hurry, be quick,
23:28 therefore that place was c the Rock of Escape.
24: 8 up and went out of the cave and c after Saul,
26:14 David c to the army and to Abner son of Ner,
29: 6 Then Achish c David and said to him,
2Sa 1: 7 he looked behind him, he saw me, and c to me.
1:15 Then David c one of the young men and said,
2:16 Therefore that place was c Helkath-hazzurim,
2:26 Then Abner c to Joab, "Is the sword
5:20 Therefore that place is c Baal-perazim.
6: 2 which is c by the name of the LORD
6: 8 so that place is c Perez-uzzah, to this day.
12:28 and it will be c by my name."
13:17 He c the young man who served him and said,
18:18 he c the pillar by his own name.
18:18 It is c Absalom's Monument to this day.
18:26 and the sentinel c to the gatekeeper and said, "See,
20:16 Then a wise woman c from the city, "Listen!
20:21 c Sheba son of Bichri, has lifted up his hand
21: 2 So the king c the Gibeonites and spoke to them.
22: 7 In my distress I c upon the LORD; to my God I c.
1Ki 7:21 he set up the pillar on the south and c it Jachin;
7:21 and he set up the pillar on the north and c it Boaz.
9:13 So they are c the land of Cabul to this day.
12: 3 And they sent and c him;
12:20 and c him to the assembly and made him king
16:24 he fortified the hill, and c the city that he built,
17:10 he c to her and said,
17:11 As she was going to bring it, he c to her and said,
18:26 c on the name of Baal from morning until noon,
20: 7 Then the king of Israel c all the elders of the land,
2Ki 3:21 were c out and were drawn up at the frontier.
4:12 When he had c her, she stood before him.
4:15 When he had c her, she stood at the door.
4:22 Then she c to her husband, and said,
4:36 "Call the Shunammite woman." So he c her.
6:11 he c his officers and said to them,
7:10 So they came and c to the gatekeepers of the city,
7:11 Then the gatekeepers c out and proclaimed it to
8: 1 for the LORD has c for a famine,
9: 1 the prophet Elisha c a member of the company
14: 7 he c it Jokthe-el, which is its name to this day.
18: 4 had made offerings to it; it was c Nehushtan.
18:18 When they c for the king,
18:28 and c out in a loud voice in the language of Judah,
1Ch 1:43 Bela son of Beor, whose city was c Dinhabah.
4:10 Jabez c on the God of Israel, saying,
11: 7 therefore it was c the city of David.
13: 6 which is c by his name.
13:11 so that place is c Perez-uzzah to this day.
14:11 Therefore that place is c Baal-perazim.
21:26 He c upon the LORD, and he answered him
22: 6 Then he c for his son Solomon and charged him
2Ch 3:17 the one on the right he c Jachin,
7:14 if my people who are c by my name humble
10: 3 They sent and c him; and Jeroboam
20:26 place has been c the Valley of Beracah to this day.
Ezr 2:61 and was c by their name).
8:17 the leader at the place c Casiphia,
Ne 5: 7 And I c a great assembly to deal with them,
5:12 And I c the priests, and made them take an oath
7:63 the daughters of Barzillai the Gileadite and was c
Est 4: 5 Then Esther c for Hathach,
4:11 to the king inside the inner court without being c,
4:11 not been c to come in to the king for thirty days."
5:10 he sent and c for his friends and his wife Zeresh,
9:26 these days are c Purim, from the word Pur.
Job 12: 4 I, who c upon God and he answered me,
31:24 or c fine gold my confidence;
Ps 18: 6 In my distress I c upon the LORD;
41: 2 they are c happy in the land.
81: 7 In distress you c, and I rescued you;
99: 6 Samuel also was among those who c on his name.
116: 4 Then I c on the name of the LORD:
118: 5 Out of my distress I c on the LORD;
138: 3 On the day I c, you answered me,
Pr 1:24 Because I have c and you refused,
3:18 those who hold her fast are c happy.
16:21 The wise of heart is c perceptive,
24: 8 to do evil will be c a mischief-maker.
SS 3: 1 I c him, but he gave no answer.
5: 6 I c him, but he gave no answer.
6: 9 The maidens saw her and c her happy;
Isa 1:26 Afterward you shall be c the city of righteousness,

Isa 4: 1 just let us be c by your name;
4: 3 in Zion and remains in Jerusalem will be c holy,
6: 3 And one c to another and said:
6: 4 the thresholds shook at the voices of those who c,
19: 18 One of these will be c the City of the Sun.
21: 8 Then the watcher c out:
22: 12 In that day the Lord GOD of hosts c to weeping
30: 7 therefore I have c her, "Rahab who sits still."
31: 4 when a band of shepherds is c out against it—
32: 5 A fool will no longer be c noble,
35: 8 and it shall be c the Holy Way;
36: 13 and c out in a loud voice in the language of Judah,
41: 9 and c from its farthest corners, saying to you,
42: 6 I have c you in righteousness,
43: 1 I have c you by name, you are mine.
43: 7 everyone who is c by my name,
44: 5 another will be c by the name of Jacob,
47: 1 For you shall no more be c tender and delicate.
47: 5 you shall no more be c the mistress of kingdoms.
48: 1 O house of Jacob, who are c by the name of Israel,
48: 8 and that from birth you were c a rebel.
48: 12 Listen to me, O Jacob, and Israel, whom I c:
48: 15 I, even I, have spoken and c him,
49: 1 The LORD c me before I was born,
50: 2 Why did no one answer when I c?
51: 2 for he was but one when I c him,
54: 5 the God of the whole earth he is c.
54: 6 For the LORD has c you like a wife forsaken
56: 7 for my house shall be c a house of prayer
58: 12 you shall be c the repairer of the breach,
61: 3 They will be c oaks of righteousness,
61: 6 but you shall be c priests of the LORD, you shall
62: 2 and you shall be c by a new name that the mouth
62: 4 but you shall be c My Delight Is in Her,
62: 12 They shall be c, "The Holy People,
62: 12 and you shall be c, "Sought Out,
63: 19 like those not c by your name.
65: 12 because, when I c, you did not answer,
66: 4 because, when I c, no one answered,
Jer 3: 4 Have you not just now c to me, "My Father,
3: 17 At that time Jerusalem shall be c the throne of
6: 30 They are c "rejected silver,"
7: 10 which is c by my name, and say, "We are safe!"—
7: 11 Has this house, which is c by my name,
7: 13 and when I c you, you did not answer,
7: 14 I will do to the house that is c by my name,
7: 30 in the house that is c by my name,
7: 32 when it will no more be c Topheth,
11: 16 The LORD once c you, "A green olive tree,
14: 9 are in the midst of us, and we are c by your name;
15: 16 for I am c by your name, O LORD, God of hosts.
19: 6 when this place shall no more be c Topheth,
23: 6 And this is the name by which he will be c:
25: 29 to bring disaster on the city that is c by my name,
30: 17 because they have c you an outcast:
33: 16 And this is the name by which it will be c:
34: 15 before me in the house that is c by my name;
35: 17 I have c to them and they have not answered.
36: 4 Then Jeremiah c Baruch son of Neriah,
La 1: 19 I c to my lovers but they deceived me;
2: 15 the city that was c the perfection of beauty,
3: 55 I c on your name, O LORD,
3: 57 You came near when I c on you;
Eze 9: 3 The LORD c to the man clothed in linen,
10: 13 they were c in my hearing "the wheelwork."
20: 29 So it is c Bamah to this day.)
39: 11 it shall be c the Valley of Hamon-gog.
Da 1: 7 Daniel he c Belteshazzar, Hananiah he c Shadrach, Mishael he c Meshach, and Azariah he c Abednego
4: 19 Then Daniel, who was c Belteshazzar,
5: 12 Now let Daniel be c, and he will give
Hos 11: 1 I loved him, and out of Egypt I c my son.
11: 2 The more I c them, the more they went from me;
Am 9: 12 the remnant of Edom and all the nations who are c
Jnh 2: 2 "I c to the LORD out of my distress,
Hag 1: 11 I have c for a drought on the land and the hills,
Zec 7: 13 Just as, when I c, they would not hear, so,
7: 13 they would not hear, so, when they c,
8: 3 Jerusalem shall be c the faithful city,
8: 3 and the mountain of the LORD of hosts shall be c
Mal 1: 4 until they are c the wicked country,
2: 5 this c for reverence, and he revered me and stood
Mt 1: 16 of whom Jesus was born, who is c the Messiah.
2: 7 Then Herod secretly c for the wise men
2: 15 "Out of Egypt I have c my son."
2: 23 There he made his home in a town c Nazareth,
2: 23 "He will be c a Nazorean."
4: 18 Simon, who is c Peter, and Andrew his brother,
4: 21 mending their nets, and he c them.
5: 9 for they will be c children of God.
5: 19 will be c least in the kingdom of heaven;
5: 19 and teaches them will be c great in the kingdom
9: 9 he saw a man c Matthew sitting at the tax booth;
10: 25 If they have c the master of the house Beelzebul,
13: 55 Is not his mother c Mary?
15: 10 Then he c the crowd to him and said to them,
15: 32 Then Jesus c his disciples to him and said,
18: 2 He c a child, whom he put among them,
20: 25 But Jesus c them to him and said,
20: 32 Jesus stood still and c them, saying,
21: 13 'My house shall be c a house of prayer';
22: 14 For many are c, but few are chosen."
23: 8 But you are not to be c rabbi,
23: 10 Nor are you to be c instructors,
26: 3 the palace of the high priest, who was c Caiaphas,
26: 14 Then one of the twelve, who was c Judas Iscariot,
26: 36 Jesus went with them to a place c Gethsemane;
Mt 27: 8 that field has been c the Field of Blood to this day.
27: 16 a notorious prisoner, c Jesus Barabbas.
27: 17 Jesus Barabbas or Jesus who is c the Messiah?"
27: 22 "Then what should I do with Jesus who is c
27: 33 to a place c Golgotha (which means Place of
Mk 1: 20 Immediately he c them;
3: 13 the mountain and c to him those whom he wanted,
3: 23 And he c them to him,
3: 31 and standing outside, they sent to him and c him.
6: 7 He c the twelve and began to send them out two
7: 14 Then he c the crowd again and said to them,
8: 1 he c his disciples and said to them,
8: 34 He c the crowd with his disciples,
9: 35 He sat down, c the twelve, and said to them,
10: 42 So Jesus c them and said to them,
10: 49 they c the blind man, saying to him, "Take heart;
11: 17 'My house shall be c a house of prayer for all
12: 43 Then he c his disciples and said to them,
14: 32 They went to a place c Gethsemane;
15: 7 Now a man c Barabbas was in prison with
15: 16 and they c together the whole cohort.
15: 22 to the place c Golgotha (which means the place of
Lk 1: 26 by God to a town in Galilee c Nazareth,
1: 32 and will be c the Son of the Most High,
1: 35 he will be c Son of God.
1: 60 But his mother said, "No; he is to be c John."
1: 76 you, child, will be c the prophet of the Most High;
2: 4 to the city of David c Bethlehem,
2: 21 and he was c Jesus, the name given by the angel
6: 13 he c his disciples and chose twelve of them,
6: 15 and Simon, who was c the Zealot,
7: 11 Soon afterwards he went to a town c Nain,
8: 2 and infirmities: Mary, c Magdalene,
8: 8 As he said this, he c out,
8: 54 he took her by the hand and c out, "Child, get up!"
9: 1 Then Jesus c the twelve together
9: 10 and withdrew privately to a city c Bethsaida.
13: 12 When Jesus saw her, he c her over and said,
15: 19 I am no longer worthy to be c your son;
15: 21 I am no longer worthy to be c your son.'
15: 26 He c one of the slaves
16: 24 He c out, 'Father Abraham, have mercy on me,
17: 13 they c out, saying, "Jesus, Master, have mercy
18: 16 But Jesus c for them and said,
19: 29 at the place c the Mount of Olives,
21: 37 the night on the Mount of Olives, as it was c.
22: 1 which is c the Passover, was near.
22: 3 Then Satan entered into Judas c Iscariot,
22: 25 and those in authority over them are c benefactors.
22: 47 suddenly a crowd came, and the one c Judas,
23: 13 Pilate then c together the chief priests, the leaders,
23: 33 When they came to the place that is c The Skull,
24: 13 of them were going to a village c Emmaus,
Jn 1: 42 to be c Cephas" (which is translated Peter).
1: 48 "I saw you under the fig tree before Philip c you."
2: 9 the steward c the bridegroom
4: 5 So he came to a Samaritan city c Sychar,
4: 25 that Messiah is coming" (who is c Christ).
5: 2 c in Hebrew Beth-zatha, which has five porticoes.
6: 1 also c the Sea of Tiberias.
9: 11 He answered, "The man c Jesus made mud,
9: 18 and had received his sight until they c the parents
9: 24 second time they c the man who had been blind,
10: 35 to whom the word of God came were c 'gods'—
11: 16 Thomas, who was c the Twin,
11: 28 she went back and c her sister Mary,
11: 47 So the chief priests and the Pharisees c a meeting
11: 54 from there to a town c Ephraim in the region near
12: 17 when he c Lazarus out of the tomb and raised him
15: 15 but I have c you friends,
19: 13 and sat on the judge's bench at a place c
19: 17 he went out to what is c The Place of the Skull, which in Hebrew is c Golgotha.
20: 24 But Thomas (who was c the Twin),
21: 2 Thomas c the Twin, Nathanael of Cana in Galilee
Ac 1: 12 to Jerusalem from the mount c Olivet,
1: 19 that the field was c in their language Hakeldama,
1: 23 So they proposed two, Joseph c Barsabbas,
3: 2 at the gate of the temple c the Beautiful Gate so
3: 11 to them in the portico c Solomon's Portico,
4: 18 So they c them and ordered them not to speak
5: 21 they c together the council and the whole body of
5: 40 and when they had c in the apostles,
6: 2 And the twelve c together the whole community
6: 9 to the synagogue of the Freedmen (as it was c),
8: 10 "This man is the power of God that is c Great."
9: 11 "Get up and go to the street c Straight,
10: 1 a centurion of the Italian Cohort, as it was c.
10: 5 to Joppa for a certain Simon who is c Peter;
10: 7 he c two of his slaves and a devout soldier from
10: 18 They c out to ask whether Simon, who was c Peter, was staying there.
10: 24 and had c together his relatives and close friends.
10: 32 to Joppa and ask for Simon, who is c Peter;
11: 13 'Send to Joppa and bring Simon, who is c Peter;
11: 26 that the disciples were first c "Christians."
13: 1 Barnabas, Simeon who was c Niger,
13: 2 and Saul for the work to which I have c them."
14: 12 Barnabas they c Zeus, and Paul they c Hermes,
14: 27 they c the church together and related all
15: 17 all the Gentiles over whom my name has been c.
15: 22 They sent Judas c Barsabbas, and Silas,
15: 37 Barnabas wanted to take with them John c Mark.
16: 10 being convinced that God had c us to proclaim
16: 29 The jailer c for lights, and rushing in,
23: 6 he c out in the council, "Brothers, I am a Pharisee,
23: 17 Paul c one of the centurions and said,
Ac 23: 18 "The prisoner Paul c me and asked me
24: 21 unless it was this one sentence that I c out
27: 8 we came to a place c Fair Havens,
27: 14 But soon a violent wind, c the northeaster,
27: 16 of a small island c Cauda we were scarcely able
28: 1 we then learned that the island was c Malta.
28: 17 Three days later he c together the local leaders of
Ro 1: 1 Paul, a servant of Jesus Christ, c to be an apostle,
1: 6 including yourselves who are c to belong
1: 7 who are c to be saints:
7: 3 be c an adulteress if she lives with another man
8: 28 who are c according to his purpose.
8: 30 And those whom he predestined he also c; and those whom he c he also justified;
9: 24 including us whom he has c,
9: 26 there they shall be c children of the living God."
1Co 1: 1 c to be an apostle of Christ Jesus by the will
1: 2 c to be saints, together with all those who
1: 9 by him you were c into the fellowship of his Son,
1: 24 but to those who are the c,
7: 15 It is to peace that God has c you.
7: 17 that the Lord has assigned, to which God c you.
7: 20 in the condition in which you were c.
7: 21 Were you a slave when c?
7: 22 For whoever was c in the Lord as a slave is
7: 22 as whoever was free when c is a slave of Christ.
7: 24 In whatever condition you were c,
14: 24 or outsider who enters is reproved by all and c
15: 9 unfit to be c an apostle,
Gal 1: 6 so quickly deserting the one who c you in
1: 15 who had set me apart before I was born and c me
5: 13 For you were c to freedom, brothers and sisters;
Eph 1: 18 the hope to which he has c you,
2: 11 c "the uncircumcision" by those who are c "the
4: 1 of the calling to which you have been c,
4: 4 just as you were c to the one hope of your calling,
Col 3: 15 to which indeed you were c in the one body.
4: 11 And Jesus who is c Justus greets you.
2Th 2: 14 For this purpose he c you
1Ti 6: 12 take hold of the eternal life, to which you were c
6: 20 and contradictions of what is falsely c knowledge;
2Ti 1: 9 who saved us and c us with a holy calling,
Heb 3: 13 as long as it is c "today,"
5: 4 but takes it only when c by God,
9: 2 this is c the Holy Place.
9: 3 the second curtain was a tent c the Holy of Holies.
9: 15 so that those who are c may receive
11: 8 when he was c to set out for a place that he was
11: 16 Therefore God is not ashamed to be c their God;
11: 24 refused to be c a son of Pharaoh's daughter,
Jas 2: 23 and he was c the friend of God.
1Pe 1: 15 Instead, as he who c you is holy,
2: 9 the mighty acts of him who c you out of darkness
2: 21 For to this you have been c,
3: 6 Thus Sarah obeyed Abraham and c him lord.
3: 9 It is for this that you were c—
5: 10 who has c you to his eternal glory in Christ,
2Pe 1: 3 the knowledge of him who c us by his own glory
1Jn 3: 1 that we should be c children of God;
Jude 1: 1 To those who are c, who are beloved in God
Rev 1: 9 was on the island c Patmos because of the word
7: 2 and he c with a loud voice to
9: 11 and in Greek he is c Apollyon.
11: 8 of the great city that is prophetically c Sodom
12: 9 that ancient serpent, who is c the Devil and Satan,
14: 18 and he c with a loud voice to him who had
16: 16 at the place that in Hebrew is c Harmagedon.
17: 14 and those with him are c and chosen and faithful."
18: 2 He c out with a mighty voice, "Fallen,
19: 11 Its rider is c Faithful and True,
19: 13 and his name is c The Word of God.
19: 17 and with a loud voice he c to all the birds that fly
Tob 2: 13 So I c her and said, "Where did you get this goat?
4: 3 Then he c his son Tobias,
5: 10 Then Tobias went out and c him, and said,
5: 17 Then he c his son and said to him, "Son,
7: 13 Then he c her mother and told her
7: 15 Raguel c his wife Edna and said to her, "Sister,
8: 9 But Raguel arose and c his servants to him,
8: 11 Raguel went into his house and c his wife,
8: 20 Then he c for Tobias and swore on oath to him
9: 1 Then Tobias c Raphael and said to him,
12: 1 Tobit c his son Tobias and said to him, "My child,
12: 5 So Tobias c him and said,
12: 6 Then Raphael c the two of them privately and said
14: 3 he c his son Tobias and the seven sons of Tobias
Jdt 2: 4 c Holofernes, the chief general of his army,
5: 2 In great anger he c together all the princes
6: 16 They c together all the elders of the town,
6: 21 all that night they c on the God of Israel for help.
9: 4 and abhorred the pollution of their blood and c
10: 2 She c her maid and went down into the house
13: 11 a distance Judith c out to the sentries at the gates,
AdE 4: 11 to the king inside the inner court without being c,
4: 11 now thirty days since I was c to go to the king.' "
9: 26 Therefore these days were c "Purim,"
16: 11 for every nation that he was c our father
Wis 7: 7 I c on God, and the spirit of wisdom came to me.
11: 4 When they were thirsty, they c upon you,
11: 25 not c forth by you have been preserved?
18: 8 by which you punished our enemies you c us
Sir 2: 10 Or has anyone c upon him and been neglected?
5: 14 Do not be c double-tongued and do not lay traps
36: 17 O Lord, on the people c by your name, on Israel,
46: 5 He c upon the Most High, the Mighty One,
46: 16 He c upon the Lord, the Mighty One,
47: 5 For he c on the Lord, the Most High,

Sir 47:18 who is c the God of Israel,
48:20 But they c upon the Lord who is merciful,
Bar 2:15 for Israel and his descendants are c by your name.
2:26 the house that is c by your name you have made
3:33 he c it, and it obeyed him, trembling;
3:34 he c them, and they said, "Here we are!"
LtJ 6:30 For how can they be c gods?
Bel 1:3 Now the Babylonians had an idol c Bel,
1:8 Then the king was angry and c the priests of Bel
1Mc 2:3 Simon c Thassi,
2:4 Judas c Maccabeus,
2:5 Eleazar c Avaran, and Jonathan c Apphus.
3:1 Then his son Judas, who was c Maccabeus,
5:16 a great assembly was c to determine what they
6:10 So he c all his Friends and said to them,
6:14 Then he c for Philip, one of his Friends,
6:43 Now Eleazar, c Avaran, saw that one of
7:37 "You chose this house to be c by your name,
8:20 who is also c Maccabeus,
10:20 be c the king's Friend and you are to take our side
11:7 with the king as far as the river c Eleutherus;
11:47 So the king c the Jews to his aid,
12:31 against the Arabs who are c Zabadeans,
12:37 and he repaired the section c Chaphenatha.
16:2 Simon c in his two eldest sons Judas and John,
16:15 in the little stronghold c Dok, which he had built;
2Mc 1:36 Nehemiah and his associates c this "nephthar,"
1:36 but by most people it is c naphtha.
3:15 before the altar in their priestly vestments and c
4:7 who was c Epiphanes, succeeded to the kingdom,
7:25 the king c the mother to him and urged her
8:1 Meanwhile Judas, who was also c Maccabeus,
8:15 he had c them by his holy and glorious name.
9:2 He had entered the city c Persepolis and attempted
10:9 the end of Antiochus, who was c Epiphanes.
10:12 Ptolemy, who was c Macron,
10:13 He heard himself c a traitor at every turn,
10:32 Timothy himself fled to a stronghold c Gazara,
12:17 to the Jews who are c Toubiani.
12:21 and also the baggage to a place c Carnaim;
12:28 But the Jews c upon the Sovereign who
12:32 After the festival c Pentecost,
12:36 Judas c upon the Lord to show himself their ally
13:23 he was dismayed, c in the Jews,
14:6 "Those of the Jews who are c Hasideans,
14:16 and engaged them in battle at a village c Dessau.
14:34 toward heaven and c upon the constant Defender
14:37 of and for his goodwill was c father of the Jews.
15:21 stretched out his hands toward heaven and c upon
15:22 He c upon him in these words:
15:31 and had c his compatriots together and stationed
15:36 which is c Adar in the Aramaic language—
1Es 3:7 to Darius and shall be c Kinsman of Darius."
4:42 You shall sit next to me, and be c my Kinsman."
4:63 up and build Jerusalem and the temple that is c
5:38 the daughters of Barzillai, and was c by his name.
6:33 may the Lord, whose name is there c upon,
8:41 I assembled them at the river c Theras,
8:92 one of the men of Israel, c out, and said to Ezra,
3Mc 4:11 to the place c Schedia,
5:7 with tears and a voice hard to silence they all c
7:17 c "rose-bearing" because of a characteristic of
2Es 1:40 who is also c the messenger of the Lord.
2:37 to him who has c you to the celestial kingdoms.
2:41 who have been c from the beginning,
3:1 I, Salathiel, who am also c Ezra.
6:49 the one you c Behemoth and the name of
6:58 we your people, whom you have c your firstborn,
7:*132* [62] O Lord, that the Most High is now c merciful,
7:*138* [68] and he is c the giver, because if he did
8:31 it is because of us sinners that you are c merciful.
8:32 then you will be c merciful.
8:44 and are c your own image because they are made
9:26 as he directed me, into the field that is c Ardat;
10:22 by which we are c has been almost profaned;
10:57 and you have been c to be with the Most High
12:24 Therefore they are c the heads of the eagle,
13:45 and that country is c Arzareth.
13:55 and c understanding your mother.
14:38 And on the next day a voice c me, saying, "Ezra,
4Mc 16:9 or have the happiness of being c grandmother.
16:16 the contest to which you are c to bear witness for

CALLING (39) [CALL]

Jos 19:47 c Leshem, Dan, after their ancestor Dan.
1Sa 3:8 Then Eli perceived that the LORD was c the boy.
3:10 the LORD came and stood there, c as before,
Est 3:14 c on all the peoples to be ready for that day.
Pr 9:15 c to those who pass by,
Isa 1:13 New moon and sabbath and c of convocation—
21:11 is c to me from Seir, "Sentinel, what of the night?
40:26 and numbers them, c them all by name;
41:4 c the generations from the beginning?
46:11 c a bird of prey from the east,
Jer 1:15 I am c all the tribes of the kingdoms of the north,
Da 8:16 c, "Gabriel, help this man understand the vision."
Am 7:4 the Lord GOD was c for a shower of fire,
Mt 2:4 and c together all the chief priests and scribes of
11:16 It is like children sitting in the marketplaces and c
27:47 they said, "This man is c for Elijah."
Mk 10:49 get up, he is c you."
15:35 they said, "Listen, he is c for Elijah."
Lk 7:32 and c to one another, 'We played the flute for you,
Jn 5:18 but was also c God his own Father,
11:28 "The Teacher is here and is c for you."
Ac 9:41 Then c the saints and widows,
22:16 and have your sins washed away, c on his name.'
Ro 11:29 for the gifts and the c of God are irrevocable.
Eph 4:1 of the c to which you have been called,
4:4 just as you were called to the one hope of your c,
2Ti 1:9 who saved us and called us with a holy c,
Heb 3:1 brothers and sisters, holy partners in a heavenly c,
Rev 6:16 c to the mountains and rocks, "Fall on us
14:15 c with a loud voice to the one who sat on
Tob 5:10 and said, "Young man, my father is c for you."
AdE 13:8 c to remembrance all the works of the Lord.
2Mc 3:22 While they were c upon the Almighty Lord
12:6 c upon God, the righteous judge,
12:15 c against the great Sovereign of the world,
14:46 c upon the Lord of life and spirit
3Mc 6:1 directed the elders around him to stop c upon
2Es 15:20 See how I am c together all the kings of the earth
4Mc 15:21 as did the voices of the children in torture c

CALLISTHENES (1)

2Mc 8:33 C and some others, who had fled

CALLS (39) [CALL]

Ge 46:33 When Pharaoh c you, and says,
1Sa 3:9 and if he c you, you shall say, 'Speak, LORD,
26:14 Abner replied, "Who are you that c to the king?"
1Ki 8:43 and do according to all that the foreigner c to you,
Ps 42:7 Deep c to deep at the thunder of your cataracts;
50:4 He c to the heavens above and to the earth,
Pr 9:3 she c from the highest places in the town,
Isa 8:12 that this people c conspiracy,
64:7 There is no one who c on your name,
Hos 7:7 none of them c upon me.
Joel 2:32 Then everyone who c on the name of the LORD
2:32 the survivors shall be those whom the LORD c.
Am 5:8 who c for the waters of the sea,
9:6 who c for the waters of the sea,
Na 2:5 He c his officers; they stumble
Mt 22:43 is it then that David by the Spirit c him Lord,
22:45 If David thus c him Lord, how can he be his son?"
Mk 12:37 David himself c him Lord;
Lk 15:6 he c together his friends and neighbors,
15:9 she c together her friends and neighbors, saying,
20:44 David thus c him Lord;
Jn 10:3 He c his own sheep by name and leads them out.
Ac 2:21 Then everyone who c on the name of
2:39 everyone whom the Lord our God c to him."
Ro 4:17 to the dead and c into existence the things that do
10:13 "Everyone who c on the name of the Lord shall
Gal 5:8 not come from the one who c you.
1Th 2:12 who c you into his own kingdom and glory.
5:24 The one who c you is faithful, and he will do this.
2Ti 2:19 and, "Let everyone who c on the name of
Rev 2:20 you tolerate that woman Jezebel, who c herself
13:18 This c for wisdom: let anyone with understanding
17:9 "This c for a mind that has wisdom:
Wis 2:13 and c himself a child of the Lord.
2:16 he c the last end of the righteous happy,
14:1 about to voyage over raging waves c upon a piece
2Mc 2:26 it is no light matter but c for sweat and loss
1Es 4:36 whole earth c upon truth, and heaven blesses her.
4Mc 14:17 warning them with their own c.

CALM (10) [CALMED, CALMNESS]

Pr 15:18 but those who are slow to anger c contention.
Eze 16:42 I will be c, and will be angry no longer.
Mt 8:26 and there was a dead c.
Mk 4:39 Then the wind ceased, and there was a dead c.
Lk 8:24 they ceased, and there was a c.
Sir 1:23 Those who are patient stay c until
39:28 and c the anger of their Maker.
48:10 to c the wrath of God before it breaks out in fury,
3Mc 2:1 and extending his hands with c dignity, prayed
4Mc 13:6 and make it c for those who sail into

CALMED (1) [CALM]

Ps 131:2 But I have c and quieted my soul,

CALMNESS (1) [CALM]

Ecc 10:4 for c will undo great offenses.

CALNEH (1)

Am 6:2 Cross over to C, and see;

CALNO (1)

Isa 10:9 Is not C like Carchemish?

CALVARY (KJV) See THE SKULL

CALVE See Index to Footnotes

CALVES‡ (23) [CALF]

1Sa 6:7 but take their c home, away from them.
6:10 and shut up their c at home.
14:32 and took sheep and oxen and c,
1Ki 12:28 So the king took counsel, and made two c of gold.
12:32 sacrificing to the c that he had made.
2Ki 10:29 the golden c that were in Bethel and in Dan.
17:16 and made for themselves cast images of two c;
2Ch 11:15 and for the c that he had made.
13:8 with you the golden c that Jeroboam made as gods
Job 21:10 their cow c and never miscarries.
Ps 68:30 the herd of bulls with the c of the peoples.
Isa 27:10 the c graze there, there they lie down,
Jer 46:21 her mercenaries in her midst are like fatted c;
Hos 13:2 People are kissing c!
Am 6:4 and eat lambs from the flock, and c from the stall;
Mic 6:6 before him with burnt offerings, with c a year old?
Mal 4:2 You shall go out leaping like c from the stall.
Mt 22:4 my oxen and my fat c have been slaughtered,
Heb 9:12 not with the blood of goats and c,
9:19 he took the blood of c and goats,
1Es 1:7 and kids, and three thousand c;
1:8 thousand six hundred sheep and three hundred c.
1:9 five thousand sheep and seven hundred c.

CALVING (1) [CALF]

Job 39:1 Do you observe the c of the deer?

CALYX (10) [CALYXES]

Ex 25:33 each with c and petals, on one branch,
25:33 each with c and petals, on the other branch—
25:35 be a c of one piece with it under the first pair
25:35 a c of one piece with it under the next pair
25:35 and a c of one piece with it under the last pair
37:19 each with c and petals, on one branch,
37:19 each with c and petals, on the other branch—
37:21 a c of one piece with it under the first pair
37:21 a c of one piece with it under the next pair
37:21 and a c of one piece with it under the last pair

CALYXES (6) [CALYX]

Ex 25:31 its c, and its petals shall be of one piece with it;
25:34 each with its c and petals.
25:36 Their c and their branches shall be of one piece
37:17 its c, and its petals were of one piece with it.
37:20 each with its c and petals.
37:22 Their c and their branches were of one piece

CAME‡ (1740) [COME]

Ge 4:15 so that no one who c upon him would kill him.
7:6 when the flood of waters c on the earth.
7:10 seven days the waters of the flood c on the earth.
8:4 the ark c to rest on the mountains of Ararat.
8:11 the dove c back to him in the evening, and there
9:10 as many as c out of the ark.
11:2 they c upon a plain in the land of Shinar
11:5 The LORD c down to see the city and the tower,
11:31 but when they c to Haran, they settled there.
13:18 and c and settled by the oaks of Mamre,
14:5 and the kings who were with him c and subdued
14:7 then they turned back and c to En-mishpat (that is,
14:13 Then one who had escaped c and told Abram
15:1 the word of the LORD c to Abram in a vision,
15:4 But the word of the LORD c to him,
15:11 And when birds of prey c down on the carcasses,
18:23 Then Abraham c near and said,
19:1 The two angels c to Sodom in the evening,
19:5 "Where are the men who c to you tonight?
19:9 And they said, "This fellow c here as an alien,
19:9 and c near the door to break it down.
19:23 The sun had risen on the earth when Lot c to Zoar.
20:3 But God c to Abimelech in a dream by night,
22:9 When they c to the place that God had shown him,
24:5 to the land from which you c?"
24:16 down to the spring, filled her jar, and c up.
24:32 So the man c into the house;
24:42 "I c today to the spring, and said, 'O LORD,
25:25 first c out red, all his body like a hairy mantle;
25:26 Afterward his brother c out,
25:29 Esau c in from the field, and he was famished.
26:32 That same day Isaac's servants c and told him
27:27 So he c near and kissed him;
27:30 his brother Esau c in from his hunting.
27:33 and I ate it all before you c,
27:35 But he said, "Your brother c deceitfully,
28:11 He c to a certain place and stayed there for
29:1 and c to the land of the people of the east.
29:9 Rachel c with her father's sheep;
29:25 When morning c, it was Leah!
30:16 When Jacob c from the field in the evening,
30:30 For you had little before I c,
30:38 the watering places, where the flocks c to drink.
30:38 And since they bred when they c to drink,
31:24 God c to Laban the Aramean in a dream by night,
32:6 saying, "We c to your brother Esau,
33:3 until he c near his brother.
33:18 Jacob c safely to the city of Shechem,
34:5 so Jacob held his peace until they c.
34:7 just as the sons of Jacob c in from the field.
34:20 and his son Shechem c to the gate of their city
34:25 took their swords and c against the city unawares,
34:27 And the other sons of Jacob c upon the slain,
35:6 Jacob c to Luz (that is, Bethel),
35:9 to Jacob again when he c from Paddan-aram,
35:27 Jacob c to his father Isaac at Mamre,
37:14 of Hebron. He c to Shechem,
37:18 and before he c near to them,
37:23 So when Joseph c to his brothers,
38:27 When the time of her delivery c,
38:28 saying, "This one c out first."
38:29 then he drew back his hand, and out c his brother;
38:30 Afterward his brother c out with
39:14 He c in to me to lie with me,
39:16 by her until his master c home,
39:17 c in to me to insult me;
40:6 When Joseph c to them in the morning,
40:10 its blossoms c out and the clusters ripened

Ge 41: 2 and there **c** up out of the Nile seven sleek
41: 3 ugly and thin, **c** up out of the Nile after them,
41:14 and changed his clothes, he **c** in before Pharaoh.
41:18 **c** up out of the Nile and fed in the reed grass.
41:19 Then seven other cows **c** up after them, poor,
41:27 The seven lean and ugly cows that **c** up
41:50 Before the years of famine **c**,
41:53 of plenty that prevailed in the land of Egypt **c** to
41:57 all the world **c** to Joseph in Egypt to buy grain,
42: 5 of Israel were among the other people who **c**
42: 6 And Joseph's brothers **c** and bowed themselves
42:29 they **c** to their father Jacob in the land of Canaan,
43:20 my lord, we **c** down the first time to buy food;
43:21 we **c** to the lodging place we opened our sacks,
43:26 When Joseph **c** home, they brought him
43:31 Then he washed his face and **c** out;
44:14 Judah and his brothers **c** to Joseph's house
45: 4 "Come closer to me." And they **c** closer.
45:25 and **c** to their father Jacob in the land of Canaan.
46: 1 with all that he had and **c** to Beer-sheba,
46: 6 and they **c** into Egypt, Jacob and all his offspring
46: 8 Jacob and his offspring, who **c** to Egypt.
46:26 the persons belonging to Jacob who **c** into Egypt,
46:27 all the persons of the house of Jacob who **c**
46:28 When they **c** to the land of Goshen,
47:15 all the Egyptians **c** to Joseph, and said,
47:18 year was ended, they **c** to him the following year,
48: 5 of Egypt before I **c** to you in Egypt, are now mine;
48: 7 For when I **c** from Paddan, Rachel, alas,
50:10 When they **c** to the threshing floor of Atad,
Ex 1: 1 the sons of Israel who **c** to Egypt with Jacob, each
1:12 so that the Egyptians **c** to dread the Israelites.
2: 5 daughter of Pharaoh **c** down to bathe at the river,
2:16 They **c** to draw water, and filled the troughs
2:17 But some shepherds **c** and drove them away.
2:17 and **c** to their defense and watered their flock.
3: 1 and **c** to Horeb, the mountain of God.
5:15 the Israelite supervisors **c** to Pharaoh and cried,
5:20 they **c** upon Moses and Aaron who were waiting
5:23 Since I first **c** to Pharaoh to speak in your name,
8: 6 and the frogs **c** up and covered the land of Egypt.
8:17 and gnats **c** on humans and animals alike;
8:24 and great swarms of flies **c** into the house
9:23 and fire **c** down on the earth.
10: 6 from the day they **c** on earth to this day.' "
10:13 morning **c**, the east wind had brought the locusts.
10:14 The locusts **c** upon all the land of Egypt
13: 3 "Remember this day on which you **c** out of Egypt,
13: 8 the LORD did for me when I **c** out of Egypt.'
14:20 It **c** between the army of Egypt and the army
15:23 When they **c** to Marah, they could not drink
15:27 Then they **c** to Elim,
16: 1 and Israel **c** to the wilderness of Sin,
16:13 In the evening quails **c** up and covered the camp;
16:22 the leaders of the congregation **c** and told Moses,
16:35 until they **c** to a habitable land;
16:35 until they **c** to the border of the land of Canaan.
17: 8 Amalek **c** and fought with Israel at Rephidim.
18: 5 **c** into the wilderness where Moses was encamped
18:12 and Aaron **c** with all the elders of Israel
19: 1 they **c** into the wilderness of Sinai.
19: 7 So Moses **c**, summoned the elders of the people,
21:13 but **c** about by an act of God,
23:15 for in it you **c** out of Egypt.
24: 3 Moses **c** and told the people all the words of
32:19 As soon as he **c** near the camp and saw the calf
32:24 and I threw it into the fire, and out **c** this calf!"
34:18 for in the month of Abib you **c** out from Egypt.
34:29 Moses **c** down from Mount Sinai.
34:29 As he **c** down from the mountain with
34:32 Afterward all the Israelites **c** near,
34:34 take the veil off, until he **c** out; and when he **c** out,
35:21 And they **c**, everyone whose heart was stirred,
35:22 So they **c**, both men and women;
36: 4 of task on the sanctuary **c**,
Lev 9:22 and he **c** down after sacrificing the sin offering,
9:23 and then **c** out and blessed the people;
9:24 Fire **c** out from the LORD and consumed
10: 2 And fire **c** out from the presence of the LORD
10: 5 They **c** forward and carried them
24:10 and whose father was an Egyptian **c** out among
Nu 3:38 any outsider who **c** near was to be put to death.
9: 6 They **c** before Moses and Aaron on that day,
10:36 And whenever it **c** to rest, he would say, "Return,
11:25 the LORD **c** down in the cloud and spoke to him,
12: 4 So the three of them **c** out.
12: 5 Then the LORD **c** down in a pillar of cloud,
12: 5 and Miriam; and they both **c** forward.
13:22 They went up into the Negeb, and **c** to Hebron;
13:23 And they **c** to the Wadi Eshcol,
13:26 And they **c** to Moses and Aaron and to all
13:27 "We **c** to the land to which you sent us;
14:45 and the Canaanites who lived in that hill country **c**
16:27 and Abiram **c** out and stood at the entrance
16:35 And fire **c** out from the LORD and consumed
16:43 Then Moses and Aaron **c** to the front of the tent
20: 1 **c** into the wilderness of Zin in the first month,
20:11 water **c** out abundantly, and the congregation
20:20 And Edom **c** out against them with a large force,
20:22 the whole congregation, **c** to Mount Hor.
20:28 Moses and Eleazar **c** down from the mountain.
21: 7 The people **c** to Moses and said,
21:23 he **c** to Jahaz, and fought against Israel.
21:28 For fire **c** out from Heshbon,
21:33 and King Og of Bashan **c** out against them,
22: 7 they **c** to Balaam, and gave him Balak's message.
22: 9 God **c** to Balaam and said,
Nu 22:16 They **c** to Balaam and said to him,
22:20 That night God **c** to Balaam and said to him,
22:39 and they **c** to Kiriath-huzoth.
23:17 When he **c** to him, he was standing
24: 2 Then the spirit of God **c** upon him,
25: 6 of the Israelites **c** and brought a Midianite woman
26: 4 Israelites, who **c** out of the land of Egypt, were:
27: 1 Then the daughters of Zelophehad **c** forward.
31:16 plague **c** among the congregation of the LORD.
32: 2 Gadites and the Reubenites **c** and spoke to Moses,
32:11 'Surely none of the people who **c** up out of Egypt,
32:16 Then they **c** up to him and said,
33: 9 They set out from Marah and **c** to Elim;
36: 1 **c** forward and spoke in the presence of Moses and
Dt 1:22 All of you **c** to me and said,
1:44 then **c** out against you and chased you as bees do.
2:23 the Caphtorim, who **c** from Caphtor,
2:32 So when Sihon **c** out against us,
3: 1 King Og of Bashan **c** out against us,
4:46 the Israelites defeated when they **c** out of Egypt.
9: 7 the LORD from the day you **c** out of the land of
Egypt until you **c** to this place.
10: 5 So I turned and **c** down from the mountain,
11: 5 until you **c** to this place;
16: 3 you **c** out of the land of Egypt in great haste,
29: 7 When you **c** to this place,
29: 7 and King Og of Bashan **c** out against us for battle,
29:16 and how we **c** through the midst of the nations
32:44 Moses **c** and recited all the words of this song in
33: 2 He said: The LORD **c** from Sinai,
33:21 he **c** at the head of the people,
Jos 2: 4 Then she said, "True, the men **c** to me,
2: 4 but I did not know where they **c** from.
2: 8 she **c** up to them on the roof
2:10 the Red Sea before you when you **c** out of Egypt,
2:23 the two men **c** down again from the hill country.
2:23 They crossed over, **c** to Joshua son of Nun,
3: 1 and they **c** to the Jordan.
4:18 of the LORD **c** up from the middle of the Jordan,
4:19 The people **c** up out of the Jordan on the tenth day
5: 4 all the males of the people who **c** out of Egypt,
5: 5 all the people who **c** out had been circumcised,
5: 6 the warriors who **c** out of Egypt, perished,
6: 1 no one **c** out and no one went in.
6: 9 the rear guard **c** after the ark,
6:11 and they **c** into the camp,
6:13 and the rear guard **c** after the ark of the LORD,
8:22 And the others **c** out from the city against them;
10: 9 So Joshua **c** upon them suddenly,
10:24 Then they **c** near and put their feet on their necks.
10:33 Then King Horam of Gezer **c** up to help Lachish;
11: 4 They **c** out, with all their troops, a great army,
11: 5 **c** and camped together at the waters of Merom,
11: 7 So Joshua **c** suddenly upon them
11:21 that time Joshua **c** and wiped out the Anakim from
14: 6 Then the people of Judah **c** to Joshua at Gilgal;
15:18 When she **c** to him, she urged him
17: 4 They **c** before the priest Eleazar and Joshua son
18: 9 then they **c** back to Joshua in the camp at Shiloh,
18:11 of the tribe of Benjamin according to its families **c**
19: 1 The second lot **c** out for Simeon,
19:10 The third lot **c** up for the tribe of Zebulun,
19:17 The fourth lot **c** out for Issachar,
19:24 The fifth lot **c** out for the tribe of Asher according
19:32 The sixth lot **c** out for the tribe of Naphtali,
19:40 The seventh lot **c** out for the tribe of Dan,
21: 1 Then the heads of the families of the Levites **c** to
21: 4 The lot **c** out for the families of the Kohathites.
21:45 of Israel had failed; all **c** to pass.
22:10 When they **c** to the region near the Jordan that lies
22:15 They **c** to the Reubenites, the Gadites,
22:17 and for which a plague **c** upon the congregation of
24: 6 of Egypt, you **c** to the sea;
24:11 When you went over the Jordan and **c** to Jericho,
Jdg 1: 5 They **c** upon Adoni-bezek at Bezek,
1:14 When she **c** to him, she urged him
3:10 The spirit of the LORD **c** upon him,
3:20 Ehud **c** to him, while he was sitting alone
3:22 of his belly; and the dirt **c** out.
3:24 After he had gone, the servants **c**.
3:31 After him **c** Shamgar son of Anath,
4: 5 and the Israelites **c** up to her for judgment.
4:18 Jael **c** out to meet Sisera, and said to him,
4:22 Then, as Barak **c** in pursuit of Sisera,
5:15 of Issachar **c** with Deborah, and Issachar faithful
5:19 "The kings **c**, they fought;
6: 5 so they wasted the land as they **c** in.
6:11 of the LORD **c** and sat under the oak at Ophrah,
6:33 and the people of the east **c** together,
7:13 and **c** to the tent, and struck it so that it fell;
7:19 the hundred who were with him **c** to the outskirts
8: 4 Then Gideon **c** to the Jordan and crossed over,
8:15 Then he **c** to the people of Succoth, and said,
9: 6 of Shechem and all Beth-millo **c** together,
9:52 Abimelech **c** to the tower, and fought against it,
9:52 and **c** near to the entrance of the tower to burn it
9:57 on them **c** the curse of Jotham son of Jerubbaal.
10: 3 After him **c** Jair the Gileadite,
10:17 and the Israelites **c** together,
11:16 but when they **c** up from Egypt,
11:16 the wilderness to the Red Sea and **c** to Kadesh.
11:29 Then the spirit of the LORD **c** upon Jephthah,
11:34 Then Jephthah **c** to his home at Mizpah;
13: 6 Then the woman **c** and told her husband,
13: 6 "A man of God **c** to me,
13: 6 I did not ask him where he **c** from,
13: 9 the angel of God **c** again to the woman as she sat
Jdg 13:10 "The man who **c** to me the other day has appeared
13:11 and **c** to the man and said to him,
14: 2 Then he **c** up, and told his father and mother,
14: 5 When he **c** to the vineyards of Timnah,
14: 9 When he **c** to his father and mother,
14:14 "Out of the eater **c** something to eat.
14:14 Out of the strong **c** something sweet."
15: 6 the Philistines **c** up, and burned her and her father.
15: 9 Then the Philistines **c** up and encamped in Judah,
15:14 When he **c** to Lehi, the Philistines **c** shouting
15:19 the hollow place that is at Lehi, and water **c**
16: 5 lords of the Philistines **c** to her and said to her,
16:18 Then the lords of the Philistines **c** up to her,
16:31 Then his brothers and all his family **c** down
17: 8 He **c** to the house of Micah in the hill country
18: 2 When they **c** to the hill country of Ephraim,
18: 7 The five men went on, and when they **c** to Laish,
18: 8 they **c** to their kinsfolk at Zorah and Eshtaol,
18:13 and **c** to the house of Micah.
18:15 So they turned in that direction and **c** to the house
18:27 and the priest who belonged to him, **c** to Laish,
19: 3 girl's father saw him and **c** with joy to meet him.
19:22 "Bring out the man who **c** into your house,
19:26 the woman **c** and fell down at the door of
19:30 since the day that the Israelites **c** up from the land
20: 1 Then all the Israelites **c** out,
20: 4 "I **c** to Gibeah that belongs to Benjamin,
20:14 The Benjaminites **c** together out of the towns
20:21 The Benjaminites **c** out of Gibeah,
20:34 There **c** against Gibeah ten thousand picked men
20:42 but the battle overtook them, and those who **c** out
21: 2 And the people **c** to Bethel,
Ru 1:19 two of them went on until they **c** to Bethlehem.
1:19 When they **c** to Bethlehem,
1:22 who **c** back with her from the country of Moab.
1:22 They **c** to Bethlehem at the beginning of
2: 3 She **c** and gleaned in the field behind the reapers.
2: 3 she **c** to the part of the field belonging to Boaz,
2: 4 Just then Boaz **c** from Bethlehem.
2: 6 "She is the Moabite who **c** back with Naomi from
2: 7 So she **c**, and she has been on her feet
2:11 and your native land and **c** to a people that you did
2:18 She picked it up and **c** into the town,
3: 7 Then she **c** stealthily and uncovered his feet,
3:14 "It must not be known that the woman **c** to
3:16 She **c** to her mother-in-law, who said,
4: 1 of whom Boaz had spoken, **c** passing by.
4:13 and she became his wife. When they **c** together,
1Sa 2:14 at Shiloh to all the Israelites who **c** there.
2:27 A man of God **c** to Eli and said to him,
3:10 Now the LORD **c** and stood there,
4: 1 And the word of Samuel **c** to all Israel.
4: 3 When the troops **c** to the camp,
4: 5 ark of the covenant of the LORD **c** into the camp,
4:12 and **c** to Shiloh the same day,
4:13 When the man **c** into the city and told the news,
4:14 Then the man **c** quickly and told Eli.
5:10 But when the ark of God **c** to Ekron,
6:14 cart **c** into the field of Joshua of Beth-shemesh,
7: 1 the people of Kiriath-jearim **c** and took up the ark
8: 4 of Israel gathered together and **c** to Samuel
9: 5 When they **c** to the land of Zuph,
9:15 Now the day before Saul **c**,
9:25 When they **c** down from the shrine into the town,
11: 4 When the messengers **c** to Gibeah of Saul,
11: 6 And the spirit of God **c** upon Saul in power
11: 7 and they **c** out as one.
11: 9 messengers **c** and told the inhabitants of Jabesh,
11:11 the morning watch they **c** into the camp and cut
12:12 that King Nahash of the Ammonites **c** against you,
13: 5 they **c** up and encamped at Michmash,
13:17 And raiders **c** out of the camp of the Philistines
14:25 All the troops **c** upon a honeycomb;
14:26 When the troops **c** upon the honeycomb,
15: 2 in opposing the Israelites when they **c** up out
15: 5 Saul **c** to the city of the Amalekites and lay in wait
15: 6 the people of Israel when they **c** up out of Egypt."
15:10 The word of the LORD **c** to Samuel:
15:13 When Samuel **c** to Saul, Saul said to him,
15:32 And Agag **c** to him haltingly.
16: 4 the LORD commanded, and **c** to Bethlehem.
16: 4 The elders of the city **c** to meet him trembling,
16: 6 When they **c**, he looked on Eliab and thought,
16:13 the spirit of the LORD **c** mightily upon David
16:21 And David **c** to Saul, and entered his service.
16:23 whenever the evil spirit from God **c** upon Saul,
17: 4 And there **c** out from the camp of the Philistines
17:16 the Philistine **c** forward and took his stand,
17:20 He **c** to the encampment as
17:23 **c** up out of the ranks of the Philistines,
17:34 and whenever a lion or a bear **c**,
17:41 The Philistine **c** on and drew near to David,
17:53 The Israelites **c** back from chasing the Philistines,
18: 6 the women **c** out of all the towns of Israel,
18:13 and David marched out and **c** in, leading the army.
18:16 it was he who marched out and **c** in leading them.
18:30 the commanders of the Philistines **c** out to battle;
18:30 and as often as they **c** out,
19: 9 Then an evil spirit from the LORD **c** upon Saul,
19:16 When the messengers **c** in, the idol was in the bed,
19:18 he **c** to Samuel at Ramah,
19:20 the spirit of God **c** upon the messengers of Saul,
19:22 He **c** to the great well that is in Secu;
19:23 and the spirit of God **c** upon him.
19:23 until he **c** to Naioth in Ramah.
20: 1 He **c** before Jonathan and said,
20:24 the new moon **c**, the king sat at the feast to eat.

1Sa 20:37 When the boy c to the place
20:38 So Jonathan's boy gathered up the arrows and c
21: 1 David c to Nob to the priest Ahimelech.
21: 1 Ahimelech c trembling to meet David,
22:11 and all of them c to the king.
23: 6 he c down with an ephod in his hand.
23:16 Saul's son Jonathan set out and c to David
23:27 a messenger c to Saul, saying, "Hurry and come;
24: 3 He c to the sheepfolds beside the road,
25: 9 When David's young men c,
25:12 and c back and told him all this.
25:20 and c down under cover of the mountain, David
25:20 David and his men c down toward her;
25:36 Abigail c to Nabal; he was holding a feast in his
25:40 When David's servants c to Abigail at Carmel,
26: 1 Then the Ziphites c to Saul at Gibeah, saying,
26: 3 When he learned that Saul c after him into
26: 5 and c to the place where Saul had encamped;
26:15 of the people c in to destroy your lord the king.
27: 9 and the clothing, and c back to Achish.
28: 4 and c and encamped at Shunem.
28: 8 They c to the woman by night.
28:21 The woman c to Saul, and when she saw
29:10 you and the servants of your lord who c with you,
30: 1 David and his men c to Ziklag on the third day,
30: 3 When David and his men c to the city,
30: 9 They c to the Wadi Besor,
30:21 Then David c to the two hundred men
30:26 When David c to Ziklag, he sent part of the spoil
31: 7 and the Philistines c and occupied them.
31: 8 next day, when the Philistines c to strip the dead,
31:12 They c to Jabesh and burned them there.
2Sa 1: 2 On the third day, a man c from Saul's camp,
1: 2 When he c to David, he fell to the ground
2: 4 Then the people of Judah c,
2:15 So they c forward and were counted
2:23 so that the spear c out at his back.
2:23 And all those who c to the place
2:24 sun was going down they c to the hill of Ammah,
2:29 and, marching the whole forenoon, they c
3:20 Abner c with twenty men to David at Hebron,
3:23 When Joab and all the army that was with him c,
3:23 it was told Joab, "Abner son of Ner c to the king,
3:24 "What have you done? Abner c to you;
3:25 You know that Abner son of Ner c to deceive you,
3:26 When Joab c out from David's presence,
3:35 the people c to persuade David to eat something
4: 4 the news about Saul and Jonathan c from Jezreel.
4: 5 the heat of the day they c to the house of Ishbaal,
4: 6 They c inside the house as though to take wheat,
5: 1 Then all the tribes of Israel c to David at Hebron,
5: 3 So all the elders of Israel c to the king at Hebron;
5:13 In Jerusalem, after he c from Hebron,
5:20 So David c to Baal-perazim,
5:22 Once again the Philistines c up,
6: 6 When they c to the threshing floor of Nacon,
6:16 As the ark of the LORD c into the city of David,
6:20 Michal the daughter of Saul c out to meet David,
7: 4 same night the word of the LORD c to Nathan:
8: 5 of Damascus c to help King Hadadezer of Zobah,
9: 6 Mephibosheth son of Jonathan son of Saul c
10: 2 David's envoys c into the land of the Ammonites,
10: 8 The Ammonites c out and drew up in battle array
10:14 from fighting against the Ammonites, and c
10:16 and they c to Helam, with Shobach
10:17 and crossed the Jordan, and c to Helam.
11: 4 and she c to him, and he lay with her.
11: 7 When Uriah c to him, David asked how Joab and
11:17 The men of the city c out and fought with Joab;
11:22 c and told David all that Joab had sent him to tell.
11:23 and c out against us in the field;
12: 1 He c to him, and said to him,
12: 4 Now there c a traveler to the rich man,
13: 6 and when the king c to see him,
13:24 Absalom c to the king, and said,
13:30 the report c to David that Absalom had killed all
14: 4 When the woman of Tekoa c to the king,
14:33 So he c to the king and prostrated himself
15: 5 Whenever people c near to do obeisance to him,
15: 6 to every Israelite who c to the king for judgment;
15:13 A messenger c to David, saying,
15:20 You c only yesterday,
15:24 Abiathar c up, and Zadok also,
15:32 When David c to the summit,
15:32 the Archite c to meet him with his coat torn
15:37 So Hushai, David's friend, c into the city,
16: 5 When King David c to Bahurim,
16: 5 the house of Saul c out whose name was Shimei son of Gera; he c out cursing.
16:15 Absalom and all the Israelites c to Jerusalem;
16:16 Hushai the Archite, David's friend, c to Absalom,
17: 6 When Hushai c to Absalom, Absalom said to him,
17:18 and c to the house of a man at Bahurim,
17:20 Absalom's servants c to the woman at the house,
17:21 After they had gone, the men c up out of the well,
17:24 Then David c to Mahanaim,
17:27 When David c to Mahanaim,
18:16 and the troops c back from pursuing Israel,
18:31 Then the Cushite c; and the Cushite said,
19: 5 Then Joab c into the house to the king, and said,
19: 8 and all the troops c before the king.
19:15 So the king c back to the Jordan;
19:15 and Judah c to Gilgal to meet the king and
19:24 Mephibosheth grandson of Saul c down to meet
19:24 from the day the king left until the day he c back
19:25 When he c from Jerusalem to meet the king,
19:41 Then all the people of Israel c to the king,
2Sa 20: 3 David c to his house at Jerusalem;
20: 8 at the large stone that is in Gibeon, Amasa c
20:12 Since he saw that all who c by him were stopping,
20:15 Joab's forces c and besieged him in Abel
20:17 He c near her; and the woman said,
21:17 But Abishai son of Zeruiah c to his aid,
22: 7 and my cry c to his ears.
22:10 He bowed the heavens, and c down;
22:19 They c upon me in the day of my calamity,
22:45 Foreigners c cringing to me;
22:46 and c trembling out of their strongholds.
23:10 people c back to him—but only to strip the dead.
24: 6 Then they c to Gilead, and to Kadesh in the land
24: 6 and they c to Dan, and from Dan they went
24: 7 and c to the fortress of Tyre and to all the cities of
24: 8 they c back to Jerusalem at the end of nine months
24:11 the word of the LORD c to the prophet Gad,
24:13 So Gad c to David and told him;
24:18 That day Gad c to David and said to him,
1Ki 1:22 with the king, the prophet Nathan c in.
1:23 When he c in before the king,
1:28 So she c into the king's presence,
1:32 When they c before the king,
1:47 Moreover the king's servants c
1:53 He c to do obeisance to King Solomon;
2: 8 but when he c down to meet me at the Jordan,
2:13 Then Adonijah son of Haggith c to Bathsheba,
2:28 When the news c to Joab—
2:30 So Benaiah c to the tent of the LORD and said
3:15 He c to Jerusalem where he stood before the ark
3:16 two women who were prostitutes c to the king
4:27 for all who c to King Solomon's table, each one
4:34 People c from all the nations to hear the wisdom
4:34 they c from all the kings of the earth
6: 1 after the Israelites c out of the land of Egypt,
6:11 Now the word of the LORD c to Solomon,
7:14 He c to King Solomon, and did all his work.
8: 3 And all the elders of Israel c,
8: 9 when they c out of the land of Egypt.
8:10 And when the priests c out of the holy place,
9:12 But when Hiram c from Tyre to see the cities
10: 1 she c to test him with hard questions.
10: 2 She c to Jerusalem with a very great retinue,
10: 2 and when she c to Solomon,
10: 7 the reports until I c and my own eyes had seen it.
10:14 The weight of gold that c to Solomon
10:15 besides that which c from the traders and from
11:18 They set out from Midian and c to Paran;
11:18 they took people with them from Paran and c
12: 3 the assembly of Israel c and said to Rehoboam,
12:12 and all the people c to Rehoboam the third day,
12:21 When Rehoboam c to Jerusalem,
12:22 the word of God c to Shemaiah the man of God:
13: 1 of God c out of Judah by the word of the LORD
13: 9 or drink water, or return by the way that you c."
13:11 One of his sons c and told him all that the man
13:12 that the man of God who c from Judah had gone.
13:14 "Are you the man of God who c from Judah?"
13:17 or return by the way that you c."
13:20 the word of the LORD c to
13:21 of God who c from Judah, "Thus says the LORD:
13:25 And they c and told it in the town where
14: 4 and c to the house of Ahijah.
14: 5 When she c, she pretended to be another woman.
14: 6 as she c in at the door, he said, "Come in,
14:17 and went away, and she c to Tirzah.
14:17 she c to the threshold of the house, the child died.
14:25 King Shishak of Egypt c up against Jerusalem;
16: 1 The word of the LORD c to Jehu son of Hanani
16: 7 the word of the LORD c by the prophet Jehu son
16:10 Zimri c in and struck him down and killed him,
17: 2 The word of the LORD c to him, saying,
17: 8 Then the word of the LORD c to him, saying,
17:10 When he c to the gate of the town,
17:22 life of the child c into him again, and he revived.
18: 1 many days the word of the LORD c to Elijah,
18:21 Elijah then c near to all the people, and said,
18:30 and all the people c closer to him.
18:31 to whom the word of the LORD c, saying,
18:36 the prophet Elijah c near and said, "O LORD,
19: 3 and c to Beer-sheba, which belongs to Judah;
19: 4 and c and sat down under a solitary broom tree.
19: 7 The angel of the LORD c a second time,
19: 9 At that place he c to a cave,
19: 9 Then the word of the LORD c to him, saying,
19:13 Then there c a voice to him that said,
20: 5 The messengers c again and said:
20:13 Then a certain prophet c up to King Ahab of Israel
20:33 So Ben-hadad c out to him;
20:43 resentful and sullen, and c to Samaria.
21: 5 His wife Jezebel c to him and said,
21:13 The two scoundrels c in and sat opposite him;
21:17 the word of the LORD c to Elijah the Tishbite,
21:28 the word of the LORD c to Elijah the Tishbite:
22: 2 But in the third year King Jehoshaphat of Judah c
22:21 a spirit c forward and stood before the LORD,
22:24 Then Zedekiah son of Chenaanah c up to Micaiah,
2Ki 1: 6 They answered him, "There c a man to meet us,
1: 7 "What sort of man was he who c to meet you
1:10 Then fire c down from heaven,
1:12 of God c down from heaven and consumed him
1:13 and c and fell on his knees before Elijah,
1:14 fire c down from heaven and consumed
2: 3 of prophets who were in Bethel c out to Elisha,
2: 4 So they c to Jericho.
2:15 They c to meet him and bowed to the ground
2:18 they c back to him (he had remained at Jericho),
2Ki 2:23 up on the way, some small boys c out of the city
2:24 Then two she-bears c out of the woods
3:15 the power of the LORD c on him.
3:24 But when they c to the camp of Israel,
3:27 And great wrath c upon Israel,
4: 7 She c and told the man of God, and he said,
4:11 One day when he c there,
4:25 and c to the man of God at Mount Carmel.
4:27 When she c to the man of God at the mountain,
4:31 He c back to meet him and told him,
4:32 When Elisha c into the house,
4:36 When she c to him, he said, "Take your son."
4:37 She c and fell at his feet, bowing to the ground;
4:39 and c and cut them up into the pot of stew,
4:42 A man c from Baal-shalishah,
5: 9 So Naaman c with his horses and chariots,
5:15 he c and stood before him and said,
5:24 When he c to the citadel, he took the bags
6: 4 When they c to the Jordan, they cut down trees.
6:14 they c by night, and surrounded the city.
6:18 When the Arameans c down against him,
6:23 the Arameans no longer c raiding into the land
6:33 the king c down to him and said,
7: 5 but when they c to the edge of the Aramean camp,
7: 8 Then they c back, entered another tent,
7:10 So they c and called to the gatekeepers of the city,
7:17 as the man of God had said when the king c down
9:11 When Jehu c back to his master's officers,
9:19 who c to them and said, "Thus says the king,
9:30 When Jehu c to Jezreel, Jezebel heard of it;
9:36 When they c back and told him, he said,
10: 8 When the messenger c and told him,
10:17 When he c to Samaria, he killed all who were left
10:21 all the worshipers of Baal c,
11: 9 and c to the priest Jehoiada.
13:21 he c to life and stood on his feet.
14:13 he c to Jerusalem, and broke down the wall
15:14 son of Gadi c up from Tirzah and c to Samaria;
15:19 King Pul of Assyria c against the land;
15:29 King Tiglath-pileser of Assyria c
16: 5 and King Pekah son of Remaliah of Israel c up
16: 6 Edomites c to Elath, where they live to this day.
16:12 king c from Damascus, the king viewed the altar.
17: 3 King Shalmaneser of Assyria c up against him;
17: 5 of Assyria invaded all the land and c to Samaria;
17:28 from Samaria c and lived in Bethel;
18: 9 King Shalmaneser of Assyria c up
18:13 King Sennacherib of Assyria c up against all
18:17 They went up and c to Jerusalem.
18:17 they c and stood by the conduit of the upper pool,
18:18 there c out to them Eliakim son of Hilkiah,
18:37 c to Hezekiah with their clothes torn and told him
19: 5 When the servants of King Hezekiah c to Isaiah,
19:28 I will turn you back on the way by which you c.
19:33 By the way that he c, by the same he shall return;
20: 1 The prophet Isaiah son of Amoz c to him,
20: 4 the word of the LORD c to him:
20:14 Then the prophet Isaiah c to King Hezekiah,
21:15 since the day their ancestors c out of Egypt,
22: 9 Then Shaphan the secretary c to the king,
23:17 the tomb of the man of God who c from Judah
23:18 the bones of the prophet who c out of Samaria.
23:34 he c to Egypt, and died there.
24: 1 In his days King Nebuchadnezzar of Babylon c up;
24: 3 this c upon Judah at the command of the LORD,
24:10 of King Nebuchadnezzar of Babylon c up
24:11 King Nebuchadnezzar of Babylon c to the city,
25: 1 of Babylon c with all his army against Jerusalem,
25: 8 a servant of the king of Babylon, c to Jerusalem.
25:23 they c with their men to Gedaliah at Mizpah,
25:25 of the royal family, c with ten men;
1Ch 2:53 from these c the Zorathites and the Eshtaolites.
2:55 These are the Kenites who c from Hammath,
4:41 c in the days of King Hezekiah of Judah,
5: 2 among his brothers and a ruler c from him,
6:31 after the ark c to rest there.
7:21 because they c down to raid their cattle.
7:22 and his brothers c to comfort him.
10: 7 and the Philistines c and occupied them.
10: 8 next day when the Philistines c to strip the dead,
11: 3 So all the elders of Israel c to the king at Hebron,
12: 1 The following are those who c to David at Ziklag,
12:16 and Judahites c to the stronghold to David.
12:18 Then the spirit c upon Amasai, chief of the Thirty,
12:19 the Manassites deserted to David when he c with
12:23 the divisions of the armed troops who c to David
12:38 c to Hebron with full intent to make David king
12:40 c bringing food on donkeys, camels, mules,
13: 9 When they c to the threshing floor of Chidon,
15:29 the ark of the covenant of the LORD c to the city
17: 3 same night the word of the LORD c to Nathan,
18: 5 of Damascus c to help King Hadadezer of Zobah,
19: 2 When David's servants c to Hanun in the land of
19: 7 who c and camped before Medeba.
19: 7 from their cities and c to battle.
19: 9 The Ammonites c out and drew up in battle array
19:15 Then Joab c to Jerusalem.
19:17 c to them, and drew up his forces against them.
20: 1 and c and besieged Rabbah.
21: 4 throughout all Israel, and c back to Jerusalem.
21:11 So Gad c to David and said to him,
21:21 David c to Ornan, Ornan looked and saw David;
22: 8 But the word of the LORD c to me, saying,
26:14 and his lot c out for the north.
26:15 Obed-edom's c out for the south,
26:16 For Shuppim and Hosah it c out for the west,
27: 1 the divisions that c and went, month after month

1Ch 27:24 yet wrath c upon Israel for this,
27:34 After Ahithophel c Jehoiada son of Benaiah,
2Ch 1:13 So Solomon c from the high place at Gibeon,
5: 4 And all the elders of Israel c,
5:10 with the people of Israel after they c out of Egypt.
5:11 when the priests c out of the holy place
7: 1 fire c down from heaven and consumed
9: 1 she c to Jerusalem to test him with hard questions,
9: 1 When she c to Solomon, she discussed
9: 6 the reports until I c and my own eyes saw it.
9:13 The weight of gold that c to Solomon
10: 3 Jeroboam and all Israel c and said to Rehoboam,
10:12 and all the people c to Rehoboam the third day,
11: 1 When Rehoboam c to Jerusalem,
11: 2 the word of the LORD c to Shemaiah the man
11:16 of Israel c after them from all the tribes of Israel
12: 2 King Shishak of Egypt c up against Jerusalem
12: 3 A countless army c with him from Egypt—
12: 4 He took the fortified cities of Judah and c as far
12: 5 Then the prophet Shemaiah c to Rehoboam and to
12: 7 the word of the LORD c to Shemaiah, saying:
12: 9 So King Shishak of Egypt c up against Jerusalem;
14: 9 the Ethiopian c out against them with an army of
14: 9 and c as far as Mareshah.
15: 1 The spirit of God c upon Azariah son of Oded.
16: 7 that time the seer Hanani c to King Asa of Judah,
18:20 a spirit c forward and stood before the LORD,
18:23 Then Zedekiah son of Chenaanah c up to Micaiah,
20: 1 c against Jehoshaphat for battle.
20: 2 Messengers c and told Jehoshaphat,
20: 4 the towns of Judah they c to seek the LORD.
20:10 whom you would not let Israel invade when they c
20:14 Then the spirit of the LORD c upon Jahaziel son
20:24 Judah c to the watchtower of the wilderness,
20:25 and his people c to take the booty from them,
20:28 They c to Jerusalem, with harps and lyres
20:29 of God c on all the kingdoms of the countries
21:12 A letter c to him from the prophet Elijah, saying:
21:17 They c up against Judah, invaded it,
21:19 his bowels c out because of the disease,
22: 1 for the troops who c with the Arabs to
22: 7 For when he c there he went out with Jehoram
23: 2 and the heads of families of Israel, and they c
24:17 after the death of Jehoiada the officials of Judah c
24:18 And wrath c upon Judah and Jerusalem
24:23 of the year the army of Aram c up against Joash.
24:23 They c to Judah and Jerusalem,
25: 7 But a man of God c to him and said, "O king,
25:14 Amaziah c from the slaughter of the Edomites,
28: 9 he went out to meet the army that c to Samaria,
28:20 So King Tilgath-pilneser of Assyria c against him,
29: 8 wrath of the LORD c upon Judah and Jerusalem,
29:17 the eighth day of the month they c to the vestibule
30:11 Zebulun humbled themselves and c to Jerusalem.
30:13 Many people c together in Jerusalem to keep
30:25 and the whole assembly that c out of Israel,
30:25 the resident aliens who c out of the land of Israel,
30:27 their prayer c to his holy dwelling in heaven.
31: 8 Hezekiah and the officials c and saw the heaps,
32: 1 King Sennacherib of Assyria c and invaded Judah
32:21 When he c into the house of his god,
32:25 wrath c upon him and upon Judah and Jerusalem.
34: 9 They c to the high priest Hilkiah and delivered
36: 6 Against him King Nebuchadnezzar of Babylon c
Ezr 2: 1 Now these were the people of the province who c
2: 2 They c with Zerubbabel, Jeshua, Nehemiah,
2:59 following were those who c up from Tel-melah,
2:68 as they c to the house of the LORD in Jerusalem,
3: 1 When the seventh month c,
4:12 that the Jews who c up from you to us have gone
5: 3 and Shethar-bozenai and their associates c to them
5:16 Then this Sheshbazzar c and laid the foundations
7: 8 They c to Jerusalem in the fifth month,
7: 9 the first day of the fifth month he c to Jerusalem,
8:13 those who c later, their names being Eliphelet,
8:32 We c to Jerusalem and remained there three days.
Ne 1: 2 Hanani, c with certain men from Judah;
2: 9 Then I c to the governors of the province Beyond
2:11 So I c to Jerusalem and was there for three days.
4:12 When the Jews who lived near them c,
4:21 the spears from break of dawn until the stars c out.
5:17 besides those who c to us from the nations
6:17 and Tobiah's letters c to them.
7: 6 These are the people of the province who c up out
7: 7 They c with Zerubbabel, Jeshua, Nehemiah,
7:61 following were those who c up from Tel-melah,
7:73 When the seventh month c—
8:13 c together to the scribe Ezra in order to study
9:13 You c down also upon Mount Sinai,
12: 1 and the Levites who c up with Zerubbabel son
12:39 and they c to a halt at the Gate of the Guard.
Est 2:12 turn c for each girl to go in to King Ahasuerus,
2:14 in the morning she c back to the second harem
2:15 the turn c for Esther daughter of Abihail the uncle
2:22 But the matter c to the knowledge of Mordecai,
4: 3 wherever the king's command and his decree c,
4: 4 Esther's maids and her eunuchs c and told her,
5: 5 So the king and Haman c to the banquet
6: 6 So Haman c in, and the king said to him,
8: 1 and Mordecai c before the king,
8:17 wherever the king's command and his edict c,
9:25 but when Esther c before the king,
Job 1: 6 the heavenly beings c to present themselves
1: 6 and Satan also c among them.
1:14 a messenger c to Job and said,
1:16 While he was still speaking, another c and said,
1:17 While he was still speaking, another c and said,
Job 1:18 While he was still speaking, another c and said,
1:19 and suddenly a great wind c across the desert,
1:21 He said, "Naked I c from my mother's womb,
2: 1 the heavenly beings c to present themselves
2: 1 and Satan also c among them to present himself
4:12 "Now a word c stealing to me,
4:14 dread c upon me, and trembling,
29:13 The blessing of the wretched c upon me,
30:26 But when I looked for good, evil c;
30:26 and when I waited for light, darkness c.
42:11 Then there c to him all his brothers and sisters
Ps 18: 9 He bowed the heavens, and c down;
18:10 he c swiftly upon the wings of the wind.
18:44 foreigners c cringing to me.
18:45 and c trembling out of their strongholds.
33: 9 For he spoke, and it c to be;
48: 4 Then the kings assembled, they c on together.
51: T *A Psalm of David, when the prophet Nathan c*
52: T *A Maskil of David, when Doeg the Edomite c*
68:17 the Lord c from Sinai into the holy place.
74: 2 Remember Mount Zion, where you c to dwell.
105:19 until what he had said c to pass,
105:23 Then Israel c to Egypt; Jacob lived
105:31 He spoke, and there c swarms of flies,
105:34 He spoke, and the locusts c,
Ecc 5:15 As they c from their mother's womb,
5:15 so they shall go again, naked as they c;
5:16 just as they c, so shall they go;
9:14 A great king c against it and besieged it,
Isa 11:16 for Israel when they c up from the land of Egypt.
14:28 In the year that King Ahaz died this oracle c:
20: 1 c to Ashdod and fought against it and took it—
23: 1 When they c in from Cyprus they learned of it.
36: 1 King Sennacherib of Assyria c up against all
36: 3 And there c out to him Eliakim son of Hilkiah,
36:22 the recorder, c to Hezekiah with their clothes torn,
37: 5 When the servants of King Hezekiah c to Isaiah,
37:24 I c to its remotest height, its densest forest.
37:29 I will turn you back on the way by which you c.
37:34 By the way that he c, by the same he shall return;
38: 1 The prophet Isaiah son of Amoz c to him,
38: 4 Then the word of the LORD c to Isaiah:
39: 3 the prophet Isaiah c to King Hezekiah and said
48: 1 and who c forth from the loins of Judah;
48: 3 then suddenly I did them and they c to pass.
48: 5 before they c to pass I announced them to you,
48:16 from the time it c to be I have been there.
50: 2 Why was no one there when I c?
64: 3 not expect, you c down, the mountains quaked
66: 7 before her pain c upon her she delivered a son.
Jer 1: 2 of the LORD c in the days of King Josiah son
1: 3 It c also in the days of King Jehoiakim son
1: 4 Now the word of the LORD c to me saying,
1:11 The word of the LORD c to me, saying,
1:13 The word of the LORD c to me a second time,
2: 1 The word of the LORD c to me, saying:
2: 3 disaster c upon them, says the LORD.
7: 1 The word that c to Jeremiah from the LORD:
7:25 From the day that your ancestors c out of the land
11: 1 The word that c to Jeremiah from the LORD:
13: 3 the word of the LORD c to me a second time,
13: 8 Then the word of the LORD c to me:
14: 1 of the LORD that c to Jeremiah concerning
16: 1 The word of the LORD c to me:
17:16 You know what c from my lips;
18: 1 The word that c to Jeremiah from the LORD:
18: 5 Then the word of the LORD c to me:
19:14 When Jeremiah c from Topheth,
21: 1 the word that c to Jeremiah from the LORD,
24: 4 Then the word of the LORD c to me:
25: 1 that c to Jeremiah concerning all the people
26: 1 this word c from the LORD:
26:10 they c up from the king's house to the house of
27: 1 this word c to Jeremiah from the LORD.
28:12 the word of the LORD c to Jeremiah:
29:30 Then the word of the LORD c to Jeremiah:
30: 1 The word that c to Jeremiah from the LORD:
32: 1 The word that c to Jeremiah from the LORD in
32: 6 Jeremiah said, The word of the LORD c to me:
32: 8 Then my cousin Hanamel c to me in the court of
32:26 The word of the LORD c to Jeremiah:
33: 1 word of the LORD c to Jeremiah a second time,
33:19 The word of the LORD c to Jeremiah:
33:23 The word of the LORD c to Jeremiah:
34: 1 The word that c to Jeremiah from the LORD,
34: 8 The word that c to Jeremiah from the LORD,
34:12 of the LORD c to Jeremiah from the LORD:
35: 1 The word that c to Jeremiah from the LORD in
35:11 But when King Nebuchadrezzar of Babylon c up
35:12 Then the word of the LORD c to Jeremiah:
36: 1 this word c to Jeremiah from the LORD:
36: 9 and all the people who c from the towns of Judah
36:14 of Neriah took the scroll in his hand and c
36:27 the word of the LORD c to Jeremiah:
37: 6 the word of the LORD c to the prophet Jeremiah:
39: 1 of Babylon and all his army c against Jerusalem
39: 3 all the officials of the king of Babylon c and sat in
39:15 the LORD c to Jeremiah while he was confined
40: 1 The word that c to Jeremiah from the LORD
40:12 and c to the land of Judah, to Gedaliah at Mizpah;
40:13 of the forces in the open country c to Gedaliah
41: 1 c with ten men to Gedaliah son of Ahikam,
41: 6 And Ishmael son of Nethaniah c out from Mizpah
41: 6 from Mizpah to meet them, weeping as he c.
41:12 They c upon him at the great pool that is
41:14 from Mizpah turned around and c back,
42: 7 of ten days the word of the LORD c to Jeremiah.
Jer 43: 7 And they c into the land of Egypt,
43: 8 word of the LORD c to Jeremiah in Tahpanhes:
44: 1 that c to Jeremiah for all the Judeans living in
46: 1 of the LORD that c to the prophet Jeremiah
47: 1 of the LORD that c to the prophet Jeremiah
49: 9 If grape-gatherers c to you,
49: 9 If thieves c by night, even they would pillage only
49:34 that c to the prophet Jeremiah concerning Elam,
52: 4 of Babylon c with all his army against Jerusalem,
La 3:57 You c near when I called on you;
Eze 1: 3 the word of the LORD c to the priest Ezekiel son
1: 4 As I looked, a stormy wind c out of the north:
1:25 And there c a voice from above the dome
3:15 I c to the exiles at Tel-abib,
3:16 the word of the LORD c to me:
6: 1 The word of the LORD c to me:
7: 1 The word of the LORD c to me:
9: 2 six men c from the direction of the upper gate,
11:14 Then the word of the LORD c to me:
12: 1 The word of the LORD c to me:
12: 8 In the morning the word of the LORD c to me:
12:17 The word of the LORD c to me:
12:21 The word of the LORD c to me:
12:26 The word of the LORD c to me:
13: 1 The word of the LORD c to me:
14: 1 Certain elders of Israel c to me and sat down
14: 2 And the word of the LORD c to me:
14:12 The word of the LORD c to me:
15: 1 The word of the LORD c to me:
16: 1 The word of the LORD c to me:
17: 1 The word of the LORD c to me:
17: 3 rich in plumage of many colors, c to the Lebanon.
17:11 Then the word of the LORD c to me:
17:12 Tell them: The king of Babylon c to Jerusalem,
18: 1 The word of the LORD c to me:
20: 1 certain elders of Israel c to consult the LORD,
20: 2 And the word of the LORD c to me:
20:45 The word of the LORD c to me:
21: 1 The word of the LORD c to me:
21: 8 And the word of the LORD c to me:
21:18 The word of the LORD c to me:
22: 1 The word of the LORD c to me:
22:17 The word of the LORD c to me:
22:23 The word of the LORD c to me:
23: 1 The word of the LORD c to me:
23:17 And the Babylonians c to her into the bed of love,
23:39 on the same day they c into my sanctuary
23:40 to whom a messenger was sent, and they c.
24: 1 the word of the LORD c to me:
24:15 The word of the LORD c to me:
24:20 The word of the LORD c to me:
25: 1 The word of the LORD c to me:
26: 1 the word of the LORD c to me:
27: 1 The word of the LORD c to me:
27:33 When your wares c from the seas,
28: 1 The word of the LORD c to me:
28:11 Moreover the word of the LORD c to me:
28:20 The word of the LORD c to me:
29: 1 the word of the LORD c to me:
29:17 the word of the LORD c to me:
30: 1 The word of the LORD c to me:
30:20 the word of the LORD c to me:
31: 1 the word of the LORD c to me:
32: 1 the word of the LORD c to me:
32:17 the word of the LORD c to me:
33: 1 The word of the LORD c to me:
33:21 someone who had escaped from Jerusalem c
33:22 upon me the evening before the fugitive c;
33:22 by the time the fugitive c to me in the morning;
33:23 The word of the LORD c to me:
34: 1 The word of the LORD c to me:
35: 1 The word of the LORD c to me:
36:16 The word of the LORD c to me:
36:20 But when they c to the nations, wherever they c,
36:21 among the nations to which they c.
36:22 among the nations to which you c.
37: 1 The hand of the LORD c upon me,
37: 7 and the bones c together, bone to its bone.
37:10 and the breath c into them, and they lived,
37:15 The word of the LORD c to me:
38: 1 The word of the LORD c to me:
43: 3 like the vision that I had seen when he c to destroy
47: 7 As I c back, I saw on the bank of the river
Da 1: 1 King Nebuchadnezzar of Babylon c to Jerusalem
2: 2 When they c in and stood before the king,
2:29 c thoughts of what would be hereafter,
3: 8 at this time certain Chaldeans c forward
3:26 Meshach, and Abednego c out from the fire.
3:27 and not even the smell of fire c from them.
4: 7 and the diviners c in, and I told them the dream,
4: 8 At last Daniel c in before me—
4:28 All this c upon King Nebuchadnezzar.
4:31 the words were still in the king's mouth, a voice c
5: 8 Then all the king's wise men c in,
5:10 c into the banqueting hall.
6: 6 So the presidents and satraps conspired and c to
6:11 The conspirators c and found Daniel praying
6:15 the conspirators c to the king and said to him,
6:20 When he c near the den where Daniel was,
7: 3 and four great beasts c up out of the sea,
7:13 And he c to the Ancient One and was presented
7:20 which c up and to make room for which three
7:22 until the Ancient One c;
8: 3 and the longer one c up second.
8: 6 It c toward the ram with the two horns
8: 8 the great horn was broken, and in its place there c
8: 9 Out of one of them c another horn, a little one,

Da 8:17 So he **c** near where I stood;
8:17 when he **c,** I became frightened and fell prostrate.
9:21 **c** to me in swift flight at the time of
9:22 He **c** and said to me, "Daniel,
10:13 So Michael, one of the chief princes, **c** to help me,
12: 1 such as has never occurred since nations first **c**
Hos 1: 1 word of the LORD that **c** to Hosea son of Beeri,
2:15 as at the time when she **c** out of the land of Egypt.
9:10 they **c** to Baal-peor, and consecrated themselves
9:15 there I **c** to hate them.
Joel 1: 1 word of the LORD that **c** to Joel son of Pethuel:
Ob 1: 5 If thieves **c** to you, if plunderers by night
1: 5 If grape-gatherers **c** to you,
Jnh 1: 1 the word of the LORD **c** to Jonah son of Amittai,
1: 4 and such a mighty storm **c** upon the sea that
1: 6 The captain **c** and said to him,
2: 7 and my prayer **c** to you, into your holy temple.
3: 1 The word of the LORD **c** to Jonah a second time,
4: 7 But when dawn **c** up the next day,
4:10 it **c** into being in a night and perished in a night.
Mic 1: 1 of the LORD that **c** to Micah of Moresheth in
7:15 in the days when you **c** out of the land of Egypt,
Hab 3: 3 God **c** from Teman, the Holy One
3: 4 rays **c** forth from his hand,
3:13 You **c** forth to save your people,
3:14 who **c** like a whirlwind to scatter us,
Zep 1: 1 the LORD that **c** to Zephaniah son of Cushi son
Hag 1: 1 the word of the LORD **c** by the prophet Haggai
1: 3 the word of the LORD **c** by the prophet Haggai,
1: 9 You have looked for much, and, lo, it **c** to little;
1:14 and they **c** and worked on the house of the LORD
2: 1 the word of the LORD **c** by the prophet Haggai,
2: 5 to the promise that I made you when you **c** out
2:10 the word of the LORD **c** by the prophet Haggai,
2:16 When one **c** to a heap of twenty measures,
2:16 when one **c** to the winevat to draw fifty measures,
2:20 of the LORD **c** a second time to Haggai on
Zec 1: 1 of the LORD **c** to the prophet Zechariah son
1: 7 of the LORD **c** to the prophet Zechariah son
2: 3 Then the angel who talked with me **c** forward,
2: 3 and another angel **c** forward to meet him,
4: 1 The angel who talked with me **c** again,
4: 8 Moreover the word of the LORD **c** to me, saying,
5: 5 the angel who talked with me **c** forward and said
6: 7 the steeds **c** out, they were impatient to get off
6: 9 The word of the LORD **c** to me:
7: 1 of the LORD **c** to Zechariah on the fourth day of
7: 4 Then the word of the LORD of hosts **c** to me:
7: 8 The word of the LORD **c** to Zechariah, saying:
7:12 Therefore great wrath **c** from the LORD of hosts.
8: 1 The word of the LORD of hosts **c** to me, saying:
8:10 from the foe for those who went out or **c** in,
8:18 The word of the LORD of hosts **c** to me, saying:
Mt 2: 1 wise men from the East **c** to Jerusalem,
3:13 Then Jesus **c** from Galilee to John at the Jordan,
3:16 just as he **c** up from the water,
4: 3 The tempter **c** and said to him,
4:11 and suddenly angels **c** and waited on him.
5: 1 and after he sat down, his disciples **c** to him.
7:25 The rain fell, the floods **c,**
7:27 The rain fell, and the floods **c,**
8: 2 and there was a leper who **c** to him and knelt
8: 5 he entered Capernaum, a centurion **c** to him,
8:28 When he **c** to the other side,
8:32 So they **c** out and entered the swine;
8:34 Then the whole town **c** out to meet Jesus;
9: 1 a boat he crossed the sea and **c** to his own town.
9:10 many tax collectors and sinners **c** and were sitting
9:14 Then the disciples of John **c** to him, saying,
9:18 suddenly a leader of the synagogue **c** in and knelt
9:20 for twelve years **c** up behind him and touched
9:23 When Jesus **c** to the leader's house and saw
9:28 he entered the house, the blind men **c** to him;
11:13 the prophets and the law prophesied until John **c;**
11:18 For John **c** neither eating nor drinking,
11:19 the Son of Man **c** eating and drinking,
12:42 because she **c** from the ends of the earth to listen
12:44 it says, 'I will return to my house from which I **c.'**
13: 4 and the birds **c** and ate them up.
13:10 Then the disciples **c** and asked him,
13:25 an enemy **c** and sowed weeds among the wheat,
13:26 So when the plants **c** up and bore grain,
13:27 the slaves of the householder **c** and said to him,
13:54 He **c** to his hometown and began to teach
14: 6 But when Herod's birthday **c,**
14:12 His disciples **c** and took the body and buried it;
14:15 it was evening, the disciples **c** to him and said,
14:23 When evening **c,** he was there alone,
14:25 the morning he **c** walking toward them on the sea.
14:29 started walking on the water, and **c** toward Jesus.
14:34 they **c** to land at Gennesaret.
15: 1 and scribes **c** to Jesus from Jerusalem and said,
15:22 then a Canaanite woman from that region **c** out
15:23 And his disciples **c** and urged him, saying,
15:25 But she **c** and knelt before him, saying, "Lord,
15:30 Great crowds **c** to him, bringing with them
16: 1 The Pharisees and Sadducees **c,**
16:13 when Jesus **c** into the district of Caesarea Philippi,
17: 7 But Jesus **c** and touched them, saying,
17:14 When they **c** to the crowd, a man **c** to him,
17:18 And Jesus rebuked the demon, and it **c** out of him,
17:19 Then the disciples **c** to Jesus privately and said,
17:24 the collectors of the temple tax **c** to Peter and said,
17:25 And when he **c** home, Jesus spoke of it first,
18: 1 At that time the disciples **c** to Jesus and asked,
18:21 Then Peter **c** and said to him, "Lord,
18:28 **c** upon one of his fellow slaves who owed him
Mt 19: 3 Some Pharisees **c** to him,
19:16 Then someone **c** to him and said, "Teacher,
20: 8 When evening **c,** the owner of the vineyard said
20: 9 When those hired about five o'clock **c,**
20:10 the first **c,** they thought they would receive more;
20:20 Then the mother of the sons of Zebedee **c** to him
20:28 as the Son of Man **c** not to be served but to serve,
21:14 The blind and the lame **c** to him in the temple,
21:23 the chief priests and the elders of the people **c**
21:32 For John **c** to you in the way of righteousness
22:11 "But when the king **c** in to see the guests,
22:23 The same day some Sadducees **c** to him,
24: 1 As Jesus **c** out of the temple and was going away,
24: 1 his disciples **c** to point out to him the buildings of
24: 3 the disciples **c** to him privately, saying, "Tell us,
24:39 until the flood **c** and swept them all away,
25:10 And while they went to buy it, the bridegroom **c,**
25:11 Later the other bridesmaids **c** also, saying, 'Lord,
25:19 of those slaves **c** and settled accounts with them.
25:20 one who had received the five talents **c** forward,
25:22 And the one with the two talents also **c** forward,
25:24 also **c** forward, saying, 'Master, I knew
26: 7 a woman **c** to him with an alabaster jar
26:17 the first day of Unleavened Bread the disciples **c**
26:40 he **c** to the disciples and found them sleeping;
26:43 Again he **c** and found them sleeping,
26:45 Then he **c** to the disciples and said to them,
26:49 At once he **c** up to Jesus and said, "Greetings,
26:50 they **c** and laid hands on Jesus and arrested him.
26:60 though many false witnesses **c** forward.
26:60 At last two **c** forward
26:69 A servant-girl **c** to him and said,
26:73 a little while the bystanders **c** up and said to Peter,
27: 1 When morning **c,** all the chief priests and
27:32 they **c** upon a man from Cyrene named Simon;
27:33 when they **c** to a place called Golgotha
27:45 darkness **c** over the whole land until three in
27:53 After his resurrection they **c** out of the tombs
27:57 there **c** a rich man from Arimathea, named Joseph,
28: 2 **c** and rolled back the stone and sat on it.
28: 9 And they **c** to him, took hold of his feet,
28:13 'His disciples **c** by night and stole him away
28:18 And Jesus **c** and said to them,
Mk 1: 9 In those days Jesus **c** from Nazareth of Galilee
1:11 And a voice **c** from heaven, "You are my Son,
1:14 Now after John was arrested, Jesus **c** to Galilee,
1:21 sabbath **c,** he entered the synagogue and taught.
1:26 and crying with a loud voice, **c** out of him.
1:31 He **c** and took her by the hand and lifted her up.
1:38 for that is what I **c** out to do."
1:40 A leper **c** to him begging him,
1:45 and people **c** to him from every quarter.
2: 3 Then some people **c,** bringing to him
2:18 and people **c** and said to him,
3: 8 they **c** to him in great numbers from Judea,
3:13 to him those whom he wanted, and they **c** to him.
3:20 and the crowd **c** together again,
3:22 And the scribes who **c** down from Jerusalem said,
3:31 Then his mother and his brothers **c;**
4: 4 and the birds **c** and ate it up.
5: 1 They **c** to the other side of the sea,
5:13 the unclean spirits **c** out and entered the swine;
5:14 people **c** to see what it was that had happened.
5:15 They **c** to Jesus and saw
5:22 the leaders of the synagogue named Jairus **c** and,
5:27 and **c** up behind him in the crowd
5:33 **c** in fear and trembling, fell down before him,
5:35 some people **c** from the leader's house to say,
5:38 they **c** to the house of the leader of the synagogue,
6: 1 He left that place and **c** to his hometown,
6:21 an opportunity **c** when Herod on his birthday gave
6:22 When his daughter Herodias **c** in and danced,
6:29 they **c** and took his body, and laid it in a tomb.
6:35 When it grew late, his disciples **c** to him and said,
6:47 When evening **c,** the boat was out on the sea,
6:48 he **c** towards them early in the morning,
6:53 they **c** to land at Gennesaret and moored the boat.
7:25 and she **c** and bowed down at his feet.
8:11 The Pharisees **c** and began to argue with him,
8:22 They **c** to Bethsaida. Some people brought a blind
9: 7 and from the cloud there **c** a voice,
9:14 When they **c** to the disciples,
9:25 When Jesus saw that a crowd **c** running together,
9:26 crying out and convulsing him terribly, it **c** out,
9:33 Then they **c** to Capernaum;
10: 2 Some Pharisees **c,** and to test him they asked,
10:35 **c** forward to him and said to him, "Teacher,
10:45 the Son of Man **c** not to be served but to serve,
10:46 They **c** to Jericho.
10:50 he sprang up and **c** to Jesus.
11:12 On the following day, when they **c** from Bethany,
11:13 When he **c** to it, he found nothing but leaves,
11:15 Then they **c** to Jerusalem.
11:19 when evening **c,** Jesus and his disciples went out
11:27 Again they **c** to Jerusalem.
11:27 and the elders **c** to him
12: 2 When the season **c,** he sent a slave to the tenants
12:14 And they **c** and said to him, "Teacher,
12:18 **c** to him and asked him a question, saying,
12:28 of the scribes **c** near and heard them disputing
12:42 poor widow **c** and put in two small copper coins,
13: 1 As he **c** out of the temple,
14: 3 a woman **c** with an alabaster jar
14:17 When it was evening, he **c** with the twelve.
14:37 He **c** and found them sleeping;
14:40 And once more he **c** and found them sleeping,
14:41 He **c** a third time and said to them,
Mk 14:45 he **c,** he went up to him at once and said, "Rabbi!"
14:66 one of the servant-girls of the high priest **c** by.
15: 8 the crowd **c** and began to ask Pilate to do for them
15:33 darkness **c** over the whole land until three in
Lk 1:28 And he **c** to her and said, "Greetings, favored one!
1:57 Now the time **c** for Elizabeth to give birth,
1:59 On the eighth day they **c** to circumcise the child,
1:65 Fear **c** over all their neighbors,
2: 6 the time **c** for her to deliver her child.
2:22 When the time **c** for their purification according to
2:27 Guided by the Spirit, Simeon **c** into the temple;
2:38 that moment she **c,** and began to praise God and
2:51 Then he went down with them and **c** to Nazareth,
3: 2 the word of God **c** to John son of Zechariah in
3: 7 John said to the crowds that **c** out to be baptized
3:12 Even tax collectors **c** to be baptized,
3:22 And a voice **c** from heaven, "You are my Son,
4:16 When he **c** to Nazareth,
4:22 and were amazed at the gracious words that **c**
4:35 down before them, he **c** out of him
4:41 Demons also **c** out of many, shouting,
5: 7 And they **c** and filled both boats,
5:18 Just then some men **c,** carrying a paralyzed man
6:13 And when day **c,** he called his disciples
6:17 He **c** down with them and stood on a level place,
6:19 for power **c** out from him and healed all of them.
7: 4 When they **c** to Jesus, they appealed
7:14 Then he **c** forward and touched the bier,
7:45 the time I **c** in she has not stopped kissing my feet.
8: 4 and people from town after town **c** to him, he said
8:19 Then his mother and his brothers **c** to him,
8:33 demons **c** out of the man and entered the swine,
8:35 Then people **c** out to see what had happened,
8:35 and when they **c** to Jesus,
8:41 Just then there **c** a man named Jairus,
8:44 She **c** up behind him and touched the fringe
8:47 that she could not remain hidden, she **c** trembling;
8:49 someone **c** from the leader's house to say,
8:51 When he **c** to the house,
9:12 and the twelve **c** to him and said,
9:34 a cloud **c** and overshadowed them;
9:35 Then from the cloud **c** a voice that said,
10:32 when he **c** to the place and saw him,
10:33 But a Samaritan while traveling **c** near him;
10:40 so she **c** to him and asked, "Lord,
11:24 it says, 'I will return to my house from which I **c.'**
11:31 because she **c** from the ends of the earth to listen
12:49 "I **c** to bring fire to the earth,
13: 6 and he **c** looking for fruit on it and found none.
13:31 that very hour some Pharisees **c** and said to him,
15:17 But when he **c** to himself he said,
15:25 and when he **c** and approached the house,
15:28 His father **c** out and began to plead with him.
15:30 But when this son of yours **c** back,
16:16 law and the prophets were in effect until John **c;**
17:27 and the flood **c** and destroyed all of them.
18:40 and when he **c** near, he asked him,
19: 5 When Jesus **c** to the place,
19:10 the Son of Man **c** to seek out and to save the lost."
19:16 The first **c** forward and said, 'Lord,
19:18 Then the second **c,** saying, 'Lord,
19:20 the other **c,** saying, 'Lord, here is your pound.
19:41 As he **c** near and saw the city, he wept over it,
20: 1 the chief priests and the scribes **c** with the elders
20: 7 that they did not know where it **c** from.
20:10 the season **c,** he sent a slave to the tenants in order
20:27 those who say there is no resurrection, **c** to him
22: 7 Then **c** the day of Unleavened Bread,
22:14 When the hour **c,** he took his place at the table,
22:39 He **c** out and went, as was his custom,
22:45 he **c** to the disciples and found them sleeping
22:47 While he was still speaking, suddenly a crowd **c,**
22:66 When day **c,** the assembly of the elders of
23:33 When they **c** to the place that is called The Skull,
23:44 and darkness **c** over the whole land until three in
23:51 He **c** from the Jewish town of Arimathea,
24: 1 at early dawn, they **c** to the tomb,
24:15 Jesus himself **c** near and went with them,
24:23 they **c** back and told us that they had indeed seen
24:28 they **c** near the village to which they were going,
Jn 1: 3 All things **c** into being through him, and without
him not one thing **c** into being.
1: 7 He **c** as a witness to testify to the light,
1: 8 but he **c** to testify to the light.
1:10 and the world **c** into being through him;
1:11 He **c** to what was his own,
1:17 grace and truth **c** through Jesus Christ.
1:31 but I **c** baptizing with water for this reason,
1:39 They **c** and saw where he was staying,
2: 9 and did not know where it **c** from
3: 2 He **c** to Jesus by night and said to him, "Rabbi,
3:26 They **c** to John and said to him, "Rabbi,
4: 5 So he **c** to a Samaritan city called Sychar,
4: 7 A Samaritan woman **c** to draw water,
4:27 Just then his disciples **c.**
4:40 So when the Samaritans **c** to him,
4:45 When he **c** to Galilee, the Galileans welcomed him,
4:46 Then he **c** again to Cana in Galilee
6:16 When evening **c,** his disciples went down to
6:23 Then some boats from Tiberias **c** near the place
6:41 "I am the bread that **c** down from heaven."
6:51 I am the living bread that **c** down from heaven.
6:58 This is the bread that **c** down from heaven,
8: 2 ⟦Early in the morning he **c** again to the temple.⟧
8: 2 ⟦All the people **c** to him and he sat down and⟧
8:42 for I **c** from God and now I am here.
9: 7 Then he went and washed and **c** back able to see.

Jn 9:39 "I **c** into this world for judgment so
10:8 All who **c** before me are thieves and bandits;
10:10 I **c** that they may have life,
10:35 to whom the word of God **c** were called 'gods'—
10:41 Many **c** to him, and they were saying,
11:32 When Mary **c** where Jesus was and saw him,
11:33 and the Jews who **c** with her also weeping,
11:38 Then Jesus, again greatly disturbed, **c** to the tomb.
11:44 The dead man **c** out, his hands and feet bound
12:1 Six days before the Passover Jesus **c** to Bethany,
12:9 they **c** not only because of Jesus but also
12:21 They **c** to Philip, who was from Bethsaida
12:28 Then a voice **c** from heaven, "I have glorified it,
12:47 for I **c** not to judge the world,
13:6 He **c** to Simon Peter, who said to him, "Lord,
16:27 and have believed that I **c** from God.
16:28 I **c** from the Father and have come into the world;
16:30 by this we believe that you **c** from God."
17:8 and know in truth that I **c** from you;
18:3 and they **c** there with lanterns and torches
18:4 **c** forward and asked them,
18:37 For this I was born, and for this I **c** into the world,
19:5 So Jesus **c** out, wearing the crown of thorns and
19:32 the soldiers **c** and broke the legs of the first and of
19:33 they **c** to Jesus and saw that he was already dead,
19:34 and at once blood and water **c** out.
19:38 so he **c** and removed his body.
19:39 who had at first come to Jesus by night, also **c**,
20:1 Mary Magdalene **c** to the tomb and saw that
20:6 Then Simon Peter **c**, following him,
20:19 Jesus **c** and stood among them and said,
20:24 was not with them when Jesus **c**.
20:26 Jesus **c** and stood among them and said,
21:8 But the other disciples **c** in the boat,
21:13 Jesus **c** and took the bread and gave it to them,
Ac 2:2 And suddenly from heaven there **c** a sound like
2:43 Awe **c** upon everyone, because many wonders
4:1 and the Sadducees **c** to them,
5:6 The young men **c** and wrapped up his body,
5:7 an interval of about three hours his wife **c** in,
5:10 When the young men **c** in they found her dead,
5:15 on some of them as he **c** by.
7:11 there **c** a famine throughout Egypt and Canaan,
7:23 it **c** into his heart to visit his relatives,
7:26 The next day he **c** to some of them
7:31 there **c** the voice of the Lord:
8:7 **c** out of many who were possessed;
8:36 As they were going along the road, they **c**
8:39 When they **c** up out of the water,
8:40 the good news to all the towns until he **c**
9:5 reply **c**, "I am Jesus, whom you are persecuting.
9:32 he **c** down also to the saints living in Lydda.
10:24 The following day they **c** to Caesarea.
10:29 So when I was sent for, I **c** without objection.
11:5 and it **c** close to me.
11:22 of this **c** to the ears of the church in Jerusalem,
11:23 When he **c** and saw the grace of God, he rejoiced,
11:27 At that time prophets **c** down from Jerusalem
12:10 they **c** before the iron gate leading into the city.
12:11 Then Peter **c** to himself and said,
12:13 a maid named Rhoda **c** to answer.
12:18 When morning **c**, there was no small commotion
12:20 So they **c** to him in a body;
13:11 Immediately mist and darkness **c** over him,
13:13 and his companions set sail from Paphos and **c**
13:14 but they went on from Perga and **c** to Antioch
13:31 and for many days he appeared to those who **c** up
14:19 But Jews **c** there from Antioch and Iconium
14:24 they passed through Pisidia and **c** to Pamphylia.
15:1 Then certain individuals **c** down from Judea
15:4 When they **c** to Jerusalem,
16:18 And it **c** out that very hour.
16:35 When morning **c**, the magistrates sent the police,
16:39 so they **c** and apologized to them.
17:1 through Amphipolis and Apollonia, they **c**
17:13 they **c** there too, to stir up and incite the crowds.
18:24 Now there **c** to Ephesus a Jew named Apollos,
19:1 Paul passed through the interior regions and **c**
19:6 the Holy Spirit **c** upon them,
19:12 and the evil spirits **c** out of them.
20:2 the believers much encouragement, he **c**
20:15 and the day after that we **c** to Miletus.
20:18 When they **c** to him, he said to them:
20:19 enduring the trials that **c** to me through the plots
21:1 we **c** by a straight course to Cos,
21:3 We **c** in sight of Cyprus;
21:8 The next day we left and **c** to Caesarea;
21:10 a prophet named Agabus **c** down from Judea.
21:11 He **c** to us and took Paul's belt,
21:16 Some of the disciples from Caesarea also **c** along
21:31 word **c** to the tribune of the cohort
21:33 Then the tribune **c**, arrested him,
21:35 When Paul **c** to the steps,
22:13 **c** to me; and standing beside me,
22:27 The tribune **c** and asked Paul, "Tell me,
23:27 I **c** with the guard and rescued him.
23:33 When they **c** to Caesarea and delivered the letter
24:1 the high priest Ananias **c** down with some elders
24:17 after some years I **c** to bring alms to my nation
24:24 when Felix **c** with his wife Drusilla,
25:23 So on the next day Agrippa and Bernice **c**
27:5 we **c** to Myra in Lycia.
27:8 we **c** to a place called Fair Havens,
28:9 the island who had diseases also **c** and were cured.
28:13 then we weighed anchor and **c** to Rhegium.
28:13 and on the second day we **c** to Puteoli.
28:14 And so we **c** to Rome.
Ac 28:15 **c** as far as the Forum of Appius
28:16 When we **c** into Rome, Paul was allowed to live
28:23 they **c** to him at his lodgings in great numbers.
28:30 at his own expense and welcomed all who **c**
Ro 5:12 just as sin **c** into the world through one man, and
death **c** through sin, and so death spread to all
5:20 But law **c** in, with the result that
7:9 but when the commandment **c**,
1Co 2:1 When I **c** to you, brothers and sisters,
2:3 And I **c** to you in weakness and in fear and
3:5 Servants through whom you **c** to believe,
11:12 For just as woman **c** from man,
15:21 For since death **c** through a human being,
2Co 2:3 And I wrote as I did, so that when I **c**,
2:12 I **c** to Troas to proclaim the good news of Christ,
3:7 **c** in glory so that the people of Israel could
3:11 for if what was set aside **c** through glory,
7:5 For even when we **c** into Macedonia,
11:9 for my needs were supplied by the friends who **c**
Gal 2:11 But when Cephas **c** to Antioch,
2:12 for until certain people **c** from James,
2:12 But after they **c**, he drew back
3:17 the law, which **c** four hundred thirty years later,
3:23 before faith **c**, we were imprisoned and guarded
3:24 the law was our disciplinarian until Christ **c**,
Eph 2:17 So he **c** and proclaimed peace
Php 2:30 because he **c** close to death for the work of Christ,
1Th 1:5 of the gospel **c** to you not in word only,
2:5 we never **c** with words of flattery or with a pretext
1Ti 1:15 that Christ Jesus **c** into the world to save sinners—
2Ti 4:16 At my first defense no one **c** to my support,
Heb 4:2 For indeed the good news **c** to us just as to them;
7:28 which **c** later than the law,
9:11 when Christ **c** as a high priest of the good things
10:5 Consequently, when Christ **c** into the world,
2Pe 1:21 because no prophecy ever **c** by human will,
1Jn 5:6 This is the one who **c** by water and blood,
Rev 1:16 and from his mouth **c** a sharp, two-edged sword,
2:8 who was dead and **c** to life:
6:2 and he **c** out conquering and to conquer.
6:4 And out **c** another horse, bright red;
6:12 I looked, and there **c** a great earthquake;
8:3 Another angel with a golden censer **c** and stood at
8:7 and there **c** hail and fire, mixed with blood,
9:3 Then from the smoke **c** locusts on the earth,
9:17 fire and smoke and sulfur **c** out of their mouths.
12:16 But the earth **c** to the help of the woman;
14:15 Another angel **c** out of the temple,
14:17 Then another angel **c** out of the temple in heaven,
14:18 Then another angel **c** out from the altar,
15:6 and out of the temple **c** the seven angels with
16:2 and painful sore **c** on those who had the mark of
16:17 and a loud voice **c** out of the temple,
16:18 And there **c** flashes of lightning, rumblings,
17:1 of the seven angels who had the seven bowls **c**
19:5 And from the throne **c** a voice saying,
19:21 the sword that **c** from his mouth;
20:4 They **c** to life and reigned with Christ
20:9 fire **c** down from heaven and consumed them.
21:9 the seven bowls full of the seven last plagues **c**
Tob 1:10 After I was carried away captive to Assyria and **c**
1:18 when he **c** fleeing from Judea in those days
3:17 of Raguel **c** down from her upper room.
4:3 and when he **c** to him he said, "My son,
6:2 the dog **c** out with him and went along with them.
7:12 When she **c** to him he took her by the hand
8:14 Then the maid **c** out and informed them
9:6 to the wedding celebration. When they **c**
10:7 Tobias **c** to him and said, "Send me back,
11:1 When they **c** near to Kaserin,
11:10 and **c** stumbling out through the courtyard door.
14:10 Ahikar **c** out into the light,
Jdt 1:14 Thus he took possession of his towns and **c**
2:25 Then he **c** to the southern borders of Japheth,
3:5 The men **c** to Holofernes and told him all this.
3:9 Then he **c** toward Esdraelon, near Dothan,
6:5 until I take revenge on this race that **c** out
6:11 the plain they went up into the hill country and **c**
6:14 Israelites **c** down from their town and found him;
7:8 and the commanders of the coastland **c** to him
8:11 They **c** to her, and she said to them, "Listen to me,
10:18 They **c** and gathered around her
10:20 the guards of Holofernes and all his servants **c** out
10:22 they told him of her, he **c** to the front of the tent,
10:23 When Judith **c** into the presence of Holofernes
12:16 Then Judith **c** in and lay down.
13:1 When evening **c**, his slaves quickly withdrew.
13:7 She **c** close to his bed,
13:10 up the mountain to Bethulia, and **c** to its gates.
14:6 When he **c** and saw the head of Holofernes in
14:13 They **c** to Holofernes' tent and said to the steward
15:5 Those in Jerusalem and all the hill country also **c**,
15:8 the Israelites who lived in Jerusalem **c** to witness
16:3 Assyrian **c** down from the mountains of the north;
16:3 he **c** with myriads of his warriors;
AdE 1:14 him in the chief seats—**c** to him
3:7 In the twelfth year of King Artaxerxes Haman **c** to
4:4 the queen's maids and eunuchs **c** and told her,
5:5 both **c** to the dinner that Esther had spoken about.
9:18 **c** together also on the fourteenth, but did not rest.
9:25 against the Jews **c** back upon himself,
10:11 and these two lots **c** to the hour and moment
11:6 Then two great dragons **c** forward,
11:10 as though from a tiny spring, there **c** a great river,
11:11 light **c**, and the sun rose,
15:8 and took her in his arms until she **c** to herself.
Wis 6:22 I will tell you what wisdom is and how she **c** to
Wis 7:7 I called on God, and the spirit of wisdom **c** to me.
7:11 All good things **c** to me along with her,
12:27 Therefore the utmost condemnation **c** upon them.
16:5 For when the terrible rage of wild animals **c**
16:10 for your mercy **c** to their help and healed them.
17:14 and which **c** upon them from the recesses
17:18 Whether there **c** a whistling wind,
18:20 and a plague **c** upon the multitude in the desert,
19:12 for, to give them relief, quails **c** up from the sea.
19:14 to receive strangers when they **c** to them,
Sir Pr:3 When I **c** to Egypt in the thirty-eighth year of
24:3 "I **c** forth from the mouth of the Most High,
27:27 and he will not know where it **c** from.
40:10 and on their account the flood **c**.
44:17 a remnant was left on the earth when the flood **c**.
47:25 until vengeance **c** upon them.
49:4 the kings of Judah **c** to an end.
50:5 as he **c** out of the house of the curtain.
50:20 Then Simon **c** down and raised his hands over
Bar 1:3 and to all the people who **c** to hear the book,
4:9 For she saw the wrath that **c** upon you from God,
Aza 1:26 But the angel of the Lord **c** down into the furnace
Sus 1:5 "Wickedness **c** forth from Babylon,
1:6 and all who had a case to be tried **c** to them there.
1:28 of her husband Joakim, the two elders **c**, full
1:30 And she **c** with her parents, her children,
1:36 this woman **c** in with two maids,
1:37 who was hiding there, **c** to her and lay with her.
Bel 1:15 During the night the priests **c** as usual,
1:16 Early in the morning the king rose and **c**,
1:40 the seventh day the king **c** to mourn for Daniel.
1:40 he **c** to the den he looked in, and there sat Daniel!
1Mc 1:1 the Macedonian, who **c** from the land of Kittim,
1:10 From them **c** forth a sinful root,
1:11 In those days certain renegades **c** out from Israel
1:20 He went up against Israel and **c** to Jerusalem with
1:29 and he **c** to Jerusalem with a large force.
1:64 Very great wrath **c** upon Israel.
2:15 the apostasy **c** to the town of Modein
2:16 Many from Israel **c** to them;
2:23 a Jew **c** forward in the sight of all to offer sacrifice
4:29 They **c** into Idumea and encamped at Beth-zur,
5:14 **c** from Galilee and made a similar report;
5:33 Then he **c** up behind them in three companies,
5:46 So they **c** to Ephron.
5:53 and encouraging the people all the way until he **c**
5:59 and his men **c** out of the town to meet them
6:3 So he **c** and tried to take the city and plunder it,
6:5 Then someone **c** to him in Persia and reported that
6:29 also **c** to him from other kingdoms and
6:31 They **c** through Idumea and encamped
7:5 Then there **c** to him all the renegade
7:10 So they marched away and **c** with a large force
7:27 So Nicanor **c** to Jerusalem with a large force,
7:29 So he **c** to Judas, and they greeted one another
7:33 of the people **c** out to greet him peaceably and
7:46 People **c** out of all the surrounding villages
8:1 they pledged friendship to those who **c** to them,
8:4 They also subdued the kings who **c** against them
9:36 of Jambri from Medeba **c** out and seized John
9:39 and the bridegroom **c** out with his friends
9:43 he **c** with a large force on the sabbath day to
9:64 Then he **c** and encamped against Bethbasi;
10:7 Then Jonathan **c** to Jerusalem and read the letter
10:57 from Egypt, he and his daughter Cleopatra, and **c**
10:67 of Demetrius **c** from Crete to the land
10:85 with those burned alive, **c** to eight thousand.
10:86 of the city **c** out to meet him with great pomp.
11:15 Alexander heard of it, he **c** against him in battle.
11:22 soon as he heard it he set out and **c** to Ptolemais;
11:44 and when they **c** to the king,
11:60 When he **c** to Askalon, the people of
12:40 and he marched out and **c** to Beth-shan.
12:41 with forty thousand picked warriors, and he **c**
13:20 this Trypho **c** to invade the country and destroy it,
15:11 and Trypho **c** in his flight to Dor,
15:32 So Athenobius, the king's Friend, **c** to Jerusalem,
15:40 So Cendebeus **c** to Jamnia and began to provoke
16:22 the men who **c** to destroy him and killed them,
2Mc 1:7 in the critical distress that **c** upon us in those years
1:14 Antiochus **c** to the place together with his Friends,
2:5 Jeremiah **c** and found a cave-dwelling,
2:6 of those who followed him **c** up intending to mark
2:10 and fire **c** down from heaven and consumed
2:10 and the fire **c** down and consumed
2:21 that **c** from heaven to those who fought bravely
3:2 it **c** about that the kings themselves honored
3:27 to the ground and deep darkness **c** over him,
4:10 When the king assented and Jason **c** to office,
4:34 Andronicus **c** to Onias, and resorting to treachery,
4:44 When the king **c** to Tyre,
5:18 from his rash act as soon as he **c** forward,
5:26 to the sword all those who **c** out to see them,
7:22 not know how you **c** into being in my womb.
7:28 And in the same way the human race **c** into being.
8:12 Word **c** to Judas concerning Nicanor's invasion;
8:19 of the occasions when help **c** to their ancestors;
8:20 by the help that **c** to them from heaven,
9:3 news **c** to him of what had happened to Nicanor
9:7 And so it **c** about that he fell out of his chariot
9:24 or any unwelcome news **c**,
9:28 **c** to the end of his life by a most pitiable fate,
10:21 word of what had happened **c** to Maccabeus,
10:24 He **c** on, intending to take Judea by storm.
10:27 and when they **c** near the enemy they halted.
10:36 Others who **c** up in the same way wheeled around
11:2 and all his cavalry and **c** against the Jews.

2Mc 12:17 from there, they **c** to Charax,
12:22 and fear **c** over the enemy at the manifestation
12:33 who **c** out with three thousand infantry
13: 1 the one hundred forty-ninth year word **c** to Judas
13: 7 By such a fate it **c** about that Menelaus
14: 1 word **c** to Judas and his men that Demetrius son
14:21 A chariot **c** forward from each army;
14:28 When this message **c** to Nicanor,
1Es 1:29 and the commanders **c** down against King Josiah.
1:40 King Nebuchadnezzar of Babylon **c** up
2:18 be known to our lord the king that the Jews who **c**
3:16 So they were summoned, and **c** in.
4:16 From women they **c**;
4:53 and that all who **c** from Babylonia to build
4:53 they and their children and all the priests who **c**.
5: 7 the Judeans who **c** up out of their sojourn in exile,
5: 8 They **c** with Zerubbabel and Jeshua, Nehemiah,
5:36 The following are those who **c** up from Tel-melah
5:44 they **c** to the temple of God that is in Jerusalem,
5:47 When the seventh month **c**,
5:57 the second month in the second year after they **c**
5:63 **c** to the building of this one with outcries
5:64 while many **c** with trumpets and a joyful noise,
5:66 they **c** to find out what the sound of
6: 3 and Sathrabuzanes and their associates **c** to them
7:10 of Israel who **c** from exile kept the passover on
8: 1 the king of the Persians, was reigning, Ezra **c**,
8: 3 This Ezra **c** up from Babylon as a scribe skilled in
8: 5 There **c** up with him to Jerusalem some of
8:61 and so we **c** to Jerusalem.
8:68 the leaders **c** to me and said,
9:55 And they **c** together.
3Mc 1: 5 it **c** about that the enemy was routed in the action,
3:16 we **c** on to Jerusalem also,
2Es 1: 4 The word of the Lord **c** to me, saying,
2:33 When I **c** to them they rejected me and refused
3:10 just as death **c** upon Adam,
3:29 I **c** here I saw ungodly deeds without number,
4:16 for the fire **c** and consumed it;
5:16 **c** to me and said, "Where have you been?
6:44 Immediately fruit **c** forth in endless abundance
7:21 For the Lord strictly commanded those who **c** into
7:21 when they **c**, what they should do to live,
9:29 when they **c** out from Egypt and when they **c**
9:47 when he grew up and I **c** to take a wife for him,
10: 3 I got up in the night and fled, and I **c** to this field,
10:13 the multitude that is now in it goes as it **c**';
10:28 who **c** to me at first?
10:29 the angel who had come to me at first **c** to me,
11:13 And after a time its reign **c** to an end,
11:14 While it was reigning its end **c** also,
12:40 and **c** to me and spoke to me, saying,
13: 5 of heaven to make war against the man who **c**
13:13 Then many people **c** to him,
13:28 that **c** to conquer him, this is the interpretation:
14: 1 suddenly a voice **c** out of a bush opposite me
4Mc 3: 8 Then when evening fell, he **c**,
4: 2 So he **c** to Apollonius, governor of Syria,
6:13 some of the king's retinue **c** to him and said,
12: 1 the seventh and youngest of all **c** forward.
13:12 "Remember whence you **c**,

CAMEL (10) [CAMEL'S, CAMELS]

Ge 24:64 she slipped quickly from the **c**,
Lev 11: 4 the **c**, for even though it chews the cud,
Dt 14: 7 the **c**, the hare, and the rock badger,
1Sa 15: 3 child and infant, ox and sheep, **c** and donkey.' "
2Ki 8: 9 all kinds of goods of Damascus, forty **c** loads.
Jer 2:23 a restive young **c** interlacing her tracks,
Mt 19:24 for a **c** to go through the eye of a needle than
23:24 You strain out a gnat but swallow a **c**!
Mk 10:25 for a **c** to go through the eye of a needle than
Lk 18:25 for a **c** to go through the eye of a needle than

CAMEL'S (5) [CAMEL]

Ge 31:34 the household gods and put them in the **c** saddle,
Mt 3: 4 of **c** hair with a leather belt around his waist,
Mk 1: 6 Now John was clothed with **c** hair,
Sir 24:15 Like cassia and **c** thorn I gave forth perfume,
2Es 15:36 and a man's thigh and a **c** hock.

CAMELS‡ (54) [CAMEL]

Ge 12:16 male and female slaves, female donkeys, and **c**.
24:10 servant took ten of his master's **c** and departed,
24:11 He made the **c** kneel down outside the city by
24:14 who shall say, 'Drink, and I will water your **c**'—
24:19 she said, "I will draw for your **c** also,
24:20 and she drew for all his **c**.
24:22 When the **c** had finished drinking,
24:30 and there he was, standing by the **c** at the spring.
24:31 the house and a place for the **c**?"
24:32 and Laban unloaded the **c**,
24:32 and gave him straw and fodder for the **c**,
24:35 male and female slaves, **c** and donkeys.
24:44 "Drink, and I will draw for your **c** also"—
24:46 and said, 'Drink, and I will also water your **c**.'
24:46 So I drank, and she also watered the **c**.
24:61 Rebekah and her maids rose up, mounted the **c**,
24:63 and looking up, he saw **c** coming.
30:43 and male and female slaves, and **c** and donkeys.
31:17 and set his children and his wives on **c**;
32: 7 and the flocks and herds and **c**,
32:15 thirty milch **c** and their colts,
37:25 with their **c** carrying gum, balm, and resin,
Ex 9: 3 the horses, the donkeys, the **c**, the herds,
Jdg 6: 5 neither they nor their **c** could be counted;
7:12 and their **c** were without number,
8:21 the crescents that were on the necks of their **c**.
8:26 and the collars that were on the necks of their **c**).
1Sa 27: 9 the **c**, and the clothing, and came back to Achish.
30:17 four hundred young men, who mounted **c** and fled.
1Ki 10: 2 with **c** bearing spices, and very much gold,
1Ch 5:21 captured their livestock: fifty thousand of their **c**,
12:40 came bringing food on donkeys, **c**, mules,
27:30 Over the **c** was Obil the Ishmaelite.
2Ch 9: 1 having a very great retinue and **c** bearing spices
14:15 and goats in abundance, and **c**.
Ezr 2:67 four hundred thirty-five **c**,
Ne 7:69 four hundred thirty-five **c**,
Job 1: 3 He had seven thousand sheep, three thousand **c**,
1:17 made a raid on the **c** and carried them off,
42:12 he had fourteen thousand sheep, six thousand **c**,
Isa 21: 7 horsemen in pairs, riders on donkeys, riders on **c**,
30: 6 and their treasures on the humps of **c**,
60: 6 A multitude of **c** shall cover you,
60: 6 the young **c** of Midian and Ephah;
Jer 49:29 carry off their **c** for yourselves,
49:32 Their **c** shall become booty,
Eze 25: 5 I will make Rabbah a pasture for **c** and Ammon
Zec 14:15 the mules, the **c**, the donkeys,
Tob 9: 2 take four servants and two **c** with you and travel
9: 5 So Raphael with the four servants and two **c** went
9: 5 then they loaded them on the **c**.
10:10 oxen and sheep, donkeys and **c**, clothing, money,
Jdt 2:17 along a vast number of **c** and donkeys and mules
1Es 5:43 There were four hundred thirty-five **c**,

CAMON (KJV) See KAMON

CAMP‡ (221) [CAMPED, CAMPING, CAMPS, ENCAMP, ENCAMPED, ENCAMPMENT, ENCAMPMENTS, ENCAMPS]

Ge 32: 2 when Jacob saw them he said, "This is God's **c**!"
32:21 and he himself spent that night in the **c**.
Ex 14: 2 and **c** in front of Pi-hahiroth, between Migdol and
14: 2 you shall **c** opposite it, by the sea.
16:13 In the evening quails came up and covered the **c**;
16:13 a layer of dew around the **c**.
19:16 that all the people who were in the **c** trembled.
19:17 Moses brought the people out of the **c**
29:14 you shall burn with fire outside the **c**;
32:17 said to Moses, "There is a noise of war in the **c**."
32:19 As soon as he came near the **c** and saw the calf
32:26 then Moses stood in the gate of the **c**,
32:27 and forth from gate to gate throughout the **c**,
33: 7 and pitch it outside the **c**, far off from the **c**;
33: 7 to the tent of meeting, which was outside the **c**.
33:11 Then he would return to the **c**;
36: 6 and word was proclaimed throughout the **c**:
Lev 4:12 he shall carry out to a clean place outside the **c**,
4:21 He shall carry the bull outside the **c**,
6:11 carry the ashes out to a clean place outside the **c**.
8:17 he burned with fire outside the **c**,
9:11 and the skin he burned with fire outside the **c**.
10: 4 the front of the sanctuary to a place outside the **c**."
10: 5 and carried them by their tunics out of the **c**,
13:46 his dwelling shall be outside the **c**.
14: 3 the priest shall go out of the **c**,
14: 8 After that he shall come into the **c**,
16:26 and afterward may come into the **c**.
16:27 shall be taken outside the **c**;
16:28 and afterward may come into the **c**.
17: 3 an ox or a lamb or a goat in the **c**,
17: 3 or slaughters it outside the **c**,
24:10 and a certain Israelite began fighting in the **c**.
24:14 Take the blasphemer outside the **c**;
24:23 and they took the blasphemer outside the **c**,
Nu 1:50 and shall **c** around the tabernacle.
1:52 The other Israelites shall **c**
1:53 but the Levites shall **c** around the tabernacle of
2: 2 The Israelites shall **c** each in their respective
2: 2 they shall **c** facing the tent of meeting
2: 3 to **c** on the east side toward the sunrise shall be of
2: 5 to **c** next to him shall be the tribe of Issachar.
2: 9 The total enrollment of the **c** of Judah,
2:12 those to **c** next to him shall be the tribe of Simeon.
2:16 The total enrollment of the **c** of Reuben,
2:17 The tent of meeting, with the **c** of the Levites,
2:17 they shall set out just as they **c**, each in position,
2:24 The total enrollment of the **c** of Ephraim,
2:27 Those to **c** next to him shall be the tribe of Asher.
2:31 The total enrollment of the **c** of Dan
3:23 the Gershonites were to **c** behind the tabernacle on
3:29 of the Kohathites were to **c** on the south side of
3:35 they were to **c** on the north side of the tabernacle.
3:38 Those who were to **c** in front of the tabernacle on
4: 5 When the **c** is to set out,
4:15 the **c** sets out, after that the Kohathites shall come
5: 2 to put out of the **c** everyone who is leprous, or has
5: 3 putting them outside the **c**;
5: 3 they must not defile their **c**,
5: 4 The Israelites did so, putting them outside the **c**;
9:17 there the Israelites would **c**.
9:18 and at the command of the LORD they would **c**.
9:18 over the tabernacle, they would remain in **c**.
9:20 of the LORD they would remain in **c**;
9:22 Israelites would remain in **c** and would not set out;
9:23 At the command of the LORD they would **c**,
10: 2 the congregation, and for breaking **c**.
Nu 10:14 The standard of the **c** of Judah set out first,
10:18 Next the standard of the **c** of Reuben set out,
10:22 Next the standard of the Ephraimite **c** set out,
10:25 Then the standard of the **c** of Dan,
10:31 you know where we should **c** in the wilderness,
10:34 over them by day when they set out from the **c**.
11: 1 and consumed some outlying parts of the **c**.
11: 9 When the dew fell on the **c** in the night,
11:26 Two men remained in the **c**, one named Eldad,
11:26 and so they prophesied in the **c**.
11:27 "Eldad and Medad are prophesying in the **c**."
11:30 Moses and the elders of Israel returned to the **c**.
11:31 from the sea and let them fall beside the **c**,
11:31 a day's journey on the other side, all around the **c**,
11:32 for themselves all around the **c**.
12:14 Let her be shut out of the **c** for seven days,
12:15 So Miriam was shut out of the **c** for seven days;
14:44 and Moses, had not left the **c**.
15:35 all the congregation shall stone him outside the **c**."
15:36 The whole congregation brought him outside the **c**
19: 3 and it shall be taken outside the **c** and slaughtered
19: 7 and afterwards he may come into the **c**;
19: 9 and deposit them outside the **c** in a clean place;
31:12 at the **c** on the plains of Moab by the Jordan
31:13 the congregation went to meet them outside the **c**.
31:19 **C** outside the **c** seven days;
31:24 afterward you may come into the **c**."
Dt 1:33 on the way to seek out a place for you to **c**,
2:14 of warriors had perished from the **c**,
2:15 to root them out from the **c**, until all had perished.
23:10 then he shall go outside the **c**;
23:10 he must not come within the **c**.
23:11 he may come back into the **c**.
23:12 You shall have a designated area outside the **c**
23:14 the LORD your God travels along with your **c**,
23:14 therefore your **c** must be holy,
29:11 your women, and the aliens who are in your **c**,
Jos 1:11 "Pass through the **c**, and command the people:
3: 2 of three days the officers went through the **c**
4: 3 down in the place where you **c** tonight.' "
5: 8 in their places in the **c** until they were healed.
6:11 and they came into the **c**,
6:11 and spent the night in the **c**.
6:14 around the city once and then returned to the **c**.
6:18 and take any of the devoted things and make the **c**
6:23 and set them outside the **c** of Israel.
8: 9 but Joshua spent that night in the **c**.
9: 6 They went to Joshua in the **c** at Gilgal,
10: 6 the Gibeonites sent to Joshua at the **c** in Gilgal,
10:15 and all Israel with him, to the **c** at Gilgal.
10:21 all the people returned safe to Joshua in the **c**
10:43 and all Israel with him, to the **c** at Gilgal.
18: 9 then they came back to Joshua in the **c** at Shiloh,
Jdg 7: 1 and the **c** of Midian was north of them,
7: 8 The **c** of Midian was below him in the valley.
7: 9 attack the **c**; for I have given it into your hand.
7:10 go down to the **c** with your servant Purah;
7:11 be strengthened to attack the **c**."
7:11 the outposts of the armed men that were in the **c**.
7:13 the **c** of Midian, and came to the tent, and struck it
7:15 he returned to the **c** of Israel, and said, "Get up;
7:17 when I come to the outskirts of the **c**, do as I do.
7:18 you also blow the trumpets around the whole **c**,
7:19 of the **c** at the beginning of the middle watch,
7:21 Every man stood in his place all around the **c**,
7:21 and all the men in **c** ran; they cried out and fled.
21: 8 that no one from Jabesh-gilead had come to the **c**,
21:12 with a man and brought them to the **c** at Shiloh,
1Sa 4: 3 When the troops came to the **c**,
4: 5 ark of the covenant of the LORD came into the **c**,
4: 6 "What does this great shouting in the **c** of
4: 6 that the ark of the LORD had come to the **c**,
4: 7 for they said, "Gods have come into the **c**."
11:11 At the morning watch they came into the **c** and cut
13:17 And raiders came out of the **c** of the Philistines
14:15 There was a panic in the **c**, in the field,
14:19 the **c** of the Philistines increased more and more;
14:21 the **c** turned and joined the Israelites who were
17: 4 the **c** of the Philistines a champion named Goliath,
17:17 and carry them quickly to the **c** to your brothers;
17:53 and they plundered their **c**.
26: 6 "Who will go down with me into the **c** to Saul?"
2Sa 1: 2 On the third day, a man came from Saul's **c**,
1: 3 "I have escaped from the **c** of Israel."
23:16 Then the three warriors broke through the **c** of
1Ki 16:16 king over Israel that day in the **c**.
2Ki 3:24 But when they came to the **c** of Israel,
6: 8 He said, "At such and such a place shall be my **c**."
7: 4 Therefore, let us desert to the Aramean **c**;
7: 5 So they arose at twilight to go to the Aramean **c**;
7: 5 but when they came to the edge of the Aramean **c**,
7: 7 and their donkeys leaving the **c** just as it was,
7: 8 these leprous men had come to the edge of the **c**,
7:10 and told them, "We went to the Aramean **c**,
7:12 the **c** to hide themselves in the open country,
7:16 and plundered the **c** of the Arameans.
19:35 down one hundred eighty-five thousand in the **c** of
1Ch 9:18 the gatekeepers of the **c** of the Levites.
9:19 as their ancestors had been in charge of the **c** of
11:18 the Three broke through the **c** of the Philistines,
2Ch 22: 1 the Arabs to the **c** had killed all the older sons.
31: 2 the gates of the **c** of the LORD and to give thanks
32:21 and commanders and officers in the **c** of the king
Ps 69:25 May their **c** be a desolation;
78:28 he let them fall within their **c**,
106:16 They were jealous of Moses in the **c**,
Isa 37:36 down one hundred eighty-five thousand in the **c** of

Am 4:10 the stench of your **c** go up into your nostrils;
Mic 4:10 for now you shall go forth from the city and **c** in
Heb 13:11 as a sacrifice for sin are burned outside the **c**.
13:13 Let us then go to him outside the **c** and bear
Rev 20: 9 of the earth and surrounded the **c** of the saints and
Jdt 6:11 the slaves took him and led him out of the **c** into
7: 1 to break **c** and move against Bethulia,
7:12 in your **c**, and keep all the men in your forces
7:13 of the nearby mountains and **c** there to keep watch
10:18 There was great excitement in the whole **c**,
12: 7 She remained in the **c** three days.
12: 7 and bathed at the spring in the **c**.
13:10 They passed through the **c**,
14: 3 the **c** and rouse the officers of the Assyrian army.
14:19 and shouts rose up throughout the **c**.
15: 5 for they were told what had happened in the **c** of
15: 6 of the people of Bethulia fell upon the Assyrian **c**
15:11 All the people plundered the **c** for thirty days.
16: 2 he sets up his **c** among his people;
Wis 19: 7 The cloud was seen overshadowing the **c**,
Sir 48:21 The Lord struck down the **c** of the Assyrians,
1Mc 3: 3 protecting the **c** by his sword.
3:41 and went to the **c** to get the Israelites for slaves.
4: 2 upon the **c** of the Jews and attack them suddenly.
4: 4 while the division was still absent from the **c**.
4: 5 When Gorgias entered the **c** of Judas by night,
4: 7 And they saw the **c** of the Gentiles,
4:13 they went out from their **c** to battle.
4:20 and that the Jews were burning the **c**,
4:23 Then Judas returned to plunder the **c**,
4:30 and gave the **c** of the Philistines into the hands
5:38 Judas sent men to spy out the **c**,
6:32 opposite the **c** of the king.
9: 6 and many slipped away from the **c**,
9:11 from the **c** and took its stand for the encounter.
11:73 to their **c**, and there they encamped.
12:26 He sent spies to their **c**,
12:27 and he stationed outposts around the **c**.
12:28 so they kindled fires in their **c** and withdrew.
12:32 Then he broke **c** and went to Damascus,
2Mc 13:14 and commonwealth, he pitched his **c** near Modein.
13:15 and killed as many as two thousand men in the **c**.
13:16 the end they filled the **c** with terror and confusion
15:22 eighty-five thousand in the **c** of Sennacherib.
4Mc 3:13 they went searching throughout the enemy **c**

CAMPAIGN (3)

1Sa 29: 6 should march out and in with me in the **c**;
Jdt 2:16 as a great army is marshaled for a **c**.
2Mc 15:17 not to carry on a **c** but to attack bravely,

CAMPED (75) [CAMP]

Ge 26:17 So Isaac departed from there and **c** in the valley
31:25 and Laban with his kinsfolk **c** in the hill country
33:18 and he **c** before the city.
Ex 13:20 They set out from Succoth, and **c** at Etham,
14: 9 they overtook them **c** by the sea, by Pi-hahiroth,
15:27 and they **c** there by the water.
17: 1 They **c** at Rephidim, but there was no water for
19: 2 the wilderness of Sinai, and **c** in the wilderness;
19: 2 Israel **c** there in front of the mountain.
Nu 2:34 They **c** by regiments, and they set out
12:16 and **c** in the wilderness of Paran.
21:10 The Israelites set out, and **c** in Oboth.
21:11 They set out from Oboth, and **c** at Iye-abarim,
21:12 From there they set out, and **c** in the Wadi Zered.
21:13 and **c** on the other side of the Arnon,
22: 1 and **c** in the plains of Moab across the Jordan
33: 5 Israelites set out from Rameses, and **c** at Succoth.
33: 6 They set out from Succoth, and **c** at Etham,
33: 7 and they **c** before Migdol.
33: 8 in the wilderness of Etham, and **c** at Marah.
33: 9 of water and seventy palm trees, and they **c** there.
33:10 They set out from Elim and **c** by the Red Sea.
33:11 from the Red Sea and **c** in the wilderness of Sin.
33:12 They set out from the wilderness of Sin and **c**
33:13 They set out from Dophkah and **c** at Alush.
33:14 They set out from Alush and **c** at Rephidim,
33:15 from Rephidim and **c** in the wilderness of Sinai.
33:16 They set out from the wilderness of Sinai and **c**
33:17 They set out from Kibroth-hattaavah and **c**
33:18 They set out from Hazeroth and **c** at Rithmah.
33:19 from Rithmah and **c** at Rimmon-perez.
33:20 They set out from Rimmon-perez and **c** at Libnah.
33:21 They set out from Libnah and **c** at Rissah.
33:22 They set out from Rissah and **c** at Kehelathah.
33:23 from Kehelathah and **c** at Mount Shepher.
33:24 They set out from Mount Shepher and **c**
33:25 They set out from Haradah and **c** at Makheloth.
33:26 They set out from Makheloth and **c** at Tahath.
33:27 They set out from Tahath and **c** at Terah.
33:28 They set out from Terah and **c** at Mithkah.
33:29 They set out from Mithkah and **c** at Hashmonah.
33:30 They set out from Hashmonah and **c** at Moseroth.
33:31 They set out from Moseroth and **c** at Bene-jaakan.
33:32 from Bene-jaakan and **c** at Hor-haggidgad.
33:33 from Hor-haggidgad and **c** at Jotbathah.
33:34 They set out from Jotbathah and **c** at Abronah.
33:35 They set out from Abronah and **c** at Ezion-geber.
33:36 from Ezion-geber and **c** in the wilderness of Zin
33:37 They set out from Kadesh and **c** at Mount Hor,
33:41 They set out from Mount Hor and **c** at Zalmonah.
33:42 They set out from Zalmonah and **c** at Punon.
33:43 They set out from Punon and **c** at Oboth.
33:44 They set out from Oboth and **c** at Iye-abarim,
33:45 They set out from Iyim and **c** at Dibon-gad.
Nu 33:46 from Dibon-gad and **c** at Almon-diblathaim.
33:47 from Almon-diblathaim and **c** in the mountains
33:48 They set out from the mountains of Abarim and **c**
33:49 they **c** by the Jordan from Beth-jeshimoth as far
Jos 3: 1 They **c** there before crossing over.
4: 8 over with them to the place where they **c**,
4:19 and they **c** in Gilgal on the east border of Jericho.
5:10 While the Israelites were **c** in Gilgal they kept
8:11 and **c** on the north side of Ai,
10: 5 up with all their armies and **c** against Gibeon,
11: 5 and came and **c** together at the waters of Merom,
Jdg 11:18 and **c** on the other side of the Arnon.
1Ch 19: 7 who came and **c** before Medeba.
Ezr 8:15 and there we **c** three days.
Ne 11:30 they **c** from Beer-sheba to the valley of Hinnom.
Tob 6: 2 and when the first night overtook them they **c** by
Jdt 2:21 and **c** opposite Bectileth near the mountain that is
3:10 he **c** between Geba and Scythopolis,
15: 3 Those who had **c** in the hills around Bethulia
1Mc 9:33 of Tekoa and **c** by the water of the pool of Asphar.
16: 4 against Cendebeus and **c** for the night in Modein.

CAMPHIRE (KJV) See HENNA

CAMPING (2) [CAMP]

Nu 24: 2 Balaam looked up and saw Israel **c** tribe by tribe.
2Sa 11:11 and my lord Joab and the servants of my lord are **c**

CAMPS‡ (11) [CAMP]

Nu 1:52 in their respective regimental **c**, by companies;
2:17 shall set out in the center of the **c**;
2:32 the total enrollment in the **c**
10: 5 the **c** on the east side shall set out;
10: 6 the **c** on the south side shall set out.
10:25 acting as the rear guard of all the **c**, set out,
Eze 4: 2 set **c** also against it, and plant battering rams
Zec 14:15 and whatever animals may be in those **c**.
Sir 14:24 who **c** near her house and fastens his tent peg
1Mc 5:41 he shows fear and **c** on the other side of the river,
2Es 1:15 I gave you **c** for your protection,

CAN‡ (628) [CANNOT]

Ge 4:13 "My punishment is greater than I **c** bear!
13:16 so that if one **c** count the dust of the earth, your offspring also **c** be counted.
17:17 "**C** a child be born to a man who is a hundred
17:17 **C** Sarah, who is ninety years old, bear a child?"
19: 2 then you **c** rise early and go on your way."
19:22 for I **c** do nothing until you arrive there."
27:37 What then **c** I do for you, my son?"
31:43 what **c** I do today about these daughters of mine,
37:30 and I, where **c** I turn?"
41:15 and there is no one who **c** interpret it.
41:15 that when you hear a dream you **c** interpret it."
41:38 "**C** we find anyone else like this—
43: 9 you **c** hold me accountable for him.
44: 1 as much as they **c** carry,
44:15 not know that one such as I **c** practice divination?"
44:16 And Judah said, "What **c** we say to my lord? What **c** we speak? How **c** we clear ourselves?
44:34 **c** I go back to my father if the boy is not with me?
46:30 Israel said to Joseph, "I **c** die now,
47:18 "We **c** not hide from my lord
Ex 4:14 I know that he **c** speak fluently;
5:11 and get straw yourselves, wherever you **c** find it;
10:21 a darkness that **c** be felt."
32:30 perhaps I **c** make atonement for your sin."
Lev 5: 3 by which one **c** become unclean—
13:12 so far as the priest **c** see,
14:22 as he **c** afford, one for a sin offering and the other
14:30 of the turtledoves or pigeons such as he **c** afford,
27: 8 to what each one making a vow **c** afford.
27:29 to destruction **c** be ransomed;
Nu 6:21 apart from what else they **c** afford.
23: 8 How **c** I curse whom God has not cursed?
23: 8 How **c** I denounce those whom the LORD has
23:10 Who **c** count the dust of Jacob,
31:23 everything that **c** withstand fire,
35:33 and no expiation **c** be made for the land
Dt 1:12 how **c** I bear the heavy burden of your disputes all
3:11 **c** still be seen in Rabbah of the Ammonites.
3:24 what god in heaven or on earth **c** perform deeds
7:17 how **c** I dispossess them?"
9: 2 "Who **c** stand up to the Anakim?"
18:21 "How **c** we recognize a word that the LORD has
19: 3 so that any homicide **c** flee to one of them.
32:39 and no one **c** deliver from my hand.
Jos 2: 5 Pursue them quickly, for you **c** overtake them."
7: 8 what **c** I say, now that Israel has turned their backs
9: 7 then how **c** we make a treaty with you?"
Jdg 6:15 He responded, "But sir, how **c** I deliver Israel?
9:33 you may deal with them as best you **c**."
14:12 If you **c** explain it to me within the seven days of
16:15 Then she said to him, "How **c** you say,
17: 9 and I am going to live wherever I **c** find a place."
18:24 How then **c** you ask me, 'What is the matter?' "
19: 9 Tomorrow you **c** get up early in the morning
1Sa 2:25 someone **c** intercede for the sinner with
2:25 who **c** make intercession?"
4: 8 Who **c** deliver us from the power
9: 7 "But if we go, what **c** we bring the man?
10:27 "How **c** this man save us?"
14: 6 for nothing **c** hinder the LORD from saving
16: 2 Samuel said, "How **c** I go?
16:17 "Provide for me someone who **c** play well,
1Sa 18: 8 what more **c** he have but the kingdom?"
25:17 he is so ill-natured that no one **c** speak to him."
26: 9 for who **c** raise his hand against
28: 2 then you shall know what your servant **c** do."
2Sa 6: 9 **c** the ark of the LORD come into my care?"
7:20 And what more **c** David say to you?
12:18 how then **c** we tell him the child is dead?
12:23 **C** I bring him back again?
15:20 while I go wherever I **c**?
19:35 **c** I discern what is pleasant and what is not?
19:35 **C** your servant taste what he eats
19:35 **C** I still listen to the voice of singing men
22:30 By you I **c** crush a troop,
22:30 and by my God I **c** leap over a wall.
22:35 so that my arms **c** bend a bow of bronze.
23:17 **C** I drink the blood of the men who went at
24: 3 while the eyes of my lord the king **c** still see it!
1Ki 3: 9 for who **c** govern this your great people?"
2Ki 4: 7 and you and your children **c** live on the rest."
4:10 so that he **c** stay there whenever he comes to us."
4:43 "How **c** I set this before a hundred people?"
6:27 How **c** I help you?
8: 1 and settle wherever you **c**;
9:22 He answered, "What peace **c** there be,
9:37 so that no one **c** say, This is Jezebel.' "
10: 4 not withstand him; how then **c** we stand?"
18:24 How then **c** you repulse a single captain among
1Ch 11:19 **C** I drink the blood of these men?
13:12 "How **c** I bring the ark of God into my care?"
17:18 And what more **c** David say to you
2Ch 1:10 for who **c** rule this great people of yours?"
13: 8 now you think that you **c** withstand the kingdom
Ezr 9:15 though no one **c** face you because of this."
Ne 2: 2 This **c** only be sadness of the heart."
Est 7: 4 but no enemy **c** compensate for this damage to
8: 6 For how **c** I bear to see the calamity that is coming
8: 6 **c** I bear to see the destruction of my kindred?"
Job 4: 2 But who **c** keep from speaking?
4:17 '**C** mortals be righteous before God?
4:17 **C** human beings be pure before their Maker?
6: 6 **C** that which is tasteless be eaten without salt,
6:26 Do you think that you **c** reprove words,
8:11 "**C** papyrus grow where there is no marsh?
8:11 **C** reeds flourish where there is no water?
9: 2 but how **c** a mortal be just before God?
9:12 He snatches away; who **c** stop him?
9:14 **c** I answer him, choosing my words with him?
9:19 If it is a matter of justice, who **c** summon him?
11: 7 "**C** you find out the deep things of God?
11: 7 **C** you find out the limit of the Almighty?
11: 8 It is higher than heaven—what **c** you do?
11: 8 Deeper than Sheol—what **c** you know?
11:10 and assembles for judgment, who **c** hinder him?
12:14 If he tears down, no one **c** rebuild;
12:14 if he shuts someone in, no one **c** open up.
13: 9 when he searches you out? Or **c** you deceive him,
14: 4 Who **c** bring a clean thing out of an unclean? No one **c**.
15: 3 or in words with which they **c** do no good?
15:14 What are mortals, that they **c** be clean?
15:14 Or those born of woman, that they **c** be righteous?
22: 2 "**C** a mortal be of use to God?
22: 2 **C** even the wisest be of service to him?
22:13 **C** he judge through the deep darkness?
22:17 and 'What **c** the Almighty do to us?'
23:13 But he stands alone and who **c** dissuade him?
25: 4 How then **c** a mortal be righteous before God?
25: 4 How **c** one born of woman be pure?
26:14 But the thunder of his power who **c** understand?"
28:17 nor **c** it be exchanged for jewels of fine gold.
28:19 nor **c** it be valued in pure gold.
33: 5 Answer me, if you **c**; set your words in order
34:29 When he is quiet, who **c** condemn?
34:29 When he hides his face, who **c** behold him,
36:23 or who **c** say, 'You have done wrong'?
36:29 **C** anyone understand the spreading of the clouds,
37:18 **C** you, like him, spread out the skies,
37:21 no one **c** look on the light when it is bright in
38:31 "**C** you bind the chains of the Pleiades,
38:32 **C** you lead forth the Mazzaroth in their season,
38:32 or **c** you guide the Bear with its children?
38:33 **C** you establish their rule on the earth?
38:34 "**C** you lift up your voice to the clouds,
38:35 **C** you send forth lightnings,
38:37 Or who **c** tilt the waterskins of the heavens,
38:39 "**C** you hunt the prey for the lion,
39: 2 **C** you number the months that they fulfill,
39:10 **C** you tie it in the furrow with ropes,
40: 9 and **c** you thunder with a voice like his?
40:14 that your own right hand **c** give you victory.
40:19 only its Maker **c** approach it with the sword.
40:24 **C** one take it with hooks or pierce its nose with
41: 1 "**C** you draw out Leviathan with a fishhook,
41: 2 **C** you put a rope in its nose,
41: 7 **C** you fill its skin with harpoons,
41:10 Who **c** stand before it?
41:11 Who **c** confront it and be safe?
41:13 Who **c** strip off its outer garment?
41:13 Who **c** penetrate its double coat of mail?
41:14 Who **c** open the doors of its face?
41:16 near to another that no air **c** come between them.
42: 2 "I know that you **c** do all things,
42: 2 and that no purpose of yours **c** be thwarted.
Ps 6: 5 in Sheol who **c** give you praise?
11: 1 how **c** you say to me, "Flee like a bird to
11: 3 what **c** the righteous do?"
18:29 By you I **c** crush a troop,

Ps 18:29 and by my God I c leap over a wall.
18:34 so that my arms c bend a bow of bronze.
19:12 But who c detect their errors?
22:17 I c count all my bones.
40: 5 none c compare with you.
40: 5 they would be more than c be counted.
44: 6 not in my bow do I trust, nor c my sword save me.
49: 7 there is no price one c give to God for it.
49: 8 the ransom of life is costly, and c never suffice
56: 4 what c flesh do to me?
56:11 What c a mere mortal do to me?
58: 9 Sooner than your pots c feel the heat of thorns,
64: 5 of laying snares secretly, thinking, "Who c see us?
64: 6 Who c search out our crimes?
73:11 And they say, "How c God know?
76: 7 c stand before you when once your anger is
78:19 saying, "C God spread a table in the wilderness?
78:20 c he also give bread, or provide meat for his
89: 6 who in the skies c be compared to the LORD?
89:48 Who c live and never see death?
89:48 Who c escape the power of Sheol?
94:20 C wicked rulers be allied with you,
106: 2 Who c utter the mighty doings of the LORD,
118: 6 What c mortals do to me?
119: 9 How c young people keep their way pure?
119:165 nothing c make them stumble.
139: 7 Where c I go from your spirit?
139: 7 Or where c I flee from your presence?
147:17 who c stand before his cold?
Pr 3:15 and nothing you desire c compare with her.
6:27 C fire be carried in the bosom
6:28 Or c one walk on hot coals without scorching
18:14 but a broken spirit—who c bear?
20: 6 but who c find one worthy of trust?
20: 9 Who c say, "I have made my heart clean;
20:24 how then c we understand our own ways?
21:30 no counsel, c avail against the LORD.
24: 6 for by wise guidance you c wage your war,
24:22 and who knows the ruin that both c bring?
25:15 and a soft tongue c break bones.
26:16 in self-esteem than seven who c answer discreetly.
30: 1 I am weary, O God. How c I prevail?
30:28 the lizard c be grasped in the hand,
31:10 A capable wife who c find?
Ecc 1: 8 All things are wearisome; more than one c express;
2:12 for what c the one do who comes after the king?
2:16 How c the wise die just like fools?
2:25 from him who c eat or who c have enjoyment?
3:14 nothing c be added to it, nor anything taken
3:22 who c bring them to see what will be after them?
4:11 but how c one keep warm alone?
4:14 One c indeed come out of prison to reign,
6:12 For who c tell them what will be after them under
7:13 who c make straight what he has made crooked?
7:24 very deep; who c find it out?
8: 4 and who c say to him, "What are you doing?"
8: 7 for who c tell them how it will be?
8:17 no one c find out what is happening under the sun.
9:12 For no one c anticipate the time of disaster.
10:14 and who c tell anyone what the future holds?
SS 8: 7 cannot quench love, neither c floods drown it.
Isa 5:29 they carry it off, and no one c rescue.
10:19 be so few that a child c write them down.
19:11 How c you say to Pharaoh, "I am one of the sages,
24:10 every house is shut up so that no one c enter.
27: 3 I guard it night and day so that no one c harm it;
29:11 If it is given to those who c read,
33:14 "Who among us c live with the devouring fire?
33:14 Who among us c live with everlasting flames?"
33:21 where no galley with oars c go,
33:21 with oars can go, nor stately ship c pass.
36: 9 How then c you repulse a single captain among
38:15 But what c I say?
43:13 there is no one who c deliver from my hand;
43:13 I work and who c hinder it?
44:10 a god or cast an image that c do no good?
44:15 Then it c be used as fuel.
44:16 "Ah, I am warm, I c feel the fire!"
49:15 C a woman forget her nursing child,
49:24 C the prey be taken from the mighty,
Jer 2:13 cracked cisterns that c hold no water.
2:23 How c you say, "I am not defiled,
2:24 Who c restrain her lust?
2:28 Let them come, if they c save you,
2:32 C a girl forget her ornaments, or a bride her attire?
5: 1 and see if you c find one person who acts justly
5: 7 How c I pardon you?
5:15 nor c you understand what they say.
8: 8 How c you say, "We are wise,
9: 7 for what else c I do with my sinful people?
11:15 C vows and sacrificial flesh avert your doom? C you then exult?
13:23 C Ethiopians change their skin
13:23 also you c do good who are accustomed to do evil.
14:22 C any idols of the nations bring rain?
14:22 Or c the heavens give showers?
15:12 C iron and bronze break iron from the north?
16:20 C mortals make for themselves gods?
17: 9 it is perverse—who c understand it?
18: 6 C I not do with you,
19:11 so that it c never be mended.
20:10 "Perhaps he c be enticed, and we c prevail against
21:13 you who say, "Who c come down against us,
21:13 or who c enter our places of refuge?"
23:24 Who c hide in secret places so
25:29 and how c you possibly avoid punishment?
30: 6 Ask now, and see, c a man bear a child?

Jer 31:37 If the heavens above c be measured,
31:37 the foundations of the earth below c be explored,
32:24 you spoke has happened, as you yourself c see.
35:13 C you not learn a lesson and obey my words?
42: 2 a few of us left out of many, as your eyes c see.
46: 6 swift cannot flee away, nor c the warrior escape;
47: 7 How c it be quiet, when the LORD has given it
48:14 c you say, "We are heroes and mighty warriors"?
49:19 Who c summon me? Who is the shepherd who c stand before me?
50:44 For who is like me? Who c summon me?
50:44 Who is the shepherd who c stand before me?
La 2:13 What c I say for you, to what compare you,
2:13 To what c I liken you, that I may comfort you,
2:13 For vast as the sea is your ruin; who c heal you?
3:37 Who c command and have it done,
3:44 with a cloud so that no prayer c pass through.
Eze 15: 5 c it ever be used for anything!
17:15 C one escape who does such things?
17:15 C he break the covenant and yet escape?
21:10 How c we make merry?
22:14 C your courage endure,
22:14 or c your hands remain strong in the days
33:10 of them; how then c we live?"
37: 3 He said to me, "Mortal, c these bones live?"
Da 1:13 You c then compare our appearance with
2: 7 then we c give its interpretation."
2: 9 I shall know that you c give me its interpretation."
2:10 on earth who c reveal what the king demands!
2:11 and no one c reveal it to the king except the gods,
2:25 the exiles from Judah a man who c tell the king
2:27 or diviners c show to the king the mystery that
4:35 There is no one who c stay his hand or say to him,
5: 7 of Babylon, "Whoever c read this writing
5:16 that you c give interpretations and solve problems.
6:15 that the king establishes c be changed."
10:17 How c my lord's servant talk with my lord?
Hos 1:10 which c be neither measured nor numbered;
4:16 c the LORD now feed them like a lamb in
11: 8 How c I give you up, Ephraim?
11: 8 How c I hand you over, O Israel?
11: 8 How c I make you like Admah?
11: 8 How c I treat you like Zeboiim?
13: 9 I will destroy you, O Israel; who c help you?
Joel 2:11 terrible indeed—who c endure it?
Am 3: 8 The Lord GOD has spoken; who c but prophesy?
7: 2 I beg you! How c Jacob stand?
7: 5 I beg you! How c Jacob stand?
Mic 6:10 C I forget the treasures of wickedness in the house
6:11 C I tolerate wicked scales and a bag
Na 1: 6 Who c stand before his indignation?
1: 6 Who c endure the heat of his anger?
Hab 2:19 "Rouse yourself!" C it teach?
Mal 3: 2 But who c endure the day of his coming,
3: 2 and who c stand when he appears?
Mt 5:13 how c its saltiness be restored?
6:24 "No one c serve two masters;
6:27 And c any of you by worrying add a single hour
7: 4 Or how c you say to your neighbor,
7:18 nor c a bad tree bear good fruit.
8: 2 "Lord, if you choose, you c make me clean."
9:15 as long as the bridegroom is with them, c they?
10:28 rather fear him who c destroy both soul and body
12:23 "C this be the Son of David?"
12:29 Or how c one enter a strong man's house
12:29 Then indeed the house c be plundered.
12:34 How c you speak good things, when you are evil?
19:11 "Not everyone c accept this teaching,
19:12 Let anyone accept this who c."
19:25 and said, "Then who c be saved?"
22:45 David thus calls him Lord, how c he be his son?"
23:33 How c you escape being sentenced to hell?
27:65 go, make it as secure as you c."
Mk 1:40 "If you choose, you c make me clean."
2: 7 Who c forgive sins but God alone?"
2:19 while the bridegroom is with them, c they?
3:23 "How c Satan cast out Satan?
3:27 But no one c enter a strong man's house
3:27 then indeed the house c be plundered.
3:29 against the Holy Spirit c never have forgiveness,
4:30 "With what c we compare the kingdom of God,
4:32 that the birds of the air c make nests in its shade."
5:31 how c you say, 'Who touched me?' "
7:15 a person that by going in c defile,
8: 4 "How c one feed these people with bread here in
8:23 he asked him, "C you see anything?"
8:24 And the man looked up and said, "I c see people,
8:37 Indeed, what c they give in return for their life?
9:23 All things c be done for the one who believes."
9:29 "This kind c come out only through prayer."
9:50 if salt has lost its saltiness, how c you season it?
10:26 and said to one another, "Then who c be saved?"
12:35 "How c the scribes say that the Messiah is the son
12:37 so how c he be his son?"
14: 7 you c show kindness to them whenever you wish;
Lk 1:34 Mary said to the angel, "How c this be,
5:12 "Lord, if you choose, you c make me clean."
5:21 Who c forgive sins but God alone?"
5:34 while the bridegroom is with them, c you?
6:39 "C a blind person guide a blind person?
6:42 Or how c you say to your neighbor, 'Friend,
12: 4 and after that c do nothing more.
12:25 And c any of you by worrying add a single hour
13: 9 but if not, you c cut it down.' "
14:33 of you c become my disciple if you do not give
14:34 how c its saltiness be restored?
16:13 No slave c serve two masters;

Lk 16:26 and no one c cross from there to us.'
17:20 not coming with things that c be observed;
18:26 Those who heard it said, "Then who c be saved?"
20:41 "How c they say that the Messiah is David's son?
20:44 so how c he be his son?"
21:30 as they sprout leaves you c see for yourselves
Jn 1:46 "C anything good come out of Nazareth?"
2:18 "What sign c you show us for doing this?"
3: 2 for no one c do these signs that you do apart from
3: 3 no one c see the kingdom of God
3: 4 "How c anyone be born after having grown old?
3: 4 C one enter a second time into the mother's womb
3: 5 no one c enter the kingdom of God
3: 9 Nicodemus said to him, "How c these things be?"
3:12 c you believe if I tell you about heavenly things?
3:27 "No one c receive anything except what has been
4:29 He cannot be the Messiah, c he?"
5:19 I tell you, the Son c do nothing on his own,
5:30 "I c do nothing on my own.
5:44 How c you believe when you accept glory
6:42 c he now say, 'I have come down from heaven'?"
6:44 No one c come to me unless drawn by
6:52 saying, "How c this man give us his flesh to eat?"
6:60 "This teaching is difficult; who c accept it?"
6:65 that no one c come to me unless it is granted by
6:68 "Lord, to whom c we go?
7:26 C it be that the authorities really know that this is
9: 4 night is coming when no one c work.
9:16 c a man who is a sinner perform such signs?"
10:21 C a demon open the eyes of the blind?"
10:29 and no one c snatch it out of the Father's hand.
10:36 c you say that the one whom
12:19 "You see, you c do nothing.
12:34 c you say that the Son of Man must be lifted up?
13:37 "Lord, why c I not follow you now?
14: 5 How c we know the way?"
14: 9 How c you say, 'Show us the Father'?
15: 4 neither c you unless you abide in me.
15: 5 because apart from me you c do nothing.
Ac 8:31 "How c I, unless someone guides me?"
8:33 Who c describe his generation?
10:47 "C anyone withhold the water
19:40 that we c give to justify this commotion."
22: 5 and the whole council of elders c testify about me.
24:11 As you c find out, it is not more than twelve days
24:13 Neither c they prove to you the charge that they
25:11 no one c turn me over to them.
27:10 I c see that the voyage will be with danger
Ro 1:19 For what c be known about God is plain to them,
6: 2 How c we who died to sin go on living in it?
7:18 I c will what is right, but I cannot do it.
9:19 For who c resist his will?"
10: 2 I c testify that they have a zeal for God,
1Co 1:15 no one c say that you were baptized in my name.
3:11 For no one c lay any foundation other than the one
6: 5 C it be that there is no one
7:21 Even if you c gain your freedom,
12: 3 and no one c say "Jesus is Lord" except by
14:16 how c anyone in the position of an outsider say
14:31 For you c all prophesy one by one,
15:12 how c some of you say there is no resurrection of
2Co 1:13 we write you nothing other than what you c read
4:18 not at what c be seen but at what cannot be seen;
4:18 for what c be seen is temporary,
8: 3 For, as I c testify, they voluntarily gave according
Gal 2:14 how c you compel the Gentiles to live like Jews?"
4: 9 how c you turn back again to the weak
4: 9 How c you want to be enslaved to them again?
Eph 3:20 accomplish abundantly far more than all we c ask
Php 2:16 of life that I c boast on the day of Christ that I did
4:13 I c do all things through him who strengthens me.
1Th 3: 9 How c we thank God enough for you in return
1Ti 3: 5 how c he take care of God's church?
5:16 so that it c assist those who are real widows.
6: 7 so that we c take nothing out of it;
6:16 whom no one has ever seen or c see;
2Ti 3: 7 and c never arrive at a knowledge of the truth.
Heb 2: 3 c we escape if we neglect so great a salvation?
10: 1 of these realities, it c never, by the same sacrifices
10:11 the same sacrifices that c never take away sins.
12:18 not come to something that c be touched,
13: 6 So we c say with confidence,
13: 6 What c anyone do to me?"
Jas 2:14 faith but do not have works? C faith save you?
3: 7 bird, of reptile and sea creature, c be tamed
3: 8 but no one c tame the tongue—
3:12 C a fig tree, my brothers and sisters, yield olives,
3:12 No more c salt water yield fresh.
Rev 5: 5 so that he c open the scroll and its seven seals."
12: 6 so that there she c be nourished
13: 4 and who c fight against it?"
13:17 no one c buy or sell who does not have the mark,
Tob 5: 2 but how c I obtain the money from him,
5:10 C you accompany him and guide him?
5:10 "I c go with him and I know all the roads,
6:13 For I know that Raguel c by no means keep her
13: 2 and there is nothing that c escape his hand.
Jdt 5:20 then we c go up and defeat them.
8:28 and there is no one who c deny your words.
10:13 by which he c go and capture all the hill country
10:19 "Who c despise these people,
11:10 nor c the sword prevail against them,
12: 3 where c we get you more of the same?
16:14 there is none that c resist your voice.
AdE 8: 6 How c I look on the ruin of my people?
8: 6 c I be safe if my ancestral nation is destroyed?"
13: 5 doing all the harm they c so that our kingdom may

AdE 13: 9 and there is no one who c oppose you
13:11 and there is no one who c resist you, the Lord.
16: 7 of those who exercise authority unworthily c
Wis 5:10 and when it has passed no trace c be found,
7:27 Although she is but one, she c do all things,
9:13 For who c learn the counsel of God?
9:13 Or who c discern what the Lord wills?
9:16 We c hardly guess at what is on earth,
11:21 and who c withstand the might of your arm?
11:23 But you are merciful to all, for you c do all things,
12:14 nor c any king or monarch confront you
14: 4 showing that you c save from every danger,
15:12 for they say one must get money however one c,
15:16 for none c form gods that are like themselves.
Sir 1: 2 of eternity—who c count them?
1: 3 and wisdom—who c search them out?
3:23 more than you c understand has been shown you.
5: 3 Do not say, "Who c have power over me?"
6:15 no amount c balance their worth.
6:32 If you are willing, my child, you c be disciplined,
7:28 how c you repay what they have given to you?
9:10 when it has aged, you c drink it with pleasure.
9:14 As much as you c, aim to know your neighbors,
10: 9 How c dust and ashes be proud?
11:23 and what further benefit c be mine?"
11:24 and what harm c come to me now?"
13: 2 How c the clay pot associate with the iron kettle?
13: 4 A rich person will exploit you if you c be of use
14:13 and reach out and give to them as much as you c.
15:15 If you choose, you c keep the commandments,
16: 3 for one c be better than a thousand,
16: 4 through one intelligent person a city c be filled
16:20 But no human mind c grasp this,
16:20 and who c comprehend his ways?
16:21 Like a tempest that no one c see,
16:22 Or who c await them?
17:31 Yet it c be eclipsed.
18: 4 and who c search out his mighty deeds?
18: 5 Who c measure his majestic power?
18: 5 And who c fully recount his mercies?
21: 2 and c destroy human lives.
21:14 like a broken jar; it c hold no knowledge.
23:18 to himself, "Who c see me?
25: 3 how c you find anything in your old age?
25: 7 I c think of nine whom I would call blessed,
25: 7 a man who c rejoice in his children;
25:11 to whom c we compare the one who has it?
26:15 and no scales c weigh the value of her chastity.
26:29 A merchant c hardly keep from wrongdoing,
28: 4 c he then seek pardon for his own sins?
29: 6 If he c pay, his creditor will hardly get back half,
30:19 For it c neither eat nor smell.
32: 8 be as one who knows and c still hold his tongue.
34: 4 From an unclean thing what c be clean?
34: 4 And from something false what c be true?
34:12 and I understand more than I c express.
35:12 and as generously as you c afford.
38:11 as much as you c afford.
38:24 the one who has little business c become wise.
38:25 How c one become wise who handles the plow,
38:32 Without them no city c be inhabited,
39:17 No one c say, 'What is this?'
39:18 and none c limit his saving power.
39:19 and nothing c be hidden from his eyes.
39:20 to the end of time he c see everything,
39:21 No one c say, 'What is this?'
39:28 and in their anger they c dislodge mountains;
39:34 No one c say, "This is not as good as that,"
42:21 Nothing c be added or taken away,
43: 3 and who c withstand its burning heat?
43:28 Where c we find the strength to praise him?
43:30 Glorify the Lord and exalt him as much as you c,
43:31 Who has seen him and c describe him?
43:31 Or who c extol him as he is?
Bar 3:35 This is our God; no other c be compared to him.
4:17 But I, how c I help you?
LtJ 6:19 though their gods c see none of them.
6:30 For how c they be called gods?
6:45 they c be nothing but what the artisans wish them
6:47 then c the things that are made by them be gods?
6:48 as to where they c hide themselves and their gods.
6:49 How then c one fail to see that these are not gods,
6:52 Who then c fail to know that they are not gods?
6:56 they c offer no resistance to king or enemy.
6:58 Anyone who c will strip them of their gold
6:66 They c neither curse nor bless kings;
6:68 for they c flee to shelter and help themselves.
Sus 1:17 and shut the garden doors so that I c bathe."
1:20 the garden doors are shut, and no one c see us.
1Mc 3:17 they said to Judas, "How c we, few as we are,
1Es 8:90 for we c no longer stand in your presence because
9:11 This is not a work we c do in one day or two,
2Es 1:21 What more c I do for you?
2: 4 But now what c I do for you?
4: 2 and do you think you c comprehend the way of
4: 4 If you c solve one of them for me,
4: 6 "Who of those that have been born c do that,
4:11 how then c your mind comprehend the way of
4:11 And how c one who is already worn out by
4:21 the earth c understand only what is on the earth,
4:21 the heavens c understand what is above the height
4:40 her womb c keep the fetus within her any longer."
4:52 I c tell you in part;
5:39 and how c I speak concerning the things
5:44 the Creator, nor c the world hold
7: 5 how c they come to the broad part
7: 8 so that only one person c walk on the path.
2Es 7:14 they c never receive those things
7:18 c endure difficult circumstances while hoping
10:32 and lo, what I have seen I saw, and c still see,
10:56 as much as your ears c hear.
13:52 as no one c explore or know what is in the depths
13:52 on earth c see my Son or those who are with him,
16: 6 C one drive off a hungry lion in the forest,
16: 7 C one turn back an arrow shot by a strong archer?
16:77 so that no one c pass through.
4Mc 1: 8 but I c demonstrate it best from the noble bravery
2: 7 a glutton, or even a drunkard c learn a better way,
2: 9 In all other matters we c recognize
2:14 through the law, c prevail even over enmity.
3: 2 No one of us c eradicate that kind of desire,
3: 2 but reason c provide a way for us not to
3: 3 No one of us c eradicate anger from the mind,
3: 3 but reason c help to deal with anger.
3: 4 No one of us c eradicate malice,
3: 4 but reason c fight at our side so that we are
3: 6 Now this c be explained more clearly by the story
3:17 For the temperate mind c conquer the drives of
3:18 it c overthrow bodily agonies even
8: 6 so I c be a benefactor to those who obey me.
8:26 when we c live in peace if we obey the king?"
9: 7 of our religion, do not suppose that you c injure us
13: 5 How then c one fail to confess the sovereignty
14:17 they do what they c to help their young by flying

CANA (4)

Jn 2: 1 the third day there was a wedding in C of Galilee,
2:11 in C of Galilee, and revealed his glory;
4:46 to C in Galilee where he had changed the water
21: 2 Nathanael of C in Galilee, the sons of Zebedee,

CANAAN (92) [CANAANITE, CANAANITES]

A. LAND OF CANAAN (67)

Ge 9:18 Ham was the father of C.
9:22 And Ham, the father of C,
9:25 "Cursed be C; lowest of slaves shall he be to his brothers."
9:26 and let C be his slave.
9:27 and let C be his slave."
10: 6 descendants of Ham: Cush, Egypt, Put, and C.
10:15 C became the father of Sidon his firstborn,
11:31 of the Chaldeans to go into the land of C; A
12: 5 and they set forth to go to the land of C. A
12: 5 When they had come to the land of C, A
13:12 Abram settled in the land of C, A
16: 3 after Abram had lived ten years in the land of C, A
17: 8 all the land of C, for a perpetual holding; A
23: 2 Hebron) in the land of C; A
23:19 Hebron) in the land of C. A
31:18 to go to his father Isaac in the land of C. A
33:18 which is in the land of C, A
35: 6 Bethel), which is in the land of C, A
36: 5 of Esau who were born to him in the land of C. A
36: 6 all the property he had acquired in the land of C; A
37: 1 as an alien, the land of C. A
42: 5 for the famine had reached the land of C. A
42: 7 They said, "From the land of C, to buy food." A
42:13 the sons of a certain man in the land of C; A
42:29 they came to their father Jacob in the land of C, A
42:32 youngest is now with our father in the land of C.' A
44: 8 we brought back to you from the land of C; A
45:17 load your animals and go back to the land of C. A
45:25 and came to their father Jacob in the land of C. A
46: 6 goods that they had acquired in the land of C, A
46:12 Zerah (but Er and Onan died in the land of C); A
46:31 who were in the land of C, have come to me. A
47: 1 have come from the land of C; A
47: 4 because the famine is severe in the land of C. A
47:13 and the land of C languished because of A
47:14 found in the land of Egypt and in the land of C, A
47:15 of Egypt and from the land of C was spent, A
48: 3 to me at Luz in the land of C, A
48: 7 Rachel, alas, died in the land of C on the way, A
49:30 near Mamre, in the land of C, A
50: 5 that I hewed out for myself in the land of C, A
50:13 They carried him to the land of C and buried A
Ex 6: 4 to give them the land of C, A
15:15 all the inhabitants of C melted away.
16:35 until they came to the border of the land of C. A
Lev 14:34 When you come into the land of C, A
18: 3 and you shall not do as they do in the land of C, A
25:38 to give you the land of C, to be your God. A
Nu 13: 2 land of C, which I am giving to the Israelites; A
13:17 Moses sent them to spy out the land of C, A
26:19 Er and Onan died in the land of C. A
32:30 among you in the land of C." A
32:32 over armed before the LORD into the land of C, A
33:40 who lived in the Negeb in the land of C, A
33:51 you cross over the Jordan into the land of C, A
34: 2 land of C (this is the land that shall fall to you A
34: 2 the land of C, defined by its boundaries), A
34:29 the inheritance for the Israelites in the land of C. A
35:10 When you cross the Jordan into the land of C, A
35:14 and three cities in the land of C, A
Dt 32:49 across from Jericho, and view the land of C, A
Jos 5:12 they ate the crops of the land of C that year. A
14: 1 that the Israelites received in the land of C, A
21: 2 they said to them at Shiloh in the land of C, A
22: 9 which is in the land of C, A
22:10 near the Jordan that lies in the land of C, A
22:11 an altar at the frontier of the land of C, A
22:32 Gadites in the land of Gilead to the land of C, A
Jos 24: 3 the River and led him through all the land of C, A
Jdg 3: 1 in Israel who had no experience of any war in C
4: 2 into the hand of King Jabin of C, who reigned
4:23 on that day God subdued King Jabin of C before
4:24 and harder on King Jabin of C,
4:24 until they destroyed King Jabin of C.
5:19 then fought the kings of C, at Taanach,
21:12 which is in the land of C. A
1Ch 1: 8 descendants of Ham: Cush, Egypt, Put, and C.
1:13 C became the father of Sidon his firstborn,
16:18 the land of C as your portion for an inheritance." A
Ps 105:11 the land of C as your portion for an inheritance." A
106:38 whom they sacrificed to the idols of C;
135:11 king of Bashan, and all the kingdoms of C—
Isa 19:18 that speak the language of C and swear allegiance
23:11 the LORD has given command concerning C
Zep 2: 5 The word of the LORD is against you, O C,
Ac 7:11 there came a famine throughout Egypt and C,
13:19 he had destroyed seven nations in the land of C, A
Jdt 5: 9 where they were living and go to the land of C. A
5:10 land of C they went down to Egypt and lived A
Bar 3:22 She has not been heard of in C, or seen in Teman;
Sus 1:56 "You offspring of C and not of Judah,
1Mc 9:37 a daughter of one of the great nobles of C,

CANAANITE (13) [CANAAN]

Ge 28: 1 "You shall not marry one of the C women.
28: 6 "You shall not marry one of the C women,"
28: 8 that the C women did not please his father Isaac,
38: 2 the daughter of a certain C whose name was Shua;
46:10 Jachin, Zohar, and Shaul, the son of a C woman.
50:11 the C inhabitants of the land saw the mourning on
Ex 6:15 Jachin, Zohar, and Shaul, the son of a C woman;
Nu 21: 1 When the C, the king of Arad,
33:40 The C, the king of Arad, who lived in the Negeb
Jos 13: 3 to the boundary of Ekron, it is reckoned as C;
1Ch 2: 3 these three the C woman Bath-shua bore to him.
Ne 9: 8 to his descendants the land of the C, the Hittite,
Mt 15:22 Just then a C woman from that region came out

CANAANITES‡ (65) [CANAAN]

Ge 10:18 Afterward the families of the C spread abroad.
10:19 And the territory of the C extended from Sidon,
12: 6 At that time the C were in the land.
13: 7 that time the C and the Perizzites lived in the land.
15:21 the C, the Girgashites, and the Jebusites."
24: 3 a wife for my son from the daughters of the C,
24:37 from the daughters of the C, in whose land I live;
34:30 to the inhabitants of the land, the C and
36: 2 Esau took his wives from the C:
Ex 3: 8 to the country of the C, the Hittites, the Amorites,
3:17 to the land of the C, the Hittites, the Amorites,
13: 5 the LORD brings you into the land of the C,
13:11 LORD has brought you into the land of the C,
23:23 the Hittites, the Perizzites, the C, the Hivites,
23:28 which shall drive out the Hivites, the C,
33: 2 and I will drive out the C, the Amorites,
34:11 I will drive out before you the Amorites, the C,
Nu 13:29 and the C live by the sea, and along the Jordan."
14:25 since the Amalekites and the C live in the valleys,
14:43 the Amalekites and the C will confront you there,
14:45 the C who lived in that hill country came down
21: 3 to the voice of Israel, and handed over the C;
Dt 1: 7 the land of the C and the Lebanon,
7: 1 the Hittites, the Girgashites, the Amorites, the C,
11:30 in the land of the C who live in the Arabah,
20:17 the Amorites, the C and the Perizzites, the Hivites
Jos 3:10 without fail will drive out from before you the C,
5: 1 and all the kings of the C by the sea,
7: 9 C and all the inhabitants of the land will hear of it,
9: 1 the Hittites, the Amorites, the C, the Perizzites,
11: 3 to the C in the east and the west,
12: 8 Amorites, C, Perizzites, Hivites, and Jebusites):
13: 4 in the south, all the land of the C,
16:10 however, drive out the C who lived in Gezer:
16:10 so the C have lived within Ephraim to this day
17:12 but the C continued to live in that land.
17:13 they put the C to forced labor,
17:16 the C who live in the plain have chariots of iron,
17:18 for you shall drive out the C,
24:11 the Perizzites, the C, the Hittites, the Girgashites,
Jdg 1: 1 "Who shall go up first for us against the C,
1: 3 that we may fight against the C;
1: 4 and the LORD gave the C and the Perizzites
1: 5 and defeated the C and the Perizzites.
1: 9 to fight against the C who lived in the hill country,
1:10 Judah went against the C who lived in Hebron
1:17 and they defeated the C who inhabited Zephath,
1:27 but the C continued to live in that land.
1:28 Israel grew strong, they put the C to forced labor,
1:29 And Ephraim did not drive out the C who lived
1:29 but the C lived among them in Gezer.
1:30 but the C lived among them,
1:32 the Asherites lived among the C, the inhabitants
1:33 but lived among the C, the inhabitants of the land;
3: 3 and all the C, and the Sidonians,
3: 5 So the Israelites lived among the C, the Hittites,
2Sa 24: 7 of Tyre and to all the cities of the Hivites and C;
1Ki 9:16 had killed the C who lived in the city,
Ezr 9: 1 from the C, the Hittites, the Perizzites,
Ne 9:24 the C, and gave them into their hands,
Eze 16: 3 and your birth were in the land of the C;
Jdt 5: 3 to them, "Tell me, you C, what people is this
5:16 They drove out before them the C, the Perizzites,
1Es 8:69 the C, the Hittites, the Perizzites, the Jebusites,
2Es 1:21 I drove out the C, the Perizzites,

CANAL (2) [CANALS]
Sir 24:30 As for me, I was like a c from a river,
24:31 And lo, my c became a river, and my river a sea.

CANALS (3) [CANAL]
Ex 7:19 over its rivers, its c, and its ponds,
8: 5 the c, and the pools, and make frogs come up on
Isa 19: 6 its c will become foul, and the branches

CANANAEAN (2)
Mt 10: 4 Simon the C, and Judas Iscariot,
Mk 3:18 and Thaddaeus, and Simon the C,

CANCEL (3) [CANCELED]
1Mc 10:33 let all officials c also the taxes on their livestock.
13:39 and c the crown tax that you owe;
4Mc 2: 8 and to lend without interest to the needy and to c

CANCELED (5) [CANCEL]
Lk 7:42 he c the debts for both of them.
7:43 the one for whom he c the greater debt."
1Mc 10:42 of the temple, this too is c, because it belongs to
11:36 not one of these grants shall be c from this time
15: 8 be c for you from henceforth and for all time.

CANDACE (1)
Ac 8:27 a court official of the C, queen of the Ethiopians,

CANDLE, CANDLESTICK, CANDLESTICKS (KJV) See LAMP, LAMPSTAND, LAMPSTANDS

CANE (4)
Ex 30:23 and two hundred fifty of aromatic c,
Isa 43:24 You have not bought me sweet c with money,
Jer 6:20 or sweet c from a distant land?
Eze 27:19 and sweet c were bartered for your merchandise.

CANKER (KJV) See GANGRENE

CANKERWORM (KJV) See LOCUST

CANNEH (1)
Eze 27:23 Haran, C, Eden, the merchants of Sheba, Asshur,

CANNOT‡ (290) [CAN, NO]
Ge 16:10 so greatly multiply your offspring that they c
19:19 but I c flee to the hills,
24:50 we c speak to you anything bad or good.
29: 8 "We c until all the flocks are gathered together,
31:35 "Let not my lord be angry that I c rise before you,
32:12 which c be counted because of their number.' "
34:14 They said to them, "We c do this thing,
44:22 We said to my lord, 'The boy c leave his father,
44:26 we said, 'We c go down.
44:26 for we c see the man's face
Ex 18:18 the task is too heavy for you; you c do it alone.
33:20 But," he said, "you c see my face;
Lev 5: 7 But if you c afford a sheep,
5:11 if you c afford two turtledoves or two pigeons,
12: 8 If she c afford a sheep,
14:21 But if he is poor and c afford so much,
14:32 who c afford the offerings for his cleansing.
27: 8 If any c afford the equivalent,
27:26 c be consecrated by anyone;
27:33 then both it and the substitute shall be holy and c
Nu 23:20 he has blessed, and I c revoke it.
31:23 and whatever c withstand fire,
Dt 28:27 scurvy, and itch, of which you c be healed.
28:35 and on the legs with grievous boils of which you c
Jos 24:19 "You c serve the LORD, for he is a holy God.
Jdg 11:35 and I c take back my vow."
14:13 But if you c explain it to me,
21:18 we c give any of our daughters to them as wives."
Ru 4: 6 "I c redeem it for myself
4: 6 of redemption yourself, for I c redeem it."
1Sa 12:21 not turn aside after useless things that c profit
17:39 Then David said to Saul, "I c walk with these;
2Sa 5: 6 thinking, "David c come in here."
14:14 we are like water spilled on the ground, which c
14:19 one c turn right or left from anything that my lord
23: 6 for they c be picked up with the hand;
1Ki 3: 8 so numerous they c be numbered or counted.
8:27 heaven and the highest heaven c contain you,
13:16 he said, "I c return with you, or go in with you;
18:12 so, when I come and tell Ahab and he c find you,
20: 9 but this thing I c do."
2Ch 2: 6 since heaven, even highest heaven, c contain him?
6:18 heaven and the highest heaven c contain you,
13:12 of your ancestors; for you c succeed."
24:20 of the LORD, so that you c prosper?
Ezr 10:13 we c stand in the open.
Ne 6: 3 "I am doing a great work and I c come down.
Est 8: 8 and sealed with the king's ring c be revoked."
Job 3:23 Why is light given to one who c see the way,
6:30 C my taste discern calamity?
9:15 Though I am innocent, I c answer him;
10:15 If I am righteous, I c lift up my head,
14: 5 you have appointed the bounds that they c pass,
19: 8 He has walled up my way so that I c pass,
22:11 or darkness so that you c see;
23: 8 or backward, I c perceive him;
23: 9 on the left he hides, and I c behold him;
23: 9 I turn to the right, but I c see him.
28:15 It c be gotten for gold,
28:15 and silver c be weighed out as its price.
28:16 It c be valued in the gold of Ophir,
28:17 Gold and glass c equal it,
28:19 The chrysolite of Ethiopia c compare with it,
33:21 Their flesh is so wasted away that it c be seen;
37: 5 he does great things that we c comprehend.
37:19 we c draw up our case because of darkness.
37:23 The Almighty—we c find him;
39:24 it c stand still at the sound of the trumpet.
41:17 they clasp each other and c be separated.
41:28 The arrow c make it flee;
Ps 33:17 and by its great might it c save.
36: 2 in their own eyes that their iniquity c be found out
38:13 like the mute, who c speak.
40:12 my iniquities have overtaken me, until I c see;
49:12 Mortals c abide in their pomp;
49:20 Mortals c abide in their pomp;
69:23 Let their eyes be darkened so that they c see,
77: 4 I am so troubled that I c speak.
88: 8 I am shut in so that I c escape;
92: 6 dullard c know, the stupid c understand this:
125: 1 which c be moved, but abides forever.
139: 6 it is so high that I c attain it.
148: 6 he fixed their bounds, which c be passed.
Pr 4:16 For they c sleep unless they have done wrong;
8:11 and all that you may desire c compare with her.
30:21 under four it c bear up:
31: 8 Speak out for those who c speak,
Ecc 1:15 What is crooked c be made straight,
1:15 and what is lacking c be counted.
3:11 yet they c find out what God has done from
8:17 to know, they c find it out.
SS 8: 7 Many waters c quench love,
Isa 1:13 I c endure solemn assemblies with iniquity.
21: 3 I am bowed down so that I c hear,
21: 3 I am dismayed so that I c see.
29:11 with the command, "Read this," they say, "We c,
29:12 And if it is given to those who c read, saying,
"Read this," they say, "We c read."
30: 5 to shame through a people that c profit them,
30: 6 to a people that c profit them.
33:19 of an obscure speech that you c comprehend,
33:19 stammering in a language that you c understand.
33:23 it c hold the mast firm in its place,
38:18 For Sheol c thank you, death c praise you;
38:18 down to the Pit c hope for your faithfulness.
41: 7 and they fasten it with nails so that it c be moved.
43:17 they lie down, they c rise, they are extinguished,
44:18 for their eyes are shut, so that they c see,
44:18 and their minds as well, so that they c understand.
44:20 and he c save himself or say,
45:20 and keep on praying to a god that c save.
46: 2 they c save the burden, but themselves go
46: 7 it c move from its place.
47:11 which you c charm away;
47:14 they c deliver themselves from the power of
50: 2 Is my hand shortened, that it c redeem?
56:10 they are all silent dogs that c bark;
57:20 wicked are like the tossing sea that c keep still;
59: 6 Their webs c serve as clothing;
59: 6 they c cover themselves with what they make.
59:14 in the public square, and uprightness c enter.
Jer 4:19 My heart is beating wildly; I c keep silent;
5:22 a perpetual barrier that it c pass;
5:22 though the waves toss, they c prevail,
5:22 though they roar, they c pass over it.
6:10 See, their ears are closed, they c listen.
8:17 adders that c be charmed, and they shall bite you,
10: 4 with hammer and nails so that it c move.
10: 5 scarecrows in a cucumber field, and they c speak;
10: 5 they have to be carried, for they c walk.
10: 5 Do not be afraid of them, for they c do evil,
10:10 and the nations c endure his indignation.
10:23 that mortals as they walk c direct their steps.
11:11 to bring disaster upon them that they c escape;
14: 9 like a mighty warrior who c give help?
20: 9 I am weary with holding it in, and I c.
23:24 in secret places so that I c see them?
24: 3 so bad that they c be eaten."
24: 8 Like the bad figs that are so bad they c be eaten,
29:17 like rotten figs that are so bad they c be eaten.
33:22 Just as the host of heaven c be numbered and the
sands of the sea c be measured,
46: 6 The swift c flee away, nor can the warrior escape;
49:23 they are troubled like the sea that c be quiet.
La 1:14 over to those whom I c withstand.
3: 7 He has walled me about so that I c escape;
Eze 3: 6 whose words you c understand.
3:25 so that you c go out among the people;
4: 8 I am putting cords on you so that you c turn
7:13 of their iniquity, they c maintain their lives.
7:19 and gold c save them on the day of the wrath of
Da 6: 8 so that it c be changed,
6: 8 the Medes and the Persians, which c be revoked."
6:12 of the Medes and Persians, which c be revoked."
Hos 2: 6 so that she c find her paths.
Mic 2: 3 an evil from which you c remove your necks;
Hab 1:13 and you c look on wrongdoing;
2:18 though the product is only an idol that c speak!
Mt 5:14 A city built on a hill c be hid.
5:36 for you c make one hair white or black.
6:24 You c serve God and wealth.
7:18 A good tree c bear bad fruit,
9:15 "The wedding guests c mourn as long as
10:28 not fear those who kill the body but c kill the soul;
16: 3 but you c interpret the signs of the times.
26:42 if this c pass unless I drink it, your will be done."
26:53 Do you think that I c appeal to my Father,
27:42 "He saved others; he c save himself.
Mk 2:19 "The wedding guests c fast while the bridegroom
2:19 the bridegroom with them, they c fast.
3:24 against itself, that kingdom c stand.
3:26 he c stand, but his end has come.
7:18 into a person from outside c defile,
15:31 "He saved others; he c save himself.
Lk 5:34 "You c make wedding guests fast while
11: 7 I c get up and give you anything.'
14:14 you will be blessed, because they c repay you,
14:20 'I have just been married, and therefore I c come.'
14:26 yes, and even life itself, c be my disciple.
14:27 Whoever does not carry the cross and follow me c
14:32 If he c, then, while the other is still far away,
16: 2 because you c be my manager any longer.'
16:13 You c serve God and wealth."
16:26 to pass from here to you c do so,
20:36 Indeed they c die anymore,
Jn 4:29 He c be the Messiah, can he?"
7: 7 The world c hate you, but it hates me
7:34 and where I am, you c come."
7:36 not find me' and 'Where I am, you c come'?"
8:21 Where I am going, you c come."
8:22 'Where I am going, you c come'?"
8:43 It is because you c accept my word.
10:35 and the scripture c be annulled—
13:33 'Where I am going, you c come.'
13:36 "Where I am going, you c follow me now;
14:17 whom the world c receive,
15: 4 as the branch c bear fruit by itself unless it abides
16:12 but you c bear them now.
Ac 4:16 through them; we c deny it.
4:20 for we c keep from speaking
15: 1 to the custom of Moses, you c be saved."
19:36 Since these things c be denied,
27:31 "Unless these men stay in the ship, you c
Ro 7:18 I can will what is right, but I c do it.
8: 7 to God's law—indeed it c,
8: 8 and those who are in the flesh c please God.
11:10 let their eyes be darkened so that they c see,
1Co 10:21 You c drink the cup of the Lord and the cup
10:21 You c partake of the table of the Lord and
12:21 The eye c say to the hand,
15:50 flesh and blood c inherit the kingdom of God,
2Co 4:18 not at what can be seen but at what c be seen;
4:18 but what c be seen is eternal.
13: 8 For we c do anything against the truth,
1Ti 5:25 and even when they are not, they c remain hidden.
2Ti 2:13 he remains faithful—for he c deny himself.
Tit 2: 8 and sound speech that c be censured;
Heb 9: 5 Of these things we c speak now in detail.
9: 9 that c perfect the conscience of the worshiper,
12:27 so that what c be shaken may remain.
12:28 we are receiving a kingdom that c be shaken,
Jas 1:13 for God c be tempted by evil
4: 2 And you covet something and c obtain it;
1Jn 3: 9 they c sin, because they have been born of God.
4:20 c love God whom they have not seen.
Rev 2: 2 I know that you c tolerate evildoers;
9:20 which c see or hear or walk.
Tob 5:10 I c see the light of heaven,
5:10 I hear people but I c see them."
9: 3 and I c violate his oath."
Jdt 6: 3 They c resist the might of our cavalry.
8:14 You c plumb the depths of the human heart
8:30 and made us take an oath that we c break.
11:10 Indeed our nation c be punished,
12: 2 But Judith said, "I c partake of them,
AdE 8: 8 at the king's command and sealed with my ring c
13: 4 that we honorably intend c be brought about.
Wis 12:25 Therefore, as though to children who c reason,
13:16 because he knows that it c help itself,
13:18 for a prosperous journey, a thing that c take a step;
16:14 but c bring back the departed spirit,
Sir 1:22 Unjust anger c be justified,
6:20 to the undisciplined; fools c remain with her.
8:17 Do not consult with fools, for they c keep a secret.
9:10 for new ones c equal them.
14:16 because in Hades one c look for luxury.
21:12 The one who is not clever c be taught,
25:18 and he c help sighing bitterly.
26: 8 arouses great anger; she c hide her shame.
29: 6 If he c pay, the borrower has robbed the other
38:33 they c expound discipline or judgment,
40:29 one's way of life c be considered a life.
43:30 for you c praise him enough.
LtJ 6: 8 but they are false and c speak.
6:12 that c save themselves from rust and corrosion.
6:15 but c defend itself from war and robbers.
6:27 If anyone sets it upright, it c move itself;
6:27 and if it is tipped over, it c straighten itself.
6:34 They c set up a king or depose one.
6:36 They c save anyone from death or rescue the weak
6:37 They c restore sight to the blind;
6:37 they c rescue one who is in distress.
6:38 They c take pity on a widow or do good to
6:40 for when they see someone who c speak,
6:41 Yet they themselves c perceive this
6:49 for they c save themselves from war or calamity?
6:53 For they c set up a king over a country
6:54 They c judge their own cause

LtJ 6:67 they c show signs in the heavens for the nations,
Aza 1:10 And now we c open our mouths;
Sus 1:22 if I do not, I c escape your hands.
Bel 1:24 "You c deny that this is a living god;
1Mc 10:72 People will tell you that you c stand before us,
2Mc 7:14 "One c but choose to die at the hands of mortals
1Es 4:17 men c exist without women.
Man 1:5 for your glorious splendor c be borne,
2Es 4:9 that you have experienced and from which you c
4:10 "You c understand the things
4:41 And I said, "No, lord, it c."
5:35 He said to me, "You c."
5:40 as you c do one of the things that were mentioned,
5:40 so you c discover my judgment,
5:44 "The creation c move faster than the Creator,
5:47 "Of course it c, but only each in its own time."
7:82 because they c now make a good repentance so
13:18 for the last days, but c attain them.
15:51 so that you c receive your mighty lovers.
4Mc 13:4 The supremacy of the mind over these c

CANOPIES See Index to Footnotes

CANOPY‡ (12)
2Sa 22:12 He made darkness around him a c, thick clouds,
1Ki 7:6 and a c in front of them.
Ps 18:11 his c thick clouds dark with water.
19:5 like a bridegroom from his wedding c,
Isa 4:5 Indeed over all the glory there will be a c.
Jer 43:10 and he will spread his royal c over them.
Eze 41:25 a c of wood in front of the vestibule outside.
Joel 2:16 Let the bridegroom leave his room, and the bride her c.
Jdt 10:21 on his bed under a c that was woven with purple
13:9 the bed and pulled down the c from the posts.
13:15 the c beneath which he lay in his drunken stupor.
16:19 and the c that she had taken for herself

CAPABILITY (1) [CAPABLE]
Sir 17:30 For not everything is within human c,

CAPABLE (3) [CAPABILITY]
Ge 47:6 and if you know that there are c men among them,
Pr 31:10 A c wife who can find?
Wis 8:15 among the people I shall show myself c,

CAPARISONED (1)
2Mc 3:25 there appeared to them a magnificently c horse,

CAPERNAUM (16)
Mt 4:13 He left Nazareth and made his home in C by
8:5 When he entered C, a centurion came to him,
11:23 And you, C, will you be exalted to heaven?
17:24 When they reached C, the collectors of
Mk 1:21 They went to C; and when the sabbath came,
2:1 When he returned to C after some days,
9:33 Then they came to C; and when he was
Lk 4:23 the things that we have heard you did at C.' "
4:31 He went down to C, a city in Galilee,
7:1 in the hearing of the people, he entered C.
10:15 And you, C, will you be exalted to heaven?
Jn 2:12 After this he went down to C with his mother,
4:46 there was a royal official whose son lay ill in C.
6:17 and started across the sea to C.
6:24 into the boats and went to C looking for Jesus.
6:59 while he was teaching in the synagogue at C.

CAPHAR-SALAMA (1)
1Mc 7:31 he went out to meet Judas in battle near C.

CAPHTOR (3) [CAPHTORIM]
Dt 2:23 the Caphtorim, who came from C,
Jer 47:4 the remnant of the coastland of C.
Am 9:7 Philistines from C and the Arameans from Kir?

CAPHTORIM (3) [CAPHTOR]
Ge 10:14 and C, from which the Philistines come.
Dt 2:23 the C, who came from Caphtor,
1Ch 1:12 and C, from whom the Philistines come.

CAPITAL (24) [CAPITALS]
1Ki 7:16 the height of the one c was five cubits,
7:16 and the height of the other c was five cubits.
7:17 seven for the one c, and seven for the other c.
7:18 he did the same with the other c.
7:20 and so with the other c.
2Ki 25:17 and on it was a bronze c;
25:17 the height of the c was three cubits;
25:17 all of bronze, were on the c all around.
2Ch 3:15 with a c of five cubits on the top of each.
Ezr 6:2 it was in Ecbatana, the c in the province of Media,
Ne 1:1 in the twentieth year, while I was in Susa the c,
Jer 52:22 Upon it was a c of bronze;
52:22 the height of the one c was five cubits;
52:22 all of bronze, encircled the top of the c.
Da 4:30 as a royal c by my mighty power and
8:2 and saw myself in Susa the c,
Zec 9:1 For to the LORD belongs the c of Aram,
AdE 2:3 to be brought to the harem in Susa, the c.
2:5 the c whose name was Mordecai son of Jair son
2:8 and many girls were gathered in Susa the c
9:12 The king said to Esther, "In Susa, the c,
AdE 9:18 The Jews who were in Susa, the c,
1Mc 3:37 and left Antioch his c in the one hundred

CAPITALS (17) [CAPITAL]
Ex 36:38 He overlaid their c and their bases with gold,
38:17 the overlaying of their c was also of silver,
38:19 the overlaying of their c and their bands of silver.
38:28 and overlaid their c and made bands for them.
1Ki 7:16 He also made two c of molten bronze,
7:17 with wreaths of chain work for the c on the tops of
7:18 to cover the c that were above the pomegranates;
7:19 Now the c that were on the tops of the pillars in
7:20 The c were on the two pillars and also above
7:41 the two bowls of the c that were on the tops of
7:41 the two bowls of the c that were on the tops of
7:42 the two bowls of the c that were on the pillars;
2Ch 4:12 the bowls, and the two c on the top of the pillars;
4:12 the two bowls of the c that were on the top of
4:13 the two bowls of the c that were on the pillars.
Am 9:1 Strike the c until the thresholds shake,
Zep 2:14 and the screech owl shall lodge on its c;

CAPPADOCIA (2)
Ac 2:9 and residents of Mesopotamia, Judea and C,
1Pe 1:1 Galatia, C, Asia, and Bithynia,

CAPTAIN‡ (52) [CAPTAINS]
Ge 37:36 one of Pharaoh's officials, the c of the guard.
39:1 an officer of Pharaoh, the c of the guard,
40:3 and he put them in custody in the house of the c of
40:4 The c of the guard charged Joseph with them,
41:10 the chief baker in custody in the house of the c of
41:12 a servant of the c of the guard.
Nu 14:4 So they said to one another, "Let us choose a c,
1Sa 22:2 and he became c over them.
2Ki 1:9 the king sent to him a c of fifty with his fifty men.
1:10 But Elijah answered the c of fifty,
1:11 Again the king sent to him another c of fifty
1:13 the king sent the c of a third fifty with his fifty.
1:13 So the third c of fifty went up,
7:2 Then the c on whose hand the king leaned said to
7:17 the c on whose hand he leaned to have charge of
7:19 the c had answered the man of God,
15:25 Pekah son of Remaliah, his c,
18:24 then can you repulse a single c among the least
25:8 Nebuzaradan, the c of the bodyguard,
25:10 the army of the Chaldeans who were with the c of
25:11 Nebuzaradan the c of the guard carried into exile
25:12 the c of the guard left some of the poorest people
25:15 of gold the c of the guard took away for the gold,
25:18 The c of the guard took the chief priest Seraiah,
25:20 Nebuzaradan the c of the guard took them,
Isa 3:3 c of fifty and dignitary, counselor
36:9 then can you repulse a single c among the least
Jer 39:9 the c of the guard exiled to Babylon the rest of
39:10 the c of the guard left in the land of Judah some of
39:11 Nebuzaradan, the c of the guard, saying,
39:13 So Nebuzaradan the c of the guard,
40:1 the c of the guard had let him go from Ramah,
40:2 The c of the guard took Jeremiah and said to him,
40:5 the c of the guard gave him an allowance of food
41:10 whom Nebuzaradan, the c of the guard,
43:6 the c of the guard had left with Gedaliah son
52:12 Nebuzaradan the c of the bodyguard who served
52:14 who were with the c of the guard,
52:15 the c of the guard carried into exile some of
52:16 the c of the guard left some of the poorest people
52:19 c of the guard took away the small bowls also,
52:24 The c of the guard took the chief priest Seraiah,
52:26 Then Nebuzaradan the c of the guard took them,
52:30 Nebuzaradan the c of the guard took into exile of
Jnh 1:6 The c came and said to him,
Ac 4:1 the priests, the c of the temple,
5:24 Now when the c of the temple and
5:26 c went with the temple police and brought them,
Jdt 14:2 set a c over them, as if you were going down to
2Mc 3:4 who had been made c of the temple,
4:28 the c of the citadel kept requesting payment—
5:24 the c of the Mysians with an army

CAPTAINS‡ (29) [CAPTAIN]
Jdg 7:25 They captured the two c of Midian,
8:3 God has given into your hands the c of Midian,
2Sa 4:2 Saul's son had two c of raiding bands;
1Ki 9:22 they were his officials, his commanders, his c,
22:31 the king of Aram had commanded the thirty-two c
22:32 When the c of the chariots saw Jehoshaphat,
22:33 the c of the chariots saw that it was not the king
2Ki 1:14 the two former c of fifty men with their fifties;
11:4 But in the seventh year Jehoiada summoned the c
11:9 The c did according to all that
11:10 The priest delivered to the c the spears and shields
11:14 with the c and the trumpeters beside the king,
11:15 the c who were set over the army,
11:19 He took the c, the Carites, the guards,
25:23 when all the c of the forces and their men heard
25:26 and the c of the forces set out and went to Egypt;
2Ch 18:30 of Aram had commanded the c of his chariots,
18:31 When the c of the chariots saw Jehoshaphat,
18:32 for when the c of the chariots saw that it was not
23:9 to the c the spears and the large and small shields
23:13 and the c and the trumpeters beside the king,
23:14 the priest Jehoiada brought out the c who were set
23:20 And he took the c, the nobles,
Job 39:25 the thunder of the c, and the shouting.
Rev 19:18 the flesh of c, the flesh of the mighty,
Jdt 14:12 who then went to the generals and the c and
1Mc 16:19 he sent letters to the c asking them to come to him
2Mc 12:19 who were c under Maccabeus,
1Es 1:9 and Joram, c over thousands, gave the Levites for

CAPTIVATE (1) [CAPTURE]
2Ti 3:6 make their way into households and c silly women,

CAPTIVATED (1) [CAPTURE]
Jdt 16:9 her beauty c his mind,

CAPTIVE‡ (65) [CAPTURE]
Ge 14:14 Abram heard that his nephew had been taken c,
Nu 21:1 he fought against Israel and took some of them c.
24:22 How long shall Asshur take you away c?"
31:9 the women of Midian and their little ones c;
Dt 21:10 over to you and you take them c,
1Sa 30:2 and taken c the women and all who were in it,
30:3 and their wives and sons and daughters taken c.
30:5 David's two wives also had been taken c,
1Ki 8:46 they are carried away c to the land of the enemy,
8:47 to which they have been taken c, and repent,
8:48 who took them c, and pray to you
2Ki 5:2 on one of their raids had taken a young girl c from
15:29 and he carried the people c to Assyria.
16:9 carrying its people c to Kir; then he killed Rezin.
24:16 The king of Babylon brought c to Babylon all
1Ch 3:17 and the sons of Jeconiah, the c: Shealtiel his son,
2Ch 6:36 that they are carried away c to a land far or near;
6:37 to which they have been taken c, and repent,
6:38 to which they were taken c,
28:5 who defeated him and took c a great number
28:8 of Israel took c two hundred thousand of their kin,
33:11 who took Manasseh c in manacles,
Ezr 2:1 from those c exiles whom King Nebuchadnezzar of Babylon had carried c to Babylonia;
Ps 106:46 to be pitied by all who held them c.
Pr 11:6 but the treacherous are taken c by their schemes.
SS 7:5 a king is held c in the tresses.
Isa 14:2 they will take c those who were their captors,
52:2 from the dust, rise up, O c Jerusalem;
52:2 the bonds from your neck, O c daughter Zion!
Jer 13:17 because the LORD's flock has been taken c.
20:4 he shall carry them c to Babylon,
22:12 where they have carried him c he shall die,
41:10 Then Ishmael took c all the rest of
41:10 of Nethaniah took them c and set out to cross over
41:14 the people whom Ishmael had carried away c
41:16 of Nethaniah had carried away c from Mizpah
43:12 and he shall burn them and carry them away c;
48:46 for your sons have been taken c,
Eze 6:9 among the nations where they are carried c,
32:9 as I carry you c among the nations,
Ac 20:22 And now, as a c to the Spirit,
Ro 7:6 dead to that which held us c,
7:23 making me c to the law of sin that dwells
2Co 10:5 and we take every thought c to obey Christ.
Eph 4:8 he ascended on high he made captivity itself a c;
Col 2:8 to it that no one takes you c through philosophy
2Ti 2:26 having been held c by him to do his will.
Rev 13:10 If you are to be taken c, into captivity you go;
Tob 1:10 After I was carried away c to Assyria and came as a c to Nineveh,
14:15 those whom King Cyaxares of Media had taken c.
Jdt 2:9 I will lead them away c to the ends of
5:18 in many battles and were led away c to
AdE 2:6 he had been taken c from Jerusalem
Sir 31:7 and every fool will be taken c by it.
1Mc 1:32 They took c the women and children,
8:10 and the Romans took c their wives and children;
10:33 of the Jews taken as a c from the land of Judah
15:40 the people and invade Judea and take the people c
2Mc 1:19 For when our ancestors were being led c to Persia,
1Es 6:16 and carried the people away c to Babylon.
2Es 1:3 who was a c in the country of the Medes in
15:63 They shall carry your children away c,
16:46 overthrow their houses, and take their children c;

CAPTIVE'S (1) [CAPTURE]
Dt 21:13 discard her c garb, and shall remain in your house

CAPTIVES (38) [CAPTURE]
Ge 31:26 carried away my daughters like c of the sword.
Nu 21:29 and his daughters c, to an Amorite king, Sihon.
31:12 the c and the booty and the spoil to Moses,
31:19 a corpse, purify yourselves and your c on the third
Dt 21:11 among the c a beautiful woman whom you desire
32:42 with the blood of the slain and the c,
Jdg 5:12 Arise, Barak, lead away your c,
2Ki 24:14 all the officials, all the warriors, ten thousand c,
1Ch 5:21 and one hundred thousand c.
2Ch 28:11 the c whom you have taken from your kindred,
28:13 "You shall not bring the c in here,
28:14 the c and the booty before the officials and all
28:15 and took the c, and with the booty they clothed all
28:17 and defeated Judah, and carried away c.
Est 2:6 the c carried away with King Jeconiah of Judah,
Ps 68:18 leading c in your train and receiving gifts
Isa 20:4 the king of Assyria lead away the Egyptians as c
49:24 or the c of a tyrant be rescued?
49:25 Even the c of the mighty shall be taken,
61:1 to proclaim liberty to the c,
Jer 40:1 in fetters along with all the c of Jerusalem

La 1: 5 her children have gone away, **c** before the foe.
Hab 1: 9 faces pressing forward; they gather **c** like sand.
Lk 4:18 to proclaim release to the **c** and recovery of sight
21:24 by the edge of the sword and be taken away as **c**
Tob 13:10 May he cheer all those within you who are **c**,
14: 4 be scattered and taken as **c** from the good land;
AdE 11: 4 He was one of the **c** whom King Nebuchadnezzar
Wis 17: 2 they themselves lay as **c** of darkness and prisoners
1Mc 9:70 with him and obtain release of the **c**.
9:72 the **c** whom he had taken previously from the land
14: 7 He gathered a host of **c**;
1Es 6: 5 for the providence of the Lord was over the **c**;
7:11 Not all of the returned **c** were purified,
7:12 the returned **c** and for their kindred the priests and
3Mc 1: 5 and many **c** also were taken.
2Es 13:40 king of the Assyrians, made **c**;
4Mc 8: 2 that others of the Hebrew **c** be brought,

CAPTIVITY‡ (42) [CAPTURE]

Dt 28:41 for they shall go into **c**.
Jdg 18:30 of the Danites until the time the land went into **c**.
2Ki 24:15 he took into **c** from Jerusalem to Babylon.
2Ch 6:37 and plead with you in the land of their **c**, saying,
6:38 with all their heart and soul in the land of their **c**,
29: 9 and our daughters and our wives are in **c** for this.
Ezr 3: 8 and all who had come to Jerusalem from the **c**.
8:35 At that time those who had come from **c**,
9: 7 to **c**, to plundering, and to utter shame,
Ne 1: 2 those who had escaped the **c**,
1: 3 in the province who escaped **c** are in great trouble
4: 4 and give them over as plunder in a land of **c**.
7: 6 the **c** of those exiles whom King Nebuchadnezzar
8:17 of those who had returned from the **c** made booths
Ps 78:61 and delivered his power to **c**,
Isa 46: 2 the burden, but themselves go into **c**.
Jer 1: 3 until the **c** of Jerusalem in the fifth month.
15: 2 and those destined for **c**, to **c**.
20: 6 and all who live in your house, shall go into **c**,
22:22 and your lovers shall go into **c**;
30:10 and your offspring from the land of their **c**.
30:16 everyone of them, shall go into **c**;
43:11 and those who are destined for **c**, to **c**,
46:27 and your offspring from the land of their **c**.
48:46 and your daughters into **c**.
La 1:18 and young men have gone into **c**.
Eze 12:11 they shall go into exile, into **c**."
30:17 and the cities themselves shall go into **c**.
30:18 and its daughter-towns shall go into **c**.
39:23 the house of Israel went into **c** for their iniquity,
Da 11:33 by sword and flame, and suffer **c** and plunder.
Am 9: 4 though they go into **c** in front of their enemies,
Na 3:10 Yet she became an exile, she went into **c**;
Eph 4: 8 he ascended on high he made **c** itself a captive;
Rev 13:10 If you are to be taken captive, into **c** you go;
Tob 1: 2 of the Assyrians was taken into **c** from Thisbe,
Jdt 8:22 The slaughter of our kindred and the **c** of the land
9: 4 up their wives for booty and their daughters to **c**,
1Es 9: 4 of those who had returned from the **c**.
2Es 16:46 in **c** and famine they will produce their children.

CAPTORS (7) [CAPTURE]

1Ki 8:47 and plead with you in the land of their **c**, saying,
8:50 and grant them compassion in the sight of their **c**,
2Ch 30: 9 your children will find compassion with their **c**,
Ps 137: 3 For there our **c** asked us for songs,
Isa 14: 2 they will take captive those who were their **c**,
Jer 50:33 all their **c** have held them fast and refuse
Mic 2: 4 Among our **c** he parcels out our fields."

CAPTURE (16) [CAPTIVATE, CAPTIVATED, CAPTIVE, CAPTIVE'S, CAPTIVES, CAPTIVITY, CAPTORS, CAPTURED, CAPTURES, CAPTURING]

Jdg 21:22 we did not **c** in battle a wife for each man.
1Sa 23:26 in on David and his men to **c** them.
2Ki 6:22 Did you **c** with your sword
Pr 6:25 and do not let her **c** you with her eyelashes;
Jer 50:46 of the **c** of Babylon the earth shall tremble,
Eze 21:23 to remembrance, bringing about their **c**.
Da 11:18 to the coastlands, and shall **c** many.
Jdt 10:13 by which he can go and **c** all the hill country
Bar 4:14 remember the **c** of my sons and daughters,
4:24 as the neighbors of Zion have now seen your **c**,
1Mc 5:11 They are preparing to come and **c** the stronghold
5:27 and **c** and destroy all these people in a single day."
5:30 carrying ladders and engines of war to **c**
9:58 and he will **c** them all in one night."
2Mc 8:36 the **c** of the people of Jerusalem proclaimed that
14:41 about to **c** the tower and were forcing the door of

CAPTURED (52) [CAPTURE]

Ge 34:29 they **c** and made their prey.
Nu 21:26 against the former king of Moab and **c** all his land
21:32 and they **c** its villages, and dispossessed
31:26 an inventory of the booty **c**,
32:39 of Machir son of Manasseh went to Gilead, **c** it,
32:41 Jair son of Manasseh went and **c** their villages,
32:42 And Nobah went and **c** Kenath and its villages,
Dt 2:34 At that time we **c** all his towns,
2:35 as well as the plunder of the towns that we had **c**.
3: 4 At that time we **c** all his towns;
Jos 6:20 ahead into the city and **c** it.
Jdg 7:25 They **c** the two captains of Midian,
1Sa 4:11 The ark of God was **c**;
4:17 are dead, and the ark of God has been **c**."
4:19 she heard the news that the ark of God was **c**,
4:21 because the ark of God had been **c** and because
4:22 for the ark of God has been **c**."
5: 1 When the Philistines **c** the ark of God,
30:20 David also **c** all the flocks and herds,
1Ki 9:16 (Pharaoh king of Egypt had gone up and **c** Gezer
2Ki 14:13 of Israel **c** King Amaziah of Judah son of Jehoash,
15:29 King Tiglath-pileser of Assyria came and **c** Ijon,
17: 6 of Hoshea the king of Assyria **c** Samaria;
18:13 against all the fortified cities of Judah and **c** them.
25: 6 Then they **c** the king and brought him up to
1Ch 5:21 They **c** their livestock: fifty thousand of their
2Ch 8: 3 Solomon went to Hamath-zobah, and **c** it.
22: 9 who was **c** while hiding in Samaria
25:12 The people of Judah **c** another ten thousand alive,
25:23 King Joash of Israel **c** King Amaziah of Judah,
Ne 9:25 And they **c** fortress cities and a rich land,
Isa 22: 3 they were **c** without the use of a bow.
22: 3 All of you who were found were **c**,
36: 1 against all the fortified cities of Judah and **c** them.
Jer 34: 3 but shall surely be **c** and handed over to him;
52: 9 Then they **c** the king, and brought him up to
Rev 19:20 And the beast was **c**, and with it
Jdt 1:14 **c** its towers, plundered its markets,
1:15 He **c** Arphaxad in the mountains of Ragau
7:27 For it would be better for us to be **c** by them.
8:21 For if we are **c**, all Judea will be **c** and our
sanctuary will be plundered;
10:13 the hill country without losing one of his men, **c**
AdE 2: 6 whom King Nebuchadnezzar of Babylon had **c**.
1Mc 1:19 They **c** the fortified cities in the land of Egypt,
5:13 enemy have **c** their wives and children and goods,
11:56 Trypho **c** the elephants and gained control
13:43 and battered and **c** one tower.
2Mc 8: 6 He **c** strategic positions and put to flight not a few
8:10 by selling the **c** Jews into slavery.
8:25 They **c** the money of those who had come
10:22 and immediately **c** the two towers.

CAPTURES (1) [CAPTURE]

Pr 16:32 one whose temper is controlled than one who **c**

CAPTURING (2) [CAPTURE]

Jos 19:47 and after **c** it and putting it to the sword,
Job 41: 9 Any hope of **c** it will be disappointed;

CARABASION (1)

1Es 9:34 **C** and Eliashib and Mamitanemus, Eliasis, Binnui,

CARAVAN (2) [CARAVANS]

Ge 37:25 a **c** of Ishmaelites coming from Gilead,
Jdg 8:11 So Gideon went up by the **c** route east of Nobah

CARAVANS (4) [CARAVAN]

Jdg 5: 6 **c** ceased and travelers kept to the byways.
Job 6:18 The **c** turn aside from their course;
6:19 The **c** of Tema look, the travelers of Sheba hope.
Isa 21:13 In the scrub of the desert plain you will lodge, O **c**

CARBUNCLE, CARBUNCLES (KJV) See JEWELS, STONES

CARCASE, CARCASES (KJV) See BODIES, CARCASSES, CORPSES

CARCASS (18) [CARCASSES]

Lev 5: 2 whether the **c** of an unclean beast or the **c** of
unclean livestock or the **c** of an unclean swarming
11:24 whoever touches the **c** of any of them shall
11:25 of the **c** of any of them shall wash his clothes and
11:27 whoever touches the **c** of any of them shall
11:28 the **c** shall wash his clothes and be unclean until
11:35 on which any part of the **c** falls shall be unclean;
11:36 whatever touches the **c** in it shall be unclean.
11:37 of their **c** falls upon any seed set aside for sowing,
11:38 on the seed and any part of their **c** falls on it,
11:39 anyone who touches its **c** shall be unclean until
11:40 Those who eat of its **c** shall wash their clothes and
11:40 the **c** shall wash their clothes and be unclean until
Jdg 14: 8 and he turned aside to see the **c** of the lion,
14: 9 that he had taken the honey from the **c** of the lion.
Ps 89:10 You crushed Rahab like a **c**;
Eze 32: 5 and fill the valleys with your **c**.

CARCASSES (7) [CARCASS]

Ge 15:11 And when birds of prey came down on the **c**,
Lev 11: 8 and their **c** you shall not touch;
11:11 and their **c** you shall regard as detestable.
26:30 I will heap your **c** on the **c** of your idols.
Dt 14: 8 and you shall not touch their **c**.
Jer 16:18 because they have polluted my land with the **c**

CARCHEMISH (4)

2Ch 35:20 of Egypt went up to fight at **C** on the Euphrates,
Isa 10: 9 Is not Calno like **C**?
Jer 46: 2 which was by the river Euphrates at **C**
1Es 1:25 went to make war at **C** on the Euphrates,

CARDERS (1)

Isa 19: 9 and the **c** and those at the loom will grow pale.

CARE‡ (95) [CARED, CAREFUL, CAREFULLY, CARELESS, CARELESSLY, CARES, CARING]

Ge 33:13 which are nursing, are a **c** to me;
39:22 The chief jailer committed to Joseph's **c** all
39:23 in Joseph's **c**, because the LORD was with him;
Ex 10:28 Take **c** that you do not see my face again,
34:12 Take **c** not to make a covenant with
Nu 7: 9 with the **c** of the holy things that had to be carried
23:12 "Must I not take **c** to say what the LORD puts
28: 2 by fire, my pleasing odor, you shall take **c** to offer
Dt 4: 9 But take **c** and watch yourselves closely,
4:15 take **c** and watch yourselves closely,
6:12 take **c** that you do not forget the LORD,
8:11 Take **c** that you do not forget
11:16 Take **c**, or you will be seduced into turning away,
12:13 Take **c** that you do not offer your burnt offerings
12:19 Take **c** that you do not neglect the Levite as long
12:30 take **c** that you are not snared into imitating them,
Jos 22: 5 Take good **c** to observe the commandment
Jdg 2:22 or not they would take **c** to walk in the way of
19:20 I will **c** for all your wants;
1Sa 25:29 be bound in the bundle of the living under the **c** of
2Sa 6: 9 can the ark of the LORD come into my **c**?"
6:10 to take the ark of the LORD into his **c** in the city
18: 3 For if we flee, they will not **c** about us.
18: 3 If half of us die, they will not **c** about us.
19:24 he had not taken **c** of his feet,
2Ki 6: 9 "Take **c** not to pass this place,
1Ch 13:12 "How can I bring the ark of God into my **c**?"
13:13 not take the ark into his **c** into the city of David;
15:13 because we did not give it proper **c**."
23:28 having the **c** of the courts and the chambers,
26:28 all dedicated gifts were in the **c** of Shelomoth
29: 8 into the **c** of Jehiel the Gershonite.
2Ch 8:18 Huram sent him, in the **c** of his servants,
13:11 and **c** for the golden lampstand so
19: 7 take **c** what you do, for there is no perversion
23:18 Jehoiada assigned the **c** of the house of
Ezr 4:22 Moreover, take **c** not to be slack in this matter;
Job 10:12 and your **c** has preserved my spirit.
21:21 For what do they **c** for their household after them,
Ps 8: 4 mortals that you **c** for them?
Pr 27:18 anyone who takes **c** of a master will be honored.
Jer 2:10 send to Kedar and examine with **c**;
17:21 of your lives, take **c** that you do not bear a burden
30:14 lovers have forgotten you; they **c** nothing for you;
40: 4 come, and I will take good **c** of you;
Zec 6:14 And the crown shall be in the **c** of Heldai,
11:16 up in the land a shepherd who does not **c** for
Mt 18:10 "Take **c** that you do not despise one
25:36 I was sick and you took **c** of me,
25:44 and did not take **c** of you?'
Mk 4:38 "Teacher, do you not **c** that we are perishing?"
Lk 10:34 brought him to an inn, and took **c** of him.
10:35 to the innkeeper, and said, 'Take **c** of him;
10:40 so she came to him and asked, "Lord, do you not **c**
12:15 And he said to them, "Take **c**!
Jn 10:13 because a hired hand does not **c** for the sheep.
Ac 24:23 and not to prevent any of his friends from taking **c**
1Co 3:10 Each builder must choose with **c** how to build
8: 9 But take **c** that this liberty of yours does
12:25 members may have the same **c** for one another.
Gal 5:15 take **c** that you are not consumed by one another.
6: 1 Take **c** that you yourselves are not tempted.
1Th 2: 8 So deeply do we **c** for you that we are determined
1Ti 3: 5 how can he take **c** of God's church?
Heb 2: 6 or mortals, that you **c** for them?
3:12 Take **c**, brothers and sisters,
4: 1 let us take **c** that none of you should seem
Jas 1:27 to **c** for orphans and widows in their distress,
Tob 2:10 and Ahikar took **c** of me for two years
Jdt 2:13 take **c** not to transgress any
12:11 the Hebrew woman who is in your **c** to join us and
AdE 4: 8 being brought up under my **c**—
16: 8 In the future we will take **c**
Wis 5:15 the Most High takes **c** of them.
6:15 on her account will soon be free from **c**,
7: 4 I was nursed with **c** in swaddling cloths.
12:13 whose **c** is for all people,
12:20 if you punished with such great **c** and indulgence
13:13 he takes and carves with **c** in his leisure,
Sir 12:11 take **c** to be on your guard against him.
13: 8 Take **c** not to be led astray and humiliated
18:19 and before you fall ill, take **c** of your health.
28:26 Take **c** not to err with your tongue,
32: 1 Take **c** of them first and then sit down;
38:30 and he takes **c** in firing the kiln.
1Mc 3:33 to take **c** of his son Antiochus until he returned.
11:37 Now therefore take **c** to make a copy of this,
2Mc 7:27 and have taken **c** of you.
1Es 2:28 the city and to take **c** that nothing more be done
6:10 and being completed with all splendor and **c**.
7: 2 supervised the holy work with very great **c**,
8:19 they shall take **c** to give him,
2Es 2:21 **c** for the injured and the weak,
9:46 And I brought him up with much **c**.
10:47 that she brought him up with much **c**,

CAREAH (KJV) See KAREAH

CARED‡ (4) [CARE]

Dt 32:10 he shielded him, **c** for him,
Jn 12: 6 (He said this not because he **c** about the poor,

Ac 27: 3 and allowed him to go to his friends to be c for.
Sir 49:15 even his bones were c for.

CAREFUL (31) [CARE]

Ex 19:12 'Be c not to go up the mountain or to touch
Dt 2: 4 be afraid of you, so, be very c
4:23 So be c not to forget the covenant that
5:32 You must therefore be c to do as
12:28 Be c to obey all these words
15: 9 Be c that you do not entertain a mean thought,
24: 8 of a leprous skin disease by being very c;
Jos 1: 7 being c to act in accordance with all the law
1: 8 so that you may be c to act in accordance with all
22: 3 but have been c to keep the charge of
23:11 Be very c, therefore, to love the LORD your God.
Jdg 13: 4 Now be c not to drink wine or strong drink,
2Ki 10:31 not c to follow the law of the LORD the God
17:37 you shall always be c to observe.
21: 8 if only they will be c to do according to all
1Ch 22:13 Then you will prosper if you are c to observe
2Ch 33: 8 be c to do all that I have commanded them,
Eze 18: 9 and is c to observe my ordinances,
18:19 and has been c to observe all my statutes,
20:19 and be c to observe my ordinances,
20:21 and were not c to observe my ordinances,
36:27 and make you follow my statutes and be c
37:24 They shall follow my ordinances and be c
Eph 5:15 Be c then how you live,
Tit 3: 8 to believe in God may be c to devote themselves
1Pe 1:10 that was to be yours made c search and inquiry,
Sir 13:13 Be on your guard and very c,
29:20 but be c not to fall yourself.
38:26 and he is c about fodder for the heifers.
38:27 and they are c to finish their work.
38:28 and he is c to complete its decoration.

CAREFULLY (16) [CARE]

Ge 43: 7 "The man questioned us c about ourselves
Ex 15:26 "If you will listen c to the voice of
Lev 22: 2 and his sons to deal c with the sacred donations of
Dt 24: 8 you shall c observe whatever
Job 13:17 Listen c to my words, and let my declaration be
21: 2 "Listen c to my words, and let this
Pr 23: 1 observe c what is before you,
Isa 55: 2 Listen c to me, and eat what is good,
Lk 1: 3 investigating everything c from the very first,
15: 8 sweep the house, and search c until she finds it?
Ac 5:35 consider c what you propose to do to these men.
17:23 For as I went through the city and looked c at
2Mc 8:31 and c stored all of them in strategic places;
2Es 9: 1 "Measure c in your mind,
16:30 some clusters may be left by those who search c
4Mc 11:18 He was c stretched tight upon it,

CARELESS (2) [CARE]

Pr 14:16 but the fool throws off restraint and is c.
Mt 12:36 to give an account for every c word you utter;

CARELESSLY (2) [CARE]

Jer 6:14 They have treated the wound of my people c,
8:11 They have treated the wound of my people c,

CARES (11) [CARE]

Ps 94:19 When the c of my heart are many,
142: 4 no refuge remains to me; no one c for me.
Ecc 5: 3 For dreams come with many c,
Jer 30:17 "It is Zion; no one c for her!"
Zec 10: 3 for the LORD of hosts c for his flock,
Mt 13:22 but the c of the world and the lure of wealth choke
Mk 4:19 but the c of the world, and the lure of wealth
Lk 8:14 they are choked by the c and riches and pleasures
Eph 5:29 but he nourishes and tenderly c for it,
1Pe 5: 7 Cast all your anxiety on him, because he c for you.
Wis 8: 9 and encouragement in c and grief.

CARESSED (2)

Eze 23: 3 their breasts were c there,
23:21 and c your young breasts.

CARGO (6)

Jnh 1: 5 They threw the c that was in the ship into the sea,
Ac 21: 3 because the ship was to unload its c there.
27:10 not only of the c and the ship,
27:18 the next day they began to throw the c overboard,
Rev 18:11 since no one buys their c anymore,
18:12 c of gold, silver, jewels

CARIA (1)

1Mc 15:23 and to C, and to Samos, and to Pamphylia,

CARING (2) [CARE]

1Th 2: 7 like a nurse tenderly c for her own children.
2Mc 11:23 the subjects of the kingdom be undisturbed in c

CARITES (2)

2Ki 11: 4 the C and of the guards and had them come to him
11:19 He took the captains, the C, the guards,

CARKAS (1)

Est 1:10 Harbona, Bigtha and Abagtha, Zethar and C,

CARMEL (29) [CARMELITE]

Jos 12:22 king of Kedesh one the king of Jokneam in C one
15:55 Maon, C, Ziph, Juttah,
19:26 on the west it touches C and Shihor-libnath,
1Sa 15:12 and Samuel was told, "Saul went to C,
25: 2 whose property was in C.
25: 2 He was shearing his sheep in C.
25: 5 and David said to the young men, "Go up to C,
25: 7 all the time they were in C.
25:40 When David's servants came to Abigail at C,
27: 3 Ahinoam of Jezreel, and Abigail of C,
30: 5 and Abigail the widow of Nabal of C.
2Sa 2: 2 and Abigail the widow of Nabal of C.
3: 3 Chileab, of Abigail the widow of Nabal of C;
23:35 Hezro of C; Paarai the Arbite;
1Ki 18:19 have all Israel assemble for me at Mount C,
18:20 and assembled the prophets at Mount C.
18:42 Elijah went up to the top of C;
2Ki 2:25 From there he went on to Mount C,
4:25 and came to the man of God at Mount C.
1Ch 11:37 Hezro of C, Naarai son of Ezbai,
SS 7: 5 Your head crowns you like C,
Isa 33: 9 and Bashan and C shake off their leaves.
35: 2 the majesty of C and Sharon.
Jer 46:18 and like C by the sea.
50:19 and it shall feed on C and in Bashan,
Am 1: 2 and the top of C dries up.
9: 3 Though they hide themselves on the top of C,
Na 1: 4 Bashan and C wither, and the bloom of Lebanon
Jdt 1: 8 and those among the nations of C and Gilead,

CARMELITE (1) [CARMEL]

1Ch 3: 1 the second Daniel, by Abigail the C;

CARMI (8) [CARMITES]

Ge 46: 9 Hanoch, Pallu, Hezron, and C.
Ex 6:14 Hanoch, Pallu, Hezron, and C;
Nu 26: 6 of C, the clan of the Carmites.
Jos 7: 1 Achan son of C son of Zabdi son of Zerah,
7:18 and Achan son of C son of Zabdi son of Zerah,
1Ch 2: 7 The sons of C: Achar, the troubler of Israel,
4: 1 sons of Judah: Perez, Hezron, C, Hur, and Shobal.
5: 3 Hanoch, Pallu, Hezron, and C.

CARMITES (1) [CARMI]

Nu 26: 6 of Carmi, the clan of the C.

CARMONIANS (1)

2Es 15:30 Also the C, raging in wrath,

CARNAIM (5)

1Mc 5:26 in Alema and Chaspho, Maked and C"—
5:43 and fled into the sacred precincts at C.
5:44 in them. Thus C was conquered;
2Mc 12:21 and also the baggage to a place called C;
12:26 Then Judas marched against C and the temple

CARNAL (KJV) See FLESH, HUMAN, MATERIAL

CARNALLY (KJV) See INTERCOURSE, [MIND ON THE] FLESH, SEXUAL RELATIONS

CARNELIAN (5)

Ex 28:17 of c, chrysolite, and emerald shall be the first row;
39:10 of c, chrysolite, and emerald was the first row;
Eze 28:13 every precious stone was your covering, c,
Rev 4: 3 And the one seated there looks like jasper and c,
21:20 the sixth c, the seventh chrysolite,

CAROUSED (1) [CAROUSING]

AdE 3:15 And while the king and Haman c together,

CAROUSING (2) [CAROUSED]

Gal 5:21 drunkenness, c, and things like these.
1Pe 4: 3 drunkenness, revels, c, and lawless idolatry.

CARPENTER (3) [CARPENTER'S, CARPENTERS]

Isa 44:13 The c stretches a line, marks it out with a stylus,
Mk 6: 3 Is not this the c, the son of Mary and brother
LtJ 6: 8 Their tongues are smoothed by the c,

CARPENTER'S (1) [CARPENTER]

Mt 13:55 Is not this the c son?

CARPENTERS (10) [CARPENTER]

2Sa 5:11 and c and masons who built David a house.
2Ki 12:11 the c and the builders who worked on the house of
22: 6 to the c, to the builders, to the masons;
1Ch 14: 1 and masons and c to build a house for him.
22:15 c, and all kinds of artisans without number,
2Ch 24:12 and they hired masons and c to restore the house
34:11 to the c and the builders to buy quarried stone,
Ezr 3: 7 So they gave money to the masons and the c,
LtJ 6:45 They are made by c and goldsmiths;
1Es 5:54 They gave money to the masons and the c,

CARPETS (2)

Jdg 5:10 you who sit on rich c and you who walk by
Eze 27:24 and in c of colored material,

CARPUS (1)

2Ti 4:13 bring the cloak that I left with C at Troas,

CARRIED‡ (190) [CARRY]

Ge 22: 6 and he himself c the fire and the knife.
31:26 c away my daughters like captives of the sword.
43:26 they brought him the present that they had c into
46: 5 and the sons of Israel c their father Jacob,
50:13 They c him to the land of Canaan and buried him
Ex 4:20 and Moses c the staff of God in his hand.
22:10 and it dies or is injured or is c off,
25:28 and the table shall be c with these.
27: 7 be on the two sides of the altar when it is c.
Lev 10: 5 They came forward and c them by their tunics out
Nu 7: 9 with the care of the holy things that had to be c on
10:17 who c the tabernacle, set out.
10:21 the Kohathites, who c the holy things, set out;
13:23 and they c it on a pole between two of them.
Dt 1:31 where you saw how the LORD your God c you,
31: 9 who c the ark of the covenant of the LORD,
31:25 Moses commanded the Levites who c the ark of
Jos 3: 3 the covenant of the LORD your God being c by
4: 8 c them over with them to the place
8:33 the levitical priests who c the ark of the covenant
Jdg 3:18 he sent the people who c the tribute on their way.
9:54 the young man who c his armor and said to him,
16: 3 and c them to the top of the hill that is in front
1Sa 14: 1 of Saul said to the young man who c his armor,
14: 6 Jonathan said to the young man who c his armor,
15:11 and has not c out my commands."
15:13 I have c out the command of the LORD."
30: 2 they killed none of them, but c them off,
2Sa 5:21 and David and his men c them away.
6: 3 They c the ark of God on a new cart,
8: 7 the gold shields that were c by the servants
15:29 and Abiathar c the ark of God back to Jerusalem,
20:12 he c Amasa from the highway into a field,
1Ki 2:26 because you c the ark of the Lord GOD
8: 3 and the priests c the ark.
8:46 they are c away captive to the land of the enemy,
9:23 who had charge of the people who c on the work.
10:11 the fleet of Hiram, which c gold from Ophir,
14:28 the guard c them and brought them back to
15:22 they c away the stones of Ramah and its timber,
17:19 c him up into the upper chamber
2Ki 4:20 He c him and brought him to his mother;
5:23 who c them in front of Gehazi.
7: 8 they went into a tent, ate and drank, c off silver,
7: 8 c off things from it, and went and hid them.
9:28 His officers c him in a chariot to Jerusalem,
15:29 and he c the people captive to Assyria.
17: 6 he c the Israelites away to Assyria.
17:11 as the nations did whom the LORD c away
17:26 "The nations that you have c away and placed in
17:27 "Send there one of the priests whom you c away
17:28 So one of the priests whom they had c away
17:33 from among whom they had been c away.
18:11 king of Assyria c the Israelites away to Assyria,
20:17 up until this day, shall be c to Babylon;
23: 4 and c their ashes to Bethel.
23:30 His servants c him dead in a chariot
24:13 He c off all the treasures of the house of
24:14 He c away all Jerusalem, all the officials,
24:15 He c away Jehoiachin to Babylon;
25:11 Nebuzaradan the captain of the guard c into exile
25:13 and c the bronze to Babylon.
1Ch 5: 6 whom King Tilgath-pilneser of Assyria c away
5:18 who c shield and sword, and drew the bow,
5:26 and he c them away, namely, the Reubenites,
8: 6 and they were c into exile to Manahath):
13: 7 They c the ark of God on a new cart,
15:15 the Levites c the ark of God on their shoulders
18: 7 the gold shields that were c by the servants
18:11 together with the silver and gold that he had c off
2Ch 5: 4 and the Levites c the ark.
6:36 that they are c away captive to a land far or near;
14: 8 from Benjamin who c shields and drew bows;
14:13 people of Judah c away a great quantity of booty.
14:15 and c away sheep and goats in abundance,
16: 6 they c away the stones of Ramah and its timber,
17:13 He c out great works in the cities of Judah.
21:17 and c away all the possessions they found
28:17 and defeated Judah, and c away captives.
29:16 and the Levites took them and c them out to
33:14 he c it around Ophel, and raised it to
35:13 and in pans, and c them quickly to all the people.
35:24 and c him in his second chariot and brought him
36: 4 but Neco took his brother Jehoahaz and c him
36: 7 Nebuchadnezzar also c some of the vessels of
Ezr 1: 7 that Nebuchadnezzar had c away from Jerusalem
2: 1 of Babylon had c captive to Babylonia;
5:12 who destroyed this house and c away the people
Ne 2: 1 I c the wine and gave it to the king.
4:17 The burden bearers c their loads in such a way
7: 6 of Babylon had c into exile;
Est 2: 6 Kish had been c away from Jerusalem among
2: 6 the captives c away with King Jeconiah of Judah,
2: 6 King Nebuchadnezzar of Babylon had c away.
Job 1:15 on them and c them off, and killed the servants
1:17 made a raid on the camels and c them off,
10:19 c from the womb to the grave.

Job 20:28 The possessions of their house will be c away,
21:32 When they are c to the grave,
Pr 6:27 be c in the bosom without burning one's clothes?
Isa 8: 4 of Samaria will be c away by the king of Assyria.
23: 7 whose feet c her to settle far away?
39: 6 up until this day, shall be c to Babylon;
46: 3 by me from your birth, c from the womb;
49:22 and your daughters shall be c on their shoulders.
53: 4 he has borne our infirmities and c our diseases;
60: 4 your daughters shall be c on their nurses' arms.
63: 9 he lifted them up and c them all the days of old.
66:12 and you shall nurse and be c on her arm,
Jer 10: 5 they have to be c, for they cannot walk.
22:12 where they have c him captive he shall die,
27:22 They shall be c to Babylon,
28: 3 of Babylon took away from this place and c
35:14 The command has been c out that Jonadab son
35:16 of Jonadab son of Rechab have c out
41:14 the people whom Ishmael had c away captive
41:16 of Nethaniah had c away captive from Mizpah
44:29 that my words against you will surely be c out:
52:15 of the guard c into exile some of the poorest of
52:17 and c all the bronze to Babylon.
La 2:17 he has c out his threat;
Eze 6: 9 among the nations where they are c captive,
17: 4 He c it to a land of trade, set it in a city of
23:14 But she c her whorings further;
23:18 When she c on her whorings so openly
30: 4 and its wealth is c away,
Da 2:35 and the wind c them away,
11:12 When the multitude has been c off,
Hos 10: 6 The thing itself shall be c to Assyria as tribute to
12: 1 they make a treaty with Assyria, and oil is c
Joel 3: 5 and have c my rich treasures into your temples.
Am 1: 6 because they c into exile entire communities,
4:10 I c away your horses; and I made the stench of
Ob 1:11 on the day that strangers c off his wealth,
Mk 2: 3 to him a paralyzed man, c by four of them.
Lk 7:12 a man who had died was being c out.
16:22 The poor man died and was c away by the angels
24:51 he withdrew from them and was c up into heaven.
Jn 20:15 she said to him, "Sir, if you have c him away,
Ac 3: 2 And a man lame from birth was being c in.
5: 6 then c him out and buried him.
5:10 they c her out and buried her beside her husband.
5:15 so that they even c out the sick into the streets,
13:29 When they had c out everything that was written
21:35 of the mob was so great that he had to be c by
Eph 3:11 that he has c out in Christ Jesus our Lord,
Heb 13: 9 not be c away by all kinds of strange teachings;
2Pe 3:17 beware that you are not c away with the error of
Jude 1:12 They are waterless clouds c along by the winds;
Rev 17: 3 So he c me away in the spirit into a wilderness,
21:10 And in the spirit he c me away to a great,
Tob 1:10 After I was c away captive to Assyria and came as
Jdt 4:12 to allow their infants to be c off and their wives to
10:22 with silver lamps c before him.
AdE 16: 4 c away by the boasts of those who know nothing
Wis 5:14 the ungodly is like thistledown c by the wind,
Sir 48:15 until they were c off as plunder from their land,
Bar 1: 8 which had been c away from the temple,
1: 9 of Babylon had c away from Jerusalem Jeconiah
2: 1 So the Lord c out the threat he spoke against us:
2:14 in the sight of those who have c us into exile;
2:24 and you have c out your threats,
4:26 they were taken away like a flock c off by
5: 6 but God will bring them back to you, c in glory,
LtJ 6:26 they are c on the shoulders of others,
Bel 1:36 by the crown of his head and c him by his hair;
1Mc 2: 9 her glorious vessels have been c into exile.
4:30 and of the man who c his armor.
2Mc 3:28 and c him away—this man who had just entered
4:19 Those who c the money, however,
5:21 So Antiochus c off eighteen hundred talents from
7:27 I c you nine months in my womb,
8:31 the rest of the spoils they c to Jerusalem.
9: 8 was brought down to earth and c in a litter,
1Es 1:13 and c them to all the people.
1:41 and c them away, and stored them in his temple
1:54 and the royal stores, and c them away to Babylon.
2:10 that Nebuchadnezzar had c away from Jerusalem
2:15 and they were c back by Sheshbazzar with
5: 7 of Babylon had c away to Babylon
6:16 and c the people away captive to Babylon.
6:26 of the house in Jerusalem and c away to Babylon,
8:60 that had been in Jerusalem c them to the temple of
3Mc 2: 7 in the depths of the sea, but c
3:18 they were c away by their traditional arrogance,
4: 6 and were c away unveiled,
5:19 while it was still night he had c out completely
6:38 So their registration was c out from
2Es 10:22 our righteous men have been c off,
4Mc 15:29 who c away the prize of the contest in your heart!

CARRIERS (1) [CARRY]

2Mc 4:20 but by the decision of its c it was applied to

CARRIES (12) [CARRY]

Lev 11:25 and whoever c any part of the carcass of any
11:28 the one who c the carcass shall wash his clothes
Nu 11:12 as a nurse c a sucking child,'
Dt 1:31 just as one c a child,
Job 21:18 and like chaff that the storm c away?
27:20 in the night a whirlwind c them off.
Isa 40:24 and the tempest c them off like stubble.
Hag 2:12 If one c consecrated meat in the fold
Rev 17: 7 with seven heads and ten horns that c her.
Jdt 12: 4 the supplies I have with me before the Lord c out
Wis 14: 1 of wood more fragile than the ship that c him.
Sir 31: 2 and a severe illness c off sleep.

CARRION (4)

Lev 11:18 the water hen, the desert owl, the c vulture,
Dt 14:17 the c vulture and the cormorant,
Isa 14:19 away from your grave, like loathsome c,
Eze 4:14 nor has c flesh come into my mouth."

CARRY (140) [CARRIED, CARRIERS, CARRIES, CARRYING]

Ge 37:25 and resin, on their way to c it down to Egypt.
42:19 The rest of you shall go and c grain for the famine
43:11 and c them down as a present to the man—
43:12 C back with you the money that was returned in
44: 1 as much as they can c,
45:27 he saw the wagons that Joseph had sent to c him,
46: 5 in the wagons that Pharaoh had sent to c him.
47:30 c me out of Egypt and bury me
50:25 you shall c up my bones from here."
Ex 13:19 then you must c my bones with you from here."
25:14 by which to c the ark.
30: 4 and they shall hold the poles with which to c it.
33:15 do not c us up from here.
37: 5 the poles into the rings on the sides of the ark, to c
37:15 He made the poles of acacia wood to c the table,
37:27 to hold the poles with which to c it.
38: 7 to c it with them; he made it hollow, with boards.
Lev 4:12 he shall c out to a clean place outside the camp,
4:21 He shall c the bull outside the camp,
6:11 c the ashes out to a clean place outside the camp.
10: 4 and c your kinsmen away from the front of
11:40 until the evening; and those who c
15:10 all who c such a thing shall wash their clothes,
Nu 1:50 they are to c the tabernacle and all its equipment,
4:15 after that the Kohathites shall come to c these,
4:15 of the tent of meeting that the Kohathites are to c.
4:25 They shall c the curtains of the tabernacle,
4:27 in all that they are to c,
4:27 to their charge all that they are to c.
4:31 This is what they are charged to c,
4:32 by name the objects that they are required to c.
11:12 to me, 'C them in your bosom, as a nurse carries
11:14 I am not able to c all this people alone,
16:46 and c it quickly to the congregation
Dt 10: 8 of Levi to c the ark of the covenant of the LORD,
17:10 C out exactly the decision that they announce
17:11 You must c out fully the law that they interpret
28:38 You shall c much seed into the field
Jos 4: 3 the place where the priests' feet stood, c them
6: 6 and have seven priests c seven trumpets
Jdg 17: 8 in the hill country of Ephraim to c on his work.
21:21 and each of you c off a wife for himself from
1Sa 17:17 and c them quickly to the camp to your brothers;
20:40 "Go and c them to the city."
28:18 and did not c out his fierce wrath against Amalek,
31: 9 to c the good news to the houses of their idols and
2Sa 13:13 As for me, where could I c my shame?
15:25 "C the ark of God back into the city.
18:19 and c tidings to the king that
18:20 Joab said to him, "You are not to c tidings today;
you may c tidings another day,
1Ki 18:12 spirit of the LORD will c you I know not where;
22:34 and c me out of the battle, for I am wounded."
2Ki 4:19 father said to his servant, "C him to his mother."
1Ch 10: 9 to c the good news to their idols and to the people.
15: 2 that no one but the Levites were to c the ark
15: 2 for the LORD had chosen them to c the ark of
15:13 Because you did not c it the first time,
23:26 so the Levites no longer need to c the tabernacle
2Ch 18:33 and c me out of the battle, for I am wounded."
20:25 for themselves until they could c no more.
29: 5 and c out the filth from the holy place.
35: 3 you need no longer c it on your shoulders.
Job 15:12 Why does your heart c you away,
24:10 though hungry, they c the sheaves;
31:36 Surely I would c it on my shoulder;
Ps 28: 9 be their shepherd, and c them forever.
37: 7 over those who c out evil devices.
49:17 For when they die they will c nothing away;
Ecc 5:15 which they may c away with their hands.
10:20 for a bird of the air may c your voice,
Isa 5:29 they growl and seize their prey, they c it off,
15: 7 they c away over the Wadi of the Willows.
30: 1 says the LORD, who c out a plan, but not mine;
30: 6 they c their riches on the backs of donkeys,
40:11 and c them in his bosom, and gently lead the
41:16 and the wind shall c them away,
44:28 and he shall c out all my purpose";
45:20 those who c about their wooden idols,
46: 1 these things you c are loaded as burdens
46: 4 even when you turn gray I will c you.
46: 4 I will c and will save.
46: 7 They lift it to their shoulders, they c it,
52:11 you who c the vessels of the LORD.
57:13 The wind will c them off,
Jer 17:22 not c a burden out of your houses on the sabbath
17:27 to c in no burden through the gates of Jerusalem
20: 4 he shall c them captive to Babylon,
20: 5 and seize them, and c them to Babylon.
43:12 and he shall burn them and c them away captive;
46: 9 Ethiopia and Put who c the shield, the Ludim,
49:29 c off their camels for yourselves,
Eze 12: 5 and c the baggage through it.
12: 6 and c it out in the dark;
12:12 he shall dig through the wall and c it through;
23:43 but they c on their sexual acts with her.
29:19 and he shall c off its wealth and despoil it
32: 9 as I c you captive among the nations,
32:20 c away both it and its hordes.
38:12 to seize spoil and c off plunder;
38:13 Have you assembled your horde to c off plunder,
38:13 to c away silver and gold,
Da 11: 8 he shall c off to Egypt as spoils of war.
11:10 and again shall c the war as far as his fortress.
Hos 5:14 I will c off, and no one shall rescue.
Mt 3:11 I am not worthy to c his sandals.
5:33 but c out the vows you have made to the Lord.'
27:32 they compelled this man to c his cross.
Mk 11:16 and he would not allow anyone to c anything
15:21 in from the country, to c his cross;
Lk 10: 4 C no purse, no bag, no sandals;
14:27 not c the cross and follow me cannot
23:26 and made him c it behind Jesus.
Jn 5:10 it is not lawful for you to c your mat."
Ac 5: 9 and they will c you out."
13:22 who will c out all my wishes.'
Gal 6: 5 For all must c their own loads.
6:17 for I c the marks of Jesus branded on my body.
2Ti 4: 5 of an evangelist, c out your ministry fully.
Heb 9: 6 into the first tent to c out their ritual duties;
Rev 17:17 into their hearts to c out his purpose by agreeing
Jdt 2:13 but c them out exactly as I have ordered you;
10: 5 up all her dishes and gave them to her to c.
13: 5 to help your heritage and to c out my design
Sir 6:25 Bend your shoulders and c her,
37: 5 yet in battle they will c his shield.
LtJ 6: 4 which people c on their shoulders,
6:62 over the whole world, they c out his command.
2Mc 3: 8 but in fact to c out the king's purpose.
4:19 to c three hundred silver drachmas for
4:23 to c the money to the king and to complete
9:10 to c the man who a little while before had thought
15:17 not to c on a campaign but to attack bravely,
15:30 to cut off Nicanor's head and arm and c them
1Es 1: 4 "You need no longer c it on your shoulders.
8:13 to c to Jerusalem the gifts for the Lord of Israel
3Mc 1: 2 determined to c out the plot he had devised,
5: 4 proceeded faithfully to c out the orders.
2Es 4:19 and the locale of the sea a place to c its waves."
15:63 They shall c your children away captive,

CARRYING (38) [CARRY]

Ge 37:25 with their camels c gum, balm, and resin,
Ex 25:27 the poles used for c the table shall be close to
32:15 c the two tablets of the covenant in his hands,
37:14 that held the poles used for c the table were close
Nu 4:10 and put it on the c frame.
4:12 and put them on the c frame.
4:49 to their several tasks of serving or c;
8:26 in the tent of meeting in c out their duties,
Jos 6: 8 the seven priests c the seven trumpets
6:13 The seven priests c the seven trumpets
1Sa 10: 3 one c three kids, another c three loaves of bread,
and another c a skin of wine.
14: 3 the priest of the LORD in Shiloh, c an ephod.
2Sa 15:24 c the ark of the covenant of God.
16: 1 c two hundred loaves of bread,
2Ki 10:30 you have done well in c out what I consider right,
16: 9 c its people captive to Kir; then he killed Rezin.
1Ch 15:26 the Levites who were c the ark of the covenant of
15:27 as also were all the Levites who were c the ark,
2Ch 28:15 and c all the feeble among them on donkeys,
Ps 126: 6 with shouts of joy, c their sheaves.
Eze 12: 7 c it on my shoulder in their sight.
Mt 9: 2 then some people were c a paralyzed man lying on
11:28 all you that are weary and are c heavy burdens,
Mk 14:13 and a man c a jar of water will meet you;
Lk 5:18 c a paralyzed man on a bed.
22:10 a man c a jar of water will meet you;
Jn 19:17 and c the cross by himself,
Ac 27:43 kept them from c out their plan.
2Co 4:10 always c in the body the death of Jesus,
Jdt 2: 1 about c out his revenge on the whole region,
AdE 15: 4 while the other followed, c her train.
Wis 18:16 c the sharp sword of your authentic command,
1Mc 5:30 c ladders and engines of war to capture
2Mc 10: 7 c ivy-wreathed wands and beautiful branches and
15: 5 he did not succeed in c out his abominable design.
4Mc 15:31 c the world in the universal flood,

CARSHENA (1)

Est 1:14 and those next to him were C,

CART (16) [CARTS]

1Sa 6: 7 a new c and two milch cows that have never borne
6: 7 and yoke the cows to the c,
6: 8 Take the ark of the LORD and place it on the c,
6:10 and yoked them to the c,
6:11 They put the ark of the LORD on the c,
6:14 c came into the field of Joshua of Beth-shemesh,
6:14 of the c and offered the cows as a burnt offering to
2Sa 6: 3 They carried the ark of God on a new c,
6: 3 the sons of Abinadab, were driving the new c
1Ch 13: 7 They carried the ark of God on a new c,
13: 7 and Uzzah and Ahio were driving the c.
Isa 5:18 who drag sin along as with c ropes,
28:27 nor is a c wheel rolled over cummin;

Isa 28:28 one drives the **c** wheel and horses over it,
Am 2:13 just as a **c** presses down when it is full of sheaves.
Sir 33: 5 The heart of a fool is like a **c** wheel,

CARTS (2) [CART]

Jdt 15:11 and hitched up her **c** and piled the things on them.
1Es 5:55 and **c** to the Sidonians and the Tyrians,

CARVE (1) [CARVED, CARVES, CARVING, CARVINGS]

Dt 10: 1 "**C** out two tablets of stone like the former ones,

CARVED (30) [CARVE]

Lev 26: 1 and erect no **c** images or pillars, and you shall
1Ki 6:29 He **c** the walls of the house all around about with **c** engravings of cherubim,
6:35 He **c** cherubim, palm trees, and open flowers,
6:35 with gold evenly applied upon the **c** work.
7:36 of its stays and on its borders he **c** cherubim,
2Ki 17:41 but also served their **c** images;
21: 7 The **c** image of Asherah that he had made he set in
2Ch 3: 7 and he **c** cherubim on the walls.
3:10 In the most holy place he made two **c** cherubim
33: 7 The **c** image of the idol that he had made he set in
34: 3 the sacred poles, and the **c** and the cast images.
34: 4 the sacred poles and the **c** and the cast images;
Ps 74: 6 they smashed all its **c** work.
Isa 42:17 those who trust in **c** images,
44:15 makes it a **c** image and bows down before it.
48: 5 not say, "My idol did them, my **c** image
Eze 23:14 she saw male figures **c** on the wall,
41:19 They were **c** on the whole temple all around;
41:20 cherubim and palm trees were **c** on the wall.
41:25 of the nave were **c** cherubim and palm trees, such as were **c** on the walls;
Na 1:14 the house of your gods I will cut off the **c** image
Wis 14:16 of monarchs **c** images were worshiped.
15:13 from earthy matter fragile vessels and **c** images.
1Mc 5:68 and the **c** images of their gods he burned with fire;
13:29 and beside the suits of armor he **c** ships,
2Es 13: 6 And I looked and saw that he **c** out for himself
13: 7 or place from which the mountain was **c**,
13:36 as you saw the mountain **c** out without hands.

CARVES (1) [CARVE]

Wis 13:13 he takes and **c** with care in his leisure,

CARVING (3) [CARVE]

Ex 31: 5 and in **c** wood, in every kind of craft.
35:33 and in **c** wood, in every kind of craft.
Isa 22:16 and **c** a habitation for yourself in the rock?

CARVINGS (3) [CARVE]

1Ki 6:18 the house had **c** of gourds and open flowers;
6:32 with **c** of cherubim, palm trees, and open flowers;
7:31 At its opening there were **c**;

CASE (81) [CASES]

Ex 18:22 let them bring every important **c** to you, but decide every minor **c** themselves.
18:26 but any minor **c** they decided themselves.
22: 9 In any **c** of disputed ownership involving ox,
22: 9 the **c** of both parties shall come before God;
Nu 27: 5 Moses brought their **c** before the LORD.
Dt 1:17 Any **c** that is too hard for you, bring to me,
6:24 so as to keep us alive, as is now the **c**.
17: 9 they shall announce to you the decision in the **c**.
19: 4 the **c** of a homicide who might flee there and live,
22:26 because this **c** is like that of someone who attacks
29:28 and cast them into another land, as is now the **c**."
Jos 20: 4 and explain the **c** to the elders of that city;
1Sa 25:39 the LORD who has judged the **c** of Nabal's insult
2Sa 20:21 That is not the **c**!
2Ch 8: 8 for forced labor, as is still the **c** today.
19:10 a **c** comes to you from your kindred who live
Ezr 9: 7 to plundering, and to utter shame, as is now the **c**.
9:15 but we have escaped as a remnant, as is now the **c**.
Job 13: 3 and I desire to argue my **c** with God.
13: 8 will you plead the **c** for God?
13:18 I have indeed prepared my **c**;
23: 4 I would lay my **c** before him,
35:14 that the **c** is before him,
36:17 "But you are obsessed with the **c** of the wicked;
37:19 we cannot draw up our **c** because of darkness.
Ps 5: 3 in the morning I plead my **c** to you, and watch.
Pr 18:17 The one who first states a **c** seems right,
25: 9 Argue your **c** with your neighbor directly,
Ecc 4: 8 **c** of solitary individuals, without sons or brothers;
Isa 3:13 The LORD rises to argue his **c**;
41:21 Set forth your **c**, says the LORD;
43:26 set forth your **c**, so that you may be proved right.
45:21 Declare and present your **c**;
Jer 12: 1 but let me put my **c** to you.
La 3:36 one's **c** is subverted —does the Lord not see it?
Eze 9: 2 with a writing **c** at his side.
9: 3 who had the writing **c** at his side;
9:11 with the writing **c** at his side, brought back word,
Mic 6: 1 Rise, plead your **c** before the mountains,
Mt 13:23 in one **c** a hundredfold, in another sixty,
19:10 "If such is the **c** of a man with his wife,
Lk 12:58 on the way make an effort to settle the **c**,
14: 8 in **c** someone more distinguished than you
14:12 in **c** they may invite you in return,
Jn 18:38 "I find no **c** against him.
19: 4 to let you know that I find no **c** against him."
19: 6 I find no **c** against him."
Ac 5:38 So in the present **c**, I tell you,
5:39 in that **c** you may even be found fighting
23:15 to make a more thorough examination of his **c**.
23:20 to inquire more thoroughly into his **c**.
24: 1 they reported their **c** against Paul to the governor.
24:22 the tribune comes down, I will decide your **c**."
25:14 Festus laid Paul's **c** before the king, saying,
28:18 there was no reason for the death penalty in my **c**.
1Co 7:15 in such a **c** the brother or sister is not bound.
9:15 so that they may be applied in my **c**.
2Co 4: 4 In their **c** the god of this world has blinded
9: 3 to have been empty in this **c**, so that you may
Gal 5:11 that **c** the offense of the cross has been removed.
Php 4:14 In any **c**, it was kind of you to share my distress.
2Ti 2: 5 And in the **c** of an athlete,
3: 9 because, as in the **c** of those two men,
Heb 6: 9 we are confident of better things in your **c**,
7: 8 In the one **c**, tithes are received
Sir 8: 2 in **c** their resources outweigh yours;
11: 9 and do not sit with sinners when they judge a **c**.
33:20 in **c** you change your mind and must ask for it.
35:25 the **c** of his people and makes them rejoice
LtJ 6:64 either to decide a **c** or to do good to anyone.
Sus 1: 6 and all who had a **c** to be tried came to them there.
2Mc 2: 8 as they were shown in the **c** of Moses,
2:29 such in my judgment is the **c** with us.
3:13 said that this money must in any **c** be confiscated
4:44 three men sent by the senate presented the **c**
6:14 the **c** of the other nations the Lord waits patiently
2Es 4:20 but why have you not judged so in your own **c**?
8:51 But think of your own **c**,
4Mc 5:21 for in either **c** the law is equally despised.
15:11 in the **c** of none of them were

CASEMENT (KJV) See LATTICE

CASES (11) [CASE]

Ex 18:19 and you should bring their **c** before God;
18:26 hard **c** they brought to Moses,
Nu 5:29 This is the law in **c** of jealousy, when a wife,
Dt 21: 5 by their decision all **c** of dispute and assault shall
2Ch 19: 8 for the LORD and to decide disputed **c**.
1Co 6: 2 are you incompetent to try trivial **c**?
6: 4 If you have ordinary **c**, then,
7: 2 But because of **c** of sexual immorality,
Sir Pr: 2 and to be indulgent in **c** where,
22:22 in these **c** any friend will take to flight.
1Es 9:17 And the **c** of the men who had foreign wives

CASIPHIA (2)

Ezr 8:17 the leader at the place called **C**,
8:17 and his colleagues the temple servants at **C**,

CASLUHIM (2)

Ge 10:14 **C**, and Caphtorim, from which
1Ch 1:12 **C**, and Caphtorim, from whom

CASPIN (1)

2Mc 12:13 inhabited by all sorts of Gentiles. Its name was **C**.

CASSIA (4)

Ex 30:24 and five hundred of **c**—measured by the
Ps 45: 8 with myrrh and aloes and **c**.
Eze 27:19 wrought iron, **c**, and sweet cane were bartered
Sir 24:15 Like **c** and camel's thorn I gave forth perfume,

CAST‡ (193) [CAST-OFF, CASTING, CASTS, DOWNCAST, OUTCAST, OUTCASTS]

Ge 21:10 "**C** out this slave woman with her son;
21:15 she **c** the child under one of the bushes.
39: 7 after a time his master's wife **c** her eyes on Joseph
Ex 15: 4 "Pharaoh's chariots and his army he **c** into the sea;
25:12 You shall **c** four rings of gold for it and put them
26:37 and you shall **c** five bases of bronze for them.
32: 4 formed it in a mold, and **c** an image of a calf;
32: 8 they have **c** for themselves an image of a calf,
34:17 You shall not make **c** idols.
34:24 For I will **c** out nations before you,
36:36 and he **c** for them four bases of silver.
37: 3 He **c** for it four rings of gold for its four feet,
37:13 He **c** for it four rings of gold,
38: 5 He **c** four rings on the four corners of
Lev 16: 8 and Aaron shall **c** lots on the two goats,
19: 4 not turn to idols or make **c** images for yourselves:
Nu 33:52 destroy all their **c** images,
Dt 9:12 they have **c** an image for themselves."
29:28 and **c** them into another land, as is now the case."
Jos 7:25 they burned them with fire, **c** stones on them,
18: 6 and I will **c** lots for you here before
18: 8 and I will **c** lots for you here before the LORD
18:10 and Joshua **c** lots for them in Shiloh before
Jdg 6:13 But now the LORD has **c** us off,
17: 3 to make an idol of **c** metal."
17: 4 who made it into an idol of **c** metal;
18:14 teraphim, and an idol of **c** metal?
18:17 to enter and take the idol of **c** metal,
18:18 into Micah's house and took the idol of **c** metal,
1Sa 12:22 For the LORD will not **c** away his people,
14:42 "**C** the lot between me and my son Jonathan."
1Ki 7:15 He **c** two pillars of bronze.
7:24 there were two rows of panels, **c** when it was **c**.
7:30 supports were **c** with wreaths at the side of each.
7:33 their rims, their spokes, and their hubs were all **c**.
7:37 all of them were **c** alike,
7:46 In the plain of the Jordan the king **c** them,
9: 7 that I have consecrated for my name I will **c** out
14: 9 and **c** images, provoking me to anger,
2Ki 17:16 and made for themselves **c** images of two calves;
19:32 or **c** up a siege ramp against it.
21:14 I will **c** off the remnant of my heritage,
1Ch 24:31 These also **c** lots corresponding to their kindred,
25: 8 And they **c** lots for their duties, small and great,
26:13 and they **c** lots by ancestral houses,
26:14 They **c** lots also for his son Zechariah,
2Ch 4: 3 there were two rows of panels, **c** when it was **c**.
4:17 In the plain of the Jordan the king **c** them,
7:20 I will **c** out of my sight,
28: 2 He even made **c** images for the Baals;
34: 3 the sacred poles, and the carved and the **c** images.
34: 4 the sacred poles and the carved and the **c** images;
Ne 9:18 when they had **c** an image of a calf for themselves
9:26 against you and **c** your law behind their backs
10:34 We have also **c** lots among the priests, the Levites,
11: 1 the rest of the people **c** lots to bring one out of ten
Est 3: 7 the twelfth year of King Ahasuerus, they **c** Pur—
9:24 against the Jews to destroy them, and had **c** Pur—
Job 6:27 You would even **c** lots over the orphan,
15:33 and **c** off their blossoms, like the olive tree.
19: 3 These ten times you have **c** reproach upon me;
30:11 they have **c** off restraint in my presence.
30:19 He has **c** me into the mire,
41:23 it is firmly **c** and immovable.
Ps 2: 3 and **c** their cords from us."
5:10 because of their many transgressions **c** them out,
17:11 they set their eyes to **c** me to the ground.
18:42 I **c** them out like the mire of the streets.
22:10 On you I was **c** from my birth,
22:18 and for my clothing they **c** lots.
27: 9 Do not **c** me off, do not forsake me,
42: 5 Why are you **c** down, O my soul,
42: 6 My soul is **c** down within me;
42:11 Why are you **c** down, O my soul,
43: 2 why have you **c** me off?
43: 5 Why are you **c** down, O my soul,
44:23 Awake, do not **c** us off forever!
50:17 and you **c** my words behind you.
51:11 Do not **c** me away from your presence,
55:22 **C** your burden on the LORD,
55:23 you, O God, will **c** them down into the lowest pit;
56: 7 in wrath **c** down the peoples, O God!
71: 9 Do not **c** me off in the time of old age;
74: 1 why do you **c** us off forever?
88:14 O LORD, why do you **c** me off?
106:19 a calf at Horeb and worshiped a **c** image.
Pr 16:33 The lot is **c** into the lap,
29:18 there is no prophecy, the people **c** off restraint,
Isa 14:19 but you are **c** out, away from your grave,
19: 8 all who **c** hooks in the Nile will lament,
25: 7 that is **c** over all peoples, the sheet that is spread
25:12 laid low, **c** to the ground, even to the dust.
34: 3 Their slain shall be **c** out,
34:17 He has **c** the lot for them,
37:33 or **c** up a siege ramp against it.
38: 8 I will make the shadow **c** by the declining sun on
38:17 for you have **c** all my sins behind your back.
41: 9 I have chosen you and not **c** you off";
42:17 who say to **c** images, "You are our gods."
44:10 a god or **c** an image that can do no good?
48: 5 and my **c** image commanded them."
54: 6 like the wife of a man's youth when she is **c** off,
Jer 6: 6 **c** up a siege ramp against Jerusalem.
7:15 And I will **c** you out of my sight, just as I **c** out all your kinsfolk,
9:19 because they have **c** down our dwellings."
22: 7 down your choicest cedars and **c** them into
22:28 and his offspring hurled out and **c** away in a land
23:33 "You are the burden, and I will **c** you off,
23:39 I will surely lift you up and **c** you away
32:24 the siege ramps have been **c** up against the city
36:30 and his dead body shall be **c** out to the heat by day
Eze 4: 2 and **c** up a ramp against it;
17:17 when ramps are **c** up and siege walls built
18:31 **C** away from you all the transgressions
19:12 it was plucked up in fury, **c** down to the ground;
20: 7 **C** away the detestable things your eyes feast on,
20: 8 not one of them **c** away
21:22 to **c** up ramps, to build siege towers.
23:35 Because you have forgotten me and **c** me
26: 8 **c** up a ramp against you,
26:12 Your stones and timber and soil they shall **c** into
28:16 so I **c** you as a profane thing from the mountain
28:17 I **c** you to the ground; I exposed you before kings,
31:11 as its wickedness deserves. I have **c** it out.
31:16 when I **c** it down to Sheol with those who go
Da 8:12 it **c** truth to the ground,
Hos 7:12 As they go, I will **c** my net over them;
13: 2 on sinning and make a **c** image for themselves,
Joel 3: 3 and **c** lots for my people,
Am 1:11 with the sword and **c** off all pity;
8: 3 dead bodies shall be many, **c** out in every place.
Ob 1:11 and foreigners entered his gates and **c** lots
Jnh 1: 7 sailors said to one another, "Come, let us **c** lots,
1: 7 So they **c** lots, and the lot fell on Jonah.
2: 3 You **c** me into the deep, into the heart of the seas,
Mic 2: 5 Therefore you will have no one to **c** the line by lot
4: 7 and those who were **c** off, a strong nation;

Mic 7:19 You will c all our sins into the depths of the sea.
Na 1:14 the carved image and the c image.
3:10 lots were c for her nobles,
Hab 2:18 a c image, a teacher of lies?
Mt 7:22 and c out demons in your name,
8:16 and he c out the spirits with a word,
8:31 The demons begged him, "If you c us out,
9:33 And when the demon had been c out,
10:1 to c them out, and to cure every disease
10:8 raise the dead, cleanse the lepers, c out demons.
12:27 If I c out demons by Beelzebul, by whom do your own exorcists c them out?
12:28 if it is by the Spirit of God that I c out demons,
17:19 "Why could we not c it out?"
17:27 go to the sea and c a hook;
Mk 1:34 with various diseases, and c out many demons;
3:15 and to have authority to c out demons.
3:23 "How can Satan c out Satan?
6:13 They c out many demons,
7:26 She begged him to c the demon out
9:18 and I asked your disciples to c it out,
9:22 It has often c him into the fire and into the water,
9:28 "Why could we not c it out?"
16:9 ⟦from whom he had c out seven demons.⟧
16:17 ⟦by using my name they will c out demons;⟧
Lk 9:40 I begged your disciples to c it out,
11:18 you say that I c out the demons by Beelzebul.
11:19 Now if I c out the demons by Beelzebul, by whom do your exorcists c them out?
11:20 it is by the finger of God that I c out the demons,
12:5 after he has killed, has authority to c into hell.
23:34 And they c lots to divide his clothing.
Jn 19:24 but c lots for it to see who will get it."
19:24 and for my clothing they c lots."
21:6 "C the net to the right side of the boat,
21:6 So they c it, and now they were not able to haul it
Ac 1:26 they c lots for them, and the lot fell on Matthias;
26:10 in prison, but I also c my vote against them
27:40 So they c off the anchors and left them in the sea.
1Pe 5:7 C all your anxiety on him, because he cares for you
2Pe 2:4 but c them into hell and committed them to chains
Rev 4:10 they c their crowns before the throne, singing,
AdE 9:24 how he made a decree and c lots to destroy them,
Wis 10:19 and c them up from the depth of the sea.
11:14 before had been c out and exposed,
Sir 37:8 He may c the lot against you
LtJ 6:24 even when they were being c, they did not feel it.
2Mc 5:8 he was c ashore in Egypt.
5:10 He who had c out many to lie unburied had no one
2Es 1:30 I will c you out from my presence.
5:7 and the Dead Sea shall c up fish;
10:22 our little ones have been c out,
14:14 c away from you the burdens of humankind,

CAST-OFF (2) [CAST]
Wis 13:12 burn the c pieces of his work to prepare his food,
13:13 But a c piece from among them,

CASTANETS (1)
2Sa 6:5 and harps and tambourines and c and cymbals.

CASTAWAY (KJV) See DISQUALIFIED

CASTIGATION (1)
2Es 15:12 because of the plague of chastisement and c that

CASTING (16) [CAST]
Ex 38:27 of silver were for c the bases of the sanctuary,
Lev 18:24 for by all these practices the nations I am c out
Dt 9:16 by c for yourselves an image of a calf;
Pr 18:18 C the lot puts an end to disputes and decides
Mt 4:18 c a net into the sea—for they were fishermen.
27:35 divided his clothing among themselves by c lots;
Mk 1:16 he saw Simon and his brother Andrew c a net into
1:39 in their synagogues and c out demons.
9:38 we saw someone c out demons in your name,
15:24 c lots to decide what each should take.
Lk 9:49 we saw someone c out demons in your name,
11:14 Now he was c out a demon that was mute;
13:32 I am c out demons and performing cures today
Jude 1:13 c up the foam of their own shame;
AdE 3:7 Haman came to a decision by c lots,
Sir 6:21 and they will not delay in c her aside.

CASTLE (2)
Pr 18:19 such quarreling is like the bars of a c.
Lk 11:21 When a strong man, fully armed, guards his c,

CASTLE[S] (KJV) See FORT, FORTRESS

CASTOR See Index to Footnotes

CASTRATE (1)
Gal 5:12 I wish those who unsettle you would c themselves!

CASTS (16) [CAST]
Dt 18:11 or one who c spells, or who consults ghosts
27:15 be anyone who makes an idol or c an image,
Job 16:11 and c me into the hands of the wicked.
20:15 God c them out of their bellies.
Ps 147:6 he c the wicked to the ground.
Pr 21:12 he c the wicked down to ruin.
Isa 26:5 He lays it low to the ground, c it to the dust.
40:19 A workman c it, and a goldsmith overlays it
40:19 and c for it silver chains.
Mt 9:34 "By the ruler of the demons he c out the demons."
12:24 that this fellow c out the demons."
12:26 If Satan c out Satan, he is divided against himself;
Mk 3:22 and by the ruler of the demons he c out demons."
Lk 11:15 "He c out demons by Beelzebul,
1Jn 4:18 but perfect love c out fear;
Tob 4:19 he c down to deepest Hades.

CASUALTIES (2)
Jdg 20:31 As before they began to inflict c on the troops,
20:39 Benjamin had begun to inflict c on the Israelites,

CATAPULT (4) [CATAPULTS]
Wis 5:22 of wrath will be hurled as from a c;
4Mc 9:26 they bound him to the torture machine and c.
11:9 the guards bound him and dragged him to the c;
18:20 the daughter of Abraham to the c and back again

CATAPULTS (3) [CATAPULT]
1Mc 6:51 machines to shoot arrows, and c.
4Mc 8:13 rack and hooks and c and caldrons,
11:26 Your fire is cold to us, and the c painless,

CATARACTS (1)
Ps 42:7 Deep calls to deep at the thunder of your c;

CATASTROPHE (1)
Jdt 8:19 and so they suffered a great c before our enemies.

CATCH‡ (17) [CATCHES, CATCHING, CAUGHT]
Nu 11:22 Are there enough fish in the sea to c for them?"
1Sa 17:35 and if it turned against me, I would c it by the jaw,
SS 2:15 C us the foxes, the little foxes,
Jer 2:34 though you did not c them breaking in.
5:26 Like fowlers they set a trap; they c human beings.
16:16 says the LORD, and they shall c them;
18:22 For they have dug a pit to c me,
Eze 19:3 and he learned to c prey; he devoured humans.
19:6 and he learned to c prey; he devoured people.
Lk 5:4 into the deep water and let down your nets for a c."
5:9 and all who were with him were amazed at the c
11:54 to c him in something he might say.
21:34 and that day c you unexpectedly,
Tob 6:4 "C hold of the fish and hang on to it!"
AdE 16:14 that by these methods he would c us undefended
Sir 27:19 and will not c him again.
Sus 1:58 Under what tree did you c them being intimate

CATCHES (3) [CATCH]
Ex 22:6 When fire breaks out and c in thorns so that
1Co 3:19 it is written, "He c the wise in their craftiness,"
Sir 34:2 As one who c at a shadow and pursues the wind,

CATCHING (1) [CATCH]
Lk 5:10 from now on you will be c people."

CATERPILLAR (4)
1Ki 8:37 if there is plague, blight, mildew, locust, or c;
2Ch 6:28 if there is plague, blight, mildew, locust, or c;
Ps 78:46 He gave their crops to the c,
Isa 33:4 Spoil was gathered as the c gathers;

CATERPILLER[S] (KJV) See LOCUST

CATHUA (1)
1Es 5:30 the descendants of C, the descendants of Geddur,

CATS (1)
LtJ 6:22 alight on their bodies and heads; and so do c.

CATTLE (68)
Ge 1:24 c and creeping things and wild animals of
1:25 and the c of every kind,
1:26 and over the birds of the air, and over the c,
2:20 The man gave names to all c,
30:29 and how your c have fared with me.
33:14 the pace of the c that are before me and according
33:17 and made booths for his c;
34:5 but his sons were with his c in the field,
36:6 and all the members of his household, his c,
47:18 and the herds of c are my lord's.
Lev 22:19 of the c or the sheep or the goats.
Nu 31:9 and they took all their c, their flocks,
32:1 and the Gadites owned a very great number of c.
32:1 and the land of Gilead was a good place for c,
32:4 is a land for c; and your servants have c."
35:3 and their pasture lands shall be for their c,
Dt 7:13 the increase of your c and the issue of your flock,
28:4 the increase of your c and the issue of your flock.
28:18 the increase of your c and the issue of your flock.
28:51 the increase of your c and the issue of your flock,
1Sa 8:16 and the best of your c and donkeys,
15:9 best of the sheep and of the c and of the fatlings,
15:14 and the lowing of c that I hear?"
15:15 the people spared the best of the sheep and the c,
15:21 But from the spoil the people took sheep and c,
1Sa 30:20 which were driven ahead of the other c;
1Ki 1:9 oxen, and fatted c by the stone Zoheleth,
1:19 He has sacrificed oxen, fatted c,
1:25 fatted c, and sheep in abundance,
4:23 and twenty pasture-fed c, one hundred sheep,
2Ki 3:17 so that you shall drink, you, your c,
1Ch 5:9 their c had multiplied in the land of Gilead.
7:21 because they came down to raid their c.
28:1 of all the property and c of the king and his sons,
2Ch 31:6 in the cities of Judah also brought in the tithe of c
32:28 and stalls for all kinds of c, and sheepfolds.
Job 18:3 Why are we counted as c?
Ps 50:10 the c on a thousand hills.
78:48 He gave over their c to the hail,
104:14 You cause the grass to grow for the c,
107:38 and he does not let their c decrease.
144:14 and may our c be heavy with young.
148:10 Wild animals and all c, creeping things
Isa 7:25 but they will become a place where c are let loose
30:23 On that day your c will graze in broad pastures;
46:1 Nebo stoops, their idols are on beasts and c;
63:14 Like c that go down into the valley,
Jer 9:10 and the lowing of c is not heard;
49:32 their herds of c a spoil.
Eze 32:13 nor shall the hoofs of c trouble them.
38:12 who are acquiring c and goods,
38:13 to take away c and goods,
Joel 1:18 of c wander about because there is no pasture
Jn 2:14 In the temple he found people selling c, sheep,
2:15 both the sheep and the c.
Rev 18:13 olive oil, choice flour and wheat, c and sheep,
Tob 1:6 the firstlings of the flock, the tithes of the c, and
Jdt 4:10 They and their wives and their children and their c
11:7 the field and the c and the birds of the air will live,
Sir 7:22 Do you have c? Look after them;
40:19 C and orchards make one prosperous;
Aza 1:59 Bless the Lord, all wild animals and c;
1Es 2:7 with gifts and with horses and c,
2:9 with silver and gold, with horses and c,
2Es 6:53 before you c, wild animals, and creeping things;
7:65 but let the c and the flocks rejoice.
8:29 the destruction of those who have the ways of c,

CAUDA (1)
Ac 27:16 of a small island called C we were scarcely able

CAUGHT‡ (60) [CATCH]
Ge 22:13 c in a thicket by its horns.
31:23 and pursued him for seven days until he c up
39:12 she c hold of his garment,
Ex 22:7 then the thief, if c, shall pay double.
22:8 If the thief is not c, the owner of the house
Nu 5:13 against her since she was not c in the act;
Dt 22:22 If a man is c lying with the wife of another man,
22:28 and they are c in the act,
24:7 If someone is c kidnaping another Israelite,
Jdg 1:6 but they pursued him, and c him,
8:14 he c a young man, one of the people of Succoth,
15:4 So Samson went and c three hundred foxes,
15:14 on his arms became like flax that has c fire,
1Sa 15:27 Saul c hold of the hem of his robe, and it tore.
2Sa 18:9 His head c fast in the oak,
2Ki 2:16 of the LORD has c him up and thrown him down
4:27 she c hold of his feet.
Job 36:8 And if they are bound in fetters and c in the cords
Ps 9:15 in the net that they hid has their own foot been c.
10:2 let them be c in the schemes they have devised.
Pr 3:26 and will keep your foot from being c.
5:22 and they are c in the toils of their sin.
6:2 c by the words of your mouth.
6:31 Yet if they are c, they will pay sevenfold;
Ecc 9:12 and like birds c in a snare,
Isa 13:15 and whoever is c will fall by the sword.
24:18 and whoever climbs out of the pit shall be c in
Jer 2:26 As a thief is shamed when c,
48:27 though he was not c among thieves;
48:44 and everyone who climbs out of the pit shall be c
50:24 You set a snare for yourself and you were c,
Eze 12:13 and he shall be c in my snare;
17:20 and he shall be c in my snare;
19:4 he was c in their pit;
19:8 he was c in their pit.
Am 3:4 from its den, if it has c nothing?
Mt 13:47 like a net that was thrown into the sea and c fish
14:31 and c him, saying to him, "You
Mk 14:51 but a linen cloth. They c hold of him,
Lk 5:5 we have worked all night long but have c nothing.
5:6 they c so many fish that their nets were beginning
Jn 8:3 ⟦brought a woman who had been c in adultery;⟧
8:4 ⟦this woman was c in the very act of committing⟧
21:3 but that night they c nothing.
21:10 "Bring some of the fish that you have just c."
Ac 27:15 the ship was c and could not be turned head-on
2Co 12:2 a person in Christ who fourteen years ago was c
12:4 was c up into Paradise and heard things that are
1Th 4:17 be c up in the clouds together with them to meet
2Pe 2:12 mere creatures of instinct, born to be c and killed.
Tob 11:6 When she c sight of him coming,
Wis 4:11 They were c up so that evil might
Sir 9:4 or you will be c by her tricks.
23:7 the one who observes it will never be c.
27:26 and whoever sets a snare will be c in it.
27:29 Those who rejoice in the fall of the godly will be c
Aza 1:25 and burned those Chaldeans who were c near
1Mc 6:24 to death as many of us as they have c,
2Mc 12:35 on horseback and was a strong man, c hold

2Mc 13:21 he was sought for, **c**, and put in prison.

CAUL[S] (KJV) See APPENDAGE, COVERING

CAULKERS (1) [CAULKING]

Eze 27:27 your mariners and your pilots, your **c**,

CAULKING (1) [CAULKERS]

Eze 27: 9 and its artisans were within you, **c** your seams;

CAUSE‡ (138) [CAUSED, CAUSES, CAUSING]

Ex 9: 9 and shall **c** festering boils on humans and animals
9:18 Tomorrow at this time I will **c** the heaviest hail
20:24 where I **c** my name to be remembered I will come
23: 8 and subverts the **c** of those who are in the right.
Lev 26:16 that waste the eyes and **c** life to pine away.
Nu 5:24 the curse shall enter her and **c** bitter pain.
5:27 the curse shall enter into her and **c** bitter pain,
35:17 in hand that could **c** death, and death ensues, is
35:18 with a weapon of wood in hand that could **c** death,
35:23 while handling any stone that could **c** death,
Dt 16:19 of the wise and subverts the **c** of those who are in
20: 8 or he might **c** the heart of his comrades to melt
28: 7 The LORD will **c** your enemies who rise
28:25 The LORD will **c** you to be defeated
Jdg 6:31 Or will you defend his **c**?
11:35 you have become the **c** of great trouble to me.
1Sa 19: 5 an innocent person by killing David without **c**?"
24:15 May he see to it, and plead my **c**,
25:31 my lord shall have no **c** of grief,
25:31 without **c** or for having saved himself.
2Sa 15: 4 Then all who had a suit or **c** might come to me,
23: 5 Will he not **c** to prosper all my help and my desire?
1Ki 2:31 the guilt for the blood that Joab shed without **c**.
8:45 and their plea, and maintain their **c**.
8:49 and their plea, maintain their **c**
8:59 maintain the **c** of his servant and the **c** of his people
17:18 and to **c** the death of my son!"
2Ki 19: 7 I will **c** him to fall by the sword
21: 8 not **c** the feet of Israel to wander any more out of
2Ch 6:35 and their plea, and maintain their **c**.
6:39 and their pleas, maintain their **c**
Ne 4: 8 and fight against Jerusalem and to **c** confusion
Job 5: 8 and to God I would commit my **c**.
9:17 and multiplies my wounds without **c**;
29:16 and I championed the **c** of the stranger.
31:13 I have rejected the **c** of my male or female slaves,
Ps 7: 4 with harm or plundered my foe without **c**,
9: 4 For you have maintained my just **c**;
17: 1 Hear a just **c**, O LORD;
22: 8 "Commit your **c** to the LORD;
35: 7 For without **c** they hid their net for me;
35: 7 without **c** they dug a pit for my life.
35:19 or those who hate me without **c** wink the eye.
35:23 Bestir yourself for my defense, for my **c**,
37: 6 and the justice of your **c** like the noonday.
38:19 Those who are my foes without **c** are mighty,
43: 1 and defend my **c** against an ungodly people;
45: 4 on victoriously for the **c** of truth and to defend
45:17 I will **c** your name to be celebrated
56: 5 All day long they seek to injure my **c**;
69: 4 of my head are those who hate me without **c**;
72: 4 May he defend the **c** of the poor of the people,
74:22 Rise up, O God, plead your **c**;
104:14 You **c** the grass to grow for the cattle,
109: 3 with words of hate, and attack me without **c**.
119:86 I am persecuted without **c**; help me!
119:154 Plead my **c** and redeem me;
119:161 Princes persecute me without **c**,
132:17 There I will **c** a horn to sprout up for David;
140:12 that the LORD maintains the **c** of the needy,
Pr 3:30 Do not quarrel with anyone without **c**,
19:26 chase away their mother are children who **c** shame
22:23 for the LORD pleads their **c** and despoils
23:11 he will plead their **c** against you.
23:29 Who has wounds without **c**?
24:28 not be a witness against your neighbor without **c**,
Isa 1:23 and the widow's **c** does not come before them.
29:21 those who **c** a person to lose a lawsuit,
30:30 the LORD will **c** his majestic voice to be heard
34: 8 a year of vindication by Zion's **c**.
37: 7 I will **c** him to fall by the sword
45: 8 and let it **c** righteousness to sprout up also;
49: 4 yet surely my **c** is with the LORD,
51:22 your God who pleads the **c** of his people:
52: 4 the Assyrian, too, has oppressed them without **c**.
52: 5 seeing that my people are taken away without **c**?
61:11 so the Lord GOD will **c** righteousness and praise
Jer 5:28 they do not judge with justice the **c** of the orphan,
11:20 for to you I have committed my **c**.
20:12 for to you I have committed my **c**.
22:16 He judged the **c** of the poor and needy;
30:13 There is no one to uphold your **c**,
33:15 that time I will **c** a righteous Branch to spring up
50:34 He will surely plead their **c**,
51:36 I am going to defend your **c** and take vengeance
La 3:51 My eyes **c** me grief at the fate of all
3:52 without **c** have hunted me like a bird;
3:58 You have taken up my **c**, O Lord,
3:59 to me, O LORD; judge my **c**.
Eze 14:23 not without **c** that I did all that I have done in it,
17: 9 **c** its fruit to rot and wither,
29:21 that day I will **c** a horn to sprout up for the house
32: 4 and will **c** all the birds of the air to settle on you,
32:12 I will **c** your hordes to fall by the swords
32:14 and **c** their streams to run like oil,
36:11 and I will **c** you to be inhabited as
36:15 and no longer shall you **c** your nation to stumble,
36:33 I will **c** the towns to be inhabited,
37: 5 I will **c** breath to enter you, and you shall live.
37: 6 and will **c** flesh to come upon you,
Da 8:24 shall **c** fearful destruction,
Zec 8:12 and I will **c** the remnant of this people
11: 6 I will **c** them, every one, to fall each into the hand
Mt 19: 3 for a man to divorce his wife for any **c**?"
Lk 17: 2 the sea than for you to **c** one of these little ones
Jn 15:25 'They hated me without a **c**.'
Ac 13:28 though they found no **c** for a sentence of death,
19:40 since there is no **c** that we can give
Ro 14:15 Do not let what you eat **c** the ruin of one
16:17 an eye on those who **c** dissensions and offenses,
1Co 8:13 Therefore, if food is a **c** of their falling,
8:13 so that I may not **c** one of them to fall.
2Co 2: 2 For if I **c** you pain,
2: 4 of heart and with many tears, not to **c** you pain,
Gal 6: 4 will become a **c** for pride.
Col 2:18 puffed up without **c** by a human way of thinking,
1Jn 2:10 and in such a person there is no **c** for stumbling.
Rev 13:15 the beast could even speak and **c** those who would
Wis 8: 5 the active **c** of all things?
14:27 not to be named is the beginning and **c** and end
Sir 5:15 In great and small matters **c** no harm,
29: 4 and **c** trouble to those who help them.
36:25 A perverse mind will **c** grief,
40:14 As a generous person has **c** to rejoice,
47:22 or **c** any of his works to perish;
LtJ 6: 4 and which **c** the heathen to fear.
6:54 They cannot judge their own **c**
1Mc 3:42 to do to the people to **c** their final destruction.
9:10 and leave no **c** to question our honor."
2Mc 4: 1 and had been the real **c** of the misfortune.
4:47 Menelaus, the **c** of all the trouble,
3Mc 7: 9 against them or **c** them any grief at all,
2Es 15: 2 and **c** them to be written on paper;
15:39 that was to **c** destruction by the east wind shall
4Mc 1:11 the **c** of the downfall of tyranny over their nation.
12:14 for having killed without **c** the contestants
16:14 O mother, soldier of God in the **c** of religion,

CAUSED‡ (58) [CAUSE]

Ge 2: 5 LORD God had not **c** it to rain upon the earth,
2:21 LORD God **c** a deep sleep to fall upon the man,
20:13 God **c** me to wander from my father's house,
39: 3 LORD **c** all that he did to prosper in his hands.
Ex 9:10 and it **c** festering boils on humans and animals.
Dt 29:24 What **c** this great display of anger?"
1Ki 14:16 which he sinned and which he **c** Israel
15:26 of his ancestor and in the sin that he **c** Israel
15:30 of Jeroboam that he committed and that he **c** Israel
15:34 the way of Jeroboam and in the sin that he **c** Israel
16: 2 and have **c** my people Israel to sin,
16:13 and that they **c** Israel to commit,
16:26 and in the sins that he **c** Israel to commit,
21:22 to anger and have **c** Israel to sin.
22:52 in the way of Jeroboam son of Nebat, who **c** Israel
2Ki 3: 3 which he **c** Israel to commit;
7: 6 For the Lord had **c** the Aramean army to hear
10:29 which he **c** Israel to commit—
10:31 which he **c** Israel to commit.
13: 2 which he **c** Israel to sin;
13: 6 which he **c** Israel to sin, but walked in them;
13:11 which he **c** Israel to sin, but he walked in them.
14:24 of Jeroboam son of Nebat, which he **c** Israel
15: 9 which he **c** Israel to sin.
15:18 of Jeroboam son of Nebat, which he **c** Israel
15:24 of Jeroboam son of Nebat, which he **c** Israel
15:28 of Jeroboam son of Nebat, which he **c** Israel
21:11 and has **c** Judah also to sin with his idols;
21:16 besides the sin that he **c** Judah to sin so
23:15 by Jeroboam son of Nebat, who **c** Israel to sin—
Job 29:13 and I **c** the widow's heart to sing for joy.
31:16 or have **c** the eyes of the widow to fail,
31:39 and **c** the death of its owners;
34:28 so that they **c** the cry of the poor to come to him,
38:12 and **c** the dawn to know its place,
Ps 60: 2 You have **c** the land to quake;
78:16 and **c** waters to flow down like rivers.
78:26 He **c** the east wind to blow in the heavens,
88: 8 You have **c** my companions to shun me;
88:18 You have **c** friend and neighbor to shun me;
105:29 and **c** their fish to die.
106:46 He **c** them to be pitied
Isa 21: 2 all the sighing she has **c** I bring to an end.
63:12 who **c** his glorious arm to march at the right hand
La 2: 8 he **c** rampart and wall to lament;
Eze 32:30 for all the terror that they **c** by their might;
Mal 2: 8 you have **c** many to stumble by your instruction;
2Co 2: 5 if anyone has **c** pain, he has **c** it not to me,
Aza 1:27 not touch them at all and **c** them no pain
1Mc 1: 9 and they **c** many evils on the earth.
3:29 and disaster that he had **c** in the land by abolishing
11:27 and **c** him to be reckoned among his chief Friends.
15:31 that you have **c** and five hundred talents more for
2Mc 3:24 and of all authority **c** so great a manifestation
2Es 3:18 and moved the world, and **c** the depths to tremble,
4Mc 3:21 against the public harmony and **c** many
4:21 and **c** Antiochus himself to make war on them.

CAUSES‡ (29) [CAUSE]

Ex 22: 5 someone **c** a field or vineyard to be grazed over,
Job 37:13 or for his land, or for love, he **c** it to happen.
37:15 and **c** the lightning of his cloud to shine?
Ps 29: 9 The voice of the LORD **c** the oaks to whirl,
Pr 10: 4 A slack hand **c** poverty, but the hand of
10:10 Whoever winks the eye **c** trouble,
16: 7 he **c** even their enemies to be at peace with them.
29:22 and the hothead **c** much transgression.
Isa 61:11 and as a garden **c** what is sown in it to spring up,
64: 2 when fire kindles brushwood and the fire **c** water
La 3:32 Although he **c** grief, he will have compassion
Eze 44:18 not bind themselves with anything that **c** sweat.
Mt 5:29 If your right eye **c** you to sin,
5:30 And if your right hand **c** you to sin,
5:32 **c** her to commit adultery;
13:41 and they will collect out of his kingdom all **c**
18: 8 "If your hand or your foot **c** you to stumble,
18: 9 And if your eye **c** you to stumble,
Mk 9:43 If your hand **c** you to stumble, cut it off;
9:45 And if your foot **c** you to stumble, cut it off;
9:47 And if your eye **c** you to stumble, tear it out;
Tit 3:10 to do with anyone who **c** divisions,
Heb 12:15 that no root of bitterness springs up and **c** trouble,
Rev 13:16 Also it **c** all, both small and great,
Wis 12:16 and your sovereignty over all **c** you to spare all.
17:13 prefers ignorance of what **c** the torment.
Sir 11:22 and quickly God **c** his blessing to flourish.
35:19 she cries out against the one who **c** them to fall?
4Mc 1:16 of divine and human matters and the **c** of these.

CAUSING (7) [CAUSE]

Lev 22:16 **c** them to bear guilt requiring a guilt offering,
1Sa 5: 9 the hand of the LORD was against the city, **c**
1Ki 16:19 and for the sin that he committed, **c** Israel to sin.
Est 1:17 **c** them to look with contempt on their husbands,
Jer 32:35 that they should do this abomination, **c** Judah
Jude 1:19 devoid of the Spirit, who are **c** divisions.
1Mc 15:35 they were **c** great damage among the people and

CAUSEWAY (KJV) See ROAD

CAUTIONED (1) [CAUTIOUS]

Mk 8:15 And he **c** them, saying, "Watch out—

CAUTIOUS (3) [CAUTIONED]

Pr 14:16 The wise are **c** and turn away from evil,
22: 5 the **c** will keep far from them.
Sir 18:27 One who is wise is **c** in everything;

CAVALRY (66)

1Ki 9:19 the cities for his chariots, the cities for his **c**,
9:22 and the commanders of his chariotry and **c**.
20:20 of Aram escaped on a horse with the **c**.
1Ch 18: 4 from him one thousand chariots, seven thousand **c**,
19: 6 of silver to hire chariots and **c** from Mesopotamia,
2Ch 8: 6 for his **c**, and whatever Solomon desired to build,
8: 9 the commanders of his chariotry and **c**.
12: 3 with twelve hundred chariots and sixty thousand **c**.
16: 8 with exceedingly many chariots and **c**?
Ezr 8:22 and **c** to protect us against the enemy on our way,
Ne 2: 9 king had sent officers of the army and **c** with me.
Isa 22: 6 Elam bore the quiver with chariots and **c**,
22: 7 and the **c** took their stand at the gates.
Eze 26: 7 king of kings, together with horses, chariots, **c**,
26:10 At the noise of **c**, wheels,
Rev 9:16 of the troops of **c** was two hundred million;
Jdt 1:13 of Arphaxad and all his **c** and all his chariots.
2: 5 thousand foot soldiers and twelve thousand **c**.
2:19 with their chariots and **c** and picked foot soldiers.
2:22 **c**, and chariots, and went up into the hill country.
6: 3 They cannot resist the might of our **c**.
7: 2 and twelve thousand **c**, not counting the baggage
7: 6 On the second day Holofernes led out all his **c**
7:20 and **c**, surrounded them for thirty-four days,
16: 3 and their **c** covered the hills.
1Mc 1:17 with chariots and elephants and **c** and with
3:39 and seven thousand **c** to go into the land of Judah
4: 1 and one thousand picked **c**,
4: 7 strong and fortified, with **c** all around it;
4:28 and five thousand **c** to subdue them.
4:31 let them be ashamed of their troops and their **c**.
6:38 The rest of the **c** were stationed on either side,
8: 6 and with **c** and chariots and a very large army.
9: 4 twenty thousand foot soldiers and two thousand **c**.
9:11 The **c** was divided into two companies,
10:73 not be able to withstand my **c** and such an army in
10:77 he mustered three thousand **c** and a large army,
10:77 he had a large troop of **c** and put confidence in it.
10:79 Now Apollonius had secretly left a thousand **c**
10:82 the phalanx in battle (for the **c** was exhausted);
10:83 and the **c** was dispersed in the plain.
12:49 Then Trypho sent troops and **c** into Galilee and
13:22 So Trypho got all his **c** ready to go,
15:13 twenty thousand warriors and eight thousand **c**.
15:38 and gave him troops of infantry and **c**.
16: 4 of the country twenty thousand warriors and **c**,
16: 5 where a large force of infantry and **c** was coming
16: 7 Then he divided the army and placed the **c** in
16: 7 for the **c** of the enemy were very numerous.
2Mc 5: 2 over all the city golden-clad **c** charging through
5: 3 of **c** drawn up, attacks and counterattacks made
10:24 and collected the **c** from Asia in no small number.
10:31 hundred were slaughtered, besides six hundred **c**.

2Mc 11: 2 about eighty thousand infantry and all his **c**
11: 4 and his thousands of **c**, and his eighty elephants.
11:11 of them and sixteen hundred **c**,
12:10 with five hundred **c** attacked them.
12:20 and two thousand five hundred **c**.
12:33 with three thousand infantry and four hundred **c**.
12:35 when one of the Thracian **c** bore down on him
13: 2 five thousand three hundred **c**,
15:20 and the **c** deployed on the flanks,
1Es 2:30 with **c** and a large number of armed troops,
5: 2 a thousand **c** to take them back to Jerusalem
8:51 the king for foot soldiers and **c** and an escort
3Mc 1: 1 to all his forces, both infantry and **c**, took

CAVE (36) [CAVE-DWELLING, CAVES]

Ge 19:30 so he lived in a **c** with his two daughters.
23: 9 so that he may give me the **c** of Machpelah,
23:11 and I give you the **c** that is in it;
23:17 with the **c** that was in it and all the trees that were
23:19 in the **c** of the field of Machpelah facing Mamre
23:20 and the **c** that is in it passed from the Hittites
25: 9 and Ishmael buried him in the **c** of Machpelah,
49:29 in the **c** in the field of Ephron the Hittite,
49:30 in the **c** in the field at Machpelah,
49:32 the field and the **c** that is in it were purchased
50:13 and buried him in the **c** of the field at Machpelah,
Jos 10:16 these five kings fled and hid themselves in the **c**
10:17 hidden in the **c** at Makkedah."
10:18 "Roll large stones against the mouth of the **c**,
10:22 Then Joshua said, "Open the mouth of the **c**,
10:22 and bring those five kings out to me from the **c**."
10:23 and brought the five kings out to him from the **c**,
10:27 down from the trees and threw them into the **c**
10:27 they set large stones against the mouth of the **c**,
1Sa 22: 1 David left there and escaped to the **c** of Adullam;
24: 3 beside the road, where there was a **c**;
24: 3 in the innermost parts of the **c**.
24: 7 Saul got up and left the **c**, and went on his way.
24: 8 up and went out of the **c** and called after Saul,
24:10 how the LORD gave you into my hand in the **c**;
2Sa 23:13 the thirty chiefs went down to join David at the **c**
1Ki 18: 4 hid them fifty to a **c**, and provided them with bread
18:13 a hundred of the LORD's prophets fifty to a **c**,
19: 9 At that place he came to a **c**,
19:13 and went out and stood at the entrance of the **c**.
1Ch 11:15 down to the rock to David at the **c** of Adullam,
Ps 57: T *A Miktam, when he fled from Saul, in the* **c**.
142: T *A Maskil of David. When he was in the* **c**.
Na 2:11 the **c** of the young lions, where the lion goes,
Jn 11:38 It was a **c**, and a stone was lying against it.
Jdt 16:23 they buried her in the **c** of her husband Manasseh;

CAVE-DWELLING (1) [CAVE, DWELL]

2Mc 2: 5 Jeremiah came and found a **c**,

CAVERNS (1)

Isa 2:21 the **c** of the rocks and the clefts in the crags,

CAVES (9) [CAVE]

Jdg 6: 2 for themselves hiding places in the mountains, **c**
1Sa 13: 6 the people hid themselves in **c** and in holes and
Isa 2:19 the **c** of the rocks and the holes of the ground,
Eze 33:27 and those who are in strongholds and in **c** shall die
Na 2:12 he has filled his **c** with prey and his dens
Heb 11:38 and in **c** and holes in the ground.
Rev 6:15 hid in the **c** and among the rocks of the mountains,
2Mc 6:11 Others who had assembled in the **c** nearby,
10: 6 they had been wandering in the mountains and **c**

CEASE‡ (40) [CEASED, CEASES, CEASING]

Ge 8:22 summer and winter, day and night, shall not **c**."
Ex 9:29 the thunder will **c**, and there will be no more hail,
Dt 15:11 there will never **c** to be some in need on the earth,
Jos 22:25 So your children might make our children **c**
1Sa 7: 8 "Do not **c** to cry out to the LORD our God for us,
2Ch 16: 5 he stopped building Ramah, and let his work **c**.
35:21 **C** opposing God, who is with me,
Ezr 4:21 issue an order that these people be made to **c**,
4:23 and by force and power made them **c**.
Est 9:28 nor should the commemoration of these days **c**
Job 3:17 There the wicked **c** from troubling,
14: 7 and that its shoots will not **c**.
Ps 46: 9 He makes wars **c** to the end of the earth;
Pr 19:27 **C** straying, my child, from the words
22:10 quarreling and abuse will **c**.
Ecc 12: 3 and the women who grind **c** working
Isa 1:16 before my eyes; **c** to do evil,
17: 1 See, Damascus will **c** to be a city,
29:20 and the scoffer shall **c** to be;
Jer 14:17 and let them not **c**, for the virgin daughter—
17: 8 and it does not **c** to bear fruit.
31:36 this fixed order were ever to **c** from my presence,
31:36 of Israel would **c** to be a nation before me forever.
Eze 45: 9 **C** your evictions of my people,
Da 9:27 the week he shall make sacrifice and offering **c**;
Am 7: 5 Then I said, "O Lord GOD, **c**, I beg you!
Ac 5:42 at home they did not **c** to teach and proclaim Jesus
20:31 remembering that for three years I did not **c** night
1Co 13: 8 as for tongues, they will **c**;
Eph 1:16 not **c** to give thanks for you as I remember you
Heb 4:10 also **c** from their labors as God did from his.
AdE 9:28 of them was never to **c** among their descendants.
Sir 23:16 of kin will never **c** until the fire burns him up.
Sir 24: 9 and for all the ages I shall not **c** to be.
Bar 2:23 I will make to **c** from the towns of Judah and from
2Mc 15: 7 But Maccabeus did not **c** to trust
3Mc 1:12 he did not **c** to maintain that he ought to enter,
3:16 who never **c** from their folly.
2Es 15:22 not **c** from those who shed innocent blood
16:67 **C** from your sins, and forget your iniquities,

CEASED (31) [CEASE]

Ge 18:11 it had **c** to be with Sarah after the manner
29:35 therefore she named him Judah; then she **c** bearing.
30: 9 When Leah saw that she had **c** bearing children,
Ex 9:33 then the thunder and the hail **c**,
9:34 that the rain and the hail and the thunder had **c**,
Jos 5:12 The manna **c** on the day they ate the produce of
Jdg 5: 6 caravans **c** and travelers kept to the byways.
Job 32: 1 So these three men **c** to answer Job,
Ps 36: 3 they have **c** to act wisely and do good.
77: 8 Has his steadfast love **c** forever?
Isa 14: 4 How the oppressor has **c**! How his insolence has **c**!
16: 4 the oppressor is no more, and destruction has **c**,
16: 9 and your grain harvest has **c**.
24: 8 the noise of the jubilant has **c**,
33: 1 you have **c** to destroy, you will be destroyed;
La 5:15 The joy of our hearts has **c**;
Jnh 1:15 and the sea **c** from its raging.
Mt 14:32 When they got into the boat, the wind **c**.
Mk 4:39 Then the wind **c**, and there was a dead calm.
6:51 he got into the boat with them and the wind **c**.
Lk 8:24 they **c**, and there was a calm.
Ac 20: 1 After the uproar had **c**, Paul sent for the disciples;
Col 1: 9 not **c** praying for you and asking that you may
Heb 10: 2 Otherwise, would they not have **c** being offered,
Wis 5:13 So we also, as soon as we were born, **c** to be,
Sir 17:28 from one who does not exist, thanksgiving has **c**;
1Mc 3:45 the flute and the harp **c** to play.
9:27 such as had not been since the time that prophets **c**
9:73 Thus the sword **c** from Israel.
4Mc 8:29 so that as soon as the tyrant had **c** counseling them

CEASES (4) [CEASE]

Pr 26:20 and where there is no whisperer, quarreling **c**.
La 3:22 of the LORD never **c**, his mercies never come to
Wis 7:10 because her radiance never **c**.
Sir 14:19 Every work decays and **c** to exist,

CEASING (7) [CEASE]

1Sa 12:23 from me that I should sin against the LORD by **c**
Ps 35:15 not know tore at me without **c**;
La 3:49 My eyes will flow without **c**, without respite,
Ro 1: 9 without **c** I remember you always in my prayers,
1Th 5:17 pray without **c**,
Rev 4: 8 Day and night without **c** they sing, "Holy, holy,
2Mc 13:12 and lying prostrate for three days without **c**,

CEDAR (53) [CEDARS, CEDARWOOD]

Nu 24: 6 like **c** trees beside the waters.
2Sa 5:11 to David, along with **c** trees, and carpenters
7: 2 "See now, I am living in a house of **c**,
7: 7 "Why have you not built me a house of **c**?"
1Ki 4:33 from the **c** that is in the Lebanon to the hyssop
5: 8 I will fulfill all your needs in the matter of **c**
5:10 for timber of **c** and cypress.
6: 9 he roofed the house with beams and planks of **c**.
6:10 and it was joined to the house with timbers of **c**.
6:15 of the house on the inside with boards of **c**;
6:16 of the house with boards of **c** from the floor to
6:18 The **c** within the house had carvings of gourds
6:18 all was **c**, no stone was seen.
6:20 He also overlaid the altar with **c**.
6:36 of dressed stone to one course of **c** beams.
7: 2 built on four rows of **c** pillars,
7: 2 with **c** beams on the pillars.
7: 3 It was roofed with **c** on the forty-five rafters,
7: 7 covered with **c** from floor to floor.
7:12 to one layer of **c** beams all around;
9:11 of Tyre having supplied Solomon with **c**
2Ki 14: 9 "A thornbush on Lebanon sent to a **c** on Lebanon,
1Ch 14: 1 with **c** logs, and masons and carpenters to build
17: 1 "I am living in a house of **c**,
17: 6 saying, Why have you not built me a house of **c**?
22: 4 and **c** logs without number—
22: 4 and Tyrians brought great quantities of **c** to David.
2Ch 1:15 and he made **c** as plentiful as the sycamore of
2: 3 and sent him **c** to build himself a house to live in.
2: 8 also **c**, cypress, and algum timber from Lebanon,
9:27 **c** as plentiful as the sycamore of the Shephelah.
25:18 "A thornbush on Lebanon sent to a **c** on Lebanon,
Ezr 3: 7 and the Tyrians to bring **c** trees from Lebanon to
Job 40:17 It makes its tail stiff like a **c**;
Ps 37:35 and towering like a **c** of Lebanon.
92:12 and grow like a **c** in Lebanon.
SS 1:17 the beams of our house are **c**, our rafters are pine.
8: 9 we will enclose her with boards of **c**.
Isa 41:19 I will put in the wilderness the **c**, the acacia,
44:14 He plants a **c** and the rain nourishes it.
Jer 22:14 paneling it with **c**, and painting it with vermilion.
22:15 Are you a king because you compete in **c**?
Eze 17: 3 He took the top of the **c**,
17:22 a sprig from the lofty top of a **c**;
17:23 and bear fruit, and become a noble **c**.
27: 5 they took a **c** from Lebanon to make a mast
31: 3 Consider Assyria, a **c** of Lebanon,
Zep 2:14 for its **c** work will be laid bare.
Zec 11: 2 Wail, O cypress, for the **c** has fallen,
Sir 24:13 "I grew tall like a **c** in Lebanon,
50:12 he was like a young **c** on Lebanon surrounded by
1Es 4:48 to bring **c** timber from Lebanon to Jerusalem,
5:55 to bring **c** logs from Lebanon and convey them

CEDARS (20) [CEDAR]

Jdg 9:15 let fire come out of the bramble and devour the **c**
1Ki 5: 6 command that **c** from the Lebanon be cut for me.
10:27 and he made **c** as numerous as the sycamores of
2Ki 19:23 I felled its tallest **c**, its choicest cypresses;
Ps 29: 5 The voice of the LORD breaks the **c**;
29: 5 the LORD breaks the **c** of Lebanon.
80:10 the mighty **c** with its branches;
104:16 the **c** of Lebanon that he planted.
148: 9 Mountains and all hills, fruit trees and all **c**!
SS 5:15 His appearance is like Lebanon, choice as the **c**.
Isa 2:13 against all the **c** of Lebanon, lofty and lifted up;
9:10 but we will put **c** in their place."
14: 8 The cypresses exult over you, the **c** of Lebanon,
37:24 I felled its tallest **c**, its choicest cypresses;
44:14 He cuts down **c** or chooses a holm tree or an oak
Jer 22: 7 they shall cut down your choicest **c** and cast them
22:23 O inhabitant of Lebanon, nested among the **c**,
Eze 31: 8 The **c** in the garden of God could not rival it,
Am 2: 9 whose height was like the height of **c**,
Zec 11: 1 O Lebanon, so that fire may devour your **c**!

CEDARWOOD (7) [CEDAR, WOOD]

Lev 14: 4 and **c** and crimson yarn and hyssop be brought for
14: 6 the living bird with the **c** and the crimson yarn and
14:49 with **c** and crimson yarn and hyssop,
14:51 the **c** and the hyssop and the crimson yarn,
14:52 and with the **c** and hyssop and crimson yarn;
Nu 19: 6 The priest shall take **c**, hyssop,
1Ki 7:11 above, cut to measure, and **c**.

CEDRON (KJV) See KIDRON

CEILING (2)

1Ki 6:15 from the floor of the house to the rafters of the **c**,
2Mc 1:16 Opening a secret door in the **c**,

CELEBRANTS (1) [CELEBRATE]

3Mc 6:31 and full of joy they apportioned to **c** the place

CELEBRATE (31) [CELEBRANTS, CELEBRATED, CELEBRATING, CELEBRATION, CELEBRATIONS]

Ex 5: 1 they may **c** a festival to me in the wilderness.' "
10: 9 because we have the LORD's festival to **c**."
12:14 You shall **c** it as a festival to the LORD;
12:47 The whole congregation of Israel shall **c** it.
12:48 to **c** the passover to the LORD, all his males shall
12:48 then he may draw near to **c** it;
Lev 23: 4 which you shall **c** at the time appointed for them.
23:37 which you shall **c** as times of holy convocation,
Nu 29:12 You shall **c** a festival to the LORD seven days.
Dt 16:15 in all your undertakings, and you shall surely **c**.
26:11 shall **c** with all the bounty that
Ne 12:27 to Jerusalem to **c** the dedication with rejoicing,
Ps 145: 7 They shall **c** the fame of your abundant goodness,
Eze 45:21 you shall **c** the festival of the passover,
Na 1:15 **C** your festivals, O Judah, fulfill your vows,
Lk 15:23 get the fatted calf and kill it, and let us eat and **c**;
15:24 And they began to **c**.
15:29 a young goat so that I might **c** with my friends.
15:32 But we had to **c** and rejoice,
1Co 5: 8 Therefore, let us **c** the festival,
Rev 11:10 over them and **c** and exchange presents,
Tob 6:13 we return from Rages we will **c** her marriage.
AdE 2:18 and the officers to **c** his marriage to Esther;
Wis 14:23 or **c** secret mysteries, or hold frenzied revels
1Mc 13:52 that every year they should **c** this day
2Mc 1:18 on the twenty-fifth day of Chislev we shall **c**
1:18 in order that you also may **c** the festival of booths
2:16 we are about to **c** the purification, we write to you.
15:36 but to **c** the thirteenth day of the twelfth month—
3Mc 6:30 that they should **c** their rescue with all joyfulness
6:33 after convening a great banquet to **c** these events,

CELEBRATED (14) [CELEBRATE]

Jdg 9:27 the grapes from their vineyards, trod them, and **c**.
Ezr 6:16 **c** the dedication of this house of God with joy.
6:22 With joy they **c** the festival
Ps 45:17 I will cause your name to be **c** in all generations;
Tob 11:18 With merriment they **c** Tobias's wedding feast
AdE 9:18 They **c** the fifteenth with joy and gladness.
9:22 was to be **c** as a time for feasting and gladness and
1Mc 4:56 So they **c** the dedication of the altar for eight days,
7:48 The people rejoiced greatly and **c** that day as
7:49 They decreed that this day should be **c** each year
10:58 and **c** her wedding at Ptolemais with great pomp,
2Mc 6: 7 and when a festival of Dionysus was **c**,
10: 6 They **c** it for eight days with rejoicing,
3Mc 7:18 There they **c** their deliverance,

CELEBRATING (5) [CELEBRATE]

AdE 9:17 **c** it with joy and gladness.
1Mc 9:37 "The family of Jambri are **c** a great wedding,
2Mc 8:33 While they were **c** the victory in the city
3Mc 5:17 the present portion of the banquet joyful by **c** all
5:36 and urged the guests to return to their **c**.

CELEBRATION‡ (8) [CELEBRATE]
2Ch 23:13 with their musical instruments leading in the **c**.
Tob 9: 2 and then bring him with you to the wedding **c**.
9: 5 and was inviting him to the wedding **c**.
9: 6 both got up early and went to the wedding **c**.
10: 7 of the wedding **c** had ended that Raguel had sworn
12: 1 When the wedding **c** was ended,
AdE 1: 4 of his kingdom and the splendor of his bountiful **c**
2Mc 6: 7 On the monthly **c** of the king's birthday,

CELEBRATIONS (1) [CELEBRATE]
Wis 19:16 having first received them with festal **c**,

CELESTIAL (1)
2Es 2:37 to him who has called you to the **c** kingdoms.

CELL (2) [CELLS]
Ac 12: 7 of the Lord appeared and a light shone in the **c**.
16:24 in the innermost **c** and fastened their feet in

CELLAR (1) [CELLARS]
Lk 11:33 "No one after lighting a lamp puts it in a **c**,

CELLARS (1) [CELLAR]
1Ch 27:27 of the vineyards for the wine **c** was Zabdi

CELLARS (KJV) See also STORES

CELLS (1) [CELL]
Jer 37:16 in the **c**, and remained there many days.

CEMETERY (2)
2Mc 9: 4 I get there I will make Jerusalem a **c** of Jews."
9:14 the ground and to make a **c**, he was now declaring

CENCHREAE (2)
Ac 18:18 At **C** he had his hair cut, for he was under a vow.
Ro 16: 1 our sister Phoebe, a deacon of the church at **C**,

CENDEBEUS (6)
1Mc 15:38 Then the king made **C** commander-in-chief of
15:40 So **C** came to Jamnia and began to provoke
16: 1 and reported to his father Simon what **C** had done.
16: 4 against **C** and camped for the night in Modein.
16: 8 and **C** and his army were put to flight;
16: 9 but John pursued them until **C** reached Kedron,

CENSER (13) [CENSERS]
Lev 10: 1 Aaron's sons, Nadab and Abihu, each took his **c**,
16:12 He shall take a **c** full of coals of fire from the altar
Nu 16:17 and let each one of you take his **c**, and put incense
16:17 each one of you present his **c** before the LORD,
16:17 you also, and Aaron, each his **c**."
16:18 So each man took his **c**,
16:46 Moses said to Aaron, "Take your **c**,
2Ch 26:19 Now he had a **c** in his hand to make offering,
Eze 8:11 Each had his **c** in his hand,
Rev 8: 3 Another angel with a golden **c** came and stood at
8: 5 Then the angel took the **c** and filled it with fire
Sir 50: 9 in the **c**, like a vessel of hammered gold studded
4Mc 7:11 For just as our father Aaron, armed with the **c**,

CENSERS (8) [CENSER]
Nu 16: 6 Do this: take **c**, Korah and all your company,
16:17 before the LORD, two hundred fifty **c**;
16:18 and they put fire in the **c** and laid incense on them,
16:37 of Aaron the priest to take the **c** out of the blaze;
16:38 the **c** of these sinners have become holy at the cost
16:39 So Eleazar the priest took the bronze **c**
1Mc 1:22 the bowls, the golden **c**, the curtain, the crowns,
1Es 2:13 one thousand silver cups, twenty-nine silver **c**,

CENSURE (2) [CENSURED]
Job 20: 3 I hear **c** that insults me,
4Mc 2:19 **c** the households of Simeon and Levi

CENSURED (1) [CENSURE]
Tit 2: 8 and sound speech that cannot be **c**;

CENSUS‡ (15)
Ex 30:12 you take a **c** of the Israelites to register them,
38:26 for everyone who was counted in the **c**,
Nu 1: 2 Take a **c** of the whole congregation of Israelites,
1:49 not take a **c** of them with the other Israelites.
4: 2 Take a **c** of the Kohathites separate from
4:22 Take a **c** of the Gershonites also,
14:29 and of all your number, included in the **c**,
26: 2 a **c** of the whole congregation of the Israelites,
26: 4 "Take a **c** of the people,
2Sa 24: 2 and take a **c** of the people,
24: 4 the presence of the king to take a **c** of the people
2Ch 2:17 a **c** of all the aliens who were residing in the land
2:17 after the **c** that his father David had taken;
Ac 5:37 at the time of the **c** and got people to follow him;
3Mc 4:17 the king that they were no longer able to take the **c**

CENTER‡ (11)
Nu 2:17 shall set out in the **c** of the camps;
1Ki 6:27 the **c** of the house were touching wing to wing.
Isa 19:19 be an altar to the LORD in the **c** of the land
66:17 following the one in the **c**, eating the flesh of pigs,
Jer 21: 4 I will bring them together into the **c** of this city.
Eze 5: 5 I have set her in the **c** of the nations,
38:12 who live at the **c** of the earth.
Da 4:10 there was a tree at the **c** of the earth,
Am 7:10 "Amos has conspired against you in the very **c** of
Rev 7:17 Lamb at the **c** of the throne will be their shepherd,
1Mc 16: 7 and placed the cavalry in the **c** of the infantry,

CENTURION (20) [CENTURIONS]
Mt 8: 5 When he entered Capernaum, a **c** came to him,
8: 8 The **c** answered, "Lord, I am not worthy
8:13 And to the **c** Jesus said, "Go;
27:54 Now when the **c** and those with him,
Mk 15:39 Now when the **c**, who stood facing him,
15:44 the **c**, he asked him whether he had been dead
15:45 When he learned from the **c** that he was dead,
Lk 7: 2 A **c** there had a slave whom he valued highly,
7: 6 the **c** sent friends to say to him, "Lord,
23:47 When the **c** saw what had taken place,
Ac 10: 1 a **c** of the Italian Cohort, as it was called.
10:22 They answered, "Cornelius, a **c**,
22:25 Paul said to the **c** who was standing by,
22:26 the **c** heard that, he went to the tribune and said
24:23 Then he ordered the **c** to keep him in custody,
27: 1 and some other prisoners to a **c** of
27: 6 the **c** found an Alexandrian ship bound for Italy
27:11 But the **c** paid more attention to the pilot and to
27:31 Paul said to the **c** and the soldiers,
27:43 but the **c**, wishing to save Paul, kept them

CENTURIONS (3) [CENTURION]
Ac 21:32 Immediately he took soldiers and **c** and ran down
23:17 Paul called one of the **c** and said,
23:23 Then he summoned two of the **c** and said,

CEPHAS (9) [=PETER]
Jn 1:42 You are to be called **C**" (which is translated Peter).
1Co 1:12 or "I belong to Apollos," or "I belong to **C**,"
3:22 or **C** or the world or life or death or the present or
9: 5 and the brothers of the Lord and **C**?
15: 5 and that he appeared to **C**, then to the twelve.
Gal 1:18 after three years I did go up to Jerusalem to visit **C**
2: 9 and when James and **C** and John,
2:11 But when **C** came to Antioch,
2:14 I said to **C** before them all, "If you, though a Jew,

CEREMONIALLY (3) [CEREMONY]
Lev 12: 2 she shall be **c** unclean seven days;
13: 3 examined him he shall pronounce him **c** unclean.
15: 2 his discharge makes him **c** unclean.

CEREMONY (1) [CEREMONIALLY]
Sir 38:16 Lay out the body with due **c**,

CERTAIN‡ (85) [CERTAINLY, CERTAINTY]
Ge 15:13 the LORD said to Abram, "Know this for **c**,
28:11 to a **c** place and stayed there for the night,
38: 1 near a **c** Adullamite whose name was Hirah.
38: 2 of a **c** Canaanite whose name was Shua;
42:13 the sons of a **c** man in the land of Canaan;
Lev 24:10 and a **c** Israelite began fighting in the camp.
25:16 for it is a **c** number of harvests that are being sold
Nu 9: 6 Now there were **c** people who were unclean
Jdg 9:53 But a **c** woman threw an upper millstone
13: 2 There was a **c** man of Zorah,
19: 1 when there was no king in Israel, a **c** Levite,
Ru 1: 1 and a **c** man of Bethlehem in Judah went to live in
1Sa 1: 1 There was a **c** man of Ramathaim,
21: 7 a **c** man of the servants of Saul was there that day,
24:11 you may know for **c** that there is no wrong
2Sa 12: 1 and said to him, "There were two men in a **c** city,
1Ki 2:37 know for **c** that you shall die;
2:42 'Know for **c** that on the day you go out and go
20:13 Then a **c** prophet came up to King Ahab of Israel
20:35 At the command of the LORD a **c** member of
22:34 a **c** man drew his bow and unknowingly struck
1Ch 16: 4 He appointed **c** of the Levites as ministers before
2Ch 13: 7 and **c** worthless scoundrels gathered around him
18:33 a **c** man drew his bow and unknowingly struck
19: 8 in Jerusalem Jehoshaphat appointed **c** Levites
28:12 Moreover, **c** chiefs of the Ephraimites,
Ne 1: 2 Hanani, came with **c** men from Judah;
11:36 And **c** divisions of the Levites
Est 3: 8 "There is a **c** people scattered and separated
Jer 26:15 Only know for **c** that if you put me to death,
Eze 14: 1 **C** elders of Israel came to me and sat down
20: 1 **c** elders of Israel came to consult the LORD,
Da 2:45 dream is **c**, and its interpretation trustworthy."
3: 8 at this time **c** Chaldeans came forward
3:12 There are **c** Jews whom you have appointed over
Mt 26:18 He said, "Go into the city to a **c** man,
Mk 14:51 A **c** young man was following him,
Lk 7:41 "A **c** creditor had two debtors;
10:38 as they went on their way, he entered a **c** village,
11: 1 He was praying in a **c** place,
18: 2 a **c** city there was a judge who neither feared God
18:18 A **c** ruler asked him, "Good Teacher,
Jn 11: 1 Now a **c** man was ill, Lazarus of Bethany,
Ac 1:14 to prayer, together with **c** women, including Mary
8: 9 a **c** man named Simon had previously practiced
9:43 in Joppa for some time with a **c** Simon,
10: 5 to Joppa for a **c** Simon who is called Peter;
13: 6 they met a **c** magician, a Jewish false prophet,
15: 1 Then **c** individuals came down from Judea
15:24 that **c** persons who have gone out from us,
16:14 A **c** woman named Lydia, a worshiper of God,
22:12 "A **c** Ananias, who was a devout man according
23: 9 and **c** scribes of the Pharisees' group stood up
24: 1 with some elders and an attorney, a **c** Tertullus,
25:19 Instead they had **c** points of disagreement
25:19 about their own religion and about a **c** Jesus,
26:26 for I am **c** that none of these things has escaped
1Co 15:31 That is as **c**, brothers and sisters,
Gal 2:12 for until **c** people came from James,
1Ti 1: 3 in Ephesus so that you may instruct **c** people not
1:19 **c** persons have suffered shipwreck in the faith;
Heb 4: 7 again he sets a **c** day—"today"—saying
Jude 1: 4 For **c** intruders have stolen in among you,
AdE 3: 8 a **c** nation scattered among the other nations
8:12 on a **c** day, the thirteenth of
13: 4 in the world there is scattered a **c** hostile people,
1Mc 1:11 In those days **c** renegades came out from Israel
11:21 But **c** renegades who hated their nation went to
11:25 Although **c** renegades of his
11:39 A **c** Trypho had formerly been one
15: 3 Whereas **c** scoundrels have gained control of
2Mc 4:40 under the leadership of a **c** Auranus,
12:13 also attacked a **c** town that was strongly fortified
12:35 But a **c** Dositheus, one of Bacenor's men,
14: 3 a **c** Alcimus, who had formerly been high priest
14:37 A **c** Razis, one of the elders of Jerusalem,
3Mc 1: 2 But a **c** Theodotus, determined to carry out
1: 3 that a **c** insignificant man should sleep in the tent;
6: 1 Then a **c** Eleazar, famous among the priests of
7: 3 **C** of our friends, frequently urging us
2Es 8:22 whose word is sure and whose utterances are **c**,
4Mc 3:11 But a **c** irrational desire for the water in
3:21 that time **c** persons attempted a revolution against
4: 1 Now there was a **c** Simon,
5: 1 in state with his counselors on a **c** high place,

CERTAINLY (27) [CERTAIN]
Lev 10:18 You should **c** have eaten it in the sanctuary,
1Sa 25:28 for the LORD will **c** make my lord a sure house,
2Sa 5:19 for I will **c** give the Philistines into your hand."
1Ki 3:26 give her the living boy; **c** do not kill him!"
2Ki 8:10 "Go, say to him, 'You shall **c** recover';
8:10 but the LORD has shown me that he shall **c** die."
8:14 "He told me that you would **c** recover."
Jer 36:16 "We **c** must report all these words to the king."
36:29 of Babylon will **c** come and destroy this land,
Mt 26:73 "**C** you are also one of them,
Mk 14:70 "**C** you are one of them; for you are a Galilean."
Lk 23:47 "**C** this man was innocent."
Ac 16:37 to discharge us in secret? **C** not!
21:22 They will **c** hear that you have come.
Ro 6: 5 we will **c** be united with him in a resurrection
2Co 11: 6 **c** in every way and in all things we have made this
Gal 2:17 then a servant of sin? **C** not!
3:21 to the promises of God? **C** not!
1Th 2:18 **c** I, Paul, wanted to again and again—
Sir 12: 2 if not by them, **c** by the Most High.
LtJ 6:46 Those who make them will **c**
2Mc 3:38 for there is **c** some power of God about the place.
7:31 will **c** not escape the hands of God.
2Es 5:45 to your servant that you will **c** give life at one time
16:54 The Lord **c** knows everything that people do;
4Mc 2: 2 **c**, that the temperate Joseph is praised,
7:16 most **c** devout reason is governor of the emotions.

CERTAINTY (3) [CERTAIN]
Jos 9:24 "Because it was told to your servants for a **c** that
Da 2: 8 "I know with **c** that you are trying to gain time,
Ac 2:36 Israel know with **c** that God has made him

CERTIFICATE (4) [CERTIFIED]
Dt 24: 1 and so he writes her a **c** of divorce,
Mt 5:31 let him give her a **c** of divorce.'
19: 7 "Why then did Moses command us to give a **c**
Mk 10: 4 "Moses allowed a man to write a **c** of dismissal

CERTIFIED (2) [CERTIFICATE]
Jn 3:33 Whoever has accepted his testimony has **c** this,
Sir 44:20 he **c** the covenant in his flesh,

CHABRIS (3)
Jdt 6:15 of the tribe of Simeon, and **C** son of Gothoniel,
8:10 to summon Uzziah and **C** and Charmis,
10: 6 with the elders of the town, **C** and Charmis.

CHADIASANS (1)
1Es 5:20 The **C** and Ammidians, four hundred twenty-two.

CHAEREAS (2)
2Mc 10:32 where **C** was commander.
10:37 who was hiding in a cistern, and his brother **C**,

CHAFF (17)
Job 13:25 a windblown leaf and pursue dry **c**?
21:18 and like **c** that the storm carries away?
41:28 slingstones, for it, are turned to **c**.
41:29 Clubs are counted as **c**; it laughs at the
Ps 1: 4 but are like **c** that the wind drives away.
35: 5 Let them be like **c** before the wind,
83:13 like whirling dust, like **c** before the wind.

Isa 17:13 chased like **c** on the mountains before the wind
29: 5 and the multitude of tyrants like flying **c**.
33:11 You conceive **c**, you bring forth stubble;
41:15 and you shall make the hills like **c**.
Jer 13:24 I will scatter you like **c** driven by the wind from
Da 2:35 were all broken in pieces and became like the **c** of
Hos 13: 3 like **c** that swirls from the threshing floor or
Zep 2: 2 before you are driven away like the drifting **c**,
Mt 3:12 but the **c** he will burn with unquenchable fire."
Lk 3:17 but the **c** he will burn with unquenchable fire."

CHAFING (1)
Sir 26: 7 A bad wife is a **c** yoke;

CHAIN (13) [CHAINED, CHAINS]
Ge 41:42 and put a gold **c** around his neck.
1Ki 7:17 of **c** work for the capitals on the tops of the pillars;
Eze 7:23 Make a **c**! For the land is full of bloody
16:11 I put bracelets on your arms, a **c** on your neck,
Da 5: 7 have a **c** of gold around his neck,
5:16 have a **c** of gold around your neck,
5:29 a **c** of gold was put around his neck,
Mk 5: 3 no one could restrain him any more, even with a **c**;
Ac 28:20 of the hope of Israel that I am bound with this **c**."
2Ti 1:16 and was not ashamed of my **c**;
Rev 20: 1 the key to the bottomless pit and a great **c**.
Wis 17:17 for with one **c** of darkness they all were bound.
1Es 1:40 with a **c** of bronze and took him away to Babylon.

CHAINED (2) [CHAIN]
2Ti 2: 9 even to the point of being **c** like a criminal.
2: 9 But the word of God is not **c**.

CHAINS (27) [CHAIN]
Ex 28:14 and two **c** of pure gold, twisted like cords;
28:14 and you shall attach the corded **c** to the settings.
28:22 You shall make for the breastpiece **c** of pure gold,
39:15 They made on the breastpiece **c** of pure gold,
1Ki 6:21 then he drew **c** of gold across,
2Ch 3: 5 and made palms and **c** on it.
3:16 He made encircling **c** and put them on the tops of
3:16 and put them on the **c**.
Job 38:31 "Can you bind the **c** of the Pleiades,
Ps 149: 8 with fetters and their nobles with **c** of iron,
Isa 40:19 and casts for it silver **c**.
45:14 they shall come over in **c** and bow down to you.
La 3: 7 he has put heavy **c** on me;
Mk 5: 4 shakles and **c**, but the **c** he wrenched apart,
Lk 8:29 under guard and bound with **c** and shackles,
Ac 8:23 in the gall of bitterness and the **c** of wickedness."
12: 6 with two **c**, was sleeping between two soldiers,
12: 7 And the **c** fell off his wrists.
16:26 and everyone's **c** were unfastened.
21:33 and ordered him to be bound with two **c**;
26:29 as I am—except for these **c**."
Eph 6:20 for which I am an ambassador in **c**.
Col 4:18 with my own hand. Remember my **c**.
Heb 11:36 and even **c** and imprisonment.
2Pe 2: 4 but cast them into hell and committed them to **c**
Jude 1: 6 in eternal **c** in deepest darkness for the judgment

CHAIR (1)
2Ki 4:10 and put there for him a bed, a table, a **c**,

CHALCOL (KJV) See CALCOL

CHALDEA (11) [CHALDEAN, CHALDEANS]
Isa 47: 1 Sit on the ground without a throne, daughter **C**!
47: 5 Sit in silence, and go into darkness, daughter **C**!
48:20 Go out from Babylon, flee from **C**,
Jer 50:10 **C** shall be plundered; all who plunder her shall be
51:24 and all the inhabitants of **C** before your very eyes
51:35 be avenged on the inhabitants of **C**,"
Eze 11:24 in a vision by the spirit of God into **C**,
16:29 You multiplied your whoring with **C**,
23:15 picture of Babylonians whose native land was **C**.
23:16 and sent messengers to them in **C**.
Jdt 5: 7 the gods of their ancestors who were in **C**.

CHALDEAN (6) [CHALDEA]
2Ki 25:24 "Do not be afraid because of the **C** officials;
Ezr 5:12 the **C**, who destroyed this house and carried away
Jer 37:11 when the **C** army had withdrawn from Jerusalem
41: 3 and the **C** soldiers who happened to be there.
Da 2:10 a thing of any magician or enchanter or **C**.
5:30 very night Belshazzar, the **C** king, was killed.

CHALDEANS (82) [CHALDEA]
Ge 11:28 in the land of his birth, in Ur of the **C**.
11:31 and they went out together from Ur of the **C** to go
15: 7 the LORD who brought you from Ur of the **C**,
2Ki 24: 2 The LORD sent against him bands of the **C**,
25: 4 though the **C** were all around the city.
25: 5 But the army of the **C** pursued the king,
25:10 All the army of the **C** who were with the captain
25:13 in the house of the LORD, the **C** broke in pieces,
25:25 the Judeans and **C** who were with him at Mizpah.
25:26 for they were afraid of the **C**.
2Ch 36:17 he brought up against them the king of the **C**,
Ne 9: 7 and brought him out of Ur of the **C** and gave him
Job 1:17 "The **C** formed three columns,
Isa 13:19 the splendor and pride of the **C**,
Isa 23:13 Look at the land of the **C**!
43:14 shouting of the **C** will be turned to lamentation.
48:14 and his arm shall be against the **C**.
Jer 21: 4 and against the **C** who are besieging you outside
21: 9 to the **C** who are besieging you shall live
22:25 of Babylon and into the hands of the **C**.
24: 5 from this place to the land of the **C**.
25:12 the land of the **C**, for their iniquity,
32: 4 the **C**, but shall surely be given into the hands of
32: 5 you fight against the **C**, you shall not succeed?"
32:24 into the hands of the **C** who are fighting against it.
32:25 the city has been given into the hands of the **C**.
32:28 I am going to give this city into the hands of the **C**
32:29 **C** who are fighting against this city shall come,
32:43 it has been given into the hands of the **C**.
33: 5 The **C** are coming in to fight and to fill them with
35:11 the army of the **C** and the army of the Arameans.'
37: 5 the **C** who were besieging Jerusalem heard news
37: 8 And the **C** shall return and fight against this city;
37: 9 saying, "The **C** will surely go away from us,"
37:10 the whole army of **C** who are fighting against you,
37:13 "You are deserting to the **C**."
37:14 I am not deserting to the **C**."
38: 2 but those who go out to the **C** shall live;
38:18 then this city shall be handed over to the **C**,
38:19 of the Judeans who have deserted to the **C**,
38:23 and your children shall be led out to the **C**,
39: 5 But the army of the **C** pursued them,
39: 8 The **C** burned the king's house and the houses of
40: 9 saying, "Do not be afraid to serve the **C**.
40:10 to represent you before the **C** who come to us;
41:18 because of the **C**; for they were afraid of them,
43: 3 to hand us over to the **C**,
50: 1 concerning the land of the **C**,
50: 8 and go out of the land of the **C**,
50:25 of hosts has a task to do in the land of the **C**.
50:35 A sword against the **C**, says the LORD,
50:45 that he has formed against the land of the **C**:
51: 4 They shall fall down slain in the land of the **C**,
51:54 A great crashing from the land of the **C**!
52: 7 though the **C** were all around the city.
52: 8 But the army of the **C** pursued the king,
52:14 All the army of the **C**,
52:17 in the house of the LORD, the **C** broke in pieces,
Eze 1: 3 in the land of the **C** by the river Chebar;
12:13 and I will bring him to Babylon, the land of the **C**,
23:14 images of the **C** portrayed in vermilion,
23:23 the Babylonians and all the **C**,
Da 1: 4 to be taught the literature and language of the **C**.
2: 2 the **C** be summoned to tell the king his dreams.
2: 4 The **C** said to the king (in Aramaic), "O king,
2: 5 king answered the **C**, "This is a public decree:
2:10 The **C** answered the king,
3: 8 at this time certain **C** came forward
4: 7 Then the magicians, the enchanters, the **C**,
5: 7 king cried aloud to bring in the enchanters, the **C**,
5:11 made him chief of the magicians, enchanters, **C**,
9: 1 who became king over the realm of the **C**—
Hab 1: 6 For I am rousing the **C**,
Ac 7: 4 he left the country of the **C** and settled in Haran.
Jdt 1: 6 Thus, many nations joined the forces of the **C**.
5: 6 These people are descended from the **C**.
Bar 1: 2 the time when the **C** took Jerusalem and burned it
LtJ 6:40 Besides, even the **C** themselves dishonor them;
Aza 1:25 and burned those **C** who were caught near
1Es 1:52 to bring against them the kings of the **C**.
4:45 when Judea was laid waste by the **C**.
6:15 Nebuchadnezzzar of Babylon, king of the **C**;

CHALDEES (KJV) See CHALDEANS

CHALKSTONES (1) [STONE]
Isa 27: 9 the stones of the altars like **c** crushed to pieces,

CHALLENGED (1)
Jer 50:24 discovered and seized, because you **c** the LORD.

CHALPHI (1)
1Mc 11:70 son of Absalom and Judas son of **C**,

CHAMBER (49) [BEDCHAMBER, CHAMBERLAIN, CHAMBERS, STORE-CHAMBERS]
Jdg 3:20 while he was sitting alone in his cool roof **c**,
3:23 and closed the doors of the roof **c** on him,
3:24 they saw that the doors of the roof **c** were locked,
3:24 "He must be relieving himself in the cool **c**."
3:25 When he still did not open the doors of the roof **c**,
16: 9 While men were lying in wait in an inner **c**,
16:12 (The men lying in wait were in an inner **c**.)
2Sa 13:10 Amnon said to Tamar, "Bring the food into the **c**,
13:10 and brought them into the **c** to Amnon her brother.
18:33 and went up to the **c** over the gate, and wept;
1Ki 17:19 up into the upper **c** where he was lodging,
17:23 from the upper **c** into the house, and gave him
22:25 on that day when you go in to hide in an inner **c**."
2Ki 1: 2 through the lattice in his upper **c** in Samaria,
4:10 Let us make a small roof **c** with walls,
4:11 he went up to the **c** and lay down there.
9: 2 and take him into an inner **c**.
23:11 by the **c** of the eunuch Nathan-melech,
23:12 The altars on the roof of the upper **c** of Ahaz,
2Ch 18:24 on that day when you go in to hide in an inner **c**."
Ezr 10: 6 and went to the **c** of Jehohanan son of Eliashib,
Job 37: 9 From its **c** comes the whirlwind,
Ps 45:13 in her **c** with gold-woven robes;
SS 3: 4 and into the **c** of her that conceived me.
8: 2 and into the **c** of the one who bore me.
Jer 35: 4 of the LORD into the **c** of the sons of Hanan son
35: 4 which was near the **c** of the officials,
35: 4 above the **c** of Maaseiah son of Shallum,
36:10 in the **c** of Gemariah son of Shaphan the secretary,
36:12 down to the king's house, into the secretary's **c**;
36:20 in the **c** of Elishama the secretary, they went to
36:21 he took it from the **c** of Elishama the secretary;
Eze 40:38 There was a **c** with its door in the vestibule of
40:45 "This **c** that faces south is for
40:46 and the **c** that faces north is for
Tob 6:14 and that they died in the bridal **c**.
6:17 When you enter the bridal **c**,
Wis 17: 4 inner **c** that held them protected them from fear,
1Mc 1:27 she who sat in the bridal **c** was mourning.
8:15 but they have built for themselves a senate **c**,
8:19 they entered the senate **c** and spoke as follows:
12: 3 So they went to Rome and entered the senate **c**
1Es 3:15 and he took his seat in the council **c**,
9: 1 the temple to the **c** of Jehohanan son of Eliashib,
3Mc 4: 6 the bridal **c** to share married life exchanged joy
2Es 5: 9 and wisdom shall withdraw into its **c**,
10: 1 that when my son entered his wedding **c**,
10:48 'My son died as he entered his wedding **c**,'
4Mc 15:25 For as in the council **c** of her own soul she saw

CHAMBERLAIN (1) [CHAMBER]
Ac 12:20 and after winning over Blastus, the king's **c**,

CHAMBERLAIN (KJV) See also CITY TREASURER, EUNUCH

CHAMBERS‡ (63) [CHAMBER]
Dt 32:25 the sword shall bereave, and in the **c** terror,
1Ki 6: 5 and he made side **c** all around.
1Ch 9:26 in charge of the **c** and the treasures of the house
9:33 in the **c** of the temple free from other service,
23:28 having the care of the courts and the **c**,
28:11 its treasuries, its upper rooms, and its inner **c**,
28:12 of the house of the LORD, all the surrounding **c**,
2Ch 3: 9 He overlaid the upper **c** with gold.
Ezr 8:29 within the **c** of the house of the LORD."
Ne 10:37 to the priests, to the **c** of the house of our God;
10:38 to the **c** of the storehouse.
12:44 On that day men were appointed over the **c** for
13: 4 who was appointed over the **c** of the house
13: 9 Then I gave orders and they cleansed the **c**,
Job 9: 9 the Pleiades and the **c** of the south;
Ps 104: 3 you set the beams of your **c** on the waters,
105:30 even in the **c** of their kings.
Pr 7:27 going down to the **c** of death.
SS 1: 4 The king has brought me into his **c**.
Isa 26:20 Come, my people, enter your **c**,
Jer 35: 2 into one of the **c**; then offer them wine to drink.
Eze 40:17 there were **c** there, and a pavement,
40:17 thirty **c** fronted on the pavement.
40:44 On the outside of the inner gateway there were **c**
41: 5 and the width of the side **c**, four cubits,
41: 6 The side **c** were in three stories, one over another,
41: 6 of the temple to serve as supports for the side **c**,
41: 7 The passageway of the side **c** widened from story
41: 8 the foundations of the side **c** measured a full reed
41: 9 of the outer wall of the side **c** was five cubits;
41: 9 the free space between the side **c** of the temple
41:10 the **c** of the court was a width of twenty cubits all
41:11 The side **c** opened onto the area left free,
42: 1 and he brought me to the **c** that were opposite
42: 3 the **c** rose gallery by gallery in three stories.
42: 4 In front of the **c** was a passage on the inner side,
42: 5 Now the upper **c** were narrower,
42: 5 from them than from the lower and middle **c** in
42: 6 for this reason the upper **c** were set back from
42: 7 There was a wall outside parallel to the **c**,
42: 7 toward the outer court, opposite the **c**,
42: 8 For the **c** on the outer court were fifty cubits long,
42: 9 the foot of these **c** ran a passage that one entered
42:10 and opposite the building, there were **c**
42:11 they were similar to the **c** on the north,
42:12 So the entrances of the **c** to the south were entered
42:13 "The north **c** and the south chambers opposite
42:13 "The north chambers and the south **c** opposite
42:13 the holy **c**, where the priests who approach
44:19 and lay them in the holy **c**;
46:19 to the north row of the holy **c** for the priests;
Am 9: 6 who builds his upper **c** in the heavens,
1Mc 4:38 They saw also the **c** of the priests in ruins.
4:57 they restored the gates and the **c** for the priests,
1Es 8:59 in Jerusalem, in the **c** of the house of our Lord."
3Mc 1:18 in their **c** rushed out with their mothers,
1:19 for marriage abandoned the bridal **c** prepared
2Es 4:35 of the righteous in their **c** ask about these matters,
4:41 "In Hades the **c** of the souls are like the womb.
5:37 the closed **c**, and bring out for me the winds shut
7:*32* and the **c** shall give up the souls
7:*95* being gathered into their **c** and guarded by angels
8:20 whose eyes are exalted and whose upper **c** are in

CHAMELEON (1)
Lev 11:30 the lizard, the sand lizard, and the **c**.

CHAMOIS (KJV) See MOUNTAIN-SHEEP

CHAMPAIGN (KJV) See ARABAH

CHAMPION (5) [CHAMPIONED]

1Sa 17: 4 the camp of the Philistines a c named Goliath,
17:23 As he talked with them, the c,
17:51 the Philistines saw that their c was dead, they fled.
Wis 18:21 For a blameless man was quick to act as their c;
4Mc 15:29 vindicator of the law and c of religion,

CHAMPIONED (1) [CHAMPION]

Job 29:16 and I c the cause of the stranger.

CHANAAN (KJV) See CANAAN

CHANCE (7)

1Sa 6: 9 it happened to us by c."
Ecc 9:11 but time and c happen to them all.
Jer 46:17 the name "Braggart who missed his c."
Lk 10:31 Now by c a priest was going down that road;
Ac 27:12 on the c that somehow they could reach Phoenix,
Heb 12:17 he was rejected, for he found no c to repent,
Wis 2: 2 For we were born by mere c,

CHANCELLOR (KJV) See ROYAL DEPUTY

CHANGE‡ (51) [CHANGED, CHANGERS, CHANGES, CHANGING]

Ge 35: 2 and purify yourselves, and c your clothes;
Ex 13:17 they may c their minds and return to Egypt."
32:12 c your mind and do not bring disaster
Nu 23:19 or a mortal, that he should c his mind.
Dt 28:24 LORD will c the rain of your land into powder,
1Sa 15:29 the Glory of Israel will not recant or c his mind;
15:29 for he is not a mortal, that he should c his mind."
2Sa 14:20 In order to c the course of affairs
Job 14:20 you c their countenance, and send them away.
Ps 46: 2 we will not fear, though the earth should c,
55:19 because they do not c, and do not fear God.
102:26 You c them like clothing, and they pass away;
110: 4 The LORD has sworn and will not c his mind,
Jer 13:23 Can Ethiopians c their skin
18: 8 I will c my mind about the disaster that I intended
18:10 then I will c my mind about the good
26: 3 that I may c my mind about the disaster
26:13 and the LORD will c his mind about the disaster
26:19 not the LORD c his mind about the disaster
Da 7:25 shall attempt to c the sacred seasons and the law;
Jnh 3: 9 God may relent and c his mind;
Zep 3: 9 At that time I will c the speech of the peoples to
3:19 and I will c their shame into praise and renown
Mal 3: 6 For I the LORD do not c;
Mt 18: 3 unless you c and become like children,
21:32 you did not c your minds and believe him.
Ac 6:14 and will c the customs that Moses handed on
Gal 4:20 with you now and could c my tone,
Heb 7:12 a c in the priesthood, there is necessarily a c in the
7:21 "The Lord has sworn and will not c his mind,
Jas 1:17 whom there is no variation or shadow due to c.
AdE 2:20 So Esther did not c her mode of life.
Wis 4:11 up so that evil might not c their understanding
12:10 and that their way of thinking would never c.
19: 2 they would c their minds and pursue them.
Sir 6: 9 And there are friends who c into enemies,
18:26 From morning to evening conditions c;
33:20 in case you c your mind and must ask for it.
43: 8 how marvelous it is in this c,
1Mc 1:49 they would forget the law and c all the ordinances.
2Mc 3:16 the c in his color disclosed the anguish of his soul.
4:46 induced the king to c his mind.
6: 9 and should kill those who did not choose to c over
11:24 not consent to our father's c to Greek customs,
3Mc 1:25 in various ways to c his arrogant mind from
3: 8 and expected that matters would c;
3:21 and we ventured to make a c,
4Mc 6:18 we should now c our course
11:25 to c our mind or to force us to eat defiling foods,
15:14 because of religion did not c her attitude.

CHANGED‡ (48) [CHANGE]

Ge 31: 7 and c my wages ten times,
31:41 and you have c my wages ten times.
41:14 When he had shaved himself and c his clothes,
Ex 10:19 LORD c the wind into a very strong west wind,
14: 5 the minds of Pharaoh and his officials were c
32:14 And the LORD c his mind about the disaster
Lev 13:55 If the diseased spot has not c color,
Nu 13:16 And Moses c the name of Hoshea son of Nun
32:38 and Baal-meon (some names being c),
1Sa 21:13 So he c his behavior before them;
2Sa 12:20 washed, anointed himself, and c his clothes.
2Ki 23:34 and c his name to Jehoiakim.
24:17 king in his place, and c his name to Zedekiah.
2Ch 36: 4 and c his name to Jehoiakim;
Est 9: 1 but which had been c to a day when
Job 38:14 It is c like clay under the seal,
Ps 77:10 that the right hand of the Most High has c."
Ecc 8: 1 and the hardness of one's countenance is c.
Jer 2:11 Has a nation c its gods,
2:11 But my people have c their glory for something
La 4: 1 the gold has grown dim, how the pure gold is c!
Da 4:16 Let his mind be c from that of a human,
6: 8 so that it cannot be c,
Da 6:15 or ordinance that the king establishes can be c."
6:17 so that nothing might be c concerning Daniel.
Hos 4: 7 they c their glory into shame.
Jnh 3:10 God c his mind about the calamity
Mt 21:29 but later he c his mind and went.
Lk 9:29 he was praying, the appearance of his face c,
Jn 4:46 in Galilee where he had c the water into wine.
Ac 28: 6 they c their minds and began to say that he was
1Co 15:51 We will not all die, but we will all be c,
15:52 be raised imperishable, and we will be c.
Heb 1:12 and like clothing they will be c.
AdE 9:22 in which their condition had been c from sorrow
15: 8 Then God c the spirit of the king to gentleness,
Wis 16:21 was c to suit everyone's liking.
16:25 Therefore at that time also, c into all forms,
19:18 For the elements c places with one another,
Sir 6:28 and she will be c into joy for you.
2Mc 6:29 before had acted toward him with goodwill now c
1Es 7:15 because he had c the will of the king of
3Mc 1: 3 by birth who later c his religion and apostatized
2Es 6:16 for they know that their end must be c."
6:26 of the earth's inhabitants shall be c and converted
8:22 at whose command they are c to wind and fire,
4Mc 4:19 Jason c the nation's way of life
6:24 and that he had not been c by their compassion,

CHANGERS (4) [CHANGE]

Mt 21:12 and he overturned the tables of the money c and
Mk 11:15 and he overturned the tables of the money c and
Jn 2:14 and doves, and the money c seated at their tables.
2:15 He also poured out the coins of the money c

CHANGES‡ (8) [CHANGE]

2Ki 5:22 please give them a talent of silver and two c
5:23 up two talents of silver in two bags, with two c
Da 2:21 He c times and seasons, deposes kings and sets
Wis 7:18 the alternations of the solstices and the c of
Sir 13:25 The heart c the countenance,
25:17 A woman's wickedness c her appearance,
27:11 but the fool c like the moon.
3Mc 5:42 the c of mind that had come about within him for

CHANGING‡ (4) [CHANGE]

Jer 2:36 How lightly you gad about, c your ways!
AdE 16: 9 by c our methods and always judging what comes
Sir 43: 6 It is the moon that marks the c seasons,
4Mc 8: 8 the Greek way of life and by c your manner

CHANNEL (4) [CHANNELS]

Job 38:25 "Who has cut a c for the torrents of rain,
SS 4:13 Your c is an orchard of pomegranates
Isa 27:12 the LORD will thresh from the c of the Euphrates
Sir 24:30 like a water c into a garden.

CHANNELS (14) [CHANNEL]

2Sa 22:16 Then the c of the sea were seen,
Job 28:10 They cut out c in the rocks,
Ps 18:15 Then the c of the sea were seen,
Isa 8: 7 above all its c and overflow all its banks;
11:15 and will split it into seven c,
Eze 29: 3 the great dragon sprawling in the midst of its c,
29: 4 and make the fish of your c stick to your scales.
29: 4 I will draw you up from your c,
29: 4 with all the fish of your c sticking to your scales.
29: 5 you and all the fish of your c;
29:10 I am against you, and against your c,
30:12 I will dry up the c, and will sell the land into
2Es 13:44 the c of the river until they had crossed over.
13:47 the Most High will stop the c of the river again,

CHANT (2) [CHANTED, CHANTING]

Eze 32:16 The women of the nations shall c it.
32:16 Over Egypt and all its hordes they shall c it,

CHANTED (1) [CHANT]

Eze 32:16 This is a lamentation; it shall be c.

CHANTING (1) [CHANT]

3Mc 6:32 They stopped their c of dirges and took up

CHAOS (6)

Job 10:22 the land of gloom and c,
Isa 24:10 The city of c is broken down,
34:11 and the plummet of c over its nobles.
45:18 did not create it a c, he formed it to be inhabited!):
45:19 not say to the offspring of Jacob, "Seek me in c."
2Es 5: 8 There shall be c also in many places,

CHAPEL (KJV) See SANCTUARY

CHAPHENATHA (1)

1Mc 12:37 and he repaired the section called C.

CHAPITER[S] (KJV) See CAPITALS, CROWN

CHARACTER (6) [CHARACTERISTIC, CHARACTERS]

Ro 5: 4 and endurance produces c, and c produces hope,
2Co 12: 7 considering the exceptional c of the revelations.
Heb 6:17 of the promise the unchangeable c of his purpose,
2Mc 5:22 by birth a Phrygian and in c more barbarous than
4Mc 15: 4 upon the c of a small child a wondrous likeness

CHARACTERISTIC (1) [CHARACTER]

3Mc 7:17 called "rose-bearing" because of a c of the place,

CHARACTERS (2) [CHARACTER]

Isa 8: 1 Take a large tablet and write on it in common c,
2Es 14:42 using c that they did not know.

CHARASHIM (KJV) See GE-HARASHIM

CHARAX (1)

2Mc 12:17 from there, they came to C, to the Jews

CHARCHEMISH (KJV) See CARCHEMISH

CHARCOAL (3)

Pr 26:21 As c is to hot embers and wood to fire,
Jn 18:18 the police had made a c fire because it was cold,
21: 9 they had gone ashore, they saw a c fire there,

CHAREA (1)

1Es 5:32 the descendants of C, the descendants of Barkos,

CHARGE (187) [CHARGED, CHARGERS, CHARGES, CHARGING]

Ge 18:19 that he may c his children and his household
24: 2 who had c of all that he had,
26: 5 Abraham obeyed my voice and kept my c,
30:35 and put them in c of his sons;
39: 4 of his house and put him in c of all that he had.
39: 6 So he left all that he had in Joseph's c;
47: 6 put them in c of my livestock."
49:33 When Jacob ended his c to his sons,
Ex 23: 7 Keep far from a false c,
Lev 8:35 keeping the LORD's c so that you do not die;
18:30 So keep my c not to commit any
22: 9 They shall keep my c, so that they may
25:15 the seller shall c you only for
Nu 3: 8 they shall be in c of all the furnishings of the tent
3:32 and to have oversight of those who had c of
3:38 having c of the rites within the sanctuary,
4:16 Eleazar son of Aaron the priest shall have c of
4:27 you shall assign to their c all that they are to carry.
9:19 the Israelites would keep the c of the LORD,
9:23 They kept the c of the LORD,
18: 8 I have given you c of the offerings made to me,
31:30 to the Levites who have c of the tabernacle of
31:47 to the Levites who had c of the tabernacle of
Dt 2: 4 and c the people as follows:
3:28 But c Joshua, and encourage and strengthen him,
11: 1 and keep his c, his decrees, his ordinances,
13:14 If the c is established that such
17: 4 and the c is proved true that such
19:15 on the evidence of two or three witnesses shall a c
20: 9 then the commanders shall take c of them.
22:20 If, however, this c is true,
23:19 not c interest on loans to another Israelite,
23:20 On loans to a foreigner you may c interest,
23:20 to another Israelite you may not c interest,
33: 3 all his holy ones were in your c;
Jos 6: 5 and all the people shall c straight ahead."
22: 3 to keep the c of the LORD your God.
Ru 2: 5 Then Boaz said to his servant who was in c of
2: 6 The servant who was in c of the reapers answered,
1Sa 7: 1 Eleazar, to have c of the ark of the LORD.
13:21 The c was two-thirds of a shekel for
14:27 But Jonathan had not heard his father c the troops
17:22 the things in c of the keeper of the baggage,
19:20 with Samuel standing in c of them,
22: 9 who was in c of Saul's servants, answered,
2Sa 3: 8 and yet you c me now with a crime
10:10 of his men he put in the c of his brother Abishai,
20:24 Adoram was in c of the forced labor;
23:23 And David put him in c of his bodyguard.
1Ki 2: 3 and keep the c of the LORD your God,
4: 6 Ahishar was in c of the palace;
4: 6 and Adoniram son of Abda was in c of
4:28 and swift steeds, each according to his c.
5:14 Adoniram was in c of the forced labor.
5:16 having c of the people who did the work.
9:23 who had c of the people who carried on the work.
11:28 that the young man was industrious he gave him c
16: 9 who was in c of the palace at Tirzah,
18: 3 who was in c of the palace.
21:10 and have them bring a c against him, saying,
21:13 and the scoundrels brought a c against Naboth,
2Ki 6: 1 the place where we live under your c is too small
7:17 the captain on whose hand he leaned to have c of
15: 5 Jotham the king's son was in c of the palace,
18:18 who was in c of the palace,
18:37 who was in c of the palace,
19: 2 And he sent Eliakim, who was in c of the palace,
1Ch 6:31 the men whom David put in c of the service
9:19 were in c of the work of the service,
9:19 as their ancestors had been in c of the camp of
9:23 and their descendants were in c of the gates of
9:26 in c of the chambers and the treasures of the house
9:27 and they had c of opening it every morning.
9:28 Some of them had c of the utensils of service,
9:31 was in c of making the flat cakes.

1Ch 9:32 Also some of their kindred of the Kohathites had c
11:25 And David put him in c of his bodyguard.
19:11 of his troops he put in the c of his brother Abishai,
22:12 when he gives you c over Israel you may keep
23: 4 "shall have c of the work in the house of
23:32 Thus they shall keep c of the tent of meeting and
26:20 Ahijah had c of the treasuries of the house of God
26:22 in c of the treasuries of the house of the LORD.
26:24 was chief officer in c of the treasuries.
26:26 and his brothers were in c of all the treasuries of
27: 2 in c of the first division in the first month;
27: 4 Dodai the Ahohite was in c of the division of
27: 6 his son Ammizabad was in c of his division.
2Ch 13:11 for we keep the c of the LORD our God,
23:18 to be in c of the house of the LORD,
24:12 The king and Jehoiada gave it to those who had c
26:21 His son Jotham was in c of the palace of the king,
31:12 The chief officer in c of them was Conaniah
31:14 was in c of the freewill offerings to God,
Ezr 1: 8 King Cyrus of Persia had them released into the c
3: 9 together took c of the workers in the house
Ne 7: 2 I gave my brother Hanani c over Jerusalem,
10:32 the obligation to c ourselves yearly one-third of
11: 9 and Judah son of Hassenuah was second in c of
11:22 the singers, in c of the work of the house of God.
12: 8 and Mattaniah, who with his associates was in c
Est 2: 3 the king's eunuch, who is in c of the women;
2: 8 who had c of the women.
2:14 who was in c of the concubines;
2:15 who had c of the women, advised.
3: 9 of silver into the hands of those who have c of
4: 8 and c her to go to the king to make supplication
Job 1:22 not sin or c God with wrongdoing.
34:13 Who gave him c over the earth and who laid
Ps 50:21 But now I rebuke you, and lay the c before you.
Isa 36: 3 who was in c of the palace,
36:22 who was in c of the palace,
37: 2 And he sent Eliakim, who was in c of the palace,
Jer 27: 4 Give them this c for their masters:
35: 8 We have obeyed the c of our ancestor Jonadab son
Eze 40:45 that faces south is for the priests who have c of
40:46 that faces north is for the priests who have c of
44: 8 And you have not kept c of my sacred offerings;
44: 8 to act for you in keeping my c in my sanctuary.
44:14 Yet I will appoint them to keep c of the temple,
44:15 who kept the c of my sanctuary when the people
44:16 to minister to me, and they shall keep my c.
48:11 the descendants of Zadok, who kept my c,
Da 6:14 the king heard the c, he was very much distressed.
Joel 2: 4 and like war-horses they c.
2: 7 Like warriors they c, like soldiers they scale
Hab 1: 8 more menacing than wolves at dusk; their horses c.
Zec 3: 7 you shall rule my house and have c of my courts,
Mt 24:45 whom his master has put in c of his household,
24:47 he will put that one in c of all his possessions.
25:21 I will put you in c of many things;
25:23 I will put you in c of many things;
27:14 But he gave him no answer, not even to a single c,
27:37 Over his head they put the c against him,
Mk 13:34 when he leaves home and puts his slaves in c,
15:26 The inscription of the c against him read,
Lk 12:42 in c of his slaves, to give them their allowance
12:44 he will put that one in c of all his possessions.
19:17 in a very small thing, take c of ten cities.'
Jn 8: 6 ⟦that they might have some c to bring against him⟧
Ac 8:27 in c of her entire treasury.
23:28 to know the c for which they accused him,
24: 9 The Jews also joined in the c by asserting
24:13 Neither can they prove to you the c that they
25:16 an opportunity to make a defense against the c.
25:18 they did not c him with any of the crimes
28:19 even though I had no c to bring against my nation.
Ro 8:33 Who will bring any c against God's elect?
1Co 9:18 of c, so as not to make full use of my rights in
2Co 11: 7 I proclaimed God's good news to you free of c?
13: 1 "Any c must be sustained by the evidence of two
1Th 5:12 and have c of you in the Lord and admonish you;
1Ti 6:13 made the good confession, I c you
Phm 1:18 or owes you anything, c that to my account.
Heb 5: 1 in c of things pertaining to God on their behalf,
1Pe 5: 2 of God that is in your c, exercising the oversight,
5: 3 Do not lord it over those in your c,
Tob 1:22 and in c of administrations of the accounts
Jdt 8:10 who was in c of all she possessed,
12:11 the eunuch who had c of his personal affairs,
14:13 to Holofernes' tent and said to the steward in c
AdE 2: 3 be entrusted to the king's eunuch who is in c of
2:14 where Gai the king's eunuch is in c of the women;
2:15 the eunuch in c of the women, had commanded.
4: 8 to c her to go in to the king and plead for his favor
13: 6 who is in c of affairs and is our second father,
Sir 26:27 *garrulous wife is like a trumpet sounding the c,*
1Mc 3:32 in c of the king's affairs from the river Euphrates
3:55 in c of thousands and hundreds and fifties
4: 8 not fear their numbers or be afraid when they c.
5:19 "Take c of this people, but do not engage in battle
7:20 He placed Alcimus in c of the country and left
9:25 Bacchides chose the godless and put them in c of
14:42 be governor over them and that he should take c
14:42 and that he should take c of the sanctuary,
2Mc 3: 7 who was in c of his affairs,
6:21 in c of that unlawful sacrifice took the man aside
10:11 appointed one Lysias to have c of the government
11: 1 who was in c of the government,
13: 2 his guardian, who had c of the government.
13:23 who had been left in c of the government,
1Es 5:58 or more years of age to have c of the work of
3Mc 5: 5 The servants in c of the Jews went out in
5:14 the person who was in c of the invitations,
6:30 in c of the revenues and ordered him to provide to
7: 7 we justly have acquitted them of every c
2Es 5:41 you have c of those who are alive at the end,

CHARGED (45) [CHARGE]

Ge 28: 1 Isaac called Jacob and blessed him, and c him,
28: 6 and that as he blessed him he c him,
40: 4 The captain of the guard c Joseph with them,
42:30 and c us with spying on the land.
45:19 You are further c to say, 'Do this:
49:29 Then he c them, saying to them,
Ex 4:28 and all the signs with which he had c him.
Nu 4:31 This is what they are c to carry,
7: 9 because they were c with the care of
Dt 1:16 I c your judges at that time:
1:18 So I c you at that time with all the things
2:37 just as the LORD our God had c.
3:18 At that time, I c you as follows:
3:21 And I c Joshua as well at that time, saying:
4: 5 See, just as the LORD my God has c me,
4:13 which he c you to observe, that is,
4:14 the LORD c me at that time to teach you statutes
6: 1 that the LORD your God c me to teach you
24: 5 with the army or be c with any related duty.
27: 1 and the elders of Israel c all the people as follows:
27:11 The same day Moses c the people as follows:
33: 4 Moses c us with the law,
Jos 6:20 so the people c straight ahead into the city
18: 8 and Joshua c those who went to write
1Sa 14:28 "Your father strictly c the troops with an oath,
21: 2 "The king has c me with a matter, and said to me,
21: 2 and with which I have c you.'
1Ki 2: 1 he c his son Solomon, saying:
2:43 and the commandment with which I c you?"
14: 6 For I am c with heavy tidings for you.
2Ki 10: 6 who were c with their upbringing.
1Ch 22: 6 for his son Solomon and c him to build a house
2Ch 19: 9 He c them: "This is how you shall act:
36:23 he has c me to build him a house at Jerusalem,
Ezr 1: 2 and he has c me to build him a house at Jerusalem
Est 2:10 for Mordecai had c her not to tell.
2:20 or her people, as Mordecai had c her;
Jer 32:13 In their presence I c Baruch, saying,
Lk 11:50 that this generation may be c with the blood of all
11:51 Yes, I tell you, it will be c against this generation.
Ac 19:40 For we are in danger of being c with rioting today,
23:29 but was c with nothing deserving death
Ro 3: 9 No, not at all; for we have already c that all,
Sus 1:43 of the wicked things that they have c against me!"
2Mc 12:37 then he c against Gorgias's troops when they were

CHARGER (KJV) See PLATE, PLATTER

CHARGERS (1) [CHARGE]

Na 2: 3 when he musters them; the c prance.

CHARGES (21) [CHARGE]

Dt 22:14 and makes up c against her, slandering her
22:17 now he has made up c against her,
Ne 5: 7 I brought c against the nobles and the officials;
Job 4:18 and his angels he c with error;
Jer 12: 1 O LORD, when I lay c against you;
18:18 Come, let us bring c against him,
Mk 15: 4 See how many c they bring against you."
Lk 16: 1 and c were brought to him
23:14 not found this man guilty of any of your c
Ac 19:38 let them bring c there against one another.
25: 7 bringing many serious c against him,
25: 9 and be tried there before me on these c?"
25:11 but if there is nothing to their c against me,
25:20 to go to Jerusalem and be tried there on these c.
25:27 a prisoner without indicating the c against him."
3Jn 1:10 to what he is doing in spreading false c against us.
1:10 And not content with those c,
1Mc 7:25 to the king and brought malicious c against them.
10:63 and proclaim that no one is to bring c against him
2Mc 4:43 C were brought against Menelaus
4:47 he acquitted of the c against him,

CHARGING (7) [CHARGE]

Ex 6:13 c them to free the Israelites from the land
Dt 4: 2 of the LORD your God with which I am c you.
Pr 28:15 or a c bear is a wicked ruler over a poor people.
Da 8: 4 the ram c westward and northward and southward.
Na 3: 3 Horsemen c, flashing sword and glittering spear,
2Mc 5: 2 over all the city golden-clad cavalry c through
3Mc 4:19 c that they had been bribed to contrive a means

CHARIOT‡ (73) [CHARIOTEER, CHARIOTEERS, CHARIOTRY, CHARIOTS]

Ge 41:43 in the c of his second-in-command;
46:29 Joseph made ready his c and went up
Ex 14: 6 So he had his c made ready,
14: 9 his c drivers and his army;
14:17 his chariots, and his c drivers.
14:18 his chariots, and his c drivers."
14:23 all of Pharaoh's horses, chariots, and c drivers.
14:25 He clogged their c wheels so that they turned
14:26 upon their chariots and c drivers."
14:28 the chariots and the c drivers, the entire army
15:19 of Pharaoh with his chariots and his c drivers went
Jdg 4:15 Sisera got down from his c and fled away on foot,
5:28 'Why is his c so long in coming?
2Sa 8: 4 David hamstrung all the c horses,
10:18 of the Arameans seven hundred c teams,
15: 1 After this Absalom got himself a c and horses,
1Ki 7:33 The wheels were made like a c wheel;
10:26 in the c cities and with the king in Jerusalem.
10:29 A c could be imported from Egypt
12:18 then hurriedly mounted his c to flee to Jerusalem.
18:44 'Harness your c and go down before
20:25 horse for horse, and c for c;
20:33 and he had him come up into the c.
22:34 so he said to the driver of his c, "Turn around,
22:35 and the king was propped up in his c facing
22:35 the wound had flowed into the bottom of the c.
22:38 They washed the c by the pool of Samaria;
2Ki 2:11 a c of fire and horses of fire separated the two
5:21 he jumped down from the c to meet him and said,
5:26 not go with you in spirit when someone left his c
8:21 and their c commanders who had surrounded him;
9:16 Then Jehu mounted his c and went to Jezreel,
9:21 And they got his c ready.
9:21 each in his c, and went to meet Jehu;
9:24 and he sank in his c.
9:27 And they shot him in the c at the ascent to Gur,
9:28 His officers carried him in a c to Jerusalem,
10:15 Jehu took him up with him into the c.
10:16 So he had him ride in his c.
23:30 His servants carried him dead in a c
1Ch 18: 4 David hamstrung all the c horses,
28:18 also his plan for the golden c of the cherubim
2Ch 1:14 in the c cities and with the king in Jerusalem.
1:17 a c for six hundred shekels of silver,
9:25 in the c cities and with the king in Jerusalem.
10:18 King Rehoboam hurriedly mounted his c to flee
18:33 so he said to the driver of his c, "Turn around,
18:34 up in his c facing the Arameans until evening;
21: 9 who had surrounded him and his c commanders.
35:24 out of the c and carried him in his second c
Ps 104: 3 you make the clouds your c,
SS 6:12 my fancy set me in a c beside my prince.
Isa 43:17 who brings out c and horse, army and warrior;
Jer 51:21 with you I smash the c and the charioteer;
Na 3: 2 galloping horse and bounding c!
Zec 6: 2 first c had red horses, the second c black horses,
6: 3 the third c white horses, and the fourth c dappled gray horses.
6: 6 The c with the black horses goes toward
9:10 He will cut off the c from Ephraim and
Ac 8:28 seated in his c, he was reading the prophet Isaiah.
8:29 "Go over to this c and join it."
8:38 He commanded the c to stop, and both of them,
Sir 48: 9 in a c with horses of fire.
49: 8 which God showed him above the c of
2Mc 9: 7 that he fell out of his c as it was rushing along,
14:21 A c came forward from each army;
1Es 1:28 Josiah, however, did not turn back to his c,
1:31 He got into his second c;
3: 6 and have a c with gold bridles,

CHARIOTEER‡ (2) [CHARIOT]

Jer 51:21 with you I smash the chariot and the c;
2Mc 9: 4 so he ordered his c to drive without stopping

CHARIOTEERS (3) [CHARIOT]

Ge 50: 9 Both chariots and c went up with him.
1Ch 19:18 and David killed seven thousand Aramean c
Eze 39:20 you shall be filled at my table with horses and c,

CHARIOTRY (3) [CHARIOT]

1Ki 9:22 and the commanders of his c and cavalry.
2Ch 8: 9 the commanders of his c and cavalry.
Ps 68:17 With mighty c, twice ten thousand,

CHARIOTS‡ (113) [CHARIOT]

Ge 50: 9 Both c and charioteers went up with him.
Ex 14: 7 six hundred picked c and all the other c of Egypt
14: 9 all Pharaoh's horses and c,
14:17 his c, and his chariot drivers.
14:18 his c, and his chariot drivers."
14:23 all of Pharaoh's horses, c, and chariot drivers.
14:26 upon their c and chariot drivers."
14:28 the c and the chariot drivers, the entire army
15: 4 "Pharaoh's c and his army he cast into the sea;
15:19 of Pharaoh with his c and his chariot drivers went
Dt 11: 4 and c, how he made the water of the Red Sea flow
20: 1 and c, an army larger than your own, you shall not
Jos 11: 4 with very many horses and c.
11: 6 and burn their c with fire."
11: 9 and burned their c with fire.
17:16 yet all the Canaanites who live in the plain have c
17:18 though they have c of iron,
24: 6 and the Egyptians pursued your ancestors with c
Jdg 1:19 because they had c of iron.
4: 3 for he had nine hundred c of iron,
4: 7 by the Wadi Kishon with his c and his troops;
4:13 Sisera called out all his c, nine hundred c of iron,
4:15 And the LORD threw Sisera and all his c
4:16 the c and the army to Harosheth-ha-goiim.
5:28 Why tarry the hoofbeats of his c?'
1Sa 8:11 and appoint them to his c and to be his horsemen, and to run before his c;
8:12 of war and the equipment of his c.
13: 5 thirty thousand c, and six thousand horsemen,
2Sa 1: 6 while the c and the horsemen drew close to him.

2Sa 8: 4 but left enough for a hundred **c**.
1Ki 1: 5 he prepared for himself **c** and horsemen,
4:26 also had forty thousand stalls of horses for his **c**,
9:19 the cities for his **c**, the cities for his cavalry,
10:26 Solomon gathered together **c** and horses;
10:26 he had fourteen hundred **c**
16: 9 But his servant Zimri, commander of half his **c**,
20: 1 with him, along with horses and **c**.
20:21 king of Israel went out, attacked the horses and **c**,
22:31 the thirty-two captains of his **c**,
22:32 When the captains of the **c** saw Jehoshaphat,
22:33 the captains of the **c** saw that it was not the king
2Ki 2:12 The **c** of Israel and its horsemen!"
5: 9 So Naaman came with his horses and **c**,
6:14 So he sent horses and **c** there and a great army;
6:15 an army with horses and **c** was all around the city.
6:17 the mountain was full of horses and **c** of fire all
7: 6 the Aramean army to hear the sound of **c**,
8:21 Then Joram crossed over to Zair with all his **c**.
10: 2 and you have at your disposal **c** and horses,
13: 7 ten **c** and ten thousand footmen;
13:14 The **c** of Israel and its horsemen!"
18:24 when you rely on Egypt for **c** and for horsemen?
19:23 'With my many **c** I have gone up the heights of
23:11 then he burned the **c** of the sun with fire.
1Ch 18: 4 David took from him one thousand **c**,
19: 6 of silver to hire **c** and cavalry from Mesopotamia,
19: 7 They hired thirty-two thousand **c** and the king
2Ch 1:14 Solomon gathered together **c** and horses;
1:14 he had fourteen hundred **c**
8: 6 and all the towns for his **c**,
9:25 Solomon had four thousand stalls for horses and **c**,
12: 3 with twelve hundred **c** and sixty thousand cavalry.
14: 9 an army of a million men and three hundred **c**,
16: 8 the Libyans a huge army with exceedingly many **c**
18:30 of Aram had commanded the captains of his **c**,
18:31 When the captains of the **c** saw Jehoshaphat,
18:32 for when the captains of the **c** saw that it was not
21: 9 over with his commanders and all his **c**.
Ps 20: 7 Some take pride in **c**, and some in horses,
SS 1: 9 my love, to a mare among Pharaoh's **c**.
Isa 2: 7 and there is no end to their **c**.
22: 6 Elam bore the quiver with **c** and cavalry,
22: 7 Your choicest valleys were full of **c**,
22:18 and there your splendid **c** shall lie,
31: 1 in **c** because they are many and in horsemen
36: 9 when you rely on Egypt for **c** and for horsemen?
37:24 'With my many **c** I have gone up the heights of
66:15 and his **c** like the whirlwind,
66:20 on horses, and in **c**, and in litters, and on mules,
Jer 4:13 He comes up like clouds, his **c** like the whirlwind;
17:25 riding in **c** and on horses, they and their officials,
22: 4 riding in **c** and on horses, they, and their servants,
46: 9 Advance, O horses, and dash madly, O **c**!
47: 3 at the clatter of his **c**,
50:37 A sword against her horses and against her **c**,
Eze 23:24 They shall come against you from the north with **c**
26: 7 king of kings, together with horses, **c**, cavalry,
26:10 wheels, and **c** your very walls shall shake,
Da 11:40 with **c** and horsemen, and with many ships.
Joel 2: 5 As with the rumbling of **c**,
Mic 1:13 Harness the steeds to the **c**,
5:10 from among you and will destroy your **c**;
Na 2: 3 on the **c** flashes on the day when he musters them;
2: 4 The **c** race madly through the streets,
2:13 and I will burn your **c** in smoke,
Hab 3: 8 when you drove your horses, your **c** to victory?
Hag 2:22 and overthrow the **c** and their riders;
Zec 6: 1 And again I looked up and saw four **c** coming out
Rev 9: 9 like the noise of many **c** with horses rushing
18:13 horses and **c**, slaves—and human lives.
Jdt 1:13 of Arphaxad and all his cavalry and all his **c**.
2:19 the whole face of the earth to the west with their **c**
2:22 cavalry, and **c**, and went up into the hill country.
7:20 The whole Assyrian army, their infantry, **c**,
1Mc 1:17 with **c** and elephants and cavalry and with
8: 6 and with cavalry and **c** and a very large army.
2Mc 13: 2 and three hundred **c** armed with scythes
3Mc 2: 7 he pursued them with **c** and a mass of troops,
6: 4 Pharaoh with his abundance of **c**,
2Es 15:29 of Arabia shall come out with many **c**,

CHARITY (5)
Ac 9:36 She was devoted to good works and acts of **c**.
Tob 1: 3 of **c** for my kindred and my people who had gone
1:16 of Shalmaneser I performed many acts of **c**
2:14 she replied to me, "Where are your acts of **c**?
Sir 31:11 and the assembly will proclaim his acts of **c**.

CHARITY (KJV) See also LOVE

CHARM (8) [CHARMED, CHARMER, CHARMERS]
Pr 31:30 **C** is deceitful, and beauty is vain,
Isa 47:11 which you cannot **c** away;
Wis 14:20 attracted by the **c** of his work,
Sir 7:19 for her **c** is worth more than gold.
26:13 A wife's **c** delights her husband,
26:15 A modest wife adds **c** to **c**,
37:21 for the Lord has withheld the gift of **c**,

CHARME (1)
1Es 5:25 The descendants of **C**, one thousand seventeen.

CHARMED (2) [CHARM]
Ecc 10:11 If the snake bites before it is **c**,
Jer 8:17 adders that cannot be **c**, and they shall bite you,

CHARMER (2) [CHARM]
Ecc 10:11 there is no advantage in a **c**.
Sir 12:13 Who pities a snake **c** when he is bitten,

CHARMERS (1) [CHARM]
Ps 58: 5 the voice of **c** or of the cunning enchanter.

CHARMIS (3)
Jdt 6:15 and Chabris son of Gothoniel, and **C** son
8:10 to summon Uzziah and Chabris and **C**,
10: 6 with the elders of the town, Chabris and **C**.

CHARRAN (KJV) See HARAN

CHARRED (3)
Eze 15: 4 both ends of it and the middle of it is **c**,
15: 5 when the fire has consumed it, and it is **c**—
1Mc 11: 4 the **c** bodies of those whom Jonathan had burned

CHASE (7) [CHASED, CHASING]
Lev 26: 7 You shall give **c** to your enemies,
26: 8 Five of you shall give **c** to a hundred,
26: 8 and a hundred of you shall give **c** to ten thousand;
Job 18:11 and **c** them at their heels.
Pr 19:26 **c** away their mother are children who cause shame
Jer 49:19 I will suddenly **c** Edom away from it;
50:44 I will suddenly **c** them away from her;

CHASED (9) [CHASE]
Dt 1:44 then came out against you and **c** you as bees do.
Jos 10:10 **c** them by the way of the ascent of Beth-horon,
11: 8 who attacked them and **c** them as far
Jdg 9:40 Abimelech **c** him, and he fled before him.
Ne 13:28 I **c** him away from me.
Job 20: 8 they will be **c** away like a vision of the night.
Isa 17:13 **c** like chaff on the mountains before the wind
La 4:19 they **c** us on the mountains,
Wis 2: 4 of a cloud, and be scattered like mist that is **c** by

CHASING (11) [CHASE]
Jos 7: 5 **c** them from outside the gate as far as Shebarim
1Sa 17:53 The Israelites came back from **c** the Philistines,
Ecc 1:14 and see, all is vanity and a **c** after wind.
1:17 I perceived that this also is but a **c** after wind.
2:11 and again, all was vanity and a **c** after wind,
2:17 for all is vanity and a **c** after wind.
2:26 This also is vanity and a **c** after wind.
4: 4 This also is vanity and a **c** after wind.
4: 6 with quiet than two handfuls with toil, and a **c**
4:16 Surely this also is vanity and a **c** after wind.
6: 9 this also is vanity and a **c** after wind.

CHASM (1) [CHASMS]
Lk 16:26 between you and us a great **c** has been fixed,

CHASMS (1) [CHASM]
4Mc 14:16 by building in precipitous **c** and in holes and tops

CHASPHO (2)
1Mc 5:26 in Alema and **C**, Maked and Carnaim"—
5:36 From there he marched on and took **C**, Maked,

CHASTE (2) [CHASTITY]
2Co 11: 2 to present you as a **c** virgin to Christ.
Tit 2: 5 **c**, good managers of the household, kind,

CHASTE (KJV) See also PURITY

CHASTENED (1) [CHASTISE]
Job 33:19 They are also **c** with pain upon their beds,

CHASTENING (2) [CHASTISE]
Isa 26:16 they poured out a prayer when your **c** was
Wis 12:22 while **c** us you scourge our enemies ten thousand

CHASTISE (4) [CHASTENED, CHASTENING, CHASTISED, CHASTISEMENT, CHASTISES]
Ps 39:11 "You **c** mortals in punishment for sin,
94:10 to humankind, does he not **c**?
Jer 30:11 I will **c** you in just measure,
46:28 I will **c** you in just measure,

CHASTISE (KJV) See also DISCIPLINE, FLOGGED, PUNISH

CHASTISED (1) [CHASTISE]
4Mc 18: 5 on earth and is being **c** after his death.

CHASTISEMENT (3) [CHASTISE]
La 4: 6 For the **c** of my people has been greater than
Sir 16:12 Great as his mercy, so also is his **c**;
2Es 15:12 because of the plague of **c** and castigation that

CHASTISES (1) [CHASTISE]
Heb 12: 6 and **c** every child whom he accepts."

CHASTISING See Index to Footnotes

CHASTITY (2) [CHASTE]
Sir 7:24 for their **c**, and do not show yourself too indulgent
26:15 and no scales can weigh the value of her **c**.

CHATTER (3)
1Ti 6:20 Avoid the profane **c** and contradictions
2Ti 2:16 Avoid profane **c**, for it will lead people into more
Sir 21:16 A fool's **c** is like a burden on a journey,

CHEAP (1) [CHEAPER]
2Es 16:21 be so **c** upon earth that people will imagine

CHEAPER (1) [CHEAP]
Wis 15:10 Their heart is ashes, their hope is **c** than dirt,

CHEAT (5) [CHEATED]
Lev 19:35 You shall not **c** in measuring length, weight,
25:14 you shall not **c** one another.
25:17 You shall not **c** one another,
Mal 1:14 be the **c** who has a male in the flock and vows
Sir 4: 1 My child, do not **c** the poor of their living,

CHEATED (1) [CHEAT]
Ge 31: 7 yet your father has **c** me and changed my wages

CHEBAR (8)
Eze 1: 1 as I was among the exiles by the river **C**,
1: 3 in the land of the Chaldeans by the river **C**;
3:15 who lived by the river **C**.
3:23 like the glory that I had seen by the river **C**;
10:15 the living creatures that I saw by the river **C**.
10:20 the God of Israel by the river **C**;
10:22 faces whose appearance I had seen by the river **C**.
43: 3 and like the vision that I had seen by the river **C**;

CHECK (1) [CHECKED, CHECKING]
Jas 3: 2 able to keep the whole body in **c** with a bridle.

CHECKED (5) [CHECK]
Lev 13: 5 that the disease is **c** and the disease has not spread
13:37 But if in his eyes the itch is **c**,
Eze 31:15 and its mighty waters were **c**.
2Mc 14:17 but had been temporarily **c** because of
4Mc 1:35 For the emotions of the appetites are restrained, **c**

CHECKER (1) [CHECKERED]
1Ki 7:17 of **c** work with wreaths of chain work for

CHECKERED (2) [CHECKER]
Ex 28: 4 a breastpiece, an ephod, a robe, a **c** tunic, a turban,
28:39 You shall make the **c** tunic of fine linen,

CHECKING (1) [CHECK]
Col 2:23 but they are of no value in **c** self-indulgence.

CHEDORLAOMER (5)
Ge 14: 1 King **C** of Elam, and King Tidal of Goiim,
14: 4 Twelve years they had served **C**,
14: 5 In the fourteenth year **C** and the kings who were
14: 9 with King **C** of Elam, King Tidal
14:17 the defeat of **C** and the kings who were with him,

CHEEK (9) [CHEEKS]
1Ki 22:24 slapped him on the **c**, and said,
2Ch 18:23 slapped him on the **c**, and said,
Job 16:10 they have struck me insolently on the **c**;
Ps 3: 7 For you strike all my enemies on the **c**;
La 3:30 to give one's **c** to the smiter,
Mic 5: 1 a rod they strike the ruler of Israel upon the **c**.
Mt 5:39 But if anyone strikes you on the right **c**,
Lk 6:29 anyone strikes you on the **c**, offer the other also;
Sir 35:18 Do not the tears of the widow run down her **c**

CHEEKS (7) [CHEEK]
SS 1:10 Your **c** are comely with ornaments,
4: 3 Your **c** are like halves of a pomegranate
5:13 His **c** are like beds of spices, yielding fragrance.
6: 7 Your **c** are like halves of a pomegranate
Isa 50: 6 and my **c** to those who pulled out the beard;
La 1: 2 in the night, with tears on her **c**;
Hos 11: 4 I was to them like those who lift infants to their **c**.

CHEER (9) [CHEERED, CHEERFUL, CHEERFULLY, CHEERFULNESS, CHEERS]
Job 9:27 I will put off my sad countenance and be of good **c**,
Ps 94:19 your consolations **c** my soul.
Ecc 2: 3 with my mind how to **c** my body with wine—
11: 9 and let your heart **c** you in the days of your youth.
Tob 8:20 and you shall **c** up my daughter,
13:10 May he **c** all those within you who are captives,

AdE 16:22 "Therefore you shall observe this with all good c
2Mc 11:26 and be of good c and go on happily in the conduct
3Mc 4: 8 in lamentations instead of good c

CHEERED (2) [CHEER]
Php 2:19 so that I may be c by news of you.
2Mc 15:11 and he c them all by relating a dream,

CHEERFUL‡ (12) [CHEER]
1Ki 21: 7 Get up, eat some food, and be c;
Pr 15:13 A glad heart makes a c countenance,
15:15 but a c heart has a continual feast.
17:22 A c heart is a good medicine,
Zec 8:19 and c festivals for the house of Judah:
2Co 9: 7 for God loves a c giver.
Jas 5:13 Are any c? They should sing songs of praise.
Sir 13:26 The sign of a happy heart is a c face,
26: 4 his heart is content, and at all times his face is c.
30:25 Those who are c and merry at table will benefit
35:11 With every gift show a c face,
4Mc 13:13 and all of them together looking at one another, c

CHEERFULLY (2) [CHEER]
Ac 24:10 "I c make my defense, knowing that
Heb 10:34 and you c accepted the plundering

CHEERFULNESS (2) [CHEER]
Ro 12: 8 in diligence; the compassionate, in c.
Sir 1:23 and then c comes back to them.

CHEERS (2) [CHEER]
Jdg 9:13 'Shall I stop producing my wine that c gods
Pr 12:25 but a good word c it up.

CHEESE‡ (2) [CHEESES]
2Sa 17:29 sheep, and c from the herd,
Job 10:10 not pour me out like milk and curdle me like c?

CHEESES (1) [CHEESE]
1Sa 17:18 also take these ten c to the commander

CHELAL (1)
Ezr 10:30 Adna, C, Benaiah, Maaseiah, Mattaniah, Bezalel,

CHELEOUDITES See Index to Footnotes

CHELLEANS (1)
Jdt 2:23 south of the country of the C.

CHELLUH (KJV) See CHELUHI

CHELOUS (1)
Jdt 1: 9 the Jordan as far as Jerusalem and Bethany and C

CHELUB (2)
1Ch 4:11 C the brother of Shuhah became the father
27:26 tilling the soil, was Ezri son of C.

CHELUBAI (1)
1Ch 2: 9 to him: Jerahmeel, Ram, and C.

CHELUHI (1)
Ezr 10:35 Benaiah, Bedeiah, C,

CHEMARIMS (KJV) See IDOLOTROUS

CHEMOSH (8)
Nu 21:29 You are undone, O people of C!
Jdg 11:24 not possess what your god C gives you
1Ki 11: 7 a high place for C the abomination of Moab,
11:33 of the Sidonians, C the god of Moab, and Milcom
2Ki 23:13 for C the abomination of Moab,
Jer 48: 7 C shall go out into exile, with his priests and
48:13 Then Moab shall be ashamed of C,
48:46 The people of C have perished,

CHENAANAH (5)
1Ki 22:11 Zedekiah son of C made for himself horns of iron,
22:24 Then Zedekiah son of C came up to Micaiah,
1Ch 7:10 Jeush, Benjamin, Ehud, C, Zethan, Tarshish,
2Ch 18:10 Zedekiah son of C made for himself horns of iron,
18:23 Then Zedekiah son of C came up to Micaiah,

CHENANI (1)
Ne 9: 4 and C stood on the stairs of the Levites

CHENANIAH (3)
1Ch 15:22 C, leader of the Levites in music,
15:27 and C the leader of the music of the singers;
26:29 C and his sons were appointed to outside duties

CHEPHAR-AMMONI (1)
Jos 18:24 C, Ophni, and Geba—twelve towns with their

CHEPHIRAH (5)
Jos 9:17 Now their cities were Gibeon, C, Beeroth,
18:26 Mizpeh, C, Mozah,
Ezr 2:25 Of Kiriatharim, C, and Beeroth,
Ne 7:29 Of Kiriath-jearim, C, and Beeroth,
1Es 5:19 Those from C and Beeroth,

CHERAN (2)
Ge 36:26 Hemdan, Eshban, Ithran, and C.
1Ch 1:41 sons of Dishon: Hamran, Eshban, Ithran, and C.

CHERETHITES (10)
1Sa 30:14 We had made a raid on the Negeb of the C and on
2Sa 8:18 of Jehoiada was over the C and the Pelethites;
15:18 All his officials passed by him; and all the C,
20: 7 Joab's men went out after him, along with the C,
20:23 Benaiah son of Jehoiada was in command of the C
1Ki 1:38 and the C and the Pelethites,
1:44 and the C and the Pelethites;
1Ch 18:17 of Jehoiada was over the C and the Pelethites;
Eze 25:16 cut off the C, and destroy the rest of the seacoast.
Zep 2: 5 inhabitants of the seacoast, you nation of the C!

CHERISH (4) [CHERISHED]
Job 36:13 "The godless in heart c anger;
Ps 55: 3 and in anger they c enmity against me.
2Mc 7:14 and to c the hope God gives of being raised again
3Mc 3:15 but should c them with clemency

CHERISHED (3) [CHERISH]
Ps 66:18 If I had c iniquity in my heart,
Eze 35: 5 Because you c an ancient enmity,
Hos 9:16 I will kill the c offspring of their womb.

CHERITH (2)
1Ki 17: 3 and hide yourself by the Wadi C,
17: 5 he went and lived by the Wadi C,

CHERUB (28) [CHERUBIM]
Ex 25:19 Make one c at the one end, and one c at the other;
37: 8 one c at the one end, and one c at the other end;
2Sa 22:11 He rode on a c, and flew;
1Ki 6:24 Five cubits was the length of one wing of the c,
6:24 five cubits the length of the other wing of the c;
6:25 The other c also measured ten cubits;
6:26 one c was ten cubits, and so was that of the other c.
6:27 a wing of the other c was touching the other wall;
2Ch 3:11 five cubits long, touched the wing of the other c;
3:12 and of this c, one wing, five cubits long, touched
3:12 was joined to the wing of the first c.
Ezr 2:59 Tel-harsha, C, Addan, and Immer,
Ne 7:61 Tel-harsha, C, Addon, and Immer,
Ps 18:10 He rode on a c, and flew;
Eze 9: 3 of Israel had gone up from the c on which it rested
10: 4 the LORD rose up from the c to the threshold of
10: 7 And a c stretched out his hand from among
10: 9 beside the cherubim, one beside each c;
10:14 the first face was that of the c,
28:14 With an anointed c as guardian I placed you;
28:16 of God, and the guardian c drove you out from
41:18 a palm tree between c and c.
41:18 Each c had two faces:
1Es 5:36 under the leadership of C, Addan, and Immer,

CHERUBIM (69) [CHERUB]
Ge 3:24 at the east of the garden of Eden he placed the c,
Ex 25:18 You shall make two c of gold;
25:19 with the mercy seat you shall make the c
25:20 The c shall spread out their wings above,
25:20 of the c shall be turned toward the mercy seat.
25:22 from between the two c that are on the ark of
26: 1 you shall make them with c skillfully worked
26:31 it shall be made with c skillfully worked into it.
36: 8 with c skillfully worked into them.
36:35 with c skillfully worked into it.
37: 7 He made two c of hammered gold;
37: 8 with the mercy seat he made the c at its two ends.
37: 9 The c spread out their wings above,
37: 9 faces of the c were turned toward the mercy seat.
Nu 7:89 the ark of the covenant from between the two c;
1Sa 4: 4 who is enthroned on the c.
2Sa 6: 2 of the LORD of hosts who is enthroned on the c.
1Ki 6:23 the inner sanctuary he made two c of olivewood,
6:25 both c had the same measure and the same form.
6:27 He put the c in the innermost part of the house;
6:27 the wings of the c were spread out so that a wing
6:28 He also overlaid the c with gold.
6:29 around about with carved engravings of c,
6:32 with carvings of c, palm trees, and open flowers;
6:32 and spread gold on the c and on the palm trees.
6:35 He carved c, palm trees, and open flowers,
7:29 in the frames were lions, oxen, and c.
7:36 of its stays and on its borders he carved c,
8: 6 underneath the wings of the c.
8: 7 c spread out their wings over the place of the ark,
8: 7 the c made a covering above the ark and its poles.
2Ki 19:15 who are enthroned above the c, you are God,
1Ch 13: 6 the LORD, who is enthroned on the c,
28:18 the golden chariot of the c that spread their wings
2Ch 3: 7 and he carved c on the walls.
3:10 In the most holy place he made two carved c
3:11 wings of the c together extended twenty cubits:
3:13 The wings of these c extended twenty cubits;
3:13 the c stood on their feet, facing the nave.
3:14 and crimson fabrics and fine linen, and worked c
5: 7 underneath the wings of the c.
2Ch 5: 8 c spread out their wings over the place of the ark,
5: 8 the c made a covering above the ark and its poles.
Ps 80: 1 You who are enthroned upon the c,
99: 1 He sits enthroned upon the c; let the earth quake!
Isa 37:16 God of Israel, who are enthroned above the c,
Eze 10: 1 of the c there appeared above them something like
10: 2 "Go within the wheelwork underneath the c;
10: 2 with burning coals from among the c,
10: 3 the c were standing on the south side of the house
10: 5 The sound of the wings of the c was heard as far
10: 6 within the wheelwork, from among the c," he went
10: 7 a cherub stretched out his hand from among the c
to the fire that was among the c,
10: 8 The c appeared to have the form of a human hand
10: 9 I looked, and there were four wheels beside the c,
10:15 The c rose up. These were the living creatures
10:16 the c moved, the wheels moved beside them;
10:16 c lifted up their wings to rise up from the earth,
10:18 of the house and stopped above the c.
10:19 The c lifted up their wings and rose up from
10:20 and I knew that they were c.
11:22 Then the c lifted up their wings,
41:18 It was formed of c and palm trees,
41:20 c and palm trees were carved on the wall.
41:25 of the nave were carved c and palm trees, such
Heb 9: 5 the c of glory overshadowing the mercy seat.
Sir 49: 8 which God showed him above the chariot of the c.
Aza 1:32 into the depths from your throne on the c,

CHESALON (1) [=JEARIM]
Jos 15:10 C), and goes down to Beth-shemesh,

CHESED (1)
Ge 22:22 C, Hazo, Pildash, Jidlaph, and Bethuel."

CHESIL (1)
Jos 15:30 Eltolad, C, Hormah,

CHESNUT (KJV) See PLANE

CHEST (9) [CHESTS]
2Ki 12: 9 Then the priest Jehoiada took a c,
12:10 that there was a great deal of money in the c,
2Ch 24: 8 So the king gave command, and they made a c,
24:10 and brought their tax and dropped it into the c
24:11 Whenever the c was brought to the king's officers
24:11 of the chief priest would come and empty the c
Da 2:32 its c and arms of silver,
Zec 13: 6 "What are these wounds on your c?"
Rev 1:13 a long robe and with a golden sash across his c.

CHESTS (3) [CHEST]
Mt 2:11 Then, opening their treasure c,
Rev 15: 6 with golden sashes across their c.
1Es 1:54 the treasure c of the Lord, and the royal stores,

CHESULLOTH (1)
Jos 19:18 Its territory included Jezreel, C, Shunem,

CHEW (7) [CHEWS]
Lev 11: 4 among those that c the cud or have divided hoofs,
11: 7 it does not c the cud; it is unclean for you.
11:26 not cleft-footed or does not c the cud is unclean
Dt 14: 7 that c the cud or have the hoof cleft you shall
14: 7 because they c the cud but do not divide the hoof;
14: 8 because it divides the hoof but does not c the cud,
Sir 31:16 and do not c greedily, or you will give offense.

CHEWS (5) [CHEW]
Lev 11: 3 that has divided hoofs and is cleft-footed and c
11: 4 the camel, for even though it c the cud,
11: 5 The rock badger, for even though it c the cud,
11: 6 The hare, for even though it c the cud,
Dt 14: 6 and c the cud, among the animals, you may eat.

CHEZIB (2)
Ge 38: 5 She was in C when she bore him.
1Es 5:31 the descendants of C, the descendants of Gazera,

CHICKENS (KJV) See BROOD

CHICKS (1)
2Es 1:30 as a hen gathers her c under her wings.

CHIDE (KJV) See ACCUSE, QUARREL, UPBRAID

CHIDON (1)
1Ch 13: 9 When they came to the threshing floor of C,

CHIEF‡ (180) [CHIEFLY, CHIEFS, CHIEFTAIN, CHIEFTAINS, COMMANDER-IN-CHIEF]
A. CHIEF PRIESTS (65)
B. CHIEF OFFICER/OFFICERS (14)
C. CHIEF PRIEST (10)

Ge 39:21 he gave him favor in the sight of the c jailer.
39:22 The c jailer committed to Joseph's care all

Ge 39:23 The **c** jailer paid no heed to anything that was
40: 2 the **c** cupbearer and the **c** baker,
40: 9 So the **c** cupbearer told his dream to Joseph,
40:16 **c** baker saw that the interpretation was favorable,
40:20 head of the **c** cupbearer and the head of the **c** baker
40:21 He restored the **c** cupbearer to his cupbearing,
40:22 but the **c** baker he hanged,
40:23 Yet the **c** cupbearer did not remember Joseph,
41: 9 Then the **c** cupbearer said to Pharaoh,
41:10 and put me and the **c** baker in custody in the house
Ex 24:11 not lay his hand on the **c** men of the people
Nu 3:32 of Aaron the priest was to be **c** over the leaders of
1Sa 21: 7 the **c** of Saul's shepherds.
2Sa 23: 8 he was **c** of the Three;
23:18 the brother of Joab, was **c** of the Thirty.
1Ki 9:23 the **c** officers who were over Solomon's work: B
2Ki 25:18 captain of the guard took the **c** priest Seraiah, C
1Ch 5: 7 the **c**, Jeiel, and Zechariah,
5:12 the **c**, Shapham the second, Janai, and Shaphat
5:15 son of Guni, was **c** in their clan;
7:40 select mighty warriors, **c** of the princes.
9:11 son of Ahitub, the **c** officer of the house of God; B
9:17 and their kindred Shallum was the **c**,
9:20 And Phinehas son of Eleazar was **c** over them
9:26 for the four **c** gatekeepers,
11: 6 "Whoever attacks the Jebusites first shall be **c**
11: 6 Joab son of Zeruiah went up first, so he became **c.**
11:11 Jashobeam, son of Hachmoni, was **c** of the Three;
11:20 Abishai, the brother of Joab, was **c** of the Thirty.
12: 3 The **c** was Ahiezer, then Joash,
12: 9 Ezer the **c**, Obadiah second, Eliab third,
12:18 Then the spirit came upon Amasai, **c** of the Thirty,
15: 5 the **c**, with one hundred twenty of his kindred;
15: 6 the **c**, with two hundred twenty of his kindred;
15: 7 Joel the **c**, with one hundred thirty of his kindred;
15: 8 Shemaiah the **c**, with two hundred of his kindred;
15: 9 Eliel the **c**, with eighty of his kindred;
15:10 Amminadab the **c**, with one hundred twelve
16: 5 Asaph was the **c**, and second to him Zechariah,
18:17 the **c** officials in the service of the king.
23: 8 Jehiel the **c**, Zetham, and Joel, three.
23:11 Jahath was the **c**, and Zizah the second;
23:16 The sons of Gershom: Shebuel the **c.**
23:17 The sons of Eliezer: Rehabiah the **c**;
23:18 The sons of Izhar: Shelomith the **c.**
23:19 Jeriah the **c**, Amariah the second,
23:20 Micah the **c** and Isshiah the second.
24: 4 Since more **c** men were found among the sons
24:21 of the sons of Rehabiah, Isshiah the **c.**
24:23 Jeriah the **c**, Amariah the second,
24:31 the **c** as well as the youngest brother.
26:10 Shimri the **c** (for though he was not the firstborn,
his father made him **c**),
26:24 was **c** officer in charge of the treasuries. B
26:31 Jerijah was **c** of the Hebronites.
27: 3 and was **c** of all the commanders of the army for
27: 4 Mikloth was the **c** officer of his division. B
27: 5 as **c**; in his division were twenty-four thousand.
27:16 Eliezer son of Zichri was **c** officer; B
2Ch 8:10 These were the **c** officers of King Solomon, B
11:22 of Maacah as **c** prince among his brothers,
19:11 Amariah the **c** priest is over you in all matters C
24: 6 So the king summoned Jehoiada the **c**,
24:11 the officer of the **c** priest would come and empty C
26:20 When the **c** priest Azariah, and all the priests, C
31:10 The **c** priest Azariah, who was of the house C
31:12 The **c** officer in charge of them was Conaniah B
31:13 of Azariah the **c** officer of the house of God. B
35: 8 and Jehiel, the **c** officers of the house of God, B
Ezr 7: 5 son of Eleazar, son of the **c** priest Aaron— C
8:29 before the **c** priests and the Levites and A
Job 29:25 I chose their way, and sat as **c**,
Ps 118:22 the builders rejected has become the **c** cornerstone.
Pr 6: 7 Without having any **c** or officer or ruler,
SS 4:14 myrrh and aloes, with all **c** spices—
Jer 20: 1 who was **c** officer in the house of the LORD, B
31: 7 and raise shouts for the **c** of the nations;
39:13 and all the **c** officers of the king of Babylon sent B
41: 1 one of the **c** officers of the king, B
52:24 captain of the guard took the **c** priest Seraiah, C
Eze 17:13 under oath (he had taken away the **c** men of
38: 2 the **c** prince of Meshech and Tubal.
38: 3 O Gog, **c** prince of Meshech and Tubal;
39: 1 O Gog, **c** prince of Meshech and Tubal!
Da 2:14 the king's **c** executioner, who had gone out
2:48 over the whole province of Babylon and **c** prefect
4: 9 **c** of the magicians, I know that you are endowed
5:11 made him **c** of the magicians, enchanters,
10:13 So Michael, one of the **c** princes, came to help me,
Mt 2: 4 calling together all the **c** priests and scribes of A
16:21 at the hands of the elders and **c** priests and A
20:18 of Man will be handed over to the **c** priests A
21:15 But when the **c** priests and the scribes saw A
21:23 the **c** priests and the elders of the people came A
21:45 **c** priests and the Pharisees heard his parables, A
26: 3 **c** priests and the elders of the people gathered A
26:14 was called Judas Iscariot, went to the **c** priests A
26:47 from the **c** priests and the elders of the people. A
26:59 the **c** priests and the whole council were looking A
27: 1 all the **c** priests and the elders of the people A
27: 3 the thirty pieces of silver to the **c** priests and A
27: 6 But the **c** priests, taking the pieces of silver, A
27:12 when he was accused by the **c** priests and elders, A
27:20 **c** priests and the elders persuaded the crowds A
27:41 In the same way the **c** priests also, A
27:62 **c** priests and the Pharisees gathered before Pilate A
28:11 into the city and told the **c** priests everything A

Mk 8:31 the **c** priests, and the scribes, and be killed, A
10:33 of Man will be handed over to the **c** priests and A
11:18 And when the **c** priests and the scribes heard it, A
11:27 As he was walking in the temple, the **c** priests, A
14: 1 The **c** priests and the scribes were looking for A
14:10 to the **c** priests in order to betray him to them. A
14:43 from the **c** priests, the scribes, and the elders. A
14:53 and all the **c** priests, the elders, A
14:55 the **c** priests and the whole council were looking A
15: 1 the **c** priests held a consultation with the elders A
15: 3 Then the **c** priests accused him of many things. A
15:10 jealousy that the **c** priests had handed him over. A
15:11 But the **c** priests stirred up the crowd A
15:31 In the same way the **c** priests, A
Lk 9:22 and be rejected by the elders, **c** priests, A
19: 2 he was a **c** tax collector and was rich.
19:47 The **c** priests, the scribes, A
20: 1 **c** priests and the scribes came with the elders A
20:19 **c** priests realized that he had told this parable A
22: 2 The **c** priests and the scribes were looking for A
22: 4 the **c** priests and officers of the temple police A
22:52 Then Jesus said to the **c** priests, A
22:66 both **c** priests and scribes, gathered together, A
23: 4 Then Pilate said to the **c** priests and the crowds, A
23:10 The **c** priests and the scribes stood by, A
23:13 Pilate then called together the **c** priests, A
24:20 how our **c** priests and leaders handed him over A
Jn 2: 8 and take it to the **c** steward."
7:32 the **c** priests and Pharisees sent temple police A
7:45 the temple police went back to the **c** priests A
11:47 the **c** priests and the Pharisees called a meeting A
11:57 the **c** priests and the Pharisees had given orders A
12:10 **c** priests planned to put Lazarus to death as well, A
18: 3 soldiers together with police from the **c** priests A
18:35 and the **c** priests have handed you over to me. A
19: 6 When the **c** priests and the police saw him, A
19:15 The **c** priests answered, "We have no king but A
19:21 Then the **c** priests of the Jews said to Pilate, A
Ac 4:23 to their friends and reported what the **c** priests A
5:24 the temple and the **c** priests heard these words, A
9:14 the **c** priests to bind all who invoke your name." A
9:21 of bringing them bound before the **c** priests?" A
14:12 because he was the **c** speaker.
22:30 and ordered the **c** priests and the entire council A
23:14 They went to the **c** priests and elders and said, A
25: 2 the **c** priests and the leaders of the Jews gave A
25:15 the **c** priests and the elders of A
26:10 with authority received from the **c** priests, A
26:12 the authority and commission of the **c** priests, A
1Pe 5: 4 And when the **c** shepherd appears,
Tob 1:22 Now Ahikar was **c** cupbearer,
Jdt 2: 4 the **c** general of his army, second only to himself,
AdE 1:14 and Malesear, who sat beside him in the **c** seats—
2:21 Now the king's eunuchs, who were **c** bodyguards,
9: 3 The **c** provincial governors, the princes,
1Mc 1:29 the king sent to the cities of Judah a **c** collector
9:11 as did all the **c** warriors.
10:65 and enrolled him among his **c** Friends,
11:27 caused him to be reckoned among his **c** Friends.
2Mc 4:50 the **c** plotter against his compatriots.
8: 9 one of the king's **c** Friends, and sent him,
10:11 and to be **c** governor of Coelesyria and Phoenicia.
1Es 1: 8 and Jehiel, the **c** officers of the temple, B
7: 2 assisting the elders of the Jews and the **c** officers B
9:39 the **c** priest and reader to bring the law of Moses C
9:40 So Ezra the **c** priest brought the law, C
9:49 Attharates said to Ezra the **c** priest and reader, C
2Es 5:16 on the second night Phaltiel, a **c** of the people,
15:16 for their king or the **c** of their leaders.

CHIEFLY (1) [CHIEF]

2Mc 8:35 having succeeded **c** in the destruction

CHIEFS‡ (20) [CHIEF]

Ex 15:15 Then the **c** of Edom were dismayed;
Nu 25: 4 "Take all the **c** of the people,
Jos 10:24 to the **c** of the warriors who had gone with him,
22:14 and with him ten **c**, one from each of
22:30 the priest Phinehas and the **c** of the congregation,
22:32 of Eleazar and the **c** returned from the Reubenites
Jdg 5:15 the **c** of Issachar came with Deborah,
20: 2 The **c** of all the people, of all the tribes of Israel,
2Sa 23:13 of the thirty **c** went down to join David at the cave
1Ch 7: 3 Obadiah, Joel, and Isshiah, five, all of them **c**;
8:28 according to their generations, **c.**
11:10 Now these are the **c** of David's warriors,
11:15 of the thirty **c** went down to the rock to David at
12:20 and Zillethai, **c** of the thousands in Manasseh.
12:32 to know what Israel ought to do, two hundred **c**,
15:16 the **c** of the Levites to appoint their kindred as
2Ch 28:12 Moreover, certain **c** of the Ephraimites,
35: 9 and Jeiel and Jozabad, the **c** of the Levites, gave
Eze 32:21 The mighty **c** shall speak of them,
Mic 3: 9 of the house of Jacob and **c** of the house of Israel,

CHIEFTAIN (1) [CHIEF]

1Ch 5: 6 he was a **c** of the Reubenites.

CHIEFTAINS (1) [CHIEF]

Jdt 7: 8 Then all the **c** of the Edomites and all the leaders

CHILD‡ (285) [CHILD'S, CHILDBEARING, CHILDBIRTH, CHILDBIRTHS, CHILDHOOD, CHILDISH, CHILDLESS, CHILDLESSNESS, CHILDREN, CHILDREN'S, GRANDCHILDREN, MAN-CHILD]

A. MY CHILD (67)
B. LITTLE CHILD (6)
C. ONLY CHILD (5)

Ge 4:25 "God has appointed for me another **c** instead
11:30 Now Sarai was barren; she had no **c.**
17:17 a **c** be born to a man who is a hundred years old?
17:17 Can Sarah, who is ninety years old, bear a **c**?"
18:13 'Shall I indeed bear a **c**, now that I am old?'
21: 8 The **c** grew, and was weaned;
21:14 putting it on her shoulder, along with the **c**,
21:15 she cast the **c** under one of the bushes.
21:16 "Do not let me look on the death of the **c.**"
44:20 and a young brother, the **c** of his old age.
Ex 2: 3 she put the **c** in it and placed it among the reeds
2: 6 When she opened it, she saw the **c.**
2: 7 from the Hebrew women to nurse the **c** for you?"
2: 9 "Take this **c** and nurse it for me,
2: 9 So the woman took the **c** and nursed it.
2:10 When the **c** grew up, she brought him
13: 8 You shall tell your **c** on that day,
13:14 When in the future your **c** asks you,
Lev 12: 2 If a woman conceives and bears a male **c**,
12: 5 a female **c**, she shall be unclean two weeks,
12: 7 This is the law for her who bears a **c**,
Nu 11:12 as a nurse carries a sucking **c**,'
Dt 1:31 just as one carries a **c**,
8: 5 then in your heart that as a parent disciplines a **c**
32:25 nursing **c** and old gray head.
Jdg 11:34 with dancing. She was his only **c**; C
Ru 4:16 Then Naomi took the **c** and laid him in her bosom,
1Sa 1:11 but will give to your servant a male **c**,
1:22 "As soon as the **c** is weaned, I will bring him,
1:24 at Shiloh; and the **c** was young.
1:25 and they brought the **c** to Eli.
1:27 For this **c** I prayed; and the LORD has granted me
4:21 She named the **c** Ichabod, meaning,
15: 3 **c** and infant, ox and sheep, camel and donkey.' "
2Sa 6:23 And Michal the daughter of Saul had no **c** to
12:14 the **c** that is born to you shall die."
12:15 The LORD struck the **c** that Uriah's wife bore
12:16 David therefore pleaded with God for the **c**;
12:18 On the seventh day the **c** died.
12:18 to tell him that the **c** was dead;
12:18 for they said, "While the **c** was still alive,
12:18 how then can we tell him the **c** is dead?
12:19 he perceived that the **c** was dead;
12:19 and David said to his servants, "Is the **c** dead?"
12:21 You fasted and wept for the **c** while it was alive;
12:21 but when the **c** died, you rose and ate food."
12:22 He said, "While the **c** was still alive,
12:22 be gracious to me, and the **c** may live.'
1Ki 3: 7 although I am only a little **c**; B
14: 3 he will tell you what shall happen to the **c.**"
14:12 When your feet enter the city, the **c** shall die.
14:17 she came to the threshold of the house, the **c** died.
17:21 Then he stretched himself upon the **c** three times,
17:22 life of the **c** came into him again, and he revived.
17:23 the **c**, brought him down from the upper chamber
2Ki 4:18 the **c** was older, he went out one day to his father
4:20 the **c** sat on her lap until noon, and he died.
4:26 Is the **c** all right?"
4:29 and lay my staff on the face of the **c.**"
4:30 Then the mother of the **c** said,
4:31 on ahead and laid the staff on the face of the **c**,
4:31 "The **c** has not awakened."
4:32 he saw the **c** lying dead on his bed.
4:34 Then he got up on the bed and lay upon the **c**,
4:34 the flesh of the **c** became warm.
4:35 the **c** sneezed seven times,
4:35 and the **c** opened his eyes.
Job 3:16 Or why was I not buried like a stillborn **c**,
24: 9 "There are those who snatch the orphan **c** from
Ps 50:20 you slander your own mother's **c.**
86:16 save the **c** of your serving girl.
116:16 I am your servant, the **c** of your serving girl.
131: 2 like a weaned **c** with its mother;
131: 2 my soul is like the weaned **c** that is with me.
Pr 1: 8 Hear, my **c**, your father's instruction, A
1:10 My **c**, if sinners entice you, do not consent. A
1:15 my **c**, do not walk in their way, keep your foot A
2: 1 My **c**, if you accept my words and treasure A
3: 1 My **c**, do not forget my teaching, A
3:11 My **c**, do not despise the LORD's discipline or A
3:21 My **c**, do not let these escape from your sight: A
4:10 Hear, my **c**, and accept my words, A
4:20 My **c**, be attentive to my words; A
5: 1 My **c**, be attentive to my wisdom; A
5: 7 And now, my **c**, listen to me, A
6: 1 My **c**, if you have given your pledge A
6: 3 So do this, my **c**, and save yourself, A
6:20 My **c**, keep your father's commandment, A
7: 1 My **c**, keep my words and store A
10: 1 A wise **c** makes a glad father,
10: 1 but a foolish **c** is a mother's grief.
10: 5 A **c** who gathers in summer is prudent,
10: 5 but a **c** who sleeps in harvest brings shame.
13: 1 A wise **c** loves discipline,
15:20 A wise **c** makes a glad father,
17: 2 over a **c** who acts shamefully,
19:13 A stupid **c** is ruin to a father,
19:27 my **c**, from the words of knowledge, A

Pr 23:15 My **c**, if your heart is wise, A
23:19 my **c**, and be wise, and direct your mind in A
23:26 My **c**, give me your heart, A
24:13 My **c**, eat honey, for it is good, A
24:21 My **c**, fear the LORD and the king, A
27:11 Be wise, my **c**, and make my heart glad, A
29: 3 A **c** who loves wisdom makes a parent glad,
29:15 but a mother is disgraced by a neglected **c**.
30: 4 And what is the name of the person's **c**?
Ecc 6: 3 I say that a stillborn **c** is better off than he.
12:12 Of anything beyond these, my **c**, beware. A
Isa 7:14 the young woman is with **c** and shall bear a son,
7:16 the **c** knows how to refuse the evil and choose
8: 4 **c** knows how to call "My father" or "My mother,"
9: 6 For a **c** has been born for us, a son given to us;
10:19 be so few that a **c** can write them down.
11: 6 and a little **c** shall lead them. B
11: 8 The nursing **c** shall play over the hole of the asp,
11: 8 the weaned **c** shall put its hand on the adder's den.
26:17 Like a woman with **c**, who writhes and cries out
26:18 with **c**, we writhed, but we gave birth only
49:15 Can a woman forget her nursing **c**,
49:15 or show no compassion for the **c** of her womb?
66:13 As a mother comforts her **c**, so I will comfort you;
Jer 4:31 anguish as of one bringing forth her first **c**,
6:26 make mourning as for an only **c**, C
20:15 "A **c** is born to you, a son," making him very glad.
30: 6 Ask now, and see, can a man bear a **c**?
31: 8 those with **c** and those in labor, together;
31:20 Is he the **c** I delight in?
44: 7 to cut off man and woman, **c** and infant,
Eze 18: 4 of the parent as well as the life of the **c** is mine:
18:20 A **c** shall not suffer for the iniquity of a parent, nor
a parent suffer for the iniquity of a **c**;
Da 11: 6 and her **c** and the one who supported her.
Hos 11: 1 When Israel was a **c**, I loved him,
Zec 12:10 as one mourns for an only **c**, C
Mt 1:18 she was found to be with **c** from the Holy Spirit.
1:20 for the **c** conceived in her is from the Holy Spirit.
2: 2 is the **c** who has been born king of the Jews?
2: 8 saying, "Go and search diligently for the **c**;
2: 9 until it stopped over the place where the **c** was.
2:11 they saw the **c** with Mary his mother;
2:13 take the **c** and his mother, and flee to Egypt,
2:13 for Herod is about to search for the **c**,
2:14 Joseph got up, took the **c** and his mother by night,
2:20 take the **c** and his mother,
2:21 Then Joseph got up, took the **c** and his mother,
7: 9 if your **c** asks for bread, will give a stone?
7:10 Or if the **c** asks for a fish, will give a snake?
10:21 and a father his **c**, and children will rise
18: 2 He called a **c**, whom he put among them,
18: 4 like this **c** is the greatest in the kingdom
18: 5 Whoever welcomes one such **c**
23:15 and you make the new convert twice as much a **c**
Mk 5:39 The **c** is not dead but sleeping."
5:40 and went in where the **c** was.
7:30 So she went home, found the **c** lying on the bed,
9:24 Immediately the father of the **c** cried out,
9:36 Then he took a little **c** and put it among them; B
9:37 "Whoever welcomes one such **c**
10:15 of God as a little **c** will never enter it." B
12:19 leaving a wife but no **c**,
13:12 and a father his **c**, and children will rise
Lk 1:35 therefore the **c** to be born will be holy;
1:41 the **c** leaped in her womb.
1:44 the **c** in my womb leaped for joy.
1:59 On the eighth day they came to circumcise the **c**,
1:66 "What then will this **c** become?"
1:76 **c**, will be called the prophet of the Most High;
1:80 The **c** grew and became strong in spirit,
2: 5 and who was expecting a **c**.
2: 6 the time came for her to deliver her **c**.
2:12 you will find a **c** wrapped in bands of cloth
2:16 and the **c** lying in the manger.
2:17 made known what had been told them about this **c**;
2:21 it was time to circumcise the **c**;
2:27 and when the parents brought in the **c** Jesus,
2:34 "This **c** is destined for the falling and the rising
2:38 and began to praise God and to speak about the **c**
2:40 **c** grew and became strong, filled with wisdom;
2:48 and his mother said to him, "**C**,
8:54 But he took her by the hand and called out, "**C**,
9:38 look at my son; he is my only **c**. C
9:47 took a little **c** and put it by his side, B
9:48 "Whoever welcomes this **c**
11:11 if your **c** asks for a fish,
11:12 Or if the **c** asks for an egg, will give a scorpion?
14: 5 "If one of you has a **c** or an ox that has fallen into
16:25 But Abraham said, '**C**, remember that
18:17 of God as a little **c** will never enter it." B
Jn 4:51 and told him that his **c** was alive.
16:21 But when her **c** is born,
Ac 7: 5 even though he had no **c**.
1Co 4:17 who is my beloved and faithful **c** in the Lord,
13:11 When I was a **c**, I spoke like a **c**, I thought like a **c**,
I reasoned like a **c**;
Gal 4: 7 So you are no longer a slave but a **c**, and if a **c**
then also an heir, through God.
4:23 the **c** of the slave, was born according to the flesh;
the other, the **c** of the free woman,
4:29 at that time the **c** who was born according to the
flesh persecuted the **c** who was born according to
4:30 "Drive out the slave and her **c**; for the **c** of the
slave will not share the inheritance with the **c**
1Ti 1: 2 To Timothy, my loyal **c** in the faith:
1:18 Timothy, my **c**, in accordance with A
2Ti 1: 2 To Timothy, my beloved **c**:
2: 1 my **c**, be strong in the grace that is in Christ A
Tit 1: 4 my loyal **c** in the faith we share:
Phm 1:10 I am appealing to you for my **c**, Onesimus, A
Heb 11:23 because they saw that the **c** was beautiful;
12: 5 "My **c**, do not regard lightly the discipline of A
12: 6 and chastises every **c** whom he accepts."
12: 7 what **c** is there whom a parent does not discipline?
1Jn 3: 8 Everyone who commits sin is a **c** of the devil;
5: 1 and everyone who loves the parent loves the **c**.
Rev 12: 4 before the woman who was about to bear a **c**,
12: 4 that he might devour her **c** as soon as it was born.
12: 5 And she gave birth to a son, a male **c**,
12: 5 But her **c** was snatched away and taken to God
12:13 the woman who had given birth to the male **c**.
Tob 2: 2 I said to my son Tobias, "Go, my **c**, A
2: 3 And I replied, "Here I am, my **c**." A
3:15 I am my father's only **c**; he has no other child C
3:15 he has no other **c** to be his heir;
4:19 So now, my **c**, remember these commandments, A
5:18 "Why is it that you have sent my **c** away? A
5:19 but let it be a ransom for our **c**.
5:21 our **c** will leave in good health and return to us
7: 7 my **c**, son of a good and noble father!" A
7:10 to you the true situation more fully, my **c**. A
7:11 But now, my **c**, eat and drink, A
7:11 May the Lord of heaven, my **c**, A
8:21 and I die. Take courage, my **c**. A
8:21 and forever. Take courage, my **c**." A
10: 4 "My **c** has perished and is no longer among A
10: 5 my **c**, the light of my eyes, A
10: 7 to deceive me! My **c** has perished." A
10: 8 said to Tobias, "Stay, my **c**, stay with me; A
10:11 he embraced Tobias and said, "Farewell, my **c**; A
10:12 Edna said to Tobias, "My **c** and dear brother, A
10:12 Go in peace, my **c**. A
11: 9 saying, "Now that I have seen you, my **c**, A
12: 1 and said to him, "My **c**, see to paying the wages A
12: 4 Tobit said, "He deserves, my **c**, A
AdE 2: 7 And he had a foster **c**,
Wis 2:13 and calls himself a **c** of the Lord.
2:18 for if the righteous man is God's **c**,
7: 1 a descendant of the first-formed **c** of earth;
8:19 As a **c** I was naturally gifted,
10: 5 in the face of his compassion for his **c**.
14:15 of his **c**, who had been suddenly taken from him;
18: 5 and one **c** had been abandoned and rescued,
18:13 they acknowledged your people to be God's **c**.
Sir 2: 1 My **c**, when you come to serve the Lord, A
3:12 My **c**, help your father in his old age, A
3:17 My **c**, perform your tasks with humility; A
4: 1 My **c**, do not cheat the poor of their living, A
6:18 My **c**, from your youth choose discipline, A
6:23 Listen, my **c**, and accept my judgment; A
6:32 If you are willing, my **c**, you can be disciplined, A
10:28 My **c**, honor yourself with humility, A
11:10 My **c**, do not busy yourself with many matters; A
14:11 My **c**, treat yourself well, A
16:24 Listen to me, my **c**, and acquire knowledge, A
18:15 My **c**, do not mix reproach with your good A
19:11 like a woman in labor with a **c**.
21: 1 Have you sinned, my **c**? A
26:19 *My* **c**, *keep sound the bloom of your youth,* A
30: 9 Pamper a **c**, and he will terrorize you;
31:22 Listen to me, my **c**, and do not disregard me, A
37:27 My **c**, test yourself while you live; A
38: 9 My **c**, when you are ill, do not delay, A
38:16 My **c**, let your tears fall for the dead, A
40:28 My **c**, do not lead the life of a beggar; A
Bar 4:15 for the aged and no pity for a **c**.
2Mc 7:28 my **c**, to look at the heaven and the earth A
1Es 1:53 old man or **c**, for he gave them all
2Es 9:43 "Your servant was barren and had no **c**,
16:38 but when the **c** comes forth from the womb,
4Mc 12: 2 he felt strong compassion for this **c** when he saw
15: 4 of a small **c** a wondrous likeness both of mind
15:12 But each **c** separately and all of them together

CHILD'S (6) [CHILD]

Ex 2: 8 So the girl went and called the **c** mother.
1Ki 17:21 let this **c** life come into him again."
Mt 2:20 for those who were seeking the **c** life are dead."
Mk 5:40 the **c** father and mother and those who were
Lk 2:33 And the **c** father and mother were amazed
8:51 John, and James, and the **c** father and mother.

CHILDBEARING‡ (2) [CHILD, BEAR]

Ge 3:16 "I will greatly increase your pangs in **c**;
1Ti 2:15 Yet she will be saved through **c**,

CHILDBIRTH (4) [CHILD, BEAR]

Ge 35:16 Rachel was in **c**, and she had hard labor.
Hos 13:13 pangs of **c** come for him, but he is an unwise son;
Gal 4:19 in the pain of **c** until Christ is formed in you,
LtJ 6:29 be touched by women in their periods or at **c**.

CHILDBIRTHS (1) [CHILD, BEAR]

4Mc 16: 7 O seven **c** all in vain, seven profitless pregnancies,

CHILDHOOD (5) [CHILD]

Pr 29:21 A slave pampered from **c** will come to a bad end.
Mk 9:21 And he said, "From **c**.
2Ti 3:15 how from **c** you have known the sacred writings
2Mc 6:23 with distinction and his excellent life even from **c**,
2Mc 15:12 and had been trained from **c** in all that belongs

CHILDISH (1) [CHILD]

1Co 13:11 when I became an adult, I put an end to **c** ways.

CHILDLESS (16) [CHILD]

Ge 15: 2 what will you give me, for I continue **c**,
Lev 20:20 to punishment; they shall die **c**.
20:21 uncovered his brother's nakedness; they shall be **c**.
1Sa 15:33 Samuel said, "As your sword has made women **c**,
so your mother shall be **c** among women."
1Ch 2:30 and Appaim; and Seled died **c**.
2:32 and Jonathan; and Jether died **c**.
Job 24:21 "They harm the **c** woman,
Jer 18:21 let their wives become **c** and widowed.
22:30 Record this man as **c**, a man who shall not succeed
Mt 22:24 Moses said, 'If a man dies **c**,
22:25 the first married, and died **c**,
Lk 20:29 the first married, and died **c**;
20:31 and so in the same way all seven died **c**.
Gal 4:27 For it is written, "Rejoice, you **c** one,
Sir 16: 3 and to die **c** better than to have ungodly children.

CHILDLESSNESS (1) [CHILD]

Wis 4: 1 Better than this is **c** with virtue,

CHILDREN‡ (740) [CHILD]

A. LITTLE CHILDREN (16)
B. CHILDREN OF *GOD (15)
C. CHILDREN'S CHILDREN (15)
D. WOMEN AND CHILDREN (10)

Ge 3:16 in pain you shall bring forth **c**,
6: 4 to the daughters of humans, who bore **c** to them.
10: 1 **c** were born to them after the flood.
10:21 To Shem also, the father of all the **c** of Eber,
10:21 the elder brother of Japheth, **c** were born.
16: 1 Now Sarai, Abram's wife, bore him no **c**.
16: 2 that the LORD has prevented me from bearing **c**;
16: 2 it may be that I shall obtain **c** by her."
18:19 that he may charge his **c** and his household
20:17 and female slaves so that they bore **c**.
21: 7 to Abraham that Sarah would nurse **c**?
22:20 "Milcah also has borne **c**, to your brother Nahor:
25: 4 All these were the **c** of Keturah.
25:22 The **c** struggled together within her;
30: 1 When Rachel saw that she bore Jacob no **c**,
30: 1 and she said to Jacob, "Give me **c**, or I shall die!"
30: 3 upon my knees and that I too may have **c**
30: 9 When Leah saw that she had ceased bearing **c**,
30:26 and my **c** for whom I have served you,
31:16 from our father belongs to us and to our **c**;
31:17 and set his **c** and his wives on camels;
31:43 the **c** are my **c**, the flocks are my flocks,
31:43 or about their **c** whom they have borne?
32:11 and kill us all, the mothers with the **c**.
32:22 his two maids, and his eleven **c**,
33: 1 the **c** among Leah and Rachel and the two maids.
33: 2 He put the maids with their **c** in front,
33: 2 with their children in front, then Leah with her **c**,
33: 5 Esau looked up and saw the women and **c**, D
33: 5 **c** whom God has graciously given your servant."
33: 6 Then the maids drew near, they and their **c**,
33: 7 and her **c** drew near and bowed down;
33:13 that the **c** are frail and that the flocks and herds,
33:14 before me and according to the pace of the **c**,
36:25 These are the **c** of Anah:
37: 3 Israel loved Joseph more than any other of his **c**,
42:36 "I am the one you have bereaved of **c**:
43:14 for me, if I am bereaved of my **c**, I am bereaved."
44:20 he alone is left of his mother's **c**,
45:10 you and your **c** and your children's children,
45:10 you and your children and your children's **c**, C
46: 9 and the **c** of Reuben: Hanoch,
46:10 The **c** of Simeon: Jemuel,
46:11 The **c** of Levi: Gershon, Kohath, and Merari.
46:12 The **c** of Judah: Er, Onan,
46:12 and the **c** of Perez were Hezron and Hamul.
46:13 **c** of Issachar: Tola, Puvah, Jashub, and Shimron.
46:14 The **c** of Zebulun: Sered, Elon, and Jahleel
46:16 The **c** of Gad: Ziphion, Haggi,
46:17 The **c** of Asher: Imnah, Ishvah,
46:17 and their sister Serah. The **c** of Beriah:
46:18 (these are the **c** of Zilpah, whom Laban gave
46:19 **c** of Jacob's wife Rachel: Joseph and Benjamin.
46:21 The **c** of Benjamin: Bela, Becher,
46:22 the **c** of Rachel, who were born to Jacob—
46:23 The **c** of Dan: Hashum.
46:24 The **c** of Naphtali: Jahzeel,
46:25 (these are the **c** of Bilhah, whom Laban gave
46:27 The **c** of Joseph, who were born to him in Egypt,
48:11 and here God has let me see your **c** also."
50: 8 Only their **c**, their flocks,
50:23 Joseph saw Ephraim's **c** of the third generation;
50:23 the **c** of Machir son of Manasseh were also born
Ex 2: 6 "This must be one of the Hebrews' **c**," she said.
10: 2 and that you may tell your **c** and grandchildren
10:24 Even your **c** may go with you."
12:24 as a perpetual ordinance for you and your **c**.
12:26 And when your **c** ask you,
12:37 about six hundred thousand men on foot, besides **c**.
13:13 among your **c** you shall redeem.
17: 3 to kill us and our **c** and livestock with thirst?"
20: 5 punishing **c** for the iniquity of parents,
21: 4 the wife and her **c** shall be her master's

Ex 21: 5 “I love my master, my wife, and my **c**;
22:24 wives shall become widows and your **c** orphans.
34: 7 the parents upon the **c** and the children’s children,
34: 7 parents upon the children and the children’s **c**, C
Lev 10:14 for they have been assigned to you and your **c**
10:15 they are to be your due and that of your **c** forever,
25:41 Then they and their **c** with them shall be free
25:46 You may keep them as a possession for your **c**
25:54 they and their **c** with them shall go free in
26:22 of your **c** and destroy your livestock;
Nu 3: 4 in the wilderness of Sinai, and they had no **c**.
5:28 she shall be immune and be able to conceive **c**.
14:18 upon the **c** to the third and the fourth generation.’
14:33 And your **c** shall be shepherds in the wilderness
16:27 together with their wives, their **c**,
26:15 The **c** of Gad by their clans:
Dt 1:39 who you thought would become booty, your **c**,
2:34 town we utterly destroyed men, women, and **c**.
3: 6 in each city utterly destroying men, women, and **c**.
3:19 Only your wives, your **c**, and your livestock—
4: 9 to your **c** and your children’s children—
4: 9 to your children and your children’s **c**— C
4:10 and may teach their **c** so”;
4:25 When you have had **c** and children’s children,
4:25 When you have had children and children’s **c**, C
5: 9 punishing **c** for the iniquity of parents,
5:29 with them and with their **c** forever!
6: 2 and your **c** and your children’s children may fear
6: 2 and your children’s **c** may fear the LORD C
6: 7 to your **c** and talk about them when you are
6:20 When your **c** ask you in time to come,
6:21 then you shall say to your **c**,
7: 4 that would turn away your **c** from following me,
11: 2 Remember today that it was not your **c** (who have
11:19 to your **c**, talking about them when you are
11:21 the days of your **c** may be multiplied in the land
12:25 all may go well with you and your **c** after you,
12:28 so that it may go well with you and with your **c**
14: 1 You are **c** of the LORD your God.
20:14 the **c**, livestock, and everything else in the town,
23: 8 The **c** of the third generation that are born
24:16 Parents shall not be put to death for their **c**, nor
shall **c** be put to death for their parents;
28:54 and to the last of his remaining **c**,
28:55 of the flesh of his **c** whom he is eating,
28:57 and the **c** that she bears,
29:11 your **c**, your women, and the aliens who are
29:22 The next generation, your **c** who rise up after you,
29:29 revealed things belong to us and to our **c** forever,
30: 2 and you and your **c** obey him with all your heart
31:12 Assemble the people—men, women, and **c**,
31:13 so that their **c**, who have not known it, may hear
32: 5 yet his degenerate **c** have dealt falsely with him,
32:20 **c** in whom there is no faithfulness.
32:43 For he will avenge the blood of his **c**,
32:46 give them as a command to your **c**,
33: 9 he ignored his kin, and did not acknowledge his **c**.
Jos 4: 6 When your **c** ask in time to come,
4:21 “When your **c** ask their parents in time to come,
4:22 then you shall let your **c** know,
5: 7 So it was their **c**, whom he raised up
14: 9 be an inheritance for you and your **c** forever,
22:24 in time to come your **c** might say to our **c**,
22:25 So your **c** might make our **c** cease to worship
22:27 that your **c** may never say to our **c** in time
24: 4 but Jacob and his **c** went down to Egypt.
24:32 from the **c** of Hamor, the father of Shechem,
Jdg 13: 2 His wife was barren, having borne no **c**.
13: 3 “Although you are barren, having borne no **c**,
Ru 4:11 May you produce **c** in Ephrathah and bestow
4:12 through the **c** that the LORD will give you
1Sa 1: 2 Peninnah had **c**, but Hannah had no **c**.
2: 5 but she who has many **c** is forlorn.
2:20 “May the LORD repay you with **c** by this woman
22:19 men and women, **c** and infants, oxen, donkeys,
30:22 except that each man may take his wife and **c**,
2Sa 12: 3 and it grew up with him and with his **c**;
1Ki 1:19 and has invited all the **c** of the king,
1:25 and has invited all the king’s **c**,
4:31 and Heman, Calcol, and Darda, **c** of Mahol;
6:13 I will dwell among the **c** of Israel,
8:25 if only your **c** look to their way,
9: 6 you turn aside from following me, you or your **c**,
11:20 Genubath was in Pharaoh’s house among the **c**
20: 3 your fairest wives and **c** also are mine.”
20: 5 to me your silver and gold, your wives and **c**’;
20: 7 for he sent to me for my wives, my **c**, my silver,
2Ki 4: 1 a creditor has come to take my two **c** as slaves.”
4: 4 go in, and shut the door behind you and your **c**,
4: 5 and shut the door behind her and her **c**;
4: 7 and you and your **c** can live on the rest.”
9:26 and for the blood of his **c** that I saw yesterday,
11: 2 among the king’s **c** who were about to be killed;
14: 6 But he did not put to death the **c** of the murderers;
14: 6 “The parents shall not be put to death for the **c**, or
the **c** be put to death for the parents;
17:31 the Sepharvites burned their **c** in the fire
17:34 that the LORD commanded the **c** of Jacob,
17:41 to this day their **c** and their children’s children
17:41 and their children’s **c** continue to do as their C
19: 3 **c** have come to the birth,
1Ch 2:18 Caleb son of Hezron had **c** by his wife Azubah,
4:27 but his brothers did not have many **c**,
6: 3 The **c** of Amram: Aaron, Moses, and Miriam.
8:40 archers, having many **c** and grandchildren,
14: 4 the names of the **c** whom he had in Jerusalem:
16:13 **c** of Jacob, his chosen ones.
1Ch 28: 8 for an inheritance to your **c** after you forever.
2Ch 6:16 if only your **c** keep to their way,
20:13 with their little ones, their wives, and their **c**.
21:14 your **c**, your wives, and all your possessions,
22:11 among the king’s **c** who were about to be killed;
24: 7 For the **c** of Athaliah, that wicked woman,
25: 4 But he did not put their **c** to death,
25: 4 “The parents shall not be put to death for the **c**, or
the **c** be put to death for the parents;
30: 9 your kindred and your **c** will find compassion
31:18 The priests were enrolled with all their little **c**, A
Ezr 6:10 and pray for the life of the king and his **c**.
8:21 our **c**, and all our possessions.
9:12 and leave it for an inheritance to your **c** forever.’
10: 1 women, and **c** gathered to him out of Israel;
10: 3 and their **c**, according to the counsel of my lord
10:44 and they sent them away with their **c**.
Ne 5: 5 our **c** are the same as their **c**;
12:43 the women and **c** also rejoiced. D
13:24 and half of their **c** spoke the language of Ashdod,
Est 3:13 young and old, women and **c**, in one day, D
8:11 that might attack them, with their **c** and women,
Job 1: 5 for Job said, “It may be that my **c** have sinned,
5: 4 Their **c** are far from safety,
8: 4 If your **c** sinned against him,
14:21 Their **c** come to honor, and they do not know it;
17: 5 the eyes of their **c** will fail.
19:18 Even young **c** despise me;
20:10 Their **c** will seek the favor of the poor,
21: 8 Their **c** are established in their presence,
21:11 like a flock, and their **c** dance around.
21:19 You say, ‘God stores up their iniquity for their **c**.’
27:14 If their **c** are multiplied, it is for the sword;
29: 5 when my **c** were around me;
38:32 or can you guide the Bear with its **c**?
42:16 and saw his **c**, and his children’s children,
42:16 and saw his children, and his children’s **c**, C
Ps 17:14 may their **c** have more than enough;
21:10 and their **c** from among humankind.
25:13 and their **c** shall possess the land.
34:11 O **c**, listen to me; I will teach you the fear of the
37:25 the righteous forsaken or their **c** begging bread.
37:26 and their **c** become a blessing.
37:28 but the **c** of the wicked shall be cut off.
69: 8 an alien to my mother’s **c**.
69:36 the **c** of his servants shall inherit it,
73:15 I would have been untrue to the circle of your **c**.
78: 4 We will not hide them from their **c**;
78: 5 he commanded our ancestors to teach to their **c**;
78: 6 that the next generation might know them, the **c**
78: 6 and rise up and tell them to their **c**,
82: 6 I say, “You are gods, **c** of the Most High,
83: 8 they are the strong arm of the **c** of Lot.
89:30 If his **c** forsake my law and do not walk according
90:16 and your glorious power to their **c**.
102:28 The **c** of your servants shall live secure;
103:13 As a father has compassion for his **c**,
103:17 and his righteousness to children’s **c**, C
105: 6 **c** of Jacob, his chosen ones.
109: 9 May his **c** be orphans, and his wife a widow.
109:10 May his **c** wander about and beg;
109:12 nor anyone to pity his orphaned **c**.
113: 9 making her the joyous mother of **c**.
115:14 the LORD give you increase, both you and your **c**.
128: 3 your **c** will be like olive shoots around your table.
128: 6 May you see your children’s **c**. C
147:13 he blesses your **c** within you.
149: 2 let the **c** of Zion rejoice in their King.
Pr 4: 1 Listen, **c**, to a father’s instruction,
7:24 And now, my **c**, listen to me,
8:32 And now, my **c**, listen to me:
13:22 good leave an inheritance to their children’s **c**, C
13:24 Those who spare the rod hate their **c**,
14:26 and one’s **c** will have a refuge.
17: 6 and the glory of **c** is their parents.
17:25 Foolish **c** are a grief to their father and bitterness
19:18 Discipline your **c** while there is hope;
19:26 chase away their mother are **c** who cause shame
20: 7 happy are the **c** who follow them!
20:11 Even **c** make themselves known by their acts,
22: 6 Train **c** in the right way, and when old,
23:13 Do not withhold discipline from your **c**;
28: 7 Those who keep the law are wise **c**,
29:17 Discipline your **c**, and they will give you rest;
31:28 Her **c** rise up and call her happy;
Ecc 5:14 though they are parents of **c**,
6: 3 man may beget a hundred **c**, and live many years;
Isa 1: 2 I reared **c** and brought them up,
1: 4 offspring who do evil, **c** who deal corruptly,
3:12 **c** are their oppressors, and women rule over them.
8:18 the **c** whom the LORD has given me are signs
13:18 their eyes will not pity **c**.
17: 3 the remnant of Aram will be like the glory of the **c**
17: 9 which they deserted because of the **c** of Israel,
29:23 For when he sees his **c**, the work of my hands,
30: 1 Oh, rebellious **c**, says the LORD,
30: 9 For they are a rebellious people, faithless **c**,
30: 9 **c** who will not hear the instruction of the LORD;
37: 3 **c** have come to the birth,
38:19 fathers make known to **c** your faithfulness.
45:11 Will you question me about my **c**,
47: 8 I shall not sit as a widow or know the loss of **c**”—
47: 9 the loss of **c** and widowhood shall come upon you
49:20 The **c** born in the time of your bereavement will
49:25 with you, and I will save your **c**.
51:18 to guide her among all the **c** she has borne;
51:18 by the hand among all the **c** she has brought up.
Isa 51:20 Your **c** have fainted, they lie at the head
54: 1 For the **c** of the desolate woman will be more than
the **c** of her that is married,
54:13 All your **c** shall be taught by the LORD,
54:13 and great shall be the prosperity of your **c**.
57: 3 But as for you, come here, you **c** of a sorceress,
57: 4 Are you not **c** of transgression,
57: 5 you that slaughter your **c** in the valleys,
59:21 or out of the mouths of your **c**,
59:21 or out of the mouths of your children’s **c**, C
60: 9 to bring your **c** from far away,
63: 8 **c** who will not deal falsely”;
65:23 not labor in vain, or bear **c** for calamity;
66: 8 as soon as Zion was in labor she delivered her **c**.
Jer 2: 9 says the LORD, and I accuse your children’s **c**. C
2:30 In vain I have struck down your **c**;
3:14 Return, O faithless **c**, says the LORD,
3:19 I thought how I would set you among my **c**,
3:21 the plaintive weeping of Israel’s **c**,
3:22 O faithless **c**, I will heal your faithlessness.
4:22 they are stupid **c**, they have no understanding.
5: 7 Your **c** have forsaken me,
6: 1 Flee for safety, O **c** of Benjamin,
6:11 Pour it out on the **c** in the street,
6:21 parents and **c** together, neighbor and friend
7:18 The **c** gather wood, the fathers kindle fire,
9:21 to cut off the **c** from the streets and the young men
10:20 my **c** have gone from me, and they are no more;
13:14 parents and **c** together, says the LORD.
17: 2 while their **c** remember their altars
18:21 Therefore give their **c** over to famine;
19: 5 of Baal to burn their **c** in the fire as burnt offerings
30:20 Their **c** shall be as of old,
31:15 Rachel is weeping for her **c**;
31:15 she refuses to be comforted for her **c**,
31:17 your **c** shall come back to their own country.
32:18 of parents into the laps of their **c** after them,
32:39 their own good and the good of their **c** after them.
35: 6 shall never drink wine, neither you nor your **c**;
38:23 All your wives and your **c** shall be led out to
40: 7 and had committed to him men, women, and **c**,
41:16 soldiers, women, **c**, and eunuchs,
43: 6 the women, the **c**, the princesses,
47: 3 parents do not turn back for **c**,
La 1: 5 her **c** have gone away, captives before the foe.
1:16 my **c** are desolate, for the enemy has prevailed.
2:19 Lift your hands to him for the lives of your **c**,
2:20 women eat their offspring, the **c** they have borne?
4: 2 The precious **c** of Zion, worth their weight
4: 4 the **c** beg for food, but no one gives them anything.
4:10 of compassionate women have boiled their own **c**;
Eze 5:10 Surely, parents shall eat their **c** in your midst,
5:10 and **c** shall eat their parents;
5:17 and they will rob you of your **c**;
9: 6 little **c** and women, but touch no one who has A
16:21 You slaughtered my **c** and delivered them up as
16:36 of the blood of your **c** that you gave to them,
16:45 who loathed her husband and her **c**;
16:45 who loathed their husbands and their **c**.
20:18 I said to their **c** in the wilderness,
20:21 But the **c** rebelled against me;
20:31 When you offer your gifts and make your **c** pass
23:37 up to them for food the **c** whom they had borne
23:39 when they had slaughtered their **c** for their idols,
36:12 No longer shall you bereave them of **c**.
36:13 and you bereave your nation of **c**,”
36:14 and no longer bereave your nation of **c**, says
37:25 their **c** and their children’s children shall live there
37:25 and their children’s **c** shall live there forever; C
47:22 among you and have begotten **c** among you.
Da 6:24 they, their **c**, and their wives.
Hos 1: 2 take for yourself a wife of whoredom and have **c**
1:10 it shall be said to them, “**C** of the living God.”
2: 4 Upon her **c** also I will have no pity,
2: 4 because they are **c** of whoredom.
4: 6 I also will forget your **c**.
5: 7 for they have borne illegitimate **c**.
9:12 Even if they bring up **c**,
9:13 now Ephraim must lead out his **c** for slaughter.
10:14 when mothers were dashed in pieces with their **c**.
11:10 he roars, his **c** shall come trembling from the west.
Joel 1: 3 Tell your **c** of it, and let your **c** tell their **c**, and
their **c** another generation.
2:16 gather the **c**, even infants at the breast.
2:23 O **c** of Zion, be glad and rejoice in
Am 2:11 of your **c** to be prophets and some of your youths
Mic 1:16 and cut off your hair for your pampered **c**;
2: 9 their young **c** you take away my glory forever.
Zec 10: 7 Their **c** shall see it and rejoice,
10: 9 and they shall rear their **c** and return.
Mal 3: 6 therefore you, O **c** of Jacob, have not perished.
3:17 as parents spare their **c** who serve them.
4: 6 He will turn the hearts of parents to their **c** and the
hearts of **c** to their parents,
Mt 2:16 and he sent and killed all the **c** in and around
2:18 Rachel weeping for her **c**;
3: 9 from these stones to raise up **c** to Abraham.
5: 9 for they will be called **c** of God. B
5:45 so that you may be **c** of your Father in heaven;
7:11 know how to give good gifts to your **c**,
10:21 and **c** will rise against parents and have them put
11:16 It is like **c** sitting in the marketplaces and calling
13:38 and the good seed are the **c** of the kingdom;
13:38 the weeds are the **c** of the evil one,
14:21 about five thousand men, besides women and **c**. D
15:38 four thousand men, besides women and **c**. D
17:25 From their **c** or from others?”

Mt 17:26 Jesus said to him, "Then the **c** are free.
18: 3 unless you change and become like **c**,
18:25 with his wife and **c** and all his possessions,
19:13 Then little **c** were being brought to him in order A
19:14 the little **c** come to me, and do not stop them; A
19:29 or brothers or sisters or father or mother or **c**
21:15 and heard the **c** crying out in the temple,
22:24 and raise up **c** for his brother.'
23:37 How often have I desired to gather your **c** together
27:25 "His blood be on us and on our **c**!"
Mk 7:27 He said to her, "Let the **c** be fed first,
10:13 People were bringing little **c** to him in order A
10:14 "Let the little **c** come to me; A
10:24 But Jesus said to them again, "**C**,
10:29 or brothers or sisters or mother or father or **c**
10:30 houses, brothers and sisters, mothers and **c**,
12:19 the man shall marry the widow and raise up **c**
12:20 the first married and, when he died, left no **c**;
12:21 the second married her and died, leaving no **c**;
12:22 none of the seven left **c**.
13:12 and **c** will rise against parents and have them put
Lk 1: 7 But they had no **c**, because Elizabeth was barren,
1:17 to turn the hearts of parents to their **c**,
3: 8 from these stones to raise up **c** to Abraham.
6:35 and you will be **c** of the Most High;
7:32 like **c** sitting in the marketplace and calling
7:35 Nevertheless, wisdom is vindicated by all her **c**."
11: 7 and my **c** are with me in bed;
11:13 know how to give good gifts to your **c**,
13:34 How often have I desired to gather your **c** together
14:26 wife and **c**, brothers and sisters, yes,
16: 8 for the **c** of this age are more shrewd in dealing
16: 8 in dealing with their own generation than are the **c**
18:16 "Let the little **c** come to me, and do not stop A
18:29 or wife or brothers or parents or **c**,
19:44 you and your **c** within you,
20:28 leaving a wife but no **c**,
20:28 the man shall marry the widow and raise up **c**
20:36 because they are like angels and are **c** of God, B
20:36 being **c** of the resurrection.
23:28 but weep for yourselves and for your **c**.
Jn 1:12 he gave power to become **c** of God, B
8:39 Jesus said to them, "If you were Abraham's **c**,
8:41 They said to him, "We are not illegitimate **c**;
11:52 but to gather into one the dispersed **c** of God. B
12:36 so that you may become **c** of light."
13:33 Little **c**, I am with you only a little longer. A
21: 5 Jesus said to them, "**C**, you have no fish,
Ac 2:39 For the promise is for you, for your **c**,
13:33 for us, their **c**, by raising Jesus;
21: 5 and all of them, with wives and **c**,
21:21 not to circumcise their **c** or observe the customs.
Ro 2:20 a corrector of the foolish, a teacher of **c**, having in
8:14 who are led by the Spirit of God are **c** of God. B
8:16 with our spirit that we are **c** of God, B
8:17 and if **c**, then heirs, heirs of God and joint heirs
8:19 eager longing for the revealing of the **c** of God; B
8:21 obtain the freedom of the glory of the **c** of God. B
9: 7 not all of Abraham's **c** are his true descendants;
9: 8 not the **c** of the flesh who are the children of God,
9: 8 the children of the flesh who are the **c** of God, B
9: 8 the **c** of the promise are counted as descendants.
9:10 when she had conceived **c** by one husband,
9:26 there they shall be called **c** of the living God."
9:27 the number of the **c** of Israel were like the sand of
1Co 4:14 but to admonish you as my beloved **c**.
7:14 Otherwise, your **c** would be unclean, but as it is,
14:20 Brothers and sisters, do not be **c** in your thinking;
2Co 6:13 I speak as to **c**—open wide your hearts also.
12:14 for **c** ought not to lay up for their parents, but
parents for their **c**.
Gal 3:26 Christ Jesus you are all **c** of God through faith. B
4: 5 so that we might receive adoption as **c**.
4: 6 And because you are **c**, God has sent the Spirit
4:19 My little **c**, for whom I am again in the pain A
4:24 is Hagar, from Mount Sinai, bearing **c** for slavery.
4:25 for she is in slavery with her **c**.
4:27 "Rejoice, you childless one, you who bear no **c**,
4:27 for the **c** of the desolate woman are more
numerous than the **c** of the one who is married."
4:28 you, my friends, are **c** of the promise, like Isaac.
4:31 So then, friends, we are **c**,
Eph 1: 5 for adoption as his **c** through Jesus Christ,
2: 3 and we were by nature **c** of wrath,
4:14 We must no longer be **c**,
5: 1 Therefore be imitators of God, as beloved **c**,
5: 8 in the Lord you are light. Live as **c** of light—
6: 1 **C**, obey your parents in the Lord, for this is right.
6: 4 And, fathers, do not provoke your **c** to anger,
Php 2:15 **c** of God without blemish in the midst of B
Col 3:20 **C**, obey your parents in everything,
3:21 Fathers, do not provoke your **c**,
1Th 2: 7 like a nurse tenderly caring for her own **c**.
2:11 with each one of you like a father with his **c**,
5: 5 for you are all **c** of light and **c** of the day;
1Ti 3: 4 keeping his **c** submissive and respectful
3:12 let them manage their **c** and their households well;
5: 4 If a widow has **c** or grandchildren,
5:10 as one who has brought up **c**, shown hospitality,
5:14 So I would have younger widows marry, bear **c**,
Tit 1: 6 married only once, whose **c** are believers,
2: 4 to love their husbands, to love their **c**,
Heb 2:10 in bringing many **c** to glory,
2:13 "Here am I and the **c** whom God has given me."
2:14 Since, therefore, the **c** share flesh and blood,
12: 5 the exhortation that addresses you as **c**—
12: 7 God is treating you as **c**;
Heb 12: 8 do not have that discipline in which all **c** share,
then you are illegitimate and not his **c**.
1Pe 1:14 Like obedient **c**, do not be conformed to
2Pe 2:14 They have hearts trained in greed. Accursed **c**!
1Jn 2: 1 My little **c**, I am writing these things to you so A
2:12 I am writing to you, little **c**, A
2:14 I write to you, **c**, because you know the Father.
2:18 **C**, it is the last hour!
2:28 And now, little **c**, abide in him, A
3: 1 that we should be called **c** of God; B
3: 2 Beloved, we are God's **c** now;
3: 7 Little **c**, let no one deceive you. A
3:10 The **c** of God and the children of the devil B
3:10 and the **c** of the devil are revealed in this way:
3:18 Little **c**, let us love, not in word or speech, A
4: 4 Little **c**, you are from God, A
5: 2 By this we know that we love the **c** of God, B
5:19 We know that we are God's **c**,
5:21 Little **c**, keep yourselves from idols. A
2Jn 1: 1 The elder to the elect lady and her **c**,
1: 4 I was overjoyed to find some of your **c** walking in
1:13 The **c** of your elect sister send you their greetings.
3Jn 1: 4 to hear that my **c** are walking in the truth.
Rev 2:23 and I will strike her **c** dead.
12:17 and went off to make war on the rest of her **c**,
21: 7 and I will be their God and they will be my **c**.
Tob 4:12 They were blessed in their **c**,
6:18 I presume that you will have **c** by her,
8:17 because you had compassion on two only **c**.
10:11 and may I see **c** of yours before I die."
10:12 and may I live long enough to see **c** of you and
13: 3 before the nations, O **c** of Israel;
13: 9 will again have mercy on the **c** of the righteous.
13:13 Go, then, and rejoice over the **c** of the righteous,
14: 3 command: "My son, take your **c**
14:8,9 So now, my **c**, I command you,
14:8,9 Your **c** are also to be commanded
14:11 So now, my **c**, see what almsgiving accomplishes,
14:12 and his wife and **c** returned to Media and settled
Jdt 4:10 and their **c** and their cattle and every resident alien
4:11 and **c** living at Jerusalem prostrated themselves
7:14 They and their wives and **c** will waste away
7:22 Their **c** were listless, and the women
7:23 the young men, the women, and the **c**,
7:27 and our wives and **c** drawing their last breath.
7:32 The women and **c** he sent home. D
9: 4 to be divided among your beloved **c** who burned
9:13 and against the house your **c** possess.
16: 4 and seize my **c** as booty,
16:12 through and wounded them like the **c** of fugitives;
AdE 7: 4 we and our **c**—male and female slaves.
13: 6 shall all—wives and **c** included—
16:16 and are **c** of the living God,
Wis 3:12 Their wives are foolish, and their **c** evil;
3:16 But **c** of adulterers will not come to maturity,
4: 6 For **c** born of unlawful unions are witnesses
5: 5 they been numbered among the **c** of God? B
12: 5 their merciless slaughter of **c**,
12:19 and you have filled your **c** with good hope,
12:21 with what strictness you have judged your **c**,
12:25 Therefore, as though to **c** who cannot reason,
13:17 about possessions and his marriage and **c**,
14:23 For whether they kill **c** in their initiations,
16:10 But your **c** were not conquered even by the fangs
16:21 manifested your sweetness toward your **c**;
16:26 that your **c**, whom you loved, O Lord, might learn
18: 4 those who had kept your **c** imprisoned,
18: 5 in punishment took away a multitude of their **c**;
18: 9 the holy **c** of good people offered sacrifices,
18:10 their piteous lament for their **c** was spread abroad.
18:12 one instant their most valued **c** had been destroyed.
19: 6 so that your **c** might be kept unharmed.
Sir 3: 1 Listen to me your father, O **c**;
3: 2 For the Lord honors a father above his **c**,
3: 2 and he confirms a mother's right over her **c**.
3: 5 in their own **c**, and when they pray they will
3: 9 a father's blessing strengthens the houses of the **c**,
3:11 it is a disgrace for **c** not to respect their mother.
4:11 Wisdom teaches her **c** and gives help
7:23 Do you have **c**? Discipline them,
14:26 who places his **c** under her shelter, and lodges
16: 1 Do not desire a multitude of worthless **c**,
16: 3 and to die childless better than to have ungodly **c**.
23: 7 my **c**, to instruction concerning the mouth;
23:23 and brought forth **c** by another man.
23:24 and her punishment will extend to her **c**.
23:25 Her **c** will not take root,
25: 7 a man who can rejoice in his **c**;
30: 1 CONCERNING C He who loves his son will whip
33:22 Better that your **c** should ask from you than that
you should look to the hand of your **c**.
39:13 Listen to me, my faithful **c**,
40: 1 and a heavy yoke is laid on the **c** of Adam,
40:15 The **c** of the ungodly put out few branches;
40:19 **C** and the building of a city establish one's name,
41: 5 The **c** of sinners are abominable **c**,
41: 6 The inheritance of the **c** of sinners will perish,
41: 7 **C** will blame an ungodly father,
41: 9 If you have **c**, calamity will be theirs;
41:14 My **c**, be true to your training and be at peace;
42: 5 and of frequent disciplining of **c**,
44: 9 they and their **c** after them.
44:11 and their inheritance with their children's **c**. C
44:12 their **c** also, for their sake.
46: 9 and his **c** obtained it for an inheritance,
46:12 those who have been honored live again in their **c**!
47:20 so that you brought wrath upon your **c**,
Sir 48:10 to turn the hearts of parents to their **c**,
51:12 *For the c of Israel, the people close to him.*
Bar 3: 4 the **c** of those who sinned before you,
4:12 I was left desolate because of the sins of my **c**,
4:19 Go, my **c**, go; for I have been left desolate.
4:21 Take courage, my **c**, cry to God,
4:25 My **c**, endure with patience the wrath
4:26 My pampered **c** have traveled rough roads;
4:27 Take courage, my **c**, and cry to God,
4:32 Wretched will be the cities that your **c** served
4:37 Look, your **c** are coming, whom you sent away;
5: 5 and see your **c** gathered from west and east at
LtJ 6:33 of their gods to clothe their wives and **c**.
Sus 1:30 And she came with her parents, her **c**,
Bel 1:10 besides their wives and **c**.
1:15 the priests came as usual, with their wives and **c**,
1:20 "I see the footprints of men and women and **c**." D
1:21 and he arrested the priests and their wives and **c**.
1Mc 1:32 They took captive the women and **c**, D
1:38 to her offspring, and her **c** forsook her.
1:60 to death the women who had their **c** circumcised,
2:38 with their wives and **c** and livestock,
2:50 Now, my **c**, show zeal for the law,
2:64 My **c**, be courageous and grow strong in the law,
3:20 and our wives and our **c**, and to despoil us;
3:45 not one of her **c** went in or out.
5:13 enemy have captured their wives and **c** and goods,
5:23 with their wives and **c**, and all they possessed,
5:45 with their wives and **c** and goods,
8:10 and the Romans took captive their wives and **c**;
13: 6 and the sanctuary and your wives and **c**,
13:45 The men in the city, with their wives and **c**,
2Mc 5:13 women, and **c**, and slaughter of young girls D
6:10 in for having circumcised their **c**.
7:34 when you raise your hand against the **c** of heaven.
8:28 distributed the rest among themselves and their **c**.
9:15 to throw out with their **c** for the wild animals and
9:20 If you and your **c** are well and your affairs are
12: 3 among them to embark, with their wives and **c**,
12:21 the women and the **c** and also the baggage to
14:25 He urged him to marry and have **c**;
15:18 Their concern for wives and **c**,
1Es 4:53 they and their **c** and all the priests who came.
6:31 to the Most High God for the king and his **c**,
8:50 and for our **c** and the livestock that were with us.
8:85 and leave it for an inheritance to your **c** forever.'
8:93 will put away all our foreign wives, with their **c**,
9:36 and they put them away together with their **c**.
3Mc 1: 4 to defend themselves and their **c**
1:20 and nurses abandoned even newborn **c** here
3:25 together with their wives and **c**,
3:27 whether old people or **c** or even infants,
5:31 "If your parents or **c** were present,
5:49 parents and **c**, mothers and daughters,
6: 3 O Father, upon the **c** of the sainted Jacob,
6:28 the **c** of the almighty and living God of heaven,
7: 2 "We ourselves and our **c** are faring well,
7: 6 always taking their part as a father does for his **c**,
2Es 1: 5 to their **c** the iniquities that they have committed
1: 5 so that they may tell their children's **c** C
1:28 or a mother her daughters or a nurse her **c**,
1:29 you should be my **c** and I should be your father?
1:34 and your sons will have no **c**,
1:37 whose **c** rejoice with gladness;
2: 2 mother who bore them says to them, 'Go, my **c**,
2: 4 Go, my **c**, and ask for mercy from the Lord.'
2: 5 as a witness in addition to the mother of the **c**,
2:15 "Mother, embrace your **c**;
2:17 Do not fear, mother of **c**, for I have chosen you,
2:19 by these I will fill your **c** with joy.
2:25 "Good nurse, nourish your **c**;
2:29 so that your **c** may not see hell.
2:30 "Rejoice, O mother, with your **c**,
2:31 Remember your **c** that sleep,
2:32 Embrace your **c** until I come,
2:41 The number of your **c**, whom you desired,
3:12 they produced **c** and peoples and many nations,
5:46 'If you bear ten **c**, why one after another?'
5:51 He replied to me, "Ask a woman who bears **c**,
6:21 **C** a year old shall speak with their voices,
6:21 to premature **c** at three and four months,
10:22 our **c** have suffered abuse,
15:25 not spare them. Depart, you faithless **c**!
15:57 Your **c** shall die of hunger,
15:63 They shall carry your **c** away captive,
16: 2 and wail for your **c**, and lament for them;
16:44 like those who will have no **c**;
16:46 overthrow their houses, and take their **c** captive;
16:46 in captivity and famine they will produce their **c**.
4Mc 2:12 It takes precedence over love for **c**,
4: 9 and **c** were imploring God in the temple to shield D
6:17 the **c** of Abraham, think so basely that out
6:22 O **c** of Abraham, die nobly for your religion!
9:18 that **c** of the Hebrews alone are invincible
14:12 up under the rackings of each one of her **c**.
14:13 how complex is a mother's love for her **c**,
14:18 to demonstrate sympathy for **c** by the example
14:20 But sympathy for her **c** did not sway the mother of
15: 1 O reason of the **c**, tyrant over the emotions!
15: 1 more desirable to the mother than her **c**!
15: 4 the emotions of parents who love their **c**?
15: 5 they are more devoted to their **c**.
15: 6 more than any other mother, loved her **c**.
15: 8 the temporary safety of her **c**.
15:11 to suffer with them out of love for her **c**,
15:15 She watched the flesh of her **c** being consumed
15:20 of **c** burned upon the flesh of other **c**,

4Mc 15:21 as did the voices of the **c** in torture calling
15:24 of seven **c** and the ingenious and various rackings,
15:25 family, parental love, and the rackings of her **c**—
15:26 and the other deliverance for her **c**.
16: 1 endured seeing her **c** tortured to death,
16: 6 bearing seven **c**, I am now the mother of none!
16: 9 Alas for my **c**, some unmarried,
16: 9 I shall not see your **c** or have the happiness
16:10 so many and beautiful **c** am a widow and alone,
17: 6 your **c** were true descendants of father Abraham.
17: 7 the seven **c** enduring their varied tortures to death
18: 1 O Israelite **c**, offspring of the seed of Abraham,
18: 6 also these principles to her **c**:
18: 9 who lived out his life with good **c**,

CHILDREN'S (20) [CHILD]
A. CHILDREN'S CHILDREN (15)

Ge 45:10 you and your children and your **c** children, A
Ex 34: 7 the parents upon the children and the **c** children, A
Dt 4: 9 to your children and your **c** children— A
4:25 When you have had children and **c** children, A
6: 2 and your children and your **c** children may fear A
2Ki 17:41 and their **c** children continue to do A
Job 42:16 and saw his children, and his **c** children, A
Ps 103:17 and his righteousness to **c** children, A
128: 6 May you see your **c** children. A
Pr 13:22 good leave an inheritance to their **c** children, A
Isa 59:21 or out of the mouths of your **c** children, A
Jer 2: 9 says the LORD, and I accuse your **c** children. A
31:29 and the **c** teeth are set on edge."
Eze 18: 2 and the **c** teeth are set on edge"?
37:25 and their **c** children shall live there forever; A
Mt 15:26 "It is not fair to take the **c** food and throw it to
Mk 7:27 for it is not fair to take the **c** food and throw it to
7:28 even the dogs under the table eat the **c** crumbs."
Sir 44:11 and their inheritance with their **c** children. A
2Es 1: 5 so that they may tell their **c** children A

CHILEAB (1)
2Sa 3: 3 **C**, of Abigail the widow of Nabal of Carmel;

CHILION (3)
Ru 1: 2 the names of his two sons were Mahlon and **C**;
1: 5 both Mahlon and **C** also died,
4: 9 to Elimelech and all that belonged to **C**

CHILMAD (1)
Eze 27:23 Asshur, and **C** traded with you.

CHIMHAM (4) [GERUTH]
2Sa 19:37 But here is your servant **C**;
19:38 The king answered, "**C** shall go over with me,
19:40 king went on to Gilgal, and **C** went on with him;
Jer 41:17 and stopped at Geruth **C** near Bethlehem,

CHIN (2)
4Mc 9:28 flayed all his flesh up to his **c**,
15:15 the flesh of the head to the **c** exposed like masks.

CHINNERETH (4) [=CHINNEROTH]
Nu 34:11 and reach the eastern slope of the sea of **C**;
Dt 3:17 from **C** down to the sea of the Arabah,
Jos 13:27 as far as the lower end of the Sea of **C**,
19:35 Zer, Hammath, Rakkath, **C**,

CHINNEROTH (3) [=CHINNERETH]
Jos 11: 2 and in the Arabah south of **C**, and in the lowland,
12: 3 and the Arabah to the Sea of **C** eastward,
1Ki 15:20 and all **C**, with all the land of Naphtali.

CHIOS (1)
Ac 20:15 and on the following day we arrived opposite **C**.

CHIP (1)
Hos 10: 7 Samaria's king shall perish like a **c** on the face of

CHIRP (1) [CHIRPED]
Isa 8:19 "Consult the ghosts and the familiar spirits that **c**

CHIRPED (1) [CHIRP]
Isa 10:14 or opened its mouth, or **c**."

CHISEL (1) [CHISELED]
Ex 20:25 for if you use a **c** upon it you profane it.

CHISELED (1) [CHISEL]
2Co 3: 7 the ministry of death, **c** in letters on stone tablets,

CHISLEU (KJV) See CHISLEV

CHISLEV (8)
Ne 1: 1 In the month of **C**, in the twentieth year,
Zec 7: 1 on the fourth day of the ninth month, which is **C**.
1Mc 1:54 Now on the fifteenth day of **C**,
4:52 which is the month of **C**,
4:59 with the twenty-fifth day of the month of **C**.
2Mc 1: 9 the festival of booths in the month of **C**,
1:18 on the twenty-fifth day of **C** we shall celebrate
10: 5 of the same month, which was **C**.

CHISLON (1)
Nu 34:21 Of the tribe of Benjamin, Elidad son of **C**.

CHISLOTH-TABOR (1) [TABOR]
Jos 19:12 toward the sunrise to the boundary of **C**;

CHITLISH (1)
Jos 15:40 Cabbon, Lahmam, **C**,

CHITTIM (KJV) See KITTIM

CHIUN (KJV) See KAIWAN

CHLOE'S (1)
1Co 1:11 by **C** people that there are quarrels among you,

CHOBA (3)
Jdt 4: 4 and to **C** and Aesora, and the valley of Salem.
15: 4 Uzziah sent men to Betomasthaim and **C**
15: 5 and cut them down as far as **C**.

CHOICE‡ (89) [CHOOSE]
Ge 18: 6 "Make ready quickly three measures of **c** flour,
24:10 taking all kinds of **c** gifts from his master;
27: 9 Go to the flock, and get me two **c** kids,
43:11 take some of the **c** fruits of the land in your bags,
49:11 to the vine and his donkey's colt to the **c** vine,
Ex 29: 2 You shall make them of **c** wheat flour.
29:40 of a measure of **c** flour mixed with one-fourth of
Lev 2: 1 the offering shall be of **c** flour;
2: 2 taking from it a handful of the **c** flour and oil,
2: 4 it shall be of **c** flour:
2: 5 it shall be of **c** flour mixed with oil, unleavened;
2: 7 it shall be made of **c** flour in oil.
2:12 to the LORD as an offering of **c** products,
5:11 of an ephah of **c** flour for a sin offering;
6:15 They shall take from it a handful of the **c** flour
6:20 of an ephah of **c** flour as a regular offering,
7:12 and cakes of **c** flour well soaked in oil.
14:10 of three-tenths of an ephah of **c** flour mixed
14:21 of **c** flour mixed with oil for a grain offering and
23:13 of an ephah of **c** flour mixed with oil, an offering
23:17 they shall be of **c** flour, baked with leaven,
24: 5 You shall take **c** flour, and bake twelve loaves
Nu 6:15 cakes of **c** flour mixed with oil
7:13 both of them full of **c** flour mixed with oil for
7:19 both of them full of **c** flour mixed with oil for
7:25 both of them full of **c** flour mixed with oil for
7:31 both of them full of **c** flour mixed with oil for
7:37 both of them full of **c** flour mixed with oil for
7:43 both of them full of **c** flour mixed with oil for
7:49 both of them full of **c** flour mixed with oil for
7:55 both of them full of **c** flour mixed with oil for
7:61 both of them full of **c** flour mixed with oil for
7:67 both of them full of **c** flour mixed with oil for
7:73 both of them full of **c** flour mixed with oil for
7:79 both of them full of **c** flour mixed with oil for
8: 8 and its grain offering of **c** flour mixed with oil,
15: 4 one-tenth of an ephah of **c** flour,
15: 6 an ephah of **c** flour mixed with one-third of a hin
15: 9 three-tenths of an ephah of **c** flour,
18:12 the **c** produce that they give to the LORD,
28: 5 of an ephah of **c** flour for a grain offering,
28: 9 of an ephah of **c** flour for a grain offering, mixed
28:12 of an ephah of **c** flour for a grain offering, mixed
28:12 and two-tenths of **c** flour for a grain offering,
28:13 of **c** flour mixed with oil as a grain offering
28:20 Their grain offering shall be of **c** flour mixed
28:28 Their grain offering shall be of **c** flour mixed
29: 3 Their grain offering shall be of **c** flour mixed
29: 9 Their grain offering shall be of **c** flour mixed
29:14 Their grain offering shall be of **c** flour mixed
Dt 12:11 all your **c** votive gifts that you vow to the LORD.
33:13 with the **c** gifts of heaven above,
33:14 with the **c** fruits of the sun, and the rich yield of
33:16 with the **c** gifts of the earth and its fullness,
1Ki 4:22 for one day was thirty cors of **c** flour,
2Ki 3:19 shall conquer every fortified city and every **c** city;
7: 1 about this time a measure of **c** meal shall be sold
7:16 So a measure of **c** meal was sold for a shekel,
7:18 and a measure of **c** meal for a shekel,
1Ch 9:29 also over the **c** flour, the wine, the oil, the incense,
21:11 "Thus says the LORD, 'Take your **c**:
23:29 the **c** flour for the grain offering,
Ne 5:18 for one day was one ox and six **c** sheep;
Pr 8:10 and knowledge rather than **c** gold;
8:19 even fine gold, and my yield than **c** silver.
10:20 The tongue of the righteous is **c** silver;
SS 5:15 His appearance is like Lebanon, **c** as the cedars.
7:13 and over our doors are all **c** fruits,
Isa 5: 2 and planted it with **c** vines;
Jer 2:21 I planted you as a **c** vine, from the purest stock.
25:34 your dispersions, and you shall fall like a **c** vessel.
Eze 16:13 You had **c** flour and honey and oil for food.
16:19 I fed you with **c** flour and oil and honey—
24: 4 and the shoulder; fill it with **c** bones.
24: 6 Empty it piece by piece, making no **c** at all.
27:24 These traded with you in **c** garments,
31:16 all the trees of Eden, the **c** and best of Lebanon,
46:14 and one-third of a hin of oil to moisten the **c** flour,
48:14 they shall not transfer this **c** portion of the land,
Hos 8:13 Though they offer **c** sacrifices,
Ac 15: 7 that in the early days God made a **c** among you,
Rev 18:13 frankincense, wine, olive oil, **c** flour and wheat,
Sir 15:14 and he left them in the power of their own free **c**.
15:15 and to act faithfully is a matter of your own **c**.
24:15 and like **c** myrrh I spread my fragrance,
35: 3 The one who returns a kindness offers **c** flour,
38:11 and a memorial portion of **c** flour,
Bel 1: 3 for it twelve bushels of **c** flour and forty sheep
1Mc 10:32 he may station in it men of his own **c** to guard it.

CHOICEST‡ (14) [CHOOSE]
Ge 23: 6 Bury your dead in the **c** of our burial places;
Ex 23:19 The **c** of the first fruits
Dt 32:14 together with the **c** wheat—
1Sa 2:29 the **c** parts of every offering of my people Israel?'
2Ki 19:23 I felled its tallest cedars, its **c** cypresses;
SS 4:13 an orchard of pomegranates with all **c** fruits,
4:16 to his garden, and eat its **c** fruits.
Isa 22: 7 Your **c** valleys were full of chariots,
37:24 I felled its tallest cedars, its **c** cypresses;
Jer 22: 7 they shall cut down your **c** cedars and cast them
48:15 **c** of his young men have gone down to slaughter,
Eze 20:40 and the **c** of your gifts,
23: 7 the **c** men of Assyria all of them;
24: 5 Take the **c** one of the flock, pile the logs under it;

CHOIRMASTER See LEADER

CHOKE (2) [CHOKED, CHOKING]
Mt 13:22 but the cares of the world and the lure of wealth **c**
Mk 4:19 the desire for other things come in and **c** the word,

CHOKED (6) [CHOKE]
Mt 13: 7 and the thorns grew up and **c** them.
Mk 4: 7 and the thorns grew up and **c** it,
Lk 8: 7 and the thorns grew with it and **c** it.
8:14 but as they go on their way, they are **c** by the cares
2Es 16:77 to those who are **c** by their sins and overwhelmed
16:77 They are like a field **c** with underbrush

CHOKING (1) [CHOKE]
Sir 51: 4 from **c** fire on every side,

CHOLER (KJV) See ENRAGED, RAGE

CHOOSE (92) [CHOICE, CHOICEST, CHOOSES, CHOOSING, CHOSE, CHOSEN]
Ex 10:26 a hoof shall be left behind, for we must **c** some
17: 9 "**C** some men for us and go out,
Lev 1:14 you shall **c** your offering from turtledoves
Nu 14: 4 So they said to one another, "Let us **c** a captain,
16: 5 the one whom he will **c** he will allow
17: 5 And the staff of the man whom I **c** shall sprout;
Dt 1:13 **C** for each of your tribes individuals who are wise,
12: 5 the LORD your God will **c** out of all your tribes
12:11 to the place that the LORD your God will **c** as
12:14 But only at the place that the LORD will **c** in one
12:18 at the place that the LORD your God will **c**,
12:21 If the place where the LORD your God will **c**
12:26 you shall bring to the place that the LORD will **c**.
14:23 the place that he will **c** as a dwelling for his name,
14:24 the place where the LORD your God will **c**
14:25 go to the place that the LORD your God will **c**;
15:20 by year at the place that the LORD will **c**.
16: 2 that the LORD will **c** as a dwelling for his name.
16: 6 But at the place that the LORD your God will **c**
16: 7 at the place that the LORD your God will **c**;
16:11 at the place that the LORD your God will **c** as
16:15 at the place that the LORD will **c**;
16:16 the LORD your God at the place that he will **c**:
17: 8 up to the place that the LORD your God will **c**,
17:10 to you from the place that the LORD will **c**,
17:15 a king whom the LORD your God will **c**.
18: 6 and comes to the place that the LORD will **c**
23:16 in any place they **c** in any one of your towns,
26: 2 to the place that the LORD your God will **c** as
30:19 **C** life so that you and your descendants may live,
31:11 the LORD your God at the place that he will **c**,
Jos 9:27 in the place that he should **c**.
24:15 **c** this day whom you will serve,
1Sa 17: 8 **C** a man for yourselves, and let him come down
2Sa 17: 1 "Let me **c** twelve thousand men,
24:12 **c** one of them, and I will do it to you."
1Ki 18:23 let them **c** one bull for themselves, cut it in pieces,
18:25 "**C** for yourselves one bull and prepare it first,
1Ch 21:10 **c** one of them, so that I may do it to you.' "
Job 7:15 so that I would **c** strangling
15: 5 and you **c** the tongue of the crafty.
34: 4 Let us **c** what is right;
34:33 For you must **c**, and not I;
Ps 16: 4 Those who **c** another god multiply their sorrows;
25:12 He will teach them the way that they should **c**.
65: 4 Happy are those whom you **c** and bring near
78:67 he did not **c** the tribe of Ephraim;
Pr 1:29 Because they hated knowledge and did not **c**
3:31 the violent and do not **c** any of their ways;
Isa 7:15 he knows how to refuse the evil and **c** the good.
7:16 child knows how to refuse the evil and **c** the good,
14: 1 on Jacob and will again **c** Israel, and will set them
56: 4 To the eunuchs who keep my sabbaths, who **c**
58: 5 Is such the fast that I **c**, a day to humble oneself?

Isa 58: 6 Is not this the fast that I **c**:
66: 4 I also will **c** to mock them, and bring
Jer 33:26 of Jacob and of my servant David and not **c** any
49:19 and I will appoint over it whomever I **c**.
50:44 and I will appoint over her whomever I **c**.
Zec 1:17 will again comfort Zion and again **c** Jerusalem.
2:12 and will again **c** Jerusalem.
Mt 8: 2 saying, "Lord, if you **c**, you can make me clean."
8: 3 and touched him, saying, "I do **c**.
20:14 I **c** to give to this last the same as I give to you.
20:15 not allowed to do what I **c** with what belongs
Mk 1:40 and kneeling he said to him, "If you **c**,
1:41 and said to him, "I do **c**.
Lk 5:12 "Lord, if you **c**, you can make me clean."
5:13 touched him, and said, "I do **c**.
Jn 6:70 Jesus answered them, "Did I not **c** you,
8:44 and you **c** to do your father's desires.
15:16 You did not **c** me but I chose you.
Ac 15:22 decided to **c** men from among their members and
15:25 we have decided unanimously to **c** representatives
1Co 3:10 Each builder must **c** with care how to build on it.
Jdt 8:15 if he does not **c** to help us within these five days,
Wis 12:18 for you have power to act whenever you **c**.
Sir 6:18 My child, from your youth **c** discipline,
15:15 If you **c**, you can keep the commandments,
15:16 stretch out your hand for whichever you **c**.
Bar 3:27 not **c** them, or give them the way to knowledge;
Sus 1:23 I **c** not to do it; I will fall into your hands, rather
1Mc 5:17 "**C** your men and go and rescue your kindred
12:45 now to their homes and **c** for yourself a few men
2Mc 5:19 But the Lord did not **c** the nation for the sake of
6: 9 and should kill those who did not **c** to change over
7:14 but **c** to die at the hands of mortals and to cherish
11:25 since we **c** that this nation also should be free
1Es 8:10 those who freely **c** to do so,
3Mc 6:10 and destroy us, Lord, by whatever fate you **c**.
2Es 7:*129* [59] '**C** life for yourself, so that you may live!'
8:56 For when they had opportunity to **c**,

CHOOSES (12) [CHOOSE]

Nu 16: 7 the man whom the LORD **c** shall be the holy one.
Isa 40:20 As a gift one **c** mulberry wood—wood that will
41:24 whoever **c** you is an abomination.
44:14 or **c** a holm tree or an oak and lets it grow strong
Mt 11:27 and anyone to whom the Son **c** to reveal him.
Lk 10:22 and anyone to whom the Son **c** to reveal him."
Jn 3: 8 The wind blows where it **c**,
Ro 9:18 So then he has mercy on whomever he **c**, and he hardens the heart of whomever he **c**.
1Co 12:11 to each one individually just as the Spirit **c**.
Tob 4:19 if he **c** otherwise, he casts down to deepest Hades.
Sir 15:17 and whichever one **c** will be given.

CHOOSING (3) [CHOOSE]

Job 9:14 then can I answer him, **c** my words with him?
Heb 11:25 **c** rather to share ill-treatment with the people
Sir 45: 4 **c** him out of all humankind.

CHOP (2)

Da 4:14 'Cut down the tree and **c** off its branches,
Mic 3: 3 and **c** them up like meat in a kettle,

CHORAL (2) [CHORUS, CHORUSES]

3Mc 6:35 arranged the aforementioned **c** group and passed
4Mc 14: 7 as the seven days of creation move in **c** dance

CHORASHAN (KJV) See BOR-ASHAN

CHORAZIN (2)

Mt 11:21 "Woe to you, **C**! Woe to you, Bethsaida!
Lk 10:13 "Woe to you, **C**! Woe to you, Bethsaida!

CHORBE (1)

1Es 5:12 The descendants of **C**, seven hundred five.

CHORES (1)

Eze 44:14 to do all its **c**, all that is to be done in it.

CHORUS (4) [CHORAL]

4Mc 8: 4 grouped about their mother as though a **c**,
13: 8 a holy **c** of religion and encouraged one another,
14: 8 a **c**, encircled the sevenfold fear of tortures
18:23 into the **c** of the fathers,

CHORUSES (1) [CHORAL]

3Mc 6:32 they formed **c** as a sign of peaceful joy.

CHOSAMAEUS (1)

1Es 9:32 and Melchias and Sabbaias and Simon **C**.

CHOSE (65) [CHOOSE]

Ge 6: 2 they took wives for themselves of all that they **c**.
13:11 So Lot **c** for himself all the plain of the Jordan,
Ex 18:25 Moses **c** able men from all Israel
Dt 4:37 he **c** their descendants after them.
7: 7 that the LORD set his heart on you and **c** you—
10:15 in love on your ancestors alone and **c** you,
33:21 He **c** the best for himself,
Jos 8: 3 Joshua **c** thirty thousand warriors
1Sa 2:28 I **c** him out of all the tribes of Israel to
13: 2 Saul **c** three thousand out of Israel;
1Sa 17:40 and **c** five smooth stones from the wadi,
2Sa 6:21 who **c** me in place of your father
10: 9 he **c** some of the picked men of Israel,
1Ki 8:16 but I **c** David to be over my people Israel.'
11:34 for the sake of my servant David whom I **c**
1Ch 19:10 he **c** some of the picked men of Israel
28: 4 of Israel **c** me from all my ancestral house to
28: 4 for he **c** Judah as leader,
2Ch 6: 5 and I **c** no one as ruler over my people Israel;
Ne 9: 7 the God who **c** Abram and brought him out of Ur
Job 29:25 I **c** their way, and sat as chief,
Ps 47: 4 He **c** our heritage for us,
78:68 but he **c** the tribe of Judah,
78:70 He **c** his servant David, and took him from
Isa 65:12 and **c** what I did not delight in.
66: 4 and **c** what did not please me.
Jer 33:24 that the LORD **c** have been rejected by him,"
Eze 20: 5 On the day when I **c** Israel,
Mk 13:20 but for the sake of the elect, whom he **c**,
Lk 6:13 he called his disciples and **c** twelve of them,
14: 7 he noticed how the guests **c** the places of honor,
Jn 15:16 You did not choose me but I **c** you.
Ac 6: 5 the whole community, and they **c** Stephen,
13:17 of this people Israel **c** our ancestors and made
15:40 But Paul **c** Silas and set out,
1Co 1:27 But God **c** what is foolish in the world to shame
1:27 God **c** what is weak in the world to shame
1:28 God **c** what is low and despised in the world,
12:18 each one of them, as he **c**.
Eph 1: 4 just as he **c** us in Christ before the foundation of
Col 1:27 To them God **c** to make known how great among
2Th 2:13 because God **c** you as the first fruits for salvation
Jdt 10:17 They **c** from their number a hundred men
11: 1 for I have never hurt anyone who **c**
Wis 7:10 and I **c** to have her rather than light,
Sir 24: 8 and my Creator **c** the place for my tent.
45:16 He **c** him out of all the living to offer sacrifice to
1Mc 1:63 They **c** to die rather than to be defiled by food or
3:38 Lysias **c** Ptolemy son of Dorymenes,
4:42 He **c** blameless priests devoted to the law,
7: 8 So the king **c** Bacchides, one of
7:37 "You **c** this house to be called by your name,
8:17 So Judas **c** Eupolemus son of John son of Accos,
9:25 Bacchides **c** the godless and put them in charge of
10:74 He **c** ten thousand men and set out
11:23 He **c** some of the elders of Israel and some of
12: 1 he **c** men and sent them to Rome to confirm
13:34 also **c** emissaries and sent them to King Demetrius
16: 4 So John **c** out of the country twenty thousand
2Mc 1:25 you **c** the ancestors and consecrated them.
3: 7 The king **c** Heliodorus, who was in charge
14:12 He immediately **c** Nicanor,
1Es 9:16 Ezra the priest **c** for himself the leading men
3Mc 2: 9 **c** this city and sanctified this place for your name,
2Es 3:13 you **c** for yourself one of them,

CHOSEN‡ (138) [CHOOSE]

Ge 18:19 for I have **c** him, that he may charge his children
Nu 1:16 These were the ones **c** from the congregation,
11:28 the assistant of Moses, one of his **c** men, said,
16: 2 leaders of the congregation, **c** from the assembly,
26: 9 **c** from the congregation, who rebelled
Dt 7: 6 the LORD your God has **c** you out of all
14: 2 the LORD has **c** out of all the peoples on earth to
18: 5 LORD your God has **c** Levi out of all your tribes,
21: 5 for the LORD your God has **c** them to minister
Jos 24:22 against yourselves that you have **c** the LORD,
Jdg 5: 8 When new gods were **c**, then war was in the gates.
10:14 Go and cry to the gods whom you have **c**;
1Sa 8:18 whom you have **c** for yourselves;
10:24 "Do you see the one whom the LORD has **c**?
12:13 See, here is the king whom you have **c**,
16: 8 He said, "Neither has the LORD **c** this one."
16: 9 And he said, "Neither has the LORD **c** this one."
16:10 "The LORD has not **c** any of these."
20:30 Do I not know that you have **c** the son of Jesse
24: 2 Saul took three thousand **c** men out of all Israel,
26: 2 with three thousand **c** men of Israel,
2Sa 6: 1 David again gathered all the **c** men of Israel,
16:18 and this people and all the Israelites have **c**,
1Ki 3: 8 in the midst of the people whom you have **c**,
8:16 I have not **c** a city from any of the tribes of Israel
8:44 to the LORD toward the city that you have **c** and
8:48 that you have **c**, and the house that I have built
11:13 and for the sake of Jerusalem, which I have **c**."
11:32 the city that I have **c** out of all the tribes of Israel.
11:36 the city where I have **c** to put my name.
12:21 one hundred eighty thousand **c** troops to fight
14:21 the city that the LORD had **c** out of all the tribes
2Ki 21: 7 which I have **c** out of all the tribes of Israel,
23:27 and I will reject this city that I have **c**, Jerusalem,
1Ch 9:22 who were **c** as gatekeepers at the thresholds,
15: 2 for the LORD had **c** them to carry the ark of
16:13 children of Jacob, his **c** ones.
16:41 of those **c** and expressly named to render thanks to
24: 6 house being **c** for Eleazar and one **c** for Ithamar.
28: 5 he has **c** my son Solomon to sit upon the throne of
28: 6 for I have **c** him to be a son to me,
28:10 for the LORD has **c** you to build a house as
29: 1 "My son Solomon, whom alone God has **c**,
2Ch 6: 5 I have not **c** a city from any of the tribes of Israel
6: 6 but I have **c** Jerusalem in order that my name may
6: 6 and I have **c** David to be over my people Israel.'
6:34 that you have **c** and the house that I have built
6:38 the city that you have **c**,
7:12 "I have heard your prayer, and have **c** this place
2Ch 7:16 For now I have **c** and consecrated this house so
11: 1 he assembled one hundred eighty thousand **c** troops
12:13 that the LORD had **c** out of all the tribes of Israel
29:11 for the LORD has **c** you to stand in his presence
33: 7 which I have **c** out of all the tribes of Israel,
Ne 1: 9 the place at which I have **c** to establish my name.'
Est 2: 9 and with seven **c** maids from the king's palace,
Ps 16: 5 The LORD is my **c** portion and my cup;
33:12 the people whom he has **c** as his heritage.
89: 3 You said, "I have made a covenant with my **c** one,
89:19 I have exalted one **c** from the people.
105: 6 children of Jacob, his **c** ones.
105:26 and Aaron whom he had **c**.
105:43 So he brought his people out with joy, his **c** ones
106: 5 that I may see the prosperity of your **c** ones,
106:23 had not Moses, his **c** one,
119:30 I have **c** the way of faithfulness;
119:173 for I have **c** your precepts.
132:13 For the LORD has **c** Zion;
135: 4 For the LORD has **c** Jacob for himself,
Pr 16:16 To get understanding is to be **c** rather than silver.
22: 1 A good name is to be **c** rather than great riches,
Isa 1:29 you shall blush for the gardens that you have **c**.
41: 8 you, Israel, my servant, Jacob, whom I have **c**,
41: 9 I have **c** you and not cast you off";
42: 1 Here is my servant, whom I uphold, my **c**,
43:10 says the LORD, and my servant whom I have **c**,
43:20 rivers in the desert, to give drink to my **c** people,
44: 1 hear, O Jacob my servant, Israel whom I have **c**!
44: 2 O Jacob my servant, Jeshurun whom I have **c**.
45: 4 For the sake of my servant Jacob, and Israel my **c**,
49: 7 the Holy One of Israel, who has **c** you."
65: 9 my **c** shall inherit it, and my servants shall settle
65:15 You shall leave your name to my **c** to use as
65:22 and my **c** shall long enjoy the work of their hands.
66: 3 These have **c** their own ways,
Hag 2:23 for I have **c** you, says the LORD of hosts.
Zec 3: 2 The LORD who has **c** Jerusalem rebuke you!
Mt 12:18 whom I have **c**, my beloved,
22:14 For many are called, but few are **c**."
Lk 1: 9 he was **c** by lot, according to the custom of
9:35 "This is my Son, my **C**; listen to him!"
10:42 Mary has **c** the better part,
18: 7 to his **c** ones who cry to him day and night?
23:35 if he is the Messiah of God, his **c** one!"
Jn 13:18 I know whom I have **c**.
15:19 but I have **c** you out of the world—
Ac 1: 2 the Holy Spirit to the apostles whom he had **c**.
1:24 Show us which one of these two you have **c**
9:15 an instrument whom I have **c** to bring my name
10:41 not to all the people but to us who were **c** by God
22:14 God of our ancestors has **c** you to know his will,
Ro 11: 5 at the present time there is a remnant, **c** by grace.
16:13 Greet Rufus, **c** in the Lord;
1Co 15:38 But God gives it a body as he has **c**,
Col 3:12 As God's **c** ones, holy and beloved,
1Th 1: 4 and sisters beloved by God, that he has **c** you,
Heb 5: 1 Every high priest **c** from among mortals is put
Jas 2: 5 not God **c** the poor in the world to be rich in faith
1Pe 1: 2 who have been **c** and destined by God the Father
2: 4 though rejected by mortals yet **c** and precious
2: 6 a cornerstone **c** and precious;
2: 9 But you are a **c** race, a royal priesthood,
5:13 **c** together with you, sends you greetings;
Rev 17:14 and those with him are called and **c** and faithful."
Tob 1: 4 This city had been **c** from among all the tribes
8:15 let all your **c** ones bless you.
13:11 the name of the **c** city will endure forever.
AdE 2: 9 as well as seven maids **c** from the palace;
16:21 for his **c** people instead of a day of destruction
Wis 9: 7 You have **c** me to be king of your people and to
Sir 47:22 he will never blot out the descendants of his **c** one,
49: 6 who set fire to the **c** city of the sanctuary,
51:12 *Give thanks to him who has **c** the sons of Zadok*
51:12 *Give thanks to him who has **c** Zion,*
1Mc 2:19 and have **c** to obey his commandments,
9:30 therefore we have **c** you today to take his place
12:16 We therefore have **c** Numenius son of Antiochus
2Mc 4:19 **c** as being Antiochian citizens from Jerusalem,
1Es 5: 1 this the heads of ancestral houses were **c** to go up,
2Es 2:15 strengthen their feet, because I have **c** you,
2:17 Do not fear, mother of children, for I have **c** you,
5:23 and from all its trees you have **c** one vine,
5:24 of the world you have **c** for yourself one region,
5:24 and from all the flowers of the world you have **c**
6:54 the people whom you have **c**.
15:53 if you had not killed my **c** people continually,
15:56 As you will do to my **c** people, says the Lord,

CHOZEBA (KJV) See COZEBA

CHRIST‡ (468) [CHRIST'S, CHRISTIAN, CHRISTIANS, MESSIAH]

A. JESUS CHRIST (138)
B. IN CHRIST (91)
C. CHRIST JESUS (86)

Mk 1: 1 The beginning of the good news of Jesus **C**, A
9:41 the name of **C** will by no means lose the reward.
Jn 1:17 grace and truth came through Jesus **C**. A
4:25 that Messiah is coming" (who is called **C**).
17: 3 and Jesus **C** whom you have sent. A
Ac 2:38 of Jesus **C** so that your sins may be forgiven; A
3: 6 in the name of Jesus **C** of Nazareth, A
4:10 in good health by the name of Jesus **C** A

Ac 8:12 the kingdom of God and the name of Jesus **C**, A
9:34 Peter said to him, "Aeneas, Jesus **C** heals you; A
10:36 preaching peace by Jesus **C**—he is Lord of all. A
10:48 to be baptized in the name of Jesus **C**. A
11:17 when we believed in the Lord Jesus **C**, A
15:26 for the sake of our Lord Jesus **C**. A
16:18 "I order you in the name of Jesus **C** to come out A
24:24 heard him speak concerning faith in **C** Jesus. BC
28:31 about the Lord Jesus **C** with all boldness and A
Ro 1: 1 Paul, a servant of Jesus **C**, called to be an A
1: 4 by resurrection from the dead, Jesus **C** our Lord, A
1: 6 who are called to belong to Jesus **C**, A
1: 7 from God our Father and the Lord Jesus **C**. A
1: 8 I thank my God through Jesus **C** for all of you, A
2:16 according to my gospel, God, through Jesus **C**, A
3:22 righteousness of God through faith in Jesus **C** A
3:24 through the redemption that is in **C** Jesus, BC
5: 1 with God through our Lord Jesus **C**, A
5: 6 at the right time **C** died for the ungodly.
5: 8 in that while we still were sinners **C** died for us.
5:11 we even boast in God through our Lord Jesus **C**, A
5:15 Jesus **C**, abounded for the many. A
5:17 in life through the one man, Jesus **C**. A
5:21 to eternal life through Jesus **C** our Lord. A
6: 3 into **C** Jesus were baptized into his death? C
6: 4 just as **C** was raised from the dead by the glory of
6: 8 But if we have died with **C**,
6: 9 We know that **C**, being raised from the dead,
6:11 to sin and alive to God in **C** Jesus. BC
6:23 gift of God is eternal life in **C** Jesus our Lord. BC
7: 4 you have died to the law through the body of **C**,
7:25 Thanks be to God through Jesus **C** our Lord! A
8: 1 for those who are in **C** Jesus. BC
8: 2 in **C** Jesus has set you free from the law of sin BC
8: 9 not have the Spirit of **C** does not belong to him.
8:10 But if **C** is in you, though the body is dead
8:11 he who raised **C** from the dead will give life
8:17 then heirs, heirs of God and joint heirs with **C**—
8:34 It is **C** Jesus, who died, yes, who was raised, C
8:35 Who will separate us from the love of **C**?
8:39 from the love of God in **C** Jesus our Lord. BC
9: 1 I am speaking the truth in **C**— B
9: 3 and cut off from **C** for the sake of my own people,
10: 4 For **C** is the end of the law so that there may
10: 6 (that is, to bring **C** down)
10: 7 (that is, to bring **C** up from the dead).
10:17 and what is heard comes through the word of **C**.
12: 5 who are many, are one body in **C**, B
13:14 Instead, put on the Lord Jesus **C**, A
14: 9 For to this end **C** died and lived again,
14:15 the ruin of one for whom **C** died.
14:18 The one who thus serves **C** is acceptable to God
15: 3 For **C** did not please himself;
15: 5 in accordance with **C** Jesus, C
15: 6 the God and Father of our Lord Jesus **C**. A
15: 7 just as **C** has welcomed you, for the glory of God.
15: 8 that **C** has become a servant of the circumcised
15:16 of **C** Jesus to the Gentiles in the priestly service C
15:17 In **C** Jesus, then, I have reason to boast BC
15:18 of anything except what **C** has accomplished
15:19 I have fully proclaimed the good news of **C**.
15:20 not where **C** has already been named,
15:29 I will come in the fullness of the blessing of **C**.
15:30 our Lord Jesus **C** and by the love of the Spirit, A
16: 3 who work with me in **C** Jesus, BC
16: 5 who was the first convert in Asia for **C**.
16: 7 and they were in **C** before I was. B
16: 9 Greet Urbanus, our co-worker in **C**, B
16:10 Greet Apelles, who is approved in **C**. B
16:16 All the churches of **C** greet you.
16:18 For such people do not serve our Lord **C**,
16:20 The grace of our Lord Jesus **C** be with you. A
16:25 to my gospel and the proclamation of Jesus **C**, A
16:27 through Jesus **C**, to whom be the glory forever! A
1Co 1: 1 to be an apostle of **C** Jesus by the will of God, C
1: 2 to those who are sanctified in **C** Jesus, BC
1: 2 the name of our Lord Jesus **C**, both their Lord A
1: 3 from God our Father and the Lord Jesus **C**. A
1: 4 of God that has been given you in **C** Jesus, BC
1: 6 just as the testimony of **C** has been strengthened
1: 7 you wait for the revealing of our Lord Jesus **C**. A
1: 8 be blameless on the day of our Lord Jesus **C**. A
1: 9 into the fellowship of his Son, Jesus **C** our Lord. A
1:10 by the name of our Lord Jesus **C**, A
1:12 or "I belong to Cephas," or "I belong to **C**."
1:13 Has **C** been divided? Was Paul crucified
1:17 For **C** did not send me to baptize but to proclaim
1:17 the cross of **C** might not be emptied of its power.
1:23 but we proclaim **C** crucified,
1:24 **C** the power of God and the wisdom of God.
1:30 He is the source of your life in **C** Jesus, BC
2: 2 to know nothing among you except Jesus **C**, A
2:16 But we have the mind of **C**.
3: 1 but rather as people of the flesh, as infants in **C**. B
3:11 that foundation is Jesus **C**. A
3:23 and you belong to **C**, and Christ belongs to God.
3:23 and you belong to Christ, and **C** belongs to God.
4: 1 as servants of **C** and stewards of God's mysteries.
4:10 We are fools for the sake of **C**,
4:10 but you are wise in **C**. B
4:15 you might have ten thousand guardians in **C**, B
4:15 in **C** Jesus I became your father through BC
4:17 to remind you of my ways in **C** Jesus, BC
5: 7 For our paschal lamb, **C**, has been sacrificed.
6:11 were justified in the name of the Lord Jesus **C** A
6:15 not know that your bodies are members of **C**?
6:15 the members of **C** and make them members of

1Co 7:22 as whoever was free when called is a slave of **C**.
8: 6 and for whom we exist, and one Lord, Jesus **C**, A
8:11 for whom **C** died are destroyed.
8:12 when it is weak, you sin against **C**.
9:12 an obstacle in the way of the gospel of **C**.
10: 4 that followed them, and the rock was **C**.
10: 9 We must not put **C** to the test,
10:16 is it not a sharing in the blood of **C**?
10:16 is it not a sharing in the body of **C**?
11: 1 Be imitators of me, as I am of **C**.
11: 3 But I want you to understand that **C** is the head
11: 3 and God is the head of **C**.
12:12 though many, are one body, so it is with **C**.
12:27 the body of **C** and individually members of it.
15: 3 that **C** died for our sins in accordance with
15:12 Now if **C** is proclaimed as raised from the dead,
15:13 then **C** has not been raised;
15:14 and if **C** has not been raised,
15:15 because we testified of God that he raised **C**—
15:16 dead are not raised, then **C** has not been raised.
15:17 If **C** has not been raised,
15:18 those also who have died in **C** have perished. B
15:19 If for this life only we have hoped in **C**, B
15:20 But in fact **C** has been raised from the dead,
15:22 so all will be made alive in **C**. B
15:23 But each in his own order: **C** the first fruits,
15:23 then at his coming those who belong to **C**.
15:31 a boast that I make in **C** Jesus our Lord. BC
15:57 the victory through our Lord Jesus **C**. A
16:24 My love be with all of you in **C** Jesus. BC
2Co 1: 1 Paul, an apostle of **C** Jesus by the will of God, C
1: 2 from God our Father and the Lord Jesus **C**. A
1: 3 be the God and Father of our Lord Jesus **C**, A
1: 5 For just as the sufferings of **C** are abundant for us,
1: 5 so also our consolation is abundant through **C**.
1:19 For the Son of God, Jesus **C**, A
1:21 But it is God who establishes us with you in **C** B
2:10 has been for your sake in the presence of **C**.
2:12 I came to Troas to proclaim the good news of **C**,
2:14 in **C** always leads us in triumphal procession, B
2:15 of **C** to God among those who are being saved
2:17 but in **C** we speak as persons of sincerity, B
3: 3 and you show that you are a letter of **C**,
3: 4 Such is the confidence that we have through **C**
3:14 since only in **C** is it set aside. B
4: 4 the light of the gospel of the glory of **C**,
4: 5 we proclaim Jesus **C** as Lord and ourselves A
4: 6 of the glory of God in the face of Jesus **C**. A
5:10 of us must appear before the judgment seat of **C**,
5:14 For the love of **C** urges us on,
5:16 we once knew **C** from a human point of view,
5:17 So if anyone is in **C**, there is a new creation: B
5:18 who reconciled us to himself through **C**,
5:19 in **C** God was reconciling the world to himself, B
5:20 So we are ambassadors for **C**,
5:20 we entreat you on behalf of **C**,
6:15 What agreement does **C** have with Beliar?
8: 9 you know the generous act of our Lord Jesus **C**, A
8:23 of the churches, the glory of **C**.
9:13 to the confession of the gospel of **C** and by
10: 1 to you by the meekness and gentleness of **C**—
10: 5 and we take every thought captive to obey **C**.
10: 7 If you are confident that you belong to **C**,
10: 7 that just as you belong to **C**, so also do we.
10:14 the way to you with the good news of **C**.
11: 2 to present you as a chaste virgin to **C**.
11: 3 from a sincere and pure devotion to **C**.
11:10 As the truth of **C** is in me,
11:13 disguising themselves as apostles of **C**.
11:23 Are they ministers of **C**?
12: 2 a person in **C** who fourteen years ago was B
12: 9 so that the power of **C** may dwell in me.
12:10 persecutions, and calamities for the sake of **C**;
12:19 We are speaking in **C** before God. B
13: 3 since you desire proof that **C** is speaking in me.
13: 5 Do you not realize that Jesus **C** is in you?— A
13:13 The grace of the Lord Jesus **C**, the love of God, A
Gal 1: 1 but through Jesus **C** and God the Father, A
1: 3 from God our Father and the Lord Jesus **C**, A
1: 6 of **C** and are turning to a different gospel—
1: 7 and want to pervert the gospel of **C**.
1:10 I would not be a servant of **C**.
1:12 but I received it through a revelation of Jesus **C**. A
1:22 by sight to the churches of Judea that are in **C**; B
2: 4 in to spy on the freedom we have in **C** Jesus, BC
2:16 works of the law but through faith in Jesus **C**. A
2:16 And we have come to believe in **C** Jesus, BC
2:16 so that we might be justified by faith in **C**, B
2:17 But if, in our effort to be justified in **C**, B
2:17 is **C** then a servant of sin?
2:19 I have been crucified with **C**;
2:20 but it is **C** who lives in me.
2:21 if justification comes through the law, then **C** died
3: 1 that Jesus **C** was publicly exhibited as crucified! A
3:13 **C** redeemed us from the curse of the law
3:14 in **C** Jesus the blessing of Abraham might BC
3:16 that is, to one person, who is **C**.
3:22 in Jesus **C** might be given to those who believe. A
3:24 the law was our disciplinarian until **C** came,
3:26 for in **C** Jesus you are all children of God BC
3:27 baptized into **C** have clothed yourselves with **C**.
3:28 for all of you are one in **C** Jesus. BC
3:29 And if you belong to **C**,
4:14 welcomed me as an angel of God, as **C** Jesus. C
4:19 in the pain of childbirth until **C** is formed in you,
5: 1 For freedom **C** has set us free.
5: 2 **C** will be of no benefit to you.

Gal 5: 4 by the law have cut yourselves off from **C**;
5: 6 For in **C** Jesus neither circumcision BC
5:24 And those who belong to **C** Jesus have crucified C
6: 2 and in this way you will fulfill the law of **C**.
6:12 that they may not be persecuted for the cross of **C**.
6:14 anything except the cross of our Lord Jesus **C**, A
6:18 grace of our Lord Jesus **C** be with your spirit, A
Eph 1: 1 Paul, an apostle of **C** Jesus by the will of God, C
1: 1 in Ephesus and are faithful in **C** Jesus: BC
1: 2 from God our Father and the Lord Jesus **C**. A
1: 3 be the God and Father of our Lord Jesus **C**, A
1: 3 in **C** with every spiritual blessing in B
1: 4 in **C** before the foundation of the world to be B
1: 5 for adoption as his children through Jesus **C**, A
1: 9 to his good pleasure that he set forth in **C**, B
1:11 In **C** we have also obtained an inheritance, B
1:12 who were the first to set our hope on **C**,
1:17 I pray that the God of our Lord Jesus **C**, A
1:20 to work in **C** when he raised him from the dead B
2: 5 made us alive together with **C**—
2: 6 with him in the heavenly places in **C** Jesus, BC
2: 7 of his grace in kindness toward us in **C** Jesus. BC
2:10 created in **C** Jesus for good works, BC
2:12 remember that you were at that time without **C**,
2:13 in **C** Jesus you who once were far off BC
2:13 brought near by the blood of **C**.
2:20 with **C** Jesus himself as the cornerstone. C
3: 1 the reason that I Paul am a prisoner for **C** Jesus C
3: 4 to perceive my understanding of the mystery of **C**.
3: 6 and sharers in the promise in **C** Jesus through BC
3: 8 the news of the boundless riches of **C**,
3:11 that he has carried out in **C** Jesus our Lord, BC
3:17 and that **C** may dwell in your hearts through faith,
3:19 to know the love of **C** that surpasses knowledge,
3:21 in the church and in **C** Jesus to all generations, BC
4:12 for building up the body of **C**,
4:13 to maturity, to the measure of the full stature of **C**.
4:15 up in every way into him who is the head, into **C**,
4:20 That is not the way you learned **C**!
4:32 as God in **C** has forgiven you. B
5: 2 as **C** loved us and gave himself up for us,
5: 5 has any inheritance in the kingdom of **C** and
5:14 Rise from the dead, and **C** will shine on you."
5:20 for everything in the name of our Lord Jesus **C**. A
5:21 Be subject to one another out of reverence for **C**.
5:23 For the husband is the head of the wife just as **C**
5:24 Just as the church is subject to **C**,
5:25 as **C** loved the church and gave himself up for her,
5:29 just as **C** does for the church,
5:32 and I am applying it to **C** and the church.
6: 5 in singleness of heart, as you obey **C**;
6: 6 and in order to please them, but as slaves of **C**,
6:23 from God the Father and the Lord Jesus **C**. A
6:24 an undying love for our Lord Jesus **C**. A
Php 1: 1 Paul and Timothy, servants of **C** Jesus, C
1: 1 To all the saints in **C** Jesus who are in Philippi, BC
1: 2 from God our Father and the Lord Jesus **C**. A
1: 6 to completion by the day of Jesus **C**. A
1: 8 for all of you with the compassion of **C** Jesus. C
1:10 in the day of **C** you may be pure and blameless,
1:11 through Jesus **C** for the glory and praise of God. A
1:13 to everyone else that my imprisonment is for **C**;
1:15 Some proclaim **C** from envy and rivalry,
1:16 These proclaim **C** out of love,
1:17 the others proclaim **C** out of selfish ambition,
1:18 Just this, that **C** is proclaimed in every way,
1:19 help of the Spirit of Jesus **C** this will turn out A
1:20 **C** will be exalted now as always in my body,
1:21 For to me, living is **C** and dying is gain.
1:23 my desire is to depart and be with **C**,
1:26 in your boasting in **C** Jesus when I come BC
1:27 in a manner worthy of the gospel of **C**,
1:29 the privilege not only of believing in **C**, but B
2: 1 If then there is any encouragement in **C**, B
2: 5 the same mind be in you that was in **C** Jesus, BC
2:11 tongue should confess that Jesus **C** is Lord, A
2:16 to the word of life that I can boast on the day of **C**
2:21 seeking their own interests, not those of Jesus **C**. A
2:30 he came close to death for the work of **C**,
3: 3 in **C** Jesus and have no confidence in the flesh BC
3: 7 those I have come to regard as loss because of **C**.
3: 8 surpassing value of knowing **C** Jesus my Lord. C
3: 8 in order that I may gain **C**
3: 9 but one that comes through faith in **C**, B
3:10 to know **C** and the power of his resurrection and
3:12 because **C** Jesus has made me his own. C
3:14 prize of the heavenly call of God in **C** Jesus. BC
3:18 For many live as enemies of the cross of **C**;
3:20 we are expecting a Savior, the Lord Jesus **C**. A
4: 7 guard your hearts and your minds in **C** Jesus. BC
4:19 according to his riches in glory in **C** Jesus. BC
4:21 Greet every saint in **C** Jesus. BC
4:23 grace of the Lord Jesus **C** be with your spirit. A
Col 1: 1 Paul, an apostle of **C** Jesus by the will of God, C
1: 2 the saints and faithful brothers and sisters in **C** B
1: 3 the Father of our Lord Jesus **C**, A
1: 4 for we have heard of your faith in **C** Jesus BC
1: 7 He is a faithful minister of **C** on your behalf,
1:27 which is **C** in you, the hope of glory.
1:28 so that we may present everyone mature in **C**. B
2: 2 of God's mystery, that is, **C** himself,
2: 5 and the firmness of your faith in **C**. B
2: 6 you therefore have received **C** Jesus the Lord, C
2: 8 of the universe, and not according to **C**.
2:11 the body of the flesh in the circumcision of **C**;
2:17 but the substance belongs to **C**.
2:20 If with **C** you died to the elemental spirits of

Col 3: 1 So if you have been raised with **C**,
3: 1 where **C** is, seated at the right hand of God.
3: 3 and your life is hidden with **C** in God.
3: 4 When **C** who is your life is revealed,
3: 11 but **C** is all and in all!
3: 15 And let the peace of **C** rule in your hearts,
3: 16 Let the word of **C** dwell in you richly;
3: 24 as your reward; you serve the Lord **C**.
4: 3 that we may declare the mystery of **C**,
4: 12 who is one of you, a servant of **C** Jesus, C
1Th 1: 1 in God the Father and the Lord Jesus **C**: A
1: 3 and steadfastness of hope in our Lord Jesus **C**. A
2: 7 we might have made demands as apostles of **C**.
2: 14 churches of God in **C** Jesus that are in Judea, BC
3: 2 for God in proclaiming the gospel of **C**,
4: 16 and the dead in **C** will rise first. B
5: 9 obtaining salvation through our Lord Jesus **C**, A
5: 18 for this is the will of God in **C** Jesus for you. BC
5: 23 blameless at the coming of our Lord Jesus **C**. A
5: 28 The grace of our Lord Jesus **C** be with you. A
2Th 1: 1 in God our Father and the Lord Jesus **C**: A
1: 2 from God our Father and the Lord Jesus **C**. A
1: 12 to the grace of our God and the Lord Jesus **C**. A
2: 1 As to the coming of our Lord Jesus **C** A
2: 14 you may obtain the glory of our Lord Jesus **C**. A
2: 16 Now may our Lord Jesus **C** himself A
3: 5 to the love of God and to the steadfastness of **C**.
3: 6 beloved, in the name of our Lord Jesus **C**, A
3: 12 in the Lord Jesus **C** to do their work quietly and A
3: 18 grace of our Lord Jesus **C** be with all of you. A
1Ti 1: 1 of **C** Jesus by the command of God our Savior C
1: 1 of God our Savior and of **C** Jesus our hope, C
1: 2 from God the Father and **C** Jesus our Lord. C
1: 12 I am grateful to **C** Jesus our Lord, C
1: 14 with the faith and love that are in **C** Jesus. BC
1: 15 that **C** Jesus came into the world to save sinners C
1: 16 Jesus **C** might display the utmost patience, A
2: 5 between God and humankind, **C** Jesus, C
3: 13 great boldness in the faith that is in **C** Jesus. BC
4: 6 you will be a good servant of **C** Jesus, C
5: 11 when their sensual desires alienate them from **C**,
5: 21 of God and of **C** Jesus and of the elect angels, C
6: 3 with the sound words of our Lord Jesus **C** and A
6: 13 who gives life to all things, and of **C** Jesus, C
6: 14 until the manifestation of our Lord Jesus **C**, A
2Ti 1: 1 Paul, an apostle of **C** Jesus by the will of God, C
1: 1 sake of the promise of life that is in **C** Jesus, BC
1: 2 from God the Father and **C** Jesus our Lord. C
1: 9 This grace was given to us in **C** Jesus before BC
1: 10 through the appearing of our Savior **C** Jesus, C
1: 13 in the faith and love that are in **C** Jesus. BC
2: 1 be strong in the grace that is in **C** Jesus; BC
2: 3 Share in suffering like a good soldier of **C** Jesus. C
2: 8 Remember Jesus **C**, raised from the dead, A
2: 10 also obtain the salvation that is in **C** Jesus, BC
3: 12 live a godly life in **C** Jesus will be persecuted. BC
3: 15 for salvation through faith in **C** Jesus. BC
4: 1 In the presence of God and of **C** Jesus, C
Tit 1: 1 Paul, a servant of God and an apostle of Jesus **C**, A
1: 4 from God the Father and **C** Jesus our Savior. C
2: 13 the glory of our great God and Savior, Jesus **C**. A
3: 6 on us richly through Jesus **C** our Savior, A
Phm 1: 1 Paul, a prisoner of **C** Jesus, C
1: 3 from God our Father and the Lord Jesus **C**. A
1: 6 the good that we may do for **C**.
1: 8 though I am bold enough in **C** to command you B
1: 9 and now also as a prisoner of **C** Jesus. C
1: 20 Refresh my heart in **C**. B
1: 23 Epaphras, my fellow prisoner in **C** Jesus, BC
1: 25 grace of the Lord Jesus **C** be with your spirit. A
Heb 3: 6 **C**, however, was faithful over God's house as
3: 14 For we have become partners of **C**,
5: 5 So also **C** did not glorify himself in becoming
6: 1 leaving behind the basic teaching about **C**,
9: 11 when **C** came as a high priest of the good things
9: 14 how much more will the blood of **C**,
9: 24 **C** did not enter a sanctuary made by human hands,
9: 28 so **C**, having been offered once to bear the sins
10: 5 Consequently, when **C** came into the world,
10: 10 through the offering of the body of Jesus **C** A
10: 12 when **C** had offered for all time a single sacrifice
11: 26 for the **C** to be greater wealth than the treasures
13: 8 Jesus **C** is the same yesterday and today A
13: 21 through Jesus **C**, to whom be the glory forever A
Jas 1: 1 James, a servant of God and of the Lord Jesus **C**, A
2: 1 in our glorious Lord Jesus **C**? A
1Pe 1: 1 Peter, an apostle of Jesus **C**, A
1: 2 to Jesus **C** and to be sprinkled with his blood: A
1: 3 be the God and Father of our Lord Jesus **C**! A
1: 3 the resurrection of Jesus **C** from the dead, A
1: 7 and glory and honor when Jesus **C** is revealed. A
1: 11 or time that the Spirit of **C** within them indicated
1: 11 in advance to the sufferings destined for **C** and
1: 13 that Jesus **C** will bring you when he is revealed. A
1: 19 but with the precious blood of **C**,
2: 5 sacrifices acceptable to God through Jesus **C**. A
2: 21 because **C** also suffered for you,
3: 15 but in your hearts sanctify **C** as Lord.
3: 16 your good conduct in **C** may be put to shame. B
3: 18 For **C** also suffered for sins once for all,
3: 21 through the resurrection of Jesus **C**, A
4: 1 Since therefore **C** suffered in the flesh,
4: 11 be glorified in all things through Jesus **C**. A
4: 14 If you are reviled for the name of **C**,
5: 1 elder myself and a witness of the sufferings of **C**,
5: 10 who has called you to his eternal glory in **C**, B
5: 14 Peace to all of you who are in **C**. B
2Pe 1: 1 Simeon Peter, a servant and apostle of Jesus **C**, A
1: 1 righteousness of our God and Savior Jesus **C**: A
1: 8 in the knowledge of our Lord Jesus **C**. A
1: 11 and Savior Jesus **C** will be richly provided A
1: 14 indeed our Lord Jesus **C** has made clear to me. A
1: 16 the power and coming of our Lord Jesus **C**, A
2: 20 the knowledge of our Lord and Savior Jesus **C**, A
3: 18 and knowledge of our Lord and Savior Jesus **C**. A
1Jn 1: 3 with the Father and with his Son Jesus **C**. A
2: 1 with the Father, Jesus **C** the righteous; A
2: 22 but the one who denies that Jesus is the **C**?
3: 23 name of his Son Jesus **C** and love one another, A
4: 2 that confesses that Jesus **C** has come in the flesh A
5: 1 that Jesus is the **C** has been born of God,
5: 6 the one who came by water and blood, Jesus **C**, A
5: 20 we are in him who is true, in his Son Jesus **C**. A
2Jn 1: 3 with us from God the Father and from Jesus **C**, A
1: 7 those who do not confess that Jesus **C** has come A
1: 9 in the teaching of **C**, but goes beyond it, does
3Jn 1: 7 for they began their journey for the sake of **C**,
Jude 1: 1 Jude, a servant of Jesus **C** and brother of James, A
1: 1 in God the Father and kept safe for Jesus **C**: A
1: 4 and deny our only Master and Lord, Jesus **C**. A
1: 17 of the apostles of our Lord Jesus **C**; A
1: 21 look forward to the mercy of our Lord Jesus **C** A
1: 25 through Jesus **C** our Lord, be glory, majesty, A
Rev 1: 1 The revelation of Jesus **C**, A
1: 2 word of God and to the testimony of Jesus **C**, A
1: 5 from Jesus **C**, the faithful witness, the firstborn A
20: 4 to life and reigned with **C** a thousand years.
20: 6 but they will be priests of God and of **C**,

CHRIST'S (4) [CHRIST]

1Co 9: 21 not free from God's law but am under **C** law) so
Eph 4: 7 according to the measure of **C** gift.
Col 1: 24 in **C** afflictions for the sake of his body,
1Pe 4: 13 rejoice insofar as you are sharing **C** sufferings,

CHRISTIAN (2) [CHRIST]

Ac 26: 28 so quickly persuading me to become a **C**?"
1Pe 4: 16 Yet if any of you suffers as a **C**,

CHRISTIANS (1) [CHRIST]

Ac 11: 26 in Antioch that the disciples were first called "**C**."

CHRISTS See Index to Footnotes

CHRONIC (2)

Lev 13: 11 it is a **c** leprous disease in the skin of his body.
Sir 30: 17 and eternal sleep than **c** sickness.

CHRYSOLITE (5)

Ex 28: 17 **c**, and emerald shall be the first row;
39: 10 row of carnelian, **c**, and emerald was the first row;
Job 28: 19 The **c** of Ethiopia cannot compare with it,
Eze 28: 13 **c**, and moonstone, beryl, onyx, and jasper,
Rev 21: 20 the sixth carnelian, the seventh **c**, the eighth beryl,

CHRYSOPRASE (1)

Rev 21: 20 the ninth topaz, the tenth **c**, the eleventh jacinth,

CHUB (KJV) See LIBYA

CHUN (KJV) See CUN

CHURCH (77) [CHURCHES]

Mt 16: 18 you are Peter, and on this rock I will build my **c**,
18: 15 "If another member of the **c** sins against you,
18: 17 member refuses to listen to them, tell it to the **c**;
18: 17 and if the offender refuses to listen even to the **c**,
18: 21 "Lord, if another member of the **c** sins against me,
Ac 5: 11 the whole **c** and all who heard of these things.
8: 1 That day a severe persecution began against the **c**
8: 3 But Saul was ravaging the **c** by entering house
9: 31 Meanwhile the **c** throughout Judea, Galilee,
11: 22 of this came to the ears of the **c** in Jerusalem,
11: 26 for an entire year they met with the **c** and taught
12: 1 upon some who belonged to the **c**.
12: 5 the **c** prayed fervently to God for him.
13: 1 the **c** at Antioch there were prophets and teachers:
14: 23 after they had appointed elders for them in each **c**,
14: 27 the **c** together and related all that God had done
15: 3 So they were sent on their way by the **c**,
15: 4 they were welcomed by the **c** and the apostles and
15: 22 with the consent of the whole **c**,
18: 22 he went up to Jerusalem and greeted the **c**,
20: 17 asking the elders of the **c** to meet him.
20: 28 to shepherd the **c** of God that he obtained with
Ro 16: 1 a deacon of the **c** at Cenchreae,
16: 5 Greet also the **c** in their house.
16: 23 Gaius, who is host to me and to the whole **c**,
1Co 1: 2 To the **c** of God that is in Corinth,
4: 17 as I teach them everywhere in every **c**.
6: 4 as judges those who have no standing in the **c**?
10: 32 Give no offense to Jews or to Greeks or to the **c**
11: 18 to begin with, when you come together as a **c**,
11: 22 Or do you show contempt for the **c** of God
12: 28 And God has appointed in the **c** first apostles,
14: 4 but those who prophesy build up the **c**.
14: 5 so that the **c** may be built up.
14: 12 strive to excel in them for building up the **c**.
14: 19 in **c** I would rather speak five words
1Co 14: 23 whole **c** comes together and all speak in tongues,
14: 28 let them be silent in **c** and speak to themselves and
14: 35 For it is shameful for a woman to speak in **c**.
15: 9 because I persecuted the **c** of God.
16: 19 together with the **c** in their house,
2Co 1: 1 To the **c** of God that is in Corinth,
Gal 1: 13 the **c** of God and was trying to destroy it.
Eph 1: 22 the head over all things for the **c**,
3: 10 the **c** the wisdom of God in its rich variety might
3: 21 in the **c** and in Christ Jesus to all generations,
5: 23 of the wife just as Christ is the head of the **c**,
5: 24 Just as the **c** is subject to Christ,
5: 25 as Christ loved the **c** and gave himself up for her,
5: 27 as to present the **c** to himself in splendor,
5: 29 just as Christ does for the **c**,
5: 32 and I am applying it to Christ and the **c**.
Php 3: 6 as to zeal, a persecutor of the **c**;
4: 15 no **c** shared with me in the matter of giving
Col 1: 18 He is the head of the body, the **c**;
1: 24 for the sake of his body, that is, the **c**.
4: 15 and to Nympha and the **c** in her house.
4: 16 have it read also in the **c** of the Laodiceans;
1Th 1: 1 the **c** of the Thessalonians in God the Father and
2Th 1: 1 the **c** of the Thessalonians in God our Father and
1Ti 3: 5 how can he take care of God's **c**?
3: 15 which is the **c** of the living God,
5: 16 let the **c** not be burdened,
6: 2 on the ground that they are members of the **c**;
Phm 1: 2 and to the **c** in your house:
Jas 5: 14 the elders of the **c** and have them pray over them,
1Pe 5: 13 Your sister **c** in Babylon, chosen together
3Jn 1: 6 they have testified to your love before the **c**.
1: 9 I have written something to the **c**;
1: 10 to do so and expels them from the **c**.
Rev 2: 1 "To the angel of the **c** in Ephesus write:
2: 8 "And to the angel of the **c** in Smyrna write:
2: 12 "And to the angel of the **c** in Pergamum write:
2: 18 "And to the angel of the **c** in Thyatira write:
3: 1 "And to the angel of the **c** in Sardis write:
3: 7 "And to the angel of the **c** in Philadelphia write:
3: 14 "And to the angel of the **c** in Laodicea write:

CHURCHES (35) [CHURCH]

Ac 15: 41 through Syria and Cilicia, strengthening the **c**.
16: 5 the **c** were strengthened in the faith and increased
Ro 16: 4 but also all the **c** of the Gentiles.
16: 16 All the **c** of Christ greet you.
1Co 7: 17 This is my rule in all the **c**.
11: 16 we have no such custom, nor do the **c** of God.
14: 33 (As in all the **c** of the saints,
14: 34 women should be silent in the **c**.
16: 1 you should follow the directions I gave to the **c**
16: 19 The **c** of Asia send greetings.
2Co 8: 1 the grace of God that has been granted to the **c**
8: 18 the brother who is famous among all the **c**
8: 19 but he has also been appointed by the **c** to travel
8: 23 as for our brothers, they are messengers of the **c**,
8: 24 Therefore openly before the **c**,
11: 8 I robbed other **c** by accepting support from them
11: 28 because of my anxiety for all the **c**.
12: 13 How have you been worse off than the other **c**,
Gal 1: 2 of God's family who are with me, To the **c**
1: 22 and I was still unknown by sight to the **c** of Judea
1Th 2: 14 became imitators of the **c** of God in Christ Jesus
2Th 1: 4 of you among the **c** of God for your steadfastness
Rev 1: 4 John to the seven **c** that are in Asia:
1: 11 in a book what you see and send it to the seven **c**,
1: 20 the seven stars are the angels of the seven **c**,
1: 20 and the seven lampstands are the seven **c**.
2: 7 an ear listen to what the Spirit is saying to the **c**.
2: 11 an ear listen to what the Spirit is saying to the **c**.
2: 17 an ear listen to what the Spirit is saying to the **c**.
2: 23 And all the **c** will know that I am the one
2: 29 an ear listen to what the Spirit is saying to the **c**.
3: 6 an ear listen to what the Spirit is saying to the **c**.
3: 13 an ear listen to what the Spirit is saying to the **c**.
3: 22 an ear listen to what the Spirit is saying to the **c**."
22: 16 to you with this testimony for the **c**.

CHURNED (1) [CHURNS]

2Es 16: 12 the sea is **c** up from the depths,

CHURNING (1) [CHURNS]

Hab 3: 15 the sea with your horses, **c** the mighty waters.

CHURNS (2) [CHURNED, CHURNING]

La 1: 20 my stomach **c**, my heart is wrung within me,
2: 11 My eyes are spent with weeping; my stomach **c**;

CHUSHAN-RISHATHAIM (KJV) See CUSHAN-RISHATHAIM

CHUSI‡ (1)

Jdt 7: 18 which is near **C** beside the Wadi Mochmur.

CHUZA (1)

Lk 8: 3 the wife of Herod's steward **C**, and Susanna,

CICADA (1)

Dt 28: 42 and the fruit of your ground the **c** shall take over.

CIELED (KJV) See PANELED, PANELING

CILICIA (15)
Ac 6: 9 and others of those from C and Asia,
15:23 of Gentile origin in Antioch and Syria and C,
15:41 He went through Syria and C,
21:39 Paul replied, "I am a Jew, from Tarsus in C,
22: 3 born in Tarsus in C, but brought up in this city at
23:34 and when he learned that he was from C,
27: 5 After we had sailed across the sea that is off C
Gal 1:21 Then I went into the regions of Syria and C,
Jdt 1: 7 those who lived in C and Damascus,
1:12 the whole territory of C and Damascus and Syria,
2:21 near the mountain that is to the north of Upper C.
2:25 He also seized the territory of C,
1Mc 11:14 Now King Alexander was in C at that time,
2Mc 4:36 When the king returned from the region of C,
4Mc 4: 2 governor of Syria, Phoenicia, and C, and said,

CINNAMON (4)
Ex 30:23 and of sweet-smelling c half as much, that is,
Pr 7:17 I have perfumed my bed with myrrh, aloes, and c.
SS 4:14 calamus and c, with all trees of frankincense,
Rev 18:13 c, spice, incense, myrrh, frankincense,

CINNEROTH (KJV) See CHINNEROTH

CIRCLE (7) [CIRCLED, CIRCLES, CIRCLING, ENCIRCLE, ENCIRCLED, ENCIRCLES, ENCIRCLING]
Job 26:10 He has described a c on the face of the waters,
Ps 73:15 I would have been untrue to the c
Pr 8:27 when he drew a c on the face of the deep,
Isa 40:22 It is he who sits above the c of the earth,
Wis 13: 2 or the c of the stars, or turbulent water,
2Es 5:42 He said to me, "I shall liken my judgment to a c;
6: 1 "At the beginning of the c of the earth,

CIRCLED (3) [CIRCLE]
Jdg 16: 2 So they c around and lay in wait for him all night
Jdt 13:10 through the camp, c around the valley, and went
1Mc 13:20 and he c around by the way to Adora.

CIRCLES (2) [CIRCLE]
Jos 15:10 and the boundary c west of Baalah to Mount Seir,
4Mc 14:17 by flying in c around them in the anguish of love,

CIRCLING (2) [CIRCLE]
Jos 6: 3 all the warriors c the city once.
6:11 ark of the LORD went around the city, c it once;

CIRCUIT (6) [CIRCUITS]
1Sa 7:16 He went on a c year by year to Bethel, Gilgal,
1Ch 11: 8 from the Millo in complete c;
Ne 12:28 from the c around Jerusalem and from the villages
Ps 19: 6 and its c to the end of them;
1Es 4:34 for it makes the c of the heavens and returns
3Mc 4:11 nor in any way claim to be inside the c of the city.

CIRCUITS (1) [CIRCUIT]
Ecc 1: 6 and on its c the wind returns.

CIRCULATED (1)
3Mc 3: 2 a hostile rumor was c against the Jewish nation

CIRCUMCISE (9) [CIRCUMCISED, CIRCUMCISING, CIRCUMCISION, CIRCUMCISIONS]
Ge 17:11 You shall c the flesh of your foreskins,
Dt 10:16 C, then, the foreskin of your heart,
30: 6 the LORD your God will c your heart and
Jos 5: 2 "Make flint knives and c the Israelites
Jer 4: 4 C yourselves to the LORD,
Lk 1:59 On the eighth day they came to c the child,
2:21 eight days had passed, it was time to c the child,
Jn 7:22 and you c a man on the sabbath.
Ac 21:21 not to c their children or observe the customs.

CIRCUMCISED‡ (60) [CIRCUMCISE]
Ge 17:10 Every male among you shall be c.
17:12 among you shall be c when he is eight days old,
17:13 and the one bought with your money must be c.
17:14 Any uncircumcised male who is not c in the flesh
17:23 and he c the flesh of their foreskins that very day,
17:24 when he was c in the flesh of his foreskin.
17:25 when he was c in the flesh of his foreskin.
17:26 very day Abraham and his son Ishmael were c;
17:27 with money from a foreigner, were c with him.
21: 4 And Abraham c his son Isaac
34:15 as we are and every male among you be c.
34:17 But if you will not listen to us and be c,
34:22 every male among us be c as they are c.
34:24 and every male was c, all who went out of
Ex 12:44 may eat of it after he has been c;
12:48 all his males shall be c;
Lev 12: 3 the eighth day the flesh of his foreskin shall be c.
Jos 5: 3 and c the Israelites at Gibeath-haaraloth.
5: 4 This is the reason why Joshua c them:
5: 5 Although all the people who came out had been c,
5: 5 after they had come out of Egypt had not been c.
5: 7 whom he raised up in their place, that Joshua c;
Jos 5: 7 because they had not been c on the way.
Jer 9:25 when I will attend to all those who are c only in
Ac 7: 8 so Abraham became the father of Isaac and c him
10:45 The c believers who had come
11: 2 the c believers criticized him,
15: 1 you are c according to the custom of Moses,
15: 5 to be c and ordered to keep the law of Moses."
16: 3 and had him c because of the Jews who were
Ro 3:30 the c on the ground of faith and the uncircumcised
4: 9 then, pronounced only on the c,
4:10 Was it before or after he had been c?
4:10 It was not after, but before he was c.
4:11 the ancestor of all who believe without being c
4:12 the ancestor of the c who are not only c but who
4:12 that our ancestor Abraham had before he was c.
15: 8 that Christ has become a servant of the c on behalf
1Co 7:18 Was anyone at the time of his call already c?
Gal 2: 3 who was with me, was not compelled to be c,
2: 7 had been entrusted with the gospel for the c
2: 8 to the c also worked through me in sending me to
2: 9 to the Gentiles and they to the c.
5: 2 am telling you that if you let yourselves be c,
5: 3 be c that he is obliged to obey the entire law.
6:12 in the flesh that try to compel you to be c—
6:13 Even the c do not themselves obey the law,
6:13 but they want you to be c so that they may boast
Php 3: 5 c on the eighth day, a member of the people
Col 2:11 also you were c with a spiritual circumcision,
3:11 c and uncircumcised, barbarian, Scythian,
Jdt 14:10 So he was c, and joined the house of Israel,
AdE 8:17 the Gentiles were c and became Jews out of fear
1Mc 1:60 to death the women who had their children c,
1:61 and their families and those who c them;
2:46 they forcibly c all the uncircumcised boys
2Mc 6:10 in for having c their children.
4Mc 4:25 because they had c their sons,

CIRCUMCISING (1) [CIRCUMCISE]
Jos 5: 8 When the c of all the nation was done,

CIRCUMCISION (27) [CIRCUMCISE]
Ex 4:26 then she said, "A bridegroom of blood by c."
Jn 7:22 Moses gave you c (it is, of course, not from Moses,
7:23 If a man receives c on the sabbath in order that
Ac 7: 8 Then he gave him the covenant of c.
Ro 2:25 C indeed is of value if you obey the law;
2:25 your c has become uncircumcision.
2:26 will not their uncircumcision be regarded as c?
2:27 that have the written code and c but break the law.
2:28 nor is true c something external and physical.
2:29 and real c is a matter of the heart—
3: 1 Or what is the value of c?
4:11 of c as a seal of the righteousness that he had
1Co 7:18 Let him not seek to remove the marks of c.
7:18 Let him not seek c.
7:19 C is nothing, and uncircumcision is nothing;
Gal 2:12 and kept himself separate for fear of the c faction.
5: 6 For in Christ Jesus neither c
5:11 if I am still preaching c?
6:15 For neither c nor uncircumcision is anything;
Eph 2:11 by those who are called "the c"—
2:11 a physical c made in the flesh by human hands—
Php 3: 3 For it is we who are the c,
Col 2:11 a spiritual c, by putting off the body of the flesh in the c of Christ;
4:11 the only ones of the c among my co-workers for
Tit 1:10 especially those of the c;
1Mc 1:15 and removed the marks of c,

CIRCUMCISIONS (1) [CIRCUMCISE]
2Es 1:31 and new moons, and c of the flesh.

CIRCUMFERENCE (3)
Jer 52:21 pillar was eighteen cubits, its c was twelve cubits;
Eze 48:35 c of the city shall be eighteen thousand cubits.
Sir 50: 3 a reservoir like the sea in c.

CIRCUMSPECT (KJV) See ATTENTIVE

CIRCUMSTANCE (1) [CIRCUMSTANCES]
Sir 41:16 for it is not good to feel shame in every c,

CIRCUMSTANCES‡ (6) [CIRCUMSTANCE]
Php 4:12 In any and all c I have learned the secret
1Th 5:18 give thanks in all c; for this is the will of God
Sir 20:11 some who have raised their heads from humble c.
29: 8 be patient with someone in humble c,
2Es 7:18 can endure difficult c while hoping
7:18 the difficult c and will never see the easier ones."

CIS (KJV) See KISH

CISTERN (22) [CISTERNS]
Lev 11:36 But a spring or a c holding water shall be clean,
2Sa 3:26 and they brought him back from the c of Sirah;
2Ki 18:31 and drink water from your own c,
Pr 5:15 Drink water from your own c,
Ecc 12: 6 and the wheel broken at the c,
Isa 30:14 or dipping water out of the c.
36:16 and drink water from your own c,
Jer 37:16 Thus Jeremiah was put in the c house, in the cells,
38: 6 So they took Jeremiah and threw him into the c
Jer 38: 6 Now there was no water in the c, but only mud,
38: 7 heard that they had put Jeremiah into the c.
38: 9 by throwing him into the c to die there of hunger,
38:10 and pull the prophet Jeremiah up from the c
38:11 which he let down to Jeremiah in the c by ropes.
38:13 up by the ropes and pulled him out of the c.
41: 7 and threw them into a c.
41: 9 the c into which Ishmael had thrown all the bodies
41: 9 the men whom he had struck down was the large c
41: 9 Ishmael son of Nethaniah filled that c
Sir 50: 3 In his days a water c was dug,
2Mc 1:19 and secretly hid it in the hollow of a dry c,
10:37 They killed Timothy, who was hiding in a c,

CISTERNS (10) [CISTERN]
Dt 6:11 hewn c that you did not hew,
1Sa 13: 6 and in holes and in rocks and in tombs and in c.
2Ch 26:10 in the wilderness and hewed out many c,
Ne 9:25 hewn c, vineyards, olive orchards,
Jer 2:13 and dug out c for themselves, cracked c that can hold no water.
14: 3 they come to the c, they find no water,
Jdt 7:21 their c were going dry,
8:31 so that the Lord may send us rain to fill our c.
Sir 48:17 the rock with iron tools, and built c for the water.

CITADEL (51) [CITADELS]
Dt 2:36 there was no c too high for us.
3: 4 there was no c that we did not take from them—
1Ki 16:18 he went into the c of the king's house;
2Ki 5:24 When he came to the c, he took the bags
10:25 and then went into the c of the temple of Baal.
15:25 in the c of the palace along with Argob and Arieh;
Ne 7: 2 along with Hananiah the commander of the c—
Est 1: 2 on his royal throne in the c of Susa,
1: 5 the king gave for all the people present in the c
2: 3 the harem in the c of Susa under custody of Hegai,
2: 5 in the c of Susa whose name was Mordecai son
2: 8 when many young women were gathered in the c
3:15 and the decree was issued in the c of Susa.
8:14 The decree was issued in the c of Susa.
9: 6 In the c of Susa the Jews killed
9:11 That very day the number of those killed in the c
9:12 The king said to Queen Esther, "In the c of Susa
Jer 30:18 and the c set on its rightful site.
1Mc 1:33 and strong towers, and it became their c.
1:36 for the c became an ambush against the sanctuary,
3:45 down, and aliens held the c;
4: 2 Men from the c were his guides.
4:41 to fight against those in the c until he had cleansed
6:18 the c kept hemming Israel in around the sanctuary.
6:20 They gathered together and besieged the c in
6:24 of our people besieged the c and became hostile
6:26 today they have encamped against the c
6:32 from the c and encamped at Beth-zechariah,
9:52 the town of Beth-zur, and Gazara, and the c, and
9:53 and put them under guard in the c at Jerusalem.
10: 6 the hostages in the c should be released to him.
10: 7 the hearing of all the people and of those in the c.
10: 9 those in the c released the hostages to Jonathan,
10:32 also my control of the c in Jerusalem and give it to
11:20 the Judeans to attack the c in Jerusalem,
11:21 to him that Jonathan was besieging the c.
11:41 that he remove the troops of the c from Jerusalem,
12:36 to erect a high barrier between the c and the city
13:21 in the c kept sending envoys to Trypho urging him
13:49 the c at Jerusalem were prevented from going in
13:50 from there and cleansed the c from its pollutions.
13:52 of the temple hill alongside the c,
14: 7 he ruled over Gazara and Beth-zur and the c,
14:36 a c from which they used to sally forth and defile
15:28 "You hold control of Joppa and Gazara and the c
2Mc 4:12 in establishing a gymnasium right under the c,
4:28 the captain of the c kept requesting payment—
5: 5 Menelaus took refuge in the c.
15:31 he sent for those who were in the c.
15:35 Judas hung Nicanor's head from the c,
4Mc 4:20 a gymnasium constructed at the very c

CITADELS (2) [CITADEL]
Ps 48: 3 Within its c God has shown himself
48:13 go through its c, that you may tell

CITIES‡ (236) [CITY]
A. CITIES OF JUDAH (32)
B. FORTIFIED CITIES (26)
C. CITIES OF REFUGE (7)

Ge 13:12 among the c of the Plain and moved his tent as far
19:25 and he overthrew those c,
19:25 and all the Plain, and all the inhabitants of the c,
19:29 it was that, when God destroyed the c of the Plain,
19:29 when he overthrew the c in which Lot had settled.
35: 5 a terror from God fell upon the c all around them,
41:35 under the authority of Pharaoh for food in the c,
41:48 and stored up food in the c;
Ex 1:11 They built supply c, Pithom and Rameses,
Lev 25:32 As for the c of the Levites,
25:32 of redemption of the houses in the c belonging
25:33 in the c of the Levites are their possession among
25:34 But the open land around their c may not be sold;
26:25 and if you withdraw within your c,
26:31 I will lay your c waste,
26:33 your land shall be a desolation, and your c
Nu 32:36 and Beth-haran, fortified c, and folds for sheep. B

Nu 35: 6 shall include the six c of refuge, C
35:11 you shall select c to be cities of refuge for you,
35:11 you shall select cities to be c of refuge for you, C
35:12 The c shall be for you a refuge from the avenger,
35:13 The c that you designate shall be six cities
35:13 you designate shall be six c of refuge for you: C
35:14 you shall designate three c beyond the Jordan,
35:14 and three c in the land of Canaan,
35:14 cities in the land of Canaan, to be c of refuge. C
35:15 These six c shall serve as refuge for the Israelites,
Dt 1:22 up and the c we will come to."
1:28 the c are large and fortified up to heaven!
4:41 on the east side of the Jordan three c
4:42 the homicide could flee to one of these c and live:
6:10 a land with fine, large c that you did not build,
9: 1 great c, fortified to the heavens,
19: 2 you shall set apart three c in the land that
19: 5 the killer may flee to one of these c and live.
19: 7 I command you: You shall set apart three c.
19: 9 then you shall add three more c to these three,
19:11 and flees into one of these c,
Jos 9:17 So the Israelites set out and reached their c on
9:17 Now their c were Gibeon, Chephirah, Beeroth,
10: 2 like one of the royal c, and was larger than Ai,
13:10 the c of King Sihon of the Amorites, who reigned
14:12 the Anakim were there, with great fortified c; B
20: 2 Appoint the c of refuge, of which I spoke to you C
20: 4 to one of these c and shall stand at the entrance of
20: 9 These were the c designated for all the Israelites,
1Sa 6:18 number of all the c of the Philistines belonging
6:18 both fortified c and unwalled villages. B
2Sa 2: 1 "Shall I go up into any of the c of Judah?" A
10:12 and for the c of our God;
12:31 Thus he did to all the c of the Ammonites.
20: 6 or he will find fortified c for himself, B
24: 7 and came to the fortress of Tyre and to all the c of
1Ki 4:13 sixty great c with walls and bronze bars);
8:37 if their enemy besieges them in any of their c;
9:11 King Solomon gave to Hiram twenty c in the land
9:12 But when Hiram came from Tyre to see the c
9:13 "What kind of c are these that you have given me,
9:19 as well as all of Solomon's storage c,
9:19 the c for his chariots, the cities for his cavalry,
9:19 the cities for his chariots, the c for his cavalry,
10:26 in the chariot c and with the king in Jerusalem.
13:32 of the high places that are in the c of Samaria,
15:20 the commanders of his armies against the c
15:23 all that he did, and the c that he built,
22:39 and all the c that he built,
2Ki 3:25 The c they overturned, and on every good piece
17: 6 the river of Gozan, and in the c of the Medes.
17:24 in the c of Samaria in place of the people of Israel;
17:24 possession of Samaria, and settled in its c.
17:26 the c of Samaria do not know the law of the god
17:29 every nation in the c in which they lived;
18:11 the river of Gozan, and in the c of the Medes,
18:13 came up against all the fortified c of Judah AB
19:25 that you should make fortified c crash into heaps B
23: 5 offerings in the high places at the c of Judah A
1Ch 6:57 To the sons of Aaron they gave the c of refuge: C
6:67 They were given the c of refuge: C
13: 2 and Levites in the c that have pasture lands,
18: 8 From Tibhath and from Cun, c of Hadadezer,
19: 7 And the Ammonites were mustered from their c
19:13 be courageous for our people and for the c
20: 3 Thus David did to all the c of the Ammonites.
27:25 Over the treasuries in the country, in the c,
2Ch 1:14 in the chariot c and with the king in Jerusalem.
8: 2 Solomon rebuilt the c that Huram had given
8: 5 fortified c, with walls, gates, and bars, B
9:25 in the chariot c and with the king in Jerusalem.
10:17 of Israel who were living in the c of Judah. A
11: 5 and he built c for defense in Judah.
11:10 fortified c that are in Judah and in Benjamin. B
11:12 He also put large shields and spears in all the c,
11:23 of Judah and Benjamin, in all the fortified c; B
12: 4 He took the fortified c of Judah and came AB
13:19 Abijah pursued Jeroboam, and took c from him:
14: 5 from all the c of Judah the high places and A
14: 6 He built fortified c in Judah while B
14: 7 He said to Judah, "Let us build these c,
14:14 They defeated all the c around Gerar,
14:14 They plundered all the c;
16: 4 the commanders of his armies against the c
17: 2 He placed forces in all the fortified c of Judah, AB
17: 2 in the c of Ephraim that his father Asa had taken.
17: 7 and Micaiah, to teach in the c of Judah. A
17: 9 around through all the c of Judah and taught A
17:12 He built fortresses and storage c in Judah.
17:13 He carried out great works in the c of Judah. A
17:19 in the fortified c throughout all Judah. B
19: 5 in the land in all the fortified c of Judah, AB
19:10 to you from your kindred who live in their c,
21: 3 together with fortified c in Judah; B
24: 5 the c of Judah and gather money from all Israel A
25:13 on the c of Judah from Samaria to Beth-horon; A
26: 6 he built c in the territory of Ashdod and elsewhere
27: 4 Moreover he built c in the hill country of Judah,
28:18 on the c in the Shephelah and the Negeb of Judah,
31: 1 to the c of Judah and broke down the pillars, A
31: 1 Then all the people of Israel returned to their c,
31: 6 the c of Judah also brought in the tithe of cattle A
31:15 in the c of the priests,
32: 1 and encamped against the fortified c, B
32:29 He likewise provided c for himself,
33:14 of the army in all the fortified c in Judah. B
Ezr 4:10 in the c of Samaria and in the rest of the province
Ne 9:25 And they captured fortress c and a rich land,
Est 9: 2 the Jews gathered in their c throughout all
Job 15:28 they will live in desolate c, in houses
Ps 9: 6 their c you have rooted out;
69:35 God will save Zion and rebuild the c of Judah; A
72:16 and may people blossom in the c like the grass of
Isa 1: 7 your c are burned with fire;
6:11 "Until c lie waste without inhabitant,
14:17 the world like a desert and overthrew its c,
14:21 the earth or cover the face of the world with c.
17: 9 On that day their strong c will be like
19:18 that day there will be five c in the land of Egypt
25: 3 c of ruthless nations will fear you.
36: 1 came up against all the fortified c of Judah AB
37:26 that you should make fortified c crash into heaps B
40: 9 say to the c of Judah, "Here is your God!" A
44:26 "It shall be inhabited," and of the c of Judah, A
61: 4 they shall repair the ruined c,
64:10 Your holy c have become a wilderness,
Jer 1:15 and against all the c of Judah. A
2:15 his c are in ruins, without inhabitant.
4: 5 and let us go into the fortified c!" B
4: 7 your c will be ruins without inhabitant.
4:16 they shout against the c of Judah. A
4:26 and all its c were laid in ruins before the LORD,
5: 6 A leopard is watching against their c;
5:17 the sword your fortified c in which you trust. B
7:34 bridegroom in the c of Judah and in the streets A
8:14 let us go into the fortified c and perish there; B
10:22 the land of the north to make the c of Judah A
11: 6 Proclaim all these words in the c of Judah, A
11:12 Then the c of Judah and the inhabitants A
20:16 like the c that the LORD overthrew without pity;
26: 2 the c of Judah that come to worship in the house A
31:21 Return, O virgin Israel, return to these your c.
32:44 and in the c of Judah, of the hill country, A
34: 1 against Jerusalem and all its c:
34: 7 the c of Judah that were left, Lachish and A
34: 7 the only fortified c of Judah that remained. AB
46: 8 let me destroy c and their inhabitants.
50:32 and I will kindle a fire in his c,
51:43 Her c have become an object of horror,
Eze 12:20 The inhabited c shall be laid waste,
26:19 like c that are not inhabited,
29:12 and her c shall be a desolation forty years
29:12 be a desolation forty years among c
30: 7 and their c shall lie among cities laid waste.
30: 7 and their cities shall lie among c laid waste.
30:17 and the c themselves shall go into captivity.
35: 9 and your c shall never be inhabited.
45: 5 as their holding for c to live in.
Hos 8:14 and Judah has multiplied fortified c; B
8:14 but I will send a fire upon his c,
11: 6 The sword rages in their c,
13:10 Where in all your c are your rulers,
Am 4: 6 I gave you cleanness of teeth in all your c,
9:14 they shall rebuild the ruined c and inhabit them;
Mic 5:11 and I will cut off the c of your land and throw
Hab 2: 8 to c and all who live in them.
2:17 to c and all who live in them.
Zep 1:16 against the fortified c and against the lofty B
3: 6 their c have been made desolate, without people,
Zec 1:12 from Jerusalem and the c of Judah, A
1:17 My c shall again overflow with prosperity;
8:20 the inhabitants of many c;
Mt 9:35 Then Jesus went about all the c and villages,
11: 1 to teach and proclaim his message in their c.
11:20 Then he began to reproach the c in which most
Mk 6:56 And wherever he went, into villages or c or farms,
Lk 4:43 of the kingdom of God to the other c also;
5:12 Once, when he was in one of the c,
8: 1 Soon afterwards he went on through c
19:17 in a very small thing, take charge of ten c.'
19:19 He said to him, 'And you, rule over five c.'
Ac 14: 6 c of Lycaonia, and to the surrounding country;
26:11 I pursued them even to foreign c.
2Pe 2: 6 and if by turning the c of Sodom and Gomorrah
Jude 1: 7 Sodom and Gomorrah and the surrounding c,
Rev 16:19 and the c of the nations fell.
AdE 9:19 in the large c keep the fifteenth day of Adar
Wis 10: 6 he escaped the fire that descended on the Five C.
Sir 28:14 destroyed strong c, and overturned the houses
46: 2 and brandished his sword against the c!
Bar 4:32 Wretched will be the c that your children served
1Mc 1:19 captured the fortified c in the land of Egypt, B
1:29 the king sent to the c of Judah a chief collector A
3: 8 He went through the c of Judah; A
9:50 to Jerusalem and built strong c in Judea:
10:71 for I have with me the power of the c.
11: 8 So King Ptolemy gained control of the coastal c
15: 4 and those who have devastated many c
15:19 against them and their c and their country,
15:28 they are c of my kingdom.
15:30 the c that you have seized and the tribute money
15:31 for the tribute money of the c.
2Mc 3: 8 of inspection of the c of Coelesyria and Phoenicia,
4:30 of Mallus revolted because their c had been given
4:32 he had sold to Tyre and the neighboring c.
6: 8 to the neighboring Greek c that they should adopt
1Es 2:22 troubling both kings and other c,
3Mc 1: 6 to visit the neighboring c and encourage them.
3:16 to the temples in the c,
4: 4 all together, by the generals in the several c,
6:41 in the c, magnanimously expressing his concern:
2Es 5:25 for yourself one river, and from all the c
15:18 Because of their pride the c shall be in confusion,
15:42 They shall destroy c and walls,
2Es 15:57 your c shall be wiped out,
15:62 They shall devour you and your c,
16:23 and its c shall be demolished.
16:47 the more they adorn their c,
16:70 in many places and in neighboring c there shall be

CITIZEN (13) [CITIZENS, CITIZENSHIP]

Lev 16:29 neither the c nor the alien who resides among you.
18:26 either the c or the alien who resides among you
19:34 with you shall be to you as the c among you;
24:22 You shall have one law for the alien and for the c:
Dt 1:16 whether c or resident alien.
Jos 8:33 All Israel, alien as well as c,
Ac 21:39 from Tarsus in Cilicia, a c of an important city;
22:25 for you to flog a Roman c who is uncondemned?"
22:26 This man is a Roman c."
22:27 "Tell me, are you a Roman c?"
22:28 Paul said, "But I was born a c."
22:29 for he realized that Paul was a Roman c and
23:27 but when I had learned that he was a Roman c,

CITIZENS‡ (20) [CITIZEN]

Lev 17:15 c or aliens, who eat what dies of itself
23:42 all that are c in Israel shall live in booths,
24:16 as c, when they blaspheme the Name, shall be put
Jos 24:11 the c of Jericho fought against you,
Jer 32:32 the c of Judah and the inhabitants of Jerusalem.
Eze 47:22 They shall be to you as c of Israel;
Lk 15:15 So he went and hired himself out to one of the c
19:14 But the c of his country hated him and sent
Ac 16:37 uncondemned, men who are Roman c,
16:38 when they heard that they were Roman c;
19:35 the town clerk had quieted the crowd, he said, "C
Eph 2:19 but you are c with the saints and also members of
Sir 10:25 Free c will serve a wise servant,
1Mc 6: 3 not because his plan had become known to the c
2Mc 4: 9 to enroll the people of Jerusalem as c of Antioch.
4:19 chosen as being Antiochian c from Jerusalem,
5:23 In his malice toward the Jewish c,
9:15 he would make, all of them, equal to c of Athens;
9:19 "To his worthy Jewish c, Antiochus their king
3Mc 1:22 of the c would not tolerate the completion

CITIZENSHIP (5) [CITIZEN]

Ac 22:28 "It cost me a large sum of money to get my c."
Php 3:20 But our c is in heaven,
3Mc 2:30 they shall have equal c with the Alexandrians."
3:21 both to deem them worthy of Alexandrian c and
3:23 they not only spurn the priceless c, but also both

CITY‡ (917) [CITIES, CITY'S, STORE-CITIES]

A. CITY OF DAVID (46)
B. HOLY CITY (19)
C. GREAT CITY (14)
D. CITY OF REFUGE (10)
E. FORTIFIED CITY (10)
F. PEOPLE OF THE CITY (9)
G. CITY OF HIS FATHER DAVID (5)

Ge 4:17 and he built a c, and named it Enoch
10:12 Nineveh and Calah; that is the great c. C
11: 4 Then they said, "Come, let us build ourselves a c,
11: 5 LORD came down to see the c and the tower,
11: 8 and they left off building the c.
18:24 Suppose there are fifty righteous within the c;
18:26 "If I find at Sodom fifty righteous in the c,
18:28 Will you destroy the whole c for lack of five?"
19: 4 But before they lay down, the men of the c,
19:12 sons, daughters, or anyone you have in the c—
19:14 for the LORD is about to destroy the c."
19:15 be consumed in the punishment of the c."
19:16 they brought him out and left him outside the c.
19:20 Look, that c is near enough to flee to,
19:21 not overthrow the c of which you have spoken.
19:22 Therefore the c was called Zoar.
23:10 of all who went in at the gate of his c,
23:18 of all who went in at the gate of his c.
24:10 and went to Aram-naharaim, to the c of Nahor.
24:11 He made the camels kneel down outside the c by
26:33 the name of the c is Beer-sheba to this day.
28:19 but the name of the c was Luz at the first.
33:18 Jacob came safely to the c of Shechem,
33:18 and he camped before the c.
34:20 the gate of their c and spoke to the men of their c,
34:24 of the c gate heeded Hamor and his son Shechem;
34:24 all who went out of the gate of his c.
34:25 and came against the c unawares,
34:27 upon the slain, and plundered the c,
34:28 and whatever was in the c and in the field.
36:32 the name of his c being Dinhabah.
36:35 the name of his c being Avith.
36:39 the name of his c being Pau;
41:48 up in every c the food from the fields around it.
44: 4 they had gone only a short distance from the c,
44:13 and they returned to the c.
Ex 9:29 "As soon as I have gone out of the c,
9:33 So Moses left Pharaoh, went out of the c,
Lev 14:40 and thrown into an unclean place outside the c.
14:41 be dumped in an unclean place outside the c.
14:45 and taken outside the c to an unclean place.
14:53 and he shall let the living bird go out of the c into
25:29 If anyone sells a dwelling house in a walled c,
25:30 that is in a walled c shall pass in perpetuity to

Lev 25:33 houses sold in a **c** belonging to them—
Nu 21:26 Heshbon was the **c** of King Sihon of the Amorites,
21:27 let the **c** of Sihon be established.
21:28 flame from the **c** of Sihon.
35:25 the slayer back to the original **c** of refuge. D
35:26 outside the bounds of the original **c** of refuge, D
35:27 outside the bounds of the **c** of refuge, D
35:28 the **c** of refuge until the death of the high priest; D
35:32 for one who has fled to a **c** of refuge, D
Dt 3: 6 in each **c** utterly destroying men, women,
19:12 of the killer's **c** shall send to have the culprit taken
22:15 the young woman's virginity to the elders of the **c**
28: 3 Blessed shall you be in the **c**,
28:16 Cursed shall you be in the **c**,
34: 3 that is, the valley of Jericho, the **c** of palm trees—
Jos 2:15 of the **c** wall and she resided within the wall itself.
3:16 the **c** that is beside Zarethan,
6: 3 You shall march around the **c**,
6: 3 all the warriors circling the **c** once.
6: 4 around the **c** seven times,
6: 5 and the wall of the **c** will fall down flat,
6: 7 "Go forward and march around the **c**;
6:11 So the ark of the LORD went around the **c**,
6:14 around the **c** once and then returned to the camp.
6:15 around the **c** in the same manner seven times.
6:15 that they marched around the **c** seven times.
6:16 For the LORD has given you the **c**.
6:17 The **c** and all that is in it shall be devoted to
6:20 so the people charged straight ahead into the **c**
6:21 by the edge of the sword all in the **c**,
6:24 They burned down the **c**, and everything in it;
6:26 the LORD be anyone who tries to build this **c**—
8: 1 over to you the king of Ai with his people, his **c**,
8: 2 Set an ambush against the **c**, behind it."
8: 4 "You shall lie in ambush against the **c**, behind it;
8: 4 do not go very far from the **c**,
8: 5 the people who are with me will approach the **c**.
8: 6 until we have drawn them away from the **c**;
8: 7 up from the ambush and seize the **c**;
8: 8 you have taken the **c**, you shall set the **c** on fire,
8:11 and drew near before the **c**,
8:12 between Bethel and Ai, to the west of the **c**.
8:13 north of the **c** and its rear guard west of the **c**.
8:14 he and all his people, the inhabitants of the **c**,
8:14 an ambush against him behind the **c**.
8:16 the people who were in the **c** were called together
8:16 they were drawn away from the **c**.
8:17 they left the **c** open, and pursued Israel.
8:18 the sword that was in his hand toward the **c**.
8:19 entered the **c**, took it, and at once set the **c** on fire.
8:20 the smoke of the **c** was rising to the sky.
8:21 and all Israel saw that the ambush had taken the **c**
8:21 the city and that the smoke of the **c** was rising,
8:22 And the others came out from the **c** against them;
8:27 and the spoil of that **c** Israel took as their booty,
8:29 threw it down at the entrance of the gate of the **c**,
10: 2 because Gibeon was a large **c**,
15:62 the C of Salt, and En-gedi:
19:29 reaching to the fortified **c** of Tyre; E
20: 4 the gate of the **c**, and explain the case to the elders of that **c**;
20: 4 then the fugitive shall be taken into the **c**,
20: 6 that **c** until there is a trial before the congregation,
21:13 Hebron, the **c** of refuge for the slayer, D
21:21 Shechem, the **c** of refuge for the slayer, D
21:27 the **c** of refuge for the slayer, D
21:32 the **c** of refuge for the slayer, D
21:38 the **c** of refuge for the slayer, D
Jdg 1: 8 They put it to the sword and set the **c** on fire.
1:16 with the people of Judah from the **c** of palms into
1:17 So the **c** was called Hormah.
1:23 to Bethel (the name of the **c** was formerly Luz).
1:24 When the spies saw a man coming out of the **c**,
1:24 they said to him, "Show us the way into the **c**,
1:25 So he showed them the way into the **c**;
1:25 and they put the **c** to the sword,
1:26 man went to the land of the Hittites and built a **c**,
3:13 and they took possession of the **c** of palms.
8:16 So he took the elders of the **c** and he took thorns
8:17 and killed the men of the **c**.
9:30 When Zebul the ruler of the **c** heard the words
9:31 and they are stirring up the **c** against you.
9:33 as soon as the sun rises, get up and rush on the **c**;
9:35 and stood in the entrance of the gate of the **c**,
9:43 he looked and saw the people coming out of the **c**,
9:44 and stood at the entrance of the gate of the **c**,
9:45 Abimelech fought against the **c** all that day;
9:45 he took the **c**, and killed the people that were in it;
9:45 and he razed the **c** and sowed it with salt.
9:51 But there was a strong tower within the **c**,
9:51 the lords of the **c** fled to it and shut themselves in;
16: 2 and lay in wait for him all night at the **c** gate.
16: 3 of the doors of the **c** gate and the two posts,
18:27 put them to the sword, and burned down the **c**.
18:28 They rebuilt the **c**, and lived in it.
18:29 They named the **c** Dan, after their ancestor Dan,
18:29 but the name of the **c** was formerly Laish.
19:11 let us turn aside to this **c** of the Jebusites,
19:12 "We will not turn aside into a **c** of foreigners,
19:15 in and sat down in the open square of the **c**,
19:17 and saw the wayfarer in the open square of the **c**,
19:22 they were enjoying themselves, the men of the **c**,
20:11 So all the men of Israel gathered against the **c**,
20:31 they were drawn away from the **c**.
20:32 "Let us retreat and draw them away from the **c**
20:37 Then they put the whole **c** to the sword.
20:38 when they sent up a cloud of smoke out of the **c**
Jdg 20:40 a column of smoke, began to rise out of the **c**,
20:40 the whole **c** going up in smoke toward the sky!
20:42 of the **c** were slaughtering them in between.
20:48 **c**, the people, the animals, and all that remained.
Ru 3:15 then he went into the **c**.
4: 2 Then Boaz took ten men of the elders of the **c**,
1Sa 4:13 When the man came into the **c** and told the news,
4:13 into the city and told the news, all the **c** cried out.
5: 9 the hand of the LORD was against the **c**,
5: 9 he struck the inhabitants of the **c**,
5:11 there was a deathly panic throughout the whole **c**.
5:12 and the cry of the **c** went up to heaven.
15: 5 Saul came to the **c** of the Amalekites and lay
16: 4 The elders of the **c** came to meet him trembling,
20: 6 of me to run to Bethlehem his **c**;
20:29 for our family is holding a sacrifice in the **c**,
20:40 "Go and carry them to the **c**."
20:42 He got up and left; and Jonathan went into the **c**.
22:19 Nob, the **c** of the priests, he put to the sword;
23:10 to destroy the **c** on my account.
27: 5 for why should your servant live in the royal **c**
28: 3 for him and buried him in Ramah, his own **c**.
30: 3 When David and his men came to the **c**,
2Sa 5: 7 which is now the **c** of David. A
5: 9 and named it the **c** of David. A
5: 9 the **c** all around from the Millo inward.
6:10 ark of the LORD into his care in the **c** of David; A
6:12 from the house of Obed-edom to the **c** of David A
6:16 the ark of the LORD came into the **c** of David, A
10: 3 not David sent his envoys to you to search the **c**,
10:14 before Abishai, and entered the **c**.
11:16 As Joab was besieging the **c**,
11:17 The men of the **c** came out and fought with Joab;
11:20 'Why did you go so near the **c** to fight?
11:25 press your attack on the **c**, and overthrow it.'
12: 1 "There were two men in a certain **c**,
12:26 of the Ammonites, and took the royal **c**.
12:27 moreover, I have taken the water **c**.
12:28 the **c**, and take it; or I myself will take the **c**,
12:30 He also brought forth the spoil of the **c**,
15: 2 and say, "From what **c** are you?"
15:12 David's counselor, from his **c** Giloh.
15:14 and attack the **c** with the edge of the sword."
15:24 until the people had all passed out of the **c**.
15:25 "Carry the ark of God back into the **c**.
15:27 go back to the **c** in peace, you and Abiathar,
15:34 But if you return to the **c** and say to Absalom,
15:37 So Hushai, David's friend, came into the **c**,
17:13 If he withdraws into a **c**,
17:13 then all Israel will bring ropes to that **c**,
17:17 for they could not risk being seen entering the **c**.
17:23 and went off home to his own **c**.
18: 3 it is better that you send us help from the **c**."
19: 3 the **c** that day as soldiers steal in who are ashamed
20:15 they threw up a siege ramp against the **c**,
20:16 Then a wise woman called from the **c**, "Listen!
20:19 you seek to destroy a **c** that is a mother in Israel;
20:21 and I will withdraw from the **c**."
20:22 and they dispersed from the **c**,
24: 5 from Aroer and from the **c** that is in the middle of
1Ki 1:41 he said, "Why is the **c** in an uproar?"
1:45 so that the **c** is in an uproar.
2:10 and was buried in the **c** of David. A
3: 1 and brought her into the **c** of David, A
8: 1 covenant of the LORD out of the **c** of David, A
8:16 not chosen a **c** from any of the tribes of Israel
8:44 the LORD toward the **c** that you have chosen and
8:48 the **c** that you have chosen,
9:16 had killed the Canaanites who lived in the **c**,
9:24 Pharaoh's daughter went up from the **c** of David A
11:27 the gap in the wall of the **c** of his father David. G
11:32 **c** that I have chosen out of all the tribes of Israel.
11:36 the **c** where I have chosen to put my name.
11:43 and was buried in the **c** of his father David; G
13:29 laid it on the donkey, and brought it back to the **c**,
14:11 Anyone belonging to Jeroboam who dies in the **c**,
14:12 When your feet enter the **c**, the child shall die.
14:21 the **c** that the LORD had chosen out of all
14:31 buried with his ancestors in the **c** of David. A
15: 8 and they buried him in the **c** of David. A
15:24 with his ancestors in the **c** of his father David; G
16: 4 Anyone belonging to Baasha who dies in the **c**
16:18 When Zimri saw that the **c** was taken,
16:24 he fortified the hill, and called the **c** that he built,
20: 2 into the **c** to King Ahab of Israel, and said to him:
20:12 And they took their positions against the **c**.
20:19 But these had already come out of the **c**:
20:30 The rest fled into the **c** of Aphek;
20:30 Ben-hadad also fled, and entered the **c** to hide.
21: 8 and the nobles who lived with Naboth in his **c**.
21:11 his **c**, the elders and the nobles who lived in his **c**,
21:13 So they took him outside the **c**,
21:24 Anyone belonging to Ahab who dies in the **c**
22:26 and return him to Amon the governor of the **c** and
22:36 the army, "Every man to his **c**, and every man
22:50 with his ancestors in the **c** of his father David; G
2Ki 2:19 Now the people of the **c** said to Elisha, F
2:19 "The location of this **c** is good, as my lord sees;
2:23 up on the way, some small boys came out of the **c**
3:19 You shall conquer every fortified **c** E
3:19 every fortified city and every choice **c**;
6:14 they came by night, and surrounded the **c**.
6:15 with horses and chariots was all around the **c**.
6:19 "This is not the way, and this is not the **c**;
6:26 as the king of Israel was walking on the **c** wall,
6:30 now since he was walking on the **c** wall,
7: 3 there were four leprous men outside the **c** gate,
2Ki 7: 4 If we say, 'Let us enter the **c**,'
7: 4 the famine is in the **c**, and we shall die there;
7:10 they came and called to the gatekeepers of the **c**,
7:12 thinking, 'When they come out of the **c**,
7:12 we shall take them alive and get into the **c**.' "
8:24 and was buried with them in the **c** of David; A
9:15 then let no one slip out of the **c** to go and tell
9:28 in his tomb with his ancestors in the **c** of David. A
10: 2 a fortified **c**, and weapons, E
10: 5 steward of the palace, and the governor of the **c**,
10: 6 seventy persons, were with the leaders of the **c**,
11:20 the **c** was quiet after Athaliah had been killed with
12:21 buried with his ancestors in the **c** of David; A
14:20 Jerusalem with his ancestors in the **c** of David. A
15: 7 buried him with his ancestors in the **c** of David; A
15:38 was buried with his ancestors in the **c** of David, A
16:20 was buried with his ancestors in the **c** of David; A
17: 9 from watchtower to fortified **c**; E
18: 8 from watchtower to fortified **c**. E
18:30 and this **c** will not be given into the hand of
19:13 the king of the **c** of Sepharvaim, the king of Hena,
19:32 He shall not come into this **c**,
19:33 he shall not come into this **c**, says the LORD.
19:34 For I will defend this **c** to save it,
20: 6 and this **c** out of the hand of the king of Assyria;
20: 6 I will defend this **c** for my own sake and
20:20 and the conduit and brought water into the **c**,
23: 8 of the gate of Joshua the governor of the **c**,
23: 8 which were on the left at the gate of the **c**.
23:17 The people of the **c** told him, F
23:27 and I will reject this **c** that I have chosen,
24:10 up to Jerusalem, and the **c** was besieged.
24:11 King Nebuchadnezzar of Babylon came to the **c**,
25: 2 So the **c** was besieged until the eleventh year
25: 3 in the **c** that there was no food for the people of
25: 4 Then a breach was made in the **c** wall;
25: 4 though the Chaldeans were all around the **c**.
25:11 the rest of the people who were left in the **c** and
25:19 from the **c** he took an officer who had been
25:19 of the king's council who were found in the **c**;
25:19 of the people of the land who were found in the **c**.
1Ch 1:43 Bela son of Beor, whose **c** was called Dinhabah.
1:46 and the name of his **c** was Avith.
1:50 the name of his **c** was Pai,
6:56 but the fields of the **c** and its villages they gave
11: 5 the stronghold of Zion, now the **c** of David. A
11: 7 therefore it was called the **c** of David. A
11: 8 He built the **c** all around, from the Millo
11: 8 and Joab repaired the rest of the **c**.
13:13 not take the ark into his care into the **c** of David; A
15: 1 David built houses for himself in the **c** of David, A
15:29 covenant of the LORD came to the **c** of David, A
19: 9 up in battle array at the entrance of the **c**,
19:15 Joab's brother, and entered the **c**.
20: 2 He also brought out the booty of the **c**,
2Ch 5: 2 covenant of the LORD out of the **c** of David, A
6: 5 not chosen a **c** from any of the tribes of Israel
6:34 toward this **c** that you have chosen and the house
6:38 the **c** that you have chosen,
8:11 the **c** of David to the house that he had built A
9:31 and was buried in the **c** of his father David; G
12:13 in Jerusalem, the **c** that the LORD had chosen out
12:16 and was buried in the **c** of David; A
14: 1 and they buried him in the **c** of David. A
15: 6 nation against nation and **c** against **c**,
16:14 he had hewn out for himself in the **c** of David. A
18:25 and return him to Amon the governor of the **c**
19: 5 the land in all the fortified cities of Judah, **c** by **c**,
21: 1 buried with his ancestors in the **c** of David; A
21:20 They buried him in the **c** of David, A
23:21 the **c** was quiet after Athaliah had been killed
24:16 And they buried him in the **c** of David among A
24:25 he died; and they buried him in the **c** of David, A
25:28 was buried with his ancestors in the **c** of David. A
27: 9 and they buried him in the **c** of David; A
28:15 to their kindred at Jericho, the **c** of palm trees.
28:25 In every **c** of Judah he made high places
28:27 and they buried him in the **c**, in Jerusalem;
29:20 assembled the officials of the **c**,
30:10 from **c** to **c** through the country of Ephraim
32: 3 the flow of the springs that were outside the **c**;
32: 5 he also strengthened the Millo in the **c** of David, A
32: 6 the gate of the **c** and spoke encouragingly to them,
32:18 in order that they might take the **c**.
32:30 down to the west side of the **c** of David. A
33:14 an outer wall for the **c** of David west of Gihon, A
33:15 and he threw them out of the **c**.
34: 8 Maaseiah the governor of the **c**,
Ezr 4:12 They are rebuilding that rebellious and wicked **c**;
4:13 if this **c** is rebuilt and the walls finished,
4:15 in the annals that this is a rebellious **c**,
4:15 On that account this **c** was laid waste.
4:16 if this **c** is rebuilt and its walls finished,
4:19 and discovered that this **c** has risen against kings
4:21 and that this **c** not be rebuilt,
Ne 2: 3 Why should my face not be sad, when the **c**,
2: 5 to the **c** of my ancestors' graves,
2: 8 and for the wall of the **c**,
3:15 the stairs that go down from the C of David. A
7: 4 The **c** was wide and large,
11: 1 of ten to live in the holy **c** Jerusalem, B
11: 9 of Hassenuah was second in charge of the **c**.
11:18 in the holy **c** were two hundred eighty-four. B
12:37 went straight up by the stairs of the **c** of David, A
13:16 Tyrians also, who lived in the **c**,
13:18 this disaster on us and on this **c**?
Est 3:15 but the **c** of Susa was thrown into confusion.

Est 4: 1 through the c, wailing with a loud and bitter cry;
4: 6 the open square of the c in front of the king's gate,
6: 9 the open square of the c, proclaiming before him:
6:11 through the open square of the c,
8:11 the king allowed the Jews who were in every c
8:15 while the c of Susa shouted and rejoiced.
8:17 In every province and in every c,
9:28 in every family, province, and c;
Job 24:12 From the c the dying groan,
29: 7 When I went out to the gate of the c,
39: 7 It scorns the tumult of the c;
Ps 31:21 to me when I was beset as a c under siege.
46: 4 There is a river whose streams make glad the c
46: 5 God is in the midst of the c;
48: 1 and greatly to be praised in the c of our God.
48: 2 in the far north, the c of the great King.
48: 8 so have we seen in the c of the LORD of hosts,
48: 8 in the c of our God,
55: 9 for I see violence and strife in the c.
59: 6 howling like dogs and prowling about the c.
59:14 howling like dogs and prowling about the c.
60: 9 Who will bring me to the fortified c? E
87: 1 On the holy mount stands the c he founded;
87: 3 Glorious things are spoken of you, O c of God.
101: 8 cutting off all evildoers from the c of the LORD.
108:10 Who will bring me to the fortified c? E
122: 3 built as a c that is bound firmly together.
127: 1 Unless the LORD guards the c,
Pr 1:21 at the entrance of the c gates she speaks:
11:10 it goes well with the righteous, the c rejoices;
11:11 By the blessing of the upright a c is exalted,
16:32 temper is controlled than one who captures a c.
18:11 The wealth of the rich is their strong c;
18:19 An ally offended is stronger than a c;
21:22 a c of warriors and brought down the stronghold
25:28 Like a c breached, without walls,
29: 8 Scoffers set a c aflame,
31:23 Her husband is known in the c gates,
31:31 and let her works praise her in the c gates.
Ecc 7:19 to the wise more than ten rulers that are in a c.
8:10 of the holy place, and were praised in the c
9:14 There was a little c with few people in it.
9:15 and he by his wisdom delivered the c.
SS 3: 2 "I will rise now and go about the c,
3: 3 sentinels found me, as they went about in the c.
5: 7 in the c the sentinels found me;
Isa 1: 8 a shelter in a cucumber field, like a besieged c.
1:21 How the faithful c has become a whore!
1:26 shall be called the c of righteousness, the faithful c.
14:31 cry, O c; melt in fear, O Philistia, all of you!
17: 1 See, Damascus will cease to be a c,
19: 2 c against city, kingdom against kingdom;
19: 2 city against c, kingdom against kingdom;
19:18 One of these will be called the C of the Sun.
22: 2 tumultuous c, exultant town?
22: 9 that there were many breaches in the c of David, A
23: 7 Is this your exultant c whose origin is from days
23:16 go about the c, you forgotten prostitute!
24:10 The c of chaos is broken down,
24:12 Desolation is left in the c,
25: 2 For you have made the c a heap,
25: 2 a heap, the fortified c a ruin; E
25: 2 the palace of aliens is a c no more,
26: 1 We have a strong c; he sets up victory
26: 5 the lofty c he lays low.
27:10 For the fortified c is solitary, E
29: 1 Ah, Ariel, Ariel, the c where David encamped!
32:13 yes, for all the joyous houses in the jubilant c.
32:14 palace will be forsaken, the populous c deserted;
32:19 and the c will be utterly laid low.
33:20 Look on Zion, the c of our appointed festivals!
36:15 this c will not be given into the hand of the king
37:13 the king of the c of Sepharvaim, the king of Hena,
37:33 He shall not come into this c,
37:34 he shall not come into this c, says the LORD.
37:35 For I will defend this c to save it,
38: 6 and this c out of the hand of the king of Assyria, and defend this c.
45:13 he shall build my c and set my exiles free,
48: 2 For they call themselves after the holy c, B
52: 1 beautiful garments, O Jerusalem, the holy c; B
60:14 they shall call you the C of the LORD,
62:12 "Sought Out, A C Not Forsaken."
66: 6 Listen, an uproar from the c!
Jer 1:18 For my part have made you today a fortified c, E
3:14 one from a c and two from a family,
6: 6 This is the c that must be punished;
8:16 the c and those who live in it.
14:18 And if I enter the c, look—those sick with famine!
17:24 and bring in no burden by the gates of this c on
17:25 by the gates of this c kings who sit on the throne
17:25 and this c shall be inhabited forever.
19: 8 I will make this c a horror, a thing to be hissed at;
19:11 So will I break this people and this c,
19:12 and to its inhabitants, making this c like Topheth.
19:15 upon this c and upon all its towns all the disaster
20: 5 I will give all the wealth of this c, all its gains,
21: 4 I will bring them together into the center of this c.
21: 6 And I will strike down the inhabitants of this c,
21: 7 and his servants, and the people in this c—
21: 9 Those who stay in this c shall die by the sword,
21:10 For I have set my face against this c for evil and
22: 6 that I will make you a desert, an uninhabited c.
22: 8 And many nations will pass by this c,
22: 8 the LORD dealt in this way with that great c?" C
23:39 and the c that I gave to you and your ancestors.
25:29 I am beginning to bring disaster on the c
Jer 26: 6 and I will make this c a curse for all the nations of
26: 9 and this c shall be desolate, without inhabitant'?"
26:11 of death because he has prophesied against this c,
26:12 to prophesy against this house and this c all
26:15 and upon this c and its inhabitants,
26:20 He prophesied against this c and against this land
27:17 Why should this c become a desolation?
27:19 and the rest of the vessels that are left in this c,
29: 7 the welfare of the c where I have sent you
29:16 and concerning all the people who live in this c,
30:18 the c shall be rebuilt upon its mound,
31:38 when the c shall be rebuilt for the LORD from
32: 3 to give this c into the hand of the king of Babylon,
32:24 the siege ramps have been cast up against the c
32:24 and the c, faced with sword, famine,
32:25 c has been given into the hands of the Chaldeans.
32:28 to give this c into the hands of the Chaldeans and
32:29 against this c shall come, set it on fire, and burn it,
32:31 This c has aroused my anger and wrath,
32:36 concerning this c of which you say,
33: 4 concerning the houses of this c and the houses of
33: 5 for I have hidden my face from this c because
33: 9 And this c shall be to me a name of joy,
34: 2 to give this c into the hand of the king of Babylon,
34:22 and will bring them back to this c;
37: 8 Chaldeans shall return and fight against this c;
37:10 they would rise up and burn this c with fire.
37:21 until all the bread of the c was gone.
38: 2 Those who stay in this c shall die by the sword,
38: 3 This c shall surely be handed over to the army of
38: 4 the soldiers who are left in this c,
38: 9 for there is no bread left in the c."
38:17 and this c shall not be burned with fire,
38:18 then this c shall be handed over to the Chaldeans,
38:23 and this c shall be burned with fire."
39: 2 a breach was made in the c.
39: 4 the c at night by way of the king's garden through
39: 9 the rest of the people who were left in the c,
39:16 to fulfill my words against this c for evil and not
41: 7 When they reached the middle of the c,
47: 2 the c and those who live in it.
49:25 How the famous c is forsaken, the joyful town!
51:31 the king of Babylon that his c is taken from end
52: 5 So the c was besieged until the eleventh year
52: 6 in the c that there was no food for the people of
52: 7 Then a breach was made in the c wall;
52: 7 the soldiers fled and went out from the c by night
52: 7 though the Chaldeans were all around the c.
52:15 the rest of the people who were left in the c and
52:25 and from the c he took an officer who had been
52:25 of the king's council who were found in the c;
52:25 of the land who were found inside the c.
La 1: 1 How lonely sits the c that once was full of people!
1:19 the c while seeking food to revive their strength.
2:11 infants and babes faint in the streets of the c.
2:12 they faint like the wounded in the streets of the c,
2:15 the c that was called the perfection of beauty,
3:51 at the fate of all the young women in my c.
5:14 The old men have left the c gate,
Eze 4: 1 On it portray a c, Jerusalem;
4: 3 as an iron wall between you and the c;
5: 2 of the hair you shall burn in the fire inside the c,
5: 2 and strike with the sword all around the c;
7:15 those in the c—famine and pestilence devour them.
7:23 the c is full of violence.
9: 1 saying, "Draw near, you executioners of the c,
9: 4 "Go through the c, through Jerusalem,
9: 5 "Pass through the c after him, and kill;
9: 7 So they went out and killed in the c.
9: 9 the land is full of bloodshed and the c full
10: 2 and scatter them over the c."
11: 2 and who give wicked counsel in this c;
11: 3 this c is the pot, and we are the meat.'
11: 6 You have killed many in this c,
11: 7 within it are the meat, and this c is the pot;
11:11 This c shall not be your pot,
11:23 of the LORD ascended from the middle of the c,
11:23 and stopped on the mountain east of the c.
17: 4 set it in a c of merchants.
21:19 make it for a fork in the road leading to a c;
22: 2 will you judge, will you judge the bloody c?
22: 3 You shall say, Thus says the Lord GOD: A c!
24: 6 Woe to the bloody c, the pot whose rust is in it,
24: 9 Woe to the bloody c! I will even make the pile
26:10 like those entering a breached c.
26:17 you have vanished from the seas, O c renowned,
26:19 When I make you a c laid waste,
30:18 the c shall be covered by a cloud,
33:21 to me and said, "The c has fallen."
39:16 (A c Hamonah is there also.)
40: 1 in the fourteenth year after the c was struck down,
40: 2 on which was a structure like a c to the south.
43: 3 that I had seen when he came to destroy the c, and
45: 6 for the c an area five thousand cubits wide,
45: 7 of the holy district and the holding of the c,
45: 7 the holy district and the holding of the c,
48:15 shall be for ordinary use for the c,
48:15 In the middle of it shall be the c;
48:17 The c shall have open land:
48:18 Its produce shall be food for the workers of the c.
48:19 The workers of the c, from all the tribes of Israel,
48:20 holy portion together with the property of the c.
48:21 of the property of the c shall belong to the prince.
48:22 and the property of the Levites and of the c,
48:30 These shall be the exits of the c:
48:31 of the c being named after the tribes of Israel.
48:35 of the c shall be eighteen thousand cubits.
Eze 48:35 And the name of the c from that time on shall be,
Da 9:16 we pray, turn away from your c Jerusalem,
9:18 at our desolation and the c that bears your name.
9:19 because your c and your people bear your name!"
9:24 for your people and your holy c: B
9:26 the prince who is to come shall destroy the c and
11:15 and take a well-fortified c.
Hos 6: 8 Gilead is a c of evildoers, tracked with blood.
Joel 2: 9 They leap upon the c, they run upon the walls;
Am 3: 6 Is a trumpet blown in a c,
3: 6 disaster befall a c, unless the LORD has done it?
4: 7 I would send rain on one c,
4: 7 and send no rain on another c;
5: 3 The c that marched out a thousand shall have
6: 8 and I will deliver up the c and all that is in it.
7:17 'Your wife shall become a prostitute in the c,
Jnh 1: 2 that great c, and cry out against it; C
3: 2 go to Nineveh, that great c, C
3: 3 Now Nineveh was an exceedingly large c,
3: 4 Jonah began to go into the c, going a day's walk.
4: 5 Jonah went out of the c and sat down east of the c,
4: 5 waiting to see what would become of the c.
4:11 not be concerned about Nineveh, that great c, C
Mic 4:10 for now you shall go forth from the c and camp in
6: 9 of the LORD cries to the c (it is sound wisdom
6: 9 Hear, O tribe and assembly of the c!
Na 2: 7 It is decreed that the c be exiled,
3: 1 C of bloodshed, utterly deceitful, full of booty—
Hab 2:12 and found a c on iniquity!"
Zep 2:15 Is this the exultant c that lived secure,
3: 1 Ah, soiled, defiled, oppressing c!
3: 7 I said, "Surely the c will fear me,
Zec 8: 3 Jerusalem shall be called the faithful c,
8: 5 of the c shall be full of boys and girls playing
8:21 the inhabitants of one c shall go to another,
14: 2 and the c shall be taken and the houses looted and
14: 2 half the c shall go into exile,
14: 2 rest of the people shall not be cut off from the c.
Mt 4: 5 the devil took him to the holy c and placed him B
5:14 A c built on a hill cannot be hid.
5:35 or by Jerusalem, for it is the c of the great King.
12:25 and no c or house divided against itself will stand.
21:10 he entered Jerusalem, the whole c was in turmoil,
21:17 He left them, went out of the c to Bethany,
21:18 In the morning, when he returned to the c,
22: 7 destroyed those murderers, and burned their c.
23:37 the c that kills the prophets
26:18 He said, "Go into the c to a certain man,
27:53 out of the tombs and entered the holy c and B
28:11 into the c and told the chief priests everything
Mk 1:33 And the whole c was gathered around the door.
5:14 The swineherds ran off and told it in the c and in
11:19 Jesus and his disciples went out of the c.
14:13 saying to them, "Go into the c,
14:16 So the disciples set out and went to the c,
Lk 2: 4 to the c of David called Bethlehem, A
2:11 is born this day in the c of David a Savior, A
4:31 He went down to Capernaum, a c in Galilee,
7:37 And a woman in the c, who was a sinner,
8:27 a man of the c who had demons met him.
8:34 they ran off and told it in the c and in the country.
8:39 throughout the c how much Jesus had done
9:10 and withdrew privately to a c called Bethsaida.
13:34 the c that kills the prophets
18: 2 "In a certain c there was a judge
18: 3 that c there was a widow who kept coming to him
19:41 As he came near and saw the c, he wept over it,
21:21 and those inside the c must leave it,
22:10 he said to them, "when you have entered the c,
23:19 for an insurrection that had taken place in the c,
24:49 the c until you have been clothed with power from
Jn 1:44 the c of Andrew and Peter.
4: 5 So he came to a Samaritan c called Sychar,
4: 8 (His disciples had gone to the c to buy food.)
4:28 woman left her water jar and went back to the c.
4:30 They left the c and were on their way to him.
4:39 Many Samaritans from that c believed in him
19:20 place where Jesus was crucified was near the c;
Ac 1:13 When they had entered the c,
4:27 in this c, in fact, both Herod and Pontius Pilate,
7:58 Then they dragged him out of the c and began
8: 5 to the c of Samaria and proclaimed the Messiah
8: 8 So there was great joy in that c.
8: 9 in the c and amazed the people of Samaria,
9: 6 But get up and enter the c,
10: 9 they were on their journey and approaching the c,
11: 5 "I was in the c of Joppa praying,
12:10 they came before the iron gate leading into the c.
13:44 the whole c gathered to hear the word of the Lord.
13:50 of high standing and the leading men of the c,
14: 4 But the residents of the c were divided;
14:13 whose temple was just outside the c,
14:19 they stoned Paul and dragged him out of the c,
14:20 he got up and went into the c.
14:21 After they had proclaimed the good news to that c
15:21 For in every c, for generations past,
15:36 the believers in every c where we proclaimed
16:12 which is a leading c of the district of Macedonia
16:12 We remained in this c for some days.
16:14 from the c of Thyatira and a dealer in purple cloth.
16:20 they said, "These men are disturbing our c;
16:39 they took them out and asked them to leave the c.
17: 5 the marketplaces they formed a mob and set the c
17: 6 and some believers before the c authorities,
17: 8 The people and the c officials were disturbed
17:16 he was deeply distressed to see that the c was full
17:23 For as I went through the c and looked carefully at

Ac 18:10 for there are many in this c who are my people."
19:29 The c was filled with the confusion;
19:35 that the c of the Ephesians is the temple keeper of
20:23 that the Holy Spirit testifies to me in every c
21: 5 with wives and children, escorted us outside the c.
21:29 the Ephesian with him in the c,
21:30 Then all the c was aroused,
21:39 a citizen of an important c;
22: 3 but brought up in this c at the feet of Gamaliel,
24:12 either in the synagogues or throughout the c.
25:23 and the prominent men of the c.
27: 8 to a place called Fair Havens, near the c of Lasea.
Ro 16:23 Erastus, the c treasurer, and our brother Quartus,
2Co 11:26 danger in the c, danger in the wilderness,
11:32 under King Aretas guarded the c of Damascus
Heb 11:10 he looked forward to the c that has foundations,
11:16 indeed, he has prepared a c for them.
12:22 But you have come to Mount Zion and to the c of
13:12 also suffered outside the c gate in order to sanctify
13:14 For here we have no lasting c,
13:14 but we are looking for the c that is to come.
Rev 3:12 and the name of the c of my God,
11: 2 nations, and they will trample over the holy c B
11: 8 of the great c that is prophetically called Sodom C
11:13 and a tenth of the c fell;
14:20 And the wine press was trodden outside the c,
16:19 The great c was split into three parts, C
17:18 The woman you saw is the great c that rules C
18:10 "Alas, alas, the great c, Babylon, the mighty C
18:10 "Alas, alas, the great city, Babylon, the mighty c!
18:16 alas, the great c, clothed in fine linen, C
18:18 "What c was like the great city?"
18:18 "What city was like the great c?" C
18:19 "Alas, alas, the great c, where all who had ships C
18:21 "With such violence Babylon the great c will C
20: 9 the camp of the saints and the beloved c.
21: 2 And I saw the holy c, the new Jerusalem, B
21:10 holy c Jerusalem coming down out of heaven B
21:14 And the wall of the c has twelve foundations,
21:15 of gold to measure the c and its gates and walls.
21:16 c lies foursquare, its length the same as its width;
21:16 and he measured the c with his rod,
21:18 wall is built of jasper, while the c is pure gold,
21:19 of the wall of the c are adorned with every jewel;
21:21 and the street of the c is pure gold,
21:22 I saw no temple in the c,
21:23 the c has no need of sun or moon to shine on it,
22: 2 through the middle of the street of the c.
22:14 to the tree of life and may enter the c by the gates.
22:19 in the tree of life and in the holy c, B
Tob 1: 4 This c had been chosen from among all the tribes
13: 9 the holy c, he afflicted you for the deeds B
13:11 the name of the chosen c will endure forever.
14:10 do not stay overnight within the confines of the c.
Jdt 1: 1 over the Assyrians in the great c of Nineveh. C
AdE 1: 2 King Artaxerxes was enthroned in the c of Susa,
1: 5 the people of various nations who lived in the c.
3:15 the c of Susa was thrown into confusion.
4: 1 then he rushed through the street of the c,
6: 9 be proclaimed through the open square of the c,
6:11 through the open square of the c,
8:11 the Jews in every c to observe their own laws,
8:17 in every c and province wherever
9: 6 the c of Susa the Jews killed five hundred people,
9:14 of the c the bodies of Haman's sons to hang up.
9:27 in every c, family, and country.
11: 3 He was a Jew living in the c of Susa, a great man,
16:24 "Every c and country, without exception,
Wis 9: 8 and an altar in the c of your habitation,
Sir 9: 7 Do not look around in the streets of a c,
9:13 and that you are walking on the c battlements.
9:18 The loud of mouth are feared in their c,
10: 2 as the ruler of the c is, so are all its inhabitants.
10: 3 but a c becomes fit to live in through
16: 4 For through one intelligent person a c can be filled
23:21 This man will be punished in the streets of the c,
24:11 Thus in the beloved c he gave me a resting place,
26: 5 Slander in the c, the gathering of a mob,
31:24 c complains of the one who is stingy with food,
36:18 Have pity on the c of your sanctuary,
36:31 a nimble robber that skips from c to c?
38:32 Without them no c can be inhabited,
40:19 and the building of a c establish one's name,
42:11 a byword in the c and the assembly of the people,
48:17 Hezekiah fortified his c, and brought water
49: 6 who set fire to the chosen c of the sanctuary,
50: 4 and fortified the c against siege.
51:12 *Give thanks to him who rebuilt his c*
Bar 4:32 be the c that received your offspring.
Aza 1: 5 the holy c of our ancestors; B
1Mc 1:30 but he suddenly fell upon the c,
1:31 He plundered the c, burned it with fire,
1:33 Then they fortified the c of David with A
2: 7 the ruin of my people, the ruin of the holy c, B
2:31 and to the troops in Jerusalem the c of David, A
6: 1 that Elymais in Persia was a c famed for its wealth
6: 3 So he came and tried to take the c and plunder it,
6:63 He found Philip in control of the c,
6:63 but he fought against him, and took the c by force.
7:24 and preventing those in the c from going out into
7:32 and the rest fled into the c of David. A
10:10 and began to rebuild and restore the c.
10:63 the c and proclaim that no one is to bring charges
10:75 but the people of the c closed its gates, F
10:76 and the people of the c became afraid and F
10:86 people of the c came out to meet him with great F
11:45 the people of the c assembled within the city, F

1Mc 11:45 the people of the city assembled within the c,
11:46 Then the people of the c seized the main streets F
11:46 the city seized the main streets of the c and began
11:47 around him and then spread out through the c;
11:48 They set fire to the c and seized a large amount
11:49 people of the c saw that the Jews had gained F
11:49 of the c as they pleased, their courage failed
11:50 make the Jews stop fighting against us and our c."
11:60 the people of the c met him and paid him honor. F
12:36 the citadel and the c to separate it from the c,
12:37 So they gathered together to rebuild the c;
13:25 and buried him in Modein, the c of his ancestors.
13:43 He made a siege engine, brought it up to the c,
13:44 The men in the siege engine leaped out into the c,
13:44 and a great tumult arose in the c.
13:45 The men in the c, with their wives and children,
13:47 But he expelled them from the c and cleansed
14:20 the c of the Spartans to the high priest Simon and
14:36 also those in the c of David in Jerusalem, A
14:37 for the safety of the country and of the c,
2Mc 1:12 drove out those who fought against the holy c. B
2:22 the c, and re-established the laws that were about
3: 1 the holy c was inhabited in unbroken peace B
3: 4 about the administration of the c market.
3: 9 by the high priest of the c,
3:14 There was no little distress throughout the whole c.
4: 2 the man who was the benefactor of the c,
4:22 the c, and ushered in with a blaze of torches and
4:36 the Jews in the c appealed to him with regard to
4:38 and led him around the whole c to that very place
4:39 in the c by Lysimachus with the connivance
4:48 so those who had spoken for the c and the villages
5: 2 the c golden-clad cavalry charging through the air,
5: 5 and suddenly made an assault on the c.
5: 5 and at last the c was being taken,
5: 8 fleeing from c to c, pursued by everyone,
5:11 he left Egypt and took the c by storm.
5:17 because of the sins of those who lived in the c,
5:26 then rushed into the c with his armed warriors
6:10 They publicly paraded them around the c,
8: 3 to have mercy on the c that was being destroyed
8:17 and the torture of the derided c, and besides,
8:33 While they were celebrating the victory in the c
9: 2 entered the c called Persepolis and attempted to
rob the temples and control the c.
9:14 that the holy c, which he was hurrying to level B
10: 1 recovered the temple and the c;
10:27 and advanced a considerable distance from the c;
10:36 in the rest of the force, and they occupied the c.
11: 2 He intended to make the c a home for Greeks,
12: 4 and this was done by public vote of the c.
12:38 Then Judas assembled his army and went to the c
13:13 and get possession of the c.
13:14 temple, c, country, and commonwealth,
15:14 and prays much for the people and the holy c— B
15:17 the c and the sanctuary and the temple were
15:19 And those who had to remain in the c were
15:37 from that time the c has been in the possession of
1Es 2:18 and are building that rebellious and wicked c,
2:19 Now if this c is built and the walls finished,
2:22 and will learn that this c was rebellious,
2:23 That is why this c was laid waste.
2:24 that if this c is built and its walls finished,
2:26 that this c from of old has fought against kings,
2:28 the c and to take care that nothing more be done
4:48 and to help him build the c.
4:53 to build the c should have their freedom,
4:56 be provided for all who guarded the c.
6: 8 to the country of Judea and entered the c
6: 9 the c of Jerusalem a great new house for the Lord,
3Mc 1:17 those who remained behind in the c were agitated
1:19 in a disorderly rush flocked together in the c.
2: 9 chose this c and sanctified this place
2:31 be exacted for maintaining the religion of their c,
3: 8 The Greeks in the c, though wronged in no way,
4: 3 What district or c, or what habitable place at all,
4:11 with a monstrous perimeter wall in front of the c,
4:11 into the c and to those from the c going out into
4:11 in any way claim to be inside the circuit of the c.
4:12 from the c frequently went out in secret
5:24 The crowds of the c had been assembled
5:41 the c is in a tumult because of its expectation;
5:44 in the c most favorable for keeping guard.
5:46 the c now being filled with countless masses
6: 5 the spear and was lifted up against your holy c, B
6:30 Then the king, when he had returned to the c,
7:16 of deliverance began their departure from the c,
2Es 3: 1 In the thirtieth year after the destruction of the c,
3:24 You commanded him to build a c for your name,
3:25 but the inhabitants of the c transgressed,
3:27 So you handed over your c to your enemies.
7: 6 There is a c built and set on a plain,
7: 9 If now the c is given to someone as an inheritance,
7:26 that the c that now is not seen shall appear,
8:52 plenty is provided, a c is built, rest is appointed,
10:18 I will not go into the c, but I will die here."
10:27 but a c was being built,
10:42 but there appeared to you a c being built)
10:44 which you now behold as a c being built.
10:46 after three thousand years Solomon built the c,
10:54 where the c of the Most High was to be revealed.
12:40 past and I had not returned to the c,
12:50 So the people went into the c, as I told them to do.
13:31 c against c, place against place,
15:17 For a person will desire to go into a c,
15:60 As they pass by they shall crush the hateful c,
16:28 For ten shall be left out of a c;

4Mc 7: 4 No c besieged with many

CITY'S (1) [CITY]

2Mc 12: 7 Then, because the c gates were closed,

CIVIC See Index to Footnotes

CLAIM (14) [CLAIMED, CLAIMING, CLAIMS]

Dt 15: 2 every creditor shall remit the c that is held against
15: 3 but you must remit your c
Ne 2:20 but you have no share or c or historic right
Job 3: 5 Let gloom and deep darkness c it.
Ecc 8:17 even though those who are wise c to know,
Jn 8:53 Who do you c to be?"
Ro 11:25 So that you may not c to be wiser than you are,
12:16 do not c to be wiser than you are.
1Co 9:12 If others share this rightful c on you,
2Co 3: 5 that we are competent of ourselves to c anything
Rev 2: 2 you have tested those who c to be apostles but are
Tob 6:12 have before all other men a hereditary c on her.
1Mc 15: 3 to lay c to the kingdom so that I may restore it
3Mc 4:11 in any way c to be inside the circuit of the city.

CLAIMED (3) [CLAIM]

2Sa 18: 8 the forest c more victims that day than the sword.
Jn 19: 7 to that law he ought to die because he has c to be
Ac 4:32 no one c private ownership of any possessions,

CLAIMING (3) [CLAIM]

Ac 5:36 c to be somebody, and a number of men,
Ro 1:22 C to be wise, they became fools;
2Ti 2:18 by c that the resurrection has already taken place.

CLAIMS (5) [CLAIM]

Dt 22: 2 and it shall remain with you until the owner c it;
2Sa 15: 3 "See, your c are good and right;
Jn 19:12 Everyone who c to be a king sets himself against
1Co 8: 2 Anyone who c to know something does not
14:37 Anyone who c to be a prophet,

CLAMOR (8)

Ps 55: 3 because of the c of the wicked.
74:23 Do not forget the c of your foes,
Isa 38:14 Like a swallow or a crane I c, I moan like a dove.
Jer 25:31 The c will resound to the ends of the earth,
51:55 laying Babylon waste, and stilling her loud c.
51:55 the sound of their c resounds;
La 2: 7 a c was raised in the house of the LORD as on
Ac 23: 9 Then a great c arose, and certain scribes of

CLAMPS (2)

1Ch 22: 3 for nails for the doors of the gates and for c,
4Mc 11:10 and fitting iron c on them,

CLAN (97) [CLANS]

Ge 36:30 c by c in the land of Seir.
Nu 3:21 the c of the Libnites and the c of the Shimeites;
3:27 To Kohath belonged the c of the Amramites,
3:27 the c of the Izharites, the c of the Hebronites,
3:27 and the c of the Uzzielites;
3:33 the c of the Mahlites and the c of the Mushites:
25:15 who was the head of a c,
26: 5 of Hanoch, the c of the Hanochites;
26: 5 of Pallu, the c of the Palluites;
26: 6 of Hezron, the c of the Hezronites;
26: 6 of Carmi, the c of the Carmites.
26:12 of Nemuel, the c of the Nemuelites;
26:12 of Jamin, the c of the Jaminites;
26:12 of Jachin, the c of the Jachinites;
26:13 of Zerah, the c of the Zerahites;
26:13 of Shaul, the c of the Shaulites.
26:15 of Zephon, the c of the Zephonites;
26:15 of Haggi, the c of the Haggites;
26:15 of Shuni, the c of the Shunites;
26:16 of Ozni, the c of the Oznites;
26:16 of Eri, the c of the Erites;
26:17 of Arod, the c of the Arodites;
26:17 of Areli, the c of the Arelites.
26:20 of Shelah, the c of the Shelanites;
26:20 of Perez, the c of the Perezites;
26:20 of Zerah, the c of the Zerahites.
26:21 of Hezron, the c of the Hezronites;
26:21 of Hamul, the c of the Hamulites.
26:23 of Tola, the c of the Tolaites;
26:23 of Puvah, the c of the Punites;
26:24 of Jashub, the c of the Jashubites;
26:24 of Shimron, the c of the Shimronites.
26:26 of Sered, the c of the Seredites;
26:26 of Elon, the c of the Elonites;
26:26 of Jahleel, the c of the Jahleelites.
26:29 of Machir, the c of the Machirites;
26:29 of Gilead, the c of the Gileadites.
26:30 of Iezer, the c of the Iezerites;
26:30 of Helek, the c of the Helekites;
26:31 and of Asriel, the c of the Asrielites;
26:31 and of Shechem, the c of the Shechemites;
26:32 and of Shemida, the c of the Shemidaites;
26:32 and of Hepher, the c of the Hepherites.
26:35 of Shuthelah, the c of the Shuthelahites;
26:35 of Becher, the c of the Becherites;
26:35 of Tahan, the c of the Tahanites.
26:36 of Eran, the c of the Eranites.

Nu 26:38 of Bela, the c of the Belaites;
26:38 of Ashbel, the c of the Ashbelites;
26:38 of Ahiram, the c of the Ahiramites;
26:39 of Shephupham, the c of the Shuphamites;
26:39 of Hupham, the c of the Huphamites.
26:40 of Ard, the c of the Ardites;
26:40 of Naaman, the c of the Naamites.
26:42 of Shuham, the c of the Shuhamites.
26:44 of Imnah, the c of the Imnites;
26:44 of Ishvi, the c of the Ishvites;
26:44 of Beriah, the c of the Beriites.
26:45 of Heber, the c of the Heberites;
26:45 of Malchiel, the c of the Malchielites.
26:48 of Jahzeel, the c of the Jahzeelites;
26:48 of Guni, the c of the Gunites;
26:49 of Jezer, the c of the Jezerites;
26:49 of Shillem, the c of the Shillemites.
26:57 of Gershon, the c of the Gershonites;
26:57 of Kohath, the c of the Kohathites;
26:57 of Merari, the c of the Merarites.
26:58 These are the clans of Levi: the c of the Libnites, the c of the Hebronites, the c of the Mahlites, the c of the Mushites, the c of the Korahites.
27: 4 be taken away from his c because he had no son?
27:11 to the nearest kinsman of his c,
36: 6 a c of their father's tribe that they are married,
36: 8 of the Israelites shall marry one from the c
36:12 in the tribe of their father's c.
Jos 7:14 the c that the LORD takes shall come near
7:17 and the c of the Zerahites was taken;
7:17 and he brought near the c of the Zerahites,
Jdg 4:17 between King Jabin of Hazor and the c of Heber
6:15 My c is the weakest in Manasseh,
9: 1 to them and to the whole c of his mother's family,
12: 9 in marriage outside his c and brought
17: 7 a young man of Bethlehem in Judah, of the c
18: 2 from the whole number of their c, from Zorah and
18:11 Six hundred men of the Danite c,
18:19 or to be priest to a tribe and c in Israel?"
1Ch 5:15 son of Guni, was chief in their c;
Isa 3: 6 a member of the c, saying, "You have a cloak;
60:22 The least of them shall become a c,
Zec 9: 7 it shall be like a c in Judah,
Sir 16: 4 but through a c of outlaws it becomes desolate.

CLANGING (2)

Ps 150: 5 Praise him with c cymbals;
1Co 13: 1 I am a noisy gong or a c cymbal.

CLANKING (1)

1Mc 6:41 by the marching of the multitude and the c

CLANS‡ (114) [CLAN]

Ge 36:15 These are the c of the sons of Esau.
36:15 the c Teman, Omar, Zepho, Kenaz,
36:16 these are the c of Eliphaz in the land of Edom;
36:17 the c Nahath, Zerah, Shammah, and Mizzah;
36:17 these are the c of Reuel in the land of Edom;
36:18 the c Jeush, Jalam, and Korah;
36:18 these are the c born of Esau's wife Oholibamah,
36:19 Edom), and these are their c.
36:21 these are the c of the Horites,
36:29 These are the c of the Horites: the c Lotan,
36:30 these are the c of the Horites,
36:40 These are the names of the c of Esau,
36:40 the c Timna, Alvah, Jetheth,
36:43 these are the c of Edom (that is, Esau,
Nu 1: 2 in their c, by ancestral houses,
1:18 They registered themselves in their c,
1:20 their lineage, in their c, by their ancestral houses,
1:22 descendants of Simeon, their lineage, in their c,
1:24 The descendants of Gad, their lineage, in their c,
1:26 The descendants of Judah, their lineage, in their c,
1:28 descendants of Issachar, their lineage, in their c,
1:30 descendants of Zebulun, their lineage, in their c,
1:32 their lineage, in their c, by their ancestral houses,
1:34 descendants of Manasseh, their lineage, in their c,
1:36 descendants of Benjamin, their lineage, in their c,
1:38 The descendants of Dan, their lineage, in their c,
1:40 The descendants of Asher, their lineage, in their c,
1:42 descendants of Naphtali, their lineage, in their c,
2:34 and they set out the same way, everyone by c,
3:15 Enroll the Levites by ancestral houses and by c.
3:18 the names of the sons of Gershon by their c:
3:19 The sons of Kohath by their c:
3:20 The sons of Merari by their c: Mahli and Mushi.
3:20 These are the c of the Levites,
3:21 these were the c of the Gershonites.
3:23 The c of the Gershonites were to camp behind
3:27 these are the c of the Kohathites.
3:29 The c of the Kohathites were to camp on
3:30 of Uzziel as head of the ancestral house of the c of
3:33 these are the c of Merari.
3:35 of the c of Merari was Zuriel son of Abihail;
3:39 at the commandment of the LORD, by their c, all
4: 2 by their c and their ancestral houses,
4:18 the c of the Kohathites be destroyed from among
4:22 by their ancestral houses and by their c;
4:24 This is the service of the c of the Gershonites,
4:28 the service of the c of the Gershonites relating to
4:29 by their c and their ancestral houses;
4:33 This is the service of the c of the Merarites,
4:34 by their c and their ancestral houses,
4:36 by c was two thousand seven hundred fifty.
4:37 the enrollment of the c of the Kohathites,
Nu 4:38 by their c and their ancestral houses,
4:40 their enrollment by their c
4:41 the enrollment of the c of the Gershonites,
4:42 The enrollment of the c of the Merarites,
4:42 by their c and their ancestral houses,
4:44 by their c was three thousand two hundred.
4:45 This is the enrollment of the c of the Merarites,
4:46 by their c and their ancestral houses,
26: 7 These are the c of the Reubenites;
26:12 The descendants of Simeon by their c:
26:14 These are the c of the Simeonites,
26:15 The children of Gad by their c:
26:18 These are the c of the Gadites:
26:20 The descendants of Judah by their c were:
26:22 These are the c of Judah:
26:23 The descendants of Issachar by their c:
26:25 These are the c of Issachar:
26:26 The descendants of Zebulun by their c:
26:27 These are the c of the Zebulunites;
26:28 sons of Joseph by their c: Manasseh and Ephraim.
26:34 These are the c of Manasseh;
26:35 the descendants of Ephraim according to their c:
26:37 These are the c of the Ephraimites:
26:37 These are the descendants of Joseph by their c.
26:38 The descendants of Benjamin by their c:
26:41 These are the descendants of Benjamin by their c;
26:42 These are the descendants of Dan by their c:
26:42 These are the c of Dan by their c.
26:43 All the c of the Shuhamites:
26:47 These are the c of the Asherites:
26:48 The descendants of Naphtali by their c:
26:50 These are the Naphtalites by their c:
26:57 This is the enrollment of the Levites by their c:
26:58 These are the c of Levi:
27: 1 a member of the Manassite c.
33:54 the land by lot according to your c;
36: 1 of the ancestral houses of the c of the descendants
36: 1 of the Josephite c, came forward and spoke in
36:12 They were married into the c of the descendants
Jos 7:14 tribe that the LORD takes shall come near by c,
7:17 He brought near the c of Judah,
13:15 to the tribe of the Reubenites according to their c.
13:28 the inheritance of the Gadites according to their c,
13:31 of Machir son of Manasseh according to their c—
22:14 the head of a family among the c of Israel.
Jdg 5:15 Among the c of Reuben there were great
5:16 Among the c of Reuben there were great
1Sa 10:19 before the LORD by your tribes and by your c."
1Ch 1:51 The c of Edom were: c Timna, Aliah, Jetheth,
1:54 Magdiel, and Iram; these are the c of Edom.
4:38 and their c increased greatly.
5:13 And their kindred according to their c:
5:24 These were the heads of their c:
5:24 mighty warriors, famous men, heads of their c.
6:19 the c of the Levites according to their ancestry.
Mic 5: 2 who are one of the little c of Judah,
Zec 12: 5 Then the c of Judah shall say to themselves,
12: 6 the c of Judah like a blazing pot on a pile of wood,
2Es 3: 7 peoples and c without number.

CLAP (8) [CLAPPED, CLAPPING, CLAPS]

Ps 47: 1 C your hands, all you peoples;
98: 8 Let the floods c their hands;
Isa 55:12 and all the trees of the field shall c their hands.
La 2:15 All who pass along the way c their hands at you;
Eze 6:11 C your hands and stamp your foot, and say,
Na 3:19 All who hear the news about you c their hands
Sir 12:18 Then he will shake his head, and c his hands,
40:13 and crash like a loud c of thunder in a storm.

CLAPPED (2) [CLAP]

2Ki 11:12 they c their hands and shouted,
Eze 25: 6 Because you have c your hands

CLAPPING (1) [CLAP]

2Es 15:53 and c your hands and talking about their death

CLAPS (2) [CLAP]

Job 27:23 It c its hands at them,
34:37 he c his hands among us,

CLASH (1) [CLASHING]

2Es 15:35 They shall c against one another

CLASHING (1) [CLASH]

Ps 150: 5 praise him with loud c cymbals!

CLASP (2) [CLASPS]

Job 41:17 they c each other and cannot be separated.
Isa 2: 6 and they c hands with foreigners.

CLASPS (9) [CLASP]

Ex 26: 6 You shall make fifty c of gold,
26: 6 and join the curtains to one another with the c,
26:11 You shall make fifty c of bronze,
26:11 and put the c into the loops,
26:33 You shall hang the curtain under the c,
35:11 its c and its frames, its bars, its pillars,
36:13 And he made fifty c of gold,
36:13 and joined the curtains one to the other with c;
36:18 He made fifty c of bronze to join the tent together

CLASSED (1) [CLASSIFY]

Lev 25:31 that have no walls around them shall be c

CLASSIFY (1) [CLASSED]

2Co 10:12 not dare to c or compare ourselves with some

CLATTER (1)

Jer 47: 3 at the c of his chariots,

CLAUDA (KJV) See CAUDA; See also Index to Footnotes

CLAUDIA (1)

2Ti 4:21 as do Pudens and Linus and C and all the brothers

CLAUDIUS (3)

Ac 11:28 and this took place during the reign of C.
18: 2 because C had ordered all Jews to leave Rome.
23:26 "C Lysias to his Excellency the governor Felix,

CLAVE (KJV) See CLUNG, CUT, DRAWN, FOLLOWED ... STEADFASTLY, HELD FAST, JOINED, SPLIT

CLAWS (3)

Da 4:33 and his nails became like birds' c.
7:19 with its teeth of iron and c of bronze,
4Mc 8:13 braziers and thumbscrews and iron c and wedges

CLAY (42)

1Ki 7:46 in the c ground between Succoth and Zarethan.
2Ch 4:17 in the c ground between Succoth and Zeredah.
Job 4:19 how much more those who live in houses of c,
10: 9 Remember that you fashioned me like c;
13:12 your defenses are defenses of c.
27:16 and pile up clothing like c—
33: 6 I too was formed from a piece of c.
38:14 It is changed like c under the seal,
Isa 29:16 Shall the potter be regarded as the c?
41:25 on rulers as on mortar, as the potter treads c.
45: 9 Does the c say to the one who fashions it,
64: 8 we are the c, and you are our potter;
Jer 18: 4 The vessel he was making of c was spoiled in
18: 6 Just like the c in the potter's hand,
43: 9 and bury them in the c pavement that is at
Da 2:33 its feet partly of iron and partly of c.
2:34 the statue on its feet of iron and c and broke them
2:35 Then the iron, the c, the bronze, the silver,
2:41 As you saw the feet and toes partly of potter's c
2:41 as you saw the iron mixed with the c.
2:42 As the toes of the feet were part iron and part c,
2:43 As you saw the iron mixed with c,
2:43 just as iron does not mix with c.
2:45 and that it crushed the iron, the bronze, the c,
Na 3:14 trample the c, tread the mortar,
Ro 9:21 Has the potter no right over the c,
2Co 4: 7 But we have this treasure in c jars,
2Ti 2:20 not only of gold and silver but also of wood and c,
Rev 2:27 as when c pots are shattered—
Wis 7: 9 and silver will be accounted as c before her.
15: 7 the same c both the vessels that serve clean uses
15: 7 the use of each of them the worker in c decides.
15: 8 these workers form a futile god from the same c—
15:10 and their lives are of less worth than c,
Sir 13: 2 How can the c pot associate with the iron kettle?
33:13 Like c in the hand of the potter,
38:30 He molds the c with his arm and makes it pliable
Bel 1: 7 for this thing is only c inside and bronze outside,
2Es 7:52 will you add to them lead and c?"
7:55 and also iron and lead and c;
7:56 and lead than iron, and c than lead.'
8: 2 it will tell you that it provides a large amount of c

CLEAN (133) [CLEANNESS, CLEANSE, CLEANSED, CLEANSES, CLEANSING]

Ge 7: 2 Take with you seven pairs of all c animals,
7: 2 and a pair of the animals that are not c,
7: 8 Of c animals, and of animals that are not c,
8:20 took of every c animal and of every c bird,
Lev 4:12 he shall carry out to a c place outside the camp,
6:11 carry the ashes out to a c place outside the camp.
7:19 for other flesh, all who are c may eat such flesh.
10:10 and between the unclean and the c;
10:14 and daughters as well may eat in any c place;
11:32 until the evening, and then it shall be c.
11:36 But a spring or a cistern holding water shall be c,
11:37 upon any seed set aside for sowing, it is c;
11:47 a distinction between the unclean and the c,
12: 7 then she shall be c from her flow of blood.
12: 8 on her behalf, and she shall be c.
13: 6 the priest shall pronounce him c;
13: 6 and he shall wash his clothes, and be c.
13:13 he shall pronounce him c of the disease;
13:13 since it has all turned white, he is c.
13:17 shall pronounce the diseased person c. He is c.
13:23 the priest shall pronounce him c.
13:28 and the priest shall pronounce him c;
13:34 the priest shall pronounce him c.
13:34 He shall wash his clothes and be c.
13:35 itch spreads in the skin after he was pronounced c,

Lev 13:37 he is **c**; and the priest shall pronounce him **c**.
13:39 that has broken out on the skin; he is **c**.
13:40 he is bald but he is **c**.
13:41 he has baldness of the forehead but he is **c**.
13:58 then be washed a second time, and it shall be **c**.
13:59 to decide whether it is **c** or unclean.
14: 4 the priest shall command that two living **c** birds
14: 7 then he shall pronounce him **c**,
14: 8 and bathe himself in water, and he shall be **c**.
14: 9 and bathe his body in water, and he shall be **c**.
14:20 on his behalf and he shall be **c**.
14:48 the priest shall pronounce the house **c**;
14:53 for the house, and it shall be **c**.
14:57 to determine when it is unclean and when it is **c**.
15: 8 one with the discharge spits on persons who are **c**,
15:13 in fresh water, and he shall be **c**.
15:28 and after that she shall be **c**.
16:30 from all your sins you shall be **c** before
17:15 until the evening; then they shall be **c**.
20:25 therefore make a distinction between the **c** animal
20:25 and between the unclean bird and the **c**;
22: 4 of the sacred donations until he is **c**.
22: 7 When the sun sets he shall be **c**;
Nu 5:28 But if the woman has not defiled herself and is **c**,
9:13 But anyone who is **c** and is not on a journey,
18:11 everyone who is **c** in your house may eat them.
18:13 everyone who is **c** in your house may eat of it.
19: 9 Then someone who is **c** shall gather up the ashes
19: 9 and deposit them outside the camp in a **c** place;
19:12 the third day and on the seventh day, and so be **c**;
19:12 and on the seventh day, they will not become **c**.
19:18 then a **c** person shall take hyssop,
19:19 The **c** person shall sprinkle the unclean ones on
19:19 and at evening they shall be **c**.
31:23 shall be passed through fire, and it shall be **c**.
31:24 on the seventh day, and you shall be **c**;
Dt 12:15 the unclean and the **c** may eat of it,
12:22 the unclean and the **c** alike may eat it.
14:11 You may eat any **c** birds.
14:20 You may eat any **c** winged creature.
15:22 the unclean and the **c** alike,
1Sa 20:26 he is not **c**, surely he is not **c**."
2Ki 5:10 your flesh shall be restored and you shall be **c**."
5:12 Could I not wash in them, and be **c**?"
5:13 when all he said to you was, 'Wash, and be **c**'?"
5:14 like the flesh of a young boy, and he was **c**.
2Ch 30:17 the passover lamb for everyone who was not **c**,
Ezr 6:20 had purified themselves; all of them were **c**.
Job 11: 4 'My conduct is pure, and I am **c** in God's sight.'
14: 4 Who can bring a **c** thing out of an unclean?
15:14 What are mortals, that they can be **c**?
15:15 and the heavens are not **c** in his sight;
17: 9 they that have **c** hands grow stronger and stronger.
33: 9 You say, 'I am **c**, without transgression;
Ps 24: 4 Those who have **c** hands and pure hearts,
51: 7 Purge me with hyssop, and I shall be **c**;
51:10 Create in me a **c** heart, O God,
73:13 All in vain I have kept my heart **c**
Pr 20: 9 Who can say, "I have made my heart **c**;
20:30 beatings make **c** the innermost parts.
Ecc 9: 2 to the good and the evil, to the **c** and the unclean,
Isa 1:16 Wash yourselves; make yourselves **c**;
28: 8 with filthy vomit; no place is **c**.
66:20 as the Israelites bring a grain offering in a **c** vessel
Jer 4:14 wash your heart **c** of wickedness so that you may
13:27 How long will it be before you are made **c**?
43:12 and he shall pick **c** the land of Egypt,
43:12 as a shepherd picks his cloak **c** of vermin;
Eze 22:26 the difference between the unclean and the **c**,
24:13 you did not become **c** from your filth;
36:25 I will sprinkle **c** water upon you,
36:25 and you shall be **c** from all your uncleannesses,
44:23 how to distinguish between the unclean and the **c**.
44:26 After he has become **c**, they shall count seven days
Zec 3: 5 And I said, "Let them put a **c** turban on his head."
3: 5 So they put a **c** turban on his head and clothed him
Mt 8: 2 saying, "Lord, if you choose, you can make me **c**."
8: 3 "I do choose. Be made **c**!"
23:25 For you **c** the outside of the cup and of the plate,
23:26 First **c** the inside of the cup, so that the outside
also may become **c**.
27:59 the body and wrapped it in a **c** linen cloth
Mk 1:40 "If you choose, you can make me **c**."
1:41 "I do choose. Be made **c**!"
1:42 the leprosy left him, and he was made **c**.
7:19 (Thus he declared all foods **c**.)
Lk 5:12 "Lord, if you choose, you can make me **c**."
5:13 and said, "I do choose. Be made **c**."
11:39 "Now you Pharisees **c** the outside of the cup and
11:41 and see, everything will be **c** for you.
17:14 And as they went, they were made **c**.
17:17 Then Jesus asked, "Were not ten made **c**?
Jn 13:10 except for the feet, but is entirely **c**.
13:10 And you are **c**, though not all of you."
13:11 for this reason he said, "Not all of you are **c**."
Ac 10:15 a second time, "What God has made **c**,
11: 9 from heaven, 'What God has made **c**, you must
Ro 14:20 Everything is indeed **c**, but it is wrong for you
1Co 5: 7 **C** out the old yeast so that you may be
Heb 10:22 with our hearts sprinkled **c** from
Jdt 7: 4 "They will now strip **c** the whole land;
Wis 15: 7 of the same clay both the vessels that serve **c** uses
Sir 34: 4 From an unclean thing what can be **c**?

CLEANING See Index to Footnotes

CLEANNESS‡ (7) [CLEAN]
2Sa 22:21 to the **c** of my hands he recompensed me.
22:25 according to my **c** in his sight.
2Ch 30:19 not in accordance with the sanctuary's rules of **c**."
Job 22:30 they will escape because of the **c** of your hands."
Ps 18:20 to the **c** of my hands he recompensed me.
18:24 according to the **c** of my hands in his sight.
Am 4: 6 I gave you **c** of teeth in all your cities,

CLEANSE‡ (31) [CLEAN]
Lev 14:52 Thus he shall **c** the house with the blood of
16:19 and **c** it and hallow it from the uncleannesses of
16:30 be made for you, to **c** you;
Nu 8: 6 the Levites from among the Israelites and **c** them.
8: 7 Thus you shall do to them, to **c** them:
8: 7 and wash their clothes, and so **c** themselves.
8:21 and Aaron made atonement for them to **c** them.
Dt 32:43 and **c** the land for his people.
2Ch 29:15 to **c** the house of the LORD.
29:16 to **c** it, and they brought out all the unclean things
Job 9:30 I wash myself with soap and **c** my hands with lye,
Ps 51: 2 and **c** me from my sin.
Pr 20:30 Blows that wound **c** away evil;
Jer 4:11 toward my poor people, not to winnow or **c**—
33: 8 I will **c** them from all the guilt of their sin
Eze 16: 4 nor were you washed with water to **c** you,
36:25 and from all your idols I will **c** you.
36:33 On the day that I **c** you from all your iniquities,
37:23 into which they have fallen, and will **c** them.
39:12 in order to **c** the land.
39:14 on the face of the land, so as to **c** it;
39:16 Thus they shall **c** the land.
43:26 for the altar and **c** it,
Zec 13: 1 to **c** them from sin and impurity.
Mt 10: 8 Cure the sick, raise the dead, **c** the lepers,
2Co 7: 1 let us **c** ourselves from every defilement of body
2Ti 2:21 All who **c** themselves of the things
Jas 4: 8 **C** your hands, you sinners, and purify your hearts,
1Jn 1: 9 and just will forgive us our sins and **c** us
Sir 38:10 and **c** your heart from all sin.
1Mc 4:36 let us go up to **c** the sanctuary and dedicate it."

CLEANSED (38) [CLEAN]
Lev 14: 4 and hyssop be brought for the one who is to be **c**.
14: 7 upon the one who is to be **c** of the leprous disease;
14: 8 The one who is to be **c** shall wash his clothes,
14:11 priest who cleanses shall set the person to be **c**,
14:14 on the lobe of the right ear of the one to be **c**,
14:17 on the lobe of the right ear of the one to be **c**,
14:18 on the head of the one to be **c**.
14:19 for the one to be **c** from his uncleanness.
14:25 on the lobe of the right ear of the one to be **c**,
14:28 on the lobe of the right ear of the one to be **c**,
14:29 on the head of the one to be **c**,
14:31 before the LORD on behalf of the one being **c**.
15:13 the one with a discharge is **c** of his discharge,
15:28 If she is **c** of her discharge,
Nu 8:15 once you have **c** them and presented them as
Jos 22:17 from which even yet we have not **c** ourselves,
2Ch 29:18 "We have **c** all the house of the LORD,
30:18 Issachar, and Zebulun, had not **c** themselves,
Ne 13: 9 Then I gave orders and they **c** the chambers,
13:30 Thus I **c** them from everything foreign,
Pr 30:12 in their own eyes yet are not **c** of their filthiness.
Isa 4: 4 and **c** the bloodstains of Jerusalem from its midst
Eze 22:24 You are a land that is not **c**,
24:13 Yet, when I **c** you in your filthy lewdness,
24:13 you shall not again be **c** until I have satisfied my
fury upon you.
Da 11:35 so that they may be refined, purified, and **c**,
12:10 Many shall be purified, **c**, and refined,
Mt 8: 3 Immediately his leprosy was **c**.
11: 5 the lepers are **c**, the deaf hear, the dead are raised,
Lk 4:27 none of them was **c** except Naaman the Syrian."
7:22 the lepers are **c**, the deaf hear, the dead are raised,
Jn 15: 3 You have already been **c** by the word
Heb 10: 2 since the worshipers, **c** once for all,
Sir 23:10 and utters the Name will never be **c** from sin.
1Mc 4:41 to fight against those in the citadel until he had **c**
4:43 and they **c** the sanctuary and removed
13:47 and **c** the houses in which the idols were located,
13:50 But he expelled them from there and **c** the citadel

CLEANSES (2) [CLEAN]
Lev 14:11 priest who **c** shall set the person to be cleansed,
1Jn 1: 7 and the blood of Jesus his Son **c** us from all sin.

CLEANSING (18) [CLEAN]
Lev 13: 7 after he has shown himself to the priest for his **c**,
14: 2 for the leprous person at the time of his **c**:
14:23 On the eighth day he shall bring them for his **c** to
14:32 who cannot afford the offerings for his **c**.
14:49 For the **c** of the house he shall take two birds,
15:13 he shall count seven days for his **c**;
Nu 6: 9 they shall shave the head on the day of their **c**;
19: 9 of the Israelites for the water for **c**.
19:13 Since water for **c** was not dashed on them,
19:20 the water for **c** has not been dashed on them,
19:21 the water for **c** shall wash his clothes,
19:21 the water for **c** shall be unclean until evening.
1Ch 23:28 the **c** of all that is holy,
Mk 1:44 and offer for your **c** what Moses commanded,
Lk 5:14 make an offering for your **c**,
Ac 15: 9 and in **c** their hearts by faith
Eph 5:26 by **c** her with the washing of water by the word,
2Pe 1: 9 and is forgetful of the **c** of past sins.

CLEAR (52) [CLEARED, CLEARING, CLEARLY, CLEARNESS, CLEARS]
Ge 44:16 How can we **c** ourselves?
Lev 24:12 until the decision of the LORD should be made **c**
26:10 and you shall have to **c** out the old to make way
Nu 15:34 because it was not **c** what should be done to him.
16:14 It is **c** you have not brought us into a land flowing
24: 3 the oracle of the man whose eye is **c**,
24:15 the oracle of the man whose eye is **c**,
Dt 7:22 The LORD your God will **c** away these nations
Jos 17:15 and **c** ground there for yourselves in the land of
17:18 you shall **c** it and possess it to its farthest borders;
2Sa 19: 6 You have made it **c** today that commanders
1Ch 28:19 he made **c** to me—the plan of all the works."
Job 15: 9 What do you understand that is not **c** to us?
Ps 19: 8 the commandment of the LORD is **c**,
19:12 **C** me from hidden faults.
Isa 18: 4 I will quietly look from my dwelling like **c** heat
25: 6 of well-aged wines strained **c**.
62:10 build up, build up the highway, **c** it of stones,
Eze 32:14 Then I will make their waters **c**,
34:18 When you drink of **c** water,
Joel 3:21 and I will not **c** the guilty,
Na 1: 3 and the LORD will by no means **c** the guilty.
Mt 3:12 and he will **c** his threshing floor
Lk 3:17 to **c** his threshing floor and to gather the wheat
Ac 23: 1 with a **c** conscience before God."
24:16 to have a **c** conscience toward God and all people.
1Co 11:19 so will it become **c** who among you are genuine.
2Co 4: 7 be made **c** that this extraordinary power belongs
7:11 what eagerness to **c** yourselves, what indignation,
1Ti 3: 9 to the mystery of the faith with a **c** conscience.
2Ti 1: 3 whom I worship with a **c** conscience,
Heb 2:16 For it is **c** that he did not come to help angels,
11:14 for people who speak in this way make it **c**
13:18 we are sure that we have a **c** conscience,
1Pe 3:16 Keep your conscience **c**, so that,
2Pe 1:14 as indeed our Lord Jesus Christ has made **c** to me.
Rev 21:11 and a radiance like a very rare jewel, like jasper, **c**
21:18 while the city is pure gold, **c** as glass.
Wis 6:22 and make knowledge of her **c**,
7:22 manifold, subtle, mobile, **c**, unpolluted, distinct,
Sir 17:19 All their works are as **c** as the sun before him,
22:13 Stay **c** of him, or you may have trouble,
22:19 and one who pricks the heart makes **c** its feelings.
24:32 and I will make it **c** from far away.
43: 1 pride of the higher realms is the **c** vault of the sky,
1Mc 12: 8 which contained a **c** declaration of alliance
2Mc 2: 9 It was also made **c** that being possessed
4:17 a fact that later events will make **c**.
6:30 "It is **c** to the Lord in his holy knowledge that,
12:40 And it became **c** to all that this was
15:35 a **c** and conspicuous sign to everyone of the help
4Mc 1: 4 also **c** that it masters the emotions that hinder one

CLEARED (4) [CLEAR]
1Sa 14:41 by the lot, but the people were **c**.
Job 37:21 when the wind has passed and **c** them.
Ps 80: 9 You **c** the ground for it;
Isa 5: 2 He dug it and **c** it of stones,

CLEARING (2) [CLEAR]
Ex 34: 7 yet by no means **c** the guilty,
Nu 14:18 but by no means **c** the guilty,

CLEARLY (17) [CLEAR]
Nu 12: 8 With him I speak face to face—**c**, not in riddles;
Dt 27: 8 on the stones all the words of this law very **c**.
1Ki 3:21 **c** it was not the son I had borne."
Jer 23:20 In the latter days you will understand it **c**.
Mt 7: 5 and then you will see **c** to take the speck out
Mk 8:25 his sight was restored, and he saw everything **c**.
Lk 6:42 and then you will see **c** to take the speck out
Jn 3:21 be **c** seen that their deeds have been done in God."
Ac 10: 3 in which he **c** saw an angel of God coming in
Col 4: 4 so that I may reveal it **c**, as I should.
Heb 6:17 to show even more **c** to the heirs of the promise
Wis 10:21 and made the tongues of infants speak **c**.
19:18 be **c** inferred from the sight of what took place.
2Mc 3:28 They recognized **c** the sovereign power of God.
3Mc 4:19 he was **c** convinced about the matter
4Mc 2: 7 unless reason is **c** lord of the emotions?
3: 6 Now this can be explained more **c** by the story

CLEARNESS (1) [CLEAR]
Ex 24:10 sapphire stone, like the very heaven for **c**.

CLEARS (1) [CLEAR]
Dt 7: 1 and he **c** away many nations before you—

CLEAVE, CLEAVED, CLEAVETH (KJV)
See CLING, CLUNG, CUT, DIVIDED, FAITHFUL, FASTENED, HELD FAST, HOLD, HOLD FAST, JOIN, REMAIN, SHRIVELED, SLASHES, SPLITS, STICK, STUCK, TEAR, UNITED

CLEFT (7) [CLEFT-FOOTED, CLEFTS]
Ex 33:22 a c of the rock, and I will cover you with my hand
Dt 14: 6 that divides the hoof and has the hoof c in two,
14: 7 the cud or have the hoof c you shall not eat these:
Jdg 15: 8 and he went down and stayed in the c of the rock
15:11 of Judah went down to the c of the rock of Etam,
SS 2:17 like a gazelle or a young stag on the c mountains.
Jer 13: 4 and hide it there in a c of the rock."

CLEFT-FOOTED (3) [CLEFT, FOOT]
Lev 11: 3 Any animal that has divided hoofs and is c
11: 7 pig, for even though it has divided hoofs and is c,
11:26 not c or does not chew the cud is unclean for you;

CLEFTS (8) [CLEFT]
SS 2:14 O my dove, in the c of the rock,
Isa 2:21 the caverns of the rocks and the c in the crags,
7:19 and in the c of the rocks,
57: 5 in the valleys, under the c of the rocks?
Jer 16:16 and out of the c of the rocks.
49:16 you who live in the c of the rock,
Ob 1: 3 you that live in the c of the rock,
2Es 16:28 in thick groves and c in the rocks.

CLEMENCY (3)
Mic 7:18 because he delights in showing c.
3Mc 3:15 should cherish them with c and great benevolence,
7: 6 and in accordance with the c that we have

CLEMENCY (KJV) See also GRACIOUSNESS

CLEMENT (1)
Php 4: 3 together with C and the rest of my co-workers,

CLEOPAS (1)
Lk 24:18 Then one of them, whose name was C,

CLEOPATRA (3)
AdE 11: 1 In the fourth year of the reign of Ptolemy and C,
1Mc 10:57 he and his daughter C, and came to Ptolemais in
10:58 and Ptolemy gave him his daughter C in marriage,

CLEOPHAS (KJV) See CLOPAS

CLERK (1)
Ac 19:35 But when the town c had quieted the crowd,

CLEVER‡ (11) [CLEVERLY, CLEVERNESS]
1Sa 25: 3 The woman was c and beautiful,
Pr 12:23 One who is c conceals knowledge,
13:16 The c do all things intelligently,
14: 8 the wisdom of the c to understand where they go,
14:15 but the c consider their steps.
14:18 but the c are crowned with knowledge.
22: 3 The c see danger and hide;
27:12 The c see danger and hide;
Sir 6:32 and if you apply yourself you will become c.
21:12 The one who is not c cannot be taught,
37:19 Some people may be c enough to teach many,

CLEVERLY (2) [CLEVER]
2Pe 1:16 not follow c devised myths when we made known
2Mc 14:31 that he had been c outwitted by the man,

CLEVERNESS (5) [CLEVER]
Sir 19:23 There is a c that is detestable,
19:25 There is a c that is exact but unjust,
21:12 but there is a c that increases bitterness.
32: 4 do not display your c at the wrong time.
34:11 but he that has traveled acquires much c.

CLIFF (3) [CLIFFS]
SS 2:14 in the clefts of the rock, in the covert of the c,
Lk 4:29 so that they might hurl him off the c.
4Mc 7: 5 For in setting his mind firm like a jutting c,

CLIFFS (1) [CLIFF]
Eze 38:20 and the c shall fall, and every wall shall tumble

CLIFT (KJV) See CLEFT

CLIMB (4) [CLIMBED, CLIMBS]
SS 7: 8 I say I will c the palm tree and lay hold
Jer 4:29 they enter thickets; they c among rocks;
Joel 2: 9 they c up into the houses,
Am 9: 2 though they c up to heaven,

CLIMBED (3) [CLIMB]
1Sa 14:13 Then Jonathan c up on his hands and feet,
Lk 19: 4 So he ran ahead and c a sycamore tree to see him,
4Mc 3:12 and taking a pitcher c over the enemy's ramparts.

CLIMBS (3) [CLIMB]
Isa 24:18 and whoever c out of the pit shall be caught in
Jer 48:44 and everyone who c out of the pit shall be caught
Jn 10: 1 by the gate but c in by another way is a thief and

CLING‡ (18) [CLINGING, CLINGS, CLUNG]
Dt 28:21 The LORD will make the pestilence c to you
28:60 and they shall c to you.
2Ki 5:27 Therefore the leprosy of Naaman shall c to you,
Job 19:20 My bones c to my skin and to my flesh,
24: 8 and c to the rock for want of shelter.
38:38 the dust runs into a mass and the clods c together?
41:23 The folds of its flesh c together;
Ps 44:25 our bodies c to the ground.
101: 3 it shall not c to me.
102: 5 of my loud groaning my bones c to my skin.
119:31 I c to your decrees, O LORD;
137: 6 Let my tongue c to the roof of my mouth,
Isa 27: 5 Or else let it c to me for protection,
Jer 13:11 of Israel and the whole house of Judah c to me,
La 4: 5 those who were brought up in purple c
Eze 3:26 and I will make your tongue c to the roof
Rev 12:11 for they did not c to life even in the face of death.
Sir 2: 3 C to him and do not depart,

CLINGING‡ (1) [CLING]
2Es 12:19 As for your seeing eight little wings c to its wings,

CLINGS (8) [CLING]
Ge 2:24 a man leaves his father and his mother and c
Ps 63: 8 My soul c to you; your right hand upholds me.
119:25 My soul c to the dust;
Jer 13:11 For as the loincloth c to one's loins,
Lk 10:11 'Even the dust of your town that c to our feet,
Heb 12: 1 let us also lay aside every weight and the sin that c
Sir 10:13 and the one who c to it pours out abominations.
1Es 4:20 and his own country, and c to his wife.

CLOAK (34) [CLOAKS]
Ex 4: 6 "Put your hand inside your c."
4: 6 He put his hand into his c;
4: 7 Then God said, "Put your hand back into your c"
4: 7 so he put his hand back into his c,
22:26 If you take your neighbor's c in pawn,
Dt 22:12 You shall make tassels on the four corners of the c
24:13 your neighbor may sleep in the c and bless you;
Ru 3: 9 spread your c over your servant,
3:15 "Bring the c you are wearing and hold it out."
1Sa 24: 4 and stealthily cut off a corner of Saul's c.
24: 5 because he had cut off a corner of Saul's c.
24:11 my father, see the corner of your c in my hand;
24:11 for by the fact that I cut off the corner of your c,
Isa 3: 6 "You have a c; you shall be our leader,
3: 7 in my house there is neither bread nor c;
Jer 43:12 as a shepherd picks his c clean of vermin;
Eze 16: 8 I spread the edge of my c over you,
Mt 5:40 to sue you and take your coat, give your c as well;
9:16 a piece of unshrunk cloth on an old c,
9:16 for the patch pulls away from the c,
9:20 up behind him and touched the fringe of his c,
9:21 "If I only touch his c, I will be made well."
14:36 that they might touch even the fringe of his c;
Mk 2:21 a piece of unshrunk cloth on an old c;
5:27 up behind him in the crowd and touched his c,
6:56 that they might touch even the fringe of his c;
10:50 So throwing off his c, he sprang up and came
15:17 And they clothed him in a purple c;
15:20 of the purple c and put his own clothes on him.
Lk 22:36 And the one who has no sword must sell his c
Ac 12: 8 "Wrap your c around you and follow me."
2Ti 4:13 bring the c that I left with Carpus at Troas,
Heb 1:12 like a c you will roll them up,
2Mc 12:35 and grasping his c was dragging him off

CLOAKS (10) [CLOAK]
Ex 12:34 with their kneading bowls wrapped up in their c
2Ki 9:13 Then hurriedly they all took their c
Isa 3:22 the mantles, the c, and the handbags;
Mt 21: 7 and put their c on them, and he sat on them.
21: 8 A very large crowd spread their c on the road,
Mk 11: 7 the colt to Jesus and threw their c on it;
11: 8 Many people spread their c on the road,
Lk 19:35 throwing their c on the colt, they set Jesus on it.
19:36 people kept spreading their c on the road.
Ac 22:23 while they were shouting, throwing off their c,

CLODS (3)
Job 21:33 The c of the valley are sweet to them;
38:38 the dust runs into a mass and the c cling together?
Joel 1:17 The seed shrivels under the c,

CLOGGED (1)
Ex 14:25 He c their chariot wheels so that they turned

CLOPAS (1)
Jn 19:25 and his mother's sister, Mary the wife of C,

CLOSE (60) [CLOSED, CLOSELY, CLOSER, CLOSEST, CLOSING, ENCLOSE, ENCLOSED, ENCLOSURE, ENCLOSURES]
Ge 46: 4 and Joseph's own hand shall c your eyes."
Ex 25:27 the poles used for carrying the table shall be c to
37:14 the poles used for carrying the table were c to
Lev 3: 9 which shall be removed c to the backbone,
20: 4 if the people of the land should ever c their eyes
Lev 21: 3 c to him because she has had no husband,
Nu 8:19 the Israelites for coming too c to the sanctuary.
Jos 2: 5 it was time to c the gate at dark, the men went out.
Jdg 19: 9 See, the day has drawn to a c.
20:34 not realize that disaster was c upon them.
20:41 for they saw that disaster was c upon them.
Ru 2: 8 but keep c to my young women.
2:21 "He even said to me, 'Stay c by my servants,
2:23 So she stayed c to the young women of Boaz,
2Sa 1: 6 the chariots and the horsemen drew c to him.
2Ki 10:11 all his leaders, c friends, and priests,
Ne 6:10 and let us c the doors of the temple,
Job 19:14 My relatives and my c friends have failed me;
Ps 17:10 They c their hearts to pity;
69:15 or the Pit c its mouth over me.
88:15 Wretched and c to death from my youth up,
88:17 from all sides they c in on me.
148:14 for the people of Israel who are c to him.
Pr 16:28 and a whisperer separates c friends.
17:28 when they c their lips, they are deemed intelligent.
18: 9 One who is slack in work is c kin to a vandal.
21:13 If you c your ear to the cry of the poor,
Isa 13:22 its time is c at hand, and its days will not be
Jer 20:10 All my c friends are watching for me to stumble.
42:16 that you dread shall follow c after you into Egypt;
La 3:56 "Do not c your ear to my cry for help,
Hab 3: 5 and plague followed c behind.
Lk 7: 2 and who was ill and c to death.
9:12 The day was drawing to a c,
Jn 1:18 who is c to the Father's heart,
Ac 10:24 and had called together his relatives and c friends.
11: 5 and it came c to me.
27:13 and began to sail past Crete, c to the shore.
Ro 7:21 that when I want to do what is good, evil lies c
1Co 8: 8 "Food will not bring us c to God."
Php 2:30 because he came c to death for the work of Christ,
1Ti 4:16 Pay c attention to yourself and to your teaching;
Tob 1:22 He was my nephew and so a c relative.
3:15 and he has no c relative or other kindred
Jdt 8:27 the Lord scourges those who are c to him in order
13: 7 She came c to his bed,
AdE 16: 7 as from investigation of matters c at hand.
Sir 11:27 and at the c of one's life one's deeds are revealed.
13:16 and people stick c to those like themselves.
16:24 and pay c attention to my words.
51:12 *For the children of Israel, the people c to him.*
51:26 it is to be found c by.
1Mc 9:16 and followed c behind Judas and his men.
12:50 and kept marching in c formation,
2Mc 4:42 the temple robber himself they killed c by
7:27 leaning c to him, she spoke
12:31 as the festival of weeks was c at hand.
15:20 and the enemy was already c at hand
2Es 2:34 at the end of the age is c at hand.
2:40 c the list of your people who are clothed in white,

CLOSED‡ (41) [CLOSE]
Ge 2:21 then he took one of his ribs and c up its place
8: 2 the deep and the windows of the heavens were c,
20:18 the LORD had c fast all the wombs of the house
Ex 14: 3 the wilderness has c in on them.'
Nu 16:33 the earth c over them, and they perished from
Jdg 3:22 and the fat c over the blade,
3:23 and c the doors of the roof chamber on him,
1Sa 1: 5 though the LORD had c her womb.
1: 6 because the LORD had c her womb.
1Ki 11:27 and c up the gap in the wall of the city
2Ki 4:21 c the door on him, and left.
4:33 So he went in and c the door on the two of them,
6:32 that you shut the door and hold it c against him.
2Ch 32:30 This same Hezekiah c the upper outlet of
Ne 4: 7 and the gaps were beginning to be c,
Job 17: 4 Since you have c their minds to understanding,
19: 6 and c his net around me.
Isa 29:10 he has c your eyes, you prophets,
32: 3 the eyes of those who have sight will not be c,
45: 1 and the gates shall not be c:
57:11 Have I not kept silent and c my eyes,
Jer 4:17 They have c in around her like watchers of a field,
6:10 See, their ears are c, they cannot listen.
La 3:54 water c over my head; I said, "I am lost."
Eze 31:15 down to Sheol I c the deep over it and covered it;
46: 1 of the inner court that faces east shall remain c on
46: 2 but the gate shall not be c until evening.
46:12 and after he has gone out the gate shall be c.
Jnh 2: 5 The waters c in over me;
2: 6 down to the land whose bars c upon me forever;
Lk 12: 3 and what you have whispered behind c doors will
Jdt 5: 1 and had c the mountain passes and fortified all
13: 1 Bagoas c the tent from outside and shut out
Sir 4:31 not let your hand be stretched out to receive and c
30:18 a mouth that is c are like offerings of food placed
1Mc 10:75 but the people of the city c its gates,
12:48 people of Ptolemais c the gates and seized him,
2Mc 1:15 they c the temple as soon as he entered it.
12: 7 Then, because the city's gates were c,
2Es 5:37 open for me the c chambers, and bring out for me
14:41 and my mouth was opened and was no longer c.

CLOSELY (11) [CLOSE]
Dt 4: 9 But take care and watch yourselves c,
4:15 take care and watch yourselves c,
Ru 3:12 there is another kinsman more c related than I.
1Sa 14:22 they too followed c after them in the battle.
1Ki 3:21 but when I looked at him c in the morning,
Job 41:15 shut up c as with a seal.

Eze 40: 4 “Mortal, look **c** and listen attentively,
44: 5 Mortal, mark well, look **c**,
Lk 14: 1 they were watching him **c**.
Ac 11: 6 As I looked at it **c** I saw four-footed animals,
Heb 12: 1 and the sin that clings so **c**,

CLOSER (6) [CLOSE]

Ge 45: 4 Then Joseph said to his brothers, “Come **c** to me.” And they came **c**.
Ex 3: 5 Then he said, “Come no **c**!
1Ki 18:30 Elijah said to all the people, “Come **c** to me”; and all the people came **c** to him.
Pr 18:24 but a true friend sticks **c** than one’s nearest kin.

CLOSEST (2) [CLOSE]

Ex 12: 4 it shall join its **c** neighbor in obtaining one;
AdE 1:14 the Persians and Medes who were **c** to the king—

CLOSET (KJV) See ROOM

CLOSING (2) [CLOSE]

1Sa 23:26 and his men were **c** in on David and his men
Ps 77: 4 You keep my eyelids from **c**;

CLOTH‡ (36) [CLOTHS, LOINCLOTH, LOINCLOTHS, SACKCLOTH, SADDLECLOTHS, WAISTCLOTH]

Lev 11:32 whether an article of wood or **c** or skin or sacking,
13:47 leprous disease appears in it, in woolen or linen **c**,
13:51 If the disease has spread in the **c**, in warp or woof,
13:56 he shall tear the spot out of the **c**, in warp or woof,
13:58 But the **c**, warp or woof, or anything of skin
13:59 the ritual for a leprous disease in a **c** of wool
15:17 of **c** or of skin on which the semen falls shall
Nu 4: 6 and spread over that a **c** all of blue,
4: 7 of the Presence they shall spread a blue **c**, and put
4: 8 then they shall spread over them a crimson **c**,
4: 9 They shall take a blue **c**, and cover the lampstand
4:11 Over the golden altar they shall spread a blue **c**,
4:12 and put them in a blue **c**,
4:13 and spread a purple **c** over it;
Dt 22:17 Then they shall spread out the **c** before the elders
1Sa 21: 9 is here wrapped in a **c** behind the ephod;
Isa 64: 6 and all our righteous deeds are like a filthy **c**.
Eze 16:10 I clothed you with embroidered **c** and with sandals
16:13 rich fabric, and embroidered **c**.
Mt 9:16 a piece of unshrunk **c** on an old cloak,
27:59 the body and wrapped it in a clean linen **c**
Mk 2:21 “No one sews a piece of unshrunk **c** on
14:51 wearing nothing but a linen **c**.
14:52 but he left the linen **c** and ran off naked.
15:46 Then Joseph bought a linen **c**,
15:46 wrapped it in the linen **c**,
Lk 2: 7 and wrapped him in bands of **c**,
2:12 you will find a child wrapped in bands of **c**
19:20 I wrapped it up in a piece of **c**,
23:53 Then he took it down, wrapped it in a linen **c**,
Jn 11:44 his hands and feet bound with strips of **c**,
11:44 and his face wrapped in a **c**.
20: 7 and the **c** that had been on Jesus’ head,
Ac 16:14 from the city of Thyatira and a dealer in purple **c**.
1Mc 4:23 and **c** dyed blue and sea purple, and great riches.
2Es 16: 2 Bind on sackcloth and **c** of goats’ hair,

CLOTHE (24) [CLOTHED, CLOTHES, CLOTHING]

Est 4: 4 she sent garments to **c** Mordecai,
Job 39:19 Do you **c** its neck with mane?
40:10 **c** yourself with glory and splendor.
Ps 65:13 the meadows **c** themselves with flocks,
132:16 Its priests I will **c** with salvation,
132:18 His enemies I will **c** with disgrace, but on him,
Pr 23:21 and drowsiness will **c** them with rags.
Isa 22:21 and will **c** him with your robe and bind your sash
50: 3 I **c** the heavens with blackness,
Eze 26:16 They shall **c** themselves with trembling,
34: 3 You eat the fat, you **c** yourselves with the wool,
Hag 1: 6 you **c** yourselves, but no one is warm;
Zec 3: 4 and I will **c** you with festal apparel.”
Mt 6:30 will he not much more **c** you—you of little faith?
Lk 12:28 how much more will he **c** you—
1Co 12:23 of the body that we think less honorable we **c**
Eph 4:24 and to **c** yourselves with the new self,
Col 3:12 **c** yourselves with compassion, kindness, humility,
3:14 Above all, **c** yourselves with love,
1Pe 5: 5 And all of you must **c** yourselves with humility
Rev 3:18 to **c** you and to keep the shame of your nakedness
LtJ 6:33 of the clothing of their gods to **c** their wives
1Mc 10:62 to take off Jonathan’s garments and to **c** him
2Es 2:20 give to the needy, defend the orphan, **c** the naked,

CLOTHED‡ (79) [CLOTHE]

Ge 3:21 of skins for the man and for his wife, and **c** them.
Lev 8: 7 fastened the sash around him, **c** him with the robe,
8:13 and **c** them with tunics, and fastened sashes
1Sa 17:38 Saul **c** David with his armor;
17:38 he put a bronze helmet on his head and **c** him with
2Sa 1:24 weep over Saul, who **c** you with crimson,
13:18 how the virgin daughters of the king were **c**
1Ki 11:29 Ahijah had **c** himself with a new garment.
1Ch 15:27 David was **c** with a robe of fine linen,
21:16 Then David and the elders, **c** in sackcloth,
2Ch 6:41 O LORD God, be **c** with salvation,
28:15 the booty they **c** all that were naked among them;
28:15 they **c** them, gave them sandals,
Est 4: 2 for no one might enter the king’s gate **c**
Job 7: 5 My flesh is **c** with worms and dirt;
8:22 Those who hate you will be **c** with shame,
10:11 You **c** me with skin and flesh,
29:14 I put on righteousness, and it **c** me;
Ps 30:11 you have taken off my sackcloth and **c** me
35:26 let those who exalt themselves against me be **c**
104: 1 You are **c** with honor and majesty,
109:18 He **c** himself with cursing as his coat,
109:29 May my accusers be **c** with dishonor;
132: 9 Let your priests be **c** with righteousness,
Pr 31:21 for all her household are **c** in crimson.
Isa 14:19 **c** with the dead, those pierced by the sword,
61:10 for he has **c** me with the garments of salvation,
Eze 9: 2 among them was a man **c** in linen,
9: 3 The LORD called to the man **c** in linen,
9:11 Then the man **c** in linen,
10: 2 He said to the man **c** in linen,
10: 6 When he commanded the man **c** in linen,
10: 7 and put it into the hands of the man **c** in linen,
16:10 I **c** you with embroidered cloth and with sandals
23: 6 **c** in blue, governors and commanders, all
23:12 warriors **c** in full armor, mounted horsemen,
31:15 I **c** Lebanon in gloom for it,
38: 4 horses and horsemen, all of them **c** in full armor,
Da 5: 7 and tell me its interpretation shall be **c** in purple,
5:16 you shall be **c** in purple,
5:29 and Daniel was **c** in purple,
10: 5 I looked up and saw a man **c** in linen,
12: 6 One of them said to the man **c** in linen,
12: 7 The man **c** in linen, who was upstream,
Na 2: 3 his soldiers are **c** in crimson.
Zec 3: 5 So they put a clean turban on his head and **c** him
Mt 6:29 even Solomon in all his glory was not **c** like one
Mk 1: 6 Now John was **c** with camel’s hair,
5:15 **c** and in his right mind, the very man who had had
15:17 And they **c** him in a purple cloak;
Lk 8:35 **c** and in his right mind.
12:27 even Solomon in all his glory was not **c** like one
24:49 in the city until you have been **c** with power from
1Co 4:11 we are poorly **c** and beaten and homeless,
2Co 5: 2 longing to be **c** with our heavenly dwelling—
5: 4 we wish not to be unclothed but to be further **c**,
Gal 3:27 as were baptized into Christ have **c** yourselves
Col 3:10 and have **c** yourselves with the new self,
Rev 1:13 **c** with a long robe and with a golden sash
3: 5 you will be **c** like them in white robes,
12: 1 a woman **c** with the sun,
16:15 Blessed is the one who stays awake and is **c**,
17: 4 The woman was **c** in purple and scarlet,
18:16 the great city, **c** in fine linen, in purple and scarlet,
19: 8 to her it has been granted to be **c** with fine linen,
19:13 He is **c** in a robe dipped in blood,
AdE 4: 2 to enter the courtyard **c** in sackcloth and ashes.
15: 6 **c** in the full array of his majesty,
Sir 40: 4 and a crown to the one who is **c** in burlap,
45: 8 He **c** him in perfect splendor,
50:11 When he put on his glorious robe and **c** himself
1Mc 1:28 and all the house of Jacob was **c** with shame.
10:64 and saw him **c** in purple, they all fled.
14:43 and that he should be **c** in purple and wear gold.
14:44 or to be **c** in purple or put on a gold buckle.
2Mc 11: 8 **c** in white and brandishing weapons of gold.
1Es 3: 6 He shall be **c** in purple, and drink from gold cups,
2Es 1:20 of the heat I **c** you with the leaves of trees.
2:40 close the list of your people who are **c** in white,

CLOTHES‡ (131) [CLOTHE]

Ge 35: 2 and purify yourselves, and change your **c**;
37:29 that Joseph was not in the pit, he tore his **c**.
41:14 When he had shaved himself and changed his **c**,
44:13 At this they tore their **c**.
Ex 19:10 tomorrow. Have them wash their **c**
19:14 the people, and they washed their **c**.
Lev 11:25 of the carcass of any of them shall wash his **c** and
11:28 the carcass shall wash his **c** and be unclean until
11:40 Those who eat of its carcass shall wash their **c** and
11:40 the carcass shall wash their **c** and be unclean until
13: 6 and he shall wash his **c**, and be clean.
13:34 He shall wash his **c** and be clean.
13:45 the leprous disease shall wear torn **c** and let
14: 8 The one who is to be cleansed shall wash his **c**,
14: 9 Then he shall wash his **c**,
14:47 and all who sleep in the house shall wash their **c**;
14:47 and all who eat in the house shall wash their **c**.
15: 5 Anyone who touches his bed shall wash his **c**,
15: 6 with the discharge has sat shall wash their **c**,
15: 7 of the one with the discharge shall wash their **c**,
15: 8 then they shall wash their **c**, and bathe in water,
15:10 and all who carry such a thing shall wash their **c**,
15:11 in water shall wash their **c**,
15:13 he shall wash his **c** and bathe his body
15:21 Whoever touches her bed shall wash his **c**,
15:22 upon which she sits shall wash his **c**, and bathe
15:27 and shall wash his **c**, and bathe in water,
16:26 for Azazel shall wash his **c** and bathe his body
16:28 The one who burns them shall wash his **c**
17:15 shall wash their **c**, and bathe themselves in water,
Nu 8: 7 with a razor and wash their **c**,
8:21 from sin and washed their **c**;
14: 6 those who had spied out the land, tore their **c**
19: 7 the priest shall wash his **c** and bathe his body
19: 8 The one who burns the heifer shall wash his **c**
19:10 of the heifer shall wash his **c** and be unclean
19:19 Then they shall wash their **c** and bathe themselves
19:21 the water for cleansing shall wash his **c**,
31:24 You must wash your **c** on the seventh day,
Dt 8: 4 The **c** on your back did not wear out
22:11 You shall not wear **c** made of wool
29: 5 The **c** on your back have not worn out,
Jos 7: 6 Then Joshua tore his **c**, and fell to the ground
9: 5 patched sandals on their feet, and worn-out **c**;
Jdg 3:16 and he fastened it on his right thigh under his **c**.
11:35 When he saw her, he tore his **c**, and said, “Alas,
17:10 a set of **c**, and your living.”
Ru 3: 3 on your best **c** and go down to the threshing floor;
1Sa 4:12 with his **c** torn and with earth upon his head.
19:13 and covered it with the **c**.
19:24 He too stripped off his **c**,
28: 8 So Saul disguised himself and put on other **c**
2Sa 1: 2 with his **c** torn and dirt on his head.
1:11 Then David took hold of his **c** and tore them;
3:31 “Tear your **c**, and put on sackcloth,
12:20 washed, anointed himself, and changed his **c**.
19:24 or trimmed his beard, or washed his **c**,
1Ki 1: 1 they covered him with **c**, he could not get warm.
21:27 he tore his **c** and put sackcloth over his bare flesh;
2Ki 2:12 he grasped his own **c** and tore them in two pieces.
5: 7 king of Israel read the letter, he tore his **c** and said,
5: 8 of God heard that the king of Israel had torn his **c**,
5: 8 “Why have you torn your **c**?
6:30 king heard the words of the woman he tore his **c**—
11:14 Athaliah tore her **c** and cried, “Treason!
18:37 came to Hezekiah with their **c** torn and told him
19: 1 When King Hezekiah heard it, he tore his **c**,
22:11 the words of the book of the law, he tore his **c**.
22:19 because you have torn your **c** and wept before me,
25:29 So Jehoiachin put aside his prison **c**.
2Ch 23:13 Athaliah tore her **c**, and cried, “Treason!
34:19 the king heard the words of the law he tore his **c**.
34:27 and have torn your **c** and wept before me,
Ne 4:23 the guard who followed me ever took off our **c**;
9:21 their **c** did not wear out and their feet did
Est 4: 1 Mordecai tore his **c** and put on sackcloth
Job 9:31 and my own **c** will abhor me.
Ps 22:18 they divide my **c** among themselves,
Pr 6:27 be carried in the bosom without burning one’s **c**?
Isa 4: 1 “We will eat our own bread and wear our own **c**;
36:22 the recorder, came to Hezekiah with their **c** torn,
37: 1 When King Hezekiah heard it, he tore his **c**,
Jer 38:11 and took from there old rags and worn-out **c**,
38:12 “Just put the rags and **c** between your armpits and
41: 5 with their beards shaved and their **c** torn,
52:33 So Jehoiachin put aside his prison **c**,
Eze 16:39 of your **c** and take your beautiful objects
23:26 of your **c** and take away your fine jewels.
27:24 in **c** of blue and embroidered work,
Zec 3: 3 Now Joshua was dressed with filthy **c** as he stood
3: 4 before him, “Take off his filthy **c**.”
Mt 6:30 But if God so **c** the grass of the field,
17: 2 and his **c** became dazzling white.
26:65 Then the high priest tore his **c** and said,
27:31 they stripped him of the robe and put his own **c**
27:35 they divided his **c** among themselves
Mk 5:28 “If I but touch his **c**, I will be made well.”
5:30 in the crowd and said, “Who touched my **c**?”
9: 3 and his **c** became dazzling white,
14:63 Then the high priest tore his **c** and said,
15:20 of the purple cloak and put his own **c** on him.
15:24 they crucified him, and divided his **c** among them,
Lk 8:27 For a long time he had worn no **c**,
8:44 up behind him and touched the fringe of his **c**,
9:29 and his **c** became dazzling white.
12:28 But if God so **c** the grass of the field,
24: 4 suddenly two men in dazzling **c** stood
Jn 19:23 they took his **c** and divided them into four parts,
19:24 “They divided my **c** among themselves,
21: 7 he put on some **c**, for he was naked,
Ac 10:30 when suddenly a man in dazzling **c** stood
14:14 they tore their **c** and rushed out into the crowd,
18: 6 in protest he shook the dust from his **c** and said
1Ti 2: 9 or with gold, pearls, or expensive **c**,
Jas 2: 2 For if a person with gold rings and in fine **c** comes
2: 2 and if a poor person in dirty **c** also comes in,
2: 3 if you take notice of the one wearing the fine **c**
5: 2 and your **c** are moth-eaten.
Rev 3: 4 in Sardis who have not soiled their **c**;
Jdt 14:16 and wept and groaned and shouted, and tore his **c**.
AdE 4: 1 he tore his **c**, put on sackcloth,
4: 4 and sent some **c** to Mordecai to put on instead
Sir 11: 4 Do not boast about wearing fine **c**,
LtJ 6:31 in their temples the priests sit with their **c** torn,
1Mc 2:14 Then Mattathias and his sons tore their **c**,
3:47 on their heads, and tore their **c**.
4:39 Then they tore their **c** and mourned
11:71 Jonathan tore his **c**, put dust on his head,
13:45 went up on the wall with their **c** torn,
1Es 4:17 Women make men’s **c**; they bring men glory;
2Es 9:38 her **c** were torn, and there were ashes on her head.

CLOTHING‡ (72) [CLOTHE]

Ge 28:20 and will give me bread to eat and **c** to wear,
Ex 3:22 and **c**, and you shall put them on your sons and
12:35 for jewelry of silver and gold, and for **c**,
21:10 **c**, or marital rights of the first wife.
22: 9 **c**, or any other loss, of which one party says,
22:27 it may be your neighbor’s only **c** to use as cover;
Lev 13:47 Concerning **c**: when a leprous disease appears in it,
13:52 the **c**, whether diseased in warp or woof, woolen

Lev 13:53 and the disease has not spread in the **c**,
14:55 for leprous diseases in **c** and houses,
Dt 10:18 providing them food and **c**.
Jos 22: 8 bronze, and iron, and with a great quantity of **c**;
1Sa 27: 9 the camels, and the **c**, and came back to Achish.
1Ki 10: 5 and the attendance of his servants, their **c**,
2Ki 5:22 a talent of silver and two changes of **c**.' "
5:23 with two changes of **c**, and gave them to two
5:26 Is this a time to accept money and to accept **c**,
7: 8 ate and drank, carried off silver, gold, and **c**,
2Ch 9: 4 and their **c**, his valets, and their **c**,
20:25 they found livestock in great numbers, goods, **c**,
Job 22: 6 and stripped the naked of their **c**.
24: 7 They lie all night naked, without **c**,
24:10 They go about naked, without **c**;
27:16 and pile up **c** like clay—
31:19 if I have seen anyone perish for lack of **c**,
Ps 22:18 and for my **c** they cast lots.
69:11 When I made sackcloth my **c**,
102:26 You change them like **c**, and they pass away;
Pr 25:20 Like a moth in **c** or a worm in wood,
27:26 the lambs will provide your **c**, and the goats
31:22 her **c** is fine linen and purple.
31:25 Strength and dignity are her **c**,
Isa 23:18 and fine **c** for those who live in the presence of
59: 6 Their webs cannot serve as **c**;
59:17 he put on garments of vengeance for **c**,
Jer 10: 9 their **c** is blue and purple;
Eze 16:13 while your **c** was of fine linen, rich fabric,
Da 7: 9 his **c** was white as snow, and the hair of his head
Joel 2:13 rend your hearts and not your **c**.
Mt 3: 4 Now John wore **c** of camel's hair with
6:25 and the body more than **c**?
6:28 And why do you worry about **c**?
7:15 in sheep's **c** but inwardly are ravenous wolves.
25:36 I was naked and you gave me **c**,
25:38 or naked and gave you **c**?
25:43 naked and you did not give me **c**,
28: 3 and his **c** white as snow.
Lk 7:25 on fine **c** and live in luxury are in royal palaces.
12:23 life is more than food, and the body more than **c**.
23:34 And they cast lots to divide his **c**.
Jn 19:24 and for my **c** they cast lots."
Ac 9:39 and other **c** that Dorcas had made while she was
16:22 of their **c** and ordered them to be beaten with rods.
20:33 I coveted no one's silver or gold or **c**.
1Ti 2: 9 and decently in suitable **c**,
6: 8 but if we have food and **c**,
Heb 1:11 they will all wear out like **c**;
1:12 and like **c** they will be changed.
1Pe 3: 3 and by wearing gold ornaments or fine **c**;
Tob 1:17 I would give my food to the hungry and my **c** to
4:16 and some of your **c** to the naked.
10:10 oxen and sheep, donkeys and camels, **c**, money,
Jdt 8: 5 around her waist and dressed in widow's **c**.
9: 2 a virgin's **c** to defile her, and exposed her thighs
16: 7 For she put away her widow's **c** to exalt
Sir 29:21 The necessities of life are water, bread, and **c**,
39:26 the blood of the grape and oil and **c**.
LtJ 6:33 The priests take some of the **c** of their gods
1Mc 11:24 and gold and **c** and numerous other gifts.
2Mc 3:33 to Heliodorus dressed in the same **c**,
2Es 2:45 "These are they who have put off mortal **c**

CLOTHS (4) [CLOTH]

Eze 16: 4 nor rubbed with salt, nor wrapped in **c**.
Lk 24:12 he saw the linen **c** by themselves;
Jn 19:40 of Jesus and wrapped it with the spices in linen **c**,
Wis 7: 4 I was nursed with care in swaddling **c**.

CLOUD (110) [CLOUDBURST, CLOUDED, CLOUDLESS, CLOUDS, DUST-CLOUD]

A. PILLAR OF CLOUD (13)

Ex 13:21 The LORD went in front of them in a pillar of **c** A
13:22 the pillar of **c** by day nor the pillar of fire A
14:19 and the pillar of **c** moved from in front of them A
14:20 And so the **c** was there with the darkness,
14:24 the LORD in the pillar of fire and **c** looked down
16:10 and the glory of the LORD appeared in the **c**.
19: 9 "I am going to come to you in a dense **c**,
19:16 as well as a thick **c** on the mountain,
24:15 and the **c** covered the mountain.
24:16 and the **c** covered it for six days;
24:16 on the seventh day he called to Moses out of the **c**.
24:18 Moses entered the **c**, and went up on
33: 9 the pillar of **c** would descend and stand at the A
33:10 When all the people saw the pillar of **c** standing A
34: 5 The LORD descended in the **c** and stood
40:34 Then the **c** covered the tent of meeting,
40:35 the tent of meeting because the **c** settled upon it,
40:36 Whenever the **c** was taken up from the tabernacle,
40:37 but if the **c** was not taken up,
40:38 the **c** of the LORD was on the tabernacle by day,
40:38 and fire was in the **c** by night,
Lev 16: 2 for I appear in the **c** upon the mercy seat.
16:13 that the **c** of the incense may cover the mercy seat
Nu 9:15 the **c** covered the tabernacle,
9:16 the **c** covered it by day and the appearance of fire
9:17 Whenever the **c** lifted from over the tent,
9:17 and in the place where the **c** settled down,
9:18 As long as the **c** rested over the tabernacle,
9:19 the **c** continued over the tabernacle many days,
9:20 Sometimes the **c** would remain a few days over
9:21 the **c** would remain from evening until morning;
Nu 9:21 and when the **c** lifted in the morning,
9:21 when the **c** lifted they would set out.
9:22 that the **c** continued over the tabernacle,
10:11 **c** lifted from over the tabernacle of the covenant.
10:12 and the **c** settled down in the wilderness of Paran.
10:34 the **c** of the LORD being over them by day
11:25 the LORD came down in the **c** and spoke to him,
12: 5 Then the LORD came down in a pillar of **c**, A
12:10 When the **c** went away from over the tent,
14:14 and your **c** stands over them and you go in front
14:14 you go in front of them, in a pillar of **c** by day A
16:42 the **c** had covered it and the glory of
Dt 1:33 in fire by night, and in the **c** by day,
5:22 out of the fire, the **c**, and the thick darkness,
31:15 the LORD appeared at the tent in a pillar of **c**; A
31:15 the pillar of **c** stood at the entrance to the tent. A
Jdg 20:38 that when they sent up a **c** of smoke out of the city
20:40 But when the **c**, a column of smoke,
1Ki 8:10 a **c** filled the house of the LORD,
8:11 not stand to minister because of the **c**;
18:44 a little **c** no bigger than
2Ch 5:13 the house of the LORD, was filled with a **c**,
5:14 not stand to minister because of the **c**;
Ne 9:12 you led them by day with a pillar of **c**, A
9:19 pillar of **c** that led them in the way did not leave A
Job 7: 9 As the **c** fades and vanishes,
26: 8 and the **c** is not torn open by them.
26: 9 and spreads over it his **c**.
30:15 and my prosperity has passed away like a **c**.
37:11 He loads the thick **c** with moisture;
37:15 and causes the lightning of his **c** to shine?
Ps 78:14 In the daytime he led them with a **c**,
99: 7 He spoke to them in the pillar of **c**; A
105:39 He spread a **c** for a covering,
Isa 4: 5 of assembly a **c** by day and smoke and the shining
18: 4 like a **c** of dew in the heat of harvest.
19: 1 LORD is riding on a swift **c** and comes to Egypt;
44:22 I have swept away your transgressions like a **c**,
60: 8 Who are these that fly like a **c**,
La 3:44 with a **c** so that no prayer can pass through.
Eze 1: 4 a great **c** with brightness around it
1:28 Like the bow in a **c** on a rainy day,
8:11 and the fragrant **c** of incense was ascending.
10: 3 and a **c** filled the inner court.
10: 4 the house was filled with the **c**,
30:18 the city shall be covered by a **c**,
32: 7 I will cover the sun with a **c**,
38: 9 you shall be like a **c** covering the land,
38:16 like a **c** covering the earth.
Hos 6: 4 Your love is like a morning **c**,
Mt 17: 5 suddenly a bright **c** overshadowed them,
17: 5 and from the **c** a voice said, "This is my Son,
Mk 9: 7 Then a **c** overshadowed them,
9: 7 and from the **c** there came a voice,
Lk 9:34 a **c** came and overshadowed them;
9:34 and they were terrified as they entered the **c**.
9:35 Then from the **c** came a voice that said,
12:54 "When you see a **c** rising in the west,
21:27 of Man coming in a **c**' with power and great glory.
Ac 1: 9 and a **c** took him out of their sight.
1Co 10: 1 that our ancestors were all under the **c**,
10: 2 and all were baptized into Moses in the **c** and in
Heb 12: 1 we are surrounded by so great a **c** of witnesses,
Rev 10: 1 wrapped in a **c**, with a rainbow over his head;
11:12 in a **c** while their enemies watched them.
14:14 Then I looked, and there was a white **c**,
14:14 and seated on the **c** was one like the Son of Man,
14:15 with a loud voice to the one who sat on the **c**,
14:16 So the one who sat on the **c** swung his sickle over
Wis 2: 4 our life will pass away like the traces of a **c**,
19: 7 The **c** was seen overshadowing the camp,
Sir 24: 4 and my throne was in a pillar of **c**. A
45: 5 and led him into the dark **c**,
2Mc 2: 8 and the glory of the Lord and the **c** will appear,
2Es 4:49 And after this a **c** full of water passed before me
4:49 drops still remained in the **c**.
7:*40* or **c** or thunder or lightning,
13:20 than to pass from the world like a **c**,
15:39 the **c** that was raised in wrath, and shall dispel it;

CLOUDBURST (1) [CLOUD]

Isa 30:30 with a **c** and tempest and hailstones.

CLOUDED (1) [CLOUD]

2Mc 1:22 and when the sun, which had been **c** over,

CLOUDLESS (1) [CLOUD]

2Sa 23: 4 like the sun rising on a **c** morning,

CLOUDS‡ (76) [CLOUD]

Ge 9:13 I have set my bow in the **c**,
9:14 When I bring **c** over the earth and the bow is seen in the **c**,
9:16 When the bow is in the **c**,
Dt 4:11 up to the very heavens, shrouded in dark **c**.
Jdg 5: 4 the **c** indeed poured water.
2Sa 22:12 He made darkness around him a canopy, thick **c**,
1Ki 18:45 while the heavens grew black with **c** and wind;
Job 3: 5 and deep darkness claim it. Let **c** settle upon it;
20: 6 and their head reaches to the **c**,
22:14 Thick **c** enwrap him, so that he does not see,
26: 8 He binds up the waters in his thick **c**,
35: 5 observe the **c**, which are higher than you.
36:29 Can anyone understand the spreading of the **c**,
37:11 the **c** scatter his lightning.
Job 37:16 Do you know the balancings of the **c**,
38: 9 when I made the **c** its garment,
38:34 "Can you lift up your voice to the **c**,
38:37 Who has the wisdom to number the **c**?
Ps 18:11 his canopy thick **c** dark with water.
18:12 before him there broke through his **c** hailstones
36: 5 extends to the heavens, your faithfulness to the **c**.
57:10 your faithfulness extends to the **c**.
68: 4 lift up a song to him who rides upon the **c**—
77:17 The **c** poured out water; the skies thundered;
97: 2 **C** and thick darkness are all around him;
104: 3 you make the **c** your chariot,
108: 4 and your faithfulness reaches to the **c**.
135: 7 He it is who makes the **c** rise at the end of
147: 8 He covers the heavens with **c**,
Pr 3:20 and the **c** drop down the dew.
16:15 his favor is like the **c** that bring the spring rain.
25:14 Like **c** and wind without rain is one who boasts of
Ecc 11: 3 When **c** are full, they empty rain on the earth;
11: 4 and whoever regards the **c** will not reap.
12: 2 and the stars are darkened and the **c** return with
Isa 5: 6 also command the **c** that they rain no rain upon it.
5:30 and the light grows dark with **c**.
14:14 I will ascend to the tops of the **c**,
25: 5 you subdued the heat with the shade of **c**;
Jer 4:13 up like **c**, his chariots like the whirlwind;
Eze 30: 3 it will be a day of **c**, a time of doom for the nations.
31: 3 and of great height, its top among the **c**.
31:10 it towered high and set its top among the **c**,
31:14 to lofty height or set their tops among the **c**,
34:12 to which they have been scattered on a day of **c**
Da 7:13 like a human being coming with the **c** of heaven.
Joel 2: 2 a day of **c** and thick darkness!
Na 1: 3 and the **c** are the dust of his feet.
Zep 1:15 a day of **c** and thick darkness,
Zec 10: 1 from the LORD who makes the storm **c**,
Mt 24:30 and they will see 'the Son of Man coming on the **c**
26:64 at the right hand of Power and coming on the **c**
Mk 13:26 Son of Man coming in **c**' with great power and
14:62 and 'coming with the **c** of heaven.' "
1Th 4:17 up in the **c** together with them to meet the Lord in
Jude 1:12 They are waterless **c** carried along by the winds;
Rev 1: 7 He is coming with the **c**;
Wis 5:21 and will leap from the **c** to the target,
Sir 13:23 they extol to the **c** what he says.
35:20 and his prayer will reach to the **c**.
35:21 The prayer of the humble pierces the **c**,
35:26 as welcome in time of distress as **c** of rain in time
43:14 and the **c** fly out like birds.
43:15 In his majesty he gives the **c** their strength,
50: 6 Like the morning star among the **c**,
50: 7 like the rainbow gleaming in splendid **c**;
50:10 and like a cypress towering in the **c**.
Bar 3:29 and taken her, and brought her down from the **c**?
LtJ 6:62 God commands the **c** to go over the whole world,
Aza 1:51 Bless the Lord, lightnings and **c**;
2Es 11: 2 and the **c** were gathered around it.
13: 3 And I saw that this man flew with the **c** of heaven;
15:34 See the **c** from the east,
15:38 heavy storm **c** shall be stirred up from the south,
15:40 Great and mighty **c**, full of wrath and tempest,

CLOVEN (KJV) See DIVIDED

CLUB (4) [CLUBS]

Pr 25:18 Like a war **c**, a sword,
Isa 10: 5 the **c** in their hands is my fury!
Jer 51:20 You are my war **c**, my weapon of battle:
Bel 1:26 and I will kill the dragon without sword or **c**."

CLUBS (6) [CLUB]

Job 41:29 **C** are counted as chaff; it laughs at the
Mt 26:47 with him was a large crowd with swords and **c**,
26:55 with swords and **c** to arrest me as though I were
Mk 14:43 with him there was a crowd with swords and **c**,
14:48 with swords and **c** to arrest me as though I were
Lk 22:52 "Have you come out with swords and **c** as

CLUE See Index to Footnotes

CLUNG (8) [CLING]

Ru 1:14 Orpah kissed her mother-in-law, but Ruth **c** to her.
2Sa 23:10 though his hand **c** to the sword.
1Ki 11: 2 Solomon **c** to these in love.
2Ki 3: 3 he **c** to the sin of Jeroboam son of Nebat,
Job 31: 7 and if any spot has **c** to my hands;
Ac 3:11 While he **c** to Peter and John,
Bar 1:20 So to this day there have **c** to us the calamities and
3: 4 so that calamities have **c** to us.

CLUSTER‡ (7) [CLUSTERS]

Nu 13:23 and cut down from there a branch with a single **c**
13:24 of the **c** that the Israelites cut down from there.
SS 1:14 a **c** of henna blossoms in the vineyards of En-gedi.
Isa 65: 8 As the wine is found in the **c**, and they say,
Mic 7: 1 finds no **c** to eat; there is no first-ripe fig
2Es 9:21 and saved for myself one grape out of a **c**,
12:42 like a **c** of grapes from the vintage,

CLUSTERS (10) [CLUSTER]

Ge 40:10 its blossoms came out and the **c** ripened
Dt 32:32 their grapes are grapes of poison, their **c** are bitter;
1Sa 25:18 one hundred **c** of raisins, and two hundred cakes

1Sa 30:12 they also gave him a piece of fig cake and two **c**
1Ch 12:40 cakes of figs, **c** of raisins, wine, oil, oxen,
SS 7: 7 and your breasts are like its **c.**
7: 8 Oh, may your breasts be like **c** of the vine,
Isa 16: 8 whose **c** once made drunk the lords of the nations,
Rev 14:18 "Use your sharp sickle and gather the **c** of the vine
2Es 16:30 some **c** may be left by those who search carefully

CNIDUS (2)
Ac 27: 7 of days and arrived with difficulty off **C,**
1Mc 15:23 and to Aradus and Gortyna and **C** and Cyprus

CO-WORKER (6) [WORK]
Ro 16: 9 Greet Urbanus, our **c** in Christ,
16:21 Timothy, my **c,** greets you;
2Co 8:23 for Titus, he is my partner and **c** in your service;
Php 2:25 my brother and **c** and fellow soldier,
1Th 3: 2 and **c** for God in proclaiming the gospel of Christ,
Phm 1: 1 To Philemon our dear friend and **c,**

CO-WORKERS (3) [WORK]
Php 4: 3 together with Clement and the rest of my **c,**
Col 4:11 the only ones of the circumcision among my **c** for
3Jn 1: 8 so that we may become **c** with the truth.

COAL (2) [COALS]
Isa 6: 6 holding a live **c** that had been taken from the altar
47:14 No **c** for warming oneself is this,

COALS‡ (22) [COAL]
Lev 16:12 a censer full of **c** of fire from the altar before
2Sa 22: 9 glowing **c** flamed forth from him.
22:13 of the brightness before him **c** of fire flamed forth.
Job 41:21 Its breath kindles **c,** and a flame comes out
Ps 11: 6 On the wicked he will rain **c** of fire and sulfur;
18: 8 glowing **c** flamed forth from him.
18:12 through his clouds hailstones and **c** of fire.
120: 4 with glowing **c** of the broom tree!
140:10 Let burning **c** fall on them!
Pr 6:28 can one walk on hot **c** without scorching the feet?
25:22 for you will heap **c** of fire on their heads,
Isa 44:12 The ironsmith fashions it and works it over the **c,**
44:19 I also baked bread on its **c,**
54:16 the smith who blows the fire of **c,** and produces
Eze 1:13 like burning **c** of fire, like torches moving to
10: 2 fill your hands with burning **c** from among
24:11 Stand it empty upon the **c,**
Ro 12:20 for by doing this you will heap burning **c**
Sir 8:10 Do not kindle the **c** of sinners,
11:32 From a spark many **c** are kindled,
2Es 16:53 for God will burn **c** of fire on the head
4Mc 9:20 the heap of **c** was being quenched by the drippings

COARSE (4)
Lev 2:14 the grain offering of your first fruits **c** new grain
2:16 of the **c** grain and oil with all its frankincense;
Sir 20:19 A **c** person is like an inappropriate story,
23:13 Do not accustom your mouth to **c,** foul language,

COAST (10) [COASTAL, COASTLAND, COASTLANDS, COASTS, SEACOAST]
Nu 34: 6 you shall have the Great Sea and its **c;**
Jos 9: 1 and in the lowland all along the **c** of the Great Sea
15:12 west boundary was the Mediterranean with its **c.**
15:47 to the Wadi of Egypt, and the Great Sea with its **c.**
Jdg 5:17 Asher sat still at the **c** of the sea,
Isa 23: 2 Be still, O inhabitants of the **c,**
23: 6 wail, O inhabitants of the **c!**
Lk 6:17 Jerusalem, and the **c** of Tyre and Sidon.
Ac 17:14 the believers immediately sent Paul away to the **c,**
27: 2 that was about to set sail to the ports along the **c**

COASTAL (2) [COAST]
1Mc 11: 8 So King Ptolemy gained control of the **c** cities
15:38 of the **c** country, and gave him troops of infantry

COASTLAND (6) [COAST, LAND]
Ge 10: 5 From these the **c** peoples spread.
Isa 20: 6 In that day the inhabitants of this **c** will say, 'See,
Jer 25:22 and the kings of the **c** across the sea;
47: 4 the remnant of the **c** of Caphtor.
Jdt 5: 2 of Ammon and all the governors of the **c,**
7: 8 the Moabites and the commanders of the **c** came

COASTLANDS (22) [COAST, LAND]
Ps 97: 1 Let the earth rejoice; let the many **c** be glad!
Isa 11:11 from Hamath, and from the **c** of the sea.
24:15 in the **c** of the sea glorify the name of the LORD,
41: 1 Listen to me in silence, O **c;**
41: 5 The **c** have seen and are afraid,
42: 4 and the **c** wait for his teaching.
42:10 the **c** and their inhabitants.
42:12 and declare his praise in the **c.**
49: 1 Listen to me, O **c,** pay attention,
51: 5 the **c** wait for me, and for my arm they hope.
59:18 to the **c** he will render requital.
60: 9 For the **c** shall wait for me,
66:19 to the **c** far away that have not heard of my fame
Jer 31:10 O nations, and declare it in the **c** far away;
Eze 26:15 Shall not the **c** shake at the sound of your fall,
26:18 Now the **c** tremble on the day of your fall;
26:18 the **c** by the sea are dismayed at your passing.
Eze 27: 3 merchant of the peoples on many **c,**
27:15 many **c** were your own special markets;
27:35 All the inhabitants of the **c** are appalled at you;
39: 6 and on those who live securely in the **c;**
Da 11:18 Afterward he shall turn to the **c,**

COASTS (5) [COAST]
Jer 2:10 Cross to the **c** of Cyprus and look,
Eze 27: 6 they made your deck of pines from the **c**
27: 7 from the **c** of Elishah was your awning.
Zep 2:11 all the **c** and islands of the nations.
Jdt 1:12 as far as the **c** of the two seas.

COAT‡ (14) [COATS]
Ex 28:32 like the opening in a **c** of mail,
39:23 in the middle of it was like the opening in a **c**
1Sa 17: 5 and he was armed with a **c** of mail;
17: 5 the weight of the **c** was five thousand shekels
17:38 on his head and clothed him with a **c** of mail.
2Sa 15:32 to meet him with his **c** torn and earth on his head.
Job 41:13 Who can penetrate its double **c** of mail?
Ps 109:18 He clothed himself with cursing as his **c,**
Jer 51: 3 and let him not array himself in his **c** of mail.
Mt 5:40 and if anyone wants to sue you and take your **c,**
24:18 the one in the field must not turn back to get a **c.**
Mk 13:16 the one in the field must not turn back to get a **c.**
Lk 6:29 and from anyone who takes away your **c** do
Wis 13:14 a **c** of red paint and coloring its surface red

COAT OF MANY COLOURS (KJV) See ROBE WITH SLEEVES

COATS (6) [COAT]
2Ch 26:14 helmets, **c** of mail, bows, and stones for slinging.
Jer 46: 4 whet your lances, put on your **c** of mail!
Lk 3:11 "Whoever has two **c** must share
Ac 7:58 and the witnesses laid their **c** at the feet of
22:20 and keeping the **c** of those who killed him.'
1Mc 6:35 a thousand men armed with **c** of mail,

COAX (2)
Jdg 14:15 "**C** your husband to explain the riddle to us,
16: 5 "**C** him, and find out what makes his strength

COCK‡ (13) [COCKCROW]
Mt 26:34 before the **c** crows, you will deny me three times."
26:74 At that moment the **c** crowed.
26:75 the **c** crows, you will deny me three times."
Mk 14:30 this day, this very night, before the **c** crows twice,
14:68 into the forecourt. Then the **c** crowed.
14:72 At that moment the **c** crowed for the second time.
14:72 "Before the **c** crows twice, you will deny me
Lk 22:34 "I tell you, Peter, the **c** will not crow this day,
22:60 while he was still speaking, the **c** crowed.
22:61 "Before the **c** crows today,
Jn 13:38 Very truly, I tell you, before the **c** crows,
18:27 and at that moment the **c** crowed.
3Mc 5:23 as soon as the **c** had crowed in the early morning,

COCKATRICE (KJV) See ADDER, VIPER

COCKCROW (1) [COCK, CROW]
Mk 13:35 in the evening, or at midnight, or at **c,** or at dawn,

COCKCROWING (KJV) See COCKCROW

COCKLE (KJV) See WEED

CODE (2)
Ro 2:27 that have the written **c** and circumcision but break
7: 6 that we are slaves not under the old written **c** but

COELESYRIA (14)
1Mc 10:69 the governor of **C,** and he assembled a large force
2Mc 3: 5 at that time was governor of **C** and Phoenicia,
3: 8 of inspection of the cities of **C** and Phoenicia,
4: 4 and governor of **C** and Phoenicia,
8: 8 the governor of **C** and Phoenicia,
10:11 of the government and to be chief governor of **C**
1Es 2:17 and the judges in **C** and Phoenicia:
2:24 you will no longer have access to **C**
2:27 and exacted tribute from **C** and Phoenicia.
4:48 the governors in **C** and Phoenicia and to those
6:29 that out of the tribute of **C** and Phoenicia a portion
7: 1 Then Sisinnes the governor of **C** and Phoenicia,
8:67 to the royal stewards and to the governors of **C**
3Mc 3:15 not rule the nations inhabiting **C** and Phoenicia by

COERCIVE (1)
4Mc 9: 6 we young men should die despising your **c** tortures,

COFFER (KJV) See BOX

COFFERS (1)
1Mc 3:28 He opened his **c** and gave a year's pay

COFFIN (1)
Ge 50:26 he was embalmed and placed in a **c** in Egypt.

COGNITIONS (KJV) See THOUGHTS

COHORT (5)
Mt 27:27 and they gathered the whole **c** around him.
Mk 15:16 and they called together the whole **c.**
Ac 10: 1 a centurion of the Italian **C,** as it was called.
21:31 to the tribune of the **c** that all Jerusalem was in
27: 1 to a centurion of the Augustan **C,**

COIN (3) [COINAGE, COINS]
Mt 17:27 and when you open its mouth, you will find a **c;**
22:19 Show me the **c** used for the tax."
Lk 15: 9 for I have found the **c** that I had lost.'

COINAGE (1) [COIN]
1Mc 15: 6 to mint your own **c** as money for your country,

COINS (5) [COIN]
Mk 12:42 poor widow came and put in two small copper **c,**
Lk 15: 8 "Or what woman having ten silver **c,**
21: 2 also saw a poor widow put in two small copper **c.**
Jn 2:15 He also poured out the **c** of the money changers
Ac 19:19 it was found to come to fifty thousand silver **c.**

COL-HOZEH (2)
Ne 3:15 Shallum son of **C,** ruler of the district of Mizpah,
11: 5 and Maaseiah son of Baruch son of **C** son

COLD‡ (23)
Ge 8:22 **c** and heat, summer and winter, day and night,
31:40 by day the heat consumed me, and the **c** by night,
Job 24: 7 without clothing, and have no covering in the **c.**
37: 9 and **c** from the scattering winds.
Ps 147:17 who can stand before his **c?**
Pr 25:13 Like the **c** of snow in the time
25:25 Like **c** water to a thirsty soul,
Jer 18:14 mountain waters run dry, the **c** flowing streams?
Na 3:17 of locusts settling on the fences on a **c** day—
Zec 14: 6 On that day there shall not be either **c** or frost.
Mt 10:42 even a cup of **c** water to one of these little ones in
24:12 the love of many will grow **c.**
Jn 18:18 a charcoal fire because it was **c,**
Ac 28: 2 Since it had begun to rain and was **c,**
2Co 11:27 often without food, **c** and naked.
Rev 3:15 you are neither **c** nor hot.
3:15 I wish that you were either **c** or hot.
3:16 because you are lukewarm, and neither **c** nor hot,
Sir 43:20 **c** north wind blows, and ice freezes on the water;
Aza 1:45 Bless the Lord, winter **c** and summer heat;
1:49 Bless the Lord, ice and **c;**
2Es 7:*41* summer or spring or heat or winter or frost or **c,**
4Mc 11:26 Your fire is **c** to us, and the catapults painless,

COLIC (1)
Sir 31:20 of sleeplessness and of nausea and **c** are with

COLLAPSE (2) [COLLAPSED, COLLAPSING]
Ps 20: 8 They will **c** and fall, but we shall rise
Isa 30:13 and about to **c,** whose crash comes suddenly,

COLLAPSED (2) [COLLAPSE]
Jdg 7:13 it turned upside down, and the tent **c.**"
AdE 15: 7 and **c** on the head of the maid who went in front

COLLAPSING (1) [COLLAPSE]
Jdt 7:22 and young men fainted from thirst and were **c** in

COLLAR (6) [COLLARS]
Job 30:18 he grasps me by the **c** of my tunic.
Ps 105:18 his neck was put in a **c** of iron;
133: 2 running down over the **c** of his robes.
Jer 29:26 to put him in the stocks and the **c.**
Sir 6:24 and your neck into her **c.**
6:29 and her **c** a glorious robe.

COLLARS (1) [COLLAR]
Jdg 8:26 and the **c** that were on the necks of their camels).

COLLEAGUES (3)
Ezr 7:18 to you and your **c** to do with the rest of the silver
8:17 to Iddo and his **c** the temple servants at Casiphia,
Zec 3: 8 high priest, you and your **c** who sit before you!

COLLECT (18) [COLLECTED, COLLECTING, COLLECTION, COLLECTIONS, COLLECTOR, COLLECTORS, COLLECTS]
1Sa 20:21 'Look, the arrows are on this side of you, **c** them,'
2Ki 6: 2 Let us go to the Jordan, and let us **c** logs there,
Ne 10:37 the Levites who **c** the tithes in all our rural towns.
Na 2: 1 gird your loins; **c** all your strength.
Hab 2: 5 and **c** all peoples as their own.
Zec 6:10 **C** silver and gold from the exiles—
Mt 13:30 **C** the weeds first and bind them in bundles to
13:41 and they will **c** out of his kingdom all causes
21:34 he sent his slaves to the tenants to **c** his produce.
Mk 8:19 many baskets full of broken pieces did you **c?**"

Mk 8:20 many baskets full of broken pieces did you **c**?"
12: 2 a slave to the tenants to **c** from them his share of
Lk 3:13 "**C** no more than the amount prescribed for you."
Heb 7: 5 a commandment in the law to **c** tithes from
Jdt 3:10 and remained for a whole month in order to **c** all
1Mc 3:31 and **c** the revenues from those regions and raise
10:30 I will not **c** them from the land of Judah or from
1Es 8:13 and to **c** for the Lord in Jerusalem all the gold

COLLECTED (21) [COLLECT]

Ge 47:14 Joseph **c** all the money to be found in the land
Jdg 11: 3 Outlaws **c** around Jephthah and went raiding
2Ki 22: 4 which the keepers of the threshold have **c** from
2Ch 24:11 they did day after day, and **c** money in abundance.
34: 9 had **c** from Manasseh and Ephraim and from all
Ecc 12:11 the **c** sayings that are given by one shepherd.
Isa 22: 9 and you **c** the waters of the lower pool.
Zec 14:14 wealth of all the surrounding nations shall be **c**—
Mt 13:40 Just as the weeds are **c** and burned up with fire,
Lk 19:23 when I returned, I could have **c** it with interest.'
Ac 19:19 of those who practiced magic **c** their books
Ro 15:28 and have delivered to them what has been **c**,
Heb 7: 6 to their ancestry, **c** tithes from Abraham
Bar 1: 6 they **c** as much money as each could give,
1Mc 13:39 and whatever other tax has been **c** in Jerusalem
shall be **c** no longer.
2Mc 2:13 and also that he founded a library and **c** the books
2:14 also **c** all the books that had been lost on account
8:27 When they had **c** the arms of the enemy
8:31 They **c** the arms of the enemy,
10:24 gathered a tremendous force of mercenaries and **c**

COLLECTING (2) [COLLECT]

1Mc 1:35 **c** the spoils of Jerusalem they stored them there,
10:30 and instead of **c** the third of the grain and the half

COLLECTION (4) [COLLECT]

Isa 57:13 When you cry out, let your **c** of idols deliver you!
1Co 16: 1 Now concerning the **c** for the saints:
2Mc 4:28 for the **c** of the revenue was his responsibility—
12:43 He also took up a **c**, man by man,

COLLECTIONS (1) [COLLECT]

1Co 16: 2 so that **c** need not be taken when I come.

COLLECTOR (8) [COLLECT]

Mt 10: 3 Thomas and Matthew the tax **c**;
18:17 let such a one be to you as a Gentile and a tax **c**.
Lk 5:27 this he went out and saw a tax **c** named Levi,
18:10 one a Pharisee and the other a tax **c**.
18:11 thieves, rogues, adulterers, or even like this tax **c**.
18:13 But the tax **c**, standing far off,
19: 2 he was a chief tax **c** and was rich.
1Mc 1:29 the king sent to the cities of Judah a chief **c**

COLLECTORS (16) [COLLECT]

Mt 5:46 Do not even the tax **c** do the same?
9:10 many tax **c** and sinners came and were sitting
9:11 "Why does your teacher eat with tax **c**
11:19 a friend of tax **c** and sinners!'
17:24 the **c** of the temple tax came to Peter and said,
21:31 the tax **c** and the prostitutes are going into
21:32 but the tax **c** and the prostitutes believed him;
Mk 2:15 many tax **c** and sinners were also sitting
2:16 that he was eating with sinners and tax **c**,
2:16 "Why does he eat with tax **c** and sinners?"
Lk 3:12 Even tax **c** came to be baptized,
5:29 of tax **c** and others sitting at the table with them.
5:30 "Why do you eat and drink with tax **c**
7:29 all the people who heard this, including the tax **c**,
7:34 a friend of tax **c** and sinners!'
15: 1 the tax **c** and sinners were coming near to listen

COLLECTS (1) [COLLECT]

Sir 14: 4 What he denies himself he **c** for others;

COLLEGE (KJV) See SECOND QUARTER

COLONNADE (4)

1Ch 26:18 for the **c** on the west there were four at the road
and two at the **c**.
2Mc 4:46 taking the king aside into a **c** as if for refreshment,
3Mc 5:23 began to move them along in the great **c**.

COLONY (2)

Ac 16:12 of the district of Macedonia and a Roman **c**.
Wis 12: 7 to you might receive a worthy **c** of the servants

COLOR (7) [COLORED, COLORFUL, COLORING, COLORS, MANY-COLORED]

Lev 13:55 If the diseased spot has not changed **c**,
Nu 11: 7 and its **c** was like the **c** of gum resin.
Rev 9:17 the riders wore breastplates the **c** of fire and
2Mc 3:16 and the change in his **c** disclosed the anguish
2Es 6:44 and flowers of inimitable **c**,
14:39 it was full of something like water, but its **c** was

COLORED (4) [COLOR]

1Ch 29: 2 antimony, **c** stones, all sorts of precious stones,
Est 1: 6 marble, mother-of-pearl, and **c** stones.
Pr 7:16 **c** spreads of Egyptian linen;
Eze 27:24 and in carpets of **c** material,

COLORFUL (1) [COLOR]

Eze 16:16 and made for yourself **c** shrines,

COLORING (1) [COLOR]

Wis 13:14 and **c** its surface red and covering every blemish

COLORS‡ (4) [COLOR]

Eze 17: 3 rich in plumage of many **c**, came to the Lebanon.
AdE 1: 6 embroidered in various **c**,
Wis 15: 4 a figure stained with varied **c**,
2Es 9:17 and as are the flowers, so are the **c**;

COLOSSAE (1)

Col 1: 2 and faithful brothers and sisters in Christ in **C**:

COLT (14) [COLTS]

Ge 49:11 Binding his foal to the vine and his donkey's **c** to
Zec 9: 9 humble and riding on a donkey, on a **c**,
Mt 21: 2 and a **c** with her; untie them and bring them to me.
21: 5 humble, and mounted on a donkey, and on a **c**,
21: 7 they brought the donkey and the **c**,
Mk 11: 2 a **c** that has never been ridden;
11: 4 They went away and found a **c** tied near a door,
11: 5 "What are you doing, untying the **c**?"
11: 7 the **c** to Jesus and threw their cloaks on it;
Lk 19:30 and as you enter it you will find tied there a **c**
19:33 As they were untying the **c**,
19:33 "Why are you untying the **c**?"
19:35 throwing their cloaks on the **c**, they set Jesus on it.
Jn 12:15 your king is coming, sitting on a donkey's **c**!"

COLTS (1) [COLT]

Ge 32:15 thirty milch camels and their **c**,

COLUMN (3) [COLUMNS]

Jdg 20:40 But when the cloud, a **c** of smoke,
SS 3: 6 from the wilderness, like a **c** of smoke, perfumed
Isa 9:18 and they swirled upward in a **c** of smoke.

COLUMNS (7) [COLUMN]

1Ki 7:18 the **c** with two rows around each latticework
Job 1:17 "The Chaldeans formed three **c**,
SS 5:15 His legs are alabaster **c**, set upon bases of gold.
Jer 36:23 As Jehudi read three or four **c**,
Joel 2:30 blood and fire and **c** of smoke.
1Mc 13:29 erecting about them great **c**,
13:29 and on the **c** he put suits of armor for

COMBAT (2)

2Ch 32: 6 He appointed **c** commanders over the people,
Pm 151: T *after he fought in single* **c** *with Goliath.*

COMBED (1)

Jdt 10: 3 She **c** her hair, put on a tiara,

COMBINE (1) [COMBINED]

2Es 15:31 if they **c** in great power and turn to pursue them,

COMBINED (2) [COMBINE]

1Ti 6: 6 in godliness **c** with contentment;
Jdt 1:16 he returned to Nineveh, he and all his **c** forces,

COME‡ (1831) [CAME, COMES, COMING, COMINGS, OUTCOME]

A. TIME TO COME (11)
B. AGE TO COME (7)
C. DAYS TO COME (6)
D. THINGS TO COME (6)

Ge 6:18 and you shall **c** into the ark, you, your sons,
6:20 two of every kind shall **c** in to you,
10:14 and Caphtorim, from which the Philistines **c**.
11: 3 And they said to one another, "**C**,
11: 4 Then they said, "**C**, let us build ourselves a city,
11: 7 **C**, let us go down, and confuse their language
12: 5 When they had **c** to the land of Canaan,
15:14 afterward they shall **c** out with great possessions.
15:16 they shall **c** back here in the fourth generation;
16: 8 where have you **c** from and where are you going?"
17: 6 and kings shall **c** from you.
17:16 kings of peoples shall **c** from her."
18: 5 since you have **c** to your servant."
18:21 according to the outcry that has **c** to me;
19: 8 for they have **c** under the shelter of my roof."
19:31 a man on earth to **c** in to us after the manner of all
19:32 **C**, let us make our father drink wine,
20:13 at every place to which we **c**, say of me,
21:18 **C**, lift up the boy and hold him fast
22: 5 we will worship, and then we will **c** back to you."
24:31 He said, "**C** in, O blessed of the LORD.
24:41 when you **c** to my kindred;
24:62 Now Isaac had **c** from Beer-lahai-roi,
26:27 Isaac said to them, "Why have you **c** to me,
27:21 Then Isaac said to Jacob, "**C** near,
27:26 his father Isaac said to him, "**C** near and kiss me,
28:21 so that I **c** again to my father's house in peace,
29: 4 "My brothers, where do you **c** from?"
30:16 and said, "You must **c** in to me;
Ge 30:33 when you **c** to look into my wages with you.
31:44 **C** now, let us make a covenant, you and I;
32:11 he may **c** and kill us all,
33:14 until I **c** to my lord in Seir."
35: 3 then **c**, let us go up to Bethel, that I may make
35:11 nation and a company of nations shall **c** from you,
37:10 Shall we indeed **c**, I and your mother
37:13 **C**, I will send you to them."
37:20 **C** now, let us kill him and throw him into one of
37:27 **C**, let us sell him to the Ishmaelites,
38:16 and said, "**C**, let me **c** in to you,"
38:16 that you may **c** in to me?"
41:29 There will **c** seven years of great plenty
41:54 and the seven years of famine began to **c**,
42: 4 for he feared that harm might **c** to him.
42: 7 "Where do you **c** from?"
42: 9 you have **c** to see the nakedness of the land!"
42:10 your servants have **c** to buy food.
42:12 "No, you have **c** to see the nakedness of the land!"
42:21 That is why this anguish has **c** upon us."
42:38 If harm should **c** to him on the journey
44:30 when I **c** to your servant my father and the boy is
44:34 to see the suffering that would **c** upon my father."
45: 4 Joseph said to his brothers, "**C** closer to me."
45: 9 **c** down to me, do not delay.
45:11 since there are five more years of famine to **c**—
45:11 and all that you have, will not **c** to poverty.'
45:16 "Joseph's brothers have **c**,"
45:18 Take your father and your households and **c**
45:19 and bring your father, and **c**.
46:31 who were in the land of Canaan, have **c** to me.
47: 1 have **c** from the land of Canaan;
47: 4 "We have **c** to reside as aliens in the land;
47: 5 "Your father and your brothers have **c** to you.
48: 2 Jacob was told, "Your son Joseph has **c** to you,"
49: 1 what will happen to you in days to **c**. C
49: 6 May I never **c** into their council;
50:24 but God will surely **c** to you,
Ex 1:10 **C**, let us deal shrewdly with them,
2:18 "How is it that you have **c** back so soon today?"
3: 5 Then he said, "**C** no closer!
3: 8 I have **c** down to deliver them from the Egyptians,
3: 9 The cry of the Israelites has now **c** to me;
3:10 So **c**, I will send you to Pharaoh
3:13 "If I **c** to the Israelites and say to them,
8: 3 they shall **c** up into your palace,
8: 4 The frogs shall **c** up on you and on your people
8: 5 and make frogs **c** up on the land of Egypt.' "
10:12 that the locusts may **c** upon it and eat every plant
11: 8 all these officials of yours shall **c** down to me,
12:25 you **c** to the land that the LORD will give you,
14:20 one did not **c** near the other all night.
14:26 so that the water may **c** back upon the Egyptians,
17: 6 Strike the rock, and water will **c** out of it,
18:15 "Because the people **c** to me to inquire of God.
18:16 they **c** to me and I decide between one person
19: 9 "I am going to **c** to you in a dense cloud,
19:11 because on the third day the LORD will **c** down
19:23 people are not permitted to **c** up to Mount Sinai;
19:24 "Go down, and **c** up bringing Aaron with you;
19:24 or the people break through to **c** up to the LORD;
20:20 for God has **c** only to test you and to put the fear
20:24 where I cause my name to be remembered I will **c**
22: 9 the case of both parties shall **c** before God;
23: 4 When you **c** upon your enemy's ox
23:27 the people against whom you shall **c**,
24: 1 Then he said to Moses, "**C** up to the LORD,
24: 2 Moses alone shall **c** near the LORD; but the others
shall not **c** near, and the people shall not **c** up with
24:12 "**C** up to me on the mountain, and wait there;
24:14 "Wait here for us, until we **c** to you again;
28:28 the breastpiece shall not **c** loose from the ephod.
28:43 they **c** near the altar to minister in the holy place;
30:12 no plague may **c** upon them for being registered.
30:20 or when they **c** near the altar to minister,
32: 1 Moses delayed to **c** down from the mountain,
32: 1 "**C**, make gods for us, who shall go before us;
32:26 on the LORD's side? **C** to me!"
34: 2 and **c** up in the morning to Mount Sinai
34: 3 No one shall **c** up with you,
34:30 and they were afraid to **c** near him.
35:10 All who are skillful among you shall **c**
36: 2 everyone whose heart was stirred to **c** to do
39:21 the breastpiece should not **c** loose from the ephod;
40:15 throughout all generations to **c**.
Lev 5: 3 and are unaware of it, when you **c** to know it,
5: 4 and are unaware of it, when you **c** to know it,
10: 4 and said to them, "**C** forward,
12: 4 not touch any holy thing, or **c** into the sanctuary,
13:16 he shall **c** to the priest;
14: 8 After that he shall **c** into the camp,
14:34 When you **c** into the land of Canaan,
14:35 the owner of the house shall **c** and tell the priest,
14:39 The priest shall **c** again on the seventh day
15:14 and **c** before the LORD to the entrance of the tent
16: 2 not to **c** just at any time into the sanctuary inside
16: 3 Thus shall Aaron **c** into the holy place:
16:24 then he shall **c** out and offer his burnt offering and
16:26 and afterward may **c** into the camp.
16:28 and afterward may **c** into the camp.
19:23 When you **c** into the land and plant all kinds
21:21 of Aaron the priest who has a blemish shall **c** near
21:21 he shall not **c** near to offer the food of his God.
21:23 But he shall not **c** near the curtain or approach
25:25 then the next of kin shall **c** and redeem what
26:32 so that your enemies who **c** to settle in it shall
Nu 1: 1 in the second year after they had **c** out of the land

Nu 4:15 after that the Kohathites shall **c** to carry these,
4:19 that they may live and not die when they **c** near to
6: 5 All the days of their nazirite vow no razor shall **c**
9: 1 of the second year after they had **c** out of the land
10:29 **c** with us, and we will treat you well;
11:13 For they **c** weeping to me and say,
11:17 I will **c** down and talk with you there;
11:23 Now you shall see whether my word will **c** true
12: 4 **"C** out, you three, to the tent of meeting."
13:33 the Nephilim (the Anakites **c** from the Nephilim);
14:30 of you shall **c** into the land in which I swore
14:35 in this wilderness they shall **c** to a full end,
15: 2 When you **c** into the land you are to inhabit,
15:18 you **c** into the land to which I am bringing you,
16:12 but they said, "We will not **c!**
16:14 of these men? We will not **c!"**
18: 5 that wrath may never again **c** upon the Israelites.
19: 7 and afterwards he may **c** into the camp;
20:18 or we will **c** out with the sword against you."
21:27 ballad singers say, **"C** to Heshbon, let it be built;
22: 5 saying, "A people has **c** out of Egypt;
22: 6 **C** now, curse this people for me,
22:11 'A people has **c** out of Egypt and has spread over
22:11 now **c,** curse them for me;
22:14 and said, "Balaam refuses to **c** with us."
22:17 **c,** curse this people for me.' "
22:20 "If the men have **c** to summon you,
22:32 I have **c** out as an adversary,
22:36 When Balak heard that Balaam had **c,**
22:37 Why did you not **c** to me?
22:38 Balaam said to Balak, "I have **c** to you now,
23: 3 Perhaps the LORD will **c** to meet me.
23: 7 **'C,** curse Jacob for me; **C,** denounce Israel!'
23:13 **"C** with me to another place
23:27 So Balak said to Balaam, **"C** now,
24:14 this people will do to your people in days to **c."** C
24:17 a star shall **c** out of Jacob,
24:24 But ships shall **c** from Kittim
27:17 who shall go out before them and **c** in
27:21 and at his word they shall **c** in,
31:14 who had **c** from service in the war.
31:24 afterward you may **c** into the camp."
32:19 because our inheritance has **c** to us on this side of
33:38 in the fortieth year after the Israelites had **c** out of
Dt 1:22 up and the cities we will **c** to."
4:30 these things have happened to you in time to **c,** A
4:45 to the Israelites when they had **c** out of Egypt,
6:20 When your children ask you in time to **c,** A
10: 1 and **c** up to me on the mountain,
11:10 not like the land of Egypt, from which you have **c,**
12: 9 not yet **c** into the rest and the possession that
14:29 may **c** and eat their fill so that
17:14 When you have **c** into the land that
18: 6 (and he may **c** whenever he wishes),
18: 9 When you **c** into the land that
20: 2 the priest shall **c** forward and speak to the troops,
20:19 in the field human beings that they should **c**
21: 2 then your elders and your judges shall **c** out
21: 5 Then the priests, the sons of Levi, shall **c** forward,
22: 6 If you **c** on a bird's nest,
23:10 he must not **c** within the camp.
23:11 he may **c** back into the camp.
26: 1 When you have **c** into the land that
26: 3 to the LORD your God that I have **c** into the land
28: 2 all these blessings shall **c** upon you
28: 6 Blessed shall you be when you **c** in,
28: 7 they shall **c** out against you one way,
28:15 then all these curses shall **c** upon you
28:19 Cursed shall you be when you **c** in,
28:24 and only dust shall **c** down upon you from the sky
28:45 All these curses shall **c** upon you,
28:52 **c** down throughout your land;
31:17 and many terrible troubles will **c** upon them.
31:17 not these troubles **c** upon us because our God is
31:21 And when many terrible troubles **c** upon them,
31:29 In time to **c** trouble will befall you, A
33:16 Let these **c** on the head of Joseph,
33:29 Your enemies shall **c** fawning to you,
Jos 2: 2 "Some Israelites have **c** here tonight to search out
2: 3 "Bring out the men who have **c** to you,
2: 3 for they have **c** only to search out the whole land."
2:16 so that the pursuers may not **c** upon you.
3: 4 do not **c** any nearer to it."
3: 8 you **c** to the edge of the waters of the Jordan,
3:15 when those who bore the ark had **c** to the Jordan,
4: 6 When your children ask in time to **c,** A
4:16 to **c** up out of the Jordan."
4:17 **"C** up out of the Jordan."
4:21 your children ask their parents in time to **c,** A
5: 4 the wilderness after they had **c** out of Egypt.
5: 5 the wilderness after they had **c** out of Egypt had
5:14 of the army of the LORD I have now **c."**
7:14 In the morning therefore you shall **c** forward tribe
7:14 tribe that the LORD takes shall **c** near by clans,
7:14 that the LORD takes shall **c** near by households,
7:14 and the household that the LORD takes shall **c**
8: 5 When they **c** out against us, as before,
8: 6 They will **c** out after us
9: 6 "We have **c** from a far country;
9: 8 And where do you **c** from?"
9: 9 "Your servants have **c** from a very far country,
9:11 **c** now, make a treaty with us." '
9:12 on the day we set out to **c** to you, but now, see,
9:20 so that wrath may not **c** upon us,
10: 4 **"C** up and help me, and let us attack Gibeon;
10: 6 **c** up to us quickly, and save us, and help us;
10:24 of the warriors who had gone with him, **"C** near,

Jos 11:20 so that they would **c** against Israel in battle,
18: 4 Then **c** back to me.
18: 8 the land and write a description of it, and **c** back
22:24 fear that in time to **c** your children might say A
22:27 may never say to our children in time to **c,** A
22:28 be said to us or to our descendants in time to **c,** A
23:14 all have **c** to pass for you,
24: 7 and made the sea **c** upon them and cover them;
Jdg 1: 3 **"C** up with me into the territory allotted to me,
1:34 they did not allow them to **c** down to the plain.
4:22 Jael went out to meet him, and said to him, **"C,**
5:23 because they did not **c** to the help of the LORD,
6: 3 the Amalekites and the people of the east would **c**
6: 5 For they and their livestock would **c** up,
6:18 Do not depart from here until I **c** to you,
7:17 when I **c** to the outskirts of the camp, do as I do.
7:24 **"C** down against the Midianites and seize
8: 9 "When I **c** back victorious,
8:21 Zebah and Zalmunna said, "You **c** and kill us;
9:10 'You **c** and reign over us.'
9:12 trees said to the vine, 'You **c** and reign over us.'
9:14 'You **c** and reign over us.'
9:15 then **c** and take refuge in my shade;
9:15 let fire **c** out of the bramble and devour the cedars
9:20 let fire **c** out from Abimelech,
9:20 and let fire **c** out from the lords of Shechem,
9:29 'Increase your army, and **c** out.' "
9:31 of Ebed and his kinsfolk have **c** to Shechem,
9:33 and when he and the troops that are with him **c** out
11: 6 They said to Jephthah, **"C** and be our commander,
11: 7 So why do you **c** to me now when you are
11:12 that you have **c** to me to fight against my land?"
12: 3 Why then have you **c** up to me this day,
13: 5 No razor is to **c** on his head,
13: 8 let the man of God whom you sent **c** to us again
13:12 Manoah said, "Now when your words **c** true,
13:17 that we may honor you when your words **c** true?"
15:10 "Why have you **c** up against us?"
15:10 They said, "We have **c** up to bind Samson,
15:12 They said to him, "We have **c** down to bind you,
16: 2 The Gazites were told, "Samson has **c** here."
16:17 "A razor has never **c** upon my head;
16:18 "This time **c** up, for he has told his whole secret
17: 9 Micah said to him, "From where do you **c?"**
18: 9 They said, **"C,** let us go up against them;
18:10 you go, you will **c** to an unsuspecting people.
18:19 Put your hand over your mouth, and **c** with us,
18:23 the matter that you **c** with such a company?"
19:11 and the servant said to his master, **"C** now,
19:13 Then he said to his servant, **"C,**
19:17 "Where are you going and where do you **c** from?"
19:18 of the hill country of Ephraim, from which I **c.**
20: 3 "Tell us, how did this criminal act **c** about?"
21: 3 why has it **c** to pass that today there should
21: 5 the tribes of Israel did not **c** up in the assembly to
21: 5 concerning whoever did not **c** up to the LORD
21: 8 the tribes of Israel who did not **c** up to the LORD
21: 8 It turned out that no one from Jabesh-gilead had **c**
21:21 when the young women of Shiloh **c** out to dance in
the dances, then **c** out of the vineyards
21:22 their fathers or their brothers **c** to complain to us,
Ru 2:12 under whose wings you have **c** for refuge!"
2:14 At mealtime Boaz said to her, **"C** here,
4: 1 So Boaz said, **"C** over, friend; sit down here."
4: 3 who has **c** back from the country of Moab,
4: 4 to you to redeem it, and I **c** after you."
1Sa 2: 3 let not arrogance **c** from your mouth;
2:13 the priest's servant would **c,**
2:15 the priest's servant would **c** and say to
2:36 in your family shall **c** to implore him for a piece
4: 3 so that he may **c** among us and save us from
4: 6 that the ark of the LORD had **c** to the camp,
4: 7 for they said, "Gods have **c** into the camp."
4:16 The man said to Eli, "I have just **c** from the battle;
6:21 **C** down and take it up to you."
7:17 Then he would **c** back to Ramah,
9: 9 **"C,** let us go to the seer";
9:10 Saul said to the boy, "Good; **c,** let us go."
9:12 Hurry; he has **c** just now to the town,
9:16 because their outcry has **c** to me."
10: 3 Then you shall go on from there further and **c** to
10: 5 After that you shall **c** to Gibeath-elohim,
10: 5 there, as you **c** to the town,
10: 8 then I will **c** down to you
10: 8 until I **c** to you and show you what you shall do."
10:11 "What has **c** over the son of Kish?
10:22 of the LORD, "Did the man **c** here?"
11: 7 "Whoever does not **c** out after Saul and Samuel,
11: 9 They said to the messengers who had **c,**
11:14 Samuel said to the people, **"C,**
13: 8 but Samuel did not **c** to Gilgal,
13:11 and that you did not **c** within the days appointed,
13:12 the Philistines will **c** down upon me at Gilgal,
14: 1 **"C,** let us go over to the Philistine garrison on
14: 6 **"C,** let us go over to the garrison
14: 9 If they say to us, 'Wait until we **c** to you,'
14:10 But if they say, **'C** up to us,' then we will go up;
14:12 **"C** up to us, and we will show you something."
14:12 Jonathan said to his armor-bearer, **"C** up after me;
14:38 Saul said, **"C** here, all you leaders of the people;
16: 2 and say, 'I have **c** to sacrifice to the LORD.'
16: 4 and said, "Do you **c** peaceably?"
16: 5 I have **c** to sacrifice to the LORD;
16: 5 sanctify yourselves and **c** with me to
17: 8 "Why have you **c** out to draw up for battle?
17: 8 and let him **c** down to me.
17:25 "Have you seen this man who has **c** up?

1Sa 17:25 Surely he has **c** up to defy Israel.
17:28 He said, "Why have you **c** down?
17:28 for you have **c** down just to see the battle."
17:43 "Am I a dog, that you **c** to me with sticks?"
17:44 The Philistine said to David, **"C** to me,
17:45 "You **c** to me with sword and spear and javelin;
but I **c** to you in the name of the LORD of hosts,
20: 9 that it was decided by my father that evil should **c**
20:11 Jonathan replied to David, **"C,**
20:21 then you are to **c,** for, as the LORD lives,
20:27 "Why has the son of Jesse not **c** to the feast,
20:29 For this reason he has not **c** to the king's table."
21:15 Shall this fellow **c** into my house?"
22: 3 "Please let my father and mother **c** to you,
23: 7 Now it was told Saul that David had **c** to Keilah.
23:10 your servant has heard that Saul seeks to **c**
23:11 now, will Saul **c** down as your servant has heard?
23:11 The LORD said, "He will **c** down."
23:15 at Horesh when he learned that Saul had **c** out
23:20 O king, whenever you wish to **c** down, do so;
23:23 and **c** back to me with sure information.
23:27 a messenger came to Saul, saying, "Hurry and **c;**
24:14 Against whom has the king of Israel **c** out?
25: 8 for we have **c** on a feast day.
25:11 give it to men who **c** from I do not know where?"
25:34 unless you had hurried and **c** to meet me,
26:10 or his day will **c** to die;
26:20 the king of Israel has **c** out to seek a single flea,
26:21 Then Saul said, "I have done wrong; **c** back,
26:22 Let one of the young men **c** over and get it.
28:10 no punishment shall **c** upon you for this thing."
31: 4 that these uncircumcised may not **c** and thrust me
2Sa 1: 3 David said to him, "Where have you **c** from?"
1: 9 He said to me, **'C,** stand over me and kill me;
1:13 to him, "Where do you **c** from?"
1:15 **"C** here and strike him down."
2:14 "Let the young men **c** forward and have a contest
2:14 Joab said, "Let them **c** forward."
3:13 when you **c** to see me."
4: 7 Now they had **c** into the house while he was lying
5: 6 who said to David, "You will not **c** in here,
5: 6 thinking, "David cannot **c** in here."
5: 8 blind and the lame shall not **c** into the house."
5:18 the Philistines had **c** and spread out in the valley
5:23 and **c** upon them opposite the balsam trees.
6: 9 "How can the ark of the LORD **c** into my care?"
7:12 who shall **c** forth from your body,
7:19 also of your servant's house for a great while to **c.**
10:11 then I will **c** and help you.
11:10 "You have just **c** from a journey.
12: 4 or herd to prepare for the wayfarer who had **c**
12: 4 and prepared that for the guest who had **c** to him."
13: 5 'Let my sister Tamar **c** and give me something
13: 6 the king, "Please let my sister Tamar **c** and make
13:11 and said to her, **"C,** lie with me, my sister."
13:35 "See, the king's sons have **c;**
13:35 as your servant said, so it has **c** about."
14:15 Now I have **c** to say this to my lord the king
14:24 he is not to **c** into my presence."
14:24 and did not **c** into the king's presence.
14:29 but Joab would not **c** to him.
14:29 He sent a second time, but Joab would not **c.**
14:32 **C** here, that I may send you to the king with
14:32 'Why have I **c** from Geshur?
15: 4 Then all who had a suit or cause might **c** to me,
17: 2 I will **c** upon him while he is weary
17:12 So we shall **c** upon him in whatever place he may
18:22 **"C** what may, let me also run after the Cushite."
18:23 **"C** what may," he said, "I will run."
19: 7 that has **c** upon you from your youth until now."
19:11 The talk of all Israel has **c** to the king.
19:16 hurried to **c** down with the people of Judah
19:20 therefore, see, I have **c** this day,
19:20 of Joseph to **c** down to meet my lord the king."
19:31 Barzillai the Gileadite had **c** down from Rogelim;
19:33 The king said to Barzillai, **"C** over with me,
20:16 Tell Joab, **'C** here, I want to speak to you.' "
21:10 not allow the birds of the air to **c** on the bodies
24:13 he asked him, "Shall three years of famine **c**
24:21 "Why has my lord the king **c** to his servant?"
1Ki 1:12 Now therefore **c,** let me give you advice.
1:14 I will **c** in after you and confirm your words."
1:21 Otherwise it will **c** to pass,
1:42 **"C** in, for you are a worthy man and
2:13 She asked, "Do you **c** peaceably?"
2:30 "The king commands, **'C** out.' "
2:33 So shall their blood **c** back on the head of Joab
3: 7 I do not know how to go out or **c** in.
8:47 yet if they **c** to their senses in the land
10:10 never again did spices **c** in such quantity as
10:12 no such almug wood has **c** or been seen
10:22 of ships of Tarshish used to **c** bringing gold,
12: 1 for all Israel had **c** to Shechem to make him king.
12: 5 "Go away for three days, then **c** again to me."
12:12 **"C** to me again the third day."
13: 7 **"C** home with me and dine,
13:10 did not return by the way that he had **c** to Bethel.
13:15 **"C** home with me and eat some food."
13:22 but have **c** back and have eaten food
13:22 your body shall not **c** to your ancestral tomb."
13:32 in the cities of Samaria, shall surely **c** to pass."
14: 6 as she came in at the door, he said, **"C** in,
14:13 he alone of Jeroboam's family shall **c** to the grave,
17:18 You have **c** to me to bring my sin
17:21 let this child's life **c** into him again."
18:12 so, when I **c** and tell Ahab and he cannot find you,
18:30 Elijah said to all the people, **"C** closer to me";

1Ki 20:17 "Men have c out from Samaria."
20:18 He said, "If they have c out for peace,
20:18 if they have c out for war, take them alive."
20:19 But these had already c out of the city:
20:22 of Israel and said to him, "C, strengthen yourself,
20:22 for in the spring the king of Aram will c up
20:33 and he had him c up into the chariot.
22:15 When he had c to the king, the king said to him,
22:27 on reduced rations of bread and water until I c
2Ki 1: 9 "O man of God, the king says, 'C down.' "
1:10 let fire c down from heaven and consume you
1:11 this is the king's order: C down quickly!"
1:12 let fire c down from heaven and consume you
2:21 from now on neither death nor miscarriage shall c
3:21 the Moabites heard that the kings had c up to fight
4: 1 creditor has c to take my two children as slaves."
4:22 to the man of God and c back again."
5: 8 Let him c to me, that he may learn that there is
5:11 "I thought that for me he would surely c out,
5:22 of prophets have just c to me from the hill country
6: 3 one of them said, "Please c with your servants."
7: 8 these leprous men had c to the edge of the camp,
7:12 thinking, 'When they c out of the city,
8: 1 and it will c on the land for seven years."
8: 7 it was told him, "The man of God has c here,"
9:11 Why did that madman c to you?"
9:12 They said, "Liar! C on, tell us!"
9:16 King Ahaziah of Judah had c down to visit Joram.
10: 6 take the heads of your master's sons and c to me
10:13 we have c down to visit the royal princes and
10:16 "C with me, and see my zeal for the LORD."
10:21 so that there was no one left who did not c.
10:25 "C in and kill them; let no one escape."
11: 4 and had them c to him in the house of the LORD.
11: 7 and your two divisions that c on duty in force on
11: 9 with those who were to c on duty on the sabbath,
14: 8 saying, "C, let us look one another in the face."
16: 7 C up, and rescue me from the hand of the king
18:23 C now, make a wager with my master the king
18:25 that I have c up against this place to destroy it?
18:31 'Make your peace with me and c out to me;
18:32 until I c and take you away to a land
19: 3 children have c to the birth,
19:28 against me and your arrogance has c to my ears,
19:32 He shall not c into this city, shoot an arrow there,
c before it with a shield,
19:33 he shall not c into this city, says the LORD.
20:14 From where did they c to you?"
20:14 "They have c from a far country, from Babylon."
23: 9 not c up to the altar of the LORD in Jerusalem,
24: 7 The king of Egypt did not c again out of his land,
1Ch 1:12 and Caphtorim, from whom the Philistines c.
9:25 to c in every seven days, in turn, to be with them;
10: 4 so that these uncircumcised may not c
11: 5 "You will not c in here."
12:17 "If you have c to me in friendship, to help me,
12:17 but if you have c to betray me to my adversaries,
12:31 who were expressly named to c
13: 2 that they may c together to us.
14: 9 the Philistines had c and made a raid in the valley
14:14 around and c on them opposite the balsam trees.
16:29 bring an offering, and c before him.
17:17 of your servant's house for a great while to c.
19: 3 Have not his servants c to you to search and
19: 9 and the kings who had c were by themselves in
29:12 Riches and honor c from you,
29:14 For all things c from you,
2Ch 1:10 now wisdom and knowledge to go out and c in
6:32 c from a distant land because of your great name,
6:32 when they c and pray toward this house,
6:37 then if they c to their senses in the land
7: 3 When all the people of Israel saw the fire c down
8:11 to which the ark of the LORD has c are holy."
9:21 the ships of Tarshish used to c bringing gold,
10: 1 for all Israel had c to Shechem to make him king.
10: 5 He said to them, "C to me again in three days."
10:12 "C to me again the third day."
11:14 and their holdings and had c to Judah
12:11 the guard would c along bearing them,
13:13 Jeroboam had sent an ambush around to c on them
14:11 in your name we have c against this multitude.
15: 5 not safe for anyone to go or c,
18:14 When he had c to the king, the king said to him,
19:10 before the LORD and wrath may not c on you
20:16 they will c up by the ascent of Ziz;
20:22 who had c against Judah, so that they were routed.
21:15 until your bowels c out, day after day,
22: 7 by God that the downfall of Ahaziah should c
23: 4 priests and Levites, who c on duty on the sabbath,
23: 8 who were to c on duty on the sabbath,
24:11 the officer of the chief priest would c and empty
24:24 Although the army of Aram had c with few men,
25:10 Then Amaziah discharged the army that had c
25:17 saying, "C, let us look one another in the face."
29:31 c near, bring sacrifices and thank offerings to
29:36 for the thing had c about suddenly.
30: 1 that they should c to the house of the LORD
30: 5 that the people should c and keep the passover to
30: 8 but yield yourselves to the LORD and c
32: 2 that Sennacherib had c and intended to fight
32: 4 "Why should the Assyrian kings c and find water
32:26 that the wrath of the LORD did not c upon them
Ezr 3: 8 and all who had c to Jerusalem from the captivity.
7:23 or wrath will c upon the realm of the king
8:35 At that time those who had c from captivity,
9:13 After all that has c upon us for our evil deeds and
10: 8 and that if any did not c within three days,
Ezr 10:14 in our towns who have taken foreign wives c
10:17 By the first day of the first month they had c to
Ne 2:10 it displeased them greatly that someone had c
2:17 C, let us rebuild the wall of Jerusalem,
4: 8 and all plotted together to c and fight
4:11 "They will not know or see anything before we c
4:12 "From all the places where they live they will c up
6: 2 "C and let us meet together in one of the villages
6: 3 "I am doing a great work and I cannot c down.
6: 3 the work stop while I leave it to c down to you?"
6: 7 So c, therefore, and let us confer together."
7: 5 of those who were the first to c back, and I found
7:65 until a priest with Urim and Thummim should c.
9:32 not treat lightly all the hardship that has c upon us,
9:33 You have been just in all that has c upon us,
13:21 From that time on they did not c on the sabbath.
13:22 that they should purify themselves and c
Est 1:12 to c at the king's command conveyed by
1:17 to be brought before him, and she did not c.'
1:19 Vashti is never again to c before King Ahasuerus;
4:11 not been called to c in to the king for thirty days."
4:14 Perhaps you have c to royal dignity for just such
5: 4 let the king and Haman c today to a banquet
5: 8 let the king and Haman c tomorrow to the banquet
5:12 "Even Queen Esther let no one but myself c with
6: 5 The king said, "Let him c in."
9:25 against the Jews should c upon his own head,
Job 1: 7 LORD said to Satan, "Where have you c from?"
2: 2 LORD said to Satan, "Where have you c from?"
2:11 of all these troubles that had c upon him, each
3: 6 let it not c into the number of the months.
3:11 c forth from the womb and expire?
3:21 but it does not c, and dig for it more than
4: 5 But now it has c to you, and you are impatient;
5: 6 For misery does not c from the earth,
5:26 You shall c to your grave in ripe old age,
6:20 they c there and are confounded.
7: 6 and c to their end without hope.
7: 9 so those who go down to Sheol do not c up;
9:32 that we should c to trial together.
13:13 and I will speak, and let c on me what may.
13:16 that the godless shall not c before him.
14:14 until my release should c.
14:21 Their children c to honor, and they do not know it;
15:21 in prosperity the destroyer will c upon them.
16:22 For when a few years have c,
17:10 But you, c back now, all of you,
19:12 His troops c on together; they have thrown
20:22 all the force of misery will c upon them.
20:25 of their gall; terrors c upon them.
21:17 How often does calamity c upon them?
22:21 in this way good will c to you.
23: 3 that I might c even to his dwelling!
23:10 when he has tested me, I shall c out like gold.
26: 4 and whose spirit has c forth from you?
28:20 "Where then does wisdom c from?
30:14 a wide breach they c; amid the crash they roll on.
30:27 days of affliction c to meet me.
34:28 to c to him, and he heard the cry of the afflicted—
38:11 'Thus far shall you c, and no farther,
38:29 From whose womb did the ice c forth,
41:16 so near to another that no air can c between them.
Ps 7: 9 O let the evil of the wicked c to an end,
14: 7 O that deliverance for Israel would c from Zion!
17: 2 From you let my vindication c;
22:19 O my help, c quickly to my aid!
24: 7 that the King of glory may c in.
24: 9 that the King of glory may c in.
27: 8 "C," my heart says, "seek his face!"
34:11 C, O children, listen to me;
35: 8 Let ruin c on them unawares.
38: 2 and your hand has c down on me.
41: 6 And when they c to see me,
42: 2 When shall I c and behold the face of God?
44:17 All this has c upon us,
44:26 Rise up, c to our help.
46: 8 C, behold the works of the LORD;
52: T *to him, "David has c to the house of Ahimelech."*
53: 6 O that deliverance for Israel would c from Zion!
55: 5 Fear and trembling c upon me,
55:15 Let death c upon them; let them go down alive
59: 4 Rouse yourself, c to my help and see!
59: 6 Each evening they c back,
59:14 Each evening they c back,
65: 2 To you all flesh shall c.
66: 5 C and see what God has done:
66:13 I will c into your house with burnt offerings;
66:16 C and hear, all you who fear God,
69: 1 O God, for the waters have c up to my neck.
69: 2 I have c into deep waters,
71:16 I will c praising the mighty deeds of
71:18 to all the generations to c.
78:16 He made streams c out of the rock,
78:39 a wind that passes and does not c again.
79: 1 the nations have c into your inheritance;
79: 8 let your compassion c speedily to meet us,
79:11 Let the groans of the prisoners c before you;
80: 2 Stir up your might, and c to save us!
83: 4 They say, "C, let us wipe them out as a nation;
86: 9 the nations you have made shall c and bow down
88: 2 let my prayer c before you;
90: 9 our years c to an end like a sigh.
91: 7 but it will not c near you.
91:10 no scourge c near your tent.
95: 1 O c, let us sing to the LORD;
95: 2 Let us c into his presence with thanksgiving;
95: 6 O c, let us worship and bow down,
Ps 96: 8 bring an offering, and c into his courts.
100: 2 c into his presence with singing.
102: 1 Hear my prayer, O LORD; let my cry c to you.
102:13 to favor it; the appointed time has c.
102:18 Let this be recorded for a generation to c,
104:20 when all the animals of the forest c creeping out.
109:17 He loved to curse; let curses c on him.
110: 3 like dew, your youth will c to you.
119:41 Let your steadfast love c to me, O LORD,
119:77 Let your mercy c to me, that I may live;
119:143 Trouble and anguish have c upon me,
119:169 Let my cry c before you, O LORD;
119:170 Let my supplication c before you;
121: 1 from where will my help c?
126: 6 shall c home with shouts of joy,
134: 1 C, bless the LORD, all you servants of
139:18 I c to the end—I am still with you.
141: 1 O LORD; c quickly to me;
144: 5 Bow your heavens, O LORD, and c down;
Pr 1:11 If they say, "C with us, let us lie in wait for blood;
1:27 when distress and anguish c upon you.
2: 6 from his mouth c knowledge and understanding;
2:10 for wisdom will c into your heart,
2:19 those who go to her never c back,
3:28 Do not say to your neighbor, "Go, and c again,
6: 3 for you have c into your neighbor's power:
6:11 and poverty will c upon you like a robber,
7:15 so now I have c out to meet you,
7:18 C, let us take our fill of love until morning;
7:20 he will not c home until full moon."
8: 6 and from my lips will c what is right;
9: 5 "C, eat of my bread and drink of
10: 8 but a babbling fool will c to ruin.
10:24 What the wicked dread will c upon them,
13: 3 those who open wide their lips c to ruin.
14: 4 abundant crops c by the strength of the ox.
20:13 Do not love sleep, or else you will c to poverty;
23:21 for the drunkard and the glutton will c to poverty,
24:25 and a good blessing will c upon them.
24:34 and poverty will c upon you like a robber,
25: 7 "C up here," than to be put lower in the presence
26:27 a stone will c back on the one who starts it rolling.
28:22 to get rich and does not know that loss is sure to c.
28:26 but those who walk in wisdom c through safely.
29:21 A slave pampered from childhood will c to
30: 4 Who has ascended to heaven and c down?
31:25 and she laughs at the time to c. A
Ecc 1:11 of people yet to c by those who c after them.
2: 1 "C now, I will make a test of pleasure;
2:16 in the days to c all will have been long forgotten. C
2:18 seeing that I must leave it to those who c after me
4: 4 and all skill in work c from one person's envy
4:14 One can indeed c out of prison to reign,
4:16 Yet those who c later will not rejoice in him.
5: 3 For dreams c with many cares,
5: 7 With many dreams c vanities and a multitude
6:10 Whatever has c to be has already been named,
7:14 that mortals may not find out anything that will c
12: 1 before the days of trouble c,
SS 2:10 "Arise, my love, my fair one, and c away;
2:12 the time of singing has c,
2:13 Arise, my love, my fair one, and c away.
3:11 c out. Look, O daughters of Zion,
4: 2 of shorn ewes that have c up from the washing,
4: 8 C with me from Lebanon, my bride;
4: 8 c with me from Lebanon.
4:16 Awake, O north wind, and c, O south wind!
4:16 Let my beloved c to his garden,
5: 1 I c to my garden, my sister, my bride;
6: 6 that have c up from the washing;
7:11 C, my beloved, let us go forth into the fields,
Isa 1:12 When you c to appear before me,
1:18 C now, let us argue it out, says the LORD:
1:23 and the widow's cause does not c before them.
2: 2 In days to c the mountain of the LORD's house C
2: 3 Many peoples shall c and say, "C,
2: 5 c, let us walk in the light of the LORD!
5:26 Here they c, swiftly, speedily!
7: 7 It shall not stand, and it shall not c to pass.
7:17 as have not c since the day that Ephraim departed
7:19 And they will all c and settle in the steep ravines,
10: 3 in the calamity that will c from far away?
10:25 a very little while my indignation will c to an end,
10:28 he has c to Aiath; he has passed
11: 1 A shoot shall c out from the stump of Jesse,
13: 5 They c from a distant land,
13: 6 it will c like destruction from the Almighty!
14: 9 up to meet you when you c;
14:24 and as I have planned, so shall it c to pass:
14:29 from the root of the snake will c forth an adder,
19:23 and the Assyrian will c into Egypt,
21: 9 Look, there they c, riders, horsemen in pairs!"
21:12 If you will inquire, inquire; c back again."
21:16 all the glory of Kedar will c to an end;
22:15 Thus says the Lord GOD of hosts: C,
26:20 C, my people, enter your chambers,
27: 6 In days to c Jacob shall take root, C
27:11 women c and make a fire of them.
27:13 the land of Egypt will c and worship the LORD
28:15 through it will not c to us;
29: 4 from low in the dust your words shall c;
29: 4 your voice shall c from the ground like the voice
29:24 those who err in spirit will c to understanding,
30: 8 it may be for the time to c as a witness forever. A
31: 4 at their noise, so the LORD of hosts will c down
32:10 the vintage will fail, the fruit harvest will not c.
35: 4 He will c with vengeance,

Isa 35: 4 He will **c** and save you."
35: 9 nor shall any ravenous beast **c** up on it;
35:10 and **c** to Zion with singing;
36: 8 **C** now, make a wager with my master the king
36:10 that I have **c** up against this land to destroy it?
36:16 'Make your peace with me and **c** out to me;
36:17 until I **c** and take you away to a land
37: 3 children have **c** to the birth,
37:29 against me and your arrogance has **c** to my ears,
37:33 He shall not **c** into this city, shoot an arrow there,
c before it with a shield,
37:34 he shall not **c** into this city, says the LORD.
39: 3 From where did they **c** to you?"
39: 3 "They have **c** to me from a far country,
41: 5 they have drawn near and **c**.
41:22 or declare to us the things to **c**. D
41:23 Tell us what is to **c** hereafter,
41:25 I stirred up one from the north, and he has **c**,
42: 9 See, the former things have **c** to pass,
42:23 who will attend and listen for the time to **c**? A
44: 7 Who has announced from of old the things to **c**? D
45:14 tall of stature, shall **c** over to you and be yours,
45:14 they shall **c** over in chains and bow down to you.
45:20 Assemble yourselves and **c** together, draw near,
45:24 all who were incensed against him shall **c** to him
47: 1 **C** down and sit in the dust,
47: 9 both these things shall **c** upon you in a moment,
47: 9 and widowhood shall **c** upon you in full measure,
47:11 But evil shall **c** upon you,
47:11 and ruin shall **c** on you suddenly,
49: 9 "**C** out," to those who are in darkness,
49:12 Lo, these shall **c** from far away, and lo,
49:18 they all gather, they **c** to you.
49:21 where then have these **c** from?"
51:11 and **c** to Zion with singing;
54:14 and from terror, for it shall not **c** near you.
55: 1 Ho, everyone who thirsts, **c** to the waters;
55: 1 and you that have no money, **c**, buy and eat!
55: 1 **C**, buy wine and milk without money and without
55: 3 Incline your ear, and **c** to me;
55:10 For as the rain and the snow **c** down from heaven,
55:13 Instead of the thorn shall **c** up the cypress;
55:13 instead of the brier shall **c** up the myrtle;
56: 1 and do what is right, for soon my salvation will **c**,
56: 9 all you wild animals in the forest, **c** to devour!
56:12 "**C**," they say, "let us get wine;
57: 3 But as for you, **c** here, you children of a sorceress,
59:19 for he will **c** like a pent-up stream that the wind of
59:20 And he will **c** to Zion as Redeemer,
60: 1 Arise, shine; for your light has **c**,
60: 3 Nations shall **c** to your light,
60: 4 they all gather together, they **c** to you;
60: 4 your sons shall **c** from far away,
60: 5 the wealth of the nations shall **c** to you.
60: 6 all those from Sheba shall **c**.
60:13 The glory of Lebanon shall **c** to you, the cypress,
60:14 of those who oppressed you shall **c** bending low
63: 4 and the year for my redeeming work had **c**.
64: 1 that you would tear open the heavens and **c** down,
65: 5 do not **c** near me, for I am too holy for you."
65:17 the former things shall not be remembered or **c**
66:15 For the LORD will **c** in fire,
66:17 vermin, and rodents, shall **c** to an end together,
66:18 and they shall **c** and shall see my glory,
66:23 all flesh shall **c** to worship before me,
Jer 1:15 and they shall **c** and all
2:27 But in the time of their trouble they say, "**C**
2:28 Let them **c**, if they can save you,
2:31 "We are free, we will **c** to you no more"?
2:37 From there also you will **c** away with your hands
3: 3 and the spring rain has not **c**;
3:16 It shall not **c** to mind, or be remembered,
3:18 and together they shall **c** from the land of
3:22 "Here we **c** to you; for you are the LORD our God.
4:16 "Besiegers **c** from a distant land;
5:12 No evil will **c** upon us, and we shall not see sword
6: 3 Shepherds with their flocks shall **c** against her.
6:26 for suddenly the destroyer will **c** upon us.
7:10 and then **c** and stand before me in this house,
7:31 nor did it **c** into my mind.
8:16 They **c** and devour the land and all that fills it,
9:17 Consider, and call for the mourning women to **c**;
9:17 send for the skilled women to **c**;
9:21 "Death has **c** up into our windows,
12:12 the bare heights in the desert spoilers have **c**;
13:18 your beautiful crown has **c** down from your head."
13:20 up your eyes and see those who **c** from the north.
13:22 "Why have these things **c** upon me?"
14: 3 they **c** to the cisterns, they find no water,
14:15 "Sword and famine shall not **c** on this land":
16:19 shall the nations **c** from the ends of the earth
17:15 "Where is the word of the LORD? Let it **c**!"
17:26 And people shall **c** from the towns of Judah and
18: 2 "**C**, go down to the potter's house,
18:18 "**C**, let us make plots against Jeremiah—
18:18 **C**, let us bring charges against him,
20:18 Why did I **c** forth from the womb to see toil
21:13 you who say, "Who can **c** down against us,
22:23 how you will groan when pangs **c** upon you,
23:17 they say, "No calamity shall **c** upon you."
25: 3 to this day, the word of the LORD has **c** to me,
25:34 for the days of your slaughter have **c**—
26: 2 the cities of Judah that **c** to worship in the house
27: 3 the hand of the envoys who have **c** to Jerusalem
29:12 when you call upon me and **c** and pray to me,
30:19 Out of them shall **c** thanksgiving,
30:21 their ruler shall **c** from their midst;
Jer 31: 6 "**C**, let us go up to Zion, to the LORD our God."
31: 9 With weeping they shall **c**,
31:12 They shall **c** and sing aloud on the height of Zion,
31:16 they shall **c** back from the land of the enemy;
31:17 your children shall **c** back to their own country.
31:18 Bring me back, let me **c** back,
32: 7 Hanamel son of your uncle Shallum is going to **c**
32:23 you have made all these disasters **c** upon them.
32:29 against this city shall **c**, set it on fire, and burn it,
33:20 day and night would not **c** at their appointed time,
35:11 "**C**, and let us go to Jerusalem for fear of the army
36: 6 in the hearing of all the people of Judah who **c** up
36: 7 It may be that their plea will **c** before the LORD,
36:14 that you read in the hearing of the people, and **c**."
36:29 of Babylon will certainly **c** and destroy this land,
37: 5 the army of Pharaoh had **c** out of Egypt;
37:19 'The king of Babylon will not **c** against you and
38:25 and they should **c** and say to you,
38:27 the officials did **c** to Jeremiah and questioned him;
40: 3 Therefore this thing has **c** upon you.
40: 4 If you wish to **c** with me to Babylon, **c**,
40: 4 not wish to **c** with me to Babylon, you need not **c**.
40:10 to represent you before the Chaldeans who **c** to us;
41: 6 he said to them, "**C** to Gedaliah son of Ahikam."
43:11 He shall **c** and ravage the land of Egypt,
44: 8 in the land of Egypt where you have **c** to settle?
44:12 the remnant of Judah who are determined to **c** to
44:14 so that none of the remnant of Judah who have **c**
44:21 Did it not **c** into his mind?
44:28 who have **c** to the land of Egypt to settle,
46:16 and one said to another, "**C**,
46:21 for the day of their calamity has **c** upon them,
46:22 and **c** against her with axes,
47: 5 Baldness has **c** upon Gaza, Ashkelon is silenced.
48: 2 "**C**, let us cut her off from being a nation!"
48: 8 The destroyer shall **c** upon every town,
48:15 The destroyer of Moab and his towns has **c** up,
48:18 **C** down from glory, and sit on the parched
48:18 For the destroyer of Moab has **c** up against you;
48:21 Judgment has **c** upon the tableland, upon Holon,
49:14 "Gather yourselves together and **c** against her,
49:36 to which the exiles from Elam shall not **c**.
50: 3 For out of the north a nation has **c** up against her;
50: 4 says the LORD, the people of Israel shall **c**,
50: 4 they shall **c** weeping as they seek
50: 5 and they shall **c** and join themselves to
50:26 **C** against her from every quarter;
50:27 Alas for them, their day has **c**,
50:31 your day has **c**, the time when I will punish you.
51: 2 They shall empty her land when they **c** against her
51:10 The LORD has brought forth our vindication; **c**,
51:13 your end has **c**, the thread of your life is cut.
51:33 yet a little while and the time of her harvest will **c**.
51:45 **C** out of her, my people!
51:48 destroyers shall **c** against them out of the north,
51:50 and let Jerusalem **c** into your mind:
51:51 have **c** into the holy places of the LORD's house.
51:53 from me destroyers would **c** upon her,
51:56 for a destroyer has **c** against her, against Babylon;
51:60 a scroll all the disasters that would **c** on Babylon,
51:61 "When you **c** to Babylon,
La 1:22 Let all their evil doing **c** before you;
3:22 his mercies never **c** to an end;
3:38 the mouth of the Most High that good and bad **c**?
3:47 panic and pitfall have **c** upon us,
4:18 our days were numbered; for our end had **c**.
Eze 4:14 nor has carrion flesh **c** into my mouth."
5: 4 from there a fire will **c** out against all the house
7: 2 The end has **c** upon the four corners of the land.
7: 6 An end has **c**, the end has come.
7: 6 An end has come, the end has **c**.
7: 7 Your doom has **c** to you, O inhabitant of the land.
7: 7 The time has **c**, the day is near—
7:12 The time has **c**, the day draws near;
11: 5 I know the things that **c** into your mind.
11:18 When they **c** there, they will remove
14: 4 and yet **c** to the prophet—
14: 4 I the LORD will answer those who **c** with
14: 7 and yet **c** to a prophet to inquire of me by him,
14:22 they will **c** out to you
16:33 to **c** to you from all around for your whorings.
21: 7 you shall say, "Because of the news that has **c**.
21:19 for the sword of the king of Babylon to **c**;
21:20 for the sword to **c** to Rabbah of the Ammonites or
21:24 because you have **c** to remembrance,
21:25 wicked prince of Israel, you whose day has **c**,
21:29 whose day has **c**, the time of final punishment.
22: 3 its time has **c**; making its idols, defiling itself.
22: 4 the appointed time of your years has **c**.
23:24 They shall **c** against you from the north
23:40 They even sent for men to **c** from far away,
24:26 one who has escaped will **c** to you to report to you
27:29 down from their ships **c** all that handle the oar.
27:36 you have **c** to a dreadful end and shall
28:19 you have **c** to a dreadful end and shall
30: 4 A sword shall **c** upon Egypt,
30: 6 and its proud might shall **c** down;
30: 9 and anguish shall **c** upon them on the day
30:18 and its proud might shall **c** to an end;
32:11 sword of the king of Babylon shall **c** against you.
32:21 "They have **c** down, they lie still,
33:28 and its proud might shall **c** to an end;
33:30 "**C** and hear what the word is that comes from
33:31 They **c** to you as people **c**,
33:33 When this comes—and **c** it will!—
35: 7 and I will cut off from it all who **c** and go.
36: 8 for they shall soon **c** home.
Eze 37: 6 and will cause flesh to **c** upon you,
37: 8 and flesh had **c** upon them,
37: 9 **C** from the four winds, O breath,
38:10 On that day thoughts will **c** into your mind,
38:13 "Have you **c** to seize spoil?
38:15 and **c** from your place out of the remotest parts of
38:16 you will **c** up against my people Israel,
39: 8 It has **c**! It has happened, says the Lord GOD.
39:17 Assemble and **c**, gather from all around to
40:46 the descendants of Levi may **c** near to the LORD
44:13 They shall not **c** near to me, to serve me as priest,
44:13 nor **c** near any of my sacred offerings,
44:15 shall **c** near to me to minister to me;
46: 8 he shall **c** in by the vestibule of the gate,
46: 9 When the people of the land **c** before the LORD
46:10 they **c** in, the prince shall **c** in with them;
Da 3: 2 the officials of the provinces to assemble and **c** to
3:26 servants of the Most High God, **c** out! **C** here!"
4:24 a decree of the Most High that has **c** upon my lord
9:13 all this calamity has **c** upon us.
9:22 now **c** out to give you wisdom and understanding.
9:23 and I have **c** to declare it,
9:26 of the prince who is to **c** shall destroy the city and
9:26 Its end shall **c** with a flood,
10:12 and I have **c** because of your words.
10:14 and have **c** to help you understand what is
10:16 because of the vision such pains have **c** upon me
10:20 Then he said, "Do you know why I have **c** to you?
10:20 the prince of Greece will **c**.
11: 6 and the daughter of the king of the south shall **c** to
11: 7 He shall **c** against the army and enter the fortress
11:15 king of the north shall **c** and throw up siegeworks,
11:17 to **c** with the strength of his whole kingdom,
11:21 he shall **c** in without warning and obtain
11:24 Without warning he shall **c** into the richest parts
11:29 "At the time appointed he shall return and **c** into
11:30 For ships of Kittim shall **c** against him,
11:41 He shall **c** into the beautiful land,
11:45 Yet he shall **c** to his end, with no one to help him.
Hos 3: 5 they shall **c** in awe to the LORD and
6: 1 "**C**, let us return to the LORD;
6: 3 he will **c** to us like the showers,
9: 4 it shall not **c** to the house of the LORD.
9: 7 The days of punishment have **c**,
9: 7 the days of recompense have **c**;
10:10 I will **c** against the wayward people
10:12 that he may **c** and rain righteousness upon you.
11: 9 and I will not **c** in wrath.
11:10 his children shall **c** trembling from the west.
11:11 They shall **c** trembling like birds from Egypt,
12:11 they shall surely **c** to nothing.
13:13 The pangs of childbirth **c** for him,
13:15 the east wind shall **c**, a blast from the LORD,
Joel 1:13 **C**, pass the night in sackcloth,
2: 2 nor will be again after them in ages to **c**.
3: 9 Let all the soldiers draw near, let them **c** up.
3:11 **C** quickly, all you nations all around,
3:12 and **c** up to the valley of Jehoshaphat;
3:18 a fountain shall **c** forth from the house of
Am 3:15 and the great houses shall **c** to an end,
4: 4 **C** to Bethel—and transgress;
5: 5 and Bethel shall **c** to nothing.
6:10 the answer will **c**, "No."
8: 2 "The end has **c** upon my people Israel;
Jnh 1: 2 for their wickedness has **c** up before me."
1: 7 The sailors said to one another, "**C**,
1: 7 on whose account this calamity has **c** upon us."
1: 8 "Tell us why this calamity has **c** upon us.
1: 8 Where do you **c** from?
1:12 of me that this great storm has **c** upon you."
4: 6 and made it **c** up over Jonah,
Mic 1: 3 and will **c** down and tread upon the high places of
1: 9 For her wound is incurable. It has **c** to Judah;
1:11 the inhabitants of Zaanan do not **c** forth;
1:12 yet disaster has **c** down from the LORD to
1:15 the glory of Israel shall **c** to Adullam.
3:11 No harm shall **c** upon us."
4: 1 In days to **c** the mountain of the LORD's house C
4: 2 and many nations shall **c** and say: "**C**, let us go up
4: 8 to you it shall **c**, the former dominion shall **c**,
5: 2 from you shall **c** forth for me one who is to rule
5: 5 Assyrians **c** into our land and tread upon our soil,
5: 6 from the Assyrians if they **c** into our land or tread
6: 6 "With what shall I **c** before the LORD,
6: 6 Shall I **c** before him with burnt offerings,
7: 4 day of their sentinels, of their punishment, has **c**;
7:12 that day they will **c** to you from Assyria to Egypt,
7:17 they shall **c** trembling out of their fortresses;
Na 2: 1 A shatterer has **c** up against you.
2: 5 they stumble as they **c** forward;
Hab 1: 8 Their horsemen **c** from far away;
1: 9 They all **c** for violence, with faces
2: 3 it will surely **c**, it will not delay.
2:16 The cup in the LORD's right hand will **c** around
2:16 and shame will **c** upon your glory!
3:16 of calamity to **c** upon the people who attack us.
Hag 1: 2 These people say the time has not yet **c** to rebuild
2: 7 so that the treasure of all nations shall **c**,
2:15 consider what will **c** to pass from this day on.
Zec 1:21 but these have **c** to terrify them,
2:10 For lo, I will **c** and dwell in your midst,
3: 8 For they are an omen of things to **c**: D
3:10 you shall invite each other to **c** under your vine
6:15 Those who are far off shall **c** and help to build
8:20 Peoples shall yet **c**, the inhabitants of many cities;
8:21 "**C**, let us go to entreat the favor of the LORD,
8:22 Many peoples and strong nations shall **c** to seek

Zec 10: 4 Out of them shall c the cornerstone,
12: 3 the nations of the earth shall c together against it.
12: 9 that day I will seek to destroy all the nations that c
14: 5 Then the LORD my God will c,
14:16 the nations that have c against Jerusalem shall go
14:18 on them shall c the plague that the LORD inflicts
14:21 that all who sacrifice may c and use them to boil
Mal 3: 1 and the Lord whom you seek will suddenly c
4: 6 so that I will not c and strike the land with a curse.
Mt 2: 2 and have c to pay him homage."
2: 6 for from you shall c a ruler who is
3: 2 "Repent, for the kingdom of heaven has c near."
3: 7 Who warned you to flee from the wrath to c?
3:14 and do you c to me?"
4:17 "Repent, for the kingdom of heaven has c near."
5:17 "Do not think that I have c to abolish the law or
5:17 I have c not to abolish but to fulfill.
5:24 and then c and offer your gift.
5:25 C to terms quickly with your accuser
6:10 Your kingdom c. Your will be done,
7:15 who c to you in sheep's clothing
8: 1 When Jesus had c down from the mountain,
8: 7 And he said to him, "I will c and cure him."
8: 8 I am not worthy to have you c under my roof;
8: 9 and he goes, and to another, 'C,' and he comes,
8:11 many will c from east and west and will eat
8:29 Have you c here to torment us before the time?"
9:13 For I have c to call not the righteous but sinners."
9:15 days will c when the bridegroom is taken away
9:18 but c and lay your hand on her, and she will live."
10: 7 'The kingdom of heaven has c near.'
10:13 If the house is worthy, let your peace c upon it;
10:34 not think that I have c to bring peace to the earth;
10:34 I have not c to bring peace, but a sword.
10:35 For I have c to set a man against his father,
11: 3 "Are you the one who is to c,
11:14 he is Elijah who is to c.
11:28 "C to me, all you that are weary
12:28 then the kingdom of God has c to you.
12:32 either in this age or in the age to c. B
13:27 Where, then, did these weeds c from?'
13:32 birds of the air c and make nests in its branches."
13:49 The angels will c out and separate the evil from
14:28 command me to c to you on the water."
14:29 He said, "C." So Peter got out of the
15:19 For out of the heart c evil intentions, murder,
16:27 the Son of Man is to c with his angels in the glory
17:10 then, do the scribes say that Elijah must c first?"
17:12 but I tell you that Elijah has already c,
18: 7 Occasions for stumbling are bound to c,
19:14 "Let the little children c to me,
19:21 and you will have treasure in heaven; then c,
21: 1 When they had c near Jerusalem
21:19 "May no fruit ever c from you again!"
21:25 Did the baptism of John c from heaven,
21:34 When the harvest time had c,
21:38 c, let us kill him and get his inheritance.'
22: 3 to the wedding banquet, but they would not c.
22: 4 c to the wedding banquet.'
23:35 that upon you may c all the righteous blood shed
23:36 all this will c upon this generation.
24: 5 For many will c in my name, saying,
24:14 and then the end will c.
24:50 of that slave will c on a day when he does
25: 6 C out to meet him.'
25:34 the king will say to those at his right hand, 'C,
26:41 and pray that you may not c into the time of trial;
26:55 "Have you c out with swords and clubs
27:40 you are the Son of God, c down from the cross."
27:42 let him c down from the cross now,
27:49 let us see whether Elijah will c to save him."
28: 6 C, see the place where he lay.
Mk 1:15 and the kingdom of God has c near;
1:24 Have you c to destroy us?
1:25 saying, "Be silent, and c out of him!"
2:17 I have c to call not the righteous but sinners."
2:20 The days will c when the bridegroom is taken away
3: 3 the man who had the withered hand, "C forward."
3:26 he cannot stand, but his end has c.
4:19 desire for other things c in and choke the word,
4:22 nor is anything secret, except to c to light.
4:29 because the harvest has c."
4:35 On that day, when evening had c, he said to them,
5: 8 For he had said to him, "C out of the man,
5:23 C and lay your hands on her,
6:31 "C away to a deserted place all by yourselves
7: 1 of the scribes who had c from Jerusalem gathered
7:15 but the things that c out are what defile."
7:21 from the human heart, that evil intentions c:
7:23 All these evil things c from within,
8: 3 and some of them have c from a great distance."
9: 1 until they see that the kingdom of God has c
9:11 "Why do the scribes say that Elijah must c first?"
9:13 But I tell you that Elijah has c,
9:25 c out of him, and never enter him again!"
9:29 "This kind can c out only through prayer."
10:14 "Let the little children c to me;
10:21 and you will have treasure in heaven; then c,
10:30 and in the age to c eternal life. B
11:23 but believe that what you say will c to pass,
11:30 Did the baptism of John c from heaven,
12: 7 c, let us kill him, and the inheritance will be ours.'
12: 9 He will c and destroy the tenants and give
13: 6 Many will c in my name and say, 'I am he!'
13: 7 this must take place, but the end is still to c.
13:33 for you do not know when the time will c.
13:35 not know when the master of the house will c,

Mk 14:38 and pray that you may not c into the time of trial;
14:41 Enough! The hour has c;
14:48 "Have you c out with swords and clubs
15:30 save yourself, and c down from the cross!"
15:32 the King of Israel, c down from the cross now,
15:36 let us see whether Elijah will c to take him down."
15:41 and there were many other women who had c up
15:42 When evening had c, and since it was the day
Lk 1:22 When he did c out, he could not speak to them,
1:35 "The Holy Spirit will c upon you,
3: 7 Who warned you to flee from the wrath to c?
4:34 Have you c to destroy us?
4:35 saying, "Be silent, and c out of him!"
4:36 the unclean spirits, and out they c!"
5: 7 in the other boat to c and help them.
5:17 near by (they had c from every village of Galilee
5:32 I have c to call not the righteous but sinners
5:35 The days will c when the bridegroom will
6: 8 to the man who had the withered hand, "C and
6:18 They had c to hear him and to be healed
7: 3 asking him to c and heal his slave.
7: 6 for I am not worthy to have you c under my roof;
7: 7 therefore I did not presume to c to you.
7: 8 and he goes, and to another, 'C,' and he comes,
7:19 "Are you the one who is to c,
7:20 When the men had c to him, they said,
7:20 'Are you the one who is to c,
7:33 For John the Baptist has c eating no bread
7:34 the Son of Man has c eating and drinking,
8:17 that will not become known and c to light.
8:29 the unclean spirit to c out of the man.
8:41 at Jesus' feet and begged him to c to his house,
9:37 when they had c down from the mountain,
9:54 to c down from heaven and consume them?"
10: 9 'The kingdom of God has c near to you.'
10:11 Yet know this: the kingdom of God has c near.'
10:35 of him; and when I c back,
11: 2 be your name. Your kingdom c.
11:20 then the kingdom of God has c to you.
12:37 and he will c and serve them.
12:46 of that slave will c on a day when he does
12:51 Do you think that I have c to bring peace to
13: 7 For three years I have c looking for fruit
13:14 c on those days and be cured,
13:25 'I do not know where you c from.'
13:27 But he will say, 'I do not know where you c from;
13:29 Then people will c from east and west,
14: 9 the host who invited both of you may c and say
14:17 'C; for everything is ready now.'
14:20 and therefore I cannot c.'
14:23 and compel people to c in,
15:27 He replied, 'Your brother has c,
15:32 this brother of yours was dead and has c to life;
16:21 even the dogs would c and lick his sores.
16:28 that they will not also c into this place of torment.'
17: 1 "Occasions for stumbling are bound to c,
17: 1 but woe to anyone by whom they c!
17: 7 among you would say to your slave who has just c
17: 7 'C here at once and take your place at the table'?
17:31 in the house must not c down to take them away;
18:16 "Let the little children c to me,
18:22 and you will have treasure in heaven; then c,
18:30 and in the age to c eternal life." B
19: 5 "Zacchaeus, hurry and c down;
19: 9 "Today salvation has c to this house,
19:13 'Do business with these until I c back.'
19:29 When he had c near Bethphage and Bethany,
19:43 Indeed, the days will c upon you,
20: 4 Did the baptism of John c from heaven,
20:16 He will c and destroy those tenants and give
21: 6 the days will c when not one stone will be left
21: 8 for many will c in my name and say, 'I am he!'
21:20 then know that its desolation has c near.
21:35 For it will c upon all who live on the face of
22:40 "Pray that you may not c into the time of trial."
22:46 and pray that you may not c into the time of trial."
22:52 and the elders who had c for him,
22:52 "Have you c out with swords and clubs as
23:42 remember me when you c into your kingdom."
23:55 The women who had c with him
Jn 1: 3 came into being. What has c into being
1:39 He said to them, "C and see."
1:46 "Can anything good c out of Nazareth?"
1:46 Philip said to him, "C and see."
2: 4 My hour has not yet c."
3: 2 that you are a teacher who has c from God;
3:19 that the light has c into the world,
3:20 For all who do evil hate the light and do not c to
3:21 But those who do what is true c to the light,
4:16 "Go, call your husband, and c back."
4:29 "C and see a man who told me everything I have
4:47 he heard that Jesus had c from Judea to Galilee,
4:47 and begged him to c down and heal his son,
4:49 "Sir, c down before my little boy dies."
5:24 and does not c under judgment,
5:29 and will c out—those who have done good,
5:40 Yet you refuse to c to me to have life.
5:43 I have c in my Father's name,
6:14 "This is indeed the prophet who is to c into
6:15 that they were about to c and take him by force
6:17 It was now dark, and Jesus had not yet c to them.
6:25 they said to him, "Rabbi, when did you c here?"
6:37 Everything that the Father gives me will c to me,
6:38 for I have c down from heaven,
6:42 can he now say, 'I have c down from heaven'?"
6:44 No one can c to me unless drawn by
6:65 "For this reason I have told you that no one can c

Jn 6:69 We have c to believe and know that you are
7: 6 Jesus said to them, "My time has not yet c,
7: 8 for my time has not yet fully c."
7:28 I have not c on my own.
7:30 because his hour had not yet c.
7:34 and where I am, you cannot c."
7:36 not find me' and 'Where I am, you cannot c'?"
7:37 he cried out, "Let anyone who is thirsty c to me,
7:41 "Surely the Messiah does not c from Galilee,
8:14 where I have c from and where I am going,
8:14 not know where I c from or where I am going.
8:20 because his hour had not yet c.
8:21 Where I am going, you cannot c."
8:22 'Where I am going, you cannot c'?"
8:42 I did not c on my own, but he sent me.
10: 9 and will c in and go out and find pasture.
11:19 and many of the Jews had c to Martha and Mary
11:30 Now Jesus had not yet c to the village,
11:34 They said to him, "Lord, c and see."
11:43 he cried with a loud voice, "Lazarus, c out!"
11:45 of the Jews therefore, who had c with Mary
11:48 the Romans will c and destroy both our holy place
11:56 Surely he will not c to the festival, will he?"
12:12 the great crowd that had c to the festival heard
12:23 hour has c for the Son of Man to be glorified.
12:27 No, it is for this reason that I have c to this hour.
12:30 Jesus answered, "This voice has c for your sake,
12:46 I have c as light into the world,
13: 1 that his hour had c to depart from this world
13: 3 and that he had c from God and was going to God,
13:33 'Where I am going, you cannot c.'
14: 3 I will c again and will take you to myself,
14:23 we will c to them and make our home with them.
15:22 If I had not c and spoken to them,
16: 7 the Advocate will not c to you;
16:13 and he will declare to you the things that are to c.
16:21 she has pain, because her hour has c.
16:28 I came from the Father and have c into the world;
16:32 The hour is coming, indeed it has c,
17: 1 up to heaven and said, "Father, the hour has c;
18:20 where all the Jews c together.
19:39 Nicodemus, who had at first c to Jesus by night,
20:29 not seen and yet have c to believe."
20:31 But these are written so that you may c to believe
21:12 Jesus said to them, "C and have breakfast."
21:22 "If it is my will that he remain until I c,
21:23 but, "If it is my will that he remain until I c,
Ac 1: 6 So when they had c together, they asked him,
1: 8 when the Holy Spirit has c upon you;
1:11 will c in the same way as you saw him go
2: 1 When the day of Pentecost had c,
3:20 of refreshing may c from the presence of the Lord,
7: 7 that they shall c out and worship me in this place.'
7:14 and all his relatives to c to him, seventy-five
7:34 and I have c down to rescue them.
7:34 C now, I will send you to Egypt.'
8:16 (for as yet the Spirit had not c upon any of them;
8:27 He had c to Jerusalem to worship
9:12 a man named Ananias c in and lay his hands
9:21 not c here for the purpose of bringing them bound
9:26 When he had c to Jerusalem,
9:38 "Please c to us without delay."
10:22 a holy angel to send for you to c to his house and
10:33 and you have been kind enough to c.
10:45 The circumcised believers who had c
14:11 "The gods have c down to us in human form!"
14:23 to the Lord in whom they had c to believe.
15:36 After some days Paul said to Barnabas, "C,
16: 7 When they had c opposite Mysia,
16: 9 "C over to Macedonia and help us."
16:15 c and stay at my home."
16:18 "I order you in the name of Jesus Christ to c out
16:36 therefore c out now and go in peace."
16:37 Let them c and take us out themselves."
17: 6 the world upside down have c here also,
18: 2 who had recently c from Italy
19: 4 the people to believe in the one who was to c
19:19 it was found to c to fifty thousand silver coins.
19:27 that this trade of ours may c into disrepute but
19:32 of them did not know why they had c together.
20:29 savage wolves will c in among you,
20:30 Some even from your own group will c distorting
21:22 They will certainly hear that you have c.
25: 5 "let those of you who have the authority c down
27:27 When the fourteenth night had c,
27:29 from the stern and prayed for day to c.
Ro 1:13 to c to you (but thus far have been prevented),
3: 8 "Let us do evil so that good may c"?
4:13 not c to Abraham or to his descendants through
5:14 who is a type of the one who was to c.
8:38 nor things present, nor things to c, nor powers, D
11:11 their stumbling salvation has c to the Gentiles,
11:25 a hardening has c upon part of Israel,
11:25 until the full number of the Gentiles has c in.
11:26 as it is written, "Out of Zion will c the Deliverer;
15:12 "The root of Jesse shall c,
15:23 as I have for many years, to c to you
15:27 for if the Gentiles have c to share
15:29 and I know that when I c to you,
15:29 I will c in the fullness of the blessing of Christ.
15:32 so that by God's will I may c to you with joy and
1Co 2: 1 I did not c proclaiming the mystery of God to you
4:19 But I will c to you soon, if the Lord wills,
4:21 Am I to c to you with a stick,
7: 5 and then c together again,
10:11 on whom the ends of the ages have c.
11:12 but all things c from God.

1Co 11:17 because when you c together it is not for the better
11:18 to begin with, when you c together as a church,
11:20 When you c together, it is not really to eat
11:33 when you c together to eat, wait for one another.
11:34 eat at home, so that when you c together,
11:34 the other things I will give instructions when I c.
13: 8 But as for prophecies, they will c to an end;
13: 8 as for knowledge, it will c to an end.
13:10 the partial will c to an end.
14: 6 if I c to you speaking in tongues,
14:26 When you c together, each one has a hymn,
15: 2 unless you have c to believe in vain.
15:11 so we proclaim and so you have c to believe.
15:21 the resurrection of the dead has also c through
15:34 C to a sober and right mind, and sin no more;
15:35 With what kind of body do they c?"
15:36 What you sow does not c to life unless it dies.
16: 2 so that collections need not be taken when I c.
16:11 so that he may c to me;
16:12 but he was not at all willing to c now.
16:12 He will c when he has the opportunity.
16:22 for the Lord. Our Lord, c!
2Co 1:15 Since I was sure of this, I wanted to c to you first,
1:16 and to c back to you from Macedonia
1:23 to spare you that I did not c again to Corinth.
3: 8 how much more will the ministry of the Spirit c
3:11 much more has the permanent c in glory!
4: 7 to God and does not c from us.
6:17 Therefore c out from them,
9: 4 if some Macedonians c with me and find
10:14 we were the first to c all the way to you with
12:14 Here I am, ready to c to you this third time.
12:20 For I fear that when I c,
12:21 I fear that when I c again,
13: 2 that if I c again, I will not be lenient—
13:10 that when I c, I may not have to be severe in using
Gal 2:16 And we have c to believe in Christ Jesus,
3:14 in Christ Jesus the blessing of Abraham might c to
3:19 until the offspring would c to whom
3:21 righteousness would indeed c through the law.
3:25 But now that faith has c,
4: 4 But when the fullness of time had c,
4: 9 Now, however, that you have c to know God,
5: 8 not c from the one who calls you.
Eph 1:17 of wisdom and revelation as you c to know him,
1:21 not only in this age but also in the age to c.
2: 7 to c he might show the immeasurable riches
4:13 until all of us c to the unity of the faith and of
4:29 Let no evil talk c out of your mouths,
Php 1:26 in your boasting in Christ Jesus when I c
1:27 whether I c and see you or am absent and hear
2:24 and I trust in the Lord that I will also c soon.
3: 7 these I have c to regard as loss because of Christ.
Col 1: 6 that has c to you. Just
1:18 that he might c to have first place in everything.
2:10 and you have c to fullness in him,
2:17 These are only a shadow of what is to c,
1Th 2:18 For we wanted to c to you—
3: 6 But Timothy has just now c to us from you,
5: 2 the day of the Lord will c like a thief in the night.
5: 3 then sudden destruction will c upon them,
5: 3 as labor pains c upon a pregnant woman,
2Th 2: 3 that day will not c unless the rebellion comes first
1Ti 1:16 making me an example to those who would c
2: 4 to be saved and to c to the knowledge of the truth.
3:14 I hope to c to you soon,
4: 8 for both the present life and the life to c.
6: 4 From these c envy, dissension, slander,
2Ti 2:25 God may perhaps grant that they will repent and c
3: 1 that in the last days distressing times will c.
4: 6 and the time of my departure has c.
4: 9 Do your best to c to me soon,
4:13 When you c, bring the cloak that I left
4:21 Do your best to c before winter.
Tit 3: 8 so that those who have c to believe in God may
3:12 or Tychicus, do your best to c to me at Nicopolis,
Heb 2:16 For it is clear that he did not c to help angels,
6: 5 the word of God and the powers of the age to c,
9:11 as a high priest of the good things that have c,
10: 1 law has only a shadow of the good things to c
10: 7 Then I said, 'See, God, I have c to do your will,
10: 9 "See, I have c to do your will."
10:37 the one who is coming will c and will not delay;
12:18 You have not c to something that can be touched,
12:22 But you have c to Mount Zion and to the city of
13:14 but we are looking for the city that is to c.
Jas 3:10 From the same mouth c blessing and cursing.
3:15 Such wisdom does not c down from above,
4: 1 and disputes among you, where do they c from?
4: 1 Do they not c from your cravings that are at war
4:13 C now, you who say, "Today
5: 1 C now, you rich people, weep and wail for
1Pe 1:21 Through him you have c to trust in God,
2: 4 C to him, a living stone, though rejected
4:17 For the time has c for judgment to begin with
2Pe 1:12 and are established in the truth that has c to you.
1:14 since I know that my death will c soon,
1:18 We ourselves heard this voice c from heaven,
3: 3 that in the last days scoffers will c,
3: 9 but all to c to repentance.
3:10 But the day of the Lord will c like a thief,
1Jn 2: 4 Whoever says, "I have c to know him,"
2:18 so now many antichrists have c.
4: 2 every spirit that confesses that Jesus Christ has c
5:20 of God has c and has given us understanding so
2Jn 1: 7 those who do not confess that Jesus Christ has c in
1:12 instead I hope to c to you and talk with you face
3Jn 1:10 So if I c, I will call attention to what he is doing
Rev 1: 4 from him who is and who was and who is to c,
1: 8 who is and who was and who is to c,
2: 5 I will c to you and remove your lampstand
2:16 I will c to you soon and make war against them
2:25 only hold fast to what you have until I c.
3: 3 If you do not wake up, I will c like a thief,
3: 3 you will not know at what hour I will c to you.
3: 9 I will make them c and bow down
3:20 I will c in to you and eat with you,
4: 1 to me like a trumpet, said, "C up here,
4: 8 who was and is and is to c."
6: 1 as with a voice of thunder, "C!"
6: 3 I heard the second living creature call out, "C!"
6: 5 I heard the third living creature call out, "C!"
6: 7 voice of the fourth living creature call out, "C!"
6:17 for the great day of their wrath has c,
7:13 robed in white, and where have they c from?"
7:14 "These are they who have c out of
9:12 There are still two woes to c.
11: 1 "C and measure the temple of God and the altar
11:12 a loud voice from heaven saying to them, "C
11:18 The nations raged, but your wrath has c,
12:10 "Now have c the salvation and the power and
12:12 for the devil has c down to you with great wrath,
13:13 even making fire c down from heaven to earth in
14: 7 for the hour of his judgment has c;
14:15 for the hour to reap has c,
15: 4 All nations will c and worship before you,
17: 1 and said to me, "C, I will show you the judgment
17: 8 because it was and is not and is to c.
17:10 one is living, and the other has not yet c;
18: 4 "C out of her, my people,
18: 8 therefore her plagues will c in a single day—
18:10 For in one hour your judgment has c."
19: 7 for the marriage of the Lamb has c,
19:17 "C, gather for the great supper of God,
20: 5 not c to life until the thousand years were ended.)
20: 8 and will c out to deceive the nations at
21: 9 "C, I will show you the bride,
22:17 The Spirit and the bride say, "C."
22:17 And let everyone who hears say, "C."
22:17 And let everyone who is thirsty c.
22:20 "Surely I am coming soon." Amen. C,
Tob 2: 2 I will wait for you, until you c back."
5: 5 Tobias said to him, "Where do you c from,
5: 5 he replied, "and I have c here to work."
5:14 kindred are good people; you c of good stock.
5:22 and he will c back in good health."
11: 5 down the road by which her son would c.
11:17 he blessed her saying, "C in, my daughter,
11:17 C in now to your home, and welcome,
11:17 C in, my daughter."
13:11 many nations will c to you from far away,
14: 4 but all will c true at their appointed times.
14: 4 be fulfilled and will c true;
14: 5 the period when the times of fulfillment shall c.
Jdt 3: 4 c and deal with them as you see fit."
5: 4 refused to c out and meet me?"
5: 5 No falsehood shall c from your servant's mouth.
5: 8 the God they had c to know,
5:19 and have c back from the places
6: 9 and none of my words shall fail to c true."
9: 5 and those that are to c.
11: 3 from them and have c over to us.
11: 3 In any event, you have c to safety.
11:18 Then I will c and tell you,
11:19 Then I will lead you through Judea, until you c
12:13 "Let this pretty girl not hesitate to c to my lord to
13: 3 for her to c out, as she did on the other days;
14: 3 Then panic will c over them,
14:13 so bold as to c down against us to give battle,
AdE 1:12 to obey him and would not c with the eunuchs.
1:19 that the queen may no longer c into his presence;
4:14 help and protection will c to the Jews
5: 4 let him and Haman c to the dinner
5: 8 let the king and Haman c to the dinner
6: 4 Now Haman had c to speak to the king
7: 4 This has c to my knowledge.
10: 4 Mordecai said, "These things have c from God;
15:10 for our law applies only to our subjects. C near."
Wis 1: 9 and a report of their words will c to the Lord,
2: 6 "C, therefore, let us enjoy the good things
3:16 But children of adulterers will not c to maturity,
4: 5 The branches will be broken off before they c
4:20 They will c with dread
6: 5 he will c upon you terribly and swiftly,
7:14 commended for the gifts that c from instruction.
8: 8 and infers the things to c;
8:13 an everlasting remembrance to those who c
12:12 Or who will c before you to plead as an advocate
14: 5 through the billows on a raft they c safely to land.
16: 4 upon those oppressors inescapable want should c,
17:12 but a giving up of the helps that c from reason;
19:13 not c upon the sinners without prior signs in
19:15 but, while punishment of some sort will c upon
Sir 1:30 because you did not c in the fear of the Lord,
2: 1 My child, when you c to serve the Lord,
3: 8 that his blessing may c upon you.
4:18 Then she will c straight back to them again
5: 7 suddenly the wrath of the Lord will c upon you,
5:13 Honor and dishonor c from speaking,
6:19 C to her like one who plows and sows,
6:26 C to her with all your soul,
11:14 poverty and wealth, c from the Lord.
11:24 "I have enough, and what harm can c to me now?"
13:22 If the rich person slips, many c to the rescue;
15: 2 She will c to meet him like a mother,
22:26 But if harm should c to me because of him,
24:19 "C to me, you who desire me,
25:23 and wounded heart c from an evil wife.
25:23 and weak knees c from the wife who does
28:12 yet both c out of your mouth.
29:26 "C here, stranger, prepare the table;
29:27 my brother has c for a visit,
31: 6 Many have c to ruin because of gold,
33:10 All human beings c from the ground,
33:15 they c in pairs, one the opposite of the other.
38:13 There may c a time when recovery lies in
40: 1 the day they c forth from their mother's womb
40: 9 c death and bloodshed and strife and sword,
41: 3 before you and those who will c after.
42:18 he sees from of old the things that are to c.
42:24 All things c in pairs, one opposite the other,
Bar 2: 7 with which the Lord threatened us have c upon us.
2:30 in the land of their exile they will c to themselves
4:14 Let the neighbors of Zion c;
4:22 and joy has c to me from the Holy One,
4:22 because of the mercy that will soon c to you
4:24 which will c to you with great glory and with
4:25 with patience the wrath that has c upon you
4:35 For fire will c upon her from the Everlasting
5: 9 with the mercy and righteousness that c from him.
LtJ 6: 3 when you have c to Babylon you will remain there
6:47 and reproach for those who c after.
Aza 1:17 for no shame will c to those who trust in you.
Sus 1: 4 to c to him because he was the most honored
1:42 and are aware of all things before they c to be;
1:50 And the rest of the elders said to him, "C,
1:52 your sins have now c home,
1Mc 1:11 from them many disasters have c upon us."
2:18 be the first to c and do what the king commands,
2:27 the law and supports the covenant c out with me!"
2:33 C out and do what the king commands,
2:34 But they said, "We will not c out,
3:20 They c against us in great insolence
4:46 the temple hill until a prophet should c to tell what
5:11 They are preparing to c and capture the stronghold
5:12 Now then, c and rescue us from their hands,
5:39 ready to c and fight against you."
6:11 I said to myself, 'To what distress I have c!
6:13 of this that these misfortunes have c upon me;
6:58 Now then let us c to terms with these people,
7:11 for they saw that they had c with a large force.
7:14 "A priest of the line of Aaron has c with the army,
7:28 I shall c with a few men to see you face to face
7:30 that Nicanor had c to him with treacherous intent,
8: 9 The Greeks planned to c and destroy them,
9: 9 and let us c back with our kindred and fight them;
9:10 If our time has c, let us die bravely
9:60 He started to c with a large force,
9:69 at the renegades who had counseled him to c into
9:72 and did not c again into their territory.
10:16 C now, we will make him our friend and ally."
10:59 Then King Alexander wrote to Jonathan to c
10:71 c down to the plain to meet us,
11: 9 He sent envoys to King Demetrius, saying, "C,
11:63 that the officers of Demetrius had c to Kadesh
12:42 When Trypho saw that he had c with a large army,
12:45 and c with me to Ptolemais.
13:21 to Trypho urging him to c to them by way of
14:22 have c to us to renew their friendship with us.
15:17 The envoys of the Jews have c to us as our friends
15:31 Otherwise we will c and make war on you."
16:19 he sent letters to the captains asking them to c
2Mc 1:15 the treasures and Antiochus had c with a few men
2:14 that had been lost on account of the war that had c
3: 9 that had been made and stated why he had c,
3:17 terror and bodily trembling had c over the man,
3:39 and destroys those who c to do it injury."
4:34 to c out from the place of sanctuary;
6: 9 therefore, the misery that had c upon them.
8: 8 to c to the aid of the king's government.
8:25 They captured the money of those who had c
9:11 and to c to his senses under the scourge of God,
9:18 for the judgment of God had justly c upon him,
12: 7 to c again and root out the whole community
14: 7 I mean the high priesthood—and have now c here,
15: 8 in mind the former times when help had c to them
15:24 of your arm may these blasphemers who c
1Es 5:56 and all who had c back to Jerusalem from exile;
8:21 not c upon the kingdom of the king and his sons.
8:78 now in some measure mercy has c to us from you,
8:86 that has happened to us has c about because
9:12 in our settlements who have foreign wives c at
3Mc 2: 5 an example to those who should c afterward.
2:10 to our petition when we c to this place and pray.
4:16 that are not able even to communicate or to c
5:26 Hermon arrived and invited him to c out,
5:27 by the unusual invitation to c out—
5:42 took no account of the changes of mind that had c
6:36 of the deliverance that had c to them through God.
7: 6 Since we have c to realize that the God of heaven
2Es 1:35 I will give your houses to a people that will c,
1:37 that is to c, whose children rejoice with gladness;
2:24 my people, because your rest will c.
2:32 Embrace your children until I c,
2:34 because he who will c at the end of
4:12 to be here than to c here and live in ungodliness,
4:14 'C, let us go and make war against the sea,
4:15 the sea also made a plan and said, 'C, let us go up
4:28 but the harvest of it has not yet c.
4:29 the field where the good has been sown will not c.
4:35 And when will the harvest of our reward c?

2Es 4:45 whether more time is to c than has passed,
4:46 but I do not know what is to c."
5:15 the angel who had c and talked with me held me
5:19 from me and do not c near me for seven days;
5:19 then you may c to me."
5:31 the angel who had c to me on
5:36 "Count up for me those who have not yet c,
5:41 or we, ourselves, or those who c after us?"
5:55 those who c after you will be smaller than you,
6:6 just as the end shall c through me alone and not
6:30 "I have c to show you these things this night.
6:45 and the arrangement of the stars to c into being;
6:54 and from him we have all c,
7:2 listen to the words that I have c to speak to you."
7:5 how can they c to the broad part unless they pass
7:16 not considered in your mind what is to c,
7:26 "For indeed the time will c,
7:26 the signs that I have foretold to you will c to pass,
7:47 I see that the world to c will bring delight to few,
7:69 And if after death we were not to c into judgment,
7:70 the world and Adam and all who have c from him,
7:75 in rest until those times c when you will renew
7:96 and shall inherit what is to c;
7:113 [43] and the beginning of the immortal age to c, B
7:114 [44] sinful indulgence has c to an end,
7:132 [62] he has mercy on those who have not yet c
7:136 [66] to those who are gone and to those yet to c—
8:1 but the world to c for the sake of only a few.
8:5 For not of your own will did you c into the world,
8:18 of the swiftness of the judgment that is to c.
8:41 all that have been sown will c up in due season,
8:43 If the farmer's seed does not c up,
8:47 For you c far short of being able
8:52 tree of life is planted, the age to c is prepared, B
9:20 in peril because of the devices of those who had c
9:25 Then I will c and talk with you."
10:9 over so many who have c into being upon her.
10:10 all have been born of her, and others will c;
10:10 and a multitude of them will c to doom.
10:15 bear bravely the troubles that have c upon you.
10:29 the angel who had c to me at first came to me,
11:10 and saw that the voice did not c from its heads,
11:39 so that the end of my times might c through them?
11:40 You, the fourth that has c,
11:43 Your insolence has c up before the Most High,
12:7 and if my prayer has indeed c up before your face,
12:32 and will c and speak with them.
12:48 but I have c to this place to pray on account of
12:49 and after these days I will c to you."
13:3 the figure of a man c up out of the heart of the sea.
13:12 the same man c down from the mountain and call
13:20 Yet it is better to c into these things,
13:25 your seeing a man c up from the heart of the sea,
13:30 of mind shall c over those who inhabit the earth.
13:34 as you saw, wishing to c and conquer him.
13:36 Zion shall c and be made manifest to all people,
13:46 and now, when they are about to c again,
13:58 and whatever things c to pass in their seasons.
14:18 and falsehood shall c near.
14:18 that you saw in the vision is already hurrying to c."
14:25 and you shall c here, and I will light in your heart
14:35 For after death the judgment will c,
14:36 But let no one c to me now,
15:27 Already calamities have c upon the whole earth,
15:29 The nations of the dragons of Arabia shall c out
15:30 with great power they shall c and engage them
15:33 and fear and trembling shall c upon their army,
15:44 They shall c to it and surround it;
15:59 you shall c and suffer fresh miseries.
16:14 and shall not return until they c over the earth.
16:18 What shall they do, when the calamities c?
16:65 You shall be put to shame when your sins c out
4Mc 4:3 "I have c here because I am loyal to
4:6 He said that he had c with the king's authority
9:31 I lighten my pain by the joys that c from virtue,
9:32 but you suffer torture by the threats that c
11:3 I have c of my own accord,
12:2 He summoned him to c nearer and tried

COMELY (2)

SS 1:10 Your cheeks are c with ornaments,
6:4 c as Jerusalem, terrible as an army with banners.

COMES‡ (328) [COME]

Ge 24:43 let the young woman who c out to draw,
24:50 "The thing c from the LORD;
32:8 "If Esau c to the one company and destroys it,
37:19 They said to one another, "Here c this dreamer.
42:15 unless your youngest brother c here!
42:22 So now there c a reckoning for his blood."
44:23 'Unless your youngest brother c down with you,
44:29 also from me, and harm c to him, you will bring
49:10 until tribute c to him; and the obedience of the
50:25 saying, "When God c to you,
Ex 1:19 and give birth before the midwife c to them."
9:19 not brought under shelter will die when the hail c
21:3 If he c in single, he shall go out single;
21:3 if he c in married, then his wife shall go out
28:35 and when he c out, so that he may not die.
29:30 when he c into the tent of meeting to minister in
32:34 Nevertheless, when the day c for punishment,
Lev 11:34 be unclean if water from any such vessel c
14:48 If the priest c and makes an inspection,
16:17 until he c out and has made atonement for himself
22:3 throughout your generations c near
25:22 until the ninth year, when its produce c in,
Nu 1:51 And any outsider who c near shall be put to death.
3:10 and any outsider who c near shall be put to death.
5:14 if a spirit of jealousy c on him, and he is jealous
5:14 or if a spirit of jealousy c on him,
5:30 a spirit of jealousy c on a man and he is jealous
11:20 until it c out of your nostrils
12:12 whose flesh is half consumed when it c out
16:29 or if a natural fate c on them,
19:14 everyone who c into the tent,
36:4 And when the jubilee of the Israelites c,
Dt 8:3 but by every word that c from the mouth of
18:6 and c to the place that the LORD will choose
19:16 a malicious witness c forward to accuse someone
23:11 When evening c, he shall wash himself
28:57 the afterbirth that c out from between her thighs,
29:22 well as the foreigner who c from a distant country,
31:11 when all Israel c to appear before
32:32 Their vine c from the vinestock of Sodom,
32:35 of their calamity is at hand, their doom c swiftly.
Jos 15:4 and c to its end at the sea.
15:11 then the boundary c to an end at the sea.
Jdg 4:20 and if anybody c and asks you, 'Is anyone here?'
11:31 then whoever c out of the doors of my house
13:14 She may not eat of anything that c from the vine.
1Sa 9:6 Whatever he says always c true.
9:13 For the people will not eat until he c,
16:11 for we will not sit down until he c here."
24:13 'Out of the wicked c forth wickedness';
2Sa 13:5 and when your father c to see you, say to him,
15:28 the fords of the wilderness until word c from you
17:3 the people back to you as a bride c home
18:27 "He is a good man, and c with good tidings."
1Ki 8:31 and c and swears before your altar in this house,
8:41 c from a distant land because of your name
8:42 when a foreigner c and prays toward this house,
2Ki 4:10 so that he can stay there whenever he c to us."
6:32 When the messenger c, see that you shut the door
1Ch 16:33 for he c to judge the earth.
29:16 for building you a house for your holy name c
2Ch 6:22 to take an oath and c and swears before your altar
13:9 Whoever c to be consecrated with a young bull
19:10 a case c to you from your kindred who live
20:9 'If disaster c upon us, the sword, judgment,
Job 3:24 For my sighing c like my bread,
3:25 Truly the thing that I fear c upon me,
3:26 I have no rest; but trouble c."
5:21 and shall not fear destruction when it c.
5:26 of grain c up to the threshing floor in its season.
14:2 c up like a flower and withers,
20:25 It is drawn forth and c out of their body,
20:25 and the glittering point c out of their gall;
27:9 Will God hear their cry when trouble c
28:5 As for the earth, out of it c bread;
33:26 he c into his presence with joy,
37:2 to the thunder of his voice and the rumbling that c
37:9 From its chamber c the whirlwind,
37:22 Out of the north c golden splendor;
41:20 Out of its nostrils c smoke,
41:21 and a flame c out of its mouth.
Ps 19:5 which c out like a bridegroom
22:25 From you c my praise in the great congregation;
30:5 but joy c with the morning.
50:3 Our God c and does not keep silence,
62:1 in silence; from him c my salvation.
75:6 the west and not from the wilderness c lifting up;
88:13 in the morning my prayer c before you.
112:10 the desire of the wicked c to nothing.
118:26 the one who c in the name of the LORD.
121:2 My help c from the LORD,
Pr 1:27 and your calamity c like a whirlwind,
7:10 Then a woman c toward him,
10:28 but the expectation of the wicked c to nothing.
11:2 When pride c, then c disgrace;
11:7 and the expectation of the godless c to nothing.
11:27 but evil c to the one who searches for it.
18:3 When wickedness c, contempt c also; and with
dishonor c disgrace.
18:17 until the other c and cross-examines.
20:4 harvest c, and there is nothing to be found.
21:5 but everyone who is hasty c only to want.
24:22 for disaster c from them suddenly,
Ecc 1:4 A generation goes, and a generation c,
2:12 for what can the one do who c after the king?
6:4 For it c into vanity and goes into darkness,
9:2 since the same fate c to all,
9:3 that the same fate c to everyone.
11:5 as you do not know how the breath c to the bones
11:8 All that c is vanity.
SS 2:8 Look, he c, leaping upon the mountains,
Isa 13:9 See, the day of the LORD c, cruel,
14:8 no one c to cut us down."
14:31 For smoke c out of the north,
16:12 when he c to his sanctuary to pray,
19:1 LORD is riding on a swift cloud and c to Egypt;
21:1 it c from the desert, from a terrible land.
21:12 The sentinel says: "Morning c, and also the night.
23:5 When the report c to Egypt,
26:21 For the LORD c out from his place to punish
28:4 whoever sees it, eats it up as soon as it c to hand.
28:29 This also c from the LORD of hosts;
30:5 everyone c to shame through a people
30:13 and about to collapse, whose crash c suddenly,
30:27 See, the name of the LORD c from far away,
34:1 the world, and all that c from it.
40:10 See, the Lord GOD c with might,
42:5 who spread out the earth and what c from it,
62:11 Say to daughter Zion, "See, your salvation c;
Isa 63:1 "Who is this that c from Edom,
Jer 4:11 A hot wind c from me out of the bare heights in
4:13 He c up like clouds, his chariots like
5:31 but what will you do when the end c?
6:20 to me is frankincense that c from Sheba,
17:6 and shall not see when relief c.
17:8 It shall not fear when heat c,
27:7 until the time of his own land c;
28:9 when the word of that prophet c true,
51:46 one year one rumor c, the next year another,
La 1:4 roads to Zion mourn, for no one c to the festivals;
Eze 7:5 Disaster after disaster! See, it c.
7:6 It has awakened against you; see, it c!
7:10 the day! See, it c! Your doom has gone out.
7:25 When anguish c, they will seek peace,
7:26 Disaster c upon disaster, rumor follows rumor;
12:22 and every vision c to nothing"?
21:7 See, it c and it will be fulfilled,"
21:22 Into his right hand c the lot for Jerusalem,
21:27 Until he c whose right it is; to him I will give it.
24:24 When this c, then you shall know that I am
33:4 and the sword c and takes them away,
33:6 and the sword c and takes any of them,
33:30 "Come and hear what the word is that c from
33:33 When this c—and come it will!—
38:18 when Gog c against the land of Israel,
Da 11:16 But he who c against him shall take
12:7 the shattering of the power of the holy people c to
Hos 4:14 thus a people without understanding c to ruin.
14:8 your faithfulness c from me.
Joel 1:15 and as destruction from the Almighty it c.
2:2 upon the mountains a great and powerful army c;
2:31 before the great and terrible day of the LORD c.
Am 5:9 so that destruction c upon the fortress.
Hab 1:4 therefore judgment c forth perverted.
Zep 2:2 there c upon you the fierce anger of the LORD,
2:2 there c upon you the day of the LORD's wrath.
Zec 9:9 your king c to you; triumphant and victorious is he,
Mal 4:1 the day that c shall burn them up,
4:5 before the great and terrible day of the LORD c.
Mt 4:4 by every word that c from the mouth of God.' "
5:37 anything more than this c from the evil one.
8:9 and to another, 'Come,' and he c, and to my slave,
10:23 the towns of Israel before the Son of Man c.
12:44 it c, it finds it empty, swept, and put in order.
13:19 the evil one c and snatches away what is sown in
15:11 but it is what c out of the mouth that defiles."
15:18 what c out of the mouth proceeds from the heart,
17:27 take the first fish that c up;
18:7 woe to the one by whom the stumbling block c!
21:9 Blessed is the one who c in the name of the Lord!
21:40 Now when the owner of the vineyard c,
23:39 the one who c in the name of the Lord.' "
24:27 the lightning c from the east and flashes as far as
25:31 "When the Son of Man c in his glory,
28:14 If this c to the governor's ears,
Mk 4:11 but for those outside, everything c in parables;
4:15 Satan immediately c and takes away the word
7:20 he said, "It is what c out of a person that defiles.
8:38 the Son of Man will also be ashamed when he c in
11:9 Blessed is the one who c in the name of the Lord!
13:36 else he may find you asleep when he c suddenly.
Lk 1:43 that the mother of my Lord c to me?
6:47 I will show you what someone is like who c
7:8 and to another, 'Come,' and he c, and to my slave,
8:12 devil c and takes away the word from their hearts,
9:26 when he c in his glory and the glory of the Father
11:25 When it c, it finds it swept and put in order.
12:33 where no thief c near and no moth destroys.
12:36 the door for him as soon as he c and knocks.
12:37 the master finds alert when he c;
12:38 If he c during the middle of the night,
13:35 you will not see me until the time c when you say,
13:35 the one who c in the name of the Lord.' "
14:10 so that when your host c, he may say to you,
14:26 "Whoever c to me and does not hate father
14:31 the one who c against him with twenty thousand?
15:6 And when he c home, he calls together his friends
18:8 the Son of Man c, will he find faith on earth?"
19:38 "Blessed is the king who c in the name of
22:18 the fruit of the vine until the kingdom of God c."
Jn 1:15 'He who c after me ranks ahead of me
1:30 'After me c a man who ranks ahead of me
3:8 you do not know where it c from or where it goes.
3:31 The one who c from above is above all;
3:31 The one who c from heaven is above all.
4:25 "When he c, he will proclaim all things to us."
4:35 'Four months more, then c the harvest'?
5:43 if another c in his own name, you will accept him.
5:44 from one another and do not seek the glory that c
6:33 that which c down from heaven and gives life to
6:35 Whoever c to me will never be hungry,
6:37 and anyone who c to me I will never drive away;
6:45 and learned from the Father c to me.
6:50 This is the bread that c down from heaven,
7:27 Messiah c, no one will know where he is from."
7:31 in him and were saying, "When the Messiah c,
7:42 that the Messiah is descended from David and c
9:29 we do not know where he c from."
9:30 You do not know where he c from,
10:10 The thief c only to steal and kill and destroy.
12:13 the one who c in the name of the Lord—
12:43 the glory that c from God.
14:6 No one c to the Father except through me.
15:26 "When the Advocate c, whom I will send to you
15:26 the Spirit of truth who c from the Father,
16:4 so that when their hour c you may remember

Jn 16: 8 And when he c, he will prove the world wrong
16:13 When the Spirit of truth c,
Ac 24:22 "When Lysias the tribune c down,
Ro 3:20 for through the law c the knowledge of sin.
9: 5 according to the flesh, c the Messiah,
10: 3 being ignorant of the righteousness that c
10: 5 concerning the righteousness that c from the law,
10: 6 But the righteousness that c from faith says,
10:17 So faith c from what is heard, and what is heard c through the word of Christ.
1Co 4: 5 the time, before the Lord c, who will bring to light
11:12 so man c through woman;
11:21 For when the time c to eat,
11:26 you proclaim the Lord's death until he c.
13:10 but when the complete c,
14:23 whole church c together and all speak in tongues,
15:24 Then c the end, when he hands over the kingdom
16:10 If Timothy c, see that he has nothing to fear
2Co 2:14 the fragrance that c from knowing him.
3:18 for this c from the Lord, the Spirit.
11: 4 For if someone c and proclaims another Jesus than
Gal 2:21 for if justification c through the law,
3:18 For if the inheritance c from the law, it no longer c from the promise;
Eph 5: 6 the wrath of God c on those who are disobedient.
Php 1:11 that c through Jesus Christ for the glory and praise
3: 9 not having a righteousness of my own that c from
3: 9 but one that c through faith in Christ,
Col 1:11 the strength that c from his glorious power,
4:10 if he c to you, welcome him.
2Th 1:10 when he c to be glorified by his saints and to
2: 3 that day will not come unless the rebellion c first
2: 6 so that he may be revealed when his time c.
1Ti 1: 5 of such instruction is love that c from a pure heart,
Heb 9:10 regulations for the body imposed until the time c
13:23 if he c in time, he will be with me when I see you.
Jas 2: 2 if a person with gold rings and in fine clothes c
2: 2 and if a poor person in dirty clothes also c in,
1Pe 2:12 and glorify God when he c to judge.
1Jn 2:16 c not from the Father but from the world.
2:21 and you know that no lie c from the truth.
2Jn 1:10 into the house or welcome anyone who c to you
Rev 3:12 the new Jerusalem that c down from my God out
11: 7 that c up from the bottomless pit will make war
17:10 and when he c, he must remain only a little while.
19:15 From his mouth c a sharp sword with which
Jdt 7:31 But if these days pass by, and no help c for us,
AdE 16: 9 and always judging what c before our eyes
Wis 2: 1 and there is no remedy when a life c to its end,
5:12 the air, thus divided, c together at once,
9: 6 be regarded as nothing without the wisdom that c
13: 5 from the greatness and beauty of created things c
14: 7 For blessed is the wood by which righteousness c.
15: 8 the time c to return the souls that were borrowed.
Sir 1:23 and then cheerfulness c back to them.
2:14 What will you do when the Lord's reckoning c?
5:14 for shame c to the thief, and severe condemnation
12: 3 No good c to one who persists in evil or
12:17 If evil c upon you, you will find him there ahead
18:20 Before judgment c, examine yourself;
21: 5 and his judgment c speedily.
26:28 and because of a third anger c over me:
27: 9 so honesty c home to those who practice it.
29:19 The sinner c to grief through surety;
30:23 and no advantage ever c from it.
38: 2 for their gift of healing c from the Most High,
39:31 their time c they never disobey his command."
41:10 Whatever c from earth returns to earth;
42:13 for from garments c the moth,
42:13 and from a woman c woman's wickedness.
43: 7 From the moon c the sign for festal days,
Bar 5: 2 on the robe of the righteousness that c from God;
LtJ 6:48 For when war or calamity c upon them,
1Mc 2:41 "Let us fight against anyone who c to attack us on
3:19 but strength c from Heaven.
8:24 If war c first to Rome or to any of their allies
8:27 if war c first to the nation of the Jews,
12:15 we have the help that c from Heaven for our aid,
16: 3 may the help that c from Heaven be with you."
1Es 4:16 the vineyards from which c wine.
4:59 "From you c the victory; from you c wisdom,
2Es 2:27 for when the day of tribulation and anguish c,
4:30 and will produce until the time of threshing c!
8: 2 but only a little dust from which gold c,
9:34 and when it c about that what was sown
12:34 and he will make them joyful until the end c,
16:38 but when the child c forth from the womb,
16:50 to her face when he c who will defend
4Mc 1:23 Fear precedes pain and sorrow c after.

COMFORT‡ (41) [COMFORTED, COMFORTER, COMFORTERS, COMFORTING, COMFORTS]

Ge 37:35 All his sons and all his daughters sought to c him;
1Ch 7:22 and his brothers came to c him.
Job 2:11 They met together to go and console and c him.
7:13 When I say, 'My bed will c me,
10:20 that I may find a little c
21:34 How then will you c me with empty nothings?
Ps 23: 4 and your staff—they c me.
71:21 You will increase my honor, and c me once again.
119:50 This is my c in my distress,
119:52 I think of your ordinances from of old, I take c,
119:76 Let your steadfast love become my c according
119:82 I ask, "When will you c me?"
Ecc 4: 1 with no one to c them!
4: 1 with no one to c them.
Isa 22: 4 not try to c me for the destruction of my beloved
40: 1 C, O c my people, says your God.
51: 3 the LORD will c Zion; he will c all her waste places,
51:19 and sword—who will c you?
57:18 I will lead them and repay them with c,
61: 2 of our God; to c all who mourn;
66:13 As a mother comforts her child, so I will c you;
Jer 16: 7 to offer c for the dead;
31:13 I will turn their mourning into joy, I will c them,
La 1: 2 among all her lovers she has no one to c her;
1: 9 her downfall was appalling, with none to c her.
1:17 but there is no one to c her;
1:21 with no one to c me.
2:13 To what can I liken you, that I may c you,
Zec 1:17 the LORD will again c Zion
Ac 9:31 the fear of the Lord and in the c of the Holy Spirit,
2Co 7:13 In this we find c.
Col 4:11 and they have been a c to me.
2Th 2:16 who loved us and through grace gave us eternal c
2:17 c your hearts and strengthen them
AdE 15:16 and all his servants tried to c her.
Sir 30:23 Indulge yourself and take c,
Bar 4:30 for the one who named you will c you.
2Es 12: 8 so that you may fully c my soul.
14:13 c the lowly among them, and instruct those

COMFORTED‡ (20) [COMFORT]

Ge 24:67 So Isaac was c after his mother's death.
37:35 but he refused to be c, and said, "No,
Ru 2:13 you have c me and spoken kindly to your servant,
Job 42:11 they showed him sympathy and c him for all
Ps 77: 2 my soul refuses to be c.
86:17 because you, LORD, have helped me and c me.
Isa 12: 1 your anger turned away, and you c me.
49:13 For the LORD has c his people,
52: 9 for the LORD has c his people,
54:11 O afflicted one, storm-tossed, and not c,
66:13 you shall be c in Jerusalem.
Jer 31:15 she refuses to be c for her children,
Mt 5: 4 "Blessed are those who mourn, for they will be c.
Lk 16:25 but now he is c here, and you are in agony.
Ac 20:12 the boy away alive and were not a little c.
AdE 15: 8 He c her with soothing words, and said to her,
Sir 38:17 then be c for your grief.
38:23 and be c for him when his spirit has departed.
48:24 and c the mourners in Zion.
49:10 for they c the people of Jacob and delivered them

COMFORTER (1) [COMFORT]

La 1:16 for a c is far from me, one to revive my courage;

COMFORTER (KJV) See also ADVOCATE

COMFORTERS (3) [COMFORT]

Job 16: 2 "I have heard many such things; miserable c are you all.
Ps 69:20 and for c, but I found none.
Na 3: 7 Where shall I seek c for you?

COMFORTING (1) [COMFORT]

Zec 1:13 replied with gracious and c words to the angel

COMFORTS (3) [COMFORT]

Job 29:25 like one who c mourners.
Isa 51:12 I, I am he who c you;
66:13 As a mother c her child, so I will comfort you;

COMING‡ (305) [COME]

A. DAYS ARE [SURELY] COMING (21)
B. TIME IS [SURELY] COMING (9)

Ge 24:13 and the daughters of the townspeople are c out
24:15 c out with her water jar on her shoulder.
24:45 there was Rebekah c out with her water jar
24:63 and looking up, he saw camels c.
29: 6 "and here is his daughter Rachel, c with
32: 6 and he is c to meet you,
33: 1 Now Jacob looked up and saw Esau c,
37:25 a caravan of Ishmaelites c from Gilead,
41:35 the food of these good years that are c,
43:25 they made the present ready for Joseph's c
Ex 4:14 even now he is c out to meet you,
9:32 for they are late in c up.)
18: 6 am c to you, with your wife and her two sons."
Nu 8:19 be no plague among the Israelites for c too close
21: 1 heard that Israel was c by the way of Atharim,
22:16 'Do not let anything hinder you from c to me;
33:40 heard of the c of the Israelites.
Dt 4:36 while you heard his words c out of the fire.
Jos 14:11 for war, and for going and c.
Jdg 1:24 When the spies saw a man c out of the city,
5:28 'Why is his chariot so long in c?
9:36 people are c down from the mountain tops!"
9:37 "Look, people are c down from Tabbur-erez,
9:37 and one company is c from the direction
9:43 he looked and saw the people c out of the city,
11:13 "Because Israel, on c from Egypt,
11:34 and there was his daughter c out to meet him
19:16 at evening there was an old man c from his work
Ru 4:11 the woman who is c into your house like Rachel
1Sa 2:31 a time is c when I will cut off your strength B
9:11 they met some girls c out to draw water,
9:14 they saw Samuel c out toward them on his way up
10: 5 to the town, you will meet a band of prophets c
11: 5 Now Saul was c from the field behind the oxen;
14:11 and the Philistines said, "Look, Hebrews are c out
14:13 and his armor-bearer, c after him, killed them.
18: 6 As they were c home, when David returned
22: 9 answered, "I saw the son of Jesse c to Nob,
25:19 "Go on ahead of me; I am c after you."
28:13 "I see a divine being c up out of the ground."
28:14 She said, "An old man is c up;
29: 6 in you from the day of your c to me until today.
2Sa 13:34 he saw many people c from the Horonaim road by
14:28 without c into the king's presence.
15:19 "Why are you also c with us?
18:25 He kept c, and drew near.
24:20 he saw the king and his servants c toward him;
1Ki 14: 5 "The wife of Jeroboam is c to inquire of you
15:17 from going out or c in to King Asa of Judah.
2Ki 4:25 When the man of God saw her c,
9:18 but he is not c back."
9:20 "He reached them, but he is not c back.
10:15 he met Jehonadab son of Rechab c to meet him;
19:27 your going out and c in,
20:17 Days are c when all that is in your house, A
1Ch 12:22 Indeed from day to day people kept c to David
2Ch 16: 1 from going out or c into the territory of King Asa
20: 2 "A great multitude is c against you from Edom,
20:11 by c to drive us out of your possession
20:12 against this great multitude that is c against us.
28:12 stood up against those who were c from the war,
35:21 I am not c against you today,
Ne 6:10 for they are c to kill you;
6:10 indeed, tonight they are c to kill you."
Est 8: 6 For how can I bear to see the calamity that is c
Ps 37:13 for he sees that their day is c.
78: 4 the c generation the glorious deeds of the LORD,
96:13 for he is c, for he is c to judge the earth.
98: 9 for he is c to judge the earth.
121: 8 and your c in from this time on and forevermore.
SS 3: 6 What is that c up from the wilderness,
8: 5 Who is that c up from the wilderness,
Isa 37:28 your going out and c in,
39: 6 Days are c when all that is in your house, A
66:18 and I am c to gather all nations and tongues;
Jer 6:22 See, a people is c from the land of the north,
7:32 Therefore, the days are surely c, says the LORD, A
8: 7 swallow, and crane observe the time of their c;
9:25 The days are surely c, says the LORD, A
10:22 Listen, it is c—a great commotion from the
16:14 Therefore, the days are surely c, says the LORD, A
19: 6 Therefore the days are surely c, says the LORD, A
23: 5 The days are surely c, says the LORD, A
23: 7 Therefore, the days are surely c, says the LORD, A
30: 3 For the days are surely c, says the LORD, A
31:27 The days are surely c, says the LORD, A
31:31 The days are surely c, says the LORD, A
31:38 The days are surely c, says the LORD, A
33: 5 The Chaldeans are c in to fight and to fill them
33:14 The days are surely c, says the LORD, A
46:13 about the c of King Nebuchadrezzar of Babylon
46:18 one is c like Tabor among the mountains,
47: 4 of the day that is c to destroy all the Philistines,
48:12 Therefore, the time is surely c, says the LORD, B
49: 2 Therefore, the time is surely c, says the LORD, B
49:19 a lion c up from the thickets of the Jordan against
50:28 of Babylon are c to declare in Zion the vengeance
50:41 Look, a people is c from the north;
50:44 a lion c up from the thickets of the Jordan against
51:47 the days are c when I will punish the images A
51:52 Therefore the time is surely c, says the LORD, B
Eze 5: 8 I, I myself, am c against you;
20: 3 Thus says the Lord GOD: Why are you c?
21: 3 I am c against you, and will draw my sword out
24:14 I the LORD have spoken; the time is c, I will act. B
30: 9 of Egypt's doom; for it is c!
33: 3 and if the sentinel sees the sword c upon the land
33: 6 if the sentinel sees the sword c and does not blow
38: 9 You shall advance, c on like a storm;
43: 2 the glory of the God of Israel was c from the east;
47: 2 and the water was c out on the south side.
Da 4:13 as I lay in bed, and there was a holy watcher, c
4:23 And whereas the king saw a holy watcher c down
7: 8 a little one c up among them;
7:13 like a human being c with the clouds of heaven.
8: 5 c across the face of the whole earth
Joel 2: 1 for the day of the LORD is c, it is near—
Am 4: 2 The time is surely c upon you, B
8:11 The time is surely c, says the Lord GOD, B
9:13 The time is surely c, says the LORD, B
Mic 1: 3 For lo, the LORD is c out of his place,
Zec 1:21 And I asked, "What are they c to do?"
5: 5 "Look up and see what this is that is c out."
5: 6 He said, "This is a basket c out."
5: 9 Then I looked up and saw two women c forward.
6: 1 And again I looked up and saw four chariots c out
14: 1 See, a day is c for the LORD,
Mal 3: 1 indeed, he is c, says the LORD of hosts.
3: 2 But who can endure the day of his c,
4: 1 See, the day is c, burning like an oven,
Mt 3: 7 But when he saw many Pharisees and Sadducees c
3:11 but one who is more powerful than I is c after me;
8:28 two demoniacs c out of the tombs met him.
16:28 before they see the Son of Man c in his kingdom."
17: 9 As they were c down the mountain,
17:11 "Elijah is indeed c and will restore all things;
21: 5 Look, your king is c to you, humble,

Mt 24: 3 and what will be the sign of your **c** and of the end
24:27 so will be the **c** of the Son of Man.
24:30 and they will see 'the Son of Man **c** on the clouds
24:37 so will be the **c** of the Son of Man.
24:39 so too will be the **c** of the Son of Man.
24:42 for you do not know on what day your Lord is **c.**
24:43 in what part of the night the thief was **c,**
24:44 for the Son of Man is **c** at an unexpected hour.
26: 2 "You know that after two days the Passover is **c,**
26:64 of Man seated at the right hand of Power and **c** on
Mk 1: 7 one who is more powerful than I is **c** after me;
1:10 And just as he was **c** up out of the water,
6:31 For many were **c** and going,
9: 9 As they were **c** down the mountain,
9:12 "Elijah is indeed **c** first to restore all things.
11:10 Blessed is the **c** kingdom of our ancestor David!
13:26 of Man **c** in clouds' with great power and glory.
14:62 and '**c** with the clouds of heaven.' "
15:21 who was **c** in from the country, to carry his cross;
Lk 3:16 but one who is more powerful than I is **c;**
9:42 While he was **c,** the demon dashed him to
12:39 the house had known at what hour the thief was **c,**
12:40 for the Son of Man is **c** at an unexpected hour."
12:45 slave says to himself, 'My master is delayed in **c,**'
15: 1 the tax collectors and sinners were **c** near to listen
17:20 by the Pharisees when the kingdom of God was **c,**
17:20 "The kingdom of God is not **c** with things that can
17:22 "The days are **c** when you will long to see one A
18: 3 In that city there was a widow who kept **c** to him
18: 5 that she may not wear me out by continually **c.**' "
21:26 and foreboding of what is **c** upon the world,
21:27 of Man **c** in a cloud' with power and great glory.
22:49 those who were around him saw what was **c,**
23:26 Simon of Cyrene, who was **c** from the country,
23:29 For the days are surely **c** when they will say, A
23:36 **c** up and offering him sour wine,
Jn 1: 9 which enlightens everyone, was **c** into the world.
1:27 the one who is **c** after me;
1:29 next day he saw Jesus **c** toward him and declared,
1:47 When Jesus saw Nathanael **c** toward him,
3:23 and people kept **c** and were being baptized
4:15 that I may never be thirsty or have to keep **c** here
4:21 the hour is **c** when you will worship
4:23 But the hour is **c,** and is now here,
4:25 "I know that Messiah is **c**" (who is called Christ).
4:54 the second sign that Jesus did after **c** from Judea
5:25 "Very truly, I tell you, the hour is **c,**
5:28 for the hour is **c** when all who are
6: 5 he looked up and saw a large crowd **c** toward him,
6:19 they saw Jesus walking on the sea and **c** near
9: 4 night is **c** when no one can work.
10:12 the wolf **c** and leaves the sheep and runs away—
11:20 When Martha heard that Jesus was **c,**
11:27 the Son of God, the one **c** into the world."
12:12 to the festival heard that Jesus was **c** to Jerusalem.
12:15 Look, your king is **c,** sitting on a donkey's colt!"
14:18 "I will not leave you orphaned; I am **c** to you.
14:28 'I am going away, and I am **c** to you.'
14:30 for the ruler of this world is **c.**
16: 2 an hour is **c** when those who kill you will think
16:25 The hour is **c** when I will no longer speak to you
16:32 The hour is **c,** indeed it has come,
17:11 but they are in the world, and I am **c** to you.
17:13 But now I am **c** to you,
19: 3 They kept **c** up to him, saying, "Hail,
Ac 2:20 before the **c** of the Lord's great and glorious day.
7:52 They killed those who foretold the **c** of
10: 3 a vision in which he clearly saw an angel of God **c**
10:11 and something like a large sheet **c** down,
10:21 what is the reason for your **c?"**
11: 5 a large sheet **c** down from heaven, being lowered
11:20 on **c** to Antioch, spoke to the Hellenists also,
13:24 before his **c** John had already proclaimed
13:25 No, but one is **c** after me;
24:25 discussed justice, self-control, and the **c** judgment,
28:21 and none of the brothers **c** here has reported
Ro 1:10 by God's will I may somehow at last succeed in **c**
15:22 that I have so often been hindered from **c** to you.
1Co 4:18 But some of you, thinking that I am not **c** to you,
15:23 then at his **c** those who belong to Christ.
16:17 the **c** of Stephanas and Fortunatus and Achaicus,
2Co 3: 5 of ourselves to claim anything as **c** from us;
7: 7 and not only by his **c,**
13: 1 This is the third time I am **c** to you.
Col 3: 6 On account of these the wrath of God is **c**
4: 9 he is **c** with Onesimus, the faithful
1Th 1:10 Jesus, who rescues us from the wrath that is **c.**
2: 1 that our **c** to you was not in vain,
2:19 of boasting before our Lord Jesus at his **c?**
3:13 be blameless before our God and Father at the **c**
4:15 who are left until the **c** of the Lord,
5:23 and blameless at the **c** of our Lord Jesus Christ.
2Th 2: 1 As to the **c** of our Lord Jesus Christ
2: 8 annihilating him by the manifestation of his **c.**
2: 9 The **c** of the lawless one is apparent in
2Ti 4: 3 For the time is **c** when people will not put up B
Heb 2: 5 Now God did not subject the **c** world,
8: 8 "The days are surely **c,** says the Lord, A
10:37 the one who is **c** will come and will not delay;
Jas 1:17 is from above, **c** down from the Father of lights,
5: 1 weep and wail for the miseries that are **c** to you.
5: 7 therefore, beloved, until the **c** of the Lord.
5: 8 for the **c** of the Lord is near.
2Pe 1:16 to you the power and **c** of our Lord Jesus Christ,
2: 6 and made them an example of what is **c** to
3: 4 "Where is the promise of his **c?**
3:12 waiting for and hastening the **c** of the day of God,
1Jn 2:18 As you have heard that antichrist is **c,**
2:28 and not be put to shame before him at his **c.**
4: 3 of which you have heard that it is **c;**
Jude 1:14 the Lord is **c** with ten thousands of his holy ones,
Rev 1: 7 He is **c** with the clouds;
3:10 that is **c** on the whole world to test the inhabitants
3:11 I am **c** soon; hold fast to what
4: 5 **C** from the throne are flashes of lightning,
9:18 and smoke and sulfur **c** out of their mouths.
10: 1 I saw another mighty angel **c** down from heaven,
11:14 The third woe is **c** very soon.
16:13 And I saw three foul spirits like frogs **c** from
16:15 ("See, I am **c** like a thief!
18: 1 this I saw another angel **c** down from heaven,
20: 1 Then I saw an angel **c** down from heaven,
21: 2 **c** down out of heaven from God,
21:10 the holy city Jerusalem **c** down out of heaven
22: 7 "See, I am **c** soon!
22:12 I am **c** soon; my reward is with me,
22:20 to these things says, "Surely I am **c** soon."
Tob 11: 6 When she caught sight of him **c,**
11: 6 your son is **c,** and the man who went with him!"
11:16 When the people of Nineveh saw him **c,**
Jdt 2: 7 for I am **c** against them in my anger,
6:12 and all the slingers kept them from **c** up
10:12 and where are you **c** from,
Wis 5:11 and afterward no sign of its **c** is found there;
Sir 38:21 Do not forget, there is no **c** back;
Bar 4:36 and see the joy that is **c** to you from God.
4:37 Look, your children are **c,** whom you sent away;
4:37 they are **c,** gathered from east and west,
1Mc 3:17 But when they saw the army **c** to meet them,
4:12 When the foreigners looked up and saw them **c**
4:19 a detachment appeared, **c** out of the hills.
4:60 to keep the Gentiles from **c** and trampling them
14:21 and we rejoiced at their **c.**
16: 5 where a large force of infantry and cavalry was **c**
2Mc 8: 6 **C** without warning, he would set fire to towns
8:16 of Gentiles who were wickedly **c** against them,
8:18 with a single nod to strike down those who are **c**
12:38 As the seventh day was **c** on,
13: 1 that Antiochus Eupator was **c** with a great army
13: 9 The king with barbarous arrogance was **c** to show
14:15 the Jews heard of Nicanor's **c** and the gathering of
15:20 When all were now looking forward to the **c** issue,
1Es 5:56 after their **c** to the temple of God in Jerusalem,
6:20 Then this Sheshbazzar, after **c** here,
3Mc 4:11 an obvious spectacle to all **c** back into the city and
4:15 **c** to an end after forty days but still uncompleted.
2Es 1:38 look with pride and see the people **c** from the east;
5: 1 lo, the days are **c** when those who inhabit A
6:18 "The days are **c** when I draw near to visit A
12:11 The eagle that you saw **c** up from the sea is
12:13 days are **c** when a kingdom shall rise on earth, A
12:17 **c** not from the eagle's heads but from the midst
13:27 as for your seeing wind and fire and a storm **c** out
13:29 The days are **c** when the Most High will deliver A
13:32 whom you saw as a man **c** up from the sea.
13:51 Why did I see the man **c** up from the heart of
16:39 the calamities will not delay in **c** upon the earth,

COMINGS (3) [COME]

2Sa 3:25 and to learn your **c** and goings and to learn all
2Ki 11: 8 Be with the king in his **c** and goings."
2Ch 23: 7 Stay with the king in his **c** and goings."

COMMAND‡ (246) [COMMANDED, COMMANDER, COMMANDER'S, COMMANDER-IN-CHIEF, COMMANDERS, COMMANDING, COMMANDMENT, COMMANDMENT'S, COMMANDMENTS, COMMANDS, SECOND-IN-COMMAND]

Ge 27: 8 Now therefore, my son, obey my word as I **c** you.
41:40 all my people shall order themselves as you **c;**
Ex 7: 2 You shall speak all that I **c** you,
27:20 You shall further **c** the Israelites
34:11 Observe what I **c** you today.
36: 6 So Moses gave **c,** and word was proclaimed
Lev 6: 9 **C** Aaron and his sons, saying:
13:54 the priest shall **c** them to wash the article in which
14: 4 the priest shall **c** that two living clean birds
14: 5 The priest shall **c** that one of the birds
14:36 The priest shall **c** that they empty the house before
14:40 the priest shall **c** that the stones in which
24: 2 **C** the people of Israel to bring you pure oil
Nu 4:27 All the service of the Gershonites shall be at the **c**
5: 2 **C** the Israelites to put out of
9: 8 so that I may hear what the LORD will **c**
9:18 the **c** of the LORD the Israelites would set out,
9:18 and at the **c** of the LORD they would camp.
9:20 the **c** of the LORD they would remain in camp;
9:20 to the **c** of the LORD they would set out.
9:23 At the **c** of the LORD they would camp,
9:23 and at the **c** of the LORD they would set out.
9:23 at the **c** of the LORD by Moses.
10:13 for the first time at the **c** of the LORD by Moses.
13: 3 according to the **c** of the LORD,
14:41 "Why do you continue to transgress the **c** of
20: 8 and **c** the rock before their eyes to yield its water.
20:24 because you rebelled against my **c** at the waters
22:18 not go beyond the **c** of the LORD my God,
23:20 See, I received a **c** to bless;
28: 2 **C** the Israelites, and say to them:
31:49 the warriors who are under our **c,**
Nu 32:28 So Moses gave **c** concerning them to Eleazar
33: 2 stage by stage, by **c** of the LORD;
33:38 Aaron the priest went up Mount Hor at the **c** of
34: 2 **C** the Israelites, and say to them:
35: 2 **C** the Israelites to give, from the inheritance
Dt 1:26 against the **c** of the LORD your God;
1:43 the **c** of the LORD and presumptuously went up
4: 2 to what I **c** you nor take away anything from it,
8: 1 that I **c** you today you must diligently observe,
9:23 against the **c** of the LORD your God,
12:11 then you shall bring everything that I **c** you to
12:14 and there you shall do everything I **c** you.
12:28 to obey all these words that I **c** you today,
12:32 must diligently observe everything that I **c** you;
15: 5 this entire commandment that I **c** you today.
15:11 to be some in need on the earth, I therefore **c** you,
15:15 for this reason I lay this **c** upon you today.
18:18 who shall speak to them everything that I **c.**
19: 7 Therefore I **c** you: You shall set apart three cities.
19: 9 that I **c** you today, by loving the LORD your God
24:18 therefore I **c** you to do this.
28: 8 The LORD will **c** the blessing upon you
31: 5 in full accord with the **c** that I have given to you.
32:46 give them as a **c** to your children,
34: 5 died there in the land of Moab, at the LORD's **c.**
Jos 1: 9 I hereby **c** you: Be strong
1:11 through the camp, and **c** the people:
1:18 whatever you **c,** shall be put to death.
3: 8 the one who shall **c** the priests who bear the ark of
4: 3 and **c** them, 'Take twelve stones from here out of
4:16 "**C** the priests who bear the ark of the covenant,
5:14 and he said to him, "What do you **c** your servant,
6:10 To the people Joshua gave this **c:**
8: 4 the **c,** "You shall lie in ambush against the city,
19:50 By **c** of the LORD they gave him the town
21: 3 So by **c** of the LORD the Israelites gave to
22: 9 of which they had taken possession by **c** of
Jdg 2: 2 But you have not obeyed my **c.**
9:29 If only this people were under my **c!**
1Sa 15:13 I have carried out the **c** of the LORD."
16:16 Let our lord now **c** the servants who attend you
2Sa 18: 2 one third under the **c** of Joab,
18: 2 one third under the **c** of Abishai son of Zeruiah,
18: 2 and one third under the **c** of Ittai the Gittite.
20:23 Now Joab was in **c** of all the army of Israel;
20:23 of Jehoiada was in **c** of the Cherethites and
1Ki 4: 4 Benaiah son of Jehoiada was in **c** of the army;
5: 6 **c** that cedars from the Lebanon be cut for me.
5:17 At the king's **c,** they quarried out great,
11:38 If you will listen to all that I **c** you,
20:35 At the **c** of the LORD a certain member of
2Ki 18:36 for the king's **c** was, "Do not answer him."
24: 3 this came upon Judah at the **c** of the LORD,
25:19 from the city he took an officer who had been in **c**
1Ch 10:13 to the LORD in that he did not keep the **c** of
12:32 and all their kindred under their **c.**
14:12 and at David's **c** they were burned.
21: 6 for the king's **c** was abhorrent to Joab.
21:17 "Was it not I who gave the **c** to count the people?
27: 6 a mighty man of the Thirty and in **c** of the Thirty;
28:21 and all the people will be wholly at your **c."**
2Ch 7:13 or **c** the locust to devour the land,
24: 8 So the king gave **c,** and they made a chest,
24:21 and by **c** of the king they stoned him to death in
26:13 Under their **c** was an army
35:10 in their divisions according to the king's **c.**
35:15 were in their place according to the **c** of David,
35:16 according to the **c** of King Josiah.
Ezr 6:14 by **c** of the God of Israel and by decree of Cyrus,
Ne 11:23 For there was a **c** from the king concerning them,
12:45 according to the **c** of David and his son Solomon.
Est 1:12 to come at the king's **c** conveyed by the eunuchs.
1:15 not performed the **c** of King Ahasuerus conveyed
3: 3 "Why do you disobey the king's **c?"**
4: 3 wherever the king's **c** and his decree came,
8:14 hurried out, urged by the king's **c.**
8:17 wherever the king's **c** and his edict came,
9: 1 the king's **c** and edict were about to be executed,
9:32 **c** of Queen Esther fixed these practices of Purim,
Job 37:15 Do you know how God lays his **c** upon them,
39:27 Is it at your **c** that the eagle mounts up
Ps 44: 4 and my God; you **c** victories for Jacob.
68:11 The Lord gives the **c;** great is the company of those
91:11 For he will **c** his angels concerning you
147:15 He sends out his **c** to the earth;
148: 8 snow and frost, stormy wind fulfilling his **c!**
Pr 8:29 so that the waters might not transgress his **c,**
Ecc 8: 2 Keep the king's **c** because of your sacred oath.
8: 5 Whoever obeys a **c** will meet no harm,
Isa 5: 6 I will also **c** the clouds that they rain no rain upon
10: 6 and against the people of my wrath I **c** him,
23:11 the LORD has given **c** concerning Canaan
29:11 If it is given to those who can read, with the **c,**
36:21 for the king's **c** was, "Do not answer him."
45:11 or **c** me concerning the work of my hands?
Jer 1: 7 and you shall speak whatever I **c** you,
1:17 stand up and tell them everything that I **c** you.
7:22 to them or **c** them concerning burnt offerings
7:23 But this **c** I gave them, "Obey my voice,
7:23 and walk only in the way that I **c** you,
7:31 which I did not **c,** nor did it come into my mind.
11: 4 saying, Listen to my voice, and do all that I **c** you.
12: 9 Is the hyena greedy for my heritage at my **c?**
14:14 nor did I **c** them or speak to them.
19: 5 which I did not **c** or decree,
26: 2 speak to them all the words that I **c** you;
29:23 in my name lying words that I did not **c** them;

Jer 32:35 though I did not c them,
34:22 I am going to c, says the LORD,
35:14 The c has been carried out that Jonadab son
35:14 for they have obeyed their ancestor's c.
35:16 of Jonadab son of Rechab have carried out the c
35:18 you have obeyed the c of your ancestor Jonadab,
39:11 King Nebuchadrezzar of Babylon gave c
52:25 from the city he took an officer who had been in c
La 3:37 Who can c and have it done,
Da 3:22 the king's c was urgent and the furnace was
3:28 They disobeyed the king's c and yielded
5:29 Then Belshazzar gave the c,
6:16 Then the king gave the c,
6:24 king gave a c, and those who had accused Daniel
Joel 2:11 Numberless are those who obey his c.
Am 9:3 there I will c the sea-serpent,
9:4 there I will c the sword, and it shall kill them;
9:9 I will c, and shake the house of Israel among all
Hab 3:9 sated were the arrows at your c.
Zec 9:10 and he shall c peace to the nations;
Mal 2:1 And now, O priests, this c is for you.
2:4 Know, then, that I have sent this c to you,
3:14 by keeping his c or by going about as mourners
Mt 4:3 c these stones to become loaves of bread."
4:6 'He will c his angels concerning you,'
14:28 if it is you, c me to come to you on the water."
19:7 "Why then did Moses c us to give a certificate
27:64 c the tomb to be made secure until the third day;
Mk 9:25 I c you, come out of him,
10:3 He answered them, "What did Moses c you?"
Lk 4:3 c this stone to become a loaf of bread."
4:10 'He will c his angels concerning you,
9:54 do you want us to c fire to come down
15:29 and I have never disobeyed your c;
Jn 10:18 I have received this c from my Father."
15:14 You are my friends if you do what I c you.
Ro 16:26 according to the c of the eternal God,
1Co 7:6 This I say by way of concession, not of c.
7:10 To the married I give this c—
7:25 Now concerning virgins, I have no c of the Lord,
14:37 that what I am writing to you is a c of the Lord.
2Co 8:8 I do not say this as a c,
1Th 4:16 For the Lord himself, with a cry of c,
5:27 I solemnly c you by the Lord that this letter
2Th 3:4 and will go on doing the things that we c.
3:6 Now we c you, beloved, in the name
3:10 even when we were with you, we gave you this c:
3:12 Now such persons we c and exhort in
1Ti 1:1 of Christ Jesus by the c of God our Savior and
6:17 c them not to be haughty,
Tit 1:3 with which I have been entrusted by the c
Phm 1:8 though I am bold enough in Christ to c you
Tob 3:6 c my spirit to be taken from me,
3:6 C, O Lord, that I be released from this distress;
3:13 C that I be released from the earth and not listen
14:3 and the seven sons of Tobias and gave this c:
14:8,9 So now, my children, I c you,
Jdt 2:3 that every one who had not obeyed his c should
AdE 3:3 "Mordecai, why do you disobey the king's c?"
3:4 that Mordecai was resisting the king's c.
8:8 for whatever is written at the king's c and sealed
Wis 9:8 You have given c to build a temple
14:16 the c of monarchs carved images were worshiped.
16:6 of deliverance to remind them of your law's c.
18:16 carrying the sharp sword of your authentic c,
Sir 24:8 "Then the Creator of all things gave me a c,
39:31 when their time comes they never disobey his c."
43:13 By his c he sends the driving snow and speeds
Bar 5:8 every fragrant tree have shaded Israel at God's c.
LtJ 6:62 to go over the whole world, they carry out his c.
1Mc 1:43 All the Gentiles accepted the c of the king.
1:50 "And whoever does not obey the c of
2:23 according to the king's c.
2:31 the king's c had gone down to the hiding places in
2:55 Joshua, because he fulfilled the c,
2:66 he shall c the army for you and fight the battle
3:1 who was called Maccabeus, took c in his place.
3:14 and his companions, who scorn the king's c."
5:19 and he gave them this c,
5:42 of the army at the stream and gave them this c,
12:23 We therefore c that our envoys report
2Mc 7:30 I will not obey the king's c,
7:30 the c of the law that was given to our ancestors
8:9 in c of no fewer than twenty thousand Gentiles
8:22 each to c a division, putting fifteen hundred men
9:8 in his superhuman arrogance that he could c
10:13 Unable to c the respect due his office,
12:20 set men in c of the divisions,
14:12 who had been in c of the elephants,
14:16 At the c of the leader,
15:5 and I c you to take up arms and finish
1Es 1:18 according to the c of King Josiah.
1:52 because of their ungodly acts he gave c to bring
4:5 and do not disobey the king's c;
6:11 'At whose c are you building this house
6:19 the c that he should take all these vessels back
6:28 "And I c that it be built completely,
7:4 and they completed it by the c of the Lord God
Man 1:3 the sea by your word of c, who confined the deep
3Mc 7:20 since at the king's c they had all
2Es 2:33 a c from the Lord on Mount Horeb to go to Israel.
8:14 with so great labor was fashioned by your c,
8:22 and at whose c they are changed to wind and fire,
8:22 whose c is strong and whose ordinance is terrible,
4Mc 7:17 "Not all have full c of their emotions,
9:11 at his c the guards brought forward the eldest,
14:11 Do not consider it amazing that reason had full c

COMMANDED‡ (427) [COMMAND]

Ge 2:16 And the LORD God c the man,
3:11 Have you eaten from the tree of which I c you not
3:17 about which I c you, 'You shall not eat of it,'
6:22 Noah did this; he did all that God c him.
7:5 And Noah did all that the LORD had c him.
7:9 went into the ark with Noah, as God had c Noah.
7:16 went in as God had c him;
21:4 when he was eight days old, as God had c him.
44:1 Then he c the steward of his house,
50:2 Joseph c the physicians in his service
Ex 1:17 they did not do as the king of Egypt c them,
1:22 Then Pharaoh c all his people,
5:6 same day Pharaoh c the taskmasters of the people,
7:6 they did just as the LORD c them.
7:10 to Pharaoh and did as the LORD had c;
7:20 Moses and Aaron did just as the LORD c.
12:28 and did just as the LORD had c Moses
12:50 the Israelites did just as the LORD had c Moses
16:16 This is what the LORD has c:
16:23 "This is what the LORD has c:
16:24 they put it aside until morning, as Moses c them;
16:32 Moses said, "This is what the LORD has c:
16:34 As the LORD c Moses, so Aaron placed it before
17:1 by stages, as the LORD c.
19:7 that the LORD had c him.
23:15 as I c you, you shall eat unleavened bread
29:35 just as I have c you;
31:6 so that they may make all that I have c you:
31:11 They shall do just as I have c you.
32:8 to turn aside from the way that I c them;
32:28 The sons of Levi did as Moses c,
34:4 up on Mount Sinai, as the LORD had c him,
34:18 as I c you, at the time appointed in the month
34:34 and told the Israelites what he had been c,
35:1 These are the things that the LORD has c you
35:4 This is the thing that the LORD has c:
35:10 and make all that the LORD has c:
35:29 for the work that the LORD had c by Moses to
36:1 in accordance with all that the LORD has c.
36:5 for doing the work that the LORD has c us
38:22 made all that the LORD c Moses;
39:1 as the LORD had c Moses.
39:5 as the LORD had c Moses.
39:7 as the LORD had c Moses.
39:21 as the LORD had c Moses.
39:26 as the LORD had c Moses.
39:29 as the LORD had c Moses.
39:31 as the LORD had c Moses.
39:32 as the LORD had c Moses.
39:42 the work just as the LORD had c Moses.
39:43 the work just as the LORD had c,
40:16 as the LORD had c him.
40:19 as the LORD had c Moses.
40:21 as the LORD had c Moses.
40:23 as the LORD had c Moses.
40:25 as the LORD had c Moses.
40:27 as the LORD had c Moses.
40:29 and the grain offering as the LORD had c Moses.
40:32 as the LORD had c Moses.
Lev 7:36 these the LORD c to be given them,
7:38 which the LORD c Moses on Mount Sinai,
7:38 when he c the people of Israel
8:4 And Moses did as the LORD c him.
8:5 "This is what the LORD has c to be done."
8:9 the holy crown, as the LORD c Moses.
8:13 on them, as the LORD c Moses.
8:17 the camp, as the LORD c Moses.
8:21 by fire to the LORD, as the LORD c Moses.
8:29 of the ram of ordination, as the LORD c Moses.
8:31 as I was c, 'Aaron and his sons shall eat it';
8:34 the LORD has c to be done to make atonement
8:35 not die; for so I am c."
8:36 and his sons did all the things that the LORD c
9:5 They brought what Moses c to the front of the tent
9:6 "This is the thing that the LORD c you to do,
9:7 for them; as the LORD has c."
9:10 into smoke on the altar, as the LORD c Moses;
9:21 before the LORD, as Moses had c.
10:1 such as he had not c them.
10:13 to the LORD; for so I am c.
10:15 that of your children forever, as the LORD has c.
10:18 have eaten it in the sanctuary, as I c."
16:34 And Moses did as the LORD had c him.
17:2 This is what the LORD has c.
24:23 people of Israel did as the LORD had c Moses.
Nu 1:19 as the LORD c Moses.
1:54 they did just as the LORD c Moses.
2:33 Just as the LORD had c Moses,
2:34 The Israelites did just as the LORD had c Moses:
3:16 according to the word of the LORD, as he was c.
3:42 among the Israelites, as the LORD c him.
3:51 as the LORD had c Moses.
4:49 by him, as the LORD c Moses.
8:3 as the LORD had c Moses.
8:20 with the Levites just as the LORD had c Moses
8:22 the LORD had c Moses concerning the Levites,
9:5 Just as the LORD had c Moses,
15:23 that the LORD has c you by Moses, from the day
15:36 just as the LORD had c Moses.
17:11 Moses did so; just as the LORD c him, so he did.
19:2 This is a statute of the law that the LORD has c:
20:9 the staff from before the LORD, as he had c him.
20:27 Moses did as the LORD had c;
26:4 and upward," as the LORD c Moses.
27:11 a statute and ordinance, as the LORD c Moses."

Nu 27:22 So Moses did as the LORD c him;
29:40 as the LORD had c Moses.
30:1 This is what the LORD has c.
30:16 the statutes that the LORD c Moses concerning
31:7 as the LORD had c Moses,
31:21 of the law that the LORD has c Moses:
31:31 the priest did as the LORD had c Moses:
31:41 to Eleazar the priest, as the LORD had c Moses.
31:47 as the LORD had c Moses.
34:13 Moses c the Israelites, saying:
34:13 the LORD has c to give to the nine tribes and to
34:29 the LORD c to apportion the inheritance for
36:2 "The LORD c my lord to give the land
36:2 and my lord was c by the LORD to give
36:5 Then Moses c the Israelites according to the word
36:10 of Zelophehad did as the LORD had c Moses.
36:13 that the LORD c through Moses to the Israelites
Dt 1:3 to the Israelites just as the LORD had c him
1:41 just as the LORD our God c us."
5:12 as the LORD your God c you.
5:15 LORD your God c you to keep the sabbath day.
5:16 as the LORD your God c you,
5:32 to do as the LORD your God has c you;
5:33 the path that the LORD your God has c you,
6:17 and his decrees, and his statutes that he has c you.
6:20 that the LORD our God has c you?"
6:24 Then the LORD c us to observe all these statutes,
6:25 as he has c us, we will be in the right."
9:12 to turn from the way that I c them;
9:16 to turn from the way that the LORD had c you.
10:5 and there they are, as the LORD c me.
12:21 and you slaughter as I have c you any of your herd
13:5 in which the LORD your God c you to walk.
18:20 in my name a word that I have not c the prophet
20:17 just as the LORD your God has c,
24:8 just as I have c them.
26:13 with your entire commandment that you c me;
26:14 doing just as you c me.
28:45 the commandments and the decrees that he c you.
29:1 the LORD c Moses to make with the Israelites in
31:10 Moses c them: "Every seventh year,
31:25 Moses c the Levites who carried the ark of
31:29 turning aside from the way that I have c you.
34:9 doing as the LORD had c Moses.
Jos 1:7 with all the law that my servant Moses c you;
1:10 Then Joshua c the officers of the people,
1:13 that Moses the servant of the LORD c you,
1:16 "All that you have c us we will do,
3:3 and c the people, "When you see the ark of
4:8 The Israelites did as Joshua c.
4:10 that the LORD c Joshua to tell the people,
4:10 according to all that Moses had c Joshua.
4:17 Joshua therefore c the priests,
6:8 As Joshua had c the people,
8:8 as the LORD has ordered; see, I have c you."
8:29 at sunset Joshua c, and they took his body down
8:31 of the LORD had c the Israelites, as it is written
8:33 Moses the servant of the LORD had c at the first,
8:35 a word of all that Moses c that Joshua did not read
9:24 that the LORD your God had c his servant Moses
10:27 At sunset Joshua c, and they took them down
10:40 as the LORD God of Israel c.
11:9 And Joshua did to them as the LORD c him;
11:12 as Moses the servant of the LORD had c.
11:15 As the LORD had c his servant Moses,
11:15 so Moses c Joshua, and so Joshua did;
11:15 of all that the LORD had c Moses.
11:20 just as the LORD had c Moses.
13:6 to Israel for an inheritance, as I have c you.
14:2 as the LORD had c Moses for the nine
14:5 The Israelites did as the LORD c Moses;
17:4 "The LORD c Moses to give us an inheritance
21:2 "The LORD c through Moses that we
21:8 as the LORD had c through Moses.
22:2 the servant of the LORD c you, and have obeyed
me in all that I have c you;
22:5 that Moses the servant of the LORD c you,
Jdg 2:20 that I c their ancestors, and have
3:4 which he c their ancestors by Moses.
13:14 She is to observe everything that I c her."
19:30 Then he c the men whom he sent, saying,
21:10 and c them, "Go, put the inhabitants
1Sa 2:29 at my sacrifices and my offerings that I c,
13:13 of the LORD your God, which he c you.
13:14 you have not kept what the LORD c you."
16:4 Samuel did what the LORD c,
17:20 took the provisions, and went as Jesse had c him.
18:22 Saul c his servants, "Speak to David in private
20:29 and my brother has c me to be there.
2Sa 4:12 So David c the young men, and they killed them;
5:25 David did just as the LORD had c him;
7:7 whom I c to shepherd my people Israel, saying,
13:28 Then Absalom c his servants,
13:28 Do not be afraid; have I not myself c you?
13:29 of Absalom did to Amnon as Absalom had c.
14:19 For it was your servant Joab who c me;
18:12 for in our hearing the king c you and Abishai
21:14 they did all that the king c.
24:19 David went up, as the LORD had c.
1Ki 2:46 Then the king c Benaiah son of Jehoiada;
8:58 and his ordinances, which he c our ancestors.
9:4 doing according to all that I have c you,
11:10 and had c him concerning this matter,
11:10 but he did not observe what the LORD c.
11:11 and my statutes that I have c you,
13:9 For thus I was c by the word of the LORD:
13:21 that the LORD your God c you,

1Ki 15: 5 not turn aside from anything that he c him all
17: 4 and I have c the ravens to feed you there."
17: 9 for I have c a widow there to feed you."
22:31 the king of Aram had c the thirty-two captains
2Ki 5:13 if the prophet had c you to do something difficult,
11: 5 He c them, "This is what you are to do:
11: 9 according to all that the priest Jehoiada c;
11:15 the priest Jehoiada c the captains who were set
14: 6 where the LORD c, "The parents shall not be put
16:15 King Ahaz c the priest Uriah, saying,
16:16 The priest Uriah did everything that King Ahaz c.
17:13 the law that I c your ancestors and that I sent
17:15 the LORD had c them that they should not do
17:27 Then the king of Assyria c,
17:34 or the law or the commandment that the LORD c
17:35 a covenant with them and c them,
18: 6 the commandments that the LORD c Moses.
18:12 all that Moses the servant of the LORD had c;
21: 8 to do according to all that I have c them,
21: 8 to all the law that my servant Moses c them."
22:12 Then the king c the priest Hilkiah,
23: 4 The king c the high priest Hilkiah,
23:21 The king c all the people,
1Ch 6:49 to all that Moses the servant of God had c.
11: 2 it was you who c the army of Israel.
14:16 David did as God had c him,
15: 2 Then David c that no one but the Levites were
15:15 Moses had c according to the word of the LORD.
15:16 David also c the chiefs of the Levites
16:15 the word that he c, for a thousand generations,
16:40 in the law of the LORD that he c Israel.
17: 6 whom I c to shepherd my people, saying,
21:18 Then the angel of the LORD c Gad to tell David
21:27 Then the LORD c the angel,
22:13 the ordinances that the LORD c Moses for Israel.
22:17 David also c all the leaders of Israel
24:19 as the LORD God of Israel had c him.
2Ch 7:17 to all that I have c you and keeping my statutes
8:14 for so David the man of God had c.
8:15 not turn away from what the king had c the priests
14: 4 and c Judah to seek the LORD,
18:30 king of Aram had c the captains of his chariots,
23: 8 according to all that the priest Jehoiada c;
25: 4 in the book of Moses, where the LORD c,
29:15 and went in as the king had c,
29:21 He c the priests the descendants of Aaron
29:24 For the king c that the burnt offering and
29:27 Then Hezekiah c that the burnt offering be offered
29:30 and the officials c the Levites to sing praises to
30: 6 as the king had c, saying, "O people of Israel,
30:12 to do what the king and the officials c by the word
31: 4 He c the people who lived in Jerusalem to give
31:11 Then Hezekiah c them to prepare store-chambers
32:12 and his altars and c Judah and Jerusalem,
33: 8 be careful to do all that I have c them,
33:16 he c Judah to serve the LORD the God of Israel.
34:20 Then the king c Hilkiah, Ahikam son of Shaphan,
35:21 and God has c me to hurry.
Ezr 4: 3 as King Cyrus of Persia has c us."
7:23 Whatever is c by the God of heaven,
9:11 which you c by your servants the prophets,
Ne 1: 7 and the ordinances that you c your servant Moses.
1: 8 the word that you c your servant Moses,
8:14 which the LORD had c by Moses,
13:19 I c that the doors should be shut and gave orders
13:22 I c the Levites that they should purify themselves
Est 1:10 he c Mehuman, Biztha, Harbona,
1:17 'King Ahasuerus c Queen Vashti to be brought
3: 2 for the king had so c concerning him.
3:12 and an edict, according to all that Haman c,
8: 9 according to all that Mordecai c,
9:14 So the king c this to be done;
Job 38:12 "Have you c the morning since your days began,
Ps 33: 9 For he spoke, and it came to be; he c,
78: 5 which he c our ancestors to teach to their children;
78:23 Yet he c the skies above, and opened the doors
105: 8 of the word that he c, for a thousand generations,
106:34 not destroy the peoples, as the LORD c them,
107:25 For he c and raised the stormy wind,
111: 9 he has c his covenant forever.
119: 4 You have c your precepts to be kept diligently.
148: 5 for he c and they were created.
Isa 13: 3 I myself have c my consecrated ones,
34:16 For the mouth of the LORD has c,
45:12 the heavens, and I c all their host.
48: 5 my carved image and my cast image c them."
Jer 11: 4 which I c your ancestors when I brought them out
11: 8 which I c them to do, but they did not.
13: 5 and hid it by the Euphrates, as the LORD c me.
13: 6 from there the loincloth that I c you to hide there."
17:22 the sabbath day holy, as I c your ancestors.
26: 8 the LORD had c him to speak to all the people,
32:23 of all you c them to do, they did nothing.
35: 6 for our ancestor Jonadab son of Rechab c us,
35: 8 son of Rechab in all that he c us,
35:10 and done all that our ancestor Jonadab c us.
35:18 and done all that he c you,
36:26 And the king c Jerahmeel the king's son
38:10 Then the king c Ebed-melech the Ethiopian,
38:27 in the very words the king had c.
50:21 do all that I have c you.
51:59 The word that the prophet Jeremiah c Seraiah son
La 1:17 the LORD has c against Jacob
Eze 9:11 saying, "I have done as you c me."
10: 6 When he c the man clothed in linen,
12: 7 I did just as I was c.
24:18 And on the next morning I did as I was c.
Eze 37: 7 So I prophesied as I had been c;
37:10 I prophesied as he c me,
Da 1: 3 Then the king c his palace master Ashpenaz
2: 2 So the king c that the magicians, the enchanters,
2:12 into a violent rage and c that all the wise men
2:46 and c that a grain offering and incense be offered
3: 4 "You are c, O peoples, nations, and languages,
3:13 Nebuchadnezzar in furious rage c that Shadrach,
4:26 it was c to leave the stump and roots of the tree,
5: 2 Belshazzar c that they bring in the vessels of gold
6:23 the king was exceedingly glad and c that Daniel
Am 2:12 and c the prophets, saying,
Na 1:14 The LORD has c concerning you:
Zec 1: 6 which I c my servants the prophets,
Mal 4: 4 and ordinances that I c him at Horeb for all Israel.
Mt 1:24 he did as the angel of the Lord c him;
8: 4 and offer the gift that Moses c,
14: 9 he c it to be given;
27:10 for the potter's field, as the Lord c me."
28:20 to obey everything that I have c you.
Mk 1:44 and offer for your cleansing what Moses c,
16: S ⟦And all that had been c them they told briefly⟧
Lk 5:14 "and show yourself to the priest, and, as Moses c,
8:29 for Jesus had c the unclean spirit to come out of
9:21 He sternly ordered and c them not to tell anyone,
17: 9 Do you thank the slave for doing what was c?
Jn 8: 5 ⟦Now in the law Moses c us to stone such women⟧
14:31 but I do as the Father has c me,
Ac 8:38 He c the chariot to stop, and both of them,
10:33 to listen to all that the Lord has c you to say."
10:42 He c us to preach to the people and to testify
13:47 For so the Lord has c us, saying,
1Co 9:14 the Lord c that those who proclaim
1Jn 3:23 just as he has c us.
2Jn 1: 4 just as we have been c by the Father.
Tob 5: 1 "I will do everything that you have c me, father;
6:16 not remember your father's orders when he c you
10:13 "I have been c by the Lord to honor you all
14:8,9 Your children are also to be c to do what is right
Jdt 5: 9 Then their God c them to leave the place
12: 1 Then he c them to bring her in
12: 7 So Holofernes c his guards not to hinder her.
AdE 1: 8 and he c his stewards to comply with his pleasure
2:10 for Mordecai had c her not to make it known.
2:15 the eunuch in charge of the women, had c.
3: 2 for so the king had c to be done.
8: 9 that he c with respect to the Jews was given
8:14 with all speed to perform what the king had c;
Sir 3:22 Reflect upon what you have been c,
7:31 and give him his portion, as you have been c:
15:20 He has not c anyone to be wicked,
24:23 the law that Moses c us as an inheritance for
48:22 as he was c by the prophet Isaiah,
Bar 2: 9 Lord is just in all the works that he has c us to do.
2:28 by your servant Moses on the day when you c him
LtJ 6: 1 to give them the message that God had c him.
Aza 1: 7 we have not kept them or done what you have c us
Sus 1:18 by the side doors to bring what they had been c;
1Mc 1:51 He appointed inspectors over all the people and c
3:39 the land of Judah and destroy it, as the king had c.
3:42 They also learned what the king had c to do to
7: 9 and he c him to take vengeance on the Israelites.
7:26 and he c him to destroy the people.
10: 6 and he c that the hostages in the citadel should
10:37 just as the king has c in the land of Judah.
10:81 But his men stood fast, as Jonathan had c,
11: 2 for King Alexander had c them to meet him,
12:17 We have c them to go also to you and greet you
12:27 Jonathan c his troops to be alert and
12:43 and c his Friends and his troops to obey him
15:39 He c him to encamp against Judea,
2Mc 5:12 He c his soldiers to cut down relentlessly
5:24 and c him to kill all the grown men and to sell
6:21 of the sacrificial meal that had been c by the king,
7: 4 and he c that the tongue of their spokesman
14:31 and c them to hand the man over.
15: 3 a sovereign in heaven who had c the keeping of
1Es 2: 4 he has c me to build him a house at Jerusalem,
4:57 he also c to be done and to be sent to Jerusalem.
5:51 as it is c in the law,
5:71 as Cyrus, the king of the Persians, has c us."
6:23 Then Darius c that search be made in
6:27 So Darius c Sisinnes the governor of Syria
6:32 He c that if anyone should transgress
8:19 have c the treasurers of Syria and Phoenicia
9:53 Levites c all the people, saying, "This day is holy;
3Mc 4:11 he c that they should be enclosed in
2Es 1:35 whom I have shown no signs will do what I have c.
3: 4 and that without help—and c the dust
3:24 You c him to build a city for your name,
5:20 as the angel Uriel had c me.
6:40 Then you c a ray of light to be brought out
6:41 and c it to divide and separate the waters,
6:42 "On the third day you c the waters to
6:45 "On the fourth day you c the brightness of the sun,
6:46 and you c them to serve humankind,
6:47 "On the fifth day you c the seventh part,
6:48 as it was c, so that therefore the nations might
6:53 "On the sixth day you c the earth to bring forth
7:21 the Lord strictly c those who came into the world,
8:10 you have c that from the members themselves
12:51 I sat in the field seven days, as the angel had c me;
14: 5 the end of the times. Then I c him, saying,
14:20 For I will go, as you have c me,
14:27 Then I went as he c me,
14:31 not keep the ways that the Most High c you.
14:37 So I took the five men, as he c me,
4Mc 8: 2 then in violent rage he c that others of

COMMANDER‡ (58) [COMMAND]

Ge 21:22 with Phicol the c of his army, said to Abraham,
21:32 Abimelech, with Phicol the c of his army,
26:26 with Ahuzzath his adviser and Phicol the c
Jos 5:14 as c of the army of the LORD I have now come."
5:15 The c of the army of the LORD said to Joshua,
Jdg 4: 2 the c of his army was Sisera,
11: 6 They said to Jephthah, "Come and be our c,
11:11 and the people made him head and c over them;
1Sa 12: 9 c of the army of King Jabin of Hazor,
14:50 name of the c of his army was Abner son of Ner,
17:18 take these ten cheeses to the c of their thousand.
17:55 he said to Abner, the c of the army, "Abner,
18:13 and made him a c of a thousand;
26: 5 with Abner son of Ner, the c of his army.
2Sa 2: 8 But Abner son of Ner, c of Saul's army,
10:16 and they came to Helam, with Shobach the c of
10:18 and wounded Shobach the c of their army,
19:13 if you are not the c of my army from now on,
23:19 of the Thirty, and became their c;
1Ki 1:19 the priest Abiathar, and Joab the c of the army;
1:25 Joab the c of the army, and the priest Abiathar,
2:32 c of the army of Israel, and Amasa son of Jether, c
11:15 Joab the c of the army went up to bury the dead,
11:21 and that Joab the c of the army was dead,
16: 9 But his servant Zimri, c of half his chariots,
16:16 therefore all Israel made Omri, the c of the army,
2Ki 4:13 on your behalf to the king or to the c of
5: 1 Naaman, c of the army of the king of Aram,
9: 5 and he announced, "I have a message for you, c."
9: 5 "For which one of us?" asked Jehu. "For you, c."
25:19 the c of the army who mustered the people of
1Ch 11: 6 the Jebusites first shall be chief and c."
11:21 of the Thirty, and became their c;
19:16 with Shophach the c of the army of Hadadezer
19:18 and also killed Shophach the c of their army.
27: 5 The third c, for the third month,
27: 8 The fifth c, for the fifth month, was Shamhuth,
27:34 Joab was c of the king's army.
2Ch 17:14 of the thousands: Adnah the c,
17:15 and next to him Jehohanan the c,
28: 7 Azrikam the c of the palace,
Ne 7: 2 along with Hananiah the c of the citadel—
Isa 55: 4 a leader and c for the peoples.
Jer 52:25 of the c of the army who mustered the people of
Da 11:18 But a c shall put an end to his insolence;
Zec 10: 4 out of them the battle bow, out of them every c.
Jdt 6: 1 Holofernes, the c of the Assyrian army,
10:13 to see Holofernes the c of your army, to give him
13:15 the c of the Assyrian army,
Sir 48:18 he sent his c and departed;
1Mc 3:13 When Seron, the c of the Syrian army,
13:42 the great high priest and c and leader of the Jews."
13:53 and so he made him c of all the forces;
14:47 to be c and ethnarch of the Jews and priests,
2Mc 4:29 the c of the Cyprian troops.
8:32 They killed the c of Timothy's forces,
10:32 especially well garrisoned, where Chaereas was c.

COMMANDER'S (1) [COMMAND]

Dt 33:21 for there a c allotment was reserved;

COMMANDER-IN-CHIEF (2) [CHIEF, COMMAND]

Isa 20: 1 the year that the c, who was sent by King Sargon
1Mc 15:38 the king made Cendebeus c of the coastal country,

COMMANDERS‡ (86) [COMMAND]

Nu 31:14 the c of thousands and the c of hundreds,
31:48 the c of thousands and the c of hundreds,
31:52 from the c of thousands and the c of hundreds,
31:54 and Eleazar the priest received the gold from the c
Dt 1:15 c of thousands, c of hundreds, c of fifties, c of tens,
20: 9 then the c shall take charge of them.
Jdg 5: 9 to the c of Israel who offered themselves willingly
5:14 from Machir marched down the c,
10:18 The c of the people of Gilead said to one another,
1Sa 8:12 for himself c of thousands and c of fifties,
18:30 Then the c of the Philistines came out to battle;
22: 7 he make you all c of thousands and c of hundreds?
29: 3 the c of the Philistines said,
29: 3 Achish said to the c of the Philistines,
29: 4 But the c of the Philistines were angry with him;
29: 4 and the c of the Philistines said to him,
29: 9 nevertheless, the c of the Philistines have said,
2Sa 18: 1 set over them c of thousands and c of hundreds.
18: 5 when the king gave orders to all the c
19: 6 that c and officers are nothing to you;
24: 2 So the king said to Joab and the c of the army,
24: 4 the king's word prevailed against Joab and the c
24: 4 and the c of the army went out from the presence
1Ki 2: 5 he dealt with the two c of the armies of Israel,
9:22 they were his officials, his c, his captains,
9:22 and the c of his chariotry and cavalry.
15:20 sent the c of his armies against the cities of Israel.
20:24 each from his post, and put c in place of them;
2Ki 8:21 and their chariot c who had surrounded him;
9: 5 He arrived while the c of the army were
1Ch 12:21 for they were all warriors and c in the army.
12:28 and twenty-two c from his own ancestral house.
12:34 Of Naphtali, a thousand c,
13: 1 David consulted with the c of the thousands and

1Ch 15:25 the elders of Israel, and the c of the thousands,
21: 2 So David said to Joab and the c of the army, "Go,
26:26 and the c of the army, had dedicated.
27: 1 the c of the thousands and the hundreds,
27: 3 of all the c of the army for the first month.
28: 1 king, the c of the thousands, the c of the hundreds,
29: 6 the c of the thousands and of the hundreds,
2Ch 1: 2 the c of the thousands and of the hundreds,
8: 9 and his officers, the c of his chariotry and cavalry.
11:11 He made the fortresses strong, and put c in them,
16: 4 sent the c of his armies against the cities of Israel.
17:14 Of Judah, the c of the thousands:
21: 9 Then Jehoram crossed over with his c
21: 9 who had surrounded him and his chariot c.
23: 1 entered into a compact with the c of the hundreds,
25: 5 by ancestral houses under c of the thousands and
26:11 the direction of Hananiah, one of the king's c.
32: 6 He appointed combat c over the people,
32:21 the mighty warriors and c and officers in the camp
33:11 Therefore the LORD brought against them the c
33:14 He also put c of the army in all the fortified cities
Isa 10: 8 For he says: "Are not my c all kings?
21: 5 Rise up, c, oil the shield!
Jer 42: 1 Then all the c of the forces,
42: 8 of Kareah and all the c of the forces who were
43: 4 the c of the forces and all the people did not obey
43: 5 and all the c of the forces took all the remnant
Eze 23: 6 in blue, governors and c, all
23:12 She lusted after the Assyrians, governors and c,
23:23 governors and c all of them, officers and warriors,
Jdt 2:14 and summoned all the c, generals,
5: 2 the princes of Moab and the c of Ammon and all
7: 8 and the c of the coastland came to him and said,
14:12 the Assyrians saw them they sent word to their c,
1Mc 5:56 and Azariah, the c of the forces,
6:28 the c of his forces and those in authority.
6:57 to the c of the forces, and to the troops, men,
6:60 The speech pleased the king and the c,
6:61 So the king and the c gave them their oath.
11:70 c of the forces of the army.
12:24 that the c of Demetrius had returned,
1Es 1:29 and the c came down against King Josiah.

COMMANDING‡ (26) [COMMAND]

Dt 4:40 which I am c you today for your own well-being
6: 2 and his commandments that I am c you,
6: 6 Keep these words that I am c you today
7:11 that I am c you today.
8:11 and his statutes, which I am c you today.
10:13 and his decrees that I am c you today,
11: 8 this entire commandment that I am c you today,
11:13 that I am c you today—
11:22 observe this entire commandment that I am c you,
11:27 of the LORD your God that I am c you today;
11:28 but turn from the way that I am c you today,
13:18 that I am c you today,
24:22 therefore I am c you to do this.
26:16 This very day the LORD your God is c you
27: 1 the entire commandment that I am c you today.
27: 4 about which I am c you today, on Mount Ebal,
27:10 and his statutes that I am c you today.
28: 1 that I am c you today,
28:13 of the LORD your God, which I am c you today,
28:14 from any of the words that I am c you today,
28:15 which I am c you today,
30: 2 just as I am c you today,
30: 8 that I am c you today,
30:11 that I am c you today is not too hard for you,
30:16 of the LORD your God that I am c you today,
2Mc 14:27 with the covenant and c him to send Maccabeus

COMMANDMENT‡ (98) [COMMAND]

Ex 24:12 the tablets of stone, with the law and the c,
34:32 in c all that the LORD had spoken with him
38:21 which were drawn up at the c of Moses,
Nu 3:39 and Aaron enrolled at the c of the LORD,
4:37 according to the c of the LORD by Moses.
4:41 and Aaron enrolled according to the c of
4:45 according to the c of the LORD by Moses.
4:49 According to the c of the LORD
15:23 from the day the LORD gave c and thereafter,
15:31 the word of the LORD and broken his c,
Dt 6: 1 Now this is the c—the statutes
6:25 If we diligently observe this entire c before
7:11 Therefore, observe diligently the c—
8: 1 This entire c that I command you today you must
11: 8 this entire c that I am commanding you today,
11:13 If you will only heed his every c
11:22 If you will diligently observe this entire c
15: 5 by diligently observing this entire c
17:20 of the community nor turning aside from the c,
19: 9 provided you diligently observe this entire c
26:13 and the widows, in accordance with your entire c
27: 1 the entire c that I am commanding you today.
30:11 this c that I am commanding you today is
Jos 15:13 According to the c of the LORD to Joshua,
17: 4 So according to the c of the LORD he gave them
22: 5 Take good care to observe the c and instruction
1Sa 12:14 and heed his voice and not rebel against the c of
12:15 but rebel against the c of the LORD,
13:13 you have not kept the c of the LORD your God,
15:24 for I have transgressed the c of the LORD
1Ki 2:43 the LORD and the c with which I charged you?"
13:21 the c that the LORD your God commanded you,
2Ki 17:34 or the c that the LORD commanded the children
17:37 the ordinances and the law and the c that he wrote
2Ch 8:13 the c of Moses for the sabbaths, the new moons,
14: 4 and to keep the law and the c.
19:10 concerning bloodshed, law or c,
29:25 the c of David and of Gad the king's seer and
29:25 the c was from the LORD through his prophets.
Ezr 10: 3 and of those who tremble at the c of our God;
Ne 12:24 according to the c of David the man of God,
13: 5 which were given by c to the Levites, singers,
Job 23:12 I have not departed from the c of his lips;
Ps 19: 8 the c of the LORD is clear, enlightening the eyes;
119:96 but your c is exceedingly broad.
119:98 Your c makes me wiser than my enemies,
Pr 6:20 My child, keep your father's c,
6:23 For the c is a lamp and the teaching a light,
13:13 but those who respect the c will be rewarded.
19:16 Those who keep the c will live;
Isa 29:13 their worship of me is a human c learned by rote;
Mt 15: 3 "And why do you break the c of God for the sake
22:36 "Teacher, which c in the law is the greatest?"
22:38 This is the greatest and first c.
Mk 7: 8 the c of God and hold to human tradition."
7: 9 "You have a fine way of rejecting the c of God
10: 5 of your hardness of heart he wrote this c for you.
12:28 he asked him, "Which c is the first of all?"
12:31 There is no other c greater than these."
Lk 23:56 On the sabbath they rested according to the c.
Jn 12:49 the Father who sent me has himself given me a c
12:50 And I know that his c is eternal life.
13:34 I give you a new c, that you love one another.
15:12 "This is my c, that you love one another
Ro 7: 8 But sin, seizing an opportunity in the c,
7: 9 from the law, but when the c came,
7:10 very c that promised life proved to be death to me.
7:11 For sin, seizing an opportunity in the c,
7:12 law is holy, and the c is holy and just and good.
7:13 the c might become sinful beyond measure.
13: 9 and any other c, are summed up in this word,
Gal 5:14 For the whole law is summed up in a single c,
Eph 6: 2 this is the first c with a promise:
1Ti 6:14 the c without spot or blame until the manifestation
Heb 7: 5 of Levi who receive the priestly office have a c in
7:18 of an earlier c because it was weak and ineffectual
9:19 For when every c had been told to all the people
2Pe 2:21 to turn back from the holy c that was passed on
3: 2 and the c of the Lord and Savior spoken
1Jn 2: 7 Beloved, I am writing you no new c, but an old c
that you have had from the beginning; the old c is
2: 8 Yet I am writing you a new c that is true in him
3:23 And this is his c, that we should believe in
4:21 The c we have from him is this:
2Jn 1: 5 not as though I were writing you a new c,
1: 6 this is the c just as you have heard it from
Sir 17:14 And he gave c to each of them concerning
35: 7 for all that you offer is in fulfillment of the c.
1Mc 2:53 Joseph in the time of his distress kept the c,
1Es 1: 6 to the c of the Lord that was given to Moses."
4:52 with the c to make seventeen offerings;
2Es 1:34 because with you they have neglected my c
2:33 to them they rejected me and refused the Lord's c.
3: 7 And you laid upon him one c of yours;
3:19 and your c to the posterity of Israel.
4Mc 13:15 before those who transgress the c of God.
16:24 of her sons to die rather than violate God's c.

COMMANDMENT'S (1) [COMMAND]

Sir 29: 9 Help the poor for the c sake,

COMMANDMENTS‡ (188) [COMMAND]

Ge 26: 5 my c, my statutes, and my laws."
Ex 15:26 and give heed to his c and keep all his statutes,
16:28 "How long will you refuse to keep my c
20: 6 of those who love me and keep my c.
34:28 on the tablets the words of the covenant, the ten c.
Lev 4: 2 of the LORD's c about things not to be done,
4:13 of the things that by the LORD's c ought not to
4:22 by c of the LORD his God ought not to be done
4:27 of the things that by the LORD's c ought not to
5:17 of the things that by the LORD's c ought not to
22:31 Thus you shall keep my c and observe them:
26: 3 and keep my c and observe them faithfully,
26:14 and do not observe all these c,
26:15 so that you will not observe all my c,
27:34 These are the c that the LORD gave to Moses for
Nu 15:22 to observe all these c that the LORD has spoken
15:39 you will remember all the c of the LORD
15:40 So you shall remember and do all my c,
36:13 These are the c and the ordinances that
Dt 4: 2 but keep the c of the LORD your God
4:13 the ten c; and he wrote them on two stone tablets.
4:40 Keep his statutes and his c,
5:10 of those who love me and keep my c.
5:29 to fear me and to keep all my c always,
5:31 you, stand here by me, and I will tell you all the c,
6: 2 and his c that I am commanding you,
6:17 You must diligently keep the c of
7: 9 with those who love him and keep his c,
8: 2 whether or not you would keep his c.
8: 6 Therefore keep the c of the LORD your God,
8:11 by failing to keep his c, his ordinances,
10: 4 the ten c that the LORD had spoken to you on
10:13 the c of the LORD your God and his decrees
11: 1 his decrees, his ordinances, and his c always.
11:27 if you obey the c of the LORD your God
11:28 if you do not obey the c of the LORD your God,
13: 4 his c you shall keep, his voice you shall obey,
13:18 of the LORD your God by keeping all his c
Dt 26:13 nor forgotten any of your c.
26:17 you to walk in his ways, to keep his statutes, his c,
26:18 as he promised you, and to keep his c;
27:10 observing his c and his statutes
28: 1 by diligently observing all his c
28: 9 if you keep the c of the LORD your God
28:13 if you obey the c of the LORD your God,
28:15 by diligently observing all his c and decrees,
28:45 the c and the decrees that he commanded you.
30: 8 the LORD, observing all his c
30:10 by observing his c and decrees that are written
30:16 If you obey the c of the LORD your God
30:16 walking in his ways, and observing his c, decrees,
Jos 22: 5 to keep his c, and to hold fast to him,
Jdg 2:17 who had obeyed the c of the LORD;
3: 4 to know whether Israel would obey the c of
1Ki 2: 3 his c, his ordinances, and his testimonies,
3:14 keeping my statutes and my c,
6:12 and keep all my c by walking in them,
8:58 and to keep his c, his statutes, and his ordinances,
8:61 walking in his statutes and keeping his c,
9: 6 not keep my c and my statutes that I have set
11:34 and who did keep my c and my statutes;
11:38 in my sight by keeping my statutes and my c,
14: 8 who kept my c and followed me with all his heart,
18:18 because you have forsaken the c of the LORD
2Ki 17:13 "Turn from your evil ways and keep my c
17:16 They rejected all the c of the LORD their God
17:19 not keep the c of the LORD their God but walked
18: 6 but kept the c that the LORD commanded Moses.
23: 3 to follow the LORD, keeping his c, his decrees,
1Ch 28: 7 if he continues resolute in keeping my c
28: 8 and search out all the c of the LORD your God;
29:19 that with single mind he may keep your c,
2Ch 7:19 if you turn aside and forsake my statutes and my c
17: 4 sought the God of his father and walked in his c,
24:20 Why do you transgress the c of the LORD,
31:21 and in accordance with the law and the c,
34:31 to follow the LORD, keeping his c, his decrees,
Ezr 7:11 of the text of the c of the LORD and his statutes
9:10 For we have forsaken your c,
9:14 shall we break your c again and intermarry with
Ne 1: 5 with those who love him and keep his c;
1: 7 failing to keep the c, the statutes,
1: 9 if you return to me and keep my c and do them,
9:13 and true laws, good statutes and c,
9:14 to them and gave them c and statutes and a law
9:16 and stiffened their necks and did not obey your c;
9:29 and did not obey your c,
9:34 the c and the warnings that you gave them.
10:29 to observe and do all the c of the LORD our Lord
Ps 78: 7 and not forget the works of God, but keep his c;
89:31 if they violate my statutes and do not keep my c,
103:18 and remember to do his c.
112: 1 who greatly delight in his c.
119: 6 having my eyes fixed on all your c.
119:10 do not let me stray from your c.
119:19 do not hide your c from me.
119:21 accursed ones, who wander from your c;
119:32 I run the way of your c,
119:35 Lead me in the path of your c, for I delight in it.
119:47 I find my delight in your c, because I love them.
119:48 I revere your c, which I love,
119:60 I hurry and do not delay to keep your c.
119:66 for I believe in your c.
119:73 give me understanding that I may learn your c.
119:86 All your c are enduring; I am persecuted without
119:115 you evildoers, that I may keep the c of my God.
119:127 Truly I love your c more than gold,
119:131 because I long for your c.
119:143 but your c are my delight.
119:151 you are near, O LORD, and all your c are true.
119:166 O LORD, and I fulfill your c.
119:172 for all your c are right.
119:176 seek out your servant, for I do not forget your c.
Pr 2: 1 if you accept my words and treasure up my c
3: 1 but let your heart keep my c;
4: 4 "Let your heart hold fast my words; keep my c,
7: 1 keep my words and store up my c with you;
7: 2 keep my c and live, keep my teachings as
10: 8 The wise of heart will heed c,
Ecc 12:13 Fear God, and keep his c;
Isa 48:18 O that you had paid attention to my c!
Da 9: 4 with those who love you and keep your c,
9: 5 turning aside from your c and ordinances.
Mt 5:19 whoever breaks one of the least of these c,
19:17 If you wish to enter into life, keep the c."
22:40 On these two c hang all the law and the prophets."
Mk 10:19 You know the c: 'You shall not murder;
Lk 1: 6 according to all the c and regulations of the Lord.
18:20 You know the c: 'You shall not commit
Jn 14:15 "If you love me, you will keep my c.
14:21 have my c and keep them are those who love me;
15:10 If you keep my c, you will abide in my love,
15:10 as I have kept my Father's c and abide in his love.
Ro 13: 9 The c, "You shall not commit adultery;
1Co 7:19 but obeying the c of God is everything.
Eph 2:15 He has abolished the law with its c
Tit 1:14 not paying attention to Jewish myths or to c
1Jn 2: 3 be sure that we know him, if we obey his c.
2: 4 but does not obey his c, is a liar,
3:22 because we obey his c and do what pleases him.
3:24 All who obey his c abide in him,
5: 2 when we love God and obey his c.
5: 3 For the love of God is this, that we obey his c.
5: 3 And his c are not burdensome,
2Jn 1: 6 And this is love, that we walk according to his c;

Rev 12:17 the **c** of God and hold the testimony of Jesus.
14:12 the **c** of God and hold fast to the faith of Jesus.
Tob 3: 4 and disobeyed your **c**.
3: 5 For we have not kept your **c** and have not walked
4: 5 my son, and refuse to sin or to transgress his **c**.
4:19 So now, my child, remember these **c**,
Wis 9: 9 and what is right according to your **c**.
Sir 1:26 If you desire wisdom, keep the **c**,
6:37 and meditate at all times on his **c**.
10:19 Those who break the **c**.
15:15 If you choose, you can keep the **c**,
23:27 nothing sweeter than to heed the **c** of the Lord.
28: 6 and death, and be true to the **c**.
28: 7 the **c**, and do not be angry with your neighbor;
29: 1 by holding out a helping hand they keep the **c**.
29:11 Lay up your treasure according to the **c** of
32:23 for this is the keeping of the **c**.
35: 2 one who heeds the **c** makes an offering
37:12 to be a keeper of the **c**,
45: 3 He gave him **c** for his people,
45: 5 and gave him the **c** face to face,
45:17 In his **c** he gave him authority and statutes
Bar 3: 9 Hear the **c** of life, O Israel;
4: 1 She is the book of the **c** of God,
4:13 they did not walk in the ways of God's **c**,
Aza 1: 7 We have not obeyed your **c**,
1Mc 2:19 and have chosen to obey his **c**,
10:14 the law and the **c**, for it served as a place
2Mc 1: 4 May he open your heart to his law and his **c**,
2: 2 not to forget the **c** of the Lord,
1Es 8: 7 from the law of the Lord or the **c**,
8:82 For we have transgressed your **c**,
3Mc 7:11 the divine **c** would never be favorably disposed
2Es 2: 1 I gave them **c** through my servants the prophets;
3:33 though they are unmindful of your **c**.
3:35 Or what nation has kept your **c** so well?
3:36 may indeed find individuals who have kept your **c**,
7:*37* whose **c** you have despised.
7:*45* Blessed are those who are alive and keep your **c**!
7:*72* they received the **c**, they did not keep them;
15:24 Alas for those who sin and do not observe my **c**,
16:76 You who keep my **c** and precepts,
4Mc 9: 1 to die rather than transgress our ancestral **c**;

COMMANDS‡ (39) [COMMAND]

Ex 8:27 and sacrifice to the LORD our God as he **c** us."
18:23 If you do this, and God so **c** you,
25:22 I will deliver to you all my **c** for the Israelites.
Nu 32:25 "Your servants will do as my lord **c**.
36: 6 LORD **c** concerning the daughters of Zelophehad,
Jdg 4: 6 "The LORD, the God of Israel, **c** you, 'Go,
1Sa 15:11 and has not carried out my **c**."
2Sa 9:11 to all that my lord the king **c** his servant,
1Ki 2:30 "The king **c**, 'Come out.' "
Job 9: 7 who **c** the sun, and it does not rise;
36:10 and **c** that they return from iniquity.
36:32 and **c** it to strike the mark.
37:12 that he **c** them on the face of the habitable world.
Ps 42: 8 By day the LORD **c** his steadfast love,
119:158 because they do not keep your **c**.
Am 6:11 the LORD **c**, and the great house shall
Zep 2: 3 all you humble of the land, who do his **c**;
Mk 1:27 He **c** even the unclean spirits, and they obey him."
13:34 and **c** the doorkeeper to be on the watch.
Lk 4:36 with authority and power he **c** the unclean spirits,
8:25 that he **c** even the winds and the water,
Jn 15:17 I am giving you these **c** so that you may love one
Ac 17:30 now he **c** all people everywhere to repent,
Col 2:22 they are simply human **c** and teachings.
1Ti 5: 7 Give these **c** as well, so that they may be
Jdt 2:13 take care not to transgress any of your lord's **c**,
Wis 19: 6 with your **c**, so that your children might
Sir 39:16 whatever he **c** will be done at the appointed time.
39:18 When he **c**, his every purpose is fulfilled,
LtJ 6:62 God **c** the clouds to go over the whole world,
1Mc 2:18 Now be the first to come and do what the king **c**,
2:33 Come out and do what the king **c**,
2:34 nor will we do what the king **c** and so profane
2:68 and obey the **c** of the law."
6:23 to live by what he said, and to follow his **c**.
9:55 so that he could no longer say a word or give **c**
2Mc 3: 7 and sent him with **c** to effect the removal of
2Es 3: 8 in your sight and rejected your **c**,
4Mc 6: 4 who faced him cried out, "Obey the king's **c**!"

COMMEMORATE (1) [COMMEMORATED, COMMEMORATION, COMMEMORATIVE]

Sir 45:11 to **c** in engraved letters each of the tribes of Israel;

COMMEMORATED (1) [COMMEMORATE]

Lev 23:24 a holy convocation **c** with trumpet blasts.

COMMEMORATION (2) [COMMEMORATE]

Est 9:28 the **c** of these days cease among their descendants.
AdE 9:28 and the **c** of them was never to cease

COMMEMORATIVE (1) [COMMEMORATE]

AdE 16:22 as a notable day among your **c** festivals,

COMMEND (12) [COMMENDABLE, COMMENDATION, COMMENDED, COMMENDING, COMMENDS]

Ecc 8:15 So I **c** enjoyment, for there is nothing better
Lk 23:46 said, "Father, into your hands I **c** my spirit."
Ac 20:32 I **c** you to God and to the message of his grace,
Ro 16: 1 I **c** to you our sister Phoebe,
1Co 11: 2 I **c** you because you remember me in everything
11:17 Now in the following instructions I do not **c** you,
11:22 What should I say to you? Should I **c** you?
11:22 In this matter I do not **c** you!
2Co 3: 1 Are we beginning to **c** ourselves again?
4: 2 by the open statement of the truth we **c** ourselves
10:12 with some of those who **c** themselves.
10:18 it is not those who **c** themselves that are approved,

COMMENDABLE (1) [COMMEND]

Php 4: 8 whatever is pleasing, whatever is **c**,

COMMENDATION (1) [COMMEND]

1Co 4: 5 Then each one will receive **c** from God.

COMMENDED (9) [COMMEND]

Job 29:11 When the ear heard, it **c** me,
Pr 12: 8 One is **c** for good sense,
Lk 16: 8 And his master **c** the dishonest manager
Ac 14:26 where they had been **c** to the grace of God for
2Co 6: 4 but as servants of God we have **c** ourselves
Heb 11:39 Yet all these, though they were **c** for their faith,
Wis 7:14 **c** for the gifts that come from instruction.
1Mc 12:43 So he received him with honor and **c** him
2Mc 9:25 whom I have often entrusted and **c** to most of you

COMMENDING (3) [COMMEND]

Ac 15:40 the believers **c** him to the grace of the Lord.
2Co 5:12 We are not **c** ourselves to you again,
12:11 Indeed you should have been the ones **c** me,

COMMENDS (1) [COMMEND]

2Co 10:18 but those whom the Lord **c**.

COMMENT (2) [COMMENTARY]

Ac 24:22 adjourned the hearing with the **c**,
2Es 7:*116* [46] answered and said, "This is my first and last **c**:

COMMENTARY (1) [COMMENT]

2Ch 24:27 are written in the **C** on the Book of the Kings.

COMMISSION (9) [COMMISSIONED, COMMISSIONERS, COMMISSIONS]

Nu 27:19 and **c** him in their sight.
Dt 31:14 in the tent of meeting, so that I may **c** him."
Jdg 6:14 from the hand of Midian; I hereby **c** you."
Ac 26:12 with the authority and **c** of the chief priests,
1Co 9:17 but if not of my own will, I am entrusted with a **c**.
Gal 1: 1 by human **c** nor from human authorities,
Eph 3: 2 of the **c** of God's grace that was given me for you,
Col 1:25 according to God's **c** that was given to me
1Es 8: 8 a copy of the written **c** from King Artaxerxes

COMMISSIONED‡ (4) [COMMISSION]

Nu 27:23 he laid his hands on him and **c** him—
Dt 31:23 Then the LORD **c** Joshua son of Nun and said,
Jdt 3: 8 he had been **c** to destroy all the gods of the land,
2Mc 1:20 Nehemiah, having been **c** by the king of Persia,

COMMISSIONERS (1) [COMMISSION]

Est 2: 3 And let the king appoint **c** in all the provinces

COMMISSIONS (1) [COMMISSION]

Ezr 8:36 also delivered the king's **c** to the king's satraps

COMMIT‡ (63) [COMMITMENT, COMMITS, COMMITTED, COMMITTING]

Ex 20:14 You shall not **c** adultery.
Lev 5:15 of you **c** a trespass and sins unintentionally in any
6: 2 and **c** a trespass against the LORD by deceiving
18:26 and **c** none of these abominations,
18:30 not to **c** any of these abominations that were done
Dt 5:18 Neither shall you **c** adultery.
1Ki 14:16 which he sinned and which he caused Israel to **c**."
15:26 and in the sin that he caused Israel to **c**.
15:30 that he committed and that he caused Israel to **c**,
15:34 and in the sin that he caused Israel to **c**.
16:13 and that they caused Israel to **c**,
16:26 and in the sins that he caused Israel to **c**,
2Ki 3: 3 which he caused Israel to **c**;
10:29 which he caused Israel to **c**—
10:31 which he caused Israel to **c**.
17:21 the LORD and made them **c** great sin.
Job 5: 8 and to God I would **c** my cause.
Ps 10:14 the helpless **c** themselves to you;
22: 8 "**C** your cause to the LORD;
31: 5 Into your hand I **c** my spirit;
37: 5 **C** your way to the LORD;
53: 1 They are corrupt, they **c** abominable acts;
Pr 16: 3 **C** your work to the LORD,
Isa 22:21 I will **c** your authority to his hand,
Jer 7: 9 Will you steal, murder, **c** adultery, swear falsely,
9: 5 they **c** iniquity and are too weary to repent.
23:14 they **c** adultery and walk in lies;
Eze 3:20 from their righteousness and **c** iniquity, and I lay
16:38 I will judge you as women who **c** adultery
18:24 and **c** iniquity and do the same abominable things
Eze 18:26 from their righteousness and **c** iniquity,
22: 9 who **c** lewdness in your midst.
23:24 and helmet, and I will **c** the judgment to them,
23:48 and not **c** lewdness as you have done.
33:13 if they trust in their righteousness and **c** iniquity,
33:18 and **c** iniquity, they shall die for it.
33:26 You depend on your swords, you **c** abominations,
Hos 4:13 and your daughters-in-law **c** adultery.
4:14 nor your daughters-in-law when they **c** adultery;
6: 9 they **c** a monstrous crime.
Mt 5:27 'You shall not **c** adultery.'
5:32 the ground of unchastity, causes her to **c** adultery;
19:18 "You shall not murder; You shall not **c** adultery;
Mk 10:19 'You shall not murder; You shall not **c** adultery;
Lk 18:20 'You shall not **c** adultery; You shall not murder;
Ro 2:22 You that forbid adultery, do you **c** adultery?
13: 9 The commandments, "You shall not **c** adultery;
2Co 11: 7 Did I **c** a sin by humbling myself so
Jas 2: 9 you **c** sin and are convicted by the law
2:11 For the one who said, "You shall not **c** adultery,"
2:11 Now if you do not **c** adultery but if you murder,
4: 2 not have it; so you **c** murder.
Rev 2:22 and those who **c** adultery with her I am throwing
Tob 12:10 but those who **c** sin and do wrong are their own worst
14: 7 but those who **c** sin and injustice will vanish
Wis 14:28 or live unrighteously, or readily **c** perjury;
Sir 7: 7 **C** no offense against the public,
7: 8 Do not **c** a sin twice;
34:26 To take away a neighbor's living is to **c** murder;
2Es 1:26 and your feet are swift to **c** murder.
2:23 **c** them to the grave and mark it,
15: 8 their ungodly acts that they impiously **c**,
16:67 and forget your iniquities, never to **c** them again;

COMMITMENT (1) [COMMIT]

Lev 24: 8 the LORD regularly as a **c** of the people of Israel,

COMMITS‡ (25) [COMMIT]

Lev 18:29 For whoever **c** any of these abominations shall
20:10 If a man **c** adultery with the wife of his neighbor,
Nu 15:28 before the LORD for the one who **c** an error,
2Sa 7:14 When he **c** iniquity, I will punish him with
Pr 6:32 But he who **c** adultery has no sense;
Eze 8:17 the house of Judah **c** the abominations done here?
18: 7 but restores to the debtor his pledge, **c** no robbery,
18:12 **c** robbery, does not restore the pledge,
18:12 lifts up his eyes to the idols, **c** abomination,
18:16 exacts no pledge, **c** no robbery,
22:11 One **c** abomination with his neighbor's wife;
Hos 1: 2 land **c** great whoredom by forsaking the LORD."
Mt 5:32 whoever marries a divorced woman **c** adultery.
19: 9 and marries another **c** adultery."
Mk 10:11 and marries another **c** adultery against her;
10:12 and marries another, she **c** adultery."
Lk 16:18 divorces his wife and marries another **c** adultery,
16:18 a woman divorced from her husband **c** adultery.
Jn 8:34 I tell you, everyone who **c** sin is a slave to sin.
1Co 6:18 Every sin that a person **c** is outside the body;
Jas 4:17 the right thing to do and fails to do it, **c** sin.
1Jn 3: 4 Everyone who **c** sin is guilty of lawlessness;
3: 8 Everyone who **c** sin is a child of the devil;
Sir 23:16 one who **c** fornication with his near
25: 2 and an old fool who **c** adultery.

COMMITTED‡ (141) [COMMIT]

Ge 34: 7 because he had **c** an outrage in Israel by lying
39:22 The chief jailer **c** to Joseph's care all
Lev 4: 3 that he has **c** a bull of the herd without blemish as
4:14 when the sin that they have **c** becomes known,
4:23 once the sin that he has **c** is made known to him,
4:28 the sin that you have **c** is made known to you,
4:28 for the sin that you have **c**.
4:35 on your behalf for the sin that you have **c**,
5: 5 you shall confess the sin that you have **c**.
5: 6 as your penalty for the sin that you have **c**,
5: 7 as your penalty for the sin that you have **c**,
5:10 on your behalf for the sin that you have **c**,
5:11 for the sin that you have **c** one-tenth of an ephah
5:13 for whichever of these sins you have **c**,
5:18 for the error that you **c** unintentionally,
6: 4 by robbery or by fraud or the deposit that was **c**
18:27 who were before you, **c** all of these abominations,
19:22 before the LORD for his sin that he **c**;
19:22 and the sin he **c** shall be forgiven him.
20:12 they have **c** perversion, their blood is upon them.
20:13 both of them have **c** an abomination;
26:40 in that they **c** treachery against me and, moreover,
Nu 5: 7 and shall confess the sin that has been **c**.
12:11 not punish us for a sin that we have so foolishly **c**.
Dt 9:18 because of all the sin you had **c**,
17: 5 that man or that woman who has **c** this crime
19:15 in connection with any offense that may be **c**.
19:20 and a crime such as this shall never again be **c**
22:21 because she **c** a disgraceful act in Israel
22:26 the young woman has not **c** an offense punishable
Jos 22:16 'What is this treachery that you have **c** against
22:31 you have not **c** this treachery against the LORD;
Jdg 9:56 Thus God repaid Abimelech for the crime he **c**
20: 6 for they have **c** a vile outrage in Israel.
20:12 "What crime is this that has been **c** among you?
1Sa 14:24 Now Saul **c** a very rash act on that day.
1Ki 8:50 and all their transgressions that they have **c**
14:22 to jealousy with their sins that they **c**,
14:24 They **c** all the abominations of the nations that
14:27 **c** them to the hands of the officers of the guard,

1Ki 15: 3 He **c** all the sins that his father did before him;
15:30 of Jeroboam that he **c** and that he caused Israel
16:13 of Baasha and the sins of his son Elah that they **c,**
16:19 because of the sins that he **c,**
16:19 and for the sin that he **c,** causing Israel to sin.
2Ki 17:22 of Israel continued in all the sins that Jeroboam **c;**
21:11 of Judah has **c** these abominations,
21:17 all that he did, and the sin that he **c,**
24: 3 for the sins of Manasseh, for all that he had **c,**
2Ch 12:10 **c** them to the hands of the officers of the guard,
34:16 "All that was **c** to your servants they are doing.
Ne 2:18 So they **c** themselves to the common good.
9:18 and had **c** great blasphemies,
9:26 and they **c** great blasphemies.
Ps 106: 6 we have **c** iniquity, have done wickedly.
Jer 2:13 for my people have **c** two evils:
5: 7 they **c** adultery and trooped to the houses
6:15 They acted shamefully, they **c** abomination;
8:12 They acted shamefully, they **c** abomination;
11:20 for to you I have **c** my cause.
16:10 that we have **c** against the LORD our God?"
20:12 for to you I have **c** my cause.
29:23 and have **c** adultery with their neighbors' wives,
37:21 and they **c** Jeremiah to the court of the guard;
40: 7 and had **c** to him men, women, and children,
41:10 had **c** to Gedaliah son of Ahikam.
44: 3 because of the wickedness that they **c,**
44: 9 which they **c** in the land of Judah and in the streets
44:22 the abominations that you **c;**
Eze 6: 9 in their own sight for the evils that they have **c,**
9: 4 and groan over all the abominations that are **c**
16:43 not **c** lewdness beyond all your abominations?
16:51 Samaria has not **c** half your sins;
16:51 you have **c** more abominations than they,
16:51 by all the abominations that you have **c.**
17:20 with him there for the treason he has **c** against me.
18:21 that they have **c** and keep all my statutes
18:22 None of the transgressions that they have **c** shall
18:24 of which they are guilty and the sin they have **c,**
18:26 for the iniquity that they have **c** they shall die.
18:27 the wickedness they have **c** and do what is lawful
18:28 the transgressions that they had **c,** they shall
18:31 from you all the transgressions that you have **c**
20:43 for all the evils that you have **c.**
22:29 of the land have practiced extortion and **c** robbery;
23:37 they have **c** adultery, and blood is on their hands;
23:37 with their idols they have **c** adultery;
33:13 but in the iniquity that they have **c** they shall die.
33:16 of the sins that they have **c** shall be remembered
33:29 because of all their abominations that they have **c.**
43: 8 by their abominations that they **c;**
44:13 of the abominations that they have **c.**
Da 9: 7 of the treachery that they have **c** against you.
Mal 2:11 abomination has been **c** in Israel and in Jerusalem;
Mt 5:28 a woman with lust has already **c** adultery with her
Mk 15: 7 in prison with the rebels who had **c** murder during
Ac 8: 3 dragging off both men and women, he **c** them
25: 8 "I have in no way **c** an offense against the law of
25:11 and have **c** something for which I deserve to die,
Ro 1:27 Men **c** shameless acts with men and received
3:25 over the sins previously **c;**
Heb 9: 7 for himself and for the sins **c** unintentionally by
Jas 5:15 and anyone who has **c** sins will be forgiven.
1Pe 2:22 "He **c** no sin, and no deceit was found
2Pe 2: 4 into hell and **c** them to chains of deepest darkness
Jude 1:15 the deeds of ungodliness that they have **c** in such
Rev 17: 2 the kings of the earth have **c** fornication,
18: 3 the kings of the earth have **c** fornication with her,
18: 9 who **c** fornication and lived in luxury with her,
Tob 3: 3 and those that my ancestors **c** before you.
Jdt 11:17 He will tell me when they have **c** their sins.
13:16 and that he **c** no sin with me,
Sir 23:23 second, she has **c** an offense against her husband;
23:23 through her fornication she has **c** adultery
27: 1 Many have **c** sin for gain,
LtJ 6: 2 Because of the sins that you have **c** before God,
Sus 1:52 which you have **c** in the past,
1Mc 2: 6 the blasphemies being **c** in Judah and Jerusalem,
13:39 We pardon any errors and offenses **c** to this day,
16:17 So he **c** an act of great treachery and returned evil
2Mc 4: 3 to such a degree that even murders were **c** by one
4:38 the whole city to that very place where he had **c**
4:39 of sacrilege had been **c** in the city by Lysimachus
8: 4 of the innocent babies and the blasphemies **c**
8:17 the lawless outrage that the Gentiles had **c** against
12:42 that had been **c** might be wholly blotted out.
13: 8 because he had **c** many sins against
1Es 1:49 of the people and of the priests **c** many acts
Man 1: 9 the sins I have **c** are more in number than the sand
3Mc 2: 4 You destroyed those who in the past **c** injustice,
2:17 not punish us for the defilement **c** by these men,
3: 9 not be left to its fate when it had **c** no offense.
2Es 1: 5 and to their children the iniquities that they have **c**
4:42 to give back those things that were **c** to them from
7:*32* up the souls that have been **c** to them.
7:72 though they had understanding, they **c** iniquity;
7:*126* [56] For while we lived and **c** iniquity we did
7:*138* [68] those who have **c** iniquities might be relieved
14:31 and your ancestors **c** iniquity and did not keep
4Mc 4: 7 that those who had **c** deposits to
4:12 For he said that he had **c** a sin deserving of death,

COMMITTING (10) [COMMIT]

Jer 3: 9 **c** adultery with stone and tree.
Eze 8: 6 that the house of Israel are **c** here,
8: 9 see the vile abominations that they are **c** here."
8:13 will see still greater abominations that they are **c.**"
33:15 and walk in the statutes of life, **c** no iniquity—
Jn 8: 4 ⟦woman was caught in the very act of **c** adultery.⟧
1Jn 5:16 or sister **c** what is not a mortal sin, you will ask,
2Mc 13:14 **c** the decision to the Creator of the world
3Mc 6:24 "You are **c** treason and surpassing tyrants
2Es 3:13 And when they were **c** iniquity in your sight,

COMMON (38) [COMMONER, COMMONWEALTH]

Lev 10:10 You are to distinguish between the holy and the **c,**
Dt 3:11 By the **c** cubit it is nine cubits long
1Sa 21: 5 even when it is a **c** journey;
1Ki 10:27 The king made silver as **c** in Jerusalem as stones,
2Ki 23: 6 the dust of it upon the graves of the **c** people.
2Ch 1:15 The king made silver and gold as **c** in Jerusalem
9:27 The king made silver as **c** in Jerusalem as stone,
11:14 The Levites had left their **c** lands
31:19 in the fields of **c** land belonging to their towns,
Ne 2:18 So they committed themselves to the **c** good.
Pr 22: 2 The rich and the poor have this in **c:**
22:29 they will serve kings; they will not serve **c** people.
29:13 The poor and the oppressor have this in **c:**
Isa 8: 1 Take a large tablet and write on it in **c** characters,
Jer 23:28 What has straw in **c** with wheat?
26:23 into the burial place of the **c** people.
Eze 22:26 between the holy and the **c,**
42:20 to make a separation between the holy and the **c.**
44:23 the difference between the holy and the **c,**
Jn 4: 9 (Jews do not share things in **c** with Samaritans.)
12: 6 the **c** purse and used to steal what was put into it.)
13:29 Some thought that, because Judas had the **c** purse,
Ac 2:44 were together and had all things in **c;**
4:32 but everything they owned was held in **c.**
1Co 3: 8 and the one who waters have a **c** purpose,
10:13 No testing has overtaken you that is not **c**
12: 7 the manifestation of the Spirit for the **c** good.
Wis 7: 3 And when I was born, I began to breathe the **c** air,
Sir 13:17 What does a wolf have in **c** with a lamb?
2Mc 8:29 they made **c** supplication and implored
11:15 Maccabeus, having regard for the **c** good,
14:25 Judas married, settled down, and shared the **c** life.
3Mc 3: 6 which was **c** talk among all;
4: 4 perceiving the **c** object of pity before their eyes,
5:32 not for an affection arising from our nurture in **c**
7:17 in accordance with the **c** desire, for seven days.
4Mc 13:22 from this **c** nurture and daily companionship,
13:25 A **c** zeal for nobility strengthened their goodwill

COMMONER (1) [COMMON]

Wis 18:11 and the **c** suffered the same loss as the king;

COMMONLY See Index to Footnotes

COMMONWEALTH‡ (3) [COMMON]

Eph 2:12 being aliens from the **c** of Israel,
2Mc 13:14 country, and **c,** he pitched his camp near Modein.
4Mc 3:20 for the temple service and recognized their **c**—

COMMOTION (6)

Jer 10:22 a great **c** from the land of the north to make
Mt 9:23 the flute players and the crowd making a **c,**
Mk 5:38 he saw a **c,** people weeping and wailing loudly.
5:39 "Why do you make a **c** and weep?
Ac 12:18 there was no small **c** among the soldiers
19:40 there is no cause that we can give to justify this **c.**"

COMMUNE (1) [COMMUNION]

Ps 77: 6 I **c** with my heart in the night;

COMMUNICATE (4) [COMMUNICATION]

Eze 44:19 on other garments, so that they may not **c** holiness
46:20 the outer court and so **c** holiness to the people."
3Mc 4:11 that they could neither **c** with the king's forces nor
4:16 not able even to **c** or to come to one's help,

COMMUNICATION (1) [COMMUNICATE]

2Mc 11:17 have delivered your signed **c** and have asked

COMMUNION (1) [COMMUNE]

2Co 13:13 and the **c** of the Holy Spirit be with all of you.

COMMUNION (KJV) See also FELLOWSHIP, SHARING

COMMUNITIES (2) [COMMUNITY]

Am 1: 6 because they carried into exile entire **c,**
1: 9 because they delivered entire **c** over to Edom,

COMMUNITY (19) [COMMUNITIES]

Dt 1:16 "Give the members of your **c** a fair hearing,
15: 2 of a neighbor who is a member of the **c,**
15: 3 on whatever any member of your **c** owes you.
15: 7 of your **c** in any of your towns within the land that
15:12 If a member of your **c,**
17:15 One of your own **c** you may set as king over you;
17:15 who is not of your own **c.**
17:20 of the **c** nor turning aside from the commandment,
18: 2 among the other members of the **c;**
Jn 21:23 the rumor spread in the **c** that this disciple would
Ac 6: 2 And the twelve called together the whole **c** of
6: 5 What they said pleased the whole **c,**
25:24 about whom the whole Jewish **c** petitioned me,
Eph 6:23 Peace be to the whole **c,** and love with faith,
1Mc 1:25 Israel mourned deeply in every **c,**
2Mc 12: 7 intending to come again and root out the whole **c**
3Mc 2:27 the Jewish **c,** and he set up a stone on the tower in
3: 9 for such a great **c** ought not be left to its fate
6:36 a public rite for these things in their whole **c** and

COMPACT (1)

2Ch 23: 1 into a **c** with the commanders of the hundreds,

COMPACTED (1)

Wis 7: 2 within the period of ten months, **c** with blood,

COMPANIES‡ (30) [COMPANY]

Ge 32: 7 and the flocks and herds and camels, into two **c,**
32:10 and now I have become two **c.**
Ex 12:17 on this very day I brought your **c** out of the land
12:41 all the **c** of the LORD went out from the land
Nu 1:52 in their respective regimental camps, by **c;**
2: 3 be of the regimental encampment of Judah by **c.**
2: 9 The total enrollment of the camp of Judah, by **c,**
2:10 be the regimental encampment of Reuben by **c.**
2:16 The total enrollment of the camp of Reuben, by **c,**
2:18 be the regimental encampment of Ephraim by **c.**
2:24 total enrollment of the camp of Ephraim, by **c,**
2:25 be the regimental encampment of Dan by **c.**
2:31 They shall set out last, by **c.**
2:32 total enrollment in the camps by their **c** was
Jdg 7:16 he divided the three hundred men into three **c,**
7:20 the three **c** blew the trumpets and broke the jars,
9:34 and lay in wait against Shechem in four **c.**
9:43 he took his troops and divided them into three **c,**
9:44 the two **c** rushed on all who were in the fields
1Sa 11:11 The next day Saul put the people in three **c.**
13:17 of the camp of the Philistines in three **c;**
Ne 12:28 The **c** of the singers gathered together from
12:31 and appointed two great **c** that gave thanks
12:40 So both **c** of those who gave thanks stood in
Eze 38: 7 you and all the **c** that are assembled around you,
Jdt 14:11 and they went out in **c** to the mountain passes.
1Mc 5:33 Then he came up behind them in three **c,**
9:11 The cavalry was divided into two **c,**
9:12 by the two **c,** the phalanx advanced to the sound
2Mc 5: 2 in **c** fully armed with lances and drawn swords—

COMPANION (12) [COMPANIONS, COMPANIONSHIP]

Jdg 14:20 And Samson's wife was given to his **c,**
15: 2 you had rejected her; so I gave her to your **c.**
15: 6 he has taken Samson's wife and given her to his **c.**
Job 30:29 I am a brother of jackals, and a **c** of ostriches.
Ps 55:13 But it is you, my equal, my **c,** my familiar friend,
55:20 My **c** laid hands on a friend and violated
119:63 I am a **c** of all who fear you,
Pr 13:20 but the **c** of fools suffers harm.
Mal 2:14 though she is your **c** and your wife by covenant.
Php 4: 3 Yes, and I ask you also, my loyal **c,**
Sir 40:23 A friend or **c** is always welcome,
Bel 1: 2 Daniel was a **c** of the king,

COMPANIONS (48) [COMPANION]

Jos 14: 8 But my **c** who went up with me made the heart of
Jdg 11:37 and bewail my virginity, my **c** and I."
11:38 So she departed, she and her **c,**
14:11 they brought thirty **c** to be with him.
2Ki 9: 2 go in and get him to leave his **c,**
Job 6:15 My **c** are treacherous like a torrent-bed,
Ps 38:11 My friends and **c** stand aloof from my affliction,
45: 7 with the oil of gladness beyond your **c;**
45:14 behind her the virgins, her **c,** follow.
88: 8 You have caused my **c** to shun me;
88:18 to shun me; my **c** are in darkness.
Pr 28: 7 but **c** of gluttons shame their parents.
SS 1: 7 beside the flocks of your **c?**
8:13 my **c** are listening for your voice; let me hear it.
Isa 1:23 Your princes are rebels and **c** of thieves.
Jer 41: 8 and did not kill them along with their **c.**
Da 2:13 they looked for Daniel and his **c,** to execute them.
2:17 Then Daniel went to his home and informed his **c,**
2:18 that Daniel and his **c** with the rest of the wise men
Mt 12: 3 when he and his **c** were hungry?
12: 4 which it was not lawful for him or his **c** to eat,
Mk 1:36 And Simon and his **c** hunted for him.
2:25 and his **c** were hungry and in need of food?
2:26 and he gave some to his **c.**"
Lk 6: 3 when he and his **c** were hungry?
6: 4 and gave some to his **c?**"
9:32 Peter and his **c** were weighed down with sleep;
24:33 the eleven and their **c** gathered together.
Ac 4:13 they were amazed and recognized them as **c**
13:13 and his **c** set sail from Paphos and came to Perga
19:29 Macedonians who were Paul's travel **c.**
20:34 with my own hands to support myself and my **c.**
26:13 shining around me and my **c.**
Heb 1: 9 with the oil of gladness beyond your **c.**"
Sir 9:16 Let the righteous be your dinner **c,**
37: 4 Some **c** rejoice in the happiness of a friend,
37: 5 Some **c** help a friend for their stomachs' sake,
42: 3 or with traveling **c,** and of dividing the inheritance
Aza 1:26 into the furnace to be with Azariah and his **c,**
1Mc 3:14 I will make war on Judas and his **c,**

1Mc 12:52 and they mourned for Jonathan and his c and were
15:15 Then Numenius and his c arrived from Rome,
2Mc 5:27 and kept himself and his c alive in the mountains
8: 1 and his c secretly entered the villages
8:12 and when he told his c of the arrival of the army,
12:11 After a hard fight, Judas and his c,
3Mc 2:25 abetted by the previously mentioned drinking c
6: 6 three c in Babylon who had voluntarily surrendered

COMPANIONSHIP (4) [COMPANION]

Wis 8:16 for c with her has no bitterness,
3Mc 2:33 and depriving them of c and mutual help.
4Mc 13:22 from this common nurture and daily c,
13:27 and c and virtuous habits had augmented

COMPANY‡ (123) [COMPANIES]

Ge 28: 3 that you may become a c of peoples.
32: 8 "If Esau comes to the one c and destroys it, then the c that is left will escape."
33: 8 "What do you mean by all this c that I met?"
35:11 a nation and a c of nations shall come from you,
48: 4 I will make of you a c of peoples,
49: 6 may I not be joined to their c—
50: 9 It was a very great c.
Ex 6:26 the Israelites out of the land of Egypt, c by c."
7: 4 and bring my people the Israelites, c by c,
12:51 the Israelites out of the land of Egypt, c by c.
Nu 1: 3 You and Aaron shall enroll them, c by c.
2: 4 with a c as enrolled of seventy-four
2: 6 with a c as enrolled of fifty-four
2: 8 with a c as enrolled of fifty-seven
2:11 a c as enrolled of forty-six thousand five hundred.
2:13 with a c as enrolled of fifty-nine
2:15 with a c as enrolled of forty-five
2:19 a c as enrolled of forty thousand five hundred.
2:21 with a c as enrolled of thirty-two
2:23 with a c as enrolled of thirty-five
2:26 with a c as enrolled of sixty-two
2:28 a c as enrolled of forty-one thousand five hundred.
2:30 with a c as enrolled of fifty-three
10:14 the camp of Judah set out first, c by c, and
10:14 the whole c was Nahshon son of Amminadab.
10:15 the c of the tribe of Issachar was Nethanel son
10:16 over the c of the tribe of Zebulun was Eliab son
10:18 of the camp of Reuben set out, c by c;
10:18 and over the whole c was Elizur son of Shedeur.
10:19 the c of the tribe of Simeon was Shelumiel son
10:20 over the c of the tribe of Gad was Eliasaph son
10:22 the Ephraimite camp set out, c by c, and
10:22 over the whole c was Elishama son of Ammihud.
10:23 the c of the tribe of Manasseh was Gamaliel son
10:24 the c of the tribe of Benjamin was Abidan son
10:25 rear guard of all the camps, set out, c by c,
10:25 the whole c was Ahiezer son of Ammishaddai.
10:26 Over the c of the tribe of Asher was Pagiel son
10:27 over the c of the tribe of Naphtali was Ahira son
10:28 of the Israelites, c by c, when they set out.
16: 5 Then he said to Korah and all his c,
16: 6 Do this: take censers, Korah and all your c,
16:11 and all your c have gathered together against
16:16 Moses said to Korah, "As for you and all your c,
16:40 so as not to become like Korah and his c—
26: 9 who rebelled against Moses and Aaron in the c
26:10 up along with Korah, when that c died,
27: 3 the c of those who gathered themselves together
27: 3 against the LORD in the c of Korah, but died
Dt 11: 6 their tents, and every living being in their c;
Jdg 9:37 and one c is coming from the direction
9:44 the c that was with him rushed forward and stood
18:23 "What is the matter that you come with such a c?"
1Sa 13:17 one c turned toward Ophrah, to the land of Shual,
13:18 another c turned toward Beth-horon,
13:18 and another c turned toward the mountain
19:20 When they saw the c of the prophets in a frenzy,
1Ki 20:35 a certain member of a c of prophets said
2Ki 2: 3 The c of prophets who were in Bethel came out
2: 5 The c of prophets who were at Jericho drew near
2: 7 Fifty men of the c of prophets also went,
2:15 the c of prophets who were at Jericho saw him at
4: 1 of a member of the c of prophets cried to Elisha,
4:38 As the c of prophets was sitting before him,
4:38 and make some stew for the c of prophets."
5:15 he returned to the man of God, he and all his c;
5:22 'Two members of a c of prophets have just come
6: 1 Now the c of prophets said to Elisha, "As you see,
9: 1 Then the prophet Elisha called a member of the c
9:17 spied the c of Jehu arriving, and said, "I see a c."
Ne 12:38 other c of those who gave thanks went to the left,
Job 15:34 For the c of the godless is barren,
16: 7 he has made desolate all my c.
34: 8 in c with evildoers and walks with the wicked?
Ps 14: 5 for God is with the c of the righteous.
22:16 a c of evildoers encircles me.
24: 6 Such is the c of those who seek him,
26: 5 I hate the c of evildoers,
49:19 they will go to the c of their ancestors,
50:18 and you keep c with adulterers.
55:14 with whom I kept pleasant c;
68:11 great is the c of those who bore the tidings:
78:49 indignation, and distress, a c of destroying angels.
106:18 Fire also broke out in their c;
111: 1 in the c of the upright, in the congregation.
141: 4 to busy myself with wicked deeds in c
Pr 29: 3 but to keep c with prostitutes is
Jer 15:17 I did not sit in the c of merrymakers,
31: 8 a great c, they shall return here.
Jer 50: 9 against Babylon a c of great nations from the land
Eze 17:17 Pharaoh with his mighty army and great c will
27:27 with all the c that is with you,
32:22 Assyria is there, and all its c,
32:23 Its c is all around its grave, all of them killed,
38: 4 a great c, all of them with shield and buckler,
Mt 14: 6 the daughter of Herodias danced before the c,
Ac 15:39 disagreement became so sharp that they parted c;
Ro 15:24 once I have enjoyed your c for a little while.
15:32 to you with joy and be refreshed in your c.
1Co 15:33 Do not be deceived: "Bad c ruins good morals."
Wis 1:16 because they are fit to belong to his c.
2:24 and those who belong to his c experience it.
6:23 nor will I travel in the c of sickly envy,
8:18 unfailing wealth, and in the experience of her c,
Sir 6:34 Stand in the c of the elders.
45:18 Dathan and Abiram and their followers and the c
1Mc 2:42 Then there united with them a c of Hasideans,
3:13 heard that Judas had gathered a large c,
3:16 Judas went out to meet him with a small c.
5:30 At dawn they looked out and saw a large c,
5:45 a very large c, to go to the land of Judah.
2Mc 1: 7 in those years after Jason and his c revolted from

COMPARABLE (1) [COMPARE]

Sir 23:12 There is a manner of speaking c to death;

COMPARE (23) [COMPARABLE, COMPARED, COMPARING, COMPARISON]

Ge 47: 9 not c with the years of the life of my ancestors
1Ki 3:13 no other king shall c with you.
Job 28:19 The chrysolite of Ethiopia cannot c with it,
Ps 40: 5 toward us; none can c with you.
Pr 3:15 and nothing you desire can c with her.
8:11 and all that you may desire cannot c with her.
SS 1: 9 I c you, my love, to a mare
Isa 40:18 or what likeness c with him?
40:25 To whom then will you c me, or who is my equal?
46: 5 and c me, as though we were alike?
La 2:13 What can I say for you, to what c you,
Eze 28: 2 though you c your mind with the mind of a god.
28: 6 Because you c your mind with the mind of a god,
Da 1:13 then c our appearance with the appearance of
1:19 no one was found to c with Daniel, Hananiah,
Mt 11:16 "But to what will I c this generation?
Mk 4:30 "With what can we c the kingdom of God,
Lk 7:31 then will I c the people of this generation,
13:18 And to what should I c it?
13:20 "To what should I c the kingdom of God?
2Co 10:12 not dare to classify or c ourselves with some
10:12 and c themselves with one another,
Sir 25:11 to whom can we c the one who has it?

COMPARED (11) [COMPARE]

Ps 89: 6 For who in the skies can be c to the LORD?
Eze 31: 8 plane trees were as nothing c with its branches;
Mt 13:24 be c to someone who sowed good seed
18:23 "For this reason the kingdom of heaven may be c
22: 2 be c to a king who gave a wedding banquet
Wis 7:29 C with the light she is found to be superior,
Sir 25:19 Any iniquity is small c to a woman's iniquity;
Bar 3:35 This is our God; no other can be c to him.
LtJ 6:63 not to be c with them in appearance or power.
2Es 6:56 and you have c their abundance to a drop from
8:47 But you have often c yourself to the unrighteous.

COMPARING‡ (1) [COMPARE]

Ro 8:18 of this present time are not worth c with the glory

COMPARISON (3) [COMPARE]

Jdg 8: 2 "What have I done now in c with you?
8: 3 what have I been able to do in c with you?"
Wis 7: 8 and I accounted wealth as nothing in c with her.

COMPASS (1) [COMPASSED]

Isa 44:13 fashions it with planes, and marks it with a c;

COMPASS (KJV) See also AROUND, CIRCLE, EXTEND HALFWAY DOWN, SURROUND

COMPASSED (1) [COMPASS]

Sir 24: 5 Alone I c the vault of heaven and traversed

COMPASSION (78) [COMPASSIONATE, COMPASSIONS]

Dt 13: 8 Show them no pity or c and do not shield them.
13:17 and show you c, and in his c multiply you,
30: 3 and have c on you, gathering you again from all
32:36 the LORD will vindicate his people, have c
Jdg 21: 6 But the Israelites had c for Benjamin their kin,
21:15 The people had c on Benjamin because
1Sa 23:21 be blessed by the LORD for showing me c!
1Ki 3:26 because c for her son burned within her—
8:50 and grant them c in the sight of their captors, so that they may have c on them
2Ki 13:23 LORD was gracious to them and had c on them;
2Ch 30: 9 and your children will find c with their captors,
36:15 he had c on his people and on his dwelling place;
36:17 and had no c on young man or young woman,
Ps 77: 9 Has he in anger shut up his c?"
79: 8 let your c come speedily to meet us,
90:13 Have c on your servants!
102:13 You will rise up and have c on Zion,
103:13 As a father has c for his children,
103:13 so the LORD has c for those who fear him.
106:45 and showed c according to the abundance
135:14 and have c on his servants.
145: 9 and his c is over all that he has made.
Isa 9:17 or c on their orphans and widows;
14: 1 But the LORD will have c on Jacob
27:11 he that made them will not have c on them,
49:13 and will have c on his suffering ones.
49:15 or show no c for the child of her womb?
54: 7 but with great c I will gather you.
54: 8 but with everlasting love I will have c on you,
54:10 says the LORD, who has c on you.
63:15 The yearning of your heart and your c?
Jer 12:15 I will again have c on them,
13:14 not pity or spare or have c when I destroy them.
21: 7 he shall not pity them, or spare them, or have c.
30:18 and have c on his dwellings;
La 3:32 he will have c according to the abundance
Eze 16: 5 to do any of these things for you out of c for you;
Da 1: 9 Now God allowed Daniel to receive favor and c
Hos 11: 8 my c grows warm and tender.
13:14 C is hidden from my eyes.
Mic 7:19 He will again have c upon us;
Zec 1:16 I have returned to Jerusalem with c;
10: 6 I will bring them back because I have c on them,
12:10 And I will pour out a spirit of c and supplication
Mt 9:36 When he saw the crowds, he had c for them,
14:14 and he had c for them and cured their sick.
15:32 "I have c for the crowd, because they have been
20:34 Moved with c, Jesus touched their eyes.
Mk 6:34 and he had c for them, because they were
8: 2 "I have c for the crowd,
Lk 7:13 the Lord saw her, he had c for her and said to her,
15:20 his father saw him and was filled with c;
Ro 9:15 and I will have c on whom I have c."
Php 1: 8 I long for all of you with the c of Christ Jesus.
2: 1 any sharing in the Spirit, any c and sympathy,
Col 3:12 clothe yourselves with c, kindness, humility,
Heb 10:34 For you had c for those who were in prison,
Tob 8:17 because you had c on two only children.
Wis 10: 5 kept him strong in the face of his c for his child.
Sir 18:13 The c of human beings is for their neighbors,
18:13 but the c of the Lord is for every living thing.
18:14 He has c on those who accept his discipline
Bar 2:27 in all your kindness and in all your great c,
1Mc 3:44 and to pray and ask for mercy and c.
2Mc 7: 6 over us and in truth has c on us,
7: 6 'And he will have c on his servants.' "
Man 1: 7 of great c, long-suffering, and very merciful,
2Es 7:*33* on the seat of judgment, and c shall pass away,
7:*136* [66] and abundant in c,
4Mc 5:12 and have c on your old age
6:24 and that he had not been changed by their c,
8:10 have c for your youth and handsome appearance.
8:20 on our youth and have c on our mother's age;
12: 2 he felt strong c for this child when he saw
12: 6 to show c on her who had been bereaved of

COMPASSIONATE (6) [COMPASSION]

Ex 22:27 I will listen, for I am c.
Ps 78:38 Yet he, being c, forgave their iniquity,
La 4:10 hands of c women have boiled their own children;
Ro 12: 8 the leader, in diligence; the c,
Jas 5:11 how the Lord is c and merciful.
Sir 2:11 For the Lord is c and merciful;

COMPASSIONS (1) [COMPASSION]

2Es 7:*136* [66] he makes his c abound more and more

COMPATRIOT See Index to Footnotes

COMPATRIOTS‡ (18)

1Th 2:14 the same things from your own c as they did from
2Mc 4: 2 the protector of his c, and a zealot for the laws.
4: 5 not accusing his c but having in view the welfare,
4:10 at once shifted his c over to the Greek way of life.
4:50 having become the chief plotter against his c.
5: 6 But Jason kept relentlessly slaughtering his c,
5: 6 of victory over enemies and not over c.
5: 8 as the executioner of his country and his c,
5:23 who lorded it over his c worse than the others did.
12: 5 When Judas heard of the cruelty visited on his c,
14: 8 and second because I have regard also for my c.
14:37 a man who loved his c and was very well thought
15:30 his youthful goodwill toward his c,
15:31 and had called his c together and stationed
3Mc 1:23 to their c to take arms and die courageously for
3:21 toward their c here, both because of their alliance
4:12 that the Jews' c from the city frequently went out
7:14 of their c who had become defiled.

COMPEL (11) [COMPELLED, COMPELS, COMPULSION]

Lk 14:23 and c people to come in,
Gal 2:14 how can you c the Gentiles to live like Jews?"
6:12 in the flesh that try to c you to be circumcised—
2Mc 6: 1 to c the Jews to forsake the laws of their ancestors
1Es 4: 6 and they c one another to pay taxes to the king.
4Mc 4:26 he himself tried through torture to c everyone in

4Mc 5: 2 to c them to eat pork and food sacrificed to idols.
5:27 be tyrannical for you to c us not only to transgress
8: 2 to c an aged man to eat defiling foods,
8: 9 you will c me to destroy each and every one
18: 5 in no way whatever was he able to c the Israelites

COMPELLED (11) [COMPEL]
Ex 3:19 that the king of Egypt will not let you go unless c
La 5:13 Young men are c to grind,
Mt 27:32 they c this man to carry his cross.
Mk 15:21 They c a passer-by, who was coming in from
Ac 28:19 Jews objected, I was c to appeal to the emperor—
Gal 2: 3 who was with me, was not c to be circumcised,
Jdt 8:30 But the people were so thirsty that they c us to do
Wis 19: 3 as fugitives those whom they had begged and c
2Mc 6: 7 they were c to wear wreathes of ivy and to walk in
7: 1 and their mother were arrested and were being c
15: 2 When the Jews who were c to follow him said,

COMPELS (1) [COMPEL]
Pr 7:21 with her smooth talk she c him.

COMPENSATE (3) [COMPENSATION]
Ex 21:26 a free person, to c for the eye.
21:27 a free person, to c for the tooth.
Est 7: 4 but no enemy can c for this damage to the king."

COMPENSATION‡ (1) [COMPENSATE]
Pr 6:35 He will accept no c, and refuses a bribe no matter

COMPETE (4) [COMPETENCE, COMPETENT, COMPETING, COMPETITION]
Jer 12: 5 how will you c with horses?
22:15 Are you a king because you c in cedar?
1Co 9:24 Do you not know that in a race the runners all c,
Wis 15: 9 but they c with workers in gold and silver,

COMPETENCE (1) [COMPETE]
2Co 3: 5 anything as coming from us; our c is from God,

COMPETENT (4) [COMPETE]
Da 1: 4 and c to serve in the king's palace;
2Co 3: 5 Not that we are c of ourselves to claim anything
3: 6 who has made us c to be ministers of a new
1Es 8:47 hand of our Lord they brought us c men of

COMPETING (2) [COMPETE]
Gal 5:26 c against one another, envying one another.
2Ti 2: 5 no one is crowned without c according to

COMPETITION (1) [COMPETE]
4Mc 17:13 the mother of the seven sons entered the c,

COMPILER (1)
2Mc 2:28 the responsibility for exact details to the c,

COMPLACENCY (1) [COMPLACENT]
Pr 1:32 and the c of fools destroys them;

COMPLACENT (4) [COMPLACENCY, COMPLACENTLY]
Dt 4:25 and become c in the land,
Isa 32: 9 you c daughters, listen to my speech.
32:10 a year you will shudder, you c ones;
32:11 you women who are at ease, shudder, you c ones;

COMPLACENTLY (1) [COMPLACENT]
Zep 1:12 I will punish the people who rest c on their dregs,

COMPLAIN (14) [COMPLAINED, COMPLAINING, COMPLAINS, COMPLAINT, COMPLAINTS]
Ex 16: 7 For what are we, that you c against us?"
Nu 14:27 long shall this wicked congregation c against me?
14:27 the complaints of the Israelites, which they c
14:36 who returned and made all the congregation c
Jdg 21:22 if their fathers or their brothers come to c to us,
Job 7:11 I will c in the bitterness of my soul.
Jer 2:29 Why do you c against me?
La 3:39 Why should any who draw breath c about
Jn 6:41 the Jews began to c about him because he said,
6:43 "Do not c among yourselves.
1Co 10:10 And do not c as some of them did,
Jdt 5:22 all the people standing around the tent began to c;
Sir 10:25 and an intelligent person will not c.
2Es 1:16 but to this day you still c.

COMPLAINED (11) [COMPLAIN]
Ge 21:25 When Abraham c to Abimelech about a well
Ex 15:24 And the people c against Moses, saying,
16: 2 of the Israelites c against Moses and Aaron in
17: 3 and the people c against Moses and said,
Nu 11: 1 when the people c in the hearing of the LORD
14: 2 And all the Israelites c against Moses and Aaron;
14:29 from twenty years old and upward, who have c
2Ki 4:19 He c to his father, "Oh, my head, my head!"
Ac 6: 1 the Hellenists c against the Hebrews
2Es 1:15 for your protection, and in them you c.
4Mc 3:12 his guards c bitterly because of the king's craving,

COMPLAINING (10) [COMPLAIN]
Ex 16: 7 because he has heard your c against the LORD.
16: 8 because the LORD has heard the c that you utter
16: 8 Your c is not against us but against the LORD."
16: 9 for he has heard your c.' "
16:12 "I have heard the c of the Israelites;
Pr 23:29 Who has strife? Who has c?
Lk 5:30 Pharisees and their scribes were c to his disciples,
Jn 6:61 being aware that his disciples were c about it,
7:12 And there was considerable c about him among
1Pe 4: 9 Be hospitable to one another without c.

COMPLAINS (1) [COMPLAIN]
Sir 31:24 The city c of the one who is stingy with food,

COMPLAINT (20) [COMPLAIN]
2Ki 6:28 But then the king asked her, "What is your c?"
Job 7:13 my couch will ease my c,'
9:27 If I say, 'I will forget my c;
10: 1 I will give free utterance to my c;
21: 4 As for me, is my c addressed to mortals?
23: 2 "Today also my c is bitter;
31:13 when they brought a c against me;
Ps 55: 2 I am troubled in my c.
55:17 and morning and at noon I utter my c and moan,
64: 1 in my c; preserve my life from the dread enemy.
142: 2 I pour out my c before him;
Da 6: 4 to find grounds for c against Daniel in connection
6: 4 But they could find no grounds for c
6: 5 not find any ground for c against this Daniel
Hab 2: 1 and what he will answer concerning my c.
Ac 18:14 be justified in accepting the c of you Jews;
19:38 and the artisans with him have a c against anyone,
Col 3:13 if anyone has a c against another,
Sir 35:17 or the widow when she pours out her c.
3Mc 5:31 who give me no ground for c and have exhibited

COMPLAINTS (5) [COMPLAIN]
Nu 14:27 I have heard the c of the Israelites,
17: 5 to the c of the Israelites that they continually make
17:10 that you may make an end of their c against me,
Ne 5: 6 when I heard their outcry and these c.
1Mc 11:25 of his nation kept making c against him,

COMPLETE‡ (52) [COMPLETED, COMPLETELY, COMPLETENESS, COMPLETES, COMPLETING, COMPLETION]
Ge 15:16 for the iniquity of the Amorites is not yet c."
29:27 C the week of this one,
Ex 5:13 taskmasters were urgent, saying, "C your work,
Lev 16:31 It is a sabbath of c rest to you,
23: 3 but the seventh day is a sabbath of c rest,
23:15 you shall count off seven weeks; they shall be c.
23:24 you shall observe a day of c rest,
23:32 It shall be to you a sabbath of c rest,
23:39 a c rest on the first day, and a c rest on the eighth day.
25: 4 the seventh year there shall be a sabbath of c rest
25: 5 it shall be a year of c rest for the land.
Dt 1:36 because of his c fidelity to the LORD."
1Ch 11: 8 from the Millo in c circuit;
Job 23:14 For he will c what he appoints for me;
36:11 and serve him, they c their days in prosperity,
Da 11:44 with great fury to bring ruin and c destruction
Zec 4: 9 his hands shall also c it.
Lk 14:28 to see whether he has enough to c it?
Jn 4:34 the will of him who sent me and to c his work.
5:36 The works that the Father has given me to c,
15:11 and that your joy may be c.
16:24 so that your joy may be c.
17:13 in the world so that they may have my joy made c
1Co 13:10 but when the c comes, the partial will come to
2Co 7:16 I rejoice, because I have c confidence in you.
8: 6 so he should also c this generous undertaking
10: 6 when your obedience is c.
Php 2: 2 make my joy c: be of the
Col 4:17 "See that you c the task that you have received in
Tit 2:10 but to show c and perfect fidelity,
Heb 13:21 make you c in everything good so
Jas 1: 4 so that you may be mature and c,
1Jn 1: 4 so that our joy may be c.
2Jn 1:12 so that our joy may be c.
Rev 6:11 be c both of their fellow servants and
Wis 15: 3 For to know you is c righteousness,
Sir Pr: 3 and night to c and publish the book
7:25 and you c a great task;
7:32 so that your blessing may be c.
26: 2 and he will c his years in peace.
34: 8 and wisdom is c in the mouth of the faithful.
38:28 and he is careful to c its decoration.
1Mc 5: 5 vowed their c destruction,
13:10 So he assembled all the warriors and hurried to c
2Mc 4:23 to carry the money to the king and to c the records
15: 1 to attack them with c safety on the day of rest.
2Es 2:41 whom you desired, is now c;
6:19 and when the humiliation of Zion is c.
6:35 to c the three weeks that had been prescribed
4Mc 4:19 and altered its form of government in c violation
15:17 who alone gave birth to such c devotion!

COMPLETED (33) [COMPLETE]
Ge 29:21 that I may go in to her, for my time is c."
29:28 Jacob did so, and c her week;
Lev 8:33 until the day when your period of ordination is c.
12: 4 until the days of her purification are c.
12: 6 When the days of her purification are c,
Nu 6: 5 the time is c for which they separate themselves to
6:13 when the time of their consecration has been c:
1Ki 9:25 So he c the house.
Est 1: 5 When these days were c, the king gave for all
Jer 25:12 Then after seventy years are c,
27: 8 until I have c its destruction by his hand.
29:10 Babylon's seventy years are c will I visit you,
Eze 4: 6 When you have c these, you shall lie down
4: 8 the other until you have c the days of your siege.
5: 2 when the days of the siege are c;
Da 11:36 He shall prosper until the period of wrath is c,
Lk 12:50 and what stress I am under until it is c!
Ac 14:26 to the grace of God for the work that they had c.
21:27 When the seven days were almost c,
Ro 15:28 when I have c this, and have delivered
Jdt 2: 4 When he had c his plan, Nebuchadnezzar,
AdE 2:12 During this time the days of beautification are c—
Sir 50:19 of the Lord was ended, and they c his ritual.
1Mc 3:49 they stirred up the nazirites who had c their days;
16:23 and the building of the walls that he c,
2Mc 9: 4 to drive without stopping until he c the journey.
1Es 4:51 for the building of the temple until it was c,
6:10 the work is prospering in their hands and being c
7: 4 and they c it by the command of the Lord God
3Mc 5:27 for which this had been so zealously c for him.
2Es 3:23 So the times passed and the years were c,
4:36 'When the number of those like yourselves is c;
4:40 when her nine months have been c,

COMPLETELY‡ (35) [COMPLETE]
Ge 20:16 all who are with you; you are c vindicated."
30:40 the striped and the c black animals in the flock
Dt 12: 2 You must demolish c all the places where
18:13 You must remain c loyal to the LORD your God.
1Ki 7:23 A line of thirty cubits would encircle it c.
8:61 devote yourselves c to the LORD our God,
9:21 whom the Israelites were unable to destroy c—
11: 6 and did not c follow the LORD,
2Ch 4: 2 A line of thirty cubits would encircle it c.
8:16 until the house of the LORD was finished c.
12:12 so as not to destroy them c;
Ps 139: 4 a word is on my tongue, O LORD, you know it c.
Pr 28: 5 but those who seek the LORD understand it c.
Isa 32:19 The forest will disappear c,
Jer 12:17 then I will c uproot it and destroy it,
14:19 Have you c rejected Judah?
La 5:20 Why have you forgotten us c?
Eze 37:11 and our hope is lost; we are cut off c.'
Zec 11:17 Let his arm be c withered,
Jn 17:23 that they may become c one,
Tob 2:10 by the white films, until I became c blind.
AdE 13: 7 and leave our government c secure
Sir 10:13 unheard-of calamities, and destroys them c.
12:11 to be sure it does not become c tarnished.
Sus 1:22 Susanna groaned and said, "I am c trapped.
1Mc 8:18 the kingdom of the Greeks was enslaving Israel c.
2Mc 4:16 and wished to imitate c became their enemies
14:46 with his blood now c drained from him,
1Es 6:28 "And I command that it be built c,
3Mc 5: 1 Then the king, c inflexible,
5:12 in his lawless purpose and was c frustrated
5:19 that while it was still night he had carried out c
5:27 he had been c overcome by incomprehension—
4Mc 9:20 The wheel was c smeared with blood,
11:10 so that he was c curled back like a scorpion,

COMPLETENESS (1) [COMPLETE]
Wis 12:17 when people doubt the c of your power,

COMPLETES (1) [COMPLETE]
Sir 43: 7 a light that wanes when it c its course.

COMPLETING (5) [COMPLETE]
Ac 12:25 after c their mission Barnabas and Saul returned
24:18 c the rite of purification, without any crowd
2Co 8:11 so that your eagerness may be matched by c it
Col 1:24 and in my flesh I am c what is lacking
Sir 37:11 or with a seasonal laborer about c his work,

COMPLETION‡ (10) [COMPLETE]
Ac 21:26 making public the c of the days of purification
Php 1: 6 a good work among you will bring it to c by
Jas 2:22 and faith was brought to c by the works.
Sir 23:20 it was known to him, and so it is since its c.
2Mc 2: 9 for the dedication and c of the temple.
1Es 1:58 of its desolation until the c of seventy years."
5:73 and uprisings they prevented the c of the building
6:20 it has not yet reached c.'
3Mc 1:22 the citizens would not tolerate the c of his plans or
2Es 11:44 they have ended, and his ages have reached c.

COMPLEX (2)
4Mc 1:25 which is the most c of all the emotions.
14:13 Observe how c is a mother's love for her children,

COMPLEXION (1)
Da 10: 8 My strength left me, and my c grew deathly pale,

COMPLY (1) [COMPLYING]
AdE 1: 8 to have it so, and he commanded his stewards to c

COMPLYING (1) [COMPLY]
Wis 19: 6 in its nature was fashioned anew, c

COMPOSED (2) [COMPOSITION]
1Ki 4:32 He c three thousand proverbs,
Sir 44: 5 those who c musical tunes, or put verses

COMPOSITION (3) [COMPOSED]
Ex 30:32 and you shall make no other like it in c;
30:37 When you make incense according to this c,
Pm 151: T *This psalm is ascribed to David as his own c*

COMPOUNDS (1)
Ex 30:33 Whoever c any like it or whoever puts any of it on

COMPREHEND (11) [COMPREHENDED, COMPREHENDS, COMPREHENSION, COMPREHENSIVE]
Job 37: 5 he does great things that we cannot c.
Isa 6: 9 'Keep listening, but do not c;
6:10 and c with their minds, and turn and be healed."
33:19 the people of an obscure speech that you cannot c,
44:18 They do not know, nor do they c;
Eph 3:18 I pray that you may have the power to c,
Jdt 8:14 and find out his mind or c his thought?
Sir 16:20 and who can c his ways?
2Es 4: 2 and do you think you can c the way of
4:11 then can your mind c the way of the Most High?
12:38 whose hearts you know are able to c

COMPREHENDED (4) [COMPREHEND]
Job 38:18 Have you c the expanse of the earth?
Col 1: 6 the day you heard it and truly c the grace of God.
3Mc 3: 1 When the impious king c this situation,
2Es 3:31 not shown to anyone how your way may be c.

COMPREHENDS (1) [COMPREHEND]
1Co 2:11 also no one c what is truly God's except the Spirit

COMPREHENSION (2) [COMPREHEND]
Sir 1:19 She rained down knowledge and discerning c,
2Es 8:21 beyond measure and whose glory is beyond c,

COMPREHENSIVE (1) [COMPREHEND]
4Mc 1:20 The two most c types of the emotions are pleasure

COMPRESSES (1)
Pr 16:30 one who c the lips brings evil to pass.

COMPULSION‡ (9) [COMPEL]
2Co 9: 7 not reluctantly or under c,
1Pe 5: 2 exercising the oversight, not under c but willingly,
Sir 20: 4 a girl is the person who does right under c.
Bel 1:30 and under c he handed Daniel over to them.
4Mc 5:13 from any transgression that arises out of c."
5:16 there is no c more powerful than our obedience
8:14 be merciful to you when you transgress under c."
8:22 for fearing the king when we are under c.
8:24 Let us not struggle against c or take hollow pride

COMPUTE (4) [COMPUTED]
Lev 25:50 They shall c with the purchaser the total from
25:52 until the jubilee year, they shall c thus:
27:18 the priest shall c the price for it according to
27:23 the priest shall c for it

COMPUTED (1) [COMPUTE]
Lev 25:27 since its sale shall be c and the difference shall

COMRADE (3) [COMRADES]
Jdg 7:13 there was a man telling a dream to his c;
7:14 And his c answered, "This is no other than
Hag 2:22 every one by the sword of a c.

COMRADES (7) [COMRADE]
Dt 20: 8 or he might cause the heart of his c to melt
Jdg 18:14 (that is, Laish) said to their c, "Do you know that
Eze 38:21 the swords of all will be against their c.
Rev 12:10 for the accuser of our c has been thrown down,
19:10 a fellow servant with you and your c who hold
22: 9 a fellow servant with you and your c the prophets,
3Mc 2:25 drinking companions and c, who were strangers

CONANIAH (3)
2Ch 31:12 chief officer in charge of them was C the Levite,
31:13 and Benaiah were overseers assisting C
35: 9 C also, and his brothers Shemaiah and Nethanel,

CONCEAL‡ (13) [CONCEALED, CONCEALS]
Ge 37:26 if we kill our brother and c his blood?
Job 14:13 that you would c me until your wrath is past,
27:11 that which is with the Almighty I will not c.
Ps 27: 5 he will c me under the cover of his tent;
Pr 10:18 Lying lips c hatred, and whoever utters slander is
25: 2 It is the glory of God to c things,
Jer 38:25 do not c it from us, or we will put you to death.
49:10 and he is not able to c himself.
50: 2 set up a banner and proclaim, do not c it, say:
Tob 12: 7 It is good to c the secret of a king,
12:11 the whole truth to you and will c nothing
12:11 'It is good to c the secret of a king,
2Es 2: 8 Assyria, who c the unrighteous within you!

CONCEALED‡ (10) [CONCEAL]
Job 28:21 and c from the birds of the air.
31:33 if I have c my transgressions as others do,
Ps 40:10 not c your steadfast love and your faithfulness
Pr 17:23 The wicked accept a c bribe to pervert the ways
21:14 and a c bribe in the bosom, strong wrath.
26:25 for there are seven abominations c within;
Jer 16:17 nor is their iniquity c from my sight.
Lk 9:45 its meaning was c from them,
Sir 11: 4 and his works are c from humankind.
16:21 so most of his works are c.

CONCEALS (4) [CONCEAL]
Pr 10: 6 but the mouth of the wicked c violence.
10:11 but the mouth of the wicked c violence.
12:23 One who is clever c knowledge,
28:13 No one who c transgressions will prosper,

CONCEDE (2) [CONCESSION, CONCESSIONS]
Isa 57:12 I will c your righteousness and your works,
4Mc 13: 1 everyone must c that devout reason is sovereign

CONCEIT (6) [CONCEITED]
Job 37:24 not regard any who are wise in their own c."
2Co 12:20 anger, selfishness, slander, gossip, c, and disorder.
Php 2: 3 Do nothing from selfish ambition or c,
1Ti 3: 6 be puffed up with c and fall into the condemnation
2Ti 3: 4 with c, lovers of pleasure rather than lovers
Sir 3:24 For their c has led many astray,

CONCEITED (2) [CONCEIT]
Gal 5:26 Let us not become c, competing against one
1Ti 6: 4 is c, understanding nothing, and has a morbid

CONCEIVE‡ (12) [CONCEIVED, CONCEIVES, CONCEIVING, CONCEPTION]
Nu 5:28 she shall be immune and be able to c children.
11:12 Did I c all this people?
Jdg 13: 3 you shall c and bear a son.
13: 5 for you shall c and bear a son.
13: 7 'You shall c and bear a son.
Ru 4:13 they came together, the LORD made her c,
Job 15:35 They c mischief and bring forth evil
Ps 7:14 how they c evil, and are pregnant with mischief,
35:20 but they c deceitful words
Isa 33:11 You c chaff, you bring forth stubble;
Mt 1:23 the virgin shall c and bear a son,
Lk 1:31 now, you will c in your womb and bear a son,

CONCEIVED (46) [CONCEIVE]
Ge 4: 1 man knew his wife Eve, and she c and bore Cain,
4:17 Cain knew his wife, and she c and bore Enoch;
16: 4 He went in to Hagar, and she c;
16: 4 and when she saw that she had c,
16: 5 and when she saw that she had c,
16:11 "Now you have c and shall bear a son;
21: 2 Sarah c and bore Abraham a son in his old age,
25:21 LORD granted his prayer, and his wife Rebekah c.
29:32 Leah c and bore a son,
29:33 She c again and bore a son, and said,
29:34 Again she c and bore a son, and said,
29:35 She c again and bore a son, and said,
30: 5 And Bilhah c and bore Jacob a son.
30: 7 Rachel's maid Bilhah c again and bore Jacob
30:17 and she c and bore Jacob a fifth son.
30:19 And Leah c again, and she bore Jacob a sixth son.
30:23 She c and bore a son, and said,
38: 3 She c and bore a son; and he named him Er.
38: 4 she c and bore a son whom she named Onan.
38:18 and went in to her, and she c by him.
Ex 2: 2 The woman c and bore a son;
1Sa 1:20 In due time Hannah c and bore a son.
2:21 she c and bore three sons and two daughters.
2Sa 11: 5 The woman c; and she sent
2Ki 4:17 The woman c and bore a son at that season,
1Ch 4:17 and she c and bore Miriam, Shammai,
7:23 and she c and bore a son;
Job 3: 3 and the night that said, 'A man-child is c.'
Ps 51: 5 I was born guilty, a sinner when my mother c me.
64: 6 We have thought out a cunningly c plot."
SS 3: 4 and into the chamber of her that c me.
Isa 8: 3 I went to the prophetess, and she c and bore a son.
Hos 1: 3 and she c and bore him a son.
1: 6 She c again and bore a daughter.
1: 8 she c and bore a son.
2: 5 she who c them has acted shamefully.
Mt 1:20 for the child c in her is from the Holy Spirit.
Lk 1:24 After those days his wife Elizabeth c,
1:36 your relative Elizabeth in her old age has also c
2:21 the name given by the angel before he was c in
Ro 9:10 when she had c children by one husband,
1Co 2: 9 nor ear heard, nor the human heart c,
Jas 1:15 when that desire has c, it gives birth to sin,
2Mc 9: 4 he c the idea of turning upon the Jews
3Mc 1:10 and c a desire to enter the sanctuary.
1:25 from the plan that he had c.

CONCEIVES (1) [CONCEIVE]
Lev 12: 2 If a woman c and bears a male child,

CONCEIVING (2) [CONCEIVE]
Isa 59: 4 they speak lies, c mischief and begetting iniquity.
59:13 c lying words and uttering them from the heart.

CONCEPTION (1) [CONCEIVE]
Hos 9:11 no birth, no pregnancy, no c!

CONCERN (16) [CONCERNED, CONCERNING, CONCERNS]
Ge 39: 6 he had no c for anything but the food that he ate.
39: 8 my master has no c about anything in the house,
Eze 36:21 But I had c for my holy name,
Jn 2: 4 "Woman, what c is that to you and to me?
Php 4:10 that now at last you have revived your c for me;
Heb 8: 9 and so I had no c for them, says the Lord.
AdE 7: 9 who gave information of c to the king;
Wis 6:17 and c for instruction is love of her,
Sir 3:22 for what is hidden is not your c.
11: 9 Do not argue about a matter that does not c you,
21:25 The lips of babblers speak of what is not their c.
38:34 and their c is for the exercise of their trade.
50:28 Happy are those who c themselves
2Mc 15:18 Their c for wives and children,
3Mc 6:41 magnanimously expressing his c:
2Es 8:38 For indeed I will not c myself about

CONCERNED (17) [CONCERN]
Da 10: 1 The word was true, and it c a great conflict.
Jnh 4:10 Then the LORD said, "You are c about the bush,
4:11 And should I not be c about Nineveh,
1Co 7:21 Do not be c about it.
9: 9 Is it for oxen that God is c?
Php 2:20 like him who will be genuinely c for your welfare.
4:10 indeed, you were c for me,
AdE 2: 1 and he no longer was c about Vashti
Wis 15: 9 But the workers are not c that mortals are destined
Sir 7:24 Be c for their chastity, and do not show
38:29 he is always deeply c over his products,
39: 1 of all the ancients, and is c with prophecies;
Bar 3:31 or is c about the path to her.
2Mc 2:29 the master builder of a new house must be c with
14: 8 first because I am genuinely c for the interests of
4Mc 1:20 of these is by nature c with both body and soul.
9:18 Hebrews alone are invincible where virtue is c."

CONCERNING‡ (240) [CONCERN]
Ge 12:20 And Pharaoh gave his men orders c him;
24: 9 of Abraham his master and swore to him c
47:26 So Joseph made it a statute c the land of Egypt,
Ex 8:12 and Moses cried out to the LORD c the frogs
25: 9 that I show you c the pattern of the tabernacle and
Lev 13:47 C clothing: when a leprous disease appears in it,
27: 2 an explicit vow to the LORD c the equivalent for
Nu 8:20 as the LORD had commanded Moses c them.
8:22 the LORD had commanded Moses c the Levites,
9: 8 that I may hear what the LORD will command c
30:12 then whatever proceeds out of her lips c her vows,
30:12 or c her pledge of herself, shall not stand.
30:16 the statutes that the LORD commanded Moses c
32:28 So Moses gave command c them to Eleazar
36: 6 the LORD commands c the daughters
Dt 2:14 as the LORD had sworn c them.
12:30 do not inquire c their gods, saying,
Jos 9:21 as the leaders had decided c them.
14: 6 to Moses the man of God in Kadesh-barnea c you
23:14 that the LORD your God promised c you;
23:15 that the LORD your God promised c
Jdg 13: 8 and teach us what we are to do c the boy who will
21: 5 For a solemn oath had been taken c whoever did
Ru 4: 7 the custom in former times in Israel c redeeming
1Sa 3:12 against Eli all that I have spoken c his house,
25:30 according to all the good that he has spoken c you,
2Sa 3: 8 you charge me now with a crime c this woman.
7:25 the word that you have spoken c your servant and
c his house,
10: 2 So David sent envoys to console him c his father.
14: 8 "Go to your house, and I will give orders c you."
18: 5 the king gave orders to all the commanders c
24:16 the LORD relented c the evil,
1Ki 2: 4 the LORD will establish his word that he spoke c
2:27 the LORD that he had spoken c the house of Eli
6:12 "C this house that you are building,
11: 2 from the nations c which the LORD had said to
11:10 and had commanded him c this matter,
14: 5 of Jeroboam is coming to inquire of you c her son;
21:23 Also c Jezebel the LORD said,
2Ki 10:10 which the LORD spoke c the house of Ahab;
17:15 the nations that were around them, c whom
19: 9 When the king heard c King Tirhakah of Ethiopia,
19:21 This is the word that the LORD has spoken c
19:32 thus says the LORD c the king of Assyria:
22:13 c the words of this book that has been found;
22:13 to do according to all that is written c us."

1Ch 11:10 according to the word of the LORD c Israel.
17:23 the word that you have spoken c your servant and c his house,
19: 2 David sent messengers to console him c his father.
21:15 the LORD took note and relented c the calamity;
22:11 as he has spoken c you.
27: 1 in all matters c the divisions that came and went,
2Ch 9:29 and in the visions of the seer Iddo c Jeroboam son
19:10 c bloodshed, law or commandment,
23: 3 as the LORD promised c the sons of David.
34:21 c the words of the book that has been found;
Ezr 6: 3 C the house of God at Jerusalem,
Ne 6: 7 also set up prophets to proclaim in Jerusalem c
11:23 For there was a command from the king c them,
11:24 was at the king's hand in all matters c the people.
13:14 Remember me, O my God, c this,
Est 3: 2 for the king had so commanded c him.
9:31 and for their descendants regulations c their fasts
Job 27:11 I will teach you c the hand of God;
41:12 "I will not keep silence c its limbs,
Ps 7: T *of David, which he sang to the LORD c Cush,*
71:10 For my enemies speak c me,
91:11 For he will command his angels c you
Ecc 2:20 to despair c all the toil of my labors under the sun,
Isa 1: 1 which he saw c Judah and Jerusalem in the days
2: 1 The word that Isaiah son of Amoz saw c Judah
5: 1 for my beloved my love-song c his vineyard:
13: 1 oracle c Babylon that Isaiah son of Amoz saw.
14:26 This is the plan that is planned c the whole earth;
15: 1 An oracle c Moab.
16:13 This was the word that the LORD spoke c Moab
17: 1 An oracle c Damascus. See,
19: 1 An oracle c Egypt. See, the LORD is riding on a
21: 1 The oracle c the wilderness of the sea.
21:11 The oracle c Dumah. One is calling to me
21:13 The oracle c the desert plain.
22: 1 The oracle c the valley of vision.
23: 1 The oracle c Tyre. Wail, O ships of Tarshish,
23:11 the LORD has given command c Canaan
29:22 who redeemed Abraham, c the house of Jacob:
30: 6 An oracle c the animals of the Negeb.
32: 6 to utter error c the LORD,
37: 9 Now the king heard c King Tirhakah of Ethiopia,
37:21 to me c King Sennacherib of Assyria,
37:22 this is the word that the LORD has spoken c him:
37:33 thus says the LORD c the king of Assyria:
45:11 or command me c the work of my hands?
Jer 7:22 or command them c burnt offerings and sacrifices.
11:21 thus says the LORD c the people of Anathoth,
12:14 the LORD c all my evil neighbors who touch
14: 1 The word of the LORD that came to Jeremiah c
14:10 Thus says the LORD c this people:
14:15 the LORD c the prophets who prophesy
16: 3 the LORD c the sons and daughters who are born
16: 3 and c the mothers who bear them and
18: 7 At one moment I may declare c a nation or
18: 8 c which I have spoken, turns from its evil,
18: 9 And at another moment I may declare c a nation
22: 6 For thus says the LORD c the house of the king
22:11 the LORD c Shallum son of King Josiah
22:18 the LORD c King Jehoiakim son of Josiah
23: 2 c the shepherds who shepherd my people:
23: 9 C the prophets: My heart is crushed within me,
23:15 thus says the LORD of hosts c the prophets:
25: 1 The word that came to Jeremiah c all the people
27:13 as the LORD has spoken c any nation that will
27:19 For thus says the LORD of hosts c the pillars,
27:21 c the vessels left in the house of the LORD,
29:16 the LORD c the king who sits on the throne
29:16 and c all the people who live in this city,
29:21 c Ahab son of Kolaiah and Zedekiah son
29:31 Thus says the LORD c Shemaiah of Nehelam:
30: 4 These are the words that the LORD spoke c
32:36 the God of Israel, c this city of which you say,
33: 4 c the houses of this city and the houses of
34: 4 Thus says the LORD c you:
36:29 And c King Jehoiakim of Judah you shall say:
36:30 thus says the LORD c King Jehoiakim of Judah:
39:11 of Babylon gave command c Jeremiah
46: 1 of the LORD that came to the prophet Jeremiah c
46: 2 C Egypt, about the army of Pharaoh Neco,
47: 1 of the LORD that came to the prophet Jeremiah c
48: 1 C Moab. Thus says the LORD of hosts,
49: 1 C the Ammonites. Thus says the LORD:
49: 7 C Edom. Thus says the LORD of hosts:
49:23 C Damascus. Hamath and Arpad
49:28 C Kedar and the kingdoms of Hazor
49:34 of the LORD that came to the prophet Jeremiah c
50: 1 The word that the LORD spoke c Babylon,
50: 1 c the land of the Chaldeans,
51:11 because his purpose c Babylon is to destroy it,
51:12 and done what he spoke c the inhabitants
51:60 all these words that are written c Babylon.
Eze 12:19 the Lord GOD c the inhabitants of Jerusalem in
13:16 the prophets of Israel who prophesied c Jerusalem
18: 2 What do you mean by repeating this proverb c
21:28 Thus says the Lord GOD c the Ammonites,
21:28 and c their reproach; say: A sword, a sword!
26: 2 because Tyre said c Jerusalem, "Aha,
36: 6 Therefore prophesy c the land of Israel,
44: 5 and listen attentively to all that I shall tell you c
44:12 therefore I have sworn c them,
Da 1:20 In every matter of wisdom and understanding c
2:18 to seek mercy from the God of heaven c
5:29 and a proclamation was made c him
6:12 they approached the king and said c the interdict,
6:17 so that nothing might be changed c Daniel.
Da 7:16 of the attendants to ask him the truth c all this.
7:19 I desired to know the truth c the fourth beast,
7:20 and c the ten horns that were on its head,
7:20 and c the other horn, which came up and
8:13 long is this vision c the regular burnt offering,
Am 1: 1 which he saw c Israel in the days of King Uzziah
7: 3 The LORD relented c this;
7: 6 The LORD relented c this;
Ob 1: 1 Thus says the Lord GOD c Edom:
Mic 1: 1 which he saw c Samaria and Jerusalem.
3: 5 LORD c the prophets who lead my people astray,
Na 1: 1 An oracle c Nineveh. The book of the vision
1:14 The LORD has commanded c you:
Hab 2: 1 and what he will answer c my complaint.
Zec 12: 1 The word of the LORD c Israel:
Mt 4: 6 it is written, 'He will command his angels c you,'
Lk 1: 4 so that you may know the truth c the things
3:15 and all were questioning in their hearts c John,
4:10 'He will command his angels c you,
Ac 1:16 the Holy Spirit through David foretold c Judas,
2:25 For David says c him, 'I saw the Lord always
18:25 and taught accurately the things c Jesus,
19:23 About that time no little disturbance broke out c
23: 6 on trial c the hope of the resurrection of the dead."
23:29 that he was accused c questions of their law,
24: 8 from him c everything of which we accuse him."
24:24 he sent for Paul and heard him speak c faith
Ro 1: 3 the gospel c his Son, who was descended
4:20 No distrust made him waver c the promise
7: 2 she is discharged from the law c the husband.
9:27 And Isaiah cries out c Israel,
10: 5 Moses writes c the righteousness that comes from
1Co 7: 1 Now c the matters about which you wrote:
7:25 Now c virgins, I have no command of the Lord,
8: 1 Now c food sacrificed to idols:
12: 1 Now c spiritual gifts, brothers and sisters,
16: 1 Now c the collection for the saints:
16:12 Now c our brother Apollos,
Col 4:10 c whom you have received instructions—
1Th 4: 9 Now c love of the brothers and sisters,
5: 1 Now c the times and the seasons,
2Th 3: 4 And we have confidence in the Lord c you,
Heb 7:16 through a legal requirement c physical descent,
1Pe 1:10 C this salvation, the prophets who prophesied of
1Jn 1: 1 and touched with our hands, c the word of life—
2:26 to you c those who would deceive you.
5:10 in the testimony that God has given c his Son.
Tob 1: 8 the ordinance decreed c it in the law of Moses and
6:13 and tonight we shall speak c the girl
14: 5 just as the prophets of Israel have said c it.
AdE 10: 5 I remember the dream that I had c these matters,
12: 2 and he informed the king c them.
Sir 17:14 And he gave commandment to each of them c
23: 7 my children, to instruction c the mouth;
30: 1 C CHILDREN He who loves his son will whip him
30:18 C FOODS Good things poured out upon
Sus 1: 5 C them the Lord had said:
1Mc 8:15 senators constantly deliberate c the people,
8:31 "C the wrongs that King Demetrius is doing
9:55 a word or give commands c his house.
11:31 This copy of the letter that we wrote c you
12:17 and deliver to you this letter from us c the renewal
12:21 It has been found in writing c the Spartans and
12:22 please write us c your welfare;
2Mc 3:36 He bore testimony to all c the deeds of
8:12 Word came to Judas c Nicanor's invasion;
11:20 And c such matters and their details,
1Es 1:24 c those who sinned and acted wickedly toward
4:54 also c their support and the priests' vestments
6: 6 from building until word could be sent to Darius c
6:22 let him send us directions c these things."
7:15 the will of the king of the Assyrians c them,
3Mc 5:30 of God his whole mind had been deranged c
2Es 4:52 "C the signs about which you ask me,
4:52 but I was not sent to tell you c your life,
5: 1 "Now c the signs: lo, the days are coming
5:39 can I speak c the things that you have asked me?"
6:34 be quick to think vain thoughts c the former times;
7:*78* Now c death, the teaching is:
7:*90* Therefore this is the teaching c them:
7:*94* the witness that he who formed them bears c
8:51 inquire c the glory of those who are like yourself,
13:22 and c those who do not survive,
15: 8 I will be silent no longer c their ungodly acts
4Mc 5:10 by holding a vain opinion c the truth,
5:29 the sacred oaths of my ancestors c the keeping of

CONCERNS (8) [CONCERN]

Lev 27: 9 If it c an animal that may be brought as
27:11 If it c any unclean animal that may not be brought
Nu 4: 4 of the Kohathites relating to the tent of meeting c
18: 7 that c the altar and the area behind the curtain.
Eze 7:13 vision c all their multitude; it shall not be revoked.
12:10 This oracle c the prince in Jerusalem and all
2Es 6:15 because the word c the end,
6:16 that the speech c them. They will tremble

CONCERT (1)

Sir 32: 5 A ruby seal in a setting of gold is a c of music at

CONCERTED (1)

3Mc 1:28 and c cry of the crowds resulted in

CONCESSION (1) [CONCEDE]

1Co 7: 6 This I say by way of c, not of command.

CONCESSIONS (1) [CONCEDE]

2Mc 4:11 He set aside the existing royal c to the Jews,

CONCISION (KJV) See MUTILATE THE FLESH

CONCLUDE (1) [CONCLUDED, CONCLUSION]

Dt 29:25 They will c, "It is because they abandoned

CONCLUDED (2) [CONCLUDE]

2Mc 14:30 c that this austerity did not spring from
3Mc 4:11 and the voyage was c as the king had decreed,

CONCLUSION (2) [CONCLUDE]

3Mc 1:26 determined to bring the aforesaid plan to a c.
3:14 as you yourselves know, it was brought to c,

CONCOCT (1)

Pr 16:27 Scoundrels c evil, and their speech is like

CONCORD (2)

4Mc 13:25 toward one another, and their c,
14: 3 and harmonious c of the seven brothers on behalf

CONCORD (KJV) See also AGREEMENT

CONCOURSE (KJV) BUSIEST, COMMOTION

CONCUBINE (24) [CONCUBINES]

Ge 22:24 Moreover, his c, whose name was Reumah,
35:22 Reuben went and lay with Bilhah his father's c;
36:12 (Timna was a c of Eliphaz, Esau's son;
Jdg 8:31 His c who was in Shechem also bore him a son,
19: 1 took to himself a c from Bethlehem in Judah.
19: 2 But his c became angry with him,
19: 9 the man with his c and his servant got up to leave,
19:10 and his c was with him.
19:24 Here are my virgin daughter and his c;
19:25 So the man seized his c, and put her out to them.
19:27 there was his c lying at the door of the house,
19:29 and grasping his c he cut her into twelve pieces,
20: 4 I and my c, to spend the night.
20: 5 and they raped my c until she died.
20: 6 Then I took my c and cut her into pieces,
2Sa 3: 7 a c whose name was Rizpah daughter of Aiah.
3: 7 "Why have you gone in to my father's c?"
21:11 told what Rizpah daughter of Aiah, the c of Saul,
1Ch 1:32 The sons of Keturah, Abraham's c:
2:46 Ephah also, Caleb's c, bore Haran, Moza,
2:48 Maacah, Caleb's c, bore Sheber and Tirhanah.
7:14 Asriel, whom his Aramean c bore;
2Mc 4:30 as a present to Antiochis, the king's c.
1Es 4:29 Yet I have seen him with Apame, the king's c,

CONCUBINES (18) [CONCUBINE]

Ge 25: 6 But to the sons of his c Abraham gave gifts,
2Sa 5:13 David took more c and wives;
15:16 except ten c whom he left behind to look after
16:21 "Go in to your father's c,
16:22 and Absalom went in to his father's c in the sight
19: 5 and the lives of your wives and your c,
20: 3 the ten c whom he had left to look after the house,
1Ki 11: 3 seven hundred princesses and three hundred c;
1Ch 3: 9 besides the sons of the c;
2Ch 11:21 wives and c (he took eighteen wives and sixty c,
Est 2:14 the king's eunuch, who was in charge of the c;
Ecc 2: 8 and delights of the flesh, and many c.
SS 6: 8 There are sixty queens and eighty c,
6: 9 the queens and c also, and they praised her.
Da 5: 2 his wives, and his c might drink from them.
5: 3 his wives, and his c drank from them.
5:23 and your c have been drinking wine from them.

CONCUPISCENCE (KJV) See COVETOUSNESS, EVIL DESIRE, LUSTFUL PASSION

CONDEMN‡ (35) [CONDEMNATION, CONDEMNED, CONDEMNING, CONDEMNS, SELF-CONDEMNED]

Job 9:20 I am innocent, my own mouth would c me;
10: 2 I will say to God, Do not c me;
34:17 Will you c one who is righteous and mighty,
34:29 When he is quiet, who can c?
40: 8 Will you c me that you may be justified?
Ps 94:21 and c the innocent to death.
109:31 to save them from those who would c them
141: 6 they are given over to those who shall c them,
Mt 12:41 up at the judgment with this generation and c it,
12:42 up at the judgment with this generation and c it,
20:18 and they will c him to death;
Mk 10:33 and they will c him to death;
Lk 6:37 do not c, and you will not be condemned.
11:31 with the people of this generation and c them,
11:32 up at the judgment with this generation and c it,
Jn 3:17 not send the Son into the world to c the world,

Jn 8:11 ⟦And Jesus said, "Neither do I c you.⟧
8:26 I have much to say about you and much to c;
Ro 2: 1 for in passing judgment on another you c yourself,
2:27 the law will c you that have the written code
8:34 Who is to c? It is Christ Jesus,
14:22 to c themselves because of what they approve.
2Co 7: 3 I do not say this to c you,
Col 2:16 not let anyone c you in matters of food and drink
1Jn 3:20 whenever our hearts c us;
3:21 Beloved, if our hearts do not c us,
Wis 2:20 Let us c him to a shameful death, for,
4:16 The righteous who have died will c
4:16 and youth that is quickly perfected will c
12:15 to c anyone who does not deserve to be punished.
Sir 10:29 Who will acquit those who c themselves?
14: 2 Happy are those whose hearts do not c them,
Sus 1:48 to c a daughter of Israel without examination and
Man 1:13 do not c me to the depths of the earth.
2Es 4:18 to justify, and which to c?"

CONDEMNATION‡ (20) [CONDEMN]

Pr 19:29 C is ready for scoffers, and flogging for the backs
Mk 12:40 They will receive the greater c."
Lk 20:47 They will receive the greater c."
23:40 since you are under the same sentence of c?
Jn 5:29 those who have done evil, to the resurrection of c.
Ro 3: 8 that good may come"? Their c is deserved!
5:16 the judgment following one trespass brought c,
5:18 just as one man's trespass led to c for all,
8: 1 There is therefore now no c for those who are
1Co 11:34 it will not be for your c.
2Co 3: 9 For if there was glory in the ministry of c,
1Ti 3: 6 be puffed up with conceit and fall into the c of
5:12 they incur c for having violated their first pledge.
Jas 5:12 so that you may not fall under c.
2Pe 2: 3 Their c, pronounced against them long ago,
Jude 1: 4 people who long ago were designated for this c
1: 9 he did not dare to bring a c of slander against him,
Wis 11:10 the ungodly as a stern king does in c.
12:27 Therefore the utmost c came upon them.
Sir 5:14 and severe c to the double-tongued.

CONDEMNED (31) [CONDEMN]

Job 9:29 I shall be c; why then do I labor in vain?
Ps 34:21 and those who hate the righteous will be c.
34:22 none of those who take refuge in him will be c.
37:33 or let them be c when they are brought to trial.
Mt 12: 7 you would not have c the guiltless.
12:37 and by your words you will be c."
27: 3 When Judas, his betrayer, saw that Jesus was c,
Mk 14:64 All of them c him as deserving death.
16:16 ⟦but the one who does not believe will be c.⟧
Lk 6:37 do not condemn, and you will not be c.
23:41 And we indeed have been c justly,
24:20 and leaders handed him over to be c to death
Jn 3:18 Those who believe in him are not c;
3:18 but those who do not believe are c already,
8:10 ⟦Has no one c you?"⟧
16:11 because the ruler of this world has been c.
Ac 26:10 against them when they were being c to death.
Ro 3: 7 why am I still being c as a sinner?
8: 3 and to deal with sin, he c sin in the flesh,
14:23 But those who have doubts are c if they eat,
1Co 11:32 we are disciplined so that we may not be c along
2Th 2:12 but took pleasure in unrighteousness will be c.
Heb 11: 7 by this he c the world and became an heir to
Jas 5: 6 You have c and murdered the righteous one,
2Pe 2: 6 to ashes he c them to extinction and made them
AdE 2: 1 and how he had c her.
Wis 17:11 a cowardly thing, c by its own testimony;
Sir 19: 5 One who rejoices in wickedness will be c,
Sus 1:41 the assembly believed them and c her to death.
1Mc 1:57 was c to death by decree of the king.
2Es 7:*115* [45] to have mercy on someone who has been c

CONDEMNING (3) [CONDEMN]

1Ki 8:32 c the guilty by bringing their conduct
Ac 13:27 they fulfilled those words by c him.
Sus 1:53 c the innocent and acquitting the guilty,

CONDEMNS (4) [CONDEMN]

Ex 22: 9 the one whom God c shall pay double to the other.
Job 15: 6 Your own mouth c you, and not I;
Pr 12: 2 but those who devise evil he c.
17:15 One who justifies the wicked and one who c

CONDENSATION (1) [CONDENSE]

2Mc 2:28 to arriving at the outlines of the c.

CONDENSE (2) [CONDENSATION]

Dt 32: 2 my speech c like the dew;
2Mc 2:23 we shall attempt to c into a single book.

CONDITION (14) [CONDITIONS]

Ge 34:15 Only on this c will we consent to you:
34:22 Only on this c will they agree to live among us,
1Sa 11: 2 "On this c I will make a treaty with you,
2Ch 24:13 and they restored the house of God to its proper c
Pr 27:23 Know well the c of your flocks,
Da 1:10 in poorer c than the other young men
1Co 7:20 of you remain in the c in which you were called.
7:21 make use of your present c now more than ever.
7:24 In whatever c you were called,
Gal 4:14 though my c put you to the test,
AdE 9:22 in which their c had been changed from sorrow
Sir 11:12 he lifts them out of their lowly c
2Mc 9:22 I do not despair of my c,
4Mc 11:11 In this c, gasping for breath and in anguish

CONDITIONS (4) [CONDITION]

2Ch 12:12 moreover, c were good in Judah.
Jer 32:11 containing the terms and c, and the open copy;
Sir 18:26 From morning to evening c change;
1Mc 6:61 On these c the Jews evacuated the stronghold.

CONDOLENCES (1)

2Sa 10: 3 because he has sent messengers with c to you?

CONDUCT‡ (35) [CONDUCTED, CONDUCTING]

1Ki 8:32 the guilty by bringing their c on their own head,
2Ch 6:23 the guilty by bringing their c on their own head,
Est 6: 9 the king wishes to honor, and let him c the man
Job 11: 4 For you say, 'My c is pure,
Ps 112: 5 who c their affairs with justice.
Pr 10:23 wise c is pleasure to a person of understanding.
14: 2 but one who is devious in c despises him.
21: 8 but the c of the pure is right.
Ecc 6: 8 the poor have who know how to c themselves
8:14 according to the c of the wicked,
8:14 according to the c of the righteous.
Eze 22:31 I have returned their c upon their heads,
36:17 their c in my sight was like the uncleanness of
36:19 with their c and their deeds I judged them.
Ro 13: 3 For rulers are not a terror to good c, but to bad.
2Co 12:18 Did we not c ourselves with the same spirit?
Col 4: 5 C yourselves wisely toward outsiders,
1Th 2:10 and blameless our c was toward you believers.
1Ti 4:12 but set the believers an example in speech and c,
2Ti 3:10 Now you have observed my teaching, my c,
1Pe 1:15 be holy yourselves in all your c;
2:12 C yourselves honorably among the Gentiles,
3: 1 be won over without a word by their wives' c,
3:16 for your good c in Christ may be put to shame.
Tob 4:14 and discipline yourself in all your c.
Sir 11:26 to reward individuals according to their c.
23:12 Such c will be far from the godly,
37:17 The mind is the root of all c;
51:19 and in my c I was strict;
1Mc 12: 4 asking them to provide for the envoys safe c to
2Mc 4:37 and wept because of the moderation and good c of
11:26 and be of good cheer and go on happily in the c
1Es 4:47 that they should give safe c to him and
2Es 10:39 He has seen your righteous c,
16:47 Those who c business, do so only

CONDUCTED (4) [CONDUCT]

Ne 13:10 the Levites and the singers, who had c the service,
Ac 17:15 Those who c Paul brought him as far as Athens;
3Mc 3: 4 they worshiped God and c themselves by his law,
4:15 therefore c with bitter haste and zealous intensity

CONDUCTING (1) [CONDUCT]

1Mc 9:37 a great wedding, and are c the bride, a daughter

CONDUIT (4)

2Ki 18:17 they came and stood by the c of the upper pool,
20:20 how he made the pool and the c and brought water
Isa 7: 3 the end of the c of the upper pool on the highway
36: 2 by the c of the upper pool on the highway to

CONEYS (1)

Ps 104:18 the rocks are a refuge for the c.

CONFECTION, CONFECTIONARIES (KJV) See PERFUMER, PERFUMERS

CONFEDERACY (KJV) See ALLIES, CONSPIRACY

CONFEDERATES (1)

Ob 1: 7 your c have prevailed against you;

CONFER (6) [CONFERENCE, CONFERRED, CONFERRING, CONFERS]

Ne 6: 7 So come, therefore, and let us c together."
Lk 22:29 and I c on you, just as my Father has conferred
Gal 1:16 I did not c with any human being,
1Mc 11:42 but I will c great honor on you and your nation,
15:28 one of his Friends, to c with him, saying,
2Mc 11:20 and my representatives to c with you.

CONFERENCE (1) [CONFER]

1Mc 11:22 not to continue the siege, but to meet him for a c

CONFERRED (7) [CONFER]

1Ki 1: 7 He c with Joab son of Zeruiah and with
Da 11:21 on whom royal majesty had not been c;
Mt 27: 1 the elders of the people c together against Jesus
Lk 22: 4 and c with the chief priests and officers of
22:29 just as my Father has c on me, a kingdom,
Ac 25:12 Then Festus, after he had c with his council,
4Mc 4:17 that if the office were c on him he would pay

CONFERRING (1) [CONFER]

Mt 27: 7 After c together, they used them to buy

CONFERS (1) [CONFER]

Sir 10: 5 and it is he who c honor upon the lawgiver.

CONFESS‡ (25) [CONFESSED, CONFESSES, CONFESSING, CONFESSION]

Lev 5: 5 you shall c the sin that you have committed.
16:21 c over it all the iniquities of the people of Israel,
26:40 But if they c their iniquity and the iniquity
Nu 5: 7 and shall c the sin that has been committed.
1Ki 8:33 but turn again to you, c your name, pray and plead
8:35 and then they pray toward this place, c your name,
2Ch 6:24 but turn again to you, c your name, pray and plead
6:26 and then they pray toward this place, c your name,
Ps 32: 5 I said, "I will c my transgressions to the LORD,"
38:18 I c my iniquity; I am sorry for my sin.
Jn 12:42 But because of the Pharisees they did not c it,
Ro 10: 9 because if you c with your lips that Jesus is Lord
15: 9 "Therefore I will c you among the Gentiles,
Php 2:11 every tongue should c that Jesus Christ is Lord,
Heb 13:15 that is, the fruit of lips that c his name.
Jas 5:16 Therefore c your sins to one another,
1Jn 1: 9 If we c our sins, he who is faithful and just
4: 3 every spirit that does not c Jesus is not from God.
4:15 God abides in those who c that Jesus is the Son
2Jn 1: 7 those who do not c that Jesus Christ has come in
Rev 3: 5 I will c your name before my Father and
Sir 4:26 Do not be ashamed to c your sins,
2Mc 6: 6 nor so much as c themselves to be Jews.
7:37 and plagues to make you c that he alone is God,
4Mc 13: 5 to c the sovereignty of right reason over emotion

CONFESSED‡ (10) [CONFESS]

Ne 9: 2 and stood and c their sins and the iniquities
Jn 1:20 He c and did not deny it, but c, "I am not the
9:22 that anyone who c Jesus to be the Messiah would
Ac 19:18 Also many of those who became believers c
Heb 11:13 They c that they were strangers and foreigners on
AdE 12: 3 and after they had c it,
Sus 1:14 the other for the reason, they c their lust.
2Es 2:45 and have c the name of God.
2:47 whom they c in the world."

CONFESSES (4) [CONFESS]

Pr 28:13 one who c and forsakes them will obtain mercy.
Ro 10:10 and one c with the mouth and so is saved.
1Jn 2:23 everyone who c the Son has the Father also.
4: 2 every spirit that c that Jesus Christ has come in

CONFESSING (4) [CONFESS]

Ne 1: 6 c the sins of the people of Israel,
Da 9:20 and c my sin and the sin of my people Israel,
Mt 3: 6 by him in the river Jordan, c their sins.
Mk 1: 5 by him in the river Jordan, c their sins.

CONFESSION (14) [CONFESS]

Jos 7:19 give glory to the LORD God of Israel and make c
Ezr 10: 1 While Ezra prayed and made c,
10:11 make c to the LORD the God of your ancestors,
Ne 9: 3 and for another fourth they made c and worshiped
Da 9: 4 I prayed to the LORD my God and made c,
2Co 9:13 the c of the gospel of Christ and by the generosity
1Ti 6:12 for which you made the good c in the presence
6:13 before Pontius Pilate made the good c,
Heb 3: 1 the apostle and high priest of our c,
4:14 Jesus, the Son of God, let us hold fast to our c.
10:23 to the c of our hope without wavering,
Bar 1:14 to make your c in the house of the Lord on
1Es 8:91 While Ezra was praying and making his c,
9: 8 then make c and give glory to the Lord the God

CONFIDENCE‡ (42) [CONFIDENT, CONFIDENTLY]

Jdg 9:26 the lords of Shechem put c in him.
2Ki 18:19 On what do you base this c of yours?
Job 4: 6 Is not your fear of God your c,
8:14 Their c is gossamer, a spider's house their trust.
11:18 And you will have c, because there is hope;
29:24 I smiled on them when they had no c;
31:24 or called fine gold my c,
Ps 62:10 Put no c in extortion, and set no vain hopes
118: 8 to take refuge in the LORD than to put c
118: 9 to take refuge in the LORD than to put c
Pr 3:26 the LORD will be your c and will keep your foot
3:32 but the upright are in his c.
11:13 but one who is trustworthy in spirit keeps a c.
14:26 In the fear of the LORD one has strong c,
Isa 36: 4 On what do you base this c of yours?
Jer 48:13 the house of Israel was ashamed of Bethel, their c.
Mic 7: 5 Put no trust in a friend, have no c in a loved one;
2Co 3: 4 the c that we have through Christ toward God.
5: 8 we do have c, and we would rather be away from
7:16 I rejoice, because I have complete c in you.
8:22 now more eager than ever because of his great c
11:17 What I am saying in regard to this boastful c,
Eph 3:12 in whom we have access to God in boldness and c
Php 3: 3 of God and boast in Christ Jesus and have no c in

Php 3: 4 too, have reason for c in the flesh.
2Th 3: 4 And we have c in the Lord concerning you,
Heb 3: 6 and we are his house if we hold firm the c and
3:14 if only we hold our first c firm to the end.
10:19 since we have c to enter the sanctuary by
10:35 Do not, therefore, abandon that c of yours;
13: 6 So we can say with c, "The Lord is my helper;
1Jn 2:28 so that when he is revealed we may have c and not
Wis 5: 1 Then the righteous will stand with great c in
Sir 26:21 *and, having c in their good descent,*
27:16 Whoever betrays secrets destroys c,
40:26 Riches and strength build up c,
1Mc 9:58 Jonathan and his men are living in quiet and c.
10:71 If you now have c in your forces,
10:77 for he had a large troop of cavalry and put c in it.
2Mc 15: 7 not cease to trust with all c that he would get help
15:11 with c in shields and spears as with the inspiration
3Mc 2: 7 through safely those who had put their c in you,

CONFIDENT (17) [CONFIDENCE]

Job 6:20 They are disappointed because they were c;
40:23 it is c though Jordan rushes against its mouth.
Ps 27: 3 though war rise up against me, yet I will be c.
Ro 15:14 I myself feel c about you, my brothers and sisters,
2Co 2: 3 for I am c about all of you,
5: 6 So we are always c;
10: 7 If you are c that you belong to Christ,
Gal 5:10 I am c about you in the Lord that you will
Php 1: 6 I am c of this, that the one who began
1:14 having been made c in the Lord
3: 4 If anyone else has reason to be c in the flesh,
Phm 1:21 C of your obedience, I am writing to you,
Heb 6: 9 beloved, we are c of better things in your case,
Jdt 2: 5 Leave my presence and take with you men c
Sir 5: 5 not be so c of forgiveness that you add sin to sin.
49:10 of Jacob and delivered them with c hope.
2Es 7:*98* and shall be c without confusion,

CONFIDENTLY‡ (3) [CONFIDENCE]

Ac 2:29 I may say to you c of our ancestor David that he
3Mc 2:32 for life they c attempted to save themselves from
5:44 and they c posted the armed forces at the places in

CONFINE (7) [CONFINED, CONFINES]

Lev 13: 4 priest shall c the diseased person for seven days.
13: 5 then the priest shall c him seven days more.
13:11 he shall not c him, for he is unclean.
13:21 the priest shall c him seven days.
13:26 the priest shall c him seven days.
13:31 the priest shall c the person with
13:33 The priest shall c the person with the itch

CONFINED (16) [CONFINE]

Ge 39:20 the place where the king's prisoners were c;
40: 3 in the prison where Joseph was c.
40: 5 who were c in the prison—
Ex 21:18 though not dead, is c to bed,
2Ki 17: 4 the king of Assyria c him and imprisoned him.
23:33 Pharaoh Neco c him at Riblah in the land
Ne 6:10 who was c to his house, he said,
Jer 32: 2 and the prophet Jeremiah was c in the court of
32: 3 where King Zedekiah of Judah had c him.
33: 1 while he was still c in the court of the guard:
39:15 of the LORD came to Jeremiah while he was c in
Sir 23:19 His fear is c to human eyes and he does not realize
Man 1: 3 who c the deep and sealed it with your terrible
3Mc 4:10 and in addition they were c under a solid deck,
5: 7 in their bonds they were forcibly c on every side.
2Es 16:58 he has c the sea in the midst of the waters;

CONFINES (1) [CONFINE]

Tob 14:10 do not stay overnight within the c of the city.

CONFIRM‡ (14) [CONFIRMATION, CONFIRMED, CONFIRMING, CONFIRMS]

Dt 8:18 so that he may c his covenant that he swore
Ru 4: 7 to c a transaction, the one took off a sandal
2Sa 7:25 c it forever; do as you have promised.
1Ki 1:14 I will come in after you and c your words."
2Ki 15:19 he might help him c his hold on the royal power.
1Ch 17:14 but I will c him in my house and
Ps 119:38 C to your servant your promise,
Ro 3: 5 But if our injustice serves to c the justice of God,
15: 8 of God in order that he might c the promises given
2Pe 1:10 be all the more eager to c your call and election,
1Mc 11:57 "I c you in the high priesthood and set you over
12: 1 to Rome to c and renew the friendship with them.
14:24 to c the alliance with the Romans.
15: 5 now therefore I c to you all the tax remissions that

CONFIRMATION (2) [CONFIRM]

Php 1: 7 both in my imprisonment and in the defense and c
Heb 6:16 and an oath given as c puts an end to all dispute.

CONFIRMED (15) [CONFIRM]

1Ki 8:26 Therefore, O God of Israel, let your word be c,
1Ch 16:17 which he c to Jacob as a statute,
2Ch 6:17 O LORD, God of Israel, let your word be c,
Ps 105:10 which he c to Jacob as a statute,
119:106 I have sworn an oath and c it,
Da 9:12 He has c his words, which he spoke against us and
Mt 18:16 that every word may be c by the evidence of two
Mk 16:20 ⟦the Lord worked with them and c the message⟧
Heb 7:20 This was c with an oath;
2Pe 1:19 So we have the prophetic message more fully c.
1Mc 11:27 He c him in the high priesthood and in
11:34 We have c as their possession both the territory
14:38 "In view of these things King Demetrius c him in
2Mc 12:25 with many words he had c his solemn promise
4Mc 18:17 He c the query of Ezekiel,

CONFIRMING (1) [CONFIRM]

Est 9:29 c this second letter about Purim.

CONFIRMS (3) [CONFIRM]

Isa 44:26 who c the word of his servant, and fulfills
Ro 9: 1 my conscience c it by the Holy Spirit—
Sir 3: 2 and he c a mother's right over her children.

CONFISCATED (2) [CONFISCATION]

Tob 1:20 Then all my property was c;
2Mc 3:13 said that this money must in any case be c for

CONFISCATION (2) [CONFISCATED]

Ezr 7:26 for death or for banishment or for c of their goods
3Mc 7:21 at all to c of their belongings by any one.

CONFLICT (3) [CONFLICTING, CONFLICTS]

Jdg 11:25 Did he ever enter into c with Israel,
12: 2 "My people and I were engaged in c with
Da 10: 1 The word was true, and it concerned a great c.

CONFLICTING (1) [CONFLICT]

Ro 2:15 and their c thoughts will accuse

CONFLICTS (2) [CONFLICT]

Jas 4: 1 Those c and disputes among you,
4: 2 so you engage in disputes and c.

CONFORMED (4) [CONFORMS]

Ro 8:29 also predestined to be c to the image of his Son,
12: 2 Do not be c to this world,
Php 3:21 of our humiliation that it may be c to the body
1Pe 1:14 do not be c to the desires that you formerly had

CONFORMS (1) [CONFORMED]

1Ti 1:11 that c to the glorious gospel of the blessed God,

CONFOUND (3) [CONFOUNDED]

Ps 14: 6 You would c the plans of the poor,
55: 9 Confuse, O Lord, c their speech;
Isa 19: 3 and I will c their plans;

CONFOUNDED‡ (12) [CONFOUND]

2Ki 19:26 shorn of strength, are dismayed and c;
Job 6:20 they come there and are c.
Ps 35: 4 be turned back and c who devise evil against me.
Isa 20: 5 be dismayed and c because of Ethiopia their hope
33: 9 Lebanon is c and withers away;
37:27 shorn of strength, are dismayed and c;
45:16 All of them are put to shame and c,
45:17 you shall not be put to shame or c to all eternity.
Jer 49:23 and Arpad are c, for they have heard bad news;
Eze 16:63 in order that you may remember and be c,
Ac 9:22 and c the Jews who lived in Damascus by proving
1Mc 3: 6 of him; all the evildoers were c;

CONFRONT (7) [CONFRONTED, CONFRONTS]

Nu 14:43 Amalekites and the Canaanites will c you there,
Dt 31:21 this song will c them as a witness,
Job 41:11 Who can c it and be safe?
Ps 17:13 Rise up, O LORD, c them, overthrow them!
Pr 17:12 to meet a she-bear robbed of its cubs than to c
Isa 50: 8 Who are my adversaries? Let them c me.
Wis 12:14 nor can any king or monarch c you

CONFRONTED (5) [CONFRONT]

Nu 16: 2 well-known men, and they c Moses.
2Sa 22: 6 the snares of death c me.
Ps 18: 5 the snares of death c me.
18:18 They c me in the day of my calamity;
Ac 6:12 then they suddenly c him, seized him,

CONFRONTS (1) [CONFRONT]

Ecc 9: 1 one does not know. Everything that c them

CONFUSE‡ (3) [CONFUSED, CONFUSES, CONFUSING, CONFUSION]

Ge 11: 7 Come, let us go down, and c their language there,
Ps 55: 9 C, O Lord, confound their speech;
Isa 3:12 and c the course of your paths.

CONFUSED (6) [CONFUSE]

Ge 11: 9 there the LORD c the language of all the earth;
Isa 28: 7 and the prophet reel with strong drink, they are c
Jer 14: 9 Why should you be like someone c,
Lk 21:25 the earth distress among nations c by the roaring
2Mc 10:30 that, c and blinded, they were thrown into disorder
1Es 8:74 "O Lord, I am ashamed and c before your face.

CONFUSES (1) [CONFUSE]

Sir 40: 5 his sleep at night c his mind.

CONFUSING (2) [CONFUSE]

Gal 1: 7 but there are some who are c you and want
5:10 whoever it is that is c you will pay the penalty.

CONFUSION (33) [CONFUSE]

Ex 23:27 and will throw into c all the people
Dt 28:28 with madness, blindness, and c of mind;
1Sa 7:10 against the Philistines and threw them into c;
14:20 so that there was very great c.
Ne 4: 8 to come and fight against Jerusalem and to cause c
Est 3:15 but the city of Susa was thrown into c.
Ps 35:26 at my calamity be put to shame and c;
40:14 to shame and c who seek to snatch away my life;
44: 7 and have put to c those who hate us.
70: 2 Let those be put to shame and c who seek my life.
Isa 9:16 and those who were led by them were left in c.
19:14 The LORD has poured into them a spirit of c;
22: 5 a day of tumult and trampling and c in the valley
34:11 He shall stretch the line of c over it,
45:16 the makers of idols go in c together.
Mic 7: 4 now their c is at hand.
Ac 19:29 The city was filled with the c;
19:32 for the assembly was in c,
Tob 4:13 For in pride there is ruin and great c.
AdE 3:15 the city of Susa was thrown into c.
11: 5 Noises and c, thunders and earthquake, tumult on
Wis 10: 5 nations in wicked agreement had been put to c,
14:26 c over what is good, forgetfulness
2Mc 4:41 threw them in wild c at Lysimachus and his men.
13:16 In the end they filled the camp with terror and c
3Mc 6:19 of the enemy and filled them with c and terror,
2Es 2: 6 so that you may bring c on them
5: 4 you shall see it thrown into c after
7:*87* because they shall utterly waste away in c and
7:*98* and shall be confident without c,
9: 3 wavering of leaders, c of princes,
15:18 Because of their pride the cities shall be in c,
16:21 the sword, famine, and great c.

CONFUTE (1) [CONFUTED]

Isa 54:17 and you shall c every tongue that rises against you

CONFUTED (1) [CONFUTE]

Job 32:12 but there was in fact no one that c Job,

CONGEALED (1)

Ex 15: 8 the deeps c in the heart of the sea.

CONGENIAL (1)

Sir 27:16 and will never find a c friend.

CONGRATULATE (4)

2Sa 8:10 to c him because he had fought against Hadadezer
1Ki 1:47 the king's servants came to c our lord King David,
1Ch 18:10 to greet him and to c him,
3Mc 1: 8 and to c him on what had happened,

CONGREGATION (153) [CONGREGATION'S, CONGREGATIONS]

A. WHOLE CONGREGATION (41)
B. ALL THE CONGREGATION (25)
C. CONGREGATION OF [THE] ISRAELITES (25)
D. CONGREGATION OF ISRAEL (13)

Ex 12: 3 Tell the whole c of Israel that on the tenth AD
12: 6 the whole assembled c of Israel shall slaughter it D
12:19 be cut off from the c of Israel, D
12:47 The whole c of Israel shall celebrate it. AD
16: 1 The whole c of the Israelites set out from Elim; AC
16: 2 The whole c of the Israelites complained AC
16: 9 "Say to the whole c of the Israelites, AC
16:10 as Aaron spoke to the whole c of the Israelites, AC
16:22 all the leaders of the c came and told Moses,
17: 1 whole c of the Israelites journeyed by stages, AC
34:31 Aaron and all the leaders of the c returned to him,
35: 1 Moses assembled all the c of the Israelites BC
35: 4 Moses said to all the c of the Israelites: BC
35:20 Then all the c of the Israelites withdrew from BC
38:25 the c who were counted was one hundred talents
Lev 4:13 If the whole c of Israel errs unintentionally AD
4:15 the c shall lay their hands on the head of the bull
8: 3 whole c at the entrance of the tent of meeting. A
8: 4 the c was assembled at the entrance of the tent
8: 5 the c, "This is what the LORD has commanded
9: 5 whole c drew near and stood before the LORD. A
10: 6 or you will die and wrath will strike all the c; B
10:17 to you that you may remove the guilt of the c,
16: 5 from the c of the people of Israel two male goats
19: 2 all the c of the people of Israel and say to them: B
24:14 and let the whole c stone him. A
24:16 the whole c shall stone the blasphemer. A
Nu 1: 2 a census of the whole c of Israelites, AC
1:16 These were the ones chosen from the c,
1:18 they assembled the whole c together. A
1:53 there may be no wrath on the c of the Israelites; C
3: 7 for the whole c in front of the tent of meeting, A
4:34 and the leaders of the c enrolled the Kohathites,
8: 9 and assemble the whole c of the Israelites. AC
8:20 and Aaron and the whole c of the Israelites did AC

Nu 10: 2 and you shall use them for summoning the **c**,
10: 3 the whole **c** shall assemble before you at A
13:26 to all the **c** of the Israelites in the wilderness BC
13:26 they brought back word to them and to all the **c**, B
14: 1 Then all the **c** raised a loud cry, B
14: 2 the whole **c** said to them, A
14: 5 before all the assembly of the **c** of the Israelites. C
14: 7 and said to all the **c** of the Israelites, BC
14:10 But the whole **c** threatened to stone them. A
14:27 long shall this wicked **c** complain against me?
14:35 to all this wicked **c** gathered together against me:
14:36 who returned and made all the **c** complain B
15:24 without the knowledge of the **c**,
15:24 the whole **c** shall offer one young bull for A
15:25 atonement for all the **c** of the Israelites, BC
15:26 All the **c** of the Israelites shall be forgiven, BC
15:33 Aaron, and to the whole **c**. A
15:35 all the **c** shall stone him outside the camp." B
15:36 The whole **c** brought him outside the camp A
16: 2 leaders of the **c**, chosen from the assembly,
16: 3 All the **c** are holy, everyone of them, B
16: 9 has separated you from the **c** of Israel, D
16: 9 and to stand before the **c** and serve them?
16:19 Then Korah assembled the whole **c** against them A
16:19 the glory of the LORD appeared to the whole **c**. A
16:21 Separate yourselves from this **c**,
16:22 and you become angry with the whole **c**?" A
16:24 Say to the **c**: Get away from the
16:26 He said to the **c**, "Turn away from the tents
16:41 the whole **c** of the Israelites rebelled AC
16:42 And when the **c** had assembled against them,
16:45 from this **c**, so that I may consume them in
16:46 and carry it quickly to the **c** and make atonement
19: 9 and they shall be kept for the **c** of the Israelites C
20: 1 The Israelites, the whole **c**, A
20: 2 Now there was no water for the **c**;
20: 8 and assemble the **c**, you and your brother Aaron,
20: 8 thus you shall provide drink for the **c**
20:11 and the **c** and their livestock drank.
20:22 the whole **c**, came to Mount Hor. A
20:27 up Mount Hor in the sight of the whole **c**. A
20:29 When all the **c** saw that Aaron had died, B
25: 6 and in the sight of the whole **c** of the Israelites, AC
25: 7 saw it, he got up and left the **c**.
26: 2 "Take a census of the whole **c** of the Israelites, AC
26: 9 the same Dathan and Abiram, chosen from the **c**,
27: 2 Eleazar the priest, the leaders, and all the **c**, B
27:14 in the wilderness of Zin when the **c** quarreled
27:16 appoint someone over the **c**
27:17 the **c** of the LORD may not be like sheep without
27:19 before Eleazar the priest and all the **c**, B
27:20 so that all the **c** of the Israelites may obey. BC
27:21 and all the Israelites with him, the whole **c**." A
27:22 before Eleazar the priest and the whole **c**; A
31:12 Eleazar the priest, and to the **c** of the Israelites, C
31:13 the leaders of the **c** went to meet them outside
31:16 that the plague came among the **c** of the LORD.
31:26 the ancestral houses of the **c** make an inventory of
31:27 the warriors who went out to battle and all the **c**. B
32: 2 to Eleazar the priest, and to the leaders of the **c**,
32: 4 that the LORD subdued before the **c** of Israel— D
35:12 not die until there is a trial before the **c**.
35:24 then the **c** shall judge between the slayer and
35:25 and the **c** shall rescue the slayer from the avenger
35:25 the **c** shall send the slayer back to the original city
Jos 9:15 and the leaders of the **c** swore an oath to them.
9:18 leaders of the **c** had sworn to them by the LORD,
9:18 Then all the **c** murmured against the leaders. B
9:19 But all the leaders said to all the **c**, B
9:21 of wood and drawers of water for all the **c**, B
9:27 and drawers of water for the **c** and for the altar of
18: 1 whole **c** of the Israelites assembled at Shiloh, AC
20: 6 until there is a trial before the **c**, until the death of
20: 9 until there was a trial before the **c**.
22:16 "Thus says the whole **c** of the LORD, A
22:17 which a plague came upon the **c** of the LORD,
22:18 be angry with the whole **c** of Israel tomorrow. AD
22:20 and wrath fell upon all the **c** of Israel? BD
22:30 When the priest Phinehas and the chiefs of the **c**,
Jdg 20: 1 the **c** assembled in one body before the LORD
21:10 So the **c** sent twelve thousand soldiers there
21:13 Then the whole **c** sent word to the Benjaminites A
21:16 So the elders of the **c** said,
1Ki 8: 5 King Solomon and all the **c** of Israel, BD
2Ch 5: 6 King Solomon and all the **c** of Israel, BD
7: 8 and all Israel with him, a very great **c**,
24: 6 on the **c** of Israel for the tent of the covenant?" D
Ezr 10: 8 they themselves banned from the **c** of the exiles.
Ps 1: 5 nor sinners in the **c** of the righteous;
22:22 in the midst of the **c** I will praise you:
22:25 From you comes my praise in the great **c**;
26:12 in the great **c** I will bless the LORD.
35:18 Then I will thank you in the great **c**;
40: 9 the glad news of deliverance in the great **c**;
40:10 and your faithfulness from the great **c**.
68:26 "Bless God in the great **c**,
74: 2 Remember your **c**, which you acquired long ago,
107:32 Let them extol him in the **c** of the people,
111: 1 in the company of the upright, in the **c**.
Jer 6:18 Therefore hear, O nations, and know, O **c**,
30:20 their **c** shall be established before me;
La 1:10 those whom you forbade to enter your **c**.
Joel 2:16 Sanctify the **c**; assemble the aged;
Ac 7:38 the **c** in the wilderness with the angel who spoke
15:30 When they gathered the **c** together,
19: 9 to believe and spoke evil of the Way before the **c**,
Heb 2:12 in the midst of the **c** I will praise you."
Sir 1:30 and overthrow you before the whole **c**, A
4: 7 Endear yourself to the **c**;
33:19 and you leaders of the **c**, pay heed!
39:10 and the **c** will proclaim his praise.
41:18 before the **c** and the people;
44:15 and the **c** proclaims their praise.
46: 7 they opposed the **c**, restrained the people from sin,
46:14 By the law of the Lord he judged the **c**,
50:13 in their hands before the whole **c** of Israel. AD
50:20 raised his hands over the whole **c** of Israelites, AC
1Mc 3:44 So the **c** assembled to be ready for battle,

CONGREGATION'S (1) [CONGREGATION]
Nu 31:43 **c** half was three hundred thirty-seven thousand five hundred sheep

CONGREGATIONS (1) [CONGREGATION]
Sir 24:23 as an inheritance for the **c** of Jacob.

CONIAH (3) [=JEHOIACHIN]
Jer 22:24 even if King **C** son of Jehoiakim of Judah were
22:28 Is this man **C** a despised broken pot,
37: 1 succeeded **C** son of Jehoiakim.

CONIES (KJV) See BADGERS, CONEYS

CONJUGAL (1)
1Co 7: 3 The husband should give to his wife her **c** rights,

CONNECTED (3) [CONNECTION]
Nu 18: 1 with you shall bear responsibility for offenses **c**
18: 1 for offenses **c** with the priesthood.
2Mc 3: 3 the expenses **c** with the service of the sacrifices.

CONNECTING (1) [CONNECTION]
Ex 36:17 and fifty loops on the edge of the other **c** curtain.

CONNECTION (5) [CONNECTED, CONNECTING]
Dt 19:15 of any crime or wrongdoing in **c** with any offense
Da 6: 4 to find grounds for complaint against Daniel in **c**
6: 5 unless we find it in **c** with the law of his God."
Heb 7:14 and in **c** with that tribe Moses said nothing
1Mc 13:15 in **c** with the offices he held,

CONNIVANCE (1)
2Mc 4:39 in the city by Lysimachus with the **c** of Menelaus,

CONONIAH (KJV) See CONANIAH

CONQUER (16) [CONQUERED, CONQUERING, CONQUEROR, CONQUERORS, CONQUERS]
2Ki 3:19 You shall **c** every fortified city
16: 5 they besieged Ahaz but could not **c** him.
Isa 7: 6 up against Judah and cut off Jerusalem and **c** it
Rev 3: 5 If you **c**, you will be clothed like them
3:12 If you **c**, I will make you a pillar in the temple
6: 2 and he came out conquering and to **c**.
11: 7 on them and **c** them and kill them,
13: 7 to make war on the saints and to **c** them.
17:14 and the Lamb will **c** them,
21: 7 Those who **c** will inherit these things,
Tob 13:12 cursed are all who **c** you and pull
1Es 4: 4 they go, and **c** mountains, walls, and towers.
2Es 5: 9 and all friends shall **c** one another;
13:28 the onrushing multitude that came to **c** him, this is
13:34 as you saw, wishing to come and **c** him.
4Mc 3:17 For the temperate mind can **c** the drives of

CONQUERED (29) [CONQUER]
Jdg 11:23 has **c** the Amorites for the benefit
11:24 that the LORD our God has **c** for our benefit?
1Ki 15:20 He **c** Ijon, Dan, Abel-beth-maacah,
2Ch 16: 4 They **c** Ijon, Dan, Abel-maim,
Jn 16:33 But take courage; I have **c** the world!"
Heb 11:33 who through faith **c** kingdoms,
1Jn 2:13 young people, because you have **c** the evil one.
4: 4 you are from God, and have **c** them;
Rev 3:21 just as I myself **c** and sat down with my Father
5: 5 of the tribe of Judah, the Root of David, has **c**, so
12:11 But they have **c** him by the blood of the Lamb and
15: 2 and those who had **c** the beast and its image and
Wis 16:10 But your children were not **c** even by the fangs
18:22 He **c** the wrath not by strength of body,
Sir 47: 6 they glorified him for the tens of thousands he **c**,
1Mc 1: 2 He fought many battles, **c** strongholds,
5:44 in them. Thus Carnaim was **c**;
8: 5 They had crushed in battle and **c** Philip,
8:10 they plundered them, **c** the land,
15:30 of the places that you have **c** outside the borders
2Es 11:40 have **c** all the beasts that have gone before;
4Mc 1:11 By their endurance they **c** the tyrant,
6:33 But now that reason has **c** the emotions,
7: 4 he **c** the besiegers with the shield
7:11 the multitude of the people and **c** the fiery angel,
13: 2 that they had been **c** by these emotions.
13: 7 **c** the tempest of the emotions.
16:14 By steadfastness you have **c** even a tyrant,
17:24 and he ravaged and **c** all his enemies.

CONQUERING (3) [CONQUER]
Isa 18: 2 near and far, a nation mighty and **c**, whose land
18: 7 near and far, a nation mighty and **c**, whose land
Rev 6: 2 and he came out **c** and to conquer.

CONQUEROR (1) [CONQUER]
Mic 1:15 I will again bring a **c** upon you,

CONQUERORS (2) [CONQUER]
Jer 8:10 and their fields to **c**, because from the least to
Ro 8:37 in all these things we are more than **c**

CONQUERS (9) [CONQUER]
1Jn 5: 4 for whatever is born of God **c** the world.
5: 4 And this is the victory that **c** the world, our faith.
5: 5 that **c** the world but the one who believes
Rev 2: 7 To everyone who **c**, I will give permission to eat
2:11 Whoever **c** will not be harmed by the second death.
2:17 To everyone who **c** I will give some of
2:26 To everyone who **c** and continues to do my works
2:28 To the one who **c** I will also give the morning star.
3:21 To the one who **c** I will give a place with me

CONSCIENCE (28) [CONSCIENCES]
1Sa 25:31 of grief, or pangs of **c**, for having shed blood
Ac 23: 1 up to this day I have lived my life with a clear **c**
24:16 Therefore I do my best always to have a clear **c**
Ro 2:15 to which their own **c** also bears witness;
9: 1 my **c** confirms it by the Holy Spirit—
13: 5 not only because of wrath but also because of **c**.
1Co 8: 7 and their **c**, being weak, is defiled.
8:10 might they not, since their **c** is weak,
8:12 and wound their **c** when it is weak,
10:25 without raising any question on the ground of **c**,
10:27 without raising any question on the ground of **c**.
10:28 one who informed you, and for the sake of **c**—
10:29 I mean the other's **c**, not your own.
10:29 be subject to the judgment of someone else's **c**?
2Co 1:12 Indeed, this is our boast, the testimony of our **c**:
4: 2 of the truth we commend ourselves to the **c**
1Ti 1: 5 a good **c**, and sincere faith.
1:19 having faith and a good **c**. By rejecting **c**, certain
3: 9 to the mystery of the faith with a clear **c**.
2Ti 1: 3 whom I worship with a clear **c**,
Heb 9: 9 and sacrifices are offered that cannot perfect the **c**
9:14 purify our **c** from dead works to worship
10:22 an evil **c** and our bodies washed with pure water.
13:18 Pray for us; we are sure that we have a clear **c**,
1Pe 3:16 Keep your **c** clear, so that,
3:21 but as an appeal to God for a good **c**,
Wis 17:11 distressed by **c**, it has always exaggerated

CONSCIENCES (4) [CONSCIENCE]
2Co 5:11 and I hope that we are also well known to your **c**.
1Ti 4: 2 through the hypocrisy of liars whose **c** are seared
Tit 1:15 Their very minds and **c** are corrupted.
Sus 1: 9 They suppressed their **c**

CONSCIENTIOUS (1)
2Ch 29:34 for the Levites were more **c** than the priests

CONSCIOUSNESS (1)
Heb 10: 2 would no longer have any **c** of sin?

CONSCRIPTED (6)
Nu 31: 5 a thousand from each tribe were **c**,
1Ki 5:13 King Solomon **c** forced labor out of all Israel;
9:15 of the forced labor that King Solomon **c** to build
9:21 these Solomon **c** for slave labor,
2Ch 2: 2 Solomon **c** seventy thousand laborers
8: 8 these Solomon **c** for forced labor,

CONSECRATE (28) [CONSECRATED, CONSECRATES, CONSECRATING, CONSECRATION]
Ex 13: 2 **C** to me all the firstborn;
19:10 to the people and **c** them today and tomorrow.
19:22 the LORD must **c** themselves or
28: 3 that they make Aaron's vestments to **c** him
28:38 that the Israelites **c** as their sacred donations;
28:41 and shall anoint them and ordain them and **c** them,
29: 1 Now this is what you shall do to them to **c** them,
29:27 You shall **c** the breast that was raised as
29:33 to ordain and **c** them, but no one else shall eat
29:36 and shall anoint it, to **c** it.
29:37 and **c** it, and the altar shall be most holy;
29:44 I will **c** the tent of meeting and the altar;
29:44 Aaron also and his sons I will **c**,
30:29 you shall **c** them, so that they may be most holy;
30:30 You shall anoint Aaron and his sons, and **c** them,
40: 9 and **c** it and all its furniture,
40:10 and **c** the altar, so that the altar shall be most holy.
40:11 also anoint the basin with its stand, and **c** it.
40:13 and you shall anoint him and **c** him,
Lev 8:11 and the basin and its base, to **c** them.
8:12 on Aaron's head and anointed him, to **c** him.
20: 7 **C** yourselves therefore, and be holy;
Nu 11:18 **C** yourselves for tomorrow,
Dt 15:19 and flock you shall **c** to the LORD your God;
Jdg 17: 3 and his mother said, "I **c** the silver to the LORD
1Ch 23:13 Aaron was set apart to **c** the most holy things,

Eze 43:26 for the altar and cleanse it, and so **c** it.
4Mc 13:13 "Let us with all our hearts **c** ourselves to God,

CONSECRATED‡ (58) [CONSECRATE]

Ex 19:14 He **c** the people, and they washed their clothes.
20:11 the LORD blessed the sabbath day and **c** it.
22:31 You shall be people **c** to me;
Lev 8:10 the tabernacle and all that was in it, and **c** them.
8:15 Thus he **c** it, to make atonement for it.
8:30 Thus he **c** Aaron and his vestments,
16:32 The priest who is anointed and **c** as priest
21:10 and who has been **c** to wear the vestments,
27:18 but if the field is **c** after the jubilee,
27:26 as a firstling belongs to the LORD, cannot be **c**
Nu 3:13 I **c** for my own all the firstborn in Israel,
6:9 defiling the **c** head, then they shall shave the head
6:12 because the **c** head was defiled.
6:18 the nazirites shall shave the **c** head at the entrance
6:18 the **c** head and put it on the fire under the sacrifice
6:19 after they have shaved the **c** head.
7:1 and had anointed and **c** it with all its furnishings,
7:1 had anointed and **c** the altar with all its utensils,
8:17 the firstborn in the land of Egypt I **c** them
18:29 the best of all of them is the part to be **c**.
1Sa 7:1 They **c** his son, Eleazar, to have charge of the ark
1Ki 8:64 the king **c** the middle of the court that was in front
9:3 I have **c** this house that you have built,
9:7 the house that I have **c** for my name I will cast out
13:33 any who wanted to be priests he **c** for
2Ch 7:7 Solomon **c** the middle of the court that was
7:16 For now I have chosen and **c** this house so
7:20 and this house, which I have **c** for my name,
13:9 to be **c** with a young bull or seven rams becomes
26:18 who are **c** to make offering.
29:31 "You have now **c** yourselves to the LORD;
29:33 The **c** offerings were six hundred bulls
31:6 the tithe of the dedicated things that had been **c** to
36:14 of the LORD that he had **c** in Jerusalem.
Ne 3:1 They **c** it and set up its doors;
3:1 they **c** it as far as the Tower of the Hundred and
Isa 13:3 I myself have commanded my **c** ones,
Jer 1:5 and before you were born I **c** you;
Eze 48:11 This shall be for the **c** priests,
Hos 9:10 and **c** themselves to a thing of shame,
Zep 1:7 a sacrifice, he has **c** his guests.
Hag 2:12 If one carries **c** meat in the fold of one's garment,
Tob 1:4 dwelling of God, had been **c** and established
Jdt 4:3 and the temple had been **c** after their profanation.
6:19 on the faces of those who are **c** to you."
11:13 which they had **c** and set aside for
Sir 45:4 For his faithfulness and meekness he **c** him,
49:7 who even in the womb had been **c** a prophet,
1Mc 4:48 the sanctuary and the interior of the temple, and **c**
2Mc 1:25 you chose the ancestors and **c** them.
2:8 that the place should be specially **c**."
15:18 and first fear was for the **c** sanctuary.
1Es 5:52 and at new moons and at all the **c** feasts.
3Mc 6:3 of your **c** portion who are perishing as foreigners
2Es 2:18 According to their counsel I have **c** and prepared
5:25 that have been built you have **c** Zion for yourself,
4Mc 17:19 "All who are **c** are under your hands."
17:20 These, then, who have been **c** for the sake of God,

CONSECRATES (6) [CONSECRATE]

Lev 27:14 If a person **c** a house to the LORD,
27:15 if the one who **c** the house wishes to redeem it,
27:16 person **c** to the LORD any inherited landholding,
27:17 If the person **c** the field as of the year of jubilee,
27:19 And if the one who **c** the field wishes to redeem it,
27:22 If someone **c** to the LORD a field

CONSECRATING (1) [CONSECRATE]

1Ch 29:5 **c** themselves today to the LORD?"

CONSECRATION (5) [CONSECRATE]

Lev 21:12 the **c** of the anointing oil of his God is upon him:
Nu 6:7 because their **c** to God is upon the head.
6:13 when the time of their **c** has been completed:
6:21 so they shall do, following the law for their **c**.
2Mc 2:17 and the kingship and the priesthood and the **c**,

CONSENT (17) [CONSENTED, CONSENTS]

Ge 34:15 Only on this condition will we **c** to you:
39:10 he would not **c** to lie beside her or to be with her.
41:44 without your **c** no one shall lift up hand or foot
Jdg 11:17 also sent to the king of Moab, but he would not **c**.
1Ki 20:8 and all the people said to him, "Do not listen or **c**."
Pr 1:10 My child, if sinners entice you, do not **c**.
Ac 5:1 with the **c** of his wife Sapphira,
15:22 with the **c** of the whole church,
23:21 They are ready now and are waiting for your **c**."
Phm 1:14 but I preferred to do nothing without your **c**,
AdE 4:4 of sackcloth; but he would not **c**.
Sus 1:20 so give your **c**, and lie with us.
2Mc 11:24 not **c** to our father's change to Greek customs,
11:35 of the king has granted you, we also give **c**.
1Es 6:22 in Jerusalem was done with the **c** of King Cyrus,
7:4 So with the **c** of Cyrus and Darius and Artaxerxes,
2Es 16:69 And those who **c** to eat shall be held in derision

CONSENTED (3) [CONSENT]

Mt 3:15 to fulfill all righteousness." Then he **c**.
Lk 22:6 So he **c** and began to look for an opportunity
1Mc 11:29 The king **c**, and wrote a letter to Jonathan

CONSENTS (2) [CONSENT]

1Co 7:12 who is an unbeliever, and she **c** to live with him,
7:13 who is an unbeliever, and he **c** to live with her,

CONSEQUENCE (1) [CONSEQUENCES, CONSEQUENTLY]

2Es 8:33 shall receive their reward in **c** of their own deeds.

CONSEQUENCES (4) [CONSEQUENCE]

Nu 9:13 such a one shall bear the **c** for the sin.
Eze 23:35 bear the **c** of your lewdness and whorings.
44:13 **c** of the abominations that they have committed.
4Mc 1:21 emotions of both pleasure and pain have many **c**.

CONSEQUENTLY (2) [CONSEQUENCE]

Heb 7:25 **C** he is able for all time to save those who approach God through him,
10:5 **C**, when Christ came into the world, he said,

CONSIDER (98) [CONSIDERABLE, CONSIDERATION, CONSIDERED, CONSIDERING, CONSIDERS]

Ex 33:13 **C** too that this nation is your people."
Dt 15:18 Do not **c** it a hardship when you send them out
32:7 Remember the days of old, **c** the years long past;
Jdg 18:14 Now therefore **c** what you will do."
19:30 **C** it, take counsel, and speak out.' "
1Sa 12:24 for **c** what great things he has done for you.
25:17 therefore know this and **c** what you should do;
2Sa 24:13 Now **c**, and decide what answer I shall return to
1Ki 8:18 'You did well to **c** building a house for my name;
20:22 and **c** well what you have to do;
2Ki 10:30 you have done well in carrying out what I **c** right,
2Ch 6:8 'You did well to **c** building a house for my name;
19:6 "**C** what you are doing, for you judge not
Job 8:8 and **c** what their ancestors have found;
11:11 when he sees iniquity, will he not **c** it?
18:2 **C**, and then we shall speak.
23:15 when I **c**, I am in dread of him.
37:14 stop and **c** the wondrous works of God.
Ps 13:3 **C** and answer me, O LORD my God!
25:18 **C** my affliction and my trouble,
25:19 **C** how many are my foes,
41:1 Happy are those who **c** the poor;
45:10 Hear, O daughter, **c** and incline your ear;
48:13 **c** well its ramparts; go through its citadels,
77:5 I **c** the days of old,
106:7 did not **c** your wonderful works;
107:43 and **c** the steadfast love of the LORD.
119:95 in wait to destroy me, but I **c** your decrees.
119:159 **C** how I love your precepts;
Pr 6:6 Go to the ant, you lazybones; **c** its ways,
14:15 but the clever **c** their steps.
Ecc 2:12 So I turned to **c** wisdom and madness and folly;
7:13 **C** the work of God; who can make straight what
7:14 and in the day of adversity **c**;
Isa 41:20 all may **c** and understand,
41:22 what they are, so that we may **c** them,
43:18 or **c** the things of old.
46:8 Remember this and **c**, recall it to mind,
64:9 Now **c**, we are all your people.
Jer 9:17 **C**, and call for the mourning women to come;
31:21 **c** well the highway, the road by which you went.
La 2:20 Look, O LORD, and **c**!
Eze 21:13 For **c**: What! If you despise the rod,
31:3 **C** Assyria, a cedar of Lebanon,
32:2 You **c** yourself a lion among the nations,
Da 9:23 So **c** the word and understand the vision:
11:36 and **c** himself greater than any god,
11:37 for he shall **c** himself greater than all.
Hos 7:2 not **c** that I remember all their wickedness.
Hag 1:5 says the LORD of hosts: **C** how you have fared.
1:7 says the LORD of hosts: **C** how you have fared.
2:15 now, **c** what will come to pass from this day on.
2:18 **C** from this day on, from the twenty-fourth day of
2:18 foundation of the LORD's temple was laid, **c**:
Mt 6:28 **C** the lilies of the field, how they grow;
Lk 11:35 **c** whether the light in you is not darkness.
12:24 **C** the ravens: they neither sow
12:27 **C** the lilies, how they grow:
14:31 will not sit down first and **c** whether he is able
Ac 5:35 **c** carefully what you propose to do to these men.
15:6 and the elders met together to **c** this matter.
26:2 "I **c** myself fortunate that it is before you,
Ro 6:11 also must **c** yourselves dead to sin and alive
8:18 I **c** that the sufferings of this present time are
1Co 1:26 **C** your own call, brothers and sisters:
10:18 **C** the people of Israel; are not those who eat
Php 3:13 Beloved, I do not **c** that I have made it my own;
Phm 1:17 So if you **c** me your partner,
Heb 3:1 holy partners in a heavenly calling, **c** that Jesus,
10:24 And let us **c** how to provoke one another to love
12:3 **C** him who endured such hostility against himself
13:7 **c** the outcome of their way of life,
Jas 1:2 of any kind, **c** it nothing but joy,
1Pe 4:16 do not **c** it a disgrace,
5:12 Through Silvanus, whom I **c** a faithful brother,
Sir 2:10 **C** the generations of old and see:
7:9 "He will **c** the great number of my gifts,
33:18 **C** that I have not labored for myself alone,
Bar 2:16 look down from your holy dwelling, and **c** us
2Mc 2:29 and decoration has to **c** only what is suitable
2Es 4:31 **C** now for yourself how much fruit of ungodliness
4:50 He said to me, "**C** it for yourself;
5:54 Therefore you also should **c** that you
7:*59* "**C** within yourself what you have thought,
7:*84* they shall **c** the torment laid up for themselves in
7:*126* [56] not **c** what we should suffer after death."
11:36 "Look in front of you and **c** what you see."
13:16 For as I **c** it in my mind,
4Mc 2:14 Do not **c** it paradoxical when reason,
5:13 For **c** this: if there is some power watching over
5:17 Therefore we **c** that we should not transgress it
8:11 Will you not **c** this, that if you disobey,
8:16 Let us **c**, on the other hand,
8:19 not fear the instruments of torture and **c** the threats
8:21 let us seriously **c** that if we disobey we are dead!
9:4 For we **c** this pity of yours,
14:11 Do not **c** it amazing that reason had full command
16:5 **C** this also: If this woman,

CONSIDERABLE (8) [CONSIDER]

Jn 7:12 And there was **c** complaining about him among
Ac 18:18 After staying there for a **c** time,
19:26 and drawn away a **c** number of people by saying
Sir Pr:1 and had acquired **c** proficiency in them,
1Mc 12:10 **c** time has passed since you sent your letter to us.
13:11 and with him a **c** army;
2Mc 10:27 up their arms and advanced a **c** distance from
3Mc 1:23 and created a **c** disturbance in the holy place;

CONSIDERATION (4) [CONSIDER]

1Co 10:28 out of **c** for the one who informed you,
1Pe 3:7 show **c** for your wives in your life together,
AdE 16:9 before our eyes with more equitable **c**.
2Mc 12:24 to whom no **c** would be shown.

CONSIDERED (39) [CONSIDER]

Ru 1:6 the LORD had **c** his people and given them food.
2Sa 4:2 for Beeroth is **c** to belong to Benjamin.
1Ki 10:21 it was not **c** as anything in the days of Solomon.
2Ch 9:20 not **c** as anything in the days of Solomon.
Ne 13:13 of Mattaniah, for they were **c** faithful;
Job 1:8 "Have you **c** my servant Job?
2:3 "Have you **c** my servant Job?
Pr 17:28 Even fools who keep silent are **c** wise;
24:32 I saw and **c** it; I looked and received instruction.
Ecc 2:11 Then I **c** all that my hands had done and
5:9 But all things **c**, this is an advantage for a land:
Isa 65:20 one who dies at a hundred years will be **c** a youth,
65:20 who falls short of a hundred will be **c** accursed.
Eze 18:28 Because they **c** and turned away from all
Lk 20:35 but those who are **c** worthy of a place in that age
Ac 5:41 that they were **c** worthy to suffer dishonor for
Ro 4:19 not weaken in faith when he **c** his own body,
4:19 or when he **c** the barrenness of Sarah's womb.
1Ti 5:17 Let the elders who rule well be **c** worthy
Heb 11:11 because he **c** him faithful who had promised.
11:19 He **c** the fact that God is able even
11:26 He **c** abuse suffered for the Christ to
Wis 2:16 We are **c** by him as something base,
8:17 When I **c** these things inwardly,
15:12 But they **c** our existence an idle game,
Sir 40:29 one's way of life cannot be **c** a life.
50:4 He **c** how to save his people from ruin,
1Mc 10:38 be annexed to Judea so that they may be **c** to be
2Mc 9:15 whom he had not **c** worth burying but had planned
11:36 as soon as you have **c** them,
14:20 When the terms had been fully **c**,
3Mc 3:15 and we **c** that we should not rule
5:50 when they **c** the help that they had received before
2Es 7:16 Why have you not **c** in your mind what is
8:49 and have not **c** yourself to be among the righteous.
9:20 So I **c** my world, and saw that it was lost.
9:45 and looked upon my low estate, and **c** my distress,
4Mc 3:15 **c** it an altogether fearful danger to his soul
8:27 of these things nor even seriously **c** them.

CONSIDERING (9) [CONSIDER]

Da 7:8 I was **c** the horns, when another horn appeared,
2Co 12:7 **c** the exceptional character of the revelations.
Wis 1:16 **c** him a friend, they pined away and made
2Mc 2:24 For **c** the flood of statistics involved and
3Mc 2:33 **c** them to be enemies of the Jewish nation,
3:11 and not **c** the might of the supreme God,
5:16 The king, after **c** this, returned to his drinking,
4Mc 4:7 indignantly protested his words, **c** it outrageous
15:5 **C** that mothers are the weaker sex and give birth

CONSIDERS (4) [CONSIDER]

Ps 90:11 Who **c** the power of your anger?
Pr 31:16 She **c** a field and buys it;
Isa 44:19 No one **c**, nor is there knowledge or discernment
Eze 18:14 **c**, and does not do likewise,

CONSIGNED (2)

Isa 38:10 I am **c** to the gates of Sheol for the rest
AdE 16:15 who were **c** to annihilation

CONSIST (4)

Isa 5:12 whose feasts **c** of lyre and harp,
Lk 12:15 for one's life does not **c** in the abundance
1Co 12:14 the body does not **c** of one member but of many.

Jdt 5: 3 and in what does their power and strength c?

CONSISTENT (3) [CONSISTENTLY]

Ac 26:20 and turn to God and do deeds c with repentance.
Tit 2: 1 as for you, teach what is c with sound doctrine.
Sir 5:10 and let your speech be c.

CONSISTENTLY (1) [CONSISTENT]

Gal 2:14 But when I saw that they were not acting c with

CONSOLATION (19) [CONSOLE]

Job 6:10 This would be my c; I would even exult
21: 2 and let this be your c.
Jer 16: 7 nor shall anyone give them the cup of c to drink
Eze 16:54 of all that you have done, becoming a c to them.
Zec 10: 2 the dreamers tell false dreams, and give empty c.
Lk 2:25 looking forward to the c of Israel,
6:24 for you have received your c.
1Co 14: 3 for their upbuilding and encouragement and c.
2Co 1: 3 the Father of mercies and the God of all c,
1: 4 with the c with which we ourselves are consoled
1: 5 so also our c is abundant through Christ.
1: 6 it is for your c and salvation;
1: 6 if we are being consoled, it is for your c,
1: 7 so also you share in our c.
7: 4 in you; I am filled with c;
7: 7 by the c with which he was consoled about you,
7:13 In addition to our own c,
Php 2: 1 any c from love, any sharing in the Spirit,
Wis 3:18 they will have no hope and no c on the day

CONSOLATIONS (3) [CONSOLE]

Job 15:11 Are the c of God too small for you,
Ps 94:19 cares of my heart are many, your c cheer my soul.
Jer 31: 9 and with c I will lead them back,

CONSOLE (13) [CONSOLATION, CONSOLATIONS, CONSOLED, CONSOLERS, CONSOLES, CONSOLING]

2Sa 10: 2 David sent envoys to c him concerning his father.
1Ch 19: 2 So David sent messengers to c him
19: 2 to Hanun in the land of the Ammonites, to c him,
Job 2:11 They met together to go and c and comfort him.
Eze 14:23 They shall c you, when you see their ways
Jn 11:19 to Martha and Mary to c them about their brother.
2Co 1: 4 be able to c those who are in any affliction with
2: 7 so now instead you should forgive and c him,
3Mc 3: 8 to c them, being grieved at the situation,
2Es 10: 2 and all my neighbors attempted to c me;
10:41 and whom you began to c
10:49 and you began to c her for what had happened.
16:23 and there shall be no one to c them;

CONSOLED (11) [CONSOLE]

2Sa 12:24 Then David c his wife Bathsheba, and went to her,
13:39 for he was now c over the death of Amnon.
Eze 14:22 you will be c for the evil that I have brought
31:16 were c in the world below.
32:31 he will be c for all his hordes—
Mt 2:18 she refused to be c, because they are no more."
2Co 1: 4 the consolation with which we ourselves are c
1: 6 if we are being c, it is for your consolation,
7: 6 c us by the arrival of Titus,
7: 7 by the consolation with which he was c about you,
2Es 10:20 and be c because of the sorrow of Jerusalem.

CONSOLERS (1) [CONSOLE]

1Ch 19: 3 "Do you think, because David has sent c to you,

CONSOLES (2) [CONSOLE]

2Co 1: 4 who c us in all our affliction,
7: 6 But God, who c the downcast,

CONSOLING (4) [CONSOLE]

Ge 27:42 and said to him, "Your brother Esau is c himself
Isa 66:11 you may nurse and be satisfied from her c breast;
Jn 11:31 The Jews who were with her in the house, c her,
2Es 10: 3 But when all of them had stopped c me,

CONSORT (1) [CONSORTS]

Ps 26: 4 nor do I c with hypocrites;

CONSORTS (1) [CONSORT]

Sir 19: 2 and the man who c with prostitutes is reckless.

CONSPICUOUS (5) [CONSPICUOUSLY]

1Ti 5:24 The sins of some people are c and precede them
5:25 So also good works are c;
1Mc 11:37 and put up in a c place on the holy mountain.' "
14:48 up in a c place in the precincts of the sanctuary,
2Mc 15:35 and c sign to everyone of the help of the Lord.

CONSPICUOUSLY (2) [CONSPICUOUS]

AdE 8:13 of the decree be posted c in all the kingdom,
4Mc 8: 2 when the tyrant was c defeated in his first attempt,

CONSPIRACY‡ (13) [CONSPIRE]

2Sa 15:12 The c grew in strength, and the people
1Ki 16:20 rest of the acts of Zimri, and the c that he made,
2Ki 12:20 His servants arose, devised a c,
14:19 They made a c against him in Jerusalem,
15:15 including the c that he made,
15:30 a c against Pekah son of Remaliah, attacked him,
2Ch 25:27 from the LORD they made a c against him
Isa 8:12 Do not call c all that this people calls c,
Jer 11: 9 C exists among the people of Judah and
Ac 23:12 a c and bound themselves by an oath neither to eat
23:13 There were more than forty who joined in this c.
2Mc 5: 7 in the end he got only disgrace from his c,

CONSPIRATOR (1) [CONSPIRE]

2Mc 14:26 since he had appointed that c against the kingdom,

CONSPIRATORS (3) [CONSPIRE]

2Sa 15:31 David was told that Ahithophel was among the c
Da 6:11 The c came and found Daniel praying
6:15 Then the c came to the king and said to him,

CONSPIRE (2) [CONSPIRACY, CONSPIRATOR, CONSPIRATORS, CONSPIRED]

Ps 2: 1 Why do the nations c, and the peoples plot
83: 5 They c with one accord; against you

CONSPIRED (27) [CONSPIRE]

Ge 37:18 before he came near to them, they c to kill him.
1Sa 22: 8 Is that why all of you have c against me?
22:13 Saul said to him, "Why have you c against me,
1Ki 15:27 of the house of Issachar, c against him;
16: 9 commander of half his chariots, c against him.
16:16 "Zimri has c, and he has killed the king";
2Ki 9:14 of Jehoshaphat son of Nimshi c against Joram.
10: 9 It was I who c against my master and killed him;
15:10 Shallum son of Jabesh c against him,
15:25 c against him with fifty of the Gileadites,
21:23 The servants of Amon c against him,
21:24 the people of the land killed all those who had c
2Ch 24:21 But they c against him, and by command of
24:25 his servants c against him because of the blood of
24:26 Those who c against him were Zabad son
33:24 His servants c against him and killed him
33:25 the people of the land killed all those who had c
Est 2:21 and c to assassinate King Ahasuerus.
6: 2 and who had c to assassinate King Ahasuerus.
Da 6: 6 the presidents and satraps c and came to the king
Am 7:10 "Amos has c against you in the very center of
Mt 12:14 But the Pharisees went out and c against him,
26: 4 and they c to arrest Jesus by stealth and kill him.
Mk 3: 6 The Pharisees went out and immediately c with
Sir 45:18 Outsiders c against him, and envied him in
Bel 1:28 they were very indignant and c against the king,
3Mc 3: 2 the Jewish nation by some who c to do them ill,

CONSTANCY (1) [CONSTANT]

Isa 40: 6 their c is like the flower of the field.

CONSTANT (3) [CONSTANCY, CONSTANTLY]

1Pe 4: 8 Above all, maintain c love for one another,
2Mc 14:34 upon the c Defender of our nation, in these words:
3Mc 5:41 and also in c danger of being plundered."

CONSTANTLY‡ (15) [CONSTANT]

Ac 1:14 All these were c devoting themselves to prayer,
8:13 he stayed c with Philip and was amazed
10: 2 to the people and prayed c to God.
Php 1: 4 c praying with joy in every one of my prayers
1Th 1: 2 for all of you and mention you in our prayers, c
2:13 We also c give thanks to God for this,
2:16 Thus they have c been filling up the measure
2Ti 1: 3 I remember you c in my prayers night and day.
AdE 13: 5 stands c in opposition to every nation,
Sir 23:10 for as a servant who is c under scrutiny will
26:24 *A shameless woman c acts disgracefully,*
1Mc 8:15 three hundred twenty senators c deliberate
12:11 We therefore remember you c on every occasion,
3Mc 3:11 that he would persevere c in his same purpose,
3:22 Since they incline c to evil,

CONSTELLATION (1) [CONSTELLATIONS]

Wis 7:29 and excels every c of the stars.

CONSTELLATIONS (3) [CONSTELLATION]

2Ki 23: 5 the moon, the c, and all the host of the heavens.
Isa 13:10 of the heavens and their c will not give their light;
Wis 7:19 the cycles of the year and the c of the stars,

CONSTERNATION (2)

Ps 116:11 I said in my c, "Everyone is a liar."
2Mc 14:17 because of the sudden c created by the enemy.

CONSTITUTED (1)

4Mc 13: 8 For they c a holy chorus of religion

CONSTRAIN (KJV) See COMPEL

CONSTRAINING (1) [CONSTRAINT]

2Mc 11:14 persuade the king, c him to be their friend.

CONSTRAINS (1) [CONSTRAINT]

Job 32:18 For I am full of words; the spirit within me c me.

CONSTRAINT (3) [CONSTRAINING, CONSTRAINS]

Job 36:16 into a broad place where there was no c,
2Mc 6: 7 under bitter c, to partake of the sacrifices;
3Mc 4: 9 driven under the c of iron bonds;

CONSTRUCTED (2) [CONSTRUCTION]

Heb 9: 2 For a tent was c, the first one,
4Mc 4:20 not only was a gymnasium c at the very citadel

CONSTRUCTION (13) [CONSTRUCTED]

Ex 36: 1 in the c of the sanctuary shall work in accordance
38:24 in all the c of the sanctuary,
1Ki 7: 8 the other court back of the hall, was of the same c.
7:28 This was the c of the stands:
Ezr 5:16 and from that time until now it has been under c,
Ne 4:16 half of my servants worked on c,
Eze 1:16 As for the appearance of the wheels and their c:
1:16 the same form, their c being something like
Jn 2:20 "This temple has been under c for forty-six years,
2Mc 2:29 a new house must be concerned with the whole c,
4:20 the decision of its carriers it was applied to the c
1Es 6:20 Although it has been in process of c from
2Es 10:54 of human c could endure in a place where the city

CONSUL (2)

1Mc 15:16 c of the Romans, to King Ptolemy, greetings.
15:22 The c wrote the same thing to King Demetrius and

CONSULT (18) [CONSULTATION, CONSULTATIONS, CONSULTED, CONSULTING, CONSULTS]

Dt 17: 9 where you shall c with the levitical priests and
1Sa 28: 8 And he said, "C a spirit for me,
Ezr 2:63 until there should be a priest to c Urim
Ps 71:10 and those who watch for my life c together.
83: 3 they c together against those you protect.
Isa 8:19 "C the ghosts and the familiar spirits that chirp
8:19 should not a people c their gods,
19: 3 they will c the idols and the spirits of the dead and
31: 1 but do not look to the Holy One of Israel or c
40:14 Whom did he c for his enlightenment,
Eze 20: 1 certain elders of Israel came to c the LORD,
20: 3 Why are you coming? To c me?
Hos 4:12 My people c a piece of wood,
Sir 8:17 Do not c with fools, for they cannot keep a secret.
9:14 aim to know your neighbors, and c with the wise.
37:10 Do not c the one who regards you with suspicion;
37:11 Do not c with a woman about her rival or with
LtJ 6:48 the priests c together as to

CONSULTATION (2) [CONSULT]

Mk 15: 1 the chief priests held a c with the elders
2Mc 14:22 so they duly held the c.

CONSULTATIONS (1) [CONSULT]

Isa 47:13 You are wearied with your many c;

CONSULTED (13) [CONSULT]

2Sa 16:23 the counsel that Ahithophel gave was as if one c
1Ki 12: 8 and c with the young men who had grown up
2Ki 22:14 in the Second Quarter, where they c her.
1Ch 10:13 moreover, he had c a medium, seeking guidance,
13: 1 David c with the commanders of the thousands
2Ch 10: 8 and c the young men who had grown up with him
Est 1:13 Then the king c the sages who knew the laws
Eze 14: 3 shall I let myself be c by them?
20: 3 I live, says the Lord GOD, I will not be c by you.
20:31 And shall I be c by you, O house of Israel?
20:31 I live, says the Lord GOD, I will not be c by you.
1Mc 3:48 into those matters about which the Gentiles c
9:59 And they went and c with him.

CONSULTING (1) [CONSULT]

2Mc 13:13 After c privately with the elders,

CONSULTS (2) [CONSULT]

Dt 18:11 or who c ghosts or spirits,
Eze 21:21 he shakes the arrows, he c the teraphim,

CONSUME‡ (43) [CONSUMED, CONSUMES, CONSUMING, CONSUMPTION]

Ge 41:30 the famine will c the land.
Ex 32:10 against them and I may c them;
32:12 and to c them from the face of the earth'?
33: 3 or I would c you on the way,
33: 5 up among you, I would c you.
Nu 16:21 so that I may c them in a moment.
16:45 so that I may c them in a moment."
25:11 that in my jealousy I did not c the Israelites.
Dt 5:25 For this great fire will c us;
28:38 for the locust shall c it.

Dt 28:51 It shall **c** the fruit of your livestock and the fruit
Jos 24:20 then he will turn and do you harm, and **c** you,
1Ki 14:10 and will **c** the house of Jeroboam,
16: 3 I will **c** Baasha and his house,
21:21 I will **c** you, and will cut off
2Ki 1:10 down from heaven and **c** you and your fifty."
1:12 down from heaven and **c** you and your fifty."
Ps 21: 9 up in his wrath, and fire will **c** them.
59:13 **c** them in wrath; **c** them until they are no more.
Ecc 4: 5 Fools fold their hands and **c** their own flesh.
10:12 but the lips of fools **c** them.
Isa 26:11 Let the fire for your adversaries **c** them.
33:11 your breath is a fire that will **c** you.
43: 2 and the flame shall not **c** you.
Jer 14:12 by famine, and by pestilence I **c** them.
Eze 15: 7 from the fire, the fire shall still **c** them;
21:28 Drawn for slaughter Polished to **c**,
Ob 1:18 they shall burn them and **c** them,
Zec 5: 4 and it shall abide in that house and **c** it,
Mt 6:19 where moth and rust **c** and where thieves break in
Lk 9:54 to come down from heaven and **c** them?"
Jn 2:17 "Zeal for your house will **c** me."
Heb 10:27 and a fury of fire that will **c** the adversaries.
Jdt 11:13 They have decided to **c** the first fruits of the grain
Wis 16:18 not **c** the creatures sent against the ungodly,
19:21 to **c** the flesh of perishable creatures that walked
Sir 27:29 and pain will **c** them before their death.
45:19 he performed wonders against them to **c** them
LtJ 6:63 to **c** mountains and woods does what it is ordered.
Bel 1:13 through which they used to go in regularly and **c**
1:21 through which they used to enter to **c** what was on
4Mc 18:14 the flame shall not **c** you.'

CONSUMED (88) [CONSUME]

Ge 19:15 else you will be **c** in the punishment of the city."
19:17 flee to the hills, or else you will be **c**."
31:40 It was like this with me: by day the heat **c** me,
Ex 3: 2 and the bush was blazing, yet it was not **c**.
15: 7 you sent out your fury, it **c** them like stubble.
22: 6 or the standing grain or the field is **c**,
Lev 9:24 the LORD and **c** the burnt offering and the fat on
10: 2 from the presence of the LORD and **c** them,
16:27 their skin and their flesh and their dung shall be **c**
19: 6 and anything left over until the third day shall be **c**
Nu 11: 1 and **c** some outlying parts of the camp.
11:33 meat was still between their teeth, before it was **c**,
12:12 whose flesh is half **c** when it comes out
16:35 And fire came out from the LORD and **c**
Dt 28:21 until it has **c** you off the land that you are entering
Jdg 6:21 the rock and **c** the meat and the unleavened cakes;
1Sa 15:18 and fight against them until they are **c**.'
2Sa 21: 5 "The man who **c** us and planned to destroy us,
22:38 and did not turn back until they were **c**.
22:39 I **c** them; I struck them down,
23: 7 And they are entirely **c** in fire on the spot.
1Ki 18:38 fire of the LORD fell and **c** the burnt offering,
2Ki 1:10 and **c** him and his fifty.
1:12 the fire of God came down from heaven and **c** him
1:14 down from heaven and **c** the two former captains
2Ch 7: 1 down from heaven and **c** the burnt offering and
Job 1:16 and **c** them; I alone have escaped to tell you."
4: 9 and by the blast of his anger they are **c**.
18:12 Their strength is **c** by hunger,
18:13 By disease their skin is **c**,
20:26 what is left in their tent will be **c**.
22:20 and what they left, the fire has **c**.'
Ps 18:37 and did not turn back until they were **c**.
69: 9 It is zeal for your house that has **c** me;
71:13 Let my accusers be put to shame and **c**;
90: 7 For we are **c** by your anger;
104:35 Let sinners be **c** from the earth,
119:20 My soul is **c** with longing for your ordinances
Pr 5:11 when your flesh and body are **c**,
Isa 1:28 and those who forsake the LORD shall be **c**.
Jer 5: 3 have **c** them, but they refused to take correction.
6:29 bellows blow fiercely, the lead is **c** by the fire;
9:16 the sword after them, until I have **c** them.
10:25 they have devoured him and **c** him,
11:16 and its branches will be **c**.
14:15 By sword and famine those prophets shall be **c**.
36:23 until the entire scroll was **c** in the fire that was in
49:37 the sword after them, until I have **c** them;
La 4:11 and kindled a fire in Zion that **c** its foundations.
Eze 5:12 of you shall die of pestilence or be **c** by famine
15: 4 when the fire has **c** both ends of it and the middle
15: 5 when the fire has **c** it, and it is charred—
19:12 its strong stem was withered; the fire **c** it.
19:14 has **c** its branches and fruit,
22:31 I have **c** them with the fire of my wrath;
24:11 its copper glow, its filth melt in it, its rust be **c**.
28:18 So I brought out fire from within you; it **c** you,
34:29 so that they shall no more be **c** with hunger in
43: 8 therefore I have **c** them in my anger.
Da 7:26 to be **c** and totally destroyed.
Na 1:10 they are **c** like dry straw.
Zep 1:18 the fire of his passion the whole earth shall be **c**;
3: 8 in the fire of my passion all the earth shall be **c**.
Ro 1:27 were **c** with passion for one another.
Gal 5:15 take care that you are not **c** by one another.
Rev 20: 9 And fire came down from heaven and **c** them.
Wis 5:13 but were **c** in our wickedness."
14:15 a father, **c** with grief at an untimely bereavement,
16:16 and hail and relentless storms, and utterly **c**
Sir 36:11 Let survivors be **c** in the fiery wrath,
LtJ 6:72 and they will finally be **c** themselves,
1Mc 6:53 from the Gentiles had **c** the last of the stores.
2Mc 1:23 sacrifice was being **c**, the priests offered prayer—
1:31 After the materials of the sacrifice had been **c**,
2:10 fire came down from heaven and **c** the sacrifices,
2:10 fire came down and **c** the whole burnt offerings.
2:11 "They were **c** because the sin offering had
3Mc 2: 5 You **c** with fire and sulfur the people
2Es 4:16 for the fire came and **c** it;
7:87 in confusion and be **c** with shame,
12:44 if we also had been **c** in the burning of Zion.
15:23 and **c** the foundations of the earth and the sinners,
16:78 It is shut off and given up to be **c** by fire.
4Mc 3:11 and inflamed him, undid and **c** him.
7: 4 his sacred life was **c** by tortures and racks,
7:12 Eleazar, though being **c** by the fire,
14:10 and it **c** their bodies quickly.
15:15 She watched the flesh of her children being **c**

CONSUMES‡ (11) [CONSUME]

Job 15:34 and fire **c** the tents of bribery.
18:13 the firstborn of Death **c** their limbs.
Ps 83:14 As fire **c** the forest, as the flame sets
97: 3 and **c** his adversaries on every side.
119:139 My zeal **c** me because my foes forget your words.
Isa 47:14 See, they are like stubble, the fire **c** them;
Hos 11: 6 sword rages in their cities, it **c** their oracle-priests,
Mt 6:20 nor rust **c** and where thieves do not break in
Rev 11: 5 fire pours from their mouth and **c** their foes;
Sir 43:21 He **c** the mountains and burns up the wilderness,
2Es 16:15 and shall not be put out until it **c** the foundations

CONSUMING (5) [CONSUME]

Job 31:12 for that would be a fire **c** down to Abaddon,
Ps 39:11 **c** like a moth what is dear to them;
Isa 9:18 wickedness burned like a fire, **c** briers and thorns;
La 2: 3 like a flaming fire in Jacob, **c** all around.
Heb 12:29 for indeed our God is a **c** fire.

CONSUMMATION (KJV) See CEASE

CONSUMPTION (3) [CONSUME]

Lev 26:16 **c** and fever that waste the eyes and cause life
Dt 28:22 The LORD will afflict you with **c**, fever,
32:24 burning **c**, bitter pestilence.

CONSUMPTION (KJV) See also DESTRUCTION

CONTACT (2)

Nu 5: 2 everyone who is unclean through **c** with a corpse;
Hag 2:13 by **c** with a dead body touches any of these,

CONTAIN‡ (5) [CONTAINED, CONTAINER, CONTAINERS, CONTAINING, CONTAINS]

1Ki 8:27 Even heaven and the highest heaven cannot **c** you,
18:32 large enough to **c** two measures of seed.
2Ch 2: 6 since heaven, even highest heaven, cannot **c** him?
6:18 Even heaven and the highest heaven cannot **c** you,
Jn 21:25 the world itself could not **c** the books that would

CONTAINED (1) [CONTAIN]

1Mc 12: 8 which **c** a clear declaration of alliance

CONTAINER (1) [CONTAIN]

Dt 23:24 but you shall not put any in a **c**.

CONTAINERS (2) [CONTAIN]

Lk 16: 7 He replied, 'A hundred **c** of wheat.'
Jdt 7:20 until all the water **c** of every inhabitant

CONTAINING (3) [CONTAIN]

Jer 32:11 **c** the terms and conditions, and the open copy;
Eze 45:11 the bath **c** one-tenth of a homer,
1Mc 6: 2 Its temple was very rich, **c** golden shields,

CONTAINS (3) [CONTAIN]

Job 28: 6 the place of sapphires, and its dust **c** gold.
Eze 12:19 because their land shall be stripped of all it **c**,
45:14 like the homer, **c** ten baths);

CONTEMN (KJV) See DESPISE, RENOUNCE

CONTEMPLATE (1)

Isa 52:15 and that which they had not heard they shall **c**.

CONTEMPORARIES (1)

2Es 5:54 that you and your **c** are smaller

CONTEMPT (39) [CONTEMPTIBLE, CONTEMPTUOUS, CONTEMPTUOUSLY]

Ge 16: 4 she looked with **c** on her mistress.
16: 5 she looked on me with **c**.
1Sa 2:17 they treated the offerings of the LORD with **c**.
2:30 and those who despise me shall be treated with **c**.
2Ch 32:17 to throw **c** on the LORD the God of Israel and
Est 1:17 causing them to look with **c** on their husbands,
1:18 and there will be no end of **c** and wrath!
Job 12: 5 Those at ease have **c** for misfortune,
12:21 He pours **c** on princes, and loosens the belt of
31:34 and the **c** of families terrified me,
Ps 31:18 against the righteous with pride and **c**.
107:40 he pours **c** on princes and makes them wander
119:22 take away from me their scorn and **c**,
123: 3 for we have had more than enough of **c**.
123: 4 have had more than enough of the **c** of the proud.
Pr 18: 1 showing **c** for all who have sound judgment.
18: 3 When wickedness comes, **c** comes also;
Isa 9: 1 In the former time he brought into **c** the land
16:14 the glory of Moab will be brought into **c**,
Jer 33:24 in such **c** that they no longer regard them as
Eze 22: 7 Father and mother are treated with **c** in you;
28:24 all their neighbors who have treated them with **c**.
28:26 all their neighbors who have treated them with **c**.
36: 5 who, with wholehearted joy and utter **c**,
Da 12: 2 and some to shame and everlasting **c**.
Mic 7: 6 the son treats the father with **c**, the daughter rises
Na 3: 6 I will throw filth at you and treat you with **c**,
Hab 2:16 You will be sated with **c** instead of glory.
Mk 9:12 through many sufferings and be treated with **c**?
Lk 18: 9 and regarded others with **c**:
23:11 Even Herod with his soldiers treated him with **c**
1Co 11:22 Or do you show **c** for the church of God
Heb 6: 6 the Son of God and are holding him up to **c**.
Wis 4:18 unrighteous will see, and will have **c** for them,
14:30 in deceit they swore unrighteously through **c**
1Mc 1:39 her sabbaths into a reproach, her honor into **c**.
2Mc 7:24 Antiochus felt that he was being treated with **c**,
2Es 9: 9 and those who have rejected them with **c** shall live
16:69 to eat shall be held in derision and **c**,

CONTEMPTIBLE (3) [CONTEMPT]

2Sa 6:22 I will make myself yet more **c** than this,
Da 11:21 a **c** person on whom royal majesty had
2Co 10:10 but his bodily presence is weak, and his speech **c**."

CONTEMPTS See Index to Footnotes

CONTEMPTUOUS (3) [CONTEMPT]

2Es 8:56 and were **c** of his law, and abandoned his ways.
12:32 and will display before them their **c** dealings.
4Mc 8:28 For they were **c** of the emotions and sovereign

CONTEMPTUOUSLY (2) [CONTEMPT]

Sir 26:28 intelligent men who are treated **c**,
4Mc 4: 9 the holy place that was being treated so **c**,

CONTEND‡ (19) [CONTENDED, CONTENDERS, CONTENDING, CONTENDS, CONTENTION, CONTENTIOUS, CONTENTIOUSNESS]

Jdg 6:31 to all who were arrayed against him, "Will you **c**
6:31 If he is a god, let him **c** for himself,
6:32 that is to say, "Let Baal **c** against him,"
Job 9: 3 If one wished to **c** with him,
10: 2 let me know why you **c** against me.
13:19 Who is there that will **c** with me?
23: 6 Would he **c** with me in the greatness
33:13 Why do you **c** against him, saying,
40: 2 "Shall a faultfinder **c** with the Almighty?
Ps 35: 1 **C**, O LORD, with those who **c** with me;
Isa 41:12 You shall seek those who **c** with you,
49:25 for I will **c** with those who **c** with you,
50: 8 Who will **c** with me? Let us stand up together.
Hos 4: 4 Yet let no one **c**, and let none accuse,
Mic 6: 2 a controversy with his people, and he will **c**
Jude 1: 3 to **c** for the faith that was once for all entrusted to
Sir 8: 1 Do not **c** with the powerful,

CONTENDED‡ (6) [CONTEND]

Ge 26:20 he called the well Esek, because they **c** with him.
Dt 33: 8 with whom you **c** at the waters of Meribah;
Ne 13:25 And I **c** with them and cursed them and beat some
Ac 23: 9 of the Pharisees' group stood up and **c**,
Jude 1: 9 But when the archangel Michael **c** with the devil
4Mc 17:13 the competition, and the brothers **c**.

CONTENDERS (1) [CONTEND]

Pr 18:18 to disputes and decides between powerful **c**.

CONTENDING (2) [CONTEND]

Eze 18: 8 executes true justice between **c** parties,
4Mc 6:21 and be despised by the tyrant as unmanly by not **c**

CONTENDS (2) [CONTEND]

Jdg 6:31 Whoever **c** for him shall be put to death
Da 10:21 There is no one with me who **c**

CONTENT (13) [CONTENTED, CONTENTMENT]

Jos 7: 7 that we had been **c** to settle beyond the Jordan!
2Ki 14:10 Be **c** with your glory, and stay at home;
2Co 12:10 Therefore I am **c** with weaknesses, insults,
Php 4:11 for I have learned to be **c** with whatever I have.
1Ti 6: 8 we will be **c** with these.
Heb 13: 5 and be **c** with what you have;
3Jn 1:10 And not **c** with those charges,
Sir 26: 4 Whether rich or poor, his heart is **c**,
29:23 Be **c** with little or much,

Sir 32:12 Amuse yourself there to your heart's **c**,
2Mc 5:15 Not **c** with this, Antiochus dared to enter
9:18 of a supplication. This was its **c**:
3Mc 2:26 He was not **c** with his uncounted licentious deeds,

CONTENTED (1) [CONTENT]

Ru 3: 7 Boaz had eaten and drunk, and he was in a **c** mood,

CONTENTION‡ (4) [CONTEND]

Pr 15:18 but those who are slow to anger calm **c**.
Jer 15:10 a man of strife and **c** to the whole land!
Hos 4: 4 and let none accuse, for with you is my **c**,
Hab 1: 3 before me; strife and **c** arise.

CONTENTIOUS (6) [CONTEND]

Ps 31:20 under your shelter from **c** tongues.
Pr 21: 9 the housetop than in a house shared with a **c** wife.
21:19 live in a desert land than with a **c** and fretful wife.
25:24 the housetop than in a house shared with a **c** wife.
27:15 dripping on a rainy day and a **c** wife are alike;
1Co 11:16 But if anyone is disposed to be **c**—

CONTENTIOUSNESS (1) [CONTEND]

4Mc 8:26 Why does such **c** excite us and such

CONTENTMENT (1) [CONTENT]

1Ti 6: 6 there is great gain in godliness combined with **c**;

CONTENTS (5)

Lev 1:16 He shall remove its crop with its **c** and throw it at
LtJ 6:59 better even the door of a house that protects its **c**,
1Mc 11:29 about all these things; its **c** were as follows:
15: 2 its **c** were as follows: "King Antiochus to Simon
2Es 16:57 he has measured the sea and its **c**;

CONTEST (9) [CONTESTANT, CONTESTANTS]

2Sa 2:14 "Let the young men come forward and have a **c**
Job 9:19 If it is a **c** of strength, he is the strong one!
Wis 4: 2 victor in the **c** for prizes that are undefiled.
10:12 in his arduous **c** she gave him the victory,
2Es 7:*127* [57] the **c** that all who are born on earth shall wage:
4Mc 11:20 being tortured he said, "O **c** befitting holiness,
15:29 who carried away the prize of the **c** in your heart!
16:16 the **c** to which you are called to bear witness for
17:11 the **c** in which they were engaged was divine,

CONTESTANT (1) [CONTEST]

4Mc 17:13 the first **c**, the mother of the seven sons entered

CONTESTANTS (1) [CONTEST]

4Mc 12:14 for having killed without cause the **c** for virtue."

CONTINGENTS (1)

Jdt 6: 1 said to Achior in the presence of all the foreign **c**:

CONTINUAL (6) [CONTINUE]

Ex 28:29 for a **c** remembrance before the LORD.
2Ch 12:15 There were **c** wars between Rehoboam
Job 33:19 and with **c** strife in their bones,
Pr 15:15 but a cheerful heart has a **c** feast.
19:13 and a wife's quarreling is a **c** dripping of rain.
27:15 A **c** dripping on a rainy day and a contentious wife

CONTINUALLY‡ (70) [CONTINUE]

Ge 6: 5 of the thoughts of their hearts was only evil **c**.
Ex 9:24 there was hail with fire flashing **c** in the midst
28:30 of the Israelites on his heart before the LORD **c**.
Nu 17: 5 to the complaints of the Israelites that they **c** make
Dt 28:29 and you shall be **c** abused and robbed,
28:33 you shall be **c** abused and crushed,
Jos 6: 9 while the trumpets blew **c**.
6:13 of the LORD passed on, blowing the trumpets **c**.
6:13 while the trumpets blew **c**.
1Ki 10: 8 who **c** attend you and hear your wisdom!
14:30 between Rehoboam and Jeroboam **c**.
1Ch 16:11 the LORD and his strength, seek his presence **c**.
2Ch 9: 7 who **c** attend you and hear your wisdom!
Ps 34: 1 his praise shall **c** be in my mouth.
40:16 may those who love your salvation say **c**,
42: 3 while people say to me **c**, "Where is your God?"
42:10 while they say to me **c**, "Where is your God?"
44: 8 In God we have boasted **c**,
50: 8 your burnt offerings are **c** before me.
69:23 and make their loins tremble **c**.
71: 6 My praise is **c** of you.
71:14 But I will hope **c**, and will praise you yet more
72:15 May prayer be made for him **c**,
73:23 I am **c** with you; you hold my right hand.
74:23 the uproar of your adversaries that goes up **c**.
105: 4 and his strength; seek his presence **c**.
109:15 Let them be before the LORD **c**,
119:44 I will keep your law **c**, forever and ever.
119:109 I hold my life in my hand **c**,
119:117 I may be safe and have regard for your statutes **c**.
140: 2 in their minds and stir up wars **c**.
141: 5 for my prayer is **c** against their wicked deeds.
Pr 6:14 perverted mind devising evil, **c** sowing discord;
Isa 9: 7 His authority shall grow **c**,
21: 8 "Upon a watchtower I stand, O Lord, **c** by day,
28:24 Do those who plow for sowing plow **c**?
Isa 28:24 Do they **c** open and harrow their ground?
49:16 your walls are **c** before me.
51:13 You fear **c** all day long because of the fury of the
52: 5 Their rulers howl, says the LORD, and **c**,
57:16 For I will not **c** accuse, nor will I always be angry;
58:11 The LORD will guide you **c**,
65: 3 a people who provoke me to my face **c**,
La 3:20 My soul **c** thinks of it and is bowed down
Eze 1: 4 with brightness around it and fire flashing forth **c**,
Hos 12: 6 and wait **c** for your God.
Mt 18:10 for, I tell you, in heaven their angels **c** see the face
Lk 18: 5 so that she may not wear me out by **c** coming.' "
24:53 and they were **c** in the temple blessing God.
Heb 9: 6 the priests go **c** into the first tent
10: 1 by the same sacrifices that are **c** offered year
13:15 let us **c** offer a sacrifice of praise to God, that is,
Tob 14: 2 giving alms and **c** blessing God
AdE 13: 4 contrary to those of every nation and **c** disregard
16:11 that he was called our father and was **c** bowed
Wis 10: 7 a **c** smoking wasteland, plants bearing fruit
Sir 20:19 **c** on the lips of the ignorant.
20:24 it is **c** on the lips of the ignorant.
37:18 and it is the tongue that **c** rules them.
45:14 be wholly burned twice every day **c**.
51:11 I will praise your name **c**,
1Mc 6: 9 because deep disappointment **c** gripped him,
15:25 **c** throwing his forces against it
Man 1:15 and I will praise you **c** all the days of my life.
3Mc 4:16 The king was greatly and **c** filled with joy,
2Es 9:25 and pray to the Most High **c**.
10: 4 but will mourn and fast **c** until I die."
10:39 and that you have sorrowed **c** for your people
15: 8 and the souls of the righteous cry out **c**.
15:53 if you had not killed my chosen people **c**,

CONTINUE‡ (69) [CONTINUAL, CONTINUALLY, CONTINUED, CONTINUES, CONTINUING, CONTINUOUS, CONTINUOUSLY]

Ge 15: 2 what will you give me, for I **c** childless,
Lev 15:25 of the discharge she shall **c** in uncleanness;
26:18 I will **c** to punish you sevenfold for your sins.
26:21 If you **c** hostile to me, and will not obey me,
26:21 I will **c** to plague you sevenfold for your sins.
26:23 not turned back to me, but **c** hostile to me,
26:24 then I too will **c** hostile to you:
26:27 despite this, you disobey me, and **c** hostile to me,
26:28 I will **c** hostile to you in fury;
Nu 14:41 "Why do you **c** to transgress the command of
34:11 and the boundary shall **c** down from Shepham
36: 8 so that all Israelites may **c** to possess
Dt 16: 8 For six days you shall **c** to eat unleavened bread,
20: 8 The officials shall **c** to address the troops, saying,
Jos 9:27 to **c** to this day, in the place that he should choose.
23:13 not **c** to drive out these nations before you;
Jdg 19:12 but we will **c** on to Gibeah."
Ru 2:13 she said, "May I **c** to find favor in your sight,
1Sa 13:14 but now your kingdom will not **c**;
2Sa 7:29 so that it may **c** forever before you;
2Ki 9:22 and sorceries of your mother Jezebel **c**?"
17:34 To this day they **c** to practice
17:41 and their children's children **c** to do
1Ch 17:27 that it may **c** forever before you.
Ne 2:14 for the animal I was riding to **c**.
Est 9:27 that without fail they would **c**
Ps 36:10 O **c** your steadfast love to those who know you,
67: 7 May God **c** to bless us;
72:17 his fame **c** as long as the sun.
89:36 His line shall **c** forever, and his throne endure
101: 7 no one who utters lies shall **c** in my presence.
Pr 23:17 but always **c** in the fear of the LORD.
Ecc 1: 7 to the place where the streams flow, there they **c**
Isa 1: 5 Why do you **c** to rebel?
Jer 42:13 But if you **c** to say, 'We will not stay in this land,'
Da 12:10 but the wicked shall **c** to act wickedly.
Zec 14: 8 it shall **c** in summer as in winter.
Jn 8:31 "If you **c** in my word, you are truly my disciples;
Ac 13:43 to them and urged them to **c** in the grace of God.
14:22 of the disciples and encouraged them to **c** in
Ro 6: 1 Should we **c** in sin in order
9:11 or bad (so that God's purpose of election might **c**,
11:22 provided you **c** in his kindness;
2Co 1:10 He who rescued us from so deadly a peril will **c**
11: 9 and will **c** to refrain from burdening you
11:12 And what I do I will also **c** to do,
Php 1:18 Yes, and I will **c** to rejoice,
1:25 and **c** with all of you for your progress and joy
Col 1:23 that you **c** securely established and steadfast in
2: 6 **c** to live your lives in him,
1Th 3: 8 we now live, if you **c** to stand firm in the Lord.
1Ti 2:15 provided they **c** in faith and love and holiness,
4:16 **c** in these things, for in doing this you will save
2Ti 3:14 **c** in what you have learned and firmly believed,
Heb 8: 9 for they did not **c** in my covenant,
13: 1 Let mutual love **c**.
2Pe 3: 4 all things **c** as they were from the beginning
Wis 16: 5 your wrath did not **c** to the end;
18:20 but the wrath did not long **c**.
Sir 44:13 Their offspring will **c** forever,
1Mc 2:20 I and my sons and my brothers will **c** to live by
10:27 Now **c** still to keep faith with us,
11:22 and he wrote Jonathan not to **c** the siege,
11:23 Jonathan heard this, he gave orders to **c** the siege.
2Mc 8:26 and for that reason they did not **c** their pursuit.
2Es 9:13 do not **c** to be curious about how the ungodly will
2Es 9:41 so that I may weep for myself and **c** to mourn,
16:71 but plundering and destroying those who **c** to fear
4Mc 5:10 you **c** to despise me to your own hurt.

CONTINUED‡ (63) [CONTINUE]

Ge 7:17 The flood **c** forty days on the earth;
8: 5 The waters **c** to abate until the tenth month;
40: 4 and they **c** for some time in custody.
Ex 5: 5 Pharaoh **c**, "Now they are more numerous than
33:21 And the LORD **c**, "See, there is a place by me
Lev 26:40 moreover, that they **c** hostile to me—
26:41 **c** hostile to them and brought them into the land
Nu 9:19 when the cloud **c** over the tabernacle many days,
9:21 they would set out, or if it **c** for a day and a night,
9:22 that the cloud **c** over the tabernacle,
21:16 From there they **c** to Beer;
32: 5 They **c**, "If we have found favor in your sight,
Jos 17:12 but the Canaanites **c** to live in that land.
Jdg 1:27 but the Canaanites **c** to live in that land.
1:35 The Amorites **c** to live in Har-heres, in Aijalon,
1Sa 1:12 As she **c** praying before the LORD,
2:26 Now the boy Samuel **c** to grow both in stature and
3:21 The LORD **c** to appear at Shiloh,
2Sa 2:27 the people would have **c** to pursue their kinsmen,
17: 8 Hushai **c**, "You know that your father
1Ki 15: 6 between Rehoboam and Jeroboam **c** all the days
22: 1 For three years Aram and Israel **c** without war.
2Ki 2:11 As they **c** walking and talking,
3:24 as they entered Moab they **c** the attack.
6:25 As the siege **c**, famine in Samaria became so great
12: 3 the people **c** to sacrifice and make offerings on
13:18 He **c**, "Take the arrows"; and he took them.
17:22 of Israel **c** in all the sins that Jeroboam committed;
17:40 but they **c** to practice their former custom.
1Ch 12:29 the majority had **c** to keep their allegiance to
21:20 with him hid themselves, Ornan **c** to thresh wheat.
2Ch 29:28 all this **c** until the burnt offering was finished.
Job 34: 1 Then Elihu **c** and said:
35: 1 Elihu **c** and said:
36: 1 Elihu **c** and said:
Jer 31: 3 therefore I have **c** my faithfulness to you.
Da 1:16 So the guard **c** to withdraw their royal rations and
1:21 Daniel **c** there until the first year of King Cyrus.
4:13 I **c** looking, in the visions of my head as I lay
6:10 he **c** to go to his house,
Hos 10: 9 O Israel; there they have **c**.
Lk 4:44 So he **c** proclaiming the message in
7:38 Then she **c** kissing his feet and anointing them
Jn 12:17 the tomb and raised him from the dead **c** to testify.
Ac 6: 7 The word of God **c** to spread;
12:16 Meanwhile Peter **c** knocking;
12:24 the word of God **c** to advance and gain adherents.
14: 7 and there they **c** proclaiming the good news.
19:10 This **c** for two years, so that all the residents
20: 7 he **c** speaking until midnight.
20:11 he **c** to converse with them until dawn;
Tob 6: 6 The two **c** on their way together until they were
6:13 He **c**, "You have every right to take her
Jdt 16:20 the people **c** feasting in Jerusalem before
1Mc 10:26 with us and have **c** your friendship with us,
2Mc 4:27 Although Menelaus **c** to hold the office,
5:27 they **c** to live on what grew wild,
8: 1 and enlisted those who had **c** in the Jewish faith,
3Mc 2:26 but even **c** with such audacity
3: 3 **c** to maintain goodwill and unswerving loyalty
5: 5 and arranged for their **c** custody through the night,
2Es 11:13 and it **c** to reign a long time.
11:28 While I **c** to look the two that remained

CONTINUES (9) [CONTINUE]

Jos 19:27 then it **c** in the north to Cabul,
1Sa 30:25 it **c** to the present day.
1Ki 12:27 If this people **c** to go up to offer sacrifices in
1Ch 28: 7 if he **c** resolute in keeping my commandments
Jer 32:20 have made yourself a name that **c** to this very day.
1Ti 5: 5 and **c** in supplications and prayers night and day;
Heb 7:24 his priesthood permanently, because he **c** forever.
Rev 2:26 To everyone who conquers and **c** to do my works
Bar 2:11 and made yourself a name that **c** to this day,

CONTINUING‡ (3) [CONTINUE]

Jos 18: 5 Judah **c** in its territory on the south,
Heb 7:23 they were prevented by death from **c** in office;
1Pe 4:19 to a faithful Creator, while **c** to do good.

CONTINUOUS (2) [CONTINUE]

Zec 14: 7 there shall be **c** day (it is known to the LORD),
3Mc 1:28 The **c**, vehement, and concerted cry of

CONTINUOUSLY‡ (1) [CONTINUE]

2Mc 3:26 on either side of him and flogged him **c**,

CONTRACT (1) [CONTRACTS]

Tob 7:13 and he wrote out a copy of a marriage **c**,

CONTRACTS (3) [CONTRACT]

Lev 13: 9 When a person **c** a leprous disease,
1Mc 13:42 people began to write in their documents and **c**,
14:43 all **c** in the country should be written in his name,

CONTRADICT (2) [CONTRADICTED, CONTRADICTION, CONTRADICTIONS]

Lk 21:15 of your opponents will be able to withstand or **c**.

Tit 1: 9 with sound doctrine and to refute those who c it.

CONTRADICTED (1) [CONTRADICT]
Ac 13:45 blaspheming, they c what was spoken by Paul.

CONTRADICTION (1) [CONTRADICT]
4Mc 7:20 No c therefore arises when some persons appear

CONTRADICTIONS (1) [CONTRADICT]
1Ti 6:20 and c of what is falsely called knowledge;

CONTRARIWISE (KJV) See CONTRARY, INSTEAD

CONTRARY (25)
Ac 15:11 On the c, we believe that we will be saved through
17: 7 They are all acting c to the decrees of the emperor,
18:13 to worship God in ways that are c to the law."
Ro 3:31 On the c, we uphold the law.
10:21 to a disobedient and c people."
11:24 c to nature, into a cultivated olive tree,
1Co 12:22 On the c, the members of the body that seem to
15:10 On the c, I worked harder than any of them—
Gal 1: 8 to you a gospel c to what we proclaimed to you,
1: 9 to you a gospel c to what you received,
2: 7 On the c, when they saw that I had been entrusted
3:12 But the law does not rest on faith; on the c,
1Ti 1:10 and whatever else is c to the sound teaching
1Pe 3: 9 but, on the c, repay with a blessing.
AdE 4:16 After that I will go to the king, c to the law,
13: 4 who have laws c to those of every nation
Wis 15: 7 the vessels that serve clean uses and those for c
19:21 on the c, failed to consume the flesh
Sir 41: 2 to one who is c, and has lost all patience!
1Mc 14:45 Whoever acts c to these decisions or rejects any
2Mc 4:11 of living and introduced new customs c to the law.
3Mc 3:22 in their innate malice they took this in a c spirit,
4Mc 2: 8 one is forced to act c to natural ways and to lend
5:26 to eat meats that would be c to this.
16:13 On the c, as though having a mind like adamant

CONTRAST (1)
Gal 5:22 By c, the fruit of the Spirit is love, joy, peace,

CONTRAVENED (1)
AdE 8: 8 and sealed with my ring cannot be c."

CONTRIBUTE (1) [CONTRIBUTED, CONTRIBUTING, CONTRIBUTION, CONTRIBUTIONS]
Ro 12:13 C to the needs of the saints;

CONTRIBUTED (7) [CONTRIBUTE]
Ex 38:29 The bronze that was c was seventy talents,
2Ch 35: 7 Then Josiah c to the people,
35: 8 His officials c willingly to the people,
Ne 7:70 Now some of the heads of ancestral houses c to
Mk 12:44 For all of them have c out of their abundance;
Lk 21: 4 for all of them have c out of their abundance,
Gal 2: 6 those leaders c nothing to me.

CONTRIBUTING (2) [CONTRIBUTE]
Dt 16:10 c a freewill offering in proportion to the blessing
Mk 12:43 in more than all those who are c to the treasury.

CONTRIBUTION (3) [CONTRIBUTE]
2Ch 31: 3 The c of the king from his own possessions was
31:14 to apportion the c reserved for the LORD and
Ne 10:39 and the sons of Levi shall bring the c of grain,

CONTRIBUTIONS (6) [CONTRIBUTE]
2Ch 31:10 "Since they began to bring the c into the house of
31:12 Faithfully they brought in the c,
Ne 10:37 and our c, the fruit of every tree,
12:44 the c, the first fruits, and the tithes,
13: 5 singers, and gatekeepers, and the c for the priests.
Eze 20:40 and there I will require your c and the choicest

CONTRITE (5) [CONTRITION]
Ps 51:17 a broken and c heart, O God, you will not despise.
Isa 57:15 also with those who are c and humble in spirit,
57:15 and to revive the heart of the c.
66: 2 to the humble and c in spirit,
Aza 1:16 a c heart and a humble spirit may we be accepted,

CONTRITION (1) [CONTRITE]
Jer 44:10 They have shown no c or fear to this day,

CONTRIVE (3) [CONTRIVED]
Ps 94:20 those who c mischief by statute?
3Mc 4:19 that they had been bribed to c a means of escape,
4Mc 10:16 C tortures, tyrant, so that you may learn

CONTRIVED (3) [CONTRIVE]
Ac 5: 4 How is it that you have c this deed in your heart?
2Mc 7:31 who have c all sorts of evil against the Hebrews,
4Mc 6:25 with maliciously c instruments,

CONTROL (33) [CONTROLLED, CONTROLLING, CONTROLS, SELF-CONTROL, SELF-CONTROLLED]
Ge 45: 1 Then Joseph could no longer c himself
Jer 10:23 that the way of human beings is not in their c,
29:26 to c any madman who plays the prophet,
Ac 27:16 to get the ship's boat under c.
1Co 7:37 but having his own desire under c,
1Th 4: 4 of you know how to c your own body in holiness
Heb 2: 8 God left nothing outside their c.
1Mc 6:56 that he was trying to seize c of the government.
6:63 He found Philip in c of the city,
7:22 They gained c of the land of Judah
8: 3 to get c of the silver and gold mines there,
8: 4 and how they had gained c of the whole region
8:16 to rule over them and to c all their land;
10:32 also my c of the citadel in Jerusalem and give it to
10:52 I crushed Demetrius and gained c of our country;
11: 8 So King Ptolemy gained c of the coastal cities
11:49 the city saw that the Jews had gained c of the city
11:56 Trypho captured the elephants and gained c
14: 6 and gained full c of the country.
15: 3 Whereas certain scoundrels have gained c of
15: 9 When we gain c of our kingdom,
15:28 "You hold c of Joppa and Gazara and the citadel
16:13 he determined to get c of the country,
2Mc 3: 6 but that it was possible for them to fall under the c
5: 7 He did not, however, gain c of the government;
9: 2 and attempted to rob the temples and c the city.
10:15 who had c of important strongholds,
3Mc 6: 5 who had already gained c of the whole world by
2Es 11:32 Moreover this head gained c of the whole earth,
4Mc 2: 6 to you all the more that reason is able to c desires.
2:20 For if reason could not c anger,
2:24 it does not c forgetfulness and ignorance?
7:18 these alone are able to c the passions of the flesh,

CONTROLLED (3) [CONTROL]
Pr 16:32 and one whose temper is c than one who captures
3Mc 1: 1 that the regions that he had c had been seized
4Mc 2:17 but c his anger by reason.

CONTROLLING (1) [CONTROL]
Ge 43:31 and c himself he said, "Serve the meal."

CONTROLS‡ (2) [CONTROL]
Sir 21:11 Whoever keeps the law c his thoughts,
4Mc 1: 9 demonstrated that reason c the emotions.

CONTROVERSIES (3) [CONTROVERSY]
Ac 26: 3 with all the customs and c of the Jews;
2Ti 2:23 Have nothing to do with stupid and senseless c;
Tit 3: 9 But avoid stupid c, genealogies, dissensions,

CONTROVERSY (4) [CONTROVERSIES]
Eze 44:24 In a c they shall act as judges,
Mic 6: 2 Hear, you mountains, the c of the LORD,
6: 2 for the LORD has a c with his people,
1Ti 6: 4 and has a morbid craving for c and for disputes

CONVENE (1) [CONVENED, CONVENING, RECONVENED]
1Mc 14:44 or to c an assembly in the country

CONVENED (2) [CONVENE]
Dt 5: 1 Moses c all Israel, and said to them:
1Mc 12:35 When Jonathan returned he c the elders of

CONVENIENT (1)
1Mc 4:46 the stones in a c place on the temple hill until

CONVENING (1) [CONVENE]
3Mc 6:33 after c a great banquet to celebrate these events,

CONVERGED (1)
1Mc 15:12 for he knew that troubles had c on him,

CONVERSATION (8) [CONVERSATIONS, CONVERSE]
Jer 38:24 "Do not let anyone else know of this c,
38:27 for the c had not been overheard.
AdE 12: 2 He overheard their c and inquired
Sir 9:15 Let your c be with intelligent people,
19: 7 Never repeat a c, and you will lose nothing at all.
22: 6 Like music in time of mourning is ill-timed c,
27: 5 so the test of a person is in his c.
27:11 The c of the godly is always wise,

CONVERSATIONS (1) [CONVERSATION]
Sir 13:11 to treat him as an equal, or trust his lengthy c;

CONVERSE (2) [CONVERSATION]
Ac 20:11 he continued to c with them until dawn;
24:26 to send for him very often and c with him.

CONVERSION (1) [CONVERT]
Ac 15: 3 they reported the c of the Gentiles,

CONVERT (4) [CONVERSION, CONVERTED, CONVERTIBLE, CONVERTS]
Mt 23:15 For you cross sea and land to make a single c,
23:15 you make the new c twice as much a child of hell
Ro 16: 5 who was the first c in Asia for Christ.
1Ti 3: 6 He must not be a recent c,

CONVERTED (2) [CONVERT]
Tob 14: 6 in the whole world will all be c and worship God
2Es 6:26 of the earth's inhabitants shall be changed and c to

CONVERTIBLE (1) [CONVERT]
Lev 5:15 c into silver by the sanctuary shekel;

CONVERTS (3) [CONVERT]
Ac 13:43 many Jews and devout c to Judaism followed Paul
1Co 16:15 of the household of Stephanas were the first c
Tob 1: 8 to the c who had attached themselves to Israel.

CONVEY (2) [CONVEYED]
Ezr 7:15 and also to c the silver and gold that the king
1Es 5:55 from Lebanon and c them in rafts to the harbor

CONVEY (KJV) See also GO, PASSAGE

CONVEYED (3) [CONVEY]
Est 1:12 to come at the king's command c by the eunuchs.
1:15 not performed the command of King Ahasuerus c
2Pe 1:17 from God the Father when that voice was c to him

CONVICT‡ (5) [CONVICTED, CONVICTION, CONVICTS]
Dt 19:15 A single witness shall not suffice to c a person
Jer 2:19 and your apostasies will c you.
Jude 1:15 and to c everyone of all the deeds of ungodliness
Wis 1: 9 to c them of their lawless deeds;
4:20 and their lawless deeds will c them to their face.

CONVICTED (3) [CONVICT]
Dt 21:22 When someone is c of a crime punishable
Jas 2: 9 and are c by the law as transgressors.
Sus 1:61 of their own mouths Daniel had c them

CONVICTION‡ (3) [CONVICT]
Ro 14:22 have as your own c before God.
1Th 1: 5 in power and in the Holy Spirit and with full c;
Heb 11: 1 the c of things not seen.

CONVICTS (2) [CONVICT]
2Sa 14:13 For in giving this decision the king c himself,
Jn 8:46 Which of you c me of sin?

CONVINCE (4) [CONVINCED, CONVINCING]
Ac 18: 4 in the synagogue and would try to c Jews
28:23 of God and trying to c them about Jesus both from
2Ti 4: 2 c, rebuke, and encourage,
4Mc 9:18 through all these tortures I will c you that children

CONVINCED (17) [CONVINCE]
Lk 16:31 neither will they be c even if someone rises from
20: 6 for they are c that John was a prophet."
Ac 5:39 against God!" They were c by him,
16:10 being c that God had called us to proclaim
26: 9 I myself was c that I ought to do many things
28:24 Some were c by what he had said,
Ro 4:21 being fully c that God was able
8:38 For I am c that neither death, nor life, nor angels,
14: 5 Let all be fully c in their own minds.
2Co 5:14 because we are c that one has died for all;
Php 1:25 Since I am c of this, I know that I will remain
Wis 16: 8 also you c our enemies that it is you who deliver
Sir 39:32 So from the beginning I have been c of all this
2Mc 13:26 c them, appeased them, gained their goodwill,
3Mc 3:24 fully c by these indications
4:19 he was clearly c about the matter
5: 5 for their continued custody through the night, c

CONVINCING (1) [CONVINCE]
Ac 1: 3 presented himself alive to them by many c proofs,

CONVOCATION (16) [CONVOCATIONS]
Lev 23: 3 a sabbath of complete rest, a holy c;
23: 7 On the first day you shall have a holy c;
23: 8 on the seventh day there shall be a holy c:
23:21 you shall hold a holy c;
23:24 a holy c commemorated with trumpet blasts.
23:27 it shall be a holy c for you:
23:35 The first day shall be a holy c;
23:36 on the eighth day you shall observe a holy c
23:37 which you shall celebrate as times of holy c,
Nu 28:18 On the first day there shall be a holy c.
28:25 And on the seventh day you shall have a holy c;
28:26 you shall have a holy c;
29: 1 of the seventh month you shall have a holy c;
29: 7 of this seventh month you shall have a holy c,
29:12 of the seventh month you shall have a holy c;

Isa 1:13 New moon and sabbath and calling of c—

CONVOCATIONS (2) [CONVOCATION]
Lev 23: 2 of the LORD that you shall proclaim as holy c,
23: 4 the LORD, the holy c, which you shall celebrate

CONVULSED (2) [CONVULSIONS]
Eze 27:35 their kings are horribly afraid, their faces are c.
Mk 9:20 When the spirit saw him, immediately it c the boy,

CONVULSES (1) [CONVULSIONS]
Lk 9:39 It c him until he foams at the mouth;

CONVULSING (2) [CONVULSIONS]
Mk 1:26 unclean spirit, c him and crying with a loud voice,
9:26 After crying out and c him terribly, it came out,

CONVULSIONS (2) [CONVULSED, CONVULSES, CONVULSING]
2Sa 1: 9 for c have seized me, and yet my life still lingers.'
Lk 9:42 the demon dashed him to the ground in c.

COOK (3) [COOKED, COOKING, COOKS]
Dt 16: 7 You shall c it and eat it at the place that
1Sa 9:23 And Samuel said to the c,
9:24 The c took up the thigh and what went with it

COOKED (2) [COOK]
2Ki 6:29 So we c my son and ate him.
4Mc 6:15 We will set before you some c meat;

COOKING (3) [COOK]
Ge 25:29 Once when Jacob was c a stew,
Zec 14:20 And the c pots in the house of the LORD shall be
14:21 and every c pot in Jerusalem and Judah shall

COOKS (1) [COOK]
1Sa 8:13 He will take your daughters to be perfumers and c

COOL (4)
Jdg 3:20 while he was sitting alone in his c roof chamber,
3:24 "He must be relieving himself in the c chamber."
Pr 17:27 one who is c in spirit has understanding.
Lk 16:24 the tip of his finger in water and c my tongue;

COOS (KJV) See COS

COPIED (1) [COPY]
Pr 25: 1 that the officials of King Hezekiah of Judah c.

COPIES (3) [COPY]
AdE 3:14 C of the document were posted in every province,
8:13 "Let c of the decree be posted conspicuously in all
1Mc 14:49 and to deposit c of them in the treasury,

COPING (1)
1Ki 7: 9 back and front, from the foundation to the c,

COPPER (9) [COPPERSMITH]
Lev 26:19 like iron and your earth like c.
Dt 8: 9 and from whose hills you may mine c.
Job 28: 2 and c is smelted from ore.
Eze 24:11 its c glow, its filth melt in it, its rust be consumed.
Mt 10: 9 Take no gold, or silver, or c in your belts,
Mk 12:42 A poor widow came and put in two small c coins,
Lk 21: 2 also saw a poor widow put in two small c coins.
Wis 15: 9 and imitate workers in c;
Sir 12:10 Never trust your enemy, for like corrosion in c,

COPPERSMITH (1) [COPPER, SMITH]
2Ti 4:14 Alexander the c did me great harm;

COPULATION (KJV) See EMISSION

COPY‡ (32) [COPIED, COPIES]
Dt 17:18 a c of this law written for him in the presence of
Jos 8:32 Joshua wrote on the stones a c of the law
22:28 'Look at this c of the altar of the LORD,
Ezr 4:11 this is a c of the letter that they sent):
4:23 when the c of King Artaxerxes' letter was read
5: 6 The c of the letter that Tattenai the governor of
7:11 This is a c of the letter that King Artaxerxes gave
Est 3:14 A c of the document was to be issued as a decree
4: 8 also gave him a c of the written decree issued
8:13 A c of the writ was to be issued as a decree
Jer 32:11 the terms and conditions, and the open c;
Heb 9:24 a mere c of the true one,
Tob 7:13 and he wrote out a c of a marriage contract,
AdE 4: 8 also gave him a c of what had been posted in Susa
13: 1 This is a c of the letter:
16: 1 The following is a c of this letter:
16:19 post a c of this letter publicly in every place,
Wis 9: 8 a c of the holy tent that you prepared from
LtJ 6: 1 A c of a letter that Jeremiah sent
1Mc 8:22 and this is a c of the letter that they wrote in reply,
11:31 This c of the letter that we wrote concerning you
11:37 Now therefore take care to make a c of this,
12: 5 This is a c of the letter that Jonathan wrote to
1Mc 12: 7 that you are our brothers, as the appended c shows.
12:19 This is a c of the letter that they sent to Onias:
14:20 This is a c of the letter that the Spartans sent:
14:23 to put a c of their words in the public archives,
14:23 a c of this to the high priest Simon.' "
14:27 This is a c of what they wrote:
15:24 a c of these things to the high priest Simon.
1Es 6: 7 A c of the letter that Sisinnes the governor
8: 8 The following is a c of the written commission

COR (2) [CORS]
Eze 45:14 one-tenth of a bath from each c (the c, like the

CORAL (3)
Job 28:18 No mention shall be made of c or of crystal;
La 4: 7 their bodies were more ruddy than c,
Eze 27:16 embroidered work, fine linen, c, and rubies.

CORBAN (1)
Mk 7:11 from me is C' (that is, an offering to God)—

CORD (20) [CORDED, CORDS, TENT-CORD]
Ge 38:18 She replied, "Your signet and your c,
38:25 the signet and the c and the staff."
Ex 28:28 by its rings to the rings of the ephod with a blue c,
28:37 You shall fasten it on the turban with a blue c;
39:21 by its rings to the rings of the ephod with a blue c,
39:31 They tied to it a blue c,
Nu 15:38 throughout their generations and to put a blue c on
Jos 2:18 and you do not tie this crimson c in the window
2:21 Then she tied the crimson c in the window.
2Sa 8: 2 measured them off with a c;
8: 2 he measured two lengths of c for those who were
1Ki 7:15 and a c of twelve cubits would encircle it;
Job 41: 1 or press down its tongue with a c?
Ecc 4:12 A threefold c is not quickly broken.
12: 6 before the silver c is snapped,
Eze 16: 4 the day you were born your navel c was not cut,
40: 3 with a linen c and a measuring reed in his hand;
47: 3 Going on eastward with a c in his hand,
Sir 6:30 and her bonds a purple c.
LtJ 6:43 as attractive as herself and her c was not broken.

CORDED (1) [CORD]
Ex 28:14 and you shall attach the c chains to the settings.

CORDS (33) [CORD]
Ex 28:14 and two chains of pure gold, twisted like c;
28:22 of pure gold, twisted like c;
28:24 You shall put the two c of gold in the two rings at
28:25 of the two c you shall attach to the two settings,
35:18 and the pegs of the court, and their c;
39:15 of pure gold, twisted like c;
39:17 and they put the two c of gold in the two rings at
39:18 of the two c they had attached to the two settings
39:40 and the screen for the gate of the court, its c,
Nu 3:26 and its c—all the service pertaining to these.
3:37 with their bases and pegs and c.
4:26 their c, and all the equipment for their service;
4:32 and c, with all their equipment
2Sa 22: 6 the c of Sheol entangled me,
Est 1: 6 with c of fine linen and purple to silver rings
Job 36: 8 if they are bound in fetters and caught in the c
38:31 or loose the c of Orion?
Ps 2: 3 and cast their c from us."
18: 4 The c of death encompassed me;
18: 5 the c of Sheol entangled me;
119:61 Though the c of the wicked ensnare me,
129: 4 he has cut the c of the wicked.
140: 5 and with c they have spread a net,
Isa 5:18 you who drag iniquity along with c of falsehood,
54: 2 lengthen your c and strengthen your stakes.
Jer 10:20 My tent is destroyed, and all my c are broken;
Eze 3:25 As for you, mortal, c shall be placed on you,
4: 8 I am putting c on you so that you cannot turn
27:24 bound with c and made secure;
Hos 11: 4 I led them with c of human kindness,
Jn 2:15 of c, he drove all of them out of the temple,
AdE 1: 6 held by c of purple linen attached to gold
LtJ 6:42 And the women, with c around them,

CORIANDER (2)
Ex 16:31 it was like c seed, white, and the taste of it was
Nu 11: 7 Now the manna was like c seed,

CORINTH (6) [CORINTHIANS]
Ac 18: 1 After this Paul left Athens and went to C.
19: 1 While Apollos was in C, Paul passed through
1Co 1: 2 To the church of God that is in C, to those who are sanctified
2Co 1: 1 To the church of God that is in C,
1:23 it was to spare you that I did not come again to C.
2Ti 4:20 Erastus remained in C; Trophimus I left ill in

CORINTHIANS (2) [CORINTH]
Ac 18: 8 of the C who heard Paul became believers
2Co 6:11 We have spoken frankly to you C;

CORMORANT (2)
Lev 11:17 the little owl, the c, the great owl,
Dt 14:17 and the desert owl, the carrion vulture and the c,

CORN (KJV) See GRAIN

CORNELIUS (8)
Ac 10: 1 In Caesarea there was a man named C,
10: 3 an angel of God coming in and saying to him, "C."
10:17 suddenly the men sent by C appeared.
10:22 They answered, "C, a centurion,
10:24 C was expecting them and had called together his
10:25 On Peter's arrival C met him,
10:30 C replied, "Four days ago at this very hour,
10:31 'C, your prayer has been heard

CORNER (30) [CORNERS, CORNERSTONE, CORNERSTONES]
Nu 15:38 and to put a blue cord on the fringe at each c.
1Sa 24: 4 Then David went and stealthily cut off a c
24: 5 because he had cut off a c of Saul's cloak.
24:11 my father, see the c of your cloak in my hand;
24:11 for by the fact that I cut off the c of your cloak,
1Ki 7:39 he set the sea on the southeast c of the house.
2Ki 14:13 from the Ephraim Gate to the C Gate,
2Ch 4:10 He set the sea at the southeast c of the house.
25:23 from the Ephraim Gate to the C Gate,
26: 9 Uzziah built towers in Jerusalem at the C Gate,
28:24 of the LORD and made himself altars in every c
Ne 3:24 the house of Azariah to the Angle and to the c.
3:31 and to the upper room of the c.
3:32 of the c and the Sheep Gate the goldsmiths and
9:22 and allotted to them every c,
Ps 144:12 our daughters like c pillars,
Pr 1:21 At the busiest c she cries out;
7: 8 passing along the street near her c,
7:12 now in the squares, and at every c she lies in wait.
21: 9 in a c of the housetop than in a house shared with
25:24 in a c of the housetop than in a house shared with
Jer 31:38 from the tower of Hananel to the C Gate.
31:40 to the c of the Horse Gate toward the east,
51:26 from you for a c and no stone for a foundation,
Eze 46:21 and in each c of the court there was a court—
Am 3:12 with the c of a couch and part of a bed.
Zec 14:10 to the place of the former gate, to the C Gate,
Ac 26:26 for this was not done in a c.
1Pe 2: 7 the very head of the c,"
Sus 1:38 We were in a c of the garden,

CORNERS (33) [CORNER]
Ex 25:26 and fasten the rings to the four c at its four legs.
26:23 You shall make two frames for c of the tabernacle
26:24 they shall form the two c.
27: 2 You shall make horns for it on its four c;
27: 4 you shall make four bronze rings at its four c.
36:28 He made two frames for c of the tabernacle in
36:29 he made two of them in this way, for the two c.
37:13 and fastened the rings to the four c at its four legs.
38: 2 He made horns for it on its four c;
38: 5 the four c of the bronze grating to hold the poles;
Nu 15:38 to make fringes on the c of their garments
Dt 22:12 You shall make tassels on the four c of the cloak
1Ki 7:30 at the four c were supports for a basin.
7:34 There were four supports at the four c
2Ch 26:15 and the c for shooting arrows and large stones.
Job 1:19 struck the four c of the house,
37: 3 and his lightning to the c of the earth.
Isa 11:12 the dispersed of Judah from the four c of the earth.
41: 9 and called from its farthest c, saying to you,
Eze 7: 2 The end has come upon the four c of the land.
41:22 its c, its base, and its walls were of wood.
43:20 and on the four c of the ledge,
45:19 the four c of the ledge of the altar,
46:21 and led me past the four c of the court;
46:22 in the four c of the court were small courts,
Zec 9:15 drenched like the c of the altar.
Mt 6: 5 and pray in the synagogues and at the street c,
Ac 10:11 being lowered to the ground by its four c.
11: 5 being lowered by its four c;
Rev 7: 1 After this I saw four angels standing at the four c
20: 8 at the four c of the earth, Gog and Magog, in order
Tob 11:13 the white films from the c of his eyes.
Sir 23:19 of human behavior and see into hidden c.

CORNERSTONE (10) [CORNER, STONE]
Job 38: 6 On what were its bases sunk, or who laid its c
Ps 118:22 that the builders rejected has become the chief c.
Isa 28:16 a tested stone, a precious c, a sure foundation:
Zec 10: 4 Out of them shall come the c,
Mt 21:42 stone that the builders rejected has become the c;
Mk 12:10 stone that the builders rejected has become the c;
Lk 20:17 that the builders rejected has become the c'?
Ac 4:11 the builders; it has become the c.'
Eph 2:20 with Christ Jesus himself as the c.
1Pe 2: 6 "See, I am laying in Zion a stone, a c chosen

CORNERSTONES (1) [CORNER, STONE]
Isa 19:13 the c of its tribes have led Egypt astray.

CORNET, CORNETS (KJV) See CASTANETS, HORN, TRUMPETS

CORNFLOOR (KJV) See THRESHING FLOOR

CORONATION (1)

2Mc 4:21 of Menestheus was sent to Egypt for the c

CORPSE‡ (21) [CORPSES]

Lev 22: 4 Whoever touches anything made unclean by a c or
Nu 5: 2 who is unclean through contact with a c;
6: 6 to the LORD they shall not go near a c.
6:11 because they incurred guilt by reason of the c.
9: 6 through touching a c, so that they could not keep
9: 7 "Although we are unclean through touching a c,
9:10 who is unclean through touching a c,
19:13 a c, the body of a human being who has died,
19:18 and on whoever touched the bone, the slain, the c,
31:19 of you has killed any person or touched a c,
Dt 21:23 his c must not remain all night upon the tree;
2Ki 9:37 the c of Jezebel shall be like dung on the field
Isa 14:19 like a c trampled underfoot.
Mt 24:28 Wherever the c is, there the vultures will gather.
Mk 9:26 it came out, and the boy was like a c,
Lk 17:37 He said to them, "Where the c is,
Rev 16: 3 and it became like the blood of a c,
Sir 34:30 If one washes after touching a c,
48: 5 You raised a c from death and from Hades,
LtJ 6:71 or like a c thrown out in the darkness.
2Es 10:30 lying there like a c, deprived

CORPSES (18) [CORPSE]

Dt 28:26 Your c shall be food for every bird of the air
2Ch 20:24 they were c lying on the ground;
Ps 110: 6 among the nations, filling them with c;
Isa 5:25 and their c were like refuse in the streets.
26:19 Your dead shall live, their c shall rise.
34: 3 and the stench of their c shall rise;
Jer 7:33 The c of this people will be food for the birds of
9:22 "Human c shall fall like dung upon the open field,
34:20 Their c shall become food for the birds of the air
Eze 6: 5 the c of the people of Israel in front of their idols;
43: 7 and by the c of their kings at their death.
43: 9 Now let them put away their idolatry and the c
Na 3: 3 heaps of c, dead bodies without end—
Wis 4:18 After this they will become dishonored c,
18:12 by the one form of death, had c too many to count.
1Mc 11: 4 and its suburbs destroyed, and the c lying about,
4Mc 15:20 and c fallen on other c,

CORRECT (5) [CORRECTING, CORRECTION, CORRECTOR, CORRECTS]

Ps 141: 5 Let the righteous strike me; let the faithful c me.
Jer 10:24 C me, O LORD, but in just measure;
Wis 12: 2 Therefore you c little by little those who trespass,
Sir 42: 8 Do not be ashamed to c the stupid or foolish or
4Mc 2:18 to c some, and to render others powerless.

CORRECTING (1) [CORRECT]

2Ti 2:25 c opponents with gentleness.

CORRECTION (8) [CORRECT]

Job 37:13 Whether for c, or for his land, or for love,
Jer 2:30 down your children; they accepted no c.
5: 3 but they refused to take c.
32:33 they would not listen and accept c.
Zep 3: 2 It has listened to no voice; it has accepted no c.
3: 7 "Surely the city will fear me, it will accept c;
2Ti 3:16 for c, and for training in righteousness,
2Es 16:19 and anguish are sent as scourges for the c

CORRECTOR (2) [CORRECT]

Ro 2:20 a c of the foolish, a teacher of children, having in
Wis 7:15 the guide even of wisdom and the c of the wise.

CORRECTS (1) [CORRECT]

Pr 9: 7 Whoever c a scoffer wins abuse;

CORRESPONDED (1) [CORRESPONDING, CORRESPONDS]

1Ch 26:16 on the ascending road. Guard c to guard.

CORRESPONDING (12) [CORRESPONDED]

Ex 24: 4 c to the twelve tribes of Israel.
28:21 with names c to the names of the sons of Israel;
38:18 five cubits high, c to the hangings of the court.
39:14 with names c to the names of the sons of Israel;
1Ch 23: 6 And David organized them in divisions c to
24:31 These also cast lots c to their kindred,
26:12 c to their leaders, had duties,
2Ch 3: 8 its length, c to the width of the house,
Eze 40:18 c to the length of the gates;
42:12 through the entrance at the head of the c passage,
45: 7 c in length to one of the tribal portions,
Wis 13: 5 and beauty of created things comes a c perception

CORRESPONDS (2) [CORRESPONDED]

Gal 4:25 Now Hagar is Mount Sinai in Arabia and c to
4:26 But the other woman c to the Jerusalem above;

CORROBORATION (1)

3Mc 5:19 But when he, with the c of his Friends,

CORROSION (2)

Sir 12:10 Never trust your enemy, for like c in copper,
LtJ 6:12 that cannot save themselves from rust and c.

CORRUPT (17) [CORRUPTED, CORRUPTIBLE, CORRUPTION, CORRUPTLY, CORRUPTS]

Ge 6:11 Now the earth was c in God's sight,
6:12 And God saw that the earth was c;
1Sa 30:22 Then all the c and worthless fellows among
2Ch 27: 2 But the people still followed c practices.
Job 15:16 how much less one who is abominable and c,
Ps 14: 1 They are c, they do abominable deeds;
53: 1 They are c, they commit abominable acts;
Eze 16:47 a very little time you were more c than they
20:44 not according to your evil ways, or c deeds,
23:11 yet she was more c than she in her lusting and
Zep 3: 7 the more eager to make all their deeds c.
Ac 2:40 saying, "Save yourselves from this c generation."
Eph 4:22 your old self, c and deluded by its lusts,
2Ti 3: 8 so these people, of c mind and counterfeit faith,
Tit 1:15 but to the c and unbelieving nothing is pure.
2Es 4:11 by the c world understand incorruption?"
9:19 have become c in their ways.

CORRUPTED (8) [CORRUPT]

Ge 6:12 for all flesh had c its ways upon the earth.
Eze 28:17 you c your wisdom for the sake of your splendor.
Hos 9: 9 They have deeply c themselves as in the days
Mal 2: 8 you have c the covenant of Levi,
2Co 7: 2 we have wronged no one, we have c no one,
Tit 1:15 Their very minds and consciences are c.
Rev 19: 2 he has judged the great whore who c the earth
4Mc 18: 8 No seducer c me on a desert plain,

CORRUPTIBLE‡ (4) [CORRUPT]

2Es 7:31 and that which is c shall perish.
7:*96* they rejoice that they have now escaped what is c
8:34 what is a c race, that you are so bitter against it?
14:13 And now renounce the life that is c,

CORRUPTION (22) [CORRUPT]

Da 6: 4 they could find no grounds for complaint or any c,
6: 4 and no negligence or c could be found in him.
Hos 7: 1 the c of Ephraim is revealed,
Ac 2:27 or let your Holy One experience c.
2:31 nor did his flesh experience c.'
13:34 no more to return to c, he has spoken in this way,
13:35 'You will not let your Holy One experience c.'
13:36 was laid beside his ancestors, and experienced c;
13:37 but he whom God raised up experienced no c.
Gal 6: 8 you will reap c from the flesh;
2Pe 1: 4 through them you may escape from the c that is in
2:19 but they themselves are slaves of c;
Wis 14:12 and the invention of them was the c of life;
14:25 theft and deceit, c, faithlessness, tumult, perjury,
Sir 28: 6 remember c and death, and be true to
2Mc 4: 7 of Onias obtained the high priesthood by c,
2Es 6:28 and c shall be overcome, and the truth,
7:*48* and has brought us into c and the ways of death,
7:*111* [41] So if now, when c has increased
7:*113* [43] in which c has passed away,
8:53 Hades has fled and c has been forgotten;
10:28 my end has become c, and my prayer a reproach."

CORRUPTLY (6) [CORRUPT]

Dt 4:16 not act c by making an idol for yourselves,
4:25 if you act c by making an idol in the form
9:12 for your people whom you have brought from Egypt have acted c.
31:29 I know that after my death you will surely act c,
Isa 1: 4 offspring who do evil, children who deal c,
Jer 6:28 they are bronze and iron, all of them act c.

CORRUPTS (1) [CORRUPT]

Ecc 7: 7 and a bribe c the heart.

CORS (9) [COR]

1Ki 4:22 Solomon's provision for one day was thirty c
4:22 of choice flour, and sixty c of meal,
5:11 Solomon in turn gave Hiram twenty thousand c
5:11 and twenty c of fine oil.
2Ch 2:10 twenty thousand c of crushed wheat,
2:10 twenty thousand c of barley,
27: 5 ten thousand c of wheat and ten thousand
Ezr 7:22 up to one hundred talents of silver, one hundred c
1Es 8:20 and likewise up to a hundred c of wheat,

COS (2)

Ac 21: 1 we came by a straight course to C,
1Mc 15:23 and to Rhodes, and to Phaselis, and to C,

COSAM (1)

Lk 3:28 son of Addi, son of C, son of Elmadam, son of Er,

COSMETIC (3) [COSMETICS]

Est 2: 3 let their c treatments be given them.
2: 9 and he quickly provided her with her c treatments
2:12 this was the regular period of their c treatment,

COSMETICS (1) [COSMETIC]

Est 2:12 and six months with perfumes and c for women.

COSMIC (1)

Eph 6:12 against the c powers of this present darkness,

COST (22) [COSTLY]

Ex 32:29 each one at the c of a son or a brother,
Nu 16:38 of these sinners have become holy at the c
Jos 6:26 At the c of his firstborn he shall lay its foundation,
6:26 at the c of his youngest he shall set up its gates!"
2Sa 24:24 to the LORD my God that c me nothing."
1Ki 16:34 at the c of Abiram his firstborn,
16:34 set up its gates at the c of his youngest son Segub,
1Ch 12:19 "He will desert to his master Saul at the c
21:24 nor offer burnt offerings that c me nothing."
Ezr 6: 4 let the c be paid from the royal treasury.
6: 8 the c is to be paid to these people,
Pr 7:23 not knowing that it will c him his life.
Lk 14:28 does not first sit down and estimate the c,
Ac 22:28 "It c me a large sum of money
LtJ 6:25 They are bought without regard to c,
Sus 1:55 This lie has c you your head,
1:59 This lie has c you also your head,
1Mc 10:44 the c of rebuilding and restoring the structures of
10:45 And let the c of rebuilding the walls of Jerusalem
10:45 and the c of rebuilding the walls in Judea,
2Mc 5: 6 the c of one's kindred is the greatest misfortune,
1Es 6:25 the c to be paid from the treasury of King Cyrus;

COSTLY (18) [COST]

Ge 24:53 to her brother and to her mother c ornaments.
1Ki 5:17 c stones in order to lay the foundation of
7: 9 All these were made of c stones,
7:10 The foundation was of c stones, huge stones,
7:11 There were c stones above, cut to measure,
2Ch 32:27 for shields, and for all kinds of c objects;
Ps 49: 8 For the ransom of life is c, and can never suffice
Pr 1:13 We shall find all kinds of c things;
20:15 There is gold, and abundance of c stones;
Da 11:38 with precious stones and c gifts.
Mt 26: 7 to him with an alabaster jar of very c ointment,
Mk 14: 3 with an alabaster jar of very c ointment of nard,
Jn 12: 3 a pound of c perfume made of pure nard,
Rev 18:12 all articles of ivory, all articles of c wood, bronze,
AdE 14: 2 and instead of c perfumes she covered her head
Wis 2: 7 Let us take our fill of c wine and perfumes,
1Mc 1:23 He took the silver and the gold, and the c vessels;
1Es 6: 9 of hewn stone, with c timber laid in the walls.

COSTS See Index to Footnotes

COTES (KJV) See STALLS

COTS (1)

Ac 5:15 and laid them on c and mats,

COTTON (2)

Est 1: 6 There were white c curtains
AdE 1: 6 with curtains of fine linen and c,

COUCH (14) [COUCHES]

Ge 49: 4 you went up onto my c!
2Sa 4: 7 while he was lying on his c in his bedchamber;
11: 2 from his c and was walking about on the roof of
11:13 and in the evening he went out to lie on his c with
Est 7: 8 on the c where Esther was reclining;
Job 7:13 my c will ease my complaint,'
17:13 if I spread my c in darkness,
Ps 6: 6 I drench my c with my weeping.
Pr 7:16 I have decked my c with coverings,
SS 1:12 While the king was on his c,
1:16 truly lovely. Our c is green;
Eze 23:41 you sat on a stately c,
Am 3:12 with the corner of a c and part of a bed.
AdE 7: 8 Haman had thrown himself on the c,

COUCHES (5) [COUCH]

Est 1: 6 There were c of gold and silver on
Ps 149: 5 let them sing for joy on their c.
Isa 57: 2 those who walk uprightly will rest on their c.
Am 6: 4 and lounge on their c, and eat lambs from
AdE 1: 6 Gold and silver c were placed on a mosaic floor

COULD (305) See Index of Articles Etc.

COUNCIL (46) [COUNCILS]

Ge 49: 6 May I never come into their c;
2Ki 9: 5 while the commanders of the army were in c,
25:19 and five men of the king's c who were found in
Job 15: 8 Have you listened in the c of God?
Ps 82: 1 God has taken his place in the divine c;
89: 7 a God feared in the c of the holy ones,
Jer 23:18 For who has stood in the c of the LORD so as
23:22 But if they had stood in my c,
52:25 and seven men of the king's c who were found in
Eze 13: 9 they shall not be in the c of my people,
Mt 5:22 you will be liable to the c;
26:59 and the whole c were looking for false testimony
Mk 14:55 the chief priests and the whole c were looking
15: 1 with the elders and scribes and the whole c.

Mk 15:43 a respected member of the **c**,
Lk 22:66 gathered together, and they brought him to their **c**.
23:50 who, though a member of the **c**,
Jn 11:47 and the Pharisees called a meeting of the **c**,
Ac 4:15 to leave the **c** while they discussed the matter
5:21 they called together the **c** and the whole body of
5:27 they had them stand before the **c**.
5:34 But a Pharisee in the **c** named Gamaliel,
5:41 As they left the **c**, they rejoiced
6:12 seized him, and brought him before the **c**.
6:15 And all who sat in the **c** looked intently at him,
22:5 and the whole **c** of elders can testify about me.
22:30 and ordered the chief priests and the entire **c**
23:1 While Paul was looking intently at the **c** he said,
23:6 he called out in the **c**, "Brothers, I am a Pharisee,
23:15 you and the **c** must notify the tribune to bring him
23:20 to ask you to bring Paul down to the **c** tomorrow,
23:28 I had him brought to their **c**.
24:20 when I stood before the **c**,
25:12 Then Festus, after he had conferred with his **c**,
1Ti 4:14 with the laying on of hands by the **c** of elders.
Jdt 6:1 the **c** had died down, Holofernes, the commander
6:17 and told them what had taken place at the **c**
11:9 "Now as for Achior's speech in your **c**,
11:14 to bring back permission from the **c** of the elders.
Sir 38:32 Yet they are not sought out for the **c** of the people,
2Mc 14:5 by Demetrius to a meeting of the **c** and was asked
1Es 2:17 and the other members of their **c**, and the judges
3:15 and he took his seat in the **c** chamber,
3Mc 1:8 Since the Jews had sent some of their **c** and elders
4Mc 15:25 For as in the **c** chamber of her own soul
17:17 and all his **c** marveled at their endurance,

COUNCILS (2) [COUNCIL]

Mt 10:17 for they will hand you over to **c** and flog you
Mk 13:9 for they will hand you over to **c**;

COUNSEL‡ (77) [COUNSELED, COUNSELING, COUNSELOR, COUNSELORS, COUNSELS]

Ex 18:19 I will give you **c**, and God be with you!
Jdg 19:30 Consider it, take **c**, and speak out.' "
20:7 all of you, give your advice and **c** here."
2Sa 15:31 turn the **c** of Ahithophel into foolishness."
15:34 then you will defeat for me the **c** of Ahithophel.
16:20 Absalom said to Ahithophel, "Give us your **c**;
16:23 the **c** that Ahithophel gave was as if one consulted
16:23 so all the **c** of Ahithophel was esteemed,
17:7 "This time the **c** that Ahithophel has given is
17:11 But my **c** is that all Israel be gathered to you,
17:14 "The **c** of Hushai the Archite is better than the **c** of Ahithophel."
17:14 For the LORD had ordained to defeat the good **c**
17:15 and so did Ahithophel **c** Absalom and the elders
17:23 When Ahithophel saw that his **c** was not followed,
1Ki 12:6 Then King Rehoboam took **c** with
12:28 So the king took **c**, and made two calves of gold.
2Ki 6:8 he took **c** with his officers.
1Ch 12:19 rulers of the Philistines took **c** and sent him away,
2Ch 10:6 Then King Rehoboam took **c** with
20:21 When he had taken **c** with the people,
25:17 Then King Amaziah of Judah took **c** and sent
30:2 in Jerusalem had taken **c** to keep the passover in
Ezr 10:3 to the **c** of my lord and of those who tremble at
Job 12:13 he has **c** and understanding.
29:21 and waited, and kept silence for my **c**.
38:2 that darkens **c** by words without knowledge?
42:3 'Who is this that hides **c** without knowledge?'
Ps 2:2 and the rulers take **c** together,
16:7 I bless the LORD who gives me **c**;
32:8 I will **c** you with my eye upon you.
33:10 The LORD brings the **c** of the nations to nothing;
33:11 The **c** of the LORD stands forever,
73:24 You guide me with your **c**,
106:13 they did not wait for his **c**.
107:11 and spurned the **c** of the Most High.
Pr 1:25 and because you have ignored all my **c**
1:30 would have none of my **c**,
12:20 but those who **c** peace have joy.
15:22 Without **c**, plans go wrong,
21:30 No wisdom, no understanding, no **c**,
Isa 8:10 Take **c** together, but it shall be brought to naught;
11:2 the spirit of **c** and might,
16:3 "Give **c**, grant justice; make your shade like night
19:11 the wise counselors of Pharaoh give stupid **c**.
28:29 he is wonderful in **c**, and excellent in wisdom.
30:2 to Egypt without asking for my **c**, to take refuge
45:21 and present your case; let them take **c** together!
Jer 18:18 not perish from the priest, nor **c** from the wise,
32:19 great in **c** and mighty in deed;
49:7 Has **c** perished from the prudent?
Eze 7:26 instruction shall perish from the priest, and **c** from
11:2 and who give wicked **c** in this city;
Da 4:27 O king, may my **c** be acceptable to you:
Eph 1:11 according to his **c** and will,
Rev 3:18 Therefore I **c** you to buy from me gold refined
Tob 4:18 and do not despise any useful **c**.
4:19 but the Lord himself will give them good **c**;
Wis 8:9 knowing that she would give me good **c**
9:13 For who can learn the **c** of God?
9:17 Who has learned your **c**,
Sir 6:23 and accept my judgment; do not reject my **c**.
19:22 nor is there prudence in the **c** of sinners.
21:13 and their **c** like a life-giving spring.
24:29 and her **c** deeper than the great abyss.
25:4 and for the aged to possess good **c**!
25:5 and understanding and **c** in the venerable!
37:7 All counselors praise the **c** they give,
37:7 but some give **c** in their own interest.
37:13 And heed the **c** of your own heart,
37:16 and **c** precedes every undertaking.
39:7 The Lord will direct his **c** and knowledge,
40:25 but good **c** is esteemed more than either.
44:3 those who gave **c** because they were intelligent;
1Mc 2:65 your brother Simeon who, I know, is wise in **c**;
2Es 2:18 to their **c** I have consecrated and prepared
4Mc 6:16 as though more bitterly tormented by this **c**,

COUNSELED (4) [COUNSEL]

2Sa 17:15 and thus and so I have **c**.
17:21 for thus and so has Ahithophel **c** against you."
Job 26:3 How you have **c** one who has no wisdom,
1Mc 9:69 at the renegades who had **c** him to come into

COUNSELING (1) [COUNSEL]

4Mc 8:29 the tyrant had ceased **c** them to eat defiling food,

COUNSELOR (16) [COUNSEL]

2Sa 15:12 he sent for Ahithophel the Gilonite, David's **c**,
1Ch 26:14 a prudent **c**, and his lot came out for the north.
27:32 Jonathan, David's uncle, was a **c**,
27:33 Ahithophel was the king's **c**,
2Ch 22:3 for his mother was his **c** in doing wickedly.
25:16 "Have we made you a royal **c**?
Isa 3:3 **c** and skillful magician and expert enchanter.
9:6 and he is named Wonderful **C**, Mighty God,
40:13 or as his **c** has instructed him?
41:28 among these there is no **c** who, when I ask,
Mic 4:9 Has your **c** perished, that pangs have seized you
Ro 11:34 Or who has been his **c**?"
Sir 37:8 Be wary of a **c**, and learn first what is his interest,
42:21 and he needs no one to be his **c**.
4Mc 9:2 to the law and to Moses our **c**.
9:3 Tyrant and **c** of lawlessness,

COUNSELORS (24) [COUNSEL]

2Ch 22:4 the death of his father they were his **c**, to his ruin.
Ezr 7:14 and his seven **c** to make inquiries about Judah
7:15 and his **c** have freely offered to the God of Israel,
7:28 to me steadfast love before the king and his **c**,
8:25 for the house of our God that the king, his **c**,
Job 3:14 with kings and **c** of the earth who rebuild ruins
12:17 He leads **c** away stripped,
Ps 119:24 Your decrees are my delight, they are my **c**.
Pr 11:14 but in an abundance of **c** there is safety.
24:6 and in abundance of **c** there is victory.
Isa 1:26 and your **c** as at the beginning.
19:11 the wise **c** of Pharaoh give stupid counsel.
Da 3:2 the **c**, the treasurers, the justices, the magistrates,
3:3 the satraps, the prefects, and the governors, the **c**,
3:24 He said to his **c**, "Was it not three men
3:27 and the king's **c** gathered together and saw that
4:36 My **c** and my lords sought me out,
6:7 the **c** and the governors are agreed that
AdE 13:3 I asked my **c** how this might be accomplished,
Sir 37:7 All **c** praise the counsel they give,
1Es 8:11 and the seven Friends who are my **c** have decided,
8:26 the king and his **c** and all his Friends and nobles.
8:55 and his **c** and the nobles and all Israel had given.
4Mc 5:1 sitting in state with his **c** on a certain high place,

COUNSELS‡ (9) [COUNSEL]

Ps 5:10 let them fall by their own **c**;
81:12 to their stubborn hearts, to follow their own **c**.
Jer 7:24 they walked in their own **c**,
Mic 6:16 and you have followed their **c**.
Na 1:11 against the LORD, who **c** wickedness.
Wis 1:9 For inquiry will be made into the **c** of the ungodly,
Sir 44:4 the people by their **c** and by their knowledge of
2Es 1:7 But they have angered me and despised my **c**.
2:1 not listen to them, and made my **c** void.

COUNT (43) [COUNTED, COUNTING, COUNTLESS, COUNTS]

Ge 13:16 so that if one can **c** the dust of the earth,
15:5 "Look toward heaven and **c** the stars, if you are able to **c** them."
Lev 15:13 he shall **c** seven days for his cleansing;
15:28 of her discharge, she shall **c** seven days,
23:15 you shall **c** off seven weeks;
23:16 You shall **c** until the day after the seventh sabbath,
25:8 You shall **c** off seven weeks of years,
Nu 3:40 from a month old and upward, and **c** their names.
23:10 Who can **c** the dust of Jacob,
Dt 16:9 shall **c** seven weeks; begin to **c** the seven weeks
2Sa 24:1 saying, "Go, **c** the people of Israel and Judah."
2Ki 5:18 may the LORD pardon your servant on one **c**:
5:18 the LORD pardon your servant on this one **c**."
22:4 and have him **c** the entire sum of the money
1Ch 9:28 to **c** them when they were brought in
21:1 and incited David to **c** the people of Israel.
21:5 Joab gave the total **c** of the people to David.
21:17 not I who gave the command to **c** the people?
27:23 David did not **c** those below twenty years of age,
27:24 Joab son of Zeruiah began to **c** them,
Job 13:24 and **c** me as your enemy?
19:15 my serving girls **c** me as a stranger;
Ps 22:17 I can **c** all my bones.
48:12 Walk about Zion, go all around it, **c** its towers,
49:18 Though in their lifetime they **c** themselves happy
56:8 You have kept **c** of my tossings;
90:12 to **c** our days that we may gain a wise heart.
119:119 All the wicked of the earth you **c** as dross;
139:18 I try to **c** them—they are more than the sand;
139:22 with perfect hatred; I **c** them my enemies.
Eze 44:26 they shall **c** seven days for him.
Mal 3:12 Then all nations will **c** you happy,
3:15 Now we **c** the arrogant happy;
Ac 20:24 But I do not **c** my life of any value to myself,
2Pe 2:13 They **c** it a pleasure to revel in the daytime.
Rev 7:9 there was a great multitude that no one could **c**,
Wis 15:9 they **c** it a glorious thing to mold counterfeit gods.
18:12 had corpses too many to **c**.
Sir 1:2 of eternity—who can **c** them?
8:12 but if you do lend anything, **c** it as a loss.
2Es 5:36 "**C** up for me those who have not yet come,

COUNTED‡ (44) [COUNT]

Ge 13:16 your offspring also can be **c**.
16:10 that they cannot be **c** for multitude."
30:33 if found with me, shall be **c** stolen."
32:12 which cannot be **c** because of their number.' "
Ex 38:25 congregation who were **c** was one hundred talents
38:26 for everyone who was **c** in the census,
Nu 31:49 "Your servants have **c** the warriors who are
Jdg 6:5 neither they nor their camels could be **c**;
1Sa 13:15 Saul **c** the people who were present with him,
2Sa 2:15 they came forward and were **c** as they passed by,
1Ki 1:21 that my son Solomon and I will be **c** offenders."
3:8 so numerous they cannot be numbered or **c**.
8:5 so many sheep and oxen that they could not be **c**
2Ki 12:10 **c** the money that was found in the house of
1Ch 23:3 The Levites, thirty years old and upward, were **c**,
2Ch 5:6 and oxen that they could not be numbered or **c**.
Ezr 1:8 who **c** them out to Sheshbazzar the prince
8:34 The total was **c** and weighed,
Job 18:3 Why are we **c** as cattle?
34:6 in spite of being right I am **c** a liar;
41:29 Clubs are **c** as chaff; it laughs at the
Ps 40:5 they would be more than can be **c**.
88:4 I am **c** among those who go down to the Pit;
109:7 let his prayer be **c** as sin.
141:2 Let my prayer be **c** as incense before you,
Pr 27:14 rising early in the morning, will be **c** as cursing.
Ecc 1:15 and what is lacking cannot be **c**.
Isa 22:10 You **c** the houses of Jerusalem,
33:18 "Where is the one who **c**?
33:18 Where is the one who **c** the towers?"
Mt 10:30 And even the hairs of your head are all **c**.
Lk 12:7 But even the hairs of your head are all **c**.
22:37 'And he was **c** among the lawless';
Ro 9:8 the children of the promise are **c** as descendants.
2Ti 4:16 May it not be **c** against them!
Tob 9:5 Gabael got up and **c** out to him the money bags,
Jdt 2:20 a multitude that could not be **c**.
5:10 so great a multitude that their race could not be **c**.
Wis 18:1 and **c** them happy for not having suffered,
Sir 42:7 you make a deposit, be sure it is **c** and weighed,
Bar 3:11 that you are **c** among those in Hades?
1Mc 5:30 and saw a large company, which could not be **c**,
1Es 8:64 The whole was **c** and weighed,
2Es 11:11 I **c** its rival wings, and there were eight of them.

COUNTENANCE‡ (21)

Ge 4:5 So Cain was very angry, and his **c** fell.
4:6 "Why are you angry, and why has your **c** fallen?
Nu 6:26 the LORD lift up his **c** upon you,
1Sa 1:18 and her **c** was sad no longer.
Job 9:27 I will put off my sad **c** and be of good cheer,'
14:20 you change their **c**, and send them away.
29:24 and the light of my **c** they did not extinguish.
Ps 10:4 In the pride of their **c** the wicked say,
44:3 and the light of your **c**, for you delighted in them.
80:16 may they perish at the rebuke of your **c**.
89:15 who walk, O LORD, in the light of your **c**;
90:8 our secret sins in the light of your **c**.
Pr 15:13 A glad heart makes a cheerful **c**,
Ecc 7:3 for by sadness of **c** the heart is made glad.
8:1 and the hardness of one's **c** is changed.
Da 8:23 a king of bold **c** shall arise, skilled in intrigue.
Jdt 16:6 of Merari with the beauty of her **c** undid him.
AdE 15:14 my lord, and your **c** is full of grace."
Sir 13:25 heart changes the **c**, either for good or for evil.
2Es 10:25 her **c** flashed like lightning,
15:63 plunder your wealth, and mar the glory of your **c**.

COUNTERATTACKS (1) [ATTACK]

2Mc 5:3 attacks and **c** made on this side and on that,

COUNTERFEIT (2)

2Ti 3:8 of corrupt mind and **c** faith, also oppose the truth.
Wis 15:9 and they count it a glorious thing to mold **c** gods.

COUNTING (8) [COUNT]

Nu 3:22 **c** all the males from a month old and upward,
3:28 **C** all the males, from a month old and upward,
3:34 **c** all the males from a month old and upward,
3:43 a month old and upward, **c** the number of names,
2Co 5:19 not **c** their trespasses against them,
Tob 9:4 For you know that my father must be **c** the days,
10:1 Tobit kept **c** how many days Tobias would need
Jdt 7:2 not **c** the baggage and the foot soldiers handling it,

COUNTLESS (7) [COUNT]

Jdg 7:12 **c** as the sand on the seashore.
2Ch 12: 3 A **c** army came with him from Egypt—
Na 3: 4 Because of the **c** debaucheries of the prostitute,
2Co 11:23 far more imprisonments, with **c** floggings,
Sir 30:15 and a robust body than **c** riches.
3Mc 5:46 with **c** masses of people crowding their way into
6: 5 Sennacherib exulting in his **c** forces,

COUNTRIES (38) [COUNTRY]

2Ki 18:35 among all the gods of the **c** have delivered their **c**
2Ch 20:29 The fear of God came on all the kingdoms of the **c**
Isa 8: 9 be dismayed; listen, all you far **c**;
36:20 among all the gods of these **c** have saved their **c**
Jer 28: 8 pestilence against many **c** and great kingdoms.
Eze 5: 5 in the center of the nations, with **c** all around her.
5: 6 the nations and the **c** all around her,
6: 8 among the nations and be scattered through the **c**.
11:16 and though I scattered them among the **c**,
11:16 for a little while in the **c** where they have gone.
11:17 from the peoples, and assemble you out of the **c**
12:15 among the nations and scatter them through the **c**.
20:23 the nations and disperse them through the **c**,
20:32 "Let us be like the nations, like the tribes of the **c**,
20:34 the **c** where you are scattered, with a mighty hand
20:41 of the **c** where you have been scattered;
22: 4 and a mockery to all the **c**.
22:15 among the nations and disperse you through the **c**,
25: 7 the peoples and will make you perish out of the **c**;
29:12 the land of Egypt a desolation among desolated **c**;
29:12 and disperse them among the **c**.
30: 7 They shall be desolated among other desolated **c**,
30:26 the nations and disperse them throughout the **c**.
32: 9 into **c** you have not known.
34:13 and gather them from the **c**, and will bring them
35:10 "These two nations and these two **c** shall be mine,
36:19 and they were dispersed through the **c**;
36:24 and gather you from all the **c**,
Da 11:40 He shall advance against **c** and pass through like
11:42 He shall stretch out his hand against the **c**,
Zec 10: 9 yet in far **c** they shall remember me,
1Mc 1: 4 He gathered a very strong army and ruled over **c**,
8: 8 the **c** of India, Media,
15:15 with letters to the kings and **c**,
15:19 therefore have decided to write to the kings and **c**
15:23 the **c**, and to Sampsames, and to the Spartans,

COUNTRY‡ (326) [COUNTRIES, COUNTRY'S, COUNTRYSIDE]

A. HILL COUNTRY (118)
HILL COUNTRY OF EPHRAIM See EPHRAIM

Ge 10:30 of Sephar, the hill **c** of the east. A
12: 1 "Go from your **c** and your kindred
12: 8 From there he moved on to the hill **c** on the east A
14: 6 the hill **c** of Seir as far as El-paran on the edge A
14: 7 Kadesh), and subdued all the **c** of the Amalekites,
14:10 fell into them, and the rest fled to the hill **c**. A
24: 4 but will go to my **c** and to my kindred and get
25: 6 from his son Isaac, eastward to the east **c**.
29:26 Laban said, "This is not done in our **c**—
30:25 that I may go to my own home and **c**.
31:21 and set his face toward the hill **c** of Gilead. A
31:23 he caught up with him in the hill **c** of Gilead. A
31:25 Now Jacob had pitched his tent in the hill **c**, A
31:25 and Laban with his kinsfolk camped in the hill **c** A
31:54 they ate bread and tarried all night in the hill **c**. A
32: 3 to his brother Esau in the land of Seir, the **c**
32: 9 'Return to your **c** and to your kindred,
36: 8 Esau settled in the hill **c** of Seir; Esau is Edom. A
36: 9 ancestor of the Edomites, in the hill **c** of Seir. A
36:35 who defeated Midian in the **c** of Moab,
41:54 There was famine in every **c**,
Ex 3: 8 to the **c** of the Canaanites, the Hittites,
8: 2 I will plague your whole **c** with frogs.
10: 4 tomorrow I will bring locusts into your **c**.
10:14 of Egypt and settled on the whole **c** of Egypt,
10:19 not a single locust was left in all the **c** of Egypt.
18:27 and he went off to his own **c**.
Lev 25:31 around them shall be classed as open **c**;
Nu 13:17 and go up into the hill **c**, A
13:29 the Jebusites, and the Amorites live in the hill **c**; A
14:40 and went up to the heights of the hill **c**, A
14:44 presumed to go up to the heights of the hill **c**, A
14:45 Canaanites who lived in that hill **c** came down A
Dt 1: 7 and go into the hill **c** of the Amorites as well as A
1: 7 the Arabah, the hill **c**, the Shephelah, the Negeb, A
1:19 on the way to the hill **c** of the Amorites, A
1:20 "You have reached the hill **c** of the Amorites, A
1:24 They set out and went up into the hill **c**, A
1:41 and thought it easy to go up into the hill **c**. A
1:43 and presumptuously went up into the hill **c**. A
1:44 in that hill **c** then came out against you A
2: 3 "You have been skirting this hill **c** long enough. A
2:37 Wadi Jabbok as well as the towns of the hill **c**, A
3:12 well as half the hill **c** of Gilead with its towns, A
3:25 that good hill **c** and the Lebanon." A
21: 1 a body is found lying in open **c**,
22:25 the man meets the engaged woman in the open **c**,
22:27 Since he found her in the open **c**,
29:22 well as the foreigner who comes from a distant **c**,
Jos 2:16 She said to them, "Go toward the hill **c**, A
2:22 into the hill **c** and stayed there three days, A
2:23 the two men came down again from the hill **c**. A
9: 1 kings who were beyond the Jordan in the hill **c** A
9: 6 "We have come from a far **c**;
9: 9 "Your servants have come from a very far **c**,
9:11 of our **c** said to us, 'Take provisions in your hand
10: 6 the Amorites who live in the hill **c** are gathered A
10:40 the hill **c** and the Negeb and the lowland and A
10:41 and all the **c** of Goshen, as far as Gibeon.
11: 2 and to the kings who were in the northern hill **c**, A
11: 3 the Perizzites, and the Jebusites in the hill **c**, A
11:16 the hill **c** and all the Negeb and all the land A
11:16 lowland and the Arabah and the hill **c** of Israel A
11:21 the hill **c**, from Hebron, from Debir, from Anab, A
11:21 from Anab, and from all the hill **c** of Judah, A
11:21 and from all the hill **c** of Israel; A
12: 8 in the hill **c**, in the lowland, in the Arabah, A
13: 6 of the hill **c** from Lebanon to Misrephoth-maim, A
14:12 So now give me this hill **c** of which A
15:48 And in the hill **c**, Shamir, Jattir, Socoh, A
16: 1 going up from Jericho into the hill **c** to Bethel; A
17:15 the hill **c** of Ephraim is too narrow for you." A
17:16 "The hill **c** is not enough for us; A
17:18 but the hill **c** shall be yours, for though it is A
18:12 then up through the hill **c** westward; A
19:50 Timnath-serah in the hill **c** of Ephraim; A
20: 7 So they set apart Kedesh in Galilee in the hill **c** A
20: 7 and Shechem in the hill **c** of Ephraim, A
20: 7 Hebron) in the hill **c** of Judah. A
21:11 that is Hebron, in the hill **c** of Judah, A
21:21 with its pasture lands in the hill **c** of Ephraim, A
24: 4 I gave Esau the hill **c** of Seir to possess, A
24:30 which is in the hill **c** of Ephraim, A
24:33 which had been given him in the hill **c** A
Jdg 1: 9 against the Canaanites who lived in the hill **c**, A
1:19 and he took possession of the hill **c**, A
1:34 pressed the Danites back into the hill **c**; A
2: 9 in the hill **c** of Ephraim, north of Mount Gaash. A
3:27 he sounded the trumpet in the hill **c** of Ephraim; A
3:27 Israelites went down with him from the hill **c**, A
4: 5 between Ramah and Bethel in the hill **c** A
7:24 throughout all the hill **c** of Ephraim, A
10: 1 who lived at Shamir in the hill **c** of Ephraim, A
11:19 'Let us pass through your land to our **c**.'
11:21 the land of the Amorites, who inhabited that **c**.
12:15 in the hill **c** of the Amalekites. A
16:24 the ravager of our **c**, who has killed many of us."
17: 1 in the hill **c** of Ephraim whose name was Micah. A
17: 8 to the house of Micah in the hill **c** of Ephraim A
18: 2 When they came to the hill **c** of Ephraim, A
18:13 From there they passed on to the hill **c** A
19: 1 in the remote parts of the hill **c** of Ephraim, A
19:16 The man was from the hill **c** of Ephraim, A
19:18 to the remote parts of the hill **c** of Ephraim, A
20:31 as well as in the open **c**,
Ru 1: 1 of Bethlehem in Judah went to live in the **c**
1: 2 They went into the **c** of Moab and remained there.
1: 6 with her daughters-in-law from the **c** of Moab,
1: 6 for she had heard in the **c** of Moab that
1:22 who came back with her from the **c** of Moab.
2: 6 with Naomi from the **c** of Moab.
4: 3 "Naomi, who has come back from the **c** of Moab,
1Sa 1: 1 a Zuphite from the hill **c** of Ephraim, A
6: 1 in the **c** of the Philistines seven months.
9: 4 the hill **c** of Ephraim and passed through A
13: 2 with Saul in Michmash and the hill **c** of Bethel, A
14:22 into hiding in the hill **c** of Ephraim heard that A
14:23 The battle spread out over the hill **c** of Ephraim. A
23:14 in the hill **c** of the Wilderness of Ziph. A
27: 5 let a place be given me in one of the **c** towns,
27: 7 The length of time that David lived in the **c** of
27:11 Such was his practice all the time he lived in the **c**
30:11 In the open **c** they found an Egyptian,
2Sa 10: 8 were by themselves in the open **c**.
15:23 whole **c** wept aloud as all the people passed by;
18: 8 The battle spread over the face of all the **c**;
20:21 But a man of the hill **c** of Ephraim, A
1Ki 4: 8 Ben-hur, in the hill **c** of Ephraim; A
4:19 the **c** of King Sihon of the Amorites and
5:15 and eighty thousand stonecutters in the hill **c**, A
11:21 "Let me depart, that I may go to my own **c**."
11:22 with me that you now seek to go to your own **c**?"
11:29 The two of them were alone in the open **c**
12:25 Jeroboam built Shechem in the hill **c** of Ephraim, A
14:11 and anyone who dies in the open **c**,
20:27 while the Arameans filled the **c**.
21:24 and anyone of his who dies in the open **c** the birds
22:36 "Every man to his city, and every man to his **c**!"
2Ki 3:20 until the **c** was filled with water.
5:22 of prophets have just come to me from the hill **c** A
7:12 the camp to hide themselves in the open **c**,
20:14 "They have come from a far **c**, from Babylon."
1Ch 1:46 who defeated Midian in the **c** of Moab,
6:67 with its pasture lands in the hill **c** of Ephraim, A
8: 8 And Shaharaim had sons in the **c** of Moab
19: 9 by themselves in the open **c**.
20: 1 ravaged the **c** of the Ammonites,
27:25 Over the treasuries in the **c**, in the cities,
2Ch 2: 2 and eighty thousand stonecutters in the hill **c**, A
2:18 eighty thousand as stonecutters in the hill **c**, A
13: 4 slope of Mount Zemaraim that is in the hill **c** A
15: 8 from the towns that he had taken in the hill **c** A
19: 4 from Beer-sheba to the hill **c** of Ephraim, A
21:11 he made high places in the hill **c** of Judah, A
27: 4 Moreover he built cities in the hill **c** of Judah, A
30:10 the couriers went from city to city through the **c**
Est 8:17 many of the peoples of the **c** professed to be Jews,
Ps 105:31 and gnats throughout their **c**.
105:33 and shattered the trees of their **c**.
Pr 25:25 so is good news from a far **c**.
Isa 1: 7 Your **c** lies desolate, your cities are burned
39: 3 "They have come to me from a far **c**,
46:11 the man for my purpose from a far **c**.
Jer 17: 3 on the mountains in the open **c**.
17:26 from the hill **c**, and from the Negeb, A
22:26 and the mother who bore you into another **c**,
31: 6 when sentinels will call in the hill **c** of Ephraim: A
31:17 your children shall come back to their own **c**.
32:44 of the hill **c**, of the Shephelah, and of the Negeb; A
33:13 In the towns of the hill **c**, of the Shephelah, A
40: 7 the forces in the open **c** and their troops heard that
40:13 and all the leaders of the forces in the open **c** came
51: 9 Forsake her, and let each of us go to our own **c**;
Eze 20:42 the **c** that I swore to give to your ancestors.
25: 9 the glory of the **c**, Beth-jeshimoth, Baal-meon,
26: 6 and its daughter-towns in the **c** shall be killed by
26: 8 Your daughter-towns in the **c** he shall put to
48:15 for dwellings and for open **c**.
Hos 10: 1 as his **c** improved, he improved his pillars.
Jnh 1: 8 Where do you come from? What is your **c**?
4: 2 while I was still in my own **c**?
Mic 1: 6 I will make Samaria a heap in the open **c**,
4:10 from the city and camp in the open **c**;
Zec 6: 6 with the black horses goes toward the north **c**,
6: 6 the white ones go toward the west **c**,
6: 6 and the dappled ones go toward the south **c**."
6: 8 those who go toward the north **c** have set my spirit
6: 8 at rest in the north **c**."
8: 7 I will save my people from the east **c** and from
8: 7 from the east country and from the west **c**;
Mal 1: 3 I have made his hill **c** a desolation and A
1: 4 until they are called the wicked **c**,
Mt 2:12 they left for their own **c** by another road.
8:28 to the **c** of the Gadarenes,
13:57 not without honor except in their own **c** and
21:33 Then he leased it to tenants and went to another **c**.
Mk 1:45 but stayed out in the **c**;
5: 1 to the **c** of the Gerasenes.
5:10 not to send them out of the **c**.
5:14 and told it in the city and in the **c**.
6:36 the surrounding **c** and villages and buy something
12: 1 then he leased it to tenants and went to another **c**.
15:21 who was coming in from the **c**, to carry his cross;
16:12 ⟦as they were walking into the **c**.⟧
Lk 1:39 went with haste to a Judean town in the hill **c**, A
1:65 about throughout the entire hill **c** of Judea. A
4:14 about him spread through all the surrounding **c**.
7:17 throughout Judea and all the surrounding **c**.
8:26 Then they arrived at the **c** of the Gerasenes,
8:34 they ran off and told it in the city and in the **c**.
8:37 of the surrounding **c** of the Gerasenes asked Jesus
15:13 and traveled to a distant **c**,
15:14 a severe famine took place throughout that **c**,
15:15 to one of the citizens of that **c**,
19:12 to a distant **c** to get royal power for himself and
19:14 of his **c** hated him and sent a delegation after him,
20: 9 and went to another **c** for a long time.
21:21 and those out in the **c** must not enter it;
23:26 Simon of Cyrene, who was coming from the **c**,
Jn 4:44 a prophet has no honor in the prophet's own **c**).
11:55 and many went up from the **c** to Jerusalem before
Ac 7: 3 'Leave your **c** and your relatives and go to
7: 4 he left the **c** of the Chaldeans and settled in Haran.
7: 4 from there to this **c** in which you are now living.
7: 6 be resident aliens in a **c** belonging to others,
12:20 their **c** depended on the king's **c** for food.
14: 6 cities of Lycaonia, and to the surrounding **c**;
Heb 11:16 it is, they desire a better **c**, that is, a heavenly one.
Tob 1: 4 When I was in my own **c**, in the land of Israel,
1:14 While in the **c** of Media I left bags
Jdt 1: 6 the people of the hill **c** and all those who lived A
2:22 cavalry, and chariots, and went up into the hill **c**. A
2:23 south of the **c** of the Chelleans.
5: 3 what people is this that lives in the hill **c**? A
5:15 the Jordan they took possession of all the hill **c**. A
5:19 and have settled in the hill **c**, A
6: 7 take you back into the hill **c** and put you in one A
6:11 the hill **c** and came to the springs below A
7: 1 to seize the passes up into the hill **c** and make A
7:18 up and encamped in the hill **c** opposite Dothan; A
10:13 by which he can go and capture all the hill **c** A
11: 2 if your people who live in the hill **c** had A
15: 2 across the plain and through the hill **c**. A
15: 5 Those in Jerusalem and all the hill **c** also came, A
15: 7 Even the villages and towns in the hill **c** and in A
16:21 her life she was honored throughout the whole **c**.
AdE 2:10 Now Esther had not disclosed her people or **c**,
2:20 Esther had not disclosed her **c**—
9:19 the **c** outside Susa keep the fourteenth of Adar as
9:27 in every city, family, and **c**.
16:24 "Every city and **c**, without exception,
Sir 8:16 and do not journey with them through lonely **c**,
46: 9 so that he went up to the hill **c**, A
48:18 In his days Sennacherib invaded the **c**;
Bar 3:10 that you are growing old in a foreign **c**,
LtJ 6:53 For they cannot set up a king over a **c** or give rain
1Mc 3:29 that the revenues from the **c** were small because of
7:20 of the **c** and left with him a force to help him;
7:24 in the city from going out into the **c**.
9:24 and the **c** went over to their side.
9:25 the godless and put them in charge of the **c**.
9:61 about fifty of the men of the **c** who were leaders
9:65 while he went out into the **c**;
9:69 to come into the **c**, and he killed many
10:38 that have been added to Judea from the **c**
10:52 I crushed Demetrius and gained control of our **c**;
10:70 assume authority against us in the hill **c**? A

1Mc 11:62 And he passed through the c as far as Damascus.
11:64 but left his brother Simon in the c.
12:25 he gave them no opportunity to invade his own c.
12:33 and marched through the c as far as Askalon and
13:20 this Trypho came to invade the c and destroy it,
13:34 with a request to grant relief to the c,
13:49 from going in and out to buy and sell in the c.
14: 6 and gained full control of the c.
14:17 that he was ruling over the c and the towns in it,
14:28 and the rulers of the nation and the elders of the c,
14:29 "Since wars often occurred in the c, Simon son
14:31 to invade their c and lay hands on their sanctuary,
14:36 so that the Gentiles were put out of the c,
14:37 in it and fortified it for the safety of the c and of
14:42 over its tasks and over the c and the weapons and
14:43 and that all contracts in the c should be written
14:44 an assembly in the c without his permission,
15: 4 to make a landing in the c so that I may proceed
15: 4 against those who have destroyed our c
15: 6 to mint your own coinage as money for your c,
15:19 against them and their cities and their c,
15:21 if any scoundrels have fled to you from their c,
15:38 of the coastal c, and gave him troops of infantry
16: 4 of the c twenty thousand warriors and cavalry,
16:13 he determined to get control of the c,
16:14 the towns of the c and attending to their needs,
16:18 and to turn over to him the towns and the c.
2Mc 4: 1 about the money against his own c,
5: 7 and fled again into the c of the Ammonites.
5: 8 as the executioner of his c and his compatriots,
5: 9 There he who had driven many from their own c
5:15 a traitor both to the laws and to his c.
8:21 to die for their laws and their c;
8:35 across the c until he reached Antioch,
9:23 when he made expeditions into the upper c,
13:10 the point of being deprived of the law and their c
13:14 temple, city, c, and commonwealth,
14: 2 and had taken possession of the c,
14: 9 may it please you to take thought for our c
14:18 and their courage in battle for their c,
15:19 being anxious over the encounter in the open c.
1Es 4:20 and his own c, and clings to his wife.
4:21 of his father or his mother or his c.
4:50 the c that they would occupy should be theirs
6: 8 to the c of Judea and entered the city of Jerusalem,
6:17 But in the first year that Cyrus reigned over the c
6:23 in Ecbatana, the fortress that is in the c of Media,
8:13 the gold and silver that may be found in the c
9:37 and the Israelites settled in Jerusalem and in the c.
3Mc 4:11 and to those from the city going out into the c,
4:18 the c, some still residing in their homes, and some
6: 1 famous among the priests of the c,
2Es 1: 3 in the c of the Medes in the reign of Artaxerxes,
5:11 One c shall ask its neighbor, 'Has righteousness,
13:45 and that c is called Arzareth.
15:57 and all your people who are in the open c shall fall
4Mc 4: 1 he fled the c with the purpose of betraying it.
4: 5 to our c accompanied by the accursed Simon and

COUNTRY'S (2) [COUNTRY]

2Mc 13: 3 not for the sake of his c welfare,
3Mc 6:25 those who faithfully kept our c fortresses,

COUNTRYSIDE (10) [COUNTRY]

Jer 13:27 your shameless prostitutions on the hills of the c.
Eze 27:28 At the sound of the cry of your pilots the c shakes,
Mk 1: 5 And people from the whole Judean c and all
Lk 9:12 they may go into the surrounding villages and c,
Jn 3:22 this Jesus and his disciples went into the Judean c,
Ac 8: 1 the apostles were scattered throughout the c
26:20 then in Jerusalem and throughout the c of Judea,
Jdt 3: 7 in the c welcomed him with garlands and dances
AdE 9:12 suppose they have done in the surrounding c?
3Mc 3: 1 was still more bitterly hostile toward those in the c;

COUNTS (7) [COUNT]

Job 19:11 and c me as his adversary.
33:10 he c me as his enemy;
41:27 It c iron as straw, and bronze as rotten wood.
Jer 33:13 under the hands of the one who c them,
Gal 5: 6 nor uncircumcision c for anything;
5: 6 the only thing that c is faith working through love.
Wis 14:30 But just penalties will overtake them on two c:

COUPLE (5)

Jdg 19: 3 He had with him his servant and a c of donkeys.
19:10 He had with him a c of saddled donkeys,
2Sa 13: 6 "Please let my sister Tamar come and make a c
16: 1 with a c of donkeys saddled,
1Ki 17:12 I am now gathering a c of sticks,

COURAGE (70) [COURAGEOUS, COURAGEOUSLY]

Jos 2:11 there was no c left in any of us because of you.
Jdg 20:22 The Israelites took c, and again formed
1Sa 4: 9 Take c, and be men, O Philistines,
2Sa 4: 1 his c failed, and all Israel was dismayed.
7:27 therefore your servant has found c
1Ch 22:13 Be strong and of good c.
28:20 "Be strong and of good c, and act.
2Ch 15: 7 But you, take c! Do not let your hands be weak,
15: 8 the prophecy of Azariah son of Oded, he took c,
23: 1 But in the seventh year Jehoiada took c,
25:11 Amaziah took c, and led out his people;
32: 7 "Be strong and of good c.
Ezr 7:28 I took c, for the hand of the LORD my God was
Ps 27:14 be strong, and let your heart take c;
31:24 Be strong, and let your heart take c,
107:26 their c melted away in their calamity;
Isa 41: 6 saying to one another, "Take c!"
Jer 4: 9 c shall fail the king and the officials;
La 1:16 a comforter is far from me, one to revive my c;
Eze 22:14 Can your c endure, or can your hands remain
Hag 2: 4 Yet now take c, O Zerubbabel, says the LORD;
2: 4 take c, O Joshua, son of Jehozadak,
2: 4 take c, all you people of the land,
Jn 16:33 But take c; I have conquered the world!"
Ac 23:11 near him and said, "Keep up your c!
27:22 I urge you now to keep up your c,
27:25 up your c, men, for I have faith in God that it will
28:15 On seeing them, Paul thanked God and took c.
1Th 2: 2 we had c in our God to declare to you the gospel
Tob 5:10 But the young man said, "Take c;
5:10 for God to heal you; take c."
7:16 wiping away the tears, she said to her, "Take c,
7:16 in place of your sorrow. Take c,
8:21 when my wife and I die. Take c,
8:21 to your wife now and forever. Take c,
11:11 he blew into his eyes, saying, "Take c, father."
Jdt 7:19 to the Lord their God, for their c failed,
7:30 Uzziah said to them, "C, my brothers and sisters!
11: 1 Then Holofernes said to her, "Take c, woman,
11: 3 you have come to safety. Take c!
AdE 14:12 in this time of our affliction, and give me c,
15: 9 "What is it, Esther? I am your husband. Take c;
Wis 8: 7 and prudence, justice and c;
Sir 45:23 in the noble c of his soul;
Bar 4: 5 Take c, my people, who perpetuate Israel's name!
4:21 Take c, my children, cry to God,
4:27 Take c, my children, and cry to God,
4:30 Take c, O Jerusalem, for the one who named you
LtJ 6:59 So it is better to be a king who shows his c,
1Mc 11:49 their c failed and they cried out to the king
2Mc 6:20 as all ought to go who have the c to refuse things
6:31 an example of nobility and a memorial of c,
7:20 she bore it with good c because of her hope in
7:21 reinforced her woman's reasoning with a man's c,
8:21 with c and made them ready to die for their laws
14:18 of the valor of Judas and his troops and their c
15:10 When he had aroused their c, he issued his orders,
15:17 and so effective in arousing valor and awaking c
15:17 the matter by fighting hand to hand with all c,
2Es 12:46 "Take c, O Israel; and do
4Mc 1: 4 and those that stand in the way of c,
1: 6 but those that are opposed to justice, c,
1:11 marveled at their c and endurance,
1:18 kinds of wisdom are rational judgment, justice, c,
5:23 and it also trains us in c,
13:11 While one said, "C, brother," another said,
15:23 a man's c in the very midst of her emotions,
17: 2 and showed the c of your faith!
17: 4 Take c, therefore, O holy-minded mother,
17:23 the c of their virtue and their endurance under

COURAGEOUS (28) [COURAGE]

Jos 1: 6 Be strong and c; for you shall put this people in
1: 7 Only be strong and very c,
1: 9 I hereby command you: Be strong and c;
1:18 Only be strong and c."
10:25 or dismayed; be strong and c;
Jdg 20:44 Eighteen thousand Benjaminites fell, all of them c
20:46 arms-bearing men, all of them c fighters.
2Sa 10:12 and let us be c for the sake of our people,
13:28 not myself commanded you? Be c and valiant."
1Ki 2: 2 to go the way of all the earth. Be strong, be c,
1Ch 19:13 be c for our people and for the cities of our God;
2Ch 17: 6 His heart was c in the ways of the LORD;
Da 10:19 you are safe. Be strong and c!"
1Co 16:13 Keep alert, stand firm in your faith, be c,
Wis 8:15 the people I shall show myself capable, and c
1Mc 2:64 My children, be c and grow strong in the law,
3:58 And Judas said, "Arm yourselves and be c.
3Mc 2:32 with a c spirit and did not abandon their religion;
4Mc 2:23 a kingdom that is temperate, just, good, and c.
6: 5 But the c and noble man, like a true Eleazar,
6:11 he amazed even his torturers by his c spirit.
6:24 When they saw that he was so c in the face of
7:23 only the wise and c are masters of their emotions.
9:21 the c youth, worthy of Abraham, did not groan,
9:23 in my struggle or renounce our c family ties.
9:26 While all were marveling at his c spirit,
15:30 and more c than men in endurance!
17:24 and this made them brave and c for infantry battle

COURAGEOUSLY (6) [COURAGE]

2Ch 19:11 Deal c, and may the LORD be with the good!"
1Mc 6:31 and burned these with fire, and fought c.
6:45 He c ran into the midst of the phalanx to reach it;
2Mc 7:10 and c stretched forth his hands,
14:43 He c ran up on the wall,
3Mc 1:23 to their compatriots to take arms and die c for

COURIERS (8)

2Ch 30: 6 So c went throughout all Israel and Judah
30:10 the c went from city to city through the country
Est 3:13 Letters were sent by c to all the king's provinces,
3:15 The c went quickly by order of the king,
8:10 by mounted c riding on fast steeds bred from
8:14 So the c, mounted on their swift royal steeds,
AdE 3:13 by c throughout all the empire of Artaxerxes
8:10 and sealed with his ring, and sent out by c.

COURSE (37) [COURSES, MIDCOURSE, WATERCOURSES]

Ge 4: 3 In the c of time Cain brought to the LORD
38:12 In c of time the wife of Judah, Shua's daughter,
1Sa 28: 1 Achish said to David, "You know, of c,
2Sa 14:20 the c of affairs your servant Joab did this.
1Ki 6:36 with three courses of dressed stone to one c
2Ch 21:19 In c of time, at the end of two years,
Ezr 6: 4 with three courses of hewn stones and one c
Job 1: 5 And when the feast days had run their c,
6:18 The caravans turn aside from their c;
Ps 19: 5 and like a strong man runs its c with joy.
Isa 3:12 and confuse the c of your paths.
Jer 2:33 How well you direct your c to seek lovers!
8: 6 All of them turn to their own c,
23:10 Their c has been evil, and their might is not right.
Joel 2: 7 Each keeps to its own c, they do not swerve from
Jn 3:24 John, of c, had not yet been thrown into prison.
7:22 Moses gave you circumcision (it is, of c,
Ac 16:11 from Troas and took a straight c to Samothrace,
20:24 if only I may finish my c and the ministry
21: 1 we came by a straight c to Cos,
Eph 2: 2 following the c of this world,
1Ti 6: 6 Of c, there is great gain in godliness combined
Heb 6:16 of c, swear by someone greater than themselves,
AdE 1: 4 during the c of one hundred eighty days,
Wis 6:22 I will trace her c from the beginning of creation,
14: 3 O Father, that steers its c,
18:14 and night in its swift c was now half gone,
Sir 19:17 and let the law of the Most High take its c.
43: 5 at his orders it hurries on its c.
43: 7 a light that wanes when it completes its c.
1Es 4:34 and heaven is high, and the sun is swift in its c,
6:25 of hewn stone and one c of new native timber;
2Es 5:47 "Of c it cannot, but only each in its own time."
8: 2 so is the c of the present world.
4Mc 1: 2 I mean, of c, rational judgment.
6:18 we should now change our c
14: 5 as though running the c toward immortality,

COURSES (8) [COURSE]

Jdg 5:20 from their c they fought against Sisera.
1Ki 6:36 the inner court with three c of dressed stone
7:12 The great court had three c of dressed stone
Ezr 6: 4 with three c of hewn stones and one course
6:18 and the Levites in their c for the service of God
SS 4: 4 Your neck is like the tower of David, built in c;
1Es 6:25 with three c of hewn stone and one course
4Mc 15: 2 Two c were open to this mother, that of religion,

COURT‡ (144) [COURTIERS, COURTS, COURTYARD, COURTYARDS, FORECOURT]

Ex 27: 9 You shall make the c of the tabernacle.
27: 9 On the south side the c shall have hangings
27:12 of the c on the west side there shall be fifty cubits
27:13 the c on the front to the east shall be fifty cubits.
27:16 of the c there shall be a screen twenty cubits long,
27:17 All the pillars around the c shall be banded
27:18 The length of the c shall be one hundred cubits,
27:19 and all its pegs and all the pegs of the c,
35:17 of the c, its pillars and its bases, and the screen for the gate of the c;
35:18 the pegs of the tabernacle and the pegs of the c,
38: 9 made the c; for the south side the hangings of the c
38:15 the gate of the c were hangings of fifteen cubits,
38:16 around the c were of fine twisted linen.
38:17 and all the pillars of the c were banded with silver.
38:18 to the c was embroidered with needlework in blue,
38:18 corresponding to the hangings of the c.
38:20 for the tabernacle and for the c all around were
38:31 all around the c, and the bases of the gate of the c,
38:31 and all the pegs around the c.
39:40 the hangings of the c, its pillars, and its bases, and the screen for the gate of the c,
40: 8 You shall set up the c all around,
40: 8 and hang up the screen for the gate of the c.
40:33 He set up the c around the tabernacle and the altar,
40:33 and put up the screen at the gate of the c.
Lev 6:16 in the c of the tent of meeting they shall eat it.
6:26 in the c of the tent of meeting.
Nu 3:26 of the c, the screen for the entrance of the c that is
3:37 also the pillars of the c all around,
4:26 the c, and the screen for the entrance of the gate
4:26 of the c that is around the tabernacle and the altar,
4:32 and the pillars of the c all around with their bases,
1Ki 6:36 the inner c with three courses of dressed stone
7: 8 in the other c back of the hall,
7: 9 and from outside to the great c.
7:12 The great c had three courses of dressed stone
7:12 so had the inner c of the house of the LORD,
8:64 the c that was in front of the house of the LORD;
2Ki 20: 4 Before Isaiah had gone out of the middle c,
2Ch 4: 9 He made the c of the priests, and the great c, and doors for the c;
6:13 and three cubits high, and had set it in the c;
7: 7 the c that was in front of the house of the LORD;
20: 5 in the house of the LORD, before the new c,
24:21 of the king they stoned him to death in the c of
29:16 in the temple of the LORD into the c of the house
Ne 3:25 the upper house of the king at the c of the guard.

Est 1: 5 in the **c** of the garden of the king's palace.
2:11 around in front of the **c** of the harem,
4:11 to the king inside the inner **c** without being called,
5: 1 on her royal robes and stood in the inner **c** of
5: 2 as the king saw Queen Esther standing in the **c**,
6: 4 The king said, "Who is in the **c**?"
6: 4 Now Haman had just entered the outer **c** of
6: 5 "Haman is there, standing in the **c**."
Pr 25: 8 do not hastily bring into **c**;
Jer 19:14 he stood in the **c** of the LORD's house and said
26: 2 Stand in the **c** of the LORD's house,
29: 2 the **c** officials, the leaders of Judah and Jerusalem,
32: 2 and the prophet Jeremiah was confined in the **c** of
32: 8 the **c** of the guard, in accordance with the word of
32:12 the Judeans who were sitting in the **c** of the guard.
33: 1 while he was still confined in the **c** of the guard:
36:10 which was in the upper **c**,
36:20 they went to the **c** of the king;
37:21 they committed Jeremiah to the **c** of the guard;
37:21 So Jeremiah remained in the **c** of the guard.
38: 6 the king's son, which was in the **c** of the guard,
38:13 And Jeremiah remained in the **c** of the guard.
38:28 And Jeremiah remained in the **c** of the guard until
39:14 and took Jeremiah from the **c** of the guard.
39:15 to Jeremiah while he was confined in the **c** of
Eze 8: 3 of the gateway of the inner **c** that faces north,
8: 7 And he brought me to the entrance of the **c**;
8:16 And he brought me into the inner **c** of the house of
10: 3 and a cloud filled the inner **c**.
10: 4 with the cloud, and the **c** was full of the brightness
10: 5 of the cherubim was heard as far as the outer **c**,
40:14 the gate next to the pilaster on every side of the **c**.
40:17 Then he brought me into the outer **c**;
40:17 and a pavement, all around the **c**;
40:19 of the lower gate to the outer front of the inner **c**,
40:20 Then he measured the gate of the outer **c**
40:23 as on the east, was a gate to the inner **c**;
40:27 There was a gate on the south of the inner **c**;
40:28 he brought me to the inner **c** by the south gate,
40:31 Its vestibule faced the outer **c**,
40:32 Then he brought me to the inner **c** on the east side,
40:34 Its vestibule faced the outer **c**,
40:37 Its vestibule faced the outer **c**,
40:44 for the singers in the inner **c**,
40:47 He measured the **c**, one hundred cubits deep,
41:10 of the **c** was a width of twenty cubits all around
42: 1 Then he led me out into the outer **c**,
42: 3 the twenty cubits that belonged to the inner **c**,
42: 3 facing the pavement that belonged to the outer **c**,
42: 6 they had no pillars like the pillars of the outer **c**;
42: 7 toward the outer **c**, opposite the chambers,
42: 8 the chambers on the outer **c** were fifty cubits long,
42: 9 the east in order to enter them from the outer **c**.
42:10 width of the passage is fixed by the wall of the **c**.
42:14 into the outer **c** without laying there the vestments
43: 5 and brought me into the inner **c**;
44:17 When they enter the gates of the inner **c**,
44:17 while they minister at the gates of the inner **c**,
44:19 When they go out into the outer **c** to the people,
44:21 when he enters the inner **c**.
44:27 into the inner **c**, to minister in the holy place,
45:19 and the posts of the gate of the inner **c**.
46: 1 the inner **c** that faces east shall remain closed on
46:20 in order not to bring them out into the outer **c** and
46:21 Then he brought me out to the outer **c**,
46:21 and led me past the four corners of the **c**;
46:21 and in each corner of the **c** there was a **c**—
46:22 in the four corners of the **c** were small courts,
Da 1: 5 that time they could be stationed in the king's **c**.
1:19 therefore they were stationed in the king's **c**.
2:49 But Daniel remained at the king's **c**.
7:10 The **c** sat in judgment, and the books were opened.
7:26 Then the **c** shall sit in judgment,
Mt 5:25 with your accuser while you are on the way to **c**
Ac 8:27 a **c** official of the Candace,
13: 1 Manaen a member of the **c** of Herod the ruler,
1Co 4: 3 that I should be judged by you or by any human **c**.
6: 1 do you dare to take it to **c** before the unrighteous,
6: 6 but a believer goes to **c** against a believer—
Jas 2: 6 Is it not they who drag you into **c**?
Rev 11: 2 but do not measure the **c** outside the temple;
AdE 3: 2 all who were at **c** used to do obeisance to Haman,
4:11 to the king inside the inner **c** without being called,
7: 4 Our antagonist brings shame on the king's **c**."
11: 3 a great man, serving in the **c** of the king.
12: 5 And the king ordered Mordecai to serve in the **c**,
Sir 50:11 he made the **c** of the sanctuary glorious.
Sus 1:49 to **c**, for these men have given false evidence
1Mc 9:54 down the wall of the inner **c** of the sanctuary.
1Es 9: 1 and went from the **c** of the temple to the chamber
4Mc 5: 4 and known to many in the tyrant's **c** because

COURTEOUS (KJV) See HUMBLE

COURTESIES (2) [COURTESY]

Sir 6: 5 and a gracious tongue multiplies **c**.
20:13 but the **c** of fools are wasted.

COURTESY (1) [COURTESIES]

Tit 3: 2 to be gentle, and to show every **c** to everyone.

COURTIERS (5) [COURT]

1Sa 8:14 and olive orchards and give them to his **c**.
8:15 and give it to his officers and his **c**.
Mk 6:21 a banquet for his **c** and officers and for the leaders
AdE 3: 3 Then the king's **c** said to Mordecai, "Mordecai,
2Mc 9:29 And Philip, one of his **c**, took his body home;

COURTS (28) [COURT]

2Ki 21: 5 of heaven in the two **c** of the house of the LORD.
23:12 that Manasseh had made in the two **c** of the house
1Ch 23:28 having the care of the **c** and the chambers,
28: 6 and my **c**, for I have chosen him to be a son
28:12 for the **c** of the house of the LORD,
2Ch 23: 5 and all the people shall be in the **c** of the house of
33: 5 of heaven in the two **c** of the house of the LORD.
Ne 8:16 in their **c** and in the **c** of the house of God,
13: 7 preparing a room for him in the **c** of the house
Ps 65: 4 and bring near to live in your **c**.
84: 2 indeed it faints for the **c** of the LORD;
84:10 day in your **c** is better than a thousand elsewhere.
92:13 they flourish in the **c** of our God.
96: 8 bring an offering, and come into his **c**.
100: 4 with thanksgiving, and his **c** with praise.
116:19 in the **c** of the house of the LORD,
135: 2 in the **c** of the house of our God.
Isa 1:12 from your hand? Trample my **c** no more;
62: 9 and those who gather it shall drink it in my holy **c**.
Eze 9: 7 "Defile the house, and fill the **c** with the slain.
46:22 in the four corners of the court were small **c**,
46:23 around each of the four **c** was a row of masonry,
Zec 3: 7 you shall rule my house and have charge of my **c**,
Ac 19:38 the **c** are open, and there are proconsuls;
Sir 38:33 nor do they understand the decisions of the **c**;
1Mc 4:38 In the **c** they saw bushes sprung up as in a thicket,
4:48 the interior of the temple, and consecrated the **c**.

COURTYARD (30) [COURT, YARD]

2Sa 17:18 who had a well in his **c**;
Mt 26:58 as far as the **c** of the high priest;
26:69 Now Peter was sitting outside in the **c**.
Mk 14:54 right into the **c** of the high priest;
14:66 While Peter was below in the **c**,
15:16 soldiers led him into the **c** of the palace (that is,
Lk 22:55 a fire in the middle of the **c** and sat down together,
Jn 18:15 he went with Jesus into the **c** of the high priest,
Tob 2: 9 into my **c** and slept by the wall of the **c**;
3:17 At the same time that Tobit returned from the **c**
7: 1 where they found him sitting beside the **c** door.
11:10 up and came stumbling out through the **c** door.
AdE 1: 5 for six days in the **c** of the royal palace,
2:11 every day Mordecai walked in the **c** of the harem,
2:19 Meanwhile Mordecai was serving in the **c**.
4: 2 because no one was allowed to enter the **c** clothed
5: 9 But when he saw Mordecai the Jew in the **c**,
5:13 as long as I see Mordecai the Jew in the **c**."
6: 4 by Mordecai, Haman was in the **c**.
6: 4 The king asked, "Who is in the **c**?"
6: 5 "Haman is standing in the **c**."
6:10 who is on duty in the **c**.
6:12 Then Mordecai returned to the **c**,
12: 1 Now Mordecai took his rest in the **c** with Gabatha
12: 1 two eunuchs of the king who kept watch in the **c**.
2Mc 14:41 the tower and were forcing the door of the **c**,
3Mc 2:27 a stone on the tower in the **c** with this inscription:
5:10 at the **c** early in the morning to report to the king
5:46 entered at about dawn into the **c**—

COURTYARDS (1) [COURT, YARD]

Ex 8:13 the frogs died in the houses, the **c**, and the fields.

COUSIN (6)

Est 2: 7 his **c**, for she had neither father nor mother;
Jer 32: 8 Then my **c** Hanamel came to me in the court of
32: 9 the field at Anathoth from my **c** Hanamel,
32:12 in the presence of my **c** Hanamel,
Col 4:10 as does Mark the **c** of Barnabas,
Tob 9: 6 for I see in Tobias the very image of my **c** Tobit."

COVENANT‡ (382) [COVENANTED, COVENANTS]

A. ARK OF THE/HIS/OUR COVENANT (58)
B. MY COVENANT (56)
C. COVENANT OF THE †LORD (38)
D. HIS COVENANT (21)
E. YOUR COVENANT (11)
F. NEW COVENANT (8)
G. BOOK OF THE COVENANT (6)

Ge 6:18 But I will establish my **c** with you; B
9: 9 I am establishing my **c** with you B
9:11 I establish my **c** with you, B
9:12 the sign of the **c** that I make between me and you
9:13 and it shall be a sign of the **c** between me and
9:15 I will remember my **c** that is between me and B
9:16 and remember the everlasting **c** between God
9:17 "This is the sign of the **c** that I have established
15:18 On that day the LORD made a **c** with Abram,
17: 2 And I will make my **c** between me and you, B
17: 4 this is my **c** with you: B
17: 7 I will establish my **c** between me and you, B
17: 7 throughout their generations, for an everlasting **c**,
17: 9 "As for you, you shall keep my **c**, B
17:10 This is my **c**, which you shall keep, B
17:11 and it shall be a sign of the **c** between me and you.
17:13 So shall my **c** be in your flesh B
17:13 be in your flesh an everlasting **c**.
17:14 from his people; he has broken my **c**." B
17:19 I will establish my **c** with him as B
17:19 as an everlasting **c** for his offspring after him
17:21 But my **c** I will establish with Isaac, B
21:27 and the two men made a **c**.
21:32 When they had made a **c** at Beer-sheba,
26:28 between you and us, and let us make a **c** with you
31:44 Come now, let us make a **c**, you and I;
Ex 2:24 God remembered his **c** with Abraham, Isaac, D
6: 4 I also established my **c** with them, B
6: 5 and I have remembered my **c**. B
16:34 so Aaron placed it before the **c**, for safekeeping.
19: 5 therefore, if you obey my voice and keep my **c**, B
23:32 You shall make no **c** with them and their gods.
24: 7 Then he took the book of the **c**, G
24: 8 "See the blood of the **c** that the LORD has made
25:16 into the ark the **c** that I shall give you.
25:21 in the ark you shall put the **c** that I shall give you.
25:22 the two cherubim that are on the ark of the **c**, A
26:33 and bring the ark of the **c** in there, A
26:34 You shall put the mercy seat on the ark of the **c** A
27:21 outside the curtain that is before the **c**,
30: 6 of the curtain that is above the ark of the **c**, A
30: 6 in front of the mercy seat that is over the **c**,
30:26 the tent of meeting and the ark of the **c**, A
30:36 the **c** in the tent of meeting where I shall meet
31: 7 the tent of meeting, and the ark of the **c**, A
31:16 throughout their generations, as a perpetual **c**.
31:18 he gave him the two tablets of the **c**,
32:15 carrying the two tablets of the **c** in his hands,
34:10 He said: I hereby make a **c**.
34:12 Take care not to make a **c** with the inhabitants of
34:15 You shall not make a **c** with the inhabitants of
34:27 in accordance with these words I have made a **c**
34:28 And he wrote on the tablets the words of the **c**,
34:29 from the mountain with the two tablets of the **c**
38:21 the **c**, which were drawn up at the commandment
39:35 the ark of the **c** with its poles and the mercy seat; A
40: 3 You shall put in it the ark of the **c**, A
40: 5 for incense before the ark of the **c**, A
40:20 He took the **c** and put it into the ark,
40:21 and screened the ark of the **c**; A
Lev 2:13 not omit from your grain offerings the salt of the **c**
16:13 the mercy seat that is upon the **c**,
24: 3 outside the curtain of the **c**,
24: 8 of the people of Israel, as a **c** forever.
26: 9 and I will maintain my **c** with you. B
26:15 all my commandments, and you break my **c**, B
26:25 executing vengeance for the **c**;
26:42 then will I remember my **c** with Jacob; B
26:42 also my **c** with Isaac and also my covenant B
26:42 also my covenant with Isaac and also my **c** B
26:44 destroy them utterly and break my **c** with them; B
26:45 the **c** with their ancestors whom I brought out of
Nu 1:50 the tabernacle of the **c**, and over all its equipment,
1:53 the tabernacle of the **c**, that there may be no wrath
1:53 the guard duty of the tabernacle of the **c**.
4: 5 and cover the ark of the **c** with it; A
7:89 the mercy seat that was on the ark of the **c** A
9:15 the cloud covered the tabernacle, the tent of the **c**;
10:11 the cloud lifted from over the tabernacle of the **c**.
10:33 with the ark of the **c** of the LORD going AC
14:44 even though the ark of the **c** of the LORD, AC
17: 4 Place them in the tent of meeting before the **c**,
17: 7 the staffs before the LORD in the tent of the **c**.
17: 8 Moses went into the tent of the **c** on the next day,
17:10 "Put back the staff of Aaron before the **c**,
18: 2 with you are in front of the tent of the **c**.
18:19 it is a **c** of salt forever before the LORD for you
25:12 say, 'I hereby grant him my **c** of peace. B
25:13 be for him and for his descendants after him a **c**
Dt 4:13 He declared to you his **c**, which he charged you D
4:23 not to forget the **c** that the LORD your God made
4:31 not forget the **c** with your ancestors that he swore
5: 2 The LORD our God made a **c** with us at Horeb.
5: 3 with our ancestors did the LORD make this **c**,
7: 2 Make no **c** with them and show them no mercy.
7: 9 the faithful God who maintains **c** loyalty
7:12 the **c** loyalty that he swore to your ancestors;
8:18 so that he may confirm his **c** that he swore D
9: 9 tablets of the **c** that the LORD made with you,
9:11 the two stone tablets, the tablets of the **c**.
9:15 the two tablets of the **c** were in my two hands.
10: 8 of Levi to carry the ark of the **c** of the LORD AC
17: 2 of the LORD your God, and transgresses his **c** D
29: 1 the **c** that the LORD commanded Moses to make
29: 1 in addition to the **c** that he had made with them
29: 9 Therefore diligently observe the words of this **c**,
29:12 to enter into the **c** of the LORD your God, sworn C
29:14 I am making this **c**, sworn by an oath,
29:21 the curses of the **c** written in this book of the law.
29:25 "It is because they abandoned the **c** of the LORD, C
31: 9 who carried the ark of the **c** of the LORD, AC
31:16 breaking my **c** that I have made with them. B
31:20 despising me and breaking my **c**. B
31:25 who carried the ark of the **c** of the LORD, AC
31:26 beside the ark of the **c** of the LORD your God; AC
33: 9 For they observed your word, and kept your **c**. E
Jos 3: 3 see the ark of the **c** of the LORD your God AC
3: 6 "Take up the ark of the **c**, A
3: 6 the ark of the **c** and went in front of the people. A
3: 8 the priests who bear the ark of the **c**, A
3:11 the ark of the **c** of the Lord of all the earth A
3:14 the priests bearing the ark of the **c** were in front A
3:17 ark of the **c** of the LORD stood on dry ground AC
4: 7 cut off in front of the ark of the **c** of the LORD AC
4: 9 of the priests bearing the ark of the **c** had stood; A
4:16 "Command the priests who bear the ark of the **c**, A
4:18 the ark the **c** of the LORD came up from the AC

Jos 6: 6 "Take up the ark of the **c**, A
6: 8 the ark of the **c** of the LORD following them. AC
7: 11 they have transgressed my **c** that I imposed B
7: 15 for having transgressed the **c** of the LORD, C
8: 33 who carried the ark of the **c** of the LORD, AC
23: 16 If you transgress the **c** of the LORD your God, C
24: 25 So Joshua made a **c** with the people that day,
Jdg 2: 1 I said, 'I will never break my **c** with you. B
2: 2 do not make a **c** with the inhabitants of this land;
2: 20 "Because this people have transgressed my **c** B
20: 27 the LORD (for the ark of the **c** of God was there A
1Sa 4: 3 the ark of the **c** of the LORD here from Shiloh, AC
4: 4 there the ark of the **c** of the LORD of hosts, AC
4: 4 were there with the ark of the **c** of God. A
4: 5 ark of the **c** of the LORD came into the camp, AC
18: 3 Then Jonathan made a **c** with David,
20: 8 for you have brought your servant into a sacred **c**
20: 16 Thus Jonathan made a **c** with the house of David,
23: 18 the two of them made a **c** before the LORD;
2Sa 3: 12 does the land belong? Make your **c** with me, E
3: 13 He said, "Good; I will make a **c** with you.
3: 21 in order that they may make a **c** with you,
5: 3 and King David made a **c** with them at Hebron
15: 24 carrying the ark of the **c** of God. A
23: 5 For he has made with me an everlasting **c**,
1Ki 3: 15 he stood before the ark of the **c** of the LORD. AC
6: 19 to set there the ark of the **c** of the LORD. AC
8: 1 to bring up the ark of the **c** of the LORD out of AC
8: 6 the priests brought the ark of the **c** of the LORD AC
8: 9 where the LORD made a **c** with the Israelites,
8: 21 in which is the **c** of the LORD that he made C
8: 23 keeping **c** and steadfast love
8: 24 **c** that you kept for your servant my father David
11: 11 and you have not kept my **c** and my statutes B
19: 10 for the Israelites have forsaken your **c**, E
19: 14 for the Israelites have forsaken your **c**, E
2Ki 11: 4 He made a **c** with them and put them under oath in
11: 12 put the crown on him, and gave him the **c**;
11: 17 a **c** between the LORD and the king and people,
13: 23 because of his **c** with Abraham, Isaac, and Jacob, D
17: 15 and his **c** that he made with their ancestors, D
17: 35 a **c** with them and commanded them,
17: 38 not forget the **c** that I have made with you.
18: 12 of the LORD their God but transgressed his **c**— D
23: 2 words of the book of the **c** that had been found G
23: 3 The king stood by the pillar and made a **c** before
23: 3 the words of this **c** that were written in this book.
23: 3 All the people joined in the **c**.
23: 21 as prescribed in this book of the **c**." G
1Ch 11: 3 and David made a **c** with them at Hebron before
15: 25 the ark of the **c** of the LORD from the house AC
15: 26 were carrying the ark of the **c** of the LORD, AC
15: 28 up the ark of the **c** of the LORD with shouting, AC
15: 29 the ark of the **c** of the LORD came to the city AC
16: 6 before the ark of the **c** of God. A
16: 15 Remember his **c** forever, the word D
16: 16 the **c** that he made with Abraham,
16: 17 to Israel as an everlasting **c**,
16: 37 ark of the **c** of the LORD to minister regularly AC
17: 1 the ark of the **c** of the LORD is under a tent." AC
22: 19 ark of the **c** of the LORD and the holy vessels AC
28: 2 the ark of the **c** of the LORD, for the footstool AC
28: 18 and covered the ark of the **c** of the LORD. AC
2Ch 5: 2 to bring up the ark of the **c** of the LORD out of AC
5: 7 the priests brought the ark of the **c** of the LORD AC
5: 10 a **c** with the people of Israel after they came out
6: 11 in which is the **c** of the LORD that he made with C
6: 14 keeping **c** in steadfast love
7: 18 as I made **c** with your father David saying,
13: 5 over Israel forever to David and his sons by a **c**
15: 12 They entered into a **c** to seek the LORD,
21: 7 not destroy the house of David because of the **c**
23: 3 Then the whole assembly made a **c** with the king
23: 11 put the crown on him, and gave him the **c**;
23: 16 Jehoiada made a **c** between himself and all
24: 6 the congregation of Israel for the tent of the **c**?"
29: 10 it is in my heart to make a **c** with the LORD,
34: 30 words of the book of the **c** that had been found G
34: 31 The king stood in his place and made a **c** before
34: 31 the words of the **c** that were written in this book.
34: 32 of Jerusalem acted according to the **c** of God,
Ezr 10: 3 a **c** with our God to send away all these wives
Ne 1: 5 and awesome God who keeps **c** and steadfast love
9: 8 with him a **c** to give to his descendants the land of
9: 32 keeping **c** and steadfast love—
13: 29 the **c** of the priests and the Levites.
Job 31: 1 "I have made a **c** with my eyes;
41: 4 a **c** with you to be taken as your servant forever?
Ps 25: 10 for those who keep his **c** and his decrees. D
25: 14 and he makes his **c** known to them. D
44: 17 or been false to your **c**. E
50: 5 who made a **c** with me by sacrifice!"
50: 16 or take my **c** on your lips? B
55: 20 on a friend and violated a **c** with me
60: T *To the leader: according to the Lily of the C.*
74: 20 Have regard for your **c**, for the dark places E
78: 10 They did not keep God's **c**,
78: 37 they were not true to his **c**. D
80: T *To the leader: on Lilies, a C. Of Asaph.*
83: 5 against you they make a **c**—
89: 3 You said, "I have made a **c** with my chosen one,
89: 28 and my **c** with him will stand firm. B
89: 34 I will not violate my **c**, B
89: 39 You have renounced the **c** with your servant;
103: 18 to those who keep his **c** and remember D
105: 8 He is mindful of his **c** forever, D
105: 9 the **c** that he made with Abraham,
Ps 105: 10 to Israel as an everlasting **c**,
106: 45 For their sake he remembered his **c**, D
111: 5 he is ever mindful of his **c**. D
111: 9 he has commanded his **c** forever. D
132: 12 If your sons keep my **c** and my decrees B
Pr 2: 17 the partner of her youth and forgets her sacred **c**;
Isa 24: 5 violated the statutes, broken the everlasting **c**.
28: 15 you have said, "We have made a **c** with death,
28: 18 Then your **c** with death will be annulled, E
42: 6 I have given you as a **c** to the people,
49: 8 I have kept you and given you as a **c** to the people,
54: 10 and my **c** of peace shall not be removed, B
55: 3 I will make with you an everlasting **c**,
56: 4 the things that please me and hold fast my **c**, B
56: 6 and do not profane it, and hold fast my **c**— B
59: 21 for me, this is my **c** with them, says the LORD: B
61: 8 and I will make an everlasting **c** with them.
Jer 3: 16 "The ark of the **c** of the LORD." AC
11: 2 Hear the words of this **c**,
11: 3 be anyone who does not heed the words of this **c**,
11: 6 Hear the words of this **c** and do them.
11: 8 So I brought upon them all the words of this **c**,
11: 10 of Israel and the house of Judah have broken the **c**
14: 21 remember and do not break your **c** with us. E
22: 9 they abandoned the **c** of the LORD their God, C
31: 31 I will make a new **c** with the house of Israel F
31: 32 not be like the **c** that I made with their ancestors
31: 32 a **c** that they broke, though I was their husband,
31: 33 But this is the **c** that I will make with the house
32: 40 I will make an everlasting **c** with them,
33: 20 If any of you could break my **c** with the day B
33: 20 with the day and my **c** with the night, B
33: 21 only then could my **c** with my servant David B
33: 21 and my **c** with my ministers the Levites. B
33: 25 if I had not established my **c** with day and night B
34: 8 a **c** with all the people in Jerusalem to make
34: 10 into the **c** that all would set free their slaves, male
34: 13 a **c** with your ancestors when I brought them out
34: 15 and you made a **c** before me in the house
34: 18 And those who transgressed my **c** and did B
34: 18 of the **c** that they made before me, I will make like
50: 5 to the LORD by an everlasting **c** that will never
Eze 16: 8 I pledged myself to you and entered into a **c**
16: 59 you who have despised the oath, breaking the **c**;
16: 60 yet I will remember my **c** with you in the days B
16: 60 and I will establish with you an everlasting **c**.
16: 61 but not on account of my **c** with you. B
16: 62 I will establish my **c** with you, B
17: 13 He took one of the royal offspring and made a **c**
17: 14 and that by keeping his **c** it might stand. D
17: 15 Can he break the **c** and yet escape?
17: 16 and whose **c** with him he broke—
17: 18 Because he despised the oath and broke the **c**,
17: 19 his head my oath that he despised, and my **c** B
20: 37 and will bring you within the bond of the **c**.
34: 25 with them a **c** of peace and banish wild animals
37: 26 I will make a **c** of peace with them;
37: 26 it shall be an everlasting **c** with them;
44: 7 have broken my **c** with all your abominations. B
Da 9: 4 keeping **c** and steadfast love
9: 27 He shall make a strong **c** with many for one week,
11: 22 and the prince of the **c** as well.
11: 28 but his heart shall be set against the holy **c**.
11: 30 be enraged and take action against the holy **c**.
11: 30 and pay heed to those who forsake the holy **c**.
11: 32 with intrigue those who violate the **c**;
Hos 2: 18 a **c** on that day with the wild animals, the birds of
6: 7 But at Adam they transgressed the **c**;
8: 1 because they have broken my **c**, B
Am 1: 9 and did not remember the **c** of kinship.
Zec 9: 11 you also, because of the blood of my **c** with you, B
11: 10 the **c** that I had made with all the peoples.
Mal 2: 4 that my **c** with Levi may hold, B
2: 5 My **c** with him was a covenant of life B
2: 5 a **c** of life and well-being, which I gave him;
2: 8 you have corrupted the **c** of Levi,
2: 10 profaning the **c** of our ancestors?
2: 14 though she is your companion and your wife by **c**.
3: 1 The messenger of the **c** in whom you delight—
Mt 26: 28 for this is my blood of the **c**,
Mk 14: 24 He said to them, "This is my blood of the **c**,
Lk 1: 72 and has remembered his holy **c**,
22: 20 "This cup that is poured out for you is the new **c** F
Ac 3: 25 and of the **c** that God gave to your ancestors,
7: 8 Then he gave him the **c** of circumcision.
Ro 11: 27 "And this is my **c** with them, B
1Co 11: 25 saying, "This cup is the new **c** in my blood. F
2Co 3: 6 ministers of a new **c**, not of letter but of spirit; F
3: 14 when they hear the reading of the old **c**,
Gal 3: 17 does not annul a **c** previously ratified by God,
Heb 7: 22 Jesus has also become the guarantee of a better **c**.
8: 6 and to that degree he is the mediator of a better **c**,
8: 7 For if that first **c** had been faultless,
8: 8 when I will establish a new **c** with the house F
8: 9 not like the **c** that I made with their ancestors,
8: 9 for they did not continue in my **c**, B
8: 10 the **c** that I will make with the house of Israel
8: 13 In speaking of "a new **c**," F
9: 1 Now even the first **c** had regulations for worship
9: 4 the ark of the **c** overlaid on all sides with gold, A
9: 4 and the tablets of the **c**;
9: 15 For this reason he is the mediator of a new **c**, F
9: 15 from the transgressions under the first **c**.
9: 18 even the first **c** was inaugurated without blood.
9: 20 the blood of the **c** that God has ordained for you."
10: 16 the **c** that I will make with them after those days,
10: 29 the blood of the **c** by which they were sanctified,
Heb 12: 24 the mediator of a new **c**, F
13: 20 by the blood of the eternal **c**,
Rev 11: 19 the ark of his **c** was seen within his temple; AD
Jdt 9: 13 against your **c**, and against your sacred house, E
Wis 1: 16 they pined away and made a **c** with him,
Sir 17: 12 He established with them an eternal **c**,
24: 23 this is the book of the **c** of the Most High God, G
28: 7 remember the **c** of the Most High,
39: 8 and will glory in the law of the Lord's **c**.
42: 2 ashamed of the law of the Most High and his **c**, D
44: 20 and entered into a **c** with him;
44: 20 he certified the **c** in his flesh,
44: 22 The blessing of all people and the **c**
45: 5 so that he might teach Jacob the **c**,
45: 7 He made an everlasting **c** with him,
45: 15 an everlasting **c** for him and for his descendants
45: 24 a **c** of friendship was established with him,
45: 25 as a **c** was established with David son of Jesse of
47: 11 he gave him a **c** of kingship and a glorious throne
Bar 2: 35 an everlasting **c** with them to be their God
Aza 1: 11 and do not annul your **c**. E
1Mc 1: 11 and make a **c** with the Gentiles around us,
1: 15 and abandoned the holy **c**.
1: 57 Anyone found possessing the book of the **c**, G
1: 63 to be defiled by food or to profane the holy **c**;
2: 20 and my brothers will continue to live by the **c**
2: 27 for the law and supports the **c** come out with me!"
2: 50 and give your lives for the **c** of our ancestors.
2: 54 received the **c** of everlasting priesthood.
4: 10 and remember his **c** with our ancestors D
11: 9 saying, "Come, let us make a **c** with each other,
2Mc 1: 2 and may he remember his **c** with Abraham D
7: 36 of ever-flowing life, under God's **c**;
14: 20 that they were of one mind, they agreed to the **c**.
14: 26 the **c** that had been made and went to Demetrius.
14: 27 the **c** and commanding him to send Maccabeus
2Es 2: 5 because they would not keep my **c**, B
2: 7 because they have despised my **c**. B
3: 15 You made an everlasting **c** with him,
7: *46* among mortals that has not transgressed your **c**? E
10: 22 the ark of our **c** has been plundered, A

COVENANTED (1) [COVENANT]

AdE 14: 8 but they have **c** with their idols

COVENANTS‡ (15) [COVENANT]

Hos 10: 4 with empty oaths they make **c**;
Ro 9: 4 and to them belong the adoption, the glory, the **c**,
Gal 4: 24 Now this is an allegory: these women are two **c**.
Eph 2: 12 and strangers to the **c** of promise,
Wis 12: 21 to whose ancestors you gave oaths and **c** full
18: 22 to the oaths and **c** given to our ancestors.
Sir 44: 12 Their descendants stand by the **c**;
44: 18 Everlasting **c** were made with him
2Mc 8: 15 for the sake of the **c** made with their ancestors,
2Es 3: 32 so believed the **c** as these tribes of Jacob?
4: 23 to destruction and the written **c** no longer exist.
5: 29 on those who believed your **c**.
7: 24 They scorned his law, and denied his **c**;
7: *83* for those who have trusted the **c** of the Most High.
8: 27 of those who have kept your **c** amid afflictions.

COVER‡ (78) [BED-COVER, COVERED, COVERING, COVERINGS, COVERS, SILVER-COVERED]

Ge 6: 14 and **c** it inside and out with pitch.
Ex 10: 5 They shall **c** the surface of the land,
21: 33 or digs a pit and does not **c** it,
22: 27 be your neighbor's only clothing to use as **c**;
26: 13 on this side and that side, to **c** it.
28: 42 linen undergarments to **c** their naked flesh;
33: 22 I will **c** you with my hand until I have passed by;
Lev 13: 45 and he shall **c** his upper lip and cry out, "Unclean,
16: 13 that the cloud of the incense may **c** the mercy seat
17: 13 that may be eaten shall pour out its blood and **c** it
Nu 4: 5 and **c** the ark of the covenant with it;
4: 8 and **c** it with a covering of fine leather,
4: 9 and **c** the lampstand for the light, with its lamps,
4: 11 and **c** it with a covering of fine leather,
4: 12 and **c** them with a covering of fine leather,
19: 15 And every open vessel with no **c** fastened
Dt 22: 12 of the cloak with which you **c** yourself.
23: 13 a hole with it and then **c** up your excrement.
27: 2 you shall set up large stones and **c** them
27: 4 on Mount Ebal, and you shall **c** them with plaster.
Jos 24: 7 and made the sea come upon them and **c** them;
1Sa 25: 20 under **c** of the mountain, David and his men came
1Ki 7: 18 around each latticework to **c** the capitals that were
7: 41 to **c** the two bowls of the capitals that were on
7: 42 to **c** the two bowls of the capitals that were on
2Ch 4: 12 and the two latticeworks to **c** the two bowls of
4: 13 to **c** the two bowls of the capitals that were on
Ne 4: 5 Do not **c** their guilt, and do not let their sin
Job 14: 17 and you would **c** over my iniquity.
16: 18 "O earth, do not **c** my blood;
21: 26 down alike in the dust, and the worms **c** them.
23: 17 and thick darkness would **c** my face!
38: 34 so that a flood of waters may **c** you?
40: 22 The lotus trees **c** it for shade;
Ps 5: 12 you **c** them with favor as with a shield.
27: 5 he will conceal me under the **c** of his tent;
91: 4 he will **c** you with his pinions,
104: 6 You **c** it with the deep as with a garment;
104: 9 so that they might not again **c** the earth.

Ps 139:11 If I say, "Surely the darkness shall **c** me,
Isa 11: 9 of the knowledge of the LORD as the waters **c**
14:21 the earth or **c** the face of the world with cities.
26:21 and will no longer **c** its slain.
58: 7 when you see the naked, to **c** them,
59: 6 they cannot **c** themselves with what they make.
60: 2 For darkness shall **c** the earth,
60: 6 A multitude of camels shall **c** you,
Jer 3:25 and let our dishonor **c** us;
14: 3 and dismayed and **c** their heads,
14: 4 the farmers are dismayed; they **c** their heads.
46: 8 It said, Let me rise, let me **c** the earth,
Eze 7:18 They shall put on sackcloth, horror shall **c** them.
12: 6 you shall **c** your face, so that you may not see
12:12 he shall **c** his face, so that he may not see the land
16:18 you took your embroidered garments to **c** them,
24: 7 not pour it out on the ground, to **c** it with earth.
24:17 not **c** your upper lip or eat the bread of mourners.
24:22 not **c** your upper lip or eat the bread of mourners.
26:10 be so many that their dust shall **c** you.
26:19 and the great waters **c** you,
32: 7 When I blot you out, I will **c** the heavens,
32: 7 I will **c** the sun with a cloud,
37: 6 and **c** you with skin, and put breath in you,
Hos 2: 9 which were to **c** her nakedness.
10: 8 They shall say to the mountains, **C** us,
Ob 1:10 to your brother Jacob, shame shall **c** you,
Mic 3: 7 they shall all **c** their lips, for there is no answer
7:10 and shame will **c** her who said to me,
Hab 2:14 as the waters **c** the sea.
Zec 5: 7 Then a leaden **c** was lifted,
Mal 2:13 You **c** the LORD's altar with tears,
Lk 23:30 and to the hills, '**C** us.'
Jas 5:20 the sinner's soul from death and will **c** a multitude
Jdt 2: 7 and will **c** the whole face of the earth with the feet
2:19 of King Nebuchadnezzar and to **c** the whole face
Wis 5:16 because with his right hand he will **c** them,
Sir 37: 3 why were you formed to **c** the land with deceit?
1Mc 9:38 they went up and hid under **c** of the mountain.

COVERED (93) [COVER]

Ge 1: 2 the earth was a formless void and darkness **c**
7:19 under the whole heaven were **c**;
9:23 and walked backward and **c** the nakedness
24:65 So she took her veil and **c** herself.
38:15 for she had **c** her face.
Ex 8: 6 and the frogs came up and **c** the land of Egypt.
10:15 They **c** the surface of the whole land,
14:28 The waters returned and **c** the chariots and
15: 5 The floods **c** them; they went down into
15:10 You blew with your wind, the sea **c** them;
16:13 In the evening quails came up and **c** the camp;
24:15 and the cloud **c** the mountain.
24:16 and the cloud **c** it for six days;
40:34 Then the cloud **c** the tent of meeting,
Lev 13:13 and if the disease has **c** all his body,
Nu 7: 3 six **c** wagons and twelve oxen,
9:15 the cloud **c** the tabernacle,
9:16 the cloud **c** it by day and the appearance of fire
16:42 the cloud had **c** it and the glory of
Jdg 4:18 and she **c** him with a rug.
4:19 a skin of milk and gave him a drink and **c** him.
1Sa 19:13 of goats' hair on its head, and **c** it with the clothes.
2Sa 15:30 with his head **c** and walking barefoot;
15:30 the people who were with him **c** their heads
19: 4 The king **c** his face, and the king cried with
19: 5 "Today you have **c** with shame the faces
1Ki 1: 1 they **c** him with clothes, he could not get warm.
6:15 he **c** them on the inside with wood;
6:15 he **c** the floor of the house with boards of cypress.
6:32 He **c** the two doors of olivewood with carvings
7: 7 **c** with cedar from floor to floor.
2Ki 3:25 of land everyone threw a stone, until it was **c**;
16:18 The **c** portal for use on the sabbath
19: 1 he tore his clothes, **c** himself with sackcloth,
19: 2 and the senior priests, **c** with sackcloth,
23:14 and **c** the sites with human bones.
1Ch 28:18 the cherubim that spread their wings and **c** the ark
2Ch 3: 5 nave he lined with cypress, **c** it with fine gold,
Ne 3:15 he rebuilt it and **c** it and set up its doors, its bolts,
Est 6:12 mourning and with his head **c**.
7: 8 the mouth of the king, they **c** Haman's face.
Job 15:27 because they have **c** their faces with their fat,
Ps 32: 1 whose transgression is forgiven, whose sin is **c**.
44:15 and shame has **c** my face
44:19 and **c** us with deep darkness.
68:13 the wings of a dove **c** with silver,
69: 7 that shame has **c** my face.
71:13 let those who seek to hurt me be **c** with scorn
80:10 The mountains were **c** with its shade,
89:45 you have **c** him with shame.
106:11 The waters **c** their adversaries;
106:17 and **c** the faction of Abiram.
140: 7 you have **c** my head in the day of battle.
Pr 11:16 but she who hates virtue is **c** with shame.
24:31 the ground was **c** with nettles,
26:26 though hatred is **c** with guile,
Ecc 6: 4 and in darkness its name is **c**;
Isa 6: 2 they **c** their faces, and with two they **c** their feet,
28: 8 All tables are **c** with filthy vomit;
29:10 you prophets, and **c** your heads, you seers.
37: 1 he tore his clothes, **c** himself with sackcloth,
37: 2 and the senior priests, **c** with sackcloth,
61:10 he has **c** me with the robe of righteousness,
Jer 51:42 she has been **c** by its tumultuous waves.
51:51 dishonor has **c** our face, for aliens have come into
Eze 1:11 the wing of another, while two **c** their bodies.
16: 8 of my cloak over you, and **c** your nakedness:
16:10 in fine linen and **c** you with rich fabric.
24: 8 so that it may not be **c**.
30:18 the city shall be **c** by a cloud,
31:15 down to Sheol I closed the deep over it and **c** it;
37: 8 upon them, and skin had **c** them;
41:16 up to the windows (now the windows were **c**),
Jnh 3: 6 removed his robe, **c** himself with sackcloth,
3: 8 and animals shall be **c** with sackcloth,
Hab 3: 3 His glory **c** the heavens, and the earth was full of
Mt 10:26 for nothing is **c** up that will not be uncovered,
Lk 5:12 there was a man **c** with leprosy.
12: 2 Nothing is **c** up that will not be uncovered,
16:20 And at his gate lay a poor man named Lazarus, **c**
Ac 7:57 But they **c** their ears,
Ro 4: 7 iniquities are forgiven, and whose sins are **c**;
Jdt 7:18 and **c** the whole face of the land.
16: 3 and their cavalry **c** the hills.
AdE 6:12 mourning and with his head **c**.
14: 2 and instead of costly perfumes she **c** her head
14: 2 that she loved to adorn she **c** with her tangled hair.
15: 6 all **c** with gold and precious stones.
Sir 16:30 With all kinds of living beings he **c** its surface,
24: 3 and **c** the earth like a mist.
1Mc 6:37 the elephants were wooden towers, strong and **c**;
2Mc 6: 5 The altar was **c** with abominable offerings

COVERING‡ (44) [COVER]

Ge 7:20 **c** them fifteen cubits deep.
8:13 and Noah removed the **c** of the ark, and looked,
Ex 26:14 a **c** of tanned rams' skins and an outer covering
26:14 a covering of tanned rams' skins and an outer **c**
35:11 its tent and its **c**, its clasps
36:19 for the tent a **c** of tanned rams' skins and an outer **c**
39:34 the **c** of tanned rams' skins and the **c** of fine leather
40:19 and put the **c** of the tent over it;
Nu 3:25 be the tabernacle, the tent with its **c**, the screen for
4: 6 then they shall put on it a **c** of fine leather,
4: 8 and cover it with a **c** of fine leather,
4:10 and they shall put it with all its utensils in a **c**
4:11 and cover it with a **c** of fine leather,
4:12 and cover them with a **c** of fine leather,
4:14 and they shall spread on it a **c** of fine leather,
4:15 and his sons have finished **c** the sanctuary and all
4:25 tent of meeting with its **c**, and the outer **c** of fine
16:38 Make them into hammered plates as a **c** for
16:39 and they were hammered out as a **c** for the altar—
1Sa 19:16 with the **c** of goats' hair on its head.
2Sa 17:19 The man's wife took a **c**, stretched it over
1Ki 8: 7 the cherubim made a **c** above the ark and its poles.
2Ch 5: 8 the cherubim made a **c** above the ark and its poles.
Job 24: 7 without clothing, and have no **c** in the cold.
26: 6 before God, and Abaddon has no **c**.
31:19 or a poor person without **c**,
Ps 18:11 He made darkness his **c** around him,
105:39 He spread a cloud for a **c**,
Pr 26:23 Like the glaze **c** an earthen vessel are smooth lips
Isa 14:11 the bed beneath you, and worms are your **c**.
22: 8 He has taken away the **c** of Judah.
28:20 and the **c** too narrow to wrap oneself in it.
50: 3 and make sackcloth their **c**.
Eze 1:23 each of the creatures had two wings **c** its body.
28:13 every precious stone was your **c**, carnelian,
38: 9 you shall be like a cloud **c** the land,
38:16 like a cloud **c** the earth.
Hos 13: 8 and will tear open the **c** of their heart;
Mal 2:16 and **c** one's garment with violence,
1Co 11:15 For her hair is given to her for a **c**.
Wis 13:14 and coloring its surface red and **c** every blemish

COVERINGS (3) [COVER]

Pr 7:16 I have decked my couch with **c**,
31:22 She makes herself **c**; her clothing is fine linen
AdE 1: 6 There were **c** of gauze, embroidered

COVERS (23) [COVER]

Ex 29:13 You shall take all the fat that **c** the entrails,
29:22 the fat tail, the fat that **c** the entrails,
Lev 3: 3 that **c** the entrails and all the fat that is around
3: 9 to the backbone, the fat that **c** the entrails, and all
3:14 that **c** the entrails, and all the fat that is around
4: 8 that **c** the entrails and all the fat that is around
7: 3 the broad tail, the fat that **c** the entrails,
9:19 the broad tail, the fat that **c** the entrails,
13:12 so that it **c** all the skin of the diseased person
Job 9:24 he **c** the eyes of its judges—
22:11 a flood of water **c** you.
26: 9 He **c** the face of the full moon,
36:30 he scatters his lightning around him and **c**
36:32 He **c** his hands with the lightning,
Ps 73: 6 violence **c** them like a garment.
84: 6 the early rain also **c** it with pools.
147: 8 He **c** the heavens with clouds,
Pr 10:12 Hatred stirs up strife, but love **c** all offenses.
Eze 18: 7 gives his bread to the hungry and **c** the naked with
18:16 but gives his bread to the hungry and **c** the naked
1Pe 4: 8 for love **c** a multitude of sins.
Sir 39:22 "His blessing **c** the dry land like a river,
40:27 and **c** a person better than any glory.

COVERT (6)

Job 38:40 or lie in wait in their **c**?
40:21 in the **c** of the reeds and in the marsh.
Ps 10: 9 they lurk in secret like a lion in its **c**;
SS 2:14 in the clefts of the rock, in the **c** of the cliff,
Isa 32: 2 from the wind, a **c** from the tempest, like streams
Jer 25:38 Like a lion he has left his **c**;

COVET (15) [COVETED, COVETOUS, COVETOUSNESS, COVETS]

Ex 20:17 You shall not **c** your neighbor's house;
20:17 you shall not **c** your neighbor's wife,
34:24 no one shall **c** your land when you go up to appear
Dt 5:21 Neither shall you **c** your neighbor's wife.
7:25 Do not **c** the silver or the gold that is on them
Jos 6:18 to **c** and take any of the devoted things and make
Pr 12:12 The wicked **c** the proceeds of wickedness,
21:26 All day long the wicked **c**,
Mic 2: 2 They **c** fields, and seize them;
Ro 7: 7 not have known what it is to **c** if the law had not said, "You shall not **c**."
13: 9 You shall not steal; You shall not **c**";
Jas 4: 2 And you **c** something and cannot obtain it;
4Mc 2: 5 "You shall not **c** your neighbor's wife or anything
2: 6 In fact, since the law has told us not to **c**,

COVETED (3) [COVET]

Jos 7:21 then I **c** them and took them.
Ac 20:33 I **c** no one's silver or gold or clothing.
1Mc 11:11 on Alexander because he **c** his kingdom.

COVETOUS (1) [COVET]

Wis 10:11 When his oppressors were **c**,

COVETOUSLY See Index to Footnotes

COVETOUSNESS‡ (4) [COVET]

Isa 57:17 Because of their wicked **c** I was angry;
Ro 1:29 with every kind of wickedness, evil, **c**,
7: 8 produced in me all kinds of **c**.
4Mc 1:26 In the soul it is boastfulness, **c**, thirst for honor,

COVETS‡ (1) [COVET]

Ps 34:12 and **c** many days to enjoy good?

COW (5) [COW'S, COWS]

Ex 34:19 the firstborn of **c** and sheep.
Nu 18:17 But the firstborn of a **c**, or the firstborn of a sheep,
Job 21:10 their **c** calves and never miscarries.
Isa 7:21 On that day one will keep alive a young **c**
11: 7 The **c** and the bear shall graze,

COW'S (1) [COW]

Eze 4:15 I will let you have **c** dung instead of human dung,

COWARD (4) [COWARDICE, COWARDLY, COWER]

Sir 34:16 or play the **c**, for he is their hope.
37:11 a **c** about war, with a merchant about business or
4Mc 10:14 not have a fire hot enough to make me play the **c**.
14: 4 the seven youths proved **c** or shrank from death,

COWARDICE (4) [COWARD]

2Ti 1: 7 for God did not give us a spirit of **c**,
1Mc 4:32 Fill them with **c**; melt the boldness of their
4Mc 6:17 so basely that out of **c** we feign a role unbecoming
6:20 that time be a laughingstock to all for our **c**,

COWARDLY (6) [COWARD]

Rev 21: 8 But as for the **c**, the faithless, the polluted,
Wis 17:11 For wickedness is a **c** thing,
2Mc 8:13 those who were **c** and distrustful
4Mc 5:31 I am not so old and **c** as not to be young in reason
8:16 if some of them had been **c** and unmanly.
13:10 Let us not be **c** in the demonstration of our piety."

COWER (3) [COWARD]

La 3:16 and made me **c** in ashes;
3Mc 6:13 And let the Gentiles **c** today in fear
4Mc 16:20 a knife and descending upon him, he did not **c**.

COWS (18) [COW]

Ge 32:15 forty **c** and ten bulls, twenty female donkeys
41: 2 up out of the Nile seven sleek and fat **c**,
41: 3 Then seven other **c**, ugly and thin,
41: 3 and stood by the other **c** on the bank of the Nile.
41: 4 and thin **c** ate up the seven sleek and fat **c**.
41:18 and seven **c**, fat and sleek, came up out of the Nile
41:19 Then seven other **c** came up after them, poor,
41:20 The thin and ugly **c** ate up the first seven fat **c**,
41:26 The seven good **c** are seven years,
41:27 The seven lean and ugly **c** that came up
1Sa 6: 7 a new cart and two milch **c** that have never borne
6: 7 and yoke the **c** to the cart,
6:10 they took two milch **c** and yoked them to the cart,
6:12 The **c** went straight in the direction
6:14 of the cart and offered the **c** as a burnt offering to
Am 4: 1 you **c** of Bashan who are on Mount Samaria,

COZ (KJV) See KOZ

COZBI (2)

Nu 25:15 Midianite woman who was killed was **C** daughter

Nu 25:18 and in the affair of **C**, the daughter of a leader

COZEBA (1)
1Ch 4:22 and the men of **C**, and Joash, and Saraph,

CRACK (1) [CRACKED, CRACKS]
Na 3: 2 The **c** of whip and rumble of wheel,

CRACKED (2) [CRACK]
Jer 2:13 **c** cisterns that can hold no water.
14: 4 because the ground is **c**.

CRACKLING (2)
Ecc 7: 6 For like the **c** of thorns under a pot,
Joel 2: 5 like the **c** of a flame of fire devouring the stubble,

CRACKNELS (KJV) See CAKES

CRACKS (1) [CRACK]
Ps 60: 2 repair the **c** in it, for it is tottering.

CRAFT (6) [CRAFTED, CRAFTILY, CRAFTINESS, CRAFTS, CRAFTY]
Ex 31: 3 intelligence, and knowledge in every kind of **c**,
31: 5 and in carving wood, in every kind of **c**.
35:31 intelligence, and knowledge in every kind of **c**,
35:33 and in carving wood, in every kind of **c**.
Isa 2:16 and against all the beautiful **c**.
AdE 16:13 and with intricate **c** and deceit asked for

CRAFTED (1) [CRAFT]
Nu 31:51 all in the form of **c** articles.

CRAFTILY (2) [CRAFT]
Ps 105:25 to deal **c** with his servants.
Ac 7:19 He dealt **c** with our race and forced our ancestors

CRAFTINESS (5) [CRAFT]
Job 5:13 He takes the wise in their own **c**;
Lk 20:23 But he perceived their **c** and said to them,
Ro 1:29 Full of envy, murder, strife, deceit, **c**,
1Co 3:19 For it is written, "He catches the wise in their **c**,"
Eph 4:14 by their **c** in deceitful scheming.

CRAFTS (1) [CRAFT]
Wis 7:16 as are all understanding and skill in **c**.

CRAFTY (7) [CRAFT]
Ge 3: 1 the serpent was more **c** than any other wild animal
2Sa 13: 3 and Jonadab was a very **c** man.
Job 5:12 He frustrates the devices of the **c**,
15: 5 and you choose the tongue of the **c**.
Ps 83: 3 They lay **c** plans against your people;
2Co 12:16 (you say) since I was **c**, I took you in by deceit.
Sir 11:29 for many are the tricks of the **c**.

CRAG (4) [CRAGS]
1Sa 14: 4 there was a rocky **c** on one side and a rocky **c** on
14: 5 One **c** rose on the north in front of Michmash,
Job 39:28 and makes its home in the fastness of the rocky **c**.

CRAGS (5) [CRAG]
Nu 23: 9 For from the top of the **c** I see him,
Dt 32:13 he nursed him with honey from the **c**,
Isa 2:21 the caverns of the rocks and the clefts in the **c**,
Jer 18:14 Does the snow of Lebanon leave the **c** of Sirion?
51:25 and roll you down from the **c**,

CRANE (2)
Isa 38:14 Like a swallow or a **c** I clamor,
Jer 8: 7 swallow, and **c** observe the time of their coming;

CRASH (8) [CRASHING]
2Ki 19:25 that you should make fortified cities **c** into heaps
Job 30:14 a wide breach they come; amid the **c** they roll on.
Ps 77:18 The **c** of your thunder was in the whirlwind;
Isa 30:13 and about to collapse, whose **c** comes suddenly,
37:26 that you should make fortified cities **c** into heaps
Zep 1:10 a loud **c** from the hills.
Wis 17:19 or the harsh **c** of rocks hurled down,
Sir 40:13 and **c** like a loud clap of thunder in a storm.

CRASHING (3) [CRASH]
Job 36:33 Its **c** tells about him; he is jealous with anger
41:25 at the **c** they are beside themselves.
Jer 51:54 A great **c** from the land of the Chaldeans!

CRATES (1)
2Mc 4:29 in the high priesthood, while Sostratus left **C**,

CRAVE (1) [CRAVED, CRAVES, CRAVING, CRAVINGS]
4Mc 1:34 when we **c** seafood and fowl and animals

CRAVED (2) [CRAVE]
Ps 78:18 in their heart by demanding the food they **c**.
78:29 for he gave them what they **c**.

CRAVES (1) [CRAVE]
Pr 13: 4 The appetite of the lazy **c**, and gets nothing,

CRAVING‡ (9) [CRAVE]
Nu 11: 4 The rabble among them had a strong **c**;
11:34 there they buried the people who had the **c**.
Ps 78:30 But before they had satisfied their **c**,
106:14 But they had a wanton **c** in the wilderness,
Pr 10: 3 but he thwarts the **c** of the wicked.
21:25 The **c** of the lazy person is fatal,
Isa 32: 6 to leave the **c** of the hungry unsatisfied,
1Ti 6: 4 a morbid **c** for controversy and for disputes
4Mc 3:12 guards complained bitterly because of the king's **c**,

CRAVINGS (1) [CRAVE]
Jas 4: 1 not come from your **c** that are at war within you?

CRAWLING (4)
Dt 32:24 with venom of things **c** in the dust.
Mic 7:17 like the **c** things of the earth;
Hab 1:14 like **c** things that have no ruler.
LtJ 6:20 when **c** creatures from the earth devour them

CREATE‡ (8) [CREATED, CREATES, CREATING, CREATION, CREATOR, NEWLY-CREATED]
Ps 51:10 **C** in me a clean heart, O God,
Isa 4: 5 Then the LORD will **c** over the whole site
45: 7 I form light and **c** darkness,
45: 7 I make weal and **c** woe;
45:18 did not **c** it a chaos, he formed it to be inhabited!):
65:17 For I am about to **c** new heavens and a new earth;
65:18 for I am about to **c** Jerusalem as a joy,
Eph 2:15 that he might **c** in himself one new humanity

CREATED‡ (103) [CREATE]
Ge 1: 1 In the beginning when God **c** the heavens and
1:21 So God **c** the great sea monsters
1:27 So God **c** humankind in his image, in the image of God he **c** them; male and female he **c** them.
2: 4 of the heavens and the earth when they were **c**.
5: 1 When God **c** humankind, he made them in
5: 2 Male and female he **c** them,
5: 2 and named them "Humankind" when they were **c**.
6: 7 from the earth the human beings I have **c**—
Dt 4:32 ever since the day that God **c** human beings on
32: 6 Is not he your father, who **c** you,
Ps 89:12 The north and the south—you **c** them;
89:47 for what vanity you have **c** all mortals!
104:30 When you send forth your spirit, they are **c**;
148: 5 for he commanded and they were **c**.
Pr 8:22 The LORD **c** me at the beginning of his work,
Isa 40:26 Lift up your eyes on high and see: Who **c** these?
41:20 the Holy One of Israel has **c** it.
42: 5 who **c** the heavens and stretched them out,
43: 1 But now thus says the LORD, he who **c** you,
43: 7 whom I **c** for my glory,
45: 8 I the LORD have **c** it.
45:12 I made the earth, and **c** humankind upon it;
45:18 who **c** the heavens (he is God!),
48: 7 They are **c** now, not long ago;
54:16 See it is I who have **c** the smith who blows the fire
54:16 I have also **c** the ravager to destroy.
Jer 31:22 For the LORD has **c** a new thing on the earth:
Eze 21:30 In the place where you were **c**,
28:13 On the day that you were **c** they were prepared.
28:15 in your ways from the day that you were **c**,
Mal 2:10 Has not one God **c** us?
Mk 13:19 the beginning of the creation that God **c** until now,
1Co 11: 9 Neither was man **c** for the sake of woman,
Eph 2:10 **c** in Christ Jesus for good works,
3: 9 for ages in God who **c** all things;
4:24 **c** according to the likeness of God
Col 1:16 in him all things in heaven and on earth were **c**,
1:16 all things have been **c** through him and for him.
1Ti 4: 3 which God **c** to be received with thanksgiving
4: 4 For everything **c** by God is good,
Heb 1: 2 through whom he also **c** the worlds.
12:27 of what is shaken—that is, **c** things—
Rev 4:11 for you **c** all things, and by your will they existed and were **c**."
10: 6 who **c** heaven and what is in it,
Jdt 13:18 who **c** the heavens and the earth,
Wis 1:14 For he **c** all things so that they might exist;
2:23 for God **c** us for incorruption,
10: 1 when he alone had been **c**;
11:17 which **c** the world out of formless matter,
13: 3 for the author of beauty **c** them.
13: 5 from the greatness and beauty of **c** things comes
14:11 because, though part of what God **c**,
Sir 1: 4 Wisdom was **c** before all other things,
1: 9 It is he who **c** her;
1:14 she is **c** with the faithful in the womb.
7:15 which was **c** by the Most High.
10:18 Pride was not **c** for human beings,
15:14 It was he who **c** humankind in the beginning,
16:26 When the Lord **c** his works from the beginning,
17: 1 The Lord **c** human beings out of earth,
18: 1 He who lives forever **c** the whole universe;
23:20 Before the universe was **c**, it was known to him,
24: 9 Before the ages, in the beginning, he **c** me,
31:13 What has been **c** more greedy than the eye?
31:27 It has been **c** to make people happy.
Sir 33:10 and humankind was **c** out of the dust.
36:20 to those whom you **c** in the beginning,
38: 1 for their services, for the Lord **c** them;
38: 4 The Lord **c** medicines out of the earth,
38:12 give the physician his place, for the Lord **c** him;
39:21 for everything has been **c** for its own purpose.
39:25 the beginning good things were **c** for the good,
39:28 "There are winds **c** for vengeance,
39:29 all these have been **c** for vengeance;
40: 1 Hard work was **c** for everyone,
40:10 All these were **c** for the wicked,
49:14 Few have ever been **c** on earth like Enoch,
49:16 but above every other **c** living being was Adam.
Bel 1: 5 who **c** heaven and earth and has dominion
2Mc 14:17 of the sudden consternation **c** by the enemy.
1Es 6:13 'We are the servants of the Lord who **c** the heaven
3Mc 1:23 and **c** a considerable disturbance in the holy place;
2: 9 you had **c** the boundless and immeasurable earth,
2Es 2:14 I set aside evil and **c** good;
5:26 the birds that have been **c** you have named
5:43 not have **c** at one time those who have been
5:44 the world hold at one time those who have been **c**
5:49 I have made the same rule for the world that I **c**."
6:41 you **c** the spirit of the firmament,
6:55 that it was for us that you **c** this world.
6:59 If the world has indeed been **c** for us,
7:*48* for a few but for almost all who have been **c**."
7:*62* of the dust like the other **c** things?
7:*139* [69] did not pardon those who were **c** by his word
8: 3 Many have been **c**, but only a few shall be saved."
8: 8 what you have **c** is preserved amid fire and water,
8: 8 the womb endures your creature that has been **c**
8: 9 the womb gives up again what has been **c** in it,
8:60 but those who were **c** have themselves defiled
9:19 but now those who have been **c** in this world,

CREATES (2) [CREATE]
Nu 16:30 But if the LORD **c** something new,
Am 4:13 lo, the one who forms the mountains, **c** the wind,

CREATING (2) [CREATE]
Isa 57:18 **c** for their mourners the fruit of the lips.
65:18 But be glad and rejoice forever in what I am **c**;

CREATION‡ (43) [CREATE]
Ge 2: 3 from all the work that he had done in **c**.
Mk 10: 6 But from the beginning of **c**,
13:19 the beginning of the **c** that God created until now,
16:15 ⟦and proclaim the good news to the whole **c**.⟧
Ro 1:20 Ever since the **c** of the world his eternal power
8:19 the **c** waits with eager longing for the revealing of
8:20 for the **c** was subjected to futility,
8:21 that the **c** itself will be set free from its bondage
8:22 that the whole **c** has been groaning in labor pains
8:23 the **c**, but we ourselves, who have the first fruits
8:39 nor depth, nor anything else in all **c**,
2Co 5:17 So if anyone is in Christ, there is a new **c**:
Gal 6:15 but a new **c** is everything!
Col 1:15 of the invisible God, the firstborn of all **c**;
Heb 9:11 (not made with hands, that is, not of this **c**),
2Pe 3: 4 as they were from the beginning of **c**!"
Rev 3:14 and true witness, the origin of God's **c**:
Tob 8: 5 Let the heavens and the whole **c** bless you forever.
Jdt 9:12 Creator of the waters, King of all your **c**,
Wis 2: 6 and make use of the **c** to the full as in youth.
5:17 and will arm all **c** to repel his enemies;
5:20 and **c** will join with him to fight
6:22 I will trace her course from the beginning of **c**,
16:24 For **c**, serving you who made it,
19: 6 For the whole **c** in its nature was fashioned anew,
Sir 16:17 for what am I in a boundless **c**?
3Mc 2: 2 and sovereign of all **c**, holy among the holy ones,
2: 7 the Ruler over the whole **c**.
6: 2 governing all **c** with mercy,
2Es 3: 5 Yet he was the **c** of your hands,
5:44 "The **c** cannot move faster than the Creator,
5:45 at one time to your **c**?
5:45 at one time and the **c** will sustain them,
5:55 a **c** that already is aging and passing the strength
5:56 through whom you will visit your **c**."
6:38 I said, "O Lord, you spoke at the beginning of **c**,
7:*75* until those times come when you will renew the **c**,
8:13 You put it to death as your **c**,
8:39 but I will rejoice over the **c** of the righteous,
8:45 for you have mercy on your own **c**."
8:47 of being able to love my **c** more than I love it.
13:26 who will himself deliver his **c**;
4Mc 14: 7 as the seven days of **c** move in choral dance

CREATOR (18) [CREATE]
Ecc 12: 1 Remember your **c** in the days of your youth,
Isa 40:28 the **C** of the ends of the earth.
43:15 I am the LORD, your Holy One, the **C** of Israel,
Ro 1:25 and served the creature rather than the **C**,
Col 3:10 in knowledge according to the image of its **c**.
1Pe 4:19 with God's will entrust themselves to a faithful **C**,
Jdt 9:12 Lord of heaven and earth, **C** of the waters,
Wis 13: 5 a corresponding perception of their **C**.
Sir 4: 6 their **C** will hear their prayer.
24: 8 "Then the **C** of all things gave me a command,
24: 8 and my **C** chose the place for my tent.
2Mc 1:24 "O Lord, Lord God, **C** of all things,
7:23 Therefore the **C** of the world,
13:14 to the **C** of the world and exhorting his troops
3Mc 2: 3 For you, the **c** of all things and the governor of all,

2Es 5:44 "The creation cannot move faster than the C,
4Mc 5:25 the nature of things the C of the world in giving us
11: 5 Is it because we revere the C of all things and live

CREATURE (43) [CREATURES]

A. LIVING CREATURE (18)

Ge 1:21 the great sea monsters and every living c A
2:19 and whatever the man called every living c, A
7:14 every bird, every winged c.
8:21 nor will I ever again destroy every living c A
9:10 and with every living c that is with you, A
9:12 between me and you and every living c that is A
9:15 that is between me and you and every living c A
9:16 every living c of all flesh that is on the earth." A
Lev 7:21 or an unclean animal or any unclean c—
11:43 not make yourselves detestable with any c
11:44 with any swarming c that moves on the earth.
11:46 every living c that moves through the waters A
11:46 the waters and every c that swarms upon the earth,
11:47 and between the living c that may be eaten and A
11:47 be eaten and the living c that may not be eaten. A
17:14 For the life of every c—
17:14 You shall not eat the blood of any c,
17:14 for the life of every c is its blood;
Dt 14:20 You may eat any clean winged c.
Job 41:33 On earth it has no equal, a c without fear.
Ecc 10:20 or some winged c tell the matter.
Eze 1:11 each c had two wings, each of which touched
47: 9 every living c that swarms will live, A
Ac 28: 4 the natives saw the c hanging from his hand,
28: 5 shook off the c into the fire and suffered no harm.
Ro 1:25 a lie and worshiped and served the c rather than
Col 1:23 which has been proclaimed to every c
Heb 4:13 And before him no c is hidden,
Jas 3: 7 and sea c, can be tamed and has been tamed by
Rev 4: 7 the first living c like a lion, A
4: 7 the second living c like an ox, A
4: 7 the third living c with a face like a human face, A
4: 7 and the fourth living c like a flying eagle. A
5:13 Then I heard every c in heaven and on earth and
6: 3 I heard the second living c call out, "Come!" A
6: 5 I heard the third living c call out, "Come!" A
6: 7 I heard the voice of the fourth living c call out, A
Sir 13:15 Every c loves its like, and every person
42:23 each c is preserved to meet a particular need.
3Mc 3:29 shall become useless for all time to any mortal c."
2Es 8: 8 the womb endures your c that has been created
8:24 and give ear to the petition of your c;
11: 6 not a single c that was on the earth.

CREATURES‡ (71) [CREATURE]

A. LIVING CREATURES (36)

Ge 1:20 "Let the waters bring forth swarms of living c, A
1:24 "Let the earth bring forth living c of every kind: A
3:14 among all animals and among all wild c;
7:21 all swarming c that swarm on the earth,
Lev 11: 2 these are the c that you may eat.
11:10 of the swarming c in the waters and among all
11:10 in the waters and among all the other living c A
11:29 These are unclean for you among the c that swarm
11:41 All c that swarm upon the earth are detestable;
11:42 all the c that swarm upon the earth,
Nu 18:15 The first issue of the womb of all c,
Ps 74:14 you gave him as food for the c of the wilderness.
104:24 the earth is full of your c.
Isa 13:21 and its houses will be full of howling c;
Eze 1: 5 the middle of it was something like four living c. A
1:13 In the middle of the living c there was A
1:13 to and fro among the living c; A
1:14 The living c darted to and fro, like a flash A
1:15 As I looked at the living c, A
1:15 I saw a wheel on the earth beside the living c, A
1:19 living c moved, the wheels moved beside them; A
1:19 the living c rose from the earth, the wheels rose. A
1:20 for the spirit of the living c was in the wheels. A
1:21 for the spirit of the living c was in the wheels. A
1:22 the heads of the living c there was something A
1:23 each of the c had two wings covering its body.
3:13 the sound of the wings of the living c brushing A
10:15 the living c that I saw by the river Chebar. A
10:17 for the spirit of the living c was in them. A
10:20 These were the living c that I saw underneath A
17:23 of its branches will nest winged c of every kind.
Ac 10:12 of four-footed c and reptiles and birds of the air.
Jas 1:18 we would become a kind of first fruits of his c.
2Pe 2:12 mere c of instinct, born to be caught and killed.
2:12 and when those c are destroyed,
Rev 4: 6 four living c, full of eyes in front and behind: A
4: 8 And the four living c, each of them A
4: 9 And whenever the living c give glory and honor A
5: 6 between the throne and the four living c and A
5: 8 the four living c and the twenty-four elders fell A
5:11 the throne and the living c and the elders; A
5:14 And the four living c said, "Amen!" A
6: 1 and I heard one of the four living c call out, A
6: 6 a voice in the midst of the four living c saying, A
7:11 and around the elders and the four living c, A
8: 9 a third of the living c in the sea died, A
14: 3 before the four living c and before the elders. A
15: 7 Then one of the four living c gave A
19: 4 the twenty-four elders and the four living c fell A
Jdt 16:14 Let all your c serve you, for you spoke,
Wis 9: 2 to have dominion over the c you have made,
11:15 you sent upon them a multitude of irrational c
12:27 in their suffering they became incensed at those c
16: 1 through such c, and were tormented by
16: 3 of appetite because of the odious c sent to them,
16:18 not consume the c sent against the ungodly,
19:19 For land animals were transformed into water c,
19:19 and c that swim moved over to the land.
19:21 the flesh of perishable c that walked among them,
Sir 11: 3 The bee is small among flying c,
40: 8 To all c, human and animal,
42:15 and all his c do his will.
43:25 In it are strange and marvelous c,
Bar 3:32 the earth for all time filled it with four-footed c;
LtJ 6:20 when crawling c from the earth devour them
Bel 1: 5 and earth and has dominion over all living c." A
2Es 5:45 If therefore all c will live at one time and
6:47 to bring forth living c, birds, and fishes; A
6:48 The dumb and lifeless water produced living c, A
6:49 "Then you kept in existence two living c; A
7:*134* [64] since they are his own c;

CREDIBLE (1)

4Mc 7: 9 by your deeds you made your words of divine philosophy c.

CREDIT (8) [CREDITED, CREDITOR, CREDITORS]

Dt 24:13 it will be to your c before the LORD your God.
Jdg 7: 2 Israel would only take the c away from me,
Lk 6:32 what c is that to you?
6:33 what c is that to you?
6:34 what c is that to you?
1Pe 2:19 For it is a c to you if, being aware of God,
2:20 for doing wrong, what c is that?
Rev 2: 6 Yet this is to your c:

CREDITED (2) [CREDIT]

Lev 7:18 nor shall it be c to the one who offers it;
Sir 3:14 and will be c to you against your sins;

CREDITOR (7) [CREDIT]

Ex 22:25 you shall not deal with them as a c;
Dt 15: 2 every c shall remit the claim that is held against
2Ki 4: 1 a c has come to take my two children as slaves."
Ps 109:11 May the c seize all that he has;
Isa 24: 2 as with the c, so with the debtor.
Lk 7:41 "A certain c had two debtors;
Sir 29: 6 If he can pay, his c will hardly get back half,

CREDITORS (2) [CREDIT]

Isa 50: 1 Or which of my c is it to whom I have sold you?
Hab 2: 7 Will not your own c suddenly rise,

CREEP (1) [CREEPING, CREEPS]

Eze 38:20 and all creeping things that c on the ground,

CREEPING (15) [CREEP]

Ge 1:24 cattle and c things and wild animals of the earth
1:26 and over every c thing that creeps upon the earth."
6: 7 with animals and c things and birds of the air,
6:20 of every c thing of the ground according
7:14 and every c thing that creeps on the earth,
7:23 human beings and animals and c things and birds
8:17 birds and animals and every c thing that creeps on
8:19 And every animal, every c thing, and every bird,
Ps 104:20 when all the animals of the forest come c out.
104:25 great and wide, c things innumerable are there,
148:10 and all cattle, c things and flying birds!
Eze 8:10 were all kinds of c things, and loathsome animals,
38:20 and all c things that creep on the ground,
Hos 2:18 the birds of the air, and the c things of the ground;
2Es 6:53 wild animals, and c things;

CREEPS (8) [CREEP]

Ge 1:25 everything that c upon the ground of every kind.
1:26 over every creeping thing that c upon the earth."
1:30 and to everything that c on the earth,
7: 8 and of everything that c on the ground,
7:14 and every creeping thing that c on the earth,
8:17 and every creeping thing that c on the earth—
9: 2 on everything that c on the ground,
Dt 4:18 the likeness of anything that c on the ground,

CRESCENS (1)

2Ti 4:10 C has gone to Galatia, Titus to Dalmatia.

CRESCENTS (3)

Jdg 8:21 the c that were on the necks of their camels.
8:26 of gold (apart from the c and the pendants and
Isa 3:18 the headbands, and the c;

CRETANS (2) [CRETE]

Ac 2:11 C and Arabs—in our own languages we hear them
Tit 1:12 "C are always liars, vicious brutes, lazy gluttons."

CRETE (7) [CRETANS]

Ac 27: 7 we sailed under the lee of C off Salmone.
27:12 It was a harbor of C,
27:13 so they weighed anchor and began to sail past C,
27:14 called the northeaster, rushed down from C.
27:21 from C and thereby avoided this damage and loss.
Tit 1: 5 I left you behind in C for this reason,
1Mc 10:67 of Demetrius came from C to the land

CRETES, CRETIANS (KJV) See CRETANS

CREW (1)

Eze 27:34 your merchandise and all your c have sunk

CRIB (2)

Job 39: 9 Will it spend the night at your c?
Isa 1: 3 and the donkey its master's c;

CRICKET (1)

Lev 11:22 the c according to its kind,

CRIED‡ (139) [CRY]

Ge 27:34 he c out with an exceedingly great and bitter cry,
39:14 and I c out with a loud voice;
39:18 but as soon as I raised my voice and c out,
41:43 and they c out in front of him, "Bow the knee!"
41:55 the people c to Pharaoh for bread.
45: 1 and he c out, "Send everyone away from me."
Ex 2:23 Israelites groaned under their slavery, and c out.
5:15 the Israelite supervisors came to Pharaoh and c,
8:12 and Moses c out to the LORD concerning
14:10 In great fear the Israelites c out to the LORD.
15:25 He c out to the LORD;
17: 4 So Moses c out to the LORD,
Nu 11: 2 But the people c out to Moses;
12:13 Moses c to the LORD, "O God, please heal her."
20:16 and when we c to the LORD, he heard our voice,
Dt 22:27 the engaged woman may have c for help,
26: 7 we c to the LORD, the God of our ancestors;
Jos 24: 7 When they c out to the LORD,
Jdg 3: 9 But when the Israelites c out to the LORD,
3:15 But when the Israelites c out to the LORD,
4: 3 Then the Israelites c out to the LORD for help;
6: 6 and the Israelites c out to the LORD for help.
6: 7 When the Israelites c to the LORD on account of
7:20 they c, "A sword for the LORD and for Gideon!"
7:21 in camp ran; they c out and fled.
9: 7 and c aloud and said to them, "Listen to me,
10:10 So the Israelites c to the LORD, saying,
10:12 you c to me, and I delivered you out of their hand.
1Sa 4:13 into the city and told the news, all the city c out.
5:10 the people of Ekron c out,
7: 9 Samuel c out to the LORD for Israel,
12: 8 then your ancestors c to the LORD and
12:10 Then they c to the LORD, and said,
15:11 and he c out to the LORD all night.
28:12 woman saw Samuel, she c out with a loud voice;
2Sa 18:28 Then Ahimaaz c out to the king, "All is well!"
19: 4 and the king c with a loud voice,
20: 1 He sounded the trumpet and c out,
22:42 they c to the LORD, but he did not answer them.
1Ki 13: 4 the king heard what the man of God c out against
17:20 He c out to the LORD, "O LORD my God,
17:21 and c out to the LORD, "O LORD my God,
18:28 Then they c aloud and, as was their custom,
20:39 As the king passed by, he c to the king and said,
22:32 against him; and Jehoshaphat c out.
2Ki 4: 1 a member of the company of prophets c to Elisha,
4:40 But while they were eating the stew, they c out,
6: 5 his ax head fell into the water; he c out,
6:26 a woman c out to him, "Help, my lord king!"
11:14 Athaliah tore her clothes and c, "Treason!
20:11 The prophet Isaiah c to the LORD;
1Ch 5:20 for they c to God in the battle,
2Ch 13:14 They c out to the LORD,
14:11 Asa c to the LORD his God, "O LORD,
18:31 Jehoshaphat c out, and the LORD helped him.
23:13 Athaliah tore her clothes and c, "Treason!
32:20 of Amoz prayed because of this and c to heaven.
Ne 9: 4 of the Levites and c out with a loud voice to
9:27 in the time of their suffering they c out to you
9:28 yet when they turned and c to you,
Job 29:12 because I delivered the poor who c,
31:38 "If my land has c out against me,
Ps 18: 6 to my God I c for help.
18:41 They c for help, but there was no one
18:41 they c to the LORD, but he did not answer them.
22: 5 To you they c, and were saved;
22:24 but heard when I c to him.
30: 2 O LORD my God, I c to you for help,
30: 8 I c, and to the LORD I made supplication:
31:22 But you heard my supplications when I c out
34: 6 This poor soul c, and was heard by the LORD,
66:17 I c aloud to him, and he was extolled
99: 6 They c to the LORD, and he answered them.
107: 6 Then they c to the LORD in their trouble,
107:13 Then they c to the LORD in their trouble,
107:19 Then they c to the LORD in their trouble,
107:28 Then they c to the LORD in their trouble,
Eze 9: 1 Then he c in my hearing with a loud voice,
9: 8 I fell prostrate on my face and c out,
11:13 Then I fell down on my face, c with a loud voice,
Da 4:14 He c aloud and said: 'Cut down the
5: 7 The king c aloud to bring in the enchanters,
6:20 he c out anxiously to Daniel, "O Daniel,
Jnh 1: 5 the mariners were afraid, and each c to his god.
1:14 Then they c out to the LORD, "Please,
2: 2 out of the belly of Sheol I c,
3: 4 And he c out, "Forty days more,
Zec 6: 8 Then he c out to me, "Lo,
Mt 14:26 And they c out in fear.

Mt 14:30 and beginning to sink, he c out, "Lord, save me!"
27:46 And about three o'clock Jesus c with a loud voice,
27:50 Then Jesus c again with a loud voice
Mk 1:24 and he c out, "What have you to do with us, Jesus
6:49 they thought it was a ghost and c out;
9:24 Immediately the father of the child c out,
10:48 but he c out even more loudly, "Son of David,
15:34 At three o'clock Jesus c out with a loud voice,
Lk 4:33 and he c out with a loud voice,
Jn 1:15 (John testified to him and c out,
7:28 Then Jesus c out as he was teaching in the temple,
7:37 he c out, "Let anyone who is thirsty come to me,
11:43 When he had said this, he c with a loud voice,
12:44 Then Jesus c aloud: "Whoever believes in me
19:12 but the Jews c out, "If you release this man,
19:15 They c out, "Away with him!
Ac 7:60 Then he knelt down and c out in a loud voice,
Rev 6:10 they c out with a loud voice,
7:10 They c out in a loud voice, saying,
18:18 and c out as they saw the smoke of her burning,
Tob 6: 3 to swallow the young man's foot, and he c out.
Jdt 4: 9 every man of Israel c out to God with great fervor,
4:12 even draped the altar with sackcloth and c out
4:15 they c out to the Lord with all their might to look
5:12 They c out to their God,
6:18 people fell down and worshiped God, and c out:
7:19 The Israelites then c out to the Lord their God,
7:23 the rulers of the town and c out with a loud voice,
7:29 and they c out to the Lord God with a loud voice.
9: 1 Judith c out to the Lord with a loud voice,
14:16 He c out with a loud voice and wept and groaned
16:11 my weak people c out, and the enemy trembled;
AdE 10: 9 this is Israel, who c out to God and were saved.
11:10 Then they c out to God;
13:18 And all Israel c out mightily,
Sir 51:10 I c out, "Lord, you are my Father;
Sus 1:24 Then Susanna c out with a loud voice,
1:42 Then Susanna c out with a loud voice, and said,
1Mc 2:27 Mattathias c out in the town with a loud voice,
3:50 and they c aloud to Heaven,
4:40 the signal was given with the trumpets, they c out
5:33 who sounded their trumpets and c aloud in prayer.
11:49 their courage failed and they c out to the king
13:45 and they c out with a loud voice,
13:50 Then they c to Simon to make peace with them,
2Mc 8: 3 to hearken to the blood that c out to him;
3Mc 5:51 and c out in a very loud voice,
2Es 10:27 I was afraid, and c with a loud voice and said,
4Mc 6: 4 while a herald who faced him c out,
6:16 more bitterly tormented by this counsel, c out:

CRIER (1) [CRY]

Sir 20:15 he opens his mouth like a town c.

CRIES (24) [CRY]

Ex 22:27 And if your neighbor c out to me, I will listen,
Job 24:12 and the throat of the wounded c for help;
Ps 32: 7 you surround me with glad c of deliverance.
Pr 1:20 Wisdom c out in the street;
1:21 At the busiest corner she c out;
8: 3 at the entrance of the portals she c out:
Isa 15: 5 My heart c out for Moab;
26:17 and c out in her pangs when she is near her time,
40: 3 A voice c out: "In the wilderness prepare the way
42:13 he c out, he shouts aloud,
46: 7 If one c out to it, it does not answer
Hos 8: 2 Israel c to me, "My God, we—
9: 7 Israel c, "The prophet is a fool,
Mic 6: 9 The voice of the LORD c to the city
Zep 1:14 day of the LORD is bitter, the warrior c aloud there.
Ro 9:27 And Isaiah c out concerning Israel,
Heb 5: 7 with loud c and tears, to the one who was able
Jas 5: 4 and the c of the harvesters have reached the ears
Jdt 14:19 and their loud c and shouts rose up throughout
Sir 35:19 she c out against the one who causes them to fall?
3Mc 1:16 and they filled the temple with c and tears;
4: 2 lamentation, and tearful c;
6:17 when the Jews observed this they raised great c
2Es 15: 8 Innocent and righteous blood c out to me,

CRIME (18) [CRIMES, CRIMINAL, CRIMINALS]

Ge 50:17 the c of your brothers and the wrong they did
50:17 Now therefore please forgive the c of the servants
Dt 17: 5 that man or that woman who has committed this c
19:15 a person of any c or wrongdoing in connection
19:20 a c such as this shall never again be committed
21:22 When someone is convicted of a c punishable
Jdg 9:56 for the c he committed against his father
20:12 "What c is this that has been committed
2Sa 3: 8 now with a c concerning this woman.
Job 31:11 For that would be a heinous c;
Ps 56: 7 so repay them for their c;
Pr 28:24 "That is no c," is partner to a thug.
Hos 6: 9 they commit a monstrous c.
Ac 18:14 "If it were a matter of c or serious villainy,
24:20 Or let these men here tell what c they had found
Sir 41:18 of a c, before a judge or magistrate;
2Mc 4:36 and the Greeks shared their hatred of the c.
4:49 even the Tyrians, showing their hatred of the c,

CRIMES (11) [CRIME]

Dt 24:16 only for their own c may persons be put to death.
Ps 64: 6 Who can search out our c?
Jer 41:11 the c that Ishmael son of Nethaniah had done,
44: 9 Have you forgotten the c of your ancestors,
44: 9 your own c and those of your wives,
Eze 7:23 For the land is full of bloody c;
Hos 12:14 so his Lord will bring his c down on him
Ac 25:18 they did not charge him with any of the c
2Mc 13: 6 of sacrilege or notorious for other c.
4Mc 11: 3 from the heavenly justice for even more c.
18:22 For these c divine justice pursued and will pursue

CRIMINAL (5) [CRIME]

Jdg 20: 3 "Tell us, how did this c act come about?"
Job 31:11 that would be a c offense;
Jn 18:30 They answered, "If this man were not a c,
2Ti 2: 9 even to the point of being chained like a c.
1Pe 4:15 let none of you suffer as a murderer, a thief, a c,

CRIMINALS (3) [CRIME]

Lk 23:32 Two others also, who were c,
23:33 they crucified Jesus there with the c,
23:39 of the c who were hanged there kept deriding him

CRIMSON (48)

Ge 38:28 midwife took and bound on his hand a c thread,
38:30 Afterward his brother came out with the c thread
Ex 25: 4 purple, and c yarns and fine linen, goats' hair,
26: 1 and blue, purple, and c yarns;
26:31 purple, and c yarns, and of fine twisted linen;
26:36 purple, and c yarns, and of fine twisted linen,
27:16 purple, and c yarns, and of fine twisted linen,
28: 5 blue, purple, and c yarns, and fine linen.
28: 6 purple, and c yarns, and of fine twisted linen,
28: 8 purple, and c yarns, and of fine twisted linen.
28:15 of gold, of blue and purple and c yarns,
28:33 purple, and c yarns, all around the lower hem,
35: 6 purple, and c yarns, and fine linen;
35:23 or purple or c yarn or fine linen or goats' hair
35:25 in blue and purple and c yarns and fine linen;
35:35 and c yarns, and in fine linen, or by a weaver—
36: 8 and blue, purple, and c yarns,
36:35 He made the curtain of blue, purple, and c yarns,
36:37 purple, and c yarns, and fine twisted linen,
38:18 purple, and c yarns and fine twisted linen.
38:23 and embroiderer in blue, purple, and c yarns,
39: 1 and c yarns they made finely worked vestments,
39: 2 purple, and c yarns, and of fine twisted linen.
39: 3 purple, and c yarns and into the fine twisted linen,
39: 5 purple, and c yarns, and of fine twisted linen;
39: 8 purple, and c yarns, and of fine twisted linen.
39:24 purple, and c yarns, and of fine twisted linen.
39:29 and c yarns, embroidered with needlework;
Lev 14: 4 and cedarwood and c yarn and hyssop be brought
14: 6 with the cedarwood and the c yarn and the hyssop,
14:49 with cedarwood and c yarn and hyssop,
14:51 the cedarwood and the hyssop and the c yarn,
14:52 and with the cedarwood and hyssop and c yarn;
Nu 4: 8 then they shall spread over them a c cloth,
19: 6 and c material, and throw them into the fire
Jos 2:18 and you do not tie this c cord in the window
2:21 Then she tied the c cord in the window.
2Sa 1:24 weep over Saul, who clothed you with c,
2Ch 2: 7 c, and blue fabrics, trained also in engraving,
2:14 and in purple, blue, and c fabrics and fine linen,
3:14 of blue and purple and c fabrics and fine linen,
Pr 31:21 for all her household are clothed in c.
SS 4: 3 Your lips are like a c thread,
Isa 1:18 they are red like c, they shall become like wool.
63: 1 from Bozrah in garments stained c?
Jer 4:30 what do you mean that you dress in c,
Na 2: 3 his soldiers are clothed in c.
Sir 45:11 with twisted c, the work of an artisan;

CRINGE (2) [CRINGING]

Ps 66: 3 of your great power, your enemies c before you.
81:15 Those who hate the LORD would c before him,

CRINGING (2) [CRINGE]

2Sa 22:45 Foreigners came c to me;
Ps 18:44 of me they obeyed me; foreigners came c to me.

CRIPPLED (6)

2Sa 4: 4 Saul's son Jonathan had a son who was c
9: 3 a son of Jonathan; he is c in his feet."
Lk 13:11 with a spirit that had c her for eighteen years.
14:13 when you give a banquet, invite the poor, the c,
14:21 the c, the blind, and the lame.'
Ac 14: 8 for he had been c from birth.

CRISIS (3)

1Co 7:26 I think that, in view of the impending c,
Sir 22:16 after due reflection will not be afraid in a c.
Bar 3: 5 in this c remember your power and your name.

CRISPUS (2)

Ac 18: 8 C, the official of the synagogue,
1Co 1:14 I thank God that I baptized none of you except C

CRITICAL (1) [CRITICIZE]

2Mc 1: 7 in the c distress that came upon us in those years

CRITICISM (1) [CRITICIZE]

Sir 38:17 to avoid c; then be comforted for your grief.

CRITICIZE (2) [CRITICAL, CRITICISM, CRITICIZED]

Sir 11: 7 examine first, and then c.
13:22 If the humble person slips, they even c him;

CRITICIZED (1) [CRITICIZE]

Ac 11: 2 the circumcised believers c him,

CROAK (1)

Zep 2:14 the raven c on the threshold;

CROCODILE‡ (1)

Lev 11:30 the land c, the lizard, the sand lizard,

CROCUS‡ (1)

Isa 35: 1 rejoice and blossom; like the c

CROOKED (21) [CROOKEDNESS]

Dt 32: 5 a perverse and c generation.
2Sa 22:27 and with the c you show yourself perverse.
Ps 18:26 and with the c you show yourself perverse.
125: 5 to their own c ways the LORD will lead away
Pr 2:15 those whose paths are c, and who are devious
4:24 Put away from you c speech,
6:12 scoundrel and a villain goes around with c speech,
8: 8 there is nothing twisted or c in them.
11:20 C minds are an abomination to the LORD,
17:20 The c of mind do not prosper,
21: 8 The way of the guilty is c,
28: 6 Better to be poor and walk in integrity than to be c
28:18 but whoever follows c ways will fall into the Pit.
Ecc 1:15 What is c cannot be made straight,
7:13 who can make straight what he has made c?
Isa 59: 8 Their roads they have made c;
La 3: 9 he has made my paths c.
Lk 3: 5 and the c shall be made straight,
Ac 13:10 not stop making c the straight paths of the Lord?
Php 2:15 in the midst of a c and perverse generation,
Wis 13:13 useful for nothing, a stick c and full of knots,

CROOKEDNESS (1) [CROOKED]

Pr 11: 3 but the c of the treacherous destroys them.

CROP (10) [CROPS]

Lev 1:16 He shall remove its c with its contents
25:15 for the remaining c years.
25:20 if we may not sow or gather in our c?
25:21 so that it will yield a c for three years.
25:22 you will be eating from the old c;
Dt 22: 9 both the c that you have sown and the yield of
1Co 9:10 in hope of a share in the c.
Heb 6: 7 a c useful to those for whom it is cultivated,
Jas 5: 7 The farmer waits for the precious c from the earth,
Sir 7: 3 and you will not reap a sevenfold c.

CROPS (12) [CROP]

Jos 5:12 they ate the c of the land of Canaan that year.
Ne 10:31 and we will forego the c of the seventh year and
Ps 78:46 He gave their c to the caterpillar,
Pr 14: 4 abundant c come by the strength of the ox.
Joel 1:11 for the c of the field are ruined.
Lk 12:17 for I have no place to store my c?'
2Ti 2: 6 to have the first share of the c.
Tob 1: 6 with the first fruits of the c and the firstlings of
Wis 16:19 to destroy the c of the unrighteous land.
16:22 that the c of their enemies were being destroyed
16:26 not the production of c that feeds humankind but
1Mc 11:34 from the c of the land and the fruit of the trees.

CROSS (92) [CROSS-EXAMINE, CROSS-EXAMINES, CROSSED, CROSSES, CROSSING, CROSSINGS, CROSSROADS]

Nu 32: 5 do not make us c the Jordan."
32:21 and all those of you who bear arms c the Jordan
32:27 but your servants will c over,
32:29 will c over the Jordan with you and the land shall
32:30 but if they will not c over with you armed,
32:32 We will c over armed before the LORD into
33:51 you c over the Jordan into the land of Canaan,
34: 4 and c to Zin, and its outer limit shall be south
34: 4 it shall go on to Hazar-addar, and c to Azmon;
35:10 When you c the Jordan into the land of Canaan,
Dt 2:13 "Now then, proceed to c over the Wadi Zered."
2:18 "Today you are going to c the boundary of Moab
2:24 "Proceed on your journey and c the Wadi Arnon.
2:29 until I c the Jordan into the land that
3:18 all your troops shall c over armed as the vanguard
3:21 to all the kingdoms into which you are about to c.
3:25 Let me c over to see the good land beyond
3:27 Look well, for you shall not c over this Jordan.
3:28 because it is he who shall c over at the head
4:14 to observe in the land that you are about to c into
4:21 and he vowed that I should not c the Jordan and
4:22 but you are going to c over to take possession of
6: 1 to observe in the land that you are about to c into
9: 1 You are about to c the Jordan today,
11:31 When you c the Jordan to go in to occupy the land
12:10 When you c over the Jordan and live in the land
27: 2 On the day that you c over the Jordan into the land

Dt 30:13 "Who will c to the other side of the sea for us,
31: 2 'You shall not c over this Jordan.'
31: 3 LORD your God himself will c over before you.
31: 3 Joshua also will c over before you,
34: 4 but you shall not c over there."
Jos 1: 2 Now proceed to c the Jordan,
1:11 for in three days you are to c over the Jordan,
1:14 But all the warriors among you shall c over armed
3:14 When the people set out from their tents to c over
22:19 c over into the LORD's land where
Jdg 3:28 and allowed no one to c over.
12: 1 "Why did you c over to fight against
1Sa 14: 8 "Now we will c over to those men
30:10 too exhausted to c the Wadi Besor.
2Sa 17:16 but by all means c over;
17:21 They said to David, "Go and c the water quickly;
19:18 as he was about to c the Jordan,
1Ki 2:37 For on the day you go out, and c the Wadi Kidron,
Isa 11:15 and make a way to c on foot;
23: 6 C over to Tarshish—wail,
23:10 C over to your own land, O ships of Tarshish;
23:12 c over to Cyprus—even there you will have no rest
51:10 of the sea a way for the redeemed to c over?
Jer 2:10 C to the coasts of Cyprus and look,
41:10 of Nethaniah took them captive and set out to c
Eze 47: 5 and it was a river that I could not c,
Am 5: 5 do not enter into Gilgal or c over to Beer-sheba;
6: 2 C over to Calneh, and see;
Mt 10:38 not take up the c and follow me is not worthy
16:24 let them deny themselves and take up their c
23:15 For you c sea and land to make a single convert,
27:32 they compelled this man to carry his c.
27:40 If you are the Son of God, come down from the c."
27:42 let him come down from the c now,
Mk 8:34 let them deny themselves and take up their c
15:21 in from the country, to carry his c;
15:30 save yourself, and come down from the c!"
15:32 the King of Israel, come down from the c now,
Lk 9:23 let them deny themselves and take up their c daily
14:27 the c and follow me cannot be my disciple.
16:26 and no one can c from there to us.'
23:26 and they laid the c on him,
Jn 19:17 and carrying the c by himself,
19:19 also had an inscription written and put on the c.
19:25 standing near the c of Jesus were his mother,
19:31 the Jews did not want the bodies left on the c
Ac 16:10 we immediately tried to c over to Macedonia,
18:27 And when he wished to c over to Achaia,
1Co 1:17 the c of Christ might not be emptied of its power.
1:18 the c is foolishness to those who are perishing,
Gal 5:11 In that case the offense of the c has been removed.
6:12 only that they may not be persecuted for the c
6:14 of anything except the c of our Lord Jesus Christ,
Eph 2:16 both groups to God in one body through the c,
Php 2: 8 obedient to the point of death—even death on a c.
3:18 For many live as enemies of the c of Christ;
Col 1:20 by making peace through the blood of his c.
2:14 He set this aside, nailing it to the c.
Heb 12: 2 of the joy that was set before him endured the c,
1Pe 2:24 He himself bore our sins in his body on the c,
1Mc 5:41 we will c over to him and defeat him."
9:48 and the enemy did not c the Jordan to attack them.
16: 6 that the soldiers were afraid to c the stream,
2Es 7:86 how some of them will c over into torments.
13:47 so that they may be able to c over.

CROSS-EXAMINE (1) [CROSS, EXAMINE]

Lk 11:53 toward him and to c him about many things,

CROSS-EXAMINES (1) [CROSS, EXAMINE]

Pr 18:17 until the other comes and c.

CROSSED‡ (62) [CROSS]

Ge 31:21 starting out he c the Euphrates,
32:10 for with only my staff I c this Jordan;
32:22 and c the ford of the Jabbok.
Dt 2:13 So we c over the Wadi Zered.
2:14 until we c the Wadi Zered was thirty-eight years,
27: 3 on them all the words of this law when you have c
27: 4 So when you have c over the Jordan,
27:12 When you have c over the Jordan,
Jos 2:23 They c over, came to Joshua son of Nun,
3:16 Then the people c over opposite Jericho.
4: 7 When it c over the Jordan,
4:10 The people c over in haste.
4:11 and the priests, c over in front of the people.
4:12 of Manasseh c over armed before the Israelites,
4:13 About forty thousand armed for war c over before
4:22 'Israel c over the Jordan here on dry ground.'
4:23 the waters of the Jordan for you until you c over,
4:23 which he dried up for us until we c over,
5: 1 the Jordan for the Israelites until they had c over,
Jdg 8: 4 Then Gideon came to the Jordan and c over,
10: 9 also c the Jordan to fight against Judah and
11:32 So Jephthah c over to the Ammonites to fight
12: 1 and they c to Zaphon and said to Jephthah,
12: 3 and c over against the Ammonites,
1Sa 13: 7 Some Hebrews c the Jordan to the land of Gad
2Sa 2:29 they c the Jordan, and, marching
10:17 he gathered all Israel together, and c the Jordan,
15:23 the king c the Wadi Kidron,
17:20 "They have c over the brook of water."
17:22 the people who were with him set out and c
17:22 by daybreak not one was left who had not c
2Sa 17:24 Absalom c the Jordan with all the men of Israel.
19:39 the people c over the Jordan, and the king c over;
24: 5 They c the Jordan, and began from Aroer and
2Ki 2: 8 until the two of them c on dry ground.
2: 9 When they had c, Elijah said to Elisha,
8:21 Then Joram c over to Zair with all his chariots.
1Ch 12:15 the men who c the Jordan in the first month,
19:17 he gathered all Israel together, c the Jordan,
2Ch 21: 9 Then Jehoram c over with his commanders
Isa 10:29 they have c over the pass, at Geba they lodge for
16: 8 their shoots once spread abroad and c over
23: 2 your messengers c over the sea
Jer 48:32 Your branches c over the sea,
Eze 47: 5 a river that could not be c.
Mt 9: 1 And after getting into a boat he c the sea and came
14:34 they had c over, they came to land at Gennesaret.
Mk 5:21 Jesus had c again in the boat to the other side,
6:53 When they had c over, they came to land
Tob 5:10 to Media and have c all its plains,
1Mc 3:37 He c the Euphrates river and went through
5: 6 Then he c over to attack the Ammonites,
5:24 Judas Maccabeus and his brother Jonathan c
5:43 Then he c over against them first,
5:52 Then they c the Jordan into the large plain
9:34 and he with all his army c the Jordan.
12:30 for they had c the Eleutherus river.
16: 6 to cross the stream, so he c over first;
16: 6 when his troops saw him, they c over after him.
3Mc 1: 2 and c over by night to the tent of Ptolemy,
2Es 13:44 the channels of the river until they had c over.

CROSSES (2) [CROSS]

Dt 9: 3 the one who c over before you as a devouring fire;
1Mc 5:40 "If he c over to us first,

CROSSING‡ (16) [CROSS]

Ge 48:14 c his hands, for Manasseh was the firstborn.
Dt 4:22 For I am going to die in this land without c over
4:26 from the land that you are c the Jordan to occupy;
11: 8 and occupy the land that you are c over to occupy,
11:11 the land that you are c over to occupy is a land
30:18 not live long in the land that you are c the Jordan
31:13 the land that you are c over the Jordan to possess."
32:47 the land that you are c over the Jordan to possess."
Jos 3: 1 They camped there before c over.
3:17 While all Israel were c over on dry ground,
3:17 until the entire nation finished c over the Jordan.
4: 1 the entire nation had finished c over the Jordan,
4:11 As soon as all the people had finished c over,
Jdg 6:33 and c the Jordan they encamped in the Valley
2Sa 19:18 while the c was taking place,
Jdt 5:15 and c over the Jordan they took possession of all

CROSSINGS (1) [CROSS]

Ob 1:14 not have stood at the c to cut off his fugitives;

CROSSROADS (2) [CROSS, ROAD]

Pr 8: 2 beside the way, at the c she takes her stand;
Jer 6:16 Stand at the c, and look, and ask for the ancient

CROUCH (4) [CROUCHED, CROUCHES]

Job 38:40 when they c in their dens,
39: 3 when they c to give birth to their offspring,
Ps 10:10 they c, and the helpless fall by their might.
Isa 10: 4 to c among the prisoners or fall among the slain?

CROUCHED (1) [CROUCH]

Nu 24: 9 He c, he lay down like a lion, and like a lioness;

CROUCHES (1) [CROUCH]

Ge 49: 9 He c down, he stretches out like a lion,

CROW (1) [COCKCROW, CROWED, CROWS]

Lk 22:34 "I tell you, Peter, the cock will not c this day,

CROWD (124) [CROWDED, CROWDING, CROWDS]

Ex 12:38 A mixed c also went up with them,
Mt 9:23 the flute players and the c making a commotion,
9:25 But when the c had been put outside,
13: 2 while the whole c stood on the beach.
14: 5 Herod wanted to put him to death, he feared the c,
14:14 When he went ashore, he saw a great c;
15:10 Then he called the c to him and said to them,
15:31 c was amazed when they saw the mute speaking,
15:32 "I have compassion for the c,
15:33 in the desert to feed so great a c?"
15:35 Then ordering the c to sit down on the ground,
17:14 When they came to the c, a man came to him,
20:29 they were leaving Jericho, a large c followed him.
20:31 The c sternly ordered them to be quiet;
21: 8 A very large c spread their cloaks on the road,
21:26 we say, 'Of human origin,' we are afraid of the c;
22:33 the c heard it, they were astounded at his teaching.
26:47 with him was a large c with swords and clubs,
27:15 to release a prisoner for the c,
27:24 the c, saying, "I am innocent of this man's blood;
Mk 2: 4 to Jesus because of the c, they removed the roof
2:13 whole c gathered around him, and he taught them.
3: 9 to have a boat ready for him because of the c, so
3:20 and the c came together again,
Mk 3:32 A c was sitting around him;
4: 1 a very large c gathered around him that he got into
4: 1 while the whole c was beside the sea on the land.
4:36 And leaving the c behind,
5:21 a great c gathered around him;
5:24 And a large c followed him and pressed in on him.
5:27 up behind him in the c and touched his cloak,
5:30 Jesus turned about in the c and said,
5:31 "You see the c pressing in on you;
6:34 As he went ashore, he saw a great c;
6:45 to Bethsaida, while he dismissed the c.
7:14 Then he called the c again and said to them,
7:17 When he had left the c and entered the house,
7:33 He took him aside in private, away from the c,
8: 1 when there was again a great c without anything
8: 2 "I have compassion for the c,
8: 6 Then he ordered the c to sit down on the ground;
8: 6 and they distributed them to the c.
8:34 He called the c with his disciples,
9:14 they saw a great c around them,
9:15 When the whole c saw him,
9:17 Someone from the c answered him, "Teacher,
9:25 When Jesus saw that a c came running together,
10:46 and a large c were leaving Jericho,
11:18 the whole c was spellbound by his teaching.
11:32 they were afraid of the c,
12:12 they wanted to arrest him, but they feared the c.
12:37 And the large c was listening to him with delight.
12:41 and watched the c putting money into the treasury.
14:43 and with him there was a c with swords and clubs,
15: 8 the c came and began to ask Pilate to do for them
15:11 up the c to have him release Barabbas
15:15 So Pilate, wishing to satisfy the c,
Lk 5: 1 c was pressing in on him to hear the word of God,
5:19 finding no way to bring him in because of the c,
5:19 the tiles into the middle of the c in front of Jesus.
5:29 a large c of tax collectors and others sitting at
6:17 a great c of his disciples and a great multitude
6:19 And all in the c were trying to touch him,
7: 9 and turning to the c that followed him, he said,
7:11 and his disciples and a large c went with him.
7:12 and with her was a large c from the town.
8: 4 When a great c gathered and people from town
8:19 but they could not reach him because of the c.
8:40 Now when Jesus returned, the c welcomed him,
9:12 "Send the c away, so that they may go into
9:16 and gave them to the disciples to set before the c.
9:37 down from the mountain, a great c met him.
9:38 Just then a man from the c shouted, "Teacher,
11:27 a woman in the c raised her voice and said to him,
12: 1 Meanwhile, when the c gathered by the thousands,
12:13 Someone in the c said to him, "Teacher,
13:14 the c, "There are six days on which work ought to
13:17 and the entire c was rejoicing at all
18:36 When he heard a c going by,
19: 3 but on account of the c he could not,
19:39 Some of the Pharisees in the c said to him,
22: 6 to betray him to them when no c was present.
22:47 While he was still speaking, suddenly a c came,
Jn 5:13 for Jesus had disappeared in the c that was there.
6: 2 A large c kept following him,
6: 5 When he looked up and saw a large c coming
6:22 the c that had stayed on the other side of
6:24 So when the c saw that neither Jesus
7:12 others were saying, "No, he is deceiving the c."
7:20 The c answered, "You have a demon!
7:31 many in the c believed in him and were saying,
7:32 The Pharisees heard the c muttering such things
7:40 When they heard these words, some in the c said,
7:43 So there was a division in the c because of him.
7:49 But this c, which does not know the law—
11:42 I have said this for the sake of the c standing here,
12: 9 the great c of the Jews learned that he was there,
12:12 the great c that had come to the festival heard
12:17 So the c that had been with him
12:18 that he had performed this sign that the c went
12:29 The c standing there heard it and said
12:34 The c answered him, "We have heard from
Ac 1:15 up among the believers (together the c numbered
2: 6 at this sound the c gathered and was bewildered,
14:14 they tore their clothes and rushed out into the c,
16:22 The c joined in attacking them,
19:30 Paul wished to go into the c,
19:33 Some of the c gave instructions to Alexander,
19:35 But when the town clerk had quieted the c,
21:27 in the temple, stirred up the whole c.
21:34 Some in the c shouted one thing, some another;
21:36 c that followed kept shouting, "Away with him!"
24:12 with anyone in the temple or stirring up a c either
24:18 without any c or disturbance.
Jdt 2:20 with them went a mixed c like a swarm of locusts,
Sir 16:28 They do not c one another,
31:14 and do not c your neighbor at the dish.
2Mc 14:43 and the c was now rushing in through the doors.
14:43 and bravely threw himself down into the c.
14:45 and his wounds were severe he ran through the c;
14:46 took them in both hands and hurled them at the c,
1Es 8:91 there gathered around him a very great c of men
3Mc 1:24 Meanwhile the c, as before,
5:48 as well as by the trampling of the c,

CROWDED (4) [CROWD]

Isa 49:19 surely now you will be too c for your inhabitants,
49:20 "The place is too c for me;
3Mc 1:20 and without a backward look they c together at
5:41 it is c with masses of people,

CROWDING (1) [CROWD]
3Mc 5:46 with countless masses of people **c** their way into

CROWDS‡ (61) [CROWD]
Mt 4:25 And great **c** followed him from Galilee,
5: 1 When Jesus saw the **c**, he went up the mountain;
7:28 the **c** were astounded at his teaching,
8: 1 down from the mountain, great **c** followed him;
8:18 Now when Jesus saw great **c** around him,
9: 8 When the **c** saw it, they were filled with awe,
9:33 and the **c** were amazed and said,
9:36 When he saw the **c**, he had compassion for them,
11: 7 Jesus began to speak to the **c** about John:
12:15 Many **c** followed him, and he cured all of them,
12:23 All the **c** were amazed and said,
12:46 While he was still speaking to the **c**,
13: 2 Such great **c** gathered around him that he got into
13:34 Jesus told the **c** all these things in parables;
13:36 Then he left the **c** and went into the house.
14:13 But when the **c** heard it,
14:15 the **c** away so that they may go into the villages
14:19 Then he ordered the **c** to sit down on the grass.
14:19 and the disciples gave them to the **c**.
14:22 ahead to the other side, while he dismissed the **c**.
14:23 And after he had dismissed the **c**,
15:30 Great **c** came to him, bringing with them the lame,
15:36 and the disciples gave them to the **c**.
15:39 After sending away the **c**,
19: 2 Large **c** followed him, and he cured them there.
21: 9 The **c** that went ahead of him and
21:11 The **c** were saying, "This is the prophet Jesus
21:46 They wanted to arrest him, but they feared the **c**,
23: 1 Then Jesus said to the **c** and to his disciples,
26:55 At that hour Jesus said to the **c**,
27:20 the elders persuaded the **c** to ask for Barabbas and
Mk 10: 1 And **c** again gathered around him;
Lk 3: 7 John said to the **c** that came out to be baptized
3:10 And the **c** asked him, "What then should we do?"
4:42 And the **c** were looking for him;
5: 3 Then he sat down and taught the **c** from the boat.
5:15 many **c** would gather to hear him and to be cured
7:24 Jesus began to speak to the **c** about John:
8:42 As he went, the **c** pressed in on him.
8:45 "Master, the **c** surround you and press in on you."
9:11 When the **c** found out about it, they followed him;
9:18 he asked them, "Who do the **c** say that I am?"
11:14 who had been mute spoke, and the **c** were amazed.
11:29 When the **c** were increasing, he began to say,
12:54 also said to the **c**, "When you see a cloud rising in
14:25 Now large **c** were traveling with him;
23: 4 Then Pilate said to the chief priests and the **c**,
23:48 And when all the **c** who had gathered there
Jn 7:12 considerable complaining about him among the **c**.
Ac 8: 6 The **c** with one accord listened eagerly
13:45 the Jews saw the **c**, they were filled with jealousy;
14:11 When the **c** saw what Paul had done,
14:13 he and the **c** wanted to offer sacrifice.
14:18 the **c** from offering sacrifice to them.
14:19 from Antioch and Iconium and won over the **c**.
17:13 they came there too, to stir up and incite the **c**.
2Mc 3:18 of their houses in **c** to make a general supplication
4:40 **c** were becoming aroused and filled with anger,
3Mc 1:28 of the **c** resulted in an immense uproar;
3: 8 and the **c** that suddenly were forming,
5:24 The **c** of the city had been assembled

CROWED‡ (6) [CROW]
Mt 26:74 At that moment the cock **c**.
Mk 14:68 into the forecourt. Then the cock **c**.
14:72 At that moment the cock **c** for the second time.
Lk 22:60 while he was still speaking, the cock **c**.
Jn 18:27 and at that moment the cock **c**.
3Mc 5:23 as soon as the cock had **c** in the early morning,

CROWN‡ (81) [CROWNED, CROWNS]
Lev 8: 9 in front, he set the golden ornament, the holy **c**,
Dt 28:35 from the sole of your foot to the **c** of your head.
2Sa 1:10 the **c** that was on his head and the armlet that was
12:30 He took the **c** of Milcom from his head;
14:25 to the **c** of his head there was no blemish in him.
1Ki 7:31 within the **c** whose height was one cubit;
2Ki 11:12 he brought out the king's son, put the **c** on him,
1Ch 20: 2 David took the **c** of Milcom from his head;
2Ch 23:11 he brought out the king's son, put the **c** on him,
Est 1:11 wearing the royal **c**, in order to show the peoples
2:17 and devotion, so that he set the royal **c**
6: 8 with a royal **c** on its head.
8:15 with a great golden **c** and a mantle of fine linen
Job 2: 7 from the sole of his foot to the **c** of his head.
19: 9 and taken the **c** from my head.
31:36 I would bind it on me like a **c**;
Ps 21: 3 you set a **c** of fine gold on his head.
65:11 You **c** the year with your bounty;
68:21 the hairy **c** of those who walk in their guilty ways.
89:19 "I have set the **c** on one who is mighty,
89:39 you have defiled his **c** in the dust.
132:18 but on him, his **c** will gleam."
Pr 4: 9 she will bestow on you a beautiful **c**."
12: 4 A good wife is the **c** of her husband,
14:24 The **c** of the wise is their wisdom,
16:31 Gray hair is a **c** of glory;
17: 6 Grandchildren are the **c** of the aged,
27:24 nor a **c** for all generations.
SS 3:11 at the **c** with which his mother crowned him on
Isa 62: 3 be a **c** of beauty in the hand of the LORD,
Jer 2:16 and Tahpanhes have broken the **c** of your head.
13:18 your beautiful **c** has come down from your head."
La 5:16 The **c** has fallen from our head;
Eze 16:12 and a beautiful **c** upon your head.
21:26 Remove the turban, take off the **c**;
Zec 6:11 Take the silver and gold and make a **c**,
6:14 And the **c** shall be in the care of Heldai, Tobijah,
9:16 like the jewels of a **c** they shall shine on his land.
Mt 27:29 and after twisting some thorns into a **c**,
Mk 15:17 twisting some thorns into a **c**, they put it on him.
Jn 19: 2 soldiers wove a **c** of thorns and put it on his head,
19: 5 wearing the **c** of thorns and the purple robe.
Php 4: 1 my joy and **c**, stand firm in the Lord in this way,
1Th 2:19 or joy or **c** of boasting before our Lord Jesus
2Ti 4: 8 on there is reserved for me the **c** of righteousness,
Jas 1:12 a one has stood the test and will receive the **c**
1Pe 5: 4 you will win the **c** of glory that never fades away.
Rev 2:10 and I will give you the **c** of life.
3:11 so that no one may seize your **c**.
6: 2 Its rider had a bow; a **c** was given to him,
12: 1 and on her head a **c** of twelve stars.
14:14 with a golden **c** on his head,
AdE 8:15 and wearing a gold **c** and a turban of purple linen.
Wis 2: 8 Let us **c** ourselves with rosebuds
5:16 a glorious **c** and a beautiful diadem from the hand
Sir 1:11 and gladness and a **c** of rejoicing.
1:18 The fear of the Lord is the **c** of wisdom,
6:31 and put her on like a splendid **c**.
11: 5 but one who was never thought of has worn a **c**.
15: 6 He will find gladness and a **c** of rejoicing,
25: 6 Rich experience is the **c** of the aged,
40: 4 and a **c** to the one who is clothed in burlap,
45:12 with a gold **c** upon his turban,
Bel 1:36 by the **c** of his head and carried him by his hair;
1Mc 6:15 He gave him the **c** and his robe and the signet,
8:14 not one of them has put on a **c** or worn purple as
10:20 He also sent him a purple robe and a golden **c**.
10:29 from payment of tribute and salt tax and **c** levies,
11:13 Ptolemy entered Antioch and put on the **c** of Asia.
11:13 the **c** of Egypt and that of Asia.
11:35 and the salt pits and the **c** taxes due to us—
11:54 to reign and put on the **c**.
12:39 to become king in Asia and put on the **c**,
13:32 putting on the **c** of Asia;
13:37 We have received the gold **c** and the palm branch
13:39 and cancel the **c** tax that you owe;
14: 5 To **c** all his honors he took Joppa for a harbor,
2Mc 14: 4 presenting to him a **c** of gold and a palm,
1Es 4:30 the **c** from the king's head and put it on her own,
2Es 2:43 and on the head of each of them he placed a **c**,
4Mc 17:15 Reverence for God was victor and gave the **c**

CROWNED‡ (11) [CROWN]
Ps 8: 5 and **c** them with glory and honor.
Pr 14:18 but the clever are **c** with knowledge.
SS 3:11 the crown with which his mother **c** him on the day
2Ti 2: 5 no one is **c** without competing according to
Heb 2: 7 you have **c** them with glory and honor,
2: 9 now **c** with glory and honor because of
Jdt 15:13 and she and those who were with her **c** themselves
Wis 4: 2 throughout all time it marches, **c** in triumph,
Sir 45:26 And now bless the Lord who has **c** you with glory.
3Mc 7:16 **c** with all sorts of very fragrant flowers,
2Es 2:45 Now they are being **c**, and receive palms."

CROWNS‡ (13) [CROWN]
Ps 103: 4 who **c** you with steadfast love and mercy,
SS 7: 5 Your head **c** you like Carmel,
Isa 23: 8 the bestower of **c**, whose merchants were princes,
Eze 23:42 and beautiful **c** upon their heads.
Rev 4: 4 with golden **c** on their heads.
4:10 they cast their **c** before the throne, singing,
9: 7 On their heads were what looked like **c** of gold;
LtJ 6: 9 People take gold and make **c** for the heads
1Mc 1: 9 They all put on **c** after his death,
1:22 the bowls, the golden censers, the curtain, the **c**,
4:57 of the temple with golden **c** and small shields;
11:13 Thus he put two **c** on his head,
2Es 2:46 "Who is that young man who is placing **c** on them

CROWS (7) [CROW]
Mt 26:34 before the cock **c**, you will deny me three times."
26:75 the cock **c**, you will deny me three times."
Mk 14:30 this day, this very night, before the cock **c** twice,
14:72 "Before the cock **c** twice,
Lk 22:61 how he had said to him, "Before the cock **c** today,
Jn 13:38 Very truly, I tell you, before the cock **c**,
LtJ 6:55 they are like **c** between heaven and earth.

CRUCIBLE (2)
Pr 17: 3 The **c** is for silver, and the furnace is for gold,
27:21 The **c** is for silver, and the furnace is for gold,

CRUCIFIED (40) [CRUCIFY]
Mt 20:19 to the Gentiles to be mocked and flogged and **c**;
26: 2 and the Son of Man will be handed over to be **c**."
27:22 All of them said, "Let him be **c**!"
27:23 But they shouted all the more, "Let him be **c**!"
27:26 after flogging Jesus, he handed him over to be **c**.
27:35 And when they had **c** him,
27:38 Then two bandits were **c** with him,
27:44 The bandits who were **c** with him also taunted him
28: 5 I know that you are looking for Jesus who was **c**.
Mk 15:15 after flogging Jesus, he handed him over to be **c**.
15:24 And they **c** him, and divided his clothes
15:25 in the morning when they **c** him.
15:27 And with him they **c** two bandits,
15:32 Those who were **c** with him also taunted him.
16: 6 you are looking for Jesus of Nazareth, who was **c**.
Lk 23:23 with loud shouts that he should be **c**;
23:33 they **c** Jesus there with the criminals,
24: 7 and be **c**, and on the third day rise again."
24:20 over to be condemned to death and **c** him.
Jn 19:16 Then he handed him over to them to be **c**.
19:18 There they **c** him, and with him two others,
19:20 the place where Jesus was **c** was near the city;
19:23 When the soldiers had **c** Jesus,
19:31 of the **c** men broken and the bodies removed.
19:32 the first and of the other who had been **c** with him.
19:41 there was a garden in the place where he was **c**,
Ac 2:23 you **c** and killed by the hands of those outside
2:36 both Lord and Messiah, this Jesus whom you **c**."
4:10 whom you **c**, whom God raised from the dead.
Ro 6: 6 We know that our old self was **c** with him so that
1Co 1:13 Was Paul **c** for you?
1:23 but we proclaim Christ **c**,
2: 2 among you except Jesus Christ, and him **c**.
2: 8 they had, they would not have **c** the Lord of glory.
2Co 13: 4 For he was **c** in weakness,
Gal 2:19 I have been **c** with Christ;
3: 1 that Jesus Christ was publicly exhibited as **c**!
5:24 to Christ Jesus have **c** the flesh with its passions
6:14 by which the world has been **c** to me,
Rev 11: 8 where also their Lord was **c**.

CRUCIFY (13) [CRUCIFIED, CRUCIFYING]
Mt 23:34 and scribes, some of whom you will kill and **c**,
27:31 Then they led him away to **c** him.
Mk 15:13 They shouted back, "**C** him!"
15:14 But they shouted all the more, "**C** him!"
15:20 Then they led him out to **c** him.
Lk 23:21 but they kept shouting, "**C**, **c** him!"
Jn 19: 6 the police saw him, they shouted, "**C** him! **C** him!"
19: 6 "Take him yourselves and **c** him;
19:10 to release you, and power to **c** you?"
19:15 "Away with him! Away with him! **C** him!"
19:15 Pilate asked them, "Shall I **c** your King?"

CRUCIFYING (1) [CRUCIFY]
Heb 6: 6 since on their own they are **c** again the Son of God

CRUDE (1)
Sir 29:22 under their own **c** roof than sumptuous food in

CRUEL (26) [CRUELLY, CRUELTIES, CRUELTY]
Ge 49: 7 for it is fierce, and their wrath, for it is **c**!
Ex 6: 9 because of their broken spirit and their **c** slavery.
Dt 32:33 the poison of serpents, the **c** venom of asps.
Job 30:21 You have turned **c** to me;
Ps 71: 4 from the grasp of the unjust and **c**.
144:11 Rescue me from the **c** sword,
Pr 11:17 but the **c** do themselves harm.
12:10 but the mercy of the wicked is **c**.
17:11 but a **c** messenger will be sent against them.
27: 4 Wrath is **c**, anger is overwhelming,
28:16 A ruler who lacks understanding is a **c** oppressor;
Ecc 9:12 Like fish taken in a **c** net,
Isa 13: 9 See, the day of the LORD comes, **c**,
27: 1 On that day the LORD with his **c** and great
Jer 6:23 they are **c** and have no mercy,
25:38 of the **c** sword, and because of his fierce anger.
50:42 they are **c** and have no mercy.
La 4: 3 but my people has become **c**,
Jdt 9:13 and bruise on those who have planned **c** things
Sir 13:12 **C** are those who do not keep your secrets;
2Mc 4:25 of a **c** tyrant and the rage of a savage wild beast.
7:27 deriding the **c** tyrant: "My son, have pity on me.
1Es 2:27 and **c** kings ruled in Jerusalem and exacted tribute
3Mc 3: 1 and put to death by the most **c** means.
4Mc 6: 8 the **c** guards rushed at him and began to kick him
18:20 with fire in his **c** caldrons,

CRUELLY (5) [CRUEL]
Jdg 4: 3 and had oppressed the Israelites **c** twenty years.
Job 39:16 It deals **c** with its young, as if they were
2Es 7:67 that we shall be preserved alive but **c** tormented?
4Mc 8: 2 they would be tortured even more **c**.
11: 1 When he too died, after being **c** tortured,

CRUELTIES (1) [CRUEL]
2Ch 16:10 And Asa inflicted **c** on some of the people at

CRUELTY (4) [CRUEL]
Na 3:19 For who has ever escaped your endless **c**?
2Mc 12: 5 Judas heard of the **c** visited on his compatriots,
3Mc 6:24 and surpassing tyrants in **c**;
7: 5 girding themselves with a **c** more savage than that

CRUMBLES (1)
Job 14:18 "But the mountain falls and **c** away,

CRUMBS (3)
Ps 147:17 He hurls down hail like **c**—
Mt 15:27 dogs eat the **c** that fall from their masters' table."
Mk 7:28 even the dogs under the table eat the children's **c**."

CRUSE (KJV) See BOWL, JUG, JAR

CRUSH (29) [CRUSHED, CRUSHES, CRUSHING]

Nu 24:17 it shall **c** the borderlands of Moab,
Dt 33:11 **c** the loins of his adversaries,
2Sa 22:30 By you I can **c** a troop,
Est 9:24 that is "the lot"—to **c** and destroy them;
Job 6: 9 that it would please God to **c** me,
39:15 forgetting that a foot may **c** them,
Ps 18:29 By you I can **c** a troop,
72: 4 give deliverance to the needy, and **c** the oppressor.
89:23 I will **c** his foes before him and strike
94: 5 They **c** your people, O LORD,
Pr 22:22 or **c** the afflicted at the gate;
27:22 **C** a fool in a mortar with a pestle along
Isa 41:15 you shall thresh the mountains and **c** them,
53:10 it was the will of the LORD to **c** him with pain.
La 1:15 a time against me to **c** my young men;
Da 2:40 it shall **c** and shatter all these.
2:44 It shall **c** all these kingdoms and bring them to
Am 4: 1 who **c** the needy, who say to their husbands,
Mt 21:44 and it will **c** anyone on whom it falls."
Mk 3: 9 so that they would not **c** him;
Lk 19:44 They will **c** you to the ground,
20:18 and it will **c** anyone on whom it falls."
Ro 16:20 God of peace will shortly **c** Satan under your feet.
Jdt 9:10 **c** their arrogance by the hand of a woman.
Sir 36:12 **C** the heads of hostile rulers who say,
1Mc 3:22 He himself will **c** them before us;
4:10 with our ancestors and **c** this army
7:42 So also **c** this army before us today;
2Es 15:60 As they pass by they shall **c** the hateful city,

CRUSHED (61) [CRUSH]

Lev 16:12 and two handfuls of **c** sweet incense,
21:20 or an itching disease or scabs or **c** testicles.
22:24 that has its testicles bruised or **c** or torn or cut,
Dt 9:21 the calf, and burned it with fire and **c** it,
23: 1 No one whose testicles are **c**
28:33 you shall be continually abused and **c**,
Jdg 5:26 she struck Sisera a blow, she **c** his head,
9:53 on Abimelech's head, and **c** his skull.
10: 8 and they **c** and oppressed the Israelites that year.
2Sa 22:43 I **c** them and stamped them down like the mire of
2Ch 2:10 twenty thousand cors of **c** wheat,
15:16 Asa cut down her image, **c** it,
Job 4:19 who are **c** like a moth.
5: 4 they are **c** in the gate,
20:19 For they have **c** and abandoned the poor,
22: 9 and the arms of the orphans you have **c**.
34:25 he overturns them in the night, and they are **c**.
Ps 34:18 and saves the **c** in spirit.
38: 8 I am utterly spent and **c**;
51: 8 let the bones that you have **c** rejoice.
74:14 You **c** the heads of Leviathan;
89:10 You **c** Rahab like a carcass;
Pr 27:22 a fool in a mortar with a pestle along with **c** grain,
Isa 27: 9 the stones of the altars like chalkstones **c**
28:28 Grain is **c** for bread, but one does
42: 4 or be **c** until he has established justice in the earth;
53: 5 But he was wounded for our transgressions, **c**
59: 5 and the **c** egg hatches out a viper.
63: 6 I **c** them in my wrath,
Jer 22:20 cry out from Abarim, for all your lovers are **c**.
23: 9 My heart is **c** within me, all my bones shake;
51:34 of Babylon has devoured me, he has **c** me;
La 3:34 all the prisoners of the land are **c** under foot,
Eze 6: 9 how I was **c** by their wanton heart
36: 3 and **c** you from all sides, so that you became
Da 2:45 and that it **c** the iron, the bronze, the clay,
Hos 5:11 Ephraim is oppressed, **c** in judgment,
Hab 3:13 You **c** the head of the wicked house,
2Co 1: 8 unbearably **c** that we despaired of life itself.
4: 8 We are afflicted in every way, but not **c**;
Sir 47: 7 he **c** their power to our own day.
1Mc 3:23 and they were **c** before him.
4:14 The Gentiles were **c**, and fled into the plain,
4:30 who **c** the attack of the mighty warrior by
4:36 and his brothers said, "See, our enemies are **c**;
5: 7 and they were **c** before him; he struck them down.
5:21 and the Gentiles were **c** before him.
7:43 The army of Nicanor was **c**,
8: 4 until they **c** them and inflicted great disaster
8: 5 They had **c** in battle and conquered Philip,
8: 6 and a very large army. He was **c** by them;
9: 7 and the battle was imminent, he was **c** in spirit,
9:15 and they **c** the right wing,
9:16 on the left wing saw that the right wing was **c**,
9:68 and he was **c** by them.
10:52 I **c** Demetrius and gained control of our country;
10:53 and he and his army were **c** by us,
12:31 and he **c** them and plundered them.
13:51 great enemy had been **c** and removed from Israel.
14:13 and the kings were **c** in those days.
3Mc 2:13 that because of our many and great sins we are **c**

CRUSHES‡ (6) [CRUSH]

Job 9:17 For he **c** me with a tempest,
Da 2:40 just as iron **c** and smashes everything,
Jdt 9: 7 not know that you are the Lord who **c** wars;
16: 2 For the Lord is a God who **c** wars;
Sir 28:17 but a blow of the tongue **c** the bones.
35:22 a warrior will not be patient until he **c** the loins of

CRUSHING (4) [CRUSH]

2Ki 23:15 He burned the high place, **c** it to dust;
Ps 143: 3 enemy has pursued me, **c** my life to the ground,
Isa 3:15 What do you mean by **c** my people,
Jer 14:17 is struck down with a **c** blow,

CRY‡ (190) [CRIED, CRIER, CRIES, CRYING, OUTCRIES, OUTCRY]

Ge 27:34 with an exceedingly great and bitter **c**,
39:15 and when he heard me raise my voice and **c** out,
Ex 2:23 Out of the slavery their **c** for help rose up to God.
3: 7 I have heard their **c** on account
3: 9 The **c** of the Israelites has now come to me;
5: 8 that is why they **c**, 'Let us go and offer sacrifice
11: 6 be a loud **c** throughout the whole land of Egypt,
12:30 and there was a loud **c** in Egypt,
14:15 LORD said to Moses, "Why do you **c** out to me?
22:23 If you do abuse them, when they **c** out to me,
22:23 I will surely heed their **c**;
Lev 13:45 and he shall cover his upper lip and **c** out,
Nu 14: 1 Then all the congregation raised a loud **c**,
Dt 15: 9 your neighbor might **c** to the LORD against you,
22:24 the young woman because she did not **c** for help
24:15 otherwise they might **c** to the LORD against you,
Jdg 10:14 Go and **c** to the gods whom you have chosen;
1Sa 5:12 and the **c** of the city went up to heaven.
7: 8 not cease to **c** out to the LORD our God for us,
8:18 in that day you will **c** out because of your king,
17:20 to the battle line, shouting the war **c**.
2Sa 22: 7 and my **c** came to his ears.
1Ki 8:28 the **c** and the prayer that your servant prays
18:27 At noon Elijah mocked them, saying, "**C** aloud!
2Ch 6:19 the **c** and the prayer that your servant prays
20: 9 and **c** to you in our distress,
Ne 9: 9 of our ancestors in Egypt and heard their **c** at
Est 4: 1 wailing with a loud and bitter **c**;
Job 3: 7 let no joyful **c** be heard in it.
19: 7 Even when I **c** out, 'Violence!'
27: 9 Will God hear their **c** when trouble comes
30:20 I **c** to you and you do not answer me;
30:24 when in disaster they **c** for help.
30:28 I stand up in the assembly and **c** for help.
34:28 that they caused the **c** of the poor to come to him,
34:28 and he heard the **c** of the afflicted—
35: 9 of the multitude of oppressions people **c** out;
35:12 There they **c** out, but he does not answer,
35:13 Surely God does not hear an empty **c**,
36:13 they do not **c** for help when he binds them.
36:19 Will your **c** avail to keep you from distress,
38:41 when its young ones **c** to God,
Ps 3: 4 I **c** aloud to the LORD,
5: 2 Listen to the sound of my **c**,
9:12 he does not forget the **c** of the afflicted.
17: 1 O LORD; attend to my **c**;
18: 6 and my **c** to him reached his ears.
22: 2 O my God, I **c** by day, but you do not answer;
27: 7 Hear, O LORD, when I **c** aloud,
28: 2 as I **c** to you for help,
34:15 and his ears are open to their **c**.
34:17 When the righteous **c** for help, the LORD hears,
39:12 O LORD, and give ear to my **c**;
40: 1 he inclined to me and heard my **c**.
57: 2 I **c** to God Most High,
61: 1 Hear my **c**, O God; listen to my prayer.
77: 1 I **c** aloud to God, aloud to God,
86: 3 O Lord, for to you do I **c** all day long.
86: 6 listen to my **c** of supplication.
88: 1 when, at night, I **c** out in your presence,
88: 2 incline your ear to my **c**.
88:13 But I, O LORD, **c** out to you;
89:26 He shall **c** to me, 'You are my Father, my God,
102: 1 Hear my prayer, O LORD; let my **c** come to you.
106:44 he regarded their distress when he heard their **c**.
119:145 With my whole heart I **c**; answer me, O LORD.
119:146 I **c** to you; save me,
119:147 I rise before dawn and **c** for help;
119:169 Let my **c** come before you, O LORD;
120: 1 In my distress I **c** to the LORD,
130: 1 Out of the depths I **c** to you, O LORD.
142: 1 With my voice I **c** to the LORD;
142: 5 I **c** to you, O LORD;
142: 6 Give heed to my **c**, for I am brought very low.
144:14 no exile, and no **c** of distress in our streets.
145:19 he also hears their **c**, and saves them.
147: 9 and to the young ravens when they **c**.
Pr 2: 3 if you indeed **c** out for insight,
8: 4 O people, I call, and my **c** is to all that live.
21:13 If you close your ear to the **c** of the poor,
21:13 you will **c** out and not be heard.
30:15 The leech has two daughters; "Give, give," they **c**.
Isa 3: 7 But the other will **c** out on that day, saying,
5: 7 righteousness, but heard a **c**!
10:30 **C** aloud, O daughter Gallim!
13: 2 On a bare hill raise a signal, **c** aloud to them;
13:22 Hyenas will **c** in its towers,
14:31 **c**, O city; melt in fear, O Philistia, all of you!
15: 4 Heshbon and Elealeh **c** out,
15: 5 the road to Horonaim they raise a **c** of destruction;
15: 8 For a **c** has gone around the land of Moab;
19:20 when they **c** to the LORD because of oppressors,
22: 5 down of walls and a **c** for help to the mountains.
30:19 surely be gracious to you at the sound of your **c**;
33: 7 the valiant **c** in the streets;
38:13 I **c** for help until morning;
40: 2 and **c** to her that she has served her term,
Isa 40: 6 A voice says, "**C** out!"
40: 6 And I said, "What shall I **c**?"
42: 2 He will not **c** or lift up his voice,
42:14 now I will **c** out like a woman in labor,
57:13 you **c** out, let your collection of idols deliver you!
58: 9 you shall **c** for help, and he will say, Here I am.
65:14 but you shall **c** out for pain of heart,
65:19 of weeping be heard in it, or the **c** of distress.
Jer 4:31 For I heard a **c** as of a woman in labor,
4:31 the **c** of daughter Zion gasping for breath,
7:16 do not raise a **c** or prayer on their behalf,
8:19 **c** of my poor people from far and wide in the land:
11:11 though they **c** out to me, I will not listen to them.
11:12 and the inhabitants of Jerusalem will go and **c** out
11:14 or lift up a **c** or prayer on their behalf,
12: 6 they are in full **c** after you;
14: 2 and the **c** of Jerusalem goes up.
14:12 Although they fast, I do not hear their **c**,
18:22 May a **c** be heard from their houses,
20: 8 For whenever I speak, I must **c** out, I must shout,
20:16 let him hear a **c** in the morning and an alarm
22:20 Go up to Lebanon, and **c** out,
22:20 **c** out from Abarim, for all your lovers are crushed.
25:34 Wail, you shepherds, and **c** out;
25:36 the **c** of the shepherds, and the wail of the lords of
30: 5 We have heard a **c** of panic, of terror,
30:15 Why do you **c** out over your hurt?
46:12 and the earth is full of your **c**;
47: 2 People shall **c** out, and all the inhabitants of the
48: 3 a **c** from Horonaim, "Desolation
48: 4 "Moab is destroyed!" her little ones **c** out.
48: 5 of Horonaim they have heard the distressing **c**
48:20 for it is broken down; wail and **c**!
48:31 Therefore I wail for Moab; I **c** out for all Moab;
48:34 Heshbon and Elealeh **c** out;
49: 3 **C** out, O daughters of Rabbah!
49:21 the sound of their **c** shall be heard at the Red Sea.
49:29 and a **c** shall go up: "Terror is all around!"
50:46 and her **c** shall be heard among the nations.
51:54 Listen!—a **c** from Babylon!
La 2:12 They **c** to their mothers, "Where is bread
2:16 they hiss, they gnash their teeth, they **c**:
2:18 **C** aloud to the Lord!
2:19 **c** out in the night, at the beginning of the watches!
3: 8 I call and **c** for help, he shuts out my prayer;
3:56 "Do not close your ear to my **c** for help,
Eze 8:18 though they **c** in my hearing with a loud voice,
21:12 **C** and wail, O mortal, for it is against my people;
21:22 to call out for slaughter, for raising the battle **c**,
27:28 of the **c** of your pilots the countryside shakes,
27:30 and wail aloud over you, and **c** bitterly.
Hos 7:14 They do not **c** to me from the heart,
Joel 1:14 and **c** out to the LORD.
1:19 To you, O LORD, I **c**.
1:20 Even the wild animals **c** to you because
Am 3: 4 Does a young lion **c** out from its den,
Jnh 1: 2 that great city, and **c** out against it;
3: 8 and they shall **c** mightily to God.
Mic 3: 4 Then they will **c** to the LORD,
3: 5 who **c** "Peace" when they have something to eat,
4: 9 Now why do you **c** aloud?
Hab 1: 2 O LORD, how long shall I **c** for help,
1: 2 Or **c** to you "Violence!" and you will not save?
2:11 The very stones will **c** out from the wall,
Zep 1:10 a **c** will be heard from the Fish Gate,
1:16 and battle **c** against the fortified cities and against
Mt 12:19 He will not wrangle or **c** aloud,
Mk 15:37 Then Jesus gave a loud **c** and breathed his last.
Lk 1:42 and exclaimed with a loud **c**,
18: 7 to his chosen ones who **c** to him day and night?
Ac 16:17 While she followed Paul and us, she would **c** out,
Ro 8:15 you have received a spirit of adoption. When we **c**,
1Th 4:16 For the Lord himself, with a **c** of command,
Jas 5: 4 which you kept back by fraud, **c** out,
Tob 13:17 and all her houses will **c**, 'Hallelujah!
AdE 4: 3 a loud **c** of mourning and lamentation among
Wis 7: 3 my first sound was a **c**, as is true of all.
18:10 But the discordant **c** of their enemies echoed back,
Sir 30: 7 and will suffer heartache at every **c**.
Bar 3: 1 soul in anguish and the wearied spirit **c** out to you.
4:20 I will **c** to the Everlasting all my days.
4:21 Take courage, my children, **c** to God,
4:27 Take courage, my children, and **c** to God,
Sus 1:44 The Lord heard her **c**.
1Mc 4:10 And now, let us **c** to Heaven,
5:31 and that the **c** of the town went up to Heaven,
9:46 **C** out now to Heaven that you may be delivered
2Mc 12:37 of their ancestors he raised the battle **c**,
3Mc 1:28 and concerted **c** of the crowds resulted in
2Es 1:17 did you not **c** out to me,
10:26 she suddenly uttered a loud and fearful **c**,
11: 7 and it uttered a **c** to its wings, saying,
15: 8 and the souls of the righteous **c** out continually.

CRYING‡ (25) [CRY]

Ge 4:10 your brother's blood is **c** out to me from
Ex 2: 6 He was **c**, and she took pity on him,
2Sa 13:19 and went away, **c** aloud as she went.
1Ki 18:26 on the name of Baal from morning until noon, **c**,
2Ki 2:12 Elisha kept watching and **c** out, "Father, father!
13:14 and wept before him, **c**, "My father, my father!
Ps 69: 3 I am weary with my **c**; my throat is parched.
Mt 3: 3 "The voice of one **c** out in the wilderness:
9:27 **c** loudly, "Have mercy on us, Son of David!"
21:15 and heard the children **c** out in the temple,
Mk 1: 3 the voice of one **c** out in the wilderness:

Mk 1:26 convulsing him and c with a loud voice,
9:26 After c out and convulsing him terribly,
Lk 3: 4 "The voice of one c out in the wilderness:
23:46 Then Jesus, c with a loud voice, said, "Father,
Jn 1:23 "I am the voice of one c out in the wilderness,
Ac 8: 7 c with loud shrieks, came out
Gal 4: 6 the Spirit of his Son into our hearts, c,
Rev 8:13 and I heard an eagle c with a loud voice as it flew
12: 2 She was pregnant and was c out in birth pangs,
14: 9 a third, followed them, c with a loud voice,
18:19 as they wept and mourned, c out, "Alas, alas,
19: 6 and like the sound of mighty thunderpeals, c out,
21: 4 mourning and c and pain will be no more,
Jdt 10: 1 Judith had stopped c out to the God of Israel,

CRYSTAL (5) [CRYSTALLINE]

Job 28:18 No mention shall be made of coral or of c;
Eze 1:22 shining like c, spread out above their heads.
Rev 4: 6 like a sea of glass, like c.
21:11 like a very rare jewel, like jasper, clear as c.
22: 1 bright as c, flowing from the throne of God and of

CRYSTALLINE (1) [CRYSTAL]

Wis 19:21 nor did they melt the c, quick-melting kind of

CUB‡ (1) [CUBS]

1Mc 3: 4 like a lion's c roaring for prey.

CUBIT‡ (39) [CUBITS]

Ge 6:16 Make a roof for the ark, and finish it to a c above;
Ex 25:10 a c and a half wide, and a c and a half high.
25:17 and a c and a half its width.
25:23 one c wide, and a c and a half high.
26:13 The c on the one side, and the c on the other side,
26:16 and a c and a half the width of each frame.
30: 2 It shall be one c long, and one c wide;
36:21 and a c and a half the width of each frame.
37: 1 a c and a half wide, and a c and a half high.
37: 6 and a c and a half its width.
37:10 one c wide, and a c and a half high.
37:25 one c long, and one c wide;
Dt 3:11 By the common c it is nine cubits long
Jdg 3:16 for himself a sword with two edges, a c in length;
1Ki 7:31 within the crown whose height was one c;
7:31 it was a c and a half wide.
7:32 and the height of a wheel was a c and a half.
7:35 of the stand there was a round band half a c high;
Eze 40: 5 each being a c and a handbreadth in length;
40: 8 the inner vestibule of the gateway, one c.
40:12 a barrier before the recesses, one c on either side;
40:42 a c and a half long, and one c and a half wide, and one c high,
43:13 (the c being one c and a handbreadth):
43:13 its base shall be one c high, and one c wide,
43:14 two cubits, with a width of one c;
43:14 four cubits, with a width of one c;
43:17 with a rim around it half a c wide,
43:17 and its surrounding base, one c.

CUBITS‡ (258) [CUBIT]

Ge 6:15 the length of the ark three hundred c, its width fifty c, and its height thirty c.
7:20 covering them fifteen c deep.
Ex 25:10 it shall be two and a half c long,
25:17 two c and a half shall be its length,
25:23 two c long, one cubit wide,
26: 2 The length of each curtain shall be twenty-eight c,
26: 2 and the width of each curtain four c;
26: 8 The length of each curtain shall be thirty c,
26: 8 and the width of each curtain four c;
26:16 Ten c shall be the length of a frame,
27: 1 five c long and five c wide;
27: 1 altar shall be square, and it shall be three c high.
27: 9 of fine twisted linen one hundred c long for
27:11 be hangings one hundred c long,
27:12 on the west side there shall be fifty c of hangings,
27:13 of the court on the front to the east shall be fifty c.
27:14 be fifteen c of hangings on the one side,
27:15 be fifteen c of hangings on the other side,
27:16 of the court there shall be a screen twenty c long,
27:18 The length of the court shall be one hundred c,
27:18 the width fifty, and the height five c,
30: 2 it shall be square, and shall be two c high;
36: 9 The length of each curtain was twenty-eight c,
36: 9 and the width of each curtain four c;
36:15 The length of each curtain was thirty c,
36:15 and the width of each curtain four c;
36:21 Ten c was the length of a frame,
37: 1 it was two and a half c long,
37: 6 two c and a half was its length,
37:10 two c long, one cubit wide,
37:25 it was square, and was two c high;
38: 1 it was five c long, and five c wide;
38: 1 it was square, and three c high.
38: 9 of fine twisted linen, one hundred c long;
38:11 north side there were hangings one hundred c long;
38:12 For the west side there were hangings fifty c long,
38:13 And for the front to the east, fifty c.
38:14 hangings for one side of the gate were fifteen c,
38:15 of the gate of the court were hangings of fifteen c,
38:18 twenty c long and, along the width of it, five c high
Nu 11:31 about two c deep on the ground.
35: 4 of the town outward a thousand c all around.
35: 5 outside the town, for the east side two thousand c,
Nu 35: 5 for the south side two thousand c,
35: 5 for the west side two thousand c,
35: 5 and for the north side two thousand c,
Dt 3:11 it is nine c long and four c wide.)
Jos 3: 4 a distance of about two thousand c;
1Sa 17: 4 of Gath, whose height was six c and a span.
1Ki 6: 2 built for the LORD was sixty c long,
6: 2 twenty c wide, and thirty c high.
6: 3 of the nave of the house was twenty c wide,
6: 3 Its depth was ten c in front of the house.
6: 6 The lowest story was five c wide, the middle one was six c wide, and the third was seven c wide;
6:10 against the whole house, each story five c high,
6:16 He built twenty c of the rear of the house
6:17 in front of the inner sanctuary, was forty c long.
6:20 interior of the inner sanctuary was twenty c long, twenty c wide, and twenty c high;
6:23 of olivewood, each ten c high.
6:24 Five c was the length of one wing of the cherub,
6:24 five c the length of the other wing of the cherub;
6:24 it was ten c from the tip of one wing to the tip of
6:25 The other cherub also measured ten c;
6:26 The height of one cherub was ten c,
7: 2 House of the Forest of the Lebanon one hundred c long, fifty c wide, and thirty c high,
7: 6 Hall of Pillars fifty c long and thirty c wide.
7:10 huge stones, stones of eight and ten c.
7:15 Eighteen c was the height of the one,
7:15 and a cord of twelve c would encircle it;
7:16 the height of the one capital was five c, and the height of the other capital was five c.
7:19 in the vestibule were of lily-work, four c high.
7:23 round, ten c from brim to brim, and five c high.
7:23 A line of thirty c would encircle it completely.
7:24 each of ten c, surrounding the sea;
7:27 was four c long, four c wide, and three c high.
7:38 each basin measured four c;
2Ki 14:13 a distance of four hundred c.
25:17 The height of the one pillar was eighteen c,
25:17 the height of the capital was three c;
1Ch 11:23 a man of great stature, five c tall.
2Ch 3: 3 the length, in c of the old standard, was sixty c, and the width twenty c.
3: 4 of the nave of the house was twenty c long,
3: 4 and its height was one hundred twenty c.
3: 8 was twenty c, and its width was twenty c;
3:11 of the cherubim together extended twenty c:
3:11 one wing of the one, five c long,
3:11 five c long, touched the wing of the other cherub;
3:12 five c long, touched the wall of the house,
3:12 and the other wing, also five c long,
3:13 The wings of these cherubim extended twenty c;
3:15 the house he made two pillars thirty-five c high, with a capital of five c on the top of each.
4: 1 He made an altar of bronze, twenty c long,
4: 1 twenty c wide, and ten c high.
4: 2 it was round, ten c from rim to rim, and five c high.
4: 2 A line of thirty c would encircle it completely.
4: 3 Under it were panels all around, each of ten c,
6:13 Solomon had made a bronze platform five c long, five c wide, and had set it in the court;
25:23 a distance of four hundred c.
Ezr 6: 3 be sixty c and its width sixty c,
Ne 3:13 and its bars, and repaired a thousand c of the wall,
Est 5:14 "Let a gallows fifty c high be made,
7: 9 stands at Haman's house, fifty c high."
Jer 52:21 the height of the one pillar was eighteen c, its circumference was twelve c;
52:22 the height of the one capital was five c;
Eze 40: 5 the man's hand was six long c, each being a cubit
40: 7 and the space between the recesses, five c;
40: 9 he measured the vestibule of the gateway, eight c; and its pilasters, two c;
40:11 the width of the opening of the gateway, ten c;
40:11 and the width of the gateway, thirteen c.
40:12 and the recesses were six c on either side.
40:13 a width of twenty-five c, from wall to wall.
40:14 He measured also the vestibule, twenty c;
40:15 of the inner vestibule of the gate was fifty c.
40:19 the outer front of the inner court, one hundred c.
40:21 its depth was fifty c, and its width twenty-five c.
40:23 he measured from gate to gate, one hundred c.
40:25 its depth was fifty c, and its width twenty-five c.
40:27 from gate to gate toward the south, one hundred c.
40:29 its depth was fifty c, and its width twenty-five c.
40:30 twenty-five c deep and five c wide.
40:33 its depth was fifty c, and its width twenty-five c.
40:36 Its depth was fifty c, and its width twenty-five c.
40:47 one hundred c deep, and one hundred c wide,
40:48 the pilasters of the vestibule, five c on either side;
40:48 and the width of the gate was fourteen c;
40:48 sidewalls of the gate were three c on either side.
40:49 The depth of the vestibule was twenty c, and the width twelve c;
41: 1 on each side six c was the width of the pilasters.
41: 2 The width of the entrance was ten c; and the sidewalls of the entrance were five c
41: 2 length of the nave, forty c, and its width, twenty c.
41: 3 the entrance, two c; and the width of the entrance, six c; and the sidewalls of the entrance, seven c.
41: 4 of the room, twenty c, and its width, twenty c,
41: 5 he measured the wall of the temple, six c thick; and the width of the side chambers, four c,
41: 8 a full reed of six long c.
41: 9 of the outer wall of the side chambers was five c;
41:10 of twenty c all around the temple on every side.
41:11 of the part that was left free was five c all around.
Eze 41:12 on the west side was seventy c wide;
41:12 wall of the building was five c thick all around, and its depth ninety c.
41:13 he measured the temple, one hundred c deep;
41:13 the building with its walls, one hundred c deep;
41:14 of the temple and the yard, one hundred c.
41:15 with its galleries on either side, one hundred c.
41:22 three c high, two c long, and two c wide;
42: 2 was one hundred c, and the width fifty c.
42: 3 the twenty c that belonged to the inner court,
42: 4 ten c wide and one hundred c deep,
42: 7 opposite the chambers, fifty c long.
42: 8 the chambers on the outer court were fifty c long,
42: 8 the temple were one hundred c long.
42:16 five hundred c by the measuring reed.
42:17 five hundred c by the measuring reed.
42:18 five hundred c by the measuring reed.
42:19 five hundred c by the measuring reed.
42:20 five hundred c long and five hundred c wide,
43:13 of the altar by c (the cubit being one cubit and
43:14 two c, with a width of one cubit;
43:14 from the smaller ledge to the larger ledge, four c,
43:15 and the altar hearth, four c;
43:16 twelve c long by twelve wide,
43:17 fourteen c long by fourteen wide,
45: 1 twenty-five thousand c long and twenty thousand c wide;
45: 2 of five hundred by five hundred c shall be for
45: 2 with fifty c for an open space around it.
45: 3 a section twenty-five thousand c long
45: 5 twenty-five thousand c long and ten thousand c wide,
45: 6 for the city an area five thousand c wide, and twenty-five thousand c long;
46:22 forty c long and thirty wide;
47: 3 the man measured one thousand c,
48: 8 twenty-five thousand c in width,
48: 9 for the LORD shall be twenty-five thousand c
48:10 an allotment measuring twenty-five thousand c on
48:10 ten thousand c in width on the western side,
48:13 an allotment twenty-five thousand c in length
48:13 The whole length shall be twenty-five thousand c
48:15 five thousand c in width and twenty-five thousand
48:16 the north side four thousand five hundred c,
48:17 on the north two hundred fifty c,
48:18 the holy portion shall be ten thousand c to
48:20 be twenty-five thousand c square,
48:21 the twenty-five thousand c of the holy portion to
48:21 and westward from the twenty-five thousand c to
48:30 to be four thousand five hundred c by measure,
48:32 which is to be four thousand five hundred c,
48:33 to be four thousand five hundred c by measure,
48:34 which is to be four thousand five hundred c,
48:35 of the city shall be eighteen thousand c.
Da 3: 1 height was sixty c and whose width was six c;
Zec 5: 2 its length is twenty c, and its width ten c."
Rev 21:17 one hundred forty-four c by human measurement,
Jdt 1: 2 with hewn stones three c thick and six c long;
1: 2 the walls seventy c high and fifty c wide.
1: 3 towers one hundred c high and sixty c wide
1: 4 gates seventy c high and forty c wide
AdE 5:14 "Let a gallows be made, fifty c high,
7: 9 at Haman's house, a gallows fifty c high."
Aza 1:24 flames poured out above the furnace forty-nine c,
2Mc 13: 5 For there is a tower there, fifty c high,
1Es 6:25 its height to be sixty c and its width sixty c,

CUBS (7) [CUB]

2Sa 17: 8 like a bear robbed of her c in the field.
Pr 17:12 to meet a she-bear robbed of its c than to confront
Eze 19: 2 She lay down among young lions, rearing her c.
19: 3 She raised up one of her c;
19: 5 took another of her c and made him a young lion.
Hos 13: 8 I will fall upon them like a bear robbed of her c,
Na 2:11 and the lion's c, with no one to disturb them?

CUCKOW (KJV) See SEA GULL

CUCUMBER (3) [CUCUMBERS]

Isa 1: 8 like a shelter in a c field, like a besieged city.
Jer 10: 5 Their idols are like scarecrows in a c field,
LtJ 6:70 Like a scarecrow in a c bed,

CUCUMBERS (1) [CUCUMBER]

Nu 11: 5 the c, the melons, the leeks, the onions,

CUD (11)

Lev 11: 3 and is cleft-footed and chews the c—
11: 4 that chew the c or have divided hoofs,
11: 4 the camel, for even though it chews the c,
11: 5 The rock badger, for even though it chews the c,
11: 6 The hare, for even though it chews the c,
11: 7 it does not chew the c; it is unclean for you.
11:26 not cleft-footed or does not chew the c is unclean
Dt 14: 6 and chews the c, among the animals, you may eat.
14: 7 the c or have the hoof cleft you shall not eat these:
14: 7 they chew the c but do not divide the hoof;
14: 8 it divides the hoof but does not chew the c,

CULPRIT (1)

Dt 19:12 to have the c taken from there and handed over to

CULT (1)
Wis 12: 5 These initiates from the midst of a heathen **c**,

CULTIVATE‡ (4) [CULTIVATED, CULTIVATION, CULTIVATOR]
Eze 48:19 from all the tribes of Israel, shall **c** it.
Sir 6:19 For when you **c** her you will toil but little,
20:28 Those who **c** the soil heap up their harvest,
2Es 16:24 No one shall be left to **c** the earth or to sow it.

CULTIVATED (4) [CULTIVATE]
Ro 11:24 contrary to nature, into a **c** olive tree,
Heb 6: 7 produces a crop useful to those for whom it is **c**,
Sir 21:23 but a **c** person remains outside.
2Es 6:42 of them might be planted and **c** and be of service

CULTIVATION (3) [CULTIVATE]
Sir 27: 6 Its fruit discloses the **c** of a tree;
27: 6 so a person's speech discloses the **c** of his mind.
2Es 8: 6 a seed for our heart and **c** of our understanding so

CULTIVATOR (1) [CULTIVATE]
4Mc 1:29 each of which the master **c**,

CUM (1)
Mk 5:41 "Talitha **c**," which means, "Little girl, get up!"

CUMBERED (KJV) See DISTRACTED

CUMI (KJV) See CUM

CUMMIN (4)
Isa 28:25 do they not scatter dill, sow **c**,
28:27 nor is a cart wheel rolled over **c**;
28:27 but dill is beaten out with a stick, and **c** with a rod.
Mt 23:23 For you tithe mint, dill, and **c**,

CUN (1)
1Ch 18: 8 From Tibhath and from **C**, cities of Hadadezer,

CUNNING (8) [CUNNINGLY]
Jos 9: 4 they on their part acted with **c**:
1Sa 23:22 for I am told that he is very **c**.
2Ki 10:19 with **c** in order to destroy the worshipers of Baal.
Ps 58: 5 the voice of charmers or of the **c** enchanter.
119:118 for their **c** is in vain.
Da 8:25 By his **c** he shall make deceit prosper
2Co 4: 2 we refuse to practice **c** or to falsify God's word;
11: 3 that as the serpent deceived Eve by its **c**,

CUNNINGLY (1) [CUNNING]
Ps 64: 6 We have thought out a **c** conceived plot."

CUP‡ (67) [CUPBEARER, CUPBEARING, CUPS, WINE-CUP]
Ge 40:11 Pharaoh's **c** was in my hand;
40:11 the grapes and pressed them into Pharaoh's **c**,
40:11 and placed the **c** in Pharaoh's hand."
40:13 and you shall place Pharaoh's **c** in his hand,
40:21 and he placed the **c** in Pharaoh's hand;
44: 2 Put my **c**, the silver **c**, in the top of the sack
44: 4 Why have you stolen my silver **c**?
44:12 and the **c** was found in Benjamin's sack.
44:16 in whose possession the **c** has been found."
44:17 the one in whose possession the **c** was found shall
2Sa 12: 3 and drink from his **c**, and lie in his bosom,
1Ki 7:26 its brim was made like the brim of a **c**,
2Ch 4: 5 its rim was made like the rim of a **c**,
Ps 11: 6 a scorching wind shall be the portion of their **c**.
16: 5 The LORD is my chosen portion and my **c**;
23: 5 you anoint my head with oil; my **c** overflows.
75: 8 of the LORD there is a **c** with foaming wine,
116:13 up the **c** of salvation and call on the name of
Pr 23:31 when it sparkles in the **c** and goes down smoothly.
Isa 51:17 at the hand of the LORD the **c** of his wrath,
51:22 I have taken from your hand the **c** of staggering;
Jer 16: 7 nor shall anyone give them the **c** of consolation
25:15 Take from my hand this **c** of the wine of wrath,
25:17 So I took the **c** from the LORD's hand,
25:28 And if they refuse to accept the **c** from your hand
49:12 not deserve to drink the **c** still have to drink it,
51: 7 Babylon was a golden **c** in the LORD's hand,
La 4:21 but to you also the **c** shall pass;
Eze 23:31 therefore I will give her **c** into your hand.
23:32 You shall drink your sister's **c**, deep and wide;
23:33 A **c** of horror and desolation is the **c** of your sister Samaria;
Hab 2:16 The **c** in the LORD's right hand will come
Zec 12: 2 I am about to make Jerusalem a **c** of reeling for all
Mt 10:42 even a **c** of cold water to one of these little ones in
20:22 Are you able to drink the **c** that I am about
20:23 He said to them, "You will indeed drink my **c**,
23:25 For you clean the outside of the **c** and of the plate,
23:26 First clean the inside of the **c**,
26:27 a **c**, and after giving thanks he gave it
26:39 if it is possible, let this **c** pass from me;
Mk 9:41 a **c** of water to drink because you bear the name
10:38 Are you able to drink the **c** that I drink,
10:39 "The **c** that I drink you will drink;
14:23 a **c**, and after giving thanks he gave it to them,
14:36 all things are possible; remove this **c** from me;
Lk 11:39 "Now you Pharisees clean the outside of the **c** and
22:17 Then he took a **c**, and after giving thanks he said,
22:20 And he did the same with the **c** after supper,
22:20 "This **c** that is poured out for you is
22:42 if you are willing, remove this **c** from me;
Jn 18:11 not to drink the **c** that the Father has given me?"
1Co 10:16 The **c** of blessing that we bless,
10:21 cannot drink the **c** of the Lord and the **c** of demons.
11:25 In the same way he took the **c** also, after supper,
11:25 saying, "This **c** is the new covenant in my blood.
11:26 For as often as you eat this bread and drink the **c**,
11:27 the **c** of the Lord in an unworthy manner will
11:28 and only then eat of the bread and drink of the **c**.
Rev 14:10 poured unmixed into the **c** of his anger,
17: 4 a golden **c** full of abominations and the impurities
18: 6 mix a double draught for her in the **c** she mixed.
AdE 1: 7 and a miniature **c** was displayed, made of ruby,
Sir 50:15 for the **c** and poured a drink offering of the blood
2Es 14:39 and a full **c** was offered to me;

CUPBEARER (11) [BEAR, CUP]
Ge 40: 1 the **c** of the king of Egypt
40: 2 the chief **c** and the chief baker,
40: 5 the **c** and the baker of the king of Egypt,
40: 9 So the chief **c** told his dream to Joseph,
40:13 just as you used to do when you were his **c**.
40:20 and lifted up the head of the chief **c** and the head
40:21 He restored the chief **c** to his cupbearing,
40:23 chief **c** did not remember Joseph, but forgot him.
41: 9 Then the chief **c** said to Pharaoh,
Ne 1:11 At the time, I was **c** to the king.
Tob 1:22 Now Ahikar was chief **c**, keeper of the signet,

CUPBEARING (1) [BEAR, CUP]
Ge 40:21 He restored the chief cupbearer to his **c**,

CUPS (20) [CUP]
Ex 25:31 its **c**, its calyxes, and its petals shall be
25:33 three **c** shaped like almond blossoms,
25:33 and three **c** shaped like almond blossoms,
25:34 the lampstand itself there shall be four **c** shaped
37:17 its **c**, its calyxes, and its petals were of one piece
37:19 three **c** shaped like almond blossoms,
37:19 and three **c** shaped like almond blossoms,
37:20 On the lampstand itself there were four **c** shaped
1Ki 7:50 the **c**, snuffers, basins, dishes for incense,
1Ch 28:17 and pure gold for the forks, the basins, and the **c**;
Isa 22:24 every small vessel, from the **c** to all the flagons.
65:11 for Fortune and fill **c** of mixed wine for Destiny;
Jer 35: 5 and **c**; and I said to them, "Have some wine."
Mk 7: 4 the washing of **c**, pots, and bronze kettles.)
AdE 1: 7 The **c** were of gold and silver,
1Mc 1:22 the **c** for drink offerings, the bowls,
11:58 to drink from gold **c** and dress in purple and wear
1Es 2:13 one thousand gold **c**, one thousand silver **c**,
3: 6 and drink from gold **c**, and sleep on a gold bed,

CURBED (1)
Ps 32: 9 whose temper must be **c** with bit and bridle,

CURDLE (1) [CURDS]
Job 10:10 not pour me out like milk and **c** me like cheese?

CURDS (9) [CURDLE]
Ge 18: 8 Then he took **c** and milk and the calf
Dt 32:14 **c** from the herd, and milk from the flock, with fat
Jdg 5:25 she brought him **c** in a lordly bowl.
2Sa 17:29 and **c**, sheep, and cheese from the herd, for David
Job 20:17 the streams flowing with honey and **c**.
Pr 30:33 For as pressing milk produces **c**,
Isa 7:15 He shall eat **c** and honey by the time he knows
7:22 and will eat **c** because of the abundance of milk
7:22 for everyone that is left in the land shall eat **c**

CURE (17) [CURED, CURES, CURING]
2Ki 5: 3 He would **c** him of his leprosy."
5: 6 that you may **c** him of his leprosy."
5: 7 that this man sends word to me to **c** a man
5:11 and would wave his hand over the spot, and **c**
Hos 5:13 But he is not able to **c** you or heal your wound.
Mt 8: 7 And he said to him, "I will come and **c** him."
10: 1 and to **c** every disease and every sickness.
10: 8 **C** the sick, raise the dead, cleanse the lepers,
12:10 "Is it lawful to **c** on the sabbath?"
17:16 but they could not **c** him."
Mk 3: 2 They watched him to see whether he would **c** him
Lk 4:23 to me this proverb, 'Doctor, **c** yourself!'
6: 7 to see whether he would **c** on the sabbath,
8:43 on physicians, no one could **c** her.
9: 1 and authority over all demons and to **c** diseases,
10: 9 **c** the sick who are there,
14: 3 "Is it lawful to **c** people on the sabbath, or not?"

CURED (29) [CURE]
Mt 4:24 epileptics, and paralytics, and he **c** them.
8:16 the spirits with a word, and **c** all who were sick.
12:15 Many crowds followed him, and he **c** all of them,
12:22 and mute; and he **c** him,
14:14 and he had compassion for them and **c** their sick.
15:30 They put them at his feet, and he **c** them,
17:18 and the boy was **c** instantly.
19: 2 Large crowds followed him, and he **c** them there.
21:14 to him in the temple, and he **c** them.
Mk 1:34 he **c** many who were sick with various diseases,
3:10 for he had **c** many,
6: 5 on a few sick people and **c** them.
6:13 anointed with oil many who were sick and **c** them.
Lk 4:40 and he laid his hands on each of them and **c** them.
5:15 to hear him and to be **c** of their diseases.
6:18 with unclean spirits were **c**.
7:21 Jesus had just then **c** many people of diseases,
8: 2 as some women who had been **c** of evil spirits
9:11 and healed those who needed to be **c**.
13:14 indignant because Jesus had **c** on the sabbath,
13:14 come on those days and be **c**,
Jn 5:10 So the Jews said to the man who had been **c**,
Ac 4:14 When they saw the man who had been **c** standing
5:16 by unclean spirits, and they were all **c**.
8: 7 many others who were paralyzed or lame were **c**.
28: 8 and **c** him by praying and putting his hands
28: 9 the island who had diseases also came and were **c**.
Tob 12: 3 he has led me back to you safely, he **c** my wife,
Wis 16:12 For neither herb nor poultice **c** them,

CURES (1) [CURE]
Lk 13:32 I am casting out demons and performing **c** today

CURING (3) [CURE]
Mt 4:23 the good news of the kingdom and **c** every disease
9:35 and **c** every disease and every sickness.
Lk 9: 6 the good news and **c** diseases everywhere.

CURIOUS (1)
2Es 9:13 to be **c** about how the ungodly will be punished;

CURLED (1)
4Mc 11:10 so that he was completely **c** back like a scorpion,

CURRENT (2)
Ge 23:16 according to the weights **c** among the merchants.
Sir 4:26 and do not try to stop the **c** of a river.

CURSE (101) [ACCURSED, CURSED, CURSES, CURSING, THRICE-ACCURSED]
Ge 8:21 "I will never again **c** the ground because
12: 3 and the one who curses you I will **c**;
27:12 and bring a **c** on myself and not a blessing."
27:13 His mother said to him, "Let your **c** be on me,
Ex 22:28 or **c** a leader of your people.
Lev 20: 9 All who **c** father or mother shall be put to death;
24:11 Israelite woman's son blasphemed the Name in a **c**.
Nu 5:18 the water of bitterness that brings the **c**.
5:19 to this water of bitterness that brings the **c**.
5:21 the priest make the woman take the oath of the **c**
5:22 that brings the **c** enter your bowels
5:24 the water of bitterness that brings the **c**,
5:24 and the water that brings the **c** shall enter her
5:27 the **c** shall enter into her and cause bitter pain,
22: 6 Come now, **c** this people for me,
22: 6 and whomever you **c** is cursed."
22:11 now come, **c** them for me;
22:12 you shall not **c** the people, for they are blessed."
22:17 come, **c** this people for me.' "
23: 7 'Come, **c** Jacob for me; Come, denounce Israel!'
23: 8 How can I **c** whom God has not cursed?
23:11 I brought you to **c** my enemies,
23:13 then **c** them for me from there."
23:25 Then Balak said to Balaam, "Do not **c** them at all,
23:27 perhaps it will please God that you may **c** them
24:10 "I summoned you to **c** my enemies,
Dt 11:26 I am setting before you today a blessing and a **c**:
11:28 and the **c**, if you do not obey the commandments
11:29 on Mount Gerizim and the **c** on Mount Ebal.
21:23 for anyone hung on a tree is under God's **c**.
23: 4 from Pethor of Mesopotamia, to **c** you.
23: 5 the LORD your God turned the **c** into a blessing
27:13 And these shall stand on Mount Ebal for the **c**:
29:27 bringing on it every **c** written in this book.
Jos 24: 9 He sent and invited Balaam son of Beor to **c** you,
Jdg 5:23 "**C** Meroz, says the angel of the LORD,
5:23 the angel of the LORD, **c** bitterly its inhabitants,
9:57 on them came the **c** of Jotham son of Jerubbaal.
17: 2 about which you uttered a **c**,
2Sa 16: 9 "Why should this dead dog **c** my lord the king?
16:10 '**C** David,' who then shall say,
16:11 Let him alone, and let him **c**;
1Ki 2: 8 a terrible **c** on the day when I went to Mahanaim;
2Ki 22:19 that they should become a desolation and a **c**,
Ne 10:29 enter into a **c** and an oath to walk in God's law,
13: 2 but hired Balaam against them to **c** them—
13: 2 yet our God turned the **c** into a blessing.
Job 1:11 and he will **c** you to your face."
2: 5 and he will **c** you to your face."
2: 9 "Do you still persist in your integrity? **C** God,
3: 8 Let those **c** it who **c** the Sea,
31:30 by asking for their lives with a **c**—
Ps 10: 3 those greedy for gain **c** and renounce the LORD.
62: 4 they bless with their mouths, but inwardly they **c**.
102: 8 those who deride me use my name for a **c**.
109:17 He loved to **c**; let curses come on him.
109:28 Let them **c**, but you will bless.
Pr 3:33 The LORD's **c** is on the house of the wicked,
11:26 The people **c** those who hold back grain,
20:20 If you **c** father or mother,

Pr 26: 2 an undeserved c goes nowhere.
28:27 but one who turns a blind eye will get many a c.
29:24 one hears the victim's c, but discloses nothing.
30:10 or the servant will c you,
30:11 There are those who c their fathers and do
Ecc 10:20 Do not c the king, even in your thoughts,
10:20 or c the rich, even in your bedroom;
Isa 8:21 be enraged and will c their king and their gods.
24: 6 Therefore a c devours the earth,
65:15 as a c, and the Lord GOD will put you to death;
Jer 15:10 nor have I borrowed, yet all of them c me.
23:10 because of the c the land mourns,
24: 9 and a c in all the places where I shall drive them.
26: 6 and I will make this city a c for all the nations of
29:22 And on account of them this c shall be used by all
44:22 a desolation and a waste and a c,
La 3:65 Give them anguish of heart; your c be on them!
Da 9:11 So the c and the oath written in the law of Moses,
Zec 5: 3 the c that goes out over the face of the whole land;
Mal 2: 2 I will send the c on you and I will c your blessings;
3: 9 cursed with a c, for you are robbing me—
4: 6 that I will not come and strike the land with a c.
Mt 26:74 Then he began to c, and he swore an oath,
Mk 14:71 But he began to c, and he swore an oath,
Lk 6:28 bless those who c you, pray for those who abuse
Ro 12:14 bless and do not c them.
Gal 3:10 on the works of the law are under a c;
3:13 from the c of the law by becoming a c for us—
Jas 3: 9 with it we c those who are made in the likeness
Sir 3: 9 but a mother's c uproots their foundations.
4: 5 and give no one reason to c you;
4: 6 for if in bitterness of soul some should c you,
23:14 and you will c the day of your birth.
28:13 C the gossips and the double-tongued,
41: 9 and when you die, a c is your lot.
41:10 so the ungodly go from c to destruction.
Bar 1:20 the calamities and the c that the Lord declared
LtJ 6:66 They can neither c nor bless kings;

CURSED (74) [CURSE]

Ge 3:14 c are you among all animals and
3:17 c is the ground because of you;
4:11 And now you are c from the ground,
5:29 that the LORD has c this one shall bring us relief
9:25 "C be Canaan; lowest of slaves shall he be to his
27:29 C be everyone who curses you,
49: 7 C be their anger, for it is fierce, and their wrath,
Lev 20: 9 having c father or mother,
Nu 22: 6 and whomever you curse is c."
23: 8 How can I curse whom God has not c?
24: 9 and c is everyone who curses you."
Dt 27:15 "C be anyone who makes an idol or casts
27:16 "C be anyone who dishonors father or mother."
27:17 "C be anyone who moves a neighbor's boundary
27:18 "C be anyone who misleads a blind person on
27:19 "C be anyone who deprives the alien, the orphan,
27:20 "C be anyone who lies with his father's wife,
27:21 "C be anyone who lies with any animal."
27:22 "C be anyone who lies with his sister,
27:23 "C be anyone who lies with his mother-in-law."
27:24 "C be anyone who strikes down a neighbor
27:25 "C be anyone who takes a bribe
27:26 "C be anyone who does not uphold the words
28:16 C shall you be in the city, and c shall you be in the
28:17 C shall be your basket and your kneading bowl.
28:18 C shall be the fruit of your womb,
28:19 C shall you be when you come in, and c shall you be when you go out.
Jos 6:26 "C before the LORD be anyone who tries
9:23 therefore you are c, and some of you shall always
Jdg 21:18 "C be anyone who gives a wife to Benjamin."
1Sa 14:24 "C be anyone who eats food before it is evening
14:28 saying, 'C be anyone who eats food this day.'
17:43 And the Philistine c David by his gods.
26:19 if it is mortals, may they be c before the LORD,
2Sa 16: 7 Shimei shouted while he c, "Out!
16:13 on the hillside opposite him and c as he went,
19:21 because he c the LORD's anointed?"
1Ki 2: 8 who c me with a terrible curse on the day
21:10 saying, 'You have c God and the king.'
21:13 saying, "Naboth c God and the king."
2Ki 2:24 he c them in the name of the LORD.
9:34 he said, "See to that c woman and bury her;
Ne 13:25 with them and c them and beat some of them
Job 1: 5 and c God in their hearts."
3: 1 After this Job opened his mouth and c the day
5: 3 but suddenly I c their dwelling.
24:18 their portion in the land is c;
Ps 37:22 but those c by him shall be cut off.
Pr 24:24 will be c by peoples, abhorred by nations;
Ecc 7:22 that many times you have yourself c others.
Jer 11: 3 C be anyone who does not heed the words
17: 5 C are those who trust in mere mortals
20:14 C be the day on which I was born!
20:15 C be the man who brought the news to my father,
Mal 1:14 C be the cheat who has a male in the flock
2: 2 indeed I have already c them,
3: 9 You are c with a curse, for you are robbing me—
Mk 11:21 The fig tree that you c has withered."
1Co 12: 3 by the Spirit of God ever says "Let Jesus be c!"
Gal 3:10 "C is everyone who does not observe and obey all
3:13 "C is everyone who hangs on a tree"—
Heb 6: 8 it is worthless and on the verge of being c;
Rev 16: 9 but they c the name of God,
16:11 and c the God of heaven because of their pains
16:21 until they c God for the plague of the hail,
Tob 13:12 C are all who speak a harsh word against you;
13:12 c are all who conquer you and pull
Sir 3:16 and whoever angers a mother is c by the Lord.
33:12 but some he c and brought low,
Bar 3: 8 to be reproached and c and punished for all
Pm 151: 6 and he c me by his idols.
4Mc 2:19 saying, "C be their anger"?

CURSES (20) [CURSE]

Ge 12: 3 and the one who c you I will curse;
27:29 Cursed be everyone who c you,
Ex 21:17 Whoever c father or mother shall be put to death.
Lev 24:15 Anyone who c God shall bear the sin.
Nu 5:23 Then the priest shall put these c in writing,
24: 9 and cursed is everyone who c you."
Dt 28:15 all these c shall come upon you and overtake you:
28:45 All these c shall come upon you,
29:20 the c written in this book will descend on them,
29:21 with all the c of the covenant written in this book
30: 1 the blessings and the c that I have set before you,
30: 7 The LORD your God will put all these c
30:19 before you life and death, blessings and c.
Jos 8:34 blessings and c, according to all that is written in
2Ch 34:24 all the c that are written in the book that was read
Ps 109:17 He loved to curse; let c come on him.
Sir 21:27 an ungodly person c an adversary, he c himself.
29: 6 he will repay him with c and reproaches,
34:29 When one prays and another c,

CURSING (18) [CURSE]

2Sa 16: 5 name was Shimei son of Gera; he came out c.
16:10 If he is c because the LORD has said to him,
16:12 and the LORD will repay me with good for this c
Ps 10: 7 Their mouths are filled with c and deceit
59:12 For the c and lies that they utter,
109:18 He clothed himself with c as his coat,
Pr 27:14 rising early in the morning, will be counted as c.
Ecc 7:21 or you may hear your servant c you;
Jer 25:18 an object of hissing and of c, as they are today;
29:18 to be an object of c, and horror, and hissing,
42:18 of execration and horror, of c and ridicule.
44: 8 and become an object of c and ridicule among all
44:12 of execration and horror, of c and ridicule.
49:13 a waste, and an object of c;
Zec 8:13 Just as you have been a c among the nations,
Ro 3:14 "Their mouths are full of c and bitterness."
Jas 3:10 From the same mouth come blessing and c.
Sir 27:14 Their c and swearing make one's hair stand

CURTAIN (57) [CURTAINS, TENT-CURTAINS]

Ex 26: 2 The length of each c shall be twenty-eight cubits,
26: 2 and the width of each c four cubits;
26: 4 on the edge of the outermost c in the first set;
26: 4 on the edge of the outermost c in the second set.
26: 5 You shall make fifty loops on the one c,
26: 5 and you shall make fifty loops on the edge of the c
26: 8 The length of each c shall be thirty cubits,
26: 8 and the width of each c four cubits;
26: 9 and the sixth c you shall double over at the front
26:10 on the edge of the c that is outermost in one set,
26:10 of the c that is outermost in the second set.
26:12 the half c that remains, shall hang over the back of
26:31 You shall make a c of blue, purple,
26:33 You shall hang the c under the clasps,
26:33 the ark of the covenant in there, within the c;
26:33 the c shall separate for you the holy place from
26:35 You shall set the table outside the c,
27:21 outside the c that is before the covenant,
30: 6 You shall place it in front of the c that is above
35:12 the mercy seat, and the c for the screen;
36: 9 The length of each c was twenty-eight cubits,
36: 9 and the width of each c four cubits;
36:11 on the edge of the outermost c of the first set;
36:11 on the edge of the outermost c of the second set;
36:12 on the one c, and he made fifty loops on the edge
36:12 on the edge of the c that was in the second set;
36:15 The length of each c was thirty cubits,
36:15 and the width of each c four cubits;
36:17 on the edge of the outermost c of the one set,
36:17 fifty loops on the edge of the other connecting c.
36:35 He made the c of blue, purple, and crimson yarns,
38:27 and the bases of the c;
39:34 and the c for the screen;
40: 3 and you shall screen the ark with the c.
40:21 and set up the c for screening,
40:22 on the north side of the tabernacle, outside the c,
40:26 in the tent of meeting before the c,
Lev 4: 6 the LORD in front of the c of the sanctuary.
4:17 before the LORD, in front of the c.
16: 2 at any time into the sanctuary inside the c before
16:12 and he shall bring it inside the c
16:15 for the people and bring its blood inside the c,
21:23 he shall not come near the c or approach the altar,
24: 3 outside the c of the covenant,
Nu 4: 5 the screening c, and cover the ark of the covenant
18: 7 that concerns the altar and the area behind the c.
2Ch 3:14 And Solomon made the c of blue and purple
Isa 40:22 who stretches out the heavens like a c,
Mt 27:51 that moment the c of the temple was torn in two,
Mk 15:38 And the c of the temple was torn in two,
Lk 23:45 and the c of the temple was torn in two.
Heb 6:19 a hope that enters the inner shrine behind the c,
9: 3 the second c was a tent called the Holy of Holies.
10:20 and living way that he opened for us through the c
Wis 17: 3 behind a dark c of forgetfulness,
Sir 50: 5 as he came out of the house of the c.
1Mc 1:22 the bowls, the golden censers, the c, the crowns,

CURTAINS (31) [CURTAIN]

Ex 26: 1 with ten c of fine twisted linen, and blue, purple,
26: 2 all the c shall be of the same size.
26: 3 Five c shall be joined to one another; and the other five c shall be joined to one another.
26: 6 and join the c to one another with the clasps,
26: 7 You shall also make c of goats' hair for a tent over the tabernacle; you shall make eleven c.
26: 8 the eleven c shall be of the same size.
26: 9 join five c by themselves, and six c by themselves,
26:12 The part that remains of the c of the tent,
26:13 of what remains in the length of the c of the tent,
36: 8 the workers made the tabernacle with ten c;
36: 9 all the c were of the same size.
36:10 He joined five c to one another, and the other five c he joined to one another.
36:13 and joined the c one to the other with clasps;
36:14 He also made c of goats' hair for a tent over the tabernacle; he made eleven c.
36:15 the eleven c were of the same size.
36:16 five c by themselves, and six c by themselves.
Nu 4:25 They shall carry the c of the tabernacle,
Est 1: 6 There were white cotton c and blue hangings tied
SS 1: 5 like the tents of Kedar, like the c of Solomon.
Isa 54: 2 and let the c of your habitations be stretched out;
Jer 4:20 my tents are destroyed, my c in a moment.
10:20 to spread my tent again, and to set up my c.
49:29 their c and all their goods;
AdE 1: 6 which was adorned with c of fine linen
1Mc 4:51 the bread on the table and hung up the c.

CUSH‡ (8) [CUSHITE]

Ge 2:13 the one that flows around the whole land of C.
10: 6 descendants of Ham: C, Egypt, Put, and Canaan.
10: 7 The descendants of C: Seba,
10: 8 C became the father of Nimrod;
1Ch 1: 8 descendants of Ham: C, Egypt, Put, and Canaan.
1: 9 The descendants of C: Seba,
1:10 C became the father of Nimrod;
Ps 7: T *which he sang to the LORD concerning C,*

CUSHAN (1)

Hab 3: 7 I saw the tents of C under affliction;

CUSHAN-RISHATHAIM (4)

Jdg 3: 8 into the hand of King C of Aram-naharaim;
3: 8 and the Israelites served C eight years.
3:10 the LORD gave King C of Aram into his hand;
3:10 and his hand prevailed over C.

CUSHI (2)

Jer 36:14 of Nethaniah son of Shelemiah son of C to say
Zep 1: 1 the LORD that came to Zephaniah son of C son

CUSHION (1)

Mk 4:38 But he was in the stern, asleep on the c;

CUSHITE‡ (10) [CUSH]

Nu 12: 1 because of the C woman whom he had married
12: 1 (for he had indeed married a C woman);
2Sa 18:21 Then Joab said to a C, "Go,
18:21 The C bowed before Joab, and ran.
18:22 "Come what may, let me also run after the C."
18:23 by the way of the Plain, and outran the C.
18:31 Then the C came; and the C said,
18:32 The king said to the C,
18:32 The C answered, "May the enemies of my lord

CUSHITES See Index to Footnotes

CUSTODY (18)

Ge 40: 3 and he put them in c in the house of the captain of
40: 4 and they continued for some time in c.
40: 7 who were with him in c in his master's house,
41:10 and put me and the chief baker in c in the house of
Lev 24:12 and they put him in c,
Nu 15:34 in c, because it was not clear what should be done
Est 2: 3 the harem in the citadel of Susa under c of Hegai,
2: 8 in the citadel of Susa in c of Hegai,
2: 8 also was taken into the king's palace and put in c
2:14 in c of Shaashgaz, the king's eunuch, who was
Eze 19: 9 into c, so that his voice should be heard no more
Ac 4: 3 So they arrested them and put them in c until
24:23 Then he ordered the centurion to keep him in c,
25:21 But when Paul had appealed to be kept in c for
Jdt 10:12 and took her into c. They asked her,
AdE 2: 8 in Susa the capital in c of Gai,
2: 8 who had c of the women.
3Mc 5: 5 and arranged for their continued c through

CUSTOM (31) [ACCUSTOM, ACCUSTOMED, CUSTOMARY, CUSTOMS]

Jdg 11:39 So there arose an Israelite c that
Ru 4: 7 Now this was the c in former times in Israel
1Ki 18:28 Then they cried aloud and, as was their c,
2Ki 11:14 by the pillar, according to c, with the captains and
17:40 but they continued to practice their former c.
2Ch 35:25 They made these a c in Israel;

Ezr 4:13 **c**, or toll, and the royal revenue will be reduced.
4:20 to whom tribute, **c**, and toll were paid.
7:24 **c**, or toll on any of the priests, the Levites,
Est 1:13 toward all who were versed in law and **c**,
9:23 Jews adopted as a **c** what they had begun to do,
9:27 as a **c** for themselves and their descendants
Ps 119:132 as is your **c** toward those who love your name.
Mk 10: 1 and, as was his **c**, he again taught them.
15: 8 to ask Pilate to do for them according to his **c**.
Lk 1: 9 according to the **c** of the priesthood,
4:16 to the synagogue on the sabbath day, as was his **c**.
22:39 He came out and went, as was his **c**,
Jn 18:39 But you have a **c** that I release someone for you at
19:40 according to the burial **c** of the Jews.
Ac 15: 1 you are circumcised according to the **c** of Moses,
17: 2 And Paul went in, as was his **c**,
25:16 the **c** of the Romans to hand over anyone before
1Co 11:16 we have no such **c**, nor do the churches of God.
Wis 14:16 Then the ungodly **c**, grown strong with time,
1Mc 1:14 in Jerusalem, according to Gentile **c**,
10:89 such as it is the **c** to give to the King's Kinsmen.
2Mc 12:38 they purified themselves according to the **c**,
14:30 was meeting him more rudely than had been his **c**,
3Mc 7: 5 a cruelty more savage than that of Scythian **c**,
4Mc 1:12 but, as my **c** is, I shall begin

CUSTOMARY (7) [CUSTOM]

Da 3:19 up seven times more than was **c**,
Lk 2:27 to do for him what was **c** under the law,
Ac 24: 4 to hear us briefly with your **c** graciousness.
Tob 3: 8 before they had been with her as is **c** for wives.
2Mc 13: 4 and to put him to death by the method that is **c** in
14: 4 and besides these some of the **c** olive branches
14:31 while the priests were offering the **c** sacrifices,

CUSTOMS (20) [CUSTOM]

2Ki 17: 8 in the **c** of the nations whom the LORD drove out
17: 8 in the **c** that the kings of Israel had introduced.
17:19 but walked in the **c** that Israel had introduced.
17:34 to practice their former **c**.
Jer 10: 3 For the **c** of the peoples are false:
Ac 6:14 and will change the **c** that Moses handed on
16:21 and are advocating **c** that are not lawful for us
21:21 not to circumcise their children or observe the **c**.
26: 3 because you are especially familiar with all the **c**
28:17 against our people or the **c** of our ancestors,
Wis 14:23 or hold frenzied revels with strange **c**,
1Mc 1:42 and that all should give up their particular **c**.
1:44 he directed them to follow **c** strange to the land,
2Mc 4:11 the lawful ways of living and introduced new **c**
6: 9 not choose to change over to Greek **c**.
11:24 not consent to our father's change to Greek **c**,
11:24 and ask that their own **c** be allowed them.
11:25 to them and that they shall live according to the **c**
3Mc 3: 2 from the observance of their **c**.
4Mc 18: 5 and to abandon their ancestral **c**,

CUT‡ (330) [CUTS, CUTTER, CUTTING, GEM-CUTTER, STONECUTTERS, STONECUTTING, WOODCUTTER]

Ge 9:11 that never again shall all flesh be **c** off by
15:10 He brought him all these and **c** them in two,
15:10 but he did not **c** the birds in two.
17:14 of his foreskin shall be **c** off from his people;
22: 3 he **c** the wood for the burnt offering,
Ex 4:25 Zipporah took a flint and **c** off her son's foreskin,
9:15 and you would have been **c** off from the earth.
12:15 the first day until the seventh day shall be **c** off
12:19 for whoever eats what is leavened shall be **c** off
29:17 Then you shall **c** the ram into its parts,
30:33 of it on an unqualified person shall be **c** off from
30:38 to use as perfume shall be **c** off from the people.
31:14 whoever does any work on it shall be **c** off from
34: 1 "**C** two tablets of stone like the former ones,
34: 4 Moses **c** two tablets of stone like the former ones;
34:13 and **c** down their sacred poles
39: 3 Gold leaf was hammered out and **c** into threads
Lev 1: 6 The burnt offering shall be flayed and **c** up
1:12 It shall be **c** up into its parts,
7:20 a state of uncleanness shall be **c** off from their kin.
7:21 you shall be **c** off from your kin.
7:25 you who eat it shall be **c** off from your kin.
7:27 Any one of you who eats any blood shall be **c** off
8:20 The ram was **c** into its parts,
17: 4 and he shall be **c** off from the people.
17: 9 shall be **c** off from the people.
17:10 and will **c** that person off from the people.
17:14 whoever eats it shall be **c** off.
18:29 of these abominations shall be **c** off
19: 8 any such person shall be **c** off from the people.
20: 3 and will **c** them off from the people,
20: 5 and will **c** them off from among their people,
20: 6 and will **c** them off from the people.
20:17 and they shall be **c** off in the sight of their people;
20:18 both of them shall be **c** off from their people.
22: 3 that person shall be **c** off from my presence:
22:24 or torn or **c**, you shall not offer to the LORD;
23:29 that entire day shall be **c** off from the people.
26:30 I will destroy your high places and **c**
Nu 9:13 shall be **c** off from the people for not presenting
13:23 and **c** down from there a branch with
13:24 of the cluster that the Israelites **c** down from there.
15:30 and shall be **c** off from among the people.
15:31 a person shall be utterly **c** off and bear the guilt.
Nu 19:13 such persons shall be **c** off from Israel.
19:20 those persons shall be **c** off from the assembly,
Dt 10: 3 **c** two tablets of stone like the former ones,
12:29 When the LORD your God has **c** off before you
19: 1 When the LORD your God has **c** off
19: 5 the forest with another to **c** wood, and when one of them swings the ax to **c** down a tree,
20:19 you must not **c** them down.
20:20 you may **c** them down for use
23: 1 or whose penis is **c** off shall be admitted to
25:12 you shall **c** off her hand; show no pity.
29:11 both those who **c** your wood
Jos 3:13 of the Jordan flowing from above shall be **c** off;
3:16 the Dead Sea, were wholly **c** off.
4: 7 that the waters of the Jordan were **c** off in front of
4: 7 the waters of the Jordan were **c** off.
7: 9 and **c** off our name from the earth.
23: 4 along with all the nations that I have already **c** off,
Jdg 1: 6 and caught him, and **c** off his thumbs and big toes.
1: 7 with their thumbs and big toes **c** off used to pick
6:25 and **c** down the sacred pole that is beside it;
6:26 of the sacred pole that you shall **c** down."
6:28 and the sacred pole beside it was **c** down,
6:30 down the altar of Baal and **c** down the sacred pole
9:48 **c** down a bundle of brushwood,
9:49 So every one of the troops **c** down a bundle
19:29 and grasping his concubine he **c** her
20: 6 Then I took my concubine and **c** her into pieces,
20:45 of them were **c** down on the main roads,
21: 6 and said, "One tribe is **c** off from Israel this day.
Ru 4:10 of the dead may not be **c** off from his kindred and
1Sa 2: 9 but the wicked shall be **c** off in darkness;
2:31 a time is coming when I will **c** off your strength
2:33 of you whom I shall not **c** off from my altar shall
5: 4 of Dagon and both his hands were lying **c** off
11: 7 and **c** them in pieces and sent them throughout all
11:11 the morning watch they came into the camp and **c**
17:46 and I will strike you down and **c** off your head;
17:51 then he **c** off his head with it.
20:15 never **c** off your faithful love from my house,
20:15 the LORD were to **c** off every one of the enemies
24: 4 Then David went and stealthily **c** off a corner
24: 5 because he had **c** off a corner of Saul's cloak.
24:11 for by the fact that I **c** off the corner of your cloak,
24:21 the LORD that you will not **c** off my descendants
28: 9 how he has **c** off the mediums and the wizards
31: 9 They **c** off his head, stripped off his armor,
2Sa 4:12 they **c** off their hands and feet,
7: 9 and have **c** off all your enemies from before you;
10: 4 **c** off their garments in the middle at their hips,
14:16 of the man who would **c** both me and my son off
14:26 When he **c** the hair of his head (for at the end of every year he used to **c** it; when it was heavy on him, he **c** it),
20:22 And they **c** off the head of Sheba son of Bichri,
1Ki 5: 6 that cedars from the Lebanon be **c** for me.
5: 6 among us who knows how to **c** timber like
7: 9 **c** according to measure, sawed with saws,
7:11 There were costly stones above, **c** to measure,
9: 7 then I will **c** Israel off from the land
13:34 so as to **c** it off and to destroy it from the face of
14:10 I will **c** off from Jeroboam every male,
14:14 who shall **c** off the house of Jeroboam today,
15:13 Asa **c** down her image and burned it at
18:23 **c** it in pieces, and lay it on the wood,
18:28 they **c** themselves with swords and lances until
18:33 Next he put the wood in order, **c** the bull in pieces,
21:21 and will **c** off from Ahab every male,
2Ki 4:39 and came and **c** them up into the pot of stew,
6: 4 When they came to the Jordan, they **c** down trees.
6: 6 When he showed him the place, he **c** off a stick,
9: 8 I will **c** off from Ahab every male, bond or free,
16:17 Then King Ahaz **c** off the frames of the stands,
18: 4 and **c** down the sacred pole.
23:14 in pieces, **c** down the sacred poles, and covered
24:13 he **c** in pieces all the vessels of gold in the temple
1Ch 17: 8 and have **c** off all your enemies before you;
19: 4 **c** off their garments in the middle at their hips,
2Ch 2:10 those who **c** the timber, twenty thousand cors
2:16 We will **c** whatever timber you need
15:16 Asa **c** down her image, crushed it
28:24 and **c** in pieces the utensils of the house of God.
32:21 And the LORD sent an angel who **c** off all
Job 4: 7 Or where were the upright **c** off?
6: 9 that he would let loose his hand and **c** me off!
8:12 While yet in flower and not **c** down,
14: 7 "For there is hope for a tree, if it is **c** down,
21:21 when the number of their months is **c** off?
22:20 'Surely our adversaries are **c** off,
24:24 they are **c** off like the heads of grain.
28:10 They **c** out channels in the rocks,
36:20 when peoples are **c** off in their place.
38:25 "Who has **c** a channel for the torrents of rain,
Ps 12: 3 May the LORD **c** off all flattering lips,
34:16 to **c** off the remembrance of them from the earth.
37: 9 For the wicked shall be **c** off,
37:22 but those cursed by him shall be **c** off.
37:28 but the children of the wicked shall be **c** off.
37:38 the posterity of the wicked shall be **c** off.
74:15 You **c** openings for springs and torrents;
75:10 All the horns of the wicked I will **c** off,
80:16 with fire, they have **c** it down;
88: 5 for they are **c** off from your hand.
89:45 You have **c** short the days of his youth;
109:13 May his posterity be **c** off;
109:15 and may his memory be **c** off from the earth.
118:10 in the name of the LORD I **c** them off!
Ps 118:11 in the name of the LORD I **c** them off!
118:12 in the name of the LORD I **c** them off!
129: 4 he has **c** the cords of the wicked.
143:12 In your steadfast love **c** off my enemies,
144:12 **c** for the building of a palace.
Pr 2:22 but the wicked will be **c** off from the land,
10:31 but the perverse tongue will be **c** off.
23:18 there is a future, and your hope will not be **c** off.
24:14 and your hope will not be **c** off.
Isa 7: 6 against Judah and **c** off Jerusalem and conquer it
9:10 the sycamores have been **c** down,
9:14 So the LORD **c** off from Israel head and tail,
10: 7 and to **c** off nations not a few.
10:33 the tallest trees will be **c** down,
11:13 the hostility of Judah shall be **c** off;
14: 8 no one comes to **c** us down."
14:12 How you are **c** down to the ground,
14:22 and will **c** off from Babylon name and remnant,
18: 5 he will **c** off the shoots with pruning hooks,
22:16 that you have **c** out a tomb here for yourself,
22:25 it will be **c** down and fall,
29:20 all those alert to do evil shall be **c** off—
33:12 like thorns **c** down, that are burned in the fire."
45: 2 the doors of bronze and **c** through the bars of iron,
48: 9 so that I may not **c** you off.
48:19 their name would never be **c** off or destroyed from
51: 9 Was it not you who **c** Rahab in pieces,
53: 8 For he was **c** off from the land of the living,
55:13 for an everlasting sign that shall not be **c** off.
56: 5 an everlasting name that shall not be **c** off.
Jer 6: 6 **C** down her trees; cast up a siege ramp against
7:28 it is **c** off from their lips.
7:29 **C** off your hair and throw it away;
9:21 to **c** off the children from the streets and
10: 3 a tree from the forest is **c** down,
11:19 let us **c** him off from the land of the living,
22: 7 they shall **c** down your choicest cedars
34:18 I will make like the calf when they **c** it in two
36:23 the king would **c** them off with a penknife
36:29 and will **c** off from it human beings and animals?
44: 7 to **c** off man and woman, child and infant,
44: 8 Will you be **c** off and become an object of cursing
46:23 They shall **c** down her forest, says the LORD,
47: 4 to **c** off from Tyre and Sidon every helper
48: 2 "Come, let us **c** her off from being a nation!"
48:25 The horn of Moab is **c** off, and his arm is broken,
48:37 For every head is shaved and every beard **c** off;
50:16 **C** off from Babylon the sower,
50:23 hammer of the whole earth is **c** down and broken!
51:13 your end has come, the thread of your life is **c**.
La 2: 3 He has **c** down in fierce anger all the might
Eze 5:11 therefore I will **c** you down;
6: 6 your incense stands **c** down,
9: 6 **C** down old men, young men and young women,
14: 8 a sign and a byword and **c** them off from the midst
14:13 and **c** off from it human beings and animals,
14:17 and I **c** off human beings and animals from it;
14:19 to **c** off humans and animals from it;
14:21 to **c** off humans and animals from it!
16: 4 the day you were born your navel cord was not **c**,
16:40 and they shall stone you and **c** you to pieces
17:17 up and siege walls built to **c** off many lives.
21: 3 will **c** off from you both righteous and wicked.
21: 4 I will **c** off from you both righteous and wicked,
23:25 They shall **c** off your nose and your ears,
23:47 and with their swords they shall **c** them down;
25: 7 I will **c** you off from the peoples
25:13 and **c** off from it humans and animals,
25:16 the Philistines, **c** off the Cherethites, and destroy
29: 8 and will **c** off from you human being and animal;
30:15 and **c** off the hordes of Thebes.
31:12 the most terrible of the nations have **c** it down
35: 7 and I will **c** off from it all who come and go.
37:11 and our hope is lost; we are **c** off completely.'
39:10 to take wood out of the field or **c** down any trees
Da 2:34 As you looked on, a stone was **c** out,
2:45 as you saw that a stone was **c** from the mountain
4:14 '**C** down the tree and chop off its branches,
4:23 '**C** down the tree and destroy it,
9:26 anointed one shall be **c** off and shall have nothing,
Hos 10:15 At dawn the king of Israel shall be utterly **c** off.
Joel 1: 5 for it is **c** off from your mouth.
1: 9 The grain offering and the drink offering are **c** off
1:16 Is not the food **c** off before our eyes,
Am 1: 5 and **c** off the inhabitants from the Valley of Aven,
1: 8 I will **c** off the inhabitants from Ashdod,
2: 3 I will **c** off the ruler from its midst,
3:14 and the horns of the altar shall be **c** off and fall to
Ob 1: 9 so that everyone from Mount Esau will be **c** off.
1:10 and you shall be **c** off forever.
1:14 at the crossings to **c** off his fugitives;
Mic 1:16 and **c** off your hair for your pampered children;
5: 9 and all your enemies shall be **c** off.
5:10 I will **c** off your horses from among you
5:11 and I will **c** off the cities of your land and throw
5:12 and I will **c** off sorceries from your hand,
5:13 and I will **c** off your images and your pillars from
Na 1:12 they will be **c** off and pass away.
1:14 of your gods I will **c** off the carved image and
1:15 shall the wicked invade you; they are utterly **c** off.
2:13 I will **c** off your prey from the earth,
3:15 the sword will **c** you off.
Hab 3:17 the flock is **c** off from the fold and there is no herd
Zep 1: 3 I will **c** off humanity from the face of the earth,
1: 4 and I will **c** off from this place every remnant
1:11 all who weigh out silver are **c** off.
3: 6 I have **c** off nations; their battlements are in ruins;

Zec 5: 3 for everyone who steals shall be **c** off according to
5: 3 be **c** off according to the writing on the other side.
9: 10 He will **c** off the chariot from Ephraim and
9: 10 and the battle bow shall be **c** off,
13: 2 I will **c** off the names of the idols from the land,
13: 8 two-thirds shall be **c** off and perish,
14: 2 rest of the people shall not be **c** off from the city.
Mal 2: 12 May the LORD **c** off from the tents
Mt 3: 10 that does not bear good fruit is **c** down and thrown
5: 30 **c** it off and throw it away;
7: 19 that does not bear good fruit is **c** down and thrown
18: 8 **c** it off and throw it away;
21: 8 and others **c** branches from the trees
24: 22 And if those days had not been **c** short,
24: 22 for the sake of the elect those days will be **c** short.
24: 51 He will **c** him in pieces and put him with
Mk 9: 43 If your hand causes you to stumble, **c** it off;
9: 45 And if your foot causes you to stumble, **c** it off;
11: 8 and others spread leafy branches that they had **c** in
13: 20 And if the Lord had not **c** short those days,
13: 20 whom he chose, he has **c** short those days.
Lk 3: 9 that does not bear good fruit is **c** down and thrown
12: 46 and will **c** him in pieces,
13: 7 and still I find none. **C** it down!
13: 9 but if not, you can **c** it down.' "
22: 50 the slave of the high priest and **c** off his right ear.
Jn 18: 10 and **c** off his right ear.
18: 26 a relative of the man whose ear Peter had **c** off,
Ac 2: 37 they were **c** to the heart and said to Peter and to
18: 18 At Cenchreae he had his hair **c**,
27: 32 Then the soldiers **c** away the ropes of the boat
Ro 9: 3 that I myself were accursed and **c** off from Christ
11: 22 otherwise you also will be **c** off.
11: 24 For if you have been **c** from what is by nature
1Co 11: 6 then she should **c** off her hair;
11: 6 for a woman to have her hair **c** off or to be shaved,
Gal 5: 4 to be justified by the law have **c** yourselves off
Tob 2: 12 when she **c** off a piece she had woven and sent it
6: 5 "**C** open the fish and take out its gall, heart,
Jdt 3: 8 Yet he demolished all their shrines and **c**
5: 22 the seacoast and Moab insisted that he should be **c**
13: 8 with all her might, and **c** off his head.
13: 18 who has guided you to **c** off the head of the leader
14: 4 the borders of Israel will pursue them and **c** them
15: 5 and **c** them down as far as Choba.
Wis 18: 23 and **c** off its way to the living.
Sir 38: 27 those who **c** the signets of seals,
Sus 1: 55 from God and will immediately **c** you in two."
1Mc 6: 6 from the armies they had **c** down;
7: 47 they **c** off Nicanor's head and the right hand
11: 17 the Arab **c** off the head of Alexander and sent it
2Mc 1: 13 they were **c** to pieces in the temple of Nanea by
1: 16 they dismembered them and **c** off their heads
5: 12 to **c** down relentlessly everyone they met and
7: 4 that the tongue of their spokesman be **c** out and
7: 4 that they scalp him and **c** off his hands and feet,
10: 30 they were thrown into disorder and **c** to pieces.
10: 35 and with savage fury **c** down everyone they met.
12: 35 down on him and **c** off his arm;
15: 30 to **c** off Nicanor's head and arm and carry them
15: 33 He **c** out the tongue of the ungodly Nicanor
1Es 4: 9 if he tells them to **c** down, they **c** down;
5: 72 **c** off their supplies, and hindered their building;
2Es 7: *114* [44] to an end, unbelief has been **c** off,
4Mc 2: 14 The fruit trees of the enemy are not **c** down,
6: 6 and his sides were being **c** to pieces.
9: 17 **C** my limbs, burn my flesh, and twist my joints;
10: 17 Antiochus gave orders to **c** out his tongue.
10: 19 See, here is my tongue; **c** it off,
12: 13 to **c** out the tongues of men who have feelings
18: 21 the pupils of their eyes and **c** out their tongues,

CUTH (1) [=CUTHAH?]
2Ki 17: 30 the people of **C** made Nergal,

CUTHA (1)
1Es 5: 32 the descendants of **C**, the descendants of Charea,

CUTHAH (1) [=CUTH?]
2Ki 17: 24 king of Assyria brought people from Babylon, **C**,

CUTS (6) [CUT]
Job 27: 8 the hope of the godless when God **c** them off,
Ps 76: 12 who **c** off the spirit of princes,
107: 16 and **c** in two the bars of iron.
Isa 38: 12 he **c** me off from the loom;
44: 14 He **c** down cedars or chooses a holm tree or
Jer 22: 14 and who **c** out windows for it,

CUTTER (1) [CUT]
Joel 2: 25 the destroyer, and the **c**, my great army,

CUTTING (14) [CUT]
Ex 31: 5 in **c** stones for setting, and in carving wood,
35: 33 in **c** stones for setting, and in carving wood,
Jdg 20: 43 **C** down the Benjaminites,
2Ch 2: 8 that your servants are skilled in **c** Lebanon timber.
Ps 101: 8 **c** off all evildoers from the city of the LORD.
Pr 26: 6 like **c** off one's foot and drinking down violence,
Isa 22: 16 **c** a tomb on the height,
Joel 1: 4 the **c** locust left, the swarming locust has eaten.
Hab 2: 10 for your house by **c** off many peoples;
Mt 26: 51 the slave of the high priest, **c** off his ear.
Mk 14: 47 the slave of the high priest, **c** off his ear.
Tob 6: 6 So after **c** open the fish
2Mc 2: 32 be foolish to lengthen the preface while **c** short
4Mc 10: 21 for you are **c** out a tongue that has been melodious

CYAMON (1)
Jdt 7: 3 as Balbaim and in length from Bethulia to **C**,

CYAXARES (1)
Tob 14: 15 those whom King **C** of Media had taken captive.

CYCLE (1) [CYCLES]
Jas 3: 6 sets on fire the **c** of nature,

CYCLES (1) [CYCLE]
Wis 7: 19 the **c** of the year and the constellations of the stars,

CYMBAL (1) [CYMBALS]
1Co 13: 1 I am a noisy gong or a clanging **c**.

CYMBALS (20) [CYMBAL]
2Sa 6: 5 and harps and tamborines and castanets and **c**.
1Ch 13: 8 and harps and tambourines and **c** and trumpets.
15: 16 on harps and lyres and **c**,
15: 19 Asaph, and Ethan were to sound bronze **c**;
15: 28 and **c**, and made loud music on harps and lyres.
16: 5 Asaph was to sound the **c**,
16: 42 and Jeduthun had with them trumpets and **c** for
25: 1 who should prophesy with lyres, harps, and **c**.
25: 6 for the music in the house of the LORD with **c**,
2Ch 5: 12 arrayed in fine linen, with **c**, harps, and lyres,
5: 13 and **c** and other musical instruments,
29: 25 the Levites in the house of the LORD with **c**,
Ezr 3: 10 and the Levites, the sons of Asaph, with **c**,
Ne 12: 27 with thanksgivings and with singing, with **c**,
Ps 150: 5 Praise him with clanging **c**;
150: 5 praise him with loud clashing **c**!
Jdt 16: 1 sing to my Lord with **c**.
1Mc 4: 54 with songs and harps and lutes and **c**.
13: 51 and with harps and **c** and stringed instruments,
1Es 5: 59 and the Levites, the sons of Asaph, with **c**,

CYPRESS (15) [CYPRESSES]
Ge 6: 14 Make yourself an ark of **c** wood;
1Ki 5: 8 in the matter of cedar and **c** timber.
5: 10 for timber of cedar and **c**.
6: 15 he covered the floor of the house with boards of **c**.
6: 34 and two doors of **c** wood;
9: 11 with cedar and **c** timber and gold,
2Ch 2: 8 **c**, and algum timber from Lebanon,
3: 5 The nave he lined with **c**,
Isa 41: 19 I will set in the desert the **c**,
55: 13 Instead of the thorn shall come up the **c**;
60: 13 The glory of Lebanon shall come to you, the **c**,
Hos 14: 8 I am like an evergreen **c**;
Zec 11: 2 Wail, O **c**, for the cedar has fallen,
Sir 24: 13 and like a **c** on the heights of Hermon.
50: 10 and like a **c** towering in the clouds.

CYPRESSES‡ (3) [CYPRESS]
2Ki 19: 23 I felled its tallest cedars, its choicest **c**;
Isa 14: 8 The **c** exult over you, the cedars of Lebanon,
37: 24 I felled its tallest cedars, its choicest **c**;

CYPRIAN (1) [CYPRUS]
2Mc 4: 29 the commander of the **C** troops.

CYPRUS (15) [CYPRIAN]
Isa 23: 1 When they came in from **C** they learned of it.
23: 12 cross over to **C**—even there you will have no rest.
Jer 2: 10 Cross to the coasts of **C** and look,
Eze 27: 6 of pines from the coasts of **C**,
Ac 4: 36 There was a Levite, a native of **C**, Joseph,
11: 19 as Phoenicia, **C**, and Antioch, and they spoke
11: 20 But among them were some men of **C**
13: 4 and from there they sailed to **C**.
15: 39 with him and sailed away to **C**.
21: 3 We came in sight of **C**;
21: 16 and brought us to the house of Mnason of **C**,
27: 4 we sailed under the lee of **C**,
1Mc 15: 23 and to Aradus and Gortyna and Cnidus and **C**
2Mc 10: 13 because he had abandoned **C**,
12: 2 in addition to these Nicanor the governor of **C**,

CYRENE (8) [CYRENIANS]
Mt 27: 32 they came upon a man from **C** named Simon;
Mk 15: 21 it was Simon of **C**, the father of Alexander
Lk 23: 26 Simon of **C**, who was coming from the country,
Ac 2: 10 Egypt and the parts of Libya belonging to **C**,
11: 20 men of Cyprus and **C** who, on coming to Antioch,
13: 1 Simeon who was called Niger, Lucius of **C**,
1Mc 15: 23 and Gortyna and Cnidus and Cyprus and **C**.
2Mc 2: 23 which has been set forth by Jason of **C**

CYRENIAN[S] (KJV) See also CYRENE

CYRENIANS (1) [CYRENE]
Ac 6: 9 the Freedmen (as it was called), **C**, Alexandrians,

CYRENIUS (KJV) See QUIRINIUS

CYRUS‡ (41)
2Ch 36: 22 In the first year of King **C** of Persia,
36: 22 up the spirit of King **C** of Persia so that he sent
36: 23 "Thus says King **C** of Persia:
Ezr 1: 1 In the first year of King **C** of Persia,
1: 1 up the spirit of King **C** of Persia so that he sent
1: 2 "Thus says King **C** of Persia:
1: 7 King **C** himself brought out the vessels of
1: 8 King **C** of Persia had them released into
3: 7 according to the grant that they had from King **C**
4: 3 as King **C** of Persia has commanded us."
4: 5 throughout the reign of King **C** of Persia and until
5: 13 However, King **C** of Babylon,
5: 14 these King **C** took out of the temple of Babylon,
5: 17 by King **C** for the rebuilding of this house of God
6: 3 the first year of his reign, King **C** issued a decree:
6: 14 and by decree of **C**, Darius, and King Artaxerxes
Isa 44: 28 who says of **C**, "He is my shepherd,
45: 1 Thus says the LORD to his anointed, to **C**,
45: 13 I have aroused **C** in righteousness,
Da 1: 21 until the first year of King **C**.
6: 28 the reign of Darius and the reign of **C** the Persian.
10: 1 of King **C** of Persia a word was revealed
Bel 1: 1 **C** the Persian succeeded to his kingdom.
1Es 2: 1 In the first year of **C** as king of the Persians,
2: 2 the spirit of King **C** of the Persians, and he made
2: 3 "Thus says **C** king of the Persians:
2: 10 King **C** also brought out the holy vessels of
2: 11 When King **C** of the Persians brought these out,
4: 44 which **C** set apart when he began
4: 57 from Babylon all the vessels that **C** had set apart;
4: 57 everything that **C** had ordered to be done,
5: 55 the decree that they had in writing from King **C** of
5: 71 as **C**, the king of the Persians,
5: 73 of the building as long as King **C** lived.
6: 17 in the first year that **C** reigned over the country
6: 17 King **C** wrote that this house should be rebuilt.
6: 18 these King **C** took out again from the temple
6: 22 with the consent of King **C**,
6: 24 of King **C**, he ordered the building of the house of
6: 25 the cost to be paid from the treasury of King **C**;
7: 4 with the consent of **C** and Darius and Artaxerxes

D

DABAREH (KJV) See DABERATH

DABBESHETH (1)
Jos 19: 11 and on to Maralah, and touches **D**,

DABERATH (3)
Jos 19: 12 from there it goes to **D**, then up to Japhia;
21: 28 with its pasture lands, **D** with its pasture lands,
1Ch 6: 72 with its pasture lands, **D** with its pasture lands,

DABRIA (1)
2Es 14: 24 and take with you Sarea, **D**, Selemia, Ethanus,

DAGGER (1)
LtJ 6: 15 Another has a **d** in its right hand, and an ax,

DAGON (15) [BETH-DAGON]
Jdg 16: 23 a great sacrifice to their god **D**, and to rejoice;
1Sa 5: 2 the ark of God and brought it into the house of **D**
and placed it beside **D**.
5: 3 of Ashdod rose early the next day, there was **D**,
5: 3 So they took **D** and put him back in his place.
5: 4 **D** had fallen on his face to the ground before
5: 4 of **D** and both his hands were lying cut off upon
5: 4 only the trunk of **D** was left to him.
5: 5 priests of **D** and all who enter the house of **D** do
not step on the threshold of **D** in Ashdod to this
5: 7 for his hand is heavy on us and on our god **D**."
1Ch 10: 10 and fastened his head in the temple of **D**.
1Mc 10: 84 the temple of **D**, and those who had taken refuge
11: 4 they showed him the burnt-out temple of **D**,

DAILY‡ (38) [DAY]
Ex 5: 13 "Complete your work, the same **d** assignment as
5: 19 "You shall not lessen your **d** number of bricks."
Nu 28: 3 two male lambs a year old without blemish, **d**,
28: 24 In the same way you shall offer **d**, for seven days,
Dt 24: 15 You shall pay them their wages **d** before sunset,
Ezr 3: 4 the **d** burnt offerings by number according to
Ne 12: 47 the days of Nehemiah all Israel gave the **d** portions
Ps 68: 19 Blessed be the Lord, who **d** bears us up;
Pr 8: 30 I was **d** his delight, rejoicing before him always,
8: 34 watching **d** at my gates, waiting beside my doors.
Jer 37: 21 of bread was given him **d** from the bakers' street,

Jer 52:34 a regular **d** allowance was given him by the king
Eze 43:25 For seven days you shall provide **d** a goat for
45:23 and a male goat **d** for a sin offering.
46:13 for a burnt offering to the LORD **d;**
Da 1: 5 a **d** portion of the royal rations of food and wine.
Mt 6:11 Give us this day our **d** bread.
20: 2 agreeing with the laborers for the usual **d** wage,
20: 9 each of them received the usual **d** wage.
20:10 but each of them also received the usual **d** wage.
20:13 did you not agree with me for the usual **d** wage?
Lk 9:23 let them deny themselves and take up their cross **d**
11: 3 Give us each day our **d** bread.
Ac 3: 2 People would lay him **d** at the gate of
6: 1 in the **d** distribution of food.
16: 5 in the faith and increased in numbers **d.**
19: 9 and argued **d** in the lecture hall of Tyrannus.
2Co 11:28 under **d** pressure because of my anxiety for all
Gal 3:15 Brothers and sisters, I give an example from **d** life:
Jas 2:15 If a brother or sister is naked and lacks **d** food,
Jdt 4:14 offered the **d** burnt offerings, the votive offerings,
12:15 from Bagoas for her **d** use in reclining.
AdE 6: 1 to his secretary to bring the book of **d** records,
1Mc 6:57 "**D** we grow weaker, our food supply is scant,
1Es 1:16 no one needed to interrupt his **d** duties,
6:30 for **d** use as the priests in Jerusalem may indicate,
2Es 4:23 but about those things that we **d** experience:
4Mc 13:22 from this common nurture and **d** companionship,

DAINTIES (2) [DAINTY]

Rev 18:14 and all your **d** and your splendor are lost to you,
Sir 31: 3 and when he rests he fills himself with his **d.**

DAINTY (1) [DAINTIES]

Job 33:20 and their appetites **d** food.

DAINTY (KJV) See also DELICACIES

DAISAN (1)

1Es 5:31 the descendants of **D,** the descendants of Noeba,

DALAIAH (KJV) See DELAIAH

DALE (KJV) See VALLEY

DALLIED (1) [DALLY]

2Mc 6: 4 who **d** with prostitutes and had intercourse

DALLY (1) [DALLIED]

Sir 9: 4 Do not **d** with a singing girl,

DALMANUTHA (1)

Mk 8:10 with his disciples and went to the district of **D.**

DALMATIA (1)

2Ti 4:10 Crescens has gone to Galatia, Titus to **D.**

DALPHON (1)

Est 9: 7 They killed Parshandatha, **D,** Aspatha,

DAMAGE (13) [DAMAGING]

Ezr 4:22 why should **d** grow to the hurt of the king?"
Est 7: 4 no enemy can compensate for this **d** to the king."
Pr 6:15 in a moment, **d** beyond repair.
Ac 27:21 from Crete and thereby avoided this **d** and loss.
Rev 6: 6 but do not **d** the olive oil and the wine!"
7: 2 four angels who had been given power to **d** earth
7: 3 "Do not **d** the earth or the sea or the trees,
9: 4 not to **d** the grass of the earth or any green growth
1Mc 7:22 of the land of Judah and did great **d** in Israel.
14:36 doing great **d** to its purity.
15:29 you have done great **d** in the land
15:35 they were causing great **d** among the people and
1Es 6:33 to hinder or **d** that house of the Lord in Jerusalem.

DAMAGING (1) [DAMAGE]

Ru 4: 6 for myself without **d** my own inheritance.

DAMARIS (1)

Ac 17:34 the Areopagite and a woman named **D,**

DAMASCUS (67)

Ge 14:15 and pursued them to Hobah, north of **D.**
15: 2 and the heir of my house is Eliezer of **D?"**
2Sa 8: 5 the Arameans of **D** came to help King Hadadezer
8: 6 David put garrisons among the Arameans of **D;**
1Ki 11:24 went to **D,** settled there, and made him king in **D.**
15:18 who resided in **D,** saying,
19:15 "Go, return on your way to the wilderness of **D;**
20:34 and you may establish bazaars for yourself in **D,**
2Ki 5:12 Are not Abana and Pharpar, the rivers of **D,**
8: 7 to **D** while King Ben-hadad of Aram was ill.
8: 9 taking a present with him, all kinds of goods of **D,**
14:28 and how he recovered for Israel **D** and Hamath,
16: 9 the king of Assyria marched up against **D,**
16:10 to **D** to meet King Tiglath-pileser of Assyria,
16:10 he saw the altar that was at **D.**
16:11 with all that King Ahaz had sent from **D,**
16:11 before King Ahaz arrived from **D.**
16:12 the king came from **D,** the king viewed the altar.
1Ch 18: 5 the Arameans of **D** came to help King Hadadezer
18: 6 Then David put garrisons in Aram of **D;**
2Ch 16: 2 who resided in **D,** saying,
24:23 and sent all the booty they took to the king of **D.**
28: 5 of his people and brought them to **D.**
28:23 For he sacrificed to the gods of **D,**
SS 7: 4 like a tower of Lebanon, overlooking **D.**
Isa 7: 8 the head of Aram is **D,** and the head of **D** is Rezin.
8: 4 of **D** and the spoil of Samaria will be carried away
10: 9 Is not Samaria like **D?**
17: 1 oracle concerning **D.** See, **D** will cease to be a city,
17: 3 and the kingdom from **D;**
Jer 49:23 Concerning **D.** Hamath
49:24 **D** has become feeble, she turned to flee,
49:27 And I will kindle a fire at the wall of **D,**
Eze 27:18 **D** traded with you for your abundant goods—
47:16 Sibraim (which lies between the border of **D** and
47:17 which is north of the border of **D,**
47:18 On the east side, between Hauran and **D;**
48: 1 as far as Hazar-enon (which is on the border of **D,**
Am 1: 3 For three transgressions of **D,** and for four,
1: 5 I will break the gate bars of **D,**
5:27 therefore I will take you into exile beyond **D,**
Zec 9: 1 against the land of Hadrach and will rest upon **D.**
Ac 9: 2 and asked him for letters to the synagogues at **D,**
9: 3 Now as he was going along and approaching **D,**
9: 8 they led him by the hand and brought him into **D.**
9:10 Now there was a disciple in **D** named Ananias.
9:19 For several days he was with the disciples in **D,**
9:22 the Jews who lived in **D** by proving that Jesus was
9:27 in **D** he had spoken boldly in the name of Jesus.
22: 5 also received letters to the brothers in **D,**
22: 6 "While I was on my way and approaching **D,**
22:10 The Lord said to me, 'Get up and go to **D;**
22:11 with me took my hand and led me to **D.**
26:12 to **D** with the authority and commission of
26:20 but declared first to those in **D,**
2Co 11:32 In **D,** the governor under King Aretas guarded the
city of **D** in order to seize me,
Gal 1:17 and afterwards I returned to **D.**
Jdt 1: 7 those who lived in Cilicia and **D,**
1:12 on the whole territory of Cilicia and **D** and Syria,
2:27 down into the plain of **D** during the wheat harvest,
15: 5 even beyond **D** and its borders.
1Mc 11:62 And he passed through the country as far as **D.**
12:32 Then he broke camp and went to **D,**

DAMNATION (KJV) See CONDEMNATION, JUDGMENT, SENTENCE

DAMSEL (KJV) See CHILD, ENGAGED WOMAN, GIRL, LITTLE GIRL, MAID, SERVANT GIRL, SLAVE GIRL, VIRGIN, WOMAN, YOUNG WOMAN

DAN‡ (58) [DANITE, DANITES, =LAISH, =LESHEM, MAHANEH-DAN]

Ge 14:14 and went in pursuit as far as **D.**
30: 6 therefore she named him **D.**
35:25 sons of Bilhah, Rachel's maid: **D** and Naphtali.
46:23 The children of **D:** Hashum.
49:16 **D** shall judge his people as one of the tribes
49:17 **D** shall be a snake by the roadside,
Ex 1: 4 **D** and Naphtali, Gad and Asher.
31: 6 of Ahisamach, of the tribe of **D;**
35:34 and Oholiab son of Ahisamach, of the tribe of **D.**
38:23 of the tribe of **D,** engraver, designer,
Lev 24:11 daughter of Dibri, of the tribe of **D—**
Nu 1:12 From **D,** Ahiezer son of Ammishaddai.
1:38 The descendants of **D,** their lineage, in their clans,
1:39 of **D** were sixty-two thousand seven hundred.
2:25 be the regimental encampment of **D** by companies.
2:31 **D** is one hundred fifty-seven thousand six hundred.
10:25 Then the standard of the camp of **D,**
13:12 from the tribe of **D,** Ammiel son of Gemalli;
26:42 These are the descendants of **D** by their clans:
26:42 These are the clans of **D** by their clans.
Dt 27:13 Reuben, Gad, Asher, Zebulun, **D,** and Naphtali.
33:22 And of **D** he said: **D** is a lion's whelp that leaps
34: 1 showed him the whole land: Gilead as far as **D,**
Jos 19:40 The seventh lot came out for the tribe of **D,**
19:47 calling Leshem, **D,** after their ancestor **D.**
19:48 This is the inheritance of the tribe of **D,**
21: 5 of Ephraim, from the tribe of **D,** and the half-tribe
21:23 Out of the tribe of **D:**
Jdg 5:17 and **D,** why did he abide with the ships?
18:29 They named the city **D,** after their ancestor **D,**
20: 1 all the Israelites came out, from **D** to Beer-sheba,
1Sa 3:20 from **D** to Beer-sheba knew that Samuel was
2Sa 3:10 of David over Israel and over Judah, from **D**
17:11 be gathered to you, from **D** to Beer-sheba,
24: 2 the tribes of Israel, from **D** to Beer-sheba, and take
24: 6 and they came to **D,** and from **D** they went around
24:15 and seventy thousand of the people died, from **D**
1Ki 4:25 from **D** even to Beer-sheba.
12:29 He set one in Bethel, and the other he put in **D.**
12:30 the one at Bethel and before the other as far as **D.**
15:20 He conquered Ijon, **D,** Abel-beth-maacah,
2Ki 10:29 the golden calves that were in Bethel and in **D.**
1Ch 2: 2 **D,** Joseph, Benjamin, Naphtali, Gad, and Asher.
21: 2 from Beer-sheba to **D,** and bring me a report,
27:22 for **D,** Azarel son of Jeroham.
2Ch 16: 4 They conquered Ijon, **D,** Abel-maim,
30: 5 to **D,** that the people should come and keep
Jer 4:15 For a voice declares from **D** and proclaims disaster
8:16 The snorting of their horses is heard from **D;**
Eze 48: 1 and extending from the east side to the west, **D,**
48: 2 Adjoining the territory of **D,**
48:32 the gate of Benjamin, and the gate of **D.**
Am 8:14 O **D,"** and, "As the way of Beer-sheba lives"—
Tob 1: 5 of Israel had erected in **D** and on all the mountains

DAN-JAAN (KJV) See DAN; See also Index to Footnotes

DANCE‡ (13) [DANCED, DANCERS, DANCES, DANCING]

Jdg 21:21 when the young women of Shiloh come out to **d** in
Job 21:11 and their children **d** around.
Ps 150: 4 Praise him with tambourine and **d;**
Ecc 3: 4 a time to mourn, and a time to **d;**
SS 6:13 as upon a **d** before two armies?
Isa 13:21 and there goat-demons will **d.**
Jer 31: 4 and go forth in the **d** of the merrymakers.
31:13 Then shall the young women rejoice in the **d,**
Mt 11:17 the flute for you, and you did not **d;**
Lk 7:32 'We played the flute for you, and you did not **d;**
Jdt 15:12 and some of them performed a **d** in her honor.
15:13 She went before all the people in the **d,**
4Mc 14: 7 as the seven days of creation move in choral **d**

DANCED (4) [DANCE]

2Sa 6:14 David **d** before the LORD with all his might;
6:21 that I have **d** before the LORD.
Mt 14: 6 the daughter of Herodias **d** before the company,
Mk 6:22 When his daughter Herodias came in and **d,**

DANCERS (2) [DANCE]

Jdg 21:23 for each of them from the **d** whom they abducted.
Ps 87: 7 Singers and **d** alike say, "All my springs are

DANCES‡ (5) [DANCE]

Jdg 21:21 women of Shiloh come out to dance in the **d,**
1Sa 21:11 Did they not sing to one another of him in **d,**
29: 5 of whom they sing to one another in **d,**
Job 41:22 In its neck abides strength, and terror **d** before it.
Jdt 3: 7 with garlands and **d** and tambourines.

DANCING (13) [DANCE]

Ex 15:20 after her with tambourines and with **d.**
32:19 near the camp and saw the calf and the **d,**
Jdg 11:34 to meet him with timbrels and with **d.**
1Sa 18: 6 singing and **d,** to meet King Saul,
30:16 eating and drinking and **d,**
2Sa 6: 5 David and all the house of Israel were **d** before
6:16 saw King David leaping and **d** before the LORD;
1Ch 13: 8 David and all Israel were **d** before God
15:29 and saw King David leaping and **d;**
Ps 30:11 You have turned my mourning into **d;**
149: 3 Let them praise his name with **d,**
La 5:15 our **d** has been turned to mourning.
Lk 15:25 and approached the house, he heard music and **d.**

DANDLED (1)

Isa 66:12 and be carried on her arm, and **d** on her knees.

DANEL See Index to Footnotes

DANGER (30) [DANGEROUS, DANGERS, ENDANGER, ENDANGERED]

1Sa 20:21 it is safe for you and there is no **d.**
30: 6 David was in great **d;**
Pr 22: 3 The clever see **d** and hide;
27:12 The clever see **d** and hide;
Lk 8:23 the boat was filling with water, and they were in **d.**
Ac 19:27 And there is **d** not only that this trade
19:40 we are in **d** of being charged with rioting today,
27:10 the voyage will be with **d** and much heavy loss,
1Co 15:30 why are we putting ourselves in **d** every hour?
2Co 11:26 in **d** from rivers, **d** from bandits, **d** from my own
people, **d** from Gentiles, **d** in the city, **d** in the
wilderness, **d** at sea, **d** from false brothers and
AdE 14: 4 for my **d** is in my hand.
Wis 14: 4 showing that you can save from every **d,**
Sir 3:26 and whoever loves **d** will perish in it.
34:13 I have often been in **d** of death,
1Mc 11:23 and some of the priests, and put himself in **d,**
14:29 exposed themselves to **d** and resisted the enemies
2Mc 15:17 city and the sanctuary and the temple were in **d.**
3Mc 5:41 and also in constant **d** of being plundered."
2Es 7: 9 unless by passing through the appointed **d?"**
7:89 and withstood **d** every hour so
12:18 and it shall be in **d** of falling;
4Mc 3:15 considered it an altogether fearful **d** to his soul
13:15 of the soul and the **d** of eternal torment lying

DANGEROUS (3) [DANGER]

Lev 26: 6 I will remove **d** animals from the land,
Ac 27: 9 much time had been lost and sailing was now **d,**
3Mc 5:33 So Hermon suffered an unexpected and **d** threat,

DANGERS (8) [DANGER]

Tob 4: 4 because she faced many **d** for you while you were
Wis 18: 9 the same things, both blessings and **d;**
Sir 43:24 Those who sail the sea tell of its **d,**
2Mc 1:11 by God out of grave **d** we thank him greatly
3Mc 6:26 and often have accepted willingly the worst of human **d?**
2Es 7:12 full of **d** and involved in great hardships.
9: 8 will survive the **d** that have been predicted,
13:19 For they shall see great **d** and much distress,

DANIEL (123) [=BELTESHAZZAR]

1Ch 3: 1 the second **D,** by Abigail the Carmelite;
Ezr 8: 2 of Phinehas, Gershom. Of Ithamar, **D.**
Ne 10: 6 **D,** Ginnethon, Baruch,
Eze 14:14 **D,** and Job, these three, were in it,
14:20 **D,** and Job were in it, as I live,
28: 3 You are indeed wiser than **D;**
Da 1: 6 Among them were **D,** Hananiah, Mishael,
1: 7 gave them other names: **D** he called Belteshazzar,
1: 8 But **D** resolved that he would not defile himself
1: 9 Now God allowed **D** to receive favor
1:10 The palace master said to **D,**
1:11 Then **D** asked the guard whom
1:11 over **D,** Hananiah, Mishael, and Azariah:
1:17 **D** also had insight into all visions and dreams.
1:19 no one was found to compare with **D,** Hananiah,
1:21 And **D** continued there until the first year
2:13 and they looked for **D** and his companions,
2:14 Then **D** responded with prudence and discretion
2:15 Arioch then explained the matter to **D.**
2:16 So **D** went in and requested that
2:17 **D** went to his home and informed his companions,
2:18 so that **D** and his companions with the rest of
2:19 mystery was revealed to **D** in a vision of the night,
2:19 and **D** blessed the God of heaven.
2:20 **D** said: "Blessed be the name of God
2:24 Therefore **D** went to Arioch,
2:25 Then Arioch quickly brought **D** before the king
2:26 The king said to **D,** whose name was Belteshazzar,
2:27 **D** answered the king, "No wise men, enchanters,
2:46 on his face, worshiped **D,** and commanded that
2:47 The king said to **D,** "Truly, your God is God
2:48 Then the king promoted **D,**
2:49 **D** made a request of the king,
2:49 But **D** remained at the king's court.
4: 8 At last **D** came in before me—
4:19 Then **D,** who was called Belteshazzar,
5:12 and solve problems were found in this **D,**
5:12 Now let **D** be called, and he will give
5:13 Then **D** was brought in before the king.
5:13 The king said to **D,** "So you are **D,**
5:17 Then **D** answered in the presence of the king,
5:29 and **D** was clothed in purple,
6: 2 and over them three presidents, including **D;**
6: 3 Soon **D** distinguished himself above all
6: 4 for complaint against **D** in connection with
6: 5 against this **D** unless we find it in connection with
6:10 **D** knew that the document had been signed,
6:11 The conspirators came and found **D** praying
6:13 Then they responded to the king, "**D,**
6:14 He was determined to save **D,**
6:16 **D** was brought and thrown into the den of lions.
6:16 The king said to **D,** "May your God,
6:17 so that nothing might be changed concerning **D.**
6:20 When he came near the den where **D** was,
6:20 he cried out anxiously to **D,** "O **D,**
6:21 **D** then said to the king, "O king, live forever!
6:23 and commanded that **D** be taken up out of the den.
6:23 So **D** was taken up out of the den,
6:24 and those who had accused **D** were brought
6:26 and fear before the God of **D:**
6:27 for he has saved **D** from the power of the lions."
6:28 So this **D** prospered during the reign of Darius and
7: 1 **D** had a dream and visions of his head as he lay
7: 2 **D,** saw in my vision by night the four winds
7:15 As for me, **D,** my spirit was troubled within me,
7:28 As for me, **D,** my thoughts greatly terrified me,
8: 1 **D,** after the one that had appeared to me at first.
8:15 I, **D,** had seen the vision, I tried to understand it.
8:27 So I, **D,** was overcome and lay sick for some days;
9: 2 **D,** perceived in the books the number of years
9:22 He came and said to me, "**D,**
10: 1 of King Cyrus of Persia a word was revealed to **D,**
10: 2 **D,** had been mourning for three weeks.
10: 7 I, **D,** alone saw the vision;
10:11 He said to me, "**D,** greatly beloved,
10:12 He said to me, "Do not fear, **D,**
12: 4 **D,** keep the words secret and the book sealed until
12: 5 Then I, **D,** looked, and two others appeared,
12: 9 He said, "Go your way, **D,**
Mt 24:15 of by the prophet **D** (let the reader understand),
Sus 1:45 up the holy spirit of a young lad named **D,**
1:51 **D** said to them, "Separate them far
1:55 And **D** said, "Very well!
1:59 **D** said to him, "Very well!
1:61 of their own mouths **D** had convicted them
1:64 that day onward **D** had a great reputation among
Bel 1: 2 **D** was a companion of the king,
1: 4 But **D** worshiped his own God.
1: 7 And **D** laughed, and said, "Do not be deceived,
1: 9 if you prove that Bel is eating them, **D** shall die,
1: 9 **D** said to the king, "Let it be done
1:10 So the king went with **D** into the temple of Bel.
1:12 otherwise **D** will, who is telling lies about us."
Bel 1:14 Then **D** ordered his servants to bring ashes,
1:16 in the morning the king rose and came, and **D**
1:17 The king said, "Are the seals unbroken, **D?**"
1:19 **D** laughed and restrained the king from going in.
1:22 king put them to death, and gave Bel over to **D,**
1:24 The king said to **D,** "You cannot deny that this is
1:25 **D** said, "I worship the Lord my God,
1:27 Then **D** took pitch, fat, and hair,
1:27 **D** said, "See what you have been worshiping!"
1:29 Going to the king, they said, "Hand **D** over to us,
1:30 and under compulsion he handed **D** over to them.
1:31 They threw **D** into the lions' den,
1:32 so that they would devour **D.**
1:34 "Take the food that you have to Babylon, to **D,**
1:37 Then Habakkuk shouted, "**D, D!**
1:38 **D** said, "You have remembered me, O God,
1:39 So **D** got up and ate.
1:40 On the seventh day the king came to mourn for **D.**
1:40 he came to the den he looked in, and there sat **D!**
1:41 the God of **D,** and there is no other besides you!"
1:42 Then he pulled **D** out, and threw into
1Mc 2:60 **D,** because of his innocence,
3Mc 6: 7 **D,** who through envious slanders was thrown
2Es 12:11 that appeared in a vision to your brother **D.**
4Mc 16: 3 The lions surrounding **D** were not so savage,
16:21 **D** the righteous was thrown to the lions,
18:13 He praised **D** in the den of the lions

DANITE (2) [DAN]

Jdg 18:11 Six hundred men of the **D** clan,
2Ch 2:14 the son of one of the **D** women,

DANITES (18) [DAN]

Nu 2:25 of the **D** shall be Ahiezer son of Ammishaddai,
7:66 of Ammishaddai, the leader of the **D:**
34:22 Of the tribe of the **D** a leader, Bukki son of Jogli.
Jos 19:47 When the territory of the **D** was lost to them,
19:47 the **D** went up and fought against Leshem,
Jdg 1:34 Amorites pressed the **D** back into the hill country;
13: 2 of the tribe of the **D,** whose name was Manoah.
18: 1 of the **D** was seeking for itself a territory to live in;
18: 2 So the **D** sent five valiant men from
18:16 While the six hundred men of the **D,**
18:22 were called out, and they overtook the **D.**
18:23 They shouted to the **D,** who turned around
18:25 And the **D** said to him,
18:26 Then the **D** went their way.
18:27 The **D,** having taken what Micah had made,
18:30 Then the **D** set up the idol for themselves.
18:30 of the **D** until the time the land went into captivity.
1Ch 12:35 Of the **D,** twenty-eight thousand six hundred

DANNAH (1)

Jos 15:49 **D,** Kiriath-sannah (that is, Debir),

DAPHNE (1)

2Mc 4:33 having first withdrawn to a place of sanctuary at **D**

DAPPLED (2)

Zec 6: 3 and the fourth chariot **d** gray horses.
6: 6 and the **d** ones go toward the south country."

DARA (1)

1Ch 2: 6 Zimri, Ethan, Heman, Calcol, and **D,** five in all.

DARDA‡ (1)

1Ki 4:31 and Heman, Calcol, and **D,** children of Mahol;

DARE (14) [DARED, DARES, DARING]

Job 41:10 No one is so fierce as to **d** to stir it up.
Jer 30:21 for who would otherwise **d** to approach me?
Mt 22:46 nor from that day did anyone **d**
Ac 7:32 Moses began to tremble and did not **d** to look.
23: 4 "Do you **d** to insult God's high priest?"
Ro 5: 7 for a good person someone might actually **d** to die.
1Co 6: 1 do you **d** to take it to court before the unrighteous,
2Co 10:12 not **d** to classify or compare ourselves with some
11:21 I also **d** to boast of that.
Php 1:14 **d** to speak the word with greater boldness and
Jude 1: 9 he did not **d** to bring a condemnation of slander
AdE 1:18 will likewise **d** to insult their husbands.
7: 5 "Who is the person that would **d** to do this thing?"
7: 8 "Will he **d** even assault my wife

DARED (10) [DARE]

Lev 26:43 because they **d** to spurn my ordinances,
Jos 10:21 no one **d** to speak against any of the Israelites.
Jer 36:29 You have **d** to burn this scroll, saying,
Mk 12:34 After that no one **d** to ask him any question.
Lk 20:40 For they no longer **d** to ask him another question.
Jn 21:12 Now none of the disciples **d** to ask him,
Ac 5:13 None of the rest **d** to join them,
2Mc 4: 2 He **d** to designate as a plotter against
5:15 Antiochus **d** to enter the most holy temple in all
2Es 13: 8 were filled with fear, and yet they **d** to fight.

DARES (2) [DARE]

Ge 49: 9 like a lioness—who **d** rouse him up?
2Co 11:21 But whatever anyone **d** to boast of—

DARICS (6)

1Ch 29: 7 of God five thousand talents and ten thousand **d**
Ezr 2:69 to the building fund sixty-one thousand **d** of gold,
8:27 twenty gold bowls worth a thousand **d,**
Ne 7:70 The governor gave to the treasury one thousand **d**
7:71 into the building fund twenty thousand **d** of gold
7:72 of the people gave was twenty thousand **d** of gold,

DARING (4) [DARE]

2Co 10: 2 when I am present I need not show boldness by **d**
Jdt 16:10 the Medes were daunted at her **d.**
2Mc 8:18 "For they trust to arms and acts of **d,**" he said,
13:18 The king, having had a taste of the **d** of the Jews,

DARIUS‡ (48)

Ezr 4: 5 of Persia and until the reign of King **D** of Persia.
4:24 the second year of the reign of King **D** of Persia.
5: 5 and they did not stop them until a report reached **D**
5: 6 in the province Beyond the River sent to King **D;**
5: 7 "To **D** the king, all peace!
6: 1 Then King **D** made a decree,
6:12 in Jerusalem. I, **D,** make a decree;
6:13 Then, according to the word sent by King **D,**
6:13 with all diligence what King **D** had ordered.
6:14 **D,** and King Artaxerxes of Persia;
6:15 in the sixth year of the reign of King **D.**
Ne 12:22 also the priests until the reign of **D** the Persian.
Da 5:31 And **D** the Mede received the kingdom,
6: 1 It pleased **D** to set over
6: 6 and came to the king and said to him, "O King **D,**
6: 9 King **D** signed the document and interdict.
6:25 Then King **D** wrote to all peoples and nations
6:28 So this Daniel prospered during the reign of **D** and
9: 1 In the first year of **D** son of Ahasuerus,
11: 1 As for me, in the first year of **D** the Mede,
Hag 1: 1 In the second year of King **D,** in the sixth month,
1:15 In the second year of King **D,**
2:10 of **D,** the word of the LORD came by
Zec 1: 1 In the eighth month, in the second year of **D,**
1: 7 the month of Shebat, in the second year of **D,**
7: 1 In the fourth year of King **D,**
1Mc 1: 1 had defeated King **D** of the Persians and
1Es 2:30 until the second year of the reign of King **D** of
3: 1 Now King **D** gave a great banquet for all that were
3: 3 and King **D** went to his bedroom;
3: 5 King **D** will give rich gifts and great honors
3: 7 and because of his wisdom he shall sit next to **D** and shall be called Kinsman of **D.**"
3: 8 and put them under the pillow of King **D,**
4:47 Then King **D** got up and kissed him,
5: 2 And **D** sent with them a thousand cavalry
5: 6 who spoke wise words before King **D** of
5:73 from building for two years, until the reign of **D.**
6: 1 Now in the second year of the reign of **D,**
6: 6 until word could be sent to **D** concerning them and
6: 7 in Syria and Phoenicia, wrote and sent to **D:**
6: 8 "To King **D,** greetings. Let it be fully
6:23 Then **D** commanded that search be made in
6:27 So **D** commanded Sisinnes the governor of Syria
6:34 King **D,** have decreed that it be done
7: 1 following the orders of King **D,**
7: 4 with the consent of Cyrus and **D** and Artaxerxes,
7: 5 in the sixth year of King **D.**

DARK (36) [DARKEN, DARKENED, DARKENS, DARKER, DARKEST, DARKNESS]

Ge 15:17 When the sun had gone down and it was **d,**
Dt 4:11 up to the very heavens, shrouded in **d** clouds.
Jos 2: 5 And when it was time to close the gate at **d,**
Ne 13:19 be **d** at the gates of Jerusalem before the sabbath,
Job 3: 9 Let the stars of its dawn be **d;**
6:16 that run **d** with ice, turbid with melting snow.
12:25 They grope in the **d** without light;
18: 6 The light is **d** in their tent,
24:16 In the **d** they dig through houses;
Ps 11: 2 to shoot in the **d** at the upright in heart.
18:11 his canopy thick clouds **d** with water.
35: 6 Let their way be **d** and slippery,
74:20 for the **d** places of the land are full of the haunts
78: 2 I will utter **d** sayings from of old,
88: 6 in the regions **d** and deep.
105:28 He sent darkness, and made the land **d;**
139:12 even the darkness is not **d** to you;
SS 1: 6 Do not gaze at me because I am **d,**
Isa 5:30 and the light grows **d** with clouds.
13:10 the sun will be **d** at its rising,
29:15 whose deeds are in the **d,** and who say,
Eze 8:12 the elders of the house of Israel are doing in the **d,**
12: 6 and carry it out in the **d;**
12: 7 I brought it out in the **d,**
12:12 on his shoulder in the **d,** and shall go out;
30:18 At Tehaphnehes the day shall be **d,**
32: 7 I will cover the heavens, and make their stars **d;**
Mt 10:27 What I say to you in the **d,** tell in the light;
Mk 1:35 In the morning, while it was still very **d,**
Lk 12: 3 Therefore whatever you have said in the **d** will
Jn 6:17 It was now **d,** and Jesus had not yet come to them.
20: 1 on the first day of the week, while it was still **d,**
2Pe 1:19 to this as to a lamp shining in a **d** place,
Wis 17: 3 behind a **d** curtain of forgetfulness,
Sir 45: 5 and led him into the **d** cloud,
2Es 12:42 and like a lamp in a **d** place,

DARKEN (2) [DARK]
Eze 32: 8 All the shining lights of the heavens I will **d**
Am 8: 9 and **d** the earth in broad daylight.

DARKENED‡ (11) [DARK]
Ps 69:23 Let their eyes be **d** so that they cannot see,
Ecc 12: 2 the moon and the stars are **d** and the clouds return
Joel 2:10 The sun and the moon are **d**,
3:15 The sun and the moon are **d**,
Mt 24:29 sun will be **d**, and the moon will not give its light;
Mk 13:24 sun will be **d**, and the moon will not give its light,
Ro 1:21 and their senseless minds were **d**.
11:10 let their eyes be **d** so that they cannot see,
Eph 4:18 They are **d** in their understanding,
Rev 8:12 so that a third of their light was **d**;
9: 2 and the air were **d** with the smoke from the shaft.

DARKENS (3) [DARK]
Job 38: 2 that **d** counsel by words without knowledge?
Am 5: 8 and **d** the day into night,
Sir 25:17 and **d** her face like that of a bear.

DARKER (1) [DARK]
Ge 49:12 his eyes are **d** than wine,

DARKEST (1) [DARK]
Ps 23: 4 though I walk through the **d** valley, I fear no evil;

DARKNESS‡ (194) [DARK]
Ge 1: 2 a formless void and **d** covered the face of the deep,
1: 4 and God separated the light from the **d**.
1: 5 and the **d** he called Night.
1:18 and to separate the light from the **d**.
15:12 and a deep and terrifying **d** descended upon him.
Ex 10:21 so that there may be **d** over the land of Egypt, a **d** that can be felt."
10:22 and there was dense **d** in all the land of Egypt
14:20 cloud was there with the **d**, and it lit up the night;
20:21 Moses drew near to the thick **d** where God was.
Dt 5:22 the cloud, and the thick **d**, and he added no more.
5:23 When you heard the voice out of the **d**,
28:29 as blind people grope in **d**, but you shall be unable
Jos 24: 7 he put **d** between you and the Egyptians,
1Sa 2: 9 but the wicked shall be cut off in **d**;
2Sa 22:10 thick **d** was under his feet.
22:12 He made **d** around him a canopy, thick clouds,
22:29 O LORD, the LORD lightens my **d**.
1Ki 8:12 LORD has said that he would dwell in thick **d**.
2Ch 6: 1 LORD has said that he would reside in thick **d**.
Job 3: 4 Let that day be **d**!
3: 5 Let gloom and deep **d** claim it.
3: 6 That night—let thick **d** seize it!
5:14 They meet with **d** in the daytime,
10:21 never to return, to the land of gloom and deep **d**,
10:22 the land of gloom and chaos, where light is like **d**."
11:17 its **d** will be like the morning.
12:22 He uncovers the deeps out of **d**,
12:22 and brings deep **d** to light.
15:22 They despair of returning from **d**,
15:23 They know that a day of **d** is ready at hand;
15:30 they will not escape from **d**;
16:16 and deep **d** is on my eyelids,
17:12 'The light,' they say, 'is near to the **d**.'
17:13 if I spread my couch in **d**,
18:18 They are thrust from light into **d**,
19: 8 and he has set **d** upon my paths.
20:26 Utter **d** is laid up for their treasures;
22:11 or **d** so that you cannot see;
22:13 Can he judge through the deep **d**?
23:17 If only I could vanish in **d**,
23:17 and thick **d** would cover my face!
24:17 For deep **d** is morning to all of them;
24:17 for they are friends with the terrors of deep **d**.
26:10 at the boundary between light and **d**.
28: 3 Miners put an end to **d**,
28: 3 to the farthest bound the ore in gloom and deep **d**.
29: 3 and by his light I walked through **d**;
30:26 and when I waited for light, **d** came.
34:22 or deep **d** where evildoers may hide themselves.
37:19 we cannot draw up our case because of **d**.
38: 9 and thick **d** its swaddling band,
38:17 or have you seen the gates of deep **d**?
38:19 and where is the place of **d**,
Ps 18: 9 thick **d** was under his feet.
18:11 He made **d** his covering around him,
18:28 the LORD, my God, lights up my **d**.
44:19 and covered us with deep **d**.
82: 5 nor understanding, they walk around in **d**;
88:12 Are your wonders known in the **d**,
88:18 to shun me; my companions are in **d**.
91: 6 or the pestilence that stalks in **d**,
97: 2 Clouds and thick **d** are all around him;
104:20 You make **d**, and it is night,
105:28 He sent **d**, and made the land dark;
107:10 Some sat in **d** and in gloom,
107:14 he brought them out of **d** and gloom,
112: 4 They rise in the **d** as a light for the upright;
139:11 If I say, "Surely the **d** shall cover me,
139:12 even the **d** is not dark to you;
139:12 for **d** is as light to you.
143: 3 making me sit in **d** like those long dead.
Pr 2:13 the paths of uprightness to walk in the ways of **d**,
4:19 The way of the wicked is like deep **d**;
Pr 7: 9 in the evening, at the time of night and **d**.
20:20 your lamp will go out in utter **d**.
Ecc 2:13 I saw that wisdom excels folly as light excels **d**.
2:14 wise have eyes in their head, but fools walk in **d**.
5:17 Besides, all their days they eat in **d**,
6: 4 For it comes into vanity and goes into **d**,
6: 4 and in **d** its name is covered;
11: 8 yet let them remember that the days of **d** will
Isa 5:20 who put **d** for light and light for **d**,
5:30 And if one look to the land—only **d** and distress;
8:22 but will see only distress and **d**,
8:22 and they will be thrust into thick **d**.
9: 2 people who walked in **d** have seen a great light;
9: 2 those who lived in a land of deep **d**—
29:18 and out of their gloom and **d** the eyes of
42: 7 from the prison those who sit in **d**.
42:16 I will turn the **d** before them into light,
45: 3 I will give you the treasures of **d** and riches hidden
45: 7 and create **d**, I make weal and create woe;
45:19 I did not speak in secret, in a land of **d**;
47: 5 Sit in silence, and go into **d**, daughter Chaldea!
49: 9 to those who are in **d**, "Show yourselves."
50:10 who walks in **d** and has no light,
58:10 then your light shall rise in the **d** and your gloom
59: 9 for light, and lo! there is **d**;
60: 2 For **d** shall cover the earth, and thick **d**
Jer 2: 6 in a land of drought and deep **d**,
2:31 or a land of thick **d**?
13:16 before he brings **d**, and before your feet stumble
13:16 he turns it into gloom and makes it deep **d**.
23:12 like slippery paths in the **d**, into which they shall
La 3: 2 and brought me into **d** without any light;
3: 6 he has made me sit in **d** like the dead of long ago.
Eze 32: 8 and put **d** on your land, says the Lord GOD.
34:12 on a day of clouds and thick **d**.
Da 2:22 he knows what is in the **d**,
Joel 2: 2 a day of **d** and gloom, a day of clouds and thick **d**!
2:31 The sun shall be turned to **d**,
Am 4:13 makes the morning **d**, and treads on the heights
5: 8 and turns deep **d** into the morning,
5:18 the day of the LORD? It is **d**, not light;
5:20 Is not the day of the LORD **d**, not light,
Mic 3: 6 without vision, and **d** to you, without revelation.
7: 8 when I sit in **d**, the LORD will be a light to me.
Na 1: 8 and will pursue his enemies into **d**.
Zep 1:15 a day of **d** and gloom,
1:15 a day of clouds and thick **d**,
Mt 4:16 the people who sat in **d** have seen a great light,
6:23 your whole body will be full of **d**.
6:23 If then the light in you is **d**, how great is the **d**!
8:12 of the kingdom will be thrown into the outer **d**,
22:13 and throw him into the outer **d**,
25:30 this worthless slave, throw him into the outer **d**,
27:45 **d** came over the whole land until three in
Mk 15:33 **d** came over the whole land until three in
Lk 1:79 to those who sit in **d** and in the shadow of death,
11:34 but if it is not healthy, your body is full of **d**.
11:35 consider whether the light in you is not **d**.
11:36 with no part of it in **d**,
22:53 But this is your hour, and the power of **d**!"
23:44 and **d** came over the whole land until three in
Jn 1: 5 The light shines in the **d**, and the **d** did not overcome it.
3:19 and people loved **d** rather than light
8:12 Whoever follows me will never walk in **d**
12:35 so that the **d** may not overtake you.
12:35 If you walk in the **d**,
12:46 in me should not remain in the **d**.
Ac 2:20 sun shall be turned to **d** and the moon to blood,
13:11 Immediately mist and **d** came over him,
26:18 to open their eyes so that they may turn from **d**
Ro 2:19 a light to those who are in **d**,
13:12 then lay aside the works of **d** and put on the armor
1Co 4: 5 who will bring to light the things now hidden in **d**
2Co 4: 6 it is the God who said, "Let light shine out of **d**,"
6:14 Or what fellowship is there between light and **d**?
Eph 5: 8 For once you were **d**, but now in
5:11 Take no part in the unfruitful works of **d**,
6:12 against the cosmic powers of this present **d**,
Col 1:13 the power of **d** and transferred us into the kingdom
1Th 5: 4 But you, beloved, are not in **d**,
5: 5 we are not of the night or of **d**.
Heb 12:18 a blazing fire, and **d**, and gloom, and a tempest,
1Pe 2: 9 the mighty acts of him who called you out of **d**
2Pe 2: 4 and committed them to chains of deepest **d** to
2:17 for them the deepest **d** has been reserved.
1Jn 1: 5 that God is light and in him there is no **d** at all.
1: 6 with him while we are walking in **d**, we lie and do
2: 8 because the **d** is passing away and
2: 9 while hating a brother or sister, is still in the **d**.
2:11 But whoever hates another believer is in the **d**, walks in the **d**, and does not know the way to go, because the **d** has brought on blindness.
Jude 1: 6 in eternal chains in deepest **d** for the judgment of
1:13 for whom the deepest **d** has been reserved forever.
Rev 16:10 and its kingdom was plunged into **d**;
Tob 4:10 from death and keeps you from going into the **D**.
5:10 I lie in **d** like the dead who no longer see the light.
14:10 but Nadab went into the eternal **d**,
AdE 11: 8 It was a day of **d** and gloom,
Wis 17: 2 they themselves lay as captives of **d** and prisoners
17:17 for with one chain of **d** they all were bound.
17:21 image of the **d** that was destined to receive them;
17:21 but still heavier than **d** were they to themselves.
18: 4 to be deprived of light and imprisoned in **d**,
19:17 when, surrounded by yawning **d**,
Sir 23:18 **D** surrounds me, the walls hide me,
LtJ 6:71 or like a corpse thrown out in the **d**.
Aza 1:48 Bless the Lord, light and **d**;
2Mc 3:27 to the ground and deep **d** came over him,
1Es 4:24 and he walks in **d**, and when he steals and robs
3Mc 4:10 so that, with their eyes in total **d**,
2Es 6:39 and **d** and silence embraced everything;
7:40 or **d** or evening or morning,
7:125 [55] but our faces shall be blacker than **d**?
14:20 For the world lies in **d**,

DARKON (2)
Ezr 2:56 Jaalah, **D**, Giddel,
Ne 7:58 of Jaala, of **D**, of Giddel,

DARLING (1)
SS 6: 9 the **d** of her mother, flawless to her that bore her.

DART (3) [DARTED]
Job 41:26 it does not avail, nor does the spear, the **d**,
Na 2: 4 their appearance is like torches, they **d**
4Mc 14:19 as though with an iron **d**,

DARTED (1) [DART]
Eze 1:14 The living creatures **d** to and fro,

DARTS (KJV) See ARROWS, CLUB, SPEARS, WEAPONS

DASH (19) [DASHED, DASHES, DASHING]
Ex 29:16 and shall take its blood and **d** it against all sides of
29:20 **d** the rest of the blood against all sides of the altar.
Lev 1:11 the priests shall **d** its blood against all sides of
3: 2 the priests shall **d** the blood against all sides of
3: 8 and Aaron's sons shall **d** its blood against all sides
3:13 the sons of Aaron shall **d** its blood against all sides
17: 6 The priest shall **d** the blood against the altar of
Nu 18:17 You shall **d** their blood on the altar,
2Ki 8:12 **d** in pieces their little ones,
16:15 then **d** against it all the blood of the burnt offering,
Ps 2: 9 and **d** them in pieces like a potter's vessel."
91:12 so that you will not **d** your foot against a stone.
137: 9 be who take your little ones and **d** them against
Jer 13:14 And I will **d** them one against another,
46: 9 Advance, O horses, and **d** madly, O chariots!
Mt 4: 6 so that you will not **d** your foot against a stone.' "
Lk 4:11 so that you will not **d** your foot against a stone.' "
Jdt 16: 4 and **d** my infants to the ground,
Wis 4:19 because he will **d** them speechless to the ground,

DASHED (22) [DASH]
Ex 24: 6 and half of the blood he **d** against the altar.
24: 8 Moses took the blood and **d** it on the people,
Lev 7: 2 its blood shall be **d** against all sides of the altar.
8:19 Moses **d** the blood against all sides of the altar.
8:24 and Moses **d** the rest of the blood against all sides
9:12 and he **d** it against all sides of the altar.
9:18 which he **d** against all sides of the altar,
Nu 19:13 Since water for cleansing was not **d** on them,
19:20 the water for cleansing has not been **d** on them,
2Ki 16:13 and **d** the blood of his offerings of well-being
2Ch 25:12 so that all of them were **d** to pieces.
29:22 priests received the blood and **d** it against the altar;
29:22 the rams and their blood was **d** against the altar;
29:22 the lambs and their blood was **d** against the altar.
30:16 the priests **d** the blood that they received from
35:11 priests **d** the blood that they received from them,
Job 16:12 he seized me by the neck and **d** me to pieces;
Isa 13:16 Their infants will be **d** to pieces before their eyes;
Hos 10:14 on the day of battle when mothers were **d** in pieces
13:16 their little ones shall be **d** in pieces,
Na 3:10 even her infants were **d** in pieces at the head
Lk 9:42 the demon **d** him to the ground in convulsions.

DASHES (2) [DASH]
Lev 7:14 it shall belong to the priest who **d** the blood of
Mk 9:18 and whenever it seizes him, it **d** him down;

DASHING (2) [DASH]
Lev 1: 5 the blood, **d** the blood against all sides of the altar
Eze 43:18 for offering burnt offerings upon it and for **d** blood

DATE (2)
Ne 2: 6 it pleased the king to send me, and I set him a **d**.
Gal 4: 2 under guardians and trustees until the **d** set by

DATHAN (12)
Nu 16: 1 along with **D** and Abiram sons of Eliab,
16:12 Moses sent for **D** and Abiram sons of Eliab;
16:24 Get away from the dwellings of Korah, **D**, and Abiram.
16:25 So Moses got up and went to **D** and Abiram;
16:27 So they got away from the dwellings of Korah, **D**,
16:27 and **D** and Abiram came out and stood at
26: 9 descendants of Eliab: Nemuel, **D**, and Abiram.
26: 9 These are the same **D** and Abiram,
Dt 11: 6 to **D** and Abiram, sons of Eliab son of Reuben,
Ps 106:17 The earth opened and swallowed up **D**,
Sir 45:18 **D** and Abiram and their followers and
4Mc 2:17 When Moses was angry with **D** and Abiram,

DATHEMA‡ (2)

1Mc 5: 9 But they fled to the stronghold of **D**,
5:29 and they went all the way to the stronghold of **D**.

DAUB (KJV) See SMEAR

DAUGHTER‡ (326) [DAUGHTER'S, DAUGHTER-IN-LAW, DAUGHTER-TOWNS, DAUGHTERS, DAUGHTERS-IN-LAW, GRANDDAUGHTER]

A. DAUGHTER ZION (26)
B. PHARAOH'S DAUGHTER; DAUGHTER OF PHARAOH (13)
C. DAUGHTER JERUSALEM (7)
D. DAUGHTER BABYLON (5)

Ge 11:29 the **d** of Haran the father of Milcah and Iscah.
20:12 the **d** of my father but not the **d** of my mother;
24:23 "Tell me whose **d** you are.
24:24 "I am the **d** of Bethuel son of Milcah,
24:47 Then I asked her, 'Whose **d** are you?'
24:47 She said, 'The **d** of Bethuel, Nahor's son,
24:48 to obtain the **d** of my master's kinsman for his son.
25:20 **d** of Bethuel the Aramean of Paddan-aram,
26:34 Judith **d** of Beeri the Hittite, and Basemath **d** of
28: 9 and took Mahalath **d** of Abraham's son Ishmael,
29: 6 "Yes," they replied, "and here is his **d** Rachel,
29:10 the **d** of his mother's brother Laban,
29:18 for your younger **d** Rachel."
29:23 in the evening he took his **d** Leah and brought her
29:24 (Laban gave his maid Zilpah to his **d** Leah to
29:28 then Laban gave him his **d** Rachel as a wife.
29:29 (Laban gave his maid Bilhah to his **d** Rachel to
30:21 Afterwards she bore a **d**, and named her Dinah.
34: 1 Now Dinah the **d** of Leah,
34: 3 And his soul was drawn to Dinah **d** of Jacob;
34: 5 Jacob heard that Shechem had defiled his **d** Dinah;
34: 7 an outrage in Israel by lying with Jacob's **d**,
34: 8 "The heart of my son Shechem longs for your **d**;
34:17 then we will take our **d** and be gone."
34:19 because he was delighted with Jacob's **d**.
36: 2 Adah **d** of Elon the Hittite, Oholibamah **d** of Anah
36: 3 and Basemath, Ishmael's **d**, sister of Nebaioth.
36:14 Oholibamah, **d** of Anah son of Zibeon:
36:18 the clans born of Esau's wife Oholibamah, the **d**
36:25 Dishon and Oholibamah **d** of Anah.
36:39 Mehetabel, the **d** of Matred, **d** of Me-zahab.
38: 2 There Judah saw the **d** of
38:12 In course of time the wife of Judah, Shua's **d**,
41:45 and he gave him Asenath **d** of Potiphera,
41:50 whom Asenath **d** of Potiphera, priest of On,
46:15 together with his **d** Dinah;
46:18 whom Laban gave to his **d** Leah;
46:20 whom Asenath **d** of Potiphera, priest of On,
46:25 whom Laban gave to his **d** Rachel,
Ex 2: 5 **d** of Pharaoh came down to bathe at the river, B
2: 7 Then his sister said to Pharaoh's **d**, B
2: 8 Pharaoh's **d** said to her, "Yes." B
2: 9 Pharaoh's **d** said to her, "Take this child B
2:10 child grew up, she brought him to Pharaoh's **d**, B
2:21 and he gave Moses his **d** Zipporah in marriage.
6:23 **d** of Amminadab and sister of Nahshon,
20:10 your son or your **d**, your male or female slave,
21: 7 When a man sells his **d** as a slave,
21: 9 he shall deal with her as with a **d**.
Lev 12: 6 whether for a son or for a **d**,
18: 9 your father's **d** or your mother's **d**,
18:10 of your son's **d** or of your daughter's **d**,
18:11 the nakedness of your father's wife's **d**,
18:17 not uncover the nakedness of a woman and her **d**,
18:17 not take her son's **d** or her daughter's **d**
19:29 Do not profane your **d** by making her a prostitute,
20:17 a **d** of his father or a **d** of his mother,
21: 2 his mother, his father, his son, his **d**, his brother;
21: 9 **d** of a priest profanes herself through prostitution,
22:12 If a priest's **d** marries a layman,
22:13 but if a priest's **d** is widowed or divorced,
24:11 now his mother's name was Shelomith, **d** of Dibri,
Nu 25:15 the Midianite woman who was killed was Cozbi **d**
25:18 the **d** of a leader of Midian, their sister;
26:46 And the name of the **d** of Asher was Serah.
26:59 name of Amram's wife was Jochebed **d** of Levi,
27: 8 then you shall pass his inheritance on to his **d**.
27: 9 If he has no **d**, then you shall give his inheritance
30:16 and a father and his **d** while she is still young and
36: 8 Every **d** who possesses an inheritance in any tribe
Dt 5:14 you, or your son or your **d**,
12:18 you together with your son and your **d**,
13: 6 or your own son or **d**, or the wife you embrace,
18:10 be found among you who makes a son or **d** pass
22:16 "I gave my **d** in marriage to this man
27:22 the **d** of his father or the **d** of his mother."
28:56 to her own son, and to her own **d**,
Jos 15:16 to him I will give my **d** Achsah as wife."
15:17 and he gave him his **d** Achsah as wife.
Jdg 1:12 I will give him my **d** Achsah as wife."
1:13 and he gave him his **d** Achsah as wife.
11:34 and there was his **d** coming out to meet him
11:34 he had no son or **d** except her.
11:35 he tore his clothes, and said, "Alas, my **d**!
11:40 of Israel would go out to lament the **d** of Jephthah
19:24 Here are my virgin **d** and his concubine;
21: 1 of us shall give his **d** in marriage to Benjamin."
Ru 2: 2 She said to her, "Go, my **d**."
Ru 2: 8 Then Boaz said to Ruth, "Now listen, my **d**,
2:22 my **d**, that you go out with his young women,
3: 1 Naomi her mother-in-law said to her, "My **d**,
3:10 "May you be blessed by the LORD, my **d**;
3:11 And now, my **d**, do not be afraid,
3:16 who said, "How did things go with you, my **d**?"
3:18 She replied, "Wait, my **d**,
1Sa 14:50 name of Saul's wife was Ahinoam **d** of Ahimaaz.
17:25 and will give him his **d** and make his family free
18:17 Saul said to David, "Here is my elder **d** Merab;
18:19 when Saul's **d** Merab should have been given
18:20 Now Saul's **d** Michal loved David.
18:27 Saul gave him his **d** Michal as a wife.
18:28 and that Saul's **d** Michal loved him,
25:44 Saul had given his **d** Michal, David's wife,
2Sa 3: 3 **d** of King Talmai of Geshur;
3: 7 a concubine whose name was Rizpah **d** of Aiah.
3:13 unless you bring Saul's **d** Michal when you come
6:16 Michal **d** of Saul looked out of the window,
6:20 But Michal the **d** of Saul came out to meet David,
6:23 the **d** of Saul had no child to the day of her death.
11: 3 It was reported, "This is Bathsheba **d** of Eliam,
12: 3 and lie in his bosom, and it was like a **d** to him.
14:27 and one **d** whose name was Tamar;
17:25 who had married Abigal **d** of Nahash,
21: 8 The king took the two sons of Rizpah **d** of Aiah,
21: 8 and the five sons of Merab **d** of Saul,
21:10 Then Rizpah the **d** of Aiah took sackcloth,
21:11 When David was told what Rizpah **d** of Aiah,
1Ki 3: 1 he took Pharaoh's **d** and brought her into the city B
4:11 in all Naphath-dor (he had Taphath, Solomon's **d**,
4:15 in Naphtali (he had taken Basemath, Solomon's **d**,
7: 8 also made a house like this hall for Pharaoh's **d**, B
9:16 and had given it as dowry to his **d**,
9:24 But Pharaoh's **d** went up from the city of David B
11: 1 along with the **d** of Pharaoh: B
15: 2 His mother's name was Maacah **d** of Abishalom.
15:10 His mother's name was Maacah **d** of Abishalom.
16:31 he took as his wife Jezebel **d** of King Ethbaal of
22:42 His mother's name was Azubah **d** of Shilhi.
2Ki 8:18 for the **d** of Ahab was his wife.
9:34 for she is a king's **d**."
11: 2 But Jehosheba, King Joram's **d**, Ahaziah's sister,
14: 9 saying, 'Give your **d** to my son for a wife';
15:33 His mother's name was Jerusha **d** of Zadok.
18: 2 His mother's name was Abi **d** of Zechariah.
19:21 she scorns you—virgin **d** Zion; A
19:21 behind your back, **d** Jerusalem. C
21:19 His mother's name was Meshullemeth **d** of Haruz
22: 1 His mother's name was Jedidah **d** of Adaiah
23:10 or a **d** pass through fire as an offering to Molech.
23:31 His mother's name was Hamutal **d** of Jeremiah
23:36 His mother's name was Zebidah **d** of Pedaiah
24: 8 His mother's name was Nehushta **d** of Elnathan
24:18 His mother's name was Hamutal **d** of Jeremiah
1Ch 1:50 Mehetabel **d** of Matred, **d** of Me-zahab.
2:21 the **d** of Machir father of Gilead, whom he married
2:35 Sheshan gave his **d** in marriage to his slave Jarha;
2:49 and the **d** of Caleb was Achsah.
3: 2 son of Maacah, **d** of King Talmai of Geshur;
3: 5 and Solomon, four by Bath-shua, **d** of Ammiel;
4:17 These are the sons of Bithiah, **d** of Pharaoh, B
7:24 His **d** was Sheerah, who built both Lower
15:29 Michal **d** of Saul looked out of the window,
2Ch 8:11 Solomon brought Pharaoh's **d** from the city B
11:18 as his wife Mahalath **d** of Jerimoth son of David,
11:18 and of Abihail **d** of Eliab son of Jesse.
11:20 After her he took Maacah **d** of Absalom,
11:21 Rehoboam loved Maacah **d** of Absalom
13: 2 His mother's name was Micaiah **d** of Uriel
20:31 His mother's name was Azubah **d** of Shilhi.
21: 6 for the **d** of Ahab was his wife.
22:11 But Jehoshabeath, the king's **d**,
22:11 **d** of King Jehoram and wife of the priest
25:18 saying, 'Give your **d** to my son for a wife';
27: 1 His mother's name was Jerushah **d** of Zadok.
29: 1 His mother's name was Abijah **d** of Zechariah.
Ne 6:18 and his son Jehohanan had married the **d**
Est 2: 7 Mordecai adopted her as his own **d**.
2:15 the turn came for Esther **d** of Abihail the uncle
2:15 who had adopted her as his own **d**,
9:29 Queen Esther **d** of Abihail,
Ps 9:14 the gates of **d** Zion, rejoice in your deliverance. A
45:10 Hear, O **d**, consider and incline your ear;
137: 8 O **d** Babylon, you devastator! D
Isa 1: 8 And **d** Zion is left like a booth in a vineyard, A
10:30 Cry aloud, O **d** Gallim!
10:32 he will shake his fist at the mount of **d** Zion, A
16: 1 by way of the desert, to the mount of **d** Zion. A
23:12 O oppressed virgin **d** Sidon;
37:22 she scorns you—virgin **d** Zion; A
37:22 behind your back, **d** Jerusalem. C
47: 1 down and sit in the dust, virgin **d** Babylon! D
47: 1 Sit on the ground without a throne, **d** Chaldea!
47: 5 Sit in silence, and go into darkness, **d** Chaldea!
52: 2 the bonds from your neck, O captive **d** Zion! A
62:11 Say to **d** Zion, "See, your salvation comes; A
Jer 4:31 the cry of **d** Zion gasping for breath, A
6: 2 I have likened **d** Zion to the loveliest pasture. A
6:23 like a warrior for battle, against you, O **d** Zion! A
14:17 and let them not cease, for the virgin **d**—
31:22 How long will you waver, O faithless **d**?
46:11 Go up to Gilead, and take balm, O virgin **d** Egypt!
46:19 Pack your bags for exile, sheltered **d** Egypt!
46:24 **D** Egypt shall be put to shame;
48:18 and sit on the parched ground, enthroned **d** Dibon!
49: 4 O faithless **d**. You trusted in your treasures,
Jer 50:42 against you, O **d** Babylon! D
51:33 **D** Babylon is like a threshing floor at the time D
52: 1 His mother's name was Hamutal **d** of Jeremiah
La 1: 6 From **d** Zion has departed all her majesty. A
1:15 as in a wine press the virgin **d** Judah.
2: 1 the Lord in his anger has humiliated **d** Zion! A
2: 2 down the strongholds of **d** Judah;
2: 4 in whom we took pride in the tent of **d** Zion; A
2: 5 multiplied in **d** Judah mourning and lamentation.
2: 8 to lay in ruins the wall of **d** Zion; A
2:10 elders of **d** Zion sit on the ground in silence; A
2:13 to what compare you, O **d** Jerusalem? C
2:13 that I may comfort you, O virgin **d** Zion? A
2:15 they hiss and wag their heads at **d** Jerusalem; C
2:18 O wall of **d** Zion! A
4:21 Rejoice and be glad, O **d** Edom,
4:22 The punishment of your iniquity, O **d** Zion, A
4:22 but your iniquity, O **d** Edom, he will punish,
Eze 14:20 they would save neither son nor **d**;
16:44 about you, "Like mother, like **d**."
16:45 You are the **d** of your mother,
22:11 another in you defiles his sister, his father's **d**.
44:25 for father or mother, however, and for son or **d**,
Da 11: 6 and the **d** of the king of the south shall come to
Hos 1: 3 So he went and took Gomer **d** of Diblaim,
1: 6 She conceived again and bore a **d**.
Mic 1:13 it was the beginning of sin to **d** Zion, A
4: 8 And you, O tower of the flock, hill of **d** Zion, A
4: 8 the sovereignty of **d** Jerusalem. C
4:10 Writhe and groan, O **d** Zion, A
4:13 Arise and thresh, O **d** Zion, A
7: 6 the **d** rises up against her mother,
Zep 3:14 Sing aloud, O **d** Zion; shout, O Israel! A
3:14 and exult with all your heart, O **d** Jerusalem! C
Zec 2: 7 Escape to Zion, you that live with **d** Babylon. D
2:10 Sing and rejoice, O **d** Zion! A
9: 9 Rejoice greatly, O **d** Zion! A
9: 9 Shout aloud, O **d** Jerusalem! C
Mal 2:11 and has married the **d** of a foreign god.
Mt 9:18 saying, "My **d** has just died;
9:22 "Take heart, **d**; your faith has made you well."
10:35 and a **d** against her mother,
10:37 and whoever loves son or **d** more than me is
14: 6 the **d** of Herodias danced before the company,
15:22 my **d** is tormented by a demon."
15:28 And her **d** was healed instantly.
21: 5 "Tell the **d** of Zion, Look, your king is coming
Mk 5:23 "My little **d** is at the point of death.
5:34 He said to her, "**D**, your faith has made you well;
5:35 from the leader's house to say, "Your **d** is dead.
6:22 When his **d** Herodias came in and danced,
7:25 but a woman whose little **d** had
7:26 She begged him to cast the demon out of her **d**.
7:29 the demon has left your **d**."
Lk 2:36 There was also a prophet, Anna the **d** of Phanuel,
8:42 for he had an only **d**,
8:48 He said to her, "**D**, your faith has made you well;
8:49 from the leader's house to say, "Your **d** is dead;
12:53 mother against **d** and **d** against mother,
13:16 a **d** of Abraham whom Satan bound
Jn 12:15 not be afraid, **d** of Zion. Look,
Ac 7:21 Pharaoh's **d** adopted him and brought him up B
Heb 11:24 refused to be called a son of Pharaoh's **d**, B
Tob 3: 7 it also happened that Sarah, the **d** of Raguel,
3: 9 May we never see a son or **d** of yours!"
3:10 'You had only one beloved **d**
3:17 and Sarah, **d** of Raguel, by giving her in marriage
3:17 Sarah **d** of Raguel came down
6:11 He is your relative, and he has a **d** named Sarah.
6:12 He has no male heir and no **d** except Sarah only,
6:13 are entitled to marry his **d**.
7: 8 and their **d** Sarah likewise wept.
7:10 brother, has the right to marry my **d** Sarah.
7:12 Then Raguel summoned his **d** Sarah.
7:16 She wept for her **d**.
7:16 she said to her, "Take courage, my **d**;
7:16 of your sorrow. Take courage, my **d**."
8:20 you shall cheer up my **d**, who has been depressed.
10: 7 that Raguel had sworn to observe for his **d**,
10:12 Then he kissed his **d** Sarah and said to her,
10:12 and said to her, "My **d**, honor your father-in-law
10:12 **d**, and may I hear a good report about you as long
10:12 to see children of you and of my **d** Sarah
10:12 In the sight of the Lord I entrust my **d** to you;
11:15 that he had married Raguel's **d** Sarah,
11:17 he blessed her saying, "Come in, my **d**,
11:17 be your God who has brought you to us, my **d**.
11:17 and blessed be you, my **d**.
11:17 with blessing and joy. Come in, my **d**."
Jdt 8: 1 the **d** of Merari son of Ox son of Joseph son
10:12 She replied, "I am a **d** of the Hebrews,
13:18 Then Uzziah said to her, "O **d**,
16: 6 but Judith **d** of Merari with the beauty of her
AdE 2: 7 he had a foster child, the **d** of his father's brother,
2:15 the time was fulfilled for Esther **d** of Aminadab,
9:29 Then Queen Esther **d** of Aminadab along
Sir 7:25 a **d** in marriage, and you complete a great task;
22: 3 and the birth of a **d** is a loss.
22: 4 A sensible **d** obtains a husband of her own,
22: 5 An impudent **d** disgraces father and husband,
26:10 Keep strict watch over a headstrong **d**, or else,
26:24 *but a modest d will even be embarrassed before*
42: 9 A **d** is a secret anxiety to her father,
42:11 Keep strict watch over a headstrong **d**,
Sus 1: 2 He married the **d** of Hilkiah, named Susanna,
1: 3 had trained their **d** according to the law of Moses.
1:29 "Send for Susanna **d** of Hilkiah,

Sus 1:48 to condemn a **d** of Israel without examination and
1:57 a **d** of Judah would not tolerate your wickedness.
1:63 and his wife praised God for their **d** Susanna,
1Mc 9:37 a **d** of one of the great nobles of Canaan,
10:54 give me now your **d** as my wife,
10:57 he and his **d** Cleopatra, and came to Ptolemais in
10:58 and Ptolemy gave him his **d** Cleopatra in marriage,
11: 9 in marriage my **d** who was Alexander's wife,
11:10 I now regret that I gave him my **d,**
11:12 So he took his **d** away from him and gave her
1Es 4:29 the **d** of the illustrious Bartacus;
4Mc 15:28 as the **d** of God-fearing Abraham she remembered
18:20 of the **d** of Abraham to the catapult and back again

DAUGHTER'S (4) [DAUGHTER]

Lev 18:10 of your son's daughter or of your **d** daughter,
18:17 not take her son's daughter or her **d** daughter
Dt 22:17 'I did not find evidence of your **d** virginity.'
22:17 But here is the evidence of my **d** virginity."

DAUGHTER-IN-LAW (19) [DAUGHTER]

Ge 11:31 and his **d** Sarai, his son Abram's wife,
38:11 Then Judah said to his **d** Tamar,
38:16 for he did not know that she was his **d.**
38:24 "Your **d** Tamar has played the whore;
Lev 18:15 You shall not uncover the nakedness of your **d:**
20:12 If a man lies with his **d,**
Ru 1:22 the Moabite, her **d,** who came back with her from
2:20 Then Naomi said to her **d,**
2:22 Naomi said to Ruth, her **d,** "It is better,
4:15 for your **d** who loves you,
1Sa 4:19 Now his **d,** the wife of Phinehas, was pregnant,
1Ch 2: 4 His **d** Tamar also bore him Perez and Zerah.
Eze 22:11 another lewdly defiles his **d;**
Mic 7: 6 the **d** against her mother-in-law;
Mt 10:35 and a **d** against her mother-in-law;
Lk 12:53 mother-in-law against her **d** and **d** against
Tob 11:16 went out to meet his **d** at the gate of Nineveh.
12:14 to heal you and Sarah your **d.**

DAUGHTER-TOWNS (3) [DAUGHTER, TOWN]

Eze 26: 6 its **d** in the country shall be killed by the sword.
26: 8 Your **d** in the country he shall put to the sword.
30:18 and its **d** shall go into captivity.

DAUGHTERS‡ (242) [DAUGHTER]

A. SONS ... DAUGHTERS (84)
B. DAUGHTERS OF JERUSALEM (8)
C. DAUGHTERS OF ZION (4)

Ge 5: 4 and he had other sons and **d.** A
5: 7 and had other sons and **d.** A
5:10 and had other sons and **d.** A
5:13 and had other sons and **d.** A
5:16 and had other sons and **d.** A
5:19 and had other sons and **d.** A
5:22 and had other sons and **d.** A
5:26 and had other sons and **d.** A
5:30 and had other sons and **d.** A
6: 1 and **d** were born to them,
6: 4 when the sons of God went in to the **d** of humans,
11:11 and had other sons and **d.** A
11:13 and had other sons and **d.** A
11:15 and had other sons and **d.** A
11:17 and had other sons and **d.** A
11:19 and had other sons and **d.** A
11:21 and had other sons and **d.** A
11:23 and had other sons and **d.** A
11:25 and had other sons and **d.** A
19: 8 Look, I have two **d** who have not known a man;
19:12 sons, **d,** or anyone you have in the city— A
19:14 who were to marry his **d,** "Up,
19:15 take your wife and your two **d** who are here,
19:16 the men seized him and his wife and his two **d** by
19:30 the hills with his two **d,** for he was afraid to stay
19:30 so he lived in a cave with his two **d.**
19:36 both the **d** of Lot became pregnant by their father.
24: 3 that you will not get a wife for my son from the **d**
24:13 and the **d** of the townspeople are coming out
24:37 from the **d** of the Canaanites, in whose land I live;
28: 2 and take as wife from there one of the **d** of Laban,
29:16 Now Laban had two **d;** the name of the
31:26 and carried away my **d** like captives of the sword.
31:28 permit me to kiss my sons and my **d** farewell? A
31:31 for I thought that you would take your **d** from me
31:41 I served you fourteen years for your two **d,**
31:43 and said to Jacob, "The **d** are my **d,**
31:43 But what can I do today about these **d** of mine,
31:50 If you ill-treat my **d,** or if you take wives in addition to my **d,**
31:55 and kissed his grandchildren and his **d**
34: 9 give your **d** to us, and take our **d** for yourselves.
34:16 Then we will give our **d** to you,
34:16 and we will take your **d** for ourselves,
34:21 take their **d** in marriage, and let us give them our **d.**
36: 6 Then Esau took his wives, his sons, his **d,** A
37:35 All his sons and all his **d** sought to comfort him; A
46: 7 his sons' sons with him, his **d,** and his sons' **d;**
46:15 in all his sons and his **d** numbered thirty-three). A
Ex 2:16 The priest of Midian had seven **d.**
2:20 He said to his **d,** "Where is he?
3:22 you shall put them on your sons and on your **d;** A
6:25 Aaron's son Eleazar married one of the **d**
Ex 10: 9 we will go with our sons and **d** and with our A
21: 4 a wife and she bears him sons or **d,** A
32: 2 your sons, and your **d,** and bring them to me." A
34:16 And you will take wives from among their **d**
34:16 and their **d** who prostitute themselves
Lev 10:14 sons and **d** as well may eat in any clean place; A
26:29 and you shall eat the flesh of your **d.**
Nu 18:11 with your sons and **d,** as a perpetual due, A
18:19 with your sons and **d,** as a perpetual due; A
21:29 He has made his sons fugitives, and his **d** captives,
26:33 Zelophehad son of Hepher had no sons, but **d:**
26:33 the names of the **d** of Zelophehad were Mahlah,
27: 1 Then the **d** of Zelophehad came forward.
27: 1 The names of his **d** were:
27: 7 **d** of Zelophehad are right in what they are saying;
36: 2 the inheritance of our brother Zelophehad to his **d.**
36: 6 the LORD commands concerning the **d**
36:10 The **d** of Zelophehad did as the LORD
36:11 Hoglah, Milcah, and Noah, the **d** of Zelophehad,
Dt 7: 3 giving your **d** to their sons or taking their **d** for your sons,
12:12 you together with your sons and your **d,** A
12:31 They would even burn their sons and their **d** in A
16:11 you and your sons and your **d,** A
16:14 you and your sons and your **d,** A
23:17 None of the **d** of Israel shall be a temple prostitute;
28:32 sons and **d** shall be given to another people, A
28:41 You shall have sons and **d,** A
28:53 sons and **d** whom the LORD your God has given A
32:19 and was jealous he spurned his sons and **d.** A
Jos 7:24 with his sons and **d,** with his oxen, donkeys, A
17: 3 of Manasseh had no sons, but only **d;**
17: 3 and these are the names of his **d:**
17: 6 because the **d** of Manasseh received an inheritance
Jdg 3: 6 and they took their **d** as wives for themselves, and their own **d** they gave to their sons;
11:40 the **d** of Israel would go out to lament the daughter
12: 9 He gave his thirty **d** in marriage outside his clan
21: 7 that we will not give them any of our **d** as wives?"
21:18 we cannot give any of our **d** to them as wives."
21:22 But neither did you incur guilt by giving your **d**
Ru 1:11 But Naomi said, "Turn back, my **d,**
1:12 Turn back, my **d,** go your way,
1:13 my **d,** it has been far more bitter for me than
1Sa 1: 4 to his wife Peninnah and to all her sons and **d;** A
2:21 she conceived and bore three sons and two **d.**
8:13 He will take your **d** to be perfumers and cooks
14:49 and the names of his two **d** were these:
30: 3 and their wives and sons and **d** taken captive. A
30: 6 people were bitter in spirit for their sons and **d.** A
30:19 sons or **d,** spoil or anything that had been taken; A
2Sa 1:20 or the **d** of the Philistines will rejoice,
1:20 the **d** of the uncircumcised will exult.
1:24 O **d** of Israel, weep over Saul,
5:13 and more sons and **d** were born to David. A
13:18 how the virgin **d** of the king were clothed
19: 5 and the lives of your sons and your **d,** A
2Ki 17:17 They made their sons and their **d** pass through fire;
1Ch 2:34 Now Sheshan had no sons, only **d;**
4:27 Shimei had sixteen sons and six **d;**
7:15 second was Zelophehad; and Zelophehad had **d.**
14: 3 David became the father of more sons and **d.** A
23:22 Eleazar died having no sons, but only **d;**
25: 5 God had given Heman fourteen sons and three **d.**
2Ch 11:21 the father of twenty-eight sons and sixty **d).**
13:21 the father of twenty-two sons and sixteen **d.**
24: 3 and he became the father of sons and **d.** A
28: 8 of their kin, women, sons, and **d;** A
29: 9 sons and our **d** and our wives are in captivity A
31:18 their sons, and their **d,** the whole multitude; A
Ezr 2:61 and Barzillai (who had married one of the **d**
9: 2 For they have taken some of their **d** as wives
9:12 Therefore do not give your **d** to their sons, neither take their **d** for your sons,
Ne 3:12 made repairs, he and his **d.**
4:14 your sons, your **d,** your wives, and your homes." A
5: 2 "With our sons and our **d,** we are many; A
5: 5 yet we are forcing our sons and **d** to be slaves, A
5: 5 and some of our **d** have been ravished;
7:63 of the **d** of Barzillai the Gileadite and was called
10:28 their wives, their sons, their **d,** A
10:30 We will not give our **d** to the peoples of the land or take their **d** for our sons;
13:25 saying, "You shall not give your **d** to their sons, or take their **d** for your sons or for yourselves.
Job 1: 2 There were born to him seven sons and three **d.**
1:13 One day when his sons and **d** were eating A
1:18 "Your sons and **d** were eating and drinking wine A
42:13 He also had seven sons and three **d.**
42:15 there were no women so beautiful as Job's **d;**
Ps 45: 9 **d** of kings are among your ladies of honor;
106:37 They sacrificed their sons and their **d** to
106:38 the blood of their sons and **d,** A
144:12 our **d** like corner pillars, cut for the building
Pr 30:15 The leech has two **d;** "Give, give," they cry.
Ecc 12: 4 and all the **d** of song are brought low;
SS 1: 5 I am black and beautiful, O **d** of Jerusalem, B
2: 7 I adjure you, O **d** of Jerusalem, B
3: 5 I adjure you, O **d** of Jerusalem, B
3:10 with love. **D** of Jerusalem, B
3:11 Look, O **d** of Zion, at King Solomon, C
5: 8 I adjure you, O **d** of Jerusalem, B
5:16 and this is my friend, O **d** of Jerusalem. B
8: 4 I adjure you, O **d** of Jerusalem, B
Isa 3:16 Because the **d** of Zion are haughty and walk C
3:17 afflict with scabs the heads of the **d** of Zion, C
4: 4 Lord has washed away the filth of the **d** of Zion C
Isa 16: 2 so are the **d** of Moab at the fords of the Arnon.
32: 9 you complacent **d,** listen to my speech.
43: 6 bring my sons from far away and my **d** from
49:22 and your **d** shall be carried on their shoulders.
56: 5 a monument and a name better than sons and **d;** A
60: 4 and your **d** shall be carried on their nurses' arms.
Jer 3:24 flocks and their herds, their sons and their **d.** A
5:17 they shall eat up your sons and your **d;** A
7:31 to burn their sons and their **d** in the fire— A
9:20 teach to your **d** a dirge, and each to her neighbor
11:22 their sons and their **d** shall die by famine; A
14:16 themselves, their wives, their sons, and their **d.** A
16: 2 nor shall you have sons or **d** in this place. A
16: 3 the sons and **d** who are born in this place, A
19: 9 the flesh of their sons and the flesh of their **d,**
29: 6 Take wives and have sons and **d;** A
29: 6 and give your **d** in marriage,
29: 6 that they may bear sons and **d;** A
32:35 to offer up their sons and **d** to Molech, A
35: 8 ourselves, our wives, our sons, or our **d,** A
41:10 the king's **d** and all the people who were left
48:46 for your sons have been taken captive, and your **d**
49: 3 Cry out, O **d** of Rabbah!
Eze 13:17 mortal, set your face against the **d** of your people,
14:16 they would save neither sons nor **d;** A
14:18 they would save neither sons nor **d,** A
14:22 sons and **d** who will be brought out; A
16:20 You took your sons and your **d,** A
16:27 and gave you up to the will of your enemies, the **d**
16:46 who lived with her **d** to the north of you;
16:46 to the south of you, is Sodom with her **d.**
16:48 your sister Sodom and her **d** have not done as you and your **d** have done.
16:49 she and her **d** had pride, excess of food,
16:53 the fortunes of Sodom and her **d** and
16:53 and the fortunes of Samaria and her **d,**
16:55 Sodom and her **d** shall return to their former state,
16:55 Samaria and her **d** shall return to their former state,
16:55 you and your **d** shall return to your former state.
16:57 a mockery to the **d** of Aram and all her neighbors,
16:57 and to the **d** of the Philistines,
16:61 and give them to you as **d,**
23: 2 there were two women, the **d** of one mother;
23: 4 They became mine, and they bore sons and **d.** A
23:10 they seized her sons and her **d;** A
23:25 They shall seize your sons and your **d,** A
23:47 they shall kill their sons and their **d,** A
24:21 sons and your **d** whom you left behind shall fall A
24:25 and also their sons and their **d,** A
32:18 with Egypt and the **d** of majestic nations,
Hos 4:13 Therefore your **d** play the whore,
4:14 I will not punish your **d** when they play the whore,
Joel 2:28 your sons and your **d** shall prophesy,
3: 8 and your **d** into the hand of the people of Judah,
Am 7:17 and your sons and your **d** shall fall by the sword,
Lk 23:28 Jesus turned to them and said, "**D** of Jerusalem, B
Ac 2:17 and your sons and your **d** shall prophesy,
21: 9 He had four unmarried **d** who had the gift
2Co 6:18 and you shall be my sons and **d,** A
1Pe 3: 6 You have become her **d** as long
Tob 4:13 the sons and **d** of your people, A
Jdt 9: 4 up their wives for booty and their **d** to captivity,
Wis 9: 7 and to be judge over your sons and **d.** A
Sir 7:24 Do you have **d?** Be concerned
Bar 2: 3 of their sons and others the flesh of their **d.**
4:10 for I have seen the exile of my sons and **d,** A
4:14 remember the capture of my sons and **d,** A
4:16 and bereaved the lonely woman of her **d.**
Sus 1:57 This is how you have been treating the **d** of Israel,
1Es 5: 1 with their wives and sons and **d,** A
5:38 of Jaddus who had married Agia, one of the **d**
8:70 For they and their descendants have married the **d**
8:84 not give your **d** in marriage to their descendants, and do not take their **d** for your descendants;
3Mc 5:49 parents and children, mothers and **d,**
2Es 1:28 as a father entreats his sons or a mother her **d** or
15:47 you have decked out your **d** for prostitution
16:33 their **d** shall mourn, because they have no help.

DAUGHTERS-IN-LAW (5) [DAUGHTER]

Ru 1: 6 to return with her **d** from the country of Moab,
1: 7 she and her two **d,** and they went on their way
1: 8 But Naomi said to her two **d,**
Hos 4:13 and your **d** commit adultery.
4:14 nor your **d** when they commit adultery;

DAUNTED (2) [DAUNTLESS]

Isa 31: 4 is not terrified by their shouting or **d** at their noise,
Jdt 16:10 the Medes were **d** at her daring.

DAUNTLESS (1) [DAUNTED]

Sir 48:24 By his **d** spirit he saw the future,

DAVID‡ (1108) [DAVID'S]

A. OF DAVID [in Psalm Titles] (72)
B. FATHER DAVID (52)
C. KING DAVID (49)
D. CITY OF DAVID (46)
E. SERVANT DAVID (32)
F. HOUSE OF DAVID (27)
G. SON OF DAVID (24)
H. CITY OF HIS FATHER DAVID (5)

Ru 4:17 he became the father of Jesse, the father of **D.**

Ru 4:22 Obed of Jesse, and Jesse of **D.**
1Sa 16:13 and the spirit of the LORD came mightily upon **D**
16:19 "Send me your son **D** who is with the sheep."
16:20 and a kid, and sent them by his son **D** to Saul.
16:21 And **D** came to Saul, and entered his service.
16:22 saying, "Let **D** remain in my service,
16:23 **D** took the lyre and played it with his hand,
17:12 Now **D** was the son of an Ephrathite of Bethlehem
17:14 **D** was the youngest; the three eldest followed Saul,
17:15 but **D** went back and forth from Saul
17:17 Jesse said to his son **D,** "Take for your brothers
17:20 **D** rose early in the morning,
17:22 **D** left the things in charge of the keeper of
17:23 as before. And **D** heard him.
17:26 **D** said to the men who stood by him,
17:28 and Eliab's anger was kindled against **D.**
17:29 **D** said, "What have I done now?
17:31 When the words that **D** spoke were heard,
17:32 **D** said to Saul, "Let no one's heart fail because
17:33 Saul said to **D,** "You are not able to go
17:34 But **D** said to Saul, "Your servant used
17:37 **D** said, "The LORD, who saved me from the paw
17:37 So Saul said to **D,** "Go, and may the LORD be
17:38 Saul clothed **D** with his armor;
17:39 **D** strapped Saul's sword over the armor,
17:39 Then **D** said to Saul, "I cannot walk with these;
17:39 to them." So **D** removed them.
17:41 The Philistine came on and drew near to **D,**
17:42 When the Philistine looked and saw **D,**
17:43 The Philistine said to **D,** "Am I a dog,
17:43 And the Philistine cursed **D** by his gods.
17:44 The Philistine said to **D,** "Come to me,
17:45 But **D** said to the Philistine,
17:48 When the Philistine drew nearer to meet **D,**
17:48 **D** ran quickly toward the battle line to meet
17:49 **D** put his hand in his bag, took out a stone,
17:50 So **D** prevailed over the Philistine with a sling and
17:51 Then **D** ran and stood over the Philistine;
17:54 **D** took the head of the Philistine and brought it
17:55 When Saul saw **D** go out against the Philistine,
17:58 And **D** answered, "I am the son
18:1 When **D** had finished speaking to Saul,
18:1 the soul of Jonathan was bound to the soul of **D,**
18:3 Then Jonathan made a covenant with **D,**
18:4 and gave it to **D,** and his armor,
18:5 **D** went out and was successful wherever Saul sent
18:6 when **D** returned from killing the Philistine,
18:7 "Saul has killed his thousands, and **D** his ten thousands."
18:8 He said, "They have ascribed to **D** ten thousands,
18:9 So Saul eyed **D** from that day on.
18:10 while **D** was playing the lyre,
18:11 for he thought, "I will pin **D** to the wall."
18:11 But **D** eluded him twice.
18:12 Saul was afraid of **D,** because the LORD was
18:13 and **D** marched out and came in, leading the army.
18:14 **D** had success in all his undertakings;
18:16 But all Israel and Judah loved **D;**
18:17 Saul said to **D,** "Here is my elder daughter Merab;
18:18 **D** said to Saul, "Who am I
18:19 to **D,** she was given to Adriel the Meholathite as
18:20 Now Saul's daughter Michal loved **D.**
18:21 Therefore Saul said to **D** a second time,
18:22 "Speak to **D** in private and say, 'See,
18:23 So Saul's servants reported these words to **D**
18:23 And **D** said, "Does it seem to you a little thing
18:24 servants of Saul told him, "This is what **D** said."
18:25 Then Saul said, "Thus shall you say to **D,**
18:25 Now Saul planned to make **D** fall by the hand of
18:26 When his servants told **D** these words,
18:26 **D** was well pleased to be the king's son-in-law.
18:27 **D** rose and went, along with his men,
18:27 and **D** brought their foreskins,
18:28 when Saul realized that the LORD was with **D,**
18:29 Saul was still more afraid of **D.**
18:30 **D** had more success than all the servants of Saul,
19:1 and with all his servants about killing **D.**
19:1 But Saul's son Jonathan took great delight in **D.**
19:2 Jonathan told **D,** "My father Saul is trying
19:4 Jonathan spoke well of **D** to his father Saul,
19:4 "The king should not sin against his servant **D,** E
19:5 an innocent person by killing **D** without cause?"
19:7 So Jonathan called **D** and related all these things
19:7 Jonathan then brought **D** to Saul,
19:8 and **D** went out to fight the Philistines.
19:9 while **D** was playing music.
19:10 Saul sought to pin **D** to the wall with the spear;
19:10 **D** fled and escaped that night.
19:12 So Michal let **D** down through the window;
19:14 When Saul sent messengers to take **D,** she said,
19:15 Saul sent the messengers to see **D** for themselves.
19:18 Now **D** fled and escaped; he came to Samuel
19:19 Saul was told, "**D** is at Naioth in Ramah."
19:20 Then Saul sent messengers to take **D.**
19:22 he asked, "Where are Samuel and **D?"**
20:1 **D** fled from Naioth in Ramah.
20:3 But **D** also swore, "Your father knows well
20:4 Then Jonathan said to **D,** "Whatever you say,
20:5 **D** said to Jonathan, "Tomorrow is the new moon,
20:6 '**D** earnestly asked leave of me to run
20:10 Then **D** said to Jonathan, "Who will tell me
20:11 Jonathan replied to **D,** "Come,
20:12 Jonathan said to **D,** "By the LORD,
20:12 if he is well disposed toward **D,**
20:15 of the enemies of **D** from the face of the earth."
20:16 a covenant with the house of **D,** F
20:16 "May the LORD seek out the enemies of **D."**

1Sa 20:17 Jonathan made **D** swear again by his love for him;
20:24 So **D** hid himself in the field.
20:28 "**D** earnestly asked leave of me to go
20:33 that it was the decision of his father to put **D**
20:34 for he was grieved for **D,**
20:35 into the field to the appointment with **D,**
20:39 only Jonathan and **D** knew the arrangement.
20:41 **D** rose from beside the stone heap
20:41 with each other; **D** wept the more.
20:42 Then Jonathan said to **D,** "Go in peace,
21:1 **D** came to Nob to the priest Ahimelech.
21:1 Ahimelech came trembling to meet **D,**
21:2 **D** said to the priest Ahimelech,
21:4 The priest answered **D,** "I have no ordinary bread
21:5 **D** answered the priest, "Indeed women have been
21:8 **D** said to Ahimelech, "Is there no spear
21:9 **D** said, "There is none like it; give it to me."
21:10 **D** rose and fled that day from Saul;
21:11 "Is this not **D** the king of the land?
21:11 killed his thousands and **D** his ten thousands'?"
21:12 **D** took these words to heart
22:1 **D** left there and escaped to the cave of Adullam;
22:3 **D** went from there to Mizpeh of Moab.
22:4 and they stayed with him all the time that **D** was in
22:5 Then the prophet Gad said to **D,**
22:5 So **D** left, and went into the forest of Hereth.
22:6 Saul heard that **D** and those who were
22:14 among all your servants is so faithful as **D?**
22:17 because their hand also is with **D;**
22:20 named Abiathar, escaped and fled after **D.**
22:21 Abiathar told **D** that Saul had killed the priests of
22:22 **D** said to Abiathar, "I knew on that day,
23:1 Now they told **D,** "The Philistines are fighting
23:2 **D** inquired of the LORD,
23:2 The LORD said to **D,** "Go and attack
23:4 Then **D** inquired of the LORD again.
23:5 So **D** and his men went to Keilah,
23:5 Thus **D** rescued the inhabitants of Keilah.
23:6 Abiathar son of Ahimelech fled to **D** at Keilah,
23:7 Now it was told Saul that **D** had come to Keilah.
23:8 to go down to Keilah, to besiege **D** and his men.
23:9 **D** learned that Saul was plotting evil against him,
23:10 **D** said, "O LORD, the God of Israel,
23:12 Then **D** said, "Will the men
23:13 Then **D** and his men, who were about six hundred,
23:13 Saul was told that **D** had escaped from Keilah,
23:14 **D** remained in the strongholds in the wilderness,
23:15 **D** was in the Wilderness of Ziph at Horesh
23:16 Saul's son Jonathan set out and came to **D**
23:18 **D** remained at Horesh, and Jonathan went home.
23:19 "**D** is hiding among us in the strongholds
23:24 **D** and his men were in the wilderness of Maon,
23:25 When **D** was told, he went down to the rock
23:25 he pursued **D** into the wilderness of Maon.
23:26 **D** and his men on the other side of the mountain.
23:26 **D** was hurrying to get away from Saul,
23:26 and his men were closing in on **D** and his men
23:28 So Saul stopped pursuing **D,**
23:29 **D** then went up from there,
24:1 he was told, "**D** is in the wilderness of En-gedi."
24:2 for **D** and his men in the direction of the Rocks of
24:3 Now **D** and his men were sitting in
24:4 The men of **D** said to him,
24:4 Then **D** went and stealthily cut off a corner
24:5 Afterward **D** was stricken to the heart
24:7 So **D** scolded his men severely and did
24:8 Afterwards **D** also rose up and went out of
24:8 **D** bowed with his face to the ground,
24:9 **D** said to Saul, "Why do you listen to the words
24:9 '**D** seeks to do you harm'?
24:16 **D** had finished speaking these words to Saul,
24:16 Saul said, "Is this your voice, my son **D?"**
24:17 He said to **D,** "You are more righteous than I;
24:22 So **D** swore this to Saul.
24:22 but **D** and his men went up to the stronghold.
25:1 Then **D** got up and went down to the wilderness
25:4 **D** heard in the wilderness that Nabal
25:5 So **D** sent ten young men;
25:5 and **D** said to the young men, "Go up to Carmel,
25:8 at hand to your servants and to your son **D.'"**
25:9 they said all this to Nabal in the name of **D;**
25:10 Nabal answered David's servants, "Who is **D?**
25:13 **D** said to his men, "Every man strap
25:13 **D** also strapped on his sword;
25:13 and about four hundred men went up after **D,**
25:14 "**D** sent messengers out of the wilderness
25:20 **D** and his men came down toward her;
25:21 Now **D** had said, "Surely it was in vain
25:22 God do so to **D** and more also,
25:23 When Abigail saw **D,** she hurried and alighted
25:23 fell before **D** on her face, bowing to the ground.
25:32 **D** said to Abigail, "Blessed be the LORD,
25:35 Then **D** received from her
25:39 When **D** heard that Nabal was dead, he said,
25:39 **D** sent and wooed Abigail, to make her his wife.
25:40 "**D** has sent us to you to take you to him
25:42 after the messengers of **D** and became his wife.
25:43 **D** also married Ahinoam of Jezreel;
26:1 saying, "**D** is in hiding on the hill of Hachilah,
26:2 to seek **D** in the Wilderness of Ziph.
26:3 But **D** remained in the wilderness.
26:4 **D** sent out spies, and learned
26:5 Then **D** set out and came to the place
26:5 and **D** saw the place where Saul lay,
26:6 Then **D** said to Ahimelech the Hittite,
26:7 So **D** and Abishai went to the army by night;
26:8 Abishai said to **D,** "God has given your enemy

1Sa 26:9 But **D** said to Abishai, "Do not destroy him;
26:10 **D** said, "As the LORD lives,
26:12 So **D** took the spear that was at Saul's head and
26:13 Then **D** went over to the other side,
26:14 **D** called to the army and to Abner son of Ner,
26:15 **D** said to Abner, "Are you not a man?
26:17 and said, "Is this your voice, my son **D?"**
26:17 **D** said, "It is my voice, my lord, O king."
26:21 my son **D,** for I will never harm you again,
26:22 **D** replied, "Here is the spear, O king!
26:25 Saul said to **D,** "Blessed be you, my son **D!**
26:25 So **D** went his way, and Saul returned to his place.
27:1 **D** said in his heart, "I shall now perish one day by
27:2 So **D** set out and went over,
27:3 **D** stayed with Achish at Gath, he and his troops,
27:3 and **D** with his two wives, Ahinoam of Jezreel,
27:4 When Saul was told that **D** had fled to Gath,
27:5 Then **D** said to Achish, "If I have found favor
27:7 The length of time that **D** lived in the country of
27:8 Now **D** and his men went up and made raids on
27:9 **D** struck the land, leaving neither man
27:10 **D** would say, "Against the Negeb of Judah,"
27:11 **D** left neither man nor woman alive to
27:11 and say, '**D** has done so and so.' "
27:12 Achish trusted **D,** thinking,
28:1 Achish said to **D,** "You know, of course,
28:2 **D** said to Achish, "Very well,
28:2 Achish said to **D,** "Very well,
28:17 and given it to your neighbor, **D.**
29:2 and **D** and his men were passing on in the rear
29:3 "Is this not **D,** the servant of King Saul of Israel,
29:5 Is this not **D,** of whom they sing to one another
29:5 and **D** his ten thousands'?"
29:6 Then Achish called **D** and said to him,
29:8 **D** said to Achish, "But what have I done?
29:9 Achish replied to **D,** "I know that you are
29:11 So **D** set out with his men early in the morning,
30:1 **D** and his men came to Ziklag on the third day,
30:3 When **D** and his men came to the city,
30:4 Then **D** and the people who were
30:6 **D** was in great danger;
30:6 **D** strengthened himself in the LORD his God.
30:7 **D** said to the priest Abiathar son of Ahimelech,
30:7 So Abiathar brought the ephod to **D.**
30:8 **D** inquired of the LORD,
30:9 So **D** set out, he and the six hundred men
30:10 But **D** went on with the pursuit,
30:11 an Egyptian, and brought him to **D.**
30:13 Then **D** said to him, "To whom do you belong?
30:15 **D** said to him, "Will you take me down
30:17 **D** attacked them from twilight until the evening of
30:18 **D** recovered all that the Amalekites had taken;
30:18 and **D** rescued his two wives.
30:19 **D** brought back everything.
30:20 **D** also captured all the flocks and herds,
30:21 Then **D** came to the two hundred men
30:21 to follow **D,** and who had been left at
30:21 to meet **D** and to meet the people who were
30:21 When **D** drew near to the people he saluted them.
30:22 among the men who had gone with **D** said,
30:23 But **D** said, "You shall not do so, my brothers,
30:26 When **D** came to Ziklag, he sent part of the spoil
30:31 all the places where **D** and his men had roamed.
2Sa 1:1 **D** had returned from defeating the Amalekites,
1:1 **D** remained two days in Ziklag.
1:2 When he came to **D,** he fell to the ground
1:3 **D** said to him, "Where have you come from?"
1:4 **D** said to him, "How did things go?
1:5 **D** asked the young man who was reporting to him,
1:11 Then **D** took hold of his clothes and tore them;
1:13 **D** said to the young man who had reported to him,
1:14 **D** said to him, "Were you not afraid
1:15 Then **D** called one of the young men and said,
1:16 **D** said to him, "Your blood be on your head;
1:17 **D** intoned this lamentation over Saul
2:1 After this **D** inquired of the LORD,
2:1 **D** said, "To which shall I go up?"
2:2 So **D** went up there, along with his two wives,
2:3 **D** brought up the men who were with him,
2:4 and there they anointed **D** king over the house
2:4 When they told **D,** "It was the people
2:5 **D** sent messengers to the people of Jabesh-gilead,
2:10 But the house of Judah followed **D.**
2:11 that **D** was king in Hebron over the house
2:13 Joab son of Zeruiah, and the servants of **D,**
2:15 and twelve of the servants of **D.**
2:17 the men of Israel were beaten by the servants of **D.**
2:31 of **D** had killed of Benjamin three hundred sixty
3:1 between the house of Saul and the house of **D;** F
3:1 **D** grew stronger and stronger,
3:2 Sons were born to **D** at Hebron:
3:5 These were born to **D** in Hebron.
3:6 between the house of Saul and the house of **D,** F
3:8 and have not given you into the hand of **D;**
3:9 For just what the LORD has sworn to **D,**
3:10 set up the throne of **D** over Israel and over Judah,
3:12 Abner sent messengers to **D** at Hebron, saying,
3:14 Then **D** sent messengers to Saul's son Ishbaal,
3:17 past you have been seeking **D** as king over you.
3:18 for the LORD has promised **D:**
3:18 Through my servant **D** I will save my people E
3:19 then Abner went to tell **D** at Hebron all that Israel
3:20 Abner came with twenty men to **D** at Hebron,
3:20 **D** made a feast for Abner and the men who were
3:21 Abner said to **D,** "Let me go and rally all Israel
3:21 **D** dismissed Abner, and he went away in peace.
3:22 Just then the servants of **D** arrived with Joab from

2Sa 3:22 But Abner was not with **D** at Hebron,
3:22 with David at Hebron, for **D** had dismissed him,
3:26 but **D** did not know about it.
3:28 Afterward, when **D** heard of it, he said,
3:31 Then **D** said to Joab and to all
3:31 And King **D** followed the bier. C
3:35 the people came to persuade **D** to eat something
3:35 but **D** swore, saying, "So may God do to me,
4: 8 They brought the head of Ishbaal to **D** at Hebron
4: 9 **D** answered Rechab and his brother Baanah,
4:12 So **D** commanded the young men,
5: 1 Then all the tribes of Israel came to **D** at Hebron,
5: 3 King **D** made a covenant with them at Hebron C
5: 3 and they anointed **D** king over Israel.
5: 4 **D** was thirty years old when he began to reign,
5: 6 who said to **D**, "You will not come in here,
5: 6 thinking, "**D** cannot come in here."
5: 7 Nevertheless **D** took the stronghold of Zion,
5: 7 which is now the city of **D**. D
5: 8 **D** had said on that day,
5: 8 the lame and the blind, those whom **D** hates."
5: 9 **D** occupied the stronghold,
5: 9 and named it the city of **D**. D
5: 9 **D** built the city all around from the Millo inward.
5:10 And **D** became greater and greater,
5:11 King Hiram of Tyre sent messengers to **D**,
5:11 and carpenters and masons who built **D** a house.
5:12 **D** then perceived that the LORD had established
5:13 **D** took more concubines and wives;
5:13 and more sons and daughters were born to **D**.
5:17 the Philistines heard that **D** had been anointed king
5:17 all the Philistines went up in search of **D**;
5:17 **D** heard about it and went down to the stronghold.
5:19 **D** inquired of the LORD,
5:19 The LORD said to **D**, "Go up;
5:20 So **D** came to Baal-perazim,
5:20 and **D** defeated them there.
5:21 and **D** and his men carried them away.
5:23 When **D** inquired of the LORD, he said,
5:25 **D** did just as the LORD had commanded him;
6: 1 **D** again gathered all the chosen men of Israel,
6: 2 **D** and all the people with him set out and went
6: 5 **D** and all the house of Israel were dancing before
6: 8 **D** was angry because the LORD had burst forth
6: 9 **D** was afraid of the LORD that day;
6:10 So **D** was unwilling to take the ark of the LORD
6:10 of the LORD into his care in the city of **D**; D
6:10 instead **D** took it to the house of Obed-edom
6:12 It was told King **D**, "The LORD has blessed C
6:12 So **D** went and brought up the ark of God from
6:12 from the house of Obed-edom to the city of **D** D
6:14 **D** danced before the LORD with all his might;
6:14 **D** was girded with a linen ephod.
6:15 So **D** and all the house of Israel brought up the ark
6:16 As the ark of the LORD came into the city of **D**, D
6:16 and saw King **D** leaping and dancing before C
6:17 inside the tent that **D** had pitched for it;
6:17 and **D** offered burnt offerings and offerings
6:18 When **D** had finished offering the burnt offerings
6:20 **D** returned to bless his household.
6:20 Michal the daughter of Saul came out to meet **D**,
6:21 **D** said to Michal, "It was before the LORD,
7: 5 Go and tell my servant **D**: E
7: 8 therefore thus you shall say to my servant **D**: E
7:17 and with all this vision, Nathan spoke to **D**.
7:18 Then King **D** went in and sat before the LORD, C
7:20 And what more can **D** say to you?
7:26 your servant **D** will be established before you. E
8: 1 **D** attacked the Philistines and subdued them;
8: 1 **D** took Metheg-ammah out of the hand of
8: 2 And the Moabites became servants to **D**
8: 3 **D** also struck down King Hadadezer son of Rehob
8: 4 **D** took from him one thousand seven hundred
8: 4 **D** hamstrung all the chariot horses,
8: 5 **D** killed twenty-two thousand men of
8: 6 Then **D** put garrisons among the Arameans
8: 6 and the Arameans became servants to **D**
8: 6 The LORD gave victory to **D** wherever he went.
8: 7 **D** took the gold shields that were carried by
8: 8 King **D** took a great amount of bronze. C
8: 9 that **D** had defeated the whole army of Hadadezer,
8:10 Toi sent his son Joram to King **D**, C
8:11 these also King **D** dedicated to the LORD, C
8:13 **D** won a name for himself.
8:14 the LORD gave victory to **D** wherever he went.
8:15 So **D** reigned over all Israel;
8:15 **D** administered justice and equity to all his people.
9: 1 **D** asked, "Is there still anyone left of the house
9: 2 and he was summoned to **D**.
9: 5 King **D** sent and brought him from the house C
9: 6 son of Jonathan son of Saul came to **D**,
9: 6 and did obeisance. **D** said,
9: 7 **D** said to him, "Do not be afraid,
10: 2 **D** said, "I will deal loyally with Hanun son
10: 2 So **D** sent envoys to console him
10: 3 that **D** is honoring your father just
10: 3 not **D** sent his envoys to you to search the city,
10: 5 When **D** was told, he sent to meet them,
10: 6 that they had become odious to **D**,
10: 7 When **D** heard of it, he sent Joab and all the army
10:17 When it was told **D**, he gathered all Israel together,
10:17 The Arameans arrayed themselves against **D**
10:18 before Israel; and **D** killed of
11: 1 **D** sent Joab with his officers and all Israel
11: 1 But **D** remained at Jerusalem.
11: 2 when **D** rose from his couch and was walking
11: 3 **D** sent someone to inquire about the woman.

2Sa 11: 4 So **D** sent messengers to get her,
11: 5 and she sent and told **D**, "I am pregnant."
11: 6 **D** sent word to Joab, "Send me Uriah the Hittite."
11: 6 And Joab sent Uriah to **D**.
11: 7 **D** asked how Joab and the people fared,
11: 8 Then **D** said to Uriah, "Go down to your house,
11:10 When they told **D**, "Uriah did not go down to his house," **D** said to Uriah,
11:11 to **D**, "The ark and Israel and Judah remain
11:12 Then **D** said to Uriah, "Remain here today also,
11:13 **D** invited him to eat and drink in his presence
11:14 In the morning **D** wrote a letter to Joab,
11:17 some of the servants of **D** among the people fell.
11:18 Then Joab sent and told **D** all the news about
11:22 came and told **D** all that Joab had sent him to tell.
11:23 to **D**, "The men gained an advantage over us,
11:25 **D** said to the messenger, "Thus you shall say
11:27 **D** sent and brought her to his house,
11:27 the thing that **D** had done displeased the LORD,
12: 1 and the LORD sent Nathan to **D**.
12: 7 Nathan said to **D**, "You are the man!
12:13 **D** said to Nathan, "I have sinned against
12:13 to **D**, "Now the LORD has put away your sin;
12:15 the child that Uriah's wife bore to **D**,
12:16 **D** therefore pleaded with God for the child;
12:16 **D** fasted, and went in and lay all night on
12:18 And the servants of **D** were afraid to tell him that
12:19 **D** saw that his servants were whispering together,
12:19 and **D** said to his servants, "Is the child dead?"
12:20 Then **D** rose from the ground, washed,
12:24 Then **D** consoled his wife Bathsheba,
12:27 Joab sent messengers to **D**, and said,
12:29 So **D** gathered all the people together and went
12:31 Then **D** and all the people returned to Jerusalem.
13: 7 Then **D** sent home to Tamar, saying,
13:21 When King **D** heard of all these things, C
13:30 to **D** that Absalom had killed all the king's sons,
13:37 **D** mourned for his son day after day.
15:13 A messenger came to **D**, saying,
15:14 Then **D** said to all his officials who were with him
15:22 **D** said to Ittai, "Go then, march on."
15:30 But **D** went up the ascent of the Mount of Olives,
15:31 **D** was told that Ahithophel was among
15:31 And **D** said, "O LORD, I pray you,
15:32 When **D** came to the summit,
15:33 **D** said to him, "If you go on with me,
16: 1 When **D** had passed a little beyond the summit,
16: 5 When King **D** came to Bahurim, C
16: 6 He threw stones at **D** and at all the servants
16: 6 at David and at all the servants of King **D**; C
16:10 'Curse **D**,' who then shall say,
16:11 **D** said to Abishai and to all his servants,
16:13 So **D** and his men went on the road,
16:23 both by **D** and by Absalom.
17: 1 and I will set out and pursue **D** tonight.
17:16 Therefore send quickly and tell **D**,
17:17 and they would go and tell King **D**; C
17:21 and went and told King **D**. C
17:21 They said to **D**, "Go and cross the water quickly;
17:22 So **D** and all the people who were with him set out
17:24 Then **D** came to Mahanaim,
17:27 When **D** came to Mahanaim,
17:29 for **D** and the people with him to eat;
18: 1 Then **D** mustered the men who were with him,
18: 2 And **D** divided the army into three groups:
18: 7 of Israel were defeated there by the servants of **D**,
18: 9 Absalom happened to meet the servants of **D**.
18:24 Now **D** was sitting between the two gates.
19:11 King **D** sent this message to the priests Zadok C
19:16 down with the people of Judah to meet King **D**; C
19:22 But **D** said, "What have I to do with you,
19:43 and in **D** also we have more than you.
20: 1 "We have no portion in **D**,
20: 2 of Israel withdrew from **D** and followed Sheba son
20: 3 **D** came to his house at Jerusalem;
20: 6 **D** said to Abishai, "Now Sheba son
20:11 "Whoever favors Joab, and whoever is for **D**,
20:21 has lifted up his hand against King **D**; C
21: 1 in the days of **D** for three years, year after year;
21: 1 and **D** inquired of the LORD,
21: 3 **D** said to the Gibeonites, "What shall I do for you?
21: 7 between **D** and Jonathan son of Saul.
21:11 When **D** was told what Rizpah daughter of Aiah,
21:12 **D** went and took the bones of Saul and the bones
21:15 and **D** went down together with his servants.
21:15 against the Philistines, and **D** grew weary.
21:16 with new weapons, said he would kill **D**.
21:22 they fell by the hands of **D** and his servants.
22: 1 **D** spoke to the LORD the words of this song on
22:51 to **D** and his descendants forever.
23: 1 Now these are the last words of **D**:
23: 1 The oracle of **D**, son of Jesse,
23: 8 These are the names of the warriors whom **D** had:
23: 9 He was with **D** when they defied
23:13 of the thirty chiefs went down to join **D** at the cave
23:14 **D** was then in the stronghold;
23:15 **D** said longingly, "O that someone would give me
23:16 that was by the gate, and brought it to **D**.
23:23 And **D** put him in charge of his bodyguard.
24: 1 and he incited **D** against them, saying, "Go,
24:10 **D** was stricken to the heart
24:10 **D** said to the LORD, "I have sinned greatly
24:11 When **D** rose in the morning,
24:12 "Go and say to **D**: Thus says the LORD:
24:13 So Gad came to **D** and told him;
24:14 Then **D** said to Gad, "I am in great distress;
24:17 **D** saw the angel who was destroying the people,

2Sa 24:18 That day Gad came to **D** and said to him,
24:19 Following Gad's instructions, **D** went up,
24:21 **D** said, "To buy the threshing floor from you
24:22 to **D**, "Let my lord the king take and offer
24:24 So **D** bought the threshing floor and the oxen
24:25 **D** built there an altar to the LORD,
1Ki 1: 1 King **D** was old and advanced in years; C
1:11 of Haggith has become king and our lord **D** does
1:13 Go in at once to King **D**, and say to him, C
1:28 King **D** answered, "Summon Bathsheba to me." C
1:31 and said, "May my lord King **D** live forever!" C
1:32 King **D** said, "Summon to me the priest Zadok, C
1:37 the throne of my lord King **D**." C
1:43 for our lord King **D** has made Solomon king; C
1:47 to congratulate our lord King **D**, C
2:10 Then **D** slept with his ancestors,
2:10 and was buried in the city of **D**. D
2:11 time that **D** reigned over Israel was forty years;
2:12 So Solomon sat on the throne of his father **D**; B
2:24 and placed me on the throne of my father **D**, B
2:26 the ark of the Lord GOD before my father **D**, B
2:32 because, without the knowledge of my father **D**, B
2:33 but to **D**, and to his descendants, and to his house,
2:44 the evil that you did to my father **D**; B
2:45 and the throne of **D** shall be established before
3: 1 and brought her into the city of **D**, D
3: 3 walking in the statutes of his father **D**; B
3: 6 to your servant my father **D**, because he walked B
3: 7 of my father **D**, although I am only a little child; B
3:14 my commandments, as your father **D** walked, B
5: 1 for Hiram had always been a friend to **D**.
5: 3 "You know that my father **D** could not build B
5: 5 as the LORD said to my father **D**, 'Your son, B
5: 7 to **D** a wise son to be over this great people."
6:12 which I made to your father **D**. B
7:51 in the things that his father **D** had dedicated, B
8: 1 of the covenant of the LORD out of the city of **D**, D
8:15 with his mouth to my father **D**, B
8:16 but I chose **D** to be over my people Israel.'
8:17 My father **D** had it in mind to build a house for B
8:18 But the LORD said to my father **D**, B
8:20 for I have risen in the place of my father **D**; B
8:24 for your servant my father **D** as you declared B
8:25 keep for your servant my father **D** B
8:26 you promised to your servant my father **D**. B
8:66 that the LORD had shown to his servant **D** and E
9: 4 before me, as **D** your father walked, with integrity
9: 5 as I promised your father **D**, saying, B
9:24 Pharaoh's daughter went up from the city of **D** D
11: 4 as was the heart of his father **D**. B
11: 6 as his father **D** had done. B
11:12 of your father **D** I will not do it in your lifetime; B
11:13 to your son, for the sake of my servant **D** and for E
11:15 For when **D** was in Edom,
11:21 that **D** slept with his ancestors and that Joab
11:24 of a marauding band, after the slaughter by **D**;
11:27 the gap in the wall of the city of his father **D**. BH
11:32 of my servant **D** and for the sake of Jerusalem, E
11:33 and my ordinances, as his father **D** did. B
11:34 for the sake of my servant **D** whom I chose E
11:36 so that my servant **D** may always have a lamp E
11:38 as **D** my servant did, I will be with you,
11:38 as I built for **D**, and I will give Israel to you.
11:39 For this reason I will punish the descendants of **D**,
11:43 and was buried in the city of his father **D**; BH
12:16 "What share do we have in **D**?
12:16 Look now to your own house, O **D**."
12:19 in rebellion against the house of **D** to this day. F
12:20 There was no one who followed the house of **D**, F
12:26 the kingdom may well revert to the house of **D**. F
13: 2 'A son shall be born to the house of **D**, F
14: 8 the kingdom away from the house of **D** to give it F
14: 8 yet you have not been like my servant **D**, E
14:31 was buried with his ancestors in the city of **D**. D
15: 3 like the heart of his father **D**. B
15: 5 **D** did what was right in the sight of the LORD,
15: 8 and they buried him in the city of **D**. D
15:11 as his father **D** had done. B
15:24 with his ancestors in the city of his father **D**; BH
22:50 with his ancestors in the city of his father **D**; BH
2Ki 8:19 for the sake of his servant **D**, E
8:24 and was buried with them in the city of **D**; D
9:28 in his tomb with his ancestors in the city of **D**. D
12:21 was buried with his ancestors in the city of **D**; D
14: 3 yet not like his ancestor **D**;
14:20 in Jerusalem with his ancestors in the city of **D**. D
15: 7 with his ancestors in the city of **D**; D
15:38 was buried with his ancestors in the city of **D**, D
16: 2 as his ancestor **D** had done,
16:20 was buried with his ancestors in the city of **D**; D
17:21 When he had torn Israel from the house of **D**, F
18: 3 of the LORD just as his ancestor **D** had done.
19:34 my own sake and for the sake of my servant **D**." E
20: 5 the God of your ancestor **D**:
21: 7 to **D** and to his son Solomon, "In this house,
22: 2 and walked in all the way of his father **D**; B
1Ch 2:15 Ozem the sixth, **D** the seventh;
3: 1 the sons of **D** who were born to him in Hebron:
4:31 These were their towns until **D** became king.
6:31 the men whom **D** put in charge of the service
7: 2 of **D** being twenty-two thousand six hundred.
9:22 **D** and the seer Samuel established them
10:14 and turned the kingdom over to **D** son of Jesse.
11: 1 Then all Israel gathered together to **D** at Hebron
11: 3 and **D** made a covenant with them at Hebron
11: 3 And they anointed **D** king over Israel,
11: 4 **D** and all Israel marched to Jerusalem,

1Ch 11: 5 The inhabitants of Jebus said to **D,**
11: 5 Nevertheless **D** took the stronghold of Zion,
11: 5 the stronghold of Zion, now the city of **D.** D
11: 6 **D** had said, "Whoever attacks
11: 7 **D** resided in the stronghold;
11: 7 therefore it was called the city of **D.** D
11: 9 And **D** became greater and greater,
11:13 He was with **D** at Pas-dammim when
11:14 and **D** took their stand in the middle of the plot,
11:15 of the thirty chiefs went down to the rock to **D** at
11:16 **D** was then in the stronghold;
11:17 **D** said longingly, "O that someone would give me
11:18 and they brought it to **D.**
11:18 But **D** would not drink of it;
11:25 And **D** put him in charge of his bodyguard.
12: 1 The following are those who came to **D** at Ziklag,
12: 8 the Gadites there went over to **D** at the stronghold
12:16 and Judahites came to the stronghold to **D.**
12:17 **D** went out to meet them and said to them,
12:18 "We are yours, O **D;** and with you, O son of Jesse!
12:18 Then **D** received them, and made them officers
12:19 the Manassites deserted to **D** when he came with
12:21 They helped **D** against the band of raiders,
12:22 Indeed from day to day people kept coming to **D**
12:23 the armed troops who came to **D** in Hebron to turn
12:31 to come and make **D** king.
12:33 to help **D** with singleness of purpose.
12:38 came to Hebron with full intent to make **D** king
12:38 of Israel were of a single mind to make **D** king.
12:39 They were there with **D** for three days,
13: 1 **D** consulted with the commanders of
13: 2 **D** said to the whole assembly of Israel,
13: 5 So **D** assembled all Israel from the Shihor
13: 6 And **D** and all Israel went up to Baalah, that is,
13: 8 **D** and all Israel were dancing before God
13:11 **D** was angry because the LORD had burst out
13:12 **D** was afraid of God that day;
13:13 So **D** did not take the ark into his care into the city
13:13 not take the ark into his care into the city of **D;** D
14: 1 King Hiram of Tyre sent messengers to **D,**
14: 2 **D** then perceived that the LORD had established
14: 3 **D** took more wives in Jerusalem,
14: 3 **D** became the father of more sons and daughters.
14: 8 the Philistines heard that **D** had been anointed king
14: 8 all the Philistines went up in search of **D;**
14: 8 and **D** heard of it and went out against them.
14:10 **D** inquired of God, "Shall I go up against
14:11 and **D** defeated them there.
14:11 **D** said, "God has burst out against my enemies
14:14 When **D** again inquired of God, God said to him,
14:16 **D** did as God had commanded him,
14:17 The fame of **D** went out into all lands,
15: 1 **D** built houses for himself in the city of David,
15: 1 David built houses for himself in the city of **D,** D
15: 2 Then **D** commanded that no one but
15: 3 **D** assembled all Israel in Jerusalem to bring up
15: 4 Then **D** gathered together the descendants
15:11 **D** summoned the priests Zadok and Abiathar,
15:16 **D** also commanded the chiefs of the Levites
15:25 So **D** and the elders of Israel,
15:27 **D** was clothed with a robe of fine linen,
15:27 and **D** wore a linen ephod.
15:29 the LORD came to the city of **D,** Michal daughter D
15:29 and saw King **D** leaping and dancing; C
16: 1 and set it inside the tent that **D** had pitched for it;
16: 2 When **D** had finished offering the burnt offerings
16: 7 on that day **D** first appointed the singing of praises
16:37 **D** left Asaph and his kinsfolk there before the ark
16:43 and **D** went home to bless his household.
17: 1 Now when **D** settled in his house,
17: 1 **D** said to the prophet Nathan,
17: 2 Nathan said to **D,** "Do all that you have in mind,
17: 4 Go and tell my servant **D:** E
17: 7 therefore thus you shall say to my servant **D:** E
17:15 and all this vision, Nathan spoke to **D.**
17:16 Then King **D** went in and sat before the LORD, C
17:18 And what more can **D** say to you
17:24 the house of your servant **D** will be established E
18: 1 **D** attacked the Philistines and subdued them;
18: 2 Moabites became subject to **D** and brought tribute.
18: 3 **D** also struck down King Hadadezer of Zobah,
18: 4 **D** took from him one thousand chariots,
18: 4 **D** hamstrung all the chariot horses,
18: 5 **D** killed twenty-two thousand Arameans.
18: 6 Then **D** put garrisons in Aram of Damascus;
18: 6 and the Arameans became subject to **D,**
18: 6 The LORD gave victory to **D** wherever he went.
18: 7 **D** took the gold shields that were carried by
18: 8 **D** took a vast quantity of bronze;
18: 9 of Hamath heard that **D** had defeated
18:10 he sent his son Hadoram to King **D,** C
18:11 these also King **D** dedicated to the LORD, C
18:13 and all the Edomites became subject to **D.**
18:13 the LORD gave victory to **D** wherever he went.
18:14 So **D** reigned over all Israel;
19: 2 **D** said, "I will deal loyally with Hanun son
19: 2 So **D** sent messengers to console him
19: 3 because **D** has sent consolers to you,
19: 5 When **D** was told about the men,
19: 6 that they had made themselves odious to **D,**
19: 8 When **D** heard of it, he sent Joab and all the army
19:17 When **D** was informed, he gathered all Israel
19:17 **D** set the battle in array against the Arameans,
19:18 and **D** killed seven thousand Aramean charioteers
19:19 they made peace with **D,** and became subject
20: 1 But **D** remained at Jerusalem.
20: 2 **D** took the crown of Milcom from his head;
1Ch 20: 3 Thus **D** did to all the cities of the Ammonites.
20: 3 Then **D** and all the people returned to Jerusalem.
20: 8 they fell by the hand of **D** and his servants.
21: 1 and incited **D** to count the people of Israel.
21: 2 **D** said to Joab and the commanders of the army,
21: 5 Joab gave the total count of the people to **D.**
21: 8 **D** said to God, "I have sinned greatly in
21:10 "Go and say to **D,** 'Thus says the LORD:
21:11 So Gad came to **D** and said to him,
21:13 Then **D** said to Gad, "I am in great distress;
21:16 **D** looked up and saw the angel of
21:16 Then **D** and the elders, clothed in sackcloth,
21:17 And **D** said to God, "Was it not I who gave
21:18 the angel of the LORD commanded Gad to tell **D**
21:19 So **D** went up following Gad's instructions,
21:21 **D** came to Ornan, Ornan looked and saw **D;**
21:21 and did obeisance to **D** with his face to the ground.
21:22 **D** said to Ornan, "Give me the site of
21:23 Then Ornan said to **D,** "Take it;
21:24 But King **D** said to Ornan, "No; C
21:25 So **D** paid Ornan six hundred shekels of gold
21:26 **D** built there an altar to the LORD
21:28 when **D** saw that the LORD had answered him at
21:30 but **D** could not go before it to inquire of God,
22: 1 Then **D** said, "Here shall be the house of
22: 2 **D** gave orders to gather together
22: 3 **D** also provided great stores of iron for nails for
22: 4 and Tyrians brought great quantities of cedar to **D.**
22: 5 For **D** said, "My son Solomon is young
22: 5 So **D** provided materials in great quantity
22: 7 **D** said to Solomon, "My son,
22:17 **D** also commanded all the leaders of Israel
23: 1 When **D** was old and full of days,
23: 2 **D** assembled all the leaders of Israel and
23: 4 "Twenty-four thousand of these," **D** said,
23: 6 And **D** organized them in divisions corresponding
23:25 For **D** said, "The LORD, the God of Israel,
23:27 to the last words of **D** these were the number of
24: 3 **D** organized them according to
24:31 in the presence of King **D,** Zadok, Ahimelech, C
25: 1 **D** and the officers of the army also set apart for
26:26 the treasuries of the dedicated gifts that King **D,** C
26:32 King **D** appointed him and his brothers, C
27:23 **D** did not count those below twenty years of age,
27:24 into the account of the Annals of King **D.** C
28: 1 **D** assembled at Jerusalem all the officials of Israel,
28: 2 Then King **D** rose to his feet and said: C
28:11 Then **D** gave his son Solomon the plan of
28:20 **D** said further to his son Solomon,
29: 1 King **D** said to the whole assembly, C
29: 9 King **D** also rejoiced greatly. C
29:10 Then **D** blessed the LORD in the presence of all
29:10 of all the assembly; **D** said:
29:20 Then **D** said to the whole assembly,
29:23 succeeding his father **D** as king; B
29:24 and also all the sons of King **D,** C
29:26 Thus **D** son of Jesse reigned over all Israel.
29:29 Now the acts of King **D,** from first to last, C
2Ch 1: 1 son of **D** established himself in his kingdom; G
1: 4 (But **D** had brought the ark of God up
1: 4 to the place that **D** had prepared for it;
1: 8 and steadfast love to my father **D,** B
1: 9 let your promise to my father **D** now be fulfilled, B
2: 3 with my father **D** and sent him cedar B
2: 7 whom my father **D** provided. B
2:12 who has given King **D** a wise son, C
2:14 the artisans of my lord, your father **D.** B
2:17 after the census that his father **D** had taken; B
3: 1 where the LORD had appeared to his father **D,** B
3: 1 at the place that **D** had designated,
5: 1 in the things that his father **D** had dedicated, B
5: 2 of the covenant of the LORD out of the city of **D,** D
6: 4 with his mouth to my father **D,** B
6: 6 and I have chosen **D** to be over my people Israel.'
6: 7 My father **D** had it in mind to build a house for B
6: 8 But the LORD said to my father **D,** B
6:10 for I have succeeded my father **D,** B
6:15 my father **D,** what you promised to him. B
6:16 keep for your servant, my father **D,** B
6:17 which you promised to your servant **D.** E
6:42 your steadfast love for your servant **D."** E
7: 6 for music to the LORD that King **D** had made C
7: 6 whenever **D** offered praises by their ministry.
7:10 the goodness that the LORD had shown to **D** and
7:17 if you walk before me, as your father **D** walked, B
7:18 as I made covenant with your father **D** saying, B
8:11 city of **D** to the house that he had built for her, D
8:11 "My wife shall not live in the house of King **D** C
8:14 According to the ordinance of his father **D,** B
8:14 for so **D** the man of God had commanded.
9:31 and was buried in the city of his father **D;** BH
10:16 "What share do we have in **D?**
10:16 Look now to your own house, O **D."**
10:19 in rebellion against the house of **D** to this day. F
11:17 for they walked for three years in the way of **D**
11:18 of Jerimoth son of **D,** and of Abihail daughter G
12:16 his ancestors and was buried in the city of **D;** D
13: 5 over Israel forever to **D** and his sons by a covenant
13: 6 a servant of Solomon son of **D,** G
13: 8 of the LORD in the hand of the sons of **D,**
14: 1 and they buried him in the city of **D.** D
16:14 that he had hewn out for himself in the city of **D.** D
21: 1 was buried with his ancestors in the city of **D;** D
21: 7 not destroy the house of **D** because of F
21: 7 because of the covenant that he had made with **D,**
21:12 "Thus says the LORD, the God of your father **D:** B
21:20 They buried him in the city of **D,** D
2Ch 23: 3 as the LORD promised concerning the sons of **D.**
23:18 to the levitical priests whom **D** had organized to be
23:18 according to the order of **D.**
24:16 buried him in the city of **D** among the kings, D
24:25 So he died; and they buried him in the city of **D,** D
25:28 he was buried with his ancestors in the city of **D.** D
27: 9 and they buried him in the city of **D;** D
28: 1 as his ancestor **D** had done,
29: 2 just as his ancestor **D** had done.
29:25 the commandment of **D** and of Gad the king's seer
29:26 The Levites stood with the instruments of **D,**
29:27 accompanied by the instruments of King **D** C
29:30 to sing praises to the LORD with the words of **D**
30:26 for since the time of Solomon son of King **D** CG
32: 5 he also strengthened the Millo in the city of **D,** D
32:30 down to the west side of the city of **D.** D
32:33 the ascent to the tombs of the descendants of **D;**
33: 7 of which God said to **D** and to his son Solomon,
33:14 the city of **D** west of Gihon, in the valley, D
34: 2 and walked in the ways of his ancestor **D;**
34: 3 he began to seek the God of his ancestor **D,**
35: 3 the holy ark in the house that Solomon son of **D,** G
35: 4 of King **D** of Israel and the written directions C
35:15 in their place according to the command of **D,**
Ezr 3:10 according to the directions of King **D** of Israel; C
8: 2 Of Ithamar, Daniel. Of **D,**
8:20 whom **D** and his officials had set apart to attend
Ne 3:15 far as the stairs that go down from the City of **D.** D
3:16 repaired from a point opposite the graves of **D,**
12:24 according to the commandment of **D** the man
12:36 with the musical instruments of **D** the man of God;
12:37 went straight up by the stairs of the city of **D,** D
12:37 at the ascent of the wall, above the house of **D,** F
12:45 to the command of **D** and his son Solomon.
12:46 For in the days of **D** and Asaph long ago
Ps 3: T *A Psalm of* ***D,*** *when he fled from his son* A
4: T *with stringed instruments. A Psalm of* ***D.*** A
5: T *To the leader: for the flutes. A Psalm of* ***D.*** A
6: T *according to The Sheminith. A Psalm of* ***D.*** A
7: T *A Shiggaion of* ***D,*** *which he sang* A
8: T *according to The Gittith. A Psalm of* ***D.*** A
9: T *according to Muth-labben. A Psalm of* ***D.*** A
11: T *To the leader. Of* ***D.*** A
12: T *according to The Sheminith. A Psalm of* ***D.*** A
13: T *To the leader. A Psalm of* ***D.*** A
14: T *To the leader. Of* ***D.*** A
15: T *A Psalm of* ***D.*** A
16: T *A Miktam of* ***D.*** A
17: T *A Prayer of* ***D.*** A
18: T *A Psalm of* ***D*** *the servant of the LORD,* A
18:50 to **D** and his descendants forever.
19: T *To the leader. A Psalm of* ***D.*** A
20: T *To the leader. A Psalm of* ***D.*** A
21: T *To the leader. A Psalm of* ***D.*** A
22: T *to The Deer of the Dawn. A Psalm of* ***D.*** A
23: T *A Psalm of* ***D.*** A
24: T *Of* ***D.*** *A Psalm.* A
25: T *Of* ***D.*** A
26: T *Of* ***D.*** A
27: T *Of* ***D.*** A
28: T *Of* ***D.*** A
29: T *A Psalm of* ***D.*** A
30: T *A Song at the dedication the temple. Of* ***D.*** A
31: T *To the leader. A Psalm of* ***D.*** A
32: T *Of* ***D.*** *A Maskil.* A
34: T *Of* ***D,*** *when he feigned madness before* A
35: T *Of* ***D.*** A
36: T *To the leader. Of* ***D,*** *the servant of the LORD.* A
37: T *Of* ***D.*** A
38: T *A Psalm of* ***D,*** *for the memorial offering.* A
39: T *To the leader: to Jeduthun. A Psalm of* ***D.*** A
40: T *To the leader. Of* ***D.*** *A Psalm.* A
41: T *To the leader. A Psalm of* ***D.*** A
51: T *To the leader. A Psalm of* ***D,*** A
52: T *To the leader. A Maskil of* ***D,*** *when Doeg* A
52: T ***"D*** *has come to the house of Ahimelech."*
53: T *according to Mahalath. A Maskil of* ***D.*** A
54: T *A Maskil of* ***D,*** *when the Ziphites went* A
54: T *told Saul,* ***"D*** *is hiding among us."*
55: T *with stringed instruments. A Maskil of* ***D.*** A
56: T *Of* ***D.*** *A Miktam,* A
57: T *Do Not Destroy. Of* ***D.*** A
58: T *Do Not Destroy. Of* ***D.*** A
59: T *Do Not Destroy. Of* ***D.*** A
60: T *A Miktam of* ***D;*** *for instruction;* A
61: T *with stringed instruments. Of* ***D.*** A
62: T *according to Jeduthun. A Psalm of* ***D.*** A
63: T *A Psalm of* ***D,*** *when he was in the Wilderness* A
64: T *To the leader. A Psalm of* ***D.*** A
65: T *To the leader. A Psalm of* ***D.*** A
68: T *To the leader. Of* ***D.*** A
69: T *To the leader: according to Lilies. Of* ***D.*** A
70: T *To the leader. Of* ***D,*** A
72:20 The prayers of **D** son of Jesse are ended.
78:70 He chose his servant **D,** and took him from E
86: T *A Prayer of* ***D.*** A
89: 3 I have sworn to my servant **D:** E
89:20 I have found my servant **D;** E
89:35 I will not lie to **D.**
89:49 which by your faithfulness you swore to **D?**
101: T *Of* ***D.*** *A Psalm.* A
103: T *Of* ***D.*** A
108: T *A Song. A Psalm of* ***D.*** A
109: T *To the leader. Of* ***D.*** *A Psalm.* A
110: T *Of* ***D.*** *A Psalm.* A
122: T *A Song of Ascents. Of* ***D.*** A
122: 5 the thrones of the house of **D.** F

Ps 124: T *A Song of Ascents. Of* **D.** A
131: T *A Song of Ascents. Of* **D.** A
132:11 to **D** a sure oath from which he will not turn back:
132:17 There I will cause a horn to sprout up for **D;**
138: T *Of* **D.** A
139: T *To the leader. Of* **D.** *A Psalm.* A
140: T *To the leader. A Psalm of* **D.** A
141: T *A Psalm of* **D.** A
142: T *A Maskil of* **D.** *When he was in the cave.* A
143: T *A Psalm of* **D.** A
144: T *Of* **D.** A
144:10 who rescues his servant **D.** E
145: T *Praise. Of* **D.** A
Pr 1: 1 proverbs of Solomon son of **D,** king of Israel: G
Ecc 1: 1 The words of the Teacher, the son of **D,** G
SS 4: 4 Your neck is like the tower of **D,** built in courses;
Isa 7: 2 the house of **D** heard that Aram had allied itself F
7:13 Then Isaiah said: "Hear then, O house of **D!** F
9: 7 for the throne of **D** and his kingdom.
16: 5 be established in steadfast love in the tent of **D,**
22: 9 that there were many breaches in the city of **D,** D
22:22 on his shoulder the key of the house of **D;** F
29: 1 Ah, Ariel, Ariel, the city where **D** encamped!
29: 3 And like **D** I will encamp against you;
37:35 my own sake and for the sake of my servant **D."** E
38: 5 the God of your ancestor **D:**
55: 3 my steadfast, sure love for **D.**
Jer 17:25 of this city kings who sit on the throne of **D,**
21:12 O house of **D!** Thus says the LORD: F
22: 2 O King of Judah sitting on the throne of **D**—
22: 4 of **D,** riding in chariots and on horses, they,
22:30 in sitting on the throne of **D,**
23: 5 when I will raise up for **D** a righteous Branch,
29:16 concerning the king who sits on the throne of **D,**
30: 9 the LORD their God and **D** their king,
33:15 a righteous Branch to spring up for **D;**
33:17 **D** shall never lack a man to sit on the throne of
33:21 only then could my covenant with my servant **D** E
33:22 so I will increase the offspring of my servant **D,** E
33:26 and of my servant **D** and not choose any E
36:30 He shall have no one to sit upon the throne of **D,**
Eze 34:23 my servant **D,** and he shall feed them: E
34:24 and my servant **D** shall be prince among them; E
37:24 My servant **D** shall be king over them; E
37:25 and my servant **D** shall be their prince forever. E
Hos 3: 5 and seek the LORD their God, and **D** their king;
Am 6: 5 and like **D** improvise on instruments of music;
9:11 of **D** that is fallen, and repair its breaches,
Zec 12: 7 of the house of **D** and the glory of the inhabitants F
12: 8 among them on that day shall be like **D,**
12: 8 and the house of **D** shall be like God, F
12:10 compassion and supplication on the house of **D** F
12:12 the family of the house of **D** by itself, F
13: 1 a fountain shall be opened for the house of **D** F
Mt 1: 1 the son of **D,** the son of Abraham. G
1: 6 and Jesse the father of King **D.** C
1: 6 **D** was the father of Solomon by the wife of Uriah,
1:17 from Abraham to **D** are fourteen generations;
1:17 and from **D** to the deportation to Babylon,
1:20 to him in a dream and said, "Joseph, son of **D,** G
9:27 crying loudly, "Have mercy on us, Son of **D!"** G
12: 3 "Have you not read what **D** did when he
12:23 "Can this be the Son of **D?"** G
15:22 Son of **D;** my daughter is tormented by a demon. G
20:30 shouted, "Lord, have mercy on us, Son of **D!"** G
20:31 "Have mercy on us, Lord, Son of **D!"** G
21: 9 "Hosanna to the Son of **D!** G
21:15 "Hosanna to the Son of **D,"** G
22:42 They said to him, "The son of **D."** G
22:43 "How is it then that **D** by the Spirit calls him Lord,
22:45 If **D** thus calls him Lord, how can he be his son?"
Mk 2:25 "Have you never read what **D** did when he
10:47 he began to shout out and say, "Jesus, Son of **D,** G
10:48 but he cried out even more loudly, "Son of **D,** G
11:10 Blessed is the coming kingdom of our ancestor **D!**
12:35 the scribes say that the Messiah is the son of **D?** G
12:36 **D** himself, by the Holy Spirit, declared,
12:37 **D** himself calls him Lord;
Lk 1:27 man whose name was Joseph, of the house of **D.** F
1:32 to him the throne of his ancestor **D**
1:69 for us in the house of his servant **D,** E
2: 4 to the city of **D** called Bethlehem,
2: 4 he was descended from the house and family of **D.**
2:11 to you is born this day in the city of **D** a Savior, D
3:31 son of Mattatha, son of Nathan, son of **D,** G
6: 3 "Have you not read what **D** did when he
18:38 shouted, "Jesus, Son of **D,** have mercy on me!" G
18:39 but he shouted even more loudly, "Son of **D,** G
20:42 For **D** himself says in the book of Psalms,
20:44 **D** thus calls him Lord; so how can he be his son?"
Jn 7:42 that the Messiah is descended from **D** and comes
7:42 the village where **D** lived?"
Ac 1:16 through **D** foretold concerning Judas, who became
2:25 For **D** says concerning him,
2:29 I may say to you confidently of our ancestor **D**
2:31 **D** spoke of the resurrection of the Messiah, saying,
2:34 For **D** did not ascend into the heavens,
4:25 by the Holy Spirit through our ancestor **D,**
7:45 And it was there until the time of **D,**
13:22 When he had removed him, he made **D** their king.
13:22 'I have found **D,** son of Jesse,
13:34 'I will give you the holy promises made to **D.'**
13:36 For **D,** after he had served the purpose of God
15:16 and I will rebuild the dwelling of **D,**
Ro 1: 3 who was descended from **D** according to the flesh
4: 6 So also **D** speaks of the blessedness of those
11: 9 And **D** says, "Let their table become a snare and
2Ti 2: 8 raised from the dead, a descendant of **D**—
Heb 4: 7 "today"—saying through **D** much later,
11:32 Jephthah, of **D** and Samuel and the prophets—
Rev 3: 7 the true one, who has the key of **D,**
5: 5 See, the Lion of the tribe of Judah, the Root of **D,**
22:16 I am the root and the descendant of **D,**
Tob 1: 4 of my ancestor Naphtali deserted the house of **D** F
Sir 45:25 a covenant was established with **D** son of Jesse of
47: 1 him Nathan rose up to prophesy in the days of **D.**
47: 2 so **D** was set apart from the Israelites.
47:22 and to **D** a root from his own family.
48:15 but with a ruler from the house of **D.** F
48:22 and he kept firmly to the ways of his ancestor **D,**
49: 4 Except for **D** and Hezekiah and Josiah,
51:12 *makes a horn to sprout for the house of* **D,** F
1Mc 1:33 city of **D** with a great strong wall and strong D
2:31 and to the troops in Jerusalem the city of **D,** D
2:57 **D,** because he was merciful,
4:30 mighty warrior by the hand of your servant **D,** E
7:32 and the rest fled into the city of **D.** D
14:36 as were also those in the city of **D** in Jerusalem, D
2Mc 2:13 and prophets, and the writings of **D,** and letters
1Es 1: 3 house that King Solomon, son of **D,** had built; G
1: 5 in accordance with the directions of King **D** C
1:15 according to the arrangement made by **D,**
5: 5 of the house of **D,** of the lineage of Phares, F
5:60 according to the directions of King **D** of Israel; C
8:29 Of the descendants of **D,** Hattush son
8:49 whom **D** and the leaders had given for the service
Pm 151: T *This psalm is ascribed to* **D**
2Es 3:23 and you raised up for yourself a servant, named **D.**
7:*108* [38] and **D** for the plague, and Solomon for those
12:32 who will arise from the offspring of **D,**
4Mc 3: 7 **D** had been attacking the Philistines all day long,
3:15 But **D,** though he was burning with thirst,
18:15 He sang to you songs of the psalmist **D,** who said,

DAVID'S (65) [DAVID]

1Sa 17:50 there was no sword in **D** hand.
17:57 On **D** return from killing the Philistine,
18:29 So Saul was **D** enemy from that time forward.
19:11 Saul sent messengers to **D** house to keep watch
19:11 **D** wife Michal told him, "If you do
20:25 by Saul's side; but **D** place was empty.
20:27 the day after the new moon, **D** place was empty.
23: 3 But **D** men said to him, "Look,
25: 9 When **D** young men came,
25:10 But Nabal answered **D** servants, "Who is David?
25:12 So **D** young men turned away,
25:40 When **D** servants came to Abigail at Carmel,
25:44 Saul had given his daughter Michal, **D** wife,
26:17 Saul recognized **D** voice, and said,
30: 5 **D** two wives also had been taken captive,
30:20 people said, "This is **D** spoil."
2Sa 2:30 of **D** servants nineteen men besides Asahel.
3: 5 Ithream, of **D** wife Eglah.
3:26 When Joab came out from **D** presence,
8:14 and all the Edomites became **D** servants.
8:18 and the Pelethites; and **D** sons were priests.
9:11 Mephibosheth ate at **D** table,
10: 2 **D** envoys came into the land of the Ammonites,
10: 4 So Hanun seized **D** envoys,
12: 5 Then **D** anger was greatly kindled against the man.
12:30 and it was placed on **D** head.
13: 1 **D** son Absalom had a beautiful sister whose name
13: 1 and **D** son Amnon fell in love with her.
13: 3 the son of **D** brother Shimeah;
13:32 But Jonadab, the son of **D** brother Shimeah, said,
15:12 he sent for Ahithophel the Gilonite, **D** counselor,
15:37 So Hushai, **D** friend, came into the city,
16:16 When Hushai the Archite, **D** friend,
19:41 and all **D** men with him?"
20:26 and Ira the Jairite was also **D** priest.
21:17 Then **D** men swore to him,
21:21 Jonathan son of **D** brother Shimei, killed him.
24:11 of the LORD came to the prophet Gad, **D** seer,
1Ki 1: 8 and **D** own warriors did not side with Adonijah.
1:38 down and had Solomon ride on King **D** mule,
2: 1 When **D** time to die drew near,
15: 4 for **D** sake the LORD his God gave him a lamp
2Ki 11:10 that had been King **D,** which were in the house of
20: 6 for my own sake and for my servant **D** sake."
1Ch 3: 9 All these were **D** sons, besides the sons of
11:10 Now these are the chiefs of **D** warriors,
11:11 This is an account of **D** mighty warriors:
14:12 and at **D** command they were burned.
18:17 and **D** sons were the chief officials in the service
19: 2 When **D** servants came to Hanun in the land of
19: 4 So Hanun seized **D** servants, shaved them,
20: 2 and it was placed on **D** head.
20: 7 Jonathan son of Shimea, **D** brother, killed him.
21: 9 The LORD spoke to Gad, **D** seer, saying,
26:31 (In the fortieth year of **D** reign search was made,
27:18 for Judah, Elihu, one of **D** brothers;
27:31 All these were stewards of King **D** property.
27:32 Jonathan, **D** uncle, was a counselor,
29:22 They made **D** son Solomon king a second time;
2Ch 23: 9 the large and small shields that had been King **D,**
Ps 132: 1 remember in **D** favor all the hardships he endured;
132:10 For your servant **D** sake do not turn away the face
Jer 13:13 the kings who sit on **D** throne, the priests,
Lk 20:41 "How can they say that the Messiah is **D** son?
4Mc 3: 6 by the story of King **D** thirst.

DAWN (37) [DAWNED, DAWNING, DAWNS]

Ex 14:27 and at **d** the sea returned to its normal depth.
Jos 6:15 On the seventh day they rose early, at **d,**
Jdg 19:25 And as the **d** began to break, they let her go.
1Sa 9:26 the break of **d** Samuel called to Saul upon the roof,
Ne 4:21 the spears from break of **d** until the stars came out.
Job 3: 9 Let the stars of its **d** be dark;
7: 4 the night is long, and I am full of tossing until **d.**
38:12 and caused the **d** to know its place,
41:18 and its eyes are like the eyelids of the **d.**
Ps 22: T *according to The Deer of the* **D.** *A Psalm of David.*
57: 8 I will awake the **d.**
108: 2 Awake, O harp and lyre! I will awake the **d.**
119:147 I rise before **d** and cry for help;
Pr 4:18 But the path of the righteous is like the light of **d,**
Ecc 11:10 for youth and the **d** of life are vanity.
SS 6:10 "Who is this that looks forth like the **d,**
Isa 8:20 Surely, those who speak like this will have no **d!**
14:12 you are fallen from heaven, O Day Star, son of **D!**
58: 8 Then your light shall break forth like the **d,**
60: 3 and kings to the brightness of your **d.**
62: 1 until her vindication shines out like the **d,**
Hos 6: 3 his appearing is as sure as the **d;**
10:15 At **d** the king of Israel shall be utterly cut off.
Jnh 4: 7 But when **d** came up the next day,
Zep 3: 5 he renders his judgment, each **d** without fail;
Mk 13:35 or at midnight, or at cockcrow, or at **d,**
Lk 1:78 the **d** from on high will break upon us,
12:38 he comes during the middle of the night, or near **d,**
24: 1 But on the first day of the week, at early **d,**
Ac 20:11 he continued to converse with them until **d;**
Jdt 14:11 as it was **d** they hung the head of Holofernes on
Sir 24:32 I will again make instruction shine forth like the **d,**
1Mc 5:30 At **d** they looked out and saw a large company,
2Mc 10:28 as **d** was breaking, the two armies joined battle,
10:35 But at **d** of the fifth day,
3Mc 5:46 entered at about **d** into the courtyard—
2Es 7:*42* or **d** or shining or brightness or light,

DAWNED (5) [DAWN]

Ge 19:15 When morning **d,** the angels urged Lot, saying,
Dt 33: 2 LORD came from Sinai, and **d** from Seir upon us;
2Ki 19:35 when morning **d,** they were all dead bodies.
Isa 37:36 when morning **d,** they were all dead bodies.
Mt 4:16 in the region and shadow of death light has **d."**

DAWNING‡ (3) [DAWN]

Mt 28: 1 the sabbath, as the first day of the week was **d,**
Wis 16:28 and must pray to you at the **d** of the light;
2Mc 13:17 This happened, just as day was **d,**

DAWNS (4) [DAWN]

Ps 46: 5 God will help it when the morning **d.**
97:11 Light **d** for the righteous, and joy for the upright
Mic 2: 1 When the morning **d,** they perform it,
2Pe 1:19 the day **d** and the morning star rises in your hearts.

DAY‡ (1750) [BIRTHDAY, DAILY, DAY'S, DAYBREAK, DAYLIGHT, DAYS, DAYS', DAYTIME, EVERYDAY, MIDDAY, NOONDAY]

A. ON THAT DAY (146)
B. SEVENTH DAY (58)
C. THIRD DAY (53)
D. FIRST DAY (51)
E. ONE DAY (46)
F. EVERY DAY (33)
G. DAY OF THE †LORD (17)
H. DAY AFTER DAY (17)
I. DAY OF ... DEATH (17)
J. DAY OF JUDGMENT (14)
K. EACH DAY (13)
L. DAY OF ... CALAMITY (12)
M. DAY OF ... WRATH (11)
N. DAY OF ... TROUBLE (10)
O. DAY OF ... DISTRESS (9)
P. DAY BY DAY (8)
Q. LAST DAY (8)
R. DAY OF THE/OUR *LORD (7)

Ge 1: 5 God called the light **D,** and
1: 5 and there was morning, the first **d.** D
1: 8 and there was morning, the second **d.**
1:13 and there was morning, the third **d.** C
1:14 be lights in the dome of the sky to separate the **d**
1:16 to rule the **d** and the lesser light to rule the night—
1:18 to rule over the **d** and over the night,
1:19 and there was morning, the fourth **d.**
1:23 and there was morning, the fifth **d.**
1:31 and there was morning, the sixth **d.**
2: 2 And on the seventh **d** God finished the work B
2: 2 the seventh **d** from all the work that he had done. B
2: 3 So God blessed the seventh **d** and hallowed it, B
2: 4 In the **d** that the LORD God made the earth and
2:17 for in the **d** that you eat of it you shall die."
7:11 on the seventeenth **d** of the month,
7:11 on that **d** all the fountains of A
7:13 On the very same **d** Noah with his sons,
8: 4 on the seventeenth **d** of the month,
8: 5 in the tenth month, on the first **d** of the month, D
8:13 in the first month, the first **d** of the month, D
8:14 on the twenty-seventh **d** of the month,

Ge 8:22 summer and winter, **d** and night, shall not cease.”
15:18 On that **d** the LORD made a covenant with A
17:23 the flesh of their foreskins that very **d**,
17:26 That very **d** Abraham and his son Ishmael were
18:1 at the entrance of his tent in the heat of the **d**.
19:34 On the next **d**, the firstborn said to the younger,
19:37 he is the ancestor of the Moabites to this **d**.
19:38 he is the ancestor of the Ammonites to this **d**.
21:8 a great feast on the **d** that Isaac was weaned.
22:4 On the third **d** Abraham looked up and saw C
22:14 as it is said to this **d**,
26:32 That same **d** Isaac's servants came and told him
26:33 the name of the city is Beer-sheba to this **d**.
27:2 I do not know the **d** of my death. I
27:45 Why should I lose both of you in one **d**?” E
30:35 But that **d** Laban removed the male goats
31:22 the third **d** Laban was told that Jacob had fled. C
31:39 whether stolen by **d** or stolen by night.
31:40 by **d** the heat consumed me, and the cold by night,
32:26 Then he said, “Let me go, for the **d** is breaking.”
32:32 to this **d** the Israelites do not eat the thigh muscle
33:13 and if they are overdriven for one **d**, E
33:16 So Esau returned that **d** on his way to Seir.
34:25 On the third **d**, when they were still in pain, C
35:3 God who answered me in the **d** of my distress O
35:20 of Rachel's tomb, which is there to this **d**.
39:10 And although she spoke to Joseph **d** after **d**, H
39:11 One **d**, however, when he went into the house E
40:20 On the third **d**, which was Pharaoh's birthday, C
42:18 On the third **d** Joseph said to them, C
47:23 “Now that I have this **d** bought you and your land
47:26 and it stands to this **d**,
48:15 who has been my shepherd all my life to this **d**,
48:20 So he blessed them that **d**, saying,
Ex 2:11 One **d**, after Moses had grown up, E
2:13 When he went out the next **d**,
5:6 That same **d** Pharaoh commanded the taskmasters
6:28 the **d** when the LORD spoke to Moses in the land
8:22 But on that **d** I will set apart the land of Goshen, A
9:6 And on the next **d** the LORD did so;
9:18 in Egypt from the **d** it was founded until now.
10:6 from the **d** they came on earth to this **d**.’ ”
10:13 an east wind upon the land all that **d** and all
10:28 for on the **d** you see my face you shall die.”
12:6 You shall keep it until the fourteenth **d**
12:14 This **d** shall be a **d** of remembrance for you.
12:15 on the first **d** you shall remove leaven D
12:15 for whoever eats leavened bread from the first **d** D
12:15 until the seventh **d** shall be cut off from Israel. B
12:16 On the first **d** you shall hold a solemn assembly, D
12:16 and on the seventh **d** a solemn assembly; B
12:17 for on this very **d** I brought your companies out of
12:17 shall observe this **d** throughout your generations
12:18 the evening of the fourteenth **d** until the evening of
12:18 until the evening of the twenty-first **d**,
12:41 of four hundred thirty years, on that very **d**, all
12:51 That very **d** the LORD brought the Israelites out
13:3 “Remember this **d** on which you came out
13:6 and on the seventh **d** there shall be a festival to B
13:8 You shall tell your child on that **d**, A
13:21 in front of them in a pillar of cloud by **d**,
13:21 so that they might travel by **d** and by night.
13:22 by **d** nor the pillar of fire by night left its place
14:30 the LORD saved Israel that **d** from the Egyptians;
16:1 and Sinai, on the fifteenth **d** of the second month
16:4 and each **d** the people shall go out K
16:4 and gather enough for that **d**.
16:5 On the sixth **d**, when they prepare what they bring
16:22 On the sixth **d** they gathered twice as much food,
16:23 ‘Tomorrow is a **d** of solemn rest,
16:26 days you shall gather it; but on the seventh **d**, B
16:27 On the seventh **d** some of the people went out B
16:29 on the sixth **d** he gives you food for two days;
16:29 do not leave your place on the seventh **d**.” B
16:30 So the people rested on the seventh **d**. B
18:13 The next **d** Moses sat as judge for the people,
19:1 the land of Egypt, on that very **d**, they came into
19:11 and prepare for the third **d**, C
19:11 because on the third **d** the LORD will come down C
19:15 he said to the people, “Prepare for the third **d**; C
19:16 On the morning of the third **d** there was thunder C
20:8 Remember the sabbath **d**, and keep it holy.
20:10 the seventh **d** is a sabbath to the LORD your God; B
20:11 and all that is in them, but rested the seventh **d**; B
20:11 LORD blessed the sabbath **d** and consecrated it.
21:21 slave survives a **d** or two, there is no punishment;
22:30 on the eighth **d** you shall give it to me.
23:12 but on the seventh **d** you shall rest, B
24:16 seventh **d** he called to Moses out of the cloud. B
29:36 every **d** you shall offer a bull as a sin offering F
29:38 two lambs a year old regularly each **d**. K
31:15 but the seventh **d** is a sabbath of solemn rest, B
31:15 whoever does any work on the sabbath **d** shall
31:17 and on the seventh **d** he rested, B
32:6 They rose early the next **d**,
32:28 about three thousand of the people fell on that **d**. A
32:29 so have brought a blessing on yourselves this **d**.”
32:30 On the next **d** Moses said to the people,
32:34 Nevertheless, when the **d** comes for punishment,
34:21 but on the seventh **d** you shall rest; B
35:2 on the seventh **d** you shall have a holy sabbath B
35:3 in all your dwellings on the sabbath **d**.
40:2 On the first **d** of the first month you shall set up D
40:17 on the first **d** of the month, D
40:37 they did not set out until the **d** that it was taken up.
40:38 cloud of the LORD was on the tabernacle by **d**,
Lev 6:20 and his sons shall offer to the LORD on the **d**
Lev 7:15 of well-being shall be eaten on the **d** it is offered;
7:16 the **d** that you offer your sacrifice, and what is left
7:16 and what is left of it shall be eaten the next **d**;
7:17 of the sacrifice shall be burned up on the third **d**. C
7:18 the third **d**, it shall not be acceptable, nor shall it C
8:33 the **d** when your period of ordination is completed.
8:35 of the tent of meeting **d** and night for seven days,
9:1 the eighth **d** Moses summoned Aaron and his sons
12:3 On the eighth **d** the flesh of his foreskin shall
13:5 The priest shall examine him on the seventh **d**, B
13:6 priest shall examine him again on the seventh **d**, B
13:27 The priest shall examine him the seventh **d**; B
13:32 the seventh **d** the priest shall examine the itch; B
13:34 the seventh **d** the priest shall examine the itch; B
13:51 He shall examine the disease on the seventh **d**. B
14:9 On the seventh **d** he shall shave all his hair: B
14:10 On the eighth **d** he shall take two male lambs
14:23 the eighth **d** he shall bring them for his cleansing
14:39 The priest shall come again on the seventh **d** B
15:14 On the eighth **d** he shall take two turtledoves
15:29 On the eighth **d** she shall take two turtledoves
16:29 In the seventh month, on the tenth **d** of the month,
16:30 For on this **d** atonement shall be made for you,
19:6 It shall be eaten on the same **d** you offer it,
19:6 on the same day you offer it, or on the next **d**;
19:6 over until the third **d** shall be consumed in fire. C
19:7 If it is eaten at all on the third **d**, C
22:27 and from the eighth **d** on it shall be acceptable as
22:28 an animal with its young on the same **d**.
22:30 It shall be eaten on the same **d**;
23:3 but the seventh **d** is a sabbath of complete rest, B
23:5 on the fourteenth **d** of the month, at twilight,
23:6 on the fifteenth **d** of the same month is the festival
23:7 On the first **d** you shall have a holy convocation; D
23:8 the seventh **d** there shall be a holy convocation: B
23:11 on the **d** after the sabbath the priest shall raise it.
23:12 On the **d** when you raise the sheaf,
23:14 that very **d**, until you have brought the offering
23:15 And from the **d** after the sabbath,
23:15 from the **d** on which you bring the sheaf of
23:16 until the **d** after the seventh sabbath, fifty days;
23:21 On that same **d** you shall make proclamation;
23:24 the seventh month, on the first **d** of the month, D
23:24 you shall observe a **d** of complete rest,
23:27 the tenth **d** of this seventh month is the day
23:27 of this seventh month is the **d** of atonement;
23:28 and you shall do no work during that entire **d**;
23:28 for it is a **d** of atonement,
23:29 not practice self-denial during that entire **d** shall
23:30 anyone who does any work during that entire **d**,
23:32 on the ninth **d** of the month at evening,
23:34 On the fifteenth **d** of this seventh month,
23:35 The first **d** shall be a holy convocation; D
23:36 the eighth **d** you shall observe a holy convocation
23:37 sacrifices and drink offerings, each on its proper **d**
23:39 Now, the fifteenth **d** of the seventh month,
23:39 a complete rest on the first **d**, D
23:39 and a complete rest on the eighth **d**.
23:40 first **d** you shall take the fruit of majestic trees, D
24:8 Every sabbath **d** Aaron shall set them in order
25:9 on the tenth **d** of the seventh month—on the **d** of
atonement—
27:23 and the assessment shall be paid as of that **d**,
Nu 1:1 on the first **d** of the second month, D
1:18 the first **d** of the second month they assembled D
6:9 then they shall shave the head on the **d**
6:9 on the seventh **d** they shall shave it. B
6:10 On the eighth **d** they shall bring two turtledoves
6:11 They shall sanctify the head that same **d**,
7:1 On the **d** when Moses had finished setting up
7:11 one leader each **d**, for the dedication of the altar. K
7:12 the first **d** was Nahshon son of Amminadab, D
7:18 On the second **d** Nethanel son of Zuar,
7:24 On the third **d** Eliab son of Helon, C
7:30 On the fourth **d** Elizur son of Shedeur,
7:36 On the fifth **d** Shelumiel son of Zurishaddai,
7:42 On the sixth **d** Eliasaph son of Deuel,
7:48 On the seventh **d** Elishama son of Ammihud, B
7:54 On the eighth **d** Gamaliel son of Pedahzur,
7:60 On the ninth **d** Abidan son of Gideoni,
7:66 On the tenth **d** Ahiezer son of Ammishaddai,
7:72 On the eleventh **d** Pagiel son of Ochran,
7:78 On the twelfth **d** Ahira son of Enan,
8:17 the **d** that I struck down all the firstborn in the land
9:3 On the fourteenth **d** of this month, at twilight,
9:5 on the fourteenth **d** of the month, at twilight,
9:6 that they could not keep the passover on that **d**. A
9:6 They came before Moses and Aaron on that **d**, A
9:11 In the second month on the fourteenth **d**,
9:15 On the **d** the tabernacle was set up,
9:16 the cloud covered it by **d** and the appearance
9:21 or if it continued for a **d** and a night,
10:11 on the twentieth **d** of the month,
10:34 over them by **d** when they set out from the camp.
11:19 You shall eat not only one **d**, or two days, E
11:32 So the people worked all that **d** and night and all
the next **d**, gathering the quails;
14:14 in front of them, in a pillar of cloud by **d** and in
14:34 for every **d** a year, you shall bear your iniquity, F
15:23 from the **d** the LORD gave commandment
15:32 a man gathering sticks on the sabbath **d**.
16:41 On the next **d**, however, the whole congregation
17:8 into the tent of the covenant on the next **d**,
19:12 the water on the third **d** and on the seventh day, C
19:12 the water on the third day and on the seventh **d**, B
19:12 if they do not purify themselves on the third **d** C
19:12 on the third day and on the seventh **d**, B
Nu 19:19 the unclean ones on the third **d** and on C
19:19 on the third day and on the seventh **d**, B
19:19 thus purifying them on the seventh **d**. B
22:30 which you have ridden all your life to this **d**?
22:41 On the next **d** Balak took Balaam and brought him
25:18 she was killed on the **d** of the plague that resulted
28:9 On the sabbath **d**: two male lambs a year old
28:16 On the fourteenth **d** of the first month there shall
28:17 And on the fifteenth **d** of this month is a festival;
28:18 On the first **d** there shall be a holy convocation. D
28:25 the seventh **d** you shall have a holy convocation; B
28:26 On the **d** of the first fruits,
29:1 On the first **d** of the seventh month you shall D
29:1 It is a **d** for you to blow the trumpets,
29:7 the tenth **d** of this seventh month you shall have
29:12 the fifteenth **d** of the seventh month you shall have
29:17 On the second **d**: twelve young bulls,
29:20 On the third **d**: eleven bulls, C
29:23 On the fourth **d**: ten bulls,
29:26 On the fifth **d**: nine bulls, two rams,
29:29 On the sixth **d**: eight bulls,
29:32 On the seventh **d**: seven bulls, B
29:35 On the eighth **d** you shall have a solemn assembly;
30:14 if her husband says nothing to her from **d** to **d**,
31:19 on the third and on the seventh **d**. B
31:24 You must wash your clothes on the seventh **d**, B
32:10 The LORD's anger was kindled on that **d** A
33:3 on the fifteenth **d** of the first month;
33:3 on the **d** after the passover
33:38 on the first **d** of the fifth month. D
Dt 1:3 on the first **d** of the eleventh month, D
1:33 in fire by night, and in the cloud by **d**,
2:22 and settle in their place even to this **d**.
2:25 This **d** I will begin to put the dread and fear of you
3:14 after himself, Havvoth-jair, as it is to this **d**.)
4:32 ever since the **d** that God created human beings on
5:12 Observe the sabbath **d** and keep it holy,
5:14 the seventh **d** is a sabbath to the LORD your God; B
5:15 your God commanded you to keep the sabbath **d**.
9:7 the LORD from the **d** you came out of the land
9:10 to you at the mountain out of the fire on the **d** of
10:4 to you on the mountain out of the fire on the **d** of
10:8 and to bless in his name, to this **d**.
11:4 so that the LORD has destroyed them to this **d**;
16:3 the **d** of your departure from the land of Egypt.
16:4 on the evening of the first **d** shall remain D
16:6 the time of **d** when you departed from Egypt.
16:8 the seventh **d** there shall be a solemn assembly B
18:16 at Horeb on the **d** of the assembly when you said:
21:16 on the **d** when he wills his possessions to his sons,
21:23 you shall bury him that same **d**,
26:16 This very **d** the LORD your God is commanding
27:2 the **d** that you cross over the Jordan into the land
27:9 This very **d** you have become the people of
27:11 The same **d** Moses charged the people as follows:
28:32 you will strain your eyes looking for them all **d**
28:66 night and **d** you shall be in dread,
29:4 But to this **d** the LORD has not given you a mind
31:17 My anger will be kindled against them in that **d**.
31:17 In that **d** they will say,
31:18 On that **d** I will surely hide my face on account A
31:22 That very **d** Moses wrote this song and taught it to
32:35 because the **d** of their calamity is at hand, L
32:48 On that very **d** the LORD addressed Moses
33:12 the High God surrounds him all **d** long—
34:6 but no one knows his burial place to this **d**.
Jos 1:8 you shall meditate on it **d** and night,
3:7 “This **d** I will begin to exalt you in the sight
4:9 and they are there to this **d**.)
4:14 On that **d** the LORD exalted Joshua in the sight A
4:19 of the Jordan on the tenth **d** of the first month,
5:9 And so that place is called Gilgal to this **d**.
5:10 in the evening on the fourteenth **d** of the month in
5:11 On the **d** after the passover, on that very **d**,
5:12 The manna ceased on the **d** they ate the produce of
6:4 On the seventh **d** you shall march around B
6:10 until the **d** I tell you to shout.
6:14 the second **d** they marched around the city once
6:15 On the seventh **d** they rose early, at dawn, B
6:15 It was only on that **d** that they marched around A
7:26 a great heap of stones that remains to this **d**.
7:26 that place to this **d** is called the Valley of Achor.
8:25 The total of those who fell that **d**,
8:28 as it is to this **d**.
8:29 which stands there to this **d**.
9:12 on the **d** we set out to come to you, but now, see,
9:17 and reached their cities on the third **d**. C
9:27 on that **d** Joshua made them hewers of wood A
9:27 for the altar of the LORD, to continue to this **d**,
10:12 On the **d** when the LORD gave the Amorites over
10:13 and did not hurry to set for about a whole **d**.
10:14 There has been no **d** like it before or since,
10:27 which remain to this very **d**.
10:28 Joshua took Makkedah on that **d**, A
10:32 and he took it on the second **d**,
10:35 and they took it that **d**, and struck it with the edge
10:35 and every person in it he utterly destroyed that **d**,
13:13 Geshur and Maacath live within Israel to this **d**.
14:9 And Moses swore on that **d**, saying, A
14:11 I am still as strong today as I was on the **d**
14:12 of which the LORD spoke on that **d**; A
14:12 you heard on that **d** how the Anakim were there, A
14:14 of Caleb son of Jephunneh the Kenizzite to this **d**,
15:63 with the people of Judah in Jerusalem to this **d**.
16:10 the Canaanites have lived within Ephraim to this **d**
22:3 to this **d**, but have been careful to keep the charge
22:29 and turn away this **d** from following the LORD

Jos 23: 8 as you have done to this **d.**
23: 9 no one has been able to withstand you to this **d.**
24:15 choose this **d** whom you will serve,
24:25 So Joshua made a covenant with the people that **d,**
Jdg 1:21 in Jerusalem among the Benjaminites to this **d.**
1:26 that is its name to this **d.**
3:30 Moab was subdued that **d** under the hand of Israel.
4:14 the **d** on which the LORD has given Sisera
4:23 on that **d** God subdued King Jabin of Canaan A
5: 1 Barak son of Abinoam sang on that **d,** saying: A
6:24 To this **d** it still stands at Ophrah,
6:27 of his family and the townspeople to do it by **d,**
6:32 on that **d** Gideon was called Jerubbaal, A
9:18 up against my father's house this **d,**
9:19 with his house this **d,** then rejoice in Abimelech,
9:42 the following **d** the people went out into the fields.
9:45 Abimelech fought against the city all that **d;**
10: 4 and are called Havvoth-jair to this **d.**
10:15 to you; but deliver us this **d!"**
12: 3 Why then have you come up to me this **d,**
13: 7 to God from birth to the **d** of his death.' " I
13:10 to me the other **d** has appeared to me."
14:15 On the fourth **d** they said to Samson's wife,
14:17 she nagged him, on the seventh **d** he told her. B
14:18 on the seventh **d** before the sun went down, B
15:19 which is at Lehi to this **d.**
16:16 she had nagged him with her words **d** after **d,** H
18:12 that place is called Mahaneh-dan to this **d;**
19: 5 On the fourth **d** they got up early in the morning,
19: 8 the fifth **d** he got up early in the morning to leave;
19: 8 So they lingered until the **d** declined,
19: 9 the **d** has worn on until it is almost evening.
19: 9 See, the **d** has drawn to a close.
19:11 When they were near Jebus, the **d** was far spent,
19:30 'Has such a thing ever happened since the **d** that
19:30 up from the land of Egypt until this **d?**
20:15 On that **d** the Benjaminites mustered A
20:21 and struck down on that **d** twenty-two thousand A
20:22 where they had formed it on the first **d.** D
20:24 against the Benjaminites the second **d.**
20:25 against them from Gibeah the second **d,**
20:26 they fasted that **d** until evening.
20:30 up against the Benjaminites on the third **d,** C
20:35 one hundred men of Benjamin that **d,**
20:46 So all who fell that **d**
21: 4 On the next **d,** the people got up early,
21: 6 and said, "One tribe is cut off from Israel this **d.**
Ru 4: 5 **d** you acquire the field from the hand of Naomi,
4:14 who has not left you this **d** without next-of-kin;
1Sa 1: 4 On the **d** when Elkanah sacrificed,
1:11 before you as a nazirite until the **d** of his death. I
2:34 both of them shall die on the same **d.**
3:12 On that **d** I will fulfill against Eli all A
4:12 and came to Shiloh the same **d,**
5: 3 When the people of Ashdod rose early the next **d,**
5: 5 on the threshold of Dagon in Ashdod to this **d.**
6:15 and presented sacrifices on that **d** to the LORD. A
6:16 they returned that **d** to Ekron.
6:18 to this **d** in the field of Joshua of Beth-shemesh.
7: 2 the **d** that the ark was lodged at Kiriath-jearim,
7: 6 They fasted that **d,** and said,
7:10 the LORD thundered with a mighty voice that **d**
8: 8 the **d** I brought them up out of Egypt to this **d,**
8:18 in that **d** you will cry out because of your king,
8:18 but the LORD will not answer you in that **d."**
9:15 Now the **d** before Saul came,
9:24 So Saul ate with Samuel that **d.**
10: 9 and all these signs were fulfilled that **d.**
11:11 The next **d** Saul put the people in three companies.
11:11 down the Ammonites until the heat of the **d;**
11:13 But Saul said, "No one shall be put to death this **d,**
12: 2 I have led you from my youth until this **d.**
12: 5 and his anointed is witness this **d,**
12:18 and the LORD sent thunder and rain that **d;**
13:22 on the **d** of the battle neither sword nor spear was
14: 1 One **d** Jonathan son of Saul said to E
14:23 So the LORD gave Israel the victory that **d.**
14:24 Now Saul committed a very rash act on that **d.** A
14:28 saying, 'Cursed be anyone who eats food this **d.'**
14:31 the Philistines that **d** from Michmash to Aijalon,
14:37 But he did not answer him that **d.**
15:28 the kingdom of Israel from you this very **d,**
15:35 not see Saul again until the **d** of his death, I
16:13 upon David from that **d** forward.
17:46 This very **d** the LORD will deliver you
17:46 the dead bodies of the Philistine army this very **d**
18: 2 Saul took him that **d** and would not let him return
18: 9 So Saul eyed David from that **d** on.
18:10 next **d** an evil spirit from God rushed upon Saul,
18:10 playing the lyre, as he did **d** by **d.** P
19:24 He lay naked all that **d** and all that night.
20:12 about this time tomorrow, or on the third **d,** C
20:19 On the **d** after tomorrow, you shall go
20:26 Saul did not say anything that **d;**
20:27 But on the second **d,** the **d** after the new moon,
20:34 in fierce anger and ate no food on the second **d** of
21: 6 be replaced by hot bread on the **d** it is taken away.
21: 7 of the servants of Saul was there that **d,** detained
21:10 David rose and fled that **d** from Saul;
22:18 on that **d** he killed eighty-five who wore A
22:22 David said to Abiathar, "I knew on that **d,** A
23:14 Saul sought him every **d,** but the LORD did F
24: 4 "Here is the **d** of which the LORD said to you,
24:10 This very **d** your eyes have seen how
24:19 with good for what you have done to me this **d.**
25: 8 for we have come on a feast **d.**
25:16 they were a wall to us both by night and by **d,**
1Sa 26:10 or his **d** will come to die;
27: 1 "I shall now perish one **d** by the hand of Saul; E
27: 6 So that **d** Achish gave him Ziklag;
27: 6 to the kings of Judah to this **d.**
28:20 for he had eaten nothing all **d** and all night.
29: 3 to me I have found no fault in him to this **d."**
29: 6 for I have found nothing wrong in you from the **d**
29: 8 in your servant from the **d** I entered your service
30: 1 and his men came to Ziklag on the third **d,** C
30:17 from twilight until the evening of the next **d.**
30:25 From that **d** forward he made it a statute and
30:25 it continues to the present **d.**
31: 6 and all his men died together on the same **d.**
31: 8 The next **d,** when the Philistines came to strip
2Sa 1: 2 On the third **d,** a man came from Saul's camp, C
2:17 The battle was very fierce that **d;**
2:32 and the **d** broke upon them at Hebron.
3:35 to eat something while it was still **d;**
3:37 So all the people and all Israel understood that **d**
3:38 a prince and a great man has fallen this **d** in Israel?
4: 3 and are there as resident aliens to this **d).**
4: 5 the heat of the **d** they came to the house of Ishbaal,
4: 8 the LORD has avenged my lord the king this **d**
5: 8 David had said on that **d,** A
6: 8 so that place is called Perez-uzzah, to this **d.**
6: 9 David was afraid of the LORD that **d;**
6:23 of Saul had no child to the **d** of her death. I
7: 6 I have not lived in a house since the **d** I brought up
7: 6 up the people of Israel from Egypt to this **d,**
11:12 Uriah remained in Jerusalem that **d.** On the next **d,**
12:18 On the seventh **d** the child died. B
13:32 from the **d** Amnon raped his sister Tamar.
13:37 David mourned for his son **d** after **d.** H
18: 7 and the slaughter there was great on that **d,** A
18: 8 forest claimed more victims that **d** than the sword.
18:18 It is called Absalom's Monument to this **d.**
18:20 you may carry tidings another **d,**
18:31 For the LORD has vindicated you this **d,**
19: 2 the victory that **d** was turned into mourning for all
19: 2 for the troops heard that **d,**
19: 3 the city that **d** as soldiers steal in who are ashamed
19:19 how your servant did wrong on the **d** my lord
19:20 therefore, see, I have come this **d,**
19:22 Shall anyone be put to death in Israel this **d?**
19:22 do I not know that I am this **d** king over Israel?"
19:24 from the **d** the king left until the **d** he came back
20: 3 So they were shut up until the **d** of their death, I
21:10 the birds of the air to come on the bodies by **d,**
21:12 on the **d** the Philistines killed Saul on Gilboa.
22: 1 the LORD the words of this song on the **d** when
22:19 They came upon me in the **d** of my calamity, L
23:10 The LORD brought about a great victory that **d.**
23:20 He also went down and killed a lion in a pit on a **d**
24:18 That **d** Gad came to David and said to him,
1Ki 1:30 so will I do this **d."**
2: 8 who cursed me with a terrible curse on the **d**
2:37 For on the **d** you go out,
2:42 on the **d** you go out and go to any place whatever,
3:18 Then on the third **d** after I gave birth, C
4:22 Solomon's provision for one **d** was thirty cors E
8: 8 they are there to this **d.**
8:16 the **d** that I brought my people Israel out of Egypt,
8:24 with your mouth and have this **d** fulfilled
8:29 that your eyes may be open night and **d**
8:59 be near to the LORD our God **d** and night,
8:59 the cause of his people Israel, as each **d** requires; K
8:61 and keeping his commandments, as at this **d."**
8:64 The same **d** the king consecrated the middle of
8:66 On the eighth **d** he sent the people away;
9:13 So they are called the land of Cabul to this **d.**
9:21 and so they are to this **d.**
10:12 or been seen to this **d.**
12:12 all the people came to Rehoboam the third **d,** C
12:12 "Come to me again the third **d."** C
12:19 in rebellion against the house of David to this **d.**
12:32 Jeroboam appointed a festival on the fifteenth **d** of
12:33 in Bethel on the fifteenth **d** in the eighth month,
13: 3 He gave a sign the same **d,** saying,
13:11 that the man of God had done that **d** in Bethel;
16:16 king over Israel that **d** in the camp
17:14 not fail until the **d** that the LORD sends rain on
18:36 let it be known this **d** that you are God in Israel,
20:29 Then on the seventh **d** the battle began; B
20:29 thousand Aramean foot soldiers in one **d.** E
22:25 "You will find out on that **d** when you go in A
22:35 The battle grew hot that **d,**
2Ki 2:22 So the water has been wholesome to this **d,**
3:20 The next **d,** about the time of
4: 8 One **d** Elisha was passing through Shunem, E
4:11 One **d** when he came there, E
4:18 went out one **d** to his father among the reapers. E
6:29 The next **d** I said to her,
7: 9 This is a **d** of good news;
8: 6 the revenue of the fields from the **d** that she left
8:15 But the next **d** he took the bed-cover and dipped it
8:22 in revolt against the rule of Judah to this **d.**
10:27 and made it a latrine to this **d.**
14: 7 he called it Jokthe-el, which is its name to this **d.**
15: 5 so that he was leprous to the **d** of his death, I
16: 6 Edomites came to Elath, where they live to this **d.**
17:23 from their own land to Assyria until this **d.**
17:34 To this **d** they continue to practice
17:41 this **d** their children and their children's children
19: 3 "Thus says Hezekiah, This **d** is a day of distress,
19: 3 "Thus says Hezekiah, This day is a **d** of distress, O
20: 5 on the third **d** you shall go up to the house of C
20: 8 up to the house of the LORD on the third **d?"** C
2Ki 20:17 which your ancestors have stored up until this **d,**
21:15 since the **d** their ancestors came out of Egypt, even to this **d."**
25: 1 in the tenth month, on the tenth **d** of the month,
25: 3 the ninth **d** of the fourth month the famine became
25: 8 on the seventh **d** of the month— B
25:27 on the twenty-seventh **d** of the month,
25:29 Every **d** of his life he dined regularly in F
25:30 a portion every **d,** as long as he lived. F
1Ch 4:41 and exterminated them to this **d,**
4:43 and they have lived there to this **d.**
5:26 Habor, Hara, and the river Gozan, to this **d.**
9:33 for they were on duty **d** and night.
10: 8 next **d** when the Philistines came to strip the dead,
11:22 He also went down and killed a lion in a pit on a **d**
12:22 Indeed from **d** to **d** people kept coming to David
13:11 so that place is called Perez-uzzah to this **d.**
13:12 David was afraid of God that **d;**
16: 7 on that **d** David first appointed the singing of A
16:23 Tell of his salvation from **d** to **d.**
16:37 before the ark as each **d** required, K
17: 5 since the **d** I brought out Israel to this very **d,**
26:17 On the east there were six Levites each **d,** K
26:17 the north four each **d,** on the south four each K
26:17 on the south four each **d,** as well as two and K
29:21 On the next **d** they offered sacrifices
29:22 before the LORD on that **d** with great joy. A
2Ch 3: 2 to build on the second **d** of the second month of
5: 9 they are there to this **d.**
6: 5 the **d** that I brought my people out of the land
6:15 with your mouth and this **d** have fulfilled
6:20 be open **d** and night toward this house,
7: 9 On the eighth **d** they held a solemn assembly;
7:10 On the twenty-third **d** of the seventh month he sent
8:13 the duty of each **d** required, offering according K
8:14 the duty of each **d** required, and the gatekeepers K
8:16 of Solomon was accomplished from the **d**
10:12 all the people came to Rehoboam the third **d,** C
10:12 "Come to me again the third **d."** C
10:19 in rebellion against the house of David to this **d.**
15:11 They sacrificed to the LORD on that **d,** A
18:24 "You will find out on that **d** when you go in A
18:34 The battle grew hot that **d,**
20:26 On the fourth **d** they assembled in the Valley
20:26 the Valley of Beracah to this **d.**
21:10 in revolt against the rule of Judah to this **d.**
21:15 until your bowels come out, **d** after **d,** H
24:11 So they did **d** after **d,** H
26:21 King Uzziah was leprous to the **d** of his death, I
28: 6 in Judah in one **d,** all of them valiant warriors, E
29:17 the first **d** of the first month, and on the eighth D
29:17 and on the eighth **d** of the month they came to
29:17 on the sixteenth **d** of the first month they finished.
30:15 on the fourteenth **d** of the second month.
30:21 Levites and the priests praised the LORD **d** by **d,** P
31:16 of the LORD as the duty of each **d** required, K
35: 1 the passover lamb on the fourteenth **d** of
35:16 all the service of the LORD was prepared that **d,**
35:25 of Josiah in their laments to this **d.**
Ezr 3: 4 to the ordinance, as required for each **d,** K
3: 6 From the first **d** of the seventh month they D
6: 9 let that be given to them **d** by **d** without fail, P
6:15 and this house was finished on the third **d** of C
6:19 On the fourteenth **d** of the first month
7: 9 On the first **d** of the first month the journey up D
7: 9 first **d** of the fifth month he came to Jerusalem, D
8:31 the twelfth **d** of the first month, to go to Jerusalem;
8:33 On the fourth **d,** within the house of our God,
9: 7 of our ancestors to this **d** we have been deep
10: 9 on the twentieth **d** of the month.
10:13 Nor is this a task for one **d** or for two, E
10:16 On the first **d** of the tenth month they sat down D
10:17 By the first **d** of the first month they had come D
Ne 1: 6 now pray before you **d** and night for your servants,
4: 2 Will they finish it in a **d?**
4: 9 a guard as a protection against them **d** and night.
4:16 From that **d** on, half of my servants worked
4:22 be a guard for us by night and may labor by **d."**
5:11 Restore to them, this very **d,** their fields,
5:18 that which was prepared for one **d** was one ox E
6:10 One **d** when I went into the house E
6:15 So the wall was finished on the twenty-fifth **d** of
8: 2 This was on the first **d** of the seventh month. D
8: 9 "This **d** is holy to the LORD your God;
8:10 for this **d** is holy to our LORD;
8:11 "Be quiet, for this **d** is holy; do not be grieved."
8:13 the second **d** the heads of ancestral houses of all
8:17 the days of Jeshua son of Nun to that **d** the people
8:18 And **d** by **d,** from the first day to the last day, P
8:18 And day by day, from the first **d** to the last day, D
8:18 And day by day, from the first day to the last **d,** Q
8:18 and on the eighth **d** there was a solemn assembly,
9: 1 on the twenty-fourth **d** of this month the people
9: 3 of the LORD their God for a fourth part of the **d,**
9:10 a name for yourself, which remains to this **d.**
9:12 you led them by **d** with a pillar of cloud,
9:19 that led them in the way did not leave them by **d,**
9:36 Here we are, slaves to this **d—**
10:31 the sabbath **d** to sell, we will not buy it from them
10:31 from them on the sabbath or on a holy **d;**
11:23 for the singers, as was required every **d.** F
12:43 They offered great sacrifices that **d** and rejoiced,
12:44 On that **d** men were appointed over the A
13: 1 On that **d** they read from the book of Moses in A
13:15 into Jerusalem on the sabbath **d;**
13:17 profaning the sabbath **d?**
13:19 from being brought in on the sabbath **d.**

Ne 13:22 to keep the sabbath **d** holy.
Est 1:10 On the seventh **d,** when the king was merry B
1:18 This very **d** the noble ladies of Persia
2:11 Every **d** Mordecai would walk around in front of F
3:4 to him **d** after **d** and he would not listen to them, H
3:7 before Haman for the **d** and for the month,
3:7 the lot fell on the thirteenth **d** of the twelfth month,
3:12 on the thirteenth **d** of the first month, and an edict,
3:13 in one **d,** the thirteenth day of the twelfth month, E
3:13 in one day, the thirteenth **d** of the twelfth month,
3:14 calling on all the peoples to be ready for that **d.**
4:16 and neither eat nor drink for three days, night or **d.**
5:1 the third **d** Esther put on her royal robes and C
5:9 Haman went out that **d** happy and in good spirits.
7:2 On the second **d,** as they were drinking wine,
8:1 On that **d** King Ahasuerus gave to Queen Esther A
8:9 the month of Sivan, on the twenty-third **d;**
8:12 on a single **d** throughout all the provinces
8:12 on the thirteenth **d** of the twelfth month,
8:13 on that **d** to take revenge on their enemies. A
9:1 which is the month of Adar, on the thirteenth **d,**
9:1 on the very **d** when the enemies of the Jews hoped
9:1 but which had been changed to a **d** when
9:11 That very **d** the number of those killed in
9:15 also on the fourteenth **d** of the month of Adar
9:17 This was on the thirteenth **d** of the month of Adar,
9:17 on the fourteenth **d** they rested and made that a **d**
9:18 in Susa gathered on the thirteenth **d** and on
9:18 and rested on the fifteenth **d,** making that a **d** of
9:19 the fourteenth **d** of the month of Adar as a **d** for
9:21 the fourteenth **d** of the month Adar and also the
fifteenth **d** of the same
Job 1:6 One **d** the heavenly beings came E
1:13 One **d** when his sons and daughters were eating E
2:1 One **d** the heavenly beings came E
3:1 After this Job opened his mouth and cursed the **d**
3:3 "Let the **d** perish in which I was born,
3:4 Let that **d** be darkness!
3:5 let the blackness of the **d** terrify it.
15:23 They know that a **d** of darkness is ready at hand;
17:12 They make night into **d;** 'The light,'
20:28 dragged off in the **d** of God's wrath. M
21:30 that the wicked are spared in the **d** of calamity, L
21:30 and are rescued in the **d** of wrath? M
24:16 by **d** they shut themselves up;
30:25 Did I not weep for those whose **d** was hard?
38:23 for the **d** of battle and war?
Ps 1:2 and on his law they meditate **d** and night.
7:11 and a God who has indignation every **d.** F
13:2 and have sorrow in my heart all **d** long?
18:T *on the d when the LORD delivered him*
18:18 They confronted me in the **d** of my calamity; L
19:2 **D** to **d** pours forth speech,
20:1 The LORD answer you in the **d** of trouble! N
22:2 O my God, I cry by **d,** but you do not answer;
25:5 for you I wait all **d** long.
27:5 he will hide me in his shelter in the **d** of trouble; N
32:3 through my groaning all **d** long.
32:4 For **d** and night your hand was heavy upon me;
35:28 and of your praise all **d** long.
37:13 for he sees that their **d** is coming.
38:6 all **d** long I go around mourning.
38:12 and meditate treachery all **d** long.
41:1 the LORD delivers them in the **d** of trouble. N
42:3 My tears have been my food **d** and night,
42:8 By **d** the LORD commands his steadfast love,
44:15 All **d** long my disgrace is before me,
44:22 Because of you we are being killed all **d** long,
50:15 Call on me in the **d** of trouble; N
52:1 done against the godly? All **d** long
55:10 **D** and night they go around it on its walls,
56:1 all **d** long foes oppress me;
56:2 my enemies trample on me all **d** long,
56:5 All **d** long they seek to injure my cause;
56:9 Then my enemies will retreat in the **d** when I call.
59:16 for me and a refuge in the **d** of my distress. O
61:8 as I pay my vows **d** after **d.** H
71:8 and with your glory all **d** long.
71:15 of your deeds of salvation all **d** long,
71:24 All **d** long my tongue will talk
72:15 and blessings invoked for him all **d** long.
73:14 For all **d** long I have been plagued,
74:16 Yours is the **d,** yours also the night;
74:22 remember how the impious scoff at you all **d** long.
77:2 In the **d** of my trouble I seek the Lord; N
78:9 turned back on the **d** of battle.
78:42 or the **d** when he redeemed them from the foe;
81:3 at the full moon, on our festal **d.**
84:10 For a **d** in your courts is better than
86:3 O Lord, for to you do I cry all **d** long.
86:7 In the **d** of my trouble I call on you, N
88:9 Every **d** I call on you, O LORD; F
88:17 They surround me like a flood all **d** long;
89:16 they exult in your name all **d** long,
91:5 or the arrow that flies by **d,**
92:T *A Song for the Sabbath D.*
95:8 as on the **d** at Massah in the wilderness,
96:2 tell of his salvation from **d** to **d.**
102:2 hide your face from me in the **d** of my distress. O
102:2 answer me speedily in the **d** when I call.
102:8 All **d** long my enemies taunt me;
109:19 like a belt that he wears every **d."** F
110:3 the **d** you lead your forces on the holy mountains.
110:5 he will shatter kings on the **d** of his wrath. M
118:24 This is the **d** that the LORD has made;
119:97 It is my meditation all **d** long.
119:164 a **d** I praise you for your righteous ordinances.
Ps 121:6 The sun shall not strike you by **d,**
136:8 over the **d,** for his steadfast love endures forever;
137:7 against the Edomites the **d** of Jerusalem's fall,
138:3 On the **d** I called, you answered me,
139:12 the night is as bright as the **d,**
140:7 you have covered my head in the **d** of battle.
145:2 Every **d** I will bless you, F
146:4 on that very **d** their plans perish.
Pr 4:18 which shines brighter and brighter until full **d.**
11:4 Riches do not profit in the **d** of wrath, M
16:4 even the wicked for the **d** of trouble. N
21:26 All **d** long the wicked covet,
21:31 The horse is made ready for the **d** of battle,
24:10 If you faint in the **d** of adversity,
27:1 for you do not know what a **d** may bring.
27:10 house of your kindred in the **d** of your calamity. L
27:15 on a rainy **d** and a contentious wife are alike;
Ecc 7:1 and the **d** of death, than the day of birth. I
7:1 and the day of death, than the **d** of birth.
7:14 In the **d** of prosperity be joyful,
7:14 and in the **d** of adversity consider;
8:8 or power over the **d** of death; I
8:16 how one's eyes see sleep neither **d** nor night,
12:3 in the **d** when the guards of the house tremble,
SS 2:17 Until the **d** breathes and the shadows flee, turn,
3:11 with which his mother crowned him on the **d**
3:11 on the **d** of the gladness of his heart.
4:6 Until the **d** breathes and the shadows flee,
8:8 on the **d** when she is spoken for?
Isa 2:11 and the LORD alone will be exalted in that **d.**
2:12 of hosts has a **d** against all that is proud and lofty,
2:17 and the LORD alone will be exalted on that **d.** A
2:20 On that **d** people will throw away to the moles A
3:7 But the other will cry out on that **d,** saying, A
3:18 In that **d** the Lord will take away the finery of
4:1 Seven women shall take hold of one man in that **d,**
4:2 On that **d** the branch of the LORD shall be A
4:5 by **d** and smoke and the shining of a flaming fire
4:6 a shade by **d** from the heat,
5:30 They will roar over it on that **d,** A
7:17 since the **d** that Ephraim departed from Judah—
7:18 On that **d** the LORD will whistle for the fly that A
7:20 On that **d** the Lord will shave with a razor hired A
7:21 On that **d** one will keep alive a young cow A
7:23 On that **d** every place where there used to be A
9:4 you have broken as on the **d** of Midian.
9:14 palm branch and reed in one **d—** E
10:3 What will you do on the **d** of punishment,
10:17 and devour his thorns and briers in one **d.** E
10:20 On that **d** the remnant of Israel and the survivors A
10:27 On that **d** his burden will be removed A
10:32 This very **d** he will halt at Nob,
11:10 On that **d** the root of Jesse shall stand as a signal A
11:11 On that **d** the Lord will extend his hand yet A
12:1 You will say in that **d:**
12:4 And you will say in that **d:**
13:6 Wail, for the **d** of the LORD is near; G
13:9 See, the **d** of the LORD comes, cruel, G
13:13 of the LORD of hosts in the **d** of his fierce anger.
14:12 How you are fallen from heaven, O **D** Star,
17:4 On that **d** the glory of Jacob will be brought low, A
17:7 On that **d** people will regard their Maker, A
17:9 On that **d** their strong cities will be like A
17:11 the **d** that you plant them, and make them blossom
17:11 yet the harvest will flee away in a **d** of grief
19:16 On that **d** the Egyptians will be like women, A
19:18 On that **d** there will be five cities in the land A
19:19 On that **d** there will be an altar to the LORD in A
19:21 and the Egyptians will know the LORD on that **d,** A
19:23 On that **d** there will be a highway from Egypt A
19:24 On that **d** Israel will be the third with Egypt A
20:6 In that **d** the inhabitants of this coastland will say,
21:8 O Lord, continually by **d,**
22:5 For the Lord GOD of hosts has a **d** of tumult
22:8 On that **d** you looked to the weapons of the A
22:12 that **d** the Lord GOD of hosts called to weeping
22:20 On that **d** I will call my servant Eliakim son A
22:25 On that **d,** says the LORD of hosts, A
23:15 that **d** Tyre will be forgotten for seventy years,
24:21 On that **d** the LORD will punish the host of A
25:9 It will be said on that **d,** Lo, this is our God; A
26:1 On that **d** this song will be sung in the land A
27:1 On that **d** the LORD with his cruel and great A
27:2 On that **d:** A pleasant vineyard, sing about it! A
27:3 I guard it night and **d** so that no one can harm it;
27:8 with his fierce blast he removed them in the **d** of
27:12 On that **d** the LORD will thresh from the channel A
27:13 And on that **d** a great trumpet will be blown, A
28:5 In that **d** the LORD of hosts will be a garland
28:19 by morning it will pass through, by **d** and by night;
29:18 On that **d** the deaf shall hear the words of a A
30:23 On that **d** your cattle will graze in broad A
30:25 on a **d** of the great slaughter, when the towers fall.
30:26 on the **d** when the LORD binds up the injuries
31:7 on that **d** all of you shall throw away your idols A
34:8 For the LORD has a **d** of vengeance,
34:10 Night and **d** it shall not be quenched;
37:3 "Thus says Hezekiah, This **d** is a day of distress,
37:3 "Thus says Hezekiah, This day is a **d** of distress, O
38:12 from **d** to night you bring me to an end;
38:13 from **d** to night you bring me to an end.
38:19 living, the living, they thank you, as I do this **d;**
39:6 which your ancestors have stored up until this **d,**
47:9 upon you in a moment, in one **d:** E
49:8 on a **d** of salvation I have helped you;
51:13 You fear continually all **d** long because of the fury
52:5 and continually, all **d** long, my name is despised.
Isa 52:6 in that **d** they shall know that it is I who speak;
58:2 Yet **d** after **d** they seek me and delight to know H
58:3 Look, you serve your own interest on your fast **d,**
58:5 the fast that I choose, a **d** to humble oneself?
58:5 a **d** acceptable to the LORD?
58:13 from pursuing your own interests on my holy **d;**
58:13 a delight and the holy **d** of the LORD honorable; G
60:11 **d** and night they shall not be shut,
60:19 The sun shall no longer be your light by **d,**
61:2 and the **d** of vengeance of our God;
62:6 all **d** and all night they shall never be silent.
63:4 For the **d** of vengeance was in my heart,
65:2 I held out my hands all **d** long to a rebellious
65:5 a fire that burns all **d** long.
66:8 Shall a land be born in one **d?** E
Jer 3:25 from our youth even to this **d;**
4:9 On that **d,** says the LORD, A
6:4 "Woe to us, for the **d** declines,
7:22 the **d** that I brought your ancestors out of the land
7:25 the **d** that your ancestors came out of the land
7:25 until this **d,** I have persistently sent all my servants
7:25 the prophets to them, **d** after **d;** H
9:1 so that I might weep **d** and night for the slain
11:5 a land flowing with milk and honey, as at this **d.**
11:7 warning them persistently, even to this **d,** saying,
12:3 and set them apart for the **d** of slaughter.
14:17 Let my eyes run down with tears night and **d,**
15:9 her sun went down while it was yet **d;**
16:13 and there you shall serve other gods **d** and night,
16:19 my refuge in the **d** of trouble, N
17:16 nor have I desired the fatal **d.**
17:17 you are my refuge in the **d** of disaster;
17:18 bring on them the **d** of disaster;
17:21 not bear a burden on the sabbath **d** or bring it in by
17:22 but keep the sabbath **d** holy,
17:24 by the gates of this city on the sabbath **d,**
17:24 but keep the sabbath **d** holy and do no work on it,
17:27 to keep the sabbath **d** holy,
17:27 the sabbath **d,** then I will kindle a fire in its gates;
18:17 not my face, in the **d** of their calamity. L
20:7 I have become a laughingstock all **d** long;
20:8 for me a reproach and derision all **d** long.
20:14 Cursed be the **d** on which I was born!
20:14 **d** when my mother bore me, let it not be blessed!
25:3 to this **d,** the word of the LORD has come to me,
25:33 by the LORD on that **d** shall extend from one end A
27:22 until the **d** when I give attention to them,
30:7 that **d** is so great there is none like it;
30:8 On that **d,** says the LORD of hosts, A
31:6 be a **d** when sentinels will call in the hill country
31:35 by **d** and the fixed order of the moon and the stars
32:20 and to this **d** in Israel and among all humankind,
32:20 a name that continues to this very **d.**
32:31 from the **d** it was built until this **d,**
33:20 If any of you could break my covenant with the **d**
33:20 with the night, so that **d** and night would not come
33:25 not established my covenant with **d** and night and
35:14 and they drink none to this **d,**
36:2 from the **d** I spoke to you,
36:6 and on a fast **d** in the hearing of the people in
36:30 and his dead body shall be cast out to the heat by **d**
38:28 of the guard until the **d** that Jerusalem was taken.
39:2 in the fourth month, on the ninth **d** of the month,
39:16 be accomplished in your presence on that **d.** A
39:17 But I will save you on that **d,** says the LORD, A
41:4 On the **d** after the murder of Gedaliah,
44:10 They have shown no contrition or fear to this **d,**
44:22 without inhabitant, as it is to this **d.**
46:10 That **d** is the day of the Lord GOD of hosts,
46:10 That day is the **d** of the Lord GOD of hosts, R
46:10 a **d** of retribution,
46:21 for the **d** of their calamity has come upon them, L
47:4 the **d** that is coming to destroy all the Philistines,
48:41 The hearts of the warriors of Moab, on that **d,** A
49:22 the heart of the warriors of Edom in that **d** shall be
49:26 and all her soldiers shall be destroyed in that **d,**
50:27 Alas for them, their **d** has come,
50:30 and all her soldiers shall be destroyed on that **d,** A
50:31 your **d** has come, the time when I will punish you.
51:2 against her from every side on the **d** of trouble. N
52:4 in the tenth month, on the tenth **d** of the month,
52:6 the ninth **d** of the fourth month the famine became
52:11 and put him in prison until the **d** of his death. I
52:12 In the fifth month, on the tenth **d** of the month—
52:31 on the twenty-fifth **d** of the month,
52:33 and every **d** of his life he dined regularly at F
52:34 as long as he lived, up to the **d** of his death. I
La 1:12 the LORD inflicted on the **d** of his fierce anger.
1:13 he has left me stunned, faint all **d** long.
1:21 Bring on the **d** you have announced,
2:1 not remembered his footstool in the **d** of his anger.
2:7 in the house of the LORD as on a **d** of festival.
2:16 Ah, this is the **d** we longed for;
2:18 Let tears stream down like a torrent **d** and night!
2:21 in the **d** of your anger you have killed them,
2:22 from all around as if for a **d** of festival;
2:22 the **d** of the anger of the LORD no one escaped
3:3 again and again, all **d** long.
3:14 the object of their taunt-songs all **d** long.
3:62 of my assailants are against me all **d** long.
Eze 1:1 in the fourth month, on the fifth **d** of the month,
1:2 On the fifth **d** of the month (it was the fifth year of
1:28 Like the bow in a cloud on a rainy **d,**
2:3 transgressed against me to this very **d.**
4:6 forty days I assign you, one **d** for each year. E
4:10 that you eat shall be twenty shekels a **d** by weight;
7:7 The time has come, the **d** is near—

Eze 7:10 See, the **d**! See, it comes! Your doom has gone out.
7:12 The time has come, the **d** draws near;
7:19 gold cannot save them on the **d** of the wrath M
8: 1 on the fifth **d** of the month, as I sat in my house,
12: 3 and go into exile by **d** in their sight;
12: 4 by **d** in their sight, as baggage for exile;
12: 7 I brought out my baggage by **d**,
13: 5 that it might stand in battle on the **d** of the LORD. G
16: 4 the **d** you were born your navel cord was not cut,
16: 5 for you were abhorred on the **d** you were born.
16:56 a byword in your mouth in the **d** of your pride,
20: 1 in the fifth month, on the tenth **d** of the month,
20: 5 On the **d** when I chose Israel,
20: 6 On that **d** I swore to them that I would bring A
20:29 So it is called Bamah to this **d**.)
20:31 you defile yourselves with all your idols to this **d**.
21:25 wicked prince of Israel, you whose **d** has come,
21:29 whose **d** has come, the time of final punishment.
22: 4 you have brought your **d** near,
22:24 not rained upon in the **d** of indignation.
23:38 they have defiled my sanctuary on the same **d**
23:39 on the same **d** they came into my sanctuary
24: 1 in the tenth month, on the tenth **d** of the month,
24: 2 write down the name of this **d**, this very **d**.
24: 2 of Babylon has laid siege to Jerusalem this very **d**.
24:25 on the **d** when I take from them their stronghold,
24:26 on that **d**, one who has escaped will come to you A
24:27 On that **d** your mouth shall be opened to A
26: 1 In the eleventh year, on the first **d** of the month, D
26:18 Now the coastlands tremble on the **d** of your fall;
27:27 into the heart of the seas on the **d** of your ruin.
28:13 the **d** that you were created they were prepared.
28:15 in your ways from the **d** that you were created,
29: 1 in the tenth month, on the twelfth **d** of the month,
29:17 in the first month, on the first **d** of the month, D
29:21 On that **d** I will cause a horn to sprout up for A
30: 2 Thus says the Lord GOD: Wail, "Alas for the **d**!"
30: 3 For a **d** is near, the day of the LORD is near;
30: 3 For a day is near, the **d** of the LORD is near; G
30: 3 it will be a **d** of clouds, a time of doom for the
30: 9 On that **d**, messengers shall go out from me A
30: 9 and anguish shall come upon them on the **d**
30:16 and Memphis face adversaries by **d**.
30:18 At Tehaphnehes the **d** shall be dark,
30:20 in the first month, on the seventh **d** of the month, B
31: 1 in the third month, on the first **d** of the month, D
31:15 On the **d** it went down to Sheol I closed the deep
32: 1 in the twelfth month, on the first **d** of the month, D
32:10 each one of them, on the **d** of your downfall.
32:17 in the first month, on the fifteenth **d** of the month,
33:21 in the tenth month, on the fifth **d** of the month,
34:12 to which they have been scattered on a **d** of clouds
36:33 the **d** that I cleanse you from all your iniquities,
38:10 On that **d** thoughts will come into your mind, A
38:14 On that **d** when my people Israel are living A
38:18 On that **d**, when Gog comes against the land A
38:19 On that **d** there shall be a great shaking in the A
39: 8 This is the **d** of which I have spoken.
39:11 On that **d** I will give to Gog a place for burial A
39:13 and it will bring them honor on the **d**
39:22 the LORD their God, from that **d** forward.
40: 1 on the tenth **d** of the month,
40: 1 the city was struck down, on that very **d**, the hand
43:18 the **d** when it is erected for offering burnt offerings
43:22 On the second **d** you shall offer a male goat
43:27 the eighth **d** onward the priests shall offer upon
44:27 On the **d** that he goes into the holy place,
45:18 In the first month, on the first **d** of the month, D
45:20 You shall do the same on the seventh **d** of B
45:21 on the fourteenth **d** of the month,
45:22 On that **d** the prince shall provide for himself A
45:25 the fifteenth **d** of the month and for the seven days
46: 1 on the sabbath **d** it shall be opened and on the **d**
46: 4 to the LORD on the sabbath **d** shall be six lambs
46: 6 the **d** of the new moon he shall offer a young bull
46:12 of well-being as he does on the sabbath **d**.
Da 6:10 to get down on his knees three times a **d** to pray
6:13 but he is saying his prayers three times a **d**."
6:19 Then, at break of **d**, the king got up and hurried to
9: 7 O Lord, but open shame, as at this **d**, falls on us,
9:15 and made your name renowned even to this **d**—
10: 4 On the twenty-fourth **d** of the first month,
10:12 for from the first **d** that you set your mind D
Hos 1: 5 On that **d** I will break the bow of Israel A
1:11 for great shall be the **d** of Jezreel.
2: 3 and expose her as in the **d** she was born,
2:16 On that **d**, says the LORD, you will call me, A
2:18 you a covenant on that **d** with the wild animals, A
2:21 On that **d** I will answer, says the LORD, A
4: 5 You shall stumble by **d**; the prophet
5: 9 Ephraim shall become a desolation in the **d**
6: 2 on the third **d** he will raise us up, C
7: 5 On the **d** of our king the officials became sick with
9: 5 What will you do on the **d** of appointed festival,
9: 5 and on the **d** of the festival of the LORD?
10:14 as Shalman destroyed Beth-arbel on the **d** of battle
12: 1 and pursues the east wind all **d** long;
Joel 1:15 Alas for the **d**! For the day of the LORD is near,
1:15 For the **d** of the LORD is near, G
2: 1 for the **d** of the LORD is coming, it is near— G
2: 2 a **d** of darkness and gloom,
2: 2 a **d** of clouds and thick darkness!
2:11 Truly the **d** of the LORD is great; G
2:31 the great and terrible **d** of the LORD comes. G
3:14 **d** of the LORD is near in the valley of decision. G
3:18 In that **d** the mountains shall drip sweet wine,
Am 1:14 with shouting on the **d** of battle,
1:14 with a storm on the **d** of the whirlwind;
2:16 among the mighty shall flee away naked in that **d**,
3:14 On the **d** I punish Israel for its transgressions,
5: 8 and darkens the **d** into night,
5:18 Alas for you who desire the **d** of the LORD! G
5:18 Why do you want the **d** of the LORD? G
5:20 Is not the **d** of the LORD darkness, not light, G
6: 3 O you that put far away the evil **d**,
8: 3 of the temple shall become wailings in that **d**,"
8: 9 On that **d**, says the Lord GOD, A
8:10 and the end of it like a bitter **d**.
8:13 In that **d** the beautiful young women and
9:11 On that **d** I will raise up the booth of David A
Ob 1: 8 On that **d**, says the LORD, A
1:11 On the **d** that you stood aside,
1:11 on the **d** that strangers carried off his wealth,
1:12 over your brother on the **d** of his misfortune;
1:12 over the people of Judah on the **d** of their ruin;
1:12 you should not have boasted on the **d** of distress. O
1:13 the gate of my people on the **d** of their calamity; L
1:13 over Judah's disaster on the **d** of his calamity; L
1:13 have looted his goods on the **d** of his calamity. L
1:14 handed over his survivors on the **d** of distress. O
1:15 the **d** of the LORD is near against all the nations. G
Jnh 4: 7 But when dawn came up the next **d**,
Mic 2: 4 On that **d** they shall take up a taunt song against A
3: 6 and the **d** shall be black over them;
4: 6 In that **d**, says the LORD,
5:10 In that **d**, says the LORD,
7: 4 **d** of their sentinels, of their punishment, has come;
7:11 A **d** for the building of your walls!
7:11 In that **d** the boundary shall be far extended.
7:12 In that **d** they will come to you from Assyria
Na 1: 7 LORD is good, a stronghold in a **d** of trouble; N
2: 3 The metal on the chariots flashes on the **d**
3:17 of locusts settling on the fences on a cold **d**—
Hab 3:16 I wait quietly for the **d** of calamity to come L
Zep 1: 7 For the **d** of the LORD is at hand; G
1: 8 on the **d** of the LORD's sacrifice I will punish
1: 9 On that **d** I will punish all who leap over A
1:10 On that **d**, says the LORD, A
1:14 The great **d** of the LORD is near, G
1:14 the sound of the **d** of the LORD is bitter, G
1:15 That **d** will be a day of wrath,
1:15 That day will be a **d** of wrath, M
1:15 a **d** of distress and anguish, O
1:15 a **d** of ruin and devastation,
1:15 a **d** of darkness and gloom,
1:15 a **d** of clouds and thick darkness,
1:16 a **d** of trumpet blast and battle cry against
1:18 able to save them on the **d** of the LORD's wrath; M
2: 2 upon you the **d** of the LORD's wrath. M
2: 3 be hidden on the **d** of the LORD's wrath. M
3: 8 for the **d** when I arise as a witness.
3:11 On that **d** you shall not be put to shame because A
3:16 On that **d** it shall be said to Jerusalem: A
3:18 as on a **d** of festival.
Hag 1: 1 in the sixth month, on the first **d** of the month, D
1:15 on the twenty-fourth **d** of the month,
2: 1 on the twenty-first **d** of the month,
2:10 On the twenty-fourth **d** of the ninth month,
2:15 consider what will come to pass from this **d** on.
2:18 from this **d** on, from the twenty-fourth **d** of the
2:18 Since the **d** that the foundation of the LORD's
2:19 From this **d** on I will bless you.
2:20 a second time to Haggai on the twenty-fourth **d** of
2:23 On that **d**, says the LORD of hosts, A
Zec 1: 7 On the twenty-fourth **d** of the eleventh month,
2:11 to the LORD on that **d**, and shall be my people; A
3: 9 I will remove the guilt of this land in a single **d**.
3:10 On that **d**, says the LORD of hosts, A
4:10 the **d** of small things shall rejoice,
6:10 and go the same **d** to the house of Josiah son
7: 1 the LORD came to Zechariah on the fourth **d** of
9:16 On that **d** the LORD their God will save them A
11:11 So it was annulled on that **d**, A
12: 3 On that **d** I will make Jerusalem a heavy stone A
12: 4 On that **d**, says the LORD, A
12: 6 On that **d** I will make the clans of Judah like A
12: 8 On that **d** the LORD will shield the inhabitants A
12: 8 so that the feeblest among them on that **d** shall A
12: 9 on that **d** I will seek to destroy all the nations A
12:11 On that **d** the mourning in Jerusalem will be as A
13: 1 On that **d** a fountain shall be opened for the A
13: 2 On that **d**, says the LORD of hosts, A
13: 4 On that **d** the prophets will be ashamed, A
14: 1 See, a **d** is coming for the LORD,
14: 3 against those nations as when he fights on a **d**
14: 4 On that **d** his feet shall stand on the Mount of
Olives, A
14: 6 On that **d** there shall not be either cold or frost. A
14: 7 And there shall be continuous **d** (it is known to
14: 7 not **d** and not night, for at evening time there shall
14: 8 On that **d** living waters shall flow out A
14: 9 on that **d** the LORD will be one and his name one. A
14:13 On that **d** a great panic from the LORD shall fall A
14:20 On that **d** there shall be inscribed on the bells of A
14:21 in the house of the LORD of hosts on that **d**. A
Mal 3: 2 But who can endure the **d** of his coming,
3:17 my special possession on the **d** when I act,
4: 1 See, the **d** is coming, burning like an oven,
4: 1 the **d** that comes shall burn them up,
4: 3 on the **d** when I act, says the LORD of hosts.
4: 5 before the great and terrible **d** of the LORD G
Mt 6:11 Give us this **d** our daily bread.
7:22 On that **d** many will say to me, 'Lord, Lord, A
10:15 Sodom and Gomorrah on the **d** of judgment J
11:22 on the **d** of judgment it will be more tolerable J
11:23 it would have remained until this **d**.
11:24 on the **d** of judgment it will be more tolerable J
12:36 **d** of judgment you will have to give an account J
13: 1 That same **d** Jesus went out of the house and sat
16:21 and be killed, and on the third **d** be raised. C
17:23 and on the third **d** he will be raised." C
20: 6 'Why are you standing here idle all **d**?'
20:12 to us who have borne the burden of the **d** and
20:19 and on the third **d** he will be raised." C
22:23 The same **d** some Sadducees came to him,
22:46 nor from that **d** did anyone dare
24:36 "But about that **d** and hour no one knows,
24:38 until the **d** Noah entered the ark,
24:42 you do not know on what **d** your Lord is coming.
24:50 on a **d** when he does not expect him and at an hour
25:13 for you know neither the **d** nor the hour.
26:17 first **d** of Unleavened Bread the disciples came D
26:29 the vine until that **d** when I drink it new with you
26:55 **D** after **d** I sat in the temple teaching, H
27: 8 the Field of Blood to this **d**.
27:62 The next **d**, that is, after the **d** of Preparation,
27:64 the tomb to be made secure until the third **d**; C
28: 1 sabbath, as the first **d** of the week was dawning, D
28:15 this story is still told among the Jews to this **d**.
Mk 2:20 and then they will fast on that **d**. A
4:27 and would sleep and rise night and **d**,
4:35 On that **d**, when evening had come, A
5: 5 Night and **d** among the tombs and on
11:12 On the following **d**, when they came
13:32 "But about that **d** or hour no one knows,
14:12 On the first **d** of Unleavened Bread, D
14:25 until that **d** when I drink it new in the kingdom
14:30 Jesus said to him, "Truly I tell you, this **d**,
14:49 **D** after **d** I was with you in the temple teaching, H
15:42 and since it was the **d** of Preparation, that is, the **d**
before the sabbath,
16: 2 And very early on the first **d** of the week, D
16: 9 ⟦after he rose early on the first **d** of the week,⟧ D
Lk 1:20 unable to speak, until the **d** these things occur."
1:59 On the eighth **d** they came to circumcise the child,
1:80 in the wilderness until the **d** he appeared publicly
2:11 to you is born this **d** in the city of David a Savior,
2:37 with fasting and prayer night and **d**.
4:16 he went to the synagogue on the sabbath **d**,
5:17 One **d**, while he was teaching, E
6:13 And when **d** came, he called his disciples
6:23 Rejoice in that **d** and leap for joy,
8:22 One **d** he got into a boat with his disciples, E
9:12 The **d** was drawing to a close,
9:22 and be killed, and on the third **d** be raised." C
9:37 On the next **d**, when they had come down from
10:12 on that **d** it will be more tolerable for Sodom A
10:35 The next **d** he took out two denarii,
11: 3 Give us each **d** our daily bread. K
12:46 on a **d** when he does not expect him and at an hour
13:14 and be cured, and not on the sabbath **d**."
13:16 be set free from this bondage on the sabbath **d**?"
13:32 and on the third **d** I finish my work. C
13:33 tomorrow, and the next **d** I must be on my way,
14: 5 not immediately pull it out on a sabbath **d**?"
16:19 and who feasted sumptuously every **d**. F
17: 4 the same person sins against you seven times a **d**,
17:24 so will the Son of Man be in his **d**.
17:27 until the **d** Noah entered the ark,
17:29 but on the **d** that Lot left Sodom,
17:30 like that on the **d** that the Son of Man is revealed.
17:31 On that **d**, anyone on the housetop who has A
18: 7 to his chosen ones who cry to him **d** and night?
18:33 and on the third **d** he will rise again." C
19:42 had only recognized on this **d** the things that make
19:47 Every **d** he was teaching in the temple. F
20: 1 One **d**, as he was teaching the people E
21:34 and that **d** catch you unexpectedly,
21:37 Every **d** he was teaching in the temple, F
22: 7 Then came the **d** of Unleavened Bread,
22:34 "I tell you, Peter, the cock will not crow this **d**,
22:53 When I was with you **d** after **d** in the temple, H
22:66 When **d** came, the assembly of the elders of
23:12 That same **d** Herod and Pilate became friends
23:54 It was the **d** of Preparation,
24: 1 But on the first **d** of the week, at early dawn, D
24: 7 and be crucified, and on the third **d** rise again." C
24:13 Now on that same **d** two of them were going to
24:21 now the third **d** since these things took place. C
24:29 almost evening and the **d** is now nearly over."
24:46 to suffer and to rise from the dead on the third **d**, C
Jn 1:29 The next **d** he saw Jesus coming toward him
1:35 The next **d** John again was standing with two
1:39 and they remained with him that **d**.
1:43 The next **d** Jesus decided to go to Galilee.
2: 1 third **d** there was a wedding in Cana of Galilee, C
5: 9 Now that **d** was a sabbath.
6:22 The next **d** the crowd that had stayed on
6:39 but raise it up on the last **d**. Q
6:40 and I will raise them up on the last **d**." Q
6:44 and I will raise that person up on the last **d**. Q
6:54 and I will raise them up on the last **d**; Q
7:37 On the last **d** of the festival, the great day, Q
7:37 On the last day of the festival, the great **d**,
8:56 that he would see my **d**;
9: 4 the works of him who sent me while it is **d**;
9:14 Now it was a sabbath **d** when Jesus made the mud
11: 9 Those who walk during the **d** do not stumble,
11:24 in the resurrection on the last **d**." Q
11:53 from that **d** on they planned to put him to death.
12: 7 She bought it so that she might keep it for the **d**

Jn 12:12 The next **d** the great crowd that had come to
12:48 on the last **d** the word that I have spoken Q
14:20 On that **d** you will know that I am in my Father, A
16:23 On that **d** you will ask nothing of me. A
16:26 On that **d** you will ask in my name. A
19:14 Now it was the **d** of Preparation for the Passover;
19:31 Since it was the **d** of Preparation,
19:31 because that sabbath was a **d** of great solemnity.
19:42 so, because it was the Jewish **d** of Preparation,
20: 1 Early on the first **d** of the week, D
20:19 When it was evening on that **d**, A
20:19 evening on that day, the first **d** of the week, D
Ac 1: 2 until the **d** when he was taken up to heaven,
1:22 the baptism of John until the **d** when he was taken
2: 1 When the **d** of Pentecost had come,
2:20 the coming of the Lord's great and glorious **d**.
2:29 and his tomb is with us to this **d**.
2:41 that **d** about three thousand persons were added.
2:46 **D** by **d**, as they spent much time together in P
2:47 And **d** by **d** the Lord added to their number P
3: 1 One **d** Peter and John were going up to the E
4: 3 and put them in custody until the next **d**,
4: 5 The next **d** their rulers, elders,
5:42 And every **d** in the temple and at home they did F
7: 8 of Isaac and circumcised him on the eighth **d**;
7:26 The next **d** he came to some of them
8: 1 That **d** a severe persecution began against
9:24 the gates **d** and night so that they might kill him;
10: 9 the next **d**, as they were on their journey
10:23 The next **d** he got up and went with them,
10:24 The following **d** they came to Caesarea.
10:40 but God raised him on the third **d** and C
12:21 On an appointed **d** Herod put on his royal robes,
13:14 on the sabbath **d** they went into the synagogue
14:20 The next **d** he went on with Barnabas to Derbe.
16:11 the following **d** to Neapolis,
16:13 On the sabbath **d** we went outside the gate by
16:16 One **d**, as we were going to the place of prayer, E
17:11 and examined the scriptures every **d** F
17:17 marketplace every **d** with those who happened F
17:31 because he has fixed a **d** on which he will have
20: 7 On the first **d** of the week, D
20: 7 since he intended to leave the next **d**,
20:15 and on the following **d** we arrived opposite Chios.
20:15 The next **d** we touched at Samos,
20:15 and the **d** after that we came to Miletus.
20:16 if possible, on the **d** of Pentecost.
20:18 the entire time from the first **d** that I set foot D
20:26 Therefore I declare to you this **d** that I am
20:31 not cease night or **d** to warn everyone with tears.
21: 1 and the next **d** to Rhodes, and from there to Patara.
21: 7 the believers and stayed with them for one **d**. E
21: 8 The next **d** we left and came to Caesarea;
21:18 The next **d** Paul went with us to visit James;
21:26 Then Paul took the men, and the next **d**,
22:30 the next **d** he released him and ordered
23: 1 up to this **d** I have lived my life with a clear
23:32 The next **d** they let the horsemen go on with him,
25: 6 the next **d** he took his seat on the tribunal
25:17 but on the next **d** took my seat on the tribunal
25:23 So on the next **d** Agrippa and Bernice came
26: 7 as they earnestly worship **d** and night.
26:22 To this **d** I have had help from God,
27: 3 The next **d** we put in at Sidon;
27:18 so violently that on the next **d** they began to throw
27:19 on the third **d** with their own hands they threw C
27:29 down four anchors from the stern and prayed for **d**
27:33 the fourteenth **d** that you have been in suspense
28:13 After one **d** there a south wind sprang up, E
28:13 and on the second **d** we came to Puteoli.
28:23 After they had set a **d** to meet with him,
Ro 2: 5 up wrath for yourself on the **d** of wrath, M
2:16 on the **d** when, according to my gospel, God,
8:36 "For your sake we are being killed all **d** long;
10:21 "All **d** long I have held out my hands to
11: 8 and ears that would not hear, down to this very **d**."
13:12 the night is far gone, the **d** is near.
13:13 let us live honorably as in the **d**,
14: 5 Some judge one **d** to be better than another, E
14: 6 Those who observe the **d**,
1Co 1: 8 be blameless on the **d** of our Lord Jesus Christ. R
3:13 for the **D** will disclose it,
4:13 the dregs of all things, to this very **d**.
5: 5 that his spirit may be saved in the **d** of the Lord. R
10: 8 and twenty-three thousand fell in a single **d**.
15: 4 that he was raised on the third **d** in accordance C
15:31 I die every **d**! That is as certain, F
16: 2 On the first **d** of every week, D
2Co 1:14 on the **d** of the Lord Jesus we are your boast R
3:14 to this very **d**, when they hear the reading of
3:15 Indeed, to this very **d** whenever Moses is read,
4:16 our inner nature is being renewed **d** by **d**. P
6: 2 and on a **d** of salvation I have helped you."
6: 2 see, now is the **d** of salvation!
11:25 for a night and a **d** I was adrift at sea;
Eph 4:30 with which you were marked with a seal for the **d**
6:13 that you may be able to withstand on that evil **d**,
Php 1: 5 of your sharing in the gospel from the first **d** D
1: 6 among you will bring it to completion by the **d**
1:10 in the **d** of Christ you may be pure and blameless,
2:16 on the **d** of Christ that I did not run in vain or labor
3: 5 on the eighth **d**, a member of the people of Israel,
Col 1: 6 from the **d** you heard it and truly comprehended
1: 9 For this reason, since the **d** we heard it,
1Th 2: 9 and **d**, so that we might not burden any of you
3:10 Night and **d** we pray most earnestly
5: 2 know very well that the **d** of the Lord will come R
1Th 5: 4 for that **d** to surprise you like a thief;
5: 5 you are all children of light and children of the **d**;
5: 8 But since we belong to the **d**, let us be sober,
2Th 1:10 by his saints and to be marveled at on that **d** A
2: 2 the effect that the **d** of the Lord is already here. R
2: 3 for that **d** will not come unless
3: 8 but with toil and labor we worked night and **d**,
1Ti 5: 5 in supplications and prayers night and **d**;
2Ti 1: 3 in my prayers night and **d**.
1:12 to guard until that **d** what I have entrusted to him.
1:18 that he will find mercy from the Lord on that **d**! A
4: 8 the righteous judge, will give me on that **d**, A
Heb 3: 8 as on the **d** of testing in the wilderness,
3:13 But exhort one another every **d**, F
4: 4 For in one place it speaks about the seventh **d** B
4: 4 God rested on the seventh **d** from all his works." B
4: 7 again he sets a certain **d**—
4: 8 God would not speak later about another **d**.
7:27 he has no need to offer sacrifices **d** after **d**, H
8: 9 on the **d** when I took them by the hand
10:11 And every priest stands **d** after **d** at his service, H
10:25 and all the more as you see the **D** approaching.
Jas 5: 5 you have fattened your hearts in a **d** of slaughter.
2Pe 1:19 until the **d** dawns and the morning star rises
2: 8 living among them **d** after **d**, H
2: 9 under punishment until the **d** of judgment J
3: 7 kept until the **d** of judgment and destruction J
3: 8 that with the Lord one **d** is like a thousand years, E
3: 8 and a thousand years are like one **d**. E
3:10 But the **d** of the Lord will come like a thief, R
3:12 for and hastening the coming of the **d** of God,
3:18 be the glory both now and to the **d** of eternity.
1Jn 4:17 that we may have boldness on the **d** of judgment, J
Jude 1: 6 for the judgment of the great **D**.
Rev 1:10 I was in the spirit on the Lord's **d**,
4: 8 **D** and night without ceasing they sing, "Holy,
6:17 for the great **d** of their wrath has come, M
7:15 and worship him **d** and night within his temple,
8:12 a third of the **d** was kept from shining,
9:15 who had been held ready for the hour, the **d**,
12:10 who accuses them **d** and night before our God.
14:11 There is no rest **d** or night for those who worship
16:14 to assemble them for battle on the great **d** of God
18: 8 therefore her plagues will come in a single **d**—
20:10 and they will be tormented **d** and night forever
21:25 Its gates will never be shut by **d**—
Tob 2:12 One **d**, the seventh of Dystrus, E
3: 7 On the same **d**, at Ecbatana in Media,
3:10 On that **d** she was grieved in spirit and wept. A
4: 1 That same **d** Tobit remembered the money
4: 9 up a good treasure for yourself against the **d**
4:14 over until the next **d** the wages of those who work
5:15 he added, "I will pay you a drachma a **d** as wages,
5:21 Your eyes will see him on the **d** when he returns
9: 4 if I delay even one **d** I will upset him very much. E
10: 1 Now, **d** by **d**, Tobit kept counting P
10: 7 She would rush out every **d** and watch F
11:17 So on that **d** there was rejoicing among all A
12:18 Bless him each and every **d**; sing his praises. F
14:10 On whatever **d** you bury your mother beside me,
Jdt 2: 1 on the twenty-second **d** of the first month,
2:10 and you shall hold them for me until the **d**
6: 5 from this **d** until I take revenge on this race
7: 1 The next **d** Holofernes ordered his whole army,
7: 2 So all their warriors marched off that **d**;
7: 6 On the second **d** Holofernes led out all his cavalry
7:21 and on no **d** did they have enough water to drink,
8: 6 the **d** before the sabbath and the sabbath itself,
8: 6 the **d** before the new moon and the day of
8: 6 before the new moon and the **d** of the new moon,
11:15 on that very **d** they will be handed over to you to
11:17 and serves the God of heaven night and **d**.
12:10 On the fourth **d** Holofernes held a banquet
12:14 it will be a joy to me until the **d** of my death." I
12:16 to seduce her from the **d** he first saw her.
12:18 because today is the greatest **d** in my whole life."
12:20 much more than he had ever drunk in any one **d** E
13:17 who have this **d** humiliated the enemies
14: 2 As soon as **d** breaks and the sun rises on the earth,
14: 8 the **d** she left until the moment she began speaking
14:10 the house of Israel, remaining so to this **d**.
16:17 on them in the **d** of judgment; J
AdE 1:10 On the seventh **d**, when the king was B
2:11 And every **d** Mordecai walked in the courtyard F
3: 4 **D** after **d** they spoke to him, H
3: 7 on one **d** to destroy the whole race of Mordecai. E
3: 7 lot fell on the fourteenth **d** of the month of Adar.
3:12 So on the thirteenth **d** of the first month
3:13 to destroy the Jewish people on a given **d**
3:14 the nations were ordered to be prepared for that **d**.
5: 4 And Esther said, "Today is a special **d** for me.
7: 2 And the second **d**, as they were drinking wine,
8: 1 that very **d** King Artaxerxes granted to Esther all
8: 9 on the twenty-third **d** of the first month,
8:12 on a certain **d**, the thirteenth of the twelfth month,
8:13 ready on that **d** to fight against their enemies." A
9: 1 Now on the thirteenth **d** of the twelfth month,
9: 2 On that same **d** the enemies of the Jews perished;
9:11 That very **d** the number of those killed
9:17 On the fourteenth **d** they rested and made that
same **d** a **d** of rest,
9:19 the fifteenth **d** of Adar as their joyful holiday,
10:11 and moment and **d** of decision before God and
11: 2 on the first **d** of Nisan, D
11: 8 It was a **d** of darkness and gloom,
11:12 seeking all **d** to understand it in every detail.
13: 6 on the fourteenth **d** of the twelfth month, Adar,
AdE 13: 7 in a single **d** go down in violence to Hades,
14:18 since the **d** that I was brought here until now,
15: 1 On the third **d**, when she ended her prayer, C
16:20 so that on the thirteenth **d** of the twelfth month,
Adar, on that very **d**, they may defend themselves
16:21 has made this **d** to be a joy for his chosen people
instead of a **d** of destruction
16:22 a notable **d** among your commemorative festivals,
Wis 3:18 and no consolation on the **d** of judgment. J
5:14 like the remembrance of a guest who stays but a **d**.
10:17 and became a shelter to them by **d**,
Sir Pr: 3 that time I have applied my skill **d** and night
1:13 on the **d** of their death they will be blessed. I
3:15 in the **d** of your distress it will be remembered O
5: 7 and do not postpone it from **d** to **d**;
5: 8 for it will not benefit you on the **d** of calamity. L
11:25 In the **d** of prosperity, adversity is forgotten,
11:25 in the **d** of adversity, prosperity is not remembered.
11:26 on the **d** of death to reward individuals according I
18:24 Think of his wrath on the **d** of death, I
23:14 and you will curse the **d** of your birth.
33: 7 Why is one **d** more important than another, E
36:10 Hasten the **d**, and remember the appointed time,
38:17 for one **d**, or two, to avoid criticism; E
38:27 by night as well as by **d**;
39:28 the **d** of reckoning they will pour out their strength
40: 1 the **d** they come forth from their mother's womb
until the **d** they return
40: 2 and anxious thought of the **d** of their death. I
40: 6 he struggles in his sleep as he did by **d**.
45:14 be wholly burned twice every **d** continually. F
46: 4 that the sun stood still and one **d** become as long E
47: 7 he crushed their power to our own **d**.
50: 8 like a green shoot on Lebanon on a summer **d**;
Bar 1: 2 on the seventh **d** of the month, B
1: 8 At the same time, on the tenth **d** of Sivan,
1:13 to this **d** the anger of the Lord and his wrath have
1:20 to this **d** there have clung to us the calamities and
2: 6 on us and our ancestors this very **d**.
2:11 and made yourself a name that continues to this **d**,
2:25 to the heat of **d** and the frost of night.
2:28 the **d** when you commanded him to write your law
3:20 Later generations have seen the light of **d**,
Aza 1:14 and are brought low this **d** in all the world because
1:15 In our **d** we have no ruler, or prophet, or leader,
Sus 1: 8 Every **d** the two elders used to see her, F
1:12 **D** after **d** they watched eagerly to see her. H
1:13 One **d** they said to each other, "Let us go home, E
1:15 while they were watching for an opportune **d**,
1:15 for it was a hot **d**.
1:28 The next **d**, when the people gathered at the house
1:62 Thus innocent blood was spared that **d**.
1:64 that **d** onward Daniel had a great reputation among
Bel 1: 3 and every **d** they provided for it twelve bushels F
1: 4 The king revered it and went every **d** to worship F
1: 6 not see how much he eats and drinks every **d**?" F
1:32 every **d** they had been given two human bodies F
1:40 seventh **d** the king came to mourn for Daniel. B
1Mc 1:54 Now on the fifteenth **d** of Chislev,
1:59 twenty-fifth **d** of the month they offered sacrifice
2:32 for battle against them on the sabbath **d**.
2:34 the king commands and so profane the sabbath **d**."
2:41 So they made this decision that **d**:
2:41 to attack us on the sabbath **d**;
3:47 that **d**, put on sackcloth and sprinkled ashes
4:25 Thus Israel had a great deliverance that **d**.
4:52 Early in the morning on the twenty-fifth **d** of
4:54 and on the very **d** that the Gentiles had profaned it,
4:59 with the twenty-fifth **d** of the month of Chislev.
5:27 and destroy all these people in a single **d**."
5:34 As many as eight thousand of them fell that **d**.
5:50 and he fought against the town all that **d** and all
5:60 as two thousand of the people of Israel fell that **d**.
5:67 On that **d** some priests, who wished to do A
7:16 he seized sixty of them and killed them in one **d**, E
7:43 in battle on the thirteenth **d** of the month of Adar.
7:48 celebrated that **d** as a **d** of great gladness.
7:49 that this **d** should be celebrated each year on the
thirteenth **d**
8:10 and enslaved them to this **d**.
8:15 every **d** three hundred twenty senators F
9:34 Bacchides found this out on the sabbath **d**,
9:43 with a large force on the sabbath **d** to the banks of
9:49 about one thousand of Bacchides' men fell that **d**.
10:30 I release them from this **d** and henceforth.
10:30 from this **d** and for all time.
10:50 and on that **d** Demetrius fell. A
10:55 "Happy was the **d** on which you returned to
11:47 killed on that **d** about one hundred thousand. A
11:48 and seized a large amount of spoil on that **d**, A
11:74 as three thousand of the foreigners fell that **d**.
13:30 in Modein; it remains to this **d**.
13:39 to this **d**, and cancel the crown tax that you owe;
13:51 On the twenty-third **d** of the second month,
13:52 that every year they should celebrate this **d**
14:27 "On the eighteenth **d** of Elul,
16: 2 the wars of Israel from our youth until this **d**,
2Mc 1:18 on the twenty-fifth **d** of Chislev we shall celebrate
3:14 So he set a **d** and went in to direct the inspection
5:25 and waited until the holy sabbath **d**;
6:11 in order to observe the seventh **d** secretly, B
6:11 in view of their regard for that most holy **d**.
7:20 she saw her seven sons perish within a single **d**,
8:26 It was the **d** before the sabbath,
8:27 for that **d** and allotted it to them as the beginning
10: 5 It happened that on the same **d** on which
10: 5 that is, on the twenty-fifth **d** of the same month,

2Mc 10:35 But at dawn of the fifth **d**,
12:38 As the seventh **d** was coming on, B
12:39 On the next **d**, as had now become necessary,
13:10 he ordered the people to call upon the Lord **d**
13:17 This happened, just as **d** was dawning,
14: 4 During that **d** he kept quiet.
14:21 leaders set a **d** on which to meet by themselves.
15: 1 to attack them with complete safety on the **d**
15: 2 for the **d** that he who sees all things has honored
15: 3 the keeping of the sabbath **d**.
15: 4 who ordered us to observe the seventh **d**," B
15:36 by public vote never to let this **d** go unobserved,
15:36 the thirteenth **d** of the twelfth month—
15:36 the **d** before Mordecai's **d**.
1Es 1: 1 he killed the passover lamb on the fourteenth **d** of
1:17 to the Lord were accomplished that **d**:
1:32 have made lamentation for him to this **d**;
4:34 of the heavens and returns to its place in one **d**. E
4:43 that you made on the **d** when you became king,
4:52 be offered on the altar every **d**, in accordance F
4:55 the Levites should be provided until the **d** when
5:51 and offered the proper sacrifices every **d**, F
7: 5 the holy house was finished by the twenty-third **d**
7:10 the passover on the fourteenth **d** of the first month,
8:61 We left the river Theras on the twelfth **d** of
8:76 and we are in great sin to this **d**.
8:77 and exile and plundering, in shame until this **d**.
8:89 for we are left as a root to this **d**.
9: 5 on the twentieth **d** of the month.
9:11 This is not a work we can do in one **d** or two, E
9:50 "This **d** is holy to the Lord"—
9:52 for the **d** is holy to the Lord;
9:53 saying, "This **d** is holy; do not be sorrowful."
3Mc 4:14 the end to be destroyed in the space of a single **d**.
5: 2 and ordered him on the following **d** to drug all
5:11 that from the beginning, night and **d**, is bestowed
5:18 to remain alive through the present **d**.
6:40 with everything by the king, until the fourteenth **d**,
7:15 In that **d** they put to death
7:15 and they kept the **d** as a joyful festival,
2Es 1:16 but to this **d** you still complain.
2:27 for when the **d** of tribulation and anguish comes,
4: 5 or call back for me the **d** that is past."
4: 9 about fire and wind and the **d**—
5: 4 and the moon during the **d**.
6:38 and said on the first **d**, D
6:41 on the second **d**, you created the spirit of
6:42 "On the third **d** you commanded the waters to C
6:44 These were made on the third **d**. C
6:45 "On the fourth **d** you commanded the brightness
6:47 "On the fifth **d** you commanded the seventh part,
6:51 that had been dried up on the third **d**, to live in it, C
6:53 the sixth **d** you commanded the earth to bring forth
7:*38* he will speak to them on the **d** of judgment— J
7:*39* a **d** that has no sun or moon or stars,
7:*102* whether on the **d** of judgment the righteous will J
7:*104* The **d** of judgment is decisive and displays to all J
7:*105* so no one shall ever pray for another on that **d**, A
7:*113* [43] But the **d** of judgment will be the end J
9:44 and every **d** during those thirty years I prayed F
9:44 to the Most High, night and **d**.
9:47 I set a **d** for the marriage feast.
10: 2 I remained quiet until the evening of the second **d**.
12:34 the **d** of judgment, of which I spoke to you at J
13:52 except in the time of his **d**.
14: 1 On the third **d**, while I was sitting under an oak, C
14:38 And on the next **d** a voice called me, saying,
15:21 Just as they have done to my elect until this **d**,
15:29 and from the **d** that they set out,
16:65 as your accusers on that **d**. A
4Mc 3: 7 David had been attacking the Philistines all **d** long,
13:20 they were brought to the light of **d**.
17:12 on that **d** virtue gave the awards and tested them A
18:20 O bitter was that **d**—and yet not bitter—

DAY'S (11) [DAY]

Nu 11:31 about a **d** journey on this side and a **d** journey
1Ki 19: 4 he himself went a **d** journey into the wilderness,
Est 9:13 also to do according to this **d** edict,
Jnh 3: 4 Jonah began to go into the city, going a **d** walk.
Lk 2:44 in the group of travelers, they went a **d** journey.
Ac 1:12 a sabbath **d** journey away.
Rev 6: 6 "A quart of wheat for a **d** pay, and three quarts of
barley for a **d** pay,
Sir 14:14 Do not deprive yourself of a **d** enjoyment;
1Mc 7:45 The Jews pursued them a **d** journey,

DAYBREAK (9) [DAY, BREAK]

Ge 32:24 and a man wrestled with him until **d**.
2Sa 17:22 by **d** not one was left who had not crossed
Lk 4:42 At **d** he departed and went into a deserted place.
Jn 21: 4 Just after **d**, Jesus stood on the beach;
Ac 5:21 the temple at **d** and went on with their teaching.
27:33 Just before **d**, Paul urged all of them
Tob 8:18 to fill in the grave before **d**.
1Mc 4: 6 At **d** Judas appeared in the plain
3Mc 5:24 and they were eagerly waiting for **d**.

DAYLIGHT (4) [DAY, LIGHT]

Ge 29: 7 He said, "Look, it is still broad **d**;
Am 8: 9 and darken the earth in broad **d**.
Jn 11: 9 "Are there not twelve hours of **d**?
Sir 33: 7 when all the **d** in the year is from the sun?

DAYSMAN (KJV) See UMPIRE

DAYSPRING (KJV) See DAWN, MORNING

DAYS[‡] (969) [DAY]

A. SEVEN DAYS (122)
B. THREE DAYS (66)
C. ALL THE DAYS (64)
D. THE DAYS OF ... LIFE (34)
E. FORTY DAYS (31)
F. DAYS ARE [SURELY] COMING (21)
G. SIX DAYS (20)
H. DAYS OF OLD (17)
I. LAST DAYS (14)
J. DAYS TO COME (6)

Ge 1:14 and let them be for signs and for seasons and for **d**
3:14 and dust you shall eat all the **d** of your life. CD
3:17 in toil you shall eat of it all the **d** of your life; CD
5: 4 The **d** of Adam after he became the father
5: 5 Thus all the **d** that Adam lived were C
5: 8 all the **d** of Seth were nine hundred twelve years; C
5:11 all the **d** of Enosh were nine hundred five years; C
5:14 all the **d** of Kenan were nine hundred and ten C
5:17 Thus all the **d** of Mahalalel were C
5:20 all the **d** of Jared were nine hundred sixty-two C
5:23 all the **d** of Enoch were three hundred sixty-five C
5:27 Thus all the **d** of Methuselah were C
5:31 Thus all the **d** of Lamech were C
6: 3 their **d** shall be one hundred twenty years."
6: 4 The Nephilim were on the earth in those **d**—
7: 4 For in seven **d** I will send rain on the earth A
7: 4 on the earth for forty **d** and forty nights; E
7:10 And after seven **d** the waters of the flood came A
7:12 The rain fell on the earth forty **d** and forty nights. E
7:17 The flood continued forty **d** on the earth; E
7:24 on the earth for one hundred fifty **d**.
8: 3 of one hundred fifty **d** the waters had abated;
8: 6 At the end of forty **d** Noah opened the window E
8:10 He waited another seven **d**, and again he sent A
8:12 waited another seven **d**, and sent out the dove; A
9:29 All the **d** of Noah were nine hundred fifty years; C
10:25 for in his **d** the earth was divided,
11:32 The **d** of Terah were two hundred five years;
14: 1 In the **d** of King Amraphel of Shinar,
17:12 be circumcised when he is eight **d** old,
21: 4 his son Isaac when he was eight **d** old,
21:34 as an alien many **d** in the land of the Philistines.
24:55 "Let the girl remain with us a while, at least ten **d**;
26: 1 the former famine that had occurred in the **d**
26:15 the wells that his father's servants had dug in the **d**
26:18 that had been dug in the **d** of his father Abraham;
27:41 **d** of mourning for my father are approaching;
29:20 and they seemed to him but a few **d** because of
30:14 In the **d** of wheat harvest Reuben went
31:23 and pursued him for seven **d** until he caught up A
35:28 Now the **d** of Isaac were one hundred eighty years.
35:29 and was gathered to his people, old and full of **d**;
37:34 and mourned for his son many **d**.
40:12 the three branches are three **d**; B
40:13 within three **d** Pharaoh will lift up your head B
40:18 the three baskets are three **d**; B
40:19 within three **d** Pharaoh will lift up your head— B
42:17 he put them all together in prison for three **d**. B
47:28 so the **d** of Jacob, the years of his life,
49: 1 tell you what will happen to you in **d** to come. J
50: 3 they spent forty **d** in doing this, E
50: 3 And the Egyptians wept for him seventy **d**.
50: 4 When the **d** of weeping for him were past,
50:10 a time of mourning for his father seven **d**. A
Ex 7:25 Seven **d** passed after the LORD had struck A
10:22 in all the land of Egypt for three **d**. B
10:23 and for three **d** they could not move from B
12:15 Seven **d** you shall eat unleavened bread; A
12:16 no work shall be done on those **d**;
12:19 seven **d** no leaven shall be found in your houses; A
13: 6 Seven **d** you shall eat unleavened bread, A
13: 7 Unleavened bread shall be eaten for seven **d**; A
15:22 They went three **d** in the wilderness B
16: 5 will be twice as much as they gather on other **d**."
16:26 Six **d** you shall gather it; G
16:29 on the sixth day he gives you food for two **d**;
20: 9 Six **d** you shall labor and do all your work. G
20:11 For in six **d** the LORD made heaven and earth, G
20:12 so that your **d** may be long in the land that
22:30 seven **d** it shall remain with its mother; A
23:12 Six **d** you shall do your work, G
23:15 for seven **d** at the appointed time in the month A
23:26 I will fulfill the number of your **d**.
24:16 and the cloud covered it for six **d**; G
24:18 on the mountain for forty **d** and forty nights. E
29:30 in his place shall wear them seven **d**, A
29:35 through seven **d** you shall ordain them. A
29:37 Seven **d** you shall make atonement for the altar, A
31:15 Six **d** shall work be done, but the seventh day is G
31:17 between me and the people of Israel that in six **d** G
34:18 Seven **d** you shall eat unleavened bread, A
34:21 Six **d** you shall work, G
34:28 with the LORD forty **d** and forty nights; E
35: 2 Six **d** shall work be done, G
Lev 8:33 the entrance of the tent of meeting for seven **d**, A
8:33 For it will take seven **d** to ordain you; A
8:35 of the tent of meeting day and night for seven **d**, A
12: 2 she shall be ceremonially unclean seven **d**; A
12: 4 of blood purification shall be thirty-three **d**;

Lev 12: 4 until the **d** of her purification are completed.
12: 5 her time of blood purification shall be sixty-six **d**.
12: 6 When the **d** of her purification are completed,
13: 4 the diseased person for seven **d**. A
13: 5 then the priest shall confine him seven **d** more. A
13:21 the priest shall confine him seven **d**. A
13:26 the priest shall confine him seven **d**. A
13:31 the person with the itching disease for seven **d**. A
13:33 the person with the itch for seven **d** more. A
13:50 and put the diseased article aside for seven **d**. A
13:54 and he shall put it aside seven **d** more. A
14: 8 but shall live outside his tent seven **d**. A
14:38 of the house and shut up the house seven **d**. A
15:13 he shall count seven **d** for his cleansing; A
15:19 she shall be in her impurity for seven **d**, A
15:24 he shall be unclean seven **d**; A
15:25 If a woman has a discharge of blood for many **d**,
15:25 all the **d** of the discharge she shall continue C
15:25 as in the **d** of her impurity, she shall be unclean.
15:26 during all the **d** of her discharge shall be treated C
15:28 of her discharge, she shall count seven **d**, A
22:27 it shall remain seven **d** with its mother, A
23: 3 Six **d** shall work be done; G
23: 6 seven **d** you shall eat unleavened bread. A
23: 8 For seven **d** you shall present A
23:16 until the day after the seventh sabbath, fifty **d**;
23:34 of this seventh month, and lasting seven **d**, A
23:36 Seven **d** you shall present the LORD's offerings A
23:39 the festival of the LORD, lasting seven **d**; A
23:40 before the LORD your God for seven **d**. A
23:41 as a festival to the LORD seven **d** in the year; A
23:42 You shall live in booths for seven **d**; A
Nu 6: 4 All their **d** as nazirites they shall eat nothing
6: 5 All the **d** of their nazirite vow no razor shall C
6: 6 All the **d** that they separate themselves to C
6: 8 All their **d** as nazirites they are holy to
6:12 and separate themselves to the LORD for their **d**
9:19 the cloud continued over the tabernacle many **d**,
9:20 Sometimes the cloud would remain a few **d** over
9:22 Whether it was two **d**, or a month,
10:10 Also on your **d** of rejoicing,
11:19 You shall eat not only one day, or two **d**, or five **d**,
or ten **d**, or twenty **d**,
12:14 would she not bear her shame for seven **d**? A
12:14 Let her be shut out of the camp for seven **d**, A
12:15 So Miriam was shut out of the camp for seven **d**; A
13:25 forty **d** they returned from spying out the land. E
14:34 to the number of the **d** in which you spied out
14:34 forty **d**, for every day a year, E
19:11 of any human being shall be unclean seven **d**. A
19:14 in the tent, shall be unclean seven **d**. A
19:16 or a grave, shall be unclean seven **d**. A
20:29 all the house of Israel mourned for Aaron thirty **d**.
24:14 to your people in **d** to come." J
28:17 seven **d** shall unleavened bread be eaten. A
28:24 the same way you shall offer daily, for seven **d**, A
29:12 a festival to the LORD seven **d**. A
31:19 Camp outside the camp seven **d**; A
Dt 1: 2 (By the way of Mount Seir it takes eleven **d**
1:46 you had stayed at Kadesh as many **d** as you did,
2: 1 and skirted Mount Seir for many **d**.
4: 9 slip from your mind all the **d** of your life; CD
5:13 Six **d** you shall labor and do all your work. G
5:16 so that your **d** may be long and that it may go well
6: 2 the LORD your God all the **d** of your life, CD
6: 2 so that your **d** may be long.
9: 9 on the mountain forty **d** and forty nights; E
9:11 of forty **d** and forty nights the LORD gave me E
9:18 the LORD as before, forty **d** and forty nights; E
9:25 the forty **d** and forty nights that I lay prostrate E
10:10 I stayed on the mountain forty **d** and forty nights, E
11:21 so that your **d** and the **d** of your children may
12: 1 has given you to occupy all the **d** that you live on C
16: 3 seven **d** you shall eat unleavened bread with it— A
16: 3 so that all the **d** of your life you may CD
16: 4 seen with you in all your territory for seven **d**; A
16: 8 six **d** you shall continue to eat unleavened bread, G
16:13 shall keep the festival of booths for seven **d**, A
16:15 Seven **d** you shall keep the festival for A
17: 9 and the judge who is in office in those **d**;
17:19 and he shall read in it all the **d** of his life, CD
19:17 priests and the judges who are in office in those **d**,
25:15 and honest measure, so that your **d** may be long in
30:20 for that means life to you and length of **d**,
32: 7 the **d** of old, consider the years long past; H
33:25 and as your **d**, so is your strength.
34: 8 for Moses in the plains of Moab thirty **d**;
Jos 1: 5 to stand against you all the **d** of your life. CD
1:11 for in three **d** you are to cross over the Jordan, B
2:16 Hide yourselves there three **d**, B
2:22 into the hill country and stayed there three **d**, B
3: 2 At the end of three **d** the officers went through B
4:14 stood in awe of Moses, all the **d** of his life. CD
6: 3 Thus you shall do for six **d**, G
6:14 They did this for six **d**. G
9:16 But when three **d** had passed after they had B
22: 3 you have not forsaken your kindred these many **d**,
24:31 Israel served the LORD all the **d** of Joshua, C
24:31 and all the **d** of the elders who outlived Joshua C
Jdg 2: 7 people worshiped the LORD all the **d** of Joshua, C
2: 7 and all the **d** of the elders who outlived Joshua, C
2:18 the hand of their enemies all the **d** of the judge; C
5: 6 "In the **d** of Shamgar son of Anath,
5: 6 the days of Shamgar son of Anath, in the **d** of Jael,
8:28 So the land had rest forty years in the **d** of Gideon.
11:40 for four **d** every year the daughters
14:12 If you can explain it to me within the seven **d** A

Jdg 14:14 But for three **d** they could not explain the riddle. B
14:17 before him the seven **d** that their feast lasted; A
15:20 in the **d** of the Philistines twenty years.
17: 6 In those **d** there was no king in Israel;
18: 1 In those **d** there was no king in Israel.
18: 1 in those **d** the tribe of the Danites was seeking
19: 1 In those **d,** when there was no king in Israel,
19: 4 and he remained with him three **d;** B
20:27 of the covenant of God was there in those **d,**
20:28 son of Aaron, ministered before it in those **d),**
21:25 In those **d** there was no king in Israel;
Ru 1: 1 In the **d** when the judges ruled,
1Sa 3: 1 The word of the LORD was rare in those **d;**
4: 1 In those **d** the Philistines mustered for war
7:13 of the LORD was against the Philistines all the **d** C
7:15 Samuel judged Israel all the **d** of his life. CD
9:20 As for your donkeys that were lost three **d** ago, B
10: 8 Seven **d** you shall wait, until I come to you A
13: 8 waited seven **d,** the time appointed by Samuel; A
13:11 and that you did not come within the **d** appointed,
14:52 against the Philistines all the **d** of Saul; C
17:12 In the **d** of Saul the man was already old
17:16 For forty **d** the Philistine came forward E
25:38 About ten **d** later the LORD struck Nabal,
28: 1 In those **d** the Philistines gathered their forces
29: 3 who has been with me now for **d** and years?
30:12 or drunk water for three **d** and three nights. B
30:13 behind because I fell sick three **d** ago. B
31:13 the tamarisk tree in Jabesh, and fasted seven **d.** A
2Sa 1: 1 David remained two **d** in Ziklag.
7:12 When your **d** are fulfilled and you lie down
14: 2 like a woman who has been mourning many **d** for
16:23 in those **d** the counsel that Ahithophel gave was as
20: 4 the men of Judah together to me within three **d,** B
20:18 Then she said, "They used to say in the old **d,**
21: 1 in the **d** of David for three years, year after year;
21: 9 They were put to death in the first **d** of harvest,
24: 8 at the end of nine months and twenty **d.**
1Ki 2:38 So Shimei lived in Jerusalem many **d.**
4:21 and served Solomon all the **d** of his life. CD
8:40 so that they may fear you all the **d** that they live C
8:65 before the LORD our God, seven **d.** A
10:21 not considered as anything in the **d** of Solomon.
11:25 all the **d** of Solomon, making trouble as Hadad C
11:34 but will make him ruler all the **d** of his life, CD
12: 5 He said to them, "Go away for three **d,** B
15: 5 he commanded him all the **d** of his life, CD
15: 6 and Jeroboam continued all the **d** of his life. CD
15:14 the heart of Asa was true to the LORD all his **d.**
15:16 between Asa and King Baasha of Israel all their **d.**
15:32 between Asa and King Baasha of Israel all their **d.**
16:15 Zimri reigned seven **d** in Tirzah. A
16:34 In his **d** Hiel of Bethel built Jericho;
17:15 as well as he and her household ate for many **d.**
18: 1 many **d** the word of the LORD came to Elijah,
19: 8 the strength of that food forty **d** and forty nights E
20:29 They encamped opposite one another seven **d.** A
21:29 I will not bring the disaster in his **d;**
21:29 but in his son's **d** I will bring the disaster
22:46 in the land in the **d** of his father Asa,
2Ki 2:17 So they sent fifty men who searched for three **d** B
3: 9 they had made a roundabout march of seven **d,** A
8:20 In his **d** Edom revolted against the rule of Judah,
10:32 In those **d** the LORD began to trim off parts
12: 2 in the sight of the LORD all his **d,**
13:22 of Aram oppressed Israel all the **d** of Jehoahaz. C
15:18 he did not depart all his **d** from any of the sins
15:29 In the **d** of King Pekah of Israel,
15:37 In those **d** the LORD began to send King Rezin
18: 4 for until those **d** the people
19:25 planned from **d** of old what now I bring to pass, H
20: 1 In those **d** Hezekiah became sick and was at
20:17 **D** are coming when all that is in your house, F
20:19 if there will be peace and security in my **d?"**
23:22 the **d** of the judges who judged Israel, or during all
23:22 or during all the **d** of the kings of Israel or C
23:29 In his **d** Pharaoh Neco king of Egypt went up to
24: 1 In his **d** King Nebuchadnezzar
1Ch 1:19 the name of the one was Peleg (for in his **d**
4:41 came in the **d** of King Hezekiah of Judah,
5:10 in the **d** of Saul they made war on the Hagrites,
5:17 All of these were enrolled by genealogies in the **d**
5:17 and in the **d** of King Jeroboam of Israel.
7: 2 of their generations, their number in the **d**
7:22 And their father Ephraim mourned many **d,**
9:25 come in every seven **d,** in turn, to be with them; A
10:12 under the oak in Jabesh, and fasted seven **d.** A
12:39 They were there with David for three **d,** B
13: 3 for we did not turn to it in the **d** of Saul."
17:11 your **d** are fulfilled to go to be with your ancestors,
21:12 or three **d** of the sword of the LORD, B
22: 9 and I will give peace and quiet to Israel in his **d.**
23: 1 When David was old and full of **d,**
29:15 our **d** on the earth are like a shadow,
29:28 He died in a good old age, full of **d,** riches,
2Ch 6:31 and walk in your ways all the **d** that they live in C
7: 8 that time Solomon held the festival for seven **d,** A
7: 9 of the altar seven **d** and the festival seven days. A
7: 9 of the altar seven days and the festival seven **d.** A
9:20 not considered as anything in the **d** of Solomon.
10: 5 He said to them, "Come to me again in three **d."** B
13:20 Jeroboam did not recover his power in the **d**
14: 1 In his **d** the land had rest for ten years.
15:17 Nevertheless the heart of Asa was true all his **d.**
20:25 They spent three **d** taking the booty, B
21: 8 In his **d** Edom revolted against the rule of Judah
24: 2 of the LORD all the **d** of the priest Jehoiada. C
2Ch 24:14 in the house of the LORD regularly all the **d** C
24:15 But Jehoiada grew old and full of **d,** and died;
26: 5 He set himself to seek God in the **d** of Zechariah,
29:17 eight **d** they sanctified the house of the LORD,
30:21 unleavened bread seven **d** with great gladness; A
30:22 people ate the food of the festival for seven **d,** A
30:23 to keep the festival for another seven **d;** A
30:23 they kept it for another seven **d** with gladness. A
32:24 In those **d** Hezekiah became sick and was at
32:26 of the LORD did not come upon them in the **d**
34:33 All his **d** they did not turn away from following
35:17 and the festival of unleavened bread seven **d.** A
35:18 like it had been kept in Israel since the **d** of
36: 9 he reigned three months and ten **d** in Jerusalem.
36:21 All the **d** that it lay desolate it kept sabbath, C
Ezr 4: 2 to him ever since the **d** of King Esar-haddon
4: 7 And in the **d** of Artaxerxes,
6:22 the festival of unleavened bread seven **d;** A
8:15 and there we camped three **d.** B
8:32 came to Jerusalem and remained there three **d.** B
9: 7 From the **d** of our ancestors
10: 8 and that if any did not come within three **d,** B
10: 9 at Jerusalem within the three **d;** B
Ne 1: 4 and wept, and mourned for **d,** fasting and praying
2:11 I came to Jerusalem and was there for three **d.** B
5:18 and every ten **d** skins of wine in abundance;
6:15 of the month Elul, in fifty-two **d.**
6:17 in those **d** the nobles of Judah sent many letters
8:17 the **d** of Jeshua son of Nun to that day the people
8:18 They kept the festival seven **d;** A
12: 7 of the priests and of their associates in the **d**
12:12 In the **d** of Joiakim the priests,
12:22 As for the Levites, in the **d** of Eliashib, Joiada,
12:23 the Book of the Annals until the **d** of Johanan son
12:26 These were in the **d** of Joiakim son of Jeshua son
12:26 and in the **d** of the governor Nehemiah and of
12:46 in the **d** of David and Asaph long ago there was
12:47 In the **d** of Zerubbabel and in the days
12:47 and in the **d** of Nehemiah all Israel gave
13:15 In those **d** I saw in Judah
13:23 those **d** also I saw Jews who had married women
Est 1: 1 This happened in the **d** of Ahasuerus,
1: 2 In those **d** when King Ahasuerus sat
1: 4 the splendor and pomp of his majesty for many **d,**
1: 4 one hundred eighty **d** in all.
1: 5 When these **d** were completed,
1: 5 a banquet lasting for seven **d,** A
2:21 In those **d,** while Mordecai was sitting at
4:11 not been called to come in to the king for thirty **d."**
4:16 neither eat nor drink for three **d,** night or day. B
9:22 as the **d** on which the Jews gained relief
9:22 **d** of feasting and gladness, **d** for sending gifts
9:26 these **d** are called Purim, from the word Pur.
9:27 to observe these two **d** every year,
9:28 These **d** should be remembered and kept
9:28 and these **d** of Purim should never fall into disuse
9:28 nor should the commemoration of these **d** cease
9:31 and giving orders that these **d** of Purim should
Job 1: 5 And when the feast **d** had run their course,
2:13 on the ground seven **d** and seven nights, A
3: 6 let it not rejoice among the **d** of the year;
7: 1 and are not their **d** like the **d** of a laborer?
7: 6 My **d** are swifter than a weaver's shuttle,
7:16 Let me alone, for my **d** are a breath.
8: 7 your latter **d** will be very great.
8: 9 for our **d** on earth are but a shadow.
9:25 "My **d** are swifter than a runner;
10: 5 Are your **d** like the **d** of mortals,
10:20 Are not the **d** of my life few? D
12:12 and understanding in length of **d?**
14: 1 born of woman, few of **d** and full of trouble,
14: 5 Since their **d** are determined,
14: 6 that they may enjoy, like laborers, their **d.**
14:14 All the **d** of my service I would wait C
15:20 The wicked writhe in pain all their **d,**
17: 1 My spirit is broken, my **d** are extinct,
17:11 My **d** are past, my plans are broken off,
21:13 They spend their **d** in prosperity,
24: 1 and why do those who know him never see his **d?**
27: 6 my heart does not reproach me for any of my **d.**
29: 2 as in the **d** when God watched over me;
29:18 and I shall multiply my **d** like the phoenix;
30:16 **d** of affliction have taken hold of me.
30:27 **d** of affliction come to meet me.
32: 7 'Let **d** speak, and many years teach wisdom.'
33:25 let him return to the **d** of his youthful vigor.'
36:11 and serve him, they complete their **d** in prosperity,
38:12 the morning since your **d** began,
38:21 and the number of your **d** is great!
42:12 the latter **d** of Job more than his beginning;
42:17 And Job died, old and full of **d.**
Ps 21: 4 length of **d** forever and ever.
23: 6 and mercy shall follow me all the **d** of my life, CD
27: 4 in the house of the LORD all the **d** of my life, CD
34:12 and covets many **d** to enjoy good?
37:18 The LORD knows the **d** of the blameless,
37:19 in the **d** of famine they have abundance.
39: 4 and what is the measure of my **d;**
39: 5 You have made my **d** a few handbreadths,
44: 1 what deeds you performed in their **d,**
44: 1 performed in their days, in the **d** of old: H
55:23 and treacherous shall not live out half their **d.**
72: 7 In his **d** may righteousness flourish
77: 5 I consider the **d** of old, H
78:33 So he made their **d** vanish like a breath,
89:45 You have cut short the **d** of his youth;
90: 9 For all our **d** pass away under your wrath;
Ps 90:10 The **d** of our life are seventy years, D
90:12 to count our **d** that we may gain a wise heart.
90:14 so that we may rejoice and be glad all our **d.**
90:15 Make us glad as many **d** as you have afflicted us,
94:13 giving them respite from **d** of trouble,
102: 3 For my **d** pass away like smoke,
102:11 My **d** are like an evening shadow;
102:23 in midcourse; he has shortened my **d.**
103:15 As for mortals, their **d** are like grass;
109: 8 May his **d** be few; may another seize his position.
128: 5 prosperity of Jerusalem all the **d** of your life. CD
139:16 In your book were written all the **d** C
143: 5 I remember the **d** of old, H
144: 4 their **d** are like a passing shadow.
Pr 3: 2 for length of **d** and years of life
9:11 For by me your **d** will be multiplied,
15:15 All the **d** of the poor are hard, C
31:12 and not harm, all the **d** of her life. CD
Ecc 2: 3 do under heaven during the few **d** of their life. D
2:16 the **d** to come all will have been long forgotten. J
2:23 For all their **d** are full of pain,
5:17 Besides, all their **d** they eat in darkness,
5:18 under the sun the few **d** of the life God gives us; D
5:20 they will scarcely brood over the **d** of their lives,
6: 3 but however many are the **d** of his years,
6:12 while they live the few **d** of their vain life, D
7:10 "Why were the former **d** better than these?"
8:13 neither will they prolong their **d** like a shadow,
8:15 the **d** of life that God gives them under the sun. D
9: 9 all the **d** of your vain life that are given you CD
11: 1 for after many **d** you will get it back.
11: 8 yet let them remember that the **d** of darkness will
11: 9 let your heart cheer you in the **d** of your youth.
12: 1 Remember your creator in the **d** of your youth,
12: 1 before the **d** of trouble come,
Isa 1: 1 concerning Judah and Jerusalem in the **d**
2: 2 In **d** to come the mountain of J
7: 1 In the **d** of Ahaz son of Jotham son of Uzziah,
7:17 on your people and on your ancestral house such **d**
13:22 and its **d** will not be prolonged.
23: 7 exultant city whose origin is from **d** of old, H
24:22 and after many **d** they will be punished.
27: 6 In **d** to come Jacob shall take root, J
30:26 like the light of seven **d,** A
37:26 I planned from **d** of old what now I bring to pass, H
38: 1 In those **d** Hezekiah became sick and was at
38:10 In the noontide of my **d** I must depart;
38:20 all the **d** of our lives, at the house of the LORD. C
39: 6 **D** are coming when all that is in your house, F
39: 8 "There will be peace and security in my **d."**
51: 9 Awake, as in **d** of old, the generations of long H
53:10 he shall see his offspring, and shall prolong his **d;**
54: 9 This is like the **d** of Noah to me:
60:20 and your **d** of mourning shall be ended.
63: 9 them up and carried them all the **d** of old. CH
63:11 Then they remembered the **d** of old, H
65:20 that lives but a few **d,** or an old person who does
65:22 like the **d** of a tree shall the **d** of my people be,
Jer 1: 2 of the LORD came in the **d** of King Josiah son
1: 3 in the **d** of King Jehoiakim son of Josiah of Judah,
2:32 my people have forgotten me, **d** without number.
3: 6 The LORD said to me in the **d** of King Josiah:
3:16 in those **d,** says the LORD,
3:18 In those **d** the house of Judah shall join the house
5:18 But even in those **d,** says the LORD,
7:32 Therefore, the **d** are surely coming, F
9:25 The **d** are surely coming, says the LORD, F
13: 6 And after many **d** the LORD said to me,
16: 9 in your **d** and before your eyes,
16:14 Therefore, the **d** are surely coming, F
19: 6 Therefore the **d** are surely coming, F
20:18 and spend my **d** in shame?
22:30 a man who shall not succeed in his **d;**
23: 5 The **d** are surely coming, says the LORD, F
23: 6 In his **d** Judah will be saved and Israel will live
23: 7 Therefore, the **d** are surely coming, F
23:20 In the latter **d** you will understand it clearly.
25:34 for the **d** of your slaughter have come—
26:18 during the **d** of King Hezekiah of Judah, said to all
30: 3 For the **d** are surely coming, says the LORD, F
30:24 In the latter **d** you will understand this.
31:27 The **d** are surely coming, says the LORD, F
31:29 In those **d** they shall no longer say:
31:31 The **d** are surely coming, says the LORD, F
31:33 the house of Israel after those **d,** says the LORD:
31:38 The **d** are surely coming, says the LORD, F
33:14 The **d** are surely coming, says the LORD, F
33:15 In those **d** and at that time I will cause
33:16 In those **d** Judah will be saved
35: 1 in the **d** of King Jehoiakim son of Josiah of Judah:
35: 7 but you shall live in tents all your **d,**
35: 7 in tents all your days, that you may live many **d** in
35: 8 to drink no wine all our **d,** ourselves, our wives,
36: 2 from the **d** of Josiah until today.
37:16 in the cells, and remained there many **d.**
42: 7 of ten **d** the word of the LORD came to Jeremiah.
46:26 Egypt shall be inhabited as in the **d** of old, H
48:47 I will restore the fortunes of Moab in the latter **d,**
49:39 in the latter **d** I will restore the fortunes of Elam,
50: 4 In those **d** and in that time, says the LORD,
50:20 In those **d** and at that time, says the LORD,
51:47 the **d** are coming when I will punish the images F
La 1: 7 in the **d** of her affliction and wandering,
1: 7 all the precious things that were hers in **d** of old. H
4:18 our **d** were numbered; for our end had come.
5:20 Why have you forsaken us these many **d?**
5:21 renew our **d** as of old—

Eze 3:15 I sat there among them, stunned, for seven **d.** A
3:16 the end of seven **d,** the word of the LORD came A
4:4 for the number of the **d** that you lie there.
4:5 For I assign to you a number of **d,**
4:5 three hundred ninety **d,** equal to the number of
4:6 forty **d** I assign you, one day for each year. E
4:8 until you have completed the **d** of your siege.
4:9 During the number of **d** that you lie on your side,
4:9 three hundred ninety **d,** you shall eat it.
5:2 when the **d** of the siege are completed;
12:22 which says, "The **d** are prolonged,
12:23 But say to them, The **d** are near,
12:25 It will no longer be delayed; but in your **d,**
16:22 and your whorings you did not remember the **d**
16:43 you have not remembered the **d** of your youth,
16:60 yet I will remember my covenant with you in the **d**
22:14 or can your hands remain strong in the **d**
23:19 remembering the **d** of her youth,
38:8 After many **d** you shall be mustered;
38:16 In the latter **d** I will bring you against my land,
38:17 in former **d** by my servants the prophets of Israel,
who in those **d** prophesied
43:25 For seven **d** you shall provide daily a goat for A
43:26 Seven **d** shall they make atonement for the altar A
43:27 When these **d** are over,
44:26 they shall count seven **d** for him. A
45:21 and for seven **d** unleavened bread shall be eaten. A
45:23 the seven **d** of the festival he shall provide A
45:23 on each of the seven **d;** A
45:25 fifteenth day of the month and for the seven **d** A
46:1 es east shall remain closed on the six working **d;**
Da 1:12 "Please test your servants for ten **d.**
1:14 to this proposal and tested them for ten **d.**
1:15 of ten **d** it was observed that they appeared better
2:28 Nebuchadnezzar what will happen at the end of **d.**
2:44 the **d** of those kings the God of heaven will set up
5:11 In the **d** of your father he was found
5:26 the **d** of your kingdom and brought it to an end;
6:7 divine or human, for thirty **d,** except to you,
6:12 divine or human, within thirty **d** except to you,
8:26 for it refers to many **d** from now."
8:27 I, Daniel, was overcome and lay sick for some **d;**
10:13 the kingdom of Persia opposed me twenty-one **d.**
10:14 to happen to your people at the end of **d.**
10:14 For there is a further vision for those **d."**
11:20 but within a few **d** he shall be broken,
11:33 for some **d,** however, they shall fall by sword
12:11 there shall be one thousand two hundred ninety **d.**
12:12 and attain the thousand three hundred thirty-five **d.**
12:13 you shall rise for your reward at the end of the **d."**
Hos 1:1 in the **d** of Kings Uzziah, Jotham, Ahaz,
1:1 in the **d** of King Jeroboam son of Joash of Israel.
2:13 I will punish her for the festival **d** of the Baals,
2:15 There she shall respond as in the **d** of her youth,
3:3 "You must remain as mine for many **d;**
3:4 the Israelites shall remain many **d** without king
3:5 to the LORD and to his goodness in the latter **d.**
6:2 After two **d** he will revive us;
9:7 The **d** of punishment have come,
9:7 the **d** of recompense have come;
9:9 They have deeply corrupted themselves as in the **d**
10:9 Since the **d** of Gibeah you have sinned, O Israel;
12:9 as in the **d** of the appointed festival.
Joel 1:2 Has such a thing happened in your **d,**
1:2 or in the **d** of your ancestors?
2:29 Even on the male and female slaves, in those **d,**
3:1 For then, in those **d** and at that time,
Am 1:1 concerning Israel in the **d** of King Uzziah of Judah
1:1 in the **d** of King Jeroboam son of Joash of Israel,
4:4 your tithes every three **d;** B
9:11 and rebuild it as in the **d** of old; H
Jnh 1:17 in the belly of the fish three **d** and three nights. B
3:4 And he cried out, "Forty **d** more, E
Mic 1:1 to Micah of Moresheth in the **d** of Kings Jotham,
4:1 In **d** to come the mountain of the LORD's house J
5:2 whose origin is from of old, from ancient **d.**
7:14 feed in Bashan and Gilead as in the **d** of old. H
7:15 in the **d** when you came out of the land of Egypt,
7:20 have sworn to our ancestors from the **d** of old. H
Hab 1:5 For a work is being done in your **d** that you would
Zep 1:1 in the **d** of King Josiah son of Amon of Judah.
Zec 8:6 to the remnant of this people in these **d,**
8:10 For before those **d** there were no wages for people
8:11 with the remnant of this people as in the former **d,**
8:15 so again I have purposed in these **d** to do good
8:23 In those **d** ten men from nations
14:5 the earthquake in the **d** of King Uzziah of Judah.
Mal 3:4 be pleasing to the LORD as in the **d** of old and H
3:7 the **d** of your ancestors you have turned aside
Mt 3:1 In those **d** John the Baptist appeared in
4:2 He fasted forty **d** and forty nights, E
9:15 **d** will come when the bridegroom is taken away
11:12 the **d** of John the Baptist until now the kingdom
12:40 Jonah was three **d** and three nights in the belly B
12:40 for three **d** and three nights the Son of Man B
15:32 with me now for three **d** and have nothing to eat; B
17:1 Six **d** later, Jesus took with him Peter and James G
23:30 'If we had lived in the **d** of our ancestors,
24:19 and to those who are nursing infants in those **d!**
24:22 And if those **d** had not been cut short,
24:22 for the sake of the elect those **d** will be cut short.
24:29 the suffering of those **d** the sun will be darkened,
24:37 For as the **d** of Noah were,
24:38 For as in those **d** before the flood they were eating
26:2 that after two **d** the Passover is coming,
26:61 the temple of God and to build it in three **d.'"** B
27:40 the temple and build it in three **d,** B
27:63 'After three **d** I will rise again.' B
Mk 1:9 In those **d** Jesus came from Nazareth of Galilee
1:13 He was in the wilderness forty **d,** E
2:1 When he returned to Capernaum after some **d,**
2:20 The **d** will come when the bridegroom is taken
8:1 In those **d** when there was again a great crowd
8:2 with me now for three **d** and have nothing to eat. B
8:31 and be killed, and after three **d** rise again. B
9:2 Six **d** later, Jesus took with him Peter and James G
9:31 and three **d** after being killed, he will rise again." B
10:34 and after three **d** he will rise again." B
13:17 and to those who are nursing infants in those **d!**
13:19 For in those **d** there will be suffering,
13:20 And if the Lord had not cut short those **d,**
13:20 whom he chose, he has cut short those **d.**
13:24 "But in those **d,** after that suffering,
14:1 It was two **d** before the Passover and the festival
14:58 and in three **d** I will build another, B
15:29 the temple and build it in three **d,** B
Lk 1:5 In the **d** of King Herod of Judea,
1:24 After those **d** his wife Elizabeth conceived,
1:39 In those **d** Mary set out and went with haste to
1:75 in holiness and righteousness before him all our **d.**
2:1 In those **d** a decree went out
2:21 After eight **d** had passed, it was time to circumcise
2:46 After three **d** they found him in the temple, B
4:2 where for forty **d** he was tempted by the devil. E
4:2 He ate nothing at all during those **d,**
5:35 The **d** will come when the bridegroom will
5:35 and then they will fast in those **d."**
6:12 Now during those **d** he went out to the mountain
9:28 Now about eight **d** after these sayings Jesus took
9:36 And they kept silent and in those **d** told no one any
9:51 When the **d** drew near for him to be taken up,
13:14 There are six **d** on which work ought to be done; G
13:14 come on those **d** and be cured,
15:13 A few **d** later the younger son gathered all he had
17:22 "The **d** are coming when you will long to see F
17:22 when you will long to see one of the **d** of the Son
17:26 Just as it was in the **d** of Noah, so too it will be in
the **d** of the Son of Man.
17:28 Likewise, just as it was in the **d** of Lot:
19:43 Indeed, the **d** will come upon you,
21:6 the **d** will come when not one stone will be left
21:22 for these are **d** of vengeance,
21:23 and to those who are nursing infants in those **d!**
23:29 For the **d** are surely coming when they will say, F
24:18 the things that have taken place there in these **d?"**
Jn 2:12 and they remained there a few **d.**
2:19 and in three **d** I will raise it up." B
2:20 and will you raise it up in three **d?"** B
4:40 and he stayed there two **d.**
4:43 When the two **d** were over,
11:6 he stayed two **d** longer in the place where he was.
11:17 that Lazarus had already been in the tomb four **d.**
11:39 a stench because he has been dead four **d."**
12:1 Six **d** before the Passover Jesus came to G
Ac 1:3 during forty **d** and speaking about the kingdom E
1:5 with the Holy Spirit not many **d** from now."
1:15 In those **d** Peter stood up among
2:17 'In the last **d** it will be, I
2:18 in those **d** I will pour out my Spirit;
3:24 and those after him, also predicted these **d.**
6:1 during those **d,** when the disciples were increasing
9:9 For three **d** he was without sight, B
9:19 several **d** he was with the disciples in Damascus,
10:30 Cornelius replied, "Four **d** ago at this very hour,
10:48 Then they invited him to stay for several **d.**
13:31 and for many **d** he appeared to those who came up
13:41 for in your **d** I am doing a work,
15:7 that in the early **d** God made a choice among you,
15:36 After some **d** Paul said to Barnabas, "Come,
16:12 We remained in this city for some **d.**
16:18 She kept doing this for many **d.**
17:2 and on three sabbath **d** argued with them from
20:6 from Philippi after the **d** of Unleavened Bread,
20:6 and in five **d** we joined them in Troas,
20:6 where we stayed for seven **d.** A
21:4 the disciples and stayed there for seven **d.** A
21:5 When our **d** there were ended,
21:10 While we were staying there for several **d,**
21:15 After these **d** we got ready and started to go up
21:26 of the **d** of purification when the sacrifice would
21:27 When the seven **d** were almost completed, A
24:1 Five **d** later the high priest Ananias came down
24:11 not more than twelve **d** since I went up to worship
24:24 Some **d** later when Felix came
25:1 Three **d** after Festus had arrived in the province, B
25:6 among them not more than eight or ten **d,** he went
25:13 After several **d** had passed,
25:14 Since they were staying there several **d,**
27:7 We sailed slowly for a number of **d** and arrived
27:20 When neither sun nor stars appeared for many **d,**
28:7 and entertained us hospitably for three **d.** B
28:12 in at Syracuse and stayed there for three **d;** B
28:14 and were invited to stay with them for seven **d.** A
28:17 Three **d** later he called together the local leaders B
Ro 14:5 while others judge all **d** to be alike.
15:4 For whatever was written in former **d** was written
Gal 1:18 to visit Cephas and stayed with him fifteen **d;**
4:10 You are observing special **d,** and months,
Eph 5:16 the most of the time, because the **d** are evil.
Php 4:15 You Philippians indeed know that in the early **d** of
2Ti 3:1 that in the last **d** distressing times will come. I
Tit 3:3 passing our **d** in malice and envy, despicable,
Heb 1:2 but in these last **d** he has spoken to us by a Son, I
5:7 In the **d** of his flesh, Jesus offered up prayers
Heb 7:3 having neither beginning of **d** nor end of life,
8:8 "The **d** are surely coming, says the Lord, F
8:10 the house of Israel after those **d,** says the Lord:
10:16 that I will make with them after those **d,** says
10:32 But recall those earlier **d** when,
11:30 after they had been encircled for seven **d.** A
Jas 5:3 You have laid up treasure for the last **d.** I
1Pe 3:10 "Those who desire life and desire to see good **d,**
3:20 when God waited patiently in the **d** of Noah,
2Pe 3:3 that in the last **d** scoffers will come, I
Rev 2:10 and for ten **d** you will have affliction.
2:13 in me even in the **d** of Antipas my witness,
9:6 And in those **d** people will seek death but will
10:7 but in the **d** when the seventh angel is
11:3 to prophesy for one thousand two hundred sixty **d,**
11:6 no rain may fall during the **d** of their prophesying,
11:9 and a half **d** members of the peoples and tribes
11:11 But after the three and a half **d,**
12:6 for one thousand two hundred sixty **d.**
Tob 1:2 who in the **d** of King Shalmaneser of
1:3 truth and righteousness all the **d** of my life. CD
1:16 In the **d** of Shalmaneser I performed many acts
1:18 from Judea in those **d** of judgment that the king
1:21 But not forty **d** passed before two E
4:3 and do not abandon her all the **d** of her life. CD
4:5 "Revere the Lord all your **d,** my son,
4:5 Live uprightly all the **d** of your life, CD
5:6 It is a journey of two **d** from Ecbatana to Rages;
8:20 "You shall not leave here for fourteen **d,**
9:4 you know that my father must be counting the **d,**
10:1 how many **d** Tobias would need for going and
10:1 when the **d** had passed and his son did not appear,
10:7 Now when the fourteen **d** of the wedding
10:12 do nothing to grieve her all the **d** of your life. CD
10:12 we all prosper together all the **d** of our lives." C
10:13 by the Lord to honor you all the **d** of my life." CD
11:18 for seven **d,** and many gifts were given A
14:7 in those **d** and are truly mindful of God will
Jdt 1:1 In those **d** Arphaxad ruled over the Medes
1:16 and feasted for one hundred twenty **d.**
2:21 three **d** from Nineveh to the plain of Bectileth, B
4:13 for the people fasted many **d** throughout Judea and
6:15 who in those **d** were Uzziah son of Micah,
7:20 and cavalry, surrounded them for thirty-four **d,**
7:30 Let us hold out for five **d** more;
7:31 But if these **d** pass by, and no help comes for us,
8:1 Now in those **d** Judith heard about these things:
8:6 She fasted all the **d** of her widowhood, C
8:6 festivals and **d** of rejoicing of the house of Israel.
8:9 to surrender the town to the Assyrians after five **d,**
8:11 the Lord turns and helps us within so many **d.**
8:15 he does not choose to help us within these five **d,**
8:18 never in our generation, nor in these present **d,**
8:18 as was done in **d** gone by.
8:33 the **d** after which you have promised to surrender
10:2 where she lived on sabbaths and on her festal **d.**
12:7 She remained in the camp three **d.** B
13:3 as she did on the other **d;**
14:8 Now tell me what you have done during these **d."**
15:11 All the people plundered the camp for thirty **d.**
16:22 she gave herself to no man all the **d** of her life CD
16:24 the house of Israel mourned her for seven **d.** A
AdE 1:1 that the following things happened in the **d**
1:2 In those **d,** when King Artaxerxes was enthroned
1:4 during the course of one hundred eighty **d,**
1:5 for six **d** in the courtyard of the royal palace, G
2:12 the **d** of beautification are completed—
2:18 a banquet lasting seven **d** for all his Friends and A
3:7 taking the **d** and the months one by one,
4:8 he said, "the **d** when you were an ordinary person,
4:11 now thirty **d** since I was called to go to the king.'"
4:16 for three **d** and nights do not eat or drink, B
9:21 the fourteenth and fifteenth **d** of Adar,
9:22 on these **d** the Jews got relief from their enemies.
9:26 Therefore these **d** were called "Purim,"
9:27 These **d** of Purim should be a memorial and kept
9:28 These **d** of Purim were to be observed for all time,
10:13 So they will observe these **d** in the month of Adar,
14:16 of my proud position, which is upon my head on **d**
14:16 and I do not wear it on the **d** when I am at leisure.
Sir 1:2 and the **d** of eternity—who can count them?
2:3 so that your last **d** may be prosperous. I
17:2 He gave them a fixed number of **d,**
18:9 The number of **d** in their life is great
18:10 so are a few years among the **d** of eternity.
18:25 in **d** of wealth think of poverty and need.
22:12 Mourning for the dead lasts seven **d,** A
22:12 for the foolish or the ungodly it lasts all the **d** C
26:1 the number of his **d** will be doubled.
33:9 Some **d** he exalted and hallowed,
33:9 and some he made ordinary **d.**
33:24 At the time when you end the **d** of your life, D
37:25 The **d** of a person's life are numbered, D
37:25 but the **d** of Israel are without number.
41:13 The **d** of a good life are numbered, D
43:7 From the moon comes the sign for festal **d,**
46:7 And in the **d** of Moses he proved his loyalty,
47:1 him Nathan rose up to prophesy in the **d** of David.
48:18 In his **d** Sennacherib invaded the country;
48:23 In Isaiah's **d** the sun went backward,
49:12 in their **d** they built the house and raised
50:3 In his **d** a water cistern was dug,
50:8 the **d** of first fruits, like lilies by a spring of water,
50:23 and may there be peace in our **d** in Israel,
50:23 as in the **d** of old. H
50:24 and may he deliver us in our **d!**
51:10 do not forsake me in the **d** of trouble,

Bar 1:11 their **d** on earth may be like the days of heaven.
1:11 their days on earth may be like the **d** of heaven.
1:12 and we shall serve them many **d** and find favor
1:14 the house of the Lord on the **d** of the festivals and
3:14 the same time discern where there is length of **d**,
4:20 I will cry to the Everlasting all my **d**.
4:35 upon her from the Everlasting for many **d**,
Aza 1:47 Bless the Lord, nights and **d**;
Sus 1:52 "You old relic of wicked **d**,
Bel 1:31 and he was there for six **d**. G
1Mc 1:11 In those **d** certain renegades came out from Israel
2:1 In those **d** Mattathias son of John son of Simeon,
2:49 Now the **d** drew near for Mattathias to die,
3:29 the laws that had existed from the earliest **d**.
3:49 up the nazirites who had completed their **d**;
4:56 for eight **d**, and joyfully offered burnt offerings;
4:59 the **d** of dedication of the altar should be observed
with joy and gladness for eight **d**,
6:9 He lay there for many **d**,
6:31 for many **d** they fought and built engines of war;
6:51 he encamped before the sanctuary for many **d**.
6:52 of war to match theirs, and fought for many **d**.
7:50 So the land of Judah had rest for a few **d**.
9:20 they mourned many **d** and said,
9:24 In those **d** a very great famine occurred,
9:64 against it for many **d** and made machines of war.
10:34 and sabbaths and new moons and appointed **d**,
10:34 and the three **d** before a festival and the three B
10:34 let them all be **d** of immunity and release for all
10:47 and they remained his allies all his **d**.
11:18 But King Ptolemy died three **d** later, B
11:20 In those **d** Jonathan assembled the Judeans
11:40 and he stayed there many **d**.
11:65 and fought against it for many **d** and hemmed it in.
12:11 both at our festivals and on other appropriate **d**,
13:26 and mourned for him many **d**.
13:43 In those **d** Simon encamped against Gazara
14:4 The land had rest all the **d** of Simon. C
14:4 as was the honor shown him, all his **d**.
14:13 and the kings were crushed in those **d**.
14:36 In his **d** things prospered in his hands,
2Mc 2:12 Likewise Solomon also kept the eight **d**.
2:16 Will you therefore please keep the **d**?
5:2 And it happened that, for almost forty **d**, E
5:14 of three **d** eighty thousand were destroyed, B
10:6 They celebrated it for eight **d** with rejoicing,
10:8 of the Jews should observe these **d** every year.
10:33 and they besieged the fort for four **d**.
12:15 or engines of war overthrew Jericho in the **d**
13:12 and lying prostrate for three **d** without ceasing, B
15:2 and hallowed above other **d**,"
1Es 1:19 and the festival of unleavened bread seven **d**. A
1:44 he reigned three months and ten **d** in Jerusalem.
4:21 With his wife he ends his **d**,
4:63 with music and rejoicing, for seven **d**. A
5:69 since the **d** of King Esar-haddon of the Assyrians,
7:14 kept the festival of unleavened bread seven **d**, A
8:41 and we encamped there three **d**, B
8:62 When we had been there three **d**, B
9:4 if any did not meet there within two or three **d**, B
9:5 at Jerusalem within three **d**; B
Man 1:15 will praise you continually all the **d** of my life. CD
3Mc 4:8 spent the remaining **d** of their marriage festival
4:15 to an end after forty **d** but still uncompleted. E
6:30 for a festival of seven **d**, A
6:36 they instituted the observance of the aforesaid **d**
6:38 of Pachon to the fourth of Epeiph, for forty **d**; E
6:38 for the fifth to the seventh of Epeiph, the three **d** B
7:17 with the common desire, for seven **d**. A
7:19 in like manner they decided to observe these **d** as
2Es 1:31 for I have rejected your festal **d**, and new moons,
2:13 pray that your **d** may be few,
4:51 "Do you think that I shall live until those **d**?
4:51 Or who will be alive in those **d**?"
5:1 lo, the **d** are coming when those who inhabit F
5:13 and weep as you do now, and fast for seven **d**, A
5:19 from me and do not come near me for seven **d**; A
5:20 So I fasted seven **d**, mourning and weeping, A
5:21 After seven **d** the thoughts A
6:18 "The **d** are coming when I draw near to visit F
6:31 you will pray again and fast again for seven **d**, A
6:35 Now after this I wept again and fasted seven **d** A
7:30 be turned back to primeval silence for seven **d**, A
7:31 After seven **d** the world that is not yet awake A
7:*84* the torment laid up for themselves in the last **d**. I
7:*95* and the glory waiting for them in the last **d**. I
7:*101* "They shall have freedom for seven **d**, A
7:*101* during these seven **d** they may see the things A
7:*107* [37] Joshua after him for Israel in the **d** of Achan,
7:*108* [38] and Samuel in the **d** of Saul,
7:*110* [40] for the people in the **d** of Sennacherib,
9:4 the Most High spoke from the **d** that were of old,
9:23 "Now, if you will let seven **d** more pass— A
9:27 After seven **d**, while I lay on the grass, A
10:59 to those who inhabit the earth in the last **d**." I
12:13 **d** are coming when a kingdom shall rise on earth, F
12:23 In its last **d** the Most High will raise I
12:28 but he also shall fall by the sword in the last **d**. I
12:32 the Most High has kept until the end of **d**,
12:39 But as for you, wait here seven **d** more, A
12:40 that the seven **d** were past and I had not returned A
12:49 and after these **d** I will come to you."
12:51 But I sat in the field seven **d**, A
12:51 and my food was of plants during those **d**.
13:1 After seven **d** I dreamed a dream in the night. A
13:16 alas for those who will be left in those **d**!
13:18 the things that are reserved for the last **d**, I
2Es 13:20 and not to see what will happen in the last **d**." I
13:29 The **d** are coming when the Most High will F
13:40 the **d** of King Hoshea, whom Shalmaneser,
13:56 that after three more **d** I will tell you other things,
13:58 And I stayed there three **d**. B
14:4 where I kept him with me many **d**.
14:22 those who want to live in the last **d** may do so." I
14:23 and tell them not to seek you for forty **d**. E
14:36 and let no one seek me for forty **d**." E
14:42 not know. They sat forty **d**; E
14:44 the forty **d**, ninety-four books were written. E
14:45 And when the forty **d** were ended, E
16:17 Who will deliver me in those **d**?
16:31 so in those **d** three or four shall be left
16:74 the **d** of tribulation are at hand,
4Mc 14:7 as the seven **d** of creation move in choral dance A
18:19 this is your life and the length of your **d**.' "

DAYS' (11) [DAY]
A. THREE DAYS' (10)

Ge 30:36 of three **d** journey between himself and Jacob, A
Ex 3:18 now go a three **d** journey into the wilderness, A
5:3 a three **d** journey into the wilderness to sacrifice A
8:27 three **d** journey into the wilderness and sacrifice A
Nu 10:33 from the mount of the LORD three **d** journey A
10:33 of the LORD going before them three **d** journey, A
33:8 a three **d** journey in the wilderness of Etham, A
1Sa 11:3 of Jabesh said to him, "Give us seven **d** respite
2Sa 24:13 Or shall there be three **d** pestilence in your land? A
Jnh 3:3 an exceedingly large city, a three **d** walk across. A
1Mc 5:24 and made three **d** journey into the wilderness. A

DAYTIME (5) [DAY, TIME]
Job 5:14 They meet with darkness in the **d**,
Ps 78:14 In the **d** he led them with a cloud,
2Pe 2:13 They count it a pleasure to revel in the **d**.
2Es 14:42 They sat forty days; they wrote during the **d**,
14:43 for me, I spoke in the **d** and was not silent at night.

DAZED (1)
Joel 1:18 even the flocks of sheep are **d**.

DAZZLED (1) [DAZZLING]
Sir 43:18 The eye is **d** by the beauty of its whiteness,

DAZZLING (5) [DAZZLED]
Mt 17:2 and his clothes became **d** white.
Mk 9:3 and his clothes became **d** white,
Lk 9:29 and his clothes became **d** white.
24:4 suddenly two men in **d** clothes stood beside them.
Ac 10:30 when suddenly a man in **d** clothes stood

DEACON‡ (1) [DEACONS]
Ro 16:1 a **d** of the church at Cenchreae,

DEACONS‡ (5) [DEACON]
Php 1:1 in Philippi, with the bishops and **d**:
1Ti 3:8 **D** likewise must be serious, not double-tongued,
3:10 prove themselves blameless, let them serve as **d**.
3:12 Let **d** be married only once,
3:13 for those who serve well as **d** gain a good standing

DEAD‡ (353) [DEADLY, DEATH, DEATH'S, DEATH-BLOW, DEATHLY, DIE, DIED, DIES, DYING]
A. RAISED FROM THE DEAD (20)
B. RESURRECTION OF/FROM THE DEAD (13)
C. DEAD SEA (10)

Ge 14:3 in the Valley of Siddim (that is, the **D** Sea). C
23:3 Abraham rose up from beside his **d**,
23:4 so that I may bury my **d** out of my sight."
23:6 Bury your **d** in the choicest of our burial places;
23:6 from you any burial ground for burying your **d**."
23:8 "If you are willing that I should bury my **d** out
23:11 of my people I give it to you; bury your **d**."
23:13 accept it from me, so that I may bury my **d** there."
23:15 between you and me? Bury your **d**."
42:38 for his brother is **d**, and he alone is left.
44:20 His brother is **d**; he alone is left
50:15 Realizing that their father was **d**,
Ex 4:19 for all those who were seeking your life are **d**."
9:7 not one of the livestock of the Israelites was **d**.
12:30 for there was not a house without someone **d**.
12:33 for they said, "We shall all be **d**."
14:30 and Israel saw the Egyptians **d** on the seashore.
21:18 though not **d**, is confined to bed,
21:34 to its owner, but keeping the **d** animal.
21:35 and the **d** animal they shall also divide.
21:36 for ox, but keep the **d** animal.
Lev 11:31 when they are **d** shall be unclean until the evening.
11:32 of them falls when they are **d** shall be unclean,
19:28 not make any gashes in your flesh for the **d**
21:1 No one shall defile himself for a **d** person
21:11 He shall not go where there is a **d** body;
Nu 14:29 your **d** bodies shall fall in this very wilderness;
14:32 for you, your **d** bodies shall fall in this wilderness.
14:33 the last of your **d** bodies lies in the wilderness.
16:48 He stood between the **d** and the living;
19:11 the **d** body of any human being shall
Nu 34:3 from the end of the **D** Sea on the east; C
34:12 and its end shall be at the **D** Sea. C
Dt 3:17 of the Arabah, the **D** Sea, with the lower slopes C
14:1 or shave your forelocks for the **d**.
18:11 or who seeks oracles from the **d**.
26:14 and I have not offered any of it to the **d**.
Jos 1:2 "My servant Moses is **d**.
3:16 the **D** Sea, were wholly cut off. C
12:3 to the sea of the Arabah, the **D** Sea, C
15:2 of the **D** Sea, from the bay that faces southward; C
15:5 And the east boundary is the **D** Sea, C
18:19 boundary ends at the northern bay of the **D** Sea, C
Jdg 3:25 There was their lord lying **d** on the floor.
4:22 and there was Sisera lying **d**,
5:27 where he sank, there he fell **d**.
9:55 When the Israelites saw that Abimelech was **d**,
Ru 1:8 as you have dealt with the **d** and with me.
2:20 not forsaken the living or the **d**!"
4:5 the widow of the **d** man, to maintain the **d** man's
4:10 to maintain the **d** man's name on his inheritance,
4:10 name of the **d** may not be cut off from his kindred
1Sa 4:17 your two sons also, Hophni and Phinehas, are **d**,
4:19 and that her father-in-law and her husband were **d**,
17:46 the **d** bodies of the Philistine army this very day to
17:51 the Philistines saw that their champion was **d**,
24:14 Whom do you pursue? A **d** dog?
25:39 When David heard that Nabal was **d**, he said,
31:5 When his armor-bearer saw that Saul was **d**,
31:7 and his sons were **d**, they forsook their towns
31:8 next day, when the Philistines came to strip the **d**,
2Sa 2:7 for Saul your lord is **d**,
4:10 Saul is **d**,' thought he was bringing good news,
9:8 that you should look upon a **d** dog such as I?"
11:21 'Your servant Uriah the Hittite is **d** too.' "
11:24 some of the king's servants are **d**;
11:24 and your servant Uriah the Hittite is **d** also."
11:26 the wife of Uriah heard that her husband was **d**,
12:18 to tell him that the child was **d**;
12:18 how then can we tell him the child is **d**?
12:19 he perceived that the child was **d**;
12:19 and David said to his servants, "Is the child **d**?"
12:19 They said, "He is **d**."
12:23 But now he is **d**; why should I fast?
13:32 the young men the king's sons; Amnon alone is **d**.
13:33 all the king's sons were **d**; for Amnon alone is **d**."
14:2 who has been mourning many days for the **d**.
14:5 I am a widow; my husband is **d**.
16:9 "Why should this **d** dog curse my lord the king?
18:20 because the king's son is **d**."
19:6 if Absalom were alive and all of us were **d** today,
19:10 whom we anointed over us, is **d** in battle.
23:10 people came back to him—but only to strip the **d**.
1Ki 3:20 and laid her **d** son at my breast.
3:21 I saw that he was **d**;
3:22 the living son is mine, and the **d** son is yours."
3:22 The first said, "No, the **d** son is yours,
3:23 and your son is **d**'; while the other says, 'Not so!
3:23 Your son is **d**, and my son is the living one.' "
11:15 the commander of the army went up to bury the **d**,
11:21 and that Joab the commander of the army was **d**,
21:14 "Naboth has been stoned; he is **d**."
21:15 that Naboth had been stoned and was **d**,
21:15 for Naboth is not alive, but **d**."
21:16 As soon as Ahab heard that Naboth was **d**,
2Ki 4:1 "Your servant my husband is **d**;
4:32 he saw the child lying **d** on his bed.
8:5 the king how Elisha had restored a **d** person to life,
11:1 Ahaziah's mother, saw that her son was **d**,
19:35 when morning dawned, they were all **d** bodies.
23:30 His servants carried him **d** in a chariot
1Ch 10:5 When his armor-bearer saw that Saul was **d**,
10:7 and his sons were **d**, they abandoned their towns
10:8 next day when the Philistines came to strip the **d**,
2Ch 22:10 Ahaziah's mother, saw that her son was **d**,
Job 1:19 and they are **d**; I alone have escaped to tell you."
Ps 31:12 I have passed out of mind like one who is **d**;
88:5 like those forsaken among the **d**,
88:10 Do you work wonders for the **d**?
106:28 and ate sacrifices offered to the **d**;
115:17 The **d** do not praise the LORD,
143:3 making me sit in darkness like those long **d**.
Pr 9:18 But they do not know that the **d** are there,
21:16 of understanding will rest in the assembly of the **d**.
Ecc 4:2 And I thought the **d**, who have already died,
9:3 and after that they go to the **d**.
9:4 for a living dog is better than a **d** lion.
9:5 that they will die, but the **d** know nothing;
10:1 **D** flies make the perfumer's ointment give off
Isa 8:19 the **d** on behalf of the living,
14:19 clothed with the **d**, those pierced by the sword,
19:3 the idols and the spirits of the **d** and the ghosts and
22:2 nor are they **d** in battle.
26:14 The **d** do not live; shades do
26:19 Your **d** shall live, their corpses shall rise.
26:19 and the earth will give birth to those long **d**.
37:36 when morning dawned, they were all **d** bodies.
59:10 among the vigorous as though we were **d**.
66:24 And they shall go out and look at the **d** bodies of
Jer 16:4 and their **d** bodies shall become food for the birds
16:7 to offer comfort for the **d**.
19:7 I will give their **d** bodies for food to the birds of
22:10 Do not weep for him who is **d**, nor bemoan him;
26:23 down with the sword and threw his **d** body into
28:16 Within this year you will be **d**,
31:40 The whole valley of the **d** bodies and the ashes,
33:5 the **d** bodies of those whom I shall strike down
36:30 and his **d** body shall be cast out to the heat by day

La 3: 6 he has made me sit in darkness like the d
Eze 24:17 Sigh, but not aloud; make no mourning for the d.
28:23 and the d shall fall in its midst,
44:25 not defile themselves by going near to a d person;
Am 6:10 And if a relative, one who burns the d,
8: 3 d bodies shall be many, cast out in every place.
Na 3: 3 piles of d, heaps of corpses, d bodies without end
Hag 2:13 by contact with a d body touches any of these,
Mt 2:20 for those who were seeking the child's life are d."
8:22 "Follow me, and let the d bury their own d."
8:26 and there was a d calm.
9:24 for the girl is not d but sleeping."
10: 8 Cure the sick, raise the d, cleanse the lepers,
11: 5 the deaf hear, the d are raised,
14: 2 he has been raised from the d, A
17: 9 the Son of Man has been raised from the d." A
22:31 And as for the resurrection of the d, B
22:32 He is God not of the d, but of the living."
23:27 but inside they are full of the bones of the d and
27:64 'He has been raised from the d,' A
28: 4 of him the guards shook and became like d men.
28: 7 'He has been raised from the d, A
Mk 4:39 Then the wind ceased, and there was a d calm.
5:35 the leader's house to say, "Your daughter is d.
5:39 The child is not d but sleeping."
6:14 "John the baptizer has been raised from the d; A
9: 9 until after the Son of Man had risen from the d.
9:10 what this rising from the d could mean.
9:26 so that most of them said, "He is d."
12:25 For when they rise from the d,
12:26 And as for the d being raised,
12:27 He is God not of the d, but of the living;
15:44 Then Pilate wondered if he were already d;
15:44 the centurion, he asked him whether he had been d
15:45 When he learned from the centurion that he was d,
Lk 7:15 The d man sat up and began to speak,
7:22 the deaf hear, the d are raised,
8:49 the leader's house to say, "Your daughter is d;
8:52 for she is not d but sleeping."
8:53 And they laughed at him, knowing that she was d.
9: 7 by some that John had been raised from the d, A
9:60 Jesus said to him, "Let the d bury their own d;
10:30 beat him, and went away, leaving him half d.
15:24 for this son of mine was d and is alive again;
15:32 this brother of yours was d and has come to life;
16:30 but if someone goes to them from the d,
16:31 be convinced even if someone rises from the d.' "
20:35 and in the resurrection from the d neither marry B
20:37 fact that the d are raised Moses himself showed,
20:38 Now he is God not of the d, but of the living;
24: 5 "Why do you look for the living among the d?
24:46 that the Messiah is to suffer and to rise from the d
Jn 2:22 After he was raised from the d, A
5:21 just as the Father raises the d and gives them life,
5:25 when the d will hear the voice of the Son of God,
11:14 Then Jesus told them plainly, "Lazarus is d.
11:39 Martha, the sister of the d man, said to him, "Lord,
11:39 a stench because he has been d four days."
11:44 The d man came out, his hands and feet bound
12: 1 whom he had raised from the d. A
12: 9 whom he had raised from the d. A
12:17 of the tomb and raised him from the d continued
19:33 they came to Jesus and saw that he was already d,
20: 9 that he must rise from the d.
21:14 to the disciples after he was raised from the d. A
Ac 3:15 whom God raised from the d. A
4: 2 that in Jesus there is the resurrection of the d. B
4:10 you crucified, whom God raised from the d. A
5:10 When the young men came in they found her d,
10:41 and drank with him after he rose from the d.
10:42 by God as judge of the living and the d.
13:30 But God raised him from the d;
13:34 As to his raising him from the d,
14:19 of the city, supposing that he was d.
17: 3 for the Messiah to suffer and to rise from the d,
17:31 to all by raising him from the d."
17:32 When they heard of the resurrection of the d, B
20: 9 three floors below and was picked up d.
23: 6 concerning the hope of the resurrection of the d. B
24:21 about the resurrection of the d that I am on trial B
26: 8 by any of you that God raises the d?
26:23 and that, by being the first to rise from the d,
28: 6 They were expecting him to swell up or drop d,
Ro 1: 4 the spirit of holiness by resurrection from the d, B
4:17 to the d and calls into existence the things that do
4:19 which was already as good as d (for he was about
4:24 in him who raised Jesus our Lord from the d,
6: 4 just as Christ was raised from the d by the glory A
6: 9 We know that Christ, being raised from the d, A
6:11 also must consider yourselves d to sin and alive
7: 4 raised from the d in order that we may bear fruit A
7: 6 d to that which held us captive,
7: 8 Apart from the law sin lies d.
8:10 though the body is d because of sin,
8:11 of him who raised Jesus from the d dwells in you,
8:11 from the d will give life to your mortal bodies also
10: 7 (that is, to bring Christ up from the d).
10: 9 in your heart that God raised him from the d,
11:15 what will their acceptance be but life from the d!
14: 9 that he might be Lord of both the d and the living.
1Co 15:12 Now if Christ is proclaimed as raised from the d, A
15:12 of you say there is no resurrection of the d? B
15:13 If there is no resurrection of the d, B
15:15 whom he did not raise if it is true that the d are
15:16 d are not raised, then Christ has not been raised.
15:20 But in fact Christ has been raised from the d, A
15:21 the resurrection of the d has also come through B
1Co 15:29 who receive baptism on behalf of the d?
15:29 If the d are not raised at all,
15:32 If the d are not raised, "Let us eat and drink,
15:35 But someone will ask, "How are the d raised?
15:42 So it is with the resurrection of the d. B
15:52 and the d will be raised imperishable,
2Co 1: 9 not on ourselves but on God who raises the d.
Gal 1: 1 who raised him from the d—
Eph 1:20 to work in Christ when he raised him from the d
2: 1 You were d through the trespasses and sins
2: 5 even when we were d through our trespasses,
5:14 Rise from the d, and Christ will shine on you."
Php 3:11 I may attain the resurrection from the d. B
Col 1:18 he is the beginning, the firstborn from the d,
2:12 who raised him from the d.
2:13 And when you were d in trespasses and
1Th 1:10 whom he raised from the d— A
4:16 and the d in Christ will rise first.
1Ti 5: 6 but the widow who lives for pleasure is d even
2Ti 2: 8 Remember Jesus Christ, raised from the d, A
4: 1 who is to judge the living and the d,
Heb 6: 1 repentance from d works and faith toward God,
6: 2 resurrection of the d, and eternal judgment. B
9:14 purify our conscience from d works to worship
11:12 from one person, and this one as good as d,
11:19 that God is able even to raise someone from the d
11:35 Women received their d by resurrection.
13:20 who brought back from the d our Lord Jesus,
Jas 2:17 So faith by itself, if it has no works, is d.
2:26 For just as the body without the spirit is d, so faith without works is also d.
1Pe 1: 3 the resurrection of Jesus Christ from the d,
1:21 who raised him from the d and gave him glory,
4: 5 to judge the living and the d.
4: 6 the gospel was proclaimed even to the d,
Jude 1:12 autumn trees without fruit, twice d, uprooted;
Rev 1: 5 the faithful witness, the firstborn of the d,
1:17 When I saw him, I fell at his feet as though d.
1:18 I was d, and see, I am alive forever and ever;
2: 8 who was d and came to life:
2:23 and I will strike her children d.
3: 1 you have a name of being alive, but you are d.
11: 8 and their d bodies will lie in the street of
11: 9 and nations will gaze at their d bodies and refuse
11:18 and the time for judging the d,
14:13 Blessed are the d who from now on die in
20: 5 (The rest of the d did not come to life until
20:12 And I saw the d, great and small,
20:12 And the d were judged according to their works,
20:13 And the sea gave up the d that were in it,
20:13 Death and Hades gave up the d that were in them,
Tob 1:17 the d body of any of my people thrown out behind
2: 8 yet here he is again burying the d!"
3: 9 Because your husbands are d?
5:10 in darkness like the d who no longer see the light.
5:10 Although still alive, I am among the d.
8:12 But if he is d, let us bury him
12:12 and likewise whenever you would bury the d.
12:13 up and leave your dinner to go and bury the d,
Jdt 2: 8 and the swelling river shall be filled with their d.
6: 4 and their fields will be full of their d.
13: 2 on his bed, for he was d drunk.
14:15 and found him sprawled on the floor d,
Wis 4:18 and an outrage among the d forever;
13:10 But miserable, with their hopes set on d things,
13:18 for life he prays to a thing that is d;
14:15 as a god what was once a d human being,
15: 5 so that they desire the lifeless form of a d image.
15:17 and what they make with lawless hands is d;
18:18 down half d, made known why they were dying;
18:23 the d had already fallen on one another in heaps,
19: 3 and were lamenting at the graves of their d,
Sir 7:33 do not withhold kindness even from the d.
10:11 For when one is d he inherits maggots and vermin
17:28 From the d, as from one who does not exist,
22:11 Weep for the d, for he has left the light behind;
22:11 Weep less bitterly for the d, for he is at rest;
22:12 Mourning for the d lasts seven days,
30: 4 When the father dies he will not seem to be d,
38:16 My child, let your tears fall for the d,
38:21 you do the d no good, and you injure yourself.
38:23 When the d is at rest, let his remembrance rest too,
48:13 Nothing was too hard for him, and when he was d,
Bar 2:17 O Lord, and see, for the d who are in Hades,
3:10 that you are defiled with the d,
LtJ 6:27 Gifts are placed before them just as before the d.
1Mc 5:51 through the town over the bodies of the d.
6:17 When Lysias learned that the king was d,
9:57 When Bacchides saw that Alcimus was d,
2Mc 5: 5 When a false rumor arose that Antiochus was d,
12:40 of each one of the d they found sacred tokens of
12:44 and foolish to pray for the d.
12:45 Therefore he made atonement for the d,
15:28 they recognized Nicanor, lying d, in full armor.
2Es 2:16 And I will raise up the d from their places,
2:23 When you find any who are d,
5: 7 and the D Sea shall cast up fish; C
7:37 to the nations that have been raised from the d, A
7:109 [39] and for the one who was d, that he might live,
16:23 And the d shall be thrown out like dung,
4Mc 4:11 down half d in the temple area that was open
8:21 that if we disobey we are d!
12:18 both in this present life and when you are d."

DEADLY (17) [DEAD]

Ex 9: 3 with a d pestilence your livestock in the field:
Ex 10:17 that at the least he remove this d thing from me."
Ps 7:13 he has prepared his d weapons,
17: 9 my d enemies who surround me.
41: 8 They think that a d thing has fastened on me,
42:10 As with a d wound in my body,
91: 3 the snare of the fowler and from the d pestilence;
Pr 12: 6 The words of the wicked are a d ambush,
26:18 a maniac who shoots d firebrands and arrows,
Jer 9: 8 Their tongue is a d arrow;
16: 4 They shall die of d diseases.
Eze 5:16 when I loose against you my d arrows of famine,
14:21 upon Jerusalem my four d acts of judgment,
Mk 16:18 ⟦if they drink any d thing, it will not hurt them;⟧
2Co 1:10 He who rescued us from so d a peril will continue
Jas 3: 8 a restless evil, full of d poison.
AdE 14: 1 Then Queen Esther, seized with d anxiety,

DEAF (14) [DEAFENS]

Ex 4:11 Who makes them mute or d, seeing or blind?
Lev 19:14 You shall not revile the d or put a stumbling block
Ps 38:13 But I am like the d, I do not hear;
58: 4 like the d adder that stops its ear,
Isa 29:18 On that day the d shall hear the words of a scroll,
35: 5 and the ears of the d unstopped;
42:18 you that are d; and you
42:19 or d like my messenger whom I send?
43: 8 yet have eyes, who are d, yet have ears!
Mic 7:16 on their mouths; their ears shall be d;
Mt 11: 5 the lame walk, the lepers are cleansed, the d hear,
Mk 7:32 a d man who had an impediment in his speech;
7:37 even makes the d to hear and the mute to speak."
Lk 7:22 the lame walk, the lepers are cleansed, the d hear,

DEAFENS (1) [DEAF]

Sir 38:28 the sound of the hammer d his ears,

DEAL‡ (77) [DEALER, DEALERS, DEALING, DEALINGS, DEALS, DEALT]

Ge 19: 9 Now we will d worse with you than with them."
21:23 not d falsely with me or with my offspring or
21:23 you will d with me and with the land
24:49 if you will d loyally and truly with my master,
47:29 under my thigh and promise to d loyally and truly
Ex 1:10 Come, let us d shrewdly with them,
8:29 not let Pharaoh again d falsely by not letting
21: 9 he shall d with her as with a daughter.
22:25 you shall not d with them as a creditor;
Lev 19:11 You shall not steal; you shall not d falsely;
22: 2 Direct Aaron and his sons to d carefully with
Nu 4:19 This is how you must d with them in order
Dt 7: 5 But this is how you must d with them:
31: 5 to you and you shall d with them in full accord
Jos 2:12 to me by the LORD that you in turn will d kindly
2:14 then we will d kindly and faithfully with you when
24:27 if you d falsely with your God."
Jdg 1:24 and we will d kindly with you."
9:33 you may d with them as best you can."
Ru 1: 8 May the LORD d kindly with you,
1Sa 18:17 let the Philistines d with him."
20: 8 Therefore d kindly with your servant,
2Sa 10: 2 "I will d loyally with Hanun son of Nahash,
18: 5 "D gently for my sake with the young man
1Ki 2: 7 D loyally, however, with the sons of Barzillai
2Ki 12:10 that there was a great d of money in the chest,
22: 7 into their hand, for they d honestly."
1Ch 19: 2 "I will d loyally with Hanun son of Nahash,
2Ch 19:11 D courageously, and may the LORD be with
Ne 5: 7 And I called a great assembly to d with them,
Job 42: 8 for I will accept his prayer not to d with you
Ps 55:12 it is not adversaries who d insolently with me—
58: 2 your hands d out violence on earth.
103:10 He does not d with us according to our sins,
105:25 to d craftily with his servants.
112: 5 It is well with those who d generously and lend,
119:17 D bountifully with your servant,
119:124 D with your servant according
142: 7 for you will d bountifully with me.
Isa 1: 4 offspring who do evil, children who d corruptly,
24:16 For the treacherous d treacherously,
24:16 the treacherous d very treacherously.
26:10 in the land of uprightness they d perversely and do
48: 8 For I knew that you would d very treacherously,
63: 8 children who will not d falsely";
Jer 18:23 d with them while you are angry.
23: 5 and he shall reign as king and d wisely,
39:12 but d with him as he may ask you."
La 1:22 and d with them as you have dealt with me
Eze 7:27 According to their way I will d with them;
16:59 I will d with you as you have done,
20:44 when I d with you for my name's sake,
22:14 in the days when I shall d with you?
23:25 in order that they may d with you in fury.
23:29 and they shall d with you in hatred,
35:11 I will d with you according to the anger and envy
35:15 because it was desolate, so I will d with you;
Da 1:13 and d with your servants according
11:39 He shall d with the strongest fortresses by the help
Hos 7: 1 for they d falsely, the thief breaks in,
Zep 3:19 I will d with all your oppressors at that time.
Zec 8:11 now I will not d with the remnant of this people as
Mt 27:19 for today I have suffered a great d because of
Jn 6:10 Now there was a great d of grass in the place;
Ac 16:16 of divination and brought her owners a great d
Ro 8: 3 and to d with sin, he condemned sin in the flesh,

1Co 7:31 and those who **d** with the world as
Heb 5: 2 to **d** gently with the ignorant and wayward,
9:10 **d** only with food and drink and various baptisms,
9:28 will appear a second time, not to **d** with sin,
Tob 3: 6 So now **d** with me as you will;
Jdt 3: 4 come and **d** with them as you see fit."
Aza 1:19 but **d** with us in your patience and
1Mc 9:29 and to **d** with those of our nation who hate us.
2Mc 6:14 but he does not **d** in this way with us,
4Mc 3: 3 but reason can help to **d** with anger.
4: 5 On receiving authority to **d** with this matter,

DEALER (1) [DEAL]
Ac 16:14 from the city of Thyatira and a **d** in purple cloth.

DEALERS (3) [DEAL]
Eze 27:21 and all the princes of Kedar were your favored **d**
27:27 your caulkers, your **d** in merchandise,
Mt 25: 9 you had better go to the **d** and buy some

DEALING (9) [DEAL]
Pr 1: 3 in wise **d**, righteousness, justice, and equity;
Isa 33: 1 and when you have stopped **d** treacherously,
66: 6 voice of the LORD, **d** retribution to his enemies!
Eze 20:27 by **d** treacherously with me.
Lk 16: 8 for the children of this age are more shrewd in **d**
2Co 13: 3 He is not weak in **d** with you,
13: 4 in **d** with you we will live with him by the power
Sir 41:18 of unjust **d**, before your partner or your friend;
42: 5 of profit from **d** with merchants,

DEALINGS (9) [DEAL]
Jdg 18: 7 they were far from the Sidonians and had no **d**
18:28 because it was far from Sidon and they had no **d**
1Sa 2:23 For I hear of your evil **d** from all these people.
Eze 36:31 and your **d** that were not good;
1Co 7:31 with the world as though they had no **d** with it.
1Pe 5: 5 with humility in your **d** with one another,
2Mc 14:30 that Nicanor was more austere in his **d** with him
2Es 12:32 will display before them their contemptuous **d**.
4Mc 5:24 so that in all our **d** we act impartially,

DEALS (7) [DEAL]
Job 15:11 or the word that **d** gently with you?
39:16 It **d** cruelly with its young,
Pr 14:35 A servant who **d** wisely has the king's favor,
17: 2 A slave who **d** wisely will rule over
Jer 6:13 and from prophet to priest, everyone **d** falsely.
8:10 from prophet to priest everyone **d** falsely.
Sir 50:22 and **d** with us according to his mercy.

DEALT (61) [DEAL]
Ge 12:16 And for her sake he **d** well with Abram;
16: 6 Then Sarai **d** harshly with her,
21: 1 The LORD **d** with Sarah as he had said,
21:23 but as I have **d** loyally with you,
33:11 because God has **d** graciously with me,
Ex 1:20 So God **d** well with the midwives;
18:11 when they **d** arrogantly with them."
21: 8 since he has **d** unfairly with her.
21:31 owner shall be **d** with according to this same rule.
Dt 32: 5 his degenerate children have **d** falsely with him,
Jos 2:12 Now then, since I have **d** kindly with you,
Jdg 9:16 if you have **d** well with Jerubbaal and his house,
9:23 lords of Shechem **d** treacherously with Abimelech.
Ru 1: 8 as you have **d** with the dead and with me.
1:20 for the Almighty has **d** bitterly with me.
1:21 when the LORD has **d** harshly with me,
1Sa 14:33 And he said, "You have **d** treacherously;
23: 5 and **d** them a heavy defeat.
24:18 Today you have explained how you have **d** well
25:31 And when the LORD has **d** well with my lord,
2Sa 10: 2 just as his father **d** loyally with me."
18:13 if I had **d** treacherously against his life
1Ki 2: 5 how he **d** with the two commanders of the armies
2Ki 10:30 with all that was in my heart have **d** with the house
12:15 to pay out to the workers, for they **d** honestly.
21: 6 and **d** with mediums and with wizards.
1Ch 19: 2 for his father **d** loyally with me."
2Ch 2: 3 "Once you **d** with my father David
11:23 He **d** wisely, and distributed some of his sons
33: 6 and **d** with mediums and with wizards.
Ne 9:33 you have **d** faithfully and we have acted wickedly;
Ps 13: 6 because he has **d** bountifully with me.
116: 7 for the LORD has **d** bountifully with you.
119:65 You have **d** well with your servant, O LORD,
147:20 He has not **d** thus with any other nation;
Isa 33: 1 with whom no one has **d** treacherously!
33: 1 you will be **d** with treacherously.
Jer 12: 6 even they have **d** treacherously with you;
22: 8 the LORD **d** in this way with that great city?"
30:14 for I have **d** you the blow of an enemy,
La 1: 2 all her friends have **d** treacherously with her,
1:22 have **d** with me because of all my transgressions;
Eze 31:11 he has **d** with it as its wickedness deserves.
39:23 because they **d** treacherously with me.
39:24 I **d** with them according to their uncleanness
Hos 5: 7 They have **d** faithlessly with the LORD;
6: 7 there they **d** faithlessly with me.
Joel 2:26 who has **d** wondrously with you.
Zec 1: 6 "The LORD of hosts has **d** with us according
Ac 7:19 He **d** craftily with our race
1Th 2:11 we **d** with each one of you like a father
Tob 8:16 you have **d** with us according to your great mercy.
Bar 2:27 Yet you have **d** with us, O Lord our God,
1Mc 1:30 he suddenly fell upon the city, **d** it a severe blow,
5: 3 He **d** them a heavy blow and humbled them
5:34 they fled before him, and he **d** them a heavy blow.
13:31 Trypho **d** treacherously with
1Es 6: 5 Yet the elders of the Jews were **d** with kindly,
3Mc 4:13 in his rage that these people be **d** with in precisely
2Es 7:72 they **d** unfaithfully with what they received.
15:52 Would I have **d** with you so violently,

DEAR (14) [DEAREST]
Ps 39:11 consuming like a moth what is **d** to them;
102:14 For your servants hold its stones **d**,
Jer 31:20 Is Ephraim my **d** son?
1Co 10:14 my **d** friends, flee from the worship of idols.
Eph 6:21 a **d** brother and a faithful minister in the Lord.
1Th 2: 8 because you have become very **d** to us.
Phm 1: 1 To Philemon our **d** friend and co-worker,
2Jn 1: 5 But now, **d** lady, I ask you,
Tob 10: 6 "Be quiet and stop worrying, my **d**; he is all right.
10: 6 Do not grieve for him, my **d**;
10:12 Edna said to Tobias, "My child and **d** brother,
Sir 37: 2 like that for death itself when a **d** friend turns into
2Es 6:58 and most **d**, have been given into their hands.
7:*103* or friends for those who are most **d**."

DEAREST (1) [DEAR]
2Es 7:*104* or a master his servant, or a friend his **d** friend,

DEARTH (KJV) See DROUGHT, FAMINE

DEATH‡ (594) [DEAD]
A. DAY OF ... DEATH (17)
B. LIFE ... DEATH (10)

Ge 21:16 "Do not let me look on the **d** of the child."
24:67 So Isaac was comforted after his mother's **d**.
25:11 After the **d** of Abraham God blessed his son Isaac.
26:11 or his wife shall be put to **d**."
26:18 for the Philistines had stopped them up after the **d**
27: 2 I do not know the day of my **d**. A
38: 7 and the LORD put him to **d**.
38:10 and he put him to **d** also.
47:29 When the time of Israel's **d** drew near,
Ex 19:12 Any who touch the mountain shall be put to **d**.
21:12 a person mortally shall be put to **d**.
21:15 Whoever strikes father or mother shall be put to **d**.
21:16 or is still held in possession, shall be put to **d**.
21:17 Whoever curses father or mother shall be put to **d**.
21:28 When an ox gores a man or a woman to **d**,
21:29 and its owner also shall be put to **d**.
22: 2 If a thief is found breaking in, and is beaten to **d**,
22:19 Whoever lies with an animal shall be put to **d**.
31:14 everyone who profanes it shall be put to **d**;
31:15 on the sabbath day shall be put to **d**.
35: 2 whoever does any work on it shall be put to **d**.
Lev 16: 1 to Moses after the **d** of the two sons of Aaron,
19:20 They shall not be put to **d**,
20: 2 of their offspring to Molech shall be put to **d**;
20: 2 the people of the land shall stone them to **d**.
20: 4 and do not put them to **d**,
20: 9 All who curse father or mother shall be put to **d**;
20:10 the adulterer and the adulteress shall be put to **d**.
20:11 both of them shall be put to **d**;
20:12 both of them shall be put to **d**;
20:13 they shall be put to **d**; their blood is upon them.
20:14 they shall be burned to **d**, both he and they,
20:15 he shall be put to **d**; and you shall kill the animal.
20:16 they shall be put to **d**, their blood is upon them.
20:27 a medium or a wizard shall be put to **d**;
20:27 they shall be stoned to **d**, their blood is upon them.
21: 9 she shall be burned to **d**.
24:16 blasphemes the name of the LORD shall be put to **d**;
24:16 when they blaspheme the Name, shall be put to **d**.
24:17 Anyone who kills a human being shall be put to **d**.
24:21 but one who kills a human being shall be put to **d**.
24:23 the camp, and stoned him to **d**.
27:29 they shall be put to **d**.
Nu 1:51 any outsider who comes near shall be put to **d**.
3:10 and any outsider who comes near shall be put to **d**.
3:38 any outsider who came near was to be put to **d**.
11:15 put me to **d** at once—
15:35 "The man shall be put to **d**;
15:36 the camp and stoned him to **d**,
16:29 If these people die a natural **d**,
18: 7 any outsider who approaches shall be put to **d**.
18:32 the holy gifts of the Israelites, on pain of **d**.
23:10 Let me die the **d** of the upright,
35:16 and **d** ensues, is a murderer;
35:16 the murderer shall be put to **d**.
35:17 that could cause **d**, and **d** ensues, is a murderer;
35:17 the murderer shall be put to **d**.
35:18 that could cause **d**, and **d** ensues, is a murderer;
35:18 the murderer shall be put to **d**.
35:19 the one who shall put the murderer to **d**;
35:20 lying in wait, and **d** ensues,
35:21 and **d** ensues, then the one who struck
35:21 the one who struck the blow shall be put to **d**;
35:21 the avenger of blood shall put the murderer to **d**,
35:23 while handling any stone that could cause **d**,
35:23 unintentionally drops it on another and **d** ensues,
35:25 until the **d** of the high priest who was anointed
35:28 in the city of refuge until the **d** of the high priest;
Nu 35:28 **d** of the high priest the slayer may return home.
35:30 the murderer shall be put to **d** on the evidence
35:30 be put to **d** on the testimony of a single witness.
35:31 of a murderer who is subject to the **d** penalty;
35:31 a murderer must be put to **d**.
35:32 to live in the land before the **d** of the high priest.
Dt 13: 5 or those who divine by dreams shall be put to **d**
13:10 Stone them to **d** for trying to turn you away from
17: 5 and you shall stone the man or woman to **d**.
17: 6 of two or three witnesses the **d** sentence shall
17: 6 be put to **d** on the evidence of only one witness.
17: 7 against the person to execute the **d** penalty,
19: 6 and overtake and put the killer to **d**,
19: 6 although a **d** sentence was not deserved,
19:12 over to the avenger of blood to be put to **d**.
21:21 Then all the men of the town shall stone him to **d**.
21:22 of a crime punishable by **d** and is executed,
22:21 and the men of her town shall stone her to **d**,
22:24 to the gate of that town and stone them to **d**,
22:26 not committed an offense punishable by **d**,
24:16 Parents shall not be put to **d** for their children,
24:16 nor shall children be put to **d** for their parents;
24:16 only for their own crimes may persons be put to **d**.
30:15 before you today life and prosperity, **d**
30:19 that I have set before you life and **d**, B
31:27 how much more after my **d**!
31:29 that after my **d** you will surely act corruptly,
33: 1 the man of God, blessed the Israelites before his **d**.
Jos 1: 1 After the **d** of Moses the servant of the LORD,
1:18 whatever you command, shall be put to **d**.
2:13 and deliver our lives from **d**."
2:19 they shall be responsible for their own **d**,
2:19 we shall bear the responsibility for their **d**.
7:25 And all Israel stoned him to **d**;
10:26 down and put them to **d**,
11:17 struck them down, and put them to **d**.
13:22 Along with the rest of those they put to **d**,
20: 6 the **d** of the one who is high priest at the time:
Jdg 1: 1 After the **d** of Joshua, the Israelites inquired of
5:18 Zebulun is a people that scorned **d**;
6:31 Whoever contends for him shall be put to **d**
13: 7 nazirite to God from birth to the day of his **d**.' " A
16:16 and pestered him, he was tired to **d**.
16:30 at his **d** were more than those he had killed
20:13 so that we may put them to **d**,
21: 5 saying, "That one shall be put to **d**."
Ru 1:17 and more as well, if even **d** parts me from you!"
2:11 the **d** of your husband has been fully told me,
1Sa 1:11 before you as a nazirite until the day of his **d**. A
11:12 Give them to us so that we may put them to **d**."
11:13 But Saul said, "No one shall be put to **d** this day,
15:32 Agag said, "Surely this is the bitterness of **d**."
15:35 not see Saul again until the day of his **d**, A
19: 6 "As the LORD lives, he shall not be put to **d**."
20: 3 there is but a step between me and **d**."
20:32 "Why should he be put to **d**?
20:33 the decision of his father to put David to **d**.
28: 9 a snare for my life to bring about my **d**?"
2Sa 1: 1 After the **d** of Saul, when David had returned
1:23 In life and in **d** they were not divided; B
6:23 of Saul had no child to the day of her **d**. A
8: 2 of cord for those who were to be put to **d**,
13:39 for he was now consoled over the **d** of Amnon.
15:21 whether for **d** or for life,
19:21 "Shall not Shimei be put to **d** for this,
19:22 Shall anyone be put to **d** in Israel this day?
19:28 For all my father's house were doomed to **d**
20: 3 So they were shut up until the day of their **d**, A
21: 1 because he put the Gibeonites to **d**."
21: 4 neither is it for us to put anyone to **d** in Israel."
21: 9 They were put to **d** in the first days of harvest,
22: 5 For the waves of **d** encompassed me,
22: 6 the snares of **d** confronted me.
1Ki 2: 8 'I will not put you to **d** with the sword.'
2:24 today Adonijah shall be put to **d**."
2:26 to your estate; for you deserve **d**.
2:26 But I will not at this time put you to **d**,
11:40 and remained in Egypt until the **d** of Solomon.
12:18 all Israel stoned him to **d**;
17:18 and to cause the **d** of my son!"
21:10 Then take him out, and stone him to **d**."
21:13 the city, and stoned him to **d**.
2Ki 1: 1 After the **d** of Ahab, Moab rebelled against Israel.
2:21 from now on neither **d** nor miscarriage shall come
4:40 "O man of God, there is **d** in the pot!"
5: 7 "Am I God, to give **d** or life,
7:17 the people trampled him to **d** in the gate,
7:20 the people trampled him to **d** in the gate.
11:16 and there she was put to **d**.
14: 6 he did not put to **d** the children of the murderers;
14: 6 "The parents shall not be put to **d** for the children,
14: 6 or the children be put to **d** for the parents;
14: 6 but all shall be put to **d** for their own sins."
14:17 the **d** of King Jehoash son of Jehoahaz of Israel.
15: 5 so that he was leprous to the day of his **d**, A
20: 1 and was at the point of **d**.
25:21 and put them to **d** at Riblah in the land of Hamath.
1Ch 2: 3 and he put him to **d**.
2:24 After the **d** of Hezron, in Caleb-ephrathah,
10:14 the LORD put him to **d** and turned the kingdom
22: 5 in great quantity before his **d**.
2Ch 10:18 the people of Israel stoned him to **d**.
15:13 should be put to **d**, whether young or old,
22: 4 after the **d** of his father they were his counselors,
22: 9 in Samaria and was brought to Jehu, and put to **d**.
23:14 "Do not put her to **d** in the house of the LORD."
23:15 and there they put her to **d**.

2Ch 24:15 he was one hundred thirty years old at his **d**.
24:17 after the **d** of Jehoiada the officials of Judah came
24:21 and by command of the king they stoned him to **d**
25: 4 But he did not put their children to **d**,
25: 4 "The parents shall not be put to **d** for the children,
25: 4 or the children be put to **d** for the parents;
25: 4 but all shall be put to **d** for their own sins."
25:16 Why should you be put to **d**?"
25:25 after the **d** of King Joash son of Jehoahaz of Israel.
26:21 King Uzziah was leprous to the day of his **d**, A
32:24 and was at the point of **d**.
32:33 of Jerusalem did him honor at his **d**.
Ezr 7:26 for **d** or for banishment or for confiscation
Est 4:11 all alike are to be put to **d**.
Job 3:21 who long for **d**, but it does not come, and dig
5:20 In famine he will redeem you from **d**,
7:15 and **d** rather than this body.
9:23 When disaster brings sudden **d**,
18:13 the firstborn of **D** consumes their limbs.
28:22 Abaddon and **D** say, 'We have heard a rumor of it
30:23 I know that you will bring me to **d**,
31:39 and caused the **d** of its owners;
33:22 and their lives to those who bring **d**.
38:17 Have the gates of **d** been revealed to you,
Ps 6: 5 For in **d** there is no remembrance of you;
9:13 the one who lifts me up from the gates of **d**,
13: 3 or I will sleep the sleep of **d**,
18: 4 The cords of **d** encompassed me;
18: 5 the snares of **d** confronted me.
22:15 you lay me in the dust of **d**.
30: 9 "What profit is there in my **d**,
33:19 to deliver their soul from **d**,
34:21 Evil brings **d** to the wicked,
49:14 **D** shall be their shepherd;
55: 4 the terrors of **d** have fallen upon me.
55:15 Let **d** come upon them; let them go down alive
56:13 For you have delivered my soul from **d**,
68:20 and to GOD, the Lord, belongs escape from **d**.
78:50 he did not spare them from **d**,
88:15 Wretched and close to **d** from my youth up,
89:48 Who can live and never see **d**?
94:21 and condemn the innocent to **d**.
107:18 and they drew near to the gates of **d**.
109:16 and needy and the brokenhearted to their **d**.
109:31 from those who would condemn them to **d**.
116: 3 The snares of **d** encompassed me;
116: 8 For you have delivered my soul from **d**,
116:15 Precious in the sight of the LORD is the **d**
118:18 but he did not give me over to **d**.
Pr 2:18 for her way leads down to **d**, and her paths to
5: 5 Her feet go down to **d**;
7:27 going down to the chambers of **d**.
8:36 all who hate me love **d**."
10: 2 but righteousness delivers from **d**.
11: 4 but righteousness delivers from **d**.
12:28 in walking its path there is no **d**.
13:14 so that one may avoid the snares of **d**.
14:12 but its end is the way to **d**.
14:27 so that one may avoid the snares of **d**.
16:14 A king's wrath is a messenger of **d**,
16:25 but in the end it is the way to **d**.
18:21 **D** and life are in the power of the tongue,
21: 6 a lying tongue is a fleeting vapor and a snare of **d**.
24:11 to **d**, those who go staggering to the slaughter;
28:17 let that killer be a fugitive until **d**;
Ecc 7: 1 and the day of **d**, than the day of birth. A
7:26 I found more bitter than **d** the woman who is
8: 8 or power over the day of **d**; A
SS 8: 6 for love is strong as **d**, passion fierce as the grave.
Isa 25: 7 he will swallow up **d** forever.
28:15 you have said, "We have made a covenant with **d**,
28:18 Then your covenant with **d** will be annulled,
38: 1 and was at the point of **d**.
38:18 For Sheol cannot thank you, **d** cannot praise you;
53:12 because he poured out himself to **d**,
65:15 and the Lord GOD will put you to **d**;
Jer 8: 3 **D** shall be preferred to life by all the remnant
9:21 "**D** has come up into our windows,
18:21 May their men meet **d** by pestilence,
21: 8 before you the way of life and the way of **d**.
26:11 of **d** because he has prophesied against this city,
26:15 Only know for certain that if you put me to **d**,
26:16 "This man does not deserve the sentence of **d**,
26:19 of Judah and all Judah actually put him to **d**?
26:21 heard his words, the king sought to put him to **d**;
26:24 over into the hands of the people to be put to **d**.
38: 4 "This man ought to be put to **d**,
38:15 "If I tell you, you will put me to **d**, will you not?
38:16 I will not put you to **d** or hand you over
38:25 do not conceal it from us, or we will put you to **d**.
52:11 and put him in prison until the day of his **d**. A
52:27 and put them to **d** at Riblah in the land of Hamath.
52:34 as long as he lived, up to the day of his **d**. A
La 1:20 in the house it is like **d**.
Eze 13:19 putting to **d** persons who should not die
18:23 Have I any pleasure in the **d** of the wicked,
18:32 For I have no pleasure in the **d** of anyone,
28: 8 you shall die a violent **d** in the heart of the seas.
28:10 You shall die the **d** of the uncircumcised by
31:14 For all of them are handed over to **d**,
33:11 I have no pleasure in the **d** of the wicked,
43: 7 and by the corpses of their kings at their **d**.
Da 7:11 And as I watched, the beast was put to **d**,
Hos 13:14 Shall I redeem them from **D**?
13:14 O **D**, where are your plagues?
Hab 2: 5 like **D** they never have enough.
Mt 2:15 and remained there until the **d** of Herod.

Mt 4:16 in the region and shadow of **d** light has dawned."
10:21 Brother will betray brother to **d**,
10:21 against parents and have them put to **d**;
14: 5 Though Herod wanted to put him to **d**,
16:28 not taste **d** before they see the Son of Man coming
20:18 and they will condemn him to **d**;
21:41 "He will put those wretches to a miserable **d**,
24: 9 over to be tortured and will put you to **d**,
26:38 he said to them, "I am deeply grieved, even to **d**;
26:59 against Jesus so that they might put him to **d**,
26:66 They answered, "He deserves **d**."
27: 1 against Jesus in order to bring about his **d**.
Mk 5:23 "My little daughter is at the point of **d**.
9: 1 there are some standing here who will not taste **d**
10:33 and they will condemn him to **d**;
13:12 Brother will betray brother to **d**,
13:12 against parents and have them put to **d**;
14:34 he said to them, "I am deeply grieved, even to **d**;
14:55 for testimony against Jesus to put him to **d**;
14:64 All of them condemned him as deserving **d**.
Lk 1:79 in darkness and in the shadow of **d**,
2:26 to him by the Holy Spirit that he would not see **d**
7: 2 and who was ill and close to **d**.
9:27 there are some standing here who will not taste **d**
21:16 and they will put some of you to **d**.
22: 2 for a way to put Jesus to **d**,
22:33 I am ready to go with you to prison and to **d**!"
23:15 Indeed, he has done nothing to deserve **d**.
23:22 in him no ground for the sentence of **d**;
23:32 were led away to be put to **d** with him.
24:20 and leaders handed him over to be condemned to **d**
Jn 4:47 for he was at the point of **d**.
5:24 but has passed from **d** to life.
8:51 whoever keeps my word will never see **d**."
8:52 'Whoever keeps my word will never taste **d**.'
11: 4 he said, "This illness does not lead to **d**;
11:13 Jesus, however, had been speaking about his **d**,
11:53 So from that day on they planned to put him to **d**.
12:10 chief priests planned to put Lazarus to **d** as well,
12:33 He said this to indicate the kind of **d** he was to die.
18:31 "We are not permitted to put anyone to **d**."
18:32 when he indicated the kind of **d** he was to die.)
21:19 the kind of **d** by which he would glorify God.)
Ac 2:24 But God raised him up, having freed him from **d**,
10:39 They put him to **d** by hanging him on a tree;
12:19 the guards and ordered them to be put to **d**.
13:28 though they found no cause for a sentence of **d**,
22: 4 to the point of **d** by binding both men and women
23:29 with nothing deserving **d** or imprisonment.
25:11 I am not trying to escape **d**;
25:25 But I found that he had done nothing deserving **d**;
26:10 when they were being condemned to **d**.
26:31 "This man is doing nothing to deserve **d**
28:18 there was no reason for the **d** penalty in my case.
Ro 4:25 who was handed over to **d** for our trespasses
5:10 we were reconciled to God through the **d**
5:12 and **d** came through sin, and so **d** spread to all
5:14 Yet **d** exercised dominion from Adam to Moses,
5:17 **d** exercised dominion through that one,
5:21 just as sin exercised dominion in **d**,
6: 3 into Christ Jesus were baptized into his **d**?
6: 4 we have been buried with him by baptism into **d**,
6: 5 if we have been united with him in a **d** like his,
6: 9 **d** no longer has dominion over him.
6:10 The **d** he died, he died to sin, once for all;
6:13 to God as those who have been brought from **d**
6:16 either of sin, which leads to **d**, or of obedience,
6:21 The end of those things is **d**.
6:23 For the wages of sin is **d**,
7: 5 were at work in our members to bear fruit for **d**.
7:10 that promised life proved to be **d** to me.
7:13 Did what is good, then, bring **d** to me?
7:13 It was sin, working **d** in me through what is good,
7:24 Who will rescue me from this body of **d**?
8: 2 from the law of sin and of **d**.
8: 6 To set the mind on the flesh is **d**,
8:13 if by the Spirit you put to **d** the deeds of the body,
8:38 For I am convinced that neither **d**, nor life,
1Co 3:22 the world or life or **d** or the present or the future—B
4: 9 though sentenced to **d**, because we have become
11:26 you proclaim the Lord's **d** until he comes.
15:21 For since **d** came through a human being,
15:26 The last enemy to be destroyed is **d**.
15:54 "**D** has been swallowed up in victory."
15:55 O **d**, is your victory? Where, O **d**, is your sting?"
15:56 sting of **d** is sin, and the power of sin is the law.
2Co 1: 9 we felt that we had received the sentence of **d** so
2:16 to the one a fragrance from **d** to **d**,
3: 7 Now if the ministry of **d**,
4:10 always carrying in the body the **d** of Jesus,
4:11 we are always being given up to **d** for Jesus' sake,
4:12 So **d** is at work in us, but life in you.
7:10 but worldly grief produces **d**.
11:23 with countless floggings, and often near **d**.
Eph 2:16 thus putting to **d** that hostility through it.
Php 1:20 whether by life or by **d**. B
2: 8 obedient to the point of **d**—even **d** on a cross.
2:30 because he came close to **d** for the work of Christ,
3:10 of his sufferings by becoming like him in his **d**,
Col 1:22 through **d**, so as to present you holy and blameless
3: 5 Put to **d**, therefore, whatever in you is earthly:
2Ti 1:10 who abolished **d** and brought life and immortality
Heb 2: 9 and honor because of the suffering of **d**,
2: 9 by the grace of God he might taste **d** for everyone.
2:14 that through **d** he might destroy the one who has
the power of **d**,
2:15 in slavery by the fear of **d**.

Heb 5: 7 to the one who was able to save him from **d**,
7:23 because they were prevented by **d** from continuing
9:15 because a **d** has occurred that redeems them from
9:16 the **d** of the one who made it must be established.
9:17 For a will takes effect only at **d**,
11: 5 so that he did not experience **d**;
11:37 They were stoned to **d**, they were sawn in two,
12:20 it shall be stoned to **d**."
Jas 1:15 when it is fully grown, gives birth to **d**.
5:20 the sinner's soul from **d** and will cover a multitude
1Pe 3:18 He was put to **d** in the flesh,
2Pe 1:14 since I know that my **d** will come soon,
1Jn 3:14 We know that we have passed from **d** to life
3:14 Whoever does not love abides in **d**.
Rev 1:18 and I have the keys of **D** and of Hades.
2:10 Be faithful until **d**, and I will give you the crown
2:11 not be harmed by the second **d**.
3: 2 strengthen what remains and is on the point of **d**,
6: 8 Its rider's name was **D**, and Hades followed
9: 6 And in those days people will seek **d** but will
9: 6 they will long to die, but **d** will flee from them.
12:11 for they did not cling to life even in the face of **d**.
20: 6 Over these the second **d** has no power,
20:13 **D** and Hades gave up the dead that were in them,
20:14 **D** and Hades were thrown into the lake of fire.
20:14 This is the second **d**, the lake of fire;
21: 4 from their eyes. **D** will be no more;
21: 8 with fire and sulfur, which is the second **d**."
Tob 1:14 Until his **d** I used to go into Media,
1:18 I also buried any whom King Sennacherib put to **d**
1:18 For in his anger he put to **d** many Israelites;
1:19 and that I was being searched for to be put to **d**,
2: 8 He has already been hunted down to be put to **d**
3: 4 So you gave us over to plunder, exile, and **d**,
4: 2 "Now I have asked for **d**.
4:10 For almsgiving delivers from **d** and keeps you
6:13 of **d** according to the decree of the book of Moses.
12: 9 from **d** and purges away every sin.
14:11 and what injustice does—it brings **d**!
Jdt 11:11 **d** will fall upon them, for a sin has overtaken them
12:14 and it will be a joy to me until the day of my **d**." A
14: 5 house of Israel and sent him to us as if to his **d**."
16:25 or for a long time after her **d**.
AdE 4: 8 has spoken against us and demands our **d**.
4: 8 to the king in our behalf, and save us from **d**."
13:18 for their **d** was before their eyes.
Wis 1:12 Do not invite **d** by the error of your life,
1:13 because God did not make **d**,
1:13 and he does not delight in the **d** of the living.
1:16 ungodly by their words and deeds summoned **d**;
2: 5 and there is no return from our **d**,
2:20 Let us condemn him to a shameful **d**, for,
2:24 but through the devil's envy **d** entered the world,
12:20 of your servants and those deserving of **d**,
16:13 For you have power over life and **d**; B
18:12 by the one form of **d**,
18:16 and stood and filled all things with **d**,
18:20 The experience of **d** touched also the righteous,
19: 5 but they themselves might meet a strange **d**.
Sir 1:13 on the day of their **d** they will be blessed. A
4:28 Fight to the **d** for truth,
8: 7 Do not rejoice over any one's **d**;
9:13 and you will not be haunted by the fear of **d**.
11:14 Good things and bad, life and **d**, B
11:26 the Lord on the day of **d** to reward individuals A
11:28 Call no one happy before his **d**;
14:12 Remember that **d** does not tarry,
15:17 Before each person are life and **d**, B
18:22 and do not wait until **d** to be released from it.
18:24 Think of his wrath on the day of **d**, A
22:11 but the life of the fool is worse than **d**.
23:12 There is a manner of speaking comparable to **d**;
26: 5 all these are worse than **d**.
26:22 *a married woman as a tower of* **d** *to her lovers.*
27:29 and pain will consume them before their **d**.
28: 6 remember corruption and **d**,
28:21 its **d** is an evil **d**, and Hades is preferable to it.
30: 5 whom in his life he looked upon with joy and at **d**,
30:17 **D** is better than a life of misery,
33:14 and life the opposite of **d**; B
33:24 in the hour of **d**, distribute your inheritance.
34:13 I have often been in danger of **d**,
37: 2 like that for **d** itself when a dear friend turns into
37:18 good and evil, life and **d**; B
38:18 For grief may result in **d**,
40: 2 and anxious thought of the day of their **d**. A
40: 5 and fear of **d**, and fury and strife.
40: 9 come **d** and bloodshed and strife and sword,
41: 1 O **d**, how bitter is the thought of you to the one
41: 2 O **d**, how welcome is your sentence
46:20 he prophesied and made known to the king his **d**,
48: 5 You raised a corpse from **d** and from Hades,
48:14 and in **d** his deeds were marvelous.
51: 6 My soul drew near to **d**, and my life was on the
51: 9 and begged for rescue from **d**.
LtJ 6:18 as though under sentence of **d**,
6:36 from **d** or rescue the weak from the strong.
Aza 1:66 the power of **d**, and delivered us from the midst of
Sus 1:22 For if I do this, it will mean **d** for me;
1:28 full of their wicked plot to have Susanna put to **d**.
1:41 assembly believed them and condemned her to **d**.
1:53 not put an innocent and righteous person to **d**.'
1:62 with the law of Moses, they put them to **d**.
Bel 1:22 Therefore the king put them to **d**,
1Mc 1: 2 and put to **d** the kings of the earth.
1: 9 They all put on crowns after his **d**,
1:57 was condemned to **d** by decree of the king.

1Mc 1:60 According to the decree, they put to d
6:24 moreover, they have put to d as many of us
9:23 the d of Judas, the renegades emerged in all parts
9:29 the d of your brother Judas there has been no one
2Mc 4:47 while he sentenced to d those unfortunate men,
6:19 welcoming d with honor rather than life
6:22 so that by doing this he might be saved from d,
6:28 to die a good d willingly and nobly for the revered
6:30 though I might have been saved from d,
6:31 in his d an example of nobility and a memorial
7:14 When he was near d, he said,
7:29 Accept d, so that in God's mercy I may get you
13:4 to put him to d by the method that is customary in
13:8 and ashes were holy, he met his d in ashes.
13:14 and exhorting his troops to fight bravely to the d
14:46 This was the manner of his d.
1Es 8:24 whether by d or some other punishment,
3Mc 1:29 because indeed all at that time preferred d to
2:28 to this are to be taken by force and put to d;
3:1 and put to d by the most cruel means.
3:25 the sure and shameful d that befits enemies.
3:27 be tortured to d with the most hateful torments,
4:8 seeing d immediately before them.
5:42 an irrevocable oath that he would send them to d
5:51 as they stood now at the gates of d.
6:29 since they now had escaped d.
6:31 those disgracefully treated and near to d,
6:31 of deliverance instead of a bitter and lamentable d,
7:5 or examination to put them to d.
7:14 to a public and shameful d any whom they met
7:15 to d more than three hundred men;
7:16 even to d and had received the full enjoyment
2Es 3:7 and immediately you appointed d for him and
3:10 just as d came upon Adam,
6:26 who from their birth have not tasted d;
7:48 has brought us into corruption and the ways of d,
7:66 or salvation promised to them after d.
7:69 And if after d we were not to come into judgment,
7:75 whether after d, as soon as everyone of us yields
7:78 Now concerning d, the teaching is:
7:92 it might not lead them astray from life into d.
7:117 [47] in sorrow now and expect punishment after d?
7:119 [49] but we have done deeds that bring d?
7:126 [56] not consider what we should suffer after d."
8:13 You put it to d as your creation,
8:31 have passed our lives in ways that bring d;
8:38 or about their d, their judgment,
8:53 illness is banished from you, and d is hidden;
9:12 these must in torment acknowledge it after d.
10:22 our priests have been burned to d,
14:34 and after d you shall obtain mercy.
14:35 For after d the judgment will come,
15:5 the sword and famine, d and destruction,
15:26 he will hand them over to d and slaughter.
15:49 bringing destruction and d.
15:53 and clapping your hands and talking about their d
4Mc 1:9 All of these, by despising sufferings that bring d,
4:12 that he had committed a sin deserving of d,
4:22 he heard that a rumor of his d had spread and that
5:37 as one who does not fear your violence even to d.
6:21 the tyrant as unmanly by not contending even to d
6:30 even in the tortures of d he resisted,
7:8 and noble sweat in sufferings even to d.
7:15 whom the faithful seal of d has perfected!
7:16 of piety an aged man despised tortures even to d,
8:18 and venture upon a disobedience that brings d?
8:25 even the law itself would arbitrarily put us to d
9:4 to be more grievous than d itself.
9:5 to terrify us by threatening us with d by torture,
9:29 "How sweet is any kind of d for the religion
10:1 When he too had endured a glorious d,
10:15 No—by the blessed d of my brothers,
12:1 thrown into the caldron, had died a blessed d,
13:1 seven brothers despised sufferings even unto d,
13:27 their brothers being maltreated and tortured to d.
14:4 the seven youths proved coward or shrank from d,
14:5 toward immortality, hastened to d by torture.
14:6 agreed to go to d for its sake.
14:19 and defend it even to the d?
15:10 so that they obeyed her even to d in keeping
15:12 and all of them together the mother urged on to d
15:19 saw in their nostrils the signs of the approach of d.
15:26 one bearing d and the other deliverance
16:1 endured seeing her children tortured to d,
16:13 and urged them on to d for the sake of religion.
17:1 about to be seized and put to d she threw herself
17:7 to d for the sake of religion?
17:10 looking to God and enduring torture even to d."
17:22 through the blood of those devout ones and their d
18:5 on earth and is being chastised after his d.
18:21 and put them to d with various tortures.

DEATH'S (1) [DEAD]
Sir 41:3 Do not fear d decree for you;

DEATH-BLOW (1) [BLOW, DEAD]
Rev 13:3 One of its heads seemed to have received a d,

DEATHLY (2) [DEAD]
1Sa 5:11 For there was a d panic throughout the whole city.
Da 10:8 and my complexion grew d pale,

DEBASE (KJV) See SENT DOWN

DEBASED (1)
Ro 1:28 to a d mind and to things that should not be done.

DEBATE (2) [DEBATED, DEBATER]
Ac 15:2 and Barnabas had no small dissension and d
15:7 After there had been much d,

DEBATED (1) [DEBATE]
Ac 17:18 Also some Epicurean and Stoic philosophers d

DEBATER (1) [DEBATE]
1Co 1:20 Where is the d of this age?

DEBAUCHERIES (2) [DEBAUCHERY]
Na 3:4 Because of the countless d of the prostitute,
3:4 who enslaves nations through her d,

DEBAUCHERY (5) [DEBAUCHERIES]
Ro 13:13 not in d and licentiousness,
Eph 5:18 Do not get drunk with wine, for that is d;
Tit 1:6 not accused of d and not rebellious.
Wis 14:26 disorder in marriages, adultery, and d.
2Mc 6:4 For the temple was filled with d and reveling by

DEBIR (14) [=KIRIATH-SANNAH, =KIRIATH-SEPHER]
Jos 10:3 and to King D of Eglon, saying,
10:38 with all Israel, turned back to D and assaulted it,
10:39 so he did to D and its king.
11:21 from Hebron, from D, from Anab,
12:13 the king of D one the king of Geder one
13:26 and from Mahanaim to the territory of D,
15:7 and the boundary goes up to D from the Valley
15:15 up against the inhabitants of D;
15:15 now the name of D formerly was Kiriath-sepher.
15:49 Dannah, Kiriath-sannah (that is, D),
21:15 with its pasture lands, D with its pasture lands,
Jdg 1:11 From there they went against the inhabitants of D
1:11 (the name of D was formerly Kiriath-sepher).
1Ch 6:58 with its pasture lands, D with its pasture lands,

DEBORAH (11)
Ge 35:8 And D, Rebekah's nurse, died,
Jdg 4:4 At that time D, a prophetess, wife of Lappidoth,
4:5 of D between Ramah and Bethel in the hill country
4:9 Then D got up and went with Barak to Kedesh.
4:10 and D went up with him.
4:14 Then D said to Barak, "Up!
5:1 D and Barak son of Abinoam sang on that day,
5:7 because you arose, D, arose as a mother in Israel.
5:12 "Awake, awake, D! Awake, awake,
5:15 of Issachar came with D, and Issachar faithful
Tob 1:8 of Moses and according to the instructions of D,

DEBT (13) [DEBTOR, DEBTORS, DEBTS, INDEBTED]
Ex 21:2 he shall go out a free person, without d.
21:11 she shall go out without d,
1Sa 22:2 and everyone who was in d,
Ne 10:31 of the seventh year and the exaction of every d.
Mt 18:27 of that slave released him and forgave him the d.
18:30 into prison until he would pay the d.
18:32 I forgave you all that d because you pleaded
18:34 over to be tortured until he would pay his entire d.
Lk 7:43 the one for whom he canceled the greater d."
1Mc 10:43 because they owe money to the king or are in d,
15:8 Every d you owe to the royal treasury
1Es 3:20 and forgets all sorrow and d.
4Mc 2:8 and to cancel the d when the seventh year arrives.

DEBTOR (3) [DEBT]
Isa 24:2 as with the creditor, so with the d.
Eze 18:7 but restores to the d his pledge,
Ro 1:14 I am a d both to Greeks and to barbarians,

DEBTORS (4) [DEBT]
Mt 6:12 as we also have forgiven our d.
Lk 7:41 "A certain creditor had two d;
16:5 So, summoning his master's d one by one,
Ro 8:12 So then, brothers and sisters, we are d,

DEBTS (6) [DEBT]
Dt 15:1 seventh year you shall grant a remission of d.
2Ki 4:7 and he said, "Go sell the oil and pay your d,
Pr 22:26 who become surety for d.
Mt 6:12 And forgive us our d, as we
Lk 7:42 he canceled the d for both of them.
1Mc 15:8 to the royal treasury and any such future d shall

DECANT (1) [DECANTERS]
Jer 48:12 when I shall send to him decanters to d him,

DECANTERS (1) [DECANT]
Jer 48:12 when I shall send to him d to decant him,

DECAPOLIS (3)
Mt 4:25 great crowds followed him from Galilee, the D,
Mk 5:20 And he went away and began to proclaim in the D
7:31 in the region of the D.

DECAY (3) [DECAYS]
Ro 8:21 from its bondage to d and will obtain the freedom
Sir 19:3 D and worms will take possession of him,
2Mc 9:9 the stench the whole army felt revulsion at his d.

DECAYS (2) [DECAY]
Sir 10:9 Even in life the human body d.
14:19 Every work d and ceases to exist,

DECEASED (3)
Dt 25:5 of the d shall not be married outside the family to
25:6 to the name of the d brother,
2Mc 4:37 of the moderation and good conduct of the d.

DECEASED (KJV) See also DEAD, DIED

DECEIT (50) [DECEITFUL, DECEITFULLY, DECEITFULNESS, DECEIVE, DECEIVED, DECEIVER, DECEIVERS, DECEIVES, DECEIVING, DECEPTION, DECEPTIONS, DECEPTIVE]
Dt 32:4 A faithful God, without d, just and upright is he;
Job 15:35 and bring forth evil and their heart prepares d."
27:4 and my tongue will not utter d.
31:5 and my foot has hurried to d—
Ps 10:7 Their mouths are filled with cursing and d
17:1 give ear to my prayer from lips free of d.
32:2 and in whose spirit there is no d.
34:13 and your lips from speaking d.
36:3 The words of their mouths are mischief and d;
50:19 and your tongue frames d.
101:7 No one who practices d shall remain in my house;
Pr 12:20 D is in the mind of those who plan evil,
20:17 Bread gained by d is sweet,
26:24 in speaking while harboring d within;
Isa 30:12 and put your trust in oppression and d,
53:9 and there was no d in his mouth.
57:4 not children of transgression, the offspring of d—
Jer 8:5 have held fast to d, they have refused to return.
9:6 Oppression upon oppression, d upon d!
9:8 it speaks d through the mouth.
14:14 and the d of their own minds.
23:26 and who prophesy the d of their own heart?
Da 8:25 By his cunning he shall make d prosper
Hos 11:12 and the house of Israel with d;
Am 8:5 and practice d with false balances,
Mic 6:12 with tongues of d in their mouths.
Mk 7:22 wickedness, d, licentiousness, envy, slander,
Jn 1:47 "Here is truly an Israelite in whom there is no d!"
Ac 13:10 full of all d and villainy,
Ro 1:29 Full of envy, murder, strife, d, craftiness,
2Co 12:16 (you say) since I was crafty, I took you in by d.
Col 2:8 through philosophy and empty d,
1Th 2:3 not spring from d or impure motives or trickery,
1Pe 2:22 and no d was found in his mouth."
3:10 from evil and their lips from speaking d;
Tob 14:10 and that much d is practiced within it,
Jdt 9:3 which was ashamed of the d they had practiced,
9:10 By the d of my lips strike down the slave with
AdE 16:13 with intricate craft and d asked for the destruction
Wis 1:5 For a holy and disciplined spirit will flee from d,
14:25 theft and d, corruption, faithlessness, tumult,
14:30 in d they swore unrighteously through contempt
Sir 1:30 and your heart was full of d.
19:26 but inwardly he is full of d.
37:3 why were you formed to cover the land with d?
Bel 1:18 O Bel, and in you there is no d at all!"
1Mc 8:28 shall keep these obligations and do so without d.
2Es 6:27 evil shall be blotted out, and d shall be quenched;
11:40 and for so long you have lived on the earth with d.

DECEITFUL (17) [DECEIT]
Ps 5:6 the LORD abhors the bloodthirsty and d.
35:20 but they conceive d words
43:1 from those who are d and unjust deliver me!
52:4 You love all words that devour, O d tongue.
109:2 For wicked and d mouths are opened against me,
120:2 O LORD, from lying lips, from a d tongue."
120:3 what more shall be done to you, you d tongue?
Pr 31:30 Charm is d, and beauty is vain,
Jer 15:18 Truly, you are to me like a d brook,
Na 3:1 City of bloodshed, utterly d, full of booty—
Zep 3:13 nor shall a d tongue be found in their mouths.
2Co 11:13 For such boasters are false apostles, d workers,
Eph 4:14 by their craftiness in d scheming.
1Ti 4:1 by paying attention to d spirits and teachings
Jdt 9:13 Make my d words bring wound and bruise
Wis 1:4 because wisdom will not enter a d soul,
4Mc 18:8 the d serpent, defile the purity of my virginity.

DECEITFULLY (10) [DECEIT]
Ge 27:35 But he said, "Your brother came d,
34:13 answered Shechem and his father Hamor d,
Jos 7:11 they have stolen, they have acted d,
Job 13:7 for God, and speak d for him?
Ps 24:4 up their souls to what is false, and do not swear d.
Pr 12:17 but a false witness speaks d.
Da 11:23 he shall act d and become strong with

Tob 14: 6 which **d** have led them into their error;
1Mc 1:30 **D** he spoke peaceable words to them,
13:17 Simon knew that they were speaking **d** to him,

DECEITFULNESS (1) [DECEIT]

Heb 3:13 that none of you may be hardened by the **d** of sin.

DECEIVE‡ (33) [DECEIT]

Ge 31:27 Why did you flee secretly and **d** me and
Jos 9:22 and said to them, "Why did you **d** us, saying,
2Sa 3:25 You know that Abner son of Ner came to **d** you,
2Ki 4:16 of God; do not **d** your servant."
18:29 Thus says the king: 'Do not let Hezekiah **d** you,
19:10 Do not let your God on whom you rely **d** you
2Ch 32:15 therefore do not let Hezekiah **d** you or mislead you
Job 13: 9 Or can you **d** him, as one person deceives another?
Pr 24:28 and do not **d** with your lips.
Isa 36:14 Thus says the king: 'Do not let Hezekiah **d** you,
37:10 Do not let your God on whom you rely **d** you
Jer 9: 5 They all **d** their neighbors,
29: 8 and the diviners who are among you **d** you,
37: 9 Thus says the LORD: Do not **d** yourselves,
Zec 13: 4 they will not put on a hairy mantle in order to **d,**
Ro 3:13 they use their tongues to **d."**
16:18 and by smooth talk and flattery they **d** the hearts
1Co 3:18 Do not **d** yourselves. If you think
Gal 6: 3 think they are something, they **d** themselves.
Eph 5: 6 Let no one **d** you with empty words,
Col 2: 4 that no one may **d** you with plausible arguments.
2Th 2: 3 Let no one **d** you in any way;
Jas 1:22 and not merely hearers who **d** themselves.
1:26 and do not bridle their tongues but **d** their hearts,
1Jn 1: 8 If we say that we have no sin, we **d** ourselves,
2:26 to you concerning those who would **d** you.
3: 7 Little children, let no one **d** you.
Rev 20: 3 so that he would **d** the nations no more,
20: 8 to **d** the nations at the four corners of the earth,
Tob 10: 7 Stop trying to **d** me!
Wis 4:11 change their understanding or guile **d** their souls.
Sir 13: 6 When he needs you he will **d** you,
2Mc 7:18 he said, "Do not **d** yourself in vain.

DECEIVED (32) [DECEIT]

Ge 29:25 Why then have you **d** me?"
31:20 And Jacob **d** Laban the Aramean,
31:26 You have **d** me, and carried away my daughters
Nu 25:18 with which they **d** you in the affair of Peor,
1Sa 19:17 "Why have you **d** me like this,
28:12 the woman said to Saul, "Why have you **d** me?
2Sa 19:26 He answered, "My lord, O king, my servant **d** me;
Job 12:16 the **d** and the deceiver are his.
Jer 4:10 how utterly you have **d** this people and Jerusalem,
49:16 and the pride of your heart have **d** you,
La 1:19 I called to my lovers but they **d** me;
Eze 14: 9 If a prophet is **d** and speaks a word, I, the LORD, have **d** that prophet,
Ob 1: 3 Your proud heart has **d** you,
1: 7 All your allies have **d** you,
Jn 7:47 "Surely you have not been **d** too, have you?
Ro 7:11 **d** me and through it killed me.
1Co 6: 9 not inherit the kingdom of God? Do not be **d!**
15:33 Do not be **d:** "Bad company ruins good morals."
2Co 11: 3 But I am afraid that as the serpent **d** Eve
Gal 6: 7 Do not be **d;** God is
1Ti 2:14 and Adam was not **d,** but the woman was **d**
2Ti 3:13 deceiving others and being **d.**
Jas 1:16 Do not be **d,** my beloved.
Rev 18:23 and all nations were **d** by your sorcery.
19:20 by which he **d** those who had received the mark of
20:10 the devil who had **d** them was thrown into the lake
Wis 12:24 they were **d** like foolish infants.
Sir 34: 7 For dreams have **d** many,
Bel 1: 7 And Daniel laughed, and said, "Do not be **d,**
2Es 10:36 —or is my mind **d,** and my soul dreaming?

DECEIVER (3) [DECEIT]

Job 12:16 the deceived and the **d** are his.
2Jn 1: 7 any such person is the **d** and the antichrist!
Rev 12: 9 the **d** of the whole world—

DECEIVERS (2) [DECEIT]

Tit 1:10 and **d,** especially those of the circumcision;
2Jn 1: 7 Many **d** have gone out into the world,

DECEIVES (3) [DECEIT]

Job 13: 9 Or can you deceive him, as one person **d** another?
Pr 26:19 so is one who **d** a neighbor and says,
Rev 13:14 it **d** the inhabitants of earth,

DECEIVING (5) [DECEIT]

Lev 6: 2 against the LORD by **d** a neighbor in a matter of
1Ki 13:18 But he was **d** him.
Job 15:31 Let them not trust in emptiness, **d** themselves;
Jn 7:12 others were saying, "No, he is **d** the crowd."
2Ti 3:13 **d** others and being deceived.

DECENTLY (2)

1Co 14:40 but all things should be done **d** and in order.
1Ti 2: 9 and **d** in suitable clothing,

DECEPTION (4) [DECEIT]

Mic 1:14 the houses of Achzib shall be a **d** to the kings
Mt 27:64 and the last **d** would be worse than the first."
2Th 2:10 of wicked **d** for those who are perishing,
2Mc 1:13 a **d** employed by the priests of the goddess Nanea.

DECEPTIONS (1) [DECEIT]

Sir 34: 8 Without such **d** the law will be fulfilled,

DECEPTIVE (6) [DECEIT]

Ex 5: 9 at it and pay no attention to **d** words."
Pr 23: 3 the ruler's delicacies, for they are **d** food.
Jer 7: 4 Do not trust in these **d** words:
7: 8 Here you are, trusting in **d** words to no avail.
La 2:14 for you false and **d** visions;
2Pe 2: 3 in their greed they will exploit you with **d** words.

DECIDE (22) [DECIDED, DECIDES, DECIDING, DECISION, DECISIONS, DECISIVE, DECISIVELY]

Ge 31:37 so that they may **d** between us two.
Ex 18:16 to me and I **d** between one person and another,
18:22 but **d** every minor case themselves.
22:11 an oath before the LORD shall **d** between the two
33: 5 and I will **d** what to do to you.' "
Lev 13:59 to **d** whether it is clean or unclean.
Dt 25: 1 and the judges **d** between them,
Jdg 11:27 **d** today for the Israelites or for the Ammonites."
2Sa 24:13 and **d** what answer I shall return to
1Ch 21:12 Now **d** what answer I shall return to
2Ch 19: 8 for the LORD and to **d** disputed cases.
Job 22:28 You will **d** on a matter,
Isa 11: 3 or **d** by what his ears hear;
11: 4 and **d** with equity for the meek of the earth;
Eze 44:24 and they shall **d** it according to my judgments.
Mk 15:24 casting lots to **d** what each should take.
Ac 24:22 the tribune comes down, I will **d** your case."
1Co 6: 5 among you wise enough to **d** between one believer
LtJ 6:64 not able either to **d** a case or to do good to anyone.
2Mc 13:13 to march out and **d** the matter by the help of God
15:17 and to **d** the matter by fighting hand to hand
4Mc 1:14 We shall **d** just what reason is

DECIDED (36) [DECIDE]

Ex 18:26 but any minor case they **d** themselves.
Jos 9:21 as the leaders had **d** concerning them.
1Sa 20: 9 that it was **d** by my father that evil should come
25:17 for evil has been **d** against our master and
2Sa 19:29 I have **d:** you and Ziba shall divide the land."
1Ki 20:40 So shall your judgment be; you yourself have **d** it."
2Ch 2: 1 Solomon **d** to build a temple for the name of
24: 4 Some time afterward Joash **d** to restore the house
Lk 1: 3 I too **d,** after investigating everything carefully
16: 4 I have **d** what to do so that,
Jn 1:43 The next day Jesus **d** to go to Galilee.
Ac 3:13 though he had **d** to release him.
15:22 **d** to choose men from among their members and
15:25 we have **d** unanimously to choose representatives
15:38 But Paul **d** not to take
20: 3 and so he **d** to return through Macedonia.
20:16 For Paul had **d** to sail past Ephesus,
25:25 and when he appealed to his Imperial Majesty, I **d**
27: 1 When it was **d** that we were to sail for Italy,
1Co 1:21 through wisdom, God **d,** through the foolishness
2: 2 For I **d** to know nothing
1Th 3: 1 we **d** to be left alone in Athens;
Tit 3:12 for I have **d** to spend the winter there.
Jdt 2: 3 They **d** that every one who had
9: 6 the things you **d** on presented themselves and said,
11:13 They have **d** to consume the first fruits of the grain
1Mc 8:26 arms, money, or ships, just as Rome has **d;**
8:28 arms, money, or ships, just as Rome has **d;**
9:69 Then he **d** to go back to his own land.
14:31 When their enemies **d** to invade their country
15:19 therefore have **d** to write to the kings and countries
2Mc 3:23 Heliodorus went on with what had been **d.**
11:36 But as to the matters that he **d** are to be referred to
1Es 8:11 the seven Friends who are my counselors have **d,**
3Mc 1: 6 Ptolemy **d** to visit the neighboring cities
7:19 in like manner they **d** to observe these days as

DECIDES (5) [DECIDE]

2Sa 15:15 to do whatever our lord the king **d."**
Pr 18:18 to disputes and **d** between powerful contenders.
Wis 15: 7 be the use of each of them the worker in clay **d.**
Sir 33:13 to be given whatever he **d.**
2Mc 15:21 he knew that it is not by arms, but as the Lord **d,**

DECIDING (3) [DECIDE]

2Mc 14:18 shrank from **d** the issue by bloodshed.
3Mc 3:21 to make a change, by **d** both to deem them worthy
6:30 **d** that they should celebrate their rescue

DECISION (30) [DECIDE]

Lev 24:12 the **d** of the LORD should be made clear to them.
Nu 27:21 for him by the **d** of the Urim before the LORD;
Dt 17: 8 If a judicial **d** is too difficult for you to make
17: 9 they shall announce to you the **d** in the case.
17:10 the **d** that they announce to you from the place that
17:11 do not turn aside from the **d** that they announce
21: 5 and by their **d** all cases of dispute and assault shall
1Sa 20:33 that it was the **d** of his father to put David to death.
2Sa 14:13 For in giving this **d** the king convicts himself,
Pr 16:33 but the **d** is the LORD's alone.
Da 4:17 the **d** is given by order of the holy ones,
Joel 3:14 Multitudes, multitudes, in the valley of **d!**
3:14 the day of the LORD is near in the valley of **d.**
Zep 3: 8 For my **d** is to gather nations,
Mk 14:64 You have heard his blasphemy! What is your **d?"**
Ac 15:19 Therefore I have reached the **d** that we should
25:21 in custody for the **d** of his Imperial Majesty,
AdE 3: 7 of King Artaxerxes Haman came to a **d**
9:31 And Mordecai and Queen Esther established this **d**
10:11 the hour and moment and day of **d** before God and
Wis 19: 3 they reached another foolish **d,**
Sir 8:14 for the **d** will favor him because of his standing.
32:17 and will find a **d** according to his liking.
1Mc 2:41 So they made this **d** that day:
2Mc 4:20 but by the **d** of its carriers it was applied to
11:25 our **d** is that their temple be restored to them and
13:14 committing the **d** to the Creator of the world
1Es 8:10 In accordance with my gracious **d,**
9: 4 in accordance with the **d** of the ruling elders,
4Mc 9:27 and they heard his noble **d.**

DECISIONS (7) [DECIDE]

Dt 16:18 and they shall render just **d** for the people.
Pr 16:10 Inspired **d** are on the lips of a king;
Ac 16: 4 to them for observance the **d** that had been reached
Sir 38:33 nor do they understand the **d** of the courts;
1Mc 14:44 to nullify any of these **d** or to oppose what he says,
14:45 Whoever acts contrary to these **d** or rejects any
14:46 the right to act in accordance with these **d.**

DECISIVE (2) [DECIDE]

2Es 7:*78* the **d** decree has gone out from the Most High that
7:*104* The day of judgment is **d** and displays to all

DECISIVELY (1) [DECIDE]

Ro 9:28 on the earth quickly and **d."**

DECK (7) [DECKED, DECKS]

Job 40:10 **"D** yourself with majesty and dignity;
Ps 65:13 the valleys **d** themselves with grain,
Jer 4:30 that you **d** yourself with ornaments of gold,
10: 4 people **d** it with silver and gold;
Eze 27: 6 they made your **d** of pines from the coasts
LtJ 6:11 They **d** their gods out with garments
3Mc 4:10 in addition they were confined under a solid **d,**

DECKED (6) [DECK]

Ps 45:13 The princess is **d** in her chamber
Pr 7:10 woman comes toward him, **d** out like a prostitute,
7:16 I have **d** my couch with coverings,
Eze 23:40 painted your eyes, and **d** yourself with ornaments;
Hos 2:13 to them and **d** herself with her ring and jewelry,
2Es 15:47 you have **d** out your daughters for prostitution

DECKEDST, DECKEST (KJV) See ADORNS, DECKED

DECKS (3) [DECK]

Ge 6:16 make it with lower, second, and third **d.**
Isa 61:10 as a bridegroom **d** himself with a garland,
2Es 16:50 when she **d** herself out, and shall accuse her

DECLARATION (3) [DECLARE]

Job 13:17 and let my **d** be in your ears.
1Mc 12: 8 which contained a clear **d** of alliance
4Mc 12: 9 Extremely pleased by the boy's **d,**

DECLARE‡ (90) [DECLARATION, DECLARED, DECLARES, DECLARING]

Ex 3:17 I **d** that I will bring you up out of the misery
Dt 5: 5 between the LORD and you to **d** to you the words
21: 7 and they shall **d:** "Our hands did
25: 9 pull his sandal off his foot, spit in his face, and **d,**
26: 3 "Today I **d** to the LORD your God
27:14 Levites shall **d** in a loud voice to all the Israelites:
30:18 I **d** to you today that you shall perish;
1Sa 12: 7 and I will **d** to you all the saving deeds of
1Ch 16:24 **D** his glory among the nations,
17:10 I **d** to you that the LORD will build you a house.
Job 12: 8 and the fish of the sea will **d** to you.
15:17 what I have seen I will **d—**
32: 6 I was timid and afraid to **d** my opinion to you.
32:10 I say, 'Listen to me; let me also **d** my opinion.'
32:17 I also will **d** my opinion.
33: 3 My words **d** the uprightness of my heart,
34:33 therefore **d** what you know.
38: 3 I will question you, and you shall **d** to me.
38:18 **D,** if you know all this.
40: 7 I will question you, and you **d** to me.
42: 4 I will question you, and you **d** to me.'
Ps 9:11 **D** his deeds among the peoples.
50: 6 The heavens **d** his righteousness,
51:15 open my lips, and my mouth will **d** your praise.
89: 2 I **d** that your steadfast love is established forever;
92: 2 to **d** your steadfast love in the morning,
96: 3 **D** his glory among the nations,
106: 2 of the LORD, or **d** all his praise?

Ps 119:13 With my lips I **d** all the ordinances of your mouth.
145: 4 and shall **d** your mighty acts.
145: 6 and I will **d** your greatness.
Isa 41:22 or **d** to us the things to come.
42: 9 and new things I now **d;**
42:12 and **d** his praise in the coastlands.
43:21 for myself so that they might **d** my praise.
44: 7 let them **d** and set it forth before me.
45:19 I the LORD speak the truth, I **d** what is right.
45:21 **D** and present your case; let them take counsel
48: 6 and will you not **d** it?
48:20 flee from Chaldea, **d** this with a shout of joy,
50: 9 Lord GOD who helps me; who will **d** me guilty?
66:19 and they shall **d** my glory among the nations.
Jer 4: 5 **D** in Judah, and proclaim in Jerusalem, and say:
5:20 **D** this in the house of Jacob, proclaim it in Judah:
9:12 so that they may **d** it?
18: 7 At one moment I may **d** concerning a nation or
18: 9 at another moment I may **d** concerning a nation or
31:10 O nations, and **d** it in the coastlands far away;
46:14 **D** in Egypt, and proclaim in Migdol;
50: 2 **D** among the nations and proclaim, set up a banner
50:28 to **d** in Zion the vengeance of the LORD our God,
51:10 let us **d** in Zion the work of the LORD our God.
Eze 22: 2 Then **d** to it all its abominable deeds.
23:36 Then **d** to them their abominable deeds.
23:45 But righteous judges shall **d** them guilty
38:19 For in my jealousy and in my blazing wrath I **d:**
40: 4 **d** all that you see to the house of Israel."
Da 4:18 Now you, Belteshazzar, **d** the interpretation,
9:23 and I have come to **d** it,
Hos 5: 9 among the tribes of Israel I **d** what is sure.
Mic 3: 5 but **d** war against those who put nothing into their
3: 8 to **d** to Jacob his transgression and to Israel his sin.
Zec 9:12 today I **d** that I will restore to you double.
Mt 7:23 Then I will **d** to them, 'I never knew you;
20:21 **"D** that these two sons of mine will sit,
Lk 8:39 and **d** how much God has done for you."
Jn 8:26 and I **d** to the world what I have heard from him."
8:38 I **d** what I have seen in the Father's presence;
16:13 and he will **d** to you the things that are to come.
16:14 because he will take what is mine and **d** it to you.
16:15 that he will take what is mine and **d** it to you.
Ac 20:26 Therefore I **d** to you this day that I am
Eph 6:20 Pray that I may **d** it boldly, as I must speak.
Col 4: 3 that we may **d** the mystery of Christ,
1Th 2: 2 we had courage in our God to **d** to you the gospel
4:15 For this we **d** to you by the word of the Lord,
Tit 2:15 **D** these things; exhort
1Jn 1: 1 We **d** to you what was from the beginning,
1: 2 and **d** to you the eternal life that was with
1: 3 we **d** to you what we have seen and heard so
Tob 12: 6 With fitting honor **d** to all people the deeds
12:11 "I will now **d** the whole truth to you
Sir 16:25 and **d** knowledge accurately.
42:15 and will **d** what I have seen.
44: 8 so that others **d** their praise.
Bar 2:18 will **d** your glory and righteousness, O Lord.
2Es 1: 5 **d** to my people their evil deeds,
6:31 I will again **d** to you greater things than these,
6:48 the nations might **d** your wondrous works.
7:*54* defer to her, and she will **d** it to you.

DECLARED‡ (53) [DECLARE]

Lev 23:44 Thus Moses **d** to the people of Israel
Dt 4:13 He **d** to you his covenant,
13: 2 the omens or the portents **d** by them take place,
1Ki 8:24 for your servant my father David as you **d** to him;
2Ki 2:15 they **d,** "The spirit of Elijah rests on Elisha."
4:17 in due time, as Elisha had **d** to her.
22:15 She **d** to them, "Thus says the LORD,
2Ch 34:23 She **d** to them, "Thus says the LORD,
36:22 a herald throughout all his kingdom and also **d** in
Ezr 1: 1 and also in a written edict **d:**
Ne 8:12 the words that were **d** to them.
Job 28:27 then he saw it and **d** it;
32: 3 though they had **d** Job to be in the wrong.
Ps 88:11 Is your steadfast love **d** in the grave,
102:21 so that the name of the LORD may be **d** in Zion,
Isa 41:26 Who **d** it from the beginning,
41:26 There was no one who **d** it, none who proclaimed,
41:27 I first have **d** it to Zion,
43: 9 Who among them **d** this, and foretold to us
43:12 I **d** and saved and proclaimed,
44: 8 have I not told you from of old and **d** it?
45:21 Who **d** it of old?
48: 3 The former things I **d** long ago,
48: 5 I **d** them to you from long ago,
48:14 Who among them has **d** these things?
Jer 44:25 in deeds what you **d** in words,
Da 4:31 "O King Nebuchadnezzar, to you it is **d:**
Mk 7:19 (Thus he **d** all foods clean.)
12:36 David himself, by the Holy Spirit, **d,**
Lk 8:47 and falling down before him, she **d** in the presence
24:25 of heart to believe all that the prophets have **d!**
Jn 1:29 next day he saw Jesus coming toward him and **d,**
13:21 saying this Jesus was troubled in spirit, and **d,**
Ac 26:20 but **d** first to those in Damascus,
Ro 1: 4 and was **d** to be Son of God with power according
Gal 3: 8 **d** the gospel beforehand to Abraham, saying,
Heb 2: 2 For if the message **d** through angels was valid,
2: 3 It was **d** at first through the Lord,
Tob 12:11 Already I have **d** it to you when I said,
Bar 1:20 the Lord **d** through his servant Moses at the time
2:20 as you **d** by your servants the prophets, saying:
2Mc 2: 7 Jeremiah learned of it, he rebuked them and **d:**
6:23 to the holy God-given law, he **d** himself quickly,
7: 6 as Moses **d** in his song that bore witness against
14:32 When they **d** on oath that they did not know where
15: 4 When they **d,** "It is the living Lord himself,
3Mc 4:17 of time the scribes **d** to the king
7: 4 for they **d** that our government would never
7:11 They **d** that those who for
2Es 7:23 they even **d** that the Most High does not exist,
8: 7 and we are a work of your hands, as you have **d.**
8:36 your righteousness and goodness will be **d,**
14: 5 the secrets of the times and **d** to him the end of

DECLARES (13) [DECLARE]

Ex 21: 5 But if the slave **d,** "I love my master, my wife,
1Sa 2:30 Therefore the LORD the God of Israel **d:**
2:30 before me forever'; but now the LORD **d:**
2Sa 7:11 Moreover the LORD **d** to you that
Job 21:31 Who **d** their way to their face,
33:23 one of a thousand, one who **d** a person upright,
36: 9 he **d** to them their work and their transgressions,
Ps 19: 2 and night to night **d** knowledge.
147:19 He **d** his word to Jacob,
Jer 4:15 For a voice **d** from Dan and proclaims disaster
Ac 2:17 be, God **d,** that I will pour out my Spirit
Sir 44:15 The assembly **d** their wisdom,
2Mc 10:26 and an adversary to their adversaries, as the law **d.**

DECLARING (7) [DECLARE]

Dt 25: 1 **d** one to be in the right and the other to be
Est 1:22 **d** that every man should be master
Isa 46:10 **d** the end from the beginning and
Ac 20:27 not shrink from **d** to you the whole purpose
1Co 14:25 **d,** "God is really among you."
2Th 2: 4 in the temple of God, **d** himself to be God.
2Mc 9:14 he was now **d** to be free;

DECLINED (4) [DECLINES, DECLINING]

Jdg 19: 8 So they lingered until the day **d,**
2Ki 20:11 by which the sun had **d** on the dial of Ahaz.
Isa 38: 8 on the dial the ten steps by which it had **d.**
Ac 18:20 When they asked him to stay longer, he **d;**

DECLINES (1) [DECLINED]

Jer 6: 4 "Woe to us, for the day **d,**

DECLINING (1) [DECLINED]

Isa 38: 8 the **d** sun on the dial of Ahaz turn back ten steps."

DECORATE (1) [DECORATED, DECORATION]

Mt 23:29 of the prophets and **d** the graves of the righteous,

DECORATED (9) [DECORATE]

Ex 28: 8 The **d** band on it shall be of
28:27 at its joining above the **d** band of the ephod.
28:28 so that it may lie on the **d** band of the ephod,
29: 5 and gird him with the **d** band of the ephod;
39: 5 The **d** band on it was of the same materials
39:20 at its joining above the **d** band of the ephod.
39:21 so that it should lie on the **d** band of the ephod,
Lev 8: 7 He then put the **d** band of the ephod around him,
1Mc 4:57 They **d** the front of the temple with golden crowns

DECORATION (4) [DECORATE]

Sir 22:17 an intelligent thought is like stucco **d** that makes
38:28 and he is careful to complete its **d.**
1Mc 1:22 and the gold **d** on the front of the temple;
2Mc 2:29 the one who undertakes its painting and **d** has

DECOY (1)

Sir 11:30 Like a **d** partridge in a cage,

DECREASE (3)

Ps 107:38 and he does not let their cattle **d.**
Jer 29: 6 multiply there, and do not **d.**
Jn 3:30 He must increase, but I must **d."**

DECREE‡ (76) [DECREED, DECREES]

Ezr 4:19 a **d,** and someone searched and discovered
4:21 and that this city not be rebuilt, until I make a **d.**
5: 3 "Who gave you a **d** to build this house and
5: 9 a **d** to build this house and to finish this structure?'
5:13 made a **d** that this house of God should be rebuilt.
5:17 to see whether a **d** was issued by King Cyrus for
6: 1 Then King Darius made a **d,**
6: 3 the first year of his reign, King Cyrus issued a **d:**
6: 8 a **d** regarding what you shall do for these elders of
6:11 Furthermore I **d** that if anyone alters this edict,
6:12 make a **d;** let it be done with all diligence."
6:14 and by **d** of Cyrus, Darius, and King Artaxerxes
7:13 I **d** that any of the people of Israel or their priests
7:21 **d** to all the treasurers in the province Beyond
Est 1:20 So when the **d** made by the king is proclaimed
3: 9 let a **d** be issued for their destruction,
3:14 A copy of the document was to be issued as a **d**
3:15 and the **d** was issued in the citadel of Susa.
4: 3 wherever the king's command and his **d** came,
4: 8 the written **d** issued in Susa for their destruction,
8:13 to be issued as a **d** in every province and published
8:14 The **d** was issued in the citadel of Susa.
9:14 a **d** was issued in Susa,
Job 28:26 a **d** for the rain, and a way for the thunderbolt;
Ps 2: 7 I will tell of the **d** of the LORD:
58: 1 Do you indeed **d** what is right,
78: 5 He established a **d** in Jacob,
81: 5 He made it a **d** in Joseph,
Pr 8:15 By me kings reign, and rulers **d** what is just;
Isa 28:22 a **d** of destruction from the Lord GOD of hosts
Jer 3: 8 Israel, I had sent her away with a **d** of divorce;
19: 5 which I did not command or **d,**
Da 2: 5 king answered the Chaldeans, "This is a public **d:**
2:13 The **d** was issued, and the wise men were about to
2:15 "Why is the **d** of the king so urgent?"
3:10 You, O king, have made a **d,**
3:29 Therefore I make a **d:** Any people,
4: 6 a **d** that all the wise men of Babylon should
4:17 The sentence is rendered by **d** of the watchers,
4:24 a **d** of the Most High that has come upon my lord
6:26 I make a **d,** that in all
Jnh 3: 7 "By the **d** of the king and his nobles:
Lk 2: 1 a **d** went out from Emperor Augustus that all
Ro 1:32 They know God's **d,** that those who practice such
Tob 1: 6 as it is prescribed for all Israel by an everlasting **d.**
6:13 the penalty of death according to the **d** of the book
7:11 She is given to you in accordance with the **d** in
7:11 with the law and **d** written in the book of Moses.
7:13 that he gave her to him as wife according to the **d**
AdE 1:19 it pleases the king, let him issue a royal **d,**
1:22 The king sent the **d** into all his kingdom,
2: 8 So, when the **d** of the king was proclaimed,
3:10 and gave it to Haman to seal the **d** that was to
8:13 "Let copies of the **d** be posted conspicuously in all
8:14 and the **d** was published also in Susa.
8:17 and province wherever the **d** was published;
9: 1 which is Adar, the **d** written by the king arrived.
9: 4 The king's **d** required that Mordecai's name
9:24 how he made a **d** and cast lots to destroy them,
9:32 Esther established it by a **d** forever,
Wis 11: 7 in rebuke for the **d** to kill the infants,
Sir 14:12 and the **d** of Hades has not been shown to you.
14:17 for the **d** from of old is, "You must die!"
16:22 For his **d** is far off."
41: 3 Do not fear death's **d** for you;
41: 4 This is the Lord's **d** for all flesh;
1Mc 1:57 was condemned to death by **d** of the king.
1:60 According to the **d,** they put to death
14:48 And they gave orders to inscribe this **d**
2Mc 6: 8 a **d** was issued to the neighboring Greek cities
1Es 5:55 the **d** that they had in writing from King Cyrus of
3Mc 4: 1 In every place, then, where this **d** arrived,
5:40 and again revoking your **d** in the matter?
2Es 7:*78* the decisive **d** has gone out from the Most High
10:16 For if you acknowledge the **d** of God to be just,
4Mc 4:23 and after he had plundered them he issued a **d** that

DECREED (29) [DECREE]

1Ki 22:23 the LORD has **d** disaster for you."
2Ki 10:20 Jehu **d,** "Sanctify a solemn assembly for Baal."
2Ch 18:22 the LORD has **d** disaster for you."
30: 5 So they **d** to make a proclamation
Est 2: 1 and what she had done and what had been **d**
Job 20:29 the heritage **d** for them by God."
Ps 122: 4 **d** for Israel, to give thanks to the name of the LORD
149: 9 to execute on them the judgment **d.**
Pr 31: 5 or else they will drink and forget what has been **d,**
Isa 10:22 Destruction is **d,** overflowing with righteousness.
10:23 Lord GOD of hosts will make a full end, as **d,**
Da 2: 8 because you see I have firmly **d:**
9:24 "Seventy weeks are **d** for your people
9:26 be war. Desolations are **d.**
9:27 until the **d** end is poured out upon the desolator."
Na 2: 7 It is **d** that the city be exiled,
1Co 2: 7 which God **d** before the ages for our glory.
Tob 1: 8 the ordinance **d** concerning it in the law of Moses
7:11 it has been **d** from heaven that she be given to you.
AdE 3: 9 let it be **d** that they are to be destroyed,
13: 6 "Therefore we have **d** that those indicated to you
1Mc 7:49 They **d** that this day should
8: 7 and **d** that he and those who would reign
13:52 Simon **d** that every year they should celebrate
2Mc 10: 8 They **d** by public edict, ratified by vote,
15:36 And they all **d** by public vote never
1Es 6:34 have **d** that it be done with all diligence
3Mc 4: 2 that had suddenly been **d** for them.
4:11 and the voyage was concluded as the king had **d,**

DECREES‡ (50) [DECREE]

Dt 4:45 These are the **d** and the statutes and ordinances
6: 2 and keep all his **d** and his commandments
6:17 the LORD your God, and his **d,** and his statutes
6:20 "What is the meaning of the **d** and the statutes and
10:13 and his **d** that I am commanding you today,
11: 1 and keep his charge, his **d,** his ordinances,
28:15 and **d,** which I am commanding you today,
28:45 by observing the commandments and the **d**
30:10 and **d** that are written in this book of the law,
30:16 and observing his commandments, **d,**
2Ki 23: 3 keeping his commandments, his **d,**
1Ch 29:19 your **d,** and your statutes, performing all of them,
2Ch 34:31 keeping his commandments, his **d,**
Ps 19: 7 **d** of the LORD are sure, making wise the simple;
25:10 for those who keep his covenant and his **d.**
78:56 They did not observe his **d,**
93: 5 Your **d** are very sure; holiness befits your house,

Ps 99: 7 they kept his **d**, and the statutes that he gave them.
119: 2 Happy are those who keep his **d**,
119:14 in the way of your **d** as much as in all riches.
119:22 for I have kept your **d**.
119:24 Your **d** are my delight, they are my counselors.
119:31 I cling to your **d**, O LORD;
119:36 Turn my heart to your **d**, and not to selfish gain.
119:46 I will also speak of your **d** before kings,
119:59 I think of your ways, I turn my feet to your **d**;
119:79 so that they may know your **d**.
119:88 so that I may keep the **d** of your mouth.
119:95 in wait to destroy me, but I consider your **d**.
119:99 for your **d** are my meditation.
119:111 Your **d** are my heritage forever;
119:119 as dross; therefore I love your **d**.
119:125 so that I may know your **d**.
119:129 Your **d** are wonderful;
119:138 You have appointed your **d** in righteousness and
119:144 Your **d** are righteous forever;
119:146 I cry to you; save me, that I may observe your **d**.
119:152 Long ago I learned from your **d**
119:157 yet I do not swerve from your **d**.
119:167 My soul keeps your **d**; I love them exceedingly.
119:168 I keep your precepts and **d**,
132:12 If your sons keep my covenant and my **d**
Isa 10: 1 Ah, you who make iniquitous **d**,
Jer 44:23 or walk in his law and in his statutes and in his **d**,
Ac 17: 7 They are all acting contrary to the **d** of
Sir 17:12 and revealed to them his **d**.
45: 5 the covenant, and Israel his **d**.
1Mc 14:22 We have recorded what they said in our public **d**,
4Mc 4:24 When, by means of his **d**,
4:26 I say, his **d** were despised by the people,

DEDAN (10) [DEDANITES]

Ge 10: 7 The descendants of Raamah: Sheba and **D**.
25: 3 Jokshan was the father of Sheba and **D**.
25: 3 The sons of **D** were Asshurim, Letushim,
1Ch 1: 9 The descendants of Raamah: Sheba and **D**.
1:32 The sons of Jokshan: Sheba and **D**.
Jer 25:23 **D**, Tema, Buz, and all who have shaven temples;
49: 8 Flee, turn back, get down low, inhabitants of **D**!
Eze 25:13 from Teman even to **D** they shall fall by
27:20 **D** traded with you in saddlecloths for riding.
38:13 Sheba and **D** and the merchants of Tarshish

DEDANITES‡ (1) [DEDAN]

Isa 21:13 the desert plain you will lodge, O caravans of **D**.

DEDICATE (6) [DEDICATED, DEDICATING, DEDICATION]

Lev 22: 2 which they **d** to me, so that they may
22: 3 which the people of Israel **d** to the LORD,
Dt 20: 5 or he might die in the battle and another **d** it.
2Ch 2: 4 the name of the LORD my God and **d** it to him
Sir 35:11 and **d** your tithe with gladness.
1Mc 4:36 let us go up to cleanse the sanctuary and **d** it."

DEDICATED (29) [DEDICATE]

Nu 18: 6 they are now yours as a gift, **d** to the LORD,
Dt 20: 5 "Has anyone built a new house but not **d** it?
2Sa 8:11 these also King David **d** to the LORD,
8:11 and gold that he **d** from all the nations he subdued,
1Ki 7:51 in the things that his father David had **d**,
8:63 So the king and all the people of Israel **d** the house
2Ki 12:18 his ancestors, the kings of Judah, had **d**,
23:11 the kings of Judah had **d** to the sun, at the entrance
1Ch 18:11 these also King David **d** to the LORD,
26:20 the house of God and the treasuries of the **d** gifts.
26:26 of all the treasuries of the **d** gifts that King David,
26:26 and the commanders of the army, had **d**.
26:27 in battles they **d** gifts for the maintenance of
26:28 and Joab son of Zeruiah had **d**—all **d** gifts
28:12 and the treasuries for **d** gifts;
2Ch 5: 1 in the things that his father David had **d**,
7: 5 So the king and all the people **d** the house of God.
24: 7 and had even used all the **d** things of the house of
31: 6 the tithe of the **d** things that had been consecrated
31:12 the tithes and the **d** things.
Isa 23:18 Her merchandise and her wages will be **d** to
42:19 Who is blind like my **d** one,
Lk 21: 5 with beautiful stones and gifts **d** to God,
2Ti 2:21 **d** and useful to the owner of the house,
Jdt 16:19 also **d** to God all the possessions of Holofernes,
1Mc 4:54 it was **d** with songs and harps and lutes
5: 1 that the altar had been rebuilt and the sanctuary **d**
3Mc 2:14 the holy place on earth **d** to your glorious name.

DEDICATING (1) [DEDICATE]

3Mc 7:20 and **d** a place of prayer at the site of the festival,

DEDICATION (19) [DEDICATE]

Nu 7:10 the **d** of the altar at the time when it was anointed;
7:11 one leader each day, for the **d** of the altar.
7:84 This was the **d** offering for the altar,
7:88 This was the **d** offering for the altar,
2Ch 7: 9 for they had observed the **d** of the altar seven days
Ezr 6:16 celebrated the **d** of this house of God with joy.
6:17 at the **d** of this house of God one hundred bulls,
Ne 12:27 at the **d** of the wall of Jerusalem they sought out
12:27 to Jerusalem to celebrate the **d** with rejoicing,
Ps 30: T *A Song at the* **d** *of the temple. Of David.*
Da 3: 2 of the provinces to assemble and come to the **d** of
Da 3: 3 assembled for the **d** of the statue
Jn 10:22 the festival of the **D** took place in Jerusalem.
1Mc 4:56 So they celebrated the **d** of the altar for eight days,
4:59 at that season the days of **d** of the altar should
2Mc 2: 9 of wisdom Solomon offered sacrifice for the **d**
2:19 and the **d** of the altar,
1Es 7: 7 the **d** of the temple of the Lord one hundred bulls,
2Es 7:*108* [38] and Solomon for those at the **d**,

DEED (36) [DO]

Ge 44:15 "What **d** is this that you have done?
Dt 11: 7 for it is your own eyes that have seen every great **d**
Jos 20: 6 to the town in which the **d** was done.' "
2Sa 12:14 by this **d** you have utterly scorned the LORD,
Est 1:17 For this **d** of the queen will be made known
Ecc 8:11 sentence against an evil **d** is not executed speedily,
12:14 For God will bring every **d** into judgment,
Isa 28:21 to do his **d**—strange is his **d**!
Jer 21: 2 perhaps the LORD will perform a wonderful **d**
32:10 I signed the **d**, sealed it, got witnesses,
32:11 Then I took the sealed **d** of purchase,
32:12 the **d** of purchase to Baruch son of Neriah son
32:12 in the presence of the witnesses who signed the **d**
32:14 both this sealed **d** of purchase and this open **d**,
32:16 After I had given the **d** of purchase to Baruch son
32:19 great in counsel and mighty in **d**;
Mt 19:16 what good **d** must I do to have eternal life?"
Mk 6: 5 And he could do no **d** of power there,
9:39 for no one who does a **d** of power in my name will
Lk 24:19 a prophet mighty in **d** and word before God and all
Ac 4: 9 of a good **d** done to someone who was sick
5: 4 is it that you have contrived this **d** in your heart?
Ro 15:18 from the Gentiles, by word and **d**,
Col 3:17 And whatever you do, in word or **d**,
Phm 1:14 in order that your good **d** might be voluntary and
Wis 3:14 the eunuch whose hands have done no lawless **d**,
Sir 3: 8 Honor your father by word and **d**,
Sus 1:63 because she was found innocent of a shameful **d**.
1Mc 5:61 thinking to do a brave **d**,
5:67 who wished to do a brave **d**, fell in battle,
2Mc 12: 3 the people of Joppa did so ungodly a **d** as this:
3Mc 1:27 and not to overlook this unlawful and haughty **d**.
3:17 but insincerely by **d**, because when we proposed
4Mc 16:14 and **d** you have proved more powerful than a man.

DEEDS‡ (217) [DO]

A. DEEDS OF POWER (12)
B. RIGHTEOUS DEEDS (11)
C. EVIL DEEDS (9)
D. GOOD DEEDS (9)
E. THE REST OF THE DEEDS (8)
F. DEEDS OF THE †LORD (7)
G. MIGHTY DEEDS (7)

Dt 3:24 on earth can perform **d** and mighty acts like yours!
11: 3 his signs and his **d** that he did in Egypt to Pharaoh,
28:20 on account of the evil of your **d**,
34:12 all the mighty **d** and all the terrifying displays G
Jdg 6:13 And where are all his wonderful **d**
Ru 2:12 May the LORD reward you for your **d**,
1Sa 12: 7 the saving **d** of the LORD that he performed F
19: 4 because his **d** have been of good service to you;
2Sa 23:20 a valiant warrior from Kabzeel, a doer of great **d**;
1Ki 2:32 The LORD will bring back his bloody **d**
2Ki 14:18 Now the rest of the **d** of Amaziah, E
15:11 Now the rest of the **d** of Zechariah are written E
15:15 Now the rest of the **d** of Shallum, E
15:21 Now the rest of the **d** of Menahem, E
15:26 Now the rest of the **d** of Pekahiah, E
20:20 The rest of the **d** of Hezekiah, all his power, E
24: 5 Now the rest of the **d** of Jehoiakim, E
1Ch 11:22 a valiant man of Kabzeel, a doer of great **d**;
16: 8 make known his **d** among the peoples.
17:19 you have done all these great **d**,
2Ch 13:22 rest of the acts of Abijah, his behavior and his **d**,
25:26 Now the rest of the **d** of Amaziah, E
32:32 the rest of the acts of Hezekiah, and his good **d**, D
35:26 the rest of the acts of Josiah and his faithful **d**
Ezr 9:13 After all that has come upon us for our evil **d** C
Ne 6:19 Also they spoke of his good **d** in my presence, D
13:14 and do not wipe out my good **d** that I have done D
Job 33:17 that he may turn them aside from their **d**,
34:11 For according to their **d** he will repay them,
Ps 9: 1 I will tell of all your wonderful **d**.
9:11 Declare his **d** among the peoples.
11: 7 he loves righteous **d**; the upright shall behold B
14: 1 They are corrupt, they do abominable **d**;
26: 7 and telling all your wondrous **d**.
28: 4 and according to the evil of their **d**;
33:15 the hearts of them all, and observes all their **d**.
40: 5 your wondrous **d** and your thoughts toward us;
44: 1 what **d** you performed in their days,
45: 4 let your right hand teach you dread **d**.
65: 3 When **d** of iniquity overwhelm us,
65: 5 By awesome **d** you answer us with deliverance,
66: 3 Say to God, "How awesome are your **d**!
66: 5 he is awesome in his **d** among mortals.
71:15 of your **d** of salvation all day long,
71:16 I will come praising the mighty **d** of G
71:17 and I still proclaim your wondrous **d**.
75: 1 People tell of your wondrous **d**.
77:11 I will call to mind the **d** of the LORD; F
77:12 and muse on your mighty **d**. G
78: 4 coming generation the glorious **d** of the LORD, F
105: 1 make known his **d** among the peoples.
Ps 106:22 and awesome **d** by the Red Sea
106:29 they provoked the LORD to anger with their **d**,
107:22 and tell of his **d** with songs of joy.
107:24 they saw the **d** of the LORD, F
111: 4 He has gained renown by his wonderful **d**;
118:17 but I shall live, and recount the **d** of the LORD. F
141: 4 to busy myself with wicked **d** in company
141: 5 my prayer is continually against their wicked **d**.
143: 5 I think about all your **d**,
145: 6 The might of your awesome **d** shall be proclaimed,
145:12 to make known to all people your mighty **d**, G
145:13 and gracious in all his **d**.
150: 2 Praise him for his mighty **d**; G
Pr 14:14 and the good, what their **d** deserve.
21: 2 All **d** are right in the sight of the doer,
24:12 And will he not repay all according to their **d**?
Ecc 1:14 I saw all the **d** that are done under the sun;
4: 3 not seen the evil **d** that are done under the sun. C
9: 1 how the righteous and the wise and their **d** are in
Isa 3: 8 their speech and their **d** are against the LORD,
5:12 but who do not regard the **d** of the LORD, F
12: 4 make known his **d** among the nations;
29:15 whose **d** are in the dark, and who say,
59: 6 and **d** of violence are in their hands.
59:18 According to their **d**, so will he repay;
63: 7 I will recount the gracious **d** of the LORD, F
64: 3 When you did awesome **d** that we did not expect,
64: 6 and all our righteous **d** are like a filthy cloth. B
Jer 5:28 They know no limits in **d** of wickedness;
11:15 when she has done vile **d**?
11:18 then you showed me their evil **d**. C
25:14 according to their **d** and the work of their hands.
32:14 Take these **d**, both this sealed deed of purchase
32:44 and **d** shall be signed and sealed and witnessed,
44:25 in **d** what you declared in words,
48:30 his boasts are false, his **d** are false.
50:29 Repay her according to her **d**;
La 3:64 Pay them back for their **d**, O LORD,
Eze 3:20 their righteous **d** that they have done shall not B
9:10 but I will bring down their **d** upon their heads."
11:21 I will bring their **d** upon their own heads,
14:22 When you see their ways and their **d**,
14:23 when you see their ways and their **d**;
16:30 the **d** of a brazen whore;
16:43 therefore, I have returned your **d** upon your head,
18:24 None of the righteous **d** that they have done B
20:43 There you shall remember your ways and all the **d**
20:44 not according to your evil ways, or corrupt **d**,
21:24 so that in all your **d** your sins appear—
22: 2 Then declare to it all its abominable **d**.
23:36 Then declare to them their abominable **d**.
33:13 none of their righteous **d** shall be remembered; B
36:17 they defiled it with their ways and their **d**;
36:19 with their conduct and their **d** I judged them.
36:31 for your iniquities and your abominable **d**.
Hos 4: 9 and repay them for their **d**.
5: 4 Their **d** do not permit them to return to their God.
7: 1 and the wicked **d** of Samaria;
7: 2 their **d** surround them, they are before my face.
9:15 of the wickedness of their **d** I will drive them out
12: 2 and repay him according to his **d**.
Joel 3: 4 I will turn your **d** back
3: 7 and I will turn your **d** back upon your own heads.
Am 8: 7 Surely I will never forget any of their **d**.
Ob 1:15 your **d** shall return on your own head.
Mic 2: 1 those who devise wickedness and evil **d** C
Zep 3: 7 the more eager to make all their **d** corrupt.
3:11 because of all the **d** by which you have rebelled
Zec 1: 4 from your evil ways and from your evil **d**." C
1: 6 with us according to our ways and **d**,
Mt 7:22 and do many **d** of power in your name?' A
11:19 Yet wisdom is vindicated by her **d**."
11:20 in which most of his **d** of power had been done, A
11:21 the **d** of power done in you had been done A
11:23 **d** of power done in you had been done A
13:54 this man get this wisdom and these **d** of power? A
13:58 And he did not do many **d** of power there, A
23: 5 They do all their **d** to be seen by others;
Mk 6: 2 What **d** of power are being done by his hands! A
Lk 10:13 the **d** of power done in you had been done in A
11:48 So you are witnesses and approve of the **d**
19:37 for all the **d** of power that they had seen, A
23:41 for we are getting what we deserve for our **d**,
Jn 3:19 rather than light because their **d** were evil.
3:20 so that their **d** may not be exposed.
3:21 be clearly seen that their **d** have been done
Ac 2:11 hear them speaking about God's **d** of power." A
2:22 a man attested to you by God with **d** of power, A
7:22 and was powerful in his words and **d**.
26:20 to God and do **d** consistent with repentance.
Ro 2: 6 For he will repay according to each one's **d**:
3:20 be justified in his sight" by **d** prescribed by
8:13 if by the Spirit you put to death the **d** of the body,
1Co 12:28 then **d** of power, then gifts of healing, A
2Co 11:15 Their end will match their **d**.
Col 1:21 and hostile in mind, doing evil **d**, C
2Ti 4:14 the Lord will pay him back for his **d**.
Tit 2:14 a people of his own who are zealous for good **d**. D
Heb 10:17 and their lawless **d** no more."
10:24 how to provoke one another to love and good **d**, D
1Pe 1:17 according to their **d**, live in reverent fear during
2:12 they may see your honorable **d** and glorify God
2Pe 2: 8 in his righteous soul by their lawless **d** that he saw
1Jn 3:12 his own **d** were evil and his brother's righteous.
2Jn 1:11 to welcome is to participate in the evil **d** of such C
Jude 1:15 and to convict everyone of all the **d** of ungodliness
Rev 14:13 from their labors, for their **d** follow them."

Rev 15: 3 “Great and amazing are your **d**,
16:11 and they did not repent of their **d**.
18: 6 and repay her double for her **d**;
19: 8 for the fine linen is the righteous **d** of the saints. B
Tob 2:14 Where are your righteous **d**? B
3: 2 O Lord, and all your **d** are just;
12: 6 With fitting honor declare to all people the **d**
12:22 and they acknowledged God for these marvelous **d**
13: 9 he afflicted you for the **d** of your hands,
Wis 1: 9 to convict them of their lawless **d**;
1:16 ungodly by their words and **d** summoned death;
4:20 and their lawless **d** will convict them to their face.
Sir 4:29 or sluggish and remiss in your **d**.
7:35 because for such **d** you will be loved.
11:27 and at the close of one's life one's **d** are revealed.
12: 1 and you will be thanked for your good **d**. D
16:12 he judges a person according to one's **d**.
16:14 everyone receives in accordance with one's **d**.
18: 4 and who can search out his mighty **d**? G
18:15 My child, do not mix reproach with your good **d**, D
20:16 and I get no thanks for my good **d**. D
32:16 and they will kindle righteous **d** like a light. B
35:24 until he repays mortals according to their **d**, and
36:10 and let people recount your mighty **d**. G
44:10 whose righteous **d** have not been forgotten; B
48: 4 glorious you were, Elijah, in your wondrous **d**!
48:14 and in death his **d** were marvelous.
Bar 2:19 of any righteous **d** of our ancestors or our kings B
2:33 turn from their stubbornness and their wicked **d**;
1Mc 2:51 “Remember the **d** of the ancestors,
3: 4 He was like a lion in his **d**,
3: 7 but he made Jacob glad by his **d**,
5:56 heard of their brave **d** and of
8: 2 the brave **d** that they were doing among the Gauls,
9:22 and his wars and the brave **d** that he did,
10:15 of the brave **d** that they had done,
16:23 of John and his wars and the brave **d** that he did,
2Mc 3:36 He bore testimony to all concerning the **d** of
1Es 1:23 **d** of Josiah were upright in the sight of the Lord,
1:49 and lawlessness beyond all the unclean **d** of all
4:39 or wicked. Everyone approves its **d**,
8:86 about because of our evil **d** and our great sins. C
3Mc 2:25 he increased in his **d** of malice,
2:26 not content with his uncounted licentious **d**,
3: 5 of life with the good **d** of upright people, D
7:22 So the supreme God perfectly performed great **d**
2Es 1: 5 declare to my people their evil **d**, C
3:28 the **d** of those who inhabit Babylon any better?
3:29 I came here I saw ungodly **d** without number,
3:31 Are the **d** of Babylon better than those of Zion?
7:*35* be manifested; righteous **d** shall awake, B
7:*35* and unrighteous **d** shall not sleep.
7:*119* [49] but we have done **d** that bring death?
8:33 in consequence of their own **d**.
14:35 and the **d** of the ungodly shall be disclosed.
15:48 You have imitated that hateful one in all her **d**
4Mc 5:38 either by words or through **d**.”
7: 9 but by your **d** you made your words
11: 6 But these **d** deserve honors, not tortures.”

DEEM (1) [DEEMED, DEEMING]

3Mc 3:21 both to **d** them worthy of Alexandrian citizenship

DEEMED (7) [DEEM]

Pr 17:28 when they close their lips, they are **d** intelligent.
Isa 32:15 and the fruitful field is **d** a forest.
Wis 17: 6 and in terror they **d** the things that they saw to
2Mc 9:21 and I have **d** it necessary to take thought for
2Es 8:30 with those who are **d** worse than wild animals,
13:14 and have **d** me worthy to have my prayer heard
4Mc 18: 3 were **d** worthy to share in a divine inheritance.

DEEMING (1) [DEEM]

Wis 12:15 **d** it alien to your power to condemn anyone who

DEEP‡ (112) [ANKLE-DEEP, DEEPER, DEEPEST, DEEPLY, DEEPS, DEPTH, DEPTHS, KNEE-DEEP]

A. THE DEEP (27)

Ge 1: 2 and darkness covered the face of the **d**, A
2:21 LORD God caused a **d** sleep to fall upon the man,
7:11 that day all the fountains of the great **d** burst forth,
7:20 covering them fifteen cubits **d**.
8: 2 the **d** and the windows of the heavens A
15:12 sun was going down, a **d** sleep fell upon Abram,
15:12 a **d** and terrifying darkness descended upon him.
49:25 blessings of the **d** that lies beneath, A
Nu 11:31 about two cubits **d** on the ground.
Dt 33:13 and of the **d** that lies beneath; A
1Sa 26:12 a **d** sleep from the LORD had fallen upon them.
Ezr 9: 7 of our ancestors to this day we have been **d**
Job 3: 5 Let gloom and **d** darkness claim it.
4:13 when **d** sleep falls on mortals,
10:21 to the land of gloom and **d** darkness,
11: 7 “Can you find out the **d** things of God?
12:22 and brings **d** darkness to light.
16:16 and **d** darkness is on my eyelids,
22:13 Can he judge through the **d** darkness?
24:17 For **d** darkness is morning to all of them;
24:17 for they are friends with the terrors of **d** darkness.
28: 3 the ore in gloom and **d** darkness.
28:14 The **d** says, 'It is not in me,' and the sea says, A
Job 33:15 when **d** sleep falls on mortals,
34:22 There is no gloom or **d** darkness
38:16 or walked in the recesses of the **d**? A
38:17 or have you seen the gates of **d** darkness?
38:30 and the face of the **d** is frozen. A
41:31 It makes the **d** boil like a pot; A
41:32 one would think the **d** to be white-haired. A
Ps 36: 1 Transgression speaks to the wicked **d**
36: 6 your judgments are like the great **d**;
42: 7 **D** calls to deep at the thunder of your cataracts;
42: 7 Deep calls to **d** at the thunder of your cataracts;
44:19 and covered us with **d** darkness.
64: 6 For the human heart and mind are **d**.
69: 2 I sink in **d** mire, where there is no foothold;
69: 2 I have come into **d** waters,
69:14 from my enemies and from the **d** waters.
69:15 or the **d** swallow me up, A
77:16 they were afraid; the very **d** trembled.
78:15 and gave them drink abundantly as from the **d**. A
80: 9 it took **d** root and filled the land.
88: 6 in the regions dark and **d**.
92: 5 Your thoughts are very **d**!
104: 6 You cover it with the **d** as with a garment; A
106: 9 he led them through the **d** as through a desert. A
107:24 his wondrous works in the **d**. A
Pr 4:19 The way of the wicked is like **d** darkness;
8:27 when he drew a circle on the face of the **d**, A
8:28 when he established the fountains of the **d**, A
18: 4 The words of the mouth are **d** waters;
19:15 Laziness brings on **d** sleep;
20: 5 The purposes in the human mind are like **d** water,
22:14 The mouth of a loose woman is a **d** pit;
23:27 prostitute is a **d** pit; an adulteress is a narrow well.
Ecc 7:24 That which is, is far off, and **d**, very **d**;
Isa 7:11 let it be **d** as Sheol or high as heaven.
9: 2 those who lived in a land of **d** darkness—
29: 4 Then **d** from the earth you shall speak,
29:10 upon you a spirit of **d** sleep;
29:15 You who hide a plan too **d** for the LORD,
30:33 its pyre made **d** and wide,
44:27 who says to the **d**, “Be dry— A
51:10 the waters of the great **d**; A
Jer 2: 6 in a land of drought and **d** darkness,
13:16 he turns it into gloom and makes it **d** darkness.
49:30 Flee, wander far away, hide in **d** places,
La 1:13 From on high he sent fire; it went **d** into my bones;
Eze 23:32 You shall drink your sister's cup, **d** and wide;
26:19 when I bring up the **d** over you, A
31: 4 The waters nourished it, the **d** made it grow tall, A
31:15 On the day it went down to Sheol I closed the **d** A
40: 6 the threshold of the gate, one reed **d**.
40: 7 each recess was one reed wide and one reed **d**;
40: 7 of the gate at the inner end was one reed **d**.
40:30 twenty-five cubits **d** and five cubits wide.
40:47 He measured the court, one hundred cubits **d**,
41:13 he measured the temple, one hundred cubits **d**;
41:13 the building with its walls, one hundred cubits **d**;
42: 4 ten cubits wide and one hundred cubits **d**,
47: 5 it was **d** enough to swim in,
Da 2:22 He reveals **d** and hidden things;
Hos 5: 2 and a pit dug **d** in Shittim;
Am 5: 8 and turns **d** darkness into the morning,
7: 4 it devoured the great **d** and was eating up the land.
Jnh 2: 3 You cast me into the **d**, into the heart of the seas, A
2: 5 waters closed in over me; the **d** surrounded me; A
Hab 3:10 the **d** gave forth its voice. A
Lk 5: 4 “Put out into the **d** water and let down your nets
Jn 4:11 “Sir, you have no bucket, and the well is **d**.
Ac 20: 9 into a **d** sleep while Paul talked still longer.
Ro 8:26 very Spirit intercedes with sighs too **d** for words.
Rev 2:24 not learned what some call 'the **d** things of Satan,'
Wis 4: 3 of their illegitimate seedlings will strike a **d** root
10:18 and led them through **d** waters;
16:11 so that they would not fall into **d** forgetfulness
Sir 22: 9 or who rouses a sleeper from **d** slumber.
43:23 By his plan he stilled the **d** and planted islands A
47:15 and you filled it with proverbs having **d** meaning.
51: 5 from the **d** belly of Hades, from an unclean tongue
1Mc 6: 9 **d** disappointment continually gripped him,
2Mc 3:27 to the ground and **d** darkness came over him,
Man 1: 3 confined the **d** and sealed it with your terrible A
3Mc 5:12 of the Lord he was overcome by so pleasant and **d**
5:47 when he had filled his impious mind with a **d** rage,
2Es 4: 7 or how many streams are at the source of the **d**, A
4: 8 'I never went down into the **d**, A
7: 3 “There is a sea set in a wide expanse so that it is **d**
7: 7 that there is fire on the right hand and **d** water on
10: 7 the mother of us all, is in **d** grief and great distress.

DEEPER (15) [DEEP]

Lev 13: 3 and the disease appears to be **d** than the skin
13: 4 and appears no **d** than the skin,
13:20 and if it appears **d** than the skin
13:21 nor is it **d** than the skin but has abated,
13:25 in the spot has turned white and it appears **d** than
13:26 and it is no **d** than the skin but has abated,
13:30 If it appears **d** than the skin and the hair
13:31 and it appears no **d** than the skin
13:32 and the itch appears to be no **d** than the skin,
13:34 in the skin and it appears to be no **d** than the skin,
14:37 and if it appears to be **d** than the surface,
Job 11: 8 **D** than Sheol—what can you know?
Pr 17:10 A rebuke strikes **d** into a discerning person than
Sir 24:29 and her counsel **d** than the great abyss.
4Mc 15: 4 because of their birth pangs have a **d** sympathy

DEEPEST (5) [DEEP]

2Pe 2: 4 and committed them to chains of **d** darkness to
2:17 for them the **d** darkness has been reserved.
Jude 1: 6 in eternal chains in **d** darkness for the judgment of
1:13 whom the **d** darkness has been reserved forever.
Tob 4:19 if he chooses otherwise, he casts down to **d** Hades.

DEEPLY (30) [DEEP]

1Sa 1:10 She was **d** distressed and prayed to the LORD,
1:15 “No, my lord, I am a woman **d** troubled;
2Sa 18:33 The king was **d** moved, and went up to
Ne 1: 7 We have offended you **d**, failing to keep
Est 4: 4 the queen was **d** distressed;
Isa 31: 6 Turn back to him whom you have **d** betrayed,
49: 7 to one **d** despised, abhorred by the nations,
66:11 that you may drink **d** with delight
Jer 31:20 Therefore I am **d** moved for him;
Hos 9: 9 They have **d** corrupted themselves as in the days
Mt 26:38 he said to them, “I am **d** grieved, even to death;
Mk 6:26 The king was **d** grieved;
8:12 And he sighed **d** in his spirit and said,
14:34 he said to them, “I am **d** grieved, even to death;
Lk 6:48 who dug **d** and laid the foundation on rock;
Jn 11:33 he was greatly disturbed in spirit and **d** moved.
Ac 17:16 he was **d** distressed to see that the city was full
1Th 2: 8 So **d** do we care for you that we are determined
1Pe 1:22 love one another **d** from the heart.
AdE 4: 4 and eunuchs came and told her, she was **d** troubled
Sir 38:29 he is always **d** concerned over his products,
Bar 2:18 but the person who is **d** grieved,
1Mc 1:25 Israel mourned **d** in every community,
2:39 they mourned for them **d**.
2:54 Phinehas our ancestor, because he was **d** zealous,
12:52 in great fear; and all Israel mourned **d**.
14:16 that Jonathan had died, and they were **d** grieved.
1Es 1:24 and how they grieved the Lord **d**,
2Es 9:38 and was **d** grieved at heart;
9:41 I am greatly embittered in spirit and **d** distressed.”

DEEPS (6) [DEEP]

Ex 15: 8 the **d** congealed in the heart of the sea.
Job 12:22 He uncovers the **d** out of darkness,
Ps 33: 7 he put the **d** in storehouses.
135: 6 in heaven and on earth, in the seas and all **d**.
148: 7 you sea monsters and all **d**,
Pr 3:20 by his knowledge the **d** broke open,

DEER‡ (13)

Dt 12:15 as they would of gazelle or **d**,
12:22 Indeed, just as gazelle or **d** is eaten,
14: 5 the **d**, the gazelle, the roebuck, the wild goat,
15:22 as you would a gazelle or **d**.
2Sa 22:34 He made my feet like the feet of **d**,
1Ki 4:23 one hundred sheep, besides **d**, gazelles, roebucks,
Job 39: 1 Do you observe the calving of the **d**?
Ps 18:33 He made my feet like the feet of a **d**,
22: T *according to The **D** of the Dawn.*
42: 1 As a **d** longs for flowing streams,
Pr 5:19 a lovely **d**, a graceful doe.
Isa 35: 6 then the lame shall leap like a **d**,
Hab 3:19 he makes my feet like the feet of a **d**,

DEFAME (1)

Lk 6:22 and **d** you on account of the Son of Man.

DEFEAT (15) [DEFEATED, DEFEATING]

Ge 14:17 After his return from the **d** of Chedorlaomer and
Nu 22: 6 perhaps I shall be able to **d** them and drive them
25:17 “Harass the Midianites, and **d** them;
Dt 7: 2 over to you and you **d** them,
9: 3 he will **d** them and subdue them before you,
Jdg 11:33 He inflicted a massive **d** on them from Aroer to
1Sa 23: 5 and dealt them a heavy **d**.
2Sa 15:34 then you will **d** for me the counsel of Ahithophel.
17:14 the LORD had ordained to **d** the good counsel
Ro 11:12 and if their **d** means riches for Gentiles,
1Co 6: 7 at all with one another is already a **d** for you.
Jdt 5:20 then we can go up and **d** them.
1Mc 5:40 for he will surely **d** us.
5:41 we will cross over to him and **d** him.”
2Mc 11:13 he pondered over the **d** that had befallen him,

DEFEATED‡ (87) [DEFEAT]

Ge 36:35 who **d** Midian in the country of Moab,
Ex 17:13 Joshua **d** Amalek and his people with the sword.
Nu 14:45 in that hill country came down and **d** them,
Dt 1: 4 after he had **d** King Sihon of the Amorites,
1:42 otherwise you will be **d** by your enemies.' ”
4:46 and the Israelites **d** when they came out of Egypt.
28: 7 against you to be **d** before you;
28:25 The LORD will cause you to be **d**
29: 7 against us for battle, but we **d** them.
Jos 10:40 So Joshua **d** the whole land,
10:41 And Joshua **d** them from Kadesh-barnea to Gaza,
12: 1 the Israelites **d**, whose land they occupied beyond
12: 6 of the LORD, and the Israelites **d** them;
12: 7 and the Israelites **d** on the west side of the Jordan,
13:12 these Moses had **d** and driven out.
13:21 whom Moses **d** with the leaders of Midian,
Jdg 1: 4 and they **d** ten thousand of them at Bezek.
1: 5 and **d** the Canaanites and the Perizzites.
1:10 and they **d** Sheshai and Ahiman and Talmai.

Jdg 1:17 and they **d** the Canaanites who inhabited Zephath,
3:13 and the Amalekites, he went and **d** Israel;
11:21 into the hand of Israel, and they **d** them;
12:4 and the men of Gilead **d** Ephraim,
20:35 The LORD **d** Benjamin before Israel;
20:36 Then the Benjaminites saw that they were **d.**
20:39 so they thought, "Surely they are **d** before us,
1Sa 4:2 Israel was **d** by the Philistines,
4:10 Israel was **d,** and they fled, everyone to his home.
13:3 Jonathan **d** the garrison of the Philistines that was
13:4 When all Israel heard that Saul had **d** the garrison
15:7 Saul **d** the Amalekites, from Havilah as far
2Sa 5:20 to Baal-perazim, and David **d** them there.
8:2 He also **d** the Moabites and,
8:9 When King Toi of Hamath heard that David had **d**
8:10 against Hadadezer and **d** him.
10:15 the Arameans saw that they had been **d** by Israel,
10:19 of Hadadezer saw that they had been **d** by Israel,
18:7 of Israel were **d** there by the servants of David,
1Ki 8:33 are **d** before an enemy but turn again to you,
20:21 and **d** the Arameans with a great slaughter.
2Ki 10:32 Hazael **d** them throughout the territory of Israel:
13:25 Three times Joash **d** him and recovered the towns
14:10 You have indeed **d** Edom,
14:12 Judah was **d** by Israel; everyone fled home.
1Ch 1:46 who **d** Midian in the country of Moab,
14:11 up to Baal-perazim, and David **d** them there.
18:2 He **d** Moab, and the Moabites became subject
18:9 When King Tou of Hamath heard that David had **d**
18:10 he had fought against Hadadezer and **d** him.
19:16 the Arameans saw that they had been **d** by Israel,
19:19 of Hadadezer saw that they had been **d** by Israel,
2Ch 6:24 are **d** before an enemy but turn again to you,
13:15 God **d** Jeroboam and all Israel before Abijah
13:17 Abijah and his army **d** them with great slaughter;
14:12 So the LORD **d** the Ethiopians before Asa and
14:14 They **d** all the cities around Gerar,
25:19 You say, 'See, I have **d** Edom,'
25:22 Judah was **d** by Israel; everyone fled home.
28:5 who **d** him and took captive a great number
28:5 who **d** him with great slaughter.
28:17 For the Edomites had again invaded and **d** Judah,
28:23 which had **d** him, and said,
Jer 37:10 Even if you **d** the whole army
46:2 and which King Nebuchadrezzar of Babylon **d** in
49:28 of Hazor that King Nebuchadrezzar of Babylon **d.**
Da 11:11 which shall, however, be **d** by his enemy.
Rev 12:8 but they were **d,** and there was no longer any place
Jdt 1:13 against King Arphaxad and **d** him in battle,
5:18 they were utterly **d** in many battles
11:11 not be **d** and his purpose frustrated,
Wis 17:13 **d** by this inward weakness,
1Mc 1:1 had **d** King Darius of the Persians and the Medes,
3:11 he went out to meet him, and he **d** and killed him.
5:43 All the Gentiles were **d** before him,
8:2 they had **d** them and forced them to pay tribute,
8:6 They also had **d** Antiochus the Great, king of Asia,
10:49 and Alexander pursued him and **d** them.
14:3 The general went and **d** the army of Demetrius,
2Mc 9:2 and Antiochus and his army were **d,**
10:24 Timothy, who had been **d** by the Jews before,
12:11 The **d** nomads begged Judas to grant them pledges
13:19 was turned back, attacked again, and was **d.**
13:22 withdrew, attacked Judas and his men, was **d;**
2Es 7:*128* [58] if they are **d** they shall suffer what you have
4Mc 8:2 the tyrant was conspicuously **d** in his first attempt,
9:30 of your tyranny being **d** by our endurance for
11:20 and in which we have not been **d!**

DEFEATING (2) [DEFEAT]

2Sa 1:1 when David had returned from **d** the Amalekites,
Heb 7:1 met Abraham as he was returning from **d** the kings

DEFECT (6) [DEFECTED, DEFECTIVE]

Nu 19:2 the Israelites to bring you a red heifer without **d,**
Dt 15:21 But if it has any **d**—any serious **d,** such as
17:1 or a sheep that has a **d,** anything seriously wrong;
Da 1:4 young men without physical **d** and handsome,
1Pe 1:19 like that of a lamb without **d** or blemish.

DEFECTED (2) [DEFECT]

2Ki 25:11 in the city and the deserters who had **d** to the king
Jer 52:15 in the city and the deserters who had **d** to the king

DEFECTIVE (1) [DEFECT]

Hos 7:16 they have become like a **d** bow;

DEFEND (35) [DEFENDED, DEFENDER, DEFENDERS, DEFENDING, DEFENDS, DEFENSE, DEFENSELESS, DEFENSES]

Jdg 6:31 Or will you **d** his cause?
2Ki 19:34 For I will **d** this city to save it,
20:6 I will **d** this city for my own sake and
Est 8:11 in every city to assemble and **d** their lives,
9:16 the king's provinces also gathered to **d** their lives,
Job 13:15 but I will **d** my ways to his face.
Ps 43:1 and **d** my cause against an ungodly people;
45:4 on victoriously for the cause of truth and to **d**
72:4 May he **d** the cause of the poor of the people,
Pr 31:9 **d** the rights of the poor and needy.
Isa 1:17 **d** the orphan, plead for the widow.
1:23 They do not **d** the orphan,
19:20 and will **d** and deliver them.
Isa 37:35 For I will **d** this city to save it,
38:6 of the hand of the king of Assyria, and **d** this city.
Jer 5:28 and they do not **d** the rights of the needy.
51:36 I am going to **d** your cause and take vengeance
Lk 12:11 about how you are to **d** yourselves or what you are
Ac 26:1 Paul stretched out his hand and began to **d** himself:
Jdt 5:21 for their Lord and God will **d** them,
6:2 of Israel because their God will **d** them?
AdE 6:13 You will not be able to **d** yourself,
8:11 to observe their own laws, to **d** themselves,
9:16 in the kingdom gathered to **d** themselves,
16:20 on that very day, they may **d** themselves
LtJ 6:15 but cannot **d** itself from war and robbers.
1Mc 8:32 we will **d** their rights and fight you on sea and
3Mc 1:4 and exhorted them to **d** themselves
1:27 to call upon him who has all power to **d** them in
2Es 2:20 give to the needy, **d** the orphan, clothe the naked,
7:*122* [52] of the Most High will **d** those who have led
13:49 he will **d** the people who remain.
16:50 to her face when he comes who will **d**
4Mc 14:19 at the time for making honeycombs **d** themselves
14:19 sting those who approach their hive and **d** it even

DEFENDED (3) [DEFEND]

2Sa 23:12 he took his stand in the middle of the plot, **d** it,
1Ch 11:14 middle of the plot, **d** it, and killed the Philistines;
Ac 7:24 he **d** the oppressed man and avenged him

DEFENDER‡ (3) [DEFEND]

2Mc 8:36 of Jerusalem proclaimed that the Jews had a **D,**
14:34 upon the constant **D** of our nation, in these words:
15:30 Then the man who was ever in body and soul the **d**

DEFENDERS (1) [DEFEND]

2Mc 10:36 up in the same way wheeled around against the **d**

DEFENDING (3) [DEFEND]

2Co 12:19 along that we have been **d** ourselves before you?
Wis 10:20 and praised with one accord your **d** hand;
2Mc 6:11 because their piety kept them from **d** themselves,

DEFENDS (2) [DEFEND]

Wis 16:17 for the universe **d** the righteous.
3Mc 7:6 to realize that the God of heaven surely **d**

DEFENSE (26) [DEFEND]

Ex 2:17 up and came to their **d** and watered their flock.
2Ch 11:5 and he built cities for **d** in Judah.
Ps 35:23 Bestir yourself for my **d,** for my cause,
48:3 Within its citadels God has shown himself a sure **d.**
Jer 33:4 a **d** against the siege ramps and before the sword:
41:9 that King Asa had made for **d** against King Baasha
Da 3:16 we have no need to present a **d** to you
Am 3:11 the land, and strip you of your **d;**
Lk 21:14 up your minds not to prepare your **d** in advance;
Ac 19:33 for silence and tried to make a **d** before the people.
22:1 listen to the **d** that I now make before you."
24:10 "I cheerfully make my **d,** knowing that
25:8 in his **d,** "I have in no way committed an offense
25:16 and had been given an opportunity to make a **d**
26:2 to make my **d** today against all the accusations of
26:24 While he was making this **d,** Festus exclaimed,
1Co 9:3 This is my **d** to those who would examine me.
Php 1:7 in my imprisonment and in the **d** and confirmation
1:16 that I have been put here for the **d** of the gospel;
2Ti 4:16 At my first **d** no one came to my support,
1Pe 3:15 to make your **d** to anyone who demands from you
Wis 6:10 those who have been taught them will find a **d.**
Sir 6:29 Then her fetters will become for you a strong **d,**
1Mc 14:10 and furnished them with the means of **d,**
2Mc 12:27 before the walls and made a vigorous **d;**
13:26 made the best possible **d,** convinced them,

DEFENSELESS (1) [DEFEND]

Ps 141:8 in you I seek refuge; do not leave me **d.**

DEFENSES (3) [DEFEND]

Job 13:12 your **d** are **d** of clay.
Ps 60:1 you have rejected us, broken our **d;**

DEFER (4) [DEFERENCE, DEFERENTIAL, DEFERRED]

Lev 19:15 not be partial to the poor or **d** to the great:
19:32 You shall rise before the aged, and **d** to the old;
Isa 48:9 For my name's sake I **d** my anger,
2Es 7:*54* **d** to her, and she will declare it to you.

DEFERENCE (6) [DEFER]

Mt 22:16 and show **d** to no one;
Mk 12:14 and show **d** to no one;
Lk 20:21 and you show **d** to no one,
1Pe 2:18 accept the authority of your masters with all **d,**
Wis 6:7 of all will not stand in awe of anyone, or show **d**
Sir 4:22 Do not show partiality, to your own harm, or **d,**

DEFERENTIAL (1) [DEFER]

Sir 29:5 and is **d** in speaking of his neighbor's money;

DEFERRED (1) [DEFER]

Pr 13:12 Hope **d** makes the heart sick,

DEFIANCE (2) [DEFY]

Job 15:25 and bid **d** to the Almighty,
3Mc 3:19 among all nations who hold their heads high in **d**

DEFIANT (2) [DEFY]

Dt 2:30 and made his heart **d** in order to hand him over
Sir 38:15 will be **d** toward the physician.

DEFIED (7) [DEFY]

1Sa 17:36 since he has **d** the armies of the living God."
17:45 the God of the armies of Israel, whom you have **d.**
2Sa 23:9 He was with David when they **d**
2Ch 13:7 around him and **d** Rehoboam son of Solomon,
Jer 50:29 for she has arrogantly **d** the LORD,
AdE 1:17 the queen had said and how she had **d** the king).
1:17 "And just as she **d** King Artaxerxes,

DEFILE (47) [DEFILED, DEFILEMENT, DEFILEMENTS, DEFILES, DEFILING]

Lev 11:43 you shall not **d** yourselves with them,
11:44 not **d** yourselves with any swarming creature
18:20 with your kinsman's wife, and **d** yourself with her.
18:23 with any animal and **d** yourself with it,
18:24 Do not **d** yourselves in any of these ways,
18:30 and not to **d** yourselves by them:
21:1 No one shall **d** himself for a dead person
21:3 he may **d** himself for her.
21:4 not **d** himself as a husband among his people and
21:11 not **d** himself even for his father or mother.
Nu 5:3 they must not **d** their camp,
6:7 should die, they may not **d** themselves;
19:13 **d** the tabernacle of the LORD;
35:34 You shall not **d** the land in which you live,
Dt 21:23 You must not **d** the land that
Isa 23:9 to **d** the pride of all glory,
30:22 Then you will **d** your silver-covered idols
Eze 9:7 Then he said to them, **"D** the house,
14:11 nor **d** themselves any more
18:6 not **d** his neighbor's wife or approach a woman
18:15 does not **d** his neighbor's wife,
20:7 and do not **d** yourselves with the idols of Egypt;
20:18 nor **d** yourselves with their idols.
20:30 Will you **d** yourselves after the manner
20:31 you **d** yourselves with all your idols to this day.
28:7 the beauty of your wisdom and **d** your splendor.
37:23 They shall never again **d** themselves
43:7 The house of Israel shall no more **d** my holy name,
44:25 not **d** themselves by going near to a dead person;
44:25 brother or unmarried sister they may **d** themselves.
Da 1:8 that he would not **d** himself with the royal rations
1:8 the palace master to allow him not to **d** himself.
Mt 15:20 These are what **d** a person,
15:20 but to eat with unwashed hands does not **d."**
Mk 7:15 a person that by going in can **d,**
7:15 but the things that come out are what **d."**
7:18 into a person from outside cannot **d,**
7:23 from within, and they **d** a person."
Jude 1:8 in the same way these dreamers also **d** the flesh,
Jdt 9:2 a virgin's clothing to **d** her, and exposed her thighs
9:8 for they intend to **d** your sanctuary,
13:16 and that he committed no sin with me, to **d**
1Mc 1:46 to **d** the sanctuary and the priests,
14:36 a citadel from which they used to sally forth and **d**
2Mc 6:25 while I **d** and disgrace my old age.
4Mc 5:36 shall not **d** the honorable mouth of my old age,
18:8 the deceitful serpent, **d** the purity of my virginity.

DEFILED‡ (73) [DEFILE]

Ge 34:5 that Shechem had **d** his daughter Dinah;
34:13 because he had **d** their sister Dinah.
34:27 because their sister had been **d.**
49:4 then you **d** it—you went up onto my couch!
Lev 18:24 before you have **d** themselves.
18:25 Thus the land became **d;**
18:27 of these abominations, and the land became **d);**
19:31 do not seek them out, to be **d** by them:
21:7 a prostitute or a woman who has been **d;**
21:14 or a woman who has been **d,** a prostitute,
Nu 5:13 so that she is undetected though she has **d** herself,
5:14 and he is jealous of his wife who has **d** herself;
5:14 though she has not **d** herself;
5:20 your husband's authority, if you have **d** yourself
5:27 if she has **d** herself and has been unfaithful
5:28 But if the woman has not **d** herself and is clean,
6:12 because the consecrated head was **d.**
19:20 for they have **d** the sanctuary of the LORD.
Dt 24:4 to be his wife after she has been **d;**
2Sa 1:21 For there the shield of the mighty was **d,**
2Ki 23:8 and **d** the high places where
23:10 He **d** Topheth, which is in the valley
23:13 king **d** the high places that were east of Jerusalem,
23:16 and burned them on the altar, and **d** it,
1Ch 5:1 he **d** his father's bed his birthright was given
Ne 13:29 O my God, because they have **d** the priesthood,
Ps 79:1 they have **d** your holy temple;
89:39 you have **d** his crown in the dust.
Isa 59:3 For your hands are **d** with blood,
Jer 2:7 But when you entered you **d** my land,
2:23 How can you say, "I am not **d,**
19:13 and the houses of the kings of Judah shall be **d** like

Jer 32:34 in the house that bears my name, and **d** it.
La 4:14 so **d** with blood that no one was able
Eze 4:14 "Ah Lord GOD! I have never **d** myself;
5:11 because you have **d** my sanctuary
20:26 I **d** them through their very gifts,
22: 4 and **d** by the idols that you have made;
23: 7 and she **d** herself with all the idols of everyone
23:13 And I saw that she was **d;**
23:17 and they **d** her with their lust;
23:17 and after she **d** herself with them,
23:38 they have **d** my sanctuary on the same day
36:17 they **d** it with their ways and their deeds;
36:18 and for the idols with which they had **d** it.
Hos 5: 3 you have played the whore; Israel is **d.**
6:10 Ephraim's whoredom is there, Israel is **d.**
9: 4 all who eat of it shall be **d;**
Zep 3: 1 Ah, soiled, **d,** oppressing city!
Mk 7: 2 of his disciples were eating with **d** hands,
7: 5 the tradition of the elders, but eat with **d** hands?"
Ac 21:28 into the temple and has **d** this holy place."
1Co 8: 7 and their conscience, being weak, is **d.**
Heb 9:13 sanctifies those who have been **d** so
12:15 and through it many become **d.**
Jude 1:23 hating even the tunic **d** by their bodies.
Rev 14: 4 not **d** themselves with women, for they are virgins;
Wis 7:25 therefore nothing **d** gains entrance into her.
11: 6 stirred up and **d** with blood
Sir 47:20 You stained your honor, and **d** your family line,
Bar 3:10 that you are **d** with the dead,
1Mc 1:37 they even **d** the sanctuary.
1:63 to be **d** by food or to profane the holy covenant;
4:43 and removed the **d** stones to an unclean place.
4:45 a lasting shame to them that the Gentiles had **d** it.
7:34 But he mocked them and derided them and **d** them
2Mc 7:34 But you, unholy wretch, you most **d** of all mortals,
14: 3 but had willfully **d** himself in the times
3Mc 7:14 of their compatriots who had become **d.**
2Es 1:26 for you have **d** your hands with blood,
8:60 but those who were created have themselves **d**
10:22 into exile, our virgins have been **d,**
4Mc 7: 6 you neither **d** your sacred teeth

DEFILEMENT (5) [DEFILE]
Jn 18:28 to avoid ritual **d** and to be able to eat the Passover.
2Co 7: 1 let us cleanse ourselves from every **d** of body and
Tob 3:14 O Master, that I am innocent of any **d** with a man,
2Mc 5:27 so that they might not share in the **d.**
3Mc 2:17 not punish us for the **d** committed by these men,

DEFILEMENTS (1) [DEFILE]
2Pe 2:20 after they have escaped the **d** of the world through

DEFILES (9) [DEFILE]
Nu 5:29 her husband's authority, goes astray and **d** herself,
Eze 18:11 upon the mountains, **d** his neighbor's wife,
22:11 another lewdly **d** his daughter-in-law;
22:11 another in you **d** his sister, his father's daughter.
33:26 and each of you **d** his neighbor's wife;
Mt 15:11 it is not what goes into the mouth that **d** a person,
15:11 but it is what comes out of the mouth that **d."**
15:18 from the heart, and this is what **d.**
Mk 7:20 he said, "It is what comes out of a person that **d.**

DEFILING (22) [DEFILE]
Lev 15:31 not die in their uncleanness by **d** my tabernacle
18:28 otherwise the land will vomit you out for **d** it,
20: 3 **d** my sanctuary and profaning my holy name.
Nu 6: 9 **d** the consecrated head, then they shall shave
Jer 7:30 in the house that is called by my name, **d** it.
Eze 22: 3 its time has come; making its idols, **d** itself.
43: 8 they were **d** my holy name by their abominations
Wis 14:26 forgetfulness of favors, **d** of souls,
4Mc 4:26 the nation to eat **d** foods and to renounce Judaism.
5: 3 If any were not willing to eat **d** food,
5:19 be a petty sin if we were to eat **d** food;
5:25 "Therefore we do not eat **d** food;
5:27 a way that you may deride us for eating **d** foods,
6:19 by setting them an example in the eating of **d** food.
7: 6 for reverence and purity, by eating **d** foods.
8: 2 to compel an aged man to eat **d** foods,
8: 2 any who ate **d** food would be freed after eating,
8:12 as to persuade them out of fear to eat the **d** food.
8:29 to eat **d** food, all with one voice together,
11:16 if you intend to torture me for not eating **d** foods,
11:25 to change our mind or force us to eat **d** foods,
13: 2 to their emotions and had eaten **d** food,

DEFINED (1)
Nu 34: 2 the land of Canaan, **d** by its boundaries),

DEFINITE (2)
Ac 2:23 to you according to the **d** plan and foreknowledge
25:26 But I have nothing **d** to write to our sovereign

DEFRAUD (3) [DEFRAUDED]
Lev 19:13 You shall not **d** your neighbor;
Mk 10:19 You shall not **d;** Honor your father and mother.' "
1Co 6: 8 you yourselves wrong and **d**—and believers at that.

DEFRAUDED (6) [DEFRAUD]
Lev 6: 2 or by robbery, or if you have **d** a neighbor,
1Sa 12: 3 Or whom have I **d?**
1Sa 12: 4 not **d** us or oppressed us or taken anything from
Lk 19: 8 and if I have **d** anyone of anything,
1Co 6: 7 Why not rather be **d?**
Sir 29: 7 but from fear of being **d** needlessly.

DEFRAYED (1)
2Mc 3: 3 even to the extent that King Seleucus of Asia **d**

DEFY (3) [DEFIANCE, DEFIANT, DEFIED, DEFYING]
1Sa 17:10 the Philistine said, "Today I **d** the ranks of Israel!
17:25 Surely he has come up to **d** Israel.
17:26 that he should **d** the armies of the living God?"

DEFYING (1) [DEFY]
Isa 3: 8 against the LORD, **d** his glorious presence.

DEGENERATE (2)
Dt 32: 5 yet his **d** children have dealt falsely with him,
Jer 2:21 How then did you turn **d** and become a wild vine?

DEGRADE (1) [DEGRADED, DEGRADES, DEGRADING]
Da 5:19 and degraded those he wanted to **d.**

DEGRADED (2) [DEGRADE]
Dt 25: 3 your neighbor will be **d** in your sight.
Da 5:19 and **d** those he wanted to degrade.

DEGRADES (1) [DEGRADE]
Sir 21:28 A whisperer **d** himself and is hated

DEGRADING (3) [DEGRADE]
Ro 1:24 to the **d** of their bodies among themselves,
1:26 For this reason God gave them up to **d** passions.
1Co 11:14 that if a man wears long hair, it is **d** to him,

DEGREE‡ (4)
2Co 3:18 the same image from one **d** of glory to another;
Heb 8: 6 to that **d** he is the mediator of a better covenant,
2Mc 4: 3 to such a **d** that even murders were committed
3Mc 5:31 and have exhibited to an extraordinary **d** a full

DEGREE, DEGREES (KJV) See also ASCENTS, HIGH RANK, INTERVALS, LOW ESTATE, LOWLY, ORDER, STEPS, STANDING

DEHAVITES (KJV) See "that is," Ezra 4:9

DEITIES (1) [DEITY]
Dt 32:17 not God, to **d** they had never known,

DEITY (2) [DEITIES]
Ac 17:29 we ought not to think that the **d** is like gold,
Col 2: 9 For in him the whole fullness of **d** dwells bodily,

DEJECTED (1) [DEJECTEDLY, DEJECTION]
Sir 25:23 **D** mind, gloomy face, and wounded heart come

DEJECTEDLY (1) [DEJECTED]
1Ki 21:27 he fasted, lay in the sackcloth, and went about **d.**

DEJECTION (1) [DEJECTED]
Jas 4: 9 be turned into mourning and your joy into **d.**

DELAIAH (8)
1Ch 3:24 Hodaviah, Eliashib, Pelaiah, Akkub, Johanan, **D,**
24:18 the twenty-third to **D,** the twenty-fourth
Ezr 2:60 the descendants of **D,** Tobiah,
Ne 6:10 the house of Shemaiah son of **D** son of Mehetabel,
7:62 the descendants of **D,** of Tobiah,
Jer 36:12 Elishama the secretary, **D** son of Shemaiah,
36:25 Even when Elnathan and **D** and Gemariah urged
1Es 5:37 the descendants of **D** son of Tobiah,

DELAY (36) [DELAYED, DELAYS]
Ge 24:56 But he said to them, "Do not **d** me,
34:19 And the young man did not **d** to do the thing,
45: 9 come down to me, do not **d.**
Ex 22:29 not **d** to make offerings from the fullness
Dt 7:10 He does not **d** but repays
Ezr 6: 8 in full and without **d,** from the royal revenue,
Ps 40:17 You are my help and my deliverer; do not **d,**
70: 5 and my deliverer; O LORD, do not **d!**
119:60 I hurry and do not **d** to keep your commandments.
Ecc 5: 4 you make a vow to God, do not **d** fulfilling it;
8: 3 do not **d** when the matter is unpleasant,
Jer 4: 6 do not **d,** for I am bringing evil from the north,
Da 9:19 O Lord, listen and act and do not **d!**
Hab 2: 3 it will surely come, it will not **d.**
Lk 1:21 and wondered at his **d** in the sanctuary.
Lk 18: 7 Will he **d** long in helping them?
Ac 9:38 "Please come to us without **d."**
16:33 he and his entire family were baptized without **d.**
22:16 And now why do you **d?**
Heb 10:37 the one who is coming will come and will not **d;**
Rev 10: 6 "There will be no more **d,**
Tob 9: 4 if I **d** even one day I will upset him very much.
Jdt 2:13 as I have ordered you; do it without **d."**
Sir 4: 3 or **d** giving to the needy.
5: 7 Do not **d** to turn back to the Lord,
6:21 and they will not **d** in casting her aside.
7:16 remember that retribution does not **d.**
35:22 Indeed, the Lord will not **d,**
38: 9 My child, when you are ill, do not **d,**
2Mc 14:27 to Antioch as a prisoner without **d.**
3Mc 5:20 without **d** prepare the elephants in the same way
5:42 that he would send them to death without **d,**
2Es 16:38 there will not be a moment's **d,**
16:39 the calamities will not **d** in coming upon the earth,
4Mc 6:23 And you, guards of the tyrant, why do you **d?"**
9: 1 "Why do you **d,** O tyrant?

DELAYED‡ (12) [DELAY]
Ge 43:10 If we had not **d,** we would now have returned
Ex 32: 1 When the people saw that Moses **d** to come down
Jdg 3:26 Ehud escaped while they **d,**
2Sa 20: 5 but he **d** beyond the set time
Eze 12:25 It will no longer be **d;**
12:28 None of my words will be **d** any longer,
Mt 24:48 wicked slave says to himself, 'My master is **d,'**
25: 5 As the bridegroom was **d,**
Lk 12:45 slave says to himself, 'My master is **d** in coming,'
1Ti 3:15 if I am **d,** you may know how one ought to behave
2Es 4:39 on account of us that the time of threshing is **d** for
16:37 The calamities draw near, and are not **d.**

DELAYS (1) [DELAY]
Sir 29: 5 but at the time for repayment he **d,**

DELECTABLE (1)
SS 7: 6 fair and pleasant you are, O loved one, **d** maiden!

DELEGATION (2)
Lk 14:32 he sends a **d** and asks for the terms of peace.
19:14 the citizens of his country hated him and sent a **d**

DELETE (1) [DELETION]
1Mc 8:30 both parties shall determine to add or **d** anything,

DELETION (1) [DELETE]
1Mc 8:30 and any addition or **d** that they may make shall

DELIBERATE‡ (3) [DELIBERATED, DELIBERATELY, DELIBERATION]
Sir 5:11 Be quick to hear, but **d** in answering.
1Mc 8:15 senators constantly **d** concerning the people,
3Mc 3:14 by the gods' **d** alliance with us in battle,

DELIBERATED (1) [DELIBERATE]
1Mc 4:44 They **d** what to do about the altar

DELIBERATELY (2) [DELIBERATE]
2Pe 3: 5 They **d** ignore this fact, that by the word
Sir 30:21 and do not distress yourself **d.**

DELIBERATION‡ (1) [DELIBERATE]
Sir 32:19 Do nothing without **d,** but when you have acted,

DELICACIES (9) [DELICACY]
Ge 49:20 and he shall provide royal **d.**
Ps 141: 4 do not let me eat of their **d.**
Pr 23: 3 Do not desire the ruler's **d,**
23: 6 of the stingy; do not desire their **d;**
Jer 51:34 he has filled his belly with my **d,**
La 4: 5 Those who feasted on **d** perish in the streets;
Jdt 12: 1 to set a table for her with some of his own **d,**
Wis 16: 3 a short time, might partake of **d.**
Sir 13: 7 He will embarrass you with his **d,**

DELICACY (2) [DELICACIES]
Wis 16: 2 a **d** to satisfy the desire of appetite;
Sir 37:29 Do not be greedy for every **d,**

DELICATE (1)
Isa 47: 1 For you shall no more be called tender and **d.**

DELICIOUS (5)
Jdg 9:11 and my **d** fruit, and go to sway over
Pr 18: 8 The words of a whisperer are like **d** morsels;
26:22 The words of a whisperer are like **d** morsels;
2Mc 15:39 while wine mixed with water is sweet and **d**
4Mc 5: 9 not to enjoy **d** things that are not shameful,

DELIGHT‡ (85) [DELIGHTED, DELIGHTFUL, DELIGHTING, DELIGHTS]
Ge 3: 6 and that it was a **d** to the eyes,
Dt 28:63 as the LORD took **d** in making you prosperous

Dt 28:63 so the LORD will take **d** in bringing you to ruin
30: 9 the LORD will again take **d** in prospering you,
1Sa 15:22 "Has the LORD as great **d** in burnt offerings
19: 1 But Saul's son Jonathan took great **d** in David.
1Ch 28: 4 and among my father's sons he took **d**
Ne 1:11 of your servants who **d** in revering your name.
Job 22:26 then you will **d** yourself in the Almighty,
27:10 Will they take **d** in the Almighty?
34: 9 'It profits one nothing to take **d** in God.'
Ps 1: 2 but their **d** is in the law of the LORD,
16: 3 they are the noble, in whom is all my **d.**
37: 4 Take **d** in the LORD, and he will give you
37:11 and **d** themselves in abundant prosperity.
40: 8 I **d** to do your will, O my God;
51:16 For you have no **d** in sacrifice;
51:19 then you will **d** in right sacrifices,
68:30 scatter the peoples who **d** in war.
111: 2 studied by all who **d** in them.
112: 1 who greatly **d** in his commandments.
119:14 I **d** in the way of your decrees as much as
119:16 I will **d** in your statutes;
119:24 Your decrees are my **d,** they are my counselors.
119:35 in the path of your commandments, for I **d** in it.
119:47 I find my **d** in your commandments,
119:70 Their hearts are fat and gross, but I **d** in your law.
119:77 for your law is my **d.**
119:92 If your law had not been my **d,**
119:143 but your commandments are my **d.**
119:174 O LORD, and your law is my **d.**
147:10 His **d** is not in the strength of the horse,
Pr 1:22 How long will scoffers **d** in their scoffing
2:14 who rejoice in doing evil and **d** in the perverseness
7:18 let us **d** ourselves with love.
8:30 and I was daily his **d,** rejoicing before him always,
11: 1 but an accurate weight is his **d.**
11:20 but those of blameless ways are his **d.**
12:22 but those who act faithfully are his **d.**
15: 8 but the prayer of the upright is his **d.**
16:13 Righteous lips are the **d** of a king,
24:25 but those who rebuke the wicked will have **d,**
29:17 they will give **d** to your heart.
SS 2: 3 With great **d** I sat in his shadow,
Isa 1:11 I do not **d** in the blood of bulls, or of lambs,
11: 3 His **d** shall be in the fear of the LORD.
13:17 who have no regard for silver and do not **d** in gold.
44: 9 and the things they **d** in do not profit;
55: 2 and **d** yourselves in rich food.
58: 2 after day they seek me and **d** to know my ways,
58: 2 they **d** to draw near to God.
58:13 a **d** and the holy day of the LORD honorable;
58:14 then you shall take **d** in the LORD,
62: 4 but you shall be called My **D** Is in Her,
65:12 and chose what I did not **d** in.
65:18 to create Jerusalem as a joy, and its people as a **d.**
65:19 I will rejoice in Jerusalem, and **d** in my people;
66: 3 and in their abominations they take **d;**
66:11 that you may drink deeply with **d**
Jer 9:24 for in these things I **d,** says the LORD.
15:16 and your words became to me a joy and the **d**
31:20 Is he the child I **d** in?
Eze 24:16 about to take away from you the **d** of your eyes;
24:21 the pride of your power, the **d** of your eyes,
24:25 the **d** of their eyes and their heart's affection,
Am 5:21 and I take no **d** in your solemn assemblies.
Mal 3: 1 The messenger of the covenant in whom you **d—**
3:12 for you will be a land of **d,**
Mk 12:37 And the large crowd was listening to him with **d.**
Ro 7:22 For I **d** in the law of God in my inmost self,
Wis 1:13 and he does not **d** in the death of the living.
3:14 and a place of great **d** in the temple of the Lord.
6:21 Therefore if you **d** in thrones and scepters,
8:18 pure **d,** and in the labors of her hands,
13: 3 If through **d** in the beauty
Sir 1:27 fidelity and humility are his **d.**
9:12 Do not **d** in what pleases the ungodly;
21:16 but **d** is found in the speech of the intelligent.
39:31 They take **d** in doing his bidding,
45:12 the work of an expert, a **d** to the eyes,
2Mc 4:12 He took **d** in establishing a gymnasium right under
2Es 7:*36* and opposite it the paradise of **d.**
7:*38* Look on this side and on that; here are **d** and rest,
7:*47* I see that the world to come will bring **d** to few,
4Mc 1:22 Thus desire precedes pleasure and **d** follows it.

DELIGHTED (12) [DELIGHT]

Ge 34:19 because he was **d** with Jacob's daughter.
Dt 30: 9 just as he **d** in prospering your ancestors,
1Sa 18:22 'See, the king is **d** with you,
2Sa 22:20 he delivered me, because he **d** in me.
1Ki 10: 9 who has **d** in you and set you on the throne
2Ch 9: 8 who has **d** in you and set you on his throne as king
Ne 9:25 and **d** themselves in your great goodness.
Est 2:14 the king **d** in her and she was summoned by name.
Ps 18:19 he delivered me, because he **d** in me.
44: 3 the light of your countenance, for you **d** in them.
Isa 1:29 you shall be ashamed of the oaks in which you **d;**
Sir 51:15 the first blossom to the ripening grape my heart **d**

DELIGHTFUL (1) [DELIGHT]

4Mc 8:23 and deprive ourselves of this **d** world?

DELIGHTING (1) [DELIGHT]

Pr 8:31 in his inhabited world and **d** in the human race.

DELIGHTS‡ (16) [DELIGHT]

Ps 5: 4 For you are not a God who **d** in wickedness;
22: 8 let him rescue the one in whom he **d!"**
35:27 who **d** in the welfare of his servant."
36: 8 and you give them drink from the river of your **d.**
37:23 when he **d** in our way;
Pr 3:12 as a father the son in whom he **d.**
Ecc 2: 8 and **d** of the flesh, and many concubines.
Isa 42: 1 whom I uphold, my chosen, in whom my soul **d;**
62: 4 the LORD **d** in you, and your land shall be married.
Mic 7:18 because he **d** in showing clemency.
Mal 2:17 in the sight of the LORD, and he **d** in them."
Sir 1:12 The fear of the Lord **d** the heart,
11:27 An hour's misery makes one forget past **d,**
24:17 Like the vine I bud forth **d,**
26:13 A wife's charm **d** her husband,
2Mc 15:39 of the story **d** the ears of those who read the work.

DELILAH (7)

Jdg 16: 4 in the valley of Sorek, whose name was **D.**
16: 6 So **D** said to Samson, "Please tell me what makes
16:10 Then **D** said to Samson, "You have mocked me
16:12 So **D** took new ropes and bound him with them,
16:13 Then **D** said to Samson,
16:14 **D** took the seven locks of his head and wove them
16:18 **D** realized that he had told her his whole secret,

DELIVER‡ (130) [DELIVERANCE, DELIVERED, DELIVERER, DELIVERING, DELIVERS, DELIVERY]

Ge 32:11 **D** me, please, from the hand of my brother,
Ex 3: 8 I have come down to **d** them from the Egyptians,
5:18 but you shall still **d** the same number of bricks."
5:23 you have done nothing at all to **d** your people."
6: 6 of the Egyptians and **d** you from slavery to them.
25:22 I will **d** to you all my commands for the Israelites.
Dt 32:39 and no one can **d** from my hand.
Jos 2:13 and **d** our lives from death."
Jdg 6:14 in this might of yours and **d** Israel from the hand
6:15 He responded, "But sir, how can I **d** Israel?
6:36 to see whether you will **d** Israel by my hand,
6:37 I shall know that you will **d** Israel by my hand,
7: 7 "With the three hundred that lapped I will **d** you,
10: 1 in the hill country of Ephraim, rose to **d** Israel.
10:11 "Did I not **d** you from the Egyptians and from
10:13 therefore I will **d** you no more.
10:14 let them **d** you in the time of your distress."
10:15 to you; but **d** us this day!"
12: 2 I called you, you did not **d** me from their hand.
12: 3 When I saw that you would not **d** me,
13: 5 It is he who shall begin to **d** Israel from the hand
1Sa 4: 8 Who can **d** us from the power
7: 3 he will **d** you out of the hand of the Philistines."
17:46 the LORD will **d** you into my hand,
2Sa 14:16 and **d** his servant from the hand of
22:28 You **d** a humble people, but your eyes are upon
1Ki 20: 5 saying, '**D** to me your silver and gold,
2Ki 3: 4 who used to **d** to the king
10:24 "Whoever allows any of those to escape whom I **d**
17:39 he will **d** you out of the hand of all your enemies."
18:29 for he will not be able to **d** you out of my hand.
18:30 The LORD will surely **d** us,
18:32 by saying, The LORD will **d** us.
18:35 the LORD should **d** Jerusalem out of my hand?' "
20: 6 I will **d** you and this city out of the hand of
2Ch 25:15 a people's gods who could not **d** their own people
Ezr 7:19 you shall **d** before the God of Jerusalem.
Job 5: 4 and there is no one to **d** them.
5:19 He will **d** you from six troubles;
10: 7 and there is no one to **d** out of your hand?
22:30 He will **d** even those who are guilty;
33:24 and says, '**D** him from going down into the Pit;
Ps 3: 7 **D** me, O my God!
6: 4 **d** me for the sake of your steadfast love.
7: 1 save me from all my pursuers, and **d** me,
17:13 By your sword **d** my life from the wicked,
18:27 For you **d** a humble people,
22: 8 "Commit your cause to the LORD; let him **d**
22:20 **D** my soul from the sword,
25:20 O guard my life, and **d** me;
31: 1 in your righteousness **d** me.
31:15 **d** me from the hand of my enemies
33:19 to **d** their soul from death,
35:10 You **d** the weak from those too strong for them,
39: 8 **D** me from all my transgressions.
40:13 Be pleased, O LORD, to **d** me;
43: 1 from those who are deceitful and unjust **d** me!
50:15 I will **d** you, and you shall glorify me."
50:22 and there will be no one to **d.**
51:14 **D** me from bloodshed, O God,
59: 1 **D** me from my enemies, O my God;
59: 2 **D** me from those who work evil;
70: 1 Be pleased, O God, to **d** me.
71: 2 In your righteousness **d** me and rescue me;
71:11 for there is no one to **d."**
74:19 not **d** the soul of your dove to the wild animals;
79: 9 **d** us, and forgive our sins, for your name's sake.
82: 4 **d** them from the hand of the wicked."
91: 3 For he will **d** you from the snare of the fowler and
91:14 Those who love me, I will **d;**
106: 4 help me when you **d** them;
109:21 because your steadfast love is good, **d** me.
119:170 **d** me according to your promise.
120: 2 "**D** me, O LORD, from lying lips,
140: 1 **D** me, O LORD, from evildoers;
144:11 and **d** me from the hand of aliens,
Ecc 8: 8 nor does wickedness **d** those who practice it.
Isa 19: 4 I will **d** the Egyptians into the hand of
19:20 and will defend and **d** them.
31: 5 he will protect and **d** it, he will spare and rescue it.
36:14 for he will not be able to **d** you.
36:15 The LORD will surely **d** us;
38: 6 I will **d** you and this city out of the hand of
43:13 there is no one who can **d** from my hand;
47:14 cannot **d** themselves from the power of the flame.
50: 2 Or have I no power to **d?**
57:13 you cry out, let your collection of idols **d** you!
66: 9 Shall I open the womb and not **d?**
Jer 1: 8 for I am with you to **d** you, says the LORD."
1:19 for I am with you, says the LORD, to **d** you.
15:20 for I am with you to save you and **d** you,
15:21 I will **d** you out of the hand of the wicked,
21:12 Execute justice in the morning, and **d** from
22: 3 Act with justice and righteousness, and **d** from
29:21 to **d** them into the hand of King Nebuchadrezzar
La 5: 8 there is no one to **d** us from their hand.
Eze 16:39 I will **d** you into their hands,
21:31 I will **d** you into brutish hands,
23:28 I will **d** you into the hands
Da 3:15 who is the god that will **d** you out of my hands?"
3:17 to **d** us from the furnace of blazing fire and out of your hand, O king, let him **d** us.
3:29 there is no other god who is able to **d** in this way."
6:16 whom you faithfully serve, **d** you!"
6:20 to **d** you from the lions?"
Am 6: 8 and I will **d** up the city and all that is in it.
Mic 5: 8 treads down and tears in pieces, with no one to **d.**
Zec 11: 6 and I will **d** no one from their hand.
Mt 27:43 let God **d** him now, if he wants to;
Lk 2: 6 the time came for her to **d** her child.
Jdt 8:33 the Lord will **d** Israel by my hand.
Wis 2:18 and will **d** him from the hand of his adversaries.
16: 8 that it is you who **d** from every evil.
Sir 50:24 and may he **d** us in our days!
Bar 2:14 and for your own sake **d** us,
4:18 upon you will **d** you from the hand
4:21 and he will **d** you from the power and hand of
LtJ 6:54 or **d** one who is wronged, for they have no power;
Aza 1:20 **D** us in accordance with your marvelous works,
1Mc 12:17 also to you and greet you and **d** to you this letter
1Es 8:17 **d** the holy vessels of the Lord that are given you
8:59 until you **d** them to the leaders of the priests and
2Es 2:30 with your children, because I will **d** you,
13:26 who will himself **d** his creation;
13:29 the Most High will **d** those who are on the earth.
14:26 and some you shall **d** in secret to the wise;
15:27 God will not **d** you, because you have sinned
16:17 Who will **d** me in those days?
16:67 so God will lead you forth and **d** you
16:74 but I will **d** you from them.

DELIVERANCE (40) [DELIVER]

Ex 14:13 and see the **d** that the LORD will accomplish
1Sa 11: 9 by the time the sun is hot, you shall have **d.'** "
11:13 for today the LORD has brought **d** to Israel."
2Ch 12: 7 but I will grant them some **d,**
Est 4:14 and **d** will rise for the Jews from another quarter,
Ps 3: 8 **D** belongs to the LORD; may your blessing be on
9:14 in the gates of daughter Zion, rejoice in your **d.**
14: 7 O that **d** for Israel would come from Zion!
22:31 and proclaim his **d** to a people yet unborn,
32: 7 you surround me with glad cries of **d.**
35: 9 in the LORD, exulting in his **d.**
40: 9 the glad news of **d** in the great congregation;
51:14 and my tongue will sing aloud of your **d.**
53: 6 O that **d** for Israel would come from Zion!
62: 7 On God rests my **d** and my honor;
65: 5 By awesome deeds you answer us with **d,**
72: 4 give **d** to the needy, and crush the oppressor.
Isa 20: 6 and to whom we fled for help and **d** from the king
46:12 you stubborn of heart, you who are far from **d:**
46:13 near my **d,** it is not far off, and my salvation will
51: 5 I will bring near my **d** swiftly,
51: 6 and my **d** will never be ended.
51: 8 but my **d** will be forever, and my salvation to all
56: 1 for soon my salvation will come, and my **d**
Jnh 2: 9 **D** belongs to the LORD!"
Php 1:19 of Jesus Christ this will turn out for my **d.**
Jdt 8:17 Therefore, while we wait for his **d,**
AdE 16:23 both now and hereafter it may represent **d** for you
Wis 16: 6 of **d** to remind them of your law's command.
18: 7 The **d** of the righteous and the destruction
1Mc 3: 6 and **d** prospered by his hand.
4:25 Thus Israel had a great **d** that day.
5:62 of those men through whom **d** was given to Israel.
3Mc 6:31 arranged for a banquet of **d** instead of a bitter
6:36 of the **d** that had come to them through God.
7:16 the full enjoyment of **d** began their departure from
7:18 There they celebrated their **d,**
7:22 God perfectly performed great deeds for their **d.**
4Mc 15:26 one bearing death and the other **d** for her children.
15:27 She did not approve the **d** that would preserve

DELIVERED‡ (119) [DELIVER]

Ge 9: 2 into your hand they are **d.**
14:20 who has **d** your enemies into your hand!"
32:16 These he **d** into the hand of his servants,
37:21 when Reuben heard it, he **d** him out of their hands,
Ex 18: 4 and **d** me from the sword of Pharaoh").

Ex 18: 8 and how the LORD had **d** them.
18:10 who has **d** you from the Egyptians and
18:11 because he **d** the people from the Egyptians,
Lev 26:25 and you shall be **d** into enemy hands.
Jdg 2:16 who **d** them out of the power
2:18 and he **d** them from the hand of their enemies all
3: 9 who **d** them, Othniel son of Kenaz,
3:31 with an oxgoad. He too **d** Israel.
6: 9 and I **d** you from the hand of the Egyptians,
7: 2 saying, 'My own hand has **d** me.'
8:22 for you have **d** us out of the hand of Midian."
10:12 and you cried to me, and I **d** you out of their hand.
2Sa 18:19 the king that the LORD has **d** him from the power
18:28 who has **d** up the men who raised their hand
19: 9 "The king **d** us from the hand of our enemies,
22: 1 on the day when the LORD **d** him from the hand
22:18 He **d** me from my strong enemy,
22:20 he **d** me, because he delighted in me.
22:44 You **d** me from strife with the peoples;
22:49 you **d** me from the violent.
1Ki 9:28 which they **d** to King Solomon.
2Ki 11:10 The priest **d** to the captains the spears and shields
12:15 an accounting from those into whose hand they **d**
18:33 of the nations ever **d** its land out of the hand of
18:34 Have they **d** Samaria out of my hand?
18:35 the gods of the countries have **d** their countries out
19:11 destroying them utterly. Shall you be **d?**
19:12 Have the gods of the nations **d** them,
22: 7 from them for the money that is **d** into their hand,
22: 9 and have **d** it into the hand of
1Ch 22:18 he has **d** the inhabitants of the land into my hand;
2Ch 23: 9 The priest Jehoiada **d** to the captains the spears
24:24 the LORD **d** into their hand a very great army,
34: 9 and **d** the money that had been brought into
34:10 They **d** it to the workers who had the oversight of
34:17 and have **d** it into the hand of the overseers and
Ezr 5:14 and they were **d** to a man named Sheshbazzar,
8:31 upon us, and he **d** us from the hand of the enemy
8:36 also **d** the king's commissions to the king's satraps
Job 8: 4 he **d** them into the power of their transgression.
29:12 because I **d** the poor who cried,
39: 3 and are **d** of their young?
Ps 18: T *the LORD **d** him from the hand of all his enemies,*
18:17 He **d** me from my strong enemy,
18:19 he **d** me, because he delighted in me.
18:43 You **d** me from strife with the peoples;
18:48 who **d** me from my enemies;
18:48 you **d** me from the violent.
22: 4 they trusted, and you **d** them.
31: 8 and have not **d** me into the hand of the enemy;
33:16 a warrior is not **d** by his great strength.
34: 4 and he answered me, and **d** me from all my fears.
54: 7 For he has **d** me from every trouble,
56:13 For you have **d** my soul from death,
69:14 be **d** from my enemies and from the deep waters.
78:61 and **d** his power to captivity,
86:13 you have **d** my soul from the depths of Sheol.
106:10 and **d** them from the hand of the enemy.
106:43 Many times he **d** them, but they were rebellious
107: 6 and he **d** them from their distress;
107:20 and **d** them from destruction.
116: 8 For you have **d** my soul from death,
Pr 11: 8 The righteous are **d** from trouble,
11: 9 but by knowledge the righteous are **d.**
Ecc 9:15 and he by his wisdom **d** the city.
Isa 36:19 Have they **d** Samaria out of my hand?
37:11 destroying them utterly. Shall you be **d?**
37:12 Have the gods of the nations **d** them,
43:28 I **d** Jacob to utter destruction,
64: 7 and have **d** us into the hand of our iniquity.
66: 7 before her pain came upon her she **d** a son.
66: 8 Shall a nation be **d** in one moment?
66: 8 as soon as Zion was in labor she **d** her children.
Jer 20:13 For he has **d** the life of the needy from the hands
La 2: 7 he has **d** into the hand of the enemy the walls
Eze 16:21 You slaughtered my children and **d** them up as
23: 9 Therefore I **d** her into the hands of her lovers,
Da 3:28 and **d** his servants who trusted in him.
12: 1 But at that time your people shall be **d,**
Am 1: 9 because they **d** entire communities over to Edom,
Ac 12:21 and **d** a public address to them.
15:30 the congregation together, they **d** the letter.
16: 4 they **d** to them for observance the decisions
23:33 When they came to Caesarea and **d** the letter to
Ro 15:28 and have **d** to them what has been collected,
Jdt 16: 2 he **d** me from the hands of my pursuers.
AdE 4:12 Hachratheus **d** her entire message to Mordecai,
Wis 10: 1 she **d** him from his transgression,
10:13 wisdom did not desert him, but **d** him from sin.
10:15 A holy people and blameless race wisdom **d** from
16:11 then were quickly **d,** so that they would not fall
19: 9 praising you, O Lord, who **d** them.
Sir 48:20 and **d** them through Isaiah.
49:10 for they comforted the people of Jacob and **d** them
51: 2 and helper and have **d** me from destruction and
51: 3 and **d** me, in the greatness of your mercy and
Aza 1:66 **d** us from the midst of the burning fiery furnace;
1:66 from the midst of the fire he has **d** us.
1Mc 2:60 was **d** from the mouth of the lions.
5:50 and the town was **d** into his hands.
7:35 Judas and his army are **d** into my hands this time,
9:46 that you may be **d** from the hands of our enemies."
12:15 and so we were **d** from our enemies,
16: 2 in our hands so that we have **d** Israel many times.
2Mc 11:15 in behalf of the Jews which Maccabeus **d** to Lysias
11:17 have **d** your signed communication
12:45 so that they might be **d** from their sin.
1Es 6:18 and they were **d** to Zerubbabel and Sheshbazzar
8: 8 from King Artaxerxes that was **d** to Ezra the priest
8:61 he **d** us from every enemy on the way,
8:62 and the gold were weighed and **d** in the house
8:67 They **d** the king's orders to the royal stewards and
2Es 7:27 Everyone who has been **d** from the evils
7:96 the straits and toil from which they have been **d,**

DELIVERER (12) [DELIVER]

Jdg 3: 9 the LORD raised up a **d** for the Israelites,
3:15 the LORD raised up for them a **d,**
18:28 There was no **d,** because it was far from Sidon
1Sa 10:27 of each of them and would not grant Israel a **d.**
2Sa 22: 2 The LORD is my rock, my fortress, and my **d,**
Ps 18: 2 The LORD is my rock, my fortress, and my **d,**
40:17 You are my help and my **d;**
70: 5 You are my help and my **d;**
140: 7 O LORD, my Lord, my strong **d,**
144: 2 my stronghold and my **d,** my shield,
Ro 11:26 as it is written, "Out of Zion will come the **D;**
3Mc 7:23 Blessed be the **D** of Israel through all times!

DELIVERING (2) [DELIVER]

Ex 18: 9 in **d** them from the Egyptians.
2Sa 18:31 **d** you from the power of all who rose up

DELIVERS (14) [DELIVER]

Ex 22: 7 When someone **d** to a neighbor money or goods
22:10 When someone **d** to another a donkey, ox, sheep,
Job 36:15 He **d** the afflicted by their affliction,
Ps 34: 7 around those who fear him, and **d** them.
41: 1 the LORD **d** them in the day of trouble.
72:12 For he **d** the needy when they call,
138: 7 and your right hand **d** me.
Pr 10: 2 but righteousness **d** from death.
11: 4 but righteousness **d** from death.
12: 6 but the speech of the upright **d** them.
Isa 41: 2 He **d** up nations to him, and tramples kings under
66: 9 shall I, the one who **d,** shut the womb?
Da 6:27 He **d** and rescues, he works signs and wonders
Tob 4:10 For almsgiving **d** from death and keeps you

DELIVERY (2) [DELIVER]

Ge 38:27 time of her **d** came, there were twins in her womb.
2Es 16:38 in the ninth month when the time of her **d** draws

DELOS (1)

1Mc 15:23 and to Sampsames, and to the Spartans, and to **D,**

DELPHON (1)

AdE 9: 7 including Pharsannestain, **D,** Phasga,

DELUDED (3) [DELUSION]

Isa 19:13 and the princes of Memphis are **d;**
44:20 He feeds on ashes; a **d** mind has led him astray,
Eph 4:22 your old self, corrupt and **d** by its lusts,

DELUDING (1) [DELUSION]

Jer 23:16 the prophets who prophesy to you; they are **d** you.

DELUGE (2) [DELUGED]

Eze 13:11 There will be a **d** of rain, great hailstones will fall,
13:13 and in my anger there shall be a **d** of rain,

DELUGED (1) [DELUGE]

2Pe 3: 6 through which the world of that time was **d**

DELUSION (7) [DELUDED, DELUDING, DELUSIONS]

Ps 62: 9 those of high estate are a **d;**
Isa 41:29 they are all a **d;** their works are nothing;
Jer 3:23 Truly the hills are a **d,**
10:15 They are worthless, a work of **d;**
18:15 they burn offerings to a **d;**
51:18 They are worthless, a work of **d;**
2Th 2:11 For this reason God sends them a powerful **d,**

DELUSIONS (1) [DELUSION]

Wis 17: 7 The **d** of their magic art lay humbled,

DEMAGOGUERY (1)

1Es 5:73 and **d** and uprisings they prevented the completion

DEMAND (8) [DEMANDED, DEMANDING, DEMANDS]

2Ki 23:35 but he taxed the land in order to meet Pharaoh's **d**
Ne 5:12 "We will restore everything and **d** nothing more
5:18 yet with all this I did not **d** the food allowance of
Eze 34:10 and I will **d** my sheep at their hand,
Lk 23:24 So Pilate gave his verdict that their **d** should
1Co 1:22 For Jews **d** signs and Greeks desire wisdom,
1Ti 4: 3 They forbid marriage and **d** abstinence
1Mc 15:35 As for Joppa and Gazara, which you **d,**

DEMANDED (7) [DEMAND]

1Ki 20: 9 All that you first **d** of your servant I will do;
2Ki 18:14 The king of Assyria **d** of King Hezekiah
Lk 12:20 This very night your life is being **d** of you.
12:48 much has been entrusted, even more will be **d.**
22:31 Satan has **d** to sift all of you like wheat,
2Mc 7:10 When it was **d,** he quickly put out his tongue
3Mc 5:18 and with sharp threats **d** to know why

DEMANDING (6) [DEMAND]

1Sa 12:17 of the LORD is great in **d** a king for yourselves."
12:19 to all our sins the evil of **d** a king for ourselves."
Ps 44:12 **d** no high price for them.
78:18 in their heart by **d** the food they craved.
Lk 11:16 to test him, kept **d** from him a sign from heaven.
23:23 But they kept urgently **d** with loud shouts

DEMANDS (7) [DEMAND]

Ex 21:22 be fined what the woman's husband **d,**
Da 2:10 on earth who can reveal what the king **d!**
Col 2:14 the record that stood against us with its legal **d.**
1Th 2: 7 we might have made **d** as apostles of Christ.
1Pe 3:15 to make your defense to anyone who **d** from you
AdE 4: 8 has spoken against us and **d** our death.
Sir 31:31 and do not distress him by making **d** of him.

DEMAS (3)

Col 4:14 Luke, the beloved physician, and **D** greet you.
2Ti 4:10 for **D,** in love with this present world,
Phm 1:24 Aristarchus, **D,** and Luke, my fellow workers.

DEMETRIUS (53)

Ac 19:24 A man named **D,** a silversmith who made silver
19:38 If therefore **D** and the artisans with him have
3Jn 1:12 Everyone has testified favorably about **D,**
1Mc 7: 1 In the one hundred fifty-first year **D** son
7: 4 and **D** took his seat on the throne of his kingdom.
8:31 "Concerning the wrongs that King **D** is doing
9: 1 When **D** heard that Nicanor
10: 2 When King **D** heard of it,
10: 3 **D** sent Jonathan a letter in peaceable words
10: 6 So **D** gave him authority to recruit troops,
10:15 of all the promises that **D** had sent to Jonathan,
10:22 **D** heard of these things he was distressed and said,
10:25 "King **D** to the nation of the Jews, greetings.
10:46 the great wrongs that **D** had done in Israel and
10:48 and encamped opposite **D.**
10:49 two kings met in battle, and the army of **D** fled,
10:50 and on that day **D** fell.
10:52 for I crushed **D** and gained control of our country;
10:67 In the one hundred sixty-fifth year **D** son
10:67 of **D** came from Crete to the land of his ancestors.
10:69 And **D** appointed Apollonius the governor
11: 9 He sent envoys to King **D,** saying, "Come,
11:12 from him and gave her to **D.**
11:19 **D** became king in the one hundred sixty-seventh
11:30 "King **D** to his brother Jonathan and to the nation
11:32 'King **D** to his father Lasthenes, greetings.
11:38 When King **D** saw that the land was quiet
11:39 that all the troops were grumbling against **D.**
11:40 also reported to Imalkue what **D** had done and told
11:40 and told of the hatred that the troops of **D** had
11:41 to King **D** the request that he remove the troops of
11:42 And **D** sent this message back to Jonathan:
11:52 So King **D** sat on the throne of his kingdom,
11:55 All the troops that **D** had discharged gathered
11:55 they fought against **D,** and he fled and was routed.
11:63 the officers of **D** had come to Kadesh in Galilee
12:24 that the commanders of **D** had returned,
12:34 over the stronghold to those whom **D** had sent.
13:34 also chose emissaries and sent them to King **D**
13:35 King **D** sent him a favorable reply to this request,
13:36 "King **D** to Simon, the high priest and friend
14: 1 hundred seventy-second year King **D** assembled
14: 2 and Media heard that **D** had invaded his territory,
14: 3 The general went and defeated the army of **D,**
14:38 "In view of these things King **D** confirmed him in
15: 1 Antiochus, son of King **D,**
15:22 The consul wrote the same thing to King **D** and
2Mc 1: 7 the reign of **D,** in the one hundred sixty-ninth year,
14: 1 and his men that **D** son of Seleucus had sailed into
14: 4 to King **D** in about the one hundred fifty-first year,
14: 5 by **D** to a meeting of the council and was asked
14:11 quickly inflamed **D** still more.
14:26 the covenant that had been made and went to **D.**

DEMOLISH (3) [DEMOLISHED]

Ex 23:24 but you shall utterly **d** them and break their pillars
Nu 33:52 and **d** all their high places.
Dt 12: 2 You must **d** completely all the places where

DEMOLISHED (8) [DEMOLISH]

2Ki 10:27 Then they **d** the pillar of Baal,
2Ch 34: 4 he **d** the incense altars that stood above them.
34: 7 and **d** all the incense altars throughout all the land
La 2:17 as he ordained long ago, he has **d** without pity;
Ro 11: 3 have killed your prophets, they have **d** your altars;
Jdt 3: 8 Yet he **d** all their shrines and cut
1Mc 9:62 he rebuilt the parts of it that had been **d,**
2Es 16:23 earth shall be left desolate, and its cities shall be **d.**

DEMON‡ (28) [DEMONIAC, DEMONIACS, DEMONIC, DEMONS, GOAT-DEMONS]

Mt 9:33 And when the **d** had been cast out,
11:18 and they say, 'He has a **d**';

Mt 15:22 my daughter is tormented by a **d**."
17:18 And Jesus rebuked the **d**, and it came out of him,
Mk 7:26 She begged him to cast the **d** out of her daughter.
7:29 the **d** has left your daughter."
7:30 found the child lying on the bed, and the **d** gone.
Lk 4:33 a man who had the spirit of an unclean **d**,
4:35 When the **d** had thrown him down before them,
7:33 and you say, 'He has a **d**';
8:29 the bonds and be driven by the **d** into the wilds.)
9:42 the **d** dashed him to the ground in convulsions.
11:14 Now he was casting out a **d** that was mute;
11:14 when the **d** had gone out,
Jn 7:20 The crowd answered, "You have a **d**!
8:48 in saying that you are a Samaritan and have a **d**?"
8:49 Jesus answered, "I do not have a **d**;
8:52 "Now we know that you have a **d**.
10:20 "He has a **d** and is out of his mind.
10:21 "These are not the words of one who has a **d**.
10:21 Can a **d** open the eyes of the blind?"
Tob 3: 8 the wicked **d** Asmodeus had killed each of them
3:17 by setting her free from the wicked **d** Asmodeus.
6: 8 in the presence of a man or woman afflicted by a **d**
6:14 I have heard people saying that it was a **d**
6:16 listen to me, brother, and say no more about this **d**.
6:18 the **d** will smell it and flee,
8: 3 so repelled the **d** that he fled to the remotest parts

DEMONIAC (4) [DEMON]

Mt 9:32 a **d** who was mute was brought to him.
12:22 they brought to him a **d** who was blind and mute;
Mk 5:15 They came to Jesus and saw the **d** sitting there,
5:16 Those who had seen what had happened to the **d**

DEMONIACS (3) [DEMON]

Mt 4:24 **d**, epileptics, and paralytics, and he cured them.
8:28 two **d** coming out of the tombs met him.
8:33 the whole story about what had happened to the **d**.

DEMONIC (1) [DEMON]

Rev 16:14 These are **d** spirits, performing signs,

DEMONS (52) [DEMON]

Dt 32:17 They sacrificed to **d**, not God,
Ps 106:37 and their daughters to the **d**;
Mt 7:22 and cast out **d** in your name,
8:16 to him many who were possessed with **d**;
8:31 The **d** begged him, "If you cast us out,
9:34 "By the ruler of the **d** he casts out the **d**."
10: 8 raise the dead, cleanse the lepers, cast out **d**.
12:24 "It is only by Beelzebul, the ruler of the **d**, that
this fellow casts out the **d**."
12:27 If I cast out **d** by Beelzebul,
12:28 But if it is by the Spirit of God that I cast out **d**,
Mk 1:32 to him all who were sick or possessed with **d**.
1:34 with various diseases, and cast out many **d**;
1:34 and he would not permit the **d** to speak,
1:39 the message in their synagogues and casting out **d**.
3:15 and to have authority to cast out **d**.
3:22 and by the ruler of the **d** he casts out **d**."
5:18 the man who had been possessed by **d** begged him
6:13 They cast out many **d**, and anointed
9:38 we saw someone casting out **d** in your name,
16: 9 ⟦from whom he had cast out seven **d**.⟧
16:17 ⟦by using my name they will cast out **d**;⟧
Lk 4:41 **D** also came out of many, shouting,
8: 2 from whom seven **d** had gone out,
8:27 a man of the city who had **d** met him.
8:30 He said, "Legion"; for many **d** had entered him.
8:32 and the **d** begged Jesus to let them enter these.
8:33 the **d** came out of the man and entered the swine,
8:35 the man from whom the **d** had gone sitting at
8:36 one who had been possessed by **d** had been healed.
8:38 the **d** had gone begged that he might be with him;
9: 1 and gave them power and authority over all **d** and
9:49 we saw someone casting out **d** in your name,
10:17 "Lord, in your name even the **d** submit to us!"
11:15 "He casts out **d** by Beelzebul, the ruler of the **d**."
11:18 —for you say that I cast out the **d** by Beelzebul.
11:19 Now if I cast out the **d** by Beelzebul,
11:20 if it is by the finger of God that I cast out the **d**,
13:32 I am casting out **d** and performing cures today
1Co 10:20 they sacrifice to **d** and not to God.
10:20 I do not want you to be partners with **d**.
10:21 the cup of the Lord and the cup of **d**.
10:21 of the table of the Lord and the table of **d**.
1Ti 4: 1 to deceitful spirits and teachings of **d**,
Jas 2:19 Even the **d** believe—and shudder.
Rev 9:20 the works of their hands or give up worshiping **d**
18: 2 It has become a dwelling place of **d**,
Bar 4: 7 the one who made you by sacrificing to **d** and not
4:35 and for a long time she will be inhabited by **d**.

DEMONSTRATE (3) [DEMONSTRATED, DEMONSTRATION]

Gal 2:18 then I **d** that I am a transgressor.
4Mc 1: 8 but I can **d** it best from the noble bravery
14:18 to **d** sympathy for children by the example

DEMONSTRATED (2) [DEMONSTRATE]

4Mc 1: 9 **d** that reason controls the emotions.
16: 2 Thus I have **d** not only that men have ruled over

DEMONSTRATION (3) [DEMONSTRATE]

1Co 2: 4 but with a **d** of the Spirit and of power,
4Mc 3:19 to a narrative **d** of temperate reason.
13:10 Let us not be cowardly in the **d** of our piety."

DEMOPHON (1)

2Mc 12: 2 as well as Hieronymus and **D**,

DEN (26) [DENS]

Isa 11: 8 weaned child shall put its hand on the adder's **d**.
Jer 7:11 become a **d** of robbers in your sight?
51:37 a **d** of jackals, an object of horror and of hissing,
Da 6: 7 O king, shall be thrown into a **d** of lions.
6:12 O king, shall be thrown into a **d** of lions?"
6:16 Daniel was brought and thrown into the **d** of lions.
6:17 stone was brought and laid on the mouth of the **d**,
6:19 the king got up and hurried to the **d** of lions.
6:20 When he came near the **d** where Daniel was,
6:23 that Daniel be taken up out of the **d**.
6:23 So Daniel was taken up out of the **d**,
6:24 and thrown into the **d** of lions—
6:24 the bottom of the **d** the lions overpowered them
Am 3: 4 Does a young lion cry out from its **d**,
Na 2:11 What became of the lions' **d**,
Mt 21:13 but you are making it a **d** of robbers."
Mk 11:17 But you have made it a **d** of robbers."
Lk 19:46 but you have made it a **d** of robbers."
Bel 1:31 They threw Daniel into the lions' **d**,
1:32 There were seven lions in the **d**,
1:34 to Babylon, to Daniel, in the lions' **d**."
1:35 and I know nothing about the **d**."
1:36 down in Babylon, right over the **d**.
1:40 When he came to the **d** he looked in,
1:42 into the **d** those who had attempted his destruction,
4Mc 18:13 He praised Daniel in the **d** of the lions

DENARII‡ (6) [DENARIUS]

Mt 18:28 of his fellow slaves who owed him a hundred **d**;
Mk 6:37 to go and buy two hundred **d** worth of bread,
14: 5 for more than three hundred **d**,
Lk 7:41 one owed five hundred **d**, and the other fifty.
10:35 The next day he took out two **d**,
Jn 12: 5 not sold for three hundred **d** and the money given

DENARIUS‡ (3) [DENARII]

Mt 22:19 And they brought him a **d**.
Mk 12:15 Bring me a **d** and let me see it."
Lk 20:24 "Show me a **d**. Whose head

DENIED (20) [DENY]

Ge 18:15 But Sarah **d**, saying, "I did not laugh";
Nu 24:11 but the LORD has **d** you any reward."
Job 6:10 for I have not **d** the words of the Holy One.
Mt 26:70 But he **d** it before all of them, saying,
26:72 Again he **d** it with an oath,
Mk 14:68 But he **d** it, saying, "I do not know
14:70 But again he **d** it.
Lk 8:45 When all **d** it, Peter said, "Master,
12: 9 before others will be **d** before the angels of God.
22:34 until you have **d** three times that you know me."
22:57 But he **d** it, saying, "Woman, I do not know him."
Jn 13:38 you will have **d** me three times.
18:25 He **d** it and said, "I am not."
18:27 Again Peter **d** it, and at that moment
Ac 8:33 In his humiliation justice was **d** him.
19:36 Since these things cannot be **d**,
1Ti 5: 8 has **d** the faith and is worse than an unbeliever.
Rev 3: 8 you have kept my word and have not **d** my name.
2Es 7:24 They scorned his law, and **d** his covenants;
7:37 'Look now, and understand whom you have **d**,

DENIES (6) [DENY]

Mt 10:33 but whoever **d** me before others,
Lk 12: 9 but whoever **d** me before others will be denied
1Jn 2:22 the liar but the one who **d** that Jesus is the Christ?
2:22 the one who **d** the Father and the Son.
2:23 No one who **d** the Son has the Father;
Sir 14: 4 What he **d** himself he collects for others;

DENOUNCE (6) [DENOUNCED]

Nu 23: 7 curse Jacob for me; Come, **d** Israel!'
23: 8 How can I **d** those whom the LORD has
Job 17: 5 Those who **d** friends for reward—
Jer 20:10 "Terror is all around! **D** him! Let us **d** him!"
2Es 12:32 He will **d** them for their ungodliness and

DENOUNCED (5) [DENOUNCE]

Nu 23: 8 can I denounce those whom the LORD has not **d**?
Da 3: 8 at this time certain Chaldeans came forward and **d**
1Co 10:30 be **d** because of that for which I give thanks?
2Mc 14:37 of the elders of Jerusalem, was **d** to Nicanor as
4Mc 9:14 and with every member disjointed he **d** the tyrant,

DENS (6) [DEN]

Job 37: 8 animals go into their lairs and remain in their **d**.
38:40 when they crouch in their **d**,
Ps 104:22 sun rises, they withdraw and lie down in their **d**.
SS 4: 8 the **d** of lions, from the mountains of leopards.
Isa 32:14 the hill and the watchtower will become **d** forever,
Na 2:12 he has filled his caves with prey and his **d**

DENSE (3) [DENSEST]

Ex 10:14 a **d** swarm of locusts as had never been before,
10:22 and there was **d** darkness in all the land of Egypt
19: 9 "I am going to come to you in a **d** cloud,

DENSEST (2) [DENSE]

2Ki 19:23 I entered its farthest retreat, its **d** forest.
Isa 37:24 I came to its remotest height, its **d** forest.

DENY (35) [DENIED, DENIES, DENYING, SELF-DENIAL]

Lev 16:29 you shall **d** yourselves, and shall do no work,
16:31 and you shall **d** yourselves; it is a statute forever.
23:27 you shall **d** yourselves and present
23:32 and you shall **d** yourselves;
Nu 29: 7 and **d** yourselves; you shall do no work.
30:13 Any vow or any binding oath to **d** herself,
Ezr 8:21 that we might **d** ourselves before our God,
Job 8:18 then it will **d** them, saying,
Pr 30: 7 do not **d** them to me before I die:
30: 9 and **d** you, and say, "Who is the LORD?"
Isa 29:21 without grounds **d** justice to the one in the right.
Mt 10:33 I also will **d** before my Father in heaven.
16:24 let them **d** themselves and take up their cross
26:34 before the cock crows, you will **d** me three times."
26:35 though I must die with you, I will not **d** you."
26:75 the cock crows, you will **d** me three times."
Mk 8:34 let them **d** themselves and take up their cross
14:30 you will **d** me three times."
14:31 though I must die with you, I will not **d** you."
14:72 you will **d** me three times."
Lk 9:23 let them **d** themselves and take up their cross daily
22:61 you will **d** me three times."
Jn 1:20 He confessed and did not **d** it, but confessed,
Ac 4:16 through them; we cannot **d** it.
2Co 11:12 in order to **d** an opportunity to those who want
2Ti 2:12 if we **d** him, he will also **d** us;
2:13 he remains faithful—for he cannot **d** himself.
Tit 1:16 but they **d** him by their actions.
2Pe 2: 1 They will even **d** the Master who bought them—
Jude 1: 4 into licentiousness and **d** our only Master
Rev 2:13 and you did not **d** your faith in me even in
Jdt 8:28 and there is no one who can **d** your words.
Bel 1:24 "You cannot **d** that this is a living god;
4Mc 6:34 It would be ridiculous to **d** it.

DENYING (2) [DENY]

Isa 59:13 and **d** the LORD, and turning away
2Ti 3: 5 to the outward form of godliness but **d** its power.

DEPART‡ (50) [DEPARTED, DEPARTING, DEPARTS, DEPARTURE]

Ge 49:10 The scepter shall not **d** from Judah,
Ex 8:29 that the swarms of flies may **d** tomorrow
18:27 Then Moses let his father-in-law **d**,
Jos 1: 8 of the law shall not **d** out of your mouth;
Jdg 6:18 Do not **d** from here until I come to you,
1Sa 10: 2 you **d** from me today you will meet two men by
16:23 and the evil spirit would **d** from him.
2Sa 12:10 therefore the sword shall never **d** from your house,
1Ki 11:21 "Let me **d**, that I may go to my own country."
2Ki 3: 3 he did not **d** from it.
13: 2 he did not **d** from them.
13: 6 not **d** from the sins of the house of Jeroboam,
13:11 not **d** from all the sins of Jeroboam son of Nebat,
14:24 not **d** from all the sins of Jeroboam son of Nebat,
15: 9 not **d** from the sins of Jeroboam son of Nebat,
15:18 he did not **d** all his days from any of the sins
15:28 not **d** from the sins of Jeroboam son of Nebat,
17:22 they did not **d** from them
18: 6 he did not **d** from following him but kept
Job 28:28 and to **d** from evil is understanding.' "
Ps 6: 8 **D** from me, all you workers of evil,
9:17 The wicked shall **d** to Sheol,
34:14 **D** from evil, and do good;
37:27 **D** from evil, and do good;
39:13 before I **d** and am no more."
55:11 and fraud do not **d** from its marketplace.
139:19 and that the bloodthirsty would **d** from me—
Pr 5: 7 and do not **d** from the words of my mouth.
17:13 not **d** from the house of one who returns evil
SS 4: 8 **D** from the peak of Amana,
Isa 11:13 The jealousy of Ephraim shall **d**,
38:10 In the noontide of my days I must **d**;
52:11 **D**, **d**, go out from there!
54:10 For the mountains may **d** and the hills be removed,
54:10 but my steadfast love shall not **d** from you,
59:21 shall not **d** out of your mouth,
Jer 43:12 and he shall **d** from there safely.
Eze 24:12 its thick rust does not **d**.
Hos 9:12 Woe to them indeed when I **d** from them!
Zec 10:11 and the scepter of Egypt shall **d**.
Mt 25:41 **d** from me into the eternal fire prepared for
Jn 13: 1 that his hour had come to **d** from this world and go
Php 1:23 my desire is to **d** and be with Christ,
Jdt 13:19 Your praise will never **d** from the hearts
Wis 19: 2 to **d** and hastily sent them out,
Sir 2: 3 Cling to him and do not **d**,
2Mc 2: 3 that the law should not **d** from their hearts.
2Es 8: 5 and against your will you **d**,
15:25 I will not spare them. **D**, you faithless children!

DEPARTED‡ (63) [DEPART]

Ge 12: 4 Abram was seventy-five years old when he **d**
14:12 who lived in Sodom, and his goods, and **d.**
21:14 And she **d,** and wandered about in the wilderness
24:10 the servant took ten of his master's camels and **d,**
26:17 So Isaac **d** from there and camped in the valley
26:31 and they **d** from him in peace.
31:55 then he **d** and returned home.
42:26 They loaded their donkeys with their grain, and **d.**
Ex 16: 1 of the second month after they had **d** from the land
Nu 12: 9 of the LORD was kindled against them, and he **d.**
22: 7 the elders of Moab and the elders of Midian **d** with
Dt 16: 6 the time of day when you **d** from Egypt.
Jos 2:21 She sent them away and they **d.**
2:22 They **d** and went into the hill country
Jdg 11:38 So she **d,** she and her companions,
19:10 he got up and **d,** and arrived opposite Jebus
21:24 So the Israelites **d** from there at that time by tribes
1Sa 4:21 meaning, "The glory has **d** from Israel,"
4:22 She said, "The glory has **d** from Israel,
6: 6 did they not let the people go, and they **d?**
16:14 Now the spirit of the LORD **d** from Saul,
18:12 the LORD was with him but had **d** from Saul.
2Sa 22:22 and have not wickedly **d** from my God.
1Ki 20:38 Then the prophet **d,** and waited for the king along
1Ch 16:43 Then all the people **d** to their homes,
19: 5 and they **d.** When David was told about the
21: 4 So Joab **d** and went throughout all Israel,
2Ch 10:16 So all Israel **d** to their tents.
21:20 He **d** with no one's regret.
Job 23:12 I have not **d** from the commandment of his lips;
Ps 18:21 and have not wickedly **d** from my God.
44:18 nor have our steps **d** from your way,
105:38 Egypt was glad when they **d,**
Isa 6: 7 your guilt has **d** and your sin is blotted out."
7:17 as have not come since the day that Ephraim **d**
Jer 29: 2 the artisans, and the smiths had **d** from Jerusalem.
La 1: 6 From daughter Zion has **d** all her majesty.
Da 4:31 The kingdom has **d** from you!
Hos 10: 5 over its glory that has **d** from it.
Mt 12:15 When Jesus became aware of this, he **d.**
27: 5 he **d;** and he went and hanged himself.
Mk 3: 7 Jesus **d** with his disciples to the sea,
Lk 1:38 Then the angel **d** from her.
4:13 he **d** from him until an opportune time.
4:42 At daybreak he **d** and went into a deserted place.
9: 6 They **d** and went through the villages,
19:32 So those who were sent **d** and found it
Jn 12:36 After Jesus had said this, he **d** and hid from them.
Ac 16:40 the brothers and sisters there, they **d.**
18:23 After spending some time there he **d** and went
Jdt 5:18 they **d** from the way he had prescribed for them,
Wis 10: 3 when an unrighteous man **d** from her in his anger,
16:14 but cannot bring back the **d** spirit,
Sir 38:17 make your mourning worthy of the **d,** for one day,
38:23 and be comforted for him when his spirit has **d.**
48:18 he sent his commander and **d;**
Bel 1:14 and sealed it with the king's signet, and **d.**
1Mc 6:10 "Sleep has **d** from my eyes and I am downhearted
3Mc 5:44 Then the Friends and officers **d** with great joy,
7:13 multitude shouted the Hallelujah and joyfully **d.**
7:20 they **d** unharmed, free, and overjoyed,
2Es 2:39 Those who have **d** from the shadow
3:22 but what was good **d,** and the evil remained.

DEPARTING (2) [DEPART]

Ge 35:18 As her soul was **d** (for she died),
Hos 9: 1 for you have played the whore, **d** from your God.

DEPARTS (2) [DEPART]

Ps 146: 4 When their breath **d,** they return to the earth;
AdE 2:14 In the evening she enters and in the morning she **d**

DEPARTURE (8) [DEPART]

Ex 12:33 The Egyptians urged the people to hasten their **d**
Dt 16: 3 of your life you may remember the day of your **d**
Lk 9:31 in glory and were speaking of his **d,**
2Ti 4: 6 and the time of my **d** has come.
2Pe 1:15 so that after my **d** you may be able at any time
Wis 3: 2 and their **d** was thought to be a disaster,
3Mc 7:10 not immediately hurry to make their **d,**
7:16 the full enjoyment of deliverance began their **d**

DEPEND (6) [DEPENDABLE, DEPENDED, DEPENDENCIES, DEPENDENT, DEPENDENTS, DEPENDS]

Job 39:11 Will you **d** on it because its strength is great,
Eze 33:26 You **d** on your swords, you commit abominations,
Mic 5: 7 not **d** upon people or wait for any mortal.
Jdt 8:24 for their lives **d** upon us, and the sanctuary—
9:11 "For your strength does not **d** on numbers,
Sir 5: 8 Do not **d** on dishonest wealth,

DEPENDABLE (1) [DEPEND]

Sir 33: 3 for such a one the law is as **d** as a divine oracle.

DEPENDED (1) [DEPEND]

Ac 12:20 their country **d** on the king's country for food.

DEPENDENCIES (1) [DEPEND]

Jos 15:45 Ekron, with its **d** and its villages;

DEPENDENT (3) [DEPEND]

Lev 25:35 If any of your kin fall into difficulty and become **d**
25:39 If any who are **d** on you become so impoverished
1Th 4:12 toward outsiders and be **d** on no one.

DEPENDENTS (2) [DEPEND]

Ge 47:12 according to the number of their **d.**
Wis 14:15 and handed on to his **d** secret rites and initiations.

DEPENDS (8) [DEPEND]

Dt 24:15 they are poor and their livelihood **d** on them;
Ro 4:16 For this reason it **d** on faith,
9:16 So it **d** not on human will or exertion,
12:18 If it is possible, so far as it **d** on you,
1Co 4:20 the kingdom of God **d** not on talk but on power.
Sir 31:20 Healthy sleep **d** on moderate eating;
38:24 The wisdom of the scribe **d** on the opportunity
1Mc 3:19 not on the size of the army that victory in battle **d,**

DEPICTED (1)

Wis 18:24 For on his long robe the whole world was **d,**

DEPLOYED (1)

2Mc 15:20 and the cavalry **d** on the flanks,

DEPORTATION (4) [DEPORTED]

Mt 1:11 at the time of the **d** to Babylon.
1:12 And after the **d** to Babylon:
1:17 and from David to the **d** to Babylon,
1:17 and from the **d** to Babylon to the Messiah,

DEPORTED (3) [DEPORTATION]

Ezr 4:10 the nations whom the great and noble Osnappar **d**
2Mc 2: 1 prophet Jeremiah ordered those who were being **d**
2: 2 instructed those who were being **d** not to forget

DEPOSE (2) [DEPOSED, DEPOSES]

LtJ 6:34 They cannot set up a king or **d** one.
1Mc 8:13 and those whom they wish they **d;**

DEPOSED (4) [DEPOSE]

2Ki 23: 5 He **d** the idolatrous priests whom the kings
2Ch 36: 3 the king of Egypt **d** him in Jerusalem and laid on
Da 5:20 he was **d** from his kingly throne,
1Es 1:35 king of Egypt **d** him from reigning in Jerusalem,

DEPOSES (1) [DEPOSE]

Da 2:21 **d** kings and sets up kings;

DEPOSIT (8) [DEPOSITED, DEPOSITS]

Lev 6: 2 by deceiving a neighbor in a matter of a **d** or
6: 4 or by fraud or the **d** that was committed to you,
Nu 19: 9 and **d** them outside the camp in a clean place;
Eze 42:13 there they shall **d** the most holy offerings—
Lk 19:21 you take what you did not **d,**
19:22 taking what I did not **d** and reaping what I did
Sir 42: 7 a **d,** be sure it is counted and weighed,
1Mc 14:49 and to **d** copies of them in the treasury,

DEPOSITED (4) [DEPOSIT]

AdE 2:23 Then the king ordered a memorandum to be **d** in
2Mc 3:15 for those who had **d** them.
1Es 6:23 in the royal archives that were **d** in Babylon.
4Mc 4: 3 that in the Jerusalem treasuries there are **d** tens

DEPOSITS (3) [DEPOSIT]

2Mc 3:10 that there were some **d** belonging to widows
3:15 upon him who had given the law about **d,**
4Mc 4: 7 that those who had committed **d** to

DEPRAVED (3) [DEPRAVITY]

1Ti 6: 5 and wrangling among those who are **d** in mind
2Pe 2:10 especially those who indulge their flesh in **d** lust,
2Mc 14:27 provoked by the false accusations of that **d** man,

DEPRAVITY (4) [DEPRAVED]

Lev 18:17 they are your flesh; it is **d.**
19:29 that the land not become prostituted and full of **d.**
20:14 If a man takes a wife and her mother also, it is **d;**
20:14 that there may be no **d** among you.

DEPRESSED (3)

1Ki 21: 5 "Why are you so **d** that you will not eat?"
Tob 8:20 you shall cheer up my daughter, who has been **d.**
2Mc 6:12 Now I urge those who read this book not to be **d**

DEPRIVE‡ (10) [DEPRIVED, DEPRIVES, DEPRIVING]

Dt 24:17 not **d** a resident alien or an orphan of justice;
Isa 5:23 and **d** the innocent of their rights!
32: 6 and to **d** the thirsty of drink.
1Co 7: 5 Do not **d** one another except perhaps by agreement
9:15 no one will **d** me of my ground for boasting!
AdE 16:12 he undertook to **d** us of our kingdom and our life,
Sir 14:14 Do not **d** yourself of a day's enjoyment;
34:27 to **d** an employee of wages is to shed blood.
3Mc 6:24 to **d** of dominion and life by secretly devising acts
4Mc 8:23 from this most pleasant life and **d** ourselves

DEPRIVED (14) [DEPRIVE]

Jer 5:25 and your sins have **d** you of good.
La 4: 9 life drains away, **d** of the produce of the field.
Ac 19:27 be **d** of her majesty that brought all Asia and
Wis 18: 4 to be **d** of light and imprisoned in darkness,
Sir 28:15 and **d** them of the fruit of their toil.
Aza 1:21 let them be disgraced and **d** of all power,
2Mc 3:29 of the divine intervention and **d** of any hope
13:10 to help those who were on the point of being **d** of
3Mc 1:12 saying, "Even if those men are **d** of this honor,
5:32 In fact you would have been **d** of life instead
6:12 the senseless insolence of the lawless are being **d**
2Es 10:23 the seal of Zion has been **d** of its glory,
10:30 **d** of my understanding, he grasped my right hand
4Mc 4: 7 to the sacred treasury should be **d** of them,

DEPRIVES (3) [DEPRIVE]

Dt 27:19 "Cursed be anyone who **d** the alien, the orphan,
Job 12:20 He **d** of speech those who are trusted,
Sir 34:25 whoever **d** them of it is a murderer.

DEPRIVING (2) [DEPRIVE]

Ecc 4: 8 they ask, "and **d** myself of pleasure?"
3Mc 2:33 and **d** them of companionship and mutual help.

DEPTH‡ (20) [DEEP]

Ex 14:27 and at dawn the sea returned to its normal **d.**
1Ki 6: 3 Its **d** was ten cubits in front of the house.
Pr 25: 3 Like the heavens for height, like the earth for **d,**
Eze 40:20 that faced north—its **d** and width.
40:21 of the first gate; its **d** was fifty cubits,
40:25 of the others; its **d** was fifty cubits,
40:29 in its vestibule; its **d** was fifty cubits,
40:33 in its vestibule; its **d** was fifty cubits,
40:36 Its **d** was fifty cubits, and its width twenty-five
40:49 The **d** of the vestibule was twenty cubits,
41: 4 He measured the **d** of the room, twenty cubits,
41:12 around, and its **d** ninety cubits.
41:15 the **d** of the building facing the yard at the west,
Mt 13: 5 since they had no **d** of soil.
18: 6 around your neck and you were drowned in the **d**
Mk 4: 5 and it sprang up quickly, since it had no **d** of soil.
Ro 8:39 nor **d,** nor anything else in all creation,
11:33 O the **d** of the riches and wisdom and knowledge
Eph 3:18 what is the breadth and length and height and **d,**
Wis 10:19 and cast them up from the **d** of the sea.

DEPTHS (33) [DEEP]

Ex 15: 5 they went down into the **d** like a stone.
Dt 32:22 and burns to the **d** of Sheol;
Ne 9:11 but you threw their pursuers into the **d,**
Ps 63: 9 to destroy my life shall go down into the **d** of
68:22 I will bring them back from the **d** of the sea,
71:20 from the **d** of the earth you will bring me up again.
86:13 you have delivered my soul from the **d** of Sheol.
88: 6 You have put me in the **d** of the Pit,
95: 4 In his hand are the **d** of the earth;
107:26 they went down to the **d;**
130: 1 Out of the **d** I cry to you, O LORD.
139:15 intricately woven in the **d** of the earth.
Pr 8:24 When there were no **d** I was brought forth,
9:18 that her guests are in the **d** of Sheol.
Isa 14:15 you are brought down to Sheol, to the **d** of the Pit.
44:23 shout, O **d** of the earth;
51:10 who made the **d** of the sea a way for the redeemed
63:13 who led them through the **d?**
La 3:55 O LORD, from the **d** of the pit;
Eze 27:34 in the **d** of the waters;
Mic 7:19 You will cast all our sins into the **d** of the sea.
Zec 10:11 and all the **d** of the Nile dried up.
1Co 2:10 the Spirit searches everything, even the **d** of God.
Jdt 8:14 You cannot plumb the **d** of the human heart
Sir 24: 5 of heaven and traversed the **d** of the abyss.
Aza 1:32 into the **d** from your throne on the cherubim,
Man 1:13 do not condemn me to the **d** of the earth.
3Mc 2: 7 you overwhelmed him in the **d** of the sea,
2Es 3:18 and moved the world, and caused the **d** to tremble,
5:25 and from all the **d** of the sea you have filled
8:23 up the **d** and whose indignation makes
13:52 as no one can explore or know what is in the **d** of
16:12 the sea is churned up from the **d,**

DEPUTED (1) [DEPUTY]

2Sa 15: 3 but there is no one **d** by the king to hear you."

DEPUTIES (3) [DEPUTY]

Jer 51:23 with you I smash governors and **d.**
51:28 with their governors and **d,**
51:57 also her governors, her **d,** and her warriors;

DEPUTY‡ (6) [DEPUTED, DEPUTIES]

1Ki 22:47 There was no king in Edom; a **d** was king.
Ezr 4: 8 Rehum the royal **d** and Shimshai the scribe wrote
4: 9 (then Rehum the royal **d,** Shimshai the scribe,
4:17 "To Rehum the royal **d** and Shimshai the scribe
2Mc 4:29 Menelaus left his own brother Lysimachus as **d** in
4:31 a man of high rank, to act as his **d.**

DERANGED (1)
3Mc 5:30 the providence of God his whole mind had been **d**

DERBE (4)
Ac 14: 6 the apostles learned of it and fled to Lystra and **D,**
14:20 The next day he went on with Barnabas to **D.**
16: 1 Paul went on also to **D** and to Lystra,
20: 4 by Gaius from **D,** and by Timothy,

DERIDE (3) [DERIDED, DERIDES, DERIDING, DERISION]
Ps 102: 8 those who **d** me use my name for a curse.
119:51 The arrogant utterly **d** me,
4Mc 5:27 a way that you may **d** us for eating defiling foods,

DERIDED (6) [DERIDE]
Ps 79: 4 mocked and **d** by those around us.
Eze 23:32 you shall be scorned and **d,** it holds so much.
Mt 27:39 Those who passed by **d** him, shaking their heads
Mk 15:29 Those who passed by **d** him,
1Mc 7:34 and **d** them and defiled them and spoke arrogantly,
2Mc 8:17 and the torture of the **d** city, and besides,

DERIDED (KJV) See also RIDICULED, SCOFFED

DERIDES (2) [DERIDE]
1Sa 2: 1 My mouth **d** my enemies,
LtJ 6:43 she **d** the woman next to her,

DERIDING (2) [DERIDE]
Lk 23:39 of the criminals who were hanged there kept **d** him
2Mc 7:27 **d** the cruel tyrant: "My son, have pity on me.

DERISION (11) [DERIDE]
Ex 32:25 to the **d** of their enemies),
Ps 2: 4 the LORD has them in **d.**
44:13 the **d** and scorn of those around us.
59: 8 you hold all the nations in **d.**
Jer 20: 8 for me a reproach and **d** all day long.
29:18 **d** among all the nations where I have driven them,
48:39 So Moab has become a **d** and a horror
Eze 36: 4 an object of **d** to the rest of the nations all around;
Tob 8:10 and we will become an object of ridicule and **d."**
Wis 5: 4 "These are persons whom we once held in **d**
2Es 16:69 And those who consent to eat shall be held in **d**

DESCEND (11) [DESCENDANT, DESCENDANTS, DESCENDED, DESCENDING, DESCENDS, DESCENT]
Ex 33: 9 of cloud would **d** and stand at the entrance of
Dt 28:43 while you shall **d** lower and lower.
29:20 All the curses written in this book will **d** on them,
Job 17:16 Shall we **d** together into the dust?"
Ps 49:14 straight to the grave they **d,**
Pr 6:15 on such a one calamity will **d** suddenly;
Isa 34: 5 in the heavens, lo, it will **d** upon Edom,
Eze 26:20 then I will thrust you down with those who **d** into
Jn 1:33 'He on whom you see the Spirit **d** and remain is
Ro 10: 7 "or 'Who will **d** into the abyss?' "
1Th 4:16 the sound of God's trumpet, will **d** from heaven,

DESCENDANT‡ (12) [DESCEND]
Lev 21:21 No **d** of Aaron the priest who has
1Ch 27: 3 He was a **d** of Perez,
Ne 10:38 And the priest, the **d** of Aaron,
Job 18:19 They have no offspring or **d** among their people,
Isa 19:11 "I am one of the sages, a **d** of ancient kings"?
Jer 35:19 Jonadab son of Rechab shall not lack a **d** to stand
Lk 1: 5 His wife was a **d** of Aaron,
Ro 11: 1 I myself am an Israelite, a **d** of Abraham,
2Ti 2: 8 raised from the dead, a **d** of David—
Rev 22:16 I am the root and the **d** of David,
Wis 7: 1 a **d** of the first-formed child of earth;
4Mc 7:12 the **d** of Aaron, Eleazar, though being consumed

DESCENDANTS‡ (463) [DESCEND]
A. HIS DESCENDANTS (38)
B. THEIR DESCENDANTS (32)
C. YOUR DESCENDANTS (27)
D. DESCENDANT[S] OF AARON (19)
E. DESCENDANTS OF ESAU (10)
F. DESCENDANT[S] OF ABRAHAM (7)

Ge 5: 1 This is the list of the **d** of Adam.
6: 9 These are the **d** of Noah.
9: 9 with you and your **d** after you, C
10: 1 These are the **d** of Noah's sons, Shem, Ham,
10: 2 The **d** of Japheth: Gomer,
10: 3 **d** of Gomer: Ashkenaz, Riphath, and Togarmah.
10: 4 The **d** of Javan: Elishah, Tarshish,
10: 5 These are the **d** of Japheth in their lands,
10: 6 The **d** of Ham: Cush, Egypt, Put, and Canaan.
10: 7 The **d** of Cush: Seba, Havilah,
10: 7 The **d** of Raamah: Sheba and Dedan.
10:20 These are the **d** of Ham, by their families,
10:22 The **d** of Shem: Elam, Asshur,
10:23 The **d** of Aram: Uz, Hul, Gether, and Mash.
Ge 10:29 all these were the **d** of Joktan.
10:31 These are the **d** of Shem, by their families,
11:10 These are the **d** of Shem.
11:27 Now these are the **d** of Terah.
15: 5 Then he said to him, "So shall your **d** be." C
15:18 saying, "To your **d** I give this land, C
25:12 These are the **d** of Ishmael, Abraham's son,
25:19 These are the **d** of Isaac, Abraham's son:
26: 3 to you and to your **d** I will give all these lands, C
36: 1 These are the **d** of Esau (that is, Edom). E
36: 9 are the **d** of Esau, ancestor of the Edomites, E
Ex 28:43 be a perpetual ordinance for him and for his **d** A
30:21 him and for his **d** throughout their generations. A
32:13 'I will multiply your **d** like the stars of heaven, C
32:13 that I have promised I will give to your **d,** C
33: 1 and Jacob, saying, 'To your **d** I will give it.' C
Lev 6:18 Every male among the **d** of Aaron shall eat of it, D
6:22 anointed from among Aaron's **d** as a successor,
24: 9 They shall be for Aaron and his **d,** A
Nu 1:20 The **d** of Reuben, Israel's firstborn, their lineage,
1:22 The **d** of Simeon, their lineage, in their clans,
1:24 The **d** of Gad, their lineage, in their clans,
1:26 The **d** of Judah, their lineage, in their clans,
1:28 The **d** of Issachar, their lineage, in their clans,
1:30 The **d** of Zebulun, their lineage, in their clans,
1:32 The **d** of Joseph, namely, the **d** of Ephraim,
1:34 The **d** of Manasseh, their lineage, in their clans,
1:36 The **d** of Benjamin, their lineage, in their clans,
1:38 The **d** of Dan, their lineage, in their clans,
1:40 The **d** of Asher, their lineage, in their clans,
1:42 The **d** of Naphtali, their lineage, in their clans,
3: 9 You shall give the Levites to Aaron and his **d;** A
3:10 you shall make a register of Aaron and his **d;** A
9:10 you or your **d** who is unclean through touching C
13:28 and besides, we saw the **d** of Anak there.
14:24 and his **d** shall possess it. A
16: 1 On son of Peleth—**d** of Reuben—
16:40 who is not of the **d** of Aaron, D
18:19 before the LORD for you and your **d** as well. C
25:13 be for him and for his **d** after him a covenant A
26: 5 The **d** of Reuben: of Hanoch,
26: 8 And the **d** of Pallu: Eliab.
26: 9 The **d** of Eliab: Nemuel, Dathan, and Abiram.
26:12 The **d** of Simeon by their clans:
26:20 The **d** of Judah by their clans were:
26:21 The **d** of Perez were: of Hezron,
26:23 The **d** of Issachar by their clans:
26:26 The **d** of Zebulun by their clans:
26:29 The **d** of Manasseh: of Machir,
26:30 These are the **d** of Gilead:
26:35 the **d** of Ephraim according to their clans:
26:36 And these are the **d** of Shuthelah:
26:37 These are the **d** of Joseph by their clans.
26:38 The **d** of Benjamin by their clans:
26:41 These are the **d** of Benjamin by their clans;
26:42 These are the **d** of Dan by their clans:
26:44 The **d** of Asher by their families:
26:45 Of the **d** of Beriah: of Heber,
26:48 The **d** of Naphtali by their clans:
32:39 The **d** of Machir son of Manasseh went to Gilead,
36: 1 the **d** of Gilead son of Machir son of Manasseh,
36: 5 "The **d** of the tribe of Joseph are right
36:12 into the clans of the **d** of Manasseh son of Joseph,
Dt 1: 8 to give to them and to their **d** after them." B
1:36 to his **d** I will give the land on which he set foot, A
2: 4 the **d** of Esau, who live in Seir. E
2: 8 the **d** of Esau who live in Seir, E
2: 9 I have given Ar as a possession to the **d** of Lot."
2:12 but the **d** of Esau dispossessed them, E
2:19 because I have given it to the **d** of Lot."
2:22 He did the same for the **d** of Esau, E
2:29 the **d** of Esau who live in Seir have done for me E
4:37 he chose their **d** after them. B
4:40 for your own well-being and that of your **d** C
10:15 their **d** after them, out of all the peoples, B
11: 9 to your ancestors to give them and to their **d,** B
17:20 he and his **d** may reign long over his kingdom A
23: 2 none of their **d** shall be admitted to the assembly B
23: 3 none of their **d** shall be admitted to the assembly B
28:46 They shall be among you and your **d** as a sign C
30: 6 and the heart of your **d,** C
30:19 Choose life so that you and your **d** may live, C
31:21 it will not be lost from the mouths of their **d.** B
34: 4 and to Jacob, saying, 'I will give it to your **d';** C
Jos 15:14 Sheshai, Ahiman, and Talmai, the **d** of Anak.
17: 2 these were the male **d** of Manasseh son of Joseph,
21: 4 So those Levites who were **d** of Aaron D
21:10 which went to the **d** of Aaron, D
21:13 To the **d** of Aaron the priest they gave Hebron, D
21:19 The towns of the **d** of Aaron— D
22:28 If this should be said to us or to our **d** in time
24:32 it became an inheritance of the **d** of Joseph.
Jdg 1:16 The **d** of Hobab the Kenite, Moses' father-in-law,
4:11 that is, the **d** of Hobab the father-in-law of Moses,
Ru 4:18 Now these are the **d** of Perez:
1Sa 6:19 The **d** of Jeconiah did not rejoice with the people
20:42 and between my **d** and your descendants,
20:42 and between my descendants and your **d,** C
24:21 the LORD that you will not cut off my **d** after me,
2Sa 21:16 Ishbi-benob, one of the **d** of the giants,
21:18 who was one of the **d** of the giants.
22:51 to David and his **d** forever. A
1Ki 2:33 head of Joab and on the head of his **d** forever; A
2:33 but to David, and to his **d,** and to his house, A
9:21 their **d** who were still left in the land, whom B
11:39 For this reason I will punish the **d** of David,
2Ki 5:27 to you, and to your **d** forever." C
2Ki 8:19 to give a lamp to him and to his **d** forever. A
17:20 The LORD rejected all the **d** of Israel;
1Ch 1: 5 The **d** of Japheth: Gomer,
1: 6 **d** of Gomer: Ashkenaz, Diphath, and Togarmah.
1: 7 The **d** of Javan: Elishah, Tarshish,
1: 8 The **d** of Ham: Cush, Egypt, Put, and Canaan.
1: 9 The **d** of Cush: Seba, Havilah,
1: 9 The **d** of Raamah: Sheba and Dedan.
1:17 The **d** of Shem: Elam, Asshur,
1:23 all these were the **d** of Joktan.
1:33 All these were the **d** of Keturah.
2:23 All these were **d** of Machir, father of Gilead.
2:33 These were the **d** of Jerahmeel.
2:50 These were the **d** of Caleb.
3:10 The **d** of Solomon: Rehoboam,
3:16 The **d** of Jehoiakim: Jeconiah his son,
7:13 The **d** of Naphtali: Jahziel,
7:13 Jahziel, Guni, Jezer, and Shallum, the **d** of Bilhah.
9:23 So they and their **d** were in charge of the gates B
15: 4 Then David gathered together the **d** of Aaron D
20: 4 who was one of the **d** of the giants;
23:28 assist the **d** of Aaron for the service of the house D
23:32 and shall attend the **d** of Aaron, their kindred, D
24: 1 The divisions of the **d** of Aaron were these. D
24:31 the **d** of Aaron, in the presence of King David, D
2Ch 8: 8 from their **d** who were still left in the land, B
13: 9 the **d** of Aaron, and the Levites, D
13:10 to the LORD who are **d** of Aaron, D
20: 7 give it forever to the **d** of your friend Abraham?
21: 7 to give a lamp to him and to his **d** forever. A
26:18 but for the priests the **d** of Aaron, D
29:21 priests the **d** of Aaron to offer them on the altar D
31:19 And for the **d** of Aaron, the priests, D
32:33 on the ascent to the tombs of the **d** of David;
35:14 the priests the **d** of Aaron were occupied D
35:14 themselves and for the priests, the **d** of Aaron. D
35:15 The singers, the **d** of Asaph,
Ezr 2: 3 the **d** of Parosh, two thousand one hundred
2: 6 Of Pahath-moab, namely the **d** of Jeshua and Joab,
2:24 The **d** of Azmaveth, forty-two.
2:29 The **d** of Nebo, fifty-two.
2:36 the **d** of Jedaiah, of the house of Jeshua,
2:40 The Levites: the **d** of Jeshua and Kadmiel,
2:40 of the **d** of Hodaviah, seventy-four.
2:41 singers: the **d** of Asaph, one hundred twenty-eight.
2:42 The **d** of the gatekeepers: of Shallum,
2:43 The temple servants: the **d** of Ziha, Hasupha,
2:55 The **d** of Solomon's servants:
2:58 All the temple servants and the **d**
2:60 the **d** of Delaiah, Tobiah,
2:61 Also, of the **d** of the priests:
2:61 the **d** of Habaiah, Hakkoz,
8: 2 Of the **d** of Phinehas, Gershom.
8: 3 of the **d** of Shecaniah. Of Parosh,
8: 4 the **d** of Pahath-moab, Eliehoenai son of Zerahiah,
8: 5 Of the **d** of Zattu, Shecaniah son of Jahaziel,
8: 6 Of the **d** of Adin, Ebed son of Jonathan,
8: 7 Of the **d** of Elam, Jeshaiah son of Athaliah,
8: 8 Of the **d** of Shephatiah, Zebadiah son of Michael,
8: 9 Of the **d** of Joab, Obadiah son of Jehiel,
8:10 Of the **d** of Bani, Shelomith son of Josiphiah,
8:11 Of the **d** of Bebai, Zechariah son of Bebai,
8:12 Of the **d** of Azgad, Johanan son of Hakkatan,
8:13 Of the **d** of Adonikam, those who came later,
8:14 Of the **d** of Bigvai, Uthai and Zaccur,
8:15 I found there none of the **d** of Levi.
8:18 of the **d** of Mahli son of Levi son of Israel,
8:19 with him Jeshaiah of the **d** of Merari, with his kin
10: 2 Shecaniah son of Jehiel, of the **d** of Elam,
10:18 There were found of the **d** of
10:18 of the **d** of Jeshua son of Jozadak and his brothers:
10:20 Of the **d** of Immer: Hanani and Zebadiah.
10:21 Of the **d** of Harim: Maaseiah,
10:22 Of the **d** of Pashhur: Elioenai,
10:25 And of Israel: of the **d** of Parosh:
10:26 Of the **d** of Elam: Mattaniah,
10:27 Of the **d** of Zattu: Elioenai,
10:28 Of the **d** of Bebai: Jehohanan,
10:29 Of the **d** of Bani: Meshullam,
10:30 Of the **d** of Pahath-moab: Adna,
10:31 Of the **d** of Harim: Eliezer,
10:33 Of the **d** of Hashum: Mattenai,
10:34 Of the **d** of Bani: Maadai, Amram, Uel,
10:38 Of the **d** of Binnui: Shimei,
10:43 Of the **d** of Nebo: Jeiel, Mattithiah,
Ne 7: 8 the **d** of Parosh, two thousand one hundred
7:11 Of Pahath-moab, namely the **d** of Jeshua and Joab,
7:34 The **d** of the other Elam,
7:39 the **d** of Jedaiah, namely the house of Jeshua,
7:43 The Levites: the **d** of Jeshua,
7:43 namely of Kadmiel of the **d** of Hodevah,
7:44 singers: the **d** of Asaph, one hundred forty-eight.
7:45 the **d** of Shallum, of Ater, of Talmon, of Akkub,
7:46 The temple servants: the **d** of Ziha, of Hasupha,
7:57 The **d** of Solomon's servants:
7:60 All the temple servants and the **d**
7:62 the **d** of Delaiah, of Tobiah,
7:63 Also, of the priests: the **d** of Hobaiah, of Hakkoz,
9: 8 with him a covenant to give to his **d** the land of A
9:23 You multiplied their **d** like the stars of heaven, B
9:24 So the **d** went in and possessed the land,
11: 3 and the **d** of Solomon's servants.
11: 4 of Shephatiah son of Mahalalel, of the **d** of Perez;
11: 6 All the **d** of Perez who lived
11:22 of the **d** of Asaph, the singers,
11:24 of the **d** of Zerah son of Judah,
12:47 set apart that which was for the **d** of Aaron. D

Est 9:27 as a custom for themselves and their **d** B
9:28 of these days cease among their **d.** B
9:31 and for their **d** regulations concerning their fasts B
10:3 and interceded for the welfare of all his **d.** A
Job 5:25 You shall know that your **d** will be many, C
Ps 18:50 to David and his **d** forever. A
77:15 the **d** of Jacob and Joseph.
89:4 'I will establish your **d** forever, C
106:27 and would disperse their **d** among the nations, B
112:2 Their **d** will be mighty in the land; B
Isa 14:20 May the **d** of evildoers nevermore be named!
44:3 I will pour my spirit upon your **d,** C
48:19 and your **d** like its grains; C
54:3 and your **d** will possess the nations and C
60:14 The **d** of those who oppressed you shall come
61:9 Their **d** shall be known among the nations, B
65:9 I will bring forth **d** from Jacob,
65:23 by the LORD—and their **d** as well. B
66:22 so shall your **d** and your name remain. C
Jer 29:32 to punish Shemaiah of Nehelam and his **d;** A
33:26 not choose any of his **d** as rulers over the A
35:14 of Rechab gave to his **d** to drink no wine; A
35:16 The **d** of Jonadab son of Rechab have carried out
Eze 2:4 The **d** are impudent and stubborn.
40:46 these are the **d** of Zadok,
40:46 among the **d** of Levi may come near to the LORD
44:15 But the levitical priests, the **d** of Zadok,
48:11 the **d** of Zadok, who kept my charge,
Mal 3:3 the **d** of Levi and refine them like gold and silver,
Mt 23:31 Thus you testify against yourselves that you are **d**
Lk 1:55 to Abraham and to his **d** forever." A
Jn 8:33 are **d** of Abraham and have never been slaves F
8:37 I know that you are **d** of Abraham; F
Ac 2:30 an oath to him that he would put one of his **d** A
3:25 You are the **d** of the prophets and of the covenant
3:25 'And in your **d** all the families of the earth shall C
7:5 to him as his possession and to his **d** after him, A
7:6 that his **d** would be resident aliens in A
13:26 "My brothers, you **d** of Abraham's family,
Ro 4:13 not come to Abraham or to his **d** through the law A
4:16 on grace and be guaranteed to all his **d,** A
4:18 "So numerous shall your **d** be." C
9:7 and not all of Abraham's children are his true **d;**
9:7 "It is through Isaac that **d** shall be named for you."
9:8 but the children of the promise are counted as **d.**
2Co 11:22 Are they **d** of Abraham? F
Gal 3:7 those who believe are the **d** of Abraham. F
Heb 2:16 not come to help angels, but the **d** of Abraham. F
7:5 And those **d** of Levi who receive
11:12 and this one as good as dead, **d** were born,
11:18 "It is through Isaac that **d** shall be named for you."
Tob 1:1 of Aduel son of Gabael son of Raphael of the **d**
4:12 a woman from among the **d** of your ancestors;
4:12 for we are the **d** of the prophets.
7:3 to the **d** of Naphtali who are exiles in Nineveh."
13:16 of my **d** should survive to see your glory
Jdt 8:32 that will go down through all generations of our **d.**
AdE 9:27 upon their **d,** and upon all who would join them, B
9:28 of them was never to cease among their **d.** B
Sir 1:15 and among their **d** she will abide faithfully. B
4:16 their **d** will also obtain her. B
44:11 their wealth will remain with their **d,** B
44:12 Their **d** stand by the covenants; B
44:23 From his **d** the Lord brought forth a godly man, A
45:13 but only his sons and his **d** in perpetuity. A
45:15 an everlasting covenant for him and for his **d** A
45:21 which he gave to him and his **d.** A
45:24 that he and his **d** should have the dignity of A
45:25 so the heritage of Aaron is for his **d** alone. A
47:22 he will never blot out the **d** of his chosen one,
Bar 2:15 for Israel and his **d** are called by your name. A
3:21 Their **d** have strayed far from her way. B
3:23 the **d** of Hagar, who seek for understanding on
Aza 1:13 to multiply their **d** like the stars of heaven and B
1Mc 1:9 and so did their **d** after them for many years; B
5:2 to destroy the **d** of Jacob who lived among them. B
5:3 But Judas made war on the **d** of Esau in Idumea, E
5:65 his brothers went out and fought the **d** of Esau E
2Mc 1:20 sent the **d** of the priests who had hidden the fire
7:17 his mighty power will torture you and your **d!"** C
1Es 5:5 the **d** of Phinehas son of Aaron;
5:9 and their leaders: the **d** of Parosh,
5:9 The **d** of Shephatiah, four hundred seventy-two.
5:10 The **d** of Arah, seven hundred fifty-six.
5:11 The **d** of Pahath-moab, of the **d** of Jeshua and Joab,
5:12 **d** of Elam, one thousand two hundred fifty-four.
5:12 The **d** of Zattu, nine hundred forty-five.
5:12 The **d** of Chorbe, seven hundred five.
5:12 The **d** of Bani, six hundred forty-eight.
5:13 The **d** of Bebai, six hundred twenty-three.
5:13 The **d** of Azgad, one thousand three hundred
5:14 The **d** of Adonikam, six hundred sixty-seven.
5:14 The **d** of Bigvai, two thousand sixty-six.
5:14 The **d** of Adin, four hundred fifty-four.
5:15 The **d** of Ater, namely of Hezekiah, ninety-two.
5:15 The **d** of Kilan and Azetas, sixty-seven.
5:15 The **d** of Azaru, four hundred thirty-two.
5:16 The **d** of Annias, one hundred one.
5:16 The **d** of Arom.
5:16 The **d** of Bezai, three hundred twenty-three.
5:16 The **d** of Arsiphurith, one hundred twelve.
5:17 The **d** of Baiterus, three thousand five.
5:17 The **d** of Bethlomon, one hundred twenty-three.
5:21 The **d** of Niphish, one hundred fifty-six.
5:22 The **d** of the other Calamolalus and Ono,
5:22 The **d** of Jerechus, three hundred forty-five.
5:23 **d** of Senaah, three thousand three hundred thirty.
1Es 5:24 The priests: the **d** of Jedaiah son of Jeshua,
5:24 of the **d** of Anasib, nine hundred seventy-two.
5:24 The **d** of Immer, one thousand and fifty-two.
5:25 The **d** of Pashhur, one thousand two hundred
5:25 The **d** of Charme, one thousand seventeen.
5:26 **d** of Jeshua and Kadmiel and Bannas and Sudias,
5:27 the **d** of Asaph, one hundred twenty-eight.
5:28 the **d** of Shallum, the **d** of Ater, the **d** of Talmon,
the **d** of Akkub, the **d** of Hatita, the **d** of Shobai
5:29 the **d** of Esau, the descendants of Hasupha, E
5:29 the **d** of Hasupha, the **d** of Tabbaoth, the **d** of
Keros, the **d** of Sua, the **d** of Padon, the **d** of
Lebanah, the **d** of Hagabah,
5:30 the **d** of Akkub, the **d** of Uthai, the **d** of Ketab, the
d of Hagab, the **d** of Subai, the **d** of Hana, the **d** of
Cathua, the **d** of Geddur,
5:31 the **d** of Jairus, the **d** of Daisan, the **d** of Noeba,
the **d** of Chezib, the **d** of Gazera, the **d** of Uzza,
the **d** of Phinoe, the **d** of Hasrah, the **d** of Basthai,
the **d** of Asnah, the **d** of Maani, the **d** of Nephisim,
the **d** of Acuph, the **d** of Hakupha, the **d** of Asur,
the **d** of Pharakim, the **d** of Bazluth,
5:32 the **d** of Mehida, the **d** of Cutha, the **d** of Charea,
the **d** of Barkos, the **d** of Serar, the **d** of Temah,
the **d** of Neziah, the **d** of Hatipha.
5:33 The **d** of Solomon's servants: the **d** of Assaphioth,
the **d** of Peruda, the **d** of Jaalah, the **d** of Lozon,
the **d** of Isdael, the **d** of Shephatiah,
5:34 the **d** of Agia, the **d** of Pochereth-hazzebaim, the **d**
of Sarothie, the **d** of Masiah, the **d** of Gas, the **d** of
Addus, the **d** of Subas, the **d** of Apherra, the **d** of
Barodis, the **d** of Shaphat, the **d** of Allon.
5:35 All the temple servants and the **d** of Solomon's
5:37 the **d** of Delaiah son of Tobiah, and the **d** of
Nekoda, six hundred fifty-two.
5:38 the **d** of Habaiah, the **d** of Hakkoz, and the **d** of
8:29 Of the **d** of Phineas, Gershom.
8:29 Of the **d** of Ithamar, Gamael.
8:29 Of the **d** of David, Hattush son of Shecaniah.
8:30 Of the **d** of Parosh, Zechariah,
8:31 the **d** of Pahath-moab, Eliehoenai son of Zerahiah,
8:32 Of the **d** of Zattu, Shecaniah son of Jahaziel,
8:32 Of the **d** of Adin, Obed son of Jonathan,
8:33 Of the **d** of Elam, Jeshaiah son of Gotholiah,
8:34 Of the **d** of Shephatiah, Zeraiah son of Michael,
8:35 Of the **d** of Joab, Obadiah son of Jehiel,
8:36 Of the **d** of Bani, Shelomith son of Josiphiah,
8:37 Of the **d** of Bebai, Zechariah son of Bebai,
8:38 Of the **d** of Azgad, Johanan son of Hakkatan,
8:39 Of the **d** of Adonikam, the last ones,
8:40 Of the **d** of Bigvai, Uthai son of Istalcurus,
8:42 When I found there none of the **d** of the priests or
8:47 of the **d** of Mahli son of Levi, son
8:47 namely Sherebiah with his **d** and kinsmen, A
8:48 of the **d** of Hananiah, and their descendants,
8:48 of the descendants of Hananiah, and their **d,** B
8:70 For they and their **d** have married the daughters B
8:84 not give your daughters in marriage to their **d,** B
8:84 and do not take their daughters for your **d;** C
9:19 of the **d** of Jeshua son of Jozadak and his kindred,
9:21 Of the **d** of Immer: Hanani
9:22 Of the **d** of Pashhur: Elioenai,
9:26 Of Israel: of the **d** of Parosh:
9:27 Of the **d** of Elam: Mattaniah
9:28 Of the **d** of Zamoth: Eliadas,
9:29 Of the **d** of Bebai: Jehohanan
9:30 Of the **d** of Mani: Olamus,
9:31 Of the **d** of Addi: Naathus
9:32 the **d** of Annan, Elionas and Asaias and Melchias
9:33 Of the **d** of Hashum: Mattenai
9:34 Of the **d** of Bani: Jeremai,
9:34 Nethaniah. Of the **d** of Ezora:
9:35 Of the **d** of Nooma: Mazitias,
3Mc 6:3 look upon the **d** of Abraham, F
6:36 in their whole community and for their **d,** B
2Es 3:7 for him and for his **d.** A
3:15 that you would never forsake his **d;** A
3:17 And when you led his **d** out of Egypt, A
3:19 to give the law to the **d** of Jacob,
3:26 as Adam and all his **d** had done, A
7:*118* [48] but ours also who are your **d.** C
9:30 O Israel, and give heed to my words, O **d** of Jacob.
4Mc 13:19 the fathers to their **d** and which was implanted B
17:6 For your children were true **d** of father Abraham. F

DESCENDED (24) [DESCEND]

Ge 15:12 and a deep and terrifying darkness **d** upon him.
Ex 19:18 because the LORD had **d** upon it in fire;
19:20 When the LORD **d** upon Mount Sinai,
34:5 LORD **d** in the cloud and stood with him there,
2Sa 21:20 he too was **d** from the giants.
21:22 These four were **d** from the giants in Gath;
1Ch 20:6 he also was **d** from the giants.
20:8 These were **d** from the giants in Gath;
Lk 2:4 he was **d** from the house and family of David.
3:22 Holy Spirit **d** upon him in bodily form like a dove.
Jn 3:13 into heaven except the one who **d** from heaven,
7:42 the scripture said that the Messiah is **d** from David
Ro 1:3 who was **d** from David according to the flesh
Eph 4:9 that he had also **d** into the lower parts of the earth?
4:10 He who **d** is the same one who ascended far
Heb 7:5 though these also are **d** from Abraham.
7:14 For it is evident that our Lord was **d** from Judah,
Jdt 5:6 These people are **d** from the Chaldeans.
Wis 10:6 he escaped the fire that **d** on the Five Cities.
10:13 She **d** with him into the dungeon,
3Mc 6:18 of fearful aspect **d,** visible to all but
2Es 3:11 and all the righteous who have **d** from him.
3:21 as were also all who were **d** from him.
6:56 As for the other nations that have **d** from Adam,

DESCENDING (8) [DESCEND]

Ge 28:12 and the angels of God were ascending and **d** on it.
Isa 30:30 to be heard and the **d** blow of his arm to be seen,
Mt 3:16 to him and he saw the Spirit of God **d** like a dove
28:2 for an angel of the Lord, **d** from heaven,
Mk 1:10 he saw the heavens torn apart and the Spirit **d** like
Jn 1:32 "I saw the Spirit **d** from heaven like a dove,
1:51 the angels of God ascending and **d** upon the Son
4Mc 16:20 a knife and **d** upon him,

DESCENDS[‡] (1) [DESCEND]

Ps 7:16 and on their own heads their violence **d.**

DESCENT (9) [DESCEND]

Ezr 2:59 they could not prove their families or their **d,**
Ne 7:61 or their **d,** whether they belonged to Israel:
9:2 Then those of Israelite **d** separated themselves
13:3 they separated from Israel all those of foreign **d.**
Jer 48:5 at the **d** of Horonaim they have heard the
Heb 7:16 a legal requirement concerning physical **d,**
Sir 26:21 *confidence in their good* **d**, *will grow great.*
43:17 and its **d** is like locusts alighting.
1Mc 3:24 They pursued them down the **d** of Beth-horon to

DESCRIBE (5) [DESCRIBED, DESCRIPTION]

Jos 18:6 You shall **d** the land in seven divisions and bring
Eze 43:10 for you, mortal, **d** the temple to the house of Israel,
Ac 8:33 Who can **d** his generation?
Wis 17:1 Great are your judgments and hard to **d;**
Sir 43:31 Who has seen him and can **d** him?

DESCRIBED (7) [DESCRIBE]

Job 26:10 He has **d** a circle on the face of the waters,
Ac 9:27 **d** for them how on the road he had seen the Lord,
12:17 and **d** for them how the Lord had brought him out
Rev 22:18 to them, God will add to that person the plagues **d**
22:19 which are **d** in this book.
Jdt 7:28 do today the things that we have **d!"**
2Es 7:*100* to see what you have **d** to me?"

DESCRIPTION (5) [DESCRIBE]

Jos 18:4 writing a **d** of it with a view to their inheritances.
18:6 the land in seven divisions and bring the **d** here
18:8 and Joshua charged those who went to write the **d**
18:8 "Go throughout the land and write a **d** of it,
18:9 the land and set down in a book a **d** of it by towns

DESCRY (KJV) See SPY

DESECRATED (2) [DESECRATION]

Ps 74:7 they **d** the dwelling place of your name,
Jdt 4:12 to be profaned and **d** to the malicious joy of

DESECRATION (1) [DESECRATED]

Jdt 8:21 and he will make us pay for its **d** with our blood.

DESERT (67) [DESERTED, DESERTERS, DESERTING, DESERTS]

Lev 11:18 the water hen, the **d** owl, the carrion vulture,
Dt 14:17 and the **d** owl, the carrion vulture and
32:10 He sustained him in a **d** land,
2Ki 7:4 Therefore, let us **d** to the Aramean camp;
1Ch 5:9 the east as far as the beginning of the **d** this side of
12:19 "He will **d** to his master Saul at the cost
Job 1:19 across the **d,** struck the four corners of the house,
24:5 Like wild asses in the **d** they go out to their toil,
38:26 on the **d,** which is empty of human life,
Ps 78:17 rebelling against the Most High in the **d.**
78:40 in the wilderness and grieved him in the **d!**
105:41 it flowed through the **d** like a river.
106:9 he led them through the deep as through a **d.**
106:14 and put God to the test in the **d;**
107:4 Some wandered in **d** wastes,
107:33 He turns rivers into a **d,**
107:35 He turns a **d** into pools of water,
Pr 21:19 a **d** land than with a contentious and fretful wife.
Isa 14:17 the world like a **d** and overthrew its cities,
16:1 by way of the **d,** to the mount of daughter Zion.
16:8 reached to Jazer and strayed to the **d;**
21:1 it comes from the **d,** from a terrible land.
21:13 The oracle concerning the **d** plain.
21:13 In the scrub of the **d** plain you will lodge,
31:9 and his officers **d** the standard in panic,"
33:9 Sharon is like a **d;** and Bashan and Carmel shake
35:1 the **d** shall rejoice and blossom;
35:6 in the wilderness, and streams in the **d;**
40:3 make straight in the **d** a highway for our God.
41:19 I will set in the **d** the cypress,
42:11 Let the **d** and its towns lift up their voice,
43:19 a way in the wilderness and rivers in the **d.**
43:20 for I give water in the wilderness, rivers in the **d,**
50:2 I make the rivers a **d;**
51:3 her **d** like the garden of the LORD;
63:13 Like a horse in the **d,** they did not stumble.

Jer 4:11 the bare heights in the **d** toward my poor people,
4:26 I looked, and lo, the fruitful land was a **d**,
5: 6 a wolf from the **d** shall destroy them.
9: 2 O that I had in the **d** a traveler's lodging place,
9:26 all those with shaven temples who live in the **d**.
12:12 the bare heights in the **d** spoilers have come;
13:24 like chaff driven by the wind from the **d**.
17: 6 They shall be like a shrub in the **d**,
22: 6 but I swear that I will make you a **d**,
25:24 the kings of the mixed peoples that live in the **d**;
38:22 that your feet are stuck in the mud, they **d** you.'
48: 6 Flee! Save yourselves! Be like a wild ass in the **d**!
50:12 a wilderness, dry land, and a **d**.
51:43 a land of drought and a **d**,
Zep 2:13 a desolation, a dry waste like the **d**.
2:14 the **d** owl and the screech owl shall lodge
Mal 1: 3 a desolation and his heritage a **d** for jackals.
Mt 15:33 to get enough bread in the **d** to feed so great
26:33 because of you, I will never **d** you."
Mk 8: 4 with bread here in the **d**?"
Lk 11:17 against itself becomes a **d**,
Jdt 2:23 and the Ishmaelites on the border of the **d**,
5:14 They drove out all the people of the **d**,
Wis 10:13 a righteous man was sold, wisdom did not **d** him,
18:20 and a plague came upon the multitude in the **d**,
1Mc 1:39 Her sanctuary became desolate like a **d**;
2:21 Far be it from us to **d** the law and the ordinances.
2Es 7:*106* [36] Moses for our ancestors who sinned in the **d**,
16:60 he has put springs of water in the **d**,
4Mc 12:16 "I do not **d** the excellent example of my brothers,
18: 8 No seducer corrupted me on a **d** plain,

DESERTED (36) [DESERT]

Lev 26:22 and your roads shall be **d**.
26:43 For the land shall be **d** by them,
1Sa 29: 3 Since he **d** to me I have found no fault in him
1Ch 12:19 Some of the Manassites **d** to David when he came
12:20 As he went to Ziklag these Manassites **d** to him:
2Ch 15: 9 for great numbers had **d** to him from Israel
Isa 7:16 before whose two kings you are in dread will be **d**.
17: 2 Her towns will be **d** forever;
17: 9 that day their strong cities will be like the **d** places
17: 9 which they **d** because of the children of Israel,
27:10 a habitation **d** and forsaken, like the wilderness;
32:14 the palace will be forsaken, the populous city **d**;
33: 8 The highways are **d**, travelers have quit the road.
Jer 38:19 of the Judeans who have **d** to the Chaldeans,
39: 9 those who had **d** to him,
Eze 36: 4 the desolate wastes and the **d** towns,
Zep 2: 4 For Gaza shall be **d**, and Ashkelon shall become
Mt 14:13 he withdrew from there in a boat to a **d** place
14:15 "This is a **d** place, and the hour is now late;
26:56 Then all the disciples **d** him and fled.
Mk 1:35 he got up and went out to a **d** place,
6:31 to a **d** place all by yourselves and rest a while."
6:32 And they went away in the boat to a **d** place
6:35 "This is a **d** place, and the hour is now very late;
14:50 All of them **d** him and fled.
Lk 4:42 At daybreak he departed and went into a **d** place.
5:16 But he would withdraw to **d** places and pray.
9:12 for we are here in a **d** place."
Ac 15:38 with them one who had **d** them in Pamphylia
2Ti 4:10 has **d** me and gone to Thessalonica;
4:16 to my support, but all **d** me.
Tob 1: 4 of my ancestor Naphtali **d** the house of David
Sir 9: 7 or wander about in its **d** sections.
1Mc 7:19 and seized many of the men who had **d** to him,
7:24 on those who had **d** and preventing those in
15:12 and his troops had **d** him.

DESERTERS (6) [DESERT]

2Ki 25:11 in the city and the **d** who had defected to the king
Jer 52:15 in the city and the **d** who had defected to the king
Mt 26:31 "You will all become **d** because of me this night;
26:33 "Though all become **d** because of you,
Mk 14:27 And Jesus said to them, "You will all become **d**;
14:29 Peter said to him, "Even though all become **d**,

DESERTING (7) [DESERT]

2Ki 25: 5 all his army was scattered, **d** him.
Isa 57: 8 for, in **d** me, you have uncovered your bed,
Jer 37:13 "You are **d** to the Chaldeans."
37:14 I am not **d** to the Chaldeans."
52: 8 and all his army was scattered, **d** him.
Jn 12:11 that many of the Jews were **d** and were believing
Gal 1: 6 that you are so quickly **d** the one who called you

DESERTS‡ (5) [DESERT]

Isa 48:21 not thirst when he led them through the **d**;
Jer 2: 6 in a land of **d** and pits,
Zec 11:17 Oh, my worthless shepherd, who **d** the flock!
Heb 11:38 They wandered in **d** and mountains,
Wis 5: 7 and we journeyed through trackless **d**,

DESERVE (20) [DESERVED, DESERVEDLY, DESERVES, DESERVING]

1Sa 26:16 As the LORD lives, you **d** to die,
1Ki 2:26 to your estate; for you **d** death.
Ps 94: 2 give to the proud what they **d**!
Pr 14:14 The perverse get what their ways **d**, and the good, what their deeds **d**.
Jer 26:16 "This man does not **d** the sentence of death,
49:12 If those who do not **d** to drink the cup still have
Mt 10:10 or a staff; for laborers **d** their food.
Lk 23:15 Indeed, he has done nothing to **d** death.
23:41 for we are getting what we **d** for our deeds,
Ac 25:11 and have committed something for which I **d**
26:31 "This man is doing nothing to **d** death
Ro 1:32 that those who practice such things **d** to die—
Rev 2:23 and I will give to each of you as your works **d**.
16: 6 It is what they **d**!"
Wis 12:15 to your power to condemn anyone who does not **d**
Sir 8: 5 remember that we all **d** punishment.
10:28 and give yourself the esteem you **d**.
2Mc 15:21 that he gains the victory for those who **d** it.
4Mc 11: 6 But these deeds **d** honors, not tortures."

DESERVED (13) [DESERVE]

Dt 19: 6 although a death sentence was not **d**,
Jdg 9:16 and have done to him as his actions **d**—
Ezr 9:13 have punished us less than our iniquities **d**
Lk 12:48 not know and did what **d** a beating will receive
Ro 3: 8 that good may come"? Their condemnation is **d**!
Heb 10:29 be **d** by those who have spurned the Son of God,
AdE 16:18 on him the punishment that he **d**.
Wis 12:26 of mild rebukes will experience the **d** judgment
16: 9 because they **d** to be punished by such things.
18: 4 For their enemies **d** to be deprived of light
19: 4 For the fate they **d** drew them on to this end,
2Mc 4:38 Lord thus repaid him with the punishment he **d**.
3Mc 7:10 of God should receive the punishment they **d**.

DESERVEDLY (2) [DESERVE]

Wis 16: 1 Therefore those people were **d** punished
4Mc 9: 9 of your bloodthirstiness toward us, will **d** undergo

DESERVES (10) [DESERVE]

Dt 25: 2 If the one in the wrong **d** to be flogged,
2Sa 12: 5 the man who has done this **d** to die;
Job 11: 6 then that God exacts of you less than your guilt **d**.
Jer 26:11 "This man **d** the sentence of death
Eze 31:11 he has dealt with it as its wickedness **d**.
Mt 26:66 They answered, "He **d** death."
Lk 10: 7 for the laborer **d** to be paid.
1Ti 5:18 and, "The laborer **d** to be paid."
Tob 12: 4 Tobit said, "He **d**, my child,
Wis 3:10 the ungodly will be punished as their reasoning **d**,

DESERVING (5) [DESERVE]

Mk 14:64 All of them condemned him as **d** death.
Ac 23:29 with nothing **d** death or imprisonment.
25:25 But I found that he had done nothing **d** death;
Wis 12:20 the enemies of your servants and those **d** of death,
4Mc 4:12 For he said that he had committed a sin **d** of death,

DESIGN (7) [DESIGNED, DESIGNER, DESIGNS]

Ex 39: 3 and into the fine twisted linen, in skilled **d**.
2Ch 2:14 and to do all sorts of engraving and execute any **d**
Est 8: 3 with him to avert the evil **d** of Haman the Agagite
Jdt 13: 5 to help your heritage and to carry out my **d**
2Mc 15: 5 not succeed in carrying out his abominable **d**.
3Mc 1:16 of this evil **d**, and they filled the temple with cries
4Mc 9:30 the arrogant **d** of your tyranny being defeated

DESIGNATE (4) [DESIGNATED, DESIGNATES]

Ex 30:16 and shall **d** it for the service of the tent of meeting;
Nu 35:13 The cities that you **d** shall be six cities of refuge
35:14 you shall **d** three cities beyond the Jordan,
2Mc 4: 2 He dared to **d** as a plotter against the government

DESIGNATED (12) [DESIGNATE]

Ex 21: 8 who **d** her for himself, then he shall let her
Lev 16:21 into the wilderness by means of someone **d** for
19:20 **d** for another man but not ransomed
Nu 1:17 Moses and Aaron took these men who had been **d**
Dt 23:12 a **d** area outside the camp to which you shall go.
Jos 20: 9 These were the cities **d** for all the Israelites,
2Ch 3: 1 at the place that David had **d**,
31:19 the people **d** by name were to distribute portions
Ezr 10:16 each of them **d** by name.
Lk 2:23 "Every firstborn male shall be **d** as holy to
Heb 5:10 having been **d** by God a high priest according to
Jude 1: 4 people who long ago were **d** for this condemnation

DESIGNATES (1) [DESIGNATE]

Ex 21: 9 If he **d** her for his son, he shall deal with her as

DESIGNED (3) [DESIGN]

Isa 14:24 As I have **d**, so shall it be;
Jdt 9: 5 You have **d** the things that are now,
2Mc 6:12 but to recognize that these punishments were **d** not

DESIGNER (3) [DESIGN]

Ex 35:35 an artisan or by a **d** or by an embroiderer in blue,
35:35 by any sort of artisan or skilled **d**.
38:23 engraver, **d**, and embroiderer in blue, purple,

DESIGNS (7) [DESIGN]

Ex 31: 4 to devise artistic **d**, to work in gold, silver,
35:32 to devise artistic **d**, to work in gold, silver,
2Co 2:11 for we are not ignorant of his **d**.
Wis 9:14 and our **d** are likely to fail;
Sir 23: 1 do not abandon me to their **d**,
1Mc 11: 8 and he kept devising wicked **d** against Alexander.
4Mc 17: 2 the violence of the tyrant, frustrated his evil **d**,

DESIRABLE (7) [DESIRE]

Pr 19:22 What is **d** in a person is loyalty,
SS 5:16 His speech is most sweet, and he is altogether **d**.
Wis 8: 5 If riches are a **d** possession in life,
Sir 1:17 she fills their whole house with **d** goods,
42:22 How **d** are all his works,
2Es 7:*57* Judge therefore which things are precious and **d**,
4Mc 15: 1 O religion, more **d** to the mother than her children!

DESIRE‡ (133) [DESIRABLE, DESIRED, DESIRES, DESIRING]

Ge 3:16 yet your **d** shall be for your husband,
4: 7 its **d** is for you, but you must master it."
Ex 15: 9 my **d** shall have its fill of them.
Dt 5:21 Neither shall you **d** your neighbor's house,
12:15 Yet whenever you **d** you may slaughter
12:20 you may eat meat whenever you have the **d**.
12:21 you may eat within your towns whenever you **d**.
14:26 sheep, wine, strong drink, or whatever you **d**.
21:11 the captives a beautiful woman whom you **d**
25: 7 if the man has no **d** to marry his brother's widow,
25: 8 If he persists, saying, "I have no **d** to marry her,"
1Sa 9:20 And on whom is all Israel's **d** fixed,
2Sa 19:38 and all that you **d** of me I will do for you."
23: 5 not cause to prosper all my help and my **d**?
1Ki 10:13 to the queen of Sheba every **d** that she expressed,
2Ch 9:12 the queen of Sheba every **d** that she expressed,
15:15 and had sought him with their whole **d**,
Job 6: 8 and that God would grant my **d**;
13: 3 and I **d** to argue my case with God.
21:14 We do not **d** to know your ways.
33:32 speak, for I **d** to justify you.
Ps 10:17 O LORD, you will hear the **d** of the meek;
20: 4 May he grant you your heart's **d**,
21: 2 You have given him his heart's **d**,
35:25 "Aha, we have our heart's **d**."
35:27 Let those who **d** my vindication shout for joy and
40: 6 Sacrifice and offering you do not **d**,
40:14 and brought to dishonor who **d** my hurt.
45:11 and the king will **d** your beauty.
51: 6 You **d** truth in the inward being;
70: 2 be turned back and brought to dishonor who **d**
73:25 there is nothing on earth that I **d** other than you.
112:10 the **d** of the wicked comes to nothing.
145:16 satisfying the **d** of every living thing.
145:19 He fulfills the **d** of all who fear him;
Pr 3:15 and nothing you **d** can compare with her.
6:25 Do not **d** her beauty in your heart,
8:11 and all that you may **d** cannot compare with her.
10:24 but the **d** of the righteous will be granted.
11:23 The **d** of the righteous ends only in good;
13: 2 but the **d** of the treacherous is for wrongdoing.
13:12 but a **d** fulfilled is a tree of life.
13:19 A **d** realized is sweet to the soul,
19: 2 **D** without knowledge is not good,
21:10 The souls of the wicked **d** evil;
23: 3 Do not **d** the ruler's delicacies,
23: 6 of the stingy; do not **d** their delicacies;
24: 1 Do not envy the wicked, nor **d** to be with them;
31: 4 or for rulers to **d** strong drink;
Ecc 6: 2 so that they lack nothing of all that they **d**,
6: 9 the sight of the eyes than the wandering of **d**;
11: 9 Follow the inclination of your heart and the **d**
12: 5 the grasshopper drags itself along and **d** fails;
SS 7:10 I am my beloved's, and his **d** is for me.
Isa 26: 8 your name and your renown are the soul's **d**.
53: 2 nothing in his appearance that we should **d** him.
57:10 You found your **d** rekindled,
Jer 34:16 whom you had set free according to their **d**,
42:22 and by pestilence in the place where you **d** to go
Eze 24:21 the delight of your eyes, and your heart's **d**;
Da 2: 3 a dream that my spirit is troubled by the **d**
Hos 6: 6 For I **d** steadfast love and not sacrifice,
Am 5:18 Alas for you who **d** the day of the LORD!
Mic 7: 3 and the powerful dictate what they **d**;
Mal 2:15 And what does the one God **d**?
Mt 9:13 Go and learn what this means, 'I **d** mercy,
12: 7 'I **d** mercy and not sacrifice,'
Mk 4:19 the **d** for other things come in and choke the word,
Jn 17:24 Father, I **d** that those also,
Ro 10: 1 my heart's **d** and prayer to God for them is
15:23 with no further place for me in these regions, I **d**,
1Co 1:22 For Jews demand signs and Greeks **d** wisdom,
7:37 being under no necessity but having his own **d**
10: 6 so that we might not **d** evil as they did.
14:35 If there is anything they **d** to know,
2Co 8:10 to do something but even to **d** to do something—
13: 3 since you **d** proof that Christ is speaking in me.
Gal 4:21 Tell me, you who **d** to be subject to the law,
Php 1:23 my **d** is to depart and be with Christ,
Col 3: 5 fornication, impurity, passion, evil **d**,
1Ti 2: 8 I **d**, then, that in every place the men should pray,
Tit 3: 8 I **d** that you insist on these things,
Heb 11:16 But as it is, they **d** a better country, that is,
Jas 1:14 But one is tempted by one's own **d**,
1:15 when that **d** has conceived, it gives birth to sin,
1Pe 3:10 "Those who **d** life and **d** to see good days,
1Jn 2:16 the **d** of the flesh, the **d** of the eyes,
2:17 And the world and its **d** are passing away,

Jude 1: 5 Now I **d** to remind you,
Rev 11: 6 with every kind of plague, as often as they **d.**
AdE 13:15 of our foes are upon us to annihilate us, and they **d**
Wis 4:12 and roving **d** perverts the innocent mind.
6:11 Therefore set your **d** on my words;
6:13 to make herself known to those who **d** her.
6:17 of wisdom is the most sincere **d** for instruction,
6:20 so the **d** for wisdom leads to a kingdom.
14: 2 For it was **d** for gain that planned that vessel,
15: 5 so that they **d** the lifeless form of a dead image.
15: 6 of hope are those who either make or **d**
15:19 so beautiful in appearance that one would **d** them,
16: 2 a delicacy to satisfy the **d** of appetite;
16:21 bread, ministering to the **d** of the one who took it,
16:25 according to the **d** of those who had need,
19:11 when **d** led them to ask for luxurious food;
Sir 1:26 If you **d** wisdom, keep the commandments,
3:29 and an attentive ear is the **d** of the wise.
6:37 and your **d** for wisdom will be granted.
16: 1 Do not **d** a multitude of worthless children,
18:31 If you allow your soul to take pleasure in base **d,**
23: 5 and remove evil **d** from me.
24:19 "Come to me, you who **d** me,
25:21 and do not **d** a woman for her possessions.
Sus 1:11 for they were ashamed to disclose their lustful **d**
1:20 We are burning with **d** for you;
2Mc 11:23 we **d** that the subjects of the kingdom
11:28 If you are well, it is as we **d.**
3Mc 1:10 and conceived a **d** to enter the sanctuary.
7: 2 great God guiding our affairs according to our **d.**
7:17 in accordance with the common **d,** for seven days.
2Es 4: 4 then I will show you the way you **d** to see,
4:43 things that you **d** to see will be disclosed to you."
15:17 For a person will **d** to go into a city,
4Mc 1:22 Thus **d** precedes pleasure and delight follows it.
2: 2 because by mental effort he overcame sexual **d.**
2: 4 frenzied urge of sexual **d,** but also over every **d.**
3: 2 No one of us can eradicate that kind of **d,**
3: 2 a way for us not to be enslaved by **d.**
3:11 But a certain irrational **d** for the water in
3:12 respecting the king's **d,** armed themselves fully,
3:16 Therefore, opposing reason to **d,**

DESIRED (33) [DESIRE]

Ge 3: 6 and that the tree was to be **d** to make one wise,
1Ki 9: 1 the king's house and all that Solomon **d** to build,
9:11 and gold, as much as he **d,** King Solomon gave
9:19 and whatever Solomon **d** to build, in Jerusalem,
2Ch 8: 6 and whatever Solomon **d** to build, in Jerusalem,
Est 1: 8 the officials of his palace to do as each one **d.**
Job 31:16 "If I have withheld anything that the poor **d,**
Ps 19:10 More to be **d** are they than gold,
68:16 at the mount that God **d** for his abode,
107:30 and he brought them to their **d** haven.
132:13 he has **d** it for his habitation:
132:14 here I will reside, for I have **d** it.
Ecc 2:10 Whatever my eyes **d** I did not keep from them;
Jer 17:16 nor have I **d** the fatal day.
Da 7:19 I **d** to know the truth concerning the fourth beast,
Mt 23:37 to it! How often have I **d**
Lk 10:24 For I tell you that many prophets and kings **d**
13:34 to it! How often have I **d**
22:15 "I have eagerly **d** to eat this Passover with you
Heb 6:17 when God **d** to show even more clearly to
10: 5 he said, "Sacrifices and offerings you have not **d,**
10: 8 "You have neither **d** nor taken pleasure
Tob 3:17 before all others who had **d** to marry her.
Jdt 16:22 Many **d** to marry her, but she gave herself
AdE 13: 2 to restore the peace **d** by all people.
Wis 8: 2 I **d** to take her for my bride,
16: 3 that those people, when they **d** food, might lose
Sir 14:14 do not let your share of **d** good pass by you.
1Mc 4: 6 not have armor and swords such as they **d.**
2Mc 15:38 that is what I myself **d;**
3Mc 5:26 that what the king **d** was ready for action.
2Es 2:41 The number of your children, whom you **d,**
8:32 For if you have **d** to have pity on us,

DESIRES‡ (41) [DESIRE]

Dt 12: 8 all of us according to our own **d,**
1Sa 18:25 'The king **d** no marriage present except
2Sa 3:21 and that you may reign over all that your heart **d."**
1Ki 11:37 and you shall reign over all that your soul **d;**
Est 5: 5 so that we may do as Esther **d."**
Job 17:11 my plans are broken off, the **d** of my heart.
23:13 What he **d,** that he does.
Ps 10: 3 For the wicked boast of the **d** of their heart,
34:12 Which of you **d** life, and covets many days
37: 4 and he will give you the **d** of your heart.
140: 8 Do not grant, O LORD, the **d** of the wicked;
Lk 5:39 And no one after drinking old wine **d** new wine,
Jn 8:44 and you choose to do your father's **d.**
Ro 13:14 for the flesh, to gratify its **d.**
Gal 5:16 I say, and do not gratify the **d** of the flesh.
5:17 For what the flesh **d** is opposed to the Spirit,
5:17 and what the Spirit **d** is opposed to the flesh;
5:24 the flesh with its passions and **d.**
Eph 2: 3 following the **d** of flesh and senses,
1Ti 2: 4 who **d** everyone to be saved and to come to
3: 1 whoever aspires to the office of bishop **d**
5:11 for when their sensual **d** alienate them from Christ,
6: 9 and are trapped by many senseless and harmful **d**
2Ti 3: 6 by their sins and swayed by all kinds of **d,**
4: 3 for themselves teachers to suit their own **d,**
1Pe 1:14 not be conformed to the **d** that you formerly had
1Pe 2:11 the **d** of the flesh that wage war against the soul.
4: 2 the rest of your earthly life no longer by human **d**
2Pe 2:18 and with licentious **d** of the flesh they entice
Tob 6:15 but it kills anyone who **d** to approach her.
AdE 5: 5 so that we may do as Esther **d."**
Sir 5: 2 and strength in pursuing the **d** of your heart.
18:30 Do not follow your base **d,**
36:27 and there is nothing he **d** more.
40:22 The eye **d** grace and beauty,
4Mc 1:31 Self-control, then, is dominance over the **d.**
1:32 Some **d** are mental, others are physical,
2: 1 And why is it amazing that the **d** of the mind for
2: 6 to you all the more that reason is able to control **d.**
3:17 the emotions and quench the flames of frenzied **d;**
5:23 so that we master all pleasures and **d,**

DESIRING‡ (4) [DESIRE]

Ro 9:22 **d** to show his wrath and to make known his power,
1Ti 1: 7 **d** to be teachers of the law,
Heb 13:18 **d** to act honorably in all things.
Wis 13: 6 while seeking God and **d** to find him.

DESIST (4)

Jdg 20:28 the Benjaminites, or shall we **d?"**
Job 14: 6 and **d,** that they may enjoy, like laborers,
Pr 23: 4 to get rich; be wise enough to **d.**
Sir 35:21 it will not **d** until the Most High responds

DESOLATE‡ (86) [DESOLATED, DESOLATES, DESOLATING, DESOLATION, DESOLATIONS, DESOLATOR]

Ge 47:19 and that the land may not become **d."**
Ex 23:29 or the land would become **d** and
Lev 26:31 will make your sanctuaries **d,**
26:34 as long as it lies **d,** while you are in the land
26:35 As long as it lies **d,**
26:43 enjoy its sabbath years by lying **d** without them,
2Sa 13:20 So Tamar remained, a **d** woman,
2Ch 36:21 All the days that it lay **d** it kept sabbath,
Job 15:28 they will live in **d** cities, in houses
16: 7 he has made **d** all my company.
30: 3 and hard hunger they gnaw the dry and **d** ground,
38:27 to satisfy the waste and **d** land,
Ps 40: 2 He drew me up from the **d** pit, out of the miry bog,
68: 6 God gives the **d** a home to live in;
Isa 1: 7 Your country lies **d,** your cities are burned
1: 7 it is **d,** as overthrown by foreigners.
5: 9 Surely many houses shall be **d,**
6:11 without people, and the land is utterly **d;**
24: 1 about to lay waste the earth and make it **d,**
49: 8 to establish the land, to apportion the **d** heritages;
49:19 and your **d** places and your devastated land—
54: 1 For the children of the **d** woman will be more than
54: 3 the nations and will settle the **d** towns.
62: 4 and your land shall no more be termed **D;**
Jer 2:12 at this, be shocked, be utterly **d,** says the LORD,
4:30 O **d** one, what do you mean that you dress
12:10 have made my pleasant portion a **d** wilderness.
12:11 They have made it a desolation; **d,**
12:11 whole land is made **d,** but no one lays it to heart.
26: 9 and this city shall be **d,** without inhabitant'?"
33:10 of Judah and the streets of Jerusalem that are **d,**
48:34 For even the waters of Nimrim have become **d.**
49: 2 it shall become a **d** mound,
51:62 and it shall be **d** forever.'
La 1: 4 all her gates are **d,** her priests groan;
1:16 my children are **d,** for the enemy has prevailed.
3:11 to pieces; he has made me **d;**
5:18 which lies **d;** jackals prowl over it.
Eze 6: 4 Your altars shall become **d,**
6:14 and make the land **d** and waste,
14:15 so that it is made **d,** and no one may pass through
14:16 be saved, but the land would be **d.**
15: 8 And I will make the land **d,**
25: 3 and over the land of Israel when it was made **d,**
25:13 and I will make it **d;**
32:15 the land of Egypt **d** and when the land is stripped
33:28 and the mountains of Israel shall be so **d**
35:12 "They are laid **d,** they are given us to devour."
35:14 As the whole earth rejoices, I will make you **d.**
35:15 because it was **d,** so I will deal with you;
35:15 you shall be **d,** Mount Seir, and all Edom, all of it.
36: 3 Because they made you **d** indeed,
36: 4 the **d** wastes and the deserted towns,
36:34 The land that was **d** shall be tilled,
36:35 "This land that was **d** has become like the garden
36:35 and **d** and ruined towns are now inhabited
36:36 and replanted that which was **d;**
Da 8:13 the transgression that makes **d,**
11:31 and set up the abomination that makes **d.**
Joel 1:17 under the clods, the storehouses are **d;**
2: 3 but after them a **d** wilderness,
2:20 and drive it into a parched and **d** land,
3:19 a desolation and Edom a **d** wilderness,
Am 7: 9 the high places of Isaac shall be made **d,**
Mic 6:13 making you **d** because of your sins.
7:13 But the earth will be **d** because of its inhabitants,
Zep 3: 6 their cities have been made **d,** without people,
Zec 7:14 Thus the land they left was **d,**
7:14 and a pleasant land was made **d.**
Mt 23:38 See, your house is left to you, **d.**
Ac 1:20 'Let his homestead become **d,**
Gal 4:27 the **d** woman are more numerous than the children
Rev 17:16 they will make her **d** and naked;
Tob 14: 4 and the whole land of Israel will be **d,**
14: 4 even Samaria and Jerusalem will be **d.**
14: 4 and it will be **d** for a while.
Sir 16: 4 but through a clan of outlaws it becomes **d.**
49: 6 and made its streets **d,** as Jeremiah had foretold.
Bar 4:12 I was left **d** because of the sins of my children,
4:19 Go, my children, go; for I have been left **d.**
1Mc 1:39 Her sanctuary became **d** like a desert;
4:38 There they saw the sanctuary **d,** the altar profaned,
2Es 1:33 "Thus says the Lord Almighty: Your house is **d;**
5: 3 and people shall see it **d.**
16:23 for the earth shall be left **d,**
16:32 The earth shall be left **d,**

DESOLATED (4) [DESOLATE]

Eze 29:12 the land of Egypt a desolation among **d** countries;
30: 7 They shall be **d** among other **d** countries,
Da 9:17 Lord, let your face shine upon your **d** sanctuary.

DESOLATES (2) [DESOLATE]

Da 9:27 and in their place shall be an abomination that **d,**
12:11 and the abomination that **d** is set up,

DESOLATING (3) [DESOLATE]

Mt 24:15 you see the **d** sacrilege standing in the holy place,
Mk 13:14 when you see the **d** sacrilege set up where it ought
1Mc 1:54 a **d** sacrilege on the altar of burnt offering.

DESOLATION‡ (62) [DESOLATE]

Lev 26:33 your land shall be a **d,** and your cities a waste.
2Ki 22:19 that they should become a **d** and a curse,
2Ch 30: 7 so that he made them a **d,** as you see.
Ps 69:25 May their camp be a **d;**
Isa 13: 9 to make the earth a **d,** and to destroy its sinners
15: 6 the waters of Nimrim are a **d;**
17: 9 of the children of Israel, and there will be **d.**
24:12 **D** is left in the city,
59: 7 **d** and destruction are in their highways.
64:10 Zion has become a wilderness, Jerusalem a **d.**
Jer 4:27 The whole land shall be a **d;**
6: 8 and make you a **d,** an uninhabited land.
9:11 and I will make the towns of Judah a **d,**
10:22 of the north to make the cities of Judah a **d,**
12:11 They have made it a **d;** desolate, it mourns to me.
22: 5 says the LORD, that this house shall become a **d.**
25:18 to make them a **d** and a waste,
27:17 Why should this city become a **d?**
32:43 It is a **d,** without human beings or animals;
34:22 towns of Judah I will make a **d** without inhabitant.
44: 2 today they are a **d,** without an inhabitant in them,
44: 6 and they became a waste and a **d,**
44:22 your land became a **d** and a waste and a curse,
48: 3 a cry from Horonaim, **"D** and great destruction!"
48: 9 her towns shall become a **d,**
50: 3 it shall make her land a **d,**
50:13 but shall be an utter **d;**
51:29 to make the land of Babylon a **d,**
Eze 5:14 a **d** and an object of mocking among the nations
12:20 and the land shall become a **d;**
23:33 of horror and of **d** is the cup of your sister Samaria;
29: 9 and the land of Egypt shall be a **d** and a waste.
29:10 I will make the land of Egypt an utter waste and **d,**
29:12 the land of Egypt a **d** among desolated countries;
29:12 be a **d** forty years among cities that are laid waste.
30:12 I will bring **d** upon the land and everything in it by
30:14 I will make Pathros a **d,** and will set fire to Zoan,
33:28 I will make the land a **d** and a waste,
33:29 a **d** and a waste because of all their abominations
35: 3 I stretch out my hand against you to make you a **d**
35: 4 I lay your towns in ruins; you shall become a **d,**
35: 7 I will make Mount Seir a waste and a **d;**
35: 9 I will make you a perpetual **d,**
36:34 the **d** that it was in the sight of all who passed by.
Da 9:18 Open your eyes and look at our **d** and the city
Hos 5: 9 Ephraim shall become a **d** in the day
Joel 3:19 a **d** and Edom a desolate wilderness,
Mic 6:16 Therefore I will make you a **d,**
Na 2:10 Devastation, **d,** and destruction!
Zep 2: 4 and Ashkelon shall become a **d;**
2:13 and he will make Nineveh a **d,**
2:15 What a **d** it has become, a lair for wild animals!
Mal 1: 3 I have made his hill country a **d** and his heritage
Lk 21:20 then know that its **d** has come near.
Jdt 8:22 of the land and the **d** of our inheritance—
Bar 2: 4 and a **d** among all the surrounding peoples,
2:23 and the whole land will be a **d** without inhabitants.
4:33 so she will be grieved at her own **d.**
1Es 1:58 of its **d** until the completion of seventy years."
8:81 the temple of our Lord, and raised Zion from **d,**
2Es 3: 2 the **d** of Zion and the wealth of those who lived
12:48 to this place to pray on account of the **d** of Zion,

DESOLATIONS‡ (2) [DESOLATE]

Ps 46: 8 see what **d** he has brought on the earth.
Da 9:26 to the end there shall be war. **D** are decreed.

DESOLATOR (1) [DESOLATE]

Da 9:27 until the decreed end is poured out upon the **d."**

DESPAIR (10) [DESPAIRED, DESPAIRING]

1Sa 27: 1 then Saul will **d** of seeking me any longer within

Job 15:22 They **d** of returning from darkness,
24:22 they rise up when they **d** of life.
Ps 69:20 Insults have broken my heart, so that I am in **d.**
Ecc 2:20 up to **d** concerning all the toil of my labors under
Isa 19: 9 The workers in flax will be in **d,**
Eze 7:27 the prince shall be wrapped in **d,**
2Co 4: 8 perplexed, but not driven to **d;**
Sir 22:21 if you draw your sword against a friend, do not **d,**
2Mc 9:22 I do not **d** of my condition,

DESPAIRED (1) [DESPAIR]
2Co 1: 8 unbearably crushed that we **d** of life itself.

DESPAIRING‡ (1) [DESPAIR]
AdE 14:19 whose might is over all, hear the voice of the **d,**

DESPERATE (7)
Dt 28:53 the **d** straits to which the enemy siege reduces you,
28:55 in the **d** straits to which the enemy
28:57 in the **d** straits to which the enemy
Job 6:26 as if the speech of the **d** were wind?
Ps 88:15 I suffer your terrors; I am **d.**
Sir 4: 3 Do not add to the troubles of the **d,**
1Mc 9:17 The battle became **d,** and many on

DESPICABLE (1) [DESPISE]
Tit 3: 3 passing our days in malice and envy, **d,**

DESPISE‡ (49) [DESPICABLE, DESPISED, DESPISES, DESPISING]
Nu 14:11 "How long will this people **d** me?
1Sa 2:30 those who **d** me shall be treated with contempt.
2Sa 19:43 Why then did you **d** us?
Job 5:17 therefore do not **d** the discipline of the Almighty.
10: 3 to **d** the work of your hands and favor the schemes
19:18 Even young children **d** me;
36: 5 "Surely God is mighty and does not **d** any;
42: 6 therefore I **d** myself, and repent in dust and ashes."
Ps 22:24 he did not **d** or abhor the affliction of the afflicted;
51:17 a broken and contrite heart, O God, you will not **d.**
69:33 and does not **d** his own that are in bonds.
73:20 on awaking you **d** their phantoms.
102:17 and will not **d** their prayer.
Pr 1: 7 fools **d** wisdom and instruction.
3:11 do not **d** the LORD's discipline or be weary
13:13 Those who **d** the word bring destruction
14:21 Those who **d** their neighbors are sinners,
15:20 but the foolish **d** their mothers.
15:32 Those who ignore instruction **d** themselves,
23: 9 who will only **d** the wisdom of your words.
23:22 and do not **d** your mother when she is old.
SS 8: 1 I would kiss you, and no one would **d** me.
Isa 33:15 who **d** the gain of oppression,
Jer 4:30 Your lovers **d** you; they seek your life.
23:17 to those who **d** the word of the LORD, "It shall
La 1: 8 all who honored her **d** her,
Eze 16:57 those all around who **d** you.
21:13 If you **d** the rod, will it not happen?
Am 5:21 I **d** your festivals, and I take no delight
Mal 1: 6 O priests, who **d** my name.
Mt 6:24 or be devoted to the one and **d** the other.
18:10 that you do not **d** one of these little ones;
Lk 16:13 or be devoted to the one and **d** the other.
Ro 2: 4 Or do you **d** the riches of his kindness
14: 3 Those who eat must not **d** those who abstain,
14:10 Or you, why do you **d** your brother or sister?
1Co 16:11 therefore let no one **d** him.
Gal 4:14 you did not scorn or **d** me,
1Th 5:20 Do not **d** the words of prophets,
1Ti 4:12 Let no one **d** your youth,
2Pe 2:10 in depraved lust, and who **d** authority.
Tob 4:18 and do not **d** any useful counsel.
Jdt 10:19 "Who can **d** these people,
Wis 3:11 those who **d** wisdom and instruction are miserable.
Sir 3:13 because you have all your faculties do not **d** him.
10:23 It is not right to **d** one who is intelligent but poor,
31:31 and do not **d** him in his merrymaking;
38: 4 and the sensible will not **d** them.
4Mc 5:10 you continue to **d** me to your own hurt.

DESPISED (67) [DESPISE]
Ge 25:34 Thus Esau **d** his birthright.
Nu 14:23 none of those who **d** me shall see it.
14:31 and they shall know the land that you have **d.**
15:31 Because of having **d** the word of the LORD
16:30 then you shall know that these men have **d**
1Sa 10:27 They **d** him and brought him no present.
15: 9 all that was **d** and worthless they utterly destroyed.
2Sa 6:16 and she **d** him in her heart.
12: 9 Why have you **d** the word of the LORD,
12:10 for you have **d** me, and have taken the wife
1Ki 11:25 he **d** Israel and reigned over Aram.
2Ki 17:15 They **d** his statutes, and his covenant that he made
1Ch 15:29 and she **d** him in her heart.
Ne 4: 4 Hear, O our God, for we are **d;**
Ps 15: 4 the wicked are **d,** but who honor those who fear
22: 6 scorned by others, and **d** by the people.
106:24 Then they **d** the pleasant land,
119:141 I am small and **d,** yet I do
Pr 1:30 of my counsel, and **d** all my reproof,
5:12 how I hated discipline, and my heart **d** reproof!
6:30 not **d** who steal only to satisfy their appetite
12: 8 but a perverse mind is **d.**
Pr 12: 9 Better to be **d** and have a servant,
Ecc 9:16 yet the poor man's wisdom is **d,**
Isa 1: 4 who have **d** the Holy One of Israel,
5:24 and have **d** the word of the Holy One of Israel.
33: 8 The treaty is broken, its oaths are **d,**
49: 7 to one deeply **d,** abhorred by the nations,
52: 5 and continually, all day long, my name is **d.**
53: 3 He was **d** and rejected by others;
53: 3 one from whom others hide their faces he was **d,**
60:14 and all who **d** you shall bow down at your feet;
Jer 22:28 Is this man Coniah a **d** broken pot,
49:15 For I will make you least among the nations, **d**
Eze 16:59 you who have **d** the oath, breaking the covenant;
17:16 whose oath he **d,** and whose covenant
17:18 Because he **d** the oath and broke the covenant,
17:19 surely return upon his head my oath that he **d,**
21:10 You have **d** the rod, and all discipline.
22: 8 You have **d** my holy things,
Ob 1: 2 among the nations; you shall be utterly **d.**
Zec 4:10 For whoever has **d** the day
Mal 1: 6 You say, "How have we **d** your name?"
1: 7 By thinking that the LORD's table may be **d.**
1:12 and the food for it may be **d.**
2: 9 so I make you **d** and abased before all the people,
1Co 1:28 God chose what is low and **d** in the world,
Jdt 11:22 on those who have **d** my lord.
14: 5 and recognize the man who **d** the house of Israel
Wis 12:24 as gods those animals that even their enemies **d;**
Sir 22: 5 and husband, and is **d** by both.
2Mc 1:27 look on those who are rejected and **d,**
2Es 1: 7 But they have angered me and **d** my counsels.
2: 7 because they have **d** my covenant.
7:*37* whose commandments you have **d.**
7:*79* the way of the Most High, who have **d** his law
8:56 For when they had opportunity to choose, they **d**
9:11 not understand but **d** it while an opportunity
4Mc 4:26 I say, his decrees were **d** by the people,
5:21 for in either case the law is equally **d.**
6:21 be **d** by the tyrant as unmanly by not contending
7:16 of piety an aged man **d** tortures even to death,
13: 1 the seven brothers **d** sufferings even unto death,
13: 9 the three youths in Assyria who **d** the same ordeal
14: 1 so that they not only **d** their agonies,
14:11 the mind of woman **d** even more diverse agonies,
16: 2 but also that a woman has **d** the fiercest tortures.

DESPISES (5) [DESPISE]
2Ki 19:21 She **d** you, she scorns you—
Pr 14: 2 but one who is devious in conduct **d** him.
15: 5 A fool **d** a parent's instruction,
Isa 37:22 She **d** you, she scorns you—
Sir 19: 1 one who **d** small things will fail little by little.

DESPISING (5) [DESPISE]
Dt 31:20 **d** me and breaking my covenant.
2Ch 36:16 **d** his words, and scoffing at his prophets,
2Mc 4:14 **D** the sanctuary and neglecting the sacrifices,
4Mc 1: 9 All of these, by **d** sufferings that bring death,
9: 6 we young men should die **d** your coercive tortures,

DESPITE (6)
Lev 26:27 But if, **d** this, you disobey me,
Job 23: 2 his hand is heavy **d** my groaning.
Isa 25:11 their pride will be laid low **d** the struggle
Sir Pr: 2 **d** our diligent labor in translating,
48:15 **D** all this the people did not repent,
4Mc 4: 1 When **d** all manner of slander he was unable

DESPITE (KJV) See also MALICE, PROFANED

DESPOIL (8) [DESPOILED, DESPOILING, DESPOILS]
1Sa 14:36 down after the Philistines by night and **d** them
Ps 17: 9 from the wicked who **d** me,
35:10 the weak and needy from those who **d** them."
Pr 22:23 and despoils of life those who **d** them.
Isa 17:14 This is the fate of those who **d** us,
Eze 29:19 he shall carry off its wealth and **d** it and plunder it;
39:10 they will **d** those who despoiled them,
1Mc 3:20 and our wives and our children, and to **d** us;

DESPOILED (7) [DESPOIL]
Ps 12: 5 "Because the poor are **d,** because the needy groan,
Isa 24: 3 The earth shall be utterly laid waste and utterly **d;**
59:15 Truth is lacking, and whoever turns from evil is **d.**
Eze 39:10 they will despoil those who **d** them,
Zec 11: 3 the wail of the shepherds, for their glory is **d!**
1Mc 5: 3 a heavy blow and humbled them and **d** them.
5:22 of the Gentiles fell, and he **d** them.

DESPOILING (1) [DESPOIL]
Jer 25:36 For the LORD is **d** their pasture,

DESPOILS (1) [DESPOIL]
Pr 22:23 for the LORD pleads their cause and **d** of life those

DESSAU (1)
2Mc 14:16 and engaged them in battle at a village called **D.**

DESTINE (1) [DESTINED, DESTINY]
Isa 65:12 I will **d** you to the sword, and all of you shall bow

DESTINED (28) [DESTINE]
Nu 24:22 yet Kain is **d** for burning.
Job 15:22 and they are **d** for the sword.
15:28 houses **d** to become heaps of ruins;
Isa 23:13 They **d** Tyre for wild animals.
Jer 15: 2 Those **d** for pestilence, to pestilence,
15: 2 and those **d** for the sword, to the sword;
15: 2 those **d** for famine, to famine,
15: 2 and those **d** for captivity, to captivity.
43:11 giving those who are **d** for pestilence, to pestilence,
43:11 and those who are **d** for captivity, to captivity,
43:11 and those who are **d** for the sword, to the sword.
Lk 2:34 "This child is **d** for the falling and the rising
Jn 17:12 one of them was lost except the one **d** to be lost,
Ac 13:48 as had been **d** for eternal life became believers.
Eph 1: 5 He **d** us for adoption as his children
1:11 having been **d** according to the purpose
1Th 3: 3 you yourselves know that this is what we are **d** for.
5: 9 For God has **d** us not for wrath but
2Th 2: 3 and the lawless one is revealed, the one **d**
1Pe 1: 2 who have been chosen and **d** by God the Father
1:11 when it testified in advance to the sufferings **d**
1:20 He was **d** before the foundation of the world,
2: 8 they disobey the word, as they were **d** to do.
Wis 15: 9 that mortals are **d** to die or that their life is brief,
17:21 image of the darkness that was **d** to receive them;
Sir 48:10 you are **d** to calm the wrath of God
49:12 a temple holy to the Lord, **d** for everlasting glory.
2Es 7:*42* by which all shall see what has been **d.**

DESTINY‡ (1) [DESTINE]
Isa 65:11 for Fortune and fill cups of mixed wine for **D;**

DESTITUTE‡ (6)
Ps 82: 3 maintain the right of the lowly and the **d.**
102:17 He will regard the prayer of the **d,**
Pr 11:16 The timid become **d,** but the aggressive gain
31: 8 for the rights of all the **d.**
Heb 11:37 they went about in skins of sheep and goats, **d,**
Sir 37:20 he will be **d** of all food,

DESTROY‡ (295) [DESTROYED, DESTROYER, DESTROYERS, DESTROYING, DESTROYS, DESTRUCTION, DESTRUCTIVE]
Ge 6:13 now I am going to **d** them along with the earth.
6:17 to **d** from under heaven all flesh in which is
8:21 nor will I ever again **d** every living creature
9:11 never again shall there be a flood to **d** the earth."
9:15 a flood to **d** all flesh.
18:28 Will you **d** the whole city for lack of five?"
18:28 he said, "I will not **d** it if I find forty-five there."
18:31 "For the sake of twenty I will not **d** it."
18:32 He answered, "For the sake of ten I will not **d** it."
19:13 For we are about to **d** this place,
19:13 and the LORD has sent us to **d** it."
19:14 for the LORD is about to **d** the city."
20: 4 so he said, "Lord, will you **d** an innocent people?
Ex 12:13 over you, and no plague shall **d** you when I strike
15: 9 I will draw my sword, my hand shall **d** them.'
Lev 23:30 such a one I will **d** from the midst of the people.
26:22 of your children and **d** your livestock;
26:30 I will **d** your high places and cut
26:44 so as to **d** them utterly and break my covenant
Nu 21: 2 then we will utterly **d** their towns."
24:19 and **d** the survivors of Ir."
32:15 and you will **d** all this people."
33:52 **d** all their figured stones, **d** all their cast images,
Dt 1:27 to hand us over to the Amorites to **d** us.
4:31 he will neither abandon you nor **d** you;
6:15 against you and he would **d** you from the face of
7: 2 then you must utterly **d** them.
7: 4 and he would **d** you quickly.
9: 3 so that you may dispossess and **d** them quickly,
9: 8 so angry with you that he was ready to **d** you.
9:14 that I may **d** them and blot out their name from
9:19 against you was so fierce that he would **d** you.
9:20 so angry with Aaron that he was ready to **d** him,
9:25 the LORD when the LORD intended to **d** you,
9:26 to the LORD and said, "Lord GOD, do not **d**
10:10 The LORD was unwilling to **d** you.
20:19 not **d** its trees by wielding an ax against them.
20:20 You may **d** only the trees that you know do
31: 3 He will **d** these nations before you,
33:27 he drove out the enemy before you, and said, "**D!**"
Jos 7: 7 to hand us over to the Amorites so as to **d** us?
7:12 unless you **d** the devoted things from among you.
9:24 and to **d** all the inhabitants of the land before you;
22:33 against them, to **d** the land where the Reubenites
Jdg 6: 4 against them and **d** the produce of the land,
1Sa 15: 3 and utterly **d** all that they have;
15: 6 or I will **d** you with them;
15: 9 and would not utterly **d** them;
15:18 'Go, utterly **d** the sinners, the Amalekites,
23:10 to **d** the city on my account.
26: 9 But David said to Abishai, "Do not **d** him;
26:15 one of the people came in to **d** your lord the king.
2Sa 1:14 to lift your hand to **d** the LORD's anointed?"
4:11 and **d** you from the earth?"

2Sa 14: 7 even if we **d** the heir as well.'
20:19 you seek to **d** a city that is a mother in Israel;
20:20 far be it, that I should swallow up or **d!**
21: 5 "The man who consumed us and planned to **d** us,
24:16 to **d** it, the LORD relented concerning the evil,
1Ki 9:21 the Israelites were unable to **d** completely—
13:34 to cut it off and to **d** it from the face of the earth.
2Ki 8:19 Yet the LORD would not **d** Judah,
10:19 with cunning in order to **d** the worshipers of Baal.
11: 1 she set about to **d** all the royal family.
13:23 Isaac, and Jacob, and would not **d** them;
18:25 that I have come up against this place to **d** it?
18:25 Go up against this land, and **d** it."
24: 2 he sent them against Judah to **d** it,
1Ch 21:15 And God sent an angel to Jerusalem to **d** it;
21:15 but when he was about to **d** it,
2Ch 12: 7 "They have humbled themselves; I will not **d** them,
12:12 so as not to **d** them completely;
20:10 and whom they avoided and did not **d**—
20:23 they all helped to **d** one another.
20:37 the LORD will **d** what you have made."
21: 7 not **d** the house of David because of the covenant
22: 7 the LORD had anointed to **d** the house of Ahab.
22:10 she set about to **d** all the royal family of the house
25:16 "I know that God has determined to **d** you,
35:21 who is with me, so that he will not **d** you."
Ezr 6:12 or to **d** this house of God in Jerusalem.
9:14 be angry with us until you **d** us without remnant
Est 3: 6 Haman plotted to **d** all the Jews,
3:13 giving orders to **d**, to kill,
7: 7 for he saw that the king had determined to **d** him.
8: 5 to **d** the Jews who are in all the provinces of
8:11 to assemble and defend their lives, to **d**, to kill,
9:24 had plotted against the Jews to **d** them,
9:24 that is "the lot"—to crush and **d** them;
Job 2: 3 to **d** him for no reason."
10: 8 and now you turn and **d** me.
14:19 so you **d** the hope of mortals.
Ps 5: 6 You **d** those who speak lies;
21:10 You will **d** their offspring from the earth,
57: T *To the leader: Do Not **D.** Of David.*
58: T *To the leader: Do Not **D.** Of David.*
59: T *To the leader: Do Not **D.** Of David.*
63: 9 But those who seek to **d** my life shall go down into
69: 4 many are those who would **d** me,
75: T *To the leader: Do Not **D.** A Psalm of Asaph.*
78:38 forgave their iniquity, and did not **d** them;
88:16 over me; your dread assaults **d** me.
101: 5 One who secretly slanders a neighbor I will **d.**
101: 8 Morning by morning I will **d** all the wicked in
106:23 Therefore he said he would **d** them—
106:34 They did not **d** the peoples,
119:95 The wicked lie in wait to **d** me,
143:12 and **d** all my adversaries, for I am your servant.
145:20 but all the wicked he will **d.**
Pr 11: 9 the godless would **d** their neighbors,
31: 3 your ways to those who **d** kings.
Ecc 5: 6 and **d** the work of your hands?
7:16 why should you **d** yourself?
Isa 10: 7 but it is in his heart to **d**, and to cut off nations
10:18 and his fruitful land the LORD will **d**,
11: 9 They will not hurt or **d** on all my holy mountain;
11:15 the LORD will utterly **d** the tongue of the sea
13: 5 and the weapons of his indignation, to **d**
13: 9 and to **d** its sinners from it.
23:11 concerning Canaan to **d** its fortresses.
25: 7 And he will **d** on this mountain the shroud
33: 1 you have ceased to **d**, you will be destroyed;
36:10 that I have come up against this land to **d** it?
36:10 Go up against this land, and **d** it."
54:16 I have also created the ravager to **d.**
65: 8 "Do not **d** it, for there is a blessing in it,"
65: 8 for my servants' sake, and not **d** them all.
65:25 They shall not hurt or **d** on all my holy mountain,
Jer 1:10 to **d** and to overthrow, to build and to plant."
5: 6 a wolf from the desert shall **d** them.
5:10 Go up through her vine-rows and **d**,
5:17 they shall **d** with the sword your fortified cities
6: 5 and let us attack by night, and **d** her palaces!"
11:19 saying, "Let us **d** the tree with its fruit,
12:17 then I will completely uproot it and **d** it,
13:14 or spare or have compassion when I **d** them.
15: 3 and the wild animals of the earth to devour and **d.**
17:18 **d** them with double destruction!
18: 7 that I will pluck up and break down and **d** it,
23: 1 Woe to the shepherds who **d** and scatter the sheep
25: 9 I will utterly **d** them, and make them an object
31:28 to overthrow, **d**, and bring evil,
36:29 of Babylon will certainly come and **d** this land,
46: 8 let me **d** cities and their inhabitants.
47: 4 of the day that is coming to **d** all the Philistines,
49:28 **D** the people of the east!
49:38 and **d** their king and officials, says the LORD.
50:21 and attack the inhabitants of Pekod and utterly **d**
50:26 pile her up like heaps of grain, and **d** her utterly;
51: 3 not spare her young men; utterly **d** her entire army.
51:11 because his purpose concerning Babylon is to **d** it,
51:20 with you I smash nations; with you I **d** kingdoms;
51:62 to **d** this place so that neither human beings
La 3:66 and **d** them from under the LORD's heavens.
Eze 5:16 which I will let loose to **d** you,
6: 3 and I will **d** your high places.
9: 8 will you **d** all who remain of Israel
13:13 and hailstones in wrath to **d** it.
14: 9 and will **d** him from the midst of my people Israel.
20:17 and I did not **d** them or make an end of them in
21:31 into brutish hands, those skillful to **d.**

Eze 22:30 so that I would not **d** it; but I found no one.
25: 7 of the countries; I will **d** you.
25:16 and **d** the rest of the seacoast.
26: 4 They shall **d** the walls of Tyre and break
26:12 down your walls and **d** your fine houses.
30:11 shall be brought in to **d** the land;
30:13 I will **d** the idols and put an end to the images
32:13 I will **d** all its livestock from
34:16 but the fat and the strong I will **d.**
43: 3 to **d** the city, and like the vision that I had seen by
Da 2:24 whom the king had appointed to **d** the wise men
2:24 "Do not **d** the wise men of Babylon;
4:23 'Cut down the tree and **d** it,
8:24 He shall **d** the powerful and the people of the holy
8:25 Without warning he shall **d** many and shall
9:26 and the troops of the prince who is to come shall **d**
11:17 In order to **d** the kingdom,
Hos 4: 5 with you by night, and I will **d** your mother.
10: 2 down their altars, and **d** their pillars.
11: 9 I will not again **d** Ephraim;
13: 9 I will **d** you, O Israel; who can help you?
Am 9: 8 and I will **d** it from the face of the earth—except
that I will not utterly **d** the house of Jacob,
Ob 1: 8 says the LORD, I will **d** the wise out of Edom,
Mic 5:10 from among you and will **d** your chariots;
5:14 from among you and **d** your towns.
Zep 2: 5 and I will **d** you until no inhabitant is left.
2:13 against the north, and **d** Assyria;
Hag 2:22 to **d** the strength of the kingdoms of the nations,
Zec 12: 9 that day I will seek to **d** all the nations that come
Mal 3:11 so that it will not **d** the produce of your soil;
Mt 2:13 Herod is about to search for the child, to **d** him."
10:28 rather fear him who can **d** both soul and body
12:14 and conspired against him, how to **d** him.
26:61 'I am able to **d** the temple of God and to build it
27:40 "You who would **d** the temple and build it
Mk 1:24 Have you come to **d** us?
3: 6 with the Herodians against him, how to **d** him.
9:22 into the fire and into the water, to **d** him;
12: 9 and **d** the tenants and give the vineyard to others.
14:58 'I will **d** this temple that is made with hands,
15:29 You who would **d** the temple and build it
Lk 4:34 Have you come to **d** us?
6: 9 to save life or to **d** it?"
20:16 He will come and **d** those tenants and give
Jn 2:19 Jesus answered them, "**D** this temple,
10:10 The thief comes only to steal and kill and **d.**
11:48 the Romans will come and **d** both our holy place
Ac 6:14 of Nazareth will **d** this place and will change
Ro 14:20 Do not, for the sake of food, **d** the work of God.
1Co 1:19 For it is written, "I will **d** the wisdom of the wise,
3:17 If anyone destroys God's temple, God will **d**
6:13 and God will **d** both one and the other.
2Co 10: 4 divine power to **d** strongholds. We **d** arguments
Gal 1:13 the church of God and was trying to **d** it.
1:23 now proclaiming the faith he once tried to **d."**
2Th 2: 8 the Lord Jesus will **d** with the breath of his mouth,
Heb 2:14 so that through death he might **d** the one who has
Jas 4:12 and judge who is able to save and to **d.**
1Jn 3: 8 to **d** the works of the devil.
Rev 11:18 and for destroying those who **d** the earth."
Jdt 3: 8 for he had been commissioned to **d** all the gods of
6: 2 He will send his forces and **d** them from the face
6: 3 we the king's servants will **d** them as one man.
7:13 of Bethulia get their water. So thirst will **d** them,
8:15 or even to **d** us in the presence of our enemies.
13: 5 to **d** the enemies who have risen up against us."
15: 4 to urge all to rush out upon the enemy to **d** them.
AdE 3: 6 plotted to **d** all the Jews under Artaxerxes' rule.
3: 7 to fix on one day to **d** the whole race of Mordecai.
3:13 the empire of Artaxerxes to **d** the Jewish people on
8: 5 the letters that Haman wrote and sent to **d** the Jews
9:24 how he made a decree and cast lots to **d** them,
10: 8 The nations are those that gathered to **d** the name
13:15 upon us to annihilate us, and they desire to **d**
13:17 do not **d** the lips of those who praise you."
14: 9 and to **d** your inheritance,
Wis 11:19 not only could the harm they did **d** people,
12: 6 you willed to **d** by the hands of our ancestors,
12: 8 as forerunners of your army to **d** them little
12: 9 or to **d** them at one blow by dread wild animals
16:19 to **d** the crops of the unrighteous land.
Sir 21: 2 Its teeth are lion's teeth, and can **d** human lives.
22:27 and my tongue may not **d** me?
28:13 for they **d** the peace of many.
36: 9 **d** the adversary and wipe out the enemy.
47:22 or **d** the family line of him who loved him.
49: 7 to pluck up and ruin and **d**,
LtJ 6:14 but is unable to **d** anyone who offends it.
Sus 1:59 so as to **d** you both."
1Mc 2:40 they will quickly **d** us from the earth."
3:20 to **d** us and our wives and our children,
3:35 a force against them to wipe out and **d** the strength
3:39 to go into the land of Judah and **d** it,
3:52 Here the Gentiles are assembled against us to **d** us;
3:58 against us to **d** us and our sanctuary.
5: 2 and they determined to **d** the descendants
5: 2 So they began to kill and **d** among the people.
5: 9 in their territory, and planned to **d** them.
5:10 Gentiles around us have gathered together to **d** us.
5:27 and capture and **d** all these people in a single day."
6:12 to **d** the inhabitants of Judah without good reason.
6:19 Judas therefore resolved to **d** them,
7:26 and he commanded him to **d** the people.
8: 9 The Greeks planned to come and **d** them,
12:49 and the Great Plain to **d** all Jonathan's soldiers.
12:53 All the nations around them tried to **d** them,

1Mc 13: 1 a large army to invade the land of Judah and **d** it,
13: 6 have gathered together out of hatred to **d** us."
13:20 this Trypho came to invade the country and **d** it,
16:22 the men who came to **d** him and killed them,
16:22 he had found out that they were seeking to **d** him.
2Mc 6:12 that these punishments were designed not to **d** but
15: 2 "Do not **d** so savagely and barbarously,
1Es 4:44 when he began to **d** Babylon,
6:33 upon, **d** every king and nation
8:88 not angry enough with us to **d** us without leaving
Man 1:13 Do not **d** me with my transgressions!
3Mc 6:10 rescue us from the hand of the enemy, and **d** us,
7:12 they might **d** those everywhere
2Es 8:14 If then you will suddenly and quickly **d** what with
12:33 when he has reproved them, then he will **d** them.
13:38 and will **d** them without effort by means of
15:11 as before, and will **d** all its land.
15:33 an enemy in ambush shall attack them and **d** one
15:40 shall rise and **d** all the earth and its inhabitants,
15:42 They shall **d** cities and walls, mountains and hills,
15:60 and shall **d** a part of your land and abolish
16:72 For they shall **d** and plunder their goods,
4Mc 8: 9 you will compel me to **d** each and every one
8:19 and this arrogance that threatens to **d** us?
17: 9 the violence of the tyrant who wished to **d** the way

DESTROYED‡ (222) [DESTROY]

Ge 13:10 before the LORD had **d** Sodom and Gomorrah.
19:29 So it was that, when God **d** the cities of the Plain,
34:30 I shall be **d**, both I and my household."
Nu 4:18 not let the tribe of the clans of the Kohathites be **d**
21: 3 and they utterly **d** them and their towns;
Dt 2:21 the LORD **d** them from before the Ammonites so
2:23 **d** them and settled in their place.)
2:34 and in each town we utterly **d** men, women,
3: 6 And we utterly **d** them, as we had done
4: 3 how the LORD your God **d** from
4:26 you will not live long on it, but will be utterly **d.**
7:20 until even the survivors and the fugitives are **d.**
7:23 and throw them into great panic, until they are **d.**
7:24 to stand against you, until you have **d** them.
11: 4 so that the LORD has **d** them to this day;
12:30 after they have been **d** before you:
28:20 until you are **d** and perish quickly,
28:24 down upon you from the sky until you are **d.**
28:45 pursuing and overtaking you until you are **d**,
28:48 an iron yoke on your neck until he has **d** you.
28:51 and the fruit of your ground until you are **d**,
28:61 the LORD will inflict on you until you are **d.**
29:23 which the LORD **d** in his fierce anger—
31: 4 and to their land, when he **d** them.
Jos 2:10 to Sihon and Og, whom you utterly **d.**
8:26 until he had utterly **d** all the inhabitants of Ai.
10: 1 how Joshua had taken Ai, and had utterly **d** it,
10:28 he utterly **d** every person in it;
10:35 and every person in it he utterly **d** that day,
10:37 and utterly **d** it with every person in it.
10:39 and utterly **d** every person in it;
10:40 but utterly **d** all that breathed,
11:14 with the edge of the sword, until they had **d** them,
11:20 in order that they might be utterly **d**,
11:21 Joshua utterly **d** them with their towns.
23:15 until he has **d** you from this good land that
24: 8 of their land, and I **d** them before you.
Jdg 4:24 until they **d** King Jabin of Canaan.
20:35 Israelites **d** twenty-five thousand one hundred men
1Sa 15: 8 utterly **d** all the people with the edge of the sword.
15: 9 all that was despised and worthless they utterly **d.**
15:15 but the rest we have utterly **d."**
15:20 and I have utterly **d** the Amalekites.
2Sa 14:11 and my son not be **d."**
22:38 I pursued my enemies and **d** them,
22:41 those who hated me, and I **d** them.
1Ki 15:29 not one that breathed, until he had **d** it,
16: 7 and also because he **d** it.
16:12 Thus Zimri **d** all the house of Baasha,
22:11 the Arameans until they are **d."**
2Ki 10:27 and **d** the temple of Baal,
13: 7 the king of Aram had **d** them and made them like
19:12 the nations that my predecessors **d**, Gozan, Haran,
19:18 and stone—and so they were **d.**
21: 3 the high places that his father Hezekiah had **d;**
21: 9 the nations had done that the LORD **d** before
1Ch 4:43 they **d** the remnant of the Amalekites
5:25 whom God had **d** before them.
2Ch 8: 8 whom the people of Israel had not **d**—
18:10 the Arameans until they are **d."**
19: 3 for you **d** the sacred poles out of the land,
24:23 **d** all the officials of the people from among them,
31: 1 until they had **d** them all.
32:14 that my ancestors utterly **d** was able
33: 9 the LORD had **d** before the people of Israel.
36:19 and **d** all its precious vessels.
Ezr 5:12 who **d** this house and carried away the people
Ne 1: 3 and its gates have been **d** by fire."
2: 3 lies waste, and its gates have been **d** by fire?"
2:13 down and its gates that had been **d** by fire.
Est 7: 4 For we have been sold, I and my people, to be **d**,
9: 6 of Susa the Jews killed and **d** five hundred people.
Job 4:20 Between morning and evening they are **d;**
8:18 If they are **d** from their place,
19:26 and after my skin has been thus **d**,
Ps 9: 5 the nations, you have **d** the wicked;
11: 3 the foundations are **d**, what can the righteous do?"
18:40 and those who hated me I **d.**
37:38 But transgressors shall be altogether **d;**

Ps 73:19 How they are **d** in a moment,
74: 3 the enemy has **d** everything in the sanctuary.
78:45 which devoured them, and frogs, which **d** them.
78:47 He **d** their vines with hail,
83:10 who were **d** at En-dor, who became dung for
Pr 14:11 The house of the wicked is **d**,
Isa 1:28 But rebels and sinners shall be **d** together,
10:27 and his yoke will be **d** from your neck.
14:20 because you have **d** your land,
23: 1 Wail, O ships of Tarshish, for your fortress is **d.**
23:14 Wail, O ships of Tarshish, for your fortress is **d.**
26:14 because you have punished and **d** them,
33: 1 Ah, you destroyer, who yourself have not been **d;**
33: 1 When you have ceased to destroy, you will be **d;**
37:12 the nations that my predecessors **d**, Gozan, Haran,
37:19 and stone—and so they were **d.**
48:19 their name would never be cut off or **d** from
Jer 4:20 Suddenly my tents are **d**, my curtains in a moment.
10:20 My tent is **d**, and all my cords are broken;
12:10 Many shepherds have **d** my vineyard,
15: 6 stretched out my hand against you and **d** you—
15: 7 I have bereaved them, I have **d** my people;
24:10 until they are utterly **d** from the land that I gave
48: 4 "Moab is **d!**" her little ones cry out.
48: 8 the valley shall perish, and the plain shall be **d,**
48:18 he has **d** your strongholds.
48:42 Moab shall be **d** as a people,
48:45 it has **d** the forehead of Moab,
49:10 His offspring are **d**, his kinsfolk
49:26 and all her soldiers shall be **d** in that day,
50:30 and all her soldiers shall be **d** on that day,
50:36 sword against her warriors, so that they may be **d!**
La 2: 2 The Lord has **d** without mercy all the dwellings
2: 5 like an enemy; he has **d** Israel;
2: 5 He has **d** all its palaces, laid in ruins
2: 6 like a garden, he has **d** his tabernacle;
2:22 those whom I bore and reared my enemy has **d.**
Eze 6: 6 your idols broken and **d**, your incense stands cut
27:32 "Who was ever **d** like Tyre in the midst of the sea?
Da 2:12 that all the wise men of Babylon be **d.**
2:44 up a kingdom that shall never be **d,**
6:26 His kingdom shall never be **d,**
7:11 its body **d** and given over to be burned with fire.
7:14 and his kingship is one that shall never be **d.**
7:26 to be consumed and totally **d.**
Hos 4: 6 My people are **d** for lack of knowledge;
10: 8 high places of Aven, the sin of Israel, shall be **d.**
10:14 and all your fortresses shall be **d,**
10:14 as Shalman **d** Beth-arbel on the day of battle
Joel 1:10 for the grain is **d**, the wine dries up,
Am 2: 9 Yet I **d** the Amorite before them,
2: 9 I **d** his fruit above, and his roots beneath.
Ob 1: 5 if plunderers by night—how you have been **d!—**
Zec 11: 3 for the thickets of the Jordan are **d!**
11: 9 what is to be **d**, let it be **d;**
Mt 9:17 and the wine is spilled, and the skins are **d;**
22: 7 He sent his troops, **d** those murderers,
Lk 5:37 and will be spilled, and the skins will be **d.**
17:27 and the flood came and **d** all of them.
17:29 it rained fire and sulfur from heaven and **d** all
Jn 11:50 for the people than to have the whole nation **d."**
Ac 13:19 he had **d** seven nations in the land of Canaan,
Ro 6: 6 with him so that the body of sin might be **d,**
1Co 8:11 for whom Christ died are **d.**
10: 9 as some of them did, and were **d** by serpents.
10:10 and were **d** by the destroyer.
15:24 after he has **d** every ruler and every authority
15:26 The last enemy to be **d** is death.
2Co 4: 9 not forsaken; struck down, but not **d;**
5: 1 For we know that if the earthly tent we live in is **d,**
2Pe 2:12 and when those creatures are **d,**
2:12 they also will be **d,**
Jude 1: 5 afterward **d** those who did not believe.
1:10 and they are **d** by those things that,
Rev 8: 9 and a third of the ships were **d.**
Tob 14:10 but Nadab fell into it himself, and was **d.**
Jdt 2: 3 not obeyed his command should be **d.**
2:24 through Mesopotamia and **d** all the fortified towns
2:27 and burned all their fields and **d** their flocks
4: 1 and how he had plundered and **d** all their temples,
4:12 and the towns they had inherited to be **d,**
5:15 by their might **d** all the inhabitants of Heshbon;
11:15 be handed over to you to be **d.**
13:14 has **d** our enemies by my hand this very night!"
AdE 3: 9 let it be decreed that they are to be **d,**
4: 1 "An innocent nation is being **d!"**
7: 4 For we have been sold, I and my people, to be **d,**
8: 6 How can I be safe if my ancestral nation is **d?"**
9:12 the capital, the Jews have **d** five hundred people.
9:16 They **d** fifteen thousand of them,
13: 6 be utterly **d** by the swords of their enemies,
16:24 accordingly shall be **d** in wrath with spear and fire.
Wis 16: 5 upon your people and they were being **d** by
16:22 the crops of their enemies were being **d** by the fire
16:27 not **d** by fire was melted when simply warmed by
18: 5 and you **d** them all together by a mighty flood.
18:12 one instant their most valued children had been **d.**
18:13 yet, when their firstborn were **d,**
Sir 6: 3 Your leaves will be devoured and your fruit **d,**
27:18 so you have **d** the friendship of your neighbor.
28:14 it has **d** strong cities, and overturned the houses
30:23 sorrow has **d** many, and no advantage ever comes
31:25 by wine-drinking, for wine has **d** many.
45:19 and in the heat of his anger they were **d;**
46: 6 and on the slope he **d** his opponents,
Bel 1:22 who **d** it and its temple.
1:28 he has **d** Bel, and killed the dragon,
1Mc 1:30 and **d** many people of Israel.
3: 8 he **d** the ungodly out of the land;
5:13 and have **d** about a thousand persons there."
5:51 He **d** every male by the edge of the sword,
7: 6 "Judas and his brothers have **d** all your Friends,
8:11 and islands, as many as ever opposed them, they **d**
9:73 and he **d** the godless out of Israel.
11: 4 and Azotus and its suburbs **d,**
15: 4 against those who have **d** our country
2Mc 4:11 and he **d** the lawful ways of living
5:14 the total of three days eighty thousand were **d,**
8: 3 the city that was being **d** and about to be leveled to
8:20 **d** one hundred twenty thousand Galatians and took
10: 2 and also **d** the sacred precincts.
10:23 he **d** more than twenty thousand in
12:19 marched out and **d** those whom Timothy had left
12:23 and **d** as many as thirty thousand.
1Es 1:56 and utterly **d** all its glorious things.
3Mc 2: 4 You **d** those who in the past committed injustice,
2: 4 whom you **d** by bringing on them
4:14 and at the end to be **d** in the space of a single day.
5:40 ordering now for a third time that they be **d,**
6: 4 you **d** together with his arrogant army
6:34 the Jews would be **d** and become food for birds,
7:15 since they had **d** the profaners.
2Es 1:11 I **d** all nations before them,
3: 9 upon the inhabitants of the world and **d** them.
3:30 those who act wickedly, and have **d** your people,
8:59 not intend that anyone should be **d;**
9:34 or what was launched or what was put in is **d,**
9:35 they are **d**, but the things that held them remain;
10:21 our altar thrown down, our temple **d;**
11:42 have **d** the homes of those who brought forth fruit,
15:18 the houses shall be **d**, and people shall be afraid.
15:45 those who survive shall serve those who have **d** it.

DESTROYER‡ (18) [DESTROY]

Ex 12:23 the **d** to enter your houses to strike you down.
Job 15:21 in prosperity the **d** will come upon them.
Isa 16: 4 be a refuge to them from the **d."**
21: 2 the betrayer betrays, and the **d** destroys.
33: 1 Ah, you **d**, who yourself have not been destroyed;
Jer 4: 7 a **d** of nations has set out;
6:26 for suddenly the **d** will come upon us.
15: 8 I have brought against the mothers of youths a **d**
48: 8 The **d** shall come upon every town,
48:15 The **d** of Moab and his towns has come up,
48:18 For the **d** of Moab has come up against you;
48:32 and your vintage the **d** has fallen.
51:56 for a **d** has come against her, against Babylon;
Joel 2:25 the hopper, the **d,** and the cutter, my great army,
1Co 10:10 and were destroyed by the **d.**
Heb 11:28 the **d** of the firstborn would not touch the firstborn
Wis 18:25 To these the **d** yielded, these he feared;
4Mc 18: 8 nor did the **d**, the deceitful serpent,

DESTROYERS (5) [DESTROY]

Isa 49:17 Your builders outdo your **d,**
Jer 15: 3 And I will appoint over them four kinds of **d,**
22: 7 I will prepare **d** against you,
51:48 for the **d** shall come against them out of the north,
51:53 from me **d** would come upon her,

DESTROYING‡ (36) [DESTROY]

Ex 21:26 strikes the eye of a male or female slave, **d** it,
Dt 2:12 **d** them and settling in their place,
2:22 by **d** the Horim before them so
3: 6 in each city utterly **d** men, women, and children.
8:20 Like the nations that the LORD is **d** before you,
13:15 utterly **d** it and everything in it—
Jos 11:11 to the sword all who were in it, utterly **d** them;
11:12 the sword, utterly **d** them, as Moses the servant of
2Sa 24:17 When David saw the angel who was **d** the people,
2Ki 19:11 of Assyria have done to all lands, **d** them utterly.
1Ch 21:12 the LORD **d** throughout all the territory of Israel.'
21:15 he said to the **d** angel, "Enough!
2Ch 20:23 the inhabitants of Mount Seir, **d** them utterly;
Est 9: 5 with the sword, slaughtering, and **d** them, and did
Ps 57: 1 until the **d** storms pass by.
78:49 indignation, and distress, a company of **d** angels.
106:23 to turn away his wrath from **d** them.
Isa 28: 2 like a storm of hail, a **d** tempest,
37:11 of Assyria have done to all lands, **d** them utterly.
Jer 46:16 to the land of our birth, because of the **d** sword."
47: 4 For the LORD is **d** the Philistines,
50:16 because of the **d** sword all of them shall return
51:25 I am against you, O **d** mountain, says the LORD,
La 2: 8 he did not withhold his hand from **d;**
Eze 9: 1 each with his **d** weapon in his hand."
22:27 shedding blood, **d** lives to get dishonest gain.
Joel 1: 4 the hopping locust left, the **d** locust has eaten.
Hab 1:17 and **d** nations without mercy?
Rev 11:18 and for **d** those who destroy the earth."
Jdt 1:15 thus **d** him once and for all.
3Mc 6:21 and began trampling and **d** them.
2Es 13:28 yet **d** the onrushing multitude that came
16:71 but plundering and **d** those who continue to fear
4Mc 1: 6 and it is not for the purpose of **d** them,
6:14 why are you so irrationally **d** yourself
11: 4 for what act of ours are you **d** us in this way?

DESTROYS (23) [DESTROY]

Ge 32: 8 "If Esau comes to the one company and **d** it,
Job 9:22 I say, he **d** both the blameless and the wicked.
12:23 He makes nations great, then **d** them;
Pr 1:32 and the complacency of fools **d** them;
6:32 he who does it **d** himself.
11: 3 but the crookedness of the treacherous **d** them.
Ecc 9:18 but one bungler **d** much good.
Isa 21: 2 the betrayer betrays, and the destroyer **d.**
Jer 51:25 says the LORD, that **d** the whole earth;
Mic 2:10 of uncleanness that **d** with a grievous destruction.
Lk 12:33 where no thief comes near and no moth **d.**
1Co 3:17 If anyone **d** God's temple,
Wis 1:11 and a lying mouth **d** the soul.
Sir 6: 4 Evil passion **d** those who have it,
10:13 unheard-of calamities, and **d** them completely.
10:16 and **d** them to the foundations of the earth.
10:17 He removes some of them and **d** them,
22:20 and one who reviles a friend **d** a friendship.
27:16 Whoever betrays secrets **d** confidence,
27:18 For as a person **d** his enemy,
35:23 until he **d** the multitude of the insolent,
2Mc 3:39 he strikes and **d** those who come to do it injury."
2Es 13:49 Therefore when he **d** the multitude of the nations

DESTRUCTION‡ (154) [DESTROY]

Ex 22:20 other than the LORD alone, shall be devoted to **d.**
Lev 27:28 that a person owns that has been devoted to **d** for
27:29 No human beings who have been devoted to **d** can
Dt 7:26 or you will be set apart for **d** like it.
7:26 for it is set apart for **d.**
13:17 not let anything devoted to **d** stick to your hand,
28:63 in bringing you to ruin and **d;**
29:23 like the **d** of Sodom and Gomorrah,
Jos 6:17 that is in it shall be devoted to the LORD for **d.**
6:18 for you, keep away from the things devoted to **d,**
6:18 and make the camp of Israel an object for **d,**
6:21 to **d** by the edge of the sword all in the city,
7:12 a thing devoted for **d** themselves.
Jdg 1:17 who inhabited Zephath, and devoted it to **d.**
21:11 that has lain with a male you shall devote to **d."**
1Sa 15:21 the best of the things devoted to **d,**
2Sa 24:16 the angel who was bringing **d** among the people,
1Ki 20:42 you have let the man go whom I had devoted to **d,**
2Ki 23:13 to the south of the Mount of **D,**
2Ch 26:16 he had become strong he grew proud, to his **d.**
Est 3: 9 let a decree be issued for their **d,**
4: 7 into the king's treasuries for the **d** of the Jews.
4: 8 of the written decree issued in Susa for their **d,**
8: 6 Or how can I bear to see the **d** of my kindred?"
Job 5:21 and shall not fear **d** when it comes.
5:22 At **d** and famine you shall laugh,
21:20 Let their own eyes see their **d,**
Ps 5: 9 in their mouths; their hearts are **d;**
37:34 you will look on the **d** of the wicked.
52: 2 you are plotting **d.**
91: 6 or the **d** that wastes at noonday.
92: 7 they are doomed to **d** forever,
107:20 and delivered them from **d.**
Pr 10:29 of the LORD is a stronghold for the upright, but **d**
13:13 Those who despise the word bring **d**
16:18 Pride goes before **d**, and a haughty spirit before
18:12 Before **d** one's heart is haughty,
19:18 do not set your heart on their **d.**
Isa 10:22 **D** is decreed, overflowing with righteousness.
10:25 and my anger will be directed to their **d.**
13: 6 it will come like **d** from the Almighty!
14:23 and I will sweep it with the broom of **d,**
15: 5 on the road to Horonaim they raise a cry of **d;**
16: 4 When the oppressor is no more, and **d** has ceased,
22: 4 to comfort me for the **d** of my beloved people.
28:22 a decree of **d** from the Lord GOD of hosts upon
30:28 to sift the nations with the sieve of **d,**
38:17 but you have held back my life from the pit of **d,**
43:28 I delivered Jacob to utter **d**, and Israel to reviling.
51:13 fury of the oppressor, who is bent on **d.**
51:19 devastation and **d**, famine and sword—
59: 7 desolation and **d** are in their highways.
60:18 devastation or **d** within your borders;
Jer 4: 6 from the north, and a great **d.**
6: 1 for evil looms out of the north, and great **d.**
6: 7 violence and **d** are heard within her;
17:18 destroy them with double **d!**
20: 8 I must cry out, I must shout, "Violence and **d!"**
27: 8 until I have completed its **d** by his hand.
48: 3 a cry from Horonaim, "Desolation and great **d!"**
50:22 The noise of battle is in the land, and great **d!**
La 2:11 on the ground because of the **d** of my people,
3:47 and pitfall have come upon us, devastation and **d.**
3:48 with rivers of tears because of the **d** of my people.
4:10 they became their food in the **d** of my people.
Eze 5:16 arrows for **d**, which I will let loose to destroy you,
25:15 and with malice of heart took revenge in **d;**
Da 8:24 in power, shall cause fearful **d**, and shall succeed
11:44 with great fury to bring ruin and complete **d**
Hos 7:13 **D** to them, for they have rebelled against me!
8: 4 and gold they made idols for their own **d.**
9: 6 For even if they escape **d,**
12:10 and through the prophets I will bring **d.**
13:14 O Sheol, where is your **d?**
Joel 1:15 and as **d** from the Almighty it comes.
Am 5: 9 who makes **d** flash out against the strong,
5: 9 so that **d** comes upon the fortress.
Mic 2:10 of uncleanness that destroys with a grievous **d.**
Na 2:10 Devastation, desolation, and **d!**
Hab 1: 3 **D** and violence are before me;
2:17 the **d** of the animals will terrify you—
Zec 14:11 for never again shall it be doomed to **d;**
Mt 7:13 gate is wide and the road is easy that leads to **d,**

Ro 9:22 the objects of wrath that are made for **d;**
1Co 5: 5 you are to hand this man over to Satan for the **d** of
Php 1:28 For them this is evidence of their **d,**
3:19 Their end is **d;** their god is the belly;
1Th 5: 3 then sudden **d** will come upon them,
2Th 1: 9 These will suffer the punishment of eternal **d,**
2: 3 the lawless one is revealed, the one destined for **d.**
1Ti 6: 9 that plunge people into ruin and **d.**
2Pe 2: 1 bringing swift **d** on themselves.
2: 3 has not been idle, and their **d** is not asleep.
3: 7 until the day of judgment and **d** of the godless.
3:16 the ignorant and unstable twist to their own **d,**
Rev 17: 8 to ascend from the bottomless pit and go to **d.**
17:11 but it belongs to the seven, and it goes to **d.**
Tob 14:15 Before he died he heard of the **d** of Nineveh,
Jdt 11:22 and bring **d** on those who have despised my lord.
13:16 that it was my face that seduced him to his **d,**
14:13 down against us to give battle, to their utter **d.**"
AdE 4: 7 the royal treasury to bring about the **d** of the Jews.
4: 8 a copy of what had been posted in Susa for their **d,**
16:13 and with intricate craft and deceit asked for the **d**
16:21 be a joy for his chosen people instead of a day of **d**
16:23 that it may be a reminder of **d** for those who plot
Wis 1:12 or bring on **d** by the works of your hands;
3: 3 and their going from us to be their **d;**
5: 7 We took our fill of the paths of lawlessness and **d,**
12:12 Who will accuse you for the **d** of nations
18: 7 The deliverance of the righteous and the **d**
Sir 9: 9 and in blood you may be plunged into **d.**
31: 6 and their **d** has met them face to face.
36:11 and may those who harm your people meet **d.**
39:30 and the sword that punishes the ungodly with **d.**
41:10 so the ungodly go from curse to **d.**
48: 6 You sent kings down to **d,** and famous men,
51: 2 and helper and have delivered me from **d** and from
51:12 for you saved me from **d** and rescued me in time
Bar 4: 6 It was not for **d** that you were sold to the nations,
4:25 but you will soon see their **d** and will tread
Bel 1:42 threw into the den those who had attempted his **d,**
1Mc 3:42 to do to the people to cause their final **d.**
4:32 let them tremble in their **d.**
5: 5 against them, vowed their complete **d,**
15:31 of silver for the **d** that you have caused
2Mc 5:13 there was massacre of young and old, **d** of boys,
8: 4 also the lawless **d** of the innocent babies and
8:35 having succeeded chiefly in the **d**
12:27 After the rout and **d** of these,
13: 6 There they all push to **d** anyone guilty of sacrilege
3Mc 4: 2 the unexpected **d** that had suddenly been decreed
5: 5 that the whole nation would experience its final **d.**
5:20 in the same way for the **d** of the lawless Jews!"
5:38 now once more for the **d** of the Jews tomorrow!"
5:47 and pitiful **d** of the aforementioned people.
6:11 not the vain-minded praise their vanities at the **d**
6:23 and saw them all fallen headlong to **d,**
6:30 in which they had expected to meet their **d.**
6:31 that had been prepared for their **d** and burial.
6:38 and their **d** was set for the fifth to the seventh
2Es 1:16 not exulted in my name at the **d** of your enemies,
3: 1 In the thirtieth year after the **d** of the city,
4:23 and the law of our ancestors has been brought to **d**
7:*131* [61] Therefore there shall not be grief at their **d,**
8:29 Do not will the **d** of those who have the ways
8:38 or about their death, their judgment, or their **d;**
10:48 this was the **d** that befell Jerusalem.
15: 5 the sword and famine, death and **d,**
15:39 that was to cause **d** by the east wind shall
15:49 bringing ruin to your houses, bringing **d** and death.
16: 2 lament for them; for your **d** is at hand.
4Mc 10:15 by the eternal **d** of the tyrant,
15:24 Although she witnessed the **d** of seven children

DESTRUCTIVE (3) [DESTROY]

Jer 51: 1 I am going to stir up a **d** wind against Babylon and
2Pe 2: 1 who will secretly bring in **d** opinions.
Wis 1:14 and there is no **d** poison in them,

DETACHMENT (2)

Jn 18: 3 So Judas brought a **d** of soldiers together
1Mc 4:19 a **d** appeared, coming out of the hills.

DETAIL (3) [DETAILED, DETAILS]

Heb 9: 5 Of these things we cannot speak now in **d.**
AdE 11:12 seeking all day to understand it in every **d.**
3Mc 4:13 not omitting any **d** of their punishment.

DETAILED (1) [DETAIL]

1Mc 4:41 Then Judas **d** men to fight against those in

DETAILS (6) [DETAIL]

2Ki 16:10 and its pattern, exact in all its **d.**
2Mc 2:28 the responsibility for exact **d** to the compiler,
2:30 and to take trouble with **d,**
11:20 And concerning such matters and their **d,**
14: 9 O king, with the **d** of this matter,
4Mc 4: 4 When Apollonius learned the **d** of these things,

DETAIN (3) [DETAINED, DETAINING]

Jdg 13:15 "Allow us to **d** you, and prepare a kid for you."
13:16 angel of the LORD said to Manoah, "If you **d** me,
Ac 24: 4 to **d** you no further, I beg you to hear us briefly

DETAINED (2) [DETAIN]

1Sa 21: 7 of the servants of Saul was there that day, **d** before
Tob 10: 2 "Is it possible that he has been **d?**

DETAINING (1) [DETAIN]

1Mc 13:15 with the offices he held, that we are **d** him.

DETECT (1) [DETECTED, DETECTS]

Ps 19:12 But who can **d** their errors?

DETECTED (2) [DETECT]

Gal 6: 1 My friends, if anyone is **d** in a transgression,
3Mc 3:29 Every place **d** sheltering a Jew is to be made

DETECTS (1) [DETECT]

Sir 36:24 so an intelligent mind **d** false words.

DETERMINATE (KJV) See DEFINITE

DETERMINATION (1) [DETERMINE]

Da 11:25 He shall stir up his power and **d** against the king of

DETERMINE (8) [DETERMINATION, DETERMINED, DETERMINES]

Ex 21:22 paying as much as the judges **d.**
22: 8 to **d** whether or not the owner had laid hands on
Lev 14:57 to **d** when it is unclean and when it is clean.
Job 34: 4 let us **d** among ourselves what is good.
Ro 2:18 and **d** what is best because you are instructed in
Php 1:10 to help you to **d** what is best,
1Mc 5:16 to **d** what they should do
8:30 If after these terms are in effect both parties shall **d**

DETERMINED (48) [DETERMINE]

Ge 6:13 "I have **d** to make an end of all flesh,
Ru 1:18 When Naomi saw that she was **d** to go with her,
1Sa 8:19 but we are **d** to have a king over us,
20: 7 he is angry, then know that evil has been **d** by him.
2Sa 13:32 This has been **d** by Absalom from
1Ki 7:47 the weight of the bronze was not **d.**
2Ki 19:25 Have you not heard that I **d** it long ago?
2Ch 4:18 so that the weight of the bronze was not **d.**
25:16 but said, "I know that God has **d** to destroy you,
Ne 9:17 but they stiffened their necks and **d** to return
Est 7: 7 for he saw that the king had **d** to destroy him.
Job 14: 5 Since their days are **d,** and the number
38: 5 Who **d** its measurements—surely you know!
Isa 37:26 Have you not heard that I **d** it long ago?
Jer 38:21 But if you are **d** not to surrender,
42:15 If you are **d** to enter Egypt and go to settle there,
42:17 All the people who have **d** to go to Egypt
44:11 I am **d** to bring disaster on you,
44:12 I will take the remnant of Judah who are **d** to come
44:25 'We are **d** to perform the vows that we have made,
La 2: 8 LORD **d** to lay in ruins the wall of daughter Zion;
Da 6:14 He was **d** to save Daniel,
11:36 for what is **d** shall be done.
Hos 5:11 because he was **d** to go after vanity.
Lk 22:22 For the Son of Man is going as it has been **d,**
Ac 5:28 and you are **d** to bring this man's blood on us."
11:29 The disciples **d** that according to their ability,
1Co 7:37 has **d** in his own mind to keep her as his fiancée,
1Th 2: 8 that we are **d** to share with you not only the gospel
Jdt 11:12 to kill their livestock and have **d** to use all
12: 4 the Lord carries out by my hand what he has **d.**"
AdE 11:12 Mordecai saw in this dream what God had **d** to do,
12: 6 **d** to injure Mordecai and his people because of
13: 2 I have **d** to settle the lives of my subjects
Wis 8: 9 Therefore I **d** to take her to live with me,
Sir 16:26 and, in making them, **d** their boundaries,
1Mc 1:16 he **d** to become king of the land of Egypt,
3:31 then he **d** to go to Persia and collect the revenues
4:59 and all the assembly of Israel **d** that every year at
5: 2 and they **d** to destroy the descendants
11:33 We have **d** to do good to the nation of the Jews,
16:13 he **d** to get control of the country,
2Mc 8:10 Nicanor **d** to make up for the king the tribute due
13:13 he **d** to march out and decide the matter by
15: 6 and arrogance had **d** to erect a public monument
15:17 they **d** not to carry on a campaign but
3Mc 1: 2 **d** to carry out the plot he had devised,
1:26 **d** to bring the aforesaid plan to a conclusion.

DETERMINES (1) [DETERMINE]

Ps 147: 4 He **d** the number of the stars;

DETERRED (1)

Sir 32:18 an insolent and proud person will not be **d** by fear.

DETEST (4) [DETESTABLE, DETESTED, DETESTS]

Nu 21: 5 and we **d** this miserable food."
Dt 7:26 You must utterly **d** and abhor it,
Wis 11:24 and **d** none of the things that you have made,
Sir 7:26 but do not trust yourself to one whom you **d.**

DETESTABLE (24) [DETEST]

Lev 11:10 that are in the waters—they are **d** to you
11:11 and **d** they shall remain.
11:11 and their carcasses you shall regard as **d.**
11:12 in the waters that does not have fins and scales is **d**
11:13 These you shall regard as **d** among the birds.
11:20 All winged insects that walk upon all fours are **d**
11:23 that have four feet are **d** to you.
11:41 All creatures that swarm upon the earth are **d;**
11:42 you shall not eat; for they are **d.**
11:43 You shall not make yourselves **d** with any creature
Dt 29:17 You have seen their **d** things,
Jer 16:18 with the carcasses of their **d** idols,
Eze 5:11 with all your **d** things and
7:20 they made their abominable images, their **d** things;
11:18 from it all its **d** things and all its abominations.
11:21 as for those whose heart goes after their **d** things
20: 7 Cast away the **d** things your eyes feast on,
20: 8 of them cast away the **d** things their eyes feasted
20:30 and go astray after their **d** things?
37:23 with their idols and their **d** things,
Hos 9:10 and became **d** like the thing they loved.
Tit 1:16 They are **d,** disobedient, unfit for any good work.
Wis 12: 4 you hated for their **d** practices,
Sir 19:23 There is a cleverness that is **d,**

DETESTED (4) [DETEST]

Zec 11: 8 with them, and they also **d** me.
Sir 20: 5 while others are **d** for being talkative.
20: 8 Whoever talks too much is **d,**
1Mc 7:26 who hated and **d** Israel, and he commanded him

DETESTS (1) [DETEST]

Sir 50:25 Two nations my soul **d,** and the third is not even

DEUEL (4)

Nu 1:14 From Gad, Eliasaph son of **D.**
7:42 On the sixth day Eliasaph son of **D,**
7:47 This was the offering of Eliasaph son of **D.**
10:20 of the tribe of Gad was Eliasaph son of **D.**

DEVASTATE (3) [DEVASTATED, DEVASTATION, DEVASTATIONS, DEVASTATOR]

Lev 26:32 I will **d** the land, so that your enemies who come
Zec 11: 6 and they shall **d** the earth,
2Es 15:30 with their tusks they shall **d** a portion of the land

DEVASTATED‡ (7) [DEVASTATE]

Isa 49:19 and your desolate places and your **d** land—
Jer 25:37 and the peaceful folds are **d,**
Joel 1:10 The fields are **d,** the ground mourns;
Na 3: 7 "Nineveh is **d;** who will bemoan her?"
1Mc 15: 4 and those who have **d** many cities in my kingdom,
15:29 You have **d** their territory,
2Es 15:60 when they return from **d** Babylon.

DEVASTATION (8) [DEVASTATE]

Dt 29:22 the **d** of that land and the afflictions with which
1Ch 21:12 or three months of **d** by your foes,
Isa 51:19 **d** and destruction, famine and sword—
60:18 **d** or destruction within your borders;
La 3:47 and pitfall have come upon us, **d** and destruction.
Da 9: 2 must be fulfilled for the **d** of Jerusalem, namely,
Na 2:10 **D,** desolation, and destruction!
Zep 1:15 a day of ruin and **d,** a day of darkness and gloom,

DEVASTATIONS (2) [DEVASTATE]

Isa 61: 4 they shall raise up the former **d;**
61: 4 the **d** of many generations.

DEVASTATOR (1) [DEVASTATE]

Ps 137: 8 O daughter Babylon, you **d!**

DEVIATED (1)

1Ti 1: 6 Some people have **d** from these and turned

DEVICES (10) [DEVISE]

Job 5:12 He frustrates the **d** of the crafty,
Ps 26:10 those in whose hands are evil **d,**
37: 7 over those who carry out evil **d.**
Pr 1:31 of their way and be sated with their own **d.**
Isa 32: 7 they devise wicked **d** to ruin the poor
65: 2 in a way that is not good, following their own **d;**
3Mc 5:45 and had been equipped with frightful **d,**
2Es 9:20 I saw that my earth was in peril because of the **d**
15:48 that hateful one in all her deeds and **d.**
4Mc 8:15 the inducements and saw the dreadful **d,**

DEVIL (36) [DEVIL'S, DEVILISH]

Mt 4: 1 into the wilderness to be tempted by the **d.**
4: 5 the **d** took him to the holy city and placed him on
4: 8 the **d** took him to a very high mountain
4:11 Then the **d** left him, and suddenly angels came
13:39 and the enemy who sowed them is the **d;**
25:41 the eternal fire prepared for the **d** and his angels;
Lk 4: 2 where for forty days he was tempted by the **d.**
4: 3 The **d** said to him, "If you are the Son of God,
4: 5 the **d** led him up and showed him in an instant all
4: 6 the **d** said to him, "To you I will give their glory
4: 9 Then the **d** took him to Jerusalem,

Lk 4:13 When the **d** had finished every test,
8:12 then the **d** comes and takes away the word
Jn 6:70 Yet one of you is a **d**."
8:44 You are from your father the **d**,
13: 2 The **d** had already put it into the heart of Judas son
Ac 10:38 and healing all who were oppressed by the **d**,
13:10 of the **d**, you enemy of all righteousness, full
Eph 4:27 and do not make room for the **d**.
6:11 be able to stand against the wiles of the **d**.
1Ti 3: 6 and fall into the condemnation of the **d**.
3: 7 not fall into disgrace and the snare of the **d**.
2Ti 2:26 and that they may escape from the snare of the **d**,
Heb 2:14 the one who has the power of death, that is, the **d**,
Jas 4: 7 Resist the **d**, and he will flee from you.
1Pe 5: 8 a roaring lion your adversary the **d** prowls around,
1Jn 3: 8 Everyone who commits sin is a child of the **d**;
3: 8 for the **d** has been sinning from the beginning.
3: 8 to destroy the works of the **d**.
3:10 and the children of the **d** are revealed in this way:
Jude 1: 9 when the archangel Michael contended with the **d**
Rev 2:10 the **d** is about to throw some of you into prison so
12: 9 that ancient serpent, who is called the **D** and Satan,
12:12 for the **d** has come down to you with great wrath,
20: 2 that ancient serpent, who is the **D** and Satan,
20:10 And the **d** who had deceived them was thrown into

DEVIL'S (1) [DEVIL]
Wis 2:24 but through the **d** envy death entered the world,

DEVILISH (1) [DEVIL]
Jas 3:15 but is earthly, unspiritual, **d**.

DEVILS (KJV) See DEMONIACS, DEMONIC SPIRITS, DEMONS, GOAT-DEMONS

DEVIOUS (4) [DEVISE]
Pr 2:15 and who are **d** in their ways.
4:24 and put **d** talk far from you.
14: 2 but one who is **d** in conduct despises him.
Jer 17: 9 The heart is **d** above all else;

DEVISE (21) [DEVICES, DEVIOUS, DEVISED, DEVISES, DEVISING]
Ex 31: 4 to **d** artistic designs, to work in gold, silver,
35:32 to **d** artistic designs, to work in gold, silver,
2Sa 14:14 he will **d** plans so as not to keep
Ps 21:11 If they plan evil against you, if they **d** mischief,
35: 4 be turned back and confounded who **d** evil
58: 2 No, in your hearts you **d** wrongs;
Pr 12: 2 but those who **d** evil he condemns.
19:21 The human mind may **d** many plans,
24: 2 for their minds **d** violence,
Isa 32: 7 they **d** wicked devices to ruin the poor
Eze 11: 2 these are the men who **d** iniquity
38:10 and you will **d** an evil scheme.
Da 11:24 He shall **d** plans against strongholds,
Mic 2: 1 Alas for those who **d** wickedness and evil deeds
Zec 7:10 do not **d** evil in your hearts against one another.
8:17 do not **d** evil in your hearts against one another,
Sir 7:12 Do not **d** a lie against your brother,
11:33 Beware of scoundrels, for they **d** evil,
13:26 but to **d** proverbs requires painful thinking.
17:31 So flesh and blood **d** evil.
3Mc 7: 9 For you should know that if we **d** any evil

DEVISED (22) [DEVISE]
1Ki 2:23 Adonijah has **d** this scheme at the risk of his life!
12:33 in the month that he alone had **d**;
2Ki 12:20 His servants arose, **d** a conspiracy,
Est 8: 3 of Haman the Agagite and the plot that he had **d**
8: 5 be written to revoke the letters **d** by Haman son
9:25 in writing that the wicked plot that he had **d**
Ps 10: 2 let them be caught in the schemes they have **d**.
Ecc 7:29 but they have **d** many schemes.
Jer 11:19 not know it was against me that they **d** schemes,
Da 11:25 for plots shall be **d** against him
Mic 6: 5 remember now what King Balak of Moab **d**,
Hab 2:10 You have **d** shame for your house
Mt 28:12 they **d** a plan to give a large sum of money to
2Pe 1:16 not follow cleverly **d** myths when we made known
AdE 9:25 but the wicked plot he had **d** against
Wis 3:14 and who has not **d** wicked things against the Lord;
1Mc 13:29 For the pyramids he **d** an elaborate setting,
2Mc 7:23 who shaped the beginning of humankind and **d**
3Mc 1: 2 determined to carry out the plot he had **d**,
5:28 a forgetfulness of the things he had previously **d**.
6:22 because of the things that he had **d** beforehand.
2Es 7:22 they **d** for themselves vain thoughts,

DEVISES (1) [DEVISE]
Pr 6:18 a heart that **d** wicked plans,

DEVISING (8) [DEVISE]
Pr 6:14 with perverted mind **d** evil,
24: 9 The **d** of folly is sin,
30:32 exalting yourself, or if you have been **d** evil,
Jer 18:11 I am a potter shaping evil against you and **d** a plan
Mic 2: 3 Now, I am **d** against this family an evil
1Mc 11: 8 and he kept **d** wicked designs against Alexander.
3Mc 5:22 as in **d** all sorts of insults for those they thought to
6:24 by secretly **d** acts of no advantage to the kingdom.

DEVOID (4)
Job 4:21 and they die **d** of wisdom.'
Jude 1:19 It is these worldly people, **d** of the Spirit,
AdE 16:10 and quite **d** of our kindliness),
Sir 16:23 Such are the thoughts of one **d** of understanding;

DEVOTE‡ (13) [DEVOTED, DEVOTEES, DEVOTES, DEVOTING, DEVOTION]
Jdg 21:11 with a male you shall **d** to destruction."
1Ki 8:61 **d** yourselves completely to the LORD our God,
2Ch 31: 4 they might **d** themselves to the law of the LORD.
Hos 4:10 they have forsaken the LORD to **d** themselves to
Mic 4:13 and shall **d** their gain to the LORD,
Ac 6: 4 will **d** ourselves to prayer and to serving
1Co 7: 5 for a set time, to **d** yourselves to prayer,
Col 4: 2 **D** yourselves to prayer, keeping alert in it
1Ti 4:15 Put these things into practice, **d** yourself to them,
Tit 3: 8 to believe in God may be careful to **d** themselves
3:14 to **d** themselves to good works in order
Sir Pr: 3 that I should myself **d** some diligence and labor to
7:20 or hired laborers who **d** themselves to their task.

DEVOTED (38) [DEVOTE]
Ex 22:20 to any god, other than the LORD alone, shall be **d**
Lev 27:21 it shall be holy to the LORD as a **d** field;
27:28 that a person owns that has been **d** to destruction
27:28 every **d** thing is most holy to the LORD.
27:29 No human beings who have been **d**
Nu 18:14 Every **d** thing in Israel shall be yours.
Dt 13:17 Do not let anything **d** to destruction stick
Jos 6:17 in it shall be **d** to the LORD for destruction.
6:18 you, keep away from the things **d** to destruction,
6:18 not to covet and take any of the **d** things and make
6:21 Then they **d** to destruction by the edge of
7: 1 the Israelites broke faith in regard to the **d** things:
7: 1 of the tribe of Judah, took some of the **d** things;
7:11 They have taken some of the **d** things;
7:12 a thing **d** for destruction themselves.
7:12 unless you destroy the **d** things from among you.
7:13 the God of Israel, "There are **d** things among you,
7:13 until you take away the **d** things from
7:15 the one who is taken as having the **d** things shall
22:20 of Zerah break faith in the matter of the **d** things,
Jdg 1:17 the Canaanites who inhabited Zephath, and **d** it
1Sa 15:21 the best of the things **d** to destruction,
1Ki 20:42 'Because you have let the man go whom I had **d**
1Ch 2: 7 who transgressed in the matter of the **d** thing;
Ne 5:16 Indeed, I **d** myself to the work on this wall,
Ps 86: 2 Preserve my life, for I am **d** to you;
Eze 44:29 and every **d** thing in Israel shall be theirs.
Mt 6:24 or be **d** to the one and despise the other.
Lk 16:13 or be **d** to the one and despise the other.
Ac 2:42 They **d** themselves to the apostles' teaching
9:36 She was **d** to good works and acts of charity.
1Co 16:15 they have **d** themselves to the service of the saints;
1Ti 5:10 and **d** herself to doing good in every way.
Sir Pr: 1 who had **d** himself especially to the reading of
46: 6 for he was a **d** follower of the Mighty One.
1Mc 4:42 He chose blameless priests **d** to the law,
2Es 13:55 for you have **d** your life to wisdom,
4Mc 15: 5 they are more **d** to their children.

DEVOTEES (1) [DEVOTE]
Isa 44:11 Look, all its **d** shall be put to shame;

DEVOTES (1) [DEVOTE]
Sir 38:34 How different the one who **d** himself to the study

DEVOTING (3) [DEVOTE]
Ac 1:14 All these were constantly **d** themselves to prayer,
Wis 14:30 about God in **d** themselves to idols,
2Mc 2:28 while **d** our effort to arriving at the outlines of

DEVOTION (9) [DEVOTE]
1Ch 29: 3 because of my **d** to the house of my God I give it
Est 2:17 of all the virgins she won his favor and **d**,
Jer 2: 2 I remember the **d** of your youth,
Ac 11:23 to remain faithful to the Lord with steadfast **d**;
1Co 7:35 but to promote good order and unhindered **d** to
2Co 11: 3 be led astray from a sincere and pure **d** to Christ.
Jdt 8: 8 for she feared God with great **d**.
4Mc 14: 6 as though moved by an immortal spirit of **d**,
15:17 who alone gave birth to such complete **d**!

DEVOUR‡ (76) [DEVOURED, DEVOURING, DEVOURS]
Ex 10: 5 They shall **d** the last remnant left you after
10: 5 and they shall **d** every tree of yours that grows in
Lev 26:38 and the land of your enemies shall **d** you.
Nu 24: 8 he shall **d** the nations that are his foes
Dt 7:16 You shall **d** all the peoples that
32:42 and my sword shall **d** flesh—
Jdg 9:15 let fire come out of the bramble and **d** the cedars
9:20 and **d** the lords of Shechem, and Beth-millo;
9:20 and from Beth-millo, and **d** Abimelech."
2Ch 7:13 or command the locust to **d** the land,
Job 20:26 a fire fanned by no one will **d** them;
Ps 27: 2 When evildoers assail me to **d** my flesh—
52: 4 You love all words that **d**, O deceitful tongue.
57: 4 down among lions that greedily **d** human prey;
Pr 30:14 to **d** the poor from off the earth,
Isa 1: 7 in your very presence aliens **d** your land;
10:17 it will burn and **d** his thorns and briers in one day.
31: 8 and a sword, not of humans, shall **d** him;
56: 9 all you wild animals in the forest, come to **d**!
Jer 5:14 and this people wood, and the fire shall **d** them.
8:16 They come and **d** the land and all that fills it,
12: 9 assemble all the wild animals; bring them to **d** her.
15: 3 and the wild animals of the earth to **d** and destroy.
17:27 it shall **d** the palaces of Jerusalem and shall not
21:14 and it shall **d** all that is around it.
30:16 Therefore all who **d** you shall be devoured,
46:10 The sword shall **d** and be sated,
46:14 for the sword shall **d** those around you."
49:27 and it shall **d** the strongholds of Ben-hadad.
50:32 and it will **d** everything around him.
Eze 7:15 famine and pestilence **d** them.
20:47 a fire in you, and it shall **d** every green tree in you
34:28 nor shall the animals of the land **d** them;
35:12 "They are laid desolate, they are given us to **d**."
36:13 Because they say to you, "You **d** people,
36:14 therefore you shall no longer **d** people
Da 7: 5 and was told, "Arise, **d** many bodies!"
7:23 it shall **d** the whole earth, and trample it down,
Hos 2:12 and the wild animals shall **d** them.
5: 7 the new moon shall **d** them along with their fields.
7: 7 of them are hot as an oven, and they **d** their rulers.
7: 9 Foreigners **d** his strength, but he does not know it;
8: 7 if it were to yield, foreigners would **d** it.
8:14 and it shall **d** his strongholds.
13: 8 there I will **d** them like a lion,
Am 1: 4 and it shall **d** the strongholds of Ben-hadad.
1: 7 fire that shall **d** its strongholds.
1:10 fire that shall **d** its strongholds.
1:12 and it shall **d** the strongholds of Bozrah.
1:14 fire that shall **d** its strongholds,
2: 2 and it shall **d** the strongholds of Kerioth,
2: 5 and it shall **d** the strongholds of Jerusalem.
5: 6 and it will **d** Bethel, with no one to quench it.
Na 2:13 and the sword shall **d** your young lions;
3:15 There the fire will **d** you,
3:15 It will **d** you like the locust.
Hab 1: 8 they fly like an eagle swift to **d**.
3:14 as if ready to **d** the poor who were in hiding.
Zec 9:15 and they shall **d** and tread down the slingers;
11: 1 O Lebanon, so that fire may **d** your cedars!
11: 9 let those that are left **d** the flesh of one another!"
12: 6 and they shall **d** to the right and to the left all
Mk 12:40 They **d** widows' houses and for the sake
Lk 20:47 They **d** widows' houses and for the sake
Gal 5:15 If, however, you bite and **d** one another,
1Pe 5: 8 looking for someone to **d**.
Rev 12: 4 so that he might **d** her child as soon as it was born.
17:16 they will **d** her flesh and burn her up with fire.
Sir 51: 3 from grinding teeth about to **d** me,
LtJ 6:20 when crawling creatures from the earth **d** them
Bel 1:32 so that they would **d** Daniel.
2Es 6:57 domineer over us and **d** us.
11:35 the head on the right side **d** the one on the left.
12:27 for the two who remained, the sword shall **d** them.
12:28 the sword of one shall **d** him who was with him;
15:62 They shall **d** you and your cities,

DEVOURED (43) [DEVOUR]
Ge 37:20 then we shall say that a wild animal has **d** him,
37:33 A wild animal has **d** him;
Nu 21:28 It **d** Ar of Moab, and swallowed up the heights
26:10 when the fire **d** two hundred fifty men;
Ps 78:45 which **d** them, and frogs, which destroyed them.
78:63 Fire **d** their young men,
79: 7 they have **d** Jacob and laid waste his habitation.
105:35 they **d** all the vegetation in their land,
Isa 1:20 you shall be **d** by the sword;
3:14 It is you who have **d** the vineyard;
5: 5 I will remove its hedge, and it shall be **d**;
9:12 and they **d** Israel with open mouth.
9:20 and they **d** on the left, but were not satisfied;
9:20 they **d** the flesh of their own kindred;
9:21 Manasseh **d** Ephraim, and Ephraim Manasseh,
Jer 2:30 Your own sword **d** your prophets like
3:24 "But from our youth the shameful thing has **d** all
10:25 for they have **d** Jacob; they have **d** him
30:16 Therefore all who devour you shall be **d**,
50: 7 All who found them have **d** them,
50:17 First the king of Assyria **d** it,
51:34 "King Nebuchadrezzar of Babylon has **d** me,
La 2:16 they cry: "We have **d** her!
Eze 16:20 and these you sacrificed to them to be **d**.
19: 3 to catch prey; he **d** humans.
19: 6 to catch prey; he **d** people.
22:25 lion tearing the prey; they have **d** human lives;
23:25 and your survivors shall be **d** by fire.
33:27 to the wild animals to be **d**;
39: 4 of every kind and to the wild animals to be **d**.
Da 7:19 and which **d** and broke in pieces,
Joel 1:19 For fire has **d** the pastures of the wilderness,
1:20 and fire has **d** the pastures of the wilderness.
Am 4: 9 the locust **d** your fig trees and your olive trees;
7: 4 and it **d** the great deep and was eating up the land.
Na 3:13 fire has **d** the bars of your gates.
Zec 9: 4 and it shall be **d** by fire.
Lk 15:30 who has **d** your property with prostitutes,
Jdt 10:12 they are about to be handed over to you to be **d**.
AdE 11:11 the lowly were exalted and **d** those held in honor.
Sir 6: 3 Your leaves will be **d** and your fruit destroyed,
2Es 11:31 the head turned with those that were with it and **d**

DEVOURER See Index to Footnotes

DEVOURING (14) [DEVOUR]
Ge 49:27 in the morning **d** the prey,
Ex 24:17 the glory of the LORD was like a **d** fire on the top
Dt 4:24 the LORD your God is a **d** fire, a jealous God.
9: 3 the one who crosses over before you as a **d** fire;
2Sa 2:26 "Is the sword to keep **d** forever?
22: 9 and **d** fire from his mouth;
Ps 18: 8 and **d** fire from his mouth;
50: 3 before him is a **d** fire,
Isa 29: 6 and the flame of a **d** fire.
30:27 and his tongue is like a **d** fire;
30:30 in furious anger and a flame of **d** fire,
33:14 "Who among us can live with the **d** fire?
Da 7: 7 It had great iron teeth and was **d**,
Joel 2: 5 like the crackling of a flame of fire **d** the stubble,

DEVOURS (11) [DEVOUR]
Nu 13:32 through as spies is a land that **d** its inhabitants;
Dt 32:22 it **d** the earth and its increase,
2Sa 11:25 for the sword **d** now one and now another;
Pr 19:28 and the mouth of the wicked **d** iniquity.
21:20 in the house of the wise, but the fool **d** it.
Isa 5:24 Therefore, as the tongue of fire **d** the stubble,
24: 6 Therefore a curse **d** the earth,
Jer 12:12 for the sword of the LORD **d** from one end of
Hos 11: 6 and **d** because of their schemes.
Joel 2: 3 Fire **d** in front of them,
Zec 11:16 but **d** the flesh of the fat ones,

DEVOUT‡ (28)
Isa 57: 1 the **d** are taken away, while no one understands.
Lk 2:25 this man was righteous and **d**,
Ac 2: 5 Now there were **d** Jews from every nation
8: 2 **D** men buried Stephen and made loud lamentation
10: 2 a **d** man who feared God with all his household;
10: 7 he called two of his slaves and a **d** soldier from
13:43 and **d** converts to Judaism followed Paul
13:50 But the Jews incited the **d** women of high standing
17: 4 the **d** Greeks and not a few of the leading women.
17:17 in the synagogue with the Jews and the **d** persons,
22:12 a **d** man according to the law and well spoken of
Tit 1: 8 a lover of goodness, prudent, upright, **d**,
Sir 11:17 The Lord's gift remains with the **d**,
12: 2 Do good to the **d**, and you will be repaid—
12: 4 Give to the **d**, but do not help the sinner.
13:17 No more has a sinner with the **d**.
4Mc 1: 1 whether **d** reason is sovereign over the emotions.
6:31 then, **d** reason is sovereign over the emotions.
7: 4 the besiegers with the shield of his **d** reason.
7:16 most certainly **d** reason is governor of
8: 1 a philosophy in accordance with **d** reason,
11:23 of tortures and enemy of those who are truly **d**.
13: 1 everyone must concede that **d** reason is sovereign
15:23 But **d** reason, giving her heart a man's courage in
16: 1 it must be admitted that **d** reason is sovereign over
16: 4 so many and such great emotions by **d** reason.
17:22 through the blood of those **d** ones and their death
18: 2 knowing that **d** reason is master of all emotions,

DEW‡ (42) [DEWS]
Ge 27:28 May God give you of the **d** of heaven,
27:39 and away from the **d** of heaven on high.
Ex 16:13 and in the morning there was a layer of **d** around
16:14 When the layer of **d** lifted,
Nu 11: 9 When the **d** fell on the camp in the night,
Dt 32: 2 my speech condense like the **d**;
33:28 where the heavens drop down **d**.
Jdg 6:37 if there is **d** on the fleece alone,
6:38 he wrung enough **d** from the fleece to fill a bowl
6:39 and on all the ground let there be **d**."
6:40 and on all the ground there was **d**.
2Sa 1:21 let there be no **d** or rain upon you,
17:12 we shall light on him as the **d** falls on the ground;
1Ki 17: 1 there shall be neither **d** nor rain these years,
Job 29:19 with the **d** all night on my branches;
29:22 and my word dropped upon them like **d**.
38:28 or who has begotten the drops of **d**?
Ps 110: 3 From the womb of the morning, like **d**,
133: 3 It is like the **d** of Hermon,
Pr 3:20 and the clouds drop down the **d**.
19:12 but his favor is like **d** on the grass.
SS 5: 2 for my head is wet with **d**,
Isa 18: 4 like a cloud of **d** in the heat of harvest.
26:19 For your **d** is a radiant dew,
26:19 For your dew is a radiant **d**,
Da 4:15 Let him be bathed with the **d** of heaven.
4:23 and let him be bathed with the **d** of heaven,
4:25 you shall be bathed with the **d** of heaven,
4:33 and his body was bathed with the **d** of heaven,
5:21 and his body was bathed with the **d** of heaven,
Hos 6: 4 like the **d** that goes away early.
13: 3 be like the morning mist or like the **d**
14: 5 I will be like the **d** to Israel;
Mic 5: 7 shall be like **d** from the LORD,
Hag 1:10 the heavens above you have withheld the **d**,
Zec 8:12 and the skies shall give their **d**;
Wis 11:22 like a drop of morning **d** that falls on the ground.
Sir 18:16 Does not the **d** give relief from the scorching heat?
43:22 the falling **d** gives refreshment from the heat.
Aza 1:42 "Bless the Lord, all rain and **d**;
3Mc 6: 6 moistening the fiery furnace with **d** and turning
2Es 7:*41* or hail or rain or **d**,

DEWS (1) [DEW]
Aza 1:46 Bless the Lord, **d** and falling snow;

DI-ZAHAB (1)
Dt 1: 1 and Tophel, Laban, Hazeroth, and **D**.

DIADEM (10) [DIADEMS]
Ex 29: 6 and put the holy **d** on the turban.
39:30 They made the rosette of the holy **d** of pure gold,
Isa 28: 5 and a **d** of beauty, to the remnant of his people;
62: 3 and a royal **d** in the hand of your God.
AdE 1:11 to proclaim her as queen and to place the **d**
2:17 so he put on her the queen's **d**.
Wis 5:16 a glorious crown and a beautiful **d** from the hand
18:24 and your majesty was on the **d** upon his head.
Sir 47: 6 when the glorious **d** was given to him.
Bar 5: 2 on your head the **d** of the glory of the Everlasting;

DIADEMS (3) [DIADEM]
Rev 12: 3 with seven heads and ten horns, and seven **d**
13: 1 and on its horns were ten **d**,
19:12 and on his head are many **d**;

DIAGNOSIS (1)
Sir 38:14 to the Lord that he grant them success in **d** and

DIAL (3)
2Ki 20:11 by which the sun had declined on the **d** of Ahaz.
Isa 38: 8 the shadow cast by the declining sun on the **d**
38: 8 on the **d** the ten steps by which it had declined.

DIALECTS (1)
Jdt 3: 8 and that all their **d** and tribes should call upon him

DIAMOND (1)
Jer 17: 1 with a **d** point it is engraved on the tablet

DIAMOND (KJV) See also MOONSTONE

DIANA (KJV) See ARTEMIS

DIBLAH See Index to Footnotes

DIBLAIM (1)
Hos 1: 3 So he went and took Gomer daughter of **D**,

DIBLATH (KJV) See RIBLAH

DIBON (11) [DIBON-GAD]
Nu 21:30 So their posterity perished from Heshbon to **D**,
32: 3 **D**, Jazer, Nimrah, Heshbon, Elealeh, Sebam,
32:34 And the Gadites rebuilt **D**, Ataroth, Aroer,
Jos 13: 9 and all the tableland from Medeba as far as **D**;
13:17 **D**, and Bamoth-baal, and Beth-baal-meon,
Ne 11:25 and in **D** and its villages,
Isa 15: 2 **D** has gone up to the temple,
15: 9 For the waters of **D** are full of blood;
15: 9 yet I will bring upon **D** even more—
Jer 48:18 on the parched ground, enthroned daughter **D**!
48:22 and **D**, and Nebo, and Beth-diblathaim,

DIBON-GAD (2) [DIBON, GAD]
Nu 33:45 They set out from Iyim and camped at **D**.
33:46 from **D** and camped at Almon-diblathaim.

DIBRI (1)
Lev 24:11 his mother's name was Shelomith, daughter of **D**,

DICTATE (1) [DICTATED, DICTATION]
Mic 7: 3 and the powerful **d** what they desire;

DICTATED (2) [DICTATE]
Jer 36:18 "He **d** all these words to me,
2Es 14:42 and by turns they wrote what was **d**,

DICTATION (6) [DICTATE]
Jer 36: 4 and Baruch wrote on a scroll at Jeremiah's **d** all
36: 6 from the scroll that you have written at my **d**.
36:17 Was it at his **d**?"
36:27 with the words that Baruch wrote at Jeremiah's **d**,
36:32 who wrote on it at Jeremiah's **d** all the words of
45: 1 in a scroll at the **d** of Jeremiah, in the fourth year

DID‡ (1552) [DO]
Ge 3: 1 He said to the woman, "**D** God say,
6:22 Noah **d** this; he **d** all that God commanded him.
7: 5 Noah **d** all that the LORD had commanded him.
8:12 and it **d** not return to him any more.
9:23 and they **d** not see their father's nakedness.
12:18 Why **d** you not tell me that she was your wife?
12:19 Why **d** you say, 'She is my sister,'
15:10 but he **d** not cut the birds in two.
18:13 LORD said to Abraham, "Why **d** Sarah laugh,
18:15 But Sarah denied, saying, "I **d** not laugh";
Ge 18:15 He said, "Oh yes, you **d** laugh."
19:33 he **d** not know when she lay down or
19:35 and he **d** not know when she lay down or
20: 5 **D** he not himself say to me, 'She is my sister'?
20: 5 I **d** this in the integrity of my heart and
20: 6 that you **d** this in the integrity of your heart;
20: 6 Therefore I **d** not let you touch her.
20:10 of, that you **d** this thing?"
20:11 Abraham said, "I **d** it because I thought,
21: 1 and the LORD **d** for Sarah as he had promised.
21:26 you **d** not tell me, and I have not heard of it
26: 9 Why then **d** you say, 'She is my sister'?"
26:22 and they **d** not quarrel over it;
27:23 He **d** not recognize him,
28: 8 the Canaanite women **d** not please his father Isaac,
28:16 and I **d** not know it!"
29:25 **D** I not serve with you for Rachel?
29:28 Jacob **d** so, and completed her week;
30:40 and **d** not put them with Laban's flock.
30:42 for the feebler of the flock he **d** not lay them there;
31: 2 And Jacob saw that Laban **d** not regard him as
favorably as he **d** before.
31: 5 not regard me as favorably as he **d** before.
31: 7 but God **d** not permit him to harm me.
31:20 in that he **d** not tell him that he intended to flee.
31:27 Why **d** you flee secretly and deceive me and
31:28 And why **d** you not permit me to kiss my sons
31:30 why **d** you steal my gods?"
31:32 Jacob **d** not know that Rachel had stolen the gods.
31:33 but he **d** not find them.
31:34 about in the tent, but **d** not find them.
31:35 So he searched, but **d** not find the household gods.
31:39 which was torn by wild beasts I **d** not bring to you;
32:25 the man saw that he **d** not prevail against Jacob,
34:19 And the young man **d** not delay to do the thing,
38:10 What he **d** was displeasing in the sight of
38:16 he **d** not know that she was his daughter-in-law.
38:26 since I **d** not give her to my son Shelah."
38:26 And he **d** not lie with her again.
39: 3 and that the LORD caused all that he **d** to prosper
39:22 he was the one who **d** it.
39:23 and whatever he **d**, the LORD made it prosper.
40:23 Yet the chief cupbearer **d** not remember Joseph,
42: 4 But Jacob **d** not send Joseph's brother Benjamin
42: 8 recognized his brothers, they **d** not recognize him.
42:21 the penalty for what we **d** to our brother;
42:22 "**D** I not tell you not to wrong the boy?
42:23 They **d** not know that Joseph understood them,
43: 6 "Why **d** you treat me so badly as to tell the man
43:17 The man **d** as Joseph said,
43:28 And they bowed their heads and **d** obeisance.
44: 2 And he **d** as Joseph told him.
45:21 The sons of Israel **d** so.
47:22 Only the land of the priests he **d** not buy;
47:22 therefore they **d** not sell their land.
47:26 land of the priests alone **d** not become Pharaoh's.
48:11 "I **d** not expect to see your face;
50:12 Thus his sons **d** for him as he had instructed them.
50:15 and pays us back in full for all the wrong that we **d**
50:17 the crime of your brothers and the wrong they **d**
Ex 1: 8 Now a new king arose over Egypt, who **d**
1:17 they **d** not do as the king
2:20 Why **d** you leave the man?
4: 1 but say, 'The LORD **d** not appear to you.' "
5:14 "Why **d** you not finish the required quantity of
bricks yesterday and today, as you **d** before?"
5:22 Why **d** you ever send me?
6: 3 'The LORD' I **d** not make myself known to them.
7: 6 Moses and Aaron **d** so; they did just
7: 6 they **d** just as the LORD commanded them.
7:10 to Pharaoh and **d** as the LORD had commanded;
7:11 **d** the same by their secret arts.
7:20 and Aaron **d** just as the LORD commanded.
7:22 magicians of Egypt **d** the same by their secret arts;
7:23 and he **d** not take even this to heart.
8: 7 But the magicians **d** the same by their secret arts,
8:13 And the LORD **d** as Moses requested:
8:17 And they **d** so; Aaron stretched out his hand
8:24 The LORD **d** so, and great swarms of flies came
8:31 And the LORD **d** as Moses asked:
9: 6 And on the next day the LORD **d** so;
9:21 Those who **d** not regard the word of
11:10 he **d** not let the people of Israel go out of his land.
12:28 and **d** just as the LORD had commanded Moses
12:50 All the Israelites **d** just as
13: 8 the LORD **d** for me when I came out of Egypt.'
13:17 God **d** not lead them by way of the land of
14: 4 that I am the LORD. And they **d** so.
14:20 one **d** not come near the other all night.
14:31 Israel saw the great work that the LORD **d**
16:15 For they **d** not know what it was.
16:17 Israelites **d** so, some gathering more, some less.
16:20 But they **d** not listen to Moses;
16:24 and it **d** not become foul,
17: 3 "Why **d** you bring us out of Egypt,
17: 6 Moses **d** so, in the sight of the elders of Israel.
17:10 So Joshua **d** as Moses told him,
18:24 So Moses listened to his father-in-law and **d** all
19: 4 You have seen what I **d** to the Egyptians,
24:11 God **d** not lay his hand on the chief men of
32:21 "What **d** this people do to you
32:28 The sons of Levi **d** as Moses commanded,
34:29 Moses **d** not know that the skin of his face shone
36:22 he **d** this for all the frames of the tabernacle.
40:16 Moses **d** everything just as
40:37 then they **d** not set out until the day
Lev 8: 4 And Moses **d** as the LORD commanded him.

Lev 8:36 Aaron and his sons **d** all the things that
10: 7 And they **d** as Moses had ordered.
10:17 "Why **d** you not eat the sin offering in
16:15 with its blood as he **d** with the blood of the bull,
16:34 And Moses **d** as the LORD had commanded him.
20:23 Because they **d** all these things, I abhorred them.
24:23 of Israel **d** as the LORD had commanded Moses.
26:35 it shall have the rest it **d** not have on your sabbaths
Nu 1:54 The Israelites **d** so; they did just
1:54 they **d** just as the LORD commanded Moses.
2:34 The Israelites **d** just as the LORD had commanded
5: 4 The Israelites **d** so, putting them outside the camp;
5: 4 LORD had spoken to Moses, so the Israelites **d.**
8: 3 Aaron **d** so; he set up its
8:20 and the whole congregation of the Israelites **d** with
8:20 the Israelites **d** with the Levites just as
8:22 concerning the Levites, so they **d** with them.
9: 5 LORD had commanded Moses, so the Israelites **d.**
11:12 **D** I conceive all this people?
11:12 **D** I give birth to them, that you should say to me,
11:20 saying, 'Why **d** we ever leave Egypt?' "
11:25 But they **d** not do so again.
12:15 and the people **d** not set out on the march
14:22 the signs that I **d** in Egypt and in the wilderness,
17:11 Moses **d** so; just as the LORD commanded him,
17:11 just as the LORD commanded him, so he **d.**
20:12 "Because you **d** not trust in me,
20:27 Moses **d** as the LORD had commanded;
21:34 to him as you **d** to King Sihon of the Amorites,
22:19 You remain here, as the others **d,**
22:34 for I **d** not know that you were standing in the road
22:37 **"D** I not send to summon you?
22:37 Why **d** you not come to me?
23: 2 Balak **d** as Balaam had said;
23:26 But Balaam answered Balak, **"D** I not tell you,
23:30 So Balak **d** as Balaam had said,
24: 1 so he **d** not go, as at other times,
24:12 **"D** I not tell your messengers whom you sent
25:11 that in my jealousy I **d** not consume the Israelites.
26:11 Notwithstanding, the sons of Korah **d** not die.
27:14 You **d** not show my holiness before their eyes at
27:22 So Moses **d** as the LORD commanded him.
30:11 and **d** not express disapproval to her,
31: 7 They **d** battle against Midian,
31:31 the priest **d** as the LORD had commanded Moses:
32: 8 Your fathers **d** this, when I sent them
36:10 The daughters of Zelophehad **d** as
Dt 1:30 as he **d** for you in Egypt before your very eyes,
1:46 you had stayed at Kadesh as many days as you **d,**
2:22 He **d** the same for the descendants of Esau,
2:37 You **d** not encroach, however,
3: 2 Do to him as you **d** to King Sihon of the Amorites,
3: 4 there was no citadel that we **d** not take
4: 3 You have seen for yourselves what the LORD **d**
4:34 as the LORD your God **d** for you in Egypt
5: 3 with our ancestors **d** the LORD make this covenant,
5: 5 because of the fire and **d** not go up the mountain.)
6:10 a land with fine, large cities that you **d** not build,
6:11 houses filled with all sorts of goods that you **d**
6:11 hewn cisterns that you **d** not hew,
6:11 vineyards and olive groves that you **d** not plant—
7:18 Just remember what the LORD your God **d**
8: 4 on your back **d** not wear out and your feet did
8: 4 on your back did not wear out and your feet **d**
8:16 in the wilderness with manna that your ancestors **d**
11: 3 that he **d** in Egypt to Pharaoh, the king of Egypt,
11: 4 what he **d** to the Egyptian army, to their horses
11: 5 what he **d** to you in the wilderness, until you came
11: 6 and what he **d** to Dathan and Abiram, sons
11: 7 that have seen every great deed that the LORD **d.**
12:30 saying, "How **d** these nations worship their gods?
21: 7 "Our hands **d** not shed this blood,
22:14 I **d** not find evidence of her virginity."
22:17 against her, saying, 'I **d** not find evidence
22:24 the young woman because she **d** not cry for help
23: 4 because they **d** not meet you with food and water
24: 9 Remember what the LORD your God **d**
25:17 Remember what Amalek **d** to you
25:18 who lagged behind you; he **d** not fear God.
28:45 because you **d** not obey the LORD your God,
28:47 Because you **d** not serve the LORD your God
28:62 because you **d** not obey the LORD your God.
29: 2 that the LORD **d** before your eyes in the land
31: 4 LORD will do to them as he **d** to Sihon and Og,
32:27 it was not the LORD who **d** all this."
33: 9 and **d** not acknowledge his children.
Jos 2: 4 but I **d** not know where they came from.
2:10 and what you **d** to the two kings of the Amorites
4: 8 The Israelites **d** as Joshua commanded.
4:23 as the LORD your God **d** to the Red Sea,
5:15 where you stand is holy." And Joshua **d** so.
6:14 They **d** this for six days.
7:20 of Israel. This is what I **d:**
7:25 Joshua said, "Why **d** you bring trouble on us?
8: 2 You shall do to Ai and its king as you **d** to Jericho
8:14 but he **d** not know that there was an ambush
8:17 There was not a man left in Ai or Bethel who **d**
8:26 For Joshua **d** not draw back his hand,
8:35 a word of all that Moses commanded that Joshua **d**
9: 9 of all that he **d** in Egypt,
9:10 and of all that he **d** to the two kings of
9:14 and **d** not ask direction from the LORD.
9:18 But the Israelites **d** not attack them,
9:22 and said to them, "Why **d** you deceive us, saying,
9:24 for our lives because of you, and **d** this thing.
9:26 This is what he **d** for them:
9:26 and they **d** not kill them.
Jos 10:13 and **d** not hurry to set for about a whole day.
10:23 They **d** so, and brought the five kings out to him
10:28 And he **d** to the king of Makkedah as he had done
10:30 and he **d** to its king as he had done to the king
10:39 so he **d** to Debir and its king.
11: 9 Joshua **d** to them as the LORD commanded him;
11:13 on mounds except Hazor, which Joshua **d** burn.
11:14 and they **d** not leave any who breathed.
11:15 so Moses commanded Joshua, and so Joshua **d;**
13:13 Yet the Israelites **d** not drive out the Geshurites or
14: 5 The Israelites **d** as the LORD commanded Moses;
16:10 They **d** not, however, drive out
17:13 but **d** not utterly drive them out.
22:20 **D** not Achan son of Zerah break faith in the matter
22:20 And he **d** not perish alone for his iniquity!' "
22:23 or if we **d** so to offer burnt offerings
22:24 We **d** it from fear that in time
24: 5 and I plagued Egypt with what I **d** in its midst;
24: 7 and your eyes saw what I **d** to Egypt.
24:13 of vineyards and oliveyards that you **d** not plant.
24:17 and who **d** those great signs in our sight.
24:31 and had known all the work that the LORD **d**
Jdg 1:21 But the Benjaminites **d** not drive out
1:27 Manasseh **d** not drive out the inhabitants
1:28 but **d** not in fact drive them out.
1:29 And Ephraim **d** not drive out
1:30 Zebulun **d** not drive out the inhabitants of Kitron,
1:31 Asher **d** not drive out the inhabitants of Acco,
1:32 for they **d** not drive them out.
1:33 Naphtali **d** not drive out the inhabitants
1:34 they **d** not allow them to come down to the plain.
2:10 who **d** not know the LORD or the work
2:11 Then the Israelites **d** what was evil in the sight of
2:17 Yet they **d** not listen even to their judges;
2:17 they **d** not follow their example.
2:22 in the way of the LORD as their ancestors **d,**
3: 7 The Israelites **d** what was evil in the sight of
3:12 The Israelites again **d** what was evil in the sight of
3:22 for he **d** not draw the sword out of his belly;
3:25 he still **d** not open the doors of the roof chamber,
4: 1 The Israelites again **d** what was evil in the sight of
5:16 Why **d** you tarry among the sheepfolds,
5:17 and Dan, why **d** he abide with the ships?
5:23 they **d** not come to the help of the LORD,
6: 1 The Israelites **d** what was evil in the sight of
6:13 **'D** not the LORD bring us up from Egypt?'
6:20 and pour out the broth." And he **d** so.
6:27 and **d** as the LORD had told him;
6:27 the townspeople to do it by day, he **d** it by night.
6:29 they were told, "Gideon son of Joash **d** it."
6:40 And God **d** so that night.
8:20 But the boy **d** not draw his sword,
8:34 Israelites **d** not remember the LORD their God,
8:35 and they **d** not exhibit loyalty to the house
9:28 **D** not the son of Jerubbaal
10: 6 The Israelites again **d** what was evil in the sight of
10: 6 the LORD, and **d** not worship him.
10:11 **"D** I not deliver you from the Egyptians and from
11:15 Israel **d** not take away the land of Moab or
11:18 They **d** not enter the territory of Moab,
11:20 But Sihon **d** not trust Israel to pass
11:25 **D** he ever enter into conflict with Israel,
11:25 or **d** he ever go to war with them?
11:26 why **d** you not recover them within that time?
11:28 the king of the Ammonites **d** not heed the message
11:39 who **d** with her according to the vow he had made.
12: 1 "Why **d** you cross over to fight against
12: 1 and **d** not call us to go with you?
12: 2 I called you, you **d** not deliver me from their hand.
13: 1 The Israelites again **d** what was evil in the sight of
13: 6 I **d** not ask him where he came from,
13: 6 and he **d** not tell me his name;
13:16 (For Manoah **d** not know that he was the angel of
13:21 of the LORD **d** not appear again to Manoah
14: 4 His father and mother **d** not know that this was
14: 6 But he **d** not tell his father
14: 9 But he **d** not tell them that he had taken the honey
15:10 to do to him as he **d** to us."
15:11 He replied, "As they **d** to me,
16:20 But he **d** not know that the LORD had left him.
17: 6 all the people **d** what was right in their own eyes
18: 4 He said to them, "Micah **d** such and such for me,
20: 3 "Tell us, how **d** this criminal act come about?"
20:34 But the Benjaminites **d** not realize
21: 5 "Which of all the tribes of Israel **d** not come up in
21: 5 concerning whoever **d** not come up to the LORD
21: 8 "Is there anyone from the tribes of Israel who **d**
21:14 but they **d** not suffice for them.
21:22 we **d** not capture in battle a wife for each man.
21:22 But neither **d** you incur guilt
21:23 The Benjaminites **d** so; they took wives
21:25 all the people **d** what was right in their own eyes.
Ru 2:11 and came to a people that you **d** not know before.
2:19 "Where **d** you glean today?
3: 6 and **d** just as her mother-in-law had instructed her.
3:16 "How **d** things go with you, my daughter?"
1Sa 1:22 But Hannah **d** not go up, for she said
2:14 This is what they **d** at Shiloh to all
3: 5 But he said, "I **d** not call; lie down again."
3: 6 But he said, "I **d** not call, my son; lie down again."
3: 7 Now Samuel **d** not yet know the LORD,
3:13 and he **d** not restrain them.
4:16 He said, "How **d** it go, my son?"
4:20 But she **d** not answer or give heed.
5:12 those who **d** not die were stricken with tumors,
6: 6 **d** they not let the people go, and they departed?
6:10 The men **d** so; they took two milch cows
1Sa 6:19 The descendants of Jeconiah **d** not rejoice with
7:13 the Philistines were subdued and **d** not again enter
8: 3 Yet his sons **d** not follow in his ways,
9: 4 but they **d** not find them.
9: 4 but they **d** not find them.
10:14 to him and to the boy, "Where **d** you go?"
10:16 he **d** not tell him anything.
10:22 So they inquired again of the LORD, **"D**
13: 8 but Samuel **d** not come to Gilgal,
13:11 that you **d** not come within the days appointed,
14: 1 But he **d** not tell his father.
14: 3 the people **d** not know that Jonathan had gone.
14:26 but they **d** not put their hands to their mouths,
14:37 But he **d** not answer him that day.
14:45 the people ransomed Jonathan, and he **d** not die.
14:48 He **d** valiantly, and struck down the Amalekites,
15: 2 'I will punish the Amalekites for what they **d**
15:19 Why then **d** you not obey the voice of the LORD?
15:19 Why **d** you swoop down on the spoil,
15:35 Samuel **d** not see Saul again until the day
16: 4 Samuel **d** what the LORD commanded,
18:10 as he **d** day by day.
20:26 Saul **d** not say anything that day;
21: 8 I **d** not bring my sword or my weapons with me,
21:11 **D** they not sing to one another of him in dances,
22:17 and **d** not disclose it to me."
23:14 but the LORD **d** not give him into his hand.
24: 7 So David scolded his men severely and **d**
24: 8 with his face to the ground, and **d** obeisance.
24:11 that I cut off the corner of your cloak, and **d**
24:18 in that you **d** not kill me when the LORD put me
25: 7 and we **d** them no harm, and they missed nothing,
25:19 But she **d** not tell her husband Nabal.
25:25 your servant, **d** not see the young men of my lord,
26:12 No one saw it, or knew it, nor **d** anyone awake;
28: 6 the LORD **d** not answer him, not by dreams,
28:14 with his face to the ground, and **d** obeisance.
28:18 Because you **d** not obey the voice of the LORD,
28:18 **d** not carry out his fierce wrath against Amalek,
30:22 "Because they **d** not go with us,
2Sa 1: 2 he fell to the ground and **d** obeisance.
1: 4 David said to him, "How **d** things go?
1:11 and all the men who were with him **d** the same.
1:22 the bow of Jonathan **d** not turn back,
3:24 why **d** you dismiss him, so that he got away?
3:26 but David **d** not know about it.
3:36 as everything the king **d** pleased all the people.
5:25 David **d** just as the LORD had commanded him;
7: 7 **d** I ever speak a word with any of the tribal leaders
9: 6 and fell on his face and **d** obeisance.
9: 8 He **d** obeisance and said, "What is your servant,
11: 9 and **d** not go down to his house.
11:10 "Uriah **d** not go down to his house,"
11:10 Why **d** you not go down to your house?"
11:13 but he **d** not go down to his house.
11:20 'Why **d** you go so near the city to fight?
11:20 **D** you not know that they would shoot from
11:21 **D** not a woman throw an upper millstone on him
11:21 Why **d** you go so near the wall?'
12: 6 the lamb fourfold, because he **d** this thing,
12:12 For you **d** it secretly; but I will do this thing
12:17 but he would not, nor **d** he eat food with them.
12:18 we spoke to him, and he **d** not listen to us;
12:31 Thus he **d** to all the cities of the Ammonites.
13:16 the other that you **d** to me."
13:29 So the servants of Absalom **d** to Amnon
14: 4 she fell on her face to the ground and **d** obeisance,
14:20 the course of affairs your servant Joab **d** this.
14:22 the ground and **d** obeisance, and blessed the king;
14:24 and **d** not come into the king's presence.
15: 6 Thus Absalom **d** to every Israelite who came to
16:17 Why **d** you not go with your friend?"
17:15 "Thus and so **d** Ahithophel counsel Absalom and
18:11 then **d** you not strike him there to the ground?
19:19 how your servant **d** wrong on the day my lord
19:25 the king said to him, "Why **d** you not go with me,
19:43 Why then **d** you despise us?
20: 3 and provided for them, but **d** not go in to them.
20:10 But Amasa **d** not notice the sword in Joab's hand;
20:10 He **d** not strike a second blow.
21:10 she **d** not allow the birds of the air to come on
21:14 they **d** all that the king commanded.
22:23 and from his statutes I **d** not turn aside.
22:38 and **d** not turn back until they were consumed.
22:39 I struck them down, so that they **d** not rise;
22:42 but he **d** not answer them.
23:17 The three warriors **d** these things.
23:19 but he **d** not attain to the Three.
23:22 Such were the things Benaiah son of Jehoiada **d,**
23:23 but he **d** not attain to the Three.
1Ki 1: 4 but the king **d** not know her sexually.
1: 8 David's own warriors **d** not side with Adonijah.
1:10 but he **d** not invite the prophet Nathan or Benaiah
1:13 and say to him, **'D** you not, my lord the king,
1:16 Bathsheba bowed and **d** obeisance to the king,
1:23 he **d** obeisance to the king,
1:26 But he **d** not invite me, your servant,
1:31 and **d** obeisance to the king, and said,
2: 5 you know also what Joab son of Zeruiah **d** to me,
2:42 **"D** I not make you swear by the LORD,
2:44 in your own heart all the evil that you **d**
5:16 having charge of the people who **d** the work.
5:18 and the Gebalites **d** the stonecutting and prepared
7:14 He came to King Solomon, and **d** all his work.
7:18 he **d** the same with the other capital.
7:40 the work that he **d** for King Solomon on the house
7:51 the work that King Solomon **d** on the house of

1Ki 8:18 'You **d** well to consider building a house
9:12 the cities that Solomon had given him, they **d**
10:7 but I **d** not believe the reports until I came
10:10 never again **d** spices come in such quantity as
11:6 So Solomon **d** what was evil in the sight of
11:6 and **d** not completely follow the LORD,
11:8 He **d** the same for all his foreign wives,
11:10 he **d** not observe what the LORD commanded.
11:25 making trouble as Hadad **d;**
11:33 and my ordinances, as his father David **d.**
11:34 and who **d** keep my commandments
11:38 as David my servant **d,** I will be with you,
11:41 all that he **d** as well as his wisdom,
12:15 So the king **d** not listen to the people,
12:32 so he **d** in Bethel, sacrificing to the calves
13:10 and **d** not return by the way that he had come
13:12 Their father said to them, "Which way **d** he go?"
13:33 this event Jeroboam **d** not turn from his evil way,
14:4 Jeroboam's wife **d** so; she set out
14:22 Judah **d** what was evil in the sight of the LORD;
14:29 the rest of the acts of Rehoboam, and all that he **d,**
15:3 He committed all the sins that his father **d**
15:5 David **d** what was right in the sight of the LORD,
15:5 and **d** not turn aside from anything
15:7 The rest of the acts of Abijam, and all that he **d,**
15:11 Asa **d** what was right in the sight of the LORD,
15:23 all that he **d,** and the cities that he built,
15:26 He **d** what was evil in the sight of the LORD,
15:31 the rest of the acts of Nadab, and all that he **d,**
15:34 He **d** what was evil in the sight of the LORD,
16:5 Now the rest of the acts of Baasha, what he **d,**
16:7 of all the evil that he **d** in the sight of the LORD,
16:11 he **d** not leave him a single male of his kindred
16:14 Now the rest of the acts of Elah, and all that he **d,**
16:25 Omri **d** what was evil in the sight of the LORD;
16:25 he **d** more evil than all who were before him.
16:27 Now the rest of the acts of Omri that he **d,**
16:30 Ahab son of Omri **d** evil in the sight of
16:33 Ahab **d** more to provoke the anger of the LORD,
17:5 and **d** according to the word of the LORD;
17:15 She went and **d** as Elijah said,
17:16 neither **d** the jug of oil fail,
18:13 not been told my lord what I **d** when Jezebel killed
18:21 The people **d** not answer him a word.
18:34 and they **d** it a second time.
18:34 and they **d** it a third time,
20:7 and I **d** not refuse him."
20:25 He heeded their voice, and **d** so.
20:34 as my father **d** in Samaria."
21:11 **d** as Jezebel had sent word to them.
22:18 "**D** I not tell you that he would
22:24 "Which way **d** the spirit of the LORD pass
22:39 Now the rest of the acts of Ahab, and all that he **d,**
22:43 he **d** not turn aside from it,
22:48 but they **d** not go, for the ships were wrecked
22:52 He **d** what was evil in the sight of the LORD,
2Ki 1:18 Now the rest of the acts of Ahaziah that he **d,**
2:17 for three days but **d** not find him.
2:18 he said to them, "**D** I not say to you, Do not go?"
3:2 He **d** what was evil in the sight of the LORD,
3:3 he **d** not depart from it.
3:25 Only at Kir-hareseth **d** the stone walls remain,
4:28 Then she said, "**D** I ask my lord for a son?
4:28 **D** I not say, Do not mislead me?"
5:26 "**D** I not go with you in spirit
6:6 Then the man of God said, "Where **d** it fall?"
6:22 **D** you capture with your sword
7:20 It **d** indeed happen to him;
8:2 up and **d** according to the word of the man of God;
8:14 who said to him, "What **d** Elisha say to you?"
8:18 He **d** what was evil in the sight of the LORD.
8:23 the rest of the acts of Joram, and all that he **d,**
9:11 Why **d** that madman come to you?"
10:21 so that there was no one left who **d** not come.
10:29 But Jehu **d** not turn aside from the sins
10:31 he **d** not turn from the sins of Jeroboam,
10:34 Now the rest of the acts of Jehu, all that he **d,**
11:9 The captains **d** according to all that
12:2 Jehoash **d** what was right in the sight of
12:15 They **d** not ask an accounting from those
12:19 Now the rest of the acts of Joash, and all that he **d,**
13:2 He **d** what was evil in the sight of the LORD,
13:2 he **d** not depart from them.
13:6 Nevertheless they **d** not depart from the sins of
13:8 the rest of the acts of Jehoahaz and all that he **d,**
13:11 also **d** what was evil in the sight of the LORD;
13:11 he **d** not depart from all the sins of Jeroboam son
13:12 Now the rest of the acts of Joash, and all that he **d,**
14:3 He **d** what was right in the sight of the LORD,
14:3 in all things he **d** as his father Joash had done.
14:6 he **d** not put to death the children of the murderers;
14:15 Now the rest of the acts that Jehoash **d,** his might,
14:24 He **d** what was evil in the sight of the LORD;
14:24 he **d** not depart from all the sins of Jeroboam son
14:28 the rest of the acts of Jeroboam, and all that he **d,**
15:3 He **d** what was right in the sight of the LORD,
15:6 the rest of the acts of Azariah, and all that he **d,**
15:9 He **d** what was evil in the sight of the LORD,
15:9 He **d** not depart from the sins of Jeroboam son
15:16 because they **d** not open it to him, he sacked it.
15:18 He **d** what was evil in the sight of the LORD;
15:18 he **d** not depart all his days from any of the sins
15:20 and **d** not stay there in the land.
15:21 rest of the deeds of Menahem, and all that he **d,**
15:24 He **d** what was evil in the sight of the LORD;
15:24 he **d** not turn away from the sins of Jeroboam son
15:26 the rest of the deeds of Pekahiah, and all that he **d,**
2Ki 15:28 He **d** what was evil in the sight of the LORD;
15:28 he **d** not depart from the sins of Jeroboam son
15:31 the rest of the acts of Pekah, and all that he **d,**
15:34 He **d** what was right in the sight of the LORD,
15:36 the rest of the acts of Jotham, and all that he **d,**
16:2 He **d** not do what was right in the sight of
16:11 just so **d** the priest Uriah build it,
16:16 The priest Uriah **d** everything
16:18 He **d** this because of the king of Assyria.
16:19 Now the rest of the acts of Ahaz that he **d,**
17:2 He **d** what was evil in the sight of the LORD,
17:9 The people of Israel secretly **d** things that were
17:11 as the nations **d** whom the LORD carried away
17:11 They **d** wicked things, provoking the LORD
17:14 who **d** not believe in the LORD their God.
17:15 that they should not do as they **d.**
17:19 Judah also **d** not keep the commandments of
17:22 they **d** not depart from them
17:25 they **d** not worship the LORD;
17:41 to do as their ancestors **d.**
18:3 He **d** what was right in the sight of the LORD just
18:6 he **d** not depart from following him but kept
18:12 because they **d** not obey the voice of
20:13 or in all his realm that Hezekiah **d** not show them.
20:14 and said to him, "What **d** these men say?
20:14 From where **d** they come to you?"
20:15 in my storehouses that I **d** not show them."
21:2 He **d** what was evil in the sight of the LORD,
21:6 He **d** much evil in the sight of the LORD,
21:9 But they **d** not listen; Manasseh misled them to do
21:11 that the Amorites **d,** who were before him,
21:16 to sin so that they **d** what was evil in the sight of
21:17 Now the rest of the acts of Manasseh, all that he **d,**
21:20 He **d** what was evil in the sight of the LORD,
21:22 and **d** not walk in the way of the LORD.
21:25 Now the rest of the acts of Amon that he **d,**
22:2 He **d** what was right in the sight of the LORD,
22:2 he **d** not turn aside to the right or to the left.
22:13 our ancestors **d** not obey the words of this book,
23:7 where the women **d** weaving for Asherah.
23:9 **d** not come up to the altar of the LORD
23:19 he **d** to them just as he had done at Bethel.
23:25 nor **d** any like him arise after him.
23:26 Still the LORD **d** not turn from the fierceness
23:28 the rest of the acts of Josiah, and all that he **d,**
23:32 He **d** what was evil in the sight of the LORD,
23:37 He **d** what was evil in the sight of the LORD,
24:5 rest of the deeds of Jehoiakim, and all that he **d,**
24:7 king of Egypt **d** not come again out of his land,
24:9 He **d** what was evil in the sight of the LORD,
24:19 He **d** what was evil in the sight of the LORD,
1Ch 4:27 but his brothers **d** not have many children,
4:27 nor **d** all their family multiply like the Judeans.
10:13 in that he **d** not keep the command of the LORD;
10:14 and **d** not seek guidance from the LORD.
11:19 The three warriors **d** these things.
11:21 but he **d** not attain to the Three.
11:24 Such were the things Benaiah son of Jehoiada **d,**
11:25 but he **d** not attain to the Three.
12:19 (Yet he **d** not help them,
13:3 for we **d** not turn to it in the days of Saul."
13:13 So David **d** not take the ark into his care into
14:16 David **d** as God had commanded him,
15:13 Because you **d** not carry it the first time,
15:13 because we **d** not give it proper care."
17:6 **d** I ever speak a word with any of the judges
17:9 down no more, as they **d** formerly,
20:3 Thus David **d** to all the cities of the Ammonites.
21:6 But he **d** not include Levi and Benjamin in
21:21 **d** obeisance to David with his face to the ground.
23:11 but Jeush and Beriah **d** not have many sons,
25:1 of those who **d** the work and of their duties was:
26:12 had duties, just as their kindred **d,**
27:23 David **d** not count those below twenty years
27:24 of Zeruiah began to count them, but **d** not finish;
27:26 Over those who **d** the work of the field,
29:6 as **d** also the leaders of the tribes,
2Ch 4:11 the work that he **d** for King Solomon on the house
5:1 Thus all the work that Solomon **d** for the house of
6:8 'You **d** well to consider building a house
8:15 They **d** not turn away from what
9:6 but I **d** not believe the reports until I came
10:15 So the king **d** not listen to the people,
12:14 He **d** evil, for he **d** not set his heart to seek
13:20 Jeroboam **d** not recover his power in the days
14:2 Asa **d** what was good and right in the sight of
16:7 and **d** not rely on the LORD your God,
16:12 yet even in his disease he **d** not seek the LORD,
17:3 he **d** not seek the Baals,
17:10 and they **d** not make war against Jehoshaphat.
18:17 "**D** I not tell you that he would
18:23 "Which way **d** the spirit of the LORD pass
20:7 **D** you not, O our God, drive out the inhabitants
20:10 and whom they avoided and **d** not destroy—
20:32 in the way of his father Asa and **d** not turn aside
20:35 with King Ahaziah of Israel, who **d** wickedly.
21:6 He **d** what was evil in the sight of the LORD.
22:4 He **d** what was evil in the sight of the LORD,
22:11 hid him from Athaliah, so that she **d** not kill him;
23:8 The Levites and all Judah **d** according to all that
23:8 for the priest Jehoiada **d** not dismiss the divisions.
24:2 Joash **d** what was right in the sight of
24:5 But the Levites **d** not act quickly.
24:11 So they **d** day after day,
24:17 the officials of Judah came and **d** obeisance to
24:22 King Joash **d** not remember the kindness
24:25 but they **d** not bury him in the tombs of the kings.
2Ch 25:2 He **d** what was right in the sight of the LORD,
25:4 But he **d** not put their children to death,
26:4 He **d** what was right in the sight of the LORD,
27:2 He **d** what was right in the sight of the LORD just
27:2 only he **d** not invade the temple of the LORD.
27:3 and **d** extensive building on the wall of Ophel.
28:1 He **d** not do what was right in the sight of
28:21 but it **d** not help him.
28:27 but they **d** not bring him into the tombs of
29:2 He **d** what was right in the sight of the LORD,
31:20 Hezekiah **d** this throughout all Judah;
31:20 he **d** what was good and right and faithful before
31:21 he **d** with all his heart; and he prospered.
32:17 the nations in other lands **d** not rescue their people
32:25 But Hezekiah **d** not respond according to
32:26 the wrath of the LORD **d** not come upon them in
32:33 and the inhabitants of Jerusalem **d** him honor
33:2 He **d** what was evil in the sight of the LORD,
33:6 He **d** much evil in the sight of the LORD,
33:9 so that they **d** more evil than the nations whom
33:22 He **d** what was evil in the sight of the LORD,
33:23 He **d** not humble himself before the LORD,
34:2 He **d** what was right in the sight of the LORD,
34:2 he **d** not turn aside to the right or to the left.
34:12 The people **d** the work faithfully.
34:13 the burden bearers and directed all who **d** work
34:21 our ancestors **d** not keep the word of the LORD,
34:33 All his days they **d** not turn away from following
35:11 while the Levites **d** the skinning.
35:12 And they **d** the same with the bulls.
35:15 they **d** not need to interrupt their service,
35:22 He **d** not listen to the words of Neco from
36:5 He **d** what was evil in the sight of
36:8 and the abominations that he **d,**
36:9 He **d** what was evil in the sight of the LORD.
36:12 He **d** what was evil in the sight of the LORD
36:12 He **d** not humble himself before
Ezr 5:5 and they **d** not stop them until
6:13 the River, Shethar-bozenai, and their associates **d**
10:6 He **d** not eat bread or drink water,
10:8 and that if any **d** not come within three days,
10:16 Then the returned exiles **d** so.
Ne 2:16 The officials **d** not know where I had gone
5:13 And the people **d** as they had promised.
5:15 But I **d** not do so, because of the fear of God.
5:18 yet with all this I **d** not demand the food allowance
6:14 O my God, according to these things that they **d,**
9:16 and **d** not obey your commandments;
9:17 and you **d** not forsake them.
9:19 you in your great mercies **d** not forsake them in
9:19 of cloud that led them in the way **d** not leave them
9:20 and **d** not withhold your manna from their mouths,
9:21 their clothes **d** not wear out and their feet **d** not
9:28 after they had rest, they again **d** evil before you,
9:29 Yet they acted presumptuously and **d**
9:31 in your great mercies you **d** not make an end
9:35 they **d** not serve you and **d** not turn from their
11:12 and their associates who **d** the work of the house,
12:45 as **d** the singers and the gatekeepers,
13:2 because they **d** not meet the Israelites with bread
13:18 **D** not your ancestors act in this way,
13:18 and **d** not our God bring all this disaster on us and
13:21 From that time on they **d** not come on the sabbath.
13:26 **D** not King Solomon of Israel sin on account
Est 1:17 to be brought before him, and she **d** not come.'
1:21 and the king **d** as Memucan proposed;
2:4 This pleased the king, and he **d** so.
2:10 Esther **d** not reveal her people or kindred,
2:14 she **d** not go in to the king again,
3:2 at the king's gate bowed down and **d** obeisance
3:2 But Mordecai **d** not bow down or do obeisance.
3:5 When Haman saw that Mordecai **d** not bow down
4:17 and **d** everything as Esther had ordered him.
9:5 and **d** as they pleased to those who hated them.
9:10 but they **d** not touch the plunder.
9:15 but they **d** not touch the plunder.
Job 1:5 This is what Job always **d.**
1:22 In all this Job **d** not sin or charge God
2:10 In all this Job **d** not sin with his lips.
2:12 When they saw him from a distance, they **d**
3:10 it **d** not shut the doors of my mother's womb,
3:11 "Why **d** I not die at birth,
10:10 **D** you not pour me out like milk and curdle me
10:18 "Why **d** you bring me forth from the womb?
20:19 they have seized a house that they **d** not build.
29:22 After I spoke they **d** not speak again,
29:24 the light of my countenance they **d** not extinguish.
30:25 **D** I not weep for those whose day was hard?
31:15 **D** not he who made me in the womb make them?
31:15 And **d** not one fashion us in the womb?
31:34 so that I kept silence, and **d** not go out of doors—
37:20 **D** anyone ever wish to be swallowed up?
38:29 From whose womb **d** the ice come forth,
42:3 Therefore I have uttered what I **d** not understand,
42:3 things too wonderful for me, which I **d** not know.
42:9 and Zophar the Naamathite went and **d** what
Ps 18:22 and his statutes I **d** not put away from me.
18:36 and my feet **d** not slip.
18:37 and **d** not turn back until they were consumed.
18:41 but he **d** not answer them.
22:24 For he **d** not despise or abhor the affliction of
22:24 he **d** not hide his face from me,
30:1 and **d** not let my foes rejoice over me.
32:5 and I **d** not hide my iniquity;
35:15 ruffians whom I **d** not know tore at me
44:3 for not by their own sword **d** they win the land,
44:3 nor **d** their own arm give them victory;

Ps 69: 4 What I **d** not steal must I now restore?
78:10 They **d** not keep God's covenant,
78:22 and **d** not trust his saving power.
78:32 they **d** not believe in his wonders.
78:38 forgave their iniquity, and **d** not destroy them;
78:38 and **d** not stir up all his wrath.
78:42 They **d** not keep in mind his power,
78:50 he **d** not spare them from death,
78:56 They **d** not observe his decrees,
78:67 he **d** not choose the tribe of Ephraim;
81:11 "But my people **d** not listen to my voice;
83: 9 Do to them as you **d** to Midian,
106: 7 **d** not consider your wonderful works;
106: 7 they **d** not remember the abundance
106:13 they **d** not wait for his counsel.
106:25 and **d** not obey the voice of the LORD.
106:34 They **d** not destroy the peoples,
106:35 with the nations and learned to do as they **d.**
109:16 For he **d** not remember to show kindness,
109:17 He **d** not like blessing; may it be far from him.
118:18 but he **d** not give me over to death.
Pr 1:29 Because they hated knowledge and **d** not choose
5:13 I **d** not listen to the voice of my teachers
23:35 they beat me, but I **d** not feel it.
24:12 "Look, we **d** not know this"—
Ecc 2:10 Whatever my eyes desired I **d** not keep from them;
2:21 to be enjoyed by another who **d** not toil for it.
SS 5: 6 I sought him, but **d** not find him;
Isa 5: 4 why **d** it yield wild grapes?
9:13 The people **d** not turn to him who struck them,
9:17 the Lord **d** not have pity on their young people,
10:24 up their staff against you as the Egyptians **d.**
10:26 and he will lift it as he **d** in Egypt.
22:11 But you **d** not look to him who **d** it,
29:16 the thing made say of its maker, "He **d** not make
39: 2 or in all his realm that Hezekiah **d** not show them.
39: 3 and said to him, "What **d** these men say?
39: 3 From where **d** they come to you?"
39: 4 in my storehouses that I **d** not show them."
40:14 Whom **d** he consult for his enlightenment,
42:25 on fire all around, but he **d** not understand;
42:25 it burned him, but he **d** not take it to heart.
43:22 Yet you **d** not call upon me, O Jacob;
45:18 he **d** not create it a chaos, he formed it to be
45:19 I **d** not speak in secret, in a land of darkness;
45:19 I **d** not say to the offspring of Jacob,
47: 7 so that you **d** not lay these things to heart
48: 3 then suddenly I **d** them and they came to pass.
48: 5 so that you would not say, "My idol **d** them,
48:21 They **d** not thirst when he led them through
50: 2 Why **d** no one answer when I called?
50: 5 and I was not rebellious, I **d** not turn backward.
50: 6 I **d** not hide my face from insult and spitting.
53: 7 and he was afflicted, yet he **d** not open his mouth;
53: 7 so he **d** not open his mouth.
54: 1 Sing, O barren one who **d** not bear;
57:10 but you **d** not say, "It is useless."
57:10 and so you **d** not weaken.
57:11 Whom **d** you dread and fear so that you lied,
57:11 and **d** not remember me or give me a thought?
58: 2 that practiced righteousness and **d** not forsake
63:13 Like a horse in the desert, they **d** not stumble.
64: 3 you **d** awesome deeds that we **d** not expect,
65: 1 I was ready to be sought out by those who **d**
65: 1 to be found by those who **d** not seek me.
65: 1 here I am," to a nation that **d** not call on my name.
65:12 because, when I called, you **d** not answer,
65:12 when I spoke, you **d** not listen,
65:12 but you **d** what was evil in my sight,
65:12 and chose what I **d** not delight in.
66: 4 no one answered, when I spoke, they **d** not listen;
66: 4 but they **d** what was evil in my sight,
66: 4 and chose what **d** not please me.
Jer 2: 5 What wrong **d** your ancestors find in me
2: 6 They **d** not say, "Where is
2: 8 The priests **d** not say, "Where is the LORD?"
2: 8 Those who handle the law **d** not know me;
2:21 **d** you turn degenerate and become a wild vine?
2:34 though you **d** not catch them breaking in.
3: 6 Have you seen what she **d**, that faithless one,
3: 7 she **d** not return, and her false sister Judah saw it.
3: 8 yet her false sister Judah **d** not fear,
3:10 for all this her false sister Judah **d** not return to me
6:15 they **d** not know how to blush.
7:12 and see what I **d** to it for the wickedness
7:13 you **d** not listen, and when I called you,
7:13 and when I called you, you **d** not answer,
7:14 just what I **d** to Shiloh.
7:22 I **d** not speak to them or command them
7:24 Yet they **d** not obey or incline their ear, but,
7:26 yet they **d** not listen to me,
7:26 They **d** worse than their ancestors **d.**
7:28 that **d** not obey the voice of the LORD their God,
7:28 and **d** not accept discipline;
7:31 I **d** not command, nor **d** it come into my mind.
8:12 they **d** not know how to blush.
10:11 The gods who **d** not make the heavens and
11: 8 Yet they **d** not obey or incline their ear,
11: 8 which I commanded them to do, but they **d** not.
11:19 And I **d** not know it was against me
14:14 I **d** not send them, nor **d** I command them
14:15 the prophets who prophesy in my name though I **d**
15: 4 of Hezekiah of Judah **d** in Jerusalem.
15: 7 they **d** not turn from their ways.
15:17 I **d** not sit in the company of merrymakers, nor **d** I rejoice;
17:11 Like the partridge hatching what it **d** not lay,
Jer 17:23 Yet they **d** not listen or incline their ear;
19: 5 which I **d** not command or decree,
19: 5 nor **d** it enter my mind.
20:17 because he **d** not kill me in the womb;
20:18 Why **d** I come forth from the womb to see toil
22:15 **D** not your father eat and drink and do justice
23:21 I **d** not send the prophets, yet they ran;
23:21 I **d** not speak to them, yet they prophesied.
23:32 when I **d** not send them or appoint them;
25: 7 Yet you **d** not listen to me, says the LORD,
26:19 **D** King Hezekiah of Judah
26:19 **D** he not fear the LORD and entreat the favor of
26:19 and **d** not the LORD change his mind about
27:20 which King Nebuchadnezzar of Babylon **d**
29: 9 I **d** not send them, says the LORD.
29:16 your kinsfolk who **d** not go out with you
29:19 because they **d** not heed my words,
29:23 and have spoken in my name lying words that I **d**
29:31 to you, though I **d** not send him,
32:23 they **d** not obey your voice or follow your law;
32:23 of all you commanded them to do, they **d** nothing.
32:32 and the people of Judah that they **d** to provoke me
32:35 I **d** not command them, nor **d** it enter my mind
34:14 But your ancestors **d** not listen to me
34:15 and **d** what was right in my sight
34:18 And those who transgressed my covenant and **d**
35:15 But you **d** not incline your ear or obey me.
36: 8 And Baruch son of Neriah **d** all that
36:17 "Tell us now, how **d** you write all these words?
36:24 was alarmed, nor **d** they tear their garments.
38: 9 these men have acted wickedly in all they **d** to
38:12 and the ropes." Jeremiah **d** so.
38:25 What **d** the king say to you?'
38:27 All the officials **d** come to Jeremiah
40: 3 against the LORD and **d** not obey his voice.
41: 8 and **d** not kill them along with their companions.
43: 2 The LORD our God **d** not send you to say,
43: 4 the commanders of the forces and all the people **d**
43: 7 for they **d** not obey the voice of the LORD.
44: 5 But they **d** not listen or incline their ear,
44:21 **d** not the LORD remember them?
44:21 **D** it not come into his mind?
44:23 and because you sinned against the LORD and **d**
46:15 Why **d** your bull not stand?
46:21 they too have turned and fled together, they **d**
50:24 O Babylon, but you **d** not know it;
52: 2 He **d** what was evil in the sight of the LORD,
La 2: 8 he **d** not withhold his hand from destroying;
4:12 The kings of the earth **d** not believe,
4:12 nor **d** any of the inhabitants of the world,
Eze 6:10 I **d** not threaten in vain to bring this disaster
10:16 the wheels at their side **d** not veer.
12: 7 I **d** just as I was commanded.
13: 7 "Says the LORD," even though I **d** not speak?
14:23 not without cause that I **d** all that I have done in it,
16:22 in all your abominations and your whorings you **d**
16:30 says the Lord GOD, that you **d** all these things,
16:49 but **d** not aid the poor and needy.
16:50 and **d** abominable things before me;
17:18 he gave his hand and yet **d** all these things,
18:18 and **d** what is not good among his people,
20: 8 nor **d** they forsake the idols of Egypt.
20:13 they **d** not observe my statutes
20:16 because they rejected my ordinances and **d**
20:17 and I **d** not destroy them or make an end of them
20:21 they **d** not follow my statutes,
23: 8 She **d** not give up her whorings
23:39 This is what they **d** in my house.
24: 7 she **d** not pour it out on the ground,
24:13 you **d** not become clean from your filth;
24:18 And on the next morning I **d** as I was commanded.
27:12 Tarshish **d** business with you out of the abundance
27:16 Edom **d** business with you because
27:21 in these they **d** business with you.
33: 5 the sound of the trumpet and **d** not take warning;
35: 6 since you **d** not hate bloodshed,
48:11 who **d** not go astray when the people of Israel went astray, as the Levites **d.**
Da 6:12 **D** you not sign an interdict,
8: 4 it **d** as it pleased and became strong.
8: 7 The ram **d** not have power to withstand it;
8:12 and kept prospering in what it **d.**
8:27 But I was dismayed by the vision and **d**
9:13 We **d** not entreat the favor of the LORD our God,
10: 7 the people who were with me **d** not see the vision,
11:38 a god whom his ancestors **d**
Hos 2: 8 She **d** not know that it was I who gave her
11: 3 but they **d** not know that I healed them.
Am 1: 9 and **d** not remember the covenant of kinship.
4: 6 yet you **d** not return to me, says the LORD.
4: 7 and the field on which it **d** not rain withered;
4: 8 yet you **d** not return to me, says the LORD.
4: 9 yet you **d** not return to me, says the LORD.
4:10 yet you **d** not return to me, says the LORD.
4:11 yet you **d** not return to me, says the LORD.
5:25 **D** you bring to me sacrifices and offerings
9: 7 **D** I not bring Israel up from the land of Egypt,
Jnh 3:10 When God saw what they **d,**
3:10 and he **d** not do it.
4:10 which you **d** not labor and which you **d** not grow;
Mic 5:15 on the nations that **d** not obey.
Hag 2:16 how **d** you fare? When one came to a
2:17 yet you **d** not return to me, says the LORD.
Zec 1: 4 But they **d** not hear or heed me, says the LORD.
1: 6 **d** they not overtake your ancestors?
8:14 and I **d** not relent, says the LORD of hosts,
Mal 2:15 **D** not one God make her?
Mt 1:24 he **d** as the angel of the Lord commanded him,
7:22 'Lord, Lord, **d** we not prophesy in your name,
7:25 and the winds blew and beat on that house, but it **d**
11: 7 "What **d** you go out into the wilderness to look at?
11: 8 What then **d** you go out to see?
11: 9 What then **d** you go out to see?
11:17 the flute for you, and you **d** not dance;
11:17 we wailed, and you **d** not mourn.'
11:20 because they **d** not repent.
12: 3 "Have you not read what David **d** when he
13: 5 where they **d** not have much soil,
13:17 but **d** not see it, and to hear what you hear, but **d** not hear it.
13:27 'Master, **d** you not sow good seed in your field?
13:27 Where, then, **d** these weeds come from?'
13:54 "Where **d** this man get this wisdom
13:56 Where then **d** this man get all this?"
13:58 And he **d** not do many deeds of power there,
14:31 "You of little faith, why **d** you doubt?"
15:23 But he **d** not answer her at all.
17:12 and they **d** not recognize him,
17:12 but they **d** to him whatever they pleased.
19: 7 then **d** Moses command us to give a certificate
20: 5 about noon and about three o'clock, he **d** the same.
20:13 **d** you not agree with me for the usual daily wage?
21: 6 disciples went and **d** as Jesus had directed them;
21:15 and the scribes saw the amazing things that he **d,**
21:20 saying, "How **d** the fig tree wither at once?"
21:25 **D** the baptism of John come from heaven,
21:25 'Why then **d** you not believe him?'
21:30 'I go, sir'; but he **d** not go.
21:31 Which of the two **d** the will of his father?"
21:32 and you **d** not believe him, but the tax collectors
21:32 you **d** not change your minds and believe him.
22:12 how **d** you get in here without a wedding robe?'
22:26 The second **d** the same, so also the third,
22:46 nor from that day **d** anyone dare
25:24 reaping where you **d** not sow, and gathering where you **d** not scatter seed;
25:26 You knew, **d** you, that I reap where I **d** not sow, and gather where I **d** not scatter?
25:40 just as you **d** it to one of the least of these who are members of my family, you **d** it to me.'
25:43 I was a stranger and you **d** not welcome me, naked and you **d** not give me clothing, sick and in prison and you **d** not visit me.'
25:44 and **d** not take care of you?'
25:45 just as you **d** not do it to one of the least of these, you **d** not do it to me.'
26:19 So the disciples **d** as Jesus had directed them,
26:55 and you **d** not arrest me.
27:12 by the chief priests and elders, he **d** not answer.
28:15 they took the money and **d** as they were directed.
Mk 2:25 "Have you never read what David **d** when he
4: 5 where it **d** not have much soil,
4:34 he **d** not speak to them except in parables,
6: 2 They said, "Where **d** this man get all this?
6:26 he **d** not want to refuse her.
6:52 for they **d** not understand about the loaves,
7:24 and **d** not want anyone to know he was there.
8:19 many baskets full of broken pieces **d** you collect?"
8:20 many baskets full of broken pieces **d** you collect?"
9: 6 He **d** not know what to say, for they were terrified.
9:13 and they **d** to him whatever they pleased,
9:30 He **d** not want anyone to know it;
9:32 But they **d** not understand what he was saying
10: 3 "What **d** Moses command you?"
11:30 **D** the baptism of John come from heaven,
11:31 he will say, 'Why then **d** you not believe him?'
14:40 and they **d** not know what to say to him.
14:49 and you **d** not arrest me.
14:56 and their testimony **d** not agree.
14:59 But even on this point their testimony **d** not agree.
14:61 But he was silent and **d** not answer.
15:23 but he **d** not take it.
16:13 [[told the rest, but they **d** not believe them.]]
Lk 1:20 But now, because you **d** not believe my words,
1:22 When he **d** come out, he could not speak to them,
2:43 but his parents **d** not know it.
2:45 When they **d** not find him,
2:49 **D** you not know that I must be
2:50 But they **d** not understand what he said to them.
4:23 that we have heard you **d** at Capernaum.' "
6: 3 "Have you not read what David **d** when he
6:10 He **d** so, and his hand was restored.
6:23 for that is what their ancestors **d** to the prophets.
6:26 that is what their ancestors **d** to the false prophets.
7: 7 therefore I **d** not presume to come to you.
7:24 "What **d** you go out into the wilderness to look at?
7:25 What then **d** you go out to see?
7:26 What then **d** you go out to see?
7:32 'We played the flute for you, and you **d** not dance;
7:32 we wailed, and you **d** not weep.'
7:46 You **d** not anoint my head with oil,
8:27 and he **d** not live in a house but in the tombs.
8:51 he **d** not allow anyone to enter with him,
9:15 They **d** so and made them all sit down.
9:45 But they **d** not understand this saying;
9:53 but they **d** not receive him,
10:24 but **d** not see it, and to hear what you hear,
10:24 and to hear what you hear, but **d** not hear it."
11:38 to see that he **d** not first wash before dinner.
11:40 **D** not the one who made the outside make the
11:52 you **d** not enter yourselves,
12:47 but **d** not prepare himself or do what was wanted,
12:48 the one who **d** not know and what deserved
13: 3 but unless you repent, you will all perish as they **d.**

Lk 13: 5 you repent, you will all perish just as they **d."**
18:34 and they **d** not grasp what was said.
19:21 you take what you **d** not deposit, and reap what
you **d** not sow.'
19:22 You knew, **d** you, that I was a harsh man, taking
what I **d** not deposit and reaping what I **d** not sow?
19:23 Why then **d** you not put my money into the bank?
19:27 as for these enemies of mine who **d** not want me to
19:44 because you **d** not recognize the time
19:48 but they **d** not find anything they could do,
20: 4 **D** the baptism of John come from heaven,
20: 5 he will say, 'Why **d** you not believe him?'
20: 7 that they **d** not know where it came from.
22:20 And he **d** the same with the cup after supper,
22:35 bag, or sandals, **d** you lack anything?"
22:53 you **d** not lay hands on me.
24: 3 but when they went in, they **d** not find the body.
24:11 and they **d** not believe them.
24:23 and when they **d** not find his body there,
24:24 but they **d** not see him."
Jn 1: 5 and the darkness **d** not overcome it.
1:10 yet the world **d** not know him.
1:11 and his own people **d** not accept him.
1:20 He confessed and **d** not deny it, but confessed,
1:31 I myself **d** not know him;
1:33 I myself **d** not know him,
1:48 "Where **d** you get to know me?"
2: 9 and **d** not know where it came from (though
2:11 Jesus **d** this, the first of his signs,
3:17 God **d** not send the Son into the world to condemn
4:38 I sent you to reap that for which you **d** not labor.
4:54 that Jesus **d** after coming from Judea to Galilee.
5:13 man who had been healed **d** not know who it was,
6:25 they said to him, "Rabbi, when **d** you come here?"
6:64 the first who were the ones that **d** not believe,
6:70 Jesus answered them, **"D** I not choose you,
7: 1 He **d** not wish to go about in Judea because
7:19 **"D** not Moses give you the law?
7:45 who asked them, "Why **d** you not arrest him?"
8:27 They **d** not understand that he was speaking
8:39 you would be doing what Abraham **d,**
8:40 This is not what Abraham **d.**
8:42 I **d** not come on my own, but he sent me.
8:52 Abraham died, and so **d** the prophets;
9:18 The Jews **d** not believe that he had been blind
9:26 They said to him, "What **d** he do to you?
9:26 How **d** he open your eyes?"
10: 6 they **d** not understand what he was saying to them.
10: 8 but the sheep **d** not listen to them.
11:40 **"D** I not tell you that if you believed,
11:45 with Mary and had seen what Jesus **d,**
11:51 He **d** not say this on his own,
12:16 His disciples **d** not understand these things at first;
12:37 they **d** not believe in him.
12:42 But because of the Pharisees they **d** not confess it,
15:16 You **d** not choose me but I chose you.
15:24 among them the works that no one else **d,**
16: 4 "I **d** not say these things to you from
18: 9 "I **d** not lose a single one
18:26 asked, **"D** I not see you in the garden with him?"
18:28 They themselves **d** not enter the headquarters,
18:34 or **d** others tell you about me?"
19:25 And that is what the soldiers **d.**
19:31 the Jews **d** not want the bodies left on the cross
19:33 they **d** not break his legs.
20: 5 but he **d** not go in.
20: 9 for as yet they **d** not understand the scripture,
20:14 but she **d** not know that it was Jesus.
20:30 Now Jesus **d** many other signs in the presence
21: 4 but the disciples **d** not know that it was Jesus.
21:13 and **d** the same with the fish.
21:23 Yet Jesus **d** not say to him that he would not die,
21:25 But there are also many other things that Jesus **d;**
Ac 1: 1 I wrote about all that Jesus **d** and taught from
2:22 and signs that God **d** through him among you,
2:31 nor **d** his flesh experience corruption.'
2:34 For David **d** not ascend into the heavens,
3: 4 Peter looked intently at him, as **d** John, and said,
3:17 that you acted in ignorance, as **d** also your rulers.
4: 7 "By what power or by what name **d** you do this?"
4:25 'Why **d** the Gentiles rage,
5: 4 it remained unsold, **d** it not remain your own?
5: 4 You **d** not lie to us but to God!"
5:22 they **d** not find them in the prison;
5:42 the temple and at home they **d** not cease to teach
6: 8 **d** great wonders and signs among the people.
7: 5 He **d** not give him any of it as a heritage,
7:25 but they **d** not understand.
7:32 Moses began to tremble and **d** not dare to look.
7:42 **'D** you offer to me slain victims
7:50 **D** not my hand make all these things?'
7:52 of the prophets **d** your ancestors not persecute?
8: 6 hearing and seeing the signs that he **d,**
9:26 for they **d** not believe that he was a disciple.
10:39 We are witnesses to all that he **d** both in Judea and
11: 3 "Why **d** you go to uncircumcised men and eat
11:30 this they **d,** sending it to the elders by Barnabas
12: 8 on your sandals." He **d** so.
12: 9 he **d** not realize that what was happening with
13:27 of Jerusalem and their leaders **d** not recognize him
15: 8 just as he **d** to us;
16: 7 but the Spirit of Jesus **d** not allow them;
17: 4 as **d** a great many of the devout Greeks and not
19: 2 **"D** you receive the Holy Spirit
19:11 God **d** extraordinary miracles through Paul,
19:32 of them **d** not know why they had come together.
20:20 I **d** not shrink from doing anything helpful,
Ac 20:27 for I **d** not shrink from declaring to you
20:31 that for three years I **d** not cease night or day
22: 9 Now those who were with me saw the light but **d**
23: 5 And Paul said, "I **d** not realize, brothers,
24:12 They **d** not find me disputing with anyone in
25:18 they **d** not charge him with any of the crimes
26:10 And that is what I **d** in Jerusalem;
27:39 In the morning they **d** not recognize the land,
Ro 1:21 they **d** not honor him as God or give thanks
1:28 And since they **d** not see fit to acknowledge God,
3:25 He **d** this to show his righteousness,
4:13 For the promise that he would inherit the world **d**
4:19 He **d** not weaken in faith
6:21 So what advantage **d** you then get from the things
7:13 **D** what is good, then, bring death to me?
8:15 For you **d** not receive a spirit of slavery
8:32 He who **d** not withhold his own Son,
9:30 Gentiles, who **d** not strive for righteousness,
9:31 who **d** strive for the righteousness that is based on
9:31 **d** not succeed in fulfilling that law.
9:32 they **d** not strive for it on the basis of faith,
10:19 Again I ask, **d** Israel not understand?
10:20 "I have been found by those who **d** not seek me;
10:20 I have shown myself to those who **d** not ask
11:21 For if God **d** not spare the natural branches,
15: 3 For Christ **d** not please himself;
1Co 1:16 (I **d** baptize also the household of Stephanas;
1:17 For Christ **d** not send me to baptize but
1:21 the world **d** not know God through wisdom,
2: 1 I **d** not come proclaiming the mystery of God
4: 7 What do you have that you **d** not receive?
10: 6 so that we might not desire evil as they **d.**
10: 7 Do not become idolaters as some of them **d;**
10: 8 in sexual immorality as some of them **d,**
10: 9 to the test, as some of them **d,** and were destroyed
10:10 And do not complain as some of them **d,**
14:36 Or **d** the word of God originate with you?
15:15 whom he **d** not raise if it is true that the dead are
2Co 1:23 to spare you that I **d** not come again to Corinth.
2: 3 And I wrote as I **d,** so that when I came,
2:13 because I **d** not find my brother Titus there.
7: 8 I do not regret it (though I **d** regret it,
7:12 it was not on account of the one who **d** the wrong,
8:15 "The one who had much **d** not have too much, and
the one who had little **d** not have too little."
11: 7 **D** I commit a sin by humbling myself so
11: 9 I **d** not burden anyone, for my needs were supplied
12:13 except that I myself **d** not burden you?
12:16 Let it be assumed that I **d** not burden you.
12:17 **D** I take advantage of you through any
12:18 Titus **d** not take advantage of you, **d** he?
12:18 **D** we not conduct ourselves with the same spirit?
12:18 **D** we not take the same steps?
13: 2 as I **d** when present on my second visit,
Gal 1:12 for I **d** not receive it from a human source,
1:16 I **d** not confer with any human being,
1:17 nor **d** I go up to Jerusalem
1:18 Then after three years I **d** go up to Jerusalem
1:19 but I **d** not see any other apostle except James
2: 5 we **d** not submit to them even for a moment,
3: 2 **D** you receive the Spirit by doing the works of
3: 4 **D** you experience so much for nothing?—
4: 8 Formerly, when you **d** not know God,
4:14 you **d** not scorn or despise me,
Php 2: 6 **d** not regard equality with God as something to
2:16 that I can boast on the day of Christ that I **d**
1Th 2: 6 nor **d** we seek praise from mortals,
2:14 from your own compatriots as they **d** from
4: 7 For God **d** not call us to impurity but in holiness.
2Th 3: 8 we **d** not eat anyone's bread without paying for it;
1Ti 1: 3 as I **d** when I was on my way to Macedonia,
2Ti 1: 3 with a clear conscience, as my ancestors **d—**
1: 7 for God **d** not give us a spirit of cowardice,
4:14 Alexander the coppersmith **d** me great harm;
Heb 1: 5 For to which of the angels **d** God ever say,
2: 5 Now God **d** not subject the coming world,
2:16 For it is clear that he **d** not come to help angels,
3:18 And to whom **d** he swear that they would
4: 2 but the message they heard **d** not benefit them,
4:10 also cease from their labors as God **d** from his.
5: 5 So also Christ **d** not glorify himself in becoming
7:27 this he **d** once for all when he offered himself.
8: 9 for they **d** not continue in my covenant,
9:24 For Christ **d** not enter a sanctuary made
11: 5 By faith Enoch was taken so that he **d**
11: 9 living in tents, as **d** Isaac and Jacob,
11:19 and figuratively speaking, he **d** receive him back.
11:31 By faith Rahab the prostitute **d** not perish
11:39 **d** not receive what was promised,
12:25 for if they **d** not escape when they refused
Jas 5:17 and for three years and six months it **d** not rain on
1Pe 2:23 When he was abused, he **d** not return abuse;
2:23 when he suffered, he **d** not threaten;
3:20 who in former times **d** not obey,
2Pe 1:16 For we **d** not follow cleverly devised myths
2: 4 if God **d** not spare the angels when they sinned,
2: 5 and if he **d** not spare the ancient world,
1Jn 2:19 but they **d** not belong to us;
3: 1 The reason the world does not know us is that it **d**
3:12 And why **d** he murder him?
Jude 1: 5 afterward destroyed those who **d** not believe.
1: 6 And the angels who **d** not keep their own position,
1: 9 he **d** not dare to bring a condemnation of slander
Rev 2: 5 repent, and do the works you **d** at first.
2:13 and you **d** not deny your faith in me even in
9:20 **d** not repent of the works of their hands or give
9:21 And they **d** not repent of their murders
Rev 12:11 they **d** not cling to life even in the face of death.
16: 9 and they **d** not repent and give him glory.
16:11 and they **d** not repent of their deeds.
20: 5 (The rest of the dead **d** not come to life until
Tob 2:10 I **d** not know that there were sparrows on the wall;
2:13 I called her and said, "Where **d** you get this goat?
2:14 But I **d** not believe her,
5: 4 but he **d** not perceive that he was an angel of God.
10: 1 the days had passed and his son **d** not appear,
12:13 And that time when you **d** not hesitate to get up
12:19 I really **d** not eat or drink anything—
14:10 what Nadab **d** to Ahikar who had reared him.
Jdt 4: 8 So the Israelites **d** as they had been ordered by
5: 7 because they **d** not wish to follow the gods
5:17 as they **d** not sin against their God they prospered,
7:15 they rebelled and **d** not receive you peaceably."
7:21 and on no day **d** they have enough water to drink,
8:25 who is putting us to the test as he **d** our ancestors.
8:26 Remember what he **d** with Abraham,
8:27 For he has not tried us with fire, as he **d** them,
9: 2 'It shall not be done'—yet they **d** it.
10:23 She prostrated herself and **d** obeisance to him,
12:10 and **d** not invite any of his officers.
13: 3 as she **d** on the other days;
14: 7 and **d** obeisance to her, and said,
14:17 and when he **d** not find her,
15: 2 they **d** not wait for one another,
16: 6 For their mighty one **d** not fall by the hands of
16: 6 nor **d** the sons of the Titans strike him down,
16: 6 nor **d** tall giants set upon him;
AdE 1:21 and the king **d** as Muchaeus had recommended.
2: 4 This pleased the king, and he **d** so.
2:20 So Esther **d** not change her mode of life.
3: 2 Mordecai, however, **d** not do obeisance.
4:17 and **d** what Esther had told him to do.
5:12 "The queen **d** not invite anyone to the dinner with
6: 3 "What honor or dignity **d** we bestow
9:16 but **d** not engage in plunder.
9:18 also on the fourteenth, but **d** not rest.
13:12 or for any love of glory that I **d** this, and refused
13:14 But I **d** this so that I might not set human glory
14: 5 and that you **d** for them all that you promised.
16:18 the one who **d** these things,
Wis 1:13 because God **d** not make death,
2:22 and they **d** not know the secret purposes of God,
4:15 Yet the peoples saw and **d** not understand,
5: 6 and the light of righteousness **d** not shine on us,
5: 6 and the sun **d** not rise upon us.
6: 4 as servants of his kingdom you **d** not rule rightly,
7: 9 Neither **d** I liken to her any priceless gem,
7:12 but I **d** not know that she was their mother.
10:13 righteous man was sold, wisdom **d** not desert him,
10:14 and when he was in prison she **d** not leave him,
11:17 **d** not lack the means to send upon them
11:19 not only could the harm they **d** destroy people,
13: 1 nor **d** they recognize the artisan while paying heed
13: 9 **d** they fail to find sooner the Lord of these things?
14:10 be punished together with the one who **d** it.
14:13 for they **d** not exist from the beginning,
14:18 of the artisan impelled even those who **d** not know
16: 5 your wrath **d** not continue to the end;
17: 5 nor **d** the brilliant flames of the stars avail
18: 1 Their enemies heard their voices but **d**
18:20 but the wrath **d** not long continue.
19:13 The punishments **d** not come upon the sinners
19:21 nor **d** they melt the crystalline,
Sir 1:30 because you **d** not come in the fear of the Lord,
16: 7 He **d** not forgive the ancient giants who revolted
16: 8 He **d** not spare the neighbors of Lot,
19:13 Question a friend; perhaps he **d** not do it;
19:13 or if he **d,** so that he may not do it again.
19:14 Question a neighbor; perhaps he **d** not say it;
24:28 The first man **d** not know wisdom fully,
31:10 the power to transgress and **d** not transgress,
31:10 and to do evil and **d** not do it?
40: 6 he struggles in his sleep as he **d** by day.
45:13 Before him such beautiful things **d** not exist.
46:11 whose hearts **d** not fall into idolatry and who **d** not
47: 4 In his youth **d** he not kill a giant,
47: 8 In all that he **d** he gave thanks to the Holy One,
48:12 in his lifetime **d** he tremble before any ruler,
48:14 In his life he **d** wonders,
48:15 Despite all this the people **d** not repent,
48:15 nor **d** they forsake their sins,
48:16 Some of them **d** what was right,
48:22 For Hezekiah **d** what was pleasing to the Lord,
49: 2 He **d** what was right by reforming the people,
Bar 1:21 We **d** not listen to the voice of the Lord our God
2:24 But we **d** not obey your voice,
3: 4 who **d** not heed the voice of the Lord their God,
3:27 God **d** not choose them, or give them the way
4:13 they **d** not walk in the ways
LtJ 6:24 even when they were being cast, they **d** not feel it.
Aza 1:27 The fire **d** not touch them at all
Sus 1:10 but they **d** not tell each other of their distress,
1:18 They **d** as she told them:
1:18 they **d** not see the elders,
1:40 We **d,** however, seize this woman and asked who
1:54 Under what tree **d** you see them being intimate
1:58 Under what tree **d** you catch them being intimate
1:61 they **d** to them as they had wickedly planned to do
1:63 and so **d** her husband Joakim and all her relatives,
1Mc 1: 9 so **d** their descendants after them for many years;
1:52 joined them, and they **d** evil in the land;
1:63 to profane the holy covenant; and they **d** die.
2:26 just as Phinehas **d** against Zimri son of Salu.
2:36 But they **d** not answer them or hurl a stone at them

1Mc 2:51 which they **d** in their generations;
4: 6 but they **d** not have armor and swords such
5:61 they **d** not listen to Judas and his brothers.
5:62 But they **d** not belong to the family of those men
6:12 But now I remember the wrong I **d** in Jerusalem.
6:59 to let them live by their laws as they **d** before;
6:59 that they became angry and **d** all these things."
7:22 of the land of Judah and **d** great damage in Israel.
9:11 as **d** all the chief warriors.
9:22 and his wars and the brave deeds that he **d,**
9:48 the enemy **d** not cross the Jordan to attack them.
9:71 He agreed, and **d** as he said;
9:72 and **d** not come again into their territory.
10: 5 the wrongs that we **d** to him and to his brothers
10:11 for better fortification; and they **d** so.
10:14 Only in Beth-zur **d** some remain who had forsaken
10:41 the government officials have not paid as they **d** in
10:46 they **d** not believe or accept them,
10:62 and to clothe him in purple, and they **d** so.
11:53 he became estranged from Jonathan and **d**
11:66 to grant them terms of peace, and he **d** so.
12:29 and his troops **d** not know it until morning,
12:30 but he **d** not overtake them,
12:46 Jonathan trusted him and **d** as he said;
13:18 "It was because Simon **d** not send him the money
13:19 Trypho broke his word and **d** not release Jonathan.
13:22 and he **d** not go because of the snow.
13:34 for all that Trypho **d** was to plunder.
13:50 to Simon to make peace with them, and he **d** so.
14:14 and **d** away with all the renegades and outlaws.
15:35 Athenobius **d** not answer him a word,
16:23 and his wars and the brave deeds that he **d,**
2Mc 1:23 and the rest responded, as **d** Nehemiah.
3: 6 they **d** not belong to the account of the sacrifices,
4:27 he **d** not pay regularly any of the money promised
5: 7 He **d** not, however, gain control of
5:17 and **d** not perceive that the Lord was angered for
5:19 But the Lord **d** not choose the nation for the sake
5:23 over his compatriots worse than the others **d.**
6: 2 as **d** the people who lived in that place.
6: 9 and should kill those who **d** not choose to change
7:28 and recognize that God **d** not make them out
8:26 for that reason they **d** not continue their pursuit.
9: 7 Yet he **d** not in any way stop his insolence,
9:18 But when his sufferings **d** not in any way abate,
11: 3 as he **d** on the sacred places of the other nations,
12: 3 the people of Joppa **d** so ungodly a deed as this:
12:18 They **d** not find Timothy in that region,
14:23 Nicanor stayed on in Jerusalem and **d** nothing out
14:30 concluded that this austerity **d** not spring from
14:32 When they declared on oath that they **d** not know
14:43 But in the heat of the struggle he **d** not hit exactly,
15: 5 Nevertheless, he **d** not succeed
15: 7 But Maccabeus **d** not cease to trust
1Es 1:11 this they **d** in the morning.
1:28 Josiah, however, **d** not turn back to his chariot,
1:28 and **d** not heed the words of the prophet Jeremiah
1:39 he **d** what was evil in the sight of the Lord.
1:44 He **d** what was evil in the sight of the Lord.
1:47 He also **d** what was evil in the sight of the Lord,
1:47 and **d** not heed the words that were spoken by
1:53 and **d** not spare young man or young woman,
7: 6 **d** according to what was written in the book
9: 2 and he **d** not eat bread or drink water,
9: 4 if any **d** not meet there within two or three days,
Man 1: 8 who **d** not sin against you,
3Mc 1: 9 and made thank offerings and **d** what was fitting
1:12 he **d** not cease to maintain that he ought to enter,
2:32 and **d** not abandon their religion;
3: 8 They **d** try to console them,
3:20 accommodated ourselves to their folly and **d**
5:22 But they **d** not so much employ the duration of
6:15 in the land of their enemies **d** I neglect them,'
7:10 On receiving this letter the Jews **d**
2Es 1:14 and **d** great wonders among you.
1:17 **d** you not cry out to me,
1:20 **d** I not split the rock so that waters flowed
1:23 I **d** not send fire on you for your blasphemies,
2: 8 remember what I **d** to Sodom and Gomorrah,
3: 4 **d** you not speak at the beginning when you planted
3: 8 they **d** ungodly things in your sight
3: 8 and you **d** not hinder them.
3:20 you **d** not take away their evil heart from them,
4: 8 neither **d** I ever ascend into heaven.'
4:23 For I **d** not wish to inquire about the ways above,
4:35 **D** not the souls of the righteous
5:35 why **d** not my mother's womb become my grave,
7:72 though they received the commandments, they **d**
7:*126* [56] and committed iniquity we **d** not consider
7:*130* [60] they **d** not believe him or the prophets
7:*137* [67] for if he **d** not make them abound, the world
7:*138* [68] because if he **d** not give out of his goodness so
7:*139* [69] if he **d** not pardon those who were created
8: 5 not of your own will **d** you come into the world,
8:59 For the Most High **d** not intend that anyone should
9:10 many as **d** not acknowledge me in their lifetime,
9:11 and **d** not understand but despised it while
9:32 they **d** not keep it and **d** not observe the statutes;
9:32 yet the fruit of the law **d** not perish—
9:33 they **d** not keep what had been sown in them.
10:32 I **d** as you directed, and went out into the field,
10:35 For I have seen what I **d** not know,
11:10 and saw that the voice **d** not come from its heads,
11:21 and others of them rose up, but **d** not hold the rule.
11:42 the walls of those who **d** you no harm.
13:51 Why **d** I see the man coming up from the heart of
14:30 the law of life, which they **d** not keep, which you
2Es 14:31 and your ancestors committed iniquity and **d**
14:42 using characters that they **d** not know.
14:48 And I **d** so.
4Mc 2:17 he **d** nothing against them in anger,
2:19 Why else **d** Jacob, our most wise father,
4: 7 and **d** all that they could to prevent it.
7: 3 in no way **d** he turn the rudder of religion
7: 4 as **d** that most holy man.
7: 9 you **d** not abandon the holiness that you praised,
9:21 worthy of Abraham, **d** not groan,
14:20 But sympathy for her children **d** not sway
15:14 because of religion **d** not change her attitude.
15:18 firstborn breathed his last, it **d** not turn you aside,
15:19 nor **d** you weep when you looked at the eyes
15:20 with many spectators of the torturings, you **d**
15:21 of swans attract the attention of their hearers as **d**
15:27 She **d** not approve the deliverance
16:12 Yet that holy and God-fearing mother **d** not wail
16:12 nor **d** she dissuade any of them from dying,
16:12 nor **d** she grieve as they were dying.
16:20 a knife and descending upon him, he **d** not cower.
17:16 Who **d** not admire the athletes of
17:20 of them our enemies **d** not rule over our nation,
18: 7 and **d** not go outside my father's house;
18: 8 nor **d** the destroyer, the deceitful serpent,
18: 9 and **d** not have the grief of bereavement.
18:18 For he **d** not forget to teach you the song

DIDRACHMA See Index to Footnotes

DIDYMUS See Index to Footnotes

DIE‡ (368) [DEAD]

Ge 2:17 for in the day that you eat of it you shall **d."**
3: 3 nor shall you touch it, or you shall **d.'** "
3: 4 the serpent said to the woman, "You will not **d;**
6:17 everything that is on the earth shall **d.**
19:19 for fear the disaster will overtake me and I **d.**
20: 3 to **d** because of the woman whom you have taken;
20: 7 know that you shall surely **d,**
25:32 Esau said, "I am about to **d;**
26: 9 "Because I thought I might **d** because of her."
27: 4 so that I may bless you before I **d."**
27: 7 I may bless you before the LORD before I **d.'**
30: 1 she said to Jacob, "Give me children, or I shall **d!"**
33:13 for one day, all the flocks will **d.**
38:11 for he feared that he too would **d,** like his brothers.
42: 2 that we may live and not **d."**
42:20 be verified, and you shall not **d."**
43: 8 so that we may live and not **d—**
44: 9 be found with any one of your servants, let him **d;**
44:22 if he should leave his father, his father would **d.'**
44:31 that the boy is not with us, he will **d;**
45:28 I must go and see him before I **d."**
46:30 Israel said to Joseph, "I can **d** now,
47:15 Why should we **d** before your eyes?
47:19 Shall we **d** before your eyes,
47:19 just give us seed, so that we may live and not **d,**
48:21 Then Israel said to Joseph, "I am about to **d,**
50: 5 he said, 'I am about to **d.**
50:24 Joseph said to his brothers, "I am about to **d;**
Ex 7:18 The fish in the river shall **d,**
9: 4 so that nothing shall **d** of all that belongs to
9:19 under shelter will **d** when the hail comes down
10:28 for on the day you see my face you shall **d."**
11: 5 Every firstborn in the land of Egypt shall **d,**
14:11 in Egypt that you have taken us away to **d** in
14:12 to serve the Egyptians than to **d** in the wilderness."
20:19 but do not let God speak to us, or we will **d."**
28:35 and when he comes out, so that he may not **d.**
28:43 or they will bring guilt on themselves and **d.**
30:20 they shall wash with water, so that they may not **d.**
30:21 so that they may not **d:**
Lev 8:35 the LORD's charge so that you do not **d;**
10: 6 or you will **d** and wrath will strike all
10: 7 the entrance of the tent of meeting, or you will **d;**
10: 9 the tent of meeting, that you may not **d;**
15:31 so that they do not **d** in their uncleanness
16: 2 the mercy seat that is upon the ark, or he will **d;**
16:13 that is upon the covenant, or he will **d.**
20:20 to punishment; they shall **d** childless.
22: 9 and **d** in the sanctuary for having profaned it:
Nu 4:15 not touch the holy things, or they will **d.**
4:19 that they may live and not **d** when they come near
4:20 for a moment; otherwise they will **d.**
6: 7 their father or mother, brother or sister, should **d,**
14:35 to a full end, and there they shall **d.**
16:29 If these people **d** a natural death,
17:10 of their complaints against me, or else they will **d."**
17:13 the tabernacle of the LORD will **d.**
18: 3 otherwise both they and you will **d.**
18:22 or else they will incur guilt and **d.**
20: 4 for us and our livestock to **d** here?
20:26 be gathered to his people, and shall **d** there."
21: 5 "Why have you brought us up out of Egypt to **d** in
23:10 Let me **d** the death of the upright,
26:11 Notwithstanding, the sons of Korah did not **d.**
26:65 "They shall **d** in the wilderness."
35:12 not **d** until there is a trial before the congregation.
Dt 4:22 to **d** in this land without crossing over the Jordan,
5:25 So now why should we **d?**
5:25 of the LORD our God any longer, we shall **d.**
9:28 he has brought them out to let them **d** in
17:12 or the judge, that person shall **d.**
18:16 or ever again see this great fire, I will **d."**
Dt 18:20 the prophet to speak—that prophet shall **d."**
20: 5 or he might **d** in the battle and another dedicate it.
20: 6 or he might **d** in the battle and another be first
20: 7 or he might **d** in the battle and another marry her."
22:22 of them shall **d,** the man who lay with the woman
22:25 then only the man who lay with her shall **d.**
24: 7 then that kidnaper shall **d.**
31:14 LORD said to Moses, "Your time to **d** is near;
32:50 you shall **d** there on the mountain that you ascend
33: 6 May Reuben live, and not **d** out,
Jos 20: 9 so as not to **d** by the hand of the avenger of blood,
Jdg 6:23 do not fear, you shall not **d."**
6:30 "Bring out your son, so that he may **d,**
13:22 And Manoah said to his wife, "We shall surely **d,**
15:18 Am I now to **d** of thirst,
16:30 Samson said, "Let me **d** with the Philistines."
Ru 1:17 Where you **d,** I will **d**—there will I be buried.
1Sa 2:33 all the members of your household shall **d** by
2:34 both of them shall **d** on the same day.
4:20 As she was about to **d,**
5:12 those who did not **d** were stricken with tumors,
12:19 so that we may not **d;**
14:39 even if it is in my son Jonathan, he shall surely **d!"**
14:43 here I am, I will **d."**
14:44 you shall surely **d,** Jonathan!"
14:45 Then the people said to Saul, "Shall Jonathan **d,**
14:45 the people ransomed Jonathan, and he did not **d.**
20: 2 "Far from it! You shall not **d.**
20:14 of the LORD; but if I **d,**
20:31 send and bring him to me, for he shall surely **d."**
22:16 The king said, "You shall surely **d,** Ahimelech,
26:10 or his day will come to **d;**
26:16 As the LORD lives, you deserve to **d,**
2Sa 3:33 saying, "Should Abner **d** as a fool dies?
11:15 so that he may be struck down and **d."**
12: 5 the man who has done this deserves to **d;**
12:13 the LORD has put away your sin; you shall not **d.**
12:14 the child that is born to you shall **d."**
14:14 We must all **d;** we are like water
18: 3 If half of us **d,** they will not care about us.
19:23 The king said to Shimei, "You shall not **d."**
19:37 so that I may **d** in my own town,
1Ki 1:52 but if wickedness is found in him, he shall **d."**
2: 1 When David's time to **d** drew near,
2:30 But he said, "No, I will **d** here."
2:37 know for certain that you shall **d;**
2:42 and go to any place whatever, you shall **d'?**
13:31 he had buried him, he said to his sons, "When I **d,**
14:12 When your feet enter the city, the child shall **d.**
17:12 that we may eat it, and **d."**
19: 4 He asked that he might **d:**
2Ki 1: 4 to which you have gone, but you shall surely **d.'** "
1: 6 to which you have gone, but shall surely **d.'** "
1:16 to which you have gone, but you shall surely **d."**
7: 3 "Why should we sit here until we **d?**
7: 4 the famine is in the city, and we shall **d** there;
7: 4 but if we sit here, we shall also **d.**
7: 4 and if they kill us, we shall but **d."**
8:10 the LORD has shown me that he shall certainly **d."**
13:14 with the illness of which he was to **d,**
18:32 that you may live and not **d.**
20: 1 Set your house in order, for you shall **d;**
2Ch 32:11 handing you over to **d** by famine and by thirst,
Job 2: 9 in your integrity? Curse God, and **d."**
3:11 "Why did I not **d** at birth,
4:21 and they **d** devoid of wisdom.'
12: 2 and wisdom will **d** with you.
13:19 For then I would be silent and **d.**
14:10 But mortals **d,** and are laid low;
14:14 If mortals **d,** will they live again?
27: 5 until I **d** I will not put away my integrity from me.
29:18 Then I thought, 'I shall **d** in my nest,
34:20 In a moment they **d;** at midnight
36:12 and **d** without knowledge.
36:14 They **d** in their youth, and their life ends in shame.
Ps 41: 5 My enemies wonder in malice when I will **d,**
49:10 When we look at the wise, they **d;**
49:17 For when they **d** they will carry nothing away;
79:11 to your great power preserve those doomed to **d.**
82: 7 you shall **d** like mortals, and fall like any prince."
102:20 to set free those who were doomed to **d;**
104:29 they **d** and return to their dust.
105:29 and caused their fish to **d.**
118:17 I shall not **d,** but I shall live,
Pr 5:23 They **d** for lack of discipline,
10:21 but fools **d** for lack of sense.
11: 7 When the wicked **d,** their hope perishes,
11:19 but whoever pursues evil will **d.**
15:10 but one who hates a rebuke will **d.**
19:16 those who are heedless of their ways will **d.**
23:13 if you beat them with a rod, they will not **d.**
30: 7 do not deny them to me before I **d:**
Ecc 2:16 How can the wise **d** just like fools?
3: 2 a time to be born, and a time to **d;**
7:17 why should you **d** before your time?
9: 5 The living know that they will **d,**
Isa 14:30 but I will make your root **d** of famine,
22:13 "Let us eat and drink, for tomorrow we **d."**
22:14 this iniquity will not be forgiven you until you **d,**
22:18 into a wide land; there you shall **d,**
38: 1 Set your house in order, for you shall **d;**
50: 2 their fish stink for lack of water, and **d** of thirst.
51: 6 and those who live on it will **d** like gnats;
51:12 then are you afraid of a mere mortal who must **d,**
51:14 they shall not **d** and go down to the Pit,
66:24 for their worm shall not **d,**
Jer 11:21 or you will **d** by our hand"—

Jer 11:22 the young men shall **d** by the sword;
11:22 their sons and their daughters shall **d** by famine;
16: 4 They shall **d** of deadly diseases.
16: 6 Both great and small shall **d** in this land;
20: 6 there you shall **d**, and there you shall be buried,
21: 6 they shall **d** of a great pestilence.
21: 9 Those who stay in this city shall **d** by the sword,
22:12 where they have carried him captive he shall **d**,
22:26 where you were not born, and there you shall **d**.
26: 8 the people laid hold of him, saying, "You shall **d**!
27:13 Why should you and your people **d** by the sword,
31:30 But all shall **d** for their own sins;
34: 4 You shall not **d** by the sword;
34: 5 you shall **d** in peace.
37:20 to the house of the secretary Jonathan to **d** there."
38: 2 Those who stay in this city shall **d** by the sword,
38: 9 by throwing him into the cistern to **d** there
38:24 of this conversation, or you will **d**.
38:26 to the house of Jonathan to **d** there.' "
42:16 into Egypt; and there you shall **d**.
42:17 to settle there shall **d** by the sword, by famine,
42:22 Be well aware, then, that you shall **d** by the sword,
44:12 they shall **d** by the sword and by famine;
Eze 3:18 If I say to the wicked, "You shall surely **d**,"
3:18 those wicked persons shall **d** for their iniquity;
3:19 they shall **d** for their iniquity;
3:20 a stumbling block before them, they shall **d**;
3:20 they shall **d** for their sin, and their righteous deeds
5:12 of you shall **d** of pestilence or be consumed
6:12 Those far off shall **d** of pestilence;
6:12 any who are left and are spared shall **d** of famine.
7:15 those in the field **d** by the sword;
12:13 not see it; and he shall **d** there.
13:19 not **d** and keeping alive persons who should
17:16 with him he broke—in Babylon he shall **d**.
18: 4 it is only the person who sins that shall **d**.
18:13 he shall surely **d**; his blood shall be upon himself.
18:17 he shall not **d** for his father's iniquity;
18:20 The person who sins shall **d**.
18:21 surely live; they shall not **d**.
18:24 and the sin they have committed, they shall **d**.
18:26 and commit iniquity, they shall **d** for it;
18:26 the iniquity that they have committed they shall **d**.
18:28 surely live; they shall not **d**.
18:31 Why will you **d**, O house of Israel?
28: 8 you shall **d** a violent death in the heart of the seas.
28:10 You shall **d** the death of the uncircumcised by
33: 8 "O wicked ones, you shall surely **d**,"
33: 8 the wicked shall **d** in their iniquity,
33: 9 the wicked shall **d** in their iniquity,
33:11 for why will you **d**, O house of Israel?
33:13 the iniquity that they have committed they shall **d**.
33:14 though I say to the wicked, "You shall surely **d**,"
33:15 they shall surely live, they shall not **d**.
33:18 and commit iniquity, they shall **d** for it.
33:27 in strongholds and in caves shall **d** by pestilence.
Am 2: 2 and Moab shall **d** amid uproar,
6: 9 If ten people remain in one house, they shall **d**.
7:11 'Jeroboam shall **d** by the sword,
7:17 you yourself shall **d** in an unclean land,
9:10 All the sinners of my people shall **d** by the sword,
Jnh 4: 3 for it is better for me to **d** than to live."
4: 8 so that he was faint and asked that he might **d**.
4: 8 He said, "It is better for me to **d** than to live."
4: 9 And he said, "Yes, angry enough to **d**."
Hab 1:12 my Holy One? You shall not **d**.
Zec 11: 9 What is to **d**, let it die;
11: 9 What is to die, let it **d**;
Mt 15: 4 of father or mother must surely **d**.'
26:35 Peter said to him, "Even though I must **d** with you,
Mk 7:10 of father or mother must surely **d**.'
14:31 "Even though I must **d** with you,
Lk 20:36 Indeed they cannot **d** anymore,
Jn 6:50 so that one may eat of it and not **d**.
8:21 but you will **d** in your sin.
8:24 I told you that you would **d** in your sins,
8:24 for you will **d** in your sins unless you believe
11:16 "Let us also go, that we may **d** with him."
11:25 Those who believe in me, even though they **d**,
11:26 and believes in me will never **d**.
11:50 to have one man **d** for the people than to have
11:51 that year he prophesied that Jesus was about to **d**
12:33 to indicate the kind of death he was to **d**.
18:14 the Jews that it was better to have one person **d** for
18:32 when he indicated the kind of death he was to **d**.)
19: 7 to that law he ought to **d** because he has claimed to
21:23 in the community that this disciple would not **d**.
21:23 Yet Jesus did not say to him that he would not **d**,
Ac 7:19 to abandon their infants so that they would **d**.
21:13 to **d** in Jerusalem for the name of the Lord Jesus."
25:11 for which I deserve to **d**, I am not trying
Ro 1:32 that those who practice such things deserve to **d**—
5: 7 rarely will anyone **d** for a righteous person—
5: 7 a good person someone might actually dare to **d**.
6: 9 being raised from the dead, will never **d** again;
8:13 for if you live according to the flesh, you will **d**;
14: 7 and we do not **d** to ourselves.
14: 8 and if we **d**, we **d** to the Lord;
14: 8 so then, whether we live or whether we **d**,
1Co 9:15 Indeed, I would rather **d** than that—
15:22 for as all **d** in Adam,
15:31 I **d** every day! That is
15:32 "Let us eat and drink, for tomorrow we **d**."
15:51 We will not all **d**, but we will all be changed,
2Co 7: 3 to **d** together and to live together.
Heb 9:27 And just as it is appointed for mortals to **d** once,
Rev 9: 6 they will long to **d**, but death will flee from them.
Rev 14:13 Blessed are the dead who from now on **d** in
Tob 3: 6 For it is better for me to **d** than to live,
3: 6 for me to **d** than to see so much distress in my life
3:10 but to pray the Lord that I may **d** and not listen
4: 2 and explain to him about the money before I **d**?"
4: 3 "My son, when I **d**, give me a proper burial.
6:14 the night when they went in to her, they would **d**.
6:15 I am afraid that I may **d** and bring my father's
8:10 "It is possible that he will **d** and we will become
8:21 the other half will be yours when my wife and I **d**.
10:11 and may I see children of yours before I **d**."
10:12 of you and of my daughter Sarah before I **d**.
11: 9 my child, I am ready to **d**."
14: 3 When he was about to **d**, he called his son Tobias
Jdt 6: 8 You will not **d** until you perish along with them.
AdE 4:16 contrary to the law, even if I must **d**."
15:10 You shall not **d**, for our law applies only
Wis 3:18 If they **d** young, they will have no hope
4: 7 the righteous, though they **d** early, will be at rest.
15: 9 not concerned that mortals are destined to **d** or
Sir 8: 7 remember that we must all **d**.
10:10 the king of today will **d** tomorrow.
14:13 Do good to friends before you **d**,
14:17 for the decree from of old is, "You must **d**!"
16: 3 to **d** childless better than to have ungodly children.
19:10 Let it **d** with you.
25:24 and because of her we all **d**.
40:28 it is better to **d** than to beg.
41: 9 and when you **d**, a curse is your lot.
Bar 4: 1 and those who forsake her will **d**.
Sus 1:43 And now I am to **d**,
Bel 1: 8 who is eating these provisions, you shall **d**.
1: 9 you prove that Bel is eating them, Daniel shall **d**,
1:12 not find that Bel has eaten it all, we will **d**;
1Mc 1:50 not obey the command of the king shall **d**."
1:63 to **d** rather than to be defiled by food or to profane
the holy covenant; and they did **d**.
2:37 "Let us all **d** in our innocence;
2:41 let us not all **d** as our kindred died
2:49 Now the days drew near for Mattathias to **d**,
3:59 for us to **d** in battle than to see the misfortunes
4:35 how ready they were either to live or to **d** nobly,
9:10 let us **d** bravely for our kindred,
2Mc 6:26 yet whether I live or **d** I shall not escape the hands
6:28 of how to **d** a good death willingly and nobly for
6:30 When he was about to **d** under the blows,
7: 2 For we are ready to **d** rather than transgress
7: 5 their mother encouraged one another to **d** nobly,
7:14 but choose to **d** at the hands of mortals and
7:18 And when he was about to **d**, he said,
8:21 and made them ready to **d** for their laws
14:42 preferring to **d** nobly rather than to fall into
3Mc 1:23 and **d** courageously for the ancestral law,
2Es 1:18 the Egyptians than to **d** in this wilderness.'
7:29 After those years my son the Messiah shall **d**,
7:*78* from the Most High that a person shall **d**,
8:58 though they knew well that they must **d**.
10: 4 but will mourn and fast continually until I **d**."
10:18 I will not go into the city, but I will **d** here."
10:34 so that I may not **d** before my time.
12:26 one of the kings shall **d** in his bed, but in agonies.
15: 4 For all unbelievers shall **d** in their unbelief.
15:57 Your children shall **d** of hunger,
16:22 those who survive the famine shall **d** by the sword.
4Mc 4:23 the ancestral law they should **d**.
6:22 O children of Abraham, **d** nobly for your religion!
7:19 do not **d** to God, but live to God.
8:11 nothing remains for you but to **d** on the rack?"
9: 1 to **d** rather than transgress our ancestral
9: 6 men should **d** despising your coercive tortures,
10: 9 When he was about to **d**, he said,
11:15 we ought likewise to **d** for the same principles.
11:22 equipped with nobility, will **d** with my brothers,
12: 4 will be miserably tortured and **d** before your time,
12:15 Then because he too was about to **d**, he said,
13: 9 let us **d** like brothers for the sake of the law;
13:17 For if we so **d**, Abraham and Isaac
16:11 I **d**, I shall have none of my sons to bury me."
16:24 to **d** rather than violate God's commandment.
16:25 that those who **d** for the sake of God live to God,

DIED‡ (304) [DEAD]

Ge 5: 5 lived were nine hundred thirty years; and he **d**.
5: 8 Seth were nine hundred twelve years; and he **d**.
5:11 of Enosh were nine hundred five years; and he **d**.
5:14 Kenan were nine hundred and ten years; and he **d**.
5:17 were eight hundred ninety-five years; and he **d**.
5:20 Jared were nine hundred sixty-two years; and he **d**.
5:27 were nine hundred sixty-nine years; and he **d**.
5:31 were seven hundred seventy-seven years; and he **d**.
7:21 And all flesh **d** that moved on the earth, birds,
7:22 in whose nostrils was the breath of life **d**.
9:29 of Noah were nine hundred fifty years; and he **d**.
11:28 Haran **d** before his father Terah in the land
11:32 two hundred five years; and Terah **d** in Haran.
23: 2 And Sarah **d** at Kiriath-arba (that is, Hebron)
25: 8 Abraham breathed his last and **d** in a good old age,
25:17 he breathed his last and **d**,
35: 8 And Deborah, Rebekah's nurse, **d**,
35:18 As her soul was departing (for she **d**),
35:19 So Rachel **d**, and she was buried on the way
35:29 he **d** and was gathered to his people,
36:33 Bela **d**, and Jobab son of Zerah
36:34 Jobab **d**, and Husham of the land of
36:35 Husham **d**, and Hadad son of Bedad,
36:36 Hadad **d**, and Samlah of Masrekah succeeded him
Ge 36:37 Samlah **d**, and Shaul of Rehoboth on
36:38 Shaul **d**, and Baal-hanan son
36:39 Baal-hanan son of Achbor **d**,
38:12 of time the wife of Judah, Shua's daughter, **d**;
46:12 Zerah (but Er and Onan **d** in the land of Canaan);
48: 7 Rachel, alas, **d** in the land of Canaan on the way,
50:16 "Your father gave this instruction before he **d**,
50:26 And Joseph **d**, being one hundred ten years old;
Ex 1: 6 Then Joseph **d**, and all his brothers,
2:23 After a long time the king of Egypt **d**.
7:21 and the fish in the river **d**.
8:13 the frogs **d** in the houses, the courtyards,
9: 6 all the livestock of the Egyptians **d**,
9: 6 but of the livestock of the Israelites not one **d**.
16: 3 "If only we had **d** by the hand of the LORD in
Lev 7:24 an animal that **d** or was torn by wild animals may
10: 2 and they **d** before the LORD.
16: 1 when they drew near before the LORD and **d**.
22: 8 That which **d** or was torn by wild animals he shall
Nu 3: 4 Nadab and Abihu **d** before the LORD
14: 2 "Would that we had **d** in the land of Egypt!
14: 2 Or would that we had **d** in this wilderness!
14:37 an unfavorable report about the land **d** by a plague
16:49 who **d** by the plague were fourteen thousand seven
16:49 besides those who **d** in the affair of Korah.
19:13 the body of a human being who has **d**,
19:16 or who has **d** naturally, or a human bone,
20: 1 Miriam **d** there, and was buried there.
20: 3 "Would that we had **d** when our kindred **d**
20:28 and Aaron **d** there on the top of the mountain.
20:29 When all the congregation saw that Aaron had **d**,
21: 6 and they bit the people, so that many Israelites **d**.
25: 9 that **d** by the plague were twenty-four thousand.
26:10 when that company **d**, when
26:19 Er and Onan **d** in the land of Canaan.
26:61 and Abihu **d** when they offered illicit fire before
27: 3 "Our father **d** in the wilderness;
27: 3 but **d** for his own sin; and he had no sons.
33:38 of the LORD and **d** there in the fortieth year after
33:39 when he **d** on Mount Hor.
Dt 2:16 as soon as all the warriors had **d** off from among
10: 6 There Aaron **d**, and there he was buried;
32:50 as your brother Aaron **d** on Mount Hor
34: 5 **d** there in the land of Moab,
34: 7 Moses was one hundred twenty years old when
he **d**;
Jos 5: 4 all the warriors, had **d** during the journey
10:11 on them as far as Azekah, and they **d**;
10:11 there were more who **d** because of the hailstones
24:29 **d**, being one hundred ten years old.
24:33 Eleazar son of Aaron **d**;
Jdg 1: 7 They brought him to Jerusalem, and he **d** there.
2: 8 **d** at the age of one hundred ten years.
2:19 But whenever the judge **d**,
2:21 of the nations that Joshua left when he **d**."
3:11 Then Othniel son of Kenaz **d**.
4: 1 in the sight of the LORD, after Ehud **d**.
4:21 fast asleep from weariness—and he **d**.
8:32 Then Gideon son of Joash **d** at a good old age,
8:33 As soon as Gideon **d**, the Israelites relapsed
9:49 all the people of the Tower of Shechem also **d**,
9:54 So the young man thrust him through, and he **d**.
10: 2 Then he **d**, and was buried at Shamir.
10: 5 Jair **d**, and was buried in Kamon.
12: 7 Then Jephthah the Gileadite **d**,
12:10 Then Ibzan **d**, and was buried at Bethlehem.
12:12 Then Elon the Zebulunite **d**,
12:15 Then Abdon son of Hillel the Pirathonite **d**,
20: 5 and they raped my concubine until she **d**.
Ru 1: 3 But Elimelech, the husband of Naomi, **d**,
1: 5 both Mahlon and Chilion also **d**,
1Sa 4:11 and the two sons of Eli, Hophni and Phinehas, **d**.
4:18 and his neck was broken and he **d**,
25: 1 Now Samuel **d**; and all Israel assembled
25:37 and his heart **d** within him; he became like a stone.
25:38 the LORD struck Nabal, and he **d**.
28: 3 Now Samuel had **d**, and all Israel had mourned
31: 5 he also fell upon his sword and **d** with him.
31: 6 and his armor-bearer and all his men **d** together on
2Sa 1: 4 but also many of the army fell and **d**;
1: 4 and Saul and his son Jonathan also **d**."
1: 5 do you know that Saul and his son Jonathan **d**?"
1:15 So he struck him down and he **d**.
2:23 He fell there, and **d** where he lay.
2:23 to the place where Asahel had fallen and **d**,
3:27 So he **d** for shedding the blood of Asahel,
4: 1 When Saul's son Ishbaal heard that Abner had **d**
6: 7 and he **d** there beside the ark of God.
10: 1 the king of the Ammonites **d**,
10:18 the commander of their army, so that he **d** there.
11:21 so that he **d** at Thebez?
12:18 On the seventh day the child **d**.
12:21 but when the child **d**, you rose and ate food."
17:23 he **d** and was buried in the tomb of his father.
18:33 Would I had **d** instead of you, O Absalom,
20:10 on the ground, and he **d**.
24:15 and seventy thousand of the people **d**,
1Ki 2:25 he struck him down, and he **d**.
2:46 and he went out and struck him down, and he **d**.
3:19 Then this woman's son **d** in the night,
14:17 she came to the threshold of the house, the child **d**.
16:18 the king's house over himself with fire, and **d**—
16:22 so Tibni **d**, and Omri became king.
22:35 the Arameans, until at evening he **d**;
22:37 So the king **d**, and was brought to Samaria;
2Ki 1:17 So he **d** according to the word of the LORD
3: 5 when Ahab **d**, the king of Moab rebelled against

2Ki 4:20 the child sat on her lap until noon, and he **d.**
8:15 and spread it over the king's face, until he **d.**
9:27 Then he fled to Megiddo, and **d** there.
12:21 his servants, who struck him down, so that he **d.**
13:20 So Elisha **d,** and they buried him.
13:24 When King Hazael of Aram **d,**
23:34 he came to Egypt, and **d** there.
25:25 they struck down Gedaliah so that he **d,**
1Ch 1:44 When Bela **d,** Jobab son of Zerah
1:45 When Jobab **d,** Husham of the land of
1:46 When Husham **d,** Hadad son of Bedad,
1:47 Hadad **d,** Samlah of Masrekah succeeded him.
1:48 When Samlah **d,** Shaul of Rehoboth on
1:49 When Shaul **d,** Baal-hanan son
1:50 When Baal-hanan **d,** Hadad succeeded him;
1:51 And Hadad **d.** The clans of Edom
2:19 When Azubah **d,** Caleb married Ephrath,
2:30 and Appaim; and Seled **d** childless.
2:32 and Jonathan; and Jether **d** childless.
10: 5 he also fell on his sword and **d.**
10: 6 Thus Saul **d;** he and his three sons and all his house **d** together.
10:13 So Saul **d** for his unfaithfulness;
13:10 and he **d** there before God.
19: 1 King Nahash of the Ammonites **d,**
23:22 Eleazar **d** having no sons, but only daughters;
24: 2 But Nadab and Abihu **d** before their father,
29:28 He **d** in a good old age, full of days, riches,
2Ch 13:20 the LORD struck him down, and he **d.**
18:34 until evening; then at sunset he **d.**
21:19 and he **d** in great agony.
24:15 But Jehoiada grew old and full of days, and **d;**
24:25 and they killed him on his bed. So he **d;**
35:24 There he **d,** and was buried in the tombs
Est 2: 7 and when her father and her mother **d,**
Job 10:18 Would that I had **d** before any eye had seen me,
42:17 And Job **d,** old and full of days.
Ecc 4: 2 And I thought the dead, who have already **d,**
Isa 6: 1 In the year that King Uzziah **d,**
14:28 In the year that King Ahaz **d** this oracle came:
Jer 28:17 in the seventh month, the prophet Hananiah **d.**
Eze 4:14 now I have never eaten what **d** of itself or was torn
11:13 I was prophesying, Pelatiah son of Benaiah **d.**
24:18 and at evening my wife **d.**
44:31 that **d** of itself or was torn by animals.
Hos 13: 1 but he incurred guilt through Baal and **d.**
Mt 2:19 When Herod **d,** an angel of
9:18 saying, "My daughter has just **d;**
22:25 the first married, and **d** childless,
22:27 Last of all, the woman herself **d.**
Mk 12:20 the first married and, when he **d,** left no children;
12:21 the second married her and **d,** leaving no children;
12:22 Last of all the woman herself **d.**
Lk 7:12 a man who had **d** was being carried out.
16:22 The poor man **d** and was carried away by
16:22 The rich man also **d** and was buried.
20:29 the first married, and **d** childless;
20:31 and so in the same way all seven **d** childless.
20:32 Finally the woman also **d.**
Jn 6:49 the manna in the wilderness, and they **d.**
6:58 not like that which your ancestors ate, and they **d.**
8:52 Abraham **d,** and so did the prophets;
8:53 Are you greater than our father Abraham, who **d?**
8:53 The prophets also **d.**
11:21 my brother would not have **d.**
11:32 my brother would not have **d."**
Ac 2:29 of our ancestor David that he both **d**
5: 5 Ananias heard these words, he fell down and **d.**
5:10 Immediately she fell down at his feet and **d.**
7: 4 After his father **d,** God had him move from there
7:15 He himself **d** there as well as our ancestors,
7:60 When he had said this, he **d.**
9:37 At that time she became ill and **d.**
12:23 and he was eaten by worms and **d.**
13:36 **d,** was laid beside his ancestors,
25:19 who had **d,** but whom Paul asserted to be alive.
Ro 5: 6 at the right time Christ **d** for the ungodly.
5: 8 in that while we still were sinners Christ **d** for us.
5:15 For if the many **d** through the one man's trespass,
6: 2 How can we who **d** to sin go on living in it?
6: 7 For whoever has **d** is freed from sin.
6: 8 But if we have **d** with Christ,
6:10 The death he **d,** he **d** to sin, once for all;
7: 4 you have **d** to the law through the body of Christ,
7:10 and I **d,** and the very commandment
8:34 It is Christ Jesus, who **d,** yes, who was raised,
14: 9 For to this end Christ **d** and lived again,
14:15 the ruin of one for whom Christ **d.**
1Co 8:11 for whom Christ **d** are destroyed.
11:30 of you are weak and ill, and some have **d.**
15: 3 that Christ **d** for our sins in accordance with
15: 6 most of whom are still alive, though some have **d.**
15:18 those also who have **d** in Christ have perished.
15:20 the first fruits of those who have **d.**
2Co 5:14 because we are convinced that one has **d** for all; therefore all have **d.**
5:15 And he **d** for all, that those who live might live
5:15 but for him who **d** and was raised for them.
Gal 2:19 the law I **d** to the law, so that I might live to God.
2:21 through the law, then Christ **d** for nothing.
Php 2:27 He was indeed so ill that he nearly **d.**
Col 2:20 If with Christ you **d** to the elemental spirits of
3: 3 for you have **d,** and your life is hidden with Christ
1Th 4:13 brothers and sisters, about those who have **d,**
4:14 For since we believe that Jesus **d** and rose again,
4:14 God will bring with him those who have **d.**
4:15 will by no means precede those who have **d.**
1Th 5:10 who **d** for us, so that whether we are awake
2Ti 2:11 If we have **d** with him, we will also live with him;
Heb 11: 4 he **d,** but through his faith he still speaks.
11:13 All of these **d** in faith without having received
2Pe 3: 4 For ever since our ancestors **d,**
Rev 8: 9 a third of the living creatures in the sea **d,**
8:11 and many **d** from the water,
16: 3 and every living thing in the sea **d.**
Tob 1: 8 for my father had **d** and left me an orphan.
1:15 But when Shalmaneser **d,**
3:15 Already seven husbands of mine have **d.**
6:14 and that they **d** in the bridal chamber.
7:11 and all **d** on the night when they went in to her.
10: 2 that Gabael has **d,** and there is no one to give him
14: 2 Tobit **d** in peace when he was one hundred twelve
14:11 Then they laid him on his bed, and he **d;**
14:12 Tobias's mother **d,** he buried her beside his father.
14:14 He **d** highly respected at the age
14:15 he **d** he heard of the destruction of Nineveh,
14:15 before he **d** he rejoiced over Nineveh,
Jdt 6: 1 by the people outside the council had **d** down,
8: 2 had **d** during the barley harvest.
8: 3 and took to his bed and **d** in his town Bethulia.
16:22 the days of her life after her husband Manasseh **d**
16:23 She **d** in Bethulia, and they buried her in the cave
16:24 Before she **d** she distributed her property
AdE 2: 7 When her parents **d,** he brought her up
Wis 3: 2 In the eyes of the foolish they seemed to have **d,**
4:16 The righteous who have **d** will condemn
Sir 37:31 Many have **d** of gluttony, but the one who guards
1Mc 1: 7 after Alexander had reigned twelve years, he **d.**
2:38 So they attacked them on the sabbath, and they **d,**
2:41 not all die as our kindred **d** in their hiding places."
2:70 He **d** in the one hundred forty-sixth year
6:16 Thus King Antiochus **d** there in
6:46 but it fell to the ground upon him and he **d.**
9:56 And Alcimus **d** at that time in great agony.
11:18 But King Ptolemy **d** three days later,
14:16 that Jonathan had **d,** and they were deeply grieved.
2Mc 4: 7 When Seleucus **d** and Antiochus,
5: 9 from their own country into exile **d** in exile,
6:31 So in this way he **d,**
7: 7 After the first brother had **d** in this way,
7: 9 because we have **d** for his laws."
7:13 After he too had **d,** they maltreated and tortured
7:40 So he **d** in his integrity,
7:41 Last of all, the mother **d,** after her sons.
13: 7 about that Menelaus the lawbreaker **d,**
1Es 1:31 and after he was brought back to Jerusalem he **d,**
2Es 10: 1 entered his wedding chamber, he fell down and **d.**
10:48 'My son **d** as he entered his wedding chamber,'
12:45 For we are no better than those who **d** there."
13:24 left are more blessed than those who have **d.**
4Mc 1: 8 from the noble bravery of those who **d** for the sake
1:10 **d** for the sake of nobility and goodness,
4:15 King Seleucus **d,** his son Antiochus Epiphanes
6:30 he said this, the holy man **d** nobly in his tortures;
10: 2 the same father begot me as well as those who **d,**
10:12 he too had **d** in a manner worthy of his brothers,
11: 1 When he too **d,** after being cruelly tortured,
11:13 he too had **d,** the sixth, a mere boy, was led in.
12: 1 thrown into the caldron, had **d** a blessed death,
12: 3 they **d** in torments because of their disobedience.
13:18 or betray the brothers who have **d** before us."
18: 9 and when these sons had grown up their father **d.**

DIES‡ (47) [DEAD]

Ge 27:10 so that he may bless you before he **d."**
Ex 21:20 with a rod and the slave **d** immediately,
21:35 someone's ox hurts the ox of another, so that it **d,**
22:10 and it **d** or is injured or is carried off,
22:14 an animal from another and it is injured or **d,**
Lev 11:39 If an animal of which you may eat **d,**
17:15 who eat what **d** of itself or what has been torn
Nu 6: 9 If someone **d** very suddenly nearby,
19:14 This is the law when someone **d** in a tent:
27: 8 You shall also say to the Israelites, "If a man **d,**
Dt 14:21 You shall not eat anything that **d** of itself;
19: 5 and strikes the other person who then **d;**
24: 3 (or the second man who married her **d**);
25: 5 and one of them **d** and has no son,
2Sa 3:33 saying, "Should Abner die as a fool **d?**
1Ki 14:11 Anyone belonging to Jeroboam who **d** in the city,
14:11 and anyone who **d** in the open country,
16: 4 Anyone belonging to Baasha who **d** in the city
16: 4 and anyone of his who **d** in the field the birds of
21:24 Anyone belonging to Ahab who **d** in the city
21:24 and anyone of his who **d** in the open country
Job 14: 8 and its stump **d** in the ground,
21:23 One **d** in full prosperity, being wholly at ease
21:25 Another **d** in bitterness of soul,
Ecc 3:19 as one **d,** so **d** the other.
Isa 59: 5 whoever eats their eggs **d,**
65:20 for one who **d** at a hundred years will
Jer 38:10 up from the cistern before he **d."**
Eze 18:18 not good among his people, he **d** for his iniquity.
Mt 22:24 Moses said, 'If a man **d** childless,
Mk 9:48 where their worm never **d,**
12:19 Moses wrote for us that 'if a man's brother **d,**
Lk 20:28 Moses wrote for us that if a man's brother **d,**
Jn 4:49 "Sir, come down before my little boy **d."**
12:24 unless a grain of wheat falls into the earth and **d,**
12:24 but if it **d,** it bears much fruit.
Ro 7: 2 if her husband **d,** she is discharged from the law
7: 3 But if her husband **d,** she is free from that law,
1Co 7:39 But if the husband **d,** she is free
1Co 15:36 What you sow does not come to life unless it **d.**
Heb 10:28 Anyone who has violated the law of Moses **d**
Tob 4: 4 when she **d,** bury her beside me in the same grave.
Sir 11:19 be until he leaves them to others and **d.**
14:18 one **d** and another is born.
23:17 he will never weary until he **d.**
30: 4 When the father **d** he will not seem to be dead,

DIFFER (2) [DIFFERED, DIFFERENCE, DIFFERENCES, DIFFERENT, DIFFERENTLY, DIFFERING, DIFFERS]

Ro 12: 6 We have gifts that **d** according to the grace given
Sir Pr: 2 and the rest of the books **d** not a little when read

DIFFERED (1) [DIFFER]

3Mc 6:26 the beginning **d** from all nations in their goodwill

DIFFERENCE (8) [DIFFER]

Lev 25:27 since its sale shall be computed and the **d** shall
2Ch 12: 8 so that they may know the **d** between serving me
14:11 there is no **d** for you between helping the mighty
Eze 22:26 neither have they taught the **d** between the unclean
44:23 They shall teach my people the **d** between the holy
Mal 3:18 Then once more you shall see the **d** between
Gal 2: 6 (what they actually were makes no **d** to me;
1Mc 3:18 of Heaven there is no **d** between saving by many

DIFFERENCES (1) [DIFFER]

3Mc 3: 7 instead they gossiped about the **d** in worship

DIFFERENT (30) [DIFFER]

Lev 19:19 You shall not let your animals breed with a **d** kind;
19:19 on a garment made of two **d** materials.
Nu 14:24 a **d** spirit and has followed me wholeheartedly,
1Sa 10: 6 along with them and be turned into a **d** person.
1Ki 18:21 long will you go limping with two **d** opinions?
Est 1: 7 of **d** kinds, and the royal wine was lavished
3: 8 their laws are **d** from those of every other people,
Isa 65:15 but to his servants he will give a **d** name.
Eze 16:34 you were **d** from other women in your whorings:
16:34 while no payment was given to you; you were **d.**
Da 7: 3 and four great beasts came up out of the sea, **d**
7: 7 It was **d** from all the beasts that preceded it,
7:19 which was **d** from all the rest,
7:23 a fourth kingdom on earth that shall be **d** from all
7:24 This one shall be **d** from the former ones,
1Co 4: 7 For who sees anything **d** in you?
7: 7 one having one kind and another a **d** kind.
14:10 There are doubtless many **d** kinds of sounds in
2Co 11: 4 if you receive a **d** spirit from the one you received,
11: 4 or a **d** gospel from the one you accepted,
Gal 1: 6 the grace of Christ and are turning to a **d** gospel—
1Ti 1: 3 not to teach any **d** doctrine,
AdE 3: 8 their laws are **d** from those of every other nation,
Wis 7: 5 For no king has had a **d** beginning of existence;
11:14 when they felt thirst in a **d** way from the righteous.
Sir 33: 8 and he appointed the **d** seasons and festivals.
33:11 and appointed their **d** ways.
38:34 How **d** the one who devotes himself to the study
2Es 5:53 the strength of youth are **d** from those born during
6:26 be changed and converted to a **d** spirit.

DIFFERENTLY (2) [DIFFER]

Php 3:15 and if you think **d** about anything,
Jdt 10: 7 in appearance and dressed **d,**

DIFFERING (1) [DIFFER]

Pr 20:23 **D** weights are an abomination to the LORD,

DIFFERS (1) [DIFFER]

1Co 15:41 indeed, star **d** from star in glory.

DIFFICULT (12) [DIFFICULTIES, DIFFICULTY]

Dt 17: 8 If a judicial decision is too **d** for you to make
2Ki 5:13 prophet had commanded you to do something **d,**
Eze 3: 5 of obscure speech and **d** language, but to the house
3: 6 of obscure speech and **d** language,
Da 2:11 The thing that the king is asking is too **d,**
4: 9 the holy gods and that no mystery is too **d** for you.
Jn 6:60 they said, "This teaching is **d;** who can accept it?"
Sir 3:21 Neither seek what is too **d** for you,
2Mc 12:21 for that place was hard to besiege and **d** of access
2Es 7:14 living pass through the **d** and futile experiences,
7:18 can endure **d** circumstances while hoping
7:18 done wickedly have suffered the **d** circumstances

DIFFICULTIES (2) [DIFFICULT]

Wis 17:11 it has always exaggerated the **d.**
1Mc 13: 3 you know also the wars and the **d** that my brothers

DIFFICULTY (10) [DIFFICULT]

Ex 14:25 so that they turned with **d.**
Lev 25:25 If anyone of your kin falls into **d** and sells a piece
25:35 of your kin fall into **d** and become dependent
25:47 and if any of your kin fall into **d** with one of them
Ac 27: 7 a number of days and arrived with **d** off Cnidus,
27: 8 with **d,** we came to a place called Fair Havens,
Wis 6:14 One who rises early to seek her will have no **d,**
2Mc 2:24 and the **d** there is for those who wish to enter upon

3Mc 5:15 And when he had with **d** roused him,
2Es 9:21 And I saw and spared some with great **d**,

DIG‡ (10) [DIGGING, DIGS, DUG]

Ex 7:24 the Egyptians had to **d** along the Nile for water
Dt 23:13 when you relieve yourself outside, you shall **d**
Job 3:21 and **d** for it more than for hidden treasures;
24:16 In the dark they **d** through houses;
Eze 8: 8 Then he said to me, "Mortal, **d** through the wall";
12: 5 **D** through the wall in their sight,
12:12 he shall **d** through the wall and carry it through;
Am 9: 2 Though they **d** into Sheol,
Lk 13: 8 until I **d** around it and put manure on it.
16: 3 I am not strong enough to **d**,

DIGGING (2) [DIG]

Ps 7:15 They make a pit, **d** it out,
Tob 8:11 When they had finished **d** the grave,

DIGNITARIES (2) [DIGNITY]

Isa 9:15 and **d** are the head, and prophets who teach lies are
Na 3:10 all her **d** were bound in fetters.

DIGNITARY (1) [DIGNITY]

Isa 3: 3 of fifty and **d**, counselor and skillful magician

DIGNITY (10) [DIGNITARIES, DIGNITARY]

Est 4:14 Perhaps you have come to royal **d** for just such
Job 40:10 "Deck yourself with majesty and **d**;
Pr 31:25 Strength and **d** are her clothing,
Hab 1: 7 their justice and **d** proceed from themselves.
1Ti 2: 2 a quiet and peaceable life in all godliness and **d**.
AdE 6: 3 "What honor or **d** did we bestow
Sir 45:24 that he and his descendants should have the **d** of
2Mc 6:23 worthy of his years and the **d** of his old age and
15:13 distinguished by his gray hair and **d**,
3Mc 2: 1 and extending his hands with calm **d**, prayed

DIGS (4) [DIG]

Ex 21:33 or **d** a pit and does not cover it,
Pr 26:27 Whoever **d** a pit will fall into it,
Ecc 10: 8 Whoever **d** a pit will fall into it;
Sir 27:26 Whoever **d** a pit will fall into it,

DIKLAH (2)

Ge 10:27 Hadoram, Uzal, **D**,
1Ch 1:21 Hadoram, Uzal, **D**,

DILAN (1)

Jos 15:38 **D**, Mizpeh, Jokthe-el,

DILIGENCE (9) [DILIGENT]

Ezr 6:12 I, Darius, make a decree; let it be done with all **d**."
6:13 with all **d** what King Darius had ordered.
7:17 you shall with all **d** buy bulls, rams, and lambs,
7:21 requires of you, let it be done with all **d**,
Ro 12: 8 in **d**; the compassionate, in cheerfulness.
Heb 6:11 And we want each one of you to show the same **d**
Sir Pr: 3 that I should myself devote some **d** and labor to
11:18 One becomes rich through **d** and self-denial,
1Es 6:34 that it be done with all **d** as here prescribed."

DILIGENT (8) [DILIGENCE, DILIGENTLY]

Pr 10: 4 but the hand of the **d** makes rich.
12:24 The hand of the **d** will rule,
12:27 but the **d** obtain precious wealth.
13: 4 while the appetite of the **d** is richly supplied.
13:24 but those who love them are **d** to discipline them.
21: 5 The plans of the **d** lead surely to abundance,
Sir Pr: 2 despite our **d** labor in translating,
38:27 each is **d** in making a great variety;

DILIGENTLY (38) [DILIGENT]

Nu 18: 7 with you shall **d** perform your priestly duties in all
Dt 4: 6 You must observe them **d**,
5: 1 you shall learn them and observe them **d**.
6: 3 Hear therefore, O Israel, and observe them **d**,
6:17 You must **d** keep the commandments of
6:25 If we **d** observe this entire commandment before
7:11 Therefore, observe **d** the commandment—
7:12 you heed these ordinances, by **d** observing them,
8: 1 that I command you today you must **d** observe,
11:22 If you will **d** observe this entire commandment
11:32 you must **d** observe all the statutes and ordinances
12: 1 and ordinances that you must **d** observe in the land
12:32 You must **d** observe everything
15: 5 by **d** observing this entire commandment
16:12 and **d** observe these statutes.
17:10 **d** observing everything they instruct you.
17:19 **d** observing all the words of this law
19: 9 provided you **d** observe this entire commandment
23:23 Whatever your lips utter you must **d** perform,
26:16 so observe them **d** with all your heart and
28: 1 by **d** observing all his commandments
28:13 commanding you today, by **d** observing them,
28:15 by **d** observing all his commandments
28:58 If you do not **d** observe all the words of this law
29: 9 Therefore **d** observe the words of this covenant,
31:12 to fear the LORD your God and to observe **d** all
32:46 that they may **d** observe all the words of this law.
Ezr 5: 8 this work is being done **d** and prospers
Ps 37:10 you look **d** for their place, they will not be there.
119: 4 You have commanded your precepts to be kept **d**.
Pr 1:28 they will seek me **d**, but will not find me.
8:17 and those who seek me **d** find me.
11:27 Whoever **d** seeks good seeks favor,
Isa 21: 7 riders on camels, let him listen **d**, very **d**."
Jer 12:16 then, if they will **d** learn the ways of my people,
Zec 6:15 if you **d** obey the voice of the LORD your God.
Mt 2: 8 saying, "Go and search **d** for the child;

DILL (4)

Isa 28:25 they have leveled its surface, do they not scatter **d**,
28:27 **D** is not threshed with a threshing sledge,
28:27 but **d** is beaten out with a stick,
Mt 23:23 For you tithe mint, **d**, and cummin,

DIM (10) [DIMLY]

Ge 27: 1 and his eyes were **d** so that he could not see,
48:10 Now the eyes of Israel were **d** with age,
1Sa 3: 2 to grow **d** so that he could not see, was lying down
1Ki 14: 4 for his eyes were **d** because of his age.
Job 17: 7 My eye has grown **d** from grief,
Ps 69: 3 My eyes grow **d** with waiting for my God.
88: 9 my eye grows **d** through sorrow.
La 4: 1 gold has grown **d**, how the pure gold is changed!
5:17 because of these things our eyes have grown **d**:
Sir 18:18 and the gift of a grudging giver makes the eyes **d**.

DIMENSIONS (6)

Eze 40:24 they had the same **d** as the others.
40:28 it was of the same **d** as the others.
40:33 and its vestibule were of the same **d** as the others;
40:35 it had the same **d** as the others.
43:13 These are the **d** of the altar by cubits
48:16 and these shall be its **d**:

DIMINISH (5) [DIMINISHED]

Ex 5: 8 do not **d** it, for they are lazy;
21:10 he shall not **d** the food, clothing,
Lev 25:16 and if the years are fewer, you shall **d** the price;
Isa 19: 6 the branches of Egypt's Nile will **d** and dry up,
Sir 18: 6 It is not possible to **d** or increase them,

DIMINISHED (2) [DIMINISH]

Ps 107:39 they are **d** and brought low through oppression,
Bar 2:34 and I will increase them, and they will not be **d**.

DIMLY (3) [DIM]

Ecc 12: 3 and those who look through the windows see **d**;
Isa 42: 3 and a **d** burning wick he will not quench;
1Co 13:12 For now we see in a mirror, **d**,

DIMNAH (1)

Jos 21:35 **D** with its pasture lands, Nahalal

DIMON See Index to Footnotes

DIMONAH (1)

Jos 15:22 Kinah, **D**, Adadah,

DINAH (7) [DINAH'S]

Ge 30:21 Afterwards she bore a daughter, and named her **D**.
34: 1 Now **D** the daughter of Leah,
34: 3 And his soul was drawn to **D** daughter of Jacob;
34: 5 that Shechem had defiled his daughter **D**;
34:13 because he had defiled their sister **D**.
34:26 and took **D** out of Shechem's house,
46:15 together with his daughter **D**;

DINAH'S (1) [DINAH]

Ge 34:25 Simeon and Levi, **D** brothers,

DINAITES (KJV) See JUDGES

DINE (6) [DINED, DINNER, DINNERWARE]

Ge 43:16 for the men are to **d** with me at noon."
43:25 for they had heard that they would **d** there.
1Ki 13: 7 "Come home with me and **d**,
Lk 11:37 a Pharisee invited him to **d** with him;
Tob 7: 9 and washed themselves and had reclined to **d**,
Sir 9: 9 Never **d** with another man's wife,

DINED (2) [DINE]

2Ki 25:29 of his life he **d** regularly in the king's presence.
Jer 52:33 of his life he **d** regularly at the king's table.

DINHABAH (2)

Ge 36:32 the name of his city being **D**.
1Ch 1:43 Bela son of Beor, whose city was called **D**.

DINNER (20) [DINE]

Pr 15:17 a **d** of vegetables where love is than a fatted ox
Mt 9:10 And as he sat at **d** in the house,
22: 4 Look, I have prepared my **d**,
Mk 2:15 And as he sat at **d** in Levi's house,
Lk 11:38 to see that he did not first wash before **d**.
14:12 "When you give a luncheon or a **d**,
14:15 One of the **d** guests, on hearing this, said to him,
14:16 "Someone gave a great **d** and invited many.
14:17 At the time for the **d** he sent his slave to say
Lk 14:24 none of those who were invited will taste my **d**.' "
Jn 12: 2 There they gave a **d** for him.
Tob 2: 1 a good **d** was prepared for me and I reclined to eat.
2: 4 Then I sprang up, left the **d** before even tasting it,
12:13 to get up and leave your **d** to go and bury the dead,
AdE 5: 4 to the **d** that I shall prepare today."
5: 5 both came to the **d** that Esther had spoken about.
5: 8 let the king and Haman come to the **d**
5:12 not invite anyone to the **d** with the king except me;
5:14 Then, go merrily with the king to the **d**."
Sir 9:16 Let the righteous be your **d** companions,

DINNERWARE (2) [DINE]

Jdt 12: 1 to bring her in where his silver **d** was kept,
15:11 the tent of Holofernes and all his silver **d**,

DIONYSIUS (1)

Ac 17:34 and became believers, including **D** the Areopagite

DIONYSUS (4)

2Mc 6: 7 and when a festival of **D** was celebrated,
6: 7 of ivy and to walk in the procession in honor of **D**.
14:33 and build here a splendid temple to **D**."
3Mc 2:29 by fire with the ivy-leaf symbol of **D**,

DIOSCORINTHIUS (1)

2Mc 11:21 one hundred forty-eighth year, **D** twenty-fourth."

DIOTREPHES (1)

3Jn 1: 9 I have written something to the church; but **D**,

DIP (12) [DIPPED, DIPPING]

Ex 12:22 **d** it in the blood that is in the basin,
Lev 4: 6 The priest shall **d** his finger in the blood
4:17 and the priest shall **d** his finger in the blood
14: 6 and **d** them and the living bird in the blood of
14:16 and **d** his right finger in the oil that is
14:51 and **d** them in the blood of the slaughtered bird
Nu 19:18 **d** it in the water, and sprinkle it on the tent,
Dt 33:24 and may he **d** his foot in oil.
Ru 2:14 and **d** your morsel in the sour wine."
Jer 13: 1 and put it on your loins, but do not **d** it in water."
Lk 16:24 and send Lazarus to **d** the tip of his finger in water
2Mc 1:20 he ordered them to **d** it out and bring it.

DIPHATH (1)

1Ch 1: 6 Ashkenaz, **D**, and Togarmah.

DIPPED (10) [DIP]

Ge 37:31 slaughtered a goat, and **d** the robe in the blood.
Lev 9: 9 and he **d** his finger in the blood and put it on
11:32 it shall be **d** into water,
Jos 3:15 and the feet of the priests bearing the ark were **d** in
1Sa 14:27 and **d** the tip of it in the honeycomb,
2Ki 8:15 and **d** it in water and spread it over the king's face,
Mt 26:23 "The one who has **d** his hand into the bowl
Jn 13:26 of bread when I have **d** it in the dish."
13:26 So when he had **d** the piece of bread,
Rev 19:13 He is clothed in a robe **d** in blood,

DIPPING‡ (2) [DIP]

Isa 30:14 or **d** water out of the cistern.
Mk 14:20 one who is **d** bread into the bowl with me.

DIRE (1)

Tob 4:13 And in idleness there is loss and **d** poverty,

DIRECT (25) [DIRECTED, DIRECTING, DIRECTION, DIRECTIONS, DIRECTLY, DIRECTS]

Lev 22: 2 **D** Aaron and his sons to deal carefully with
1Sa 7: 3 **D** your heart to the LORD, and serve him only,
1Ch 15:22 leader of the Levites in music, was to **d** the music,
29:18 and **d** their hearts toward you.
Job 11:13 "If you **d** your heart rightly,
Ps 74: 3 **D** your steps to the perpetual ruins;
119:128 Truly I **d** my steps by all your precepts;
Pr 23:19 and be wise, and **d** your mind in the way.
Jer 2:33 How well you **d** your course to seek lovers!
5:31 and the priests rule as the prophets **d**;
10:23 that mortals as they walk cannot **d** their steps.
Eze 23:25 I will **d** my indignation against you,
26: 9 He shall **d** the shock of his battering rams
1Th 3:11 and Father himself and our Lord Jesus **d** our way
2Th 3: 5 May the Lord **d** your hearts to the love of God and
Jdt 11: 7 of him who has sent you to **d** every living being!
12: 8 she prayed the Lord God of Israel to **d** her way for
Sir 6:17 Those who fear the Lord **d** their friendship aright,
25:26 If she does not go as you **d**,
37:15 to the Most High that he may **d** your way in truth.
38:10 Give up your faults and **d** your hands rightly,
39: 7 The Lord will **d** his counsel and knowledge,
2Mc 3:14 So he set a day and went in to **d** the inspection
2Es 13:26 and he will **d** those who are left.
4Mc 14: 9 not only heard the **d** word of threat,

DIRECTED (26) [DIRECT]

Nu 27:23 as the LORD had **d** through Moses.
2Ki 23: 1 Then the king **d** that all the elders of Judah
2Ch 32:30 the upper outlet of the waters of Gihon and **d** them

2Ch 34:13 and **d** all who did work in every kind of service;
Job 32:14 He has not **d** his words against me,
Isa 10:25 and my anger will be **d** to their destruction.
40:13 Who has **d** the spirit of the LORD,
Eze 21:16 Wherever your edge is **d.**
Mt 21: 6 The disciples went and did as Jesus had **d** them;
26:19 So the disciples did as Jesus had **d** them,
28:15 So they took the money and did as they were **d.**
28:16 to the mountain to which Jesus had **d** them.
Lk 8:55 Then he **d** them to give her something to eat.
Ac 7:44 as God **d** when he spoke to Moses,
10:22 was **d** by a holy angel to send for you to come
22:24 the tribune **d** that he was to be brought into
1Th 4:11 and to work with your hands, as we **d** you,
Tit 1: 5 in every town, as I **d** you:
AdE 16:16 who has **d** the kingdom both for us and
Wis 6: 9 To you then, O monarchs, my words are **d,**
Sir 51:20 I **d** my soul to her, and in purity I found her.
1Mc 1:44 he **d** them to follow customs strange to the land,
10:11 He **d** those who were doing the work to build
3Mc 6: 1 **d** the elders around him to stop calling upon
2Es 9:26 So I went, as he **d** me,
10:32 I did as you **d,** and went out into the field, and lo,

DIRECTING (1) [DIRECT]
Ne 2: 8 **d** him to give me timber to make beams for

DIRECTION (38) [DIRECT]
Ge 10:19 in the **d** of Gerar, as far as Gaza, and in the **d** of Sodom, Gomorrah,
10:30 in which they lived extended from Mesha in the **d**
13:10 like the land of Egypt, in the **d** of Zoar;
25:18 which is opposite Egypt in the **d** of Assyria;
Ex 38:21 of the Levites being under the **d** of Ithamar son of
Nu 7: 8 under the **d** of Ithamar son of Aaron the priest.
Dt 1:40 in the **d** of the Red Sea."
2: 1 in the **d** of the Red Sea,"
33: 3 they marched at your heels, accepted **d** from you.
Jos 8:15 and fled in the **d** of the wilderness.
9:14 and did not ask **d** from the LORD.
12: 3 and in the **d** of Beth-jeshimoth,
18:13 the boundary passes along southward in the **d**
18:14 Then the boundary goes in another **d,**
18:17 in a northerly **d** going on to En-shemesh,
19:12 from Sarid it goes in the other **d** eastward toward
Jdg 9:37 and one company is coming from the **d**
18:15 that **d** and came to the house of the young Levite,
20:42 from the Israelites in the **d** of the wilderness;
1Sa 6:12 the **d** of Beth-shemesh along one highway, lowing
24: 2 and went to look for David and his men in the **d** of
1Ki 18: 6 Ahab went in one **d** by himself,
18: 6 and Obadiah went in another **d** by himself.
2Ki 3:20 suddenly water began to flow from the **d** of Edom,
9:27 he fled in the **d** of Beth-haggan.
25: 4 They went in the **d** of the Arabah.
1Ch 25: 2 sons of Asaph, under the **d** of Asaph,
25: 2 who prophesied under the **d** of the king.
25: 3 six, under the **d** of their father Jeduthun,
25: 6 the **d** of their father for the music in the house of
28:19 "All this, in writing at the LORD's **d,**
2Ch 26:11 the officer Maaseiah, under the **d** of Hananiah, one
Jer 52: 7 They went in the **d** of the Arabah.
Eze 8: 5 lift up your eyes now in the **d** of the north."
9: 2 And six men came from the **d** of the upper gate,
10:11 but in whatever **d** the front wheel faced,
2Mc 12:22 In their flight they rushed headlong in every **d,**

DIRECTIONS (10) [DIRECT]
2Ch 35: 4 following the written **d** of King David of Israel
35: 4 of Israel and the written **d** of his son Solomon.
Ezr 3:10 according to the **d** of King David of Israel;
Eze 1:17 they moved in any of the four **d** without veering
10:11 they moved in any of the four **d** without veering
1Co 16: 1 you should follow the **d** I gave to the churches
1Es 1: 5 the **d** of King David of Israel and the magnificence
5:49 with the **d** in the book of Moses the man of God.
5:60 according to the **d** of King David of Israel;
6:22 let him send us **d** concerning these things."

DIRECTLY (3) [DIRECT]
2Sa 3:19 Abner also spoke **d** to the Benjaminites;
Pr 4:25 Let your eyes look **d** forward,
25: 9 Argue your case with your neighbor **d,**

DIRECTS (4) [DIRECT]
Pr 16: 9 but the LORD **d** the steps.
Jas 3: 4 the will of the pilot **d.**
1Mc 4:47 Then they took unhewn stones, as the law **d,**
4:53 as the law **d,** on the new altar of burnt offering

DIRGE (3) [DIRGES]
Jer 9:18 let them quickly raise a **d** over us,
9:20 teach to your daughters a **d,**
1Mc 9:41 and the voice of their musicians into a funeral **d.**

DIRGES (2) [DIRGE]
3Mc 5:25 and mournful **d** implored the supreme God
6:32 They stopped their chanting of **d** and took up

DIRT (6) [DIRTY]
Jdg 3:22 of his belly; and the **d** came out.
2Sa 1: 2 with his clothes torn and **d** on his head.
Job 7: 5 My flesh is clothed with worms and **d;**
Zec 9: 3 and gold like the **d** of the streets.
1Pe 3:21 not as a removal of **d** from the body,
Wis 15:10 Their heart is ashes, their hope is cheaper than **d,**

DIRTY (2) [DIRT]
Jas 2: 2 and if a poor person in **d** clothes also comes in,
Sir 13: 1 Whoever touches pitch gets **d,**

DISABLED (2)
Pr 26: 7 The legs of a **d** person hang limp;
2Mc 8:24 and wounded and **d** most of Nicanor's army,

DISADVANTAGE See Index to Footnotes

DISAGREED (1) [DISAGREEMENT]
Ac 28:25 So they **d** with each other;

DISAGREEMENT (3) [DISAGREED]
Ac 15:39 The **d** became so sharp that they parted company;
25:19 of **d** with him about their own religion and about
2Mc 3: 4 a **d** with the high priest about the administration of

DISALLOW (KJV) See DISAPPROVAL

DISANNUL, DISANNULLED (KJV) See ABROGATION, ANNUL, CONDEMN, NULLIFY

DISAPPEAR (9) [DISAPPEARED, DISAPPEARS]
Job 6:17 In time of heat they **d;**
Isa 17: 3 The fortress will **d** from Ephraim,
32:19 The forest will **d** completely,
Heb 8:13 And what is obsolete and growing old will soon **d.**
Jas 1:10 because the rich will **d** like a flower in the field.
Sir 39: 9 His memory will not **d,** and his name will live
2Es 11:16 I announce this to you before you **d.**
11:33 and saw the head in the middle suddenly **d,**
11:45 Therefore you, eagle, will surely **d,**

DISAPPEARED (14) [DISAPPEAR]
Nu 32:13 in the sight of the LORD had **d.**
Ps 12: 1 the faithful have **d** from humankind.
Mic 7: 2 The faithful have **d** from the land,
Jn 5:13 for Jesus had **d** in the crowd that was there.
Ac 5:36 and all who followed him were dispersed and **d.**
2Es 11:13 And after a time its reign came to an end, and it **d,**
11:14 so that it **d** like the first.
11:18 the rule as the earlier ones had done, and it also **d.**
11:20 of them that ruled, yet **d** suddenly;
11:22 the twelve wings and the two little wings had **d,**
11:26 As I kept looking, one was set up, but suddenly **d;**
11:27 and this **d** more quickly than the first.
12: 2 and saw that the remaining head had **d.**
12:26 As for your seeing that the large head **d,**

DISAPPEARS (2) [DISAPPEAR]
Lev 13:58 or anything of skin from which the disease **d**
Sir 12: 9 but in adversity even one's friend **d.**

DISAPPOINT (1) [DISAPPOINTED, DISAPPOINTMENT]
Ro 5: 5 and hope does not **d** us,

DISAPPOINTED (4) [DISAPPOINT]
Job 6:20 They are **d** because they were confident;
41: 9 Any hope of capturing it will be **d;**
Sir 2:10 has anyone trusted in the Lord and been **d?**
51:18 and I shall never be **d.**

DISAPPOINTMENT (4) [DISAPPOINT]
1Mc 6: 1 and in great **d** left there to return to Babylon.
6: 8 He took to his bed and became sick from **d,**
6: 9 because deep **d** continually gripped him,
6:13 here I am, perishing of bitter **d** in a strange land."

DISAPPROVAL (4)
Nu 30: 5 But if her father expresses **d** to her at the time
30: 5 because her father had expressed to her his **d.**
30: 8 he expresses **d** to her, then he shall nullify the vow
30:11 and did not express **d** to her,

DISARMED (1)
Col 2:15 He **d** the rulers and authorities and made

DISASTER‡ (84) [DISASTERS]
Ge 19:19 for fear the **d** will overtake me and I die.
Ex 32:12 change your mind and do not bring **d**
32:14 about the **d** that he planned to bring on his people.
Dt 28:20 The LORD will send upon you **d,** panic,
29:19 we go our own stubborn ways" (thus bringing **d**
Jdg 20:34 the Benjaminites did not realize that **d** was close
20:41 for they saw that **d** was close upon them.
2Sa 15:14 and bring **d** down upon us,
16: 8 See, **d** has overtaken you;
19: 7 for you than any **d** that has come upon you
1Ki 9: 9 the LORD has brought this **d** upon them.' "
21:21 I will bring **d** on you;
21:29 I will not bring the **d** in his days;
21:29 in his son's days I will bring the **d** on his house."
22: 8 anything favorable about me, but only **d."**
22:18 anything favorable about me, but only **d?"**
22:23 the LORD has decreed **d** for you."
2Ki 22:16 I will indeed bring **d** on this place and
22:20 your eyes shall not see all the **d** that I will bring
1Ch 7:23 because **d** had befallen his house.
2Ch 18: 7 anything favorable about me, but only **d."**
18:17 anything favorable about me, but only **d?"**
18:22 the LORD has decreed **d** for you."
20: 9 'If **d** comes upon us, the sword, judgment,
34:24 I will indeed bring **d** upon this place and
34:28 your eyes shall not see all the **d** that I will bring
Ne 13:18 not our God bring all this **d** on us and on this city?
Job 9:23 When **d** brings sudden death,
30:24 when in **d** they cry for help.
31: 3 and **d** the workers of iniquity?
Pr 1:33 be secure and will live at ease, without dread of **d."**
24:22 for **d** comes from them suddenly,
Ecc 9:12 For no one can anticipate the time of **d.**
11: 2 for you do not know what **d** may happen on earth.
Isa 31: 2 Yet he too is wise and brings **d;**
47:11 **d** shall fall upon you, which you will not be able
Jer 1:14 the north **d** shall break out on all the inhabitants of
2: 3 **d** came upon them, says the LORD.
4:15 from Dan and proclaims **d** from Mount Ephraim.
4:20 **D** overtakes **d,** the whole land is laid waste.
6:19 I am going to bring **d** on this people,
11:11 to bring **d** upon them that they cannot escape;
11:23 For I will bring **d** upon the people of Anathoth,
17:17 you are my refuge in the day of **d;**
17:18 bring on them the day of **d;**
18: 8 I will change my mind about the **d** that I intended
19: 3 I am going to bring such **d** upon this place that
19:15 upon all its towns all the **d** that I have pronounced
23:12 for I will bring **d** upon them in the year
25:29 I am beginning to bring **d** on the city that is called
25:32 See, **d** is spreading from nation to nation,
26: 3 about the **d** that I intend to bring on them because
26:13 and the LORD will change his mind about the **d**
26:19 about the **d** that he had pronounced against them?
26:19 But we are about to bring great **d** on ourselves!"
32:42 as I have brought all this great **d** upon this people,
35:17 and on all the inhabitants of Jerusalem every **d**
40: 2 LORD your God threatened this place with this **d;**
42:10 I am sorry for the **d** that I have brought upon you.
42:17 they shall have no remnant or survivor from the **d**
44: 2 the **d** that I have brought on Jerusalem and on all
44:11 I am determined to bring **d** on you,
44:23 that this **d** has befallen you,
45: 5 for I am going to bring **d** upon all flesh,
49:37 I will bring **d** upon them, my fierce anger,
Eze 6:10 not threaten in vain to bring this **d** upon them.
7: 5 Thus says the Lord GOD: **D** after **d!**
7:26 **D** comes upon **d,** rumor follows rumor;
Am 3: 6 Does **d** befall a city, unless the LORD has done it?
Ob 1:13 not have joined in the gloating over Judah's **d** on
Mic 1:12 yet **d** has come down from the LORD to the gate
Zep 3:15 you shall fear **d** no more.
3:18 I will remove **d** from you,
Zec 1:15 I was only a little angry, they made the **d** worse.
8:14 Just as I purposed to bring **d** upon you,
Wis 3: 2 and their departure was thought to be a **d,**
18:21 he withstood the anger and put an end to the **d,**
Sir 29:12 and it will rescue you from every **d;**
1Mc 3:29 because of the dissension and **d** that he had caused
8: 4 until they crushed them and inflicted great **d**
2Mc 4:16 For this reason heavy **d** overtook them,

DISASTERS (11) [DISASTER]
Dt 32:23 I will heap **d** upon them, spend my arrows
Jer 19: 8 be horrified and will hiss because of all its **d.**
32:23 you have made all these **d** come upon them.
36: 3 be that when the house of Judah hears of all the **d**
36:31 all the **d** with which I have threatened them—
49:17 be horrified and will hiss because of all its **d.**
51:60 in a scroll all the **d** that would come on Babylon,
51:64 because of the **d** that I am bringing on her.' "
1Mc 1:11 since we separated from them many **d** have come
2Es 12:43 Are not the **d** that have befallen us enough?
4Mc 3:21 and caused many and various **d.**

DISBELIEVE (1) [DISBELIEVED, DISBELIEVING]
2Es 16:36 receive it and do not **d** what the Lord says.

DISBELIEVED (1) [DISBELIEVE]
Wis 18:13 they had **d** everything because of their magic arts,

DISBELIEVING (1) [DISBELIEVE]
Lk 24:41 While in their joy they were **d** and still wondering,

DISCARD (1)
Dt 21:13 **d** her captive's garb, and shall remain

DISCERN (12) [DISCERNED, DISCERNING, DISCERNMENT]
Dt 32:29 they would **d** what the end would be.
2Sa 19:35 can I **d** what is pleasant and what is not?
1Ki 3: 9 able to **d** between good and evil;
3:11 for yourself understanding to **d** what is right,
Job 4:16 It stood still, but I could not **d** its appearance.

Job 6:30 Cannot my taste **d** calamity?
38:20 to its territory and that you may **d** the paths
Ps 139: 2 you **d** my thoughts from far away.
Ro 12: 2 so that you may **d** what is the will of God—
1Co 2:15 Those who are spiritual **d** all things,
Wis 9:13 Or who can **d** what the Lord wills?
Bar 3:14 at the same time **d** where there is length of days,

DISCERNED (3) [DISCERN]
1Co 2:14 to understand them because they are spiritually **d**.
Wis 2:22 nor **d** the prize for blameless souls;
6:12 and she is easily **d** by those who love her,

DISCERNING (14) [DISCERN]
Ge 41:33 let Pharaoh select a man who is **d** and wise,
41:39 there is no one so **d** and wise as you.
Dt 1:13 **d**, and reputable to be your leaders."
4: 6 "Surely this great nation is a wise and **d** people!"
2Sa 14:17 the king is like the angel of God, **d** good and evil.
1Ki 3:12 Indeed I give you a wise and **d** mind;
Pr 1: 5 and gain in learning, and the **d** acquire skill,
17:10 into a **d** person than a hundred blows into a fool.
17:24 The **d** person looks to wisdom,
Isa 29:14 and the discernment of the **d** shall be hidden.
Hos 14: 9 those who are **d** know them.
1Co 1:19 and the discernment of the **d** I will thwart."
11:29 For all who eat and drink without **d** the body,
Sir 1:19 down knowledge and **d** comprehension,

DISCERNMENT (7) [DISCERN]
Dt 4: 6 this will show your wisdom and **d** to the peoples,
1Ki 4:29 God gave Solomon very great wisdom, **d**,
Job 12:20 and takes away the **d** of the elders.
Isa 29:14 and the **d** of the discerning shall be hidden.
44:19 nor is there knowledge or **d** to say,
1Co 1:19 and the **d** of the discerning I will thwart."
12:10 to another prophecy, to another the **d** of spirits,

DISCHARGE (33) [DISCHARGED, DISCHARGING]
Lev 15: 2 When any man has a **d** from his member, his **d** makes him ceremonially unclean.
15: 3 The uncleanness of his **d** is this: whether his member flows with his **d**,
15: 4 on which the one with the **d** lies shall be unclean;
15: 6 the one with the **d** has sat shall wash their clothes,
15: 7 of the one with the **d** shall wash their clothes,
15: 8 the one with the **d** spits on persons who are clean,
15: 9 on which the one with the **d** rides shall be unclean.
15:11 the **d** touches without his having rinsed his hands
15:12 that the one with the **d** touches shall be broken;
15:13 the one with a **d** is cleansed of his **d**,
15:15 on his behalf before the LORD for his **d**.
15:19 a **d** of blood that is her regular **d** from her body,
15:25 If a woman has a **d** of blood for many days,
15:25 or if she has a **d** beyond the time of her impurity,
15:25 of the **d** she shall continue in uncleanness;
15:26 of her **d** shall be treated as the bed of her impurity;
15:28 If she is cleansed of her **d**,
15:30 on her behalf before the LORD for her unclean **d**.
15:32 This is the ritual for those who have a **d**:
15:33 for anyone, male or female, who has a **d**,
22: 4 or suffers a **d** may eat of the sacred donations
22:22 or maimed, or having a **d** or an itch or scabs—
Nu 5: 2 a **d**, and everyone who is unclean through contact
5:21 the LORD makes your uterus drop, your womb **d**;
5:22 curse enter your bowels and make your womb **d**,
5:27 and her womb shall **d**, her uterus drop,
2Sa 3:29 of Joab never be without one who has a **d**,
Ecc 8: 8 there is no **d** from the battle,
Ac 16:37 and now are they going to **d** us in secret?

DISCHARGED (4) [DISCHARGE]
2Ch 25:10 Then Amaziah **d** the army that had come to him
Ro 7: 2 she is **d** from the law concerning the husband.
7: 6 But now we are **d** from the law,
1Mc 11:55 All the troops that Demetrius had **d** gathered

DISCHARGING (1) [DISCHARGE]
Lev 15: 3 or his member is stopped from **d**,

DISCIPLE (30) [DISCIPLES, DISCIPLES']
Mt 10:24 "A **d** is not above the teacher,
10:25 it is enough for the **d** to be like the teacher,
10:42 to one of these little ones in the name of a **d**—
27:57 named Joseph, who was also a **d** of Jesus.
Lk 6:40 A **d** is not above the teacher,
14:26 yes, and even life itself, cannot be my **d**.
14:27 not carry the cross and follow me cannot be my **d**.
14:33 none of you can become my **d** if you do not give
17: 3 If another **d** sins, you must rebuke the offender,
Jn 9:28 Then they reviled him, saying, "You are his **d**,
18:15 Simon Peter and another **d** followed Jesus.
18:15 Since that **d** was known to the high priest,
18:16 So the other **d**, who was known to the high priest,
19:26 and the **d** whom he loved standing beside her,
19:27 Then he said to the **d**, "Here is your mother."
19:27 from that hour the **d** took her into his own home.
19:38 Joseph of Arimathea, who was a **d** of Jesus,
20: 2 she ran and went to Simon Peter and the other **d**,
20: 3 and the other **d** set out and went toward the tomb.
20: 4 the other **d** outran Peter and reached the tomb first.
20: 8 Then the other **d**, who reached the tomb first,
Jn 21: 7 **d** whom Jesus loved said to Peter, "It is the Lord!"
21:20 and saw the **d** whom Jesus loved following them;
21:23 in the community that this **d** would not die.
21:24 This is the **d** who is testifying to these things
Ac 9:10 Now there was a **d** in Damascus named Ananias.
9:26 for they did not believe that he was a **d**.
9:36 in Joppa there was a **d** whose name was Tabitha,
16: 1 where there was a **d** named Timothy,
21:16 an early **d**, with whom we were to stay.

DISCIPLES‡ (241) [DISCIPLE]
Isa 8:16 seal the teaching among my **d**.
Mt 5: 1 and after he sat down, his **d** came to him.
8:21 Another of his **d** said to him, "Lord,
8:23 when he got into the boat, his **d** followed him.
9:10 and were sitting with him and his **d**.
9:11 When the Pharisees saw this, they said to his **d**,
9:14 Then the **d** of John came to him, saying,
9:14 but your **d** do not fast?"
9:19 And Jesus got up and followed him, with his **d**.
9:37 Then he said to his **d**, "The harvest is plentiful,
10: 1 Then Jesus summoned his twelve **d**
11: 1 when Jesus had finished instructing his twelve **d**,
11: 2 he sent word by his **d**
12: 1 his **d** were hungry, and they began to pluck heads
12: 2 your **d** are doing what is not lawful to do on
12:49 And pointing to his **d**, he said,
13:10 Then the **d** came and asked him,
13:36 And his **d** approached him, saying,
14:12 His **d** came and took the body and buried it;
14:15 When it was evening, the **d** came to him and said,
14:19 to the **d**, and the **d** gave them to the crowds.
14:22 Immediately he made the **d** get into the boat
14:26 But when the **d** saw him walking on the sea,
15: 2 "Why do your **d** break the tradition of the elders?
15:12 Then the **d** approached and said to him,
15:23 And his **d** came and urged him, saying,
15:32 Then Jesus called his **d** to him and said,
15:33 The **d** said to him, "Where are we
15:36 to the **d**, and the **d** gave them to the crowds.
16: 5 When the **d** reached the other side,
16:13 he asked his **d**, "Who do people say that the Son
16:20 the **d** not to tell anyone that he was the Messiah.
16:21 to show his **d** that he must go to Jerusalem
16:24 Then Jesus told his **d**, "If any want
17: 6 When the **d** heard this, they fell to the ground
17:10 And the **d** asked him, "Why, then,
17:13 the **d** understood that he was speaking to them
17:16 And I brought him to your **d**,
17:19 Then the **d** came to Jesus privately and said,
18: 1 At that time the **d** came to Jesus and asked,
19:10 His **d** said to him, "If such is the case of a man
19:13 The **d** spoke sternly to those who brought them;
19:23 Then Jesus said to his **d**, "Truly I tell you,
19:25 the **d** heard this, they were greatly astounded
20:17 he took the twelve **d** aside by themselves,
21: 1 at the Mount of Olives, Jesus sent two **d**,
21: 6 The **d** went and did as Jesus had directed them;
21:20 When the **d** saw it, they were amazed, saying,
22:16 So they sent their **d** to him,
23: 1 Then Jesus said to the crowds and to his **d**,
24: 1 his **d** came to point out to him the buildings of
24: 3 the **d** came to him privately, saying, "Tell us,
26: 1 finished saying all these things, he said to his **d**,
26: 8 But when the **d** saw it, they were angry and said,
26:17 On the first day of Unleavened Bread the **d** came
26:18 the Passover at your house with my **d**.' "
26:19 So the **d** did as Jesus had directed them,
26:26 and after blessing it he broke it, gave it to the **d**,
26:35 And so said all the **d**.
26:36 and he said to his **d**,
26:40 Then he came to the **d** and found them sleeping;
26:45 Then he came to the **d** and said to them,
26:56 Then all the **d** deserted him and fled.
27:64 otherwise his **d** may go and steal him away,
28: 7 Then go quickly and tell his **d**,
28: 8 and ran to tell his **d**.
28:13 'His **d** came by night and stole him away
28:16 Now the eleven **d** went to Galilee,
28:19 Go therefore and make **d** of all nations,
Mk 2:15 and sinners were also sitting with Jesus and his **d**—
2:16 with sinners and tax collectors, they said to his **d**,
2:18 Now John's **d** and the Pharisees were fasting;
2:18 "Why do John's **d** and the **d** of the Pharisees fast, but your **d** do not fast?"
2:23 as they made their way his **d** began to pluck heads
3: 7 Jesus departed with his **d** to the sea,
3: 9 He told his **d** to have a boat ready for him because
4:34 but he explained everything in private to his **d**.
5:31 And his **d** said to him, "You see
6: 1 to his hometown, and his **d** followed him.
6:29 When his **d** heard about it,
6:35 When it grew late, his **d** came to him and said,
6:41 and gave them to his **d** to set before the people;
6:45 Immediately he made his **d** get into the boat
7: 2 that some of his **d** were eating with defiled hands,
7: 5 "Why do your **d** not live according to the tradition
7:17 his **d** asked him about the parable.
8: 1 he called his **d** and said to them,
8: 4 His **d** replied, "How can one feed these people
8: 6 and gave them to his **d** to distribute;
8:10 with his **d** and went to the district of Dalmanutha.
8:14 Now the **d** had forgotten to bring any bread;
8:27 on with his **d** to the villages of Caesarea Philippi;
8:27 and on the way he asked his **d**,
8:33 But turning and looking at his **d**,
Mk 8:34 He called the crowd with his **d**, and said to them,
9:14 When they came to the **d**,
9:18 and I asked your **d** to cast it out,
9:28 his **d** asked him privately,
9:31 for he was teaching his **d**,
10:10 the house the **d** asked him again about this matter.
10:13 and the **d** spoke sternly to them.
10:23 Then Jesus looked around and said to his **d**,
10:24 And the **d** were perplexed at these words.
10:46 and his **d** and a large crowd were leaving Jericho,
11: 1 Mount of Olives, he sent two of his **d**
11:14 And his **d** heard it.
11:19 evening came, Jesus and his **d** went out of the city.
12:43 Then he called his **d** and said to them,
13: 1 one of his **d** said to him, "Look, Teacher,
14:12 the Passover lamb is sacrificed, his **d** said to him,
14:13 So he sent two of his **d**, saying to them,
14:14 where I may eat the Passover with my **d**?'
14:16 So the **d** set out and went to the city,
14:32 and he said to his **d**, "Sit here while I pray."
16: 7 tell his **d** and Peter that he is going ahead of you
Lk 5:30 and their scribes were complaining to his **d**,
5:33 said to him, "John's **d**, like the **d** of the Pharisees, frequently fast and pray, but your **d** eat and drink.
6: 1 his **d** plucked some heads of grain,
6:13 he called his **d** and chose twelve of them,
6:17 with a great crowd of his **d** and a great multitude
6:20 Then he looked up at his **d** and said:
7:11 and his **d** and a large crowd went with him.
7:18 The **d** of John reported all these things to him.
7:18 So John summoned two of his **d**
8: 9 Then his **d** asked him what this parable meant.
8:22 One day he got into a boat with his **d**,
9:14 And he said to his **d**,
9:16 and gave them to the **d** to set before the crowd.
9:18 with only the **d** near him, he asked them,
9:40 I begged your **d** to cast it out, but they could not."
9:43 at all that he was doing, he said to his **d**,
9:54 When his **d** James and John saw it, they said,
10:23 Then turning to the **d**, Jesus said to them privately,
11: 1 and after he had finished, one of his **d** said to him, "Lord, teach us to pray, as John taught his **d**."
12: 1 he began to speak first to his **d**,
12:22 He said to his **d**, "Therefore I tell you,
16: 1 Then Jesus said to the **d**,
17: 1 to his **d**, "Occasions for stumbling are bound
17:22 Then he said to the **d**,
18:15 the **d** saw it, they sternly ordered them not to do it.
19:29 he sent two of the **d**,
19:37 of the **d** began to praise God joyfully with
19:39 "Teacher, order your **d** to stop."
20:45 In the hearing of all the people he said to the **d**,
22:11 where I may eat the Passover with my **d**?" '
22:39 of Olives; and the **d** followed him.
22:45 he came to the **d** and found them sleeping because
Jn 1:35 John again was standing with two of his **d**,
1:37 two **d** heard him say this, and they followed Jesus.
2: 2 and his **d** had also been invited to the wedding.
2:11 and his **d** believed in him.
2:12 and his **d**; and they remained there a few days.
2:17 His **d** remembered that it was written,
2:22 his **d** remembered that he had said this;
3:22 and his **d** went into the Judean countryside,
3:25 about purification arose between John's **d** and
4: 1 "Jesus is making and baptizing more **d** than John"
4: 2 it was not Jesus himself but his **d** who baptized—
4: 8 (His **d** had gone to the city to buy food.)
4:27 Just then his **d** came.
4:31 Meanwhile the **d** were urging him, "Rabbi,
4:33 So the **d** said to one another,
6: 3 up the mountain and sat down there with his **d**.
6: 8 One of his **d**, Andrew, Simon Peter's brother,
6:12 When they were satisfied, he told his **d**,
6:16 When evening came, his **d** went down to the sea,
6:22 that Jesus had not got into the boat with his **d**,
6:22 but that his **d** had gone away alone.
6:24 crowd saw that neither Jesus nor his **d** were there,
6:60 When many of his **d** heard it, they said,
6:61 being aware that his **d** were complaining about it,
6:66 of his **d** turned back and no longer went about
7: 3 that your **d** also may see the works you are doing;
8:31 "If you continue in my word, you are truly my **d**;
9: 2 His **d** asked him, "Rabbi, who sinned,
9:27 Do you also want to become his **d**?"
9:28 "You are his disciple, but we are **d** of Moses.
11: 7 this he said to the **d**, "Let us go to Judea again."
11: 8 The **d** said to him, "Rabbi,
11:12 The **d** said to him, "Lord, if he has fallen asleep,
11:16 who was called the Twin, said to his fellow **d**,
11:54 and he remained there with the **d**.
12: 4 of his **d** (the one who was about to betray him),
12:16 His **d** did not understand these things at first;
13:22 The **d** looked at one another,
13:23 One of his **d**—the one whom Jesus loved—
13:35 By this everyone will know that you are my **d**,
15: 8 that you bear much fruit and become my **d**.
16:17 Then some of his **d** said to one another,
16:29 His **d** said, "Yes, now you are speaking plainly,
18: 1 he went out with his **d** across the Kidron valley to
18: 1 which he and his **d** entered.
18: 2 because Jesus often met there with his **d**.
18:17 "You are not also one of this man's **d**, are you?"
18:19 Then the high priest questioned Jesus about his **d**
18:25 They asked him, "You are not also one of his **d**,
20:10 Then the **d** returned to their homes.
20:18 Mary Magdalene went and announced to the **d**,
20:19 the **d** had met were locked for fear of the Jews,

Jn 20:20 Then the **d** rejoiced when they saw the Lord.
20:25 So the other **d** told him, “We have seen the Lord.”
20:26 A week later his **d** were again in the house,
20:30 in the presence of his **d,**
21: 1 to the **d** by the Sea of Tiberias;
21: 2 the sons of Zebedee, and two others of his **d.**
21: 4 but the **d** did not know that it was Jesus.
21: 8 But the other **d** came in the boat,
21:12 none of the **d** dared to ask him, “Who are you?”
21:14 that Jesus appeared to the **d** after he was raised
Ac 6: 1 when the **d** were increasing in number,
6: 2 the whole community of the **d** and said,
6: 7 number of the **d** increased greatly in Jerusalem,
9: 1 still breathing threats and murder against the **d** of
9:19 For several days he was with the **d** in Damascus,
9:25 but his **d** took him by night and let him down
9:26 he attempted to join the **d;**
9:38 Since Lydda was near Joppa, the **d,**
11:26 in Antioch that the **d** were first called “Christians.”
11:29 The **d** determined that according to their ability,
13:52 the **d** were filled with joy and with the Holy Spirit.
14:20 But when the **d** surrounded him,
14:21 the good news to that city and had made many **d,**
14:22 the souls of the **d** and encouraged them to continue
14:28 And they stayed there with the **d** for some time.
15:10 the neck of the **d** a yoke that neither our ancestors
18:23 of Galatia and Phrygia, strengthening all the **d.**
18:27 the believers encouraged him and wrote to the **d**
19: 1 and came to Ephesus, where he found some **d.**
19: 9 he left them, taking the **d** with him,
19:30 but the **d** would not let him;
20: 1 After the uproar had ceased, Paul sent for the **d;**
20:30 the truth in order to entice the **d** to follow them.
21: 4 up the **d** and stayed there for seven days.
21:16 Some of the **d** from Caesarea also came along

DISCIPLES’ (1) [DISCIPLE]
Jn 13: 5 and began to wash the **d** feet and to wipe them

DISCIPLINARIAN (2) [DISCIPLINE]
Gal 3:24 Therefore the law was our **d** until Christ came,
3:25 faith has come, we are no longer subject to a **d,**

DISCIPLINE‡ (58) [DISCIPLINARIAN, DISCIPLINED, DISCIPLINES, DISCIPLINING, SELF-DISCIPLINE, WELL-DISCIPLINED]
Dt 4:36 From heaven he made you hear his voice to **d** you.
11: 2 not known or seen the **d** of the LORD your God),
21:18 who does not heed them when they **d** him,
1Ki 12:11 but I will **d** you with scorpions.’ ”
12:14 but I will **d** you with scorpions.”
2Ch 10:11 but I will **d** you with scorpions.’ ”
10:14 but I will **d** you with scorpions.”
Job 5:17 therefore do not despise the **d** of the Almighty.
Ps 6: 1 or **d** me in your wrath.
38: 1 or **d** me in your wrath.
50:17 you hate **d,** and you cast my words behind you.
94:12 Happy are those whom you **d,** O LORD,
Pr 3:11 do not despise the LORD’s **d** or be weary
5:12 how I hated **d,** and my heart despised reproof!
5:23 They die for lack of **d,**
6:23 and the reproofs of **d** are the way of life,
12: 1 Whoever loves **d** loves knowledge,
13: 1 A wise child loves **d,** but a scoffer does not listen
13:24 but those who love them are diligent to **d** them.
15:10 There is severe **d** for one who forsakes the way,
19:18 **D** your children while there is hope;
22:15 but the rod of **d** drives it far away.
23:13 Do not withhold **d** from your children;
29:17 **D** your children, and they will give you rest;
Jer 7:28 of the LORD their God, and did not accept **d;**
31:18 “You disciplined me, and I took the **d;**
Eze 21:10 You have despised the rod, and all **d.**
Hos 7:12 I will **d** them according to the report made
Eph 6: 4 bring them up in the **d** and instruction of the Lord.
Heb 12: 5 “My child, do not regard lightly the **d** of the Lord,
12: 7 Endure trials for the sake of **d.**
12: 7 for what child is there whom a parent does not **d?**
12: 8 you do not have that **d** in which all children share,
12: 9 Moreover, we had human parents to **d** us,
12:11 **d** always seems painful rather than pleasant at
1Pe 1:13 prepare your minds for action; **d** yourselves;
4: 7 therefore be serious and **d** yourselves for the sake
5: 8 **D** yourselves, keep alert.
Rev 3:19 I reprove and **d** those whom I love.
Tob 4:14 and **d** yourself in all your conduct.
Sir 1:27 For the fear of the Lord is wisdom and **d,**
4:17 will torment them by her **d** until she trusts them,
6:18 My child, from your youth choose **d,**
7:23 **D** them, and make them obedient from their youth.
8: 8 because from them you will learn **d** and how
16:25 I will impart **d** precisely
18:14 He has compassion on those who accept his **d**
22: 6 but a thrashing and **d** are at all times wisdom.
23: 2 and the **d** of wisdom over my mind,
23: 7 D OF THE TONGUE Listen, my children,
30:13 **D** your son and make his yoke heavy,
32:14 The one who seeks God will accept his **d,**
33:25 bread and **d** and work for a slave.
38:33 they cannot expound **d** or judgment,
2Mc 6:12 not to destroy but to **d** our people.
7:33 for a little while, to rebuke and **d** us, he will again
2Es 14:34 then, will rule over your minds and **d** your hearts,
4Mc 13:22 from both general education and our **d** in the law

DISCIPLINED (14) [DISCIPLINE]
1Ki 12:11 My father **d** you with whips,
12:14 my father **d** you with whips,
2Ch 10:11 My father **d** you with whips,
10:14 my father **d** you with whips,
Pr 29:19 By mere words servants are not **d,**
Jer 31:18 “You **d** me, and I took the discipline;
1Co 11:32 we are **d** so that we may not be condemned along
Heb 12:10 they **d** us for a short time as seemed best to them,
Wis 1: 5 For a holy and **d** spirit will flee from deceit,
3: 5 Having been **d** a little, they will receive great good,
11: 9 though they were being **d** in mercy,
Sir 6:32 If you are willing, my child, you can be **d,**
23:15 to using abusive language will never become **d**
2Mc 10: 4 they might be **d** by him with forbearance and not

DISCIPLINES (7) [DISCIPLINE]
Dt 8: 5 Know then in your heart that as a parent **d** a child
8: 5 a child so the LORD your God **d** you.
Ps 94:10 He who **d** the nations, he who teaches knowledge
Heb 12: 6 for the Lord **d** those whom he loves,
12:10 but he **d** us for our good,
Sir 30: 2 He who **d** his son will profit by him,
2Mc 6:16 Although he **d** us with calamities,

DISCIPLINING (1) [DISCIPLINE]
Sir 42: 5 and of frequent **d** of children,

DISCLOSE (10) [DISCLOSED, DISCLOSES, DISCLOSING, DISCLOSURE]
1Sa 20:12 shall I not then send and **d** it to you?
20:13 if I do not **d** it to you, and send you away,
22:17 they knew that he fled, and did not **d** it to me.”
Pr 25: 9 and do not **d** another’s secret;
Isa 26:21 the earth will **d** the blood shed on it,
Da 7:16 So he said that he would **d** to me the interpretation
1Co 3:13 for the Day will **d** it,
4: 5 now hidden in darkness and will **d** the purposes of
Sus 1:11 for they were ashamed to **d** their lustful desire
2Mc 2: 8 Then the Lord will **d** these things,

DISCLOSED (18) [DISCLOSE]
Da 2:28 in heaven who reveals mysteries, and he has **d**
2:29 the revealer of mysteries **d** to you what is to be.
Mk 4:22 For there is nothing hidden, except to be **d;**
Lk 8:17 For nothing is hidden that will not be **d,**
Ac 19:18 became believers confessed and **d** their practices.
Ro 3:21 the righteousness of God has been **d,**
16:26 but is now **d,** and through
1Co 14:25 After the secrets of the unbeliever’s heart are **d,**
Heb 9: 8 yet been **d** as long as the first tent is still standing.
2Pe 3:10 earth and everything that is done on it will be **d.**
AdE 2:10 Now Esther had not **d** her people or country,
2:20 Esther had not **d** her country—
1Mc 7:31 When Nicanor learned that his plan had been **d,**
2Mc 3:16 the change in his color **d** the anguish of his soul.
2Es 4:43 the things that you desire to see will be **d** to you.”
7:26 and the land that now is hidden shall be **d.**
7:*36* and the furnace of hell shall be **d,**
14:35 and the deeds of the ungodly shall be **d.**

DISCLOSES (6) [DISCLOSE]
1Sa 22: 8 No one **d** to me when my son makes a league with
22: 8 or **d** to me that my son has stirred up my servant
Pr 29:24 one hears the victim’s curse, but **d** nothing.
Sir 27: 6 Its fruit **d** the cultivation of a tree;
27: 6 so a person’s speech **d** the cultivation of his mind.
42:19 He **d** what has been and what is to be,

DISCLOSING (1) [DISCLOSE]
1Sa 20: 2 either great or small without **d** it to me;

DISCLOSURE (2) [DISCLOSE]
Sir 22:22 But as for reviling, arrogance, **d** of secrets,
2Mc 3: 9 he told about the **d** that had been made

DISCOMFITED, DISCOMFITURE (KJV)
See CONFUSION, DEFEATED, FORCED LABOR, PANIC, ROUTED

DISCOMFORT (1)
Jnh 4: 6 to save him from his **d;**

DISCONTENTED (1)
1Sa 22: 2 and everyone who was **d** gathered to him;

DISCONTINUED (1)
Ezr 4:24 the house of God in Jerusalem stopped and was **d**

DISCORD (3) [DISCORDANT]
Pr 6:14 mind devising evil, continually sowing **d;**
6:19 and one who sows **d** in a family.
Sir 28: 9 and the sinner disrupts friendships and sows **d**

DISCORDANT (1) [DISCORD]
Wis 18:10 But the **d** cry of their enemies echoed back,

DISCOURAGE (1) [DISCOURAGED, DISCOURAGING]
Nu 32: 7 Why will you **d** the hearts of the Israelites

DISCOURAGED (5) [DISCOURAGE]
Nu 32: 9 they **d** the hearts of the Israelites from going into
2Sa 17: 2 I will come upon him while he is weary and **d,**
Ezr 4: 4 Then the people of the land **d** the people of Judah,
Isa 54: 4 do not be **d,** for you will not suffer disgrace;
1Mc 4:27 When he heard it, he was perplexed and **d,**

DISCOURAGING (1) [DISCOURAGE]
Jer 38: 4 he is **d** the soldiers who are left in this city,

DISCOURSE (5)
Job 27: 1 Job again took up his **d** and said:
29: 1 Job again took up his **d** and said:
Sir 6:35 Be ready to listen to every godly **d,**
8: 8 Do not slight the **d** of the sages,
8: 9 Do not ignore the **d** of the aged,

DISCOVER (3) [DISCOVERED]
Ezr 4:15 You will **d** in the annals that this is
Ps 44:21 would not God **d** this?
2Es 5:40 so you cannot **d** my judgment,

DISCOVERED (5) [DISCOVER]
2Ki 12: 5 the house wherever any need of repairs is **d.”**
Ezr 4:19 and **d** that this city has risen against kings
Ne 13: 7 then **d** the wrong that Eliashib had done on behalf
Jer 31:19 and after I was **d,** I struck my thigh;
50:24 **d** and seized, because you challenged the LORD.

DISCREDITED (1)
Tit 2: 5 so that the word of God may not be **d.**

DISCREET (1) [DISCRETION]
Sir 21:24 the **d** would be grieved by the disgrace.

DISCREETLY (1) [DISCRETION]
Pr 26:16 in self-esteem than seven who can answer **d.**

DISCRETION (7) [DISCREET, DISCREETLY]
1Ch 22:12 may the LORD grant you **d** and understanding,
2Ch 2:12 endowed with **d** and understanding,
Ezr 8:18 they brought us a man of **d,**
Pr 8:12 live with prudence, and I attain knowledge and **d.**
Da 2:14 Daniel responded with prudence and **d** to Arioch,
Sir 17: 6 **D** and tongue and eyes, ears and a mind
1Mc 8:30 they shall do so at their **d,**

DISCUS-THROWING (1) [THROW]
2Mc 4:14 in the wrestling arena after the signal for the **d,**

DISCUSS (3) [DISCUSSED, DISCUSSING, DISCUSSION]
Ac 15: 2 up to Jerusalem to **d** this question with the apostles
2Mc 2:30 to **d** matters from every side,
4Mc 1: 1 subject that I am about to **d** is most philosophical,

DISCUSSED (6) [DISCUSS]
2Ch 9: 1 she **d** with him all that was on her mind.
Lk 6:11 and **d** with one another what they might do
20: 5 They **d** it with one another, saying, “If we say,
20:14 they **d** it among themselves and said,
Ac 4:15 to leave the council while they **d** the matter
24:25 And as he **d** justice, self-control,

DISCUSSING (4) [DISCUSS]
Mk 2: 8 in his spirit that they were **d** these questions
Lk 24:15 While they were talking and **d,**
24:17 “What are you **d** with each other
Jn 16:19 “Are you **d** among yourselves what I meant

DISCUSSION (6) [DISCUSS]
Da 5:10 when she heard the **d** of the king and his lords,
Jn 3:25 Now a **d** about purification arose
Ac 18:19 into the synagogue and had a **d** with the Jews.
20: 7 Paul was holding a **d** with them;
Sir 9:15 let all your **d** be about the law of the Most High.
37:16 **D** is the beginning of every work,

DISDAIN (4) [DISDAINED, DISDAINING]
Tob 4:13 and in your heart do not **d** your kindred,
Jdt 8:20 we hope that he will not **d** us or any of our nation.
Sir 8: 6 Do not **d** one who is old,
2Mc 7:11 and because of his laws I **d** them,

DISDAINED (5) [DISDAIN]
1Sa 17:42 the Philistine looked and saw David, he **d** him,
Job 30: 1 whose fathers I would have **d** to set with the dogs
Jer 30:19 I will make them honored, and they shall not be **d.**
3Mc 3:22 in a contrary spirit, and **d** what is good.
4Mc 15: 8 of God she **d** the temporary safety of her children.

DISDAINFULLY See Index to Footnotes

DISDAINING (1) [DISDAIN]
2Mc 4:15 **d** the honors prized by their ancestors and putting

DISEASE‡ (79) [DISEASED, DISEASES]
Lev 13: 2 it turns into a leprous **d** on the skin of his body,
13: 3 priest shall examine the **d** on the skin of his body,
13: 3 and the **d** appears to be deeper than the skin of his body, it is a leprous **d**;
13: 5 if he sees that the **d** is checked and the **d** has
13: 6 the **d** has abated and the **d** has not spread in
13: 8 shall pronounce him unclean; it is a leprous **d**.
13: 9 When a person contracts a leprous **d**,
13:11 it is a chronic leprous **d** in the skin of his body.
13:12 But if the **d** breaks out in the skin,
13:13 and if the **d** has covered all his body, he shall pronounce him clean of the **d**;
13:15 Raw flesh is unclean, for it is a leprous **d**.
13:17 and if the **d** has turned white,
13:20 this is a leprous **d**, broken out in the boil.
13:25 deeper than the skin, it is a leprous **d**;
13:25 This is a leprous **d**.
13:27 This is a leprous **d**.
13:29 man or woman has a **d** on the head or in the beard,
13:30 the priest shall examine the **d**.
13:30 it is an itch, a leprous **d** of the head or the beard.
13:31 If the priest examines the itching **d**,
13:31 the person with the itching **d** for seven days.
13:42 it is a leprous **d** breaking out on his bald head
13:43 on his bald forehead, which resembles a leprous **d**
13:44 the **d** is on his head.
13:45 the leprous **d** shall wear torn clothes and let
13:46 He shall remain unclean as long as he has the **d**;
13:47 when a leprous **d** appears in it,
13:49 if the **d** shows greenish or reddish in the garment,
13:49 it is a leprous **d** and shall be shown to the priest.
13:50 The priest shall examine the **d**,
13:51 He shall examine the **d** on the seventh day.
13:51 If the **d** has spread in the cloth, in warp or woof,
13:51 this is a spreading leprous **d**; it is unclean.
13:52 or anything of skin, for it is a spreading leprous **d**;
13:53 and the **d** has not spread in the clothing,
13:54 to wash the article in which the **d** appears,
13:55 though the **d** has not spread, it is unclean;
13:56 and the **d** has abated after it is washed,
13:57 with fire that in which the **d** appears.
13:58 or anything of skin from which the **d** disappears
13:59 This is the ritual for a leprous **d** in a cloth of wool
14: 3 If the **d** is healed in the leprous person,
14: 7 the one who is to be cleansed of the leprous **d**;
14:32 This is the ritual for the one who has a leprous **d**,
14:34 and I put a leprous **d** in a house in the land
14:35 to me to be some sort of **d** in my house."
14:36 the house before the priest goes to examine the **d**,
14:37 He shall examine the **d**;
14:37 if the **d** is in the walls of the house with greenish
14:39 if the **d** has spread in the walls of the house,
14:40 that the stones in which the **d** appears be taken out
14:43 If the **d** breaks out again in the house,
14:44 if the **d** has spread in the house,
14:44 it is a spreading leprous **d** in the house;
14:48 and the **d** has not spread in the house after
14:48 shall pronounce the house clean; the **d** is healed.
14:54 This is the ritual for any leprous **d**: for an itch,
21:20 or a man with a blemish in his eyes or an itching **d**
22: 4 No one of Aaron's offspring who has a leprous **d**
Dt 24: 8 Guard against an outbreak of a leprous skin **d**
2Ch 16:12 in his feet, and his **d** became severe;
16:12 yet even in his **d** he did not seek the LORD,
21:15 a severe sickness with a **d** of your bowels,
21:15 day after day, because of the **d**."
21:18 in his bowels with an incurable **d**.
21:19 his bowels came out because of the **d**,
26:19 the priests a leprous **d** broke out on his forehead,
Job 18:13 By **d** their skin is consumed,
Ps 106:15 but sent a wasting **d** among them.
Mt 4:23 the good news of the kingdom and curing every **d**
9:35 and curing every **d** and every sickness.
10: 1 and to cure every **d** and every sickness.
Mk 5:29 she felt in her body that she was healed of her **d**.
5:34 go in peace, and be healed of your **d**."
2Es 3:22 Thus the **d** became permanent;

DISEASED (13) [DISEASE]
Lev 13: 3 the **d** area has turned white and the disease appears
13: 4 priest shall confine the **d** person for seven days.
13:12 that it covers all the skin of the **d** person from head
13:17 the priest shall pronounce the **d** person clean.
13:22 the priest shall pronounce him unclean; it is **d**.
13:42 or the bald forehead a reddish-white **d** spot,
13:43 the **d** swelling is reddish-white on his bald head or
13:50 and put the **d** article aside for seven days.
13:52 whether **d** in warp or woof, woolen or linen,
13:55 the **d** article after it has been washed.
13:55 If the **d** spot has not changed color,
1Ki 15:23 But in his old age he was **d** in his feet.
2Ch 16:12 In the thirty-ninth year of his reign Asa was **d**

DISEASES (20) [DISEASE]
Ex 15:26 not bring upon you any of the **d** that I brought
Lev 14:55 for leprous **d** in clothing and houses,
14:57 This is the ritual for leprous **d**.
Dt 7:15 all the dread **d** of Egypt that you experienced,
28:60 He will bring back upon you all the **d** of Egypt,
Ps 103: 3 forgives all your iniquity, who heals all your **d**,
Isa 53: 4 he has borne our infirmities and carried our **d**;
Jer 16: 4 They shall die of deadly **d**.
Mt 4:24 those who were afflicted with various **d** and pains,
8:17 "He took our infirmities and bore our **d**."
Mk 1:34 And he cured many who were sick with various **d**,
3:10 that all who had **d** pressed upon him to touch him.
Lk 4:40 with various kinds of **d** brought them to him;
5:15 to hear him and to be cured of their **d**.
6:18 to hear him and to be healed of their **d**;
7:21 Jesus had just then cured many people of **d**,
9: 1 and authority over all demons and to cure **d**,
9: 6 bringing the good news and curing **d** everywhere.
Ac 19:12 their **d** left them, and the evil spirits came out
28: 9 on the island who had **d** also came and were cured.

DISFIGURE (1)
Mt 6:16 for they **d** their faces so as to show others

DISFIGURED See Index to Footnotes

DISGORGE (1)
Jer 51:44 and make him **d** what he has swallowed.

DISGRACE (73) [DISGRACED, DISGRACEFUL, DISGRACEFULLY, DISGRACES]
Ge 34:14 for that would be a **d** to us.
Lev 20:17 and she sees his nakedness, it is a **d**,
Jos 5: 9 "Today I have rolled away from you the **d**
Jdg 20:10 of Benjamin for all the **d** that they have done
1Sa 11: 2 and thus put **d** upon all Israel."
2Ki 19: 3 This day is a day of distress, of rebuke, and of **d**;
2Ch 32:21 So he returned in **d** to his own land.
Ne 2:17 so that we may no longer suffer **d**."
Job 10:15 for I am filled with **d** and look upon my affliction.
Ps 44:15 All day long my **d** is before me,
71:13 to hurt me be covered with scorn and **d**.
78:66 he put them to everlasting **d**.
83:17 and dismayed forever; let them perish in **d**.
119:39 Turn away the **d** that I dread,
132:18 His enemies I will clothe with **d**, but on him,
Pr 3:35 The wise will inherit honor, but stubborn fools, **d**.
6:33 and his **d** will not be wiped away.
11: 2 When pride comes, then comes **d**;
13:18 and **d** are for the one who ignores instruction,
18: 3 and with dishonor comes **d**.
Isa 4: 1 by your name; take away our **d**."
22:18 O you **d** to your master's house!
25: 8 and the **d** of his people he will take away from all
30: 5 nor profit, but shame and **d**.
37: 3 This day is a day of distress, of rebuke, and of **d**;
54: 4 do not be discouraged, for you will not suffer **d**;
54: 4 **d** of your widowhood you will remember no more.
Jer 23:40 upon you everlasting **d** and perpetual shame,
24: 9 a **d**, a byword, a taunt, and a curse in all the places
25: 9 of horror and of hissing, and an everlasting **d**.
31:19 I was dismayed because I bore the **d** of my youth."
La 5: 1 what has befallen us; look, and see our **d**!
Eze 16:52 Bear your **d**, you also, for you have brought about
16:52 So be ashamed, you also, and bear your **d**,
16:54 in order that you may bear your **d** and be ashamed
22: 4 Therefore I have made you a **d** before the nations,
36:15 no longer shall you bear the **d** of the peoples;
36:30 so that you may never again suffer the **d** of famine
Da 9:16 Jerusalem and your people have become a **d**
Mic 2: 6 of such things; **d** will not overtake us."
Mt 1:19 and unwilling to expose her to public **d**,
Lk 1:25 on me and took away the **d** I have endured
14: 9 then in **d** you would start to take the lowest place.
1Ti 3: 7 he may not fall into **d** and the snare of the devil.
1Pe 4:16 do not consider it a **d**,
Tob 3:15 O Lord, to take my life, hear me in my **d**."
Jdt 1:11 sent back his messengers empty-handed and in **d**.
1:14 plundered its markets, and turned its glory into **d**.
8:22 and we shall be an offense and a **d** in the eyes
9: 2 and polluted her womb to **d** her;
12:12 For it would be a **d** if we let such a woman go
14:18 One Hebrew woman has brought **d** on the house
Sir 3:11 it is a **d** for children not to respect their mother.
6: 9 and tell of the quarrel to your **d**.
7: 7 and do not **d** yourself among the people.
20:26 A liar's way leads to **d**,
21:24 the discreet would be grieved by the **d**.
22: 1 and every one hisses at his **d**.
22: 3 It is a **d** to be the father of an undisciplined son,
23:26 behind an accursed memory and her **d** will never
25:22 There is wrath and impudence and great **d** when
41: 6 and on their offspring will be a perpetual **d**.
41: 7 for they suffer **d** because of him.
42:14 it is woman who brings shame and **d**.
47: 4 and take away the people's **d**,
1Mc 4:58 and the **d** brought by the Gentiles was removed.
10:70 I have fallen into ridicule and **d** because of you.
2Mc 5: 7 in the end he got only **d** from his conspiracy,
6:25 while I defile and **d** my old age.
Pm 151: 7 and took away **d** from the people of Israel.
3Mc 2:27 to inflict public **d** on the Jewish community,
6:34 groaned as they themselves were overcome by **d**,
2Es 4:23 over to the Gentiles in **d**;

DISGRACED (12) [DISGRACE]
1Sa 20:34 and because his father had **d** him.
Ps 71:24 to do me harm have been put to shame, and **d**.
Pr 29:15 but a mother is **d** by a neglected child.
Isa 41:11 against you shall be ashamed and **d**;
Isa 50: 7 therefore I have not been **d**;
Jer 15: 9 she has been shamed and **d**.
50:12 and she who bore you shall be **d**.
Mic 3: 7 the seers shall be **d**, and the diviners put to shame;
2Co 7:14 about you to him, I was not **d**;
Tob 3:15 not **d** my name or the name of my father in
Sir 11: 6 Many rulers have been utterly **d**,
Aza 1:21 let them be **d** and deprived of all power,

DISGRACEFUL (3) [DISGRACE]
Dt 22:21 because she committed a **d** act in Israel
1Co 11: 6 if it is **d** for a woman to have her hair cut off or to
2Mc 11:12 and Lysias himself escaped by **d** flight.

DISGRACEFULLY (3) [DISGRACE]
Pr 13: 5 but the wicked act shamefully and **d**.
Sir 26:24 *A shameless woman constantly acts d,*
3Mc 6:31 Accordingly those **d** treated and near to death,

DISGRACES (3) [DISGRACE]
1Co 11: 4 with something on his head **d** his head,
11: 5 or prophesies with her head unveiled **d** her head—
Sir 22: 5 An impudent daughter **d** father and husband,

DISGUISE (4) [DISGUISED, DISGUISES, DISGUISING]
1Ki 14: 2 Jeroboam said to his wife, "Go, **d** yourself,
22:30 "I will **d** myself and go into battle,
2Ch 18:29 "I will **d** myself and go into battle,
2Co 11:15 also **d** themselves as ministers of righteousness.

DISGUISED (4) [DISGUISE]
1Sa 28: 8 So Saul **d** himself and put on other clothes
1Ki 22:30 the king of Israel **d** himself and went into battle.
2Ch 18:29 king of Israel **d** himself, and they went into battle.
35:22 but **d** himself in order to fight with him.

DISGUISES (2) [DISGUISE]
Job 24:15 'No eye will see me'; and he **d** his face.
2Co 11:14 Even Satan **d** himself as an angel of light.

DISGUISING (2) [DISGUISE]
1Ki 20:38 **d** himself with a bandage over his eyes.
2Co 11:13 **d** themselves as apostles of Christ.

DISGUST (6) [DISGUSTING]
Ps 119:158 I look at the faithless with **d**,
Jer 6: 8 O Jerusalem, or I shall turn from you in **d**,
Eze 23:17 she turned from them in **d**.
23:18 I turned in **d** from her,
23:22 from whom you turned in **d**, and I will bring them
23:28 the hands of those from whom you turned in **d**;

DISGUSTING (1) [DISGUST]
Jer 23:13 In the prophets of Samaria I saw a **d** thing:

DISH (20) [DISHES]
Nu 7:14 one golden **d** weighing ten shekels, full of incense;
7:20 one golden **d** weighing ten shekels, full of incense;
7:26 one golden **d** weighing ten shekels, full of incense;
7:32 one golden **d** weighing ten shekels, full of incense;
7:38 one golden **d** weighing ten shekels, full of incense;
7:44 one golden **d** weighing ten shekels, full of incense;
7:50 one golden **d** weighing ten shekels, full of incense;
7:56 one golden **d** weighing ten shekels, full of incense;
7:62 one golden **d** weighing ten shekels, full of incense;
7:68 one golden **d** weighing ten shekels, full of incense;
7:74 one golden **d** weighing ten shekels, full of incense;
7:80 one golden **d** weighing ten shekels, full of incense;
2Ki 21:13 I will wipe Jerusalem as one wipes a **d**,
Pr 19:24 The lazy person buries a hand in the **d**,
26:15 The lazy person buries a hand in the **d**,
Lk 11:39 the outside of the cup and of the **d**,
Jn 13:26 of bread when I have dipped it in the **d**."
Sir 31:14 and do not crowd your neighbor at the **d**.
LtJ 6:17 just as someone's **d** is useless when it is broken,
2Es 9:34 or the sea a ship, or any **d** food or drink,

DISHAN (5)
Ge 36:21 Ezer, and **D**; these are the clans of the
36:28 These are the sons of **D**: Uz and Aran.
36:30 Ezer, and **D**; these are the clans of the
1Ch 1:38 Shobal, Zibeon, Anah, Dishon, Ezer, and **D**.
1:42 The sons of **D**: Uz and Aran.

DISHEARTENED (3) [HEART]
Dt 20: 8 saying, "Is anyone afraid or **d**?
Eze 13:22 Because you have **d** the righteous falsely, although I have not **d** them,

DISHES (9) [DISH]
Ex 25:29 You shall make its plates and **d** for incense,
37:16 its plates and **d** for incense,
Nu 4: 7 and put on it the plates, the **d** for incense,
7:84 twelve silver basins, twelve golden **d**,
7:86 the twelve golden **d**, full of incense,
7:86 of the **d** being one hundred twenty shekels;
1Ki 7:50 basins, **d** for incense, and firepans, of pure gold;
2Ki 25:14 the shovels, the snuffers, the **d** for incense,
Jdt 10: 5 then she wrapped up all her **d** and gave them

DISHEVEL (3) [DISHEVELED]
Lev 10: 6 not **d** your hair, and do not tear your vestments,
21:10 shall not **d** his hair, nor tear his vestments.
Nu 5:18 before the LORD, **d** the woman's hair, and place

DISHEVELED (2) [DISHEVEL]
Lev 13:45 and let the hair of his head be **d;**
3Mc 1: 4 the troops with wailing and tears, her locks all **d,**

DISHON‡ (7)
Ge 36:21 **D,** Ezer, and Dishan; these are the clans of the
36:25 **D** and Oholibamah daughter of Anah.
36:26 These are the sons of **D:**
36:30 **D,** Ezer, and Dishan; these are the clans of the
1Ch 1:38 The sons of Seir: Lotan, Shobal, Zibeon, Anah, **D,**
1:41 The sons of Anah: **D.**
1:41 sons of **D:** Hamran, Eshban, Ithran, and Cheran.

DISHONEST (12) [DISHONESTLY]
Ex 18:21 are trustworthy, and hate **d** gain;
Jer 22:17 But your eyes and heart are only on your **d** gain,
Eze 22:13 at the **d** gain you have made,
22:27 shedding blood, destroying lives to get **d** gain.
Mic 6:11 and a bag of **d** weights?
Lk 16: 8 the **d** manager because he had acted shrewdly;
16: 9 make friends for yourselves by means of **d** wealth
16:10 and whoever is **d** in a very little is **d** also
16:11 then you have not been faithful with the **d** wealth,
Sir 5: 8 Do not depend on **d** wealth,
35:15 and do not rely on a **d** sacrifice;

DISHONESTLY (1) [DISHONEST]
Dt 25:16 For all who do such things, all who act **d,**

DISHONOR (29) [DISHONORED, DISHONORING, DISHONORS]
Ezr 4:14 and it is not fitting for us to witness the king's **d,**
Ps 35: 4 be put to shame and **d** who seek after my life.
35:26 against me be clothed with shame and **d.**
40:14 and brought to **d** who desire my hurt.
69:19 the insults I receive, and my shame and **d;**
70: 2 be turned back and brought to **d** who desire
109:29 May my accusers be clothed with **d;**
Pr 6:33 He will get wounds and **d,**
18: 3 and with **d** comes disgrace.
Isa 61: 7 and **d** was proclaimed as their lot,
Jer 3:25 and let our **d** cover us;
14:21 do not **d** your glorious throne;
20:11 Their eternal **d** will never be forgotten.
51:51 **d** has covered our face, for aliens have come into
La 2: 2 to the ground in **d** the kingdom and its rulers.
Jn 8:49 but I honor my Father, and you **d** me.
Ac 5:41 that they were considered worthy to suffer **d** for
Ro 2:23 do you **d** God by breaking the law?
1Co 15:43 It is sown in **d,** it is raised in glory.
2Co 6: 8 in honor and **d,** in ill repute
Jdt 8:23 but the Lord our God will turn it to **d.**
Sir 1:30 or you may fall and bring **d** upon yourself.
3:10 for your father's **d** is no glory to you.
5:13 Honor and **d** come from speaking,
10:29 And who will honor those who **d** themselves?
29: 6 and instead of glory will repay him with **d.**
LtJ 6:40 Besides, even the Chaldeans themselves **d** them;
1Mc 1:40 Her **d** now grew as great as her glory;
2Mc 3:18 the holy place was about to be brought into **d.**

DISHONORED (6) [DISHONOR]
Dt 21:14 not treat her as a slave, since you have **d** her.
Ps 69: 6 do not let those who seek you be **d** because of me,
Jas 2: 6 But you have **d** the poor.
Wis 4:18 After this they will become **d** corpses,
Sir 10:31 And one **d** in wealth, how much more in poverty!
2Es 5:28 and **d** the one root beyond the others,

DISHONORING (1) [DISHONOR]
Sir 3:10 Do not glorify yourself by **d** your father,

DISHONORS (2) [DISHONOR]
Dt 27:16 "Cursed be anyone who **d** father or mother."
Sir 26:26 *but if she **d** him in her pride she will be known*

DISINHERIT (1)
Nu 14:12 I will strike them with pestilence and **d** them,

DISJOINTED (3)
4Mc 9:14 and with every member **d** he denounced the tyrant,
10: 5 they **d** his hands and feet with their instruments,
11:10 and all his members were **d.**

DISLIKED (7) [DISLIKES]
Dt 21:15 one of them loved and the other **d,**
21:15 if both the loved and the **d** have borne him sons,
21:15 the firstborn being the son of the one who is **d,**
21:16 as the firstborn in preference to the son of the **d,**
21:17 of the one who is **d,** giving him a double portion
Pr 14:20 The poor are **d** even by their neighbors,
Sir 42: 9 or if married, for fear she may be **d;**

DISLIKES‡ (3) [DISLIKED]
Dt 22:13 a woman, but after going in to her, he **d** her
22:16 in marriage to this man but he **d** her;
24: 3 Then suppose the second man **d** her,

DISLOCATED (2) [JOINT-DISLOCATORS]
4Mc 9:13 around this, his limbs were **d,**
10: 8 and while his vertebrae were being **d** by this,

DISLODGE (1)
Sir 39:28 and in their anger they can **d** mountains;

DISLOYAL‡ (1) [DISLOYALTY]
2Mc 14:26 He told him that Nicanor was **d** to the government,

DISLOYALTY (1) [DISLOYAL]
Hos 14: 4 I will heal their **d;** I will love them freely,

DISMAL (2)
Mt 6:16 "And whenever you fast, do not look **d,**
Wis 17: 4 and **d** phantoms with gloomy faces appeared.

DISMAY (5) [DISMAYED]
Pr 21:15 it is a joy to the righteous, but **d** to evildoers.
Jer 8:21 I mourn, and **d** has taken hold of me.
Eze 4:16 and they shall drink water by measure and in **d.**
4:17 they will look at one another in **d,**
12:19 and drink their water in **d,**

DISMAYED (55) [DISMAY]
Ge 42:35 father saw their bundles of money, they were **d.**
45: 3 so **d** were they at his presence.
Ex 15:15 Then the chiefs of Edom were **d;**
Dt 1:21 do not fear or be **d.**"
31: 8 Do not fear or be **d.**"
Jos 1: 9 do not be frightened or **d,**
8: 1 the LORD said to Joshua, "Do not fear or be **d;**
10:25 And Joshua said to them, "Do not be afraid or **d;**
Jdg 20:41 and the Benjaminites were **d,**
1Sa 17:11 they were **d** and greatly afraid.
2Sa 4: 1 his courage failed, and all Israel was **d.**
2Ki 19:26 shorn of strength, are **d** and confounded;
1Ch 22:13 Do not be afraid or **d.**
28:20 Do not be afraid or **d;**
2Ch 20:15 'Do not fear or be **d** at this great multitude;
20:17 Do not fear or be **d;**
32: 7 or **d** before the king of Assyria and all the horde
Job 4: 5 it touches you, and you are **d.**
21: 6 When I think of it I am **d,**
32:15 "They are **d,** they answer no more;
39:22 It laughs at fear, and is not **d;**
Ps 30: 7 you hid your face; I was **d.**
83:17 Let them be put to shame and **d** forever;
104:29 When you hide your face, they are **d;**
Isa 8: 9 Band together, you peoples, and be **d;**
8: 9 gird yourselves and be **d;** gird yourselves and be **d!**
13: 8 and they will be **d.** Pangs
19:10 Its weavers will be **d,** and all who work
20: 5 And they shall be **d** and confounded because
21: 3 I am **d** so that I cannot see.
37:27 shorn of strength, are **d** and confounded;
51: 7 and do not be **d** when they revile you.
Jer 8: 9 they shall be **d** and taken;
10: 2 or be **d** at the signs of the heavens;
10: 2 for the nations are **d** at them.
14: 3 They are ashamed and **d** and cover their heads,
14: 4 the farmers are **d;** they cover their heads.
17:18 let them be **d,** but do not let me be dismayed;
17:18 let them be dismayed, but do not let me be **d;**
22:22 be ashamed and **d** because of all your wickedness.
23: 4 or be **d,** nor shall any be missing, says the LORD.
30:10 says the LORD, and do not be **d,** O Israel;
31:19 I was **d** because I bore the disgrace of my youth."
46:27 have no fear, my servant Jacob, and do not be **d,**
50: 2 Bel is put to shame, Merodach is **d.**
50: 2 Her images are put to shame, her idols are **d.**
Eze 2: 6 and do not be **d** at their looks,
3: 9 do not fear them or be **d** at their looks,
26:18 the coastlands by the sea are **d** at your passing.
36:32 Be ashamed and **d** for your ways,
Da 8:27 I was **d** by the vision and did not understand it.
Joel 1:11 Be **d,** you farmers, wail, you vinedressers,
Jdt 14:19 they tore their tunics and were greatly **d,**
2Mc 13:23 he was **d,** called in the Jews,

DISMEMBERED (1) [DISMEMBERING]
2Mc 1:16 they **d** them and cut off their heads

DISMEMBERING (1) [DISMEMBERED]
4Mc 10: 5 **d** him by prying his limbs from their sockets,

DISMISS (6) [DISMISSAL, DISMISSED, DISMISSING]
2Sa 3:24 why did you **d** him, so that he got away?
2Ch 23: 8 for the priest Jehoiada did not **d** the divisions.
Mt 1:19 to public disgrace, planned to **d** her quietly.
Sir 7:19 Do not **d** a wise and good wife,
1Mc 12:45 **D** them now to their homes and choose
2Mc 7: 9 you **d** us from this present life,

DISMISSAL (4) [DISMISS]
Mt 19: 7 to give a certificate of **d** and to divorce her?"
Mk 10: 4 "Moses allowed a man to write a certificate of **d**
3Mc 6:37 asking for **d** to their homes.
6:40 on which also they made the petition for their **d.**

DISMISSED (18) [DISMISS]
Jdg 2: 6 When Joshua **d** the people,
2Sa 3:21 So David **d** Abner, and he went away in peace.
3:22 not with David at Hebron, for David had **d** him,
3:23 and he has **d** him, and he has gone away in peace."
2Ki 5:24 he **d** the men, and they left.
Mt 14:22 on ahead to the other side, while he **d** the crowds.
14:23 And after he had **d** the crowds,
Mk 6:45 to Bethsaida, while he **d** the crowd.
Lk 16: 4 when I am **d** as manager,
Ac 18:16 And he **d** them from the tribunal.
19:41 When he had said this, he **d** the assembly.
23:22 So the tribune **d** the young man, ordering him,
Jdt 7:32 Then he **d** the people to their various posts,
Sus 1:36 shut the garden doors, and **d** the maids.
1Mc 11:38 he **d** all his troops, all of them to their own homes,
2Mc 14:23 but **d** the flocks of people that had gathered.
3Mc 5:34 by one sullenly slipped away and **d**
2Es 9:39 I **d** the thoughts with which I had been engaged,

DISMISSING (1) [DISMISS]
Lk 2:29 now you are **d** your servant in peace,

DISMOUNTED (2)
Jos 15:18 As she **d** from her donkey, Caleb said to her,
Jdg 1:14 As she **d** from her donkey, Caleb said to her,

DISOBEDIENCE‡ (10) [DISOBEY]
Ro 5:19 by the one man's **d** the many were made sinners,
11:30 but have now received mercy because of their **d,**
11:32 For God has imprisoned all in **d** so that he may
2Co 10: 6 We are ready to punish every **d**
Heb 2: 2 every transgression or **d** received a just penalty,
4: 6 the good news failed to enter because of **d,**
4:11 so that no one may fall through such **d** as theirs.
4Mc 8: 9 But if by **d** you rouse my anger,
8:18 and venture upon a **d** that brings death?
12: 3 for they died in torments because of their **d.**

DISOBEDIENT‡ (18) [DISOBEY]
Ne 9:26 "Nevertheless they were **d** and rebelled
Lk 1:17 and the **d** to the wisdom of the righteous,
Ac 26:19 King Agrippa, I was not **d** to the heavenly vision,
Ro 10:21 "All day long I have held out my hands to a **d** and
11:30 Just as you were once **d** to God but have
11:31 so they have now been **d** in order that,
Eph 2: 2 spirit that is now at work among those who are **d.**
5: 6 the wrath of God comes on those who are **d.**
Col 3: 6 the wrath of God is coming on those who are **d.**
1Ti 1: 9 not for the innocent but for the lawless and **d,**
2Ti 3: 2 arrogant, abusive, **d** to their parents, ungrateful,
Tit 1:16 They are detestable, **d,** unfit for any good work.
3: 3 For we ourselves were once foolish, **d,** led astray,
Heb 3:18 if not to those who were **d?**
11:31 not perish with those who were **d,**
Sir 16: 6 and in a **d** nation wrath blazes up.
Bar 1:19 we have been **d** to the Lord our God,
4Mc 9:10 as at those who are **d,** but also infuriated,

DISOBEY (16) [DISOBEDIENCE, DISOBEDIENT, DISOBEYED, DISOBEYING, DISOBEYS]
Lev 26:27 But if, despite this, you **d** me,
Dt 17:12 for anyone who presumes to **d** the priest appointed
Est 3: 3 "Why do you **d** the king's command?"
Pr 24:21 and do not **d** either of them;
1Pe 2: 8 They stumble because they **d** the word,
AdE 3: 3 "Mordecai, why do you **d** the king's command?"
Sir 1:28 Do not **d** the fear of the Lord;
2:15 Those who fear the Lord do not **d** his words,
16:28 and they never **d** his word.
20:12 or else he will become stubborn and **d** you,
39:31 their time comes they never **d** his command."
1Es 4: 5 and do not **d** the king's command;
4:11 to attend to his own affairs, nor do they **d** him.
4Mc 8: 6 Just as I am able to punish those who **d** my orders,
8:11 Will you not consider this, that if you **d,**
8:21 let us seriously consider that if we **d** we are dead!

DISOBEYED (9) [DISOBEY]
1Ki 13:21 Because you have **d** the word of the LORD,
13:26 the man of God who **d** the word of the LORD;
Da 3:28 They **d** the king's command and yielded
9:14 for we have **d** his voice.
Lk 15:29 and I have never **d** your command;
Tob 3: 4 and **d** your commandments.
Jdt 2: 6 because they **d** my orders.
Sir 23:23 For first of all, she has **d** the law of the Most High;
Bar 1:18 We have **d** him, and have not heeded the voice of

DISOBEYING (1) [DISOBEY]
Jer 42:13 thus **d** the voice of the LORD your God

DISOBEYS (2) [DISOBEY]
Jos 1:18 against your orders and **d** your words,
Jn 3:36 whoever **d** the Son will not see life,

DISORDER (7) [DISORDERLY, DISORDERS]
1Co 14:33 for God is a God not of **d** but of peace.
2Co 12:20 anger, selfishness, slander, gossip, conceit, and **d.**
Jas 3:16 there will also be **d** and wickedness of every kind.
Wis 14:26 sexual perversion, **d** in marriages, adultery,
2Mc 9: 1 Antiochus had retreated in **d** from the region
10:30 they were thrown into **d** and cut to pieces.
3Mc 3:24 if a sudden **d** later arises against us,

DISORDERLY (1) [DISORDER]
3Mc 1:19 in a **d** rush flocked together in the city.

DISORDERS (1) [DISORDER]
Wis 17: 8 the fears and **d** of a sick soul were sick themselves

DISORGANIZED (1)
2Es 15:32 then these shall be **d** and silenced by their power,

DISOWNED (1)
La 2: 7 The Lord has scorned his altar, **d** his sanctuary;

DISPATCHED (3)
2Ki 6:32 So he **d** a man from his presence.
2Ch 2:13 "I have **d** Huram-abi, a skilled artisan,
2Mc 4:38 and there he **d** the bloodthirsty fellow.

DISPEL (2)
2Es 15:39 the cloud that was raised in wrath, and shall **d** it;
4Mc 5:11 **d** your futile reasonings, adopt a mind appropriate

DISPENSATION (KJV) See COMMISSION

DISPENSES (1)
Pr 15: 2 The tongue of the wise **d** knowledge,

DISPERSE (9) [DISPERSED, DISPERSION, DISPERSIONS]
1Sa 14:34 Saul said, **"D** yourselves among the troops,
Ps 106:27 and would **d** their descendants among the nations,
Eze 12:15 when I **d** them among the nations and scatter them
20:23 the nations and **d** them through the countries,
22:15 I will scatter you among the nations and **d** you
29:12 and **d** them among the countries.
30:23 and **d** them throughout the lands.
30:26 the nations and **d** them throughout the countries.
3Mc 2:19 Wipe away our sins and **d** our errors,

DISPERSED (9) [DISPERSE]
2Sa 20:22 So he blew the trumpet, and they **d** from the city,
Isa 11:12 the **d** of Judah from the four corners of the earth.
Eze 36:19 and they were **d** through the countries;
Jn 11:52 but to gather into one the **d** children of God.
Ac 5:36 and all who followed him were **d** and disappeared.
Tob 3: 4 among all the nations among whom you have **d** us.
Wis 5:14 it is **d** like smoke before the wind,
Sir 51:12 *Give thanks to him who gathers the* **d** *of Israel,*
1Mc 10:83 and the cavalry was **d** in the plain.

DISPERSION (3) [DISPERSE]
Jn 7:35 to the **D** among the Greeks and teach the Greeks?
Jas 1: 1 To the twelve tribes in the **D:** Greetings.
1Pe 1: 1 To the exiles of the **D** in Pontus, Galatia,

DISPERSIONS (1) [DISPERSE]
Jer 25:34 and your **d,** and you shall fall like a choice vessel.

DISPLAY (14) [DISPLAYED, DISPLAYS]
Dt 26: 8 with a terrifying **d** of power,
29:24 What caused this great **d** of anger?"
Isa 61: 3 the planting of the LORD, to **d** his glory.
Eze 36:23 through you I **d** my holiness before their eyes.
38:16 O Gog, I **d** my holiness before their eyes.
38:23 So I will **d** my greatness and my holiness
39:21 I will **d** my glory among the nations;
1Ti 1:16 Jesus Christ might **d** the utmost patience,
AdE 1:11 and to have her **d** her beauty to all the governors
Sir 7: 5 or **d** your wisdom before the king.
10:26 a **d** of your wisdom when you do your work,
32: 4 do not **d** your cleverness at the wrong time.
2Es 12:32 will **d** before them their contemptuous dealings.
4Mc 8: 5 not to **d** the same madness as that of

DISPLAYED (8) [DISPLAY]
Dt 6:22 The LORD **d** before our eyes great
Est 1: 4 while he **d** the great wealth of his kingdom and
Ps 77:14 you have **d** your might among the peoples.
78:43 when he **d** his signs in Egypt,
Eze 39:27 and through them have **d** my holiness in the sight
AdE 1: 4 when he had **d** to them the riches of his kingdom
1: 7 and a miniature cup was **d,** made of ruby,
1Mc 7:47 brought them and **d** them just outside Jerusalem.

DISPLAYS (4) [DISPLAY]
Dt 4:34 and by terrifying **d** of power,
34:12 the terrifying **d** of power that Moses performed in
Pr 13:16 do all things intelligently, but the fool **d** folly.
2Es 7:*104* The day of judgment is decisive and **d** to all

DISPLEASE (2) [DISPLEASED, DISPLEASING, DISPLEASURE]
1Sa 29: 7 do nothing to **d** the lords of the Philistines."
1Th 2:15 they **d** God and oppose everyone

DISPLEASED (12) [DISPLEASE]
Ge 48:17 on the head of Ephraim, it **d** him;
Nu 11:10 the LORD became very angry, and Moses was **d.**
1Sa 8: 6 But the thing **d** Samuel when they said,
18: 8 Saul was very angry, for this saying **d** him.
2Sa 11:27 But the thing that David had done **d** the LORD,
1Ki 1: 6 His father had never at any time **d** him by asking,
1Ch 21: 7 God was **d** with this thing, and he struck Israel.
Ne 2:10 it **d** them greatly that someone had come to seek
Pr 24:18 or else the LORD will see it and be **d,**
Isa 59:15 and it **d** him that there was no justice.
2Mc 4:35 were grieved and **d** at the unjust murder of
14:27 stating that he was **d** with the covenant

DISPLEASING (3) [DISPLEASE]
Ge 38:10 What he did was **d** in the sight of the LORD,
Nu 22:34 therefore, if it is **d** to you, I will return home."
Jnh 4: 1 this was very **d** to Jonah, and he became angry.

DISPLEASURE (1) [DISPLEASE]
Nu 14:34 forty years, and you shall know my **d."**

DISPOSAL (2) [DISPOSED]
2Ki 10: 2 and you have at your **d** chariots and horses,
Ac 5: 4 after it was sold, were not the proceeds at your **d?**

DISPOSED (11) [DISPOSAL, DISPOSITION, ILL-DISPOSED, WELL-DISPOSED]
1Sa 20:12 or on the third day, if he is well **d** toward David,
Zec 11: 8 In one month I **d** of the three shepherds,
1Co 10:27 an unbeliever invites you to a meal and you are **d**
11:16 But if anyone is **d** to be contentious—
Sir Pr: 3 to gain learning and are **d** to live according to
Bar 4:28 For just as you were **d** to go astray from God,
2Mc 5:25 he pretended to be peaceably **d** and waited until
12:31 they thanked them and exhorted them to be well **d**
1Es 8:11 Let as many as are so **d,** therefore, leave with you,
3Mc 3:23 among them who are sincerely **d** toward us;
7:11 be favorably **d** toward the king's government.

DISPOSITION (1) [DISPOSED]
Jdt 8:29 for your heart's **d** is right.

DISPOSSESS (11) [DISPOSSESSED, DISPOSSESSING]
Dt 2:21 so that they could **d** them and settle in their place.
2:22 so that they could **d** them and settle in their place
7:17 are more numerous than I; how can I **d** them?"
9: 1 in and **d** nations larger and mightier than you,
9: 3 so that you may **d** and destroy them quickly,
11:23 and you will **d** nations larger
12: 2 about to **d** served their gods,
12:29 the nations whom you are about to enter to **d** them,
18:14 that you are about to **d** do give heed to soothsayers
31: 3 before you, and you shall **d** them.
Jer 49: 2 then Israel shall **d** those who dispossessed him,

DISPOSSESSED (11) [DISPOSSESS]
Nu 21:32 and **d** the Amorites who were there.
32:39 captured it, and **d** the Amorites who were there;
Dt 2:12 but the descendants of Esau **d** them,
12:29 when you have **d** them and live in their land,
19: 1 and you have **d** them and settled in their towns and
Jer 49: 1 Why then has Milcom **d** Gad,
49: 2 then Israel shall dispossess those who **d** him,
Eze 46:18 that none of my people shall be **d** of their holding.
Ob 1:17 Jacob shall take possession of those who **d** them.
Ac 7:45 in turn brought it in with Joshua when they **d**
Sir 16: 9 on those **d** because of their sins;

DISPOSSESSED (KJV) See also CONQUERED

DISPOSSESSING (2) [DISPOSSESS]
Dt 9: 4 of these nations that the LORD is **d** them
9: 5 of these nations the LORD your God is **d** them

DISPUTE (11) [DISPUTED, DISPUTES, DISPUTING]
Ex 18:16 When they have a **d,** they come to me and I decide
24:14 whoever has a **d** may go to them."
Dt 17: 8 any such matters of **d** in your towns—
19:17 parties to the **d** shall appear before the LORD,
21: 5 by their decision all cases of **d** and assault shall
25: 1 Suppose two persons have a **d** and enter
Ecc 6:10 they are not able to **d** with those who are stronger.
Lk 22:24 A **d** also arose among them as to which one
Heb 6:16 an oath given as confirmation puts an end to all **d.**
7: 7 It is beyond **d** that the inferior is blessed by
Sir 28:11 and a hasty **d** sheds blood.

DISPUTED (4) [DISPUTE]
Ex 22: 9 In any case of **d** ownership involving ox, donkey,
2Ch 19: 8 for the LORD and to decide **d** cases.
Jn 6:52 The Jews then **d** among themselves, saying,
Jude 1: 9 with the devil and **d** about the body of Moses,

DISPUTES (7) [DISPUTE]
Dt 1:12 But how can I bear the heavy burden of your **d** all
Pr 17: 9 but one who dwells on **d** will alienate a friend.
18:18 to **d** and decides between powerful contenders.
2Co 7: 5 **d** without and fears within.
1Ti 6: 4 and has a morbid craving for controversy and for **d**
Jas 4: 1 Those conflicts and **d** among you,
4: 2 so you engage in **d** and conflicts.

DISPUTING (3) [DISPUTE]
2Sa 19: 9 All the people were **d** throughout all the tribes
Mk 12:28 One of the scribes came near and heard them **d**
Ac 24:12 not find me **d** with anyone in the temple or stirring

DISQUALIFIED (1) [DISQUALIFY]
1Co 9:27 proclaiming to others I myself should not be **d.**

DISQUALIFY (1) [DISQUALIFIED]
Col 2:18 Do not let anyone **d** you,

DISQUIETED (3)
Ps 42: 5 O my soul, and why are you **d** within me?
42:11 O my soul, and why are you **d** within me?
43: 5 O my soul, and why are you **d** within me?

DISREGARD (4) [DISREGARDED, DISREGARDING, DISREGARDS]
Jdt 11:10 Therefore, lord and master, do not **d** what he said,
AdE 13: 4 contrary to those of every nation and continually **d**
Sir 31:22 Listen to me, my child, and do not **d** me,
4Mc 15:23 strengthened her to **d,** for the time,

DISREGARDED (10) [DISREGARD]
1Ki 12: 8 But he **d** the advice that the older men gave him,
12:13 He **d** the advice that the older men had given him
Isa 33: 8 its oaths are despised, its obligation is **d.**
40:27 and my right is **d** by my God"?
Eze 22:26 and they have **d** my sabbaths,
Jdt 1:11 But all who lived in the whole region **d**
Wis 3:10 those who **d** the righteous and rebelled against
2Es 7:20 that the law of God that is set before them be **d!**
4Mc 4:24 that all his threats and punishments were being **d**
15:24 this noble mother **d** all these because of faith

DISREGARDING (2) [DISREGARD]
Heb 12: 2 the cross, **d** its shame, and has taken his seat at
2Mc 5:17 that this was the reason he was **d** the holy place.

DISREGARDS (2) [DISREGARD]
Sir 14: 8 he turns away and **d** people.
23:11 his sin remains on him, and if he **d** it,

DISREPUTABLE (1) [DISREPUTE]
Job 30: 8 **d** brood, they have been whipped out of the land.

DISREPUTE (2) [DISREPUTABLE]
Ac 19:27 of ours may come into **d** but also that the temple
1Co 4:10 You are held in honor, but we in **d.**

DISRESPECTFUL (1)
1Ti 6: 2 be **d** to them on the ground that they are members

DISRUPTS (1)
Sir 28: 9 and the sinner **d** friendships and sows discord

DISSEMBLED, DISSIMULATION (KJV) See ACTED DECEITFULLY, CONSORT WITH HYPOCRICY, FATAL MISTAKE, HYPOCRICY

DISSEMBLES (1)
Pr 26:24 An enemy **d** in speaking

DISSENSION (6) [DISSENSIONS]
Ac 15: 2 after Paul and Barnabas had no small **d** and debate
23: 7 **d** began between the Pharisees and the Sadducees,
23:10 When the **d** became violent, the tribune,
1Co 12:25 that there may be no **d** within the body,
1Ti 6: 4 From these come envy, **d,** slander,
1Mc 3:29 of the **d** and disaster that he had caused in the land

DISSENSIONS (3) [DISSENSION]
Ro 16:17 to keep an eye on those who cause **d** and offenses,
Gal 5:20 enmities, strife, jealousy, anger, quarrels, **d,**
Tit 3: 9 But avoid stupid controversies, genealogies, **d,**

DISSIPATION (3)
Lk 21:34 so that your hearts are not weighed down with **d**
1Pe 4: 4 in the same excesses of **d,**
2Pe 2:13 reveling in their **d** while they feast with you.

DISSOLUTE (1)
Lk 15:13 and there he squandered his property in **d** living.

DISSOLVE (1) [DISSOLVED, DISSOLVES]
Wis 2: 3 and the spirit will **d** like empty air.

DISSOLVED (4) [DISSOLVE]
2Pe 3:10 and the elements will be **d** with fire,
3:11 Since all these things are to be **d** in this way,
3:12 of which the heavens will be set ablaze and **d**,
4Mc 14: 8 encircled the sevenfold fear of tortures and **d** it.

DISSOLVES‡ (1) [DISSOLVE]
Ps 58: 8 Let them be like the snail that **d** into slime;

DISSUADE (3)
Job 23:13 But he stands alone and who can **d** him?
1Mc 9: 9 But they tried to **d** him, saying,
4Mc 16:12 nor did she **d** any of them from dying,

DISTAFF (1)
Pr 31:19 She puts her hands to the **d**,

DISTANCE (46) [DISTANCES, DISTANT]
Ge 21:16 about the **d** of a bowshot;
22: 3 to the place in the **d** that God had shown him.
30:36 a **d** of three days' journey between himself
35:16 and when they were still some **d** from Ephrath,
36: 6 he moved to a land some **d** from his brother Jacob.
37:18 They saw him from a **d**,
44: 4 When they had gone only a short **d** from the city,
48: 7 while there was still some **d** to go to Ephrath;
Ex 2: 4 His sister stood at a **d**,
20:18 they were afraid and trembled and stood at a **d**,
20:21 Then the people stood at a **d**,
24: 1 of the elders of Israel, and worship at a **d**.
Dt 11:30 they are beyond the Jordan, some **d** to the west,
14:24 the **d** is so great that you are unable to transport it,
19: 6 But if the **d** is too great,
32:52 Although you may view the land from a **d**,
Jos 3: 4 a **d** of about two thousand cubits;
Jdg 18:22 When they were some **d** from the home of Micah,
1Sa 26:13 with a great **d** between them.
2Ki 2: 7 and stood at some **d** from them,
2:15 of prophets who were at Jericho saw him at a **d**,
5:19 But when Naaman had gone from him a short **d**,
14:13 a **d** of four hundred cubits.
2Ch 25:23 a **d** of four hundred cubits.
Job 2:12 When they saw him from a **d**,
39:25 From a **d** it smells the battle,
Isa 59:14 and righteousness stands at a **d**;
Eze 40:19 Then he measured the **d** from the inner front of
Mt 8:30 Now a large herd of swine was feeding at some **d**
26:58 But Peter was following him at a **d**,
27:55 also there, looking on from a **d**;
Mk 5: 6 When he saw Jesus from a **d**,
8: 3 and some of them have come from a great **d**."
11:13 Seeing in the **d** a fig tree in leaf,
14:54 Peter had followed him at a **d**,
15:40 There were also women looking on from a **d**;
Lk 17:12 ten lepers approached him. Keeping their **d**,
22:54 But Peter was following at a **d**.
23:49 stood at a **d**, watching these things.
Heb 11:13 but from a **d** they saw and greeted them.
Rev 14:20 for a **d** of about two hundred miles.
Jdt 13:11 a **d** Judith called out to the sentries at the gates,
Wis 14:17 since they lived at a **d**,
Sir 27:22 and those who know him will keep their **d**.
2Mc 8:25 After pursuing them for some **d**,
10:27 up their arms and advanced a considerable **d** from

DISTANCES (2) [DISTANCE]
Dt 19: 3 the **d** and divide into three regions the land that
21: 2 and your judges shall come out to measure the **d** to

DISTANT (14) [DISTANCE]
Dt 29:22 well as the foreigner who comes from a **d** country,
1Ki 8:41 comes from a **d** land because of your name
2Ch 6:32 come from a **d** land because of your great name,
Isa 13: 5 They come from a **d** land,
Jer 4:16 "Besiegers come from a **d** land;
6:20 or sweet cane from a **d** land?
51:50 Remember the LORD in a **d** land,
Eze 12:27 he prophesies for **d** times."
Lk 15:13 and traveled to a **d** country,
19:12 to a **d** country to get royal power for himself and
Bar 4:15 For he brought a **d** nation against them,
1Mc 8: 4 even though the place was far **d** from them.
2Mc 12: 9 of the light was seen in Jerusalem, thirty miles **d**.
2Es 13:41 of the nations and go to a more **d** region,

DISTILL‡ (1) [DISTILLING, DISTILLS]
SS 4:11 Your lips **d** nectar, my bride;

DISTILLING (1) [DISTILL]
SS 5:13 His lips are lilies, **d** liquid myrrh.

DISTILLS (1) [DISTILL]
Job 36:27 he **d** his mist in rain,

DISTINCT (3) [DISTINCTION, DISTINCTIONS, DISTINCTLY]
Ex 33:16 In this way, we shall be **d**, I and your people,
1Co 14: 7 If they do not give **d** notes,
Wis 7:22 clear, unpolluted, **d**, invulnerable, loving the good,

DISTINCTION (13) [DISTINCT]
Ex 8:23 Thus I will make a **d** between my people
9: 4 the LORD will make a **d** between the livestock
11: 7 so that you may know that the LORD makes a **d**
Lev 11:47 to make a **d** between the unclean and the clean,
20:25 a **d** between the clean animal and the unclean,
Est 6: 3 "What honor or **d** has been bestowed on Mordecai
Eze 22:26 they have made no **d** between the holy and
Ac 11:12 to go with them and not to make a **d** between them
15: 9 in cleansing their hearts by faith he has made no **d**
Ro 3:22 for all who believe. For there is no **d**,
10:12 For there is no **d** between Jew and Greek;
Sir 45:12 a **d** to be prized, the work of an expert,
2Mc 6:23 with **d** and his excellent life even from childhood,

DISTINCTIONS (1) [DISTINCT]
Jas 2: 4 have you not made **d** among yourselves,

DISTINCTLY (1) [DISTINCT]
Isa 32: 4 tongues of stammerers will speak readily and **d**.

DISTINGUISH (4) [DISTINGUISHED]
Lev 10:10 You are to **d** between the holy and the common,
Ezr 3:13 not **d** the sound of the joyful shout from the sound
Eze 44:23 and show them how to **d** between the unclean and
Heb 5:14 by practice to **d** good from evil.

DISTINGUISHED (10) [DISTINGUISH]
Nu 22:15 more numerous and more **d** than these.
SS 5:10 and ruddy, **d** among ten thousand.
Da 6: 3 Soon Daniel **d** himself above all
Lk 14: 8 in case someone more **d** than you has been invited
AdE 13: 3 who excels among us in sound judgment, and is **d**
Sir 33: 8 By the Lord's wisdom they were **d**,
33:11 In the fullness of his knowledge the Lord **d** them
38: 3 The skill of physicians makes them **d**,
1Mc 3:32 He left Lysias, a **d** man of royal lineage,
2Mc 15:13 **d** by his gray hair and dignity,

DISTORT (1) [DISTORTED, DISTORTING]
Dt 16:19 You must not **d** justice; you must

DISTORTED (1) [DISTORT]
Da 3:19 Meshach, and Abednego that his face was **d**.

DISTORTING (1) [DISTORT]
Ac 20:30 even from your own group will come **d** the truth

DISTRACTED (2)
Lk 10:40 But Martha was **d** by her many tasks;
10:41 Martha, you are worried and **d** by many things;

DISTRACTS See Index to Footnotes

DISTRAUGHT (1)
Ps 55: 2 in my complaint. I am **d**

DISTRESS‡ (113) [DISTRESSED, DISTRESSES, DISTRESSING]
A. TIME OF ... DISTRESS (11)
B. DAY OF ... DISTRESS (9)
C. GREAT DISTRESS (9)

Ge 35: 3 the God who answered me in the day of my **d** B
Dt 4:30 In your **d**, when all these things have happened
Jdg 2:15 and they were in great **d**. C
10:14 let them deliver you in the time of your **d**." A
1Sa 2:32 Then in **d** you will look with greedy eye on all
13: 6 When the Israelites saw that they were in **d** (for
22: 2 Everyone who was in **d**, and everyone who was
28:15 Saul answered, "I am in great **d**, C
2Sa 16:12 It may be that the LORD will look on my **d**,
22: 7 In my **d** I called upon the LORD;
24:14 Then David said to Gad, "I am in great **d**; C
2Ki 4:27 "Let her alone, for she is in bitter **d**;
14:26 the LORD saw that the **d** of Israel was very bitter;
19: 3 day is a day of **d**, of rebuke, and of disgrace; B
1Ch 21:13 Then David said to Gad, "I am in great **d**; C
2Ch 15: 4 but when in their **d** they turned to the LORD,
15: 6 for God troubled them with every sort of **d**.
20: 9 and cry to you in our **d**,
28:22 In the time of his **d** he became yet more faithless A
33:12 in **d** he entreated the favor of the LORD his God
Ne 9: 9 the **d** of our ancestors in Egypt and heard their cry
9:37 at their pleasure, and we are in great **d**." C
Job 15:24 **d** and anguish terrify them;
20:22 In full sufficiency they will be in **d**;
36:16 He also allured you out of **d** into a broad place
36:19 Will your cry avail to keep you from **d**,
Ps 4: 1 You gave me room when I was in **d**.
18: 6 In my **d** I called upon the LORD;
25:17 and bring me out of my **d**.
31: 9 Be gracious to me, O LORD, for I am in **d**;
32: 6 at a time of **d**, the rush of mighty waters shall A
39: 2 to no avail; my **d** grew worse,
59:16 fortress for me and a refuge in the day of my **d**. B
69:17 for I am in **d**—make haste to answer me.
78:49 and **d**, a company of destroying angels.
81: 7 In **d** you called, and I rescued you;
102: 2 not hide your face from me in the day of my **d**. B
106:44 he regarded their **d** when he heard their cry.
107: 6 and he delivered them from their **d**;
107:13 and he saved them from their **d**;
107:19 and he saved them from their **d**;
107:28 and he brought them out from their **d**;
107:41 but he raises up the needy out of **d**,
116: 3 on me; I suffered **d** and anguish.
118: 5 Out of my **d** I called on the LORD;
119:50 This is my comfort in my **d**,
120: 1 In my **d** I cry to the LORD,
144:14 no exile, and no cry of **d** in our streets.
Pr 1:27 when **d** and anguish come upon you.
31: 6 and wine to those in bitter **d**;
Isa 5:30 to the land—only darkness and **d**;
8:22 but will see only **d** and darkness,
25: 4 a refuge to the needy in their **d**,
26:16 O LORD, in **d** they sought you,
29: 2 Yet I will **d** Ariel, and there shall be moaning
29: 7 and who **d** her, shall be like a dream,
30: 6 Through a land of trouble and **d**,
37: 3 day is a day of **d**, of rebuke, and of disgrace; B
63: 9 in all their **d**. It was no messenger
65:19 of weeping be heard in it, or the cry of **d**.
Jer 10:18 and I will bring **d** on them,
15:11 on you in a time of trouble and in a time of **d**. A
19: 9 and in the **d** with which their enemies
30: 7 it is a time of **d** for Jacob; A
La 1: 3 in the midst of her **d**.
Hos 5:15 In their **d** they will beg my favor:
Ob 1:12 you should not have boasted on the day of **d**. B
1:14 over his survivors on the day of **d**. B
Jnh 2: 2 "I called to the LORD out of my **d**,
Zep 1:15 will be a day of wrath, a day of **d** and anguish, B
1:17 I will bring such **d** upon people
Zec 10:11 They shall pass through the sea of **d**,
Mt 8: 6 at home paralyzed, in terrible **d**."
Lk 21:23 For there will be great **d** on the earth and wrath C
21:25 the earth **d** among nations confused by the roaring
Ro 2: 9 be anguish and **d** for everyone who does evil,
8:35 Will hardship, or **d**, or persecution, or famine,
1Co 7:28 Yet those who marry will experience **d** in this life,
2Co 2: 4 For I wrote you out of much **d** and anguish
Php 4:14 In any case, it was kind of you to share my **d**.
1Th 3: 7 and sisters, during all our **d**
Jas 1:27 to care for orphans and widows in their **d**,
Rev 2:22 into great **d**, unless they repent of her doings; C
Tob 3: 6 Command, O Lord, that I be released from this **d**;
3: 6 For it is better for me to die than to see so much **d**
3:10 but she hanged herself because of her **d**.'
Jdt 4:13 and had regard for their **d**;
AdE 9:22 sorrow into gladness and from a time of **d** to A
11: 8 of tribulation and **d**, affliction and great tumult on
14: 2 on the garments of **d** and mourning, and instead
Sir 2:11 he forgives sins and saves in time of **d**. A
3:15 in the day of your **d** it will be remembered B
4: 4 Do not reject a suppliant in **d**,
22:23 Stand by him in time of **d**, A
30:21 and do not **d** yourself deliberately.
31:20 The **d** of sleeplessness and of nausea and colic
31:31 and do not **d** him by making demands of him.
35:26 as welcome in time of **d** as clouds of rain in time A
LtJ 6:37 they cannot rescue one who is in **d**.
Aza 1:27 at all and caused them no pain or **d**.
Sus 1:10 but they did not tell each other of their **d**,
1Mc 2:53 in the time of his **d** kept the commandment, A
5:16 in **d** and were being attacked by enemies.
6:11 I said to myself, 'To what **d** I have come!
9:27 So there was great **d** in Israel, C
13: 5 from me to spare my life in any time of **d**, A
2Mc 1: 7 in the critical **d** that came upon us in those years
3:14 There was no little **d** throughout the whole city.
15:19 to remain in the city were in no little **d**,
2Es 6:37 and my soul was in **d**.
9:45 and considered my **d**, and gave me a son.
10: 7 the mother of us all, is in deep grief and great **d**. C
13:19 For they shall see great dangers and much **d**,

DISTRESSED‡ (26) [DISTRESS]
Ge 21:12 "Do not be **d** because of the boy and because
32: 7 Then Jacob was greatly afraid and **d**;
45: 5 And now do not be **d**, or angry with yourselves,
Jdg 10: 9 so that Israel was greatly **d**.
1Sa 1:10 She was deeply **d** and prayed to the LORD,
2Sa 1:26 I am **d** for you, my brother Jonathan;
Est 4: 4 and told her, the queen was deeply **d**;
Isa 8:21 through the land, greatly **d** and hungry;
La 1:20 See, O LORD, how **d** I am;
Da 4:19 was severely **d** for a while.
6:14 the king heard the charge, he was very much **d**.
Mt 17:23 And they were greatly **d**.
18:31 they were greatly **d**, and they went and reported
26:22 And they became greatly **d** and began to say
Mk 14:19 to be **d** and to say to him one after another,
14:33 and began to be **d** and agitated.
Ac 17:16 he was deeply **d** to see that the city was full
Php 2:26 and has been **d** because you heard that he was ill.
2Pe 2: 7 a righteous man greatly **d** by the licentiousness of
Tob 13:10 and love all those within you who are **d**,
Wis 11:11 Whether absent or present, they were equally **d**,
17:11 **d** by conscience, it has always exaggerated

1Mc 10:22 Demetrius heard of these things he was **d** and said,
10:68 he was greatly **d** and returned to Antioch.
2Es 9:41 for I am greatly embittered in spirit and deeply **d.**"
10:50 that you are sincerely grieved and profoundly **d**

DISTRESSES (1) [DISTRESS]
1Sa 10:19 from all your calamities and your **d;**

DISTRESSING (3) [DISTRESS]
Ge 21:11 The matter was very **d** to Abraham on account
Jer 48:5 the descent of Horonaim they have heard the **d** cry
2Ti 3:1 that in the last days **d** times will come.

DISTRIBUTE (13) [DISTRIBUTED, DISTRIBUTING, DISTRIBUTION]
2Ch 31:15 to **d** the portions to their kindred,
31:19 the people designated by name were to **d** portions
35:12 that they might **d** them according to the groupings
Ne 13:13 and their duty was to **d** to their associates.
Job 21:17 How often does God **d** pains in his anger?
Da 11:39 and shall **d** the land for a price.
Mk 8:6 and gave them to his disciples to **d;**
Lk 18:22 Sell all that you own and **d** the money to the poor,
Ac 2:45 they would sell their possessions and goods and **d**
Tob 1:7 up a second tenth in money and go and **d** it
Sir 33:24 in the hour of death, **d** your inheritance.
37:6 not be unmindful of him when you **d** your spoils.
1Mc 3:36 and **d** their land by lot.

DISTRIBUTED‡ (18) [DISTRIBUTE]
Jos 13:32 the inheritances that Moses **d** in the plains
14:1 of the families of the tribes of the Israelites **d**
19:51 the Israelites **d** by lot at Shiloh before the LORD,
2Sa 6:19 and **d** food among all the people,
1Ch 16:3 and he **d** to every person in Israel—
2Ch 11:23 and **d** some of his sons through all the districts
Job 38:24 What is the way to the place where the light is **d,**
Ps 112:9 They have **d** freely, they have given to the poor;
Mk 8:6 and they **d** them to the crowd.
8:7 he ordered that these too should be **d.**
Jn 6:11 he **d** them to those who were seated;
Ac 4:35 and it was **d** to each as any had need.
Heb 2:4 by gifts of the Holy Spirit, **d** according to his will.
Jdt 15:12 in her hands and **d** them to the women who were
16:24 Before she died she **d** her property
Sir 44:23 and **d** them among twelve tribes.
1Mc 6:35 They **d** the animals among the phalanxes;
2Mc 8:28 **d** the rest among themselves and their children.

DISTRIBUTING (1) [DISTRIBUTE]
Jos 19:49 When they had finished **d** the several territories of

DISTRIBUTION (1) [DISTRIBUTE]
Ac 6:1 in the daily **d** of food.

DISTRICT (28) [DISTRICTS]
1Ki 20:14 By the young men who serve the **d** governors."
20:15 the young men who serve the **d** governors,
20:17 the **d** governors went out first.
20:19 the young men who serve the **d** governors,
Ne 3:9 ruler of half the **d** of Jerusalem, made repairs.
3:12 ruler of half the **d** of Jerusalem, made repairs,
3:14 ruler of the **d** of Beth-haccherem,
3:15 of the **d** of Mizpah, repaired the Fountain Gate;
3:16 ruler of half the **d** of Beth-zur,
3:17 ruler of half the **d** of Keilah, made repairs for his **d.**
3:18 son of Henadad, ruler of half the **d** of Keilah;
Eze 45:1 for the LORD a portion of the land as a holy **d,**
45:3 In the holy **d** you shall measure off
45:6 the holy **d** you shall assign as a holding for the city
45:7 on both sides of the holy **d** and the holding of
45:7 alongside the holy **d** and the holding of the city,
Mt 2:22 he went away to the **d** of Galilee.
9:26 And the report of this spread throughout that **d.**
9:31 and spread the news about him throughout that **d.**
15:21 Jesus left that place and went away to the **d**
16:13 when Jesus came into the **d** of Caesarea Philippi,
Mk 8:10 into the boat with his disciples and went to the **d**
Ac 16:12 which is a leading city of the **d** of Macedonia and
Jdt 4:4 So they sent word to every **d** of Samaria,
5:5 about this people that lives in the mountain **d**
LtJ 6:14 One of them holds a scepter, like a **d** judge,
3Mc 4:3 What **d** or city, or what habitable place at all,

DISTRICTS (7) [DISTRICT]
2Ch 11:23 and distributed some of his sons through all the **d**
1Mc 10:30 the three **d** added to it from Samaria and Galilee,
10:38 for the three **d** that have been added to Judea from
11:28 the king to free Judea and the three **d** of Samaria
11:34 the territory of Judea and the three **d** of Aphairema
11:57 in the high priesthood and set you over the four **d**
3Mc 3:12 to his generals and soldiers in Egypt and all its **d,**

DISTRUST (2) [DISTRUSTFUL]
Ro 4:20 No **d** made him waver concerning the promise
Wis 1:2 and manifests himself to those who do not **d** him.

DISTRUSTFUL (1) [DISTRUST]
2Mc 8:13 and **d** of God's justice ran off and got away.

DISTURB (2) [DISTURBANCE, DISTURBANCES, DISTURBED, DISTURBING]
Na 2:11 and the lion's cubs, with no one to **d** them?
Ac 15:24 to **d** you and have unsettled your minds,

DISTURBANCE (6) [DISTURB]
Ac 19:23 that time no little **d** broke out concerning the Way.
24:18 the rite of purification, without any crowd or **d.**
Jdt 6:1 When the **d** made by the people outside
2Mc 3:30 which a little while before was full of fear and **d,**
11:25 that this nation also should be free from **d,**
3Mc 1:23 and created a considerable **d** in the holy place;

DISTURBANCES (1) [DISTURB]
2Ch 15:5 for great **d** afflicted all the inhabitants of the lands.

DISTURBED (10) [DISTURB]
1Sa 28:15 "Why have you **d** me by bringing me up?"
2Sa 7:10 in their own place, and be **d** no more;
1Ch 17:9 in their own place, and be **d** no more;
Ps 4:4 When you are **d,** do not sin;
Jn 11:33 he was greatly **d** in spirit and deeply moved.
11:38 Then Jesus, again greatly **d,** came to the tomb.
Ac 17:8 and the city officials were **d** when they heard this,
Wis 18:19 the dreams that **d** them forewarned them of this,
2Es 5:33 "Are you greatly **d** in mind over Israel?
7:15 why are you **d,** seeing that you are to perish?

DISTURBING (2) [DISTURB]
Ac 16:20 they said, "These men are **d** our city;
Wis 17:9 For even if nothing **d** frightened them, yet,

DISUSE (1)
Est 9:28 of Purim should never fall into **d** among the Jews,

DIVERS, DIVERSE (KJV) See also DIFFERENT, DIFFERING, EMBROIDERED, KINDS, QUANTITIES, SWARMS

DIVERSE (3)
Pr 20:10 **D** weights and diverse measures are both alike
20:10 and **d** measures are both alike an abomination to
4Mc 14:11 the mind of woman despised even more **d** agonies,

DIVEST (1)
2Es 14:14 and **d** yourself now of your weak nature;

DIVESTED See Index to Footnotes

DIVIDE (33) [DIVIDED, DIVIDES, DIVIDING, DIVISION, DIVISIONS]
Ge 49:7 I will **d** them in Jacob, and scatter them in Israel.
Ex 14:16 and stretch out your hand over the sea and **d** it,
15:9 'I will pursue, I will overtake, I will **d** the spoil,
21:35 then they shall sell the live ox and **d** the price of it;
21:35 and the dead animal they shall also **d.**
Nu 31:27 **D** the booty into two parts,
Dt 14:7 because they chew the cud but do not **d** the hoof;
19:3 the distances and **d** into three regions the land that
Jos 13:7 Now therefore **d** this land for an inheritance to
18:5 They shall **d** it into seven portions,
22:8 **d** the spoil of your enemies with your kindred."
2Sa 19:29 I have decided: you and Ziba shall **d** the land."
1Ki 3:25 The king said, "**D** the living boy in two;
3:26 be neither mine nor yours; **d** it."
Job 27:17 and the innocent will **d** the silver.
41:6 Will they **d** it up among the merchants?
Ps 22:18 they **d** my clothes among themselves,
60:6 "With exultation I will **d** up Shechem,
68:12 The women at home **d** the spoil,
108:7 "With exultation I will **d** up Shechem,
Pr 16:19 of a lowly spirit among the poor than to **d** the spoil
Ecc 11:2 **D** your means seven ways, or even eight,
Isa 18:2 and conquering, whose land the rivers **d.**
18:7 whose land the rivers **d,** to Mount Zion,
53:12 and he shall **d** the spoil with the strong;
Eze 5:1 then take balances for weighing, and **d** the hair.
47:13 These are the boundaries by which you shall **d**
47:14 You shall **d** it equally; I swore to give
47:21 So you shall **d** this land among you according to
Lk 12:13 tell my brother to **d** the family inheritance
22:17 "Take this and **d** it among yourselves;
23:34 And they cast lots to **d** his clothing.
2Es 6:41 and commanded it to **d** and separate the waters,

DIVIDED‡ (71) [DIVIDE]
Ge 10:25 for in his days the earth was **d,**
14:15 He **d** his forces against them by night,
25:23 and two peoples born of you shall be **d;**
32:7 and he **d** the people that were with him,
33:1 So he **d** the children among Leah and Rachel and
Ex 12:4 the lamb shall be **d** in proportion to the number
14:21 into dry land; and the waters were **d.**
Lev 11:3 Any animal that has **d** hoofs and is cleft-footed
11:4 among those that chew the cud or have **d** hoofs,
11:4 it does not have **d** hoofs; it is unclean for you.
11:5 it does not have **d** hoofs; it is unclean for you.
Lev 11:6 it does not have **d** hoofs; it is unclean for you.
11:7 for even though it has **d** hoofs and is cleft-footed,
11:26 that has **d** hoofs but is not cleft-footed or does
Dt 32:8 when he **d** humankind, he fixed the boundaries of
Jdg 7:16 he **d** the three hundred men into three companies,
9:43 and **d** them into three companies,
2Sa 1:23 In life and in death they were not **d;**
18:2 And David **d** the army into three groups:
1Ki 16:21 Then the people of Israel were **d** into two parts;
18:6 they **d** the land between them to pass through it;
1Ch 1:19 (for in his days the earth was **d**),
Ne 9:11 And you **d** the sea before them,
Ps 74:13 You **d** the sea by your might;
78:13 He **d** the sea and let them pass through it,
136:13 who **d** the Red Sea in two,
Isa 33:23 Then prey and spoil in abundance will be **d;**
63:12 who **d** the waters before them to make for himself
Eze 37:22 never again shall they be **d** into two kingdoms.
Da 2:41 it shall be a **d** kingdom;
5:28 your kingdom is **d** and given to the Medes
11:4 be broken and **d** toward the four winds of heaven,
Joel 3:2 among the nations. They have **d** my land,
Zec 14:1 plunder taken from you will be **d** in your midst.
Mt 12:25 "Every kingdom **d** against itself is laid waste,
12:25 and no city or house **d** against itself will stand.
12:26 If Satan casts out Satan, he is **d** against himself;
27:35 they **d** his clothes among themselves
Mk 3:24 If a kingdom is **d** against itself,
3:25 And if a house is **d** against itself,
3:26 And if Satan has risen up against himself and is **d,**
6:41 and he **d** the two fish among them all.
15:24 they crucified him, and **d** his clothes among them,
Lk 11:17 "Every kingdom **d** against itself becomes a desert,
11:18 If Satan also is **d** against himself,
12:52 From now on five in one household will be **d,**
12:53 they will be **d:** father against son
15:12 So he **d** his property between them.
Jn 9:16 a sinner perform such signs?" And they were **d.**
10:19 Again the Jews were **d** because of these words.
19:23 they took his clothes and **d** them into four parts,
19:24 "They **d** my clothes among themselves,
Ac 2:3 **D** tongues, as of fire, appeared among them,
14:4 But the residents of the city were **d;**
23:7 and the Sadducees, and the assembly was **d.**
1Co 1:13 Has Christ been **d?** Was Paul crucified
7:34 and his interests are **d.**
Tob 5:3 and I gave him my bond. I **d** his in two;
Jdt 9:4 to be **d** among your beloved children who burned
Wis 5:12 when an arrow is shot at a target, the air, thus **d,**
Sir 1:28 do not approach him with a **d** mind.
14:15 and what you acquired by toil to be **d** by lot?
44:23 he **d** his portions, and distributed them among
47:21 because the sovereignty was **d** and
1Mc 1:6 and **d** his kingdom among them
9:11 The cavalry was **d** into two companies,
16:7 Then he **d** the army and placed the cavalry in
2Mc 8:21 then he **d** his army into four parts.
8:30 and they **d** a very large amount of plunder,
2Es 1:21 I **d** fertile lands among you;
14:11 For the age is **d** into twelve parts,

DIVIDES (5) [DIVIDE]
Ge 2:10 and from there it **d** and becomes four branches.
Dt 14:6 Any animal that **d** the hoof and has the hoof cleft
14:8 because it **d** the hoof but does not chew the cud,
Lk 11:22 in which he trusted and **d** his plunder.
Heb 4:12 piercing until it **d** soul from spirit,

DIVIDING (7) [DIVIDE]
Ge 49:27 and at evening **d** the spoil."
Jos 19:51 So they finished **d** the land.
Jdg 5:30 'Are they not finding and **d** the spoil?—
Isa 9:3 as people exult when **d** plunder.
Eph 2:14 into one and has broken down the **d** wall,
Sir 42:3 and of **d** the inheritance of friends;
2Es 6:7 "What will be the **d** of the times?

DIVINATION (17) [DIVINE]
Ge 30:27 by **d** that the LORD has blessed me because
44:5 Does he not indeed use it for **d?**
44:15 not know that one such as I can practice **d?**"
Nu 22:7 the elders of Midian departed with the fees for **d**
23:23 Surely there is no enchantment against Jacob, no **d**
Dt 18:10 or who practices **d,** or is a soothsayer, or an augur,
Jos 13:22 to the sword Balaam son of Beor, who practiced **d.**
1Sa 15:23 For rebellion is no less a sin than **d,**
2Ki 17:17 through fire; they used **d** and augury;
Jer 14:14 worthless **d,** and the deceit of their own minds.
Eze 12:24 be any false vision or flattering **d** within the house
13:6 They have envisioned falsehood and lying **d;**
13:7 not seen a false vision or uttered a lying **d,**
13:23 you shall no longer see false visions or practice **d;**
21:21 at the fork in the two roads, to use **d;**
21:23 But to them it will seem like a false **d;**
Ac 16:16 of **d** and brought her owners a great deal of money

DIVINATIONS (2) [DIVINE]
Eze 13:9 prophets who see false visions and utter lying **d;**
Sir 34:5 **D** and omens and dreams are unreal,

DIVINE‡ (50) [DIVINATION, DIVINATIONS, DIVINER, DIVINERS, DIVINING, DIVINITIES]
Ex 31:3 and I have filled him with **d** spirit,

Ex 35:31 he has filled him with **d** spirit,
Dt 13: 1 or those who **d** by dreams appear among you
13: 3 of those prophets or those who **d** by dreams;
13: 5 But those prophets or those who **d** by dreams shall
1Sa 28:13 "I see a **d** being coming up out of the ground."
Ps 82: 1 God has taken his place in the **d** council;
Da 6: 7 **d** or human, for thirty days, except to you, O king,
6:12 that anyone who prays to anyone, **d** or human,
Mt 16:23 for you are setting your mind not on **d** things but
Mk 8:33 For you are setting your mind not on **d** things but
Lk 2:52 and in **d** and human favor.
Ro 1:20 of the world his eternal power and **d** nature,
3:25 because in his **d** forbearance he had passed over
11: 4 But what is the **d** reply to him?
2Co 10: 4 but they have **d** power to destroy strongholds.
11: 2 I feel a **d** jealousy for you,
1Ti 1: 4 the **d** training that is known by faith.
Heb 1:14 Are not all angels spirits in the **d** service,
2Pe 1: 3 His **d** power has given us everything needed
1: 4 and may become participants of the **d** nature.
Wis 18: 9 and with one accord agreed to the **d** law,
Sir 33: 3 such a one the law is as dependable as a **d** oracle.
2Mc 3:29 of the **d** intervention and deprived of any hope
4:17 to show irreverence to the **d** laws—
3Mc 7:11 the **d** commandments would never
4Mc 1:16 of **d** and human matters and the causes of these.
1:17 by which we learn **d** matters reverently
4:13 by human treachery and not by **d** justice.
4:21 The **d** justice was angered by these acts
5:16 to govern our lives by the **d** law,
5:18 not truly **d** and we had wrongly held it to
5:18 and we had wrongly held it to be **d**,
6:21 by not contending even to death for our **d** law.
7: 7 in harmony with the law and philosopher of **d** life!
7: 9 you made your words of **d** philosophy credible.
8:22 **d** justice will excuse us for fearing the king
9: 9 from the **d** justice eternal torment by fire."
9:15 but because I protect the **d** law."
9:32 the judgments of the **d** wrath."
10:21 a tongue that has been melodious with **d** hymns."
11:27 not the guards of the tyrant but those of the **d** law
13:16 the full armor of self-control, which is **d** reason.
13:19 the **d** and all-wise Providence has bequeathed
17:11 the contest in which they were engaged was **d**,
17:16 not admire the athletes of the **d** legislation?
17:18 now stand before the **d** throne and live the life
17:22 **d** Providence preserved Israel
18: 3 were deemed worthy to share in a **d** inheritance.
18:22 For these crimes **d** justice pursued and will pursue

DIVINER (1) [DIVINE]

Isa 3: 2 judge and prophet, **d** and elder,

DIVINERS‡ (13) [DIVINE]

Dt 18:14 to dispossess do give heed to soothsayers and **d**,
1Sa 6: 2 Philistines called for the priests and the **d** and said,
Isa 2: 6 Indeed they are full of **d** from the east and
44:25 the omens of liars, and makes fools of **d**;
Jer 27: 9 therefore, must not listen to your prophets, your **d**,
29: 8 and the **d** who are among you deceive you,
50:36 A sword against the **d**, so
Da 2:27 or **d** can show to the king the mystery that
4: 7 the enchanters, the Chaldeans, and the **d** came in,
5: 7 the Chaldeans, and the **d**;
5:11 enchanters, Chaldeans, and **d**,
Mic 3: 7 and the **d** put to shame;
Zec 10: 2 For the teraphim utter nonsense, and the **d** see lies;

DIVINING (3) [DIVINE]

Eze 21:29 Offering false visions for you, **d** lies for you,
22:28 seeing false visions and **d** lies for them, saying,
Hos 4:12 and their **d** rod gives them oracles.

DIVINITIES (1) [DIVINE]

Ac 17:18 "He seems to be a proclaimer of foreign **d**."

DIVISION‡ (27) [DIVIDE]

1Ch 27: 1 each **d** numbering twenty-four thousand:
27: 2 in charge of the first **d** in the first month;
27: 2 in his **d** were twenty-four thousand.
27: 4 Dodai the Ahohite was in charge of the **d** of
27: 4 Mikloth was the chief officer of his **d**.
27: 4 In his **d** were twenty-four thousand.
27: 5 in his **d** were twenty-four thousand.
27: 6 his son Ammizabad was in charge of his **d**.
27: 7 in his **d** were twenty-four thousand.
27: 8 in his **d** were twenty-four thousand.
27: 9 in his **d** were twenty-four thousand.
27:10 in his **d** were twenty-four thousand.
27:11 in his **d** were twenty-four thousand.
27:12 in his **d** were twenty-four thousand.
27:13 in his **d** were twenty-four thousand.
27:14 in his **d** were twenty-four thousand.
27:15 in his **d** were twenty-four thousand.
2Ch 31: 2 **d** by **d**, everyone according to his service,
35: 5 be Levites for each **d** of an ancestral house.
Lk 12:51 No, I tell you, but rather **d**!
Jn 7:43 So there was a **d** in the crowd because of him.
1Mc 4: 1 and this **d** moved out by night
4: 4 while the **d** was still absent from the camp.
2Mc 8:22 each to command a **d**, putting fifteen hundred men
8:23 then, leading the first **d** himself,
12:22 But when Judas's first **d** appeared,

DIVISIONS (35) [DIVIDE]

Nu 1:16 the heads of the **d** of Israel.
Jos 18: 6 the land in seven **d** and bring the description here
18: 9 in a book a description of it by towns in seven **d**;
2Ki 11: 7 and your two **d** that come on duty in force on
1Ch 12:23 of the **d** of the armed troops who came to David
23: 6 And David organized them in **d** corresponding to
24: 1 The **d** of the descendants of Aaron were these.
26: 1 As for the **d** of the gatekeepers:
26:12 These **d** of the gatekeepers,
26:19 the **d** of the gatekeepers among the Korahites and
27: 1 the king in all matters concerning the **d** that came
28: 1 the officers of the **d** that served the king,
28:13 for the **d** of the priests and of the Levites, and all
28:21 Here are the **d** of the priests and the Levites for all
2Ch 5:11 sanctified themselves, without regard to their **d**,
8:14 he appointed the **d** of the priests for their service,
8:14 and the gatekeepers in their **d** for the several gates;
23: 8 for the priest Jehoiada did not dismiss the **d**.
26:11 in **d** according to the numbers in the muster made
31: 2 Hezekiah appointed the **d** of the priests and of
31:15 old and young alike, by **d**,
31:16 according to their offices, by their **d**.
31:17 according to their offices, by their **d**.
35: 4 by your ancestral houses by your **d**,
35:10 in their **d** according to the king's command.
Ezr 6:18 Then they set the priests in their **d** and the Levites
Ne 11:36 And certain **d** of the Levites in Judah were joined
1Co 1:10 be in agreement and that there be no **d** among you,
11:18 I hear that there are **d** among you;
Tit 3:10 to do with anyone who causes **d**,
Jude 1:19 devoid of the Spirit, who are causing **d**.
Jdt 2:15 the picked troops by **d** as his lord had ordered him
2Mc 12:20 But Maccabeus arranged his army in **d**,
12:20 set men in command of the **d**,
1Es 1: 2 having placed the priests according to their **d**,

DIVORCE (17) [DIVORCED, DIVORCES]

Dt 22:19 not be permitted to **d** her as long as he lives.
22:29 not be permitted to **d** her as long as he lives.
24: 1 and so he writes her a certificate of **d**,
24: 3 writes her a bill of **d**, puts it in her hand,
Isa 50: 1 Where is your mother's bill of **d**
Jer 3: 8 Israel, I had sent her away with a decree of **d**;
Mal 2:16 For I hate **d**, says the LORD, the God of Israel,
Mt 5:31 let him give her a certificate of **d**.'
19: 3 for a man to **d** his wife for any cause?"
19: 7 to give a certificate of dismissal and to **d** her?"
19: 8 that Moses allowed you to **d** your wives,
Mk 10: 2 "Is it lawful for a man to **d** his wife?"
10: 4 to write a certificate of dismissal and to **d** her."
1Co 7:11 and that the husband should not **d** his wife.
7:12 to live with him, he should not **d** her.
7:13 to live with her, she should not **d** him.
Sir 7:26 you have a wife who pleases you? Do not **d** her;

DIVORCED‡ (7) [DIVORCE]

Lev 21: 7 neither shall they marry a woman **d**
21:14 or a **d** woman, or a woman who has been defiled,
22:13 but if a priest's daughter is widowed or **d**,
Nu 30: 9 (But every vow of a widow or of a **d** woman,
Eze 44:22 They shall not marry a widow, or a **d** woman,
Mt 5:32 whoever marries a **d** woman commits adultery.
Lk 16:18 marries a woman **d** from her husband commits

DIVORCES (7) [DIVORCE]

Jer 3: 1 If a man **d** his wife and she goes from him
Mt 5:31 "It was also said, 'Whoever **d** his wife,
5:32 But I say to you that anyone who **d** his wife,
19: 9 And I say to you, whoever **d** his wife,
Mk 10:11 to them, "Whoever **d** his wife and marries another
10:12 and if she **d** her husband and marries another,
Lk 16:18 "Anyone who **d** his wife

DIVULGE (1)

Sir 8:18 for you do not know what they will **d**.

DO‡ (3312) [DEED, DEEDS, DID, DOER, DOERS, DOES, DOING, DOINGS, DONE, EVILDOING, EVILDOER, EVILDOERS, OUTDO, WRONGDOER, WRONGDOERS, WRONGDOING, WRONGDOINGS]

Ge 4: 7 If you **d** well, will you not be accepted?
4: 7 And if you **d** not **d** well, sin is lurking at the door;
4: 9 "I **d** not know; am I my brother's keeper?"
11: 6 and this is only the beginning of what they will **d**;
11: 6 that they propose to **d** will now be impossible
15: 1 "**D** not be afraid, Abram, I am your shield;
16: 6 **d** to her as you please."
18: 3 **d** not pass by your servant.
18: 5 So they said, "**D** as you have said."
18:17 "Shall I hide from Abraham what I am about to **d**,
18:25 Far be it from you to **d** such a thing,
18:25 Shall not the Judge of all the earth **d** what is just?"
18:29 "For the sake of forty I will not **d** it."
18:30 he said, "Oh **d** not let the Lord be angry if I speak.
18:30 He answered, "I will not **d** it, if I find thirty there."
18:32 "Oh **d** not let the Lord be angry
19: 7 "I beg you, my brothers, **d** not act so wickedly.
19: 8 and **d** to them as you please; only **d** nothing to
19:17 **d** not look back or stop anywhere in the Plain;
19:22 for I can **d** nothing until you arrive there."
20: 7 But if you **d** not restore her,
20:13 I said to her, 'This is the kindness you must **d** me:
21:12 "**D** not be distressed because of the boy and
21:12 whatever Sarah says to you, **d** as she tells you,
21:16 "**D** not let me look on the death of the child."
21:17 "What troubles you, Hagar? **D** not be afraid;
21:22 "God is with you in all that you **d**;
21:26 "I **d** not know who has done this;
22:12 "**D** not lay your hand on the boy or do anything
22:12 not lay your hand on the boy or **d** anything to him;
24: 6 "See to it that you **d** not take my son back there.
24:31 Why **d** you stand outside when I have prepared
24:56 But he said to them, "**D** not delay me,
25:22 and she said, "If it is to be this way, why **d** I live?"
26: 2 "**D** not go down to Egypt;
26:24 **d** not be afraid, for I am with you
26:29 so that you will **d** us no harm,
27: 2 I **d** not know the day of my death.
27:37 What then can I **d** for you, my son?"
29: 4 "My brothers, where **d** you come from?"
29: 5 "**D** you know Laban son of Nahor?"
29: 5 of Nahor?" They said, "We **d**."
30:31 if you will **d** this for me,
31:16 now then, **d** whatever God has said to you."
31:29 It is in my power to **d** you harm;
31:43 what can I **d** today about these daughters of mine,
32: 9 and I will **d** you good,'
32:12 Yet you have said, 'I will surely **d** you good,
32:17 and asks you, 'To whom **d** you belong?
32:32 to this day the Israelites **d** not eat the thigh muscle
33: 8 "What **d** you mean by all this company
34:14 They said to them, "We cannot **d** this thing,
34:19 And the young man did not delay to **d** the thing,
35:17 the midwife said to her, "**D** not be afraid;
39: 9 How then could I **d** this great wickedness,
39:11 when he went into the house to **d** his work,
40: 8 "**D** not interpretations belong to God?
40:13 just as you used to **d** when you were his cupbearer.
40:14 please **d** me the kindness to make mention of me
41:25 God has revealed to Pharaoh what he is about to **d**.
41:28 God has shown to Pharaoh what he is about to **d**.
41:55 what he says to you, **d**."
42: 1 "Why **d** you keep looking at one another?
42: 7 "Where **d** you come from?"
42:18 "**D** this and you will live, for I fear God:
42:20 And they agreed to **d** so.
42:37 "You may kill my two sons if I **d**
43: 9 If I **d** not bring him back to you and set him
43:11 "If it must be so, then **d** this:
43:22 We **d** not know who put our money in our sacks."
43:23 He replied, "Rest assured, **d** not be afraid;
44: 7 from your servants that they should **d** such a thing!
44:15 **D** you not know that one such
44:17 But he said, "Far be it from me that I should **d** so!
44:18 and **d** not be angry with your servant;
44:32 saying, 'If I **d** not bring him back to you,
45: 5 And now **d** not be distressed,
45: 9 come down to me, **d** not delay.
45:17 "Say to your brothers, '**D** this:
45:19 You are further charged to say, '**D** this:
45:24 "**D** not quarrel along the way."
46: 3 **d** not be afraid to go down to Egypt,
47: 9 They **d** not compare with the years of the life
47:29 **D** not bury me in Egypt.
47:30 He answered, "I will **d** as you have said."
50: 6 and bury your father, as he made you swear to **d**."
50:19 But Joseph said to them, "**D** not be afraid!
50:20 Even though you intended to **d** harm to me,
Ex 1:17 not **d** as the king of Egypt commanded them,
2:13 "Why **d** you strike your fellow Hebrew?"
2:14 **D** you mean to kill me as you killed
4: 1 suppose they **d** not believe me or listen to me,
4:15 and will teach you what you shall **d**.
5: 2 I **d** not know the LORD,
5: 8 **d** not diminish it, for they are lazy;
5:15 "Why **d** you treat your servants like this?
6: 1 "Now you shall see what I will **d** to Pharaoh:
8:26 But Moses said, "It would not be right to **d** so;
8:28 provided you **d** not go very far away.
8:29 only **d** not let Pharaoh again deal falsely by
9: 5 "Tomorrow the LORD will **d** this thing in
9:30 I know that you **d** not yet fear the LORD God.
10: 7 **d** you not yet understand that Egypt is ruined?"
10:17 **D** forgive my sin just this once,
10:28 Take care that you **d** not see my face again,
12: 9 **D** not eat any of it raw or boiled in water,
12:26 'What **d** you mean by this observance?'
13:13 if you **d** not redeem it, you must break its neck.
14:13 But Moses said to the people, "**D** not be afraid,
14:15 LORD said to Moses, "Why **d** you cry out to me?
15:26 and **d** what is right in his sight,
16:29 **d** not leave your place on the seventh day."
17: 2 Moses said to them, "Why **d** you quarrel with me?
17: 2 Why **d** you test the LORD?"
17: 4 "What shall I **d** with this people?
18:14 Why **d** you sit alone, while all the people stand
18:18 task is too heavy for you; you cannot **d** it alone.
18:20 the way they are to go and the things they are to **d**.
18:23 If you **d** this, and God so commands you,
19: 8 "Everything that the LORD has spoken we will **d**."
19:15 **d** not go near a woman."
19:24 but **d** not let either the priests or the people break
20: 9 Six days you shall labor and **d** all your work.
20:10 you shall not **d** any work—
20:19 but **d** not let God speak to us, or we will die."
20:20 Moses said to the people, "**D** not be afraid;
20:20 and to put the fear of him upon you so that you **d**

Ex 20:25 **d** not build it of hewn stones;
21: 7 she shall not go out as the male slaves **d.**
21:11 And if he does not **d** these three things for her,
22: 1 thief shall make restitution, but if unable to **d** so,
22:23 If you **d** abuse them, when they cry out to me,
22:30 You shall **d** the same with your oxen and
23: 7 and **d** not kill the innocent and those in the right,
23:11 You shall **d** the same with your vineyard,
23:12 Six days you shall **d** your work,
23:13 **D** not invoke the names of other gods;
23:13 **d** not let them be heard on your lips.
23:21 **d** not rebel against him, for he will
23:22 But if you listen attentively to his voice and **d** all
24: 3 the words that the LORD has spoken we will **d.**"
24: 7 "All that the LORD has spoken we will **d,**
29: 1 Now this is what you shall **d** to them
29:35 Thus you shall **d** to Aaron and to his sons,
31:11 They shall **d** just as I have commanded you.
32: 1 we **d** not know what has become of him."
32:12 change your mind and **d** not bring disaster
32:21 "What did this people **d** to you
32:22 "**D** not let the anger of my lord burn hot;
32:23 we **d** not know what has become of him.'
33: 5 and I will decide what to **d** to you.' "
33:15 **d** not carry us up from here.
33:17 "I will **d** the very thing that you have asked;
34: 3 and **d** not let anyone be seen throughout all
34: 3 and **d** not let flocks or herds graze in front of
34:10 for it is an awesome thing that I will **d** with you.
35: 1 that the LORD has commanded you to **d:**
35:35 to **d** every kind of work done by an artisan or by
36: 1 to know how to **d** any work in the construction of
36: 2 everyone whose heart was stirred to come to **d**
36: 5 the work that the LORD has commanded us to **d.**"
36: 7 brought was more than enough to **d** all the work.
Lev 4:13 and they **d** any one of the things that by
4:20 He shall **d** with the bull just as is done with
4:20 he shall **d** the same with this.
6: 3 of the various things that one may **d**
6: 7 the things that one may **d** and incur guilt thereby.
8:35 keeping the LORD's charge so that you **d**
9: 6 the thing that the LORD commanded you to **d,**
10: 6 "**D** not dishevel your hair, and **d** not tear your
15:31 so that they **d** not die in their uncleanness
16:15 and **d** with its blood as he did with the blood of
16:16 and so he shall **d** for the tent of meeting,
16:29 you shall deny yourselves, and shall **d** no work,
17:16 if they **d** not wash themselves or bathe their body,
18: 3 You shall not **d** as they **d** in the land of Egypt,
18: 3 you shall not **d** as they **d** in the land of Canaan,
18:24 **D** not defile yourselves in any of these ways,
19: 4 **D** not turn to idols or make cast images
19:29 **D** not profane your daughter by making her
19:31 **D** not turn to mediums or wizards;
19:31 **d** not seek them out, to be defiled by them:
20: 4 and **d** not put them to death,
22:24 such you shall not **d** within your land,
23: 3 a holy convocation; you shall **d** no work:
23:28 and you shall **d** no work during that entire day;
23:31 You shall **d** no work: it is a statute forever
25:26 then prospers and finds sufficient means to **d** so,
25:36 **D** not take interest in advance or otherwise make
26:14 and **d** not observe all these commandments,
26:16 I in turn will **d** this to you:
Nu 3: 8 to the duties for the Israelites as they **d** service at
4: 3 all who qualify to **d** work relating to the tent
4:23 all who qualify to **d** work in the tent of meeting.
4:26 and they shall **d** all that needs to be done
4:27 and in all that they have to **d;**
4:30 everyone who qualifies to **d** the work of the tent
4:47 everyone who qualified to **d** the work of service
6:21 with whatever vow they take, so they shall **d,**
8: 7 Thus you shall **d** to them, to cleanse them:
8:11 that they may **d** the service of the LORD.
8:15 Thereafter the Levites may go in to **d** service at
8:19 to **d** the service for the Israelites at the tent
8:22 Thereafter the Levites went in to **d** their service in
8:24 to **d** duty in the service of the tent of meeting;
8:26 Thus you shall **d** with the Levites
9:14 to the LORD shall **d** so according to the statute of
10:31 "**D** not leave us, for you know
10:32 the same we will **d** for you."
11:15 and **d** not let me see my misery."
11:25 But they did not **d** so again.
12:11 **d** not punish us for a sin that we have
12:12 **D** not let her be like one stillborn,
14: 9 Only, **d** not rebel against the LORD;
14: 9 and **d** not fear the people of the land,
14: 9 with us; **d** not fear them."
14:20 LORD said, "I **d** forgive, just as you have asked;
14:28 "I will **d** to you the very things I heard you say:
14:35 I the LORD have spoken; surely I will **d** thus
14:41 "Why **d** you continue to transgress the command
14:42 **D** not go up, for the LORD is not with you;
14:42 **d** not let yourselves be struck down
15:12 so you shall **d** with each and every one.
15:13 Every native Israelite shall **d** these things
15:14 a pleasing odor to the LORD, shall **d** as you **d.**
15:39 the commandments of the LORD and **d** them,
15:40 you shall remember and **d** all my commandments,
16: 3 then **d** you exalt yourselves above the assembly of
16: 6 **D** this: take censers, Korah and all your company,
16:28 that the LORD has sent me to **d** all these works;
19:12 but if they **d** not purify themselves on the third day
19:13 and **d** not purify themselves,
19:20 Any who are unclean but **d** not purify themselves,
21:34 LORD said to Moses, "**D** not be afraid of him;

Nu 21:34 You shall **d** to him as you did to King Sihon of
22:16 '**D** not let anything hinder you from coming
22:17 surely **d** you great honor, and whatever you say to me I will **d;**
22:18 the command of the LORD my God, to **d** less
22:20 but **d** only what I tell you to **d.**"
22:38 but **d** I have power to say just anything?
23:19 Has he promised, and will he not **d** it?
23:25 Balak said to Balaam, "**D** not curse them at all,
23:25 and **d** not bless them at all."
23:26 that is what I must **d**'?"
24:13 to **d** either good or bad of my own will;
24:14 let me advise you what this people will **d**
29: 7 and deny yourselves; you shall **d** no work.
30: 2 he shall **d** according to all that proceeds out
32: 5 **d** not make us cross the Jordan."
32:20 So Moses said to them, "If you **d** this—
32:23 But if you **d** not **d** this,
32:24 but **d** what you have promised."
32:25 "Your servants will **d** as my lord commands.
32:27 to **d** battle for the LORD, just as my lord orders."
32:31 to your servants, so we will **d.**
33:55 if you **d** not drive out the inhabitants of the land
33:56 And I will **d** to you as I thought to **d** to them.
Dt 1:18 at that time with all the things that you should **d.**
1:21 **d** not fear or be dismayed."
1:39 who today **d** not yet know right from wrong,
1:42 "Say to them, '**D** not go up and **d** not fight,
1:44 against you and chased you as bees **d.**
2: 9 "**D** not harass Moab or engage them in battle,
2:19 **d** not harass them or engage them in battle,
3: 2 The LORD said to me, "**D** not fear him,
3: 2 **D** to him as you did to King Sihon of
3:21 so the LORD will **d** to all the kingdoms
3:22 **D** not fear them, for it is
4:16 so that you **d** not act corruptly by making an idol
4:19 **d** not be led astray and bow down to them
5:13 Six days you shall labor and **d** all your work.
5:14 you shall not **d** any work—
5:27 and we will listen and **d** it."
5:31 so that they may **d** them in the land
5:32 to **d** as the LORD your God has commanded you;
6:12 take care that you **d** not forget the LORD,
6:14 **D** not follow other gods, any of the gods of
6:16 **D** not put the LORD your God to the test,
6:18 **D** what is right and good in the sight of
7: 3 **D** not intermarry with them,
7:18 **d** not be afraid of them.
7:19 The LORD your God will **d** the same to all
7:25 **D** not covet the silver or the gold that is on them
7:26 **D** not bring an abhorrent thing into your house,
8:11 that you **d** not forget the LORD your God,
8:14 then **d** not exalt yourself, forgetting
8:16 and in the end to **d** you good.
8:17 **D** not say to yourself, "My power and the might
8:19 If you **d** forget the LORD your God
9: 4 **d** not say to yourself, "It is because
9: 7 Remember and **d** not forget how you provoked
9:26 the LORD and said, "Lord GOD, **d** not destroy
10:16 and **d** not be stubborn any longer.
11:28 if you **d** not obey the commandments of
12:13 Take care that you **d** not offer your burnt offerings
12:14 and there you shall **d** everything I command you.
12:19 Take care that you **d** not neglect the Levite as long
12:23 Only be sure that you **d** not eat the blood;
12:24 **D** not eat it; you shall pour it out on the
12:25 **D** not eat it, so that all may go well with you
12:25 you **d** what is right in the sight of the LORD.
12:30 **d** not inquire concerning their gods, saying,
12:30 I also want to **d** the same."
12:31 not **d** the same for the LORD your God,
12:32 **d** not add to it or take anything from it.
13: 8 Show them no pity or compassion and **d**
13:11 and never again **d** any such wickedness.
13:17 **D** not let anything devoted to destruction stick
14: 7 they chew the cud but **d** not divide the hoof;
14:27 Levites resident in your towns, **d** not neglect them,
15: 7 **d** not be hard-hearted or tight-fisted
15: 9 Be careful that you **d** not entertain a mean thought,
15:10 Give liberally and be ungrudging when you **d** so,
15:17 You shall **d** the same with regard
15:18 **D** not consider it a hardship
15:18 LORD your God will bless you in all that you **d.**
15:19 not **d** work with your firstling ox nor shear
16: 8 when you shall **d** no work.
17:11 **d** not turn aside from the decision
18:14 about to dispossess **d** give heed to soothsayers
18:14 the LORD your God does not permit you to **d** so.
18:22 **d** not be frightened by it.
19:19 then you shall **d** to the false witness just as the false witness had meant to **d** to the other.
20: 3 Today you are drawing near to **d** battle
20: 3 **D** not lose heart, or be afraid, or panic,
20:18 not teach you to **d** all the abhorrent things that they **d** for their gods,
20:20 You may destroy only the trees that you know **d**
21: 8 **d** not let the guilt of innocent blood remain in
21: 9 because you must **d** what is right in the sight of
22: 2 If the owner does not reside near you or you **d**
22: 3 You shall **d** the same with a neighbor's donkey;
22: 3 you shall **d** the same with a neighbor's garment;
22: 3 and you shall **d** the same with anything else
22:26 You shall **d** nothing to the young woman;
23:21 **d** not postpone fulfilling it;
24:18 therefore I command you to **d** this.
24:20 you beat your olive trees, **d** not strip what is left;
24:21 **d** not glean what is left;

Dt 24:22 therefore I am commanding you to **d** this.
25:16 For all who **d** such things, all who act dishonestly,
25:19 under heaven; **d** not forget.
28:14 and if you **d** not turn aside from any of the words
28:20 and frustration in everything you attempt to **d,**
28:32 for them all day but be powerless to **d** anything.
28:33 A people whom you **d** not know shall eat up
28:49 a nation whose language you **d** not understand,
28:58 If you **d** not diligently observe all the words
29: 9 that you may succeed in everything that you **d.**
30:17 But if your heart turns away and you **d** not hear,
31: 4 LORD will **d** to them as he did to Sihon and Og,
31: 8 **D** not fear or be dismayed."
31:21 For I know what they are inclined to **d** even now,
31:29 you will **d** what is evil in the sight of the LORD,
32: 6 **D** you thus repay the LORD,
33:11 so that they **d** not rise again.
Jos 1: 7 **d** not turn from it to the right hand or to the left,
1: 9 **d** not be frightened or dismayed,
1:16 "All that you have commanded us we will **d,**
2: 5 Where the men went I **d** not know.
2:14 If you **d** not tell this business of ours,
2:18 and you **d** not tie this crimson cord in the window
2:18 and you **d** not gather into your house your father
3: 4 **d** not come any nearer to it."
3: 5 tomorrow the LORD will **d** wonders among you."
4: 6 'What **d** those stones mean to you?'
4:21 'What **d** these stones mean?'
5:14 "What **d** you command your servant, my lord?"
6: 3 Thus you shall **d** for six days,
7: 3 **d** not make the whole people toil up there."
7: 9 Then what will you **d** for your great name?"
7:19 **d** not hide it from me."
8: 1 "**D** not fear or be dismayed;
8: 2 You shall **d** to Ai and its king as you did to Jericho
8: 4 **d** not go very far from the city,
9: 8 And where **d** you come from?"
9:20 This is what we will **d** to them:
9:25 **d** as it seems good and right in your sight to **d** to us
10: 6 saying, "**D** not abandon your servants;
10: 8 The LORD said to Joshua, "**D** not fear them,
10:19 but **d** not stay there yourselves;
10:19 **D** not let them enter their towns,
10:25 Joshua said to them, "**D** not be afraid or dismayed;
10:25 for thus the LORD will **d** to all the enemies
11: 6 LORD said to Joshua, "**D** not be afraid of them,
15:18 Caleb said to her, "What **d** you wish?"
16:10 to this day but have been made to **d** forced labor.
22:19 only **d** not rebel against the LORD,
22:22 of faith toward the LORD, **d** not spare us today
22:24 'What have you to **d** with the LORD,
22:27 that we **d** perform the service of the LORD
23: 6 to observe and **d** all that is written in the book of
24:20 then he will turn and **d** you harm,
Jdg 1:14 Caleb said to her, "What **d** you wish?"
2: 2 **d** not make a covenant with the inhabitants
6:18 **D** not depart from here until I come to you,
6:23 **d** not fear, you shall not die."
6:27 of his family and the townspeople to **d** it by day,
6:39 "**D** not let your anger burn against me,
7:17 "Look at me, and **d** the same;
7:17 I come to the outskirts of the camp, **d** as I **d.**
8: 3 what have I been able to **d** in comparison
8: 6 "**D** you already have in your possession the hands
8:15 '**D** you already have in your possession the hands
9:48 "What you have seen me **d, d** quickly,
10:15 **d** to us whatever seems good to you;
11: 7 So why **d** you come to me now when you are
11:10 we will surely **d** as you say."
11:23 **D** you intend to take their place?
11:36 **d** to me according to what has gone out
13: 8 to **d** concerning the boy who will be born."
13:12 of life; what is he to **d?**"
13:18 "Why **d** you ask my name?
14:10 as the young men were accustomed to **d.**
14:16 you **d** not really love me.
15: 3 "This time, when I **d** mischief to the Philistines,
15: 7 Samson said to them, "If this is what you **d,**
15:10 to **d** to him as he did to us."
15:11 "**D** you not know that the Philistines are rulers
17: 9 Micah said to him, "From where **d** you come?"
18: 8 they said to them, "What **d** you report?"
18: 9 and it is very good. Will you **d** nothing?
18: 9 **D** not be slow to go,
18:14 "**D** you know that in these buildings there are
18:14 Now therefore consider what you will **d.**"
19:12 who **d** not belong to the people of Israel;
19:17 are you going and where **d** you come from?"
19:20 only **d** not spend the night in the square."
19:23 "No, my brothers, **d** not act so wickedly.
19:23 this man is my guest, **d** not **d** this vile thing.
19:24 Ravish them and **d** whatever you want to them;
19:24 but against this man **d** not **d** such a vile thing."
20: 9 But now this is what we will **d** to Gibeah:
21: 7 What shall we **d** for wives for those who are left,
21:11 This is what you shall **d;**
21:16 "What shall we **d** for wives for those who are left,
Ru 1:11 **D** I still have sons in my womb
1:16 "**D** not press me to leave you or to turn back
1:17 May the LORD **d** thus and so to me,
2: 8 **d** not go to glean in another field or leave this one,
2:15 the standing sheaves, and **d** not reproach her.
2:16 the bundles, and leave them for her to glean, and **d**
3: 3 but **d** not make yourself known to the man
3: 4 and he will tell you what to **d.**"
3: 5 She said to her, "All that you tell me I will **d.**"
3:11 **d** not be afraid, I will **d** for you all that you ask,

Ru 3:13 as next-of-kin for you, good; let him **d** it.
3:17 for he said, '**D** not go back to your mother-in-law
1Sa 1: 8 "Hannah, why **d** you weep? Why **d** you not eat?
1:16 **D** not regard your servant as a worthless woman,
1:23 "**D** what seems best to you,
2:23 He said to them, "Why **d** you **d** such things?
2:35 who shall **d** according to what is in my heart and
3:11 I am about to **d** something in Israel that will make
3:17 **D** not hide it from me.
3:17 May God **d** so to you and more also,
3:18 let him **d** what seems good to him."
4:20 "**D** not be afraid, for you have borne a son."
5: 5 and all who enter the house of Dagon **d** not step on
5: 8 "What shall we **d** with the ark of the God
6: 2 "What shall we **d** with the ark of the LORD?
6: 3 "If you send away the ark of the God of Israel, **d**
7: 8 "**D** not cease to cry out to the LORD our God
8: 5 and your sons **d** not follow in your ways;
10: 2 What shall I **d** about my son?'
10: 7 these signs meet you, **d** whatever you see fit to **d,**
10: 8 to you and show you what you shall **d.**"
10:24 "**D** you see the one whom the LORD has chosen?
11:10 you may **d** to us whatever seems good to you."
12:16 and see this great thing that the LORD will **d**
12:20 And Samuel said to the people, "**D** not be afraid;
12:20 yet **d** not turn aside from following the LORD,
12:21 and **d** not turn aside after useless things
12:25 But if you still **d** wickedly,
14: 7 "**D** all that your mind inclines to.
14:34 and **d** not sin against the LORD by eating with
14:36 They said, "**D** whatever seems good to you."
14:40 people said to Saul, "**D** what seems good to you."
14:44 Saul said, "God **d** so to me and more also;
15: 3 **d** not spare them, but kill both man and woman,
15:19 and **d** what was evil in the sight of the LORD?"
16: 3 and I will show you what you shall **d;**
16: 4 and said, "**D** you come peaceably?"
16: 7 "**D** not look on his appearance or on the height
17:55 "As your soul lives, O king, I **d** not know."
19:11 "If you **d** not save your life tonight,
20: 3 and he thinks, '**D** not let Jonathan know this,
20: 4 "Whatever you say, I will **d** for you."
20:13 But if my father intends to **d** you harm, the LORD
d so to Jonathan, and more also, if I **d** not disclose
20:30 **D** I not know that you have chosen the son
20:38 "Hurry, be quick, **d** not linger."
21:15 **D** I lack madmen, that you have brought this
22: 3 until I know what God will **d** for me."
22: 5 "**D** not remain in the stronghold;
22:14 and is quick to **d** your bidding,
22:15 **D** not let the king impute anything to his servant
22:23 Stay with me, and **d** not be afraid;
23:17 He said to him, "**D** not be afraid;
23:20 O king, whenever you wish to come down, **d** so;
24: 4 and you shall **d** to him as it seems good to you.' "
24: 6 "The LORD forbid that I should **d** this thing
24: 9 "Why **d** you listen to the words of those who say,
24: 9 'David seeks to **d** you harm'?
24:14 of Israel come out? Whom **d** you pursue?
25:11 to men who come from I **d** not know where?"
25:17 know this and consider what you should **d;**
25:22 God **d** so to David and more also,
25:25 **d** not take seriously this ill-natured fellow, Nabal;
25:26 now let your enemies and those who seek to **d** evil
26: 9 But David said to Abishai, "**D** not destroy him;
26:20 therefore, **d** not let my blood fall to the ground,
26:25 You will **d** many things and will succeed in them."
28: 2 then you shall know what your servant can **d.**"
28:13 king said to her, "Have no fear; what **d** you see?"
28:15 I have summoned you to tell me what I should **d.**"
28:16 Samuel said, "Why then **d** you ask me,
29: 6 Nevertheless the lords **d** not approve of you.
29: 7 **d** nothing to displease the lords of the Philistines."
29:10 As for the evil report, **d** not take it to heart,
30:13 Then David said to him, "To whom **d** you belong?
30:23 But David said, "You shall not **d** so, my brothers,
2Sa 1: 5 **d** you know that Saul and his son Jonathan died?"
1:13 "Where **d** you come from?"
2:26 **D** you not know that the end will be bitter?
3: 9 So may God **d** to Abner and so may he add to it!
3:19 and the whole house of Benjamin were ready to **d.**
3:35 but David swore, saying, "So may God **d** to me,
3:38 "**D** you not know that a prince and
7: 3 "Go, **d** all that you have in mind;
7:25 confirm it forever; **d** as you have promised.
9: 7 David said to him, "**D** not be afraid,
9:11 commands his servant, so your servant will **d.**"
10: 3 to their lord Hanun, "**D** you really think
10:12 and may the LORD **d** what seems good to him."
11:11 and as your soul lives, I will not **d** such a thing."
11:25 '**D** not let this matter trouble you,
12: 9 to **d** what is evil in his sight?
12:12 but I will **d** this thing before all Israel,
12:18 He may **d** himself some harm."
13: 2 and it seemed impossible to Amnon to **d** anything
13:12 "No, my brother, **d** not force me;
13:12 **d** not **d** anything so vile!
13:20 **d** not take this to heart."
13:28 then kill him. **D** not be afraid;
13:33 **d** not let my lord the king take it to heart,
14: 2 **d** not anoint yourself with oil,
14:18 "**D** not withhold from me anything I ask you."
15: 5 Whenever people came near to **d** obeisance
15:15 "Your servants are ready to **d** whatever our lord
15:26 let him **d** to me what seems good to him."
16: 4 now yours." Ziba said, "I **d** obeisance;
16:10 But the king said, "What have I to **d** with you,
2Sa 16:20 "Give us your counsel; what shall we **d?**"
17: 6 shall we **d** as he advises?
17:16 '**D** not lodge tonight at the fords of the wilderness,
18: 4 "Whatever seems best to you I will **d.**"
18:20 but today you shall not **d** so,
18:29 but I **d** not know what it was."
18:32 and all who rise up to **d** you harm,
19: 7 for I swear by the LORD, if you **d** not go,
19:10 therefore why **d** you say nothing about bringing
19:13 So may God **d** to me, and more,
19:18 over the king's household, and to **d** his pleasure.
19:22 But David said, "What have I to **d** with you,
19:22 **d** I not know that I am this day king over Israel?"
19:27 **d** therefore what seems good to you.
19:37 and **d** for him whatever seems good to you."
19:38 and I will **d** for him whatever seems good to you;
19:38 and all that you desire of me I will **d** for you."
20: 6 of Bichri will **d** us more harm than Absalom;
21: 3 "What shall I **d** for you?
21: 4 "What **d** you say that I should **d** for you?"
21:17 so that you **d** not quench the lamp of Israel."
22:37 and my feet **d** not slip;
23:17 "The LORD forbid that I should **d** this.
24: 3 But why does my lord the king want to **d** this?"
24:12 choose one of them, and I will **d** it to you."
1Ki 1:16 and the king said, "What **d** you wish?"
1:18 though you, my lord the king, **d** not know it.
1:30 so will I **d** this day."
1:53 He came to **d** obeisance to King Solomon;
2: 3 so that you may prosper in all that you **d**
2: 6 **d** not let his gray head go down to Sheol in peace.
2: 9 **d** not hold him guiltless, for you are a wise man;
2: 9 you will know what you ought to **d** to him,
2:13 She asked, "**D** you come peaceably?"
2:16 to make of you; **d** not refuse me."
2:20 to make of you; **d** not refuse me."
2:22 "And why **d** you ask Abishag the Shunammite
2:23 "So may God **d** to me, and more also,
2:31 The king replied to him, "**D** as he has said,
2:36 and **d** not go out from there to any place whatever.
2:38 my lord the king has said, so will your servant **d.**"
3: 7 I **d** not know how to go out or come in.
3:12 I now **d** according to your word.
3:26 give her the living boy; certainly **d** not kill him!"
3:27 Give the first woman the living boy; **d** not kill him.
8:43 **d** according to all that the foreigner calls to you,
8:43 as **d** your people Israel, and so that they may know
9: 6 and **d** not keep my commandments
11:12 Yet for the sake of your father David I will not **d** it
11:22 "What **d** you lack with me that you now seek to go
11:22 And he said, "No, **d** let me go."
11:38 and **d** what is right in my sight
12: 6 "How **d** you advise me to answer this people?"
12: 9 to them, "What **d** you advise
12:16 "What share **d** we have in David?
14: 6 why **d** you pretend to be another?
17:13 "**D** not be afraid; go and **d** as you have said;
18:34 Then he said, "**D** it a second time";
18:34 Again he said, "**D** it a third time";
18:40 **d** not let one of them escape."
19: 2 saying, "So may the gods **d** to me, and more also,
19: 2 if I **d** not make your life like the life of one
20: 8 the people said to him, "**D** not listen or consent."
20: 9 that you first demanded of your servant I will **d;**
20: 9 but this thing I cannot **d.**"
20:10 "The gods **d** so to me, and more also,
20:22 and consider well what you have to **d;**
20:24 Also **d** this: remove the kings,
21: 7 "**D** you now govern Israel?
21:20 Because you have sold yourself to **d** what is evil in
21:25 who sold himself to **d** what was evil in the sight of
22: 3 "**D** you know that Ramoth-gilead belongs to us,
22:22 and you shall succeed; go out and **d** it.'
2Ki 1:15 **d** not be afraid of him."
2: 3 to Elisha, and said to him, "**D** you know that today
2: 5 to Elisha, and said to him, "**D** you know that today
2: 9 "Tell me what I may **d** for you,
2:16 He responded, "No, **d** not send them."
2:18 he said to them, "Did I not say to you, **D** not go?"
3:13 "What have I to **d** with you?
4: 2 Elisha said to her, "What shall I **d** for you?
4: 2 Tell me, what **d** you have in the house?"
4:16 **d** not deceive your servant."
4:24 **d** not hold back for me unless I tell you."
4:28 Did I not say, **D** not mislead me?"
4:29 and if anyone greets you, **d** not answer;
5:13 to **d** something difficult, would you
5:18 when I **d** bow down in the house of Rimmon,
6: 2 to live." He answered, "**D** so."
6:15 master! What shall we **d?**"
6:16 He replied, "**D** not be afraid,
6:31 "So may God **d** to me, and more,
8:12 the evil that you will **d** to the people of Israel;
8:13 that he should **d** this great thing?"
9: 3 Then open the door and flee; **d** not linger."
9:18 Jehu responded, "What have you to **d** with peace?
9:19 Jehu answered, "What have you to **d** with peace?
10: 5 we will **d** anything you say.
10: 5 **d** whatever you think right."
11: 5 He commanded them, "This is what you are to **d:**
12: 7 Now therefore **d** not accept any more money
16: 2 He did not **d** what was right in the sight of
17:12 to them, "You shall not **d** this."
17:15 that they should not **d** as they did.
17:17 and they sold themselves to **d** evil in the sight of
17:26 and placed in the cities of Samaria **d** not know
17:26 they **d** not know the law of the god of the land."
2Ki 17:34 They **d** not worship the LORD and they **d** not
follow the statutes
17:41 and their children's children continue to **d**
18:19 On what **d** you base this confidence of yours?
18:20 **D** you think that mere words are strategy
18:20 On whom **d** you now rely,
18:26 **d** not speak to us in the language of Judah within
18:29 '**D** not let Hezekiah deceive you,
18:30 **D** not let Hezekiah make you rely on the LORD
18:31 **D** not listen to Hezekiah;
18:32 **D** not listen to Hezekiah when he misleads you
18:36 for the king's command was, "**D** not answer him."
19: 6 **D** not be afraid because of the words
19:10 **D** not let your God on whom you rely deceive you
19:31 The zeal of the LORD of hosts will **d** this.
20: 9 the LORD will **d** the thing that he has promised:
21: 8 to **d** according to all that I have commanded them,
21: 9 to **d** more evil than the nations had done that
22:13 to **d** according to all that is written concerning us."
25:24 "**D** not be afraid because of the Chaldean officials;
1Ch 11:19 "My God forbid that I should **d** this.
12:32 to know what Israel ought to **d,**
13: 4 The whole assembly agreed to **d** so,
16:22 "**D** not touch my anointed ones; **d** my prophets no
17: 2 "**D** all that you have in mind, for God is with you."
17:23 and **d** as you have promised.
19: 3 "**D** you think, because David has sent consolers
19:13 and may the LORD **d** what seems good to him."
21:10 choose one of them, so that I may **d** it to you.' "
21:17 but **d** not let your people be plagued!"
21:23 let my lord the king **d** what seems good to him;
22:13 **D** not be afraid or dismayed.
23:24 from twenty years old and upward who were to **d**
28:20 **D** not be afraid or dismayed;
2Ch 2:14 to **d** all sorts of engraving and execute any design
6:33 and **d** whatever the foreigners ask of you,
6:33 as **d** your people Israel, and that they may know
6:42 O LORD God, **d** not reject your anointed one.
7:11 all that Solomon had planned to **d** in the house of
10: 6 "How **d** you advise me to answer this people?"
10: 9 to them, "What **d** you advise
10:16 "What share **d** we have in David?
13: 5 **D** you not know that the LORD God
13:12 O Israelites, **d** not fight against the LORD,
15: 7 **D** not let your hands be weak,
18:21 and you shall succeed; go out and **d** it.'
19: 7 take care what you **d,** for there is no perversion
19:10 **D** so, and you will not incur guilt.
20: 6 **D** you not rule over all the kingdoms of
20:12 We **d** not know what to **d,**
20:15 '**D** not fear or be dismayed at this great multitude;
20:17 **D** not fear or be dismayed;
23: 4 This is what you are to **d:**
23: 6 **D** not let anyone enter the house of
23:14 "**D** not put her to death in the house of
24:20 Why **d** you transgress the commandments of
25: 7 "O king, **d** not let the army of Israel go with you,
25: 9 "But what shall we **d** about the hundred talents
28: 1 not **d** what was right in the sight of the LORD,
29:11 My sons, **d** not now be negligent,
30: 7 **D** not be like your ancestors and your kindred,
30: 8 **D** not now be stiff-necked as your ancestors were,
30:12 to **d** what the king and the officials commanded by
32: 7 **D** not be afraid or dismayed before the king
32:13 **D** you not know what I
32:15 Now therefore **d** not let Hezekiah deceive you
32:15 in this fashion, and **d** not believe him, for no god
33: 8 be careful to **d** all that I have commanded them,
35:21 "What have I to **d** with you, king of Judah?
Ezr 4: 2 for we worship your God as you **d,**
6: 8 a decree regarding what you shall **d**
7:10 and to **d** it, and to teach the statutes and ordinances
7:18 and your colleagues to **d** with the rest of the silver
7:18 you may **d,** according to the will of your God.
7:25 and you shall teach those who **d** not know them.
9:12 Therefore **d** not give your daughters to their sons,
10: 4 with you; be strong, and **d** it."
10: 5 all Israel swear that they would **d** as had been said.
10:11 the God of your ancestors, and **d** his will;
10:12 we must **d** as you have said.
Ne 1: 9 to me and keep my commandments and **d** them,
2: 4 Then the king said to me, "What **d** you request?"
2:12 into my heart to **d** for Jerusalem.
2:16 the officials, and the rest that were to **d** the work.
4: 5 **D** not cover their guilt, and **d** not let their sin be
4:14 "**D** not be afraid of them.
5:12 We will **d** as you say."
5:12 made them take an oath to **d** as they had promised.
5:15 But I did not **d** so, because of the fear of God.
6: 2 But they intended to **d** me harm.
8: 9 to the LORD your God; **d** not mourn or weep."
8:10 and **d** not be grieved, for the joy of
8:11 for this day is holy; **d** not be grieved."
9:24 to **d** with them as they pleased.
9:32 **d** not treat lightly all the hardship that has come
10:29 and to observe and **d** all the commandments of
13:14 and **d** not wipe out my good deeds
13:21 "Why **d** you spend the night in front of the wall?
13:21 If you **d** so again, I will lay hands on you."
13:27 Shall we then listen to you and **d** all this great evil
Est 1: 8 the officials of his palace to **d** as each one desired.
3: 2 But Mordecai did not bow down or **d** obeisance.
3: 3 "Why **d** you disobey the king's command?"
3: 5 that Mordecai did not bow down or **d** obeisance
3: 8 and they **d** not keep the king's laws,
3:11 to **d** with them as it seems good to you."
4:13 to reply to Esther, "**D** not think that in

Est 4:16 I and my maids will also fast as you **d.**
5:5 so that we may **d** as Esther desires."
5:8 and then I will **d** as the king has said."
6:10 and **d** so to the Jew Mordecai who sits at
7:5 and where is he, who has presumed to **d** this?"
9:13 in Susa be allowed tomorrow also to **d** according
9:23 as a custom what they had begun to **d,**
Job 1:12 only **d** not stretch out your hand against him!"
2:9 "**D** you still persist in your integrity?
3:18 they **d** not hear the voice of the taskmaster.
5:17 **d** not despise the discipline of the Almighty.
6:26 **D** you think that you can reprove words,
7:1 "**D** not human beings have a hard service on earth,
7:9 so those who go down to Sheol **d** not come up;
7:10 nor **d** their places know them any more.
7:20 If I sin, what **d** I **d** to you,
7:21 Why **d** you not pardon my transgression
9:5 and they **d** not know it, when he overturns them
9:11 Look, he passes by me, and I **d** not see him;
9:11 he moves on, but I **d** not perceive him.
9:16 I **d** not believe that he would listen to my voice.
9:21 I **d** not know myself; I loathe my life.
9:29 I shall be condemned; why then **d** I labor in vain?
10:2 I will say to God, **D** not condemn me;
10:4 **D** you have eyes of flesh?
10:4 **D** you see as humans see?
10:14 you watch me, and **d** not acquit me of my iniquity.
11:8 It is higher than heaven—what can you **d?**
11:14 and **d** not let wickedness reside in your tents.
13:21 and **d** not let dread of you terrify me.
13:24 Why **d** you hide your face,
14:3 **D** you fix your eyes on such a one?
14:3 **D** you bring me into judgment with you?
14:12 so mortals lie down and **d** not rise again;
14:21 and they **d** not know it;
15:3 or in words with which they can **d** no good?
15:8 And **d** you limit wisdom to yourself?
15:9 What **d** you know that we **d** not know?
15:9 What **d** you understand that is not clear to us?
15:12 and why **d** your eyes flash,
16:4 I also could talk as you **d,** if you were in my place;
16:18 "O earth, **d** not cover my blood;
18:21 such is the place of those who **d** not know God."
19:22 Why **d** you, like God, pursue me,
20:4 **D** you not know this from of old,
21:7 Why **d** the wicked live on, reach old age,
21:14 We **d** not desire to know your ways.
21:15 And what profit **d** we get if we pray to him?'
21:21 what **d** they care for their household after them,
21:29 and **d** you not accept their testimony,
22:17 and 'What can the Almighty **d** to us?'
24:1 why **d** those who know him never see his days?
24:13 and **d** not stay in its paths.
24:16 they **d** not know the light.
24:21 and **d** no good to the widow.
26:14 and how small a whisper **d** we hear of him!
27:19 They go to bed with wealth, but will **d** so no more;
28:13 Mortals **d** not know the way to it,
30:10 they **d** not hesitate to spit at the sight of me.
30:20 I cry to you and you **d** not answer me;
31:14 what then shall I **d** when God rises up?
31:33 if I have concealed my transgressions as others **d,**
32:13 Yet **d** not say, 'We have found wisdom;
32:16 And am I to wait, because they **d** not speak,
32:22 For I **d** not know how to flatter—
33:13 Why **d** you contend against him, saying,
33:14 and in two, though people **d** not perceive it.
34:10 far be it from God that he should **d** wickedness,
34:10 and from the Almighty that he should **d** wrong.
34:12 Of a truth, God will not **d** wickedly,
34:32 teach me what I **d** not see;
34:32 if I have done iniquity, I will **d** it no more'?
35:2 "**D** you think this to be just?
35:6 what **d** you accomplish against him?
35:6 what **d** you **d** to him?
35:7 If you are righteous, what **d** you give to him;
35:14 much less when you say that you **d** not see him,
36:12 But if they **d** not listen,
36:13 they **d** not cry for help when he binds them.
36:18 and **d** not let the greatness of
36:20 **D** not long for the night,
36:21 **D** not turn to iniquity;
36:26 Surely God is great, and we **d** not know him;
37:15 **D** you know how God lays his command
37:16 **D** you know the balancings of the clouds,
38:33 **D** you know the ordinances of the heavens?
39:1 "**D** you know when the mountain goats give birth?
39:1 **D** you observe the calving of the deer?
39:2 and **d** you know the time when they give birth,
39:4 they go forth, and **d** not return to them.
39:12 **D** you have faith in it that it will return,
39:19 "**D** you give the horse its might?
39:19 **D** you clothe its neck with mane?
39:20 **D** you make it leap like the locust?
41:8 you will not **d** it again!
42:2 "I know that you can **d** all things,
Ps 1:1 Happy are those who **d** not follow the advice of
1:3 and their leaves **d** not wither.
1:3 In all that they **d,** they prosper.
2:1 Why **d** the nations conspire,
4:4 When you are disturbed, **d** not sin;
6:1 **d** not rebuke me in your anger,
9:19 O LORD! **D** not let mortals prevail;
10:1 O LORD, **d** you stand far off?
10:1 Why **d** you hide yourself in times of trouble?
10:12 **d** not forget the oppressed.
10:13 Why **d** the wicked renounce God,
Ps 10:14 But you **d** see! Indeed you note trouble
10:18 to **d** justice for the orphan and the oppressed,
11:3 what can the righteous **d?"**
14:1 They are corrupt, they **d** abominable deeds;
14:4 and **d** not call upon the LORD?
15:2 Those who walk blamelessly, and **d** what is right,
15:3 who **d** not slander with their tongue,
15:3 and **d** no evil to their friends,
15:5 who **d** not lend money at interest,
15:5 and **d** not take a bribe against the innocent.
15:5 Those who **d** these things shall never be moved.
16:10 For you **d** not give me up to Sheol,
17:4 As for what others **d,** by the word
19:13 **d** not let them have dominion over me.
22:2 O my God, I cry by day, but you **d** not answer;
22:11 **D** not be far from me,
22:19 But you, O LORD, **d** not be far away!
24:4 who **d** not lift up their souls to what is false,
24:4 and **d** not swear deceitfully.
25:2 **d** not let me be put to shame;
25:2 **d** not let my enemies exult over me.
25:3 **D** not let those who wait for you be put to shame;
25:7 **D** not remember the sins of my youth
25:20 **d** not let me be put to shame,
26:4 I **d** not sit with the worthless,
26:4 nor **d** I consort with hypocrites;
26:9 **D** not sweep me away with sinners,
27:8 Your face, LORD, **d** I seek.
27:9 **D** not hide your face from me.
27:9 **D** not turn your servant away in anger,
27:9 **D** not cast me off, **d** not forsake me,
27:12 **D** not give me up to the will of my adversaries,
28:1 my rock, **d** not refuse to hear me,
28:3 **D** not drag me away with the wicked,
28:5 they **d** not regard the works of the LORD,
31:1 **d** not let me ever be put to shame;
31:17 **D** not let me be put to shame, O LORD,
32:9 **D** not be like a horse or a mule,
34:14 Depart from evil, and **d** good;
35:11 they ask me about things I **d** not know.
35:19 **D** not let my treacherous enemies rejoice over me,
35:20 For they **d** not speak peace,
35:22 You have seen, O LORD; **d** not be silent!
35:22 O Lord, **d** not be far from me!
35:24 and **d** not let them rejoice over me.
35:25 **D** not let them say to themselves, "Aha,
35:25 **D** not let them say, "We have swallowed you up."
36:3 they have ceased to act wisely and **d** good.
36:4 not good; they **d** not reject evil.
36:11 **D** not let the foot of the arrogant tread on me,
37:1 **D** not fret because of the wicked;
37:1 **d** not be envious of wrongdoers,
37:3 Trust in the LORD, and **d** good;
37:7 **d** not fret over those who prosper in their way,
37:8 **D** not fret—it leads only to evil.
37:21 The wicked borrow, and **d** not pay back,
37:27 Depart from evil, and **d** good;
37:31 in their hearts; their steps **d** not slip.
38:1 **d** not rebuke me in your anger,
38:13 But I am like the deaf, I **d** not hear;
38:16 For I pray, "Only **d** not let them rejoice over me,
38:21 **D** not forsake me, O LORD;
38:21 O my God, **d** not be far from me;
39:6 they heap up, and **d** not know who will gather.
39:7 "And now, O Lord, what **d** I wait for?
39:8 **D** not make me the scorn of the fool.
39:9 I am silent; I **d** not open my mouth,
39:12 **d** not hold your peace at my tears.
40:4 who **d** not turn to the proud,
40:6 Sacrifice and offering you **d** not desire,
40:8 I delight to **d** your will, O my God;
40:11 **D** not, O LORD, withhold your mercy from me;
40:17 You are my help and my deliverer; **d** not delay,
41:2 You **d** not give them up to the will
44:6 in my bow **d** I trust, nor can my sword save me.
44:23 Why **d** you sleep, O Lord?
44:23 Awake, **d** not cast us off forever!
44:24 Why **d** you hide your face?
44:24 Why **d** you forget our affliction and oppression?
49:16 **D** not be afraid when some become rich,
49:18 for you are praised when you **d** well
50:8 Not for your sacrifices **d** I rebuke you;
50:13 **D** I eat the flesh of bulls,
51:11 **D** not cast me away from your presence,
51:11 and **d** not take your holy spirit from me.
51:18 **D** good to Zion in your good pleasure;
52:1 Why **d** you boast, O mighty one, of mischief done
53:4 and **d** not call upon God?
54:3 they **d** not set God before them.
55:1 **d** not hide yourself from my supplication.
55:11 and fraud **d** not depart from its marketplace.
55:19 because they **d** not change, and **d** not fear God.
56:4 what can flesh **d** to me?
56:11 What can a mere mortal **d** to me?
57:T *To the leader:* ***D*** *Not Destroy. Of David.*
58:T *To the leader:* ***D*** *Not Destroy. Of David.*
58:1 **D** you indeed decree what is right,
58:1 **D** you judge people fairly?
59:T *To the leader:* ***D*** *Not Destroy. Of David.*
59:11 **D** not kill them, or my people may forget;
59:15 and growl if they **d** not get their fill.
60:10 You **d** not go out, O God, with our armies.
60:12 With God we shall **d** valiantly;
62:10 if riches increase, **d** not set your heart on them.
68:16 Why **d** you look with envy,
69:6 **D** not let those who hope in you be put to shame
69:6 **d** not let those who seek you be dishonored
Ps 69:15 **D** not let the flood sweep over me,
69:17 **D** not hide your face from your servant,
70:5 and my deliverer; O LORD, **d** not delay!
71:9 **D** not cast me off in the time of old age;
71:9 **d** not forsake me when my strength is spent.
71:12 O God, **d** not be far from me;
71:18 **d** not forsake me, until I proclaim your might to all
71:24 for those who tried to **d** me harm have been put
74:1 why **d** you cast us off forever?
74:9 We **d** not see our emblems;
74:11 Why **d** you hold back your hand;
74:11 why **d** you keep your hand in your bosom?
74:19 **D** not deliver the soul of your dove to
74:19 **d** not forget the life of your poor forever.
74:21 **D** not let the downtrodden be put to shame;
74:23 **D** not forget the clamor of your foes,
75:T *To the leader:* ***D*** *Not Destroy.*
75:4 "**D** not boast," and to the wicked, "**D** not lift up
75:5 **d** not lift up your horn on high,
79:6 Pour out your anger on the nations that **d**
79:6 and on the kingdoms that **d** not call on your name.
79:8 **D** not remember against us the iniquities
83:1 O God, **d** not keep silence;
83:1 **d** not hold your peace or be still, O God!
83:9 **D** to them as you did to Midian,
86:3 O Lord, for to you **d** I cry all day long.
86:10 For you are great and **d** wondrous things;
86:14 and they **d** not set you before them.
88:10 **D** you work wonders for the dead?
88:10 **D** the shades rise up to praise you?
88:14 O LORD, why **d** you cast me off?
88:14 Why **d** you hide your face from me?
89:30 If his children forsake my law and **d** not walk
89:31 and **d** not keep my commandments,
95:8 **D** not harden your hearts, as at Meribah,
95:10 and they **d** not regard my ways."
102:2 **D** not hide your face from me in the day
102:24 "**d** not take me away at the mid-point of my life,
103:2 O my soul, and **d** not forget all his benefits—
103:18 and remember to **d** his commandments.
103:20 you mighty ones who **d** his bidding,
103:21 all his hosts, his ministers that **d** his will.
105:15 "**D** not touch my anointed ones; **d** my prophets no
106:3 who **d** righteousness at all times.
106:35 but they mingled with the nations and learned to **d**
108:11 You **d** not go out, O God, with our armies.
108:13 With God we shall **d** valiantly;
109:1 **D** not be silent, O God of my praise.
109:12 May there be no one to **d** him a kindness,
109:14 and **d** not let the sin of his mother be blotted out.
115:5 have mouths, but **d** not speak; eyes, but **d** not see.
115:6 have ears, but **d** not hear; noses, but **d** not smell.
115:7 have hands, but **d** not feel; feet, but **d** not walk;
115:17 The dead **d** not praise the LORD,
115:17 nor **d** any that go down into silence.
118:6 With the LORD on my side I **d** not fear.
118:6 What can mortals **d** to me?
119:3 who also **d** no wrong, but walk in his ways.
119:8 will observe your statutes; **d** not utterly forsake me.
119:10 **d** not let me stray from your commandments.
119:19 **d** not hide your commandments from me.
119:43 **D** not take the word of truth utterly out
119:51 but I **d** not turn away from your law.
119:60 and **d** not delay to keep your commandments.
119:61 I **d** not forget your law.
119:68 You are good and **d** good; teach me your statutes.
119:102 I **d** not turn away from your ordinances,
119:109 but I **d** not forget your law.
119:110 but I **d** not stray from your precepts.
119:121 **d** not leave me to my oppressors.
119:122 **d** not let the godless oppress me.
119:141 yet I **d** not forget your precepts.
119:153 for I **d** not forget your law.
119:155 for they **d** not seek your statutes.
119:157 yet I **d** not swerve from your decrees.
119:158 because they **d** not keep your commands.
119:176 for I **d** not forget your commandments.
125:3 not stretch out their hands to **d** wrong.
125:4 **D** good, O LORD, to those who are good,
129:7 with which reapers **d** not fill their hands or binders
129:8 while those who pass by **d** not say,
131:1 I **d** not occupy myself with things too great
132:10 For your servant David's sake **d** not turn away
135:16 They have mouths, but they **d** not speak;
135:16 they have eyes, but they **d** not see;
135:17 but they **d** not hear, and there is no breath
137:6 if I **d** not remember you,
137:6 if I **d** not set Jerusalem above my highest joy.
138:8 **D** not forsake the work of your hands.
139:21 **D** I not hate those who hate you, O LORD?
139:21 And **d** I not loathe those who rise up against you?
140:8 **D** not grant, O LORD, the desires of the wicked;
140:8 **d** not further their evil plot.
140:11 **D** not let the slanderer be established in the land;
141:4 **D** not turn my heart to any evil,
141:4 **d** not let me eat of their delicacies.
141:8 **d** not leave me defenseless.
143:2 **D** not enter into judgment with your servant,
143:7 **D** not hide your face from me,
143:10 Teach me to **d** your will, for you are my God.
146:3 **D** not put your trust in princes, in mortals,
147:20 they **d** not know his ordinances.
Pr 1:8 and **d** not reject your mother's teaching;
1:10 My child, if sinners entice you, **d** not consent.
1:15 **d** not walk in their way, keep your foot
2:19 nor **d** they regain the paths of life.
3:1 My child, **d** not forget my teaching,

Pr 3: 3 **D** not let loyalty and faithfulness forsake you;
3: 5 and **d** not rely on your own insight.
3: 7 **D** not be wise in your own eyes;
3:11 **d** not despise the LORD's discipline or be weary
3:21 My child, **d** not let these escape from your sight:
3:25 **D** not be afraid of sudden panic,
3:27 **D** not withhold good from those to whom it is due,
3:27 when it is in your power to **d** it.
3:28 **D** not say to your neighbor, "Go, and come again,
3:29 **D** not plan harm against your
3:30 **D** not quarrel with anyone without cause,
3:31 **D** not envy the violent and do not choose any
3:31 the violent and **d** not choose any of their ways;
4: 2 **d** not forsake my teaching.
4: 5 Get wisdom; get insight: **d** not forget,
4: 6 **D** not forsake her, and she will keep you;
4:13 **d** not let go; guard her, for she is your life.
4:14 **D** not enter the path of the wicked,
4:14 and **d** not walk in the way of evildoers.
4:15 **d** not go on it; turn away from it and pass on.
4:19 they **d** not know what they stumble over.
4:21 **D** not let them escape from your sight;
4:27 **D** not swerve to the right or to the left;
5: 7 and **d** not depart from the words of my mouth.
5: 8 and **d** not go near the door of her house;
6: 3 So **d** this, my child, and save yourself,
6:20 and **d** not forsake your mother's teaching.
6:25 **D** not desire her beauty in your heart,
6:25 and **d** not let her capture you with her eyelashes;
7:11 her feet **d** not stay at home;
7:25 **D** not let your hearts turn aside to her ways;
7:25 **d** not stray into her paths.
8:33 Hear instruction and be wise, and **d** not neglect it.
9:18 But they **d** not know that the dead are there,
10: 2 Treasures gained by wickedness **d** not profit,
11: 4 Riches **d** not profit in the day of wrath,
11:15 but there is safety in refusing to **d** so.
11:17 but the cruel **d** themselves harm.
12:27 The lazy **d** not roast their game,
13:16 The clever **d** all things intelligently,
14: 7 for there you **d** not find words of knowledge.
14:22 **D** they not err that plan evil?
15:12 Scoffers **d** not like to be rebuked;
16:12 It is an abomination to kings to **d** evil,
17:20 The crooked of mind **d** not prosper,
19:18 **d** not set your heart on their destruction.
19:19 you will only have to **d** it again.
19:26 Those who **d** violence to their father
20:11 by whether what they **d** is pure and right.
20:13 **D** not love sleep, or else you will come to poverty;
20:19 therefore **d** not associate with a babbler.
20:22 **D** not say, "I will repay evil";
21: 3 To **d** righteousness and justice is more acceptable
21: 7 because they refuse to **d** what is just.
21:26 but the righteous give and **d** not hold back.
22:22 **D** not rob the poor because they are poor,
22:24 and **d** not associate with hotheads,
22:26 **D** not be one of those who give pledges,
22:28 **D** not remove the ancient landmark
22:29 **D** you see those who are skillful in their work?
23: 3 **D** not desire the ruler's delicacies,
23: 4 **D** not wear yourself out to get rich;
23: 6 **D** not eat the bread of the stingy;
23: 6 **d** not desire their delicacies;
23: 7 they say to you; but they **d** not mean it.
23: 9 **D** not speak in the hearing of a fool,
23:10 **D** not remove an ancient landmark or encroach on
23:13 **D** not withhold discipline from your children;
23:17 **D** not let your heart envy sinners,
23:20 **D** not be among winebibbers,
23:22 and **d** not despise your mother when she is old.
23:23 Buy truth, and **d** not sell it;
23:31 **D** not look at wine when it is red,
24: 1 **D** not envy the wicked, nor desire to be with them;
24: 7 in the gate they **d** not open their mouths.
24: 8 to **d** evil will be called a mischief-maker.
24:15 **D** not lie in wait like an outlaw against the home
24:15 **d** no violence to the place where
24:17 **D** not rejoice when your enemies fall,
24:17 **d** not let your heart be glad when they stumble,
24:19 **D** not fret because of evildoers.
24:19 of evildoers. **D** not envy the wicked;
24:21 and **d** not disobey either of them;
24:28 **D** not be a witness against your neighbor
24:28 and **d** not deceive with your lips.
24:29 **D** not say, "I will do to others as they have done
24:29 "I will **d** to others as they have done to me;
25: 6 **D** not put yourself forward in the king's presence
25: 8 **d** not hastily bring into court;
25: 8 for what will you **d** in the end,
25: 9 and **d** not disclose another's secret;
26: 4 **D** not answer fools according to their folly,
26:12 **D** you see persons wise in their own eyes?
26:25 when an enemy speaks graciously, **d** not believe it,
27: 1 **D** not boast about tomorrow,
27: 1 for you **d** not know what a day may bring.
27:10 **D** not forsake your friend or the friend
27:10 **d** not go to the house of your kindred in the day
27:24 for riches **d** not last forever,
28: 5 The evil **d** not understand justice,
28:21 yet for a piece of bread a person may **d** wrong.
29:20 **D** you see someone who is hasty in speech?
30: 2 I **d** not have human understanding.
30: 6 **D** not add to his words, or else he will rebuke you,
30: 7 **d** not deny them to me before I die:
30:10 **D** not slander a servant to a master,
30:11 There are those who curse their fathers and **d**

Pr 30:18 for me; four I **d** not understand:
31: 3 **D** not give your strength to women,
Ecc 1: 3 What **d** people gain from all the toil
2: 3 to **d** under heaven during the few days of their life.
2:12 for what can the one **d** who comes after the king?
2:22 What **d** mortals get from all the toil and strain
2:23 even at night their minds **d** not rest.
5: 1 for they **d** not know how to keep from doing evil.
5: 4 you make a vow to God, **d** not delay fulfilling it;
5: 6 **D** not let your mouth lead you into sin,
5: 6 and **d** not say before the messenger that it was
5: 8 **d** not be amazed at the matter;
5:16 what gain **d** they have from toiling for the wind?
6: 6 **d** not all go to one place?
6: 8 And what **d** the poor have who know how
7: 9 **D** not be quick to anger,
7:10 **D** not say, "Why were the former days better
7:16 **D** not be too righteous, and **d** not act too wise;
7:17 **D** not be too wicked, and **d** not be a fool;
7:20 so righteous as to **d** good without ever sinning.
7:21 **D** not give heed to everything that people say,
8: 3 **D** not be terrified; go from his
8: 3 **d** not delay when the matter is unpleasant,
8: 7 Indeed, they **d** not know what is to be,
8:11 the human heart is fully set to **d** evil.
8:12 Though sinners **d** evil a hundred times
8:13 because they **d** not stand in fear before God.
9: 2 to those who sacrifice and those who **d**
9: 7 for God has long ago approved what you **d.**
9: 8 **d** not let oil be lacking on your head.
9:10 Whatever your hand finds to **d, d** with your might;
10: 4 the ruler rises against you, **d** not leave your post,
10:15 for they **d** not even know the way to town.
10:20 **D** not curse the king, even in your thoughts,
11: 2 for you **d** not know what disaster may happen
11: 5 Just as you **d** not know how the breath comes to
11: 5 so you **d** not know the work of God,
11: 6 and at evening **d** not let your hands be idle;
11: 6 for you **d** not know which will prosper,
SS 1: 4 love more than wine; rightly **d** they love you.
1: 6 **D** not gaze at me because I am dark,
1: 8 If you **d** not know, O fairest among women,
2: 7 **d** not stir up or awaken love until it is ready!
3: 5 **d** not stir up or awaken love until it is ready!
8: 4 **d** not stir up or awaken love until it is ready!
8: 8 What shall we **d** for our sister,
Isa 1: 3 Israel does not know, my people **d** not understand.
1: 4 offspring who **d** evil, children who deal corruptly,
1: 5 Why **d** you seek further beatings?
1: 5 Why **d** you continue to rebel?
1:11 I **d** not delight in the blood of bulls, or of lambs,
1:16 before my eyes; cease to **d** evil,
1:17 learn to **d** good; seek justice,
1:23 They **d** not defend the orphan,
2: 9 and everyone is brought low—**d** not forgive them!
3: 9 they proclaim their sin like Sodom, they **d**
3:15 What **d** you mean by crushing my people,
5: 4 to **d** for my vineyard that I have not done in it?
5: 5 now I will tell you what I will **d** to my vineyard.
5:12 but who **d** not regard the deeds of the LORD,
6: 9 'Keep listening, but **d** not comprehend;
6: 9 keep looking, but **d** not understand.'
7: 4 Take heed, be quiet, **d** not fear,
7: 4 and **d** not let your heart be faint because
7: 9 If you **d** not stand firm in faith,
8:12 **D** not call conspiracy all that this people calls
8:12 and **d** not fear what it fears, or be in dread.
9: 7 The zeal of the LORD of hosts will **d** this.
10: 3 What will you **d** on the day of punishment,
10:11 not **d** to Jerusalem and her idols what I have done
10:24 O my people, who live in Zion, **d** not be afraid of
13:17 who have no regard for silver and **d** not delight
14:29 **D** not rejoice, all you Philistines, that the rod
16: 3 hide the outcasts, **d** not betray the fugitive;
16: 5 and is swift to **d** what is right.
19:15 will be able to **d** anything for Egypt.
22: 1 What **d** you mean that you have gone up,
22: 4 **d** not try to comfort me for the destruction of my
22:16 What right **d** you have here?
24: 9 No longer **d** they drink wine with singing;
26:10 they **d** not learn righteousness,
26:10 and **d** not see the majesty of the LORD.
26:11 your hand is lifted up, but they **d** not see it.
26:14 The dead **d** not live; shades **d** not rise—
28:21 to **d** his deed—strange is his deed!
28:22 **d** not scoff, or your bonds will be made stronger;
28:24 **D** those who plow for sowing plow continually?
28:24 **D** they continually open and harrow their ground?
28:25 **d** they not scatter dill, sow cummin,
29:14 so I will again **d** amazing things with this people,
29:20 all those alert to **d** evil shall be cut off—
30:10 who say to the seers, "**D** not see";
30:10 "**D** not prophesy to us what is right;
31: 1 but **d** not look to the Holy One of Israel or consult
35: 4 to those who are of a fearful heart, "Be strong, **d**
36: 4 On what **d** you base this confidence of yours?
36: 5 **D** you think that mere words are strategy
36: 5 On whom **d** you now rely,
36:11 **d** not speak to us in the language of Judah within
36:14 '**D** not let Hezekiah deceive you,
36:15 **D** not let Hezekiah make you rely on the LORD
36:16 **D** not listen to Hezekiah;
36:18 **D** not let Hezekiah mislead you by saying,
36:21 for the king's command was, "**D** not answer him."
37: 6 **D** not be afraid because of the words
37:10 **D** not let your God on whom you rely deceive you
37:32 The zeal of the LORD of hosts will **d** this.

Isa 38: 7 the LORD will **d** this thing that he has promised:
38:19 living, the living, they thank you, as I **d** this day;
40: 9 herald of good tidings, lift it up, **d** not fear;
40:27 Why **d** you say, O Jacob, and speak, O Israel,
41:10 **d** not fear, for I am with you, **d** not be afraid,
41:13 it is I who say to you, "**D** not fear,
41:14 **D** not fear, you worm Jacob, you insect Israel!
41:23 **d** good, or **d** harm, that we may be afraid
42:16 I will lead the blind by a road they **d** not know,
42:16 These are the things I will **d,**
43: 1 **D** not fear, for I have redeemed you;
43: 5 **D** not fear, for I am with you;
43: 6 and to the south, "**D** not withhold;
43:18 **D** not remember the former things,
43:19 I am about to **d** a new thing;
43:19 now it springs forth, **d** you not perceive it?
44: 2 **D** not fear, O Jacob my servant,
44: 8 **D** not fear, or be afraid;
44: 9 and the things they delight in **d** not profit;
44:10 a god or cast an image that can **d** no good?
44:18 They **d** not know, nor **d** they comprehend;
45: 4 I surname you, though you **d** not know me.
45: 5 I arm you, though you **d** not know me,
45: 7 I the LORD **d** all these things.
46:11 I have planned, and I will **d** it.
48:11 For my own sake, for my own sake, I **d** it,
51: 7 **d** not fear the reproach of others,
51: 7 and **d** not be dismayed when they revile you.
54: 2 be stretched out; **d** not hold back;
54: 4 **D** not fear, for you will not be ashamed;
54: 4 **d** not be discouraged, for you will
55: 2 Why **d** you spend your money for that which is
55: 5 See, you shall call nations that you **d** not know,
55: 5 and nations that **d** not know you shall run to you,
55:10 and **d** not return there until they have watered
56: 1 Maintain justice, and **d** what is right,
56: 3 **D** not let the foreigner joined to the LORD say,
56: 3 and **d** not let the eunuch say, "I am just a dry tree."
56: 6 and **d** not profane it, and hold fast my covenant—
57: 4 Against whom **d** you open your mouth wide
57:11 and so you **d** not fear me?
58: 1 Shout out, **d** not hold back!
58: 3 "Why **d** we fast, but you **d** not see?
58: 3 Why humble ourselves, but you **d** not notice?"
58: 4 as you **d** today will not make your voice heard
59: 8 The way of peace they **d** not know,
63:17 **d** you make us stray from your ways
63:17 so that we **d** not fear you?
63:19 We have long been like those whom you **d**
64: 5 You meet those who gladly **d** right,
64: 9 **D** not be exceedingly angry, O LORD,
64: 9 O LORD, and **d** not remember iniquity forever.
65: 5 **d** not come near me, for I am too holy for you."
65: 8 "**D** not destroy it, for there is a blessing in it,"
65: 8 so I will **d** for my servants' sake,
Jer 1: 6 Truly I **d** not know how to speak,
1: 7 LORD said to me, "**D** not say, 'I am only a boy';
1: 8 **D** not be afraid of them,
1:11 saying, "Jeremiah, what **d** you see?"
1:13 saying, "What **d** you see?"
1:17 **D** not break down before them,
2: 8 and went after things that **d** not profit.
2:18 What then **d** you gain by going to Egypt,
2:18 Or what **d** you gain by going to Assyria,
2:29 Why **d** you complain against me?
2:31 Why then **d** my people say, "We are free,
4: 1 from my presence, and **d** not waver,
4: 3 and **d** not sow among thorns.
4: 6 **d** not delay, for I am bringing evil from the north,
4:22 "For my people are foolish, they **d** not know me;
4:22 but **d** not know how to **d** good."
4:30 what **d** you mean that you dress in crimson,
5: 3 O LORD, **d** your eyes not look for truth?
5: 4 for they **d** not know the way of the LORD,
5:10 but **d** not make a full end;
5:12 and have said, "He will **d** nothing.
5:15 a nation whose language you **d** not know,
5:21 but **d** not see, who have ears, but **d** not hear.
5:22 **D** you not fear me?
5:22 says the LORD; **D** you not tremble before me?
5:24 They **d** not say in their hearts,
5:28 they **d** not judge with justice the cause of
5:28 and they **d** not defend the rights of the needy.
5:31 but what will you **d** when the end comes?
6:25 **D** not go out into the field, or walk on the road;
7: 4 **D** not trust in these deceptive words:
7: 6 if you **d** not oppress the alien,
7: 6 if you **d** not go after other gods to your own hurt,
7:14 I will **d** to the house that is called by my name,
7:16 As for you, **d** not pray for this people,
7:16 **d** not raise a cry or prayer on their behalf,
7:16 and **d** not intercede with me,
7:17 **D** you not see what they are doing in the towns
8: 4 When people fall, **d** they not get up again?
8: 4 If they go astray, **d** they not turn back?
8: 6 but they **d** not speak honestly;
8: 7 but my people **d** not know the ordinance of
8:14 Why **d** we sit still?
9: 3 and they **d** not know me, says the LORD.
9: 7 for what else can I **d** with my sinful people?
9:23 **D** not let the wise boast in their wisdom,
9:23 **d** not let the mighty boast in their might,
9:23 **d** not let the wealthy boast in their wealth;
10: 2 **D** not learn the way of the nations,
10: 5 **D** not be afraid of them, for they cannot **d** evil, nor is it in them to **d** good.
10:21 and **d** not inquire of the LORD;

Jer 10:25 that **d** not know you, and on the peoples that **d** not call on your name;
11: 4 Listen to my voice, and **d** all that I command you.
11: 6 Hear the words of this covenant and **d** them.
11: 8 which I commanded them to **d,** but they did not.
11:14 As for you, **d** not pray for this people,
12: 1 Why **d** all who are treacherous thrive?
12: 6 **d** not believe them, though they speak friendly
13: 1 and put it on your loins, but **d** not dip it in water."
13:12 **"D** you think we **d** not know
13:15 **d** not be haughty, for the LORD has spoken.
13:23 you can **d** good who are accustomed to **d** evil.
14: 9 by your name; **d** not forsake us!
14:11 **D** not pray for the welfare of this people.
14:12 Although they fast, I **d** not hear their cry,
14:12 and grain offering, I **d** not accept them;
14:21 **D** not spurn us, for your name's sake;
14:21 **d** not dishonor your glorious throne;
14:21 remember and **d** not break your covenant with us.
14:22 for it is you who **d** all this.
15:14 in a land that you **d** not know,
15:15 In your forbearance **d** not take me away;
16: 5 **D** not enter the house of mourning,
17: 4 in a land that you **d** not know,
17:17 **D** not become a terror to me;
17:18 but **d** not let me be shamed;
17:18 but **d** not let me be dismayed;
17:21 that you **d** not bear a burden on the sabbath day
17:22 And **d** not carry a burden out of your houses on the sabbath or **d** any work,
17:24 but keep the sabbath day holy and **d** no work on it,
17:27 But if you **d** not listen to me,
18: 6 Can I not **d** with you,
18:10 about the good that I had intended to **d** to it.
18:14 **D** the mountain waters run dry,
18:23 **D** not forgive their iniquity,
18:23 **d** not blot out their sin from your sight.
19:12 Thus will I **d** to this place, says the LORD,
22: 3 And **d** no wrong or violence to the alien,
22:10 **D** not weep for him who is dead, nor bemoan him;
22:15 Did not your father eat and drink and **d** justice
22:28 and cast away in a land that they **d** not know?
23:16 **D** not listen to the words of
23:24 **D** I not fill heaven and earth?
23:32 so they **d** not profit this people at all,
24: 3 LORD said to me, "What **d** you see, Jeremiah?"
25: 6 **d** not go after other gods to serve
25: 6 and **d** not provoke me to anger with the work
25: 6 Then I will **d** you no harm."
26: 2 **d** not hold back a word.
26:14 **D** with me as seems good and right to you.
27:14 **D** not listen to the words of
27:16 **D** not listen to the words
27:17 **D** not listen to them; serve the king of Babylon
28: 6 "Amen! May the LORD **d** so;
29: 6 multiply there, and **d** not decrease.
29: 8 **D** not let the prophets and the diviners who are
29: 8 and **d** not listen to the dreams that they dream,
29:32 to see the good that I am going to **d** to my people,
30: 6 then **d** I see every man with his hands on his loins
30:10 says the LORD, and **d** not be dismayed, O Israel;
30:15 Why **d** you cry out over your hurt?
32: 3 Zedekiah had said, "Why **d** you prophesy and say:
32:23 of all you commanded them to **d,**
32:35 that they should **d** this abomination,
33: 9 of the earth who shall hear of all the good that I **d**
35:15 and **d** not go after other gods to serve them,
36: 3 of Judah hears of all the disasters that I intend to **d**
37: 9 Thus says the LORD: **D** not deceive yourselves,
37:20 to my plea, and **d** not send me back to the house of
38:14 **d** not hide anything from me."
38:18 if you **d** not surrender to the officials of the king
38:24 **"D** not let anyone else know of this conversation,
38:25 **d** not conceal it from us,
39:12 look after him well and **d** him no harm,
40: 4 but if you **d** not wish to come with me to Babylon,
40: 9 saying, **"D** not be afraid to serve the Chaldeans.
40:16 **"D** not **d** such a thing,
41: 8 **"D** not kill us, for we have stores of wheat, barley,
42: 3 where we should go and what we should **d."**
42: 5 against us if we **d** not act according to everything
42:11 **D** not be afraid of the king of Babylon,
42:11 **d** not be afraid of him, says the LORD,
42:19 O remnant of Judah, **D** not go to Egypt.
42:20 tell us and we will **d** it.'
43: 2 **'D** not go to Egypt to settle there';
43: 9 Let the Judeans see you **d** it,
44: 4 not to **d** this abominable thing that I hate!"
44: 8 Why **d** you provoke me to anger with the works
44:17 Instead, we will **d** everything that we have vowed,
44:17 used to **d** in the towns of Judah and in the streets
44:19 **d** you think that we made cakes for her,
45: 5 And you, **d** you seek great things for yourself? **D** not seek them;
46: 5 Why **d** I see them terrified?
46: 5 They **d** not look back—terror is all around!
46:27 my servant Jacob, and **d** not be dismayed,
47: 3 parents **d** not turn back for children,
49: 4 Why **d** you boast in your strength?
49:12 If those who **d** not deserve to drink
50: 2 set up a banner and proclaim, **d** not conceal it, say:
50:15 take vengeance on her, **d** to her as she has done.
50:21 **d** all that I have commanded you.
50:25 the Lord GOD of hosts has a task to **d** in the land
50:29 just as she has done, **d** to her—
51: 3 **D** not spare her young men;
51: 6 **D** not perish because of her guilt,
Jer 51:46 **D** not be fainthearted or fearful at
51:50 You survivors of the sword, go, **d** not linger!
La 3:56 **"D** not close your ear to my cry for help,
3:57 on you; you said, **"D** not fear!"
4:15 "Away! Away! **D** not touch!"
Eze 2: 6 And you, O mortal, **d** not be afraid of them,
2: 6 and **d** not be afraid of their words,
2: 6 **d** not be afraid of their words,
2: 6 and **d** not be dismayed at their looks,
2: 8 **d** not be rebellious like that rebellious house;
3: 9 **d** not fear them or be dismayed at their looks,
3:19 and they **d** not turn from their wickedness,
3:21 and they **d** not sin, they shall surely live,
5: 9 I will **d** to you what I have never yet done,
5: 9 and the like of which I will never **d** again.
8: 6 "Mortal, **d** you see what they are doing,
12: 2 who have eyes to see but **d** not see,
12: 2 who have ears to hear but **d** not hear;
12: 4 as those **d** who go into exile.
16: 5 to **d** any of these things for you out of compassion
17:12 **D** you not know what these things mean?
18: 2 What **d** you mean by repeating this proverb
18:14 considers, and does not **d** likewise,
18:21 and keep all my statutes and **d** what is lawful
18:24 **d** the same abominable things that the wicked **d,**
18:27 and **d** what is lawful and right,
20: 7 **d** not defile yourselves with the idols of Egypt;
20:18 **D** not follow the statutes of your parents,
21: 7 And when they say to you, "Why **d** you moan?"
22:14 I the LORD have spoken, and I will **d** it.
24:17 **d** not cover your upper lip or eat the bread
24:22 And you shall **d** as I have done;
24:24 you shall **d** just as he has done.
32:19 "Whom **d** you surpass in beauty?
32:27 And they **d** not lie with the fallen warriors
33: 4 then if any who hear the sound of the trumpet **d**
33: 8 and you **d** not speak to warn the wicked to turn
33: 9 and they **d** not turn from their ways,
33:14 yet if they turn from their sin and **d** what is lawful
33:19 and **d** what is lawful and right, they shall live by it.
33:32 they hear what you say, but they will not **d** it.
34: 3 but you **d** not feed the sheep.
36:11 and will **d** more good to you than ever before.
36:36 I, the LORD, have spoken, and I will **d** it.
36:37 I will also let the house of Israel ask me to **d** this
44:14 to **d** all its chores, all that is to be done in it.
45: 9 and **d** what is just and right.
45:20 You shall **d** the same on the seventh day of
Da 2: 5 if you **d** not tell me both the dream
2: 6 if you **d** tell me the dream and its interpretation,
2: 9 if you **d** not tell me the dream,
2:24 **"D** not destroy the wise men of Babylon;
3:12 They **d** not serve your gods and they do
3:12 not serve your gods and they **d** not worship
3:14 you **d** not serve my gods and you **d** not worship
3:15 But if you **d** not worship,
4:19 **d** not let the dream or
5:10 **D** not let your thoughts terrify you
5:23 wood, and stone, which **d** not see or hear or know;
9:18 We **d** not present our supplication before you on
9:19 O Lord, listen and act and **d** not delay!
10:12 He said to me, **"D** not fear, Daniel,
10:19 He said, **"D** not fear, greatly beloved, you are safe.
10:20 he said, **"D** you know why I have come to you?
11:11 the south shall go out and **d** battle against the king
11:24 the richest parts of the province and **d** what none
Hos 4:15 O Israel, **d** not let Judah become guilty.
4:15 **D** not enter into Gilgal, or go up to Beth-aven,
4:15 and **d** not swear, "As the LORD lives."
5: 4 Their deeds **d** not permit them to return
5: 4 and they **d** not know the LORD.
6: 4 What shall I **d** with you, O Ephraim?
6: 4 What shall I **d** with you, O Judah?
7: 2 But they **d** not consider
7:10 yet they **d** not return to the LORD their God,
7:14 They **d** not cry to me from the heart,
9: 1 **D** not rejoice, O Israel!
9: 1 **D** not exult as other nations **d;**
9: 5 What will you **d** on the day of appointed festival,
10: 3 "We have no king, for we **d** not fear the LORD,
10: 3 what could he **d** for us?"
14: 8 O Ephraim, what have I to **d** with idols?
Joel 2: 7 they **d** not swerve from their paths.
2: 8 They **d** not jostle one another,
2:17 and **d** not make your heritage a mockery,
2:21 **D** not fear, O soil; be glad
2:22 **D** not fear, you animals of the field,
Am 3: 3 **D** two walk together unless they have made
3:10 They **d** not know how to **d** right,
4: 5 for so you love to **d,** O people of Israel!
4:12 Therefore thus I will **d** to you, O Israel;
4:12 because I will **d** this to you,
5: 5 but **d** not seek Bethel, and **d** not enter into Gilgal
5:18 Why **d** you want the day of the LORD?
6:12 **D** horses run on rocks?
7: 8 the LORD said to me, "Amos, what **d** you see?"
7:16 You say, **'D** not prophesy against Israel,
7:16 and **d** not preach against the house of Isaac.'
8: 2 He said, "Amos, what **d** you see?"
Jnh 1: 6 the god will spare us a thought so that we **d**
1: 8 Where **d** you come from?
1:11 Then they said to him, "What shall we **d** to you,
1:14 **d** not let us perish on account of this man's life.
1:14 **D** not make us guilty of innocent blood;
3: 9 he may turn from his fierce anger, so that we **d**
3:10 and he did not **d** it.
4:11 a hundred and twenty thousand persons who **d**
Mic 1:11 the inhabitants of Zaanan **d** not come forth;
2: 6 **"D** not preach"—thus they preach—
2: 7 **D** not my words **d** good to one who walks uprightly?
4: 9 Now why **d** you cry aloud?
4:12 But they **d** not know the thoughts of the LORD;
4:12 they **d** not understand his plan,
5: 7 which **d** not depend upon people or wait
6: 8 the LORD require of you but to **d** justice,
7: 3 Their hands are skilled to **d** evil;
7: 8 **D** not rejoice over me, O my enemy;
Na 1: 9 Why **d** you plot against the LORD?
Hab 1: 3 Why **d** you make me see wrongdoing and look
1:13 why **d** you look on the treacherous,
2: 5 wealth is treacherous; the arrogant **d** not endure.
Zep 1:12 "The LORD will not **d** good, nor will he **d** harm."
2: 3 all you humble of the land, who **d** his commands;
3:13 they shall **d** no wrong and utter no lies,
3:16 **D** not fear, O Zion; **d** not let your hands grow weak
Hag 2: 5 My spirit abides among you; **d** not fear.
2:19 **D** the vine, the fig tree, the pomegranate,
Zec 1: 4 **D** not be like your ancestors,
1: 5 And the prophets, **d** they live forever?
1: 6 just as he planned to **d."**
1:21 And I asked, "What are they coming to **d?"**
4: 2 He said to me, "What **d** you see?"
4: 5 **"D** you not know what these are?"
4:13 He said to me, **"D** you not know what these are?"
5: 2 And he said to me, "What **d** you see?"
7: 6 **d** you not eat and drink only for yourselves?
7:10 **d** not oppress the widow, the orphan, the alien,
7:10 and **d** not devise evil in your hearts
8:13 **D** not be afraid, but let your hands be strong.
8:15 to **d** good to Jerusalem and to the house of Judah; **d** not be afraid.
8:16 These are the things that you shall **d:**
8:17 **d** not devise evil in your hearts
9: 1 as **d** all the tribes of Israel;
14:17 the families of the earth **d** not go up to Jerusalem
14:18 of Egypt **d** not go up and present themselves,
14:18 the LORD inflicts on the nations that **d** not go up
14:19 and the punishment of all the nations that **d** not go
Mal 2: 2 because you **d** not lay it to heart.
2:13 And this you **d** as well:
2:15 and **d** not let anyone be faithless to the wife
2:16 So take heed to yourselves and **d** not be faithless.
2:17 "All who **d** evil are good in the sight of
3: 5 and **d** not fear me, says the LORD of hosts.
3: 6 For I the LORD **d** not change;
3:14 What **d** we profit by keeping his command or
Mt 1:20 But just when he had resolved to **d** this,
1:20 **d** not be afraid to take Mary as your wife,
3: 9 **D** not presume to say to yourselves,
3:14 and **d** you come to me?"
4: 7 **'D** not put the Lord your God to the test.' "
5:17 **"D** not think that I have come to abolish the law or
5:19 and teaches others to **d** the same,
5:34 But I say to you, **D** not swear at all,
5:36 And **d** not swear by your head,
5:39 But I say to you, **D** not resist an evildoer.
5:42 and **d** not refuse anyone who wants to borrow
5:46 love those who love you, what reward **d** you have?
5:46 **D** not even the tax collectors **d** the same?
5:47 **D** not even the Gentiles **d** the same?
6: 2 **d** not sound a trumpet before you,
6: 2 hypocrites **d** in the synagogues and in the streets,
6: 3 But when you give alms, **d**
6: 5 whenever you pray, **d** not be like the hypocrites;
6: 7 **d** not heap up empty phrases as the Gentiles **d;**
6: 8 **D** not be like them, for your Father knows what
6:13 And **d** not bring us to the time of trial,
6:15 but if you **d** not forgive others,
6:16 "And whenever you fast, **d** not look dismal,
6:19 **"D** not store up for yourselves treasures on earth,
6:20 nor rust consumes and where thieves **d** not break
6:25 "Therefore I tell you, **d** not worry about your life,
6:28 And why **d** you worry about clothing?
6:31 **d** not worry, saying, 'What will we eat?'
6:34 "So **d** not worry about tomorrow,
7: 1 **"D** not judge, so that you may not be judged.
7: 3 Why **d** you see the speck in your neighbor's eye,
7: 3 but **d** not notice the log in your own eye?
7: 6 **"D** not give what is holy to dogs;
7: 6 and **d** not throw your pearls before swine,
7:12 "In everything **d** to others as you would have them **d** to you;
7:22 and **d** many deeds of power in your name?'
8: 3 and touched him, saying, "I **d** choose.
8: 9 'Come,' and he comes, and to my slave, **'D** this,'
8:29 "What have you to **d** with us, Son of God?
9: 4 said, "Why **d** you think evil in your hearts?
9:14 "Why **d** we and the Pharisees fast often, but your disciples **d** not fast?"
9:28 **"D** you believe that I am able to **d** this?"
10:19 **d** not worry about how you are to speak
10:28 **D** not fear those who kill the body but cannot kill
10:31 So **d** not be afraid; you are of more
10:34 **"D** not think that I have come to bring peace to
12: 2 your disciples are doing what is not lawful to **d** on
12:12 So it is lawful to **d** good on the sabbath."
12:27 by whom **d** your own exorcists cast them out?
13:10 "Why **d** you speak to them in parables?"
13:13 in parables is that 'seeing they **d** not perceive,
13:13 and hearing they **d** not listen,
13:13 not listen, nor **d** they understand.'
13:28 'Then **d** you want us to go and gather them?'
13:58 And he did not **d** many deeds of power there,

Mt 14:27 it is I; **d** not be afraid."
15: 2 "Why **d** your disciples break the tradition of
15: 2 For they **d** not wash their hands before they eat."
15: 3 "And why **d** you break the commandment of God
15: 9 in vain **d** they worship me,
15:12 "**D** you know that the Pharisees took offense
15:17 **D** you not see that whatever goes into
15:32 and I **d** not want to send them away hungry,
16: 9 **D** you still not perceive?
16: 9 **D** you not remember the five loaves for
16:13 "Who **d** people say that the Son of Man is?"
16:15 He said to them, "But who **d** you say that I am?"
17: 7 saying, "Get up and **d** not be afraid."
17:10 **d** the scribes say that Elijah must come first?"
17:25 Jesus spoke of it first, asking, "What **d** you think,
17:25 From whom **d** kings of the earth take toll
17:27 However, so that we **d** not give offense to them,
18:10 that you **d** not despise one of these little ones;
18:12 What **d** you think? If a shepherd has a hundred
18:35 So my heavenly Father will also **d** to every one
18:35 if you **d** not forgive your brother or sister
19:14 the little children come to me, and **d**
19:16 what good deed must I **d** to have eternal life?"
19:17 "Why **d** you ask me about what is good?
19:20 "I have kept all these; what **d** I still lack?"
20:15 not allowed to **d** what I choose with what belongs
20:21 And he said to her, "What **d** you want?"
20:22 "You **d** not know what you are asking.
20:32 saying, "What **d** you want me to **d** for you?"
21:16 "**D** you hear what these are saying?"
21:21 "Truly I tell you, if you have faith and **d** not doubt,
21:21 only will you **d** what has been done to the fig tree,
21:24 also tell you by what authority I **d** these things.
21:27 So they answered Jesus, "We **d** not know."
21:28 "What **d** you think? A man had two sons;
21:40 what will he **d** to those tenants?"
22:16 for you **d** not regard people with partiality.
22:42 "What **d** you think of the Messiah?
23: 3 **d** whatever they teach you and follow it; but **d** not
d as they **d**, for they **d** not practice what they teach.
23: 5 They **d** all their deeds to be seen by others;
23:13 For you **d** not go in yourselves,
24: 2 he asked them, "You see all these, **d** you not?
24:23 or 'There he is!'—**d** not believe it.
24:26 He is in the wilderness,' **d** not go out.
24:26 He is in the inner rooms,' **d** not believe it.
24:42 you **d** not know on what day your Lord is coming.
25:12 he replied, 'Truly I tell you, I **d** not know you.'
25:45 just as you did not **d** it to one of the least of these,
you did not **d** it to me.'
26:10 said to them, "Why **d** you trouble the woman?
26:17 "Where **d** you want us to make the preparations
26:50 "Friend, **d** what you are here to **d**."
26:53 **D** you think that I cannot appeal to my Father,
26:65 Why **d** we still need witnesses?
26:70 saying, "I **d** not know what you are talking about."
26:72 "I **d** not know the man."
26:74 and he swore an oath, "I **d** not know the man!"
27:13 "**D** you not hear how many accusations they make
27:17 "Whom **d** you want me to release for you,
27:19 "Have nothing to **d** with that innocent man,
27:21 of the two **d** you want me to release for you?"
27:22 "Then what should I **d** with Jesus who is called
27:24 So when Pilate saw that he could **d** nothing,
28: 5 But the angel said to the women, "**D** not be afraid;
28:10 Then Jesus said to them, "**D** not be afraid;
Mk 1:24 "What have you to **d** with us, Jesus of Nazareth?
1:38 for that is what I came out to **d**."
1:41 and said to him, "I **d** choose.
2: 8 "Why **d** you raise such questions in your hearts?
2:18 to him, "Why **d** John's disciples and the disciples
of the Pharisees fast, but your disciples **d** not fast?"
3: 4 to **d** good or to **d** harm on the sabbath,
4:13 "**D** you not understand this parable?
4:38 "Teacher, **d** you not care that we are perishing?"
5: 7 "What have you to **d** with me, Jesus,
5: 7 I adjure you by God, **d** not torment me."
5:36 "**D** not fear, only believe."
5:39 "Why **d** you make a commotion and weep?
6: 5 And he could **d** no deed of power there,
6:50 it is I; **d** not be afraid."
7: 3 **d** not eat unless they thoroughly wash their hands,
7: 4 and they **d** not eat anything from the market
7: 5 "Why **d** your disciples not live according to
7: 7 in vain **d** they worship me,
7:13 And you **d** many things like this."
7:18 "Then **d** you also fail to understand?
7:18 **D** you not see that whatever goes into a person
8: 5 He asked them, "How many loaves **d** you have?"
8:17 **D** you still not perceive or understand?
8:18 **D** you have eyes, and fail to see?
8:18 **D** you have ears, and fail to hear?
8:18 And **d** you not remember?
8:21 Then he said to them, "**D** you not yet understand?"
8:26 saying, "**D** not even go into the village."
8:27 "Who **d** people say that I am?"
8:29 He asked them, "But who **d** you say that I am?"
9:11 Then they asked him, "Why **d** the scribes say
9:18 to cast it out, but they could not **d** so."
9:22 but if you are able to **d** anything,
9:39 But Jesus said, "**D** not stop him;
10:14 Let the little children come to me; **d** not stop them;
10:17 what must I **d** to inherit eternal life?"
10:18 Jesus said to him, "Why **d** you call me good?
10:35 we want you to **d** for us whatever we ask of you."
10:36 "What is it you want me to **d** for you?"
10:38 "You **d** not know what you are asking.
Mk 10:51 "What **d** you want me to **d** for you?"
11:23 and if you **d** not doubt in your heart,
11:28 Who gave you this authority to **d** them?"
11:29 I will tell you by what authority I **d** these things.
11:33 So they answered Jesus, "We **d** not know."
12: 9 What then will the owner of the vineyard **d**?
12:14 for you **d** not regard people with partiality,
13: 2 Jesus asked him, "**D** you see these great buildings?
13: 7 When you hear of wars and rumors of wars, **d** not
13:11 **d** not worry beforehand about what you are to say;
13:21 There he is!'—**d** not believe it.
13:33 for you **d** not know when the time will come.
13:35 for you **d** not know when the master of
14: 6 Jesus said, "Let her alone; why **d** you trouble her?
14:12 "Where **d** you want us to go and make
14:63 "Why **d** we still need witnesses?
14:68 But he denied it, saying, "I **d** not know
14:71 "I **d** not know this man you are talking about."
15: 8 to ask Pilate to **d** for them according to his custom.
15: 9 "**D** you want me to release for you the King of
15:12 "Then what **d** you wish me to **d** with the man
16: 6 But he said to them, "**D** not be alarmed;
Lk 1:13 But the angel said to him, "**D** not be afraid,
1:30 The angel said to her, "**D** not be afraid, Mary,
2:10 But the angel said to them, "**D** not be afraid;
2:27 to **d** for him what was customary under the law,
3: 8 **D** not begin to say to yourselves,
3:10 the crowds asked him, "What then should we **d**?"
3:11 and whoever has food must **d** likewise."
3:12 and they asked him, "Teacher, what should we **d**?"
3:14 "And we, what should we **d**?"
3:14 "**D** not extort money from anyone by threats
4:12 '**D** not put the Lord your God to the test.' "
4:23 '**D** here also in your hometown the things
4:34 What have you to **d** with us, Jesus of Nazareth?
5:10 Then Jesus said to Simon, "**D** not be afraid;
5:13 touched him, and said, "I **d** choose.
5:22 "Why **d** you raise such questions in your hearts?
5:30 "Why **d** you eat and drink with tax collectors
6: 9 is it lawful to **d** good or to **d** harm on the sabbath,
6:11 and discussed with one another what they might **d**
6:27 Love your enemies, **d** good to those who hate you,
6:29 and from anyone who takes away your coat **d**
6:30 and if anyone takes away your goods, **d** not ask
6:31 **D** to others as you would have them **d** to you.
6:33 If you **d** good to those who **d** good to you,
6:33 For even sinners **d** the same.
6:35 But love your enemies, **d** good, and lend,
6:37 "**D** not judge, and you will not be judged;
6:37 **d** not condemn, and you will not be condemned.
6:41 Why **d** you see the speck in your neighbor's eye,
6:41 but **d** not notice the log in your own eye?
6:42 you yourself **d** not see the log in your own eye?
6:46 "Why **d** you call me 'Lord, Lord,' and **d** not **d**
what I tell you?
7: 4 "He is worthy of having you **d** this for him,
7: 6 "Lord, **d** not trouble yourself,
7: 8 'Come,' and he comes, and to my slave, '**D** this,'
7:13 for her and said to her, "**D** not weep."
7:44 he said to Simon, "**D** you see this woman?
8:18 and from those who **d** not have,
8:21 the word of God and **d** it."
8:28 "What have you to **d** with me, Jesus,
8:28 I beg you, **d** not torment me"—
8:49 **d** not trouble the teacher any longer."
8:50 When Jesus heard this, he replied, "**D** not fear.
8:52 "**D** not weep; for she is not dead but sleeping."
9: 5 Wherever they **d** not welcome you,
9:18 he asked them, "Who **d** the crowds say that I am?"
9:20 He said to them, "But who **d** you say that I am?"
9:50 But Jesus said to him, "**D** not stop him;
9:54 **d** you want us to command fire to come down
10: 7 **D** not move about from house to house.
10:10 But whenever you enter a town and they **d**
10:20 Nevertheless, **d** not rejoice at this,
10:25 he said, "what must I **d** to inherit eternal life?"
10:26 What **d** you read there?"
10:28 "You have given the right answer; **d** this,
10:36 Which of these three, **d** you think,
10:37 Jesus said to him, "Go and **d** likewise."
10:40 **d** you not care that my sister has left me to **d** all
11: 4 And **d** not bring us to the time of trial."
11: 7 And he answers from within, '**D** not bother me;
11:19 by whom **d** your exorcists cast them out?
11:46 and you yourselves **d** not lift a finger to ease them.
12: 4 my friends, **d** not fear those who kill the body,
12: 4 and after that can **d** nothing more.
12: 7 hairs of your head are all counted. **D** not be afraid;
12:11 **d** not worry about how you are
12:17 And he thought to himself, 'What should I **d**,
12:18 Then he said, 'I will **d** this:
12:22 "Therefore I tell you, **d** not worry about your life,
12:26 then you are not able to **d** so small a thing as that,
12:26 why **d** you worry about the rest?
12:29 And **d** not keep striving for what you are to eat
12:29 to eat and what you are to drink, and **d**
12:32 "**D** not be afraid, little flock,
12:33 Make purses for yourselves that **d** not wear out,
12:47 but did not prepare himself or **d** what was wanted,
12:51 **D** you think that I have come to bring peace to
12:56 but why **d** you not know how to interpret
12:57 why **d** you not judge for yourselves what is right?
13: 2 "**D** you think that because these Galileans suffered
13: 4 **d** you think that they were worse offenders than all
13:25 'I **d** not know where you come from.'
13:27 he will say, 'I **d** not know where you come from;
14: 8 **d** not sit down at the place of honor,
Lk 14:12 **d** not invite your friends or your brothers
14:33 of you can become my disciple if you **d** not give
16: 3 Then the manager said to himself, 'What will I **d**,
16: 4 I have decided what to **d** so that,
16: 5 'How much **d** you owe my master?'
16: 7 he asked another, 'And how much **d** you owe?'
16:26 to pass from here to you cannot **d** so,
16:31 'If they **d** not listen to Moses and the prophets,
17: 9 **D** you thank the slave for doing what was
17:10 you have done all that you were ordered to **d**,
17:23 **D** not go, **d** not set off in pursuit.
18:15 they sternly ordered them not to **d** it.
18:16 and said, "Let the little children come to me, and **d**
18:18 what must I **d** to inherit eternal life?"
18:19 Jesus said to him, "Why **d** you call me good?
18:41 "What **d** you want me to **d** for you?"
19:13 '**D** business with these until I come back.'
19:14 saying, 'We **d** not want this man to rule over us.'
19:48 but they did not find anything they could **d**,
20:13 the owner of the vineyard said, 'What shall I **d**?
20:15 then will the owner of the vineyard **d** to them?
21: 8 **D** not go after them.
21: 9 "When you hear of wars and insurrections, **d** not
22: 9 **d** you want us to make preparations for it?"
22:19 **D** this in remembrance of me."
22:23 which one of them it could be who would **d** this.
22:57 he denied it, saying, "Woman, I **d** not know him."
22:60 "Man, I **d** not know what you are talking about!"
22:71 they said, "What further testimony **d** we need?
23:28 "Daughters of Jerusalem, **d** not weep for me,
23:31 For if they **d** this when the wood is green,
23:34 ⟦for they **d** not know what they are doing."⟧
23:40 other rebuked him, saying, "**D** you not fear God,
24: 5 "Why **d** you look for the living among the dead?
24:38 and why **d** doubts arise in your hearts?
Jn 1:22 What **d** you say about yourself?"
1:26 Among you stands one whom you **d** not know,
1:50 "**D** you believe because I told you that I saw you
2: 5 "**D** whatever he tells you."
3: 2 for no one can **d** these signs that you **d** apart from
3: 7 **D** not be astonished that I said to you,
3: 8 but you **d** not know where it comes from or
3:10 and yet you **d** not understand these things?
3:11 yet you **d** not receive our testimony.
3:12 If I have told you about earthly things and you **d**
3:18 those who **d** not believe are condemned already,
3:20 For all who **d** evil hate the light and **d** not come
3:21 But those who **d** what is true come to the light,
4: 9 (Jews **d** not share things in common
4:11 Where **d** you get that living water?
4:22 You worship what you **d** not know;
4:27 but no one said, "What **d** you want?"
4:32 "I have food to eat that you **d** not know about."
4:34 "My food is to **d** the will of him who sent me and
4:35 **D** you not say, 'Four months more,
5: 6 he said to him, "**D** you want to be made well?"
5:14 **D** not sin any more, so that nothing worse happens
5:19 I tell you, the Son can **d** nothing on his own,
5:28 **D** not be astonished at this;
5:30 "I can **d** nothing on my own.
5:30 because I seek to **d** not my own will but the will
5:38 and you **d** not have his word abiding in you,
5:38 because you **d** not believe him whom he has sent.
5:41 I **d** not accept glory from human beings.
5:42 I know that you **d** not have the love of God in you.
5:43 and you **d** not accept me;
5:44 when you accept glory from one another and **d**
5:45 **D** not think that I will accuse you before
5:47 But if you **d** not believe what he wrote,
6: 6 for he himself knew what he was going to **d**.
6:20 But he said to them, "It is I; **d** not be afraid."
6:27 **D** not work for the food that perishes,
6:28 "What must we **d** to perform the works of God?"
6:36 But I said to you that you have seen me and yet **d**
6:38 not to **d** my own will,
6:43 "**D** not complain among yourselves.
6:64 But among you there are some who **d** not believe."
6:67 "**D** you also wish to go away?"
7: 4 If you **d** these things, show yourself to the world."
7:17 to **d** the will of God will know whether
7:24 **D** not judge by appearances,
7:28 one who sent me is true, and you **d** not know him.
7:31 will he **d** more signs than this man has done?"
8: 5 ⟦Now what **d** you say?"⟧
8:11 ⟦And Jesus said, "Neither **d** I condemn you.⟧
8:11 ⟦Go your way, and from now on **d** not sin again."⟧
8:14 but you **d** not know where I come from or
8:16 Yet even if I **d** judge, my judgment is valid;
8:25 Jesus said to them, "Why **d** I speak to you at all?
8:28 and that I **d** nothing on my own,
8:29 for I always **d** what is pleasing to him."
8:33 What **d** you mean by saying,
8:38 for you, you should **d** what you have heard from
8:43 Why **d** you not understand what I say?
8:44 and you choose to **d** your father's desires.
8:45 But because I tell the truth, you **d** not believe me.
8:46 If I tell the truth, why **d** you not believe me?
8:47 The reason you **d** not hear them is that you are not
8:49 Jesus answered, "I **d** not have a demon;
8:50 Yet I **d** not seek my own glory;
8:53 Who **d** you claim to be?"
8:55 though you **d** not know him.
8:55 if I would say that I **d** not know him,
8:55 But I **d** know him and I keep his word.
9:12 He said, "I **d** not know."
9:17 "What **d** you say about him?
9:21 but we **d** not know how it is that now he sees,

Jn 9:21 nor **d** we know who opened his eyes.
9:25 "I **d** not know whether he is a sinner.
9:25 One thing I **d** know, that though I was blind,
9:26 They said to him, "What did he **d** to you?
9:27 Why **d** you want to hear it again?
9:27 **D** you also want to become his disciples?"
9:29 we **d** not know where he comes from."
9:30 You **d** not know where he comes from,
9:33 this man were not from God, he could **d** nothing."
9:35 he said, **"D** you believe in the Son of Man?"
9:39 for judgment so that those who **d** not see may see,
9:39 and those who **d** see may become blind."
10: 5 because they **d** not know the voice of strangers."
10:16 I have other sheep that **d** not belong to this fold.
10:25 "I have told you, and you **d** not believe.
10:25 works that I **d** in my Father's name testify to me;
10:26 but you **d** not believe, because you do not belong
10:26 because you **d** not belong to my sheep.
10:37 If I am not doing the works of my Father, then **d**
10:38 But if I **d** them, even though you **d** not believe me,
11: 9 Those who walk during the day **d** not stumble,
11:26 in me will never die. **D** you believe this?"
11:47 and said, "What are we to **d?**
11:50 You **d** not understand that it is better for you
11:56 as they stood in the temple, "What **d** you think?
12: 8 but you **d** not always have me."
12:15 **"D** not be afraid, daughter
12:19 "You see, you can **d** nothing.
12:35 you **d** not know where you are going.
12:47 I **d** not judge anyone who hears my words
13: 7 "You **d** not know now what I am doing,
13:12 **"D** you know what I have done to you?
13:15 that you also should **d** as I have done to you.
13:17 you are blessed if you **d** them.
13:27 **"D** quickly what you are going to **d."**
14: 1 **"D** not let your hearts be troubled.
14: 5 "Lord, we **d** not know where you are going.
14: 7 now on you **d** know him and have seen him."
14: 9 Philip, and you still **d** not know me?
14:10 **D** you not believe that I am in the Father and
14:10 words that I say to you I **d** not speak on my own;
14:11 but if you **d** not, then believe me because of
14:12 the one who believes in me will also **d** the works
14:12 in me will also do the works that I **d** and,
14:12 in fact, will **d** greater works than these,
14:13 I will **d** whatever you ask in my name,
14:14 If in my name you ask me for anything, I will **d** it.
14:27 I **d** not give to you as the world gives.
14:27 **D** not let your hearts be troubled,
14:27 and **d** not let them be afraid.
14:31 but I **d** as the Father has commanded me,
15: 5 because apart from me you can **d** nothing.
15:14 You are my friends if you **d** what I command you.
15:15 I **d** not call you servants any longer,
15:19 Because you **d** not belong to the world,
15:21 But they will **d** all these things to you on account
15:21 because they **d** not know him who sent me.
16: 3 And they will **d** this because they have not known
16: 7 for if I **d** not go away,
16: 9 about sin, because they **d** not believe in me;
16:18 We **d** not know what he is talking about."
16:26 I **d** not say to you that I will ask the Father
16:30 and **d** not need to have anyone question you;
16:31 Jesus answered them, **"D** you now believe?
17: 4 by finishing the work that you gave me to **d.**
17:14 and the world has hated them because they **d**
17:14 just as I **d** not belong to the world.
17:16 They **d** not belong to the world,
17:16 just as I **d** not belong to the world.
18:21 Why **d** you ask me?
18:23 if I have spoken rightly, why **d** you strike me?"
18:29 "What accusation **d** you bring against this man?"
18:34 Jesus answered, **"D** you ask this on your own,
18:39 **D** you want me to release for you the King of
19:10 **"D** you refuse to speak to me?
19:10 **D** you not know that I have power to release you,
19:21 **"D** not write, 'The King of the Jews,' but,
20: 2 and we **d** not know where they have laid him."
20:13 and I **d** not know where they have laid him."
20:17 Jesus said to her, **"D** not hold on to me,
20:27 **D** not doubt but believe."
21:15 **d** you love me more than these?"
21:16 "Simon son of John, **d** you love me?"
21:17 "Simon son of John, **d** you love me?"
21:17 to him the third time, **"D** you love me?"
21:18 around you and take you where you **d** not wish
Ac 1:11 why **d** you stand looking up toward heaven?
2:37 "Brothers, what should we **d?"**
3:12 "You Israelites, why **d** you wonder at this,
3:12 or why **d** you stare at us,
4: 7 "By what power or by what name did you **d** this?"
4:16 They said, "What will we **d** with them?
4:28 to **d** whatever your hand
5:35 consider carefully what you propose to **d**
7:26 why **d** you wrong each other?'
7:28 **D** you want to kill me as you killed
7:40 we **d** not know what has happened to him.'
7:51 just as your ancestors used to **d.**
7:60 "Lord, **d** not hold this sin against them."
8:30 **"D** you understand what you are reading?"
9: 4 "Saul, Saul, why **d** you persecute me?"
9: 6 and you will be told what you are to **d."**
13:25 he said, 'What **d** you suppose that I am?
15:29 If you keep yourselves from these, you will **d** well.
16:28 **"D** not harm yourself, for we are all here."
16:30 "Sirs, what must I **d** to be saved?"
18: 9 **"D** not be afraid, but speak and **d** not be silent;

Ac 18:15 I **d** not wish to be a judge of these matters."
19:36 you ought to be quiet and **d** nothing rash.
20:10 and said, **"D** not be alarmed, for his life is in him."
20:24 But I **d** not count my life of any value to myself,
21:23 So **d** what we tell you.
21:37 The tribune replied, **"D** you know Greek?
22:10 I asked, 'What am I to **d,** Lord?'
22:10 that has been assigned to you to **d.'**
22:16 And now why **d** you delay?
22:26 "What are you about to **d?**
23: 4 **"D** you dare to insult God's high priest?"
23:15 to **d** away with him before he arrives."
23:21 But **d** not be persuaded by them,
24:16 Therefore I **d** my best always to have
25: 9 But Festus, wishing to **d** the Jews a favor,
25: 9 **"D** you wish to go up to Jerusalem and
26: 9 that I ought to **d** many things against the name
26:20 to God and **d** deeds consistent with repentance.
26:27 King Agrippa, **d** you believe the prophets?
27:24 and he said, **'D** not be afraid, Paul;
Ro 1:32 yet they not only **d** them but
2: 2 that God's judgment on those who **d** such things is
2: 3 **D** you imagine, whoever you are,
2: 3 that when you judge those who **d** such things
2: 3 yet **d** them yourself, you will escape the judgment
2: 4 Or **d** you despise the riches of his kindness
2: 4 **D** you not realize that God's kindness is meant
2:14 When Gentiles, who **d** not possess the law,
2:14 **d** instinctively what the law requires, these,
2:21 While you preach against stealing, **d** you steal?
2:22 You that forbid adultery, **d** you commit adultery?
2:22 You that abhor idols, **d** you rob temples?
2:23 **d** you dishonor God by breaking the law?
3: 8 "Let us **d** evil so that good may come"?
3:31 **D** we then overthrow the law by this faith?
4:17 and calls into existence the things that **d** not exist.
4:21 that God was able to **d** what he had promised.
6: 3 **D** you not know that all
6:12 **d** not let sin exercise dominion
6:16 **D** you not know that if you present yourselves
7: 1 **D** you not know, brothers and sisters—
7:15 I **d** not understand my own actions.
7:15 I **d** not **d** what I want, but I **d** the very thing I hate.
7:16 Now if I **d** what I **d** not want,
7:17 But in fact it is no longer I that **d** it,
7:18 I can will what is right, but I cannot **d** it.
7:19 For I **d** not **d** the good I want, but the evil I **d** not
want is what I **d.**
7:20 if I **d** what I **d** not want, it is no longer I that **d** it,
7:21 to be a law that when I want to **d** what is good,
8: 3 weakened by the flesh, could not **d:**
8:25 But if we hope for what we **d** not see,
8:26 for we **d** not know how to pray as we ought,
10: 6 **"D** not say in your heart,
11: 2 **D** you not know what the scripture says of Elijah,
11:18 **d** not boast over the branches.
11:18 If you **d** boast, remember that it is not you
11:20 So **d** not become proud, but stand in awe.
11:23 those of Israel, if they **d** not persist in unbelief,
12: 2 **D** not be conformed to this world,
12:11 **D** not lag in zeal, be ardent in spirit,
12:14 bless and **d** not curse them.
12:16 **d** not be haughty, but associate with the lowly;
12:16 **d** not claim to be wiser than you are.
12:17 **D** not repay anyone evil for evil,
12:21 **D** not be overcome by evil,
13: 3 **D** you wish to have no fear of the authority?
13: 3 **d** what is good, and you will receive its approval;
13: 4 But if you **d** what is wrong, you should be afraid,
14: 7 We **d** not live to ourselves, and we **d** not die to
14:10 Why **d** you pass judgment on your brother
14:10 Or you, why **d** you despise your brother or sister?
14:15 **D** not let what you eat cause the ruin of one
14:16 So **d** not let your good be spoken of as evil.
14:20 **D** not, for the sake of food,
14:21 not to eat meat or drink wine or **d** anything
14:23 because they **d** not act from faith;
15:20 so that I **d** not build on someone else's foundation,
15:24 For I **d** hope to see you on my journey and to
15:27 They were pleased to **d** this,
16:18 For such people **d** not serve our Lord Christ,
16:21 so **d** Lucius and Jason and Sosipater, my relatives.
1Co 1:16 I **d** not know whether I baptized anyone else.)
2: 6 Yet among the mature we **d** speak wisdom,
2:14 Those who are unspiritual **d** not receive the gifts
3:16 **D** you not know that you are God's temple and
3:18 **D** not deceive yourselves.
4: 3 I **d** not even judge myself.
4: 5 **d** not pronounce judgment before the time,
4: 7 What **d** you have that you did not receive?
4: 7 why **d** you boast as if it were not a gift?
4:15 you **d** not have many fathers.
5: 6 **D** you not know that a little yeast leavens
5:11 **D** not even eat with such a one.
5:12 For what have I to **d** with judging those outside?
6: 1 **d** you dare to take it to court before
6: 2 **D** you not know that the saints will judge
6: 3 **D** you not know that we are to judge angels—
6: 4 If you have ordinary cases, then, **d** you appoint
6: 9 **D** you not know that wrongdoers will not inherit
6: 9 **D** not be deceived!
6:15 **D** you not know that your bodies are members
6:16 **D** you not know that whoever is united to
6:19 Or **d** you not know that your body is a temple of
7: 5 **D** not deprive one another except perhaps
7:21 **D** not be concerned about it.
7:23 **d** not become slaves of human masters.

1Co 7:27 **D** not seek to be free.
7:27 **D** not seek a wife.
7:28 But if you marry, you **d** not sin,
7:37 to keep her as his fiancée, he will **d** well.
7:38 and he who refrains from marriage will **d** better.
8: 8 We are no worse off if we **d** not eat, and no better
off if we **d.**
9: 4 **D** we not have the right to our food and drink?
9: 5 **D** we not have the right to be accompanied by
9: 5 as **d** the other apostles and the brothers of the Lord
9: 8 **D** I say this on human authority?
9:12 If others share this rightful claim on you, **d**
9:13 **D** you not know that those who are employed in
9:16 and woe to me if I **d** not proclaim the gospel!
9:17 For if I **d** this of my own will, I have a reward;
9:23 I **d** it all for the sake of the gospel,
9:24 **D** you not know that in a race
9:25 they **d** it to receive a perishable wreath,
9:26 So I **d** not run aimlessly, nor **d** I box as though
10: 1 I **d** not want you to be unaware,
10: 7 **D** not become idolaters as some of them did;
10:10 And **d** not complain as some of them did,
10:12 watch out that you **d** not fall.
10:19 What **d** I imply then?
10:20 I **d** not want you to be partners with demons.
10:24 **D** not seek your own advantage,
10:28 then **d** not eat it, out of consideration for
10:31 whatever you **d, d** everything for the glory of God.
10:33 just as I try to please everyone in everything I **d,**
11:16 nor **d** the churches of God.
11:17 in the following instructions I **d** not commend you,
11:22 **D** you not have homes to eat and drink in?
11:22 Or **d** you show contempt for the church of God
11:22 In this matter I **d** not commend you!
11:24 **D** this in remembrance of me."
11:25 **D** this, as often as you drink it,
12: 1 I **d** not want you to be uninformed.
12:15 I **d** not belong to the body,"
12:16 I **d** not belong to the body,"
12:24 whereas our more respectable members **d**
12:29 Are all teachers? **D** all work miracles?
12:30 **D** all possess gifts of healing? **D** all speak in
tongues? **D** all interpret?
13: 1 of mortals and of angels, but **d** not have love,
13: 2 so as to remove mountains, but **d** not have love,
13: 3 but **d** not have love, I gain nothing.
14: 2 in a tongue **d** not speak to other people but to God;
14: 7 If they **d** not give distinct notes,
14:11 If then I **d** not know the meaning of a sound,
14:15 What should I **d** then?
14:20 **d** not be children in your thinking;
14:39 and **d** not forbid speaking in tongues;
15:29 what will those people **d** who receive baptism
15:33 **D** not be deceived: "Bad company ruins good
15:35 With what kind of body **d** they come?"
15:37 you **d** not sow the body that is to be,
16: 7 I **d** not want to see you now just in passing,
16:14 Let all that you **d** be done in love.
2Co 1: 8 We **d** not want you to be unaware,
1:17 Was I vacillating when I wanted to **d** this?
1:17 **D** I make my plans according
1:24 I **d** not mean to imply that we lord it
2:11 And we **d** this so that we may not be outwitted
3: 1 Surely we **d** not need, as some **d,**
3: 1 of recommendation to you or from you, **d** we?
4: 1 that we are engaged in this ministry, we **d**
4: 5 For we **d** not proclaim ourselves;
4:16 So we **d** not lose heart.
5: 8 Yes, we **d** have confidence,
6:14 **D** not be mismatched with unbelievers.
7: 3 I **d** not say this to condemn you,
7: 8 I **d** not regret it (though I did regret it,
8: 8 I **d** not say this as a command,
8:10 not only to **d** something but even to desire to **d**
something—
8:13 I **d** not mean that there should be relief for others
8:21 to **d** what is right not only in the Lord's sight but
10: 3 we **d** not wage war according to human standards;
10: 7 that just as you belong to Christ, so also **d** we.
10: 9 I **d** not want to seem as though I am trying
10:11 we will also **d** when present.
10:12 We **d** not dare to classify or compare ourselves
10:12 they **d** not show good sense.
10:15 We **d** not boast beyond limits, that is,
11: 1 in a little foolishness. **D** bear with me!
11:11 Because I **d** not love you?
11:11 not love you? God knows I **d!**
11:12 And what I **d** I will also continue to **d,**
11:16 but if you **d,** then accept me as a fool,
11:31 knows that I **d** not lie.
12: 2 in the body or out of the body I **d** not know;
12: 3 in the body or out of the body I **d** not know;
12:14 because I **d** not want what is yours but you;
12:19 Everything we **d,** beloved, is for the sake of
13: 5 **D** you not realize that Jesus Christ is in you?—
13: 7 that you may not **d** anything wrong—
13: 7 but that you may **d** what is right,
13: 8 For we cannot **d** anything against the truth,
Gal 1:20 In what I am writing to you, before God, I **d**
2:10 which was actually what I was eager to **d.**
2:21 I **d** not nullify the grace of God;
5: 1 and **d** not submit again to a yoke of slavery.
5:13 only **d** not use your freedom as an opportunity
5:16 I say, and **d** not gratify the desires of the flesh.
5:21 those who **d** such things will not inherit
6: 7 **D** not be deceived; God is
6: 9 if we **d** not give up.

Gal 6:13 the circumcised **d** not themselves obey the law,
Eph 1:16 I **d** not cease to give thanks for you
4:26 Be angry but **d** not sin; **d** not let the sun go down
4:27 and **d** not make room for the devil.
4:30 And **d** not grieve the Holy Spirit of God,
5: 7 Therefore **d** not be associated with them.
5:12 even to mention what such people **d** secretly;
5:17 So **d** not be foolish, but understand what the will
5:18 **D** not get drunk with wine, for that is debauchery;
5:28 as they **d** their own bodies.
6: 4 And, fathers, **d** not provoke your children to anger,
6: 8 knowing that whatever good we **d,**
6: 9 And, masters, **d** the same to them.
Php 1:22 and I **d** not know which I prefer.
2: 3 **D** nothing from selfish ambition or conceit,
2:14 **D** all things without murmuring and arguing,
3:13 I **d** not consider that I have made it my own;
3:13 but this one thing I **d:**
4: 6 **D** not worry about anything,
4:13 I can **d** all things through him who strengthens me.
Col 2:16 Therefore **d** not let anyone condemn you
2:18 **D** not let anyone disqualify you,
2:20 why **d** you live as if you still belonged to
2:20 Why **d** you submit to regulations,
2:21 **"D** not handle, **D** not taste, **D** not touch"?
3: 9 **D** not lie to one another,
3:17 whatever you **d,** in word or deed, **d** everything in the name of the Lord Jesus,
3:21 Fathers, **d** not provoke your children,
1Th 2: 8 So deeply **d** we care for you
4: 1 you are doing), you should **d** so more and more.
4: 5 like the Gentiles who **d** not know God;
4: 9 you **d** not need to have anyone write to you,
4:10 and indeed you **d** love all the brothers and sisters
4:10 But we urge you, beloved, to **d** so more and more,
4:13 But we **d** not want you to be uninformed,
4:13 you may not grieve as others **d** who have no hope.
5: 1 you **d** not need to have anything written to you.
5: 6 So then let us not fall asleep as others **d,**
5:15 always seek to **d** good to one another and to all.
5:19 **D** not quench the Spirit.
5:20 **D** not despise the words of prophets,
5:24 one who calls you is faithful, and he will **d** this.
2Th 1: 8 inflicting vengeance on those who **d** not know God and on those who **d** not obey
2: 5 **D** you not remember that I told you these things
3: 9 This was not because we **d** not have that right,
3:12 the Lord Jesus Christ to **d** their work quietly and
3:13 **d** not be weary in doing what is right.
3:14 of those who **d** not obey what we say in this letter;
3:14 have nothing to **d** with them,
3:15 **D** not regard them as enemies,
1Ti 4: 7 to **d** with profane myths and old wives' tales.
4:14 **D** not neglect the gift that is in you,
5: 1 **D** not speak harshly to an older man,
5:22 **D** not ordain anyone hastily,
5:22 and **d** not participate in the sins of others;
6:18 They are to **d** good, to be rich in good works,
2Ti 1: 8 **D** not be ashamed, then, of the testimony
1:12 and for this reason I suffer as I **d.**
2:15 **D** your best to present yourself to God
2:23 to **d** with stupid and senseless controversies;
2:26 having been held captive by him to **d** his will.
4: 5 endure suffering, **d** the work of an evangelist,
4: 9 **D** your best to come to me soon,
4:21 **D** your best to come before winter.
4:21 as **d** Pudens and Linus and Claudia and all
Tit 3:10 to **d** with anyone who causes divisions,
3:12 **d** your best to come to me at Nicopolis,
Phm 1: 6 when you perceive all the good that we may **d**
1: 8 in Christ to command you to **d** your duty,
1: 9 and I, Paul, **d** this as an old man,
1:14 but I preferred to **d** nothing without your consent,
1:21 knowing that you will **d** even more than I say.
1:24 and so **d** Mark, Aristarchus, Demas,
Heb 2: 1 so that we **d** not drift away from it.
2: 8 we **d** not yet see everything in subjection to them,
2: 9 but we **d** see Jesus, who for a little
3: 8 **d** not harden your hearts as in the rebellion,
3:15 **d** not harden your hearts as in the rebellion."
4: 7 if you hear his voice, **d** not harden your hearts."
4:15 For we **d** not have a high priest who is unable
6: 3 And we will **d** this, if God permits.
6:10 for his sake in serving the saints, as you still **d.**
10: 7 Then I said, 'See, God, I have come to **d** your will,
10: 9 "See, I have come to **d** your will."
10:29 How much worse punishment **d** you think will
10:35 **D** not, therefore, abandon that confidence
11:29 Egyptians attempted to **d** so they were drowned.
12: 5 **d** not regard lightly the discipline of the Lord,
12: 8 If you **d** not have that discipline
12:25 See that you **d** not refuse the one who is speaking;
13: 2 **D** not neglect to show hospitality to strangers,
13: 6 What can anyone **d** to me?"
13: 9 **D** not be carried away by all kinds
13:16 **D** not neglect to **d** good and to share what you
13:17 Let them **d** this with joy and not with sighing—
13:19 I urge you all the more to **d** this,
13:21 in everything good so that you may **d** his will,
Jas 1:16 **D** not be deceived, my beloved.
1:26 **d** not bridle their tongues but deceive their hearts,
2: 1 **d** you with your acts of favoritism really believe
2: 8 You **d** well if you really fulfill the royal law
2:11 if you **d** not commit adultery but if you murder,
2:14 if you say you have faith but **d** not have works?
2:16 and yet you **d** not supply their bodily needs,
2:19 You believe that God is one; you **d** well.
Jas 2:20 **D** you want to be shown, you senseless person,
3:14 **d** not be boastful and false to the truth.
4: 1 where **d** they come from?
4: 1 **D** they not come from your cravings that are
4: 2 You want something and **d** not have it;
4: 2 You **d** not have, because you **d** not ask.
4: 3 You ask and **d** not receive,
4: 4 **D** you not know that friendship with
4: 5 Or **d** you suppose that it is for nothing that
4:11 **D** not speak evil against one another,
4:14 you **d** not even know what tomorrow will bring.
4:15 we will live and **d** this or that."
4:17 who knows the right thing to **d** and fails to **d** it,
5: 9 Beloved, **d** not grumble against one another,
5:12 Above all, my beloved, **d** not swear,
1Pe 1: 8 and even though you **d** not see him now,
1:14 **d** not be conformed to the desires
2: 7 but for those who **d** not believe,
2: 8 as they were destined to **d.**
2:14 to punish those who **d** wrong and to praise those who **d** right.
2:16 yet **d** not use your freedom as a pretext for evil.
2:20 if you endure when you **d** right and suffer for it,
3: 1 so that, even if some of them **d** not obey the word,
3: 3 **D** not adorn yourselves outwardly
3: 6 as long as you **d** what is good
3: 9 **D** not repay evil for evil or abuse for abuse;
3:11 let them turn away from evil and **d** good;
3:12 the face of the Lord is against those who **d** evil."
3:13 if you are eager to **d** what is good?
3:14 But even if you **d** suffer for doing what is right,
3:14 **D** not fear what they fear, and **d** not be intimidated,
3:16 yet **d** it with gentleness and reverence.
4: 3 in doing what the Gentiles like to **d,**
4:11 Whoever speaks must **d** so as one speaking
4:11 whoever serves must **d** so with the strength
4:12 **d** not be surprised at the fiery ordeal
4:16 **d** not consider it a disgrace,
4:17 be the end for those who **d** not obey the gospel
4:19 while continuing to **d** good.
5: 2 as God would have you **d** it—
5: 3 **D** not lord it over those in your charge,
2Pe 1:10 for if you **d** this, you will never stumble.
1:19 You will **d** well to be attentive to this as to
2:11 **d** not bring against them a slanderous judgment
2:12 They slander what they **d** not understand,
3: 8 But **d** not ignore this one fact, beloved,
3:16 as they **d** the other scriptures.
1Jn 1: 6 we lie and **d** not **d** what is true;
2:15 **D** not love the world or the things in the world.
2:17 but those who **d** the will of God live forever.
2:21 not because you **d** not know the truth,
2:27 and so you **d** not need anyone to teach you.
3: 2 What we **d** know is this:
3: 9 Those who have been born of God **d** not sin,
3:10 all who **d** not **d** what is right are not from God,
3:10 are those who **d** not love their brothers and sisters.
3:13 **D** not be astonished, brothers and sisters,
3:15 that murderers **d** not have eternal life abiding
3:21 Beloved, if our hearts **d** not condemn us,
3:22 obey his commandments and **d** what pleases him.
4: 1 Beloved, **d** not believe every spirit,
4:14 and **d** testify that the Father has sent his Son as
4:18 for fear has to **d** with punishment,
4:20 for those who **d** not love a brother
5:10 Those who **d** not believe in God have made him
5:16 I **d** not say that you should pray about that.
5:18 We know that those who are born of God **d**
2Jn 1: 7 into the world, those who **d** not confess
1: 8 so that you **d** not lose what we have worked for,
1:10 **D** not receive into the house
3Jn 1: 5 you **d** faithfully whatever you **d** for the friends,
1: 6 You will **d** well to send them on in
1:10 and even prevents those who want to **d** so
1:11 **d** not imitate what is evil but imitate what is good.
Jude 1:10 But these people slander whatever they **d**
Rev 1:17 But he placed his right hand on me, saying, **"D** not
2: 5 repent, and **d** the works you did at first.
2:10 **D** not fear what you are about to suffer.
2:24 who **d** not hold this teaching,
2:24 to you I say, I **d** not lay on you any other burden;
2:26 to **d** my works to the end, I will give authority
3: 3 If you **d** not wake up, I will come like a thief,
3:17 You **d** not realize that you are wretched, pitiable,
5: 5 Then one of the elders said to me, **"D** not weep.
6: 6 but **d** not damage the olive oil and the wine!"
7: 3 **"D** not damage the earth or the sea or the trees,
9: 4 but only those people who **d** not have the seal
10: 4 and **d** not write it down."
11: 2 but **d** not measure the court outside the temple;
18: 4 my people, so that you **d** not take part in her sins,
18: 4 and so that you **d** not share in her plagues;
19:10 but he said to me, "You must not **d** that!
22: 9 but he said to me, "You must not **d** that!
22:10 **"D** not seal up the words of the prophecy
22:11 Let the evildoer still **d** evil,
22:11 and the righteous still **d** right,
Tob 3: 3 **D** not punish me for my sins and
3: 6 release me to go to the eternal home, and **d** not,
3: 9 Why **d** you beat us?
4: 2 Why **d** I not call my son Tobias and explain to him
4: 3 and **d** not abandon her all the days of her life.
4: 3 **D** whatever pleases her, and **d** not grieve her
4: 5 and **d** not walk in the ways of wrongdoing;
4: 7 and **d** not let your eye begrudge the gift
4: 7 **D** not turn your face away
4: 8 if few, **d** not be afraid to give according to
Tob 4:12 **d** not marry a foreign woman,
4:13 and in your heart **d** not disdain your kindred,
4:14 **"D** not keep over until the next day the wages
4:14 "Watch yourself, my son, in everything you **d,**
4:15 And what you hate, **d** not **d** to anyone.
4:15 **D** not drink wine to excess or let drunkenness go
4:16 **d** not let your eye begrudge your giving of alms.
4:18 Seek advice from every wise person and **d**
4:19 and **d** not let them be erased from your heart.
4:21 **D** not be afraid, my son,
4:21 from every sin and **d** what is good in the sight of
5: 1 "I will **d** everything that you have commanded me,
5: 2 since he does not know me and I **d** not know him?
5: 2 Also, I **d** not know the roads to Media,
5: 5 Tobias said to him, "Where **d** you come from,
5: 5 **"D** you know the way to go to Media?"
5: 7 for I **d** need you to travel with me,
5: 8 but **d** not take too long."
5:12 He replied, "Why **d** you need to know my tribe?"
5:14 **D** not feel bitter toward me, brother,
5:16 "I will go with him; so **d** not fear.
5:19 **D** not heap money upon money,
5:21 Tobit said to her, **"D** not worry;
5:21 **D** not fear for them, my sister.
6:16 **"D** you not remember your father's orders
6:18 **D** not be afraid, for she was set apart for you
7: 4 **"D** you know our kinsman Tobit?"
7:11 So Raguel said, "I will **d** so.
10: 6 **D** not grieve for him, my dear;
10: 7 for I know that my father and mother **d** not believe
10:12 **d** nothing to grieve her all the days of your life.
12: 2 It would **d** no harm to give him half of
12: 6 **D** not be slow to acknowledge him.
12: 7 **D** good and evil will not overtake you.
12:10 and **d** wrong are their own worst enemies.
12:17 But he said to them, **"D** not be afraid;
13: 6 to **d** what is true before him,
13: 6 you sinners, and **d** what is right before him;
14:8,9 serve God faithfully and **d** what is pleasing
14:8,9 be commanded to **d** what is right and to give alms,
14:8,9 now, my son, leave Nineveh; **d** not remain here.
14:10 **d** not stay overnight within the confines of
Jdt 2:13 as I have ordered you; **d** it without delay."
2:15 by divisions as his lord had ordered him to **d,**
3: 2 **D** with us whatever you will.
3: 3 **d** with them as you please.
5: 3 What towns **d** they inhabit?
6: 9 then **d** not look downcast!
6:17 that Holofernes had boasted he would **d** against
7:10 **d** not rely on their spears but on the height of
7:11 **d** not fight against them in regular formation,
7:16 and he gave orders to **d** as they had said.
7:28 **d** today the things that we have described!"
7:31 and no help comes for us, I will **d** as you say."
8:14 how **d** you expect to search out God,
8:14 No, my brothers, **d** not anger the Lord our God.
8:16 **D** not try to bind the purposes of
8:30 to **d** for them what we have promised,
8:32 I am about to **d** something that will go down
8:34 Only, **d** not try to find out what I am doing;
8:34 until I have finished what I am about to **d."**
9: 7 They **d** not know that you are
9: 9 a widow, the strong hand to **d** what I plan.
10:12 They asked her, "To what people **d** you belong,
11: 1 woman, and **d** not be afraid in your heart,
11: 4 all will treat you well, as they **d** the servants
11: 7 only **d** human beings serve him because of you,
11:10 lord and master, **d** not disregard what he said,
11:11 to anger when they **d** what is wrong.
11:23 If you **d** as you have said,
12:12 If we **d** not seduce her, she will laugh at us."
12:14 Whatever pleases him I will **d** at once,
13:10 as they were accustomed to **d** for prayer.
14: 2 against the Assyrian outpost; only **d** not go down.
14: 5 But before you **d** all this,
AdE 3: 2 So all who were at court used to **d** obeisance
3: 2 Mordecai, however, did not **d** obeisance.
3: 3 why **d** you disobey the king's command?"
3: 8 and they **d** not keep the laws of the king.
3:11 and **d** whatever you want with that nation."
4:13 **d** not say to yourself that you alone among all
4:16 for three days and nights **d** not eat or drink,
4:17 and did what Esther had told him to **d.**
5: 3 The king said to her, "What **d** you wish, Esther?
5: 5 so that we may **d** as Esther desires."
5: 8 and tomorrow I will **d** as I have done today."
6: 6 "What shall I **d** for the person whom I wish
6:10 **D** just as you have said for Mordecai the Jew,
7: 5 the person that would dare to **d** this thing?"
8: 7 against the Jews, what else **d** you request?
9:12 What **d** you suppose they have done in
9:13 "Let the Jews be allowed to **d** the same tomorrow.
11:12 in this dream what God had determined to **d,**
13:14 and I will not **d** these things in pride.
13:16 **D** not neglect your portion,
13:17 **d** not destroy the lips of those who praise you."
14:11 **d** not surrender your scepter to what has no being;
14:11 and **d** not let them laugh at our downfall;
14:16 I **d** not wear it on the days when I am at leisure.
16: 2 the more proud **d** they become,
16:17 "You will therefore **d** well not to put in execution
Wis 1: 2 he is found by those who **d** not put him to the test,
1: 2 manifests himself to those who **d** not distrust him.
1:12 **D** not invite death by the error of your life,
7:13 I **d** not hide her wealth,
7:27 Although she is but one, she can **d** all things,
9: 4 and **d** not reject me from among your servants.

Wis 11:23 you are merciful to all, for you can **d** all things,
Sir 1:28 **D** not disobey the fear of the Lord;
1:28 **d** not approach him with a divided mind.
1:29 **D** not be a hypocrite before others,
1:30 **D** not exalt yourself, or you may fall
2: 2 and **d** not be impetuous in time of calamity.
2: 3 Cling to him and **d** not depart,
2: 7 **d** not stray, or else you may fall.
2:14 will you **d** when the Lord's reckoning comes?
2:15 Those who fear the Lord **d** not disobey his words,
3:10 **D** not glorify yourself by dishonoring your father,
3:12 and **d** not grieve him as long as he lives;
3:13 you have all your faculties **d** not despise him.
3:23 **D** not meddle in matters that are beyond you,
4: 1 My child, **d** not cheat the poor of their living,
4: 1 and **d** not keep needy eyes waiting.
4: 2 **D** not grieve the hungry, or anger one in need.
4: 3 **D** not add to the troubles of the desperate,
4: 4 **D** not reject a suppliant in distress,
4: 5 **D** not avert your eye from the needy,
4: 9 and **d** not be hesitant in giving a verdict.
4:20 and **d** not be ashamed to be yourself.
4:22 **D** not show partiality, to your own harm,
4:23 **D** not refrain from speaking at the proper moment,
4:23 and **d** not hide your wisdom.
4:26 **D** not be ashamed to confess your sins,
4:26 and **d** not try to stop the current of a river.
4:27 **D** not subject yourself to a fool,
4:29 **D** not be reckless in your speech,
4:30 **D** not be like a lion in your home,
4:31 **D** not let your hand be stretched out to receive
5: 1 **D** not rely on your wealth, or say,
5: 2 **D** not follow your inclination and strength
5: 3 **D** not say, "Who can have power over me?"
5: 4 **D** not say, "I sinned, yet what has happened
5: 5 **D** not be so confident of forgiveness
5: 6 **D** not say, "His mercy is great,
5: 7 **D** not delay to turn back to the Lord,
5: 7 and **d** not postpone it from day to day;
5: 8 **D** not depend on dishonest wealth,
5: 9 **D** not winnow in every wind, or follow every path.
5:14 **D** not be called double-tongued and **d** not lay traps
6: 1 and **d** not become an enemy instead of a friend;
6: 2 **D** not fall into the grip of passion,
6: 7 and **d** not trust them hastily.
6:23 and accept my judgment; **d** not reject my counsel.
6:25 and **d** not fret under her bonds.
6:27 and when you get hold of her, **d** not let her go.
7: 1 **D** no evil, and evil will never overtake you.
7: 3 **D** not sow in the furrows of injustice,
7: 4 **D** not seek from the Lord high office,
7: 5 **D** not assert your righteousness before the Lord,
7: 6 **D** not seek to become a judge,
7: 7 and **d** not disgrace yourself among the people.
7: 8 **D** not commit a sin twice;
7: 9 **D** not say, "He will consider the great number
7:10 **D** not grow weary when you pray;
7:10 **d** not neglect to give alms.
7:11 **D** not ridicule a person who is embittered in spirit,
7:12 **D** not devise a lie against your brother,
7:12 or **d** the same to a friend.
7:14 **D** not babble in the assembly of the elders,
7:14 and **d** not repeat yourself when you pray.
7:15 **D** not hate hard labor or farm work,
7:16 **D** not enroll in the ranks of sinners;
7:18 **D** not exchange a friend for money,
7:19 **D** not dismiss a wise and good wife,
7:20 **D** not abuse slaves who work faithfully,
7:21 **d** not withhold from them their freedom.
7:22 **D** you have cattle?
7:23 **D** you have children? Discipline them,
7:24 **D** you have daughters?
7:24 and **d** not show yourself too indulgent with them.
7:26 **D** you have a wife who pleases you? **D** not divorce
7:26 but **d** not trust yourself to one whom you detest.
7:27 and **d** not forget the birth pangs of your mother.
7:30 and **d** not neglect his ministers.
7:33 **d** not withhold kindness even from the dead.
7:34 **D** not avoid those who weep,
7:35 **D** not hesitate to visit the sick,
7:36 In all you **d**, remember the end of your life,
8: 1 **D** not contend with the powerful,
8: 2 **D** not quarrel with the rich,
8: 3 **D** not argue with the loud of mouth,
8: 3 and **d** not heap wood on their fire.
8: 4 **D** not make fun of one who is ill-bred,
8: 5 **D** not reproach one who is turning away from sin;
8: 6 **D** not disdain one who is old,
8: 7 **D** not rejoice over any one's death;
8: 8 **D** not slight the discourse of the sages,
8: 9 **D** not ignore the discourse of the aged,
8:10 **D** not kindle the coals of sinners,
8:11 **D** not let the insolent bring you to your feet,
8:12 **D** not lend to one who is stronger than you;
8:12 but if you **d** lend anything, count it as a loss.
8:13 **D** not give surety beyond your means;
8:14 **D** not go to law against a judge,
8:15 **D** not go traveling with the reckless,
8:16 **D** not pick a fight with the quick-tempered,
8:16 **d** not journey with them through lonely country,
8:17 **D** not consult with fools, for they cannot keep
8:18 In the presence of strangers **d** nothing that is to
8:18 for you **d** not know what they will divulge.
8:19 **D** not reveal your thoughts to anyone,
9: 1 **D** not be jealous of the wife of your bosom,
9: 2 **D** not give yourself to a woman
9: 3 **D** not go near a loose woman,
Sir 9: 4 **D** not dally with a singing girl,
9: 5 **D** not look intently at a virgin,
9: 6 **D** not give yourself to prostitutes,
9: 7 **D** not look around in the streets of a city,
9: 8 and **d** not gaze at beauty belonging to another;
9:10 **D** not abandon old friends,
9:11 **D** not envy the success of sinners,
9:11 for you **d** not know what their end will be like.
9:12 **D** not delight in what pleases the ungodly;
10: 6 **D** not get angry with your neighbor
10: 6 and **d** not resort to acts of insolence.
10:26 **D** not make a display of your wisdom when you **d** your work,
10:26 and **d** not boast when you are in need.
11: 2 **D** not praise individuals for their good looks,
11: 4 **D** not boast about wearing fine clothes,
11: 4 and **d** not exalt yourself when you are honored;
11: 7 **D** not find fault before you investigate;
11: 8 **D** not answer before you listen,
11: 8 and **d** not interrupt when another is speaking.
11: 9 **D** not argue about a matter that does
11: 9 and **d** not sit with sinners when they judge a case.
11:10 My child, **d** not busy yourself with many matters;
11:21 **D** not wonder at the works of a sinner,
11:23 **D** not say, "What **d** I need,
11:24 **D** not say, "I have enough,
11:29 **D** not invite everyone into your home,
12: 1 If you **d** good, know to whom you **d** it,
12: 2 **D** good to the devout, and you will be repaid—
12: 4 Give to the devout, but **d** not help the sinner.
12: 5 **D** good to the humble, but **d** not give to the ungodly;
12: 5 hold back their bread, and **d** not give it to them,
12: 7 but **d** not help the sinner.
12:12 **D** not put him next to you,
12:12 **D** not let him sit at your right hand,
13: 2 **D** not lift a weight too heavy for you,
13: 6 to you kindly and say, "What **d** you need?"
13:10 **D** not be forward, or you may be rebuffed;
13:10 **d** not stand aloof, or you will be forgotten.
13:11 **D** not try to treat him as an equal,
13:12 Cruel are those who **d** not keep your secrets;
14: 1 Happy are those who **d** not blunder with their lips,
14: 2 Happy are those whose hearts **d**
14:13 **D** good to friends before you die,
14:14 **D** not deprive yourself of a day's enjoyment;
14:14 **d** not let your share of desired good pass by you.
15: 1 Whoever fears the Lord will **d** this,
15:11 **D** not say, "It was the Lord's doing
15:11 for he does not **d** what he hates.
15:12 **D** not say, "It was he who led me astray";
16: 1 **D** not desire a multitude of worthless children,
16: 1 and **d** not rejoice in ungodly offspring.
16: 2 If they multiply, **d** not rejoice in them,
16: 3 **D** not trust in their survival,
16:17 **D** not say, "I am hidden from the Lord,
16:27 and they **d** not abandon their tasks.
16:28 They **d** not crowd one another,
18:15 **d** not mix reproach with your good deeds,
18:22 and **d** not wait until death to be released from it.
18:23 **d** not be like one who puts the Lord to the test.
18:30 **D** not follow your base desires,
18:32 **D** not revel in great luxury,
18:33 **D** not become a beggar by feasting
19: 8 With friend or foe **d** not report it,
19: 8 unless it would be a sin for you, **d** not reveal it;
19:13 Question a friend; perhaps he did not **d** it;
19:13 or if he did, so that he may not **d** it again.
19:15 so **d** not believe everything you hear.
19:28 nevertheless **d** evil when he finds the opportunity.
21: 1 **D** so no more, but ask forgiveness for your
22:13 **D** not talk much with a senseless person or visit
22:21 **d** not despair, for there is a way back.
22:22 **d** not worry, for reconciliation is possible.
23: 1 **d** not abandon me to their designs,
23: 1 and **d** not let me fall because of them!
23: 4 **d** not give me haughty eyes,
23: 6 and **d** not give me over to shameless passion.
23: 9 **D** not accustom your mouth to oaths,
23:13 **D** not accustom your mouth to coarse,
25:21 **D** not be ensnared by a woman's beauty,
25:21 and **d** not desire a woman for her possessions.
26:11 and **d** not be surprised if she sins against you.
26:19 *and **d** not give your strength to strangers.*
27: 4 so **d** a person's faults when he speaks.
27: 7 **D** not praise anyone before he speaks,
27:17 if you betray his secrets, **d** not follow after him.
27:20 **D** not go after him, for he is too far off,
28: 7 and **d** not be angry with your neighbor;
29: 8 and **d** not keep him waiting for your alms.
29: 9 in their need **d** not send them away empty-handed.
29:10 and **d** not let it rust under a stone and be lost.
29:15 **D** not forget the kindness of your guarantor,
30:10 **D** not laugh with him, or you will have sorrow
30:11 and **d** not ignore his errors.
30:21 **D** not give yourself over to sorrow,
30:21 and **d** not distress yourself deliberately.
31:10 and to **d** evil and did not **d** it?
31:12 **D** not be greedy at it, and **d** not say,
31:14 **D** not reach out your hand for everything you see,
31:14 and **d** not crowd your neighbor at the dish.
31:16 and **d** not chew greedily, or you will give offense.
31:17 and **d** not be insatiable, or you will give offense.
31:18 **d** not help yourself before they do.
31:18 do not help yourself before they **d**.
31:22 Listen to me, my child, and **d** not disregard me,
31:22 In everything you **d** be moderate,
Sir 31:25 **D** not try to prove your strength by wine-drinking,
31:31 **D** not reprove your neighbor at a banquet of wine,
31:31 and **d** not despise him in his merrymaking;
31:31 and **d** not distress him by making demands of him.
32: 1 If they make you master of the feast, **d**
32: 3 and **d** not interrupt the music.
32: 4 Where there is entertainment, **d** not pour out talk;
32: 4 **d** not display your cleverness at the wrong time.
32: 9 Among the great **d** not act as their equal;
32: 9 and when another is speaking, **d** not babble.
32:11 Leave in good time and **d** not be the last;
32:11 go home quickly and **d** not linger.
32:12 but **d** not sin through proud speech.
32:19 **D** nothing without deliberation,
32:19 but when you have acted, **d** not regret it.
32:20 **D** not go on a path full of hazards,
32:20 and **d** not stumble at an obstacle twice.
32:21 **D** not be overconfident on a smooth road,
33:20 **d** not give power over yourself,
33:20 and **d** not give your property to another,
33:21 **d** not let anyone take your place.
33:23 Excel in all that you **d**;
33:30 **D** not be overbearing toward anyone,
33:30 toward anyone, and **d** nothing unjust.
34:28 what **d** they gain but hard work?
35: 6 **D** not appear before the Lord empty-handed,
35:10 and **d** not stint the first fruits of your hands.
35:14 **D** not offer him a bribe, for he will not accept it;
35:15 and **d** not rely on a dishonest sacrifice;
35:18 **D** not the tears of the widow run down her cheek
37: 6 **D** not forget a friend during the battle,
37: 6 and **d** not be unmindful of him
37:10 **D** not consult the one who regards you
37:11 **D** not consult with a woman about her rival or
37:27 see what is bad for you and **d** not give in to it.
37:29 **D** not be greedy for every delicacy,
37:29 and **d** not eat without restraint;
38: 9 My child, when you are ill, **d** not delay,
38:12 **d** not let him leave you, for you need him.
38:16 and **d** not neglect the burial.
38:20 **D** not give your heart to grief;
38:21 **D** not forget, there is no coming back;
38:21 you **d** the dead no good, and you injure yourself.
38:33 nor **d** they attain eminence in the public assembly.
38:33 They **d** not sit in the judge's seat,
38:33 nor **d** they understand the decisions of the courts;
40:28 My child, **d** not lead the life of a beggar;
41: 3 **D** not fear death's decree for you;
41:22 and **d** not approach her bed;
41:22 and **d** not be insulting after making a gift.
42: 1 Of the following things **d** not be ashamed,
42: 1 and **d** not sin to save face:
42: 2 **D** not be ashamed of the law of the Most High
42: 8 **D** not be ashamed to correct the stupid or foolish
42:12 **D** not let her parade her beauty before any man,
42:15 and all his creatures **d** his will.
43:17 so **d** the storm from the north and the whirlwind.
43:30 summon all your strength, and **d** not grow weary,
51:10 **d** not forsake me in the days of trouble,
51:24 Why **d** you say you are lacking in these things,
51:24 and why **d** you endure such great thirst?
51:30 **D** your work in good time,
Bar 2: 9 in all the works that he has commanded us to **d**.
3: 5 **D** not remember the iniquities of our ancestors,
4: 3 **D** not give your glory to another,
LtJ 6:16 not gods; so **d** not fear them.
6:20 them and their robes. They **d** not notice
6:22 on their bodies and heads; and so **d** cats.
6:23 not gods; so **d** not fear them.
6:29 by these things that they are not gods, **d**
6:32 They howl and shout before their gods as some **d**
6:38 They cannot take pity on a widow or **d** good to
6:60 and when sent to **d** a service, they are obedient.
6:64 either to decide a case or to **d** good to anyone.
6:65 Since you know then that they are not gods, **d**
6:69 that they are gods; therefore **d** not fear them.
Aza 1:11 For your name's sake **d** not give us up forever,
1:11 and **d** not annul your covenant.
1:12 **D** not withdraw your mercy from us,
1:19 **D** not put us to shame,
1:21 Let all who **d** harm to your servants be put
Sus 1:22 For if I **d** this, it will mean death for me;
1:22 if I **d** not, I cannot escape your hands.
1:23 I choose not to **d** it;
1:61 to them as they had wickedly planned to **d**
Bel 1: 4 king said to him, "Why **d** you not worship Bel?"
1: 5 "Because I **d** not revere idols made with hands,
1: 6 "**D** you not think that Bel is a living god?
1: 6 **D** you not see how much he eats
1: 7 And Daniel laughed, and said, "**D** not be deceived,
1: 8 you **d** not tell me who is eating these provisions,
1:12 if you **d** not find that Bel has eaten it all,
1Mc 1:15 with the Gentiles and sold themselves to **d** evil.
2:18 the first to come and **d** what the king commands,
2:33 Come out and **d** what the king commands,
2:34 nor will we **d** what the king commands and
2:40 "If we all **d** as our kindred have done and refuse
2:62 **D** not fear the words of sinners,
3:22 as for you, **d** not be afraid of them."
3:42 also learned what the king had commanded to **d** to
3:50 saying, "What shall we **d** with these?
3:53 if you **d** not help us?"
3:60 But as his will in heaven may be, so shall he **d**."
4: 8 "**D** not fear their numbers or be afraid
4:17 "**D** not be greedy for plunder,
4:44 They deliberated what to **d** about the altar
4:46 a prophet should come to tell what to **d** with them.

1Mc 5:16 to determine what they should **d**
5:19 but **d** not engage in battle with the Gentiles
5:48 No one will **d** you harm;
5:61 thinking to **d** a brave deed,
5:67 who wished to **d** a brave deed, fell in battle,
6:22 "How long will you fail to **d** justice and
6:27 they will **d** still greater things,
7: 3 he said, **"D** not let me see their faces!"
8:28 and they shall keep these obligations and **d** so
8:30 they shall **d** so at their discretion,
9: 9 saying, "We **d** not have the strength.
9:10 from us to **d** such a thing as to flee from them.
9:60 but they were unable to **d** it,
10:27 and we will repay you with good for what you **d**
10:56 And now I will **d** for you as you wrote,
10:58 at Ptolemais with great pomp, as kings **d.**
10:70 Why **d** you assume authority against us in
11:33 We have determined to **d** good to the nation of
11:42 only will I **d** these things for you and your nation,
11:43 you will **d** well to send me men who will help me,
12:40 He feared that Jonathan might not permit him to **d**
13: 9 and all that you say to us we will **d."**
13:46 **"D** not treat us according to our wicked acts but
16:13 against Simon and his sons, to **d** away with them.
16:19 He sent other troops to Gazara to **d** away
2Mc 1: 2 May God **d** good to you,
1: 3 a heart to worship him and to **d** his will with
3:39 and destroys those who come to **d** it injury."
5:27 in the mountains as wild animals **d;**
7: 2 said, "What **d** you intend to ask and learn from us?
7:16 also are mortal, you **d** what you please.
7:16 But **d** not think that God has forsaken our people.
7:18 he said, **"D** not deceive yourself in vain.
7:19 But **d** not think that you will go unpunished
7:22 "I **d** not know how you came into being
7:29 **D** not fear this butcher, but prove worthy
7:34 **d** not be elated in vain and puffed up
9:22 I **d** not despair of my condition,
11:24 that the Jews **d** not consent to our father's change
11:26 You will **d** well, therefore,
14:33 "If you **d** not hand Judas over to me as a prisoner,
14:40 that by arresting him he would **d** them an injury.
15: 2 **"D** not destroy so savagely and barbarously,
15:38 that was the best I could **d.**
1Es 1:17 So the things that had to **d** with the sacrifices to
1:26 "What have we to **d** with each other,
1:27 Stand aside, and **d** not oppose the Lord."
3:23 they **d** not remember what they have done.
3:24 since it forces people to **d** these things?"
4: 4 to make war on one another, they **d** it;
4: 5 and **d** not disobey the king's command;
4: 6 Likewise those who **d** not serve in the army
4:11 to his own affairs, nor **d** they disobey him.
4:22 **"D** you not labor and toil,
4:28 And now **d** you not believe me?
4:28 **D** not all lands fear to touch him?
4:32 since they **d** such things?"
5:69 as you **d** and we have been sacrificing to him ever
5:70 "You have nothing to **d** with us in building
6:21 Now therefore, O king, if it seems wise to **d** so,
8:10 those who freely choose to **d** so,
8:16 Whatever you and your kindred are minded to **d**
8:23 and you shall teach it to those who **d** not know it.
8:84 Therefore **d** not give your daughters in marriage
8:84 **d** not take their daughters for your descendants;
8:85 **d** not seek ever to have peace with them,
8:96 of all Israel swear that they would **d** this.
9: 9 and **d** his will; separate yourselves from the
9:10 "We will **d** as you have said.
9:11 This is not a work we can **d** in one day or two,
9:52 **d** not be sorrowful, for the Lord will exalt you."
9:53 "This day is holy; **d** not be sorrowful."
Man 1:13 **D** not destroy me with my transgressions!
1:13 **D** not be angry with me forever or store up evil
1:13 **d** not condemn me to the depths of the earth.
3Mc 2:17 **D** not punish us for the defilement committed
2:28 "None of those who **d** not sacrifice shall enter
3: 2 by some who conspired to **d** them ill,
2Es 1:21 What more can I **d** for you?
1:24 "What shall I **d** to you, O Jacob?
1:30 But now, what shall I **d** to you?
1:35 shown no signs will **d** what I have commanded.
1:37 though they **d** not see me with bodily eyes,
2: 4 But now what can I **d** for you?
2: 9 That is what I will **d** to those who have
2:17 **D** not fear, mother of children,
2:21 **d** not ridicule the lame, protect the maimed,
2:27 **D** not be anxious, for when the day of tribulation
2:28 they shall not be able to **d** anything against you,
4: 2 and **d** you think you can comprehend the way of
4: 6 "Who of those that have been born can **d** that,
4:25 But what will he **d** for his name that is invoked
4:34 **"D** not be in a greater hurry than the Most High.
4:42 so also **d** these places hasten
4:46 but I **d** not know what is to come."
4:51 **"D** you think that I shall live until those days?
4:52 to tell you concerning your life, for I **d** not know.
5: 6 the earth **d** not expect,
5: 7 the many **d** not know shall make his voice heard
5:13 and weep as you **d** now, and fast for seven days,
5:17 Or **d** you not know that Israel has been entrusted
5:18 therefore and eat some bread, and **d** not forsake us,
5:19 from me and **d** not come near me for seven days;
5:33 Or **d** you love him more than his Maker does?"
5:40 "Just as you cannot **d** one of the things
5:41 but what will those **d** who lived before me, or we,
6:15 while the voice is speaking, **d** not be terrified;
2Es 6:33 'Believe and **d** not be afraid!
6:34 **D** not be quick to think vain thoughts concerning
6:59 why **d** we not possess our world as an inheritance?
7:21 when they came, what they should **d** to live,
7:*66* they **d** not look for a judgment, and they **d** not
7:*76* but **d** not include yourself
7:*106* [36] then **d** we find that first Abraham prayed for
8:26 O **d** not look on the sins of your people,
8:27 **D** not take note of the endeavors
8:28 **D** not think of those who have lived wickedly
8:29 **D** not will the destruction of those who have
8:30 **D** not be angry with those
8:47 to the unrighteous. Never **d** so!
8:55 Therefore **d** not ask any more questions about
8:63 a great number of the signs that you will **d** in
8:63 you have not shown me when you will **d** them."
9:13 **d** not continue to be curious about how
9:23 **d** not, however, fast during them,
10: 6 **d** you not see our mourning,
10:18 She said to me, "I will not **d** so;
10:20 **"D** not **d** that, but let yourself be persuaded—
10:34 I said, "Speak, my lord; only **d** not forsake me,
10:35 and I hear what I **d** not understand
10:42 (you **d** not now see the form of a woman,
10:55 "Therefore **d** not be afraid,
10:55 and **d** not let your heart be terrified;
10:59 in those dream visions what the Most High will **d**
11: 8 **"D** not all watch at the same time;
12:46 and **d** not be sorrowful, O house of Jacob;
12:50 the people went into the city, as I told them to **d.**
13:22 and concerning those who **d** not survive,
14:22 those who want to live in the last days may **d** so."
15: 3 **D** not fear the plots against you,
15: 3 and **d** not be troubled by the unbelief
15:17 and shall not be able to **d** so.
15:21 so I will **d,** and will repay into their bosom.
15:24 and **d** not observe my commandments, says
15:25 **D** not pollute my sanctuary.
15:56 As you will **d** to my chosen people, says the Lord,
so God will **d** to you,
16:18 What shall they **d,** when the calamities come?
16:36 receive it and **d** not disbelieve what the Lord says.
16:44 and those who **d** not marry,
16:47 **d** so only to have it plundered;
16:51 Therefore **d** not be like her or her works.
16:54 Lord certainly knows everything that people **d;**
16:66 What will you **d?**
16:75 **D** not fear or doubt, for God is your guide.
4Mc 2:14 **D** not consider it paradoxical when reason,
5:10 that you will **d** something even more senseless if,
5:19 Therefore **d** not suppose that it would be
5:25 "Therefore we **d** not eat defiling food;
5:33 I **d** not so pity my old age as to break
6:23 And you, guards of the tyrant, why **d** you delay?"
7:19 **d** not die to God, but live to God.
8: 5 Not only **d** I advise you not to display
8:18 why **d** we take pleasure in vain resolves
8:23 Why **d** we banish ourselves
9: 1 "Why **d** you delay, O tyrant?
9: 3 for us **d** not pity us more than we pity ourselves.
9: 7 and if you take our lives because of our religion, **d**
9:23 **"D** not leave your post in my struggle
9:30 To the tyrant he said, **"D** you not think,
10: 2 **"D** you not know that the same father begot me
10: 3 I **d** not renounce the noble kinship that binds me
10:13 **d** not give way to the same insanity
10:14 "You **d** not have a fire hot enough
12: 4 You too, if you **d** not obey,
12:16 "I **d** not desert the excellent example
13:18 **"D** not put us to shame, brother,
14:11 **D** not consider it amazing
14:17 they **d** what they can to help their young by flying
15: 4 a deeper sympathy toward their offspring than **d**
16:25 as **d** Abraham and Isaac and Jacob and all
18:16 'There is a tree of life for those who **d** his will.'

DOBRATH See Index to Footnotes

DOCTOR (1)

Lk 4:23 will quote to me this proverb, **'D,** cure yourself!'

DOCTRINE (6) [DOCTRINES]

Eph 4:14 to and fro and blown about by every wind of **d,**
1Ti 1: 3 not to teach any different **d,**
2Ti 4: 3 when people will not put up with sound **d,**
Tit 1: 9 so that he may be able both to preach with sound **d**
2: 1 as for you, teach what is consistent with sound **d.**
2:10 in everything they may be an ornament to the **d**

DOCTRINES (2) [DOCTRINE]

Mt 15: 9 teaching human precepts as **d.'"**
Mk 7: 7 teaching human precepts as **d.'**

DOCUMENT (9) [DOCUMENTS]

Ne 9:38 and on that sealed **d** are inscribed the names
10: 1 Upon the sealed **d** are the names of Nehemiah
Est 3:14 A copy of the **d** was to be issued as a decree
Isa 29:11 for you like the words of a sealed **d.**
Da 6: 8 O king, establish the interdict and sign the **d,**
6: 9 Therefore King Darius signed the **d** and interdict.
6:10 Although Daniel knew that the **d** had been signed,
AdE 3:14 Copies of the **d** were posted in every province,
2Mc 2: 4 It was also in the same **d** that the prophet,

DOCUMENTS (2) [DOCUMENT]

Ezr 6: 1 the archives where the **d** were stored in Babylon.
1Mc 13:42 the people began to write in their **d** and contracts,

DODAI (1)

1Ch 27: 4 **D** the Ahohite was in charge of the division of

DODANIM See Index to Footnotes

DODAVAHU (1)

2Ch 20:37 of **D** of Mareshah prophesied against Jehoshaphat,

DODO (5)

Jdg 10: 1 After Abimelech, Tola son of Puah son of **D,**
2Sa 23: 9 among the three warriors was Eleazar son of **D** son
23:24 Elhanan son of **D** of Bethlehem;
1Ch 11:12 among the three warriors was Eleazar son of **D,**
11:26 Elhanan son of **D** of Bethlehem,

DOE (3) [DOES]

Ge 49:21 Naphtali is a **d** let loose that bears lovely fawns.
Pr 5:19 a lovely deer, a graceful **d.**
Jer 14: 5 Even the **d** in the field forsakes her newborn fawn

DOEG (7)

1Sa 21: 7 his name was **D** the Edomite,
22: 9 **D** the Edomite, who was in charge
22:18 Then the king said to **D,** "You, Doeg,
22:18 Then the king said to Doeg, "You, **D,**
22:18 **D** the Edomite turned and attacked the priests;
22:22 when **D** the Edomite was there,
Ps 52: T *A Maskil of David, when* **D** *the Edomite came*

DOER (4) [DO]

2Sa 23:20 a valiant warrior from Kabzeel, a **d** of great deeds;
1Ch 11:22 of Jehoiada was a valiant man of Kabzeel, a **d**
Pr 21: 2 All deeds are right in the sight of the **d,**
Jas 4:11 you are not a **d** of the law but a judge.

DOERS (5) [DO]

Ro 2:13 but the **d** of the law who will be justified.
Jas 1:22 But be **d** of the word,
1:23 For if any are hearers of the word and not **d,**
1:25 being not hearers who forget but **d** who act—
2Es 6:19 from the **d** of iniquity the penalty of their iniquity,

DOES‡ (530) [DO, DOE]

Ge 31: 5 that your father **d** not regard me as favorably
44: 5 **D** he not indeed use it for divination?
44: 7 "Why **d** my lord speak such words as these?
Ex 7: 4 When Pharaoh **d** not listen to you,
13:14 the future your child asks you, 'What **d** this mean?'
21: 8 If she **d** not please her master,
21:11 And if he **d** not do these three things for her,
21:33 or digs a pit and **d** not cover it,
31:14 whoever **d** any work on it shall be cut off from
31:15 whoever **d** any work on the sabbath day shall
32:11 why **d** your wrath burn hot against your people,
35: 2 whoever **d** any work on it shall be put to death.
Lev 4: 2 about things not to be done, and **d** any one
5: 1 **d** not speak up, you are subject to punishment.
11: 4 it **d** not have divided hoofs; it is unclean for you.
11: 5 it **d** not have divided hoofs; it is unclean for you.
11: 6 it **d** not have divided hoofs; it is unclean for you.
11: 7 it **d** not chew the cud; it is unclean for you.
11:10 or the streams that **d** not have fins and scales,
11:12 that **d** not have fins and scales is detestable to you.
11:26 that has divided hoofs but is not cleft-footed or **d**
13:23 if the spot remains in one place and **d** not spread,
13:28 if the spot remains in one place and **d** not spread in
17: 4 and **d** not bring it to the entrance of the tent
17: 9 and **d** not bring it to the entrance of the tent
23:29 For anyone who **d** not practice self-denial during
23:30 anyone who **d** any work during that entire day,
Nu 10:32 whatever good the LORD **d** for us,
23:24 It **d** not lie down until it has eaten the prey
24:18 of its enemies, while Israel **d** valiantly.
24:23 "Alas, who shall live when God **d** this?
Dt 7:10 He **d** not delay but repays
8: 3 in order to make you understand that one **d**
10:12 what **d** the LORD your God require of you?
14: 8 because it divides the hoof but **d** not chew the cud,
14:10 And whatever **d** not have fins and scales you shall
17: 2 a man or woman who **d** what is evil in the sight of
18:12 whoever **d** these things is abhorrent to the LORD;
18:14 the LORD your God **d** not permit you to do so.
18:19 Anyone who **d** not heed the words that
18:22 of the LORD but the thing **d** not take place
20:12 If it **d** not submit to you peacefully,
21:18 who **d** not heed them when they discipline him,
22: 2 If the owner **d** not reside near you or you do
22: 5 for whoever **d** such things is abhorrent to
24: 1 but she **d** not please him
25: 9 the man who **d** not build up his brother's house."
27:26 be anyone who **d** not uphold the words of this law
28:56 that she **d** not venture to set the sole of her foot on
Jdg 11:27 the one who **d** me wrong by making war on me.
Ru 2: 5 "To whom **d** this young woman belong?"
1Sa 2: 9 for not by might **d** one prevail.
4: 6 "What **d** this great shouting in the camp of
11: 7 "Whoever **d** not come out after Saul and Samuel,
16: 7 for the LORD **d** not see as mortals see;

1Sa 17:47 that all this assembly may know that the LORD **d**
18:23 "**D** it seem to you a little thing to become
20: 2 My father **d** nothing either great or small
26:18 he added, "Why **d** my lord pursue his servant?
2Sa 3:12 saying, "To whom **d** the land belong?
3:39 The LORD pay back the one who **d** wickedly
14:13 the king **d** not bring his banished one home again.
24: 3 But why **d** my lord the king want to do this?"
1Ki 1:11 of Haggith has become king and our lord David **d**
8:46 for there is no one who **d** not sin—
2Ki 8:12 Hazael asked, "Why **d** my lord weep?"
2Ch 6:36 for there is no one who **d** not sin—
Ne 5:13 from property who **d** not perform this promise.
Est 5:13 Yet all this **d** me no good so long as I see
Job 1: 9 "**D** Job fear God for nothing?
3:21 but it **d** not come, and dig for it more than
5: 6 For misery **d** not come from the earth,
5: 6 nor **d** trouble sprout from the ground;
5: 9 He **d** great things and unsearchable,
6: 5 **D** the wild ass bray over its grass,
6:25 But your reproof, what **d** it reprove?
8: 3 **D** God pervert justice?
8: 3 Or **d** the Almighty pervert the right?
9: 7 the sun, and it **d** not rise;
9:10 who **d** great things beyond understanding,
10: 3 **D** it seem good to you to oppress,
12: 3 Who **d** not know such things as these?
12: 9 Who among all these **d** not know that the hand of
12:11 **D** not the ear test words as the palate tastes food?
14: 2 flees like a shadow and **d** not last.
15:12 Why **d** your heart carry you away,
16:21 as one **d** for a neighbor.
18: 5 and the flame of their fire **d** not shine.
21:17 How often **d** calamity come upon them?
21:17 How often **d** God distribute pains in his anger?
22:13 Therefore you say, 'What **d** God know?
22:14 Thick clouds enwrap him, so that he **d** not see,
23:13 What he desires, that he **d**.
24:19 so **d** Sheol those who have sinned.
25: 3 Upon whom **d** his light not arise?
27: 6 my heart **d** not reproach me for any of my days.
28:20 "Where then **d** wisdom come from?
30:24 "Surely one **d** not turn against the needy,
31: 3 **D** not calamity befall the unrighteous,
31: 4 **D** he not see my ways, and number all my steps?
33:29 "God indeed **d** all these things, twice, three times,
35: 7 or what **d** he receive from your hand?
35:12 There they cry out, but he **d** not answer,
35:13 Surely God **d** not hear an empty cry,
35:13 nor **d** the Almighty regard it.
35:15 And now, because his anger **d** not punish,
35:15 and he **d** not greatly heed transgression,
36: 5 "Surely God is mighty and **d** not despise any;
36: 6 He **d** not keep the wicked alive,
36: 7 He **d** not withdraw his eyes from the righteous,
36:18 Beware that wrath **d** not entice you into scoffing,
37: 4 he thunders with his majestic voice and he **d**
37: 5 he **d** great things that we cannot comprehend.
37:24 he **d** not regard any who are wise
39: 7 it **d** not hear the shouts of the driver.
39:22 it **d** not turn back from the sword.
41:26 Though the sword reaches it, it **d** not avail,
41:26 sword reaches it, it does not avail, nor **d** the spear,
Ps 7:12 If one **d** not repent, God will whet his sword;
9:12 he **d** not forget the cry of the afflicted.
14: 1 there is no one who **d** good.
14: 3 there is no one who **d** good, no, not one.
17: 3 my mouth **d** not transgress.
38:14 Truly, I am like one who **d** not hear,
50: 3 Our God comes and **d** not keep silence,
53: 1 there is no one who **d** good.
53: 3 there is no one who **d** good, no, not one.
58: 5 so that it **d** not hear the voice of charmers or of
69:33 and **d** not despise his own that are in bonds.
72:18 the God of Israel, who alone **d** wondrous things.
74: 1 Why **d** your anger smoke against the sheep
78:39 a wind that passes and **d** not come again.
84:11 No good thing **d** the LORD withhold
94: 7 and they say, "The LORD **d** not see;
94: 7 the God of Jacob **d** not perceive."
94: 9 He who planted the ear, **d** he not hear?
94: 9 He who formed the eye, **d** he not see?
94:10 to humankind, **d** he not chastise?
103:10 He **d** not deal with us according to our sins,
107:38 and he **d** not let their cattle decrease.
115: 3 in the heavens; he **d** whatever he pleases.
118:15 "The right hand of the LORD **d** valiantly;
118:16 the right hand of the LORD **d** valiantly."
135: 6 Whatever the LORD pleases he **d**,
136: 4 who alone **d** great wonders,
Pr 5: 6 She **d** not keep straight to the path of life;
5: 6 her ways wander, and she **d** not know it.
6:32 he who **d** it destroys himself.
8: 1 **D** not wisdom call, and **d** not understanding raise
10: 3 The LORD **d** not let the righteous go hungry,
13: 1 but a scoffer **d** not listen to rebuke.
14: 5 A faithful witness **d** not lie,
16:10 his mouth **d** not sin in judgment.
20: 4 The lazy person **d** not plow in season;
24:12 **d** not he who weighs the heart perceive it?
24:12 **D** not he who keeps watch over your soul know it?
26: 7 so **d** a proverb in the mouth of a fool.
26:14 door turns on its hinges, so **d** a lazy person in bed.
28:22 a hurry to get rich and **d** not know that loss is sure
30:30 which is mightiest among wild animals and **d**
31:12 She **d** him good, and not harm,
31:18 Her lamp **d** not go out at night.
Pr 31:27 and **d** not eat the bread of idleness.
Ecc 3:14 I know that whatever God **d** endures forever;
4:10 but woe to one who is alone and falls and **d**
6: 2 yet God **d** not enable them to enjoy these things,
6: 3 if he **d** not enjoy life's good things,
8: 3 for he **d** whatever he pleases.
8: 8 nor **d** wickedness deliver those who practice it.
9: 1 whether it is love or hate one **d** not know.
10:10 If the iron is blunt, and one **d** not whet the edge,
SS 2: 7 by the gazelles or the wild **d**:
3: 5 by the gazelles or the wild **d**:
Isa 1: 3 Israel **d** not know, my people do not understand.
1:23 and the widow's cause **d** not come before them.
10: 7 nor **d** he have this in mind;
28:28 but one **d** not thresh it forever;
28:28 one drives the cart wheel and horses over it, but **d**
31: 2 he **d** not call back his words,
40:28 He **d** not faint or grow weary;
42:20 He sees many things, but **d** not observe them;
42:20 his ears are open, but he **d** not hear.
45: 9 **D** the clay say to the one who fashions it,
46: 7 it **d** not answer or save anyone from trouble.
55: 2 and your labor for that which **d** not satisfy?
56: 2 Happy is the mortal who **d** this,
59: 2 from you so that he **d** not hear.
59: 9 and righteousness **d** not reach us;
63:16 though Abraham **d** not know us and Israel **d** not
65:20 or an old person who **d** not live out a lifetime;
Jer 2:11 for something that **d** not profit.
11: 3 Cursed be anyone who **d** not heed the words
12: 1 Why **d** the way of the guilty prosper?
14:10 therefore the LORD **d** not accept them,
14:19 **D** your heart loathe Zion?
17: 8 and it **d** not cease to bear fruit.
18:10 but if it **d** evil in my sight,
18:14 **D** the snow of Lebanon leave the crags of Sirion?
22:13 and **d** not give them their wages;
26:16 "This man **d** not deserve the sentence of death,
50: 9 a skilled warrior who **d** not return empty-handed.
La 3:33 for he **d** not willingly afflict or grieve anyone.
3:36 one's cause is subverted—**d** the Lord not see it?
Eze 8:12 For they say, 'The LORD **d** not see us,
9: 9 and the LORD **d** not see.'
15: 2 **d** the wood of the vine surpass all other wood—
15: 3 **D** one take a peg from it on which
17:15 Can one escape who **d** such things?
18: 5 man is righteous and **d** what is lawful and right—
18: 6 if he **d** not eat upon the mountains or lift
18: 6 **d** not defile his neighbor's wife or approach
18: 7 **d** not oppress anyone, but restores to
18: 8 **d** not take advance or accrued interest,
18:11 who **d** any of these things
18:11 of these things (though his father **d** none of them),
18:12 commits robbery, **d** not restore the pledge,
18:14 considers, and **d** not do likewise,
18:15 who **d** not eat upon the mountains or lift
18:15 **d** not defile his neighbor's wife,
18:16 **d** not wrong anyone, exacts no pledge,
24:12 its thick rust **d** not depart.
33: 6 the sentinel sees the sword coming and **d** not blow
46:12 of well-being as he **d** on the sabbath day.
Da 2:43 just as iron **d** not mix with clay.
3: 6 Whoever **d** not fall down
3:11 and whoever **d** not fall down and worship shall
4:35 and he **d** what he wills with the host of heaven and
8:24 and shall succeed in what he **d**.
Hos 7: 4 whose baker **d** not need to stir the fire,
7: 9 but he **d** not know it;
7: 9 gray hairs are sprinkled upon him, but he **d** not
7:16 They turn to that which **d** not profit;
8:13 the LORD **d** not accept them.
11: 7 but he **d** not raise them up at all.
13:13 for at the proper time he **d** not present himself at
Am 3: 4 **D** a lion roar in the forest, when it has no prey?
3: 4 **D** a young lion cry out from its den,
3: 5 **D** a bird fall into a snare on the earth,
3: 5 **D** a snare spring up from the ground,
3: 6 **D** disaster befall a city, unless the LORD has done
3: 7 Surely the Lord GOD **d** nothing,
6:12 **D** one plow the sea with oxen?
9:12 says the LORD who **d** this.
Mic 6: 8 what **d** the LORD require of you but to do justice,
7:18 He **d** not retain his anger forever,
Hab 2: 3 it speaks of the end, and **d** not lie.
3:17 fig tree **d** not blossom, and no fruit is on the vines;
Zep 3: 5 The LORD within it is righteous; he **d** no wrong.
Hag 2: 3 How **d** it look to you now?
2:12 or oil, or any kind of food, **d** it become holy?
2:13 of these, **d** it become unclean?"
Zec 11:16 now raising up in the land a shepherd who **d**
Mal 2:12 from the tents of Jacob anyone who **d** this—
2:14 You ask, "Why **d** he not?"
2:15 And what **d** the one God desire?
3:18 one who serves God and one who **d** not serve him.
Mt 3:10 that **d** not bear good fruit is cut down and thrown
4: 4 "It is written, 'One **d** not live by bread alone,
5:19 but whoever **d** them and teaches them will
7:19 that **d** not bear good fruit is cut down and thrown
7:21 the one who **d** the will of my Father in heaven.
7:26 of mine and **d** not act on them will be like
8: 9 and to my slave, 'Do this,' and the slave **d** it."
9:11 "Why **d** your teacher eat with tax collectors
10:38 and whoever **d** not take up the cross
12:30 and whoever **d** not gather with me scatters.
12:50 For whoever **d** the will of my Father
13:19 the word of the kingdom and **d** not understand it,
15:20 but to eat with unwashed hands **d** not defile."
Mt 17:24 "**D** your teacher not pay the temple tax?"
17:25 He said, "Yes, he **d**."
18:12 **d** he not leave the ninety-nine on the mountains
24:50 on a day when he **d** not expect him and at an hour
that he **d** not know.
Mk 2: 7 "Why **d** this fellow speak in this way?
2:16 "Why **d** he eat with tax collectors and sinners?"
3:35 Whoever **d** the will of God is my brother
4:27 and day, and the seed would sprout and grow, he **d**
8:12 "Why **d** this generation ask for a sign?
9:39 for no one who **d** a deed of power in my name will
10:15 whoever **d** not receive the kingdom of God as
16:16 ⟦the one who **d** not believe will be condemned.⟧
Lk 3: 9 that **d** not bear good fruit is cut down and thrown
4: 4 "It is written, 'One **d** not live by bread alone.' "
6:43 nor again **d** a bad tree bear good fruit;
6:49 and **d** not act is like a man who built a house on
7: 8 and to my slave, 'Do this,' and the slave **d** it."
8:14 and their fruit **d** not mature.
9:25 What **d** it profit them if they gain the whole world,
9:49 because he **d** not follow with us."
11:23 and whoever **d** not gather with me scatters.
12:15 for one's life **d** not consist in the abundance
12:46 on a day when he **d** not expect him and at an hour
that he **d** not know,
13:15 **D** not each of you on the sabbath untie his ox
14:26 "Whoever comes to me and **d** not hate father
14:27 Whoever **d** not carry the cross
14:28 **d** not first sit down and estimate the cost,
15: 4 **d** not leave the ninety-nine in the wilderness
15: 8 if she loses one of them, **d** not light a lamp,
18:17 whoever **d** not receive the kingdom of God as
20:17 "What then **d** this text mean:
20:24 Whose head and whose title **d** it bear?"
24:18 the only stranger in Jerusalem who **d** not know
24:39 for a ghost **d** not have flesh and bones as you see
Jn 5:19 for whatever the Father **d**, the Son **d** likewise.
5:23 Anyone who **d** not honor the Son **d** not honor
5:24 and **d** not come under judgment,
6:61 said to them, "**D** this offend you?
7:15 saying, "How **d** this man have such learning,
7:35 **d** this man intend to go that we will not find him?
7:35 **D** he intend to go to the Dispersion among
7:36 What **d** he mean by saying,
7:41 Surely the Messiah **d** not come from Galilee, **d** he?
7:49 But this crowd, which **d** not know the law—
7:51 "Our law **d** not judge people
7:51 a hearing to find out what they are doing, **d** it?"
8:35 The slave **d** not have a permanent place in
8:41 You are indeed doing what your father **d**."
8:44 a murderer from the beginning and **d** not stand in
9:16 for he **d** not observe the sabbath."
9:19 How then **d** he now see?"
9:31 We know that God **d** not listen to sinners,
9:31 but he **d** listen to one who worships him
10: 1 anyone who **d** not enter the sheepfold by the gate
10:12 who is not the shepherd and **d** not own the sheep,
10:13 The hired hand runs away because a hired hand **d**
11: 4 he said, "This illness **d** not lead to death;
12:47 I do not judge anyone who hears my words and **d**
12:48 and **d** not receive my word has a judge;
13:10 "One who has bathed **d** not need to wash,
13:19 before it occurs, so that when it **d** occur,
14:10 but the Father who dwells in me **d** his works.
14:24 Whoever **d** not love me **d** not keep my words;
14:29 so that when it **d** occur, you may believe.
15: 6 Whoever **d** not abide in me is thrown away like
15:15 the servant **d** not know what the master is doing;
16:17 "What **d** he mean by saying to us, 'A little while,
16:18 "What **d** he mean by this 'a little while'?
17:25 "Righteous Father, the world **d** not know you,
Ac 2:12 saying to one another, "What **d** this mean?"
3:23 that everyone who **d** not listen to that prophet will
7:48 Yet the Most High **d** not dwell in houses made
8:32 so he **d** not open his mouth.
8:34 may I ask you, **d** the prophet say this,
10:35 and **d** what is right is acceptable to him.
13:40 that what the prophets said **d** not happen to you:
17:18 Some said, "What **d** this babbler want to say?"
17:24 **d** not live in shrines made by human hands,
19:35 that **d** not know that the city of the Ephesians is
Ro 2: 9 be anguish and distress for everyone who **d** evil,
2:10 and honor and peace for everyone who **d** good,
4: 3 For what **d** the scripture say?
5: 5 and hope **d** not disappoint us,
8: 7 it **d** not submit to God's law—
8: 9 Anyone who **d** not have the Spirit of Christ **d** not
belong to him.
9:19 "Why then **d** he still find fault?
10: 5 "the person who **d** these things will live by them."
10: 8 But what **d** it say?
13: 4 for the authority **d** not bear the sword in vain!
13:10 Love **d** no wrong to a neighbor;
14:23 for whatever **d** not proceed from faith is sin.
1Co 7: 4 the wife **d** not have authority over her own body,
but the husband **d**; likewise the husband **d** not
have authority over his own body, but the wife **d**.
7:11 if she **d** separate, let her remain unmarried or else
7:28 and if a virgin marries, she **d** not sin.
7:38 So then, he who marries his fiancée d well;
8: 2 Anyone who claims to know something **d** not
8: 9 that this liberty of yours **d** not somehow become
9: 7 Who plants a vineyard and **d** not eat any
9: 7 Or who tends a flock and **d** not get any of its milk?
9: 8 **D** not the law also say the same?
9:10 Or **d** he not speak entirely for our sake?
11:14 **D** not nature itself teach you that if

1Co 12:14 body **d** not consist of one member but of many.
13: 5 It **d** not insist on its own way;
13: 6 it **d** not rejoice in wrongdoing,
14:16 the outsider **d** not know what you are saying?
14:38 Anyone who **d** not recognize this is not to
15:27 that this **d** not include the one who put all things
15:36 What you sow **d** not come to life unless it dies.
15:50 nor **d** the perishable inherit the imperishable.
2Co 3: 9 much more **d** the ministry of justification abound
4: 7 to God and **d** not come from us.
6:15 What agreement **d** Christ have with Beliar?
6:15 Or what **d** a believer share with an unbeliever?
8:12 not according to what one **d** not have.
Gal 3: 5 **d** God supply you with the Spirit
3:10 for it is written, "Cursed is everyone who **d**
3:12 But the law **d** not rest on faith;
3:12 "Whoever **d** the works of the law will live
3:16 it **d** not say, "And to offsprings," as of many;
3:17 **d** not annul a covenant previously ratified by God,
4:30 But what **d** the scripture say?
5: 8 Such persuasion **d** not come from
Eph 4: 9 what **d** it mean but that he had also descended into
5:29 just as Christ **d** for the church,
Php 1:18 What **d** it matter? Just this,
Col 4:10 as **d** Mark the cousin of Barnabas,
1Th 2: 3 For our appeal **d** not spring from deceit
1Ti 3: 5 for if someone **d** not know how
5: 8 And whoever **d** not provide for relatives,
6: 3 Whoever teaches otherwise and **d** not agree with
2Ti 2: 6 It is the farmer who **d** the work who ought to have
2:14 to avoid wrangling over words, which **d** no good
Heb 5: 4 And one **d** not presume to take this honor,
7: 6 But this man, who **d** not belong to their ancestry,
12: 7 for what child is there whom a parent **d**
Jas 1:20 for your anger **d** not produce God's righteousness.
3:11 **D** a spring pour forth from the same opening
3:15 Such wisdom **d** not come down from above,
5: 6 the righteous one, who **d** not resist you.
1Pe 4: 6 they might live in the spirit as God **d.**
5:13 and so **d** my son Mark.
2Pe 3:16 speaking of this as he **d** in all his letters.
1Jn 2: 1 But if anyone **d** sin, we have an advocate with
2: 4 but **d** not obey his commandments, is a liar, and in
such a person the truth **d** not exist;
2:11 and **d** not know the way to go,
2:29 that everyone who **d** right has been born of him.
3: 1 The reason the world **d** not know us is that it did
3: 7 Everyone who **d** what is right is righteous,
3:14 Whoever **d** not love abides in death.
3:17 How **d** God's love abide in anyone who has
4: 3 and every spirit that **d** not confess Jesus is not
4: 6 and whoever is not from God **d** not listen to us.
4: 8 Whoever **d** not love **d** not know God,
5:12 whoever **d** not have the Son of God **d** not have life.
5:18 and the evil one **d** not touch them.
2Jn 1: 9 Everyone who **d** not abide in the teaching of
Christ, but goes beyond it, **d** not have God;
1:10 or welcome anyone who comes to you and **d**
3Jn 1: 9 **d** not acknowledge our authority.
1:11 Whoever **d** good is from God; whoever **d** evil has
not seen God.
Rev 13:17 no one can buy or sell who **d** not have the mark,
Tob 5: 2 since he **d** not know me and I do not know him?
6:15 It **d** not harm her, but it kills anyone who desires
14:11 and what injustice **d**—it brings death!
Jdt 5: 3 and in what **d** their power and strength consist?
8:15 he **d** not choose to help us within these five days,
9:11 "For your strength **d** not depend on numbers,
AdE 2:14 and she **d** not go in to the king again
16:24 that **d** not act accordingly shall be destroyed
Wis 1:10 and the sound of grumbling **d** not go unheard.
1:13 and he **d** not delight in the death of the living.
3:15 and the root of understanding **d** not fail.
6:23 for envy **d** not associate with wisdom.
7:30 but against wisdom evil **d** not prevail.
10: 7 plants bearing fruit that **d** not ripen,
11:10 For you tested them as a parent **d** in warning,
11:10 but you examined the ungodly as a stern king **d**
12:15 to condemn anyone who **d** not deserve to
Sir Pr: 2 For what was originally expressed in Hebrew **d**
4:10 and he will love you more than **d** your mother.
7:16 remember that retribution **d** not delay.
11: 9 not argue about a matter that **d** not concern you,
11:19 he **d** not know how long it will be
12: 3 to one who persists in evil or to one who **d**
12:11 to be sure it **d** not become completely tarnished.
13: 3 A rich person **d** wrong, and even adds insults;
13:17 What **d** a wolf have in common with a lamb?
14: 7 If ever he **d** good, it is by mistake;
14:12 Remember that death **d** not tarry,
15:11 for he **d** not do what he hates.
17:28 From the dead, as from one who **d** not exist,
18:16 **D** not the dew give relief from the scorching heat?
18:17 Indeed, **d** not a word surpass a good gift?
19: 1 The one who **d** this will not become rich;
19: 4 and one who sins **d** wrong to oneself.
20: 4 is the person who **d** right under compulsion.
20:20 for he **d** not tell it at the proper time.
23:19 to human eyes and he **d** not realize that the eyes of
25: 8 the one who **d** not plow with ox and ass together.
25: 8 Happy is the one who **d** not sin with the tongue,
25:23 from the wife who **d** not make her husband happy.
25:26 If she **d** not go as you direct,
27:10 A lion lies in wait for prey; so **d** sin for evildoers.
27:27 If a person **d** evil, it will roll back upon him,
28: 3 **D** anyone harbor anger against another,
31: 8 and who **d** not go after gold.
Sir 31:19 He **d** not breathe heavily when in bed.
33:30 and if he **d** not obey, make his fetters heavy.
34:18 To whom **d** he look? And who is his support?
34:23 nor for a multitude of sacrifices **d** he forgive sins.
34:31 and goes again and **d** the same things,
35:22 and **d** justice for the righteous,
42:14 of a man than a woman who **d** good;
LtJ 6:34 Whether one **d** evil to them or good,
6:35 if one makes a vow to them and **d** not keep it,
6:63 and woods **d** what it is ordered.
1Mc 1:50 "And whoever **d** not obey the command of
2Mc 6:14 but he **d** not deal in this way with us,
6:16 he **d** not forsake his own people.
1Es 4:35 Is not the one who **d** these things great?
4:39 but it **d** what is righteous instead of anything
3Mc 7: 6 always taking their part as a father **d**
2Es 2:15 bring them up with gladness, as **d** a dove;
4:29 and if the place where the evil has been sown **d**
5:11 or anyone who **d** right, passed through you?'
5:33 Or do you love him more than his Maker **d?"**
5:49 For as an infant **d** not bring forth,
5:49 and a woman who has become old **d**
7:23 they even declared that the Most High **d** not exist,
7:*67* What **d** it profit us that we shall be preserved alive
7:*104* Just as now a father **d** not send his son,
7:*112* [42] the full glory **d** not remain in it;
8:43 If the farmer's seed **d** not come up,
9:37 however, **d** not perish but survives in its glory."
13:57 the Most High for the wonders that he **d** from time
16:16 as an arrow shot by a mighty archer **d** not return,
16:42 let the one who **d** business be like one who will
4Mc 1: 6 For reason **d** not rule its own emotions,
2:24 it **d** not control forgetfulness and ignorance?
3: 5 For reason **d** not uproot the emotions
5: 7 it **d** not seem to me that you are a philosopher
5:37 as one who **d** not fear your violence even to death.
8:26 Why **d** such contentiousness excite us and such
17: 5 with the stars, **d** not stand so august as you, who,

DOG‡ (17) [DOG'S, DOGGED, DOGS]

Ex 11: 7 But not a **d** shall growl at any of the Israelites—
Jdg 7: 5 as a **d** laps, you shall put to one side;
1Sa 17:43 The Philistine said to David, "Am I a **d,**
24:14 Whom do you pursue? A dead **d?**
2Sa 9: 8 that you should look upon a dead **d** such as I?"
16: 9 "Why should this dead **d** curse my lord the king?
2Ki 8:13 "What is your servant, who is a mere **d,**
Ps 22:20 my life from the power of the **d!**
Pr 26:11 a **d** that returns to its vomit is a fool who reverts
26:17 a passing **d** by the ears is one who meddles in
Ecc 9: 4 for a living **d** is better than a dead lion.
2Pe 2:22 "The **d** turns back to its own vomit," and,
Tob 6: 2 **d** came out with him and went along with them.
11: 4 And the **d** went along behind them.
Jdt 11:19 and no **d** will so much as growl at you.
Sir 13:18 What peace is there between a hyena and a **d?**
26:25 *A headstrong wife is regarded as a **d,***

DOG'S (2) [DOG]

2Sa 3: 8 he said, "Am I a **d** head for Judah?
Isa 66: 3 like one who breaks a **d** neck;

DOGGED (1) [DOG]

La 4:18 They **d** our steps so that we could not walk

DOGS (26) [DOG]

Ex 22:31 you shall throw it to the **d.**
1Ki 14:11 to Jeroboam who dies in the city, the **d** shall eat;
16: 4 to Baasha who dies in the city the **d** shall eat;
21:19 the place where **d** licked up the blood of Naboth,
21:19 **d** will also lick up your blood."
21:23 **d** shall eat Jezebel within the bounds of Jezreel.'
21:24 to Ahab who dies in the city the **d** shall eat;
22:38 the **d** licked up his blood,
2Ki 9:10 The **d** shall eat Jezebel in the territory of Jezreel,
9:36 'In the territory of Jezreel the **d** shall eat the flesh
Job 30: 1 to set with the **d** of my flock.
Ps 22:16 For **d** are all around me;
59: 6 howling like **d** and prowling about the city.
59:14 howling like **d** and prowling about the city.
68:23 so that the tongues of your **d** may have their share
Isa 56:10 they are all silent **d** that cannot bark;
56:11 **d** have a mighty appetite; they never have enough.
Jer 15: 3 the sword to kill, the **d** to drag away,
Mt 7: 6 "Do not give what is holy to **d;**
15:26 to take the children's food and throw it to the **d."**
15:27 yet even the **d** eat the crumbs that fall
Mk 7:27 to take the children's food and throw it to the **d."**
7:28 the **d** under the table eat the children's crumbs."
Lk 16:21 even the **d** would come and lick his sores.
Php 3: 2 Beware of the **d,** beware of the evil workers,
Rev 22:15 the **d** and sorcerers and fornicators and murderers

DOING‡ (192) [DO]

Ge 18:19 to keep the way of the LORD by **d** righteousness
31:12 for I have seen all that Laban is **d** to you.
44: 5 You have done wrong in **d** this.' "
50: 3 they spent forty days in **d** this,
50:20 to preserve a numerous people, as he is **d** today.
Ex 15:11 awesome in splendor, **d** wonders?
18:14 When Moses' father-in-law saw all that he was **d**
18:14 "What is this that you are **d** for the people?
18:17 "What you are **d** is not good.
36: 3 that the Israelites had brought for **d** the work on
Ex 36: 4 that all the artisans who were **d** every sort of task
36: 5 for **d** the work that the LORD has commanded us
Lev 4:22 **d** unintentionally any one of all the things that
4:27 among you sins unintentionally in **d** any one of
5:17 **d** any of the things that by
18: 5 by **d** so one shall live: I am the LORD.
Nu 3: 7 **d** service at the tabernacle;
7: 5 that they may be used in **d** the service of the tent
Dt 4:25 thus **d** what is evil in the sight of
8:18 that he swore to your ancestors, as he is **d** today.
9:18 the LORD by **d** what was evil in his sight.
12:28 because you will be **d** what is good and right in
13:18 **d** what is right in the sight of the LORD
26:14 **d** just as you commanded me.
34: 9 **d** as the LORD had commanded Moses.
Jos 8: 8 **d** as the LORD has ordered;
10: 1 **d** to Ai and its king as he had done to Jericho
11:20 For it was the LORD's **d** to harden their hearts so
Jdg 18: 3 What are you **d** in this place?
18:18 the priest said to them, "What are you **d?"**
1Sa 2:22 He heard all that his sons were **d** to all Israel,
8: 8 so also they are **d** to you.
22: 8 to lie in wait, as he is **d** today."
22:13 to lie in wait, as he is **d** today?"
29: 3 "What are these Hebrews **d** here?"
2Sa 3:25 and goings and to learn all that you are **d."**
7:23 **d** great and awesome things for them,
1Ki 9: 4 **d** according to all that I have commanded you,
11:33 **d** what is right in my sight
14: 8 **d** only that which was right in my sight,
16:19 **d** evil in the sight of the LORD,
19: 9 saying, "What are you **d** here, Elijah?"
19:13 "What are you **d** here, Elijah?"
22: 3 yet we are **d** nothing to take it out of the hand of
22:43 **d** what was right in the sight of the LORD;
2Ki 7: 9 they said to one another, "What we are **d** is wrong.
8:27 **d** what was evil in the sight of the LORD,
1Ch 6:49 **d** all the work of the most holy place,
2Ch 7:17 **d** according to all that I have commanded you
19: 6 "Consider what you are **d,**
20:32 **d** what was right in the sight of the LORD.
22: 3 for his mother was his counselor in **d** wickedly.
25:20 But Amaziah would not listen—it was God's **d,**
34:16 that was committed to your servants they are **d.**
Ne 2:16 not know where I had gone or what I was **d;**
2:19 saying, "What is this that you are **d?**
4: 2 "What are these feeble Jews **d?**
5: 9 So I said, "The thing that you are **d** is not good.
6: 3 "I am **d** a great work and I cannot come down.
13:17 "What is this evil thing that you are **d,**
Job 9:12 Who will say to him, 'What are you **d?'**
15: 4 But you are **d** away with the fear of God,
Ps 69:10 they insulted me for **d** so.
107:23 **d** business on the mighty waters;
118:23 This is the LORD's **d;** it is marvelous in our
Pr 2:14 in **d** evil and delight in the perverseness of evil;
10:23 **D** wrong is like sport to a fool,
Ecc 2:11 and the toil I had spent in **d** it,
5: 1 for they do not know how to keep from **d** evil.
8: 4 and who can say to him, "What are you **d?"**
Isa 52: 5 Now therefore what am I **d** here, says the LORD,
56: 2 not profaning it, and refrains from **d** any evil.
Jer 4:22 They are skilled in **d** evil,
7:10 only to go on **d** all these abominations?
7:17 not see what they are **d** in the towns of Judah and
32:40 never to draw back from **d** good to them;
32:41 I will rejoice in **d** good to them,
44: 7 Why are you **d** such great harm to yourselves,
48:10 the one who is slack in **d** the work of the LORD;
La 1:22 Let all their evil **d** come before you;
Eze 8: 6 "Mortal, do you see what they are **d,**
8:12 the elders of the house of Israel are **d** in the dark,
12: 9 said to you, "What are you **d?"**
Da 4:35 or say to him, "What are you **d?"**
Jnh 1: 6 "What are you **d** sound asleep?
Mt 5:47 what more are you **d** than others?
6: 3 let your left hand know what your right hand is **d,**
11: 2 John heard in prison what the Messiah was **d,**
12: 2 your disciples are **d** what is not lawful to do on
20:13 'Friend, I am **d** you no wrong;
21:23 "By what authority are you **d** these things,
21:27 by what authority I am **d** these things.
21:42 the Lord's **d,** and it is amazing in our eyes'?
Mk 2:24 why are they **d** what is not lawful on the sabbath?"
3: 8 hearing all that he was **d,**
7:12 then you no longer permit **d** anything for a father
11: 3 If anyone says to you, 'Why are you **d** this?'
11: 5 "What are you **d,** untying the colt?"
11:28 "By what authority are you **d** these things?
11:33 by what authority I am **d** these things."
12:11 the Lord's **d,** and it is amazing in our eyes'?
Lk 6: 2 "Why are you **d** what is not lawful on
9:43 While everyone was amazed at all that he was **d,**
13:17 at all the wonderful things that he was **d.**
17: 9 the slave for **d** what was commanded?
20: 2 "Tell us, by what authority are you **d** these things?
20: 8 by what authority I am **d** these things."
23:34 ⟦for they do not know what they are **d."**⟧
Jn 2:18 "What sign can you show us for **d** this?"
2:23 because they saw the signs that he was **d.**
5:16 because he was **d** such things on the sabbath.
5:19 but only what he sees the Father **d;**
5:20 the Son and shows him all that he himself is **d;**
5:36 the very works that I am **d,**
6: 2 they saw the signs that he was **d** for the sick.
7: 3 also may see the works you are **d;**
7:51 a hearing to find out what they are **d,**

Jn 8:39 you would be **d** what Abraham did,
8:41 You are indeed **d** what your father does."
10:37 If I am not **d** the works of my Father,
13: 7 "You do not know now what I am **d,**
15:15 the servant does not know what the master is **d;**
16: 2 that by **d** so they are offering worship to God.
Ac 10:38 about **d** good and healing all who were oppressed
13:41 for in your days I am **d** a work,
14:15 why are you **d** this? We are mortals just like you,
14:17 not left himself without a witness in **d** good—
15:36 the word of the Lord and see how they are **d."**
16:18 She kept **d** this for many days.
19:14 of a Jewish high priest named Sceva were **d** this.
20:20 I did not shrink from **d** anything helpful,
21:13 Then Paul answered, "What are you **d,**
24:18 While I was **d** this, they found me in the temple,
26:31 "This man is **d** nothing to deserve death
Ro 2: 1 because you, the judge, are **d** the very same things.
2: 7 to those who by patiently **d** good seek for glory
12:20 for by **d** this you will heap burning coals
1Co 9: 7 the expenses for **d** military service?
16:10 for he is **d** the work of the Lord just as I am;
2Co 8:11 now finish **d** it, so that your eagerness may
Gal 2:16 and not by **d** the works of the law,
3: 2 Did you receive the Spirit by **d** the works of
3: 5 and work miracles among you by your **d** the works
5:17 to prevent you from **d** what you want.
6: 9 So let us not grow weary in **d** what is right,
Eph 2: 8 and this is not your own **d;**
6: 6 **d** the will of God from the heart.
6:21 you also may know how I am and what I am **d,**
Php 1:28 And this is God's **d.**
4: 9 on **d** the things that you have learned and received
Col 1:21 and hostile in mind, **d** evil deeds,
1Th 4: 1 you are **d),** you should do so more and more.
5:11 and build up each other, as indeed you are **d.**
2Th 3: 4 are **d** and will go on **d** the things that we command.
3:11 mere busybodies, not **d** any work.
3:13 do not be weary in **d** what is right.
1Ti 4:16 continue in these things, for in **d** this you will save
5:10 and devoted herself to **d** good in every way.
5:21 **d** nothing on the basis of partiality.
Heb 13: 2 for by **d** that some have entertained angels
Jas 1:25 they will be blessed in their **d.**
4:13 **d** business and making money."
1Pe 2:15 that by **d** right you should silence the ignorance of
2:20 If you endure when you are beaten for **d** wrong,
3:14 you do suffer for **d** what is right, you are blessed.
3:17 For it is better to suffer for **d** good,
3:17 than to suffer for **d** evil.
4: 3 You have already spent enough time in **d** what
2Pe 2:13 suffering the penalty for **d** wrong.
2:15 who loved the wages of **d** wrong,
3Jn 1:10 to what he is **d** in spreading false charges
Tob 2: 8 to be put to death for **d** this, and he ran away;
Jdt 8:34 Only, do not try to find out what I am **d;**
11:14 even the people in Jerusalem have been **d** this,
AdE 3: 5 that Mordecai was not **d** obeisance to him,
13: 5 **d** all the harm they can so that our kingdom may
Wis 11:13 they perceived it was the Lord's **d.**
18: 2 previously wronged, were **d** them no injury;
Sir 15:11 Do not say, "It was the Lord's **d** that I fell away";
39:31 They take delight in **d** his bidding,
Bar 1:22 and **d** what is evil in the sight of the Lord our God.
1Mc 8: 2 the brave deeds that they were **d** among the Gauls,
8:31 "Concerning the wrongs that King Demetrius is **d**
10:11 He directed those who were **d** the work to build
14:36 **d** great damage to its purity.
2Mc 6:22 so that by **d** this he might be saved from death,
12:43 In **d** this he acted very well and honorably,
3Mc 1: 7 By **d** this, and by endowing their sacred enclosures
7: 8 with no one in any place **d** them harm at all
2Es 3:26 in everything **d** just as Adam
4Mc 4:13 although otherwise he had scruples about **d** so,

DOINGS (26) [DO]

Ps 106: 2 Who can utter the mighty **d** of the LORD,
106:39 and prostituted themselves in their **d.**
145:17 and kind in all his **d.**
Isa 1:16 remove the evil of your **d** from before my eyes;
19:14 in all its **d** as a drunkard staggers around in vomit.
Jer 4: 4 because of the evil of your **d.**
4:18 Your ways and your **d** have brought this upon you.
7: 3 Amend your ways and your **d,**
7: 5 For if you truly amend your ways and your **d,**
17:10 according to the fruit of their **d.**
18:11 and amend your ways and your **d.**
21:12 with no one to quench it, because of your evil **d.**
21:14 I will punish you according to the fruit of your **d,**
23: 2 So I will attend to you for your evil **d,**
23:22 and from the evil of their **d.**
25: 5 from your evil way and wicked **d,**
26: 3 to bring on them because of their evil **d.**
26:13 Now therefore amend your ways and your **d,**
32:19 to their ways and according to the fruit of their **d.**
35:15 and amend your **d,** and do not go after other gods
44:22 the sight of your evil **d,** the abominations
Eze 24:14 to your ways and your **d** I will judge you,
Mic 2: 7 Is the LORD's patience exhausted? Are these his **d?**
7:13 for the fruit of their **d.**
Rev 2:22 unless they repent of her **d;**
2Es 15: 6 and their harmful **d** have reached their limit.

DOK (1)

1Mc 16:15 the little stronghold called **D,** which he had built;

DOLE (1)

Lev 26:26 and they shall **d** out your bread by weight;

DOLEFUL (KJV) See HOWLING, BITTER

DOLT (1)

Ps 49:10 fool and **d** perish together and leave their wealth

DOMAIN (1)

Sir 24:11 and in Jerusalem was my **d.**

DOME‡ (16)

Ge 1: 6 "Let there be a **d** in the midst of the waters,
1: 7 made the **d** and separated the waters that were
under the **d** from the waters that were above the **d.**
1: 8 God called the **d** Sky.
1:14 the **d** of the sky to separate the day from the night;
1:15 in the **d** of the sky to give light upon the earth."
1:17 God set them in the **d** of the sky to give light upon
1:20 and let birds fly above the earth across the **d** of
Job 22:14 and he walks on the **d** of heaven.'
Eze 1:22 the living creatures there was something like a **d,**
1:23 the **d** their wings were stretched out straight, one
1:25 a voice from above the **d** over their heads;
1:26 above the **d** over their heads there was something
10: 1 and above the **d** that was over the heads of
2Es 16:59 like a **d** and made it secure upon the waters;

DOMESTIC (4)

Ge 7:14 and all **d** animals of every kind,
7:21 birds, **d** animals, wild animals,
8: 1 and all the **d** animals that were with him in the ark.
9:10 the birds, the **d** animals, and every animal of

DOMINANCE (2) [DOMINATE]

4Mc 1:31 Self-control, then, is **d** over the desires.
6:34 to acknowledge the **d** of reason when it masters

DOMINANT (1) [DOMINATE]

4Mc 1: 7 from many and various examples that reason is **d**

DOMINATE (1) [DOMINANCE, DOMINANT, DOMINATED, DOMINATION, DOMINEER, DOMINION, DOMINIONS]

4Mc 5:38 but you shall not **d** my religious principles,

DOMINATED (3) [DOMINATE]

1Co 6:12 but I will not be **d** by anything.
2Es 11:32 and with much oppression **d** its inhabitants;
4Mc 7:20 therefore arises when some persons appear to be **d**

DOMINATION (3) [DOMINATE]

4Mc 1:34 we abstain because of **d** by reason.
3:18 by nobility of reason spurn all **d** by the emotions.
6:32 we would have testified to their **d.**

DOMINEER (1) [DOMINATE]

2Es 6:57 **d** over us and devour us.

DOMINION‡ (54) [DOMINATE]

Ge 1:26 and let them have **d** over the fish of the sea,
1:28 and have **d** over the fish of the sea and over
37: 8 Are you indeed to have **d** over us?"
Jdg 14: 4 At that time the Philistines had **d** over Israel.
1Ki 4:24 For he had **d** over all the region west of
9:19 in Lebanon, and in all the land of his **d.**
2Ch 8: 6 in Lebanon, and in all the land of his **d.**
Ne 9:28 so that they had **d** over them;
Job 25: 2 "**D** and fear are with God;
Ps 8: 6 You have given them **d** over the works
19:13 do not let them have **d** over me.
22:28 For **d** belongs to the LORD,
72: 8 May he have **d** from sea to sea,
103:22 all his works, in all places of his **d.**
114: 2 Judah became God's sanctuary, Israel his **d.**
119:133 and never let iniquity have **d** over me.
145:13 and your **d** endures throughout all generations.
Jer 34: 1 and all the peoples under his **d** were fighting
51:28 and every land under their **d.**
Eze 30:18 when I break there the **d** of Egypt,
Da 6:26 in all my royal **d** people should tremble and fear
6:26 and his **d** has no end.
7: 6 and **d** was given to it.
7:12 for the rest of the beasts, their **d** was taken away,
7:14 To him was given **d** and glory and kingship,
7:14 His **d** is an everlasting **d** that shall not pass away,
7:26 and his **d** shall be taken away,
7:27 and **d** and the greatness of the kingdoms under
11: 3 who shall rule with great **d** and take action
11: 4 nor according to the **d** with which he ruled;
Mic 4: 8 to you it shall come, the former **d** shall come,
Zec 9:10 his **d** shall be from sea to sea,
Ro 5:14 Yet death exercised **d** from Adam to Moses,
5:17 death exercised **d** through that one,
5:17 and the free gift of righteousness exercise **d** in life
5:21 just as sin exercised **d** in death,
5:21 also exercise **d** through justification leading
6: 9 death no longer has **d** over him.
6:12 do not let sin exercise **d** in your mortal bodies,
6:14 For sin will have no **d** over you,
Eph 1:21 far above all rule and authority and power and **d,**
1Ti 6:16 to him be honor and eternal **d.**
Rev 1: 6 to him be glory and **d** forever and ever.
AdE 14:12 O King of the gods and Master of all **d!**
Wis 1:14 and the **d** of Hades is not on earth.
6: 3 For your **d** was given you from the Lord,
9: 2 to have **d** over the creatures you have made,
Sir 16:27 and their **d** for all generations.
17: 4 and gave them **d** over beasts and birds.
Bel 1: 5 and earth and has **d** over all living creatures."
1Mc 8:24 to Rome or to any of their allies in all their **d,**
3Mc 6:24 to deprive of **d** and life by secretly devising acts
2Es 3:28 Is that why it has gained **d** over Zion?

DOMINIONS (2) [DOMINATE]

Da 7:27 and all **d** shall serve and obey them."
Col 1:16 whether thrones or **d** or rulers or powers—

DONATION (7) [DONATIONS, DONORS]

Lev 22:14 If a man eats of the sacred **d** unintentionally,
22:14 and give the sacred **d** to the priest.
27:23 a sacred **d** to the LORD.
Nu 15:19 you shall present a **d** to the LORD.
15:20 of dough you shall present a loaf as a **d;**
15:20 you shall present it just as you present a **d** from
15:21 to the LORD a **d** from the first of your batch

DONATIONS (19) [DONATION]

Ex 28:38 that the Israelites consecrate as their sacred **d;**
Lev 22: 2 and his sons to deal carefully with the sacred **d** of
22: 3 the sacred **d,** which the people of Israel dedicate to
22: 4 or suffers a discharge may eat of the sacred **d**
22: 6 of the sacred **d** unless he has washed his body
22: 7 and afterward he may eat of the sacred **d,**
22:10 No lay person shall eat of the sacred **d.**
22:10 of the priest shall eat of the sacred **d;**
22:12 she shall not eat of the offering of the sacred **d;**
22:15 No one shall profane the sacred **d** of the people
22:16 a guilt offering, by eating their sacred **d:**
Nu 5: 9 Among all the sacred **d** of the Israelites,
5:10 The sacred **d** of all are their own;
Dt 12: 6 your tithes and your **d,** your votive gifts,
12:11 and your sacrifices, your tithes and your **d,**
12:17 your freewill offerings, or your **d;**
12:26 But the sacred **d** that are due from you,
2Ki 12: 4 "All the money offered as sacred **d** that is brought
Ne 10:33 the appointed festivals, the sacred **d,**

DONE‡ (623) [DO]

Ge 2: 2 the work that he had **d,**
2: 2 on the seventh day from all the work that he had **d.**
2: 3 on it God rested from all the work that he had **d**
3:13 "What is this that you have **d?"**
3:14 "Because you have **d** this,
4:10 And the LORD said, "What have you **d?**
8:21 again destroy every living creature as I have **d.**
9:24 and knew what his youngest son had **d** to him,
12:18 and said, "What is this you have **d** to me?
16: 5 "May the wrong **d** to me be on you!
18:21 and see whether they have **d** altogether according
20: 9 and said to him, "What have you **d** to us?
20: 9 You have **d** things to me that ought not to be **d."**
21:26 "I do not know who has **d** this;
22:16 Because you have **d** this, and have
24:66 the servant told Isaac all the things that he had **d.**
26:10 Abimelech said, "What is this you have **d** to us?
26:29 just as we have not touched you and have **d**
27:19 I have **d** as you told me;
27:45 and he forgets what you have **d** to him;
28:15 until I have **d** what I have promised you."
29:25 "What is this you have **d** to me?
29:26 Laban said, "This is not **d** in our country—
31:26 Laban said to Jacob, "What have you **d?**
31:28 What you have **d** is foolish.
34: 7 for such a thing ought not to be **d.**
39:22 and whatever was **d** there,
40:15 also I have **d** nothing that they should have put me
41:21 that they had **d** so, for they were still as ugly
42:25 This was **d** for them.
42:28 saying, "What is this that God has **d** to us?"
44: 5 You have **d** wrong in doing this.' "
44:15 "What deed is this that you have **d?**
Ex 1:18 "Why have you **d** this, and allowed the boys
3:16 I have given heed to you and to what has been **d**
5:23 you have **d** nothing at all to deliver your people."
10: 2 of the Egyptians and what signs I have **d**
12:16 no work shall be **d** on those days;
12:35 The Israelites had **d** as Moses told them;
14: 5 and they said, "What have we **d,**
14:11 What have you **d** to us, bringing us out of Egypt?
18: 1 that God had **d** for Moses and for his people Israel,
18: 8 the LORD had **d** to Pharaoh and to the Egyptians
18: 9 for all the good that the LORD had **d** to Israel,
31:15 Six days shall work be **d,** but the seventh day is
35: 2 be **d,** but on the seventh day you shall have
35:29 the LORD had commanded by Moses to be **d,**
35:35 with skill to do every kind of work **d** by an artisan
39:32 the Israelites had **d** everything just as
39:42 The Israelites had **d** all of the work just as
39:43 When Moses saw that they had **d** all the work just
Lev 4: 2 about things not to be **d,** and does any one
4:13 by the LORD's commandments ought not to be **d**
4:20 He shall do with the bull just as is **d** with the bull
4:22 of the LORD his God ought not to be **d**
4:27 by the LORD's commandments ought not to be **d**

Lev 5:17 the LORD's commandments ought not to be **d**,
8: 5 "This is what the LORD has commanded to be **d**."
8:34 been **d** today, the LORD has commanded to be **d**
18:30 of these abominations that were **d** before you,
23: 3 Six days shall work be **d**;
Nu 3:38 whatever had to be **d** for the Israelites;
4:26 and they shall do all that needs to be **d** with regard
14:11 in spite of all the signs that I have **d** among them?
15:11 Thus it shall be **d** for each ox or ram,
15:24 if it was **d** unintentionally without the knowledge
15:34 because it was not clear what should be **d** to him.
22: 2 of Zippor saw all that Israel had **d** to the Amorites.
22:28 and it said to Balaam, "What have I **d** to you,
23:11 Balak said to Balaam, "What have you **d** to me?
23:11 but now you have **d** nothing but bless them."
23:23 be said of Jacob and Israel, 'See what God has **d**!'
32:13 until all the generation that had **d** evil in the sight
Dt 2:12 as Israel has **d** in the land that
2:29 as the descendants of Esau who live in Seir have **d**
2:30 in order to hand him over to you, as he has now **d**.
3: 6 as we had **d** to King Sihon of Heshbon,
3:21 the LORD your God has **d** to these two kings;
10:10 as I had **d** the first time.
10:21 who has **d** for you these great and awesome things
12:31 that the LORD hates they have **d** for their gods.
13:14 an abhorrent thing has been **d** among you,
25: 9 "This is what is **d** to the man who does not build
29:24 "Why has the LORD **d** thus to this land?
31:18 of all the evil they have **d** by turning to other gods.
Jos 5: 8 When the circumcising of all the nation was **d**,
7:15 and for having **d** an outrageous thing in Israel.' "
7:19 Tell me now what you have **d**;
9: 3 the inhabitants of Gibeon heard what Joshua had **d**
10: 1 and its king as he had **d** to Jericho and its king,
10:28 And he did to the king of Makkedah as he had **d** to
10:30 to its king as he had **d** to the king of Jericho.
10:32 and every person in it, as he had **d** to Libnah.
10:35 in it he utterly destroyed that day, as he had **d**
10:37 he left no one remaining, just as he had **d** to Eglon,
10:39 just as he had **d** to Hebron, and,
10:39 and, as he had **d** to Libnah and its king,
20: 6 to the town in which the deed was **d**.' "
23: 3 the LORD your God has **d** to all these nations
23: 8 as you have **d** to this day.
24:20 and consume you, after having **d** you good."
Jdg 1: 7 as I have **d**, so God has paid me back."
2: 2 See what you have **d**!
2: 7 the great work that the LORD had **d** for Israel.
2:10 the LORD or the work that he had **d** for Israel.
3:12 against Israel, because they had **d** what was evil in
6:29 So they said to one another, "Who has **d** this?"
8: 1 Ephraimites said to him, "What have you **d** to us,
8: 2 "What have I **d** now in comparison with you?
8:35 in return for all the good that he had **d** to Israel.
9:16 and have **d** to him as his actions deserved—
9:24 so that the violence **d** to the seventy sons
9:48 you have seen me do, do quickly, as I have **d**."
11:37 she said to her father, "Let this thing be **d** for me:
14: 6 not tell his father or his mother what he had **d**.
15: 6 Then the Philistines asked, "Who has **d** this?"
15:11 What then have you **d** to us?"
15:11 "As they did to me, so I have **d** to them."
20:10 of Benjamin for all the disgrace that they have **d**
Ru 2:11 "All that you have **d** for your mother-in-law since
3:16 Then she told her all that the man had **d** for her,
1Sa 6: 9 then it is he who has **d** us this great harm;
8: 8 Just as they have **d** to me,
11: 7 so shall it be **d** to his oxen!"
12:17 that the wickedness that you have **d** in the sight of
12:20 you have **d** all this evil, yet do not turn aside
12:24 for consider what great things he has **d** for you.
13:11 Samuel said, "What have you **d**?"
13:13 Samuel said to Saul, "You have **d** foolishly;
14:43 Saul said to Jonathan, "Tell me what you have **d**."
17:26 be **d** for the man who kills this Philistine,
17:27 "So shall it be **d** for the man who kills him."
17:29 David said, "What have I **d** now?
19:18 and told him all that Saul had **d** to him.
20: 1 before Jonathan and said, "What have I **d**?
20:32 to death? What has he **d**?"
24:19 with good for what you have **d** to me this day.
25:30 When the LORD has **d** to my lord according
26:16 This thing that you have **d** is not good.
26:18 For what have I **d**?
26:21 Then Saul said, "I have **d** wrong;
27:11 and say, 'David has **d** so and so.' "
28: 9 "Surely you know what Saul has **d**,
28:17 The LORD has **d** to you just as he spoke by me;
28:18 therefore the LORD has **d** this thing to you today.
29: 8 David said to Achish, "But what have I **d**?
29:10 for you have **d** well before me.
31:11 of Jabesh-gilead heard what the Philistines had **d**
2Sa 2: 6 because you have **d** this thing.
3:24 to the king and said, "What have you **d**?
11:27 the thing that David had **d** displeased the LORD,
12: 5 the man who has **d** this deserves to die;
12:21 "What is this thing that you have **d**?
13:12 for such a thing is not **d** in Israel;
16:10 who then shall say, 'Why have you **d** so?' "
21:11 the concubine of Saul, had **d**,
24:10 "I have sinned greatly in what I have **d**.
24:10 for I have **d** very foolishly."
24:17 "I alone have sinned, and I alone have **d** wickedly;
24:17 but these sheep, what have they **d**?
1Ki 1: 6 "Why have you **d** thus and so?"
8:47 saying, 'We have sinned, and have **d** wrong;
9: 8 'Why has the LORD **d** such a thing to this land
1Ki 11: 6 as his father David had **d**.
13:11 that the man of God had **d** that day in Bethel;
14: 9 but you have **d** evil above all those who were
14:22 more than all that their ancestors had **d**.
15:11 as his father David had **d**.
18:36 and that I have **d** all these things at your bidding.
19: 1 Ahab told Jezebel all that Elijah had **d**,
19:20 for what have I **d** to you?"
21:26 in going after idols, as the Amorites had **d**, whom
22:53 the God of Israel, to anger, just as his father had **d**.
2Ki 4:13 what may be **d** for you?
4:14 He said, "What then may be **d** for her?"
5:13 would you not have **d** it?
8: 4 "Tell me all the great things that Elisha has **d**."
8:18 as the house of Ahab had **d**,
8:27 as the house of Ahab had **d**,
10:10 for the LORD has **d** what he said
10:30 "Because you have **d** well
14: 3 in all things he did as his father Joash had **d**.
15: 3 just as his father Amaziah had **d**.
15: 9 in the sight of the LORD, as his ancestors had **d**.
15:34 just as his father Uzziah had **d**.
16: 2 as his ancestor David had **d**,
17: 4 as he had **d** year by year;
18: 3 of the LORD just as his ancestor David had **d**.
18:14 of Assyria at Lachish, saying, "I have **d** wrong;
19:11 you have heard what the kings of Assyria have **d**
20: 3 and have **d** what is good in your sight."
21: 3 made a sacred pole, as King Ahab of Israel had **d**,
21: 9 the nations had **d** that the LORD destroyed before
21:11 has **d** things more wicked than all that
21:15 because they have **d** what is evil in my sight
21:20 as his father Manasseh had **d**.
23:17 and predicted these things that you have **d** against
23:19 he did to them just as he had **d** at Bethel.
23:32 just as his ancestors had **d**.
23:37 just as all his ancestors had **d**.
24: 9 just as his father had **d**.
24:19 the sight of the LORD, just as Jehoiakim had **d**.
1Ch 10:11 that the Philistines had **d** to Saul,
12:17 though my hands have **d** no wrong,
16:12 Remember the wonderful works he has **d**,
17:19 you have **d** all these great deeds,
21: 8 "I have sinned greatly in that I have **d** this thing.
21: 8 for I have **d** very foolishly."
21:17 It is I who have sinned and **d** very wickedly.
21:17 But these sheep, what have they **d**?
29: 5 and for all the work to be **d** by artisans,
2Ch 6:37 saying, 'We have sinned, and have **d** wrong;
7:21 'Why has the LORD **d** such a thing to this land
16: 9 You have **d** foolishly in this;
21: 6 as the house of Ahab had **d**;
22: 4 as the house of Ahab had **d**;
24:16 because he had **d** good in Israel,
25:16 because you have **d** this and have not listened
26: 4 just as his father Amaziah had **d**.
26:18 Go out of the sanctuary; for you have **d** wrong,
27: 2 of the LORD just as his father Uzziah had **d**—
28: 1 as his ancestor David had **d**,
29: 2 just as his ancestor David had **d**.
29: 6 and have **d** what was evil in the sight of
29:36 the people rejoiced because of what God had **d** for
32:13 Do you not know what I and my ancestors have **d**
32:25 not respond according to the benefit **d** to him,
32:31 to him to inquire about the sign that had been **d** in
33:22 as his father Manasseh had **d**.
Ezr 5: 8 this work is being **d** diligently and prospers
6:12 let it be **d** with all diligence."
7:21 requires of you, let it be **d** with all diligence,
7:23 be **d** with zeal for the house of the God of heaven,
9: 1 After these things had been **d**,
10: 3 and let it be **d** according to the law.
Ne 5:19 O my God, all that I have **d** for this people.
6: 8 saying, "No such things as you say have been **d**;
6: 9 and it will not be **d**."
8:17 to that day the people of Israel had not **d** so.
13: 7 the wrong that Eliashib had **d** on behalf of Tobiah,
13:14 and do not wipe out my good deeds that I have **d**
Est 1:15 what is to be **d** to Queen Vashti because she has
1:16 "Not only has Queen Vashti **d** wrong to the king,
2: 1 and what she had **d** and what had been decreed
4: 1 When Mordecai learned all that had been **d**,
6: 3 "Nothing has been **d** for him."
6: 6 be **d** for the man whom the king wishes to honor?"
6: 9 be **d** for the man whom the king wishes
6:11 be **d** for the man whom the king wishes to honor."
9:12 What have they **d** in the rest of
9:14 So the king commanded this to be **d**;
Job 6:29 Turn, I pray, let no wrong be **d**.
12: 9 not know that the hand of the LORD has **d** this?
21:31 and who repays them for what they have **d**?
34:32 if I have **d** iniquity, I will do it no more'?
36:23 or who can say, 'You have **d** wrong'?
42: 8 of me what is right, as my servant Job has **d**."
Ps 7: 3 O LORD my God, if I have **d** this,
22:31 saying that he has **d** it.
33: 4 and all his work is **d** in faithfulness.
39: 9 for it is you who have **d** it.
50:21 These things you have **d** and I have been silent;
51: 4 have I sinned, and **d** what is evil in your sight,
52: 1 O mighty one, of mischief **d** against the godly?
52: 9 because of what you have **d**.
58:10 righteous will rejoice when they see vengeance **d**;
64: 9 and ponder what he has **d**.
66: 5 Come and see what God has **d**:
66:16 and I will tell what he has **d** for me.
68:28 O God, as you have **d** for us before.
Ps 69: 5 the wrongs I have **d** are not hidden from you.
71:19 You who have **d** great things, O God,
78: 4 and his might, and the wonders that he has **d**.
78:11 They forgot what he had **d**,
98: 1 for he has **d** marvelous things.
105: 5 Remember the wonderful works he has **d**,
106: 6 we have committed iniquity, have **d** wickedly.
106:21 their Savior, who had **d** great things in Egypt,
109:27 you, O LORD, have **d** it.
119:121 I have **d** what is just and right;
120: 3 what more shall be **d** to you, you deceitful tongue?
126: 2 "The LORD has **d** great things for them."
126: 3 LORD has **d** great things for us, and we rejoiced.
137: 8 be who pay you back what you have **d** to us!
Pr 3:30 when no harm has been **d** to you.
4:16 For they cannot sleep unless they have **d** wrong;
21:15 When justice is **d**, it is a joy to the righteous,
24:29 "I will do to others as they have **d** to me;
24:29 I will pay them back for what they have **d**."
30:20 and says, "I have **d** no wrong."
31:29 "Many women have **d** excellently,
Ecc 1: 9 and what has been **d** is what will be **d**;
1:13 to search out by wisdom all that is **d** under heaven;
1:14 I saw all the deeds that are **d** under the sun;
2:11 Then I considered all that my hands had **d** and
2:12 Only what has already been **d**.
2:17 what is **d** under the sun was grievous to me;
3:11 yet they cannot find out what God has **d** from
3:14 God has **d** this, so that all should stand in awe
4: 3 not seen the evil deeds that are **d** under the sun.
8: 9 applying my mind to all that is **d** under the sun,
8:10 in the city where they had **d** such things.
8:16 and to see the business that is **d** on earth,
Isa 3:11 for what their hands have **d** shall be **d** to them.
5: 4 to do for my vineyard that I have not **d** in it?
10:11 not do to Jerusalem and her idols what I have **d**
10:13 "By the strength of my hand I have **d** it,
12: 5 to the LORD, for he has **d** gloriously;
20: 2 and he had **d** so, walking naked and barefoot.
25: 1 for you have **d** wonderful things,
26:12 all that we have **d**, you have **d** for us.
33:13 Hear, you who are far away, what I have **d**;
37:11 you have heard what the kings of Assyria have **d**
38: 3 and have **d** what is good in your sight."
38:15 For he has spoken to me, and he himself has **d** it.
41: 4 Who has performed and **d** this,
41:20 that the hand of the LORD has **d** this,
44:23 Sing, O heavens, for the LORD has **d** it;
46:10 and from ancient times things not yet **d**,
53: 9 although he had **d** no violence,
63: 7 because of all that the LORD has **d** for us,
Jer 2:23 in the valley; know what you have **d**—
3: 5 but you have **d** all the evil that you could.
3: 7 "After she has **d** all this she will return to me";
5:13 Thus shall it be **d** to them!
5:19 "Why has the LORD our God **d** all these things
7:13 And now, because you have **d** all these things,
7:30 For the people of Judah have **d** evil in my sight,
8: 6 of wickedness, saying, "What have I **d**!"
11:15 when she has **d** vile deeds?
11:17 the house of Israel and the house of Judah have **d**,
18: 6 O house of Israel, just as this potter has **d**?
18:13 The virgin Israel has **d** a most horrible thing.
21: 2 a wonderful deed for us, as he has often **d**,
30:15 I have **d** these things to you.
31:37 the offspring of Israel because of all they have **d**,
32:30 of Israel and the people of Judah have **d** nothing
32:30 of Israel have **d** nothing but provoke me to anger
35:10 and have obeyed and **d** all
35:18 and **d** all that he commanded you,
37:18 "What wrong have I **d** to you or your servants
40: 3 and has **d** as he said,
41:11 the crimes that Ishmael son of Nethaniah had **d**,
50:15 take vengeance on her, do to her as she has **d**.
50:29 just as she has **d**, do to her—
51:12 the LORD has both planned and **d** what he spoke
51:24 for all the wrong that they have **d** in Zion,
52: 2 the sight of the LORD, just as Jehoiakim had **d**.
La 1:21 they are glad that you have **d** it.
2:17 The LORD has **d** what he purposed,
2:20 To whom have you **d** this?
3:37 Who can command and have it **d**,
3:59 You have seen the wrong **d** to me, O LORD;
Eze 3:20 and their righteous deeds that they have **d** shall not
5: 9 I will do to you what I have never yet **d**,
8:17 of Judah commits the abominations **d** here?
9:11 saying, "I have **d** as you commanded me."
12:11 as I have **d**, so shall it be **d** to them;
14:23 not without cause that I did all that I have **d** in it,
16:48 your sister Sodom and her daughters have not **d**
16:48 not done as you and your daughters have **d**.
16:54 and be ashamed of all that you have **d**,
16:59 I will deal with you as you have **d**,
16:63 when I forgive you all that you have **d**,
18:13 He has **d** all these abominable things;
18:14 a son who sees all the sins that his father has **d**,
18:19 When the son has **d** what is lawful and right,
18:22 the righteousness that they have **d** they shall live.
18:24 None of the righteous deeds that they have **d** shall
22:26 Its priests have **d** violence to my teaching
23:38 Moreover this they have **d** to me:
23:48 and not commit lewdness as you have **d**.
24:22 And you shall do as I have **d**;
24:24 you shall do just as he has **d**.
33:16 they have **d** what is lawful and right,
43:11 When they are ashamed of all that they have **d**,
44:14 to do all its chores, all that is to be **d** in it.

Da 6:10 just as he had **d** previously.
6:22 and also before you, O king, I have **d** no wrong."
9: 5 we have sinned and **d** wrong,
9:12 that what has been **d** against Jerusalem has never before been **d** under
9:14 the LORD our God is right in all that he has **d;**
9:15 we have sinned, we have **d** wickedly.
11:24 and do what none of his predecessors had ever **d,**
11:36 for what is determined shall be **d.**
Hos 10:15 Thus it shall be **d** to you, O Bethel,
Joel 2:20 Surely he has **d** great things!
2:21 for the LORD has **d** great things!
3:19 because of the violence **d** to the people of Judah,
Am 3: 6 unless the LORD has **d** it?
Ob 1:10 the slaughter and violence **d** to your brother Jacob,
1:15 As you have **d,** it shall be **d** to you;
Jnh 1:10 and said to him, "What is this that you have **d!"**
1:14 for you, O LORD, have **d** as it pleased you."
Mic 6: 3 "O my people, what have I **d** to you?
Hab 1: 5 For a work is being **d** in your days that you would
2:17 the violence **d** to Lebanon will overwhelm you;
Zep 3: 4 they have **d** violence to the law.
Zec 7: 3 as I have **d** for so many years?"
Mt 6: 4 so that your alms may be **d** in secret;
6:10 Your will be **d,** on earth as it is in heaven.
8:13 let it be **d** for you according to your faith."
9:29 "According to your faith let it be **d** to you."
11:20 in which most of his deeds of power had been **d,**
11:21 the deeds of power **d** in you had been **d** in Tyre
11:23 deeds of power **d** in you had been **d** in Sodom,
13:28 He answered, 'An enemy has **d** this.'
15:28 Let it be **d** for you as you wish."
16:27 then he will repay everyone for what has been **d.**
18:19 it will be **d** for you by my Father in heaven.
21:21 only will you do what has been **d** to the fig tree,
21:21 'Be lifted up and thrown into the sea,' it will be **d.**
25:21 His master said to him, 'Well **d,**
25:23 His master said to him, 'Well **d,**
26:13 what she has **d** will be told in remembrance
26:42 if this cannot pass unless I drink it, your will be **d."**
27:23 Then he asked, "Why, what evil has he **d?"**
Mk 5:19 and tell them how much the Lord has **d** for you,
5:20 in the Decapolis how much Jesus had **d** for him;
5:32 He looked all around to see who had **d** it.
6: 2 What deeds of power are being **d** by his hands!
6:30 and told him all that they had **d** and taught.
7:37 saying, "He has **d** everything well;
9:23 All things can be **d** for the one who believes."
11:23 it will be **d** for you.
14: 8 She has **d** what she could;
14: 9 what she has **d** will be told in remembrance
15:14 Pilate asked them, "Why, what evil has he **d?"**
Lk 1:25 the Lord has **d** for me when he looked favorably
1:49 for the Mighty One has **d** great things for me,
3:19 because of all the evil things that Herod had **d,**
4:35 of him without having **d** him any harm.
5: 6 When they had **d** this, they caught so many fish
8:39 and declare how much God has **d** for you."
8:39 throughout the city how much Jesus had **d** for him.
9:10 the apostles told Jesus all they had **d.**
10:13 the deeds of power **d** in you had been **d** in Tyre
13:14 "There are six days on which work ought to be **d;**
14:22 the slave said, 'Sir, what you ordered has been **d,**
17:10 when you have **d** all that you were ordered to do,
17:10 we have **d** only what we ought to have **d!'"**
19:17 He said to him, 'Well **d,** good slave!
22:42 yet, not my will but yours be **d."**
23:15 Indeed, he has **d** nothing to deserve death.
23:22 "Why, what evil has he **d?**
23:41 but this man has **d** nothing wrong."
Jn 3:21 be clearly seen that their deeds have been **d**
4:29 a man who told me everything I have ever **d!**
4:39 "He told me everything I have ever **d.**"
4:45 since they had seen all that he had **d** in Jerusalem
5:29 those who have **d** good, to the resurrection of life,
5:29 and those who have **d** evil,
6:14 When the people saw the sign that he had **d,**
7:31 will he do more signs than this man has **d?"**
11:46 to the Pharisees and told them what he had **d.**
12:16 of him and had been **d** to him.
13:12 "Do you know what I have **d** to you?
13:15 that you also should do as I have **d** to you.
15: 7 and it will be **d** for you.
15:24 not **d** among them the works that no one else did,
18:35 to me. What have you **d?"**
Ac 2:43 because many wonders and signs were being **d** by
4: 9 of a good deed **d** to someone who was sick
4:16 that a notable sign has been **d** through them;
5:12 and wonders were **d** among the people through
9:13 much evil he has **d** to your saints in Jerusalem;
14: 3 of his grace by granting signs and wonders to be **d**
14:11 When the crowds saw what Paul had **d,**
14:27 the church together and related all that God had **d**
15: 4 and they reported all that God had **d** with them.
15:12 and wonders that God had **d** through them among
21:14 to say, "The Lord's will be **d."**
21:19 he related one by one the things that God had **d**
21:22 What then is to be **d?**
21:33 he inquired who he was and what he had **d.**
25:10 I have **d** no wrong to the Jews,
25:25 But I found that he had **d** nothing deserving death;
26:26 for this was not **d** in a corner.
28:17 though I had **d** nothing against our people or
Ro 1:28 a debased mind and to things that should not be **d.**
8: 3 For God has **d** what the law,
9:11 before they had been born or had **d** anything good
9:23 if he has **d** so in order to make known the riches
1Co 3:13 and the fire will test what sort of work each has **d.**
5: 2 that he who has **d** this would have been removed
5: 4 the Lord Jesus on the man who has **d** such a thing.
14:26 What should be **d** then, my friends?
14:26 Let all things be **d** for building up.
14:40 but all things should be **d** decently and in order.
16:14 Let all that you do be **d** in love.
2Co 5:10 for what has been **d** in the body,
10:16 of work already **d** in someone else's sphere
Gal 4:12 You have **d** me no wrong.
Eph 6:13 and having **d** everything, to stand firm.
Col 3:23 as **d** for the Lord and not for your masters,
3:25 be paid back for whatever wrong has been **d,**
Tit 1: 5 you should put in order what remained to be **d,**
3: 5 of any works of righteousness that we had **d,**
Heb 10:36 so that when you have **d** the will of God,
Jas 3:13 Show by your good life that your works are **d**
2Pe 3:10 and everything that is **d** on it will be disclosed.
Rev 16:17 from the throne, saying, "It is **d!"**
20:13 and all were judged according to what they had **d.**
21: 6 Then he said to me, "It is **d!**
Tob 12: 6 the living for the good things he has **d** for you.
13: 6 So now see what he has **d** for you;
14:15 Tobias praised God for all he had **d** to the people
Jdt 4: 1 the king of the Assyrians, had **d** to the nations,
6: 2 as you have **d** today and tell us not to make war
7:24 You have **d** us a great injury in not making peace
8:18 as was **d** in days gone by.
9: 2 for you said, 'It shall not be **d'**—yet they did it.
9: 5 "For you have **d** these things and those that went
10:10 When they had **d** this, Judith went out,
11:22 "God has **d** well to send you ahead of the people,
13:11 against our enemies, as he has **d** today!"
14: 8 Now tell me what you have **d** during these days."
14: 8 in the presence of the people all that she had **d,**
14:10 When Achior saw all that the God of Israel had **d,**
15: 8 to witness the good things that the Lord had **d**
15:10 You have **d** all this with your own hand;
15:10 you have **d** great good to Israel,
AdE 1:15 and told him what must be **d** to Queen Vashti for
2:20 just as she had **d** when she was with him.
3: 2 for so the king had commanded to be **d.**
4: 1 When Mordecai learned of all that had been **d,**
5: 8 and tomorrow I will do as I have **d** today."
6: 3 "You have not **d** anything for him."
6: 9 be **d** to everyone whom the king honors.' "
6:11 be **d** to everyone whom the king wishes to honor."
9:12 What do you suppose they have **d** in
9:12 Whatever more you ask will be **d** for you."
9:14 So he permitted this to be **d,**
9:29 the Jew wrote down what they had **d,**
10: 9 God has **d** great signs and wonders,
Wis 3:14 the eunuch whose hands have **d** no lawless deed,
12:12 For who will say, "What have you **d?"**
14:10 for what was **d** will be punished together with
Sir 12: 5 as much evil for all the good you have **d** to them.
28: 2 Forgive your neighbor the wrong he has **d,**
31: 9 For he has **d** wonders among his people.
39:16 and whatever he commands will be **d** at
Bar 2: 2 Under the whole heaven there has not been **d** the
2: 2 not been done the like of what he has **d**
2:12 we have been ungodly, we have **d** wrong,
LtJ 6:44 Whatever is **d** for these idols is false.
Aza 1: 4 For you are just in all you have **d;**
1: 7 not kept them or **d** what you have commanded us
1: 8 and all that you have **d** to us,
1: 8 you have **d** by a true judgment.
Sus 1:43 though I have **d** none of the wicked things
Bel 1: 9 "Let it be **d** as you have said."
1Mc 2:18 and those that are left in Jerusalem have **d.**
2:40 "If we all do as our kindred have **d** and refuse
2:67 and avenge the wrong **d** to your people.
3:34 and gave him orders about all that he wanted **d.**
4:60 and trampling them down as they had **d** before.
7:23 the wrongs that Alcimus and those with him had **d**
7:23 it was more than the Gentiles had **d.**
8: 3 and what they had **d** in the land of Spain
10:15 of the brave deeds that they had **d,**
10:23 "What is this that we have **d?**
10:46 the great wrongs that Demetrius had **d** in Israel
11: 5 They also told the king what Jonathan had **d,**
11:40 He also reported to Imalkue what Demetrius had **d**
11:53 not repay the favors that Jonathan had **d** him,
13: 3 of my father have **d** for the laws and the sanctuary;
14:35 because he had **d** all these things and because of
15:29 you have **d** great damage in the land,
16: 1 to his father Simon what Cendebeus had **d.**
2Mc 1:22 When this had been **d** and some time had passed,
1:32 When this was **d,** a flame blazed up;
3:12 be **d** to those people who had trusted in
7: 8 as the first brother had **d.**
8:29 they had **d** this, they made common supplication
9: 4 the injury **d** by those who had put him to flight;
10: 4 When they had **d** this, they fell prostrate
10:12 to the Jews because of the wrong that had been **d**
11:31 be molested in any way for what may have been **d**
12: 4 and this was **d** by public vote of the city.
13: 9 that had been **d** in his father's time.
14:28 when the man had **d** no wrong.
15:38 if it is poorly **d** and mediocre,
1Es 1:32 it was ordained that this should always be **d**
1:33 and the things that he had **d** before,
2:28 the city and to take care that nothing more be **d**
3:23 they do not remember what they have **d.**
4:57 had ordered to be **d,** he also commanded to be **d**
6:22 of the house of the Lord in Jerusalem was **d** with
6:34 that it be **d** with all diligence as here prescribed."
1Es 8:68 After these things had been **d,**
Man 1:10 and have **d** what is evil in your sight,
3Mc 2: 3 and you judge those who have **d** anything
5:17 When this was **d** he urged them to give themselves
2Es 1:34 and have **d** what is evil in my sight.
2: 3 the Lord God and have **d** what is evil in my sight.
3:25 This was **d** for many years;
3:26 as Adam and all his descendants had **d,**
6:43 your word went forth, and at once the work was **d.**
6:47 and fishes; and so it was **d.**
7:18 but those who have **d** wickedly have suffered
7:*118* [48] O Adam, what have you **d?**
7:*119* [49] but we have **d** deeds that bring death?
8:35 there is no one who has not **d** wrong.
11:18 and held the rule as the earlier ones had **d,**
11:33 just as the wings had **d.**
12:41 and what harm have we **d** you,
14:21 things which have been **d** or will be **d**
15:21 Just as they have **d** to my elect until this day,

DONKEY‡ (77) [DONKEY'S, DONKEYS]

Ge 22: 3 Abraham rose early in the morning, saddled his **d,**
22: 5 to his young men, "Stay here with the **d;**
42:27 of them opened his sack to give his **d** fodder at
44:13 Then each one loaded his **d,**
49:14 a strong **d,** lying down between the sheepfolds;
Ex 4:20 on a **d** and went back to the land of Egypt;
13:13 every firstborn **d** you shall redeem with a sheep;
20:17 or **d,** or anything that belongs to your neighbor.
21:33 and an ox or a **d** falls into it,
22: 4 When the animal, whether ox or **d** or sheep,
22: 9 In any case of disputed ownership involving ox, **d,**
22:10 When someone delivers to another a **d,** ox, sheep,
23: 4 upon your enemy's ox or **d** going astray,
23: 5 the **d** of one who hates you lying under its burden
23:12 so that your ox and your **d** may have relief,
34:20 The firstborn of a **d** you shall redeem with a lamb,
Nu 16:15 I have not taken one **d** from them,
22:21 So Balaam got up in the morning, saddled his **d,**
22:22 Now he was riding on the **d,**
22:23 The **d** saw the angel of the LORD standing in
22:23 the **d** turned off the road, and went into the field;
22:23 Balaam struck the **d,** to turn it back onto the road.
22:25 When the **d** saw the angel of the LORD,
22:27 When the **d** saw the angel of the LORD,
22:27 and he struck the **d** with his staff.
22:28 Then the LORD opened the mouth of the **d,**
22:29 Balaam said to the **d,** "Because you have made
22:30 But the **d** said to Balaam, "Am I not your **d,**
22:32 "Why have you struck your **d** these three times?
22:33 The **d** saw me, and turned away
Dt 5:14 or your ox or your **d,** or any of your livestock,
5:21 or **d,** or anything that belongs to your neighbor.
22: 3 You shall do the same with a neighbor's **d;**
22: 4 not see your neighbor's **d** or ox fallen on the road
22:10 not plow with an ox and a **d** yoked together.
28:31 Your **d** shall be stolen in front of you,
Jos 15:18 As she dismounted from her **d,** Caleb said to her,
Jdg 1:14 As she dismounted from her **d,** Caleb said to her,
6: 4 and no sheep or ox or **d.**
15:15 Then he found a fresh jawbone of a **d,**
15:16 And Samson said, "With the jawbone of a **d,**
15:16 the jawbone of a **d** I have slain a thousand men."
19:28 Then he put her on the **d;**
1Sa 12: 3 Or whose **d** have I taken?
15: 3 child and infant, ox and sheep, camel and **d.' "**
16:20 Jesse took a **d** loaded with bread, a skin of wine,
25:20 the **d** and came down under cover of the mountain,
25:23 she hurried and alighted from the **d,**
25:42 Abigail got up hurriedly and rode away on a **d;**
2Sa 17:23 he saddled his **d** and went off home
19:26 for your servant said to him, 'Saddle a **d** for me,
1Ki 2:40 Shimei arose and saddled a **d,** and went to Achish
13:13 Then he said to his sons, "Saddle a **d** for me."
13:13 So they saddled a **d** for him, and he mounted it.
13:23 they saddled for him a **d** belonging to
13:24 and the **d** stood beside it;
13:27 Then he said to his sons, "Saddle a **d** for me."
13:28 with the **d** and the lion standing beside the body.
13:28 The lion had not eaten the body or attacked the **d.**
13:29 laid it on the **d,** and brought it back to the city,
2Ki 4:24 Then she saddled the **d** and said to her servant,
Job 24: 3 They drive away the **d** of the orphan;
Pr 26: 3 A whip for the horse, a bridle for the **d,**
Isa 1: 3 ox knows its owner, and the **d** its master's crib;
32:20 who let the ox and the **d** range freely.
Jer 22:19 With the burial of a **d** he shall be buried—
Zec 9: 9 humble and riding on a **d,** on a colt, the foal of a **d.**
Mt 21: 2 and immediately you will find a **d** tied,
21: 5 and mounted on a **d,** and on a colt, the foal of a **d."**
21: 7 they brought the **d** and the colt,
Lk 13:15 the sabbath untie his ox or his **d** from the manger,
Jn 12:14 Jesus found a young **d** and sat on it;
2Pe 2:16 a speechless **d** spoke with a human voice
Sir 33:25 Fodder and a stick and burdens for a **d;**

DONKEY'S (3) [DONKEY]

Ge 49:11 Binding his foal to the vine and his **d** colt to
2Ki 6:25 in Samaria became so great that a **d** head was sold
Jn 12:15 Look, your king is coming, sitting on a **d** colt!"

DONKEYS (66) [DONKEY]

Ge 12:16 male **d,** male and female slaves, female **d,**
24:35 male and female slaves, camels and **d.**
30:43 and male and female slaves, and camels and **d.**

Ge 32: 5 **d,** flocks, male and female slaves;
32:15 twenty female **d** and ten male **d.**
34:28 They took their flocks and their herds, their **d,**
36:24 as he pastured the **d** of his father Zibeon.
42:26 They loaded their **d** with their grain, and departed.
43:18 to make slaves of us and take our **d."**
43:24 and when he had given their **d** fodder,
44: 3 the men were sent away with their **d.**
45:23 ten **d** loaded with the good things of Egypt,
45:23 and ten female **d** loaded with grain, bread,
47:17 the flocks, the herds, and the **d.**
Ex 9: 3 horses, the **d,** the camels, the herds, and the flocks.
Nu 31:28 whether persons, oxen, **d,** sheep, or goats.
31:30 whether persons, oxen, **d,** sheep, or goats—
31:34 sixty-one thousand **d,**
31:39 The **d** were thirty thousand five hundred,
31:45 thirty thousand five hundred **d,**
Jos 6:21 young and old, oxen, sheep, and **d.**
7:24 with his sons and daughters, with his oxen, **d,**
9: 4 and took worn-out sacks for their **d,**
Jdg 5:10 "Tell of it, you who ride on white **d,**
10: 4 He had thirty sons who rode on thirty **d;**
12:14 and thirty grandsons, who rode on seventy **d;**
19: 3 He had with him his servant and a couple of **d.**
19:10 He had with him a couple of saddled **d,**
19:19 We your servants have straw and fodder for our **d,**
19:21 So he brought him into his house, and fed the **d;**
1Sa 8:16 and the best of your cattle and **d,**
9: 3 Now the **d** of Kish, Saul's father, had strayed.
9: 3 go and look for the **d."**
9: 5 or my father will stop worrying about the **d**
9:20 As for your **d** that were lost three days ago,
10: 2 'The **d** that you went to seek are found,
10:14 And he replied, "To seek the **d;**
10:16 "He told us that the **d** had been found."
22:19 men and women, children and infants, oxen, **d,**
25:18 figs. She loaded them on **d**
27: 9 the oxen, the **d,** the camels, and the clothing,
2Sa 16: 1 with a couple of **d** saddled,
16: 2 "The **d** are for the king's household to ride,
2Ki 4:22 "Send me one of the servants and one of the **d,**
7: 7 and their **d** leaving the camp just as it was,
7:10 the **d** tied, and the tents as they were."
1Ch 5:21 two hundred fifty thousand sheep, two thousand **d,**
12:40 came bringing food on **d,** camels, mules,
27:30 Over the **d** was Jehdeiah the Meronothite.
2Ch 28:15 and carrying all the feeble among them on **d,**
Ezr 2:67 and six thousand seven hundred twenty **d.**
Ne 7:69 and six thousand seven hundred twenty **d.**
13:15 bringing in heaps of grain and loading them on **d;**
Job 1: 3 five hundred yoke of oxen, five hundred **d,**
1:14 "The oxen were plowing and the **d** were feeding
42:12 a thousand yoke of oxen, and a thousand **d.**
Isa 21: 7 he sees riders, horsemen in pairs, riders on **d,**
30: 6 they carry their riches on the backs of **d,**
30:24 the oxen and **d** that till the ground will eat silage,
Eze 23:20 whose members were like those of **d,**
Zec 14:15 the mules, the camels, the **d,**
Tob 10:10 oxen and sheep, **d** and camels, clothing, money,
Jdt 2:17 along a vast number of camels and **d** and mules
1Es 5:43 and five thousand five hundred twenty-five **d.**

DONORS (2) [DONATION]

2Ki 12: 5 let the priests receive from each of the **d;**
12: 7 from your **d** but hand it over for the repair of

DOOM‡ (12) [DOOMED]

Dt 32:35 of their calamity is at hand, their **d** comes swiftly.
Ps 81:15 and their **d** would last forever.
92:11 my ears have heard the **d** of my evil assailants.
Jer 4:18 This is your **d;** how bitter it is!
11:15 Can vows and sacrificial flesh avert your **d?**
48:16 near at hand and his **d** approaches swiftly.
Eze 7: 7 Your **d** has come to you, O inhabitant of the land.
7:10 Your **d** has gone out.
30: 3 a time of **d** for the nations.
30: 9 upon them on the day of Egypt's **d;**
3Mc 5: 2 so that the Jews might meet their **d.**
2Es 10:10 and a multitude of them will come to **d.**

DOOMED (16) [DOOM]

2Sa 19:28 For all my father's house were **d** to death
2Ki 18:27 who are **d** with you to eat their own dung and
Ps 79:11 according to your great power preserve those **d**
92: 7 they are **d** to destruction forever,
102:20 to set free those who were **d** to die;
Isa 34: 2 he has **d** them, has given them over for slaughter.
34: 5 upon the people I have **d** to judgment.
36:12 who are **d** with you to eat their own dung
Jer 8:14 for the LORD our God has **d** us to perish,
Zec 11: 4 Be a shepherd of the flock **d** to slaughter.
11: 7 I became the shepherd of the flock **d** to slaughter.
14:11 for never again shall it be **d** to destruction;
1Co 2: 6 of this age or of the rulers of this age, who are **d**
Wis 18:15 into the midst of the land that was **d,**
Sir 16: 9 He showed no pity on the **d** nation,
3Mc 5:22 of insults for those they thought to be **d.**

DOOR‡ (90) [DOORKEEPER, DOORKEEPERS, DOORPOST, DOORPOSTS, DOORS, DOORSTEP, DOORWAYS]

Ge 4: 7 And if you do not do well, sin is lurking at the **d;**
6:16 and put the **d** of the ark in its side;
19: 6 Lot went out of the **d** to the men, shut the **d** after
19: 9 and came near the **d** to break it down.
19:10 into the house with them, and shut the **d.**
19:11 with blindness the men who were at the **d** of
19:11 so that they were unable to find the **d.**
Ex 12:22 None of you shall go outside the **d** of your house
12:23 the LORD will pass over that **d** and will not allow
21: 6 He shall be brought to the **d** or the doorpost;
Lev 14:38 the priest shall go outside to the **d** of the house
Dt 15:17 an awl and thrust it through his earlobe into the **d,**
Jdg 19:22 and started pounding on the **d.**
19:26 at the **d** of the man's house where her master was,
19:27 there was his concubine lying at the **d** of
2Sa 13:17 and bolt the **d** after her."
13:18 his servant put her out, and bolted the **d** after her.
1Ki 6:34 the two leaves of the one **d** were folding,
6:34 and the two leaves of the other **d** were folding.
14: 6 as she came in at the **d,** he said, "Come in,
14:27 who kept the **d** of the king's house.
2Ki 4: 4 and shut the **d** behind you and your children,
4: 5 and shut the **d** behind her and her children;
4:15 When he had called her, she stood at the **d.**
4:21 closed the **d** on him, and left.
4:33 So he went in and closed the **d** on the two of them,
6:32 that you shut the **d** and hold it closed against him.
9: 3 Then open the **d** and flee; do not linger."
9:10 Then he opened the **d** and fled.
2Ch 12:10 who kept the **d** of the king's house.
Ne 3:20 to the **d** of the house of the high priest Eliashib.
3:21 of Hakkoz repaired another section from the **d** of
Job 31: 9 and I have lain in wait at my neighbor's **d;**
Ps 141: 3 keep watch over the **d** of my lips.
Pr 5: 8 and do not go near the **d** of her house;
9:14 She sits at the **d** of her house,
26:14 **d** turns on its hinges, so does a lazy person in bed.
SS 8: 9 but if she is a **d,** we will enclose her with boards
Isa 57: 8 Behind the **d** and the doorpost you have set
Eze 40:38 There was a chamber with its **d** in the vestibule of
41:11 one **d** toward the north, and another **d** toward the
41:17 to the space above the **d,**
41:20 from the floor to the area above the **d,**
41:23 The nave and the holy place had each a double **d.**
41:24 two swinging leaves for each **d.**
Da 3:26 the **d** of the furnace of blazing fire and said,
Hos 2:15 and make the Valley of Achor a **d** of hope.
Mt 6: 6 the **d** and pray to your Father who is in secret;
7: 7 knock, and the **d** will be opened for you.
7: 8 for everyone who knocks, the **d** will be opened.
25:10 into the wedding banquet; and the **d** was shut.
27:60 a great stone to the **d** of the tomb and went away.
Mk 1:33 And the whole city was gathered around the **d.**
2: 2 not even in front of the **d;**
11: 4 They went away and found a colt tied near a **d,**
15:46 He then rolled a stone against the **d** of the tomb.
Lk 11: 7 the **d** has already been locked,
11: 9 knock, and the **d** will be opened for you.
11:10 for everyone who knocks, the **d** will be opened.
12:36 the **d** for him as soon as he comes and knocks.
13:24 "Strive to enter through the narrow **d;**
13:25 the owner of the house has got up and shut the **d,**
13:25 you begin to stand outside and to knock at the **d,**
Ac 5: 9 those who have buried your husband are at the **d,**
12: 6 while guards in front of the **d** were keeping watch
14:27 how he had opened a **d** of faith for the Gentiles.
18: 7 his house was next **d** to the synagogue.
1Co 16: 9 for a wide **d** for effective work has opened to me,
2Co 2:12 a **d** was opened for me in the Lord;
Col 4: 3 as well that God will open to us a **d** for the word,
Rev 3: 8 Look, I have set before you an open **d,**
3:20 I am standing at the **d,** knocking;
3:20 if you hear my voice and open the **d,**
4: 1 this I looked, and there in heaven a **d** stood open!
Tob 7: 1 they found him sitting beside the courtyard **d.**
8: 4 parents had gone out and shut the **d** of the room,
8:13 they sent the maid, lit a lamp, and opened the **d;**
11:10 and came stumbling out through the courtyard **d.**
Wis 19:17 just as were those at the **d** of the righteous man—
Sir 21:23 A boor peers into the house from the **d,**
21:24 It is ill-mannered for a person to listen at a **d;**
28:25 so make a **d** and a bolt for your mouth.
LtJ 6:59 even the **d** of a house that protects its contents,
Sus 1:26 in at the side **d** to see what had happened to her.
Bel 1:11 and shut the **d** and seal it with your signet.
1:14 shut the **d** and sealed it with the king's signet,
2Mc 1:16 Opening a secret **d** in the ceiling,
14:41 the tower and were forcing the **d** of the courtyard,

DOORKEEPER (2) [DOOR, KEEP]

Ps 84:10 a **d** in the house of my God than live in the tents
Mk 13:34 and commands the **d** to be on the watch.

DOORKEEPERS (1) [DOOR, KEEP]

Ezr 7:24 the Levites, the singers, the **d,** the temple servants,

DOORPOST (3) [DOOR, POST]

Ex 21: 6 He shall be brought to the door or the **d;**
1Sa 1: 9 the seat beside the **d** of the temple of the LORD.
Isa 57: 8 the door and the **d** you have set up your symbol;

DOORPOSTS (13) [DOOR, POST]

Ex 12: 7 and put it on the two **d** and the lintel of the houses
12:22 the lintel and the two **d** with the blood in the basin.
12:23 he sees the blood on the lintel and on the two **d,**
Dt 6: 9 and write them on the **d** of your house and
11:20 on the **d** of your house and on your gates,
1Ki 6:31 the lintel and the **d** were five-sided.
6:33 So also he made for the entrance to the nave **d**
7: 5 All the doorways and **d** had four-sided frames,
2Ki 18:16 the **d** that King Hezekiah of Judah had overlaid
Eze 41:21 The **d** of the nave were square.
43: 8 by my threshold and their **d** beside my doorposts,
43: 8 by my threshold and their doorposts beside my **d,**
45:19 the blood of the sin offering and put it on the **d** of

DOORS (86) [DOOR]

Jos 2:19 of you go out of the **d** of your house into the street,
Jdg 3:23 and closed the **d** of the roof chamber on him,
3:24 that the **d** of the roof chamber were locked,
3:25 he still did not open the **d** of the roof chamber,
11:31 then whoever comes out of the **d** of my house
16: 3 of the **d** of the city gate and the two posts,
19:27 opened the **d** of the house,
1Sa 3:15 then he opened the **d** of the house of the LORD.
21:13 He scratched marks on the **d** of the gate,
1Ki 6:31 For the entrance to the inner sanctuary he made **d**
6:32 the two **d** of olivewood with carvings of cherubim,
6:34 and two **d** of cypress wood;
7:50 the sockets for the **d** of the innermost part of
7:50 and for the **d** of the nave of the temple, of gold.
2Ki 18:16 At that time Hezekiah stripped the gold from the **d**
1Ch 22: 3 for nails for the **d** of the gates and for clamps,
2Ch 3: 7 its beams, its thresholds, its walls, and its **d;**
4: 9 and the great court, and **d** for the court;
4: 9 he overlaid their **d** with bronze.
4:22 the inner **d** to the most holy place and the **d** of
28:24 He shut up the **d** of the house of the LORD
29: 3 he opened the **d** of the house of the LORD
29: 7 They also shut the **d** of the vestibule and put out
Ne 3: 1 They consecrated it and set up its **d;**
3: 3 they laid its beams and set up its **d,** its bolts,
3: 6 they laid its beams and set up its **d,** its bolts,
3:13 they rebuilt it and set up its **d,** its bolts,
3:14 he rebuilt it and set up its **d,** its bolts, and its bars.
3:15 he rebuilt it and covered it and set up its **d,**
6: 1 up to that time I had not set up the **d** in the gates),
6:10 and let us close the **d** of the temple,
7: 1 the wall had been built and I had set up the **d,**
7: 3 let them shut and bar the **d.**
13:19 that the **d** should be shut and gave orders
Job 3:10 it did not shut the **d** of my mother's womb,
31:32 I have opened my **d** to the traveler—
31:34 so that I kept silence, and did not go out of **d—**
38: 8 "Or who shut in the sea with **d** when it burst out
38:10 and prescribed bounds for it, and set bars and **d,**
41:14 Who can open the **d** of its face?
Ps 24: 7 and be lifted up, O ancient **d!**
24: 9 and be lifted up, O ancient **d!**
78:23 and opened the **d** of heaven;
107:16 For he shatters the **d** of bronze,
Pr 8:34 watching daily at my gates, waiting beside my **d.**
18:16 A gift opens **d;** it gives access to the great.
Ecc 12: 4 when the **d** on the street are shut, and the sound of
SS 7:13 and over our **d** are all choice fruits,
Isa 26:20 enter your chambers, and shut your **d** behind you;
45: 1 open **d** before him—and the gates shall not be
45: 2 in pieces the **d** of bronze and cut through the bars
Eze 33:30 and at the **d** of the houses, say to one another,
41:24 The **d** had two leaves apiece,
41:25 On the **d** of the nave were carved cherubim
42:11 with the same exits and arrangements and **d.**
Mic 7: 5 guard the **d** of your mouth from her who lies
Zec 11: 1 Open your **d,** O Lebanon,
Mal 1:10 that someone among you would shut the temple **d,**
Lk 12: 3 and what you have whispered behind closed **d** will
Jn 20:19 and the **d** of the house where
20:26 Although the **d** were shut,
Ac 5:19 the night an angel of the Lord opened the prison **d,**
5:23 and the guards standing at the **d,**
16:26 and immediately all the **d** were opened
16:27 the jailer woke up and saw the prison **d** wide open,
21:30 and immediately the **d** were shut.
Jas 5: 9 See, the Judge is standing at the **d!**
AdE 15: 6 When she had gone through all the **d,**
Wis 19:17 of them tried to find the way through their own **d.**
Sir 14:23 through her windows and listens at her **d;**
LtJ 6:18 so the priests make their temples secure with **d**
Sus 1:17 and shut the garden **d** so that I can bathe."
1:18 the **d** of the garden and went out by the side **d**
1:20 They said, "Look, the garden **d** are shut,
1:25 And one of them ran and opened the garden **d.**
1:36 shut the garden **d,** and dismissed the maids.
1:39 and he opened the **d** and got away.
Bel 1:18 As soon as the **d** were opened,
1:21 the secret **d** through which they used to enter
1Mc 1:55 and offered incense at the **d** of the houses and in
4:57 for the priests, and fitted them with **d.**
2Mc 14:41 they ordered that fire be brought and the **d** burned.
14:43 and the crowd was now rushing in through the **d.**
1Es 4:49 or treasurer should forcibly enter their **d;**

DOORSTEP (1) [DOOR, STEP]

Sir 6:36 let your foot wear out his **d.**

DOORWAYS (1) [DOOR, WAY]

1Ki 7: 5 All the **d** and doorposts had four-sided frames,

DOPHKAH (2)

Nu 33:12 from the wilderness of Sin and camped at **D.**
33:13 They set out from **D** and camped at Alush.

DOR (7) [NAPHATH-DOR, NAPHOTH-DOR]
Jos 12:23 of **D** in Naphath-dor one the king of Goiim
17:11 the inhabitants of **D** and its villages,
Jdg 1:27 or the inhabitants of **D** and its villages,
1Ch 7:29 Megiddo and its towns, **D** and its towns.
1Mc 15:11 and Trypho came in his flight to **D,**
15:13 So Antiochus encamped against **D,**
15:25 King Antiochus besieged **D** for the second time,

DORCAS (2) [=TABITHA]
Ac 9:36 whose name was Tabitha, which in Greek is **D.**
9:39 and other clothing that **D** had made while she was

DORYMENES (2)
1Mc 3:38 Lysias chose Ptolemy son of **D,**
2Mc 4:45 a substantial bribe to Ptolemy son of **D** to win over

DOSITHEUS (5)
AdE 11:1 **D,** who said that he was a priest and a Levite,
2Mc 12:19 **D** and Sosipater, who were captains
12:24 into the hands of **D** and Sosipater and their men.
12:35 But a certain **D,** one of Bacenor's men,
3Mc 1:3 But **D,** known as the son of Drimylus,

DOTED (KJV) See LUSTED

DOTHAN (8)
Ge 37:17 for I heard them say, 'Let us go to **D.'** "
37:17 after his brothers, and found them at **D.**
2Ki 6:13 He was told, "He is in **D."**
Jdt 3:9 Then he came toward Esdraelon, near **D,**
4:6 which faces Esdraelon opposite the plain near **D,**
7:3 in breadth over **D** as far as Balbaim and in length
7:18 up and encamped in the hill country opposite **D;**
8:3 with his ancestors in the field between **D**

DOUBLE‡ (27) [DOUBLE-MINDED, DOUBLE-TONGUED, DOUBLED, DOUBLING, DOUBLY]
Ge 43:12 Take **d** the money with you.
43:15 and they took **d** the money with them,
Ex 22:4 in the thief's possession, the thief shall pay **d.**
22:7 then the thief, if caught, shall pay **d.**
22:9 one whom God condemns shall pay **d** to the other.
26:9 and the sixth curtain you shall **d** over at the front
39:9 It was square; the breastpiece was made **d,**
Dt 3:5 **d** gates, and bars, besides a great many villages.
21:17 giving him a **d** portion of all that he has;
1Sa 1:5 but to Hannah he gave a **d** portion,
2Ki 2:9 "Please let me inherit a **d** share of your spirit."
Job 41:13 Who can penetrate its **d** coat of mail?
Ps 12:2 with flattering lips and a **d** heart they speak.
Isa 40:2 that she has received from the LORD's hand **d**
61:7 Because their shame was **d,**
61:7 therefore they shall possess a **d** portion;
Jer 17:18 destroy them with **d** destruction!
Eze 41:23 The nave and the holy place had each a **d** door.
Hos 10:10 when they are punished for their **d** iniquity.
Zec 9:12 today I declare that I will restore to you **d.**
2Co 1:15 so that you might have a **d** favor;
1Ti 5:17 of **d** honor, especially those who labor
Rev 18:6 and repay her **d** for her deeds;
18:6 mix a **d** draught for her in the cup she mixed.
Sir 2:12 and to the sinner who walks a **d** path!
20:10 and the gift to be paid back **d.**
50:2 He laid the foundations for the high **d** walls,

DOUBLE-MINDED (3) [DOUBLE, MIND]
Ps 119:113 I hate the **d,** but I love your law.
Jas 1:7,8 being **d** and unstable in every way,
4:8 you sinners, and purify your hearts, you **d.**

DOUBLE-TONGUED‡ (5) [DOUBLE, TONGUE]
1Ti 3:8 Deacons likewise must be serious, not **d,**
Sir 5:14 be called **d** and do not lay traps with your tongue;
5:14 and severe condemnation to the **d.**
6:1 so it is with the **d** sinner.
28:13 Curse the gossips and the **d,**

DOUBLED (4) [DOUBLE]
Ex 28:16 It shall be square and **d,**
39:9 a span in length and a span in width when **d.**
Sir 26:1 the number of his days will be **d.**
26:26 *for the number of his years will be* **d.**

DOUBLING (1) [DOUBLE]
Ge 41:32 And the **d** of Pharaoh's dream means that

DOUBLY (2) [DOUBLE]
Jer 16:18 And I will **d** repay their iniquity and their sin,
Sir 23:11 and if he disregards it, he sins **d;**

DOUBT (11) [DOUBTED, DOUBTER, DOUBTING, DOUBTLESS, DOUBTS]
Ge 37:33 Joseph is without **d** torn to pieces."
Dt 28:66 Your life shall hang in **d** before you;
Job 12:2 "No **d** you are the people,
Mt 14:31 "You of little faith, why did you **d?"**
Mt 21:21 "Truly I tell you, if you have faith and do not **d,**
Mk 11:23 and if you do not **d** in your heart,
Jn 20:27 Do not **d** but believe."
Gal 1:13 no **d,** of my earlier life in Judaism.
1Ti 3:16 Without any **d,** the mystery
Wis 12:17 when people **d** the completeness of your power,
2Es 16:75 Do not fear or **d,** for God is your guide.

DOUBTED (1) [DOUBT]
Mt 28:17 they saw him, they worshiped him; but some **d.**

DOUBTER (1) [DOUBT]
Jas 1:7,8 for the **d,** being double-minded and unstable

DOUBTING (1) [DOUBT]
Jas 1:6 never **d,** for the one who doubts is like a wave of

DOUBTLESS (2) [DOUBT]
Lk 4:23 **"D** you will quote to me this proverb, 'Doctor,
1Co 14:10 There are **d** many different kinds of sounds in

DOUBTS (3) [DOUBT]
Lk 24:38 and why do **d** arise in your hearts?
Ro 14:23 But those who have **d** are condemned if they eat,
Jas 1:6 for the one who **d** is like a wave of the sea,

DOUGH (12)
Ex 12:34 So the people took their **d** before it was leavened,
12:39 of the **d** that they had brought out of Egypt;
Nu 15:20 From your first batch of **d** you shall present a loaf
15:21 a donation from the first of your batch of **d.**
2Sa 13:8 She took **d,** kneaded it, made cakes in his sight,
Ne 10:37 the first of our **d,** and our contributions, the fruit
Jer 7:18 the fathers kindle fire, and the women knead **d,**
Eze 44:30 also give to the priests the first of your **d,**
Hos 7:4 from the kneading of the **d** until it is leavened.
Ro 11:16 If the part of the **d** offered as first fruits is holy,
1Co 5:6 that a little yeast leavens the whole batch of **d?**
Gal 5:9 A little yeast leavens the whole batch of **d.**

DOVE (21) [DOVE'S, DOVES]
Ge 8:8 Then he sent out the **d** from him,
8:9 but the **d** found no place to set its foot,
8:10 and again he sent out the **d** from the ark;
8:11 the **d** came back to him in the evening, and there
8:12 he waited another seven days, and sent out the **d;**
Ps 55:6 And I say, "O that I had wings like a **d!**
56:T *according to The* **D** *on Far-off Terebinths.*
68:13 the wings of a **d** covered with silver,
74:19 not deliver the soul of your **d** to the wild animals;
SS 2:14 O my **d,** in the clefts of the rock,
5:2 "Open to me, my sister, my love, my **d,**
6:9 My **d,** my perfect one, is the only one,
Isa 38:14 a swallow or a crane I clamor, I moan like a **d.**
Jer 48:28 Be like the **d** that nests on the sides of the mouth
Hos 7:11 Ephraim has become like a **d,**
Mt 3:16 the Spirit of God descending like a **d** and alighting
Mk 1:10 and the Spirit descending like a **d** on him.
Lk 3:22 upon him in bodily form like a **d.**
Jn 1:32 "I saw the Spirit descending from heaven like a **d,**
2Es 2:15 bring them up with gladness, as does a **d;**
5:26 for yourself one **d,** and from all the flocks

DOVE'S (1) [DOVE]
2Ki 6:25 and one-fourth of a kab of **d** dung for five shekels

DOVES (13) [DOVE]
SS 1:15 you are beautiful; your eyes are **d.**
4:1 Your eyes are **d** behind your veil.
5:12 His eyes are like **d** beside springs of water,
Isa 59:11 like **d** we moan mournfully.
60:8 and like **d** to their windows?
Eze 7:16 be found on the mountains like **d** of the valleys,
Hos 11:11 and like **d** from the land of Assyria;
Na 2:7 moaning like **d** and beating their breasts.
Mt 10:16 so be wise as serpents and innocent as **d.**
21:12 and the seats of those who sold **d.**
Mk 11:15 and the seats of those who sold **d;**
Jn 2:14 he found people selling cattle, sheep, and **d,**
2:16 He told those who were selling the **d,**

DOWN‡ (1349) [DOWNCAST, DOWNFALL, DOWNHEARTED, DOWNTRODDEN, DOWNWARD]
A. DOWN FROM HEAVEN (30)
B. DOWN TO EGYPT (13)

Ge 11:5 The LORD came **d** to see the city and the tower,
11:7 let us go **d,** and confuse their language there,
12:10 Abram went **d** to Egypt to reside there B
15:11 And when birds of prey came **d** on the carcasses,
15:12 As the sun was going **d,**
15:17 When the sun had gone **d** and it was dark,
18:2 and bowed **d** to the ground.
18:21 I must go **d** and see whether they have done
19:1 and bowed **d** with his face to the ground.
19:4 But before they lay **d,** the men of the city,
19:9 and came near the door to break it **d.**
19:28 and he looked **d** toward Sodom and Gomorrah and
19:33 he did not know when she lay **d** or when she rose.
19:35 he did not know when she lay **d** or when she rose.
Ge 21:16 she went and sat **d** opposite him a good way off,
23:12 Abraham bowed **d** before the people of the land.
24:11 He made the camels kneel **d** outside the city by
24:16 She went **d** to the spring, filled her jar,
24:45 and she went **d** to the spring, and drew.
24:46 She quickly let **d** her jar from her shoulder,
25:18 he settled **d** alongside of all his people.
26:2 "Do not go **d** to Egypt; B
27:29 Let peoples serve you, and nations bow **d** to you.
27:29 and may your mother's sons bow **d** to you.
28:11 he put it under his head and lay **d** in that place.
33:6 they and their children, and bowed **d;**
33:7 and her children drew near and bowed **d;**
33:7 and Rachel drew near, and they bowed **d.**
37:7 and bowed **d** to my sheaf."
37:9 the moon, and eleven stars were bowing **d** to me."
37:25 Then they sat **d** to eat;
37:25 and resin, on their way to carry it **d** to Egypt. B
37:35 "No, I shall go **d** to Sheol to my son, mourning."
38:1 at that time that Judah went **d** from his brothers
38:14 and sat **d** at the entrance to Enaim,
39:1 Now Joseph was taken **d** to Egypt, and Potiphar, B
39:1 from the Ishmaelites who had brought him **d** there.
42:2 go **d** and buy grain for us there,
42:3 of Joseph's brothers went **d** to buy grain in Egypt.
42:38 But he said, "My son shall not go **d** with you,
42:38 you would bring **d** my gray hairs with sorrow
43:4 we will go **d** and buy you food;
43:5 we will not go **d,** for the man said to us,
43:7 that he would say, 'Bring your brother **d'?"**
43:11 and carry them **d** as a present to the man—
43:15 Then they went on their way **d** to Egypt, B
43:20 my lord, we came **d** the first time to buy food;
43:22 Moreover we have brought **d**
44:21 you said to your servants, 'Bring him **d** to me,
44:23 'Unless your youngest brother comes **d** with you,
44:26 we said, 'We cannot go **d.**
44:26 if our youngest brother goes with us, we will go **d;**
44:29 you will bring **d** my gray hairs in sorrow to Sheol.'
44:31 and your servants will bring **d** the gray hairs
45:9 come **d** to me, do not delay.
45:13 Hurry and bring my father **d** here."
46:3 do not be afraid to go **d** to Egypt, B
46:4 I myself will go **d** with you to Egypt,
47:30 When I lie **d** with my ancestors,
49:8 your father's sons shall bow **d** before you.
49:9 He crouches **d,** he stretches out like a lion,
49:14 lying **d** between the sheepfolds;
50:18 Then his brothers also wept, fell **d** before him,
Ex 2:5 daughter of Pharaoh came **d** to bathe at the river,
2:15 and sat **d** by a well.
3:8 I have come **d** to deliver them from the Egyptians,
4:31 they bowed **d** and worshiped.
7:9 'Take your staff and throw it **d** before Pharaoh,
7:10 Aaron threw **d** his staff before Pharaoh
7:12 Each one threw **d** his staff,
9:19 under shelter will die when the hail comes **d**
9:23 and fire came **d** on the earth.
9:25 The hail struck **d** everything that was in
9:25 the hail also struck **d** all the plants of the field,
9:33 and the rain no longer poured **d** on the earth.
11:8 all these officials of yours shall come **d** to me,
12:12 I will strike **d** every firstborn in the land of Egypt,
12:23 For the LORD will pass through to strike **d**
12:23 the destroyer to enter your houses to strike you **d.**
12:27 he struck **d** the Egyptians but spared our houses.' "
12:27 And the people bowed **d** and worshiped.
12:29 At midnight the LORD struck **d** all the firstborn
14:24 the LORD in the pillar of fire and cloud looked **d**
15:5 they went **d** into the depths like a stone.
18:7 he bowed **d** and kissed him;
19:11 because on the third day the LORD will come **d**
19:14 So Moses went **d** from the mountain to the people.
19:21 "Go **d** and warn the people not to break through to
19:24 The LORD said to him, "Go **d,**
19:25 So Moses went **d** to the people and told them.
20:5 You shall not bow **d** to them or worship them;
22:26 you shall restore it before the sun goes **d;**
23:24 you shall not bow **d** to their gods,
24:4 And Moses wrote **d** all the words of the LORD.
27:5 of the altar so that the net shall extend halfway **d**
32:1 the people saw that Moses delayed to come **d** from
32:6 people sat **d** to eat and drink, and rose up to revel.
32:7 The LORD said to Moses, "Go **d** at once!
32:15 Then Moses turned and went **d** from the mountain,
33:10 all the people would rise and bow **d,** all of them,
34:13 You shall tear **d** their altars, break their pillars,
34:13 and cut **d** their sacred poles
34:29 Moses came **d** from Mount Sinai.
34:29 As he came **d** from the mountain with
38:4 under its ledge, extending halfway **d.**
Lev 9:22 and he came **d** after sacrificing the sin offering,
14:45 He shall have the house torn **d,**
17:13 who hunts **d** an animal or bird that may
26:6 I will grant peace in the land, and you shall lie **d,**
26:17 and you shall be struck **d** by your enemies;
26:30 I will destroy your high places and cut **d**
Nu 1:51 tabernacle is to set out, the Levites shall take it **d;**
4:5 and take **d** the screening curtain, and cover the ark
8:17 the day that I struck **d** all the firstborn in the land
9:17 and in the place where the cloud settled **d,**
10:12 and the cloud settled **d** in the wilderness of Paran.
10:17 Then the tabernacle was taken **d,**
11:17 I will come **d** and talk with you there;
11:25 the LORD came **d** in the cloud and spoke to him,
12:5 Then the LORD came **d** in a pillar of cloud,
13:23 and cut **d** from there a branch with a single cluster

Nu 13:24 of the cluster that the Israelites cut **d** from there.
14:42 not let yourselves be struck **d** before your enemies.
14:45 in that hill country came **d** and defeated them,
16:30 and they go **d** alive into Sheol,
16:33 that belonged to them went **d** alive into Sheol;
20:15 how our ancestors went **d** to Egypt, and we lived B
20:28 Moses and Eleazar came **d** from the mountain.
22:27 the donkey saw the angel of the LORD, it lay **d**
22:31 and he bowed **d,** falling on his face.
23:24 not lie **d** until it has eaten the prey and drunk
24: 4 who sees the vision of the Almighty, who falls **d,**
24: 9 He crouched, he lay **d** like a lion,
24:16 who sees the vision of the Almighty, who falls **d,**
25: 2 and the people ate and bowed **d** to their gods.
33: 2 Moses wrote **d** their starting points, stage by stage,
33: 4 whom the LORD had struck **d** among them.
34:11 and the boundary shall continue **d** from Shepham
34:11 and the boundary shall go **d,**
34:12 and the boundary shall go **d** to the Jordan,
Dt 1:25 which they brought **d** to us.
1:44 They beat you **d** in Seir as far as Hormah.
2:33 and we struck him **d,** along with his offspring
3: 3 We struck him **d** until not
3:17 from Chinnereth **d** to the sea of the Arabah,
4:19 be led astray and bow **d** to them and serve them,
5: 9 You shall not bow **d** to them or worship them;
6: 7 when you lie **d** and when you rise.
7: 5 break **d** their altars, smash their pillars, hew **d**
their sacred poles,
9:12 "Get up, go **d** quickly from here,
9:15 So I turned and went **d** from the mountain,
9:21 of it into the stream that runs **d** the mountain.
10: 5 So I turned and came **d** from the mountain,
10:22 Your ancestors went **d** to Egypt seventy persons; B
11:19 when you lie **d** and when you rise.
12: 3 Break **d** their altars, smash their pillars,
12: 3 and hew **d** the idols of their gods,
19: 5 when one of them swings the ax to cut **d** a tree,
20:19 you must not cut them **d.**
20:20 you may cut them **d** for use in building siegeworks
21: 1 and it is not known who struck the person **d,**
21: 4 the elders of that town shall bring the heifer **d** to
25: 2 that person lie **d** and be beaten in his presence
25:18 and struck **d** all who lagged behind you;
26: 4 from your hand and sets it **d** before the altar of
26: 5 he went **d** into Egypt and lived there as an alien,
26:10 You shall set it **d** before the LORD your God and
bow **d** before
26:15 Look **d** from your holy habitation, from heaven,
27:24 be anyone who strikes **d** a neighbor in secret."
28:24 and only dust shall come **d** upon you from the sky
28:49 to swoop **d** on you like an eagle,
28:52 come **d** throughout your land;
30:17 but are led astray to bow **d** to other gods
31: 9 Then Moses wrote **d** this law,
31:16 "Soon you will lie **d** with your ancestors.
31:24 When Moses had finished writing **d** in a book
33:28 where the heavens drop **d** dew.
Jos 2:15 she let them **d** by a rope through the window,
2:18 in the window through which you let us **d,**
2:23 the two men came **d** again from the hill country.
4: 3 lay them **d** in the place where you camp tonight.' "
4: 8 to the place where they camped, and laid them **d**
6: 5 and the wall of the city will fall **d** flat,
6:20 they raised a great shout, and the wall fell **d** flat;
6:24 They burned **d** the city, and everything in it;
8:21 then they turned back and struck **d** the men of Ai.
8:22 on the other; and Israel struck them **d**
8:29 and they took his body **d** from the tree,
8:29 threw it **d** at the entrance of the gate of the city,
10:10 struck them **d** as far as Azekah and Makkedah.
10:11 while they were going **d** the slope of Beth-horon,
10:11 the LORD threw **d** huge stones from heaven
10:26 Afterward Joshua struck them **d** and put them
10:27 and they took them **d** from the trees
11: 8 of Mizpeh. They struck them **d,**
11:10 and struck its king **d** with the sword.
11:14 but all the people they struck **d** with the edge of
11:17 He took all their kings, struck them **d,**
15:10 Chesalon), and goes **d** to Beth-shemesh,
16: 3 then it goes **d** westward to the territory of
16: 7 it goes **d** from Janoah to Ataroth and to Naarah,
17: 9 Then the boundary went **d** to the Wadi Kanah.
18: 9 So the men went and traversed the land and set **d**
18:13 then the boundary goes **d** to Ataroth-addar,
18:16 the boundary goes **d** to the border of the mountain
18:16 and it then goes **d** the valley of Hinnom,
18:17 it goes **d** to the Stone of Bohan, Reuben's son;
18:18 the slope of Beth-arabah it goes **d** to the Arabah;
22: 3 not forsaken your kindred these many days, **d**
23: 7 or serve them, or bow yourselves **d** to them,
23:16 and go and serve other gods and bow **d** to them,
24: 4 but Jacob and his children went **d** to Egypt. B
Jdg 1: 9 Afterward the people of Judah went **d** to fight
1:34 they did not allow them to come **d** to the plain.
2: 2 of this land; tear **d** their altars.'
2:12 around them, and bowed **d** to them;
2:17 they lusted after other gods and bowed **d** to them.
2:19 worshiping them and bowing **d** to them.
3:27 Israelites went **d** with him from the hill country,
3:28 So they went **d** after him,
4:14 So Barak went **d** from Mount Tabor
4:15 Sisera got **d** from his chariot and fled away
4:21 until it went **d** into the ground—
5:11 **d** to the gates marched the people of the LORD.
5:13 Then **d** marched the remnant of the noble;
5:13 the LORD marched **d** for him against the mighty.
Jdg 5:14 from Machir marched **d** the commanders,
5:17 settling **d** by his landings.
6:16 and you shall strike **d** the Midianites,
6:25 pull **d** the altar of Baal that belongs to your father,
6:25 and cut **d** the sacred pole that is beside it;
6:26 the wood of the sacred pole that you shall cut **d."**
6:28 the altar of Baal was broken **d,**
6:28 and the sacred pole beside it was cut **d,**
6:30 for he has pulled **d** the altar of Baal and cut **d**
6:31 because his altar has been pulled **d."**
6:32 because he pulled **d** his altar.
7: 4 take them **d** to the water and I will sift them out
7: 5 So he brought the troops **d** to the water;
7: 5 all those who kneel **d** to drink,
7: 6 but all the rest of the troops knelt **d** to drink water.
7:10 go **d** to the camp with your servant Purah;
7:11 Then he went **d** with his servant Purah to
7:13 it turned upside **d,** and the tent collapsed."
7:24 "Come **d** against the Midianites and seize
8: 9 I will break **d** this tower."
8:17 He also broke **d** the tower of Penuel,
9:36 people are coming **d** from the mountain tops!"
9:37 "Look, people are coming **d** from Tabbur-erez,
9:48 cut **d** a bundle of brushwood,
9:49 So every one of the troops cut **d** a bundle
12: 1 We will burn your house **d** over you!"
14: 1 Once Samson went **d** to Timnah,
14: 5 Then Samson went **d** with his father and mother
14: 7 Then he went **d** and talked with the woman,
14:10 His father went **d** to the woman,
14:18 to him on the seventh day before the sun went **d,**
14:19 and he went **d** to Ashkelon.
15: 8 He struck them **d** hip and thigh
15: 8 and he went **d** and stayed in the cleft of the rock
15:11 of Judah went **d** to the cleft of the rock of Etam,
15:12 They said to him, "We have come **d** to bind you,
15:15 reached **d** and took it, and with it he killed
16:21 They brought him **d** to Gaza and bound him
16:31 Then his brothers and all his family came **d**
18:27 put them to the sword, and burned **d** the city.
19:14 and the sun went **d** on them near Gibeah,
19:15 He went in and sat **d** in the open square of the city,
19:26 the woman came and fell **d** at the door of
20:21 and struck **d** on that day twenty-two thousand of
20:25 and struck **d** eighteen thousand of the Israelites,
20:43 Cutting **d** the Benjaminites,
20:43 from Nohah and trod them **d** as far as a place east
20:45 of them were cut **d** on the main roads,
Ru 3: 3 and put on your best clothes and go **d** to
3: 4 When he lies **d,** observe the place where he lies;
3: 4 then, go and uncover his feet and lie **d;**
3: 6 So she went **d** to the threshing floor and did just
3: 7 he went to lie **d** at the end of the heap of grain.
3: 7 and uncovered his feet, and lay **d.**
3:13 Lie **d** until the morning."
4: 1 up to the gate and sat **d** there than the next-of-kin,
4: 1 So Boaz said, "Come over, friend; sit **d** here."
4: 1 And he went over and sat **d.**
4: 2 and said, "Sit **d** here"; so they sat **d.**
1Sa 2: 6 he brings **d** to Sheol and raises up.
3: 2 was lying **d** in his room;
3: 3 Samuel was lying **d** in the temple of the LORD,
3: 5 But he said, "I did not call; lie **d** again."
3: 5 So he went and lay **d.**
3: 6 But he said, "I did not call, my son; lie **d** again."
3: 9 Therefore Eli said to Samuel, "Go, lie **d;**
3: 9 So Samuel went and lay **d** in his place.
6:15 The Levites took **d** the ark of the LORD and
6:18 beside which they set **d** the ark of the LORD,
6:21 Come **d** and take it up to you."
7:11 and struck them **d** as far as beyond Beth-car.
9:25 When they came **d** from the shrine into the town,
9:25 and he lay **d** to sleep.
9:27 As they were going **d** to the outskirts of the town,
10: 5 you will meet a band of prophets coming **d** from
10: 8 And you shall go **d** to Gilgal ahead of me;
10: 8 then I will come **d** to you
11:11 and cut **d** the Ammonites until the heat of the day;
13:12 the Philistines will come **d** upon me at Gilgal,
13:18 toward the mountain that looks **d** upon the valley
13:20 so all the Israelites went **d** to the Philistines
14:31 After they had struck **d** the Philistines that day
14:36 "Let us go **d** after the Philistines by night
14:37 "Shall I go **d** after the Philistines?
14:48 He did valiantly, and struck **d** the Amalekites,
15:12 and on returning he passed on **d** to Gilgal."
15:19 Why did you swoop **d** on the spoil,
16:11 for we will not sit **d** until he comes here."
17: 8 and let him come **d** to me.
17:28 He said, "Why have you come **d?**
17:28 for you have come **d** just to see the battle."
17:35 and struck it **d,** rescuing the lamb from its mouth;
17:35 I would catch it by the jaw, strike it **d,** and kill it.
17:46 and I will strike you **d** and cut off your head;
17:49 and he fell face **d** on the ground.
17:50 striking **d** the Philistine and killing him;
19:12 So Michal let David **d** through the window;
20:19 you shall go a long way **d;**
21:13 and let his spittle run **d** his beard.
22: 1 and all his father's house heard of it, they went **d**
23: 4 The LORD answered him, "Yes, go **d** to Keilah;
23: 6 he came **d** with an ephod in his hand.
23: 8 to go **d** to Keilah, to besiege David and his men.
23:11 now, will Saul come **d** as your servant has heard?
23:11 The LORD said, "He will come **d."**
23:20 O king, whenever you wish to come **d,** do so;
23:25 he went **d** to the rock and stayed in the wilderness
1Sa 25: 1 Then David got up and went **d** to the wilderness
25:20 and came **d** under cover of the mountain, David
and his men came **d** toward her;
25:41 and bowed **d,** with her face to the ground,
26: 2 So Saul rose and went **d** to the Wilderness of Ziph,
26: 6 "Who will go **d** with me into the camp to Saul?"
26: 6 Abishai said, "I will go **d** with you."
26:10 the LORD will strike him **d;**
26:10 or he will go **d** into battle and perish.
29: 4 he shall not go **d** with us to battle,
30: 1 They had attacked Ziklag, burned it **d,**
30: 3 to the city, they found it burned **d,** and their wives
30:14 of Caleb; and we burned Ziklag **d."**
30:15 "Will you take me **d** to this raiding party?"
30:15 and I will take you **d** to them."
30:16 When he had taken him **d,**
30:24 of the one who goes **d** into the battle shall be
2Sa 1:15 "Come here and strike him **d."**
1:15 So he struck him **d** and he died.
2:16 in his opponent's side; so they fell **d** together.
2:24 sun was going **d** they came to the hill of Ammah,
3:35 or anything else before the sun goes **d!"**
5: 8 "Whoever would strike **d** the Jebusites,
5:17 David heard about it and went **d** to the stronghold.
5:24 before you to strike **d** the army of the Philistines."
5:25 and he struck **d** the Philistines from Geba all
7:12 When your days are fulfilled and you lie **d**
8: 2 making them lie **d** on the ground,
8: 3 David also struck **d** King Hadadezer son of Rehob
11: 8 Then David said to Uriah, "Go **d** to your house,
11: 9 and did not go **d** to his house.
11:10 they told David, "Uriah did not go **d** to his house,"
11:10 Why did you not go **d** to your house?"
11:13 but he did not go **d** to his house.
11:15 so that he may be struck **d** and die."
12: 9 You have struck **d** Uriah the Hittite with
13: 5 Jonadab said to him, "Lie **d** on your bed,
13: 6 So Amnon lay **d,** and pretended to be ill;
13: 8 her brother Amnon's house, where he was lying **d.**
15:14 and bring disaster **d** upon us,
15:24 They set **d** the ark of God,
17: 2 I will strike **d** only the king,
17:18 and they went **d** into it.
19:16 hurried to come **d** with the people of Judah
19:17 rushed **d** to the Jordan ahead of the king,
19:18 Shimei son of Gera fell **d** before the king,
19:20 of Joseph to come **d** to meet my lord the king."
19:24 Mephibosheth grandson of Saul came **d** to meet
19:31 Barzillai the Gileadite had come **d** from Rogelim;
20:15 Joab's forces were battering the wall to break it **d.**
21:15 and David went **d** together with his servants.
22:10 He bowed the heavens, and came **d;**
22:28 your eyes are upon the haughty to bring them **d.**
22:39 I struck them **d,** so that they did not rise;
22:43 I crushed them and stamped them **d** like the mire
22:48 the God who gave me vengeance and brought **d**
23:10 He struck **d** the Philistines
23:13 of the thirty chiefs went **d** to join David at the cave
23:20 he struck **d** two sons of Ariel of Moab.
23:20 He also went **d** and killed a lion in a pit on a day
24:20 When Araunah looked **d,** he saw the king
1Ki 1:25 For today he has gone **d** and has sacrificed oxen,
1:33 and bring him **d** to Gihon.
1:38 went **d** and had Solomon ride
1:53 Then King Solomon sent to have him brought **d**
2: 6 but do not let his gray head go **d** to Sheol in peace.
2: 8 but when he came **d** to meet me at the Jordan,
2: 9 to do to him, and you must bring his gray head **d**
2:19 The king rose to meet her, and bowed **d** to her;
2:25 he struck him **d,** and he died.
2:29 saying, "Go, strike him **d."**
2:31 "Do as he has said, strike him **d** and bury him;
2:34 of Jehoiada went up and struck him **d**
2:46 and he went out and struck him **d,** and he died.
5: 9 My servants shall bring it **d** to the sea from
9:16 up and captured Gezer and burned it **d,** had killed
13: 3 'The altar shall be torn **d,**
13: 5 The altar also was torn **d,**
15:13 Asa cut **d** her image and burned it at
15:27 and Baasha struck him **d** at Gibbethon,
16:10 Zimri came in and struck him **d** and killed him,
16:18 he burned **d** the king's house over himself
17:23 brought him **d** from the upper chamber into
18:30 the altar of the LORD that had been thrown **d;**
18:40 and Elijah brought them **d** to the Wadi Kishon,
18:42 there he bowed himself **d** upon the earth
18:44 'Harness your chariot and go **d** before
19: 4 and came and sat **d** under a solitary broom tree.
19: 5 Then he lay **d** under the broom tree and fell asleep.
19: 6 He ate and drank, and lay **d** again.
19:10 thrown **d** your altars, and killed your prophets with
19:14 thrown **d** your altars, and killed your prophets with
21: 4 He lay **d** on his bed, turned away his face,
21:16 to go **d** to the vineyard of Naboth the Jezreelite,
21:18 Go **d** to meet King Ahab of Israel, who rules
22: 2 the third year King Jehoshaphat of Judah came **d**
2Ki 1: 9 "O man of God, the king says, 'Come **d.'** "
1:10 let fire come **d** from heaven and consume you A
1:10 Then fire came **d** from heaven, A
1:11 this is the king's order: Come **d** quickly!"
1:12 let fire come **d** from heaven and consume you A
1:12 of God came **d** from heaven and consumed him A
1:14 fire came **d** from heaven and consumed A
1:15 "Go **d** with him; do not be afraid of him."
1:15 So he set out and went **d** with him to the king,
2: 2 So they went **d** to Bethel.
2:16 the LORD has caught him up and thrown him **d**

2Ki 3:12 and Jehoshaphat and the king of Edom went **d**
4:11 he went up to the chamber and lay **d** there.
4:35 He got **d**, walked once to and fro in the room,
5:14 So he went **d** and immersed himself seven times in
5:18 and I bow **d** in the house of Rimmon,
5:18 when I do bow **d** in the house of Rimmon,
5:21 he jumped **d** from the chariot to meet him
6:4 When they came to the Jordan, they cut **d** trees.
6:9 because the Arameans are going **d** there."
6:18 When the Arameans came **d** against him,
6:33 the king came **d** to him and said,
7:17 as the man of God had said when the king came **d**
8:29 King Ahaziah son of Jehoram of Judah went **d**
9:7 You shall strike **d** the house of your master Ahab,
9:16 King Ahaziah of Judah had come **d** to visit Joram.
9:33 He said, "Throw her **d**."
9:33 "Throw her down." So they threw her **d**;
10:9 but who struck **d** all these?
10:13 we have come **d** to visit the royal princes and
11:18 the land went to the house of Baal, and tore it **d**;
11:19 then they brought the king **d** from the house of
12:20 on the way that goes **d** to Silla.
12:21 his servants, who struck him **d**, so that he died.
13:14 King Joash of Israel went **d** to him,
13:19 then you would have struck **d** Aram
13:19 but now you will strike **d** Aram only three times."
14:9 of Lebanon passed by and trampled **d**
14:13 to Jerusalem, and broke **d** the wall of Jerusalem
15:10 and struck him **d** in public and killed him,
15:14 he struck **d** Shallum son of Jabesh in Samaria
18:4 He removed the high places, broke **d** the pillars, and cut **d** the sacred pole.
19:35 and struck **d** one hundred eighty-five thousand in
21:13 wiping it and turning it upside **d**.
23:7 He broke **d** the houses of
23:8 he broke **d** the high places of the gates that were at
23:12 he pulled **d** from there and broke in pieces,
23:14 in pieces, cut **d** the sacred poles, and covered
23:15 he pulled **d** that altar along with the high place.
25:9 every great house he burned **d**.
25:10 of the guard broke **d** the walls around Jerusalem.
25:21 The king of Babylon struck them **d** and put them
25:25 they struck **d** Gedaliah so that he died,
1Ch 7:21 because they came **d** to raid their cattle.
11:15 of the thirty chiefs went **d** to the rock to David at
11:22 he struck **d** two sons of Ariel of Moab.
11:22 He also went **d** and killed a lion in a pit on a day
13:10 he struck him **d** because he put out his hand to
14:15 before you to strike **d** the army of the Philistines."
14:16 and they struck **d** the Philistine army from Gibeon
17:9 and evildoers shall wear them **d** no more,
18:3 David also struck **d** King Hadadezer of Zobah,
2Ch 6:27 and send **d** rain upon your land,
7:1 fire came **d** from heaven and consumed A
7:3 When all the people of Israel saw the fire come **d**
7:3 they bowed **d** on the pavement with their faces to
13:20 the LORD struck him **d**, and he died.
14:3 broke **d** the pillars, hewed **d** the sacred poles,
15:16 Asa cut **d** her image, crushed it,
18:2 After some years he went **d** to Ahab in Samaria.
20:16 Tomorrow go **d** against them;
20:18 Jehoshaphat bowed **d** with his face to the ground,
20:18 and the inhabitants of Jerusalem fell **d** before
22:6 of King Jehoram of Judah went **d** to see Joram son
23:17 to the house of Baal, and tore it **d**;
23:20 and they brought the king **d** from the house of
25:8 or God will fling you **d** before the enemy;
25:11 and struck **d** ten thousand men of Seir.
25:12 and threw them **d** from the top of Sela,
25:18 of Lebanon passed by and trampled **d**
25:23 he brought him to Jerusalem, and broke **d** the wall
26:6 and broke **d** the wall of Gath and the wall
29:29 and all who were present with him bowed **d**
29:30 and they bowed **d** and worshiped.
31:1 broke **d** the pillars, hewed **d** the sacred poles, and pulled **d** the high places and the altars
32:5 and built up the entire wall that was broken **d**,
32:21 of his own sons struck him **d** there with the sword.
32:30 of Gihon and directed them **d** to the west side of
33:3 that his father Hezekiah had pulled **d**,
34:4 In his presence they pulled **d** the altars of
34:4 He broke **d** the sacred poles and the carved and
34:7 he broke **d** the altars, beat the sacred poles and
36:19 broke **d** the wall of Jerusalem,
Ezr 5:10 so that we might write **d** the names of the men
10:1 weeping and throwing himself **d** before the house
10:16 the tenth month they sat **d** to examine the matter.
Ne 1:3 the wall of Jerusalem is broken **d**,
1:4 When I heard these words I sat **d** and wept,
2:13 of Jerusalem that had been broken **d** and its gates
3:15 far as the stairs that go **d** from the City of David.
4:3 any fox going up on it would break it **d**!"
6:3 "I am doing a great work and I cannot come **d**.
6:3 the work stop while I leave it to come **d** to you?"
9:13 You came **d** also upon Mount Sinai,
Est 3:2 at the king's gate bowed **d** and did obeisance
3:2 But Mordecai did not bow **d** or do obeisance.
3:5 When Haman saw that Mordecai did not bow **d**
3:15 The king and Haman sat **d** to drink;
9:5 the Jews struck **d** all their enemies with the sword,
9:31 just as they had laid **d** for themselves and
Job 1:7 and from walking up and **d** on it."
2:2 and from walking up and **d** on it."
3:13 Now I would be lying **d** and quiet;
7:4 When I lie **d** I say, 'When shall I rise?'
7:9 so those who go **d** to Sheol do not come up;
8:12 While yet in flower and not cut **d**,
Job 11:19 You will lie **d**, and no one will make you afraid;
12:14 If he tears **d**, no one can rebuild;
14:7 "For there is hope for a tree, if it is cut **d**,
14:12 so mortals lie **d** and do not rise again;
17:3 "Lay **d** a pledge for me with yourself;
17:16 Will it go **d** to the bars of Sheol?
18:7 and their own schemes throw them **d**.
19:10 He breaks me **d** on every side, and I am gone,
19:23 "O that my words were written **d**!
20:11 once full of youth, will lie **d** in the dust with them.
20:15 They swallow **d** riches and vomit them up again;
20:18 and will not swallow it **d**;
21:13 and in peace they go **d** to Sheol.
21:26 They lie **d** alike in the dust,
26:12 by his understanding he struck **d** Rahab.
31:12 for that would be a fire consuming **d** to Abaddon,
33:24 and says, 'Deliver him from going **d** into the Pit;
33:28 He has redeemed my soul from going **d** to the Pit,
36:28 which the skies pour **d** and drop
40:12 tread **d** the wicked where they stand.
41:1 or press **d** its tongue with a cord?
Ps 3:5 I lie **d** and sleep; I wake again,
4:8 I will both lie **d** and sleep in peace;
4:8 for you alone, O LORD, make me lie **d** in safety.
5:7 I will bow **d** toward your holy temple in awe
14:2 The LORD looks **d** from heaven on humankind A
17:11 They track me **d**; now they surround me;
18:9 He bowed the heavens, and came **d**;
18:16 He reached **d** from on high, he took me;
18:27 but the haughty eyes you bring **d**.
18:38 I struck them **d**, so that they were not able to rise;
22:29 indeed, shall all who sleep in the earth bow **d**;
22:29 before him shall bow all who go **d** to the dust,
23:2 He makes me lie **d** in green pastures;
28:1 I shall be like those who go **d** to the Pit.
28:5 he will break them **d** and build them up no more.
30:3 restored me to life from among those gone **d** to
30:9 if I go **d** to the Pit?
33:13 The LORD looks **d** from heaven; A
35:14 bowed **d** and in mourning.
36:12 they are thrust **d**, unable to rise.
37:14 and bend their bows to bring **d** the poor and needy,
38:2 and your hand has come **d** on me.
38:6 I am utterly bowed **d** and prostrate;
39:10 I am worn **d** by the blows of your hand.
42:5 Why are you cast **d**, O my soul,
42:6 My soul is cast **d** within me;
42:11 Why are you cast **d**, O my soul,
43:5 Why are you cast **d**, O my soul,
44:5 Through you we push **d** our foes;
44:5 through your name we tread **d** our assailants.
44:25 For we sink **d** to the dust;
49:17 their wealth will not go **d** after them.
52:5 But God will break you **d** forever;
53:2 God looks **d** from heaven on humankind to see A
55:15 let them go **d** alive to Sheol;
55:23 you, O God, will cast them **d** into the lowest pit;
56:7 in wrath cast **d** the peoples, O God!
57:4 I lie **d** among lions that greedily devour human
57:6 They set a net for my steps; my soul was bowed **d**.
58:7 like grass let them be trodden **d** and wither.
59:11 and bring them **d**, O Lord, our shield.
60:12 it is he who will tread **d** our foes.
62:4 Their only plan is to bring **d** a person
63:9 But those who seek to destroy my life shall go **d**
68:8 the heavens poured **d** rain at the presence of God,
69:26 For they persecute those whom you have struck **d**,
72:9 May his foes bow **d** before him,
72:11 May all kings fall **d** before him,
75:7 putting **d** one and lifting up another.
75:8 the wicked of the earth shall drain it **d** to the dregs.
78:16 and caused waters to flow **d** like rivers.
78:24 he rained **d** on them manna to eat,
80:12 Why then have you broken **d** its walls,
80:14 look **d** from heaven, and see; A
80:16 They have burned it with fire, they have cut it **d**;
81:9 you shall not bow **d** to a foreign god.
85:11 and righteousness will look **d** from the sky.
86:9 the nations you have made shall come and bow **d**
88:4 I am counted among those who go **d** to the Pit;
89:23 before him and strike **d** those who hate him.
95:6 O come, let us worship and bow **d**,
97:7 all gods bow **d** before him.
102:19 that he looked **d** from his holy height,
104:8 ran **d** to the valleys to the place that you appointed
104:22 the sun rises, they withdraw and lie **d** in their dens.
105:36 He struck **d** all the firstborn in their land,
107:12 Their hearts were bowed **d** with hard labor;
107:12 they fell **d**, with no one to help.
107:23 Some went **d** to the sea in ships,
107:26 they went **d** to the depths;
108:13 it is he who will tread **d** our foes.
113:6 who looks far **d** on the heavens and the earth?
115:17 nor do any that go **d** into silence.
133:2 running **d** upon the beard, on the beard of Aaron,
133:2 running **d** over the collar of his robes.
135:8 He it was who struck **d** the firstborn of Egypt,
135:10 He struck **d** many nations
136:17 who struck **d** great kings,
137:1 there we sat **d** and there we wept
137:7 said, "Tear it **d**! Tear it **d**! **D** to its foundations!"
138:2 I bow **d** toward your holy temple and give thanks
139:2 You know when I sit **d** and when I rise up;
139:3 You search out my path and my lying **d**,
140:11 let evil speedily hunt **d** the violent!
143:7 or I shall be like those who go **d** to the Pit.
144:5 Bow your heavens, O LORD, and come **d**;
Ps 145:14 and raises up all who are bowed **d**.
146:8 The LORD lifts up those who are bowed **d**;
147:17 He hurls **d** hail like crumbs—
Pr 1:12 like those who go **d** to the Pit.
2:18 for her way leads **d** to death, and her paths to
3:20 and the clouds drop **d** the dew.
3:24 If you sit **d**, you will not be afraid;
3:24 when you lie **d**, your sleep will be sweet.
5:5 Her feet go **d** to death;
6:22 when you lie **d**, they will watch over you;
7:27 going **d** to the chambers of death.
12:25 Anxiety weighs **d** the human heart,
14:1 but the foolish tears it **d** with her own hands.
14:19 The evil bow **d** before the good,
15:25 The LORD tears **d** the house of the proud,
18:8 they go **d** into the inner parts of the body.
21:12 he casts the wicked **d** to ruin.
21:22 a city of warriors and brought **d** the stronghold
23:1 When you sit **d** to eat with a ruler,
23:31 when it sparkles in the cup and goes **d** smoothly.
23:34 You will be like one who lies **d** in the midst of
24:31 and its stone wall was broken **d**.
26:6 like cutting off one's foot and drinking **d** violence,
26:22 they go **d** into the inner parts of the body.
30:4 Who has ascended to heaven and come **d**?
Ecc 1:5 The sun rises and the sun goes **d**,
3:3 a time to break **d**, and a time to build up;
SS 1:7 where you make it lie **d** at noon;
4:1 moving **d** the slopes of Gilead.
6:2 My beloved has gone **d** to his garden,
6:5 moving **d** the slopes of Gilead.
6:11 I went **d** to the nut orchard,
7:9 and your kisses like the best wine that goes **d**
Isa 2:8 they bow **d** to the work of their hands,
5:5 I will break **d** its wall, and it shall be trampled **d**.
5:14 the nobility of Jerusalem and her multitude go **d**,
5:15 People are bowed **d**, everyone is brought low,
5:24 and as dry grass sinks **d** in the flame,
9:10 the sycamores have been cut **d**,
10:6 and to tread them **d** like the mire of the streets.
10:13 a bull I have brought **d** those who sat on thrones.
10:19 be so few that a child can write them **d**.
10:33 the tallest trees will be cut **d**,
10:34 He will hack **d** the thickets of the forest with
11:6 the leopard shall lie **d** with the kid,
11:7 their young shall lie **d** together;
11:14 But they shall swoop **d** on the backs of
13:20 shepherds will not make their flocks lie **d** there.
13:21 But wild animals will lie **d** there,
14:6 that struck **d** the peoples in wrath
14:8 no one comes to cut us **d**."
14:11 Your pomp is brought **d** to Sheol,
14:12 How you are cut **d** to the ground,
14:15 But you are brought **d** to Sheol,
14:19 who go **d** to the stones of the Pit,
14:30 and the needy lie **d** in safety;
17:2 they will be places for flocks, which will lie **d**,
21:3 I am bowed **d** so that I cannot hear,
22:5 a battering **d** of walls and a cry for help
22:10 and you broke **d** the houses to fortify the wall.
22:19 and you will be pulled **d** from your post.
22:25 it will be cut **d** and fall,
23:13 they tore **d** her palaces, they made her a ruin.
24:10 The city of chaos is broken **d**,
25:10 The Moabites shall be trodden **d** in their place as straw is trodden **d** in a dung-pit.
25:12 high fortifications of his walls will be brought **d**,
27:7 struck them **d** as he struck **d** those who struck them
27:10 the calves graze there, there they lie **d**,
28:2 with his hand he will hurl them **d** to the earth.
28:18 through you will be beaten **d** by it.
29:16 You turn things upside **d**!
30:2 to go **d** to Egypt without asking for my counsel, B
31:1 those who go **d** to Egypt for help and who rely B
31:4 of hosts will come **d** to fight upon Mount Zion and
33:12 like thorns cut **d**, that are burned in the fire."
37:28 I know your rising up and your sitting **d**,
37:36 Then the angel of the LORD set out and struck **d**
38:18 those who go **d** to the Pit cannot hope
43:14 For your sake I will send to Babylon and break **d**
43:17 they lie **d**, they cannot rise, they are extinguished,
44:14 He cuts **d** cedars or chooses a holm tree or an oak
44:15 makes it a carved image and bows **d** before it.
44:17 his idol, bows **d** to it and worships it;
44:19 Shall I fall **d** before a block of wood?"
45:8 from above, and let the skies rain **d** righteousness;
45:14 they shall come over in chains and bow **d** to you.
46:1 Bel bows **d**, Nebo stoops,
46:2 They stoop, they bow **d** together;
46:6 then they fall **d** and worship!
47:1 Come **d** and sit in the dust,
49:10 neither scorching wind nor sun shall strike them **d**,
49:23 With their faces to the ground they shall bow **d**
50:11 you shall lie **d** in torment.
51:14 they shall not die and go **d** to the Pit,
51:23 "Bow **d**, that we may walk on you";
52:4 my people went **d** into Egypt to reside there
53:4 yet we accounted him stricken, struck **d** by God,
55:10 as the rain and the snow come **d** from heaven, A
56:10 dreaming, lying **d**, loving to slumber.
57:9 you sent your envoys far away, and sent **d** even
58:5 Is it to bow **d** the head like a bulrush,
60:10 for in my wrath I struck you **d**,
60:14 and all who despised you shall bow **d** at your feet;
60:20 Your sun shall no more go **d**,
63:6 I trampled **d** peoples in my anger,
63:14 Like cattle that go **d** into the valley,

Isa 63:15 Look **d** from heaven and see, A
63:18 our adversaries have trampled **d** your sanctuary.
64: 1 that you would tear open the heavens and come **d,**
64: 3 not expect, you came **d,** the mountains quaked
65:10 and the Valley of Achor a place for herds to lie **d,**
65:12 and all of you shall bow **d** to the slaughter;
Jer 1:10 to pluck up and to pull **d,**
1:17 Do not break **d** before them,
2:30 In vain I have struck **d** your children;
3:25 Let us lie **d** in our shame,
6: 6 Cut **d** her trees; cast up a siege ramp against
9:18 so that our eyes may run **d** with tears,
9:19 because they have cast **d** our dwellings."
10: 3 a tree from the forest is cut **d,**
12: 5 And if in a safe land you fall **d,**
12:10 they have trampled **d** my portion,
13:17 my eyes will weep bitterly and run **d** with tears,
13:18 your beautiful crown has come **d** from your head."
14:17 Let my eyes run **d** with tears night and day,
14:17 is struck **d** with a crushing blow,
14:19 Why have you struck us **d** so
15: 9 her sun went **d** while it was yet day;
15:15 and bring **d** retribution for me on my persecutors.
18: 2 go **d** to the potter's house,
18: 3 So I went **d** to the potter's house,
18: 7 that I will pluck up and break **d** and destroy it,
21: 6 And I will strike **d** the inhabitants of this city,
21: 7 He shall strike them **d** with the edge of the sword;
21:13 you who say, "Who can come **d** against us,
22: 1 Go **d** to the house of the king of Judah,
22: 7 they shall cut **d** your choicest cedars and cast them
24: 6 I will build them up, and not tear them **d;**
26:23 who struck him **d** with the sword
31:28 over them to pluck up and break **d,**
33: 4 the houses of the kings of Judah that were torn **d**
33: 5 the dead bodies of those whom I shall strike **d**
36:12 he went **d** to the king's house,
36:15 And they said to him, "Sit **d** and read it to us."
38: 6 letting Jeremiah **d** by ropes.
38:11 which he let **d** to Jeremiah in the cistern by ropes.
39: 8 and broke **d** the walls of Jerusalem.
41: 2 and the ten men with him got up and struck **d**
41: 9 the bodies of the men whom he had struck **d** was
42:10 then I will build you up and not pull you **d;**
45: 4 I am going to break **d** what I have built,
46: 5 their warriors are beaten **d,** and have fled in haste.
46:15 because the LORD thrust him **d.**
46:23 They shall cut **d** her forest, says the LORD,
48: 1 the fortress is put to shame and broken **d;**
48:15 and the choicest of his young men have gone **d**
48:18 Come **d** from glory, and sit on the parched ground,
48:20 Moab is put to shame, for it is broken **d;**
48:40 Look, he shall swoop **d** like an eagle,
49: 8 Flee, turn back, get **d** low, inhabitants of Dedan!
49:16 from there I will bring you **d,** says the LORD.
49:22 he shall mount up and swoop **d** like an eagle,
50:15 her bulwarks have fallen, her walls are thrown **d."**
50:23 hammer of the whole earth is cut **d** and broken!
50:27 Kill all her bulls, let them go **d** to the slaughter.
51: 4 They shall fall **d** slain in the land of the Chaldeans,
51:25 and roll you **d** from the crags,
51:40 I will bring them **d** like lambs to the slaughter,
52:13 every great house he burned **d.**
52:14 broke **d** all the walls around Jerusalem.
52:27 And the king of Babylon struck them **d,**
La 2: 1 has thrown **d** from heaven to earth the splendor A
2: 2 in his wrath he has broken **d** the strongholds
2: 2 he has brought **d** to the ground in dishonor
2: 3 He has cut **d** in fierce anger all the might of Israel;
2: 6 He has broken **d** his booth like a garden,
2:18 Let tears stream **d** like a torrent day and night!
3:20 My soul continually thinks of it and is bowed **d**
3:50 until the LORD from heaven looks **d** and sees.
Eze 1:24 when they stopped, they let **d** their wings.
1:25 when they stopped, they let **d** their wings.
4: 6 you shall lie **d** a second time,
5:11 therefore I will cut you **d;**
6: 4 and I will throw **d** your slain in front of your idols.
6: 6 your incense stands cut **d,**
9: 6 Cut **d** old men, young men and young women,
9:10 but I will bring **d** their deeds upon their heads."
11:13 Then I fell **d** on my face, cried with a loud voice,
13:14 I will break **d** the wall that you have smeared
13:18 Will you hunt **d** lives among my people,
13:20 the lives that you hunt **d** like birds.
14: 1 Certain elders of Israel came to me and sat **d**
16:39 throw **d** your platform and break **d** your lofty
19: 2 She lay **d** among young lions, rearing her cubs.
19:12 But it was plucked up in fury, cast **d** to the ground;
20: 1 of Israel came to consult the LORD, and sat **d**
23:47 and with their swords they shall cut them **d;**
24: 2 write **d** the name of this day, this very day.
24:16 nor shall your tears run **d.**
26: 4 They shall destroy the walls of Tyre and break **d**
26: 9 against your walls and break **d** your towers
26:12 they shall break **d** your walls
26:16 Then all the princes of the sea shall step **d**
26:20 Then I will thrust you **d** with those who descend
26:20 with those who go **d** to the Pit,
27:29 and **d** from their ships come all that handle the oar.
28: 8 They shall thrust you **d** to the Pit,
30: 4 and its foundations are torn **d.**
30: 6 and its proud might shall come **d;**
31: 7 for its roots went **d** to abundant water.
31:12 from the most terrible of the nations have cut it **d**
31:14 with those who go **d** to the Pit.
31:15 the day it went **d** to Sheol I closed the deep over it
Eze 31:16 when I cast it **d** to Sheol with those who go **d**
31:17 They also went **d** to Sheol with it,
31:18 Now you shall be brought **d** with the trees of Eden
32:15 when I strike **d** all who live in it,
32:18 wail over the hordes of Egypt, and send them **d,**
32:18 to the world below, with those who go **d** to the Pit.
32:19 "Whom do you surpass in beauty? Go **d!**
32:21 "They have come **d,** they lie still,
32:24 who went **d** uncircumcised into the world below,
32:24 They bear their shame with those who go **d** to
32:25 and they bear their shame with those who go **d** to
32:27 with the fallen warriors of long ago who went **d**
32:29 with those who go **d** to the Pit.
32:30 who have gone **d** in shame with the slain,
32:30 bear their shame with those who go **d** to the Pit.
34:14 there they shall lie **d** in good grazing land,
34:15 and I will make them lie **d,** says the Lord GOD.
34:18 but you must tread **d** with your feet the rest
34:26 and I will send **d** the showers in their season;
37: 1 the spirit of the LORD and set me **d** in the middle
38:20 and the mountains shall be thrown **d,**
38:22 and I will pour **d** torrential rains and hailstones,
39:10 to take wood out of the field or cut **d** any trees in
40: 1 in the fourteenth year after the city was struck **d,**
40: 2 and set me **d** upon a very high mountain,
43:11 and write it **d** in their sight,
46: 2 and he shall bow **d** at the threshold of the gate.
46: 3 of the land shall bow **d** at the entrance of that gate
47: 1 the water was flowing **d** from below the south end
47: 8 the eastern region and goes **d** into the Arabah;
Da 3: 5 you are to fall **d** and worship the golden statue
3: 6 not fall **d** and worship shall immediately
3: 7 and languages fell **d** and worshiped
3:10 shall fall **d** and worship the golden statue,
3:11 and whoever does not fall **d** and worship shall
3:15 and entire musical ensemble to fall **d** and worship
3:23 Shadrach, Meshach, and Abednego, fell **d,** bound,
4:13 a holy watcher, coming **d** from heaven. A
4:14 'Cut **d** the tree and chop off its branches,
4:23 holy watcher coming **d** from heaven and saying, A
4:23 'Cut **d** the tree and destroy it,
6:10 and to get **d** on his knees three times a day to pray
6:14 the sun went **d** he made every effort to rescue him.
7: 1 Then he wrote **d** the dream:
7:23 it shall devour the whole earth, and trample it **d,**
7:24 and shall put **d** three kings.
8: 7 it threw the ram **d** to the ground and trampled
8:10 It threw **d** to the earth some of the host and some
Hos 2:18 and I will make you lie **d** in safety.
6: 1 he has struck **d,** and he will bind us up.
7:12 I will bring them **d** like birds of the air;
10: 2 The LORD will break **d** their altars,
11: 4 I bent **d** to them and fed them.
12:14 so his Lord will bring his crimes **d** on him
Joel 1: 7 it has stripped off their bark and thrown it **d;**
2:23 he has poured **d** for you abundant rain,
3: 2 I will gather all the nations and bring them **d** to
3: 3 and sold girls for wine, and drunk it **d.**
3:11 Bring **d** your warriors, O LORD.
Am 2: 8 they lay themselves **d** beside every altar
2:13 So, I will press you **d** in your place,
2:13 just as a cart presses **d** when it is full of sheaves.
3:15 I will tear **d** the winter house as well as
5:24 But let justice roll **d** like waters,
6: 2 then go **d** to Gath of the Philistines.
8: 9 I will make the sun go **d** at noon,
9: 2 from there I will bring them **d.**
Ob 1: 3 "Who will bring me **d** to the ground?"
1: 4 from there I will bring you **d,** says the LORD.
1:16 they shall drink and gulp **d,**
Jnh 1: 3 He went **d** to Joppa and found a ship going
1: 5 had gone **d** into the hold of the ship and had lain
1: 5 down into the hold of the ship and had lain **d,**
1:11 that the sea may quiet **d** for us?"
1:12 then the sea will quiet **d** for you;
2: 6 I went **d** to the land whose bars closed upon me
4: 5 Then Jonah went out of the city and sat **d** east of
4: 8 and the sun beat **d** on the head of Jonah so
Mic 1: 3 and will come **d** and tread upon the high places of
1: 4 like waters poured **d** a steep place.
1: 6 I will pour **d** her stones into the valley,
1:12 yet disaster has come **d** from the LORD
3: 6 The sun shall go **d** upon the prophets,
5: 8 treads **d** and tears in pieces, with no one to deliver.
5:11 of your land and throw **d** all your strongholds;
5:13 and you shall bow **d** no more to the work
6:13 Therefore I have begun to strike you **d,**
7:10 she will be trodden **d** like the mire of the streets.
Zep 1: 5 those who bow **d** on the roofs to the host of
1: 5 those who bow **d** and swear to the LORD,
2: 7 the houses of Ashkelon they shall lie **d** at evening.
2:11 and to him shall bow **d,** each in its place,
2:14 Herds shall lie **d** in it, every wild animal;
3:13 Then they will pasture and lie **d,**
Zec 1:21 to terrify them, to strike **d** the horns of the nations
5: 8 and pressed the leaden weight **d** on its mouth.
5:11 they will set the basket **d** there on its base."
9:15 and they shall devour and tread **d** the slingers;
10:11 and the waves of the sea shall be struck **d,**
Mal 1: 4 They may build, but I will tear **d,**
3:10 the windows of heaven for you and pour **d** for you
4: 3 And you shall tread **d** the wicked,
Mt 2:11 and they knelt **d** and paid him homage.
3:10 that does not bear good fruit is cut **d** and thrown
4: 6 "If you are the Son of God, throw yourself **d;**
4: 9 if you will fall **d** and worship me."
5: 1 and after he sat **d,** his disciples came to him.
Mt 7:19 that does not bear good fruit is cut **d** and thrown
8: 1 When Jesus had come **d** from the mountain,
8:32 the whole herd rushed **d** the steep bank into
11:23 No, you will be brought **d** to Hades.
13:48 they drew it ashore, sat **d,**
14:19 Then he ordered the crowds to sit **d** on the grass.
15:29 and he went up the mountain, where he sat **d.**
15:35 Then ordering the crowd to sit **d** on the ground,
17: 9 As they were coming **d** the mountain,
18:29 Then his fellow slave fell **d** and pleaded with him,
22:26 so also the third, **d** to the seventh.
24: 2 upon another; all will be thrown **d."**
24:17 on the housetop must not go **d** to take what is in
27: 5 Throwing **d** the pieces of silver in the temple,
27:36 then they sat **d** there and kept watch over him.
27:40 If you are the Son of God, come **d** from the cross."
27:42 let him come **d** from the cross now,
Mk 1: 7 I am not worthy to stoop **d** and untie the thong
2: 4 they let **d** the mat on which the paralytic lay.
3:11 they fell **d** before him and shouted,
3:22 And the scribes who came **d** from Jerusalem said,
5: 6 he ran and bowed **d** before him;
5:13 rushed **d** the steep bank into the sea,
5:33 fell **d** before him, and told him the whole truth.
6:39 Then he ordered them to get all the people to sit **d**
6:40 So they sat **d** in groups of hundreds and of fifties.
7:25 and she came and bowed **d** at his feet.
8: 6 Then he ordered the crowd to sit **d** on the ground;
9: 9 As they were coming **d** the mountain,
9:18 and whenever it seizes him, it dashes him **d;**
9:35 He sat **d,** called the twelve, and said to them,
12:41 He sat **d** opposite the treasury,
13: 2 upon another; all will be thrown **d."**
13:15 not go **d** or enter the house to take anything away;
14:72 And he broke **d** and wept.
15:19 spat upon him, and knelt **d** in homage to him.
15:30 save yourself, and come **d** from the cross!"
15:32 the King of Israel, come **d** from the cross now,
15:36 let us see whether Elijah will come to take him **d."**
15:46 Joseph bought a linen cloth, and taking **d** the body,
16:19 ⟦into heaven and sat **d** at the right hand of God.⟧
Lk 1: 1 to set **d** an orderly account of the events
1:52 He has brought **d** the powerful from their thrones,
2:51 Then he went **d** with them and came to Nazareth,
3: 9 that does not bear good fruit is cut **d** and thrown
4: 9 throw yourself **d** from here,
4:20 gave it back to the attendant, and sat **d.**
4:31 He went **d** to Capernaum, a city in Galilee,
4:35 When the demon had thrown him **d** before them,
5: 3 Then he sat **d** and taught the crowds from the boat.
5: 4 "Put out into the deep water and let **d** your nets for
5: 5 Yet if you say so, I will let **d** the nets."
5: 8 when Simon Peter saw it, he fell **d** at Jesus' knees,
5:19 up on the roof and let him **d** with his bed through
6:17 He came **d** with them and stood on a level place,
6:38 A good measure, pressed **d,** shaken together,
8:23 A windstorm swept **d** on the lake,
8:28 he fell **d** before him and shouted at the top
8:33 and the herd rushed **d** the steep bank into the lake
8:47 and falling **d** before him, she declared in
9:14 "Make them sit **d** in groups of about fifty each."
9:15 They did so and made them all sit **d.**
9:32 and his companions were weighed **d** with sleep;
9:37 when they had come **d** from the mountain,
9:54 to come **d** from heaven and consume them?" A
10:15 No, you will be brought **d** to Hades.
10:30 "A man was going **d** from Jerusalem to Jericho,
10:31 Now by chance a priest was going **d** that road;
12:18 I will pull **d** my barns and build larger ones,
12:37 he will fasten his belt and have them sit **d** to eat,
13: 7 and still I find none. Cut it **d!**
13: 9 but if not, you can cut it **d.' "**
14: 8 do not sit **d** at the place of honor,
14:10 you are invited, go and sit **d** at the lowest place,
14:28 does not first sit **d** and estimate the cost,
14:31 will not sit **d** first and consider whether he is able
16: 6 He said to him, 'Take your bill, sit **d** quickly,
17:31 in the house must not come **d** to take them away;
18:14 this man went **d** to his home justified rather than
19: 5 "Zacchaeus, hurry and come **d;**
19: 6 So he hurried **d** and was happy to welcome him.
19:37 now approaching the path **d** from the Mount
21: 6 upon another; all will be thrown **d."**
21:34 "Be on guard so that your hearts are not weighed **d**
22:41 from them about a stone's throw, knelt **d,**
22:44 ⟦like great drops of blood falling **d** on the ground.⟧
22:55 in the middle of the courtyard and sat **d** together,
23:53 Then he took it **d,** wrapped it in a linen cloth,
Jn 2:12 this he went **d** to Capernaum with his mother,
4:47 and begged him to come **d** and heal his son,
4:49 "Sir, come **d** before my little boy dies."
4:51 As he was going **d,** his slaves met him
5: 7 someone else steps **d** ahead of me."
6: 3 up the mountain and sat **d** there with his disciples.
6:10 Jesus said, "Make the people sit **d."**
6:10 so they sat **d,** about five thousand in all.
6:16 evening came, his disciples went **d** to the sea,
6:33 that which comes **d** from heaven and gives life A
6:38 for I have come **d** from heaven, A
6:41 "I am the bread that came **d** from heaven." A
6:42 can he now say, 'I have come **d** from heaven'?" A
6:50 This is the bread that comes **d** from heaven, A
6:51 I am the living bread that came **d** from heaven. A
6:58 This is the bread that came **d** from heaven, A
8: 2 ⟦All the people came to him and he sat **d** and⟧
8: 6 ⟦Jesus bent **d** and wrote with his finger on⟧
8: 8 ⟦once again he bent **d** and wrote on the ground.⟧

Jn 10:11 The good shepherd lays **d** his life for the sheep.
10:15 And I lay **d** my life for the sheep.
10:17 because I lay **d** my life in order to take it up again.
10:18 but I lay it **d** of my own accord.
10:18 I have power to lay it **d,**
13:37 I will lay **d** my life for you."
13:38 Jesus answered, "Will you lay **d** your life for me?
15:13 to lay **d** one's life for one's friends.
20: 5 He bent **d** to look in and saw
21:25 if every one of them were written **d,**
Ac 5: 5 Ananias heard these words, he fell **d** and died.
5:10 Immediately she fell **d** at his feet and died.
7:15 so Jacob went **d** to Egypt. B
7:24 the oppressed man and avenged him by striking **d**
7:34 and I have come **d** to rescue them.
7:60 Then he knelt **d** and cried out in a loud voice,
8: 5 Philip went **d** to the city of Samaria
8:15 The two went **d** and prayed for them
8:26 up and go toward the south to the road that goes **d**
8:38 went **d** into the water, and Philip baptized him.
9:25 but his disciples took him by night and let him **d**
9:30 they brought him **d** to Caesarea and sent him off
9:32 he came **d** also to the saints living in Lydda.
9:40 and then he knelt **d** and prayed.
10:11 and something like a large sheet coming **d,**
10:20 get up, go **d,** and go with them without hesitation;
10:21 So Peter went **d** to the men and said,
11: 5 like a large sheet coming **d** from heaven, A
11:27 At that time prophets came **d** from Jerusalem
12:19 Then Peter went **d** from Judea to Caesarea
12:23 an angel of the Lord struck him **d,**
13: 4 So, being sent out by the Holy Spirit, they went **d**
13:14 into the synagogue and sat **d.**
13:29 they took him **d** from the tree and laid him in
14:11 "The gods have come **d** to us in human form!"
14:25 the word in Perga, they went **d** to Attalia.
15: 1 Then certain individuals came **d** from Judea
15:30 So they were sent off and went **d** to Antioch.
16: 8 so, passing by Mysia, they went **d** to Troas.
16:13 and we sat **d** and spoke to
16:29 he fell **d** trembling before Paul and Silas.
17: 6 the world upside **d** have come here also,
18:22 and then went **d** to Antioch.
20:10 But Paul went **d,** and bending over him took him
20:36 he knelt **d** with them all and prayed.
21: 5 There we knelt **d** on the beach and prayed
21:10 a prophet named Agabus came **d** from Judea.
21:32 and centurions and ran **d** to them.
22:30 He brought Paul **d** and had him stand before them.
23:10 ordered the soldiers to go **d,** take him by force,
23:15 the council must notify the tribune to bring him **d**
23:20 "The Jews have agreed to ask you to bring Paul **d**
24: 1 the high priest Ananias came **d** with some elders
24:14 believing everything laid **d** according to the law
24:22 "When Lysias the tribune comes **d,**
25: 5 "let those of you who have the authority come **d**
25: 6 not more than eight or ten days, he went **d**
25: 7 the Jews who had gone **d**
27:14 called the northeaster, rushed **d** from Crete.
27:29 they let **d** four anchors from the stern and prayed
Ro 10: 6 (that is, to bring Christ **d**)
11: 8 that would not see and ears that would not hear, **d**
1Co 10: 5 and they were struck **d** in the wilderness.
10: 7 as it is written, "The people sat **d** to eat and drink,
10:11 and they were written **d** to instruct us,
14:25 person will bow **d** before God and worship him,
2Co 4: 9 struck **d,** but not destroyed;
10: 8 for building you up and not for tearing you **d,**
11:33 but I was let **d** in a basket through a window in
13:10 for building up and not for tearing **d.**
Gal 2:18 I build up again the very things that I once tore **d,**
Eph 2:14 into one and has broken **d** the dividing wall,
4:26 do not let the sun go **d** on your anger,
1Ti 1: 9 This means understanding that the law is laid **d** not
Tit 2:15 Let no one look **d** on you.
Heb 1: 3 he sat **d** at the right hand of the Majesty on high,
10:12 "he sat **d** at the right hand of God,"
Jas 1:17 is from above, coming **d** from the Father of lights,
3:15 Such wisdom does not come **d** from above,
1Jn 3:16 that he laid **d** his life for us—
3:16 and we ought to lay **d** our lives for one another.
Rev 3: 9 I will make them come and bow **d**
3:12 the new Jerusalem that comes **d** from my God out
3:21 as I myself conquered and sat **d** with my Father
5:14 And the elders fell **d** and worshiped.
10: 1 another mighty angel coming **d** from heaven, A
10: 4 and do not write it **d."**
12: 4 His tail swept **d** a third of the stars of heaven
12: 9 The great dragon was thrown **d,**
12: 9 he was thrown **d** to the earth, and his angels were
thrown **d** with him.
12:10 the accuser of our comrades has been thrown **d,**
12:12 for the devil has come **d** to you with great wrath,
12:13 dragon saw that he had been thrown **d** to the earth,
13:13 even making fire come **d** from heaven to earth A
18: 1 this I saw another angel coming **d** from heaven, A
18:21 be thrown **d,** and will be found no more;
19: 4 and the four living creatures fell **d**
19:10 Then I fell **d** at his feet to worship him,
19:15 to strike **d** the nations, and he will rule them with
20: 1 Then I saw an angel coming **d** from heaven, A
20: 9 And fire came **d** from heaven and consumed A
21: 2 coming **d** out of heaven from God,
21:10 and showed me the holy city Jerusalem coming **d**
22: 8 I fell **d** to worship at the feet of
Tob 2: 8 He has already been hunted **d** to be put to death
3:10 And I shall bring my father in his old age **d**
3:17 of Raguel came **d** from her upper room.
4:19 he chooses otherwise, he casts **d** to deepest Hades.
6: 3 Then the young man went **d** to wash his feet in
6:15 and mother's life **d** to their grave, grieving
11: 5 Meanwhile Anna sat looking intently **d** the road
12:16 they fell face **d,** for they were afraid.
12:20 Write **d** all these things that have happened
13: 2 he leads **d** to Hades in the lowest regions of
13:12 cursed are all who conquer you and pull **d**
14:10 while still alive, brought **d** into the earth?
Jdt 1:15 in the mountains of Ragau and struck him **d**
2:27 Then he went **d** into the plain of Damascus during
3: 6 Then he went **d** to the seacoast with his army
3: 8 Yet he demolished all their shrines and cut **d**
5:10 of Canaan they went **d** to Egypt and lived there B
6: 1 by the people outside the council had died **d,**
6:14 Israelites came **d** from their town and found him;
6:18 people fell **d** and worshiped God, and cried out:
8:32 I am about to do something that will go **d**
9: 3 and you struck **d** slaves along with princes,
9: 8 and bring **d** their power in your anger;
9:10 of my lips strike **d** the slave with the prince and
10: 2 She called her maid and went **d** into the house
10: 8 She bowed **d** to God.
10:10 until she had gone **d** the mountain and passed
10:15 "You have saved your life by hurrying **d**
12:16 Then Judith came in and lay **d.**
13: 6 and took **d** his sword that hung there.
13: 9 Next she rolled his body off the bed and pulled **d**
13:12 they hurried **d** to the town gate and summoned
13:15 Lord has struck him **d** by the hand of a woman.
13:17 They bowed **d** and worshiped God,
14: 2 set a captain over them, as if you were going **d** to
14: 2 against the Assyrian outpost; only do not go **d.**
14: 4 of Israel will pursue them and cut them **d**
14: 6 he fell **d** on his face in a faint.
14:13 so bold as to come **d** against us to give battle,
15: 5 and cut them **d** as far as Choba.
16: 3 Assyrian came **d** from the mountains of the north;
16: 6 nor did the sons of the Titans strike him **d,**
AdE 9:29 along with Mordecai the Jew wrote **d**
13: 7 and remain so may in a single day go **d** in violence
13:12 and refused to bow **d** to this proud Haman;
13:14 and I will not bow **d** to anyone but you,
16:11 and was continually bowed **d** to by all as
Wis 9:15 for a perishable body weighs **d** the soul,
13:11 A skilled woodcutter may saw **d** a tree easy
16:13 you lead mortals **d** to the gates of Hades
17:16 And whoever was there fell **d,**
17:19 or the harsh crash of rocks hurled **d,**
18:18 and one here and another there, hurled **d** half dead,
Sir 1:19 She rained **d** knowledge
8:16 where no help is at hand, they will strike you **d.**
9: 2 not give yourself to a woman and let her trample **d**
12:11 Even if he humbles himself and walks bowed **d,**
13:23 And should he stumble, they even push him **d.**
19:26 There is the villain bowed **d** in mourning,
28:16 nor will they settle **d** in peace.
30:12 Bow **d** his neck in his youth,
32: 1 Take care of them first and then sit **d;**
34:28 When one builds and another tears **d,**
35:18 Do not the tears of the widow run **d** her cheek
38:19 but the life of the poor weighs **d** the heart.
41: 2 worn **d** by age and anxious about everything;
42:16 The sun looks **d** on everything with its light,
43:17 He scatters the snow like birds flying **d,**
47: 4 when he whirled the stone in the sling and struck **d**
47: 5 and he gave strength to his right arm to strike **d**
48: 3 and also three times brought **d** fire.
48: 6 You sent kings **d** to destruction, and famous men,
48:21 The Lord struck **d** the camp of the Assyrians,
50:20 Then Simon came **d** and raised his hands over
50:21 and they bowed **d** in worship a second time,
Bar 2: 5 They were brought **d** and not raised up,
2:16 O Lord, look **d** from your holy dwelling,
3:19 They have vanished and gone **d** to Hades,
3:29 and taken her, and brought her **d** from the clouds?
Aza 1:26 the angel of the Lord came **d** into the furnace to be
Bel 1:36 the speed of the wind he set him **d** in Babylon,
1Mc 1:31 and tore **d** its houses and its surrounding walls.
2:25 and he tore **d** the altar.
2:29 and justice went **d** to the wilderness to live there,
2:31 the king's command had gone **d** to
2:44 and struck **d** sinners in their anger and renegades
2:45 and his friends went around and tore **d** the altars;
2:47 They hunted **d** the arrogant,
3:24 They pursued them **d** the descent of Beth-horon to
3:45 The sanctuary was trampled **d,**
3:51 Your sanctuary is trampled **d** and profaned,
4:33 Strike them **d** with the sword
4:40 and fell face **d** on the ground.
4:45 And they thought it best to tear it **d,**
4:45 So they tore **d** the altar,
4:60 the Gentiles from coming and trampling them **d**
5: 7 before him; he struck them **d.**
5:65 and tore **d** its strongholds and burned its towers
5:68 he tore **d** their altars, and the carved images
6: 6 from the armies they had cut **d;**
6: 7 that they had torn **d** the abomination
6:62 the oath he had sworn and gave orders to tear **d**
7:41 and struck **d** one hundred eighty-five thousand of
7:44 they threw **d** their arms and fled.
8:10 conquered the land, tore **d** their strongholds,
9:54 Alcimus gave orders to tear **d** the wall of
9:54 He tore **d** the work of the prophets!
9:55 But he only began to tear it **d,**
9:66 He struck **d** Odomera and his kindred and
1Mc 10:71 come **d** to the plain to meet us,
11:51 And they threw **d** their arms and made peace.
16:14 and he went **d** to Jericho with his sons Mattathias
2Mc 1:16 they threw stones and struck **d** the leader
2:10 and fire came **d** from heaven and consumed A
2:10 and the fire came **d** and consumed
5:12 to cut **d** relentlessly everyone they met and
6:10 and then hurled them **d** headlong from the wall.
8:18 with a single nod to strike **d** those who are coming
9: 8 was brought **d** to earth and carried in a litter,
10: 2 they tore **d** the altars that had been built in
10:35 and with savage fury cut **d** everyone they met.
12:35 when one of the Thracian cavalry bore **d** on him
14:25 so Judas married, settled **d,**
14:33 of God to the ground and tear **d** the altar,
14:43 and bravely threw himself **d** into the crowd.
15:16 with which you will strike **d** your adversaries."
15:24 against your holy people be struck **d."**
1Es 1:29 and the commanders came **d** against King Josiah.
1:55 broke **d** the walls of Jerusalem,
4: 9 if he tells them to cut **d,** they cut **d;**
6:16 and they pulled **d** the house,
8:71 and sat **d** in anxiety and grief.
8:73 and kneeling **d** and stretching out my hands to
Man 1:10 I am weighted **d** with many an iron fetter,
3Mc 2:18 'We have trampled **d** the house of the sanctuary as
2:18 as the houses of the abominations are trampled **d.'**
6: 7 who through envious slanders was thrown **d** into
2Es 1:10 I struck **d** Pharaoh with his servants
3:18 You bent **d** the heavens and shook the earth,
4: 8 'I never went **d** into the deep,
4:49 before me and poured **d** a heavy and violent rain,
10: 1 entered his wedding chamber, he fell **d** and died.
10:21 our altar thrown **d,** our temple destroyed;
13:12 the same man come **d** from the mountain and call
15:61 You shall be broken **d** by them like stubble,
16:76 must not let your sins weigh you **d,**
4Mc 2:14 The fruit trees of the enemy are not cut **d,**
4:11 Then Apollonius fell **d** half dead in
6:25 threw him **d,** and poured stinking liquids

DOWNCAST (5) [DOWN, CAST]

Ge 40: 7 "Why are your faces **d** today?"
Pr 17:22 but a **d** spirit dries up the bones.
2Co 7: 6 But God, who consoles the **d,**
Jdt 6: 9 that they will not be taken, then do not look **d!**
3Mc 2:20 the mouth of those who are **d** and broken in spirit,

DOWNFALL‡ (18) [DOWN, FALL]

2Ch 22: 7 by God that the **d** of Ahaziah should come about
Est 6:13 "If Mordecai, before whom your **d** has begun,
Ps 92:11 My eyes have seen the **d** of my enemies;
140: 4 from the violent who have planned my **d.**
Pr 29:16 but the righteous will look upon their **d.**
La 1: 7 the foe looked on mocking over her **d.**
1: 9 her **d** was appalling, with none to comfort her.
Eze 32:10 each one of them, on the day of your **d.**
Mic 7:10 My eyes will see her **d;** now she will be trodden
AdE 14:11 and do not let them laugh at our **d;**
Sir 4:22 to your own harm, or deference, to your **d.**
5:13 and the tongue of mortals may be their **d.**
13:13 for you are walking about with your own **d.**
20:18 the **d** of the wicked will occur just as speedily.
25: 7 a man who lives to see the **d** of his foes.
3Mc 2:14 In our **d** this audacious
4Mc 1:11 the cause of the **d** of tyranny over their nation.
11:25 to eat defiling foods, is not this your **d?**

DOWNHEARTED (1) [DOWN, HEART]

1Mc 6:10 "Sleep has departed from my eyes and I am **d**

DOWNSITTING (KJV) See SIT DOWN

DOWNTRODDEN (2) [DOWN, TREAD]

Ps 74:21 Do not let the **d** be put to shame;
147: 6 The LORD lifts up the **d;**

DOWNWARD (5) [DOWN]

Jos 18:16 of the slope of the Jebusites, and **d** to En-rogel;
2Ki 19:30 of the house of Judah shall again take root **d,**
Ecc 3:21 and the spirit of animals goes **d** to the earth?
Isa 37:31 of the house of Judah shall again take root **d,**
Eze 1:27 and **d** from what looked like

DOWNWARD (KJV) See also BELOW

DOWRY (3)

Ge 30:20 Leah said, "God has endowed me with a good **d;**
1Ki 9:16 and had given it as **d** to his daughter,
2Mc 1:14 to secure most of its treasures as a **d.**

DOWRY (KJV) See also BRIDE-PRICE, MARRIAGE PRESENT

DRACHMA (1) [DRACHMAS]

Tob 5:15 Then he added, "I will pay you a **d** a day as wages,

DRACHMAS‡ (4) [DRACHMA]

2Mc 4:19 to carry three hundred silver **d** for the sacrifice
10:20 and on receiving seventy thousand **d** let some
12:43 to the amount of two thousand **d** of silver,

3Mc 3:28 and also two thousand **d** from the royal treasury,

DRAG (9) [DRAGGED, DRAGGING, DRAGNET, DRAGS]

2Sa 17:13 and we shall **d** it into the valley,
Ps 7:2 they will **d** me away, with no one to rescue.
10:9 they seize the poor and **d** them off in their net.
28:3 Do not **d** me away with the wicked,
Isa 5:18 you who **d** iniquity along with cords of falsehood,
5:18 who **d** sin along as with cart ropes,
Jer 15:3 the sword to kill, the dogs to **d** away,
Jas 2:6 Is it not they who **d** you into court?
2Es 16:68 they shall **d** some of you away and force you

DRAGGED‡ (17) [DRAG]

Job 20:28 **d** off in the day of God's wrath.
Jer 22:19 **d** off and thrown out beyond the gates
49:20 Surely the little ones of the flock shall be **d** away;
50:45 Surely the little ones of the flock shall be **d** away;
Mt 10:18 be **d** before governors and kings because of me,
Lk 12:58 or you may be **d** before the judge,
Ac 7:58 they **d** him out of the city and began to stone him;
14:19 Then they stoned Paul and **d** him out of the city,
16:19 and Silas and **d** them into the marketplace before
17:6 they **d** Jason and some believers before
21:30 They seized Paul and **d** him out of the temple,
3Mc 2:23 that he would lose his life, quickly **d** him out,
4:7 In bonds and in public view they were violently **d**
4Mc 6:1 the guards who were standing by **d** him violently
10:12 they **d** in the fourth, saying,
11:9 the guards bound him and **d** him to the catapult;
13:18 to each of the brothers who were being **d** away,

DRAGGING (4) [DRAG]

Jn 21:8 **d** the net full of fish,
Ac 8:3 **d** off both men and women,
19:29 **d** with them Gaius and Aristarchus,
2Mc 12:35 grasping his cloak was **d** him off by main strength,

DRAGNET (1) [DRAG, NET]

Eze 32:3 and I will haul you up in my **d**.

DRAGON‡ (25) [DRAGON'S, DRAGONS]

Job 7:12 Am I the Sea, or the **D**,
Isa 27:1 and he will kill the **d** that is in the sea.
51:9 in pieces, who pierced the **d**?
Eze 29:3 the great **d** sprawling in the midst of its channels,
32:2 but you are like a **d** in the seas;
Rev 12:3 a great red **d**, with seven heads and ten horns,
12:4 the **d** stood before the woman who was about
12:7 Michael and his angels fought against the **d**.
12:7 The **d** and his angels fought back,
12:9 The great **d** was thrown down,
12:13 **d** saw that he had been thrown down to the earth,
12:16 the river that the **d** had poured from his mouth.
12:17 Then the **d** was angry with the woman,
12:18 the **d** took his stand on the sand of the seashore.
13:2 And the **d** gave it his power and his throne
13:4 the **d**, for he had given his authority to the beast,
13:11 it had two horns like a lamb and it spoke like a **d**.
16:13 like frogs coming from the mouth of the **d**,
20:2 He seized the **d**, that ancient serpent,
Sir 25:16 with a lion and a **d** than live with an evil woman.
Bel 1:23 Now in that place there was a great **d**,
1:26 and I will kill the **d** without sword or club."
1:27 which he fed to the **d**.
1:27 The **d** ate them, and burst open.
1:28 he has destroyed Bel, and killed the **d**,

DRAGON'S (1) [DRAGON]

Ne 2:13 by night by the Valley Gate past the **D** Spring and

DRAGONS (5) [DRAGON]

Ps 74:13 you broke the heads of the **d** in the waters.
AdE 10:7 The two **d** are Haman and myself.
11:6 Then two great **d** came forward,
2Es 15:29 the **d** of Arabia shall come out with many chariots,
15:31 And then the **d**, remembering their origin,

DRAGONS (KJV) See also JACKALS, SEA MONSTERS, SERPENTS

DRAGS (2) [DRAG]

Ecc 12:5 the grasshopper **d** itself along and desire fails;
Hab 1:15 he **d** them out with his net,

DRAIN (3) [DRAINED, DRAINS]

Ps 75:8 and all the wicked of the earth shall **d** it down to
Eze 23:34 you shall drink it and **d** it out, and gnaw its sherds,
Sir 13:5 he will **d** your resources without a qualm.

DRAINED‡ (5) [DRAIN]

Lev 1:15 its blood shall be **d** out against the side of the altar.
5:9 of the blood shall be **d** out at the base of the altar;
Isa 1:6 they have not been **d**, or bound up,
Sir 13:7 until he has **d** you two or three times,
2Mc 14:46 with his blood now completely **d** from him,

DRAINS (1) [DRAIN]

La 4:9 whose life **d** away, deprived of the produce of

DRAMS (KJV) See DARICS

DRANK‡ (50) [DRINK]

Ge 9:21 He **d** some of the wine and became drunk,
24:46 So I **d**, and she also watered the camels.
24:54 he and the men who were with him ate and **d**,
25:34 and he ate and **d**, and rose and went his way.
26:30 So he made them a feast, and they ate and **d**.
27:25 and he brought him wine, and he **d**.
43:34 So they **d** and were merry with him.
Ex 24:11 also they beheld God, and they ate and **d**.
34:28 he neither ate bread nor **d** water.
Nu 20:11 and the congregation and their livestock **d**.
Dt 9:9 I neither ate bread nor **d** water.
9:18 I neither ate bread nor **d** water,
32:14 you **d** fine wine from the blood of grapes.
32:38 and **d** the wine of their libations?
Jdg 9:27 they went into the temple of their god, ate and **d**,
15:19 When he **d**, his spirit returned, and he revived.
19:4 so they ate and **d**, and he stayed there.
19:6 So the two men sat and ate and **d** together;
19:8 and the two of them ate and **d**.
19:21 they washed their feet, and ate and **d**.
1Sa 1:18 ate and **d** with her husband,
1Ki 4:20 they ate and **d** and were happy.
13:19 and ate food and **d** water in his house.
17:6 and he **d** from the wadi.
19:6 He ate and **d**, and lay down again.
19:8 He got up, and ate and **d**;
2Ki 6:23 after they ate and **d**, he sent them on their way,
7:8 they went into a tent, ate and **d**, carried off silver,
9:34 Then he went in and ate and **d**;
19:24 I dug wells and **d** foreign waters,
1Ch 29:22 and they ate and **d** before the LORD on that day
Isa 37:25 I dug wells and **d** waters,
Jer 51:7 nations **d** of her wine, and so the nations went mad.
Da 5:3 his wives, and his concubines **d** from them.
5:4 They **d** the wine and praised the gods of gold
Mk 14:23 and all of them **d** from it.
Lk 13:26 you will begin to say, 'We ate and **d** with you,
Jn 4:12 and with his sons and his flocks **d** from it?"
Ac 9:9 without sight, and neither ate nor **d**.
10:41 and who ate and **d** with him after he rose from
1Co 10:4 and all **d** the same spiritual drink.
10:4 they **d** from the spiritual rock that followed them,
Jdt 12:19 and ate and **d** before him.
12:20 and **d** a great quantity of wine,
AdE 1:7 such as the king himself **d**.
Bel 1:7 and it never ate or **d** anything."
1:15 and they ate and **d** everything.
1Es 3:3 They ate and **d**, and
2Es 14:40 I took it and **d**; and
4Mc 13:21 they **d** milk from the same fountains.

DRAPED (1)

Jdt 4:12 They even **d** the altar with sackcloth and cried out

DRAUGHT (2) [DRAUGHTS]

Ps 75:8 pour a **d** from it, and all the wicked of the earth
Rev 18:6 mix a double **d** for her in the cup she mixed.

DRAUGHT (KJV) See also CATCH, LATRINE, SEWER

DRAUGHTS (1) [DRAUGHT]

3Mc 5:45 by the very fragrant **d** of wine mixed

DRAW‡ (78) [DRAWERS, DRAWING, DRAWN, DRAWS, DREW, WELL-DRAWN]

Ge 24:11 the time when women go out to **d** water.
24:13 of the townspeople are coming out to **d** water.
24:19 she said, "I will **d** for your camels also,
24:20 into the trough and ran again to the well to **d**,
24:43 let the young woman who comes out to **d**,
24:44 "Drink, and I will **d** for your camels also"—
Ex 2:16 They came to **d** water, and filled the troughs
12:48 then he may **d** near to celebrate it;
15:9 I will **d** my sword, my hand shall destroy them.'
16:9 the whole congregation of the Israelites, '**D** near
Lev 9:7 "**D** near to the altar and sacrifice your sin offering
21:18 For no one who has a blemish shall **d** near,
Dt 20:10 When you **d** near to a town to fight against it,
29:11 and those who **d** your water—
Jos 3:9 "**D** near and hear the words of
8:26 For Joshua did not **d** back his hand,
Jdg 3:22 for he did not **d** the sword out of his belly;
4:7 I will **d** out Sisera, the general of Jabin's army,
8:20 But the boy did not **d** his sword, for he was afraid,
9:54 "**D** your sword and kill me,
20:23 of the LORD, "Shall we again **d** near to battle
20:32 and **d** them away from the city toward the roads."
1Sa 9:11 they met some girls coming out to **d** water,
14:36 But the priest said, "Let us **d** near to God here."
17:8 "Why have you come out to **d** up for battle?
31:4 "**D** your sword and thrust me through with it,
2Sa 11:15 and then **d** back from him,
24:9 soldiers able to **d** the sword, and those
1Ki 13:4 against him withered so that he could not **d** it back
2Ki 13:16 Then he said to the king of Israel, "**D** the bow";
1Ch 10:4 Saul said to his armor-bearer, "**D** your sword,
Job 33:22 Their souls **d** near the Pit,
37:19 we cannot **d** up our case because of darkness.
41:1 "Can you **d** out Leviathan with a fishhook,
Ps 35:3 **D** the spear and javelin against my pursuers;
37:14 The wicked **d** the sword and bend their bows
69:18 **D** near to me, redeem me,
119:150 Those who persecute me with evil purpose **d** near;
Pr 20:5 but the intelligent will **d** them out.
Ecc 5:1 to **d** near to listen is better than
12:1 and the years **d** near when you will say,
SS 1:4 **D** me after you, let us make haste.
Isa 12:3 With joy you will **d** water from the wells
29:13 Because these people **d** near with their mouths
34:1 **D** near, O nations, to hear; O peoples, give heed!
41:1 let us together **d** near for judgment.
45:20 Assemble yourselves and come together, **d** near,
48:16 **D** near to me, hear this!
58:2 they delight to **d** near to God.
66:19 and Lud—which **d** the bow—
Jer 32:40 never to **d** back from doing good to them;
46:9 the Ludim, who **d** the bow.
La 3:39 Why should any who **d** breath complain about
Eze 9:1 saying, "**D** near, you executioners of the city,
21:3 and will **d** my sword out of its sheath,
28:7 they shall **d** their swords against the beauty
29:4 I will **d** you up from your channels,
30:11 and they shall **d** their swords against Egypt,
43:19 who **d** near to me to minister to me,
Joel 3:9 Let all the soldiers **d** near, let them come up.
Na 3:14 **D** water for the siege, strengthen your forts;
Hag 2:16 when one came to the winevat to **d** fifty measures,
Mal 3:5 Then I will **d** near to you for judgment;
Jn 2:8 He said to them, "Now **d** some out,
4:7 A Samaritan woman came to **d** water,
4:15 be thirsty or have to keep coming here to **d** water."
12:32 will **d** all people to myself."
Jas 4:8 **D** near to God, and he will **d** near to you.
Wis 15:15 nor nostrils with which to **d** breath,
Sir 22:21 Even if you **d** your sword against a friend,
33:4 **d** upon your training, and give your answer.
51:23 **D** near to me, you who are uneducated,
1Es 3:22 and before long they **d** their swords.
2Es 6:18 when I **d** near to visit the inhabitants of the earth,
7:29 and all who **d** human breath.
15:15 For the sword and misery **d** near them,
16:37 The calamities **d** near, and are not delayed.

DRAWERS (3) [DRAW]

Jos 9:21 of wood and **d** of water for all the congregation,
9:23 of wood and **d** of water for the house of my God."
9:27 that day Joshua made them hewers of wood and **d**

DRAWING (7) [DRAW]

Dt 20:3 Today you are **d** near to do battle
Lk 9:12 The day was **d** to a close,
21:28 because your redemption is **d** near."
Jdt 7:27 and our wives and children **d** their last breath.
Sir 42:5 and of **d** of blood from the back of a wicked slave.
3Mc 5:49 at their breasts who were **d** their last milk.
2Es 8:61 Therefore my judgment is now **d** near;

DRAWN (31) [DRAW]

Ge 34:3 And his soul was **d** to Dinah daughter of Jacob;
Ex 38:21 which were **d** up at the commandment of Moses,
Nu 22:23 with a **d** sword in his hand;
22:31 with his **d** sword in his hand;
Jos 5:13 and saw a man standing before him with a **d** sword
8:6 after us until we have **d** them away from the city;
8:16 and as they pursued Joshua they were **d** away from
Jdg 19:9 See, the day has **d** to a close.
20:31 they were **d** away from the city.
Ru 2:9 and drink from what the young men have **d**."
2Ki 3:21 were called out and were **d** up at the frontier.
1Ch 21:16 a **d** sword stretched out over Jerusalem.
Job 20:25 It is **d** forth and comes out of their body,
Ps 30:1 O LORD, for you have **d** me up,
55:21 but in fact were **d** swords.
Isa 21:15 they have fled from the swords, from the **d** sword,
41:5 they have **d** near and come.
Eze 21:5 the LORD have **d** my sword out of its sheath;
21:28 **D** for slaughter Polished to consume,
Joel 2:5 like a powerful army **d** up for battle,
Mic 5:6 and the land of Nimrod with the **d** sword;
Zep 3:2 it has not **d** near to its God.
Jn 2:9 (though the servants who had **d** the water knew),
6:44 to me unless **d** by the Father who sent me;
Ac 19:26 and **d** away a considerable number of people
Tob 6:18 and his heart was **d** to her.
1Mc 4:21 and when they also saw the army of Judas **d** up in
12:26 the enemy were being **d** up in formation to attack
2Mc 5:2 with lances and **d** swords—
5:3 of cavalry **d** up, attacks and counterattacks made
15:20 at hand with their army **d** up for battle,

DRAWS (6) [DRAW]

Job 36:27 For he **d** up the drops of water;
Ps 88:3 and my life **d** near to Sheol.
Eze 7:12 The time has come, the day **d** near;
2Es 12:21 when the middle of its time **d** near;
16:38 in the ninth month when the time of her delivery **d**
4Mc 14:13 which **d** everything toward an emotion felt

DREAD (48) [DREADFUL]

Ge 9:2 The fear and **d** of you shall rest on every animal of
Ex 1:12 so that the Egyptians came to **d** the Israelites.
15:16 Terror and **d** fell upon them;
Nu 22:3 Moab was in great **d** of the people,

Dt 1:29 I said to you, "Have no **d** or fear of them.
2:25 the **d** and fear of you upon the peoples everywhere
7:15 all the **d** diseases of Egypt that you experienced,
7:21 Have no **d** of them, for the LORD your God,
11:25 and **d** of you on all the land on which you set foot,
20: 3 or be afraid, or panic, or be in **d** of them;
28:60 of which you were in **d**,
28:66 night and day you shall be in **d**,
28:67 of the **d** that your heart shall feel and the sights
31: 6 Be strong and bold; have no fear or **d** of them,
Jos 2: 9 and that **d** of you has fallen on us,
1Sa 11: 7 Then the **d** of the LORD fell upon the people,
Ezr 3: 3 because they were in **d** of the neighboring peoples,
Job 3:25 and what I **d** befalls me.
4:14 **d** came upon me, and trembling,
9:34 and not let **d** of him terrify me,
13:11 and the **d** of him fall upon you?
13:21 and do not let **d** of you terrify me.
23:15 when I consider, I am in **d** of him.
Ps 31:11 an object of **d** to my acquaintances;
45: 4 let your right hand teach you **d** deeds.
64: 1 preserve my life from the **d** enemy.
88:16 your **d** assaults destroy me.
105:38 for **d** of them had fallen upon it.
119:39 Turn away the disgrace that I **d**,
Pr 1:33 and will live at ease, without **d** of disaster."
10:24 What the wicked **d** will come upon them,
20: 2 **d** anger of a king is like the growling of a lion;
Isa 7:16 the land before whose two kings you are in **d** will
8:12 and do not fear what it fears, or be in **d**.
8:13 let him be your fear, and let him be your **d**.
57:11 Whom did you **d** and fear so that you lied,
Jer 20:11 But the LORD is with me like a **d** warrior;
39:17 not be handed over to those whom you **d**.
42:16 that you **d** shall follow close after you into Egypt;
Mic 7:17 they shall turn in **d** to the LORD our God,
Hab 1: 7 **D** and fearsome are they; their justice
Jdt 2:28 and **d** of him fell upon all the people who lived
Wis 4:20 with **d** when their sins are reckoned up,
8:15 **d** monarchs will be afraid of me when they hear
10:16 and withstood **d** kings with wonders and signs.
12: 9 at one blow by **d** wild animals or your stern word.
Sir 4:17 she will bring fear and **d** upon them,
1Mc 7:18 Then the fear and **d** of them fell on all the people,

DREADFUL (10) [DREAD]

Eze 26:21 I will bring you to a **d** end,
27:36 to a **d** end and shall be no more forever."
28:19 to a **d** end and shall be no more forever.
Da 7: 7 terrifying and **d** and exceedingly strong.
Lk 21:11 and there will be **d** portents and great signs
Wis 5: 2 they will be shaken with **d** fear,
17: 6 Nothing was shining through to them except a **d**,
18:17 in **d** dreams greatly troubled them,
4Mc 8: 9 of you with **d** punishments through tortures.
8:15 the inducements and saw the **d** devices,

DREAM (79) [DREAMED, DREAMER, DREAMERS, DREAMING, DREAMS]

Ge 20: 3 But God came to Abimelech in a **d** by night,
20: 6 Then God said to him in the **d**, "Yes,
31:10 of the flock I once had a **d** in which I looked up
31:11 Then the angel of God said to me in the **d**,
31:24 God came to Laban the Aramean in a **d** by night,
37: 5 Once Joseph had a **d**, and when he told it
37: 6 He said to them, "Listen to this **d** that I dreamed.
37: 9 He had another **d**, and told it to his brothers,
37: 9 saying, "Look, I have had another **d**:
37:10 "What kind of **d** is this that you have had?
40: 5 each his own **d**, and each dream
40: 5 and each **d** with its own meaning.
40: 9 So the chief cupbearer told his **d** to Joseph,
40: 9 "In my **d** there was a vine before me,
40:16 he said to Joseph, "I also had a **d**:
41: 7 Pharaoh awoke, and it was a **d**.
41:11 he and I, each having a **d** with its own meaning.
41:12 giving an interpretation to each according to his **d**.
41:15 And Pharaoh said to Joseph, "I have had a **d**,
41:15 that when you hear a **d** you can interpret it."
41:17 "In my **d** I was standing on the banks of the Nile;
41:22 a second time and I saw in my **d** seven ears
41:32 And the doubling of Pharaoh's **d** means that
Jdg 7:13 there was a man telling a **d** to his comrade;
7:13 and he said, "I had a **d**,
7:15 of the **d** and its interpretation, he worshiped;
1Ki 3: 5 At Gibeon the LORD appeared to Solomon in a **d**
3:15 Then Solomon awoke; it had been a **d**.
Job 20: 8 They will fly away like a **d**, and not be found;
33:15 In a **d**, in a vision of the night,
Ps 73:20 They are like a **d** when one awakes;
90: 5 You sweep them away; they are like a **d**,
126: 1 we were like those who **d**.
Isa 29: 7 and who distress her, shall be like a **d**,
Jer 23:28 Let the prophet who has a **d** tell the **d**,
29: 8 and do not listen to the dreams that they **d**,
Da 2: 3 "I have had such a **d** that my spirit is troubled by
2: 4 Tell your servants the **d**, and we will reveal
2: 5 you do not tell me both the **d** and its interpretation,
2: 6 But if you do tell me the **d** and its interpretation,
2: 6 Therefore tell me the **d** and its interpretation."
2: 7 "Let the king first tell his servants the **d**,
2: 9 if you do not tell me the **d**,
2: 9 Therefore, tell me the **d**, and I shall know
2:26 "Are you able to tell me the **d** that I have seen
2:28 Your **d** and the visions of your head as you lay
Da 2:36 the **d**; now we will tell the king its interpretation.
2:45 **d** is certain, and its interpretation trustworthy."
4: 5 I saw a **d** that frightened me;
4: 6 that they might tell me the interpretation of the **d**.
4: 7 and the diviners came in, and I told them the **d**,
4: 8 and I told him the **d**:
4: 9 Hear the **d** that I saw; tell me its interpretation.
4:18 This is the **d** that I, King Nebuchadnezzar, saw.
4:19 do not let the **d** or the interpretation terrify you."
4:19 "My lord, may the **d** be for those who hate you,
7: 1 Daniel had a **d** and visions of his head as he lay
7: 1 Then he wrote down the **d**:
Joel 2:28 your old men shall **d** dreams,
Mt 1:20 angel of the Lord appeared to him in a **d** and said,
2:12 having been warned in a **d** not to return to Herod,
2:13 the Lord appeared to Joseph in a **d** and said, "Get
2:19 of the Lord suddenly appeared in a **d** to Joseph
2:22 And after being warned in a **d**,
27:19 a great deal because of a **d** about him."
Ac 2:17 and your old men shall **d** dreams.
AdE 10: 5 the **d** that I had concerning these matters,
11: 2 of the tribe of Benjamin, had a **d**.
11: 4 of Judea. And this was his **d**:
11:12 Mordecai saw in this **d** what God had determined
2Mc 15:11 and he cheered them all by relating a **d**,
2Es 10:59 in those **d** visions what the Most High will do
11: 1 On the second night I had a **d**:
12:35 This is the **d** that you saw,
13: 1 After seven days I dreamed a **d** in the night.
13:15 now show me the interpretation of this **d** also.
13:53 This is the interpretation of the **d** that you saw.
4Mc 6: 5 was unmoved, as though being tortured in a **d**;

DREAMED (11) [DREAM]

Ge 28:12 he **d** that there was a ladder set up on the earth,
37: 6 He said to them, "Listen to this dream that I **d**.
40: 5 One night they both **d**—the cupbearer
41: 1 Pharaoh **d** that he was standing by the Nile,
41: 5 Then he fell asleep and **d** a second time;
41:11 We **d** on the same night, he and I,
42: 9 Joseph also remembered the dreams that he had **d**
Jer 23:25 saying, "I have **d**, I have **d**!"
Da 2: 1 Nebuchadnezzar **d** such dreams
2Es 13: 1 After seven days I **d** a dream in the night.

DREAMER (1) [DREAM]

Ge 37:19 They said to one another, "Here comes this **d**.

DREAMERS (3) [DREAM]

Jer 27: 9 your **d**, your soothsayers, or your sorcerers,
Zec 10: 2 the **d** tell false dreams, and give empty consolation.
Jude 1: 8 Yet in the same way these **d** also defile the flesh,

DREAMING (2) [DREAM]

Isa 56:10 **d**, lying down, loving to slumber.
2Es 10:36 or is my mind deceived, and my soul **d**?

DREAMS‡ (38) [DREAM]

Ge 37: 8 So they hated him even more because of his **d**
37:20 and we shall see what will become of his **d**."
40: 8 They said to him, "We have had **d**,
41: 8 and all its wise men. Pharaoh told them his **d**,
41:12 When we told him, he interpreted our **d** to us,
41:25 "Pharaoh's **d** are one and the same;
41:26 the seven good ears are seven years; the **d** are one.
42: 9 also remembered the **d** that he had dreamed
Nu 12: 6 I speak to them in **d**.
Dt 13: 1 by **d** appear among you and promise you omens
13: 3 of those prophets or those who divine by **d**;
13: 5 But those prophets or those who divine by **d** shall
1Sa 28: 6 the LORD did not answer him, not by **d**,
28:15 either by prophets or by **d**;
Job 7:14 you scare me with **d** and terrify me with visions,
Ecc 5: 3 For **d** come with many cares,
5: 7 With many **d** come vanities and a multitude
Isa 29: 8 as when a hungry person **d** of eating and wakes
29: 8 a thirsty person **d** of drinking and wakes up faint,
Jer 23:27 to make my people forget my name by their **d**
23:32 See, I am against those who prophesy lying **d**,
29: 8 and do not listen to the **d** that they dream,
Da 1:17 Daniel also had insight into all visions and **d**.
2: 1 Nebuchadnezzar dreamed such **d**
2: 2 the Chaldeans be summoned to tell the king his **d**.
5:12 and understanding to interpret **d**, explain riddles,
Joel 2:28 your old men shall dream **d**,
Zec 10: 2 dreamers tell false **d**, and give empty consolation.
Ac 2:17 and your old men shall dream **d**.
Wis 18:17 in dreadful **d** greatly troubled them,
18:19 the **d** that disturbed them forewarned them of this,
Sir 34: 1 and **d** give wings to fools.
34: 2 so is anyone who believes in **d**.
34: 3 What is seen in **d** is but a reflection,
34: 5 Divinations and omens and **d** are unreal,
34: 7 For **d** have deceived many,
2Es 13:19 and much distress, as these **d** show.
14: 8 the **d** that you have seen, and the interpretations

DREGS (5)

Ps 75: 8 of the earth shall drain it down to the **d**.
Isa 51:17 who have drunk to the **d** the bowl of staggering.
Jer 48:11 settled like wine on its **d**;
Zep 1:12 the people who rest complacently on their **d**,
1Co 4:13 the **d** of all things, to this very day.

DRENCH (4) [DRENCHED, DRENCHES]

Ps 6: 6 I **d** my couch with my weeping.
Isa 16: 9 I **d** you with my tears, O Heshbon and Elealeh;
Eze 32: 6 I will **d** the land with your flowing blood up to
Sir 24:31 "I will water my garden and **d** my flower-beds."

DRENCHED (1) [DRENCH]

Zec 9:15 **d** like the corners of the altar.

DRENCHES (1) [DRENCH]

Sir 39:22 and **d** it like a flood.

DRESS (7) [DRESSED, DRESSER, DRESSES, VINEDRESSERS]

Dt 28:39 You shall plant vineyards and **d** them,
Isa 61: 5 foreigners shall till your land and **d** your vines;
Jer 4:30 what do you mean that you **d** in crimson,
Zep 1: 8 and the king's sons and all who **d** themselves
1Ti 2: 9 also that the women should **d** themselves modestly
Jdt 12:15 to **d** herself in all her woman's finery.
1Mc 11:58 to drink from gold cups and **d** in purple and wear

DRESSED (23) [DRESS]

1Sa 25:18 two skins of wine, five sheep ready **d**,
1Ki 5:17 to lay the foundation of the house with **d** stones.
6:36 the inner court with three courses of **d** stone
7:12 of **d** stone to one layer of cedar beams all around;
1Ch 22: 2 to prepare **d** stones for building the house of God.
Isa 9:10 but we will build with **d** stones;
Joel 1: 8 like a virgin **d** in sackcloth for the husband
Zec 3: 3 Now Joshua was **d** with filthy clothes as he stood
Mt 11: 8 Someone **d** in soft robes?
Mk 16: 5 **d** in a white robe, sitting on the right side;
Lk 7:25 Someone **d** in soft robes?
12:35 "Be **d** for action and have your lamps lit;
16:19 a rich man who was **d** in purple and fine linen
Jn 19: 2 and they **d** him in a purple robe.
Rev 3: 4 they will walk with me, **d** in white,
4: 4 and seated on the thrones are twenty-four elders, **d**
Jdt 8: 5 around her waist and **d** in widow's clothing.
10: 3 and **d** herself in the festive attire that she used
10: 7 in appearance and **d** differently,
AdE 8:15 Mordecai went out **d** in the royal robe and wearing
LtJ 6:12 When they have been **d** in purple robes,
2Mc 3:26 gloriously beautiful and splendidly **d**,
3:33 to Heliodorus **d** in the same clothing,

DRESSER (1) [DRESS]

Am 7:14 but I am a herdsman, and a **d** of sycamore trees,

DRESSES (1) [DRESS]

Ex 30: 7 when he **d** the lamps he shall offer it,

DREW (76) [DRAW]

Ge 24:20 and she **d** for all his camels.
24:45 and she went down to the spring, and **d**.
33: 6 Then the maids **d** near, they and their children,
33: 7 and her children **d** near and bowed down;
33: 7 and finally Joseph and Rachel **d** near,
37:28 they **d** Joseph up, lifting him out of the pit,
38:29 But just then he **d** back his hand,
47:29 When the time of Israel's death **d** near,
49:33 he **d** up his feet into the bed, breathed his last,
Ex 2:10 "because," she said, "I **d** him out of the water."
2:19 he even **d** water for us and watered the flock."
4: 3 and Moses **d** back from it.
14:10 As Pharaoh **d** near, the Israelites looked back,
20:21 while Moses **d** near to the thick darkness
Lev 9: 5 the whole congregation **d** near and stood before
9: 8 Aaron **d** near to the altar,
16: 1 when they **d** near before the LORD and died.
Jos 8:11 and **d** near before the city,
Jdg 20:20 and the Israelites **d** up the battle line against them
20:33 the Israelites **d** back its battle line to Baal-tamar,
1Sa 4: 2 The Philistines **d** up in line against Israel,
7: 6 and **d** water and poured it out before the LORD.
7:10 the Philistines **d** near to attack Israel;
17:21 Israel and the Philistines **d** up for battle,
17:40 and he **d** near to the Philistine.
17:41 The Philistine came on and **d** near to David,
17:48 When the Philistine **d** nearer to meet David,
17:51 he grasped his sword, **d** it out of its sheath,
30:21 When David **d** near to the people he saluted them.
2Sa 1: 6 the chariots and the horsemen **d** close to him.
10: 8 and **d** up in battle array at the entrance of the gate;
18:25 He kept coming, and **d** near.
22:17 he took me, he **d** me out of mighty waters.
23:16 **d** water from the well of Bethlehem that was by
1Ki 2: 1 When David's time to die **d** near,
6:21 then he **d** chains of gold across,
22:34 a certain man **d** his bow and unknowingly struck
2Ki 2: 5 of prophets who were at Jericho **d** near to Elisha,
9:24 Jehu **d** his bow with all his strength,
13:16 "Draw the bow"; and he **d** it.
16:12 Then the king **d** near to the altar, went up on it,
1Ch 5:18 who carried shield and sword, and **d** the bow,
11:18 and **d** water from the well of Bethlehem that was
19: 9 and **d** up in battle array at the entrance of the city,
19:17 came to them, and **d** up his forces against them.
21: 5 men who **d** the sword,
21: 5 four hundred seventy thousand who **d** the sword.
2Ch 13: 3 and Jeroboam **d** up his line of battle against him

2Ch 14: 8 from Benjamin who carried shields and **d** bows;
14:10 and they **d** up their lines of battle in the valley
18:31 God **d** them away from him,
18:33 a certain man **d** his bow and unknowingly struck
Ps 18:16 he **d** me out of mighty waters.
40: 2 He **d** me up from the desolate pit,
107:18 and they **d** near to the gates of death.
Pr 8:27 when he **d** a circle on the face of the deep,
Jer 38:13 Then they **d** Jeremiah up by the ropes
La 4:18 in our streets; our end **d** near;
Mt 13:48 they **d** it ashore, sat down,
26:51 **d** it, and struck the slave of the high priest,
Mk 14:47 of those who stood near **d** his sword and struck
Lk 9:51 When the days **d** near for him to be taken up,
Jn 18:10 Then Simon Peter, who had a sword, **d** it,
Ac 7:17 the time **d** near for the fulfillment of the promise
16:27 he **d** his sword and was about to kill himself,
22:29 about to examine him **d** back from him;
23:19 **d** him aside privately, and asked,
Gal 2:12 he **d** back and kept himself separate for fear of
Tob 6: 4 So the young man grasped the fish and **d** it up on
Wis 19: 4 For the fate they deserved **d** them on to this end,
Sir 51: 6 My soul **d** near to death, and my life was on the
1Mc 2:49 Now the days **d** near for Mattathias to die,
5:40 Judas and his army **d** near to the stream of water,
2Mc 10:25 As he **d** near, Maccabeus
14:44 But as they quickly **d** back,
Pm 151: 7 But I **d** his own sword;

DRIED (32) [DRY]

Ge 8: 7 and fro until the waters were **d** up from the earth.
8:13 the waters were **d** up from the earth;
Nu 6: 3 not drink any grape juice or eat grapes, fresh or **d.**
11: 6 but now our strength is **d** up,
Jos 2:10 For we have heard how the LORD **d** up the water
4:23 For the LORD your God **d** up the waters of
4:23 which he **d** up for us until we crossed over,
5: 1 that the LORD had **d** up the waters of the Jordan
Jdg 16: 7 with seven fresh bowstrings that are not **d** out,
16: 8 that had not **d** out, and she bound him
1Ki 17: 7 wadi **d** up, because there was no rain in the land.
2Ki 19:24 I **d** up with the sole of my foot all the streams
Ps 22:15 my mouth is **d** up like a potsherd,
32: 4 my strength was **d** up as by the heat of summer.
74:15 you **d** up ever-flowing streams.
Isa 19: 5 The waters of the Nile will be **d** up,
37:25 I **d** up with the sole of my foot all the streams
51:10 Was it not you who **d** up the sea,
Jer 23:10 and the pastures of the wilderness are **d** up.
50:38 drought against her waters, that they may be **d** up!
Eze 19:12 the east wind **d** it up; its fruit was stripped off,
37:11 They say, 'Our bones are **d** up,
Hos 9:16 Ephraim is stricken, their root is **d** up,
Joel 1:12 all the trees of the field are **d** up;
1:20 to you because the watercourses are **d** up,
Zec 10:11 and all the depths of the Nile **d** up.
Lk 7:44 with her tears and **d** them with her hair.
Rev 16:12 and its water was **d** up in order to prepare the way
Jdt 5:13 Then God **d** up the Red Sea before them,
10: 5 and filled a bag with roasted grain, **d** fig cakes,
2Es 6:42 six parts you **d** up and kept so that some
6:51 that had been **d** up on the third day, to live in it,

DRIES (8) [DRY]

Job 14:11 and a river wastes away and **d** up,
Pr 17:22 but a downcast spirit **d** up the bones.
Isa 24: 4 The earth **d** up and withers,
24: 7 The wine **d** up, the vine languishes,
Joel 1:10 the grain is destroyed, the wine **d** up, the oil fails.
Am 1: 2 and the top of Carmel **d** up.
Na 1: 4 and he **d** up all the rivers;
2Es 8:23 whose look **d** up the depths

DRIFT (1) [ADRIFT, DRIFTING]

Heb 2: 1 so that we do not **d** away from it.

DRIFTING (2) [DRIFT]

Zep 2: 2 before you are driven away like the **d** chaff,
Ac 27:27 as we were **d** across the sea of Adria,

DRIMYLUS (1)

3Mc 1: 3 But Dositheus, known as the son of **D,**

DRINK‡ (383) [DRANK, DRINKING, DRINKS, DRUNK, DRUNKARD, DRUNKARDS, DRUNKEN, DRUNKENNESS, WINE-DRINKERS, WINE-DRINKING]

A. DRINK OFFERING (32)
B. DRINK OFFERINGS (27)
C. STRONG DRINK (21)

Ge 19:32 Come, let us make our father **d** wine,
19:33 So they made their father **d** wine that night;
19:34 let us make him **d** wine tonight also;
19:35 So they made their father **d** wine that night also;
21:19 and gave the boy a **d.**
24:14 'Please offer your jar that I may **d,'**
24:14 **'D,** and I will water your camels'—
24:18 **"D,** my lord," she said,
24:18 upon her hand and gave him a **d.**
24:19 When she had finished giving him a **d,** she said,
Ge 24:43 "Please give me a little water from your jar to **d,"**
24:44 **"D,** and I will draw for your camels also"—
24:45 I said to her, 'Please let me **d.'**
24:46 and said, **'D,** and I will also water your camels.'
30:38 the watering places, where the flocks came to **d.**
30:38 And since they bred when they came to **d,**
35:14 and he poured out a **d** offering on it, A
Ex 7:18 and the Egyptians shall be unable to **d** water from
7:21 so that the Egyptians could not **d** its water,
7:24 to dig along the Nile for water to **d,**
7:24 for they could not **d** the water of the river.
15:23 not **d** the water of Marah because it was bitter.
15:24 saying, "What shall we **d?"**
17: 1 but there was no water for the people to **d.**
17: 2 and said, "Give us water to **d."**
17: 6 so that the people may **d."**
25:29 and bowls with which to pour **d** offerings; B
29:40 and one-fourth of a hin of wine for a **d** offering. A
29:41 with it a grain offering and its **d** offering, A
30: 9 and you shall not pour a **d** offering on it. A
32: 6 people sat down to eat and **d,** and rose up to revel.
32:20 and made the Israelites **d** it.
37:16 and flagons with which to pour **d** offerings. B
Lev 10: 9 **D** no wine or strong drink, neither you
10: 9 Drink no wine or strong **d,** neither you C
23:13 and the **d** offering with it shall be of wine, A
23:18 with their grain offering and their **d** offerings, B
23:37 sacrifices and **d** offerings, B
Nu 4: 7 the bowls, and the flagons for the **d** offering; A
5:24 He shall make the woman **d** the water of bitterness
5:26 and afterward shall make the woman **d** the water.
5:27 When he has made her **d** the water, then,
6: 3 separate themselves from wine and strong **d;** C
6: 3 they shall **d** no wine vinegar or other vinegar,
6: 3 and shall not **d** any grape juice or eat grapes,
6:15 with their grain offering and their **d** offerings. B
6:17 the accompanying grain offering and **d** offering. A
6:20 After that the nazirites may **d** wine.
15: 5 of wine as a **d** offering with the burnt offering A
15: 7 as a **d** offering you shall offer one-third of a hin A
15:10 shall present as a **d** offering half a hin of wine, A
15:24 with its grain offering and its **d** offering, A
20: 5 and there is no water to **d."**
20: 8 thus you shall provide **d** for the congregation
20:17 or **d** water from any well;
20:19 and if we **d** of your water, we and our livestock,
21:22 we will not **d** the water of any well;
28: 7 Its **d** offering shall be one-fourth of a hin A
28: 7 in the sanctuary you shall pour out a **d** offering A
28: 7 a drink offering of strong **d** to the LORD. C
28: 8 a grain offering and a **d** offering like the one A
28: 9 mixed with oil, and its **d** offering— A
28:10 to the regular burnt offering and its **d** offering. A
28:14 Their **d** offerings shall be half a hin of wine for B
28:15 to the regular burnt offering and its **d** offering. A
28:24 to the regular burnt offering and its **d** offering. A
28:31 you shall offer them and their **d** offering. A
29: 6 and their **d** offerings, according to the ordinance B
29:11 and its grain offering, and their **d** offerings. B
29:16 its grain offering and its **d** offering. A
29:18 grain offering and the **d** offerings for the bulls, B
29:19 and its grain offering, and their **d** offerings. B
29:21 grain offering and the **d** offerings for the bulls, B
29:22 and its grain offering and its **d** offering. A
29:24 grain offering and the **d** offerings for the bulls, B
29:25 its grain offering and its **d** offering. A
29:27 grain offering and the **d** offerings for the bulls, B
29:28 and its grain offering and its **d** offering. A
29:30 grain offering and the **d** offerings for the bulls, B
29:31 its grain offering, and its **d** offerings. B
29:33 grain offering and the **d** offerings for the bulls, B
29:34 its grain offering, and its **d** offering. A
29:37 grain offering and the **d** offerings for the bull, B
29:38 and its grain offering and its **d** offering. A
29:39 **d** offerings, and your offerings of well-being. B
33:14 where there was no water for the people to **d.**
Dt 2: 6 from them for money, so that you may **d.**
2:28 and supply me water for money, so that I may **d.**
14:26 oxen, sheep, wine, strong **d,** C
28:39 you shall neither **d** the wine nor gather the grapes,
29: 6 and you have not drunk wine or strong **d**— C
Jdg 4:19 he said to her, "Please give me a little water to **d;**
4:19 a skin of milk and gave him a **d** and covered him.
7: 5 all those who kneel down to **d,**
7: 6 but all the rest of the troops knelt down to **d** water.
13: 4 Now be careful not to **d** wine or strong drink,
13: 4 Now be careful not to drink wine or strong **d,** C
13: 7 So then **d** no wine or strong drink,
13: 7 So then drink no wine or strong **d,** C
13:14 She is not to **d** wine or strong drink,
13:14 She is not to drink wine or strong **d,** C
Ru 2: 9 and **d** from what the young men have drawn."
1Sa 1:11 He shall **d** neither wine nor intoxicants,
1:15 I have drunk neither wine nor strong **d,** C
30:11 they gave him water to **d;**
2Sa 11:11 shall I then go to my house, to eat and to **d,**
11:13 to eat and **d** in his presence and made him drunk;
12: 3 and **d** from his cup, and lie in his bosom,
16: 2 wine is for those to **d** who faint in the wilderness."
23:15 "O that someone would give me water to **d** from
23:16 But he would not **d** of it;
23:17 Can I **d** the blood of the men who went at the risk
23:17 Therefore he would not **d** it.
1Ki 13: 8 nor will I eat food or **d** water in this place.
13: 9 You shall not eat food, or **d** water,
13:16 will I eat food or **d** water with you in this place;
13:17 You shall not eat food or **d** water there,
1Ki 13:18 so that he may eat food and **d** water.
13:22 'Eat no food, and **d** no water,'
17: 4 You shall **d** from the wadi,
17:10 a little water in a vessel, so that I may **d."**
18:41 Elijah said to Ahab, "Go up, eat and **d;**
18:42 So Ahab went up to eat and to **d.**
2Ki 3:17 so that you shall **d,** you, your cattle,
6:22 and water before them so that they may eat and **d;**
16:13 and his grain offering, poured his **d** offering, A
16:15 their grain offering, and their **d** offering; A
18:27 to eat their own dung and to **d** their own urine?"
18:31 and **d** water from your own cistern,
1Ch 11:17 "O that someone would give me water to **d** from
11:18 But David would not **d** of it;
11:19 Can I **d** the blood of these men?
11:19 Therefore he would not **d** it.
2Ch 28:15 provided them with food and **d,**
29:35 were the **d** offerings for the burnt offerings. B
Ezr 3: 7 the masons and the carpenters, and food, **d,** and oil
7:17 and their grain offerings and their **d** offerings, B
10: 6 He did not eat bread or **d** water,
Ne 8:10 the fat and **d** sweet wine and send portions of them
8:12 And all the people went their way to eat and **d** and
Est 3:15 The king and Haman sat down to **d;**
4:16 and neither eat nor **d** for three days, night or day.
Job 1: 4 and invite their three sisters to eat and **d**
21:20 and let them **d** of the wrath of the Almighty.
22: 7 You have given no water to the weary to **d,**
Ps 16: 4 their **d** offerings of blood I will not pour out B
36: 8 you give them **d** from the river of your delights.
50:13 Do I eat the flesh of bulls, or **d** the blood of goats?
60: 3 you have given us wine to **d** that made us reel.
69:21 and for my thirst they gave me vinegar to **d.**
78:15 and gave them **d** abundantly as from the deep.
78:44 so that they could not **d** of their streams.
80: 5 and given them tears to **d** in full measure.
102: 9 I eat ashes like bread, and mingle tears with my **d,**
104:11 giving **d** to every wild animal;
110: 7 He will **d** from the stream by the path;
Pr 4:17 For they eat the bread of wickedness and **d**
5:15 **D** water from your own cistern,
9: 5 eat of my bread and **d** of the wine I have mixed.
20: 1 Wine is a mocker, strong **d** a brawler, C
23: 7 in the throat, so are they. "Eat and **d!"**
23:35 I will seek another **d."**
25:21 and if they are thirsty, give them water to **d;**
31: 4 O Lemuel, it is not for kings to **d** wine,
31: 4 or for rulers to desire strong **d;** C
31: 5 else they will **d** and forget what has been decreed,
31: 6 Give strong **d** to one who is perishing, C
31: 7 let them **d** and forget their poverty,
Ecc 2:24 for mortals than to eat and **d,**
3:13 that all should eat and **d** and take pleasure
5:18 it is fitting to eat and **d** and find enjoyment in all
8:15 and **d,** and enjoy themselves,
9: 7 and **d** your wine with a merry heart;
SS 5: 1 I **d** my wine with my milk.
5: 1 Eat, friends, **d,** and be drunk with love.
8: 2 I would give you spiced wine to **d,**
Isa 5:11 in the morning in pursuit of strong **d,** C
5:22 in drinking wine and valiant at mixing **d,**
21: 5 they spread the rugs, they eat, they **d.**
22:13 "Let us eat and **d,** for tomorrow we die."
24: 9 No longer do they **d** wine with singing;
24: 9 strong **d** is bitter to those who drink it. C
24: 9 strong drink is bitter to those who **d** it.
28: 7 also reel with wine and stagger with strong **d;** C
28: 7 the priest and the prophet reel with strong **d,** C
28: 7 they stagger with strong **d;** C
29: 9 stagger, but not from strong **d!** C
32: 6 and to deprive the thirsty of **d.**
36:12 to eat their own dung and **d** their own urine?"
36:16 and **d** water from your own cistern,
43:20 rivers in the desert, to give **d** to my chosen people,
51:22 you shall **d** no more from the bowl of my wrath.
56:12 let us fill ourselves with strong **d.** C
57: 6 to them you have poured out a **d** offering, A
62: 8 for your enemies, and foreigners shall not **d**
62: 9 those who gather it shall **d** it in my holy courts.
65:13 my servants shall **d,** but you shall be thirsty;
66:11 that you may **d** deeply with delight
Jer 2:18 to **d** the waters of the Nile?
2:18 to **d** the waters of the Euphrates?
7:18 and they pour out **d** offerings to other gods, B
8:14 and has given us poisoned water to **d,**
9:15 and giving them poisonous water to **d.**
16: 7 the cup of consolation to **d** for their fathers
16: 8 the house of feasting to sit with them, to eat and **d.**
22:15 Did not your father eat and **d** and do justice
23:15 and give them poisoned water to **d;**
25:15 and make all the nations to whom I send you **d** it.
25:16 They shall **d** and stagger and go out of their minds
25:17 the nations to whom the LORD sent me **d** it:
25:26 And after them the king of Sheshach shall **d.**
25:27 **D,** get drunk and vomit, fall and rise no more,
25:28 they refuse to accept the cup from your hand to **d,**
25:28 Thus says the LORD of hosts: You must **d!**
35: 2 then offer them wine to **d.**
35: 6 But they answered, "We will **d** no wine,
35: 6 'You shall never **d** wine, neither you
35: 8 to **d** no wine all our days, ourselves, our wives,
35:14 of Rechab gave to his descendants to **d** no wine;
35:14 and they **d** none to this day,
46:10 and **d** its fill of their blood.
49:12 who do not deserve to **d** the cup still have to **d** it,
49:12 You shall not go unpunished; you must **d** it.
51:39 I will set out their **d** and make them drunk,

La 5: 4 We must pay for the water we **d**;
Eze 4:11 you shall **d** water by measure, one-sixth of a hin;
4:11 at fixed times you shall **d**.
4:16 and they shall **d** water by measure and in dismay.
12:18 **d** your water with trembling and with fearfulness;
12:19 and **d** their water in dismay,
20:28 and there they poured out their **d** offerings. B
23:32 You shall **d** your sister's cup, deep and wide;
23:34 you shall **d** it and drain it out, and gnaw its sherds,
25: 4 and they shall **d** your milk.
31:14 that no trees that **d** water may reach up to them
34:18 When you **d** of clear water,
34:19 and **d** what you have fouled with your feet?
39:17 and you shall eat flesh and **d** blood.
39:18 and **d** the blood of the princes of the earth—
39:19 and **d** blood until you are drunk,
44:21 No priest shall **d** wine when he enters
45:17 and **d** offerings, at the festivals, the new moons, B
Da 1:10 he has appointed your food and your **d**.
1:12 Let us be given vegetables to eat and water to **d**.
1:16 and the wine they were to **d**,
5: 2 his wives, and his concubines might **d** from them.
Hos 2: 5 my wool and my flax, my oil and my **d**."
9: 4 not pour **d** offerings of wine to the LORD, B
Joel 1: 9 The grain offering and the **d** offering are cut off A
1:13 Grain offering and **d** offering are withheld from A
2:14 a grain offering and a **d** offering for the LORD, A
Am 2: 8 and in the house of their God they **d** wine bought
2:12 But you made the nazirites **d** wine,
4: 1 say to their husbands, "Bring something to **d**!"
4: 8 or three towns wandered to one town to **d** water,
5:11 but you shall not **d** their wine.
6: 6 who **d** wine from bowls, and anoint themselves
9:14 they shall plant vineyards and **d** their wine,
Ob 1:16 all the nations around you shall **d**;
1:16 they shall **d** and gulp down,
Jnh 3: 7 They shall not feed, nor shall they **d** water.
Mic 2:11 "I will preach to you of wine and strong **d**," C
6:15 you shall tread grapes, but not **d** wine.
Hab 2:15 "Alas for you who make your neighbors **d**,
2:16 **D**, you yourself, and stagger!
Zep 1:13 they shall not **d** wine from them.
Hag 1: 6 you **d**, but you never have your fill;
Zec 7: 6 And when you eat and when you **d**,
7: 6 do you not eat and **d** only for yourselves?
9:15 they shall **d** their blood like wine,
Mt 6:25 what you will eat or what you will **d**,
6:31 or 'What will we **d**?'
20:22 Are you able to **d** the cup that I am about to **d**?"
20:23 He said to them, "You will indeed **d** my cup,
25:35 I was thirsty and you gave me something to **d**,
25:37 or thirsty and gave you something to **d**?
25:42 I was thirsty and you gave me nothing to **d**,
26:27 saying, "**D** from it, all of you;
26:29 I will never again **d** of this fruit of the vine until that day when I **d** it new with you
26:42 if this cannot pass unless I **d** it, your will be done."
27:34 they offered him wine to **d**, mixed with gall;
27:34 but when he tasted it, he would not **d** it.
27:48 put it on a stick, and gave it to him to **d**.
Mk 9:41 a cup of water to **d** because you bear the name
10:38 Are you able to **d** the cup that I **d**,
10:39 "The cup that I **d** you will **d**;
14:25 I will never again **d** of the fruit of the vine until that day when I **d** it new in the kingdom of God."
15:36 put it on a stick, and gave it to him to **d**, saying,
16:18 ⟦and if they **d** any deadly thing,⟧
Lk 1:15 He must never **d** wine or strong drink;
1:15 He must never drink wine or strong **d**; C
5:30 "Why do you eat and **d** with tax collectors
5:33 but your disciples eat and **d**.
12:19 for many years; relax, eat, **d**,
12:29 for what you are to eat and what you are to **d**,
12:45 men and women, and to eat and **d** and get drunk,
17: 8 put on your apron and serve me while I eat and **d**;
17: 8 later you may eat and **d**'?
22:18 from now on I will not **d** of the fruit of the vine
22:30 you may eat and **d** at my table in my kingdom,
Jn 4: 7 and Jesus said to her, "Give me a **d**."
4: 9 a Jew, ask a **d** of me, a woman of Samaria?"
4:10 and who it is that is saying to you, 'Give me a **d**,'
4:14 but those who **d** of the water
6:53 the flesh of the Son of Man and **d** his blood,
6:54 and **d** my blood have eternal life,
6:55 for my flesh is true food and my blood is true **d**.
6:56 Those who eat my flesh and **d** my blood abide
7:38 and let the one who believes in me **d**.
18:11 not to **d** the cup that the Father has given me?"
Ac 23:12 to eat nor **d** until they had killed Paul.
23:21 by an oath neither to eat nor **d** until they kill him.
Ro 12:20 if they are thirsty, give them something to **d**;
14:17 and **d** but righteousness and peace and joy in
14:21 it is good not to eat meat or **d** wine or do anything
1Co 9: 4 Do we not have the right to our food and **d**?
10: 4 and all drank the same spiritual **d**.
10: 7 as it is written, "The people sat down to eat and **d**,
10:21 You cannot **d** the cup of the Lord and the cup
10:31 So, whether you eat or **d**, or whatever you do,
11:22 Do you not have homes to eat and **d** in?
11:25 Do this, as often as you **d** it,
11:26 For as often as you eat this bread and **d** the cup,
11:28 and only then eat of the bread and **d** of the cup.
11:29 For all who eat and **d** without discerning the body,
11:29 eat and **d** judgment against themselves.
12:13 and we were all made to **d** of one Spirit.
15:32 "Let us eat and **d**, for tomorrow we die."
Col 2:16 in matters of food and **d** or of observing festivals,
1Ti 5:23 No longer **d** only water, but take a little wine for
Tit 2: 3 not to be slanderers or slaves to **d**;
Heb 9:10 deal only with food and **d** and various baptisms,
Rev 14: 8 She has made all nations **d** of the wine of
14:10 they will also **d** the wine of God's wrath,
16: 6 you have given them blood to **d**.
Tob 4:15 Do not **d** wine to excess or let drunkenness go
7:10 "Eat and **d**, and be merry tonight.
7:11 But now, my child, eat and **d**,
7:11 "I will neither eat nor **d** anything until you settle
7:14 Then they began to eat and **d**.
12:19 I really did not eat or **d** anything—
Jdt 7:21 and on no day did they have enough water to **d**,
12: 1 and with some of his own wine to **d**.
12:11 in your care to join us and to eat and **d** with us.
12:17 "Have a **d** and be merry with us!"
12:18 Judith said, "I will gladly **d**, my lord,
AdE 4:16 for three days and nights do not eat or **d**,
7: 1 the king and Haman went in to **d** with the queen.
Sir 9:10 when it has aged, you can **d** it with pleasure.
15: 3 and give him the water of wisdom to **d**.
24:21 and those who **d** of me will thirst for more.
29:25 the host and provide **d** without being thanked,
50:15 for the cup and poured a **d** offering of the blood A
1Mc 1:22 the cups for **d** offerings, the bowls, B
1:45 and sacrifices and **d** offerings in the sanctuary, B
11:58 to **d** from gold cups and dress in purple and wear
2Mc 15:39 For just as it is harmful to **d** wine alone, or, again,
15:39 or, again, to **d** water alone,
1Es 3: 6 and **d** from gold cups, and sleep on a gold bed,
3:18 It leads astray the minds of all who **d** it.
3:22 When people **d** they forget to be friendly
5:54 to the masons and the carpenters, and food and **d**
9: 2 and he did not eat bread or **d** water,
9:51 eat the fat and **d** the sweet,
9:54 to eat and **d** and enjoy themselves,
3Mc 5: 2 maddened by the lavish abundance of **d**,
2Es 8: 4 "Then **d** your fill of understanding, O my soul,
8: 4 O my soul, and **d** wisdom, O my heart.
9:24 and taste no meat and **d** no wine,
9:34 or the sea a ship, or any dish food or **d**,
10: 4 I will neither eat nor **d**,
14:38 open your mouth and **d** what I give you to drink."
14:38 open your mouth and drink what I give you to **d**."
15:58 for bread and **d** their own blood in thirst for water.
4Mc 3:14 and from it boldly brought the king a **d**.
3:15 to his soul to **d** what was regarded as equivalent
3:16 he poured out the **d** as an offering to God.

DRINKING (44) [DRINK]

Ge 24:19 until they have finished **d**."
24:22 When the camels had finished **d**,
Ru 3: 3 to the man until he has finished eating and **d**.
1Sa 30:16 eating and **d** and dancing,
1Ki 1:25 who are now eating and **d** before him, and saying,
10:21 All King Solomon's **d** vessels were of gold,
16: 9 **d** himself drunk in the house of Arza,
20:12 now he had been **d** with the kings in the booths—
20:16 Ben-hadad was **d** himself drunk in the booths,
1Ch 12:39 eating and **d**, for their kindred had provided
2Ch 9:20 All King Solomon's **d** vessels were of gold,
Est 1: 8 **D** was by flagons, without restraint;
5: 6 While they were **d** wine, the king said to Esther,
7: 2 On the second day, as they were **d** wine,
Job 1:13 and **d** wine in the eldest brother's house,
1:18 "Your sons and daughters were eating and **d** wine
Pr 26: 6 like cutting off one's foot and **d** down violence,
Isa 5:22 you who are heroes in **d** wine and valiant
22:13 and slaughtering sheep, eating meat and **d** wine.
29: 8 or a thirsty person dreams of **d** and wakes up faint,
Da 5: 1 and he was **d** wine in the presence of the thousand.
5:23 and your concubines have been **d** wine from them.
Hos 4:18 their **d** is ended, they indulge in sexual orgies;
Mt 11:18 For John came neither eating nor **d**, and they say,
11:19 the Son of Man came eating and **d**,
24:38 before the flood they were eating and **d**,
Lk 5:39 And no one after **d** old wine desires new wine,
7:33 and **d** no wine, and you say, 'He has a demon';
7:34 the Son of Man has come eating and **d**,
10: 7 eating and **d** whatever they provide,
17:27 and **d**, and marrying and being given in marriage,
17:28 they were eating and **d**, buying and selling,
Tob 8: 1 When they had finished eating and **d** they wanted
8:20 but shall stay here eating and **d** with me;
Jdt 7:21 for their **d** water was rationed.
12:13 and to enjoy **d** wine with us,
AdE 1: 5 the festivity the king gave a **d** party for the people
1: 8 The **d** was not according to a fixed rule;
1: 9 Queen Vashti gave a **d** party for the women in
5: 6 While they were **d** wine, the king said to Esther,
7: 2 And the second day, as they were **d** wine,
3Mc 2:25 by the previously mentioned **d** companions
5:16 The king, after considering this, returned to his **d**,
6:36 as a festival, not for **d** and gluttony,

DRINKS (14) [DRINK]

Ge 44: 5 Is it not from this that my lord **d**?
2Sa 19:35 Can your servant taste what he eats or what he **d**?
Est 1: 7 **D** were served in golden goblets,
Job 6: 4 in me; my spirit **d** their poison;
15:16 one who **d** iniquity like water!
34: 7 who **d** up scoffing like water,
Isa 44:12 he **d** no water and is faint.
Mt 24:49 and eats and **d** with drunkards,
Jn 4:13 "Everyone who **d** of this water will
1Co 11:27 eats the bread or **d** the cup of the Lord in
Heb 6: 7 Ground that **d** up the rain falling on it repeatedly,
Sir 26:12 As a thirsty traveler opens his mouth and **d**
Bel 1: 6 not see how much he eats and **d** every day?"
1Es 4:10 Furthermore, he reclines, he eats and **d** and sleeps,

DRIP (4) [DRIPPED, DRIPPING, DRIPPINGS]

Pr 5: 3 For the lips of a loose woman **d** honey,
Joel 3:18 In that day the mountains shall **d** sweet wine,
Am 9:13 the mountains shall **d** sweet wine,
2Es 5: 5 Blood shall **d** from wood,

DRIPPED (1) [DRIP]

SS 5: 5 and my hands **d** with myrrh,

DRIPPING (3) [DRIP]

1Sa 14:26 upon the honeycomb, the honey was **d** out;
Pr 19:13 and a wife's quarreling is a continual **d** of rain.
27:15 A continual **d** on a rainy day and

DRIPPINGS (3) [DRIP]

Ps 19:10 sweeter also than honey, and **d** of the honeycomb.
Pr 24:13 the **d** of the honeycomb are sweet to your taste.
4Mc 9:20 and the heap of coals was being quenched by the **d**

DRIVE (67) [DRIVEN, DRIVER, DRIVERS, DRIVES, DRIVING, DROVE]

Ex 6: 1 by a mighty hand he will **d** them out of his land."
11: 1 indeed, when he lets you go, he will **d** you away.
23:28 which shall **d** out the Hivites, the Canaanites,
23:29 I will not **d** them out from before you in one year,
23:30 Little by little I will **d** them out from before you,
23:31 and you shall **d** them out before you.
33: 2 and I will **d** out the Canaanites, the Amorites,
34:11 See, I will **d** out before you the Amorites,
Nu 22: 6 perhaps I shall be able to defeat them and **d** them
22:11 be able to fight against them and **d** them out.' "
33:52 you shall **d** out all the inhabitants of the land from
33:55 if you do not **d** out the inhabitants of the land from
Dt 11:23 the LORD will **d** out all these nations before you,
Jos 3:10 the living God who without fail will **d** out from
13: 6 I will myself **d** them out from before the Israelites;
13:13 Yet the Israelites did not **d** out the Geshurites or
14:12 and I shall **d** them out, as the LORD said."
15:63 the people of Judah could not **d** out the Jebusites,
16:10 however, **d** out the Canaanites who lived in Gezer:
17:13 but did not utterly **d** them out.
17:18 for you shall **d** out the Canaanites,
23: 5 and **d** them out of your sight;
23:13 not continue to **d** out these nations before you;
Jdg 1:19 but could not **d** out the inhabitants of the plain,
1:21 not **d** out the Jebusites who lived in Jerusalem;
1:27 not **d** out the inhabitants of Beth-shean
1:28 but did not in fact **d** them out.
1:29 not **d** out the Canaanites who lived in Gezer;
1:30 Zebulun did not **d** out the inhabitants of Kitron,
1:31 Asher did not **d** out the inhabitants of Acco,
1:32 for they did not **d** them out.
1:33 not **d** out the inhabitants of Beth-shemesh,
2: 3 So now I say, I will not **d** them out before you;
2:21 I will no longer **d** out before them any of
2Ch 20: 7 **d** out the inhabitants of this land
20:11 by coming to **d** us out of your possession
Job 24: 3 They **d** away the donkey of the orphan;
Ps 36:11 or the hand of the wicked **d** me away.
68: 2 As smoke is driven away, so **d** them away;
Pr 22:10 **D** out a scoffer, and strife goes out;
Jer 24: 9 and a curse in all the places where I shall **d** them.
27:10 I will **d** you out, and you will perish.
27:15 the result that I will **d** you out and you will perish,
Eze 4:13 among the nations to which I will **d** them."
8: 6 to **d** me far from my sanctuary?
39: 2 I will turn you around and **d** you forward,
Hos 9:15 of the wickedness of their deeds I will **d** them out
Joel 2:20 and **d** it into a parched and desolate land,
Mic 2: 9 of my people you **d** out from their pleasant houses;
Mk 11:15 and began to **d** out those who were selling
Lk 19:45 to **d** out those who were selling things there;
Jn 6:37 and anyone who comes to me I will never **d** away;
1Co 5:13 "**D** out the wicked person from among you."
Gal 4:30 "**D** out the slave and her child;
Jas 3: 4 so large that it takes strong winds to **d** them,
Jdt 11:19 You will **d** them like sheep that have no shepherd,
Wis 17: 8 For those who promised to **d** off the fears
Sir 8:19 or you may **d** away your happiness.
38:20 **d** it away, and remember your own end.
2Mc 9: 4 so he ordered his charioteer to **d** without stopping
9: 7 and giving orders to **d** even faster.
3Mc 5: 2 and plenty of unmixed wine, and to **d** them in,
2Es 1:33 I will **d** you out as the wind drives straw;
16: 5 and who is there to **d** them away?
16: 6 Can one **d** off a hungry lion in the forest,
16: 8 and who will **d** them away?
16:72 and **d** them out of house and home.

DRIVEN (66) [DRIVE]

Ge 4:14 Today you have **d** me away from the soil,
Ex 10:11 And they were **d** out from Pharaoh's presence.
12:39 they were **d** out of Egypt and could not wait,
Lev 26:36 the sound of a **d** leaf shall put them to flight,
Nu 32:21 until he has **d** out his enemies from before him
Dt 28:34 and **d** mad by the sight that your eyes shall see.
30: 1 the nations where the LORD your God has **d** you,

Jos 13:12 these Moses had defeated and **d** out.
23: 9 For the LORD has **d** out before you great
1Sa 26:19 before the LORD, for they have **d** me out today
30:20 which were **d** ahead of the other cattle;
2Ch 13: 9 Have you not **d** out the priests of the LORD,
Job 6:13 and any resource is **d** from me.
18:18 and **d** out of the world.
30: 5 They are **d** out from society;
Ps 31:22 "I am **d** far from your sight."
68: 2 As smoke is **d** away, so drive them away;
109:10 may they be **d** out of the ruins they inhabit.
Pr 27:22 but the folly will not be **d** out.
Isa 19: 7 all that is sown by the Nile will dry up, be **d** away,
27:13 in the land of Assyria and those who were **d** out to
41: 2 like **d** stubble with his bow.
Jer 8: 3 in all the places where I have **d** them,
13:24 I will scatter you like chaff **d** by the wind from
16:15 and out of all the lands where he had **d** them."
23: 2 and have **d** them away, and you have not attended
23: 3 of all the lands where I have **d** them,
23: 8 and out of all the lands where he had **d** them."
23:12 into which they shall be **d** and fall;
29:14 the nations and all the places where I have **d** you,
29:18 among all the nations where I have **d** them,
43: 5 from all the nations to which they had been **d**—
50:17 Israel is a hunted sheep **d** away by lions.
La 3: 2 he has **d** and brought me into darkness
5: 5 With a yoke on our necks we are hard **d**;
Da 4:25 You shall be **d** away from human society,
4:32 You shall be **d** away from human society,
4:33 He was **d** away from human society,
5:21 He was **d** from human society,
9: 7 in all the lands to which you have **d** them,
Ob 1: 7 they have **d** you to the border;
Jnh 2: 4 Then I said, 'I am **d** away from your sight;
Mic 4: 6 the lame and gather those who have been **d** away,
Zep 2: 2 before you are **d** away like the drifting chaff,
2: 4 Ashdod's people shall be **d** out at noon,
Lk 8:29 the bonds and be **d** by the demon into the wilds.)
Jn 9:35 Jesus heard that they had **d** him out,
12:31 now the ruler of this world will be **d** out.
Ac 27:15 we gave way to it and were **d**.
27:17 they lowered the sea anchor and so were **d**.
28: 3 **d** out by the heat, fastened itself on his hand.
2Co 4: 8 perplexed, but not **d** to despair;
Jas 1: 6 **d** and tossed by the wind;
2Pe 2:17 These are waterless springs and mists **d** by
Wis 5:14 and like a light frost **d** away by a storm;
17:15 and now were **d** by monstrous specters,
Sir 27: 2 a stake is **d** firmly into a fissure between stones,
28:15 Slander has **d** virtuous women from their homes,
29:18 it has **d** the influential into exile,
1Mc 7: 6 and have **d** us out of our land.
2Mc 4:26 was **d** as a fugitive into the land of Ammon.
5: 9 There he who had **d** many from their own country
3Mc 4: 5 by the violence with which they were **d** in such
4: 9 **d** under the constraint of iron bonds;
6:25 Who has **d** from their homes those who faithfully
2Es 15:39 the east wind shall be **d** violently toward the south

DRIVER (4) [DRIVE]

1Ki 22:34 so he said to the **d** of his chariot, "Turn around,
2Ch 18:33 so he said to the **d** of his chariot, "Turn around,
Job 39: 7 it does not hear the shouts of the **d**.
1Mc 6:37 from there, and also its Indian **d**.

DRIVERS (7) [DRIVE]

Ex 14: 9 his chariot **d** and his army;
14:17 his chariots, and his chariot **d**.
14:18 his chariots, and his chariot **d**."
14:23 all of Pharaoh's horses, chariots, and chariot **d**.
14:26 upon their chariots and chariot **d**."
14:28 the chariots and the chariot **d**, the entire army
15:19 of Pharaoh with his chariots and his chariot **d** went

DRIVES‡ (11) [DRIVE]

2Ki 9:20 for he **d** like a maniac."
Ps 1: 4 but are like chaff that the wind **d** away.
Pr 20:26 and **d** the wheel over them.
22:15 but the rod of discipline **d** it far away.
Isa 28:28 one **d** the cart wheel and horses over it,
59:19 a pent-up stream that the wind of the LORD **d** on.
Sir 31: 1 and anxiety about it **d** away sleep.
38:25 who **d** oxen and is occupied with their work,
39:23 But his wrath **d** out the nations,
2Es 1:33 I will drive you out as the wind **d** straw;
4Mc 3:17 For the temperate mind can conquer the **d** of

DRIVING (13) [DRIVE]

Lev 20:23 the practices of the nation that I am **d** out
Dt 4:38 **d** out before you nations greater
18:12 the LORD your God is **d** them out before you.
33:17 **d** them to the ends of the earth;
Jdg 2:23 not **d** them out at once,
2Sa 6: 3 the sons of Abinadab, were **d** the new cart
7:23 by **d** out before his people nations and their gods?
2Ki 9:20 It looks like the **d** of Jehu son of Nimshi;
1Ch 13: 7 and Uzzah and Ahio were **d** the cart.
17:21 for great and terrible things, in **d** out nations
Ps 35: 5 with the angel of the LORD **d** them on.
Ac 26:24 Too much learning is **d** you insane!"
Sir 43:13 By his command he sends the **d** snow and speeds

DROMEDARIES (1)

Isa 66:20 and on **d**, to my holy mountain Jerusalem,

DROMEDARIES, DROMEDARY (KJV)

See CAMEL, CAMELS, HORSE, STEED

DROOPING (2) [DROOPS]

Heb 12:12 lift your **d** hands and strengthen your weak knees,
Sir 25:23 **D** hands and weak knees come from the wife who

DROOPS (1) [DROOPING]

Joel 1:12 The vine withers, the fig tree **d**.

DROP (18) [DROPPED, DROPPINGS, DROPS]

Nu 5:21 when the LORD makes your uterus **d**,
5:22 and make your womb discharge, your uterus **d**!"
5:27 and her womb shall discharge, her uterus **d**,
Dt 28:40 for your olives shall **d** off.
32: 2 May my teaching **d** like the rain,
33:28 where the heavens **d** down dew.
Jdg 2:19 not **d** any of their practices or their stubborn ways.
Ne 6: 9 thinking, "Their hands will **d** from the work,
Job 29:17 and made them **d** their prey from their teeth.
36:28 down and **d** upon mortals abundantly.
Pr 3:20 and the clouds **d** down the dew.
Isa 40:15 Even the nations are like a **d** from a bucket,
Eze 39: 3 will make your arrows **d** out of your right hand.
Ac 28: 6 They were expecting him to swell up or **d** dead,
Wis 11:22 like a **d** of morning dew that falls on the ground.
Sir 18:10 Like a **d** of water from the sea and a grain of sand,
2Es 6:56 and you have compared their abundance to a **d**
9:16 as a wave is greater than a **d** of water."

DROPPED (4) [DROP]

2Ch 24:10 the people rejoiced and brought their tax and **d** it
Job 29:22 and my word **d** upon them like dew.
Lk 16:17 than for one stroke of a letter in the law to be **d**.
Rev 16:21 about a hundred pounds, **d** from heaven on people,

DROPPINGS (1) [DROP]

Tob 2:10 their fresh **d** fell into my eyes

DROPS (11) [DROP]

Nu 35:23 unintentionally **d** it on another and death ensues,
Job 36:27 For he draws up the **d** of water;
38:28 or who has begotten the **d** of dew?
SS 5: 2 my locks with the **d** of the night."
Lk 22:44 ⟦like great **d** of blood falling down on the ground.⟧
Rev 6:13 as the fig tree **d** its winter fruit when shaken by
Sir 1: 2 The sand of the sea, the **d** of rain,
2Es 4:49 **d** still remained in the cloud.
4:50 for just as the rain is more than the **d**,
4:50 but **d** and smoke remained."
4Mc 10: 8 around and **d** of blood flowing from his entrails.

DROPSY (1)

Lk 14: 2 in front of him, there was a man who had **d**.

DROSS‡ (7)

Ps 119:119 All the wicked of the earth you count as **d**;
Pr 25: 4 Take away the **d** from the silver,
Isa 1:22 Your silver has become **d**,
1:25 I will smelt away your **d** as with lye
Eze 22:18 the house of Israel has become **d** to me;
22:18 In the smelter they have become **d**.
22:19 Because you have all become **d**,

DROUGHT‡ (11)

Dt 28:22 with fiery heat and **d**, and with blight and mildew;
1Ki 18: 1 in the third year of the **d**, saying, "Go,
Job 24:19 **D** and heat snatch away the snow waters;
Jer 2: 6 in a land of **d** and deep darkness,
14: 1 that came to Jeremiah concerning the **d**:
17: 8 in the year of **d** it is not anxious,
50:38 A **d** against her waters, that they may be dried up!
51:43 a land of **d** and a desert,
Hos 13: 5 in the wilderness, in the land of **d**.
Hag 1:11 And I have called for a **d** on the land and the hills,
Sir 35:26 in time of distress as clouds of rain in time of **d**.

DROVE (55) [DRIVE, DROVES]

Ge 3:24 He **d** out the man;
15:11 down on the carcasses, Abram **d** them away.
31:18 and he **d** away all his livestock,
32:16 every **d** by itself, and said to his servants,
32:16 and put a space between **d** and **d**."
Ex 2:17 But some shepherds came and **d** them away.
10:19 the locusts and **d** them into the Red Sea;
14:21 The LORD **d** the sea back by
Dt 33:27 he **d** out the enemy before you, and said,
Jos 15:14 Caleb **d** out from there the three sons of Anak:
24:12 which **d** out before you the two kings of
24:18 and the LORD **d** out before us all the peoples,
Jdg 1:20 and he **d** out from it the three sons of Anak.
4:21 went softly to him and **d** the peg into his temple,
6: 9 and **d** them out before you,
9:41 and Zebul **d** out Gaal and his kinsfolk,
11: 2 his wife's sons grew up, they **d** Jephthah away,
11: 7 not the very ones who rejected me and **d** me out
2Sa 11:23 but we **d** them back to the entrance of the gate.
1Ki 14:24 that the LORD **d** out before the people of Israel.
21:26 whom the LORD **d** out before the Israelites.)
2Ki 16: 3 of the nations whom the LORD **d** out before
16: 6 and **d** the Judeans from Elath;
17: 8 the customs of the nations whom the LORD **d** out
17:21 Jeroboam **d** Israel from following the LORD
21: 2 that the LORD **d** out before the people of Israel.
2Ch 28: 3 of the nations whom the LORD **d** out before
33: 2 of the nations whom the LORD **d** out before
Ps 34: T *so that he d him out, and he went away.*
44: 2 you with your own hand **d** out the nations,
78:55 He **d** out nations before them;
80: 8 you **d** out the nations and planted it.
Jer 32:37 to gather them from all the lands to which I **d** them
Eze 28:16 of God, and the guardian cherub **d** you out from
Hab 3: 8 when you **d** your horses, your chariots to victory?
Mt 21:12 and **d** out all who were selling and buying in
Mk 1:12 Spirit immediately **d** him out into the wilderness.
Lk 4:29 They got up, **d** him out of the town,
Jn 2:15 he **d** all of them out of the temple,
9:34 And they **d** him out.
Ac 7:45 when they dispossessed the nations that God **d** out
13:50 and **d** them out of their region.
1Th 2:15 both the Lord Jesus and the prophets, and **d** us out;
Jdt 5: 8 their ancestors **d** them out from the presence
5:12 So the Egyptians **d** them out of their sight.
5:14 They **d** out all the people of the desert,
5:16 They **d** out before them the Canaanites,
Sir 47:23 Rehoboam, whose policy **d** the people to revolt.
Aza 1:26 and **d** the fiery flame out of the furnace,
1Mc 1:53 they **d** Israel into hiding in every place
7:46 and they outflanked the enemy and **d** them back
13:11 he **d** out its occupants and remained there.
2Mc 1:12 he **d** out those who fought against the holy city.
2Es 1:21 I **d** out the Canaanites, the Perizzites,

DROVES (2) [DROVE]

Ge 30:40 and he put his own **d** apart,
32:19 and the third and all who followed the **d**,

DROWN (1) [DROWNED, DROWNING]

SS 8: 7 waters cannot quench love, neither can floods **d** it.

DROWNED (6) [DROWN]

Mt 18: 6 around your neck and you were **d** in the depth of
Mk 5:13 the steep bank into the sea, and were **d** in the sea.
Lk 8:33 down the steep bank into the lake and was **d**.
Heb 11:29 the Egyptians attempted to do so they were **d**.
Wis 10:19 but she **d** their enemies, and cast them up from
2Mc 12: 4 people of Joppa took them out to sea and **d** them,

DROWNING (1) [DROWN]

3Mc 6: 4 with his arrogant army by **d** them in the sea,

DROWSINESS (1) [DROWSY]

Pr 23:21 and **d** will clothe them with rags.

DROWSY (2) [DROWSINESS]

Mt 25: 5 all of them became **d** and slept.
Sir 22:10 Whoever tells a story to a fool tells it to a **d** man;

DRUG (1) [DRUGGED]

3Mc 5: 2 and ordered him on the following day to **d** all

DRUGGED (1) [DRUG]

3Mc 5:10 when he had **d** the pitiless elephants

DRUM (4) [DRUMS]

Da 3: 5 lyre, trigon, harp, **d**, and entire musical ensemble,
3: 7 lyre, trigon, harp, **d**, and entire musical ensemble,
3:10 lyre, trigon, harp, **d**, and entire musical ensemble,
3:15 lyre, trigon, harp, **d**, and entire musical ensemble

DRUMS (1) [DRUM]

1Es 5: 2 with the music of **d** and flutes;

DRUNK (54) [DRINK]

Ge 9:21 He drank some of the wine and became **d**,
Lev 11:34 be **d** shall be unclean if it was in any such vessel.
Nu 23:24 down until it has eaten the prey and **d** the blood of
Dt 29: 6 and you have not **d** wine or strong drink—
32:42 I will make my arrows **d** with blood,
Ru 3: 7 When Boaz had eaten and **d**,
1Sa 1: 9 After they had eaten and **d** at Shiloh,
1:13 therefore Eli thought she was **d**.
1:15 I have **d** neither wine nor strong drink,
25:36 within him, for he was very **d**;
30:12 or **d** water for three days and three nights.
2Sa 11:13 to eat and drink in his presence and made him **d**;
1Ki 13:22 and **d** water in the place of which he said to you,
13:23 After the man of God had eaten food and had **d**,
16: 9 drinking himself **d** in the house of Arza,
20:16 Ben-hadad was drinking himself **d** in the booths,
SS 5: 1 Eat, friends, drink, and be **d** with love.
Isa 16: 8 whose clusters once made **d** the lords of
29: 9 Be **d**, but not from wine; stagger, but not from
34: 5 When my sword has **d** its fill in the heavens, lo,
49:26 they shall be **d** with their own blood as with wine.
51:17 you who have **d** at the hand of the LORD the cup
51:17 who have **d** to the dregs the bowl of staggering.
51:21 hear this, you who are wounded, who are **d**,

Jer 25:27 Drink, get **d** and vomit, fall and rise no more,
48:26 Make him **d**, because he magnified himself
51:39 I will set out their drink and make them **d**,
51:57 I will make her officials and her sages **d**,
La 4:21 you shall become **d** and strip yourself bare.
Eze 39:19 and drink blood until you are **d**,
Joel 3:3 and sold girls for wine, and **d** it down.
Ob 1:16 For as you have **d** on my holy mountain,
Na 1:10 like drunkards they are **d**;
Hab 2:15 pouring out your wrath until they are **d**,
Lk 12:45 men and women, and to eat and drink and get **d**,
Jn 2:10 the inferior wine after the guests have become **d**.
Ac 2:15 Indeed, these are not **d**, as you suppose,
1Co 11:21 and one goes hungry and another becomes **d**.
Eph 5:18 Do not get **d** with wine, for that is debauchery;
1Th 5:7 and those who are **d** get **d** at night.
Rev 17:2 the inhabitants of the earth have become **d**."
17:6 And I saw that the woman was **d** with the blood of
18:3 For all the nations have **d** of the wine of the wrath
Jdt 6:4 their mountains will be **d** with their blood,
12:20 much more than he had ever **d** in any one day
13:2 on his bed, for he was dead **d**.
AdE 14:17 and I have not honored the king's feast or **d**
Sir 31:28 Wine **d** at the proper time and
31:29 Wine **d** to excess leads to bitterness of spirit,
1Mc 16:16 When Simon and his sons were **d**,
2Mc 7:36 a brief suffering have **d** of ever-flowing life,
2Es 14:40 I took it and drank; and when I had **d** it,
15:53 and talking about their death when you were **d**?

DRUNKARD‡ (13) [DRINK]

Dt 21:20 He is a glutton and a **d**."
Job 12:25 he makes them stagger like a **d**.
Pr 23:21 for the **d** and the glutton will come to poverty,
26:9 the hand of a **d** is a proverb in the mouth of a fool.
26:10 one who hires a passing fool or **d**.
Isa 19:14 in all its doings as a **d** staggers around in vomit.
24:20 The earth staggers like a **d**, it sways like a hut;
Jer 23:9 have become like a **d**, like one overcome by wine,
Mt 11:19 and they say, 'Look, a glutton and a **d**,
Lk 7:34 and you say, 'Look, a glutton and a **d**,
1Co 5:11 or is an idolater, reviler, **d**, or robber.
1Ti 3:3 a **d**, not violent but gentle, not quarrelsome,
4Mc 2:7 a glutton, or even a **d** can learn a better way,

DRUNKARDS (8) [DRINK]

Ps 69:12 and the **d** make songs about me.
107:27 they reeled and staggered like **d**,
Isa 28:1 Ah, the proud garland of the **d** of Ephraim,
28:3 under foot will be the proud garland of the **d**
Joel 1:5 Wake up, you **d**, and weep;
Na 1:10 they are entangled, like **d** they are drunk;
Mt 24:49 and eats and drinks with **d**,
1Co 6:10 the greedy, **d**, revilers, robbers—

DRUNKEN (6) [DRINK]

1Sa 1:14 long will you make a **d** spectacle of yourself?
Jer 51:7 in the LORD's hand, making all the earth **d**;
Eze 23:42 of the rabble brought in **d** from the wilderness;
Na 3:11 You also will be **d**, you will go into hiding;
Jdt 13:15 the canopy beneath which he lay in his **d** stupor.
Sir 26:8 A **d** wife arouses great anger;

DRUNKENNESS (9) [DRINK]

Ecc 10:17 at the proper time—for strength, and not for **d**!
Jer 13:13 and all the inhabitants of Jerusalem—with **d**.
Eze 23:33 You shall be filled with **d** and sorrow.
Lk 21:34 with dissipation and **d** and the worries of this life,
Ro 13:13 the day, not in reveling and **d**, not in debauchery
Gal 5:21 **d**, carousing, and things like these.
1Pe 4:3 living in licentiousness, passions, **d**, revels,
Tob 4:15 Do not drink wine to excess or let **d** go with you
Sir 31:30 **D** increases the anger of a fool to his own hurt,

DRUSILLA (1)

Ac 24:24 Some days later when Felix came with his wife **D**,

DRY‡ (81) [DRIED, DRIES, DRYING]

Ge 1:9 and let the **d** land appear."
1:10 God called the **d** land Earth,
7:22 everything on **d** land in whose nostrils was
8:14 of the month, the earth was **d**.
Ex 4:9 from the Nile and pour it on the **d** ground;
4:9 from the Nile will become blood on the **d** ground."
14:16 that the Israelites may go into the sea on **d** ground.
14:21 and turned the sea into **d** land;
14:22 The Israelites went into the sea on **d** ground,
14:29 the Israelites walked on **d** ground through the sea,
15:19 the Israelites walked through the sea on **d** ground.
Lev 7:10 every other grain offering, mixed with oil or **d**,
Dt 29:19 (thus bringing disaster on moist and **d** alike)—
Jos 3:17 While all Israel were crossing over on **d** ground,
3:17 of the LORD stood on **d** ground in the middle of
4:18 and the soles of the priests' feet touched **d** ground,
4:22 'Israel crossed over the Jordan here on **d** ground.'
9:5 and all their provisions were **d** and moldy.
9:12 but now, see, it is **d** and moldy;
Jdg 6:37 and it is **d** on all the ground,
6:39 let it be **d** only on the fleece,
6:40 It was **d** on the fleece only,
2Ki 2:8 until the two of them crossed on **d** ground.
Ne 9:11 so that they passed through the sea on **d** land,
Job 12:15 If he withholds the waters, they **d** up;
13:25 a windblown leaf and pursue **d** chaff?
15:30 the flame will **d** up their shoots,
18:16 Their roots **d** up beneath,
30:3 Through want and hard hunger they gnaw the **d**
Ps 63:1 as in a **d** and weary land where there is no water.
66:6 He turned the sea into **d** land;
95:5 The sea is his, for he made it, and the **d** land,
106:9 He rebuked the Red Sea, and it became **d**;
Pr 17:1 a **d** morsel with quiet than a house full of feasting
Isa 5:24 and as **d** grass sinks down in the flame,
19:5 and the river will be parched and **d**;
19:6 branches of Egypt's Nile will diminish and **d** up,
19:7 and all that is sown by the Nile will **d** up,
25:5 in a **d** place, you subdued the heat with the shade
27:11 When its boughs are **d**, they are broken;
32:2 like streams of water in a **d** place,
35:1 The wilderness and the **d** land shall be glad,
41:18 and the **d** land springs of water.
42:15 and **d** up all their herbage;
42:15 I will turn the rivers into islands, and **d** up
44:3 and streams on the **d** ground;
44:27 who says to the deep, "Be **d**—
44:27 I will **d** up your rivers";
50:2 By my rebuke I **d** up the sea,
53:2 and like a root out of **d** ground;
56:3 and do not let the eunuch say, "I am just a **d** tree."
Jer 18:14 Do the mountain waters run **d**,
50:12 a wilderness, **d** land, and a desert.
51:36 I will **d** up her sea and make her fountain dry;
51:36 I will dry up her sea and make her fountain **d**;
La 4:8 it has become as **d** as wood.
Eze 17:24 I **d** up the green tree and make the dry tree flourish.
17:24 up the green tree and make the **d** tree flourish.
19:13 into a **d** and thirsty land.
20:47 in you and every **d** tree;
30:12 I will **d** up the channels, and will sell the land into
37:2 in the valley, and they were very **d**.
37:4 O **d** bones, hear the word of the LORD.
Hos 9:14 Give them a miscarrying womb and **d** breasts.
13:15 his fountain shall **d** up, his spring shall be parched.
Jnh 1:9 who made the sea and the **d** land."
2:10 and it spewed Jonah out upon the **d** land.
Na 1:4 He rebukes the sea and makes it **d**,
1:10 they are consumed like **d** straw.
Zep 2:13 and he will make Nineveh a desolation, a **d** waste
Hag 2:6 and the earth and the sea and the **d** land;
Lk 7:38 to bathe his feet with her tears and to **d** them
23:31 what will happen when it is **d**?"
Heb 11:29 through the Red Sea as if it were **d** land,
Jdt 7:21 their cisterns were going **d**,
Wis 4:19 they will be left utterly **d** and barren,
19:7 **d** land emerging where water had stood before,
Sir 39:22 "His blessing covers the **d** land like a river,
40:13 The wealth of the unjust will **d** up like a river,
2Mc 1:19 and secretly hid it in the hollow of a **d** cistern,
4Mc 18:17 'Shall these **d** bones live?'

DRYING (1) [DRY]

Ge 8:13 and saw that the face of the ground was **d**.

DRYSHOD (KJV) See ON FOOT

DUE (64)

Ge 18:10 one said, "I will surely return to you in **d** season,
18:14 At the set time I will return to you, in **d** season,
Ex 22:15 if it was hired, only the hiring fee is **d**.
23:6 You shall not pervert the justice **d** to your poor
Lev 6:18 as their perpetual **d** throughout your generations,
6:22 a perpetual **d**—to be turned entirely into smoke.
7:34 as a perpetual **d** from the people of Israel.
7:36 as a perpetual **d** from the people of Israel
10:13 because it is your **d** and your sons' due,
10:13 because it is your due and your sons' **d**,
10:15 to be your **d** and that of your children forever,
24:9 the offerings by fire to the LORD, a perpetual **d**.
Nu 18:8 to you and your sons as a priestly portion **d** you
18:11 a perpetual **d**, whatever is set aside from the gifts
18:19 with your sons and daughters, as a perpetual **d**;
18:29 you shall set apart every offering **d** to the LORD;
Dt 12:26 But the sacred donations that are **d** from you,
18:3 This shall be the priests' **d** from the people,
1Sa 1:20 In **d** time Hannah conceived and bore a son.
1Ki 10:1 (fame **d** to the name of the LORD),
2Ki 4:16 He said, "At this season, in **d** time,
4:17 in **d** time, as Elisha had declared to her.
1Ch 6:32 and they performed their service in **d** order.
16:29 Ascribe to the LORD the glory **d** his name;
2Ch 31:4 to give the portion **d** to the priests and the Levites,
Ps 7:17 to the LORD the thanks **d** to his righteousness,
28:4 render them their **d** reward.
65:1 Praise is **d** to you, O God, in Zion;
90:11 Your wrath is as great as the fear that is **d** you.
96:8 Ascribe to the LORD the glory **d** his name;
104:27 to you to give them their food in **d** season;
145:15 and you give them their food in **d** season.
Pr 3:27 Do not withhold good from those to whom it is **d**,
11:24 others withhold what is **d**, and only suffer want.
Jer 10:7 of the nations? For that is your **d**;
51:6 he is repaying her what is **d**.
Mal 1:6 If then I am a father, where is the honor **d** me?
1:6 And if I am a master, where is the respect **d** me?
Ro 1:27 in their own persons the **d** penalty for their error.
4:4 not reckoned as a gift but as something **d**.
13:7 Pay to all what is **d** them—taxes to whom taxes
are **d**, revenue to whom revenue is **d**, respect to
whom respect is **d**, honor to whom honor is **d**.
Tit 1:3 in **d** time he revealed his word through
Jas 1:17 with whom there is no variation or shadow **d**
1Pe 5:6 so that he may exalt you in **d** time.
Tob 12:11 but to reveal with **d** honor the works of God.'
Wis 14:22 but though living in great strife **d** to ignorance,
Sir 22:16 the mind firmly resolved after **d** reflection will not
29:2 repay your neighbor when a loan falls **d**.
38:16 Lay out the body with **d** ceremony,
1Mc 10:36 be given them that is **d** to all the forces of the king.
11:35 other payments henceforth **d** to us of the tithes,
and the taxes **d** to us, and the salt pits and the
crown taxes **d** to us—
2Mc 8:10 up for the king the tribute **d** to the Romans,
10:13 Unable to command the respect **d** his office,
2Es 8:41 all that have been sown will come up in **d** season,
8:43 because it has not received your rain in **d** season,
10:16 you will receive your son back in **d** time,
11:20 and in **d** time the wings that followed also rose up
14:32 in **d** time he took from you what he had given.

DUG‡ (33) [DIG]

Ge 21:30 be a witness for me that I **d** this well."
26:15 the wells that his father's servants had **d** in
26:18 Isaac **d** again the wells of water that had been **d** in
26:19 But when Isaac's servants **d** in the valley
26:21 Then they **d** another well,
26:22 He moved from there and **d** another well,
26:25 And there Isaac's servants **d** a well.
26:32 and told him about the well that they had **d**,
Nu 21:18 that the nobles of the people **d**, with the scepter,
2Ki 19:24 I **d** wells and drank foreign waters,
Ps 35:7 without cause they **d** a pit for my life.
57:6 They **d** a pit in my path,
94:13 until a pit is **d** for the wicked.
119:85 The arrogant have **d** pitfalls for me;
Isa 5:2 He **d** it and cleared it of stones,
37:25 I **d** wells and drank waters,
51:1 and to the quarry from which you were **d**.
Jer 2:13 and **d** out cisterns for themselves,
13:7 Then I went to the Euphrates, and **d**,
18:20 Yet they have **d** a pit for my life.
18:22 For they have **d** a pit to catch me,
Eze 8:8 when I **d** through the wall, there was an entrance.
12:7 and in the evening I **d** through the wall
Hos 5:2 and a pit **d** deep in Shittim;
Mt 21:33 **d** a wine press in it, and built a watchtower.
25:18 the one talent went off and **d** a hole in the ground
Mk 2:4 and after having **d** through it,
12:1 **d** a pit for the wine press, and built a watchtower;
Lk 6:48 who **d** deeply and laid the foundation on rock;
Tob 2:7 sun had set, I went and **d** a grave and buried him.
8:9 and they went and **d** a grave,
Sir 50:3 In his days a water cistern was **d**,

DUKE[S] (KJV) See CLANS

DULCIMER (KJV) See DRUM

DULL (6) [DULLARD, DULLEST]

Lev 13:39 the spots on the skin of the body are of a **d** white,
Isa 6:10 Make the mind of this people **d**,
59:1 nor his ear too **d** to hear.
Mt 13:15 For this people's heart has grown **d**,
Ac 28:27 For this people's heart has grown **d**,
Heb 5:11 since you have become **d** in understanding.

DULLARD (1) [DULL]

Ps 92:6 **d** cannot know, the stupid cannot understand this:

DULLEST (1) [DULL]

Ps 94:8 Understand, O **d** of the people;

DULY (1)

2Mc 14:22 so they **d** held the consultation.

DUMAH (4)

Ge 25:14 Mishma, **D**, Massa,
Jos 15:52 Arab, **D**, Eshan,
1Ch 1:30 Mishma, **D**, Massa, Hadad, Tema,
Isa 21:11 The oracle concerning **D**. One is calling to me

DUMB (1)

2Es 6:48 The **d** and lifeless water produced living creatures,

DUMB (KJV) See also KEEPS ... FROM SPEAKING, MUTE, SILENT, SPEECHLESS, UNABLE TO SPEAK

DUMBFOUNDED (1)

Ps 31:17 let them go **d** to Sheol.

DUMPED (1)

Lev 14:41 and the plaster that is scraped off shall be **d** in

DUNG (29) [DUNG-PIT, DUNGHILL, DUNGHILLS]

Ex 29:14 But the flesh of the bull, and its skin, and its **d**,
Lev 4:11 as well as its head, its legs, its entrails, and its **d**—
8:17 But the bull itself, its skin and flesh and its **d**,
16:27 and their flesh and their **d** shall be consumed

Nu 19: 5 its skin, its flesh, and its blood, with its **d**,
1Ki 14:10 just as one burns up **d** until it is all gone.
2Ki 6:25 of a kab of dove's **d** for five shekels of silver.
9:37 the corpse of Jezebel shall be like **d** on the field in
18:27 who are doomed with you to eat their own **d** and
Ne 2:13 past the Dragon's Spring and to the **D** Gate,
3:13 a thousand cubits of the wall, as far as the **D** Gate.
3:14 of Beth-haccherem, repaired the **D** Gate;
12:31 One went to the right on the wall to the **D** Gate;
Job 20: 7 they will perish forever like their own **d**;
Ps 83:10 who became **d** for the ground.
Isa 36:12 to eat their own **d** and drink their own urine?"
Jer 8: 2 they shall be like **d** on the surface of the ground.
9:22 "Human corpses shall fall like **d** upon
16: 4 they shall become like **d** on the surface of
25:33 they shall become **d** on the surface of the ground.
Eze 4:12 baking it in their sight on human **d**.
4:15 I will let you have cow's **d** instead of human **d**,
Zep 1:17 be poured out like dust, and their flesh like **d**.
Mal 2: 3 and spread **d** on your faces, the **d** of your offerings,
AdE 14: 2 and **d**, and she utterly humbled her body;
1Mc 2:62 for their splendor will turn into **d** and worms.
2Es 16:23 And the dead shall be thrown out like **d**,

DUNG-PIT (1) [DUNG, PIT]

Isa 25:10 in their place as straw is trodden down in a **d**.

DUNGEON (5)

Ge 40:15 that they should have put me into the **d**."
41:14 and he was hurriedly brought out of the **d**.
Ex 12:29 to the firstborn of the prisoner who was in the **d**,
Isa 42: 7 to bring out the prisoners from the **d**,
Wis 10:13 She descended with him into the **d**,

DUNGHILL (1) [DUNG, HILL]

Ezr 6:11 The house shall be made a **d**.

DUNGHILL (KJV) See also ASH HEAP, DUNG-PIT, MANURE PILE, RUINS

DUNGHILLS (1) [DUNG, HILL]

Sir 22: 2 The idler is like the filth of **d**;

DURA (1)

Da 3: 1 up on the plain of **D** in the province of Babylon.

DURATION (1) [DURING]

3Mc 5:22 not so much employ the **d** of the night in sleep as

DURETH (KJV) See ENDURES

DURING‡ (86) [DURATION]

Ge 31:10 **D** the mating of the flock I once had a dream
41:34 of the land of Egypt **d** the seven plenteous years.
41:47 **D** the seven plenteous years
47: 9 of the life of my ancestors **d** their long sojourn."
Lev 15:20 upon which she lies **d** her impurity shall
15:26 Every bed on which she lies **d** all the days
23:28 and you shall do no work **d** that entire day;
23:29 For anyone who does not practice self-denial **d**
23:30 And anyone who does any work **d** that entire day,
25: 6 You may eat what the land yields **d** its sabbath—
Dt 16:14 Rejoice **d** your festival, you and your sons
31:10 in the scheduled year of remission, **d** the festival
Jos 5: 4 of Egypt, all the warriors, had died **d** the journey
Jdg 16:30 at his death were more than those he had killed **d**
1Ki 4:25 **D** Solomon's lifetime Judah and Israel lived
2Ki 23:22 or **d** all the days of the kings of Israel or of
2Ch 8: 1 **d** which Solomon had built the house of
29:19 the utensils that King Ahaz repudiated **d** his reign
Ne 2:12 I got up **d** the night, I and a few men with me;
5: 3 and our houses in order to get grain **d** the famine."
8:14 that the people of Israel should live in booths **d**
Ecc 2: 3 to do under heaven **d** the few days of their life.
Jer 26:18 who prophesied **d** the days of King Hezekiah
Eze 4: 9 **D** the number of days that you lie on your side,
18: 6 or approach a woman **d** her menstrual period,
36:38 the flock at Jerusalem **d** her appointed festivals,
45:23 And **d** the seven days of
Da 6:28 So this Daniel prospered **d** the reign of Darius and
Mt 26: 5 But they said, "Not **d** the festival,
Mk 14: 2 for they said, "Not **d** the festival, or there may be
15: 7 with the rebels who had committed murder **d**
Lk 3: 2 **d** the high priesthood of Annas and Caiaphas,
4: 2 He ate nothing at all **d** those days,
6:12 **d** those days he went out to the mountain to pray;
12:38 If he comes **d** the middle of the night,
16:25 that **d** your lifetime you received your good things,
Jn 2:23 When he was in Jerusalem **d** the Passover festival,
11: 9 Those who walk **d** the day do not stumble,
13: 2 to betray him. And **d** supper
19:31 the Jews did not want the bodies left on the cross **d**
Ac 1: 3 appearing to them **d** forty days and speaking about
1:21 So one of the men who have accompanied us **d** all
5:19 But **d** the night an angel of the Lord opened
6: 1 Now **d** those days, when the disciples were
7: 6 who would enslave them and mistreat them **d**
11:28 and this took place **d** the reign of Claudius.
12: 3 (This was **d** the festival of Unleavened Bread.)
13:17 and made the people great **d** their stay in the land
16: 9 **D** the night Paul had a vision:
23:31 and brought him **d** the night to Antipatris.
Ro 7: 1 on a person only **d** that person's lifetime?
2Co 8: 2 for **d** a severe ordeal of affliction,
1Th 3: 7 For this reason, brothers and sisters, **d**
2Th 1: 4 and faith **d** all your persecutions and the afflictions
Phm 1:10 whose father I have become **d** my imprisonment.
1:13 of service to me in your place **d** my imprisonment
Heb 9: 9 **d** which gifts and sacrifices are offered
1Pe 1:17 live in reverent fear **d** the time of your exile.
3:20 **d** the building of the ark, in which a few, that is,
Rev 11: 6 no rain may fall **d** the days of their prophesying,
Tob 2: 1 Then **d** the reign of Esar-haddon I returned home,
Jdt 2:27 Then he went down into the plain of Damascus **d**
8: 2 had died **d** the barley harvest.
14: 8 Now tell me what you have done **d** these days."
16:25 among the Israelites **d** the lifetime of Judith,
AdE 1: 4 and the splendor of his bountiful celebration **d**
2:12 **D** this time the days of beautification are
Sir Pr: 3 **D** that time I have applied my skill day and night
37: 6 Do not forget a friend **d** the battle,
Bel 1:15 **D** the night the priests came as usual,
2Mc 10: 6 **d** the festival of booths, they had been wandering
14: 4 **D** that day he kept quiet.
3Mc 4:10 they would undergo treatment befitting traitors **d**
7:19 as a joyous festival **d** the time of their stay.
2Es 3:29 and my soul has seen many sinners **d**
5: 4 to shine at night, and the moon **d** the day.
5:53 of youth are different from those born **d** the time
7:89 **D** the time that they lived in it,
7:101 so that **d** these seven days they may see the things
9:23 do not, however, fast **d** them,
9:44 and every day **d** those thirty years I prayed to
12:51 and my food was of plants **d** those days.
14:42 They sat forty days; they wrote **d** the daytime,
14:44 **d** the forty days, ninety-four books were written.
4Mc 6:20 a little while and **d** that time be a laughingstock
13:20 of time and was shaped **d** the same period of time;

DURST (KJV) See AFRAID, DARE, DARED, PRESUMED

DUSK (2)

Job 24:14 The murderer rises at **d** to kill the poor and needy,
Hab 1: 8 more menacing than wolves at **d**;

DUST‡ (127) [DUST-CLOUD]

A. DUST OF THE EARTH (13)

Ge 2: 7 the **d** of the ground, and breathed into his nostrils
3:14 and **d** you shall eat all the days of your life.
3:19 you are **d**, and to dust you shall return."
3:19 you are dust, and to **d** you shall return."
13:16 I will make your offspring like the **d** of the earth; A
13:16 so that if one can count the **d** of the earth, A
18:27 I who am but **d** and ashes.
28:14 like the **d** of the earth, and you shall spread A
Ex 8:16 out your staff and strike the **d** of the earth, A
8:17 the **d** of the earth, and gnats came on humans A
8:17 all the **d** of the earth turned into gnats A
9: 9 It shall become fine **d** all over the land of Egypt,
Nu 5:17 and take some of the **d** that is on the floor of
23:10 Who can count the **d** of Jacob,
Dt 9:21 grinding it thoroughly, until it was reduced to **d**;
9:21 and I threw the **d** of it into the stream that runs
28:24 and only **d** shall come down upon you from
32:24 with venom of things crawling in the **d**.
Jos 7: 6 and they put **d** on their heads.
1Sa 2: 8 He raises up the poor from the **d**;
2Sa 16:13 throwing stones and flinging **d** at him.
22:43 I beat them fine like the **d** of the earth, A
1Ki 16: 2 the **d** and made you leader over my people Israel,
18:38 the wood, the stones, and the **d**,
20:10 the **d** of Samaria will provide a handful for each of
2Ki 13: 7 and made them like the **d** at threshing.
23: 6 beat it to **d** and threw the **d** of it upon the graves
23:15 He burned the high place, crushing it to **d**;
2Ch 1: 9 over a people as numerous as the **d** of the earth. A
34: 4 he made **d** of them and scattered it over the graves
Job 2:12 they tore their robes and threw **d** in the air
4:19 whose foundation is in the **d**,
10: 9 and will you turn me to **d** again?
16:15 and have laid my strength in the **d**.
17:16 Shall we descend together into the **d**?"
20:11 will lie down in the **d** with them.
21:26 They lie down alike in the **d**,
22:24 if you treat gold like **d**,
27:16 Though they heap up silver like **d**,
28: 6 the place of sapphires, and its **d** contains gold.
30:19 and I have become like **d** and ashes.
34:15 and all mortals return to **d**.
38:38 **d** runs into a mass and the clods cling together?
40:13 Hide them all in the **d** together;
42: 6 and repent in **d** and ashes."
Ps 7: 5 and lay my soul in the **d**.
18:42 I beat them fine, like **d** before the wind;
22:15 you lay me in the **d** of death.
22:29 before him shall bow all who go down to the **d**,
30: 9 Will the **d** praise you? Will it tell of your faithfulness?
44:25 For we sink down to the **d**;
72: 9 and his enemies lick the **d**.
78:27 upon them like **d**, winged birds like the sand of
83:13 O my God, make them like whirling **d**,
89:39 you have defiled his crown in the **d**.
90: 3 You turn us back to **d**, and say, "Turn back,
102:14 and have pity on its **d**.
103:14 he remembers that we are **d**.
Ps 104:29 they die and return to their **d**.
113: 7 He raises the poor from the **d**,
119:25 My soul clings to the **d**;
Ecc 3:20 all are from the **d**, and all turn to **d** again.
12: 7 and the **d** returns to the earth as it was,
Isa 2:10 and hide in the **d** from the terror of the LORD,
5:24 and their blossom go up like **d**;
17:13 on the mountains before the wind and whirling **d**
25:12 laid low, cast to the ground, even to the **d**.
26: 5 He lays it low to the ground, casts it to the **d**.
26:19 O dwellers in the **d**, awake and sing for joy!
29: 4 from low in the **d** your words shall come;
29: 4 and your speech shall whisper out of the **d**.
29: 5 the multitude of your foes shall be like small **d**,
40:12 enclosed the **d** of the earth in a measure, A
40:15 and are accounted as **d** on the scales;
40:15 see, he takes up the isles like fine **d**.
41: 2 he makes them like **d** with his sword,
47: 1 Come down and sit in the **d**,
49:23 and lick the **d** of your feet.
52: 2 Shake yourself from the **d**, rise up,
65:25 but the serpent—its food shall be **d**!
La 2:10 they have thrown **d** on their heads and put
3:29 to put one's mouth to the **d** (there may yet
Eze 26:10 be so many that their **d** shall cover you.
27:30 They throw **d** on their heads and wallow in ashes;
Da 12: 2 Many of those who sleep in the **d** of the earth A
Am 2: 7 the head of the poor into the **d** of the earth, A
Mic 1:10 in Beth-leaphrah roll yourselves in the **d**.
7:17 they shall lick **d** like a snake,
Na 1: 3 and the clouds are the **d** of his feet.
Zep 1:17 their blood shall be poured out like **d**,
Zec 9: 3 and heaped up silver like **d**,
Mt 10:14 the **d** from your feet as you leave that house
Mk 6:11 shake off the **d** that is on your feet as a testimony
Lk 9: 5 that town shake the **d** off your feet as a testimony
10:11 'Even the **d** of your town that clings to our feet,
Ac 13:51 So they shook the **d** off their feet in protest
18: 6 in protest he shook the **d** from his clothes and said
22:23 and tossing **d** into the air,
1Co 15:47 The first man was from the earth, a man of **d**;
15:48 was the man of **d**, so are those who are of the **d**;
15:49 Just as we have borne the image of the man of **d**,
Rev 18:19 And they threw **d** on their heads,
Tob 3: 6 from the face of the earth and become **d**.
Jdt 2:20 like the **d** of the earth— A
Sir 10: 9 How can **d** and ashes be proud?
17:32 but all human beings are **d** and ashes.
33:10 and humankind was created out of the **d**.
40: 3 on a splendid throne to the one who grovels in **d**
44:21 make him as numerous as the **d** of the earth, A
LtJ 6:13 their faces are wiped because of the **d** from
6:18 of the **d** raised by the feet of those who enter.
1Mc 2:63 because they will have returned to the **d**,
11:71 Jonathan tore his clothes, put **d** on his head,
2Mc 10:25 Maccabeus and his men sprinkled **d** on their heads
14:15 they sprinkled **d** on their heads and prayed
3Mc 1:18 sprinkled their hair with **d**,
5:48 the **d** raised by the elephants going out at the gate
2Es 3: 4 and that without help—and commanded the **d**
7:32 and the **d** those who rest there in silence;
7:62 of the **d** like the other created things?
7:63 For it would have been better if the **d** itself had
8: 2 but only a little **d** from which gold comes,
13:11 the innumerable multitude but only the **d** of ashes
15:44 then the **d** and smoke shall reach the sky,

DUST-CLOUD (1) [CLOUD, DUST]

Nu 23:10 or number the **d** of Israel?

DUTIES (23) [DUTY]

Nu 3: 7 They shall perform **d** for him and for
3: 8 to the **d** for the Israelites as they do service at
3:28 attending to the **d** of the sanctuary.
8:26 in the tent of meeting in carrying out their **d**,
8:26 with the Levites in assigning their **d**.
16: 9 to perform the **d** of the LORD's tabernacle,
18: 3 They shall perform **d** for you and for
18: 4 They are attached to you in order to perform the **d**
18: 5 the **d** of the sanctuary and the **d** of the altar,
18: 7 with you shall diligently perform your priestly **d**
1Sa 2:13 or for the **d** of the priests to the people.
10:25 the people the rights and **d** of the kingship;
1Ch 24: 3 according to the appointed **d** in their service.
25: 1 list of those who did the work and of their **d** was:
25: 8 And they cast lots for their **d**, small and great,
26:12 corresponding to their leaders, had **d**,
26:29 and his sons were appointed to outside **d** for Israel,
Ne 13:30 and I established the **d** of the priests and Levites,
1Ti 6: 2 Teach and urge these **d**.
Heb 9: 6 into the first tent to carry out their ritual **d**;
Sir 32: 2 when you have fulfilled all your **d**,
1Es 1:16 no one needed to interrupt his daily **d**,

DUTY (32) [DUTIES]

Ge 38: 8 "Go in to your brother's wife and perform the **d** of
Nu 1:53 the guard **d** of the tabernacle of the covenant.
8:24 and upward they shall begin to do **d** in the service
8:25 the age of fifty years they shall retire from the **d** of
Dt 24: 5 with the army or be charged with any related **d**.
25: 5 performing the **d** of a husband's brother to her,
25: 7 not perform the **d** of a husband's brother to me."
2Ki 11: 5 those who go off **d** on the sabbath and guard
11: 7 and your two divisions that come on **d** in force on
11: 9 each brought his men who were to go off **d** on

2Ki 11: 9 with those who were to come on **d** on the sabbath,
1Ch 9:27 for on them lay the **d** of watching,
9:33 for they were on **d** day and night.
23:28 "but their **d** shall be to assist the descendants
24:19 These had as their appointed **d** in their service
2Ch 5:13 It was the **d** of the trumpeters and singers
8:13 as the **d** of each day required, offering according
8:14 as the **d** of each day required, and the gatekeepers
23: 4 who come on **d** on the sabbath,
23: 8 who were to come on **d** on the sabbath,
23: 8 with those who were to go off **d** on the sabbath;
31:16 all who entered the house of the LORD as the **d**
Ezr 10: 4 Take action, for it is your **d**, and we are with you;
Ne 13:13 and their **d** was to distribute to their associates.
Ecc 12:13 for that is the whole **d** of everyone.
Lk 1: 8 as priest before God and his section was on **d**,
Col 3:20 for this is your acceptable **d** in the Lord.
1Ti 5: 4 they should first learn their religious **d**
Phm 1: 8 in Christ to command you to do your **d**,
AdE 6:10 who is on **d** in the courtyard.
Sus 1: 9 from looking to Heaven or remembering their **d**
2Mc 2:30 It is the **d** of the original historian to occupy

DWARF (1)

Lev 21:20 or a hunchback, or a **d**, or a man with a blemish

DWELL (35) [CAVE-DWELLING, DWELLERS, DWELLING, DWELLINGS, DWELLS, DWELT, TENT-DWELLING]

Ex 25: 8 so that I may **d** among them.
29:45 I will **d** among the Israelites,
29:46 of the land of Egypt that I might **d** among them;
Nu 5: 3 not defile their camp, where I **d** among them.
35:34 the land in which you live, in which I also **d**;
35:34 for I the LORD **d** among the Israelites.
1Ki 6:13 I will **d** among the children of Israel,
8:12 LORD has said that he would **d** in thick darkness.
8:13 a place for you to **d** in forever."
8:27 "But will God indeed **d** on the earth?
Ps 15: 1 Who may **d** on your holy hill?
23: 6 and I shall **d** in the house of
26: 8 O LORD, I love the house in which you **d**,
74: 2 Remember Mount Zion, where you came to **d**.
85: 9 that his glory may **d** in our land.
SS 8:13 O you who **d** in the gardens,
Isa 32:16 Then justice will **d** in the wilderness,
57:15 I **d** in the high and holy place,
Jer 7: 3 and let me **d** with you in this place.
7: 7 then I will **d** with you in this place,
7:12 where I made my name **d** at first,
Joel 3:17 the LORD your God, **d** in Zion,
Zec 2:10 For lo, I will come and **d** in your midst,
2:11 and I will **d** in your midst.
8: 3 and will **d** in the midst of Jerusalem;
Ac 7:48 Yet the Most High does not **d** in houses made
2Co 12: 9 so that the power of Christ may **d** in me.
Eph 3:17 and that Christ may **d** in your hearts through faith,
Col 1:19 in him all the fullness of God was pleased to **d**,
3:16 Let the word of Christ **d** in you richly;
Jas 4: 5 for the spirit that he has made to **d** in us"?
Rev 12:12 you heavens and those who **d** in them!
13: 6 that is, those who **d** in heaven.
21: 3 He will **d** with them as their God;
Wis 1: 4 or **d** in a body enslaved to sin.

DWELLERS (1) [DWELL]

Isa 26:19 O **d** in the dust, awake and sing for joy!

DWELLING‡ (67) [DWELL]

Lev 13:46 his **d** shall be outside the camp.
25:29 If anyone sells a **d** house in a walled city,
26:11 I will place my **d** in your midst,
Nu 24:21 "Enduring is your **d** place,
Dt 12:11 that the LORD your God will choose as a **d**
14:23 the place that he will choose as a **d** for his name,
16: 2 that the LORD will choose as a **d** for his name.
16: 6 that the LORD your God will choose as a **d**
16:11 that the LORD your God will choose as a **d**
26: 2 that the LORD your God will choose as a **d**
1Ki 8:30 O hear in heaven your **d** place; heed and forgive.
8:39 in heaven your **d** place, forgive, act, and render
8:43 then hear in heaven your **d** place,
8:49 in heaven your **d** place their prayer and their plea,
1Ch 6:54 These are their **d** places according
2Ch 6:21 may you hear from heaven your **d** place;
6:30 from heaven, your **d** place, forgive, and render
6:33 may you hear from heaven your **d** place,
6:39 then hear from heaven your **d** place their prayer
29: 6 and have turned away their faces from the **d** of
30:27 their prayer came to his holy **d** in heaven.
36:15 on his people and on his **d** place;
Ezr 7:15 to the God of Israel, whose **d** is in Jerusalem,
Job 5: 3 but suddenly I cursed their **d**.
23: 3 that I might come even to his **d**!
38:19 "Where is the way to the **d** of light,
39: 6 the salt land for its **d** place?
Ps 43: 3 let them bring me to your holy hill and to your **d**.
49:11 their **d** places to all generations,
68:10 your flock found a **d** in it;
74: 7 they desecrated the **d** place of your name,
76: 2 in Salem, his **d** place in Zion.
78:60 He abandoned his **d** at Shiloh,
84: 1 How lovely is your **d** place, O LORD of hosts!
90: 1 Lord, you have been our **d** place in all generations.
Ps 91: 9 the Most High your **d** place,
120: 6 Too long have I had my **d**
132: 5 a **d** place for the Mighty One of Jacob."
132: 7 "Let us go to his **d** place;
Isa 11:10 and his **d** shall be glorious.
18: 4 I will quietly look from my **d** like clear heat
38:12 My **d** is plucked up and removed from me like
Eze 37:27 My **d** place shall be with them;
Da 2:11 whose **d** is not with mortals."
4:25 and your **d** shall be with the wild animals.
4:32 and your **d** shall be with the animals of the field.
5:21 His **d** was with the wild asses,
Ob 1: 3 whose **d** is in the heights.
Zec 2:13 for he has roused himself from his holy **d**.
Jn 14: 2 In my Father's house there are many **d** places.
Ac 7:46 that he might find a **d** place for the house of Jacob.
15:16 and I will rebuild the **d** of David, which has fallen;
2Co 5: 2 longing to be clothed with our heavenly **d**—
Eph 2:22 also are built together spiritually into a **d** place
Col 2:18 of angels, **d** on visions, puffed up without cause by
Jude 1: 6 not keep their own position, but left their proper **d**,
Rev 13: 6 blaspheming his name and his **d**, that is,
18: 2 It has become a **d** place of demons,
Tob 1: 4 the temple, the **d** of God, had been consecrated
Sir 24: 8 He said, 'Make your **d** in Jacob,
36:18 Jerusalem, the place of your **d**.
Bar 2:16 O Lord, look down from your holy **d**,
1Mc 1:38 she became a **d** of strangers;
2Mc 3:39 For he who has his **d** in heaven watches over
1Es 1:50 he would have spared them and his **d** place.
3Mc 2:15 For your **d** is the heaven of heavens,
2Es 5:38 to know these things except he whose **d** is not

DWELLINGS (16) [DWELL]

Ex 35: 3 You shall kindle no fire in all your **d** on
Nu 16:24 Get away from the **d** of Korah, Dathan,
16:27 So they got away from the **d** of Korah, Dathan,
Job 18:21 Surely such are the **d** of the ungodly,
Ps 78:28 within their camp, all around their **d**.
87: 2 the gates of Zion more than all the **d** of Jacob.
Isa 32:18 in secure **d**, and in quiet resting places.
Jer 9:19 because they have cast down our **d**."
30:18 and have compassion on his **d**;
La 2: 2 The Lord has destroyed without mercy all the **d**
Eze 48:15 for **d** and for open country.
Hab 1: 6 the breadth of the earth to seize **d** not their own.
Mt 17: 4 if you wish, I will make three **d** here, one for you,
Mk 9: 5 let us make three **d**, one for you, one for Moses,
Lk 9:33 let us make three **d**, one for you, one for Moses,
2Es 4: 7 'How many **d** are in the heart of the sea,

DWELLS (22) [DWELL]

Dt 33:16 and the favor of the one who **d** on Sinai.
Job 17: 2 and my eye **d** on their provocation.
Ps 9:11 Sing praises to the LORD, who **d** in Zion.
Pr 17: 9 but one who **d** on disputes will alienate a friend.
Isa 8:18 from the LORD of hosts, who **d** on Mount Zion.
33: 5 The LORD is exalted, he **d** on high;
Da 2:22 he knows what is in the darkness, and light **d**
Joel 3:21 for the LORD **d** in Zion.
Mt 23:21 swears by it and by the one who **d** in it;
Jn 14:10 but the Father who **d** in me does his works.
Ro 7:17 but sin that **d** within me.
7:18 For I know that nothing good **d** within me, that is,
7:20 it is no longer I that do it, but sin that **d** within me.
7:23 making me captive to the law of sin that **d**
8: 9 since the Spirit of God **d** in you.
8:11 the Spirit of him who raised Jesus from the dead **d**
8:11 to your mortal bodies also through his Spirit that **d**
1Co 3:16 that you are God's temple and that God's Spirit **d**
Col 2: 9 For in him the whole fullness of deity **d** bodily,
1Ti 6:16 It is he alone who has immortality and **d**
Sir 14:27 and **d** in the midst of her glory.
1Es 2: 5 he is the Lord who **d** in Jerusalem,

DWELT (2) [DWELL]

Ps 78:60 the tent where he **d** among mortals,
Sir 24: 4 I **d** in the highest heavens,

DWINDLE (1) [DWINDLED]

Pr 13:11 Wealth hastily gotten will **d**,

DWINDLED (1) [DWINDLE]

Isa 24: 6 inhabitants of the earth **d**, and few people are left.

DYED (5)

Jdg 5:30 spoil of **d** stuffs for Sisera, spoil of **d** stuffs
embroidered, two pieces of **d** work embroidered
Job 38:14 and it is **d** like a garment.
1Mc 4:23 and cloth **d** blue and sea purple, and great riches.

DYING (18) [DEAD]

2Ch 16:13 **d** in the forty-first year of his reign.
24:22 As he was **d**, he said, "May the LORD see
Job 24:12 From the city the **d** groan,
Isa 5:13 their nobles are **d** of hunger,
Lk 8:42 about twelve years old, who was **d**.
15:17 but here I am **d** of hunger!
Jn 11:37 of the blind man have kept this man from **d**?"
2Co 6: 9 yet are well known; as **d**, and see—
Php 1:21 For to me, living is Christ and **d** is gain.
Heb 11:21 when **d**, blessed each of the sons of Joseph,
Jdt 7:27 not witness our little ones **d** before our eyes,
Wis 18:18 made known why they were **d**;
1Mc 1: 5 After this he fell sick and perceived that he was **d**.
6: 9 and he realized that he was **d**.
4Mc 6:27 I am **d** in burning torments for the sake of the law.
12:14 they by **d** nobly fulfilled their service to God,
16:12 nor did she dissuade any of them from **d**,
16:12 nor did she grieve as they were **d**.

DYNASTY (1)

3Mc 3: 3 and unswerving loyalty toward the **d**;

DYSENTERY (1)

Ac 28: 8 of Publius lay sick in bed with fever and **d**.

DYSTRUS (1)

Tob 2:12 One day, the seventh of **D**,

E

EACH‡ (477)

A. EACH OF YOU (34)
B. EACH OTHER (33)
C. EACH OF THEM (27)
D. EACH DAY (13)
E. EACH OF US (10)

Ge 9: 5 **e** one for the blood of another,
13:11 thus they separated from **e** other. B
15:10 laying **e** half over against the other;
40: 5 **e** his own dream, and each dream
40: 5 and **e** dream with its own meaning.
41:11 he and I, **e** having a dream with its own meaning.
41:12 an interpretation to **e** according to his dream.
42:35 there in **e** one's sack was his bag of money.
43:21 and there was **e** one's money in the top of his sack,
44: 1 and put **e** man's money in the top of his sack.
44:11 **e** one quickly lowered his sack to the ground,
44:11 to the ground, and **e** opened his sack.
44:13 Then **e** one loaded his donkey,
45:22 To **e** one of them he gave a set of garments;
49:28 blessing **e** one of them with a suitable blessing.
Ex 1: 1 the sons of Israel who came to Egypt with Jacob, **e**
3:22 **e** woman shall ask her neighbor
7:12 **E** one threw down his staff,
12: 3 of this month they are to take a lamb for **e** family,
12: 3 a lamb for each family, a lamb for **e** household.
16: 4 and **e** day the people shall go out D
16:16 'Gather as much of it as **e** of you needs, A
16:18 they gathered as much as **e** of them needed. C
16:21 by morning they gathered it, as much as **e** needed;
16:29 **e** of you stay where you are; A
18: 7 **e** asked after the other's welfare,
25:33 **e** with calyx and petals, on one branch,
25:33 **e** with calyx and petals, on the other branch—
25:34 **e** with its calyxes and petals.
26: 2 length of **e** curtain shall be twenty-eight cubits,
26: 2 and the width of **e** curtain four cubits;
26: 8 The length of **e** curtain shall be thirty cubits,
26: 8 and the width of **e** curtain four cubits;
26:16 and a cubit and a half the width of **e** frame.
26:17 be two pegs in **e** frame to fit the frames together;
28:21 **e** engraved with its name, for the twelve tribes.
29:38 two lambs a year old regularly **e** day. D
30:13 This is what **e** one who is registered shall give:
30:14 **E** one who is registered, from twenty years old
30:34 with pure frankincense (an equal part of **e**),
32:27 'Put your sword on your side, **e** of you! A
32:27 and **e** of you kill your brother, your friend, A
32:29 **e** one at the cost of a son or a brother,
33: 8 all the people would rise and stand, **e** of them, C
36: 4 **e** from the task being performed,
36: 9 The length of **e** curtain was twenty-eight cubits,
36: 9 and the width of **e** curtain four cubits;
36:15 The length of **e** curtain was thirty cubits,
36:15 and the width of **e** curtain four cubits;
36:21 and a cubit and a half the width of **e** frame.
36:22 **E** frame had two pegs for fitting together;
37:19 **e** with calyx and petals, on one branch,
37:19 **e** with calyx and petals, on the other branch—
37:20 **e** with its calyxes and petals.
38:15 on **e** side of the gate of the court were hangings
39:14 they were like signets, **e** engraved with its name,
40:36 Israelites would set out on **e** stage of their journey;
40:38 of all the house of Israel at **e** stage of their journey.
Lev 7:14 From this you shall offer one cake from **e** offering,
8:15 and with his finger put some on **e** of the horns of
10: 1 Aaron's sons, Nadab and Abihu, **e** took his censer,
16:18 and put it on **e** of the horns of the altar.
19: 3 You shall **e** revere your mother and father,
23:17 **e** made of two-tenths of an ephah;
23:37 and drink offerings, **e** on its proper day—
24: 5 two-tenths of an ephah shall be in **e** loaf.
24: 7 You shall put pure frankincense with **e** row,
27: 8 according to what **e** one making a vow can afford.
Nu 1: 4 A man from **e** tribe shall be with you,

Nu 1: 4 e man the head of his ancestral house.
1:44 twelve men, e representing his ancestral house.
2: 2 The Israelites shall camp e in their respective
2:17 they shall set out just as they camp, e in position,
4:19 Aaron and his sons shall go in and assign e to
7: 3 and for e one an ox;
7: 5 to e according to his service.
7:11 one leader e day, for the dedication of the altar. D
7:85 e silver plate weighing one hundred thirty shekels
7:85 and e basin seventy, all the silver of
13: 2 from e of their ancestral tribes you shall send
15: 5 with the burnt offering or the sacrifice, for e lamb.
15:11 Thus it shall be done for e ox or ram,
15:11 or for e of the male lambs or the kids.
15:12 so you shall do with e and every one.
15:38 and to put a blue cord on the fringe at e corner.
16:17 and let e one of you take his censer,
16:17 e one of you present his censer before the LORD,
16:17 you also, and Aaron, e his censer."
16:18 So e man took his censer,
17: 2 from them, one for e ancestral house, from all
17: 2 Write e man's name on his staff,
17: 3 be one staff for the head of e ancestral house.
17: 6 all their leaders gave him staffs, one for e leader,
17: 9 and they looked, and e man took his staff.
23: 2 and Balaam offered a bull and a ram on e altar.
23: 4 and have offered a bull and a ram on e altar."
23:14 and offered a bull and a ram on e altar.
23:30 and offered a bull and a ram on e altar.
25: 5 "E of you shall kill any of your people who A
28: 7 be one-fourth of a hin for e lamb;
28:12 mixed with oil, for e bull;
28:21 one-tenth shall you offer for e of the seven lambs;
28:28 three-tenths of an ephah for e bull,
28:29 one-tenth for e of the seven lambs;
29: 4 and one-tenth for e of the seven lambs;
29:10 one-tenth for e of the seven lambs;
29:14 three-tenths of an ephah for e of the thirteen bulls,
29:14 two-tenths for e of the two rams,
29:15 and one-tenth for e of the fourteen lambs;
31: 4 You shall send a thousand from e of the tribes
31: 5 a thousand from e tribe were conscripted,
31: 6 a thousand from e tribe, along with Phinehas son
31:50 what e of us found, articles of gold, E
35: 8 e, in proportion to the inheritance that it obtains,
36: 9 for e of the tribes of the Israelites
Dt 1:13 for e of your tribes individuals who are wise,
1:23 and I selected twelve of you, one from e tribe.
2:34 and in e town we utterly destroyed men, women,
3: 6 in e city utterly destroying men, women,
3:20 then e of you may return to the property A
Jos 3:12 from the tribes of Israel, one from e tribe.
4: 2 from the people, one from e tribe,
4: 4 whom he had appointed, one from e tribe.
4: 5 and e of you take up a stone on his shoulder, A
4: 5 one for e of the tribes of the Israelites,
18: 4 Provide three men from e tribe,
18:10 the land to the Israelites, to e a portion.
21:42 E of these towns had its pasture lands around it;
22:14 one from e of the tribal families of Israel,
Jdg 8:24 e of you give me an earring he has taken A
8:25 e threw into it an earring he had taken as booty.
15: 4 and put a torch between e pair of tails.
16: 5 and we will e give you eleven hundred pieces
21:21 then come out of the vineyards and e of you A
21:22 we did not capture in battle a wife for e man.
21:23 they took wives for e of them from C
Ru 1: 8 "Go back e of you to your mother's house. A
1: 9 e of you in the house of your husband." A
1Sa 2:19 for him a little robe and take it to him e year,
8:22 to the people of Israel, "E of you return home." A
10:27 would gouge out the right eye of e of them C
20:41 He bowed three times, and they kissed e other, B
20:41 they kissed each other, and wept with e other; B
30:22 except that e man may take his wife and children,
2Sa 2:16 E grasped his opponent by the head,
6:19 both men and women, to e a cake of bread,
10: 4 shaved off half the beard of e,
13:29 and e mounted his mule and fled.
21:20 who had six fingers on e hand,
21:20 and six toes on e foot, twenty-four in number;
1Ki 4: 7 e one had to make provision for one month in
4:27 e one in his month; they let nothing be lacking.
4:28 for the horses and swift steeds, e according
6:10 against the whole house, e story five cubits high,
6:23 of olivewood, e ten cubits high.
6:33 to the nave doorposts of olivewood, four-sided e,
7: 3 fifteen in e row, which were on the pillars.
7: 4 facing e other in the three rows. B
7: 5 opposite, facing e other in the three rows. B
7:18 the columns with two rows around e latticework
7:24 e of ten cubits, surrounding the sea;
7:25 The hindquarters of e were toward the inside.
7:27 e stand was four cubits long, four cubits wide,
7:30 E stand had four bronze wheels and axles
7:30 supports were cast with wreaths at the side of e.
7:34 at the four corners of e stand;
7:36 where e had space, with wreaths all around.
7:38 of bronze; e basin held forty baths,
7:38 e basin measured four cubits;
7:38 there was a basin for e of the ten stands.
7:42 two rows of pomegranates for e latticework,
8:59 the cause of his people Israel, as e day requires; D
10:16 of gold went into e large shield.
10:17 three minas of gold went into e shield;
10:19 and on e side of the seat were arm rests
10:20 one on e end of a step on the six steps.
1Ki 20:10 the dust of Samaria will provide a handful for e of
20:20 E killed his man; the Arameans fled
20:24 Also do this: remove the kings, e from his post,
22:17 let e one go home in peace.' "
2Ki 4: 4 when e is full, set it aside."
6: 2 and let us collect logs there, one for e of us, E
9:21 e in his chariot, and went to meet Jehu;
11: 8 the king, e with weapons in hand;
11: 9 e brought his men who were to go off duty on
12: 4 the money for which e person is assessed—
12: 5 let the priests receive from e of the donors;
15:20 fifty shekels of silver from e one,
1Ch 9:32 to prepare them for e sabbath.
16: 3 to e a loaf of bread, a portion of meat,
16:37 before the ark as e day required, D
20: 6 who had six fingers on e hand,
20: 6 and six toes on e foot, twenty-four in number;
26:17 On the east there were six Levites e day, D
26:17 the north four e day, on the south four each day, D
26:17 on the south four e day, as well as two and two D
27: 1 e division numbering twenty-four thousand:
28:14 weight of gold for all golden vessels for e service,
28:14 the weight of silver vessels for e service,
28:15 the weight of gold for e lampstand and its lamps,
28:15 according to the use of e in the service,
28:16 weight of gold for e table for the rows of bread,
28:17 for the golden bowls and the weight of e;
28:17 for the silver bowls and the weight of e;
2Ch 3:15 with a capital of five cubits on the top of e.
4: 3 Under it were panels all around, e of ten cubits,
4: 4 The hindquarters of e were toward the inside.
4:13 two rows of pomegranates for e latticework,
8:13 as the duty of e day required, offering D
8:14 the priests as the duty of e day required, D
9:15 of beaten gold went into e large shield.
9:16 three hundred shekels of gold went into e shield;
9:18 and on e side of the seat were arm rests
9:19 one on e end of a step on the six steps.
10:16 E of you to your tents, O Israel! A
18:16 let e one go home in peace.' "
23: 7 e with his weapons in his hand;
23: 8 e brought his men, who were to come on duty on
31:16 of the LORD as the duty of e day required, D
35: 5 be Levites for e division of an ancestral house.
35:15 The gatekeepers were at e gate;
Ezr 3: 4 according to the ordinance, as required for e day, D
6: 5 and brought back to the temple in Jerusalem, e
10:16 e of them designated by name. C
Ne 3:28 e one opposite his own house.
4:15 we all returned to the wall, e to his work.
4:17 that e labored on the work with one hand and with
4:18 And e of the builders had his sword strapped
4:23 e kept his weapon in his right hand.
7: 6 they returned to Jerusalem and Judah, e
8:16 e on the roofs of their houses,
13:30 the duties of the priests and Levites, e in his work;
Est 1: 8 the officials of his palace to do as e one desired.
2:12 turn came for e girl to go in to King Ahasuerus,
Job 2:11 e of them set out from his home— C
41:17 They clasp e other and cannot be separated. B
42:11 and e of them gave him a piece of money and C
Ps 12: 2 They utter lies to e other; B
59: 6 E evening they come back,
59:14 E evening they come back,
85:10 righteousness and peace will kiss e other. B
119:148 My eyes are awake before e watch of the night,
SS 3: 8 e with his sword at his thigh because of alarms
8:11 e one was to bring for its fruit a thousand pieces
Isa 6: 2 above him; e had six wings:
14:18 of the nations lie in glory, e in his own tomb;
32: 2 E will be like a hiding place from the wind,
34:14 goat-demons shall call to e other; B
34:15 the buzzards shall gather, e one with its mate.
41: 6 E one helps the other, saying to one another,
47:13 and at e new moon predict what shall befall you.
Jer 5: 8 e neighing for his neighbor's wife.
9:20 and e to her neighbor a lament.
18:12 e of us will act according to the stubbornness E
31:34 or say to e other, "Know the LORD," B
34:14 "Every seventh year e of you A
34:16 around and profaned my name when e of you A
49: 5 e headlong, with no one to gather the fugitives.
51: 6 the midst of Babylon, save your lives, e of you! A
51: 9 and let e of us go to our own country; E
51:45 e of you, from the fierce anger of the LORD! A
Eze 1: 6 E had four faces,
1: 6 and e of them had four wings. C
1: 9 e of them moved straight ahead, C
1:11 e creature had two wings, e of which touched
1:12 E moved straight ahead; wherever the spirit would
1:15 one for e of the four of them.
1:23 e of the creatures had two wings covering its body.
4: 6 forty days I assign you, one day for e year.
8:11 E had his censer in his hand,
8:12 e in his room of images?
9: 1 e with his destroying weapon in his hand."
9: 2 e with his weapon for slaughter in his hand;
10: 9 beside the cherubim, one beside e cherub;
10:14 E one had four faces: the first face was
10:21 E had four faces, e four wings,
10:22 E one moved straight ahead.
32:10 e one of them, on the day of your downfall.
33:26 and e of you defiles his neighbor's wife; A
33:30 say to one another, e to a neighbor,
40: 5 e being a cubit and a handbreadth in length;
40: 7 and e recess was one reed wide and one reed deep;
41: 1 on e side six cubits was the width of the pilasters.
Eze 41: 6 one over another, thirty in e story.
41:18 and cherub. E cherub had two faces:
41:23 The nave and the holy place had e a double door.
41:24 two swinging leaves for e door.
45:13 one-sixth of an ephah from e homer of wheat,
45:13 and one-sixth of an ephah from e homer of barley,
45:14 one-tenth of a bath from e cor (the cor,
45:23 on e of the seven days;
45:24 as a grain offering an ephah for e bull,
45:24 an ephah for e ram, and a hin of oil to e ephah.
46: 5 together with a hin of oil to e ephah.
46: 7 together with a hin of oil to e ephah.
46:21 and in e corner of the court there was a court—
46:23 around e of the four courts was a row of masonry,
Joel 2: 7 E keeps to its own course,
2: 8 e keeps to its own track;
Am 4: 3 in the wall you shall leave, e one straight ahead;
Jnh 1: 5 the mariners were afraid, and e cried to his god.
Mic 4: 5 For all the peoples walk, e in the name of its god,
7: 2 and they hunt e other with nets. B
Zep 2:11 and to him shall bow down, e in its place,
3: 5 he renders his judgment, e dawn without fail;
Zec 3:10 you shall invite e other to come under your vine B
4: 2 there are seven lamps on it, with seven lips on e of
8: 4 e with staff in hand because of their great age.
11: 6 every one, to fall e into the hand of a neighbor,
11: 6 and e into the hand of the king;
12:12 The land shall mourn, e family by itself;
12:14 e by itself, and their wives by themselves.
13: 5 but e of them will say, "I am no prophet, I am C
14:13 so that e will seize the hand of a neighbor,
Mt 20: 9 e of them received the usual daily wage. C
20:10 but e of them also received the usual daily wage. C
25:15 to another one, to e according to his ability.
Mk 13:34 e with his work, and commands the doorkeeper to
15:24 casting lots to decide what e should take.
Lk 4:40 he laid his hands on e of them and cured them. C
6:44 for e tree is known by its own fruit.
9:14 "Make them sit down in groups of about fifty e."
11: 3 Give us e day our daily bread. D
13:15 Does not e of you on the sabbath untie his ox A
23:12 and Pilate became friends with e other; B
24:14 and talking with e other about all these things B
24:17 "What are you discussing with e other B
24:32 They said to e other, "Were not our hearts B
Jn 2: 6 e holding twenty or thirty gallons.
6: 7 not buy enough bread for e of them to get C
7:53 ⟦Then e of them went home,⟧ C
16:32 e one to his home, and you will leave me alone.
19:23 and divided them into four parts, one for e soldier.
Ac 2: 3 and a tongue rested on e of them. C
2: 6 because e one heard them speaking in the native
language of e.
2: 8 And how is it that we hear, e of us, E
3:26 by turning e of you from your wicked ways." A
4:35 and it was distributed to e as any had need.
7:26 why do you wrong e other?' B
11:29 e would send relief to the believers living in Judea;
14:23 they had appointed elders for them in e church,
17:27 though indeed he is not far from e one of us.
21:26 when the sacrifice would be made for e of them. C
28:25 So they disagreed with e other; B
Ro 1:12 be mutually encouraged by e other's faith,
2: 6 For he will repay according to e one's deeds:
12: 3 e according to the measure of faith
14:12 So then, e of us will be accountable to God. E
15: 2 E of us must please our neighbor for E
1Co 1:12 What I mean is that e of you says, A
3: 5 as the Lord assigned to e.
3: 8 e will receive wages according to the labor of e.
3:10 E builder must choose with care how to build
3:13 the work of e builder will become visible,
3:13 and the fire will test what sort of work e has done.
4: 5 Then e one will receive commendation from God.
7: 2 e man should have his own wife and e woman her
own husband.
7: 7 But e has a particular gift from God,
7:17 let e of you lead the life that A
7:20 Let e of you remain in the condition A
11:21 e of you goes ahead with your own supper, A
12: 7 To e is given the manifestation of the Spirit for
12:11 to e one individually just as the Spirit chooses.
12:18 e one of them, as he chose.
14:26 When you come together, e one has a hymn,
14:27 and e in turn; and let one interpret.
15:23 But e in his own order:
15:38 and to e kind of seed its own body.
16: 2 e of you is to put aside A
2Co 5:10 so that e may receive recompense
9: 7 E of you must give as you have made A
Gal 5:17 for these are opposed to e other, B
Eph 4: 7 But e of us was given grace according to E
4:16 as e part is working properly,
5:33 E of you, however, should love his wife A
Php 2: 4 Let e of you look not to your own interests, A
Col 3:13 a complaint against another, forgive e other; B
1Th 2:11 with e one of you like a father with his children,
4: 4 that e one of you know how
5:11 encourage one another and build up e other, B
Heb 6:11 And we want e one of you to show
8:11 shall not teach one another or say to e other, B
11:21 when dying, blessed e of the sons of Joseph,
1Pe 4:10 with whatever gift e of you has received. A
3Jn 1:15 Greet the friends there, e by name.
Rev 2:23 I will give to e of you as your works deserve. A
4: 6 Around the throne, and on e side of the throne,
4: 8 four living creatures, e of them with six wings, C

Rev 5: 8 e holding a harp and golden bowls full of incense,
6:11 They were e given a white robe and told to rest
16:21 e weighing about a hundred pounds,
21:21 e of the gates is a single pearl,
22: 2 producing its fruit e month;
Tob 3: 8 wicked demon Asmodeus had killed e of them C
5: 3 we e took one part, and I put one with the money.
12:18 Bless him e and every day; sing his praises.
Jdt 12: 7 She went out e night to the valley of Bethulia,
14: 2 e of you take up your weapons, A
AdE 3:12 governors were addressed e in his own language.
8: 9 to e province in its own language.
Wis 15: 7 and laboriously molds e vessel for our service,
15: 7 the use of e of them the worker in clay decides. C
19:18 while e note remains the same.
Sir 15:17 Before e person are life and death,
17:14 And he gave commandment to e of them C
38:27 e is diligent in making a great variety;
42:23 e creature is preserved to meet a particular need.
42:25 E supplements the virtues of the other.
43:26 Because of him e of his messengers succeeds,
45:11 to commemorate in engraved letters e of the tribes
Bar 1: 6 they collected as much money as e could give,
2: 8 e of us, from the thoughts of our wicked hearts. E
Sus 1:10 but they did not tell e other of their distress, B
1:13 One day they said to e other, "Let us go home, B
1:13 So they both left and parted from e other. B
1:14 and when e pressed the other for the reason,
1:51 "Separate them far from e other, B
1:52 When they were separated from e other, B
1:54 did you see them being intimate with e other?" B
1:58 did you catch them being intimate with e other?" B
1Mc 1: 8 Then his officers began to rule, e in his own place.
6:35 with e elephant they stationed a thousand men
6:35 picked horsemen were assigned to e beast.
6:37 they were fastened on e animal by special harness,
6:37 on e were four armed men who fought from there,
7:49 be celebrated e year on the thirteenth day of Adar.
8:16 They trust one man e year to rule over them and
10:71 and let us match strength with e other there, B
11: 3 as a garrison in e town.
11: 9 "Come, let us make a covenant with e other, B
11:34 that the king formerly received from them e year,
2Mc 7:21 She encouraged e of them in the language C
7:22 I who set in order the elements within e of you. A
8:22 and Joseph and Jonathan, e to command
8:22 putting fifteen hundred men under e.
9:26 e of you, toward me and my son. A
12:40 of e one of the dead they found sacred tokens of
13: 2 E of them had a Greek force C
14:21 A chariot came forward from e army;
15:11 armed e of them not so much with confidence C
1Es 1:16 The gatekeepers were at e gate;
1:26 "What have we to do with e other, B
2: 6 let e of you, wherever you may live, be helped A
3: 5 "Let e of us state what one thing is strongest; E
3: 8 Then e wrote his own statement,
5: 8 and the rest of Judea, e to his own town.
7: 9 and the gatekeepers were at e gate.
9:13 with the elders and judges of e place,
3Mc 1: 4 to give them e two minas of gold if they won
5:49 to lamentation and groans they kissed e other, B
2Es 2:43 and on the head of e of them he placed a crown, C
4:19 I answered and said, "E made a foolish plan,
5:47 "Of course it cannot, but only e in its own time."
11: 8 let e sleep in its own place, and watch in its turn;
16:61 and put a heart in the midst of e body,
16:61 gave e person breath and life and understanding
4Mc 1:20 and e of these is by nature concerned with
1:29 e of which the master cultivator,
5: 2 to seize e and every Hebrew and to compel them
6: 3 they had tied his arms on e side they flogged him,
8: 5 with favorable feelings I admire e and every one
8: 9 you will compel me to destroy e and every one
9:11 and arms with thongs on e side.
13:13 E of them and all of them together looking C
13:18 to e of the brothers who were being dragged away,
13:20 There e of the brothers spent the same length
14:12 up under the rackings of e one of her children.
15: 7 the many pains she suffered with e of them C
15:12 But e child separately and all of them together
15:19 at the eyes of e one in his tortures gazing boldly at
16:24 the seven encouraged and persuaded e of her sons

EAGER (18) [EAGERLY, EAGERNESS]

Ps 17:12 They are like a lion e to tear,
Zep 3: 7 were the more e to make all their deeds corrupt.
Ac 20:16 he was e to be in Jerusalem, if possible,
Ro 8:19 the creation waits with e longing for the revealing
1Co 14:12 since you are e for spiritual gifts,
14:39 So, my friends, be e to prophesy,
2Co 8:17 but since he is more e than ever,
8:22 and found e in many matters,
8:22 but who is now more e than ever because
Gal 2:10 which was actually what I was e to do.
Php 1:20 It is my e expectation and hope that I will not
2:28 I am the more e to send him, therefore,
1Pe 3:13 Now who will harm you if you are e
2Pe 1:10 be all the more e to confirm your call and election,
Sir 18:14 on those who accept his discipline and who are e
2Mc 15: 9 he made them the more e.
3Mc 1: 8 the more e to visit them as soon as possible.
5:29 "O king, according to your e purpose."

EAGERLY (17) [EAGER]

Pr 7:15 to seek you e, and I have found you!
La 4:17 were watching e for a nation that could not save.
Lk 22:15 "I have e desired to eat this Passover with you
Ac 8: 6 with one accord listened e to what was said
8:10 from the least to the greatest, listened to him e,
8:11 And they listened e to him because for
16:14 The Lord opened her heart to listen e
17:11 for they welcomed the message very e
Gal 5: 5 by faith, we e wait for the hope of righteousness.
2Ti 1:17 he e searched for me and found me
Heb 9:28 but to save those who are e waiting for him.
1Pe 5: 2 not for sordid gain but e.
Jude 1: 3 while e preparing to write to you about
Sus 1:12 Day after day they watched e to see her.
1Mc 1:13 and some of the people e went to the king,
2Mc 11: 7 Then they e rushed off together.
3Mc 5:24 and they were e waiting for daybreak.

EAGERNESS (9) [EAGER]

Ro 1:15 hence my e to proclaim the gospel to you
2Co 7:11 what e to clear yourselves, what indignation,
8: 7 in faith, in speech, in knowledge, in utmost e,
8:11 so that your e may be matched by completing it
8:12 if the e is there, the gift is acceptable according
8:16 be to God who put in the heart of Titus the same e
9: 2 for I know your e, which is the subject
1Th 2:17 we longed with great e to see you face to face.
1Ti 6:10 and in their e to be rich some have wandered away

EAGLE (31) [EAGLE'S, EAGLES, EAGLES']

Lev 11:13 the e, the vulture, the osprey,
Dt 14:12 But these are the ones that you shall not eat: the e,
28:49 to swoop down on you like an e,
32:11 As an e stirs up its nest, and hovers over its young;
Job 9:26 like an e swooping on the prey.
39:27 that the e mounts up and makes its nest on high?
Pr 23: 5 flying like an e toward heaven.
30:19 the way of an e in the sky,
Jer 48:40 Look, he shall swoop down like an e,
49:22 he shall mount up and swoop down like an e,
Eze 1:10 of an ox on the left side, and the face of an e;
10:14 the third that of a lion, and the fourth that of an e.
17: 3 A great e, with great wings and long pinions,
17: 7 There was another great e,
Ob 1: 4 Though you soar aloft like the e,
Mic 1:16 make yourselves as bald as the e,
Hab 1: 8 they fly like an e swift to devour.
Rev 4: 7 and the fourth living creature like a flying e.
8:13 and I heard an e crying with a loud voice as it flew
12:14 the woman was given the two wings of the great e,
2Es 11: 1 from the sea an e that had twelve feathered wings
11: 5 Then I saw that the e flew with its wings,
11: 7 Then I saw the e rise upon its talons,
11:37 and I heard how it uttered a human voice to the e,
11:45 Therefore you, e, will surely disappear,
12: 1 While the lion was saying these words to the e,
12: 3 The whole body of the e was burned,
12:11 The e that you saw coming up from the sea is
12:24 Therefore they are called the heads of the e,
12:31 to the e and reproving him for his unrighteousness,
14:18 the e that you saw in the vision is already hurrying

EAGLE'S (5) [EAGLE]

Ps 103: 5 so that your youth is renewed like the e.
Jer 49:16 Although you make your nest as high as the e,
2Es 11:23 the e body except the three heads that were at rest
12:17 the e heads but from the midst of its body, this is
12:30 the Most High has kept for the e end;

EAGLES (4) [EAGLE]

2Sa 1:23 were swifter than e, they were stronger than lions.
Isa 40:31 they shall mount up with wings like e,
Jer 4:13 his horses are swifter than e—
La 4:19 Our pursuers were swifter than the e in the heavens

EAGLES' (3) [EAGLE]

Ex 19: 4 I bore you on e wings and brought you to myself.
Da 4:33 as long as e feathers and his nails became
7: 4 The first was like a lion and had e wings.

EAR‡ (100) [EARLOBE, EARRING, EARRINGS, EARS]

Ex 9:31 for the barley was in the e and the flax was in bud.
21: 6 and his master shall pierce his e with an awl;
29:20 on the lobe of Aaron's right e and on the lobes of
Lev 8:23 on the lobe of Aaron's right e and on the thumb
14:14 on the lobe of the right e of the one to be cleansed,
14:17 on the lobe of the right e of the one to be cleansed,
14:25 on the lobe of the right e of the one to be cleansed,
14:28 on the lobe of the right e of the one to be cleansed,
Dt 32: 1 Give e, O heavens, and I will speak;
Jdg 5: 3 "Hear, O kings; give e, O princes;
2Ki 19:16 Incline your e, O LORD, and hear;
Ne 1: 6 let your e be attentive and your eyes open to hear
1:11 let your e be attentive to the prayer
Job 4:12 my e received the whisper of it.
12:11 Does not the e test words as the palate tastes food?
13: 1 my e has heard and understood it.
29:11 When the e heard, it commended me,
34: 2 you wise men, and give e to me, you who know;
34: 3 for the e tests words as the palate tastes food.
36:15 and opens their e by adversity.
42: 5 I had heard of you by the hearing of the e,
Ps 5: 1 Give e to my words, O LORD;
10:17 will strengthen their heart, you will incline your e
17: 1 give e to my prayer from lips free of deceit.
17: 6 incline your e to me, hear my words.
31: 2 Incline your e to me; rescue me speedily.
39:12 O LORD, and give e to my cry;
40: 6 but you have given me an open e.
45:10 Hear, O daughter, consider and incline your e;
49: 1 give e, all inhabitants of the world,
49: 4 I will incline my e to a proverb;
54: 2 give e to the words of my mouth.
55: 1 Give e to my prayer, O God;
58: 4 like the deaf adder that stops its e,
71: 2 incline your e to me and save me.
78: 1 Give e, O my people, to my teaching;
80: 1 Give e, O Shepherd of Israel, you who lead Joseph
84: 8 O LORD God of hosts, hear my prayer; give e,
86: 1 Incline your e, O LORD, and answer me,
86: 6 Give e, O LORD, to my prayer;
88: 2 incline your e to my cry.
94: 9 He who planted the e, does he not hear?
102: 2 Incline your e to me; answer me speedily
116: 2 Because he inclined his e to me,
140: 6 give e, O LORD, to the voice
141: 1 give e to my voice when I call to you.
143: 1 give e to my supplications in your faithfulness;
Pr 2: 2 making your e attentive to wisdom
4:20 incline your e to my sayings.
5: 1 incline your e to my understanding,
5:13 of my teachers or incline my e to my instructors.
15:31 The e that heeds wholesome admonition will lodge
18:15 and the e of the wise seeks knowledge.
20:12 The hearing e and the seeing eye—
21:13 If you close your e to the cry of the poor,
22:17 Incline your e and hear my words,
23:12 to instruction and your e to words of knowledge.
25:12 of gold is a wise rebuke to a listening e.
Ecc 1: 8 or the e filled with hearing.
Isa 37:17 Incline your e, O LORD, and hear;
48: 8 from of old your e has not been opened.
50: 4 wakens my e to listen as those who are taught.
50: 5 The Lord GOD has opened my e,
55: 3 Incline your e, and come to me;
59: 1 nor his e too dull to hear.
64: 4 past no one has heard, no e has perceived,
Jer 7:24 Yet they did not obey or incline their e, but,
11: 8 Yet they did not obey or incline their e,
13:15 Hear and give e; do not be haughty,
17:23 Yet they did not listen or incline their e;
35:15 But you did not incline your e or obey me.
44: 5 But they did not listen or incline their e,
La 3:56 "Do not close your e to my cry for help,
Da 9:18 Incline your e, O my God, and hear.
Joel 1: 2 O elders, give e, all inhabitants of the land!
Am 3:12 the mouth of the lion two legs, or a piece of an e,
Mt 26:51 the slave of the high priest, cutting off his e.
Mk 14:47 the slave of the high priest, cutting off his e.
Lk 22:50 the slave of the high priest and cut off his right e.
22:51 And he touched his e and healed him.
Jn 18:10 and cut off his right e.
18:26 a relative of the man whose e Peter had cut off,
1Co 2: 9 it is written, "What no eye has seen, nor e heard,
12:16 And if the e would say, "Because I am not an eye,
Rev 2: 7 who has an e listen to what the Spirit is saying to
2:11 who has an e listen to what the Spirit is saying to
2:17 who has an e listen to what the Spirit is saying to
2:29 who has an e listen to what the Spirit is saying to
3: 6 who has an e listen to what the Spirit is saying to
3:13 who has an e listen to what the Spirit is saying to
3:22 who has an e listen to what the Spirit is saying to
13: 9 Let anyone who has an e listen:
Wis 1:10 because a jealous e hears all things,
6: 2 Give e, you that rule over multitudes,
Sir 3:29 and an attentive e is the desire of the wise.
16: 5 my e has heard things more striking than these.
51:16 I inclined my e a little and received her,
Bar 2:16 Incline your e, O Lord, and hear;
3: 9 give e, and learn wisdom!
2Es 8:24 and give e to the petition of your creature;

EARED, EARING (KJV) See PLOWED, PLOWING

EARLIER (11) [EARLY]

1Sa 20:19 go to the place where you hid yourself e,
2Sa 13:18 of the king were clothed in e times.)
2Ch 17: 3 because he walked in the e ways of his father;
Jer 34: 5 the e kings who preceded you,
Da 7: 8 three of the e horns were plucked up by the roots.
Jn 10:40 to the place where John had been baptizing e,
Gal 1:13 You have heard, no doubt, of my e life in Judaism.
1Ti 1:18 in accordance with the prophecies made e
Heb 7:18 of an e commandment because it was weak
10:32 But recall those e days when,
2Es 11:18 and held the rule as the e ones had done,

EARLIEST (1) [EARLY]

1Mc 3:29 the laws that had existed from the e days.

EARLOBE (1) [EAR]

Dt 15:17 an awl and thrust it through his e into the door,

EARLY‡ (88) [EARLIER, EARLIEST]

Ge 19: 2 then you can rise e and go on your way."
19:27 Abraham went e in the morning to the place

Ge 20: 8 So Abimelech rose **e** in the morning,
21:14 So Abraham rose **e** in the morning,
22: 3 So Abraham rose **e** in the morning,
26:31 In the morning they rose **e** and exchanged oaths;
28:18 So Jacob rose **e** in the morning,
31:55 **E** in the morning Laban rose up,
Ex 8:20 "Rise **e** in the morning and present yourself
9:13 "Rise up **e** in the morning and present yourself
24: 4 He rose **e** in the morning,
32: 6 They rose **e** the next day,
34: 4 and he rose **e** in the morning and went up
Nu 14:40 They rose **e** in the morning and went up to
Dt 11:14 the **e** rain and the later rain,
Jos 3: 1 **E** in the morning Joshua rose and set out
6:12 Then Joshua rose **e** in the morning,
6:15 On the seventh day they rose **e**, at dawn,
7:16 So Joshua rose **e** in the morning,
8:10 In the morning Joshua rose **e** and mustered
8:14 hurried out **e** in the morning to
Jdg 6:28 When the townspeople rose **e** in the morning,
6:38 he rose **e** next morning and squeezed the fleece,
7: 1 the troops that were with him rose **e** and encamped
9:33 Then **e** in the morning, as soon as the sun rises,
19: 5 On the fourth day they got up **e** in the morning,
19: 8 the fifth day he got up **e** in the morning to leave;
19: 9 Tomorrow you can get up **e** in the morning
21: 4 On the next day, the people got up **e**,
Ru 2: 7 and she has been on her feet from **e** this morning
1Sa 1:19 They rose **e** in the morning and worshiped before
5: 3 When the people of Ashdod rose **e** the next day,
5: 4 But when they rose **e** on the next morning,
15:12 Samuel rose **e** in the morning to meet Saul,
17:20 David rose **e** in the morning,
29:10 Now then rise **e** in the morning,
29:10 Start **e** in the morning, and leave as soon
29:11 So David set out with his men **e** in the morning,
2Sa 15: 2 Absalom used to rise **e** and stand beside the road
2Ki 3:22 When they rose **e** in the morning,
6:15 When an attendant of the man of God rose **e** in
2Ch 20:20 They rose **e** in the morning and went out into
29:20 Then King Hezekiah rose **e**,
Ne 8: 3 the square before the Water Gate from **e** morning
Job 1: 5 and he would rise **e** in the morning
Ps 84: 6 the **e** rain also covers it with pools.
127: 2 It is in vain that you rise up **e** and go late to rest,
Pr 27:14 rising **e** in the morning, will be counted as cursing.
SS 7:12 let us go out **e** to the vineyards,
Isa 5:11 you who rise **e** in the morning in pursuit
Hos 6: 4 like the dew that goes away **e**.
13: 3 the morning mist or like the dew that goes away **e**,
Joel 2:23 for he has given the **e** rain for your vindication,
2:23 the **e** and the later rain, as before.
Mt 14:25 And **e** in the morning he came walking
20: 1 like a landowner who went out **e** in the morning
Mk 6:48 he came towards them **e** in the morning,
16: 2 And very **e** on the first day of the week,
16: 9 ⟦Now after he rose **e** on the first day of the week,⟧
Lk 21:38 the people would get up **e** in the morning to listen
24: 1 But on the first day of the week, at **e** dawn,
24:22 They were at the tomb **e** this morning,
Jn 8: 2 ⟦**E** in the morning he came again to the temple.⟧
18:28 It was **e** in the morning.
20: 1 **E** on the first day of the week,
Ac 15: 7 that in the **e** days God made a choice among you,
21:16 an **e** disciple, with whom we were to stay.
Php 4:15 You Philippians indeed know that in the **e** days of
Jas 5: 7 with it until it receives the **e** and the late rains.
Tob 9: 6 both got up **e** and went to the wedding celebration.
Wis 4: 7 the righteous, though they die **e**, will be at rest.
6:14 One who rises **e** to seek her will have no difficulty,
Sir 4:12 and those who seek her from **e** morning are filled
6:36 If you see an intelligent person, rise **e** to visit him;
31:20 on moderate eating; he rises **e**,
32:14 and those who rise **e** to seek him will find favor.
39: 5 to rise **e** to seek the Lord who made him,
47:10 and the sanctuary resounded from **e** morning.
Bel 1:16 **E** in the morning the king rose and came,
1Mc 3:58 Be ready **e** in the morning to fight
4:52 **E** in the morning on the twenty-fifth day of
6:33 **E** in the morning the king set out
10:80 at his men from **e** morning until late afternoon.
11:67 **E** in the morning they marched to the plain
16: 5 **E** in the morning they started out and marched into
1Es 9:41 from **e** morning until midday, in the presence of
3Mc 5:10 the courtyard **e** in the morning to report to the king
5:23 as soon as the cock had crowed in the **e** morning,

EARN (6) [EARNED]

Pr 11:18 The wicked **e** no real gain,
Am 7:12 flee away to the land of Judah, **e** your bread there,
Hag 1: 6 and you that **e** wages earn wages to put them into
1: 6 and you that earn wages **e** wages to put them into
1Co 16: 2 to put aside and save whatever extra you **e**,
2Th 3:12 to do their work quietly and to **e** their own living.

EARNED (1) [EARN]

Tob 2:11 also, my wife Anna **e** money at women's work.

EARNEST (4) [EARNESTLY, EARNESTNESS]

Ro 15:30 to join me in **e** prayer to God on my behalf,
Rev 3:19 Be **e**, therefore, and repent.
3Mc 3:10 and to exert more **e** efforts for their assistance.
4Mc 1: 1 to advise you to pay **e** attention to philosophy.

EARNESTLY‡ (11) [EARNEST]

1Sa 20: 6 'David **e** asked leave of me to run
20:28 "David **e** asked leave of me to go to Bethlehem;
Ps 78:34 they repented and sought God **e**.
Isa 26: 9 my spirit within me **e** seeks you.
Mk 5:10 He begged him **e** not to send them out of
Lk 7: 4 When they came to Jesus, they appealed to him **e**,
22:44 ⟦In his anguish he prayed more **e**,⟧
Ac 26: 7 as they **e** worship day and night.
2Co 8: 4 begging us **e** for the privilege of sharing
1Th 3:10 and day we pray most **e** that we may see you face
Man 1:13 I **e** implore you, forgive me, O Lord, forgive me!

EARNESTNESS (2) [EARNEST]

2Co 7:11 see what **e** this godly grief has produced in you,
8: 8 the genuineness of your love against the **e**

EARRING (2) [EAR, RING]

Jdg 8:24 each of you give me an **e** he has taken as booty."
8:25 and each threw into it an **e** he had taken as booty.

EARRINGS (6) [EAR, RING]

Ex 35:22 of a willing heart brought brooches and **e**
Nu 31:50 armlets and bracelets, signet rings, **e**,
Jdg 8:24 (For the enemy had golden **e**,
8:26 The weight of the golden **e**
Eze 16:12 on your nose, **e** in your ears, and a beautiful crown
Jdt 10: 4 bracelets, rings, **e**, and all her other jewelry.

EARS‡ (109) [EAR]

Ge 35: 4 and the rings that were in their **e**;
41: 5 seven **e** of grain, plump and good,
41: 6 Then seven **e**, thin and blighted by the east wind,
41: 7 thin **e** swallowed up the seven plump and full **e**.
41:22 a second time and I saw in my dream seven **e**
41:23 and seven **e**, withered, thin, and blighted by
41:24 and the thin **e** swallowed up the seven good **e**.
41:26 and the seven good **e** are seven years;
41:27 as are the seven empty **e** blighted by the east wind.
44:18 a word in my lord's **e**, and do not be angry
Ex 29:20 of Aaron's right ear and on the lobes of the right **e**
32: 2 the gold rings that are on the **e** of your wives,
32: 3 all the people took off the gold rings from their **e**,
Lev 2:14 of your first fruits coarse new grain from fresh **e**,
8:24 of the blood on the lobes of their right **e** and on
23:14 You shall eat no bread or parched grain or fresh **e**
Dt 23:25 you may pluck the **e** with your hand,
29: 4 or eyes to see, or **e** to hear.
Ru 2: 2 "Let me go to the field and glean among the **e**
1Sa 3:11 to do something in Israel that will make both **e**
8:21 he repeated them in the **e** of the LORD.
15:14 "What then is this bleating of sheep in my **e**,
25:24 please let your servant speak in your **e**,
2Sa 7:22 according to all that we have heard with our **e**.
22: 7 and my cry came to his **e**.
2Ki 4:42 twenty loaves of barley and fresh **e** of grain
19:28 against me and your arrogance has come to my **e**,
21:12 that the **e** of everyone who hears of it will tingle.
1Ch 17:20 according to all that we have heard with our **e**.
2Ch 6:40 and your **e** attentive to prayer from this place.
7:15 Now my eyes will be open and my **e** attentive to
Ne 8: 3 the **e** of all the people were attentive to the book of
Job 13:17 and let my declaration be in your **e**.
15:21 Terrifying sounds are in their **e**;
28:22 'We have heard a rumor of it with our **e**.'
33:16 then he opens their **e**, and terrifies them
36:10 He opens their **e** to instruction,
Ps 18: 6 and my cry to him reached his **e**.
34:15 and his **e** are open to their cry.
44: 1 We have heard with our **e**,
78: 1 incline your **e** to the words of my mouth.
92:11 my **e** have heard the doom of my evil assailants.
115: 6 They have **e**, but do not hear;
130: 2 Let your **e** be attentive to the voice of my
135:17 they have **e**, but they do not hear,
Pr 26:17 the **e** is one who meddles in the quarrel of another.
Isa 6:10 and stop their **e**, and shut their eyes,
6:10 not look with their eyes, and listen with their **e**,
11: 3 or decide by what his **e** hear;
17: 5 harvest the **e**, as when one gleans the **e** of grain
22:14 The LORD of hosts has revealed himself in my **e**:
30:21 your **e** shall hear a word behind you, saying,
32: 3 and the **e** of those who have hearing will listen.
33:15 who stop their **e** from hearing of bloodshed
35: 5 and the **e** of the deaf unstopped;
37:29 against me and your arrogance has come to my **e**,
42:20 his **e** are open, but he does not hear.
43: 8 yet have eyes, who are deaf, yet have **e**!
Jer 5:21 but do not see, who have **e**, but do not hear.
6:10 See, their **e** are closed, they cannot listen.
9:20 and let your **e** receive the word of his mouth;
19: 3 that the **e** of everyone who hears of it will tingle.
25: 4 you have neither listened nor inclined your **e**
26:11 as you have heard with your own **e**."
26:15 to you to speak all these words in your **e**."
34:14 not listen to me or incline their **e** to me.
Eze 3:10 to you receive in your heart and hear with your **e**;
12: 2 who have **e** to hear but do not hear;
16:12 a ring on your nose, earrings in your **e**, and
23:25 They shall cut off your nose and your **e**,
Mic 7:16 on their mouths; their **e** shall be deaf;
Zec 7:11 and stopped their **e** in order not to hear.
Mt 11:15 Let anyone with **e** listen!
13: 9 Let anyone with **e** listen!"
13:15 and their **e** are hard of hearing,
13:15 not look with their eyes, and listen with their **e**,
13:16 blessed are your eyes, for they see, and your **e**,
13:43 Let anyone with **e** listen!
28:14 If this comes to the governor's **e**,
Mk 4: 9 And he said, "Let anyone with **e** to hear listen!"
4:23 Let anyone with **e** to hear listen!"
7:33 and put his fingers into his **e**,
7:35 And immediately his **e** were opened,
8:18 Do you have **e**, and fail to hear?
Lk 8: 8 he called out, "Let anyone with **e** to hear listen!"
9:44 "Let these words sink into your **e**:
14:35 Let anyone with **e** to hear listen!"
Ac 7:51 uncircumcised in heart and **e**,
7:57 But they covered their **e**, and with
11:22 of this came to the **e** of the church in Jerusalem,
28:27 and their **e** are hard of hearing,
28:27 not look with their eyes, and listen with their **e**,
Ro 11: 8 eyes that would not see and **e** that would not hear,
2Ti 4: 3 up with sound doctrine, but having itching **e**,
Jas 5: 4 and the cries of the harvesters have reached the **e**
1Pe 3:12 and his **e** are open to their prayer.
Wis 15:15 nor **e** with which to hear, nor fingers to feel with,
Sir 17: 6 **e** and a mind for thinking he gave them.
17:13 and their **e** heard the glory of his voice.
21: 5 The prayer of the poor goes from their lips to the **e**
27:14 and their quarrels make others stop their **e**.
38:28 the sound of the hammer deafens his **e**,
Bar 2:31 I will give them a heart that obeys and **e** that hear;
2Mc 15:39 of the story delights the **e** of those who read
2Es 10:56 as much as your **e** can hear.
15: 1 in the **e** of my people the words of the prophecy

EARTH‡ (1051) [EARTH'S, EARTHEN, EARTHENWARE, EARTHLY, EARTHQUAKE, EARTHQUAKES, EARTHWORKS, EARTHY]

A. ALL THE EARTH (65)
B. HEAVEN ... EARTH (64)
C. WHOLE EARTH (42)
D. ENDS OF THE EARTH (39)
E. KINGS OF THE EARTH (26)
F. INHABITANTS OF THE EARTH (19)
G. FOUNDATION[S] OF THE EARTH (16)
H. HEAVENS AND ... EARTH (17)
I. END OF THE EARTH (14)
J. KINGDOMS OF THE EARTH (14)
K. DUST OF THE EARTH (13)
L. PEOPLES OF THE EARTH (9)
M. EARTH ... HEAVEN (8)

Ge 1: 1 when God created the heavens and the **e**, H
1: 2 the **e** was a formless void and darkness covered
1:10 God called the dry land **E**,
1:11 Then God said, "Let the **e** put forth vegetation:
1:11 and fruit trees of every kind on **e** that bear fruit
1:12 The **e** brought forth vegetation:
1:15 in the dome of the sky to give light upon the **e**."
1:17 in the dome of the sky to give light upon the **e**,
1:20 and let birds fly above the **e** across the dome of
1:22 and let birds multiply on the **e**."
1:24 the **e** bring forth living creatures of every kind:
1:24 and creeping things and wild animals of the **e**
1:25 God made the wild animals of the **e** of every kind,
1:26 and over all the wild animals of the **e**,
1:26 over every creeping thing that creeps upon the **e**."
1:28 and fill the **e** and subdue it;
1:28 and over every living thing that moves upon the **e**."
1:29 upon the face of all the **e**, and every tree A
1:30 And to every beast of the **e**,
1:30 and to everything that creeps on the **e**,
2: 1 Thus the heavens and the **e** were finished, H
2: 4 are the generations of the heavens and the **e** H
2: 4 that the LORD God made the **e** and the heavens,
2: 5 the **e** and no herb of the field had yet sprung up—
2: 5 LORD God had not caused it to rain upon the **e**,
2: 6 the **e**, and water the whole face of the ground—
4:12 you will be a fugitive and a wanderer on the **e**."
4:14 I shall be a fugitive and a wanderer on the **e**,
6: 4 The Nephilim were on the **e** in those days—
6: 5 the wickedness of humankind was great in the **e**,
6: 6 that he had made humankind on the **e**,
6: 7 from the **e** the human beings I have created—
6:11 Now the **e** was corrupt in God's sight,
6:11 and the **e** was filled with violence.
6:12 And God saw that the **e** was corrupt;
6:12 for all flesh had corrupted its ways upon the **e**.
6:13 for the **e** is filled with violence because of them;
6:13 now I am going to destroy them along with the **e**.
6:17 I am going to bring a flood of waters on the **e**,
6:17 everything that is on the **e** shall die.
7: 3 to keep their kind alive on the face of all the **e**. A
7: 4 For in seven days I will send rain on the **e**
7: 6 when the flood of waters came on the **e**.
7:10 seven days the waters of the flood came on the **e**.
7:12 The rain fell on the **e** forty days and forty nights.
7:14 and every creeping thing that creeps on the **e**,
7:17 The flood continued forty days on the **e**;
7:17 and bore up the ark, and it rose high above the **e**.
7:18 waters swelled and increased greatly on the **e**;
7:19 The waters swelled so mightily on the **e** that all
7:21 And all flesh died that moved on the **e**, birds,
7:21 all swarming creatures that swarm on the **e**,
7:23 they were blotted out from the **e**.
7:24 waters swelled on the **e** for one hundred fifty days.

Ge 8: 1 And God made a wind blow over the e,
8: 3 and the waters gradually receded from the e.
8: 7 and fro until the waters were dried up from the e.
8: 9 the waters were still on the face of the whole e. C
8:11 that the waters had subsided from the e.
8:13 the waters were dried up from the e;
8:14 of the month, the e was dry.
8:17 and every creeping thing that creeps on the e—
8:17 so that they may abound on the e,
8:17 and be fruitful and multiply on the e."
8:19 and every bird, everything that moves on the e,
8:22 As long as the e endures, seedtime and harvest,
9: 1 "Be fruitful and multiply, and fill the e.
9: 2 the e, and on every bird of the air, on everything
9: 7 abound on the e and multiply in it."
9:10 and every animal of the e with you,
9:11 never again shall there be a flood to destroy the e."
9:13 be a sign of the covenant between me and the e.
9:14 over the e and the bow is seen in the clouds,
9:16 of all flesh that is on the e."
9:17 between me and all flesh that is on the e."
9:19 and from these the whole e was peopled. C
10: 8 he was the first on e to become a mighty warrior.
10:25 for in his days the e was divided,
10:32 from these the nations spread abroad on the e after
11: 1 whole e had one language and the same words. C
11: 4 scattered abroad upon the face of the whole e." C
11: 8 from there over the face of all the e, A
11: 9 the LORD confused the language of all the e; A
11: 9 over the face of all the e. A
12: 3 in you all the families of the e shall be blessed."
13:16 I will make your offspring like the dust of the e; K
13:16 so that if one can count the dust of the e, K
14:19 by God Most High, maker of heaven and e; B
14:22 God Most High, maker of heaven and e, B
18:18 and all the nations of the e shall be blessed in him?
18:25 Shall not the Judge of all the e do what is just?" A
19:23 The sun had risen on the e when Lot came to Zoar.
19:31 a man on e to come in to us after the manner of all
22:18 the nations of the e gain blessing for themselves,
24: 3 the LORD, the God of heaven and e, B
26: 4 and all the nations of the e shall gain blessing
26:15 the Philistines had stopped up and filled with e all
27:28 and of the fatness of the e,
27:39 away from the fatness of the e shall your home be,
28:12 he dreamed that there was a ladder set up on the e,
28:14 your offspring shall be like the dust of the e, K
28:14 the e shall be blessed in you and in your offspring.
41:47 the e produced abundantly.
45: 7 before you to preserve for you a remnant on e,
48:12 and he bowed himself with his face to the e.
48:16 and let them grow into a multitude on the e."
Ex 8:16 out your staff and strike the dust of the e, K
8:17 the dust of the e, and gnats came on humans K
8:17 all the dust of the e turned into gnats K
9:14 that there is no one like me in all the e. A
9:15 and you would have been cut off from the e.
9:16 and to make my name resound through all the e. A
9:23 and fire came down on the e.
9:29 so that you may know that the e is the LORD's.
9:33 and the rain no longer poured down on the e.
10: 6 from the day they came on e to this day.' "
15:12 your right hand, the e swallowed them.
19: 5 Indeed, the whole e is mine, C
20: 4 or that is on the e beneath,
20: 4 or that is in the water under the e.
20:11 For in six days the LORD made heaven and e, B
20:24 of e and sacrifice on it your burnt offerings
31:17 that in six days the LORD made heaven and e, B
32:12 and to consume them from the face of the e'?
33:16 from every people on the face of the e."
34: 8 And Moses quickly bowed his head toward the e,
34:10 not been performed in all the e or in any nation; A
Lev 11:29 among the creatures that swarm upon the e:
11:41 All creatures that swarm upon the e are detestable;
11:42 all the creatures that swarm upon the e,
11:44 with any swarming creature that moves on the e.
11:46 and every creature that swarms upon the e,
17:13 shall pour out its blood and cover it with e.
26:19 and I will make your sky like iron and your e
Nu 12: 3 more so than anyone else on the face of the e.
14:21 as all the e shall be filled with the glory of the A
16:32 The e opened its mouth and swallowed them up,
16:33 the e closed over them, and they perished from
16:34 for they said, "The e will swallow us too!"
22: 5 they have spread over the face of the e,
22:11 of Egypt and has spread over the face of the e;
26:10 and the e opened its mouth and swallowed them
Dt 3:24 what god in heaven or on e can perform deeds B
4:10 on the e, and may teach their children so";
4:17 the likeness of any animal that is on the e,
4:18 likeness of any fish that is in the water under the e.
4:26 I call heaven and e to witness against you today B
4:32 the day that God created human beings on the e;
4:36 On e he showed you his great fire,
4:39 in heaven above and on the e beneath; B
5: 8 or that is on the e beneath,
5: 8 or that is in the water under the e.
6:15 and he would destroy you from the face of the e.
7: 6 of all the peoples on e to be his people,
10:14 the e with all that is in it,
11: 6 the e opened its mouth and swallowed them up,
11:21 as long as the heavens are above the e.
12: 1 to occupy all the days that you live on the e.
13: 7 from one end of the e to the other, I
14: 2 the LORD has chosen out of all the peoples on e
15:11 there will never cease to be some in need on the e,

Dt 28: 1 above all the nations of the e;
28:10 peoples of the e shall see that you are called by L
28:23 and the e under you iron.
28:25 an object of horror to all the kingdoms of the e. J
28:26 for every bird of the air and animal of the e,
28:49 from the end of the e, I
28:64 from one end of the e to the other; I
30:19 I call heaven and e to witness against you today B
31:28 in their hearing and call heaven and e to witness B
32: 1 let the e hear the words of my mouth.
32:22 it devours the e and its increase,
33:16 with the choice gifts of the e and its fullness,
33:17 driving them to the ends of the e; D
Jos 2:11 in heaven above and on e below.
3:11 the Lord of all the e is going to pass before you A
3:13 Lord of all the e, rest in the waters of the Jordan, A
4:24 the peoples of the e may know that the hand of L
5:14 And Joshua fell on his face to the e and worshiped,
7: 9 and surround us, and cut off our name from the e.
23:14 "And now I am about to go the way of all the e, A
Jdg 5: 4 the e trembled, and the heavens poured,
18: 7 quiet and unsuspecting, lacking nothing on e,
18:10 a place where there is no lack of anything on e."
1Sa 2: 8 For the pillars of the e are the LORD's,
2:10 The LORD will judge the ends of the e; D
4: 5 a mighty shout, so that the e resounded.
4:12 with his clothes torn and with e upon his head.
14:15 the e quaked; and it became a very great panic.
17:46 of the air and to the wild animals of the e,
17:46 all the e may know that there is a God in Israel, A
20:15 of the enemies of David from the face of the e."
20:31 For as long as the son of Jesse lives upon the e,
2Sa 4:11 and destroy you from the e?"
7: 9 like the name of the great ones of the e.
7:23 on e whose God went to redeem it as a people,
14: 7 nor remnant on the face of the e."
14:20 of God to know all things that are on the e."
15:32 to meet him with his coat torn and e on his head.
18: 9 and he was left hanging between heaven and e, B
22: 8 Then the e reeled and rocked;
22:43 I beat them fine like the dust of the e, K
1Ki 1:40 so that the e quaked at their noise.
2: 2 "I am about to go the way of all the e. A
4:34 the kings of the e who had heard of his wisdom. E
8:23 like you in heaven above or on e beneath, B
8:27 "But will God indeed dwell on the e?
8:43 all the peoples of the e may know your name L
8:53 from among all the peoples of the e, L
8:60 so that all the peoples of the e may know that L
10:23 King Solomon excelled all the kings of the e E
10:24 The whole e sought the presence of Solomon C
13:34 to cut it off and to destroy it from the face of the e.
17:14 until the day that the LORD sends rain on the e."
18: 1 I will send rain on the e."
18:42 upon the e and put his face between his knees.
2Ki 5:15 that there is no God in all the e except in Israel; A
5:17 please let two mule-loads of e be given
10:10 fall to the e nothing of the word of the LORD,
19:15 you alone, of all the kingdoms of the e; J
19:15 you have made heaven and e. B
19:19 all the kingdoms of the e may know that you, J
1Ch 1:10 he was the first to be a mighty one on the e.
1:19 (for in his days the e was divided),
16:14 his judgments are in all the e. A
16:23 Sing to the LORD, all the e. A
16:30 tremble before him, all the e. A
16:31 Let the heavens be glad, and let the e rejoice,
16:33 for he comes to judge the e.
17: 8 like the name of the great ones of the e.
17:21 the e whom God went to redeem to be his people,
21:16 of the LORD standing between e and heaven, M
22: 8 you have shed so much blood in my sight on the e.
29:11 all that is in the heavens and on the e is yours; H
29:15 our days on the e are like a shadow,
29:30 and Israel and all the kingdoms of the e. J
2Ch 1: 9 over a people as numerous as the dust of the e. K
2:12 of Israel, who made heaven and e, B
6:14 there is no God like you, in heaven or on e, B
6:18 "But will God indeed reside with mortals on e?
6:33 all the peoples of the e may know your name L
9:22 King Solomon excelled all the kings of the e E
9:23 kings of the e sought the presence of Solomon E
16: 9 eyes of the LORD range throughout the entire e,
32:19 if he were like the gods of the peoples of the e, L
36:23 has given me all the kingdoms of the e, J
Ezr 1: 2 has given me all the kingdoms of the e, J
5:11 We are the servants of the God of heaven and e, B
Ne 9: 1 and with e on their heads.
9: 6 with all their host, the e and all that is on it,
Job 1: 7 "From going to and fro on the e,
1: 8 There is no one like him on the e,
2: 2 "From going to and fro on the e,
2: 3 There is no one like him on the e,
3:14 of the e who rebuild ruins for themselves,
5: 6 For misery does not come from the e,
5:10 He gives rain on the e and sends waters on
5:22 and shall not fear the wild animals of the e.
5:25 and your offspring like the grass of the e.
7: 1 "Do not human beings have a hard service on e,
7:21 For now I shall lie in the e;
8: 9 for our days on e are but a shadow.
8:19 and out of the e still others will spring.
9: 6 the e out of its place, and its pillars tremble;
9:24 The e is given into the hand of the wicked;
11: 9 Its measure is longer than the e,
12: 8 ask the plants of the e, and they will teach you;
12:24 He strips understanding from the leaders of the e,

Job 14: 8 Though its root grows old in the e,
14:19 the torrents wash away the soil of the e;
15:29 nor will they strike root in the e;
16:18 "O e, do not cover my blood;
18: 4 shall the e be forsaken because of you,
18:17 Their memory perishes from the e,
19:25 and that at the last he will stand upon the e;
20: 4 ever since mortals were placed on e,
20:27 and the e will rise up against them.
24: 4 the poor of the e all hide themselves.
26: 7 and hangs the e upon nothing.
28: 2 Iron is taken out of the e,
28: 5 As for the e, out of it comes bread;
28:24 For he looks to the ends of the e, D
34:13 over the e and who laid on him the whole world?
35:11 who teaches us more than the animals of the e,
37: 3 and his lightning to the corners of the e.
37: 6 For to the snow he says, 'Fall on the e';
37:17 you whose garments are hot when the e is still
38: 4 were you when I laid the foundation of the e? G
38:13 so that it might take hold of the skirts of the e,
38:18 Have you comprehended the expanse of the e?
38:24 or where the east wind is scattered upon the e?
38:33 Can you establish their rule on the e?
39:14 For it leaves its eggs to the e,
41:33 On e it has no equal, a creature without fear.
Ps 2: 2 The kings of the e set themselves, E
2: 8 and the ends of the e your possession. D
2:10 O kings, be wise; be warned, O rulers of the e.
8: 1 how majestic is your name in all the e! A
8: 9 how majestic is your name in all the e! A
10:18 so that those from e may strike terror no more.
18: 7 Then the e reeled and rocked;
19: 4 yet their voice goes out through all the e, A
21:10 You will destroy their offspring from the e,
22:27 All the ends of the e shall remember and turn D
22:29 indeed, shall all who sleep in the e bow down;
24: 1 The e is the LORD's and all that is in it,
33: 5 the e is full of the steadfast love of the LORD.
33: 8 Let all the e fear the LORD; A
33:14 he watches all the inhabitants of the e— F
34:16 to cut off the remembrance of them from the e.
45:16 you will make them princes in all the e. A
46: 2 we will not fear, though the e should change,
46: 6 he utters his voice, the e melts.
46: 8 see what desolations he has brought on the e.
46: 9 He makes wars cease to the end of the e; I
46:10 I am exalted in the e."
47: 2 is awesome, a great king over all the e. A
47: 7 For God is the king of all the e; A
47: 9 For the shields of the e belong to God;
48: 2 is the joy of all the e, Mount Zion, A
48:10 like your praise, reaches to the ends of the e. D
50: 1 and summons the e from the rising of the sun
50: 4 He calls to the heavens above and to the e,
57: 5 Let your glory be over all the e. A
57:11 Let your glory be over all the e. A
58: 2 your hands deal out violence on e.
58:11 surely there is a God who judges on e."
59:13 to the ends of the e that God rules over Jacob. D
61: 2 From the end of the e I call to you, I
63: 9 down into the depths of the e;
65: 5 you are the hope of all the ends of the e and of D
65: 9 You visit the e and water it, you greatly enrich it;
66: 1 Make a joyful noise to God, all the e; A
66: 4 All the e worships you; they sing praises to you, A
67: 2 that your way may be known upon e,
67: 4 with equity and guide the nations upon e.
67: 6 The e has yielded its increase;
67: 7 let all the ends of the e revere him. D
68: 8 the e quaked, the heavens poured down rain at
68:32 Sing to God, O kingdoms of the e; J
69:34 Let heaven and e praise him, B
71:20 from the depths of the e you will bring me up
72: 6 like showers that water the e.
72: 8 and from the River to the ends of the e. D
72:19 may his glory fill the whole e. C
73: 9 and their tongues range over the e.
73:25 there is nothing on e that I desire other than you.
74:12 working salvation in the e.
74:17 You have fixed all the bounds of the e;
75: 3 When the e totters, with all its inhabitants,
75: 8 and all the wicked of the e shall drain it down to
76: 8 the e feared and was still
76: 9 to save all the oppressed of the e.
76:12 who inspires fear in the kings of the e. E
77:18 the e trembled and shook.
78:69 like the e, which he has founded forever.
79: 2 flesh of your faithful to the wild animals of the e.
82: 5 all the foundations of the e are shaken. G
82: 8 Rise up, O God, judge the e;
83:18 are the Most High over all the e. A
89:11 The heavens are yours, the e also is yours;
89:27 the highest of the kings of the e. E
90: 2 or ever you had formed the e and the world,
94: 2 Rise up, O judge of the e;
95: 4 In his hand are the depths of the e;
96: 1 sing to the LORD, all the e. A
96: 9 tremble before him, all the e. A
96:11 Let the heavens be glad, and let the e rejoice;
96:13 for he is coming, for he is coming to judge the e.
97: 1 Let the e rejoice; let the many coastlands be glad!
97: 4 up the world; the e sees and trembles.
97: 5 before the Lord of all the e. A
97: 9 For you, O LORD, are most high over all the e; A
98: 3 ends of the e have seen the victory of our God. D
98: 4 Make a joyful noise to the LORD, all the e; A

Ps 98: 9 for he is coming to judge the e.
99: 1 upon the cherubim; let the e quake!
100: 1 Make a joyful noise to the LORD, all the e. A
102: 15 and all the kings of the e your glory. E
102: 19 from heaven the LORD looked at the e, B
102: 25 Long ago you laid the foundation of the e, G
103: 11 For as the heavens are high above the e,
104: 5 You set the e on its foundations,
104: 9 so that they might not again cover the e.
104: 13 the e is satisfied with the fruit of your work.
104: 14 to bring forth food from the e,
104: 24 the e is full of your creatures.
104: 32 who looks on the e and it trembles,
104: 35 Let sinners be consumed from the e,
105: 7 his judgments are in all the e. A
106: 17 The e opened and swallowed up Dathan,
108: 5 and let your glory be over all the e. A
109: 15 and may his memory be cut off from the e.
110: 6 he will shatter heads over the wide e.
113: 6 who looks far down on the heavens and the e? H
114: 7 Tremble, O e, at the presence of the LORD,
115: 15 by the LORD, who made heaven and e. B
115: 16 but the e he has given to human beings.
119: 64 The e, O LORD, is full of your steadfast love;
119: 87 They have almost made an end of me on e;
119: 90 you have established the e, and it stands fast.
119: 119 All the wicked of the e you count as dross;
121: 2 from the LORD, who made heaven and e. B
124: 8 the name of the LORD, who made heaven and e. B
134: 3 May the LORD, maker of heaven and e, B
135: 6 in heaven and on e, in the seas and all deeps. B
135: 7 the clouds rise at the end of the e; I
136: 6 who spread out the e on the waters,
138: 4 All the kings of the e shall praise you, O LORD, E
139: 15 intricately woven in the depths of the e.
146: 4 When their breath departs, they return to the e;
146: 6 who made heaven and e, the sea, and all that is B
147: 8 the heavens with clouds, prepares rain for the e,
147: 15 He sends out his command to the e;
148: 7 Praise the LORD from the e,
148: 11 Kings of the e and all peoples, E
148: 11 princes and all rulers of the e!
148: 13 his glory is above e and heaven. M
Pr 3: 19 The LORD by wisdom founded the e;
8: 23 at the first, before the beginning of the e.
8: 26 when he had not yet made e and fields,
8: 29 when he marked out the foundations of the e, G
11: 31 If the righteous are repaid on e,
17: 24 but the eyes of a fool to the ends of the e. D
25: 3 Like the heavens for height, like the e for depth,
30: 4 Who has established all the ends of the e? D
30: 14 to devour the poor from off the e,
30: 16 the barren womb, the e ever thirsty for water,
30: 21 Under three things the e trembles;
30: 24 Four things on e are small,
Ecc 1: 4 and a generation comes, but the e remains forever.
3: 21 and the spirit of animals goes downward to the e?
5: 2 and you upon e; therefore let your words be few.
7: 20 Surely there is no one on e so righteous as
8: 14 There is a vanity that takes place on e,
8: 16 and to see the business that is done on e,
11: 2 you do not know what disaster may happen on e.
11: 3 When clouds are full, they empty rain on the e;
12: 7 and the dust returns to the e as it was,
SS 2: 12 The flowers appear on the e;
Isa 1: 2 Hear, O heavens, and listen, O e;
2: 19 when he rises to terrify the e.
2: 21 when he rises to terrify the e.
5: 26 and whistle for a people at the ends of the e; D
6: 3 the whole e is full of his glory." C
8: 22 or they will look to the e, but will see only distress
10: 14 so I have gathered all the e; A
10: 23 a full end, as decreed, in all the e. A
11: 4 and decide with equity for the meek of the e;
11: 4 he shall strike the e with the rod of his mouth,
11: 9 the e will be full of the knowledge of the LORD
11: 12 of Judah from the four corners of the e.
12: 5 let this be known in all the e. A
13: 5 of his indignation, to destroy the whole e. C
13: 9 to make the e a desolation,
13: 13 and the e will be shaken out of its place,
14: 7 The whole e is at rest and quiet; C
14: 9 all who were leaders of the e;
14: 16 "Is this the man who made the e tremble,
14: 21 the e or cover the face of the world with cities.
14: 26 the plan that is planned concerning the whole e; C
18: 3 you who live on the e,
18: 6 of the mountains and to the animals of the e.
18: 6 and all the animals of the e will winter on them.
19: 24 a blessing in the midst of the e,
23: 8 whose traders were the honored of the e?
23: 9 to shame all the honored of the e.
23: 17 the kingdoms of the world on the face of the e.
24: 1 about to lay waste the e and make it desolate,
24: 3 e shall be utterly laid waste and utterly despoiled;
24: 4 The e dries up and withers,
24: 4 the heavens languish together with the e.
24: 5 The e lies polluted under its inhabitants;
24: 6 Therefore a curse devours the e,
24: 6 therefore the inhabitants of the e dwindled, F
24: 11 the gladness of the e is banished.
24: 13 For thus it shall be on the e and among the nations,
24: 16 From the ends of the e we hear songs of praise, D
24: 17 and the snare are upon you, O inhabitant of the e!
24: 18 and the foundations of the e tremble. G
24: 19 The e is utterly broken, the e is torn asunder, the e is violently shaken.
Isa 24: 20 The e staggers like a drunkard, it sways like a hut;
24: 21 and on e the kings of the earth.
24: 21 and on earth the kings of the e. E
25: 8 of his people he will take away from all the e, A
26: 9 For when your judgments are in the e,
26: 18 We have won no victories on e,
26: 19 and the e will give birth to those long dead.
26: 21 punish the inhabitants of the e for their iniquity; F
26: 21 the e will disclose the blood shed on it,
28: 2 with his hand he will hurl them down to the e.
29: 4 Then deep from the e you shall speak,
34: 1 Let the e hear, and all that fills it;
37: 16 you alone, of all the kingdoms of the e; J
37: 16 you have made heaven and e. B
37: 20 all the kingdoms of the e may know that you J
40: 12 enclosed the dust of the e in a measure, K
40: 21 not understood from the foundations of the e? G
40: 22 It is he who sits above the circle of the e,
40: 23 and makes the rulers of the e as nothing.
40: 24 scarcely has their stem taken root in the e,
40: 28 the Creator of the ends of the e. D
41: 5 the ends of the e tremble; D
41: 9 you whom I took from the ends of the e, D
42: 4 until he has established justice in the e;
42: 5 who spread out the e and what comes from it,
42: 10 his praise from the end of the e! I
43: 6 and my daughters from the end of the e— I
44: 23 shout, O depths of the e;
44: 24 who by myself spread out the e;
45: 8 let the e open, that salvation may spring up,
45: 12 I made the e, and created humankind upon it;
45: 18 who formed the e and made it (he established it;
45: 22 Turn to me and be saved, all the ends of the e! D
48: 13 My hand laid the foundation of the e, G
48: 20 proclaim it, send it forth to the end of the e; I
49: 6 that my salvation may reach to the end of the e." I
49: 13 Sing for joy, O heavens, and exult, O e;
51: 6 and look at the e beneath;
51: 6 the e will wear out like a garment,
51: 13 the heavens and laid the foundations of the e. G
51: 16 the heavens and laying the foundations of the e, G
52: 10 and all the ends of the e shall see the salvation D
54: 5 the God of the whole e he is called. C
54: 9 of Noah would never again go over the e,
55: 9 For as the heavens are higher than the e,
55: 10 do not return there until they have watered the e,
58: 14 I will make you ride upon the heights of the e;
60: 2 For darkness shall cover the e,
61: 11 For as the e brings forth its shoots,
62: 7 and makes it renowned throughout the e.
62: 11 The LORD has proclaimed to the end of the e: I
63: 6 and I poured out their lifeblood on the e."
65: 17 I am about to create new heavens and a new e; H
66: 1 Heaven is my throne and the e is my footstool;
66: 22 For as the new heavens and the new e, H
Jer 4: 23 I looked on the e, and lo, it was waste and void;
4: 28 Because of this the e shall mourn,
6: 19 O e; I am going to bring
6: 22 from the farthest parts of the e.
7: 33 and for the animals of the e;
9: 24 justice, and righteousness in the e,
10: 10 At his wrath the e quakes,
10: 11 not make the heavens and the e shall perish H
10: 11 the heavens and the earth shall perish from the e
10: 12 It is he who made the e by his power,
10: 13 he makes the mist rise from the ends of the e. D
15: 3 of the air and the wild animals of the e to devour
15: 4 a horror to all the kingdoms of the e because J
16: 4 of the air and for the wild animals of the e.
16: 19 the nations come from the ends of the e and say: D
19: 7 of the air and to the wild animals of the e.
23: 24 Do I not fill heaven and e? B
24: 9 an evil thing, to all the kingdoms of the e— J
25: 26 of the world that are on the face of the e.
25: 29 a sword against all the inhabitants of the e, F
25: 30 against all the inhabitants of the e. F
25: 31 The clamor will resound to the ends of the e, D
25: 32 from the farthest parts of the e!
25: 33 on that day shall extend from one end of the e to I
26: 6 a curse for all the nations of the e.
27: 5 and my outstretched arm have made the e,
27: 5 with the people and animals that are on the e,
28: 16 I am going to send you off the face of the e.
29: 18 a horror to all the kingdoms of the e, J
31: 8 and gather them from the farthest parts of the e,
31: 22 For the LORD has created a new thing on the e:
31: 37 the foundations of the e below can be explored, G
32: 17 the heavens and the e by your great power and H
33: 2 the e, the LORD who formed it to establish it—
33: 9 before all the nations of the e who shall hear of all
33: 25 and night and the ordinances of heaven and e, B
34: 1 and all the kingdoms of the e and all the peoples J
34: 17 a horror to all the kingdoms of the e. J
34: 20 the birds of the air and the wild animals of the e.
44: 8 and ridicule among all the nations of the e?
46: 8 It said, Let me rise, let me cover the e,
46: 12 and the e is full of your cry;
49: 21 At the sound of their fall the e shall tremble;
50: 23 hammer of the whole e is cut down and broken! C
50: 34 that he may give rest to the e,
50: 41 from the farthest parts of the e.
50: 46 of the capture of Babylon the e shall tremble,
51: 7 in the LORD's hand, making all the e drunken; A
51: 15 It is he who made the e by his power,
51: 16 he makes the mist rise from the ends of the e. D
51: 25 says the LORD, that destroys the whole e; C
51: 41 the pride of the whole e seized! C
Jer 51: 48 Then the heavens and the e, and all that is in H
51: 49 slain of all the e have fallen because of Babylon. A
La 2: 1 down from heaven to e the splendor of Israel; B
2: 15 the perfection of beauty, the joy of all the e?" A
4: 12 The kings of the e did not believe, E
Eze 1: 15 I saw a wheel on the e beside the living creatures,
1: 19 living creatures rose from the e, the wheels rose.
1: 21 and when they rose from the e,
7: 21 to the wicked of the e as plunder;
8: 3 the spirit lifted me up between e and heaven, M
10: 16 up their wings to rise up from the e,
10: 19 the e in my sight as they went out with the wheels
21: 32 your blood shall enter the e;
24: 7 not pour it out on the ground, to cover it with e.
27: 33 merchandise you enriched the kings of the e. E
28: 18 to ashes on the e in the sight of all who saw you.
29: 5 of the e and to the birds of the air I have given you
31: 12 the peoples of the e went away from its shade L
32: 4 wild animals of the whole e gorge themselves C
34: 6 my sheep were scattered over all the face of the e,
34: 27 and the e shall yield its increase.
35: 14 the whole e rejoices, I will make you desolate. C
38: 12 who live at the center of the e.
38: 16 like a cloud covering the e.
38: 20 and all human beings that are on the face of the e,
39: 18 and drink the blood of the princes of the e—
43: 2 and the e shone with his glory.
Da 2: 10 on e who can reveal what the king demands!
2: 35 a great mountain and filled the whole e. C
2: 39 which shall rule over the whole e. C
4: 1 nations, and languages that live throughout the e:
4: 10 there was a tree at the center of the e,
4: 11 and it was visible to the ends of the whole e. C
4: 15 with the animals of the field in the grass of the e.
4: 20 and was visible to the end of the whole e, C
4: 22 and your sovereignty to the ends of the e. D
4: 35 the inhabitants of the e are accounted as nothing, F
4: 35 the host of heaven and the inhabitants of the e. F
6: 27 he works signs and wonders in heaven and on e; B
7: 17 four kings shall arise out of the e.
7: 23 be a fourth kingdom on e that shall be different
7: 23 it shall devour the whole e, and trample it down, C
8: 5 across the face of the whole e without touching C
8: 10 It threw down to the e some of the host and some
12: 2 those who sleep in the dust of the e shall awake, K
Hos 2: 21 the heavens and they shall answer the e;
2: 22 the e shall answer the grain, the wine, and the oil,
6: 3 like the spring rains that water the e."
Joel 2: 10 The e quakes before them, the heavens tremble.
2: 30 I will show portents in the heavens and on the e, H
3: 16 and the heavens and the e shake. H
Am 2: 7 into the dust of the e, and push the afflicted out K
3: 2 of all the families of the e;
3: 5 Does a bird fall into a snare on the e,
4: 13 and treads on the heights of the e—
5: 8 and pours them out on the surface of the e,
8: 9 and darken the e in broad daylight.
9: 5 GOD of hosts, he who touches the e and it melts,
9: 6 and founds his vault upon the e;
9: 6 and pours them out upon the surface of the e—
9: 8 and I will destroy it from the face of the e—
Mic 1: 2 listen, O e, and all that is in it;
1: 3 down and tread upon the high places of the e.
4: 13 their wealth to the Lord of the whole e. C
5: 4 for now he shall be great to the ends of the e; D
6: 2 and you enduring foundations of the e; G
7: 13 the e will be desolate because of its inhabitants,
7: 17 like the crawling things of the e;
Na 1: 5 the e heaves before him, the world and all who
2: 13 I will cut off your prey from the e,
Hab 1: 6 through the breadth of the e to seize dwellings
1: 10 and heap up e to take it.
2: 8 of human bloodshed, and violence to the e,
2: 14 the e will be filled with the knowledge of the glory
2: 17 of human bloodshed and violence to the e,
2: 20 let all the e keep silence before him! A
3: 3 and the e was full of his praise.
3: 6 He stopped and shook the e;
3: 9 You split the e with rivers.
3: 12 In fury you trod the e,
Zep 1: 2 from the face of the e,
1: 3 I will cut off humanity from the face of the e,
1: 18 of his passion the whole e shall be consumed; C
1: 18 of all the inhabitants of the e. F
2: 11 he will shrivel all the gods of the e,
3: 8 fire of my passion all the e shall be consumed. A
3: 19 into praise and renown in all the e. A
3: 20 and praised among all the peoples of the e, L
Hag 1: 10 and the e has withheld its produce.
2: 6 I will shake the heavens and the e H
2: 21 I am about to shake the heavens and the e, H
Zec 1: 10 the LORD has sent to patrol the e."
1: 11 "We have patrolled the e, and lo,
1: 11 and lo, the whole e remains at peace." C
4: 10 which range through the whole e." C
4: 14 by the Lord of the whole e." C
5: 9 and they lifted up the basket between e and sky.
6: 5 before the LORD of all the e. A
6: 7 they were impatient to get off and patrol the e.
6: 7 And he said, "Go, patrol the e."
6: 7 So they patrolled the e.
9: 10 and from the River to the ends of the e. D
11: 6 on the inhabitants of the e, F
11: 6 and they shall devastate the e,
12: 1 who stretched out the heavens and founded the e
12: 3 the nations of the e shall come together against it.
14: 9 And the LORD will become king over all the e; A

Zec 14:17 of the families of the e do not go up to Jerusalem
Mt 5: 5 "Blessed are the meek, for they will inherit the e.
5:13 "You are the salt of the e;
5:18 truly I tell you, until heaven and e pass away, B
5:35 or by the e, for it is his footstool, or by Jerusalem,
6:10 Your will be done, on e as it is in heaven. M
6:19 "Do not store up for yourselves treasures on e,
9: 6 of Man has authority on e to forgive sins"—
10:34 not think that I have come to bring peace to the e;
11:25 "I thank you, Father, Lord of heaven and e, B
12:40 the Son of Man will be in the heart of the e.
12:42 she came from the ends of the e to listen D
16:19 whatever you bind on e will be bound in heaven,
16:19 whatever you loose on e will be loosed in heaven."
17:25 From whom do kings of the e take toll or tribute? E
18:18 whatever you bind on e will be bound in heaven,
18:18 whatever you loose on e will be loosed in heaven.
18:19 if two of you agree on e about anything you ask,
23: 9 And call no one your father on e,
23:35 the righteous blood shed on e,
24:30 and then all the tribes of the e will mourn,
24:35 Heaven and e will pass away, B
27:51 The e shook, and the rocks were split.
28:18 All authority in heaven and on e has been given B
Mk 2:10 of Man has authority on e to forgive sins"—
4:28 The e produces of itself, first the stalk,
4:31 is the smallest of all the seeds on e;
9: 3 such as no one on e could bleach them.
13:27 from the ends of the e to the ends of heaven. D
13:31 Heaven and e will pass away, B
Lk 2:14 and on e peace among those whom he favors!"
5:24 of Man has authority on e to forgive sins"—
10:21 "I thank you, Father, Lord of heaven and e, B
11:31 he came from the ends of the e to listen D
12:49 "I came to bring fire to the e,
12:51 that I have come to bring peace to the e?
12:56 You know how to interpret the appearance of e
16:17 But it is easier for heaven and e to pass away, B
18: 8 the Son of Man comes, will he find faith on e?"
21:23 For there will be great distress on the e and wrath
21:25 and on the e distress among nations confused by
21:33 Heaven and e will pass away, B
21:35 upon all who live on the face of the whole e. C
Jn 3:31 the one who is of the e belongs to the earth
3:31 the one who is of the earth belongs to the e
12:24 unless a grain of wheat falls into the e and dies,
12:32 And I, when I am lifted up from the e,
17: 4 on e by finishing the work that you gave me to do.
Ac 1: 8 all Judea and Samaria, and to the ends of the e." D
2:19 in the heaven above and signs on the e below,
3:25 in your descendants all the families of the e shall
4:24 Sovereign Lord, who made the heaven and the e, B
4:26 The kings of the e took their stand, E
7:49 and the e is my footstool.
8:33 For his life is taken away from the e."
13:47 you may bring salvation to the ends of the e.' " D
14:15 who made the heaven and the e and the sea B
17:24 he who is Lord of heaven and e, B
17:26 to inhabit the whole e, and he allotted the times C
22:22 "Away with such a fellow from the e!
Ro 9:17 that my name may be proclaimed in all the e." A
9:28 the Lord will execute his sentence on the e quickly
10:18 for "Their voice has gone out to all the e, A
1Co 8: 5 there may be so-called gods in heaven or on e— B
10:26 for "the e and its fullness are the Lord's."
15:47 The first man was from the e, a man of dust;
Eph 1:10 things in heaven and things on e.
3:15 in heaven and on e takes its name. B
4: 9 also descended into the lower parts of the e?
6: 3 be well with you and you may live long on the e."
Php 2:10 in heaven and on e and under the earth, B
2:10 in heaven and on earth and under the e,
Col 1:16 all things in heaven and on e were created, B
1:20 whether on e or in heaven, M
3: 2 not on things that are on e,
Heb 1:10 And, "In the beginning, Lord, you founded the e,
8: 4 Now if he were on e,
11:13 that they were strangers and foreigners on the e,
12:25 when they refused the one who warned them on e,
12:26 At that time his voice shook the e;
12:26 shake not only the e but also the heaven." M
Jas 5: 5 You have lived on the e in luxury and in pleasure;
5: 7 The farmer waits for the precious crop from the e,
5:12 either by heaven or by e or by any other oath, B
5:17 three years and six months it did not rain on the e.
5:18 the heaven gave rain and the e yielded its harvest.
2Pe 3: 5 and an e was formed out of water and by means
3: 7 the present heavens and e have been reserved H
3:10 and the e and everything that is done on it will
3:13 we wait for new heavens and a new e, H
Rev 1: 5 and the ruler of the kings of the e. E
1: 7 and on his account all the tribes of the e will wail.
3:10 the whole world to test the inhabitants of the e. F
5: 3 And no one in heaven or on e or under B
5: 3 on earth or under the e was able to open the scroll
5: 6 the seven spirits of God sent out into all the e. A
5:10 and they will reign on e."
5:13 Then I heard every creature in heaven and on e B
5:13 and under the e and in the sea, and all that is in
6: 4 its rider was permitted to take peace from the e,
6: 8 they were given authority over a fourth of the e,
6: 8 and pestilence, and by the wild animals of the e.
6:10 avenge our blood on the inhabitants of the e?" F
6:13 to the e as the fig tree drops its winter fruit
6:15 kings of the e and the magnates and the generals E
7: 1 at the four corners of the e,
7: 1 the e so that no wind could blow on e or sea or
Rev 7: 2 who had been given power to damage e and sea,
7: 3 "Do not damage the e or the sea or the trees,
8: 5 with fire from the altar and threw it on the e;
8: 7 mixed with blood, and they were hurled to the e;
8: 7 and a third of the e was burned up,
8:13 "Woe, woe, woe to the inhabitants of the e, F
9: 1 and I saw a star that had fallen from heaven to e, B
9: 3 Then from the smoke came locusts on the e,
9: 3 like the authority of scorpions of the e.
9: 4 the grass of the e or any green growth or any tree,
10: 6 the e and what is in it, and the sea and what is in it:
11: 4 that stand before the Lord of the e.
11: 6 and to strike the e with every kind of plague,
11:10 and the inhabitants of the e will gloat over them F
11:10 a torment to the inhabitants of the e. F
11:18 and for destroying those who destroy the e."
12: 4 of the stars of heaven and threw them to the e.
12: 9 he was thrown down to the e,
12:12 But woe to the e and the sea,
12:13 that he had been thrown down to the e,
12:16 But the e came to the help of the woman;
13: 3 In amazement the whole e followed the beast. C
13: 8 and all the inhabitants of the e will worship it, F
13:11 Then I saw another beast that rose out of the e;
13:12 the e and its inhabitants worship the first beast,
13:13 making fire come down from heaven to e in B
13:14 it deceives the inhabitants of e,
14: 3 who have been redeemed from the e.
14: 6 to proclaim to those who live on the e—
14: 7 and worship him who made heaven and e, B
14:15 because the harvest of the e is fully ripe."
14:16 on the cloud swung his sickle over the e,
14:16 over the earth, and the e was reaped.
14:18 and gather the clusters of the vine of the e,
14:19 the angel swung his sickle over the e and gathered
14:19 over the earth and gathered the vintage of the e,
16: 1 and pour out on the e the seven bowls of the wrath
16: 2 the first angel went and poured his bowl on the e,
16:18 as had not occurred since people were upon the e,
17: 2 the kings of the e have committed fornication, E
17: 2 the inhabitants of the e have become drunk." F
17: 8 And the inhabitants of the e, F
17:18 the great city that rules over the kings of the e." E
18: 1 and the e was made bright with his splendor.
18: 3 the kings of the e have committed fornication E
18: 3 and the merchants of the e have grown rich from
18: 9 the kings of the e, who committed fornication E
18:11 the merchants of the e weep and mourn for her,
18:23 for your merchants were the magnates of the e,
18:24 and of all who have been slaughtered on e."
19: 2 he has judged the great whore who corrupted the e
19:19 and the kings of the e with their armies gathered E
20: 8 the four corners of the e, Gog and Magog, in order
20: 9 of the e and surrounded the camp of the saints and
20:11 the e and the heaven fled from his presence, M
21: 1 Then I saw a new heaven and a new e; B
21: 1 the first heaven and the first e had passed away, B
21:24 the kings of the e will bring their glory into it. E
Tob 3: 6 so that I may be released from the face of the e
3:13 the e and not listen to such reproaches any more.
10:13 praising the Lord of heaven and e, King over all, B
13: 2 down to Hades in the lowest regions of the e,
13:11 A bright light will shine to all the ends of the e; D
13:11 of the remotest parts of the e to your holy name,
14: 7 and injustice will vanish from all the e. A
14:10 while still alive, brought down into the e?
Jdt 2: 5 the lord of the whole e: C
2: 7 Tell them to prepare e and water,
2: 7 and will cover the whole face of the e with the feet
2: 9 to the ends of the whole e. C
2:19 of the e to the west with their chariots and cavalry
2:20 like the dust of the e— K
6: 2 and destroy them from the face of the e.
6: 4 says King Nebuchadnezzar, lord of the whole e. C
7:28 witness against you heaven and e and our God, B
9:12 Lord of heaven and e, Creator of the waters, B
11: 1 to serve Nebuchadnezzar, king of all the e. A
11: 7 the life of Nebuchadnezzar, king of the whole e, C
11:21 one end of the e to the other looks so beautiful I
13:18 the Most High God above all other women on e;
13:18 who created the heavens and the e, H
14: 2 As soon as day breaks and the sun rises on the e,
AdE 11: 5 thunders and earthquake, tumult on the e!
11: 8 affliction and great tumult on the e!
13:10 made heaven and e and every wonderful thing B
Wis 1: 1 Love righteousness, you rulers of the e,
1:14 and the dominion of Hades is not on e.
5:23 Lawlessness will lay waste the whole e, C
6: 1 learn, O judges of the ends of the e. D
7: 1 a descendant of the first-formed child of e;
7: 3 and fell upon the kindred e;
8: 1 She reaches mightily from one end of the e to I
9:16 We can hardly guess at what is on e,
9:18 And thus the paths of those on e were set right,
10: 4 When the e was flooded because of him,
15: 7 the soft e and laboriously molds each vessel
15: 8 of e a short time before and after a little while go
15: 8 while go to the e from which all mortals are taken,
18:16 and touched heaven while standing on the e.
19:10 of producing animals the e brought forth gnats,
Sir 1: 3 The height of heaven, the breadth of the e,
10: 4 government of the e is in the hand of the Lord,
10:16 and destroys them to the foundations of the e. G
10:17 and erases the memory of them from the e.
16:18 the abyss and the e, tremble at his visitation!
16:19 the foundations of the e quiver and quake G
16:29 Then the Lord looked upon the e,
Sir 17: 1 The Lord created human beings out of e,
17: 2 granted them authority over everything on the e.
24: 3 and covered the e like a mist.
24: 6 Over waves of the sea, over all the e, A
36:22 and all who are on the e will know that you are
38: 4 The Lord created medicines out of the e,
38: 8 and from him health spreads over all the e. A
39:31 always ready for his service on e;
40:11 All that is of e returns to e,
41:10 Whatever comes from e returns to e;
43:17 The voice of his thunder rebukes the e;
43:19 He pours frost over the e like salt,
44:17 a remnant was left on the e when the flood came.
44:21 as numerous as the dust of the e, K
44:21 and from the Euphrates to the ends of the e. D
47:15 Your influence spread throughout the e,
48:15 and were scattered over all the e. A
49:14 Few have ever been created on e like Enoch,
49:14 for he was taken up from the e.
51: 9 And I sent up my prayer from the e,
Bar 1:11 their days on e may be like the days of heaven.
2:15 all the e may know that you are the Lord A
3:16 and those who lorded it over the animals on e;
3:20 and have lived upon the e;
3:23 who seek for understanding on the e,
3:32 The one who prepared the e for all time filled it
3:37 Afterward she appeared on e and lived
LtJ 6:20 when crawling creatures from the e devour them
6:55 they are like crows between heaven and e. B
Aza 1:52 "Let the e bless the Lord;
1:60 "Bless the Lord, all people on e;
Bel 1: 5 who created heaven and e and has dominion B
1Mc 1: 2 and put to death the kings of the e. E
1: 3 He advanced to the ends of the e, D
1: 3 When the e became quiet before him,
1: 9 and they caused many evils on the e.
2:37 heaven and e testify for us B
2:40 they will quickly destroy us from the e."
3: 9 He was renowned to the ends of the e; D
8: 4 from the ends of the e, until they crushed them D
9:13 The e was shaken by the noise of the armies,
14:10 until his renown spread to the ends of the e. D
15: 9 your glory will become manifest in all the e." A
2Mc 7:28 look at the heaven and the e and see everything B
9: 8 was brought down to e and carried in a litter,
13: 7 without even burial in the e.
15: 5 "But I am a sovereign also, on e,
1Es 4:34 The e is vast, and heaven is high, M
4:36 whole e calls upon truth, and heaven blesses her. C
6:13 of the Lord who created the heaven and the e. B
8:77 over to the kings of the e, E
Man 1: 2 you who made heaven and e with all their order; B
1:13 do not condemn me to the depths of the e.
3Mc 1:29 also the walls and the whole e around echoed, C
2: 9 the boundless and immeasurable e, chose this city
2:14 to violate the holy place on e dedicated
2Es 2: 7 let their names be blotted out from the e,
2:14 Call, O call heaven and e to witness: B
2:31 I will bring them out of the hiding places of the e,
3: 4 not speak at the beginning when you planted the e
3: 6 your right hand had planted before the e appeared.
3:12 "When those who lived on e began to multiply,
3:18 You bent down the heavens and shook the e,
3:35 the inhabitants of the e not sinned in your sight? F
4:21 the e can understand only what is on the earth,
4:21 the earth can understand only what is on the e,
4:39 on account of the sins of those who inhabit the e."
5: 1 when those who inhabit the e shall be seized
5: 6 the e do not expect,
5:10 and unrestraint shall increase on e.
5:23 from every forest of the e and
5:48 of the e to those who from time to time are sown
6: 1 "At the beginning of the circle of the e,
6:15 and the foundations of the e will understand G
6:18 when I draw near to visit the inhabitants of the e, F
6:24 the e and those who inhabit it shall be terrified,
6:38 'Let heaven and e be made,' B
6:42 to be gathered together in a seventh part of the e;
6:53 the e to bring forth before you cattle, wild animals,
7:*32* The e shall give up those who are asleep in it,
7:*54* "Not only that, but ask the e and she will tell you;
7:*62* "O e, what have you brought forth,
7:*72* therefore, those who live on e shall be tormented,
7:*116* [46] it would have been better if the e had
7:*127* [57] contest that all who are born on e shall wage:
8: 2 Just as, when you ask the e,
8:17 for I see the failings of us who inhabit the e;
9:20 I saw that my e was in peril because of the devices
10: 9 the e, and she will tell you that it is she who ought
10:13 it is with the e according to the way of the e—
10:14 the e also has from the beginning given her fruit,
10:26 so that the e shook at the sound.
10:59 the Most High will do to those who inhabit the e in
11: 2 I saw it spread its wings over the whole e, C
11: 5 it reigned over the e and over those who inhabit it.
11: 6 not a single creature that was on the e.
11:12 and it reigned over all the e. A
11:16 you who have ruled the e all this time;
11:32 this head gained control of the whole e, C
11:34 in like manner ruled over the e and its inhabitants.
11:40 and over all the e with grievous oppression; A
11:40 for so long you have lived on the e with deceit.
11:41 You have judged the e, but not with truth,
11:46 so that the whole e, freed from your violence, C
12: 3 and the e was exceedingly terrified.
12:13 days are coming when a kingdom shall rise on e,
12:23 many things in it, and shall rule the e

2Es 13:29 the Most High will deliver those who are on the **e.**
13:30 of mind shall come over those who inhabit the **e.**
13:52 on **e** can see my Son or those who are with him,
15:20 how I am calling together all the kings of the **e** E
15:22 from those who shed innocent blood on **e.**
15:23 consumed the foundations of the **e** and G
15:27 Already calamities have come upon the whole **e,** C
15:29 their hissing shall spread over the **e,**
15:35 a heavy tempest on the **e,** and their own tempest;
15:37 there shall be fear and great trembling on the **e;**
15:40 rise and destroy all the **e** and its inhabitants, A
16:12 The **e** and its foundations quake,
16:14 and shall not return until they come over the **e.**
16:15 until it consumes the foundations of the **e.** G
16:16 calamities that are sent upon the **e** shall not return.
16:21 be so cheap upon **e** that people will imagine
16:21 and then calamities shall spring up on the **e**—
16:22 of those who live on the **e** shall perish by famine;
16:23 for the **e** shall be left desolate,
16:24 No one shall be left to cultivate the **e** or to sow it.
16:32 The **e** shall be left desolate,
16:39 the calamities will not delay in coming upon the **e,**
16:40 of the calamities be like strangers on the **e.**
16:50 the one who searches out every sin on **e.**
16:52 from the **e,** and righteousness will reign
16:55 He said, "Let the **e** be made," and it was made,
16:58 by his word he has suspended the **e** over the water.
16:60 so as to send rivers from the heights to water the **e.**
4Mc 18:5 The tyrant Antiochus was both punished on **e**

EARTH'S‡ (4) [EARTH]

Ps 65:8 Those who live at **e** farthest bounds are awed
Rev 17:5 mother of whores and of **e** abominations."
2Es 6:26 the **e** inhabitants shall be changed and converted to
10:12 if you say to me, 'My lamentation is not like the **e,**

EARTHEN (10) [EARTH]

Lev 6:28 An **e** vessel in which it was boiled shall be broken;
11:33 And if any of them falls into any **e** vessel,
14:5 be slaughtered over fresh water in an **e** vessel.
14:50 of the birds over fresh water in an **e** vessel,
15:12 Any **e** vessel that the one with
Nu 5:17 the priest shall take holy water in an **e** vessel,
2Sa 17:28 and **e** vessels, wheat, barley, meal, parched grain,
Pr 26:23 Like the glaze covering an **e** vessel are smooth lips
Isa 45:9 to you who strive with your Maker, **e** vessels with
La 4:2 how they are reckoned as **e** pots,

EARTHENWARE (3) [EARTH]

Jer 19:1 Thus said the LORD: Go and buy a potter's **e** jug.
32:14 and put them in an **e** jar,
2Es 8:2 a large amount of clay from which **e** is made,

EARTHLY (14) [EARTH]

Ge 47:9 "The years of my **e** sojourn are one hundred thirty;
Jn 3:12 If I have told you about **e** things and you do
3:31 to the earth and speaks about **e** things.
1Co 15:40 There are both heavenly bodies and **e** bodies,
15:40 and that of the **e** is another.
2Co 1:12 not by **e** wisdom but by the grace of God—
5:1 we know that if the **e** tent we live in is destroyed,
Eph 6:5 obey your **e** masters with fear and trembling,
Php 3:19 their minds are set on **e** things.
Col 3:5 Put to death, therefore, whatever in you is **e:**
3:22 Slaves, obey your **e** masters in everything,
Heb 9:1 for worship and an **e** sanctuary.
Jas 3:15 but is **e,** unspiritual, devilish.
1Pe 4:2 the rest of your **e** life no longer by human desires

EARTHQUAKE (20) [EARTH, QUAKE]

1Ki 19:11 after the wind an **e,** but the LORD was not in the **e;**
19:12 after the **e** a fire, but the LORD was not in the fire;
Isa 29:6 of hosts with thunder and **e** and great noise,
Am 1:1 of Joash of Israel, two years before the **e.**
Zec 14:5 as you fled from the **e** in the days of King Uzziah
Mt 27:54 saw the **e** and what took place,
28:2 And suddenly there was a great **e;**
Ac 16:26 Suddenly there was an **e,** so violent that
Rev 6:12 I looked, and there came a great **e;**
8:5 rumblings, flashes of lightning, and an **e.**
11:13 At that moment there was a great **e,**
11:13 seven thousand people were killed in the **e,**
11:19 rumblings, peals of thunder, an **e,** and heavy hail.
16:18 rumblings, peals of thunder, and a violent **e,**
16:18 upon the earth, so violent was that **e.**
AdE 11:5 thunders and **e,** tumult on the earth!
Sir 22:16 into a building is not loosened by an **e;**
2Es 3:19 through the four gates of fire and **e** and wind
4Mc 17:3 you held firm and unswerving against the **e** of

EARTHQUAKES‡ (4) [EARTH, QUAKE]

Mt 24:7 and there will be famines and **e** in various places:
Mk 13:8 there will be **e** in various places;
Lk 21:11 there will be great **e,** and in various places famines
2Es 9:3 So when there shall appear in the world **e,**

EARTHWORKS (1) [EARTH]

2Mc 12:13 a certain town that was strongly fortified with **e**

EARTHY (2) [EARTH]

Wis 9:15 and this **e** tent burdens the thoughtful mind.
15:13 from **e** matter fragile vessels and carved images.

EASE‡ (21) [EASIER, EASILY, EASY]

Dt 28:65 Among those nations you shall find no **e,**
Job 3:18 There the prisoners are at **e** together;
3:26 I am not at **e,** nor am I quiet;
7:13 my couch will **e** my complaint,'
12:5 Those at **e** have contempt for misfortune,
16:12 I was at **e,** and he broke me in two;
21:23 being wholly at **e** and secure,
Ps 73:12 always at **e,** they increase in riches.
123:4 of the scorn of those who are at **e,**
Pr 1:33 to me will be secure and will live at **e,**
Isa 32:9 Rise up, you women who are at **e,** hear my voice;
32:11 Tremble, you women who are at **e,** shudder,
Jer 30:10 Jacob shall return and have quiet and **e,**
46:27 Jacob shall return and have quiet and **e,**
48:11 Moab has been at **e** from his youth,
49:31 Rise up, advance against a nation at **e,**
Eze 16:49 excess of food, and prosperous **e,**
Da 4:4 at **e** in my home and prospering in my palace.
Am 6:1 Alas for those who are at **e** in Zion,
Zec 1:15 with the nations that are at **e;**
Lk 11:46 and you yourselves do not lift a finger to **e** them.

EASIER‡ (11) [EASE]

Ex 18:22 So it will be **e** for you,
Mt 9:5 For which is **e,** to say, 'Your sins are forgiven,'
19:24 it is **e** for a camel to go through the eye of
Mk 2:9 Which is **e,** to say to the paralytic,
10:25 It is **e** for a camel to go through the eye of
Lk 5:23 Which is **e,** to say, 'Your sins are forgiven you,'
16:17 But it is **e** for heaven and earth to pass away,
18:25 it is **e** for a camel to go through the eye of
Sir 22:15 a piece of iron are **e** to bear than a stupid person.
2Es 7:18 difficult circumstances while hoping for **e** ones;
7:18 and will never see the **e** ones."

EASILY‡ (3) [EASE]

Ge 26:10 of the people might **e** have lain with your wife,
Wis 6:12 and she is **e** discerned by those who love her,
3Mc 5:13 and again implored him who is **e** reconciled

EAST‡ (195) [EASTERN, EASTWARD, NORTHEASTER, SOUTHEAST]

A. EAST SIDE (31)
B. EAST WIND (19)
C. PEOPLE OF THE EAST (11)

Ge 2:8 LORD God planted a garden in Eden, in the **e;**
2:14 the third river is Tigris, which flows **e** of Assyria.
3:24 and at the **e** of the garden of Eden he placed
4:16 and settled in the land of Nod, **e** of Eden.
10:30 the hill country of the **e.**
11:2 And as they migrated from the **e,**
12:8 the **e** of Bethel, and pitched his tent, with Bethel
12:8 with Bethel on the west and Ai on the **e;**
23:17 which was to the **e** of Mamre,
25:6 eastward to the **e** country.
25:9 in the field of Ephron son of Zohar the Hittite, **e**
28:14 to the west and to the **e** and to the north and to
29:1 and came to the land of the people of the **e.** C
41:6 Then seven ears, thin and blighted by the **e** wind, B
41:23 and blighted by the **e** wind, sprouting after them; B
41:27 are the seven empty ears blighted by the **e** wind. B
Ex 10:13 the LORD brought an **e** wind upon the land all B
10:13 the **e** wind had brought the locusts. B
14:21 by a strong **e** wind all night, and turned the sea B
27:13 the court on the front to the **e** shall be fifty cubits.
38:13 And for the front to the **e,** fifty cubits.
Lev 1:16 with its contents and throw it at the **e** side of A
Nu 2:3 to camp on the **e** side toward the sunrise shall be A
3:38 to camp in front of the tabernacle on the **e**—
3:38 in front of the tent of meeting toward the **e**—
10:5 the camps on the **e** side shall set out; A
32:19 to us on this side of the Jordan to the **e.**"
34:3 from the end of the Dead Sea on the **e;**
34:11 from Shepham to Riblah on the **e** side of Ain; A
35:5 for the **e** side two thousand cubits, A
Dt 3:17 with the lower slopes of Pisgah on the **e.**
3:27 to the north, to the south, and to the **e.**
4:41 on the **e** side of the Jordan three cities A
4:49 the Arabah on the **e** side of the Jordan as far as A
Jos 1:15 the LORD gave you beyond the Jordan to the **e.**"
4:19 they camped in Gilgal on the **e** border of Jericho.
7:2 which is near Beth-aven, **e** of Bethel,
11:3 to the Canaanites in the **e** and the west,
12:1 the **e,** from the Wadi Arnon to Mount Hermon,
13:3 which is **e** of Egypt, northward to the boundary
13:5 and all Lebanon, toward the **e,**
13:25 to Aroer, which is **e** of Rabbah,
13:32 beyond the Jordan **e** of Jericho.
15:5 And the **e** boundary is the Dead Sea,
16:1 **e** of the waters of Jericho, into the wilderness,
16:5 of their inheritance on the **e** was Ataroth-addar
16:6 then on the **e** the boundary makes a turn
16:6 and passes along beyond it on the **e** to Janoah,
17:7 to Michmethath, which is **e** of Shechem;
17:10 the north Asher is reached, and on the **e** Issachar.
19:11 then the wadi that is **e** of Jokneam;
19:13 along on the **e** toward the sunrise to Gath-hepher,
19:34 and Judah on the **e** at the Jordan.
20:8 And beyond the Jordan **e** of Jericho,
Jdg 6:3 the people of the **e** would come up against them. C
6:33 and the people of the **e** came together, C
7:12 the Amalekites and all the people of the **e** lay C
8:10 of all the army of the people of the **e;** C
8:11 up by the caravan route **e** of Nobah and Jogbehah,
11:18 arrived on the **e** side of the land of Moab, A
20:43 from Nohah and trod them down as far as a place **e**
21:19 on the **e** of the highway that goes up from Bethel
1Sa 13:5 and encamped at Michmash, to the **e** of Beth-aven.
15:7 from Havilah as far as Shur, which is **e** of Egypt.
1Ki 4:30 the wisdom of all the people of the **e,** C
7:25 and three facing **e;** the sea was set on them.
11:7 on the mountain **e** of Jerusalem.
17:3 which is **e** of the Jordan.
17:5 he went and lived by the Wadi Cherith, which is **e**
2Ki 23:13 The king defiled the high places that were **e**
1Ch 4:39 to the **e** side of the valley, A
5:9 the **e** as far as the beginning of the desert this side
5:10 in their tents throughout all the region **e** of Gilead.
6:78 on the **e** side of the Jordan, A
9:18 in the king's gate on the **e** side. A
9:24 The gatekeepers were on the four sides, **e,** west,
12:15 to the **e** and to the west.
26:14 The lot for the **e** fell to Shelemiah.
26:17 On the **e** there were six Levites each day,
2Ch 4:4 and three facing **e;** the sea was set on them.
5:12 with cymbals, harps, and lyres, stood **e** of the altar
29:4 and assembled them in the square on the **e.**
31:14 Kore son of Imnah the Levite, keeper of the **e** gate,
Ne 3:26 up to a point opposite the Water Gate on the **e** and
3:29 the keeper of the **E** Gate, made repairs.
12:37 to the Water Gate on the **e.**
Job 1:3 man was the greatest of all the people of the **e.** C
15:2 and fill themselves with the **e** wind? B
18:20 and horror seizes those of the **e.**
27:21 The **e** wind lifts them up and they are gone; B
38:24 or where the **e** wind is scattered upon the earth? B
Ps 48:7 as when an **e** wind shatters the ships of Tarshish. B
75:6 For not from the **e** or from the west and not from
78:26 He caused the **e** wind to blow in the heavens, B
103:12 as far as the **e** is from the west,
107:3 from the **e** and from the west,
Isa 2:6 from the **e** and of soothsayers like the Philistines,
9:12 Arameans on the **e** and the Philistines on the west,
11:14 together they shall plunder the people of the **e.** C
24:15 Therefore in the **e** give glory to the LORD;
27:8 in the day of the **e** wind. B
41:2 Who has roused a victor from the **e,**
43:5 I will bring your offspring from the **e,**
46:11 calling a bird of prey from the **e,**
59:19 and those in the **e,** his glory;
Jer 18:17 Like the wind from the **e,**
31:40 to the corner of the Horse Gate toward the **e,**
49:28 Destroy the people of the **e!** C
Eze 8:16 and their faces toward the **e,**
8:16 prostrating themselves to the sun toward the **e.**
10:19 They stopped at the entrance of the **e** gate of
11:1 the **e** gate of the house of the house of the LORD, which faces **e.**
11:23 and stopped on the mountain **e** of the city.
17:10 When the **e** wind strikes it, B
19:12 the **e** wind dried it up; its fruit was stripped off, B
25:4 over to the people of the **e** for a possession. C
25:10 along with Ammon to the people of the **e** as C
27:26 **e** wind has wrecked you in the heart of the seas. B
39:11 the Valley of the Travelers **e** of the sea;
40:6 Then he went into the gateway facing **e,**
40:10 on either side of the **e** gate;
40:22 as those of the gate that faced toward the **e.**
40:23 Opposite the gate on the north, as on the **e,**
40:32 he brought me to the inner court on the **e** side, A
40:44 the other at the side of the **e** gate facing north.
41:14 the width of the **e** front of the temple and the yard,
42:9 that one entered from the **e** in order to enter them
42:12 from the **e,** along the matching wall.
42:15 he led me out by the gate that faces **e,**
42:16 He measured the **e** side with the measuring reed, A
43:1 Then he brought me to the gate, the gate facing **e.**
43:2 glory of the God of Israel was coming from the **e;**
43:4 the temple by the gate facing **e,**
43:17 Its steps shall face **e.**
44:1 which faces **e;** and it was shut.
45:7 on the west and on the **e,**
46:1 the inner court that faces **e** shall remain closed on
46:12 the gate facing **e** shall be opened for him;
47:1 the temple toward the **e** (for the temple faced east);
47:1 toward the east (for the temple faced **e);**
47:2 to the outer gate that faces toward the **e;**
47:18 On the **e** side, between Hauran and Damascus; A
47:18 This shall be the **e** side. A
48:1 and extending from the **e** side to the west, Dan, A
48:2 from the **e** side to the west, Asher, one portion. A
48:3 the **e** side to the west, Naphtali, one portion. A
48:4 the **e** side to the west, Manasseh, one portion. A
48:5 the **e** side to the west, Ephraim, one portion. A
48:6 from the **e** side to the west, Reuben, one portion. A
48:7 from the **e** side to the west, Judah, one portion. A
48:8 from the **e** side to the west, A
48:8 from the **e** side to the west, A
48:16 the **e** side four thousand five hundred, A
48:17 on the **e** two hundred fifty,
48:18 be ten thousand cubits to the **e,**
48:21 of the holy portion to the **e** border,
48:23 the **e** side to the west, Benjamin, one portion. A
48:24 the **e** side to the west, Simeon, one portion. A
48:25 the **e** side to the west, Issachar, one portion. A
48:26 the **e** side to the west, Zebulun, one portion. A
48:27 the **e** side to the west, Gad, one portion. A
48:32 On the **e** side, which is to A
Da 8:9 toward the **e,** and toward the beautiful land.

Da 11:44 reports from the e and the north shall alarm him,
Hos 12: 1 and pursues the e wind all day long; B
13:15 the e wind shall come, a blast from the LORD, B
Am 8:12 from sea to sea, and from north to e;
Jnh 4: 5 Then Jonah went out of the city and sat down e of
4: 8 the sun rose, God prepared a sultry e wind, B
Zec 8: 7 I will save my people from the e country and from
14: 4 which lies before Jerusalem on the e;
14: 4 the Mount of Olives shall be split in two from e
Mt 2: 1 wise men from the E came to Jerusalem,
8:11 many will come from e and west and will eat
24:27 For as the lightning comes from the e and flashes
Mk 16: S ⟦through them, from e to west, the sacred⟧
Lk 13:29 Then people will come from e and west,
Rev 16:12 to prepare the way for the kings from the e.
21:13 on the e three gates, on the north three gates,
Jdt 7:18 of their men toward the south and the e,
Bar 4:36 Look toward the e, O Jerusalem,
4:37 they are coming, gathered from e and west,
5: 5 look toward the e, and see your children gathered
5: 5 and see your children gathered from west and e at
1Mc 12:37 part of the wall on the valley to the e had fallen,
1Es 5:47 in the square before the first gate toward the e.
9:38 in the open square before the e gate of the temple;
2Es 1:11 scattered in the e the peoples of two provinces,
1:38 with pride and see the people coming from the e;
15:20 from the e and from Lebanon;
15:28 What a terrifying sight, appearing from the e!
15:34 See the clouds from the e,
15:39 the winds from the e shall prevail over the cloud
15:39 that was to cause destruction by the e wind shall B

EASTER (KJV) See PASSOVER

EASTERN (11) [EAST]

Nu 23: 7 the king of Moab from the e mountains:
34:10 You shall mark out your e boundary
34:11 and reach the e slope of the sea of Chinnereth;
Dt 4:47 the two kings of the Amorites on the e side of
Jos 18:20 The Jordan forms its boundary on the e side.
Eze 45: 7 and extending from the western to the e boundary
47: 8 "This water flows toward the e region and goes
47:18 to the e sea and as far as Tamar.
48:10 ten thousand in width on the e side,
Joel 2:20 into the e sea, and its rear into the western sea;
Zec 14: 8 to the e sea and half of them to the western sea;

EASTWARD‡ (17) [EAST]

Ge 13:11 the plain of the Jordan, and Lot journeyed e;
13:14 northward and southward and e and westward;
25: 6 and he sent them away from his son Isaac, e to
Nu 34:15 beyond the Jordan at Jericho e,
Jos 11: 8 and e as far as the valley of Mizpeh.
12: 1 to Mount Hermon, with all the Arabah e:
12: 3 and the Arabah to the Sea of Chinneroth e, and in
13: 8 which Moses gave them, beyond the Jordan e,
13:27 as far as the lower end of the Sea of Chinnereth, e
18: 7 beyond the Jordan e, which Moses the servant of
19:12 from Sarid it goes in the other direction e toward
19:27 then it turns e, goes to Beth-dagon,
1Ki 17: 3 "Go from here and turn e,
2Ki 10:33 the Jordan e, all the land of Gilead, the Gadites,
13:17 he said, "Open the window e"; and he opened it.
1Ch 7:28 and e Naaran, and westward Gezer and its towns,
Eze 47: 3 Going on e with a cord in his hand,

EASY (13) [EASE]

Dt 1:41 and thought it e to go up into the hill country.
31:17 from them; they will become e prey,
Pr 14: 6 but knowledge is e for one who understands.
Mt 7:13 for the gate is wide and the road is e that leads
11:30 For my yoke is e, and my burden is light."
Jdt 4: 7 and it would be e to stop any who tried to enter,
7:10 for it is not e to reach the tops of their mountains.
Wis 13:11 A skilled woodcutter may saw down a tree e
Sir 11:21 for it is e in the sight of the Lord to make
11:26 For it is e for the Lord on the day of death
1Mc 3:18 "It is e for many to be hemmed in by few,
2Mc 2:25 to make it e for those who are inclined
2:27 just as it is not e for one who prepares a banquet

EAT‡ (591) [ATE, EATEN, EATER, EATERS, EATING, EATS, MOTH-EATEN, OVEREATING]

A. SHALL EAT (107)
B. NOT EAT (70)
C. MAY EAT (60)

Ge 2:16 "You may freely e of every tree of the garden;
2:17 the knowledge of good and evil you shall not e, B
2:17 for in the day that you e of it you shall die."
3: 1 'You shall not e from any tree in the garden'?" B
3: 2 "We may e of the fruit of the trees in the garden; C
3: 3 not e of the fruit of the tree that is in the middle B
3: 5 for God knows that when you e of it your eyes
3:11 the tree of which I commanded you not to e?"
3:14 and dust you shall e all the days of your life. A
3:17 not e of it,' cursed is the ground because of you; B
3:17 in toil you shall e of it all the days of your life; A
3:18 and you shall e the plants of the field. A
3:19 of your face you shall e bread until you return to A
3:22 and e, and live forever"—
9: 4 Only, you shall not e flesh with its life, that is, B
24:33 Then food was set before him to e;
Ge 24:33 he said, "I will not e until I have told my errand." B
25:30 "Let me e some of that red stuff,
27: 4 such as I like, and bring it to me to e,
27: 7 and prepare for me savory food to e,
27:10 and you shall take it to your father to e,
27:19 now sit up and e of my game,
27:25 that I may e of my son's game and bless you." C
27:31 "Let my father sit up and e of his son's game,
28:20 and will give me bread to e and clothing to wear,
31:54 on the height and called his kinsfolk to e bread;
32:32 this day the Israelites do not e the thigh muscle B
37:25 Then they sat down to e;
40:19 and the birds will e the flesh from you."
43:32 the Egyptians could not e with the Hebrews, B
Ex 10:12 the locusts may come upon it and e every plant in
12: 4 in proportion to the number of people who e of it.
12: 7 and the lintel of the houses in which they e it.
12: 8 They shall e the lamb that same night; A
12: 8 they shall e it roasted over the fire A
12: 9 Do not e any of it raw or boiled in water, B
12:11 This is how you shall e it: A
12:11 and you shall e it hurriedly. A
12:15 Seven days you shall e unleavened bread; A
12:16 only what everyone must e,
12:18 you shall e unleavened bread. A
12:20 You shall e nothing leavened; A
12:20 your settlements you shall e unleavened bread. A
12:43 no foreigner shall e of it, A
12:44 any slave who has been purchased may e of it C
12:45 no bound or hired servant may e of it. C
12:48 But no uncircumcised person shall e of it; A
13: 6 Seven days you shall e unleavened bread, A
16: 8 the LORD gives you meat to e in the evening
16:12 say to them, 'At twilight you shall e meat, A
16:15 "It is the bread that the LORD has given you to e.
16:25 "E it today, for today is a sabbath to the LORD;
18:12 of Israel to e bread with Moses' father-in-law in
22:31 you shall not e any meat that is mangled B
23:11 so that the poor of your people may e; C
23:11 and what they leave the wild animals may e. C
23:15 commanded you, you shall e unleavened bread A
29:32 Aaron and his sons shall e the flesh of the ram A
29:33 They themselves shall e the food A
29:33 but no one else shall e of them, A
32: 6 and the people sat down to e and drink,
34:15 and you will e of the sacrifice.
34:18 Seven days you shall e unleavened bread, A
Lev 3:17 you must not e any fat or any blood. B
6:16 Aaron and his sons shall e what is left of it; A
6:16 in the court of the tent of meeting they shall e it. A
6:18 among the descendants of Aaron shall e of it, A
6:26 priest who offers it as a sin offering shall e of it; A
6:29 Every male among the priests shall e of it; A
7: 6 Every male among the priests shall e of it; A
7:19 all who are clean may e such flesh. C
7:20 But those who e flesh from the LORD's sacrifice
7:23 You shall e no fat of ox or sheep or goat. A
7:24 but you must not e it. B
7:25 you who e it shall be cut off from your kin.
7:26 You must not e any blood whatever, B
8:31 and e it there with the bread that is in the basket
8:31 'Aaron and his sons shall e it'; A
10:12 and e it unleavened beside the altar,
10:13 shall e it in a holy place, because it is your due A
10:14 and daughters as well may e in any clean place; C
10:17 not e the sin offering in the sacred area? B
11: 2 these are the creatures that you may e. C
11: 3 and chews the cud—such you may e. C
11: 4 you shall not e the following: B
11: 8 Of their flesh you shall not e, B
11: 9 These you may e, of all that are in the waters. C
11: 9 in the streams—such you may e. C
11:11 Of their flesh you shall not e, B
11:21 you may e those that have jointed legs C
11:22 Of them you may e: the locust according to C
11:39 If an animal of which you may e dies, C
11:40 Those who e of its carcass shall wash their clothes
11:42 you shall not e; for they are detestable. B
14:47 all who e in the house shall wash their clothes.
17:12 No person among you shall e blood, A
17:12 shall any alien who resides among you e blood.
17:14 You shall not e the blood of any creature, B
17:15 who e what dies of itself or what has been torn
19: 8 All who e it shall be subject to punishment,
19:25 But in the fifth year you may e of their fruit, C
19:26 You shall not e anything with its blood. B
21:22 He may e the food of his God, C
22: 4 a leprous disease or suffers a discharge may e C
22: 6 be unclean until evening and shall not e of B
22: 7 and afterward he may e of the sacred donations, C
22: 8 wild animals he shall not e, becoming unclean B
22:10 No lay person shall e of the sacred donations. A
22:10 No bound or hired servant of the priest shall e A
22:11 the person may e of them; C
22:11 that are born in his house may e of his food. C
22:12 not e of the offering of the sacred donations; B
22:13 as in her youth, she may e of her father's food. C
22:13 No lay person shall e of it. A
23: 6 seven days you shall e unleavened bread. A
23:14 You shall e no bread or parched grain or fresh A
24: 9 who shall e them in a holy place, A
25: 6 You may e what the land yields C
25:12 you shall e only what the field itself produces. A
25:19 and you will e your fill and live on it securely.
25:20 What shall we e in the seventh year,
25:22 when its produce comes in, you shall e the old. A
26: 5 you shall e your bread to the full, A
Lev 26:10 You shall e old grain long stored, A
26:16 for your enemies shall e it. A
26:26 and though you e, you shall not be satisfied.
26:29 You shall e the flesh of your sons, A
26:29 and you shall e the flesh of your daughters. A
Nu 6: 3 and shall not drink any grape juice or e grapes,
6: 4 as nazirites they shall e nothing that is produced A
9:11 they shall e it with unleavened bread A
11: 4 and said, "If only we had meat to e!
11: 5 We remember the fish we used to e in Egypt
11:13 to me and say, 'Give us meat to e!'
11:18 for tomorrow, and you shall e meat; A
11:18 saying, 'If only we had meat to e!
11:18 the LORD will give you meat, and you shall e. A
11:19 You shall e not only one day, or two days, A
11:21 that they may e for a whole month'! C
15:19 whenever you e of the bread of the land,
18:10 As a most holy thing you shall e it; A
18:10 every male may e it; it shall be holy to you. C
18:11 everyone who is clean in your house may e C
18:13 everyone who is clean in your house may e of it. C
18:31 You may e it in any place, C
Dt 2: 6 from them for money, so that you may e; C
2:28 shall sell me food for money, so that I may e, C
4:28 nor hear, nor e, nor smell.
8: 9 a land where you may e bread without scarcity, C
8:10 You shall e your fill and bless A
11:15 and you will e your fill.
12: 7 And you shall e there in the presence of A
12:15 and e meat within any of your towns,
12:15 the unclean and the clean may e of it, C
12:16 The blood, however, you must not e; B
12:17 Nor may you e within your towns the tithe
12:18 these you shall e in the presence of A
12:20 and you say, "I am going to e some meat,"
12:20 because you wish to e meat,
12:20 you may e meat whenever you have the desire. C
12:21 that the LORD has given you, then you may e C
12:22 just as gazelle or deer is eaten, so you may e it; C
12:22 the unclean and the clean alike may e it. C
12:23 Only be sure that you do not e the blood; B
12:23 and you shall not e the life with the meat. B
12:24 Do not e it; you shall pour it out on the B
12:25 Do not e it, so that all may go well with you B
12:27 of the LORD your God, but the meat you may e. C
14: 3 You shall not e any abhorrent thing. B
14: 4 These are the animals you may e: C
14: 6 chews the cud, among the animals, you may e. C
14: 7 cud or have the hoof cleft you shall not e these: B
14: 8 You shall not e their meat, B
14: 9 Of all that live in water you may e these: C
14: 9 whatever has fins and scales you may e. C
14:10 not have fins and scales you shall not e; B
14:11 You may e any clean birds. C
14:12 But these are the ones that you shall not e: B
14:20 You may e any clean winged creature. C
14:21 You shall not e anything that dies of itself; B
14:21 to aliens residing in your towns for them to e,
14:23 you shall e the tithe of your grain, your wine, A
14:26 And you shall e there in the presence of A
14:29 may come and e their fill so that
15:20 You shall e it, you together with your household, A
15:22 within your towns you may e it, C
15:23 Its blood, however, you must not e; B
16: 3 You must not e with it anything leavened. B
16: 3 seven days you shall e unleavened bread with it A
16: 7 You shall cook it and e it at the place that
16: 8 six days you shall continue to e unleavened bread,
18: 1 They may e the sacrifices that are C
18: 8 They shall have equal portions to e,
23:24 you may e your fill of grapes, C
26:12 so that they may e their fill within your towns, C
27: 7 of well-being, and e them there, rejoicing before
28:31 but you shall not e of it. B
28:33 not know shall e up the fruit of your ground and A
28:39 for the worm shall e them. A
28:53 you will e the fruit of your womb,
Jos 24:13 you e the fruit of vineyards and oliveyards
Jdg 13: 4 or strong drink, or to e anything unclean,
13: 7 and e nothing unclean, for the boy shall be
13:14 She may not e of anything that comes from B
13:14 or strong drink, or e any unclean thing.
13:16 "If you detain me, I will not e your food; B
14:14 "Out of the eater came something to e.
Ru 2:14 "Come here, and e some of this bread,
1Sa 1: 7 Therefore Hannah wept and would not e. B
1: 8 Why do you not e? B
2:36 that I may e a morsel of bread.' " C
9:13 before he goes up to the shrine to e;
9:13 For the people will not e until he comes, B
9:13 afterward those e who are invited.
9:19 for today you shall e with me, A
9:24 what was kept is set before you. E;
9:24 so that you might e with the guests."
14:34 and slaughter them here, and e;
20:24 the new moon came, the king sat at the feast to e.
28:22 E, that you may have strength when you go
28:23 He refused, and said, "I will not e." B
2Sa 3:35 the people came to persuade David to e something
9: 7 and you yourself shall e at my table always." A
9:10 that your master's grandson may have food to e;
9:10 master's grandson Mephibosheth shall always e
11:11 shall I then go to my house, to e and to drink,
11:13 David invited him to e and drink in his presence
12: 3 it used to e of his meager fare,
12:17 but he would not, nor did he e food with them.
13: 5 and give me something to e,

2Sa 13: 5 so that I may see it and **e** it from her hand.' "
13: 6 so that I may **e** from her hand." C
13: 9 and set them out before him, but he refused to **e.**
13:10 so that I may **e** from your hand." C
13:11 But when she brought them near him to **e,**
16: 2 bread and summer fruit for the young men to **e,**
17:29 for David and the people with him to **e;**
19:28 but you set your servant among those who **e**
1Ki 2: 7 and let them be among those who **e** at your table;
13: 8 nor will I **e** food or drink water in this place.
13: 9 You shall not **e** food, or drink water, B
13:15 "Come home with me and **e** some food."
13:16 will I **e** food or drink water with you in this place;
13:17 You shall not **e** food or drink water there, B
13:18 with you into your house so that he may **e** food C
13:22 '**E** no food, and drink no water,'
14:11 who dies in the city, the dogs shall **e;** A
14:11 the birds of the air shall **e;** A
16: 4 to Baasha who dies in the city the dogs shall **e;** A
16: 4 in the field the birds of the air shall **e."** A
17:12 that we may **e** it, and die." C
18:19 and the four hundred prophets of Asherah, who **e**
18:41 Elijah said to Ahab, "Go up, **e** and drink;
18:42 So Ahab went up to **e** and to drink.
19: 5 and said to him, "Get up and **e."**
19: 7 touched him, and said, "Get up and **e,**
21: 4 turned away his face, and would not **e.** B
21: 5 "Why are you so depressed that you will not **e?"** B
21: 7 Get up, **e** some food, and be cheerful;
21:23 dogs shall **e** Jezebel within the bounds of A
21:24 to Ahab who dies in the city the dogs shall **e;** A
21:24 in the open country the birds of the air shall **e."** A
2Ki 4:40 They served some for the men to **e.**
4:40 They could not **e** it. B
4:41 and said, "Serve the people and let them **e."**
4:42 Elisha said, "Give it to the people and let them **e."**
4:43 he repeated, "Give it to the people and let them **e,**
4:43 'They shall **e** and have some left.' " A
6:22 food and water before them so that they may **e** C
6:28 up your son; we will **e** him today,
6:28 and we will **e** my son tomorrow.'
6:29 'Give up your son and we will **e** him.'
7: 2 but you shall not **e** from it." B
7:19 but you shall not **e** from it." B
9:10 dogs shall **e** Jezebel in the territory of Jezreel, A
9:36 territory of Jezreel the dogs shall **e** the flesh A
18:27 who are doomed with you to **e** their own dung and
18:31 then every one of you will **e** from your own vine
19:29 This year you shall **e** what grows of itself, A
19:29 reap, plant vineyards, and **e** their fruit.
2Ch 31:10 we have had enough to **e** and have plenty to spare;
Ezr 9:12 that you may be strong and **e** the good of the land
10: 6 He did not **e** bread or drink water, B
Ne 5: 2 so that we may **e** and stay alive." C
8:10 **e** the fat and drink sweet wine and send portions
8:12 And all the people went their way to **e** and drink
Est 4:16 and neither **e** nor drink for three days,
Job 1: 4 and invite their three sisters to **e** and drink
5: 5 The hungry **e** their harvest,
27:14 and their offspring have not enough to **e.**
31: 8 then let me sow, and another **e;**
Ps 14: 4 the evildoers who **e** up my people as they **e** bread,
22:26 The poor shall **e** and be satisfied; A
50:13 Do I **e** the flesh of bulls,
53: 4 who **e** up my people as they eat bread,
53: 4 who eat up my people as they **e** bread,
78:24 he rained down on them manna to **e,**
102: 4 I am too wasted to **e** my bread.
102: 9 For I **e** ashes like bread,
128: 2 You shall **e** the fruit of the labor of your hands; A
141: 4 do not let me **e** of their delicacies.
Pr 1:31 therefore they shall **e** the fruit of their way and A
4:17 For they **e** the bread of wickedness and drink
9: 5 **e** of my bread and drink of the wine I have mixed.
13: 2 of their words good persons **e** good things,
18:21 and those who love it will **e** its fruits.
23: 1 When you sit down to **e** with a ruler,
23: 6 Do not **e** the bread of the stingy; B
23: 7 so are they. "**E** and drink!"
24:13 My child, **e** honey, for it is good,
25:16 If you have found honey, **e** only enough for you,
25:21 If your enemies are hungry, give them bread to **e;**
25:27 It is not good to **e** much honey,
27:18 Anyone who tends a fig tree will **e** its fruit,
31:27 and does not **e** the bread of idleness. B
Ecc 2:24 There is nothing better for mortals than to **e**
2:25 from him who can **e** or who can have enjoyment?
3:13 that all should **e** and drink and take pleasure
5:11 When goods increase, those who **e** them increase;
5:12 whether they **e** little or much;
5:17 Besides, all their days they **e** in darkness,
5:18 it is fitting to **e** and drink and find enjoyment in all
8:15 for people under the sun than to **e,**
9: 7 Go, **e** your bread with enjoyment,
SS 4:16 to his garden, and **e** its choicest fruits.
5: 1 I **e** my honeycomb with my honey,
5: 1 **E,** friends, drink, and be drunk with love.
Isa 1:19 you shall **e** the good of the land; A
3:10 for they shall **e** the fruit of their labors. A
4: 1 "We will **e** our own bread
7:15 shall **e** curds and honey by the time he knows A
7:22 and will **e** curds because of the abundance of milk
7:22 for everyone that is left in the land shall **e** curds A
11: 7 and the lion shall **e** straw like the ox. A
21: 5 they spread the rugs, they **e,** they drink.
22:13 "Let us **e** and drink, for tomorrow we die."
30:24 oxen and donkeys that till the ground will **e** silage,

Isa 36:12 to **e** their own dung and drink their own urine?"
36:16 then everyone of you will **e** from your own vine
37:30 This year **e** what grows of itself,
37:30 reap, plant vineyards, and **e** their fruit.
49:26 I will make your oppressors **e** their own flesh,
50: 9 the moth will **e** them up.
51: 8 For the moth will **e** them up like a garment,
51: 8 and the worm will **e** them like wool;
55: 1 and you that have no money, come, buy and **e!**
55: 2 Listen carefully to me, and **e** what is good,
62: 9 but those who garner it shall **e** it and praise A
65: 4 who **e** swine's flesh, with broth of abominable
65:13 My servants shall **e,** but you shall be hungry; A
65:21 they shall plant vineyards and **e** their fruit.
65:22 they shall not plant and another **e;**
65:25 the lion shall **e** straw like the ox; A
Jer 2: 7 a plentiful land to **e** its fruits and its good things.
5:17 They shall **e** up your harvest and your food; A
5:17 they shall **e** up your sons and your daughters; A
5:17 they shall **e** up your flocks and your herds; A
5:17 they shall **e** up your vines and your fig trees; A
7:21 Add your burnt offerings to your sacrifices, and **e**
16: 8 into the house of feasting to sit with them, to **e**
19: 9 And I will make them **e** the flesh of their sons and
19: 9 shall **e** the flesh of their neighbors in the siege, A
22:15 Did not your father **e** and drink and do justice
23:15 "I am going to make them **e** wormwood,
29: 5 plant gardens and **e** what they produce.
29:28 and plant gardens and **e** what they produce."
La 2:20 Should women **e** their offspring,
Eze 2: 8 open your mouth and **e** what I give you.
3: 1 He said to me, O mortal, **e** what is offered to you;
3: 1 **e** this scroll, and go, speak to the house of Israel.
3: 2 and he gave me the scroll to **e.**
3: 3 **e** this scroll that I give you and fill your stomach
4: 9 three hundred ninety days, you shall **e** it. A
4:10 that you shall be twenty shekels a day by weight; A
4:10 at fixed times you shall **e** it. A
4:12 You shall **e** it as a barley-cake, A
4:13 "Thus shall the people of Israel **e** their bread,
4:16 shall **e** bread by weight and with fearfulness; A
5:10 parents shall **e** their children in your midst, A
5:10 and children shall **e** their parents; A
12:18 **e** your bread with quaking,
12:19 They shall **e** their bread with fearfulness, A
18: 6 not **e** upon the mountains or lift up his eyes to B
18:15 not **e** upon the mountains or lift up his eyes to B
22: 9 those in you who **e** upon the mountains,
24:17 do not cover your upper lip or **e** the bread
24:22 you shall not cover your upper lip or **e** the bread
25: 4 in your midst; they shall **e** your fruit, A
33:25 You **e** flesh with the blood,
34: 3 You **e** the fat, you clothe yourselves with the wool,
34:19 And must my sheep **e** what you have trodden
39:17 and you shall **e** flesh and drink blood. A
39:18 You shall **e** the flesh of the mighty, A
39:19 You shall **e** fat until you are filled, A
42:13 the priests who approach the LORD shall **e** A
44: 3 may sit in it to **e** food before the LORD;
44:29 They shall **e** the grain offering, the sin offering, A
44:31 The priests shall not **e** of anything, B
Da 1:12 Let us be given vegetables to **e** and water to drink.
1:13 with the appearance of the young men who **e**
4:25 You shall be made to **e** grass like oxen,
4:32 You shall be made to **e** grass like oxen,
11:26 by those who **e** of the royal rations.
Hos 4:10 They shall **e,** but not be satisfied; A
8:13 they offer choice sacrifices, though they **e** flesh,
9: 3 and in Assyria they shall **e** unclean food. A
9: 4 all who **e** of it shall be defiled;
Joel 2:26 You shall **e** in plenty and be satisfied, A
Am 6: 4 and **e** lambs from the flock,
9:14 and they shall make gardens and **e** their fruit.
Mic 3: 3 who **e** the flesh of my people,
3: 5 who cry "Peace" when they have something to **e,**
6:14 You shall **e,** but not be satisfied, A
7: 1 finds no cluster to **e;** there is no first-ripe fig
Hag 1: 6 you **e,** but you never have enough;
Zec 7: 6 And when you **e** and when you drink,
7: 6 do you not **e** and drink only for yourselves? B
Mt 6:25 what you will **e** or what you will drink,
6:31 do not worry, saying, 'What will we **e?'**
8:11 and will **e** with Abraham and Isaac and Jacob in
9:11 "Why does your teacher **e** with tax collectors
12: 1 and they began to pluck heads of grain and to **e.**
12: 4 not lawful for him or his companions to **e,**
14:16 you give them something to **e."**
15: 2 For they do not wash their hands before they **e."**
15:20 but to **e** with unwashed hands does not defile."
15:27 yet even the dogs **e** the crumbs that fall
15:32 with me now for three days and have nothing to **e;**
26:17 the preparations for you to **e** the Passover?"
26:26 gave it to the disciples, and said, "Take, **e;**
Mk 2:16 "Why does he **e** with tax collectors and sinners?"
2:26 which it is not lawful for any but the priests to **e,**
3:20 so that they could not even **e.**
5:43 and told them to give her something to **e.**
6:31 and they had no leisure even to **e.**
6:36 and buy something for themselves to **e."**
6:37 "You give them something to **e."**
6:37 and give it to them to **e?"**
7: 3 not **e** unless they thoroughly wash their hands, B
7: 4 and they do not **e** anything from the market B
7: 5 but **e** with defiled hands?"
7:28 the dogs under the table **e** the children's crumbs."
8: 1 a great crowd without anything to **e,**
8: 2 with me now for three days and have nothing to **e.**

Mk 11:14 "May no one ever **e** fruit from you again."
14:12 to go and make the preparations for you to **e**
14:14 where I may **e** the Passover with my disciples?' C
Lk 5:30 "Why do you **e** and drink with tax collectors
5:33 but your disciples **e** and drink.
6: 4 which it is not lawful for any but the priests to **e,**
7:36 One of the Pharisees asked Jesus to **e** with him,
8:55 Then he directed them to give her something to **e.**
9:13 he said to them, "You give them something to **e."**
10: 8 **e** what is set before you;
12:19 relax, **e,** drink, be merry.'
12:22 do not worry about your life, what you will **e,**
12:29 for what you are to **e** and what you are to drink,
12:37 he will fasten his belt and have them sit down to **e,**
12:45 men and women, and to **e** and drink and get drunk,
13:29 and will **e** in the kingdom of God.
14: 1 the house of a leader of the Pharisees to **e** a meal
14:15 "Blessed is anyone who will **e** bread in
15:23 and let us **e** and celebrate;
17: 8 on your apron and serve me while I **e** and drink;
17: 8 later you may **e** and drink'? C
22: 8 the Passover meal for us that we may **e** it." C
22:11 where I may **e** the Passover with my disciples?" ' C
22:15 "I have eagerly desired to **e** this Passover with you
22:16 not **e** it until it is fulfilled in the kingdom of God B
22:30 you may **e** and drink at my table in my kingdom, C
24:41 he said to them, "Have you anything here to **e?"**
Jn 4:31 disciples were urging him, "Rabbi, **e** something."
4:32 "I have food to **e** that you do not know about."
4:33 "Surely no one has brought him something to **e?"**
6: 5 are we to buy bread for these people to **e?"**
6:31 'He gave them bread from heaven to **e.'** "
6:50 so that one may **e** of it and not die. C
6:52 saying, "How can this man give us his flesh to **e?"**
6:53 unless you **e** the flesh of the Son of Man
6:54 Those who **e** my flesh
6:56 Those who **e** my flesh and drink my blood abide
18:28 so as to avoid ritual defilement and to be able to **e**
Ac 10:10 He became hungry and wanted something to **e;**
10:13 he heard a voice saying, "Get up, Peter; kill and **e."**
11: 3 "Why did you go to uncircumcised men and **e**
11: 7 'Get up, Peter; kill and **e.'**
23:12 and bound themselves by an oath neither to **e**
23:21 an oath neither to **e** nor drink until they kill him.
27:35 he broke it and began to **e.**
Ro 14: 2 while the weak **e** only vegetables.
14: 3 Those who **e** must not despise those who abstain,
14: 3 not pass judgment on those who **e;**
14: 6 Also those who **e,** eat in honor of the Lord,
14: 6 Also those who eat, **e** in honor of the Lord,
14:15 or sister is being injured by what you **e,**
14:15 Do not let what you **e** cause the ruin of one
14:20 for you to make others fall by what you **e;**
14:21 not to **e** meat or drink wine or do anything
14:23 those who have doubts are condemned if they **e,**
1Co 5:11 Do not even **e** with such a one.
8: 7 they still think of the food they **e** as food offered to
8: 8 We are no worse off if we do not **e,** B
8:13 food is a cause of their falling, I will never **e** meat,
9: 7 Who plants a vineyard and does not **e** any B
10: 7 it is written, "The people sat down to **e** and drink,
10:18 not those who **e** the sacrifices partners in the altar?
10:25 **E** whatever is sold in the meat market
10:27 **e** whatever is set before you
10:28 then do not **e** it, out of consideration for B
10:31 So, whether you **e** or drink, or whatever you do,
11:20 it is not really to **e** the Lord's supper.
11:21 For when the time comes to **e,**
11:22 Do you not have homes to **e** and drink in?
11:26 For as often as you **e** this bread and drink the cup,
11:28 and only then **e** of the bread and drink of the cup.
11:29 all who **e** and drink without discerning the body,
11:29 **e** and drink judgment against themselves.
11:33 when you come together to **e,**
11:34 If you are hungry, **e** at home,
15:32 "Let us **e** and drink, for tomorrow we die."
Gal 2:12 he used to **e** with the Gentiles.
2Th 3: 8 did not **e** anyone's bread without paying for it; B
3:10 Anyone unwilling to work should not **e.** B
Heb 13:10 in the tent have no right to **e.**
Jas 2:16 keep warm and **e** your fill,"
5: 3 and it will **e** your flesh like fire.
Rev 2: 7 I will give permission to **e** from the tree of life
2:14 of Israel, so that they would **e** food sacrificed
2:20 to practice fornication and to **e** food sacrificed
3:20 I will come in to you and **e** with you,
10: 9 and he said to me, "Take it, and **e;**
19:18 to **e** the flesh of kings, the flesh of captains,
Tob 1: 8 and we would **e** it according to
2: 1 for me and I reclined to **e.**
2: 2 and he shall **e** together with me. A
2:13 for we have no right to **e** anything stolen."
7:10 "**E** and drink, and be merry tonight.
7:11 But now, my child, **e** and drink,
7:11 "I will neither **e** nor drink anything until you settle
7:14 Then they began to **e** and drink.
12:19 I really did not **e** or drink anything— B
Jdt 11:12 that God by his laws has forbidden them to **e.**
12:11 in your care to join us and to **e** and drink with us.
AdE 4:16 for three days and nights do not **e** or drink, B
Wis 4: 5 and their fruit will be useless, not ripe enough to **e,**
13:12 of his work to prepare his food, and **e** his fill.
16: 2 and you prepared quails to **e,**
16:20 from heaven with bread ready to **e,**
Sir 6:19 and soon you will **e** of her produce.
20:16 Those who **e** my bread are evil-tongued."
24:19 you who desire me, and **e** your fill of my fruits.

Sir 24:21 Those who e of me will hunger for more,
29:26 let me e what you have there."
30:19 For it can neither e nor smell.
31:16 E what is set before you like
37:29 and do not e without restraint; B
45:21 for they e the sacrifices of the Lord,
1Mc 1:62 in their hearts not to e unclean food.
2Mc 6:18 to open his mouth to e swine's flesh.
7: 7 "Will you e rather than have your body punished
9:15 to e, he would make, all of them, equal to citizens
1Es 8:85 so that you may be strong and e the good things of
9: 2 and he did not e bread or drink water, B
9:51 e the fat and drink the sweet,
9:54 to e and drink and enjoy themselves,
2Es 5:18 Rise therefore and e some bread,
7:*104* to be ill or sleep or e or be healed in his place,
9:24 and e only of the flowers of the field,
9:24 and drink no wine, but e only flowers,
10: 4 I will neither e nor drink,
15:58 and they shall e their own flesh in hunger A
16:68 and force you to e what was sacrificed to idols.
16:69 to e shall be held in derision and contempt,
4Mc 4:26 to e defiling foods and to renounce Judaism.
5: 2 and to compel them to e pork and food sacrificed
5: 3 If any were not willing to e defiling food,
5:14 in this fashion to e meat unlawfully,
5:19 be a petty sin if we were to e defiling food;
5:25 "Therefore we do not e defiling food; B
5:26 to e what will be most suitable for our lives,
5:26 but he has forbidden us to e meats that would be
5:27 but also to e in such a way that you may deride us
6:15 save yourself by pretending to e pork."
8: 2 to compel an aged man to e defiling foods,
8:12 to persuade them out of fear to e the defiling food.
8:29 to e defiling food, all with one voice together,
9:16 "Agree to e so that you may be released from
9:27 they inquired if he were willing to e,
11:13 the tyrant inquired whether he was willing to e and
11:25 or to force us to e defiling foods,

EATEN‡ (94) [EAT]

Ge 3:11 Have you e from the tree
3:17 have e of the tree about which I commanded you,
6:21 Also take with you every kind of food that is e,
14:24 but what the young men have e, and the share of
31:38 and I have not e the rams of your flocks.
41:21 when they had e them no one would have known
43: 2 when they had e up the grain that they had brought
Ex 12:46 It shall be e in one house;
13: 3 no leavened bread shall be e.
13: 7 Unleavened bread shall be e for seven days;
21:28 the ox shall be stoned, and its flesh shall not be e;
29:34 it shall not be e, because it is holy.
Lev 6:16 it shall be e as unleavened cakes in a holy place;
6:23 be wholly burned; it shall not be e.
6:26 it shall be e in a holy place,
6:30 be e from which any blood is brought into the tent
7: 6 it shall be e in a holy place; it is most holy.
7:15 of well-being shall be e on the day it is offered;
7:16 be e on the day that you offer your sacrifice,
7:16 and what is left of it shall be e the next day;
7:18 of the flesh of your sacrifice of well-being is e on
7:19 that touches any unclean thing shall not be e;
10:18 You should certainly have e it in the sanctuary,
10:19 If I had e the sin offering today,
11:13 among the birds. They shall not be e;
11:34 Any food that could be e shall be unclean if water
11:41 upon the earth are detestable; they shall not be e.
11:47 be e and the living creature that may not be e.
17:13 that may be e shall pour out its blood and cover it
19: 6 It shall be e on the same day you offer it,
19: 7 it is e at all on the third day, it is an abomination;
19:23 be forbidden to you, it must not be e.
22:30 It shall be e on the same day;
Nu 23:24 down until it has e the prey and drunk the blood of
28:17 seven days shall unleavened bread be e.
Dt 6:11 and when you have e your fill,
8:12 When you have e your fill
12:22 Indeed, just as gazelle or deer is e,
14:19 for you; they shall not be e.
26:14 I have not e of it while in mourning;
29: 6 not e bread, and you have not drunk wine
31:20 and they have e their fill and grown fat,
Ru 3: 7 When Boaz had e and drunk,
1Sa 1: 9 After they had e and drunk at Shiloh,
14:30 How much better if today the troops had e freely
28:20 for he had e nothing all day and all night.
30:12 When he had e, his spirit revived;
30:12 not e bread or drunk water for three days
2Sa 19:42 Have we e at all at the king's expense?
1Ki 13:22 and have e food and drunk water in the place
13:23 After the man of God had e food and had drunk,
13:28 lion had not e the body or attacked the donkey.
Ezr 6:21 It was e by the people of Israel who had returned
Job 6: 6 Can that which is tasteless be e without salt,
20:21 There was nothing left after they had e;
31:17 or have e my morsel alone, and the orphan has not
e from it—
31:39 if I have e its yield without payment, and caused
Pr 9:17 and bread e in secret is pleasant."
23: 8 You will vomit up the little you have e,
30:17 be pecked out by the ravens of the valley and e by
Isa 44:19 I roasted meat and have e.
Jer 24: 2 so bad that they could not be e.
24: 3 so bad that they cannot be e."
24: 8 Like the bad figs that are so bad they cannot be e,
Jer 29:17 like rotten figs that are so bad they cannot be e.
31:29 "The parents have e sour grapes,
Eze 4:14 now I have never e what died of itself or was torn
18: 2 "The parents have e sour grapes,
45:21 and for seven days unleavened bread shall be e.
Da 10: 3 I had e no rich food,
Hos 10:13 you have e the fruit of lies.
Joel 1: 4 the swarming locust has e.
1: 4 the swarming locust left, the hopping locust has e,
1: 4 the destroying locust has e.
2:25 for the years that the swarming locust has e,
Mt 15:38 Those who had e were four thousand men,
Mk 6:44 and those who had e the loaves numbered five thousand men.
Jn 6:13 left by those who had e, they filled twelve baskets.
6:23 near the place where they had e the bread after
Ac 10:14 for I have never e anything that is profane
12:23 and he was e by worms and died.
20:11 and after he had broken bread and e,
27:33 and remaining without food, having e nothing.
Rev 10:10 but when I had e it, my stomach was made bitter.
AdE 14:17 And your servant has not e at Haman's table,
LtJ 6:20 are e away when crawling creatures from
Bel 1:12 if you do not find that Bel has e it all, we will die;
1:42 and they were instantly e before his eyes.
1Mc 3:17 And we are faint, for we have e nothing today."
2Mc 2:11 because the sin offering had not been e."
2Es 6:52 you have kept them to be e by whom you wish,
4Mc 13: 2 to their emotions and had e defiling food,

EATER (3) [EAT]

Jdg 14:14 "Out of the e came something to eat.
Isa 55:10 giving seed to the sower and bread to the e,
Na 3:12 if shaken they fall into the mouth of the e.

EATERS (1) [EAT]

Pr 23:20 or among gluttonous e of meat;

EATING‡ (59) [EAT]

Ge 40:17 the birds were e it out of the basket on my head."
Lev 22:16 by e their sacred donations:
25:22 you will be e from the old crop;
Dt 28:55 of the flesh of his children whom he is e,
28:57 she is e them in secret for lack of anything else,
Jdg 14: 9 and went on, e as he went.
Ru 3: 3 to the man until he has finished e and drinking.
1Sa 14:33 the troops are sinning against the LORD by e
14:34 not sin against the LORD by e with the blood.' "
30:16 e and drinking and dancing,
1Ki 1:25 who are now e and drinking before him,
2Ki 4:40 But while they were e the stew, they cried out,
1Ch 12:39 e and drinking, for their kindred had provided
Job 1:13 One day when his sons and daughters were e
1:18 and daughters were e and drinking wine
Ps 127: 2 e the bread of anxious toil;
Isa 22:13 e meat and drinking wine.
29: 8 as when a hungry person dreams of e and wakes
66:17 following the one in the center, e the flesh of pigs,
Da 1:15 and fatter than all the young men who had been e
Am 7: 2 When they had finished e the grass of the land,
7: 4 it devoured the great deep and was e up the land.
Mt 11:18 For John came neither e nor drinking,
11:19 the Son of Man came e and drinking,
24:38 For as in those days before the flood they were e
26:21 while they were e, he said, "Truly I tell you, one
26:26 While they were e, Jesus took a loaf of bread,
Mk 2:16 of the Pharisees saw that he was e with sinners
7: 2 they noticed that some of his disciples were e
14:18 And when they had taken their places and were e,
14:18 one of you will betray me, one who is e with me."
14:22 While they were e, he took a loaf of bread,
Lk 7:33 For John the Baptist has come e no bread
7:34 the Son of Man has come e and drinking,
7:37 that he was e in the Pharisee's house,
10: 7 e and drinking whatever they provide,
15:16 with the pods that the pigs were e;
17:27 They were e and drinking,
17:28 they were e and drinking, buying and selling,
Ro 14: 2 Some believe in e anything,
1Co 8: 4 Hence, as to the e of food offered to idols,
8:10 who possess knowledge, e in the temple of an idol,
8:10 be encouraged to the point of e food sacrificed
Tob 1:11 but I kept myself from e the food of the Gentiles.
8: 1 When they had finished e
8:20 but shall stay here e and drinking with me;
Sir 31:20 Healthy sleep depends on moderate e;
Bel 1: 8 "If you do not tell me who is e these provisions,
1: 9 But if you prove that Bel is e them,
2Mc 6:21 that he was e the flesh of the sacrificial meal
7:42 about the e of sacrifices and the extreme tortures.
4Mc 1:27 indiscriminate e, gluttony,
5: 6 I would advise you to save yourself by e pork,
5: 8 why should you abhor e the very excellent meat
5:27 a way that you may deride us for e defiling foods,
6:19 to the young by setting them an example in the e
7: 6 for reverence and purity, by e defiling foods.
8: 2 any who ate defiling food would be freed after e,
11:16 if you intend to torture me for not e defiling foods,

EATS (29) [EAT]

Ex 12:15 from your houses, for whoever e leavened bread
12:19 for whoever e what is leavened shall be cut off
Lev 7:18 and the one who e of it shall incur guilt.
7:21 e flesh from the LORD's sacrifice of well-being,
7:25 If any one of you e the fat from an animal
7:27 Any one of you who e any blood shall be cut off
Lev 17:10 of the aliens who reside among them e any blood,
17:10 I will set my face against that person who e blood,
17:14 whoever e it shall be cut off.
22:14 If a man e of the sacred donation unintentionally,
1Sa 14:24 "Cursed be anyone who e food before it is evening
14:28 saying, 'Cursed be anyone who e food this day.'
2Sa 19:35 Can your servant taste what he e
Job 40:15 it e grass like an ox.
Ps 106:20 of God for the image of an ox that e grass.
Pr 30:20 This is the way of an adulteress: she e,
Isa 28: 4 e it up as soon as it comes to hand.
44:16 over this half he roasts meat, e it and is satisfied.
59: 5 whoever e their eggs dies,
Jer 31:30 the teeth of everyone who e sour grapes shall
Eze 18:11 who e upon the mountains,
Mt 24:49 and e and drinks with drunkards,
Lk 15: 2 "This fellow welcomes sinners and e with them."
Jn 6:51 Whoever e of this bread will live forever;
6:57 so whoever e me will live because of me.
6:58 But the one who e this bread will live forever."
1Co 11:27 e the bread or drinks the cup of the Lord in
Bel 1: 6 not see how much he e and drinks every day?"
1Es 4:10 he reclines, he e and drinks and sleeps,

EBAL (8)

Ge 36:23 Alvan, Manahath, E, Shepho, and Onam.
Dt 11:29 on Mount Gerizim and the curse on Mount E.
27: 4 on Mount E, and you shall cover them
27:13 And these shall stand on Mount E for the curse:
Jos 8:30 Joshua built on Mount E an altar to the LORD,
8:33 and half of them in front of Mount E,
1Ch 1:22 E, Abimael, Sheba,
1:40 Alian, Manahath, E, Shephi, and Onam.

EBBING (2)

Jer 49: 4 Your strength is e, O faithless daughter.
Jnh 2: 7 As my life was e away, I remembered the LORD;

EBED (6)

Jdg 9:26 of E moved into Shechem with his kinsfolk,
9:28 Gaal son of E said, "Who is Abimelech,
9:30 of the city heard the words of Gaal son of E,
9:31 of E and his kinsfolk have come to Shechem,
9:35 of E went out and stood in the entrance of the gate
Ezr 8: 6 Of the descendants of Adin, E son of Jonathan,

EBED-MELECH (6)

Jer 38: 7 E the Ethiopian, a eunuch in the king's house,
38: 8 So E left the king's house and spoke to the king,
38:10 Then the king commanded E the Ethiopian,
38:11 So E took the men with him and went to the house
38:12 Then E the Ethiopian said to Jeremiah,
39:16 Go and say to E the Ethiopian:

EBENEZER (3)

1Sa 4: 1 they encamped at E, and the Philistines encamped
5: 1 they brought it from E to Ashdod;
7:12 between Mizpah and Jeshanah, and named it E;

EBER (16)

Ge 10:21 To Shem also, the father of all the children of E,
10:24 and Shelah became the father of E.
10:25 To E were born two sons:
11:14 he became the father of E;
11:15 after the birth of E four hundred three years,
11:16 When E had lived thirty-four years,
11:17 and E lived after the birth
Nu 24:24 from Kittim and shall afflict Asshur and E;
1Ch 1:18 and Shelah became the father of E.
1:19 To E were born two sons:
1:25 E, Peleg, Reu;
5:13 Meshullam, Sheba, Jorai, Jacan, Zia, and E, seven.
8:12 The sons of Elpaal: E, Misham, and Shemed,
8:22 Ishpan, E, Eliel,
Ne 12:20 of Sallai, Kallai; of Amok, E;
Lk 3:35 son of Reu, son of Peleg, son of E, son of Shelah,

EBEZ (1)

Jos 19:20 Rabbith, Kishion, E,

EBIASAPH (3)

1Ch 6:23 Elkanah his son, E his son, Assir his son,
6:37 son of Assir, son of E, son of Korah,
9:19 Shallum son of Kore, son of E, son of Korah,

EBONY (1)

Eze 27:15 they brought you in payment ivory tusks and e.

EBRON (1)

Jos 19:28 E, Rehob, Hammon, Kanah, as far as Great Sidon;

EBRONAH (KJV) See ABRONAH

ECBATANA‡ (13)

Ezr 6: 2 in E, the capital in the province of Media,
Tob 3: 7 On the same day, at E in Media,
5: 6 It is a journey of two days from E to Rages;
5: 6 while E is in the middle of the plain."
6:10 he entered Media and already was approaching E,
7: 1 Now when they entered E, Tobias said to him,
14:12 and children returned to Media and settled in E

Tob 14:13 and buried them in **E** of Media.
Jdt 1: 1 In those days Arphaxad ruled over the Medes in **E.**
1: 2 around **E** with hewn stones three cubits thick
1:14 of his towns and came to **E,**
2Mc 9: 3 in **E,** news came to him of what had happened
1Es 6:23 in **E,** the fortress that is in the country of Media,

ECHO (1) [ECHOED]
Wis 17:19 an **e** thrown back from a hollow of the mountains,

ECHOED (2) [ECHO]
Wis 18:10 But the discordant cry of their enemies **e** back,
3Mc 1:29 but also the walls and the whole earth around **e,**

ECLIPSED‡ (1)
Sir 17:31 Yet it can be **e.**

ED (KJV) See WITNESS

EDDINUS (1)
1Es 1:15 Zechariah, and **E,** who represented the king.

EDEN (19) [BETH-EDEN]
Ge 2: 8 the LORD God planted a garden in **E,** in the east;
2:10 A river flows out of **E** to water the garden,
2:15 and put him in the garden of **E** to till it and keep it.
3:23 LORD God sent him forth from the garden of **E,**
3:24 the east of the garden of **E** he placed the cherubim,
4:16 and settled in the land of Nod, east of **E.**
2Ki 19:12 and the people of **E** who were in Telassar?
2Ch 29:12 Joah son of Zimmah, and **E** son of Joah;
31:15 **E,** Miniamin, Jeshua, Shemaiah, Amariah,
Isa 37:12 and the people of **E** who were in Telassar?
51: 3 and will make her wilderness like **E,**
Eze 27:23 Haran, Canneh, **E,** the merchants of Sheba,
28:13 You were in **E,** the garden of God;
31: 9 of all the trees of **E** that were in the garden of God.
31:16 and all the trees of **E,**
31:18 Which among the trees of **E** was like you in glory
31:18 down with the trees of **E** to the world below;
36:35 that was desolate has become like the garden of **E;**
Joel 2: 3 Before them the land is like the garden of **E,**

EDER (5)
Ge 35:21 and pitched his tent beyond the tower of **E.**
Jos 15:21 toward the boundary of Edom, were Kabzeel, **E,**
1Ch 8:15 Zebadiah, Arad, **E,**
23:23 The sons of Mushi: Mahli, **E,** and Jeremoth, three.
24:30 The sons of Mushi: Mahli, **E,** and Jerimoth.

EDGE (57) [EDGES, TWO-EDGED]
Ge 14: 6 the hill country of Seir as far as El-paran on the **e**
Ex 13:20 and camped at Etham, on the **e** of the wilderness.
19:12 not to go up the mountain or to touch the **e** of it.
26: 4 on the **e** of the outermost curtain in the first set;
26: 4 on the **e** of the outermost curtain in the second set.
26: 5 on the **e** of the curtain that is in the second set;
26:10 on the **e** of the curtain that is outermost in one set,
26:10 on the **e** of the curtain that is outermost in
28:26 on its inside **e** next to the ephod.
36:11 on the **e** of the outermost curtain of the first set;
36:11 on the **e** of the outermost curtain of the second set;
36:12 on the **e** of the curtain that was in the second set;
36:17 on the **e** of the outermost curtain of the one set,
36:17 fifty loops on the **e** of the other connecting curtain.
39:19 on its inside **e** next to the ephod.
Nu 20:16 a town on the **e** of your territory.
33: 6 which is on the **e** of the wilderness.
33:37 on the **e** of the land of Edom.
Dt 2:36 From Aroer on the **e** of the Wadi Arnon (including
3:12 that is on the **e** of the Wadi Arnon,
4:48 which is on the **e** of the Wadi Arnon,
Jos 3: 8 you come to the **e** of the waters of the Jordan,
3:15 the priests bearing the ark were dipped in the **e** of
6:21 to destruction by the **e** of the sword all in the city,
8:24 to the very last had fallen by the **e** of the sword
8:24 and attacked it with the **e** of the sword.
10:28 and struck it and its king with the **e** of the sword;
10:30 and he struck it with the **e** of the sword,
10:32 and struck it with the **e** of the sword,
10:35 and struck it with the **e** of the sword;
10:37 and struck it with the **e** of the sword,
10:39 they struck them with the **e** of the sword,
11:12 and struck them with the **e** of the sword,
11:14 but all the people they struck down with the **e** of
12: 2 which is on the **e** of the Wadi Arnon,
13: 9 which is on the **e** of the Wadi Arnon,
13:16 which is on the **e** of the Wadi Arnon,
1Sa 15: 8 but utterly destroyed all the people with the **e** of
2Sa 15:14 and attack the city with the **e** of the sword."
2Ki 7: 5 but when they came to the **e** of the Aramean camp,
7: 8 these leprous men had come to the **e** of the camp,
Job 1:15 and killed the servants with the **e** of the sword;
1:17 and killed the servants with the **e** of the sword;
Ps 89:43 you have turned back the **e** of his sword,
Ecc 10:10 If the iron is blunt, and one does not whet the **e,**
Jer 21: 7 He shall strike them down with the **e** of the sword;
31:29 and the children's teeth are set on **e."**
31:30 of everyone who eats sour grapes shall be set on **e.**
Eze 16: 8 I spread the **e** of my cloak over you,
18: 2 and the children's teeth are set on **e"?**
21:16 Wherever your **e** is directed.
43:13 with a rim of one span around its **e.**
Lk 21:24 the **e** of the sword and be taken away as captives
Heb 11:34 escaped the **e** of the sword,
Sir 28:18 Many have fallen by the **e** of the sword,
1Mc 5:28 and killed every male by the **e** of the sword;
5:51 He destroyed every male by the **e** of the sword,

EDGES (11) [EDGE]
Ex 28: 7 to its two **e,** so that it may
28:23 put the two rings on the two **e** of the breastpiece.
28:24 of gold in the two rings at the **e** of the breastpiece;
39: 4 joined to it at its two **e.**
39:16 put the two rings on the two **e** of the breastpiece;
39:17 of gold in the two rings at the **e** of the breastpiece.
Lev 19: 9 you shall not reap to the very **e** of your field,
19:27 not round off the hair on your temples or mar the **e**
21: 5 or shave off the **e** of their beards,
23:22 you shall not reap to the very **e** of your field,
Jdg 3:16 Ehud made for himself a sword with two **e,**

EDICT‡ (13)
2Ch 36:22 and also declared in a written **e:**
Ezr 1: 1 and also in a written **e** declared:
6:11 Furthermore I decree that if anyone alters this **e,**
Est 2: 8 when the king's order and his **e** were proclaimed,
3:12 and an **e,** according to all that Haman commanded,
8: 8 for an **e** written in the name of the king and sealed
8: 9 and an **e** was written, according to all
8:17 wherever the king's command and his **e** came,
9: 1 king's command and **e** were about to be executed,
9:13 also to do according to this day's **e,**
Heb 11:23 and they were not afraid of the king's **e.**
AdE 8:10 The **e** was written with the king's authority
2Mc 10: 8 They decreed by public **e,** ratified by vote,

EDNA (7)
Tob 7: 2 He said to his wife **E,**
7: 3 Then **E** questioned them, saying,
7: 8 His wife **E** also wept for him,
7:15 Raguel called his wife **E** and said to her, "Sister,
8:21 I am your father and **E** is your mother,
10:12 Then **E** said to Tobias, "My child
10:13 Finally, he blessed Raguel and his wife **E,**

EDOM‡ (98) [EDOMITE, EDOMITES, =ESAU]
Ge 25:30 (Therefore he was called **E.**)
32: 3 in the land of Seir, the country of **E,**
36: 1 These are the descendants of Esau (that is, **E**).
36: 8 Esau settled in the hill country of Seir; Esau is **E.**
36:16 these are the clans of Eliphaz in the land of **E;**
36:17 these are the clans of Reuel in the land of **E;**
36:19 These are the sons of Esau (that is, **E**),
36:21 the sons of Seir in the land of **E.**
36:31 These are the kings who reigned in the land of **E,**
36:32 Bela son of Beor reigned in **E,**
36:43 are the clans of **E** (that is, Esau, the father of **E**),
Ex 15:15 Then the chiefs of **E** were dismayed;
Nu 20:14 to the king of **E,** "Thus says your brother Israel:
20:18 But **E** said to him, "You shall not pass through,
20:20 And **E** came out against them with a large force,
20:21 Thus **E** refused to give Israel passage
20:23 on the border of the land of **E,**
21: 4 to go around the land of **E;**
24:18 **E** will become a possession,
33:37 on the edge of the land of **E.**
34: 3 from the wilderness of Zin along the side of **E.**
Jos 15: 1 to the boundary of **E,** to the wilderness of Zin at
15:21 toward the boundary of **E,** were Kabzeel, Eder,
Jdg 5: 4 when you marched from the region of **E,**
11:17 Israel then sent messengers to the king of **E,**
11:17 but the king of **E** would not listen.
11:18 went around the land of **E** and the land of Moab,
1Sa 14:47 against Moab, against the Ammonites, against **E,**
2Sa 8:12 from **E,** Moab, the Ammonites,
8:14 He put garrisons in **E;** throughout all **E** he put
1Ki 9:26 on the shore of the Red Sea, in the land of **E.**
11:14 he was of the royal house in **E.**
11:15 For when David was in **E,**
11:15 he killed every male in **E**
11:16 until he had eliminated every male in **E**);
22:47 There was no king in **E;** a deputy was king.
2Ki 3: 8 "By the way of the wilderness of **E.**"
3: 9 the king of Judah, and the king of **E** set out;
3:12 of Israel and Jehoshaphat and the king of **E** went
3:20 to flow from the direction of **E,**
3:26 opposite the king of **E;** but they could not.
8:20 In his days **E** revolted against the rule of Judah,
8:22 So **E** has been in revolt against the rule of Judah
14:10 You have indeed defeated **E,**
16: 6 the king of **E** recovered Elath for **E,** and drove
1Ch 1:43 These are the kings who reigned in the land of **E**
1:51 And Hadad died. The clans of **E** were:
1:54 Magdiel, and Iram; these are the clans of **E.**
18:11 from **E,** Moab, the Ammonites, the Philistines,
18:13 He put garrisons in **E;**
2Ch 8:17 and Eloth on the shore of the sea, in the land of **E.**
20: 2 "A great multitude is coming against you from **E,**
21: 8 In his days **E** revolted against the rule of Judah
21:10 So **E** has been in revolt against the rule of Judah
25:19 You say, 'See, I have defeated **E,**'
25:20 because they had sought the gods of **E.**
Ps 60: 8 Moab is my washbasin; on **E** I hurl my shoe;
60: 9 Who will lead me to **E?**
83: 6 the tents of **E** and the Ishmaelites,
Ps 108: 9 Moab is my washbasin; on **E** I hurl my shoe;
108:10 Who will lead me to **E?**
Isa 11:14 They shall put forth their hand against **E**
34: 5 lo, it will descend upon **E,**
34: 6 a great slaughter in the land of **E.**
34: 9 And the streams of **E** shall be turned into pitch,
63: 1 "Who is this that comes from **E,**
Jer 9:26 Judah, **E,** the Ammonites, Moab,
25:21 **E,** Moab, and the Ammonites;
27: 3 Send word to the king of **E,** the king of Moab,
40:11 in Moab and among the Ammonites and in **E** and
49: 7 Concerning **E.** Thus says the LORD of hosts:
49:17 **E** shall become an object of horror;
49:19 I will suddenly chase **E** away from it;
49:20 the LORD has made against **E** and the purposes
49:22 the warriors of **E** in that day shall be like the heart
La 4:21 Rejoice and be glad, O daughter **E,**
4:22 but your iniquity, O daughter **E,** he will punish,
Eze 25:12 Because **E** acted revengefully against the house
25:13 I will stretch out my hand against **E,**
25:14 I will lay my vengeance upon **E** by the hand
25:14 and they shall act in **E** according to my anger and
27:16 **E** did business with you because
32:29 **E** is there, its kings and all its princes,
35:15 you shall be desolate, Mount Seir, and all **E,**
36: 5 against the rest of the nations, and against all **E,**
Da 11:41 but **E** and Moab and the main part of
Joel 3:19 a desolation and **E** a desolate wilderness,
Am 1: 6 to hand them over to **E.**
1: 9 they delivered entire communities over to **E,**
1:11 For three transgressions of **E,** and for four,
2: 1 he burned to lime the bones of the king of **E.**
9:12 the remnant of **E** and all the nations who are called
Ob 1: 1 Thus says the Lord GOD concerning **E:**
1: 8 says the LORD, I will destroy the wise out of **E,**
Mal 1: 4 If **E** says, "We are shattered but we will rebuild

EDOMITE (7) [EDOM]
1Sa 21: 7 his name was Doeg the **E,**
22: 9 Doeg the **E,** who was in charge of Saul's servants,
22:18 Doeg the **E** turned and attacked the priests;
22:22 "I knew on that day, when Doeg the **E** was there,
1Ki 11: 1 Moabite, Ammonite, **E,** Sidonian,
11:14 Hadad the **E;** he was of the royal house in Edom.
Ps 52: T *A Maskil of David, when Doeg the **E** came*

EDOMITES (19) [EDOM]
Ge 36: 9 ancestor of the **E,** in the hill country of Seir.
Dt 23: 7 You shall not abhor any of the **E,**
2Sa 8:13 he killed eighteen thousand **E** in the Valley
8:14 and all the **E** became David's servants.
1Ki 11:17 with some **E** who were servants of his father.
2Ki 8:21 He set out by night and attacked the **E**
14: 7 He killed ten thousand **E** in the Valley of Salt
16: 6 the **E** came to Elath, where they live to this day.
1Ch 18:12 Abishai son of Zeruiah killed eighteen thousand **E**
18:13 and all the **E** became subject to David.
2Ch 21: 9 He set out by night and attacked the **E,**
25:14 after Amaziah came from the slaughter of the **E,**
28:17 For the **E** had again invaded and defeated Judah,
Ps 60: T *on his return killed twelve thousand **E***
137: 7 against the **E** the day of Jerusalem's fall,
Jdt 7: 8 Then all the chieftains of the **E** and all the leaders
7:18 And the **E** and Ammonites went up and encamped
1Es 4:45 which the **E** burned when Judea was laid waste by
8:69 the Moabites, the Egyptians, and the **E.**

EDREI (8)
Nu 21:33 he and all his people, to battle at **E.**
Dt 1: 4 who reigned in Ashtaroth and in **E.**
3: 1 he and all his people, for battle at **E.**
3:10 and all of Bashan, as far as Salecah and **E,**
Jos 12: 4 who lived at Ashtaroth and at **E**
13:12 and in **E** (he alone was left of the survivors of
13:31 and **E,** the towns of the kingdom of Og in Bashan;
19:37 Kedesh, **E,** En-hazor,

EDUCATED (4) [EDUCATES, EDUCATION]
Da 1: 5 They were to be **e** for three years,
Ac 22: 3 **e** strictly according to our ancestral law,
Sir 34: 9 An **e** person knows many things,
4Mc 13:24 Since they had been **e** by the same law and trained

EDUCATES (1) [EDUCATED]
Sir 10: 1 A wise magistrate **e** his people,

EDUCATION‡ (5) [EDUCATED]
Sir 4:24 and **e** through the words of the tongue.
21:19 To a senseless person **e** is fetters on his feet,
21:21 To the sensible person **e** is like a golden ornament,
4Mc 1:17 This, in turn, is **e** in the law,
13:22 from both general **e** and our discipline in the law

EDUTH See Index to Footnotes

EFFECT (17) [EFFECTIVE]
2Ch 34:22 in the Second Quarter) and spoke to her to that **e.**
Pr 19:19 if you **e** a rescue, you will only have to do it again.
Isa 32:17 The **e** of righteousness will be peace,
Lk 16:16 law and the prophets were in **e** until John came;
Ac 23:25 He wrote a letter to this **e:**
Ro 5:16 the free gift is not like the **e** of the one man's sin.
2Th 2: 2 to the **e** that the day of the Lord is already here.

Heb 9:17 For a will takes **e** only at death,
Jas 1: 4 and let endurance have its full **e,**
Tob 7:13 to the **e** that he gave her to him as wife according
Wis 14: 5 of your wisdom should not be without **e;**
16:17 the fire had still greater **e,**
1Mc 8:30 in **e** both parties shall determine to add
12: 2 also sent letters to the same **e** to the Spartans and
2Mc 1:24 The prayer was to this **e:**
3: 7 and sent him with commands to **e** the removal of
11:16 letter written to the Jews by Lysias was to this **e:**

EFFECTIVE‡ (7) [EFFECT]

Ro 3:25 of atonement by his blood, **e** through faith.
1Co 16: 9 for a wide door for **e** work has opened to me,
Phm 1: 6 of your faith may become **e** when you perceive all
Jas 5:16 The prayer of the righteous is powerful and **e.**
Wis 8: 6 And if understanding is **e,**
Sir 22:27 and an **e** seal upon my lips,
2Mc 15:17 and so **e** in arousing valor and awaking courage in

EFFECTS See Index to Footnotes

EFFEMINATE (KJV) See MALE PROSTITUTES

EFFORT (13) [EFFORTS]

Da 6:14 the sun went down he made every **e** to rescue him.
Lk 12:58 on the way make an **e** to settle the case,
Gal 2:17 But if, in our **e** to be justified in Christ,
Eph 4: 3 making every **e** to maintain the unity of the Spirit
Tit 3:13 Make every **e** to send Zenas the lawyer
Heb 4:11 Let us therefore make every **e** to enter that rest,
2Pe 1: 5 you must make every **e** to support your faith
1:15 And I will make every **e** so that
2Mc 2:28 while devoting our **e** to arriving at the outlines of
1Es 6:28 and that full **e** be made
2Es 7:92 with great **e** to overcome the evil thought
13:38 and will destroy them without **e** by means of
4Mc 2: 2 because by mental **e** he overcame sexual desire.

EFFORTS (1) [EFFORT]

3Mc 3:10 and to exert more earnest **e** for their assistance.

EGG (2) [EGGS]

Isa 59: 5 and the crushed **e** hatches out a viper.
Lk 11:12 Or if the child asks for an **e,** will give a scorpion?

EGGS (6) [EGG]

Dt 22: 6 in any tree or on the ground, with fledglings or **e,**
22: 6 the mother sitting on the fledglings or on the **e,**
Job 39:14 For it leaves its **e** to the earth,
Isa 10:14 and as one gathers **e** that have been forsaken,
59: 5 They hatch adders' **e,** and weave the spider's web;
59: 5 whoever eats their **e** dies, and the crushed egg

EGLAH (2)

2Sa 3: 5 Ithream, of David's wife **E.**
1Ch 3: 3 the sixth Ithream, by his wife **E;**

EGLAIM (1)

Isa 15: 8 the wailing reaches to **E,** the wailing reaches to

EGLATH-SHELISHIYAH (2)

Isa 15: 5 his fugitives flee to Zoar, to **E.**
Jer 48:34 from Zoar to Horonaim and **E.**

EGLON (13) [EGLON'S]

Jos 10: 3 to King Japhia of Lachish, and to King Debir of **E,**
10: 5 the king of Lachish, and the king of **E**—
10:23 the king of Lachish, and the king of **E.**
10:34 on with all Israel to **E;**
10:36 Joshua went up with all Israel from **E** to Hebron;
10:37 he left no one remaining, just as he had done to **E,**
12:12 the king of **E** one the king of Gezer one
15:39 Lachish, Bozkath, **E,**
Jdg 3:12 and the LORD strengthened King **E** of Moab
3:14 Israelites served King **E** of Moab eighteen years.
3:15 Israelites sent tribute by him to King **E** of Moab.
3:17 Then he presented the tribute to King **E** of Moab.
3:17 Now **E** was a very fat man.

EGLON'S (1) [EGLON]

Jdg 3:21 and thrust it into **E** belly;

EGREBEH (1)

Jdt 7:18 toward the south and the east, toward **E,**

EGYPT‡ (675) [EGYPT'S, EGYPTIAN, EGYPTIAN'S, EGYPTIANS]

A. LAND OF EGYPT (233)
B. OUT OF EGYPT (61)
C. KING OF EGYPT (48)
D. DOWN TO EGYPT (13)
E. WADI OF EGYPT (9)

Ge 10: 6 descendants of Ham: Cush, **E,** Put, and Canaan.
10:13 **E** became the father of Ludim, Anamim, Lehabim,
12:10 Abram went down to **E** to reside there as D
12:11 When he was about to enter **E,**
12:14 When Abram entered **E** the Egyptians saw that
13: 1 So Abram went up from **E,** he and his wife,
13:10 like the land of **E,** in the direction of Zoar; A
15:18 from the river of **E** to the great river,
21:21 mother got a wife for him from the land of **E.** A
25:18 which is opposite **E** in the direction of Assyria;
26: 2 "Do not go down to **E;** D
37:25 and resin, on their way to carry it down to **E.** D
37:28 And they took Joseph to **E.**
37:36 the Midianites had sold him in **E** to Potiphar,
39: 1 Now Joseph was taken down to **E,** and Potiphar, D
40: 1 the king of **E** and his baker offended their lord C
40: 1 and his baker offended their lord the king of **E.** C
40: 5 the cupbearer and the baker of the king of **E,** C
41: 8 so he sent and called for all the magicians of **E**
41:19 in all the land of **E.** A
41:29 of great plenty throughout all the land of **E.** A
41:30 all the plenty will be forgotten in the land of **E;** A
41:33 and set him over the land of **E.** A
41:34 the land of **E** during the seven plenteous years. A
41:36 of famine that are to befall the land of **E,** A
41:41 "See, I have set you over all the land of **E.**" A
41:43 Thus he set him over all the land of **E.** A
41:44 up hand or foot in all the land of **E.**" A
41:45 Thus Joseph gained authority over the land of **E.** A
41:46 he entered the service of Pharaoh king of **E.** C
41:46 and went through all the land of **E.** A
41:48 when there was plenty in the land of **E,** and A
41:53 of plenty that prevailed in the land of **E** came to A
41:54 but throughout the land of **E** there was bread. A
41:55 When all the land of **E** was famished, A
41:56 for the famine was severe in the land of **E.** A
41:57 all the world came to Joseph in **E** to buy grain,
42: 1 When Jacob learned that there was grain in **E,**
42: 2 I have heard," he said, "that there is grain in **E;**
42: 3 of Joseph's brothers went down to buy grain in **E.**
43: 2 up the grain that they had brought from **E,**
43:15 Then they went on their way down to **E,** D
45: 4 "I am your brother, Joseph, whom you sold into **E.**
45: 8 of all his house and ruler over all the land of **E.** A
45: 9 God has made me lord of all **E;**
45:13 how greatly I am honored in **E,**
45:18 so that I may give you the best of the land of **E,** A
45:19 wagons from the land of **E** for your little ones A
45:20 for the best of all the land of **E** is yours.' " A
45:23 ten donkeys loaded with the good things of **E,**
45:25 went up out of **E** and came to their father Jacob B
45:26 He is even ruler over all the land of **E.**" A
46: 3 do not be afraid to go down to **E,** D
46: 4 I myself will go down with you to **E,**
46: 6 in the land of Canaan, and they came into **E,** Jacob
46: 7 all his offspring he brought with him into **E.**
46: 8 Jacob and his offspring, who came to **E.**
46:20 the land of **E** were born Manasseh and Ephraim, A
46:26 the persons belonging to Jacob who came into **E,**
46:27 children of Joseph, who were born to him in **E,**
46:27 the house of Jacob who came into **E** were seventy.
47: 6 The land of **E** is before you; A
47:11 and granted them a holding in the land of **E,** A
47:13 the land of **E** and the land of Canaan languished A
47:14 the land of **E** and in the land of Canaan, A
47:15 the money from the land of **E** and from the land A
47:20 So Joseph bought all the land of **E** for Pharaoh. A
47:21 he made slaves of them from one end of **E** to
47:26 made it a statute concerning the land of **E,** A
47:27 Thus Israel settled in the land of **E,** A
47:28 Jacob lived in the land of **E** seventeen years; A
47:29 Do not bury me in **E.**
47:30 out of **E** and bury me in their burial place." B
48: 5 two sons born to you in the land of **E** A
48: 5 before I came to you in **E,** are now mine;
50: 7 and all the elders of the land of **E,** A
50:14 to **E** with his brothers and all who had gone up
50:22 So Joseph remained in **E,**
50:26 he was embalmed and placed in a coffin in **E.**
Ex 1: 1 the sons of Israel who came to **E** with Jacob, each
1: 5 Joseph was already in **E.**
1: 8 new king arose over **E,** who did not know Joseph.
1:15 The king of **E** said to the Hebrew midwives, C
1:17 did not do as the king of **E** commanded them, C
1:18 the king of **E** summoned the midwives and said C
2:23 After a long time the king of **E** died. C
3: 7 the misery of my people who are in **E;**
3:10 to bring my people, the Israelites, out of **E.**" B
3:11 and bring the Israelites out of **E?**" B
3:12 when you have brought the people out of **E,** B
3:16 to you and to what has been done to you in **E.**
3:17 that I will bring you up out of the misery of **E,**
3:18 Israel shall go to the king of **E** and say to him, C
3:19 king of **E** will not let you go unless compelled C
3:20 So I will stretch out my hand and strike **E**
4:18 "Please let me go back to my kindred in **E**
4:19 LORD said to Moses in Midian, "Go back to **E;**
4:20 on a donkey and went back to the land of **E;** A
4:21 LORD said to Moses, "When you go back to **E,**
5: 4 the king of **E** said to them, "Moses and Aaron, C
5:12 the people scattered throughout the land of **E,** A
6:11 king of **E** to let the Israelites go out of his land." C
6:13 the Israelites and Pharaoh king of **E,** C
6:13 to free the Israelites from the land of **E.** A
6:26 "Bring the Israelites out of the land of **E,** A
6:27 to Pharaoh king of **E** to bring the Israelites out C
6:27 of Egypt to bring the Israelites out of **E,** B
6:28 when the LORD spoke to Moses in the land of **E,** A
6:29 tell Pharaoh king of **E** all that I am speaking C
7: 3 and wonders in the land of **E.** A
7: 4 I will lay my hand upon **E** and bring my people
Ex 7: 4 out of the land of **E** by great acts of judgment. A
7: 5 when I stretch out my hand against **E** and bring
7:11 and they also, the magicians of **E,**
7:19 and stretch out your hand over the waters of **E**—
7:19 be blood throughout the whole land of **E,** A
7:21 there was blood throughout the whole land of **E.** A
7:22 magicians of **E** did the same by their secret arts;
8: 5 and make frogs come up on the land of **E.**' " A
8: 6 Aaron stretched out his hand over the waters of **E;**
8: 6 the frogs came up and covered the land of **E.** A
8: 7 and brought frogs up on the land of **E.** A
8:16 throughout the whole land of **E.**' " A
8:17 into gnats throughout the whole land of **E.** A
8:24 in all of **E** the land was ruined because of the flies.
9: 4 the livestock of Israel and the livestock of **E,**
9: 9 It shall become fine dust all over the land of **E,** A
9: 9 and animals throughout the whole land of **E.**" A
9:18 the heaviest hail to fall that has ever fallen in **E**
9:22 so that hail may fall on the whole land of **E,** A
9:22 and all the plants of the field in the land of **E.**" A
9:23 And the LORD rained hail on the land of **E;** A
9:24 in all the land of **E** since it became a nation. A
9:25 in the open field throughout all the land of **E,** A
10: 7 do you not yet understand that **E** is ruined?"
10:12 "Stretch out your hand over the land of **E,** A
10:13 Moses stretched out his staff over the land of **E,** A
10:14 the land of **E** and settled on the whole country A
10:14 of Egypt and settled on the whole country of **E,**
10:15 no tree, no plant in the field, in all the land of **E.** A
10:19 not a single locust was left in all the country of **E.**
10:21 that there may be darkness over the land of **E,** A
10:22 there was dense darkness in all the land of **E** A
11: 1 upon Pharaoh and upon **E;**
11: 3 a man of great importance in the land of **E,** A
11: 4 About midnight I will go out through **E.**
11: 5 Every firstborn in the land of **E** shall die, A
11: 6 be a loud cry throughout the whole land of **E,** A
11: 7 that the LORD makes a distinction between **E**
11: 9 be multiplied in the land of **E.**" A
12: 1 LORD said to Moses and Aaron in the land of **E:** A
12:12 For I will pass through the land of **E** that night, A
12:12 strike down every firstborn in the land of **E,** A
12:12 on all the gods of **E** I will execute judgments:
12:13 when I strike the land of **E.** A
12:17 I brought your companies out of the land of **E:** A
12:27 he passed over the houses of the Israelites in **E,**
12:29 down all the firstborn in the land of **E,** A
12:30 and there was a loud cry in **E,**
12:39 of the dough that they had brought out of **E;** B
12:39 they were driven out of **E** and could not wait, B
12:40 in **E** was four hundred thirty years.
12:41 of the LORD went out from the land of **E.** A
12:42 to bring them out of the land of **E.** A
12:51 the Israelites out of the land of **E,** A
13: 3 Remember this day on which you came out of **E,** B
13: 8 the LORD did for me when I came out of **E.**' B
13: 9 a strong hand the LORD brought you out of **E.** B
13:14 of hand the LORD brought us out of **E,** B
13:15 the LORD killed all the firstborn in the land of **E,** A
13:16 of hand the LORD brought us out of **E.**" B
13:17 they may change their minds and return to **E.**"
13:18 up out of the land of **E** prepared for battle. A
14: 5 the king of **E** was told that the people had fled, C
14: 7 the other chariots of **E** with officers over all
14: 8 Pharaoh king of **E** and he pursued the Israelites, C
14:11 "Was it because there were no graves in **E**
14:11 What have you done to us, bringing us out of **E?** B
14:12 Is this not the very thing we told you in **E,**
14:20 between the army of **E** and the army of Israel.
14:25 for the LORD is fighting for them against **E.**"
16: 1 after they had departed from the land of **E.** A
16: 3 in the land of **E,** when we sat by the fleshpots A
16: 6 the LORD who brought you out of the land of **E,** A
16:32 when I brought you out of the land of **E.**' " A
17: 3 "Why did you bring us out of **E,** B
18: 1 how the LORD had brought Israel out of **E.** B
19: 1 after the Israelites had gone out of the land of **E,** A
20: 2 who brought you out of the land of **E,** A
22:21 for you were aliens in the land of **E.** A
23: 9 for you were aliens in the land of **E.** A
23:15 for in it you came out of **E.** B
29:46 of the land of **E** that I might dwell among them; A
32: 1 the man who brought us up out of the land of **E,** A
32: 4 who brought you up out of the land of **E!**" A
32: 7 whom you brought up out of the land of **E,** A
32: 8 who brought you up out of the land of **E!**' " A
32:11 brought out of the land of **E** with great power A
32:23 the man who brought us up out of the land of **E,** A
33: 1 up out of the land of **E,** A
34:18 for in the month of Abib you came out from **E.**
Lev 11:45 up from the land of **E,** to be your God; A
18: 3 You shall not do as they do in the land of **E,** A
19:34 for you were aliens in the land of **E:** A
19:36 who brought you out of the land of **E.** A
22:33 I who brought you out of the land of **E** to A
23:43 when I brought them out of the land of **E:** A
25:38 who brought you out of the land of **E,** A
25:42 whom I brought out of the land of **E;** A
25:55 servants whom I brought out from the land of **E:** A
26:13 of the land of **E,** to be their slaves no more; A
26:45 out of the land of **E** in the sight of the nations, A
Nu 1: 1 after they had come out of the land of **E,** saying: A
3:13 when I killed all the firstborn in the land of **E,** A
8:17 the firstborn in the land of **E** I consecrated them A
9: 1 after they had come out of the land of **E,** saying: A
11: 5 to eat in **E** for nothing, the cucumbers, the melons,
11:18 Surely it was better for us in **E.**'

Nu 11:20 saying, 'Why did we ever leave E?' "
13:22 (Hebron was built seven years before Zoan in E.)
14: 2 "Would that we had died in the land of E! A
14: 3 would it not be better for us to go back to E?"
14: 4 "Let us choose a captain, and go back to E."
14:19 as you have pardoned this people, from E even
14:22 and the signs that I did in E and in the wilderness,
15:41 who brought you out of the land of E, A
20: 5 Why have you brought us up out of E, B
20:15 our ancestors went down to E, and we lived D
20:15 and we lived in E a long time;
20:16 and sent an angel and brought us out of E; B
21: 5 "Why have you brought us up out of E to die in B
22: 5 saying, "A people has come out of E; B
22:11 'A people has come out of E and has spread B
23:22 God, who brings them out of E, B
24: 8 God who brings him out of E, B
26: 4 Israelites, who came out of the land of E, were: A
26:59 who was born to Levi in E;
32:11 none of the people who came up out of E, B
33: 1 by which the Israelites went out of the land of E A
33:38 after the Israelites had come out of the land of E, A
34: 5 shall turn from Azmon to the Wadi of E, E
Dt 1:27 that he has brought us out of the land of E, A
1:30 just as he did for you in E before your very eyes,
4:20 brought you out of the iron-smelter, out of E, B
4:34 as the LORD your God did for you in E
4:37 He brought you out of E with his own presence, B
4:45 to the Israelites when they had come out of E, B
4:46 the Israelites defeated when they came out of E. B
5: 6 who brought you out of the land of E, A
5:15 that you were a slave in the land of E, A
6:12 who brought you out of the land of E, A
6:21 "We were Pharaoh's slaves in E,
6:21 LORD brought us out of E with a mighty hand. B
6:22 and awesome signs and wonders against E,
7: 8 from the hand of Pharaoh king of E. C
7:15 all the dread diseases of E that you experienced,
7:18 the LORD your God did to Pharaoh and to all E,
8:14 who brought you out of the land of E, A
9: 7 of the land of E until you came to this place. A
9:12 from E have acted corruptly.
9:26 whom you brought out of E with a mighty hand. B
10:19 for you were strangers in the land of E. A
10:22 Your ancestors went down to E seventy persons; D
11: 3 his signs and his deeds that he did in E to Pharaoh,
11: 3 the king of E, and to all his land; C
11:10 to enter to occupy is not like the land of E, A
13: 5 the land of E and redeemed you from the house A
13:10 who brought you out of the land of E, A
15:15 that you were a slave in the land of E, A
16: 1 the LORD your God brought you out of E B
16: 3 you came out of the land of E in great haste, A
16: 3 the day of your departure from the land of E. A
16: 6 the time of day when you departed from E.
16:12 Remember that you were a slave in E,
17:16 the people to E in order to acquire more horses,
20: 1 who brought you up from the land of E. A
23: 4 with food and water on your journey out of E, B
24: 9 to Miriam on your journey out of E. B
24:18 in E and the LORD your God redeemed you
24:22 that you were a slave in the land of E; A
25:17 to you on your journey out of E, B
26: 5 he went down into E and lived there as an alien,
26: 8 brought us out of E with a mighty hand and B
28:27 The LORD will afflict you with the boils of E,
28:60 He will bring back upon you all the diseases of E,
28:68 The LORD will bring you back in ships to E,
29: 2 the LORD did before your eyes in the land of E, A
29:16 You know how we lived in the land of E, A
29:25 when he brought them out of the land of E. A
34:11 the LORD sent him to perform in the land of E, A
Jos 2:10 Red Sea before you when you came out of E, B
5: 4 all the males of the people who came out of E, B
5: 4 the wilderness after they had come out of E. B
5: 5 the wilderness after they had come out of E had B
5: 6 the warriors who came out of E, perished, B
5: 9 from you the disgrace of E."
9: 9 of all that he did in E,
13: 3 which is east of E, northward to the boundary
15: 4 goes out by the Wadi of E, E
15:47 the Wadi of E, and the Great Sea with its coast. E
24: 4 but Jacob and his children went down to E. D
24: 5 and I plagued E with what I did in its midst;
24: 6 When I brought your ancestors out of E, B
24: 7 and your eyes saw what I did to E.
24:14 beyond the River and in E,
24:17 and our ancestors up from the land of E, A
24:32 which the Israelites had brought up from E,
Jdg 2: 1 and said, "I brought you up from E,
2:12 who had brought them out of the land of E; A
6: 8 up from E, and brought you out of the house
6:13 saying, 'Did not the LORD bring us up from E?'
11:13 "Because Israel, on coming from E,
11:16 but when they came up from E,
19:30 that the Israelites came up from the land of E A
1Sa 2:27 of your ancestor in E when they were slaves to
8: 8 the day I brought them up out of E to this day, B
10:18 the God of Israel, 'I brought up Israel out of E, B
12: 6 your ancestors up out of the land of E. A
12: 8 into E and the Egyptians oppressed them,
12: 8 who brought forth your ancestors out of E, B
15: 2 the Israelites when they came up out of E. B
15: 6 people of Israel when they came up out of E." B
15: 7 from Havilah as far as Shur, which is east of E.
27: 8 on the way to Shur and on to the land of E. A
30:13 He said, "I am a young man of E,
2Sa 7: 6 the day I brought up the people of Israel from E
1Ki 3: 1 a marriage alliance with Pharaoh king of E; C
4:21 even to the border of E;
4:30 and all the wisdom of E.
6: 1 after the Israelites came out of the land of E, A
8: 9 when they came out of the land of E. A
8:16 the day that I brought my people Israel out of E, B
8:21 when he brought them out of the land of E." A
8:51 which you brought out of E, B
8:53 when you brought our ancestors out of E, B
8:65 people from Lebo-hamath to the Wadi of E— E
9: 9 who brought their ancestors out of the land of E, A
9:16 king of E had gone up and captured Gezer C
10:28 Solomon's import of horses was from E and Kue,
10:29 from E for six hundred shekels of silver,
11:17 to E with some Edomites who were servants
11:18 with them from Paran and came to E,
11:18 to Pharaoh king of E, who gave him a house, C
11:21 in E that David slept with his ancestors and
11:40 but Jeroboam promptly fled to E,
11:40 to Egypt, to King Shishak of E,
11:40 and remained in E until the death of Solomon.
12: 2 of Nebat heard of it (for he was still in E,
12: 2 then Jeroboam returned from E.
12:28 who brought you up out of the land of E." A
14:25 King Shishak of E came up against Jerusalem;
2Ki 7: 6 the kings of the Hittites and the kings of E to fight
17: 4 for he had sent messengers to King So of E,
17: 7 the land of E from under the hand of Pharaoh A
17: 7 from under the hand of Pharaoh king of E. C
17:36 of the land of E with great power and with A
18:21 See, you are relying now on E,
18:21 Pharaoh king of E to all who rely on him. C
18:24 when you rely on E for chariots and for horsemen?
19:24 up with the sole of my foot all the streams of E.'
21:15 since the day their ancestors came out of E, B
23:29 In his days Pharaoh Neco king of E went up to C
23:34 he came to E, and died there.
24: 7 king of E did not come again out of his land, C
24: 7 that belonged to the king of E from the Wadi C
24: 7 from the Wadi of E to the River Euphrates. E
25:26 the captains of the forces set out and went to E;
1Ch 1: 8 descendants of Ham: Cush, E, Put, and Canaan.
1:11 E became the father of Ludim, Anamim, Lehabim,
13: 5 from the Shihor of E to Lebo-hamath,
17:21 before your people whom you redeemed from E?
2Ch 1:16 Solomon's horses were imported from E and Kue;
1:17 They imported from E, and then exported,
5:10 the people of Israel after they came out of E. B
6: 5 the land of E, I have not chosen a city from any A
7: 8 from Lebo-hamath to the Wadi of E. E
7:22 of the land of E, and they adopted other gods, A
9:26 and to the border of E.
9:28 Horses were imported for Solomon from E and
10: 2 of Nebat heard of it (for he was in E,
10: 2 then Jeroboam returned from E.
12: 2 King Shishak of E came up against Jerusalem
12: 3 A countless army came with him from E—
12: 9 So King Shishak of E came up against Jerusalem;
20:10 the land of E, and whom they avoided and did A
26: 8 and his fame spread even to the border of E,
35:20 King Neco of E went up to fight at Carchemish on
36: 3 the king of E deposed him in Jerusalem and laid C
36: 4 king of E made his brother Eliakim king over C
36: 4 took his brother Jehoahaz and carried him to E.
Ne 9: 9 "And you saw the distress of our ancestors in E
9:17 and determined to return to their slavery in E.
9:18 'This is your God who brought you up out of E,' B
Ps 68:31 Let bronze be brought from E;
78:12 in the land of E, in the fields A
78:43 when he displayed his signs in E,
78:51 He struck all the firstborn in E,
80: 8 You brought a vine out of E; B
81: 5 when he went out over the land of E. A
81:10 who brought you up out of the land of E. A
105:23 Then Israel came to E; Jacob lived
105:38 E was glad when they departed,
106: 7 Our ancestors, when they were in E,
106:21 their Savior, who had done great things in E,
114: 1 When Israel went out from E,
136: 8 He it was who struck down the firstborn of E,
135: 9 O E, against Pharaoh and all his servants.
136:10 who struck E through their firstborn,
Isa 7:18 the fly that is at the sources of the streams of E,
10:26 and he will lift it as he did in E.
11:11 from E, from Pathros, from Ethiopia, from Elam,
11:15 the tongue of the sea of E;
11:16 for Israel when they came up from the land of E. A
19: 1 An oracle concerning E.
19: 1 LORD is riding on a swift cloud and comes to E;
19: 1 the idols of E will tremble at his presence,
19:12 the LORD of hosts has planned against E.
19:13 the cornerstones of its tribes have led E astray.
19:14 and they have made E stagger in all its doings as
19:15 will be able to do anything for E.
19:18 the land of E that speak the language of Canaan A
19:19 to the LORD in the center of the land of E, A
19:20 a witness to the LORD of hosts in the land of E; A
19:22 The LORD will strike E, striking and healing;
19:23 On that day there will be a highway from E
19:23 and the Assyrian will come into E,
19:24 On that day Israel will be the third with E
19:25 saying, "Blessed be E my people,
20: 3 for three years as a sign and a portent against E
20: 4 with buttocks uncovered, to the shame of E.
20: 5 of Ethiopia their hope and of E their boast.
23: 5 When the report comes to E,
Isa 27:12 the channel of the Euphrates to the Wadi of E, E
27:13 the land of E will come and worship the LORD A
30: 2 go down to E without asking for my counsel, D
30: 2 and to seek shelter in the shadow of E;
30: 3 the shelter in the shadow of E your humiliation.
31: 1 those who go down to E for help and who rely D
36: 6 See, you are relying on E,
36: 6 Pharaoh king of E to all who rely on him. C
36: 9 when you rely on E for chariots and for horsemen?
37:25 up with the sole of my foot all the streams of E.'
43: 3 I give E as your ransom, Ethiopia and Seba
45:14 The wealth of E and the merchandise of Ethiopia,
52: 4 my people went down into E to reside there
Jer 2: 6 the LORD who brought us up from the land of E, A
2:18 What then do you gain by going to E,
2:36 You shall be put to shame by E as you were put
7:22 I brought your ancestors out of the land of E, A
7:25 that your ancestors came out of the land of E A
9:26 E, Judah, Edom, the Ammonites, Moab,
11: 4 when I brought them out of the land of E, A
11: 7 when I brought them up out of the land of E, A
16:14 the people of Israel up out of the land of E," A
23: 7 the people of Israel up out of the land of E," A
24: 8 and those who live in the land of E. A
25:19 Pharaoh king of E, his servants, his officials, C
26:21 he was afraid and fled and escaped to E.
26:22 of Achbor and men with him to E,
26:23 and they took Uriah from E and brought him
31:32 by the hand to bring them out of the land of E— A
32:20 You showed signs and wonders in the land of E, A
32:21 out of the land of E with signs and wonders, A
34:13 when I brought them out of the land of E, A
37: 5 the army of Pharaoh had come out of E; B
37: 7 is going to return to its own land, to E.
41:17 near Bethlehem, intending to go to E
42:14 'No, we will go to the land of E, A
42:15 If you are determined to enter E and go
42:16 shall overtake you there, in the land of E; A
42:16 that you dread shall follow close after you into E;
42:17 to go to E to settle there shall die by the sword,
42:18 be poured out on you when you go to E.
42:19 O remnant of Judah, Do not go to E.
43: 2 'Do not go to E to settle there';
43: 7 And they came into the land of E, A
43:11 He shall come and ravage the land of E, A
43:12 a fire in the temples of the gods of E;
43:12 and he shall pick clean the land of E, A
43:13 which is in the land of E; A
43:13 temples of the gods of E he shall burn with fire.
44: 1 for all the Judeans living in the land of E, A
44: 8 in the land of E where you have come to settle? A
44:12 to land of E to settle, and they shall perish, A
44:12 in the land of E they shall fall; A
44:13 I will punish those who live in the land of E, A
44:14 in the land of E shall escape or survive or return A
44:15 the people who lived in Pathros in the land of E, A
44:24 all you Judeans who are in the land of E, A
44:26 all you Judeans who live in the land of E: A
44:26 any of the people of Judah in all the land of E, A
44:27 of Judah who are in the land of E shall perish by A
44:28 land of E to the land of Judah, few in number; A
44:28 who have come to the land of E to settle, A
44:30 I am going to give Pharaoh Hophra, king of E, C
46: 2 Concerning E, about the army of Pharaoh Neco,
46: 2 about the army of Pharaoh Neco, king of E, C
46: 8 E rises like the Nile, like rivers
46:11 and take balm, O virgin daughter E!
46:13 of Babylon to attack the land of E: A
46:14 Declare in E, and proclaim in Migdol;
46:17 Give Pharaoh, king of E, the name "Braggart C
46:19 Pack your bags for exile, sheltered daughter E!
46:20 A beautiful heifer is E—a gadfly from the
46:24 Daughter E shall be put to shame;
46:25 and Pharaoh, and E and her gods and her kings,
46:26 Afterward E shall be inhabited as in the days
La 5: 6 We have made a pact with E and Assyria,
Eze 17:15 against him by sending ambassadors to E,
19: 4 they brought him with hooks to the land of E. A
20: 5 making myself known to them in the land of E A
20: 6 the land of E into a land that I had searched out A
20: 7 and do not defile yourselves with the idols of E;
20: 8 nor did they forsake the idols of E.
20: 8 against them in the midst of the land of E. A
20: 9 to them in bringing them out of the land of E. A
20:10 land of E and brought them into the wilderness. A
20:36 in the wilderness of the land of E, A
23: 3 they played the whore in E;
23: 8 up her whorings that she had practiced since E;
23:19 when she played the whore in the land of E A
23:27 and your whoring brought from the land of E; A
23:27 or remember E any more.
27: 7 Of fine embroidered linen from E was your sail,
29: 2 set your face against Pharaoh king of E, C
29: 2 and prophesy against him and against all E;
29: 3 I am against you, Pharaoh king of E, C
29: 6 Then all the inhabitants of E shall know that I am
29: 9 the land of E shall be a desolation and a waste. A
29:10 and I will make the land of E an utter waste A
29:12 the land of E a desolation among desolated A
29:14 the fortunes of E, and bring them back to the land
29:19 land of E to King Nebuchadrezzar of Babylon; A
29:20 land of E as his payment for which he labored, A
30: 4 A sword shall come upon E,
30: 4 the slain fall in E, and its wealth is carried away,
30: 6 Those who support E shall fall,
30: 8 when I have set fire to E,
30:10 I will put an end to the hordes of E,

Eze 30:11 and they shall draw their swords against E,
30:13 shall no longer be a prince in the land of E; A
30:13 so I will put fear in the land of E. A
30:15 upon Pelusium, the stronghold of E, and cut off
30:16 I will set fire to E;
30:18 when I break there the dominion of E,
30:19 Thus I will execute acts of judgment on E.
30:21 I have broken the arm of Pharaoh king of E; C
30:22 I am against Pharaoh king of E, C
30:25 He shall stretch it out against the land of E, A
31: 2 say to Pharaoh king of E and to his hordes: C
32: 2 raise a lamentation over Pharaoh king of E, C
32:12 They shall bring to ruin the pride of E,
32:15 make the land of E desolate and when the land A
32:16 Over E and all its hordes they shall chant it,
32:18 wail over the hordes of E, and send them down,
32:18 with E and the daughters of majestic nations,
32:20 E has been handed over to the sword;
47:19 from there along the Wadi of E to the Great Sea. E
48:28 from there along the Wadi of E to the Great Sea. E
Da 9:15 who brought your people out of the land of E A
11: 8 he shall carry off to E as spoils of war.
11:42 and the land of E shall not escape. A
11:43 and all the riches of E;
Hos 2:15 at the time when she came out of the land of E. A
7:11 they call upon E, they go to Assyria.
7:16 So much for their babbling in the land of E. A
8:13 and punish their sins; they shall return to E.
9: 3 but Ephraim shall return to E,
9: 6 if they escape destruction, E shall gather them,
11: 1 I loved him, and out of E I called my son. B
11: 5 They shall return to the land of E, A
11:11 They shall come trembling like birds from E,
12: 1 a treaty with Assyria, and oil is carried to E.
12: 9 I am the LORD your God from the land of E; A
12:13 a prophet the LORD brought Israel up from E,
13: 4 the LORD your God ever since the land of E; A
Joel 3:19 E shall become a desolation and Edom
Am 2:10 Also I brought you up out of the land of E, A
3: 1 that I brought up out of the land of E: A
3: 9 and to the strongholds in the land of E, and say, A
4:10 among you a pestilence after the manner of E;
8: 8 about and sink again, like the Nile of E?
9: 5 and sinks again, like the Nile of E;
9: 7 Did I not bring Israel up from the land of E, A
Mic 6: 4 For I brought you up from the land of E, A
7:12 that day they will come to you from Assyria to E,
7:12 and from E to the River, from sea to sea
7:15 in the days when you came out of the land of E, A
Na 3: 9 Ethiopia was her strength, E too,
Hag 2: 5 that I made you when you came out of E. B
Zec 10:10 I will bring them home from the land of E, A
10:11 and the scepter of E shall depart.
14:18 family of E do not go up and present themselves,
14:19 of E and the punishment of all the nations that do
Mt 2:13 and flee to E, and remain there until I tell you;
2:14 the child and his mother by night, and went to E,
2:15 "Out of E I have called my son." B
2:19 in a dream to Joseph in E and said,
Ac 2:10 E and the parts of Libya belonging to Cyrene,
7: 9 patriarchs, jealous of Joseph, sold him into E;
7:10 king of E, who appointed him ruler over Egypt C
7:10 who appointed him ruler over E and
7:11 there came a famine throughout E and Canaan,
7:12 But when Jacob heard that there was grain in E,
7:15 so Jacob went down to E. D
7:17 our people in E increased and multiplied
7:18 not known Joseph ruled over E.
7:34 the mistreatment of my people who are in E
7:34 Come now, I will send you to E.'
7:36 having performed wonders and signs in E,
7:39 and in their hearts they turned back to E,
7:40 this Moses who led us out from the land of E, A
13:17 people great during their stay in the land of E, A
Heb 3:16 not all those who left E under the leadership
8: 9 by the hand to lead them out of the land of E; A
11:26 to be greater wealth than the treasures of E,
11:27 By faith he left E, unafraid of the king's anger;
Jude 1: 5 for all saved a people out of the land of E, A
Rev 11: 8 that is prophetically called Sodom and E,
Tob 8: 3 the demon that he fled to the remotest parts of E.
Jdt 1: 9 and Chelous and Kadesh and the river of E,
1:10 all who lived in E as far as the borders of Ethiopia.
1:12 and all Judea, and every one in E,
5:10 of Canaan they went down to E and lived there D
5:11 So the king of E became hostile to them; C
5:12 the whole land of E with incurable plagues. A
6: 5 on this race that came out of E. B
AdE 11: 1 to E the preceding Letter about Purim,
13:16 for yourself out of the land of E. A
Sir Pr: 3 When I came to E in the thirty-eighth year of
Bar 1:19 Lord brought our ancestors out of the land of E A
1:20 he brought our ancestors out of the land of E A
2:11 the land of E with a mighty hand and with signs A
1Mc 1:16 he determined to become king of the land of E, A
1:17 So he invaded E with a strong force,
1:18 He engaged King Ptolemy of E in battle,
1:19 captured the fortified cities in the land of E, A
1:19 and he plundered the land of E. A
1:20 After subduing E, Antiochus returned in
2:53 the commandment, and became lord of E.
3:32 from the river Euphrates to the borders of E.
10:51 Ptolemy king of E with the following message: C
10:57 So Ptolemy set out from E,
11: 1 Then the king of E gathered great forces, C
11:13 the crown of E and that of Asia.
11:59 from the Ladder of Tyre to the borders of E.
2Mc 1: 1 To their Jewish kindred in E,
1:10 and to the Jews in E, Greetings and good health.
4:21 of Menestheus was sent to E for the coronation
5: 1 Antiochus made his second invasion of E.
5: 8 he was cast ashore in E.
5:11 he left E and took the city by storm.
9:29 he withdrew to Ptolemy Philometor in E.
1Es 1:25 it happened that Pharaoh, king of E, C
1:26 And the king of E sent word to him saying, C
1:35 king of E deposed him from reigning in C
1:37 The king of E made his brother Jehoiakim king C
1:38 and brought him back from E.
3Mc 2:25 in E, he increased in his deeds of malice, abetted
3:12 in E and all its districts, greetings and good health:
3:20 "But we, when we arrived in E victorious,
4:18 the task was impossible for all the generals in E.
6: 4 the former ruler of this E,
7: 1 "King Ptolemy Philopator to the generals in E
2Es 1: 7 not I who brought them out of the land of E, A
3:17 And when you led his descendants out of E, B
9:29 in the wilderness when they came out from E and
14: 3 to Moses when my people were in bondage in E;
14: 4 and I sent him and led my people out of E; B
14:29 At first our ancestors lived as aliens in E,
15:10 allow them to live any longer in the land of E, A
15:11 and will strike E with plagues, as before,
15:12 Let E mourn, and its foundations,
16: 1 Woe to you, E and Syria!
4Mc 4:22 For when he was warring against Ptolemy in E,

EGYPT'S (3) [EGYPT]

Isa 19: 6 the branches of E Nile will diminish and dry up,
30: 7 For E help is worthless and empty,
Eze 30: 9 upon them on the day of E doom;

EGYPTIAN‡ (26) [EGYPT]

Ge 16: 1 She had an E slave-girl whose name was Hagar,
16: 3 Abram's wife, took Hagar the E, her slave-girl,
21: 9 But Sarah saw the son of Hagar the E,
25:12 whom Hagar the E, Sarah's slave-girl,
39: 1 the captain of the guard, an E,
39: 2 he was in the house of his E master.
Ex 1:19 the Hebrew women are not like the E women;
2:11 He saw an E beating a Hebrew,
2:12 and seeing no one he killed the E and hid him in
2:14 Do you mean to kill me as you killed the E?"
2:19 They said, "An E helped us against the shepherds;
14:24 of fire and cloud looked down upon the E army,
14:24 and threw the E army into panic.
Lev 24:10 an Israelite and whose father was an E came out
Dt 11: 4 to the E army, to their horses and chariots,
1Sa 30:11 In the open country they found an E,
2Sa 23:21 And he killed an E, a handsome man.
23:21 The E had a spear in his hand;
1Ch 2:34 Sheshan had an E slave, whose name was Jarha.
11:23 And he killed an E, a man of great stature,
11:23 E had in his hand a spear like a weaver's beam;
Pr 7:16 colored spreads of E linen;
Isa 19:23 the E into Assyria, and the Egyptians will worship
Ac 7:24 and avenged him by striking down the E.
7:28 to kill me as you killed the E yesterday?'
21:38 not the E who recently stirred up a revolt and led

EGYPTIAN'S (3) [EGYPT]

Ge 39: 5 the LORD blessed the E house for Joseph's sake;
2Sa 23:21 snatched the spear out of the E hand,
1Ch 11:23 snatched the spear out of the E hand,

EGYPTIANS‡ (104) [EGYPT]

Ge 12:12 the E see you, they will say, 'This is his wife';
12:14 the E saw that the woman was very beautiful.
41:55 Pharaoh said to all the E, "Go to Joseph;
41:56 and sold to the E, for the famine was severe in
43:32 the E who ate with him by themselves, because
the E could not eat with the Hebrews, for that is an
abomination to the E.
45: 2 And he wept so loudly that the E heard it,
46:34 because all shepherds are abhorrent to the E."
47:15 all the E came to Joseph, and said, "Give us food!
47:20 All the E sold their fields,
50: 3 And the E wept for him seventy days.
50:11 "This is a grievous mourning on the part of the E."
Ex 1:12 so that the E came to dread the Israelites.
1:13 The E became ruthless in imposing tasks on
3: 8 and I have come down to deliver them from the E,
3: 9 I have also seen how the E oppress them.
3:21 I will bring this people into such favor with the E
3:22 and so you shall plunder the E."
6: 5 of the Israelites whom the E are holding as slaves,
6: 6 the burdens of the E and deliver you from slavery
6: 7 who has freed you from the burdens of the E.
7: 5 The E shall know that I am the LORD,
7:18 E shall be unable to drink water from the Nile.' "
7:21 river stank so that the E could not drink its water,
7:24 the E had to dig along the Nile for water to drink,
8:21 and the houses of the E shall be filled with swarms
8:26 to the LORD our God are offensive to the E.
8:26 in the sight of the E sacrifices that are offensive
9: 6 all the livestock of the E died,
9:11 boils afflicted the magicians as well as all the E.
10: 2 and grandchildren how I have made fools of the E
10: 6 the houses of all your officials and of all the E—
11: 3 LORD gave the people favor in the sight of the E.
12:23 LORD will pass through to strike down the E;
12:27 he struck down the E but spared our houses.' "
Ex 12:30 he and all his officials and all the E;
12:33 The E urged the people to hasten their departure
12:35 they had asked the E for jewelry of silver
12:36 the people favor in the sight of the E,
12:36 And so they plundered the E.
14: 4 and the E shall know that I am the LORD.
14: 9 The E pursued them, all Pharaoh's horses
14:10 and there were the E advancing on them.
14:12 'Let us alone and let us serve the E'?
14:12 for us to serve the E than to die in the wilderness."
14:13 E whom you see today you shall never see again.
14:17 of the E so that they will go in after them;
14:18 And the E shall know that I am the LORD,
14:23 The E pursued, and went into the sea after them,
14:25 The E said, "Let us flee from the Israelites,
14:26 so that the water may come back upon the E,
14:27 As the E fled before it,
14:27 the LORD tossed the E into the sea.
14:30 Thus the LORD saved Israel that day from the E;
14:30 and Israel saw the E dead on the seashore.
14:31 the great work that the LORD did against the E.
15:26 of the diseases that I brought upon the E;
18: 8 that the LORD had done to Pharaoh and to the E
18: 9 in delivering them from the E.
18:10 who has delivered you from the E and
18:11 because he delivered the people from the E,
19: 4 You have seen what I did to the E,
32:12 Why should the E say, 'It was with evil intent
Nu 14:13 "Then the E will hear of it,
20:15 and the E oppressed us and our ancestors;
33: 3 in the sight of all the E,
33: 4 while the E were burying all their firstborn,
Dt 23: 7 You shall not abhor any of the E,
26: 6 When the E treated us harshly and afflicted us,
Jos 24: 6 and the E pursued your ancestors with chariots
24: 7 he put darkness between you and the E,
Jdg 6: 9 and I delivered you from the hand of the E, and
10:11 not deliver you from the E and from the Amorites,
1Sa 4: 8 the E with every sort of plague in the wilderness.
6: 6 Why should you harden your hearts as the E
10:18 and I rescued you from the hand of the E and from
12: 8 Jacob went into Egypt and the E oppressed them,
Ezr 9: 1 the Jebusites, the Ammonites, the Moabites, the E,
Isa 10:24 and lift up their staff against you as the E did.
19: 1 and the heart of the E will melt within them.
19: 2 I will stir up E against E,
19: 3 the spirit of the E within them will be emptied out,
19: 4 I will deliver the E into the hand of a hard master;
19:16 On that day the E will be like women,
19:17 the land of Judah will become a terror to the E;
19:21 The LORD will make himself known to the E;
19:21 and the E will know the LORD on that day,
19:23 and the E will worship with the Assyrians.
20: 4 the king of Assyria lead away the E as captives
31: 3 The E are human, and not God;
Eze 16:26 You played the whore with the E,
23:21 when the E fondled your bosom
29:12 I will scatter the E among the nations,
29:13 of forty years I will gather the E from the peoples
29:16 The E shall never again be the reliance of
30:23 I will scatter the E among the nations,
30:26 the E among the nations and disperse them
Ac 7:22 of the E and was powerful in his words and deeds.
Heb 11:29 when the E attempted to do so they were drowned.
Jdt 5:12 So the E drove them out of their sight.
1Es 8:69 the Perizzites, the Jebusites, the Moabites, the E,
2Es 1:18 for us to serve the E than to die in this wilderness.'

EHI (1)

Ge 46:21 Bela, Becher, Ashbel, Gera, Naaman, E, Rosh,

EHUD‡ (10)

Jdg 3:15 E son of Gera, the Benjaminite, a left-handed man.
3:16 E made for himself a sword with two edges,
3:18 When E had finished presenting the tribute,
3:20 E came to him, while he was sitting alone
3:21 Then E reached with his left hand,
3:23 Then E went out into the vestibule,
3:26 E escaped while they delayed,
4: 1 in the sight of the LORD, after E died.
1Ch 7:10 Jeush, Benjamin, E, Chenaanah, Zethan, Tarshish,
8: 6 the sons of E (they were heads of ancestral houses

EIGHT (68) [EIGHTH]

Ge 5: 4 the father of Seth were e hundred years;
5: 7 after the birth of Enosh e hundred seven years,
5:10 after the birth of Kenan e hundred fifteen years,
5:13 Kenan lived after the birth of Mahalalel e hundred
5:16 after the birth of Jared e hundred thirty years,
5:17 of Mahalalel were e hundred ninety-five years;
5:19 after the birth of Enoch e hundred years,
17:12 be circumcised when he is e days old,
21: 4 when he was e days old,
22:23 These e Milcah bore to Nahor, Abraham's brother.
Ex 26:25 And so there shall be e frames,
36:30 There were e frames with their bases of silver:
Nu 2:24 is one hundred e thousand one hundred.
3:28 there were e thousand six hundred,
4:48 enrollment was e thousand five hundred eighty.
7: 8 four wagons and e oxen he gave to the Merarites,
29:29 On the sixth day: e bulls, two rams,
Jdg 3: 8 the Israelites served Cushan-rishathaim e years.
12:14 on seventy donkeys; he judged Israel e years.
1Sa 17:12 named Jesse, who had e sons.
2Sa 23: 8 against e hundred whom he killed at one time.

2Sa 24: 9 in Israel there were **e** hundred thousand soldiers
1Ki 7:10 huge stones, stones of **e** and ten cubits.
2Ki 8:17 and he reigned **e** years in Jerusalem.
22: 1 Josiah was **e** years old when he began to reign;
1Ch 12:24 numbered six thousand **e** hundred armed troops.
12:30 Of the Ephraimites, twenty thousand **e** hundred,
24: 4 and **e** of the sons of Ithamar.
2Ch 13: 3 with **e** hundred thousand picked mighty warriors.
21: 5 he reigned **e** years in Jerusalem.
21:20 he reigned **e** years in Jerusalem.
29:17 for **e** days they sanctified the house of the LORD,
34: 1 Josiah was **e** years old when he began to reign;
36: 9 Jehoiachin was **e** years old when he began
Ezr 2: 6 two thousand **e** hundred twelve.
Ne 7:11 two thousand **e** hundred eighteen.
7:13 Of Zattu, **e** hundred forty-five.
11:12 the work of the house, **e** hundred twenty-two;
Ecc 11: 2 Divide your means seven ways, or even **e**,
Jer 41:15 of Nethaniah escaped from Johanan with **e** men,
52:29 from Jerusalem **e** hundred thirty-two persons;
Eze 40: 9 he measured the vestibule of the gateway, **e** cubits;
40:31 and its stairway had **e** steps.
40:34 and its stairway had **e** steps.
40:37 and its stairway had **e** steps.
40:41 of the gate, **e** tables, on which the sacrifices were
Mic 5: 5 against them seven shepherds and **e** installed
Lk 2:21 After **e** days had passed, it was time to circumcise
9:28 Now about **e** days after these sayings Jesus took
Ac 9:33 who had been bedridden for **e** years,
25: 6 among them not more than **e** or ten days, he went
1Pe 3:20 that is, **e** persons, were saved through water.
1Mc 3:24 **e** hundred of them fell, and the rest fled into
4:56 for **e** days, and joyfully offered burnt offerings;
4:59 be observed with joy and gladness for **e** days,
5:20 and **e** thousand to Judas for Gilead.
5:34 As many as **e** thousand of them fell that day.
9: 6 until no more than **e** hundred of them were left.
10:85 with those burned alive, came to **e** thousand.
15:13 thousand warriors and **e** thousand cavalry.
2Mc 2:12 Likewise Solomon also kept the **e** days.
8:20 when **e** thousand Jews fought along
8:20 Macedonians were hard pressed, the **e** thousand,
10: 6 They celebrated it for **e** days with rejoicing,
1Es 5:11 two thousand **e** hundred twelve.
2Es 11:11 I counted its rival wings, and there were **e** of them.
12:19 for your seeing **e** little wings clinging to its wings,
12:20 **E** kings shall arise in it, whose times shall be short

EIGHTEEN (25) [EIGHTEENTH]

Ge 14:14 born in his house, three hundred **e** of them,
Jdg 3:14 the Israelites served King Eglon of Moab **e** years.
10: 8 For **e** years they oppressed all the Israelites
20:25 and struck down **e** thousand of the Israelites,
20:44 **E** thousand Benjaminites fell,
2Sa 8:13 he killed **e** thousand Edomites in the Valley
1Ki 7:15 **E** cubits was the height of the one,
2Ki 24: 8 Jehoiachin was **e** years old when he began
25:17 The height of the one pillar was **e** cubits,
1Ch 12:31 Of the half-tribe of Manasseh, **e** thousand,
18:12 Abishai son of Zeruiah killed **e** thousand Edomites
26: 9 Meshelemiah had sons and brothers, able men, **e**.
29: 7 **e** thousand talents of bronze,
2Ch 11:21 and concubines (he took **e** wives
Ezr 8: 9 and with him two hundred **e** males.
8:18 namely Sherebiah, with his sons and kin, **e**;
Ne 7:11 two thousand eight hundred **e**.
Jer 52:21 pillars, the height of the one pillar was **e** cubits,
Eze 48:35 of the city shall be **e** thousand cubits.
Lk 13: 4 Or those **e** who were killed when the tower
13:11 with a spirit that had crippled her for **e** years.
13:16 of Abraham whom Satan bound for **e** long years,
2Mc 5:21 So Antiochus carried off **e** hundred talents from
1Es 1:43 when he was made king he was **e** years old,
8:47 with his descendants and kinsmen, **e**;

EIGHTEENTH (14) [EIGHTEEN]

1Ki 15: 1 Now in the **e** year of King Jeroboam son of Nebat,
2Ki 3: 1 In the **e** year of King Jehoshaphat of Judah,
22: 3 In the **e** year of King Josiah,
23:23 the **e** year of King Josiah this passover was kept to
1Ch 24:15 the seventeenth to Hezir, the **e** to Happizzez,
25:25 the **e**, to Hanani, his sons and his brothers, twelve;
2Ch 13: 1 In the **e** year of King Jeroboam,
34: 8 In the **e** year of his reign,
35:19 In the **e** year of the reign
Jer 32: 1 which was the **e** year of Nebuchadrezzar.
52:29 in the **e** year of Nebuchadrezzar he took into exile
Jdt 2: 1 In the **e** year, on the twenty-second day of
1Mc 14:27 "On the **e** day of Elul,
1Es 1:22 In the **e** year of the reign

EIGHTH (37) [EIGHT]

Ex 22:30 on the **e** day you shall give it to me.
Lev 9: 1 the **e** day Moses summoned Aaron and his sons
12: 3 On the **e** day the flesh of his foreskin shall
14:10 On the **e** day he shall take two male lambs
14:23 On the **e** day he shall bring them for his cleansing
15:14 On the **e** day he shall take two turtledoves
15:29 On the **e** day she shall take two turtledoves
22:27 and from the **e** day on it shall be acceptable as
23:36 on the **e** day you shall observe a holy convocation
23:39 and a complete rest on the **e** day.
25:22 When you sow in the **e** year,
Nu 6:10 On the **e** day they shall bring two turtledoves
7:54 On the **e** day Gamaliel son of Pedahzur,
Nu 29:35 On the **e** day you shall have a solemn assembly;
1Ki 6:38 in the month of Bul, which is the **e** month,
8:66 On the **e** day he sent the people away;
12:32 on the fifteenth day of the **e** month like the festival
12:33 on the fifteenth day in the **e** month, in the month
2Ki 24:12 of Babylon took him prisoner in the **e** year
1Ch 12:12 Johanan **e**, Elzabad ninth,
24:10 the seventh to Hakkoz, the **e** to Abijah,
25:15 the **e** to Jeshaiah, his sons and his brothers, twelve;
26: 5 Peullethai the **e**; for God blessed him.
27:11 **E**, for the eighth month, was Sibbecai
27:11 for the **e** month, was Sibbecai the Hushathite,
2Ch 7: 9 On the **e** day they held a solemn assembly;
29:17 the **e** day of the month they came to the vestibule
34: 3 For in the **e** year of his reign,
Ne 8:18 and on the **e** day there was a solemn assembly,
Eze 43:27 from the **e** day onward the priests shall offer upon
Zec 1: 1 In the **e** month, in the second year of Darius,
Lk 1:59 On the **e** day they came to circumcise the child,
Ac 7: 8 of Isaac and circumcised him on the **e** day;
Php 3: 5 circumcised on the **e** day, a member of the people
Rev 17:11 it is an **e** but it belongs to the seven,
21:20 the seventh chrysolite, the **e** beryl, the ninth topaz,
2Es 6:36 the **e** night my heart was troubled within me again,

EIGHTIETH (1) [EIGHTY]

1Ki 6: 1 In the four hundred **e** year after

EIGHTY (29) [EIGHTIETH]

Ge 35:28 Now the days of Isaac were one hundred **e** years.
Ex 7: 7 Moses was **e** years old and Aaron eighty-three
Nu 4:48 their enrollment was eight thousand five hundred **e**.
Jdg 3:30 And the land had rest **e** years.
2Sa 19:32 Barzillai was a very aged man, **e** years old.
19:35 Today I am **e** years old;
1Ki 5:15 and **e** thousand stonecutters in the hill country,
12:21 one hundred **e** thousand chosen troops to fight
2Ki 6:25 a donkey's head was sold for **e** shekels of silver,
10:24 Now Jehu had stationed **e** men outside, saying,
1Ch 15: 9 Eliel the chief, with **e** of his kindred;
2Ch 2: 2 and **e** thousand stonecutters in the hill country,
2:18 **e** thousand as stonecutters in the hill country,
11: 1 assembled one hundred **e** thousand chosen troops
14: 8 and two hundred **e** thousand troops
17:15 with two hundred **e** thousand,
17:18 with one hundred **e** thousand armed for war.
26:17 with **e** priests of the LORD who were men
Ezr 8: 8 Zebadiah son of Michael, and with him **e** males.
Est 1: 4 one hundred **e** days in all.
Ps 90:10 days of our life are seventy years, or perhaps **e**,
SS 6: 8 There are sixty queens and **e** concubines,
Jer 41: 5 **e** men arrived from Shechem and Shiloh
Lk 16: 7 He said to him, 'Take your bill and make it **e**.'
AdE 1: 4 during the course of one hundred **e** days,
2Mc 4: 8 and from another source of revenue **e** talents.
5:14 the total of three days **e** thousand were destroyed,
11: 2 about **e** thousand infantry and all his cavalry
11: 4 and his thousands of cavalry, and his **e** elephants.

EIGHTY-EIGHT (2) [EIGHTY-EIGHTH]

1Ch 25: 7 of whom were skillful, numbered two hundred **e**.
Ne 7:26 of Bethlehem and Netophah, one hundred **e**.

EIGHTY-EIGHTH (1) [EIGHTY-EIGHT]

2Mc 1: 9 in the one hundred **e** year.

EIGHTY-FIVE (7)

Jos 14:10 and here I am today, **e** years old.
1Sa 22:18 on that day he killed **e** who wore the linen ephod.
2Ki 19:35 down one hundred **e** thousand in the camp of
Isa 37:36 down one hundred **e** thousand in the camp of
1Mc 7:41 down one hundred **e** thousand of the Assyrians.
2Mc 8:19 when one hundred **e** thousand perished,
15:22 and he killed fully one hundred **e** thousand in

EIGHTY-FOUR (2)

Ne 11:18 the Levites in the holy city were two hundred **e**.
Lk 2:37 then as a widow to the age of **e**.

EIGHTY-SEVEN (2)

Ge 5:25 When Methuselah had lived one hundred **e** years,
1Ch 7: 5 of Issachar were in all **e** thousand mighty warriors,

EIGHTY-SIX (2)

Ge 16:16 Abram was **e** years old
Nu 2: 9 is one hundred **e** thousand four hundred.

EIGHTY-THREE (1)

Ex 7: 7 and Aaron **e** when they spoke to Pharaoh.

EIGHTY-TWO (2)

Ge 5:26 after the birth of Lamech seven hundred **e** years,
5:28 When Lamech had lived one hundred **e** years,

EITHER (83)

Ge 24:49 that I may turn **e** to the right hand or to the left."
31:24 that you say not a word to Jacob, **e** good or bad."
Ex 19:24 not let **e** the priests or the people break through
Lev 7:26 **e** of bird or of animal, in any of your settlements.
13:59 **e** in warp or woof, or in anything of skin,
18:26 **e** the citizen or the alien who resides among you
27:10 **e** good for bad or bad for good;
Nu 6: 2 When **e** men or women make a special vow,
18: 3 not approach **e** the utensils of the sanctuary or
22:24 with a wall on **e** side.
22:26 where there was no way to turn **e** to the right or to
24:13 to do **e** good or bad of my own will;
Dt 17:11 **e** to the right or to the left.
17:20 **e** to the right or to the left,
28:14 **e** to the right or to the left,
1Sa 20: 2 My father does nothing **e** great or small
20:27 the son of Jesse not come to the feast, **e** yesterday
28:15 **e** by prophets or by dreams;
1Ki 18:27 **e** he is meditating, or he has wandered away,
1Ch 12: 2 and sling stones with **e** the right hand or the left;
21:12 **e** three years of famine;
Pr 24:21 and do not disobey **e** of them;
Isa 17: 8 **e** the sacred poles or the altars of incense.
Eze 40:10 There were three recesses on **e** side of
40:10 and the pilasters on **e** side were of the same size.
40:12 a barrier before the recesses, one cubit on **e** side;
40:12 and the recesses were six cubits on **e** side.
40:21 Its recesses, three on **e** side,
40:26 It had palm trees on its pilasters, one on **e** side.
40:34 and it had palm trees on its pilasters, on **e** side;
40:37 and it had palm trees on its pilasters, on **e** side;
40:39 the vestibule of the gate were two tables on **e** side,
40:48 the pilasters of the vestibule, five cubits on **e** side;
40:48 sidewalls of the gate were three cubits on **e** side.
40:49 there were pillars beside the pilasters on **e** side.
41: 2 the sidewalls of the entrance were five cubits on **e**
41:15 together with its galleries on **e** side,
41:26 and palm trees on **e** side,
46:12 **e** a burnt offering or offerings of well-being as
Zec 14: 6 On that day there shall not be **e** cold or frost.
Mt 5:34 But I say to you, Do not swear at all, **e** by heaven,
6:24 for a slave will **e** hate the one and love the other,
12:32 **e** in this age or in the age to come.
12:33 "**E** make the tree good, and its fruit good;
Lk 16:13 for a slave will **e** hate the one and love the other,
Jn 19:18 one on **e** side, with Jesus between them.
Ac 24:12 with anyone in the temple or stirring up a crowd **e**
Ro 6:16 you are slaves of the one whom you obey, **e** of sin,
2Th 2: 2 **e** by spirit or by word or by letter,
2:15 **e** by word of mouth or by our letter.
1Ti 1: 7 without understanding **e** what they are saying or
Jas 5:12 **e** by heaven or by earth or by any other oath,
1Jn 3: 6 no one who sins has **e** seen him or known him.
Rev 3:15 I wish that you were **e** cold or hot.
22: 2 On **e** side of the river is the tree of life
Jdt 13: 4 everyone went out, and no one, **e** small or great,
Wis 13: 2 but they supposed that **e** fire or wind or swift air,
14:24 they no longer keep **e** their lives
14:24 but they **e** treacherously kill one another,
14:28 For their worshipers **e** rave in exultation,
15: 6 and fit for such objects of hope are those who **e**
Sir 13:25 **e** for good or for evil.
20:30 and unseen treasure, of what value is **e**?
40:18 but better than **e** is finding a treasure.
40:19 but better than **e** is the one who finds wisdom.
40:19 but a blameless wife is accounted better than **e**.
40:20 but the love of friends is better than **e**.
40:21 but a pleasant voice is better than **e**.
40:22 but the green shoots of grain more than **e**.
40:23 but a sensible wife is better than **e**.
40:24 but almsgiving rescues better than **e**.
40:25 but good counsel is esteemed more than **e**.
40:26 but the fear of the Lord is better than **e**.
41:14 and unseen treasure—of what value is **e**?
LtJ 6:35 Likewise they are not able to give **e** wealth
6:64 for they are not able **e** to decide a case or
1Mc 4:35 and how ready they were **e** to live or to die nobly,
6:38 The rest of the cavalry were stationed on **e** side,
2Mc 3:26 on **e** side of him and flogged him continuously,
1Es 8:24 by death or some other punishment, **e** fine
4Mc 5:20 in matters **e** small or great is of equal seriousness,
5:21 for in **e** case the law is equally despised.
5:38 **e** by words or through deeds."

EKER (1)

1Ch 2:27 of Jerahmeel: Maaz, Jamin, and **E**.

EKRON (25)

Jos 13: 3 northward to the boundary of **E**,
13: 3 Ashkelon, Gath, and **E**), and those of the Avvim,
15:11 of the hill north of **E**, then the boundary bends
15:45 **E**, with its dependencies and its villages;
15:46 from **E** to the sea, all that were near Ashdod,
19:43 Elon, Timnah, **E**,
Jdg 1:18 with its territory, and **E** with its territory.
1Sa 5:10 So they sent the ark of the God of Israel to **E**.
5:10 But when the ark of God came to **E**,
5:10 the people of **E** cried out,
6:16 they returned that day to **E**.
6:17 one for Ashkelon, one for Gath, one for **E**;
7:14 from Israel were restored to Israel, from **E**
17:52 the Philistines as far as Gath and the gates of **E**,
17:52 on the way from Shaaraim as far as Gath and **E**.
2Ki 1: 2 "Go, inquire of Baal-zebub, the god of **E**,
1: 3 to inquire of Baal-zebub, the god of **E**?'
1: 6 to inquire of Baal-zebub, the god of **E**?
1:16 to inquire of Baal-zebub, the god of **E**,—
Jer 25:20 Ashkelon, Gaza, **E**, and the remnant of Ashdod;
Am 1: 8 I will turn my hand against **E**,
Zep 2: 4 be driven out at noon, and **E** shall be uprooted.
Zec 9: 5 **E** also, because its hopes are withered.
9: 7 and **E** shall be like the Jebusites.
1Mc 10:89 He also gave him **E** and all its environs

EL See Index to Footnotes

EL-BERITH (1)
Jdg 9:46 they entered the stronghold of the temple of **E.**

EL-BETHEL (1) [BETHEL]
Ge 35: 7 and there he built an altar and called the place **E,**

EL-ELOHE-ISRAEL (1) [ISRAEL]
Ge 33:20 There he erected an altar and called it **E.**

EL-PARAN (1) [PARAN]
Ge 14: 6 the hill country of Seir as far as **E** on the edge of

EL-ROI (1)
Ge 16:13 the LORD who spoke to her, "You are **E**";

ELA (1)
1Ki 4:18 Shimei son of **E,** in Benjamin;

ELABORATE (1)
1Mc 13:29 For the pyramids he devised an **e** setting,

ELAH (16)
Ge 36:41 Oholibamah, **E,** Pinon,
1Sa 17: 2 and encamped in the valley of **E,**
17:19 and all the men of Israel, were in the valley of **E,**
21: 9 whom you killed in the valley of **E,**
1Ki 16: 6 and his son **E** succeeded him.
16: 8 **E** son of Baasha began to reign over Israel
16:13 of all the sins of Baasha and the sins of his son **E**
16:14 Now the rest of the acts of **E,** and all that he did,
2Ki 15:30 of **E** made a conspiracy against Pekah son
17: 1 Hoshea son of **E** began to reign in Samaria
18: 1 the third year of King Hoshea son of **E** of Israel,
18: 9 the seventh year of King Hoshea son of **E**
1Ch 1:52 Oholibamah, **E,** Pinon,
4:15 Iru, **E,** and Naam; and the son of Elah: Kenaz.
4:15 and Naam; and the son of **E:**
9: 8 **E** son of Uzzi, son of Michri,

ELAM (32) [ELAMITES]
Ge 10:22 **E,** Asshur, Arpachshad, Lud, and Aram.
14: 1 King Arioch of Ellasar, King Chedorlaomer of **E,**
14: 9 with King Chedorlaomer of **E,**
1Ch 1:17 The descendants of Shem: **E,** Asshur, Arpachshad,
8:24 Hananiah, **E,** Anthothijah,
26: 3 **E** the fifth, Jehohanan the sixth, Eliehoenai
Ezr 2: 7 Of **E,** one thousand two hundred fifty-four.
2:31 the other **E,** one thousand two hundred fifty-four.
8: 7 Of the descendants of **E,** Jeshaiah son of Athaliah,
10: 2 Shecaniah son of Jehiel, of the descendants of **E,**
10:26 Of the descendants of **E:** Mattaniah,
Ne 7:12 Of **E,** one thousand two hundred fifty-four.
7:34 The descendants of the other **E,**
10:14 Parosh, Pahath-moab, **E,** Zattu, Bani,
12:42 Eleazar, Uzzi, Jehohanan, Malchijah, **E,** and Ezer.
Isa 11:11 from Pathros, from Ethiopia, from **E,** from Shinar,
21: 2 Go up, O **E,** lay siege, O Media;
22: 6 **E** bore the quiver with chariots and cavalry,
Jer 25:25 all the kings of **E,** and all the kings of Media;
49:34 that came to the prophet Jeremiah concerning **E,**
49:35 I am going to break the bow of **E,**
49:36 upon **E** the four winds from the four quarters
49:36 be no nation to which the exiles from **E** shall
49:37 I will terrify **E** before their enemies,
49:38 and I will set my throne in **E,**
49:39 in the latter days I will restore the fortunes of **E,**
Eze 32:24 **E** is there, and all its hordes around its grave;
32:25 They have made **E** a bed among the slain
Da 8: 2 in the province of **E,** and I was by the river Ulai.
1Es 5:12 of **E,** one thousand two hundred fifty-four.
8:33 the descendants of **E,** Jeshaiah son of Gotholiah,
9:27 Of the descendants of **E:** Mattaniah

ELAMITES (2) [ELAM]
Ezr 4: 9 the Babylonians, the people of Susa, that is, the **E,**
Ac 2: 9 Medes, **E,** and residents of Mesopotamia,

ELAPSED (2)
Lev 25:29 be redeemed until a year has **e** since its sale;
25:30 If it is not redeemed before a full year has **e,**

ELASA (1)
1Mc 9: 5 Now Judas was encamped in **E,**

ELASAH (2)
Ezr 10:22 Maaseiah, Ishmael, Nethanel, Jozabad, and **E.**
Jer 29: 3 of **E** son of Shaphan and Gemariah son of Hilkiah,

ELATED‡ (7)
2Co 12: 7 Therefore, to keep me from being too **e,**
12: 7 to keep me from being too **e.**
AdE 13: 2 of the whole world (not **e** with presumption
2Mc 5:17 Antiochus was **e** in spirit, and did not perceive that
5:21 and walk on the sea, because his mind was **e.**
7:34 not be **e** in vain and puffed up by uncertain hopes,
11: 4 but was **e** with his ten thousands of infantry,

ELATH (5)
Dt 2: 8 and leaving behind **E** and Ezion-geber.
2Ki 14:22 He rebuilt **E** and restored it to Judah,
16: 6 that time the king of Edom recovered **E** for Edom,
16: 6 and drove the Judeans from **E;**
16: 6 Edomites came to **E,** where they live to this day.

ELBOW (1) [ELBOWS]
Sir 41:19 and of leaning on your **e** at meals;

ELBOWS (1) [ELBOW]
4Mc 10: 6 and breaking his fingers and arms and legs and **e.**

ELDAAH (2)
Ge 25: 4 Epher, Hanoch, Abida, and **E.**
1Ch 1:33 Ephah, Epher, Hanoch, Abida, and **E.**

ELDAD (2)
Nu 11:26 Two men remained in the camp, one named **E,**
11:27 "**E** and Medad are prophesying in the camp."

ELDER‡ (22) [ELDERS, ELDEST]
Ge 10:21 the **e** brother of Japheth, children were born.
25:23 the **e** shall serve the younger."
27: 1 he called his **e** son Esau and said to him,
27:15 Rebekah took the best garments of her **e** son Esau,
27:42 the words of her **e** son Esau were told to Rebekah;
29:16 the name of the **e** was Leah,
1Sa 18:17 Saul said to David, "Here is my **e** daughter Merab;
1Ki 2:22 For he is my **e** brother;
Isa 3: 2 judge and prophet, diviner and **e,**
3: 5 the youth will be insolent to the **e,**
Eze 16:46 Your **e** sister is Samaria, who lived
16:61 both your **e** and your younger,
23: 4 of the **e** and Oholibah the name of her sister.
Lk 15:25 "Now his **e** son was in the field;
Ro 9:12 "The **e** shall serve the younger."
1Ti 5:19 Never accept any accusation against an **e** except
1Pe 5: 1 **e** myself and a witness of the sufferings of Christ,
2Jn 1: 1 The **e** to the elect lady and her children,
3Jn 1: 1 The **e** to the beloved Gaius, whom I love in truth.
Sus 1:50 for God has given you the standing of an **e.**"
4Mc 7:10 O aged man, more powerful than tortures; O **e,**
16:14 of God in the cause of religion, **e** and woman!

ELDERS (235) [ELDER]
A. ELDERS OF ISRAEL (33)
B. ELDERS OF THE/MY PEOPLE (14)
C. ELDERS OF THE JEWS (9)

Ge 50: 7 the servants of Pharaoh, the **e** of his household,
50: 7 and all the **e** of the land of Egypt,
Ex 3:16 and assemble the **e** of Israel, and say to them, A
3:18 the **e** of Israel shall go to the king of Egypt A
4:29 and Aaron went and assembled all the **e** of
12:21 Moses called all the **e** of Israel and said to them, A
17: 5 and take some of the **e** of Israel with you; A
17: 6 Moses did so, in the sight of the **e** of Israel. A
18:12 and Aaron came with all the **e** of Israel A
19: 7 So Moses came, summoned the **e** of the people, B
24: 1 and Abihu, and seventy of the **e** of Israel, A
24: 9 and Abihu, and seventy of the **e** of Israel went A
24:14 To the **e** he had said, "Wait here for us,
Lev 4:15 The **e** of the congregation shall lay their hands on
9: 1 and his sons and the **e** of Israel. A
Nu 11:16 "Gather for me seventy of the **e** of Israel, A
11:16 to be the **e** of the people and officers over them; B
11:24 and he gathered seventy **e** of the people, B
11:25 that was on him and put it on the seventy **e;**
11:30 Moses and the **e** of Israel returned to the camp. A
16:25 the **e** of Israel followed him. A
22: 4 And Moab said to the **e** of Midian,
22: 7 the **e** of Moab and the elders of Midian departed
22: 7 the elders of Moab and the **e** of Midian departed
Dt 5:23 all the heads of your tribes and your **e;**
19:12 then the **e** of the killer's city shall send to have
21: 2 then your **e** and your judges shall come out
21: 3 The **e** of the town nearest the body shall take
21: 4 the **e** of that town shall bring the heifer down to
21: 6 All the **e** of that town nearest
21:19 and bring him out to the **e** of his town at the gate
21:20 They shall say to the **e** of his town,
22:15 of the young woman's virginity to the **e** of the city
22:16 The father of the young woman shall say to the **e:**
22:17 Then they shall spread out the cloth before the **e** of
22:18 **e** of that town shall take the man and punish him;
25: 7 then his brother's widow shall go up to the **e** at
25: 8 **e** of his town shall summon him and speak to him.
25: 9 up to him in the presence of the **e,**
27: 1 the **e** of Israel charged all the people as follows: A
29:10 the leaders of your tribes, your **e,**
31: 9 and to all the **e** of Israel. A
31:28 to me all the **e** of your tribes and your officials,
32: 7 your **e,** and they will tell you.
Jos 7: 6 he and the **e** of Israel; A
8:10 with the **e** of Israel, before the people to Ai. A
8:33 with their **e** and officers and their judges,
9:11 So our **e** and all the inhabitants of our country said
20: 4 and explain the case to the **e** of that city;
23: 2 their **e** and heads, their judges and officers,
24: 1 and summoned the **e,** the heads, the judges,
24:31 of the **e** who outlived Joshua and had known all
Jdg 2: 7 and all the days of the **e** who outlived Joshua,
8:14 he listed for him the officials and **e** of Succoth,
8:16 So he took the **e** of the city and he took thorns of
11: 5 the **e** of Gilead went to bring Jephthah from
11: 7 But Jephthah said to the **e** of Gilead,
11: 8 The **e** of Gilead said to Jephthah, "Nevertheless,
11: 9 Jephthah said to the **e** of Gilead,
11:10 And the **e** of Gilead said to Jephthah,
11:11 So Jephthah went with the **e** of Gilead,
21:16 So the **e** of the congregation said,
Ru 4: 2 Then Boaz took ten men of the **e** of the city,
4: 4 and in the presence of the **e** of my people. B
4: 9 Then Boaz said to the **e** and all the people,
4:11 along with the **e,** said, "We are witnesses.
1Sa 4: 3 the troops came to the camp, the **e** of Israel said, A
8: 4 Then all the **e** of Israel gathered together and A
11: 3 The **e** of Jabesh said to him,
15:30 yet honor me now before the **e** of my people and B
16: 4 The **e** of the city came to meet him trembling,
30:26 the **e** of Judah, saying, "Here is a present for you
2Sa 3:17 Abner sent word to the **e** of Israel, saying, A
5: 3 So all the **e** of Israel came to the king at Hebron; A
12:17 The **e** of his house stood beside him,
17: 4 advice pleased Absalom and all the **e** of Israel. A
17:15 Ahithophel counsel Absalom and the **e** of Israel; A
19:11 "Say to the **e** of Judah,
1Ki 8: 1 Then Solomon assembled the **e** of Israel and all A
8: 3 And all the **e** of Israel came, A
20: 7 Then the king of Israel called all the **e** of the land,
20: 8 Then all the **e** and all the people said to him,
21: 8 to the **e** and the nobles who lived with Naboth
21:11 the **e** and the nobles who lived in his city,
2Ki 6:32 and the **e** were sitting with him.
6:32 Before the messenger arrived, Elisha said to the **e,**
10: 1 to the **e,** and to the guardians of the sons of Ahab,
10: 5 along with the **e** and the guardians,
23: 1 the **e** of Judah and Jerusalem should be gathered
1Ch 11: 3 So all the **e** of Israel came to the king at Hebron, A
15:25 So David and the **e** of Israel, A
21:16 Then David and the **e,** clothed in sackcloth,
2Ch 5: 2 Then Solomon assembled the **e** of Israel and all A
5: 4 And all the **e** of Israel came, A
34:29 the king sent word and gathered together all the **e**
Ezr 5: 5 the eye of their God was upon the **e** of the Jews, C
5: 9 Then we spoke to those **e** and asked them,
6: 7 the Jews and the **e** of the Jews rebuild this house C
6: 8 what you shall do for these **e** of the Jews C
6:14 So the **e** of the Jews built and prospered, C
10: 8 of the officials and the **e** all their property should
10:14 and with them the **e** and judges of every town,
Job 12:20 and takes away the discernment of the **e.**
Ps 105:22 and to teach his **e** wisdom.
107:32 and praise him in the assembly of the **e.**
Pr 31:23 taking his seat among the **e** of the land.
Isa 3:14 into judgment with the **e** and princes of his people:
9:15 **e** and dignitaries are the head,
24:23 and before his **e** he will manifest his glory.
Jer 19: 1 **e** of the people and some of the senior priests, B
26:17 And some of the **e** of the land arose and said to all
29: 1 from Jerusalem to the remaining **e** among
La 1:19 my priests and **e** perished in the city
2:10 **e** of daughter Zion sit on the ground in silence;
4:16 to the priests, no favor to the **e.**
5:12 no respect is shown to the **e.**
Eze 7:26 from the priest, and counsel from the **e.**
8: 1 with the **e** of Judah sitting before me,
8:11 them stood seventy of the **e** of the house of Israel,
8:12 the **e** of the house of Israel are doing in the dark,
9: 6 So they began with the **e** who were in front of
14: 1 Certain **e** of Israel came to me and sat down A
20: 1 certain **e** of Israel came to consult the LORD, A
20: 3 speak to the **e** of Israel, and say to them: A
27: 9 The **e** of Gebal and its artisans were within you,
Joel 1: 2 O **e,** give ear, all inhabitants of the land!
1:14 Gather the **e** and all the inhabitants of the land
Mt 15: 2 Why do your disciples break the tradition of the **e?**
16:21 at the hands of the **e** and chief priests and scribes,
21:23 the chief priests and the **e** of the people came B
26: 3 the chief priests and the **e** of the people gathered B
26:47 from the chief priests and the **e** of the people. B
26:57 in whose house the scribes and the **e** had gathered.
27: 1 and the **e** of the people conferred together B
27: 3 of silver to the chief priests and the **e.**
27:12 when he was accused by the chief priests and **e,**
27:20 the chief priests and the **e** persuaded the crowds
27:41 along with the scribes and **e,** were mocking him,
28:12 After the priests had assembled with the **e,**
Mk 7: 3 thus observing the tradition of the **e;**
7: 5 not live according to the tradition of the **e,**
8:31 and be rejected by the **e,** the chief priests,
11:27 and the **e** came to him
14:43 from the chief priests, the scribes, and the **e.**
14:53 and all the chief priests, the **e,**
15: 1 the chief priests held a consultation with the **e**
Lk 7: 3 he sent some Jewish **e** to him,
9:22 and be rejected by the **e,** chief priests, and scribes,
20: 1 the chief priests and the scribes came with the **e**
22:52 and the **e** who had come for him,
22:66 day came, the assembly of the **e** of the people, B
Jn 8: 9 ⟦went away, one by one, beginning with the **e;**⟧
Ac 4: 5 The next day their rulers, **e,**
4: 8 said to them, "Rulers of the people and **e,**
4:23 the chief priests and the **e** had said to them.
5:21 council and the whole body of the **e** of Israel, A
6:12 They stirred up the people as well as the **e** and
11:30 sending it to the **e** by Barnabas and Saul.
14:23 after they had appointed **e** for them in each church,
15: 2 to discuss this question with the apostles and the **e.**

Ac 15: 4 by the church and the apostles and the e,
15: 6 and the e met together to consider this matter.
15:22 Then the apostles and the e,
15:23 "The brothers, both the apostles and the e,
16: 4 by the apostles and e who were in Jerusalem.
20:17 asking the e of the church to meet him.
21:18 and all the e were present.
22: 5 and the whole council of e can testify about me.
23:14 They went to the chief priests and e and said,
24: 1 the high priest Ananias came down with some e
25:15 chief priests and the e of the Jews informed me C
1Ti 4:14 with the laying on of hands by the council of e.
5:17 Let the e who rule well be considered worthy
Tit 1: 5 and should appoint e in every town,
Jas 5:14 the e of the church and have them pray over them,
1Pe 5: 1 I exhort the e among you
5: 5 who are younger must accept the authority of the e.
Rev 4: 4 and seated on the thrones are twenty-four e,
4:10 the twenty-four e fall before the one who is seated
5: 5 Then one of the e said to me, "Do not weep.
5: 6 and the four living creatures and among the e
5: 8 the four living creatures and the twenty-four e fell
5:11 the throne and the living creatures and the e;
5:14 And the e fell down and worshiped.
7:11 and around the e and the four living creatures,
7:13 Then one of the e addressed me, saying,
11:16 Then the twenty-four e who sit on their thrones
14: 3 before the four living creatures and before the e.
19: 4 the twenty-four e and the four living creatures fell
Jdt 6:16 They called together all the e of the town,
6:21 to his own house and gave a banquet for the e;
7:23 and said before all the e,
8:10 to summon Uzziah and Chabris and Charmis, the e
10: 6 and found Uzziah standing there with the e of
11:14 to bring back permission from the council of the e.
13:12 to the town gate and summoned the e of the town.
15: 8 the e of the Israelites who lived in Jerusalem came
Wis 8:10 the multitudes and honor in the presence of the e,
Sir 6:34 Stand in the company of the e.
7:14 Do not babble in the assembly of the e,
Bar 1: 4 and to the e, and to all the people, small and great,
Sus 1: 5 That year two e from the people were appointed
1: 5 from Babylon, from e who were judges,
1: 8 Every day the two e used to see her,
1:16 No one was there except the two e,
1:18 they did not see the e, because they were hiding.
1:19 the two e got up and ran to her.
1:24 and the two e shouted against her.
1:27 And when the e told their story,
1:28 the house of her husband Joakim, the two e came,
1:34 Then the two e stood up before the people
1:36 The e said, "While we were walking in
1:41 Because they were e of the people and judges, B
1:50 And the rest of the e said to him, "Come,
1:61 And they took action against the two e,
1Mc 1:26 rulers and e groaned, young women
7:33 the sanctuary and some of the e of the people B
11:23 He chose some of the e of Israel and some of A
12:35 returned he convened the e of the people B
13:36 and to the e and nation of the Jews, greetings.
14:20 the Spartans to the high priest Simon and to the e
14:28 the e of the country, the following was proclaimed
2Mc 13:13 After consulting privately with the e,
14:37 A certain Razis, one of the e of Jerusalem,
1Es 6: 5 Yet the e of the Jews were dealt with kindly, C
6: 8 found the e of the Jews, who had been in exile, C
6:11 Then we asked these e, 'At whose
6:27 the e of the Jews to build this house of the Lord C
7: 2 assisting the e of the Jews and the chief officers C
9: 4 in accordance with the decision of the ruling e,
9:13 with the e and judges of each place,
3Mc 1: 8 the Jews had sent some of their council and e
1:23 being barely restrained by the old men and the e,
1:25 while the e near the king tried in various ways
6: 1 directed the e around him to stop calling upon

ELDEST (9) [ELDER]

Ge 44:12 with the e and ending with the youngest;
1Sa 17:13 The three e sons of Jesse had followed Saul to
17:14 David was the youngest; the three e followed Saul,
17:28 His e brother Eliab heard him talking to the men;
Job 1:13 and drinking wine in the e brother's house,
1:18 and drinking wine in their e brother's house,
1Mc 16: 2 Simon called in his two e sons Judas and John,
4Mc 9:11 at his command the guards brought forward the e,
9:26 the guards brought in the next e,

ELEAD (1)

1Ch 7:21 Shuthelah his son, and Ezer and E.

ELEADAH (1)

1Ch 7:20 and Bered his son, Tahath his son, E his son,

ELEALEH (5)

Nu 32: 3 Dibon, Jazer, Nimrah, Heshbon, E, Sebam, Nebo,
32:37 And the Reubenites rebuilt Heshbon, E,
Isa 15: 4 Heshbon and E cry out, their voices are heard
16: 9 I drench you with my tears, O Heshbon and E;
Jer 48:34 Heshbon and E cry out;

ELEASAH (4)

1Ch 2:39 the father of Helez, and Helez of E.
2:40 E became the father of Sismai,
8:37 Raphah was his son, E his son, Azel his son.
9:43 and Rephaiah was his son, E his son, Azel his son.

ELEAZAR (102) [=AVARAN]

Ex 6:23 and she bore him Nadab, Abihu, E, and Ithamar.
6:25 Aaron's son E married one of the daughters
28: 1 Nadab and Abihu, E and Ithamar.
Lev 10: 6 to Aaron and to his sons E and Ithamar, "Do
10:12 and to his remaining sons, E and Ithamar:
10:16 He was angry with E and Ithamar,
Nu 3: 2 Nadab the firstborn, and Abihu, E, and Ithamar;
3: 4 E and Ithamar served as priests in the lifetime
3:32 E son of Aaron the priest was to be chief over
4:16 E son of Aaron the priest shall have charge of
16:37 Tell E son of Aaron the priest to take
16:39 So E the priest took the bronze censers
19: 3 You shall give it to the priest E,
19: 4 The priest E shall take some of its blood
20:25 Take Aaron and his son E,
20:26 and put them on his son E.
20:28 and put them on his son E;
20:28 Moses and E came down from the mountain.
25: 7 When Phinehas son of E, son of Aaron the priest,
25:11 "Phinehas son of E, son of Aaron
26: 1 the plague the LORD said to Moses and to E son
26: 3 and E the priest spoke with them in the plains
26:60 To Aaron were born Nadab, Abihu, E,
26:63 These were those enrolled by Moses and E
27: 2 They stood before Moses, E the priest, the leaders,
27:19 before E the priest and all the congregation,
27:21 But he shall stand before E the priest,
27:22 before E the priest and the whole congregation;
31: 6 along with Phinehas son of E the priest,
31:12 to Moses, to E the priest, and to the congregation
31:13 E the priest, and all the leaders of
31:21 E the priest said to the troops who had gone
31:26 "You and E the priest and the heads of
31:29 Take it from their half and give it to E the priest as
31:31 Then Moses and E the priest did as
31:41 the offering for the LORD, to E the priest,
31:51 and E the priest received the gold from them,
31:54 So Moses and E the priest received the gold from
32: 2 and the Reubenites came and spoke to Moses, to E
32:28 So Moses gave command concerning them to E
34:17 the priest E and Joshua son of Nun.
Dt 10: 6 his son E succeeded him as priest.
Jos 14: 1 which the priest E, and Joshua son of Nun,
17: 4 before the priest E and Joshua son of Nun and
19:51 the priest E and Joshua son of Nun and the heads
21: 1 the families of the Levites came to the priest E and
22:13 the priest Phinehas son of E to the Reubenites and
22:31 of E said to the Reubenites and the Gadites and
22:32 of E and the chiefs returned from the Reubenites
24:33 E son of Aaron died; and they buried him
Jdg 20:28 and Phinehas son of E, son of Aaron, ministered
1Sa 7: 1 They consecrated his son, E,
2Sa 23: 9 among the three warriors was E son of Dodo son
1Ch 6: 3 The sons of Aaron: Nadab, Abihu, E, and Ithamar.
6: 4 E became the father of Phinehas,
6:50 E his son, Phinehas his son, Abishua his son,
9:20 And Phinehas son of E was chief over them
11:12 among the three warriors was E son of Dodo,
23:21 The sons of Mahli: E and Kish.
23:22 E died having no sons, but only daughters;
24: 1 The sons of Aaron: Nadab, Abihu, E, and Ithamar.
24: 2 so E and Ithamar became the priests.
24: 3 Along with Zadok of the sons of E,
24: 4 the sons of E than among the sons of Ithamar,
24: 4 of ancestral houses of the sons of E,
24: 5 among both the sons of E and the sons of Ithamar.
24: 6 one ancestral house being chosen for E
24:28 Of Mahli: E, who had no sons.
Ezr 7: 5 son of E, son of the chief priest Aaron—
8:33 and with him was E son of Phinehas,
10:25 Ramiah, Izziah, Malchijah, Mijamin, E,
Ne 12:42 Shemaiah, E, Uzzi, Jehohanan, Malchijah, Elam,
Mt 1:15 and Eliud the father of E,
1:15 and E the father of Matthan,
Sir 45:23 of E ranks third in glory for being zealous in
50:27 Jesus son of E son of Sirach of Jerusalem,
1Mc 2: 5 E called Avaran, and Jonathan called Apphus.
6:43 Now E, called Avaran, saw that one of
8:17 of Accos, and Jason son of E, and sent them
2Mc 6:18 E, one of the scribes in high position,
6:24 "for many of the young might suppose that E
8:23 he appointed E to read aloud from the holy book,
1Es 8: 2 of Abishua son of Phineas son of E son of Aaron
8:63 with him was E son of Phinehas,
9:26 Ramiah, Izziah, Malchijah, Mijamin, and E,
3Mc 6: 1 Then a certain E, famous among the priests of
6:16 Just as E was ending his prayer,
2Es 1: 2 of Borith son of Abishua son of Phinehas son of E
4Mc 1: 8 E and the seven brothers and their mother.
5: 4 one man, E by name, leader of the flock,
5:14 E asked to have a word.
6: 1 When E in this manner had made eloquent
6: 5 But the courageous and noble man, like a true E,
6:14 "E, why are you so irrationally destroying yourself
6:16 But E, as though more bitterly tormented
7: 1 of our father E steered the ship of religion over
7: 5 our father E broke the maddening waves of
7:10 O supreme king over the passions, E!
7:12 E, though being consumed by the fire,
9: 5 a short time ago you learned nothing from E.
16:15 you stood and watched E being tortured,
17:13 E was the first contestant,

ELECT (19) [ELECTION]

Mt 24:22 for the sake of the e those days will be cut short.
24:24 to lead astray, if possible, even the e.
24:31 and they will gather his e from the four winds,
Mk 13:20 but for the sake of the e, whom he chose,
13:22 to lead astray, if possible, the e.
13:27 and gather his e from the four winds,
Ro 8:33 Who will bring any charge against God's e?
11: 7 The e obtained it, but the rest were hardened,
1Ti 5:21 of God and of Christ Jesus and of the e angels,
2Ti 2:10 I endure everything for the sake of the e,
Tit 1: 1 the faith of God's e and the knowledge of the truth
2Jn 1: 1 The elder to the e lady and her children,
1:13 children of your e sister send you their greetings.
Wis 3: 9 and he watches over his e.
4:15 that God's grace and mercy are with his e,
Sir 46: 1 as his name implies, a great savior of God's e,
2Es 15:21 Just as they have done to my e until this day,
16:73 Then the tested quality of my e shall be manifest,
16:74 Listen, my e ones, says the Lord;

ELECTION (3) [ELECT]

Ro 9:11 or bad (so that God's purpose of e might continue,
11:28 but as regards e they are beloved,
2Pe 1:10 be all the more eager to confirm your call and e,

ELEGANT (1)

Lk 23:11 then he put an e robe on him,

ELEMENTAL (4) [ELEMENTS]

Gal 4: 3 we were enslaved to the e spirits of the world.
4: 9 to the weak and beggarly e spirits?
Col 2: 8 according to the e spirits of the universe,
2:20 If with Christ you died to the e spirits of

ELEMENTS‡ (7) [ELEMENTAL]

Heb 5:12 you need someone to teach you again the basic e
2Pe 3:10 and the e will be dissolved with fire,
3:12 and the e will melt with fire?
Wis 7:17 the structure of the world and the activity of the e;
19:18 For the e changed places with one another,
2Mc 7:22 nor I who set in order the e within each of you.
4Mc 12:13 like yours and are made of the same e as you,

ELEPHANT (4) [ELEPHANTS]

1Mc 6:35 with each e they stationed a thousand men armed
6:46 He got under the e, stabbed it from beneath,
2Mc 13:15 He stabbed the leading e and its rider.
3Mc 5:45 with frightful devices, the e keeper

ELEPHANTS (19) [ELEPHANT]

1Mc 1:17 with chariots and e and cavalry and with
3:34 over to Lysias half of his forces and the e,
6:30 and thirty-two e accustomed to war.
6:34 the e the juice of grapes and mulberries,
6:37 On the e were wooden towers, strong and covered;
8: 6 to fight against them with one hundred twenty e
11:56 Trypho captured the e and gained control
2Mc 11: 4 and his thousands of cavalry, and his eighty e.
13: 2 twenty-two e, and three hundred chariots armed
14:12 who had been in command of the e,
15:20 the e strategically stationed and
15:21 and the savagery of the e, stretched out his hands
3Mc 5: 1 so he summoned Hermon, keeper of the e,
5: 2 ordered him on the following day to drug all the e
5: 4 And Hermon, keeper of the e,
5:10 the pitiless e until they had been filled with
5:20 without delay prepare the e in the same way for
5:38 Equip the e now once more for the destruction of
5:48 the Jews saw the dust raised by the e going out at

ELEUTHERUS (2)

1Mc 11: 7 with the king as far as the river called E;
12:30 for they had crossed the E river.

ELEVATE (2) [ELEVATED, ELEVATION]

Nu 5:25 and shall e the grain offering before the LORD
6:20 the priest shall e them as an elevation offering

ELEVATED (5) [ELEVATE]

Lev 10:14 But the breast that is e and the thigh that is raised,
10:15 the breast that is e they shall bring, together with
14:21 for a guilt offering to be e, to make atonement
Nu 6:20 for the priest, together with the breast that is e and
18:18 the breast that is e and as the right thigh are yours.

ELEVATION (22) [ELEVATE]

A. ELEVATION OFFERING[S] (21)

Ex 29:24 and raise them as an e offering before the LORD. A
29:26 Aaron's ordination and raise it as an e offering A
29:27 as an e offering and the thigh that was raised as A
29:27 the thigh that was raised as an e offering from A
Lev 7:30 so that the breast may be raised as an e offering A
7:34 For I have taken the breast of the e offering, A
8:27 raised them as an e offering before the LORD. A
8:29 took the breast and raised it as an e offering A
9:21 right thigh Aaron raised as an e offering before A
10:15 to raise for an e offering before the LORD; A
14:12 and raise them as an e offering before the LORD. A
14:24 the priest shall raise them as an e offering before A

Lev 23:15 the **e** offering, you shall count off seven weeks; A
23:17 bread as an **e** offering, each made of two-tenths A
23:20 the first fruits as an **e** offering before the LORD, A
Nu 6:20 priest shall elevate them as an **e** offering before A
8:11 the LORD as an **e** offering from the Israelites, A
8:13 and you shall present them as an **e** offering to A
8:15 and presented them as an **e** offering. A
8:21 Aaron presented them as an **e** offering before A
18:11 the gifts of all the **e** offerings of the Israelites; A
Ps 48:2 in **e**, is the joy of all the earth, Mount Zion,

ELEVEN‡ (25) [ELEVENTH]

Ge 32:22 his two maids, and his **e** children,
37:9 the moon, and **e** stars were bowing down to me."
Ex 26:7 you shall make **e** curtains.
26:8 the **e** curtains shall be of the same size.
36:14 over the tabernacle; he made **e** curtains.
36:15 the **e** curtains were of the same size.
Nu 29:20 On the third day: **e** bulls, two rams,
Dt 1:2 (By the way of Mount Seir it takes **e** days
Jos 15:51 **e** towns with their villages.
Jdg 16:5 we will each give you **e** hundred pieces of silver."
17:2 "The **e** hundred pieces of silver that were taken
17:3 Then he returned the **e** hundred pieces of silver
2Ki 23:36 he reigned **e** years in Jerusalem.
24:18 he reigned **e** years in Jerusalem.
2Ch 36:5 he reigned **e** years in Jerusalem.
36:11 he reigned **e** years in Jerusalem.
Jer 52:1 he reigned **e** years in Jerusalem.
Mt 28:16 Now the **e** disciples went to Galilee,
Mk 16:14 ⟦the **e** themselves as they were sitting at the table;⟧
Lk 24:9 they told all this to the **e** and to all the rest.
24:33 the **e** and their companions gathered together.
Ac 1:26 and he was added to the **e** apostles.
2:14 But Peter, standing with the **e**,
2Mc 11:11 and laid low **e** thousand of them
1Es 1:46 and he reigned **e** years.

ELEVENTH (19) [ELEVEN]

Nu 7:72 On the **e** day Pagiel son of Ochran,
Dt 1:3 In the fortieth year, on the first day of the **e** month,
1Ki 6:38 In the **e** year, in the month of Bul,
2Ki 9:29 In the **e** year of Joram son of Ahab,
25:2 So the city was besieged until the **e** year
1Ch 12:13 Jeremiah tenth, Machbannai **e**.
24:12 the **e** to Eliashib, the twelfth to Jakim,
25:18 the **e** to Azarel, his sons and his brothers, twelve;
27:14 **E**, for the eleventh month,
27:14 Eleventh, for the **e** month,
Jer 1:3 until the end of the **e** year of King Zedekiah son
39:2 in the **e** year of Zedekiah,
52:5 So the city was besieged until the **e** year
Eze 26:1 In the **e** year, on the first day of the month,
30:20 In the **e** year, in the first month,
31:1 In the **e** year, in the third month,
Zec 1:7 On the twenty-fourth day of the **e** month,
Rev 21:20 the tenth chrysoprase, the **e** jacinth,
1Mc 16:14 in the **e** month, which is the month of Shebat.

ELHANAN (4)

2Sa 21:19 and **E** son of Jaare-oregim, the Bethlehemite,
23:24 **E** son of Dodo of Bethlehem;
1Ch 11:26 **E** son of Dodo of Bethlehem,
20:5 and **E** son of Jair killed Lahmi the brother

ELI‡ (37) [ELI'S, ELOI]

1Sa 1:3 where the two sons of **E**, Hophni and Phinehas,
1:9 Now **E** the priest was sitting on the seat beside
1:12 before the LORD, **E** observed her mouth.
1:13 therefore **E** thought she was drunk.
1:14 So **E** said to her, "How long will you make
1:17 Then **E** answered, "Go in peace;
1:25 and they brought the child to **E**.
2:11 in the presence of the priest **E**.
2:12 Now the sons of **E** were scoundrels;
2:20 Then **E** would bless Elkanah and his wife, and say,
2:22 Now **E** was very old.
2:27 A man of God came to **E** and said to him,
3:1 boy Samuel was ministering to the LORD under **E**.
3:2 At that time **E**, whose eyesight had begun
3:5 ran to **E**, and said, "Here I am, for you called me."
3:6 Samuel got up and went to **E**, and said,
3:8 And he got up and went to **E**, and said,
3:8 **E** perceived that the LORD was calling the boy.
3:9 Therefore **E** said to Samuel, "Go, lie down;
3:12 On that day I will fulfill against **E** all
3:14 the house of **E** that the iniquity of Eli's house shall
3:15 Samuel was afraid to tell the vision to **E**.
3:16 But **E** called Samuel and said, "Samuel, my son."
3:17 **E** said, "What was it that he told you?
4:4 The two sons of **E**, Hophni and Phinehas,
4:11 and the two sons of **E**, Hophni and Phinehas, died.
4:13 **E** was sitting upon his seat by the road watching,
4:14 When **E** heard the sound of the outcry, he said,
4:14 Then the man came quickly and told **E**.
4:15 **E** was ninety-eight years old and his eyes were set,
4:16 man said to **E**, "I have just come from the battle;
4:18 **E** fell over backward from his seat by the side of
14:3 Ichabod's brother, son of Phinehas son of **E**,
1Ki 2:27 that he had spoken concerning the house of **E**
Mt 27:46 **"E, E,** lema sabachthani?"
2Es 1:2 son of Ahijah son of Phinehas son of **E** son

ELI'S (1) [ELI]

1Sa 3:14 the house of Eli that the iniquity of **E** house shall

ELI-ZAPHAN (1)

Nu 34:25 Of the tribe of the Zebulunites a leader, **E** son

ELIAB (21) [ELIAB'S]

Nu 1:9 From Zebulun, **E** son of Helon.
2:7 leader of the Zebulunites shall be **E** son of Helon,
7:24 On the third day **E** son of Helon,
7:29 This was the offering of **E** son of Helon.
10:16 the company of the tribe of Zebulun was **E** son
16:1 along with Dathan and Abiram sons of **E**,
16:12 Moses sent for Dathan and Abiram sons of **E**;
26:8 And the descendants of Pallu: **E**.
26:9 descendants of **E**: Nemuel, Dathan, and Abiram.
Dt 11:6 of **E** son of Reuben, how in the midst of all Israel
1Sa 16:6 When they came, he looked on **E** and thought,
17:13 of his three sons who went to the battle were **E**
17:28 His eldest brother **E** heard him talking to the men;
1Ch 2:13 Jesse became the father of **E** his firstborn,
6:27 **E** his son, Jeroham his son, Elkanah his son.
12:9 Ezer the chief, Obadiah second, **E** third,
15:18 Shemiramoth, Jehiel, Unni, **E**, Benaiah, Maaseiah,
15:20 Aziel, Shemiramoth, Jehiel, Unni, **E**, Maaseiah,
16:5 Mattithiah, **E**, Benaiah, Obed-edom, and Jeiel,
2Ch 11:18 and of Abihail daughter of **E** son of Jesse.
Jdt 8:1 of **E** son of Nathanael son of Salamiel son

ELIAB'S (1) [ELIAB]

1Sa 17:28 and **E** anger was kindled against David.

ELIADA (4)

2Sa 5:16 Elishama, **E**, and Eliphelet.
1Ki 11:23 Rezon son of **E**, who had fled from his master,
1Ch 3:8 Elishama, **E**, and Eliphelet, nine.
2Ch 17:17 Of Benjamin: **E**, a mighty warrior,

ELIADAS (1)

1Es 9:28 Of the descendants of Zamoth: **E**, Eliashib,

ELIAH (KJV) See ELIJAH

ELIAHBA (2)

2Sa 23:32 **E** of Shaalbon; the sons of Jashen: Jonathan
1Ch 11:33 Azmaveth of Baharum, **E** of Shaalbon,

ELIAKIM (15) [=JEHOIAKIM]

2Ki 18:18 there came out to them **E** son of Hilkiah,
18:26 Then **E** son of Hilkiah, and Shebnah,
18:37 Then **E** son of Hilkiah, who was in charge of
19:2 And he sent **E**, who was in charge of the palace,
23:34 Pharaoh Neco made **E** son of Josiah king in place
2Ch 36:4 of Egypt made his brother **E** king over Judah
Ne 12:41 and the priests **E**, Maaseiah,
Isa 22:20 that day I will call my servant **E** son of Hilkiah,
36:3 And there came out to him **E** son of Hilkiah,
36:11 Then **E**, Shebna, and Joah said to the Rabshakeh,
36:22 Then **E** son of Hilkiah, who was in charge of
37:2 And he sent **E**, who was in charge of the palace,
Mt 1:13 and Abiud the father of **E**,
1:13 and **E** the father of Azor,
Lk 3:30 son of Joseph, son of Jonam, son of **E**,

ELIALIS (1)

1Es 9:34 Eliasis, Binnui, **E**, Shimei, Shelemiah, Nethaniah.

ELIAM (2)

2Sa 11:3 It was reported, "This is Bathsheba daughter of **E**,
23:34 **E** son of Ahithophel the Gilonite;

ELIAS (KJV) See ELIJAH

ELIASAPH (6)

Nu 1:14 From Gad, **E** son of Deuel.
2:14 The leader of the Gadites shall be **E** son of Reuel,
3:24 with **E** son of Lael as head of the ancestral house
7:42 On the sixth day **E** son of Deuel,
7:47 This was the offering of **E** son of Deuel.
10:20 over the company of the tribe of Gad was **E** son

ELIASHIB (21)

1Ch 3:24 Hodaviah, **E**, Pelaiah, Akkub, Johanan, Delaiah,
24:12 the eleventh to **E**, the twelfth to Jakim,
Ezr 10:6 and went to the chamber of Jehohanan son of **E**,
10:24 Of the singers: **E**. Of the gatekeepers:
10:27 Elioenai, **E**, Mattaniah, Jeremoth, Zabad,
10:36 Vaniah, Meremoth, **E**,
Ne 3:1 Then the high priest **E** set to work
3:20 to the door of the house of the high priest **E**.
3:21 the house of **E** to the end of the house of **E**.
12:10 Joiakim the father of **E**, **E** the father of Joiada,
12:22 As for the Levites, in the days of **E**, Joiada,
12:23 of the Annals until the days of Johanan son of **E**.
13:4 Now before this, the priest **E**,
13:7 the wrong that **E** had done on behalf of Tobiah,
13:28 the high priest **E**, was the son-in-law of Sanballat
1Es 9:1 the temple to the chamber of Jehohanan son of **E**,
9:24 Of the temple singers: **E** and Zaccur.
9:28 Of the descendants of Zamoth: Eliadas, **E**,
1Es 9:34 Carabasion and **E** and Mamitanemus, Eliasis,

ELIASIS (1)

1Es 9:34 **E**, Binnui, Elialis, Shimei, Shelemiah, Nethaniah.

ELIATHAH (2)

1Ch 25:4 Hananiah, Hanani, **E**, Giddalti, and Romamti-ezer,
25:27 to **E**, his sons and his brothers, twelve;

ELIDAD (1)

Nu 34:21 Of the tribe of Benjamin, **E** son of Chislon.

ELIEHOENAI (3)

1Ch 26:3 Elam the fifth, Jehohanan the sixth, **E** the seventh.
Ezr 8:4 Of the descendants of Pahath-moab, **E** son
1Es 8:31 Of the descendants of Pahath-moab, **E** son

ELIEL (10)

1Ch 5:24 Epher, Ishi, **E**, Azriel, Jeremiah, Hodaviah,
6:34 son of Jeroham, son of **E**, son of Toah,
8:20 Elienai, Zillethai, **E**,
8:22 Ishpan, Eber, **E**,
11:46 **E** the Mahavite, and Jeribai and Joshaviah sons
11:47 **E**, and Obed, and Jaasiel the Mezobaite.
12:11 Attai sixth, **E** seventh,
15:9 **E** the chief, with eighty of his kindred;
15:11 and the Levites Uriel, Asaiah, Joel, Shemaiah, **E**,
2Ch 31:13 Asahel, Jerimoth, Jozabad, **E**, Ismachiah, Mahath,

ELIENAI (1)

1Ch 8:20 **E**, Zillethai, Eliel,

ELIEZAR (2)

1Es 8:43 I sent word to **E**, Iduel, Maasmas,
9:19 Maaseiah, **E**, Jarib, and Jodan.

ELIEZER (15)

Ge 15:2 and the heir of my house is **E** of Damascus?"
Ex 18:4 the name of the other, **E** (for he said, "The God
1Ch 7:8 The sons of Becher: Zemirah, Joash, **E**, Elioenai,
15:24 Amasai, Zechariah, Benaiah, and **E**, the priests,
23:15 The sons of Moses: Gershom and **E**.
23:17 The sons of **E**: Rehabiah the chief;
23:17 **E** had no other sons, but the sons
26:25 from **E** were his son Rehabiah, his son Jeshaiah,
27:16 **E** son of Zichri was chief officer;
2Ch 20:37 Then **E** son of Dodavahu of Mareshah prophesied
Ezr 8:16 Then I sent for **E**, Ariel, Shemaiah, Elnathan,
10:18 Maaseiah, **E**, Jarib, and Gedaliah.
10:23 Kelaiah (that is, Kelita), Pethahiah, Judah, and **E**.
10:31 **E**, Isshijah, Malchijah, Shemaiah, Shimeon,
Lk 3:29 son of **E**, son of Jorim, son of Matthat,

ELIHOENAI (KJV) See ELIEHOENAI

ELIHOREPH (1)

1Ki 4:3 **E** and Ahijah sons of Shisha were secretaries;

ELIHU (11)

1Sa 1:1 of Jeroham son of **E** son of Tohu son of Zuph,
1Ch 12:20 Adnah, Jozabad, Jediael, Michael, Jozabad, **E**,
26:7 whose brothers were able men, **E** and Semachiah.
27:18 **E**, one of David's brothers;
Job 32:2 Then **E** son of Barachel the Buzite,
32:4 Now **E** had waited to speak to Job,
32:5 But when **E** saw that there was no answer in
32:6 **E** son of Barachel the Buzite answered:
34:1 Then **E** continued and said:
35:1 **E** continued and said:
36:1 **E** continued and said:

ELIJAH‡ (109)

1Ki 17:1 Now **E** the Tishbite, of Tishbe in Gilead,
17:13 **E** said to her, "Do not be afraid;
17:15 She went and did as **E** said,
17:16 to the word of the LORD that he spoke by **E**.
17:18 She then said to **E**, "What have you against me,
17:22 The LORD listened to the voice of **E**;
17:23 **E** took the child, brought him down from
17:23 then **E** said, "See, your son is alive."
17:24 So the woman said to **E**,
18:1 many days the word of the LORD came to **E**,
18:2 So **E** went to present himself to Ahab.
18:7 As Obadiah was on the way, **E** met him;
18:7 fell on his face, and said, "Is it you, my lord **E**?"
18:8 Go, tell your lord that **E** is here."
18:11 now you say, 'Go, tell your lord that **E** is here.'
18:14 now you say, 'Go, tell your lord that **E** is here';
18:15 **E** said, "As the LORD of hosts lives,
18:16 and Ahab went to meet **E**.
18:17 When Ahab saw **E**, Ahab said to him, "Is it you,
18:21 **E** then came near to all the people, and said,
18:22 Then **E** said to the people, "I, even I only,
18:25 Then **E** said to the prophets of Baal,
18:27 At noon **E** mocked them, saying, "Cry aloud!
18:30 **E** said to all the people, "Come closer to me";
18:31 **E** took twelve stones, according to the number of
18:36 the prophet **E** came near and said, "O LORD,
18:40 **E** said to them, "Seize the prophets of Baal;
18:40 and **E** brought them down to the Wadi Kishon,
18:41 **E** said to Ahab, "Go up, eat and drink;

1Ki 18:42 E went up to the top of Carmel;
18:46 But the hand of the LORD was on E;
19: 1 Ahab told Jezebel all that E had done,
19: 2 Then Jezebel sent a messenger to E, saying,
19: 9 saying, "What are you doing here, E?"
19:13 When E heard it, he wrapped his face
19:13 "What are you doing here, E?"
19:19 E passed by him and threw his mantle over him.
19:20 He left the oxen, ran after E, and said,
19:20 Then E said to him, "Go back again;
19:21 he set out and followed E, and became his servant.
21:17 the word of the LORD came to E the Tishbite,
21:20 Ahab said to E, "Have you found me,
21:28 the word of the LORD came to E the Tishbite:
2Ki 1: 3 But the angel of the LORD said to E the Tishbite,
1: 4 but you shall surely die.' " So E went.
1: 8 He said, "It is E the Tishbite."
1: 9 to E, who was sitting on the top of a hill, and said
1:10 But E answered the captain of fifty,
1:12 But E answered them, "If I am a man of God,
1:13 and came and fell on his knees before E,
1:15 Then the angel of the LORD said to E,
1:17 to the word of the LORD that E had spoken.
2: 1 the LORD was about to take E up to heaven by
2: 1 E and Elisha were on their way from Gilgal.
2: 2 E said to Elisha, "Stay here;
2: 4 E said to him, "Elisha, stay here;
2: 6 Then E said to him, "Stay here;
2: 8 Then E took his mantle and rolled it up,
2: 9 When they had crossed, E said to Elisha,
2:11 and E ascended in a whirlwind into heaven.
2:13 He picked up the mantle of E that had fallen
2:14 He took the mantle of E that had fallen from him,
2:14 saying, "Where is the LORD, the God of E?"
2:15 they declared, "The spirit of E rests on Elisha."
3:11 who used to pour water on the hands of E,
9:36 which he spoke by his servant E the Tishbite,
10:10 LORD has done what he said through his servant E.
10:17 to the word of the LORD that he spoke to E.
1Ch 8:27 E, and Zichri were the sons of Jeroham.
2Ch 21:12 A letter came to him from the prophet E, saying:
Ezr 10:21 Maaseiah, E, Shemaiah, Jehiel, and Uzziah.
10:26 Zechariah, Jehiel, Abdi, Jeremoth, and E.
Mal 4: 5 the prophet E before the great and terrible day of
Mt 11:14 he is E who is to come.
16:14 "Some say John the Baptist, but others E,
17: 3 Suddenly there appeared to them Moses and E,
17: 4 one for you, one for Moses, and one for E."
17:10 then, do the scribes say that E must come first?"
17:11 "E is indeed coming and will restore all things;
17:12 but I tell you that E has already come,
27:47 they said, "This man is calling for E."
27:49 let us see whether E will come to save him."
Mk 6:15 But others said, "It is E."
8:28 E; and still others, one of the prophets."
9: 4 And there appeared to them E with Moses,
9: 5 one for you, one for Moses, and one for E."
9:11 "Why do the scribes say that E must come first?"
9:12 "E is indeed coming first to restore all things.
9:13 But I tell you that E has come,
15:35 they said, "Listen, he is calling for E."
15:36 let us see whether E will come to take him down."
Lk 1:17 the spirit and power of E he will go before him,
4:25 there were many widows in Israel in the time of E,
4:26 yet E was sent to none of them except to a widow
9: 8 by some that E had appeared,
9:19 They answered, "John the Baptist; but others, E;
9:30 Suddenly they saw two men, Moses and E,
9:33 one for you, one for Moses, and one for E"—
Jn 1:21 "What then? Are you E?"
1:25 if you are neither the Messiah, nor E, nor
Ro 11: 2 Do you not know what the scripture says of E,
Jas 5:17 E was a human being like us,
Jdt 8: 1 of Ahitub son of E son of Hilkiah son of Eliab son
Sir 48: 1 Then E arose, a prophet like fire,
48: 4 glorious you were, E, in your wondrous deeds!
48:12 When E was enveloped in the whirlwind,
1Mc 2:58 E, because of great zeal for the law,
1Es 9:27 Jezrielus and Abdi, and Jeremoth and E.
2Es 7:109 [39] and E for those who received the rain,

ELIKA (1)
2Sa 23:25 Shammah of Harod; E of Harod;

ELIM (6)
Ex 15:27 to E, where there were twelve springs of water
16: 1 of the Israelites set out from E;
16: 1 which is between E and Sinai,
Nu 33: 9 They set out from Marah and came to E;
33: 9 at E there were twelve springs of water
33:10 They set out from E and camped by the Red Sea.

ELIMELECH (6)
Ru 1: 2 of the man was E and the name of his wife Naomi,
1: 3 But E, the husband of Naomi, died,
2: 1 of the family of E, whose name was Boaz.
2: 3 who was of the family of E.
4: 3 the parcel of land that belonged to our kinsman E.
4: 9 that belonged to E and all that belonged to Chilion

ELIMINATED (1)
1Ki 11:16 until he had e every male in Edom);

ELIOENAI (8)
1Ch 3:23 sons of Neariah: E, Hizkiah, and Azrikam, three.
3:24 The sons of E: Hodaviah, Eliashib,
4:36 E, Jaakobah, Jeshohaiah, Asaiah,
7: 8 The sons of Becher: Zemirah, Joash, Eliezer, E,
Ezr 10:22 Of the descendants of Pashhur: E, Maaseiah,
10:27 E, Eliashib, Mattaniah, Jeremoth, Zabad,
Ne 12:41 Miniamin, Micaiah, E, Zechariah, and Hananiah,
1Es 9:22 Of the descendants of Pashhur: E, Maaseiah,

ELIONAS (1)
1Es 9:32 E and Asaias and Melchias and Sabbaias

ELIPHAL (1)
1Ch 11:35 Ahiam son of Sachar the Hararite, E son of Ur,

ELIPHAZ (15)
Ge 36: 4 Adah bore E to Esau; Basemath bore Reuel;
36:10 E son of Adah the wife of Esau;
36:11 The sons of E were Teman, Omar, Zepho, Gatam,
36:12 (Timna was a concubine of E, Esau's son;
36:12 Esau's son; she bore Amalek to E.)
36:15 The sons of E the firstborn of Esau:
36:16 these are the clans of E in the land of Edom;
1Ch 1:35 sons of Esau: E, Reuel, Jeush, Jalam, and Korah.
1:36 The sons of E: Teman, Omar,
Job 2:11 E the Temanite, Bildad the Shuhite,
4: 1 Then E the Temanite answered:
15: 1 Then E the Temanite answered:
22: 1 Then E the Temanite answered:
42: 7 the LORD said to E the Temanite:
42: 9 So E the Temanite and Bildad the Shuhite

ELIPHELEHU (2)
1Ch 15:18 Benaiah, Maaseiah, Mattithiah, E, and Mikneiah,
15:21 E, Mikneiah, Obed-edom, Jeiel,

ELIPHELET (10)
2Sa 5:16 Elishama, Eliada, and E.
23:34 E son of Ahasbai of Maacah;
1Ch 3: 6 then Ibhar, Elishama, E,
3: 8 Elishama, Eliada, and E, nine.
8:39 Jeush the second, and E the third.
14: 7 Elishama, Beeliada, and E.
Ezr 8:13 those who came later, their names being E, Jeuel,
10:33 Mattenai, Mattattah, Zabad, E, Jeremai,
1Es 8:39 their names being E, Jeuel, and Shemaiah,
9:33 and Mattattah and Zabad and E and Manasseh

ELISABETH (KJV) See ELIZABETH

ELISEUS (KJV) See ELISHA

ELISHA (63) [ELISHA'S]
1Ki 19:16 and you shall anoint E son of Shaphat
19:17 from the sword of Jehu, E shall kill.
19:19 he set out from there, and found E son of Shaphat,
2Ki 2: 1 Elijah and E were on their way from Gilgal.
2: 2 Elijah said to E, "Stay here;
2: 2 But E said, "As the LORD lives,
2: 3 of prophets who were in Bethel came out to E,
2: 4 Elijah said to him, "E, stay here;
2: 5 of prophets who were at Jericho drew near to E,
2: 9 When they had crossed, Elijah said to E,
2: 9 E said, "Please let me inherit a double share
2:12 E kept watching and crying out, "Father, father!
2:14 to the one side and to the other, and E went over.
2:15 they declared, "The spirit of Elijah rests on E."
2:19 Now the people of the city said to E,
2:22 according to the word that E spoke.
3:11 the servants of the king of Israel answered, "E son
3:13 E said to the king of Israel,
3:14 E said, "As the LORD of hosts lives,
4: 1 a member of the company of prophets cried to E,
4: 2 E said to her, "What shall I do for you?
4: 8 One day E was passing through Shunem,
4:17 in due time, as E had declared to her.
4:32 When E came into the house,
4:36 E summoned Gehazi and said,
4:38 When E returned to Gilgal,
4:42 E said, "Give it to the people and let them eat."
5: 8 But when E the man of God heard that the king
5:10 E sent a messenger to him, saying, "Go,
5:20 the servant of E the man of God, thought,
5:25 E said to him, "Where have you been, Gehazi?"
6: 1 Now the company of prophets said to E,
6:12 It is E, the prophet in Israel,
6:17 Then E prayed: "O LORD,
6:17 of horses and chariots of fire all around E.
6:18 E prayed to the LORD, and said,
6:18 So he struck them with blindness as E had asked.
6:19 E said to them, "This is not the way,
6:20 As soon as they entered Samaria, E said,
6:21 When the king of Israel saw them he said to E,
6:31 of E son of Shaphat stays on his shoulders today."
6:32 Now E was sitting in his house,
6:32 Before the messenger arrived, E said to the elders,
7: 1 But E said, "Hear the word of the LORD:
8: 1 Now E had said to the woman whose son he had
8: 4 "Tell me all the great things that E has done."
8: 5 the king how E had restored a dead person to life,
8: 5 and here is her son whom E restored to life."
2Ki 8: 7 E went to Damascus while King Ben-hadad
8:10 E said to him, "Go, say to him,
8:13 E answered, "The LORD has shown me
8:14 Then he left E, and went to his master Ben-hadad,
8:14 who said to him, "What did E say to you?"
9: 1 the prophet E called a member of the company
13:14 Now when E had fallen sick with the illness
13:15 E said to him, "Take a bow and arrows";
13:16 E laid his hands on the king's hands.
13:17 E said, "Shoot"; and he shot.
13:20 So E died, and they buried him.
13:21 and the man was thrown into the grave of E;
13:21 as soon as the man touched the bones of E,
Lk 4:27 in Israel in the time of the prophet E,
Sir 48:12 E was filled with his spirit.

ELISHA'S (1) [ELISHA]
2Ki 5: 9 and halted at the entrance of E house.

ELISHAH (3)
Ge 10: 4 E, Tarshish, Kittim, and Rodanim.
1Ch 1: 7 E, Tarshish, Kittim, and Rodanim.
Eze 27: 7 and purple from the coasts of E was your awning.

ELISHAMA (17)
Nu 1:10 from Ephraim, E son of Ammihud;
2:18 The leader of the people of Ephraim shall be E son
7:48 On the seventh day E son of Ammihud,
7:53 This was the offering of E son of Ammihud.
10:22 over the whole company was E son of Ammihud.
2Sa 5:16 E, Eliada, and Eliphelet.
2Ki 25:25 Ishmael son of Nethaniah son of E,
1Ch 2:41 the father of Jekamiah, and Jekamiah of E.
3: 6 then Ibhar, E, Eliphelet,
3: 8 E, Eliada, and Eliphelet, nine.
7:26 Ladan his son, Ammihud his son, E his son,
14: 7 E, Beeliada, and Eliphelet.
2Ch 17: 8 and with these Levites, the priests E and Jehoram.
Jer 36:12 E the secretary, Delaiah son of Shemaiah,
36:20 in the chamber of E the secretary, they went to
36:21 he took it from the chamber of E the secretary;
41: 1 Ishmael son of Nethaniah son of E,

ELISHAPHAT (1)
2Ch 23: 1 Maaseiah son of Adaiah, and E son of Zichri.

ELISHEBA (1)
Ex 6:23 Aaron married E, daughter of Amminadab

ELISHUA (2)
2Sa 5:15 Ibhar, E, Nepheg, Japhia,
1Ch 14: 5 Ibhar, E, and Elpelet;

ELITE (1)
2Ki 24:15 his officials, and the e of the land,

ELIUD (2)
Mt 1:14 and Achim the father of E,
1:15 and E the father of Eleazar,

ELIZABETH‡ (9)
Lk 1: 5 a descendant of Aaron, and her name was E.
1: 7 But they had no children, because E was barren,
1:13 Your wife E will bear you a son,
1:24 After those days his wife E conceived,
1:36 your relative E in her old age has also conceived
1:40 she entered the house of Zechariah and greeted E.
1:41 When E heard Mary's greeting,
1:41 And E was filled with the Holy Spirit
1:57 time came for E to give birth, and she bore a son.

ELIZAPHAN (3)
Nu 3:30 with E son of Uzziel as head of
1Ch 15: 8 of E, Shemaiah the chief, with two hundred
2Ch 29:13 and of the sons of E, Shimri and Jeuel;

ELIZUR (5)
Nu 1: 5 From Reuben, E son of Shedeur.
2:10 of the Reubenites shall be E son of Shedeur,
7:30 On the fourth day E son of Shedeur,
7:35 This was the offering of E son of Shedeur.
10:18 over the whole company was E son of Shedeur.

ELKANAH (20)
Ex 6:24 The sons of Korah: Assir, E, and Abiasaph;
1Sa 1: 1 whose name was E son of Jeroham son
1: 4 On the day when E sacrificed,
1: 8 Her husband E said to her, "Hannah,
1:19 E knew his wife Hannah,
1:21 The man E and all his household went up to offer
1:23 Her husband E said to her,
2:11 Then E went home to Ramah,
2:20 Then Eli would bless E and his wife, and say,
1Ch 6:23 E his son, Ebiasaph his son, Assir his son,
6:25 The sons of E: Amasai and Ahimoth,
6:26 E his son, Zophai his son, Nahath his son,
6:27 Eliab his son, Jeroham his son, E his son.
6:34 son of E, son of Jeroham, son of Eliel, son
6:35 son of E, son of Mahath, son of Amasai,
6:36 son of E, son of Joel, son of Azariah, son
9:16 and Berechiah son of Asa, son of E,

1Ch 12: 6 **E,** Isshiah, Azarel, Joezer, and Jashobeam,
15:23 Berechiah and **E** were to be gatekeepers for
2Ch 28: 7 and **E** the next in authority to the king.

ELKIAH (1)
Jdt 8: 1 of Ox son of Joseph son of Oziel son of **E** son

ELKOSH (1)
Na 1: 1 The book of the vision of Nahum of **E.**

ELLASAR (2)
Ge 14: 1 King Arioch of **E,** King Chedorlaomer of Elam,
14: 9 King Amraphel of Shinar, and King Arioch of **E,**

ELMADAM (1)
Lk 3:28 son of Addi, son of Cosam, son of **E,** son of Er,

ELNAAM (1)
1Ch 11:46 and Jeribai and Joshaviah sons of **E,**

ELNATHAN (9)
2Ki 24: 8 His mother's name was Nehushta daughter of **E**
Ezr 8:16 Then I sent for Eliezer, Ariel, Shemaiah, **E,** Jarib,
8:16 Shemaiah, Elnathan, Jarib, **E,** Nathan, Zechariah,
8:16 who were leaders, and for Joiarib and **E,**
Jer 26:22 Then King Jehoiakim sent **E** son of Achbor
36:12 **E** son of Achbor, Gemariah son of Shaphan,
36:25 when **E** and Delaiah and Gemariah urged the king
1Es 8:44 **E,** Shemaiah, Jarib, Nathan, Elnathan, Zechariah,
8:44 Jarib, Nathan, **E,** Zechariah, and Meshullam,

ELOHIM See Index to Footnotes

ELOI (2) [ELI]
Mk 15:34 with a loud voice, **"E, E,** lema sabachthani?"

ELON (7) [ELONITES]
Ge 26:34 and Basemath daughter of **E** the Hittite;
36: 2 Adah daughter of **E** the Hittite,
46:14 The children of Zebulun: Sered, **E,** and Jahleel
Nu 26:26 of **E,** the clan of the Elonites;
Jos 19:43 **E,** Timnah, Ekron,
Jdg 12:11 After him **E** the Zebulunite judged Israel;
12:12 Then **E** the Zebulunite died,

ELON-BETH-HANAN (1)
1Ki 4: 9 in Makaz, Shaalbim, Beth-shemesh, and **E;**

ELON-BEZAANANNIM (1)
Jdg 4:11 and had encamped as far away as **E,**

ELON-MEONENIM (1)
Jdg 9:37 one company is coming from the direction of **E."**

ELONITES (1) [ELON]
Nu 26:26 of Elon, the clan of the **E;**

ELOQUENT (5)
Ex 4:10 "O my Lord, I have never been **e,**
Ac 18:24 He was an **e** man, well-versed in the scriptures.
1Co 1:17 but to proclaim the gospel, and not with **e** wisdom,
AdE 14:13 Put **e** speech in my mouth before the lion,
4Mc 6: 1 When Eleazar in this manner had made **e** response

ELOTH (3)
1Ki 9:26 which is near **E** on the shore of the Red Sea,
2Ch 8:17 Then Solomon went to Ezion-geber and **E** on
26: 2 He rebuilt **E** and restored it to Judah,

ELPAAL (3)
1Ch 8:11 He also had sons by Hushim: Abitub and **E.**
8:12 The sons of **E:** Eber, Misham,
8:18 Ishmerai, Izliah, and Jobab were the sons of **E.**

ELPELET (1)
1Ch 14: 5 Ibhar, Elishua, and **E;**

ELSE‡ (89) [ELSE'S, ELSEWHERE]
Ge 19:12 the men said to Lot, "Have you anyone **e** here?
19:15 or **e** you will be consumed in the punishment of
19:17 flee to the hills, or **e** you will be consumed."
26: 7 to say, "My wife," thinking, "or **e** the men of
31:50 though no one **e** is with us,
39:11 and while no one **e** was in the house,
41:38 "Can we find anyone **e** like this—
42:16 or **e,** as Pharaoh lives, surely you are spies."
Ex 4:13 But he said, "O my Lord, please send someone **e."**
22:27 in what **e** shall that person sleep?
29:33 but no one **e** shall eat of them,
36: 6 or woman is to make anything **e** as an offering for
Lev 6: 5 or anything **e** about which you have sworn falsely,
27:20 or if it has been sold to someone **e,**
Nu 6:21 apart from what **e** they can afford.
12: 3 more so than anyone **e** on the face of the earth.
17:10 of their complaints against me, or **e** they will die."
18:22 or **e** they will incur guilt and die.
Dt 17:17 or **e** his heart will turn away;
20:14 and everything **e** in the town, all its spoil.
Dt 22: 3 the same with anything **e** that your neighbor loses
28:55 because nothing **e** remains to him,
28:57 she is eating them in secret for lack of anything **e,**
Jdg 16: 7 then I shall become weak, and be like anyone **e."**
16:11 then I shall become weak, and be like anyone **e."**
16:13 then I shall become weak, and be like anyone **e."**
16:17 I would become weak, and be like anyone **e."**
18:25 or **e** hot-tempered fellows will attack you,
1Sa 9: 2 he stood head and shoulders above everyone **e.**
29: 4 **e** he may become an adversary to us in the battle.
2Sa 3:35 and more, if I taste bread or anything **e** before
13:25 or **e** we will be burdensome to you."
1Ki 3:18 there was no one **e** with us in the house,
4:31 He was wiser than anyone **e,**
20:39 or **e** you shall pay a talent of silver.'
21: 6 'Give me your vineyard for money; or **e,**
Ezr 7:20 whatever **e** is required for the house of your God,
Ps 32: 9 **e** it will not stay near you.
Pr 4: 7 Get wisdom, and whatever **e** you get, get insight.
20:13 Do not love sleep, or **e** you will come to poverty;
24:18 or **e** the LORD will see it and be displeased,
25:10 or **e** someone who hears you will bring shame
25:16 eat only enough for you, or **e,** having too much,
30: 6 Do not add to his words, or **e** he will rebuke you,
31: 5 **e** they will drink and forget what has been decreed,
Isa 27: 5 Or **e** let it cling to me for protection,
Jer 4: 4 or **e** my wrath will go forth like fire,
9: 7 for what **e** can I do with my sinful people?
17: 9 The heart is devious above all **e;**
21:12 or **e** my wrath will go forth like fire, and burn,
38:24 "Do not let anyone **e** know of this conversation,
40:15 and no one **e** will know.
Da 5:17 or give your rewards to someone **e!**
Am 6:10 in the innermost parts of the house, "Is anyone **e**
Zep 2:15 that said to itself, "I am, and there is no one **e"?**
Mk 13:36 or **e** he may find you asleep
Lk 22:58 A little later someone **e,** on seeing him, said,
Jn 5: 7 someone **e** steps down ahead of me."
10:29 What my Father has given me is greater than all **e,**
15:24 not done among them the works that no one **e** did,
21:18 and someone **e** will fasten a belt around you
Ac 4:12 There is salvation in no one **e,**
8:34 about himself or about someone **e?"**
Ro 8:32 will he not with him also give us everything **e?**
8:39 nor depth, nor anything **e** in all creation,
1Co 1:16 I do not know whether I baptized anyone **e.)**
3:10 and someone **e** is building on it.
7:11 let her remain unmarried or **e** be reconciled
14:30 a revelation is made to someone **e** sitting nearby,
Eph 2: 3 by nature children of wrath, like everyone **e.**
Php 1:13 to everyone **e** that my imprisonment is for Christ;
3: 4 If anyone **e** has reason to be confident in the flesh,
1Ti 1:10 and whatever **e** is contrary to the sound teaching
AdE 2: 3 and let ointments and whatever **e** they need
8: 7 against the Jews, what **e** do you request?
Wis 7: 1 I also am mortal, like everyone **e,**
10:12 that godliness is more powerful than anything **e.**
Sir 2: 7 do not stray, or **e** you may fall.
12:12 or **e** he may try to take your own seat,
26:10 or **e,** when she finds liberty,
30:12 or **e** he will become stubborn and disobey you,
Bel 1:29 or **e** we will kill you and your household."
1Mc 15:31 or **e** pay me five hundred talents of silver for
1Es 4: 5 whatever spoil they take and everything **e.**
8:18 And whatever **e** occurs to you as necessary for
3Mc 6:30 both wines and everything **e** needed for a festival
2Es 6:10 seek for nothing **e,** Ezra, between the heel and
7:*116* [46] or **e,** when it had produced him,
4Mc 2:19 Why **e** did Jacob, our most wise father,

ELSE'S (5) [ELSE]
Ex 22: 5 or lets livestock loose to graze in someone **e** field,
Ro 15:20 so that I do not build on someone **e** foundation,
1Co 2:15 they are themselves subject to no one **e** scrutiny.
10:29 to the judgment of someone **e** conscience?
2Co 10:16 of work already done in someone **e** sphere

ELSEWHERE (2) [ELSE, WHERE]
2Ch 26: 6 he built cities in the territory of Ashdod and **e**
Ps 84:10 a day in your courts is better than a thousand **e.**

ELTEKE (1) [=ELTEKEH]
Jos 21:23 Out of the tribe of Dan: **E** with its pasture lands,

ELTEKEH (1) [=ELTEKE]
Jos 19:44 **E,** Gibbethon, Baalath,

ELTEKON (1)
Jos 15:59 Beth-anoth, and **E:** six towns with their villages.

ELTOLAD (2)
Jos 15:30 **E,** Chesil, Hormah,
19: 4 **E,** Bethul, Hormah,

ELUDED (3) [ELUDING]
1Sa 18:11 But David **e** him twice.
19:10 he **e** Saul, so that he struck the spear into the wall.
1Mc 9:47 but he **e** him and went to the rear.

ELUDING (1) [ELUDED]
4Mc 3:13 **E** the sentinels at the gates,

ELUL (2)
Ne 6:15 on the twenty-fifth day of the month **E,**
1Mc 14:27 "On the eighteenth day of **E,**

ELUZAI (1)
1Ch 12: 5 **E,** Jerimoth, Bealiah, Shemariah, Shephatiah

ELYMAIS (2)
Tob 2:10 of me for two years before he went to **E.**
1Mc 6: 1 through the upper provinces when he heard that **E**

ELYMAS (1) [=BAR-JESUS]
Ac 13: 8 But the magician **E** (for that is the translation

ELYMEANS (1)
Jdt 1: 6 and, on the plain, Arioch, king of the **E.**

ELYON See Index to Footnotes

ELZABAD (2)
1Ch 12:12 Johanan eighth, **E** ninth,
26: 7 Othni, Rephael, Obed, and **E,**

ELZAPHAN (2)
Ex 6:22 The sons of Uzziel: Mishael, **E,** and Sithri.
Lev 10: 4 Moses summoned Mishael and **E,**

EMADABUN (1)
1Es 5:58 and the sons of Jeshua **E** and the sons of Joda son

EMANATION (1)
Wis 7:25 and a pure **e** of the glory of the Almighty;

EMATHIS (1)
1Es 9:29 Jehohanan and Hananiah and Zabbai and **E.**

EMBALM (1) [EMBALMED, EMBALMING]
Ge 50: 2 the physicians in his service to **e** his father.

EMBALMED (2) [EMBALM]
Ge 50: 2 So the physicians **e** Israel;
50:26 he was **e** and placed in a coffin in Egypt.

EMBALMING (1) [EMBALM]
Ge 50: 3 for that is the time required for **e.**

EMBARK (1) [EMBARKATION, EMBARKED, EMBARKING]
2Mc 12: 3 they invited the Jews who lived among them to **e,**

EMBARKATION (1) [EMBARK]
3Mc 4: 7 along as far as the place of **e.**

EMBARKED (2) [EMBARK]
1Mc 15:37 Meanwhile Trypho **e** on a ship and escaped
2Mc 5: 9 having **e** to go to the Lacedaemonians in hope

EMBARKING (1) [EMBARK]
Ac 27: 2 **E** on a ship of Adramyttium that was about

EMBARRASS (1) [EMBARRASSED]
Sir 13: 7 He will **e** you with his delicacies,

EMBARRASSED‡ (3) [EMBARRASS]
Jdg 3:25 So they waited until they were **e.**
Ezr 9: 6 I am too ashamed and **e** to lift my face to you,
Sir 26:24 *but a modest daughter will even be* **e** *before her*

EMBER (1) [EMBERS]
2Sa 14: 7 Thus they would quench my one remaining **e,**

EMBERS (3) [EMBER]
Pr 26:21 As charcoal is to hot **e** and wood to fire,
Tob 6:17 and put them on the **e** of the incense.
8: 2 the bag where he had them and put them on the **e**

EMBITTERED (4) [BITTER]
Ps 73:21 When my soul was **e,** when I was pricked in heart,
Sir 7:11 Do not ridicule a person who is **e** in spirit,
1Mc 3: 7 He **e** many kings, but he made Jacob glad
2Es 9:41 for I am greatly **e** in spirit and deeply distressed."

EMBLEM (3) [EMBLEMS]
Ex 13:16 a sign on your hand and as an **e** on your forehead
Dt 6: 8 fix them as an **e** on your forehead,
11:18 and fix them as an **e** on your forehead.

EMBLEMS (2) [EMBLEM]
Ps 74: 4 they set up their **e** there.
74: 9 We do not see our **e;**

EMBODIMENT (1)
Ro 2:20 having in the law the **e** of knowledge and truth,

EMBRACE (9) [EMBRACED, EMBRACES, EMBRACING]
Ge 16: 5 I gave my slave-girl to your **e**,
Dt 13: 6 or the wife you **e**, or your most intimate friend—
2Ki 4:16 "At this season, in due time, you shall **e** a son."
Pr 4: 8 she will honor you if you **e** her.
5:20 by another woman and **e** the bosom of
Ecc 3: 5 a time to **e**, and a time to refrain from embracing;
Mic 7: 5 of your mouth from her who lies in your **e**;
2Es 2:15 **e** your children; bring them up with
2:32 **E** your children until I come,

EMBRACED (11) [EMBRACE]
Ge 29:13 he **e** him and kissed him,
33: 4 But Esau ran to meet him, and **e** him,
48:10 and he kissed them and **e** them.
1Ki 9: 9 **e** other gods, worshiping them and serving them;
SS 2: 6 and that his right hand **e** me!
8: 3 and that his right hand **e** me!
Ac 20:37 they **e** Paul and kissed him,
Tob 7: 7 He then **e** his kinsman Tobias and wept.
10:11 he **e** Tobias and said, "Farewell, my child;
AdE 15:12 he **e** her, and said, "Speak to me."
2Es 6:39 and darkness and silence **e** everything;

EMBRACES (3) [EMBRACE]
Dt 28:54 to the wife whom he **e**,
28:56 will begrudge food to the husband whom she **e**,
4Mc 13:21 From such **e** brotherly-loving souls are nourished;

EMBRACING (5) [EMBRACE]
Ecc 3: 5 a time to embrace, and a time to refrain from **e**;
Sir 30:20 and groans as a eunuch groans when **e** a girl.
Sus 1:39 Although we saw them **e**,
3Mc 5:49 **e** relatives and falling into one another's arms—
4Mc 1:24 is an emotion **e** pleasure and pain.

EMBROIDERED (16) [EMBROIDERER]
Ex 26:36 and of fine twisted linen, **e** with needlework.
27:16 and of fine twisted linen, **e** with needlework;
28:39 and you shall make a sash **e** with needlework.
36:37 and fine twisted linen, **e** with needlework;
38:18 the entrance to the court was **e** with needlework
39:29 purple, and crimson yarns, **e** with needlework;
Jdg 5:30 of dyed stuffs for Sisera, spoil of dyed stuffs **e**,
5:30 two pieces of dyed work **e** for my neck as spoil?'
Eze 16:10 with **e** cloth and with sandals of fine leather;
16:13 of fine linen, rich fabric, and **e** cloth.
16:18 and you took your **e** garments to cover them,
26:16 and strip off their **e** garments.
27: 7 Of fine **e** linen from Egypt was your sail,
27:16 purple, **e** work, fine linen, coral, and rubies.
27:24 in clothes of blue and **e** work,
AdE 1: 6 of gauze, **e** in various colors, with roses arranged

EMBROIDERER (3) [EMBROIDERED]
Ex 35:35 or by an **e** in blue, purple, and crimson yarns,
38:23 designer, and **e** in blue, purple, and crimson yarns,
Sir 45:10 of gold and violet and purple, the work of an **e**;

EMBROIDERY See Index to Footnotes

EMEK-KEZIZ (1)
Jos 18:21 to their families were Jericho, Beth-hoglah, **E**,

EMERALD (8) [EMERALDS]
Ex 28:17 chrysolite, and **e** shall be the first row;
39:10 chrysolite, and **e** was the first row;
Eze 28:13 onyx, and jasper, sapphire, turquoise, and **e**;
Rev 4: 3 around the throne is a rainbow that looks like an **e**.
21:19 the second sapphire, the third agate, the fourth **e**,
Tob 13:16 of Jerusalem will be built with sapphire and **e**,
AdE 1: 6 on a mosaic floor of **e**,
Sir 32: 6 A seal of **e** in a rich setting of gold is the melody

EMERALDS (1) [EMERALD]
Jdt 10:21 **e** and other precious stones.

EMERGED (2) [EMERGING]
1Mc 9:23 the renegades **e** in all parts of Israel;
11:69 in ambush **e** from their places and joined battle.

EMERGING (1) [EMERGED]
Wis 19: 7 and dry land **e** where water had stood before,

EMERODS (KJV) See TUMORS, ULCERS

EMIM (3) [REPHAIM]
Ge 14: 5 the Zuzim in Ham, the **E** in Shaveh-kiriathaim,
Dt 2:10 (The **E**—a large and numerous people,
2:11 though the Moabites call them **E**.

EMINENCE (1) [EMINENT, EMINENTLY]
Sir 38:33 nor do they attain **e** in the public assembly.

EMINENT‡ (1) [EMINENCE]
Sir 10:22 The rich, and the **e**, and the poor—

EMINENT (KJV) See also LOFTY

EMINENTLY (1) [EMINENCE]
2Mc 13: 8 And this was **e** just;

EMISSARIES (1)
1Mc 13:34 also chose **e** and sent them to King Demetrius with

EMISSION (6)
Lev 15:16 If a man has an **e** of semen,
15:18 If a man lies with a woman and has an **e** of semen,
15:32 for him who has an **e** of semen,
22: 4 by a corpse or a man who has had an **e** of semen,
Dt 23:10 of you becomes unclean because of a nocturnal **e**,
Eze 23:20 and whose **e** was like that of stallions.

EMMANUEL (1) [=IMMANUEL]
Mt 1:23 name him **E**," which means, "God is with us."

EMMAUS (5)
Lk 24:13 of them were going to a village called **E**,
1Mc 3:40 they arrived they encamped near **E** in the plain.
3:57 and encamped to the south of **E**.
4: 3 to attack the king's force in **E**
9:50 the fortress in Jericho, and **E**, and Beth-horon,

EMMOR (KJV) See HAMOR

EMOTION (4) [EMOTIONS]
4Mc 1:14 We shall decide just what reason is and what **e** is,
1:24 is an **e** embracing pleasure and pain.
13: 5 to confess the sovereignty of right reason over **e**
14:13 which draws everything toward an **e** felt

EMOTIONS‡ (55) [EMOTION]
4Mc 1: 1 whether devout reason is sovereign over the **e**.
1: 3 it is evident that reason rules over those **e**
1: 4 it is also clear that it masters the **e** that hinder one
1: 5 Some might perhaps ask, "If reason rules the **e**,
1: 6 For reason does not rule its own **e**,
1: 7 that reason is dominant over the **e**,
1: 9 demonstrated that reason controls the **e**.
1:13 is whether reason is sovereign over the **e**.
1:14 how many kinds of **e** there are,
1:19 since by means of it reason rules over the **e**.
1:20 of the **e** are pleasure and pain;
1:21 The **e** of both pleasure
1:25 which is the most complex of all the **e**.
1:29 and so tames the jungle of habits and **e**.
1:30 but over the **e** it is sovereign.
1:30 that rational judgment is sovereign over the **e**
1:35 For the **e** of the appetites are restrained,
2: 6 Just so it is with the **e** that hinder one from justice.
2: 7 unless reason is clearly lord of the **e**?
2: 9 we can recognize that reason rules the **e**.
2:15 that reason rules even the more violent **e**:
2:16 the temperate mind repels all these malicious **e**,
2:18 temperate mind is able to get the better of the **e**,
2:21 he planted in them **e** and inclinations,
2:24 one might say, that if reason is master of the **e**,
3: 1 it is evident that reason rules not over its own **e**,
3: 5 reason does not uproot the **e** but is their antagonist.
3:17 the temperate mind can conquer the drives of the **e**
3:18 of reason spurn all domination by the **e**.
6:31 then, devout reason is sovereign over the **e**.
6:32 For if the **e** had prevailed over reason,
6:33 But now that reason has conquered the **e**,
7: 1 the ship of religion over the sea of the **e**,
7: 5 the maddening waves of the **e**.
7:16 most certainly devout reason is governor of the **e**.
7:17 "Not all have full command of their **e**,
7:20 by their **e** because of the weakness of their reason.
7:22 not be able to overcome the **e** through godliness?
7:23 the wise and courageous are masters of their **e**.
8:28 For they were contemptuous of the **e**
13: 1 that devout reason is sovereign over the **e**.
13: 2 to their **e** and had eaten defiling food,
13: 2 that they had been conquered by these **e**.
13: 3 they prevailed over their **e**.
13: 4 for the brothers mastered both **e** and pains.
13: 7 conquered the tempest of the **e**.
14: 1 but also mastered the **e** of brotherly love.
15: 1 O reason of the children, tyrant over the **e**!
15: 4 the **e** of parents who love their children?
15:23 a man's courage in the very midst of her **e**,
15:32 by the flood of your **e** and the violent winds,
16: 1 that devout reason is sovereign over the **e**.
16: 2 not only that men have ruled over the **e**,
16: 4 But the mother quenched so many and such great **e**
18: 2 knowing that devout reason is master of all **e**,

EMPEROR (23) [EMPIRE]
Mt 22:17 Is it lawful to pay taxes to the **e**, or not?"
22:21 therefore to the **e** the things that are the emperor's,
Mk 12:14 Is it lawful to pay taxes to the **e**, or not?
12:17 "Give to the **e** the things that are the emperor's,
Lk 2: 1 In those days a decree went out from **E** Augustus
3: 1 In the fifteenth year of the reign of **E** Tiberius,
20:22 Is it lawful for us to pay taxes to the **e**, or not?"
20:25 give to the **e** the things that are the emperor's,
23: 2 forbidding us to pay taxes to the **e**,
Jn 19:12 you are no friend of the **e**.
19:12 to be a king sets himself against the **e**."
19:15 "We have no king but the **e**."
Ac 17: 7 They are all acting contrary to the decrees of the **e**,
25: 8 or against the temple, or against the **e**."
25:11 I appeal to the **e**."
25:12 replied, "You have appealed to the **e**; to the **e** you will go."
25:21 to be held until I could send him to the **e**."
26:32 if he had not appealed to the **e**."
27:24 you must stand before the **e**;
28:19 Jews objected, I was compelled to appeal to the **e**
1Pe 2:13 whether of the **e** as supreme,
2:17 the family of believers. Fear God. Honor the **e**.

EMPEROR'S (8) [EMPIRE]
Mt 22:21 They answered, "The **e**."
22:21 therefore to the emperor the things that are the **e**,
Mk 12:16 and whose title?" They answered, "The **e**."
12:17 "Give to the emperor the things that are the **e**,
Lk 20:24 and whose title does it bear?" They said, "The **e**."
20:25 give to the emperor the things that are the **e**,
Ac 25:10 Paul said, "I am appealing to the **e** tribunal;
Php 4:22 especially those of the **e** household.

EMPIRE (2) [EMPEROR, EMPEROR'S, IMPERIAL]
AdE 3:13 the **e** of Artaxerxes to destroy the Jewish people
4:11 of the **e** know that if any man or woman goes to

EMPLOY (1) [EMPLOYED, EMPLOYEE, EMPLOYERS]
3Mc 5:22 not so much **e** the duration of the night in sleep as

EMPLOYED (3) [EMPLOY]
1Co 9:13 Do you not know that those who are **e** in
2Mc 1:13 a deception **e** by the priests of the goddess Nanea.
1Es 8:22 or gatekeepers or temple servants or persons **e**

EMPLOYEE (1) [EMPLOY]
Sir 34:27 to deprive an **e** of wages is to shed blood.

EMPLOYERS (1) [EMPLOY]
Pr 10:26 and smoke to the eyes, so are the lazy to their **e**.

EMPOWERED (1) [POWER]
Sir 42:17 The Lord has not **e** even his holy ones

EMPTIED (10) [EMPTY]
Ge 24:20 So she quickly **e** her jar into the trough
1Ki 17:14 not be **e** and the jug of oil will not fail until the day
17:16 The jar of meal was not **e**,
2Ki 22: 9 "Your servants have **e** out the money
2Ch 34:17 They have **e** out the money that was found in
Ne 5:13 Thus may they be shaken out and **e**."
Isa 19: 3 of the Egyptians within them will be **e** out,
Jer 48:11 he has not been **e** from vessel to vessel,
1Co 1:17 that the cross of Christ might not be **e** of its power.
Php 2: 7 but **e** himself, taking the form of a slave,

EMPTINESS (5) [EMPTY]
Job 7: 3 so I am allotted months of **e**,
15:31 Let them not trust in **e**, deceiving themselves;
15:31 for **e** will be their recompense.
Isa 6:12 and vast is the **e** in the midst of the land.
40:17 by him as less than nothing and **e**.

EMPTY‡ (47) [EMPTIED, EMPTINESS, EMPTY-HANDED, EMPTYING]
Ge 37:24 The pit was **e**; there was no water in it.
41:27 as are the seven **e** ears blighted by the east wind.
Lev 14:36 The priest shall command that they **e** the house
Jdg 7:16 and **e** jars, with torches inside the jars,
Ru 1:21 but the LORD has brought me back **e**;
1Sa 6: 3 the ark of the God of Israel, do not send it **e**, but
20:18 you will be missed, because your place will be **e**
20:25 by Saul's side; but David's place was **e**.
20:27 the day after the new moon, David's place was **e**.
2Sa 1:22 nor the sword of Saul return **e**.
2Ki 4: 3 **e** vessels and not just a few.
2Ch 24:11 and **e** the chest and take it and return it to its place.
Job 21:34 How then will you comfort me with **e** nothings?
35:13 Surely God does not hear an **e** cry,
35:16 Job opens his mouth in **e** talk,
38:26 on the desert, which is **e** of human life,
Ps 41: 6 when they come to see me, they utter **e** words,
94:11 that they are but an **e** breath.
Pr 13:25 but the belly of the wicked is **e**.
Ecc 11: 3 When clouds are full, they **e** rain on the earth;
Isa 30: 7 For Egypt's help is worthless and **e**,
41:29 their works are nothing; their images are **e** wind.
55:11 it shall not return to me **e**,
59: 4 they rely on **e** pleas, they speak lies,
Jer 14: 3 they find no water, they return with their vessels **e**.
48:12 and **e** his vessels, and break his jars in pieces.
51: 2 They shall **e** her land when they come against her
51:34 he has made me an **e** vessel,
Eze 24: 6 **E** it piece by piece, making no choice at all.
24:11 Stand it **e** upon the coals,
Hos 10: 4 with **e** oaths they make covenants;
Mic 2:11 If someone were to go about uttering **e** falsehoods,
Zec 10: 2 dreamers tell false dreams, and give **e** consolation.

Mt 6: 7 do not heap up **e** phrases as the Gentiles do;
12:44 it comes, it finds it **e**, swept, and put in order.
Lk 1:53 and sent the rich away **e**.
2Co 9: 3 to have been **e** in this case, so that you may
Eph 5: 6 Let no one deceive you with **e** words,
Col 2: 8 through philosophy and **e** deceit,
Jdt 7:20 of every inhabitant of Bethulia were **e**;
Wis 2: 3 and the spirit will dissolve like **e** air.
Sir 29: 5 and pays back with **e** promises,
2Mc 14:44 and he fell in the middle of the **e** space.
3Mc 5:43 to him would quickly render it forever **e**
2Es 6:22 full storehouses shall suddenly be found to be **e**;
7:25 is the reason, Ezra, that **e** things are for the **e**,

EMPTY-HANDED (15) [EMPTY, HAND]

Ge 31:42 surely now you would have sent me away **e**.
Ex 3:21 when you go, you will not go **e**;
23:15 No one shall appear before me **e**.
34:20 No one shall appear before me **e**.
Dt 15:13 you shall not send him out **e**.
16:16 They shall not appear before the LORD **e**;
Ru 3:17 'Do not go back to your mother-in-law **e**.' "
Job 22: 9 You have sent widows away **e**,
Jer 50: 9 of a skilled warrior who does not return **e**.
Mk 12: 3 and beat him, and sent him away **e**.
Lk 20:10 but the tenants beat him and sent him away **e**.
20:11 one also they beat and insulted and sent away **e**.
Jdt 1:11 they sent back his messengers **e** and in disgrace.
Sir 29: 9 and in their need do not send them away **e**.
35: 6 Do not appear before the Lord **e**,

EMPTYING (2) [EMPTY]

Ge 42:35 As they were **e** their sacks,
Hab 1:17 Is he then to keep on **e** his net,

EMULATION (KJV) See JEALOUS

EN-DOR (2) [=ENDOR]

Jos 17:11 the inhabitants of **E** and its villages,
Ps 83:10 who were destroyed at **E**,

EN-EGLAIM (1)

Eze 47:10 beside the sea from En-gedi to **E**;

EN-GANNIM (3)

Jos 15:34 Zanoah, **E**, Tappuah, Enam,
19:21 Remeth, **E**, En-haddah, Beth-pazzez;
21:29 **E** with its pasture lands—

EN-GEDI (7) [=HAZAZON-TAMAR]

Jos 15:62 and **E**: six towns with their villages.
1Sa 23:29 and lived in the strongholds of **E**.
24: 1 he was told, "David is in the wilderness of **E**."
2Ch 20: 2 already they are at Hazazon-tamar" (that is, **E**).
SS 1:14 a cluster of henna blossoms in the vineyards of **E**.
Eze 47:10 People will stand fishing beside the sea from **E**
Sir 24:14 I grew tall like a palm tree in **E**,

EN-HADDAH (1)

Jos 19:21 Remeth, En-gannim, **E**, Beth-pazzez;

EN-HAKKORE (1)

Jdg 15:19 it was named **E**, which is at Lehi to this day.

EN-HAZOR (1)

Jos 19:37 Kedesh, Edrei, **E**,

EN-MISHPAT (1) [=KADESH]

Ge 14: 7 then they turned back and came to **E** (that is,

EN-RIMMON (1) [RIMMON]

Ne 11:29 in **E**, in Zorah, in Jarmuth,

EN-ROGEL (4)

Jos 15: 7 along to the waters of En-shemesh, and ends at **E**;
18:16 of the slope of the Jebusites, and downward to **E**;
2Sa 17:17 Jonathan and Ahimaaz were waiting at **E**;
1Ki 1: 9 which is beside **E**, and he invited all his brothers,

EN-SHEMESH (2)

Jos 15: 7 and the boundary passes along to the waters of **E**,
18:17 in a northerly direction going on to **E**, and

EN-TAPPUAH (1) [TAPPUAH]

Jos 17: 7 along southward to the inhabitants of **E**.

ENABLE (2) [ABLE]

Ecc 6: 2 yet God does not **e** them to enjoy these things,
Eph 3: 4 of which will **e** you to perceive my understanding

ENABLED (3) [ABLE]

2Ch 20:27 LORD had **e** them to rejoice over their enemies.
Ac 7:10 and **e** him to win favor and to show wisdom
Col 1:12 who has **e** you to share in the inheritance of

ENABLES (2) [ABLE]

Ecc 5:19 and possessions and whom he **e** to enjoy them,
Php 3:21 also **e** him to make all things subject to himself.

ENABLING (2) [ABLE]

Nu 35:32 **e** the fugitive to return to live in the land before
Php 2:13 **e** you both to will and to work

ENACTED (1) [ENACTS]

Heb 8: 6 which has been **e** through better promises.

ENACTS (1) [ENACTED]

AdE 1:20 Let whatever law the king **e** be proclaimed

ENAIM (2)

Ge 38:14 and sat down at the entrance to **E**,
38:21 "Where is the temple prostitute who was at **E** by

ENAM (1)

Jos 15:34 Zanoah, En-gannim, Tappuah, **E**,

ENAMORED (1)

Wis 8: 2 and became **e** of her beauty.

ENAN (5)

Nu 1:15 From Naphtali, Ahira son of **E**.
2:29 leader of the Naphtalites shall be Ahira son of **E**,
7:78 On the twelfth day Ahira son of **E**,
7:83 This was the offering of Ahira son of **E**.
10:27 of the tribe of Naphtali was Ahira son of **E**.

ENCAMP (10) [CAMP]

Jdg 6: 4 They would **e** against them and destroy
2Sa 12:28 and **e** against the city, and take it;
Job 19:12 they have thrown up siegeworks against me, and **e**
Ps 27: 3 an army **e** against me, my heart shall not fear;
Isa 29: 3 And like David I will **e** against you;
Jer 50:29 **E** all around her; let no one escape.
Zec 9: 8 Then I will **e** at my house as a guard,
1Mc 5:42 and gave them this command, "Permit no one to **e**,
5:49 to the army that all should **e** where they were.
15:39 He commanded him to **e** against Judea,

ENCAMPED‡ (71) [CAMP]

Ex 18: 5 the wilderness where Moses was **e** at the mountain
Dt 23: 9 When you are **e** against your
Jdg 4:11 and had **e** as far away as Elon-bezaanannim,
6:33 crossing the Jordan they **e** in the Valley of Jezreel.
7: 1 the troops that were with him rose early and **e**
9:50 Abimelech went to Thebez, and **e** against Thebez,
10:17 the Ammonites were called to arms, and they **e**
10:17 the Israelites came together, and they **e** at Mizpah.
11:20 and **e** at Jahaz, and fought with Israel.
15: 9 Then the Philistines came up and **e** in Judah,
18:12 and went up and **e** at Kiriath-jearim in Judah.
20:19 Then the Israelites got up in the morning, and **e**
1Sa 4: 1 they **e** at Ebenezer, and the Philistines **e** at Aphek.
13: 5 they came up and **e** at Michmash,
13:16 but the Philistines **e** at Michmash.
17: 1 and **e** between Socoh and Azekah,
17: 2 Saul and the Israelites gathered and **e** in the valley
26: 3 Saul **e** on the hill of Hachilah,
26: 5 and came to the place where Saul had **e**;
26: 5 while the army was **e** around him.
28: 4 Philistines assembled, and came and **e** at Shunem.
28: 4 Saul gathered all Israel, and they **e** at Gilboa.
29: 1 Israelites were **e** by the fountain that is in Jezreel.
2Sa 17:26 The Israelites and Absalom **e** in the land of Gilead.
23:13 band of Philistines was **e** in the valley of Rephaim.
1Ki 16:15 Now the troops were **e** against Gibbethon,
16:16 and the troops who were **e** heard it said,
20:27 of Israel **e** opposite them like two little flocks
20:29 They **e** opposite one another seven days.
1Ch 11:15 while the army of Philistines was **e** in the valley
2Ch 32: 1 of Assyria came and invaded Judah and **e** against
Isa 29: 1 Ah, Ariel, Ariel, the city where David **e**!
Jdt 7: 3 They **e** in the valley near Bethulia,
7:17 and they **e** in the valley and seized
7:18 And the Edomites and Ammonites went up and **e**
7:18 The rest of the Assyrian army **e** in the plain,
1Mc 2:32 they **e** opposite them and prepared for battle
3:40 they arrived they **e** near Emmaus in the plain.
3:42 and that the forces were **e** in their territory.
3:57 army marched out and **e** to the south of Emmaus.
4:29 They came into Idumea and **e** at Beth-zur,
5: 5 in their towers; and he **e** against them,
5:37 and **e** opposite Raphon, on the other side of
5:39 and they are **e** across the stream,
5:50 So the men of the forces **e**,
6:26 today they have **e** against the citadel in Jerusalem
6:31 through Idumea and **e** against Beth-zur,
6:32 Then Judas marched away from the citadel and **e**
6:48 and the king **e** in Judea and at Mount Zion.
6:51 Then he **e** before the sanctuary for many days.
7:19 Then Bacchides withdrew from Jerusalem and **e**
7:39 Now Nicanor went out from Jerusalem and **e**
7:40 Judas **e** in Adasa with three thousand men.
9: 2 They went by the road that leads to Gilgal and **e**
9: 3 of the one hundred fifty-second year they **e**
9: 5 Now Judas was **e** in Elasa,
9:64 Then he came and **e** against Bethbasi;
10:48 and **e** opposite Demetrius.
10:69 he assembled a large force and **e** against Jamnia.
10:75 He **e** before Joppa, but the people of
10:86 Then Jonathan left there and **e** against Askalon,
11:65 Simon **e** before Beth-zur and fought against it
1Mc 11:67 and his army **e** by the waters of Gennesaret.
11:73 to their camp, and there they **e**.
13:13 Simon **e** in Adida, facing the plain.
13:43 In those days Simon **e** against Gazara
15:13 So Antiochus **e** against Dor,
1Es 8:41 and we **e** there three days, and I inspected them.
3Mc 1: 1 where the army of Antiochus was **e**.
4Mc 3: 8 the whole army of our ancestors had **e**.

ENCAMPMENT (8) [CAMP]

Nu 2: 3 the sunrise shall be of the regimental **e** of Judah
2:10 the south side shall be the regimental **e** of Reuben
2:18 the west side shall be the regimental **e** of Ephraim
2:25 On the north side shall be the regimental **e** of Dan
Jos 8:13 the main **e** that was north of the city
1Sa 17:20 the **e** as the army was going forth to the battle line,
26: 5 Saul was lying within the **e**,
26: 7 there Saul lay sleeping within the **e**,

ENCAMPMENTS (5) [CAMP]

Ge 25:16 by their villages and by their **e**,
Nu 24: 5 how fair are your tents, O Jacob, your **e**, O Israel!
31:10 and all their **e**, they burned,
Eze 25: 4 They shall set their **e** among you
Jdt 3: 3 and our flocks and herds and all our **e** lie

ENCAMPS‡ (1) [CAMP]

Ps 34: 7 angel of the LORD **e** around those who fear him,

ENCHANTER (3) [ENCHANTERS, ENCHANTMENT, ENCHANTMENTS]

Ps 58: 5 not hear the voice of charmers or of the cunning **e**.
Isa 3: 3 counselor and skillful magician and expert **e**.
Da 2:10 has ever asked such a thing of any magician or **e**

ENCHANTERS (7) [ENCHANTER]

Da 1:20 the magicians and **e** in his whole kingdom.
2: 2 So the king commanded that the magicians, the **e**,
2:27 Daniel answered the king, "No wise men, **e**,
4: 7 Then the magicians, the **e**, the Chaldeans,
5: 7 The king cried aloud to bring in the **e**,
5:11 made him chief of the magicians, **e**, Chaldeans,
5:15 Now the wise men, the **e**, have been brought in

ENCHANTMENT (1) [ENCHANTER]

Nu 23:23 Surely there is no **e** against Jacob,

ENCHANTMENTS (2) [ENCHANTER]

Isa 47: 9 and the great power of your **e**.
47:12 Stand fast in your **e** and your many sorceries,

ENCIRCLE (5) [CIRCLE]

1Ki 7:15 and a cord of twelve cubits would **e** it;
7:23 A line of thirty cubits would **e** it completely.
2Ch 4: 2 A line of thirty cubits would **e** it completely.
Ps 22:12 Many bulls **e** me, strong bulls
1Mc 10:11 the walls and **e** Mount Zion with squared stones,

ENCIRCLED‡ (7) [CIRCLE]

SS 7: 2 Your belly is a heap of wheat, **e** with lilies.
Jer 52:22 all of bronze, **e** the top of the capital.
Heb 11:30 of Jericho fell after they had been **e** for seven days.
Sir 45: 9 And he **e** him with pomegranates,
1Mc 12:13 ourselves, many trials and many wars have **e** us;
3Mc 4: 8 their necks **e** with ropes instead of garlands,
4Mc 14: 8 **e** the sevenfold fear of tortures and dissolved it.

ENCIRCLES (2) [CIRCLE]

Ps 22:16 a company of evildoers **e** me.
Sir 43:12 It **e** the sky with its glorious arc;

ENCIRCLING (2) [CIRCLE]

2Ch 3:16 He made **e** chains and put them on the tops of
Jer 52:23 the pomegranates **e** the latticework numbered

ENCLOSE (1) [CLOSE]

SS 8: 9 if she is a door, we will **e** her with boards of cedar.

ENCLOSED (6) [CLOSE]

Ex 39: 6 **e** in settings of gold filigree and engraved like
39:13 they were **e** in settings of gold filigree.
Isa 40:12 **e** the dust of the earth in a measure,
Eze 1:27 something that looked like fire **e** all around;
2Mc 1:34 and **e** the place and made it sacred.
3Mc 4:11 be **e** in the hippodrome that had been built with

ENCLOSURE (1) [CLOSE]

Sir 50: 2 the high retaining walls for the temple **e**.

ENCLOSURES (1) [CLOSE]

3Mc 1: 7 and by endowing their sacred **e** with gifts,

ENCOMPASSED (5) [ENCOMPASSES]

2Sa 22: 5 For the waves of death **e** me,
Ps 18: 4 The cords of death **e** me;
40:12 For evils have **e** me without number;
116: 3 The snares of death **e** me;
3Mc 6:26 Who is it that has so lawlessly **e**

ENCOMPASSES (1) [ENCOMPASSED]

Jer 31:22 on the earth: a woman e a man.

ENCOUNTER (2) [ENCOUNTERED, ENCOUNTERS]

1Mc 9:11 from the camp and took its stand for the e.
2Mc 15:19 being anxious over the e in the open country.

ENCOUNTERED (3) [ENCOUNTER]

1Mc 5:25 They e the Nabateans, who met them peaceably
2Mc 10:17 and slaughtered those whom they e,
14:17 Simon, the brother of Judas, had e Nicanor,

ENCOUNTERS (1) [ENCOUNTER]

2Mc 8:30 In e with the forces of Timothy

ENCOURAGE‡ (17) [ENCOURAGED, ENCOURAGEMENT, ENCOURAGES, ENCOURAGING, ENCOURAGINGLY]

Dt 1:38 e him, for he is the one who will secure Israel's
3:28 But charge Joshua, and e and strengthen him,
2Sa 11:25 and overthrow it.' And e him."
Job 16: 5 I could e you with my mouth,
Ac 15:32 said much to e and strengthen the believers.
Eph 6:22 to let you know how we are, and to e your hearts.
Col 4: 8 how we are and that he may e your hearts;
1Th 3: 2 to strengthen and e you for the sake of your faith,
4:18 Therefore e one another with these words.
5:11 Therefore e one another and build up each other,
5:14 to admonish the idlers, e the faint hearted,
2Ti 4: 2 and e, with the utmost patience in teaching.
Tit 2: 4 so that they may e the young women
1Pe 5:12 to e you and to testify that this is the true grace
Sir 13: 6 and will smile at you and e you;
2Mc 11:32 And I have also sent Menelaus to e you.
3Mc 1: 6 to visit the neighboring cities and e them.

ENCOURAGED (22) [ENCOURAGE]

2Ch 32: 8 The people were e by the words of King Hezekiah
35: 2 He appointed the priests to their offices and e them
Eze 13:22 and you have e the wicked not to turn
Ac 14:22 of the disciples and e them to continue in the faith,
16:40 they had seen and e the brothers and sisters there,
18:27 the believers e him and wrote to the disciples
27:36 all of them were e and took food for themselves.
Ro 1:12 so that we may be mutually e by each other's faith,
1Co 8:10 be e to the point of eating food sacrificed to idols?
14:31 so that all may learn and all be e.
Col 2: 2 I want their hearts to be e and united in love,
1Th 3: 7 and persecution we have been e about you
Heb 6:18 we who have taken refuge might be strongly e
1Mc 12:50 and they e one another and kept marching
13: 3 he e them, saying to them,
2Mc 7: 5 but the brothers and their mother e one another
7:21 She e each of them in the language
15:17 E by the words of Judas,
1Es 8:27 I was e by the help of the Lord my God,
4Mc 13: 8 a holy chorus of religion and e one another,
14: 1 Furthermore, they e them to face the torture,
16:24 of the seven e and persuaded each of her sons

ENCOURAGEMENT (10) [ENCOURAGE]

Ac 4:36 the name Barnabas (which means "son of e").
20: 2 and had given the believers much e,
Ro 15: 4 and by the e of the scriptures we might have hope.
15: 5 of steadfastness and e grant you to live in harmony
1Co 14: 3 for their upbuilding and e and consolation.
Php 2: 1 If then there is any e in Christ,
Phm 1: 7 I have indeed received much joy and e
Wis 8: 9 that she would give me good counsel and e
1Mc 10:24 of e and promise them honor and gifts,
12: 9 we have as e the holy books that are in our hands,

ENCOURAGES (3) [ENCOURAGE]

Isa 41: 7 The artisan e the goldsmith,
41: 7 the hammer e the one who strikes the anvil, saying
Sir 17:24 and he e those who are losing hope.

ENCOURAGING (6) [ENCOURAGE]

Ac 20: 1 e them and saying farewell, he left for Macedonia.
1Th 2:12 and e you and pleading that you lead a life worthy
Heb 10:25 as is the habit of some, but e one another,
1Mc 5:53 and e the people all the way until he came to
2Mc 15: 9 E them from the law and the prophets,
2Es 10: 3 e me to be quiet, I got up in the night and fled,

ENCOURAGINGLY (2) [ENCOURAGE]

2Ch 30:22 Hezekiah spoke e to all the Levites who showed
32: 6 in the square at the gate of the city and spoke e

ENCROACH (2)

Dt 2:37 You did not e, however, on the land of
Pr 23:10 not remove an ancient landmark or e on the fields

ENCRUSTED (1)

SS 5:14 His body is ivory work, e with sapphires.

END‡ (359) [ENDED, ENDING, ENDLESS, ENDS]

A. PUT AN END TO (18)
B. MADE/MAKE AN END (15)
C. END OF THE EARTH (14)
D. END OF THE/THIS AGE (10)

Ge 6:13 "I have determined to make an e of all flesh, B
8: 3 At the e of one hundred fifty days
8: 6 At the e of forty days Noah opened the window of
23: 9 it is at the e of his field.
41:53 that prevailed in the land of Egypt came to an e;
47:21 he made slaves of them from one e of Egypt to
Ex 12:41 At the e of four hundred thirty years,
23:16 the festival of ingathering at the e of the year,
25:19 Make one cherub at the one e,
26:28 shall pass through from e to e.
36:33 He made the middle bar to pass through from e
36:33 through from end to e halfway up the frames.
37: 8 at the one e, and one cherub at the other end;
37: 8 and one cherub at the other e;
Nu 13:25 the e of forty days they returned from spying out
14:35 in this wilderness they shall come to a full e,
17:10 may make an e of their complaints against me, B
23:10 and let my e be like his!"
24:20 but its e is to perish forever."
34: 3 Your southern boundary shall begin from the e of
34: 9 and its e shall be at Hazar-enan;
34:12 and its e shall be at the Dead Sea.
Dt 4:32 ask from one e of heaven to the other:
7:22 you will not be able to make a quick e of them,
8:16 and in the e to do you good.
9:11 At the e of forty days and forty nights
11:12 from the beginning of the year to the e of the year.
13: 7 from one e of the earth to the other, C
28:49 from the e of the earth, C
28:64 from one e of the earth to the other; C
31:24 down in a book the words of this law to the very e,
31:30 to the very e, in the hearing of the whole assembly
32:20 I will see what their e will be;
32:29 they would discern what the e would be.
Jos 3: 2 At the e of three days the officers went through
13:27 as far as the lower e of the Sea of Chinnereth,
15: 2 And their south boundary ran from the e of
15: 4 and comes to its e at the sea.
15: 8 at the northern e of the valley of Rephaim;
15:11 then the boundary comes to an e at the sea.
18:16 which is at the north e of the valley of Rephaim;
18:19 at the south e of the Jordan:
Jdg 11:39 At the e of two months, she returned to her father,
Ru 2:23 until the e of the barley and wheat harvests;
3: 7 he went to lie down at the e of the heap of grain.
1Sa 3:12 concerning his house, from beginning to e.
2Sa 2:26 Do you not know that the e will be bitter?
14:26 of his head (for at the e of every year he used
15: 7 At the e of four years Absalom said to the king,
24: 8 at the e of nine months and twenty days.
1Ki 2:39 But it happened at the e of three years that two
9:10 At the e of twenty years,
10:20 one on each e of a step on the six steps.
2Ki 8: 3 At the e of the seven years,
13:17 Arameans in Aphek until you have made an e B
13:19 down Aram until you had made an e of it, B
18:10 and at the e of three years,
21:16 until he had filled Jerusalem from one e
2Ch 8: 1 At the e of twenty years,
9:19 one on each e of a step on the six steps.
20:16 you will find them at the e of the valley,
20:23 they had made an e of the inhabitants of Seir, B
21:19 In course of time, at the e of two years,
24:23 At the e of the year the army of Aram came up
Ezr 9:11 from e to e with their uncleanness.
10:17 of the first month they had come to the e of all
Ne 3:21 from the door of the house of Eliashib to the e of
9:31 in your great mercies you did not make an e B
Est 1:18 and there will be no e of contempt and wrath!
Job 5:13 the schemes of the wily are brought to a quick e.
6:11 And what is my e, that I should be patient?
7: 6 and come to their e without hope.
22: 5 There is no e to your iniquities.
28: 3 Miners put an e to darkness, A
32:22 or my Maker would soon put an e to me! A
Ps 7: 9 O let the evil of the wicked come to an e,
19: 4 and their words to the e of the world.
19: 6 Its rising is from the e of the heavens,
19: 6 and its circuit to the e of them;
39: 4 let me know my e, and what is the measure
46: 9 He makes wars cease to the e of the earth; C
49:13 the e of those who are pleased with their lot.
54: 5 In your faithfulness, put an e to them. A
61: 2 From the e of the earth I call to you, C
73:17 of God; then I perceived their e.
73:27 you put an e to those who are false to you. A
77: 8 Are his promises at an e for all time?
90: 9 our years come to an e like a sigh.
102:27 but you are the same, and your years have no e.
107:27 and were at their wits' e.
112: 8 in the e they will look in triumph on their foes.
119:33 and I will observe it to the e.
119:87 They have almost made an e of me on earth; B
119:112 to perform your statutes forever, to the e.
135: 7 who makes the clouds rise at the e of the earth; C
139:18 I come to the e—I am still with you.
Pr 1:19 Such is the e of all who are greedy for gain;
5: 4 but in the e she is bitter as wormwood,
5:11 and at the e of your life you will groan,
Pr 14:12 but its e is the way to death.
14:13 and the e of joy is grief.
16:25 but in the e it is the way to death.
18:18 Casting the lot puts an e to disputes and decides
20:21 in the beginning will not be blessed in the e.
25: 8 for what will you do in the e,
25:10 and your ill repute will have no e.
29:21 from childhood will come to a bad e.
Ecc 3:11 from the beginning to the e.
4: 8 yet there is no e to all their toil,
4:16 there was no e to all those people whom he led.
7: 2 for this is the e of everyone,
7: 8 Better is the e of a thing than its beginning;
12:12 Of making many books there is no e,
12:13 The e of the matter; all has been heard.
Isa 2: 7 and there is no e to their treasures;
2: 7 and there is no e to their chariots.
7: 3 at the e of the conduit of the upper pool on
10:23 For the Lord GOD of hosts will make a full e,
10:25 while my indignation will come to an e,
13: 5 from the e of the heavens,
13:11 I will put an e to the pride of the arrogant, A
21: 2 all the sighing she has caused I bring to an e.
21:16 all the glory of Kedar will come to an e;
23:15 At the e of seventy years, it will happen to Tyre as
23:17 At the e of seventy years,
38:12 from day to night you bring me to an e;
38:13 from day to night you bring me to an e.
42:10 his praise from the e of the earth! C
43: 6 and my daughters from the e of the earth— C
46:10 declaring the e from the beginning and
47: 7 not lay these things to heart or remember their e.
48:20 proclaim it, send it forth to the e of the earth; C
49: 6 my salvation may reach to the e of the earth." C
62:11 The LORD has proclaimed to the e of the earth: C
66:17 vermin, and rodents, shall come to an e together,
Jer 1: 3 the e of the eleventh year of King Zedekiah son
3: 5 will he be indignant to the e?"
4:27 yet I will not make a full e.
5:10 but do not make a full e;
5:18 says the LORD, I will not make a full e of you.
5:31 but what will you do when the e comes?
7:34 an e the sound of mirth and gladness, the voice of
12:12 for the sword of the LORD devours from one e of
17:11 and at their e they will prove to be fools.
25:33 on that day shall extend from one e of the earth C
30:11 I will make an e of all the nations B
30:11 but of you I will not make an e. B
42: 7 At the e of ten days the word of the LORD came
44:11 to bring all Judah to an e.
46:28 I will make an e of all the nations B
46:28 but I will not make an e of you! B
48:35 And I will bring to an e in Moab, says the LORD,
50:17 and now at the e King Nebuchadrezzar
51:13 your e has come, the thread of your life is cut.
51:31 the king of Babylon that his city is taken from e
51:31 of Babylon that his city is taken from end to e:
La 3:22 his mercies never come to an e;
4:18 in our streets; our e drew near;
4:18 our days were numbered; for our e had come.
Eze 3:16 the e of seven days, the word of the LORD came
7: 2 to the land of Israel: An e!
7: 2 The e has come upon the four corners of the land.
7: 3 e is upon you, I will let loose my anger upon you;
7: 6 An e has come, the end has come.
7: 6 An end has come, the e has come.
7:24 I will put an e to the arrogance of the strong, A
11:13 will you make a full e of the remnant of Israel?"
12:23 I will put an e to this proverb, A
20:13 to make an e of them. B
20:17 and I did not destroy them or make an e of them B
23:27 So I will put an e to your lewdness A
23:48 Thus will I put an e to lewdness in the land, A
26:21 I will bring you to a dreadful e,
27:36 to a dreadful e and shall be no more forever."
28:19 to a dreadful e and shall be no more forever.
29:13 At the e of forty years I will gather the Egyptians
30:10 I will put an e to the hordes of Egypt, A
30:13 will destroy the idols and put an e to the images A
30:18 and its proud might shall come to an e;
33:28 and its proud might shall come to an e;
40: 7 of the gate at the inner e was one reed deep.
40: 9 and the vestibule of the gate was at the inner e.
40:15 From the front of the gate at the entrance to the e
44: 6 of Israel, let there be an e to all your abominations
46:19 and there I saw a place at the extreme western e
47: 1 down from below the south e of the threshold of
Da 1: 5 so that at the e of that time they could be stationed
1:15 At the e of ten days it was observed
1:18 At the e of the time that the king had set for them
2:28 to King Nebuchadnezzar what will happen at the e
2:44 and bring them to an e, and it shall stand forever;
4:20 and was visible to the e of the whole earth,
4:29 the e of twelve months he was walking on the roof
5:26 the days of your kingdom and brought it to an e;
6:26 and his dominion has no e.
8:17 O mortal, that the vision is for the time of the e."
8:19 for it refers to the appointed time of the e.
8:23 At the e of their rule,
9:24 to finish the transgression, to put an e to sin, A
9:26 Its e shall come with a flood,
9:26 and to the e there shall be war.
9:27 the decreed e is poured out upon the desolator."
10:14 to happen to your people at the e of days.
11:18 But a commander shall put an e to his insolence; A
11:27 for there remains an e at the time appointed.
11:35 purified, and cleansed, until the time of the e,

Da 11:40 of the e king of the south shall attack him.
11:45 he shall come to his e, with no one to help him.
12: 4 and the book sealed until the time of the e.
12: 6 long shall it be until the e of these wonders?"
12: 7 of the power of the holy people comes to an e,
12: 9 to remain secret and sealed until the time of the e.
12:13 you shall rise for your reward at the e of the days."
Hos 1: 4 for the blood of Jezreel, and I will put an e A
2:11 I will put an e to all her mirth, her festivals, A
Am 3:15 and the great houses shall come to an e,
8: 2 "The e has come upon my people Israel;
8:10 and the e of it like a bitter day.
Na 1: 8 He will make a full e of his adversaries,
1: 9 He will make an e; no adversary will rise up B
2: 9 There is no e of treasure! An abundance of every
3: 1 full of booty—no e to the plunder!
3: 3 bodies without e—they stumble over the bodies!
Hab 2: 3 it speaks of the e, and does not lie.
Zep 1:18 a terrible e he will make of all the inhabitants of
Zec 9: 6 and I will make an e of the pride of Philistia. B
Mt 10:22 But the one who endures to the e will be saved.
13:39 the harvest is the e of the age, D
13:40 so will it be at the e of the age. D
13:49 So it will be at the e of the age. D
24: 3 sign of your coming and of the e of the age?" D
24: 6 for this must take place, but the e is not yet.
24:13 But the one who endures to the e will be saved.
24:14 and then the e will come.
24:31 from one e of heaven to the other.
26:58 with the guards in order to see how this would e.
28:20 I am with you always, to the e of the age." D
Mk 3:26 he cannot stand, but his e has come.
13: 7 this must take place, but the e is still to come.
13:13 But the one who endures to the e will be saved.
Lk 1:33 and of his kingdom there will be no e."
21: 9 but the e will not follow immediately."
Jn 13: 1 he loved them to the e.
Ro 6:21 The e of those things is death.
6:22 The e is eternal life.
10: 4 the e of the law so that there may be righteousness
14: 9 For to this e Christ died and lived again,
1Co 1: 8 He will also strengthen you to the e,
13: 8 But as for prophecies, they will come to an e;
13: 8 as for knowledge, it will come to an e.
13:10 the partial will come to an e.
13:11 I became an adult, I put an e to childish ways. A
15:24 the e, when he hands over the kingdom to God
2Co 1:13 I hope you will understand until the e—
3:13 to keep the people of Israel from gazing at the e of
11:15 Their e will match their deeds.
Eph 6:18 To that e keep alert and always persevere
Php 3:19 Their e is destruction; their god is the belly;
2Th 1:11 To this e we always pray for you,
1Ti 4:10 For to this e we toil and struggle,
Heb 1:12 But you are the same, and your years will never e."
3:14 if only we hold our first confidence firm to the e.
6: 8 its e is to be burned over.
6:11 to realize the full assurance of hope to the very e,
6:16 oath given as confirmation puts an e to all dispute.
7: 3 having neither beginning of days nor e of life,
9:26 at the e of the age to remove sin by the sacrifice D
11:22 By faith Joseph, at the e of his life,
1Pe 1:20 but was revealed at the e of the ages for your sake.
4: 7 The e of all things is near;
4:17 be the e for those who do not obey the gospel
Rev 2:26 to do my works to the e, I will give authority over
21: 6 the Alpha and the Omega, the beginning and the e.
22:13 the first and the last, the beginning and the e."
Jdt 11:21 "No other woman from one e of the earth to C
AdE 1: 5 the e of the festivity the king gave a drinking party
14:13 that there may be an e of him and those who agree
Wis 2: 1 and there is no remedy when a life comes to its e,
2:16 he calls the last e of the righteous happy,
2:17 and let us test what will happen at the e of his life;
3:19 For the e of an unrighteous generation is grievous.
4:17 For they will see the e of the wise,
5: 4 that their lives were madness and that their e was
7:18 the beginning and e and middle of times,
8: 1 She reaches mightily from one e of the earth to C
11:14 at the e of the events they marveled at him,
14:14 and therefore their speedy e has been planned.
14:27 not to be named is the beginning and cause and e
16: 5 your wrath did not continue to the e;
18:21 withstood the anger and put an e to the disaster, A
19: 1 ungodly were assailed to the e by pitiless anger,
19: 4 For the fate they deserved drew them on to this e,
Sir 1:13 Those who fear the Lord will have a happy e;
3:26 A stubborn mind will fare badly at the e,
7:36 In all you do, remember the e of your life,
9:11 for you do not know what their e will be like.
14: 7 and in the e he reveals his meanness.
18:12 He sees and recognizes that their e is miserable;
21: 9 and their e is a blazing fire.
21:10 but at its e is the pit of Hades.
22:10 and at the e he will say, "What is it?"
27:14 and swearing make one's hair stand on e,
28: 6 Remember the e of your life, and set enmity aside;
30:10 and in the e you will gnash your teeth.
31:22 and in the e you will appreciate my words.
33:24 At the time when you e the days of your life,
38:20 drive it away, and remember your own e.
39:20 to the e of time he can see everything,
48:25 He revealed what was to occur to the e of time,
49: 4 the kings of Judah came to an e.
51:14 and I will search for her until the e.
Bar 3:17 and there is no e to their getting;
2Mc 5: 7 in the e he got only disgrace from his conspiracy,
2Mc 5: 8 Finally he met a miserable e.
7:38 and through me and my brothers to bring to an e
9:28 came to the e of his life by a most pitiable fate,
10: 9 Such then was the e of Antiochus,
13:16 In the e they filled the camp with terror
15:37 So I will here e my story.
15:39 And here will be the e.
1Es 9:17 to an e by the new moon of the first month.
3Mc 1: 2 intending single-handed to kill him and thereby e
4:14 the e to be destroyed in the space of a single day.
4:15 to an e after forty days but still uncompleted.
5:49 the e of their most miserable suspense,
6:32 Putting an e to all mourning and wailing,
2Es 2:34 because he who will come at the e of the age D
3:14 and to him alone you revealed the e of the times,
4:26 because the age is hurrying swiftly to its e.
5:41 you have charge of those who are alive at the e,
6: 6 just as the e shall come through me alone and not
6: 7 the e of the first age and the beginning of the D
6: 9 Now Esau is the e of this age, D
6:10 and the e of a person is the heel;
6:15 because the word concerns the e,
6:16 for they know that their e must be changed."
6:25 and shall see my salvation and the e of my world.
7:*112* [42] "This present world is not the e;
7:*113* [43] the day of judgment will be the e of this age D
7:*114* [44] sinful indulgence has come to an e,
8:54 the e the treasure of immortality is made manifest.
9: 5 the beginning is evident, and the e manifest;
9: 6 and the e in penalties and in signs.
10:28 my e has become corruption,
11:13 And after a time its reign came to an e,
11:14 While it was reigning its e came also,
11:39 that the e of my times might come through them?
12: 6 the Most High that he may strengthen me to the e."
12: 9 the e of the times and the last events of the times."
12:21 be kept for the time when its e approaches,
12:21 but two shall be kept until the e.
12:30 the Most High has kept for the eagle's e;
12:32 the Most High has kept until the e of days,
12:34 and he will make them joyful until the e comes,
14: 5 of the times and declared to him the e of the times.
4Mc 4:24 any way to put an e to the people's observance A
11:15 Since to this e we were born and bred,

ENDANGER (1) [DANGER]

Da 1:10 you would e my head with the king."

ENDANGERED (1) [DANGER]

Ecc 10: 9 and whoever splits logs will be e by them.

ENDEAR (1)

Sir 4: 7 E yourself to the congregation;

ENDEAVOR (1) [ENDEAVORED, ENDEAVORS]

2Mc 11:19 I will e in the future to help promote your welfare.

ENDEAVORED (1) [ENDEAVOR]

2Mc 10:15 and e to keep up the war.

ENDEAVORS (2) [ENDEAVOR]

2Es 8:27 not take note of the e of those who act wickedly,
8:27 of those who act wickedly, but of the e

ENDEAVOUR (KJV) See MAKE EVERY EFFORT

ENDED‡ (34) [END]

Ge 47:18 When that year was e, they came to him
49:33 When Jacob e his charge to his sons,
Dt 34: 8 then the period of mourning for Moses was e.
Jos 19:33 and it e at the Jordan;
1Sa 10:13 When his prophetic frenzy had e, he went home.
2Ch 7: 1 When Solomon had e his prayer,
Job 31:40 The words of Job are e.
Ps 72:20 The prayers of David son of Jesse are e.
Isa 24:13 as at the gleaning when the grape harvest is e.
51: 6 and my deliverance will never be e.
60:20 and your days of mourning shall be e.
Jer 8:20 "The harvest is past, the summer is e,
Hos 4:18 their drinking is e, they indulge in sexual orgies;
Lk 1:23 his time of service was e, he went to his home.
2:43 When the festival was e and they started to return,
Ac 21: 5 When our days there were e,
Rev 15: 1 for with them the wrath of God is e.
15: 8 until the seven plagues of the seven angels were e.
20: 3 until the thousand years were e.
20: 5 not come to life until the thousand years were e.)
20: 7 When the thousand years are e,
Tob 10: 7 the fourteen days of the wedding celebration had e
12: 1 When the wedding celebration was e,
14: 1 So e Tobit's words of praise.
Jdt 10: 1 and had e all these words,
AdE 15: 1 On the third day, when she e her prayer,
Sir 50:19 until the order of worship of the Lord was e,
2Mc 10:13 he took poison and e his life.
15:24 With these words he e his prayer.
2Es 10:22 and our rejoicing has been e;
11:44 at his times; now they have e,
14: 9 with those who are like you, until the times are e.
14:45 And when the forty days were e,
4Mc 12:19 he flung himself into the braziers and so e his life.

ENDING (4) [END]

Ge 44:12 beginning with the eldest and e with the youngest;
Jos 16: 7 and touches Jericho, e at the Jordan.
Gal 3: 3 are you now e with the flesh?
3Mc 6:16 Just as Eleazar was e his prayer,

ENDLESS (5) [END]

Isa 9: 7 and there shall be e peace for the throne of David
Na 3:19 For who has ever escaped your e cruelty?
1Ti 1: 4 with myths and e genealogies
2Es 6:44 Immediately fruit came forth in e abundance and
4Mc 17:12 The prize was immortality in e life.

ENDOR (1) [=EN-DOR]

1Sa 28: 7 servants said to him, "There is a medium at E."

ENDOWED (12) [ENDOWING]

Ge 30:20 Leah said, "God has e me with a good dowry;
Ex 28: 3 whom I have e with skill,
2Ch 2:12 e with discretion and understanding,
2:13 a skilled artisan, e with understanding,
Da 1: 4 e with knowledge and insight,
4: 8 and who is e with a spirit of the holy gods—
4: 9 I know that you are e with a spirit of the holy gods
4:18 for you are e with a spirit of the holy gods."
5:11 a man in your kingdom who is e with a spirit of
Sir 17: 3 He e them with strength like his own,
44: 6 rich men e with resources, living peacefully
2Es 4:22 why have I been e with the power

ENDOWING (2) [ENDOWED]

Pr 8:21 e with wealth those who love me,
3Mc 1: 7 and by e their sacred enclosures with gifts,

ENDS (75) [END]

A. ENDS OF THE EARTH (39)

Ex 25:18 at the two e of the mercy seat.
25:19 the cherubim at its two e.
28:25 the two e of the two cords you shall attach to
28:26 and put them at the two e of the breastpiece,
37: 7 at the two e of the mercy seat he made them,
37: 8 the mercy seat he made the cherubim at its two e.
39:18 Two e of the two cords they had attached to
39:19 and put them at the two e of the breastpiece,
Dt 30: 4 Even if you are exiled to the e of the world,
33:17 driving them to the e of the earth; A
Jos 15: 7 to the waters of En-shemesh, and e at En-rogel;
16: 3 then to Gezer, and it e at the sea.
16: 8 to the Wadi Kanah, and e at the sea.
17: 9 along the north side of the wadi and e at the sea.
18:12 and it e at the wilderness of Beth-aven.
18:14 and it e at Kiriath-baal (that is, Kiriath-jearim),
18:19 boundary e at the northern bay of the Dead Sea,
19:14 and it e at the valley of Iphtah-el;
19:22 and its boundary e at the Jordan—
19:29 the boundary turns to Hosah, and it e at the sea;
1Sa 2:10 The LORD will judge the e of the earth; A
1Ki 8: 8 the e of the poles were seen from the holy place
2Ch 5: 9 the e of the poles were seen from the holy place
Job 28:24 For he looks to the e of the earth, A
36:14 They die in their youth, and their life e in shame.
Ps 2: 8 and the e of the earth your possession. A
22:27 All the e of the earth shall remember and turn to A
48:10 like your praise, reaches to the e of the earth. A
59:13 to the e of the earth that God rules over Jacob. A
65: 5 you are the hope of all the e of the earth and of A
67: 7 let all the e of the earth revere him. A
72: 8 and from the River to the e of the earth. A
98: 3 e of the earth have seen the victory of our God. A
Pr 10:28 The hope of the righteous e in gladness,
11:23 The desire of the righteous e only in good;
17:24 but the eyes of a fool to the e of the earth. A
30: 4 Who has established all the e of the earth? A
Ecc 10:13 and their talk e in wicked madness;
Isa 5:26 and whistle for a people at the e of the earth; A
24:16 From the e of the earth we hear songs of praise, A
40:28 the Creator of the e of the earth. A
41: 5 the e of the earth tremble; A
41: 9 you whom I took from the e of the earth, A
45:22 Turn to me and be saved, all the e of the earth! A
52:10 and all the e of the earth shall see the salvation A
Jer 10:13 he makes the mist rise from the e of the earth. A
16:19 nations come from the e of the earth and say: A
25:31 The clamor will resound to the e of the earth, A
51:16 he makes the mist rise from the e of the earth. A
Eze 15: 4 the fire has consumed both e of it and the middle
Da 4:11 and it was visible to the e of the whole earth.
4:22 and your sovereignty to the e of the earth. A
7:28 Here the account e.
Mic 5: 4 for now he shall be great to the e of the earth; A
Zec 9:10 and from the River to the e of the earth. A
Mt 12:42 she came from the e of the earth to listen A
Mk 13:27 from the e of the earth to the ends of heaven. A
13:27 from the ends of the earth to the e of heaven.
Lk 11:31 she came from the e of the earth to listen A
Ac 1: 8 all Judea and Samaria, and to the e of the earth." A
13:47 you may bring salvation to the e of the earth.' " A
Ro 10:18 and their words to the e of the world."
1Co 10:11 on whom the e of the ages have come.
13: 8 Love never e. But as for prophecies,
Tob 13:11 A bright light will shine to all the e of the earth; A

Jdt 2: 9 I will lead them away captive to the **e** of
Wis 6: 1 learn, O judges of the **e** of the earth. A
Sir 11:28 by how he **e**, a person becomes known.
44:21 and from the Euphrates to the **e** of the earth. A
1Mc 1: 3 He advanced to the **e** of the earth, A
3: 9 He was renowned to the **e** of the earth; A
8: 4 from the **e** of the earth, until they crushed them A
14:10 until his renown spread to the **e** of the earth. A
1Es 4:21 With his wife he **e** his days,
2Es 16:13 and when they are shot to the **e** of the world will

ENDURANCE‡ (32) [ENDURE]

Lk 8:15 and bear fruit with patient **e**.
21:19 By your **e** you will gain your souls.
Ro 5: 3 knowing that suffering produces **e**,
5: 4 and **e** produces character,
2Co 6: 4 through great **e**, in afflictions, hardships,
1Ti 6:11 pursue righteousness, godliness, faith, love, **e**,
Tit 2: 2 prudent, and sound in faith, in love, and in **e**.
Heb 10:36 For you need **e**, so that when you have done
Jas 1: 3 that the testing of your faith produces **e**;
1: 4 and let **e** have its full effect,
5:11 Indeed we call blessed those who showed **e**.
5:11 You have heard of the **e** of Job,
2Pe 1: 6 with self-control, and self-control with **e**,
1: 6 and self-control with endurance, and **e**
Rev 1: 9 the persecution and the kingdom and the patient **e**,
2: 2 your toil and your patient **e**.
2:19 your love, faith, service, and patient **e**.
3:10 Because you have kept my word of patient **e**,
13:10 Here is a call for the **e** and faith of the saints.
14:12 Here is a call for the **e** of the saints,
4Mc 1:11 marveled at their courage and **e**,
1:11 By their **e** they conquered the tyrant,
6:13 partly out of admiration for his **e**,
7: 9 to the law through your glorious **e**,
9: 8 For we, through this severe suffering and **e**,
9:30 of your tyranny being defeated by our **e** for
11:12 an opportunity to show our **e** for the law."
15:30 and more courageous than men in **e**!
17:12 the awards and tested them for their **e**.
17:17 and all his council marveled at their **e**,
17:23 when he saw the courage of their virtue and their **e**
17:23 to his soldiers as an example for their own **e**,

ENDURE (55) [ENDURANCE, ENDURED, ENDURES, ENDURING]

Ex 18:23 then you will be able to **e**,
Job 8:15 if one lays hold of it, it will not **e**.
15:29 and their wealth will not **e**,
20:21 therefore their prosperity will not **e**.
Ps 61: 6 may his years **e** to all generations!
72:17 May his name **e** forever, his fame continue as long
89:29 and his throne as long as the heavens **e**.
89:36 and his throne **e** before me like the sun.
102:24 you whose years **e** throughout all generations."
102:26 They will perish, but you **e**;
104:31 May the glory of the LORD **e** forever;
119:84 How long must your servant **e**?
Pr 12:19 Truthful lips **e** forever,
18:14 The human spirit will **e** sickness;
Isa 1:13 I cannot **e** solemn assemblies with iniquity.
Jer 10:10 and the nations cannot **e** his indignation.
Eze 22:14 Can your courage **e**, or can your hands remain
Da 11: 6 and his offspring shall not **e**.
Joel 2:11 terrible indeed—who can **e** it?
Na 1: 6 Who can **e** the heat of his anger?
Hab 2: 5 wealth is treacherous; the arrogant do not **e**.
Mal 3: 2 But who can **e** the day of his coming,
Mk 4:17 But they have no root, and **e** only for a while;
Lk 17:25 But first he must **e** much suffering and be rejected
Jn 3:36 the Son will not see life, but must **e** God's wrath.
1Co 4:12 When reviled, we bless; when persecuted, we **e**;
9:12 but we **e** anything rather than put an obstacle in
10:13 the way out so that you may be able to **e** it.
2Co 1: 6 which you experience when you patiently **e**
Gal 4:27 you who **e** no birth pangs;
Col 1:11 be prepared to **e** everything with patience,
2Ti 2:10 Therefore I **e** everything for the sake of the elect,
2:12 if we **e**, we will also reign with him;
4: 5 As for you, always be sober, **e** suffering,
Heb 12: 7 **E** trials for the sake of discipline.
12:20 (For they could not **e** the order that was given,
1Pe 2:19 you **e** pain while suffering unjustly.
2:20 If you **e** when you are beaten for doing wrong,
2:20 But if you **e** when you do right and suffer for it,
Tob 13:11 the name of the chosen city will **e** forever.
Sir 37:23 and the fruits of his good sense will **e**.
45:15 and for his descendants as long as the heavens **e**,
45:26 that their glory may **e** through all their generations.
51:24 and why do you **e** such great thirst?
Bar 4:25 **e** with patience the wrath that has come upon you
2Mc 2:27 of many we will gladly **e** the uncomfortable toil,
9:12 And when he could not **e** his own stench,
2Es 1: 9 How long shall I **e** them,
3:30 because I have seen how you **e** those who sin,
7:18 can **e** difficult circumstances while hoping
10:54 because no work of human construction could **e** in
4Mc 5:23 so that we **e** any suffering willingly;
6: 7 to the ground because his body could not **e**
7:22 and knows that it is blessed to **e** any suffering for
16:19 you ought to **e** any suffering for the sake of God.

ENDURED (28) [ENDURE]

1Ki 2:26 you shared in all the hardships my father **e**."
Job 34:31 has anyone said to God, 'I have **e** punishment;
Ps 107:17 and because of their iniquities **e** affliction;
132: 1 remember in David's favor all the hardships he **e**;
Mk 5:26 She had **e** much under many physicians,
Lk 1:25 on me and took away the disgrace I have **e**
Ro 9:22 has **e** with much patience the objects of wrath
2Ti 3:11 and Lystra. What persecutions I **e**!
Heb 6:15 And thus Abraham, having patiently **e**,
10:32 you **e** a hard struggle with sufferings,
12: 2 for the sake of the joy that was set before him **e**
12: 3 Consider him who **e** such hostility against himself
13:13 to him outside the camp and bear the abuse he **e**.
Wis 11:25 would anything have **e** if you had not willed it?
17:17 they were seized, and **e** the inescapable fate;
Sir 51: 3 from the many troubles I **e**,
1Mc 10:15 and of the troubles that they had **e**.
2Mc 9:28 having **e** the more intense suffering,
4Mc 6: 9 and scorned the punishment and **e** the tortures.
9:22 by fire into immortality, he nobly **e** the rackings.
9:28 But he steadfastly **e** this agony and said,
10: 1 When he too had **e** a glorious death,
13:27 those who were left **e** for the sake of religion,
15:31 in the universal flood, stoutly **e** the waves,
15:32 **e** nobly and withstood the wintry storms
16: 1 **e** seeing her children tortured to death,
16: 8 In vain, my sons, I **e** many birth pangs for you,
16:21 into the fiery furnace and **e** it for the sake of God.

ENDURES (90) [ENDURE]

A. STEADFAST LOVE ENDURES FOREVER (43)
B. HIS MERCY ENDURES FOREVER (17)

Ge 8:22 As long as the earth **e**, seedtime and harvest,
1Ch 16:34 for his steadfast love **e** forever. A
16:41 for his steadfast love **e** forever. A
2Ch 5:13 "For he is good, for his steadfast love **e** forever," A
7: 3 "For he is good, for his steadfast love **e** forever." A
7: 6 for his steadfast love **e** forever— A
20:21 for his steadfast love **e** forever." A
Ezr 3:11 for his steadfast love **e** forever toward Israel." A
Ps 45: 6 Your throne, O God, **e** forever and ever.
72: 5 May he live while the sun **e**,
100: 5 his steadfast love **e** forever, A
102:12 your name **e** to all generations.
106: 1 for his steadfast love **e** forever. A
107: 1 for his steadfast love **e** forever. A
111: 3 and his righteousness **e** forever.
111:10 have a good understanding. His praise **e** forever.
112: 3 and their righteousness **e** forever.
112: 9 their righteousness **e** forever;
117: 2 and the faithfulness of the LORD **e** forever.
118: 1 his steadfast love **e** forever! A
118: 2 Let Israel say, "His steadfast love **e** forever." A
118: 3 "His steadfast love **e** forever." A
118: 4 "His steadfast love **e** forever." A
118:29 for he is good, for his steadfast love **e** forever. A
119:90 Your faithfulness **e** to all generations;
119:160 every one of your righteous ordinances **e** forever.
135:13 Your name, O LORD, **e** forever, your renown,
136: 1 for he is good, for his steadfast love **e** forever. A
136: 2 for his steadfast love **e** forever. A
136: 3 for his steadfast love **e** forever; A
136: 4 for his steadfast love **e** forever; A
136: 5 for his steadfast love **e** forever; A
136: 6 for his steadfast love **e** forever; A
136: 7 for his steadfast love **e** forever; A
136: 8 for his steadfast love **e** forever; A
136: 9 for his steadfast love **e** forever; A
136:10 for his steadfast love **e** forever; A
136:11 for his steadfast love **e** forever; A
136:12 for his steadfast love **e** forever; A
136:13 for his steadfast love **e** forever; A
136:14 for his steadfast love **e** forever; A
136:15 for his steadfast love **e** forever; A
136:16 for his steadfast love **e** forever; A
136:17 for his steadfast love **e** forever; A
136:18 for his steadfast love **e** forever; A
136:19 for his steadfast love **e** forever; A
136:20 king of Bashan, for his steadfast love **e** forever; A
136:21 for his steadfast love **e** forever, A
136:22 for his steadfast love **e** forever. A
136:23 for his steadfast love **e** forever; A
136:24 for his steadfast love **e** forever; A
136:25 for his steadfast love **e** forever. A
136:26 for his steadfast love **e** forever. A
138: 8 your steadfast love, O LORD, **e** forever. A
145:13 and your dominion **e** throughout all generations.
Ecc 3:14 I know that whatever God does **e** forever;
Jer 33:11 for his steadfast love **e** forever!" A
La 5:19 your throne **e** to all generations.
Da 4:34 and his kingdom **e** from generation to generation.
Mt 10:22 But the one who **e** to the end will be saved.
13:21 but **e** only for a while,
24:13 But the one who **e** to the end will be saved.
Mk 13:13 But the one who **e** to the end will be saved.
Jn 6:27 but for the food that **e** for eternal life,
1Co 13: 7 believes all things, hopes all things, **e** all things.
2Co 9: 9 his righteousness **e** forever."
Jas 1:12 Blessed is anyone who **e** temptation.
1Pe 1:25 but the word of the Lord **e** forever."
Sir 40:17 a garden of blessings, and almsgiving **e** forever.
51:12 *for his mercy **e** forever;* B
51:12 *for his mercy **e** forever;* B
51:12 *for his mercy **e** forever;* B
51:12 *for his mercy **e** forever;* B
51:12 *for his mercy **e** forever;* B
Ps 51:12 *for his mercy **e** forever;* B
51:12 *for his mercy **e** forever;* B
51:12 *for his mercy **e** forever;* B
51:12 *for his mercy **e** forever;* B
51:12 *for his mercy **e** forever;* B
51:12 *for his mercy **e** forever;* B
51:12 *for his mercy **e** forever;* B
51:12 *for his mercy **e** forever;* B
51:12 *for his mercy **e** forever;* B
Bar 4: 1 the commandments of God, the law that **e** forever.
Aza 1:67 for he is good, for his mercy **e** forever. B
1:68 and give thanks to him, for his mercy **e** forever." B
1Mc 4:24 "For he is good, for his mercy **e** forever." B
1Es 4:38 But truth **e** and is strong forever,
2Es 8: 8 the womb **e** your creature that has been created
4Mc 16:17 aged man **e** such agonies for the sake of religion,

ENDURING‡ (20) [ENDURE]

Nu 24:21 "**E** is your dwelling place,
1Ki 11:38 and will build you an **e** house, as I built for David,
Ps 19: 9 the fear of the LORD is pure, **e** forever;
89:37 an **e** witness in the skies."
119:86 All your commandments are **e**;
Pr 8:18 and honor are with me, **e** wealth and prosperity.
Ecc 2:16 there is no **e** remembrance of the wise or of fools,
Jer 5:15 It is an **e** nation, it is an ancient nation,
Da 6:26 For he is the living God, **e** forever.
Mic 6: 2 and you **e** foundations of the earth;
Ac 20:19 **e** the trials that came to me through the plots of
2Th 1: 4 and the afflictions that you are **e**.
1Pe 1:23 through the living and **e** word of God.
Rev 2: 3 I also know that you are **e** patiently and bearing up
2Mc 6:30 from death, I am **e** terrible sufferings in my body
7:36 after **e** a brief suffering have drunk
4Mc 9: 6 of their religion lived piously while **e** torture,
17: 4 maintaining firm an **e** hope in God.
17: 7 the seven children **e** their varied tortures to death
17:10 looking to God and **e** torture even to death."

ENEMESSAROS See Index to Footnotes

ENEMIES‡ (339) [ENEMY]

A. YOUR ENEMIES (89)
B. THEIR ENEMIES (80)
C. MY ENEMIES (46)
D. OUR ENEMIES (40)
E. HIS ENEMIES (32)

Ge 14:20 who has delivered your **e** into your hand!" A
22:17 your offspring shall possess the gate of their **e**, B
49: 8 your hand shall be on the neck of your **e**; A
Ex 1:10 join our **e** and fight against us and escape from D
23:22 be an enemy to your **e** and a foe to your foes. A
23:27 I will make all your **e** turn their backs to you. A
32:25 to the derision of their **e**), B
Lev 26: 7 You shall give chase to your **e**, A
26: 8 your **e** shall fall before you by the sword. A
26:16 for your **e** shall eat it. A
26:17 and you shall be struck down by your **e**; A
26:32 so that your **e** who come to settle in it shall A
26:34 while you are in the land of your **e**; A
26:36 into their hearts in the lands of their **e**; B
26:37 you shall have no power to stand against your **e**. A
26:38 and the land of your **e** shall devour you. A
26:39 in the land of your **e** because of their iniquities; A
26:41 and brought them into the land of their **e**; B
26:44 for all that, when they are in the land of their **e**, B
Nu 10: 9 the LORD your God and be saved from your **e**. A
10:35 "Arise, O LORD, let your **e** be scattered, A
14:42 not let yourselves be struck down before your **e**. A
23:11 I brought you to curse my **e**, C
24:10 "I summoned you to curse my **e**, C
24:18 Seir a possession of its **e**,
32:21 until he has driven out his **e** from before him E
35:23 and death ensues, though they were not **e**,
Dt 1:42 otherwise you will be defeated by your **e**.' " A
6:19 thrusting out all your **e** from before you, A
12:10 when he gives you rest from your **e** all around A
20: 1 When you go out to war against your **e**, A
20: 3 near to do battle against your **e**. A
20: 4 to fight for you against your **e**, A
20:14 You may enjoy the spoil of your **e**, A
21:10 When you go out to war against your **e**, A
23: 9 against your **e** you shall guard A
23:14 to save you and to hand over your **e** to you, A
25:19 from all your **e** on every hand, in the land that A
28: 7 The LORD will cause your **e** who rise A
28:25 to be defeated before your **e**; A
28:31 Your sheep shall be given to your **e**, A
28:48 therefore you shall serve your **e** whom A
28:68 for sale to your **e** as male and female slaves, A
30: 7 your God will put all these curses on your **e** A
32:31 like our Rock; our **e** are fools. D
33:29 Your **e** shall come fawning to you, A
Jos 7: 8 now that Israel has turned their backs to their **e**! B
7:12 the Israelites are unable to stand before their **e**; B
7:12 they turn their backs to their **e**, B
7:13 to stand before your **e** until you take away A
10:13 until the nation took vengeance on their **e**. B
10:19 pursue your **e**, and attack them from the rear. A
10:25 for thus the LORD will do to all the **e**
21:44 not one of all their **e** had withstood them, B
21:44 the LORD had given all their **e** into their hands. B
22: 8 divide the spoil of your **e** with your kindred." A
23: 1 to Israel from all their **e** all around, B

Jdg 2:14 he sold them into the power of their **e** all around, B
2:14 so that they could no longer withstand their **e**. B
2:18 and he delivered them from the hand of their **e** B
3:28 for the LORD has given your **e** the Moabites A
5:31 "So perish all your **e**, O LORD! A
8:34 had rescued them from the hand of all their **e** B
11:36 LORD has given you vengeance against your **e**, A
1Sa 2:1 My mouth derides my **e**, because I rejoice C
4:3 and save us from the power of our **e**." D
10:1 from the hand of their **e** all around. B
12:10 but now rescue us out of the hand of our **e**, D
12:11 and rescued you out of the hand of your **e** A
14:24 and I have been avenged on my **e**." C
14:30 of the spoil taken from their **e**; B
14:47 he fought against all his **e** on every side— E
18:25 that he may be avenged on the king's **e**.' "
20:15 if the LORD were to cut off every one of the **e**
20:16 saying, "May the LORD seek out the **e** of David."
25:26 now let your **e** and those who seek to do evil A
25:29 of your **e** he shall sling out as from the hollow A
29:8 and fight against the **e** of my lord the king?"
30:26 "Here is a present for you from the spoil of the **e**
2Sa 3:18 the hand of the Philistines, and from all their **e**." B
5:20 LORD has burst forth against my **e** before me, C
7:1 and the LORD had given him rest from all his **e** E
7:9 and have cut off all your **e** from before you; A
7:11 and I will give you rest from all your **e**. A
18:19 from the power of his **e**." E
18:32 Cushite answered, "May the **e** of my lord the king,
19:9 "The king delivered us from the hand of our **e**, D
22:1 from the hand of all his **e**, E
22:4 and I am saved from my **e**. C
22:38 I pursued my **e** and destroyed them, C
22:41 You made my **e** turn their backs to me, C
22:49 who brought me out from my **e**; C
1Ki 3:11 or for the life of your **e**, A
5:3 of the warfare with which his **e** surrounded him, E
8:48 of their **e**, who took them captive, B
2Ki 17:39 will deliver you out of the hand of all your **e**." A
21:14 and give them into the hand of their **e**; B
21:14 shall become a prey and a spoil to all their **e**, B
1Ch 14:11 "God has burst out against my **e** by my hand, C
17:8 and have cut off all your **e** before you; A
17:10 and I will subdue all your **e**. A
21:12 while the sword of your **e** overtakes you; A
22:9 will give him peace from all his **e** on every side; E
2Ch 6:28 if their **e** besiege them in any of the settlements B
6:34 "If your people go out to battle against their **e**, B
20:27 LORD had enabled them to rejoice over their **e**. B
20:29 that the LORD had fought against the **e** of Israel.
32:22 of Assyria and from the hand of all his **e**; E
Ne 4:11 And our **e** said, "They will not know D
4:15 our **e** heard that their plot was known to us, D
5:9 to prevent the taunts of the nations our **e**? D
6:1 to the rest of our **e** that I had built the wall D
6:16 And when all our **e** heard of it, D
9:27 you gave them into the hands of their **e**, B
9:27 from the hands of their **e**. B
9:28 and you abandoned them to the hands of their **e**, B
Est 8:13 be ready on that day to take revenge on their **e**. B
9:1 the **e** of the Jews hoped to gain power over them,
9:5 the Jews struck down all their **e** with the sword, B
9:16 and gained relief from their **e**, B
9:22 on which the Jews gained relief from their **e**, B
Ps 3:7 For you strike all my **e** on the cheek; C
5:8 O LORD, in your righteousness because of my **e**; C
6:10 my **e** shall be ashamed and struck with terror; C
7:6 lift yourself up against the fury of my **e**; C
9:3 When my **e** turned back, they stumbled C
9:6 The **e** have vanished in everlasting ruins;
17:9 my deadly **e** who surround me.
18:T *delivered him from the hand of all his e,* E
18:3 so I shall be saved from my **e**. C
18:37 I pursued my **e** and overtook them; C
18:40 You made my **e** turn their backs to me, C
18:48 who delivered me from my **e**; C
21:8 Your hand will find out all your **e**; A
23:5 a table before me in the presence of my **e**; C
25:2 do not let my **e** exult over me. C
27:6 my head is lifted up above my **e** all around me, C
27:11 and lead me on a level path because of my **e**. C
31:15 deliver me from the hand of my **e** and C
35:19 Do not let my treacherous **e** rejoice over me,
37:20 **e** of the LORD are like the glory of the pastures;
41:2 You do not give them up to the will of their **e**. B
41:5 My **e** wonder in malice when I will die, C
44:10 and our **e** have gotten spoil. D
45:5 Your arrows are sharp in the heart of the king's **e**;
54:5 He will repay my **e** for their evil. C
54:7 and my eye has looked in triumph on my **e**. C
55:12 It is not **e** who taunt me—
56:2 my **e** trample on me all day long, C
56:9 Then my **e** will retreat in the day when I call. C
59:1 Deliver me from my **e**, O my God; C
59:10 my God will let me look in triumph on my **e**. C
66:3 of your great power, your **e** cringe before you. A
68:1 Let God rise up, let his **e** be scattered; E
68:21 But God will shatter the heads of his **e**, E
69:4 my **e** who accuse me falsely. C
69:14 delivered from my **e** and from the deep waters. C
69:18 redeem me, set me free because of my **e**. C
71:10 For my **e** speak concerning me, C
72:9 and his **e** lick the dust. E
78:53 but the sea overwhelmed their **e**. B
80:6 our **e** laugh among themselves. D
81:14 Then I would quickly subdue their **e**, B
83:2 Even now your **e** are in tumult; A

Ps 89:10 you scattered your **e** with your mighty arm. A
89:42 you have made all his **e** rejoice. E
89:51 with which your **e** taunt, O LORD, A
92:9 your **e**, O LORD, for your enemies shall perish; A
92:9 your enemies, O LORD, for your **e** shall perish; A
92:11 My eyes have seen the downfall of my **e**; C
102:8 All day long my **e** taunt me; C
106:42 Their **e** oppressed them, and they were brought B
110:1 until I make your **e** your footstool." A
119:98 Your commandment makes me wiser than my **e**, C
124:2 on our side, when our **e** attacked us, D
127:5 not be put to shame when he speaks with his **e** E
132:18 His **e** I will clothe with disgrace, but on him, E
138:7 you preserve me against the wrath of my **e**; C
139:22 with perfect hatred; I count them my **e**. C
143:9 Save me, O LORD, from my **e**; C
143:12 In your steadfast love cut off my **e**, C
Pr 16:7 he causes even their **e** to be at peace with them. B
24:17 Do not rejoice when your **e** fall, A
25:21 If your **e** are hungry, give them bread to eat; A
Isa 1:24 Ah, I will pour out my wrath on my **e**, C
9:11 against them, and stirred up their **e**, B
59:18 wrath to his adversaries, requital to his **e**; E
62:8 for your **e**, and foreigners shall not drink A
66:6 voice of the LORD, dealing retribution to his **e**! E
66:14 and his indignation is against his **e**. E
Jer 12:7 the beloved of my heart into the hands of her **e**.
15:9 them I will give to the sword before their **e**, B
15:11 surely I have imposed **e** on you in a time of trouble
15:14 I will make you serve your **e** in a land that you A
17:4 and I will make you serve your **e** in a land A
19:7 will make them fall by the sword before their **e**, B
19:9 and in the distress with which their **e** B
20:4 by the sword of their **e** while you look on. B
20:5 of the kings of Judah into the hand of their **e**, B
21:7 of Babylon, into the hands of their **e**, B
34:20 over to their **e** and to those who seek their lives. B
34:21 over to their **e** and to those who seek their lives. B
44:30 into the hands of his **e**, those who seek his life, E
46:22 for her **e** march in force,
49:37 I will terrify Elam before their **e**, B
50:7 and their **e** have said, "We are not guilty, B
La 1:2 with her, they have become her **e**.
1:5 Her foes have become the masters, her **e** prosper,
1:10 **E** have stretched out their hands
1:21 All my **e** heard of my trouble; C
2:16 All your **e** open their mouths against you; A
2:22 You invited my **e** from all around as if for a day C
3:46 All our **e** have opened their mouths against us; D
3:52 Those who were my **e** without cause C
Eze 16:27 and gave you up to the will of your **e**, A
Da 4:19 and its interpretation for your **e**! A
Am 9:4 though they go into captivity in front of their **e**, B
Mic 4:10 from the hands of your **e**. A
5:9 and all your **e** shall be cut off. A
7:6 your **e** are members of your own household. A
Na 1:2 on his adversaries and rages against his **e**. E
1:8 and will pursue his **e** into darkness. E
Zep 3:15 he has turned away your **e**. A
Mt 5:44 Love your **e** and pray for those who persecute A
22:44 until I put your **e** under your feet" '? A
Mk 12:36 until I put your **e** under your feet." ' A
Lk 1:71 from our **e** and from the hand of all who hate us. D
1:74 being rescued from the hands of our **e**, D
6:27 "But I say to you that listen, Love your **e**, A
6:35 But love your **e**, do good, and lend, A
19:27 But as for these **e** of mine who did not want me to
19:43 when your **e** will set up ramparts around you A
20:43 until I make your **e** your footstool." ' A
23:12 before this they had been **e**.
Ac 2:35 until I make your **e** your footstool." ' A
Ro 5:10 For if while we were **e**,
11:28 regards the gospel they are **e** of God for your sake;
12:20 No, "if your **e** are hungry, feed them; A
1Co 15:25 For he must reign until he has put all his **e** E
Eph 6:12 For our struggle is not against **e** of blood and flesh,
Php 3:18 For many live as **e** of the cross of Christ;
2Th 3:15 Do not regard them as **e**,
Heb 1:13 at my right hand until I make your **e** a footstool A
10:13 and since then has been waiting "until his **e** E
Rev 11:12 to heaven in a cloud while their **e** watched them. B
Tob 12:10 and do wrong are their own worst **e**.
Jdt 5:18 and their towns were occupied by their **e**. B
7:19 because all their **e** had surrounded them, B
8:11 promising to surrender the town to our **e** D
8:15 or even to destroy us in the presence of our **e**. D
8:19 so they suffered a great catastrophe before our **e**. D
8:33 to surrender the town to our **e**, D
8:35 to take vengeance on our **e**." D
13:5 to destroy the **e** who have risen up against us."
13:11 in Israel and his strength against our **e**, D
13:14 has destroyed our **e** by my hand this very night!" D
13:17 who have this day humiliated the **e**
13:18 to cut off the head of the leader of our **e**. D
AdE 8:11 act as they wished against their opponents and **e**
8:13 be ready on that day to fight against their **e**." B
9:2 On that same day the **e** of the Jews perished;
9:16 and got relief from their **e**. B
9:22 for on these days the Jews got relief from their **e**. B
13:6 be utterly destroyed by the swords of their **e**, B
14:6 and you have handed us over to our **e** D
Wis 5:17 and will arm all creation to repel his **e**; E
10:12 She protected him from his **e**, E
10:19 but she drowned their **e**, and cast them up from B
11:3 They withstood their **e** and fought off their foes. B
11:5 the very things by which their **e** were punished, B
11:8 at that time how you punished their **e**. B

Wis 12:20 the **e** of your servants and those deserving
12:22 you scourge our **e** ten thousand times more, D
12:24 as gods those animals that even their **e** despised; B
15:14 are all the **e** who oppressed your people.
16:4 how their **e** were being tormented. B
16:8 you convinced our **e** that it is you who deliver D
16:22 that the crops of their **e** were being destroyed by B
18:1 Their **e** heard their voices but did B
18:4 For their **e** deserved to be deprived of light B
18:7 and the destruction of their **e** were expected B
18:8 by which you punished our **e** you called us D
18:10 But the discordant cry of their **e** echoed back, B
Sir 6:4 and makes them the laughingstock of their **e**. B
6:9 And there are friends who change into **e**,
6:13 Keep away from your **e**, and be on guard A
12:9 One's **e** are friendly when one prospers,
18:31 it will make you the laughingstock of your **e**. A
25:14 And any vengeance, but not the vengeance of **e**!
30:3 He who teaches his son will make his **e** envious, E
30:6 He has left behind him an avenger against his **e**, E
42:11 or she may make you a laughingstock to your **e**, A
45:2 and made him great, to the terror of his **e**. E
46:1 to take vengeance on the **e** that rose against them,
46:5 when **e** pressed him on every side,
46:16 when his **e** pressed him on every side, E
47:7 For he wiped out his **e** on every side, E
51:8 for you and save them from the hand of their **e**. B
Bar 3:10 why is it that you are in the land of your **e**, A
4:6 over to your **e** because you angered God. A
4:18 will deliver you from the hand of your **e**. A
5:6 from you on foot, led away by their **e**; B
Aza 1:9 You have handed us over to our **e**, D
1Mc 4:18 But stand now against our **e** and fight them, D
4:36 and his brothers said, "See, our **e** are crushed; D
5:16 in distress and were being attacked by **e**.
8:28 And to their **e** there shall not be given grain, B
9:8 "Let us get up and go against our **e**. D
9:29 like him to go against our **e** and Bacchides, D
9:46 you may be delivered from the hands of our **e**." D
10:26 and have not sided with our **e**, D
12:15 and so we were delivered from our **e**, D
12:15 from our enemies, and our **e** were humbled. D
14:26 they have fought and repulsed Israel's **e**
14:29 the **e** of their nation, in order that their sanctuary
14:31 When their **e** decided to invade their country B
15:33 at one time had been unjustly taken by our **e**. D
2Mc 4:16 and wished to imitate completely became their **e** B
5:6 that he was setting up trophies of victory over **e**
10:21 by setting their **e** free to fight against them. B
10:26 gracious to them and to be an enemy to their **e** B
12:28 with power shatters the might of his **e**, E
1Es 5:66 the **e** of the tribe of Judah and Benjamin heard it,
3Mc 2:13 subjected to our **e**, and overtaken by D
2:33 considering them to be **e** of the Jewish nation,
3:24 behind our backs as traitors and barbarous **e**,
3:25 to suffer the sure and shameful death that befits **e**.
4:4 of their **e**, perceiving the common object of pity B
6:6 and turning the flame against all their **e**. B
6:15 were in the land of their **e** did I neglect them,' B
7:21 also possessed greater prestige among their **e**, B
2Es 1:11 and Sidon; I killed all their **e**. B
1:16 in my name at the destruction of your **e**, A
3:27 So you handed over your city to your **e**. A
3:30 destroyed your people, and protected your **e**, A
6:24 that time friends shall make war on friends like **e**,
4Mc 2:14 the property of **e** from marauders and helps raise
17:20 our **e** did not rule over our nation, D
17:24 and he ravaged and conquered all his **e**. E

ENEMIES' (1) [ENEMY]

Eze 39:27 the peoples and gathered them from their **e** lands,

ENEMY[‡] (170) [ENEMIES, ENEMIES', ENEMY'S, ENMITIES, ENMITY]

A. THE ENEMY (96)
B. MY ENEMY (10)
C. YOUR ENEMY (10)

Ge 14:11 the **e** took all the goods of Sodom and A
Ex 15:6 your right hand, O LORD, shattered the **e**. A
15:9 The **e** said, 'I will pursue, I will overtake, A
23:22 be an **e** to your enemies and a foe to your foes.
Lev 26:25 and you shall be delivered into **e** hands.
Dt 28:53 to which the **e** siege reduces you, A
28:55 the **e** siege will reduce you in all your towns. A
28:57 which the **e** siege will reduce you in your towns. A
32:27 the **e**, for their adversaries might misunderstand A
32:42 the slain and the captives, from the long-haired **e**.
33:27 he drove out the **e** before you, and said, A
Jdg 8:24 (For the **e** had golden earrings, A
16:23 "Our god has given Samson our **e** into our hand."
16:24 they said, "Our god has given our **e** into our hand,
1Sa 18:29 So Saul was David's **e** from that time forward.
19:17 and let my **e** go, so that he has escaped?" B
24:4 'I will give your **e** into your hand, C
24:19 For who has ever found an **e**,
24:19 and sent the **e** safely away? A
26:8 "God has given your **e** into your hand today; C
28:16 LORD has turned from you and become your **e**? C
2Sa 4:8 "Here is the head of Ishbaal, son of Saul, your **e**, C
22:18 He delivered me from my strong **e**,
1Ki 8:33 are defeated before an **e** but turn again to you,
8:37 if their **e** besieges them in any of their cities;
8:44 "If your people go out to battle against their **e**,
8:46 you are angry with them and give them to an **e**,

1Ki 8:46 are carried away captive to the land of the e, A
21:20 "Have you found me, O my e?" B
2Ch 6:24 are defeated before an e but turn again to you,
6:36 you are angry with them and give them to an e,
25: 8 or God will fling you down before the e; A
26:13 to help the king against the e. A
Ezr 8:22 cavalry to protect us against the e on our way, A
8:31 from the hand of the e and from ambushes along A
Est 3:10 Haman son of Hammedatha the Agagite, the e A
7: 4 no e can compensate for this damage to the king."
7: 6 Esther said, "A foe and e, this wicked Haman!"
8: 1 the house of Haman, the e of the Jews; A
9:10 Haman son of Hammedatha, the e of the Jews; A
9:24 the Agagite, the e of all the Jews, had plotted A
Job 13:24 and count me as your e? C
27: 7 "May my e be like the wicked, B
33:10 he counts me as his e;
Ps 7: 5 then let the e pursue and overtake me, A
8: 2 to silence the e and the avenger. A
13: 2 How long shall my e be exalted over me? B
13: 4 and my e will say, "I have prevailed"; B
18:17 He delivered me from my strong e,
31: 8 and have not delivered me into the hand of the e; A
41:11 because my e has not triumphed over me. B
42: 9 about mournfully because the e oppresses me?" A
43: 2 because of the oppression of the e? A
44:16 at the sight of the e and the avenger. A
55: 3 by the noise of the e, A
61: 3 a strong tower against the e. A
64: 1 preserve my life from the dread e.
74: 3 the e has destroyed everything in the sanctuary. A
74:10 Is the e to revile your name forever? A
74:18 Remember this, O LORD, how the e scoffs, A
89:22 The e shall not outwit him, A
106:10 and delivered them from the hand of the e. A
143: 3 For the e has pursued me, A
Pr 26:24 An e dissembles in speaking
26:25 when an e speaks graciously, do not believe it,
27: 6 but profuse are the kisses of an e.
Isa 63:10 therefore he became their e;
Jer 6:25 for the e has a sword, terror is on every side." A
18:17 I will scatter them before the e. A
30:14 for I have dealt you the blow of an e,
31:16 they shall come back from the land of the e; A
44:30 his e who sought his life."
La 1: 9 look at my affliction, for the e has triumphed!" A
1:16 my children are desolate, for the e has prevailed. A
2: 3 from them in the face of the e; A
2: 4 He has bent his bow like an e,
2: 5 The Lord has become like an e;
2: 7 he has delivered into the hand of the e the walls A
2:17 he has made the e rejoice over you, A
2:22 whom I bore and reared my e has destroyed. B
4:12 that foe or e could enter the gates of Jerusalem.
Eze 36: 2 Because the e said of you, "Aha!" A
Da 11:11 which shall, however, be defeated by his e.
Hos 8: 3 has spurned the good; the e shall pursue him. A
Mic 2: 8 But you rise up against my people as an e;
7: 8 Do not rejoice over me, O my e; B
7:10 Then my e will see, and shame will cover her B
Na 3:11 you will seek a refuge from the e. A
Hab 1:15 The e brings all of them up with a hook; A
Mt 5:43 'You shall love your neighbor and hate your e.' C
13:25 an e came and sowed weeds among the wheat,
13:28 He answered, 'An e has done this.'
13:39 and the e who sowed them is the devil; A
Lk 10:19 and over all the power of the e; A
Ac 13:10 "You son of the devil, you e of all righteousness,
1Co 15:26 The last e to be destroyed is death.
Gal 4:16 now become your e by telling you the truth? C
Jas 4: 4 to be a friend of the world becomes an e of God.
Jdt 15: 4 urge all to rush out upon the e to destroy them. A
15: 5 with one accord they fell upon the e, A
15: 5 in the camp of the e. A
16:11 my weak people cried out, and the e trembled; A
16:11 and the e were turned back. A
AdE 7: 6 Esther said, "Our e is this evil man Haman!"
9:10 the Bougean, the e of the Jews— A
Sir 6: 1 and do not become an e instead of a friend;
12: 8 nor is an e hidden in adversity.
12:10 Never trust your e, for like corrosion in copper, C
12:16 An e speaks sweetly with his lips,
12:16 an e may have tears in his eyes,
20:23 and so makes an e for nothing.
23: 3 and my e may rejoice over me. B
27:18 For as a person destroys his e,
29: 6 and he has needlessly made him an e;
29:13 it will fight for you against the e. A
36: 9 destroy the adversary and wipe out the e. A
37: 2 for death itself when a dear friend turns into an e?
46:18 he subdued the leaders of the e and all the rulers A
Bar 4:21 from the power and hand of the e. A
4:25 Your e has overtaken you, C
4:26 like a flock carried off by the e. A
LtJ 6:56 Besides, they can offer no resistance to king or e.
1Mc 2: 7 and to live there when it was given over to the e, A
2:35 Then the e quickly attacked them. A
5:13 the e have captured their wives and children A
5:27 the e are getting ready to attack A
6:38 to harass the e while being themselves protected A
7:29 but the e were preparing to kidnap Judas. A
7:46 and they outflanked the e and drove them back A
8:23 and may sword and e be far from them.
8:26 To the e that makes war they shall not give A
9: 6 When they saw the huge number of the e forces, A
9:48 and the e did not cross the Jordan to attack them. A
11:72 Then he turned back to the battle against the e A
1Mc 12:26 that the e were being drawn up in formation A
12:28 When the e heard that Jonathan A
13:51 great e had been crushed and removed from Israel.
14:33 formerly the arms of the e had been stored, A
14:34 where the e formerly lived. A
16: 7 for the cavalry of the e were very numerous. A
2Mc 3:38 "If you have any e or plotter
8: 6 and put to flight not a few of the e. A
8:16 and exhorted them not to be frightened by the e A
8:24 they killed more than nine thousand of the e, A
8:27 arms of the e and stripped them of their spoils, A
8:31 They collected the arms of the e, A
10:26 be gracious to them and to be an e to their enemies
10:27 and when they came near the e they halted. A
10:29 there appeared to the e from heaven A
10:30 showered arrows and thunderbolts on the e, A
11:11 They hurled themselves like lions against the e, A
12:22 and fear came over the e at the manifestation A
13:21 gave secret information to the e; A
14:17 of the sudden consternation created by the e. A
14:22 to prevent sudden treachery on the part of the e; A
15:20 and the e was already close at hand A
15:26 his troops met the e in battle with invocations A
1Es 4: 4 and if he sends them out against the e, they go, A
8:61 he delivered us from every e on the way,
3Mc 1: 5 it came about that the e was routed in the action, A
2:30 In order that he might not appear to be an e of all,
6:10 rescue us from the hand of the e, and destroy us, A
6:19 the e and filled them with confusion and terror, A
2Es 15:33 of the Assyrians an e in ambush shall attack them
4Mc 2:14 The fruit trees of the e are not cut down, A
3:13 they went searching throughout the e camp A
8:10 Even I, your e, have compassion for your youth C
9:15 e of heavenly justice, savage of mind,
11:23 of tortures and e of those who are truly devout.
18: 4 of the law in the homeland they ravaged the e. A

ENEMY'S‡ (5) [ENEMY]

Ex 23: 4 you come upon your e ox or donkey going astray,
Pr 26:26 the e wickedness will be exposed in the assembly.
1Mc 10:81 and the e horses grew tired.
4Mc 3:11 in the e territory tormented and inflamed him,
3:12 and taking a pitcher climbed over the e ramparts.

ENENEUS (1)

1Es 5: 8 Resaiah, E, Mordecai, Beelsarus, Aspharasus,

ENERGY (1)

Col 1:29 the e that he powerfully inspires within me.

ENFORCE (1) [ENFORCING]

Da 6: 7 that the king should establish an ordinance and e

ENFORCING (1) [ENFORCE]

1Mc 2:15 The king's officers who were e the apostasy came

ENGAGE (10) [ENGAGED, ENGAGEMENT, ENGAGING]

Dt 2: 5 not to e in battle with them,
2: 9 "Do not harass Moab or e them in battle,
2:19 do not harass them or e them in battle,
20: 2 Before you e in battle, the priest shall come
1Ki 20:27 they went out to e them;
Eze 21:16 Attack to the right! E to the left!
Jas 4: 2 so you e in disputes and conflicts.
AdE 9:16 but did not e in plunder.
1Mc 5:19 not e in battle with the Gentiles until we return."
2Es 15:30 and with great power they shall come and e them

ENGAGED (27) [ENGAGE]

Ex 22:16 a man seduces a virgin who is not e to be married,
Dt 20: 7 Has anyone become e to a woman but not
22:23 a virgin already e to be married,
22:25 if the man meets the e woman in the open country,
22:27 the e woman may have cried for help,
22:28 If a man meets a virgin who is not e,
28:30 You shall become e to a woman,
Jdg 12: 2 "My people and I were e in conflict with
2Sa 2:28 they no longer pursued Israel or e
3:14 to whom I became e at the price
2Ch 13: 3 Abijah e in battle, having an army
24:13 So those who were e in the work labored,
Mt 1:18 When his mother Mary had been e to Joseph,
Lk 1:27 to a virgin e to a man whose name was Joseph,
2: 5 to whom he was e and who was expecting a child.
2Co 4: 1 it is by God's mercy that we are e in this ministry,
Wis 19: 3 For while they were still e in mourning,
1Mc 1:18 He e King Ptolemy of Egypt in battle,
4:14 and e in battle. The Gentiles were crushed,
5: 7 He e in many battles with them,
10:78 and the armies e in battle.
10:82 Then Simon brought forward his force and e
2Mc 14:16 they set out from there immediately and e them
3Mc 1:24 Meanwhile the crowd, as before, was e in prayer,
2Es 9:39 I dismissed the thoughts with which I had been e,
10: 5 I broke off the reflections with which I was still e,
4Mc 17:11 Truly the contest in which they were e was divine,

ENGAGEMENT (1) [ENGAGE]

Tob 6:13 concerning the girl and arrange her e to you.

ENGAGING (1) [ENGAGE]

Dt 2:24 Begin to take possession by e him in battle.

ENGINE (2) [ENGINES]

1Mc 13:43 He made a siege e, brought it up to the city,
13:44 The men in the siege e leaped out into the city,

ENGINES (9) [ENGINE]

1Mc 5:30 carrying ladders and e of war to capture
6:20 and he built siege towers and other e of war.
6:31 and for many days they fought and built e of war;
6:51 e of war to throw fire and stones,
6:52 The Jews also made e of war to match theirs,
11:20 and he built many e of war to use against it.
15:25 against it and making e of war;
2Mc 12:15 or e of war overthrew Jericho in the days
12:27 and great stores of war e and missiles were there.

ENGRAFTED (KJV) See IMPLANTED

ENGRAVE (4) [ENGRAVED, ENGRAVER, ENGRAVES, ENGRAVING, ENGRAVINGS]

Ex 28: 9 and e on them the names of the sons of Israel,
28:11 so you shall e the two stones with the names of
28:36 You shall make a rosette of pure gold, and e on it,
Zec 3: 9 I will e its inscription, says the LORD of hosts,

ENGRAVED (9) [ENGRAVE]

Ex 28:21 they shall be like signets, each e with its name,
32:16 of God, and the writing was the writing of God, e
39: 6 enclosed in settings of gold filigree and e like
39:14 they were like signets, each e with its name,
Job 19:24 that with an iron pen and with lead they were e on
Jer 17: 1 a diamond point it is e on the tablet of their hearts,
Wis 18:24 of the ancestors were e on the four rows of stones,
Sir 45:11 with precious stones e like seals,
45:11 of a jeweler, to commemorate in e letters each of

ENGRAVER (1) [ENGRAVE]

Ex 38:23 e, designer, and embroiderer in blue, purple,

ENGRAVES (1) [ENGRAVE]

Ex 28:11 As a gem-cutter e signets,

ENGRAVING (4) [ENGRAVE]

Ex 28:36 like the e of a signet, "Holy to the LORD."
39:30 like the e of a signet, "Holy to the LORD."
2Ch 2: 7 crimson, and blue fabrics, trained also in e,
2:14 and to do all sorts of e and execute any design

ENGRAVINGS (3) [ENGRAVE]

Ex 39: 6 of gold filigree and engraved like the e of a signet,
1Ki 6:29 of the house all around about with carved e
Eze 28:13 and worked in gold were your settings and your e.

ENHANCE (2) [ENHANCES]

2Mc 5:16 that other kings had made to e the glory and honor
3Mc 2:31 to e their reputation by their future association

ENHANCES (1) [ENHANCE]

2Mc 15:39 and delicious and e one's enjoyment,

ENJOIN[ED] (KJV) See also COMMAND, DIRECTED, ORDAINED, PRESCRIBED

ENJOINED (2) [ENJOINING]

Jos 23:16 the covenant of the LORD your God, which he e
Est 9:31 the Jew Mordecai and Queen Esther e on the Jews,

ENJOINING (1) [ENJOINED]

Est 9:21 e them that they should keep the fourteenth day of

ENJOY† (40) [ENJOYED, ENJOYING, ENJOYMENT, ENJOYS]

Ge 45:18 and you may e the fat of the land.'
Lev 26:34 Then the land shall e its sabbath years as long
26:34 then the land shall rest, and e its sabbath years.
26:43 e its sabbath years by lying desolate without them,
Dt 20: 6 in the battle and another be first to e its fruit.
20:14 You may e the spoil of your enemies,
28:30 You shall plant a vineyard, but not e its fruit.
Jdg 19: 6 "Why not spend the night and e yourself?"
19: 9 Spend the night here and e yourself.
Ne 9:36 the land that you gave to our ancestors to e its fruit
Job 14: 6 and desist, that they may e, like laborers,
Ps 34:12 and covets many days to e good?
37: 3 so you will live in the land, and e security.
Pr 14: 9 but the upright e God's favor.
28:16 but one who hates unjust gain will e a long life.
Ecc 2: 1 I will make a test of pleasure; e yourself."
3:12 to be happy and e themselves as long as they live;
3:22 that all should e their work, for that is their lot;
5:19 and possessions and whom he enables to e them,
6: 2 yet God does not enable them to e these things,
6: 3 if he does not e life's good things, or has no burial,
6: 6 yet e no good—do not all go to one place?
8:15 and drink, and e themselves,
9: 9 E life with the wife whom you love,

Isa 61: 6 you shall e the wealth of the nations,
65:22 my chosen shall long e the work of their hands.
Jer 31: 5 the planters shall plant, and shall e the fruit.
Heb 11:25 the people of God than to e the fleeting pleasures
Tob 12: 9 Those who give alms will e a full life,
Jdt 12:13 and to e drinking wine with us,
Wis 2: 6 therefore, let us e the good things that exist,
Sir 14: 5 He will not e his own riches.
41: 1 and still is vigorous enough to e food!
2Mc 11:31 for the Jews to e their own food and laws,
1Es 9:54 to eat and drink and e themselves,
2Es 7:95 they understand the rest that they now e,
7:96 the spacious liberty that they are to receive and e
4Mc 5: 9 not to e delicious things that are not shameful,
8: 5 also exhort you to yield to me and e my friendship.
8: 8 E your youth by adopting the Greek way of life

ENJOYED (7) [ENJOY]
Dt 20: 6 a vineyard but not yet e its fruit?
Ecc 2:21 and skill must leave all to be e by another who did
Ac 24: 2 because of you we have long e peace,
Ro 15:24 once I have e your company for a little while.
AdE 16:11 e so fully the goodwill that we have
1Es 1:58 "Until the land has e its sabbaths,
4Mc 16:18 a share in the world and have e life,

ENJOYING (3) [ENJOY]
Jdg 19:22 While they were e themselves, the men of the city,
Sir 13: 8 and humiliated when you are e yourself.
4Mc 3:20 a time when our ancestors were e profound peace

ENJOYMENT (13) [ENJOY]
Job 20:18 from the profit of their trading they will get no e.
Ecc 2:24 and find e in their toil.
2:25 apart from him who can eat or who can have e?
5:18 it is fitting to eat and drink and find e in all the toil
5:19 and to accept their lot and find e in their toil—
8:15 So I commend e, for there is nothing better
9: 7 Go, eat your bread with e,
1Ti 6:17 with everything for our e.
Wis 2: 9 everywhere let us leave signs of e,
Sir 14:14 Do not deprive yourself of a day's e;
2Mc 15:39 and delicious and enhances one's e,
3Mc 7:16 to God even to death and had received the full e
4Mc 2: 1 for the e of beauty are rendered powerless?

ENJOYS (2) [ENJOY]
Ecc 6: 2 to enjoy these things, but a stranger e them.
Sir 37:28 for everyone, and no one e everything.

ENLARGE (6) [LARGE]
Ex 34:24 before you, and e your borders;
1Ch 4:10 "Oh that you would bless me and e my border,
Ps 119:32 for you e my understanding.
Isa 54: 2 E the site of your tent, and let the curtains
Jer 4:30 that you e your eyes with paint?
Am 1:13 in Gilead in order to e their territory.

ENLARGED‡ (3) [LARGE]
Isa 5:14 Therefore Sheol has e its appetite
26:15 you have e all the borders of the land.
2Co 10:15 our sphere of action among you may be greatly e,

ENLARGEMENT (1) [LARGE]
Dt 33:20 Blessed be the e of Gad! Gad lives like a lion;

ENLARGES (3) [LARGE]
Dt 12:20 When the LORD your God e your territory,
19: 8 If the LORD your God e your territory,
Job 12:23 he e nations, then leads them away.

ENLIGHTEN (1) [LIGHT]
Sir 45:17 and to e Israel with his law.

ENLIGHTENED (5) [LIGHT]
Ro 10: 2 that they have a zeal for God, but it is not e.
Eph 1:18 with the eyes of your heart e,
Heb 6: 4 to repentance those who have once been e,
10:32 after you had been e, you endured a hard struggle
2Es 13:53 And you alone have been e about this,

ENLIGHTENING (1) [LIGHT]
Ps 19: 8 commandment of the LORD is clear, e the eyes;

ENLIGHTENMENT (3) [LIGHT]
Isa 40:14 Whom did he consult for his e,
Da 5:11 In the days of your father he was found to have e,
5:14 and that e, understanding,

ENLIGHTENS (1) [LIGHT]
Jn 1: 9 The true light, which e everyone,

ENLISTED (2) [ENLISTING]
1Mc 4:35 he withdrew to Antioch and e mercenaries in order
2Mc 8: 1 and e those who had continued in the Jewish faith,

ENLISTING (1) [ENLISTED]
2Ti 2: 4 the soldier's aim is to please the e officer.

ENMITIES (1) [ENEMY]
Gal 5:20 e, strife, jealousy, anger, quarrels, dissensions,

ENMITY‡ (16) [ENEMY]
Ge 3:15 I will put e between you and the woman,
Nu 35:21 or in e strikes another with the hand,
35:22 if someone pushes another suddenly without e,
Dt 4:42 the two not having been at e before;
19: 4 when the two had not been at e before:
19: 6 since the two had not been at e before.
19:11 at e with another lies in wait and attacks and takes
Jos 20: 5 there having been no e between them before.
Ps 55: 3 and in anger they cherish e against me.
Eze 35: 5 Because you cherished an ancient e,
Jas 4: 4 that friendship with the world is e with God?
Sir 28: 6 Remember the end of your life, and set e aside;
1Mc 11:12 and their e became manifest.
2Mc 14:39 wishing to exhibit the e that he had for the Jews,
3Mc 4: 1 for the inveterate e that had long ago been
4Mc 2:14 through the law, can prevail even over e.

ENOCH‡ (16)
Ge 4:17 and she conceived and bore E;
4:17 he built a city, and named it E after his son Enoch.
4:17 he built a city, and named it Enoch after his son E.
4:18 To E was born Irad; and Irad was the father of
5:18 hundred sixty-two years he became the father of E.
5:19 after the birth of E eight hundred years,
5:21 When E had lived sixty-five years,
5:22 E walked with God after the birth
5:23 the days of E were three hundred sixty-five years.
5:24 E walked with God; then he was no more,
1Ch 1: 3 E, Methuselah, Lamech;
Lk 3:37 son of E, son of Jared, son of Mahalaleel,
Heb 11: 5 By faith E was taken so that he did
Jude 1:14 It was also about these that E,
Sir 44:16 E pleased the Lord and was taken up,
49:14 Few have ever been created on earth like E,

ENOS (1) [=ENOSH]
Lk 3:38 son of E, son of Seth, son of Adam, son of God.

ENOSH (8) [=ENOS]
Ge 4:26 To Seth also a son was born, and he named him E.
5: 6 he became the father of E.
5: 7 after the birth of E eight hundred seven years,
5: 9 When E had lived ninety years,
5:10 E lived after the birth of Kenan
5:11 the days of E were nine hundred five years;
1Ch 1: 1 Adam, Seth, E;
Sir 49:16 Shem and Seth and E were honored,

ENOUGH (95)
Ge 19:20 Look, that city is near e to flee to,
33: 9 But Esau said, "I have e, my brother;
34:21 for the land is large e for them;
45:28 Israel said, "E! My son Joseph is still alive.
Ex 9:28 E of God's thunder and hail!
16: 4 and each day the people shall go out and gather e
36: 5 "The people are bringing much more than e
36: 7 for what they had already brought was more than e
Nu 11:22 Are there e flocks and herds to slaughter for them?
11:22 Are there e fish in the sea to catch for them?"
Dt 1: 6 saying, "You have stayed long e at this mountain.
2: 3 "You have been skirting this hill country long e.
3:26 The LORD said to me, "E from you!
15: 8 willingly lending e to meet the need,
Jos 17:16 "The hill country is not e for us;
22:17 Have we not had e of the sin at Peor from which
Jdg 6:38 he wrung e dew from the fleece to fill a bowl
2Sa 8: 4 but left e for a hundred chariots.
24:16 "It is e; now stay your hand."
1Ki 12:28 "You have gone up to Jerusalem long e.
18:32 large e to contain two measures of seed.
19: 4 He asked that he might die: "It is e;
1Ch 21:15 he said to the destroying angel, "E!
2Ch 31:10 we have had e to eat and have plenty to spare;
Job 27:14 and their offspring have not e to eat.
Ps 17:14 may their children have more than e;
123: 3 for we have had more than e of contempt.
Pr 13:25 The righteous have e to satisfy their appetite,
23: 4 to get rich; be wise e to desist.
25:16 If you have found honey, eat only e for you,
27:27 there will be e goats' milk for your food,
30:15 things are never satisfied; four never say, "E":
30:16 and the fire that never says, "E."
Isa 1:11 I have had e of burnt offerings of rams and the fat
40:16 Lebanon would not provide fuel e,
40:16 nor are its animals e for a burnt offering.
56:11 dogs have a mighty appetite; they never have e.
Jer 9:12 Who is wise e to understand this?
37:20 be good e to listen to my plea,
42: 2 "Be good e to listen to our plea,
La 5: 6 a pact with Egypt and Assyria, to get e bread.
Eze 8:17 Is it not bad e that the house of Judah commits
16:20 As if your whorings were not e!
34:18 Is it not e for you to feed on the good pasture,
45: 9 Thus says the Lord GOD: E, O princes of Israel!
47: 5 it was deep e to swim in,
Jnh 4: 9 And he said, "Yes, angry e to die."
Na 2:12 The lion has torn e for his whelps
Hab 2: 5 like Death they never have e.
Hag 1: 6 you eat, but you never have e;
Mt 6:34 Today's trouble is e for today.
Mt 10:25 it is e for the disciple to be like the teacher,
15:33 "Where are we to get e bread in the desert to feed
25: 9 there will not be e for you and for us;
Mk 14:41 "Are you still sleeping and taking your rest? E!
Lk 14:28 to see whether he has e to complete it?
15:17 of my father's hired hands have bread e and
16: 3 I am not strong e to dig, and I am ashamed to beg.
22:38 He replied, "It is e."
Jn 6: 7 not buy e bread for each of them to get a little."
Ac 10:33 and you have been kind e to come.
1Co 6: 5 be that there is no one among you wise e to decide
14:17 For you may give thanks well e,
2Co 2: 6 This punishment by the majority is e for such
9: 8 so that by always having e of everything,
11: 4 you submit to it readily e.
Php 4:18 I have been paid in full and have more than e;
1Th 3: 9 How can we thank God e for you in return for all
Phm 1: 8 though I am bold e in Christ to command you
1Pe 4: 3 You have already spent e time in doing what
Tob 5: 9 and whether he is trustworthy e to go with you."
5:20 the life that is given to us by the Lord is e for us."
10:12 and may I live long e to see children of you and
Jdt 4: 7 wide e for only two at a time to pass.
7:21 and on no day did they have e water to drink,
12: 2 I will have e with the things I brought with me."
Wis 4: 5 and their fruit will be useless, not ripe e to eat,
14:22 not e for them to err about the knowledge of God,
18:25 for merely to test the wrath was e.
Sir 5: 1 Do not rely on your wealth, or say, "I have e."
11:24 "I have e, and what harm can come to me now?"
12:16 an opportunity he will never have e of your blood.
20: 1 there is the person who is wise e to keep silent.
37:19 Some people may be clever e to teach many,
39:11 and if he goes to rest, it is e for him.
41: 1 and still is vigorous e to enjoy food!
43:27 We could say more but could never say e;
43:30 for you cannot praise him e.
1Mc 2:33 They said to them, "E of this!
2Mc 7:42 Let this be e, then, about the eating of sacrifices
1Es 8:88 not angry e with us to destroy us without leaving
3Mc 3: 8 were not strong e to help them,
2Es 12:43 Are not the disasters that have befallen us e?
4Mc 10:14 not have a fire hot e to make me play the coward.
15:11 of none of them were the various tortures strong e

ENQUIRE, ENQUIRED, ENQUIREST, ENQUIRY (KJV) See ASKED, ASKING, CALL, CONSULT, DISCUSSING, FIND OUT, INQUIRE, INQUIRY, INQUIRING, LOOK, QUESTIONED, SOUGHT

ENRAGED (19) [RAGE]
Ge 39:19 the way your servant treated me," he became e.
2Sa 17: 8 and his men are warriors, and that they are e, like
Ne 4: 1 he was angry and greatly e,
Est 1:12 At this the king was e,
Isa 8:21 be e and will curse their king and their gods.
34: 2 For the LORD is e against all the nations,
Jer 37:15 The officials were e at Jeremiah,
Eze 16:43 but have e me with all these things;
Da 8: 7 It was e against it and struck the ram,
11:30 be e and take action against the holy covenant.
Mt 22: 7 The king was e. He sent his troops,
Ac 5:33 they were e and wanted to kill them.
7:54 they became e and ground their teeth at Stephen.
19:28 When they heard this, they were e and shouted,
26:11 and since I was so furiously e at them,
Bel 1:21 Then the king was e, and he arrested the priests
1Mc 6:28 The king was e when he heard this.
3Mc 3: 1 not only was he e against those Jews who lived
4Mc 10: 5 E by the man's boldness, they disjointed his hands

ENRICH (3) [RICH]
1Sa 17:25 The king will greatly e the man who kills him,
Ps 65: 9 You visit the earth and water it, you greatly e it;
Pr 22:16 Oppressing the poor in order to e oneself,

ENRICHED (5) [RICH]
Pr 11:25 A generous person will be e,
28:25 but whoever trusts in the LORD will be e.
Eze 27:33 with your abundant wealth and merchandise you e
1Co 1: 5 for in every way you have been e in him, in speech
2Co 9:11 be e in every way for your great generosity,

ENRICHES (1) [RICH]
Sir 35: 8 The offering of the righteous e the altar,

ENROLL (10) [ENROLLED, ENROLLMENT]
Nu 1: 3 You and Aaron shall e them,
1:49 Only the tribe of Levi you shall not e,
3:15 E the Levites by ancestral houses and by clans.
3:15 You shall e every male from a month old
3:40 E all the firstborn males of the Israelites,
4:23 up to fifty years old you shall e them,
4:29 you shall e them by their clans
4:30 up to fifty years old you shall e them,
Sir 7:16 Do not e in the ranks of sinners;
2Mc 4: 9 to e the people of Jerusalem as citizens of Antioch.

ENROLLED (79) [ENROLL]
Nu 1:19 So he e them in the wilderness of Sinai.
1:21 those e of the tribe of Reuben

Nu 1:23 those e of the tribe of Simeon
1:25 those e of the tribe of Gad
1:27 those e of the tribe of Judah
1:29 those e of the tribe of Issachar
1:31 those e of the tribe of Zebulun
1:33 those e of the tribe of Ephraim
1:35 those e of the tribe of Manasseh
1:37 those e of the tribe of Benjamin
1:39 those e of the tribe of Dan
1:41 those e of the tribe of Asher
1:43 those e of the tribe of Naphtali
1:44 These are those who were e,
1:44 and Aaron e with the help of the leaders of Israel,
2: 4 as e of seventy-four thousand six hundred.
2: 6 as e of fifty-four thousand four hundred.
2: 8 as e of fifty-seven thousand four hundred.
2:11 a company as e of forty-six thousand five hundred.
2:13 as e of fifty-nine thousand three hundred.
2:15 as e of forty-five thousand six hundred fifty.
2:19 a company as e of forty thousand five hundred.
2:21 as e of thirty-two thousand two hundred.
2:23 as e of thirty-five thousand four hundred.
2:26 as e of sixty-two thousand seven hundred.
2:28 as e of forty-one thousand five hundred.
2:30 as e of fifty-three thousand four hundred.
2:33 the Levites were not e among the other Israelites.
3:16 So Moses e them according to the word of
3:39 and Aaron e at the commandment of the LORD,
3:42 So Moses e all the firstborn among the Israelites,
4:34 the leaders of the congregation e the Kohathites,
4:37 and Aaron e according to the commandment of
4:41 and Aaron e according to the commandment of
4:45 and Aaron e according to the commandment of
4:46 All those who were e of the Levites,
4:46 and Aaron and the leaders of Israel e,
4:49 thus they were e by him,
7: 2 who were over those who were e, made offerings.
26: 7 e was forty-three thousand seven hundred thirty.
26:18 of those e was forty thousand five hundred.
26:22 of those e was seventy-six thousand five hundred.
26:25 sixty-four thousand three hundred e.
26:27 of those e was sixty thousand five hundred.
26:34 of those e was fifty-two thousand seven hundred.
26:37 of those e was thirty-two thousand five hundred.
26:41 of those e was forty-five thousand six hundred.
26:43 sixty-four thousand four hundred e.
26:47 of those e was fifty-three thousand four hundred.
26:50 of those e was forty-five thousand four hundred.
26:51 This was the number of the Israelites e:
26:62 The number of those e was twenty-three thousand,
26:62 for they were not e among the Israelites
26:63 These were those e by Moses and Eleazar
26:63 who e the Israelites in the plains of Moab by
26:64 not one of those e by Moses and Aaron the priest,
26:64 who had e the Israelites in the wilderness of Sinai.
1Ch 5: 1 not e in the genealogy according to the birthright;
5:17 All of these were e by genealogies in the days
7: 5 in all eighty-seven thousand mighty warriors, e
7:40 Their number e by genealogies, for service in war,
9: 1 So all Israel was e by genealogies;
9:22 They were e by genealogies in their villages.
23:11 so they were e as a single family.
23:24 of families as they were e according to the number
2Ch 31:16 except those e by genealogy,
31:18 The priests were e with all their little children,
31:19 and to everyone among the Levites who was e.
Ne 7: 5 the nobles and the officials and the people to be e
7:64 These sought their registration among those e in
Ps 69:28 let them not be e among the righteous.
Eze 13: 9 nor be e in the register of the house of Israel,
Heb 12:23 the assembly of the firstborn who are e in heaven,
1Mc 8:20 so that we may be e as your allies and friends."
10:36 "Let Jews be e in the king's forces to the number
10:65 Thus the king honored him and e him
13:40 any of you are qualified to be e in our bodyguard,
13:40 let them be e, and let there be peace between us."
1Es 8:30 Zechariah, and with him a hundred fifty men e.

ENROLLMENT (24) [ENROLL]

Nu 2: 9 The total e of the camp of Judah, by companies,
2:16 The total e of the camp of Reuben, by companies,
2:24 The total e of the camp of Ephraim, by companies,
2:31 The total e of the camp of Dan
2:32 the e of the Israelites by their ancestral houses;
2:32 the total e in the camps by their companies
3:22 Their e, counting all the males from a month old
3:34 Their e, counting all the males from a month old
3:39 The total e of the Levites whom Moses
3:43 The total e, all the firstborn males from
4:36 e by clans was two thousand seven hundred fifty.
4:37 This was the e of the clans of the Kohathites,
4:38 The e of the Gershonites, by their clans
4:40 their e by their clans and their ancestral houses
4:41 This was the e of the clans of the Gershonites,
4:42 The e of the clans of the Merarites,
4:44 e by their clans was three thousand two hundred.
4:45 This is the e of the clans of the Merarites,
4:48 their e was eight thousand five hundred eighty.
26:54 be given its inheritance according to its e.
26:57 This is the e of the Levites by their clans:
1Ch 7: 7 mighty warriors; and their e
7: 9 and their e by genealogies,
2Ch 31:17 The e of the priests was according

ENSAMPLE (KJV) See EXAMPLE

ENSEMBLE (4)

Da 3: 5 pipe, lyre, trigon, harp, drum, and entire musical e,
3: 7 pipe, lyre, trigon, harp, drum, and entire musical e,
3:10 pipe, lyre, trigon, harp, drum, and entire musical e,
3:15 and entire musical e to fall down and worship

ENSIGN (2) [ENSIGNS]

Isa 62:10 clear it of stones, lift up an e over the peoples.
Eze 27: 7 from Egypt was your sail, serving as your e;

ENSIGNS (1) [ENSIGN]

Nu 2: 2 under e by their ancestral houses;

ENSLAVE (3) [SLAVE]

Ac 7: 6 who would e them and mistreat them
1Co 9:27 but I punish my body and e it,
Gal 2: 4 so that they might e us—

ENSLAVED (13) [SLAVE]

Jer 34:10 male or female, so that they would not be e again;
Eze 34:27 save them from the hands of those who e them.
Ro 6: 6 and we might no longer be e to sin.
6:22 that you have been freed from sin and e to God,
Gal 4: 3 we were e to the elemental spirits of the world.
4: 8 you were e to beings that by nature are not gods.
4: 9 How can you want to be e to them again?
Wis 1: 4 or dwell in a body e to sin.
1Mc 8:10 the land, tore down their strongholds, and e them
8:11 as ever opposed them, they destroyed and e;
3Mc 2: 6 Pharaoh who had e your holy people Israel.
2Es 10:22 our young men have been e
4Mc 3: 2 but reason can provide a way for us not to be e

ENSLAVES (1) [SLAVE]

Na 3: 4 who e nations through her debaucheries,

ENSLAVING (2) [SLAVE]

Dt 24: 7 If someone is caught kidnaping another Israelite, e
1Mc 8:18 of the Greeks was e Israel completely.

ENSNARE (4) [SNARE]

Job 34:30 or those who e the people.
Ps 35: 8 And let the net that they hid e them;
119:61 cords of the wicked e me, I do not forget your law.
Pr 5:22 The iniquities of the wicked e them,

ENSNARED (3) [SNARE]

Dt 7:25 because you could be e by it;
Pr 12:13 The evil are e by the transgression of their lips,
Sir 25:21 Do not be e by a woman's beauty,

ENSUE (KJV) See PURSUE

ENSUES (6)

Nu 35:16 and death e, is a murderer;
35:17 and death e, is a murderer;
35:18 and death e, is a murderer;
35:20 lying in wait, and death e,
35:21 and death e, then the one who struck
35:23 unintentionally drops it on another and death e,

ENTANGLE (1) [ENTANGLED, TANGLED]

Pr 22:25 you may learn their ways and e yourself in a snare.

ENTANGLED (7) [ENTANGLE]

2Sa 22: 6 the cords of Sheol e me,
Ps 18: 5 the cords of Sheol e me;
Na 1:10 Like thorns they are e, like drunkards
2Ti 2: 4 in the army gets e in everyday affairs;
2Pe 2:20 they are again e in them and overpowered,
3Mc 6:10 our lives have become e in impieties in our exile,
2Es 7:*68* For all who have been born are e in iniquities,

ENTER (201) [ENTERED, ENTERING, ENTERS, ENTRANCE, ENTRANCES, ENTRIES, ENTRY]

Ge 12:11 When he was about to e Egypt,
Ex 12:23 the destroyer to e your houses to strike you down.
40:35 to e the tent of meeting because the cloud settled
Lev 10: 9 when you e the tent of meeting,
14:46 All who e the house while it is shut up shall
16:23 Then Aaron shall e the tent of meeting,
23:10 When you e the land that I am giving you
25: 2 When you e the land that I am giving you,
Nu 5:22 that brings the curse e your bowels
5:24 and the water that brings the curse shall e her
5:27 the curse shall e into her and cause bitter pain,
20:24 not e the land that I have given to the Israelites,
34: 2 When you e the land of Canaan (this is the land
Dt 1:37 saying, "You also shall not e there.
1:38 Joshua son of Nun, your assistant, shall e there;
1:39 not yet know right from wrong, they shall e there;
4: 1 so that you may live to e and occupy the land that
4: 5 in the land that you are about to e and occupy.
4:21 the Jordan and that I should not e the good land
7: 1 to e and occupy, and he clears away many nations
11:10 about to e to occupy is not like the land of Egypt,
12:29 before you the nations whom you are about to e
23:20 in the land that you are about to e and possess.
Dt 25: 1 Suppose two persons have a dispute and e
27: 3 when you have crossed over, to e the land that
29:12 to e into the covenant of the LORD your God,
30:18 that you are crossing the Jordan to e and possess.
32:52 the land from a distance, you shall not e it—
Jos 10:19 Do not let them e their towns,
Jdg 11:18 They did not e the territory of Moab,
11:25 Did he ever e into conflict with Israel,
18: 9 but e in and possess the land.
18:17 to spy out the land proceeded to e and take the idol
1Sa 5: 5 and all who e the house of Dagon do not step on
7:13 the Philistines were subdued and did not again e
9:13 As soon as you e the town, you will find him,
12: 7 so that I may e into judgment with you before
1Ki 1:35 Let him e and sit on my throne;
11: 2 "You shall not e into marriage with them,
14:12 When your feet e the city, the child shall die.
2Ki 7: 4 If we say, 'Let us e the city,'
1Ch 24:19 in their service to e the house of the LORD
2Ch 7: 2 The priests could not e the house of the LORD,
23: 6 not let anyone e the house of the LORD except
23: 6 they may e, for they are holy,
23:19 that no one should e who was in any way unclean.
Ne 9:23 into the land that you had told their ancestors to e
10:29 e into a curse and an oath to walk in God's law,
13: 1 or Moabite should ever e the assembly of God,
Est 4: 2 for no one might e the king's gate clothed
Ps 5: 7 of your steadfast love, will e your house,
37:15 their sword shall e their own heart,
45:15 With joy and gladness they are led along as they e
95:11 in my anger I swore, "They shall not e my rest."
100: 4 E his gates with thanksgiving,
118:19 that I may e through them and give thanks to
118:20 the righteous shall e through it.
132: 3 "I will not e my house or get into my bed;
143: 2 Do not e into judgment with your servant,
Pr 4:14 Do not e the path of the wicked,
Isa 2:10 E into the rock, and hide in the dust from
2:19 E the caves of the rocks and the holes of
2:21 to e the caverns of the rocks and the clefts in
13: 2 the hand for them to e the gates of the nobles.
24:10 every house is shut up so that no one can e.
26: 2 that the righteous nation that keeps faith may e in.
26:20 Come, my people, e your chambers,
52: 1 and the unclean shall e you no more.
57: 2 and they e into peace; those who walk uprightly
59:14 in the public square, and uprightness cannot e.
Jer 4:29 every town takes to flight; they e thickets;
7: 2 you that e these gates to worship the LORD.
14:18 And if I e the city, look—those sick with famine!
16: 5 Do not e the house of mourning, or go to lament,
17:19 the People's Gate, by which the kings of Judah e
17:20 the inhabitants of Jerusalem, who e by these gates.
17:25 then there shall e by the gates
19: 5 nor did it e my mind.
21:13 or who can e our places of refuge?"
22: 2 and your people who e these gates.
22: 4 of this house shall e kings who sit on the throne
32:35 nor did it e my mind
42:15 If you are determined to e Egypt and go
La 1:10 those whom you forbade to e your congregation.
4:12 that foe or enemy could e the gates of Jerusalem.
Eze 7:22 the violent shall e it, they shall profane it.
13: 9 nor shall they e the land of Israel;
17:20 to Babylon and e into judgment with him there for
20:35 there I will e into judgment with you face to face.
20:36 so I will e into judgment with you,
20:38 but they shall not e the land of Israel.
21:32 your blood shall e the earth;
37: 5 I will cause breath to e you, and you shall live.
38:22 and bloodshed I will e into judgment with him;
42: 9 that one entered from the east in order to e them
42:14 When the priests e the holy place,
44: 2 it shall not be opened, and no one shall e by it;
44: 3 he shall e by way of the vestibule of the gate,
44: 9 among the people of Israel, shall e my sanctuary.
44:16 It is they who shall e my sanctuary,
44:17 When they e the gates of the inner court,
46: 2 The prince shall e by the vestibule of the gate
Da 11: 7 the army and e the fortress of the king of the north,
Hos 4:15 Do not e into Gilgal, or go up to Beth-aven,
Joel 2: 9 they e through the windows like a thief.
3: 2 and I will e into judgment with them there,
Am 5: 5 do not e into Gilgal or cross over to Beer-sheba;
Zec 5: 4 and it shall e the house of the thief,
Mt 5:20 you will never e the kingdom of heaven.
7:13 "E through the narrow gate;
7:21 'Lord, Lord,' will e the kingdom of heaven,
10: 5 and e no town of the Samaritans,
10:11 Whatever town or village you e,
10:12 As you e the house, greet it.
12:29 Or how can one e a strong man's house
12:45 and they e and live there;
18: 3 you will never e the kingdom of heaven.
18: 8 to e life maimed or lame than to have two hands
18: 9 to e life with one eye than to have two eyes and to
19:17 you wish to e into life, keep the commandments."
19:23 it will be hard for a rich person to e the kingdom
19:24 for someone who is rich to e the kingdom of God."
25:21 e into the joy of your master.'
25:23 e into the joy of your master.'
Mk 3:27 But no one can e a strong man's house
5:12 into the swine; let us e them."
6:10 He said to them, "Wherever you e a house,
9:25 come out of him, and never e him again!"
9:43 to e life maimed than to have two hands and to go
9:45 for you to e life lame than to have two feet and to

Mk 9:47 for you to **e** the kingdom of God with one eye than
10:15 of God as a little child will never **e** it."
10:23 be for those who have wealth to **e** the kingdom
10:24 "Children, how hard it is to **e** the kingdom of God!
10:25 for someone who is rich to **e** the kingdom of God."
11: 2 and immediately as you **e** it,
13:15 not go down or **e** the house to take anything away;
Lk 1: 9 to **e** the sanctuary of the Lord and offer incense.
8:16 so that those who **e** may see the light.
8:32 and the demons begged Jesus to let them **e** these.
8:51 he did not allow anyone to **e** with him,
9: 4 Whatever house you **e**, stay there,
10: 5 Whatever house you **e**, first say,
10: 8 Whenever you **e** a town
10:10 But whenever you **e** a town and they do
11:26 and they **e** and live there;
11:33 but on the lampstand so that those who **e** may see
11:52 of knowledge; you did not **e** yourselves,
13:24 "Strive to **e** through the narrow door;
13:24 many, I tell you, will try to **e** and will not be able.
16:16 and everyone tries to **e** it by force.
18:17 of God as a little child will never **e** it."
18:24 "How hard it is for those who have wealth to **e**
18:25 for someone who is rich to **e** the kingdom of God."
19:30 and as you **e** it you will find tied there a colt
21:21 and those out in the country must not **e** it;
24:26 the Messiah should suffer these things and then **e**
Jn 3: 4 Can one **e** a second time into the mother's womb
3: 5 no one can **e** the kingdom of God
10: 1 anyone who does not **e** the sheepfold by the gate
18:28 They themselves did not **e** the headquarters,
Ac 9: 6 But get up and **e** the city,
14:22 "It is through many persecutions that we must **e**
1Co 14:23 and outsiders or unbelievers **e**,
Heb 3:11 in my anger I swore, 'They will not **e** my rest.' "
3:18 that they would not **e** his rest,
3:19 that they were unable to **e** because of unbelief.
4: 3 For we who have believed **e** that rest,
4: 3 'They shall not **e** my rest,' "
4: 5 "They shall not **e** my rest."
4: 6 Since therefore it remains open for some to **e** it,
4: 6 the good news failed to **e** because of disobedience,
4:10 for those who **e** God's rest also cease
4:11 Let us therefore make every effort to **e** that rest,
9:24 not **e** a sanctuary made by human hands,
10:19 since we have confidence to **e** the sanctuary by
Rev 15: 8 and no one could **e** the temple until
21:27 But nothing unclean will **e** it,
22:14 to the tree of life and may **e** the city by the gates.
Tob 6:17 When you **e** the bridal chamber,
12:15 of the seven angels who stand ready and **e** before
Jdt 4: 7 and it would be easy to stop any who tried to **e**,
AdE 4: 2 to **e** the courtyard clothed in sackcloth and ashes.
Wis 1: 4 because wisdom will not **e** a deceitful soul,
8:16 When I **e** my house, I shall find rest with her;
LtJ 6:18 of the dust raised by the feet of those who **e**.
Bel 1:21 through which they used to **e** to consume what was
1Mc 5:42 but make them all **e** the battle."
15:14 and permitted no one to leave or **e** it.
2Mc 2:24 the difficulty there is for those who wish to **e** upon
5:15 Antiochus dared to **e** the most holy temple in all
13:13 the king's army could **e** Judea and get possession
1Es 4:49 or treasurer should forcibly **e** their doors;
3Mc 1:10 and conceived a desire to **e** the sanctuary.
1:11 members of their own nation were allowed to **e**,
1:12 he did not cease to maintain that he ought to **e**,
1:15 the king said, "why should not I at least **e**,
2:28 not sacrifice shall **e** their sanctuaries,
3:17 because when we proposed to **e** their inner temple
2Es 7:*80* such spirits shall not **e** into habitations,
7:*123* [53] but we shall not **e** it

ENTERED‡ (148) [ENTER]

Ge 7:13 and Noah's wife and the three wives of his sons **e**
7:16 And those that **e**, male and female of all flesh,
12:14 When Abram **e** Egypt the Egyptians saw that
19: 3 so they turned aside to him and **e** his house;
31:33 And he went out of Leah's tent, and **e** Rachel's.
41:46 Joseph was thirty years old when he **e** the service
Ex 19: 2 **e** the wilderness of Sinai, and camped in
24:18 Moses **e** the cloud, and went up on the mountain.
33: 9 When Moses **e** the tent, the pillar
Lev 9:23 Moses and Aaron **e** the tent of meeting,
Jos 2: 1 **e** the house of a prostitute whose name was Rahab,
2: 3 to you, who **e** your house, for they have come only
8:19 They **e** the city, took it, and at once set the city
10:20 when the survivors had **e** into the fortified towns,
Jdg 9:46 they **e** the stronghold of the temple of El-berith.
19:29 When he had **e** his house, he took a knife,
1Sa 10:27 from the Ammonites and had **e** Jabesh-gilead.
16:21 And David came to Saul, and **e** his service.
29: 8 in your servant from the day I **e** your service until
2Sa 10:14 they likewise fled before Abishai, and **e** the city.
1Ki 20:30 Ben-hadad also fled, and **e** the city to hide.
2Ki 3:24 as they **e** Moab they continued the attack.
6:20 As soon as they **e** Samaria, Elisha said,
7: 8 Then they came back, **e** another tent,
8: 9 When he **e** and stood before him, he said,
9:31 As Jehu **e** the gate, she said, "Is it peace, Zimri,
10:21 They **e** the temple of Baal,
10:23 Then Jehu **e** the temple of Baal
12: 9 beside the altar on the right side as one **e** the house
19:23 I **e** its farthest retreat, its densest forest.
1Ch 19:15 Joab's brother, and **e** the city.
27:24 for this, and the number was not **e** into the account
2Ch 15:12 They **e** into a covenant to seek the LORD,
2Ch 23: 1 and **e** into a compact with the commanders of
26:16 and **e** the temple of the LORD to make offering
31:16 all who **e** the house of the LORD as the duty
Ne 2:15 Then I turned back and **e** by the Valley Gate,
Est 6: 4 Now Haman had just **e** the outer court of
Job 38:16 "Have you **e** into the springs of the sea,
38:22 "Have you **e** the storehouses of the snow,
Jer 2: 7 But when you **e** you defiled my land,
9:21 into our windows, it has **e** our palaces, to cut off
32:23 and they **e** and took possession of it.
34:10 all the officials and all the people who had **e** into
52:12 the king of Babylon, **e** Jerusalem.
Eze 2: 2 a spirit **e** into me and set me on my feet;
3:24 The spirit **e** into me, and set me on my feet;
16: 8 I pledged myself to you and **e** into a covenant
20:36 As I **e** into judgment with your ancestors in
27:19 and Javan from Uzal **e** into trade for your wares;
42: 9 the foot of these chambers ran a passage that one **e**
42:12 the entrances of the chambers to the south were **e**
43: 4 of the LORD **e** the temple by the gate facing east,
44: 2 for the LORD, the God of Israel, has **e** by it;
46: 9 not return by way of the gate by which they **e**,
Da 10: 3 no meat or wine had **e** my mouth,
Ob 1:11 foreigners **e** his gates and cast lots for Jerusalem,
1:13 You should not have **e** the gate of my people on
Mt 8: 5 When he **e** Capernaum, a centurion came to him,
8:14 When Jesus **e** Peter's house,
8:32 So they came out and **e** the swine;
9:28 When he **e** the house, the blind men came to him;
12: 4 He **e** the house of God and ate the bread of
12: 9 He left that place and **e** their synagogue;
21:10 When he **e** Jerusalem, the whole city was
21:12 Then Jesus **e** the temple
21:23 When he **e** the temple, the chief priests and
24:38 until the day Noah **e** the ark,
27:53 of the tombs and **e** the holy city and appeared
Mk 1:21 the sabbath came, he **e** the synagogue and taught.
1:29 they **e** the house of Simon and Andrew,
2:26 He **e** the house of God,
3: 1 Again he **e** the synagogue,
5:13 And the unclean spirits came out and **e** the swine;
5:39 When he had **e**, he said to them,
7:17 When he had left the crowd and **e** the house,
7:24 He **e** a house and did not want anyone
9:28 When he had **e** the house,
11:11 Then he **e** Jerusalem and went into the temple;
11:15 And he **e** the temple and began
16: 5 As they **e** the tomb, they saw a young man,
Lk 1:40 where she **e** the house of Zechariah
4:38 After leaving the synagogue he **e** Simon's house.
6: 4 He **e** the house of God and took and ate the bread
6: 6 On another sabbath he **e** the synagogue and taught,
7: 1 in the hearing of the people, he **e** Capernaum.
7:44 "Do you see this woman? I **e** your house;
8:30 He said, "Legion"; for many demons had **e** him.
8:33 the demons came out of the man and **e** the swine,
9:34 and they were terrified as they **e** the cloud.
9:52 On their way they **e** a village of the Samaritans
10:38 as they went on their way, he **e** a certain village,
17:12 As he **e** a village, ten lepers approached him.
17:27 until the day Noah **e** the ark,
19: 1 He **e** Jericho and was passing through it.
19:45 Then he **e** the temple and began
22: 3 Then Satan **e** into Judas called Iscariot,
22:10 he said to them, "when you have **e** the city,
Jn 4:38 and you have **e** into their labor."
13:27 he received the piece of bread, Satan **e** into him.
18: 1 which he and his disciples **e**.
18:33 Then Pilate **e** the headquarters again,
19: 9 He **e** his headquarters again and asked Jesus,
Ac 1:13 When they had **e** the city,
3: 8 and he **e** the temple with them,
5:21 they **e** the temple at daybreak and went on
9:17 So Ananias went and **e** the house.
11: 8 nothing profane or unclean has ever **e** my mouth.'
11:12 and we **e** the man's house.
19: 8 He **e** the synagogue and
21:26 he **e** the temple with them,
25:23 and they **e** the audience hall with
Heb 6:20 a forerunner on our behalf, has **e**,
9:12 he **e** once for all into the Holy Place,
9:24 but he **e** into heaven itself,
Rev 11:11 the breath of life from God **e** them,
Tob 6:10 When he **e** Media and already was approaching
7: 1 Now when they **e** Ecbatana, Tobias said to him,
Wis 2:24 but through the devil's envy death **e** the world,
3:13 who has not **e** into a sinful union;
8:20 or rather, being good, I **e** an undefiled body.
10:16 She **e** the soul of a servant of the Lord,
14:14 For through human vanity they **e** the world,
Sir 44:20 and **e** into a covenant with him;
Bar 3:15 And who has **e** her storehouses?
1Mc 1:21 He arrogantly **e** the sanctuary and took
4: 5 When Gorgias **e** the camp of Judas by night,
6:62 But when the king **e** Mount Zion and saw what
8:19 they **e** the senate chamber and spoke as follows:
10:83 They fled to Azotus and **e** Beth-dagon,
11: 3 But when Ptolemy **e** the towns he stationed forces
11:13 Ptolemy **e** Antioch and put on the crown of Asia.
12: 3 So they went to Rome and **e** the senate chamber
12:48 But when Jonathan **e** Ptolemais,
12:48 they killed with the sword all who had **e** with him.
13:47 and then **e** it with hymns and praise.
13:51 the Jews **e** it with praise and palm branches,
2Mc 1:15 they closed the temple as soon as he **e** it.
3:28 this man who had just **e** the aforesaid treasury with
8: 1 and his companions secretly **e** the villages
2Mc 9: 2 He had **e** the city called Persepolis and attempted
1Es 6: 8 to the country of Judea and **e** the city of Jerusalem,
3Mc 1:13 he inquired why, when he **e** every other temple,
4: 6 And young women who had just **e**
5:46 **e** at about dawn into the courtyard—
2Es 10: 1 that when my son **e** his wedding chamber,
10:48 'My son died as he **e** his wedding chamber,'
4Mc 17:13 the mother of the seven sons **e** the competition,

ENTERING (21) [ENTER]

Dt 11:29 into the land that you are **e** to occupy,
28:21 the land that you are **e** to possess.
28:63 be plucked off the land that you are **e** to possess.
30:16 in the land that you are **e** to possess.
1Sa 9:14 As they were **e** the town,
23: 7 in by **e** a town that has gates and bars."
2Sa 15:37 just as Absalom was **e** Jerusalem.
17:17 for they could not risk being seen **e** the city.
Ezr 9:11 that you are **e** to possess is a land unclean with
Jer 25:31 he is **e** into judgment with all flesh,
36: 5 "I am prevented from **e** the house of the LORD;
Eze 26:10 he enters your gates like those **e** a breached city.
Mt 2:11 On **e** the house, they saw the child
Lk 11:52 and you hindered those who were **e**."
Ac 3: 2 that he could ask for alms from those **e** the temple.
8: 3 But Saul was ravaging the church by **e** house
Heb 4: 1 while the promise of **e** his rest is still open,
1Mc 7: 2 As he was **e** the royal palace of his ancestors,
1Es 8:83 'The land that you are **e** to take possession of is
3Mc 1: 9 upon **e** the place and being impressed
3:18 their traditional arrogance, and excluded us from **e**;

ENTERS‡ (23) [ENTER]

Lev 16:17 of meeting from the time he **e** to make atonement
Dt 24: 1 Suppose a man **e** into marriage with a woman,
2Ch 23: 7 and whoever **e** the house shall be killed.
Job 22: 4 and **e** into judgment with you?
Isa 3:14 The LORD **e** into judgment with the elders
Eze 26:10 he **e** your gates like those entering a breached city.
44:21 No priest shall drink wine when he **e**
46: 8 the prince **e**, he shall come in by the vestibule of
46: 9 whoever **e** by the north gate
46: 9 and whoever **e** by the south gate shall go out by
47: 8 and when it **e** the sea, the sea of stagnant waters,
Hab 3:16 Rottenness **e** into my bones,
Mt 15:17 that whatever goes into the mouth **e** the stomach,
Mk 7:19 since it **e**, not the heart but the stomach,
14:14 and wherever he **e**, say to the owner of the house,
Lk 22:10 follow him into the house he **e**
Jn 10: 2 one who **e** by the gate is the shepherd of the sheep.
10: 9 Whoever **e** by me will be saved,
1Co 14:24 an unbeliever or outsider who **e** is reproved by all
Heb 6:19 a hope that **e** the inner shrine behind the curtain,
9:25 as the high priest **e** the Holy Place year after year
AdE 2:14 the evening she **e** and in the morning she departs
Sir 4:13 and the Lord blesses the place she **e**.

ENTERTAIN (2) [ENTERTAINED, ENTERTAINMENT]

Dt 15: 9 Be careful that you do not **e** a mean thought,
Jdg 16:25 they said, "Call Samson, and let him **e** us."

ENTERTAINED (3) [ENTERTAIN]

Ac 17: 7 and Jason has **e** them as guests.
28: 7 who received us and **e** us hospitably
Heb 13: 2 that some have **e** angels without knowing it.

ENTERTAINMENT (1) [ENTERTAIN]

Sir 32: 4 Where there is **e**, do not pour out talk;

ENTHRONED (20) [THRONE]

1Sa 4: 4 who is **e** on the cherubim.
2Sa 6: 2 of the LORD of hosts who is **e** on the cherubim.
2Ki 19:15 who are **e** above the cherubim, you are God,
1Ch 13: 6 the LORD, who is **e** on the cherubim,
Ps 9: 7 But the LORD sits **e** forever,
22: 3 Yet you are holy, **e** on the praises of Israel.
29:10 The LORD sits **e** over the flood;
29:10 the LORD sits **e** as king forever.
33:14 From where he sits **e** he watches all the inhabitants
55:19 God, who is **e** from of old, *Selah*
61: 7 May he be **e** forever before God;
80: 1 You who are **e** upon the cherubim,
99: 1 He sits **e** upon the cherubim; let the earth quake!
102:12 But you, O LORD, are **e** forever;
123: 1 O you who are **e** in the heavens!
Isa 37:16 God of Israel, who are **e** above the cherubim,
Jer 48:18 and sit on the parched ground, **e** daughter Dibon!
AdE 1: 2 when King Artaxerxes was **e** in the city of Susa,
Bar 3: 3 you are **e** forever, and we are perishing forever.
4Mc 2:22 the same time he **e** the mind among the senses as

ENTHRONES (1) [THRONE]

Sir 10:14 and **e** the lowly in their place.

ENTHUSIASM (2)

Ac 18:25 and he spoke with burning **e** and taught accurately
Eph 6: 7 Render service with **e**, as to the Lord and not

ENTICE (13) [ENTICED, ENTICES]

1Ki 22:20 And the LORD said, 'Who will **e** Ahab,
22:21 before the LORD, saying, 'I will **e** him.'

1Ki 22:22 Then the LORD said, 'You are to **e** him,
2Ch 18:19 the LORD said, 'Who will **e** King Ahab of Israel,
18:20 before the LORD, saying, 'I will **e** him.'
18:21 Then the LORD said, 'You are to **e** him,
Job 36:18 Beware that wrath does not **e** you into scoffing,
Pr 1:10 My child, if sinners **e** you, do not consent.
16:29 The violent **e** their neighbors,
Ac 20:30 the truth in order to **e** the disciples to follow them.
2Pe 2:14 for sin. They **e** unsteady souls.
2:18 of the flesh they **e** people who have just escaped
Jdt 10:4 to **e** the eyes of all the men who might see her.

ENTICED (7) [ENTICE]

Job 31:9 "If my heart has been **e** by a woman,
31:27 and my heart has been secretly **e**,
Jer 20:7 O LORD, you have **e** me, and I was **e**;
20:10 "Perhaps he can be **e**, and we can prevail
1Co 12:2 you were **e** and led astray to idols that could
Jas 1:14 being lured and **e** by it;

ENTICES (1) [ENTICE]

Dt 13:6 If anyone secretly **e** you—even if it is your brother,

ENTIRE (54) [ENTIRELY]

Ex 14:28 the **e** army of Pharaoh that had followed them into
Lev 23:28 and you shall do no work during that **e** day;
23:29 during that **e** day shall be cut off from the people.
23:30 And anyone who does any work during that **e** day,
Nu 5:30 and the priest shall apply this **e** law to her.
Dt 2:14 the **e** generation of warriors had perished from
4:8 as this **e** law that I am setting before you today?
6:25 If we diligently observe this **e** commandment
8:1 This **e** commandment that I command you today
11:8 then, this **e** commandment that I am commanding
11:22 If you will diligently observe this **e** commandment
15:5 by diligently observing this **e** commandment
19:9 you diligently observe this **e** commandment
26:13 in accordance with your **e** commandment
27:1 Keep the **e** commandment
34:11 against Pharaoh and all his servants and his **e** land,
Jos 3:17 the **e** nation finished crossing over the Jordan.
4:1 the **e** nation had finished crossing over the Jordan,
1Ki 7:1 and he finished his **e** house.
11:13 I will not, however, tear away the **e** kingdom;
2Ki 6:24 of Aram mustered his **e** army;
22:4 the **e** sum of the money that has been brought into
2Ch 16:9 eyes of the LORD range throughout the **e** earth,
32:5 and built up the **e** wall that was broken down,
Jer 36:23 until the **e** scroll was consumed in the fire that was
51:3 utterly destroy her **e** army.
Eze 10:12 Their **e** body, their rims, their spokes, their wings,
43:11 all its ordinances and its **e** plan and all its laws;
43:11 so that they may observe and follow the **e** plan
45:1 it shall be holy throughout its **e** extent.
Da 3:5 lyre, trigon, harp, drum, and **e** musical ensemble,
3:7 lyre, trigon, harp, drum, and **e** musical ensemble,
3:10 lyre, trigon, harp, drum, and **e** musical ensemble,
3:15 and **e** musical ensemble to fall down and worship
Am 1:6 because they carried into exile **e** communities,
1:9 they delivered **e** communities over to Edom,
Mt 18:34 over to be tortured until he would pay his **e** debt.
Lk 1:65 about throughout the **e** hill country of Judea.
13:17 and the **e** crowd was rejoicing at all
Ac 2:2 and it filled the **e** house where they were sitting.
2:36 the **e** house of Israel know with certainty
8:27 in charge of her **e** treasury.
11:14 a message by which you and your **e** household will
11:26 for an **e** year they met with the church and taught
16:33 he and his **e** family were baptized without delay.
16:34 and his **e** household rejoiced that he had become
20:18 the **e** time from the first day that I set foot in Asia,
22:30 and ordered the chief priests and the **e** council
Gal 5:3 that he is obliged to obey the **e** law.
Tob 1:21 and he had authority over the **e** administration.
AdE 4:12 Hachratheus delivered her **e** message to Mordecai,
1Mc 3:40 So they set out with their **e** force,
3Mc 4:14 The **e** race was to be registered individually,
4Mc 2:19 and Levi for their irrational slaughter of the **e** tribe

ENTIRELY (8) [ENTIRE]

Lev 6:22 to be turned **e** into smoke.
2Sa 23:7 And they are **e** consumed in fire on the spot.
Jn 9:34 They answered him, "You were born **e** in sins,
13:10 except for the feet, but is **e** clean.
1Co 9:10 Or does he not speak **e** for our sake?
Eph 5:4 **E** out of place is obscene, silly, and vulgar talk;
1Th 5:23 May the God of peace himself sanctify you **e**;
4Mc 3:1 But this argument is **e** ridiculous;

ENTITLED (2)

Tob 3:17 For Tobias was **e** to have her
6:13 are **e** to marry his daughter.

ENTRAILS‡ (26)

Ex 29:13 You shall take all the fat that covers the **e**,
29:17 and wash its **e** and its legs,
29:22 the fat tail, the fat that covers the **e**,
Lev 1:9 but its **e** and its legs shall be washed with water.
1:13 but the **e** and the legs shall be washed with water.
3:3 covers the **e** and all the fat that is around the **e**;
3:9 covers the **e**, and all the fat that is around the **e**;
3:14 covers the **e**, and all the fat that is around the **e**;
4:8 covers the **e** and all the fat that is around the **e**;
4:11 as well as its head, its legs, its **e**, and its dung—
Lev 7:3 the broad tail, the fat that covers the **e**,
8:16 Moses took all the fat that was around the **e**,
8:21 after the **e** and the legs were washed with water,
8:25 the broad tail, all the fat that was around the **e**,
9:14 He washed the **e** and the legs and,
9:19 the broad tail, the fat that covers the **e**,
2Sa 20:10 in the belly so that his **e** poured out on the ground,
Pr 7:23 until an arrow pierces its **e**.
2Mc 14:46 he tore out his **e**, took them in both hands
4Mc 5:30 not even if you gouge out my eyes and burn my **e**.
10:8 around and drops of blood flowing from his **e**.
11:19 pierced his ribs so that his **e** were burned through.

ENTRANCE‡ (138) [ENTER]

Ge 18:1 as he sat at the **e** of his tent in the heat of the day.
18:2 he saw them, he ran from the tent **e** to meet them,
18:10 And Sarah was listening at the tent **e** behind him.
38:14 and sat down at the **e** to Enaim,
43:19 of Joseph's house and spoke with him at the **e** to
Ex 26:36 You shall make a screen for the **e** of the tent,
29:4 You shall bring Aaron and his sons to the **e** of
29:11 at the **e** of the tent of meeting,
29:32 at the **e** of the tent of meeting.
29:42 at the **e** of the tent of meeting before the LORD,
33:8 at the **e** of their tents and watch Moses
33:9 of cloud would descend and stand at the **e** of
33:10 the people saw the pillar of cloud standing at the **e**
33:10 all of them, at the **e** of their tent.
35:15 the screen for the **e**, the entrance of the tabernacle;
35:15 the screen for the entrance, the **e** of the tabernacle;
36:37 He also made a screen for the **e** to the tent, of blue,
38:8 from the mirrors of the women who served at the **e**
38:18 The screen for the **e** to the court was embroidered
38:30 with it he made the bases for the **e** of the tent
39:38 and the screen for the **e** of the tent;
40:5 and set up the screen for the **e** of the tabernacle.
40:6 of burnt offering before the **e** of the tabernacle of
40:12 Then you shall bring Aaron and his sons to the **e**
40:28 in place the screen for the **e** of the tabernacle.
40:29 the altar of burnt offering at the **e** of the tabernacle
Lev 1:3 you shall bring it to the **e** of the tent of meeting,
1:5 of the altar that is at the **e** of the tent of meeting.
3:2 on the head of the offering and slaughter it at the **e**
4:4 to the **e** of the tent of meeting before the LORD
4:7 which is at the **e** of the tent of meeting.
4:18 the altar of burnt offering that is at the **e** of the tent
8:3 and assemble the whole congregation at the **e** of
8:4 the congregation was assembled at the **e** of the tent
8:31 "Boil the flesh at the **e** of the tent of meeting,
8:33 the **e** of the tent of meeting for seven days,
8:35 at the **e** of the tent of meeting day and night
10:7 the **e** of the tent of meeting, or you will die;
12:6 the **e** of the tent of meeting a lamb in its first year
14:11 before the LORD, at the **e** of the tent of meeting.
14:23 to the **e** of the tent of meeting, before the LORD;
15:14 before the LORD to the **e** of the tent of meeting
15:29 or two pigeons and bring them to the priest to the **e**
16:7 and set them before the LORD at the **e** of the tent
17:4 to the **e** of the tent of meeting, to present it as
17:5 to the priest at the **e** of the tent of meeting,
17:6 against the altar of the LORD at the **e** of the tent
17:9 does not bring it to the **e** of the tent of meeting,
19:21 at the **e** of the tent of meeting,
Nu 3:25 the screen for the **e** of the tent of meeting,
3:26 the **e** of the court that is around the tabernacle and
4:25 and the screen for the **e** of the tent of meeting,
4:26 the screen for the **e** of the gate of the court that is
6:10 or two young pigeons to the priest at the **e** of
6:13 be brought to the **e** of the tent of meeting,
6:18 the consecrated head at the **e** of the tent
10:3 before you at the **e** of the tent of meeting.
12:5 and stood at the **e** of the tent,
16:18 the **e** of the tent of meeting with Moses and Aaron.
16:19 the whole congregation against them at the **e** of
16:27 and Abiram came out and stood at the **e**
16:50 Aaron returned to Moses at the **e** of the tent
20:6 from the assembly to the **e** of the tent of meeting;
25:6 they were weeping at the **e** of the tent of meeting.
27:2 at the **e** of the tent of meeting, and they said,
Dt 22:21 the young woman out to the **e** of her father's house
31:15 the pillar of cloud stood at the **e** to the tent.
Jos 8:29 threw it down at the **e** of the gate of the city,
19:51 at the **e** of the tent of meeting.
20:4 of these cities and shall stand at the **e** of the gate of
Jdg 4:20 He said to her, "Stand at the **e** of the tent,
9:35 of Ebed went out and stood in the **e** of the gate of
9:40 Many fell wounded, up to the **e** of the gate.
9:44 with him rushed forward and stood at the **e** of
9:52 came near to the **e** of the tower to burn it with fire.
18:16 stood by the **e** of the gate,
18:17 the **e** of the gate with the six hundred men armed
1Sa 2:22 how they lay with the women who served at the **e**
2Sa 10:8 and drew up in battle array at the **e** of the gate;
11:9 But Uriah slept at the **e** of the king's house with all
11:23 but we drove them back to the **e** of the gate.
1Ki 6:8 The **e** for the middle story was on the south side of
6:31 For the **e** to the inner sanctuary he made doors
6:33 So also he made for the **e** to the nave doorposts
18:46 up his loins and ran in front of Ahab to the **e**
19:13 in his mantle and went out and stood at the **e** of
22:10 the threshing floor at the **e** of the gate of Samaria;
2Ki 5:9 and halted at the **e** of Elisha's house.
10:8 "Lay them in two heaps at the **e** of the gate until
11:16 she went through the horses' **e** to the king's house,
16:18 the outer **e** for the king he removed from the house
23:8 down the high places of the gates that were at the **e**
2Ki 23:11 at the **e** to the house of the LORD,
1Ch 4:39 They journeyed to the **e** of Gedor,
9:19 of the camp of the LORD, guardians of the **e**.
9:21 of Meshelemiah was gatekeeper at the **e** of the tent
19:9 and drew up in battle array at the **e** of the city,
2Ch 4:22 As for the **e** to the temple:
18:9 and they were sitting at the threshing floor at the **e**
23:13 there was the king standing by his pillar at the **e**,
23:15 into the **e** of the Horse Gate of the king's house,
33:14 in the valley, reaching the **e** at the Fish Gate;
Est 4:2 he went up to the **e** of the king's gate,
5:1 on his royal throne inside the palace opposite the **e**
Ps 74:5 At the upper **e** they hacked the wooden trellis
Pr 1:21 at the **e** of the city gates she speaks:
8:3 at the **e** of the portals she cries out:
Jer 1:15 of them shall set their thrones at the **e** of the gates
38:14 and received him at the third **e** of the temple of
43:9 and bury them in the clay pavement that is at the **e**
Eze 8:3 of God to Jerusalem, to the **e** of the gateway of
8:5 and there, north of the altar gate, in the **e**,
8:7 And he brought me to the **e** of the court;
8:8 and when I dug through the wall, there was an **e**.
8:14 the **e** of the north gate of the house of the LORD;
8:16 there, at the **e** of the temple of the LORD,
10:19 They stopped at the **e** of the east gate of the house
11:1 There, at the **e** of the gateway,
27:3 which sits at the **e** to the sea,
40:15 the gate at the **e** to the end of the inner vestibule of
40:40 at the **e** of the north gate were two tables;
41:2 The width of the **e** was ten cubits; and the
sidewalls of the **e** were five cubits on either side.
41:3 the pilasters of the **e**, two cubits; and the width of
the **e**, six cubits; and the sidewalls of the **e**, seven
42:12 the south were entered through the **e** at the head of
46:3 The people of the land shall bow down at the **e** of
46:19 Then he brought me through the **e**,
47:1 Then he brought me back to the **e** of the temple;
Mk 16:3 "Who will roll away the stone for us from the **e** to
Ac 23:16 he went and gained **e** to the barracks and told Paul.
Wis 7:6 there is for all one **e** into life, and one way out.
7:25 therefore nothing defiled gains **e** into her.
Bel 1:13 for beneath the table they had made a hidden **e**,
2Mc 2:5 then he sealed up the **e**.
2Es 7:4 but it has an **e** set in a narrow place,
7:7 the **e** to it is narrow and set in a precipitous place,

ENTRANCES‡ (7) [ENTER]

Nu 11:10 all at the **e** of their tents.
Eze 42:4 and its **e** were on the north.
42:12 So the **e** of the chambers to the south were entered
43:11 its exits and its **e**, and its whole form—
2Es 4:7 or which are the **e** of paradise?'
7:12 And so the **e** of this world were made narrow
7:13 But the **e** of the greater world are broad and safe,

ENTRAP (1) [TRAP]

Mt 22:15 Then the Pharisees went and plotted to **e** him

ENTREAT (13) [ENTREATED, ENTREATIES, ENTREATS, ENTREATY]

Ge 23:8 hear me, and **e** for me Ephron son of Zohar,
1Ki 13:6 "**E** now the favor of the LORD your God,
Est 4:8 to the king to make supplication to him and **e** him
Job 11:19 and no one will make you afraid; many will **e** your favor.
Jer 26:19 not fear the LORD and **e** the favor of the LORD,
Da 9:13 We did not **e** the favor of the LORD our God,
Zec 7:2 to **e** the favor of the LORD,
8:21 "Come, let us go to **e** the favor of the LORD,
8:22 and to **e** the favor of the LORD.
2Co 5:20 we **e** you on behalf of Christ,
3Mc 6:14 of infants and their parents **e** you with tears.
2Es 7:*102* to intercede for the ungodly or to **e** the Most High
12:6 now **e** the Most High that he may strengthen me to

ENTREATED (10) [ENTREAT]

Dt 3:23 At that time, too, I **e** the LORD, saying:
Jdg 13:8 Then Manoah **e** the LORD, and said, "O, LORD,
1Sa 13:12 and I have not **e** the favor of the LORD';
1Ki 13:6 So the man of God **e** the LORD;
2Ki 1:13 and **e** him, "O man of God, please let my life,
13:4 But Jehoahaz **e** the LORD,
2Ch 33:12 in distress he **e** the favor of the LORD his God
Bar 2:8 not **e** the favor of the Lord by turning away,
3Mc 1:16 in all their vestments prostrated themselves and **e**
2Es 1:28 Have I not **e** you as a father entreats his sons or

ENTREATIES (1) [ENTREAT]

Pr 18:23 The poor use **e**, but the rich answer roughly.

ENTREATS (2) [ENTREAT]

Wis 13:18 for aid he **e** a thing that is utterly inexperienced;
2Es 1:28 as a father **e** his sons or a mother her daughters or

ENTREATY‡ (6) [ENTREAT]

1Ch 5:20 and he granted their **e** because they trusted in him.
2Ch 33:13 He prayed to him, and God received his **e**,
33:19 His prayer, and how God received his **e**,
Ezr 8:23 and he listened to our **e**.
1Mc 11:49 and they cried out to the king with this **e**:
3Mc 5:9 So their **e** ascended fervently to heaven.

ENTRIES (1) [ENTER]
Ezr 2:62 for their **e** in the genealogical records,

ENTRIES (KJV) See also DOORS, ENTRANCE, GATEWAY

ENTRUST (7) [TRUST]
Lk 16:11 who will **e** to you the true riches?
Jn 2:24 But Jesus on his part would not **e** himself to them,
2Ti 2: 2 from me through many witnesses **e**
1Pe 4:19 with God's will **e** themselves to a faithful Creator,
Tob 10:12 In the sight of the Lord I **e** my daughter to you;
Sir 50:24 May he **e** to us his mercy,
2Mc 7:24 that he would take him for his Friend and **e** him

ENTRUSTED (29) [TRUST]
Nu 12: 7 with my servant Moses; he is **e** with all my house.
SS 8:11 he **e** the vineyard to keepers;
Jer 39:14 They **e** him to Gedaliah son of Ahikam son
Mt 25:14 summoned his slaves and **e** his property to them;
Lk 12:48 and from the one to whom much has been **e,**
Ac 14:23 with prayer and fasting they **e** them to the Lord
Ro 3: 2 in the first place the Jews were **e** with the oracles
6:17 to the form of teaching to which you were **e,**
1Co 9:17 if not of my own will, I am **e** with a commission.
Gal 2: 7 when they saw that I had been **e** with the gospel
2: 7 just as Peter had been **e** with the gospel for
1Th 2: 4 but just as we have been approved by God to be **e**
1Ti 1:11 the glorious gospel of the blessed God, which he **e**
6:20 Timothy, guard what has been **e** to you.
2Ti 1:12 that he is able to guard until that day what I have **e**
1:14 Guard the good treasure **e** to you,
Tit 1: 3 through the proclamation with which I have been **e**
1Pe 2:23 but he **e** himself to the one who judges justly.
Jude 1: 3 to contend for the faith that was once for all **e** to
AdE 2: 3 be **e** to the king's eunuch who is in charge of
16: 5 of friends who have been **e** with the administration
2Mc 3:22 that he would keep what had been **e** safe
3:22 and secure for those who had **e** it,
9:25 whom I have often **e** and commended to most
10:13 which Philometor had **e** to him,
3Mc 3:21 with us and the myriad affairs liberally **e** to them
2Es 2:37 Receive what the Lord has **e** to you and be joyful,
5:17 not know that Israel has been **e** to you in the land
7:*94* the law with which they were **e.**

ENTRUSTING (1) [TRUST]
2Co 5:19 and **e** the message of reconciliation to us.

ENTRY (5) [ENTER]
Jer 19: 2 of the son of Hinnom at the **e** of the Potsherd Gate,
26:10 the **e** of the New Gate of the house of the LORD.
36:10 at the **e** of the New Gate of the LORD's house.
2Pe 1:11 **e** into the eternal kingdom of our Lord
Jdt 14:14 Bagoas went in and knocked at the **e** of the tent,

ENTRY (KJV) See also DOORS, ENTRANCE, GATEWAY

ENVELOPED (3)
La 3: 5 he has besieged and **e** me with bitterness
Wis 18:14 For while gentle silence **e** all things,
Sir 48:12 When Elijah was **e** in the whirlwind,

ENVIABLE (1) [ENVY]
2Mc 7:24 with oaths that he would make him rich and **e**

ENVIED (3) [ENVY]
Ge 26:14 so that the Philistines **e** him.
30: 1 that she bore Jacob no children, she **e** her sister;
Sir 45:18 and **e** him in the wilderness,

ENVIOUS‡ (6) [ENVY]
Ps 37: 1 do not be **e** of wrongdoers,
73: 3 For I was **e** of the arrogant;
Mt 20:15 Or are you **e** because I am generous?'
1Co 13: 4 love is not **e** or boastful or arrogant
Sir 30: 3 He who teaches his son will make his enemies **e,**
3Mc 6: 7 who through **e** slanders was thrown down into

ENVIRONS (3)
1Mc 10:31 Jerusalem and its **e,** its tithes and its revenues,
10:89 also gave him Ekron and all its **e** as his possession.
14:36 to sally forth and defile the **e** of the sanctuary,

ENVISIONED (2)
Eze 13: 6 They have **e** falsehood and lying divination;
13: 8 Because you have uttered falsehood and **e** lies,

ENVOY (2) [ENVOYS]
Pr 13:17 A bad messenger brings trouble, but a faithful **e,**
1Mc 12: 8 Onias welcomed the **e** with honor,

ENVOYS (26) [ENVOY]
2Sa 10: 2 David sent **e** to console him concerning his father.
10: 2 David's **e** came into the land of the Ammonites,
10: 3 Has not David sent his **e** to you to search the city,
10: 4 So Hanun seized David's **e,**
2Ki 20:12 of Baladan of Babylon sent **e** with letters and
2Ch 32:31 in the matter of the **e** of the officials of Babylon,
35:21 But Neco sent **e** to him, saying,
Ezr 4: 9 and the rest of their associates, the judges, the **e,**
5: 6 and his associates the **e** who were in the province
6: 6 the **e** in the province Beyond the River,
Isa 30: 4 his officials are at Zoan and his **e** reach Hanes,
33: 7 the **e** of peace weep bitterly.
39: 1 of Baladan of Babylon sent **e** with letters and
57: 9 sent your **e** far away, and sent down even to Sheol.
Jer 27: 3 by the hand of the **e** who have come to Jerusalem
1Mc 11: 9 He sent **e** to King Demetrius, saying, "Come,
12: 4 asking them to provide for the **e** safe conduct to
12:23 We therefore command that our **e** report
13:14 so he sent **e** to him and said,
13:21 in the citadel kept sending **e** to Trypho urging him
14:21 The **e** who were sent to our people have told us
14:22 of Antiochus and Antipater son of Jason, **e** of
14:40 Romans had received the **e** of Simon with honor.
15:17 The **e** of the Jews have come to us as our friends
2Mc 4:19 the vile Jason sent **e,** chosen
11:34 **e** of the Romans, to the people of the Jews,

ENVY (25) [ENVIABLE, ENVIED, ENVIOUS, ENVYING]
Ps 68:16 Why do you look with **e,**
Pr 3:31 Do not **e** the violent and do not choose any
23:17 Do not let your heart **e** sinners,
24: 1 Do not **e** the wicked, nor desire to be with them;
24:19 of evildoers. Do not **e** the wicked;
Ecc 4: 4 and all skill in work come from one person's **e**
9: 6 and their hate and their **e** have already perished;
Eze 31: 9 the **e** of all the trees of Eden that were in
35:11 I will deal with you according to the anger and **e**
Mk 7:22 wickedness, deceit, licentiousness, **e,** slander,
Ro 1:29 Full of **e,** murder, strife, deceit, craftiness,
Gal 5:21 **e,** drunkenness, carousing, and things
Php 1:15 Some proclaim Christ from **e** and rivalry,
1Ti 6: 4 From these come **e,** dissension, slander,
Tit 3: 3 passing our days in malice and **e,** despicable,
Jas 3:14 But if you have bitter **e** and selfish ambition
3:16 For where there is **e** and selfish ambition,
1Pe 2: 1 and all guile, insincerity, **e,** and all slander.
Wis 2:24 but through the devil's **e** death entered the world,
6:23 nor will I travel in the company of sickly **e,**
6:23 for **e** does not associate with wisdom.
Sir 9:11 Do not **e** the success of sinners,
40: 5 there is anger and **e** and trouble and unrest,
1Mc 8:16 and there is no **e** or jealousy among them.
2Es 2:28 The nations shall **e** you, but they shall not be able

ENVYING (1) [ENVY]
Gal 5:26 competing against one another, **e** one another.

ENWRAP (1) [WRAP]
Job 22:14 Thick clouds **e** him, so that he does not see,

EPAENETUS (1)
Ro 16: 5 Greet my beloved **E,** who was the first convert

EPAPHRAS (3)
Col 1: 7 you learned from **E,** our beloved fellow servant.
4:12 **E,** who is one of you, a servant of Christ Jesus,
Phm 1:23 **E,** my fellow prisoner in Christ Jesus,

EPAPHRODITUS (2)
Php 2:25 Still, I think it necessary to send to you **E**—
4:18 now that I have received from **E** the gifts you sent,

EPEIPH (2)
3Mc 6:38 from the twenty-fifth of Pachon to the fourth of **E,**
6:38 for the fifth to the seventh of **E,**

EPHAH‡ (49)
Ge 25: 4 The sons of Midian were **E,** Epher, Hanoch,
Ex 16:36 An omer is a tenth of an **e.**
Lev 5:11 the sin that you have committed one-tenth of an **e**
6:20 of an **e** of choice flour as a regular offering,
14:10 of three-tenths of an **e** of choice flour mixed
14:21 and one-tenth of an **e** of choice flour mixed
19:36 honest weights, an honest **e,** and an honest hin:
23:13 of an **e** of choice flour mixed with oil, an offering
23:17 each made of two-tenths of an **e;**
24: 5 two-tenths of an **e** shall be in each loaf.
Nu 5:15 one-tenth of an **e** of barley flour.
15: 4 one-tenth of an **e** of choice flour,
15: 6 an **e** of choice flour mixed with one-third of a hin
15: 9 three-tenths of an **e** of choice flour,
28: 5 of an **e** of choice flour for a grain offering,
28: 9 a year old without blemish, and two-tenths of an **e**
28:12 of an **e** of choice flour for a grain offering, mixed
28:20 three-tenths of an **e** shall you offer for a bull,
28:28 three-tenths of an **e** for each bull,
29: 3 three-tenths of one **e** for the bull,
29: 9 three-tenths of an **e** for the bull,
29:14 three-tenths of an **e** for each of the thirteen bulls,
Jdg 6:19 and unleavened cakes from an **e** of flour;
Ru 2:17 and it was about an **e** of barley.
1Sa 1:24 along with a three-year-old bull, an **e** of flour,
17:17 "Take for your brothers an **e** of this parched grain
1Ch 1:33 **E,** Epher, Hanoch, Abida, and Eldaah.
2:46 **E** also, Caleb's concubine, bore Haran, Moza,
2:47 Regem, Jotham, Geshan, Pelet, **E,** and Shaaph.
Isa 5:10 and a homer of seed shall yield a mere **e.**
Isa 60: 6 the young camels of Midian and **E;**
Eze 45:10 You shall have honest balances, an honest **e,**
45:11 The **e** and the bath shall be of the same measure,
45:11 and the **e** one-tenth of a homer;
45:13 one-sixth of an **e** from each homer of wheat,
45:13 and one-sixth of an **e** from each homer of barley,
45:24 He shall provide as a grain offering an **e**
45:24 an **e** for each ram, and a hin of oil to each **e.**
46: 5 and the grain offering with the ram shall be an **e,**
46: 5 together with a hin of oil to each **e.**
46: 7 a grain offering he shall provide an **e** with the bull
46: 7 an ephah with the bull and an **e** with the ram,
46: 7 together with a hin of oil to each **e.**
46:11 the grain offering with a young bull shall be an **e,**
46:11 and with a ram an **e,**
46:11 together with a hin of oil to an **e.**
46:14 of an **e,** and one-third of a hin of oil to moisten
Am 8: 5 We will make the **e** small and the shekel great,

EPHAI (1)
Jer 40: 8 the sons of **E** the Netophathite,

EPHER (4)
Ge 25: 4 The sons of Midian were Ephah, **E,** Hanoch,
1Ch 1:33 Ephah, **E,** Hanoch, Abida, and Eldaah.
4:17 The sons of Ezrah: Jether, Mered, **E,** and Jalon.
5:24 These were the heads of their clans: **E,** Ishi, Eliel,

EPHES-DAMMIM (1)
1Sa 17: 1 and encamped between Socoh and Azekah, in **E.**

EPHESIAN (1) [EPHESUS]
Ac 21:29 For they had previously seen Trophimus the **E**

EPHESIANS (3) [EPHESUS]
Ac 19:28 "Great is Artemis of the **E!**"
19:34 "Great is Artemis of the **E!**"
19:35 the **E** is the temple keeper of the great Artemis

EPHESUS‡ (17) [EPHESIAN, EPHESIANS]
Ac 18:19 When they reached **E,** he left them there,
18:21 Then he set sail from **E.**
18:24 Now there came to **E** a Jew named Apollos,
19: 1 through the interior regions and came to **E,**
19:17 When this became known to all residents of **E,**
19:26 and hear that not only in **E** but in almost the whole
19:35 of **E,** who is there that does not know that the city
20:16 For Paul had decided to sail past **E,**
20:17 From Miletus he sent a message to **E,**
1Co 15:32 with wild animals at **E,** what would I have gained
16: 8 But I will stay in **E** until Pentecost,
Eph 1: 1 To the saints who are in **E** and are faithful
1Ti 1: 3 in **E** so that you may instruct certain people not
2Ti 1:18 how much service he rendered in **E.**
4:12 I have sent Tychicus to **E.**
Rev 1:11 to **E,** to Smyrna, to Pergamum, to Thyatira,
2: 1 "To the angel of the church in **E** write:

EPHLAL (2)
1Ch 2:37 Zabad became the father of **E,** and **E** of Obed.

EPHOD‡ (53)
Ex 25: 7 and gems to be set in the **e** and for the breastpiece.
28: 4 a breastpiece, an **e,** a robe, a checkered tunic,
28: 6 They shall make the **e** of gold, of blue, purple,
28:12 of the **e,** as stones of remembrance for the sons
28:15 you shall make it in the style of the **e;**
28:25 so attach it in front to the shoulder-pieces of the **e.**
28:26 on its inside edge next to the **e.**
28:27 the lower part of the two shoulder-pieces of the **e,** at its joining above the decorated band of the **e.**
28:28 by its rings to the rings of the **e** with a blue cord, so that it may lie on the decorated band of the **e,**
28:28 the breastpiece shall not come loose from the **e.**
28:31 You shall make the robe of the **e** all of blue.
29: 5 put on Aaron the tunic and the robe of the **e,** and the **e,** and the breastpiece, and gird him with the decorated band of the **e;**
35: 9 and onyx stones and gems to be set in the **e** and
35:27 and gems to be set in the **e** and the breastpiece,
39: 2 He made the **e** of gold, of blue, purple,
39: 4 They made for the **e** shoulder-pieces,
39: 7 He set them on the shoulder-pieces of the **e,**
39: 8 in skilled work, like the work of the **e,** of gold,
39:18 in front to the shoulder-pieces of the **e.**
39:19 on its inside edge next to the **e.**
39:20 the lower part of the two shoulder-pieces of the **e,** at its joining above the decorated band of the **e.**
39:21 by its rings to the rings of the **e** with a blue cord, so that it should lie on the decorated band of the **e,**
39:21 the breastpiece should not come loose from the **e;**
39:22 also made the robe of the **e** woven all of blue yarn;
Lev 8: 7 clothed him with the robe, and put the **e** on him.
8: 7 then put the decorated band of the **e** around him, tying the **e** to him with it.
Nu 34:23 of the Manassites a leader, Hanniel son of **E,**
Jdg 8:27 Gideon made an **e** of it and put it in his town,
17: 5 and he made an **e** and teraphim,
18:14 that in these buildings there are an **e,**
18:17 to enter and take the idol of cast metal, the **e,** and
18:18 the **e,** and the teraphim, the priest said to them,
18:20 He took the **e,** the teraphim, and the idol,
1Sa 2:18 a boy wearing a linen **e.**

1Sa 2:28 to offer incense, to wear an **e** before me;
14: 3 the priest of the LORD in Shiloh, carrying an **e.**
21: 9 is here wrapped in a cloth behind the **e;**
22:18 that day he killed eighty-five who wore the linen **e.**
23: 6 he came down with an **e** in his hand.
23: 9 he said to the priest Abiathar, "Bring the **e** here."
30: 7 of Ahimelech, "Bring me the **e.**"
30: 7 So Abiathar brought the **e** to David.
2Sa 6:14 David was girded with a linen **e.**
1Ch 15:27 and David wore a linen **e.**
Hos 3: 4 without sacrifice or pillar, without **e** or teraphim.
Sir 45: 8 the linen undergarments, the long robe, and the **e.**

EPHPHATHA (1)

Mk 7:34 he sighed and said to him, "**E,**" that is,

EPHRAIM (162) [EPHRAIM'S, EPHRAIMITE, EPHRAIMITES]

A. HILL COUNTRY OF EPHRAIM (31)
B. TRIBE OF EPHRAIM (6)

Ge 41:52 The second he named **E,**
46:20 in the land of Egypt were born Manasseh and **E,**
48: 1 he took with him his two sons, Manasseh and **E.**
48: 5 **E** and Manasseh shall be mine,
48:13 **E** in his right hand toward Israel's left,
48:14 and laid it on the head of **E,**
48:17 that his father laid his right hand on the head of **E,**
48:20 'God make you like **E** and like Manasseh.' "
48:20 So he put **E** ahead of Manasseh.
Nu 1:10 from **E,** Elishama son of Ammihud;
1:32 the descendants of **E,** their lineage, in their clans,
1:33 the tribe of **E** were forty thousand five hundred. B
2:18 be the regimental encampment of **E** by companies.
2:18 of **E** shall be Elishama son of Ammihud,
2:24 The total enrollment of the camp of **E,**
13: 8 from the tribe of **E,** Hoshea son of Nun; B
26:28 sons of Joseph by their clans: Manasseh and **E.**
26:35 the descendants of **E** according to their clans:
Dt 33:17 such are the myriads of **E,**
34: 2 the land of **E** and Manasseh,
Jos 14: 4 of Joseph were two tribes, Manasseh and **E;**
16: 4 Manasseh and **E**—received their inheritance.
16:10 so the Canaanites have lived within **E** to this day
17: 9 among the towns of Manasseh, belong to **E.**
17:15 the hill country of **E** is too narrow for you." A
17:17 to **E** and Manasseh, "You are indeed
19:50 Timnath-serah in the hill country of **E;** A
20: 7 and Shechem in the hill country of **E,** A
21: 5 from the families of the tribe of **E,** B
21:20 towns allotted to them were out of the tribe of **E.** B
21:21 with its pasture lands in the hill country of **E,** A
24:30 which is in the hill country of **E,** A
24:33 had been given him in the hill country of **E.** A
Jdg 1:29 And **E** did not drive out the Canaanites who lived
2: 9 in the hill country of **E,** north of Mount Gaash. A
3:27 he sounded the trumpet in the hill country of **E;** A
4: 5 and Bethel in the hill country of **E;** A
5:14 From **E** they set out into the valley, following you,
7:24 throughout all the hill country of **E,** A
7:24 So all the men of **E** were called out,
8: 2 the grapes of **E** better than the vintage of Abiezer?
10: 1 who lived at Shamir in the hill country of **E,** A
10: 9 and against Benjamin and against the house of **E;**
12: 1 The men of **E** were called to arms,
12: 4 the men of Gilead and fought with **E;**
12: 4 and the men of Gilead defeated **E,**
12: 4 because they said, "You are fugitives from **E,**
12: 4 in the heart of **E** and Manasseh."
12: 5 Whenever one of the fugitives of **E** said,
12:15 and was buried at Pirathon in the land of **E,**
17: 1 in the hill country of **E** whose name was Micah. A
17: 8 house of Micah in the hill country of **E** to carry A
18: 2 When they came to the hill country of **E,** A
18:13 there they passed on to the hill country of **E,** A
19: 1 in the remote parts of the hill country of **E,** A
19:16 The man was from the hill country of **E,** A
19:18 to the remote parts of the hill country of **E,** A
1Sa 1: 1 a Zuphite from the hill country of **E,** A
9: 4 He passed through the hill country of **E** and A
14:22 into hiding in the hill country of **E** heard that A
14:23 The battle spread out over the hill country of **E.** A
2Sa 2: 9 Jezreel, **E,** Benjamin, and over all Israel.
13:23 which is near **E,** and Absalom invited all
18: 6 and the battle was fought in the forest of **E.**
20:21 But a man of the hill country of **E,** A
1Ki 4: 8 Ben-hur, in the hill country of **E;** A
12:25 Jeroboam built Shechem in the hill country of **E,** A
2Ki 5:22 to me from the hill country of **E;** A
14:13 of Jerusalem from the **E** Gate to the Corner Gate,
1Ch 6:66 of their territory out of the tribe of **E.** B
6:67 with its pasture lands in the hill country of **E,** A
7:20 The sons of **E:** Shuthelah,
7:22 And their father **E** mourned many days,
7:23 **E** went in to his wife, and she conceived and bore
9: 3 And some of the people of Judah, Benjamin, **E,**
2Ch 13: 4 that is in the hill country of **E,** A
15: 8 that he had taken in the hill country of **E.** A
15: 9 and those from **E,** Manasseh,
17: 2 and in the cities of **E** that his father Asa had taken.
19: 4 from Beer-sheba to the hill country of **E,** A
25:10 the army that had come to him from **E,**
25:23 of Jerusalem from the **E** Gate to the Corner Gate,
28: 7 And Zichri, a mighty warrior of **E,**
30: 1 and wrote letters also to **E** and Manasseh,
2Ch 30:10 through the country of **E** and Manasseh, and as far
30:18 a multitude of the people, many of them from **E,**
31: 1 throughout all Judah and Benjamin, and in **E**
34: 6 In the towns of Manasseh, **E,** and Simeon,
34: 9 had collected from Manasseh and **E** and from all
Ne 8:16 the Water Gate and in the square at the Gate of **E.**
12:39 and above the Gate of **E,** and by the Old Gate,
Ps 60: 7 **E** is my helmet; Judah is my scepter.
78:67 he did not choose the tribe of **E;** B
80: 2 before **E** and Benjamin and Manasseh.
108: 8 Gilead is mine; Manasseh is mine; **E** is my helmet;
Isa 7: 2 of David heard that Aram had allied itself with **E,**
7: 5 with **E** and the son of Remaliah—
7: 8 (Within sixty-five years **E** will be shattered,
7: 9 The head of **E** is Samaria,
7:17 as have not come since the day that **E** departed
9: 9 **E** and the inhabitants of Samaria—
9:21 Manasseh devoured **E,** and Ephraim Manasseh,
9:21 and **E** Manasseh, and together they were
11:13 The jealousy of **E** shall depart,
11:13 **E** shall not be jealous of Judah,
11:13 and Judah shall not be hostile towards **E.**
17: 3 The fortress will disappear from **E,**
28: 1 Ah, the proud garland of the drunkards of **E,**
28: 3 be the proud garland of the drunkards of **E.**
Jer 4:15 from Dan and proclaims disaster from Mount **E.**
7:15 I cast out all your kinsfolk, all the offspring of **E.**
31: 6 when sentinels will call in the hill country of **E:** A
31: 9 a father to Israel, and **E** is my firstborn.
31:18 Indeed I heard **E** pleading:
31:20 Is **E** my dear son?
50:19 and on the hills of **E** and in Gilead its hunger shall
Eze 37:16 "For Joseph (the stick of **E**) and all the house
37:19 the stick of Joseph (which is in the hand of **E**) and
48: 5 from the east side to the west, **E,** one portion.
48: 6 Adjoining the territory of **E,**
Hos 4:17 **E** is joined to idols—let him alone.
5: 3 I know **E,** and Israel is not hidden from me;
5: 3 for now, O **E,** you have played the whore;
5: 5 against him; **E** stumbles in his guilt;
5: 9 **E** shall become a desolation in the day
5:11 **E** is oppressed, crushed in judgment,
5:12 Therefore I am like maggots to **E,**
5:13 When **E** saw his sickness, and Judah his wound,
5:13 then **E** went to Assyria, and sent to the great king.
5:14 For I will be like a lion to **E,**
6: 4 What shall I do with you, O **E?**
7: 1 the corruption of **E** is revealed,
7: 8 **E** mixes himself with the peoples;
7: 8 **E** is a cake not turned.
7:11 **E** has become like a dove, silly and without sense;
8: 9 **E** has bargained for lovers.
8:11 When **E** multiplied altars to expiate sin,
9: 3 but **E** shall return to Egypt,
9: 8 The prophet is a sentinel for my God over **E,**
9:13 Once I saw **E** as a young palm planted in
9:13 but now **E** must lead out his children for slaughter.
9:16 **E** is stricken, their root is dried up,
10: 6 **E** shall be put to shame, and Israel shall be
10:11 **E** was a trained heifer that loved to thresh,
10:11 but I will make **E** break the ground;
11: 3 Yet it was I who taught **E** to walk,
11: 8 How can I give you up, **E?**
11: 9 I will not again destroy **E;**
11:12 **E** has surrounded me with lies,
12: 1 **E** herds the wind, and pursues
12: 8 **E** has said, "Ah, I am rich,
12:14 **E** has given bitter offense,
13: 1 When **E** spoke, there was trembling;
14: 8 O **E,** what have I to do with idols?
Ob 1:19 they shall possess the land of **E** and the land
Zec 9:10 from **E** and the war horse from Jerusalem;
9:13 I have made **E** its arrow.
10: 7 Then the people of **E** shall become like warriors,
Jn 11:54 a town called **E** in the region near the wilderness;
Jdt 6: 2 Achior and you mercenaries of **E,**
Sir 47:21 and a rebel kingdom arose out of **E.**
47:23 of Nebat led Israel into sin and started **E**

EPHRAIM'S (6) [EPHRAIM]

Ge 48:17 to remove it from **E** head to Manasseh's head.
50:23 Joseph saw **E** children of the third generation;
Jos 17:10 the south is **E** and that to the north is Manasseh's,
Hos 6:10 **E** whoredom is there, Israel is defiled.
9:11 **E** glory shall fly away like a bird—
13:12 **E** iniquity is bound up; his sin is kept in store.

EPHRAIMITE (4) [EPHRAIM]

Nu 10:22 Next the standard of the **E** camp set out,
Jdg 12: 5 of Gilead would say to him, "Are you an **E?**"
1Sa 1: 1 of Elihu son of Tohu son of Zuph, an **E.**
1Ki 11:26 Jeroboam son of Nebat, an **E** of Zeredah,

EPHRAIMITES (17) [EPHRAIM]

Nu 7:48 of Ammihud, the leader of the **E:**
26:37 These are the clans of the **E:**
34:24 and of the tribe of the **E** a leader,
Jos 16: 5 territory of the **E** by their families was as follows:
16: 8 Such is the inheritance of the tribe of the **E**
16: 9 that were set apart for the **E** within the inheritance
17: 8 on the boundary of Manasseh belonged to the **E.**
Jdg 8: 1 Then the **E** said to him,
12: 5 the fords of the Jordan against the **E.**
12: 6 Forty-two thousand of the **E** fell at that time.
1Ch 12:30 Of the **E,** twenty thousand eight hundred,
1Ch 27:10 was Helez the Pelonite, of the **E;**
27:14 was Benaiah of Pirathon, of the **E;**
27:20 for the **E,** Hoshea son of Azaziah;
2Ch 25: 7 for the LORD is not with Israel—all these **E.**
28:12 Moreover, certain chiefs of the **E,**
Ps 78: 9 The **E,** armed with the bow,

EPHRAIN (KJV) See EPHRON; See also Index to Footnotes

EPHRATH (5) [BETHLEHEM, EPHRATHAH, EPHRATHITE, EPHRATHITES]

Ge 35:16 and when they were still some distance from **E,**
35:19 and she was buried on the way to **E** (that is,
48: 7 while there was still some distance to go to **E;**
48: 7 and I buried her there on the way to **E**" (that is,
1Ch 2:19 Azubah died, Caleb married **E,** who bore him Hur.

EPHRATHAH (5) [CALEB-EPHRATHAH, EPHRATH]

Ru 4:11 May you produce children in **E** and bestow a name
1Ch 2:50 The sons of Hur the firstborn of **E:**
4: 4 These were the sons of Hur, the firstborn of **E,**
Ps 132: 6 We heard of it in **E;**
Mic 5: 2 But you, O Bethlehem of **E,**

EPHRATHITE (1) [EPHRATH]

1Sa 17:12 David was the son of an **E** of Bethlehem in Judah,

EPHRATHITES (1) [EPHRATH]

Ru 1: 2 they were **E** from Bethlehem in Judah.

EPHRON (17)

Ge 23: 8 hear me, and entreat for me **E** son of Zohar,
23:10 Now **E** was sitting among the Hittites;
23:10 and **E** the Hittite answered Abraham in the hearing
23:13 to **E** in the hearing of the people of the land,
23:14 **E** answered Abraham,
23:16 Abraham agreed with **E;**
23:16 for **E** the silver that he had named in the hearing of
23:17 So the field of **E** in Machpelah,
25: 9 in the field of **E** son of Zohar the Hittite,
49:29 in the cave in the field of **E** the Hittite,
49:30 the field that Abraham bought from **E** the Hittite
50:13 which Abraham bought as a burial site from **E**
Jos 15: 9 and from there to the towns of Mount **E;**
18:15 and the boundary goes from there to **E,**
2Ch 13:19 with its villages and **E** with its villages.
1Mc 5:46 So they came to **E.**
2Mc 12:27 he marched also against **E,**

EPICUREAN (1)

Ac 17:18 some **E** and Stoic philosophers debated with him.

EPILEPTIC (1) [EPILEPTICS]

Mt 17:15 for he is an **e** and he suffers terribly;

EPILEPTICS (1) [EPILEPTIC]

Mt 4:24 demoniacs, **e,** and paralytics, and he cured them.

EPIPHANES (7)

1Mc 1:10 From them came forth a sinful root, Antiochus **E,**
10: 1 In the one hundred sixtieth year Alexander **E,**
2Mc 2:20 the wars against Antiochus **E** and his son Eupator,
4: 7 Seleucus died and Antiochus, who was called **E,**
10: 9 then was the end of Antiochus, who was called **E.**
10:13 and had gone over to Antiochus **E.**
4Mc 4:15 his son Antiochus **E** succeeded to the throne,

EPIPHANY See Index to Footnotes

EPISODE (1)

2Mc 3:40 This was the outcome of the **e** of Heliodorus and

EPISTLE (KJV) See LETTER

EQUAL (31) [EQUALITY, EQUALLY, EQUALS]

Ex 22:17 he shall pay an amount **e** to the bride-price
30:34 sweet spices with pure frankincense (an **e** part
Dt 18: 8 They shall have **e** portions to eat,
1Ch 12:14 least **e** to a hundred and the greatest to a thousand.
Job 28:17 Gold and glass cannot **e** it,
41:33 On earth it has no **e,** a creature without fear.
Ps 55:13 But it is you, my **e,** my companion,
Isa 40:25 then will you compare me, or who is my **e?**
46: 5 To whom will you liken me and make me **e,**
Eze 4: 5 **e** to the number of the years of their punishment;
31: 8 nor the fir trees **e** its boughs;
48: 8 and in length **e** to one of the tribal portions,
Mt 20:12 and you have made them **e** to us who have borne
Jn 5:18 thereby making himself **e** to God.
Rev 21:16 its length and width and height are **e.**
Sir 2:17 for **e** to his majesty is his mercy,
2:17 and **e** to his name are his works.
9:10 for new ones cannot **e** them.
13:11 Do not try to treat him as an **e,**

Sir 32: 9 Among the great do not act as their **e;**
45: 2 He made him **e** in glory to the holy ones,
48: 4 Whose glory is **e** to yours?
50:29 they will be **e** to anything,
2Mc 8:30 and also to the aged, shares **e** to their own.
9:12 mortals should not think that they are **e** to God."
9:15 all of them, **e** to citizens of Athens;
1Es 3:19 It makes **e** the mind of the king and the orphan,
3Mc 2:30 the mysteries, they shall have **e** citizenship with
4Mc 5:20 in matters either small or great is of **e** seriousness,
11:14 but I am their **e** in mind.
13:21 When they were born after an **e** time of gestation,

EQUALITY (1) [EQUAL]
Php 2: 6 did not regard **e** with God as something to

EQUALLY (5) [EQUAL]
Lev 7:10 shall belong to all the sons of Aaron **e.**
Eze 47:14 You shall divide it **e;** I swore to give
Wis 11:11 Whether absent or present, they were **e** distressed,
14: 9 For **e** hateful to God are the ungodly
4Mc 5:21 for in either case the law is **e** despised.

EQUALS (1) [EQUAL]
2Co 11:12 to be recognized as our **e** in what they boast about.

EQUIP (3) [EQUIPMENT, EQUIPPED]
Eph 4:12 to **e** the saints for the work of ministry,
1Mc 10: 6 to **e** them with arms, and to become his ally;
3Mc 5:38 **E** the elephants now once more for the destruction

EQUIPMENT (9) [EQUIP]
Nu 1:50 and over all its **e,** and over all that belongs to it;
1:50 they are to carry the tabernacle and all its **e,**
4:26 and their cords, and all the **e** for their service;
4:32 with all their **e** and all their related service;
1Sa 8:12 and to make his implements of war and the **e**
1Ki 19:21 using the **e** from the oxen, he boiled their flesh,
2Ki 7:15 the whole way was littered with garments and **e**
2Ch 4:16 and all the **e** for these Huram-abi made
1Mc 15:26 silver and gold and a large amount of military **e.**

EQUIPPED (14) [EQUIP]
1Ch 12:33 **e** for battle with all the weapons of war,
12:35 twenty-eight thousand six hundred **e** for battle.
SS 3: 8 all **e** with swords and expert in war,
Jer 6:23 they ride on horses, **e** like a warrior for battle,
Eph 4:16 by every ligament with which it is **e,**
2Ti 3:17 to God may be proficient, **e** for every good work.
Rev 9: 7 In appearance the locusts were like horses **e**
1Mc 6:43 that one of the animals was **e** with royal armor.
10:21 and he recruited troops and **e** them with arms
15: 3 a host of mercenary troops and have **e** warships,
2Mc 10:18 in two very strong towers well **e** to withstand
3Mc 5:23 Hermon, having **e** the animals,
5:45 of wine mixed with frankincense and had been **e**
4Mc 11:22 I also, **e** with nobility, will die with my brothers,

EQUITABLE (1) [EQUITY]
AdE 16: 9 before our eyes with more **e** consideration.

EQUITY (14) [EQUITABLE]
2Sa 8:15 David administered justice and **e** to all his people.
1Ch 18:14 and he administered justice and **e** to all his people.
Ps 9: 8 he judges the peoples with **e.**
45: 6 Your royal scepter is a scepter of **e;**
67: 4 for you judge the peoples with **e** and guide
75: 2 At the set time that I appoint I will judge with **e.**
96:10 He will judge the peoples with **e."**
98: 9 with righteousness, and the peoples with **e.**
99: 4 lover of justice, you have established **e;**
Pr 1: 3 righteousness, justice, and **e;**
2: 9 and justice and **e,** every good path;
29:14 If a king judges the poor with **e,**
Isa 11: 4 and decide with **e** for the meek of the earth;
Mic 3: 9 who abhor justice and pervert all **e,**

EQUIVALENT (12)
Lev 5:18 or the **e,** as a guilt offering;
6: 6 a ram without blemish from the flock, or its **e,**
27: 2 an explicit vow to the LORD concerning the **e** for
27: 3 the **e** for a male shall be:
27: 3 to sixty years of age the **e** shall be fifty shekels
27: 4 If the person is a female, the **e** is thirty shekels.
27: 5 the **e** is twenty shekels for a male and ten shekels
27: 6 the **e** for a male is five shekels of silver,
27: 6 and for a female the **e** is three shekels of silver.
27: 7 then the **e** for a male is fifteen shekels,
27: 8 If any cannot afford the **e,**
4Mc 3:15 to his soul to drink what was regarded as **e**

ER (11)
Ge 38: 3 and bore a son; and he named him **E.**
38: 6 Judah took a wife for **E** his firstborn;
38: 7 But **E,** Judah's firstborn, was wicked in the sight
46:12 The children of Judah: **E,** Onan, Shelah, Perez,
46:12 (but **E** and Onan died in the land of Canaan);
Nu 26:19 The sons of Judah: **E** and Onan;
26:19 **E** and Onan died in the land of Canaan.
1Ch 2: 3 The sons of Judah: **E,** Onan, and Shelah;
2: 3 Now **E,** Judah's firstborn,
4:21 **E** father of Lecah, Laadah father of Mareshah,
Lk 3:28 son of Cosam, son of Elmadam, son of **E,**

ERADICATE (3)
4Mc 3: 2 No one of us can **e** that kind of desire,
3: 3 No one of us can **e** anger from the mind,
3: 4 No one of us can **e** malice,

ERAN (1) [ERANITES]
Nu 26:36 of **E,** the clan of the Eranites.

ERANITES (1) [ERAN]
Nu 26:36 of Eran, the clan of the **E.**

ERASED (1) [ERASES, ERASING]
Tob 4:19 and do not let them be **e** from your heart.

ERASES (1) [ERASED]
Sir 10:17 and **e** the memory of them from the earth.

ERASING (1) [ERASED]
Col 2:14 **e** the record that stood against us

ERASTUS (3)
Ac 19:22 So he sent two of his helpers, Timothy and **E,**
Ro 16:23 **E,** the city treasurer, and our brother Quartus,
2Ti 4:20 **E** remained in Corinth; Trophimus I left ill

ERECH (2)
Ge 10:10 The beginning of his kingdom was Babel, **E,**
Ezr 4: 9 the Persians, the people of **E,** the Babylonians,

ERECT (12) [ERECTED, ERECTING, ERECTION]
Ex 26:30 Then you shall **e** the tabernacle according to
Lev 26: 1 and **e** no carved images or pillars, and you shall
26:13 the bars of your yoke and made you walk **e.**
2Sa 24:18 and **e** an altar to the LORD on the threshing floor
1Ch 21:18 and **e** an altar to the LORD on the threshing floor
Ezr 2:68 to **e** it on its site.
Heb 8: 5 for Moses, when he was about to **e** the tent,
1Mc 12:36 to **e** a high barrier between the citadel and the city
2Mc 15: 6 to **e** a public monument of victory over Judas
1Es 5:44 they would **e** the house on its site,
9:46 When he opened the law, they all stood **e.**
2Es 2:38 stand **e** and see the number

ERECTED (12) [ERECT]
Ge 33:20 There he **e** an altar and called it El-Elohe-Israel.
1Ki 16:32 He **e** an altar for Baal in the house of Baal,
2Ki 21: 3 he **e** altars for Baal, made a sacred pole,
23:15 the high place **e** by Jeroboam son of Nebat,
2Ch 33: 3 and **e** altars to the Baals, made sacred poles,
Isa 23:13 They **e** their siege towers,
Eze 43:18 On the day when it is **e** for offering burnt offerings
Tob 1: 5 the calf that King Jeroboam of Israel had **e** in Dan
1Mc 1:54 they **e** a desolating sacrilege on the altar
6: 7 down the abomination that he had **e** on the altar
13:28 He also **e** seven pyramids, opposite one another,
1Es 5:50 And they **e** the altar in its place,

ERECTING (1) [ERECT]
1Mc 13:29 **e** about them great columns,

ERECTION (1) [ERECT]
1Es 5:62 the Lord for the **e** of the house of the Lord.

ERI (2) [ERITES]
Ge 46:16 Ziphion, Haggi, Shuni, Ezbon, **E,** Arodi,
Nu 26:16 of **E,** the clan of the Erites;

ERITES (1) [ERI]
Nu 26:16 of Eri, the clan of the **E;**

ERR (6) [ERRED, ERROR, ERRORS, ERRS]
Ps 58: 3 they **e** from their birth, speaking lies.
Pr 14:22 Do they not **e** that plan evil?
Isa 28: 7 they **e** in vision, they stumble in giving judgment.
29:24 those who **e** in spirit will come to understanding,
Wis 14:22 not enough for them to **e** about the knowledge
Sir 28:26 Take care not to **e** with your tongue,

ERRAND (1)
Ge 24:33 but he said, "I will not eat until I have told my **e."**

ERRAND (KJV) See also MESSAGE

ERRED (1) [ERR]
Job 19: 4 it is true that I have **e,** my error remains with me.

ERROR‡ (20) [ERR]
Lev 5:18 for the **e** that you committed unintentionally,
Nu 15:25 before the LORD, for their **e.**
15:26 because the whole people was involved in the **e.**
15:28 before the LORD for the one who commits an **e,**
15:29 the same law for anyone who acts in **e.**
Job 4:18 and his angels he charges with **e;**
19: 4 it is true that I have erred, my **e** remains with me.
Ecc 10: 5 as great an **e** as if it proceeded from the ruler:
Isa 32: 6 to utter **e** concerning the LORD,
Eze 45:20 for anyone who has sinned through **e** or ignorance;
Ro 1:27 in their own persons the due penalty for their **e.**
2Pe 2:18 from those who live in **e.**
3:17 beware that you are not carried away with the **e** of
1Jn 4: 6 the spirit of truth and the spirit of **e.**
Jude 1:11 and abandon themselves to Balaam's **e** for
Tob 14: 6 which deceitfully have led them into their **e;**
Wis 1:12 Do not invite death by the **e** of your life,
12:24 For they went far astray on the paths of **e,**
Sir 23:11 If he swears in **e,** his sin remains on him,
1Es 9:20 and to offer rams in expiation of their **e.**

ERRORS (5) [ERR]
Ps 19:12 But who can detect their **e?**
Sir 23: 2 so as not to spare me in my **e,**
30:11 and do not ignore his **e.**
1Mc 13:39 We pardon any **e** and offenses committed
3Mc 2:19 Wipe away our sins and disperse our **e,**

ERRS (1) [ERR]
Lev 4:13 the whole congregation of Israel **e** unintentionally

ERUPTION (5)
Lev 13: 2 on the skin of his body a swelling or an **e** or a spot,
13: 6 priest shall pronounce him clean; it is only an **e;**
13: 7 But if the **e** spreads in the skin
13: 8 and if the **e** has spread in the skin,
14:56 and for a swelling or an **e** or a spot,

ESAIAS (KJV) See ISAIAH

ESAR-HADDON (7)
2Ki 19:37 His son **E** succeeded him.
Ezr 4: 2 of King **E** of Assyria who brought us here."
Isa 37:38 His son **E** succeeded him.
Tob 1:21 and his son **E** reigned after him.
1:22 of Assyria; so **E** reappointed him.
2: 1 Then during the reign of **E** I returned home,
1Es 5:69 since the days of King **E** of the Assyrians,

ESAU (98) [=EDOM, ESAU'S]
Ge 25:25 like a hairy mantle; so they named him **E.**
25:27 When the boys grew up, **E** was a skillful hunter,
25:28 Isaac loved **E,** because he was fond of game;
25:29 **E** came in from the field, and he was famished.
25:30 **E** said to Jacob, "Let me eat some of that red stuff,
25:32 **E** said, "I am about to die;
25:34 Then Jacob gave **E** bread and lentil stew,
25:34 Thus **E** despised his birthright.
26:34 When **E** was forty years old,
27: 1 he called his elder son **E** and said to him,
27: 5 when Isaac spoke to his son **E.**
27: 5 **E** went to the field to hunt for game and bring it,
27: 6 "I heard your father say to your brother **E,**
27:11 "Look, my brother **E** is a hairy man,
27:15 the best garments of her elder son **E,** which were
27:19 Jacob said to his father, "I am **E** your firstborn.
27:21 to know whether you are really my son **E** or not."
27:22 but the hands are the hands of **E."**
27:24 He said, "Are you really my son **E?"**
27:30 his brother **E** came in from his hunting.
27:32 He answered, "I am your firstborn son, **E."**
27:34 When **E** heard his father's words,
27:36 **E** said, "Is he not rightly named Jacob?
27:37 answered **E,** "I have already made him your lord,
27:38 **E** said to his father, "Have you only one blessing,
27:38 And **E** lifted up his voice and wept.
27:41 Now **E** hated Jacob because of the blessing
27:41 and **E** said to himself, "The days of mourning
27:42 the words of her elder son **E** were told to Rebekah;
27:42 "Your brother **E** is consoling himself by planning
28: 6 Now **E** saw that Isaac had blessed Jacob
28: 8 So when **E** saw that the Canaanite women did
28: 9 **E** went to Ishmael and took Mahalath daughter
32: 3 Jacob sent messengers before him to his brother **E**
32: 4 "Thus you shall say to my lord **E:**
32: 6 saying, "We came to your brother **E,**
32: 8 "If **E** comes to the one company and destroys it,
32:11 from the hand of my brother, from the hand of **E,**
32:13 with him he took a present for his brother **E,**
32:17 "When **E** my brother meets you, and asks you,
32:18 they are a present sent to my lord **E;**
32:19 the same thing to **E** when you meet him,
33: 1 Now Jacob looked up and saw **E** coming,
33: 4 But **E** ran to meet him, and embraced him,
33: 5 **E** looked up and saw the women and children,
33: 8 **E** said, "What do you mean by all this company
33: 9 But **E** said, "I have enough, my brother;
33:12 Then **E** said, "Let us journey on our way,
33:15 So **E** said, "Let me leave with you some of
33:16 So **E** returned that day on his way to Seir.
35: 1 to you when you fled from your brother **E."**
35:29 and his sons **E** and Jacob buried him.
36: 1 These are the descendants of **E** (that is, Edom).
36: 2 **E** took his wives from the Canaanites:
36: 4 Adah bore Eliphaz to **E;** Basemath bore Reuel;
36: 5 of **E** who were born to him in the land of Canaan.
36: 6 Then **E** took his wives, his sons, his daughters,
36: 8 **E** settled in the hill country of Seir; **E** is Edom.
36: 9 These are the descendants of **E,**
36:10 Eliphaz son of Adah the wife of **E;**
36:14 she bore to **E** Jeush, Jalam, and Korah.
36:15 These are the clans of the sons of **E.**

Ge 36:15 The sons of Eliphaz the firstborn of **E**:
36:19 These are the sons of **E** (that is, Edom),
36:40 These are the names of the clans of **E**,
36:43 these are the clans of Edom (that is, **E**,
Dt 2: 4 the descendants of **E**, who live in Seir.
2: 5 I have given Mount Seir to **E** as a possession.
2: 8 the descendants of **E** who live in Seir,
2:12 but the descendants of **E** dispossessed them,
2:22 He did the same for the descendants of **E**,
2:29 as the descendants of **E** who live in Seir have done
Jos 24: 4 and to Isaac I gave Jacob and **E**.
24: 4 I gave **E** the hill country of Seir to possess,
1Ch 1:34 The sons of Isaac: **E** and Israel.
1:35 The sons of **E**: Eliphaz, Reuel,
Jer 49: 8 For I will bring the calamity of **E** upon him,
49:10 But as for me, I have stripped **E** bare,
Ob 1: 6 **E** has been pillaged, his treasures searched out!
1: 8 and understanding out of Mount **E**.
1: 9 so that everyone from Mount **E** will be cut off.
1:18 and the house of **E** stubble;
1:18 and there shall be no survivor of the house of **E**;
1:19 Those of the Negeb shall possess Mount **E**,
1:21 up to Mount Zion to rule Mount **E**;
Mal 1: 2 Is not **E** Jacob's brother?
1: 3 but I have hated **E**; I have made his hill country
Ro 9:13 "I have loved Jacob, but I have hated **E**."
Heb 11:20 for the future on Jacob and **E**.
12:16 See to it that no one becomes like **E**,
1Mc 5: 3 But Judas made war on the descendants of **E**
5:65 and fought the descendants of **E** in the land to
1Es 5:29 the descendants of **E**, the descendants of Hasupha,
2Es 3:15 and to Isaac you gave Jacob and **E**.
3:16 for yourself, but **E** you rejected;
6: 8 because from him were born Jacob and **E**,
6: 9 Now **E** is the end of this age,

ESAU'S (14) [ESAU]

Ge 25:26 with his hand gripping **E** heel;
27:23 his hands were hairy like his brother **E** hands;
28: 5 the brother of Rebekah, Jacob's and **E** mother.
36:10 These are the names of **E** sons:
36:10 Reuel, the son of **E** wife Basemath.
36:12 (Timna was a concubine of Eliphaz, **E** son;
36:12 These were the sons of Adah, **E** wife.
36:13 These were the sons of **E** wife, Basemath.
36:14 These were the sons of **E** wife Oholibamah,
36:17 These are the sons of **E** son Reuel:
36:17 they are the sons of **E** wife Basemath.
36:18 These are the sons of **E** wife Oholibamah:
36:18 these are the clans born of **E** wife Oholibamah,
2Es 6: 8 for Jacob's hand held **E** heel from the beginning.

ESCAPE‡ (92) [ESCAPED, ESCAPES, ESCAPING]

Ge 7: 7 and his sons' wives went into the ark to **e**
19:20 and it is a little one. Let me **e** there—
19:22 **e** there, for I can do nothing
32: 8 then the company that is left will **e**."
Ex 1:10 join our enemies and fight against us and **e** from
Lev 26:37 as if to **e** a sword, though no one pursues;
1Sa 23:28 therefore that place was called the Rock of **E**.
27: 1 there is nothing better for me than to **e** to the land
27: 1 and I shall **e** out of his hand."
2Sa 15:14 or there will be no **e** for us from Absalom.
20: 6 or he will find fortified cities for himself, and **e**
1Ki 18:40 do not let one of them **e**."
2Ki 10:24 "Whoever allows any of those to **e** whom I deliver
10:25 and kill them; let no one **e**."
Est 4:13 in the king's palace you will **e** any more than all
Job 11:20 all way of **e** will be lost to them,
15:30 they will not **e** from darkness;
20:20 in their greed they let nothing **e**.
22:30 they will **e** because of the cleanness
Ps 68:20 and to GOD, the Lord, belongs **e** from death.
88: 8 I am shut in so that I cannot **e**;
89:48 Who can **e** the power of Sheol?
141:10 the wicked fall into their own nets, while I alone **e**.
Pr 3:21 My child, do not let these **e** from your sight.
4:21 Do not let them **e** from your sight;
11:21 but those who are righteous will **e**.
12:13 but the righteous **e** from trouble.
19: 5 and a liar will not **e**.
Isa 15: 9 a lion for those of Moab who **e**,
20: 6 And we, how shall we **e**?' "
Jer 11:11 to bring disaster upon them that they cannot **e**;
25:35 and there shall be no **e** for the lords of the flock.
32: 4 not **e** out of the hands of the Chaldeans, but shall
34: 3 And you yourself shall not **e** from his hand,
38:18 and you yourself shall not **e** from their hand."
38:23 and you yourself shall not **e** from their hand,
44:14 in the land of Egypt shall **e** or survive or return to
44:28 And those who **e** the sword shall return from
46: 6 The swift cannot flee away, nor can the warrior **e**;
48: 8 upon every town, and no town shall **e**;
50:29 Encamp all around her; let no one **e**.
La 3: 7 He has walled me about so that I cannot **e**;
Eze 6: 8 Some of you shall **e** the sword among the nations
6: 9 Those of you who **e** shall remember me among
7:16 If any survivors **e**, they shall be found on
12:16 But I will let a few of them **e** from the sword,
15: 7 although they **e** from the fire,
17:15 Can one **e** who does such things?
17:15 Can he break the covenant and yet **e**?
17:18 and yet did all these things, he shall not **e**.
Da 11:41 and the main part of the Ammonites shall **e**
11:42 and the land of Egypt shall not **e**.
Hos 9: 6 For even if they **e** destruction,
Joel 2:32 and in Jerusalem there shall be those who **e**,
Am 9: 1 of them shall flee away, not one of them shall **e**.
Ob 1:17 But on Mount Zion there shall be those that **e**,
Zec 2: 7 **E** to Zion, you that live with daughter Babylon.
Mal 3:15 but when they put God to the test they **e**."
Mt 23:33 How can you **e** being sentenced to hell?
Mk 7:24 Yet he could not **e** notice,
Lk 21:36 that you may have the strength to **e** all these things
Ac 25:11 I am not trying to **e** death;
27:30 the sailors tried to **e** from the ship and had lowered
27:42 so that none might swim away and **e**;
Ro 2: 3 you will **e** the judgment of God?
1Th 5: 3 and there will be no **e**!
2Ti 2:26 and that they may **e** from the snare of the devil,
Heb 2: 3 how can we **e** if we neglect so great a salvation?
12:25 not **e** when they refused the one who warned them
on earth, how much less will we **e** if we reject
2Pe 1: 4 that through them you may **e** from the corruption
Tob 13: 2 and there is nothing that can **e** his hand.
Jdt 7:19 and there was no way of **e** from them.
AdE 4:11 there is no **e** for that person.
4:13 that you alone among all the Jews will **e** alive.
16: 4 even assume that they will **e** the evil-hating justice
Wis 1: 8 not **e** notice, and justice, when it punishes, will
16:15 To **e** from your hand is impossible;
Sir 6:35 and let no wise proverbs **e** you.
11:10 and by fleeing you will not **e**.
16:13 The sinner will not **e** with plunder,
27:19 And as you allow a bird to **e** from your hand,
LtJ 6:55 their priests will flee and **e**,
Sus 1:22 if I do not, I cannot **e** your hands.
1Mc 2:43 to **e** their troubles joined them
2Mc 6:26 yet whether I live or die I shall not **e** the hands of
7:31 will certainly not **e** the hands of God.
3Mc 4:19 that they had been bribed to contrive a means of **e**,
2Es 4:42 as a woman who is in labor makes haste to **e**
9: 7 be that all who will be saved and will be able to **e**
14:15 and hurry to **e** from these times.
4Mc 9:32 You will not **e**, you most abominable tyrant,

ESCAPED (66) [ESCAPE]

Ge 14:13 one who had **e** came and told Abram the Hebrew,
Dt 23:15 Slaves who have **e** to you from their owners shall
Jos 8:22 down until no one was left who survived or **e**.
Jdg 3:26 Ehud **e** while they delayed,
3:26 and passed beyond the sculptured stones, and **e**
3:29 able-bodied men; no one **e**.
1Sa 10:27 But there were seven thousand men who had **e**
19:10 David fled and **e** that night.
19:12 through the window; he fled away and **e**.
19:17 and let my enemy go, so that he has **e**?"
19:18 Now David fled and **e**; he came to Samuel
22: 1 David left there and **e** to the cave of Adullam;
22:20 named Abiathar, **e** and fled after David.
23:13 When Saul was told that David had **e** from Keilah,
30:17 of the next day. Not one of them **e**,
2Sa 1: 3 He said to him, "I have **e** from the camp of Israel."
4: 6 then Rechab and his brother Baanah **e**.
1Ki 20:20 but King Ben-hadad of Aram **e** on a horse with
2Ki 13: 5 so that they **e** from the hand of the Arameans;
19:37 and they **e** into the land of Ararat.
1Ch 4:43 the remnant of the Amalekites that had **e**,
2Ch 16: 7 the army of the king of Aram has **e** you.
20:24 on the ground; no one had **e**.
30: 6 to the remnant of you who have **e** from the hand of
36:20 He took into exile in Babylon those who had **e**
Ezr 9:15 but we have **e** as a remnant, as is now the case.
Ne 1: 2 those who had **e** the captivity,
1: 3 in the province who **e** captivity are in great trouble
Job 1:15 I alone have **e** to tell you."
1:16 I alone have **e** to tell you."
1:17 I alone have **e** to tell you."
1:19 I alone have **e** to tell you."
19:20 and I have **e** by the skin of my teeth.
Ps 124: 7 We have **e** like a bird from the snare of
124: 7 the snare is broken, and we have **e**.
Isa 37:38 and they **e** into the land of Ararat.
Jer 26:21 he was afraid and fled and **e** to Egypt.
41:15 But Ishmael son of Nethaniah **e** from Johanan
La 2:22 and on the day of the anger of the LORD no one **e**
Eze 24:26 one who has **e** will come to you to report to you
24:27 be opened to the one who has **e**,
33:21 someone who had **e** from Jerusalem came to me
Na 3:19 For who has ever **e** your endless cruelty?
Jn 10:39 but he **e** from their hands.
Ac 16:27 since he supposed that the prisoners had **e**.
26:26 that none of these things has **e** his notice,
28: 4 though he has **e** from the sea,
2Co 11:33 in a basket through a window in the wall, and **e**
Heb 11:34 **e** the edge of the sword,
2Pe 2:18 of the flesh they entice people who have just **e**
2:20 after they have **e** the defilements of the world
Tob 14:10 Ahikar **e** the fatal trap that Nadab had set for him,
Wis 10: 6 he **e** the fire that descended on the Five Cities.
15:19 but they have **e** both the praise of God
Sir 27:20 and has **e** like a gazelle from a snare.
34:13 but have **e** because of these experiences.
40: 6 by the visions of his mind like one who has **e** from
1Mc 4:26 Those of the foreigners who **e** went and reported
6:21 of the garrison **e** from the siege and some of
15:37 Meanwhile Trypho embarked on a ship and **e**
2Mc 7:35 You have not yet **e** the judgment of the almighty,
11:12 and Lysias himself **e** by disgraceful flight.
12:35 so Gorgias **e** and reached Marisa.
3Mc 5:13 the Jews, since they had **e** the appointed hour,
6:29 since they now had **e** death.
2Es 7:96 now **e** what is corruptible and shall inherit what is

ESCAPES (6) [ESCAPE]

Lev 4:13 of Israel errs unintentionally and the matter **e**
1Ki 19:17 Whoever **e** from the sword of Hazael,
19:17 and whoever **e** from the sword of Jehu,
Ecc 7:26 one who pleases God **e** her,
Joel 2: 3 a desolate wilderness, and nothing **e** them.
Sir 42:20 No thought **e** him, and nothing is hidden from him.

ESCAPING (1) [ESCAPE]

Jer 48:19 Ask the man fleeing and the woman **e**;

ESCHEW (KJV) See TURN AWAY FROM

ESCORT (5) [ESCORTED]

2Sa 19:31 he went on with the king to the Jordan, to **e** him
Jdt 10:15 some of us will **e** you and hand you over to him.
AdE 1:11 to **e** the queen to him in order to proclaim her
1Mc 9:37 from Nadabath with a large **e**."
1Es 8:51 the king for foot soldiers and cavalry and an **e**

ESCORTED (1) [ESCORT]

Ac 21: 5 with wives and children, **e** us outside the city.

ESDRAELON (4)

Jdt 1: 8 and Upper Galilee and the great plain of **E**,
3: 9 Then he came toward **E**, near Dothan,
4: 6 which faces **E** opposite the plain near Dothan,
7: 3 from Bethulia to Cyamon, which faces **E**.

ESDRIS (1)

2Mc 12:36 As **E** and his men had been fighting for

ESEK (1)

Ge 26:20 So he called the well **E**,

ESH-BAAL (2) [=ISHBAAL]

1Ch 8:33 Saul of Jonathan, Malchishua, Abinadab, and **E**;
9:39 Saul of Jonathan, Malchishua, Abinadab, and **E**;

ESHAN (1)

Jos 15:52 Arab, Dumah, **E**,

ESHBAN (2)

Ge 36:26 Hemdan, **E**, Ithran, and Cheran.
1Ch 1:41 sons of Dishon: Hamran, **E**, Ithran, and Cheran.

ESHCOL (6)

Ge 14:13 brother of **E** and of Aner;
14:24 of the men who went with me—Aner, **E**,
Nu 13:23 And they came to the Wadi **E**,
13:24 That place was called the Wadi **E**,
32: 9 they went up to the Wadi **E** and saw the land,
Dt 1:24 they reached the Valley of **E** they spied it out

ESHEAN (KJV) See ESHAN

ESHEK (1)

1Ch 8:39 The sons of his brother **E**:

ESHKALONITES (KJV) See ASHKELON

ESHTAOL (7) [ESHTAOLITES]

Jos 15:33 And in the Lowland, **E**, Zorah, Ashnah,
19:41 The territory of its inheritance included Zorah, **E**,
Jdg 13:25 to stir him in Mahaneh-dan, between Zorah and **E**.
16:31 and buried him between Zorah and **E** in the tomb
18: 2 and from **E**, to spy out the land and to explore it;
18: 8 When they came to their kinsfolk at Zorah and **E**,
18:11 set out from Zorah and **E**,

ESHTAOLITES (1) [ESHTAOL]

1Ch 2:53 from these came the Zorathites and the **E**.

ESHTEMOA (5)

Jos 21:14 with its pasture lands, **E** with its pasture lands,
1Sa 30:28 in Aroer, in Siphmoth, in **E**,
1Ch 4:17 Shammai, and Ishbah father of **E**.
4:19 were the fathers of Keilah the Garmite and **E**
6:57 Jattir, **E** with its pasture lands,

ESHTEMOH (1)

Jos 15:50 Anab, **E**, Anim,

ESHTON (2)

1Ch 4:11 who was the father of **E**.
4:12 **E** became the father of Beth-rapha, Paseah,

ESLI (1)

Lk 3:25 son of Nahum, son of **E**, son of Naggai,

ESPECIALLY (19) [SPECIAL]

Jos 2: 1 saying, "Go, view the land, **e** Jericho."
Jn 19:31 **e** because that sabbath was a day

Ac 20:38 grieving e because of what he had said,
25:26 and e before you, King Agrippa, so that,
26: 3 because you are e familiar with all the customs
1Co 14: 1 and e that you may prophesy.
Gal 6:10 and e for those of the family of faith.
Php 4:22 e those of the emperor's household.
1Ti 4:10 the Savior of all people, e of those who believe.
5: 8 and e for family members,
5:17 e those who labor in preaching and teaching;
Tit 1:10 e those of the circumcision;
Phm 1:16 e to me but how much more to you,
2Pe 2:10 —e those who indulge their flesh in depraved lust,
Sir Pr: 1 who had devoted himself e to the reading of
2Mc 7:20 The mother was e admirable and worthy
10:32 to a stronghold called Gazara, e well garrisoned,
3Mc 5: 3 of his Friends and of the army who were e hostile
4Mc 15: 4 E is this true of mothers,

ESPIED, ESPY (KJV) See SAW, SEARCHED OUT, WATCH, SPY

ESPOUSALS, ESPOUSED (KJV) See BRIDE, ENGAGED, PROMISED, WEDDING

ESROM (KJV) See HEZRON

ESSENTIAL (2) [ESSENTIALS]

2Mc 4:23 the king and to complete the records of e business.
4Mc 1: 2 For the subject is e to everyone

ESSENTIALS (1) [ESSENTIAL]

Ac 15:28 to impose on you no further burden than these e:

ESTABLISH‡ (46) [ESTABLISHED, ESTABLISHES, ESTABLISHING, ESTABLISHMENT, RE-ESTABLISHED]

Ge 6:18 But I will e my covenant with you;
9:11 I e my covenant with you,
17: 7 I will e my covenant between me and you,
17:19 I will e my covenant with him as
17:21 But my covenant I will e with Isaac,
Dt 28: 9 The LORD will e you as his holy people,
29:13 in order that he may e you today as his people,
1Sa 1:23 may the LORD e his word."
2Sa 7:12 and I will e his kingdom.
7:13 and I will e the throne of his kingdom forever.
1Ki 2: 4 Then the LORD will e his word that he spoke
6:12 then I will e my promise with you,
9: 5 then I will e your royal throne over Israel forever,
20:34 and you may e bazaars for yourself in Damascus,
1Ch 17:11 one of your own sons, and I will e his kingdom.
17:12 and I will e his throne forever.
22:10 and I will e his royal throne in Israel forever.'
28: 7 I will e his kingdom forever
2Ch 7:18 then I will e your royal throne,
9: 8 your God loved Israel and would e them forever,
Ne 1: 9 to the place at which I have chosen to e my name.'
Job 38:33 Can you e their rule on the earth?
Ps 7: 9 an end, but e the righteous, you who test the minds
76: 9 when God rose up to e judgment,
87: 5 for the Most High himself will e it.
89: 4 'I will e your descendants forever,
89:29 I will e his line forever,
107:36 and they e a town to live in;
Isa 9: 7 He will e and uphold it with justice and
49: 8 to e the land, to apportion the desolate heritages;
Jer 33: 2 the LORD who formed it to e it—
Eze 16:60 and I will e with you an everlasting covenant.
16:62 I will e my covenant with you,
Da 6: 7 and the governors are agreed that the king should e
6: 8 O king, e the interdict and sign the document,
Am 5:15 Hate evil and love good, and e justice in the gate;
Ro 10: 3 and seeking to e their own,
Heb 8: 8 when I will e a new covenant with the house
10: 9 He abolishes the first in order to e the second.
1Pe 5:10 support, strengthen, and e you.
Sir 40:19 Children and the building of a city e one's name,
1Mc 8:17 sent them to Rome to e friendship and alliance,
8:20 of the Jews have sent us to you to e alliance
10:54 now therefore let us e friendship with one another;
2Mc 4: 9 to e by his authority a gymnasium and a body
4:11 on the mission to e friendship and alliance with

ESTABLISHED‡ (115) [ESTABLISH]

Ge 9:17 the sign of the covenant that I have e between me
Ex 6: 4 I also e my covenant with them,
15:17 the sanctuary, O LORD, that your hands have e.
Lev 26:46 that the LORD e between himself and the people
Nu 21:27 let the city of Sihon be e.
Dt 13:14 If the charge is e that such
32: 6 who created you, who made you and e you?
1Sa 13:13 The LORD would have e your kingdom
20:31 neither you nor your kingdom shall be e.
24:20 that the kingdom of Israel shall be e in your hand.
2Sa 5:12 then perceived that the LORD had e him king
7:16 your throne shall be e forever.
7:24 And you e your people Israel for yourself to
7:26 house of your servant David will be e before you.
1Ki 2:12 and his kingdom was firmly e.
2:24 who has e me and placed me on the throne
1Ki 2:45 of David shall be e before the LORD forever."
2:46 So the kingdom was e in the hand of Solomon.
2Ki 23:24 so that he e the words of the law that were written
1Ch 9:22 and the seer Samuel e them in their office of trust.
14: 2 then perceived that the LORD had e him as king
16:30 The world is firmly e; it shall never be moved.
17:14 and his throne shall be e forever.
17:23 let it be e forever, and do as you have promised.
17:24 Thus your name will be e and magnified forever in
17:24 of your servant David will be e in your presence.
24:19 the LORD according to the procedure e for them
2Ch 1: 1 Solomon son of David e himself in his kingdom;
12: 1 the rule of Rehoboam was e and he grew strong,
12:13 So King Rehoboam e himself in Jerusalem
17: 5 Therefore the LORD e the kingdom in his hand.
20:20 in the LORD your God and you will be e;
21: 4 the throne of his father and was e,
Ezr 6:12 God who has e his name there overthrow any king
Ne 13:30 and I e the duties of the priests and Levites,
Est 9:27 the Jews e and accepted as a custom
Job 21: 8 Their children are e in their presence,
22:28 and it will be e for you,
28:27 he e it, and searched it out.
Ps 8: 3 the moon and the stars that you have e;
9: 7 he has e his throne for judgment.
24: 2 and e it on the rivers.
30: 7 O LORD, you had e me as a strong mountain;
65: 6 By your strength you e the mountains;
74:16 you e the luminaries and the sun.
76: 2 His abode has been e in Salem,
78: 5 He e a decree in Jacob, and appointed a law
89: 2 I declare that your steadfast love is e forever;
89:37 It shall be e forever like the moon,
93: 1 He has e the world;
93: 2 your throne is e from of old;
96:10 The world is firmly e; it shall never be moved.
99: 4 Mighty King, lover of justice, you have e equity;
102:28 their offspring shall be e in your presence.
103:19 The LORD has e his throne in the heavens,
111: 8 They are e forever and ever,
119:90 you have e the earth, and it stands fast.
119:152 from your decrees that you have e them forever.
140:11 Do not let the slanderer be e in the land;
148: 6 He e them forever and ever;
Pr 3:19 by understanding he e the heavens;
8:27 When he e the heavens, I was there,
8:28 when he e the fountains of the deep,
10:25 but the righteous are e forever.
16: 3 and your plans will be e.
16:12 for the throne is e by righteousness.
19:21 but it is the purpose of the LORD that will be e.
20:18 Plans are e by taking advice;
24: 3 and by understanding it is e;
25: 5 and his throne will be e in righteousness.
29:14 his throne will be e forever.
30: 4 Who has e all the ends of the earth?
Isa 2: 2 of the LORD's house shall be e as the highest of
16: 5 then a throne shall be e in steadfast love in the tent
42: 4 not grow faint or be crushed until he has e justice
45:18 who formed the earth and made it (he e it;
54:14 In righteousness you shall be e;
Jer 10:12 who e the world by his wisdom,
30:20 their congregation shall be e before me;
33:25 if I had not e my covenant with day and night and
51:15 who e the world by his wisdom,
Da 2:38 and whom he has e as ruler over them all—
Mic 4: 1 of the LORD's house shall be e as the highest of
Hab 1:12 and you, O Rock, have e them for punishment.
Col 1:23 that you continue securely e and steadfast in
2: 7 rooted and built up in him and e in the faith,
Heb 9:16 the death of the one who made it must be e.
2Pe 1:12 though you know them already and are e in
Tob 1: 4 and e for all generations forever.
AdE 9:26 what had befallen them, Mordecai e this festival,
9:31 And Mordecai and Queen Esther e this decision
9:32 Esther e it by a decree forever,
Sir 17:12 He e with them an eternal covenant,
24:10 and so I was e in Zion.
31:11 be e, and the assembly will proclaim his acts
42:17 which the Lord the Almighty has e so that
45:24 a covenant of friendship was e with him,
45:25 Just as a covenant was e with David son of Jesse
46:13 of the Lord, he e the kingdom and anointed rulers
1Mc 1:16 When Antiochus saw that his kingdom was e,
10:52 on the throne of my ancestors, and e my rule—
14:11 He e peace in the land,
14:18 and alliance that they had e with his brothers Judas
14:26 and repulsed Israel's enemies and e its freedom."
2Mc 13: 3 because he thought that he would be e in office.
14:15 and prayed to him who e his own people forever
3Mc 3: 5 they were e in good repute with everyone.
3:26 for the remaining time the government will be e
7: 4 that our government would never be firmly e
2Es 6: 3 and before the powers of movements were e,
6: 4 and before the footstool of Zion was e,
8:23 and whose truth is e forever—
8:52 goodness is e and wisdom perfected beforehand.
4Mc 5:25 for since we believe that the law was e by God,
13:23 sympathy and brotherly affection had been so e,

ESTABLISHES‡ (4) [ESTABLISH]

Ps 48: 8 in the city of our God, which God e forever.
Isa 62: 7 until he e Jerusalem and makes it renowned
Da 6:15 that no interdict or ordinance that the king e can
2Co 1:21 But it is God who e us with you in Christ

ESTABLISHING (3) [ESTABLISH]

Ge 9: 9 I am e my covenant with you
1Ki 15: 4 setting up his son after him, and e Jerusalem;
2Mc 4:12 He took delight in e a gymnasium right under

ESTABLISHMENT (1) [ESTABLISH]

2Ch 36:20 to him and to his sons until the e of the kingdom

ESTATE (8)

1Ki 2:26 "Go to Anathoth, to your e; for you deserve death.
Ps 62: 9 Those of low e are but a breath, those of high e are a delusion;
136:23 It is he who remembered us in our low e,
Pr 20:21 An e quickly acquired in the beginning will not
Jdt 8: 7 and she maintained this e.
16:21 Judith went to Bethulia, and remained on her e.
2Es 9:45 and looked upon my low e,

ESTEEM (5) [ESTEEMED, SELF-ESTEEM]

Ne 6:16 and fell greatly in their own e;
Ac 5:13 but the people held them in high e.
1Th 5:13 e them very highly in love because of their work.
Sir 10:28 and give yourself the e you deserve.
2Mc 9:21 I remember with affection your e and goodwill.

ESTEEMED‡ (2) [ESTEEM]

2Sa 16:23 so all the counsel of Ahithophel was e,
Sir 40:25 but good counsel is e more than either.

ESTHER (95) [ESTHER'S]

Est 2: 7 Mordecai had brought up Hadassah, that is E,
2: 8 E also was taken into the king's palace and put
2:10 E did not reveal her people or kindred,
2:11 to learn how E was and how she fared.
2:15 the turn came for E daughter of Abihail the uncle
2:15 Now E was admired by all who saw her.
2:16 When E was taken to King Ahasuerus
2:17 the king loved E more than all the other women;
2:20 Now E had not revealed her kindred or her people,
2:20 for E obeyed Mordecai just as
2:22 he told it to Queen E, and E told the king in the
4: 5 Then E called for Hathach,
4: 8 that he might show it to E, explain it to her,
4: 9 Hathach went and told E what Mordecai had said.
4:10 Then E spoke to Hathach and gave him a message
4:12 When they told Mordecai what E had said,
4:13 Mordecai told them to reply to E,
4:15 Then E said in reply to Mordecai,
4:17 and did everything as E had ordered him.
5: 1 the third day E put on her royal robes and stood in
5: 2 as the king saw Queen E standing in the court,
5: 2 E approached and touched the top of the scepter.
5: 3 The king said to her, "What is it, Queen E?
5: 4 Then E said, "If it pleases the king,
5: 5 so that we may do as E desires."
5: 5 to the banquet that E had prepared.
5: 6 While they were drinking wine, the king said to E,
5: 7 Then E said, "This is my petition and request:
5:12 "Even Queen E let no one but myself come with
6:14 to the banquet that E had prepared.
7: 1 king and Haman went in to feast with Queen E.
7: 2 the king again said to E, "What is your petition,
7: 2 "What is your petition, Queen E?
7: 3 Then Queen E answered,
7: 5 Then King Ahasuerus said to Queen E,
7: 6 E said, "A foe and enemy, this wicked Haman!"
7: 7 but Haman stayed to beg his life from Queen E,
7: 8 on the couch where E was reclining;
8: 1 to Queen E the house of Haman, the enemy of
8: 1 for E had told what he was to her.
8: 2 So E set Mordecai over the house of Haman.
8: 3 Then E spoke again to the king;
8: 4 The king held out the golden scepter to E,
8: 5 and E rose and stood before the king.
8: 7 Then King Ahasuerus said to Queen E and to
8: 7 "See, I have given E the house of Haman,
9:12 The king said to Queen E,
9:13 E said, "If it pleases the king,
9:25 but when E came before the king,
9:29 Queen E daughter of Abihail,
9:31 Jew Mordecai and Queen E enjoined on the Jews,
9:32 The command of Queen E fixed these practices
AdE 2: 7 Aminadab, and her name was E.
2: 8 E also was brought to Gai,
2:10 Now E had not disclosed her people or country,
2:11 to see what would happen to E.
2:15 the time was fulfilled for E daughter of Aminadab,
2:15 Now E found favor in the eyes of all who saw her.
2:16 So E went in to King Artaxerxes in
2:17 the king loved E and she found favor beyond all
2:18 and the officers to celebrate his marriage to E;
2:20 E had not disclosed her country—
2:20 So E did not change her mode of life.
2:22 and he warned E, who in turn revealed the plot to
4: 5 Then E summoned Hachratheus,
4: 8 in Susa for their destruction, to show to E;
4: 9 Hachratheus went in and told E all these things.
4:13 to her, "E, do not say to yourself that you alone
4:15 Then E gave the messenger this answer
4:17 and did what E had told him to do.
5: 3 The king said to her, "What do you wish, E?
5: 4 And E said, "Today is a special day for me.
5: 5 so that we may do as E desires."
5: 5 both came to the dinner that E had spoken about.

AdE 5: 6 the king said to **E,** "What is it, Queen **E?**
6:14 to the banquet that **E** had prepared.
7: 2 the king said, "What is it, Queen **E?**
7: 6 **E** said, "Our enemy is this evil man Haman!"
8: 1 On that very day King Artaxerxes granted to **E** all
8: 1 for **E** had told the king that he was related to her.
8: 2 and **E** set Mordecai over everything
8: 4 The king extended his golden scepter to **E,**
8: 5 **E** said, "If it pleases you,
8: 7 The king said to **E,** "Now that I have granted all
9:12 The king said to **E,** "In Susa, the capital,
9:13 And **E** said to the king,
9:29 Then Queen **E** daughter of Aminadab along
9:31 and Queen **E** established this decision
9:32 **E** established it by a decree forever,
10: 6 the river is **E,** whom the king married
14: 1 Then Queen **E,** seized with deadly anxiety,
15: 9 "What is it, **E?** I am your husband. Take courage;
16:13 and of **E,** the blameless partner of our kingdom,

ESTHER'S (2) [ESTHER]

Est 2:18 to all his officials and ministers—"**E** banquet."
4: 4 When **E** maids and her eunuchs came and told her,

ESTIMATE (1)

Lk 14:28 does not first sit down and **e** the cost,

ESTRANGED (9)

Job 19:13 and my acquaintances are wholly **e** from me.
Isa 1: 4 the Holy One of Israel, who are utterly **e!**
Eze 14: 5 all of whom are **e** from me through their idols.
Col 1:21 And you who were once **e** and hostile in mind,
1Mc 11:12 He was **e** from Alexander,
11:53 he became **e** from Jonathan and did not repay
12:10 so that we may not become **e** from you,
15:27 with Simon, and became **e** from him.
2Es 6: 5 the imaginations of those who now sin were **e,** and

ESYELUS See Index to Footnotes

ETAM (5)

Jdg 15: 8 down and stayed in the cleft of the rock of **E.**
15:11 of Judah went down to the cleft of the rock of **E,**
1Ch 4: 3 These were the sons of **E:**
4:32 And their villages were **E,** Ain, Rimmon, Tochen,
2Ch 11: 6 He built up Bethlehem, **E,** Tekoa,

ETERNAL[‡] (94) [ETERNITY]

A. ETERNAL LIFE (44)

Ge 49:26 the blessings of the **e** mountains, the bounties of
Ecc 12: 5 because all must go to their **e** home,
Jer 20:11 Their **e** dishonor will never be forgotten.
Hab 3: 6 The **e** mountains were shattered;
Mt 18: 8 or two feet and to be thrown into the **e** fire.
19:16 what good deed must I do to have **e** life?" A
19:29 receive a hundredfold, and will inherit **e** life. A
25:41 the **e** fire prepared for the devil and his angels;
25:46 And these will go away into **e** punishment,
25:46 but the righteous into **e** life." A
Mk 3:29 but is guilty of an **e** sin"—
10:17 "Good Teacher, what must I do to inherit **e** life?" A
10:30 and in the age to come **e** life. A
16: S ⟦and imperishable proclamation of **e** salvation.⟧
Lk 10:25 he said, "what must I do to inherit **e** life?" A
16: 9 they may welcome you into the **e** homes.
18:18 "Good Teacher, what must I do to inherit **e** life?" A
18:30 and in the age to come **e** life." A
Jn 3:15 that whoever believes in him may have **e** life. A
3:16 in him may not perish but may have **e** life. A
3:36 Whoever believes in the Son has **e** life; A
4:14 in them a spring of water gushing up to **e** life." A
4:36 and is gathering fruit for **e** life, A
5:24 and believes him who sent me has **e** life, A
5:39 because you think that in them you have **e** life; A
6:27 but for the food that endures for **e** life, A
6:40 the Son and believe in him may have **e** life, A
6:47 truly, I tell you, whoever believes has **e** life. A
6:54 and drink my blood have **e** life, A
6:68 You have the words of **e** life. A
10:28 I give them **e** life, and they will never perish. A
12:25 in this world will keep it for **e** life. A
12:50 And I know that his commandment is **e** life. A
17: 2 to give **e** life to all whom you have given him. A
17: 3 And this is **e** life, that they may know you, A
Ac 13:46 and judge yourselves to be unworthy of **e** life, A
13:48 as had been destined for **e** life became believers. A
Ro 1:20 Ever since the creation of the world his **e** power
2: 7 and honor and immortality, he will give **e** life; A
5:21 to **e** life through Jesus Christ our Lord. A
6:22 The end is **e** life. A
6:23 free gift of God is **e** life in Christ Jesus our Lord. A
16:26 according to the command of the **e** God,
2Co 4:17 for an **e** weight of glory beyond all measure,
4:18 but what cannot be seen is **e.**
5: 1 a house not made with hands, **e** in the heavens.
Gal 6: 8 you will reap **e** life from the Spirit. A
Eph 3:11 This was in accordance with the **e** purpose
2Th 1: 9 These will suffer the punishment of **e** destruction,
2:16 who loved us and through grace gave us **e** comfort
1Ti 1:16 to believe in him for **e** life. A
6:12 take hold of the **e** life, A
6:16 to him be honor and **e** dominion.
2Ti 2:10 the salvation that is in Christ Jesus, with **e** glory.
Tit 1: 2 of **e** life that God, who never lies, promised A
3: 7 according to the hope of **e** life. A
Heb 5: 9 the source of **e** salvation for all who obey him,
6: 2 resurrection of the dead, and **e** judgment.
9:12 thus obtaining **e** redemption.
9:14 the **e** Spirit offered himself without blemish
9:15 the promised **e** inheritance,
13:20 by the blood of the **e** covenant,
1Pe 5:10 who has called you to his **e** glory in Christ,
2Pe 1:11 entry into the **e** kingdom of our Lord
1Jn 1: 2 and declare to you the **e** life that was with A
2:25 And this is what he has promised us, **e** life. A
3:15 murderers do not have **e** life abiding in them. A
5:11 God gave us **e** life, and this life is in his Son. A
5:13 so that you may know that you have **e** life. A
5:20 He is the true God and **e** life. A
Jude 1: 6 in **e** chains in deepest darkness for the judgment of
1: 7 an example by undergoing a punishment of **e** fire.
1:21 of our Lord Jesus Christ that leads to **e** life. A
Rev 14: 6 with an **e** gospel to proclaim to those who live on
Tob 3: 6 release me to go to the **e** home, and do not,
14: 7 and in righteousness they will praise the **e** God.
14:10 but Nadab went into the **e** darkness,
Wis 7:26 For she is a reflection of **e** light,
17: 2 shut in under their roofs, exiles from **e** providence.
Sir 1:15 She made among human beings an **e** foundation,
16:27 he arranged his works in an **e** order,
17:12 He established with them an **e** covenant,
30:17 and **e** sleep than chronic sickness.
46:19 Before the time of his **e** sleep,
Sus 1:42 "O **e** God, you know what is secret and are aware
2Mc 1:25 you alone are just and almighty and **e.**
3Mc 6:12 O **E** One, who have all might and all power,
7:16 of their ancestors, the **e** Savior of Israel, in words
4Mc 9: 9 from the divine justice **e** torment by fire."
10:15 by the **e** destruction of the tyrant,
12:12 justice has laid up for you intense and **e** fire
13:15 of **e** torment lying before those who transgress
15: 3 the religion that preserves them for **e** life A
17:18 the divine throne and live the life of **e** blessedness.

ETERNITY (9) [ETERNAL]

Isa 45:17 not be put to shame or confounded to all **e.**
57:15 thus says the high and lofty one who inhabits **e,**
2Pe 3:18 To him be the glory both now and to the day of **e.**
Wis 2:23 and made us in the image of his own **e,**
Sir 1: 2 sand of the sea, the drops of rain, and the days of **e**
1: 4 and prudent understanding from **e.**
18:10 so are a few years among the days of **e.**
42:21 he is from all **e** one and the same.
2Es 8:20 you who inhabit **e,** whose eyes are exalted

ETH-KAZIN (1)

Jos 19:13 to **E,** and going on to Rimmon it bends

ETHAM (4)

Ex 13:20 They set out from Succoth, and camped at **E,**
Nu 33: 6 They set out from Succoth, and camped at **E,**
33: 7 They set out from **E,** and turned back
33: 8 went a three days' journey in the wilderness of **E,**

ETHAN (7) [ETHAN'S]

1Ki 4:31 wiser than **E** the Ezrahite, and Heman, Calcol,
1Ch 2: 6 Zimri, **E,** Heman, Calcol, and Dara, five in all.
6:42 son of **E,** son of Zimmah, son of Shimei,
6:44 **E** son of Kishi, son of Abdi, son of Malluch,
15:17 their kindred, **E** son of Kushaiah;
15:19 Asaph, and **E** were to sound bronze cymbals;
Ps 89: T *A Maskil of **E** the Ezrahite.*

ETHAN'S (1) [ETHAN]

1Ch 2: 8 and **E** son was Azariah.

ETHANIM (1)

1Ki 8: 2 to King Solomon at the festival in the month **E,**

ETHANUS (1)

2Es 14:24 and take with you Sarea, Dabria, Selemia, **E,**

ETHBAAL (1)

1Ki 16:31 he took as his wife Jezebel daughter of King **E** of

ETHER (2)

Jos 15:42 Libnah, **E,** Ashan,
19: 7 Rimmon, **E,** and Ashan—

ETHIOPIA[‡] (27) [ETHIOPIAN, ETHIOPIANS]

2Ki 19: 9 the king heard concerning King Tirhakah of **E,**
Est 1: 1 hundred twenty-seven provinces from India to **E.**
8: 9 and the officials of the provinces from India to **E,**
Job 28:19 The chrysolite of **E** cannot compare with it,
Ps 68:31 let **E** hasten to stretch out its hands to God.
87: 4 Philistia too, and Tyre, with **E**—
Isa 11:11 from Assyria, from Egypt, from Pathros, from **E,**
18: 1 Ah, land of whirring wings beyond the rivers of **E,**
20: 3 as a sign and a portent against Egypt and **E,**
20: 5 because of **E** their hope and of Egypt their boast.
37: 9 the king heard concerning King Tirhakah of **E,**
43: 3 **E** and Seba in exchange for you.
45:14 The wealth of Egypt and the merchandise of **E,**
Jer 46: 9 **E** and Put who carry the shield, the Ludim,
Eze 29:10 from Migdol to Syene, as far as the border of **E.**
Eze 30: 4 and anguish shall be in **E,**
30: 5 **E,** and Put, and Lud, and all Arabia, and Libya,
38: 5 Persia, **E,** and Put are with them,
Na 3: 9 **E** was her strength, Egypt too,
Zep 3:10 From beyond the rivers of **E** my suppliants,
Jdt 1:10 all who lived in Egypt as far as the borders of **E.**
AdE 1: 1 hundred twenty-seven provinces from India to **E.**
3:12 the governors in every province from India to **E.**
8: 9 and governors of the provinces from Media to **E,**
13: 1 from India to **E** and to the officials under them:
16: 1 to the governors of the provinces from India to **E,**
1Es 3: 2 hundred twenty-seven satrapies from India to **E.**

ETHIOPIAN (6) [ETHIOPIA]

2Ch 14: 9 Zerah the **E** came out against them with an army
Jer 38: 7 Ebed-melech the **E,** a eunuch in the king's house,
38:10 Then the king commanded Ebed-melech the **E,**
38:12 Then Ebed-melech the **E** said to Jeremiah,
39:16 Go and say to Ebed-melech the **E:**
Ac 8:27 Now there was an **E** eunuch,

ETHIOPIANS (13) [ETHIOPIA]

2Ch 12: 3 from Egypt—Libyans, Sukkiim, and **E.**
14:12 So the LORD defeated the **E** before Asa and before Judah, and the **E** fled.
14:13 and the **E** fell until no one remained alive;
16: 8 Were not the **E** and the Libyans a huge army
21:16 and of the Arabs who are near the **E.**
Isa 20: 4 the Egyptians as captives and the **E** as exiles,
Jer 13:23 Can **E** change their skin or leopards their spots?
Eze 30: 9 from me in ships to terrify the unsuspecting **E;**
Da 11:43 and the Libyans and the **E** shall follow in his train.
Am 9: 7 Are you not like the **E** to me, O people of Israel?
Zep 2:12 You also, O **E,** shall be killed by my sword.
Ac 8:27 queen of the **E,** in charge of her entire treasury.

ETHNAN (1)

1Ch 4: 7 The sons of Helah: Zereth, Izhar, and **E.**

ETHNARCH[‡] (3)

1Mc 14:47 to be commander and **e** of the Jews and priests,
15: 1 the priest and **e** of the Jews, and to all the nation;
15: 2 the high priest and **e** and to the nation of the Jews,

ETHNI (1)

1Ch 6:41 son of **E,** son of Zerah, son of Adaiah,

EUBULUS (1)

2Ti 4:21 **E** sends greetings to you, as do Pudens and Linus

EUERGETES (1)

Sir Pr: 3 to Egypt in the thirty-eighth year of the reign of **E**

EUMENES (1)

1Mc 8: 8 These they took from him and gave to King **E.**

EUNICE (1)

2Ti 1: 5 in your grandmother Lois and your mother **E** and

EUNUCH (19) [EUNUCHS]

2Ki 23:11 by the chamber of the **e** Nathan-melech,
Est 2: 3 the king's **e,** who is in charge of the women;
2:14 the king's **e,** who was in charge of the concubines;
2:15 for nothing except what Hegai the king's **e,**
Isa 56: 3 and do not let the **e** say, "I am just a dry tree."
Jer 38: 7 a **e** in the king's house,
Ac 8:27 Now there was an Ethiopian **e,**
8:34 The **e** asked Philip, "About whom, may I ask you,
8:36 and the **e** said, "Look, here is water!
8:38 Philip and the **e,** went down into the water,
8:39 **e** saw him no more, and went on his way rejoicing.
Jdt 12:11 the **e** who had charge of his personal affairs,
AdE 2: 3 be entrusted to the king's **e** who is in charge of
2:14 where Gai the king's **e** is in charge of the women;
2:15 the **e** in charge of the women, had commanded.
4: 5 the **e** who attended her, and ordered him
Wis 3:14 the **e** whose hands have done no lawless deed,
Sir 20: 4 Like a **e** lusting to violate a girl is
30:20 and groans as a **e** groans when embracing a girl.

EUNUCHS (32) [EUNUCH]

2Ki 9:32 Two or three **e** looked out at him.
20:18 be **e** in the palace of the king of Babylon."
Est 1:10 Zethar and Carkas, the seven **e** who attended him,
1:12 to come at the king's command conveyed by the **e.**
1:15 of King Ahasuerus conveyed by the **e?"**
2:21 two of the king's **e,** who guarded the threshold,
4: 4 When Esther's maids and her **e** came and told her,
4: 5 Esther called for Hathach, one of the king's **e,**
6: 2 two of the king's **e,** who guarded the threshold,
6:14 the king's **e** arrived and hurried Haman off to
7: 9 Harbona, one of the **e** in attendance on the king,
Isa 39: 7 be **e** in the palace of the king of Babylon."
56: 4 To the **e** who keep my sabbaths,
Jer 34:19 the officials of Jerusalem, the **e,** the priests,
41:16 soldiers, women, children, and **e,**
Mt 19:12 For there are **e** who have been so from birth,
19:12 and there are **e** who have been made **e**
19:12 there are **e** who have made themselves **e**
AdE 1:10 the seven **e** who served King Artaxerxes,
1:12 to obey him and would not come with the **e.**
1:15 the order that the king had sent her by the **e.**

AdE 2:21 Now the king's **e**, who were chief bodyguards,
2:23 He investigated the two **e** and hanged them.
4: 4 When the queen's maids and **e** came and told her,
6: 2 the king about the two royal **e** who were on guard
6:14 the **e** arrived and hurriedly brought Haman to
7: 9 Then Bugathan, one of the **e**, said to the king,
12: 1 two **e** of the king who kept watch in the courtyard.
12: 3 Then the king examined the two **e**,
12: 6 and his people because of the two **e** of the king.

EUODIA (1)

Php 4: 2 I urge **E** and I urge Syntyche to be of

EUPATOR (5)

1Mc 6:17 from boyhood; he named him **E**.
2Mc 2:20 against Antiochus Epiphanes and his son **E**,
10:10 we will tell what took place under Antiochus **E**,
10:13 As a result he was accused before **E** by
13: 1 to Judas and his men that Antiochus **E** was coming

EUPHRATES (45)

Ge 2:14 And the fourth river is the **E**.
15:18 the river of Egypt to the great river, the river **E**,
31:21 starting out he crossed the **E**,
36:37 and Shaul of Rehoboth on the **E** succeeded him
Ex 23:31 and from the wilderness to the **E**;
Nu 22: 5 which is on the **E**, in the land of Amaw,
Dt 1: 7 as far as the great river, the river **E**.
11:24 the river **E**, to the Western Sea.
Jos 1: 4 the river **E**, all the land of the Hittites,
24: 2 lived beyond the **E** and served other gods.
2Sa 8: 3 as he went to restore his monument at the river **E**.
10:16 the Arameans who were beyond the **E**;
1Ki 4:21 from the **E** to the land of the Philistines,
4:24 the region west of the **E** from Tiphsah to Gaza,
4:24 over all the kings west of the **E**;
14:15 and scatter them beyond the **E**,
2Ki 23:29 up to the king of Assyria to the river **E**.
24: 7 of Egypt from the Wadi of Egypt to the River **E**.
1Ch 1:48 Shaul of Rehoboth on the **E** succeeded him.
5: 9 as the beginning of the desert this side of the **E**,
18: 3 as he went to set up a monument at the river **E**.
19:16 the Arameans who were beyond the **E**,
2Ch 9:26 the kings from the **E** to the land of the Philistines,
35:20 of Egypt went up to fight at Carchemish on the **E**,
Isa 27:12 the LORD will thresh from the channel of the **E**
Jer 2:18 to drink the waters of the **E**?
13: 4 and go now to the **E**,
13: 5 So I went, and hid it by the **E**,
13: 6 the LORD said to me, "Go now to the **E**, and take
13: 7 Then I went to the **E**, and dug,
46: 2 which was by the river **E** at Carchemish
46: 6 in the north by the river **E** they have stumbled
46:10 a sacrifice in the land of the north by the river **E**.
51:63 and throw it into the middle of the **E**,
Rev 9:14 the four angels who are bound at the great river **E**."
16:12 sixth angel poured his bowl on the great river **E**,
Jdt 1: 6 and all those who lived along the **E**,
2:24 the **E** and passed through Mesopotamia
Sir 24:26 It runs over, like the **E**, with understanding,
44:21 an inheritance from sea to sea and from the **E** to the
1Mc 3:32 of the king's affairs from the river **E** to the borders
3:37 the **E** river and went through the upper provinces.
1Es 1:25 went to make war at Carchemish on the **E**,
1:27 for my war is at the **E**.
2Es 13:43 they went in by the narrow passages of the **E** river.

EUPOLEMUS (2)

1Mc 8:17 So Judas chose **E** son of John son of Accos,
2Mc 4:11 secured through John the father of **E**,

EUROCLYDON (KJV) See NORTHEASTER

EUTYCHUS (1)

Ac 20: 9 A young man named **E**, who was sitting in

EVACUATED (2)

1Mc 6:49 with the people of Beth-zur, and they **e** the town
6:61 On these conditions the Jews **e** the stronghold.

EVANGELIST (2) [EVANGELISTS]

Ac 21: 8 and we went into the house of Philip the **e**,
2Ti 4: 5 do the work of an **e**, carry out your ministry fully.

EVANGELISTS (1) [EVANGELIST]

Eph 4:11 some prophets, some **e**, some pastors and teachers,

EVE (5)

Ge 3:20 The man named his wife **E**,
4: 1 Now the man knew his wife **E**,
2Co 11: 3 But I am afraid that as the serpent deceived **E**
1Ti 2:13 For Adam was formed first, then **E**;
Tob 8: 6 him you made his wife **E** as a helper and support.

EVEN (612) [EVENLY] See Index of Articles Etc.

EVENING‡ (155) [EVENINGS, EVENTIDE]

A. UNTIL [THE] EVENING (53)
B. IN THE EVENING (24)
C. MORNING ... EVENING (16)
D. EVENING ... MORNING (12)

Ge 1: 5 there was **e** and there was morning, the first day. D
1: 8 And there was **e** and there was morning, D
1:13 was **e** and there was morning, the third day. D
1:19 was **e** and there was morning, the fourth day. D
1:23 was **e** and there was morning, the fifth day. D
1:31 was **e** and there was morning, the sixth day. D
3: 8 in the garden at the time of the **e** breeze,
8:11 and the dove came back to him in the **e**, and B
19: 1 The two angels came to Sodom in the **e**, B
24:11 it was toward **e**, the time when women go out
24:63 Isaac went out in the **e** to walk in the field; B
29:23 in the **e** he took his daughter Leah and brought B
30:16 When Jacob came from the field in the **e**, B
49:27 and at **e** dividing the spoil."
Ex 12:18 from the **e** of the fourteenth day until the evening
12:18 until the **e** of the twenty-first day, A
16: 6 "In the **e** you shall know that it was B
16: 8 "When the LORD gives you meat to eat in the **e** B
16:13 In the **e** quails came up and covered the camp; B
18:13 stood around him from morning until **e**. AC
18:14 around you from morning until **e**?" AC
27:21 and his sons shall tend it from **e** to morning D
29:39 and the other lamb you shall offer in the **e**; B
29:41 And the other lamb you shall offer in the **e**, B
30: 8 and when Aaron sets up the lamps in the **e**, B
Lev 6:20 half of it in the morning and half in the **e**. BC
11:24 of any of them shall be unclean until the **e**, A
11:25 and be unclean until the **e**. A
11:27 of any of them shall be unclean until the **e**, A
11:28 and be unclean until the **e**; A
11:31 when they are dead shall be unclean until the **e**. A
11:32 and it shall be unclean until the **e**, A
11:39 touches its carcass shall be unclean until the **e**. A
11:40 and be unclean until the **e**; A
11:40 and be unclean until the **e**. A
14:46 while it is shut up shall be unclean until the **e**; A
15: 5 and bathe in water, and be unclean until the **e**. A
15: 6 and bathe in water, and be unclean until the **e**. A
15: 7 and bathe in water, and be unclean until the **e**. A
15: 8 and bathe in water, and be unclean until the **e**. A
15:10 that was under him shall be unclean until the **e**, A
15:10 and bathe in water, and be unclean until the **e**. A
15:11 and bathe in water, and be unclean until the **e**. A
15:16 and be unclean until the **e**. A
15:17 and be unclean until the **e**. A
15:18 and be unclean until the **e**. A
15:19 whoever touches her shall be unclean until the **e**. A
15:21 and bathe in water, and be unclean until the **e**. A
15:22 and bathe in water, and be unclean until the **e**; A
15:23 he touches it he shall be unclean until the **e**. A
15:27 and bathe in water, and be unclean until the **e**. A
17:15 and be unclean until the **e**; A
22: 6 until **e** and shall not eat of the sacred donations A
23:32 on the ninth day of the month at **e**,
23:32 from **e** to evening you shall keep your sabbath.
23:32 from evening to **e** you shall keep your sabbath.
24: 3 from **e** to morning before the LORD regularly; D
Nu 9:15 from **e** until morning it was over the tabernacle, D
9:21 the cloud would remain from **e** until morning; D
19: 7 but the priest shall remain unclean until **e**. A
19: 8 he shall remain unclean until **e**. A
19:10 shall wash his clothes and be unclean until **e**. A
19:19 and at **e** they shall be clean.
19:21 the water for cleansing shall be unclean until **e**. A
19:22 anyone who touches it shall be unclean until **e**. A
Dt 16: 4 on the **e** of the first day shall remain until morning.
16: 6 in the **e** at sunset, the time of day when B
23:11 When **e** comes, he shall wash himself with water,
28:67 In the morning you shall say, "If only it were **e**!"
28:67 at **e** you shall say, "If only it were morning!"—
Jos 5:10 in the **e** on the fourteenth day of the month in B
7: 6 the ark of the LORD until the **e**, he and the elders A
8:29 And he hanged the king of Ai on a tree until **e**; A
10:26 And they hung on the trees until **e**. A
Jdg 19: 9 "Look, the day has worn on until it is almost **e**.
19:16 at **e** there was an old man coming from his work
20:23 up and wept before the LORD until the **e**; A
20:26 they fasted that day until **e**. A
21: 2 and sat there until **e** before God, A
Ru 2:17 So she gleaned in the field until **e**. A
1Sa 14:24 "Cursed be anyone who eats food before it is **e**
17:16 and took his stand, morning and **e**. C
20: 5 so that I may hide in the field until the third **e**.
30:17 David attacked them from twilight until the **e** of A
2Sa 1:12 fasted until **e** for Saul and for his son Jonathan, A
11:13 and in the **e** he went out to lie on his couch with B
1Ki 17: 6 and bread and meat in the **e**; B
22:35 the Arameans, until at **e** he died; A
2Ki 16:15 the **e** grain offering, and the king's burnt offering,
1Ch 16:40 morning and **e**, according to all that is written C
23:30 and praising the LORD, and likewise at **e**,
2Ch 2: 4 and for burnt offerings morning and **e**, C
13:11 every morning and every **e** burnt offerings C
13:11 so that its lamps may burn every **e**;
18:34 up in his chariot facing the Arameans until **e**; A
31: 3 the burnt offerings of morning and **e**, C
Ezr 3: 3 upon it to the LORD, morning and **e**. C
9: 4 while I sat appalled until the **e** sacrifice. A
9: 5 At the **e** sacrifice I got up from my fasting,
Est 2:14 In the **e** she went in; B
Job 4:20 Between morning and **e** they are destroyed; C
Ps 55:17 **E** and morning and at noon I utter my complaint D
59: 6 Each **e** they come back, howling like dogs
59:14 Each **e** they come back, howling like dogs
65: 8 the gateways of the morning and the **e** shout C
90: 6 in the **e** it fades and withers. B
102:11 My days are like an **e** shadow;
104:23 to their work and to their labor until the **e**. A
109:23 I am gone like a shadow at **e**;
141: 2 and the lifting up of my hands as an **e** sacrifice.
Pr 7: 9 in the **e**, at the time of night and darkness. B
Ecc 11: 6 and at **e** do not let your hands be idle;
Isa 5:11 who linger in the **e** to be inflamed by wine, B
17:14 At **e** time, lo, terror!
Jer 6: 4 for the day declines, the shadows of **e** lengthen!"
Eze 12: 4 and you shall go out yourself at **e** in their sight,
12: 7 in the **e** I dug through the wall with my own B
24:18 in the morning, and at **e** my wife died. C
33:22 the hand of the LORD had been upon me the **e**
46: 2 but the gate shall not be closed until **e**. A
Da 9:21 to me in swift flight at the time of the **e** sacrifice.
Zep 2: 7 in the houses of Ashkelon they shall lie down at **e**.
3: 3 its judges are **e** wolves that leave nothing until
Zec 14: 7 for at **e** time there shall be light.
Mt 8:16 That **e** they brought to him
14:15 When it was **e**, the disciples came to him and said,
14:23 When **e** came, he was there alone,
16: 2 He answered them, "When it is **e**, you say,
20: 8 When **e** came, the owner of the vineyard said
26:20 When it was **e**, he took his place with the twelve;
27:57 When it was **e**, there came a rich man
Mk 1:32 That **e**, at sundown, they brought
4:35 On that day, when **e** had come, he said to them,
6:47 When **e** came, the boat was out on the sea,
11:19 And when **e** came, Jesus and his disciples went out
13:35 in the **e**, or at midnight, or at cockcrow, B
14:17 When it was **e**, he came with the twelve.
15:42 When **e** had come, and since it was the day
Lk 24:29 it is almost **e** and the day is now nearly over."
Jn 6:16 When **e** came, his disciples went down to the sea,
20:19 When it was **e** on that day,
Ac 4: 3 in custody until the next day, for it was already **e**.
28:23 From morning until **e** he explained the matter AC
Jdt 9: 1 when the **e** incense was being offered in the house
12: 9 in the tent until she ate her food toward **e**.
13: 1 When **e** came, his slaves quickly withdrew.
AdE 2:14 In the **e** she enters and in the morning she B
Sir 18:26 From morning to **e** conditions change; C
1Mc 9:13 and the battle raged from morning until **e**. AC
1Es 5:50 and burnt offerings to the Lord morning and **e**. C
8:72 and I sat grief-stricken until the **e** sacrifice. A
3Mc 5: 5 the Jews went out in the **e** and bound the hands B
2Es 7:*40* or darkness or **e** or morning, D
10: 2 I remained quiet until the **e** of the second day. A
4Mc 3: 8 Then when **e** fell, he came,

EVENINGS‡ (2) [EVENING]

Da 8:14 "For two thousand three hundred **e** and mornings;
8:26 the **e** and the mornings that has been told is true.

EVENLY (1) [EVEN]

1Ki 6:35 with gold **e** applied upon the carved work.

EVENT (3) [EVENTS]

Ex 1:10 or they will increase and, in the **e** of war,
1Ki 13:33 this **e** Jeroboam did not turn from his evil way,
Jdt 11: 3 In any **e**, you have come to safety.

EVENT (KJV) See also FATE

EVENTIDE (1) [EVENING]

Isa 24:11 all joy has reached its **e**;

EVENTS (12) [EVENT]

1Ki 21: 1 Later the following **e** took place:
1Ch 29:30 and of the **e** that befell him and Israel and all
Lk 1: 1 an orderly account of the **e** that have been fulfilled
Heb 11: 7 warned by God about **e** as yet unseen,
AdE 3: 1 these **e** King Artaxerxes promoted Haman son
Wis 11:14 at the end of the **e** they marveled at him,
19:10 For they still recalled the **e** of their sojourn,
1Mc 7:33 After these **e** Nicanor went up to Mount Zion.
2Mc 4:17 a fact that later **e** will make clear.
1Es 1:24 the **e** of his reign have been recorded—
3Mc 6:33 convening a great banquet to celebrate these **e**,
2Es 12: 9 to be shown the end of the times and the last **e** of

EVER‡ (163) [EVER-FLOWING, EVERGREEN, EVERLASTING, EVERMORE, FOREVER, FOREVERMORE]

A. FOREVER AND EVER (46)

Ge 8:21 nor will I **e** again destroy every living creature
21: 7 "Who would **e** have said to Abraham
Ex 5:22 Why did you **e** send me?
9:18 the heaviest hail to fall that has **e** fallen in Egypt
10:10 if **e** I let your little ones go with you!
10:14 of locusts as had never been before, nor **e** shall
11: 6 such as has never been or will **e** be again.
15:18 The LORD will reign forever and **e**." A
19: 9 when I speak with you and so trust you **e** after."
Lev 13:14 if raw flesh **e** appears on him, he shall be unclean;
20: 4 if the people of the land should **e** close their eyes

Nu 11:20 saying, 'Why did we e leave Egypt?' "
Dt 4:32 e since the day that God created human beings on
4:32 has anything so great as this e happened or has its
4:32 or has its like e been heard of?
4:33 Has any people e heard the voice of
4:34 Or has any god e attempted to go and take a nation
18:16 or e again see this great fire, I will die."
Jos 6:25 Her family has lived in Israel e since.
Jdg 11:25 Did he e enter into conflict with Israel,
11:25 or did he e go to war with them?
19:30 'Has such a thing e happened since the day that
1Sa 2:32 and no one in your family shall e live to old age.
24:19 For who has e found an enemy,
2Sa 7: 7 did I e speak a word with any of the tribal leaders
1Ki 10:20 Nothing like it was e made in any kingdom.
2Ki 18:33 the nations e delivered its land out of the hand of
1Ch 17: 6 did I e speak a word with any of the judges
29:10 the God of our ancestor Israel, forever and e. A
Ezr 4: 2 to him e since the days of King Esar-haddon
Ne 4:23 the guard who followed me e took off our clothes;
13: 1 or Moabite should e enter the assembly of God,
Job 4: 7 "Think now, who that was innocent e perished?
20: 4 e since mortals were placed on earth,
29:20 and my bow e new in my hand.'
31:31 of my tent e said, 'O that we might be sated
37:20 Did anyone e wish to be swallowed up?
Ps 5:11 let them e sing for joy.
9: 5 you have blotted out their name forever and e. A
10:16 The LORD is king forever and e; A
21: 4 length of days forever and e. A
25:15 My eyes are e toward the LORD,
31: 1 do not let me e be put to shame;
37:26 They are e giving liberally and lending,
38:17 For I am ready to fall, and my pain is e with me.
45: 6 Your throne, O God, endures forever and e. A
45:17 the peoples will praise you forever and e. A
48:14 our God forever and e. A
51: 3 and my sin is e before me.
52: 8 I trust in the steadfast love of God forever and e. A
84: 4 in your house, e singing your praise.
90: 2 or e you had formed the earth and the world,
111: 5 he is e mindful of his covenant.
111: 8 They are established forever and e, A
119:44 I will keep your law continually, forever and e. A
145: 1 and bless your name forever and e. A
145: 2 and praise your name forever and e. A
145:21 all flesh will bless his holy name forever and e. A
148: 6 He established them forever and e; A
Pr 30:16 the barren womb, the earth e thirsty for water,
Ecc 7:20 so righteous as to do good without e sinning.
Isa 34:10 no one shall pass through it forever and e. A
Jer 2:10 see if there has e been such a thing.
6: 7 sickness and wounds are e before me.
7: 7 I gave of old to your ancestors forever and e. A
15:10 Woe is me, my mother, that you e bore me,
23:26 Will the hearts of the prophets e turn back—
31:36 this fixed order were e to cease from my presence,
35: 7 nor shall you e build a house, or sow seed;
La 4:17 Our eyes failed, e watching vainly for help;
Eze 15: 5 can it e be used for anything!
16:16 nothing like this has e been or e shall be.
27:32 "Who was e destroyed like Tyre in the midst of
36:11 and will do more good to you than e before.
Da 2:10 has e asked such a thing of any magician
7:18 possess the kingdom forever—forever and e." A
11:24 and do what none of his predecessors had e done,
12: 3 like the stars forever and e. A
Hos 13: 4 the LORD your God e since the land of Egypt;
Mic 4: 5 in the name of the LORD our God forever and e. A
Na 3:19 For who has e escaped your endless cruelty?
Mal 3: 7 E since the days of your ancestors you have turned
Mt 21:19 "May no fruit e come from you again!"
Mk 11:14 "May no one e eat fruit from you again."
Lk 5:15 more than e the word about Jesus spread abroad;
23:53 a rock-hewn tomb where no one had e been laid.
Jn 1:18 No one has e seen God.
4:29 a man who told me everything I have e done!
4:39 "He told me everything I have e done."
19: 8 when Pilate heard this, he was more afraid than e.
19:41 a new tomb in which no one had e been laid.
Ac 5:14 Yet more than e believers were added to the Lord,
11: 8 or unclean has e entered my mouth.'
20:25 will e see my face again.
Ro 1:20 E since the creation of the world his eternal power
1Co 7:21 of your present condition now more than e.
12: 3 by the Spirit of God e says "Let Jesus be cursed!"
2Co 8:17 but since he is more eager than e,
8:22 but who is now more eager than e because
Gal 1: 5 to whom be the glory forever and e. Amen. A
Eph 3:21 in Christ Jesus to all generations, forever and e. A
5:29 For no one e hates his own body,
Php 4:20 To our God and Father be glory forever and e. A
1Ti 1:17 the only God, be honor and glory forever and e. A
6:16 whom no one has e seen or can see;
2Ti 4:18 To him be the glory forever and e. A
Heb 1: 5 For to which of the angels did God e say,
1: 8 "Your throne, O God, is forever and e, A
1:13 But to which of the angels has he e said,
7:13 from which no one has e served at the altar.
13:21 to whom be the glory forever and e. A
1Pe 4:11 the glory and the power forever and e. A
5:11 To him be the power forever and e. Amen. A
2Pe 1:21 because no prophecy e came by human will,
3: 4 For e since our ancestors died,
1Jn 4:12 No one has e seen God;
Rev 1: 6 to him be glory and dominion forever and e. A
1:18 I was dead, and see, I am alive forever and e; A
Rev 4: 9 on the throne, who lives forever and e, A
4:10 and worship the one who lives forever and e; A
5:13 and honor and glory and might forever and e!" A
7:12 power and might be to our God forever and e! A
10: 6 and swore by him who lives forever and e, A
11:15 and he will reign forever and e." A
14:11 smoke of their torment goes up forever and e. A
15: 7 of the wrath of God, who lives forever and e; A
19: 3 The smoke goes up from her forever and e." A
20:10 be tormented day and night forever and e. A
22: 5 and they will reign forever and e. A
Tob 13:17 blessed will bless the holy name forever and e." A
14:15 and he blessed the Lord God forever and e. A
Jdt 11: 3 You will live tonight and e after.
12:20 much more than he had e drunk in any one day
16:25 No one e again spread terror among the Israelites
AdE 14: 5 E since I was born I have heard in the tribe
Wis 3: 1 and no torment will e touch them.
Sir 14: 7 If e he does good, it is by mistake;
17:19 and his eyes are e upon their ways.
20:26 and his shame is e with him.
30:23 and no advantage e comes from it.
31: 4 and if e he rests he becomes needy.
42:25 Who could e tire of seeing his glory?
45:13 No outsider e put them on,
46: 3 Who before him e stood so firm?
49:14 Few have e been created on earth like Enoch,
49:15 Nor was anyone e born like Joseph;
Sus 1:27 nothing like this had e been said about Susanna.
1Mc 8:11 as many as e opposed them,
2Mc 8:14 by the ungodly Nicanor before he e met them,
10: 4 but that, if they should e sin,
13:10 now if e to help those who were on the point
15:30 the man who was e in body and soul the defender
1Es 4:38 and lives and prevails forever and e. A
5:69 as you do and we have been sacrificing to him e
8:72 And all who were e moved at the word of the Lord
8:85 do not seek e to have peace with them,
2Es 4: 8 neither did I e ascend into heaven.'
7:*105* so no one shall e pray for another on that day,
13:41 where no human beings had e lived,
16:20 or e be mindful of the scourges.
4Mc 7: 4 with many ingenious war machines has e held out
18:24 to whom be glory forever and e. Amen. A

EVER-FLOWING (4) [EVER, FLOW]

Ps 74:15 and torrents; you dried up e streams.
Am 5:24 and righteousness like an e stream.
Wis 11: 6 Instead of the fountain of an e river,
2Mc 7:36 a brief suffering have drunk of e life,

EVERGREEN (2) [EVER, GREEN]

Hos 14: 8 I am like an e cypress; your faithfulness comes
Sus 1:58 He answered, "Under an e oak."

EVERLASTING‡ (96) [EVER, LAST]

Ge 9:16 and remember the e covenant between God
17: 7 throughout their generations, for an e covenant,
17:13 shall my covenant be in your flesh an e covenant.
17:19 as an e covenant for his offspring after him.
21:33 on the name of the LORD, the E God.
49:26 the bounties of the e hills;
Lev 16:34 This shall be an e statute for you,
Dt 33:15 and the abundance of the e hills;
2Sa 23: 5 For he has made with me an e covenant,
1Ch 16:17 to Israel as an e covenant,
16:36 the God of Israel, from e to e."
Ne 9: 5 Stand up and bless the LORD your God from e to e.
Ps 9: 6 The enemies have vanished in e ruins;
41:13 the God of Israel, from e to e.
76: 4 more majestic than the e mountains.
78:66 he put them to e disgrace.
90: 2 from e to e you are God.
93: 2 throne is established from of old; you are from e.
103:17 But the steadfast love of the LORD is from e to e
105:10 to Israel as an e covenant,
106:48 the God of Israel, from e to e.
119:142 Your righteousness is an e righteousness,
139:24 and lead me in the way e.
145:13 Your kingdom is an e kingdom,
Isa 9: 6 Mighty God, E Father, Prince of Peace.
24: 5 violated the statutes, broken the e covenant.
26: 4 for in the LORD GOD you have an e rock.
33:14 Who among us can live with e flames?"
35:10 e joy shall be upon their heads;
40:28 The LORD is the e God, the Creator of the ends of
45:17 But Israel is saved by the LORD with e salvation;
51:11 e joy shall be upon their heads;
54: 8 but with e love I will have compassion on you,
55: 3 I will make with you an e covenant, my steadfast,
55:13 for an e sign that shall not be cut off.
56: 5 I will give them an e name that shall not be cut off.
60:19 but the LORD will be your e light,
60:20 for the LORD will be your e light,
61: 7 shall possess a double portion; e joy shall be theirs.
61: 8 and I will make an e covenant with them.
63:12 before them to make for himself an e name,
Jer 10:10 he is the living God and the e King.
23:40 upon you e disgrace and perpetual shame,
25: 9 of horror and of hissing, and an e disgrace.
25:12 says the LORD, making the land an e waste.
31: 3 I have loved you with an e love;
32:40 I will make an e covenant with them,
49:33 Hazor shall become a lair of jackals, an e waste;
50: 5 to the LORD by an e covenant that will never
Eze 16:60 and I will establish with you an e covenant.
37:26 it shall be an e covenant with them;
Da 4: 3 His kingdom is an e kingdom,
4:34 For his sovereignty is an e sovereignty,
7:14 His dominion is an e dominion that shall
7:27 their kingdom shall be an e kingdom,
9:24 to bring in e righteousness,
12: 2 in the dust of the earth shall awake, some to e life,
and some to shame and e contempt.
Hab 3: 6 along his ancient pathways the e hills sank low.
Tob 1: 6 as it is prescribed for all Israel by an e decree.
AdE 14: 5 among all their forebears, for an e inheritance,
Wis 8:13 and leave an e remembrance to those who come
10:14 and she gave him e honor.
Sir 15: 6 and will inherit an e name.
43: 6 governing the times, their e sign.
44:18 E covenants were made with him
45: 7 He made an e covenant with him,
45:15 an e covenant for him and for his descendants
49:12 a temple holy to the Lord, destined for e glory.
Bar 2:35 an e covenant with them to be their God
4: 8 You forgot the e God, who brought you up,
4:10 which the E brought upon them.
4:14 which the E brought upon them.
4:20 I will cry to the E all my days.
4:22 For I have put my hope in the E to save you,
4:22 that will soon come to you from your e savior.
4:24 with great glory and with the splendor of the E.
4:29 upon you will bring you e joy with your salvation.
4:35 fire will come upon her from the E for many days,
5: 2 put on your head the diadem of the glory of the E;
5: 7 and the e hills be made low and the valleys filled
1Mc 2:51 and you will receive great honor and an e name.
2:54 received the covenant of e priesthood.
6:44 and to win for himself an e name.
2Mc 7: 9 of the universe will raise us up to an e renewal
2Es 2:11 and will give to these others the e habitations,
2:34 he will give you e rest,
3:15 You made an e covenant with him,
7:*120* [50] that an e hope has been promised to us,
4Mc 10:15 and by the e life of the pious,

EVERMORE (3) [EVER]

Ps 35:27 and say e, "Great is the LORD,
70: 4 Let those who love your salvation say e,
Bar 5: 4 For God will give you e the name,

EVERY‡ (820) [EVERYBODY, EVERYDAY, EVERYONE, EVERYONE'S, EVERYTHING, EVERYWHERE]

A. EVERY KIND (39)
B. EVERY ONE (39)
C. ON EVERY SIDE (34)
D. EVERY DAY (33)
E. EVERY MALE (28)
F. IN EVERY WAY (22)
G. EVERY MAN (14)
H. EVERY NATION (13)
I. EVERY MORNING (12)
J. EVERY TREE (12)
K. EVERY GREEN TREE (11)
L. EVERY YEAR (11)

Ge 1:11 and fruit trees of e kind on earth that bear fruit A
1:12 plants yielding seed of e kind, A
1:12 trees of e kind bearing fruit with the seed in it. A
1:21 the great sea monsters and e living creature
1:21 of e kind, with which the waters swarm, A
1:21 and e winged bird of every kind.
1:21 and every winged bird of e kind. A
1:24 the earth bring forth living creatures of e kind: A
1:24 and wild animals of the earth of e kind." A
1:25 made the wild animals of the earth of e kind, A
1:25 and the cattle of e kind, A
1:25 that creeps upon the ground of e kind. A
1:26 over e creeping thing that creeps upon the earth."
1:28 and over the birds of the air and over e living thing
1:29 I have given you e plant yielding seed that is upon
1:29 and e tree with seed in its fruit; J
1:30 And to e beast of the earth,
1:30 to every beast of the earth, and to e bird of the air,
1:30 I have given e green plant for food."
2: 9 of the ground the LORD God made to grow e tree J
2:16 "You may freely eat of e tree of the garden; J
2:19 of the ground the LORD God formed e animal of
2:19 of the field and e bird of the air, and brought them
2:19 and whatever the man called e living creature,
2:20 and to e animal of the field;
6: 5 and that e inclination of the thoughts
6:19 And of e living thing, of all flesh,
6:19 you shall bring two of e kind into the ark, A
6:20 of e creeping thing of the ground according
6:20 two of e kind shall come in to you, A
6:21 Also take with you e kind of food that is eaten, A
7: 4 and e living thing that I have made I will blot out
7:14 they and e wild animal of every kind,
7:14 they and every wild animal of e kind, A
7:14 and all domestic animals of e kind, A
7:14 and e creeping thing that creeps on the earth,
7:14 and e bird of every kind—
7:14 and every bird of e kind— A
7:14 e bird, e winged creature.
7:23 He blotted out e living thing that was on the face
8:17 Bring out with you e living thing that is with you
8:17 birds and animals and e creeping thing that creeps

Ge 8:19 And **e** animal, **e** creeping thing, and **e** bird,
8:20 and took of **e** clean animal and of **e** clean bird,
8:21 nor will I ever again destroy **e** living creature
9: 2 The fear and dread of you shall rest on **e** animal of
9: 2 and on **e** bird of the air,
9: 3 **E** moving thing that lives shall be food for you;
9: 5 from **e** animal I will require it and
9:10 and with **e** living creature that is with you,
9:10 and **e** animal of the earth with you,
9:12 between me and you and **e** living creature that is
9:15 that is between me and you and **e** living creature
9:16 between God and **e** living creature of all flesh
17:10 **E** male among you shall be circumcised. E
17:12 Throughout your generations **e** male E
17:23 **e** male among the men of Abraham's house, E
20:13 at **e** place to which we come, say of me,
30:32 removing from it **e** speckled and spotted sheep
30:32 and **e** black lamb, and the spotted and speckled
30:33 **E** one that is not speckled and spotted among B
30:35 **e** one that had white on it, B
30:35 and **e** lamb that was black,
32:16 **e** drove by itself, and said to his servants,
34:15 as we are and **e** male among you be circumcised. E
34:22 that **e** male among us be circumcised E
34:24 and **e** male was circumcised, E
41:48 up in **e** city the food from the fields around it.
41:54 There was famine in **e** country,
42:25 to return **e** man's money to his sack,
Ex 1:14 hard service in mortar and brick and in **e** kind A
1:22 "**E** boy that is born to the Hebrews you shall throw
1:22 but you shall let **e** girl live."
9:19 **e** human or animal that is in the open field and is
9:25 and shattered **e** tree in the field. J
10: 5 and they shall devour **e** tree of yours that grows J
10:12 that the locusts may come upon it and eat **e** plant
11: 2 Tell the people that **e** man is to ask his neighbor G
11: 2 and **e** woman is to ask her neighbor for objects
11: 5 **E** firstborn in the land of Egypt shall die,
12:12 I will strike down **e** firstborn in the land of Egypt,
13:13 **e** firstborn donkey you shall redeem with a sheep;
13:13 **E** firstborn male among your children you shall
13:15 to the LORD **e** male that first opens the womb, E
13:15 but **e** firstborn of my sons I redeem.'
18:22 let them bring **e** important case to you, but decide **e** minor case themselves.
20:24 in **e** place where I cause my name to
27:19 All the utensils of the tabernacle for **e** use,
29:36 Also **e** day you shall offer a bull as a sin offering D
30: 7 **e** morning when he dresses the lamps I
31: 3 intelligence, and knowledge in **e** kind of craft, A
31: 5 and in carving wood, in **e** kind of craft. A
33:16 from **e** people on the face of the earth."
35:31 intelligence, and knowledge in **e** kind of craft, A
35:33 and in carving wood, in **e** kind of craft. A
35:35 with skill to do **e** kind of work done by an artisan A
36: 1 Bezalel and Oholiab and **e** skillful one to whom
36: 2 then called Bezalel and Oholiab and **e** skillful one
36: 3 kept bringing him freewill offerings **e** morning, I
36: 4 that all the artisans who were doing **e** sort of task
36:30 sixteen bases, under **e** frame two bases.
Lev 6:12 **E** morning the priest shall add wood to it, I
6:18 **E** male among the descendants of Aaron shall E
6:23 **E** grain offering of a priest shall be wholly burned;
6:29 **E** male among the priests shall eat of it; E
7: 6 **E** male among the priests shall eat of it; E
7: 9 And **e** grain offering baked in the oven,
7:10 But **e** other grain offering, mixed with oil or dry,
11:15 **e** raven of any kind;
11:26 **E** animal that has divided hoofs but is
11:46 and bird and **e** living creature that moves through the waters and **e** creature that swarms
15: 4 **E** bed on which the one with
15:12 and **e** vessel of wood shall be rinsed in water.
15:24 and **e** bed on which he lies shall be unclean.
15:26 **E** bed on which she lies during all the days
17:14 For the life of **e** creature—
17:14 for the life of **e** creature is its blood;
24: 8 **E** sabbath day Aaron shall set them in order before
25:10 you shall return, **e** one of you, B
25:10 to your property and **e** one of you to your family. B
25:13 **e** one of you, to your property. B
27:28 **e** devoted thing is most holy to the LORD.
27:32 **e** tenth one that passes under the shepherd's staff,
Nu 1: 2 to the number of names, **e** male individually; E
1:20 **e** male from twenty years old and upward, E
1:22 **e** male from twenty years old and upward, E
2: 2 the tent of meeting on **e** side. C
3:15 You shall enroll **e** male from a month old E
5: 9 **e** gift that they bring to the priest shall be his.
7: 3 a wagon for **e** two of the leaders,
13: 2 **e** one a leader among them." B
14:34 for **e** day a year, you shall bear your iniquity, D
15:12 so you shall do with **e** one. B
15:13 **E** native Israelite shall do these things in this way,
18: 9 **e** offering of theirs that they render to me as
18:10 **e** male may eat it; it shall be holy to you. E
18:14 **E** devoted thing in Israel shall be yours.
18:21 To the Levites I have given **e** tithe in Israel for
18:29 you shall set apart **e** offering due to the LORD;
19:15 And **e** open vessel with no cover fastened
26:54 **e** tribe shall be given its inheritance according
26:62 **e** male one month old and up; E
28:10 this is the burnt offering for **e** sabbath,
28:13 with oil as a grain offering for **e** lamb—
28:14 This is the burnt offering of **e** month throughout
30: 9 (But **e** vow of a widow or of a divorced woman,
31: 7 LORD had commanded Moses, and killed **e** male. E
Nu 31:17 Now therefore, kill **e** male among the little ones, E
31:17 and kill **e** woman who has known a man
31:20 You shall purify **e** garment, every article of skin,
31:20 You shall purify every garment, **e** article of skin,
31:20 of goats' hair, and **e** article of wood."
31:28 one item out of **e** five hundred, whether persons,
31:30 the Israelites' half you shall take one out of **e** fifty,
31:47 From the Israelites' half Moses took one of **e** fifty,
34:18 You shall take one leader of **e** tribe to apportion
36: 8 **E** daughter who possesses an inheritance
Dt 7:15 The LORD will turn away from you **e** illness;
8: 3 but by **e** word that comes from the mouth of
11: 6 their tents, and **e** living being in their company;
11: 7 for it is your own eyes that have seen **e** great deed
11:13 If you will only heed his **e** commandment
11:24 **E** place on which you set foot shall be yours;
12: 2 on the hills, and under **e** leafy tree.
12:31 because **e** abhorrent thing that
14:14 **e** raven of any kind;
14:28 **E** third year you shall bring out the full tithe
15: 1 **E** seventh year you shall grant a remission
15: 2 **e** creditor shall remit the claim that is held against
15:19 **E** firstling male born of your herd
25:19 from all your enemies on **e** hand, in the land that
28:26 Your corpses shall be food for **e** bird of the air
28:61 **E** other malady and affliction,
29:27 bringing on it **e** curse written in this book.
31:10 Moses commanded them: "**E** seventh year,
Jos 1: 3 **E** place that the sole of your foot will tread
10:28 he utterly destroyed **e** person in it;
10:30 with the edge of the sword, and **e** person in it;
10:32 and **e** person in it, as he had done to Libnah.
10:35 and **e** person in it he utterly destroyed that day,
10:37 and its king and its towns, and **e** person in it;
10:37 and utterly destroyed it with **e** person in it.
10:39 and utterly destroyed **e** person in it;
21:44 on **e** side just as he had sworn to their ancestors; C
22:14 **e** one of them the head of a family among B
Jdg 5:30 A girl or two for **e** man; G
6:16 and you shall strike down the Midianites, **e** one B
7:21 **E** man stood in his place all around the camp, G
7:22 the LORD set **e** man's sword against his fellow
8:18 **e** one of them; they resembled the sons of a king. B
8:34 from the hand of all their enemies on **e** side; C
9:49 So **e** one of the troops cut down a bundle B
11:40 for four days **e** year the daughters L
20:16 **e** one could sling a stone at a hair, and not miss. B
21:11 **e** male and every woman that has lain with E
21:11 every male and **e** woman that has lain with
1Sa 2:29 of **e** offering of my people Israel?'
4: 8 the gods who struck the Egyptians with **e** sort
12:11 of the hand of your enemies on **e** side; C
14:20 and **e** sword was against the other,
14:47 he fought against all his enemies on **e** side— C
20:15 if the LORD were to cut off **e** one of the enemies B
22: 7 of Jesse give **e** one of you fields and vineyards, B
23:14 Saul sought him **e** day, but the LORD did D
25:13 "**E** man strap on his sword!" G
25:13 And **e** one of them strapped on his sword; B
27: 3 he and his troops, **e** man with his household, G
2Sa 2: 3 up the men who were with him, **e** one B
4: 9 who has redeemed my life out of **e** adversity,
14:26 of his head (for at the end of **e** year he used L
15: 6 to **e** Israelite who came to the king for judgment;
1Ki 1:29 who has saved my life from **e** adversity,
5: 4 the LORD my God has given me rest on **e** side; C
5:10 So Hiram supplied Solomon's **e** need for timber
8:39 for only you know what is in **e** human heart—
10:13 to the queen of Sheba **e** desire that she expressed,
10:22 Once **e** three years the fleet of ships
10:25 **E** one of them brought a present, B
11:15 he killed **e** male in Edom E
11:16 until he had eliminated **e** male in Edom); E
14:10 I will cut off from Jeroboam **e** male, E
14:23 on **e** high hill and under every green tree;
14:23 on every high hill and under **e** green tree; K
19:18 and **e** mouth that has not kissed him."
21:21 and will cut off from Ahab **e** male, bond or free, E
22:36 "**E** man to his city, and every man to his G
22:36 man to his city, and **e** man to his country!" G
2Ki 3:19 You shall conquer **e** fortified city and **e** choice city;
3:19 **e** good tree you shall fell,
3:19 **e** good piece of land you shall ruin with stones."
3:25 on **e** good piece of land everyone threw a stone,
3:25 **e** spring of water they stopped up,
3:25 and **e** good tree they felled.
9: 8 I will cut off from Ahab **e** male, bond or free, E
11:11 **e** man with his weapons in his hand, G
11:11 to guard the king on **e** side. C
16: 4 on the hills, and under **e** green tree. K
17:10 on **e** high hill and under every green tree;
17:10 on every high hill and under **e** green tree; K
17:13 the LORD warned Israel and Judah by **e** prophet
17:13 and Judah by every prophet and **e** seer,
17:29 But **e** nation still made gods of its own H
17:29 **e** nation in the cities in which they lived; H
18:31 then **e** one of you will eat from your own vine B
25: 9 **e** great house he burned down.
25:29 **E** day of his life he dined regularly in D
25:30 a portion **e** day, as long as he lived. D
1Ch 9:25 to come in **e** seven days, in turn, to be with them;
9:27 and they had charge of opening it **e** morning. I
13: 1 the thousands and of the hundreds, with **e** leader.
16: 3 and he distributed to **e** person in Israel—
22: 9 from all his enemies on **e** side; C
22:18 Has he not given you peace on **e** side? C
23:30 And they shall stand **e** morning, I
1Ch 28: 9 for the LORD searches **e** mind,
28: 9 and understands **e** plan and thought.
28:21 in all the work will be **e** volunteer who has skill
2Ch 9:12 the queen of Sheba **e** desire that she expressed,
9:21 once **e** three years the ships of Tarshish used
9:24 **E** one of them brought a present, B
13:11 They offer to the LORD **e** morning I
13:11 and **e** evening burnt offerings and fragrant incense,
13:11 so that its lamps may burn **e** evening;
14: 7 and he has given us peace on **e** side." C
15: 6 for God troubled them with **e** sort of distress.
28: 4 on the hills, and under **e** green tree. K
28:24 of the LORD and made himself altars in **e** corner
28:25 In **e** city of Judah he made high places
31:19 to distribute portions to **e** male among the priests E
31:21 And **e** work that he undertook in the service of
32:22 he gave them rest on **e** side. C
34:13 directed all who did work in **e** kind of service; A
Ezr 10:14 and with them the elders and judges of **e** town,
Ne 4:22 "Let **e** man and his servant pass the night G
5:18 and **e** ten days skins of wine in abundance;
9:22 and allotted to them **e** corner,
10:31 of the seventh year and the exaction of **e** debt.
10:35 of **e** tree, year by year, to the house of the LORD; J
10:37 and our contributions, the fruit of **e** tree, J
11:23 for the singers, as was required **e** day. D
Est 1:22 to **e** province in its own script and to **e** people
1:22 that **e** man should be master in his own house. G
2:11 **E** day Mordecai would walk around in front of D
3: 8 from those of **e** other people,
3:12 to **e** province in its own script and **e** people in its own language;
3:14 as a decree in **e** province by proclamation,
4: 3 In **e** province, wherever the king's command
8: 9 to **e** province in its own script and to every people
8: 9 to every province in its own script and to **e** people
8:11 the king allowed the Jews who were in **e** city
8:13 the writ was to be issued as a decree in **e** province
8:17 In **e** province and in **e** city,
9:27 to observe these two days **e** year, L
9:28 throughout **e** generation, in every family, province,
9:28 in **e** family, province, and city;
Job 1:10 and his house and all that he has, on **e** side? C
7:18 visit them **e** morning, test them every moment? I
7:18 visit them every morning, test them **e** moment?
12:10 In his hand is the life of **e** living thing and
12:10 and the breath of **e** human being.
18:11 Terrors frighten them on **e** side, C
19:10 He breaks me down on **e** side, and I am gone, C
28:10 and their eyes see **e** precious thing.
39: 8 and it searches after **e** green thing.
Ps 6: 6 **e** night I flood my bed with tears;
7:11 and a God who has indignation **e** day. D
12: 8 On **e** side the wicked prowl, C
34: 6 and was saved from **e** trouble.
50:10 For **e** wild animal of the forest is mine,
54: 7 For he has delivered me from **e** trouble,
73:14 and am punished **e** morning. I
77:17 your arrows flashed on **e** side. C
88: 9 **E** day I call on you, O LORD; D
97: 3 and consumes his adversaries on **e** side. C
104:11 giving drink to **e** wild animal;
105:16 and broke **e** staff of bread,
109:19 like a belt that he wears **e** day." D
118:11 They surrounded me, surrounded me on **e** side; C
119:101 I hold back my feet from **e** evil way,
119:104 therefore I hate **e** false way.
119:128 by all your precepts; I hate **e** false way.
119:160 of your word is truth; and **e** one B
144:13 May our barns be filled, with produce of **e** kind; A
145: 2 **E** day I will bless you, D
145:16 satisfying the desire of **e** living thing.
Pr 2: 9 and justice and equity, **e** good path;
7:12 now in the squares, and at **e** corner she lies in wait.
15: 3 The eyes of the LORD are in **e** place,
20: 3 but **e** fool is quick to quarrel.
20:27 the lamp of the LORD, searching **e** inmost part.
30: 5 **E** word of God proves true;
Ecc 3: 1 and a time for **e** matter under heaven:
3:17 for he has appointed a time for **e** matter,
3:17 a time for every matter, and for **e** work.
8: 6 For **e** matter has its time and way,
10:19 wine gladdens life, and money meets **e** need.
12:14 For God will bring **e** deed into judgment,
12:14 including **e** secret thing, whether good or evil.
Isa 2:15 against **e** high tower, and against **e** fortified wall;
7:23 On that day **e** place where there used to be
9:17 and an evildoer, and **e** mouth spoke folly.
13: 7 and **e** human heart will melt,
15: 2 On **e** head is baldness, **e** beard is shorn;
22:24 **e** small vessel, from the cups to all the flagons.
24:10 **e** house is shut up so that no one can enter.
27: 3 I, the LORD, am its keeper; **e** moment I water it.
30:25 On **e** lofty mountain and **e** high hill there will
30:32 And **e** stroke of the staff of punishment that
32:20 Happy will you be who sow beside **e** stream,
33: 2 Be our arm **e** morning, our salvation in the time I
40: 4 **E** valley shall be lifted up,
40: 4 and **e** mountain and hill be made low;
44:23 O mountains, O forest, and **e** tree in it! J
45:23 "To me **e** knee shall bow, **e** tongue shall swear."
51:20 they lie at the head of **e** street like an antelope in
54:17 and you shall confute **e** tongue that rises
57: 5 with lust among the oaks, under **e** green tree; K
57:14 remove **e** obstruction from my people's way."
58: 6 to let the oppressed go free, and to break **e** yoke?
Jer 2:20 On **e** high hill and under every green tree

Jer 2:20 and under **e** green tree you sprawled and played K
3: 6 up on **e** high hill and under every green tree,
3: 6 up on every high hill and under **e** green tree, K
3:13 among strangers under **e** green tree, K
4:29 At the noise of horseman and archer **e** town takes
6:25 for the enemy has a sword, terror is on **e** side." C
9: 4 and **e** neighbor goes around like a slanderer.
12: 4 and the grass of **e** field wither?
13:12 **E** wine-jar should be filled with wine.
13:12 that **e** wine-jar should be filled with wine?"
16:12 **e** one of you, following your stubborn evil will, B
16:16 shall hunt them from **e** mountain and **e** hill,
17: 2 beside **e** green tree, and on the high hills, K
30: 6 do I see **e** man with his hands on his loins G
30: 6 Why has **e** face turned pale?
34:14 "**E** seventh year each of you
35:17 and on all the inhabitants of Jerusalem **e** disaster
45: 5 as a prize of war in **e** place to which you may go."
47: 4 from Tyre and Sidon **e** helper that remains.
48: 8 The destroyer shall come upon **e** town,
48:37 For **e** head is shaved and **e** beard cut off;
49:32 scatter to **e** wind those who have shaven temples,
49:32 and I will bring calamity against them from **e** side,
50:26 Come against her from **e** quarter;
51: 2 when they come against her from **e** side on the day
51:28 and **e** land under their dominion.
52:13 **e** great house he burned down.
52:33 and **e** day of his life he dined regularly at D
La 2:19 who faint for hunger at the head of **e** street.
3:23 are new **e** morning; great is your faithfulness. I
4: 1 sacred stones lie scattered at the head of **e** street.
Eze 5:10 any of you who survive I will scatter to **e** wind.
5:12 to **e** wind and will unsheathe the sword after them.
6:13 on **e** high hill, on all the mountain tops,
6:13 under **e** green tree, and under every leafy oak, K
6:13 under every green tree, and under **e** leafy oak,
12:14 I will scatter to **e** wind all who are around him,
12:22 and **e** vision comes to nothing"?
12:23 The days are near, and the fulfillment of **e** vision.
13:18 make veils for the heads of persons of **e** height,
16:24 and made yourself a lofty place in **e** square;
16:25 at the head of **e** street you built your lofty place
16:25 offering yourself to **e** passer-by,
16:31 building your platform at the head of **e** street,
16:31 and making your lofty place in **e** square!
17:21 and the survivors shall be scattered to **e** wind;
17:23 Under it **e** kind of bird will live; A
17:23 branches will nest winged creatures of **e** kind. A
20: 7 **e** one of you, and do not defile yourselves with B
20:47 in you, and it shall devour **e** green tree in you K
20:47 in you and **e** dry tree;
21: 7 **E** heart will melt and all hands will be feeble,
21: 7 **e** spirit will faint and all knees will turn to water.
23:22 and I will bring them against you from **e** side:
23:24 they shall set themselves against you on **e** side C
26:16 they shall tremble **e** moment,
27:18 because of your great wealth of **e** kind— A
28:13 **e** precious stone was your covering, carnelian,
28:23 by the sword that is against it on **e** side. C
29:18 **e** head was made bald and **e** shoulder was rubbed
32:10 they shall tremble **e** moment for their lives,
34: 6 over all the mountains and on **e** high hill;
37:21 and will gather them from **e** quarter,
38:20 and **e** wall shall tumble to the ground.
39: 4 **e** kind and to the wild animals to be devoured. A
39:17 the birds of **e** kind and to all the wild animals: A
40:14 gate next to the pilaster on **e** side of the court. C
41:10 of twenty cubits all around the temple on **e** side. C
44:29 and **e** devoted thing in Israel shall be theirs.
44:30 and **e** offering of all kinds from all your offerings,
45:15 and one sheep from **e** flock of two hundred,
47: 9 **e** living creature that swarms will live,
47:12 but they will bear fresh fruit **e** month,
Da 1: 4 versed in **e** branch of wisdom,
1:17 and skill in **e** aspect of literature and wisdom;
1:20 In **e** matter of wisdom and understanding
6:14 the sun went down he made **e** effort to rescue him.
6:25 of **e** language throughout the whole world:
Hos 9:15 **E** evil of theirs began at Gilgal;
13:15 It shall strip his treasury of **e** precious thing.
Am 2: 8 down beside **e** altar on garments taken in pledge;
4: 4 bring your sacrifices **e** morning, I
4: 4 sacrifices every morning, your tithes **e** three days;
8: 3 "the dead bodies shall be many, cast out in **e** place.
8:10 sackcloth on all loins, and baldness on **e** head;
Na 2: 9 An abundance of **e** precious thing!"
3:10 in pieces at the head of **e** street;
Hab 1:10 They laugh at **e** fortress, and heap up earth to take
Zep 1: 4 and I will cut off from this place **e** remnant of Baal
2:14 Herds shall lie down in it, **e** wild animal;
3: 5 **E** morning he renders his judgment, I
Hag 2:14 and so with **e** work of their hands;
2:22 **e** one by the sword of a comrade. B
Zec 8:23 from nations of **e** language shall take hold of
10: 4 out of them **e** commander.
11: 6 **e** one, to fall each into the hand of a neighbor, B
12: 4 says the LORD, I will strike **e** horse with panic,
12: 4 I strike **e** horse of the peoples with blindness.
13: 4 On that day the prophets will be ashamed, **e** one, B
14:21 and **e** cooking pot in Jerusalem and Judah shall
Mal 1:11 and in **e** place incense is offered to my name,
Mt 3:10 **e** tree therefore that does not bear good fruit is J
4: 4 by **e** word that comes from the mouth of God.' "
4:23 and curing **e** disease and **e** sickness among
7:17 In the same way, **e** good tree bears good fruit,
7:19 **E** tree that does not bear good fruit is cut down J
9:35 and curing **e** disease and **e** sickness.

Mt 10: 1 and to cure **e** disease and **e** sickness.
12:25 "**E** kingdom divided against itself is laid waste,
12:31 people will be forgiven for **e** sin and blasphemy,
12:36 to give an account for **e** careless word you utter;
13:47 into the sea and caught fish of **e** kind; A
13:52 "Therefore **e** scribe who has been trained for
15:13 "**E** plant that my heavenly Father has
18:16 so that **e** word may be confirmed by the evidence
18:35 my heavenly Father will also do to **e** one of you, B
Mk 1:45 and people came to him from **e** quarter.
Lk 2:23 "**E** firstborn male shall be designated as holy to
2:41 Now **e** year his parents went to Jerusalem for L
3: 5 **E** valley shall be filled, and **e** mountain and hill
3: 9 **e** tree therefore that does not bear good fruit is J
4:13 When the devil had finished **e** test,
4:37 And a report about him began to reach **e** place in
5:17 near by (they had come from **e** village of Galilee
10: 1 and sent them on ahead of him in pairs to **e** town
11:17 "**E** kingdom divided against itself becomes
16:19 fine linen and who feasted sumptuously **e** day. D
19:43 and hem you in on **e** side. C
19:47 **E** day he was teaching in the temple. D
21:37 **E** day he was teaching in the temple, D
Jn 15: 2 He removes **e** branch in me that bears no fruit.
15: 2 **E** branch that bears fruit he prunes
21:25 if **e** one of them were written down, B
Ac 2: 5 from **e** nation under heaven living in Jerusalem. H
2:38 and be baptized **e** one of you in the name B
5:42 And **e** day in the temple and at home they did D
10:35 but in **e** nation anyone who fears him H
13:27 the words of the prophets that are read **e** sabbath,
15:21 For in **e** city, for generations past,
15:21 for he has been read aloud **e** sabbath in
15:36 the believers in **e** city where we proclaimed
17:11 and examined the scriptures **e** day D
17:17 the marketplace **e** day with those who happened D
17:22 I see how extremely religious you are in **e** way. F
18: 4 **E** sabbath he would argue in the synagogue
20:23 except that the Holy Spirit testifies to me in **e** city
22:19 that in **e** synagogue I imprisoned
24: 3 in **e** way and everywhere with utmost gratitude. F
Ro 1:29 They were filled with **e** kind of wickedness, evil, A
3: 2 Much, in **e** way. For in the first place the Jews F
3:19 so that **e** mouth may be silenced,
13: 1 Let **e** person be subject to
14:11 "As I live, says the Lord, **e** knee shall bow to me,
14:11 and **e** tongue shall give praise to God."
1Co 1: 2 with all those who in **e** place call on the name
1: 5 in **e** way you have been enriched in him, F
1: 5 in speech and knowledge of **e** kind— A
4:17 as I teach them everywhere in **e** church.
6:18 **E** sin that a person commits is outside the body;
11: 3 to understand that Christ is the head of **e** man, G
15:24 after he has destroyed **e** ruler and **e** authority
15:30 why are we putting ourselves in danger **e** hour?
15:31 I die **e** day! That is as certain, D
16: 2 On the first day of **e** week,
2Co 1:20 For in him **e** one of God's promises is a "Yes." B
2:14 and through us spreads in **e** place the fragrance
4: 8 We are afflicted in **e** way, but not crushed; F
6: 4 of God we have commended ourselves in **e** way: F
7: 1 let us cleanse ourselves from **e** defilement of body
7: 5 but we were afflicted in **e** way— F
7:11 At **e** point you have proved yourselves guiltless in
9: 8 And God is able to provide you with **e** blessing
9: 8 you may share abundantly in **e** good work.
9:11 be enriched in **e** way for your great generosity, F
10: 5 and **e** proud obstacle raised up against
10: 5 and we take **e** thought captive to obey Christ.
10: 6 We are ready to punish **e** disobedience
11: 6 in **e** way and in all things we have made this F
Gal 5: 3 Once again I testify to **e** man who lets himself G
Eph 1: 3 with **e** spiritual blessing in the heavenly places,
1:21 and above **e** name that is named,
3:15 from whom **e** family in heaven and
4: 3 making **e** effort to maintain the unity of the Spirit
4:14 to and fro and blown about by **e** wind of doctrine,
4:15 we must grow up in **e** way into him who is F
4:16 by **e** ligament with which it is equipped,
4:19 greedy to practice **e** kind of impurity A
6:18 the Spirit at all times in **e** prayer and supplication.
Php 1: 3 I thank my God **e** time I remember you,
1: 4 praying with joy in **e** one of my prayers B
1:18 Just this, that Christ is proclaimed in **e** way, F
2: 9 and gave him the name that is above **e** name,
2:10 so that at the name of Jesus **e** knee should bend,
2:11 **e** tongue should confess that Jesus Christ is Lord,
4:19 And my God will fully satisfy **e** need of yours
4:21 Greet **e** saint in Christ Jesus.
Col 1:10 in **e** good work and as you grow in the knowledge
1:23 which has been proclaimed to **e** creature
2:10 who is the head of **e** ruler and authority.
1Th 1: 8 in **e** place your faith in God has become known,
5:22 abstain from **e** form of evil.
2Th 1:11 by his power **e** good resolve and work of faith,
2: 4 and exalts himself above **e** so-called god or object
2:10 and **e** kind of wicked deception A
2:17 and strengthen them in **e** good work and word.
3:17 This is the mark in **e** letter of mine;
1Ti 2: 8 I desire, then, that in **e** place the men should pray,
3: 4 and respectful in **e** way— F
4: 8 godliness is valuable in **e** way, F
5:10 and devoted herself to doing good in **e** way. F
2Ti 2:21 to the owner of the house, ready for **e** good work.
3:17 equipped for **e** good work.
4:18 The Lord will rescue me from **e** evil attack
Tit 1: 5 and should appoint elders in **e** town,

Tit 2: 9 and to give satisfaction in **e** respect;
3: 1 to be obedient, to be ready for **e** good work,
3: 2 to be gentle, and to show **e** courtesy to everyone.
3:13 Make **e** effort to send Zenas the lawyer
Heb 2: 2 and **e** transgression or disobedience received
2:17 to become like his brothers and sisters in **e** respect,
3: 4 (For **e** house is built by someone,
3:13 But exhort one another **e** day, D
4:11 Let us therefore make **e** effort to enter that rest,
4:15 but we have one who in **e** respect has been tested
5: 1 **E** high priest chosen from among mortals is put
8: 3 For **e** high priest is appointed to offer gifts
9:19 For when **e** commandment had been told to all
10:11 And **e** priest stands day after day at his service,
12: 1 let us also lay aside **e** weight and the sin that clings
12: 6 and chastises **e** child whom he accepts."
Jas 1:7,8 being double-minded and unstable in **e** way, F
1:17 **E** generous act of giving, with **e** perfect gift,
3: 7 For **e** species of beast and bird,
3:16 also be disorder and wickedness of **e** kind. A
1Pe 2:13 the authority of **e** human institution,
2Pe 1: 5 you must make **e** effort to support your faith
1:15 And I will make **e** effort so that
1Jn 4: 1 Beloved, do not believe **e** spirit,
4: 2 **e** spirit that confesses that Jesus Christ has come in
4: 3 and **e** spirit that does not confess Jesus is not
Rev 1: 7 **e** eye will see him, even those who pierced him;
5: 9 from **e** tribe and language and people and nation;
5:13 Then I heard **e** creature in heaven and on earth and
6:14 **e** mountain and island was removed from its place.
7: 4 sealed out of **e** tribe of the people of Israel:
7: 9 from **e** nation, from all tribes and peoples H
7:17 and God will wipe away **e** tear from their eyes."
11: 6 and to strike the earth with **e** kind of plague, A
13: 7 over **e** tribe and people and language and nation,
14: 6 to **e** nation and tribe and language and people. H
16: 3 and **e** living thing in the sea died.
16:20 And **e** island fled away, and no mountains were to
18: 2 a haunt of **e** foul spirit, a haunt of **e** foul bird, a
haunt of **e** foul and hateful beast.
21: 4 he will wipe **e** tear from their eyes.
21:19 of the wall of the city are adorned with **e** jewel;
Tob 4:12 "Beware, my son, of **e** kind of fornication. A
4:18 Seek advice from **e** wise person and do
4:21 from **e** sin and do what is good in the sight of
6: 8 and **e** affliction will flee away and never remain
6:13 "You have **e** right to take her in marriage.
8:15 "Blessed are you, O God, with **e** pure blessing;
10: 7 She would rush out **e** day and watch D
12: 9 from death and purges away **e** sin.
12:18 Bless him each and **e** day; sing his praises. D
13: 4 Exalt him in the presence of **e** living being,
Jdt 1:12 and all Judea, and **e** one in Egypt, B
2: 3 They decided that **e** one who had B
4: 4 So they sent word to **e** district of Samaria,
4: 9 **e** man of Israel cried out to God with great G
4:10 and **e** resident alien and hired laborer
7:20 until all the water containers of **e** inhabitant
9:14 and **e** tribe know and understand that you are God,
11: 7 of him who has sent you to direct **e** living being!
11:17 but **e** night your servant will go out into the valley
14: 2 and let **e** able-bodied man go out of the town;
14: 7 and said, "Blessed are you in **e** tent of Judah!
14: 7 In **e** nation those who hear your name will H
15: 2 with one impulse all rushed out and fled by **e** path
16:16 **e** sacrifice as a fragrant offering is a small thing,
AdE 1:22 to **e** province in its own language,
1:22 so that in **e** house respect would be shown
1:22 every house respect would be shown to **e** husband.
2:11 And **e** day Mordecai walked in the courtyard of D
3: 8 from those of **e** other nation,
3:12 the governors in **e** province from India to Ethiopia.
3:14 Copies of the document were posted in **e** province,
4: 3 And in **e** province where the king's proclamation
8:11 the Jews in **e** city to observe their own laws,
8:17 in **e** city and province wherever
9:27 in **e** city, family, and country.
11: 7 At their roaring **e** nation prepared for war, H
11:12 seeking all day to understand it in **e** detail.
13: 4 to those of **e** nation and continually disregard H
13: 5 stands constantly in opposition to **e** nation, H
13:10 and earth and **e** wonderful thing under heaven.
14: 2 **e** part that she loved to adorn she covered
16:11 so fully the goodwill that we have for **e** nation H
16:19 post a copy of this letter publicly in **e** place,
16:24 "**E** city and country, without exception,
Wis 6:16 and meets them in **e** thought.
7:27 in **e** generation she passes into holy souls
7:29 and excels **e** constellation of the stars.
13:14 and covering **e** blemish in it with paint;
14: 4 showing that you can save from **e** danger,
14:27 the beginning and cause and end of **e** evil.
16: 8 that it is you who deliver from **e** evil.
16:20 providing **e** pleasure and suited to every taste.
16:20 providing every pleasure and suited to **e** taste.
Sir 5: 9 Do not winnow in **e** wind, or follow **e** path.
6:35 Be ready to listen to **e** godly discourse,
10: 6 Do not get angry with your neighbor for **e** injury,
13:15 **E** creature loves its like, and **e** person the neighbor.
14:19 **E** work decays and ceases to exist,
15:19 and he knows **e** human action.
16:14 He makes room for **e** act of mercy;
17:17 He appointed a ruler for **e** nation, H
18:13 the compassion of the Lord is for **e** living thing.
18:28 **E** intelligent person knows wisdom,
22: 1 and **e** one hisses at his disgrace. B
23:19 they look upon **e** aspect of human behavior

Sir 24: 6 and over **e** people and nation I have held sway.
26:12 of **e** tent peg and open her quiver to the arrow.
26:27 *e person who lives like this lives in the anarchy*
29: 3 and on **e** occasion you will find what you need.
29:12 and it will rescue you from **e** disaster;
30: 7 and will suffer heartache at **e** cry.
31: 7 and **e** fool will be taken captive by it.
31:15 and in **e** matter be thoughtful.
32:23 Guard yourself in **e** act, for this is the keeping of
35:11 With **e** gift show a cheerful face,
37: 1 **E** friend says, "I too am a friend";
37:16 Discussion is the beginning of **e** work,
37:16 and counsel precedes **e** undertaking.
37:29 Do not be greedy for **e** delicacy,
38:27 So too is **e** artisan and master artisan who labors
39:18 When he commands, his **e** purpose is fulfilled,
39:33 and he will supply **e** need in its time.
41:16 for it is not good to feel shame in **e** circumstance,
41:16 nor is **e** kind of abashment to be approved. A
43:20 it settles on **e** pool of water,
45:14 be wholly burned twice **e** day continually. D
46: 5 when enemies pressed him on **e** side, C
46:16 when his enemies pressed him on **e** side, C
47: 7 For he wiped out his enemies on **e** side, C
47:25 For they sought out **e** kind of wickedness, A
48:12 and marvels with **e** utterance of his mouth.
49: 1 his memory is as sweet as honey to **e** mouth,
49:16 but above **e** other created living being was Adam.
51: 4 from choking fire on **e** side, C
51: 7 They surrounded me on **e** side, C
Bar 5: 7 For God has ordered that **e** high mountain and
5: 8 The woods and **e** fragrant tree have shaded Israel
LtJ 6:18 on **e** side against anyone who has offended C
6:61 and the wind likewise blows in **e** land.
6:71 a thornbush in a garden on which **e** bird perches;
Sus 1: 8 **E** day the two elders used to see her, D
Bel 1: 3 and **e** day they provided for it twelve bushels D
1: 4 The king revered it and went **e** day to worship it. D
1: 6 not see how much he eats and drinks **e** day?" D
1:32 **e** day they had been given two human bodies D
1Mc 1:25 Israel mourned deeply in **e** community,
1:27 **E** bridegroom took up the lament;
1:37 On **e** side of the sanctuary they shed innocent C
1:53 into hiding in **e** place of refuge they had.
2:27 "Let **e** one who is zealous for the law and B
4:59 that **e** year at that season the days of dedication L
5:28 and killed **e** male by the edge of the sword; E
5:35 and he killed **e** male in it, plundered it, E
5:51 He destroyed **e** male by the edge of the sword, E
6:18 in **e** way to harm them and strengthen the F
8: 4 the rest paid them tribute **e** year. L
8:15 **e** day three hundred twenty senators constantly D
10:42 of silver that my officials have received **e** year L
12: 4 Romans gave them letters to the people in **e** place,
12:11 therefore remember you constantly on **e** occasion,
13:10 and he fortified it on **e** side. C
13:20 along opposite him to **e** place he went.
13:52 that **e** year they should celebrate this day L
14:35 He sought in **e** way to exalt his people. F
15: 8 **E** debt you owe to the royal treasury
2Mc 1:17 Blessed in **e** way be our God, F
1:25 You rescue Israel from **e** evil;
2:30 to discuss matters from **e** side,
9: 7 fall was so hard as to torture **e** limb of his body.
9:11 for he was tortured with pain **e** moment.
9:17 and would visit **e** inhabited place to proclaim
10: 8 of the Jews should observe these days **e** year. L
10:13 He heard himself called a traitor at **e** turn,
10:14 and at **e** turn kept attacking the Jews.
11: 3 and to put up the high priesthood for sale **e** year. L
11:15 For the king granted **e** request in behalf of
12:22 In their flight they rushed headlong in **e** direction,
1Es 1:33 and **e** one of the acts of Josiah, and his splendor, B
3:20 It turns **e** thought to feasting and mirth,
4:15 Women gave birth to the king and to **e** people
4:52 to be offered on the altar **e** day, in accordance D
5:51 and offered the proper sacrifices **e** day, D
6:30 regularly **e** year, without quibbling, L
6:33 upon, destroy **e** king and nation
8:52 and will support them in **e** way." F
8:61 he delivered us from **e** enemy on the way,
3Mc 1:13 he inquired why, when he entered **e** other temple,
3:23 in **e** situation, in accordance
3:24 that they are ill-disposed toward us in **e** way, F
3:29 **E** place detected sheltering a Jew is to
4: 1 In **e** place, then, where this decree arrived,
5: 7 bonds they were forcibly confined on **e** side. C
5:51 over **e** power to manifest himself and be merciful
6: 1 throughout his life had been adorned with **e** virtue,
6:25 and foolishly gathered **e** one of them here? B
7: 7 we justly have acquitted them of **e** charge
7: 9 not a mortal but the Ruler over **e** power,
2Es 3: 8 And **e** nation walked after its own will; H
5:23 from **e** forest of the earth and
5:34 for **e** hour I suffer agonies of heart,
7:89 and withstood danger **e** hour so
8: 6 by which **e** mortal who bears the likeness of
9:44 **E** hour and every day during those thirty years
9:44 and **e** day during those thirty years I prayed D
12:49 Now go to your homes, **e** one of you, B
15: 6 because iniquity has spread throughout **e** land,
15:40 and shall pour out upon **e** high and lofty place
16:29 or four olives may be left on **e** tree, J
16:39 and pains will seize it on **e** side. C
16:50 the one who searches out **e** sin on earth.
4Mc 2: 4 of sexual desire, but also over **e** desire.
5: 2 ordered the guards to seize each and **e** Hebrew and
4Mc 8: 3 modest, noble, and accomplished in **e** way— F
8: 5 with favorable feelings I admire each and **e** one B
8: 9 you will compel me to destroy each and **e** one B
9:14 with **e** member disjointed he denounced the tyrant,
15:32 from **e** side by the flood of your emotions and
18: 1 obey this law and exercise piety in **e** way, F

EVERYBODY (2) [EVERY]

Pr 26:10 Like an archer who wounds **e** is one who hires
Mt 13:25 but while **e** was asleep, an enemy came

EVERYDAY (1) [EVERY, DAY]

2Ti 2: 4 in the army gets entangled in **e** affairs;

EVERYONE‡ (296) [EVERY, ONE]

Ge 16:12 his hand against **e**, and everyone's hand against
21: 6 **e** who hears will laugh with me."
27:29 Cursed be **e** who curses you, and blessed be **e** who blesses you!"
45: 1 and he cried out, "Send **e** away from me."
Ex 12:16 only what **e** must eat, that alone may be prepared
31:14 **e** who profanes it shall be put to death;
33: 7 And **e** who sought the LORD would go out to
35:21 And they came, **e** whose heart was stirred,
35:21 and **e** whose spirit was willing,
35:22 **e** bringing an offering of gold to the LORD.
35:23 And **e** who possessed blue or purple
35:24 **E** who could make an offering of silver
35:24 and **e** who possessed acacia wood of any use in
36: 2 **e** whose heart was stirred to come to do the work;
38:26 for **e** who was counted in the census,
Lev 11:26 **e** who touches one of them shall be unclean.
Nu 1: 3 **e** in Israel able to go to war.
1:20 twenty years old and upward, **e** able to go to war:
1:22 twenty years old and upward, **e** able to go to war:
1:24 twenty years old and upward, **e** able to go to war:
1:26 twenty years old and upward, **e** able to go to war:
1:28 twenty years old and upward, **e** able to go to war:
1:30 twenty years old and upward, **e** able to go to war:
1:32 twenty years old and upward, **e** able to go to war:
1:34 twenty years old and upward, **e** able to go to war:
1:36 twenty years old and upward, **e** able to go to war:
1:38 twenty years old and upward, **e** able to go to war:
1:40 twenty years old and upward, **e** able to go to war:
1:42 twenty years old and upward, **e** able to go to war:
1:45 twenty years old and upward, **e** able to go to war
2:34 and they set out the same way, **e** by clans,
4:30 **e** who qualifies to do the work of the tent
4:35 **e** who qualified for work relating to the tent
4:39 **e** who qualified for work relating to the tent
4:43 **e** who qualified for work relating to the tent
4:47 **e** who qualified to do the work of service and
5: 2 of the camp **e** who is leprous, or has a discharge,
5: 2 **e** who is unclean through contact with a corpse;
16: 3 All the congregation are holy, **e** of them,
16:32 **e** who belonged to Korah and all their goods.
17:13 **E** who approaches the tabernacle of
18:11 **e** who is clean in your house may eat them.
18:13 **e** who is clean in your house may eat of it.
19:14 **e** who comes into the tent,
19:14 and **e** who is in the tent,
21: 8 and **e** who is bitten shall look at it and live."
24: 9 Blessed is **e** who blesses you, and cursed is **e** who curses you."
26: 2 **e** in Israel able to go to war."
32:27 **e** armed for war, to do battle for the LORD,
32:29 **e** armed for battle before the LORD,
Dt 4: 3 from among you **e** who followed the Baal of Peor,
1Sa 2:36 **E** who is left in your family shall come
4:10 Israel was defeated, and they fled, **e** to his home.
9: 2 he stood head and shoulders above **e** else.
22: 2 **E** who was in distress, and **e** who was in debt, and **e** who was discontented gathered to him;
26:23 The LORD rewards **e** for his righteousness
2Sa 13: 9 Amnon said, "Send out **e** from me."
13: 9 So **e** went out from him.
20: 1 **E** to your tents, O Israel!"
1Ki 9: 8 **e** passing by it will be astonished, and will hiss;
12:24 Let **e** go home, for this thing is from me."
2Ki 3:25 and on every good piece of land **e** threw a stone,
14:12 Judah was defeated by Israel; **e** fled home.
21:12 and Judah such evil that the ears of **e** who hears
2Ch 7:21 now exalted, **e** passing by will be astonished,
11: 4 Let **e** return home, for this thing is from me."
23:10 a guard for the king, **e** with weapon in hand,
25:22 Judah was defeated by Israel; **e** fled home.
30:17 to slaughter the passover lamb for **e** who was
31: 2 division by division, **e** according to his service,
31:19 to every male among the priests and to **e** among
Ezr 1: 5 **e** whose spirit God had stirred—
3: 5 the offerings of **e** who made a freewill offering to
Ne 5:13 "So may God shake out **e** from house and
Job 21:33 **e** will follow after, and those who went
36:25 **e** watches it from far away.
Ps 31:19 for those who take refuge in you, in the sight of **e**!
39: 5 Surely **e** stands as a mere breath.
39: 6 Surely **e** goes about like a shadow.
39:11 surely **e** is a mere breath.
64: 9 Then **e** will fear; they will tell what God has
84:12 O LORD of hosts, happy is **e** who trusts in you.
116:11 I said in my consternation, "**E** is a liar."
128: 1 Happy is **e** who fears the LORD,
Pr 19: 6 and **e** is a friend to a giver of gifts.
21: 5 but **e** who is hasty comes only to want.
Ecc 3:10 I have seen the business that God has given to **e** to
Ecc 7: 2 the end of **e**, and the living will lay it to heart.
9: 3 that the same fate comes to **e**.
10: 3 they lack sense, and show to **e** that they are fools.
12:13 for that is the whole duty of **e**.
Isa 1:23 **E** loves a bribe and runs after gifts.
2: 9 so people are humbled, and **e** is brought low—
2:11 and the pride of **e** shall be humbled;
2:17 and the pride of **e** shall be brought low;
3: 5 **e** by another and **e** by a neighbor;
4: 3 **e** who has been recorded for life in Jerusalem,
5:15 People are bowed down, **e** is brought low,
6:12 until the LORD sends **e** far away,
7:22 **e** that is left in the land shall eat curds and honey.
9:17 for **e** was godless and an evildoer,
15: 3 the housetops and in the squares **e** wails and melts
16: 7 Therefore let Moab wail, let **e** wail for Moab.
19:17 **e** to whom it is mentioned will fear because of
30: 5 **e** comes to shame through a people
36:16 then **e** of you will eat from your own vine
43: 7 **e** who is called by my name,
55: 1 Ho, **e** who thirsts, come to the waters;
Jer 5: 6 **e** who goes out of them shall be torn in pieces—
6:13 **e** is greedy for unjust gain;
6:13 and from prophet to priest, **e** deals falsely.
8:10 the least to the greatest **e** is greedy for unjust gain;
8:10 from prophet to priest **e** deals falsely.
10:14 **E** is stupid and without knowledge;
11: 8 but **e** walked in the stubbornness of an evil will.
12:15 to their heritage and to their land, **e** of them.
19: 3 that the ears of **e** who hears of it will tingle.
19: 8 **e** who passes by it will be horrified and will hiss
20: 7 become a laughingstock all day long; **e** mocks me.
25: 5 **e** of you, from your evil way and wicked doings,
30:16 **e** of them, shall go into captivity;
31:30 the teeth of **e** who eats sour grapes shall be set
35:15 saying, 'Turn now **e** of you from your evil way,
43: 6 and **e** whom Nebuzaradan the captain of
44:12 of Egypt to settle, and they shall perish, **e**;
48:44 **E** who flees from the terror shall fall into the pit,
48:44 and **e** who climbs out of the pit shall be caught in
49:17 **e** who passes by it will be horrified and will hiss
50:13 **e** who passes by Babylon shall be appalled
51:17 **E** is stupid and without knowledge;
Eze 16:44 **e** who uses proverbs will use this proverb
20:11 by whose observance **e** shall live.
20:13 by whose observance **e** shall live;
20:21 by whose observance **e** shall live;
20:39 Go serve your idols, **e** of you now and hereafter,
22: 6 princes of Israel in you, **e** according to his power,
23: 7 and she defiled herself with all the idols of **e**
Da 3:10 that **e** who hears the sound of the horn, pipe, lyre,
12: 1 **e** who is found written in the book.
Joel 2:32 Then **e** who calls on the name of the LORD shall
Am 8: 8 and **e** mourn who lives in it,
Ob 1: 9 so that **e** from Mount Esau will be cut off.
Jnh 3: 5 they proclaimed a fast, and **e**, great and small,
Hab 2: 6 Shall not **e** taunt such people and,
Zep 2:15 **E** who passes by it hisses and shakes the fist.
Zec 5: 3 for **e** who steals shall be cut off according to
5: 3 and **e** who swears falsely shall be cut off according
10: 1 the vegetation in the field to **e**.
Mt 5:28 But I say to you that **e** who looks at a woman
5:42 Give to **e** who begs from you,
7: 8 For **e** who asks receives, and **e** who searches finds, and for **e** who knocks, the door will be opened.
7:21 "Not **e** who says to me, 'Lord, Lord,'
7:24 "**E** then who hears these words of mine and acts
7:26 And **e** who hears these words of mine and does
10:32 "**E** therefore who acknowledges me before others,
16:27 and then he will repay **e** for what has been done.
19:11 he said to them, "Not **e** can accept this teaching,
19:29 And **e** who has left houses or brothers or sisters
22: 9 and invite **e** you find to the wedding banquet.'
Mk 1:37 they said to him, "**E** is searching for you."
5:20 for him; and **e** was amazed.
9:49 "For **e** will be salted with fire.
Lk 4:15 to teach in their synagogues and was praised by **e**.
6:30 Give to **e** who begs from you;
6:40 but **e** who is fully qualified will be like the teacher.
9:43 While **e** was amazed at all that he was doing,
11: 4 for we ourselves forgive **e** indebted to us.
11:10 For **e** who asks receives, and **e** who searches finds, and for **e** who knocks, the door will be opened.
12: 8 I tell you, **e** who acknowledges me before others,
12:10 And **e** who speaks a word against the Son
12:41 "Lord, are you telling this parable for us or for **e**?"
12:48 From **e** to whom much has been given,
16:16 and **e** tries to enter it by force.
20:18 **E** who falls on that stone will be broken to pieces;
Jn 1: 9 The true light, which enlightens **e**,
2:10 "**E** serves the good wine first,
2:25 for he himself knew what was in **e**.
3: 8 So it is with **e** who is born of the Spirit."
3:16 so that **e** who believes in him may not perish
4:13 "**E** who drinks of this water will be thirsty again,
6:45 **E** who has heard and learned from
8:34 I tell you, **e** who commits sin is a slave to sin.
11:26 and **e** who lives and believes in me will never die.
11:48 If we let him go on like this, **e** will believe in him,
12:46 so that **e** who believes in me should not remain in
13:35 By this **e** will know that you are my disciples,
18:37 **E** who belongs to the truth listens to my voice."
19:12 **E** who claims to be a king sets himself against
Ac 2:21 Then **e** who calls on the name of the Lord shall
2:39 **e** whom the Lord our God calls to him."
2:43 Awe came upon **e**, because many wonders
3:23 be that **e** who does not listen to that prophet will

Ac 10:43 the prophets testify about him that **e** who believes
13:39 by this Jesus **e** who believes is set free
19:17 both Jews and Greeks, **e** was awestruck;
20:31 not cease night or day to warn **e** with tears.
21:28 This is the man who is teaching **e** everywhere
Ro 1:16 the power of God for salvation to **e** who has faith,
2: 9 be anguish and distress for **e** who does evil,
2:10 glory and honor and peace for **e** who does good,
3: 4 Although **e** is a liar, let God be proved true,
10: 4 be righteousness for **e** who believes.
10:13 "**E** who calls on the name of the Lord shall
12: 3 For by the grace given to me I say to **e** among you
1Co 8: 7 It is not **e**, however, who has this knowledge.
10:13 that is not common to **e**.
10:33 just as I try to please **e** in everything I do,
12: 6 it is the same God who activates all of them in **e**.
16:16 and of **e** who works and toils with them.
2Co 4: 2 to the conscience of **e** in the sight of God.
Gal 3:10 for it is written, "Cursed is **e** who does not observe
3:13 it is written, "Cursed is **e** who hangs on a tree"—
Eph 2: 3 by nature children of wrath, like **e** else.
3: 9 and to make **e** see what is the plan of
Php 1:13 throughout the whole imperial guard and to **e** else
4: 5 Let your gentleness be known to **e**.
Col 1:28 warning **e** and teaching **e** in all wisdom,
1:28 so that we may present **e** mature in Christ.
4: 6 so that you may know how you ought to answer **e**.
1Th 2:15 they displease God and oppose **e**
2Th 1: 3 the love of **e** of you for one another is increasing.
1Ti 2: 1 intercessions, and thanksgivings be made for **e**,
2: 4 who desires **e** to be saved and to come to
2Ti 2:19 and, "Let **e** who calls on the name of
2:24 not be quarrelsome but kindly to **e**,
3: 9 their folly will become plain to **e**.
3:17 so that **e** who belongs to God may be proficient,
Tit 3: 2 to be gentle, and to show every courtesy to **e**.
3: 8 these things are excellent and profitable to **e**.
Heb 2: 9 that by the grace of God he might taste death for **e**.
5:13 for **e** who lives on milk,
12:14 Pursue peace with **e**, and the holiness
Jas 1:19 let **e** be quick to listen, slow to speak,
1Pe 2:17 Honor **e**. Love the family of believers.
4: 6 they had been judged in the flesh as **e** is judged,
1Jn 2:23 **e** who confesses the Son has the Father also.
2:29 that **e** who does right has been born of him.
3: 4 **E** who commits sin is guilty of lawlessness;
3: 7 **E** who does what is right is righteous,
3: 8 **E** who commits sin is a child of the devil;
4: 7 **e** who loves is born of God and knows God.
5: 1 **E** who believes that Jesus is
5: 1 and **e** who loves the parent loves the child.
2Jn 1: 9 **E** who does not abide in the teaching of Christ,
3Jn 1:12 **E** has testified favorably about Demetrius,
Jude 1:15 and to convict **e** of all the deeds of ungodliness
Rev 2: 7 To **e** who conquers, I will give permission to eat
2:17 To **e** who conquers I will give some of
2:26 To **e** who conquers and continues to do my works
6:15 the generals and the rich and the powerful, and **e**,
13: 8 **e** whose name has not been written from
22:15 and **e** who loves and practices falsehood.
22:17 And let **e** who hears say, "Come."
22:17 And let **e** who is thirsty come.
22:18 I warn **e** who hears the words of the prophecy
Tob 1:10 **e** of my kindred and my people ate the food of
Jdt 2:18 for **e**, and a huge amount of gold and silver from
2:25 and killed **e** who resisted him.
13: 4 So **e** went out, and no one, either small or great,
15: 3 Then the Israelites, **e** that was a soldier,
AdE 6: 9 be done to **e** whom the king honors.' "
6:11 "Thus shall it be done to **e** whom the king wishes
Wis 7: 1 I also am mortal, like **e** else,
Sir 11:29 Do not invite **e** into your home,
16:14 **e** receives in accordance with one's deeds.
37:28 For not everything is good for **e**,
40: 1 Hard work was created for **e**,
42: 1 and will find favor with **e**.
1Mc 1:52 Many of the people, **e** who forsook the law,
2:19 to obey his commandments, **e** of them abandoning
10:33 And **e** of the Jews taken as a captive from the land
2Mc 1:23 the priests offered prayer—the priests and **e**.
5: 4 Therefore **e** prayed that the apparition might prove
5: 8 pursued by **e**, hated as a rebel against the laws,
5:12 to cut down relentlessly **e** they met and
10:35 the wall and with savage fury cut down **e** they met.
15:35 and conspicuous sign to **e** of the help of the Lord.
1Es 3:21 and makes **e** talk in millions.
4:39 or wicked. **E** approves its deeds,
3Mc 3: 5 they were established in good repute with **e**.
2Es 7:27 **E** who has been delivered from the evils
7:75 as soon as **e** of us yields up the soul,
16:53 of fire on the head of **e** who says,
4Mc 1: 2 subject is essential to **e** who is seeking knowledge,
4:26 to compel **e** in the nation to eat defiling foods and
13: 1 **e** must concede that devout reason is sovereign

EVERYONE'S (8) [EVERY, ONE]

Ge 16:12 a man, with his hand against everyone, and **e** hand
1Sa 11: 2 namely that I gouge out **e** right eye,
Job 37: 7 serves as a sign on **e** hand,
Jer 23:36 for the burden is **e** own word,
Ac 1:24 they prayed and said, "Lord, you know **e** heart.
16:26 and **e** chains were unfastened.
Rev 22:12 to repay according to **e** work.
Wis 16:21 was changed to suit **e** liking.

EVERYTHING‡ (233) [EVERY, THING]

Ge 1:25 and **e** that creeps upon the ground of every kind.
1:30 and to **e** that creeps on the earth, **e** that has the breath of life,
1:31 God saw **e** that he had made, and indeed,
6:17 **e** that is on the earth shall die.
7: 8 and of birds, and of **e** that creeps on the ground,
7:22 **e** on dry land in whose nostrils was the breath
8:19 and every bird, **e** that moves on the earth,
9: 2 on **e** that creeps on the ground,
9: 3 just as I gave you the green plants, I give you **e**.
14:20 And Abram gave him one tenth of **e**.
32:23 and likewise **e** that he had.
33:11 and because I have **e** I want."
39: 8 and he has put **e** that he has in my hand.
Ex 9:19 and **e** that you have in the open field brought to
9:25 The hail struck down **e** that was in the open field
19: 8 "**E** that the LORD has spoken we will do."
39:32 the Israelites had done **e** just as
40:16 Moses did **e** just as the LORD had commanded him.
Lev 11: 9 **E** in the waters that has fins and scales,
11:12 **E** in the waters that does not have fins
11:35 **E** on which any part of the carcass falls shall
15: 4 and **e** on which he sits shall be unclean.
15:17 **E** made of cloth or of skin on which
15:20 **E** upon which she lies during her impurity shall
15:20 **e** also upon which she sits shall be unclean.
15:26 and **e** on which she sits shall be unclean,
Nu 15:23 **e** that the LORD has commanded you by Moses,
29:40 So Moses told the Israelites **e** just as
31:20 **e** made of goats' hair, and every article of wood."
31:23 **e** that can withstand fire, shall be passed
Dt 2:36 The LORD our God gave **e** to us.
3:21 "Your own eyes have seen **e** that
5:27 Then tell us **e** that the LORD our God tells you,
12:11 then you shall bring **e** that I command you to
12:14 and there you shall do **e** I command you.
12:32 You must diligently observe **e**
13:15 utterly destroying it and **e** in it—
17:10 diligently observing **e** they instruct you.
18:18 who shall speak to them **e** that I command.
20:14 the children, livestock, and **e** else in the town,
28:20 panic, and frustration in **e** you attempt to do,
28:47 and with gladness of heart for the abundance of **e**,
28:48 in hunger and thirst, in nakedness and lack of **e**.
29: 9 in order that you may succeed in **e** that you do.
Jos 4:10 the middle of the Jordan, until **e** was finished that
6:24 They burned down the city, and **e** in it;
Jdg 11:24 And should we not be the ones to possess **e** that
13:14 She is to observe **e** that I commanded her."
1Sa 3:18 So Samuel told him **e** and hid nothing from him.
30:19 that had been taken; David brought back **e**.
2Sa 3:36 just as **e** the king did pleased all the people.
15:36 and by them you shall report to me **e** you hear."
1Ki 14:26 of the king's house; he took **e**.
2Ki 5:21 the chariot to meet him and said, "Is **e** all right?"
9:11 they said to him, "Is **e** all right?
16:16 priest Uriah did **e** that King Ahaz commanded.
1Ch 10:11 But when all Jabesh-gilead heard **e** that
16:32 let the field exult, and **e** in it.
26:32 of the Manassites for **e** pertaining to God and for
2Ch 12: 9 of the king's house; he took **e**.
31: 5 and they brought in abundantly the tithe of **e**.
Ezr 8:34 and the weight of **e** was recorded.
Ne 5:12 "We will restore **e** and demand nothing more
13:30 Thus I cleansed them from **e** foreign,
Est 4:17 and did **e** as Esther had ordered him.
6:13 and all his friends **e** that had happened to him,
Job 28:24 and sees **e** under the heavens.
41:34 It surveys **e** that is lofty;
Ps 69:34 the seas and **e** that moves in them.
74: 3 the enemy has destroyed **e** in the sanctuary.
96:12 the field exult, and **e** in it.
138: 2 have exalted your name and your word above **e**.
150: 6 Let **e** that breathes praise the LORD!
Pr 14:15 The simple believe **e**, but the clever consider
16: 4 The LORD has made **e** for its purpose,
24:27 get **e** ready for you in the field;
Ecc 3: 1 For **e** there is a season, and a time for every matter
3:11 He has made **e** suitable for its time;
7:15 In my vain life I have seen **e**;
7:21 Do not give heed to **e** that people say,
9: 1 hate one does not know. **E** that confronts them
11: 5 not know the work of God, who makes **e**.
Jer 1:17 stand up and tell them **e** that I command you.
25:13 that I have uttered against it, **e** written in this book,
42: 5 according to **e** that the LORD your God sends us
44:17 Instead, we will do **e** that we have vowed,
44:18 we have lacked **e** and have perished by the sword
50:32 and it will devour **e** around him.
Eze 7:14 They have blown the horn and made **e** ready;
30:12 upon the land and **e** in it by the hand of foreigners;
47: 9 and **e** will live where the river goes.
Da 2:40 just as iron crushes and smashes **e**,
Zep 1: 2 I will utterly sweep away **e** from the face of
Mt 7:12 "In **e** do to others as you would have them do
18:26 'Have patience with me, and I will pay you **e**.'
19:27 "Look, we have left **e** and followed you.
22: 4 and **e** is ready; come to the wedding banquet.'
23:20 swears by it and by **e** on it;
28:11 and told the chief priests **e** that had happened.
28:20 to obey **e** that I have commanded you.
Mk 4:11 but for those outside, **e** comes in parables;
4:34 but he explained **e** in private to his disciples.
7:37 saying, "He has done **e** well;
8:25 and his sight was restored, and he saw **e** clearly.
Mk 10:28 "Look, we have left **e** and followed you."
11:11 and when he had looked around at **e**,
12:44 but she out of her poverty has put in **e** she had,
13:23 But be alert; I have already told you **e**.
14:16 and found **e** as he had told them;
Lk 1: 3 after investigating **e** carefully from the very first,
2:39 When they had finished **e** required by the law of
5:11 they left **e** and followed him.
5:28 And he got up, left **e**, and followed him.
11:41 and see, **e** will be clean for you.
14:17 'Come; for **e** is ready now.'
15:14 When he had spent **e**, a severe famine took place
18:31 and **e** that is written about the Son of Man by
22:13 So they went and found **e** as he had told them;
24:44 that **e** written about me in the law of Moses,
Jn 4:29 and see a man who told me **e** I have ever done!
4:39 "He told me **e** I have ever done."
6:37 **E** that the Father gives me will come to me,
10:41 but **e** that John said about this man was true."
14:26 the Father will send in my name, will teach you **e**,
15:15 to you **e** that I have heard from my Father.
17: 7 they know that **e** you have given me is from you;
21:17 And he said to him, "Lord, you know **e**;
Ac 4:24 the heaven and the earth, the sea, and **e** in them,
4:32 but **e** they owned was held in common.
10: 8 and after telling them **e**, he sent them to Joppa.
11:10 then **e** was pulled up again to heaven.
13:29 they had carried out **e** that was written about him,
17:24 The God who made the world and **e** in it,
22:10 there you will be told **e** that has been assigned
24: 8 from him concerning **e** of which we accuse him."
24:14 believing **e** laid down according to the law
Ro 8:32 will he not with him also give us **e** else?
14:20 **E** is indeed clean, but it is wrong for you
1Co 2:10 for the Spirit searches **e**, even the depths of God.
7:19 but obeying the commandments of God is **e**.
10:31 or whatever you do, do **e** for the glory of God.
10:33 just as I try to please everyone in **e** I do,
11: 2 I commend you because you remember me in **e**
2Co 2: 9 and to know whether you are obedient in **e**.
4:15 Yes, **e** is for your sake, so that grace,
5:17 **e** old has passed away; see, **e** has become new!
6:10 as having nothing, and yet possessing **e**.
7:14 but just as **e** we said to you was true,
8: 7 Now as you excel in **e**—
9: 8 so that by always having enough of **e**,
12:19 **E** we do, beloved, is for the sake
Gal 6:15 but a new creation is **e**!
Eph 5:13 but **e** exposed by the light becomes visible,
5:14 for **e** that becomes visible is light.
5:20 to God the Father at all times and for **e** in the name
5:24 so also wives ought to be, in **e**, to their husbands.
6:13 and having done **e**, to stand firm.
6:21 and what I am doing, Tychicus will tell you **e**.
Php 3: 8 I regard **e** as loss because of the surpassing value
4: 6 but in **e** by prayer and supplication
Col 1:11 may you be prepared to endure **e** with patience,
1:18 so that he might come to have first place in **e**.
3:14 which binds **e** together in perfect harmony.
3:17 do **e** in the name of the Lord Jesus,
3:20 Children, obey your parents in **e**,
3:22 Slaves, obey your earthly masters in **e**,
4: 9 They will tell you about **e** here.
4:12 that you may stand mature and fully assured in **e**
1Th 5:21 but test **e**; hold fast to what is good;
1Ti 4: 4 For **e** created by God is good,
6:17 but rather on God who richly provides us with **e**
2Ti 2:10 Therefore I endure **e** for the sake of the elect,
Tit 2:10 that in **e** they may be an ornament to the doctrine
Heb 2: 8 As it is, we do not yet see **e** in subjection to them,
7: 2 and to him Abraham apportioned "one-tenth of **e**."
8: 5 "See that you make **e** according to the pattern
9:22 under the law almost **e** is purified with blood,
13:21 in **e** good so that you may do his will,
2Pe 1: 3 His divine power has given us **e** needed for life
3:10 the earth and **e** that is done on it will be disclosed.
1Jn 3:20 for God is greater than our hearts, and he knows **e**.
Tob 1:13 and I used to buy **e** he needed.
4:14 "Watch yourself, my son, in **e** you do,
5: 1 "I will do **e** that you have commanded me, father;
14: 4 **e** that was spoken by the prophets of Israel,
Jdt 4: 1 When the Israelites living in Judea heard of **e**
8:25 of **e** let us give thanks to the Lord our God,
AdE 8: 2 Esther set Mordecai over **e** that had been Haman's.
16: 4 the evil-hating justice of God, who always sees **e**.
Wis 18:13 they had disbelieved **e** because of their magic arts,
19:22 For in **e**, O Lord, you have exalted
Sir 15:18 he is mighty in power and sees **e**;
17: 2 but granted them authority over **e** on the earth.
17:30 For not **e** is within human capability,
18:27 One who is wise is cautious in **e**;
19:15 so do not believe **e** you hear.
25:11 Fear of the Lord surpasses **e**;
31:14 Do not reach out your hand for **e** you see,
31:22 In **e** you do be moderate, and no sickness will
37:28 For not **e** is good for everyone,
37:28 for everyone, and no one enjoys **e**.
39:20 the beginning to the end of time he can see **e**,
39:21 for **e** has been created for its own purpose.
39:34 for **e** proves good in its appointed time.
41: 1 to worry about and is prosperous in **e**,
41: 2 worn down by age and anxious about **e**;
42:16 The sun looks down on **e** with its light,
Bel 1:15 and they ate and drank **e**.
1Mc 1:48 to make themselves abominable by **e** unclean
2Mc 7:28 to look at the heaven and the earth and see **e** that is
10:23 Having success at arms in **e** he undertook,

2Mc 11:14 and persuaded them to settle **e** on just terms,
11:18 the king of **e** that needed to be brought before him,
1Es 2: 9 their neighbors helped them with **e**,
4: 5 if they win the victory, they bring **e** to the king—
4: 5 whatever spoil they take and **e** else.
4:22 and bring **e** and give it to women?
4:57 **e** that Cyrus had ordered to be done,
8:64 and the weight of **e** was recorded at that very time.
3Mc 2:25 who were strangers to **e** just.
5:42 a Phalaris in **e** and filled with madness,
6:30 and **e** else needed for a festival of seven days,
6:40 they feasted, being provided with **e** by the king,
7: 9 in **e** and inescapably as an antagonist
2Es 3:26 in **e** doing just as Adam
6:39 and darkness and silence embraced **e**;
9: 5 For just as with **e** that has occurred in the world,
13: 3 **e** under his gaze trembled,
14:22 and I will write **e** that has happened in the world
16:54 The Lord certainly knows **e** that people do;
4Mc 14:13 which draws **e** toward an emotion felt

EVERYWHERE (18) [EVERY, WHERE]

Ge 13:10 of the Jordan was well watered **e** like the garden of
Dt 2:25 to put the dread and fear of you upon the peoples **e**
4:19 to all the peoples **e** under heaven.
Mk 16:20 ⟦they went out and proclaimed the good news **e**,⟧
Lk 9: 6 bringing the good news and curing diseases **e**.
Ac 17:30 now he commands all people **e** to repent,
21:28 This is the man who is teaching everyone **e**
24: 3 in every way and **e** with utmost gratitude.
28:22 to this sect we know that **e** it is spoken against."
1Co 4:17 as I teach them **e** in every church.
2Th 3: 1 of the Lord may spread rapidly and be glorified **e**,
Wis 2: 9 **e** let us leave signs of enjoyment,
Sir 50:22 bless the God of all, who **e** works great wonders,
Bar 5: 3 for God will show your splendor **e** under heaven.
2Mc 2:18 on us and will gather us from **e** under heaven
8: 7 And talk of his valor spread **e**.
3Mc 4: 2 **e** their hearts were burning,
7:12 they might destroy those **e** in his kingdom

EVI (2)

Nu 31: 8 They killed the kings of Midian: **E**, Rekem, Zur,
Jos 13:21 **E** and Rekem and Zur and Hur and Reba,

EVICTIONS (1)

Eze 45: 9 Cease your **e** of my people, says the Lord GOD.

EVIDENCE (23) [EVIDENT]

Ex 22:13 If it was mangled by beasts, let it be brought as **e**;
Nu 35:30 the murderer shall be put to death on the **e**
Dt 17: 6 On the **e** of two or three witnesses
17: 6 not be put to death on the **e** of only one witness.
19:15 on the **e** of two or three witnesses shall a charge
22:14 I lay with her, I did not find **e** of her virginity."
22:15 the **e** of the young woman's virginity to the elders
22:17 'I did not find **e** of your daughter's virginity.'
22:17 But here is the **e** of my daughter's virginity."
22:20 **e** of the young woman's virginity was not found,
Pr 12:17 Whoever speaks the truth gives honest **e**,
Mt 18:16 that every word may be confirmed by the **e** of two
2Co 13: 1 be sustained by the **e** of two or three witnesses."
Php 1:28 For them this is **e** of their destruction,
2Th 1: 5 This is **e** of the righteous judgment of God,
1Ti 5:19 an elder except on the **e** of two or three witnesses.
Jas 5: 3 and their rust will be **e** against you,
Tob 5: 2 What **e** am I to give him so that he will recognize
Wis 5:11 no **e** of its passage is found;
10: 7 **E** of their wickedness still remains:
LtJ 6:69 So we have no **e** whatever that they are gods;
Sus 1:43 that these men have given false **e** against me.
1:49 for these men have given false **e** against her."

EVIDENT (10) [EVIDENCE]

Jer 44:23 this disaster has befallen you, as is still **e** today."
2Co 11: 6 in every way and in all things we have made this **e**
Gal 3:11 Now it is **e** that no one is justified before God by
Heb 7:14 it is **e** that our Lord was descended from Judah,
LtJ 6:16 From this it is **e** that they are not gods;
3Mc 4: 1 in their minds was now made **e** and outspoken.
2Es 9: 5 the beginning is **e**, and the end manifest;
4Mc 1: 3 it is **e** that reason rules over those emotions
2:15 It is **e** that reason rules even
3: 1 it is **e** that reason rules not over its own emotions,

EVIL‡ (535) [EVIL-HATING, EVIL-TONGUED, EVILDOER, EVILDOERS, EVILDOING, EVILS]

A. EVIL IN THE SIGHT OF THE †LORD (53)
B. GOOD ... EVIL (22)
C. FROM EVIL (17)
D. EVIL ... GOOD (17)
E. THE EVIL ONE (12)
F. EVIL SPIRIT (11)
G. EVIL WAYS (10)
H. EVIL DEEDS (9)
I. EVIL WAY (7)
J. EVIL SPIRITS (4)

Ge 2: 9 and the tree of the knowledge of good and **e**. B
2:17 the tree of the knowledge of good and **e** you B
3: 5 and you will be like God, knowing good and **e**." B
3:22 like one of us, knowing good and **e**; B
6: 5 the thoughts of their hearts was only **e** continually.
8:21 the inclination of the human heart is **e** from youth;
44: 4 to them, 'Why have you returned **e** for good? D
Ex 10:10 Plainly, you have some **e** purpose in mind.
32:12 with **e** intent that he brought them out to kill them
32:22 you know the people, that they are bent on **e**.
Nu 32:13 that had done **e** in the sight of the LORD A
Dt 1:35 not one of this **e** generation—
4:25 thus doing what is **e** in the sight of the LORD A
9:18 the LORD by doing what was **e** in his sight.
13: 5 So you shall purge the **e** from your midst.
17: 2 who does what is **e** in the sight of the LORD A
17: 7 So you shall purge the **e** from your midst.
17:12 So you shall purge the **e** from Israel.
19:19 So you shall purge the **e** from your midst.
21:21 So you shall purge the **e** from your midst;
22:21 So you shall purge the **e** from your midst.
22:22 So you shall purge the **e** from Israel.
22:24 So you shall purge the **e** from your midst.
24: 7 So you shall purge the **e** from your midst.
28:20 on account of the **e** of your deeds,
31:18 on account of all the **e** they have done by turning
31:29 you will do what is **e** in the sight of the LORD, A
Jdg 2:11 Israelites did what was **e** in the sight of the LORD A
3: 7 Israelites did what was **e** in the sight of the LORD A
3:12 again did what was **e** in the sight of the LORD; A
3:12 had done what was **e** in the sight of the LORD. A
4: 1 again did what was **e** in the sight of the LORD, A
6: 1 did what was **e** in the sight of the LORD, A
9:23 But God sent an **e** spirit between Abimelech and F
10: 6 again did what was **e** in the sight of the LORD, A
13: 1 again did what was **e** in the sight of the LORD, A
20:13 and purge the **e** from Israel."
1Sa 2:23 For I hear of your **e** dealings from all these people.
12:19 the **e** of demanding a king for ourselves."
12:20 you have done all this **e**, yet do not turn aside
15:19 and do what was **e** in the sight of the LORD?" A
16:14 and an **e** spirit from the LORD tormented him. F
16:15 See now, an **e** spirit from God is tormenting you. F
16:16 and when the **e** spirit from God is upon you, F
16:23 whenever the **e** spirit from God came upon Saul, F
16:23 and the **e** spirit would depart from him. F
17:28 I know your presumption and the **e** of your heart;
18:10 next day an **e** spirit from God rushed upon Saul, F
19: 9 Then an **e** spirit from the LORD came upon Saul, F
20: 7 then know that **e** has been determined by him.
20: 9 by my father that **e** should come upon you,
23: 9 David learned that Saul was plotting **e** against him,
24:17 whereas I have repaid you **e**.
25:17 for **e** has been decided against our master and
25:21 but he has returned me **e** for good. D
25:26 now let your enemies and those who seek to do **e**
25:28 and **e** shall not be found in you so long as you live.
25:39 and has kept back his servant from **e**; C
29:10 As for the **e** report, do not take it to heart,
2Sa 12: 9 to do what is **e** in his sight?
14:17 like the angel of God, discerning good and **e**. B
24:16 the LORD relented concerning the **e**,
1Ki 2:44 "You know in your own heart all the **e** that you did
2:44 LORD will bring back your **e** on your own head.
3: 9 able to discern between good and **e**; B
11: 6 did what was **e** in the sight of the LORD, A
13:33 this event Jeroboam did not turn from his **e** way, I
14: 9 but you have done **e** above all those who were
14:10 I will bring **e** upon the house of Jeroboam.
14:22 Judah did what was **e** in the sight of the LORD; A
15:26 He did what was **e** in the sight of the LORD, A
15:34 He did what was **e** in the sight of the LORD, A
16: 7 of all the **e** that he did in the sight of the LORD,
16:19 doing **e** in the sight of the LORD, A
16:25 Omri did what was **e** in the sight of the LORD; A
16:25 he did more **e** than all who were before him.
16:30 Ahab son of Omri did **e** in the sight of the LORD A
21:20 to do what is **e** in the sight of the LORD, A
21:25 to do what was **e** in the sight of the LORD, A
22:52 He did what was **e** in the sight of the LORD, A
2Ki 3: 2 He did what was **e** in the sight of the LORD, A
8:12 the **e** that you will do to the people of Israel;
8:18 He did what was **e** in the sight of the LORD. A
8:27 doing what was **e** in the sight of the LORD, A
13: 2 He did what was **e** in the sight of the LORD, A
13:11 He also did what was **e** in the sight of the LORD; A
14:24 He did what was **e** in the sight of the LORD; A
15: 9 He did what was **e** in the sight of the LORD, A
15:18 He did what was **e** in the sight of the LORD; A
15:24 He did what was **e** in the sight of the LORD; A
15:28 He did what was **e** in the sight of the LORD; A
17: 2 He did what was **e** in the sight of the LORD, A
17:13 from your **e** ways and keep my commandments G
17:17 themselves to do **e** in the sight of the LORD, A
21: 2 He did what was **e** in the sight of the LORD, A
21: 6 He did much **e** in the sight of the LORD, A
21: 9 to do more **e** than the nations had done that
21:12 I am bringing upon Jerusalem and Judah such **e**
21:15 because they have done what is **e** in my sight
21:16 they did what was **e** in the sight of the LORD. A
21:20 He did what was **e** in the sight of the LORD, A
23:32 He did what was **e** in the sight of the LORD, A
23:37 He did what was **e** in the sight of the LORD, A
24: 9 He did what was **e** in the sight of the LORD, A
24:19 He did what was **e** in the sight of the LORD, A
2Ch 12:14 He did **e**, for he did not set his heart to seek
21: 6 He did what was **e** in the sight of the LORD. A
22: 4 He did what was **e** in the sight of the LORD, A
29: 6 done what was **e** in the sight of the LORD A
33: 2 He did what was **e** in the sight of the LORD, A
33: 6 He did much **e** in the sight of the LORD, A
2Ch 33: 9 so that they did more **e** than the nations whom
33:22 He did what was **e** in the sight of the LORD, A
36: 5 He did what was **e** in the sight of the LORD A
36: 9 He did what was **e** in the sight of the LORD. A
36:12 He did what was **e** in the sight of the LORD A
Ezr 9:13 After all that has come upon us for our **e** deeds H
Ne 9:28 after they had rest, they again did **e** before you,
13:17 "What is this **e** thing that you are doing,
13:27 to you and do all this great **e** and act treacherously
Est 8: 3 the **e** design of Haman the Agagite and the plot
Job 1: 1 one who feared God and turned away from **e**. C
1: 8 man who fears God and turns away from **e**." C
2: 3 man who fears God and turns away from **e**. C
15:35 and bring forth **e** and their heart prepares deceit."
28:28 and to depart from **e** is understanding.' " C
30:26 But when I looked for good, **e** came; B
31:29 or exulted when **e** overtook them—
42:11 the **e** that the LORD had brought upon him;
Ps 5: 4 **e** will not sojourn with you.
6: 8 Depart from me, all you workers of **e**,
7: 9 O let the **e** of the wicked come to an end,
7:14 See how they conceive **e**, and are pregnant
15: 3 and do no **e** to their friends,
21:11 If they plan **e** against you, if they devise mischief,
23: 4 I walk through the darkest valley, I fear no **e**;
26:10 those in whose hands are **e** devices,
28: 3 with those who are workers of **e**,
28: 4 and according to the **e** of their deeds;
34:13 Keep your tongue from **e**, C
34:14 Depart from **e**, and do good; CD
34:21 **E** brings death to the wicked,
35: 4 be turned back and confounded who devise **e**
35:12 They repay me **e** for good; my soul is forlorn. D
36: 4 not good; they do not reject **e**.
37: 7 over those who carry out **e** devices.
37: 8 Do not fret—it leads only to **e**.
37:19 they are not put to shame in **e** times,
37:27 Depart from **e**, and do good; CD
38:20 Those who render me **e** for good D
50:19 "You give your mouth free rein for **e**,
51: 4 have I sinned, and done what is **e** in your sight,
52: 3 You love **e** more than good,
54: 5 He will repay my enemies for their **e**.
55:15 for **e** is in their homes and in their hearts.
56: 5 all their thoughts are against me for **e**.
59: 2 Deliver me from those who work **e**;
59: 5 spare none of those who treacherously plot **e**.
64: 5 They hold fast to their **e** purpose;
90:15 and as many years as we have seen **e**.
91:10 no **e** shall befall you, no scourge come
92:11 my ears have heard the doom of my **e** assailants.
97:10 The LORD loves those who hate **e**;
101: 4 I will know nothing of **e**.
109: 5 So they reward me **e** for good, D
109:20 of those who speak **e** against my life.
112: 7 They are not afraid of **e** tidings;
119:101 I hold back my feet from every **e** way, I
119:150 with **e** purpose draw near;
121: 7 The LORD will keep you from all **e**;
139:20 and lift themselves up against you for **e**!
140: 2 who plan **e** things in their minds and stir
140: 8 do not further their **e** plot.
140:11 let **e** speedily hunt down the violent!
141: 4 Do not turn my heart to any **e**,
Pr 1:16 for their feet run to **e**,
2:12 It will save you from the way of **e**,
2:14 in doing **e** and delight in the perverseness of evil;
2:14 in doing evil and delight in the perverseness of **e**;
3: 7 fear the LORD, and turn away from **e**. C
4:27 turn your foot away from **e**. C
6:14 with perverted mind devising **e**,
6:18 feet that hurry to run to **e**,
8:13 The fear of the LORD is hatred of **e**.
8:13 and the way of **e** and perverted speech I hate.
11:19 but whoever pursues **e** will die.
11:27 but **e** comes to the one who searches for it.
12: 2 but those who devise **e** he condemns.
12:13 **e** are ensnared by the transgression of their lips,
12:20 Deceit is in the mind of those who plan **e**,
13:19 to turn away from **e** is an abomination to fools. C
14:16 The wise are cautious and turn away from **e**, C
14:19 The **e** bow down before the good, D
14:22 Do they not err that plan **e**?
15: 3 keeping watch on the **e** and the good. D
15:26 **E** plans are an abomination to the LORD,
15:28 but the mouth of the wicked pours out **e**.
16: 6 and by the fear of the LORD one avoids **e**.
16:12 It is an abomination to kings to do **e**,
16:17 The highway of the upright avoids **e**;
16:27 Scoundrels concoct **e**, and their speech is like
16:30 one who compresses the lips brings **e** to pass.
17:11 **E** people seek only rebellion,
17:13 **E** will not depart from the house
17:13 from the house of one who returns **e** for good. D
20: 8 of judgment winnows all **e** with his eyes.
20:22 Do not say, "I will repay **e**";
20:30 Blows that wound cleanse away **e**;
21:10 The souls of the wicked desire **e**;
21:27 how much more when brought with **e** intent.
24: 8 to do **e** will be called a mischief-maker.
24:20 for the **e** have no future;
26:23 an earthen vessel are smooth lips with an **e** heart.
28: 5 The **e** do not understand justice,
28:10 **e** ways will fall into pits of their own making, G
29: 6 In the transgression of the **e** there is a snare,
30:32 exalting yourself, or if you have been devising **e**,
Ecc 2:21 This also is vanity and a great **e**.

Ecc 4: 3 not seen the e deeds that are done under the sun. H
5: 1 for they do not know how to keep from doing e.
6: 1 There is an e that I have seen under the sun,
8: 11 against an e deed is not executed speedily,
8: 11 the human heart is fully set to do e.
8: 12 Though sinners do e a hundred times
9: 2 the good and the e, to the clean and the unclean, B
9: 3 This is an e in all that happens under the sun,
9: 3 Moreover, the hearts of all are full of e;
10: 5 There is an e that I have seen under the sun,
12: 14 including every secret thing, whether good or e. B
Isa 1: 4 offspring who do e, children who deal corruptly,
1: 16 remove the e of your doings from before my eyes;
1: 16 before my eyes; cease to do e,
3: 9 For they have brought e on themselves.
5: 20 Ah, you who call e good and good evil, D
5: 20 Ah, you who call evil good and good e, B
7: 5 has plotted e against you, saying,
7: 15 the time he knows how to refuse the e and choose
7: 16 the child knows how to refuse the e and choose
13: 11 I will punish the world for its e,
29: 20 all those alert to do e shall be cut off—
32: 7 The villainies of villains are e;
33: 15 and shut their eyes from looking on e,
47: 11 But e shall come upon you,
56: 2 not profaning it, and refrains from doing any e.
58: 9 the pointing of the finger, the speaking of e,
59: 7 to e, and they rush to shed innocent blood;
59: 15 and whoever turns from e is despoiled. C
65: 12 but you did what was e in my sight,
66: 4 but they did what was e in my sight,
Jer 2: 19 and see that it is e and bitter for you to forsake
3: 5 but you have done all the e that you could.
3: 17 shall no longer stubbornly follow their own e will.
4: 4 because of the e of your doings.
4: 6 do not delay, for I am bringing e from the north,
4: 14 How long shall your e schemes lodge within you?
4: 22 They are skilled in doing e,
5: 12 No e will come upon us, and we shall not see
6: 1 for e looms out of the north, and great destruction.
7: 24 but, in the stubbornness of their e will,
7: 30 For the people of Judah have done e in my sight,
8: 3 by all the remnant that remains of this e family
9: 3 for they proceed from e to evil, C
9: 3 for they proceed from evil to e,
10: 5 Do not be afraid of them, for they cannot do e,
11: 8 everyone walked in the stubbornness of an e will.
11: 17 who planted you, has pronounced e against you,
11: 17 of the e that the house of Israel and the house
11: 18 then you showed me their e deeds. H
12: 14 concerning all my e neighbors who touch
13: 10 This e people, who refuse to hear my words,
13: 23 also you can do good who are accustomed to do e.
16: 10 the LORD pronounced all this great e against us?
16: 12 every one of you, following your stubborn e will,
18: 8 concerning which I have spoken, turns from its e,
18: 10 but if it does e in my sight,
18: 11 a potter shaping e against you and devising a plan
18: 11 Turn now, all of you from your e way, I
18: 12 according to the stubbornness of our e will."
18: 20 Is e a recompense for good?
21: 10 For I have set my face against this city for e and
21: 12 with no one to quench it, because of your e doings.
23: 2 So I will attend to you for your e doings,
23: 10 course has been e, and their might is not right.
23: 22 they would have turned them from their e way, I
23: 22 and from the e of their doings.
24: 9 I will make them a horror, an e thing,
25: 5 from your e way and wicked doings, I
26: 3 all of them, and will turn from their e way, I
26: 3 to bring on them because of their e doings.
31: 28 to overthrow, destroy, and bring e,
32: 30 and the people of Judah have done nothing but e
32: 32 of all the e of the people of Israel and the people
35: 15 'Turn now everyone of you from your e way, I
36: 3 all of them may turn from their e ways, G
36: 7 and that all of them will turn from their e ways, G
39: 16 to fulfill my words against this city for e and not
44: 22 the sight of your e doings, the abominations
48: 2 In Heshbon they planned e against her:
52: 2 He did what was e in the sight of the LORD, A
La 1: 22 Let all their e doing come before you;
Eze 14: 22 you will be consoled for the e that I have brought
20: 44 not according to your e ways, or corrupt deeds, G
33: 11 turn back, turn back from your e ways; G
36: 31 Then you shall remember your e ways, G
38: 10 and you will devise an e scheme.
Da 11: 27 The two kings, their minds bent on e,
12: 4 be running back and forth, and e shall increase."
Hos 7: 15 yet they plot e against me.
9: 15 Every e of theirs began at Gilgal;
Am 5: 13 for it is an e time.
5: 14 Seek good and not e, that you may live; B
5: 15 Hate e and love good, and establish justice in D
6: 3 O you that put far away the e day,
9: 10 who say, "E shall not overtake or meet us."
Jnh 3: 8 from their e ways and from the violence that is G
3: 10 how they turned from their e ways, G
Mic 2: 1 for those who devise wickedness and e deeds H
2: 3 an e from which you cannot remove your necks;
2: 3 for it will be an e time.
3: 2 and love the e, who tear the skin off my people,
7: 3 Their hands are skilled to do e;
Na 1: 11 From you one has gone out who plots e against
Hab 1: 13 Your eyes are too pure to behold e,
2: 9 "Alas for you who get e gain for your houses,
Zec 1: 4 from your e ways and from your evil deeds." G

Zec 1: 4 from your evil ways and from your e deeds." H
7: 10 do not devise e in your hearts against one another.
8: 17 do not devise e in your hearts against one another,
Mal 2: 17 "All who do e are good in the sight of the LORD, D
Mt 5: 11 and utter all kinds of e against you falsely
5: 37 anything more than this comes from the e one. E
5: 45 he makes his sun rise on the e and on the good,
6: 13 but rescue us from the e one. E
7: 11 then, who are e, know how to give good gifts
9: 4 said, "Why do you think e in your hearts?
12: 34 How can you speak good things, when you are e?
12: 35 e person brings e things out of an e treasure.
12: 39 "An e and adulterous generation asks for a sign,
12: 45 along seven other spirits more e than itself,
12: 45 So will it be also with this e generation."
13: 19 the e one comes and snatches away what is sown E
13: 38 the weeds are the children of the e one, E
13: 49 The angels will come out and separate the e from
15: 4 'Whoever speaks e of father or mother must
15: 19 For out of the heart come e intentions, murder,
16: 4 An e and adulterous generation asks for a sign,
27: 23 Then he asked, "Why, what e has he done?"
Mk 7: 10 and, 'Whoever speaks e of father or mother must
7: 21 from the human heart, that e intentions come:
7: 23 All these e things come from within,
9: 39 in my name will be able soon afterward to speak e
15: 14 Pilate asked them, "Why, what e has he done?"
Lk 3: 19 because of all the e things that Herod had done,
6: 45 and the e person out of e treasure produces e;
7: 21 of diseases, plagues, and e spirits, J
8: 2 as some women who had been cured of e spirits J
11: 13 then, who are e, know how to give good gifts
11: 26 and brings seven other spirits more e than itself,
11: 29 "This generation is an e generation;
16: 25 and Lazarus in like manner e things;
23: 22 "Why, what e has he done?
Jn 3: 19 because their deeds were e.
3: 20 For all who do e hate the light and do not come to
5: 29 and those who have done e,
7: 7 because I testify against it that its works are e.
17: 15 but I ask you to protect them from the e one. E
Ac 9: 13 much e he has done to your saints in Jerusalem;
19: 9 and spoke e of the Way before the congregation,
19: 12 and the e spirits came out of them. J
19: 13 of the Lord Jesus over those who had e spirits, J
19: 15 But the e spirit said to them in reply, F
19: 16 Then the man with the e spirit leaped on them, F
23: 5 for it is written, 'You shall not speak e of a leader
28: 21 or spoken anything e about you.
Ro 1: 29 They were filled with every kind of wickedness, e,
1: 30 boastful, inventors of e, rebellious toward parents,
2: 9 be anguish and distress for everyone who does e,
3: 8 "Let us do e so that good may come"? D
7: 19 but the e I do not want is what I do.
7: 21 that when I want to do what is good, e lies close B
12: 9 hate what is e, hold fast to what is good;
12: 17 Do not repay anyone e for e,
12: 21 Do not be overcome by e,
12: 21 but overcome e with good. D
14: 16 So do not let your good be spoken of as e.
16: 19 be wise in what is good and guileless in what is e.
1Co 5: 8 not with the old yeast, the yeast of malice and e,
10: 6 so that we might not desire e as they did.
14: 20 rather, be infants in e, but in thinking be adults.
2Co 5: 10 in the body, whether good or e. B
Gal 1: 4 for our sins to set us free from the present e age,
Eph 4: 29 Let no e talk come out of your mouths,
5: 16 the most of the time, because the days are e.
6: 12 the spiritual forces of e in the heavenly places.
6: 13 so that you may be able to withstand on that e day,
6: 16 to quench all the flaming arrows of the e one. E
Php 3: 2 Beware of the dogs, beware of the e workers,
Col 1: 21 and hostile in mind, doing e deeds, H
3: 5 fornication, impurity, passion, e desire,
1Th 5: 15 See that none of you repays e for e,
5: 22 abstain from every form of e.
2Th 3: 2 that we may be rescued from wicked and e people;
3: 3 and guard you from the e one. E
1Ti 6: 10 For the love of money is a root of all kinds of e,
2Ti 4: 18 The Lord will rescue me from every e attack
Tit 2: 8 having nothing e to say of us.
3: 2 to speak e of no one,
Heb 3: 12 that none of you may have an e,
5: 14 by practice to distinguish good from e. BC
10: 22 clean from an e conscience and our bodies washed
Jas 1: 13 be tempted by e and he himself tempts no one.
2: 4 and become judges with e thoughts?
3: 8 a restless e, full of deadly poison.
4: 11 Do not speak e against one another,
4: 11 Whoever speaks e against another
4: 11 speaks e against the law and judges the law;
4: 16 in your arrogance; all such boasting is e.
1Pe 2: 16 yet do not use your freedom as a pretext for e.
3: 9 Do not repay e for e or abuse for abuse;
3: 10 let them keep their tongues from e and their lips C
3: 11 let them turn away from e and do good; CD
3: 12 But the face of the Lord is against those who do e."
3: 17 than to suffer for doing e.
1Jn 2: 13 because you have conquered the e one. E
2: 14 and you have overcome the e one. E
3: 12 must not be like Cain who was from the e one E
3: 12 his own deeds were e and his brother's righteous.
5: 18 and the e one does not touch them. E
5: 19 whole world lies under the power of the e one. E
2Jn 1: 11 to welcome is to participate in the e deeds of H
3Jn 1: 11 do not imitate what is e but imitate what is good.
1: 11 whoever does e has not seen God.

Rev 22: 11 Let the evildoer still do e,
Tob 6: 8 a man or woman afflicted by a demon or e spirit, F
12: 7 Do good and e will not overtake you. B
Jdt 7: 15 Thus you will pay them back with e,
AdE 7: 6 Esther said, "Our enemy is this e man Haman!"
8: 3 to avert all the e that Haman had planned against
16: 6 of their e natures beguile the sincere goodwill
Wis 3: 12 Their wives are foolish, and their children e;
4: 6 of unlawful unions are witnesses of e
4: 11 up so that e might not change their understanding
7: 30 but against wisdom e does not prevail.
12: 10 not unaware that their origin was e
14: 27 the beginning and cause and end of every e.
15: 4 For neither has the e intent of human art misled us,
15: 6 Lovers of e things and fit for such objects
16: 8 that it is you who deliver from every e.
Sir 3: 28 for an e plant has taken root in him.
4: 20 Watch for the opportune time, and beware of e,
6: 4 E passion destroys those who have it,
7: 1 Do no e, and evil will never overtake you.
7: 1 Do no evil, and e will never overtake you.
9: 1 or you will teach her an e lesson to your own hurt.
11: 31 for they lie in wait, turning good into e, B
11: 33 Beware of scoundrels, for they devise e,
12: 3 to one who persists in e or to one who does
12: 5 as much e for all the good you have done to them.
12: 17 If e comes upon you, you will find him there
13: 24 poverty is e only in the opinion of the ungodly.
13: 25 either for good or for e. B
14: 8 The miser is an e person;
17: 7 and showed them good and e. B
17: 14 He said to them, "Beware of all e."
17: 31 So flesh and blood devise e.
18: 8 What is good in them, and what is e? B
19: 6 but one who hates gossip has less e.
19: 28 nevertheless do e when he finds the opportunity.
23: 5 and remove e desire from me.
25: 16 a lion and a dragon than live with an e woman.
25: 23 and wounded heart come from an e wife.
25: 25 and no boldness of speech to an e wife.
27: 27 If a person does e, it will roll back upon him,
28: 21 its death is an e death,
31: 10 and to do e and did not do it?
33: 1 No e will befall the one who fears the Lord,
33: 14 Good is the opposite of e, B
33: 29 for idleness teaches much e.
37: 3 O inclination to e, why were you formed to cover
37: 18 good and e, life and death; B
39: 4 in foreign lands and learns what is good and e B
Bar 1: 22 by serving other gods and doing what is e in
LtJ 6: 34 Whether one does e to them or good,
1Mc 1: 15 with the Gentiles and sold themselves to do e.
1: 36 an e adversary of Israel at all times.
1: 52 joined them, and they did e in the land;
16: 17 an act of great treachery and returned e for good. D
2Mc 1: 5 and may he not forsake you in time of e.
1: 25 You rescue Israel from every e;
6: 3 Harsh and utterly grievous was the onslaught of e.
7: 31 who have contrived all sorts of e against
8: 4 and to show his hatred of e.
1Es 1: 39 he did what was e in the sight of the Lord.
1: 44 He did what was e in the sight of the Lord.
1: 47 He also did what was e in the sight of the Lord,
8: 86 about because of our e deeds and our great sins. H
Man 1: 10 and have done what is e in your sight,
1: 13 not be angry with me forever or store up e for me;
3Mc 1: 16 the violence of this e design, and they filled
2: 26 that he framed e reports in the various localities;
3: 22 Since they incline constantly to e,
5: 8 with vengeance the e plot against them and in
7: 9 For you should know that if we devise any e
2Es 1: 5 declare to my people their e deeds, H
1: 34 and have done what is e in my sight.
2: 3 the Lord God and have done what is e in my sight.
2: 14 I set aside e and created good;
3: 20 you did not take away their e heart from them,
3: 21 For the first Adam, burdened with an e heart,
3: 22 in the hearts of the people along with the e root;
3: 22 but what was good departed, and the e remained.
3: 26 for they also had the e heart,
4: 4 and will teach you why the heart is e."
4: 28 For the e about which you ask me has been sown,
4: 29 and if the place where the e has been sown does
4: 30 a grain of e seed was sown in Adam's heart from
4: 31 of ungodliness a grain of e seed has produced.
4: 33 Why are our years few and e?"
6: 27 For e shall be blotted out, and deceit shall
7: 12 they are few and e, full of dangers and involved
7: *48* For an e heart has grown up in us,
7: 92 with great effort to overcome the e thought
8: 53 The root of e is sealed up from you,
11: 45 your most e little wings, your malicious heads,
11: 45 your malicious heads, your most e talons,
13: 38 to their face with their e thoughts and the torments
4Mc 6: 14 destroying yourself through these e things?
17: 2 the violence of the tyrant, frustrated his e designs,

EVIL-HATING (1) [EVIL, HATE]

AdE 16: 4 even assume that they will escape the e justice

EVIL-MERODACH (2)

2Ki 25: 27 King E of Babylon, in the year that he began
Jer 52: 31 King E of Babylon, in the year he began to reign,

EVIL-TONGUED (1) [EVIL, TONGUE]
Sir 20:16 Those who eat my bread are **e**."

EVILDOER (5) [DO, EVIL]
Ps 52: 6 and fear, and will laugh at the **e**, saying,
Pr 17: 4 An **e** listens to wicked lips;
Isa 9:17 for everyone was godless and an **e**,
Mt 5:39 But I say to you, Do not resist an **e**.
Rev 22:11 Let the **e** still do evil, and the filthy still be filthy,

EVILDOERS (46) [DO, EVIL]
2Sa 7:10 and **e** shall afflict them no more, as formerly,
1Ch 17: 9 and **e** shall wear them down no more,
Job 8:20 nor take the hand of **e**.
34: 8 in company with **e** and walks with the wicked?
34:22 or deep darkness where **e** may hide themselves.
35:12 but he does not answer, because of the pride of **e**.
Ps 5: 5 before your eyes; you hate all **e**.
10:15 Break the arm of the wicked and **e**;
14: 4 all the **e** who eat up my people as they eat bread,
22:16 a company of **e** encircles me.
26: 5 I hate the company of **e**,
27: 2 When **e** assail me to devour my flesh—
34:16 The face of the LORD is against **e**,
36:12 There the **e** lie prostrate; they are thrust down,
53: 4 Have they no knowledge, those **e**,
64: 2 of the wicked, from the scheming of **e**,
92: 7 the wicked sprout like grass and all **e** flourish,
92: 9 your enemies shall perish; all **e** shall be scattered.
94: 4 They pour out their arrogant words; all the **e** boast.
94:16 Who stands up for me against **e**?
101: 8 cutting off all **e** from the city of the LORD.
119:115 Go away from me, you **e**,
125: 5 the LORD will lead away with **e**.
140: 1 Deliver me, O LORD, from **e**;
141: 9 and from the snares of **e**.
Pr 4:14 and do not walk in the way of **e**.
10:29 a stronghold for the upright, but destruction for **e**.
21:15 it is a joy to the righteous, but dismay to **e**.
24:19 Do not fret because of **e**. Do not envy the wicked;
Isa 14:20 May the descendants of **e** nevermore be named!
31: 2 but will rise against the house of the **e**,
Jer 20:13 the life of the needy from the hands of **e**.
23:14 they strengthen the hands of **e**,
Eze 30:12 and will sell the land into the hand of **e**;
Hos 6: 8 Gilead is a city of **e**, tracked with blood.
Mal 3:15 **e** not only prosper, but when they put God to
4: 1 when all the arrogant and all **e** will be stubble;
Mt 7:23 go away from me, you **e**.'
13:41 of his kingdom all causes of sin and all **e**,
Lk 13:27 go away from me, all you **e**!'
1Pe 2:12 so that, though they malign you as **e**,
Rev 2: 2 I know that you cannot tolerate **e**;
AdE 14:19 and save us from the hands of **e**.
16:15 by this thrice-accursed man, are not **e**,
Sir 27:10 A lion lies in wait for prey; so does sin for **e**.
1Mc 3: 6 all the **e** were confounded;

EVILDOING (4) [DO, EVIL]
1Sa 25:39 the LORD has returned the **e** of Nabal
Pr 14:32 The wicked are overthrown by their **e**,
Ecc 7:15 wicked people who prolong their life in their **e**.
Wis 5:23 and **e** will overturn the thrones of rulers.

EVILS (17) [EVIL]
Ps 40:12 For **e** have encompassed me without number;
Jer 2:13 for my people have committed two **e**:
Eze 6: 9 be loathsome in their own sight for the **e**
20:43 and you shall loathe yourselves for all the **e**
AdE 10: 9 the Lord has rescued us from all these **e**;
11: 9 they feared the **e** that threatened them,
Wis 14:22 they call such great **e** peace.
Sir 39:27 but for sinners they turn into **e**.
1Mc 1: 9 and they caused many **e** on the earth.
2Mc 2:18 for he has rescued us from great **e** and has purified
3Mc 2:12 and rescued them from great **e**,
2Es 1: 8 the hair of your head and hurl all **e** upon them,
7:27 the **e** that I have foretold shall see my wonders.
14:16 For **e** worse than those that you have
14:17 the more shall **e** be increased upon its inhabitants.
15: 5 says the Lord, I am bringing **e** upon the world,
15:49 I will send **e** upon you:

EWE (6) [EWES]
Ge 21:28 Abraham set apart seven **e** lambs of the flock.
21:29 of these seven **e** lambs that you have set apart?"
21:30 "These seven **e** lambs you shall accept
Lev 14:10 and one **e** lamb in its first year without blemish,
Nu 6:14 one **e** lamb a year old without blemish as
2Sa 12: 3 but the poor man had nothing but one little **e** lamb,

EWES (5) [EWE]
Ge 31:38 your **e** and your female goats have not miscarried,
32:14 two hundred **e** and twenty rams,
Ps 78:71 from tending the nursing **e** he brought him to be
SS 4: 2 of shorn **e** that have come up from the washing,
6: 6 Your teeth are like a flock of **e**,

EXACT (9) [EXACTED, EXACTING, EXACTION, EXACTIONS, EXACTLY, EXACTS]
Ex 22:25 you shall not **e** interest from them.
Dt 15: 3 Of a foreigner you may **e** it,
2Ki 16:10 and its pattern, **e** in all its details.
Est 4: 7 and the **e** sum of money that Haman had promised
Mt 2: 7 for the wise men and learned from them the **e** time
Heb 1: 3 the reflection of God's glory and the **e** imprint
Sir 19:25 There is a cleverness that is **e** but unjust,
1Mc 10:35 to **e** anything from them or annoy any of them
2Mc 2:28 the responsibility for **e** details to the compiler,

EXACTED (5) [EXACT]
2Ki 15:20 Menahem **e** the money from Israel, that is,
23:35 He **e** the silver and the gold from the people of
Job 22: 6 For you have **e** pledges from your family
1Es 2:27 and cruel kings ruled in Jerusalem and **e** tribute
3Mc 2:31 to be **e** for maintaining the religion of their city,

EXACTING (3) [EXACT]
Dt 15: 2 the claim that is held against a neighbor, not **e** it of
Ne 5:11 wine, and oil that you have been **e** from them."
Tob 3: 5 now your many judgments are true in **e** penalty

EXACTION (1) [EXACT]
Ne 10:31 of the seventh year and the **e** of every debt.

EXACTIONS (1) [EXACT]
Pr 29: 4 but one who makes heavy **e** ruins it.

EXACTLY (8) [EXACT]
Dt 5:33 You must follow **e** the path that
17:10 Carry out **e** the decision that they announce to you
1Sa 23:22 find out **e** where he is,
Jer 26:20 against this land in words **e** like those of Jeremiah.
Ac 27:25 in God that it will be **e** as I have been told.
Jdt 2:13 but carry them out **e** as I have ordered you;
Sir Pr: 2 not have **e** the same sense when translated
2Mc 14:43 But in the heat of the struggle he did not hit **e**,

EXACTS (2) [EXACT]
Job 11: 6 that God **e** of you less than your guilt deserves.
Eze 18:16 **e** no pledge, commits no robbery,

EXAGGERATE (1) [EXAGGERATED]
2Co 2: 5 to some extent—not to **e** it—to all of you.

EXAGGERATED (1) [EXAGGERATE]
Wis 17:11 it has always **e** the difficulties.

EXALT (67) [EXALTATION, EXALTED, EXALTING, EXALTS]
Ex 15: 2 my father's God, and I will **e** him.
Nu 16: 3 then do you **e** yourselves above the assembly of
Dt 8:14 then do not **e** yourself, forgetting
Jos 3: 7 "This day I will begin to **e** you in the sight
1Sa 2:10 and **e** the power of his anointed."
1Ch 25: 5 according to the promise of God to **e** him;
Ps 34: 3 and let us **e** his name together.
35:26 let those who **e** themselves against me be clothed
37:34 and he will **e** you to inherit the land;
66: 7 let the rebellious not **e** themselves.
Pr 4: 8 Prize her highly, and she will **e** you;
Isa 25: 1 I will **e** you, I will praise your name;
Eze 21:26 **E** that which is low, abase that which is high.
29:15 and never again **e** itself above the nations;
Da 11:36 shall **e** himself and consider himself greater than
Mt 23:12 All who **e** themselves will be humbled,
Lk 14:11 For all who **e** themselves will be humbled,
18:14 for all who **e** themselves will be humbled,
Jas 4:10 before the Lord, and he will **e** you.
1Pe 5: 6 so that he may **e** you in due time.
Tob 13: 4 **E** him in the presence of every living being,
13: 6 and **e** the King of the ages.
13: 7 As for me, I **e** my God,
Jdt 16: 1 **e** him, and call upon his name.
16: 7 For she put away her widow's clothing to **e**
Sir 1:30 not **e** yourself, or you may fall and bring dishonor
11: 4 and do not **e** yourself when you are honored;
15: 5 She will **e** him above his neighbors,
32: 1 of the feast, do not **e** yourself;
43:30 Glorify the Lord and **e** him as much as you can,
43:30 When you **e** him, summon all your strength,
44:21 and **e** his offspring like the stars,
47: 5 and to **e** the power of his people.
Aza 1:35 sing praise to him and highly **e** him forever.
1:36 sing praise to him and highly **e** him forever.
1:37 sing praise to him and highly **e** him forever.
1:38 sing praise to him and highly **e** him forever.
1:39 sing praise to him and highly **e** him forever.
1:40 sing praise to him and highly **e** him forever.
1:41 sing praise to him and highly **e** him forever.
1:42 sing praise to him and highly **e** him forever.
1:43 sing praise to him and highly **e** him forever.
1:44 sing praise to him and highly **e** him forever.
1:45 sing praise to him and highly **e** him forever.
1:46 sing praise to him and highly **e** him forever.
1:47 sing praise to him and highly **e** him forever.
1:48 sing praise to him and highly **e** him forever.
1:49 sing praise to him and highly **e** him forever.
1:50 sing praise to him and highly **e** him forever.
1:51 sing praise to him and highly **e** him forever.
1:52 sing praise to him and highly **e** him forever.
1:53 sing praise to him and highly **e** him forever.
1:54 sing praise to him and highly **e** him forever.
Aza 1:55 sing praise to him and highly **e** him forever.
1:56 sing praise to him and highly **e** him forever.
1:57 sing praise to him and highly **e** him forever.
1:58 sing praise to him and highly **e** him forever.
1:59 sing praise to him and highly **e** him forever.
1:60 sing praise to him and highly **e** him forever.
1:61 sing praise to him and highly **e** him forever.
1:62 sing praise to him and highly **e** him forever.
1:63 sing praise to him and highly **e** him forever.
1:64 sing praise to him and highly **e** him forever.
1:65 sing praise to him and highly **e** him forever.
1:66 sing praise to him and highly **e** him forever.
1Mc 14:35 He sought in every way to **e** his people.
1Es 9:52 and do not be sorrowful, for the Lord will **e** you."

EXALTATION (2) [EXALT]
Jdt 13: 4 look in this hour on the work of my hands for the **e**
1Mc 1:40 her **e** was turned into mourning.

EXALTED‡ (90) [EXALT]
Lev 21:10 The priest who is **e** above his fellows,
Nu 24: 7 and his kingdom shall be **e**.
Jos 4:14 the LORD **e** Joshua in the sight of all Israel;
1Sa 2: 1 my strength is **e** in my God.
2Sa 5:12 and that he had **e** his kingdom for the sake
22:47 Blessed be my rock, and **e** be my God,
22:49 you **e** me above my adversaries,
23: 1 son of Jesse, the oracle of the man whom God **e**,
1Ki 1: 5 Now Adonijah son of Haggith **e** himself, saying,
8:13 I have built you an **e** house,
14: 7 Because I **e** you from among the people,
16: 2 "Since I **e** you out of the dust and made you leader
1Ch 14: 2 and that his kingdom was highly **e** for the sake
29:11 O LORD, and you are **e** as head above all.
29:25 LORD highly **e** Solomon in the sight of all Israel,
2Ch 6: 2 I have built you an **e** house,
7:21 And regarding this house, now **e**,
32:23 so that he was **e** in the sight of all nations from
Ne 9: 5 which is **e** above all blessing and praise."
Job 24:24 They are **e** a little while, and then are gone;
36: 7 on the throne he sets them forever, and they are **e**.
36:22 See, God is **e** in his power;
Ps 12: 8 as vileness is **e** among humankind.
13: 2 How long shall my enemy be **e** over me?
18:46 and **e** be the God of my salvation,
18:48 indeed, you **e** me above my adversaries;
21:13 Be **e**, O LORD, in your strength!
46:10 I am **e** among the nations, I am **e** in the earth."
47: 9 shields of the earth belong to God; he is highly **e**.
57: 5 Be **e**, O God, above the heavens.
57:11 Be **e**, O God, above the heavens.
75:10 but the horns of the righteous shall be **e**.
89:17 by your favor our horn is **e**.
89:19 I have **e** one chosen from the people.
89:24 and in my name his horn shall be **e**.
89:42 You have **e** the right hand of his foes;
92:10 But you have **e** my horn like that of the wild ox;
97: 9 you are **e** far above all gods.
99: 2 he is **e** over all the peoples.
108: 5 Be **e**, O God, above the heavens,
112: 9 their horn is **e** in honor.
118:16 the right hand of the LORD is **e**;
138: 2 for you have **e** your name and your word
148:13 for his name alone is **e**;
Pr 11:11 By the blessing of the upright a city is **e**,
Isa 2:11 and the LORD alone will be **e** in that day.
2:17 and the LORD alone will be **e** on that day.
5:16 But the LORD of hosts is **e** by justice,
12: 4 proclaim that his name is **e**.
33: 5 The LORD is **e**, he dwells on high;
33:10 "now I will lift myself up; now I will be **e**.
52:13 he shall be **e** and lifted up, and shall be very high.
Jer 17:12 O glorious throne, **e** from the beginning,
La 2:17 and **e** the might of your foes.
Da 5:23 You have **e** yourself against the Lord of heaven!
11:12 multitude has been carried off, his heart shall be **e**,
Hos 13: 1 there was trembling; he was **e** in Israel;
Hab 3:11 the moon stood still in its **e** place,
Zec 12: 7 the inhabitants of Jerusalem may not be **e** over that
Mt 11:23 Capernaum, will you be **e** to heaven?
23:12 and all who humble themselves will be **e**.
Lk 10:15 Capernaum, will you be **e** to heaven?
14:11 and those who humble themselves will be **e**."
18:14 but all who humble themselves will be **e**."
Ac 2:33 Being therefore **e** at the right hand of God,
5:31 God **e** him at his right hand as Leader and Savior
2Co 11: 7 a sin by humbling myself so that you might be **e**,
Php 1:20 Christ will be **e** now as always in my body,
2: 9 also highly **e** him and gave him the name that is
Heb 7:26 separated from sinners, and **e** above the heavens.
Jdt 10: 8 of Israel may glory and Jerusalem may be **e**."
AdE 11:11 lowly were **e** and devoured those held in honor.
Wis 19:22 O Lord, you have **e** and glorified your people,
Sir 33: 9 Some days he **e** and hallowed,
33:12 and **e**, and some he made holy and brought near
45: 6 He **e** Aaron, a holy man like Moses
47:11 Lord took away his sins, and **e** his power forever;
Aza 1:29 and to be praised and highly **e** forever;
1:30 and to be highly praised and highly **e** forever.
1:32 and to be praised and highly **e** forever.
1:33 and to be extolled and highly **e** forever.
1Mc 1: 3 the earth became quiet before him, he was **e**,
2:63 Today they will be **e**, but tomorrow they will not
8:13 and they have been greatly **e**.
11:26 he **e** him in the presence of all his Friends.
3Mc 2:21 scourged him who had **e** himself in insolence

3Mc 6: 4 e with lawless insolence and boastful tongue,
2Es 2:43 but he was more e than they.
8:20 whose eyes are e and whose upper chambers are in

EXALTING (3) [EXALT]
Ex 9:17 You are still e yourself against my people,
Dt 17:20 neither e himself above other members of
Pr 30:32 If you have been foolish, e yourself,

EXALTS‡ (5) [EXALT]
1Sa 2: 7 he brings low, he also e.
Pr 14:29 but one who has a hasty temper e folly.
14:34 Righteousness e a nation, but sin is a reproach
2Th 2: 4 and e himself above every so-called god or object
Sir 7:11 for there is One who humbles and e.

EXAMINATION‡ (11) [EXAMINE]
Lev 13: 8 The priest shall make an e,
13:10 The priest shall make an e,
13:13 then the priest shall make an e, and if
13:20 The priest shall make an e,
13:39 an e, and if the spots on the skin of the body are of
13:53 If the priest makes an e,
13:56 If the priest makes an e,
14: 3 and the priest shall make an e.
Ac 23:15 that you want to make a more thorough e
Sus 1:48 a daughter of Israel without e and without learning
3Mc 7: 5 they tried without any inquiry or e to put them

EXAMINE (28) [CROSS-EXAMINE, CROSS-EXAMINED, EXAMINATION, EXAMINED, EXAMINES, EXAMINING]
Lev 13: 3 priest shall e the disease on the skin of his body,
13: 5 The priest shall e him on the seventh day,
13: 6 The priest shall e him again on the seventh day,
13:15 the priest shall e the raw flesh
13:17 the priest shall e him,
13:25 the priest shall e it. If the hair in the
13:27 The priest shall e him the seventh day;
13:30 the priest shall e the disease.
13:32 On the seventh day the priest shall e the itch;
13:34 On the seventh day the priest shall e the itch;
13:36 the priest shall e him. If the itch has spread in the
13:43 The priest shall e him; if the diseased swelling is
13:50 The priest shall e the disease,
13:51 He shall e the disease on the seventh day.
13:55 The priest shall e the diseased article
14:36 before the priest goes to e the disease, or all that is
14:37 He shall e the disease; if the disease is in the
Ezr 10:16 the first day of the tenth month they sat down to e
Jer 2:10 send to Kedar and e with care;
La 3:40 Let us test and e our ways,
Ac 22:29 about to e him drew back from him;
1Co 9: 3 This is my defense to those who would e me.
11:28 E yourselves, and only then eat of the bread
2Co 13: 5 E yourselves to see whether you are living in
Sir 11: 7 Do not find fault before you investigate; e first,
18:20 Before judgment comes, e yourself;
Sus 1:51 from each other, and I will e them."
2Es 16:64 The Lord will strictly e all their works,

EXAMINED (9) [EXAMINE]
Lev 13: 3 priest has e him he shall pronounce him
Lk 23:14 and here I have e him in your presence and have
Ac 12:19 he e the guards and ordered them to be put
17:11 for they welcomed the message very eagerly and e
22:24 and ordered him to be e by flogging,
25:26 King Agrippa, so that, after we have e him,
28:18 When they had e me, the Romans wanted
AdE 12: 3 Then the king e the two eunuchs,
Wis 11:10 but you e the ungodly as a stern king does

EXAMINES (7) [EXAMINE]
Lev 13:21 But if the priest e it and the hair on it is not white,
13:26 the priest e it and the hair in the spot is not white,
13:31 If the priest e the itching disease,
Ps 11: 4 His eyes behold, his gaze e humankind.
Pr 5:21 and he e all their paths.
Wis 3:13 she will have fruit when God e souls.
4: 6 of evil against their parents when God e them.

EXAMINING (3) [EXAMINE]
Ecc 9: 1 All this I laid to heart, e it all,
Ac 24: 8 By e him yourself you will be able to learn
Sir 13:11 and while he smiles he will be e you.

EXAMPLE (30) [EXAMPLES]
Jdg 2:17 they did not follow their e.
Ecc 9:13 I have also seen this e of wisdom under the sun,
Jn 13:15 For I have set you an e,
Ac 20:35 an e that by such work we must support the weak,
Ro 4:12 not only circumcised but who also follow the e of
1Co 10:11 These things happened to them to serve as an e,
Gal 3:15 Brothers and sisters, I give an e from daily life:
Php 3:17 according to the e you have in us.
Col 2:15 the rulers and authorities and made a public e
1Th 1: 7 so that you became an e to all the believers
2Th 3: 9 but in order to give you an e to imitate.
1Ti 1:16 an e to those who would come to believe in him
4:12 but set the believers an e in speech and conduct,
Jas 5:10 As an e of suffering and patience, beloved,
1Pe 2:21 leaving you an e, so that you should follow
2Pe 2: 6 and made them an e of what is coming to
Jude 1: 7 as an e by undergoing a punishment of eternal fire.
Jdt 8:24 my brothers, let us set an e for our kindred,
AdE 14:11 and make an e of him who began this against us.
Sir 44:16 an e of repentance to all generations.
2Mc 6:10 For e, two women were brought in
6:28 and leave to the young a noble e of how to die
6:31 in his death an e of nobility and a memorial
3Mc 2: 5 an e to those who should come afterward.
2Es 7: 6 Another e: There is a city built
4Mc 6:19 by setting them an e in the eating of defiling food.
12:16 "I do not desert the excellent e of my brothers,
14:15 For e, among birds, the ones that are tame
14:18 to demonstrate sympathy for children by the e
17:23 to his soldiers as an e for their own endurance,

EXAMPLES (3) [EXAMPLE]
1Co 10: 6 Now these things occurred as e for us,
1Pe 5: 3 but be e to the flock.
4Mc 1: 7 from many and various e that reason is dominant

EXASPERATED (1)
2Mc 7:39 and handled him worse than the others, being e

EXCEEDING (1) [EXCEEDINGLY]
Ps 43: 4 I will go to the altar of God, to God my e joy;

EXCEEDINGLY‡ (32) [EXCEEDING, EXCEEDS, EXCESS, EXCESSES, EXCESSIVE]
Ge 17: 2 and will make you e numerous."
17: 6 I will make you e fruitful;
17:20 and make him fruitful and e numerous;
27:34 he cried out with an e great and bitter cry,
30:43 Thus the man grew e rich, and had large flocks,
47:27 and were fruitful and multiplied e.
Ex 1: 7 they multiplied and grew e strong,
Nu 14: 7 that we went through as spies is an e good land.
1Ch 22: 5 to be built for the LORD must be e magnificent,
2Ch 1: 1 with him and made him e great.
16: 8 and the Libyans a huge army with e many chariots
36:14 and the people also were e unfaithful, following all
Job 3:22 who rejoice e, and are glad when they find
Ps 119:96 but your commandment is e broad.
119:167 My soul keeps your decrees; I love them e.
Pr 30:24 Four things on earth are small, yet they are e wise:
Isa 47: 6 on the aged you made your yoke e heavy.
64: 9 Do not be e angry, O LORD,
Eze 9: 9 guilt of the house of Israel and Judah is e great;
16:13 You grew e beautiful, fit to be a queen.
Da 6:23 the king was e glad and commanded that Daniel
7: 7 terrifying and dreadful and e strong.
7:19 which was different from all the rest, e terrifying,
8: 8 Then the male goat grew e great;
8: 9 a little one, which grew e great toward the south,
Jnh 3: 3 Now Nineveh was an e large city,
Sir 43:11 it is e beautiful in its brightness.
2Mc 8:30 and got possession of some e high strongholds,
3Mc 2:23 panic-stricken in their e great fear.
2Es 10:25 her face suddenly began to shine e;
12: 3 and the earth was e terrified.
15:34 Their appearance is e threatening,

EXCEEDS (1) [EXCEEDINGLY]
Mt 5:20 unless your righteousness e that of the scribes

EXCEL (5) [EXCELLED, EXCELLENCE, EXCELLENCY, EXCELLENT, EXCELLENTLY, EXCELLING, EXCELS]
Ge 49: 4 you shall no longer e because you went
1Co 14:12 strive to e in them for building up the church.
2Co 8: 7 Now as you e in everything—
8: 7 to e also in this generous undertaking.
Sir 33:23 E in all that you do;

EXCELLED‡ (2) [EXCEL]
1Ki 10:23 Thus King Solomon e all the kings of the earth
2Ch 9:22 Thus King Solomon e all the kings of the earth

EXCELLENCE (3) [EXCEL]
Php 4: 8 if there is any e and if there is anything worthy
2Mc 15:12 from childhood in all that belongs to e,
3Mc 1: 9 and being impressed by its e and its beauty,

EXCELLENCY‡ (4) [EXCEL]
Ac 23:26 "Claudius Lysias to his E the governor Felix,
24: 2 E, because of you we have long enjoyed peace,
26: 7 It is for this hope, your E,
26:13 your E, I saw a light from heaven,

EXCELLENT (20) [EXCEL]
Isa 28:29 he is wonderful in counsel, and e in wisdom.
Da 5:12 because an e spirit, knowledge, and understanding
5:14 understanding, and e wisdom are found in you.
6: 3 and satraps because an e spirit was in him,
Lk 1: 3 an orderly account for you, most e Theophilus,
Ac 26:25 most e Festus, but I am speaking the sober truth.
1Co 12:31 And I will show you a still more e way.
Tit 3: 8 these things are e and profitable to everyone.
Heb 1: 4 as the name he has inherited is more e than theirs.
Heb 8: 6 But Jesus has now obtained a more e ministry,
Jas 2: 7 Is it not they who blaspheme the e name
Tob 4:11 is an e offering in the presence of the Most High.
AdE 6:10 "You have made an e suggestion!
16:16 for us and for our ancestors in the most e order.
Sir 14:25 and so occupies an e lodging place;
32: 2 and receive a wreath for your e leadership.
2Mc 1:35 the king favored he exchanged many e gifts.
6:23 that he had reached with distinction and his e life
4Mc 5: 8 why should you abhor eating the very e meat
12:16 "I do not desert the e example of my brothers,

EXCELLENTLY (1) [EXCEL]
Pr 31:29 "Many women have done e,

EXCELLING (3) [EXCEL]
Ge 49: 3 first fruits of my vigor, e in rank and e in power.
1Co 15:58 immovable, always e in the work of the Lord,

EXCELS (4) [EXCEL]
Ecc 2:13 I saw that wisdom e folly as light e darkness.
AdE 13: 3 who e among us in sound judgment,
Wis 7:29 and e every constellation of the stars.

EXCEPT‡ (107) [EXCEPTION, EXCEPTIONAL]
Ge 39: 9 nor has he kept back anything from me e yourself,
Ex 21:19 e to pay for the loss of time,
Lev 21: 2 e for his nearest kin: his mother,
Nu 14:30 e Caleb son of Jephunneh and Joshua son of Nun.
26:65 e Caleb son of Jephunneh and Joshua son of Nun.
32:12 none e Caleb son of Jephunneh the Kenizzite
35:33 e by the blood of the one who shed it.
Dt 1:36 e Caleb son of Jephunneh.
Jos 11:13 of the towns that stood on mounds e Hazor,
11:19 e the Hivites, the inhabitants of Gibeon;
Jdg 11:34 he had no son or daughter e her.
1Sa 18:25 'The king desires no marriage present e
21: 6 for there was no bread there e the bread of
21: 9 take it, for there is none here e that one."
30:17 one of them escaped, e four hundred young men,
30:22 e that each man may take his wife and children,
2Sa 15:16 e ten concubines whom he left behind to look after
22:32 And who is a rock, e our God?
1Ki 8: 9 There was nothing in the ark e the two tablets
12:20 e the tribe of Judah alone.
15: 5 e in the matter of Uriah the Hittite.
17: 1 be neither dew nor rain these years, e
2Ki 4: 2 in the house, e a jar of oil."
5:15 "Now I know that there is no God in all the earth e
5:17 or sacrifice to any god e the LORD.
24:14 no one remained, e the poorest people of the land.
2Ch 2: 6 e as a place to make offerings before him?
5:10 in the ark e the two tablets that Moses put there
21:17 so that no son was left to him e Jehoahaz,
23: 6 Do not let anyone enter the house of the LORD e
28:10 But what have you e sins against
31:16 e those enrolled by genealogy,
Est 2:15 for nothing e what Hegai the king's eunuch,
Ps 18:31 For who is God e the LORD?
Jer 44:14 they shall not go back, e some fugitives.
Da 2:11 and no one can reveal it to the king e the gods,
3:28 and worship any god e their own God.
6: 7 divine or human, for thirty days, e to you, O king,
6:12 divine or human, within thirty days e to you,
10:21 against these princes e Michael,
Am 9: 8 e that I will not utterly destroy the house of Jacob,
Mt 5:32 e on the ground of unchastity,
11:27 and no one knows the Son e the Father, and no one knows the Father e the Son
12:39 be given to it e the sign of the prophet Jonah.
13:57 not without honor e in their own country and
16: 4 but no sign will be given to it e the sign of Jonah."
17: 8 they saw no one e Jesus himself alone.
19: 9 whoever divorces his wife, e for unchastity,
Mk 4:22 For there is nothing hidden, e to be disclosed;
4:22 nor is anything secret, e to come to light.
4:34 he did not speak to them e in parables,
5:37 He allowed no one to follow him e Peter, James,
6: 4 e in their hometown, and among their own kin,
6: 5 e that he laid his hands on a few sick people
6: 8 to take nothing for their journey e a staff;
Lk 4:26 yet Elijah was sent to none of them e to a widow
4:27 none of them was cleansed e Naaman the Syrian."
8:51 he did not allow anyone to enter with him, e Peter,
10:22 and no one knows who the Son is e the Father, or who the Father is e the Son
11:29 but no sign will be given to it e the sign of Jonah.
17:18 to return and give praise to God e this foreigner?"
Jn 3:13 into heaven e the one who descended from heaven,
3:27 No one can receive anything e what has been given
6:46 that anyone has seen the Father e the one who is
13:10 e for the feet, but is entirely clean.
14: 6 No one comes to the Father e through me.
17:12 one of them was lost e the one destined to be lost,
Ac 8: 1 and all e the apostles were scattered throughout
11:19 and they spoke the word to no one e Jews.
20:23 e that the Holy Spirit testifies to me in every city
21:14 we remained silent e to say,
26:29 as I am—e for these chains."
Ro 13: 1 for there is no authority e from God,
13: 8 Owe no one anything, e to love one another;
15:18 of anything e what Christ has accomplished
1Co 1:14 I thank God that I baptized none of you e Crispus

1Co 2: 2 to know nothing among you e Jesus Christ,
2: 11 what human being knows what is truly human e
2: 11 So also no one comprehends what is truly God's e
7: 5 not deprive one another e perhaps by agreement
12: 3 and no one can say "Jesus is Lord" e by
2Co 12: 5 but on my own behalf I will not boast, e
12: 13 e that I myself did not burden you?
Gal 1: 19 but I did not see any other apostle e James
6: 14 of anything e the cross of our Lord Jesus Christ,
Php 4: 15 in the matter of giving and receiving, e you alone.
1Ti 5: 19 Never accept any accusation against an elder e on
Rev 2: 17 that no one knows e the one who receives it.
14: 3 No one could learn that song e
Tob 1: 20 not taken into the royal treasury e my wife Anna
6: 12 He has no male heir and no daughter e Sarah only,
7: 10 For no one e you, brother,
Jdt 6: 2 What god is there e Nebuchadnezzar?
8: 6 e the day before the sabbath and the sabbath itself,
AdE 5: 12 not invite anyone to the dinner with the king e me;
14: 18 e in you, O Lord God of Abraham.
Wis 17: 6 Nothing was shining through to them e a dreadful,
Sir 22: 14 And what is its name e "Fool"?
49: 4 E for David and Hezekiah and Josiah,
Sus 1: 16 No one was there e the two elders,
1Mc 11: 38 e the foreign troops that he had recruited from
11: 70 of them was left e Mattathias son of Absalom
2Es 5: 38 to know these things e he whose dwelling is not
11: 23 the eagle's body e the three heads that were at rest
13: 52 e in the time of his day.

EXCEPTION (1) [EXCEPT]
AdE 16: 24 "Every city and country, without e,

EXCEPTIONAL (1) [EXCEPT]
2Co 12: 7 even considering the e character of the revelations.

EXCESS (4) [EXCEEDINGLY]
Nu 3: 48 and his sons the money by which the e number
Eze 16: 49 she and her daughters had pride, e of food,
Tob 4: 15 not drink wine to e or let drunkenness go with you
Sir 31: 29 Wine drunk to e leads to bitterness of spirit,

EXCESSES (1) [EXCEEDINGLY]
1Pe 4: 4 that you no longer join them in the same e

EXCESSIVE (1) [EXCEEDINGLY]
2Co 2: 7 so that he may not be overwhelmed by e sorrow.

EXCHANGE‡ (13) [EXCHANGED, EXCHANGING]
Ge 47: 14 in e for the grain that they bought;
47: 16 and I will give you food in e for your livestock,
47: 17 and Joseph gave them food in e for the horses,
47: 17 That year he supplied them with food in e
47: 19 Buy us and our land in e for food.
Isa 43: 3 Ethiopia and Seba in e for you.
43: 4 nations in e for your life.
Eze 48: 14 They shall not sell or e any of it;
Da 11: 27 shall sit at one table and e lies.
Rev 11: 10 over them and celebrate and e presents,
Sir 7: 18 Do not e a friend for money,
3Mc 2: 32 in e for life they confidently attempted
4Mc 6: 29 and take my life in e for theirs."

EXCHANGED (15) [EXCHANGE]
Ge 26: 31 In the morning they rose early and e oaths;
Lev 27: 10 Another shall not be e or substituted for it,
Job 28: 17 nor can it be e for jewels of fine gold.
Ps 106: 20 They e the glory of God for the image of an ox
Eze 27: 12 silver, iron, tin, and lead they e for your wares.
27: 13 they e human beings and vessels of bronze
27: 14 Beth-togarmah e for your wares horses,
27: 16 they e for your wares turquoise, purple,
27: 17 they e for your merchandise wheat from Minnith,
27: 22 they e for your wares the best of all kinds
Ro 1: 23 and they e the glory of the immortal God
1: 25 because they e the truth about God for a lie
1: 26 Their women e natural intercourse for unnatural,
2Mc 1: 35 the king favored he e many excellent gifts.
3Mc 4: 6 the bridal chamber to share married life e joy

EXCHANGING (1) [EXCHANGE]
Ru 4: 7 in Israel concerning redeeming and e:

EXCITE (1) [EXCITED, EXCITEMENT]
4Mc 8: 26 Why does such contentiousness e us and such

EXCITED (1) [EXCITE]
2Mc 14: 27 The king became e and, provoked by

EXCITEMENT (1) [EXCITE]
Jdt 10: 18 There was great e in the whole camp,

EXCLAIMED‡ (3)
Lk 1: 42 and e with a loud cry, "Blessed are you among
Jn 1: 36 he e, "Look, here is the Lamb of God!"
Ac 26: 24 While he was making this defense, Festus e,

EXCLUDE (2) [EXCLUDED]
Lk 6: 22 and when they e you, revile you,
Gal 4: 17 they want to e you, so that you may make much

EXCLUDED (7) [EXCLUDE]
2Ch 26: 21 for he was e from the house of the LORD.
Ezr 2: 62 and so they were e from the priesthood as unclean;
Ne 7: 64 so they were e from the priesthood as unclean;
Eze 44: 5 and all those who are to be e from the sanctuary.
Ro 3: 27 Then what becomes of boasting? It is e.
1Es 5: 39 they were e from serving as priests.
3Mc 3: 18 by their traditional arrogance, and e us

EXCREMENT (1)
Dt 23: 13 a hole with it and then cover up your e.

EXCRUCIATINGLY (1)
4Mc 14: 10 What could be more e painful than this?

EXCUSE (6) [EXCUSED, EXCUSES]
Jn 15: 22 but now they have no e for their sin.
Ro 1: 20 things he has made. So they are without e;
2: 1 Therefore you have no e, whoever you are,
2: 15 conflicting thoughts will accuse or perhaps e them
4Mc 5: 13 it will e you from any transgression that arises out
8: 22 divine justice will e us for fearing the king

EXCUSED‡ (1) [EXCUSE]
Wis 13: 8 Yet again, not even they are to be e;

EXCUSES (1) [EXCUSE]
Lk 14: 18 But they all alike began to make e.

EXECRATION (4)
Nu 5: 21 an e and an oath among your people,
5: 27 the woman shall become an e among her people.
Jer 42: 18 You shall become an object of e and horror,
44: 12 and they shall become an object of e and horror,

EXECUTE (37) [EXECUTED, EXECUTES, EXECUTING, EXECUTION, EXECUTIONER, EXECUTIONERS]
Ex 12: 12 on all the gods of Egypt I will e judgments:
Nu 31: 3 to e the LORD's vengeance on Midian.
35: 19 the avenger of blood shall e the sentence.
Dt 13: 9 be first against them to e them,
17: 7 against the person to e the death penalty,
1Ki 3: 28 that the wisdom of God was in him, to e justice.
10: 9 he has made you king to e justice
2Ch 2: 14 and to do all sorts of engraving and e any design
9: 8 that you may e justice and righteousness."
20: 12 O our God, will you not e judgment upon them?
Ps 110: 6 He will e judgment among the nations,
149: 7 to e vengeance on the nations and punishment on
149: 9 to e on them the judgment decreed.
Isa 13: 3 my proudly exulting ones, to e my anger.
66: 16 For by fire will the LORD e judgment,
Jer 21: 12 E justice in the morning, and deliver from the hand
23: 5 and shall e justice and righteousness in the land.
33: 15 he shall e justice and righteousness in the land.
Eze 5: 8 I will e judgments among you in the sight of
5: 10 I will e judgments on you,
5: 15 when I e judgments on you in anger and fury,
11: 9 and e judgments upon you.
16: 41 They shall burn your houses and e judgments
25: 11 and I will e judgments upon Moab.
25: 17 I will e great vengeance on them
28: 22 when I e judgments in it, and manifest my holiness
28: 26 in safety, when I e judgments
30: 14 and will e acts of judgment on Thebes.
30: 19 Thus I will e acts of judgment on Egypt.
Da 2: 13 for Daniel and his companions, to e them.
2: 14 who had gone out to e the wise men of Babylon;
Hos 11: 9 I will not e my fierce anger;
Mic 5: 15 And in anger and wrath I will e vengeance on
Jn 5: 27 and he has given him authority to e judgment,
Ro 9: 28 the Lord will e his sentence on the earth quickly
13: 4 the servant of God to e wrath on the wrongdoer.
Jude 1: 15 to e judgment on all, and to convict everyone of all

EXECUTED (18) [EXECUTE]
Nu 33: 4 The LORD e judgments even against their gods.
Dt 17: 6 or three witnesses the death sentence shall be e;
21: 22 of a crime punishable by death and is e,
33: 21 he e the justice of the LORD,
2Ch 24: 24 Thus they e judgment on Joash.
Ezr 7: 26 let judgment be strictly e on them,
Est 9: 1 the king's command and edict were about to be e,
Ps 9: 16 LORD has made himself known, he has e judgment;
99: 4 you have e justice and righteousness in Jacob.
Ecc 8: 11 sentence against an evil deed is not e speedily,
Jer 23: 20 of the LORD will not turn back until he has e
30: 24 of the LORD will not turn back until he has e
Eze 20: 24 because they had not e my ordinances,
23: 10 Judgment was e upon her,
39: 21 all the nations shall see my judgment that I have e,
Da 2: 13 and the wise men were about to be e;
Tob 1: 18 of heaven e upon him because of his blasphemies.
Aza 1: 5 You have e true judgments in all you have brought

EXECUTES (7) [EXECUTE]
Dt 10: 18 who e justice for the orphan and the widow,
Ps 75: 7 but it is God who e judgment,
Ps 140: 12 and e justice for the poor.
146: 7 who e justice for the oppressed;
Eze 18: 8 e true justice between contending parties,
Mic 7: 9 until he takes my side and e judgment for me.
Sir 35: 22 and does justice for the righteous, and e judgment.

EXECUTING (2) [EXECUTE]
Lev 26: 25 e vengeance for the covenant;
2Ch 22: 8 When Jehu was e judgment on the house of Ahab,

EXECUTION (4) [EXECUTE]
Ex 21: 14 you shall take the killer from my altar for e.
AdE 12: 3 they were led away to e.
16: 17 therefore do well not to put in e the letters sent
Sus 1: 45 Just as she was being led off to e,

EXECUTIONER (2) [EXECUTE]
Da 2: 14 the king's chief e, who had gone out to execute
2Mc 5: 8 as the e of his country and his compatriots,

EXECUTIONERS (1) [EXECUTE]
Eze 9: 1 saying, "Draw near, you e of the city,

EXEMPT (2)
1Ki 15: 22 a proclamation to all Judah, none was e:
1Mc 10: 29 "I now free you and e all the Jews from payment

EXERCISE (9) [EXERCISED, EXERCISES, EXERCISING]
Ro 5: 17 the free gift of righteousness e dominion in life
5: 21 also e dominion through justification leading
6: 12 do not let sin e dominion in your mortal bodies,
1Co 9: 25 Athletes e self-control in all things;
Rev 13: 5 it was allowed to e authority for forty-two months.
AdE 16: 7 of those who e authority unworthily can be seen,
Sir 38: 34 and their concern is for the e of their trade.
3Mc 3: 18 but they were spared the e of our power because of
4Mc 18: 1 obey this law and e piety in every way,

EXERCISED (5) [EXERCISE]
1Ch 26: 6 his son Shemaiah sons were born who e authority
2Ch 8: 10 who e authority over the people.
Ro 5: 14 Yet death e dominion from Adam to Moses,
5: 17 death e dominion through that one,
5: 21 just as sin e dominion in death,

EXERCISES (2) [EXERCISE]
Ecc 8: 9 while one person e authority over another to
Rev 13: 12 It e all the authority of the first beast on its behalf,

EXERCISING‡ (1) [EXERCISE]
1Pe 5: 2 e the oversight, not under compulsion

EXERT (1) [EXERTED, EXERTION, EXERTS]
3Mc 3: 10 and to e more earnest efforts for their assistance.

EXERTED (1) [EXERT]
Ecc 10: 10 then more strength must be e;

EXERTION (1) [EXERT]
Ro 9: 16 So it depends not on human will or e,

EXERTS (1) [EXERT]
Wis 16: 24 e itself to punish the unrighteous,

EXHAUST (1) [EXHAUSTED, EXHAUSTION, EXHAUSTIVE]
Jer 51: 58 The peoples e themselves for nothing,

EXHAUSTED (12) [EXHAUST]
Jdg 8: 4 and the three hundred who were with him, e
8: 5 of bread to my followers, for they are e,
8: 15 we should give bread to your troops who are e?' "
1Sa 30: 10 too e to cross the Wadi Besor.
30: 21 to the two hundred men who had been too e
Isa 40: 30 and the young will fall e;
Jer 48: 45 In the shadow of Heshbon fugitives stop e;
Mic 2: 7 Is the LORD's patience e?
Jdt 11: 12 Since their food supply is e
1Mc 3: 29 Then he saw that the money in the treasury was e,
10: 82 the phalanx in battle (for the cavalry was e);
4Mc 3: 8 when evening fell, he came, sweating and quite e,

EXHAUSTION (2) [EXHAUST]
Jdt 7: 25 to be strewn before them in thirst and e.
2Es 5: 35 not see the travail of Jacob and the e of the people

EXHAUSTIVE (1) [EXHAUST]
2Mc 2: 31 for brevity of expression and to forego e treatment.

EXHIBIT (2) [EXHIBITED]
Jdg 8: 35 not e loyalty to the house of Jerubbaal (that is,
2Mc 14: 39 wishing to e the enmity that he had for the Jews,

EXHIBITED (3) [EXHIBIT]
1Co 4: 9 For I think that God has e us apostles as last of all,

Gal 3: 1 before your eyes that Jesus Christ was publicly **e**
3Mc 5:31 who give me no ground for complaint and have **e**

EXHORT (5) [EXHORTATION, EXHORTATIONS, EXHORTED, EXHORTER, EXHORTING]
2Th 3:12 Now such persons we command and **e** in
Tit 2:15 **e** and reprove with all authority.
Heb 3:13 But **e** one another every day,
1Pe 5: 1 I **e** the elders among you
4Mc 8: 5 also **e** you to yield to me and enjoy my friendship.

EXHORTATION (5) [EXHORT]
Ac 13:15 if you have any word of **e** for the people, give it."
15:31 When its members read it, they rejoiced at the **e**.
Ro 12: 8 the exhorter, in **e**; the giver,
Heb 12: 5 And you have forgotten the **e** that addresses you
13:22 brothers and sisters, bear with my word of **e**,

EXHORTATIONS (2) [EXHORT]
Lk 3:18 with many other **e**, he proclaimed the good news
4Mc 6: 1 to the **e** of the tyrant,

EXHORTED (11) [EXHORT]
Ac 2:40 with many other arguments and **e** them,
11:23 and he **e** them all to remain faithful to the Lord
2Mc 2: 3 And with other similar words he **e** them that
8:16 and **e** them not to be frightened by the enemy and
12:31 they thanked them and **e** them to be well disposed
12:42 The noble Judas **e** the people
13:12 Judas **e** them and ordered them to stand ready.
15: 8 He **e** his troops not to fear the attack of
3Mc 1: 4 and **e** them to defend themselves and their children
4Mc 8:17 and **e** us to accept kind treatment if we obey him,
12: 7 his mother had **e** him in the Hebrew language,

EXHORTER (1) [EXHORT]
Ro 12: 8 the **e**, in exhortation; the giver, in generosity;

EXHORTING (2) [EXHORT]
1Ti 4:13 to the public reading of scripture, to **e**,
2Mc 13:14 and **e** his troops to fight bravely to the death for

EXILE‡ (94) [EXILE'S, EXILED, EXILES]
2Sa 15:19 you are a foreigner, and also an **e** from your home.
2Ki 25:11 the captain of the guard carried into **e** the rest of
25:21 So Judah went into **e** out of its land.
25:27 the thirty-seventh year of the **e** of King Jehoiachin
1Ch 5: 6 of Assyria carried away into **e**;
5:22 And they lived in their territory until the **e**.
6:15 Jehozadak went into **e** when the LORD sent Judah and Jerusalem into **e**
8: 6 and they were carried into **e** to Manahath):
9: 1 into **e** in Babylon because of their unfaithfulness.
2Ch 36:20 He took into **e** in Babylon those who had escaped
Ezr 6:21 by the people of Israel who had returned from **e**,
Ne 7: 6 of Babylon had carried into **e**;
Ps 144:14 May there be no breach in the walls, no **e**,
Isa 5:13 Therefore my people go into **e** without knowledge;
27: 8 By expulsion, by **e** you struggled against them;
Jer 13:19 all Judah is taken into **e**, wholly taken into exile.
13:19 all Judah is taken into exile, wholly taken into **e**.
24: 1 into **e** from Jerusalem King Jeconiah son
27:20 not take away when he took into **e** from Jerusalem
29: 1 whom Nebuchadnezzar had taken into **e**
29: 4 the exiles whom I have sent into **e** from Jerusalem
29: 7 of the city where I have sent you into **e**,
29:14 to the place from which I sent you into **e**.
29:16 your kinsfolk who did not go out with you into **e**:
40: 7 the land who had not been taken into **e** to Babylon,
43: 3 that they may kill us or take us into **e** in Babylon."
46:19 Pack your bags for **e**, sheltered daughter Egypt!
48: 7 Chemosh shall go out into **e**,
48:11 from vessel to vessel, nor has he gone into **e**;
49: 3 For Milcom shall go into **e**,
52:15 of the guard carried into **e** some of the poorest of
52:27 So Judah went into **e** out of its land.
52:28 of the people whom Nebuchadrezzar took into **e**:
52:29 of Nebuchadrezzar he took into **e** from Jerusalem
52:30 Nebuzaradan the captain of the guard took into **e**
52:31 the thirty-seventh year of the **e** of King Jehoiachin
La 1: 3 into **e** with suffering and hard servitude;
4:22 is accomplished, he will keep you in **e** no longer;
Eze 1: 2 the fifth year of the **e** of King Jehoiachin),
12: 3 and go into **e** by day in their sight;
12: 3 like an **e** from your place to another place
12: 4 by day in their sight, as baggage for **e**;
12: 4 as those do who go into **e**.
12: 7 as baggage for **e**, and in the evening I dug through
12:11 they shall go into **e**, into captivity."
25: 3 and over the house of Judah when it went into **e**;
33:21 In the twelfth year of our **e**, in the tenth month,
39:28 the LORD their God because I sent them into **e**
40: 1 In the twenty-fifth year of our **e**,
Am 1: 5 and the people of Aram shall go into **e** to Kir,
1: 6 because they carried into **e** entire communities,
1:15 then their king shall go into **e**,
5: 5 for Gilgal shall surely go into **e**,
5:27 therefore I will take you into **e** beyond Damascus,
6: 7 Therefore they shall now be the first to go into **e**,
7:11 and Israel must go into **e** away from his land.' "
7:17 Israel shall surely go into **e** away from its land.' "
Mic 1:16 for they have gone from you into **e**.
Na 3:10 Yet she became an **e**, she went into captivity;
Zec 14: 2 half the city shall go into **e**,
1Pe 1:17 live in reverent fear during the time of your **e**.
Tob 1: 3 in **e** to Nineveh in the land of the Assyrians.
3: 4 So you gave us over to plunder, **e**, and death,
3:15 or the name of my father in the land of my **e**.
13: 6 In the land of my **e** I acknowledge him,
14: 5 After this they all will return from their **e**
Jdt 4: 3 For they had only recently returned from **e**,
Sir 29:18 it has driven the influential into **e**,
Bar 2:14 in the sight of those who have carried us into **e**;
2:30 in the land of their **e** they will come to themselves
2:32 they will praise me in the land of their **e**,
3: 7 and we will praise you in our **e**,
3: 8 we are today in our **e** where you have scattered us,
4:10 for I have seen the **e** of my sons and daughters,
1Mc 2: 9 her glorious vessels have been carried into **e**.
2Mc 5: 9 from their own country into **e** died in **e**,
1Es 5: 7 the Judeans who came up out of their sojourn in **e**,
5:56 and all who had come back to Jerusalem from **e**;
5:67 from **e** were building the temple for the Lord God
6: 8 the elders of the Jews, who had been in **e**,
6:28 to help those who have returned from the **e**
7: 6 of those who returned from **e** who joined them,
7:10 from **e** kept the passover on the fourteenth day of
7:13 people of Israel who had returned from **e** ate it,
8:65 from **e** offered sacrifices to the Lord,
8:77 to the sword and **e** and plundering,
9: 3 from **e** that they should assemble at Jerusalem,
9:15 And those who had returned from **e** acted
3Mc 6:10 in impieties in our **e**, rescue us from the hand of
2Es 5:17 to you in the land of their **e**?
10:22 our Levites have gone into **e**,
13:40 that were taken away from their own land into **e** in

EXILE'S (1) [EXILE]
Eze 12: 3 mortal, prepare for yourself an **e** baggage,

EXILED (8) [EXILE]
Dt 30: 4 Even if you are **e** to the ends of the world,
2Ki 17:23 So Israel was **e** from their own land to Assyria
Isa 49:21 I was bereaved and barren, **e** and put away—
Jer 39: 9 the captain of the guard **e** to Babylon the rest of
40: 1 of Jerusalem and Judah who were being **e**
Na 2: 7 It is decreed that the city be **e**,
Sir 47:24 until they were **e** from their land.
2Mc 1:33 in the place where the **e** priests had hidden the fire,

EXILES (44) [EXILE]
Ezr 1:11 **e** were brought up from Babylonia to Jerusalem.
2: 1 from those captive **e** whom King Nebuchadnezzar
4: 1 that the returned **e** were building a temple to
6:16 and the rest of the returned **e**,
6:19 of the first month the returned **e** kept the passover.
6:20 the passover lamb for all the returned **e**,
8:35 the returned **e**, offered burnt offerings to the God
9: 4 because of the faithlessness of the returned **e**,
10: 6 he was mourning over the faithlessness of the **e**.
10: 7 to all the returned **e** that they should assemble
10: 8 from the congregation of the **e**.
10:16 Then the returned **e** did so.
Ne 7: 6 of those **e** whom King Nebuchadnezzar
Isa 20: 4 the Egyptians as captives and the Ethiopians as **e**,
45:13 he shall build my city and set my **e** free,
Jer 24: 5 so I will regard as good the **e** from Judah,
28: 4 and all the **e** from Judah who went to Babylon,
28: 6 of the house of the LORD, and all the **e**.
29: 1 to the remaining elders among the **e**,
29: 4 the **e** whom I have sent into exile from Jerusalem
29:20 all you **e** whom I sent away from Jerusalem
29:22 be used by all the **e** from Judah in Babylon:
29:31 Send to all the **e**, saying, Thus says the LORD
49:36 be no nation to which the **e** from Elam shall
Eze 1: 1 as I was among the **e** by the river Chebar,
3:11 then go to the **e**, to your people, and speak
3:15 I came to the **e** at Tel-abib,
11:15 your kinsfolk, your own kin, your fellow **e**,
11:24 a vision by the spirit of God into Chaldea, to the **e**.
11:25 the **e** all the things that the LORD had shown me.
Da 2:25 the **e** from Judah a man who can tell the king
5:13 "So you are Daniel, one of the **e** of Judah,
6:13 one of the **e** from Judah, pays no attention to you,
Ob 1:20 The **e** of the Israelites who are in Halah
1:20 and the **e** of Jerusalem who are in Sepharad
Zec 6:10 Collect silver and gold from the **e**—
1Pe 1: 1 To the **e** of the Dispersion in Pontus, Galatia,
2:11 and **e** to abstain from the desires of the flesh
Tob 2: 2 of our people among the **e** in Nineveh,
7: 3 to the descendants of Naphtali who are **e**
Wis 17: 2 **e** from eternal providence.
LtJ 6: 1 to those who were to be taken to Babylon as **e** by
6: 2 be taken to Babylon as **e** by Nebuchadnezzar,
1Es 2:15 by Sheshbazzar with the returning **e** from Babylon

EXIST‡ (18) [EXISTED, EXISTENCE, EXISTING, EXISTS]
Ro 4:17 and calls into existence the things that do not **e**.
13: 1 and those authorities that **e** have been instituted
1Co 8: 6 from whom are all things and for whom we **e**,
8: 6 whom are all things and through whom we **e**.
Heb 2:10 for whom and through whom all things **e**,
1Jn 2: 4 is a liar, and in such a person the truth does not **e**;
Wis 1:14 For he created all things so that they might **e**;
2: 6 therefore, let us enjoy the good things that **e**,
11:24 For you love all things that **e**,
14:13 for they did not **e** from the beginning,
Sir 14:19 Every work decays and ceases to **e**,
17:28 From the dead, as from one who does not **e**,
45:13 Before him such beautiful things did not **e**.
1Es 4:17 men cannot **e** without women.
2Es 4:23 and the written covenants no longer **e**.
7:23 they even declared that the Most High does not **e**,
8: 7 For you alone **e**, and we are a work of your hands,
9:18 now **e**, before the world was made for them to live

EXISTED‡ (9) [EXIST]
Ps 139:16 when none of them as yet **e**.
Jn 17: 5 that I had in your presence before the world **e**.
2Pe 3: 5 that by the word of God heavens **e** long ago and
Rev 4:11 and by your will they **e** and were created."
Sir 44: 9 they have perished as though they had never **e**;
1Mc 3:29 in the land by abolishing the laws that had **e** from
2Mc 7:28 that God did not make them out of things that **e**.
2Es 8:35 among those who have **e** there is no one who has
9:18 and no one opposed me then, for no one **e**;

EXISTENCE (6) [EXIST]
Da 12: 1 since nations first came into **e**.
Ac 17:26 of their **e** and the boundaries of the places
Ro 4:17 to the dead and calls into **e** the things that do
Wis 7: 5 For no king has had a different beginning of **e**;
15:12 But they considered our **e** an idle game,
2Es 6:49 "Then you kept in **e** two living creatures;

EXISTING (1) [EXIST]
2Mc 4:11 He set aside the **e** royal concessions to the Jews,

EXISTS (8) [EXIST]
Ps 119:89 The LORD **e** forever; your word is firmly fixed in heaven.
Jer 11: 9 Conspiracy **e** among the people of Judah and
1Co 8: 4 we know that "no idol in the world really **e**,"
Heb 11: 6 that he **e** and that he rewards those who seek him.
Wis 7:17 of what **e**, to know the structure of the world and
8: 6 who more than she is fashioner of what **e**?
13: 1 the one who **e**, nor did they recognize the artisan
4Mc 1:25 In pleasure there **e** even a malevolent tendency,

EXITS (4)
Eze 42:11 with the same **e** and arrangements and doors.
43:11 its **e** and its entrances, and its whole form—
48:30 These shall be the **e** of the city:
2Es 4: 7 or which are the **e** of Hades,

EXODUS (1)
Heb 11:22 of the **e** of the Israelites and gave instructions

EXONERATION (1)
Ge 20:16 it is your **e** before all who are with you;

EXORBITANT (1)
Pr 28: 8 One who augments wealth by **e** interest gathers it

EXORCISTS (3)
Mt 12:27 by whom do your own **e** cast them out?
Lk 11:19 by whom do your **e** cast them out?
Ac 19:13 Then some itinerant Jewish **e** tried to use the name

EXPANSE (2)
Job 38:18 Have you comprehended the **e** of the earth?
2Es 7: 3 "There is a sea set in a wide **e** so that it is deep

EXPECT (11) [EXPECTANTLY, EXPECTATION, EXPECTATIONS, EXPECTED, EXPECTING]
Ge 48:11 Israel said to Joseph, "I did not **e** to see your face;
Isa 64: 3 When you did awesome deeds that we did not **e**,
Mt 24:50 on a day when he does not **e** him and at an hour
Lk 12:46 on a day when he does not **e** him and at an hour
Jas 1:7,8 must not **e** to receive anything from the Lord.
Jdt 8:14 how do you **e** to search out God,
Wis 12:22 and when we are judged, we may **e** mercy.
14:29 in lifeless idols they swear wicked oaths and **e**
Sir 28: 3 and **e** healing from the Lord?
2Es 5: 6 not **e**, and the birds shall fly away together;
7:*117* [47] that they live in sorrow now and **e** punishment

EXPECTANTLY (2) [EXPECT]
Mk 15:43 who was also himself waiting **e** for the kingdom
Lk 23:51 and he was waiting **e** for the kingdom of God.

EXPECTATION‡ (6) [EXPECT]
Pr 10:28 but the **e** of the wicked comes to nothing.
11: 7 and the **e** of the godless comes to nothing.
11:23 the **e** of the wicked in wrath.
Lk 3:15 As the people were filled with **e**,
Php 1:20 It is my eager **e** and hope that I will not be put
3Mc 5:41 As a result the city is in a tumult because of its **e**;

EXPECTATIONS (1) [EXPECT]
4Mc 4:14 So Apollonius, having been saved beyond all **e**,

EXPECTED (10) [EXPECT]
1Ki 2:15 and that all Israel **e** me to reign;
Isa 5: 2 he **e** it to yield grapes, but it yielded wild grapes.
5: 4 I **e** it to yield grapes, why did it yield wild grapes?
5: 7 he **e** justice, but saw bloodshed;
2Co 8: 5 and this, not merely as we **e**;
Tob 8:16 It has not turned out as I **e**,
Wis 18: 7 and the destruction of their enemies were **e**
3Mc 2:31 since they **e** to enhance their reputation
3: 8 and **e** that matters would change;
6:30 in which they had **e** to meet their destruction.

EXPECTING (12) [EXPECT]
Lk 2: 5 to whom he was engaged and who was **e** a child.
6:35 do good, and lend, **e** nothing in return.
Ac 3: 5 **e** to receive something from them.
10:24 was **e** them and had called together his relatives
12:11 and from all that the Jewish people were **e**."
25:18 not charge him with any of the crimes that I was **e**.
28: 6 They were **e** him to swell up or drop dead,
1Co 16:11 for I am **e** him with the brothers.
Php 3:20 and it is from there that we are **e** a Savior,
2Mc 8:11 not **e** the judgment from the Almighty that was
12:37 against Gorgias's troops when they were not **e** it,
12:44 not **e** that those who had fallen would rise again,

EXPEDIENT (1)
AdE 3: 8 It is not **e** for the king to tolerate them.

EXPEDIENT (KJV) See also ADVANTAGE, APPROPRIATE, BENEFICIAL, BETTER, GAINED

EXPEDITED (1) [EXPEDITION]
AdE 3:15 The matter was **e** also in Susa.

EXPEDITION (5) [EXPEDITED, EXPEDITIONS]
1Sa 21: 5 from us as always when I go on an **e**;
23:13 from Keilah, he gave up the **e**.
2Ch 11: 4 the word of the LORD and turned back from the **e**
1Mc 9:68 for his plan and his **e** had been in vain.
3Mc 3:14 When our **e** took place in Asia,

EXPEDITIONS (1) [EXPEDITION]
2Mc 9:23 when he made **e** into the upper country,

EXPELLED (6) [EXPELS, EXPULSION]
1Sa 28: 3 Saul had **e** the mediums and the wizards from
2Ki 24:20 and Judah so angered the LORD that he **e** them
Jer 52: 3 and Judah so angered the LORD that he **e** them
1Mc 13:47 But he **e** them from the city and cleansed
13:50 But he **e** them from there and cleansed the citadel
1Es 9: 4 be seized for sacrifice and the men themselves **e**

EXPELS (1) [EXPELLED]
3Jn 1:10 even prevents those who want to do so and **e** them

EXPEND (1) [EXPENSE]
2Mc 4:19 but to **e** it for another purpose.

EXPENDED (1) [EXPENSE]
Eze 29:18 from Tyre to pay for the labor that he had **e**

EXPENSE (4) [EXPEND, EXPENDED, EXPENSES, EXPENSIVE]
2Sa 19:42 Have we eaten at all at the king's **e**?
Ac 28:30 at his own **e** and welcomed all who came to him,
Sir 18:32 or you may become impoverished by its **e**.
3Mc 4: 1 a feast at public **e** was arranged for the Gentiles

EXPENSES (6) [EXPENSE]
1Co 9: 7 at any time pays the **e** for doing military service?
Tob 5:15 as well as **e** for yourself and my son.
1Mc 3:30 not have such funds as he had before for his **e** and
10:39 to meet the necessary **e** of the sanctuary.
2Mc 3: 3 the **e** connected with the service of the sacrifices.
9:16 the **e** incurred for the sacrifices he would provide

EXPENSIVE (1) [EXPENSE]
1Ti 2: 9 or with gold, pearls, or **e** clothes,

EXPERIENCE‡ (23) [EXPERIENCED, EXPERIENCES]
Jdg 3: 1 to test all those in Israel who had no **e** of any war
3: 2 to teach those who had no **e** of it before):
Ecc 1:16 and my mind has had great **e** of wisdom
Ac 2:27 or let your Holy One **e** corruption.
2:31 nor did his flesh **e** corruption.'
13:35 'You will not let your Holy One **e** corruption.'
1Co 7:28 Yet those who marry will **e** distress in this life,
2Co 1: 6 which you **e** when you patiently endure
Gal 3: 4 Did you **e** so much for nothing?—
Heb 11: 5 so that he did not **e** death;
Wis 2:24 and those who belong to his company **e** it.
8: 8 And if anyone longs for wide **e**,
8:18 unfailing wealth, and in the **e** of her company,
12:26 not heeded the warning of mild rebukes will **e**
Wis 18:20 The **e** of death touched also the righteous,
19: 5 that your people might **e** an incredible journey,
Sir 25: 6 Rich **e** is the crown of the aged,
34: 9 one with much **e** knows what he is talking about.
36:25 but a person with **e** will pay him back.
2Mc 8: 9 a general and a man of **e** in military service.
3Mc 5: 5 that the whole nation would **e** its final destruction.
2Es 4:23 but about those things that we daily **e**:
4Mc 1:24 Anger, as a person will see by reflecting on this **e**,

EXPERIENCED (9) [EXPERIENCE]
Dt 7:15 all the dread diseases of Egypt that you **e**,
1Ch 12: 8 in the wilderness mighty and **e** warriors, expert
Ac 13:36 was laid beside his ancestors, and **e** corruption;
13:37 but he whom God raised up **e** no corruption.
2Co 1: 8 brothers and sisters, of the affliction we **e** in Asia;
AdE 9:26 and because of what they had **e** in this affair
Sir 21:22 but an **e** person waits respectfully outside.
3Mc 6:33 for the unexpected rescue that he had **e**.
2Es 4: 9 things that you have **e** and from which you cannot

EXPERIENCES (2) [EXPERIENCE]
Sir 34:13 but have escaped because of these **e**.
2Es 7:14 the living pass through the difficult and futile **e**,

EXPERT (8)
Ge 21:20 and became an **e** with the bow.
2Sa 17: 8 Besides, your father is **e** in war;
1Ch 5:18 **e** in war, forty-four thousand seven hundred sixty,
12: 8 **e** with shield and spear, whose faces were like
SS 3: 8 all equipped with swords and **e** in war,
Isa 3: 3 counselor and skillful magician and **e** enchanter.
Sir 45:12 a distinction to be prized, the work of an **e**,
Bar 3:26 who were famous of old, great in stature, **e** in war.

EXPIATE (1) [EXPIATED, EXPIATION]
Hos 8:11 When Ephraim multiplied altars to **e** sin,

EXPIATED (2) [EXPIATE]
1Sa 3:14 of Eli that the iniquity of Eli's house shall not be **e**
Isa 27: 9 Therefore by this the guilt of Jacob will be **e**,

EXPIATION (3) [EXPIATE]
Nu 35:33 and no **e** can be made for the land,
2Sa 21: 3 How shall I make **e**, that you may bless
1Es 9:20 and to offer rams in **e** of their error.

EXPIRE (3) [EXPIRED]
Job 3:11 come forth from the womb and **e**?
14:10 humans **e**, and where are they?
4Mc 6:26 now burned to his very bones and about to **e**,

EXPIRED (2) [EXPIRE]
1Sa 18:26 be the king's son-in-law. Before the time had **e**,
4Mc 15:18 at you piteously nor when the third **e**;

EXPIRED (KJV) See also COMPLETED, ENDED, FULFILLED, OVER, PASSED, SPRING

EXPLAIN (26) [EXPLAINED, EXPLAINING, EXPLANATION]
Ge 41:24 there was no one who could **e** it to me."
Jos 20: 4 and **e** the case to the elders of that city;
Jdg 14:12 If you can **e** it to me within the seven days of
14:13 But if you cannot **e** it to me,
14:14 But for three days they could not **e** the riddle.
14:15 "Coax your husband to **e** the riddle to us,
1Ki 10: 3 from the king that he could not **e** to her.
2Ch 9: 2 from Solomon that he could not **e** to her.
Est 4: 8 that he might show it to Esther, **e** it to her,
Isa 28: 9 and to whom will he **e** the message?
Da 5:12 and understanding to interpret dreams, **e** riddles,
Mt 13:36 "**E** to us the parable of the weeds of the field."
15:15 But Peter said to him, "**E** this parable to us."
Ac 11: 4 Then Peter began to **e** it to them, step by step,
Heb 5:11 About this we have much to say that is hard to **e**,
Tob 4: 2 Why do I not call my son Tobias and **e** to him
4:20 let me **e** to you that I left ten talents of silver
7:10 But let me **e** to you the true situation more fully,
1Es 3:16 and they shall **e** their statements."
3:17 "**E** to us what you have written."
2Es 5:37 and then I will **e** to you the travail that you ask
10:32 and can still see, I am unable to **e**."
12:12 But it was not explained to him as I now **e** to you
13:21 also **e** to you the things that you have mentioned.
13:51 I said, "O sovereign Lord, **e** this to me:
13:56 and **e** weighty and wondrous matters to you."

EXPLAINED (13) [EXPLAIN]
Jdg 14:16 but you have not **e** it to me."
14:17 Then she **e** the riddle to her people.
14:19 the festal garments to those who had **e** the riddle.
1Sa 24:18 Today you have **e** how you have dealt well
Da 2:15 Arioch then **e** the matter to Daniel.
Mk 4:34 but he **e** everything in private to his disciples.
Ac 18:26 and Aquila heard him, they took him aside and **e**
28:23 From morning until evening he **e** the matter
Tob 10: 7 I have already **e** to you how I left him."
2Mc 3:10 The high priest **e** that there were some deposits
2Es 12:12 not **e** to him as I now explain to you or have **e** it.
4Mc 3: 6 Now this can be **e** more clearly by the story

EXPLAINING (3) [EXPLAIN]
Ac 17: 3 **e** and proving that it was necessary for the Messiah
2Ti 2:15 rightly **e** the word of truth.
1Es 9:48 at the same time **e** what was read.

EXPLANATION (2) [EXPLAIN]
2Es 7:*51* while the ungodly abound, hear the **e** for this.
10:37 Now therefore I beg you to give your servant an **e**

EXPLICIT (1)
Lev 27: 2 an **e** vow to the LORD concerning the equivalent

EXPLOIT (3) [EXPLOITED, EXPLOITS]
1Th 4: 6 no one wrong or **e** a brother or sister in this matter,
2Pe 2: 3 And in their greed they will **e** you
Sir 13: 4 rich person will **e** you if you can be of use to him,

EXPLOITED (2) [EXPLOIT]
Php 2: 6 not regard equality with God as something to be **e**,
Jdt 5:11 he **e** them and forced them to make bricks.

EXPLOITS (2) [EXPLOIT]
Job 10:16 you repeat your **e** against me.
Jas 3: 5 tongue is a small member, yet it boasts of great **e**.

EXPLORE (4) [EXPLORED]
Dt 1:22 "Let us send men ahead of us to **e** the land for us
Jdg 18: 2 to spy out the land and to **e** it;
18: 2 and they said to them, "Go, **e** the land."
2Es 13:52 "Just as no one can **e** or know what is in the depths

EXPLORED (1) [EXPLORE]
Jer 31:37 and the foundations of the earth below can be **e**,

EXPORTED (3)
1Ki 10:29 the king's traders they were **e** to all the kings of
2Ch 1:17 They imported from Egypt, and then **e**,
1:17 so through them these were **e** to all the kings of

EXPOSE (3) [EXPOSED, EXPOSES, EXPOSING]
Hos 2: 3 or I will strip her naked and **e** her as in
Mt 1:19 being a righteous man and unwilling to **e** her
Eph 5:11 of darkness, but instead **e** them.

EXPOSED‡ (15) [EXPOSE]
Ex 20:26 so that your nakedness may not be **e** on it."
Pr 26:26 the enemy's wickedness will be **e** in the assembly.
La 2:14 not **e** your iniquity to restore your fortunes,
Eze 23:29 and the nakedness of your whorings shall be **e**.
28:17 I **e** you before kings, to feast their eyes on you.
Jn 3:20 so that their deeds may not be **e**.
Eph 5:13 but everything **e** by the light becomes visible,
Heb 10:33 sometimes being publicly **e** to abuse
Rev 16:15 not going about naked and **e** to shame.")
Jdt 9: 2 and **e** her thighs to put her to shame,
Wis 11:14 before had been cast out and **e**,
Sir 28:19 who has not been **e** to its anger,
1Mc 14:29 **e** themselves to danger and resisted the enemies
2Mc 4:33 he publicly **e** them, having first withdrawn to
4Mc 15:15 and the flesh of the head to the chin **e** like masks.

EXPOSES (1) [EXPOSE]
Wis 1: 3 and when his power is tested, it **e** the foolish;

EXPOSING (1) [EXPOSE]
Ge 30:37 **e** the white of the rods.

EXPOUND (2)
Dt 1: 5 Moses undertook to **e** this law as follows:
Sir 38:33 they cannot **e** discipline or judgment,

EXPRESS (5) [EXPRESSED, EXPRESSES, EXPRESSING, EXPRESSION, EXPRESSLY]
Nu 30:11 and did not **e** disapproval to her,
Ecc 1: 8 All things are wearisome; more than one can **e**;
Sir 34:12 and I understand more than I can **e**.
39:12 I have more on my mind to **e**;
4Mc 15: 4 In what manner might I **e** the emotions

EXPRESSED (5) [EXPRESS]
Nu 30: 5 because her father had **e** to her his disapproval.
1Ki 10:13 to the queen of Sheba every desire that she **e**,
2Ch 9:12 the queen of Sheba every desire that she **e**,
Sir Pr: 2 For what was originally **e** in Hebrew does
4Mc 18: 6 The mother of seven sons **e** also these principles

EXPRESSES (2) [EXPRESS]
Nu 30: 5 But if her father **e** disapproval to her at the time
30: 8 he **e** disapproval to her, then he shall nullify

EXPRESSING (2) [EXPRESS]
Pr 18: 2 but only in **e** personal opinion.

3Mc 6:41 magnanimously **e** his concern:

EXPRESSION (1) [EXPRESS]
2Mc 2:31 for brevity of **e** and to forego exhaustive treatment.

EXPRESSLY (3) [EXPRESS]
1Ch 12:31 who were **e** named to come and make David king.
16:41 of those chosen and **e** named to render thanks to
1Ti 4: 1 Now the Spirit **e** says that

EXPULSION (2) [EXPELLED]
Isa 27: 8 By **e**, by exile you struggled against them;
3Mc 4: 4 of life and shed tears at the most miserable **e**

EXTEND (10) [EXTENDED, EXTENDING, EXTENDS, EXTENSIVE, EXTENT]
Ex 27: 5 the ledge of the altar so that the net shall **e** halfway
Nu 21:15 and the slopes of the wadis that **e** to the seat of Ar,
34: 3 your south sector shall **e** from the wilderness
34: 9 the boundary shall **e** to Ziphron, and its end shall
Dt 11:24 your territory shall **e** from the wilderness to
Isa 11:11 that day the Lord will **e** his hand yet a second time
66:12 I will **e** prosperity to her like a river,
Jer 25:33 by the LORD on that day shall **e** from one end of
Ro 12:13 of the saints; **e** hospitality to strangers.
Sir 23:24 and her punishment will **e** to her children.

EXTENDED (12) [EXTEND]
Ge 10:19 And the territory of the Canaanites **e** from Sidon,
10:30 The territory in which they lived **e** from Mesha in
Jos 13:30 Their territory **e** from Mahanaim,
1Sa 14:27 so he **e** the staff that was in his hand,
2Ch 3:11 wings of the cherubim together **e** twenty cubits:
3:13 The wings of these cherubim **e** twenty cubits;
Ezr 7:28 and who **e** to me steadfast love before the king
9: 9 but has **e** to us his steadfast love before the kings
Mic 7:11 In that day the boundary shall be far **e**.
AdE 8: 4 The king **e** his golden scepter to Esther,
1Mc 3: 3 He **e** the glory of his people.
14: 6 He **e** the borders of his nation,

EXTENDING (5) [EXTEND]
Ex 38: 4 under its ledge, **e** halfway down.
Eze 45: 7 and **e** from the western to the eastern boundary
48: 1 and **e** from the east side to the west, Dan,
48:21 **E** from the twenty-five thousand cubits of
3Mc 2: 1 and **e** his hands with calm dignity, prayed

EXTENDS (5) [EXTEND]
Nu 21:13 in the wilderness that **e** from the boundary of
Jos 15: 9 then the boundary **e** from the top of the mountain
Ps 36: 5 Your steadfast love, O LORD, **e** to the heavens,
57:10 your faithfulness **e** to the clouds.
2Co 4:15 so that grace, as it **e** to more and more people,

EXTENSIVE (1) [EXTEND]
2Ch 27: 3 and did **e** building on the wall of Ophel.

EXTENT‡ (8) [EXTEND]
Jdg 20: 6 throughout the whole **e** of Israel's territory;
Eze 45: 1 it shall be holy throughout its entire **e**.
1Co 11:18 and to some **e** I believe it.
2Co 2: 5 but to some **e**—not to exaggerate it—to all of you.
AdE 13: 2 and open to travel throughout all its **e**,
2Mc 3: 3 even to the **e** that King Seleucus of Asia defrayed
3:11 an **e** the impious Simon had misrepresented
4Mc 4:25 even to the **e** that women, because they had

EXTERMINATED (3)
Jos 11:20 and might receive no mercy, but be **e**,
1Ki 22:46 in the land in the days of his father Asa, he **e**.
1Ch 4:41 and **e** them to this day, and settled in their place,

EXTERNAL (2)
Ro 2:28 nor is true circumcision something **e** and physical.
4Mc 6:34 of reason when it masters even **e** agonies.

EXTINCT (1) [EXTINCTION]
Job 17: 1 My spirit is broken, my days are **e**,

EXTINCT (KJV) See also EXTINGUISHED

EXTINCTION‡ (1) [EXTINCT]
2Pe 2: 6 to **e** and made them an example of what is coming

EXTINGUISH (1) [EXTINGUISHED, EXTINGUISHES]
Job 29:24 and the light of my countenance they did not **e**.

EXTINGUISHED‡ (3) [EXTINGUISH]
Isa 43:17 they lie down, they cannot rise, they are **e**,
Wis 2: 3 when it is **e**, the body will turn to ashes,
2Es 7:*61* they are set on fire and burn hotly, and are **e**."

EXTINGUISHES (1) [EXTINGUISH]
Sir 3:30 water **e** a blazing fire, so almsgiving atones for sin.

EXTOL (15) [EXTOLLED, EXTOLLING]
2Sa 22:50 For this I will **e** you, O LORD,
Job 36:24 "Remember to **e** his work,
Ps 18:49 For this I will **e** you, O LORD,
30: 1 I will **e** you, O LORD, for you have drawn me up,
89:16 your name all day long, and **e** your righteousness.
99: 5 **E** the LORD our God; worship at his footstool.
99: 9 **E** the LORD our God, and worship
107:32 Let them **e** him in the congregation of the people,
117: 1 **E** him, all you peoples!
118:28 you are my God, I will **e** you.
145: 1 I will **e** you, my God and King,
SS 1: 4 we will **e** your love more than wine;
Da 4:37 praise and **e** and honor the King of heaven,
Sir 13:23 they **e** to the clouds what he says.
43:31 Or who can **e** him as he is?

EXTOLLED (4) [EXTOL]
Ps 66:17 I cried aloud to him, and he was **e** with my tongue.
Aza 1:31 and to be **e** and highly glorified forever.
1:33 and to be **e** and highly exalted forever.
2Mc 4:24 **e** him with an air of authority,

EXTOLLING (1) [EXTOL]
Ac 10:46 they heard them speaking in tongues and **e** God.

EXTORT (1) [EXTORTED, EXTORTION]
Lk 3:14 "Do not **e** money from anyone by threats

EXTORTED (1) [EXTORT]
Eze 22:29 and have **e** from the alien without redress.

EXTORTION (6) [EXTORT]
Ps 62:10 Put no confidence in **e**, and set no vain hopes
Eze 18:18 As for his father, because he practiced **e**,
22: 7 the alien residing within you suffers **e**;
22:12 and make gain of your neighbors by **e**;
22:29 the land have practiced **e** and committed robbery;
2Co 9: 5 it may be ready as a voluntary gift and not as an **e**.

EXTRA (3)
Lk 9: 3 nor money—not even an **e** tunic.
1Co 16: 2 to put aside and save whatever **e** you earn,
Tob 12: 3 How much **e** shall I give him as a bonus?"

EXTRAORDINARY (4)
Da 2:31 This statue was huge, its brilliance **e**;
Ac 19:11 God did **e** miracles through Paul,
2Co 4: 7 that it may be made clear that this **e** power belongs
3Mc 5:31 an **e** degree a full and firm loyalty to my ancestors.

EXTREME (7) [EXTREMELY]
Jos 15:21 to the tribe of the people of Judah in the **e** South,
Eze 46:19 there I saw a place at the **e** western end of them.
2Co 8: 2 and their **e** poverty have overflowed in a wealth
2Mc 4:13 There was such an **e** of Hellenization and increase
7:42 about the eating of sacrifices and the **e** tortures.
3Mc 7:22 of it restored it to them with **e** fear.
4Mc 3:18 even when they are **e**, and by nobility

EXTREMELY (4) [EXTREME]
Zec 1:15 And I am **e** angry with the nations that are at ease;
Ac 17:22 I see how **e** religious you are in every way.
4Mc 3:10 but the king was **e** thirsty,
12: 9 **E** pleased by the boy's declaration,

EXULT‡ (30) [EXULTANT, EXULTATION, EXULTED, EXULTING, EXULTS]
2Sa 1:20 the daughters of the uncircumcised will **e**.
1Ch 16:32 let the field **e**, and everything in it.
Job 6:10 I would even **e** in unrelenting pain;
Ps 5:11 so that those who love your name may **e** in you.
9: 2 I will be glad and **e** in you;
25: 2 do not let my enemies **e** over me.
31: 7 I will **e** and rejoice in your steadfast love
63:11 all who swear by him shall **e**,
68: 3 be joyful; let them **e** before God;
89:16 they **e** in your name all day long,
94: 3 how long shall the wicked **e**?
96:12 let the field **e**, and everything
149: 5 Let the faithful **e** in glory;
SS 1: 4 We will **e** and rejoice in you;
Isa 5:14 her throng and all who **e** in her.
9: 3 as people **e** when dividing plunder.
14: 8 The cypresses **e** over you, the cedars of Lebanon,
23:12 You will **e** no longer, O oppressed virgin daughter
29:19 neediest people shall **e** in the Holy One of Israel.
49:13 Sing for joy, O heavens, and **e**, O earth;
61:10 my whole being shall **e** in my God;
Jer 11:15 sacrificial flesh avert your doom? Can you then **e**?
50:11 Though you rejoice, though you **e**,
Hos 9: 1 Do not **e** as other nations do;
Hab 3:18 I will **e** in the God of my salvation.
Zep 3:14 Rejoice and **e** with all your heart,
3:17 he will **e** over you with loud singing
Zec 10: 7 their hearts shall **e** in the LORD.
Rev 19: 7 Let us rejoice and **e** and give him the glory,
3Mc 2:17 the transgressors will boast in their wrath and **e** in

EXULTANT (5) [EXULT]
Ps 68: 4 his name is the LORD—be **e** before him.
Isa 22: 2 that are full of shoutings, tumultuous city, **e** town?
23: 7 Is this your **e** city whose origin is from days
Zep 2:15 Is this the **e** city that lived secure,
3:11 from your midst your proudly **e** ones,

EXULTATION‡ (4) [EXULT]
Ps 60: 6 "With **e** I will divide up Shechem,
108: 7 "With **e** I will divide up Shechem,
Wis 14:28 For their worshipers either rave in **e**,
Sir 1:11 The fear of the Lord is glory and **e**,

EXULTED (2) [EXULT]
Job 31:29 or **e** when evil overtook them—
2Es 1:16 You have not **e** in my name at the destruction

EXULTING (5) [EXULT]
Job 20: 5 that the **e** of the wicked is short,
Ps 35: 9 Then my soul shall rejoice in the LORD, **e**
Isa 13: 3 have summoned my warriors, my proudly **e** ones,
3Mc 6: 5 Sennacherib **e** in his countless forces,
2Es 15:53 **e** and clapping your hands and talking

EXULTS (5) [EXULT]
1Sa 2: 1 "My heart **e** in the LORD;
Job 39:21 It paws violently, **e** mightily;
Ps 21: 1 O LORD, and in your help how greatly he **e**!
28: 7 so I am helped, and my heart **e**,
Hab 1:15 in his seine; so he rejoices and **e**.

EYE‡ (109) [EYEBROWS, EYED, EYELASHES, EYELIDS, EYES, EYESIGHT, EYEWITNESSES]
Ex 21:24 **e** for **e**, tooth for tooth, hand for hand, foot
21:26 slaveowner strikes the **e** of a male or female slave,
21:26 a free person, to compensate for the **e**.
Lev 24:20 **e** for **e**, tooth for tooth;
Nu 24: 3 the oracle of the man whose **e** is clear,
24:15 the oracle of the man whose **e** is clear,
Dt 19:21 life for life, **e** for **e**, tooth for tooth,
32:10 cared for him, guarded him as the apple of his **e**.
Jdg 18: 6 mission you are on is under the **e** of the LORD."
1Sa 2:29 with greedy **e** at my sacrifices and my offerings
2:32 Then in distress you will look with greedy **e** on all
10:27 He would gouge out the right **e** of each of them
10:27 across the Jordan whose right **e** Nahash,
11: 2 namely that I gouge out everyone's right **e**,
Ezr 5: 5 the **e** of their God was upon the elders of the Jews,
Job 7: 7 my **e** will never again see good.
7: 8 The **e** that beholds me will see me no more;
10:18 Would that I had died before any **e** had seen me,
13: 1 "Look, my **e** has seen all this,
16:20 My friends scorn me; my **e** pours out tears to God,
17: 2 and my **e** dwells on their provocation.
17: 7 My **e** has grown dim from grief,
20: 9 The **e** that saw them will see them no more,
24:15 The **e** of the adulterer also waits for the twilight,
24:15 'No **e** will see me'; and he disguises his face.
28: 7 and the falcon's **e** has not seen it.
29:11 ear heard, it commended me, and when the **e** saw,
42: 5 but now my **e** sees you;
Ps 17: 8 Guard me as the apple of the **e**;
31: 9 my **e** wastes away from grief,
32: 8 I will counsel you with my **e** upon you.
33:18 the **e** of the LORD is on those who fear him,
35:19 or those who hate me without cause wink the **e**.
54: 7 and my **e** has looked in triumph on my enemies.
88: 9 my **e** grows dim through sorrow.
94: 9 He who formed the **e**, does he not see?
Pr 7: 2 keep my teachings as the apple of your **e**;
10:10 Whoever winks the **e** causes trouble,
20:12 The hearing ear and the seeing **e**—
28:27 but one who turns a blind **e** will get many a curse.
30:17 The **e** that mocks a father and scorns to obey
Ecc 1: 8 the **e** is not satisfied with seeing,
Isa 64: 4 no **e** has seen any God besides you,
Jer 32: 4 with him face to face and see him **e** to **e**;
34: 3 king of Babylon **e** to **e** and speak with him face
Eze 5:11 my **e** will not spare, and I will have no pity.
7: 4 My **e** will not spare you, I will have no pity.
7: 9 My **e** will not spare; I will have no pity.
8:18 my **e** will not spare, nor will I have pity;
9: 5 your **e** shall not spare, and you shall show no pity.
9:10 As for me, my **e** will not spare,
16: 5 No **e** pitied you, to do any of these things
20:17 Nevertheless my **e** spared them,
Zec 2: 8 one who touches you touches the apple of my **e**.
11:17 May the sword strike his arm and his right **e**!
11:17 his right **e** utterly blinded!
12: 4 But on the house of Judah I will keep a watchful **e**,
Mt 5:29 If your right **e** causes you to sin,
5:38 'An **e** for an **e** and a tooth for a tooth.'
6:22 "The **e** is the lamp of the body.
6:22 if your **e** is healthy, your whole body will be full
6:23 but if your **e** is unhealthy,
7: 3 Why do you see the speck in your neighbor's **e**, but do not notice the log in your own **e**?
7: 4 'Let me take the speck out of your **e**,' while the log is in your own **e**?
7: 5 first take the log out of your own **e**,
7: 5 to take the speck out of your neighbor's **e**.
18: 9 And if your **e** causes you to stumble,
18: 9 with one **e** than to have two eyes and to be thrown
19:24 for a camel to go through the **e** of a needle than
Mk 9:47 And if your **e** causes you to stumble, tear it out;

Mk 9:47 with one e than to have two eyes and to be thrown
10:25 for a camel to go through the e of a needle than
Lk 6:41 Why do you see the speck in your neighbor's e,
but do not notice the log in your own e?
6:42 'Friend, let me take out the speck in your e,'
6:42 you yourself do not see the log in your own e?
6:42 first take the log out of your own e,
6:42 to take the speck out of your neighbor's e.
11:34 Your e is the lamp of your body.
11:34 your e is healthy, your whole body is full of light;
18:25 for a camel to go through the e of a needle than
Ro 16:17 an e on those who cause dissensions and offenses,
1Co 2: 9 But, as it is written, "What no e has seen,
12:16 And if the ear would say, "Because I am not an e,
12:17 If the whole body were an e,
12:21 The e cannot say to the hand,
15:52 in the twinkling of an e, at the last trumpet.
Rev 1: 7 every e will see him, even those who pierced him;
Tob 4: 7 not let your e begrudge the gift when you make it.
4:16 do not let your e begrudge your giving of alms.
Sir 4: 5 Do not avert your e from the needy,
14: 9 The e of the greedy person is not satisfied
16: 5 Many such things my e has seen,
17:22 a person's kindness like the apple of his e.
22:19 One who pricks the e brings tears,
26:11 Be on guard against her impudent e,
27:22 Whoever winks the e plots mischief,
31:13 Remember that a greedy e is a bad thing.
31:13 What has been created more greedy than the e?
40:22 The e desires grace and beauty,
43:18 The e is dazzled by the beauty of its whiteness,

EYEBROWS (1) [EYE, BROW]

Lev 14: 9 of head, beard, e; he shall shave all his hair.

EYED (1) [EYE]

1Sa 18: 9 So Saul e David from that day on.

EYELASHES (1) [EYE]

Pr 6:25 and do not let her capture you with her e;

EYELIDS (9) [EYE]

Job 3: 9 may it not see the e of the morning—
16:16 and deep darkness is on my e,
41:18 and its eyes are like the e of the dawn.
Ps 77: 4 You keep my e from closing;
132: 4 not give sleep to my eyes or slumber to my e,
Pr 6: 4 Give your eyes no sleep and your e no slumber;
30:13 how lofty are their eyes, how high their e lift!
Jer 9:18 and our e flow with water.
Sir 26: 9 betrays an unchaste wife; her e give her away.

EYES‡ (479) [EYE]

Ge 3: 5 for God knows that when you eat of it your e will
3: 6 and that it was a delight to the e,
3: 7 Then the e of both were opened,
13:14 "Raise your e now, and look from the place
21:19 God opened her e and she saw a well of water.
27: 1 and his e were dim so that he could not see,
29:17 Leah's e were lovely, and Rachel was graceful
30:41 Jacob laid the rods in the troughs before the e of
31:40 and my sleep fled from my e.
39: 7 after a time his master's wife cast her e on Joseph
42:24 and had him bound before their e.
44:21 so that I may set my e on him.'
45:12 now your e and the e of my brother Benjamin see
46: 4 and Joseph's own hand shall close your e."
47:15 Why should we die before your e?
47:19 Shall we die before your e, both we and our land?
48:10 Now the e of Israel were dim with age,
49:12 his e are darker than wine,
Ex 40:38 before the e of all the house of Israel at each stage
Lev 13:37 But if in his e the itch is checked,
20: 4 if the people of the land should ever close their e
21:20 a man with a blemish in his e or an itching disease
26:16 that waste the e and cause life to pine away.
Nu 10:31 and you will serve as e for us.
15:39 follow the lust of your own heart and your own e.
16:14 Would you put out the e of these men?
20: 8 command the rock before their e to yield its water.
20:12 to show my holiness before the e of the Israelites,
22:31 Then the LORD opened the e of Balaam,
24: 4 who falls down, but with e uncovered:
24:16 who falls down, but with his e uncovered:
27:14 not show my holiness before their e at the waters."
33:55 be as barbs in your e and thorns in your sides;
Dt 1:30 just as he did for you in Egypt before your very e,
3:21 "Your own e have seen everything that
4: 9 the things that your e have seen nor to let them slip
4:34 for you in Egypt before your very e?
6:22 before our e great and awesome signs and wonders
7:19 the great trials that your e saw,
9:17 smashing them before your e.
10:21 and awesome things that your own e have seen.
11: 7 for it is your own e that have seen every great deed
11:12 The e of the LORD your God are always on it,
16:19 for a bribe blinds the e of the wise and subverts
28:31 Your ox shall be butchered before your e,
28:32 you will strain your e looking for them all day but
28:34 and driven mad by the sight that your e shall see.
28:65 failing e, and a languishing spirit.
28:67 and the sights that your e shall see.
29: 2 the LORD did before your e in the land of Egypt,
29: 3 the great trials that your e saw,
Dt 29: 4 or e to see, or ears to hear.
34: 4 I have let you see it with your e,
Jos 23:13 a scourge on your sides, and thorns in your e,
24: 7 and your e saw what I did to Egypt.
Jdg 16:21 So the Philistines seized him and gouged out his e.
16:28 the Philistines for my two e."
17: 6 all the people did what was right in their own e.
21:25 all the people did what was right in their own e.
Ru 2: 9 Keep your e on the field that is being reaped,
1Sa 2:33 be spared to weep out his e and grieve his heart;
4:15 Eli was ninety-eight years old and his e were set,
12: 3 a bribe to blind my e with it?
12:16 that the LORD will do before your e.
14:27 to his mouth; and his e brightened.
14:29 how my e have brightened because I tasted a little
15:17 Samuel said, "Though you are little in your own e,
16:12 Now he was ruddy, and had beautiful e,
24:10 This very day your e have seen how
2Sa 6:20 uncovering himself today before the e
6:22 and I will be abased in my own e;
7:19 this was a small thing in your e, O Lord GOD;
12:11 and I will take your wives before your e,
15:25 If I find favor in the e of the LORD,
22:28 your e are upon the haughty to bring them down.
24: 3 while the e of my lord the king can still see it!
1Ki 1:20 the e of all Israel are on you
8:29 that your e may be open night and day
8:52 Let your e be open to the plea of your servant,
9: 3 my e and my heart will be there for all time.
10: 7 the reports until I came and my own e had seen it.
14: 4 for his e were dim because of his age.
20:38 disguising himself with a bandage over his e.
20:41 he quickly took the bandage away from his e.
2Ki 4:34 his e upon his e, and his hands upon his hands;
4:35 and the child opened his e.
6:17 "O LORD, please open his e that he may see."
6:17 LORD opened the e of the servant, and he saw;
6:20 open the e of these men so that they may see."
6:20 The LORD opened their e,
7: 2 But he said, "You shall see it with your own e,
7:19 "You shall see it with your own e,
9:30 she painted her e, and adorned her head,
19:16 open your e, O LORD, and see;
19:22 and haughtily lifted your e?
22:20 your e shall not see all the disaster that I will bring
25: 7 before his e, then put out the eyes of Zedekiah;
25: 7 then put out the e of Zedekiah;
2Ch 6:20 May your e be open day and night
6:40 let your e be open and your ears attentive to prayer
7:15 Now my e will be open and my ears attentive to
7:16 my e and my heart will be there for all time.
9: 6 the reports until I came and my own e saw it.
16: 9 e of the LORD range throughout the entire earth,
20:12 We do not know what to do, but our e are on you."
29: 8 and of hissing, as you see with your own e.
34:28 your e shall not see all the disaster that I will bring
Ezr 9: 8 in order that he may brighten our e and grant us
Ne 1: 6 and your e open to hear the prayer of your servant
Job 3:10 and hide trouble from my e.
4:16 A form was before my e;
7: 8 while your e are upon me, I shall be gone.
9:24 he covers the e of its judges—
10: 4 Do you have e of flesh?
11:20 But the e of the wicked will fail;
14: 3 Do you fix your e on such a one?
15:12 and why do your e flash,
16: 9 my adversary sharpens his e against me.
17: 5 the e of their children will fail.
19:15 I have become an alien in their e.
19:27 and my e shall behold, and not another.
21: 8 and their offspring before their e.
21:20 Let their own e see their destruction,
24:23 his e are upon their ways.
27:19 they open their e, and it is gone.
28:10 and their e see every precious thing.
28:21 It is hidden from the e of all living,
29:15 I was e to the blind, and feet to the lame.
31: 1 "I have made a covenant with my e;
31: 7 and my heart has followed my e,
31:16 or have caused the e of the widow to fail,
32: 1 because he was righteous in his own e.
34:21 "For his e are upon the ways of mortals,
36: 7 He does not withdraw his e from the righteous,
39:29 its e see it from far away.
41:18 and its e are like the eyelids of the dawn.
Ps 5: 5 The boastful will not stand before your e;
6: 7 My e waste away because of grief;
10: 8 Their e stealthily watch for the helpless;
11: 4 His e behold, his gaze examines humankind.
13: 3 Give light to my e, or I will sleep the sleep
15: 4 in whose e the wicked are despised,
17: 2 let your e see the right.
17:11 they set their e to cast me to the ground.
18:27 but the haughty e you bring down.
19: 8 of the LORD is clear, enlightening the e;
25:15 My e are ever toward the LORD,
26: 3 For your steadfast love is before my e,
34:15 The e of the LORD are on the righteous,
35:21 they say, "Aha, Aha, our e have seen it."
36: 1 there is no fear of God before their e.
36: 2 For they flatter themselves in their own e
38:10 as for the light of my e—it also has gone from me.
66: 7 whose e keep watch on the nations—
69: 3 My e grow dim with waiting for my God.
69:23 Let their e be darkened so that they cannot see,
73: 7 Their e swell out with fatness;
79:10 be known among the nations before our e.
Ps 91: 8 with your e and see the punishment of the wicked.
92:11 My e have seen the downfall of my enemies;
101: 3 I will not set before my e anything that is base.
115: 5 They have mouths, but do not speak; e,
116: 8 my e from tears, my feet from stumbling.
118:23 it is marvelous in our e.
119: 6 having my e fixed on all your commandments.
119:15 and fix my e on your ways.
119:18 Open my e, so that I may behold wondrous things
119:37 Turn my e from looking at vanities;
119:82 My e fail with watching for your promise;
119:123 My e fail from watching for your salvation,
119:136 My e shed streams of tears because your law is
119:148 My e are awake before each watch of the night,
121: 1 I lift up my e to the hills—
123: 1 To you I lift up my e,
123: 2 the e of servants look to the hand of their master,
123: 2 as the e of a maid to the hand of her mistress,
123: 2 so our e look to the LORD our God,
131: 1 my e are not raised too high;
132: 4 not give sleep to my e or slumber to my eyelids,
135:16 they have e, but they do not see;
139:16 Your e beheld my unformed substance.
141: 8 my e are turned toward you, O GOD, my Lord;
145:15 The e of all look to you,
146: 8 the LORD opens the e of the blind.
Pr 3: 7 Do not be wise in your own e;
4:25 Let your e look directly forward,
5:21 For human ways are under the e of the LORD,
6: 4 Give your e no sleep and your eyelids no slumber;
6:13 winking the e, shuffling the feet, pointing
6:17 haughty e, a lying tongue, and hands
10:26 Like vinegar to the teeth, and smoke to the e,
15: 3 The e of the LORD are in every place,
15:30 The light of the e rejoices the heart,
16: 2 All one's ways may be pure in one's own e,
16:30 One who winks the e plans perverse things;
17: 8 like a magic stone in the e of those who give it;
17:24 but the e of a fool to the ends of the earth.
20: 8 the throne of judgment winnows all evil with his e.
20:13 open your e, and you will have plenty of bread.
21: 4 Haughty e and a proud heart—
21:10 their neighbors find no mercy in their e.
22:12 The e of the LORD keep watch over knowledge,
23: 5 When your e light upon it, it is gone;
23:26 and let your e observe my ways.
23:29 Who has redness of e?
23:33 Your e will see strange things,
25: 7 of a noble. What your e have seen
26: 5 or they will be wise in their own e.
26:12 Do you see persons wise in their own e?
27:20 and human e are never satisfied.
29:13 the LORD gives light to the e of both.
30:12 There are those who are pure in their own e yet are
30:13 how lofty are their e, how high their eyelids lift!
Ecc 2:10 Whatever my e desired I did not keep from them;
2:14 The wise have e in their head,
4: 8 and their e are never satisfied with riches.
5:11 but to see them with his e?
6: 9 the sight of the e than the wandering of desire;
8:16 how one's e see sleep neither day nor night,
11: 7 and it is pleasant for the e to see the sun.
11: 9 of your heart and the desire of your e,
SS 1:15 you are beautiful; your e are doves.
4: 1 Your e are doves behind your veil.
4: 9 with a glance of your e,
5:12 His e are like doves beside springs of water,
6: 5 Turn away your e from me,
7: 4 Your e are pools in Heshbon,
8:10 then I was in his e as one who brings peace.
Isa 1:15 I will hide my e from you;
1:16 remove the evil of your doings from before my e;
2:11 The haughty e of people shall be brought low,
3:16 glancing wantonly with their e,
5:15 and the e of the haughty are humbled.
5:21 Ah, you who are wise in your own e,
6: 5 my e have seen the King, the LORD of hosts!"
6:10 and stop their ears, and shut their e,
6:10 so that they may not look with their e,
11: 3 He shall not judge by what his e see,
13:16 be dashed to pieces before their e;
13:18 their e will not pity children.
17: 7 and their e will look to the Holy One of Israel;
29:10 he has closed your e, you prophets,
29:18 and out of their gloom and darkness the e of
30:20 but your e shall see your Teacher.
32: 3 the e of those who have sight will not be closed,
33:15 of bloodshed and shut their e from looking on evil,
33:17 Your e will see the king in his beauty;
33:20 Your e will see Jerusalem, a quiet habitation,
35: 5 Then the e of the blind shall be opened,
37:17 open your e, O LORD, and see;
37:23 and haughtily lifted your e?
38:14 My e are weary with looking upward.
40:26 Lift up your e on high and see: Who created these?
42: 7 to open the e that are blind,
43: 8 Bring forth the people who are blind, yet have e,
44:18 for their e are shut, so that they cannot see,
49:18 Lift up your e all around and see;
51: 6 Lift up your e to the heavens,
52:10 The LORD has bared his holy arm before the e
57:11 Have I not kept silent and closed my e,
59:10 groping like those who have no e;
60: 4 Lift up your e and look around;
Jer 4:30 that you enlarge your e with paint?
5: 3 O LORD, do your e not look for truth?
5:21 O foolish and senseless people, who have e,

Jer 9: 1 and my **e** a fountain of tears,
9:18 so that our **e** may run down with tears,
13:17 my **e** will weep bitterly and run down with tears,
13:20 up your **e** and see those who come from the north.
14: 6 their **e** fail because there is no herbage.
14:17 Let my **e** run down with tears night and day,
16: 9 in your days and before your **e**,
16:17 For my **e** are on all their ways;
22:17 your **e** and heart are only on your dishonest gain,
24: 6 I will set my **e** upon them for good,
29:21 and he shall kill them before your **e**.
31:16 Keep your voice from weeping, and your **e**
32:19 whose **e** are open to all the ways of mortals,
39: 6 the sons of Zedekiah at Riblah before his **e**;
39: 7 He put out the **e** of Zedekiah,
42: 2 a few of us left out of many, as your **e** can see.
51:24 of Chaldea before your very **e** for all the wrong
52:10 the sons of Zedekiah before his **e**,
52:11 He put out the **e** of Zedekiah,
La 1:16 For these things I weep; my **e** flow with tears;
2:11 My **e** are spent with weeping;
2:18 Give yourself no rest, your **e** no respite!
3:48 My **e** flow with rivers of tears because of
3:49 My **e** will flow without ceasing, without respite,
3:51 My **e** cause me grief at the fate of all
4:17 Our **e** failed, ever watching vainly for help;
5:17 because of these things our **e** have grown dim:
Eze 1:18 for the rims of all four were full of **e** all around.
6: 9 and their wanton **e** that turned after their idols.
8: 5 lift up your **e** now in the direction of the north."
8: 5 So I lifted up my **e** toward the north, and there,
10:12 were full of **e** all around.
12: 2 who have **e** to see but do not see,
12:12 so that he may not see the land with his **e**.
18: 6 upon the mountains or lift up his **e** to the idols of
18:12 lifts up his **e** to the idols, commits abomination,
18:15 upon the mountains or lift up his **e** to the idols of
20: 7 Cast away the detestable things your **e** feast on,
20: 8 the detestable things their **e** feasted on,
20:24 and their **e** were set on their ancestors' idols.
21: 6 with breaking heart and bitter grief before their **e**.
23:40 For them you bathed yourself, painted your **e**,
24:16 about to take away from you the delight of your **e**;
24:21 the pride of your power, the delight of your **e**,
24:25 the delight of their **e** and their heart's affection,
28:17 I exposed you before kings, to feast their **e** on you.
33:25 and lift up your **e** to your idols, and shed blood;
36:23 through you I display my holiness before their **e**.
37:20 in your hand before their **e**,
38:16 O Gog, I display my holiness before their **e**.
38:23 and make myself known in the **e** of many nations.
Da 4:34 I, Nebuchadnezzar, lifted my **e** to heaven,
7: 8 There were **e** like human **e** in this horn,
7:20 horn that had **e** and a mouth that spoke arrogantly,
8: 5 The goat had a horn between its **e**.
8:21 and the great horn between its **e** is the first king.
9:18 Open your **e** and look at our desolation and
10: 6 his face like lightning, his **e** like flaming torches,
Hos 13:14 Compassion is hidden from my **e**.
Joel 1:16 Is not the food cut off before our **e**,
Am 9: 4 I will fix my **e** on them for harm and not for good.
9: 8 **e** of the Lord GOD are upon the sinful kingdom,
Mic 4:11 and let our **e** gaze upon Zion."
7:10 My **e** will see her downfall;
Hab 1:13 Your **e** are too pure to behold evil,
Zep 3:20 when I restore your fortunes before your **e**,
Zec 4:10 "These seven are the **e** of the LORD,
9: 8 for now I have seen with my own **e**.
14:12 their **e** shall rot in their sockets,
Mal 1: 5 Your own **e** shall see this, and you shall say,
Mt 9:29 Then he touched their **e** and said,
9:30 And their **e** were opened.
13:15 and they have shut their **e**;
13:15 so that they might not look with their **e**,
13:16 But blessed are your **e**, for they see, and your ears,
18: 9 to have two **e** and to be thrown into the hell of fire.
20:33 They said to him, "Lord, let our **e** be opened."
20:34 Moved with compassion, Jesus touched their **e**.
21:42 and it is amazing in our **e**'?
26:43 and found them sleeping, for their **e** were heavy.
Mk 8:18 Do you have **e**, and fail to see?
8:23 when he had put saliva on his **e** and laid his hands
8:25 Then Jesus laid his hands on his **e** again;
9:47 with one eye than to have two **e** and to be thrown
12:11 and it is amazing in our **e**'?"
14:40 for their **e** were very heavy;
Lk 2:30 for my **e** have seen your salvation,
4:20 The **e** of all in the synagogue were fixed on him.
10:23 "Blessed are the **e** that see what you see!
19:42 But now they are hidden from your **e**.
24:16 but their **e** were kept from recognizing him.
24:31 their **e** were opened, and they recognized him;
Jn 9: 6 with the saliva and spread the mud on the man's **e**,
9:10 "Then how were your **e** opened?"
9:11 spread it on my **e**, and said to me,
9:14 when Jesus made the mud and opened his **e**.
9:15 He said to them, "He put mud on my **e**.
9:17 It was your **e** he opened."
9:21 nor do we know who opened his **e**.
9:26 How did he open your **e**?"
9:30 and yet he opened my **e**.
9:32 that anyone opened the **e** of a person born blind.
10:21 Can a demon open the **e** of the blind?"
11:37 the **e** of the blind man have kept this man
12:40 "He has blinded their **e** and hardened their heart,
12:40 so that they might not look with their **e**,
Ac 9: 8 and though his **e** were open, he could see nothing;
Ac 9:18 immediately something like scales fell from his **e**,
9:40 she opened her **e**, and seeing Peter, she sat up.
26:18 to open their **e** so that they may turn from darkness
28:27 and they have shut their **e**;
28:27 so that they might not look with their **e**,
Ro 3:18 "There is no fear of God before their **e**."
11: 8 **e** that would not see and ears that would not hear,
11:10 let their **e** be darkened so that they cannot see,
2Co 10: 7 Look at what is before your **e**.
Gal 3: 1 was before your **e** that Jesus Christ was publicly
4:15 you would have torn out your **e** and given them
Eph 1:18 with the **e** of your heart enlightened,
Heb 4:13 but all are naked and laid bare to the **e** of the one
1Pe 3:12 For the **e** of the Lord are on the righteous,
2Pe 2:14 They have **e** full of adultery, insatiable for sin.
1Jn 1: 1 what we have seen with our **e**,
2:16 the desire of the flesh, the desire of the **e**,
Rev 1:14 his **e** were like a flame of fire,
2:18 who has **e** like a flame of fire,
3:18 and salve to anoint your **e** so that you may see.
4: 6 full of **e** in front and behind:
4: 8 are full of **e** all around and inside.
5: 6 having seven horns and seven **e**,
7:17 and God will wipe away every tear from their **e**."
19:12 His **e** are like a flame of fire,
21: 4 he will wipe every tear from their **e**.
Tob 2:10 into my **e** and produced white films.
3:12 I turn my face to you, and raise my **e** toward you.
3:17 Tobit, by removing the white films from his **e**,
3:17 so that he might see God's light with his **e**;
5:21 Your **e** will see him on the day when he returns
6: 9 a person's **e** where white films have appeared
6: 9 upon the white films, and the **e** will be healed."
10: 5 the light of my **e**, that I let you make the journey."
11: 7 "I know that his **e** will be opened.
11: 8 Smear the gall of the fish on his **e**;
11: 8 the white films shrink and peel off from his **e**,
11:11 and holding him firmly, he blew into his **e**, saying,
11:11 With this he applied the medicine on his **e**,
11:13 the white films from the corners of his **e**.
11:14 "I see you, my son, the light of my **e**!"
Jdt 7:27 not witness our little ones dying before our **e**,
8:22 and we shall be an offense and a disgrace in the **e**
10: 4 to entice the **e** of all the men who might see her.
10:14 she was in their **e** marvelously beautiful—
16: 9 Her sandal ravished his **e**,
AdE 2:15 Esther found favor in the **e** of all who saw her.
13:15 for the **e** of our foes are upon us to annihilate us,
13:18 for their death was before their **e**.
16: 9 before our **e** with more equitable consideration.
Wis 3: 2 In the **e** of the foolish they seemed to have died,
11:18 or flash terrible sparks from their **e**;
15:15 these have neither the use of their **e** to see with,
Sir 3:25 Without **e** there is no light;
4: 1 and do not keep needy **e** waiting.
9: 8 Turn away your **e** from a shapely woman,
10:20 the Lord are worthy of honor in his **e**.
11:12 but the **e** of the Lord look kindly upon them;
12:16 an enemy may have tears in his **e**,
15:19 his **e** are on those who fear him,
17: 6 Discretion and tongue and **e**,
17:13 Their **e** saw his glorious majesty,
17:15 they will not be hid from his **e**.
17:19 and his **e** are ever upon their ways.
18:18 and the gift of a grudging giver makes the **e** dim.
20:29 Favors and gifts blind the **e** of the wise;
23: 4 do not give me haughty **e**,
23:19 to human **e** and he does not realize that the **e** of
27: 1 and those who seek to get rich will avert their **e**.
30:20 he sees with his **e** and groans as a eunuch groans
34:19 The **e** of the Lord are on those who love him,
34:20 He lifts up the soul and makes the **e** sparkle;
34:24 a son before his father's **e** is the person who offers
38:28 and his **e** are on the pattern of the object.
39:19 and nothing can be hidden from his **e**.
43: 4 and its bright rays blind the **e**.
45:12 the work of an expert, a delight to the **e**,
51:27 See with your own **e** that I have labored but little
Bar 1:12 The Lord will give us strength, and light to our **e**;
2:17 open your **e**, O Lord, and see; for the dead who are
2:18 with failing **e** and famished soul,
3:14 and life, where there is light for the **e**, and peace.
LtJ 6:18 Their **e** are full of the dust raised by the feet
Sus 1: 9 and turned away their **e** from looking to Heaven
1:32 so that they might feast their **e** on her beauty.
Bel 1:42 and they were instantly eaten before his **e**.
1Mc 6:10 from my **e** and I am downhearted with worry.
2Mc 3:36 which he had seen with his own **e**.
8:17 keeping before their **e** the lawless outrage that
12:42 with their own **e** what had happened as the result
3Mc 4: 4 the common object of pity before their **e**,
4:10 so that, with their **e** in total darkness,
5:33 and his **e** wavered and his face fell.
5:47 with invulnerable heart and with his own **e**,
2Es 1:37 though they do not see me with bodily **e**,
8:20 you who inhabit eternity, whose **e** are exalted
10:55 as far as it is possible for your **e** to see it,
4Mc 4: 1 of slander he was unable to injure Onias in the **e** of
5:30 even if you gouge out my **e** and burn my entrails.
6: 6 yet while the old man's **e** were raised to heaven,
6:26 he lifted up his **e** to God and said,
15:19 at the **e** of each one in his tortures gazing boldly at
18:21 the pupils of their **e** and cut out their tongues,

EYESIGHT (3) [EYE, SEE]

1Sa 3: 2 whose **e** had begun to grow dim so that he could
Tob 5:10 I am a man without **e**;
14: 2 He was sixty-two years old when he lost his **e**,

EYEWITNESSES (2) [EYE, WITNESS]

Lk 1: 2 by those who from the beginning were **e**
2Pe 1:16 but we had been **e** of his majesty.

EYING See Index to Footnotes

EZBAI (1)

1Ch 11:37 Hezro of Carmel, Naarai son of **E**,

EZBON (2)

Ge 46:16 Ziphion, Haggi, Shuni, **E**, Eri, Arodi, and Areli.
1Ch 7: 7 The sons of Bela: **E**, Uzzi, Uzziel, Jerimoth,

EZEKIAS (KJV) See HEZEKIAH

EZEKIEL (4)

Eze 1: 3 of the LORD came to the priest **E** son of Buzi,
24:24 Thus **E** shall be a sign to you;
Sir 49: 8 It was **E** who saw the vision of glory,
4Mc 18:17 He confirmed the query of **E**,

EZEM (3)

Jos 15:29 Baalah, Iim, **E**,
19: 3 Hazar-shual, Balah, **E**,
1Ch 4:29 Bilhah, **E**, Tolad,

EZER‡ (10)

Ge 36:21 **E**, and Dishan; these are the clans of the
36:27 These are the sons of **E**:
36:30 **E**, and Dishan; these are the clans of the
1Ch 1:38 Lotan, Shobal, Zibeon, Anah, Dishon, **E**,
1:42 The sons of **E**: Bilhan, Zaavan, and Jaakan.
4: 4 and **E** the father of Hushah.
7:21 Shuthelah his son, and **E** and Elead.
12: 9 **E** the chief, Obadiah second, Eliab third,
Ne 3:19 next to him **E** son of Jeshua,
12:42 Eleazar, Uzzi, Jehohanan, Malchijah, Elam, and **E**.

EZION-GEBER (7)

Nu 33:35 They set out from Abronah and camped at **E**.
33:36 They set out from **E** and camped in the wilderness
Dt 2: 8 and leaving behind Elath and **E**.
1Ki 9:26 King Solomon built a fleet of ships at **E**,
22:48 they did not go, for the ships were wrecked at **E**.
2Ch 8:17 Then Solomon went to **E** and Eloth on the shore of
20:36 they built the ships in **E**.

EZORA (1)

1Es 9:34 Nethaniah. Of the descendants of **E**:

EZRA‡ (60) [EZRA'S]

Ezr 7: 1 **E** son of Seraiah, son of Azariah, son of Hilkiah,
7: 6 this **E** went up from Babylonia.
7:10 **E** had set his heart to study the law of the LORD,
7:11 to the priest **E**, the scribe, a scholar of the text of
7:12 king of kings, to the priest **E**,
7:21 Whatever the priest **E**, the scribe of the law of
7:25 "And you, **E**, according to the God-given wisdom
10: 1 While **E** prayed and made confession,
10: 2 of the descendants of Elam, addressed **E**, saying,
10: 5 Then **E** stood up and made the leading priests,
10: 6 Then **E** withdrew from before the house of God,
10:10 Then **E** the priest stood up and said to them,
10:16 **E** the priest selected men, heads of families,
Ne 8: 1 the scribe **E** to bring the book of the law of Moses,
8: 2 the priest **E** brought the law before the assembly,
8: 4 The scribe **E** stood on a wooden platform
8: 5 **E** opened the book in the sight of all the people,
8: 6 Then **E** blessed the LORD, the great God,
8: 9 who was the governor, and **E** the priest and scribe,
8:13 the scribe **E** in order to study the words of the law.
9: 6 And **E** said: "You are the LORD,
12: 1 and Jeshua: Seraiah, Jeremiah, **E**,
12:13 of **E**, Meshullam; of Amariah, Jehohanan;
12:26 of the governor Nehemiah and of the priest **E**,
12:33 and Azariah, **E**, Meshullam,
12:36 and the scribe **E** went in front of them.
1Es 8: 1 the king of the Persians, was reigning, **E** came,
8: 3 This **E** came up from Babylon as a scribe skilled
8: 7 For **E** possessed great knowledge,
8: 8 to **E** the priest and reader of the law of the Lord:
8: 9 to **E** the priest and reader of the law of the Lord,
8:19 that whatever **E** the priest and reader of the law of
8:23 "And you, **E**, according to the wisdom of God,
8:25 Then **E** the scribe said, "Blessed be the Lord
8:91 While **E** was praying and making his confession,
8:92 one of the men of Israel, called out, and said to **E**,
8:96 Then **E** rose up and made the leaders of the priests
9: 1 Then **E** set out and went from the court of
9: 7 Then **E** stood up and said to them,
9:16 **E** the priest chose for himself the leading men
9:39 they told **E** the chief priest and reader to bring
9:40 So **E** the chief priest brought the law,
9:42 **E** the priest and reader of the law stood on
9:45 Then **E** took up the book of the law in the sight of
9:46 And **E** blessed the Lord God Most High,
9:49 Attharates said to **E** the chief priest and reader,
2Es 1: 1 of the prophet **E** son of Seraiah son of Azariah son
2:10 Thus says the Lord to **E**:

2Es 2:33 **E,** received a command from the Lord
2:42 **E,** saw on Mount Zion a great multitude
3: 1 I, Salathiel, who am also called **E.**
6:10 nothing else, **E,** between the heel and the hand, **E!"**
7: 2 **E,** and listen to the words that I have come
7:25 **E,** that empty things are for the empty,
7:*49* He answered me and said, "Listen to me, **E,**
8: 2 But I tell you a parable, **E.**
14: 1 of a bush opposite me and said, **"E, E!"**
14:38 And on the next day a voice called me, saying, **"E,**

EZRA'S (1) [EZRA]

2Es 8:19 The beginning of the words of **E** prayer,

EZRAH (1) [EZRAHITE]

1Ch 4:17 The sons of **E:** Jether, Mered, Epher, and Jalon.

EZRAHITE (3) [EZRAH]

1Ki 4:31 wiser than Ethan the **E,** and Heman, Calcol,
Ps 88: T *A Maskil of Heman the* **E.**
89: T *A Maskil of Ethan the* **E.**

EZRI (1)

1Ch 27:26 tilling the soil, was **E** son of Chelub.

F

FABLES (KJV) See MYTHS

FABRIC (3) [FABRICS]

Eze 16:10 in fine linen and covered you with rich **f.**
16:13 while your clothing was of fine linen, rich **f,**
Sir 38:34 But they maintain the **f** of the world,

FABRICATE (1)

Sir 51: 2 by a slanderous tongue, from lips that **f** lies.

FABRICS (3) [FABRIC]

2Ch 2: 7 crimson, and blue **f,** trained also in engraving,
2:14 and in purple, blue, and crimson **f** and fine linen,
3:14 of blue and purple and crimson **f** and fine linen,

FACE‡ (398) [FACED, FACES, FACING, GRIM-FACED]

A. HID/HIDDEN/HIDE/HIDES/HIDING ... FACE (30)
B. SET ... FACE (25)
C. FACE TO FACE (23)
D. FACE TO THE GROUND (20)

Ge 1: 2 a formless void and darkness covered the **f** of
1: 2 a wind from God swept over the **f** of the waters.
1:29 that is upon the **f** of all the earth, and every tree
2: 6 and water the whole **f** of the ground—
3:19 of your **f** you shall eat bread until you return to
4:14 and I shall be hidden from your **f;**
6: 1 people began to multiply on the **f** of the ground,
7: 3 to keep their kind alive on the **f** of all the earth.
7: 4 that I have made I will blot out from the **f** of
7:18 and the ark floated on the **f** of the waters.
7:23 He blotted out every living thing that was on the **f**
8: 8 the waters had subsided from the **f** of the ground;
8: 9 the waters were still on the **f** of the whole earth.
8:13 and saw that the **f** of the ground was drying.
11: 4 otherwise we shall be scattered abroad upon the **f**
11: 8 from there over the **f** of all the earth,
11: 9 the LORD scattered them abroad over the **f** of all
17: 3 Then Abram fell on his **f;** and God said to him,
17:17 Then Abraham fell on his **f** and laughed,
19: 1 and bowed down with his **f** to the ground. D
31:21 and set his **f** toward the hill country of Gilead. B
32:20 and afterwards I shall see his **f;**
32:30 saying, "For I have seen God **f** to **f,** C
33:10 truly to see your **f** is like seeing the face of God—
33:10 truly to see your face is like seeing the **f** of God—
38:15 for she had covered her **f.**
43: 3 'You shall not see my **f** unless your brother is
43: 5 for the man said to us, 'You shall not see my **f,**
43:31 Then he washed his **f** and came out;
44:23 you shall see my **f** no more.'
44:26 the man's **f** unless our youngest brother is
48:11 "I did not expect to see your **f;**
48:12 and he bowed himself with his **f** to the earth.
50: 1 Then Joseph threw himself on his father's **f**
Ex 3: 6 Moses hid his **f,** for he was afraid to look at God. A
10:28 Take care that you do not see my **f** again,
10:28 for on the day you see my **f** you shall die."
10:29 I will never see your **f** again."
13:17 for God thought, "If the people **f** war,
25:20 They shall **f** one to another;
32:12 and to consume them from the **f** of the earth'?
33:11 Thus the LORD used to speak to Moses **f** to **f,** C
33:16 from every people on the **f** of the earth."
Ex 33:20 But," he said, "you cannot see my **f;**
33:23 but my **f** shall not be seen."
34:29 Moses did not know that the skin of his **f** shone
34:30 the skin of his **f** was shining,
34:33 he put a veil on his **f;**
34:35 the Israelites would see the **f** of Moses,
34:35 that the skin of his **f** was shining;
34:35 and Moses would put the veil on his **f** again,
Lev 17:10 will set my **f** against that person who eats blood, B
20: 3 I myself will set my **f** against them, B
20: 5 I myself will set my **f** against them and B
20: 6 I will set my **f** against them, B
21:18 or one who has a mutilated **f** or a limb too long,
26:17 I will set my **f** against you, B
Nu 6:25 the LORD make his **f** to shine upon you,
12: 3 more so than anyone else on the **f** of the earth.
12: 8 With him I speak **f** to **f**— C
12:14 "If her father had but spit in her **f,**
14:14 for you, O LORD, are seen **f** to **f,** C
16: 4 When Moses heard it, he fell on his **f.**
22: 5 they have spread over the **f** of the earth,
22:11 of Egypt and has spread over the **f** of the earth;
22:31 and he bowed down, falling on his **f.**
24: 1 but set his **f** toward the wilderness. B
Dt 5: 4 LORD spoke with you **f** to **f** at the mountain, C
6:15 and he would destroy you from the **f** of the earth.
25: 9 pull his sandal off his foot, spit in his **f,**
31:17 I will forsake them and hide my **f** from them; A
31:18 that day I will surely hide my **f** on account of all A
32:20 He said: I will hide my **f** from them, A
34:10 whom the LORD knew **f** to **f.** C
Jos 5:14 Joshua fell on his **f** to the earth and worshiped,
7: 6 the ground on his **f** before the ark of the LORD
7:10 Why have you fallen upon your **f?**
Jdg 6:22 For I have seen the angel of the LORD **f** to **f."** C
Ru 2:10 Then she fell prostrate, with her **f** to the ground, D
1Sa 5: 3 fallen on his **f** to the ground before the ark of D
5: 4 Dagon had fallen on his **f** to the ground before D
17:49 and he fell **f** down on the ground.
20:15 of the enemies of David from the **f** of the earth."
20:41 and prostrated himself with his **f** to the ground. D
24: 8 David bowed with his **f** to the ground, D
25:23 fell before David on her **f,** bowing to the ground.
25:41 with her **f** to the ground, and said, D
28:14 and he bowed with his **f** to the ground, D
2Sa 2:22 then could I show my **f** to your brother Joab?"
9: 6 and fell on his **f** and did obeisance.
14: 4 she fell on her **f** to the ground and did obeisance, D
14: 7 to my husband neither name nor remnant on the **f**
14:22 Joab prostrated himself with his **f** to the ground D
14:33 and prostrated himself with his **f** to the ground D
18: 8 The battle spread over the **f** of all the country;
18:28 himself before the king with his **f** to the ground, D
19: 4 The king covered his **f,** and the king cried with
24:20 himself before the king with his **f** to the ground. D
1Ki 1:23 to the king, with his **f** to the ground. D
1:31 Then Bathsheba bowed with her **f** to the ground, D
13:34 so as to cut it off and to destroy it from the **f** of
18: 7 Obadiah recognized him, fell on his **f,** and said,
18:42 upon the earth and put his **f** between his knees.
19:13 he wrapped his **f** in his mantle and went out
21: 4 He lay down on his bed, turned away his **f,**
2Ki 4:29 and lay my staff on the **f** of the child."
4:31 Gehazi went on ahead and laid the staff on the **f**
8:15 in water and spread it over the king's **f,**
12:17 when Hazael set his **f** to go up against Jerusalem, B
14: 8 saying, "Come, let us look one another in the **f."**
20: 2 Then Hezekiah turned his **f** to the wall and prayed
1Ch 21:21 did obeisance to David with his **f** to the ground. D
2Ch 7:14 pray, seek my **f,** and turn from their wicked ways,
20:18 bowed down with his **f** to the ground, D
25:17 saying, "Come, let us look one another in the **f."**
30: 9 and will not turn away his **f** from you,
Ezr 9: 6 I am too ashamed and embarrassed to lift my **f**
9:15 though no one can **f** you because of this."
Ne 2: 2 So the king said to me, "Why is your **f** sad,
2: 3 Why should my **f** not be sad, when the city,
4: 5 they have hurled insults in the **f** of the builders.
Est 7: 8 the mouth of the king, they covered Haman's **f.**
Job 1:11 and he will curse you to your **f."**
2: 5 and he will curse you to your **f."**
4:15 A spirit glided past my **f;**
6:28 for I will not lie to your **f.**
11:15 then you will lift up your **f** without blemish;
13:15 but I will defend my ways to his **f.**
13:20 then I will not hide myself from your **f:**
13:24 Why do you hide your **f,** A
16: 8 up against me, and it testifies to my **f.**
16:16 My **f** is red with weeping,
21:31 Who declares their way to their **f,**
22:26 and lift up your **f** to God.
23:17 and thick darkness would cover my **f!**
24:15 'No eye will see me'; and he disguises his **f.**
24:18 "Swift are they on the **f** of the waters;
26: 9 He covers the **f** of the full moon,
26:10 He has described a circle on the **f** of the waters,
34:29 When he hides his **f,** who can behold him, A
37:12 to accomplish all that he commands them on the **f**
38:30 and the **f** of the deep is frozen.
41:14 Who can open the doors of its **f?**
Ps 4: 6 Let the light of your **f** shine on us, O LORD!"
10:11 he has hidden his **f,** he will never see it." A
11: 7 the upright shall behold his **f.**
13: 1 How long will you hide your **f** from me? A
17:15 As for me, I shall behold your **f** in righteousness;
22:24 he did not hide his **f** from me, A
24: 6 who seek the **f** of the God of Jacob.
Ps 27: 8 "Come," my heart says, "seek his **f!"**
27: 8 Your **f,** LORD, do I seek.
27: 9 Do not hide your **f** from me. A
30: 7 you hid your **f;** I was dismayed. A
31:16 Let your **f** shine upon your servant;
34:16 The **f** of the LORD is against evildoers,
42: 2 When shall I come and behold the **f** of God?
44:15 and shame has covered my **f**
44:24 Why do you hide your **f?** A
51: 9 Hide your **f** from my sins, A
67: 1 to us and bless us and make his **f** to shine upon us,
69: 7 that shame has covered my **f.**
69:17 Do not hide your **f** from your servant, A
80: 3 let your **f** shine, that we may be saved.
80: 7 let your **f** shine, that we may be saved.
80:19 let your **f** shine, that we may be saved.
84: 9 look on the **f** of your anointed.
88:14 Why do you hide your **f** from me? A
102: 2 hide your **f** from me in the day of my distress. A
104:15 oil to make the **f** shine, and bread to strengthen
104:29 When you hide your **f,** they are dismayed; A
104:30 and you renew the **f** of the ground.
119:135 Make your **f** shine upon your servant,
132:10 not turn away the **f** of your anointed one.
143: 7 Do not hide your **f** from me, A
Pr 7:13 and with impudent **f** she says to him:
8:27 when he drew a circle on the **f** of the deep,
16:15 In the light of a king's **f** there is life,
21:29 The wicked put on a bold **f,**
27:19 Just as water reflects the **f,**
Ecc 8: 1 Wisdom makes one's **f** shine,
SS 2:14 let me see your **f,** let me hear your voice;
2:14 for your voice is sweet, and your **f** is lovely.
Isa 3:15 by grinding the **f** of the poor?
8:17 who is hiding his **f** from the house of Jacob, A
14:21 the earth or cover the **f** of the world with cities.
23:17 the kingdoms of the world on the **f** of the earth.
29:22 no longer shall his **f** grow pale.
38: 2 Then Hezekiah turned his **f** to the wall,
50: 6 I did not hide my **f** from insult and spitting. A
50: 7 therefore I have set my **f** like flint, B
54: 8 In overflowing wrath for a moment I hid my **f** A
59: 2 and your sins have hidden his **f** from you so A
64: 7 for you have hidden your **f** from us, A
65: 3 a people who provoke me to my **f** continually,
Jer 13:26 I myself will lift up your skirts over your **f,**
17:16 from my lips; it was before your **f.**
18:17 I will show them my back, not my **f,**
21:10 For I have set my **f** against this city for evil and B
25:26 and all the kingdoms of the world that are on the **f**
28:16 I am going to send you off the **f** of the earth.
30: 6 Why has every **f** turned pale?
32: 4 and shall speak with him **f** to **f** and see him eye C
33: 5 for I have hidden my **f** from this city because A
34: 3 Babylon eye to eye and speak with him **f** to **f;** C
51:51 dishonor has covered our **f,**
La 1: 8 she herself groans, and turns her **f** away.
2: 3 from them in the **f** of the enemy;
Eze 1:10 the four had the **f** of a human being,
1:10 the **f** of a lion on the right side,
1:10 the **f** of an ox on the left side,
1:10 of an ox on the left side, and the **f** of an eagle;
1:28 When I saw it, I fell on my **f,**
3: 8 See, I have made your **f** hard against their faces,
3:23 and I fell on my **f.**
4: 3 set your **f** toward it, and let it be in a state B
4: 7 You shall set your **f** toward the siege B
6: 2 set your **f** toward the mountains of Israel, B
7:22 I will avert my **f** from them,
9: 8 I fell prostrate on my **f** and cried out,
10:14 the first **f** was that of the cherub,
10:14 the second **f** was that of a human being,
11:13 Then I fell down on my **f,** cried with a loud voice,
12: 6 you shall cover your **f,** so that you may not see
12:12 he shall cover his **f,** so that he may not see
13:17 set your **f** against the daughters of your people, B
14: 8 I will set my **f** against them; B
15: 7 I will set my **f** against them; B
15: 7 when I set my **f** against them. B
20:35 there I will enter into judgment with you **f** to **f.** C
20:46 set your **f** toward the south, B
21: 2 set your **f** toward Jerusalem and preach against B
25: 2 set your **f** toward the Ammonites and prophesy B
28:21 set your **f** toward Sidon, and prophesy against it, B
29: 2 set your **f** against Pharaoh king of Egypt, B
30:16 and Memphis **f** adversaries by day.
34: 6 my sheep were scattered over all the **f** of
35: 2 set your **f** against Mount Seir, B
38: 2 set your **f** toward Gog, of the land of Magog, B
38:20 and all human beings that are on the **f** of the earth,
39:14 and bury any invaders who remain on the **f** of
39:23 So I hid my **f** from them and gave them into A
39:24 and hid my **f** from them. A
39:29 and I will never again hide my **f** from them, A
41:19 a human **f** turned toward the palm tree on
41:19 the **f** of a young lion turned toward the palm tree
43: 3 and I fell upon my **f.**
43:17 Its steps shall **f** east.
44: 4 and I fell upon my **f.**
Da 2:46 Then King Nebuchadnezzar fell on his **f,**
3:19 Meshach, and Abednego that his **f** was distorted.
5: 6 Then the king's **f** turned pale,
5: 9 became greatly terrified and his **f** turned pale,
5:10 let your thoughts terrify you or your **f** grow pale.
7:28 thoughts greatly terrified me, and my **f** turned pale;
8: 5 across the **f** of the whole earth without touching
8:18 I fell into a trance, **f** to the ground; D

Da 9:17 let your **f** shine upon your desolated sanctuary.
10: 6 His body was like beryl, his **f** like lightning,
10: 9 I fell into a trance, **f** to the ground. D
10:15 I turned my **f** toward the ground
Hos 2: 2 that she put away her whoring from her **f,**
5:15 until they acknowledge their guilt and seek my **f.**
7: 2 their deeds surround them, they are before my **f.**
10: 7 Samaria's king shall perish like a chip on the **f** of
Am 9: 8 from the **f** of the earth —except that I will
Mic 3: 4 he will hide his **f** from them at that time, A
Na 3: 5 and will lift up your skirts over your **f;**
Zep 1: 2 I will utterly sweep away everything from the **f** of
1: 3 I will cut off humanity from the **f** of the earth,
Zec 5: 3 "This is the curse that goes out over the **f** of
Mt 6:17 you fast, put oil on your head and wash your **f,**
17: 2 and his **f** shone like the sun,
18:10 in heaven their angels continually see the **f**
26:67 Then they spat in his **f** and struck him;
Lk 5:12 with his **f** to the ground and begged him, D
9:29 he was praying, the appearance of his **f** changed,
9:51 he set his **f** to go to Jerusalem. B
9:53 because his **f** was set toward Jerusalem.
21:35 For it will come upon all who live on the **f** of
Jn 11:44 and his **f** wrapped in a cloth.
16:33 In the world you **f** persecution.
18:22 the police standing nearby struck Jesus on the **f,**
19: 3 and striking him on the **f.**
Ac 6:15 they saw that his **f** was like the face of an angel.
6:15 they saw that his face was like the **f** of an angel.
20:25 will ever see my **f** again.
25:16 before the accused had met the accusers **f** to **f** C
1Co 13:12 dimly, but then we will see **f** to **f.** C
2Co 3: 7 of Israel could not gaze at Moses' **f** because of
3: 7 at Moses' face because of the glory of his **f,**
3:13 over his **f** to keep the people of Israel from gazing
4: 6 of the knowledge of the glory of God in the **f**
10: 1 I who am humble when **f** to **f** with you, C
11:20 or puts on airs, or gives you a slap in the **f.**
Gal 2:11 Cephas came to Antioch, I opposed him to his **f,**
Col 2: 1 and for all who have not seen me **f** to **f.** C
1Th 2:17 we longed with great eagerness to see you **f** to **f.** C
3:10 that we may see you **f** to **f** and restore C
Jas 1: 2 whenever you **f** trials of any kind,
1Pe 3:12 the **f** of the Lord is against those who do evil."
2Jn 1:12 I hope to come to you and talk with you **f** to **f,** C
3Jn 1:14 and we will talk together **f** to **f.** C
Rev 1:16 and his **f** was like the sun shining with full force.
4: 7 third living creature with a **f** like a human face,
4: 7 third living creature with a face like a human **f,**
6:16 on us and hide us from the **f** of the one seated on
10: 1 his **f** was like the sun,
12:11 for they did not cling to life even in the **f** of death.
22: 4 they will see his **f,** and his name will be
Tob 2: 9 and my **f** was uncovered because of the heat.
3: 6 from me, so that I may be released from the **f** of
3: 6 and do not, O Lord, turn your **f** away from me.
3:12 And now, Lord, I turn my **f** to you,
4: 7 not turn your **f** away from anyone who is poor,
4: 7 the **f** of God will not be turned away from you.
12:16 they fell **f** down, for they were afraid.
13: 6 to you and will no longer hide his **f** from you. A
14:10 to his **f** for this shameful treatment.
Jdt 2: 7 and will cover the whole **f** of the earth with
2:19 of King Nebuchadnezzar and to cover the whole **f**
6: 2 and destroy them from the **f** of the earth.
6: 5 you shall not see my **f** again from this day
7:18 and covered the whole **f** of the land.
10:14 the men heard her words, and observed her **f—**
10:23 they all marveled at the beauty of her **f.**
13:16 I swear that it was my **f** that seduced him
14: 6 he fell down on his **f** in a faint.
16: 7 She anointed her **f** with perfume;
AdE 7: 8 Haman, when he heard, turned away his **f.**
15: 7 Lifting his **f,** flushed with splendor,
Wis 4:20 their lawless deeds will convict them to their **f.**
10: 5 and kept him strong in the **f** of his compassion
Sir 4: 4 or turn your **f** away from the poor.
12:18 and whisper much, and show his true **f.**
13:26 The sign of a happy heart is a cheerful **f,**
18:24 of vengeance when he turns away his **f.**
19:27 He hides his **f** and pretends not to hear, A
19:29 a sensible person is known when first met, **f** to **f.** C
25:17 and darkens her **f** like that of a bear.
25:23 Dejected mind, gloomy **f,**
26: 4 and at all times his **f** is cheerful.
26:17 so is a beautiful **f** on a stately figure.
28: 1 The vengeful will **f** the Lord's vengeance,
31: 6 and their destruction has met them **f** to **f.** C
34: 3 the likeness of a **f** looking at itself.
35:11 With every gift show a cheerful **f,**
36:27 A woman's beauty lights up a man's **f,**
42: 1 and do not sin to save **f:**
45: 5 and gave him the commandments **f** to **f,** C
51: 2 the **f** of my adversaries you have been my helper
1Mc 4:40 and fell **f** down on the ground.
7:28 I shall come with a few men to see you **f** to **f** C
11:68 but they themselves met him **f** to **f.** C
2Mc 3:16 for his **f** and the change in his color disclosed
1Es 4:58 he lifted up his **f** to heaven toward Jerusalem,
8:74 I am ashamed and confused before your **f.**
3Mc 5:33 and his eyes wavered and his **f** fell.
6:15 O Lord, and have not turned your **f** from us;
6:18 and true God revealed his holy **f** and opened
2Es 1:31 I will turn my **f** from you;
4:11 When I heard this, I fell on my **f**
5:16 And why is your **f** sad?
6:20 the books shall be opened before the **f** of
7:*97* when it is shown them how their **f** is to shine like
7:*98* to see the **f** of him whom they served in life and
10:25 her **f** suddenly began to shine exceedingly;
12: 7 if my prayer has indeed come up before your **f,**
13: 3 and wherever he turned his **f** to look,
13:38 to their **f** with their evil thoughts and the torments
15:54 Beautify your **f!**
16:50 to her **f** when he comes who will defend
4Mc 6:11 with his **f** bathed in sweat,
6:24 When they saw that he was so courageous in the **f**
14: 1 they encouraged them to **f** the torture,

FACED (16) [FACE]

Ex 37: 9 They **f** one another;
2Ki 14:11 of Judah **f** one another in battle at Beth-shemesh,
2Ch 25:21 of Judah **f** one another in battle at Beth-shemesh,
Est 9:26 and of what they had **f** in this matter,
Job 31:23 and I could not have **f** his majesty.
Jer 32:24 and the city, **f** with sword, famine, and pestilence,
Eze 10:11 but in whatever direction the front wheel **f,**
40:20 the gate of the outer court that **f** north—
40:22 of the same size as those of the gate that **f** toward
40:31 Its vestibule **f** the outer court,
40:34 Its vestibule **f** the outer court,
40:37 Its vestibule **f** the outer court,
47: 1 the temple toward the east (for the temple **f** east);
Tob 4: 4 because she **f** many dangers for you
1Mc 4:61 the people might have a stronghold that **f** Idumea.
4Mc 6: 4 while a herald who **f** him cried out,

FACES‡ (86) [FACE]

Ge 9:23 their **f** were turned away,
30:40 and set the **f** of the flocks toward the striped and
40: 7 "Why are your **f** downcast today?"
42: 6 and bowed themselves before him with their **f** to
Ex 25:20 the **f** of the cherubim shall be turned toward
37: 9 the **f** of the cherubim were turned toward
Lev 9:24 they shouted and fell on their **f.**
Nu 14: 5 and Aaron fell on their **f** before all the assembly
16:22 They fell on their **f,** and said, "O God,
16:45 And they fell on their **f.**
20: 6 on their **f,** and the glory of the LORD appeared
33: 7 to Pi-hahiroth, which **f** Baal-zephon;
Jos 15: 2 from the bay that **f** southward;
Jdg 13:20 and they fell on their **f** to the ground.
2Sa 19: 5 "Today you have covered with shame the **f**
1Ki 18:39 all the people saw it, they fell on their **f** and said,
1Ch 12: 8 whose **f** were like the **f** of lions,
21:16 clothed in sackcloth, fell on their **f.**
2Ch 7: 3 they bowed down on the pavement with their **f** to
29: 6 and have turned away their **f** from the dwelling of
Ne 8: 6 and worshiped the LORD with their **f** to
Job 15:27 because they have covered their **f** with their fat,
40:13 bind their **f** in the world below.
Ps 21:12 you will aim at their **f** with your bows.
34: 5 so your **f** shall never be ashamed.
83:16 Fill their **f** with shame,
Isa 3: 9 The look on their **f** bears witness against them;
6: 2 with two they covered their **f,**
8:21 They will turn their **f** upward,
13: 8 at one another; their **f** will be aflame.
25: 8 Lord GOD will wipe away the tears from all **f,**
49:23 With their **f** to the ground they shall bow down
53: 3 from whom others hide their **f** he was despised,
Jer 2:27 they have turned their backs to me, and not their **f.**
5: 3 They have made their **f** harder than rock;
32:33 They have turned their backs to me, not their **f;**
50: 5 with **f** turned toward it, and they shall come
Eze 1: 6 Each had four **f,** and each of them had four wings.
1: 8 And the four had their **f** and their wings thus:
1:10 As for the appearance of their **f:**
1:11 such were their **f.**
3: 8 See, I have made your face hard against their **f,**
7:18 Shame shall be on all **f,** baldness on all their heads.
8: 3 of the gateway of the inner court that **f** north,
8:16 and their **f** toward the east,
9: 2 which **f** north, each with his weapon for slaughter
10:14 Each one had four **f:** the first face was
10:21 Each had four **f,** each four wings,
10:22 As for what their **f** were like,
10:22 they were the same **f** whose appearance I had seen
11: 1 of the house of the LORD, which **f** east.
14: 6 and turn away your **f** from all your abominations.
20:47 all **f** from south to north shall be scorched by it.
27:35 kings are horribly afraid, their **f** are convulsed.
40:45 that **f** south is for the priests who have charge of
40:46 that **f** north is for the priests who have charge of
41:18 and cherub. Each cherub had two **f:**
42:15 he led me out by the gate that **f** east,
44: 1 which **f** east; and it was shut.
46: 1 the inner court that **f** east shall remain closed on
47: 2 the outside to the outer gate that **f** toward the east;
Joel 2: 6 them peoples are in anguish, all **f** grow pale.
Na 2:10 all loins quake, all **f** grow pale!
Hab 1: 9 for violence, with **f** pressing forward;
Mal 2: 3 and spread dung on your **f,**
Mt 6:16 for they disfigure their **f** so as to show others
Lk 24: 5 The women were terrified and bowed their **f** to
2Co 3:18 And all of us, with unveiled **f,**
Rev 7:11 on their **f** before the throne and worshiped God,
9: 7 their **f** were like human **f,**
11:16 before God fell on their **f** and worshiped God,
Jdt 4: 6 which **f** Esdraelon opposite the plain near Dothan,
6:19 on the **f** of those who are consecrated to you."
7: 3 from Bethulia to Cyamon, which **f** Esdraelon.
Wis 17: 4 and dismal phantoms with gloomy **f** appeared.
Sir 50:17 to the ground on their **f** to worship their Lord,
LtJ 6:13 their **f** are wiped because of the dust from
6:21 when their **f** have been blackened by the smoke of
1Mc 4:55 on their **f** and worshiped and blessed Heaven,
7: 3 he said, "Do not let me see their **f!**"
2Mc 7: 6 that bore witness against the people to their **f,**
1Es 4:24 he **f** lions, and he walks in darkness,
2Es 7:*125* [55] that the **f** of those who practiced self-control
7:*125* [55] but our **f** shall be blacker than darkness?

FACETS (1)

Zec 3: 9 on a single stone with seven **f,**

FACING‡ (34) [FACE]

Ge 23:19 in the cave of the field of Machpelah **f** Mamre
Nu 2: 2 they shall camp **f** the tent of meeting
Jos 8:14 in the morning to the meeting place **f** the Arabah
1Ki 7: 4 **f** each other in the three rows.
7: 5 opposite, **f** each other in the three rows.
7:25 It stood on twelve oxen, three **f** north, three **f** west, three **f** south, and three **f** east;
8:54 he arose from **f** the altar of the LORD,
22:35 and the king was propped up in his chariot **f**
2Ch 3:13 the cherubim stood on their feet, **f** the nave.
4: 4 It stood on twelve oxen, three **f** north, three **f** west, three **f** south, and three **f** east;
18:34 up in his chariot **f** the Arameans until evening;
Ne 8: 3 He read from it **f** the square before the Water Gate
Eze 40: 6 Then he went into the gateway **f** east,
40:44 one at the side of the north gate **f** south, the other at the side of the east gate **f** north.
41:12 The building that was **f** the temple yard on
41:15 the depth of the building **f** the yard at the west,
41:16 **F** the threshold the temple was paneled
42: 3 **f** the pavement that belonged to the outer court,
43: 1 Then he brought me to the gate, the gate **f** east.
43: 4 the LORD entered the temple by the gate **f** east,
46:12 the gate **f** east shall be opened for him;
Mk 15:39 Now when the centurion, who stood **f** him,
Ac 27:12 **f** southwest and northwest.
Jdt 2:25 to the southern borders of Japheth, **f** Arabia.
3: 9 near Dothan, **f** the great ridge of Judea;
1Mc 13:13 Simon encamped in Adida, **f** the plain.
3Mc 2: 1 Then the high priest Simon, **f** the sanctuary,

FACT (37) [FACTS]

Ge 40:15 in **f** I was stolen out of the land of the Hebrews;
Dt 3:11 In **f** his bed, an iron bed,
Jos 9:22 while in **f** you are living among us?
Jdg 1:28 but did not in **f** drive them out.
1Sa 24:11 for by the **f** that I cut off the corner of your cloak,
Job 16:19 Even now, in **f,** my witness is in heaven,
32:12 but there was in **f** no one that confuted Job,
Ps 55:21 but in **f** were drawn swords.
Jer 8: 8 and the law of the LORD is with us," when, in **f,**
Da 2:10 In **f** no king, however great and powerful,
Lk 17:21 For, in **f,** the kingdom of God is among you."
18:34 in **f,** what he said was hidden from them,
20:37 **f** that the dead are raised Moses himself showed,
Jn 14:12 in **f,** will do greater works than these,
Ac 4:27 in **f,** both Herod and Pontius Pilate,
24: 5 We have, in **f,** found this man a pestilent fellow,
25: 3 in **f,** planning an ambush to kill him along
Ro 7:17 But in **f** it is no longer I that do it,
8:17 if, in **f,** we suffer with him so that we may also
1Co 6: 7 In **f,** to have lawsuits at all
8: 5 as in **f** there are many gods and many lords—
15:20 But in **f** Christ has been raised from the dead,
Gal 4:24 One woman, in **f,** is Hagar, from Mount Sinai,
1Th 3: 4 In **f,** when we were with you,
4: 1 how you ought to live and to please God (as, in **f,**
Heb 11:19 the **f** that God is able even to raise someone from
2Pe 3: 5 They deliberately ignore this **f,**
3: 8 But do not ignore this one **f,** beloved,
2Mc 3: 8 but in **f** to carry out the king's purpose.
4:17 a **f** that later events will make clear.
6:13 In **f,** it is a sign of great kindness not to let
13:25 in **f** they were so angry that they wanted
3Mc 5:32 In **f** you would have been deprived of life instead
4Mc 2: 6 In **f,** since the law has told us not to covet,
6:11 in **f,** with his face bathed in sweat,
13: 3 But in **f** it was not so.
17:20 also by the **f** that because of them our enemies did

FACTION (2) [FACTIONS]

Ps 106:17 and covered the **f** of Abiram.
Gal 2:12 for fear of the circumcision **f.**

FACTIONS (2) [FACTION]

1Co 11:19 Indeed, there have to be **f** among you,
Gal 5:20 strife, jealousy, anger, quarrels, dissensions, **f,**

FACTORS (1)

4Mc 15:11 though so many **f** influenced the mother to suffer

FACTORY See Index to Footnotes

FACTS (3) [FACT]

Ac 21:34 as he could not learn the **f** because of the uproar,
Sus 1:48 without examination and without learning the **f?**
2Mc 3:11 the impious Simon had misrepresented the **f.**

FACULTIES‡ (2)
Heb 5:14 for those whose **f** have been trained by practice
Sir 3:13 because you have all your **f** do not despise him.

FADE (4) [FADED, FADES, FADING]
Job 24:24 they wither and **f** like the mallow;
Ps 37: 2 for they will soon **f** like the grass,
Isa 64: 6 We all **f** like a leaf, and our iniquities, like the wind
Eze 17: 9 its fresh sprouting leaves to **f**?

FADED (1) [FADE]
1Mc 1:26 the beauty of the women **f**.

FADES (7) [FADE]
Job 7: 9 As the cloud **f** and vanishes,
Ps 90: 6 in the evening it **f** and withers.
Isa 40: 7 The grass withers, the flower **f**,
40: 8 The grass withers, the flower **f**;
51:12 a human being who **f** like grass?
Na 1: 4 and the bloom of Lebanon **f**.
1Pe 5: 4 you will win the crown of glory that never **f** away.

FADING (2) [FADE]
Isa 28: 1 and the **f** flower of its glorious beauty,
28: 4 And the **f** flower of its glorious beauty,

FAIL (62) [FAILED, FAILING, FAILINGS, FAILS, FAILURE, FAILURES]
Nu 15:22 But if you unintentionally **f**
Dt 31: 6 he will not **f** you or forsake you."
31: 8 he will not **f** you or forsake you.
Jos 1: 5 I will not **f** you or forsake you.
3:10 the living God who without **f** will drive out from
1Sa 17:32 "Let no one's heart **f** because of him;
20: 5 and I should not **f** to sit with the king at the meal;
1Ki 2: 4 there shall not **f** you a successor on the throne
8:25 'There shall never **f** you a successor before me
9: 5 'There shall not **f** you a successor on the throne
17:14 not **f** until the day that the LORD sends rain on
17:16 neither did the jug of oil **f**,
1Ch 28:20 He will not **f** you or forsake you,
2Ch 6:16 'There shall never **f** you a successor before me
Ezr 6: 9 let that be given to them day by day without **f**,
Est 9:27 that without **f** they would continue
Job 11:20 But the eyes of the wicked will **f**;
14:11 As waters **f** from a lake,
17: 5 the eyes of their children will **f**.
21:10 Their bull breeds without **f**;
31:16 or have caused the eyes of the widow to **f**,
Ps 73:26 My flesh and my heart may **f**,
119:82 My eyes **f** with watching for your promise;
119:123 My eyes **f** from watching for your salvation,
Pr 22: 8 and the rod of anger will **f**.
Isa 32:10 the vintage will **f**, the fruit harvest will not come.
58:11 like a spring of water, whose waters never **f**.
Jer 4: 9 courage shall **f** the king and the officials;
14: 6 their eyes **f** because there is no herbage.
15:18 to me like a deceitful brook, like waters that **f**.
25:35 Flight shall **f** the shepherds,
Eze 47:12 Their leaves will not wither nor their fruit **f**,
Da 11:14 up in order to fulfill the vision, but they shall **f**.
Hos 9: 2 and the new wine shall **f** them.
Zep 3: 5 he renders his judgment, each dawn without **f**;
Mt 16:11 How could you **f** to perceive that I was
Mk 7:18 "Then do you also **f** to understand?
8:18 Do you have eyes, and **f** to see?
8:18 Do you have ears, and **f** to hear?
Lk 22:32 for you that your own faith may not **f**;
Ac 5:38 or this undertaking is of human origin, it will **f**;
2Co 13: 5 unless, indeed, you **f** to meet the test!
Heb 11:32 For time would **f** me to tell of Gideon, Barak,
Tob 14: 4 None of all their words will **f**,
14: 4 not a single word of the prophecies will **f**.
Jdt 6: 9 and none of my words shall **f** to come true."
11: 6 and my lord will not **f** to achieve his purposes.
AdE 9:27 all who would join them, to observe it without **f**.
Wis 2: 9 Let none of us **f** to share in our revelry;
3:15 and the root of understanding does not **f**.
9:14 and our designs are likely to **f**;
13: 9 did they **f** to find sooner the Lord of these things?
Sir 19: 1 one who despises small things will **f** little
29:14 one who has lost all sense of shame will **f** him.
37:12 and who will grieve with you if you **f**.
40:14 so lawbreakers will utterly **f**.
LtJ 6:49 How then can one **f** to see that these are not gods,
6:52 Who then can **f** to know that they are not gods?
1Mc 6:22 "How long will you **f** to do justice and
2Es 2:32 my springs run over, and my grace will not **f**."
15:13 because their seed shall **f** to grow
4Mc 13: 5 How then can one **f** to confess the sovereignty

FAILED (26) [FAIL]
Jos 21:45 the LORD had made to the house of Israel had **f**;
23:14 that not one thing has **f** of all the good things that
23:14 to pass for you, not one of them has **f**.
2Sa 4: 1 his courage **f**, and all Israel was dismayed.
1Ki 8:56 not one word has **f** of all his good promise,
Job 19:14 My relatives and my close friends have **f** me;
SS 5: 6 My soul **f** me when he spoke.
Jer 51:30 their strength has **f**, they have become women;
La 4:17 Our eyes **f**, ever watching vainly for help;
Joel 1:17 the granaries are ruined because the grain has **f**.
Lk 23:45 while the sun's light **f**;
Ro 9: 6 It is not as though the word of God had **f**.
11: 7 Israel **f** to obtain what it was seeking.
2Co 13: 6 I hope you will find out that we have not **f**.
13: 7 though we may seem to have **f**.
Heb 4: 1 that none of you should seem to have **f** to reach it.
4: 6 the good news **f** to enter because of disobedience,
Jdt 7:19 to the Lord their God, for their courage **f**,
AdE 10: 5 and none of them has **f** to be fulfilled.
Wis 15:11 because they **f** to know the one who formed them
19:21 **f** to consume the flesh of perishable creatures
1Mc 11:49 their courage **f** and they cried out to the king
3Mc 5:12 by so pleasant and deep a sleep that he quite **f**
2Es 3:29 during these thirty years. And my heart **f** me,
4: 2 understanding has utterly **f** regarding this world,
7:*120* [50] but we have miserably **f**?

FAILING (8) [FAIL]
Dt 8:11 by **f** to keep his commandments, his ordinances,
28:65 **f** eyes, and a languishing spirit.
32:51 by **f** to maintain my holiness among the Israelites.
Ne 1: 7 **f** to keep the commandments, the statutes,
4:10 "The strength of the burden bearers is **f**,
Sir 41: 2 to one who is needy and **f** in strength, worn down
Bar 2:18 with **f** eyes and famished soul,
2Es 5:53 during the time of old age, when the womb is **f**.'

FAILINGS (2) [FAIL]
Ro 15: 1 We who are strong ought to put up with the **f** of
2Es 8:17 for I see the **f** of us who inhabit the earth;

FAILS (14) [FAIL]
Ps 31:10 my strength **f** because of my misery,
38:10 My heart throbs, my strength **f** me;
40:12 the hairs of my head, and my heart **f** me.
143: 7 Answer me quickly, O LORD; my spirit **f**.
Ecc 12: 5 the grasshopper drags itself along and desire **f**;
Isa 15: 6 the grass is withered, the new growth **f**,
44:12 he becomes hungry and his strength **f**,
Joel 1:10 the grain is destroyed, the wine dries up, the oil **f**.
Hab 3:17 produce of the olive **f** and the fields yield no food;
Heb 12:15 See to it that no one **f** to obtain the grace of God;
Jas 2:10 but **f** in one point has become accountable for all
4:17 who knows the right thing to do and **f** to do it,
Tob 14:11 But now my breath **f** me."
Sir 3:13 even if his mind **f**, be patient with him;

FAILURE (1) [FAIL]
Sir 20: 3 the one who admits his fault will be kept from **f**.

FAILURES (1) [FAIL]
Wis 10: 8 so that their **f** could never go unnoticed.

FAIN (KJV) See GLADLY, HEADLONG

FAINT (44) [FAINTED, FAINTHEARTED, FAINTING, FAINTNESS, FAINTS]
Dt 25:18 when you were **f** and weary,
1Sa 14:28 And so the troops are **f**."
14:31 to Aijalon, the troops were very **f**;
2Sa 16: 2 for those to drink who **f** in the wilderness."
Job 23:16 God has made my heart **f**;
Ps 61: 2 of the earth I call to you, when my heart is **f**.
102: T *when f and pleading before the LORD.*
142: 3 When my spirit is **f**, you know my way.
Pr 24:10 If you **f** in the day of adversity,
SS 2: 5 for I am **f** with love.
5: 8 tell him this: I am **f** with love.
Isa 1: 5 The whole head is sick, and the whole heart **f**.
7: 4 be **f** because of these two smoldering stumps
29: 8 thirsty person dreams of drinking and wakes up **f**,
40:28 He does not **f** or grow weary;
40:29 He gives power to the **f**,
40:30 Even youths will **f** and be weary,
40:31 they shall walk and not **f**.
42: 4 He will not grow **f** or be crushed
44:12 he drinks no water and is **f**.
57:16 for then the spirits would grow **f** before me,
61: 3 the mantle of praise instead of a **f** spirit.
Jer 31:25 and all who are **f** I will replenish.
La 1:13 he has left me stunned, **f** all day long.
1:22 for my groans are many and my heart is **f**.
2:11 infants and babes **f** in the streets of the city.
2:12 they **f** like the wounded in the streets of the city,
2:19 who **f** for hunger at the head of every street.
Eze 21: 7 every spirit will **f** and all knees will turn to water.
Am 8:13 and the young men shall **f** for thirst.
Jnh 4: 8 on the head of Jonah so that he was **f** and asked
Na 2:10 Hearts **f** and knees tremble, all loins quake,
Mt 15:32 for they might **f** on the way."
Mk 8: 3 they will **f** on the way—
Lk 21:26 People will **f** from fear and foreboding
1Th 5:14 to admonish the idlers, encourage the **f** hearted,
Jdt 8: 9 because they were **f** for lack of water,
8:31 Then we will no longer feel **f** from thirst."
14: 6 he fell down on his face in a **f**.
AdE 15: 7 The queen faltered, and turned pale and **f**,
1Mc 1:26 young women and young men became **f**,
3:17 And we are **f**, for we have eaten nothing today."
9: 8 He became **f**, but he said to those who were left,
2Mc 3:24 and became **f** with terror.

FAINTED (6) [FAINT]
Ps 107: 5 hungry and thirsty, their soul **f** within them.
Isa 51:20 Your children have **f**, they lie at the head
Eze 31:15 and all the trees of the field **f** because of it.
Jdt 7:22 and young men **f** from thirst and were collapsing
AdE 15:15 And while she was speaking, she **f** and fell.
2Es 5:14 and my soul was so troubled that it **f**.

FAINTHEARTED (4) [FAINT, HEART]
Jer 51:46 be **f** or fearful at the rumors heard in the land—
Sir 2:13 Woe to the **f** who have no trust!
1Mc 3:56 or were planting a vineyard, or were **f**,
4Mc 16: 5 If this woman, though a mother, had been **f**,

FAINTING (1) [FAINT]
Jer 4:31 I am **f** before killers!"

FAINTNESS (1) [FAINT]
Lev 26:36 I will send **f** into their hearts in the lands

FAINTS (5) [FAINT]
Job 19:27 My heart **f** within me!
Ps 63: 1 my flesh **f** for you, as in a dry and weary land
77: 3 I meditate, and my spirit **f**.
84: 2 indeed it **f** for the courts of the LORD;
143: 4 Therefore my spirit **f** within me;

FAIR (26) [FAIREST, FAIRLY]
Ge 6: 2 the sons of God saw that they were **f**;
24:16 The girl was very **f** to look upon, a virgin,
Nu 24: 5 how **f** are your tents, O Jacob,
Dt 1:16 the members of your community a **f** hearing,
1Ki 2:38 And Shimei said to the king, "The sentence is **f**;
2:42 And you said to me, 'The sentence is **f**; I accept.'
Est 1:11 for she was **f** to behold.
2: 7 the girl was **f** and beautiful,
Job 26:13 By his wind the heavens were made **f**;
Pr 1: 9 for they are a **f** garland for your head,
4: 9 She will place on your head a **f** garland;
SS 2:10 "Arise, my love, my **f** one, and come away;
2:13 Arise, my love, my **f** one, and come away.
6:10 **f** as the moon, bright as the sun,
7: 6 How **f** and pleasant you are, O loved one,
Jer 11:16 "A green olive tree, **f** with goodly fruit";
Eze 31: 3 with **f** branches and forest shade,
Hos 10:11 and I spared her **f** neck;
Mt 15:26 "It is not **f** to take the children's food and throw it
16: 2 you say, 'It will be **f** weather, for the sky is red.'
Mk 7:27 not **f** to take the children's food and throw it to
Ac 27: 8 we came to a place called **F** Havens,
2Co 8:13 but it is a question of a **f** balance between
8:14 in order that there may be a **f** balance.
Sir 3:15 like frost in **f** weather, your sins will melt away.
24:14 like a **f** olive tree in the field,

FAIR HAVENS See FAIR, HAVENS

FAIREST (4) [FAIR]
1Ki 20: 3 your **f** wives and children also are mine."
SS 1: 8 If you do not know, O **f** among women,
5: 9 more than another beloved, O **f** among women?
6: 1 has your beloved gone, O **f** among women?

FAIRLY (2) [FAIR]
Ps 58: 1 Do you judge people **f**?
Col 4: 1 Masters, treat your slaves justly and **f**,

FAIRS (KJV) See WARES

FAITH‡ (275) [FAITHFUL, FAITHFULLY, FAITHFULNESS, FAITHLESS, FAITHLESSLY, FAITHLESSNESS]
A. BY ... FAITH (39)
B. THE FAITH (36)
C. IN ... FAITH (32)
D. THROUGH ... FAITH (20)
E. LITTLE FAITH (6)

Nu 5: 6 breaking **f** with the LORD,
Dt 32:51 both of you broke **f** with me among the Israelites
Jos 2:12 Give me a sign of good **f**
7: 1 Israelites broke **f** in regard to the devoted things:
22:20 Did not Achan son of Zerah break **f** in the matter
22:22 in rebellion or in breach of **f** toward the LORD,
Jdg 9:15 'If in good **f** you are anointing me king over you, C
9:16 if you acted in good **f** and honor C
9:19 in good **f** and honor with Jerubbaal and C
Ezr 10: 2 "We have broken **f** with our God
Job 39:12 Do you have **f** in it that it will return,
Ps 78:22 because they had no **f** in God,
106:24 having no **f** in his promise.
116:10 I kept my **f**, even when I said,
146: 6 in them; who keeps **f** forever;
Isa 7: 9 If you do not stand firm in **f**, C
26: 2 that the righteous nation that keeps **f** may enter in.
Hab 2: 4 but the righteous live by their **f**. A
Mt 6:30 not much more clothe you—you of little **f**? E
8:10 in no one in Israel have I found such **f**.
8:13 let it be done for you according to your **f**."
8:26 "Why are you afraid, you of little **f**?" E
9: 2 When Jesus saw their **f**, he said to the paralytic,
9:22 your **f** has made you well."
9:29 "According to your **f** let it be done to you."

Mt 14:31 “You of little **f**, why did you doubt?” E
15:28 Jesus answered her, “Woman, great is your **f**!
16: 8 becoming aware of it, Jesus said, “You of little **f**, E
17:20 He said to them, “Because of your little **f**. E
17:20 if you have **f** the size of a mustard seed,
21:21 “Truly I tell you, if you have **f** and do not doubt,
21:22 Whatever you ask for in prayer with **f**,
23:23 of the law: justice and mercy and **f**.
Mk 2: 5 When Jesus saw their **f**, he said to the paralytic,
4:40 Have you still no **f**?”
5:34 “Daughter, your **f** has made you well;
10:52 your **f** has made you well.”
11:22 Jesus answered them, “Have **f** in God.
16:14 ⟦and he upbraided them for their lack of **f**⟧
Lk 5:20 When he saw their **f**, he said, “Friend,
7: 9 “I tell you, not even in Israel have I found such **f**.”
7:50 he said to the woman, “Your **f** has saved you;
8:25 He said to them, “Where is your **f**?”
8:48 your **f** has made you well; go in peace.”
12:28 much more will he clothe you—you of little **f**! E
17: 5 The apostles said to the Lord, “Increase our **f**!”
17: 6 “If you had **f** the size of a mustard seed,
17:19 your **f** has made you well.”
18: 8 the Son of Man comes, will he find **f** on earth?”
18:42 “Receive your sight; your **f** has saved you.”
22:32 but I have prayed for you that your own **f** may
Ac 3:16 And by **f** in his name, his name itself A
3:16 and the **f** that is through Jesus has given him B
6: 5 a man full of **f** and the Holy Spirit,
6: 7 of the priests became obedient to the **f**. B
11:24 full of the Holy Spirit and of **f**.
13: 8 and tried to turn the proconsul away from the **f**. B
14: 9 looking at him intently and seeing that he had **f** to
14:22 and encouraged them to continue in the **f**, BC
14:27 how he had opened a door of **f** for the Gentiles.
15: 9 by **f** he has made no distinction between them A
16: 5 So the churches were strengthened in the **f** BC
20:21 and Greeks about repentance toward God and **f**
24:24 he sent for Paul and heard him speak concerning **f**
26:18 a place among those who are sanctified by **f** A
27:25 for I have **f** in God that it will be exactly
Ro 1: 5 and apostleship to bring about the obedience of **f**
1: 8 your **f** is proclaimed throughout the world.
1:12 be mutually encouraged by each other’s **f**,
1:16 of God for salvation to everyone who has **f**,
1:17 the righteousness of God is revealed through **f** D
1:17 of God is revealed through faith for **f**;
1:17 “The one who is righteous will live by **f**.” A
3:22 righteousness of God through **f** in Jesus Christ D
3:25 of atonement by his blood, effective through **f**. D
3:26 and that he justifies the one who has **f** in Jesus.
3:27 No, but by the law of **f**.
3:28 For we hold that a person is justified by **f** apart A
3:30 on the ground of **f** and the uncircumcised through that same **f**.
3:31 Do we then overthrow the law by this **f**? A
4: 5 such **f** is reckoned as righteousness.
4: 9 “**F** was reckoned to Abraham as righteousness.”
4:11 he had by **f** while he was still uncircumcised. A
4:12 but who also follow the example of the **f** B
4:13 the law but through the righteousness of **f**.
4:14 **f** is null and the promise is void.
4:16 For this reason it depends on **f**,
4:16 the **f** of Abraham (for he is the father of all of us, B
4:19 in **f** when he considered his own body, C
4:20 he grew strong in his **f** as he gave glory to God, C
4:22 his **f** “was reckoned to him as righteousness.”
5: 1 Therefore, since we are justified by **f**, A
9:30 have attained it, that is, righteousness through **f**; D
9:32 Because they did not strive for it on the basis of **f**,
10: 6 But the righteousness that comes from **f** says,
10: 8 the word of **f** that we proclaim);
10:17 So **f** comes from what is heard,
11:20 but you stand only through **f**. D
12: 3 to the measure of **f** that God has assigned.
12: 6 prophecy, in proportion to **f**;
14: 1 Welcome those who are weak in **f**, C
14:22 The **f** that you have, have as your own B
14:23 because they do not act from **f**;
14:23 for whatever does not proceed from **f** is sin.
16:26 to bring about the obedience of **f**—
1Co 2: 5 that your **f** might rest not on human wisdom but
12: 9 to another **f** by the same Spirit,
13: 2 and if I have all **f**, so as to remove mountains,
13:13 And now **f**, hope, and love abide, these three;
15:14 in vain and your **f** has been in vain.
15:17 your **f** is futile and you are still in your sins.
16:13 Keep alert, stand firm in your **f**, be courageous, C
2Co 1:24 not mean to imply that we lord it over your **f**;
1:24 because you stand firm in the **f**. BC
4:13 But just as we have the same spirit of **f** that is
5: 7 for we walk by **f**, not by sight. A
8: 7 Now as you excel in everything—in **f**, in speech, C
10:15 but our hope is that, as your **f** increases,
13: 5 to see whether you are living in the **f**. BC
Gal 1:23 now proclaiming the **f** he once tried to destroy.” B
2:16 works of the law but through **f** in Jesus Christ. D
2:16 so that we might be justified by **f** in Christ, A
2:20 live in the flesh I live by **f** in the Son of God, A
3: 8 that God would justify the Gentiles by **f**, A
3:11 for “The one who is righteous will live by **f**.” A
3:12 But the law does not rest on **f**;
3:14 the promise of the Spirit through **f**. D
3:22 through **f** in Jesus Christ might be given D
3:23 before **f** came, we were imprisoned and guarded
3:23 and guarded under the law until **f** would
3:24 so that we might be justified by **f**. A
Gal 3:25 But now that **f** has come,
3:26 Jesus you are all children of God through **f**. D
5: 5 For through the Spirit, by **f**, A
5: 6 only thing that counts is **f** working through love.
6:10 and especially for those of the family of **f**.
Eph 1:15 of your **f** in the Lord Jesus and your love
2: 8 For by grace you have been saved through **f**, D
3:12 in boldness and confidence through **f** in him. D
3:17 that Christ may dwell in your hearts through **f**, D
4: 5 one Lord, one **f**, one baptism,
4:13 unity of the **f** and of the knowledge of the Son B
6:16 With all of these, take the shield of **f**,
6:23 the whole community, and love with **f**, from God
Php 1:25 with all of you for your progress and joy in **f**, C
1:27 striving side by side with one mind for the **f** of B
2:17 of your **f**, I am glad and rejoice with all of you—
3: 9 but one that comes through **f** in Christ, D
3: 9 the righteousness from God based on **f**.
Col 1: 4 for we have heard of your **f** in Christ Jesus and of
1:23 and steadfast in the **f**, without shifting BC
2: 5 to see your morale and the firmness of your **f**
2: 7 and built up in him and established in the **f**, BC
2:12 also raised with him through **f** in the power D
1Th 1: 3 of **f** and labor of love and steadfastness of hope
1: 8 in every place your **f** in God has become known,
3: 2 and encourage you for the sake of your **f**,
3: 5 I sent to find out about your **f**;
3: 6 has brought us the good news of your **f** and love.
3: 7 about you through your **f**. D
3:10 to face and restore whatever is lacking in your **f**. C
5: 8 and put on the breastplate of **f** and love,
2Th 1: 3 as is right, because your **f** is growing abundantly,
1: 4 the churches of God for your steadfastness and **f**
1:11 by his power every good resolve and work of **f**,
3: 2 and evil people; for not all have **f**.
1Ti 1: 2 my loyal child in the **f**: BC
1: 4 the divine training that is known by **f**. A
1: 5 a good conscience, and sincere **f**.
1:14 overflowed for me with the **f** and love B
1:19 having **f** and a good conscience.
1:19 persons have suffered shipwreck in the **f**; BC
2: 7 a teacher of the Gentiles in **f** and truth. C
2:15 they continue in **f** and love and holiness, C
3: 9 they must hold fast to the mystery of the **f** with B
3:13 great boldness in the **f** that is in Christ Jesus. BC
4: 1 the **f** by paying attention to deceitful spirits B
4: 6 on the words of the **f** and of the sound teaching B
4:12 an example in speech and conduct, in love, in **f**, C
5: 8 has denied the **f** and is worse than an unbeliever. B
6:10 to be rich some have wandered away from the **f** B
6:11 pursue righteousness, godliness, **f**, love,
6:12 Fight the good fight of the **f**; B
6:21 the mark as regards the **f**. B
2Ti 1: 5 I am reminded of your sincere **f**,
1: 5 a **f** that lived first in your grandmother Lois
1:13 in the **f** and love that are in Christ Jesus. BC
2:18 They are upsetting the **f** of some. B
2:22 **f**, love, and peace, along with those who call on
3: 8 so these people, of corrupt mind and counterfeit **f**,
3:10 my conduct, my aim in life, my **f**, my patience,
3:15 are able to instruct you for salvation through **f** D
4: 7 I have finished the race, I have kept the **f**. B
Tit 1: 1 sake of the **f** of God’s elect and the knowledge B
1: 4 my loyal child in the **f** we share: BC
1:13 so that they may become sound in the **f**, BC
2: 2 and sound in **f**, in love, and in endurance. C
3:15 Greet those who love us in the **f**. BC
Phm 1: 5 for all the saints and your **f** toward the Lord Jesus.
1: 6 that the sharing of your **f** may become effective
Heb 4: 2 were not united by **f** with those who listened. A
6: 1 repentance from dead works and **f** toward God,
6:12 through **f** and patience inherit the promises. D
10:22 with a true heart in full assurance of **f**,
10:38 but my righteous one will live by **f**. A
10:39 but among those who have **f** and so are saved.
11: 1 Now **f** is the assurance of things hoped for,
11: 2 Indeed, by **f** our ancestors received approval. A
11: 3 By **f** we understand that the worlds were A
11: 4 By **f** Abel offered to God A
11: 4 he died, but through his **f** he still speaks D
11: 5 By **f** Enoch was taken so that he did A
11: 6 And without **f** it is impossible to please God,
11: 7 By **f** Noah, warned by God about events as A
11: 7 to the righteousness that is in accordance with **f**.
11: 8 By **f** Abraham obeyed when he was called A
11: 9 By **f** he stayed for a time in A
11:11 By **f** he received power of procreation, A
11:13 All of these died in **f** without having received C
11:17 By **f** Abraham, when put to the test, A
11:20 By **f** Isaac invoked blessings for the future A
11:21 By **f** Jacob, when dying, blessed each of the sons A
11:22 By **f** Joseph, at the end of his life, A
11:23 By **f** Moses was hidden by his parents A
11:24 By **f** Moses, when he was grown up, A
11:27 By **f** he left Egypt, unafraid of the king’s anger; A
11:28 By **f** he kept the Passover and the sprinkling A
11:29 By **f** the people passed through the Red Sea as A
11:30 By **f** the walls of Jericho fell A
11:31 By **f** Rahab the prostitute did not perish A
11:33 who through **f** conquered kingdoms, D
11:39 though they were commended for their **f**,
12: 2 to Jesus the pioneer and perfecter of our **f**,
13: 7 of their way of life, and imitate their **f**.
Jas 1: 3 that the testing of your **f** produces endurance;
1: 6 But ask in **f**, never doubting, C
2: 5 poor in the world to be rich in **f** and to be heirs C
2:14 if you say you have **f** but do not have works?
Jas 2:14 not have works? Can **f** save you?
2:17 So **f** by itself, if it has no works, is dead.
2:18 someone will say, “You have **f** and I have works.”
2:18 Show me your **f** apart from your works,
2:18 and I by my works will show you my **f**.
2:20 that **f** apart from works is barren?
2:22 You see that **f** was active along with his works,
2:22 and **f** was brought to completion by the works.
2:24 person is justified by works and not by **f** alone. A
2:26 so **f** without works is also dead.
5:15 The prayer of **f** will save the sick,
1Pe 1: 5 the power of God through **f** for a salvation ready D
1: 7 so that the genuineness of your **f**—
1: 9 for you are receiving the outcome of your **f**,
1:21 so that your **f** and hope are set on God.
5: 9 Resist him, steadfast in your **f**, C
2Pe 1: 1 a **f** as precious as ours through the righteousness
1: 5 you must make every effort to support your **f**
1Jn 5: 4 this is the victory that conquers the world, our **f**.
Jude 1: 3 contend for the **f** that was once for all entrusted B
1:20 build yourselves up on your most holy **f**;
Rev 2:13 and you did not deny your **f** in me even in
2:19 your love, **f**, service, and patient endurance.
13:10 Here is a call for the endurance and **f** of the saints.
14:12 commandments of God and hold fast to the **f** B
Sir 27:17 Love your friend and keep **f** with him;
40:12 but good **f** will last forever.
1Mc 10:27 Now continue still to keep **f** with us,
2Mc 8: 1 in the Jewish **f**, and so they gathered
2Es 5: 1 and the land shall be barren of **f**.
6: 5 those who stored up treasures of **f** were sealed—
9: 7 on account of the **f** by which they have believed, B
13:23 who have works and **f** toward the Almighty.
4Mc 15:24 mother disregarded all these because of **f** in God.
16:22 You too must have the same **f** in God and not
17: 2 and showed the courage of your **f**!

FAITHFUL‡ (117) [FAITH]

Dt 7: 9 the **f** God who maintains covenant loyalty
32: 4 A **f** God, without deceit, just and upright is he;
Jdg 5:15 and Issachar **f** to Barak;
1Sa 2: 9 “He will guard the feet of his **f** ones,
2:35 I will raise up for myself a **f** priest,
20:14 I am still alive, show me the **f** love of the LORD;
20:15 never cut off your **f** love from my house,
22:14 “Who among all your servants is so **f** as David?
2Sa 20:19 of those who are peaceable and **f** in Israel;
2Ch 6:41 and let your **f** rejoice in your goodness.
31:18 for they were **f** in keeping themselves holy.
31:20 he did what was good and right and **f** before
35:26 and his **f** deeds in accordance with what is written
Ne 7: 2 he was a **f** man and feared God more than many.
9: 8 and you found his heart **f** before you, and made
13:13 for they were considered **f**;
Ps 4: 3 that the LORD has set apart the **f** for himself;
12: 1 the **f** have disappeared from humankind.
16:10 or let your **f** one see the Pit.
30: 4 Sing praises to the LORD, O you his **f** ones,
31: 5 you have redeemed me, O LORD, **f** God.
31:23 The LORD preserves the **f**,
32: 6 Therefore let all who are **f** offer prayer to you;
37:28 he will not forsake his **f** ones.
50: 5 “Gather to me my **f** ones,
52: 9 In the presence of the **f** I will proclaim your name,
69:13 your steadfast love, answer me. With your **f** help
78: 8 whose spirit was not **f** to God.
79: 2 the flesh of your **f** to the wild animals of the earth.
85: 8 to his **f**, to those who turn to him in their hearts.
89:19 you spoke in a vision to your **f** one, and said:
97:10 he guards the lives of his **f**;
101: 6 I will look with favor on the **f** in the land,
111: 7 The works of his hands are **f** and just;
116:15 the sight of the LORD is the death of his **f** ones.
132: 9 and let your **f** shout for joy.
132:16 and its **f** will shout for joy.
141: 5 Let the righteous strike me; let the **f** correct me.
145:10 O LORD, and all your **f** shall bless you.
145:13 The LORD is **f** in all his words,
148:14 for all his **f**, for the people of Israel who are close
149: 1 his praise in the assembly of the **f**.
149: 5 Let the **f** exult in glory;
149: 9 This is glory for all his **f** ones.
Pr 2: 8 of justice and preserving the way of his **f** ones.
13:17 A bad messenger brings trouble, but a **f** envoy,
14: 5 A **f** witness does not lie,
25:13 of snow in the time of harvest are **f** messengers
28:20 The **f** will abound with blessings,
Isa 1:21 How the **f** city has become a whore!
1:26 be called the city of righteousness, the **f** city.
25: 1 plans formed of old, **f** and sure.
49: 7 because of the LORD, who is **f**,
Jer 42: 5 be a true and **f** witness against us if we do not act
Da 6: 4 because he was **f**, and no negligence
Hos 11:12 and is **f** to the Holy One.
Mic 7: 2 The **f** have disappeared from the land,
Zec 8: 3 Jerusalem shall be called the **f** city,
Mt 24:45 “Who then is the **f** and wise slave,
Lk 12:42 And the Lord said, “Who then is the **f**
16:10 “Whoever is **f** in a very little is **f** also
16:11 you have not been **f** with the dishonest wealth,
16:12 you have not been **f** with what belongs to another,
Ac 11:23 and he exhorted them all to remain **f** to the Lord
16:15 “If you have judged me to be **f** to the Lord,
1Co 1: 9 God is **f**; by him you were called into the
4:17 who is my beloved and **f** child in the Lord,
10:13 God is **f**, and he will not let you be tested

2Co 1:18 As surely as God is **f**,
Eph 1: 1 To the saints who are in Ephesus and are **f**
6:21 He is a dear brother and a **f** minister in the Lord.
Col 1: 2 To the saints and **f** brothers and sisters in Christ
1: 7 He is a **f** minister of Christ on your behalf,
4: 7 he is a beloved brother, a **f** minister,
4: 9 the **f** and beloved brother, who is one of you.
1Th 5:24 The one who calls you is **f**, and he will do this.
2Th 3: 3 But the Lord is **f**; he will strengthen you
1Ti 1:12 he judged me **f** and appointed me to his service,
3:11 not slanderers, but temperate, **f** in all things.
2Ti 2: 2 to **f** people who will be able to teach others
2:13 he remains **f**—for he cannot deny himself.
Heb 2:17 so that he might be a merciful and **f** high priest in
3: 2 was **f** to the one who appointed him,
3: 2 just as Moses also "was **f** in all God's house."
3: 5 Now Moses was **f** in all God's house as a servant,
3: 6 Christ, however, was **f** over God's house as a son,
10:23 for he who has promised is **f**.
11:11 because he considered him **f** who had promised.
1Pe 4:19 with God's will entrust themselves to a **f** Creator,
5:12 Through Silvanus, whom I consider a **f** brother,
1Jn 1: 9 he who is **f** and just will forgive us our sins
Rev 1: 5 the **f** witness, the firstborn of the dead,
2:10 Be **f** until death, and I will give you the crown
2:13 my **f** one, who was killed among you,
3:14 The words of the Amen, the **f** and true witness,
17:14 and those with him are called and chosen and **f**."
19:11 Its rider is called **F** and True,
Wis 3: 9 and the **f** will abide with him in love,
Sir 1:14 she is created with the **f** in the womb.
4:16 If they remain **f**, they will inherit her;
6:14 **F** friends are a sturdy shelter:
6:15 **F** friends are beyond price;
6:16 **F** friends are life-saving medicine;
34: 8 and wisdom is complete in the mouth of the **f**.
37:13 for no one is more **f** to you than it is.
39:13 Listen to me, my **f** children,
39:24 To the **f** his ways are straight,
44:20 and when he was tested he proved **f**.
1Mc 2:52 Was not Abraham found **f** when tested,
3:13 of **f** soldiers who stayed with him and went out
7: 8 a great man in the kingdom and was **f** to the king.
7:17 of your **f** ones and their blood they poured out all
2Mc 1: 2 with Abraham and Isaac and Jacob, his **f** servants.
1Es 8:89 O Lord of Israel, you are **f**;
3Mc 2:11 And indeed you are **f** and true.
4Mc 7:15 whom the **f** seal of death has perfected!

FAITHFULLY (22) [FAITH]

Lev 25:18 and **f** keep my ordinances,
26: 3 and keep my commandments and observe them **f**,
Jos 2:14 then we will deal kindly and **f** with you when
1Sa 12:24 and serve him **f** with all your heart;
2Ch 31:12 **F** they brought in the contributions,
31:15 and Shecaniah were **f** assisting him in the cities of
34:12 The people did the work **f**.
Ne 9:33 for you have dealt **f** and we have acted wickedly;
Pr 12:22 but those who act **f** are his delight.
Isa 42: 3 he will **f** bring forth justice.
61: 8 I will **f** give them their recompense,
Jer 23:28 let the one who has my word speak my word **f**.
Eze 18: 9 and is careful to observe my ordinances, acting **f**—
Da 6:16 "May your God, whom you **f** serve, deliver you!"
6:20 has your God whom you **f** serve been able
3Jn 1: 5 you do **f** whatever you do for the friends,
Tob 14:8,9 serve God **f** and do what is pleasing in his sight.
Sir 1:15 and among their descendants she will abide **f**.
7:20 Do not abuse slaves who work **f**,
15:15 and to act **f** is a matter of your own choice.
3Mc 5: 4 proceeded **f** to carry out the orders.
6:25 those who **f** kept our country's fortresses,

FAITHFULNESS‡ (80) [FAITH]

A. STEADFAST LOVE AND ... FAITHFULNESS (16)

Ge 24:27 has not forsaken his steadfast love and his **f** A
32:10 steadfast love and all the **f** that you have shown A
Ex 34: 6 and abounding in steadfast love and **f**, A
Dt 32:20 children in whom there is no **f**.
Jos 24:14 and serve him in sincerity and in **f**;
1Sa 26:23 for his righteousness and his **f**;
2Sa 2: 6 may the LORD show steadfast love and **f** to you! A
15:20 and may the LORD show steadfast love and **f** A
1Ki 2: 4 in **f** with all their heart and with all their soul,
3: 6 because he walked before you in **f**,
2Ki 20: 3 I have walked before you in **f** with a whole heart,
2Ch 19: 9 in the fear of the LORD, in **f**,
32: 1 After these things and these acts of **f**,
Ps 25:10 the paths of the LORD are steadfast love and **f**, A
26: 3 and I walk in **f** to you.
30: 9 Will it tell of your **f**?
33: 4 and all his work is done in **f**.
36: 5 extends to the heavens, your **f** to the clouds.
40:10 I have spoken of your **f** and your salvation;
40:10 not concealed your steadfast love and your **f** A
40:11 steadfast love and your **f** keep me safe forever. A
54: 5 In your **f**, put an end to them.
57: 3 God will send forth his steadfast love and his **f**. A
57:10 your **f** extends to the clouds.
61: 7 appoint steadfast love and **f** to watch over him! A
71:22 I will also praise you with the harp for your **f**,
85:10 Steadfast love and **f** will meet; A
85:11 **F** will spring up from the ground,
86:15 to anger and abounding in steadfast love and **f**. A
88:11 in the grave, or your **f** in Abaddon?
Ps 89: 1 with my mouth I will proclaim your **f**
89: 2 your **f** is as firm as the heavens.
89: 5 your **f** in the assembly of the holy ones.
89: 8 O LORD? Your **f** surrounds you.
89:14 steadfast love and **f** go before you. A
89:24 My **f** and steadfast love shall be with him;
89:33 or be false to my **f**.
89:49 which by your **f** you swore to David?
91: 4 his **f** is a shield and buckler.
92: 2 in the morning, and your **f** by night,
98: 3 He has remembered his steadfast love and **f** to A
100: 5 and his **f** to all generations.
108: 4 and your **f** reaches to the clouds.
111: 8 to be performed with **f** and uprightness.
115: 1 for the sake of your steadfast love and your **f**. A
117: 2 and the **f** of the LORD endures forever.
119:30 I have chosen the way of **f**;
119:75 and that in **f** you have humbled me.
119:90 Your **f** endures to all generations;
119:138 in righteousness and in all **f**.
138: 2 to your name for your steadfast love and your **f**; A
143: 1 give ear to my supplications in your **f**;
Pr 3: 3 Do not let loyalty and **f** forsake you;
14:22 Those who plan good find loyalty and **f**.
16: 6 By loyalty and **f** iniquity is atoned for,
20:28 Loyalty and **f** preserve the king,
Isa 11: 5 and **f** the belt around his loins.
16: 5 and on it shall sit in **f** a ruler who seeks justice
38: 3 I have walked before you in **f** with a whole heart,
38:18 down to the Pit cannot hope for your **f**.
38:19 fathers make known to children your **f**.
65:16 a blessing in the land shall bless by the God of **f**,
65:16 an oath in the land shall swear by the God of **f**;
Jer 31: 3 therefore I have continued my **f** to you.
32:41 and I will plant them in this land in **f**,
La 3:23 they are new every morning; great is your **f**.
Hos 2:20 I will take you for my wife in **f**;
4: 1 There is no **f** or loyalty, and no knowledge of God
14: 8 like an evergreen cypress; your **f** comes from me.
Mic 7:20 You will show **f** to Jacob and unswerving loyalty
Zec 8: 8 in **f** and in righteousness.
Ro 3: 3 Will their faithlessness nullify the **f** of God?
Gal 5:22 joy, peace, patience, kindness, generosity, **f**,
3Jn 1: 3 of the friends arrived and testified to your **f** to
Wis 3:14 for special favor will be shown him for his **f**,
Sir 45: 4 For his **f** and meekness he consecrated him,
46:15 By his **f** he was proved to be a prophet,
1Mc 14:35 "The people saw Simon's **f** and the glory
2Es 6:28 **f** shall flourish, and corruption shall be overcome,
7:34 truth shall stand, and **f** shall grow strong.

FAITHLESS (36) [FAITH]

2Ch 28:19 without restraint in Judah and had been **f** to
28:22 In the time of his distress he became yet more **f** to
29:19 when he was **f**, we have made ready
30: 7 who were **f** to the LORD God of their ancestors,
Ps 78:57 but turned away and were **f** like their ancestors;
119:158 I look at the **f** with disgust,
Pr 13:15 but the way of the **f** is their ruin.
21:18 and the **f** for the upright.
22:12 but he overthrows the words of the **f**.
23:28 like a robber and increases the number of the **f**.
25:19 a lame foot is trust in a **f** person in time of trouble.
Isa 30: 9 For they are a rebellious people, **f** children,
Jer 3: 6 Have you seen what she did, that **f** one, Israel,
3: 8 She saw that for all the adulteries of that **f** one,
3:11 **F** Israel has shown herself less guilty than false Judah.
3:12 Return, **f** Israel, says the LORD.
3:14 Return, O **f** children, says the LORD,
3:20 Instead, as a **f** wife leaves her husband,
3:20 so you have been **f** to me, O house of Israel,
3:22 O **f** children, I will heal your faithlessness.
5:11 and the house of Judah have been utterly **f** to me,
31:22 How long will you waver, O **f** daughter?
49: 4 O **f** daughter. You trusted in your treasures, saying,
Zep 3: 4 Its prophets are reckless, **f** persons;
Mal 2:10 Why then are we **f** to one another,
2:11 Judah has been **f**, and abomination has been
2:14 to whom you have been **f**,
2:15 do not let anyone be **f** to the wife of his youth.
2:16 So take heed to yourselves and do not be **f**.
Mt 17:17 Jesus answered, "You **f** and perverse generation,
Mk 9:19 He answered them, "You **f** generation,
Lk 9:41 Jesus answered, "You **f** and perverse generation,
Ro 1:31 foolish, **f**, heartless, ruthless.
2Ti 2:13 if we are **f**, he remains faithful—
Rev 21: 8 But as for the cowardly, the **f**, the polluted,
2Es 15:25 not spare them. Depart, you **f** children!

FAITHLESSLY (4) [FAITH]

Eze 14:13 when a land sins against me by acting **f**,
15: 8 because they have acted **f**, says the Lord GOD.
Hos 5: 7 They have dealt **f** with the LORD;
6: 7 there they dealt **f** with me.

FAITHLESSNESS (8) [FAITH]

Nu 14:33 and shall suffer for your **f**,
2Ch 33:19 all his sin and his **f**,
Ezr 9: 2 and in this **f** the officials and leaders have led
9: 4 because of the **f** of the returned exiles,
10: 6 for he was mourning over the **f** of the exiles.
Jer 3:22 O faithless children, I will heal your **f**.
Ro 3: 3 Will their **f** nullify the faithfulness of God?
Wis 14:25 theft and deceit, corruption, **f**, tumult, perjury,

FALCON'S (1)

Job 28: 7 and the **f** eye has not seen it.

FALL‡ (265) [DOWNFALL, FALLEN, FALLING, FALLS, FELL, FELLED, FELLING]

Ge 2:21 So the LORD God caused a deep sleep to **f** upon
43:18 so that he may have an opportunity to **f** upon us,
Ex 5: 3 or he will **f** upon us with pestilence or sword."
9:18 the heaviest hail to **f** that has ever fallen in Egypt
9:22 so that hail may **f** on the whole land of Egypt,
Lev 25:35 If any of your kin **f** into difficulty
25:47 and if any of your kin **f** into difficulty with one
26: 7 and they shall **f** before you by the sword.
26: 8 your enemies shall **f** before you by the sword.
26:36 and they shall **f** though no one pursues.
Nu 11: 9 the manna would **f** with it.
11:31 and it brought quails from the sea and let them **f**
14: 3 Why is the LORD bringing us into this land to **f**
14:29 your dead bodies shall **f** in this very wilderness;
14:32 you, your dead bodies shall **f** in this wilderness.
14:43 and you shall **f** by the sword;
34: 2 of Canaan (this is the land that shall **f** to you for
Dt 22: 8 if anyone should **f** from it.
Jos 6: 5 and the wall of the city will **f** down flat,
Jdg 9:57 the wickedness of the people of Shechem **f** back
15:18 and **f** into the hands of the uncircumcised?"
16:19 She let him **f** asleep on her lap;
1Sa 3:19 and let none of his words **f** to the ground.
14:45 not one hair of his head shall **f** to the ground;
18:25 Now Saul planned to make David **f** by the hand of
26:20 therefore, do not let my blood **f** to the ground,
2Sa 3:29 May the guilt **f** on the head of Joab,
14:11 not one hair of your son shall **f** to the ground."
17: 9 And when some of our troops **f** at the first attack,
24:14 let us **f** into the hand of the LORD,
24:14 but let me not **f** into human hands."
1Ki 1:52 not one of his hairs shall **f** to the ground;
22:20 so that he may go up and **f** at Ramoth-gilead?'
2Ki 6: 6 Then the man of God said, "Where did it **f**?"
9:18 to do with with peace? **F** in behind me."
9:19 to do with with peace? **F** in behind me."
10:10 that there shall **f** to the earth nothing of the word
14:10 for why should you provoke trouble so that you **f**,
19: 7 to **f** by the sword in his own land.' "
1Ch 21:13 let me **f** into the hand of the LORD,
21:13 but let me not **f** into human hands."
2Ch 18:19 so that he may go up and **f** at Ramoth-gilead?'
25:19 why should you provoke trouble so that you **f**,
Est 6:13 but will surely **f** before him."
9:28 and these days of Purim should never **f** into disuse
Job 13:11 and the dread of him **f** upon you?
31:22 then let my shoulder blade **f** from my shoulder,
37: 6 For to the snow he says, '**F** on the earth';
Ps 5:10 let them **f** by their own counsels;
7:15 and **f** into the hole that they have made.
10:10 they crouch, and the helpless **f** by their might.
20: 8 They will collapse and **f**,
27: 2 and foes—they shall stumble and **f**.
35: 8 let them **f** in it—to their ruin.
37:24 we shall not **f** headlong, for the LORD holds us
38:17 For I am ready to **f**, and my pain is ever with me.
45: 5 of the king's enemies; the peoples **f** under you.
72:11 May all kings **f** down before him,
73:18 you make them **f** to ruin.
78:28 he let them **f** within their camp,
82: 7 you shall die like mortals, and **f** like any prince."
91: 7 A thousand may **f** at your side,
101: 3 I hate the work of those who **f** away;
106:26 and swore to them that he would make them **f** in
137: 7 against the Edomites the day of Jerusalem's **f**,
140:10 Let burning coals **f** on them!
141:10 Let the wicked **f** into their own nets,
144:15 Happy are the people to whom such blessings **f**;
Pr 11: 5 but the wicked **f** by their own wickedness.
16:18 and a haughty spirit before a **f**.
17:20 and the perverse of tongue **f** into calamity.
24:16 for though they **f** seven times, they will rise again;
24:17 Do not rejoice when your enemies **f**,
26:27 Whoever digs a pit will **f** into it,
28:10 into evil ways will **f** into pits of their own making,
28:14 but one who is hard-hearted will **f** into calamity.
28:18 whoever follows crooked ways will **f** into the Pit.
Ecc 4:10 For if they **f**, one will lift up the other;
10: 8 Whoever digs a pit will **f** into it;
Isa 3:25 Your men shall **f** by the sword and your warriors
8:15 they shall **f** and be broken;
10: 4 as not to crouch among the prisoners or **f** among
10:34 and Lebanon with its majestic trees will **f**.
13:15 and whoever is caught will **f** by the sword.
22:25 it will be cut down and **f**,
24:18 Whoever flees at the sound of the terror shall **f**
28:13 in order that they may go, and **f** backward,
30:25 on a day of the great slaughter, when the towers **f**.
31: 3 the helper will stumble, and the one helped will **f**,
31: 8 the Assyrian shall **f** by a sword, not of mortals;
33:23 even the lame will **f** to plundering.
34: 7 Wild oxen shall **f** with them,
37: 7 to **f** by the sword in his own land.' "
40:30 and the young will **f** exhausted;
44:19 Shall I **f** down before a block of wood?"
46: 6 then they **f** down and worship!
47:11 disaster shall **f** upon you,
54:15 whoever stirs up strife with you shall **f** because
Jer 6:15 Therefore they shall **f** among those who **f**;

Jer 6:24 of them, our hands **f** helpless;
8:4 When people **f**, do they not get up again?
8:12 Therefore they shall **f** among those who **f**;
9:22 "Human corpses shall **f** like dung upon the open
12:5 And if in a safe land you **f** down,
15:8 I have made anguish and terror **f**
19:7 and will make them **f** by the sword
20:4 and they shall **f** by the sword of their enemies
23:12 into which they shall be driven and **f**;
25:27 Drink, get drunk and vomit, **f** and rise no more,
25:34 and you shall **f** like a choice vessel.
39:18 and you shall not **f** by the sword;
44:12 in the land of Egypt they shall **f**;
48:9 Set aside salt for Moab, for she will surely **f**;
48:44 Everyone who flees from the terror shall **f** into
49:21 At the sound of their **f** the earth shall tremble;
49:26 Therefore her young men shall **f** in her squares,
50:30 Therefore her young men shall **f** in her squares,
50:32 The arrogant one shall stumble and **f**,
51:4 They shall **f** down slain in the land of
51:47 and all her slain shall **f** in her midst.
51:49 Babylon must **f** for the slain of Israel,
Eze 5:12 one third shall **f** by the sword around you;
6:7 The slain shall **f** in your midst;
6:11 For they shall **f** by the sword, by famine,
6:12 those nearby shall **f** by the sword;
11:10 You shall **f** by the sword;
13:11 to those who smear whitewash on it that it shall **f**.
13:11 be a deluge of rain, great hailstones will **f**,
17:21 All the pick of his troops shall **f** by the sword,
21:14 Let the sword **f** twice, thrice;
23:25 and your survivors shall **f** by the sword.
24:21 and your daughters whom you left behind shall **f**
25:13 from Teman even to Dedan they shall **f** by
26:11 and your strong pillars shall **f** to the ground.
26:15 not the coastlands shake at the sound of your **f**,
26:18 Now the coastlands tremble on the day of your **f**;
28:23 and the dead shall **f** in its midst,
29:5 you shall **f** in the open field,
30:4 when the slain **f** in Egypt,
30:5 and the people of the allied land shall **f** with them
30:6 Those who support Egypt shall **f**,
30:6 from Migdol to Syene they shall **f** within it by
30:17 The young men of On and of Pi-beseth shall **f** by
30:22 and I will make the sword **f** from his hand.
30:25 but the arms of Pharaoh shall **f**.
31:16 I made the nations quake at the sound of its **f**,
32:12 I will cause your hordes to **f** by the swords
32:20 They shall **f** among those who are killed by
33:27 surely those who are in the waste places shall **f** by
35:8 those killed with the sword shall **f**.
38:11 I will **f** upon the quiet people who live in safety,
38:20 and the cliffs shall **f**, and every wall shall tumble
39:4 You shall **f** upon the mountains of Israel,
39:5 You shall **f** in the open field;
47:14 and this land shall **f** to you as your inheritance.
Da 1:2 The Lord let King Jehoiakim of Judah **f**
3:5 you are to **f** down and worship the golden statue
3:6 not **f** down and worship shall immediately
3:10 shall **f** down and worship the golden statue,
3:11 and whoever does not **f** down and worship shall
3:15 and entire musical ensemble to **f** down
11:19 but he shall stumble and **f**, and shall not be found.
11:26 be swept away, and many shall **f** slain.
11:33 however, they shall **f** by sword and flame,
11:34 When they **f** victim, they shall receive
11:35 Some of the wise shall **f**,
11:41 and tens of thousands shall **f** victim,
Hos 7:16 their officials shall **f** by the sword because of
10:8 Cover us, and to the hills, **F** on us.
13:8 I will **f** upon them like a bear robbed of her cubs,
13:16 they shall **f** by the sword,
Am 3:5 Does a bird **f** into a snare on the earth,
3:14 and the horns of the altar shall be cut off and **f** to
7:17 the city, and your sons and your daughters shall **f**
8:14 they shall **f**, and never rise again.
9:9 but no pebble shall **f** to the ground.
Mic 7:8 Do not rejoice over me, O my enemy; when I **f**,
Na 3:12 if shaken they **f** into the mouth of the eater.
Hag 2:22 and the horses and their riders shall **f**,
Zec 11:6 every one, to **f** each into the hand of a neighbor,
14:13 the LORD shall **f** on them, so that each will seize
14:15 a plague like this plague shall **f** on the horses,
Mt 4:9 if you will **f** down and worship me."
7:25 but it did not **f**, because it had been founded
7:27 and it fell—and great was its **f**!"
10:29 Yet not one of them will **f** to the ground apart
15:14 both will **f** into a pit."
15:27 the crumbs that **f** from their masters' table."
24:10 Then many will **f** away,
24:29 the stars will **f** from heaven,
Mk 4:17 immediately they **f** away.
Lk 6:39 Will not both **f** into a pit?
8:13 for a while and in a time of testing **f** away.
10:18 "I watched Satan **f** from heaven like a flash
21:24 they will **f** by the edge of the sword and
23:30 they will begin to say to the mountains, '**F** on us';
Ac 5:15 in order that Peter's shadow might **f** on some
Ro 3:23 all have sinned and **f** short of the glory of God;
8:15 not receive a spirit of slavery to **f** back into fear,
9:33 a rock that will make them **f**,
11:11 So I ask, have they stumbled so as to **f**?
14:4 It is before their own lord that they stand or **f**.
14:20 for you to make others **f** by what you eat;
1Co 8:13 so that I may not cause one of them to **f**.
10:12 watch out that you do not **f**.
1Th 5:6 So then let us not **f** asleep as others do,
1Ti 3:6 up with conceit and **f** into the condemnation of
3:7 so that he may not **f** into disgrace and the snare of
6:9 But those who want to be rich **f** into temptation
Heb 4:11 no one may **f** through such disobedience as theirs.
10:31 It is a fearful thing to **f** into the hands of
Jas 5:12 so that you may not **f** under condemnation.
1Pe 2:8 and a rock that makes them **f**."
Rev 4:10 the twenty-four elders **f** before
6:16 "**F** on us and hide us from the face of
11:6 so that no rain may **f** during the days
Jdt 6:6 and you shall **f** among their wounded.
7:11 and not a man of your army will **f**.
11:11 and his purpose frustrated, death will **f**
16:6 For their mighty one did not **f** by the hands of
AdE 6:13 to be humiliated before him, you will surely **f**.
Wis 11:20 people could **f** at a single breath when pursued
13:16 He takes thought for it, so that it may not **f**,
16:11 so that they would not **f** into deep forgetfulness
Sir 1:30 or you may **f** and bring dishonor upon yourself.
2:7 do not stray, or else you may **f**.
2:17 Let us **f** into the hands of the Lord,
3:31 when they **f** they will find support.
6:2 Do not **f** into the grip of passion,
8:1 or you may **f** into their hands.
9:3 or you will **f** into her snares.
15:4 He will lean on her and not **f**,
18:19 and before you **f** ill, take care of your health.
22:27 so that I may not **f** because of them,
23:1 and do not let me **f** because of them!
23:3 and I may **f** before my adversaries,
27:26 Whoever digs a pit will **f** into it,
27:29 in the **f** of the godly will be caught in a snare,
28:23 Those who forsake the Lord will **f** into its power;
28:26 and **f** victim to one lying in wait.
29:20 but be careful not to **f** yourself.
35:19 against the one who causes them to **f**?
38:16 My child, let your tears **f** for the dead,
46:11 whose hearts did not **f** into idolatry and who did
Bar 4:31 and who rejoiced at your **f**.
4:33 For just as she rejoiced at your **f** and was glad
Sus 1:23 I choose not to do it; I will **f** into your hands,
1Mc 4:2 to **f** upon the camp of the Jews
7:38 and let them **f** by the sword;
7:43 and he himself was the first to **f** in the battle.
2Mc 3:6 that it was possible for them to **f** under the control
9:7 **f** was so hard as to torture every limb of his body.
10:4 the Lord that they might never again **f**
12:45 that is laid up for those who **f** asleep in godliness,
13:11 to let the people who had just begun to revive **f**
14:42 preferring to die nobly rather than to **f** into
2Es 5:5 the peoples shall be troubled, and the stars shall **f**.
7:*118* [48] you who sinned, the **f** was not yours alone,
12:18 nevertheless it shall not **f** then,
12:28 but he also shall **f** by the sword in the last days.
13:23 at that time will protect those who **f** into peril,
15:57 and you shall **f** by the sword;
15:57 in the open country shall **f** by the sword.

FALLEN‡ (104) [FALL]

Ge 4:6 and why has your countenance **f**?
Ex 9:18 the heaviest hail to fall that has ever **f** in Egypt
9:24 such heavy hail as had never **f** in all the land
Lev 19:10 or gather the **f** grapes of your vineyard;
Dt 22:4 You shall not see your neighbor's donkey or ox **f**
Jos 2:9 and that dread of you has **f** on us,
7:10 Why have you **f** upon your face?
8:24 when all of them to the very last had **f** by the edge
Jdg 8:10 hundred twenty thousand men bearing arms had **f**.
1Sa 5:3 **f** on his face to the ground before the ark of
5:4 Dagon had **f** on his face to the ground before
20:37 to the place where Jonathan's arrow had **f**,
26:12 a deep sleep from the LORD had **f** upon them.
31:8 and his three sons **f** on Mount Gilboa.
2Sa 1:10 for I knew that he could not live after he had **f**.
1:12 because they had **f** by the sword.
1:19 How the mighty have **f**!
1:25 How the mighty have **f** in the midst of the battle!
1:27 mighty have **f**, and the weapons of war perished!
2:23 to the place where Asahel had **f** and died,
3:34 as one falls before the wicked you have **f**."
3:38 a prince and a great man has **f** this day in Israel?
23:20 a lion in a pit on a day when snow had **f**.
2Ki 1:2 Ahaziah had **f** through the lattice
2:13 He picked up the mantle of Elijah that had **f**
2:14 He took the mantle of Elijah that had **f** from him,
13:14 Now when Elisha had **f** sick with the illness
1Ch 10:8 they found Saul and his sons **f** on Mount Gilboa.
11:22 a lion in a pit on a day when snow had **f**.
2Ch 29:9 Our fathers have **f** by the sword and our sons
Est 8:17 because the fear of the Jews had **f** upon them.
9:2 because the fear of them had **f** upon all peoples.
9:3 because the fear of Mordecai had **f** upon them.
Ps 16:6 boundary lines have **f** for me in pleasant places;
53:3 They have all **f** away, they are all alike perverse;
55:4 the terrors of death have **f** upon me.
57:6 but they have **f** into it themselves.
69:9 the insults of those who insult you have **f** on me.
105:38 for dread of them had **f** upon it.
119:56 This blessing has **f** to me,
Isa 3:8 For Jerusalem has stumbled and Judah has **f**,
9:10 "The bricks have **f**, but we will build
14:12 you are **f** from heaven, O Day Star, son of Dawn!
21:9 Then he responded, "**F**, **f** is Babylon;
Jer 46:5 Why do I see them terrified? They have **f** back;
46:6 by the river Euphrates they have stumbled and **f**.
46:12 against warrior; both have **f** together.
48:32 and your vintage the destroyer has **f**.
50:15 her bulwarks have **f**, her walls are thrown down."
51:8 Suddenly Babylon has **f** and is shattered;
51:44 the wall of Babylon has **f**.
51:49 slain of all the earth have **f** because of Babylon.
La 2:21 my young women and my young men have **f** by
5:16 The crown has **f** from our head;
Eze 31:12 and in all the valleys its branches have **f**,
31:13 On its **f** trunk settle all the birds of the air,
32:22 all of them killed, **f** by the sword.
32:23 all of them killed, **f** by the sword,
32:24 all of them killed, **f** by the sword,
32:27 not lie with the **f** warriors of long ago who went
33:21 to me and said, "The city has **f**."
37:23 from all the apostasies into which they have **f**,
Hos 7:7 All their kings have **f**; none of them calls upon me.
Am 5:2 **F**, no more to rise, is maiden Israel;
9:11 that is **f**, and repair its breaches, and raise
Zec 11:2 Wail, O cypress, for the cedar has **f**,
Mt 27:52 of the saints who had **f** asleep were raised.
Lk 14:5 "If one of you has a child or an ox that has **f** into
Jn 11:11 he told them, "Our friend Lazarus has **f** asleep,
11:12 disciples said to him, "Lord, if he has **f** asleep,
Ac 15:16 the dwelling of David, which has **f**;
26:14 When we had all **f** to the ground,
Ro 11:22 severity toward those who have **f**,
15:3 insults of those who insult you have **f** on me."
Gal 5:4 you have **f** away from grace.
Heb 6:6 and then have **f** away,
Rev 2:5 Remember then from what you have **f**;
9:1 and I saw a star that had **f** from heaven to earth,
14:8 saying, "**F**, **f** is Babylon the great!
17:10 of whom five have **f**, one is living,
18:2 a mighty voice, "**F**, **f** is Babylon the great!
Wis 18:23 the dead had already **f** on one another in heaps,
Sir 28:18 Many have **f** by the edge of the sword,
28:18 but not as many as have **f** because of the tongue.
46:20 Even after he had **f** asleep,
49:13 he raised our **f** walls, and set up gates and bars,
1Mc 5:12 for many of us have **f**,
5:54 not one of them had **f**.
7:44 When his army saw that Nicanor had **f**,
9:1 that Nicanor and his army had **f** in battle,
9:21 "How is the mighty **f**, the savior of Israel!"
10:70 I have **f** into ridicule and disgrace because of you.
12:37 part of the wall on the valley to the east had **f**,
2Mc 7:38 an end the wrath of the Almighty that has justly **f**
12:39 the bodies of the **f** and to bring them back to lie
12:40 to all that this was the reason these men had **f**.
12:42 as the result of the sin of those who had **f**.
12:44 that those who had **f** would rise again,
3Mc 6:23 and saw them all **f** headlong to destruction,
4Mc 2:14 from marauders and helps raise up what has **f**.
15:20 and corpses **f** on other corpses,

FALLING (22) [FALL]

Nu 22:31 and he bowed down, **f** on his face.
Ps 56:13 from **f**, so that I may walk before God in the light
118:13 I was pushed hard, so that I was **f**,
145:14 The LORD upholds all who are **f**,
Mk 13:25 and the stars will be **f** from heaven,
Lk 2:34 "This child is destined for the **f** and the rising
8:47 and **f** down before him, she declared in
22:44 ⟦like great drops of blood **f** down on the ground.⟧
Ac 1:18 and **f** headlong, he burst open in the middle
10:25 and **f** at his feet, worshiped him.
1Co 8:13 Therefore, if food is a cause of their **f**,
Heb 6:7 Ground that drinks up the rain **f** on it repeatedly,
Jude 1:24 Now to him who is able to keep you from **f**,
AdE 8:3 she spoke once again to the king and, **f** at his feet,
Sir 18:21 Before **f** ill, humble yourself;
34:19 a guard against stumbling and a help against **f**.
43:22 the **f** dew gives refreshment from the heat.
Aza 1:46 Bless the Lord, dews and **f** snow;
2Mc 10:26 **F** upon the steps before the altar,
3Mc 5:49 and **f** into one another's arms—
2Es 12:18 and it shall be in danger of **f**;
4Mc 9:20 of flesh were **f** off the axles of the machine.

FALLOW (3)

Ex 23:11 and lie **f**, so that the poor of your people may eat;
Jer 4:3 Break up your **f** ground, and do not sow among
Hos 10:12 reap steadfast love; break up your **f** ground;

FALLOWDEER (KJV) See ROE BUCKS

FALLS‡ (53) [FALL]

Ge 49:17 bites the horse's heels so that its rider **f** backward.
Ex 21:33 and an ox or a donkey **f** into it,
Lev 11:32 of them **f** when they are dead shall be unclean,
11:33 And if any of them **f** into any earthen vessel,
11:35 on which any part of the carcass **f** shall
11:37 of their carcass **f** upon any seed set aside
11:38 on the seed and any part of their carcass **f** on it,
15:17 on which the semen **f** shall be washed with water,
15:24 any man lies with her, and her impurity **f** on him,
25:25 If anyone of your kin **f** into difficulty and sells
Nu 24:4 who sees the vision of the Almighty, who **f** down,
24:16 who sees the vision of the Almighty, who **f** down,
33:54 to the person on whom the lot **f**;
Dt 20:20 the town that makes war with you, until it **f**.
2Sa 3:29 or who holds a spindle, or who **f** by the sword,
3:34 as one **f** before the wicked you have fallen."
17:12 we shall light on him as the dew **f** on the ground;
Job 4:13 when deep sleep **f** on mortals,

Job 14:18 "But the mountain **f** and crumbles away,
30:30 My skin turns black and **f** from me,
33:15 when deep sleep **f** on mortals,
Ps 72: 6 May he be like rain that **f** on the mown grass,
133: 3 which **f** on the mountains of Zion.
Pr 11:14 Where there is no guidance, a nation **f**,
14:35 but his wrath **f** on one who acts shamefully.
22:14 he with whom the LORD is angry **f** into it.
Ecc 4:10 but woe to one who is alone and **f** and does
9:12 when it suddenly **f** upon them.
11: 3 whether a tree **f** to the south or to the north,
11: 3 in the place where the tree **f**, there it will lie.
Isa 24:20 its transgression lies heavy upon it, and it **f**,
65:20 a youth, and one who **f** short of a hundred will
Eze 13:12 When the wall **f**, will it not be said to you,
13:14 when it **f**, you shall perish within it;
Da 9: 7 O Lord, but open shame, as at this day, **f** on us,
9: 8 Open shame, O LORD, **f** on us, our kings,
Mt 12:11 "Suppose one of you has only one sheep and it **f**
13:21 that person immediately **f** away.
17:15 he often **f** into the fire and often into the water.
21:44 one who **f** on this stone will be broken to pieces;
21:44 and it will crush anyone on whom it **f**."
Lk 11:17 against itself becomes a desert, and house **f**
20:18 Everyone who **f** on that stone will be broken
20:18 and it will crush anyone on whom it **f**."
Jn 12:24 unless a grain of wheat **f** into the earth and dies,
Jas 1:11 its flower **f**, and its beauty perishes.
1Pe 1:24 The grass withers, and the flower **f**,
Wis 6: 5 severe judgment **f** on those in high places.
11:22 like a drop of morning dew that **f** on the ground.
Sir 13:21 but when the humble **f**, he is pushed away even
29: 2 repay your neighbor when a loan **f** due.
43:18 and the mind is amazed as it **f**.
LtJ 6:27 if any of these gods **f** to the ground,

FALSE (111) [FALSEHOOD, FALSEHOODS, FALSELY, FALSIFY]

A. FALSE WITNESS[ES] (19)
B. FALSE PROPHET[S] (11)

Ex 20:16 not bear **f** witness against your neighbor. A
23: 1 You shall not spread a **f** report.
23: 7 Keep far from a **f** charge,
Dt 5:20 Neither shall you bear **f** witness A
19:18 If the witness is a **f** witness, A
19:19 then you shall do to the **f** witness just as A
19:19 as the **f** witness had meant to do to the other. A
2Ki 17:15 They went after **f** idols and became false;
17:15 They went after false idols and became **f**;
2Ch 26:16 For he was **f** to the LORD his God,
Job 31:28 for I should have been **f** to God above.
36: 4 For truly my words are not **f**;
Ps 24: 4 who do not lift up their souls to what is **f**,
27:12 for **f** witnesses have risen against me, A
40: 4 to those who go astray after **f** gods.
44:17 or been **f** to your covenant.
73:27 you put an end to those who are **f** to you.
89:33 or be **f** to my faithfulness.
119:29 Put **f** ways far from me;
119:104 therefore I hate every **f** way.
119:128 by all your precepts; I hate every **f** way.
144: 8 and whose right hands are **f**.
144:11 and whose right hands are **f**.
Pr 11: 1 A **f** balance is an abomination to the LORD,
12:17 but a **f** witness speaks deceitfully. A
14: 5 but a **f** witness breathes out lies. A
17: 7 still less is **f** speech to a ruler.
19: 5 A **f** witness will not go unpunished, A
19: 9 A **f** witness will not go unpunished, A
20:23 and **f** scales are not good.
21:28 A **f** witness will perish, A
25:18 a sharp arrow is one who bears **f** witness against A
Isa 16: 6 and his insolence; his boasts are **f**.
Jer 3: 7 she did not return, and her **f** sister Judah saw it.
3: 8 yet her **f** sister Judah did not fear,
3:10 for all this her **f** sister Judah did not return to me
3:11 Israel has shown herself less guilty than **f** Judah.
8: 8 the **f** pen of the scribes has made it into a lie?
10: 3 For the customs of the peoples are **f**:
10:14 their images are **f**, and there is no breath in them.
48:30 his boasts are **f**, his deeds are **f**.
51:17 their images are **f**, and there is no breath in them.
La 2:14 Your prophets have seen for you **f** and deceptive
2:14 but have seen oracles for you that are **f**
Eze 12:24 be any **f** vision or flattering divination within
13: 7 not seen a **f** vision or uttered a lying divination,
13: 9 be against the prophets who see **f** visions
13:23 therefore you shall no longer see **f** visions
21:23 But to them it will seem like a **f** divination;
21:29 Offering **f** visions for you, divining lies for you,
22:28 seeing **f** visions and divining lies for them,
Hos 10: 2 Their heart is **f**; now they must bear their guilt.
12: 7 A trader, in whose hands are **f** balances,
Am 8: 5 and practice deceit with **f** balances,
Zec 8:17 against one another, and love no **f** oath;
10: 2 the dreamers tell **f** dreams,
Mt 7:15 "Beware of **f** prophets, who come to you B
15:19 adultery, fornication, theft, **f** witness, slander. A
19:18 You shall not bear **f** witness; A
24:11 many **f** prophets will arise and lead many astray. B
24:24 For **f** messiahs and false prophets will appear
24:24 For false messiahs and **f** prophets will appear B
26:59 the whole council were looking for **f** testimony
26:60 though many **f** witnesses came forward. A
Mk 10:19 You shall not bear **f** witness; A
13:22 **F** messiahs and false prophets will appear
13:22 and **f** prophets will appear and produce signs B
14:56 For many gave **f** testimony against him,
14:57 Some stood up and gave **f** testimony against him,
Lk 3:14 from anyone by threats or **f** accusation,
6:26 that is what their ancestors did to the **f** prophets. B
18:20 You shall not bear **f** witness; A
Jn 7:18 and there is nothing **f** in him.
Ac 6:13 They set up **f** witnesses who said, A
13: 6 they met a certain magician, a Jewish **f** prophet, B
2Co 11:13 For such boasters are **f** apostles,
11:26 danger at sea, danger from **f** brothers and sisters;
Gal 2: 4 But because of **f** believers secretly brought in,
Php 1:18 whether out of **f** motives or true;
2Th 2:11 leading them to believe what is **f**,
Heb 6:18 in which it is impossible that God would prove **f**,
Jas 3:14 do not be boastful and **f** to the truth.
2Pe 2: 1 But **f** prophets also arose among the people, B
2: 1 just as there will be **f** teachers among you,
1Jn 4: 1 many **f** prophets have gone out into the world. B
3Jn 1:10 to what he is doing in spreading **f** charges
Rev 2: 2 and have found them to be **f**.
16:13 and from the mouth of the **f** prophet. B
19:20 the **f** prophet who had performed in its presence B
20:10 where the beast and the **f** prophet were, B
Jdt 11: 5 I will say nothing **f** to my lord this night.
AdE 16: 6 by the **f** trickery of their evil natures beguile
Wis 10:14 Those who accused him she showed to be **f**,
Sir 23:11 if he swears a **f** oath, he will not be justified,
26: 5 and **f** accusation—all these are worse than death.
34: 1 The senseless have vain and **f** hopes,
34: 4 And from something **f** what can be true?
36:24 so an intelligent mind detects **f** words.
LtJ 6: 8 but they are **f** and cannot speak.
6:44 Whatever is done for these idols is **f**.
6:50 it will afterward be known that they are **f**.
6:59 than to be these **f** gods;
6:59 that protects its contents, than these **f** gods;
6:59 also a wooden pillar in a palace, than these **f** gods.
Sus 1:43 that these men have given **f** evidence against me.
1:49 for these men have given **f** evidence against her."
1:61 of their own mouths Daniel had convicted them of bearing **f** witness; A
2Mc 5: 5 When a **f** rumor arose that Antiochus was dead,
14:27 by the **f** accusations of that depraved man,
4Mc 5:34 I will not play **f** to you, O law that trained me,

FALSEHOOD (20) [FALSE]

Job 21:34 There is nothing left of your answers but **f**."
27: 4 my lips will not speak **f**,
31: 5 "If I have walked with **f**, and my foot has hurried
Ps 62: 4 of prominence. They take pleasure in **f**;
119:163 I hate and abhor **f**, but I love your law.
Pr 13: 5 The righteous hate **f**, but the wicked act shamefully
29:12 a ruler listens to **f**, all his officials will be wicked.
30: 8 Remove far from me **f** and lying;
Isa 5:18 Ah, you who drag iniquity along with cords of **f**,
28:15 and in **f** we have taken shelter";
Jer 9: 3 they have grown strong in the land for **f**,
Eze 13: 6 They have envisioned **f** and lying divination;
13: 8 Because you have uttered **f** and envisioned lies,
Hos 12: 1 they multiply **f** and violence;
Ro 3: 7 my **f** God's truthfulness abounds to his glory,
Eph 4:25 then, putting away **f**, let all of us speak the truth
Rev 21:27 nor anyone who practices abomination or **f**,
22:15 and everyone who loves and practices **f**.
Jdt 5: 5 No **f** shall come from your servant's mouth.
2Es 14:18 Truth shall go farther away, and **f** shall come near.

FALSEHOODS (1) [FALSE]

Mic 2:11 If someone were to go about uttering empty **f**,

FALSELY‡ (29) [FALSE]

Ge 21:23 not deal **f** with me or with my offspring or
Ex 8:29 only do not let Pharaoh again deal **f** by not letting
Lev 6: 3 if you swear **f** regarding any of the various things
6: 5 or anything else about which you have sworn **f**,
19:11 You shall not steal; you shall not deal **f**;
19:12 And you shall not swear **f** by my name,
Dt 19:18 having testified **f** against another,
32: 5 yet his degenerate children have dealt **f** with him,
Jos 24:27 if you deal **f** with your God."
Job 13: 7 Will you speak **f** for God,
Ps 69: 4 my enemies who accuse me **f**.
Pr 6:19 a lying witness who testifies **f**,
Isa 63: 8 children who will not deal **f**";
Jer 5: 2 they say, "As the LORD lives," yet they swear **f**.
5:12 They have spoken **f** of the LORD, and have said,
5:31 the prophets prophesy **f**, and the priests rule as
6:13 and from prophet to priest, everyone deals **f**.
7: 9 Will you steal, murder, commit adultery, swear **f**,
8:10 from prophet to priest everyone deals **f**.
20: 6 to whom you have prophesied **f**.
27:15 but they are prophesying **f** in my name,
Eze 13:22 Because you have disheartened the righteous **f**,
Hos 7: 1 for they deal **f**, the thief breaks in,
Zec 5: 3 on one side, and everyone who swears **f** shall
5: 4 the house of anyone who swears **f** by my name;
Mal 3: 5 against the adulterers, against those who swear **f**,
Mt 5:11 and utter all kinds of evil against you **f**
5:33 to those of ancient times, 'You shall not swear **f**,
1Ti 6:20 and contradictions of what is **f** called knowledge;

FALSIFY (1) [FALSE]

2Co 4: 2 we refuse to practice cunning or to **f** God's word;

FALTER (1) [FALTERED]

Sir 12:15 He stands by you for a while, but if you **f**,

FALTERED‡ (1) [FALTER]

AdE 15: 7 The queen **f**, and turned pale and faint,

FAME (22) [FAMED, FAMOUS]

Dt 26:19 in praise and in **f** and in honor;
Jos 6:27 and his **f** was in all the land.
1Sa 18:30 so that his **f** became very great.
1Ki 4:31 his **f** spread throughout all
10: 1 the queen of Sheba heard of the **f** of Solomon,
10: 1 (**f** due to the name of the LORD),
1Ch 14:17 The **f** of David went out into all lands,
2Ch 9: 1 the queen of Sheba heard of the **f** of Solomon,
26: 8 and his **f** spread even to the border of Egypt,
26:15 and large stones. And his **f** spread far,
Est 9: 4 and his **f** spread throughout all the provinces as
Ps 72:17 his **f** continue as long as the sun.
145: 7 the **f** of your abundant goodness,
Isa 66:19 that have not heard of my **f** or seen my glory;
Eze 16:14 Your **f** spread among the nations on account
16:15 and played the whore because of your **f**,
Mt 4:24 So his **f** spread throughout all Syria,
Mk 1:28 At once his **f** began to spread throughout
Sir 47:16 Your **f** reached to far-off islands,
1Mc 3:26 His **f** reached the king, and the Gentiles talked of
8: 1 Now Judas heard of the **f** of the Romans,
8:12 as many as have heard of their **f** have feared them.

FAMED (1) [FAME]

1Mc 6: 1 when he heard that Elymais in Persia was a city **f**

FAMILIAR (8)

1Ki 9:27 sailors who were **f** with the sea,
2Ch 8:18 ships and servants **f** with the sea.
Ps 55:13 it is you, my equal, my companion, my **f** friend,
Isa 8:19 the ghosts and the **f** spirits that chirp and mutter;
19: 3 of the dead and the ghosts and the **f** spirits;
Ac 26: 3 because you are especially **f** with all the customs
Tob 5:10 and I am **f** with its mountains and all of its roads."
Sir Pr: 1 so that by becoming **f** also with his book

FAMILIES (121) [FAMILY]

Ge 8:19 went out of the ark by **f**.
10: 5 with their own language, by their **f**,
10:18 Afterward the **f** of the Canaanites spread abroad.
10:20 These are the descendants of Ham, by their **f**,
10:31 These are the descendants of Shem, by their **f**,
10:32 These are the **f** of Noah's sons,
12: 3 and in you all the **f** of the earth shall be blessed."
28:14 and all the **f** of the earth shall be blessed in you
36:40 to their **f** and their localities by their names:
Ex 1:21 the midwives feared God, he gave them **f**.
6:14 these are the **f** of Reuben.
6:15 these are the **f** of Simeon.
6:17 sons of Gershon: Libni and Shimei, by their **f**.
6:19 the **f** of the Levites according to their genealogies.
6:24 these are the **f** of the Korahites.
6:25 of the ancestral houses of the Levites by their **f**.
12:21 "Go, select lambs for your **f**,
Lev 25:45 and from their **f** that are with you,
Nu 11:10 the people weeping throughout their **f**,
26:44 The descendants of Asher by their **f**:
Jos 13:23 according to their **f** with their towns and villages.
13:24 to the tribe of the Gadites, according to their **f**.
13:29 of the Manassites according to their **f**.
14: 1 of the **f** of the tribes of the Israelites distributed
15: 1 of Judah according to their **f** reached southward to
15:12 the people of Judah according to their **f**.
15:20 of the people of Judah according to their **f**.
16: 5 The territory of the Ephraimites by their **f** was
16: 8 of the tribe of the Ephraimites by their **f**,
17: 2 by their **f**, Abiezer, Helek, Asriel, Shechem,
17: 2 of Manasseh son of Joseph, by their **f**.
18:11 the tribe of Benjamin according to its **f** came up,
18:20 the tribe of Benjamin, according to its **f**, boundary
18:21 of Benjamin according to their **f** were Jericho,
18:28 of the tribe of Benjamin according to its **f**.
19: 1 for the tribe of Simeon, according to its **f**;
19: 8 of the tribe of Simeon according to its **f**.
19:10 up for the tribe of Zebulun, according to its **f**.
19:16 according to its **f**—these towns with their villages.
19:17 for the tribe of Issachar, according to its **f**.
19:23 according to its **f**—the towns with their villages.
19:24 for the tribe of Asher according to its **f**.
19:31 of the tribe of Asher according to its **f**—
19:32 for the tribe of Naphtali, according to its **f**.
19:39 of the tribe of Naphtali according to its **f**—
19:40 for the tribe of Dan, according to its **f**.
19:48 of the tribe of Dan, according to their **f**—
19:51 and Joshua son of Nun and the heads of the **f** of
21: 1 the **f** of the Levites came to the priest Eleazar and
21: 1 and to Joshua son of Nun and to the heads of the **f**
21: 4 The lot came out for the **f** of the Kohathites.
21: 5 by lot ten towns from the **f** of the tribe
21: 6 by lot thirteen towns from the **f** of the tribe
21: 7 according to their **f** received twelve towns from
21:10 one of the **f** of the Kohathites who belonged to
21:20 of the Kohathites belonging to the Kohathite **f** of
21:26 the **f** of the rest of the Kohathites were ten in all,
21:27 To the Gershonites, one of the **f** of the Levites,
21:33 of the several **f** of the Gershonites were
21:34 To the rest of the Levites—the Merarite **f**—

Jos 21:40 As for the towns of the several Merarite f, that is,
21:40 that is, the remainder of the f of the Levites,
22:14 one from each of the tribal f of Israel,
22:21 of Manasseh said in answer to the heads of the f
22:30 the heads of the f of Israel who were with him,
Jdg 21:24 from there at that time by tribes and f,
1Sa 9:21 the humblest of all the f of the tribe of Benjamin.
10:21 He brought the tribe of Benjamin near by its f,
1Ch 2:53 And the f of Kiriath-jearim:
2:55 The f also of the scribes that lived at Jabez:
4:2 These were the f of the Zorathites.
4:8 Zobebah, and the f of Aharhel son of Harum.
4:21 the f of the guild of linen workers at Beth-ashbea;
4:38 these mentioned by name were leaders in their f,
5:7 And his kindred by their f,
6:54 to the sons of Aaron of the f of Kohathites—
6:60 All their towns throughout their f were thirteen.
6:62 to their f were allotted thirteen towns out of
6:63 to their f were allotted twelve towns out of
6:66 of the f of the sons of Kohath had towns
6:70 for the rest of the f of the Kohathites.
7:5 Their kindred belonging to all the f
9:9 of f according to their ancestral houses.
15:12 "You are the heads of f of the Levites;
16:28 Ascribe to the LORD, O f of the peoples,
23:9 These were the heads of f of Ladan.
23:24 the heads of f as they were enrolled according to
26:21 the heads of f belonging to Ladan the Gershonite:
26:26 the heads of f, and the officers of the thousands
26:32 of ability, heads of f, to have the oversight of
27:1 the heads of f, the commanders of the thousands
2Ch 1:2 and all the leaders of all Israel, the heads of f.
19:8 and priests and heads of f of Israel,
23:2 and the heads of f of Israel,
Ezr 1:5 The heads of the f of Judah and Benjamin,
2:59 they could not prove their f or their descent,
2:68 some of the heads of f made freewill offerings for
3:12 many of the priests and Levites and heads of f,
4:2 they approached Zerubbabel and the heads of f
4:3 the rest of the heads of f in Israel said to them,
8:29 the chief priests and the Levites and the heads of f
10:16 selected men, heads of f, according to their f,
Ne 4:13 I stationed the people according to their f,
Job 31:34 and the contempt of f terrified me,
Ps 22:27 all the f of the nations shall worship before him.
96:7 Ascribe to the LORD, O f of the peoples,
107:41 and makes their f like flocks.
Jer 2:4 and all the f of the house of Israel.
31:1 I will be the God of all the f of Israel,
33:24 not observed how these people say, "The two f
Am 3:2 You only have I known of all the f of the earth;
Zec 12:14 and all the f that are left,
14:17 of the f of the earth do not go up to Jerusalem
Ac 3:25 in your descendants all the f of the earth shall
Tit 1:11 since they are upsetting whole f by teaching
1Mc 1:61 and their f and those who circumcised them;
1Es 1:4 prepare yourselves by your f and kindred,
2:8 Then arose the heads of f of the tribes of Judah
5:44 Some of the heads of f,
3Mc 3:27 the most hateful torments, together with their f.

FAMILY‡ (125) [FAMILIES]

Ge 34:19 Now he was the most honored of all his f.
37:2 This is the story of the f of Jacob.
Ex 12:3 of this month they are to take a lamb for each f,
Lev 20:5 against them and against their f,
25:10 to your property and every one of you to your f.
25:41 they shall go back to their own f and return
25:47 or to a branch of the alien's f,
25:49 or anyone of their f who is
Nu 25:6 and brought a Midianite woman into his f,
Dt 18:8 they have income from the sale of f possessions.
25:5 of the deceased shall not be married outside the f
25:10 Throughout Israel his f shall be known as
29:18 be that there is among you a man or woman, or a f
Jos 2:12 that you in turn will deal kindly with my f.
2:18 your brothers, and all your f.
6:25 with her f and all who belonged to her,
6:25 Her f has lived in Israel ever since.
7:17 f by f, and Zabdi was taken.
22:14 every one of them the head of a f among the clans
Jdg 1:25 but they let the man and all his f go.
6:15 and I am the least in my f."
6:27 of his f and the townspeople to do it by day,
8:27 and it became a snare to Gideon and to his f.
9:1 to them and to the whole clan of his mother's f,
16:31 Then his brothers and all his f came down
Ru 2:1 of the f of Elimelech, whose name was Boaz.
2:3 who was of the f of Elimelech.
1Sa 2:27 'I revealed myself to the f of your ancestor
2:28 to the f of your ancestor all my offerings by fire
2:30 'I promised that your f and the f of your ancestor
2:31 and the strength of your ancestor's f,
2:31 so that no one in your f will live to old age.
2:32 and no one in your f shall ever live to old age.
2:36 in your f shall come to implore him for a piece
9:21 and my f is the humblest of all the families of
10:21 and the f of the Matrites was taken by lot.
10:21 Finally he brought the f of the Matrites near man
17:25 and will give him his daughter and make his f free
18:18 my father's f in Israel, that I should be son-in-law
20:6 for there is a yearly sacrifice there for all the f.'
20:29 for our f is holding a sacrifice in the city,
2Sa 14:7 Now the whole f has risen against your servant.
16:5 a man of the f of the house
1Ki 14:13 he alone of Jeroboam's f shall come to the grave,
2Ki 11:1 she set about to destroy all the royal f.
25:25 of the royal f, came with ten men;
1Ch 4:27 nor did all their f multiply like the Judeans.
6:61 of the Kohathites were given by lot out of the f of
23:11 so they were enrolled as a single f.
26:31 of whatever genealogy or f,
2Ch 22:10 she set about to destroy all the royal f of the house
Ezr 8:1 These are their f heads, and this is the genealogy
Ne 1:6 Both I and my f have sinned.
Est 4:14 but you and your father's f will perish.
9:28 in every f, province, and city;
Job 19:13 "He has put my f far from me,
19:17 I am loathsome to my own f.
22:6 For you have exacted pledges from your f
32:2 Elihu son of Barachel the Buzite, of the f of Ram,
Pr 6:19 and one who sows discord in a f.
17:2 and will share the inheritance as one of the f.
Jer 3:14 I will take you, one from a city and two from a f,
8:3 to life by all the remnant that remains of this evil f
12:6 For even your kinsfolk and your own f,
41:1 of Nethaniah son of Elishama, of the royal f, one
Eze 43:19 you shall give to the levitical priests of the f
Da 1:3 to bring some of the Israelites of the royal f and of
Am 3:1 the whole f that I brought up out of the land
Mic 2:3 Now, I am devising against this f an evil
Zec 11:14 annulling the f ties between Judah and Israel.
12:12 The land shall mourn, each f by itself;
12:12 the f of the house of David by itself,
12:12 the f of the house of Nathan by itself,
12:13 the f of the house of Levi by itself,
12:13 the f of the Shimeites by itself,
14:18 f of Egypt do not go up and present themselves,
Mt 25:40 of the least of these who are members of my f,
Mk 3:21 When his f heard it, they went out to restrain him,
Lk 2:4 he was descended from the house and f of David.
12:13 tell my brother to divide the f inheritance
Ac 4:6 and all who were of the high-priestly f.
7:13 and Joseph's f became known to Pharaoh.
13:26 "My brothers, you descendants of Abraham's f,
16:33 he and his entire f were baptized without delay.
Ro 8:29 that he might be the firstborn within a large f.
16:10 Greet those who belong to the f of Aristobulus.
16:11 in the Lord who belong to the f of Narcissus.
1Co 8:12 But when you thus sin against members of your f,
Gal 1:2 and all the members of God's f who are with me,
6:10 and especially for those of the f of faith.
Eph 3:15 from whom every f in heaven and
1Ti 5:4 to their own f and make some repayment
5:8 and especially for f members,
1Pe 2:17 Love the f of believers.
Tob 1:9 a member of our own f,
5:9 about his f and to what tribe he belongs,
5:11 "Brother, of what f are you and from what tribe?
Jdt 8:2 who belonged to her tribe and f,
8:18 has there been any tribe or f or people or town
AdE 4:14 but you and your father's f will perish.
9:27 in every city, f, and country.
14:5 since I was born I have heard in the tribe of my f
Sir 10:20 Among f members their leader is worthy
11:34 and will make you a stranger to your own f.
47:20 You stained your honor, and defiled your f line,
47:22 or destroy the f line of him who loved him.
47:22 and to David a root from his own f.
1Mc 2:1 a priest of the f of Joarib,
5:62 But they did not belong to the f of those men
9:36 But the f of Jambri from Medeba came out
9:37 "The f of Jambri are celebrating a great wedding,
12:10 we have undertaken to send to renew our f ties
12:17 from us concerning the renewal of our f ties.
12:21 and the Jews that they are brothers and are of the f
2Mc 1:10 who is of the f of the anointed priests,
15:14 the f of Israel and prays much for the people and
3Mc 6:8 watched over and restored unharmed to all his f.
4Mc 5:4 He was a man of priestly f, learned in the law,
9:23 in my struggle or renounce our courageous f ties.
10:15 I will not renounce our noble f ties.
13:19 You are not ignorant of the affection of f ties,
13:27 of f ties, those who were left endured for the sake
15:25 nature, f, parental love, and the rackings

FAMINE (123) [FAMINES]

Ge 12:10 Now there was a f in the land.
12:10 for the f was severe in the land.
26:1 Now there was a f in the land,
26:1 besides the former f that had occurred in the days
41:27 They are seven years of f.
41:30 After them there will arise seven years of f,
41:30 the f will consume the land.
41:31 in the land because of the f that will follow,
41:36 a reserve for the land against the seven years of f
41:36 so that the land may not perish through the f."
41:50 Before the years of f came, Joseph had two sons,
41:54 and the seven years of f began to come,
41:54 There was f in every country,
41:56 And since the f had spread over all the land,
41:56 for the f was severe in the land of Egypt.
41:57 the f became severe throughout the world.
42:5 for the f had reached the land of Canaan.
42:19 The rest of you shall go and carry grain for the f
42:33 take grain for the f of your households,
43:1 Now the f was severe in the land.
45:6 For the f has been in the land these two years;
45:11 since there are five more years of f to come—
47:4 for your servants' flocks because the f is severe in
47:13 for the f was very severe.
47:13 the land of Canaan languished because of the f.
Ge 47:20 because the f was severe upon them;
Ru 1:1 there was a f in the land,
2Sa 21:1 there was a f in the days of David for three years,
24:13 "Shall three years of f come to you on your land?
1Ki 8:37 "If there is f in the land, if there is plague, blight,
18:2 The f was severe in Samaria.
2Ki 4:38 there was a f in the land.
6:25 f in Samaria became so great that
7:4 we say, 'Let us enter the city,' the f is in the city,
8:1 for the LORD has called for a f,
25:3 On the ninth day of the fourth month the f became
1Ch 21:12 either three years of f;
2Ch 6:28 "If there is f in the land, if there is plague, blight,
20:9 the sword, judgment, or pestilence, or f,
32:11 handing you over to die by f and by thirst,
Ne 5:3 and our houses in order to get grain during the f."
Job 5:20 In f he will redeem you from death,
5:22 At destruction and f you shall laugh,
Ps 33:19 and to keep them alive in f.
37:19 in the days of f they have abundance.
105:16 When he summoned f against the land,
Isa 14:30 but I will make your root die of f,
51:19 devastation and destruction, f and sword—
Jer 5:12 and we shall not see sword or f."
11:22 their sons and their daughters shall die by f;
14:12 by f, and by pestilence I consume them.
14:13 not see the sword, nor shall you have f,
14:15 "Sword and f shall not come on this land":
14:15 By sword and f those prophets shall be consumed.
14:16 the streets of Jerusalem, victims of f and sword.
14:18 And if I enter the city, look—those sick with f!
15:2 those destined for f, to f,
16:4 They shall perish by the sword and by f,
18:21 Therefore give their children over to f;
21:7 those who survive the pestilence, sword, and f—
21:9 in this city shall die by the sword, by f, and
24:10 And I will send sword, f,
27:8 with f, and with pestilence, says the LORD,
27:13 by f, and by pestilence, as the LORD has spoken
28:8 and me from ancient times prophesied war, f,
29:17 I am going to let loose on them sword, f,
29:18 I will pursue them with the sword, with f,
32:24 and the city, faced with sword, f, and pestilence,
32:36 of the king of Babylon by the sword, by f, and
34:17 a release to the sword, to pestilence, and to f.
38:2 in this city shall die by the sword, by f, and
42:16 the f that you dread shall follow close after you
42:17 to settle there shall die by the sword, by f, and
42:22 then, that you shall die by the sword, by f,
44:12 by the sword and by f they shall perish;
44:12 they shall die by the sword and by f;
44:13 with the sword, with f, and with pestilence,
44:18 and have perished by the sword and by f."
44:27 of Egypt shall perish by the sword and by f,
52:6 On the ninth day of the fourth month the f became
La 5:10 as an oven from the scorching heat of f.
Eze 5:12 of you shall die of pestilence or be consumed by f
5:16 when I loose against you my deadly arrows of f,
5:16 and when I bring more and more f upon you,
5:17 I will send f and wild animals against you,
6:11 For they shall fall by the sword, by f,
6:12 and any who are left and are spared shall die of f.
7:15 The sword is outside, pestilence and f are inside;
7:15 f and pestilence devour them.
12:16 from f and pestilence, so that they may tell
14:13 and break its staff of bread and send f upon it,
14:21 sword, f, wild animals, and pestilence,
36:29 and make it abundant and lay no f upon you.
36:30 that you may never again suffer the disgrace of f
Am 8:11 when I will send a f on the land;
8:11 not a f of bread, or a thirst for water,
Lk 4:25 and there was a severe f over all the land;
15:14 a severe f took place throughout that country,
Ac 7:11 there came a f throughout Egypt and Canaan,
11:28 that there would be a severe f over all the world;
Ro 8:35 Will hardship, or distress, or persecution, or f,
Rev 6:8 to kill with sword, f, and pestilence,
18:8 pestilence and mourning and f—
Tob 4:13 because idleness is the mother of f.
Jdt 5:10 a f spread over the land of Canaan they went
7:14 and children will waste away with f,
Sir 39:29 Fire and hail and f and pestilence,
40:9 calamities and f and ruin and plague.
48:2 He brought a f upon them,
Bar 2:25 by f and sword and pestilence.
1Mc 6:54 for the f proved too much for them.
9:24 In those days a very great f occurred,
13:49 and many of them perished from f.
2Es 15:5 the sword and f, death and destruction,
15:49 widowhood, poverty, f, sword, and pestilence,
16:18 the beginning of f, when many shall perish;
16:19 F and plague, tribulation and anguish are sent
16:21 the sword, f, and great confusion.
16:22 of those who live on the earth shall perish by f;
16:22 those who survive the f shall die by the sword.
16:34 and their husbands shall perish of f.
16:46 in captivity and f they will produce their children.

FAMINES (3) [FAMINE]

Mt 24:7 there will be f and earthquakes in various places:
Mk 13:8 in various places; there will be f.
Lk 21:11 and in various places f and plagues;

FAMISHED (7)

Ge 25:29 Esau came in from the field, and he was f.
25:30 "Let me eat some of that red stuff, for I am f!"

Ge 41:55 When all the land of Egypt was f,
Jdg 8: 4 with him, exhausted and f.
Mt 4: 2 and forty nights, and afterwards he was f.
Lk 4: 2 and when they were over, he was f.
Bar 2:18 with failing eyes and f soul,

FAMOUS (13) [FAME]

1Ki 1:47 the name of Solomon more f than yours,
1Ch 5:24 Hodaviah, and Jahdiel, mighty warriors, f men,
22: 5 f and glorified throughout all lands;
Ps 136:18 and killed f kings, for his steadfast love endures
Jer 49:25 How the f city is forsaken, the joyful town!
2Co 8:18 With him we are sending the brother who is f
Jdt 16:23 She became more and more f,
Sir 39: 2 of the f and penetrates the subtleties of parables;
44: 1 now sing the praises of f men,
48: 6 You sent kings down to destruction, and f men,
Bar 3:26 The giants were born there, who were f of old,
2Mc 2:22 the temple f throughout the world, and liberated
3Mc 6: 1 f among the priests of the country,

FAN (1) [FANNED, FANNING]

4Mc 5:32 Therefore get your torture wheels ready and f

FANCY (1)

SS 6:12 my f set me in a chariot beside my prince.

FANFARE (1)

Sir 50:16 they sounded a mighty f as a reminder before the Most High.

FANGS (5)

Job 29:17 I broke the f of the unrighteous,
Ps 58: 6 tear out the f of the young lions, O LORD!
Joel 1: 6 and it has the f of a lioness.
Wis 16:10 even by the f of venomous serpents,
Sir 39:30 the f of wild animals and scorpions and vipers,

FANNED (1) [FAN]

Job 20:26 a fire f by no one will devour them;

FANNING (1) [FAN]

4Mc 9:19 f the flames they tightened the wheel further.

FANTASIES (2)

Da 4: 5 my f in bed and the visions
Sir 34: 5 and like a woman in labor, the mind has f.

FAR‡ (336) [FAR-OFF]

Ge 10:19 as f as Gaza, and in the direction of Sodom,
10:19 Gomorrah, Admah, and Zeboiim, as f as Lasha.
13: 3 He journeyed on by stages from the Negeb as f
13:12 of the Plain and moved his tent as f as Sodom.
14: 6 as f as El-paran on the edge of the wilderness;
14:14 and went in pursuit as f as Dan.
18:25 F be it from you to do such a thing,
18:25 F be that from you!
22: 4 up and saw the place f away.
44: 7 F be it from your servants
44:17 But he said, "F be it from me that I should do so!
Ex 8:28 provided you do not go very f away.
23: 7 Keep f from a false charge,
33: 7 and pitch it outside the camp, f off from the camp;
Lev 13:12 so f as the priest can see,
Nu 14:45 pursuing them as f as Hormah.
16: 3 and said to them, "You have gone too f!
16: 7 You Levites have gone too f!"
16:37 then scatter the fire f and wide.
21:24 as f as to the Ammonites;
21:26 and captured all his land as f as the Arnon.
24: 6 Like palm groves that stretch f away,
33:49 from Beth-jeshimoth as f as Abel-shittim in
Dt 1: 7 as f as the great river, the river Euphrates.
1:44 They beat you down in Seir as f as Hormah.
2:36 the town that is in the wadi itself) as f as Gilead,
3:10 and all of Bashan, as f as Salecah and Edrei,
3:14 of Argob as f as the border of the Geshurites and
3:16 the Gadites I gave the territory from Gilead as f as
4:48 as f as Mount Sirion (that is, Hermon),
4:49 the Arabah on the east side of the Jordan as f as
12:21 to put his name is too f from you,
13: 7 whether near you or f away from you,
14:24 to set his name is too f away from you,
20:15 Thus you shall treat all the towns that are very f
28:49 The LORD will bring a nation from f away,
30:11 nor is it too f away.
34: 1 showed him the whole land: Gilead as f as Dan,
34: 2 all the land of Judah as f as the Western Sea,
34: 3 of palm trees—as f as Zoar.
Jos 1: 4 From the wilderness and the Lebanon as f as
2: 7 on the way to the Jordan as f as the fords.
3:16 rising up in a single heap f off at Adam,
7: 5 as f as Shebarim and killing them on the slope.
8: 4 do not go very f from the city,
9: 6 "We have come from a f country;
9: 9 "Your servants have come from a very f country,
9:22 saying, 'We are very f from you,'
10:10 struck them down as f as Azekah and Makkedah.
10:11 down huge stones from heaven on them as f
10:41 and all the country of Goshen, as f as Gibeon.
11: 8 as f as Great Sidon and Misrephoth-maim,
11: 8 and eastward as f as the valley of Mizpeh.
Jos 11:17 as f as Baal-gad in the valley
12: 2 the middle of the valley as f as the river Jabbok,
13: 9 and all the tableland from Medeba as f as Dibon;
13:10 as f as the boundary of the Ammonites;
13:27 as f as the lower end of the Sea of Chinnereth,
16: 3 as f as the territory of Lower Beth-horon,
16: 5 on the east was Ataroth-addar as f
19: 8 with all the villages all around these towns as f
19:10 boundary of its inheritance reached as f as Sarid;
19:28 Rehob, Hammon, Kanah, as f as Great Sidon;
19:33 and Adami-nekeb, and Jabneel, as f as Lakkum;
22:29 F be it from us that we should rebel against
24:16 "F be it from us that we should forsake
Jdg 3: 3 from Mount Baal-hermon as f as Lebo-hamath.
4:11 had encamped as f away as Elon-bezaanannim,
6: 4 as f as the neighborhood of Gaza,
7:22 the army fled as f as Beth-shittah toward Zererah,
7:22 as f as the border of Abel-meholah, by Tabbath.
7:24 as f as Beth-barah, and also the Jordan."
7:24 and they seized the waters as f as Beth-barah,
11:33 twenty towns, and as f as Abel-keramim.
18: 7 they were f from the Sidonians
18:28 because it was f from Sidon
19:11 When they were near Jebus, the day was f spent,
20:43 and trod them down as f as a place east of Gibeah.
20:45 and they were pursued as f as Gidom,
Ru 1:13 it has been f more bitter for me than for you,
1Sa 2:30 now the LORD declares: 'F be it from me;
6:12 the lords of the Philistines went after them as f as
7:11 and struck them down as f as beyond Beth-car.
7:12 for he said, "Thus f the LORD has helped us."
12:23 f be it from me that I should sin against
14:45 this great victory in Israel? F from it!
15: 7 from Havilah as f as Shur, which is east of Egypt.
17:52 the Philistines as f as Gath and the gates of Ekron,
17:52 the way from Shaaraim as f as Gath and Ekron.
20: 2 He said to him, "F from it!
20: 9 Jonathan said, "F be it from you!
26:13 and stood on top of a hill f away,
2Sa 7:18 that you have brought me thus f?
20:20 Joab answered, "F be it from me, f be it,
1Ki 4:12 as f as the other side of Jokmeam;
8:46 to the land of the enemy, f off or near;
10: 7 your wisdom and prosperity f surpass the report
12:30 the one at Bethel and before the other as f as Dan.
2Ki 2: 2 for the LORD has sent me as f as Bethel."
7:15 So they went after them as f as the Jordan;
14:25 from Lebo-hamath as f as the Sea of the Arabah,
18: 8 the Philistines as f as Gaza and its territory,
19:23 to the f recesses of Lebanon;
20:14 "They have come from a f country,
1Ch 4:33 that were around these towns as f as Baal.
5: 8 who lived in Aroer, as f as Nebo and Baal-meon.
5: 9 He also lived to the east as f as the beginning of
5:11 beside them in the land of Bashan as f as Salecah:
7:28 as f as Ayyah and its towns;
12:40 as f away as Issachar and Zebulun and Naphtali,
17:16 that you have brought me thus f?
29: 2 so f as I was able, the gold for the things of gold,
2Ch 6:36 they are carried away captive to a land f or near;
9: 6 you f surpass the report that I had heard.
12: 4 He took the fortified cities of Judah and came as f
14: 9 and came as f as Mareshah.
14:13 the army with him pursued them as f as Gerar,
26:15 and large stones. And his fame spread f,
30:10 of Ephraim and Manasseh, and as f as Zebulun;
34: 6 and as f as Naphtali, in their ruins all around,
Ezr 3:13 so loudly that the sound was heard f away.
Ne 3: 1 as f as the Tower of the Hundred and as f as the
3: 8 they restored Jerusalem as f as the Broad Wall.
3:13 and repaired a thousand cubits of the wall, as f as
3:15 of the Pool of Shelah of the king's garden, as f as
3:16 as f as the artificial pool and the house of
3:27 the great projecting tower as f as the wall
3:31 as f as the house of the temple servants and of
4:19 we are separated f from one another on the wall.
5: 8 "As f as we were able,
12:43 The joy of Jerusalem was heard f away.
Est 9:20 the provinces of King Ahasuerus, both near and f,
Job 5: 4 Their children are f from safety,
11:14 If iniquity is in your hand, put it f away,
13:21 withdraw your hand f from me,
19:13 "He has put my family f from me,
27: 5 F be it from me to say that you are right;
34:10 f be it from God that he should do wickedness,
36: 3 I will bring my knowledge from f away,
36:25 everyone watches it from f away.
38:11 'Thus f shall you come, and no farther,
39:29 its eyes see it from f away.
Ps 10: 1 O LORD, do you stand f off?
22: 1 Why are you so f from helping me,
22:11 Do not be f from me,
22:19 But you, O LORD, do not be f away!
31:22 "I am driven f from your sight."
35:22 O Lord, do not be f from me!
38:11 and my neighbors stand f off.
38:21 O my God, do not be f from me;
48: 2 in the f north, the city of the great King.
55: 7 I would flee f away; I would lodge in the
71:12 O God, do not be f from me;
73:27 Indeed, those who are f from you will perish;
97: 9 you are exalted f above all gods.
101: 4 Perverseness of heart shall be f from me;
103:12 as f as the east is from the west,
103:12 so f he removes our transgressions from us.
109:17 He did not like blessing; may it be f from him.
113: 6 who looks f down on the heavens and the earth?
Ps 119:29 Put false ways f from me;
119:150 they are f from your law.
119:155 Salvation is f from the wicked,
138: 6 but the haughty he perceives from f away.
139: 2 you discern my thoughts from f away.
Pr 4:24 and put devious talk f from you.
5: 8 Keep your way f from her,
15:29 The LORD is f from the wicked,
22: 5 the cautious will keep f from them.
22:15 but the rod of discipline drives it f away.
25:25 so is good news from a f country.
27:10 who is nearby than kindred who are f away.
30: 8 Remove f from me falsehood and lying;
31:10 She is f more precious than jewels.
31:14 she brings her food from f away.
Ecc 7:23 I said, "I will be wise," but it was f from me.
7:24 That which is, is f off, and deep, very deep;
Isa 5:26 He will raise a signal for a nation f away,
6:12 until the LORD sends everyone f away,
8: 9 listen, all you f countries;
10: 3 in the calamity that will come from f away?
15: 4 their voices are heard as f as Jahaz;
17:13 and they will flee f away,
18: 2 to a people feared near and f,
18: 7 from a people feared near and f,
22: 3 though they had fled f away.
23: 7 whose feet carried her to settle f away?
29:13 while their hearts are f from me,
30:27 See, the name of the LORD comes from f away,
33:13 Hear, you who are f away, what I have done;
33:17 they will behold a land that stretches f away.
37:24 to the f recesses of Lebanon;
39: 3 "They have come to me from a f country,
43: 6 from f away and my daughters from the end of
46:11 the man for my purpose from a f country.
46:12 you who are f from deliverance:
46:13 it is not f off, and my salvation will not tarry;
49: 1 pay attention, you peoples from f away!
49:12 Lo, these shall come from f away, and lo,
49:19 and those who swallowed you up will be f away.
54:14 you shall be f from oppression,
57: 9 you sent your envoys f away,
57:19 Peace, peace, to the f and the near,
59: 9 Therefore justice is f from us,
59:11 for salvation, but it is f from us.
60: 4 your sons shall come from f away,
60: 9 to bring your children from f away,
66:19 and Javan, to the coastlands f away that have
Jer 2: 5 in me that they went f from me,
5:15 to bring upon you a nation from f away,
8:19 of my poor people from f and wide in the land:
12: 2 near in their mouths yet f from their hearts.
23:23 says the LORD, and not a God f off?
25:26 f and near, one after another,
27:10 that you will be removed f from your land;
30:10 for I am going to save you from f away,
31: 3 the LORD appeared to him from f away.
31:10 O nations, and declare it in the coastlands f away;
31:40 and all the fields as f as the Wadi Kidron,
46:27 for I am going to save you from f away,
48:24 and all the towns of the land of Moab, f and near.
48:32 over the sea, reached as f as Jazer;
48:34 as f as Jahaz they utter their voice,
48:47 Thus f is the judgment on Moab.
49:30 Flee, wander f away, hide in deep places,
51:64 Thus f are the words of Jeremiah.
La 1:16 comforter is f from me, one to revive my courage;
Eze 6:12 Those f off shall die of pestilence;
8: 6 to drive me f from my sanctuary?
10: 5 of the cherubim was heard as f as the outer court,
11:15 "They have gone f from the LORD;
11:16 I removed them f away among the nations,
22: 5 near and those who are f from you will mock you,
23:40 They even sent for men to come from f away,
29:10 as f as the border of Ethiopia.
34:21 with your horns until you scattered them f
43: 9 and the corpses of their kings f from me,
44:10 But the Levites who went f from me,
47:16 and the border of Hamath), as f as Hazer-hatticon,
47:18 to the eastern sea and as f as Tamar.
47:19 it shall run from Tamar as f as the waters
48: 1 from Lebo-hamath, as f as Hazar-enon (which is
Da 9: 7 those who are near and those who are f away,
11: 2 The fourth shall be f richer than all of them,
11:10 and again shall carry the war as f as his fortress.
Joel 2:20 I will remove the northern army f from you,
3: 6 removing them f from their own border.
3: 8 to a nation f away; for the LORD has spoken.
Am 6: 3 O you that put f away the evil day,
Ob 1:20 in Halah shall possess Phoenicia as f
Mic 4: 3 and shall arbitrate between strong nations f away;
7:11 In that day the boundary shall be f extended.
Hab 1: 8 Their horsemen come from f away;
Zec 6:15 Those who are f off shall come and help to build
10: 9 yet in f countries they shall remember me,
Mt 14:24 battered by the waves, was f from the land,
15: 8 but their hearts are f from me;
24:27 the lightning comes from the east and flashes as f
26:58 as f as the courtyard of the high priest;
Mk 7: 6 but their hearts are f from me;
12:34 "You are not f from the kingdom of God."
Lk 7: 6 but when he was not f from the house,
14:32 If he cannot, then, while the other is still f away,
15:20 But while he was still f off,
16:23 up and saw Abraham f away with Lazarus
18:13 But the tax collector, standing f off,
24:50 Then he led them out as f as Bethany, and,

Jn 21: 8 for they were not **f** from the land,
Ac 2:39 for your children, and for all who are **f** away,
11:19 that took place over Stephen traveled as **f**
13: 6 When they had gone through the whole island as **f**
17:15 Those who conducted Paul brought him as **f**
17:27 though indeed he is not **f** from each one of us.
22:21 'Go, for I will send you **f** away to the Gentiles.' "
28:15 as **f** as the Forum of Appius and Three Taverns
Ro 1:13 to come to you (but thus **f** have been prevented),
12:18 If it is possible, so **f** as it depends on you,
13:12 the night is **f** gone, the day is near.
15:19 as **f** around as Illyricum I have fully proclaimed
2Co 10:13 to reach out even as **f** as you.
11:23 with **f** greater labors, far more imprisonments,
11:23 with far greater labors, **f** more imprisonments,
Gal 1:14 for I was **f** more zealous for the traditions
Eph 1:21 **f** above all rule and authority and power
2:13 in Christ Jesus you who once were **f** off have been brought near
2:17 and proclaimed peace to you who were **f** off
3:20 accomplish abundantly **f** more than all we can ask
4:10 the same one who ascended **f** above all
Php 1:23 to depart and be with Christ, for that is **f** better;
Rev 18:10 they will stand **f** off, in fear of her torment,
18:15 who gained wealth from her, will stand **f** off,
18:17 and all whose trade is on the sea, stood **f** off
Tob 13:11 many nations will come to you from **f** away,
Jdt 1: 9 beyond the Jordan as **f** as Jerusalem and Bethany
1:10 and all who lived in Egypt as **f** as the borders
1:12 as **f** as the coasts of the two seas.
2:24 the fortified towns along the brook Abron, as **f** as
7: 3 and they spread out in breadth over Dothan as **f**
15: 5 and cut them down as **f** as Choba.
AdE 4: 2 He got as **f** as the king's gate,
9:20 in the kingdom of Artaxerxes both near and **f**,
Wis 12:24 For they went **f** astray on the paths of error,
14:17 they imagined their appearance **f** away,
Sir 9:13 Keep **f** from those who have power to kill,
15: 8 She is **f** from arrogance, and liars will never think
16:22 For his decree is **f** off."
23:12 Such conduct will be **f** from the godly,
24:32 and I will make it clear from **f** away.
27:20 Do not go after him, for he is too **f** off,
30:23 and remove sorrow **f** from you,
Bar 3:21 Their descendants have strayed **f** from her way.
LtJ 6:73 such a person will be **f** above reproach.
Sus 1:51 "Separate them **f** from each other,
1Mc 2:21 **F** be it from us to desert the law and
7:45 from Adasa as **f** as Gazara,
8: 4 even though the place was **f** distant from them.
8:12 They have subdued kings **f** and near,
8:23 and may sword and enemy be **f** from them.
9:10 "**F** be it from us to do such a thing as to flee
9:15 and he pursued them as **f** as Mount Azotus.
11: 7 with the king as **f** as the river called Eleutherus;
11: 8 of the coastal cities as **f** as Seleucia by the sea,
11:62 he passed through the country as **f** as Damascus.
11:73 and joined him in the pursuit as **f** as Kadesh,
12:33 and marched through the country as **f** as Askalon
13: 5 **f** be it from me to spare my life in any time
14:16 It was heard in Rome, and as **f** away as Sparta,
2Mc 13: 9 to show the Jews things **f** worse than those
1Es 5:65 so that the sound was heard **f** away;
3Mc 4: 7 along as **f** as the place of embarkation.
2Es 4:50 so the quantity that passed was **f** greater;
7:*48* of perdition and removed us **f** from life—
8:47 For you come **f** short of being able
10:55 as **f** as it is possible for your eyes to see it,

FAR-OFF (2) [FAR]

Ps 56: T *according to The Dove on F Terebinths. Of David.*
Sir 47:16 Your fame reached to **f** islands,

FARE (7) [FARED, FARING]

Ge 18:25 so that the righteous **f** as the wicked!
1Sa 17:18 See how your brothers **f**, and bring some token
2Sa 12: 3 it used to eat of his meager **f**,
Jer 12: 5 how will you **f** in the thickets of the Jordan?
Jnh 1: 3 so he paid his **f** and went on board,
Hag 2:16 how did you **f**? When one came to a heap
Sir 3:26 A stubborn mind will **f** badly at the end,

FARED (6) [FARE]

Ge 30:29 and how your cattle have **f** with me.
2Sa 11: 7 David asked how Joab and the people **f**,
Est 2:11 to learn how Esther was and how she **f**.
Hag 1: 5 Consider how you have **f**.
1: 7 Consider how you have **f**.
Ro 9:29 we would have **f** like Sodom and been made

FAREWELL‡ (17)

Ge 31:28 to kiss my sons and my daughters **f**?
Mk 6:46 After saying **f** to them, he went up on
Lk 9:61 but let me first say **f** to those at my home."
Ac 15:29 from these, you will do well. **F**."
18:18 Paul said **f** to the believers and sailed for Syria,
20: 1 and after encouraging them and saying **f**,
21: 6 and said **f** to one another.
2Co 2:13 So I said **f** to them and went on to Macedonia.
13:11 Finally, brothers and sisters, **f**.
Tob 10:11 he embraced Tobias and said, "**F**, my child;
10:12 Then he bade them **f** and let them go.
12: 5 of all that you brought back, and **f**."
2Mc 3:35 and having bidden Onias **f**,
11:21 **F**. The one hundred forty-eighth year,
11:33 **F**. The one hundred forty-eighth year,
11:38 **F**. The one hundred forty-eighth year,
3Mc 7: 9 as an antagonist to avenge such acts. **F**."

FARING (2) [FARE]

3Mc 3:13 "I myself and our government are **f** well.
7: 2 "We ourselves and our children are **f** well,

FARM (2) [FARMER, FARMER'S, FARMERS, FARMING, FARMS]

Mt 22: 5 they made light of it and went away, one to his **f**,
Sir 7:15 Do not hate hard labor or **f** work,

FARMER (4) [FARM]

2Ti 2: 6 It is the **f** who does the work who ought to have
Jas 5: 7 The **f** waits for the precious crop from the earth,
2Es 8:41 as the **f** sows many seeds in the ground and plants
9:17 and as is the **f**, so is the threshing floor.

FARMER'S (2) [FARM]

2Es 8:43 If the **f** seed does not come up,
8:44 have you also made them like the **f** seed?

FARMERS (8) [FARM]

2Ch 26:10 and he had **f** and vinedressers in the hills and in
Jer 14: 4 the **f** are dismayed; they cover their heads.
31:24 and the **f** and those who wander with their flocks.
51:23 with you I smash **f** and their teams;
Joel 1:11 Be dismayed, you **f**, wail, you vinedressers,
Am 5:16 They shall call the **f** to mourning,
Wis 17:17 for whether they were **f** or shepherds
2Es 15:13 Let the **f** that till the ground mourn,

FARMING (1) [FARM]

2Mc 12: 1 and the Jews went about their **f**.

FARMS (1) [FARM]

Mk 6:56 And wherever he went, into villages or cities or **f**,

FARTHER (9) [FARTHEST]

Job 38:11 'Thus far shall you come, and no **f**,
Jer 31:39 And the measuring line shall go out **f**,
Mt 26:39 a little **f**, he threw himself on the ground
Mk 1:19 As he went a little **f**,
14:35 a little **f**, he threw himself on the ground
Ac 27:28 a little **f** on they took soundings again
1Mc 10:77 and went to Azotus as though he were going **f**.
2Es 14:18 Truth shall go **f** away,
14:33 you are here, and your people are **f** in the interior.

FARTHEST (14) [FARTHER]

Nu 22:36 at the **f** point of the boundary.
Jos 15: 1 to the wilderness of Zin at the **f** south.
17:18 you shall clear it and possess it to its **f** borders;
2Ki 19:23 I entered its **f** retreat, its densest forest.
Ne 1: 9 though your outcasts are under the **f** skies,
Job 28: 3 the **f** bound the ore in gloom and deep darkness.
Ps 65: 5 of all the ends of the earth and of the **f** seas.
65: 8 Those who live at earth's **f** bounds are awed
139: 9 of the morning and settle at the **f** limits of the sea,
Isa 41: 9 and called from its **f** corners, saying to you,
Jer 6:22 the north, a great nation is stirring from the **f** parts
25:32 and a great tempest is stirring from the **f** parts of
31: 8 and gather them from the **f** parts of the earth,
50:41 and many kings are stirring from the **f** parts of

FARTHING (KJV) See PENNY

FASCINATION (1)

Wis 4:12 For the **f** of wickedness obscures what is good,

FASHION (8) [FASHIONED, FASHIONER, FASHIONING, FASHIONS]

2Ch 32:15 or mislead you in this **f**,
Job 31:15 And did not one **f** us in the womb?
Isa 44:10 Who would **f** a god or cast an image
2Mc 15:13 Then in the same **f** another appeared,
1Es 4:12 since he is to be obeyed in this **f**?"
3Mc 4:13 be dealt with in precisely the same **f** as the others,
4Mc 5:14 tyrant urged him in this **f** to eat meat unlawfully,
10: 7 with their fingernails in a Scythian **f**.

FASHIONED‡ (11) [FASHION]

Job 10: 8 Your hands **f** and made me;
10: 9 Remember that you **f** me like clay;
Ps 119:73 Your hands have made and **f** me;
Isa 54:17 No weapon that is **f** against you shall prosper,
Wis 13:10 gold and silver **f** with skill,
19: 6 For the whole creation in its nature was **f** anew,
Pm 151: 2 My hands made a harp; my fingers **f** a lyre.
2Es 8: 8 because you give life to the body that is now **f** in
8:11 that what has been **f** may be nourished for a time;
8:14 with so great labor was **f** by your command,
4Mc 2:21 Now when God **f** human beings,

FASHIONER (2) [FASHION]

Wis 7:22 the **f** of all things, taught me.
8: 6 who more than she is **f** of what exists?

FASHIONING (2) [FASHION]

Wis 15: 7 **f** out of the same clay both the vessels
2Es 8:38 For indeed I will not concern myself about the **f**

FASHIONS (4) [FASHION]

Ps 33:15 he who **f** the hearts of them all,
Isa 44:12 The ironsmith **f** it and works it over the coals,
44:13 **f** it with planes, and marks it with a compass;
45: 9 Does the clay say to the one who **f** it,

FAST‡ (99) [FASTED, FASTER, FASTING, FASTNESS, FASTS]

Ge 20:18 For the LORD had closed **f** all the wombs of
21:18 lift up the boy and hold him **f** with your hand,
Dt 4: 4 while those of you who held **f** to
10:20 to him you shall hold **f**,
11:22 walking in all his ways, and holding **f** to him,
13: 4 him you shall serve, and to him you shall hold **f**.
30:20 obeying him, and holding **f** to him;
Jos 22: 5 to keep his commandments, and to hold **f** to him,
23: 8 but hold **f** to the LORD your God,
Jdg 4:21 he was lying **f** asleep from weariness—
2Sa 12:23 But now he is dead; why should I **f**?
18: 9 His head caught **f** in the oak,
1Ki 21: 9 She wrote in the letters, "Proclaim a **f**,
21:12 a **f** and seated Naboth at the head of the assembly.
2Ki 18: 6 For he held **f** to the LORD;
2Ch 20: 3 and proclaimed a **f** throughout all Judah.
Ezr 8:21 Then I proclaimed a **f** there, at the river Ahava,
Est 4:16 and hold a **f** on my behalf,
4:16 I and my maids will also **f** as you do.
8:10 by mounted couriers riding on **f** steeds bred from
Job 23:11 My foot has held **f** to his steps;
27: 6 I hold **f** my righteousness, and will not let it go;
37:10 and the broad waters are frozen **f**.
Ps 17: 5 My steps have held **f** to your paths;
64: 5 They hold **f** to their evil purpose;
119:90 you have established the earth, and it stands **f**.
139:10 and your right hand shall hold me **f**.
Pr 3:18 those who hold her **f** are called happy.
4: 4 and said to me, "Let your heart hold **f** my words;
Isa 47:12 Stand **f** in your enchantments
56: 2 the one who holds it **f**, who keeps the sabbath,
56: 4 the things that please me and hold **f** my covenant,
56: 6 and do not profane it, and hold **f** my covenant—
58: 3 "Why do we **f**, but you do not see?
58: 3 Look, you serve your own interest on your **f** day,
58: 4 you **f** only to quarrel and to fight and to strike
58: 5 Is such the **f** that I choose,
58: 5 you call this a **f**, a day acceptable to the LORD?
58: 6 Is not this the **f** that I choose:
Jer 8: 5 They have held **f** to deceit,
14:12 Although they **f**, I do not hear their cry,
36: 6 and on a **f** day in the hearing of the people in
36: 9 to Jerusalem proclaimed a **f** before the LORD.
50:33 all their captors have held them **f** and refuse
Da 6:12 The king answered, "The thing stands **f**,
Hos 12: 6 you, return to your God, hold **f** to love and justice,
Joel 1:14 Sanctify a **f**, call a solemn assembly.
2:15 Blow the trumpet in Zion; sanctify a **f**;
Jnh 1: 5 of the ship and had lain down, and was **f** asleep.
3: 5 they proclaimed a **f**, and everyone,
Zep 1:14 of the LORD is near, near and hastening **f**;
Zec 8:19 The **f** of the fourth month, and the **f** of the fifth, and the **f** of the seventh, and the **f** of the tenth,
Mt 6:16 "And whenever you **f**, do not look dismal,
6:17 But when you **f**, put oil on your head
9:14 saying, "Why do we and the Pharisees **f** often, but your disciples do not **f**?"
9:15 from them, and then they will **f**.
Mk 2:18 and the disciples of the Pharisees **f**, but your disciples do not **f**?"
2:19 The wedding guests cannot **f** while the bridegroom
2:19 the bridegroom with them, they cannot **f**.
2:20 and then they will **f** on that day.
Lk 5:33 like the disciples of the Pharisees, frequently **f**
5:34 "You cannot make wedding guests **f** while
5:35 and then they will **f** in those days."
8:15 hold it **f** in an honest and good heart,
18:12 I **f** twice a week; I give a tenth of all my income.'
Ac 27: 9 because even the **F** had already gone by,
Ro 12: 9 hate what is evil, hold **f** to what is good;
Php 2:16 It is by your holding **f** to the word of life
3:16 Only let us hold **f** to what we have attained.
Col 2:19 and not holding **f** to the head,
1Th 5:21 but test everything; hold **f** to what is good;
2Th 2:15 and hold **f** to the traditions that you were taught
1Ti 3: 9 they must hold **f** to the mystery of the faith with
Heb 4:14 the Son of God, let us hold **f** to our confession.
10:23 Let us hold **f** to the confession of our hope
1Pe 5:12 that this is the true grace of God. Stand **f** in it.
Rev 2:13 Yet you are holding **f** to my name,
2:25 only hold **f** to what you have until I come.
3:11 I am coming soon; hold **f** to what you have,
14:12 the commandments of God and hold **f** to the faith
AdE 4:16 "Go and gather all the Jews who are in Susa and **f**
Sir 1:19 she heightened the glory of those who held her **f**.
4:13 Whoever holds her **f** inherits glory,
49: 9 also mentioned Job who held **f** to all the ways
Bar 4: 1 All who hold her **f** will live,
1Mc 10:81 But his men stood **f**, as Jonathan had commanded,
1Es 8:50 There I proclaimed a **f** for the young men
8:73 Then I rose from my **f**,
3Mc 7:16 But those who had held **f** to God even to death
2Es 5:13 and weep as you do now, and **f** for seven days,

2Es 6:31 you will pray again and **f** again for seven days,
9:23 do not, however, **f** during them,
10: 4 but will mourn and **f** continually until I die."
4Mc 11:27 therefore, unconquered, we hold **f** to reason."

FASTED (19) [FAST]

Jdg 20:26 they **f** that day until evening.
1Sa 7: 6 They **f** that day, and said,
31:13 the tamarisk tree in Jabesh, and **f** seven days.
2Sa 1:12 **f** until evening for Saul and for his son Jonathan,
12:16 David **f**, and went in and lay all night on
12:21 You **f** and wept for the child while it was alive;
12:22 "While the child was still alive, I **f** and wept;
1Ki 21:27 he **f**, lay in the sackcloth,
1Ch 10:12 under the oak in Jabesh, and **f** seven days.
Ezr 8:23 So we **f** and petitioned our God for this,
Zec 7: 5 When you **f** and lamented in the fifth month and
7: 5 for these seventy years, was it for me that you **f**?
Mt 4: 2 He **f** forty days and forty nights,
Jdt 4:13 for the people **f** many days throughout Judea and
8: 6 She **f** all the days of her widowhood,
Bar 1: 5 they wept, and **f**, and prayed before the Lord;
1Mc 3:47 They **f** that day, put on sackcloth
2Es 5:20 So I **f** seven days, mourning and weeping,
6:35 Now after this I wept again and **f** seven days in

FASTEN (12) [FASTENED, FASTENS]

Ex 25:26 and **f** the rings to the four corners at its four legs.
28:37 You shall **f** it on the turban with a blue cord;
39:31 to **f** it on the turban above;
Lev 16: 4 **f** the linen sash, and wear the linen turban;
Isa 22:23 I will **f** him like a peg in a secure place,
41: 7 and they **f** it with nails so that it cannot be moved.
Jer 10: 4 they **f** it with hammer and nails so
Lk 12:37 he will **f** his belt and have them sit down to eat,
Jn 21:18 you used to **f** your own belt and
21:18 and someone else will **f** a belt around you
Ac 12: 8 "**F** your belt and put on your sandals."
Eph 6:14 and **f** the belt of truth around your waist,

FASTENED (18) [FASTEN]

Ex 37:13 and **f** the rings to the four corners at its four legs.
Lev 8: 7 He put the tunic on him, **f** the sash around him,
8:13 and **f** sashes around them,
Nu 19:15 every open vessel with no cover **f** on it is unclean.
Jdg 3:16 and he **f** it on his right thigh under his clothes.
1Sa 31:10 and they **f** his body to the wall of Beth-shan.
2Sa 20: 8 and over it was a belt with a sword in its sheath **f**
1Ch 10:10 and **f** his head in the temple of Dagon.
Ps 41: 8 They think that a deadly thing has **f** on me,
Isa 22:25 the peg that was **f** in a secure place will give way;
La 1:14 by his hand they were **f** together;
Eze 40:43 one handbreadth long, **f** all around the inside.
Mt 18: 6 if a great millstone were **f** around your neck
Ac 16:24 in the innermost cell and **f** their feet in the stocks.
28: 3 driven out by the heat, **f** itself on his hand.
Jdt 16: 8 she **f** her hair with a tiara and put on a linen gown
1Mc 6:37 they were **f** on each animal by special harness,
3Mc 4: 9 some were **f** by the neck to the benches of

FASTENS (2) [FASTEN]

Wis 13:15 and sets it in the wall, and **f** it there with iron.
Sir 14:24 near her house and **f** his tent peg to her walls;

FASTER (2) [FAST]

2Mc 9: 7 and giving orders to drive even **f**.
2Es 5:44 "The creation cannot move **f** than the Creator,

FASTING‡ (21) [FAST]

Ezr 9: 5 At the evening sacrifice I got up from my **f**,
Ne 1: 4 **f** and praying before the God of heaven.
9: 1 of Israel were assembled with **f** and in sackcloth,
Est 4: 3 with **f** and weeping and lamenting,
Ps 35:13 I wore sackcloth; I afflicted myself with **f**.
69:10 When I humbled my soul with **f**,
109:24 My knees are weak through **f**;
Isa 58: 4 Such **f** as you do today will not make your voice
Da 6:18 the king went to his palace and spent the night **f**;
9: 3 and supplication with **f** and sackcloth and ashes.
Joel 2:12 with **f**, with weeping, and with mourning;
Mt 6:16 so as to show others that they are **f**.
6:18 so that your **f** may be seen not by others but
Mk 2:18 Now John's disciples and the Pharisees were **f**;
Lk 2:37 but worshiped there with **f** and prayer night
Ac 13: 2 While they were worshiping the Lord and **f**,
13: 3 after **f** and praying they laid their hands on them
14:23 with prayer and **f** they entrusted them to the Lord
Tob 12: 8 with **f** is good, but better than both is almsgiving
Jdt 4: 9 and they humbled themselves with much **f**.
2Mc 13:12 and **f** and lying prostrate for three days

FASTNESS (1) [FAST]

Job 39:28 It lives on the rock and makes its home in the **f** of

FASTS (2) [FAST]

Est 9:31 concerning their **f** and their lamentations.
Sir 34:31 So if one **f** for his sins,

FAT‡ (109) [FATLING, FATLINGS, FATNESS, FATTED, FATTENED, FATTENING, FATTER]

Ge 4: 4 of the firstlings of his flock, their **f** portions.
Ge 41: 2 up out of the Nile seven sleek and **f** cows,
41: 4 and thin cows ate up the seven sleek and **f** cows.
41:18 **f** and sleek, came up out of the Nile and fed in
41:20 thin and ugly cows ate up the first seven **f** cows,
45:18 and you may enjoy the **f** of the land.'
Ex 23:18 let the **f** of my festival remain until the morning.
29:13 You shall take all the **f** that covers the entrails,
29:13 and the two kidneys with the **f** that is on them,
29:22 take the **f** of the ram, the **f** tail, the **f** that covers the
29:22 the two kidneys with the **f** that is on them,
Lev 3: 3 the **f** that covers the entrails and all the **f** that is
3: 4 two kidneys with the **f** that is on them at the loins,
3: 9 You shall present its **f** from the sacrifice
3: 9 the **f** that covers the entrails, and all the **f** that is
3:10 two kidneys with the **f** that is on them at the loins,
3:14 the **f** that covers the entrails, and all the **f** that is
3:15 two kidneys with the **f** that is on them at the loins,
3:16 All **f** is the LORD's.
3:17 you must not eat any **f** or any blood.
4: 8 He shall remove all the **f** from the bull
4: 8 the **f** that covers the entrails and all the **f** that is
4: 9 two kidneys with the **f** that is on them at the loins;
4:19 He shall remove all its **f** and turn it into smoke on
4:26 All its **f** he shall turn into smoke on the altar,
4:26 like the **f** of the sacrifice of well-being.
4:31 He shall remove all its **f**,
4:31 the **f** is removed from the offering of well-being,
4:35 You shall remove all its **f**,
4:35 as the **f** of the sheep is removed from the sacrifice
6:12 and turn into smoke the **f** pieces of the offerings
7: 3 All its **f** shall be offered:
7: 3 the broad tail, the **f** that covers the entrails,
7: 4 two kidneys with the **f** that is on them at the loins,
7:23 You shall eat no **f** of ox or sheep or goat.
7:24 The **f** of an animal that died or was torn
7:25 If any one of you eats the **f** from an animal
7:30 you shall bring the **f** with the breast,
7:31 The priest shall turn the **f** into smoke on the altar,
7:33 the sons of Aaron who offers the blood and **f** of
8:16 Moses took all the **f** that was around the entrails,
8:16 and the two kidneys with their **f**,
8:25 He took the **f**—the broad tail, all the **f** that was
8:25 and the two kidneys with their **f**—
8:26 and placed them on the **f** and on the right thigh.
9:10 the **f**, the kidneys, and the appendage of the liver
9:19 and the **f** of the ox and of the ram—
9:19 the broad tail, the **f** that covers the entrails,
9:19 the two kidneys and the **f** on them,
9:20 They first laid the **f** on the breasts,
9:20 and the **f** was turned into smoke on the altar;
9:24 and consumed the burnt offering and the **f** on
10:15 together with the offerings by fire of the **f**,
16:25 The **f** of the sin offering he shall turn into smoke
17: 6 the **f** into smoke as a pleasing odor to the LORD,
Nu 18:17 and shall turn their **f** into smoke as an offering
Dt 31:20 and they have eaten their fill and grown **f**,
32:14 with **f** of lambs and rams;
32:15 Jacob ate his fill; Jeshurun grew **f**, and kicked.
32:15 You grew **f**, bloated, and gorged!
32:38 who ate the **f** of their sacrifices,
Jdg 3:17 Now Eglon was a very **f** man.
3:22 and the **f** closed over the blade,
5: 7 they grew **f** on plunder, because you arose,
1Sa 2: 5 but those who were hungry are **f** with spoil.
2:15 Moreover, before the **f** was burned,
2:16 if the man said to him, "Let them burn the **f** first,
15:22 and to heed than the **f** of rams.
2Sa 1:22 from the **f** of the mighty,
1Ki 4:23 ten **f** oxen, and twenty pasture-fed cattle,
8:64 and the **f** pieces of the sacrifices of well-being,
8:64 and the **f** pieces of the sacrifices of well-being.
2Ch 7: 7 for there he offered the burnt offerings and the **f**
7: 7 and the grain offering and the **f** parts.
29:35 of burnt offerings there was the **f** of the offerings
35:14 the burnt offerings and the **f** parts until night;
Ne 8:10 eat the **f** and drink sweet wine and send portions
9:25 so they ate, and were filled and became **f**,
Job 15:27 because they have covered their faces with their **f**,
15:27 and gathered **f** upon their loins,
Ps 119:70 Their hearts are **f** and gross,
Isa 1:11 of burnt offerings of rams and the **f** of fed beasts;
17: 4 and the **f** of his flesh will grow lean.
34: 6 it is sated with blood, it is gorged with **f**,
34: 6 with the **f** of the kidneys of rams.
34: 7 and their soil made rich with **f**.
43:24 or satisfied me with the **f** of your sacrifices.
Jer 5:28 they have grown **f** and sleek.
Eze 34: 3 You eat the **f**, you clothe yourselves with
34:16 but the **f** and the strong I will destroy.
34:20 I myself will judge between the **f** sheep and
39:19 You shall eat **f** until you are filled,
44: 7 when you offer to me my food, the **f** and
44:15 and they shall attend me to offer me the **f** and
Zec 11:16 but devours the flesh of the **f** ones,
Mt 22: 4 my oxen and my **f** calves have been slaughtered,
Jdt 16:16 and the **f** of all whole burnt offerings to you is
Sir 47: 2 the **f** is set apart from the offering of well-being,
Aza 1:17 or with tens of thousands of **f** lambs;
Bel 1:27 Then Daniel took pitch, **f**, and hair,
1Es 1:14 the priests were offering the **f** until nightfall;
9:51 eat the **f** and drink the sweet,

FATAL (5)

Pr 21:25 The craving of the lazy person is **f**,
Jer 17:16 nor have I desired the **f** day.
42:20 that you have made a **f** mistake.
Tob 14:10 Ahikar escaped the **f** trap that Nadab had set
4Mc 8:26 and such a **f** stubbornness please us,

FATE‡ (23)

Nu 16:29 or if a natural **f** comes on them,
1Sa 2:34 The **f** of your two sons, Hophni and Phinehas,
2Ki 7:13 since those left here will suffer the **f** of
Job 18:20 They of the west are appalled at their **f**,
Ps 49:13 Such is the **f** of the foolhardy,
Ecc 2:14 Yet I perceived that the same **f** befalls all of them.
3:19 **f** of humans and the **f** of animals is the same;
9: 2 since the same **f** comes to all,
9: 3 that the same **f** comes to everyone.
Isa 17:14 This is the **f** of those who despoil us,
Jer 49:20 surely their fold shall be appalled at their **f**.
50:45 surely their fold shall be appalled at their **f**.
La 3:51 at the **f** of all the young women in my city.
Wis 17:17 they were seized, and endured the inescapable **f**;
19: 4 For the **f** they deserved drew them on to this end,
Sir 38:22 Remember his **f**, for yours is like it;
2Mc 9:28 came to the end of his life by a most pitiable **f**,
13: 7 By such a **f** it came about that Menelaus
3Mc 3: 9 be left to its **f** when it had committed no offense.
5: 8 in a glorious manifestation rescue them from the **f**
6:10 and destroy us, Lord, by whatever **f** you choose.
2Es 3:10 And the same **f** befell all of them:

FATHER‡ (1125) [FATHER'S, FATHER-IN-LAW, FATHERLESS, FATHERS, FATHERS', GRANDFATHER, GRANDFATHER'S]

A. BECAME THE FATHER OF (84)
B. FATHER ... MOTHER (69)
C. FATHER DAVID (52)
D. WAS THE FATHER OF (19)
E. *GOD THE FATHER (15)
F. FATHER IN HEAVEN (14)
G. FATHER ABRAHAM (13)
H. *GOD AND FATHER (13)
I. *GOD OUR FATHER (11)
J. HEAVENLY FATHER (7)

Ge 2:24 a man leaves his **f** and his mother and clings
4:18 and Irad was the **f** of Mehujael, D
4:18 and Mehujael the **f** of Methushael,
4:18 and Methushael the **f** of Lamech.
5: 3 he became the **f** of a son in his likeness, A
5: 4 The days of Adam after he became the **f** A
5: 6 he became the **f** of Enosh. A
5: 9 he became the **f** of Kenan. A
5:12 he became the **f** of Mahalalel. A
5:15 he became the **f** of Jared. A
5:18 he became the **f** of Enoch. A
5:21 he became the **f** of Methuselah. A
5:25 he became the **f** of Lamech. A
5:28 he became the **f** of a son; A
5:32 Noah became the **f** of Shem, Ham, and Japheth. A
9:18 Ham was the **f** of Canaan. D
9:22 And Ham, the **f** of Canaan,
9:22 the father of Canaan, saw the nakedness of his **f**,
9:23 and covered the nakedness of their **f**;
10: 8 Cush became the **f** of Nimrod; A
10:13 Egypt became the **f** of Ludim, Anamim, A
10:15 Canaan became the **f** of Sidon his firstborn, A
10:21 To Shem also, the **f** of all the children of Eber,
10:24 Arpachshad became the **f** of Shelah; A
10:24 and Shelah became the **f** of Eber. A
10:26 Joktan became the **f** of Almodad, Sheleph, A
11:10 he became the **f** of Arpachshad two years after A
11:12 he became the **f** of Shelah; A
11:14 he became the **f** of Eber; A
11:16 he became the **f** of Peleg; A
11:18 he became the **f** of Reu; A
11:20 he became the **f** of Serug; A
11:22 he became the **f** of Nahor; A
11:24 he became the **f** of Terah; A
11:26 he became the **f** of Abram, Nahor, and Haran. A
11:27 Terah was the **f** of Abram, Nahor, and Haran; D
11:27 and Haran was the **f** of Lot. D
11:28 before his **f** Terah in the land of his birth,
11:29 the daughter of Haran the **f** of Milcah and Iscah.
17:20 he shall be the **f** of twelve princes,
19:31 the firstborn said to the younger, "Our **f** is old,
19:32 Come, let us make our **f** drink wine,
19:32 so that we may preserve offspring through our **f**."
19:33 So they made their **f** drink wine that night;
19:33 and the firstborn went in, and lay with her **f**;
19:34 "Look, I lay last night with my **f**;
19:34 so that we may preserve offspring through our **f**."
19:35 So they made their **f** drink wine that night also;
19:36 the daughters of Lot became pregnant by their **f**.
20:12 of my **f** but not the daughter of my mother;
22: 7 Isaac said to his **f** Abraham, "Father!" G
22: 7 Isaac said to his father Abraham, "**F**!"
22:21 Buz his brother, Kemuel the **f** of Aram,
22:23 Bethuel became the **f** of Rebekah. A
25: 3 Jokshan was the **f** of Sheba and Dedan. D
25:19 Abraham was the **f** of Isaac, D
26: 3 the oath that I swore to your **f** Abraham. G
26:15 in the days of his **f** Abraham.) G
26:18 that had been dug in the days of his **f** Abraham; G
26:18 he gave them the names that his **f** had given them.
26:24 "I am the God of your **f** Abraham; G
27: 6 "I heard your **f** say to your brother Esau,
27: 9 I may prepare from them savory food for your **f**,

Ge 27:10 and you shall take it to your **f** to eat,
27:12 Perhaps my **f** will feel me,
27:14 mother prepared savory food, such as his **f** loved.
27:18 So he went in to his **f**, and said, "My **f**";
27:19 Jacob said to his **f**, "I am Esau your firstborn.
27:22 So Jacob went up to his **f** Isaac,
27:26 Then his **f** Isaac said to him,
27:30 from the presence of his **f** Isaac,
27:31 and brought it to his **f**.
27:31 And he said to his **f**, "Let my **f** sit up and eat
27:32 His **f** Isaac said to him, "Who are you?"
27:34 and said to his **f**, "Bless me, me also, **f**!"
27:38 Esau said to his **f**, "Have you only one blessing, **f**?
27:38 Bless me, me also, **f**!"
27:39 Then his **f** Isaac answered him:
27:41 of the blessing with which his **f** had blessed him,
27:41 "The days of mourning for my **f** are approaching;
28: 2 to the house of Bethuel, your mother's **f**;
28: 7 and that Jacob had obeyed his **f** and his mother
28: 8 the Canaanite women did not please his **f** Isaac,
28:13 the God of Abraham your **f** and the God of Isaac;
29:12 and she ran and told her **f**.
31: 1 from what belonged to our **f**."
31: 5 "I see that your **f** does not regard me as favorably
31: 5 But the God of my **f** has been with me.
31: 6 that I have served your **f** with all my strength;
31: 7 yet your **f** has cheated me
31: 9 Thus God has taken away the livestock of your **f**,
31:16 that God has taken away from our **f** belongs to us
31:18 to go to his **f** Isaac in the land of Canaan.
31:29 but the God of your **f** spoke to me last night,
31:35 And she said to her **f**,
31:42 If the God of my **f**,
31:53 the God of their **f**—"judge between us."
31:53 So Jacob swore by the Fear of his **f** Isaac,
32: 9 of my **f** Abraham and God of my father Isaac, G
32: 9 of my father Abraham and God of my **f** Isaac,
33:19 And from the sons of Hamor, Shechem's **f**,
34: 4 So Shechem spoke to his **f** Hamor, saying,
34: 6 And Hamor the **f** of Shechem went out to Jacob
34:11 Shechem also said to her **f** and to her brothers,
34:13 and his **f** Hamor deceitfully,
35:18 but his **f** called him Benjamin.
35:27 Jacob came to his **f** Isaac at Mamre,
36:24 as he pastured the donkeys of his **f** Zibeon.
36:43 the clans of Edom (that is, Esau, the **f** of Edom),
37: 1 Jacob settled in the land where his **f** had lived as
37: 2 and Joseph brought a bad report of them to their **f**.
37: 4 that their **f** loved him more than all his brothers,
37:10 But when he told it to his **f** and to his brothers,
37:10 his **f** rebuked him, and said to him,
37:11 but his **f** kept the matter in mind.
37:22 of their hand and restore him to his **f**.
37:32 to their **f**, and they said, "This we have found;
37:35 Thus his **f** bewailed him.
42:13 the youngest, however, is now with our **f**,
42:29 they came to their **f** Jacob in the land of Canaan,
42:32 We are twelve brothers, sons of our **f**;
42:32 youngest is now with our **f** in the land of Canaan.'
42:35 they and their **f** saw their bundles of money,
42:36 And their **f** Jacob said to them,
42:37 Then Reuben said to his **f**,
43: 2 their **f** said to them, "Go again,
43: 7 saying, 'Is your **f** still alive?
43: 8 Then Judah said to his **f** Israel,
43:11 Then their **f** Israel said to them, "If it must be so,
43:23 of your **f** must have put treasure in your sacks
43:27 "Is your **f** well, the old man of whom you spoke?
43:28 They said, "Your servant our **f** is well;
44:17 but as for you, go up in peace to your **f**."
44:19 saying, 'Have you a **f** or a brother?'
44:20 And we said to my lord, 'We have a **f**,
44:20 of his mother's children, and his **f** loves him.'
44:22 We said to my lord, 'The boy cannot leave his **f**,
44:22 for if he should leave his **f**, his **f** would die.'
44:24 to your servant my **f** we told him the words
44:25 And when our **f** said, 'Go again,
44:27 Then your servant my **f** said to us,
44:30 when I come to your servant my **f** and the boy is
44:31 the gray hairs of your servant our **f** with sorrow
44:32 your servant became surety for the boy to my **f**,
44:32 the blame in the sight of my **f** all my life.'
44:34 can I go back to my **f** if the boy is not with me?
44:34 to see the suffering that would come upon my **f**."
45: 3 Is my **f** still alive?"
45: 8 he has made me a **f** to Pharaoh,
45: 9 Hurry and go up to my **f** and say to him,
45:13 You must tell my **f** how greatly I am honored
45:13 Hurry and bring my **f** down here."
45:18 Take your **f** and your households and come to me,
45:19 and bring your **f**, and come.
45:23 To his **f** he sent the following:
45:23 bread, and provision for his **f** on the journey.
45:25 and came to their **f** Jacob in the land of Canaan.
45:27 the spirit of their **f** Jacob revived.
46: 1 he offered sacrifices to the God of his **f** Isaac.
46: 3 Then he said, "I am God, the God of your **f**;
46: 5 and the sons of Israel carried their **f** Jacob,
46:29 and went up to meet his **f** Israel in Goshen.
47: 1 "My **f** and my brothers, with their flocks
47: 5 "Your **f** and your brothers have come to you.
47: 6 settle your **f** and your brothers in the best part of
47: 7 Then Joseph brought in his **f** Jacob,
47:11 Joseph settled his **f** and his brothers,
47:12 And Joseph provided his **f**, his brothers,
48: 1 After this Joseph was told, "Your **f** is ill."
48: 9 Joseph said to his **f**, "They are my sons,

Ge 48:17 When Joseph saw that his **f** laid his right hand on
48:18 Joseph said to his **f**, "Not so, my **f**!
48:19 his **f** refused, and said, "I know, my son, I know;
49: 2 of Jacob; listen to Israel your **f**.
49:25 by the God of your **f**,
49:26 of your **f** are stronger than the blessings of
49:28 and this is what their **f** said to them
50: 2 the physicians in his service to embalm his **f**.
50: 5 My **f** made me swear an oath;
50: 5 therefore let me go up, so that I may bury my **f**;
50: 6 Pharaoh answered, "Go up, and bury your **f**,
50: 7 So Joseph went up to bury his **f**.
50:10 a time of mourning for his **f** seven days.
50:14 After he had buried his **f**,
50:14 and all who had gone up with him to bury his **f**.
50:15 Realizing that their **f** was dead,
50:16 "Your **f** gave this instruction before he died,
50:17 the crime of the servants of the God of your **f**."
Ex 2:18 When they returned to their **f** Reuel, he said,
3: 6 He said further, "I am the God of your **f**,
18: 4 "The God of my **f** was my help,
20:12 Honor your **f** and your mother, B
21:15 strikes **f** or mother shall be put to death. B
21:17 curses **f** or mother shall be put to death. B
22:17 But if her **f** refuses to give her to him,
40:15 as you anointed their **f**, that they may serve me
Lev 18: 7 You shall not uncover the nakedness of your **f**,
18: 8 it is the nakedness of your **f**.
18:11 begotten by your **f**, since she is your sister.
19: 3 You shall each revere your mother and **f**,
20: 9 All who curse **f** or mother shall be put to death; B
20: 9 having cursed **f** or mother, B
20:17 a daughter of his **f** or a daughter of his mother,
21: 2 his mother, his **f**, his son, his daughter,
21: 9 she profanes her **f**; she shall be burned to death.
21:11 not defile himself even for his **f** or mother. B
24:10 and whose **f** was an Egyptian came out among
Nu 3: 4 as priests in the lifetime of their **f** Aaron.
6: 7 Even if their **f** or mother, brother or sister, B
12:14 "If her **f** had but spit in her face,
26:29 and Machir was the **f** of Gilead; D
26:58 Now Kohath was the **f** of Amram. D
27: 3 "Our **f** died in the wilderness;
27: 4 the name of our **f** be taken away from his clan
27: 7 and pass the inheritance of their **f** on to them.
27:11 And if his **f** has no brothers,
30: 4 and her **f** hears of her vow or her pledge
30: 5 if her **f** expresses disapproval to her at the time
30: 5 her **f** had expressed to her his disapproval.
30:16 and a **f** and his daughter while she is still young
Dt 5:16 Honor your **f** and your mother, B
21:13 mourning for her **f** and mother; B
21:18 son who will not obey his **f** and mother, B
21:19 then his **f** and his mother shall take hold of him B
22:15 The **f** of the young woman and her mother shall
22:16 The **f** of the young woman shall say to the elders:
22:19 the young woman's **f**) because he has slandered
22:29 of silver to the young woman's **f**,
27:16 "Cursed be anyone who dishonors **f** or mother." B
27:22 whether the daughter of his **f** or the daughter
32: 6 Is not he your **f**, who created you,
32: 7 ask your **f**, and he will inform you;
33: 9 said of his **f** and mother, "I regard them not"; B
Jos 2:13 that you will spare my **f** and mother, B
2:18 not gather into your house your **f** and mother, B
6:23 along with her **f**, her mother, her brothers, B
15:13 that is, Hebron (Arba was the **f** of Anak). D
15:18 she urged him to ask her **f** for a field.
17: 1 the **f** of Gilead, were allotted Gilead and Bashan,
17: 4 an inheritance among the kinsmen of their **f**.
21:11 They gave them Kiriath-arba (Arba being the **f**
24: 3 Then I took your **f** Abraham from beyond G
24:32 **f** of Shechem, for one hundred pieces of money;
Jdg 1:14 she urged him to ask her **f** for a field.
6:25 pull down the altar of Baal that belongs to your **f**,
8:32 of his **f** Joash at Ophrah of the Abiezrites.
9:17 for my **f** fought for you, and risked his life,
9:28 and Zebul his officer serve the men of Hamor **f**
9:56 against his **f** in killing his seventy brothers;
11: 1 Gilead was the **f** of Jephthah. D
11:36 to him, "My **f**, if you have opened your mouth to
11:37 she said to her **f**, "Let this thing be done for me:
11:39 At the end of two months, she returned to her **f**,
14: 2 Then he came up, and told his **f** and mother, B
14: 3 But his **f** and mother said to him, B
14: 3 But Samson said to his **f**, "Get her for me,
14: 4 His **f** and mother did not know that this was B
14: 5 Then Samson went down with his **f** and mother B
14: 6 not tell his **f** or his mother what he had done. B
14: 9 When he came to his **f** and mother, B
14:10 His **f** went down to the woman,
14:16 "Look, I have not told my **f** or my mother. B
15: 1 But her **f** would not allow him to go in.
15: 2 Her **f** said, "I was sure that you had rejected her;
15: 6 the Philistines came up, and burned her and her **f**.
16:31 and Eshtaol in the tomb of his **f** Manoah.
17:10 "Stay with me, and be to me a **f** and a priest,
18:19 and come with us, and be to us a **f** and a priest.
19: 3 girl's **f** saw him and came with joy to meet him.
19: 4 His father-in-law, the girl's **f**, made him stay,
19: 5 but the girl's **f** said to his son-in-law,
19: 6 and the girl's **f** said to the man,
19: 8 and the girl's **f** said, "Fortify yourself."
19: 9 his father-in-law, the girl's **f**, said to him, "Look,
Ru 2:11 and how you left your **f** and mother B
4:17 he became the **f** of Jesse, the father of David. A
4:17 he became the father of Jesse, the **f** of David.

Ru 4:18 Perez became the **f** of Hezron, A
1Sa 2:25 But they would not listen to the voice of their **f**;
9: 3 Now the donkeys of Kish, Saul's **f**, had strayed.
9: 5 or my **f** will stop worrying about the donkeys
10: 2 and now your **f** has stopped worrying about them
10:12 man of the place answered, "And who is their **f**?"
14: 1 But he did not tell his **f**.
14:27 But Jonathan had not heard his **f** charge the troops
14:28 "Your **f** strictly charged the troops with an oath,
14:29 Then Jonathan said, "My **f** has troubled the land;
14:51 Kish was the **f** of Saul, D
14:51 and Ner the **f** of Abner was the son of Abiel.
17:34 "Your servant used to keep sheep for his **f**;
19: 2 "My **f** Saul is trying to kill you;
19: 3 and stand beside my **f** in the field where you are,
19: 3 and I will speak to my **f** about you;
19: 4 Jonathan spoke well of David to his **f** Saul,
20: 1 And what is my sin against your **f** that he is trying
20: 2 My **f** does nothing either great or small
20: 2 and why should my **f** hide this from me?
20: 3 "Your **f** knows well that you like me;
20: 6 If your **f** misses me at all, then say,
20: 8 why should you bring me to your **f**?"
20: 9 that it was decided by my **f** that evil should come
20:10 "Who will tell me if your **f** answers you harshly?"
20:12 When I have sounded out my **f**,
20:13 But if my **f** intends to do you harm,
20:13 as he has been with my **f**.
20:32 Then Jonathan answered his **f** Saul,
20:33 so Jonathan knew that it was the decision of his **f**
20:34 and because his **f** had disgraced him.
22: 3 "Please let my **f** and mother come to you, B
23:17 for the hand of my **f** Saul shall not find you;
23:17 my **f** Saul also knows that this is so."
24:11 my **f**, see the corner of your cloak in my hand;
2Sa 2:32 up Asahel and buried him in the tomb of his **f**,
3: 8 of your **f** Saul, to his brothers, and to his friends,
6:21 in place of your **f** and all his household,
7:14 I will be a **f** to him, and he shall be a son to me.
9: 7 for the sake of your **f** Jonathan;
10: 2 just as his **f** dealt loyally with me."
10: 2 to console him concerning his **f**.
10: 3 that David is honoring your **f** just
13: 5 and when your **f** comes to see you, say to him,
16:19 Just as I have served your **f**, so I will serve you."
16:21 that you have made yourself odious to your **f**,
17: 8 "You know that your **f** and his men are warriors,
17: 8 Besides, your **f** is expert in war;
17:10 for all Israel knows that your **f** is a warrior,
17:23 he died and was buried in the tomb of his **f**.
19:37 near the graves of my **f** and my mother. B
21:14 in the tomb of his **f** Kish;
1Ki 1: 6 His **f** had never at any time displeased him
2:12 So Solomon sat on the throne of his **f** David; C
2:24 and placed me on the throne of my **f** David, C
2:26 the ark of the Lord GOD before my **f** David, C
2:26 you shared in all the hardships my **f** endured."
2:32 because, without the knowledge of my **f** David, C
2:44 the evil that you did to my **f** David; C
3: 3 walking in the statutes of his **f** David; C
3: 6 to your servant my **f** David, because he walked C
3: 7 of my **f** David, although I am only a little child; C
3:14 and my commandments, as your **f** David walked, C
5: 1 that they had anointed him king in place of his **f**;
5: 3 "You know that my **f** David could not build C
5: 5 as the LORD said to my **f** David, 'Your son, C
6:12 which I made to your **f** David. C
7:14 whose **f**, a man of Tyre, had been an artisan
7:51 in the things that his **f** David had dedicated, C
8:15 with his mouth to my **f** David, C
8:17 My **f** David had it in mind to build a house for C
8:18 But the LORD said to my **f** David, C
8:20 for I have risen in the place of my **f** David; C
8:24 for your servant my **f** David as you declared C
8:25 keep for your servant my **f** David C
8:26 which you promised to your servant my **f** David. C
9: 4 before me, as David your **f** walked, with integrity
9: 5 as I promised your **f** David, saying, C
11: 4 as was the heart of his **f** David. C
11: 6 as his **f** David had done. C
11:12 of your **f** David I will not do it in your lifetime; C
11:17 with some Edomites who were servants of his **f**.
11:27 up the gap in the wall of the city of his **f** David. C
11:33 and my ordinances, as his **f** David did. C
11:43 and was buried in the city of his **f** David; C
12: 4 "Your **f** made our yoke heavy.
12: 4 of your **f** and his heavy yoke that he placed on us,
12: 6 the older men who had attended his **f** Solomon
12: 9 'Lighten the yoke that your **f** put on us'?"
12:10 'Your **f** made our yoke heavy,
12:11 Now, whereas my **f** laid on you a heavy yoke,
12:11 My **f** disciplined you with whips,
12:14 "My **f** made your yoke heavy,
12:14 my **f** disciplined you with whips,
13:11 that he had spoken to the king, they told to their **f**.
13:12 Their **f** said to them, "Which way did he go?"
15: 3 He committed all the sins that his **f** did
15: 3 like the heart of his **f** David. C
15:11 as his **f** David had done. C
15:15 the votive gifts of his **f** and his own votive gifts—
15:19 like that between my **f** and your **f**:
15:24 with his ancestors in the city of his **f** David; C
19:20 and said, "Let me kiss my **f** and my mother, B
20:34 the towns that my **f** took from your **f**;
20:34 in Damascus, as my **f** did in Samaria."
22:43 He walked in all the way of his **f** Asa;
22:46 in the land in the days of his **f** Asa,

1Ki 22:50 with his ancestors in the city of his f David; C
22:52 and walked in the way of his f and mother, B
22:53 the God of Israel, to anger, just as his f had done.
2Ki 2:12 Elisha kept watching and crying out, "F, f!
3: 2 though not like his f and mother, B
3: 2 he removed the pillar of Baal that his f had made.
4:18 he went out one day to his f among the reapers.
4:19 He complained to his f, "Oh, my head, my head!"
4:19 f said to his servant, "Carry him to his mother."
5:13 But his servants approached and said to him, "F,
6:21 the king of Israel saw them he said to Elisha, "F,
9:25 and I rode side by side behind his f Ahab how
13:14 and wept before him, crying, "My f, my f!
13:25 the towns that he had taken from his f Jehoahaz
14: 3 in all things he did as his f Joash had done.
14: 5 he killed his servants who had murdered his f
14:21 and made him king to succeed his f Amaziah.
15: 3 just as his f Amaziah had done.
15:34 just as his f Uzziah had done.
21: 3 the high places that his f Hezekiah had destroyed;
21:20 as his f Manasseh had done.
21:21 He walked in all the way in which his f walked,
21:21 served the idols that his f served,
22: 2 and walked in all the way of his f David; C
23:30 and made him king in place of his f.
23:34 of Josiah king in place of his f Josiah,
24: 9 just as his f had done.
1Ch 1:10 Cush became the f of Nimrod; A
1:11 Egypt became the f of Ludim, Anamim, A
1:13 Canaan became the f of Sidon his firstborn, A
1:18 Arpachshad became the f of Shelah; A
1:18 and Shelah became the f of Eber. A
1:20 Joktan became the f of Almodad, Sheleph, A
1:34 Abraham became the f of Isaac. A
2:10 Ram became the f of Amminadab, A
2:10 and Amminadab became the f of Nahshon, A
2:11 Nahshon became the f of Salma, Salma of Boaz, A
2:13 Jesse became the f of Eliab his firstborn, A
2:17 and the f of Amasa was Jether the Ishmaelite.
2:20 Hur became the f of Uri, A
2:20 and Uri became the f of Bezalel. A
2:21 of Machir f of Gilead, whom he married
2:22 and Segub became the f of Jair, A
2:23 All these were descendants of Machir, f of Gilead.
2:24 of Hezron bore him Ashhur, f of Tekoa.
2:36 Attai became the f of Nathan, A
2:37 Zabad became the f of Ephlal, A
2:38 Obed became the f of Jehu, and Jehu of Azariah. A
2:39 Azariah became the f of Helez, A
2:40 Eleasah became the f of Sismai, A
2:41 Shallum became the f of Jekamiah, A
2:42 Mesha his firstborn, who was f of Ziph.
2:42 The sons of Mareshah f of Hebron.
2:44 Shema became f of Raham, f of Jorkeam;
2:44 and Rekem became the f of Shammai. A
2:45 and Maon was the f of Beth-zur. D
2:46 and Haran became the f of Gazez. A
2:49 She also bore Shaaph f of Madmannah,
2:49 Sheva f of Machbenah and f of Gibea;
2:50 Shobal f of Kiriath-jearim,
2:51 Salma f of Bethlehem, and Hareph f of Beth-gader.
2:52 Shobal f of Kiriath-jearim had other sons:
2:55 f of the house of Rechab.
4: 2 Reaiah son of Shobal became the f of Jahath, A
4: 2 and Jahath became the f of Ahumai and Lahad. A
4: 4 and Penuel was the f of Gedor, D
4: 4 and Ezer the f of Hushah.
4: 4 the firstborn of Ephrathah, the f of Bethlehem.
4: 5 Ashhur f of Tekoa had two wives,
4: 8 Koz became the f of Anub, Zobebah, A
4:11 the brother of Shuhah became the f of Mehir, A
4:11 who was the f of Eshton. D
4:12 Eshton became the f of Beth-rapha, Paseah, A
4:12 Paseah, and Tehinnah the f of Ir-nahash.
4:14 Meonothai became the f of Ophrah; A
4:14 and Seraiah became the f of Joab father A
4:14 Joab f of Ge-harashim, so-called because
4:17 Shammai, and Ishbah f of Eshtemoa.
4:18 And his Judean wife bore Jered f of Gedor,
4:18 Heber f of Soco, and Jekuthiel f of Zanoah.
4:21 Er f of Lecah, Laadah f of Mareshah,
6: 4 Eleazar became the f of Phinehas, A
6:11 Azariah became the f of Amariah, A
7:14 she bore Machir the f of Gilead.
7:22 And their f Ephraim mourned many days,
7:31 Heber and Malchiel, who was the f of Birzaith. D
7:32 Heber became the f of Japhlet, Shomer, Hotham, A
8: 1 Benjamin became the f of Bela his firstborn, A
8: 7 Heglam, who became the f of Uzza and Ahihud. A
8:29 Jeiel the f of Gibeon lived in Gibeon,
8:32 who became the f of Shimeah. A
8:33 Ner became the f of Kish, Kish of Saul, A
8:34 and Merib-baal became the f of Micah. A
8:36 Ahaz became the f of Jehoaddah; A
8:36 and Jehoaddah became the f of Alemeth, A
8:36 Zimri became the f of Moza. A
8:37 Moza became the f of Binea; A
9:35 In Gibeon lived the f of Gibeon, Jeiel,
9:38 and Mikloth became the f of Shimeam; A
9:39 Ner became the f of Kish, Kish of Saul, A
9:40 and Merib-baal became the f of Micah. A
9:42 Ahaz became the f of Jarah, and Jarah of A
9:42 and Zimri became the f of Moza. A
9:43 Moza became the f of Binea; A
14: 3 David became the f of more sons and daughters. A
17:13 I will be a f to him, and he shall be a son to me.
19: 2 for his f dealt loyally with me."
1Ch 19: 2 to console him concerning his f.
19: 3 that he is honoring your f?
22:10 He shall be a son to me, and I will be a f to him,
24: 2 But Nadab and Abihu died before their f,
25: 3 six, under the direction of their f Jeduthun,
25: 6 of their f for the music in the house of the LORD
26:10 not the firstborn, his f made him chief),
28: 6 and I will be a f to him.
28: 9 you, my son Solomon, know the God of your f,
29:23 succeeding his f David as king; C
2Ch 1: 8 and steadfast love to my f David, C
1: 9 let your promise to my f David now be fulfilled, C
2: 3 with my f David and sent him cedar C
2: 7 whom my f David provided. C
2:14 of one of the Danite women, his f a Tyrian.
2:14 the artisans of my lord, your f David. C
2:17 after the census that his f David had taken; C
3: 1 where the LORD had appeared to his f David, C
5: 1 in the things that his f David had dedicated, C
6: 4 with his mouth to my f David, C
6: 7 My f David had it in mind to build a house for C
6: 8 But the LORD said to my f David, C
6:10 for I have succeeded my f David, C
6:15 my f David, what you promised to him. C
6:16 my f David, that which you promised him, C
7:17 if you walk before me, as your f David walked, C
7:18 as I made covenant with your f David saying, C
8:14 According to the ordinance of his f David, C
9:31 and was buried in the city of his f David; C
10: 4 "Your f made our yoke heavy.
10: 4 of your f and his heavy yoke that he placed on us,
10: 6 the older men who had attended his f Solomon
10: 9 'Lighten the yoke that your f put on us'?"
10:10 'Your f made our yoke heavy,
10:11 Now, whereas my f laid on you a heavy yoke,
10:11 My f disciplined you with whips,
10:14 "My f made your yoke heavy, but I will add to it;
10:14 my f disciplined you with whips,
11:21 became the f of twenty-eight sons and sixty A
13:21 became the f of twenty-two sons and sixteen A
15:18 the votive gifts of his f and his own votive gifts—
16: 3 like that between my f and your f;
17: 2 in the cities of Ephraim that his f Asa had taken.
17: 3 because he walked in the earlier ways of his f;
17: 4 of his f and walked in his commandments,
20:32 in the way of his f Asa and did not turn aside
21: 3 Their f gave them many gifts, of silver, gold,
21: 4 When Jehoram had ascended the throne of his f
21:12 "Thus says the LORD, the God of your f David: C
21:12 of your f Jehoshaphat or in the ways of King Asa
22: 4 after the death of his f they were his counselors,
24: 3 and he became the f of sons and daughters. A
24:22 Zechariah's f, had shown him, but killed his son.
25: 3 he killed his servants who had murdered his f
26: 1 and made him king to succeed his f Amaziah.
26: 4 just as his f Amaziah had done.
27: 2 of the LORD just as his f Uzziah had done—
33: 3 the high places that his f Hezekiah had pulled
33:22 as his f Manasseh had done.
33:22 to all the images that his f Manasseh had made,
33:23 as his f Manasseh had humbled himself,
36: 1 and made him king to succeed his f in Jerusalem.
Ne 12:10 Jeshua was the f of Joiakim, D
12:10 Joiakim the f of Eliashib,
12:10 the father of Eliashib, Eliashib the f of Joiada,
12:11 Joiada the f of Jonathan, and Jonathan the f of
Est 2: 7 his cousin, for she had neither f nor mother; B
2: 7 and when her f and her mother died, B
Job 15:10 the aged are on our side, those older than your f.
17:14 'You are my f,' and to the worm, 'My mother,'
29:16 I was a f to the needy,
31:18 from my youth I reared the orphan like a f, and
38:28 "Has the rain a f, or who has begotten the drops
42:15 and their f gave them an inheritance along
Ps 27:10 If my f and mother forsake me, B
68: 5 F of orphans and protector of widows is God
89:26 He shall cry to me, 'You are my F, my God,
103:13 As a f has compassion for his children,
109:14 May the iniquity of his f be remembered before
Pr 3:12 as a f the son in whom he delights.
4: 3 When I was a son with my f, tender,
10: 1 A wise child makes a glad f,
15:20 A wise child makes a glad f,
17:25 to their f and bitterness to her who bore them.
19:13 A stupid child is ruin to a f,
19:26 violence to their f and chase away their mother B
20:20 If you curse f or mother, B
23:22 Listen to your f who begot you,
23:24 The f of the righteous will greatly rejoice;
23:25 Let your f and mother be glad; B
28:24 Anyone who robs f or mother and says, B
30:17 a f and scorns to obey a mother will be pecked out
Isa 8: 4 child knows how to call "My f" or "My mother,"
9: 6 Mighty God, Everlasting F, Prince of Peace.
14:21 for his sons because of the guilt of their f.
22:21 and he shall be a f to the inhabitants of Jerusalem
45:10 Woe to anyone who says to a f,
51: 2 to Abraham your f and to Sarah who bore you;
63:16 For you are our f, though Abraham does
63:16 you, O LORD, are our f;
64: 8 Yet, O LORD, you are our F;
Jer 2:27 "You are my f," and to a stone,
3: 4 Have you not just now called to me, "My F,
3:19 And I thought you would call me, My F,
20:15 Cursed be the man who brought the news to my f,
22:11 who succeeded his f Josiah,
22:15 Did not your f eat and drink and do justice
Jer 31: 9 for I have become a f to Israel,
Eze 16: 3 your f was an Amorite, and your mother a Hittite.
16:45 Your mother was a Hittite and your f an Amorite.
18:11 of these things (though his f does none of them),
18:14 a son who sees all the sins that his f has done,
18:18 As for his f, because he practiced extortion,
18:19 not the son suffer for the iniquity of the f?"
22: 7 F and mother are treated with contempt in you; B
44:25 for f or mother, however, and for son or B
Da 5: 2 that his f Nebuchadnezzar had taken out of
5:11 of your f he was found to have enlightenment,
5:11 Your f, King Nebuchadnezzar,
5:13 whom my f the king brought from Judah?
5:18 God gave your f Nebuchadnezzar kingship,
Am 2: 7 f and son go in to the same girl,
Mic 7: 6 the f with contempt, the daughter rises up
Mal 1: 6 A son honors his f, and servants their master.
1: 6 If then I am a f, where is the honor due me?
2:10 Have we not all one f?
Mt 1: 2 Abraham was the f of Isaac, D
1: 2 and Isaac the f of Jacob,
1: 2 and Jacob the f of Judah and his brothers,
1: 3 and Judah the f of Perez and Zerah by Tamar,
1: 3 and Perez the f of Hezron,
1: 3 and Hezron the f of Aram,
1: 4 and Aram the f of Aminadab,
1: 4 and Aminadab the f of Nahshon,
1: 4 and Nahshon the f of Salmon,
1: 5 and Salmon the f of Boaz by Rahab,
1: 5 and Boaz the f of Obed by Ruth,
1: 5 and Obed the f of Jesse,
1: 6 and Jesse the f of King David.
1: 6 David was the f of Solomon by the wife of Uriah, D
1: 7 and Solomon the f of Rehoboam,
1: 7 and Rehoboam the f of Abijah,
1: 7 and Abijah the f of Asaph,
1: 8 and Asaph the f of Jehoshaphat,
1: 8 and Jehoshaphat the f of Joram,
1: 8 and Joram the f of Uzziah,
1: 9 and Uzziah the f of Jotham,
1: 9 and Jotham the f of Ahaz,
1: 9 and Ahaz the f of Hezekiah,
1:10 and Hezekiah the f of Manasseh,
1:10 and Manasseh the f of Amos,
1:10 and Amos the f of Josiah,
1:11 and Josiah the f of Jechoniah and his brothers,
1:12 Jechoniah was the f of Salathiel, D
1:12 and Salathiel the f of Zerubbabel,
1:13 and Zerubbabel the f of Abiud,
1:13 and Abiud the f of Eliakim,
1:13 and Eliakim the f of Azor,
1:14 and Azor the f of Zadok,
1:14 and Zadok the f of Achim,
1:14 and Achim the f of Eliud,
1:15 and Eliud the f of Eleazar,
1:15 and Eleazar the f of Matthan,
1:15 and Matthan the f of Jacob,
1:16 and Jacob the f of Joseph the husband of Mary,
2:22 over Judea in place of his f Herod,
4:21 in the boat with their f Zebedee,
4:22 Immediately they left the boat and their f,
5:16 and give glory to your F in heaven. F
5:45 so that you may be children of your F in heaven; F
5:48 therefore, as your heavenly F is perfect. J
6: 1 then you have no reward from your F in heaven. F
6: 4 and your F who sees in secret will reward you.
6: 6 the door and pray to your F who is in secret;
6: 6 and your F who sees in secret will reward you.
6: 8 your F knows what you need before you ask him.
6: 9 Our F in heaven, hallowed be your name. F
6:14 your heavenly F will also forgive you; J
6:15 neither will your F forgive your trespasses.
6:18 not by others but by your F who is in secret;
6:18 and your F who sees in secret will reward you.
6:26 and yet your heavenly F feeds them. J
6:32 and indeed your heavenly F knows J
7:11 how much more will your F in heaven give F
7:21 the one who does the will of my F in heaven. F
8:21 "Lord, first let me go and bury my f."
10:20 but the Spirit of your F speaking through you.
10:21 a f his child, and children will rise against parents
10:29 of them will fall to the ground apart from your F.
10:32 I also will acknowledge before my F in heaven; F
10:33 I also will deny before my F in heaven. F
10:35 For I have come to set a man against his f,
10:37 Whoever loves f or mother more than me is B
11:25 At that time Jesus said, "I thank you, F,
11:26 yes, F, for such was your gracious will.
11:27 All things have been handed over to me by my F;
11:27 and no one knows the Son except the F, and no one knows the F except the Son
12:50 of my F in heaven is my brother and sister F
13:43 like the sun in the kingdom of their F.
15: 4 For God said, 'Honor your f and your mother,' B
15: 4 'Whoever speaks evil of f or mother must B
15: 5 But you say that whoever tells f or mother, B
15: 5 then that person need not honor the f.
15:13 that my heavenly F has not planted will J
16:17 not revealed this to you, but my F in heaven. F
16:27 to come with his angels in the glory of his F,
18:10 the face of my F in heaven. F
18:14 So it is not the will of your F in heaven that one F
18:19 it will be done for you by my F in heaven. F
18:35 my heavenly F will also do to every one of you, J
19: 5 a man shall leave his f and mother and be joined B
19:19 Honor your f and mother; B
19:29 or brothers or sisters or f or mother or children B

Mt 20:23 for those for whom it has been prepared by my F."
21:30 The f went to the second and said the same;
21:31 Which of the two did the will of his f?"
23: 9 And call no one your f on earth,
23: 9 for you have one F—the one in heaven.
24:36 nor the Son, but only the F.
25:34 'Come, you that are blessed by my F,
26:39 "My F, if it is possible, let this cup pass from me;
26:42 "My F, if this cannot pass unless I drink it,
26:53 Do you think that I cannot appeal to my F,
28:19 of the F and of the Son and of the Holy Spirit,
Mk 1:20 and they left their f Zebedee in the boat with
5:40 the child's f and mother and those who were B
7:10 For Moses said, 'Honor your f and your mother'; B
7:10 and, 'Whoever speaks evil of f or mother must B
7:11 But you say that if anyone tells f or mother, B
7:12 permit doing anything for a f or mother, B
8:38 be ashamed when he comes in the glory of his F
9:21 the f, "How long has this been happening
9:24 Immediately the f of the child cried out,
10: 7 a man shall leave his f and mother and be joined B
10:19 Honor your f and mother.'" B
10:29 or brothers or sisters or mother or f or children
11:25 so that your F in heaven may also forgive you F
13:12 a f his child, and children will rise against parents
13:32 nor the Son, but only the F.
14:36 He said, "Abba, F, for you all things are possible;
15:21 the f of Alexander and Rufus.
Lk 1:59 to name him Zechariah after his f.
1:62 to his f to find out what name he wanted
1:67 Then his f Zechariah was filled with
2:33 And the child's f and mother were amazed B
2:48 your f and I have been searching for you
6:36 Be merciful, just as your F is merciful.
8:51 John, and James, and the child's f and mother. B
9:26 when he comes in his glory and the glory of the F
9:42 healed the boy, and gave him back to his f.
9:59 But he said, "Lord, first let me go and bury my f."
10:21 "I thank you, F, Lord of heaven and earth,
10:21 yes, F, for such was your gracious will.
10:22 All things have been handed over to me by my F;
10:22 and no one knows who the Son is except the F, or
who the F is except the Son
11: 2 F, hallowed be your name.
11:13 how much more will the heavenly F give J
12:30 and your F knows that you need them.
12:53 f against son and son against father,
12:53 father against son and son against f,
14:26 comes to me and does not hate f and mother, B
15:12 The younger of them said to his f, 'F,
15:18 I will get up and go to my f, and I will say to him,
15:18 "F, I have sinned against heaven and before you;
15:20 So he set off and went to his f.
15:20 his f saw him and was filled with compassion;
15:21 Then the son said to him, 'F,
15:22 f said to his slaves, 'Quickly, bring out a robe—
15:27 and your f has killed the fatted calf,
15:28 His f came out and began to plead with him.
15:29 But he answered his f, 'Listen!
15:31 Then the f said to him, 'Son,
16:24 He called out, 'F Abraham, have mercy on me, G
16:27 f, I beg you to send him to my father's house—
16:30 He said, 'No, f Abraham; G
18:20 Honor your f and mother.'" B
22:29 just as my F has conferred on me, a kingdom,
22:42 "F, if you are willing, remove this cup from me;
23:34 ⟦Then Jesus said, "F, forgive them;⟧
23:46 Then Jesus, crying with a loud voice, said, "F,
24:49 see, I am sending upon you what my F promised;
Jn 3:35 The F loves the Son and has placed all things
4:21 the F neither on this mountain nor in Jerusalem.
4:23 the true worshipers will worship the F in spirit
4:23 for the F seeks such as these to worship him.
4:53 The f realized that this was the hour
5:17 But Jesus answered them, "My F is still working,
5:18 but was also calling God his own F,
5:19 but only what he sees the F doing;
5:19 for whatever the F does, the Son does likewise.
5:20 The F loves the Son and shows him all
5:21 just as the F raises the dead and gives them life
5:22 The F judges no one but has given all judgment to
5:23 all may honor the Son just as they honor the F.
5:23 the Son does not honor the F who sent him.
5:26 For just as the F has life in himself,
5:36 The works that the F has given me to complete,
5:36 testify on my behalf that the F has sent me.
5:37 F who sent me has himself testified on my behalf.
5:45 Do not think that I will accuse you before the F;
6:27 For it is on him that God the F has set his seal." E
6:32 but it is my F who gives you the true bread
6:37 Everything that the F gives me will come to me,
6:40 This is indeed the will of my F,
6:42 the son of Joseph, whose f and mother we know? B
6:44 to me unless drawn by the F who sent me;
6:45 and learned from the F comes to me.
6:46 that anyone has seen the F except the one who is
6:46 from God; he has seen the F.
6:57 Just as the living F sent me,
6:57 and I live because of the F,
6:65 to me unless it is granted by the F."
8:16 but I and the F who sent me.
8:18 and the F who sent me testifies on my behalf."
8:19 Then they said to him, "Where is your F?"
8:19 Jesus answered, "You know neither me nor my F.
8:19 If you knew me, you would know my F also."
8:27 that he was speaking to them about the F.
8:28 but I speak these things as the F instructed me.
Jn 8:38 you should do what you have heard from the F."
8:39 They answered him, "Abraham is our f."
8:41 You are indeed doing what your f does."
8:41 we have one f, God himself."
8:42 Jesus said to them, "If God were your F,
8:44 You are from your f the devil,
8:44 for he is a liar and the f of lies.
8:49 but I honor my F, and you dishonor me.
8:53 Are you greater than our f Abraham, who died? G
8:54 It is my F who glorifies me, he of whom you say,
10:15 just as the F knows me and I know the F.
10:17 For this reason the F loves me,
10:18 I have received this command from my F."
10:29 What my F has given me is greater than all else,
10:30 The F and I are one."
10:32 "I have shown you many good works from the F.
10:36 the one whom the F has sanctified and sent into
10:37 If I am not doing the works of my F,
10:38 understand that the F is in me and I am in the F."
11:41 And Jesus looked upward and said, "F,
12:26 Whoever serves me, the F will honor.
12:27 what should I say—'F, save me from this hour'?
12:28 F, glorify your name."
12:49 but the F who sent me has himself given me
12:50 therefore, I speak just as the F has told me."
13: 1 to depart from this world and go to the F.
13: 3 that the F had given all things into his hands,
14: 6 No one comes to the F except through me.
14: 7 If you know me, you will know my F also.
14: 8 Philip said to him, "Lord, show us the F,
14: 9 Whoever has seen me has seen the F.
14: 9 How can you say, 'Show us the F'?
14:10 that I am in the F and the F is in me?
14:10 but the F who dwells in me does his works.
14:11 Believe me that I am in the F and the F is in me;
14:12 because I am going to the F.
14:13 so that the F may be glorified in the Son.
14:16 And I will ask the F,
14:20 On that day you will know that I am in my F,
14:21 and those who love me will be loved by my F,
14:23 and my F will love them,
14:24 but is from the F who sent me.
14:26 whom the F will send in my name,
14:28 you would rejoice that I am going to the F,
14:28 because the F is greater than I.
14:31 but I do as the F has commanded me,
14:31 so that the world may know that I love the F.
15: 1 "I am the true vine, and my F is the vinegrower.
15: 8 My F is glorified by this,
15: 9 As the F has loved me, so I have loved you;
15:15 to you everything that I have heard from my F.
15:16 so that the F will give you whatever you ask him
15:23 Whoever hates me hates my F also.
15:24 now they have seen and hated both me and my F.
15:26 whom I will send to you from the F,
15:26 the Spirit of truth who comes from the F,
16: 3 because they have not known the F or me.
16:10 to the F and you will see me no longer;
16:15 All that the F has is mine.
16:17 and 'Because I am going to the F'?"
16:23 if you ask anything of the F in my name,
16:25 but will tell you plainly of the F.
16:26 not say to you that I will ask the F on your behalf;
16:27 for the F himself loves you,
16:28 I came from the F and have come into the world;
16:28 I am leaving the world and am going to the F."
16:32 Yet I am not alone because the F is with me.
17: 1 he looked up to heaven and said, "F,
17: 5 F, glorify me in your own presence with the glory
17:11 Holy F, protect them in your name
17:21 As you, F, are in me and I am in you,
17:24 F, I desire that those also,
17:25 "Righteous F, the world does not know you,
18:11 not to drink the cup that the F has given me?"
20:17 because I have not yet ascended to the F.
20:17 'I am ascending to my F and your F,
20:21 As the F has sent me, so I send you."
Ac 1: 4 but to wait there for the promise of the F.
1: 7 or periods that the F has set by his own authority.
2:33 and having received from the F the promise of
7: 4 After his f died, God had him move from there
7: 8 And so Abraham became the f of Isaac A
7: 8 and Isaac became the f of Jacob, A
7:14 and invited his f Jacob and all his relatives
7:29 There he became the f of two sons. A
16: 1 but his f was a Greek.
16: 3 for they all knew that his f was a Greek.
28: 8 It so happened that the f of Publius lay sick in bed
Ro 1: 7 Grace to you and peace from God our F and I
4:16 the faith of Abraham (for he is the f of all of us,
4:17 "I have made you the f of many nations")—
4:18 that he would become "the f of many nations,"
6: 4 from the dead by the glory of the F,
8:15 of adoption. When we cry, "Abba! F!"
15: 6 the God and F of our Lord Jesus Christ. H
1Co 1: 3 Grace to you and peace from God our F and I
4:15 in Christ Jesus I became your f through
8: 6 the F, from whom are all things and
15:24 when he hands over the kingdom to God the F, E
2Co 1: 2 Grace to you and peace from God our F and I
1: 3 be the God and F of our Lord Jesus Christ, H
1: 3 the F of mercies and the God of all consolation,
6:18 and I will be your f,
11:31 The God and F of the Lord Jesus (blessed be he H
Gal 1: 1 but through Jesus Christ and God the F, E
1: 3 Grace to you and peace from God our F and I
1: 4 according to the will of our God and F, H
Gal 4: 2 and trustees until the date set by the f.
4: 6 into our hearts, crying, "Abba! F!"
Eph 1: 2 Grace to you and peace from God our F and I
1: 3 be the God and F of our Lord Jesus Christ, H
1:17 the God of our Lord Jesus Christ, the F of glory,
2:18 him both of us have access in one Spirit to the F.
3:14 For this reason I bow my knees before the F,
4: 6 one God and F of all, H
5:20 giving thanks to God the F at all times and E
5:31 this reason a man will leave his f and mother B
6: 2 "Honor your f and mother"— B
6:23 from God the F and the Lord Jesus Christ. E
Php 1: 2 Grace to you and peace from God our F and I
2:11 to the glory of God the F. E
2:22 a son with a f he has served with me in the work
4:20 To our God and F be glory forever and ever. H
Col 1: 2 Grace to you and peace from God our F. I
1: 3 the F of our Lord Jesus Christ,
1:12 giving thanks to the F, who has enabled you
3:17 giving thanks to God the F through him. E
1Th 1: 1 the church of the Thessalonians in God the F E
1: 3 remembering before our God and F your work H
2:11 with each one of you like a f with his children,
3:11 may our God and F himself and our Lord Jesus H
3:13 blameless before our God and F at the coming H
2Th 1: 1 the church of the Thessalonians in God our F I
1: 2 Grace to you and peace from God our F and I
2:16 and God our F, who loved us and I
1Ti 1: 2 peace from God the F and Christ Jesus our Lord. E
1: 9 those who kill their f or mother, for murderers, B
5: 1 but speak to him as to a f,
2Ti 1: 2 peace from God the F and Christ Jesus our Lord. E
Tit 1: 4 from God the F and Christ Jesus our Savior. E
Phm 1: 3 Grace to you and peace from God our F and I
1:10 whose f I have become during my imprisonment.
Heb 1: 5 "I will be his F, and he will be my Son"?
2:11 and those who are sanctified all have one F.
7: 3 Without f, without mother, without genealogy,
12: 9 even more willing to be subject to the F of spirits
Jas 1:17 is from above, coming down from the F of lights,
1:27 that is pure and undefiled before God, the F,
3: 9 With it we bless the Lord and F,
1Pe 1: 2 have been chosen and destined by God the F E
1: 3 be the God and F of our Lord Jesus Christ! H
1:17 as F the one who judges all people impartially
2Pe 1:17 For he received honor and glory from God the F E
1Jn 1: 2 that was with the F and was revealed to us—
1: 3 and truly our fellowship is with the F and
2: 1 anyone does sin, we have an advocate with the F,
2:14 I write to you, children, because you know the F.
2:15 love of the F is not in those who love the world;
2:16 comes not from the F but from the world.
2:22 the one who denies the F and the Son.
2:23 No one who denies the Son has the F;
2:23 everyone who confesses the Son has the F also.
2:24 then you will abide in the Son and in the F.
3: 1 See what love the F has given us,
4:14 the F has sent his Son as the Savior of the world.
2Jn 1: 3 be with us from God the F and from Jesus Christ, E
1: 4 just as we have been commanded by the F.
1: 9 whoever abides in the teaching has both the F and
Jude 1: 1 who are beloved in God the F and kept safe E
Rev 1: 6 priests serving his God and F, H
2:28 even as I also received authority from my F.
3: 5 I will confess your name before my F and
3:21 as I myself conquered and sat down with my F
Tob 1: 8 the mother of my f Tobiel,
1: 8 for my f had died and left me an orphan.
1: 9 I became the f of a son whom I named Tobias. A
2: 3 When he had returned he said, "F!"
2: 3 Then he went on to say, "Look, f,
3:10 "Never shall they reproach my f, saying to him,
3:10 And I shall bring my f in his old age down
3:15 not disgraced my name or the name of my f in
5: 1 Then Tobias answered his f Tobit,
5: 1 that you have commanded me, f;
5: 7 young man, until I go in and tell my f;
5: 9 Tobias went in to tell his f Tobit and said to him,
5:10 and said, "Young man, my f is calling for you."
5:17 he kissed his f and mother. B
6:12 and very beautiful, and her f is a good man."
6:13 tonight I will speak to her f about the girl,
6:15 So now, since I am the only son my f has,
7: 5 And Tobias added, "He is my f!"
7: 7 my child, son of a good and noble f!"
7:12 Take her and bring her safely to your f.
8:21 of what I own and return in safety to your f;
8:21 I am your f and Edna is your mother,
9: 4 you know that my f must be counting the days,
9: 6 "Good and noble son of a f good and noble,
9: 6 and to your wife's f and mother. B
10: 7 for I know that my f and mother do not believe B
10: 7 of you, f, to let me go so that I may return
10: 7 to let me go so that I may return to my own f.
10: 8 to your f Tobit and they will inform him
10: 9 I beg you to send me back to my f."
11: 2 "You are aware of how we left your f.
11: 6 she caught sight of him coming, she said to his f,
11: 7 before he had approached his f,
11: 8 and your f will regain his sight and see the light."
11:11 he blew into his eyes, saying, "Take courage, f."
11:15 to his f that his journey had been successful,
11:17 Blessed be your f and your mother, B
12: 2 He replied, "F, how much shall I pay him?
13: 4 he is our F and he is God forever.
14:12 Tobias's mother died, he buried her beside his f.
14:13 the property of Raguel and that of his f Tobit.

Jdt 9:12 Please, please, God of my f,
AdE 2:15 the brother of Mordecai's f, to go in to the king,
13:6 who is in charge of affairs and is our second f,
16:11 for every nation that he was called our f
Wis 2:16 and boasts that God is his f.
9:12 and shall be worthy of the throne of my f.
10:1 Wisdom protected the first-formed f of the world,
14:3 O F, that steers its course,
14:15 For a f, consumed with grief at
Sir 3:1 Listen to me your f, O children;
3:2 For the Lord honors a f above his children,
3:3 Those who honor their f atone for sins,
3:5 Those who honor their f will have joy
3:6 Those who respect their f will have long life,
3:8 Honor your f by word and deed,
3:10 Do not glorify yourself by dishonoring your f,
3:11 The glory of one's f is one's own glory,
3:12 My child, help your f in his old age,
3:14 For kindness to a f will not be forgotten,
3:16 Whoever forsakes a f is like a blasphemer,
4:10 Be a f to orphans, and be like a husband
7:27 With all your heart honor your f,
22:3 It is a disgrace to be the f of an undisciplined son,
22:4 but one who acts shamefully is a grief to her f.
22:5 An impudent daughter disgraces f and husband,
23:1 O Lord, F and Master of my life,
23:4 O Lord, F and God of my life,
23:14 Remember your f and mother when you sit B
30:4 When the f dies he will not seem to be dead,
41:7 Children will blame an ungodly f,
41:17 of sexual immorality, before your f or mother; B
42:9 A daughter is a secret anxiety to her f,
44:19 Abraham was the great f of a multitude
44:22 same assurance for the sake of his f Abraham. G
51:10 I cried out, "Lord, you are my F;
1Mc 2:65 to him; he shall be your f.
3:2 and all who had joined his f helped him;
6:23 We were happy to serve your f,
11:32 'King Demetrius to his f Lasthenes, greetings.
11:40 to become king in place of his f.
13:3 of my f have done for the laws and the sanctuary;
13:27 over the tomb of his f and his brothers;
13:28 for his f and mother and four brothers. B
14:26 and the house of his f have stood firm;
16:1 to his f Simon what Cendebeus had done.
16:21 ahead and reported to John at Gazara that his f
16:24 the time that he became high priest after his f.
2Mc 4:11 secured through John the f of Eupolemus,
9:23 but I observed that my f,
11:23 Now that our f has gone on to the gods,
14:37 of and for his goodwill was called f of the Jews.
1Es 1:34 and made him king in succession to his f Josiah.
4:20 A man leaves his own f, who brought him up,
4:21 with no thought of his f or his mother B
4:25 man loves his wife more than his f or his mother. B
3Mc 2:21 the first F of all, holy among the holy ones,
5:7 their merciful God and F, H
6:3 O F, upon the children of the sainted Jacob,
6:8 sea-born monster, you, F,
7:6 always taking their part as a f does
2Es 1:28 Have I not entreated you as a f entreats his sons or
1:29 be my children and I should be your f?
1:38 f, look with pride and see the people coming from
2:5 upon you, f, as a witness in addition to the mother
7:*104* Just as now a f does not send his son,
7:*104* or a son his f, or a master his servant,
4Mc 2:19 Why else did Jacob, our most wise f,
7:1 of our f Eleazar steered the ship of religion over
7:5 our f Eleazar broke the maddening waves of
7:9 f, strengthened our loyalty to the law
7:11 For just as our f Aaron, armed with the censer,
10:2 the same f begot me as well as those who died,
13:12 the f by whose hand Isaac would have submitted
16:20 For his sake also our f Abraham was zealous G
17:6 children were true descendants of f Abraham. G
18:9 and when these sons had grown up their f died.

FATHER See also ANCESTOR

FATHER'S‡ (150) [FATHER]

A. FATHER'S HOUSE (52)

Ge 9:23 and they did not see their f nakedness.
12:1 your f house to the land that I will show you. A
20:13 God caused me to wander from my f house, A
24:7 took me from my f house and from the land A
24:23 Is there room in your f house for us to spend A
24:38 but you shall go to my f house, A
24:40 for my son from my kindred, from my f house. A
26:15 with earth all the wells that his f servants had dug
27:34 When Esau heard his f words,
28:21 so that I come again to my f house in peace, A
29:9 Rachel came with her f sheep; for she kept them.
29:12 And Jacob told Rachel that he was her f kinsman,
31:1 "Jacob has taken all that was our f;
31:14 or inheritance left to us in our f house? A
31:19 and Rachel stole her f household gods.
31:30 because you longed greatly for your f house, A
35:22 Reuben went and lay with Bilhah his f concubine;
37:2 to the sons of Bilhah and Zilpah, his f wives;
37:12 Now his brothers went to pasture their f flock
38:11 in your f house until my son Shelah grows up" A
38:11 So Tamar went to live in her f house. A
41:51 forget all my hardship and all my f house." A
46:31 Joseph said to his brothers and to his f household,
46:31 'My brothers and my f household,
Ge 47:12 his brothers, and all his f household with food,
48:12 Then Joseph removed them from his f knees,
48:17 so he took his f hand,
49:4 because you went up onto your f bed;
49:8 your f sons shall bow down before you.
50:1 Then Joseph threw himself on his f face and wept
50:8 his brothers, and his f household.
50:22 Joseph remained in Egypt, he and his f household;
Ex 2:16 and filled the troughs to water their f flock.
6:20 Amram married Jochebed his f sister
15:2 this is my God, and I will praise him, my f God,
Lev 16:32 as priest in his f place shall make atonement,
18:8 not uncover the nakedness of your f wife;
18:9 your f daughter or your mother's daughter,
18:11 the nakedness of your f wife's daughter,
18:12 not uncover the nakedness of your f sister;
18:12 of your father's sister; she is your f flesh.
18:14 the nakedness of your f brother, that is, you shall
20:11 with his f wife has uncovered his f nakedness;
20:19 of your mother's sister or of your f sister,
22:13 without offspring, and returns to her f house, A
22:13 as in her youth, she may eat of her f food.
Nu 27:4 Give to us a possession among our f brothers."
27:7 among their f brothers and pass the inheritance
27:10 you shall give his inheritance to his f brothers.
30:3 while within her f house, in her youth, A
30:16 while she is still young and in her f house. A
36:6 be into a clan of their f tribe that they are married,
36:8 from the clan of her f tribe,
36:11 married sons of their f brothers.
36:12 in the tribe of their f clan.
Dt 13:6 it is your brother, your f son or your mother's son,
22:21 to the entrance of her f house and the men A
22:21 in Israel by prostituting herself in her f house. A
22:30 A man shall not marry his f wife,
22:30 thereby violating his f rights.
27:20 "Cursed be anyone who lies with his f wife,
27:20 because he has violated his f rights."
Jdg 6:25 night the LORD said to him, "Take your f bull,
9:5 He went to his f house at Ophrah, A
9:18 you have risen up against my f house this day, A
11:2 "You shall not inherit anything in our f house; A
11:7 and drove me out of my f house? A
14:15 or we will burn you and your f house with fire. A
14:19 In hot anger he went back to his f house. A
19:2 from him to her f house at Bethlehem in Judah, A
19:3 When he reached her f house, A
1Sa 17:15 from Saul to feed his f sheep at Bethlehem.
18:2 and would not let him return to his f house. A
18:18 my f family in Israel, that I should be son-in-law
22:1 when his brothers and all his f house heard of it, A
22:11 for all his f house, the priests who were at Nob; A
22:15 to his servant or to any member of my f house; A
22:16 Ahimelech, you and all your f house." A
22:22 am responsible for the lives of all your f house. A
24:21 will not wipe out my name from my f house." A
2Sa 3:7 "Why have you gone in to my f concubine?"
3:29 and on all his f house; A
14:9 my lord the king, and on my f house; A
15:34 as I have been your f servant in time past,
16:21 "Go in to your f concubines,
16:22 in to his f concubines in the sight of all Israel.
19:28 For all my f house were doomed to death A
24:17 I pray, be against me and against my f house." A
1Ki 2:31 thus take away from me and from my f house A
12:10 'My little finger is thicker than my f loins.
18:18 but you have, and your f house, A
2Ki 3:13 Go to your f prophets or to your mother's."
10:3 set him on his f throne,
1Ch 5:1 he defiled his f bed his birthright was given
21:17 be against me and against my f house; A
28:4 and in the house of Judah my f house, A
28:4 and among my f sons he took delight
2Ch 10:10 'My little finger is thicker than my f loins.
21:13 members of your f house, A
Est 4:14 but you and your f family will perish.
Ps 45:10 forget your people and your f house, A
Pr 1:8 Hear, my child, your f instruction,
4:1 Listen, children, to a f instruction,
6:20 My child, keep your f commandment,
Eze 18:17 he shall not die for his f iniquity;
22:11 another in you defiles his sister, his f daughter.
Mt 26:29 when I drink it new with you in my F kingdom."
Lk 2:49 you not know that I must be in my F house?" A
12:32 for it is your F good pleasure to give you
15:17 of my f hired hands have bread enough and
16:27 father, I beg you to send him to my f house— A
Jn 1:14 the glory as of a f only son,
1:18 It is God the only Son, who is close to the F heart,
2:16 Stop making my F house a marketplace!" A
5:43 I have come in my F name,
8:38 I declare what I have seen in the F presence;
8:44 and you choose to do your f desires.
10:25 The works that I do in my F name testify to me;
10:29 and no one can snatch it out of the F hand.
14:2 In my F house there are many dwelling places. A
15:10 as I have kept my F commandments and abide
Ac 7:20 three months he was brought up in his f house; A
1Co 5:1 for a man is living with his f wife.
2Jn 1:3 the F Son, in truth and love.
Rev 14:1 and his F name written on their foreheads.
Tob 3:7 was reproached by one of her f maids.
3:10 When she had gone up to her f upper room,
3:15 I am my f only child; he has no other child
4:12 who is not of your f tribe;
6:12 Also it is right for you to inherit her f possessions.
6:15 that I may die and bring my f and mother's life
Tob 6:16 "Do you not remember your f orders
6:16 to take a wife from your f house? A
6:18 related through his f lineage,
AdE 2:7 he had a foster child, the daughter of his f brother,
4:14 but you and your f family will perish.
Sir 3:9 a f blessing strengthens the houses of the children,
3:10 for your f dishonor is no glory to you.
34:24 a son before his f eyes is the person who offers
42:10 be seduced and become pregnant in her f house; A
1Mc 11:9 and you shall reign over your f kingdom.
16:2 "My brothers and I and my f house have fought A
2Mc 11:24 not consent to our f change to Greek customs,
13:9 that had been done in his f time.
Pm 151:1 and the youngest in my f house; A
151:1 in my father's house; I tended my f sheep.
151:4 and took me from my f sheep,
4Mc 16:20 and when Isaac saw his f hand wielding a knife
18:7 a pure virgin and did not go outside my f house; A

FATHER-IN-LAW (30) [FATHER]

Ge 38:13 "Your f is going up to Timnah
38:25 she was being brought out, she sent word to her f,
Ex 3:1 Moses was keeping the flock of his f Jethro,
4:18 Moses went back to his f Jethro and said to him,
18:1 Jethro, the priest of Midian, Moses' f,
18:2 his f Jethro took her back,
18:5 Moses' f, came into the wilderness
18:6 He sent word to Moses, "I, your f Jethro,
18:7 Moses went out to meet his f;
18:8 Then Moses told his f all that
18:12 Moses' f, brought a burnt offering and sacrifices
18:12 to eat bread with Moses' f in the presence of God.
18:14 Moses' f saw all that he was doing for the people,
18:15 Moses said to his f, "Because the people come
18:17 Moses' f said to him, "What you are doing is
18:24 So Moses listened to his f and did all
18:27 Then Moses let his f depart,
Nu 10:29 Moses' f, "We are setting out for the place
Jdg 1:16 The descendants of Hobab the Kenite, Moses' f,
4:11 that is, the descendants of Hobab the f of Moses,
19:4 His f, the girl's father, made him stay,
19:7 his f kept urging him until he spent
19:9 his f, the girl's father, said to him, "Look,
1Sa 4:19 and that her f and her husband were dead,
4:21 of God had been captured and because of her f
Jn 18:13 who was the f of Caiaphas,
Tob 10:12 honor your f and your mother-in-law,
14:12 and settled in Ecbatana with Raguel his f.
1Mc 10:56 and I will become your f, as you have said."
11:2 since he was Alexander's f.

FATHERHOOD See Index to Footnotes

FATHERLESS (1) [FATHER]

La 5:3 We have become orphans, f;

FATHERS‡ (27) [FATHER]

Nu 32:8 Your f did this, when I sent them
32:14 a brood of sinners, have risen in place of your f,
Jdg 21:22 if their f or their brothers come to complain to us,
1Ch 4:19 were the f of Keilah the Garmite and Eshtemoa
2Ch 29:9 Our f have fallen by the sword and our sons
Job 30:1 whose f I would have disdained to set with
Pr 30:11 There are those who curse their f and do
Isa 38:19 f make known to children your faithfulness.
49:23 Kings shall be your foster f,
Jer 7:18 The children gather wood, the f kindle fire,
16:3 and the f who beget them in this land:
16:7 of consolation to drink for their f or their mothers.
Zec 13:3 their f and mothers who bore them will say
13:3 of the LORD"; and their f
Ac 7:2 Stephen replied: "Brothers and f, listen to me.
22:1 and f, listen to the defense that I now make
1Co 4:15 you do not have many f.
Eph 6:4 And, f, do not provoke your children to anger,
Col 3:21 F, do not provoke your children,
1Jn 2:13 to you, f, because you know him who is from
2:14 I write to you, f, because you know him who is
3Mc 2:12 when our f were oppressed you helped them
2Es 7:*103* f for sons or sons for parents,
4Mc 13:17 and all the f will praise us."
13:19 through the f to their descendants
15:4 toward their offspring than do the f.
18:23 into the chorus of the f,

FATHERS See also ANCESTORS

FATHERS' (1) [FATHER]

Eze 22:10 In you they uncover their f nakedness;

FATFLESHED (KJV) See FAT

FATHOM (2) [FATHOMS]

Sir 18:6 nor is it possible to f the wonders of the Lord.
24:28 nor will the last one f her.

FATHOMS (2) [FATHOM]

Ac 27:28 So they took soundings and found twenty f;
27:28 on they took soundings again and found fifteen f.

FATLING (2) [FAT]

2Sa 6:13 he sacrificed an ox and a f.

Isa 11: 6 the calf and the lion and the **f** together,

FATLINGS (5) [FAT]

1Sa 15: 9 the best of the sheep and of the cattle and of the **f,**
Ps 66:15 I will offer to you burnt offerings of **f,**
Isa 5:17 **f** and kids shall feed among the ruins.
Eze 34: 3 with the wool, you slaughter the **f;**
39:18 and of goats, of bulls, all of them **f** of Bashan.

FATNESS‡ (5) [FAT]

Ge 27:28 and of the **f** of the earth,
27:39 away from the **f** of the earth shall your home be,
Job 36:16 and what was set on your table was full of **f.**
Ps 73: 7 Their eyes swell out with **f;**
Jer 31:14 I will give the priests their fill of **f,**

FATTED (11) [FAT]

1Sa 28:24 Now the woman had a **f** calf in the house.
1Ki 1: 9 oxen, and **f** cattle by the stone Zoheleth,
1:19 He has sacrificed oxen, **f** cattle,
1:25 **f** cattle, and sheep in abundance,
4:23 besides deer, gazelles, roebucks, and **f** fowl.
Pr 15:17 of vegetables where love is than a **f** ox and hatred
Jer 46:21 her mercenaries in her midst are like **f** calves;
Am 5:22 of your **f** animals I will not look upon.
Lk 15:23 And get the **f** calf and kill it,
15:27 and your father has killed the **f** calf,
15:30 you killed the **f** calf for him!'

FATTENED (1) [FAT]

Jas 5: 5 you have **f** your hearts in a day of slaughter.

FATTENING (1) [FAT]

1Sa 2:29 by **f** yourselves on the choicest parts

FATTER (1) [FAT]

Da 1:15 and **f** than all the young men who had been eating

FAULT (11) [FAULTFINDER, FAULTLESS, FAULTS]

1Sa 29: 3 Since he deserted to me I have found no **f** in him
Ps 59: 4 for no **f** of mine, they run
73:10 and find no **f** in them.
Mal 1: 9 be gracious to us. The **f** is yours.
Mt 18:15 and point out the **f** when the two of you are alone.
Ro 9:19 "Why then does he still find **f?**
2Co 6: 3 so that no **f** may be found with our ministry,
Heb 8: 8 God finds **f** with them when he says:
Sir 11: 7 Do not find **f** before you investigate;
20: 3 the one who admits his **f** will be kept from failure.
29: 5 and finds **f** with the time.

FAULTFINDER (1) [FAULT, FIND]

Job 40: 2 "Shall a **f** contend with the Almighty?

FAULTLESS (1) [FAULT]

Heb 8: 7 For if that first covenant had been **f,**

FAULTS (5) [FAULT]

Ge 41: 9 to Pharaoh, "I remember my **f** today.
Ps 19:12 Clear me from hidden **f.**
Sir 27: 4 so do a person's **f** when he speaks.
28: 7 the covenant of the Most High, and overlook **f.**
38:10 Give up your **f** and direct your hands rightly,

FAVOR‡ (169) [FAVORABLE, FAVORABLY, FAVORED, FAVORITE, FAVORITISM, FAVORS]

Ge 6: 8 But Noah found **f** in the sight of the LORD.
18: 3 He said, "My lord, if I find **f** with you,
19:19 your servant has found **f** with you,
19:21 He said to him, "Very well, I grant you this **f** too
32: 5 in order that I may find **f** in your sight.' "
33: 8 Jacob answered, "To find **f** with my lord."
33:10 Jacob said, "No, please; if I find **f** with you,
33:10 since you have received me with such **f.**
34:11 "Let me find **f** with you,
39: 4 So Joseph found **f** in his sight and attended him;
39:21 he gave him **f** in the sight of the chief jailer.
47:29 "If I have found **f** with you,
50: 4 "If now I have found **f** with you,
Ex 3:21 I will bring this people into such **f** with
11: 3 The LORD gave the people **f** in the sight of
12:36 and the LORD had given the people **f** in the sight
28:38 in order that they may find **f** before the LORD.
33:12 and you have also found **f** in my sight.'
33:13 Now if I have found **f** in your sight,
33:13 so that I may know you and find **f** in your sight.
33:16 shall it be known that I have found **f** in your sight,
33:17 for you have found **f** in my sight,
34: 9 He said, "If now I have found **f** in your sight,
Lev 26: 9 I will look with **f** upon you and make you fruitful
26:45 but I will remember in their **f** the covenant
Nu 11:11 Why have I not found **f** in your sight,
11:15 if I have found **f** in your sight—
32: 5 They continued, "If we have found **f** in your sight,
Dt 28:50 to the old or **f** to the young.
33:16 and the **f** of the one who dwells on Sinai.
33:23 Naphtali, sated with **f,** full of the blessing
Jdg 6:17 he said to him, "If now I have found **f** with you,
Ru 2: 2 behind someone in whose sight I may find **f."**
2:10 "Why have I found **f** in your sight,
2:13 she said, "May I continue to find **f** in your sight,
1Sa 1:18 she said, "Let your servant find **f** in your sight."
2:26 both in stature and in **f** with the LORD and with
13:12 and I have not entreated the **f** of the LORD';
16:22 for he has found **f** in my sight."
20:29 So now, if I have found **f** in your sight,
25: 8 Therefore let my young men find **f** in your sight;
27: 5 "If I have found **f** in your sight,
2Sa 14:22 "Today your servant knows that I have found **f**
15:25 If I find **f** in the eyes of the LORD,
16: 4 let me find **f** in your sight, my lord the king."
1Ki 11:19 Hadad found great **f** in the sight of Pharaoh,
13: 6 "Entreat now the **f** of the LORD your God,
2Ki 5: 1 was a great man and in high **f** with his master,
2Ch 33:12 While he was in distress he entreated the **f** of
Ezr 9: 8 But now for a brief moment **f** has been shown by
Ne 2: 5 and if your servant has found **f** with you,
13:22 Remember this also in my **f,** O my God,
Est 2: 9 The girl pleased him and won his **f,**
2:17 of all the virgins she won his **f** and devotion,
5: 2 she won his **f** and he held out to her
5: 8 If I have won the king's **f,**
7: 3 Queen Esther answered, "If I have won your **f,**
8: 5 "If it pleases the king, and if I have won his **f,**
Job 10: 3 of your hands and **f** the schemes of the wicked?
11:19 will make you afraid; many will entreat your **f.**
20:10 Their children will seek the **f** of the poor,
Ps 5:12 you cover them with **f** as with a shield.
20: 3 and regard with **f** your burnt sacrifices.
30: 5 his **f** is for a lifetime.
30: 7 By your **f,** O LORD, you had established me as
45:12 the people of Tyre will seek your **f** with gifts,
84:11 and shield; he bestows **f** and honor.
86:17 Show me a sign of your **f,**
89:17 by your **f** our horn is exalted.
90:17 Let the **f** of the Lord our God be upon us,
101: 6 I will look with **f** on the faithful in the land,
102:13 for it is time to **f** it; the appointed time has come.
106: 4 O LORD, when you show **f** to your people;
119:58 I implore your **f** with all my heart;
132: 1 in David's **f** all the hardships he endured;
Pr 3: 4 So you will find **f** and good repute in the sight
3:34 but to the humble he shows **f.**
8:35 For whoever finds me finds life and obtains **f**
11:27 Whoever diligently seeks good seeks **f,**
12: 2 The good obtain **f** from the LORD,
13:15 Good sense wins **f,** but the way of
14: 9 but the upright enjoy God's **f.**
14:35 A servant who deals wisely has the king's **f,**
16:15 his **f** is like the clouds that bring the spring rain.
18:22 and obtains **f** from the LORD.
19: 6 Many seek the **f** of the generous,
19:12 but his **f** is like dew on the grass.
22: 1 and **f** is better than silver or gold.
28:23 will afterward find more **f** than one who flatters
29:26 Many seek the **f** of a ruler,
Ecc 9:11 nor riches to the intelligent, nor **f** to the skillful;
10:12 Words spoken by the wise bring them **f,**
Isa 26:10 If **f** is shown to the wicked,
27:11 he that formed them will show them no **f.**
49: 8 In a time of **f** I have answered you,
60:10 but in my **f** I have had mercy on you.
61: 2 of the LORD's **f,** and the day of vengeance
63: 7 and the great **f** to the house of Israel
Jer 16:13 for I will show you no **f.**
26:19 Did he not fear the LORD and entreat the **f** of
52:31 showed **f** to King Jehoiachin of Judah
La 4:16 no honor was shown to the priests, no **f** to
Da 1: 9 Now God allowed Daniel to receive **f**
9:13 We did not entreat the **f** of the LORD our God,
Hos 5:15 In their distress they will beg my **f:**
12: 4 he wept and sought his **f;**
Zec 7: 2 to entreat the **f** of the LORD,
8:21 "Come, let us go to entreat the **f** of the LORD,
8:22 and to entreat the **f** of the LORD.
11: 7 one I named **F,** the other I named Unity,
11:10 I took my staff **F** and broke it,
Mal 1: 8 will he be pleased with you or show you **f?**
1: 9 And now implore the **f** of God,
1: 9 Will he show **f** to any of you?
2:13 the offering or accepts it with **f** at your hand.
Mt 20:20 and kneeling before him, she asked a **f** of him.
Lk 1:30 Mary, for you have found **f** with God.
1:48 for he has looked with **f** on the lowliness
2:40 and the **f** of God was upon him.
2:52 and in divine and human **f.**
4:19 to proclaim the year of the Lord's **f."**
Ac 7:10 and enabled him to win **f** and to show wisdom
7:46 who found **f** with God and asked
24:27 and since he wanted to grant the Jews a **f,**
25: 3 as a **f** to them against Paul,
25: 9 But Festus, wishing to do the Jews a **f,**
27:12 the majority was in **f** of putting to sea from there,
1Co 4: 6 so that none of you will be puffed up in **f** of one
2Co 1:15 so that you might have a double **f;**
Tob 1:13 the Most High gave me **f** and good standing
13: 6 with **f** upon you and show you mercy.'
Jdt 4:15 to the Lord with all their might to look with **f** on
8:23 For our slavery will not bring us into **f,**
10: 8 of our ancestors grant you **f** and fulfill your plans,
AdE 2: 9 The girl pleased him and won his **f,**
2: 9 he treated her and her maids with special **f** in
2:15 Esther found **f** in the eyes of all who saw her.
2:17 the king loved Esther and she found **f** beyond all
4: 8 to go in to the king and plead for his **f** in behalf of
AdE 5: 8 if I have found **f** in the sight of the king,
7: 3 "If I have found **f** with the king,
8: 5 "If it pleases you, and if I have found **f,**
Wis 3:14 special **f** will be shown him for his faithfulness,
Sir 3:15 of your distress it will be remembered in your **f;**
3:18 so you will find **f** in the sight of the Lord.
4:21 and there is a shame that is glory and **f.**
8:14 the decision will **f** him because of his standing.
11:17 and his **f** brings lasting success.
32:14 and those who rise early to seek him will find **f.**
42: 1 and will find **f** with everyone.
44:23 who found **f** in the sight of all
Bar 1:12 and we shall serve them many days and find **f**
2: 8 not entreated the **f** of the Lord by turning away,
2:14 and grant us **f** in the sight
1Mc 4:10 to see whether he will **f** us
10:60 and gold and many gifts, and found **f** with them.
11:24 And he won his **f.**
1Es 8: 4 for he found **f** before the king in all his requests.
8:80 he brought us into **f** with the kings of the Persians,
3Mc 1: 4 matters were turning out rather in **f** of Antiochus,
2Es 4:44 "If I have found **f** in your sight,
5:56 O Lord, if I have found **f** in your sight,
6:11 "O sovereign Lord, if I have found **f** in your sight,
7:*75* "If I have found **f** in your sight, O Lord,
7:*102* "If I have found **f** in your sight,
7:*104* "Since you have found **f** in my sight,
8:42 "If I have found **f** in your sight, let me speak.
12: 7 "O sovereign Lord, if I have found **f** in your sight,
14:22 If then I have found **f** with you,

FAVORABLE (16) [FAVOR]

Ge 40:16 the chief baker saw that the interpretation was **f,**
41:16 God will give Pharaoh a **f** answer."
1Ki 22: 8 for he never prophesies anything **f** about me,
22:13 the words of the prophets with one accord are **f** to
22:18 not tell you that he would not prophesy anything **f**
2Ch 18: 7 for he never prophesies anything **f** about me,
18:12 the words of the prophets with one accord are **f** to
18:17 not tell you that he would not prophesy anything **f**
Ps 77: 7 the Lord spurn forever, and never again be **f?**
85: 1 you were **f** to your land;
Eze 16:52 about for your sisters a more **f** judgment;
2Ti 4: 2 be persistent whether the time is **f** or unfavorable;
1Mc 12: 1 when Jonathan saw that the time was **f** for him,
13:35 King Demetrius sent him a **f** reply to this request,
3Mc 5:44 at the places in the city most **f** for keeping guard.
4Mc 8: 5 with **f** feelings I admire each and every one

FAVORABLY (12) [FAVOR]

Ge 31: 2 And Jacob saw that Laban did not regard him as **f**
31: 5 "I see that your father does not regard me as **f**
2Sa 24:23 "May the LORD your God respond **f** to you."
1Ki 22:13 be like the word of one of them, and speak **f."**
2Ch 18:12 be like the word of one of them, and speak **f."**
Lk 1:25 the Lord has done for me when he looked **f** on me
1:68 he has looked **f** on his people and redeemed them.
7:16 and "God has looked **f** on his people!"
Ac 15:14 Simeon has related how God first looked **f** on
3Jn 1:12 Everyone has testified **f** about Demetrius,
Tob 3: 3 now, O Lord, remember me and look **f** upon me.
3Mc 7:11 be **f** disposed toward the king's government.

FAVORED (5) [FAVOR]

Job 22: 8 The powerful possess the land, and the **f** live in it.
Eze 27:21 the princes of Kedar were your **f** dealers in lambs,
Lk 1:28 And he came to her and said, "Greetings, **f** one!
1Mc 10:47 They **f** Alexander, because he had been the first
2Mc 1:35 the king **f** he exchanged many excellent gifts.

FAVORITE (4) [FAVOR]

Dt 33: 3 Indeed, O **f** among peoples,
33:24 may he be the **f** of his brothers,
2Sa 23: 1 the **f** of the Strong One of Israel:
Pr 4: 3 tender, and my mother's **f,**

FAVORITISM (1) [FAVOR]

Jas 2: 1 do you with your acts of **f** really believe

FAVORS (10) [FAVOR]

2Sa 20:11 "Whoever **f** Joab, and whoever is for David,
Jer 3:13 and scattered your **f** among strangers
Eze 23: 7 She bestowed her **f** upon them,
Lk 2:14 and on earth peace among those whom he **f!"**
Wis 14:26 forgetfulness of **f,** defiling of souls,
Sir 3:31 Those who repay **f** give thought to the future;
19:25 and there are people who abuse **f** to gain a verdict.
20:29 **F** and gifts blind the eyes of the wise;
1Mc 11:53 not repay the **f** that Jonathan had done him,
4Mc 11:12 they are splendid **f** that you grant us

FAWN (1) [FAWNS]

Jer 14: 5 Even the doe in the field forsakes her newborn **f**

FAWNING (1)

Dt 33:29 Your enemies shall come **f** to you,

FAWNS (3) [FAWN]

Ge 49:21 Naphtali is a doe let loose that bears lovely **f.**
SS 4: 5 Your two breasts are like two **f,**
7: 3 Your two breasts are like two **f,**

FEAR‡ (438) [AFRAID, FEARED, FEARFUL, FEARFULLY, FEARFULNESS, FEARING, FEARS, FEARSOME, GOD-FEARING]

A. DO NOT FEAR (58)
B. FEAR THE †LORD (28)
C. FEAR OF THE †LORD (24)
D. FEAR OF THE *LORD (24)
E. FEAR THE *LORD (23)
F. FEAR [YOUR] *GOD (20)
G. FEAR OF ... *GOD (13)
H. FEAR AND ... TREMBLING (10)

Ge 9: 2 The f and dread of you shall rest on every animal
19:19 for f the disaster will overtake me and I die.
20:11 There is no f of God at all in this place, G
22:12 for now I know that you f God, F
31:42 the God of Abraham and the F of Isaac,
31:53 So Jacob swore by the F of his father Isaac,
42:18 "Do this and you will live, for I f God: F
44:34 I f to see the suffering that would come
50:21 So have no f; I myself will provide
Ex 9:30 I know that you do not yet f the LORD God." B
14:10 In great f the Israelites cried out to the LORD.
18:21 men who f God, are trustworthy, F
20:20 God has come only to test you and to put the f of
Lev 19:14 you shall f your God: I am the LORD. F
19:32 and you shall f your God: I am the LORD. F
25:17 but you shall f your God; F
25:36 but f your God; let them live with you. F
25:43 over them with harshness, but shall f your God. F
Nu 14: 9 and do not f the people of the land, A
14: 9 and the LORD is with us; do not f them." A
22: 3 Moab was overcome with f of the people
Dt 1:21 do not f or be dismayed." A
1:29 I said to you, "Have no dread or f of them.
2:25 This day I will begin to put the dread and f of you
3: 2 The LORD said to me, "Do not f him, A
3:22 Do not f them, for it is the LORD your God who A
4:10 that they may learn to f me as long as they live on
5:29 If only they had such a mind as this, to f me and
6: 2 and your children's children may f the LORD B
6:13 The LORD your God you shall f; B
6:24 to f the LORD our God, for our lasting good, B
10:12 Only to f the LORD your God, B
10:20 You shall f the LORD your God; B
11:25 the LORD your God will put the f and dread
13: 4 your God you shall follow, him alone you shall f,
14:23 you may learn to f the LORD your God always. B
17:19 so that he may learn to f the LORD his God, B
25:18 behind you; he did not f God.
31: 6 Be strong and bold; have no f or dread of them,
31: 8 Do not f or be dismayed." A
31:12 and learn to f the LORD your God and B
31:13 may hear and learn to f the LORD your God, B
Jos 2: 9 all the inhabitants of the land melt in f before you.
2:24 all the inhabitants of the land melt in f before us."
4:24 so that you may f the LORD your God forever." B
8: 1 LORD said to Joshua, "Do not f or be dismayed; A
9:24 so we were in great f for our lives because of you,
10: 8 The LORD said to Joshua, "Do not f them, A
22:24 We did it from f that in time
Jdg 4:18 turn aside to me; have no f."
6:23 do not f, you shall not die." A
7:10 But if you f to attack, go down to the camp
9:21 where he remained for f of his brother Abimelech.
1Sa 12:14 If you will f the LORD and serve him B
12:24 Only f the LORD, and serve him faithfully B
28:13 king said to her, "Have no f; what do you see?"
28:20 filled with f because of the words of Samuel;
2Sa 17:10 like the heart of a lion, will utterly melt with f;
23: 3 rules over people justly, ruling in the f of God, G
1Ki 8:40 so that they may f you all the days that they live
8:43 of the earth may know your name and f you,
1Ch 14:17 the LORD brought the f of him on all nations.
2Ch 6:31 Thus may they f you and walk in your ways all
6:33 of the earth may know your name and f you,
14:14 for the f of the LORD was on them. C
17:10 The f of the LORD fell on all the kingdoms of C
19: 7 Now, let the f of the LORD be upon you; C
19: 9 in the f of the LORD, in faithfulness, C
20:15 'Do not f or be dismayed at this great multitude; A
20:17 Do not f or be dismayed; A
20:29 The f of God came on all the kingdoms of G
26: 5 who instructed him in the f of God; G
Ne 5: 9 Should you not walk in the f of our God, G
5:15 But I did not do so, because of the f of God. G
Est 8:17 because the f of the Jews had fallen upon them.
9: 2 because the f of them had fallen upon all peoples.
9: 3 because the f of Mordecai had fallen upon them.
Job 1: 9 "Does Job f God for nothing? F
3:25 Truly the thing that I f comes upon me,
4: 6 Is not your f of God your confidence, G
5:21 and shall not f destruction when it comes.
5:22 and shall not f the wild animals of the earth.
6:14 from a friend forsake the f of the Almighty.
9:35 then I would speak without f of him,
11:15 you will be secure, and will not f.
15: 4 But you are doing away with the f of God, G
21: 9 Their houses are safe from f,
25: 2 "Dominion and f are with God;
28:28 he said to humankind, 'Truly, the f of the Lord, D
31:34 because I stood in great f of the multitude,
33: 7 No f of me need terrify you;
37:24 Therefore mortals f him; he does
39:16 though its labor should be in vain, yet it has no f;
Job 39:22 It laughs at f, and is not dismayed;
41:33 On earth it has no equal, a creature without f.
Ps 2:11 Serve the LORD with f, with trembling
9:20 Put them in f, O LORD;
15: 4 but who honor those who f the LORD; B
19: 9 the f of the LORD is pure, enduring forever; C
22:23 You who f the LORD, praise him! B
22:25 my vows I will pay before those who f him.
23: 4 I walk through the darkest valley, I f no evil;
25:12 Who are they that f the LORD? B
25:14 friendship of the LORD is for those who f him,
27: 1 and my salvation; whom shall I f?
27: 3 an army encamp against me, my heart shall not f;
31:19 that you have laid up for those who f you,
33: 8 Let all the earth f the LORD; B
33:18 the eye of the LORD is on those who f him,
34: 7 of the LORD encamps around those who f him,
34: 9 O f the LORD, you his holy ones, B
34: 9 for those who f him have no want.
34:11 I will teach you the f of the LORD. C
36: 1 there is no f of God before their eyes. G
40: 3 Many will see and f, and put their trust in the LORD
46: 2 not f, though the earth should change,
49: 5 Why should I f in times of trouble,
52: 6 and f, and will laugh at the evildoer, saying,
55: 5 F and trembling come upon me, H
55:19 because they do not change, and do not f God. A
60: 4 You have set up a banner for those who f you,
61: 5 the heritage of those who f your name.
64: 4 they shoot suddenly and without f.
64: 9 Then everyone will f; they will tell what God
66:16 and hear, all you who f God, F
76:12 who inspires f in the kings of the earth.
85: 9 his salvation is at hand for those who f him,
90:11 Your wrath is as great as the f that is due you.
91: 5 You will not f the terror of the night,
102:15 The nations will f the name of the LORD,
103:11 great is his steadfast love toward those who f him;
103:13 the LORD has compassion for those who f him.
103:17 to everlasting on those who f him,
111: 5 He provides food for those who f him;
111:10 The f of the LORD is the beginning of wisdom; C
112: 1 Happy are those who f the LORD, B
115:11 You who f the LORD, trust in the LORD! B
115:13 he will bless those who f the LORD, B
118: 4 Let those who f the LORD say, B
118: 6 With the LORD on my side I do not f. A
119:38 which is for those who f you.
119:63 I am a companion of all who f you,
119:74 Those who f you shall see me and rejoice,
119:79 Let those who f you turn to me,
119:120 My flesh trembles for f of you,
135:20 You that f the LORD, bless the LORD! B
145:19 He fulfills the desire of all who f him;
147:11 but the LORD takes pleasure in those who f him,
Pr 1: 7 f of the LORD is the beginning of knowledge; C
1:29 and did not choose the f of the LORD, C
2: 5 then you will understand the f of the LORD C
3: 7 f the LORD, and turn away from evil. B
8:13 The f of the LORD is hatred of evil. C
9:10 The f of the LORD is the beginning of wisdom, C
10:27 The f of the LORD prolongs life, C
14: 2 Those who walk uprightly f the LORD, B
14:26 In the f of the LORD one has strong confidence, C
14:27 The f of the LORD is a fountain of life, C
15:16 a little with the f of the LORD than great treasure C
15:33 The f of the LORD is instruction in wisdom, C
16: 6 and by the f of the LORD one avoids evil. C
19:23 The f of the LORD is life indeed; C
22: 4 and f of the LORD is riches and honor and life. C
23:17 but always continue in the f of the LORD. C
24:21 My child, f the LORD and the king, B
28:14 Happy is the one who is never without f,
29:25 The f of others lays a snare,
Ecc 5: 7 and a multitude of words; but f God. F
8:12 I know that it will be well with those who f God, F
8:12 because they stand in f before him,
8:13 because they do not stand in f before God.
12:13 F God, and keep his commandments; F
Isa 7: 4 Take heed, be quiet, do not f, A
7:25 you will not go there for f of briers and thorns;
8: 6 melt in f before Rezin and the son of Remaliah;
8:12 and do not f what it fears, or be in dread. A
8:13 let him be your f, and let him be your dread.
11: 2 the spirit of knowledge and the f of the LORD. C
11: 3 His delight shall be in the f of the LORD. C
14:31 melt in f, O Philistia, all of you!
19:16 and tremble with f before the hand that
19:17 to whom it is mentioned will f because of the plan
25: 3 cities of ruthless nations will f you.
33: 6 the f of the LORD is Zion's treasure. C
35: 4 of a fearful heart, "Be strong, do not f! A
40: 9 herald of good tidings, lift it up, do not f; A
41:10 do not f, for I am with you, do not be afraid, A
41:13 it is I who say to you, "Do not f, I will help you." A
41:14 Do not f, you worm Jacob, you insect Israel! A
43: 1 Do not f, for I have redeemed you; A
43: 5 Do not f, for I am with you; A
44: 2 Do not f, O Jacob my servant, A
44: 8 Do not f, or be afraid; A
51: 7 do not f the reproach of others, A
51:13 You f continually all day long because of the fury
54: 4 Do not f, for you will not be ashamed; A
54:14 be far from oppression, for you shall not f;
57:11 Whom did you dread and f so that you lied,
57:11 and so you do not f me? A
59:19 those in the west shall f the name of the LORD,
Isa 63:17 so that we do not f you? A
66: 4 and bring upon them what they f;
Jer 2:19 the f of me is not in you,
3: 8 yet her false sister Judah did not f,
5:22 Do you not f me?
5:24 "Let us f the LORD our God, B
10: 7 Who would not f you, O King of the nations?
17: 8 It shall not f when heat comes,
23: 4 and they shall not f any longer, or be dismayed,
26:19 Did he not f the LORD and entreat the favor of B
30:10 But as for you, have no f, my servant Jacob,
32:39 that they may f me for all time,
32:40 and I will put the f of me in their hearts,
33: 9 they shall f and tremble because of all the good
35:11 for f of the army of the Chaldeans and the army of
42:16 then the sword that you f shall overtake you there,
44:10 They have shown no contrition or f to this day,
46:27 But as for you, have no f, my servant Jacob,
46:28 As for you, have no f, my servant Jacob,
49:23 in f, they are troubled like the sea that cannot
La 3:57 on you; you said, "Do not f!" A
Eze 3: 9 do not f them or be dismayed at their looks, A
30:13 so I will put f in the land of Egypt.
Da 6:26 and f before the God of Daniel:
10:12 He said to me, "Do not f, Daniel, A
10:19 He said, "Do not f, greatly beloved, you are safe. A
Hos 10: 3 "We have no king, for we do not f the LORD, AB
Joel 2:21 Do not f, O soil; be glad A
2:22 Do not f, you animals of the field, A
Am 3: 8 The lion has roared; who will not f?
Mic 6: 9 to the city (it is sound wisdom to f your name):
7:17 and they shall stand in f of you.
Zep 3: 7 I said, "Surely the city will f me,
3:15 you shall f disaster no more.
3:16 Do not f, O Zion; do not let your hands A
Hag 2: 5 My spirit abides among you; do not f. A
Mal 3: 5 and do not f me, says the LORD of hosts. A
Mt 10:26 "So have no f of them;
10:28 Do not f those who kill the body but cannot kill A
10:28 rather f him who can destroy both soul and body
14:26 And they cried out in f.
17: 6 they fell to the ground and were overcome by f.
28: 4 For f of him the guards shook and became
28: 8 So they left the tomb quickly with f and great joy,
Mk 5:33 came in f and trembling, fell down before him, H
5:36 to the leader of the synagogue, "Do not f, A
Lk 1:12 he was terrified; and f overwhelmed him.
1:50 His mercy is for those who f him from generation
1:65 F came over all their neighbors,
1:74 might serve him without f,
7:16 F seized all of them; and they glorified God,
8:37 for they were seized with great f.
8:50 When Jesus heard this, he replied, "Do not f. A
12: 4 my friends, do not f those who kill the body, A
12: 5 But I will warn you whom to f:
12: 5 But I will warn you whom to fear: f him who,
12: 5 Yes, I tell you, f him!
18: 4 I have no f of God and no respect for anyone, G
21:26 from f and foreboding of what is coming upon
23:40 other rebuked him, saying, "Do you not f God,
Jn 7:13 Yet no one would speak openly about him for f of
12:42 for f that they would be put out of the synagogue;
19:38 though a secret one because of his f of the Jews,
20:19 where the disciples had met were locked for f of
Ac 5: 5 And great f seized all who heard of it.
5:11 And great f seized the whole church
9:31 Living in the f of the Lord and in the comfort D
13:16 "You Israelites, and others who f God, listen. F
13:26 of Abraham's family, and others who f God, F
Ro 3:18 "There is no f of God before their eyes." G
8:15 not receive a spirit of slavery to fall back into f,
13: 3 Do you wish to have no f of the authority?
1Co 2: 3 in weakness and in f and in much trembling. H
16:10 see that he has nothing to f among you,
2Co 5:11 Therefore, knowing the f of the Lord, D
7: 1 making holiness perfect in the f of God. G
7:15 how you welcomed him with f and trembling. H
12:20 For I f that when I come,
12:20 I f that there may perhaps be quarreling, jealousy,
12:21 I f that when I come again,
Gal 2:12 he drew back and kept himself separate for f of
Eph 6: 5 obey your earthly masters with f and trembling, H
Php 1:14 the word with greater boldness and without f.
2:12 your own salvation with f and trembling; H
1Ti 5:20 so that the rest also may stand in f.
Heb 2:15 in slavery by the f of death.
12:21 the sight that Moses said, "I tremble with f.")
1Pe 1:17 live in reverent f during the time of your exile.
2:17 Love the family of believers. F God. F
3:14 Do not f what they fear, A
3:14 Do not fear what they f,
1Jn 4:18 There is no f in love,
4:18 but perfect love casts out f;
4:18 for f has to do with punishment,
Jude 1:12 while they feast with you without f,
1:23 and have mercy on still others with f,
Rev 2:10 Do not f what you are about to suffer. A
11:18 the prophets and saints and all who f your name,
14: 7 "F God and give him glory, F
15: 4 Lord, who will not f and glorify your name?
18:10 in f of her torment, and say, "Alas, alas,
18:15 in f of her torment, weeping and mourning aloud,
19: 5 and all who f him, small and great."
Tob 4:21 You have great wealth if you f God and flee F
5:16 "I will go with him; so do not f. A
5:21 Do not f for them, my sister. A
Jdt 2:28 So f and dread of him fell upon all

Jdt 10:16 you stand before him, have no f in your heart,
15: 2 Overcome with f and trembling, H
16:15 But to those who f you you show mercy.
AdE 2:20 but she was to f God and keep his laws, F
8:17 and became Jews out of f of the Jews.
9: 3 because f of Mordecai weighed upon them.
14:19 And save me from my f!"
15: 5 as if beloved, but her heart was frozen with f.
15:13 and my heart was shaken with f at your glory.
Wis 5: 2 they will be shaken with dreadful f,
12:11 through f of anyone that you left them unpunished
17: 4 that held them protected them from f,
17: 8 a sick soul were sick themselves with ridiculous f.
17:10 they perished in trembling f,
17:12 For f is nothing but a giving up of the helps
17:15 for sudden and unexpected f overwhelmed them.
Sir 1:11 The f of the Lord is glory and exultation, D
1:12 The f of the Lord delights the heart, D
1:13 Those who f the Lord will have a happy end; E
1:14 To f the Lord is the beginning of wisdom; E
1:16 To f the Lord is fullness of wisdom; E
1:18 The f of the Lord is the crown of wisdom, D
1:20 To f the Lord is the root of wisdom, E
1:27 For the f of the Lord is wisdom and discipline, D
1:28 Do not disobey the f of the Lord; D
1:30 because you did not come in the f of the Lord, D
2: 7 You who f the Lord, wait for his mercy; E
2: 8 You who f the Lord, trust in him, E
2: 9 You who f the Lord, hope for good things, E
2:10 Or has anyone persevered in the f of the Lord D
2:15 Those who f the Lord do not disobey his words, E
2:16 Those who f the Lord seek to please him, E
2:17 Those who f the Lord prepare their hearts, E
4:17 she will bring f and dread upon them,
6:16 and those who f the Lord will find them. E
6:17 who f the Lord direct their friendship aright, E
7:29 With all your soul f the Lord, E
7:31 F the Lord and honor the priest, E
9:13 and you will not be haunted by the f of death.
9:16 and let your glory be in the f of the Lord. D
10:19 Those who f the Lord. E
10:20 but those who f the Lord are worthy of honor E
10:22 their glory is the f of the Lord. D
15:13 such things are not loved by those who f him.
15:19 his eyes are on those who f him,
16: 2 unless the f of the Lord is in them. D
17: 4 He put the f of them in all living beings,
17: 8 He put the f of him into their hearts to show them
19:20 The whole of wisdom is f of the Lord, D
21: 6 but those who f the Lord repent in their heart. E
21:11 the fulfillment of the f of the Lord is wisdom. D
22:18 a fool's resolve will not stand firm against any f.
23:19 His f is confined to human eyes and he does
23:27 that nothing is better than the f of the Lord, D
25: 6 and their boast is the f of the Lord. D
25:11 F of the Lord surpasses everything; D
26: 5 and of a fourth I am in great f:
26:25 *but one who has a of shame will f the Lord.* E
27: 3 If a person is not steadfast in the f of the Lord, D
29: 7 but from f of being defrauded needlessly.
32:16 Those who f the Lord will form true judgments, E
32:18 and proud person will not be deterred by f.
34:14 The spirit of those who f the Lord will live, E
34:16 Those who f the Lord will not be timid, E
36: 2 and put all the nations in f of you.
40: 2 Perplexities and f of heart are theirs,
40: 5 and f of death, and fury and strife.
40:26 but the f of the Lord is better than either. D
40:26 There is no want in the f of the Lord, D
40:27 The f of the Lord is like a garden of blessing, D
41: 3 Do not f death's decree for you; A
42: 9 when she is young, for f she may not marry,
42: 9 or if married, for f she may be disliked;
42:10 for f she may be seduced and become pregnant
42:10 or having a husband, for f she may go astray, or,
42:10 or, though married, for f she may be barren.
45:23 in glory for being zealous in the f of the Lord, D
50:29 for the f of the Lord is their path. D
Bar 3: 7 the f of you in our hearts so that we would call
LtJ 6: 4 and which cause the heathen to f.
6: 5 or of letting f for these gods possess you
6:16 not gods; so do not f them. A
6:23 not gods; so do not f them. A
6:29 that they are not gods, do not f them. A
6:65 then that they are not gods, do not f them. A
6:69 that they are gods; therefore do not f them. A
Aza 1:18 we f you and seek your presence.
Sus 1:57 and they were intimate with you through f;
1Mc 2:62 Do not f the words of sinners, A
3: 6 Lawbreakers shrank back for f of him;
4: 8 "Do not f their numbers or be afraid when they A
5:41 But if he shows f and camps on the other side of
7:18 the f and dread of them fell on all the people,
12:52 and his companions and were in great f;
13: 2 and he saw that the people were trembling with f.
2Mc 3:30 a little while before was full of f and disturbance,
6:30 to suffer these things because I f him."
7:29 Do not f this butcher, but prove worthy A
8:16 not to be frightened by the enemy and not to f
12:22 and f came over the enemy at the manifestation
15: 8 He exhorted his troops not to f the attack of
15:18 and first f was for the consecrated sanctuary.
1Es 4:28 Do not all lands f to touch him?
3Mc 2:23 panic-stricken in their exceedingly great f.
6:13 And let the Gentiles cower today in f
7:22 of it restored it to them with extreme f.
2Es 2:17 Do not f, mother of children, A
7:79 and hated those who f God— F
7:87 and shall wither with f at seeing the glory of
7:98 and shall be glad without f,
10:38 and tell you about the things that you f;
12: 3 I woke up in great perplexity of mind and great f,
12: 5 a little strength is left in me, because of the great f
13: 8 were filled with f, and yet they dared to fight.
15: 3 Do not f the plots against you, A
15:29 so that all who hear them will f and tremble.
15:33 and f and trembling shall come upon their army, H
15:37 there shall be f and great trembling on the earth; H
16:67 Indeed, God is the judge; f him!
16:70 be a great uprising against those who f the Lord. E
16:71 and destroying those who continue to f the Lord. E
16:75 Do not f or doubt, for God is your guide. A
4Mc 1: 4 namely anger, f, and pain.
1:23 F precedes pain and sorrow comes after.
4:10 instilling in them great f and trembling. H
5:37 one who does not f your violence even to death.
8:12 to persuade them out of f to eat the defiling food.
8:19 not f the instruments of torture and consider
13:14 Let us not f him who thinks he is killing us,
14: 8 the sevenfold f of tortures and dissolved it.
15: 8 the f of God she disdained the temporary safety G

FEARED‡ (43) [FEAR]

Ge 38:11 for he f that he too would die, like his brothers.
42: 4 for he f that harm might come to him.
Ex 1:17 But the midwives f God; they did
1:21 the midwives f God, he gave them families.
9:20 Those officials of Pharaoh who f the word of
14:31 So the people f the LORD and believed in
Dt 32:17 whom your ancestors had not f.
32:27 but I f provocation by the enemy,
1Sa 12:18 all the people greatly f the LORD and Samuel.
14:26 not put their hands to their mouths, for they f
15:24 because I f the people and obeyed their voice.
2Sa 3:11 not answer Abner another word, because he f him.
2Ki 4: 1 and you know that your servant f the LORD,
Ne 7: 2 he was a faithful man and f God more than many.
Job 1: 1 one who f God and turned away from evil.
Ps 76: 8 the earth f and was still
89: 7 a God f in the council of the holy ones,
Isa 18: 2 to a people f near and far,
18: 7 from a people f near and far,
Eze 11: 8 You have f the sword;
Da 5:19 nations, and languages trembled and f before him.
Jnh 1:16 Then the men f the LORD even more,
Hag 1:12 and the people f the LORD.
Mt 14: 5 Herod wanted to put him to death, he f the crowd,
21:46 They wanted to arrest him, but they f the crowds,
Mk 6:20 for Herod f John, knowing that he was a righteous
12:12 they wanted to arrest him, but they f the crowd.
Lk 18: 2 a certain city there was a judge who neither f God
20:19 to lay hands on him at that very hour, but they f
Ac 10: 2 a devout man who f God with all his household;
Jdt 2:28 in Azotus and Ascalon f him greatly.
8: 8 for she f God with great devotion.
AdE 9: 2 no one resisted, because they f them.
11: 9 they f the evils that threatened them,
Wis 18:25 To these the destroyer yielded, these he f;
Sir 1: 8 There is but one who is wise, greatly to be f,
9:18 The loud of mouth are f in their city,
Sus 1: 2 a very beautiful woman and one who f the Lord.
1Mc 3:25 Then Judas and his brothers began to be f,
3:30 He f that he might not have such funds as he had
8:12 as many as have heard of their fame have f them.
12:40 He f that Jonathan might not permit him to do so,
2Es 8:28 that you are to be f.

FEARFUL (10) [FEAR]

Jdg 7: 3 'Whoever is f and trembling,
Isa 35: 4 Say to those who are of a f heart, "Be strong,
Jer 51:46 Do not be fainthearted or f at the rumors heard in
Da 8:24 shall cause f destruction, and shall succeed
Heb 10:27 but a f prospect of judgment,
10:31 a f thing to fall into the hands of the living God.
Rev 16:21 for the plague of the hail, so f was that plague.
3Mc 6:18 of f aspect descended, visible to all but
2Es 10:26 she suddenly uttered a loud and f cry,
4Mc 3:15 considered it an altogether f danger to his soul

FEARFULLY (1) [FEAR]

Ps 139:14 I praise you, for I am f and wonderfully made.

FEARFULNESS (3) [FEAR]

Eze 4:16 they shall eat bread by weight and with f;
12:18 and drink your water with trembling and with f;
12:19 They shall eat their bread with f,

FEARING (12) [FEAR]

Dt 8: 6 by walking in his ways and by f him.
28:58 f this glorious and awesome name,
1Ki 1:50 f Solomon, got up and went to grasp the horns of
Ac 23:10 the tribune, f that they would tear Paul to pieces,
27:17 then, f that they would run on the Syrtis,
27:29 F that we might run on the rocks,
Col 3:22 but wholeheartedly, f the Lord.
2Mc 3:32 f that the king might get the notion
9:29 then, f the son of Antiochus,
3Mc 2:23 and f that he would lose his life,
4Mc 8:22 for f the king when we are under compulsion.
8:25 to death for f the instruments of torture.

FEARS‡ (24) [FEAR]

Job 1: 8 and upright man who f God and turns away
2: 3 and upright man who f God and turns away
Ps 34: 4 and delivered me from all my f.
128: 1 Happy is everyone who f the LORD,
128: 4 Thus shall the man be blessed who f the LORD.
Pr 31:30 but a woman who f the LORD is to be praised.
Ecc 7:18 for the one who f God shall succeed with both.
Isa 8:12 and do not fear what it f, or be in dread.
50:10 among you f the LORD and obeys the voice
Ac 10:35 but in every nation anyone who f him
2Co 7: 5 disputes without and f within.
1Pe 3: 6 as you do what is good and never let f alarm you.
1Jn 4:18 and whoever f has not reached perfection in love.
Jdt 16:16 but whoever f the Lord is great forever.
Wis 17: 8 For those who promised to drive off the f
18:17 and unexpected f assailed them;
Sir 10:24 of them is greater than the one who f the Lord.
15: 1 Whoever f the Lord will do this,
25:10 But none is superior to the one who f the Lord.
26: 3 be granted among the blessings of the man who f
26:23 *a pious wife is given to the man who f the Lord.*
33: 1 No evil will befall the one who f the Lord,
34:17 Happy is the soul that f the Lord!
40: 7 astonished that his f were groundless.

FEARSOME (1) [FEAR]

Hab 1: 7 Dread and f are they; their justice

FEAST‡ (44) [FEASTED, FEASTING, FEASTS, LOVE-FEASTS]

Ge 19: 3 and he made them a f,
21: 8 a great f on the day that Isaac was weaned.
26:30 So he made them a f, and they ate and drank.
29:22 the people of the place, and made a f.
40:20 he made a f for all his servants,
Jdg 14:10 a f there as the young men were accustomed
14:12 to me within the seven days of the f,
14:17 before him the seven days that their f lasted;
1Sa 20:24 the new moon came, the king sat at the f to eat.
20:27 "Why has the son of Jesse not come to the f,
25: 8 for we have come on a f day.
25:36 he was holding a f in his house, like the f of a king.
2Sa 3:20 David made a f for Abner and the men who were
13:27 Absalom made a f like a king's f.
1Ki 3:15 and provided a f for all his servants.
2Ki 6:23 So he prepared for them a great f;
Est 7: 1 king and Haman went in to f with Queen Esther.
7: 7 The king rose from the f in wrath and went into
Job 1: 5 And when the f days had run their course,
Ps 36: 8 They f on the abundance of your house,
63: 5 My soul is satisfied as with a rich f,
Pr 15:15 but a cheerful heart has a continual f.
Ecc 10:16 and your princes f in the morning!
10:17 and your princes f at the proper time—
Isa 25: 6 of hosts will make for all peoples a f of rich food,
25: 6 a feast of rich food, a f of well-aged wines,
Eze 20: 7 Cast away the detestable things your eyes f on,
28:17 I exposed you before kings, to f their eyes on you.
39:17 to the sacrificial f that I am preparing for you,
39:17 a great sacrificial f on the mountains of Israel,
39:19 at the sacrificial f that I am preparing for you.
2Pe 2:13 reveling in their dissipation while they f with you.
Jude 1:12 while they f with you without fear,
Tob 11:18 merriment they celebrated Tobias's wedding f
AdE 14:17 and I have not honored the king's f or drunk
Sir 11:19 and now I shall f on my goods!"
32: 1 If they make you master of the f,
Sus 1:32 so that they might f their eyes on her beauty.
3Mc 4: 1 a f at public expense was arranged for
5:31 a rich f for the savage animals instead of the Jews,
2Es 2:38 the number of those who have been sealed at the f
9:47 I set a day for the marriage f.

FEASTED (6) [FEAST]

La 4: 5 Those who f on delicacies perish in the streets;
Eze 20: 8 the detestable things their eyes f on,
Lk 16:19 and fine linen and who f sumptuously every day.
Jdt 1:16 and there he and his forces rested and f
1Es 4:63 they f, with music and rejoicing, for seven days.
3Mc 6:40 Then they f, being provided with everything by

FEASTING (16) [FEAST]

1Ki 1:41 with him heard it as they finished f.
Est 9:17 and made that a day of f and gladness.
9:18 making that a day of f and gladness.
9:19 of the month of Adar as a day for gladness and f,
9:22 they should make them days of f and gladness,
Pr 17: 1 a dry morsel with quiet than a house full of f
Ecc 7: 2 of mourning than to go to the house of f;
Jer 16: 8 not go into the house of f to sit with them,
Jdt 16:20 the people continued f in Jerusalem before
AdE 9:22 a time for f and gladness and for sending presents
13:17 turn our mourning into f that we may live
Wis 12: 5 and their sacrificial f on human flesh and blood.
Sir 18:33 not become a beggar by f with borrowed money,
1Es 3:20 It turns every thought to f and mirth,
3Mc 5: 3 he had given these orders he returned to his f,
6:35 in f to the accompaniment of joyous thanksgiving

FEASTS‡ (7) [FEAST]

Job 1: 4 to go and hold f in one another's houses in turn;
Ecc 10:19 F are made for laughter; wine gladdens life,

Isa 5:12 whose **f** consist of lyre and harp,
Am 8:10 I will turn your **f** into mourning,
1Mc 1:39 her **f** were turned into mourning,
1Es 5:52 and at new moons and at all the consecrated **f**.
3Mc 4:16 organizing **f** in honor of all his idols,

FEATHERED (1) [FEATHERS]
2Es 11: 1 an eagle that had twelve **f** wings and three heads.

FEATHERS (1) [FEATHERED]
Da 4:33 as long as eagles' **f** and his nails became

FED (20) [FEED]
Ge 41:18 came up out of the Nile and **f** in the reed grass.
Ex 16:32 that they may see the food with which I **f** you in
Dt 8:16 and **f** you in the wilderness with manna
32:13 and **f** him with produce of the field;
Jdg 19:21 he brought him into his house, and **f** the donkeys;
Ps 80: 5 You have **f** them with the bread of tears,
Isa 1:11 of burnt offerings of rams and the fat of **f** beasts;
Jer 5: 7 When I **f** them to the full,
Eze 16:19 I **f** you with choice flour and oil and honey—
34: 8 but the shepherds have **f** themselves, and have not **f** my sheep;
Da 4:12 and from it all living beings were **f**.
5:21 he was **f** grass like oxen,
Hos 11: 4 I bent down to them and **f** them.
13: 5 It was I who **f** you in the wilderness,
13: 6 When I **f** them, they were satisfied;
Mk 7:27 He said to her, "Let the children be **f** first,
1Co 3: 2 I **f** you with milk, not solid food,
Wis 16:23 in order that the righteous might be **f**,
Bel 1:27 which he **f** to the dragon.

FEE (3) [FEES]
Ex 22:15 if it was hired, only the hiring **f** is due.
Dt 23:18 not bring the **f** of a prostitute or the wages of
Pr 6:26 for a prostitute's **f** is only a loaf of bread,

FEEBLE (14) [FEEBLER, FEEBLEST]
1Sa 2: 4 but the **f** gird on strength.
2Ch 28:15 and carrying all the **f** among them on donkeys,
36:17 the aged or the **f**; he gave them all into his hand.
Ne 4: 2 "What are these **f** Jews doing?
Job 4: 4 and you have made firm the **f** knees.
Isa 13: 7 Therefore all hands will be **f**,
16:14 and those who survive will be very few and **f**.
35: 3 and make firm the **f** knees.
Jer 47: 3 not turn back for children, so **f** are their hands,
49:24 Damascus has become **f**, she turned to flee,
Eze 7:17 All hands shall grow **f**, all knees turn to water.
21: 7 Every heart will melt and all hands will be **f**,
Bar 2:18 who walks bowed and **f**, with failing eyes
4Mc 7:13 his muscles flabby, his sinews **f**,

FEEBLER (2) [FEEBLE]
Ge 30:42 but for the **f** of the flock he did not lay them there;
30:42 so the **f** were Laban's, and the stronger Jacob's.

FEEBLEST (1) [FEEBLE]
Zec 12: 8 the **f** among them on that day shall be like David,

FEED‡ (45) [FED, FEEDING, FEEDS, PASTURE-FED, WELL-FED]
Ge 30:31 I will again **f** your flock and keep it:
1Sa 17:15 from Saul to **f** his father's sheep at Bethlehem.
1Ki 17: 4 and I have commanded the ravens to **f** you there."
17: 9 for I have commanded a widow there to **f** you."
22:27 and **f** him on reduced rations of bread and water
2Ch 18:26 and **f** him on reduced rations of bread and water
Ps 80:13 and all that move in the field **f** on it.
81:16 I would **f** you with the finest of the wheat,
Pr 10:21 The lips of the righteous **f** many,
15:14 but the mouths of fools **f** on folly.
30: 8 **f** me with the food that I need,
SS 4: 5 twins of a gazelle, that **f** among the lilies.
Isa 5:17 fatlings and kids shall **f** among the ruins.
40:11 He will **f** his flock like a shepherd;
49: 9 They shall **f** along the ways,
58:14 I will **f** you with the heritage
61: 5 Strangers shall stand and **f** your flocks,
65:25 The wolf and the lamb shall **f** together,
Jer 3:15 who will **f** you with knowledge
50:19 and it shall **f** on Carmel and in Bashan,
Eze 34: 2 Should not shepherds **f** the sheep?
34: 3 but you do not **f** the sheep.
34:10 no longer shall the shepherds **f** themselves.
34:13 and I will **f** them on the mountains of Israel,
34:14 I will **f** them with good pasture,
34:14 and they shall **f** on rich pasture on the mountains
34:16 I will **f** them with justice.
34:18 Is it not enough for you to **f** on the good pasture,
34:23 my servant David, and he shall **f** them:
34:23 he shall **f** them and be their shepherd.
Hos 4: 8 They **f** on the sin of my people;
4:16 now **f** them like a lamb in a broad pasture?
9: 2 Threshing floor and wine vat shall not **f** them,
Jnh 3: 7 They shall not **f**, nor shall they drink water.
Mic 5: 4 And he shall stand and **f** his flock in the strength
7:14 let them **f** in Bashan and Gilead as in the days
Hab 2:13 the LORD of hosts that peoples labor only to **f**
Mt 15:33 to get enough bread in the desert to **f** so great
Mk 8: 4 "How can one **f** these people with bread here in
Lk 15:15 who sent him to his fields to **f** the pigs.
Jn 21:15 Jesus said to him, "**F** my lambs."
21:17 Jesus said to him, "**F** my sheep.
Ro 12:20 No, "if your enemies are hungry, **f** them;
Sir 15: 3 She will **f** him with the bread of learning,
2Mc 15:33 and said that he would **f** it piecemeal to the birds

FEEDING‡ (10) [FEED]
Dt 8: 3 then by **f** you with manna,
Job 1:14 "The oxen were plowing and the donkeys were **f**
Jer 9:15 I am **f** this people with wormwood,
Eze 34: 2 of Israel who have been **f** yourselves!
34:10 and put a stop to their **f** the sheep;
Mt 8:30 Now a large herd of swine was **f** at some distance
Mk 5:11 there on the hillside a great herd of swine was **f**;
Lk 8:32 there on the hillside a large herd of swine was **f**;
Jude 1:12 with you without fear, **f** themselves.
Sir 13:19 likewise the poor are **f** grounds for the rich.

FEEDS (4) [FEED]
Isa 44:20 He **f** on ashes; a deluded mind has led him astray,
Mt 6:26 and yet your heavenly Father **f** them.
Lk 12:24 nor barn, and yet God **f** them.
Wis 16:26 not the production of crops that **f** humankind but

FEEL (22) [FEELINGS, FEELS, FELT]
Ge 27:12 Perhaps my father will **f** me,
27:21 Isaac said to Jacob, "Come near, that I may **f** you,
Dt 28:67 of the dread that your heart shall **f** and the sights
Jdg 16:26 "Let me **f** the pillars on which the house rests,
1Sa 16:16 he will play it, and you will **f** better."
16:23 and Saul would be relieved and **f** better,
Job 14:22 They **f** only the pain of their own bodies,
Ps 58: 9 Sooner than your pots can **f** the heat of thorns,
115: 7 They have hands, but do not **f**;
Pr 23:35 they beat me, but I did not **f** it.
Isa 44:16 "Ah, I am warm, I can **f** the fire!"
Jer 10:18 on them, so that they shall **f** it.
Am 6: 1 and for those who **f** secure on Mount Samaria,
Ro 15:14 I myself **f** confident about you,
2Co 11: 2 I **f** a divine jealousy for you,
1Th 3: 9 the joy that we **f** before our God because of you?
Tob 5:14 Do not **f** bitter toward me, brother,
Jdt 8:31 Then we will no longer **f** faint from thirst."
Wis 15:15 nor ears with which to hear, nor fingers to **f** with,
Sir 41:16 it is not good to **f** shame in every circumstance,
LtJ 6:24 even when they were being cast, they did not **f** it.
1Es 3:21 It makes all hearts **f** rich,

FEELINGS‡ (5) [FEEL]
Wis 1: 6 because God is witness of their inmost **f**,
Sir 22:19 and one who pricks the heart makes clear its **f**.
31:15 Judge your neighbor's **f** by your own,
4Mc 8: 5 with favorable **f** I admire each and every one
12:13 of men who have **f** like yours and are made of

FEELS (3) [FEEL]
Sir 20:21 so when he rests he **f** no remorse.
31:20 he rises early, and **f** fit.
2Es 13: 4 as wax melts when it **f** the fire.

FEES (1) [FEE]
Nu 22: 7 and the elders of Midian departed with the **f**

FEET‡ (272) [FOOT]
Ge 18: 4 Let a little water be brought, and wash your **f**,
19: 2 and spend the night, and wash your **f**;
24:32 and water to wash his **f** and the **f** of the men
43:24 and they had washed their **f**,
49:10 nor the ruler's staff from between his **f**,
49:33 he drew up his **f** into the bed, breathed his last,
Ex 3: 5 Remove the sandals from your **f**,
4:25 and touched Moses' **f** with it, and said,
12:11 your loins girded, your sandals on your **f**,
24:10 Under his **f** there was something like a pavement
25:12 of gold for it and put them on its four **f**,
29:20 and on the big toes of their right **f**,
30:19 and his sons shall wash their hands and their **f**.
30:21 They shall wash their hands and their **f**,
37: 3 He cast for it four rings of gold for its four **f**,
40:31 and his sons washed their hands and their **f**.
Lev 8:24 and on the big toes of their right **f**;
11:21 that have jointed legs above their **f**,
11:23 that have four **f** are detestable to you.
11:42 or whatever has many **f**, all the creatures
Dt 8: 4 on your back did not wear out and your **f** did
29: 5 and the sandals on your **f** have not worn out;
Jos 3:13 the soles of the **f** of the priests who bear the ark of
3:15 the **f** of the priests bearing the ark were dipped in
4: 3 from the place where the priests' **f** stood,
4: 9 the place where the **f** of the priests bearing the ark
4:18 and the soles of the priests' **f** touched dry ground,
5:15 "Remove the sandals from your **f**,
9: 5 patched sandals on their **f**, and worn-out clothes;
10:24 put your **f** on the necks of these kings."
10:24 they came near and put their **f** on their necks.
Jdg 5:27 he fell, he lay still at her **f**; at her **f** he sank, he fell;
19:21 they washed their **f**, and ate and drank.
Ru 2: 7 and she has been on her **f** from early this morning
3: 4 then, go and uncover his **f** and lie down;
3: 7 Then she came stealthily and uncovered his **f**,
3: 8 and turned over, and there, lying at his **f**,
3:14 So she lay at his **f** until morning,
1Sa 2: 9 "He will guard the **f** of his faithful ones,
14:13 Then Jonathan climbed up on his hands and **f**,
25:24 She fell at his **f** and said, "Upon me alone,
25:41 a slave to wash the **f** of the servants of my lord."
2Sa 3:34 not bound, your **f** were not fettered;
4: 4 a son who was crippled in his **f**.
4:12 they cut off their hands and **f**,
9: 3 he is crippled in his **f**."
9:13 Now he was lame in both his **f**.
11: 8 "Go down to your house, and wash your **f**."
19:24 he had not taken care of his **f**,
22:10 thick darkness was under his **f**.
22:34 He made my **f** like the **f** of deer,
22:37 and my **f** do not slip;
22:39 not rise; they fell under my **f**.
1Ki 2: 5 and on the sandals on his **f**.
5: 3 until the LORD put them under the soles of his **f**.
14: 6 But when Ahijah heard the sound of her **f**,
14:12 When your **f** enter the city, the child shall die.
15:23 But in his old age he was diseased in his **f**.
2Ki 4:27 she caught hold of his **f**.
4:37 She came and fell at his **f**, bowing to the ground;
6:32 Is not the sound of his master's **f** behind him?"
9:35 they found no more of her than the skull and the **f**
13:21 he came to life and stood on his **f**.
21: 8 the **f** of Israel to wander any more out of the land
1Ch 28: 2 Then King David rose to his **f** and said:
2Ch 3:13 the cherubim stood on their **f**, facing the nave.
16:12 in his **f**, and his disease became severe;
33: 8 I will never again remove the **f** of Israel from
Ne 9:21 their clothes did not wear out and their **f** did
Est 8: 3 at his **f**, weeping and pleading with him to avert
Job 12: 5 but it is ready for those whose **f** are unstable.
13:27 You put my **f** in the stocks,
13:27 you set a bound to the soles of my **f**.
18: 8 For they are thrust into a net by their own **f**,
29:15 I was eyes to the blind, and **f** to the lame.
33:11 he puts my **f** in the stocks,
Ps 2:12 kiss his **f**, or he will be angry, and you will perish
8: 6 you have put all things under their **f**,
17: 5 to your paths; my **f** have not slipped.
18: 9 thick darkness was under his **f**.
18:33 He made my **f** like the **f** of a deer,
18:36 and my **f** did not slip.
18:38 not able to rise; they fell under my **f**.
22:16 My hands and **f** have shriveled;
25:15 for he will pluck my **f** out of the net.
31: 8 you have set my **f** in a broad place.
40: 2 out of the miry bog, and set my **f** upon a rock,
47: 3 under us, and nations under our **f**.
56:13 and my **f** from falling, so that I may walk
58:10 they will bathe their **f** in the blood of the wicked.
66: 9 and has not let our **f** slip.
68:23 so that you may bathe your **f** in blood,
73: 2 But as for me, my **f** had almost stumbled;
105:18 His **f** were hurt with fetters,
115: 7 They have hands, but do not feel; **f**,
116: 8 my eyes from tears, my **f** from stumbling.
119:59 I think of your ways, I turn my **f** to your decrees;
119:101 I hold back my **f** from every evil way,
119:105 Your word is a lamp to my **f** and a light
122: 2 Our **f** are standing within your gates,
Pr 1:16 for their **f** run to evil,
4:26 Keep straight the path of your **f**,
5: 5 Her **f** go down to death;
6:13 shuffling the **f**, pointing the fingers,
6:18 **f** that hurry to run to evil,
6:28 on hot coals without scorching the **f**?
7:11 her **f** do not stay at home;
29: 5 a neighbor is spreading a net for the neighbor's **f**.
SS 5: 3 I had bathed my **f**; how could I soil them?
7: 1 graceful are your **f** in sandals, O queenly maiden!
Isa 3:16 mincing along as they go, tinkling with their **f**;
6: 2 and with two they covered their **f**,
7:20 the head and the hair of the **f**,
20: 2 from your loins and take your sandals off your **f**,"
23: 7 whose **f** carried her to settle far away?
26: 6 The foot tramples it, the **f** of the poor,
41: 3 scarcely touching the path with his **f**.
49:23 and lick the dust of your **f**.
52: 7 How beautiful upon the mountains are the **f** of
59: 7 Their **f** run to evil, and they rush
60:13 and I will glorify where my **f** rest.
60:14 all who despised you shall bow down at your **f**;
Jer 2:25 Keep your **f** from going unshod and your throat
13:16 your **f** stumble on the mountains at twilight;
14:10 they have not restrained their **f**;
18:22 and laid snares for my **f**.
38:22 that your **f** are stuck in the mud, they desert you.'
La 1:13 he spread a net for my **f**;
Eze 1: 7 soles of their **f** were like the sole of a calf's foot;
2: 1 He said to me: O mortal, stand up on your **f**,
2: 2 a spirit entered into me and set me on my **f**;
3:24 The spirit entered into me, and set me on my **f**;
24:17 and put your sandals on your **f**;
24:23 be on your heads and your sandals on your **f**;
25: 6 and stamped your **f** and rejoiced with all
32: 2 trouble the water with your **f**,
34:18 but you must tread down with your **f** the rest
34:18 must you foul the rest with your **f**?
34:19 with your **f**, and drink what you have fouled with your **f**?
37:10 and stood on their **f**, a vast multitude.
43: 7 of my throne and the place for the soles of my **f**,
Da 2:33 its **f** partly of iron and partly of clay.
2:34 the statue on its **f** of iron and clay and broke them
2:41 As you saw the **f** and toes partly of potter's clay

Da 2:42 As the toes of the **f** were part iron and part clay,
7: 4 from the ground and made to stand on two **f** like
7: 7 and stamping what was left with its **f.**
7:19 and stamped what was left with its **f;**
8:18 then he touched me and set me on my **f.**
10:11 Stand on your **f,** for I have now been sent to you."
Na 1: 3 and the clouds are the dust of his **f.**
1:15 the **f** of one who brings good tidings,
Hab 3:19 he makes my **f** like the feet of a deer,
3:19 he makes my feet like the **f** of a deer,
Zec 14: 4 that day his **f** shall stand on the Mount of Olives,
14:12 their flesh shall rot while they are still on their **f;**
Mal 4: 3 for they will be ashes under the soles of your **f,**
Mt 10:14 from your **f** as you leave that house or town.
15:30 They put them at his **f,** and he cured them,
18: 8 to have two hands or two **f** and to be thrown into
22:44 until I put your enemies under your **f"** '?
28: 9 And they came to him, took hold of his **f,**
Mk 5:22 and, when he saw him, fell at his **f**
6:11 shake off the dust that is on your **f** as a testimony
7:25 and she came and bowed down at his **f.**
9:45 for you to enter life lame than to have two **f** and
12:36 until I put your enemies under your **f."** '
Lk 1:79 to guide our **f** into the way of peace."
7:38 She stood behind him at his **f,** weeping,
7:38 to bathe his **f** with her tears and to dry them
7:38 Then she continued kissing his **f**
7:44 for my **f,** but she has bathed my **f** with her tears
7:45 in she has not stopped kissing my **f.**
7:46 but she has anointed my **f** with ointment.
8:35 from whom the demons had gone sitting at the **f**
8:41 at Jesus' **f** and begged him to come to his house,
9: 5 that town shake the dust off your **f** as a testimony
10:11 'Even the dust of your town that clings to our **f,**
10:39 at the Lord's **f** and listened to what he was saying.
15:22 put a ring on his finger and sandals on his **f.**
17:16 He prostrated himself at Jesus' **f** and thanked him.
24:39 Look at my hands and my **f;**
24:40 he showed them his hands and his **f.**
Jn 11: 2 with perfume and wiped his **f** with her hair;
11:32 she knelt at his **f** and said to him, "Lord,
11:44 his hands and **f** bound with strips of cloth,
12: 3 anointed Jesus' **f,** and wiped them with her hair.
13: 5 into a basin and began to wash the disciples' **f** and
13: 6 "Lord, are you going to wash my **f?"**
13: 8 Peter said to him, "You will never wash my **f."**
13: 9 not my **f** only but also my hands and my head!"
13:10 except for the **f,** but is entirely clean.
13:12 After he had washed their **f,** had put on his robe,
13:14 your **f,** you also ought to wash one another's **f.**
20:12 one at the head and the other at the **f.**
Ac 3: 7 immediately his **f** and ankles were made strong.
4:35 They laid it at the apostles' **f.**
4:37 and laid it at the apostles' **f.**
5: 2 brought only a part and laid it at the apostles' **f.**
5: 9 the **f** of those who have buried your husband are
5:10 Immediately she fell down at his **f** and died.
7:33 'Take off the sandals from your **f,**
7:58 and the witnesses laid their coats at the **f** of
10:25 and falling at his **f,** worshiped him.
13:25 to untie the thong of the sandals on his **f.'**
13:51 So they shook the dust off their **f** in protest
14: 8 a man sitting who could not use his **f**
14:10 "Stand upright on your **f."**
16:24 in the innermost cell and fastened their **f** in
21:11 bound his own **f** and hands with it, and said,
22: 3 but brought up in this city at the **f** of Gamaliel,
26:16 But get up and stand on your **f;**
Ro 3:15 "Their **f** are swift to shed blood;
10:15 the **f** of those who bring good news!"
16:20 of peace will shortly crush Satan under your **f.**
1Co 12:21 nor again the head to the **f,**
15:25 until he has put all his enemies under his **f.**
15:27 "God has put all things in subjection under his **f."**
Eph 1:22 under his **f** and has made him the head
6:15 for your **f** put on whatever will make you ready
1Ti 5:10 washed the saints' **f,** helped the afflicted,
Heb 1:13 until I make your enemies a footstool for your **f"?**
2: 8 subjecting all things under their **f."**
10:13 be made a footstool for his **f."**
12:13 and make straight paths for your **f,**
Jas 2: 3 "Stand there," or, "Sit at my **f,"**
Rev 1:15 his **f** were like burnished bronze,
1:17 When I saw him, I fell at his **f** as though dead.
2:18 and whose **f** are like burnished bronze:
3: 9 and bow down before your **f,**
11:11 and they stood on their **f,**
12: 1 with the moon under her **f,**
13: 2 its **f** were like a bear's,
19:10 Then I fell down at his **f** to worship him,
22: 8 to worship at the **f** of the angel who showed them
Tob 6: 3 Then the young man went down to wash his **f** in
Jdt 2: 7 the whole face of the earth with the **f**
10: 4 She put sandals on her **f,** and put on her anklets,
14: 7 they raised him up he threw himself at Judith's **f,**
AdE 8: 3 falling at his **f,** she asked him to avert all the evil
13:13 to kiss the soles of his **f** to save Israel!
Wis 14:11 for human souls and a trap for the **f** of the foolish.
15:15 and their **f** are of no use for walking.
Sir 6:24 Put your **f** into her fetters,
8:11 Do not let the insolent bring you to your **f,**
21:19 To a senseless person education is fetters on his **f,**
25:20 A sandy ascent for the **f** of the aged—
26:18 so are shapely legs and steadfast **f.**
38:29 at his work and turning the wheel with his **f;**
38:30 with his arm and makes it pliable with his **f;**
LtJ 6:18 of the dust raised by the **f** of those who enter.
LtJ 6:26 Having no **f,** they are carried on the shoulders
2Mc 7: 4 that they scalp him and cut off his hands and **f,**
3Mc 4: 9 others had their **f** secured by unbreakable fetters,
5:42 mangled by the knees and **f** of the animals,
2Es 1:26 and your **f** are swift to commit murder.
2:15 strengthen their **f,** because I have chosen you,
2:25 nourish your children; strengthen their **f.**
5:15 and strengthened me and set me on my **f.**
6:13 "Rise to your **f** and you will hear a full,
6:17 When I heard this, I got to my **f** and listened;
10:30 and strengthened me and set me on my **f,**
14: 2 I answered, "Here I am, Lord," and I rose to my **f.**
4Mc 10: 5 they disjointed his hands and **f**
14: 6 and **f** are moved in harmony with the guidance of

FEIGN (1) [FEIGNED]

4Mc 6:17 that out of cowardice we **f** a role unbecoming

FEIGNED (1) [FEIGN]

Ps 34: T *Of David, when he* **f** *madness before Abimelech,*

FELIX (8)

Ac 23:24 and take him safely to **F** the governor."
23:26 to his Excellency the governor **F,**
24:22 But **F,** who was rather well informed about
24:24 when **F** came with his wife Drusilla,
24:25 **F** became frightened and said,
24:27 **F** was succeeded by Porcius Festus;
24:27 to grant the Jews a favor, **F** left Paul in prison.
25:14 "There is a man here who was left in prison by **F.**

FELL‡ (272) [FALL]

Ge 4: 5 So Cain was very angry, and his countenance **f.**
7:12 The rain **f** on the earth forty days and forty nights.
14:10 as the kings of Sodom and Gomorrah fled, some **f**
15:12 sun was going down, a deep sleep **f** upon Abram,
17: 3 Then Abram **f** on his face; and God said to him,
17:17 Then Abraham **f** on his face and laughed,
33: 4 and **f** on his neck and kissed him, and they wept.
35: 5 terror from God **f** upon the cities all around them,
41: 5 Then he **f** asleep and dreamed a second time;
41:22 I **f** asleep a second time and I saw
44:14 and they **f** to the ground before him.
45:14 he **f** upon his brother Benjamin's neck and wept,
46:29 He presented himself to him, **f** on his neck,
50:18 Then his brothers also wept, **f** down before him,
Ex 15:16 Terror and dread **f** upon them;
32:28 about three thousand of the people **f** on that day.
Lev 9:24 they shouted and **f** on their faces.
16: 9 Aaron shall present the goat on which the lot **f** for
16:10 the lot **f** for Azazel shall be presented alive before
Nu 11: 9 When the dew **f** on the camp in the night,
14: 5 and Aaron **f** on their faces before all the assembly
16: 4 When Moses heard it, he **f** on his face.
16:22 They **f** on their faces, and said, "O God,
16:45 And they **f** on their faces.
20: 6 they **f** on their faces, and the glory of
Jos 5:14 Joshua **f** on his face to the earth and worshiped,
6:20 they raised a great shout, and the wall **f** down flat;
7: 6 and **f** to the ground on his face before the ark of
8:25 The total of those who **f** that day,
11: 7 by the waters of Merom, and **f** upon them.
17: 5 Thus there **f** to Manasseh ten portions,
18:11 and the territory allotted to it **f** between the tribe
21:10 since the lot **f** to them first.
22:20 and wrath **f** upon all the congregation of Israel?
Jdg 4:16 All the army of Sisera **f** by the sword;
5:27 He sank, he **f,** he lay still at her feet; at her feet he
sank, he **f;** where he sank, there he **f** dead.
7:13 and came to the tent, and struck it so that it **f;**
9:40 Many **f** wounded, up to the entrance of the gate.
12: 6 Forty-two thousand of the Ephraimites **f** at
13:20 and they **f** on their faces to the ground.
16: 4 After this he **f** in love with a woman in the valley
16:30 and the house **f** on the lords and all
19:26 the woman came and **f** down at the door of
20:44 Eighteen thousand Benjaminites **f,**
20:46 So all who **f** that day
Ru 2:10 Then she **f** prostrate, with her face to the ground,
1Sa 4:10 for there **f** of Israel thirty thousand foot soldiers.
4:18 Eli **f** over backward from his seat by the side of
10:10 and he **f** into a prophetic frenzy along with them.
11: 7 Then the dread of the LORD **f** upon the people,
14:13 The Philistines **f** before Jonathan,
17:49 and he **f** face down on the ground.
17:52 so that the wounded Philistines **f** on the way
19:20 and they also **f** into a prophetic frenzy.
19:21 and they also **f** into a frenzy.
19:21 and they also **f** into a frenzy.
19:23 As he was going, he **f** into a prophetic frenzy,
19:24 and he too **f** into a frenzy before Samuel.
25:23 **f** before David on her face, bowing to the ground.
25:24 She **f** at his feet and said, "Upon me alone,
28:20 Immediately Saul **f** full length on the ground,
30:13 behind because I **f** sick three days ago.
31: 1 and many **f** on Mount Gilboa.
31: 4 So Saul took his own sword and **f** upon it.
31: 5 he also **f** upon his sword and died with him.
2Sa 1: 2 he **f** to the ground and did obeisance.
1: 4 but also many of the army **f** and died;
2:16 in his opponent's side; so they **f** down together.
2:23 He **f** there, and died where he lay.
4: 4 it happened that he **f** and became lame.
9: 6 and **f** on his face and did obeisance.
11:17 of the servants of David among the people **f.**
2Sa 13: 1 and David's son Amnon **f** in love with her.
14: 4 she **f** on her face to the ground and did obeisance,
19:18 Shimei son of Gera **f** down before the king,
20: 8 as he went forward it **f** out.
21:10 from the beginning of harvest until rain **f** on them
21:22 they **f** by the hands of David and his servants.
22:39 not rise; they **f** under my feet.
1Ki 14: 1 At that time Abijah son of Jeroboam **f** sick.
18: 7 Obadiah recognized him, **f** on his face, and said,
18:38 of the LORD **f** and consumed the burnt offering,
18:39 they **f** on their faces and said,
19: 5 he lay down under the broom tree and **f** asleep.
20:30 and the wall **f** on twenty-seven thousand men
2Ki 1:13 and came and **f** on his knees before Elijah,
3:19 every good tree you shall **f,**
4:37 She came and **f** at his feet, bowing to the ground;
6: 5 one was felling a log, his ax head **f** into the water;
1Ch 5:10 of Saul they made war on the Hagrites, who **f**
5:22 Many **f** slain, because the war was of God.
6:54 for the lot **f** to them first—
10: 1 and **f** slain on Mount Gilboa.
10: 4 So Saul took his own sword and **f** on it.
10: 5 he also **f** on his sword and died.
20: 8 they **f** by the hand of David and his servants.
21:14 and seventy thousand persons **f** in Israel.
21:16 clothed in sackcloth, **f** on their faces.
24: 7 The first lot **f** to Jehoiarib, the second to Jedaiah,
25: 9 The first lot **f** for Asaph to Joseph;
26:14 The lot for the east **f** to Shelemiah.
2Ch 13:17 five hundred thousand picked men of Israel **f** slain.
14:13 and the Ethiopians **f** until no one remained alive;
17:10 of the LORD **f** on all the kingdoms of the lands
20:18 and all Judah and the inhabitants of Jerusalem **f**
25:13 **f** on the cities of Judah from Samaria
Ezr 9: 5 with my garments and my mantle torn, and **f**
Ne 6:16 all the nations around us were afraid and **f** greatly
Est 3: 7 lot **f** on the thirteenth day of the twelfth month,
8: 3 she **f** at his feet, weeping and pleading with him
Job 1:15 and the Sabeans **f** on them and carried them off,
1:16 of God **f** from heaven and burned up the sheep
1:19 and it **f** on the young people, and they are dead;
1:20 and **f** on the ground and worshiped.
Ps 18:38 to rise; they **f** under my feet.
68:14 When the Almighty scattered kings there, snow **f**
78:64 Their priests **f** by the sword,
107:12 they **f** down, with no one to help.
Isa 9: 8 Lord sent a word against Jacob, and it **f** on Israel;
Jer 46:16 Your multitude stumbled and **f,**
46:22 against her with axes, like those who **f** trees.
50:43 of them, and his hands **f** helpless;
La 1: 7 When her people **f** into the hand of the foe,
Eze 1:28 When I saw it, I **f** on my face,
3:23 and I **f** on my face.
8: 1 the hand of the Lord GOD **f** upon me there.
9: 8 I **f** prostrate on my face and cried out,
11: 5 Then the spirit of the LORD **f** upon me,
11:13 Then I **f** down on my face,
39:23 and they all **f** by the sword.
43: 3 and I **f** upon my face.
44: 4 and I **f** upon my face.
Da 2:46 Then King Nebuchadnezzar **f** on his face,
3: 7 and languages **f** down and worshiped
3:23 **f** down, bound, into the furnace of blazing fire.
7:20 and to make room for which three of them **f** out—
8:17 he came, I became frightened and **f** prostrate.
8:18 As he was speaking to me, I **f** into a trance,
10: 7 though a great trembling **f** upon them,
10: 9 I heard the sound of his words, I **f** into a trance,
Jnh 1: 7 So they cast lots, and the lot **f** on Jonah.
Mt 7:25 The rain **f,** the floods came,
7:27 The rain **f,** and the floods came,
7:27 and it **f**—and great was its fall!"
13: 4 And as he sowed, some seeds **f** on the path,
13: 5 Other seeds **f** on rocky ground,
13: 7 Other seeds **f** among thorns,
13: 8 Other seeds **f** on good soil
17: 6 they **f** to the ground and were overcome by fear.
18:26 So the slave **f** on his knees before him, saying,
18:29 his fellow slave **f** down and pleaded with him,
Mk 3:11 they **f** down before him and shouted,
4: 4 And as he sowed, some seed **f** on the path,
4: 5 Other seed **f** on rocky ground,
4: 7 Other seed **f** among thorns,
4: 8 Other seed **f** into good soil
5:22 and, when he saw him, **f** at his feet
5:33 **f** down before him, and told him the whole truth.
9:20 and he **f** on the ground and rolled about,
Lk 5: 8 Simon Peter saw it, he **f** down at Jesus' knees,
6:49 When the river burst against it, immediately it **f,**
8: 5 some **f** on the path and was trampled on,
8: 6 Some **f** on the rock;
8: 7 Some **f** among thorns, and the thorns grew with it
8: 8 Some **f** into good soil, and when it grew,
8:14 As for what **f** among the thorns,
8:23 and while they were sailing he **f** asleep.
8:28 he **f** down before him and shouted at the top
8:41 He **f** at Jesus' feet and begged him to come
10:30 and **f** into the hands of robbers, who stripped him,
10:36 was a neighbor to the man who **f** into the hands of
13: 4 when the tower of Siloam **f** on them—
16:21 who longed to satisfy his hunger with what **f** from
Jn 18: 6 "I am he," they stepped back and **f** to the ground.
Ac 1:26 they cast lots for them, and the lot **f** on Matthias;
5: 5 Ananias heard these words, he **f** down and died.
5:10 Immediately she **f** down at his feet and died.
9: 4 He **f** to the ground and heard a voice saying
9:18 And immediately something like scales **f**

Ac 10:10 while it was being prepared, he **f** into a trance.
10:44 the Holy Spirit **f** upon all who heard the word.
11:15 the Holy Spirit **f** upon them just as it had upon us
12: 7 And the chains **f** off his wrists.
16:29 he **f** down trembling before Paul and Silas.
19:35 of the great Artemis and of the statue that **f**
20: 9 he **f** to the ground three floors below
22: 7 I **f** to the ground and heard a voice saying to me,
22:17 while I was praying in the temple, I **f** into a trance
1Co 10: 8 and twenty-three thousand **f** in a single day.
Heb 3:17 whose bodies **f** in the wilderness?
11:30 of Jericho **f** after they had been encircled
Rev 1:17 When I saw him, I **f** at his feet as though dead.
5: 8 and the twenty-four elders **f** before the Lamb,
5:14 And the elders **f** down and worshiped.
6:13 and the stars of the sky **f** to the earth as
7:11 and they **f** on their faces before the throne
8:10 and a great star **f** from heaven,
8:10 and it **f** on a third of the rivers and on the springs
11:13 and a tenth of the city **f;**
11:16 before God **f** on their faces and worshiped God,
16:19 and the cities of the nations **f.**
19: 4 and the four living creatures **f** down
19:10 Then I **f** down at his feet to worship him,
22: 8 I **f** down to worship at the feet of the angel
Tob 2:10 their fresh droppings **f** into my eyes
12:16 they **f** face down, for they were afraid.
14:10 but Nadab **f** into it himself, and was destroyed.
Jdt 2:28 and dread of him **f** upon all the people who lived
6:18 people **f** down and worshiped God, and cried out:
14: 6 he **f** down on his face in a faint.
15: 5 with one accord they **f** upon the enemy,
15: 6 the people of Bethulia **f** upon the Assyrian camp
AdE 3: 7 lot **f** on the fourteenth day of the month of Adar.
15:15 And while she was speaking, she fainted and **f.**
Wis 7: 3 and **f** upon the kindred earth;
8:19 and a good soul **f** to my lot;
17:16 And whoever was there **f** down,
Sir 15:11 "It was the Lord's doing that I **f** away";
50:17 the people together quickly **f** to the ground
1Mc 1: 5 this he **f** sick and perceived that he was dying.
1:18 and many were wounded and **f.**
1:30 but he suddenly **f** upon the city,
3:11 Many were wounded and **f**, and the rest fled.
3:24 eight hundred of them **f**, and the rest fled into
3:25 and terror **f** on the Gentiles all around them.
4:15 and all those in the rear **f** by the sword.
4:15 and three thousand of them **f.**
4:34 there **f** of the army of Lysias five thousand men;
they **f** in action.
4:40 and **f** face down on the ground.
4:55 All the people **f** on their faces and worshiped
5:22 as many as three thousand of the Gentiles **f**,
5:34 As many as eight thousand of them **f** that day.
5:60 as two thousand of the people of Israel **f** that day.
5:67 **f** in battle, for they went out to battle unwisely.
6:42 and six hundred of the king's army **f.**
6:46 but it **f** to the ground upon him and he died.
7:18 the fear and dread of them **f** on all the people,
7:32 About five hundred of the army of Nicanor **f**,
7:46 so that they all **f** by the sword;
8:10 Many of them were wounded and **f**,
9:17 and many on both sides were wounded and **f.**
9:18 Judas also **f**, and the rest fled.
9:40 Many were wounded and **f**,
9:49 about one thousand of Bacchides' men **f** that day.
10:50 and on that day Demetrius **f.**
10:85 The number of those who **f** by the sword,
11:74 As many as three thousand of the foreigners **f**
13:22 but that night a very heavy snow **f**,
16: 8 many of them **f** wounded and the rest fled into
16:10 and about two thousand of them **f.**
2Mc 3:27 When he suddenly **f** to the ground
7: 3 The king **f** into a rage,
7:39 The king **f** into a rage,
9: 7 that he **f** out of his chariot as it was rushing along,
10: 4 they **f** prostrate and implored the Lord
12:24 Timothy himself **f** into the hands of Dositheus
12:34 it happened that a few of the Jews **f.**
14:41 Being surrounded, Razis **f** upon his own sword,
14:44 and he **f** in the middle of the empty space.
1Es 1:24 so that the words of the Lord **f** upon Israel.
9:47 and **f** to the ground and worshiped the Lord.
3Mc 5:33 and his eyes wavered and his face **f.**
2Es 4:11 When I heard this, I **f** on my face
10: 1 when my son entered his wedding chamber, he **f**
13:11 and **f** on the onrushing multitude
4Mc 3: 8 Then when evening **f**, he came,
4:11 Then Apollonius **f** down half dead in
6: 7 Although he **f** to the ground
6: 8 in the side to make him get up again after he **f.**

FELLED (5) [FALL]

2Ki 3:25 and every good tree they **f.**
19:23 I **f** its tallest cedars, its choicest cypresses;
Isa 6:13 oak whose stump remains standing when it is **f."**
37:24 I **f** its tallest cedars, its choicest cypresses;
Zec 11: 2 oaks of Bashan, for the thick forest has been **f!**

FELLING (1) [FALL]

2Ki 6: 5 as one was **f** a log, his ax head fell into the water;

FELLOW (51) [FELLOW-LEVITES, FELLOWS, FELLOWSHIP]

Ge 19: 9 And they said, "This **f** came here as an alien,
Ex 2:13 "Why do you strike your **f** Hebrew?"
10: 7 "How long shall this **f** be a snare to us?
Lev 25:46 but as for your **f** Israelites,
Jos 22: 7 beside their **f** Israelites in the land west of
Jdg 7:22 the LORD set every man's sword against his **f**
1Sa 21:15 that you have brought this **f** to play the madman
21:15 Shall this **f** come into my house?"
25:21 in vain that I protected all that this **f** has in
25:25 My lord, do not take seriously this ill-natured **f,**
29: 4 For how could this **f** reconcile himself to his lord?
2Sa 6:20 any vulgar **f** might shamelessly uncover himself!"
1Ki 22:27 Put this **f** in prison, and feed him
2Ch 18:26 Put this **f** in prison, and feed him
Ezr 3: 2 Then Jeshua son of Jozadak, with his **f** priests,
6:20 for their **f** priests, and for themselves.
Ne 3: 1 with his **f** priests and rebuilt the Sheep Gate.
Isa 22:17 LORD is about to hurl you away violently, my **f.**
Eze 11:15 your kinsfolk, your own kin, your **f** exiles,
Mt 12:24 that this **f** casts out the demons."
18:28 of his **f** slaves who owed him a hundred denarii;
18:29 Then his **f** slave fell down and pleaded with him,
18:31 When his **f** slaves saw what had happened,
18:33 Should you not have had mercy on your **f** slave,
24:49 and he begins to beat his **f** slaves,
26:61 "This **f** said, 'I am able to destroy the temple
Mk 2: 7 "Why does this **f** speak in this way?
Lk 14:30 'This **f** began to build and was not able to finish.'
15: 2 "This **f** welcomes sinners and eats with them."
23:18 they all shouted out together, "Away with this **f!**
Jn 11:16 who was called the Twin, said to his **f** disciples,
Ac 2:29 "**F** Israelites, I may say to you confidently
5:35 Then he said to them, "**F** Israelites,
21:28 "**F** Israelites, help! This is the man who
22:22 "Away with such a **f** from the earth!
24: 5 We have, in fact, found this man a pestilent **f,**
Eph 3: 6 the Gentiles have become **f** heirs,
Php 2:25 my brother and co-worker and **f** soldier,
Col 1: 7 from Epaphras, our beloved **f** servant.
4: 7 a faithful minister, and a **f** servant in the Lord.
4:10 Aristarchus my **f** prisoner greets you,
Phm 1: 2 to Archippus our **f** soldier,
1:23 Epaphras, my **f** prisoner in Christ Jesus,
1:24 Aristarchus, Demas, and Luke, my **f** workers.
Rev 6:11 of their **f** servants and of their brothers and sisters,
19:10 a **f** servant with you and your comrades who hold
22: 9 I am a **f** servant with you and your comrades
Sir 13:23 poor person speaks and they say, "Who is this **f?"**
2Mc 4:38 and there he dispatched the bloodthirsty **f.**
9:13 Then the abominable **f** made a vow to the Lord,
1Es 5:48 Then Jeshua son of Jozadak, with his **f** priests,

FELLOW-LEVITES (1) [FELLOW, LEVI]

Dt 18: 7 like all his **f** who stand to minister there before

FELLOWCITIZENS (KJV) See CITIZEN

FELLOWLABOURER (KJV) See CO-WORKER

FELLOWPRISONER (KJV) See FELLOW PRISONER

FELLOWSERVANT (KJV) See FELLOW SLAVE

FELLOWSOLDIER (KJV) See FELLOW SOLDIER

FELLOWWORKERS (KJV) See CO-WORKERS

FELLOWS (6) [FELLOW]

Lev 21:10 The priest who is exalted above his **f,**
Jdg 9: 4 Abimelech hired worthless and reckless **f,**
18:25 among us or else hot-tempered **f** will attack you,
1Sa 10:27 But some worthless **f** said,
30:22 and worthless **f** among the men who had gone
4Mc 8:14 "Be afraid, young **f;** whatever justice you revere

FELLOWSHIP (8) [FELLOW]

Ac 2:42 to the apostles' teaching and **f,**
1Co 1: 9 by him you were called into the **f** of his Son,
2Co 6:14 Or what **f** is there between light and darkness?
Gal 2: 9 they gave to Barnabas and me the right hand of **f,**
1Jn 1: 3 and heard so that you also may have **f** with us; and
truly our **f** is with the Father and with his Son
1: 6 that we have **f** with him while we are walking
1: 7 we have **f** with one another,

FELT (21) [FEEL]

Ge 27:22 who **f** him and said, "The voice is Jacob's voice,
31:34 Laban **f** all about in the tent,
31:37 Although you have **f** about through all my goods,
Ex 10:21 a darkness that can be **f."**
2Sa 13:15 even greater than the lust he had **f** for her.
18:12 if I **f** in my hand the weight of a thousand pieces
1Ch 19: 5 for they **f** greatly humiliated.
Isa 47:10 You **f** secure in your wickedness;
Jer 5: 3 You have struck them, but they **f** no anguish;
Mk 5:29 and she **f** in her body that she was healed
Jn 21:17 Peter **f** hurt because he said to him the third time,
2Co 1: 9 we **f** that we had received the sentence of death so
7: 9 for you **f** a godly grief,
Gal 4:15 What has become of the goodwill you **f?**
Wis 11:14 they **f** thirst in a different way from the righteous.
Sus 1:27 the servants **f** very much ashamed,
2Mc 7:24 Antiochus **f** that he was being treated
9: 9 because of the stench the whole army **f** revulsion
4Mc 12: 2 he **f** strong compassion for this child when he saw
14:13 which draws everything toward an emotion **f**
15: 9 she **f** a greater tenderness toward them.

FEMALE (77)

Ge 1:27 male and **f** he created them.
5: 2 Male and **f** he created them,
6:19 they shall be male and **f.**
7: 3 of the air also, male and **f**, to keep their kind alive
7: 9 male and **f**, went into the ark with Noah,
7:16 And those that entered, male and **f** of all flesh,
12:16 male donkeys, male and **f** slaves, **f** donkeys,
15: 9 a **f** goat three years old, a ram three years old,
20:14 and oxen, and male and **f** slaves, and gave them
20:17 and also healed his wife and **f** slaves so
24:35 male and **f** slaves, camels and donkeys.
30:35 and all the **f** goats that were speckled and spotted,
30:43 and male and **f** slaves, and camels and donkeys.
31:38 your ewes and your **f** goats have not miscarried,
32: 5 donkeys, flocks, male and **f** slaves;
32:14 two hundred **f** goats and twenty male goats,
32:15 twenty **f** donkeys and ten male donkeys.
45:23 and ten **f** donkeys loaded with grain, bread,
Ex 11: 5 on his throne to the firstborn of the **f** slave who is
20:10 your son or your daughter, your male or **f** slave,
20:17 or male or **f** slave, or ox, or donkey,
21:20 When a slaveowner strikes a male or **f** slave with
21:26 a slaveowner strikes the eye of a male or **f** slave,
21:27 the owner knocks out a tooth of a male or **f** slave,
21:32 If the ox gores a male or **f** slave,
22:18 You shall not permit a **f** sorcerer to live.
Lev 3: 1 of the herd, whether male or **f**, you shall offer one
3: 6 male or **f,** you shall offer one without blemish.
4:28 a **f** goat without blemish as your offering,
4:32 you shall bring a **f** without blemish.
5: 6 a **f** from the flock, a sheep or a goat,
12: 5 a **f** child, she shall be unclean two weeks,
12: 7 the law for her who bears a child, male or **f.**
15:33 for anyone, male or **f**, who has a discharge,
25: 6 you, your male and **f** slaves,
25:44 As for the male and **f** slaves whom you may have,
25:44 that you may acquire male and **f** slaves.
27: 4 the person is a **f**, the equivalent is thirty shekels.
27: 5 for a male and ten shekels for a **f.**
27: 6 for a **f** the equivalent is three shekels of silver.
27: 7 and for a **f** ten shekels.
Nu 5: 3 both male and **f**, putting them outside the camp;
15:27 a **f** goat a year old for a sin offering.
Dt 4:16 the likeness of male or **f,**
5:14 or your daughter, or your male or **f** slave,
5:14 your male and **f** slave may rest as well as you.
5:21 or field, or male or **f** slave, or ox, or donkey,
12:12 and your daughters, your male and **f** slaves,
12:18 your male and **f** slaves, and the Levites resident
15:17 You shall do the same with regard to your **f** slave.
16:11 and **f** slaves, the Levites resident in your towns,
16:14 your male and **f** slaves, as well as the Levites,
28:68 for sale to your enemies as male and **f** slaves,
1Sa 8:16 He will take your male and **f** slaves,
2Ki 5:26 sheep and oxen, and male and **f** slaves?
2Ch 28:10 male and **f**, as your slaves.
Ezr 2:65 besides their male and **f** servants,
2:65 and they had two hundred male and **f** singers.
Ne 7:67 besides their male and **f** slaves,
7:67 had two hundred forty-five singers, male and **f.**
Job 31:13 I have rejected the cause of my male or **f** slaves,
Ecc 2: 7 I bought male and **f** slaves,
Isa 14: 2 as male and **f** slaves in the LORD's land;
Jer 34: 9 and **f**, so that no one should hold another Judean
34:10 or **f**, so that they would not be enslaved again;
34:11 the male and **f** slaves they had set free,
34:16 of you took back your male and **f** slaves,
Joel 2:29 Even on the male and **f** slaves, in those days,
Mt 19: 4 at the beginning 'made them male and **f**,'
Mk 10: 6 'God made them male and **f.'**
Gal 3:28 there is no longer male and **f;**
Tob 10:10 male and **f** slaves, oxen and sheep,
AdE 7: 4 and our children—male and **f** slaves.
1Es 5: 1 and their male and **f** servants, and their livestock.
5:41 besides male and **f** servants,
5:42 **f** servants were seven thousand three hundred

FENCE (6) [FENCED, FENCES]

Job 1:10 a **f** around him and his house and all that he has,
Ps 62: 3 as you would a leaning wall, a tottering **f?**
Mt 21:33 put a **f** around it, dug a wine press in it,
Mk 12: 1 "A man planted a vineyard, put a **f** around it,
Sir 28:24 As you **f** in your property with thorns,
36:30 there is no **f**, the property will be plundered;

FENCED (1) [FENCE]

Job 3:23 who cannot see the way, whom God has **f** in?

FENCED (KJV) See also FORTIFIED, FORTRESS, KNIT, USES, WALLED

FENCES (2) [FENCE]
Na 3:17 settling on the **f** on a cold day—
Sir 22:18 **F** set on a high place will not stand firm against

FERTILE (5)
2Ch 26:10 and vinedressers in the hills and in the **f** lands,
Isa 5: 1 My beloved had a vineyard on a very **f** hill.
Eze 17: 5 he took a seed from the land, placed it in **f** soil;
Sir 26:20 *a f field within the whole plain,*
2Es 1:21 I divided **f** lands among you;

FERVENT (2) [FERVENTLY, FERVOR]
Sir 38:17 Let your weeping be bitter and your wailing **f**;
4Mc 13:26 they could make their brotherly love more **f**

FERVENTLY (4) [FERVENT]
Ac 12: 5 the church prayed **f** to God for him.
Jas 5:17 and he prayed **f** that it might not rain,
Jdt 4:12 praying **f** to the God of Israel not
3Mc 5: 9 So their entreaty ascended **f** to heaven.

FERVOR (1) [FERVENT]
Jdt 4: 9 every man of Israel cried out to God with great **f**,

FESTAL (14) [FESTIVAL]
Jdg 14:12 thirty linen garments and thirty **f** garments.
14:13 thirty linen garments and thirty **f** garments."
14:19 gave the **f** garments to those who had explained
Ps 81: 3 at the full moon, on our **f** day.
89:15 Happy are the people who know the **f** shout,
118:27 Bind the **f** procession with branches,
Isa 3:22 **f** robes, the mantles, the cloaks, and the handbags;
Zec 3: 4 and I will clothe you with **f** apparel."
Heb 12:22 and to innumerable angels in **f** gathering,
Jdt 10: 2 where she lived on sabbaths and on her **f** days.
Wis 19:16 having first received them with **f** celebrations,
Sir 43: 7 From the moon comes the sign for **f** days,
50: 6 like the full moon at the **f** season;
2Es 1:31 for I have rejected your **f** days, and new moons,

FESTER (1) [FESTERING]
Ps 38: 5 My wounds grow foul and **f** because

FESTERING (2) [FESTER]
Ex 9: 9 and shall cause **f** boils on humans and animals
9:10 and it caused **f** boils on humans and animals.

FESTIVAL‡ (123) [FESTAL, FESTIVALS, FESTIVE, FESTIVITY]
A. FESTIVAL OF BOOTHS (16)
B. FESTIVAL OF UNLEAVENED BREAD (15)
C. FESTIVAL OF WEEKS (7)

Ex 5: 1 they may celebrate a **f** to me in the wilderness.'"
10: 9 because we have the LORD's **f** to celebrate."
12:14 You shall celebrate it as a **f** to the LORD;
12:17 You shall observe the **f** of unleavened bread, B
13: 6 the seventh day there shall be a **f** to the LORD.
23:14 Three times in the year you shall hold a **f** for me.
23:15 You shall observe the **f** of unleavened bread; B
23:16 You shall observe the **f** of harvest,
23:16 You shall observe the **f** of ingathering at the end
23:18 or let the fat of my **f** remain until the morning.
32: 5 "Tomorrow shall be a **f** to the LORD."
34:18 You shall keep the **f** of unleavened bread. B
34:22 You shall observe the **f** of weeks, C
34:22 and the **f** of ingathering at the turn of the year.
34:25 and the sacrifice of the **f** of the passover shall not
Lev 23: 6 of the same month is the **f** of unleavened bread B
23:34 there shall be the **f** of booths to the LORD. A
23:39 you shall keep the **f** of the LORD,
23:41 You shall keep it as a **f** to the LORD seven days
Nu 28:17 And on the fifteenth day of this month is a **f**;
28:26 to the LORD at your **f** of weeks, you shall have C
29:12 You shall celebrate a **f** to the LORD seven days.
Dt 16:10 the **f** of weeks for the LORD your God, C
16:13 You shall keep the **f** of booths for seven days, A
16:14 Rejoice during your **f**, you and your sons
16:15 the **f** for the LORD your God at the place that
16:16 at the **f** of unleavened bread, B
16:16 at the **f** of weeks, and at the festival of booths. C
16:16 at the festival of weeks, and at the **f** of booths. A
31:10 year of remission, during the **f** of booths, A
Jdg 21:19 yearly **f** of the LORD is taking place at Shiloh,
1Ki 8: 2 to King Solomon at the **f** in the month Ethanim,
8:65 So Solomon held the **f** at that time,
12:32 a **f** on the fifteenth day of the eighth month like
the **f** that was in Judah,
12:33 he appointed a **f** for the people of Israel,
2Ki 23:16 when Jeroboam stood by the altar at the **f**;
2Ch 5: 3 the Israelites assembled before the king at the **f**
7: 8 At that time Solomon held the **f** for seven days,
7: 9 of the altar seven days and the **f** seven days.
8:13 the **f** of unleavened bread, the festival of weeks, B
8:13 the festival of unleavened bread, the **f** of weeks, C
8:13 the festival of weeks, and the **f** of booths. A
30:13 in Jerusalem to keep the **f** of unleavened bread B
30:21 at Jerusalem kept the **f** of unleavened bread B
30:22 So the people ate the food of the **f** for seven days,
30:23 the whole assembly agreed together to keep the **f**
35:17 and the **f** of unleavened bread seven days. B
Ezr 3: 4 And they kept the **f** of booths, as prescribed, A
Ezr 6:22 the **f** of unleavened bread seven days; B
Ne 8:14 of Israel should live in booths during the **f** of
8:18 They kept the **f** seven days;
Est 8:17 and joy among the Jews, a **f** and a holiday.
Ps 42: 4 and songs of thanksgiving, a multitude keeping **f**.
Isa 30:29 a song as in the night when a holy **f** is kept;
La 2: 6 the LORD has abolished in Zion **f** and sabbath,
2: 7 in the house of the LORD as on a day of **f**.
2:22 from all around as if for a day of **f**;
Eze 45:21 you shall celebrate the **f** of the passover,
45:23 during the seven days of the **f** he shall provide as
45:25 of the month and for the seven days of the **f**,
Da 5: 1 King Belshazzar made a great **f** for a thousand
Hos 2:13 I will punish her for the **f** days of the Baals,
9: 5 What will you do on the day of appointed **f**,
9: 5 and on the day of the **f** of the LORD?
12: 9 as in the days of the appointed **f**.
Zep 3:18 as on a day of **f**.
Zec 14:16 the LORD of hosts, and to keep the **f** of booths. A
14:18 that do not go up to keep the **f** of booths. A
14:19 that do not go up to keep the **f** of booths. A
Mt 26: 5 But they said, "Not during the **f**,
27:15 at the **f** the governor was accustomed to release
Mk 14: 1 the Passover and the **f** of Unleavened Bread. B
14: 2 for they said, "Not during the **f**, or there may be
15: 6 at the **f** he used to release a prisoner for them,
Lk 2:41 to Jerusalem for the **f** of the Passover.
2:42 they went up as usual for the **f**.
2:43 When the **f** was ended and they started to return,
22: 1 Now the **f** of Unleavened Bread, B
Jn 2:23 When he was in Jerusalem during the Passover **f**,
4:45 that he had done in Jerusalem at the **f**;
4:45 for they too had gone to the **f**.
5: 1 After this there was a **f** of the Jews,
6: 4 Now the Passover, the **f** of the Jews, was near.
7: 2 Now the Jewish **f** of Booths was near. A
7: 8 Go to the **f** yourselves.
7: 8 I am not going to this **f**,
7:10 But after his brothers had gone to the **f**,
7:11 Jews were looking for him at the **f** and saying,
7:14 the middle of the **f** Jesus went up into the temple
7:37 On the last day of the **f**, the great day,
10:22 the **f** of the Dedication took place in Jerusalem.
11:56 Surely he will not come to the **f**, will he?"
12:12 to the **f** heard that Jesus was coming to Jerusalem.
12:20 up to worship at the **f** were some Greeks.
13: 1 Now before the **f** of the Passover,
13:29 "Buy what we need for the **f**";
Ac 12: 3 (This was during the **f** of Unleavened Bread.) B
1Co 5: 8 Therefore, let us celebrate the **f**,
Tob 2: 1 At our **f** of Pentecost, which is the sacred festival
2: 1 which is the sacred **f** of weeks, C
AdE 9:26 Mordecai established this **f**,
Wis 15:12 and life a **f** held for profit,
1Mc 10:21 the one hundred sixtieth year, at the **f** of booths, A
10:34 and the three days before a **f** and the three after
10:34 three days before a festival and the three after a **f**—
2Mc 1: 9 And now see that you keep the **f** of booths in A
1:18 also may celebrate the **f** of booths and the A
1:18 and the **f** of the fire given when Nehemiah,
6: 7 and when a **f** of Dionysus was celebrated,
10: 6 in the manner of the **f** of booths, A
10: 6 during the **f** of booths, they had been wandering A
12:31 as the **f** of weeks was close at hand. C
12:32 After the **f** called Pentecost,
1Es 1:19 and the **f** of unleavened bread seven days. B
5:51 They kept the **f** of booths, A
7:14 also kept the **f** of unleavened bread seven days, B
3Mc 4: 8 spent the remaining days of their marriage **f**
6:30 and everything else needed for a **f** of seven days,
6:36 the observance of the aforesaid days as a **f**,
7:15 and they kept the day as a joyful **f**,
7:19 as a joyous **f** during the time of their stay.
7:20 a place of prayer at the site of the **f**,

FESTIVALS (41) [FESTIVAL]
A. APPOINTED FESTIVALS (19)

Lev 23: 2 These are the appointed **f** of the LORD A
23: 2 as holy convocations, my appointed **f**. A
23: 4 These are the appointed **f** of the LORD, A
23:37 These are the appointed **f** of the LORD, A
23:44 the people of Israel the appointed **f** of the LORD. A
Nu 10:10 on your days of rejoicing, at your appointed **f**, A
15: 3 or as a freewill offering or at your appointed **f**— A
29:39 to the LORD at your appointed **f**, A
1Ch 23:31 new moons, and appointed **f**, A
2Ch 2: 4 and the appointed **f** of the LORD our God, A
8:13 the new moons, and the three annual **f**—
31: 3 the new moons, and the appointed **f**, A
Ezr 3: 5 at the new moon and at all the sacred **f** of
Ne 10:33 the sabbaths, the new moons, the appointed **f**, A
Isa 1:14 and your appointed **f** my soul hates; A
29: 1 Add year to year; let the **f** run their round.
33:20 Look on Zion, the city of our appointed **f**! A
La 1: 4 roads to Zion mourn, for no one comes to the **f**;
Eze 36:38 the flock at Jerusalem during her appointed **f**, A
44:24 and my statutes regarding all my appointed **f**, A
45:17 and drink offerings, at the **f**, the new moons,
45:17 all the appointed **f** of the house of Israel: A
46: 9 the LORD at the appointed **f**, whoever enters by A
46:11 the **f** and the appointed seasons the grain offering
Hos 2:11 I will put an end to all her mirth, her **f**,
2:11 her sabbaths, and all her appointed **f**. A
Am 5:21 I despise your **f**, and I take no delight
Na 1:15 Celebrate your **f**, O Judah, fulfill your vows,
Zec 8:19 and cheerful **f** for the house of Judah:
Col 2:16 in matters of food and drink or of observing **f**,
Tob 1: 6 But I alone went often to Jerusalem for the **f**,
2: 6 "Your **f** shall be turned into mourning,
Jdt 8: 6 the **f** and days of rejoicing of the house of Israel.
AdE 16:22 as a notable day among your commemorative **f**,
Sir 33: 8 and he appointed the different seasons and **f**.
47:10 He gave beauty to the **f**,
Bar 1:14 in the house of the Lord on the days of the **f** and
1Mc 1:45 to profane sabbaths and **f**,
10:34 "All the **f** and sabbaths and new moons
12:11 both at our **f** and on other appropriate days,
2Mc 6: 6 nor observe the **f** of their ancestors,

FESTIVE (1) [FESTIVAL]
Jdt 10: 3 and dressed herself in the **f** attire that she used

FESTIVITY (2) [FESTIVAL]
Isa 22:13 but instead there was joy and **f**,
AdE 1: 5 the **f** the king gave a drinking party for the people

FESTUS (13)
Ac 24:27 Felix was succeeded by Porcius **F**;
25: 1 Three days after **F** had arrived in the province,
25: 4 **F** replied that Paul was being kept at Caesarea,
25: 9 But **F**, wishing to do the Jews a favor, asked Paul,
25:12 Then **F**, after he had conferred with his council,
25:13 and Bernice arrived at Caesarea to welcome **F**.
25:14 **F** laid Paul's case before the king, saying,
25:22 Agrippa said to **F**, "I would like to hear
25:23 Then **F** gave the order and Paul was brought in.
25:24 And **F** said, "King Agrippa and all here present
26:24 While he was making this defense, **F** exclaimed,
26:25 "I am not out of my mind, most excellent **F**,
26:32 to **F**, "This man could have been set free if he had

FETCH[ED] (KJV) See BRING, CHANGE, GET, GO, SEIZE, TAKE

FETTER (1) [FETTERED, FETTERS]
Man 1:10 I am weighted down with many an iron **f**,

FETTERED (1) [FETTER]
2Sa 3:34 Your hands were not bound, your feet were not **f**;

FETTERS (23) [FETTER]
2Ki 25: 7 they bound him in **f** and took him to Babylon.
2Ch 33:11 bound him with **f**, and brought him to Babylon.
36: 6 and bound him with **f** to take him to Babylon.
Job 36: 8 And if they are bound in **f** and caught in the cords
Ps 105:18 His feet were hurt with **f**,
149: 8 with **f** and their nobles with chains of iron,
Ecc 7:26 and nets, whose hands are **f**;
Jer 39: 7 and bound him in **f** to take him to Babylon.
40: 1 in **f** along with all the captives of Jerusalem
40: 4 I have just released you today from the **f**
52:11 of Zedekiah, and bound him in **f**, and the king
Na 3:10 all her dignitaries were bound in **f**.
Sir 6:24 Put your feet into her **f**,
6:29 Then her **f** will become for you a strong defense,
21:19 To a senseless person education is **f** on his feet,
28:19 and has not been bound with its **f**.
28:20 and its **f** are **f** of bronze;
33:30 and if he does not obey, make his **f** heavy.
1Mc 3:41 in immense amounts, and **f**, and went to the camp
3Mc 3:25 and bound securely with iron **f**,
4: 9 others had their feet secured by unbreakable **f**,
4Mc 12: 2 when he saw that he was already in **f**.

FETUS (1)
2Es 4:40 her womb can keep the **f** within her any longer."

FEVER (10)
Lev 26:16 and **f** that waste the eyes and cause life
Dt 28:22 The LORD will afflict you with consumption, **f**,
Mt 8:14 he saw his mother-in-law lying in bed with a **f**;
8:15 and the **f** left her, and she got up and began
Mk 1:30 Now Simon's mother-in-law was in bed with a **f**,
1:31 Then the **f** left her, and she began to serve them.
Lk 4:38 from a high **f**, and they asked him
4:39 Then he stood over her and rebuked the **f**,
Jn 4:52 "Yesterday at one in the afternoon the **f** left him."
Ac 28: 8 of Publius lay sick in bed with **f** and dysentery.

FEW‡ (105) [FEWER, FEWEST]
Ge 29:20 and they seemed to him but a **f** days because of
34:30 my numbers are **f**, and if they gather themselves
47: 9 **f** and hard have been the years of my life.
Lev 25:52 and if **f** years remain until the jubilee year,
26:22 they shall make you **f** in number,
Nu 9:20 Sometimes the cloud would remain a **f** days over
13:18 whether they are **f** or many,
35: 8 and from the smaller tribes you shall take **f**;
Dt 4:27 a **f** of you will be left among the nations where
26: 5 **f** in number, and there he became a great nation,
28:62 you shall be left **f** in number,
33: 6 and not die out, even though his numbers are **f**.
Jos 7: 3 so **f**, do not make the whole people toil
1Sa 14: 6 the LORD from saving by many or by **f**."
17:28 With whom have you left those **f** sheep in
2Ki 4: 3 empty vessels and not just a **f**.
1Ch 16:19 When they were **f** in number, of little account,

2Ch 24:24 Although the army of Aram had come with f men,
29:34 But the priests were too f and could not skin all
30:11 Only a f from Asher, Manasseh,
Ne 2:12 I got up during the night, I and a f men with me;
7: 4 within it were f and no houses had been built.
Job 10:20 Are not the days of my life f?
14: 1 born of woman, f of days and full of trouble,
16:22 For when a f years have come,
Ps 39: 5 You have made my days a f handbreadths,
105:12 When they were f in number, of little account,
109: 8 May his days be f; may another seize his position.
Ecc 2: 3 to do under heaven during the f days of their life.
5: 2 therefore let your words be f.
5:18 under the sun the f days of the life God gives us;
6:12 while they live the f days of their vain life,
9:14 There was a little city with f people in it.
12: 3 because they are f, and those who look through
Isa 1: 9 the LORD of hosts had not left us a f survivors,
10: 7 and to cut off nations not a f.
10:19 The remnant of the trees of his forest will be so f
16:14 and those who survive will be very f and feeble.
21:17 the remaining bows of Kedar's warriors will be f;
24: 6 of the earth dwindled, and f people are left.
65:20 that lives but a f days, or an old person who does
Jer 30:19 I will make them many, and they shall not be f;
42: 2 For there are only a f of us left out of many,
44:28 from the land of Egypt to the land of Judah, f
Eze 12:16 But I will let a f of them escape from the sword,
Da 11:20 but within a f days he shall be broken,
Mt 7:14 and there are f who find it.
9:37 "The harvest is plentiful, but the laborers are f;
15:34 They said, "Seven, and a f small fish."
22:14 For many are called, but f are chosen."
25:21 you have been trustworthy in a f things,
25:23 you have been trustworthy in a f things,
Mk 6: 5 except that he laid his hands on a f sick people
8: 7 They had also a f small fish;
Lk 10: 2 "The harvest is plentiful, but the laborers are f;
13:23 "Lord, will only a f be saved?"
15:13 A f days later the younger son gathered all he had
Jn 2:12 and they remained there a f days.
Ac 17: 4 a great many of the devout Greeks and not a f of
17:12 not a f Greek women and men of high standing.
Eph 3: 3 as I wrote above in a f words,
1Pe 3:20 during the building of the ark, in which a f,
Rev 2:14 But I have a f things against you:
3: 4 Yet you have still a f persons in Sardis who have
Tob 4: 8 if f, do not be afraid to give according to
Sir 18:10 so are a f years among the days of eternity.
20:13 wise make themselves beloved by only f words,
32: 8 Be brief; say much in f words;
34:10 An inexperienced person knows f things,
40:15 The children of the ungodly put out f branches;
43:32 for I have seen but f of his works.
48: 2 and by his zeal he made them f in number.
48:15 The people were left very f in number,
49:14 F have ever been created on earth like Enoch,
Bar 2:13 for we are left, f in number,
1Mc 3:17 they said to Judas, "How can we, f as we are,
3:18 "It is easy for many to be hemmed in by f,
3:18 between saving by many or by f.
6:54 Only a f men were left in the sanctuary;
7: 1 sailed with a f men to a town by the sea,
7:28 I shall come with a f men to see you face to face
7:50 So the land of Judah had rest for a f days.
9: 9 and fight them; we are too f."
9:65 and he went with only a f men.
12:45 and choose for yourself a f men to stay with you,
15:10 so that there were only a f with Trypho.
2Mc 1:15 a f men inside the wall of the sacred precinct,
2:21 though f in number they seized the whole land
8: 6 and put to flight not a f of the enemy.
12:34 it happened that a f of the Jews fell.
14:30 So he gathered not a f of his men,
3Mc 3:23 by speech and by silence they abominate those f
2Es 2:13 pray that your days may be f,
4:33 Why are our years f and evil?"
7:12 they are f and evil, full of dangers and involved
7:*47* that the world to come will bring delight to f,
7:*48* for a f but for almost all who have been created."
7:*51* that the righteous are not many but f,
7:*52* "If you have just a f precious stones,
7:*60* for I will rejoice over the f who shall be saved,
7:*140* [70] left only very f of the innumerable multitude."
8: 1 but the world to come for the sake of only a f.
8: 3 but only a f shall be saved."
8:62 but only to you and a f like you."
10:57 to be with the Most High as f have been.

FEWER (6) [FEW]

Lev 25:16 you shall increase the price, and if the years are f,
Sir 28: 8 Refrain from strife, and your sins will be f;
Aza 1:14 we, O Lord, have become f than any other nation,
2Mc 5: 5 Jason took no f than a thousand men
8: 9 of no f than twenty thousand Gentiles
10:17 killing no f than twenty thousand.

FEWEST (1) [FEW]

Dt 7: 7 for you were the f of all peoples.

FIANCÉE (3)

1Co 7:36 that he is not behaving properly toward his f,
7:37 in his own mind to keep her as his f,
7:38 So then, he who marries his f does well;

FIBER (1)

Jdg 16: 9 as a strand of f snaps when it touches the fire.

FIDELITY (5)

Dt 1:36 because of his complete f to the LORD."
Da 9:13 turning from our iniquities and reflecting on his f.
Tit 2:10 but to show complete and perfect f,
AdE 13: 3 and steadfast f, and has attained the second place
Sir 1:27 f and humility are his delight.

FIELD‡ (266) [BATTLEFIELD, FIELDS, GRAINFIELDS]

Ge 2: 5 of the f was yet in the earth and no herb of
2: 5 the earth and no herb of the f had yet sprung up—
2:19 the f and every bird of the air, and brought them
2:20 and to every animal of the f;
3:18 and you shall eat the plants of the f.
4: 8 "Let us go out to the f."
4: 8 And when they were in the f,
23: 9 it is at the end of his f.
23:11 I give you the f, and I give you the cave that is
23:13 I will give the price of the f;
23:17 So the f of Ephron in Machpelah,
23:17 the f with the cave that was in it and all the trees
that were in the f,
23:19 in the cave of the f of Machpelah facing Mamre
23:20 The f and the cave that is in it passed from
24:63 Isaac went out in the evening to walk in the f;
24:65 walking in the f to meet us?"
25: 9 in the f of Ephron son of Zohar the Hittite,
25:10 the f that Abraham purchased from the Hittites.
25:27 a man of the f, while Jacob was a quiet man,
25:29 Esau came in from the f, and he was famished.
27: 3 your quiver and your bow, and go out to the f,
27: 5 Esau went to the f to hunt for game and bring it,
27:27 like the smell of a f that the LORD has blessed.
29: 2 in the f and three flocks of sheep lying there
30:14 and found mandrakes in the f,
30:16 When Jacob came from the f in the evening,
31: 4 and Leah into the f where his flock was,
34: 5 but his sons were with his cattle in the f,
34: 7 just as the sons of Jacob came in from the f.
34:28 and whatever was in the city and in the f.
37: 7 There we were, binding sheaves in the f.
39: 5 the LORD was on all that he had, in house and f.
47:24 as seed for the f and as food for yourselves
49:29 in the cave in the f of Ephron the Hittite,
49:30 in the cave in the f at Machpelah,
49:30 in the f that Abraham bought from Ephron
49:32 the f and the cave that is in it were purchased
50:13 and buried him in the cave of the f at Machpelah,
50:13 the f near Mamre, which Abraham bought as
Ex 1:14 in mortar and brick and in every kind of f labor.
9: 3 with a deadly pestilence your livestock in the f:
9:19 in the open f brought to a secure place;
9:19 every human or animal that is in the open f and is
9:21 and livestock in the open f.
9:22 on humans and animals and all the plants of the f
9:25 in the open f throughout all the land of Egypt,
9:25 the hail also struck down all the plants of the f,
9:25 and shattered every tree in the f.
10: 5 of yours that grows in the f.
10:15 nothing green was left, no tree, no plant in the f,
16:25 today you will not find it in the f.
22: 5 someone causes a f or vineyard to be grazed over,
22: 5 lets livestock loose to graze in someone else's f,
22: 5 from the best in the owner's f or vineyard.
22: 6 or the standing grain or the f is consumed,
22:31 that is mangled by beasts in the f;
23:16 of what you sow in the f.
23:16 you gather in from the f the fruit of your labor.
Lev 14: 7 and he shall let the living bird go into the open f.
14:53 the living bird go out of the city into the open f;
17: 5 that they offer in the open f,
19: 9 you shall not reap to the very edges of your f,
19:19 you shall not sow your f with two kinds of seed;
23:22 you shall not reap to the very edges of your f,
25: 3 Six years you shall sow your f,
25: 4 you shall not sow your f or prune your vineyard.
25:12 you shall eat only what the f itself produces.
26: 4 and the trees of the f shall yield their fruit.
27:17 person consecrates the f as of the year of jubilee,
27:18 but if the f is consecrated after the jubilee,
27:19 the one who consecrates the f wishes to redeem it,
27:20 but if the f is not redeemed,
27:21 But when the f is released in the jubilee, it shall be
holy to the LORD as a devoted f;
27:22 to the LORD a f that has been purchased,
27:24 In the year of jubilee the f shall return to the one
Nu 19:16 in the open f touches one who has been killed by
20:17 We will not pass through f or vineyard,
21:22 we will not turn aside into f or vineyard;
22: 4 as an ox licks up the grass of the f."
22:23 donkey turned off the road, and went into the f;
23:14 So he took him to the f of Zophim,
Dt 5:21 or f, or male or female slave, or ox, or donkey,
14:22 of your seed that is brought in yearly from the f.
20:19 in the f human beings that they should come
24:19 harvest in your f and forget a sheaf in the f,
28: 3 and blessed shall you be in the f.
28:16 and cursed shall you be in the f.
28:38 You shall carry much seed into the f
32:13 and fed him with produce of the f;
Jos 15:18 she urged him to ask her father for a f.
Jdg 1:14 she urged him to ask her father for a f.
Jdg 5:18 Naphtali too, on the heights of the f.
9:27 They went out into the f and gathered the grapes
13: 9 to the woman as she sat in the f;
19:16 an old man coming from his work in the f.
Ru 2: 2 "Let me go to the f and glean among the ears
2: 3 She came and gleaned in the f behind the reapers.
2: 3 she came to the part of the f belonging to Boaz,
2: 8 do not go to glean in another f or leave this one,
2: 9 Keep your eyes on the f that is being reaped,
2:17 So she gleaned in the f until evening.
2:22 otherwise you might be bothered in another f."
4: 5 day you acquire the f from the hand of Naomi,
1Sa 4: 2 who killed about four thousand men on the f
6:14 cart came into the f of Joshua of Beth-shemesh,
6:18 to this day in the f of Joshua of Beth-shemesh.
11: 5 Saul was coming from the f behind the oxen;
14:15 There was a panic in the camp, in the f,
17:44 of the air and to the wild animals of the f."
19: 3 and stand beside my father in the f where you are,
20: 5 so that I may hide in the f until the third evening.
20:11 "Come, let us go out into the f."
20:11 So they both went out into the f.
20:24 So David hid himself in the f.
20:35 In the morning Jonathan went out into the f to
2Sa 11:11 of my lord are camping in the open f;
11:23 and came out against us in the f;
14: 6 and they fought with one another in the f;
14:30 Joab's f is next to mine, and he has barley there;
14:30 So Absalom's servants set the f on fire.
14:31 "Why have your servants set my f on fire?"
17: 8 like a bear robbed of her cubs in the f.
18: 6 So the army went out into the f against Israel;
20:12 he carried Amasa from the highway into a f,
1Ki 16: 4 and anyone of his who dies in the f the birds of
2Ki 4:39 One of them went out into the f to gather herbs;
9:37 the corpse of Jezebel shall be like dung on the f in
18:17 which is on the highway to the Fuller's F.
19:26 they have become like plants of the f and
1Ch 16:32 let the f exult, and everything in it.
27:26 Over those who did the work of the f,
2Ch 26:23 near his ancestors in the burial f that belonged to
31: 5 to wine, oil, honey, and of all the produce of the f;
Job 5:23 For you shall be in league with the stones of the f,
24: 6 a f not their own and they glean in the vineyard of
Ps 8: 7 all sheep and oxen, and also the beasts of the f,
50:11 and all that moves in the f is mine.
72:16 in the cities like the grass of the f.
80:13 and all that move in the f feed on it.
96:12 let the f exult, and everything
103:15 they flourish like a flower of the f;
Pr 13:23 The f of the poor may yield much food,
24:27 get everything ready for you in the f;
24:30 I passed by the f of one who was lazy,
27:26 and the goats the price of a f;
31:16 She considers a f and buys it;
Ecc 5: 9 a king for a plowed f.
Isa 1: 8 like a shelter in a cucumber f, like a besieged city.
5: 8 you who join house to house, who add f to f,
7: 3 the upper pool on the highway to the Fuller's F,
16:10 and gladness are taken away from the fruitful f;
29:17 become a fruitful f, and the fruitful f be regarded
32:15 becomes a fruitful f, and the fruitful f is deemed a
32:16 and righteousness abide in the fruitful f.
36: 2 the upper pool on the highway to the Fuller's F.
37:27 they have become like plants of the f and
40: 6 their constancy is like the flower of the f.
55:12 and all the trees of the f shall clap their hands.
Jer 4:17 in around her like watchers of a f,
6:25 Do not go out into the f, or walk on the road;
7:20 on the trees of the f and the fruit of the ground;
9:22 like dung upon the open f,
10: 5 Their idols are like scarecrows in a cucumber f,
12: 4 and the grass of every f wither?
14: 5 Even the doe in the f forsakes her newborn fawn
14:18 If I go out into the f, look—
26:18 Zion shall be plowed as a f;
27: 6 even the wild animals of the f to serve him.
32: 7 "Buy my f that is at Anathoth,
32: 8 "Buy my f that is at Anathoth in the land
32: 9 the f at Anathoth from my cousin Hanamel,
32:25 "Buy the f for money and get witnesses"—
35: 9 We have no vineyard or f or seed;
La 4: 9 deprived of the produce of the f.
Eze 7:15 those in the f die by the sword;
16: 5 but you were thrown out in the open f,
16: 7 and grow up like a plant of the f."
17:24 the trees of the f shall know that I am the LORD.
29: 5 you shall fall in the open f,
31: 4 sending forth its streams to all the trees of the f.
31: 5 So it towered high above all the trees of the f;
31: 6 the animals of the f gave birth to their young;
31:15 and all the trees of the f fainted because of it.
32: 4 on the open f I will fling you,
33:27 in the open f I will give to the wild animals to
34:27 The trees of the f shall yield their fruit,
36:30 of the tree and the produce of the f abundant,
38:20 and the birds of the air, and the animals of the f,
39: 5 You shall fall in the open f;
39:10 to take wood out of the f or cut down any trees in
Da 2:38 the wild animals of the f, and the birds of the air,
4:12 The animals of the f found shade under it,
4:15 in the tender grass of the f.
4:15 with the animals of the f in the grass of the earth.
4:21 under which animals of the f lived,
4:23 in the grass of the f;
4:23 and let his lot be with the animals of the f,
4:32 your dwelling shall be with the animals of the f.

Hos 10: 4 up like poisonous weeds in the furrows of the f.
12:11 be like stone heaps on the furrows of the f.
Joel 1:11 for the crops of the f are ruined.
1:12 all the trees of the f are dried up;
1:19 and flames have burned all the trees of the f.
2:22 Do not fear, you animals of the f,
Am 4: 7 one f would be rained upon,
4: 7 and the f on which it did not rain withered;
Mic 3:12 because of you Zion shall be plowed as a f;
Zec 10: 1 the vegetation in the f to everyone.
Mal 3:11 and your vine in the f shall not be barren,
Mt 6:28 Consider the lilies of the f, how they grow;
6:30 But if God so clothes the grass of the f,
13:24 to someone who sowed good seed in his f;
13:27 'Master, did you not sow good seed in your f?
13:31 that someone took and sowed in his f;
13:36 "Explain to us the parable of the weeds of the f."
13:38 the f is the world, and the good seed are
13:44 kingdom of heaven is like treasure hidden in a f,
13:44 and sells all that he has and buys that f.
24:18 the one in the f must not turn back to get a coat.
24:40 Then two will be in the f;
27: 7 to buy the potter's f as a place to bury foreigners.
27: 8 this reason that f has been called the F of Blood
27:10 and they gave them for the potter's f,
Mk 13:16 the one in the f must not turn back to get a coat.
Lk 12:28 But if God so clothes the grass of the f,
15:25 "Now his elder son was in the f;
17: 7 in from plowing or tending sheep in the f,
17:31 and likewise anyone in the f must not turn back.
Ac 1:18 (Now this man acquired a f with the reward
1:19 that the f was called in their language Hakeldama,
that is, F of Blood.)
4:37 He sold a f that belonged to him,
1Co 3: 9 you are God's f, God's building.
2Co 10:13 will keep within the f that God has assigned to us,
Jas 1:10 the rich will disappear like a flower in the f.
1:11 with its scorching heat and withers the f;
Jdt 8: 3 in the f, he was overcome by the burning heat,
8: 3 So they buried him with his ancestors in the f
11: 7 the animals of the f and the cattle and the birds of
Sir 24:14 like a fair olive tree in the f,
26:20 *Seek a fertile f within the whole plain,*
Bel 1:33 and was going into the f to take it to the reapers.
2Es 4:29 f where the good has been sown will not come.
7:*65* but let the wild animals of the f be glad;
9:17 He answered me and said, "As is the f,
9:24 into a f of flowers where no house has been built,
9:24 and eat only of the flowers of the f,
9:26 as he directed me, into the f that is called Ardat;
9:26 among the flowers and ate of the plants of the f,
10: 3 I got up in the night and fled, and I came to this f,
10:32 I did as you directed, and went out into the f,
10:51 to remain in the f where no house had been built,
10:53 to go into the f where there was no foundation
12:51 But I sat in the f seven days,
12:51 and I ate only of the flowers of the f,
13:57 Then I got up and walked in the f,
14:37 as he commanded me, and we proceeded to the f,
16:28 and two, out of the f,
16:77 They are like a f choked with underbrush

FIELDS (67) [FIELD]

Ge 37:15 and a man found him wandering in the f;
41:48 up in every city the food from the f around it.
47:20 All the Egyptians sold their f,
Ex 8:13 frogs died in the houses, the courtyards, and the f.
Nu 16:14 or given us an inheritance of f and vineyards.
Dt 11:15 and he will give grass in your f for your livestock,
Jos 21:12 the f of the town and its villages had been given
Jdg 9:32 and lie in wait in the f.
9:42 the following day the people went out into the f.
9:43 and lay in wait in the f.
9:44 on all who were in the f and killed them.
1Sa 8:14 He will take the best of your f and vineyards
22: 7 of Jesse give every one of you f and vineyards,
25:15 we never missed anything when we were in the f,
2Sa 1:21 be no dew or rain upon you, nor bounteous f!
2Ki 8: 6 together with all the revenue of the f from the day
23: 4 he burned them outside Jerusalem in the f of
1Ch 6:56 but the f of the city and its villages they gave
2Ch 31:19 in the f of common land belonging to their towns,
Ne 5: 3 "We are having to pledge our f, our vineyards,
5: 4 to borrow money on our f and vineyards to pay
5: 5 and our f and vineyards now belong to others."
5:11 Restore to them, this very day, their f,
11:25 And as for the villages, with their f,
11:30 Lachish and its f, and Azekah and its villages.
12:44 for the Levites from the f belonging to the towns;
13:10 the service, had gone back to their f.
Job 5:10 on the earth and sends waters on the f;
Ps 78:12 in the land of Egypt, in the f of Zoan.
78:43 and his miracles in the f of Zoan.
107:37 they sow f, and plant vineyards, and get
132: 6 we found it in the f of Jaar.
144:13 by tens of thousands in our f,
Pr 8:26 when he had not yet made earth and f,
23:10 an ancient landmark or encroach on the f
SS 7:11 Come, my beloved, let us go forth into the f,
Isa 16: 8 For the f of Heshbon languish,
32:12 Beat your breasts for the pleasant f,
Jer 6:12 their f and wives together;
8:10 to others and their f to conquerors,
31:40 and all the f as far as the Wadi Kidron,
32:15 Houses and f and vineyards shall again be bought
32:43 F shall be bought in this land
Jer 32:44 F shall be bought for money,
39:10 and gave them vineyards and f at the same time.
41: 8 barley, oil, and honey hidden in the f."
Hos 5: 7 new moon shall devour them along with their f.
Joel 1:10 The f are devastated, the ground mourns;
Mic 2: 2 They covet f, and seize them;
2: 4 Among our captors he parcels out our f."
Hab 3:17 produce of the olive fails and the f yield no food;
Mt 19:29 or sisters or father or mother or children or f,
Mk 10:29 or sisters or mother or father or children or f,
10:30 mothers and children, and f with persecutions—
11: 8 that they had cut in the f.
Lk 2: 8 In that region there were shepherds living in the f,
15:15 who sent him to his f to feed the pigs.
Jn 4:35 and see how the f are ripe for harvesting.
Jas 5: 4 The wages of the laborers who mowed your f,
Jdt 2:27 and burned all their f and destroyed their flocks
3: 3 and all our land and all our wheat f and our flocks
4: 5 since their f had recently been harvested.
6: 4 and their f will be full of their dead.
8: 7 livestock, and f; and she maintained this estate.
1Mc 16:10 They also fled into the towers that were in the f
2Es 15:41 so that all the f and all the streams shall be filled
16:32 and its f shall be plowed up,

FIERCE (47) [FIERCELY, FIERCENESS, FIERCER, FIERCEST]

Ge 49: 7 Cursed be their anger, for it is f, and their wrath,
Ex 32:12 of the earth'? Turn from your f wrath;
Nu 25: 4 that the f anger of the LORD may turn away
32:14 to increase the LORD's f anger against Israel!
Dt 9:19 against you was so f that he would destroy you.
13:17 so that the LORD may turn from his f anger
29:23 which the LORD destroyed in his f anger—
Jdg 20:34 of all Israel, and the battle was f.
1Sa 20:34 in f anger and ate no food on the second day of
28:18 and did not carry out his f wrath against Amalek,
2Sa 2:17 The battle was very f that day;
2Ch 25:10 and returned home in f anger.
28:11 for the f wrath of the LORD is upon you."
28:13 and there is f wrath against Israel."
29:10 so that his f anger may turn away from us.
30: 8 so that his f anger may turn away from you.
Ezr 10:14 the f wrath of our God on this account is averted
Job 4:10 The roar of the lion, the voice of the f lion,
20:23 to the full God will send his f anger into them,
41:10 No one is so f as to dare to stir it up.
Ps 78:49 He let loose on them his f anger, wrath,
SS 8: 6 for love is strong as death, passion f as the grave.
Isa 7: 4 because of the f anger of Rezin and Aram and
13: 9 cruel, with wrath and f anger,
13:13 of the LORD of hosts in the day of his f anger.
19: 4 a f king will rule over them, says the Sovereign,
27: 8 with his f blast he removed them in the day of
Jer 4: 8 "The f anger of the LORD has not turned away
4:26 in ruins before the LORD, before his f anger.
12:13 of their harvests because of the f anger of
25:37 because of the f anger of the LORD.
25:38 and because of his f anger.
30:24 The f anger of the LORD will not turn back
49:37 I will bring disaster upon them, my f anger,
51:45 each of you, from the f anger of the LORD!
La 1:12 the LORD inflicted on the day of his f anger.
2: 3 He has cut down in f anger all the might of Israel;
2: 6 in his f indignation has spurned king and priest.
Hos 11: 9 I will not execute my f anger;
Jnh 3: 9 he may turn from his f anger,
Hab 1: 6 that f and impetuous nation,
Zep 2: 2 there comes upon you the f anger of the LORD,
Mt 8:28 They were so f that no one could pass that way.
Rev 16: 9 they were scorched by the f heat,
AdE 15: 7 flushed with splendor, he looked at her in f anger.
1Mc 6:47 the Jews saw the royal might and the f attack of
2Mc 10:29 When the battle became f,

FIERCELY (2) [FIERCE]

Ge 49:23 The archers f attacked him;
Jer 6:29 bellows blow f, the lead is consumed by the fire;

FIERCENESS (2) [FIERCE]

2Ki 23:26 Still the LORD did not turn from the f of his great
Job 39:24 With f and rage it swallows the ground;

FIERCER (2) [FIERCE]

2Sa 19:43 But the words of the people of Judah were f than
4Mc 7:10 more powerful than tortures; O elder, f than fire;

FIERCEST (1) [FIERCE]

4Mc 16: 2 but also that a woman has despised the f tortures.

FIERY‡ (17) [FIRE]

Dt 28:22 fever, inflammation, with f heat and drought,
Ps 7:13 making his arrows f shafts.
21: 9 You will make them like a f furnace
78:14 and all night long with a f light.
Isa 14:29 and its fruit will be a flying f serpent.
Da 7: 9 his throne was f flames, and its wheels were
1Pe 4:12 not be surprised at the f ordeal that is taking place
Wis 11:18 or such as breathe out f breath,
Sir 36:11 Let survivors be consumed in the f wrath,
43: 4 it breathes out f vapors, and its bright rays blind
Aza 1:26 and drove the f flame out of the furnace,
1:66 from the midst of the burning f furnace;
3Mc 6: 6 moistening the f furnace with dew and turning
4Mc 7:11 of the people and conquered the f angel,
13: 5 in those who were not turned back by f agonies?
16: 3 the raging f furnace of Mishael so intensely hot,
16:21 the f furnace and endured it for the sake of God.

FIFTEEN‡ (23) [FIFTEENTH]

Ge 5:10 after the birth of Kenan eight hundred f years,
7:20 covering them f cubits deep.
Ex 27:14 be f cubits of hangings on the one side,
27:15 be f cubits of hangings on the other side,
38:14 hangings for one side of the gate were f cubits,
38:15 of the gate of the court were hangings of f cubits,
Lev 27: 7 then the equivalent for a male is f shekels,
Jdg 8:10 about f thousand men, all who were left of all
2Sa 9:10 Now Ziba had f sons and twenty servants.
19:17 with his f sons and his twenty servants,
1Ki 7: 3 f in each row, which were on the pillars.
2Ki 14:17 King Amaziah son of Joash of Judah lived f years
20: 6 I will add f years to your life.
2Ch 25:25 lived f years after the death of King Joash son
Isa 38: 5 I will add f years to your life.
Eze 45:12 and f shekels shall make a mina for you.
Hos 3: 2 So I bought her for f shekels of silver and a homer
Ac 27:28 on they took soundings again and found f fathoms.
Gal 1:18 to visit Cephas and stayed with him f days;
Rev 21:16 the city with his rod, f hundred miles;
AdE 9:16 They destroyed f thousand of them,
1Mc 10:40 I also grant f thousand shekels of silver yearly out
2Mc 8:22 putting f hundred men under each.

FIFTEENTH‡ (25) [FIFTEEN]

Ex 16: 1 and Sinai, on the f day of the second month
Lev 23: 6 and on the f day of the same month is the festival
23:34 On the f day of this seventh month,
23:39 Now, the f day of the seventh month,
Nu 28:17 And on the f day of this month is a festival;
29:12 On the f day of the seventh month you shall have
33: 3 on the f day of the first month;
1Ki 12:32 on the f day of the eighth month like the festival
12:33 the altar that he had made in Bethel on the f day
2Ki 14:23 the f year of King Amaziah son of Joash of Judah,
1Ch 24:14 the f to Bilgah, the sixteenth to Immer,
25:22 to the f, to Jeremoth, his sons
2Ch 15:10 the third month of the f year of the reign of Asa.
Est 9:18 and rested on the f day,
9:21 of the month Adar and also the f day of
Eze 32:17 in the first month, on the f day of the month,
45:25 on the f day of the month and for the seven days
Lk 3: 1 In the f year of the reign of Emperor Tiberius,
AdE 9:18 They celebrated the f with joy and gladness.
9:19 the f day of Adar as their joyful holiday,
9:21 that they should keep the fourteenth and f days
10:13 on the fourteenth and f of that month,
1Mc 1:54 Now on the f day of Chislev,
2Mc 11:33 The one hundred forty-eighth year, Xanthicus f."
11:38 The one hundred forty-eighth year, Xanthicus f."

FIFTH (55) [FIVE]

Ge 1:23 and there was morning, the f day.
30:17 and she conceived and bore Jacob a f son.
47:26 that Pharaoh should have the f.
Lev 19:25 But in the f year you may eat of their fruit,
Nu 5: 7 for the wrong, adding one f to it, and giving it to
7:36 On the f day Shelumiel son of Zurishaddai,
29:26 On the f day: nine bulls, two rams,
33:38 on the first day of the f month.
Jos 19:24 The f lot came out for the tribe of Asher
Jdg 19: 8 the f day he got up early in the morning to leave;
2Sa 3: 4 the f, Shephatiah son of Abital;
1Ki 14:25 In the f year of King Rehoboam,
2Ki 8:16 In the f year of King Joram son of Ahab of Israel,
25: 8 In the f month, on the seventh day of the month—
1Ch 2:14 Nethanel the fourth, Raddai the f,
3: 3 the f Shephatiah, by Abital;
8: 2 Nohah the fourth, and Rapha the f.
12:10 Mishmannah fourth, Jeremiah f,
24: 9 the f to Malchijah, the sixth to Mijamin,
25:12 f to Nethaniah, his sons and his brothers, twelve;
26: 3 Elam the f, Jehohanan the sixth, Eliehoenai
26: 4 Joah the third, Sachar the fourth, Nethanel the f,
27: 8 The f commander, for the f month,
2Ch 12: 2 In the f year of King Rehoboam,
Ezr 7: 8 They came to Jerusalem in the f month,
7: 9 the first day of the f month he came to Jerusalem,
Ne 6: 5 for the f time sent his servant to me with
Jer 1: 3 until the captivity of Jerusalem in the f month.
28: 1 in the f month of the fourth year,
36: 9 In the f year of King Jehoiakim son of Josiah
52:12 In the f month, on the tenth day of the month—
Eze 1: 1 in the fourth month, on the f day of the month,
1: 2 On the f day of the month (it was the f year of
8: 1 on the f day of the month, as I sat in my house,
20: 1 In the seventh year, in the f month,
33:21 in the tenth month, on the f day of the month,
Zec 7: 3 and practice abstinence in the f month,
7: 5 When you fasted and lamented in the f month and
8:19 The fast of the fourth month, and the fast of the f,
Rev 6: 9 When he opened the f seal,
9: 1 And the f angel blew his trumpet,
16:10 f angel poured his bowl on the throne of the beast,
21:20 the f onyx, the sixth carnelian,
Bar 1: 2 in the f year, on the seventh day of the month,
2Mc 7:15 Next they brought forward the f
10:35 But at dawn of the f day,

1Es 8: 6 in the f month (this was the king's seventh year);
8: 6 in Jerusalem on the new moon of the f month,
3Mc 6:38 and their destruction was set for the f to
2Es 6:47 "On the f day you commanded the seventh part,
7:85 The f way, they shall see how the habitations of
7:96 The f order, they rejoice that they have
4Mc 11: 1 after being cruelly tortured, the f leaped up,

FIFTIES (7) [FIFTY]

Ex 18:21 over them as officers over thousands, hundreds, f
18:25 as officers over thousands, hundreds, f, and tens.
Dt 1:15 commanders of hundreds, commanders of f,
1Sa 8:12 of thousands and commanders of f,
2Ki 1:14 the two former captains of fifty men with their f;
Mk 6:40 So they sat down in groups of hundreds and of f.
1Mc 3:55 in charge of thousands and hundreds and f

FIFTIETH (4) [FIFTY]

Lev 25:10 the f year and you shall proclaim liberty
25:11 That f year shall be a jubilee for you:
2Ki 15:23 In the f year of King Azariah of Judah,
1Mc 6:20 and besieged the citadel in the one hundred f year;

FIFTY‡ (132) [FIFTIES, FIFTIETH]

Ge 6:15 its width f cubits, and its height thirty cubits.
7:24 on the earth for one hundred f days.
8: 3 of one hundred f days the waters had abated;
9:28 After the flood Noah lived three hundred f years.
9:29 All the days of Noah were nine hundred f years;
18:24 Suppose there are f righteous within the city;
18:24 and not forgive it for the f righteous who are in it?
18:26 "If I find at Sodom f righteous in the city,
18:28 Suppose five of the f righteous are lacking?
Ex 26: 5 You shall make f loops on the one curtain,
26: 5 and you shall make f loops on the edge of
26: 6 You shall make f clasps of gold,
26:10 You shall make f loops on the edge of the curtain
26:10 and f loops on the edge of the curtain
26:11 You shall make f clasps of bronze,
27:12 of the court on the west side there shall be f cubits
27:13 the court on the front to the east shall be f cubits.
27:18 the width f, and the height five cubits,
30:23 as much, that is, two hundred f,
30:23 and two hundred f of aromatic cane,
36:12 he made f loops on the one curtain,
36:12 and he made f loops on the edge of the curtain
36:13 And he made f clasps of gold,
36:17 He made f loops on the edge of
36:17 and f loops on the edge of
36:18 He made f clasps of bronze to join
38:12 the west side there were hangings f cubits long,
38:13 And for the front to the east, f cubits.
38:26 for six hundred three thousand, five hundred f men.
Lev 23:16 until the day after the seventh sabbath, f days;
27: 3 of age the equivalent shall be f shekels of silver
27:16 f shekels of silver to a homer of barley seed.
Nu 1:25 of Gad were forty-five thousand six hundred f.
1:46 was six hundred three thousand five hundred f.
2:15 as enrolled of forty-five thousand six hundred f.
2:16 is one hundred fifty-one thousand four hundred f.
2:32 was six hundred three thousand five hundred f.
4: 3 from thirty years old up to f years old,
4:23 up to f years old you shall enroll them,
4:30 up to f years old you shall enroll them,
4:35 up to f years old, everyone who qualified
4:36 by clans was two thousand seven hundred f.
4:39 up to f years old, everyone who qualified
4:43 up to f years old, everyone who qualified
4:47 from thirty years old up to f years old,
8:25 the age of f years they shall retire from the duty of
16: 2 two hundred f Israelite men,
16:17 before the LORD, two hundred f censers;
16:35 and consumed the two hundred f men offering
26:10 when the fire devoured two hundred f men;
31:30 the Israelites' half you shall take one out of every f,
31:47 the Israelites' half Moses took one of every f,
31:52 was sixteen thousand seven hundred f shekels.
Dt 22:29 the man who lay with her shall give f shekels
Jos 7:21 and a bar of gold weighing f shekels,
2Sa 15: 1 and f men to run ahead of him.
24:24 the threshing floor and the oxen for f shekels
1Ki 1: 5 and f men to run before him.
7: 2 f cubits wide, and thirty cubits high,
7: 6 of Pillars f cubits long and thirty cubits wide.
9:23 five hundred f, who had charge of
10:29 and a horse for one hundred f;
18: 4 hid them f to a cave,
18:13 how I hid a hundred of the LORD's prophets f to
18:19 with the four hundred f prophets of Baal and
18:22 but Baal's prophets number four hundred f.
2Ki 1: 9 king sent to him a captain of f with his f men.
1:10 But Elijah answered the captain of f,
1:10 down from heaven and consume you and your f."
1:10 and consumed him and his f.
1:11 the king sent to him another captain of f with his f.
1:12 down from heaven and consume you and your f."
1:12 down from heaven and consumed him and his f.
1:13 the king sent the captain of a third f with his f.
1:13 So the third captain of f went up,
1:13 and the life of these f servants of yours,
1:14 the two former captains of f men with their fifties;
2: 7 F men of the company of prophets also went,
2:16 we have f strong men among your servants;
2:17 So they sent f men who searched for three days
13: 7 an army of not more than f horsemen, ten chariots
2Ki 15:20 f shekels of silver from each one,
15:25 conspired against him with f of the Gileadites,
1Ch 5:21 f thousand of their camels, two hundred f thousand
8:40 and grandchildren, one hundred f.
12:33 Of Zebulun, f thousand seasoned troops,
2Ch 1:17 and a horse for one hundred f;
3: 9 The weight of the nails was f shekels of gold.
8:10 the chief officers of King Solomon, two hundred f
8:18 and imported from there four hundred f talents
Ezr 8: 3 with whom were registered one hundred f males.
8: 6 Ebed son of Jonathan, and with him f males.
8:26 I weighed out into their hand six hundred f talents
Ne 5:17 there were at my table one hundred f people,
7:70 f basins, and five hundred thirty priestly robes.
Est 5:14 "Let a gallows f cubits high be made,
7: 9 stands at Haman's house, f cubits high."
Isa 3: 3 captain of f and dignitary,
Eze 40:15 of the inner vestibule of the gate was f cubits.
40:21 of the first gate; its depth was f cubits,
40:25 of the others; its depth was f cubits,
40:29 in its vestibule; its depth was f cubits,
40:33 in its vestibule; its depth was f cubits,
40:36 Its depth was f cubits,
42: 2 was one hundred cubits, and the width f cubits.
42: 7 opposite the chambers, f cubits long.
42: 8 chambers on the outer court were f cubits long,
45: 2 with f cubits for an open space around it.
48:17 on the north two hundred f cubits,
48:17 on the south two hundred f,
48:17 on the east two hundred f,
48:17 on the west two hundred f.
Hag 2:16 one came to the winevat to draw f measures,
Lk 7:41 one owed five hundred denarii, and the other f.
9:14 "Make them sit down in groups of about f each."
16: 6 'Take your bill, sit down quickly, and make it f.'
Jn 8:57 the Jews said to him, "You are not yet f years old,
Ac 13:20 for about four hundred f years.
19:19 it was found to come to f thousand silver coins.
Jdt 1: 2 the walls seventy cubits high and f cubits wide.
AdE 5:14 "Let a gallows be made, f cubits high,
7: 9 at Haman's house, a gallows f cubits high."
1Mc 9:61 And Jonathan's men seized about f of the men of
2Mc 4: 9 to this he promised to pay one hundred f more
13: 5 For there is a tower there, f cubits high,
1Es 8:30 and with him a hundred f men enrolled.
8:32 and with him two hundred f men.
8:56 I weighed and gave to them six hundred f talents

FIFTY-EIGHT‡ (1)

1Es 5:18 Those from Anathoth, one hundred f.

FIFTY-FIRST (2) [FIFTY-ONE]

1Mc 7: 1 In the one hundred f year Demetrius son
2Mc 14: 4 in about the one hundred f year,

FIFTY-FIVE (4)

2Ki 21: 1 he reigned f years in Jerusalem.
2Ch 33: 1 he reigned f years in Jerusalem.
Ne 7:20 Of Adin, six hundred f.
1Es 5:18 Those from Netophah, f.

FIFTY-FOUR (9)

Nu 1:29 of Issachar were f thousand four hundred.
2: 6 as enrolled of f thousand four hundred.
Ezr 2: 7 Of Elam, one thousand two hundred f.
2:15 Of Adin, four hundred f.
2:31 Of the other Elam, one thousand two hundred f.
Ne 7:12 Of Elam, one thousand two hundred f.
7:34 one thousand two hundred f.
1Es 5:12 one thousand two hundred f.
5:14 The descendants of Adin, four hundred f.

FIFTY-NINE (2)

Nu 1:23 of Simeon were f thousand three hundred.
2:13 as enrolled of f thousand three hundred.

FIFTY-ONE (1) [FIFTY-FIRST]

Nu 2:16 is one hundred f thousand four hundred fifty.

FIFTY-SECOND (2) [FIFTY-TWO]

2Ki 15:27 In the f year of King Azariah of Judah,
1Mc 9: 3 of the one hundred f year they encamped

FIFTY-SEVEN (3)

Nu 1:31 of Zebulun were f thousand four hundred.
2: 8 as enrolled of f thousand four hundred.
2:31 of Dan is one hundred f thousand six hundred.

FIFTY-SIX (6)

1Ch 9: 9 according to their generations, nine hundred f.
Ezr 2:14 Of Bigvai, two thousand f.
2:22 The people of Netophah, f.
2:30 Of Magbish, one hundred f.
1Es 5:10 The descendants of Arah, seven hundred f.
5:21 The descendants of Niphish, one hundred f.

FIFTY-THIRD (1) [FIFTY-THREE]

1Mc 9:54 In the one hundred and f year,

FIFTY-THREE (5) [FIFTY-THIRD]

Nu 1:43 of Naphtali were f thousand four hundred.
2:30 as enrolled of f thousand four hundred.
Nu 26:47 of those enrolled was f thousand four hundred.
2Ch 2:17 to be one hundred f thousand six hundred.
Jn 21:11 full of large fish, a hundred f of them;

FIFTY-TWO (13) [FIFTY-SECOND]

Nu 26:34 of those enrolled was f thousand seven hundred.
2Ki 15: 2 and he reigned f years in Jerusalem.
2Ch 26: 3 and he reigned f years in Jerusalem.
Ezr 2:29 The descendants of Nebo, f.
2:37 Of Immer, one thousand f.
2:60 Tobiah, and Nekoda, six hundred f.
Ne 6:15 the twenty-fifth day of the month Elul, in f days.
7:10 Of Arah, six hundred f.
7:33 Of the other Nebo, f.
7:40 Of Immer, one thousand f.
1Es 5:21 Those from Betolio, f.
5:24 The descendants of Immer, one thousand and f.
5:37 and the descendants of Nekoda, six hundred f.

FIG (45) [FIGS]

Ge 3: 7 and they sewed f leaves together
Dt 8: 8 of vines and f trees and pomegranates,
Jdg 9:10 Then the trees said to the f tree,
9:11 But the f tree answered them,
1Sa 30:12 also gave him a piece of f cake and two clusters
1Ki 4:25 all of them under their vines and f trees.
2Ki 18:31 from your own vine and your own f tree,
Ps 105:33 He struck their vines and f trees,
Pr 27:18 Anyone who tends a f tree will eat its fruit,
SS 2:13 The f tree puts forth its figs,
Isa 28: 4 will be like a first-ripe f before the summer;
34: 4 or fruit withering on a f tree.
36:16 from your own vine and your own f tree
Jer 5:17 they shall eat up your vines and your f trees;
8:13 nor figs on the f tree;
Hos 2:12 I will lay waste her vines and her f trees,
9:10 Like the first fruit on the f tree, in its first season,
Joel 1: 7 and splintered my f trees;
1:12 The vine withers, the f tree droops.
2:22 the f tree and vine give their full yield.
Am 4: 9 locust devoured your f trees and your olive trees;
Mic 4: 4 under their own vines and under their own f trees,
7: 1 there is no first-ripe f for which I hunger.
Na 3:12 All your fortresses are like f trees
Hab 3:17 Though the f tree does not blossom,
Hag 2:19 Do the vine, the f tree, the pomegranate,
Zec 3:10 to come under your vine and f tree."
Mt 21:19 And seeing a f tree by the side of the road,
21:19 And the f tree withered at once.
21:20 saying, "How did the f tree wither at once?"
21:21 only will you do what has been done to the f tree,
24:32 "From the f tree learn its lesson:
Mk 11:13 Seeing in the distance a f tree in leaf,
11:20 they saw the f tree withered away to its roots.
11:21 The f tree that you cursed has withered."
13:28 "From the f tree learn its lesson:
Lk 13: 6 "A man had a f tree planted in his vineyard;
13: 7 for fruit on this f tree,
21:29 "Look at the f tree and all the trees;
Jn 1:48 under the f tree before Philip called you."
1:50 because I told you that I saw you under the f tree?
Jas 3:12 Can a f tree, my brothers and sisters, yield olives,
Rev 6:13 as the f tree drops its winter fruit when shaken by
Jdt 10: 5 and filled a bag with roasted grain, dried f cakes,
1Mc 14:12 the people sat under their own vines and f trees,

FIGHT (143) [FIGHTERS, FIGHTING, FIGHTS, FOUGHT]

Ex 1:10 join our enemies and f against us and escape from
14:14 The LORD will f for you,
17: 9 to Joshua, "Choose some men for us and go out, f
Nu 22:11 be able to f against them and drive them out.' "
Dt 1:30 is the one who will f for you,
1:41 We are ready to go up and f,
1:42 "Say to them, 'Do not go up and do not f,
20: 4 to f for you against your enemies,
20:10 When you draw near to a town to f against it,
25:11 If men get into a f with one another,
Jos 9: 2 with one accord to f Joshua and Israel.
10:25 to all the enemies against whom you f."
11: 5 and camped together at the waters of Merom, to f
24: 9 set out to f against Israel.
Jdg 1: 1 for us against the Canaanites, to f against them?"
1: 3 that we may f against the Canaanites;
1: 9 Afterward the people of Judah went down to f
8: 1 when you went to f against the Midianites?"
9:38 Go out now and f with them."
10: 9 also crossed the Jordan to f against Judah and
10:18 "Who will begin the f against the Ammonites?
11: 6 so that we may f with the Ammonites."
11: 8 you may go with us and f with the Ammonites,
11: 9 "If you bring me home again to f with
11:12 that you have come to me to f against my land?"
11:32 So Jephthah crossed over to the Ammonites to f
12: 1 "Why did you cross over to f against
12: 3 then have you come up to me this day, to f
1Sa 4: 9 as they have been to you; be men and f."
8:20 and go out before us and f our battles."
13: 5 The Philistines mustered to f with Israel,
15:18 and f against them until they are consumed.'
17: 9 If he is able to f with me and kill me,
17:10 Give me a man, that we may f together."
17:32 your servant will go and f with this Philistine."
17:33 not able to go against this Philistine to f with him;
18:17 be valiant for me and f the LORD's battles."

1Sa 19: 8 and David went out to **f** the Philistines.
28: 1 the Philistines gathered their forces for war, to **f**
29: 8 and **f** against the enemies of my lord the king?"
2Sa 11:20 'Why did you go so near the city to **f**?
1Ki 12:21 one hundred eighty thousand chosen troops to **f**
12:24 up or **f** against your kindred the people of Israel.
20:23 but let us **f** against them in the plain,
20:25 then we will **f** against them in the plain,
20:26 and went up to Aphek to **f** against Israel.
22:31 "**F** with no one small or great,
22:32 So they turned to **f** against him;
2Ki 3:21 that the kings had come up to **f** against them,
7: 6 of the Hittites and the kings of Egypt to **f**
10: 3 and **f** for your master's house."
13:17 For you shall **f** the Arameans in Aphek
19: 9 "See, he has set out to **f** against you,"
2Ch 11: 1 of Judah and Benjamin to **f** against Israel,
11: 4 You shall not go up or **f** against your kindred.
13:12 O Israelites, do not **f** against the LORD,
18:30 "**F** with no one small or great,
18:31 So they turned to **f** against him;
20:17 This battle is not for you to **f**;
32: 2 that Sennacherib had come and intended to **f**
32: 8 to help us and to **f** our battles."
35:20 King Neco of Egypt went up to **f** at Carchemish
35:22 but disguised himself in order to **f** with him.
Ne 4: 8 and **f** against Jerusalem and to cause confusion
4:14 who is great and awesome, and **f** for your kin,
4:20 Our God will **f** for us."
Ps 35: 1 **f** against those who **f** against me!
56: 2 on me all day long, for many **f** against me.
Isa 19: 2 and they will **f**, one against the other,
29: 7 multitude of all the nations that **f** against Ariel,
29: 7 all that **f** against her and her stronghold,
29: 8 so shall the multitude of all the nations be that **f**
30:32 battling with brandished arm he will **f** with him.
31: 4 of hosts will come down to **f** upon Mount Zion
37: 9 "He has set out to **f** against you."
58: 4 to quarrel and to **f** and to strike with a wicked fist.
Jer 1:19 They will **f** against you;
15:20 they will **f** against you, but they shall not prevail
21: 5 I myself will **f** against you with outstretched hand
32: 5 though you **f** against the Chaldeans,
33: 5 The Chaldeans are coming in to **f** and to fill them
34:22 and they will **f** against it, and take it,
37: 8 the Chaldeans shall return and **f** against this city;
41:12 and went to **f** against Ishmael son of Nethaniah.
Da 10:20 I must return to **f** against the prince of Persia,
Zec 10: 5 they shall **f**, for the LORD is with them,
14: 3 and **f** against those nations as when he fights on
14:14 even Judah will **f** at Jerusalem.
1Ti 1:18 that by following them you may **f** the good **f**,
6:12 **F** the good **f** of the faith;
2Ti 4: 7 I have fought the good **f**, I have finished the race,
Rev 13: 4 "Who is like the beast, and who can **f** against it?"
Jdt 7:11 do not **f** against them in regular formation,
AdE 8:13 be ready on that day to **f** against their enemies."
11: 6 two great dragons came forward, both ready to **f**,
11: 7 to **f** against the righteous nation.
Wis 5:20 with him to **f** against his frenzied foes.
Sir 4:28 **F** to the death for truth, and the Lord God will **f**
8:16 Do not pick a **f** with the quick-tempered,
29:13 it will **f** for you against the enemy.
1Mc 2:40 and refuse to **f** with the Gentiles for our lives and
2:41 "Let us **f** against anyone who comes to attack us
2:66 for you and **f** the battle against the peoples.
3:10 and a large force from Samaria to **f** against Israel.
3:17 **f** against so great and so strong a multitude?
3:21 but we **f** for our lives and our laws.
3:43 and **f** for our people and the sanctuary."
3:58 to **f** with these Gentiles who have assembled
4:18 But stand now against our enemies and **f** them,
4:41 Then Judas detailed men to **f** against those in
5:32 "**F** today for your kindred!"
5:39 ready to come and **f** against you."
8: 6 who went to **f** against them
8:32 we will defend their rights and **f** you on sea and
9: 8 We may have the strength to **f** them."
9: 9 and let us come back with our kindred and **f** them;
9:30 as our ruler and leader, to **f** our battle."
9:44 "Let us get up now and **f** for our lives,
11:46 the main streets of the city and began to **f**.
12:51 When their pursuers saw that they would **f**
13: 9 **F** our battles, and all that you say
14:13 No one was left in the land to **f** them,
15:26 to Antiochus two thousand picked troops, to **f**
16: 3 and go out and **f** for our nation,
2Mc 7:19 that you will go unpunished for having tried to **f**
8:16 against them, but to **f** nobly,
10:16 and imploring God to **f** on their side,
10:21 by setting their enemies free to **f** against them.
10:28 while the other made rage their leader in the **f**.
12:11 After a hard **f**, Judas and his companions,
13:14 of the world and exhorting his troops to **f** bravely
1Es 1:28 but tried to **f** with him,
3Mc 1: 4 When a bitter **f** resulted,
2Es 13: 8 were filled with fear, and yet they dared to **f**.
13:11 on the onrushing multitude that was prepared to **f**,
15:15 and nation shall rise up to **f** against nation,
4Mc 3: 4 but reason can **f** at our side so that we are
9:24 **F** the sacred and noble battle for religion.
16:16 **F** zealously for our ancestral law.

FIGHTERS (2) [FIGHT]

Jdg 20:44 all of them courageous **f**.
20:46 all of them courageous **f**.

FIGHTING (41) [FIGHT]

Ex 2:13 he went out the next day, he saw two Hebrews **f**;
14:25 for the LORD is **f** for them against Egypt."
21:22 When people who are **f** injure a pregnant woman
Lev 24:10 and a certain Israelite began **f** in the camp.
Jos 8: 1 take all the **f** men with you, and go up now to Ai.
8: 3 and all the **f** men set out to go up against Ai.
8:11 All the **f** men who were with him went up,
10: 7 he and all the **f** force with him,
11: 7 upon them with all his **f** force,
1Sa 14:52 There was hard **f** against the Philistines all
17:19 were in the valley of Elah, **f** with the Philistines.
23: 1 "The Philistines are **f** against Keilah,
25:28 because my lord is **f** the battles of the LORD;
2Sa 10:14 Joab returned from **f** against the Ammonites,
11:15 "Set Uriah in the forefront of the hardest **f**,
11:18 Joab sent and told David all the news about the **f**;
11:19 the king all the news about the **f**,
2Ki 19: 8 and found the king of Assyria **f** against Libnah;
1Ch 7: 4 were units of the **f** force, thirty-six thousand,
Isa 37: 8 and found the king of Assyria **f** against Libnah;
Jer 21: 4 with which you are **f** against the king of Babylon
32:24 the hands of the Chaldeans who are **f** against it.
32:29 Chaldeans who are **f** against this city shall come,
34: 1 and all the peoples under his dominion were **f**
34: 7 the king of Babylon was **f** against Jerusalem and
37:10 the whole army of Chaldeans who are **f**
51:30 The warriors of Babylon have given up **f**,
Jn 18:36 be **f** to keep me from being handed over to
Ac 5:39 that case you may even be found **f** against God!"
Jdt 7: 2 **f** forces numbered one hundred seventy thousand
AdE 14:13 turn his heart to hate the man who is **f** against us,
Sir 46: 6 that he was **f** in the sight of the Lord;
1Mc 6:57 the place against which we are **f** is strong,
7:28 "Let there be no **f** between you and me;
11:41 for they kept **f** against Israel.
11:50 and make the Jews stop **f** against us and our city."
13:47 an agreement with them and stopped **f**
2Mc 5:14 forty thousand in hand-to-hand **f**,
12:36 As Esdris and his men had been **f** for a long time
15:17 the matter by **f** hand to hand with all courage,
15:27 **f** with their hands and praying to God

FIGHTS (3) [FIGHT]

Dt 3:22 for it is the LORD your God who **f** for you."
Jos 23:10 since it is the LORD your God who **f** for you,
Zec 14: 3 and fight against those nations as when he **f** on

FIGS (25) [FIG]

Nu 13:23 They also brought some pomegranates and **f**.
20: 5 It is no place for grain, or **f**, or vines,
1Sa 25:18 and two hundred cakes of **f**.
2Ki 20: 7 Then Isaiah said, "Bring a lump of **f**.
1Ch 12:40 abundant provisions of meal, cakes of **f**,
Ne 13:15 and also wine, grapes, **f**, and all kinds of burdens,
SS 2:13 The fig tree puts forth its **f**,
Isa 38:21 Now Isaiah had said, "Let them take a lump of **f**,
Jer 8:13 nor **f** on the fig tree;
24: 1 The LORD showed me two baskets of **f** placed
24: 2 One basket had very good **f**, like first-ripe **f**,
24: 2 but the other basket had very bad **f**,
24: 3 "**F**, the good **f** very good, and the bad **f** very bad,
24: 5 Like these good **f**, so I will regard as good
24: 8 the bad **f** that are so bad they cannot be eaten,
29:17 like rotten **f** that are so bad they cannot be eaten.
Na 3:12 like fig trees with first-ripe **f**—
Mt 7:16 from thorns, or **f** from thistles?
Mk 11:13 for it was not the season for **f**.
Lk 6:44 **F** are not gathered from thorns,
Jas 3:12 yield olives, or a grapevine **f**?
Tob 1: 7 wine, olive oil, pomegranates, **f**,

FIGURATIVELY (1)

Heb 11:19 and **f** speaking, he did receive him back.

FIGURE (8) [FIGURED, FIGUREHEAD, FIGURES]

Dt 4:16 in the form of any **f**—
Pr 1: 6 to understand a proverb and a **f**,
Eze 8: 2 and there was a **f** that looked like a human being;
Jn 10: 6 Jesus used this **f** of speech with them,
16:29 not in any **f** of speech!
Wis 15: 4 a **f** stained with varied colors,
Sir 26:17 so is a beautiful face on a stately **f**.
2Es 13: 3 the **f** of a man come up out of the heart of the sea.

FIGURED (2) [FIGURE]

Lev 26: 1 and you shall not place **f** stones in your land,
Nu 33:52 from before you, destroy all their **f** stones,

FIGUREHEAD (1) [FIGURE, HEAD]

Ac 28:11 Alexandrian ship with the Twin Brothers as its **f**.

FIGURES (4) [FIGURE]

1Sa 6: 8 and put in a box at its side the **f** of gold,
Eze 23:14 she saw male **f** carved on the wall,
Jn 16:25 "I have said these things to you in **f** of speech.
16:25 when I will no longer speak to you in **f**,

FILIGREE (7)

Ex 28:11 you shall mount them in settings of gold **f**.
28:13 You shall make settings of gold **f**,
28:20 they shall be set in gold **f**.
39: 6 enclosed in settings of gold **f** and engraved like
39:13 they were enclosed in settings of gold **f**.
39:16 of gold **f** and two gold rings, and put the two rings
39:18 to the two settings of **f**;

FILL‡ (82) [FILLED, FILLING, FILLS, FULL, FULL-TONED, FULLNESS, FULLY]

Ge 1:22 "Be fruitful and multiply and **f** the waters in
1:28 and **f** the earth and subdue it;
9: 1 "Be fruitful and multiply, and **f** the earth.
42:25 Joseph then gave orders to **f** their bags with grain,
44: 1 "**F** the men's sacks with food,
Ex 10: 6 They shall **f** your houses,
15: 9 my desire shall have its **f** of them.
16: 3 we sat by the fleshpots and ate our **f** of bread;
16: 8 in the evening and your **f** of bread in the morning,
16:12 and in the morning you shall have your **f** of bread;
Lev 25:19 and you will eat your **f** and live on it securely.
Dt 6:11 that you did not **f**, hewn cisterns that you did
6:11 and when you have eaten your **f**,
8:10 You shall eat your **f** and bless
8:12 When you have eaten your **f**
11:15 and you will eat your **f**.
14:29 may come and eat their **f** so that
23:24 you may eat your **f** of grapes,
26:12 so that they may eat their **f** within your towns,
31:20 and they have eaten their **f** and grown fat,
32:15 Jacob ate his **f**; Jeshurun grew fat, and kicked.
Jdg 6:38 he wrung enough dew from the fleece to **f** a bowl
1Sa 16: 1 **F** your horn with oil and set out;
1Ki 18:33 "**F** four jars with water and pour it on
Job 3:15 who **f** their houses with silver.
8:21 He will yet **f** your mouth with laughter,
15: 2 and **f** themselves with the east wind?
20:23 To **f** their belly to the full God will send his fierce
23: 4 and **f** my mouth with arguments.
41: 7 Can you **f** its skin with harpoons,
Ps 59:15 and growl if they do not get their **f**.
72:19 may his glory **f** the whole earth.
81:10 Open your mouth wide and I will **f** it.
83:16 **F** their faces with shame,
123: 4 Our soul has had more than its **f** of the scorn
129: 7 with which reapers do not **f** their hands or binders
Pr 1:13 we shall **f** our houses with booty.
5:10 and strangers will take their **f** of your wealth,
7:18 Come, let us take our **f** of love until morning;
Isa 8: 8 and its outspread wings will **f** the breadth
27: 6 and **f** the whole world with fruit.
34: 5 When my sword has drunk its **f** in the heavens, lo,
56:12 let us **f** ourselves with strong drink.
65:11 for Fortune and **f** cups of mixed wine for Destiny;
Jer 13:13 I am about to **f** all the inhabitants of this land—
23:24 Do I not **f** heaven and earth?
31:14 I will give the priests their **f** of fatness,
33: 5 in to fight and to **f** them with the dead bodies
46:10 and drink its **f** of their blood.
51:11 Sharpen the arrows! **F** the quivers!
51:14 I will **f** you with troops like a swarm of locusts,
Eze 3: 3 eat this scroll that I give you and **f** your stomach
7:19 not satisfy their hunger or **f** their stomachs with it.
8:17 Must they **f** the land with violence,
9: 7 "Defile the house, and **f** the courts with the slain.
10: 2 **f** your hands with burning coals from among
24: 4 and the shoulder; **f** it with choice bones.
30:11 and **f** the land with the slain.
32: 5 and **f** the valleys with your carcass.
35: 8 I will **f** its mountains with the slain;
Zep 1: 9 who **f** their master's house with violence
Hag 1: 6 you drink, but you never have your **f**;
2: 7 and I will **f** this house with splendor,
Mt 23:32 **F** up, then, the measure of your ancestors.
Jn 2: 7 Jesus said to them, "**F** the jars with water."
6:26 but because you ate your **f** of the loaves.
Ro 15:13 May the God of hope **f** you with all joy and peace
Eph 4:10 so that he might **f** all things.)
Jas 2:16 keep warm and eat your **f**,"
Tob 8:18 Then he ordered his servants to **f** in the grave
Jdt 2: 8 Their wounded shall **f** their ravines and gullies,
8:31 so that the Lord may send us rain to **f** our cisterns.
Wis 2: 7 Let us take our **f** of costly wine and perfumes,
5: 7 We took our **f** of the paths of lawlessness
13:12 of his work to prepare his food, and eat his **f**.
19: 4 in order that they might **f** up the punishment
Sir 24:19 you who desire me, and eat your **f** of my fruits.
36:19 **F** Zion with your majesty,
1Mc 4:32 **F** them with cowardice; melt the boldness of their
2Es 2:19 by these I will **f** your children with joy.
4:32 how great a threshing floor they will **f**!"
8: 4 "Then drink your **f** of understanding, O my soul,

FILLED‡ (184) [FILL]

Ge 6:11 and the earth was **f** with violence.
6:13 for the earth is **f** with violence because of them;
21:19 She went, and **f** the skin with water,
24:16 She went down to the spring, **f** her jar,
26:15 the Philistines had stopped up and **f** with earth all
Ex 1: 7 so that the land was **f** with them.
2:16 and **f** the troughs to water their father's flock.
8:21 of the Egyptians shall be **f** with swarms of flies;
31: 3 and I have **f** him with divine spirit,
35:31 he has **f** him with divine spirit,
35:35 He has **f** them with skill to do every kind
40:34 and the glory of the LORD **f** the tabernacle.
40:35 and the glory of the LORD **f** the tabernacle.

Nu 14:21 the earth shall be f with the glory of the LORD—
Dt 6:11 houses f with all sorts of goods that you did
Jos 9:13 these wineskins were new when we f them,
1Sa 28:20 f with fear because of the words of Samuel;
1Ki 8:10 a cloud f the house of the LORD,
8:11 glory of the LORD f the house of the LORD.
18:35 and f the trench also with water.
20:27 while the Arameans f the country.
2Ki 3:17 but the wadi shall be f with water,
3:20 until the country was f with water.
10:21 until the temple of Baal was f from wall to wall.
21:16 until he had f Jerusalem from one end to another,
24:4 for he f Jerusalem with innocent blood,
2Ch 5:13 the house of the LORD, was f with a cloud,
5:14 for the glory of the LORD f the house of God.
7:1 and the glory of the LORD f the temple.
7:2 the glory of the LORD f the LORD's house.
16:14 on a bier that had been f with various kinds
Ezr 9:11 They have f it from end to end
Ne 9:25 and took possession of houses f with all sorts
9:25 so they ate, and were f and became fat,
Job 10:15 I am f with disgrace and look upon my affliction.
22:18 Yet he f their houses with good things—
Ps 10:7 Their mouths are f with cursing and deceit
17:14 May their bellies be f with what you have stored
38:7 For my loins are f with burning,
48:10 Your right hand is f with victory.
71:8 My mouth is f with your praise,
78:29 And they ate and were well f,
80:9 it took deep root and f the land.
104:28 you open your hand, they are f with good things.
126:2 Then our mouth was f with laughter,
144:13 May our barns be f, with produce of every kind;
Pr 3:10 then your barns will be f with plenty,
12:14 the fruit of the mouth one is f with good things,
12:21 but the wicked are f with trouble.
19:23 f with it one rests secure and suffers no harm.
24:4 by knowledge the rooms are f with all precious
Ecc 1:8 not satisfied with seeing, or the ear f with hearing.
Isa 2:7 Their land is f with silver and gold,
2:7 their land is f with horses,
2:8 Their land is f with idols;
6:1 and the hem of his robe f the temple.
6:4 and the house f with smoke.
21:3 Therefore my loins are f with anguish;
25:6 of rich food f with marrow,
33:5 he f Zion with justice and righteousness;
Jer 13:12 Every wine-jar should be f with wine.
13:12 that every wine-jar should be f with wine?"
15:17 for you had f me with indignation.
16:18 have f my inheritance with their abominations.
19:4 and because they have f this place with the blood
41:9 Ishmael son of Nethaniah f that cistern
51:34 he has f his belly with my delicacies,
La 3:15 He has f me with bitterness,
3:30 to give one's cheek to the smiter, and be f
Eze 10:3 and a cloud f the inner court.
10:4 the house was f with the cloud,
11:6 and have f its streets with the slain.
23:33 You shall be f with drunkenness and sorrow.
27:25 So you were f and heavily laden in the heart of
28:16 In the abundance of your trade you were f
32:6 and the watercourses will be f with you.
36:38 shall the ruined towns be f with flocks of people.
39:19 You shall eat fat until you are f,
39:20 be f at my table with horses and charioteers,
43:5 and the glory of the LORD f the temple.
44:4 glory of the LORD f the temple of the LORD;
Da 2:35 the statue became a great mountain and f
3:19 Then Nebuchadnezzar was so f with rage
Mic 3:8 But as for me, I am f with power,
Na 2:12 he has f his caves with prey and his dens
Hab 2:14 the earth will be f with the knowledge of the glory
Mt 5:6 and thirst for righteousness, for they will be f.
9:8 When the crowds saw it, they were f with awe,
14:20 And all ate and were f;
15:37 And all of them ate and were f;
22:10 so the wedding hall was f with guests.
27:48 f it with sour wine, put it on a stick,
Mk 4:41 And they were f with great awe and said
6:42 And all ate and were f;
8:8 They ate and were f;
15:36 And someone ran, f a sponge with sour wine,
Lk 1:15 before his birth he will be f with the Holy Spirit.
1:41 And Elizabeth was f with the Holy Spirit
1:53 he has f the hungry with good things,
1:67 Then his father Zechariah was f with
2:40 child grew and became strong, f with wisdom;
3:5 Every valley shall be f, and every mountain
3:15 As the people were f with expectation,
4:14 Then Jesus, f with the power of the Spirit,
4:28 all in the synagogue were f with rage.
5:7 And they came and f both boats,
5:26 and they glorified God and were f with awe,
6:11 But they were f with fury and discussed
6:21 you who are hungry now, for you will be f.
9:17 And all ate and were f.
14:23 so that my house may be f.
15:16 He would gladly have f himself with the pods that
15:20 his father saw him and was f with compassion;
Jn 2:7 And they f them up to the brim.
6:13 left by those who had eaten, they f twelve baskets.
12:3 house was f with the fragrance of the perfume.
16:6 to you, sorrow has f your hearts.
Ac 2:2 and it f the entire house where they were sitting.
2:4 All of them were f with the Holy Spirit and began
2:13 "They are f with new wine."
3:10 and they were f with wonder and amazement
4:8 Then Peter, f with the Holy Spirit, said to them,
4:31 and they were all f with the Holy Spirit and spoke
5:3 "why has Satan f your heart to lie to
5:17 the sect of the Sadducees), being f with jealousy,
5:28 yet here you have f Jerusalem with your teaching
7:55 But f with the Holy Spirit,
9:17 so that you may regain your sight and be f with
13:9 Saul, also known as Paul, f with the Holy Spirit,
13:45 Jews saw the crowds, they were f with jealousy;
13:52 disciples were f with joy and with the Holy Spirit.
19:29 The city was f with the confusion;
Ro 1:29 They were f with every kind of wickedness, evil,
15:14 of goodness, f with all knowledge, and able
2Co 7:4 in you; I am f with consolation;
Eph 3:19 so that you may be f with all the fullness of God.
5:18 but be f with the Spirit,
Col 1:9 and asking that you may be f with the knowledge
2Ti 1:4 I long to see you so that I may be f with joy.
Rev 8:5 Then the angel took the censer and f it with fire
15:8 and the temple was f with smoke from the glory
Jdt 2:8 and the swelling river shall be f with their dead.
10:5 and f a bag with roasted grain, dried fig cakes,
AdE 5:9 the Jew in the courtyard, he was f with anger.
Wis 1:7 Because the spirit of the Lord has f the world,
12:19 and you have f your children with good hope,
18:16 and stood and f all things with death,
Sir 2:16 and those who love him are f with his law.
4:12 and those who seek her from early morning are f
16:4 one intelligent person a city can be f with people,
16:29 and f it with his good things.
17:7 He f them with knowledge and understanding,
23:11 for his house will be f with calamities.
32:15 The one who seeks the law will be f with it,
33:17 and like a grape-picker I f my wine press.
39:6 he will be f with the spirit of understanding;
47:15 and you f it with proverbs having deep meaning.
48:12 Elisha was f with his spirit.
Bar 3:32 The one who prepared the earth for all time f it
5:7 the everlasting hills be made low and the valleys f
2Mc 3:30 was f with joy and gladness,
4:37 Antiochus was grieved at heart and f with pity,
4:40 crowds were becoming aroused and f with anger,
6:4 the temple was f with debauchery and reveling by
7:21 of their ancestors. F with a noble spirit,
8:21 With these words he f them with courage
9:7 but was even more f with arrogance,
13:16 the end they f the camp with terror and confusion
1Es 8:83 and they have f it with their uncleanness.
3Mc 1:16 and they f the temple with cries and tears;
1:18 and f the streets with groans and lamentations.
4:3 not f with mourning and wailing for them?
4:16 The king was greatly and continually f with joy,
5:1 was f with overpowering anger and wrath;
5:10 the pitiless elephants until they had been f with
5:30 But at these words he was f with
5:42 a Phalaris in everything and f with madness,
5:46 the city now being f with countless masses
5:47 when he had f his impious mind with a deep rage,
6:19 the forces of the enemy and f them with confusion
2Es 5:25 and from all the depths of the sea you have f
13:8 were f with fear, and yet they dared to fight.
15:41 so that all the fields and all the streams shall be f
4Mc 15:20 when you saw the place f with many spectators of

FILLET[ED] (KJV) See CIRCUMFERENCE

FILLING (5) [FILL]

Ps 110:6 among the nations, f them with corpses;
Pr 8:21 those who love me, and f their treasuries.
Lk 8:23 and the boat was f with water,
Ac 14:17 and f you with food and your hearts with joy."
1Th 2:16 Thus they have constantly been f up the measure

FILLS (15) [FILL]

1Ch 16:32 Let the sea roar, and all that f it;
Job 9:18 not let me get my breath, but f me with bitterness.
Ps 96:11 let the sea roar, and all that f it;
98:7 Let the sea roar, and all that f it;
107:9 and the hungry he f with good things.
147:14 he f you with the finest of wheat.
Isa 34:1 Let the earth hear, and all that f it;
42:10 Let the sea roar and all that f it,
Jer 8:16 They come and devour the land and all that f it,
47:2 they shall overflow the land and all that f it,
Eze 32:15 and when the land is stripped of all that f it,
Eph 1:23 the fullness of him who f all in all.
Sir 1:17 she f their whole house with desirable goods,
31:3 and when he rests he f himself with his dainties.
32:13 who f you with his good gifts.

FILMS (7)

Tob 2:10 into my eyes and produced white f.
2:10 the more my vision was obscured by the white f,
3:17 Tobit, by removing the white f from his eyes,
6:9 a person's eyes where white f have appeared
6:9 blow upon them, upon the white f,
11:8 the white f shrink and peel off from his eyes,
11:13 with both his hands he peeled off the white f from

FILTH (9) [FILTHINESS, FILTHY]

2Ch 29:5 and carry out the f from the holy place.
Job 9:31 yet you will plunge me into f,
Isa 4:4 the Lord has washed away the f of the daughters
La 3:45 You have made us f and rubbish among
Eze 24:11 its f melt in it, its rust be consumed.
24:13 you did not become clean from your f;
Na 3:6 I will throw f at you and treat you with contempt,
Mt 23:27 of the bones of the dead and of all kinds of f.
Sir 22:2 The idler is like the f of dunghills;

FILTHINESS (2) [FILTH]

Pr 30:12 in their own eyes yet are not cleansed of their f.
Eze 22:15 and I will purge your f out of you.

FILTHY‡ (12) [FILTH]

Dt 29:17 the f idols of wood and stone, of silver and gold,
Isa 28:8 All tables are covered with f vomit;
30:22 You will scatter them like f rags;
64:6 and all our righteous deeds are like a f cloth.
La 1:17 Jerusalem has become a f thing among them.
Eze 24:13 Yet, when I cleansed you in your f lewdness,
Zec 3:3 with f clothes as he stood before the angel.
3:4 before him, "Take off his f clothes."
Rev 22:11 and the f still be f,
AdE 14:16 I abhor it like a f rag,
Sir 22:1 The idler is like a f stone,

FINAL (6) [FINALLY]

Eze 21:25 whose day has come, the time of f punishment,
21:29 whose day has come, the time of f punishment.
35:5 at the time of their f punishment;
Sir 43:27 let the f word be: "He is the all."
1Mc 3:42 to do to the people to cause their f destruction.
3Mc 5:5 whole nation would experience its f destruction.

FINALLY‡ (18) [FINAL]

Ge 33:7 and f Joseph and Rachel drew near,
Jdg 16:16 F, after she had nagged him with her words day
1Sa 10:21 F he brought the family of the Matrites near man
Mt 21:37 F he sent his son to them, saying,
Mk 12:6 F he sent him to them, saying,
Lk 20:32 F the woman also died.
2Co 13:11 F, brothers and sisters, farewell.
Eph 6:10 F, be strong in the Lord and in the strength
Php 3:1 F, my brothers and sisters, rejoice in the Lord.
4:8 F, beloved, whatever is true,
1Th 4:1 F, brothers and sisters, we ask and urge you in
2Th 3:1 F, brothers and sisters, pray for us,
1Pe 3:8 F, all of you, have unity of spirit, sympathy,
Tob 10:13 F, he blessed Raguel and his wife Edna, and said,
Wis 3:17 and f their old age will be without honor.
Sir 13:7 and f he will laugh at you.
LtJ 6:72 and they will f be consumed themselves,
2Mc 5:8 F he met a miserable end.

FIND (255) [FAULTFINDER, FINDING, FINDS, FOUND]

Ge 18:3 He said, "My lord, if I f favor with you,
18:26 "If I f at Sodom fifty righteous in the city,
18:28 "I will not destroy it if I f forty-five there."
18:30 He answered, "I will not do it, if I f thirty there."
19:11 so that they were unable to f the door.
31:32 anyone with whom you f your gods shall not live.
31:33 but he did not f them.
31:34 Laban felt all about in the tent, but did not f them.
31:35 So he searched, but did not f the household gods.
32:5 in order that I may f favor in your sight.' "
33:8 Jacob answered, "To f favor with my lord."
33:10 Jacob said, "No, please; if I f favor with you,
34:11 "Let me f favor with you,
38:20 the pledge from the woman, he could not f her.
38:23 you see, I sent this kid, and you could not f her."
41:38 "Can we f anyone else like this—
Ex 5:11 and get straw yourselves, wherever you can f it;
16:25 today you will not f it in the field.
28:38 in order that they may f favor before the LORD.
33:13 so that I may know you and f favor in your sight.
Lev 23:11 that you may f acceptance;
Nu 32:23 and be sure your sin will f you out.
Dt 4:29 and you will f him if you search after him
22:3 that your neighbor loses and you f.
22:14 I did not f evidence of her virginity."
22:17 'I did not f evidence of your daughter's virginity.'
28:29 but you shall be unable to f your way;
28:65 Among those nations you shall f no ease,
Jdg 14:12 within the seven days of the feast, and f it out,
16:5 and f out what makes his strength so great,
17:8 to live wherever he could f a place.
17:9 and I am going to live wherever I can f a place."
Ru 1:9 The LORD grant that you may f security,
2:2 behind someone in whose sight I may f favor."
2:13 she said, "May I continue to f favor in your sight,
1Sa 1:18 she said, "Let your servant f favor in your sight."
9:4 but they did not f them.
9:4 but they did not f them.
9:13 As soon as you enter the town, you will f him,
14:38 and let us f out how this sin has arisen today.
20:21 I will send the boy, saying, 'Go, f the arrows.'
20:36 "Run and f the arrows that I shoot."
23:17 for the hand of my father Saul shall not f you;
23:22 f out exactly where he is,
25:8 Therefore let my young men f favor in your sight;
2Sa 15:25 If I f favor in the eyes of the LORD,
16:4 let me f favor in your sight, my lord the king."
17:20 when they had searched and could not f them,
20:6 or he will f fortified cities for himself,
1Ki 18:5 perhaps we may f grass to keep the horses

1Ki 18:12 when I come and tell Ahab and he cannot **f** you,
22:25 "You will **f** out on that day when you go in
2Ki 2:17 for three days but did not **f** him.
6:13 He said, "Go and **f** where he is;
7:13 let us send and **f** out."
7:14 after the Aramean army, saying, "Go and **f** out."
2Ch 18:24 "You will **f** out on that day when you go in
20:16 you will **f** them at the end of the valley,
30: 9 your kindred and your children will **f** compassion
32: 4 the Assyrian kings come and **f** water
Ezr 7:16 and gold that you shall **f** in the whole province
Ne 5: 8 They were silent, and could not **f** a word to say.
Job 3:22 and are glad when they **f** the grave?
10:20 that I may **f** a little comfort
11: 7 "Can you **f** out the deep things of God?
11: 7 Can you **f** out the limit of the Almighty?
16:18 let my outcry **f** no resting place.
17:10 and I shall not **f** a sensible person among you.
23: 3 Oh, that I knew where I might **f** him,
32:20 I must speak, so that I may **f** relief;
37:23 The Almighty—we cannot **f** him;
Ps 10:15 seek out their wickedness until you **f** none.
17: 3 if you test me, you will **f** no wickedness in me;
21: 8 Your hand will **f** out all your enemies;
21: 8 your right hand will **f** out those who hate you.
22: 2 and by night, but **f** no rest.
55: 8 to **f** a shelter for myself from the raging wind
61: 4 **f** refuge under the shelter of your wings.
73:10 and **f** no fault in them.
91: 4 and under his wings you will **f** refuge;
119:47 I **f** my delight in your commandments,
132: 5 until I **f** a place for the LORD,
Pr 1:13 We shall **f** all kinds of costly things;
1:28 they will seek me diligently, but will not **f** me.
2: 5 of the LORD and **f** the knowledge of God.
3: 4 So you will **f** favor and good repute in the sight
3:13 Happy are those who **f** wisdom,
4:22 For they are life to those who **f** them,
8: 9 and right to those who **f** knowledge.
8:17 and those who seek me diligently **f** me.
14: 7 for there you do not **f** words of knowledge.
14:22 Those who plan good **f** loyalty and faithfulness.
14:32 but the righteous **f** a refuge in their integrity.
20: 6 but who can **f** one worthy of trust?
21:10 their neighbors **f** no mercy in their eyes.
21:21 and kindness will **f** life and honor.
24:14 if you **f** it, you will find a future,
24:14 if you find it, you will **f** a future,
28:23 will afterward **f** more favor than one who flatters
31:10 A capable wife who can **f**?
Ecc 2:24 and **f** enjoyment in their toil.
3:11 yet they cannot **f** out what God has done from
5:18 it is fitting to eat and drink and **f** enjoyment in all
5:19 to accept their lot and **f** enjoyment in their toil—
7:14 that mortals may not **f** out anything that will come
7:24 very deep; who can **f** it out?
7:27 adding one thing to another to **f** the sum,
8:17 no one can **f** out what is happening under the sun.
8:17 they will not **f** it out;
8:17 to know, they cannot **f** it out.
12:10 The Teacher sought to **f** pleasing words,
SS 5: 6 I sought him, but did not **f** him;
5: 8 O daughters of Jerusalem, if you **f** my beloved,
Isa 14:32 the needy among his people will **f** refuge in her."
34:14 there too Lilith shall repose, and **f** a place to rest.
41:12 but you shall not **f** them;
53:11 he shall **f** satisfaction through his knowledge.
Jer 2: 5 What wrong did your ancestors **f** in me
2:24 in her month they will **f** her.
5: 1 and see if you can **f** one person who acts justly
6:16 and walk in it, and **f** rest for your souls.
8:15 We look for peace, but **f** no good,
14: 3 they **f** no water, they return with their vessels
14:19 We look for peace, but **f** no good;
29: 7 for in its welfare you will **f** your welfare.
29:13 When you search for me, you will **f** me;
29:14 I will let you **f** me,
45: 3 I am weary with my groaning, and I **f** no rest."
La 1: 6 like stags that **f** no pasture;
Eze 28:24 of Israel shall no longer **f** a pricking brier or
Da 6: 4 the presidents and the satraps tried to **f** grounds
6: 4 But they could **f** no grounds for complaint
6: 5 not **f** any ground for complaint against this Daniel
unless we **f** it in connection with the law
Hos 2: 6 so that she cannot **f** her paths.
2: 7 and she shall seek them, but shall not **f** them.
5: 6 they will not **f** him; he has withdrawn from them.
Am 8:12 the word of the LORD, but they shall not **f** it.
Mt 7: 7 be given you; search, and you will **f**;
7:14 and there are few who **f** it.
10:11 **f** out who in it is worthy,
10:39 Those who **f** their life will lose it, and those who
lose their life for my sake will **f** it.
11:29 and you will **f** rest for your souls.
16:25 and those who lose their life for my sake will **f** it.
17:27 and when you open its mouth, you will **f** a coin;
21: 2 and immediately you will **f** a donkey tied,
22: 9 invite everyone you **f** to the wedding banquet.'
24:46 Blessed is that slave whom his master will **f**
Mk 11: 2 you will **f** tied there a colt
11:13 to see whether perhaps he would **f** anything on it.
13:36 or else he may **f** you asleep
Lk 1:62 to **f** out what name he wanted to give him.
2:12 you will **f** a child wrapped in bands of cloth
2:45 When they did not **f** him,
6: 7 so that they might **f** an accusation against him.
11: 9 be given you; search, and you will **f**;
Lk 12:43 Blessed is that slave whom his master will **f**
13: 7 for fruit on this fig tree, and still I **f** none.
18: 8 the Son of Man comes, will he **f** faith on earth?"
19:15 so that he might **f** out what they had gained
19:30 and as you enter it you will **f** tied there a colt
19:48 but they did not **f** anything they could do,
23: 4 "I **f** no basis for an accusation against this man."
24: 3 but when they went in, they did not **f** the body.
24:23 and when they did not **f** his body there,
Jn 7:34 You will search for me, but you will not **f** me;
7:35 does this man intend to go that we will not **f** him?
7:36 for me and you will not **f** me' and 'Where I am,
7:51 a hearing to **f** out what they are doing,
10: 9 and will come in and go out and **f** pasture.
18:38 "I **f** no case against him.
19: 4 to let you know that I **f** no case against him."
19: 6 I **f** no case against him."
21: 6 to the right side of the boat, and you will **f** some."
Ac 5:22 they did not **f** them in the prison;
7:11 and our ancestors could **f** no food.
7:46 and asked that he might **f** a dwelling place for
12:19 Herod had searched for him and could not **f** him,
17: 6 When they could not **f** them,
17:27 for God and perhaps grope for him and **f** him—
22:24 to **f** out the reason for this outcry against him.
22:30 to **f** out what Paul was being accused of by
23: 9 "We **f** nothing wrong with this man.
24:11 As you can **f** out, it is not more than twelve days
24:12 not **f** me disputing with anyone in the temple
Ro 7:21 So I **f** it to be a law that when I want
9:19 "Why then does he still **f** fault?
1Co 4:19 and I will **f** out not the talk
2Co 2:13 not rest because I did not **f** my brother Titus there.
7:13 In this we **f** comfort.
9: 4 with me and **f** that you are not ready, we would
12:20 I may **f** you not as I wish, and that you may **f** me
13: 6 I hope you will **f** out that we have not failed.
Eph 5:10 Try to **f** out what is pleasing to the Lord.
1Th 3: 5 I sent to **f** out about your faith;
2Ti 1:18 the Lord grant that he will **f** mercy from the Lord
Heb 4:16 so that we may receive mercy and **f** grace to help
2Jn 1: 4 to **f** some of your children walking in the truth,
Jude 1: 3 I **f** it necessary to write and appeal to you
Rev 9: 6 those days people will seek death but will not **f** it;
Tob 1:18 Sennacherib looked for them he could not **f** them.
2: 2 and bring whatever poor person you may **f**
5: 3 **f** yourself a trustworthy man to go with you,
8: 7 Grant that she and I may **f** mercy and
Jdt 5:20 against their God and we **f** out their offense,
8:14 and **f** out his mind or comprehend his thought?
8:34 Only, do not try to **f** out what I am doing;
14: 3 into the tent of Holofernes and will not **f** him.
14:17 and when he did not **f** her,
AdE 16:15 "But we **f** that the Jews,
Wis 2:19 so that we may **f** out how gentle he is,
6:10 those who have been taught them will **f** a defense.
8:16 When I enter my house, I shall **f** rest with her;
9:16 and what is at hand we **f** with labor;
13: 6 while seeking God and desiring to **f** him.
13: 9 did they fail to **f** sooner the Lord of these things?
19:17 by yawning darkness, all of them tried to **f**
Sir 3:18 so you will **f** favor in the sight of the Lord.
3:31 when they fall they will **f** support.
6:16 and those who fear the Lord will **f** them.
6:18 when you have gray hair you will still **f** wisdom.
6:28 For at last you will **f** the rest she gives,
11: 7 Do not **f** fault before you investigate;
12:17 you will **f** him there ahead of you;
15: 6 He will **f** gladness and a crown of rejoicing,
18:20 and at the time of scrutiny you will **f** forgiveness.
22:13 Avoid him and you will **f** rest,
25: 3 how can you **f** anything in your old age?
27:16 and will never **f** a congenial friend.
28:16 Those who pay heed to slander will not **f** rest,
29: 3 and on every occasion you will **f** what you need.
32:14 and those who rise early to seek him will **f** favor.
32:17 and will **f** a decision according to his liking.
33:26 Set your slave to work, and you will **f** rest;
42: 1 and will **f** favor with everyone.
43:28 Where can we **f** the strength to praise him?
Bar 1:12 and we shall serve them many days and **f** favor
Aza 1:15 to make an offering before you and to **f** mercy.
Sus 1:14 for a time when they could **f** her alone.
Bel 1:12 if you do not **f** that Bel has eaten it all,
1Mc 10:16 So he said, "Shall we **f** another such man?
11:16 Alexander fled into Arabia to **f** protection there,
11:42 on you and your nation, if I **f** an opportunity.
2Mc 2: 6 up intending to mark the way, but could not **f** it.
12:18 They did not **f** Timothy in that region,
14:10 it is impossible for the government to **f** peace."
1Es 2:22 You will **f** in the annals what has been written
5:66 to **f** out what the sound of the trumpets meant.
2Es 2:23 When you **f** any who are dead,
3:36 **f** individuals who have kept your commandments,
3:36 but nations you will not **f.**"
7:*106* [36] "How then do we **f** that first Abraham prayed
14:22 so that people may be able to **f** the path,

FINDING‡ (9) [FIND]

Jdg 5:30 'Are they not **f** and dividing the spoil?—
Ps 107: 4 **f** no way to an inhabited town;
Mt 13:46 on **f** one pearl of great value,
Lk 5:19 **f** no way to bring him in because of the crowd,
11:24 a resting place, but not **f** any, it says, 'I will return
Ac 4:21 **f** no way to punish them because of the people,
Sir 40:18 but better than either is **f** a treasure.
2Mc 5: 9 in hope of **f** protection because of their kinship.
5:25 then, **f** the Jews not at work,

FINDS‡ (37) [FIND]

Lev 25:26 but then prospers and **f** sufficient means to do so,
Dt 24: 1 because he **f** something objectionable about her,
Job 24:20 The womb forgets them; the worm **f** them sweet;
33:10 Look, he **f** occasions against me,
Ps 84: 3 Even the sparrow **f** a home,
119:162 I rejoice at your word like one who **f** great spoil.
Pr 8:35 For whoever **f** me **f** life and obtains favor
12: 3 No one **f** security by wickedness,
18:22 He who **f** a wife **f** a good thing,
Ecc 6: 5 yet it **f** rest rather than he.
9:10 Whatever your hand **f** to do, do with your might;
La 1: 3 now among the nations, and **f** no resting place;
Hos 14: 3 In you the orphan **f** mercy."
Mic 7: 1 **f** no cluster to eat; there is no first-ripe fig
Mt 7: 8 and everyone who searches **f**,
12:43 for a resting place, but it **f** none.
12:44 it comes, it **f** it empty, swept, and put in order.
18:13 And if he **f** it, truly I tell you,
Lk 11:10 and everyone who searches **f**,
11:25 When it comes, it **f** it swept and put in order.
12:37 Blessed are those slaves whom the master **f** alert
12:38 and **f** them so, blessed are those slaves.
15: 4 and go after the one that is lost until he **f** it?
15: 8 and search carefully until she **f** it?
Heb 8: 8 God **f** fault with them when he says:
Sir 6:14 whoever **f** one has found a treasure.
12:16 if he **f** an opportunity he will never have enough
18:28 and praises the one who **f** her.
19:28 nevertheless do evil when he **f** the opportunity.
25: 9 Happy is the one who **f** a friend,
25:10 How great is the one who **f** wisdom!
26:10 or else, when she **f** liberty, she will make use of it.
29: 5 and pays back with empty promises, and **f** fault
40:19 but better than either is the one who **f** wisdom.
2Mc 2: 1 One **f** in the records that

FINE (110) [FINED, FINELY, FINERY, FINES, FINEST]

A. FINE LINEN (32)
B. FINE TWISTED LINEN (22)
C. FINE LEATHER (14)
D. FINE GOLD (11)

Ge 41:42 he arrayed him in garments of **f** linen, A
Ex 2: 2 and when she saw that he was a **f** baby,
9: 9 It shall become **f** dust all over the land of Egypt,
16:14 of the wilderness was a **f** flaky substance,
16:14 as **f** as frost on the ground.
25: 4 and crimson yarns and **f** linen, goats' hair, A
25: 5 tanned rams' skins, **f** leather, acacia wood, C
26: 1 tabernacle with ten curtains of **f** twisted linen, B
26:14 and an outer covering of **f** leather. C
26:31 purple, and crimson yarns, and of **f** twisted linen; B
26:36 purple, and crimson yarns, and of **f** twisted linen, B
27: 9 of **f** twisted linen one hundred cubits long for B
27:16 purple, and crimson yarns, and of **f** twisted linen, B
27:18 with hangings of **f** twisted linen and bases B
28: 5 blue, purple, and crimson yarns, and **f** linen. A
28: 6 purple, and crimson yarns, and of **f** twisted linen, B
28: 8 purple, and crimson yarns, and of **f** twisted linen. B
28:15 and of **f** twisted linen you shall make it. B
28:39 You shall make the checkered tunic of **f** linen, A
28:39 and you shall make a turban of **f** linen, A
35: 6 purple, and crimson yarns, and **f** linen; A
35: 7 tanned rams' skins, and **f** leather; acacia wood, C
35:23 purple or crimson yarn or **f** linen or goats' hair A
35:23 or goats' hair or tanned rams' skins or **f** leather, C
35:25 blue and purple and crimson yarns and **f** linen; A
35:35 purple, and crimson yarns, and in **f** linen, A
36: 8 they were made of **f** twisted linen, and blue, B
36:19 and an outer covering of **f** leather. C
36:35 purple, and crimson yarns, and **f** twisted linen, B
36:37 purple, and crimson yarns, and **f** twisted linen, B
38: 9 the hangings of the court were of **f** twisted linen, B
38:16 around the court were of **f** twisted linen. B
38:18 purple, and crimson yarns and **f** twisted linen. B
38:23 purple, and crimson yarns, and in **f** linen. A
39: 2 purple, and crimson yarns, and of **f** twisted linen. B
39: 3 and crimson yarns and into the **f** twisted linen, B
39: 5 purple, and crimson yarns, and of **f** twisted linen; B
39: 8 purple, and crimson yarns, and of **f** twisted linen. B
39:24 purple, and crimson yarns, and of **f** twisted linen. B
39:27 They also made the tunics, woven of **f** linen, A
39:28 and the turban of **f** linen, A
39:28 and the headdresses of **f** linen, A
39:28 and the linen undergarments of **f** twisted linen, B
39:29 the sash of **f** twisted linen, and of blue, purple, B
39:34 and the covering of **f** leather, and the curtain for C
Nu 4: 6 then they shall put on it a covering of **f** leather, C
4: 8 and cover it with a covering of **f** leather, C
4:10 with all its utensils in a covering of **f** leather, C
4:11 and cover it with a covering of **f** leather, C
4:12 and cover them with a covering of **f** leather, C
4:14 they shall spread on it a covering of **f** leather, C
4:25 the outer covering of **f** leather that is on top of it, C
Dt 6:10 a land with **f**, large cities that you did not build,
8:12 and have built **f** houses and live in them,
22:19 they shall **f** him one hundred shekels
32:14 you drank **f** wine from the blood of grapes.
2Sa 22:43 I beat them **f** like the dust of the earth,
1Ki 5:11 and twenty cors of **f** oil.

1Ch 15:27 David was clothed with a robe of **f** linen, A
2Ch 2:14 blue, and crimson fabrics and **f** linen, A
3: 5 he lined with cypress, covered it with **f** gold, D
3: 8 he overlaid it with six hundred talents of **f** gold. D
3:14 and purple and crimson fabrics and **f** linen, A
5:12 arrayed in **f** linen, with cymbals, harps, and A
Ezr 8:27 and two vessels of **f** polished bronze as precious
Est 1: 6 with cords of **f** linen and purple to silver rings A
8:15 a great golden crown and a mantle of **f** linen A
Job 28:17 nor can it be exchanged for jewels of **f** gold. D
31:24 or called **f** gold my confidence; D
Ps 18:42 I beat them **f**, like dust before the wind;
19:10 be desired are they than gold, even much **f** gold; D
21: 3 you set a crown of **f** gold on his head. D
119:127 more than gold, more than **f** gold. D
Pr 8:19 My fruit is better than gold, even **f** gold, D
17: 7 **F** speech is not becoming to a fool;
17:26 To impose a **f** on the innocent is not right,
31:22 her clothing is **f** linen and purple. A
Isa 13:12 I will make mortals more rare than **f** gold, D
23:18 and **f** clothing for those who live in the presence
40:15 see, he takes up the isles like **f** dust.
La 4: 2 worth their weight in **f** gold— D
Eze 16:10 and with sandals of **f** leather; C
16:10 in **f** linen and covered you with rich fabric. A
16:13 while your clothing was of **f** linen, rich fabric, A
23:26 of your clothes and take away your **f** jewels.
26:12 down your walls and destroy your **f** houses.
27: 7 Of **f** embroidered linen from Egypt was your sail,
27:16 embroidered work, **f** linen, coral, and rubies. A
Da 2:32 The head of that statue was of **f** gold, D
Mt 13:45 of heaven is like a merchant in search of **f** pearls;
Mk 7: 9 "You have a **f** way of rejecting the commandment
Lk 7:25 those who put on **f** clothing and live in luxury are
16:19 rich man who was dressed in purple and **f** linen A
Jas 2: 2 if a person with gold rings and in **f** clothes comes
2: 3 if you take notice of the one wearing the **f** clothes
1Pe 3: 3 and by wearing gold ornaments or **f** clothing;
Rev 18:12 and pearls, **f** linen, purple, silk and scarlet, A
18:16 clothed in **f** linen, in purple and scarlet, A
19: 8 to be clothed with **f** linen, bright and pure"— A
19: 8 the **f** linen is the righteous deeds of the saints. A
19:14 And the armies of heaven, wearing **f** linen, A
Jdt 10: 5 dried fig cakes, and **f** bread;
AdE 1: 6 which was adorned with curtains of **f** linen A
6: 8 king's servants bring out the **f** linen robe that A
Sir 11: 4 Do not boast about wearing **f** clothes,
26:20 *sow it with your own seed, trusting in your **f** stock.*
Sus 1: 4 and had a **f** garden adjoining his house;
1Es 3: 6 turban of **f** linen, and a necklace around his neck; A
8:24 either **f** or imprisonment."
8:57 and twelve bronze vessels of **f** bronze

FINED (2) [FINE]

Ex 21:22 be **f** what the woman's husband demands,
1Es 1:36 and **f** the nation one hundred talents of silver

FINELY (4) [FINE]

Ex 31:10 and the **f** worked vestments,
35:19 the **f** worked vestments for ministering in
39: 1 and crimson yarns they made **f** worked vestments,
39:41 the **f** worked vestments for ministering in

FINERY (2) [FINE]

Isa 3:18 the Lord will take away the **f** of the anklets,
Jdt 12:15 to dress herself in all her woman's **f**.

FINES (1) [FINE]

Am 2: 8 they drink wine bought with **f** they imposed.

FINEST (9) [FINE]

Ex 30:23 Take the **f** spices: of liquid myrrh
Dt 33:15 with the **f** produce of the ancient mountains,
1Ki 10:18 and overlaid it with the **f** gold.
Ps 81:16 I would feed you with the **f** of the wheat,
147:14 he fills you with the **f** of wheat.
SS 5:11 His head is the **f** gold;
Am 6: 6 and anoint themselves with the **f** oils,
2Mc 3: 2 and glorified the temple with the **f** presents,
9:16 he would adorn with the **f** offerings;

FINGER (29) [FINGERNAILS, FINGERS]

Ex 8:19 magicians said to Pharaoh, "This is the **f** of God!"
29:12 and put it on the horns of the altar with your **f**,
31:18 tablets of stone, written with the **f** of God.
Lev 4: 6 The priest shall dip his **f** in the blood
4:17 and the priest shall dip his **f** in the blood
4:25 the sin offering with his **f** and put it on the horns
4:30 The priest shall take some of its blood with his **f**
4:34 the sin offering with his **f** and put it on the horns
8:15 and with his **f** put some on each of the horns of
9: 9 and he dipped his **f** in the blood and put it on
14:16 and dip his right **f** in the oil that is in his left hand
14:16 and sprinkle some oil with his **f** seven times
14:27 and shall sprinkle with his right **f** some of the oil
16:14 with his **f** on the front of the mercy seat,
16:14 the blood with his **f** seven times.
16:19 of the blood on it with his **f** seven times.
Nu 19: 4 with his **f** and sprinkle it seven times towards
Dt 9:10 the two stone tablets written with the **f** of God;
1Ki 12:10 'My little **f** is thicker than my father's loins.
2Ch 10:10 'My little **f** is thicker than my father's loins.
Isa 58: 9 the pointing of the **f**, the speaking of evil,
Mt 23: 4 but they themselves are unwilling to lift a **f**
Lk 11:20 if it is by the **f** of God that I cast out the demons,
11:46 and you yourselves do not lift a **f** to ease them.
15:22 put a ring on his **f** and sandals on his feet.
16:24 to dip the tip of his **f** in water and cool my tongue;
Jn 8: 6 ⟦down and wrote with his **f** on the ground.⟧
20:25 and put my **f** in the mark of the nails and my hand
20:27 "Put your **f** here and see my hands.

FINGERNAILS (1) [FINGER]

4Mc 10: 7 and scalped him with their **f** in a Scythian fashion.

FINGERS (17) [FINGER]

2Sa 21:20 who had six **f** on each hand,
1Ch 20: 6 who had six **f** on each hand,
Ps 8: 3 When I look at your heavens, the work of your **f**,
144: 1 who trains my hands for war, and my **f** for battle;
Pr 6:13 shuffling the feet, pointing the **f**,
7: 3 bind them on your **f**, write them on the tablet
SS 5: 5 my **f** with liquid myrrh, upon the handles of the
Isa 2: 8 to what their own **f** have made.
17: 8 they will not look to what their own **f** have made,
59: 3 For your hands are defiled with blood, and your **f**
Jer 52:21 it was hollow and its thickness was four **f**.
Da 5: 5 the **f** of a human hand appeared and began writing
Mk 7:33 away from the crowd, and put his **f** into his ears,
Wis 15:15 nor ears with which to hear, nor **f** to feel with,
Pm 151: 2 My hands made a harp; my **f** fashioned a lyre.
4Mc 10: 6 and breaking his **f** and arms and legs and elbows.
15:15 their toes and **f** scattered on the ground,

FINING POT (KJV) See CRUCIBLE

FINISH‡ (16) [FINISHED, FINISHING]

Ge 6:16 Make a roof for the ark, and **f** it to a cubit above;
Ex 5:14 not **f** the required quantity of bricks yesterday
1Ch 27:24 of Zeruiah began to count them, but did not **f**;
Ezr 5: 3 to build this house and to **f** this structure?"
5: 9 to build this house and to **f** this structure?'
Ne 4: 2 Will they **f** it in a day?
Jer 51:63 When you **f** reading this scroll, tie a stone to it,
Da 9:24 to **f** the transgression, to put an end to sin,
Lk 13:32 and on the third day I **f** my work.
14:29 when he has laid a foundation and is not able to **f**,
14:30 'This fellow began to build and was not able to **f**.'
Ac 20:24 if only I may **f** my course and the ministry
2Co 8:11 now **f** doing it, so that your eagerness may
Sir 38:27 and they are careful to **f** their work.
38:30 he sets his heart to **f** the glazing,
2Mc 15: 5 to take up arms and **f** the king's business."

FINISHED (119) [FINISH]

Ge 2: 1 Thus the heavens and the earth were **f**,
2: 2 the seventh day God **f** the work that he had done,
17:22 And when he had **f** talking with him,
18:33 when he had **f** speaking to Abraham;
24:15 Before he had **f** speaking, there was Rebekah,
24:19 When she had **f** giving him a drink, she said,
24:19 until they have **f** drinking."
24:22 When the camels had **f** drinking,
24:45 "Before I had **f** speaking in my heart,
27:30 As soon as Isaac had **f** blessing Jacob,
Ex 31:18 God **f** speaking with Moses on Mount Sinai,
34:33 When Moses had **f** speaking with them,
39:32 of the tabernacle of the tent of meeting was **f**;
40:33 So Moses **f** the work.
Lev 16:20 When he has **f** atoning for the holy place and
Nu 4:15 and his sons have **f** covering the sanctuary and all
7: 1 when Moses had **f** setting up the tabernacle,
16:31 As soon as he **f** speaking all these words,
Dt 20: 9 When the officials have **f** addressing the troops,
26:12 When you have **f** paying all the tithe
31: 1 Moses had **f** speaking all these words to all Israel,
31:24 When Moses had **f** writing down in a book
32:45 Moses had **f** reciting all these words to all Israel,
Jos 3:17 until the entire nation **f** crossing over the Jordan.
4: 1 the entire nation had **f** crossing over the Jordan,
4:10 until everything was **f** that
4:11 As soon as all the people had **f** crossing over,
8:24 When Israel had **f** slaughtering all the inhabitants
10:20 When Joshua and the Israelites had **f** inflicting
19:49 When they had **f** distributing
19:51 So they **f** dividing the land.
Jdg 3:18 When Ehud had **f** presenting the tribute,
15:17 he had **f** speaking, he threw away the jawbone;
Ru 2:21 until they have **f** all my harvest.' "
3: 3 to the man until he has **f** eating and drinking.
1Sa 13:10 As soon as he had **f** offering the burnt offering,
18: 1 When David had **f** speaking to Saul,
24:16 When David had **f** speaking these words to Saul,
2Sa 6:18 When David had **f** offering the burnt offerings
11:19 "When you have **f** telling the king all the news
13:36 As soon as he had **f** speaking,
1Ki 1:41 with him heard it as they **f** feasting.
3: 1 of David, until he had **f** building his own house
6: 7 The house was built with stone **f** at the quarry,
6: 9 So he built the house, and **f** it;
6:14 So Solomon built the house, and **f** it.
6:38 the house was **f** in all its parts,
7: 1 and he **f** his entire house.
7:22 Thus the work of the pillars was **f**.
7:40 So Hiram **f** all the work that he did
7:51 on the house of the LORD was **f**.
8:54 Now when Solomon **f** offering all this prayer
9: 1 When Solomon had **f** building the house of
2Ki 10:25 As soon as he had **f** presenting the burnt offering,
1Ch 16: 2 When David had **f** offering the burnt offerings
28:20 for the service of the house of the LORD is **f**.
2Ch 4:11 Thus Huram **f** the work that he did
5: 1 for the house of the LORD was **f**.
7:11 Thus Solomon **f** the house of the LORD and
8:16 until the house of the LORD was **f** completely.
24:14 When they had **f**, they brought the rest of
29:17 and on the sixteenth day of the first month they **f**.
29:28 all this continued until the burnt offering was **f**.
29:29 When the offering was **f**,
29:34 the Levites, helped them until the work was **f**—
31: 1 Now when all this was **f**,
31: 7 and **f** them in the seventh month.
Ezr 4:13 if this city is rebuilt and the walls **f**,
4:16 if this city is rebuilt and its walls **f**,
5:11 which a great king of Israel built and **f**.
5:16 under construction, and it is not yet **f**.'
6:14 They **f** their building by command of the God
6:15 and this house was **f** on the third day of the month
Ne 6:15 So the wall was **f** on the twenty-fifth day of
Isa 10:12 When the Lord has **f** all his work on Mount Zion
Jer 26: 8 And when Jeremiah had **f** speaking all that
43: 1 When Jeremiah **f** speaking to all
Eze 42:15 he had **f** measuring the interior of the temple area,
43:23 When you have **f** purifying it,
Am 7: 2 When they had **f** eating the grass of the land,
Mt 7:28 Now when Jesus had **f** saying these things,
11: 1 when Jesus had **f** instructing his twelve disciples,
13:53 Jesus had **f** these parables, he left that place.
19: 1 When Jesus had **f** saying these things,
26: 1 When Jesus had **f** saying all these things,
Lk 2:39 When they had **f** everything required by the law
4:13 When the devil had **f** every test,
5: 4 When he had **f** speaking, he said to Simon,
7: 1 After Jesus had **f** all his sayings in the hearing of
11: 1 and after he had **f**, one of his disciples said
Jn 19:28 After this, when Jesus knew that all was now **f**,
19:30 Jesus had received the wine, he said, "It is **f**."
21:15 When they had **f** breakfast,
Ac 15:13 After they **f** speaking, James replied,
20:36 When he had **f** speaking, he knelt down
21: 7 When we had **f** the voyage from Tyre,
2Ti 4: 7 I have fought the good fight, I have **f** the race,
Heb 4: 3 his works were **f** at the foundation of the world.
1Pe 4: 1 (for whoever has suffered in the flesh has **f**
Rev 11: 7 When they have **f** their testimony,
Tob 8: 1 When they had **f** eating and drinking they wanted
8:11 When they had **f** digging the grave,
Jdt 5:22 When Achior had **f** saying these things,
8:34 not tell you until I have **f** what I am about to do."
14: 9 When she had **f**, the people raised a great shout
Sir 18: 7 When human beings have **f**,
38: 8 God's works will never be **f**;
1Mc 2:23 When he had **f** speaking these words,
3:23 When he **f** speaking, he rushed suddenly
4:51 Thus they **f** all the work they had undertaken.
1Es 2:19 Now if this city is built and the walls **f**,
2:24 that if this city is built and its walls **f**,
4:55 when the temple would be **f** and Jerusalem built.
6:14 of Israel who was great and strong, and it was **f**.
6:28 until the house of the Lord is **f**;
7: 5 the holy house was **f** by the twenty-third day of
2Es 7: When I had **f** speaking these words,
14:25 be put out until what you are about to write is **f**.
14:26 you have **f**, some things you shall make public,

FINISHING (8) [FINISH]

Ezr 4:12 they are **f** the walls and repairing the foundations.
Jn 17: 4 on earth by **f** the work that you gave me to do.
Ac 13:25 And as John was **f** his work, he said,
Sir 38:28 He sets his heart on **f** his handiwork,
50:14 **F** the service at the altars,
1Mc 4:19 Just as Judas was **f** this speech,
1Es 6: 4 and this roof and **f** all the other things?
6: 4 And who are the builders that are **f** these things?"

FINS (5)

Lev 11: 9 Everything in the waters that has **f** and scales,
11:10 or the streams that does not have **f** and scales,
11:12 Everything in the waters that does not have **f**
Dt 14: 9 whatever has **f** and scales you may eat.
14:10 not have **f** and scales you shall not eat;

FIR (3)

Ps 104:17 the stork has its home in the **f** trees.
Eze 27: 5 They made all your planks of **f** trees from Senir;
31: 8 nor the **f** trees equal its boughs;

FIR-TREES See Index to Footnotes

FIRE‡ (659) [FIERY, FIRE-BREATHING, FIRE-QUENCHING, FIREBRANDS, FIRED, FIRELIGHT, FIREPANS, FIRES, FIRING]

A. OFFERING BY FIRE (43)
B. OFFERINGS BY FIRE (20)
C. OUT OF ... FIRE (11)
D. DEVOURING FIRE (10)
E. PILLAR OF FIRE (8)

Ge 15:17 a smoking **f** pot and a flaming torch passed
19:24 and Gomorrah sulfur and **f** from the LORD out

Ge 22: 6 and he himself carried the f and the knife.
22: 7 He said, "The f and the wood are here,
Ex 3: 2 the LORD appeared to him in a flame of f out of
9:23 and f came down on the earth.
9:24 with f flashing continually in the midst of it,
12: 8 over the f with unleavened bread and bitter herbs.
12: 9 but roasted over the f, with its head, legs,
13:21 and in a pillar of f by night, to give them light, E
13:22 nor the pillar of f by night left its place in front E
14:24 At the morning watch the LORD in the pillar of f E
19:18 because the LORD had descended upon it in f;
22: 6 When f breaks out and catches in thorns so that
22: 6 one who started the f shall make full restitution.
24:17 of the LORD was like a devouring f on the top of D
29:14 you shall burn with f outside the camp;
29:18 an offering by f to the LORD. A
29:25 it is an offering by f to the LORD. A
29:34 then you shall burn the remainder with f;
29:41 an offering by f to the LORD. A
30:20 to make an offering by f to the LORD, A
32:20 burned it with f, ground it to powder,
32:24 so they gave it to me, and I threw it into the f,
35: 3 You shall kindle no f in all your dwellings on
40:38 and f was in the cloud by night,
Lev 1: 7 The sons of the priest Aaron shall put f on
1: 7 on the altar and arrange wood on the f.
1: 8 on the wood that is on the f on the altar;
1: 9 an offering by f of pleasing odor to the LORD. A
1:12 on the wood that is on the f on the altar;
1:13 an offering by f of pleasing odor to the LORD. A
1:17 on the wood that is on the f;
1:17 an offering by f of pleasing odor to the LORD. A
2: 2 an offering by f of pleasing odor to the LORD. A
2: 3 most holy part of the offerings by f to the LORD. B
2: 9 an offering by f of pleasing odor to the LORD. A
2:10 it is a most holy part of the offerings by f to B
2:11 into smoke as an offering by f to the LORD. A
2:14 from fresh ears, parched with f.
2:16 it is an offering by f to the LORD. A
3: 3 as an offering by f to the LORD, A
3: 5 the burnt offering that is on the wood on the f,
3: 5 an offering by f of pleasing odor to the LORD. A
3: 9 as an offering by f to the LORD: A
3:11 on the altar as a food offering by f to the LORD. A
3:14 as an offering by f to the LORD, A
3:16 into smoke on the altar as a food offering by f A
4:12 to the ash heap, and shall burn it on a wood f;
4:35 with the offerings by f to the LORD. B
5:12 with the offerings by f to the LORD; B
6: 9 while the f on the altar shall be kept burning.
6:10 the f has reduced the burnt offering on the altar,
6:12 The f on the altar shall be kept burning;
6:13 A perpetual f shall be kept burning on the altar;
6:17 as their portion of my offerings by f; B
6:18 from the LORD's offerings by f; B
6:30 it shall be burned with f.
7: 5 on the altar as an offering by f to the LORD; A
7:25 animal of which an offering by f may be made A
7:30 the LORD's offering by f; A
7:35 and to his sons from the offerings made by f
8:17 he burned with f outside the camp,
8:21 an offering by f to the LORD, A
8:28 an offering by f to the LORD. A
8:32 of the flesh and the bread you shall burn with f.
9:11 and the skin he burned with f outside the camp.
9:24 F came out from the LORD and consumed
10: 1 Nadab and Abihu, each took his censer, put f in it,
10: 1 and they offered unholy f before the LORD,
10: 2 And f came out from the presence of the LORD
10:12 that is left from the LORD's offerings by f, B
10:13 from the offerings by f to the LORD; B
10:15 together with the offerings by f of the fat, B
13:52 it shall be burned in f.
13:55 you shall burn it in f,
13:57 with f that in which the disease appears.
16:12 a censer full of coals of f from the altar before
16:13 and put the incense on the f before the LORD,
16:27 and their dung shall be consumed in f.
19: 6 over until the third day shall be consumed in f.
21: 6 for they offer the LORD's offerings by f, B
21:21 near to offer the LORD's offerings by f; B
22:22 or put any of them on the altar as offerings by f B
22:27 be acceptable as the LORD's offering by f. A
23: 8 the LORD's offerings by f; B
23:13 an offering by f of pleasing odor to the LORD; A
23:18 an offering by f of pleasing odor to the LORD. A
23:25 and you shall present the LORD's offering by f. A
23:27 and present the LORD's offering by f; A
23:36 the LORD's offerings by f; B
23:36 and present the LORD's offerings by f; B
23:37 for presenting to the LORD offerings by f— B
24: 7 as an offering by f to the LORD. A
24: 9 for him from the offerings by f to the LORD, B
Nu 3: 4 when they offered illicit f before the LORD in
6:18 the consecrated head and put it on the f under
9:15 having the appearance of f.
9:16 by day and the appearance of f by night.
11: 1 Then the f of the LORD burned against them,
11: 2 Moses prayed to the LORD, and the f abated.
11: 3 because the f of the LORD burned against them.
14:14 in a pillar of cloud by day and in a pillar of f E
15: 3 and you make an offering by f to the LORD from A
15:10 as an offering by f, a pleasing odor to the LORD. A
15:13 in presenting an offering by f, A
15:14 and wishes to offer an offering by f, A
15:25 an offering by f to the LORD, A
16: 7 and tomorrow put f in them, and lay incense

Nu 16:18 they put f in the censers and laid incense on them,
16:35 And f came out from the LORD and consumed
16:37 then scatter the f far and wide.
16:46 put f on it from the altar and lay incense on it,
18: 9 from the most holy things, reserved from the f:
18:17 an offering by f for a pleasing odor to the LORD; A
19: 6 into the f in which the heifer is burning.
21:28 For f came out from Heshbon,
21:30 and we laid waste until f spread to Medeba."
26:10 when the f devoured two hundred fifty men;
26:61 and Abihu died when they offered illicit f before
28: 2 My offering, the food for my offerings by f, B
28: 3 This is the offering by f that you shall offer to A
28: 6 an offering by f to the LORD. A
28: 8 you shall offer it as an offering by f, A
28:13 an offering by f to the LORD. A
28:19 You shall offer an offering by f, A
28:24 for seven days, the food of an offering by f, A
29: 6 a pleasing odor, an offering by f to the LORD. A
29:13 You shall offer a burnt offering, an offering by f, A
29:36 You shall offer a burnt offering, an offering by f, A
31:23 everything that can withstand f,
31:23 shall be passed through f, and it shall be clean.
31:23 and whatever cannot withstand f,
Dt 1:33 in f by night, and in the cloud by day,
4:12 Then the LORD spoke to you out of the f. C
4:15 the LORD spoke to you at Horeb out of the f, C
4:24 LORD your God is a devouring f, a jealous God. D
4:33 the voice of a god speaking out of a f, C
4:36 On earth he showed you his great f,
4:36 while you heard his words coming out of the f. C
5: 4 face to face at the mountain, out of the f. C
5: 5 because of the f and did not go up the mountain.)
5:22 out of the f, the cloud, and the thick darkness, C
5:23 while the mountain was burning with f,
5:24 and we have heard his voice out of the f. C
5:25 For this great f will consume us;
5:26 the voice of the living God speaking out of f, C
7: 5 and burn their idols with f.
7:25 The images of their gods you shall burn with f.
9: 3 over before you as a devouring f; D
9:10 to you at the mountain out of the f on the day C
9:21 the calf, and burned it with f and crushed it,
10: 4 to you on the mountain out of the f on the day C
12: 3 smash their pillars, burn their sacred poles with f,
12:31 even burn their sons and their daughters in the f
13:16 then burn the town and all its spoil with f,
18:10 a son or daughter pass through f,
18:16 or ever again see this great f, I will die."
32:22 For a f is kindled by my anger,
32:22 and sets on f the foundations of the mountains.
Jos 7:15 the devoted things shall be burned with f,
7:25 they burned them with f, cast stones on them,
8: 8 you shall set the city on f,
8:19 took it, and at once set the city on f.
11: 6 and burn their chariots with f."
11: 9 and burned their chariots with f.
11:11 and he burned Hazor with f.
13:14 the offerings by f to the LORD God B
Jdg 1: 8 They put it to the sword and set the city on f.
6:21 and f sprang up from the rock and consumed
9:15 if not, let f come out of the bramble and devour
9:20 let f come out from Abimelech,
9:20 and let f come out from the lords of Shechem,
9:49 and they set the stronghold on f over them,
9:52 near to the entrance of the tower to burn it with f.
14:15 we will burn you and your father's house with f.
15: 5 When he had set f to the torches,
15:14 on his arms became like flax that has caught f,
16: 9 as a strand of fiber snaps when it touches the f.
20:48 Also the remaining towns they set on f.
1Sa 2:28 the family of your ancestor all my offerings by f B
2Sa 14:30 go and set it on f."
14:30 So Absalom's servants set the field on f.
14:31 "Why have your servants set my field on f?"
22: 9 and devouring f from his mouth; D
22:13 the brightness before him coals of f flamed forth.
23: 7 And they are entirely consumed in f on the spot.
1Ki 16:18 the king's house over himself with f, and died—
18:23 and lay it on the wood, but put no f to it;
18:23 the other bull and lay it on the wood, but put no f
18:24 the god who answers by f is indeed God."
18:25 call on the name of your god, but put no f to it."
18:38 Then the f of the LORD fell and consumed
19:12 after the earthquake a f, but the LORD was not in
the f; and after the f a sound of sheer silence.
2Ki 1:10 let f come down from heaven and consume you
1:10 Then f came down from heaven,
1:12 let f come down from heaven and consume you
1:12 Then the f of God came down from heaven
1:14 f came down from heaven and consumed
2:11 a chariot of f and horses of f separated the two
6:17 of horses and chariots of f all around Elisha.
8:12 you will set their fortresses on f,
16: 3 He even made his son pass through f,
17:17 and their daughters pass through f;
17:31 the Sepharvites burned their children in the f
19:18 into the f, though they were no gods but the work
21: 6 He made his son pass through f;
23:10 a son or a daughter pass through f as an offering
23:11 then he burned the chariots of the sun with f.
1Ch 21:26 with f from heaven on the altar of burnt offering.
2Ch 7: 1 f came down from heaven and consumed
7: 3 the f come down and the glory of the LORD on
16:14 and they made a very great f in his honor.
21:19 His people made no f in his honor,
28: 3 and made his sons pass through f,

2Ch 33: 6 He made his son pass through f in the valley of
35:13 They roasted the passover lamb with f according
36:19 burned all its palaces with f,
Ne 1: 3 and its gates have been destroyed by f."
2: 3 and its gates have been destroyed by f?"
2:13 down and its gates that had been destroyed by f.
9:12 and by night with a pillar of f, E
9:19 nor the pillar of f by night that gave them light E
Job 1:16 "The f of God fell from heaven and burned up
15:34 and f consumes the tents of bribery.
18: 5 and the flame of their f does not shine.
20:26 a f fanned by no one will devour them;
22:20 and what they left, the f has consumed.'
28: 5 but underneath it is turned up as by f.
31:12 that would be a f consuming down to Abaddon,
41:19 its mouth go flaming torches; sparks of f leap out.
Ps 11: 6 On the wicked he will rain coals of f and sulfur;
18: 8 and devouring f from his mouth; D
18:12 through his clouds hailstones and coals of f.
21: 9 and f will consume them.
29: 7 The voice of the LORD flashes forth flames of f.
39: 3 While I mused, the f burned;
46: 9 he burns the shields with f.
50: 3 before him is a devouring f, D
66:12 we went through f and through water;
68: 2 as wax melts before the f,
74: 7 They set your sanctuary on f;
78:21 a f was kindled against Jacob,
78:63 F devoured their young men,
79: 5 Will your jealous wrath burn like f?
80:16 They have burned it with f, they have cut it down;
83:14 As f consumes the forest,
89:46 How long will your wrath burn like f?
97: 3 F goes before him, and consumes his adversaries
104: 4 f and flame your ministers.
105:39 and f to give light by night.
106:18 F also broke out in their company;
118:12 they blazed like a f of thorns;
148: 8 f and hail, snow and frost,
Pr 6:27 Can f be carried in the bosom
16:27 and their speech is like a scorching f.
25:22 for you will heap coals of f on their heads,
26:20 For lack of wood the f goes out,
26:21 As charcoal is to hot embers and wood to f,
30:16 and the f that never says, "Enough."
SS 8: 6 Its flashes are flashes of f, a raging flame.
Isa 1: 7 your cities are burned with f;
4: 5 by day and smoke and the shining of a flaming f
5:24 Therefore, as the tongue of f devours the stubble,
9: 5 in blood shall be burned as fuel for the f.
9:18 For wickedness burned like a f,
9:19 and the people became like fuel for the f;
10:16 a burning will be kindled, like the burning of f.
10:17 The light of Israel will become a f,
26:11 Let the f for your adversaries consume them.
27:11 women come and make a f of them.
29: 6 and the flame of a devouring f. D
30:14 not a sherd is found for taking f from the hearth,
30:27 and his tongue is like a devouring f; D
30:30 in furious anger and a flame of devouring f, D
30:33 with f and wood in abundance;
31: 9 says the LORD, whose f is in Zion,
33:11 your breath is a f that will consume you.
33:12 like thorns cut down, that are burned in the f."
33:14 "Who among us can live with the devouring f? D
37:19 into the f, though they were no gods, but the work
42:25 it set him on f all around,
43: 2 when you walk through f you shall not be burned,
44:15 he kindles a f and bakes bread.
44:16 Half of it he burns in the f;
44:16 "Ah, I am warm, I can feel the f!"
44:19 "Half of it I burned in the f;
47:14 See, they are like stubble, the f consumes them;
47:14 for warming oneself is this, no f to sit before!
50:11 all of you are kindlers of f, lighters of firebrands.
50:11 Walk in the flame of your f,
54:16 the smith who blows the f of coals, and produces
64: 2 when f kindles brushwood and the f causes water
64:11 has been burned by f, and all our pleasant places
65: 5 a f that burns all day long.
66:15 For the LORD will come in f,
66:15 and his rebuke in flames of f.
66:16 For by f will the LORD execute judgment,
66:24 their f shall not be quenched,
Jer 4: 4 or else my wrath will go forth like f,
5:14 I am now making my words in your mouth a f,
5:14 and the f shall devour them.
6:29 the lead is consumed by the f;
7:18 The children gather wood, the fathers kindle f,
7:31 to burn their sons and their daughters in the f—
11:16 with the roar of a great tempest he will set f to it,
15:14 in my anger a f is kindled that shall burn forever.
17: 4 in my anger a f is kindled that shall burn forever.
17:27 then I will kindle a f in its gates;
19: 5 to burn their children in the f as burnt offerings
20: 9 within me there is something like a burning f shut
21:10 and he shall burn it with f.
21:12 or else my wrath will go forth like f, and burn,
21:14 I will kindle a f in its forest,
22: 7 and cast them into the f.
23:29 Is not my word like f, says the LORD,
29:22 whom the king of Babylon roasted in the f,"
32:29 set it on f, and burn it,
34: 2 and he shall burn it with f.
34:22 and take it, and burn it with f.
36:22 there was a f burning in the brazier before him.
36:23 with a penknife and throw them into the f in

Jer 36:23 the entire scroll was consumed in the **f** that was in
36:32 that King Jehoiakim of Judah had burned in the **f**;
37: 8 they shall take it and burn it with **f**.
37:10 they would rise up and burn this city with **f**.
38:17 and this city shall not be burned with **f**,
38:18 and they shall burn it with **f**,
38:23 and this city shall be burned with **f**."
43:12 He shall kindle a **f** in the temples of the gods
43:13 temples of the gods of Egypt he shall burn with **f**.
48:45 for a **f** has gone out from Heshbon,
49: 2 and its villages shall be burned with **f**;
49:27 And I will kindle a **f** at the wall of Damascus,
50:32 and I will kindle a **f** in his cities,
51:30 her buildings are set on **f**, her bars are broken.
51:32 the marshes have been burned with **f**,
51:58 and her high gates shall be burned with **f**.
51:58 and the nations weary themselves only for **f**.
La 1:13 From on high he sent **f**;
2: 3 he has burned like a flaming **f** in Jacob,
2: 4 he has poured out his fury like **f**.
4:11 kindled a **f** in Zion that consumed its foundations.
Eze 1: 4 around it and **f** flashing forth continually,
1: 4 and in the middle of the **f**,
1:13 like burning coals of **f**, like torches moving to
1:13 **f** was bright, and lightning issued from the **f**.
1:27 something that looked like **f** enclosed all around;
1:27 I saw something that looked like **f**,
5: 2 One third of the hair you shall burn in the **f** inside
5: 4 throw them into the **f** and burn them up;
5: 4 from there a **f** will come out against all the house
8: 2 below what appeared to be its loins it was **f**,
10: 6 "Take **f** from within the wheelwork,
10: 7 from among the cherubim to the **f** that was among
15: 4 It is put in the **f** for fuel;
15: 4 the **f** has consumed both ends of it and the middle
15: 5 when the **f** has consumed it, and it is charred—
15: 6 which I have given to the **f** for fuel,
15: 7 although they escape from the **f**,
15: 7 the **f** shall still consume them;
19:12 its strong stem was withered; the **f** consumed it.
19:14 And **f** has gone out from its stem,
20:31 and make your children pass through the **f**,
20:47 I will kindle a **f** in you,
21:31 with the **f** of my wrath I will blow upon you.
21:32 You shall be fuel for the **f**,
22:20 to blow the **f** upon them in order to melt them;
22:21 I will gather you and blow upon you with the **f**
22:31 I have consumed them with the **f** of my wrath;
23:25 and your survivors shall be devoured by **f**.
24:10 Heap up the logs, kindle the **f**;
24:12 To the **f** with its rust!
28:14 you walked among the stones of **f**.
28:16 from among the stones of **f**.
28:18 So I brought out **f** from within you;
30: 8 when I have set **f** to Egypt,
30:14 and will set **f** to Zoan,
30:16 I will set **f** to Egypt;
38:22 down torrential rains and hailstones, **f** and sulfur,
39: 6 I will send **f** on Magog and
Da 3: 6 be thrown into a furnace of blazing **f**."
3:11 be thrown into a furnace of blazing **f**.
3:15 be thrown into a furnace of blazing **f**,
3:17 to deliver us from the furnace of blazing **f** and out
3:20 and to throw them into the furnace of blazing **f**.
3:21 they were thrown into the furnace of blazing **f**.
3:23 fell down, bound, into the furnace of blazing **f**.
3:24 not three men that we threw bound into the **f**?"
3:25 walking in the middle of the **f**,
3:26 the door of the furnace of blazing **f** and said,
3:26 Meshach, and Abednego came out from the **f**.
3:27 that the **f** had not had any power over the bodies
3:27 and not even the smell of **f** came from them.
7: 9 and its wheels were burning **f**.
7:10 of **f** issued and flowed out from his presence.
7:11 and given over to be burned with **f**.
Hos 7: 4 whose baker does not need to stir the **f**,
7: 6 in the morning it blazes like a flaming **f**.
8:14 but I will send a **f** upon his cities,
Joel 1:19 For **f** has devoured the pastures of the wilderness,
1:20 and **f** has devoured the pastures of the wilderness.
2: 3 **F** devours in front of them,
2: 5 like the crackling of a flame of **f** devouring
2:30 blood and **f** and columns of smoke.
Am 1: 4 So I will send a **f** on the house of Hazael,
1: 7 So I will send a **f** on the wall of Gaza, **f** that shall
devour its strongholds.
1:10 So I will send a **f** on the wall of Tyre, **f** that shall
devour its strongholds.
1:12 So I will send a **f** on Teman,
1:14 So I will kindle a **f** against the wall of Rabbah,
1:14 **f** that shall devour its strongholds,
2: 2 So I will send a **f** on Moab,
2: 5 So I will send a **f** on Judah,
4:11 and you were like a brand snatched from the **f**;
5: 6 against the house of Joseph like **f**,
7: 4 the Lord GOD was calling for a shower of **f**,
Ob 1:18 The house of Jacob shall be a **f**,
Mic 1: 4 like wax near the **f**, like waters poured down
1: 7 all her wages shall be burned with **f**,
Na 1: 6 His wrath is poured out like **f**,
3:13 **f** has devoured the bars of your gates.
3:15 There the **f** will devour you,
Zep 1:18 in the **f** of his passion the whole earth shall be
3: 8 for in the **f** of my passion all the earth shall
Zec 2: 5 For I will be a wall of **f** all around it,
3: 2 Is not this man a brand plucked from the **f**?"
9: 4 and it shall be devoured by **f**.

Zec 11: 1 O Lebanon, so that **f** may devour your cedars!
13: 9 And I will put this third into the **f**,
Mal 1:10 so that you would not kindle **f** on my altar in vain!
3: 2 For he is like a refiner's **f** and like fullers' soap;
Mt 3:10 down and thrown into the **f**.
3:11 He will baptize you with the Holy Spirit and **f**.
3:12 but the chaff he will burn with unquenchable **f**."
5:22 'You fool,' you will be liable to the hell of **f**.
7:19 down and thrown into the **f**.
13:40 as the weeds are collected and burned up with **f**,
13:42 and they will throw them into the furnace of **f**,
13:50 and throw them into the furnace of **f**,
17:15 he often falls into the **f** and often into the water.
18: 8 or two feet and to be thrown into the eternal **f**.
18: 9 and to be thrown into the hell of **f**.
25:41 the eternal **f** prepared for the devil and his angels;
Mk 9:22 It has often cast him into the **f** and into the water,
9:43 and to go to hell, to the unquenchable **f**.
9:48 and the **f** is never quenched.
9:49 "For everyone will be salted with **f**.
14:54 warming himself at the **f**.
Lk 3: 9 down and thrown into the **f**."
3:16 He will baptize you with the Holy Spirit and **f**.
3:17 but the chaff he will burn with unquenchable **f**."
9:54 do you want us to command **f** to come down
12:49 "I came to bring **f** to the earth,
17:29 it rained **f** and sulfur from heaven
22:55 When they had kindled a **f** in the middle of
Jn 15: 6 such branches are gathered, thrown into the **f**,
18:18 the slaves and the police had made a charcoal **f**
21: 9 they had gone ashore, they saw a charcoal **f** there,
Ac 2: 3 Divided tongues, as of **f**, appeared among them,
2:19 blood, and **f**, and smoky mist.
28: 2 they kindled a **f** and welcomed all of us around it.
28: 3 of brushwood and was putting it on the **f**,
28: 5 the creature into the **f** and suffered no harm.
1Co 3:13 because it will be revealed with **f**,
3:13 the **f** will test what sort of work each has done.
3:15 the builder will be saved, but only as through **f**.
2Th 1: 8 in flaming **f**, inflicting vengeance on those who
Heb 1: 7 and his servants flames of **f**."
10:27 and a fury of **f** that will consume the adversaries.
11:34 quenched raging **f**, escaped the edge of the sword,
12:18 a blazing **f**, and darkness, and gloom,
12:29 for indeed our God is a consuming **f**.
Jas 3: 5 How great a forest is set ablaze by a small **f**!
3: 6 And the tongue is a **f**.
3: 6 sets on **f** the cycle of nature, and is itself set on **f**
by hell.
5: 3 and it will eat your flesh like **f**.
1Pe 1: 7 though perishable, is tested by **f**—
2Pe 3: 7 and earth have been reserved for **f**,
3:10 and the elements will be dissolved with **f**,
3:12 and the elements will melt with **f**?
Jude 1: 7 by undergoing a punishment of eternal **f**.
1:23 save others by snatching them out of the **f**; C
Rev 1:14 his eyes were like a flame of **f**,
2:18 who has eyes like a flame of **f**,
3:18 to buy from me gold refined by **f** so that you may
8: 5 Then the angel took the censer and filled it with **f**
8: 7 and there came hail and **f**, mixed with blood,
8: 8 burning with **f**, was thrown into the sea.
9:17 the riders wore breastplates the color of **f** and
9:17 **f** and smoke and sulfur came out of their mouths.
9:18 by the **f** and smoke and sulfur coming out
10: 1 and his legs like pillars of **f**.
11: 5 **f** pours from their mouth and consumes their foes;
13:13 even making **f** come down from heaven to earth
14:10 be tormented with **f** and sulfur in the presence of
14:18 the angel who has authority over **f**,
15: 2 to be a sea of glass mixed with **f**,
16: 8 and it was allowed to scorch them with **f**;
17:16 they will devour her flesh and burn her up with **f**.
18: 8 and she will be burned with **f**;
19:12 His eyes are like a flame of **f**,
19:20 These two were thrown alive into the lake of **f**
20: 9 **f** came down from heaven and consumed them.
20:10 into the lake of **f** and sulfur,
20:14 Death and Hades were thrown into the lake of **f**.
20:14 This is the second death, the lake of **f**;
20:15 in the book of life was thrown into the lake of **f**.
21: 8 their place will be in the lake that burns with **f**
Tob 13:12 and set your homes on **f**.
Jdt 8:27 For he has not tried us with **f**, as he did them,
13:13 Then they lit a **f** to give light,
16:17 he will send **f** and worms into their flesh;
AdE 16:24 be destroyed in wrath with spear and **f**.
Wis 10: 6 the **f** that descended on the Five Cities.
13: 2 they supposed that either **f** or wind or swift air,
16:16 and utterly consumed by **f**.
16:17 the **f** had still greater effect,
16:19 the midst of water it burned more intensely than **f**,
16:22 Snow and ice withstood **f** without melting,
16:22 of their enemies were being destroyed by the **f**
16:23 whereas the **f**, in order that the righteous might
16:27 For what was not destroyed by **f** was melted
17: 5 And no power of **f** was able to give light,
17: 6 through to them except a dreadful, self-kindled **f**,
18: 3 Therefore you provided a flaming pillar of **f** as E
19:20 **F** even in water retained its normal power,
Sir 2: 5 For gold is tested in the **f**,
3:30 As water extinguishes a blazing **f**,
7:17 for the punishment of the ungodly is **f** and worms.
8: 3 and do not heap wood on their **f**.
8:10 or you may be burned in their flaming **f**.
9: 8 and by it passion is kindled like a **f**.
15:16 He has placed before you **f** and water;

Sir 16: 6 In an assembly of sinners a **f** is kindled,
21: 9 and their end is a blazing **f**.
22:24 vapor and smoke of the furnace precede the **f**;
23:16 a **f** will not be quenched until it burns itself out;
23:16 of kin will never cease until the **f** burns him up.
28:10 In proportion to the fuel, so will the **f** burn,
28:11 A hasty quarrel kindles a **f**,
38:28 the breath of the **f** melts his flesh,
39:26 and **f** and iron and salt and wheat flour and milk
39:29 **F** and hail and famine and pestilence,
40:30 but it kindles a **f** inside him.
43:21 and withers the tender grass like **f**.
45:19 against them to consume them in flaming **f**.
48: 1 Then Elijah arose, a prophet like **f**,
48: 3 and also three times brought down **f**.
48: 9 You were taken up by a whirlwind of **f**, in a
chariot with horses of **f**.
49: 6 who set **f** to the chosen city of the sanctuary,
50: 9 like **f** and incense in the censer, like a vessel
51: 4 from choking **f** on every side, and from the midst
of **f** that I had not kindled,
Bar 1: 2 the Chaldeans took Jerusalem and burned it with **f**.
4:35 For **f** will come upon her from the Everlasting
LtJ 6:55 When **f** breaks out in a temple
6:63 And the **f** sent from above to consume mountains
Aza 1: 2 Then Azariah stood still in the **f** and prayed aloud:
1:27 The **f** did not touch them at all
1:44 Bless the Lord, **f** and heat;
1:66 from the midst of the **f** he has delivered us.
1Mc 1:31 He plundered the city, burned it with **f**,
1:56 to pieces and burned with **f**.
5: 5 and burned with **f** their towers and all who were
5:28 then he seized all its spoils and burned it with **f**.
5:35 plundered it, and burned it with **f**.
5:44 the town and burned the sacred precincts with **f**,
5:68 the carved images of their gods he burned with **f**;
6:31 but the Jews sallied out and burned these with **f**,
6:51 engines of war to throw **f** and stones,
9:67 and his men sallied out from the town and set **f** to
10:84 in it, he burned with **f**.
11:48 They set **f** to the city and seized a large amount
11:61 and burned its suburbs with **f** and plundered them.
16:10 and John burned it with **f**,
2Mc 1:18 and the festival of the **f** given when Nehemiah,
1:19 the pious priests of that time took some of the **f** of
1:20 of the priests who had hidden the **f** to get it.
1:20 when they reported to us that they had not found **f**
1:22 a great **f** blazed up, so that all marveled.
1:33 where the exiled priests had hidden the **f**,
2: 1 to take some of the **f**,
2:10 and **f** came down from heaven and consumed
2:10 and the **f** came down and consumed
7: 5 the king ordered them to take him to the **f**,
8: 6 he would set **f** to towns and villages.
8:33 they burned those who had set **f** to
9: 7 breathing **f** in his rage against the Jews,
10: 3 then, striking **f** out of flint, they offered sacrifices,
10:36 against the defenders and set **f** to the towers;
12: 6 He set **f** to the harbor by night, burned the boats,
12: 9 the Jamnites by night and set **f** to the harbor and
13: 8 against the altar whose **f** and ashes were holy,
14:41 that **f** be brought and the doors burned.
1Es 1:12 They roasted the passover lamb with **f**,
1:55 burned their towers with **f**,
6:24 where they sacrifice with perpetual **f**;
3Mc 2: 5 You consumed with **f** and sulfur the people
2:29 on their bodies by **f** with the ivy-leaf symbol
3:29 to be made unapproachable and burned with **f**,
5:43 and rapidly level it to the ground with **f** and spear,
2Es 1:14 I provided light for you from a pillar of **f**, E
1:23 I did not send **f** on you for your blasphemies,
3:19 Your glory passed through the four gates of **f**
4: 5 he said to me, "Go, weigh for me the weight of **f**,
4: 9 But now I have asked you only about **f** and wind
4:16 for the **f** came and consumed it;
4:50 and the **f** is greater than the smoke,
5: 8 also in many places, **f** shall often break out,
7: 7 that there is **f** on the right hand and deep water on
7: 8 that is, between the **f** and the water,
7:*38* and there are **f** and torments.'
7:*61* they are set on **f** and burn hotly,
8: 8 what you have created is preserved amid **f**
8:22 to wind and **f**, whose word is sure
13: 4 as wax melts when it feels the **f**.
13:10 from his mouth something like a stream of **f**,
13:11 of **f** and the flaming breath and the great storm,
13:27 and **f** and a storm coming out of his mouth,
13:38 of the law (which was symbolized by the **f**).
14:39 of something like water, but its color was like **f**.
15:23 And a **f** went forth from his wrath,
15:41 **f** and hail and flying swords and floods of water,
15:61 and they shall be like **f** to you.
15:62 with **f** all your forests and your fruitful trees.
16: 4 A **f** has been sent upon you,
16: 6 or quench a **f** in the stubble once it has started
16: 9 **F** will go forth from his wrath,
16:15 The **f** is kindled, and shall not be put out
16:53 for God will burn coals of **f** on the head
16:73 like gold that is tested by **f**.
16:78 It is shut off and given up to be consumed by **f**.
4Mc 5:32 and fan the **f** more vehemently!
6:24 the guards brought him to the **f**.
7:10 powerful than tortures; O elder, fiercer than **f**;
7:12 Eleazar, though being consumed by the **f**,
9: 9 from the divine justice eternal torment by **f**."
9:19 While he was saying these things, they spread **f**
9:22 but as though transformed by **f** into immortality,

4Mc 10:14 "You do not have a **f** hot enough to make me play
11:19 that had been heated in the **f,**
11:26 Your **f** is cold to us, and the catapults painless,
12:12 justice has laid up for you intense and eternal **f**
14: 9 and in agonies of **f** at that.
14:10 For the power of **f** is intense and swift,
15:15 the flesh of her children being consumed by **f,**
18:12 Azariah, and Mishael in the **f.**
18:14 which says, 'Even though you go through the **f,**
18:20 when that bitter tyrant of the Greeks quenched **f**
18:20 of the Greeks quenched fire with **f**

FIRE-BREATHING (1) [BREATH, FIRE]

3Mc 6:34 and their **f** boldness was ignominiously quenched.

FIRE-QUENCHING (1) [FIRE, QUENCH]

Wis 19:20 and water forgot its **f** nature.

FIREBRANDS (3) [BRAND, FIRE]

Pr 26:18 Like a maniac who shoots deadly **f** and arrows,
Isa 7: 4 because of these two smoldering stumps of **f,**
50:11 But all of you are kindlers of fire, lighters of **f.**

FIRED (1) [FIRE]

2Mc 10:35 **f** with anger because of the blasphemies,

FIRELIGHT (1) [FIRE, LIGHT]

Lk 22:56 Then a servant-girl, seeing him in the **f,**

FIREPANS (7) [FIRE, PAN]

Ex 27: 3 and shovels and basins and forks and **f;**
38: 3 and the **f:** all its utensils he made of bronze.
Nu 4:14 the **f,** the forks, the shovels, and the basins,
1Ki 7:50 basins, dishes for incense, and **f,** of pure gold;
2Ki 25:15 as well as the **f** and the basins.
2Ch 4:22 basins, ladles, and **f,** of pure gold.
Jer 52:19 the **f,** the basins, the pots, the lampstands,

FIRES (8) [FIRE]

2Ch 21:19 like the **f** made for his ancestors.
Eze 39: 9 of Israel will go out and make **f** of the weapons
39: 9 and they will make **f** of them for seven years.
39:10 for they will make their **f** of the weapons;
Jdt 7: 5 and when they had kindled **f** on their towers,
1Mc 12:28 so they kindled **f** in their camp and withdrew.
12:29 for they saw the **f** burning.
2Mc 10:36 they kindled **f** and burned the blasphemers alive.

FIRING (1) [FIRE]

Sir 38:30 and he takes care in **f** the kiln.

FIRKINS (KJV) See GALLONS

FIRM‡ (45) [FIRMLY, FIRMNESS]

Ex 14:13 "Do not be afraid, stand **f,**
Ne 9:38 of all this we make a **f** agreement in writing,
Job 4: 4 and you have made **f** the feeble knees.
Ps 33: 9 he commanded, and it stood **f.**
37:23 Our steps are made **f** by the LORD,
89: 2 your faithfulness is as **f** as the heavens.
89:28 and my covenant with him will stand **f.**
112: 7 their hearts are **f,** secure in the LORD.
Pr 8:28 when he made **f** the skies above,
Isa 7: 9 If you do not stand **f** in faith,
22:17 He will seize **f** hold on you,
33:23 it cannot hold the mast **f** in its place,
35: 3 and make **f** the feeble knees.
Da 11:32 the people who are loyal to their God shall stand **f**
1Co 7:37 But if someone stands **f** in his resolve,
16:13 Keep alert, stand **f** in your faith, be courageous,
2Co 1:24 because you stand **f** in the faith.
Gal 5: 1 Stand **f,** therefore, and do not submit again to
Eph 6:13 and having done everything, to stand **f.**
Php 1:27 I will know that you are standing **f** in one spirit,
4: 1 my joy and crown, stand **f** in the Lord in this way,
1Th 3: 8 if you continue to stand **f** in the Lord.
2Th 2:15 stand **f** and hold fast to the traditions
2Ti 2:19 But God's **f** foundation stands,
Tit 1: 9 a **f** grasp of the word that is trustworthy
Heb 3: 6 and we are his house if we hold **f** the confidence
3:14 if only we hold our first confidence **f** to the end.
Wis 4: 3 a deep root or take a **f** hold.
Sir 5:10 Stand **f** for what you know,
22:18 Fences set on a high place will not stand **f** against
22:18 a timid mind with a fool's resolve will not stand **f**
40:25 Gold and silver make one stand **f,**
42:17 so that the universe may stand **f** in his glory.
45:23 and standing **f,** when the people turned away,
46: 3 Who before him ever stood so **f?**
1Mc 1:62 in Israel stood **f** and were resolved in their hearts
14:26 and the house of his father have stood **f;**
3Mc 2: 9 a **f** foundation for the glory of your great
5:31 to an extraordinary degree a full and **f** loyalty
7: 7 the friendly and **f** goodwill that they had
2Es 4:17 for the sand stood **f** and blocked it.
4Mc 7: 5 For in setting his mind **f** like a jutting cliff,
7:13 his body no longer tense and **f,**
17: 3 you held **f** and unswerving against the earthquake
17: 4 maintaining **f** an enduring hope in God.

FIRMAMENT (6) [FIRMAMENTS]

Ps 19: 1 and the **f** proclaims his handiwork.
Ps 150: 1 praise him in his mighty **f!**
Aza 1:34 Blessed are you in the **f** of heaven,
2Es 4: 7 or how many streams are above the **f,**
6:20 the books shall be opened before the face of the **f,**
6:41 on the second day, you created the spirit of the **f,**

FIRMAMENT (KJV) See also DOME, SKY

FIRMAMENTS (1) [FIRMAMENT]

2Es 6: 4 and before the measures of the **f** were named,

FIRMLY‡ (23) [FIRM]

1Ki 2:12 and his kingdom was **f** established.
2Ki 14: 5 As soon as the royal power was **f**
1Ch 16:30 world is **f** established; it shall never be moved.
2Ch 25: 3 As soon as the royal power was **f**
Job 41:23 it is **f** cast and immovable.
Ps 96:10 world is **f** established; it shall never be moved.
119:89 your word is **f** fixed in heaven.
122: 3 built as a city that is bound **f** together.
Ecc 12:11 and like nails **f** fixed are the collected sayings
Da 2: 8 because you see I have **f** decreed:
1Co 15: 2 if you hold **f** to the message that I proclaimed
2Ti 3:14 continue in what you have learned and **f** believed,
Tob 11:11 and holding him **f,** he blew into his eyes, saying,
Jdt 14:10 the God of Israel had done, he believed **f** in God.
Sir 22:16 A wooden beam **f** bonded into a building is
22:16 so the mind **f** resolved after due reflection will not
27: 2 a stake is driven **f** into a fissure between stones,
48:22 and he kept **f** to the ways of his ancestor David,
1Mc 15:34 we are **f** holding the inheritance of our ancestors.
3Mc 2:32 But the majority acted **f** with a courageous spirit
5:42 and he **f** swore an irrevocable oath
7: 4 that our government would never be **f** established
4Mc 17: 5 stand in honor before God and are **f** set in heaven

FIRMNESS (1) [FIRM]

Col 2: 5 to see your morale and the **f** of your faith

FIRST‡ (518) [FIRST-FORMED, FIRST-RIPE, FIRSTBORN, FIRSTLING, FIRSTLINGS, ONE]

A. FIRST DAY (51)
B. FIRST MONTH (42)
C. FIRST FRUITS (39)
D. FIRST YEAR (17)
E. FROM FIRST TO LAST (8)

Ge 1: 5 and there was morning, the **f** day. A
2:11 The name of the **f** is Pishon;
8: 5 in the tenth month, on the **f** day of the month, A
8:13 In the six hundred **f** year, in the first month,
8:13 In the six hundred first year, in the **f** month, B
8:13 in the first month, the **f** day of the month, A
9:20 a man of the soil, was the **f** to plant a vineyard.
10: 8 he was the **f** on earth to become a mighty warrior.
13: 4 to the place where he had made an altar at the **f;**
25:25 **f** came out red, all his body like a hairy mantle;
25:31 Jacob said, "**F** sell me your birthright."
25:33 Jacob said, "Swear to me **f.**"
28:19 but the name of the city was Luz at the **f.**
38:28 saying, "This one came out **f.**"
41:20 thin and ugly cows ate up the **f** seven fat cows,
43:18 replaced in our sacks the **f** time,
43:20 my lord, we came down the **f** time to buy food;
49: 3 my might and the **f** fruits of my vigor, C
Ex 4: 8 "If they will not believe you or heed the **f** sign,
5:23 Since I **f** came to Pharaoh to speak in your name,
12: 2 it shall be the **f** month of the year for you. B
12:15 on the **f** day you shall remove leaven A
12:15 for whoever eats leavened bread from the **f** day A
12:16 On the **f** day you shall hold a solemn assembly, A
12:18 In the **f** month, from the evening of B
13: 2 the **f** to open the womb among the Israelites,
13:12 you shall set apart to the LORD all that **f** opens
13:15 to the LORD every male that **f** opens the womb,
21:10 clothing, or marital rights of the **f** wife,
23:16 of the **f** fruits of your labor, C
23:19 of the **f** fruits of your ground you shall bring C
25:35 the **f** pair of branches, a calyx of one piece with it
26: 4 on the edge of the outermost curtain in the **f** set;
26:19 two bases under the **f** frame for its two pegs,
26:21 two bases under the **f** frame,
26:24 but joined at the top, at the **f** ring;
26:25 two bases under the **f** frame,
28:17 chrysolite, and emerald shall be the **f** row;
29:40 and with the **f** lamb one-tenth of a measure
34:19 All that **f** opens the womb is mine,
34:22 the **f** fruits of wheat harvest, C
34:26 of the **f** fruits of your ground you shall bring to C
36:11 on the edge of the outermost curtain of the **f** set;
36:24 two bases under the **f** frame for its two pegs,
36:26 two bases under the **f** frame and two bases under
36:29 but joined at the top, at the **f** ring;
37:21 of one piece with it under the **f** pair of branches,
39:10 chrysolite, and emerald was the **f** row;
40: 2 On the **f** day of the first month you shall set up A
40: 2 of the **f** month you shall set up the tabernacle of B
40:17 In the **f** month in the second year, B
40:17 on the **f** day of the month, A
Lev 2:14 a grain offering of **f** fruits to the LORD, C
2:14 grain offering of your **f** fruits coarse new grain C
4:21 and burn it as he burned the **f** bull;
5: 8 who shall offer **f** the one for the sin offering,
Lev 9:15 and presented it as a sin offering like the **f** one.
9:20 They **f** laid the fat on the breasts,
12: 6 of the tent of meeting a lamb in its **f** year for D
14:10 and one ewe lamb in its **f** year without blemish, D
23: 5 the **f** month, on the fourteenth day of the month, B
23: 7 On the **f** day you shall have a holy convocation; A
23:10 of the **f** fruits of your harvest to the priest. C
23:17 baked with leaven, as **f** fruits to the LORD. C
23:20 the bread of the **f** fruits as an elevation offering C
23:24 In the seventh month, on the **f** day of the month, A
23:35 The **f** day shall be a holy convocation; A
23:39 a complete rest on the **f** day, A
23:40 **f** day you shall take the fruit of majestic trees, A
Nu 1: 1 on the **f** day of the second month, A
1:18 the **f** day of the second month they assembled A
2: 9 They shall set out **f** on the march.
7:12 the **f** day was Nahshon son of Amminadab, A
9: 1 in the **f** month of the second year B
9: 5 They kept the passover in the **f** month, B
10:13 They set out for the **f** time at the command of
10:14 The standard of the camp of Judah set out **f,**
13:20 Now it was the season of the **f** ripe grapes.
15:20 From your **f** batch of dough you shall present
15:21 to the LORD a donation from the **f** of your batch
18:13 The **f** fruits of all that is in their land, C
18:15 The **f** issue of the womb of all creatures,
20: 1 came into the wilderness of Zin in the **f** month, B
24:20 "**F** among the nations was Amalek,
28:16 of the **f** month there shall be a passover offering B
28:18 On the **f** day there shall be a holy convocation. A
28:26 On the day of the **f** fruits, C
29: 1 On the **f** day of the seventh month you shall A
33: 3 They set out from Rameses in the **f** month, B
33: 3 on the fifteenth day of the **f** month; B
33:38 on the **f** day of the fifth month. A
Dt 1: 3 on the **f** day of the eleventh month, A
10:10 as I had done the **f** time.
13: 9 your own hand shall be **f** against them
16: 4 on the evening of the **f** day shall remain A
16: 9 the seven weeks from the time the sickle is **f** put
17: 7 The hands of the witnesses shall be the **f** raised
18: 4 The **f** fruits of your grain, your wine, and your C
18: 4 as well as the **f** of the fleece of your sheep,
20: 6 in the battle and another be **f** to enjoy its fruit.
21:17 since he is the **f** issue of his virility,
24: 4 her **f** husband, who sent her away,
26: 2 you shall take some of the **f** of all the fruit of
26:10 I bring the **f** of the fruit of the ground that you,
Jos 4:19 of the Jordan on the tenth day of the **f** month, B
8:33 of the LORD had commanded at the **f,**
21:10 since the lot fell to them **f.**
Jdg 1: 1 "Who shall go up **f** for us against the Canaanites,
20:18 "Which of us shall go up **f** to battle against
20:18 And the LORD answered, "Judah shall go up **f.**"
20:22 where they had formed it on the **f** day. A
20:39 before us, as in the **f** battle."
Ru 3:10 of your loyalty is better than the **f;**
1Sa 2:16 if the man said to him, "Let them burn the fat **f,**
14:14 In that **f** slaughter Jonathan
14:35 it was the **f** altar that he built to the LORD.
22:15 the **f** time that I have inquired of God for him?
2Sa 17: 9 And when some of our troops fall at the **f** attack,
18:27 of the **f** one is like the running of Ahimaaz son
19:20 therefore, see, I have come this day, the **f** of all
19:43 not the **f** to speak of bringing back our king?"
21: 9 They were put to death in the **f** days of harvest,
1Ki 1:51 'Let King Solomon swear to me **f** that he will
3:22 The **f** said, "No, the dead son is yours,
3:27 "Give the **f** woman the living boy; do not kill him.
17:13 but **f** make me a little cake of it and bring it to me,
18:25 "Choose for yourselves one bull and prepare it **f,**
18:30 **F** he repaired the altar of the LORD
20: 9 All that you **f** demanded of your servant I will do;
20:17 the district governors went out **f.**
22: 5 "Inquire **f** for the word of the LORD."
2Ki 4:42 food from the **f** fruits to the man of God: C
17:25 When they **f** settled there,
1Ch 1:10 he was the **f** to be a mighty one on the earth.
6:54 for the lot fell to them **f**—
9: 2 Now the **f** to live again in their possessions
11: 6 "Whoever attacks the Jebusites **f** shall be chief
11: 6 And Joab son of Zeruiah went up **f,**
12:15 the men who crossed the Jordan in the **f** month, B
15:13 Because you did not carry it the **f** time,
16: 7 that day David **f** appointed the singing of praises
24: 7 The **f** lot fell to Jehoiarib, the second to Jedaiah,
25: 9 The **f** lot fell for Asaph to Joseph;
27: 2 in charge of the **f** division in the first month;
27: 2 in charge of the first division in the **f** month; B
27: 3 the commanders of the army for the **f** month. B
29:29 Now the acts of King David, from **f** to last, E
2Ch 3:12 was joined to the wing of the **f** cherub.
9:29 the rest of the acts of Solomon, from **f** to last, E
12:15 Now the acts of Rehoboam, from **f** to last, E
16:11 The acts of Asa, from **f** to last, E
18: 4 "Inquire **f** for the word of the LORD."
20:34 the rest of the acts of Jehoshaphat, from **f** to last, E
25:26 the rest of the deeds of Amaziah, from **f** to last, E
26:22 Now the rest of the acts of Uzziah, from **f** to last, E
28:26 rest of his acts and all his ways, from **f** to last, E
29: 3 In the **f** year of his reign, in the first month, D
29: 3 In the first year of his reign, in the **f** month, B
29:17 the **f** day of the first month, and on the eighth A
29:17 first day of the **f** month, and on the eighth day B
29:17 the sixteenth day of the **f** month they finished. B
31: 5 people of Israel gave in abundance the **f** fruits C
35: 1 on the fourteenth day of the **f** month. B

2Ch 35:27 and his acts, f and last, are written in the Book
36:22 In the f year of King Cyrus of Persia, D
Ezr 1: 1 In the f year of King Cyrus of Persia, D
3: 6 From the f day of the seventh month they A
3:12 old people who had seen the f house
5:13 Cyrus of Babylon, in the f year of his reign, D
6: 3 In the f year of his reign, D
6:19 f month the returned exiles kept the passover. B
7: 9 On the f day of the first month the journey up A
7: 9 On the first day of the f month the journey up B
7: 9 f day of the fifth month he came to Jerusalem, A
8:31 twelfth day of the f month, to go to Jerusalem; B
10:16 On the f day of the tenth month they sat down A
10:17 By the f day of the first month they had come to A
10:17 By the first day of the f month they had come to B
Ne 7: 5 of those who were the f to come back, and I found
8: 2 This was on the f day of the seventh month. A
8:18 And day by day, from the f day to the last day, A
10:35 to bring the f fruits of our soil and the first fruits C
10:35 our soil and the f fruits of all fruit of every tree, C
10:37 the f of our dough, and our contributions, the fruit
12:44 the contributions, the f fruits, and the tithes, C
13:31 at appointed times, and for the f fruits. C
Est 1:14 and sat f in the kingdom):
3: 7 In the f month, which is the month of Nisan, B
3:12 the thirteenth day of the f month, and an edict, B
Job 40:19 "It is the f of the great acts of God—
42:14 He named the f Jemimah, the second Keziah,
Ps 78:51 the f issue of their strength in the tents of Ham.
105:36 the f issue of all their strength.
Pr 3: 9 with your substance and with the f fruits C
8:22 the f of his acts of long ago.
8:23 Ages ago I was set up, at the f,
8:26 or the world's f bits of soil.
18:17 The one who f states a case seems right,
Isa 1:26 And I will restore your judges as at the f,
41: 4 I, the LORD, am f, and will be with the last.
41:27 I f have declared it to Zion,
43:27 Your f ancestor sinned,
44: 6 I am the f and I am the last;
48:12 I am the f, and I am the last.
60: 9 the ships of Tarshish f, to bring your children
Jer 2: 3 the f fruits of his harvest. C
4:31 anguish as of one bringing forth her f child,
7:12 where I made my name dwell at f,
25: 1 the f year of King Nebuchadrezzar of Babylon), D
33: 7 and rebuild them as they were at f.
33:11 For I will restore the fortunes of the land as at f,
36:28 on it all the former words that were in the f scroll,
50:17 F the king of Assyria devoured it,
Eze 10:14 the f face was that of the cherub,
26: 1 In the eleventh year, on the f day of the month, A
29:17 In the twenty-seventh year, in the f month, B
29:17 in the first month, on the f day of the month, A
30:20 In the eleventh year, in the f month, B
31: 1 in the third month, on the f day of the month, A
32: 1 in the twelfth month, on the f day of the month, A
32:17 In the twelfth year, in the f month, B
40:21 of the same size as those of the f gate;
44:30 The f of all the first fruits of all kinds,
44:30 The first of all the f fruits of all kinds, C
44:30 also give to the priests the f of your dough,
45:18 In the f month, on the first day of the month, B
45:18 In the first month, on the f day of the month, A
45:21 In the f month, on the fourteenth day of B
Da 1:21 And Daniel continued there until the f year D
2: 7 "Let the king f tell his servants the dream,
7: 1 In the f year of King Belshazzar of Babylon, D
7: 4 The f was like a lion and had eagles' wings.
8: 1 Daniel, after the one that had appeared to me at f.
8:21 and the great horn between its eyes is the f king.
9: 1 In the f year of Darius son of Ahasuerus, D
9: 2 in the f year of his reign, D
10: 4 On the twenty-fourth day of the f month, B
10:12 for from the f day that you set your mind A
11: 1 As for me, in the f year of Darius the Mede, D
12: 1 such as has never occurred since nations f came
Hos 1: 2 When the LORD f spoke through Hosea,
2: 7 "I will go and return to my f husband,
9:10 Like the f fruit on the fig tree, in its f season,
Am 6: 1 the notables of the f of the nations,
6: 7 Therefore they shall now be the f to go into exile,
Hag 1: 1 in the sixth month, on the f day of the month, A
Zec 6: 2 The f chariot had red horses,
12: 7 LORD will give victory to the tents of Judah f,
Mt 5:24 f be reconciled to your brother or sister,
6:33 But strive f for the kingdom of God
7: 5 You hypocrite, f take the log out of your own eye,
8:21 "Lord, f let me go and bury my father."
10: 2 These are the names of the twelve apostles: f,
12:29 without f tying up the strong man?
12:45 the last state of that person is worse than the f.
13:30 Collect the weeds f and bind them in bundles to
17:10 then, do the scribes say that Elijah must come f?"
17:25 And when he came home, Jesus spoke of it f,
17:27 take the f fish that comes up;
19:30 many who are f will be last, and the last will be f.
20: 8 beginning with the last and then going to the f.'
20:10 the f came, they thought they would receive more;
20:16 So the last will be f, and the f will be last."
20:27 and whoever wishes to be f among you must
21:28 A man had two sons; he went to the f and said,
21:31 They said, "The f."
21:36 Again he sent other slaves, more than the f;
22:25 the f married, and died childless,
22:38 This is the greatest and f commandment.
23:26 F clean the inside of the cup,
Mt 26:17 the f day of Unleavened Bread the disciples A
27:64 and the last deception would be worse than the f."
28: 1 sabbath, as the f day of the week was dawning, A
Mk 3:27 and plunder his property without f tying up
4:28 The earth produces of itself, f the stalk,
7:27 He said to her, "Let the children be fed f,
9:11 the scribes say that Elijah must come f?"
9:12 "Elijah is indeed coming f to restore all things.
9:35 to be f must be last of all and servant of all."
10:31 But many who are f will be last,
10:31 and the last will be f."
10:44 and whoever wishes to be f among you must
12:20 the f married and, when he died, left no children;
12:28 "Which commandment is the f of all?"
12:29 Jesus answered, "The f is, 'Hear, O Israel:
13:10 good news must f be proclaimed to all nations.
14:12 On the f day of Unleavened Bread, A
16: 2 And very early on the f day of the week, A
16: 9 ⟦after he rose early on the f day of the week,⟧ A
16: 9 ⟦he appeared f to Mary Magdalene,⟧
Lk 1: 3 investigating everything carefully from the very f,
2: 2 This was the f registration and was taken
6:42 You hypocrite, f take the log out of your own eye,
9:59 he said, "Lord, f let me go and bury my father."
9:61 but let me f say farewell to those at my home."
10: 5 Whatever house you enter, f say,
11:26 the last state of that person is worse than the f."
11:38 to see that he did not f wash before dinner.
12: 1 he began to speak f to his disciples,
13:30 some are last who will be f, and some are f who will be last."
14:18 The f said to him, 'I have bought a piece of land,
14:28 does not f sit down and estimate the cost,
14:31 not sit down f and consider whether he is able
16: 5 his master's debtors one by one, he asked the f,
17:25 But f he must endure much suffering and
19:16 The f came forward and said, 'Lord,
20:29 the f married, and died childless;
21: 9 for these things must take place f,
24: 1 But on the f day of the week, at early dawn, A
Jn 1:41 He f found his brother Simon and said to him,
2:10 "Everyone serves the good wine f,
2:11 Jesus did this, the f of his signs,
6:64 from the f who were the ones that did not believe,
7:51 not judge people without f giving them a hearing
8: 7 ⟦among you who is without sin be the f to throw⟧
12:16 His disciples did not understand these things at f;
18:13 F they took him to Annas,
19:32 Then the soldiers came and broke the legs of the f
19:39 Nicodemus, who had at f come to Jesus by night,
20: 1 Early on the f day of the week, A
20: 4 other disciple outran Peter and reached the tomb f.
20: 8 Then the other disciple, who reached the tomb f,
20:19 evening on that day, the f day of the week, A
Ac 1: 1 In the f book, Theophilus,
3:26 God raised up his servant, he sent him f to you,
7:12 he sent our ancestors there on their f visit.
11:26 that the disciples were f called "Christians."
12:10 After they had passed the f and the second guard,
13:46 that the word of God should be spoken f to you.
15:14 Simeon has related how God f looked favorably
18:19 but f he himself went into the synagogue and had
20: 7 On the f day of the week, A
20:18 the entire time from the f day that I set foot A
26:20 but declared f to those in Damascus,
26:23 and that, by being the f to rise from the dead,
27:43 to jump overboard f and make for the land,
Ro 1: 8 F, I thank my God through Jesus Christ for all
1:16 to the Jew f and also to the Greek.
2: 9 the Jew f and also the Greek,
2:10 the Jew f and also the Greek.
3: 2 For in the f place the Jews were entrusted with
8:23 who have the f fruits of the Spirit, C
10:19 F Moses says, "I will make you jealous
11:16 If the part of the dough offered as f fruits is holy, C
16: 5 who was the f convert in Asia for Christ.
1Co 12:28 And God has appointed in the church f apostles,
14:30 let the f person be silent.
15: 3 For I handed on to you as of f importance what I
15:20 the f fruits of those who have died. C
15:23 But each in his own order: Christ the f fruits, C
15:45 Thus it is written, "The f man, Adam,
15:46 But it is not the spiritual that is f, but the physical,
15:47 The f man was from the earth, a man of dust;
16: 2 On the f day of every week, A
16:15 of the household of Stephanas were the f converts
2Co 1:15 I was sure of this, I wanted to come to you f,
1:22 in our hearts as a f installment.
8: 5 they gave themselves f to the Lord and,
10:14 we were the f to come all the way to you with
Gal 4:13 because of a physical infirmity that I f announced
Eph 1:12 who were the f to set our hope on Christ,
6: 2 this is the f commandment with a promise:
Php 1: 5 of your sharing in the gospel from the f day A
Col 1:18 that he might come to have f place in everything.
1Th 4:16 and the dead in Christ will rise f.
2Th 2: 3 not come unless the rebellion comes f and
2:13 the f fruits for salvation through sanctification C
1Ti 2: 1 F of all, then, I urge that supplications, prayers,
2:13 For Adam was formed f, then Eve;
3:10 And let them f be tested;
5: 4 they should f learn their religious duty
5:12 for having violated their f pledge.
2Ti 1: 5 a faith that lived f in your grandmother Lois
2: 6 the work who ought to have the f share of
4:16 At my f defense no one came to my support,
Tit 3:10 After a f and second admonition,
Heb 2: 3 It was declared at f through the Lord,
3:14 if only we hold our f confidence firm to the end.
7: 2 in the f place, means "king of righteousness";
7:27 f for his own sins, and then for those of
8: 7 For if that f covenant had been faultless,
8:13 he has made the f one obsolete.
9: 1 even the f covenant had regulations for worship
9: 2 For a tent was constructed, the f one,
9: 6 into the f tent to carry out their ritual duties;
9: 8 as long as the f tent is still standing.
9:15 from the transgressions under the f covenant.
9:18 Hence not even the f covenant was inaugurated
10: 9 He abolishes the f in order to establish the second.
Jas 1:18 so that we would become a kind of f fruits C
3:17 But the wisdom from above is f pure,
2Pe 1:20 F of all you must understand this,
2:20 last state has become worse for them than the f.
3: 3 F of all you must understand this,
1Jn 4:19 We love because he f loved us.
3Jn 1: 9 but Diotrephes, who likes to put himself f,
Rev 1:17 I am the f and the last,
2: 4 that you have abandoned the love you had at f.
2: 5 repent, and do the works you did at f.
2: 8 These are the words of the f and the last,
2:19 I know that your last works are greater than the f.
4: 1 the f voice, which I had heard speaking to me like
4: 7 the f living creature like a lion,
8: 7 The f angel blew his trumpet,
9:12 The f woe has passed.
13:12 It exercises all the authority of the f beast
13:12 the earth and its inhabitants worship the f beast,
14: 4 humankind as f fruits for God and the Lamb, C
16: 2 the f angel went and poured his bowl on the earth,
20: 5 This is the f resurrection.
20: 6 and holy are those who share in the f resurrection.
21: 1 the f heaven and the f earth had passed away,
21: 4 for the f things have passed away."
21:19 the f was jasper, the second sapphire,
22:13 I am the Alpha and the Omega, the f and the last,
Tob 1: 6 I would hurry off to Jerusalem with the f fruits C
1: 6 and the f shearings of the sheep.
4:12 F of all, marry a woman from among
5:10 So he went in to him, and Tobit greeted him f.
6: 2 and when the f night overtook them they camped
6:18 both of you must f stand up and pray,
7: 1 They greeted him f, and he replied,
14: 5 not like the f one until the period when the times
Jdt 2: 1 on the twenty-second day of the f month, B
8:29 not the f time your wisdom has been shown,
11:13 to consume the f fruits of the grain and the tithes C
12:16 to seduce her from the day he f saw her.
AdE 3:12 So on the thirteenth day of the f month B
5:11 he had advanced him to be the f in the kingdom.
8: 9 twenty-third day of the f month, that is, Nisan, B
11: 2 on the f day of Nisan, A
Wis 7: 3 my f sound was a cry, as is true of all.
19:16 having f received them with festal celebrations,
Sir 4:17 at f she will walk with them on tortuous paths;
7:31 the f fruits, the guilt offering, C
7:31 and the f fruits of the holy things. C
11: 7 examine f, and then criticize.
19:29 and a sensible person is known when f met,
23:23 For f of all, she has disobeyed the law of
24:25 and like the Tigris at the time of the f fruits. C
24:28 The f man did not know wisdom fully,
31:17 Be the f to stop, as befits good manners,
32: 1 Take care of them f and then sit down;
33:17 by the blessing of the Lord I arrived f,
35:10 and do not stint the f fruits of your hands. C
37: 8 and learn f what is his interest,
45:20 he allotted to him the best of the f fruits, C
45:20 and prepared bread of f fruits in abundance; C
50: 8 days of f fruits, like lilies by a spring of water, C
51:15 From the f blossom to the ripening grape my heart
51:20 With her I gained understanding from the f;
1Mc 2:18 be the f to come and do what the king commands,
3:49 and the f fruits and the tithes, and they stirred up C
5:40 "If he crosses over to us f,
5:43 Then he crossed over against them f,
6: 2 Macedonian king who f reigned over the Greeks.
6: 6 that Lysias had gone f with a strong force,
7:13 The Hasideans were f among the Israelites
7:43 and he himself was the f to fall in the battle.
8:24 If war comes f to Rome or to any of their allies
8:27 if war comes f to the nation of the Jews,
9: 3 In the f month of the one hundred fifty-second B
10: 4 "Let us act f to make peace with him
10:41 not paid as they did in the f years,
10:47 the f to speak peaceable words to them,
13:42 "In the f year of Simon the great high priest D
16: 6 to cross the stream, so he crossed over f;
2Mc 4:33 having f withdrawn to a place of sanctuary
7: 7 After the f brother had died in this way,
7: 8 as the f brother had done.
8:23 then, leading the f division himself,
11: 7 Maccabeus himself was the f to take up arms,
12:22 But when Judas's f division appeared,
14: 8 f because I am genuinely concerned for
15:18 and f fear was for the consecrated sanctuary.
1Es 1: 1 on the fourteenth day of the f month, B
2: 1 In the f year of Cyrus as king of the Persians, D
3:10 The f wrote, "Wine is strongest."
3:17 Then the f, who had spoken of the strength
5: 6 in the month of Nisan, the f month. B
5:47 a single purpose in the square before the f gate
6:17 in the f year that Cyrus reigned over the country D
6:24 the f year of the reign of King Cyrus, he ordered D

1Es 7:10 passover on the fourteenth day of the f month, B
8: 6 on the new moon of the f month and arrived B
8:61 river Theras on the twelfth day of the f month; B
9:17 to an end by the new moon of the f month. B
3Mc 2:21 the f Father of all, holy among the holy ones,
2Es 2:23 and I will give you the f place in my resurrection.
3:21 For the f Adam, burdened with an evil heart,
5:42 so for those who are f there is no haste."
6: 7 the end of the f age and the beginning of the age
6:38 and said on the f day, A
7:30 as it was at the f beginnings,
7:*70* he f prepared the judgment and the things
7:*78* f of all it adores the glory of the Most High.
7:*81* The f way, because they have scorned the law of
7:*91* F of all, they shall see with great joy the glory
7:*92* The f order, because they have striven
7:*106* [36] "How then do we find that f Abraham prayed
7:*116* [46] "This is my f and last comment:
10:28 who came to me at f?
10:29 the angel who had come to me at f came to me,
11:14 so that it disappeared like the f.
11:27 and this disappeared more quickly than the f.
12:33 For f he will bring them alive
14:29 At f our ancestors lived as aliens in Egypt,
14:45 the twenty-four books that you wrote f, and let
4Mc 1:30 now, f of all, that rational judgment is sovereign
6: 2 F they stripped the old man,
8: 2 in his f attempt, being unable to compel
17: 7 would not those who f beheld it have shuddered
17:13 Eleazar was the f contestant,

FIRST-FORMED (2) [FIRST, FORM]

Wis 7: 1 a descendant of the f child of earth;
10: 1 Wisdom protected the f father of the world,

FIRST-RIPE (4) [FIRST, RIPE]

Isa 28: 4 will be like a f fig before the summer;
Jer 24: 2 One basket had very good figs, like f figs,
Mic 7: 1 there is no f fig for which I hunger.
Na 3:12 All your fortresses are like fig trees with f figs—

FIRSTBEGOTTEN (KJV) See FIRSTBORN

FIRSTBORN‡ (140) [BEAR, FIRST]

A. ALL THE FIRSTBORN (22)

Ge 10:15 Canaan became the father of Sidon his f,
19:31 And the f said to the younger, "Our father is old,
19:33 and the f went in, and lay with her father;
19:34 On the next day, the f said to the younger, "Look,
19:37 The f bore a son, and named him Moab;
22:21 Uz the f, Buz his brother, Kemuel the father
25:13 Nebaioth, the f of Ishmael;
27:19 Jacob said to his father, "I am Esau your f.
27:32 He answered, "I am your f son, Esau."
29:26 giving the younger before the f.
35:23 The sons of Leah: Reuben (Jacob's f), Simeon,
36:15 The sons of Eliphaz the f of Esau:
38: 6 Judah took a wife for Er his f;
38: 7 Judah's f, was wicked in the sight of the LORD,
41:51 Joseph named the f Manasseh, "For," he said,
43:33 the f according to his birthright and the youngest
46: 8 to Egypt. Reuben, Jacob's f,
48:14 crossing his hands, for Manasseh was the f.
48:18 this one is the f, put your right hand on his head."
49: 3 you are my f, my might and the first fruits
Ex 4:22 'Thus says the LORD: Israel is my f son.
4:23 now I will kill your f son.' "
6:14 the sons of Reuben, the f of Israel:
11: 5 Every f in the land of Egypt shall die,
11: 5 from the f of Pharaoh who sits on his throne to the f of the female slave
11: 5 and all the f of the livestock. A
12:12 I will strike down every f in the land of Egypt,
12:29 At midnight the LORD struck down all the f in A
12:29 from the f of Pharaoh who sat on his throne to the f of the prisoner
12:29 and all the f of the livestock. A
13: 2 Consecrate to me all the f; A
13:12 All the f of your livestock that are males shall be A
13:13 every f donkey you shall redeem with a sheep;
13:13 f male among your children you shall redeem.
13:15 the LORD killed all the f in the land of Egypt, A
13:15 from human f to the f of animals.
13:15 but every f of my sons I redeem.'
22:29 The f of your sons you shall give to me.
34:19 all your male livestock, the f of cow and sheep.
34:20 The f of a donkey you shall redeem with a lamb,
34:20 All the f of your sons you shall redeem. A
Nu 1:20 The descendants of Reuben, Israel's f,
3: 2 Nadab the f, and Abihu, Eleazar, and Ithamar;
3:12 the Israelites as substitutes for all the f that open A
3:13 for all the f are mine; A
3:13 when I killed all the f in the land of Egypt, A
3:13 I consecrated for my own all the f in Israel, A
3:40 Enroll all the f males of the Israelites, A
3:41 as substitutes for all the f among the Israelites, A
3:41 for all the f among the livestock of the Israelites. A
3:42 So Moses enrolled all the f among the Israelites, A
3:43 all the f males from a month old and upward, A
3:45 all the f among the Israelites, and the livestock A
3:46 of the two hundred seventy-three of the f of
3:50 from the f of the Israelites he took the money,
8:16 in place of all that open the womb, the f of all
8:17 For all the f among the Israelites are mine, A
Nu 8:17 the day that I struck down all the f in the land A
8:18 but I have taken the Levites in place of all the f A
18:15 but the f of human beings you shall redeem,
18:15 and the f of unclean animals you shall redeem.
18:17 the f of a cow, or the f of a sheep, or the f of a goat,
26: 5 the f of Israel. The descendants of Reuben:
33: 4 while the Egyptians were burying all their f,
Dt 21:15 the f being the son of the one who is disliked,
21:16 not permitted to treat the son of the loved as the f
21:16 to the son of the disliked, who is the f.
21:17 as f the son of the one who is disliked, giving him
21:17 the right of the f is his.
25: 6 the f whom she bears shall succeed to the name of
33:17 A f bull—majesty is his!
Jos 6:26 At the cost of his f he shall lay its foundation,
17: 1 for he was the f of Joseph.
17: 1 To Machir the f of Manasseh,
Jdg 8:20 So he said to Jether his f, "Go kill them!"
1Sa 8: 2 The name of his f son was Joel,
14:49 the name of the f was Merab,
17:13 to the battle were Eliab the f,
2Sa 3: 2 his f was Amnon, of Ahinoam of Jezreel;
13:21 because he loved him, for he was his f.
1Ki 16:34 he laid its foundation at the cost of Abiram his f,
2Ki 3:27 Then he took his f son who was to succeed him,
1Ch 1:13 Canaan became the father of Sidon his f,
1:29 the f of Ishmael, Nebaioth;
2: 3 Judah's f, was wicked in the sight of the LORD,
2:13 Jesse became the father of Eliab his f,
2:25 The sons of Jerahmeel, the f of Hezron:
2:25 Ram his f, Bunah, Oren, Ozem, and Ahijah.
2:27 The sons of Ram, the f of Jerahmeel:
2:42 Mesha his f, who was father of Ziph.
2:50 The sons of Hur the f of Ephrathah:
3: 1 the f Amnon, by Ahinoam the Jezreelite;
3:15 Johanan the f, the second Jehoiakim,
4: 4 These were the sons of Hur, the f of Ephrathah,
5: 1 The sons of Reuben the f of Israel.
5: 1 was the f, but because he defiled his father's bed
5: 3 The sons of Reuben, the f of Israel:
6:28 The sons of Samuel: Joel his f, the second Abijah.
8: 1 Benjamin became the father of Bela his f,
8:30 His f son: Abdon, then Zur, Kish, Baal, Nadab,
8:39 The sons of his brother Eshek: Ulam his f,
9: 5 And of the Shilonites: Asaiah the f, and his sons.
9:31 one of the Levites, the f of Shallum the Korahite,
9:36 His f son was Abdon, then Zur, Kish, Baal, Ner,
26: 2 Meshelemiah had sons: Zechariah the f,
26: 4 Shemaiah the f, Jehozabad the second,
26:10 Shimri the chief (for though he was not the f,
2Ch 21: 3 the kingdom to Jehoram, because he was the f.
Ne 10:36 the f of our sons and of our livestock,
Job 15: 7 "Are you the f of the human race?
18:13 the f of Death consumes their limbs.
Ps 78:51 He struck all the f in Egypt, A
89:27 I will make him the f,
105:36 He struck down all the f in their land, A
135: 8 He it was who struck down the f of Egypt,
136:10 who struck Egypt through their f,
Isa 14:30 The f of the poor will graze,
Jer 31: 9 a father to Israel, and Ephraim is my f.
Eze 20:26 in their offering up all their f,
Mic 6: 7 Shall I give my f for my transgression,
Zec 12:10 and weep bitterly over him, as one weeps over a f.
Lk 2: 7 And she gave birth to her f son and wrapped him
2:23 "Every f male shall be designated as holy to
Ro 8:29 that he might be the f within a large family.
Col 1:15 of the invisible God, the f of all creation;
1:18 he is the beginning, the f from the dead,
Heb 1: 6 And again, when he brings the f into the world,
11:28 of the f would not touch the firstborn of Israel.
11:28 of the firstborn would not touch the f of Israel.
12:23 the assembly of the f who are enrolled in heaven,
Rev 1: 5 the faithful witness, the f of the dead,
Wis 18:13 yet, when their f were destroyed,
Sir 36:17 on Israel, whom you have named your f,
2Es 6:58 we your people, whom you have called your f,
4Mc 15:18 When the f breathed his last,

FIRSTLING (5) [FIRST]

Lev 27:26 A f of animals, however, which as
27:26 however, which as a f belongs to the LORD,
Dt 15:19 Every f male born of your herd
15:19 not do work with your f ox nor shear the f of your

FIRSTLING (KJV) See also FIRSTBORN

FIRSTLINGS (6) [FIRST]

Ge 4: 4 and Abel for his part brought of the f of his flock,
Dt 12: 6 and the f of your herds and flocks.
12:17 and your oil, the f of your herds and your flocks,
14:23 as well as the f of your herd and flock,
Ne 10:36 and the f of our herds and of our flocks;
Tob 1: 6 the first fruits of the crops and the f of the flock,

FISH (77) [FISH'S, FISHERMEN, FISHES, FISHHOOK, FISHHOOKS, FISHING]

Ge 1:26 and let them have dominion over the f of the sea,
1:28 and have dominion over the f of the sea and over
9: 2 and on all the f of the sea;
Ex 7:18 The f in the river shall die,
7:21 and the f in the river died.
Nu 11: 5 We remember the f we used to eat in Egypt
11:22 Are there enough f in the sea to catch for them?"
Dt 4:18 the likeness of any f that is in the water under
1Ki 4:33 and birds, and reptiles, and f.
2Ch 33:14 in the valley, reaching the entrance at the F Gate;
Ne 3: 3 The sons of Hassenaah built the F Gate;
12:39 and by the F Gate and the Tower of Hananel and
13:16 in f and all kinds of merchandise and sold them
Job 12: 8 and the f of the sea will declare to you.
Ps 8: 8 and the f of the sea,
105:29 and caused their f to die.
Ecc 9:12 Like f taken in a cruel net,
Isa 19: 8 Those who f will mourn; all who cast hooks in the
50: 2 their f stink for lack of water, and die of thirst.
Eze 29: 4 make the f of your channels stick to your scales.
29: 4 the f of your channels sticking to your scales.
29: 5 you and all the f of your channels;
38:20 the f of the sea, and the birds of the air,
47: 9 and there will be very many f,
47:10 its f will be of a great many kinds, like the f of the Great Sea.
Hos 4: 3 even the f of the sea are perishing.
Jnh 1:17 LORD provided a large f to swallow up Jonah;
1:17 in the belly of the f three days and three nights.
2: 1 to the LORD his God from the belly of the f,
2:10 Then the LORD spoke to the f,
Hab 1:14 You have made people like the f of the sea,
Zep 1: 3 I will sweep away the birds of the air and the f of
1:10 a cry will be heard from the F Gate,
Mt 4:19 "Follow me, and I will make you f for people."
7:10 Or if the child asks for a f, will give a snake?
13:47 a net that was thrown into the sea and caught f
14:17 "We have nothing here but five loaves and two f."
14:19 Taking the five loaves and the two f,
15:34 They said, "Seven, and a few small f."
15:36 he took the seven loaves and the f;
17:27 take the first f that comes up;
Mk 1:17 "Follow me and I will make you f for people."
6:38 they had found out, they said, "Five, and two f."
6:41 Taking the five loaves and the two f,
6:41 and he divided the two f among them all.
6:43 of broken pieces and of the f.
8: 7 They had also a few small f;
Lk 5: 6 so many f that their nets were beginning to break.
5: 9 with him were amazed at the catch of f
9:13 "We have no more than five loaves and two f—
9:16 And taking the five loaves and the two f,
11:11 if your child asks for a f, will give a snake instead of a f?
24:42 They gave him a piece of broiled f,
Jn 6: 9 a boy here who has five barley loaves and two f.
6:11 so also the f, as much as they wanted.
21: 5 Jesus said to them, "Children, you have no f,
21: 6 to haul it in because there were so many f.
21: 8 dragging the net full of f,
21: 9 they saw a charcoal fire there, with f on it,
21:10 "Bring some of the f that you have just caught."
21:11 full of large f, a hundred fifty-three of them;
21:13 and did the same with the f.
1Co 15:39 another for birds, and another for f.
Tob 6: 3 Suddenly a large f leaped up from the water
6: 4 "Catch hold of the f and hang on to it!"
6: 4 So the young man grasped the f and drew it up on
6: 5 "Cut open the f and take out its gall, heart,
6: 6 the f the young man gathered together the gall,
6: 6 then he roasted and ate some of the f,
8: 3 odor of the f so repelled the demon that he fled to
11: 8 Smear the gall of the f on his eyes;
11:11 with the gall of the f in his hand,
Wis 19:10 and instead of f the river spewed out vast numbers
2Es 5: 7 and the Dead Sea shall cast up f;
16:12 the f with them shall be troubled at the presence

FISH'S (4) [FISH]

Tob 6: 7 what medicinal value is there in the f heart
6: 8 He replied, "As for the f heart and liver,
6:17 take some of the f liver and heart,
8: 2 and he took the f liver and heart out of the bag

FISHERMEN (4) [FISH, MAN]

Jer 16:16 I am now sending for many f, says the LORD,
Mt 4:18 into the sea—for they were f.
Mk 1:16 into the sea—for they were f.
Lk 5: 2 the f had gone out of them

FISHES (1) [FISH]

2Es 6:47 to bring forth living creatures, birds, and f;

FISHHOOK (1) [FISH, HOOK]

Job 41: 1 "Can you draw out Leviathan with a f,

FISHHOOKS (1) [FISH, HOOK]

Am 4: 2 even the last of you with f.

FISHING (3) [FISH]

Job 41: 7 or its head with f spears?
Eze 47:10 People will stand f beside the sea from En-gedi
Jn 21: 3 Simon Peter said to them, "I am going f."

FISHPOOL (KJV) See POOL

FISSURE (1)

Sir 27: 2 a stake is driven firmly into a f between stones,

FIST (5) [TIGHT-FISTED]

Ex 21:18 and one strikes the other with a stone or f so that
Isa 10:32 he will shake his f at the mount of daughter Zion,
58: 4 and to fight and to strike with a wicked f.
Zep 2:15 by it hisses and shakes the f.
Sir 48:18 he shook his f against Zion,

FIT (17) [FITLY, FITNESS, FITTED, FITTING, FITTINGLY]

Ex 26:17 There shall be two pegs in each frame to f
1Sa 10: 7 these signs meet you, do whatever you see f to do,
2Ki 24:16 one thousand, all of them strong and f for war.
2Ch 25: 5 they were three hundred thousand picked troops f
26:11 Uzziah had an army of soldiers, f for war,
Isa 54:16 and produces a weapon f for its purpose;
Eze 16:13 You grew exceedingly beautiful, f to be a queen.
Lk 9:62 to the plow and looks back is f for the kingdom
14:35 It is f neither for the soil nor for the manure pile;
Ro 1:28 And since they did not see f to acknowledge God,
Jdt 3: 4 come and deal with them as you see f."
Wis 1:16 because they are f to belong to his company.
15: 6 and f for such objects of hope are those who
Sir 10: 3 but a city becomes f to live in through
30:14 healthy, and f than rich and afflicted in body.
31:20 he rises early, and feels f.
36:29 a helper f for him and a pillar of support.

FITCHES (KJV) See DILL, SPELT

FITLY (2) [FIT]

Pr 25:11 A word f spoken is like apples of gold in a setting
SS 5:12 beside springs of water, bathed in milk, f set.

FITNESS (1) [FIT]

Sir 30:15 Health and f are better than any gold,

FITTED (3) [FIT]

2Sa 21:16 and who was f out with new weapons,
Ps 11: 2 they have f their arrow to the string,
1Mc 4:57 and the chambers for the priests, and f them

FITTING (19) [FIT]

Ex 36:22 Each frame had two pegs for f together;
Ezr 4:14 of the palace and it is not f for us to witness
Ps 147: 1 for he is gracious, and a song of praise is f.
Pr 19:10 It is not f for a fool to live in luxury,
26: 1 so honor is not f for a fool.
Ecc 5:18 it is f to eat and drink and find enjoyment in all
Ro 16: 2 that you may welcome her in the Lord as is f for
Col 3:18 be subject to your husbands, as is f in the Lord.
Heb 2:10 It was f that God, for whom and
7:26 it was f that we should have such a high priest,
Tob 12: 6 With f honor declare to all people the deeds
12: 7 and with f honor to acknowledge him.
Sir 33:30 Set him to work, as is f for him,
3Mc 1: 9 and made thank offerings and did what was f for
7:13 When they had applauded him in f manner,
4Mc 1:10 On this anniversary it is f for me to praise
9: 6 it would be even more f
9:26 in the next eldest, and after f themselves
11:10 and f iron clamps on them,

FITTINGLY (1) [FIT]

2Mc 15:12 who spoke f and had been trained from childhood

FIVE‡ (293) [FIFTH, FIVE-SIDED, ONE-FIFTH]

Ge 5: 6 When Seth had lived one hundred f years,
5:11 the days of Enosh were nine hundred f years;
5:30 the birth of Noah f hundred ninety-five years,
5:32 After Noah was f hundred years old,
11:11 after the birth of Arpachshad f hundred years,
11:32 The days of Terah were two hundred f years;
14: 9 and King Arioch of Ellasar, four kings against f.
18:28 Suppose f of the fifty righteous are lacking?
18:28 Will you destroy the whole city for lack of f?"
43:34 but Benjamin's portion was f times as much
45: 6 and there are f more years in which there will
45:11 since there are f more years of famine to come—
45:22 of silver and f sets of garments.
47: 2 From among his brothers he took f men
Ex 22: 1 the thief shall pay f oxen for an ox,
26: 3 F curtains shall be joined to one another;
26: 3 the other f curtains shall be joined to one another.
26: 9 You shall join f curtains by themselves,
26:26 f for the frames of the one side of the tabernacle,
26:27 and f bars for the frames of the other side of
26:27 and f bars for the frames of the side of
26:37 You shall make for the screen f pillars of acacia,
26:37 and you shall cast f bases of bronze for them.
27: 1 f cubits long and f cubits wide;
27:18 the width fifty, and the height f cubits,
30:23 of liquid myrrh f hundred shekels,
30:24 and f hundred of cassia—
36:10 He joined f curtains to one another,
36:10 and the other f curtains he joined to one another.
36:16 He joined f curtains by themselves,
36:31 f for the frames of the one side of the tabernacle,
36:32 and f bars for the frames of the other side of
36:32 and f bars for the frames of the tabernacle at
36:38 and its f pillars with their hooks.
36:38 but their f bases were of bronze.
Ex 38: 1 it was f cubits long, and f cubits wide;
38:18 along the width of it, f cubits high,
38:26 six hundred three thousand, f hundred fifty men.
Lev 26: 8 F of you shall give chase to a hundred,
27: 5 If the age is from f to twenty years of age,
27: 6 If the age is from one month to f years,
27: 6 the equivalent for a male is f shekels of silver,
Nu 1:21 of Reuben were forty-six thousand f hundred.
1:33 of Ephraim were forty thousand f hundred.
1:41 of Asher were forty-one thousand f hundred.
1:46 six hundred three thousand f hundred fifty.
2:11 as enrolled of forty-six thousand f hundred.
2:19 as enrolled of forty thousand f hundred.
2:28 as enrolled of forty-one thousand f hundred.
2:32 six hundred three thousand f hundred fifty.
3:22 was seven thousand f hundred.
3:47 you shall accept f shekels apiece,
4:48 enrollment was eight thousand f hundred eighty.
7:17 f rams, f male goats, and f male lambs a year old.
7:23 f rams, f male goats, and f male lambs a year old.
7:29 f rams, f male goats, and f male lambs a year old.
7:35 f rams, f male goats, and f male lambs a year old.
7:41 f rams, f male goats, and f male lambs a year old.
7:47 f rams, f male goats, and f male lambs a year old.
7:53 f rams, f male goats, and f male lambs a year old.
7:59 f rams, f male goats, and f male lambs a year old.
7:65 f rams, f male goats, and f male lambs a year old.
7:71 f rams, f male goats, and f male lambs a year old.
7:77 f rams, f male goats, and f male lambs a year old.
7:83 f rams, f male goats, and f male lambs a year old.
11:19 or f days, or ten days, or twenty days,
18:16 you shall fix at f shekels of silver,
26:18 of those enrolled was forty thousand f hundred.
26:22 enrolled was seventy-six thousand f hundred.
26:27 of those enrolled was sixty thousand f hundred.
26:37 those enrolled was thirty-two thousand f hundred.
31: 8 Zur, Hur, and Reba, the f kings of Midian,
31:28 one item out of every f hundred, whether persons,
31:36 three hundred thirty-seven thousand f hundred
31:39 The donkeys were thirty thousand f hundred,
31:43 three hundred thirty-seven thousand f hundred
31:45 thirty thousand f hundred donkeys,
Jos 8:12 Taking about f thousand men,
10: 5 Then the f kings of the Amorites—
10:16 these f kings fled and hid themselves in the cave
10:17 it was told Joshua, "The f kings have been found,
10:22 and bring those f kings out to me from the cave."
10:23 and brought the f kings out to him from the cave,
10:26 and he hung them on f trees.
13: 3 there are f rulers of the Philistines, those of Gaza,
Jdg 3: 3 the f lords of the Philistines,
18: 2 So the Danites sent f valiant men from
18: 7 The f men went on, and when they came to Laish,
18:14 f men who had gone to spy out the land (that is,
18:17 the f men who had gone to spy out
20:45 f thousand of them were cut down on
1Sa 6: 4 "F gold tumors and five gold mice,
6: 4 "Five gold tumors and f gold mice,
6:16 When the f lords of the Philistines saw it,
6:18 of the Philistines belonging to the f lords,
17: 5 the weight of the coat was f thousand shekels
17:40 and chose f smooth stones from the wadi,
21: 3 Give me f loaves of bread, or whatever is here."
25:18 f sheep ready dressed, f measures of parched grain,
25:42 on a donkey; her f maids attended her.
2Sa 4: 4 He was f years old when the news about Saul
21: 8 and the f sons of Merab daughter of Saul,
24: 9 and those of Judah were f hundred thousand.
1Ki 4:32 and his songs numbered a thousand and f.
6: 6 The lowest story was f cubits wide,
6:10 against the whole house, each story f cubits high,
6:24 F cubits was the length of one wing of the cherub,
6:24 f cubits the length of the other wing of the cherub;
7:16 the height of the one capital was f cubits, and the height of the other capital was f cubits.
7:23 ten cubits from brim to brim, and f cubits high.
7:39 He set f of the stands on the south side of
7:39 and f on the north side of the house;
7:49 f on the south side and f on the north,
9:23 f hundred fifty, who had charge of
2Ki 6:25 of a kab of dove's dung for f shekels of silver.
7:13 "Let some men take f of the remaining horses,
13:19 and said, "You should have struck f or six times;
25:19 and f men of the king's council who were found
1Ch 2: 4 Judah had f sons in all.
2: 6 Zimri, Ethan, Heman, Calcol, and Dara, f in all.
3:20 Ohel, Berechiah, Hasadiah, and Jushab-hesed, f.
4:32 Ain, Rimmon, Tochen, and Ashan, f towns,
4:42 some of them, f hundred men of the Simeonites,
7: 3 Michael, Obadiah, Joel, and Isshiah, f,
7: 7 Ezbon, Uzzi, Uzziel, Jerimoth, and Iri, f,
11:23 a man of great stature, f cubits tall.
29: 7 the service of the house of God f thousand talents
2Ch 3:11 one wing of the one, f cubits long,
3:11 and its other wing, f cubits long,
3:12 f cubits long, touched the wall of the house, and the other wing, also f cubits long,
3:15 with a capital of f cubits on the top of each.
4: 2 ten cubits from rim to rim, and f cubits high.
4: 6 and set f on the right side, and f on the left.
4: 7 f on the south side and f on the north.
4: 8 f on the right side and f on the left.
6:13 a bronze platform f cubits long, f cubits wide,
13:17 f hundred thousand picked men of Israel fell slain.
26:13 of three hundred seven thousand f hundred,
35: 9 the passover offerings f thousand lambs and kids and f hundred bulls.
Ezr 1:11 and silver vessels was f thousand four hundred.
2:69 f thousand minas of silver,
Ne 7:70 fifty basins, and f hundred thirty priestly robes.
Est 9: 6 the Jews killed and destroyed f hundred people.
9:12 of Susa the Jews have killed f hundred people and
Job 1: 3 f hundred yoke of oxen, f hundred donkeys,
Isa 17: 6 four or f on the branches of a fruit tree,
19:18 that day there will be f cities in the land of Egypt
30:17 at the threat of f you shall flee,
Jer 52:22 the height of the one capital was f cubits;
Eze 40: 7 and the space between the recesses, f cubits;
40:30 twenty-five cubits deep and f cubits wide.
40:48 the pilasters of the vestibule, f cubits on
41: 2 and the sidewalls of the entrance were f cubits on
41: 9 the outer wall of the side chambers was f cubits;
41:11 the part that was left free was f cubits all around.
41:12 wall of the building was f cubits thick all around,
42:16 f hundred cubits by the measuring reed.
42:17 f hundred cubits by the measuring reed.
42:18 f hundred cubits by the measuring reed.
42:19 f hundred cubits by the measuring reed.
42:20 a wall around it, f hundred cubits long
42:20 and f hundred cubits wide,
45: 2 of f hundred by f hundred cubits shall be for
45: 6 for the city an area f thousand cubits wide,
48:15 f thousand cubits in width
48:16 the north side four thousand f hundred cubits,
48:16 the south side four thousand f hundred,
48:16 the east side four thousand f hundred,
48:16 and the west side four thousand and f hundred.
48:30 to be four thousand f hundred cubits by measure,
48:32 which is to be four thousand f hundred cubits,
48:33 to be four thousand f hundred cubits by measure,
48:34 which is to be four thousand f hundred cubits,
Mt 14:17 "We have nothing here but f loaves and two fish."
14:19 Taking the f loaves and the two fish,
14:21 And those who ate were about f thousand men,
16: 9 not remember the f loaves for the f thousand,
20: 6 And about f o'clock he went out
20: 9 When those hired about f o'clock came,
25: 2 F of them were foolish, and five were wise.
25: 2 Five of them were foolish, and f were wise.
25:15 to one he gave f talents,
25:16 The one who had received the f talents went off and traded with them, and made f more talents.
25:20 had received the f talents came forward, bringing f more talents, saying, 'Master, you handed over to me f talents; see, I have made f more talents.'
Mk 6:38 they had found out, they said, "F, and two fish."
6:41 Taking the f loaves and the two fish,
6:44 the loaves numbered f thousand men.
8:19 When I broke the f loaves for the f thousand,
Lk 1:24 and for f months she remained in seclusion.
7:41 one owed f hundred denarii, and the other fifty.
9:13 "We have no more than f loaves and two fish—
9:14 For there were about f thousand men.
9:16 And taking the f loaves and the two fish,
12: 6 Are not f sparrows sold for two pennies?
12:52 From now on f in one household will be divided,
14:19 Another said, 'I have bought f yoke of oxen,
16:28 for I have f brothers—
19:18 saying, 'Lord, your pound has made f pounds.'
19:19 He said to him, 'And you, rule over f cities.'
Jn 4:18 for you have had f husbands,
5: 2 in Hebrew Beth-zatha, which has f porticoes.
6: 9 a boy here who has f barley loaves and two fish.
6:10 so they sat down, about f thousand in all.
6:13 and from the fragments of the f barley loaves,
Ac 4: 4 and they numbered about f thousand.
20: 6 and in f days we joined them in Troas,
24: 1 F days later the high priest Ananias came down
1Co 14:19 in church I would rather speak f words
15: 6 Then he appeared to more than f hundred brothers
2Co 11:24 F times I have received from the Jews
Rev 9: 5 They were allowed to torture them for f months,
9:10 to harm people for f months.
17:10 of whom f have fallen, one is living,
Jdt 7:17 together with f thousand Assyrians,
7:30 Let us hold out for f days more;
8: 9 the town to the Assyrians after f days,
8:15 he does not choose to help us within these f days,
16:23 reaching the age of one hundred f.
AdE 9: 6 the city of Susa the Jews killed f hundred people,
9:12 the Jews have destroyed f hundred people.
Wis 10: 6 he escaped the fire that descended on the F Cities.
1Mc 2: 2 He had f sons, John surnamed Gaddi,
4: 1 Now Gorgias took f thousand infantry
4:28 and f thousand cavalry to subdue them.
4:34 there fell of the army of Lysias f thousand men;
6:35 and f hundred picked horsemen were assigned
7:32 About f hundred of the army of Nicanor fell,
10:42 the f thousand shekels of silver
15:31 or else pay me f hundred talents of silver for
15:31 and f hundred talents more for the tribute money
2Mc 2:23 by Jason of Cyrene in f volumes,
10:29 to the enemy from heaven f resplendent men
10:31 Twenty thousand f hundred were slaughtered,
11: 5 a fortified place about f stadia from Jerusalem,
12:10 against Timothy, at least f thousand Arabs
12:10 with f hundred cavalry attacked them.
12:20 and two thousand f hundred cavalry.
13: 2 f thousand three hundred cavalry,
14:39 sent more than f hundred soldiers to arrest him;
1Es 1: 9 the Levites for the passover f thousand sheep
2:14 f thousand four hundred sixty-nine,
5:12 The descendants of Chorbe, seven hundred f.
5:17 The descendants of Baiterus, three thousand f.

1Es 5:43 and **f** thousand **f** hundred twenty-five donkeys.
5:45 **f** thousand minas of silver,
3Mc 5: 2 to drug all the elephants—**f** hundred in number—
2Es 14:24 these **f**, who are trained to write rapidly;
14:37 So I took the **f** men, as he commanded me,
14:42 the Most High gave understanding to the **f** men,

FIVE-SIDED (1) [FIVE, SIDE]

1Ki 6:31 the lintel and the doorposts were **f.**

FIX (8) [FIXED]

Nu 18:16 you shall **f** at five shekels of silver,
Dt 6: 8 **f** them as an emblem on your forehead,
11:18 and **f** them as an emblem on your forehead.
Job 14: 3 Do you **f** your eyes on such a one?
Ps 119:15 and **f** my eyes on your ways.
Am 9: 4 and I will **f** my eyes on them for harm and not
AdE 3: 7 to **f** on one day to destroy the whole race
Wis 6:15 To **f** one's thought on her

FIXED (25) [FIX]

Ge 41:32 of Pharaoh's dream means that the thing is **f**
47:22 for the priests had a **f** allowance from Pharaoh,
Dt 32: 8 he **f** the boundaries of the peoples according to
1Sa 9:20 And on whom is all Israel's desire **f,**
2Ki 8:11 He **f** his gaze and stared at him,
Est 9:32 The command of Queen Esther **f** these practices
Ps 74:17 You have **f** all the bounds of the earth;
119: 6 having my eyes **f** on all your commandments.
119:89 your word is firmly **f** in heaven.
148: 6 he **f** their bounds, which cannot be passed.
Ecc 12:11 and like nails firmly **f** are the collected sayings
Jer 31:35 who gives the sun for light by day and the **f** order
31:36 this **f** order were ever to cease from my presence,
Eze 4:10 at **f** times you shall eat it.
4:11 at **f** times you shall drink.
42:10 width of the passage is **f** by the wall of the court.
45:14 and as the **f** portion of oil, one-tenth of a bath
Lk 4:20 The eyes of all in the synagogue were **f** on him.
16:26 between you and us a great chasm has been **f,**
Ac 3: 5 And he **f** his attention on them,
17:31 because he has **f** a day on which he will have
AdE 1: 8 The drinking was not according to a **f** rule;
Sir 17: 2 He gave them a **f** number of days,
49: 3 He kept his heart **f** on the Lord;
2Es 16:56 At his word the stars were **f** in their places,

FLABBY (1)

4Mc 7:13 his body no longer tense and firm, his muscles **f,**

FLAG (KJV) See REED

FLAGONS (5)

Ex 25:29 and its **f** and bowls with which
37:16 and **f** with which to pour drink offerings.
Nu 4: 7 the bowls, and the **f** for the drink offering;
Est 1: 8 Drinking was by **f,** without restraint;
Isa 22:24 every small vessel, from the cups to all the **f.**

FLAGSTAFF (1)

Isa 30:17 until you are left like a **f** on the top of a mountain,

FLAILING (2)

Eze 16: 6 and saw you **f** about in your blood,
16:22 of your youth, when you were naked and bare, **f**

FLAKY (1)

Ex 16:14 of the wilderness was a fine **f** substance,

FLAME (38) [AFLAME, FLAMED, FLAMES, FLAMING]

Ex 3: 2 of the LORD appeared to him in a **f** of fire out of
Nu 21:28 **f** from the city of Sihon.
Jdg 13:20 When the **f** went up toward heaven from the altar,
13:20 the angel of the LORD ascended in the **f** of
Job 15:30 the **f** will dry up their shoots,
18: 5 and the **f** of their fire does not shine.
41:21 and a **f** comes out of its mouth.
Ps 83:14 as the **f** sets the mountains ablaze,
104: 4 winds your messengers, fire and **f** your ministers.
106:18 the **f** burned up the wicked.
SS 8: 6 Its flashes are flashes of fire, a raging **f.**
Isa 5:24 and as dry grass sinks down in the **f,**
10:17 and his Holy One a **f;**
29: 6 and the **f** of a devouring fire.
30:30 in furious anger and a **f** of devouring fire,
43: 2 and the **f** shall not consume you.
47:14 from the power of the **f.**
50:11 Walk in the **f** of your fire,
Jer 48:45 a **f** from the house of Sihon;
Eze 20:47 the blazing **f** shall not be quenched,
Da 11:33 however, they shall fall by sword and **f,**
Joel 2: 3 and behind them a **f** burns.
2: 5 the crackling of a **f** of fire devouring the stubble,
Ob 1:18 of Joseph a **f,** and the house of Esau stubble;
Ac 7:30 in the **f** of a burning bush.
Rev 1:14 his eyes were like a **f** of fire,
2:18 who has eyes like a **f** of fire,
19:12 His eyes are like a **f** of fire,
Wis 10:17 and a starry **f** through the night.
16:18 At one time the **f** was restrained,
Sir 28:22 they will not be burned in its **f.**
Aza 1:26 and drove the fiery **f** out of the furnace,
1Mc 2:59 and Mishael believed and were saved from the **f.**
2Mc 1:32 When this was done, a **f** blazed up;
3Mc 6: 6 the fiery furnace with dew and turning the **f**
2Es 4:48 and when the **f** had gone by I looked, and lo,
7:61 and are similar to a **f** and smoke—
4Mc 18:14 the **f** shall not consume you.'

FLAMED (3) [FLAME]

2Sa 22: 9 glowing coals **f** forth from him.
22:13 of the brightness before him coals of fire **f** forth.
Ps 18: 8 glowing coals **f** forth from him.

FLAMES‡ (18) [FLAME]

Ps 29: 7 The voice of the LORD flashes forth **f** of fire.
Isa 33:14 Who among us can live with everlasting **f?"**
66:15 and his rebuke in **f** of fire.
Da 3:22 the raging **f** killed the men who lifted Shadrach,
7: 9 his throne was fiery **f,** and its wheels were burning
Joel 1:19 and **f** have burned all the trees of the field.
Hab 2:13 of hosts that peoples labor only to feed the **f,**
Lk 16:24 for I am in agony in these **f.'**
Heb 1: 7 and his servants **f** of fire."
Wis 17: 5 nor did the brilliant **f** of the stars avail to illumine
19:21 **F,** on the contrary, failed to consume the flesh
Aza 1: 1 They walked around in the midst of the **f,**
1:24 **f** poured out above the furnace forty-nine cubits,
3Mc 6: 6 to the **f** so as not to serve vain things,
2Es 13:38 to be tortured (which were symbolized by the **f**),
4Mc 3:17 the emotions and quench the **f** of frenzied desires;
9:19 fanning the **f** they tightened the wheel further.
17: 1 into the **f** so that no one might touch her body.

FLAMING (18) [FLAME]

Ge 3:24 a sword **f** and turning to guard the way to the tree
15:17 and a **f** torch passed between these pieces.
Job 41:19 From its mouth go **f** torches;
Isa 4: 5 and smoke and the shining of a **f** fire by night.
La 2: 3 he has burned like a **f** fire in Jacob,
Da 10: 6 his face like lightning, his eyes like **f** torches,
Hos 7: 6 in the morning it blazes like a **f** fire.
Zec 12: 6 like a **f** torch among sheaves;
Eph 6:16 be able to quench all the **f** arrows of the evil one.
2Th 1: 8 in **f** fire, inflicting vengeance on those who do
Rev 4: 5 and in front of the throne burn seven **f** torches,
Wis 18: 3 Therefore you provided a **f** pillar of fire as a guide
Sir 8:10 or you may be burned in their **f** fire.
45:19 against them to consume them in **f** fire.
1Mc 6:39 with them and gleamed like **f** torches.
2Es 4:48 and lo, a **f** furnace passed by before me,
13:10 and from his lips a **f** breath,
13:11 stream of fire and the **f** breath and the great storm,

FLANK (2) [FLANKED, FLANKS, OUTFLANKED]

Eze 25: 9 the **f** of Moab from the towns on its frontier,
34:21 Because you pushed with **f** and shoulder,

FLANKED (1) [FLANK]

1Mc 9:12 **F** by the two companies, the phalanx advanced to

FLANKS (2) [FLANK]

1Mc 6:38 on the two **f** of the army,
2Mc 15:20 and the cavalry deployed on the **f,**

FLAP (1)

Job 39:13 "The ostrich's wings **f** wildly,

FLASH (11) [FLASHED, FLASHES, FLASHING]

Job 15:12 and why do your eyes **f,**
41:18 Its sneezes **f** forth light, and its eyes are like
Ps 144: 6 Make the lightning **f** and scatter them;
Eze 1:14 The living creatures darted to and fro, like a **f**
21:10 honed to **f** like lightning!
21:28 for slaughter Polished to consume, to **f**
Am 5: 9 who makes destruction **f** out against the strong,
Lk 10:18 "I watched Satan fall from heaven like a **f**
Wis 11:18 or **f** terrible sparks from their eyes;
2Mc 5: 3 the **f** of golden trappings, and armor of all kinds.
2Es 16:10 He will **f** lightning, and who will not be afraid?

FLASHED (6) [FLASH]

Ps 18:14 he **f** forth lightnings, and routed them.
77:17 your arrows **f** on every side.
105:32 and lightning that **f** through their land.
Ac 9: 3 suddenly a light from heaven **f** around him.
Wis 16:22 that blazed in the hail and **f** in the showers of rain;
2Es 10:25 her countenance **f** like lightning,

FLASHES (12) [FLASH]

Ps 29: 7 The voice of the LORD **f** forth flames of fire.
SS 8: 6 Its **f** are **f** of fire, a raging flame.
Na 2: 3 the chariots **f** on the day when he musters them;
Mt 24:27 the lightning comes from the east and **f** as far as
Lk 17:24 the lightning **f** and lights up the sky from one side
Rev 4: 5 Coming from the throne are **f** of lightning,
8: 5 rumblings, **f** of lightning, and an earthquake.
11:19 and there were **f** of lightning, rumblings,
16:18 And there came **f** of lightning, rumblings,
LtJ 6:61 So also the lightning, when it **f,** is widely seen;
2Es 6: 2 and before the **f** of lightning shone,

FLASHING (9) [FLASH]

Ex 9:24 there was hail with fire **f** continually in the midst
Dt 32:41 when I whet my **f** sword, and my hand takes hold
Job 39:23 Upon it rattle the quiver, the **f** spear,
Ps 76: 3 There he broke the **f** arrows, the shield, the sword,
Eze 1: 4 around it and fire **f** forth continually,
21:15 Ah! It is made for **f,** it is polished for slaughter.
Na 3: 3 Horsemen charging, **f** sword and glittering spear,
Hab 3:11 at the gleam of your **f** spear.
4Mc 4:10 with lightning **f** from their weapons appeared

FLASK (3) [FLASKS]

2Ki 9: 1 take this **f** of oil in your hand,
9: 3 Then take the **f** of oil, pour it on his head, and say,
Jdt 10: 5 She gave her maid a skin of wine and a **f** of oil,

FLASKS (1) [FLASK]

Mt 25: 4 but the wise took **f** of oil with their lamps.

FLAT (3)

Jos 6: 5 and the wall of the city will fall down **f,**
6:20 and the wall fell down **f;**
1Ch 9:31 was in charge of making the **f** cakes.

FLATTER (4) [FLATTERED, FLATTERING, FLATTERS, FLATTERY]

Job 32:22 For I do not know how to **f—**
Ps 5: 9 they **f** with their tongues.
36: 2 For they **f** themselves in their own eyes
Wis 14:17 so that by their zeal they might **f** the absent one as

FLATTERED (1) [FLATTER]

Ps 78:36 But they **f** him with their mouths;

FLATTERING (5) [FLATTER]

Ps 12: 2 with **f** lips and a double heart they speak.
12: 3 May the LORD cut off all **f** lips,
Pr 26:28 and a **f** mouth works ruin.
Eze 12:24 or **f** divination within the house of Israel.
Jude 1:16 **f** people to their own advantage.

FLATTERS (3) [FLATTER]

Pr 28:23 will afterward find more favor than one who **f**
29: 5 Whoever **f** a neighbor is spreading a net for
1Es 4:31 if she loses her temper with him, he **f** her,

FLATTERY (4) [FLATTER]

Job 32:21 I will not show partiality to any person or use **f**
Eze 33:31 For **f** is on their lips,
Ro 16:18 and by smooth talk and **f** they deceive the hearts
1Th 2: 5 we never came with words of **f** or with a pretext

FLAUNTED (1)

Eze 23:18 on her whorings so openly and **f** her nakedness,

FLAVOR (2)

Job 6: 6 or is there any **f** in the juice of mallows?
Jer 48:11 his **f** has remained and his aroma is unspoiled.

FLAW (1) [FLAWLESS]

SS 4: 7 there is no **f** in you.

FLAWLESS (1) [FLAW]

SS 6: 9 the darling of her mother, **f** to her that bore her.

FLAX (8)

Ex 9:31 (Now the **f** and the barley were ruined, for the barley was in the ear and the **f** was in bud.
Jos 2: 6 up to the roof and hidden them with the stalks of **f**
Jdg 15:14 and the ropes that were on his arms became like **f**
Pr 31:13 She seeks wool and **f,** and works
Isa 19: 9 The workers in **f** will be in despair,
Hos 2: 5 my wool and my **f,** my oil and my drink."
2: 9 and I will take away my wool and my **f,**

FLAY (1) [FLAYED]

Mic 3: 3 **f** their skin off them, break their bones in pieces,

FLAY (KJV) See also SKIN

FLAYED (2) [FLAY]

Lev 1: 6 burnt offering shall be **f** and cut up into its parts.
4Mc 9:28 **f** all his flesh up to his chin,

FLEA (2)

1Sa 24:14 A dead dog? A single **f?**
26:20 the king of Israel has come out to seek a single **f,**

FLED‡ (184) [FLEE]

Ge 14:10 and as the kings of Sodom and Gomorrah **f,**
14:10 and the rest **f** to the hill country.
31:21 So he **f** with all that he had;
31:22 On the third day Laban was told that Jacob had **f.**
31:40 and my sleep **f** from my eyes.
35: 1 to the God who appeared to you when you **f**
35: 7 that God had revealed himself to him when he **f**

Ge 39:12 But he left his garment in her hand, and f
39:13 in her hand and had f outside,
39:15 he left his garment beside me, and f outside."
39:18 he left his garment beside me, and f outside."
Ex 2:15 But Moses f from Pharaoh.
14:5 the king of Egypt was told that the people had f,
14:27 As the Egyptians f before it,
Nu 16:34 All Israel around them f at their outcry,
35:32 Nor shall you accept ransom for one who has f to
Jos 7:4 and they f before the men of Ai.
8:15 and f in the direction of the wilderness.
8:20 for the people who f to the wilderness turned back
10:11 As they f before Israel, while they were going
10:16 these five kings f and hid themselves in the cave
Jdg 1:6 Adoni-bezek f; but they pursued him,
4:15 Sisera got down from his chariot and f away
4:17 Now Sisera had f away on foot to the tent
7:21 in camp ran; they cried out and f.
7:22 the army f as far as Beth-shittah toward Zererah,
8:12 Zebah and Zalmunna f;
9:21 Then Jotham ran away and f, going to Beer,
9:40 Abimelech chased him, and he f before him.
9:51 the lords of the city f to it and shut themselves in;
11:3 Then Jephthah f from his brothers and lived in
20:45 When they turned and f toward the wilderness to
20:47 and f toward the wilderness to the rock
1Sa 4:10 Israel was defeated, and they f,
4:16 I f from the battle today."
4:17 "Israel has f before the Philistines,
17:24 f from him and were very much afraid.
17:51 that their champion was dead, they f.
19:8 so that they f before him.
19:10 David f and escaped that night.
19:12 through the window; he f away and escaped.
19:18 Now David f and escaped;
20:1 David f from Naioth in Ramah.
21:10 David rose and f that day from Saul;
22:17 they knew that he f, and did not disclose it
22:20 named Abiathar, escaped and f after David.
23:6 Abiathar son of Ahimelech f to David at Keilah,
27:4 When Saul was told that David had f to Gath,
30:17 who mounted camels and f.
31:1 and the men of Israel f before the Philistines,
31:7 the Jordan saw that the men of Israel had f and
31:7 they forsook their towns and f;
2Sa 1:4 He answered, "The army f from the battle,
4:3 (Now the people of Beeroth had f to Gittaim
4:4 His nurse picked him up and f;
10:13 against the Arameans; and they f before him.
10:14 When the Ammonites saw that the Arameans f,
10:14 they likewise f before Abishai,
10:18 The Arameans f before Israel;
13:29 and each mounted his mule and f.
13:34 But Absalom f. When the young man
13:37 But Absalom f, and went to Talmai son
13:38 Absalom, having f to Geshur,
18:17 Meanwhile all the Israelites f to their homes.
19:8 Meanwhile, all the Israelites had f to their homes.
19:9 now he has f out of the land because of Absalom.
23:11 and the army f from the Philistines.
1Ki 2:7 for with such loyalty they met me when I f
2:28 Joab f to the tent of the LORD and grasped
2:29 "Joab has f to the tent of the LORD and now is
11:17 but Hadad f to Egypt with some
11:23 Rezon son of Eliada, who had f from his master,
11:40 but Jeroboam promptly f to Egypt,
12:2 where he had f from King Solomon),
19:3 Then he was afraid; he got up and f for his life,
20:20 the Arameans f and Israel pursued them,
20:30 The rest f into the city of Aphek;
20:30 Ben-hadad also f, and entered the city to hide.
2Ki 3:24 up and attacked the Moabites, who f before them;
7:7 So they f away in the twilight
7:7 the camp just as it was, and f for their lives.
8:21 who had surrounded him; but his army f home.
9:10 Then he opened the door and f.
9:23 Then Joram reined about and f,
9:27 he f in the direction of Beth-haggan.
9:27 Then he f to Megiddo, and died there.
14:12 Judah was defeated by Israel; everyone f home.
14:19 a conspiracy against him in Jerusalem, and he f
25:4 the king with all the soldiers f by night by the way
1Ch 10:1 and the men of Israel f before the Philistines,
10:7 in the valley saw that the army had f and that Saul
10:7 they abandoned their towns and f;
11:13 Now the people had f from the Philistines,
19:14 for battle; and they f before him.
19:15 When the Ammonites saw that the Arameans f,
19:15 they likewise f before Abishai, Joab's brother,
19:18 The Arameans f before Israel;
2Ch 10:2 where he had f from King Solomon),
13:16 The Israelites f before Judah,
14:12 and before Judah, and the Ethiopians f.
25:22 Judah was defeated by Israel; everyone f home.
25:27 a conspiracy against him in Jerusalem, and he f
Ps 3:T *A Psalm of David, when he f from his son*
57:T *A Miktam, when he f from Saul,*
114:3 The sea looked and f; Jordan turned back.
143:9 I have f to you for refuge.
Isa 10:29 Ramah trembles, Gibeah of Saul has f.
20:6 and to whom we f for help and deliverance from
21:15 For they have f from the swords,
22:3 Your rulers have all f together;
22:3 though they had f far away.
33:3 At the sound of tumult, peoples f;
38:15 my sleep has f because of the bitterness of my soul.
Jer 4:25 and all the birds of the air had f.
Jer 9:10 both the birds of the air and the animals have f
26:21 he was afraid and f and escaped to Egypt.
39:4 they f, going out of the city at night by way of
46:5 their warriors are beaten down, and have f
46:15 Why has Apis f? Why did your bull
46:21 they too have turned and f together,
52:7 the soldiers f and went out from the city by night
La 1:6 they f without strength before the pursuer.
Da 6:18 no food was brought to him, and sleep f
10:7 and they f and hid themselves.
Hos 12:12 Jacob f to the land of Aram,
Am 5:19 if someone f from a lion, and was met by a bear;
Jnh 4:2 That is why I f to Tarshish at the beginning;
Zec 14:5 and you shall flee as you f from the earthquake in
Mt 26:56 Then all the disciples deserted him and f.
Mk 14:50 All of them deserted him and f.
16:8 So they went out and f from the tomb,
Ac 7:29 Moses f and became a resident alien in the land
14:6 of it and f to Lystra and Derbe, cities of Lycaonia,
19:16 that they f out of the house naked and wounded.
Rev 12:6 and the woman f into the wilderness,
16:20 And every island f away,
20:11 the earth and the heaven f from his presence,
Tob 1:21 and they f to the mountains of Ararat,
8:3 the demon that he f to the remotest parts of Egypt.
Jdt 5:8 So they f to Mesopotamia,
11:3 But now tell me why you have f from them
11:16 when I, your slave, learned all this, I f from them.
15:2 and f by every path across the plain and through
AdE 14:1 seized with deadly anxiety, f to the Lord.
Wis 10:10 When a righteous man f from his brother's wrath,
1Mc 1:18 and Ptolemy turned and f before him,
1:38 Because of them the residents of Jerusalem f;
2:28 and his sons f to the hills and left all that they had
2:44 the survivors f to the Gentiles for safety.
3:11 Many were wounded and fell, and the rest f.
3:24 and the rest f into the land of the Philistines.
4:14 The Gentiles were crushed, and f into the plain,
4:22 they all f into the land of the Philistines.
5:9 But they f to the stronghold of Dathema,
5:11 and capture the stronghold to which we have f,
5:34 of Timothy realized that it was Maccabeus, they f
5:43 and f into the sacred precincts at Carnaim.
6:4 So he f and in great disappointment left there
6:6 but had turned and f before the Jews;
7:32 and the rest f into the city of David.
7:44 they threw down their arms and f.
9:18 Judas also fell, and the rest f.
9:33 and they f into the wilderness of Tekoa
9:40 and the rest f to the mountain;
10:12 in the strongholds that Bacchides had built f;
10:49 and the army of Demetrius f,
10:64 and saw him clothed in purple, they all f.
10:82 they were overwhelmed by him and f,
10:83 They f to Azotus and entered Beth-dagon,
11:16 Alexander f into Arabia to find protection there,
11:46 But the king f into the palace.
11:55 against Demetrius, and he f and was routed.
11:70 All the men with Jonathan f;
11:72 against the enemy and routed them, and they f.
15:21 any scoundrels have f to you from their country,
16:8 many of them fell wounded and the rest f into
16:10 They also f into the towers that were in the fields
2Mc 5:7 and f again into the country of the Ammonites.
8:33 who had f into one little house;
10:32 Timothy himself f to a stronghold called Gazara,
14:14 who had f before Judas, flocked to join Nicanor,
2Es 8:53 Hades has f and corruption has been forgotten;
10:3 I got up in the night and f,
4Mc 4:1 he f the country with the purpose of betraying it.

FLEDGLINGS (2)

Dt 22:6 in any tree or on the ground, with f or eggs,
22:6 with the mother sitting on the f or on the eggs,

FLEE (111) [FLED, FLEEING, FLEES]

Ge 19:17 they said, "F for your life;
19:17 f to the hills, or else you will be consumed."
19:19 but I cannot f to the hills,
19:20 Look, that city is near enough to f to,
27:43 f at once to my brother Laban in Haran,
31:20 in that he did not tell him that he intended to f.
31:27 Why did you f secretly and deceive me and
Ex 14:25 The Egyptians said, "Let us f from the Israelites,
21:13 for you a place to which the killer may f.
Lev 26:17 and you shall f though no one pursues you.
26:36 and they shall f as one flees from the sword,
Nu 10:35 and your foes f before you."
35:6 where you shall permit a slayer to f,
35:11 a person without intent may f there.
35:15 a person without intent may f there.
Dt 4:42 to which a homicide could f,
4:42 homicide could f to one of these cities and live:
19:3 so that any homicide can f to one of them.
19:4 the case of a homicide who might f there and live,
19:5 the killer may f to one of these cities and live.
28:7 and f before you seven ways.
28:25 you shall go out against them one way and f
Jos 8:5 as before, we shall f from them.
8:6 as before.' While we f from them,
8:20 They had no power to f this way or that,
20:3 a person without intent or by mistake may f there;
20:4 The slayer shall f to one of these cities
20:9 a person without intent could f there,
2Sa 4:4 and, in her haste to f,
15:14 Let us f, or there will be no escape for us
2Sa 17:2 and all the people who are with him will f.
18:3 For if we f, they will not care about us.
19:3 as soldiers steal in who are ashamed when they f
24:13 Or will you f three months before your foes
1Ki 12:18 then hurriedly mounted his chariot to f
2Ki 9:3 Then open the door and f; do not linger."
2Ch 10:18 King Rehoboam hurriedly mounted his chariot to f
Job 9:25 they f away, they see no good.
20:24 They will f from an iron weapon;
27:22 they f from its power in headlong flight.
41:28 The arrow cannot make it f;
Ps 11:1 "F like a bird to the mountains;
31:11 those who see me in the street f from me.
55:7 I would f far away; I would lodge in the
68:1 let those who hate him f before him.
68:12 "The kings of the armies, they f, they f!"
104:7 At your rebuke they f; at the
114:5 Why is it, O sea, that you f?
139:7 Or where can I f from your presence?
Pr 28:1 The wicked f when no one pursues,
SS 2:17 Until the day breathes and the shadows f, turn,
4:6 Until the day breathes and the shadows f,
Isa 10:3 To whom will you f for help,
10:31 the inhabitants of Gebim f for safety.
13:14 and all will f to their own lands.
15:5 his fugitives f to Zoar, to Eglath-shelishiyah.
17:11 yet the harvest will f away in a day of grief
17:13 but he will rebuke them, and they will f far away,
30:16 We will f upon horses"—therefore you shall flee!
30:16 upon horses"—therefore you shall f!
30:17 A thousand shall f at the threat of one,
30:17 at the threat of five you shall f,
31:8 he shall f from the sword,
35:10 and sorrow and sighing shall f away.
48:20 Go out from Babylon, f from Chaldea,
51:11 and sorrow and sighing shall f away.
Jer 4:6 Raise a standard toward Zion, f for safety,
6:1 F for safety, O children of Benjamin,
46:6 swift cannot f away, nor can the warrior escape;
48:6 F! Save yourselves!
49:8 F, turn back, get down low, inhabitants of Dedan!
49:24 Damascus has become feeble, she turned to f,
49:30 F, wander far away, hide in deep places,
50:3 both human beings and animals shall f away.
50:8 F from Babylon, and go out of the land of
50:16 and all of them shall f to their own land.
51:6 F from the midst of Babylon, save your lives,
Da 4:14 Let the animals f from beneath it and the birds
Am 2:16 among the mighty shall f away naked in that day,
7:12 f away to the land of Judah, earn your bread there,
9:1 not one of them shall f away,
Jnh 1:3 to f to Tarshish from the presence of the LORD.
Zec 2:6 F from the land of the north, says the LORD;
14:5 And you shall f by the valley of
14:5 and you shall f as you fled from the earthquake in
Mt 2:13 and f to Egypt, and remain there until I tell you;
3:7 Who warned you to f from the wrath to come?
10:23 they persecute you in one town, f to the next;
24:16 then those in Judea must f to the mountains;
Mk 13:14 then those in Judea must f to the mountains;
Lk 3:7 Who warned you to f from the wrath to come?
21:21 Then those in Judea must f to the mountains,
1Co 10:14 my dear friends, f from the worship of idols.
Jas 4:7 Resist the devil, and he will f from you.
Rev 9:6 they will long to die, but death will f from them.
Tob 4:21 You have great wealth if you fear God and f
6:8 and every affliction will f away and never remain
6:18 the demon will smell it and f,
Jdt 14:3 and they will f before you.
Wis 1:5 a holy and disciplined spirit will f from deceit,
Sir 21:2 F from sin as from a snake;
LtJ 6:55 their priests will f and escape,
6:68 for they can f to shelter and help themselves.
1Mc 9:10 be it from us to do such a thing as to f from them.
10:73 where there is no stone or pebble, or place to f."
2Mc 8:24 and forced them all to f.
11:11 and forced all the rest to f.
2Es 2:36 F from the shadow of this age,
15:32 and silenced by their power, and shall turn and f.
16:41 Let the one who sells be like one who will f;

FLEE, FLEETH (KJV) See also BE OFF, FLIGHT, FLY, FUGITIVE, HURRIED, RUN AWAY, RUNNING AWAY, SHRINK FROM

FLEECE (9)

Dt 18:4 as well as the first of the f of your sheep,
Jdg 6:37 to lay a f of wool on the threshing floor;
6:37 if there is dew on the f alone,
6:38 he rose early next morning and squeezed the f,
6:38 he wrung enough dew from the f to fill a bowl
6:39 please, make trial with the f just once more;
6:39 let it be dry only on the f,
6:40 It was dry on the f only,
Job 31:20 and who was not warmed with the f of my sheep;

FLEEING (11) [FLEE]

Jos 8:6 for they will say, 'They are f from us, as before.'
1Sa 14:22 of Ephraim heard that the Philistines were f,
Job 26:13 his hand pierced the f serpent.
Isa 27:1 the f serpent, Leviathan the twisting serpent,
Jer 48:19 Ask the man f and the woman escaping;
Jnh 1:10 For the men knew that he was f from the presence
Tob 1:18 to death when he came f from Judea in those days

Jdt 10:12 but I am **f** from them,
Sir 11:10 and by **f** you will not escape.
1Mc 11:73 When his men who were **f** saw this,
2Mc 5: 8 **f** from city to city, pursued by everyone,

FLEES (5) [FLEE]

Lev 26:36 and they shall flee as one **f** from the sword,
Dt 19:11 and **f** into one of these cities,
Job 14: 2 **f** like a shadow and does not last.
Isa 24:18 Whoever **f** at the sound of the terror shall fall into
Jer 48:44 Everyone who **f** from the terror shall fall into

FLEET (10) [FLEETING]

1Ki 9:26 King Solomon built a **f** of ships at Ezion-geber,
9:27 Hiram sent his servants with the **f**,
10:11 Moreover, the **f** of Hiram,
10:22 the king had a **f** of ships of Tarshish at sea with
10:22 of ships of Tarshish at sea with the **f** of Hiram.
10:22 Once every three years the **f** of ships
1Mc 1:17 and elephants and cavalry and with a large **f**.
2Mc 12: 9 by night and set fire to the harbor and the **f**,
14: 1 the harbor of Tripolis with a strong army and a **f**,
3Mc 7:17 a characteristic of the place, the **f** waited for them,

FLEETING (5) [FLEET]

Ps 39: 4 let me know how **f** my life is.
Pr 21: 6 a lying tongue is a **f** vapor and a snare of death.
Heb 11:25 the people of God than to enjoy the **f** pleasures
Wis 16:27 when simply warmed by a **f** ray of the sun,
Sir 41:11 The human body is a **f** thing,

FLESH‡ (322) [FLESHLY, FLESHPOTS]

A. ALL FLESH (37)
B. ONE FLESH (8)

Ge 2:21 of his ribs and closed up its place with **f**.
2:23 at last is bone of my bones and **f** of my flesh;
2:23 at last is bone of my bones and flesh of my **f**;
2:24 and clings to his wife, and they become one **f**. B
6: 3 not abide in mortals forever, for they are **f**;
6:12 for all **f** had corrupted its ways upon the earth. A
6:13 "I have determined to make an end of all **f**, A
6:17 under heaven all **f** in which is the breath of life; A
6:19 And of every living thing, of all **f**, A
7:15 and two of all **f** in which there was the breath A
7:16 And those that entered, male and female of all **f**, A
7:21 And all **f** died that moved on the earth, birds, A
8:17 that is with you of all **f**— A
9: 4 Only, you shall not eat **f** with its life, that is,
9:11 never again shall all **f** be cut off by the waters A
9:15 and you and every living creature of all **f**; A
9:15 a flood to destroy all **f**. A
9:16 between God and every living creature of all **f** A
9:17 that I have established between me and all **f** A
17:11 You shall circumcise the **f** of your foreskins,
17:13 be in your **f** an everlasting covenant.
17:14 not circumcised in the **f** of his foreskin shall
17:23 and he circumcised the **f** of their foreskins
17:24 when he was circumcised in the **f** of his foreskin.
17:25 when he was circumcised in the **f** of his foreskin.
29:14 "Surely you are my bone and my **f**!"
37:27 for he is our brother, our own **f**."
40:19 and the birds will eat the **f** from you."
Ex 21:28 the ox shall be stoned, and its **f** shall not be eaten;
28:42 linen undergarments to cover their naked **f**;
29:14 But the **f** of the bull, and its skin, and its dung,
29:31 and boil its **f** in a holy place;
29:32 the **f** of the ram and the bread that is in the basket,
29:34 If any of the **f** for the ordination, or of the bread,
Lev 4:11 But the skin of the bull and all its **f**,
6:27 Whatever touches its **f** shall become holy;
7:15 And the **f** of your thanksgiving sacrifice
7:17 of the **f** of the sacrifice shall be burned up on
7:18 of the **f** of your sacrifice of well-being is eaten on
7:19 **F** that touches any unclean thing shall not
7:19 As for other **f**, all who are clean may eat such **f**.
7:20 But those who eat **f** from the LORD's sacrifice
7:21 eats **f** from the LORD's sacrifice of well-being,
8:17 But the bull itself, its skin and **f** and its dung,
8:31 "Boil the **f** at the entrance of the tent of meeting,
8:32 of the **f** and the bread you shall burn with fire.
9:11 and the **f** and the skin he burned with fire outside
11: 8 Of their **f** you shall not eat,
11:11 Of their **f** you shall not eat,
12: 3 On the eighth day the **f** of his foreskin shall
13:10 and there is quick raw **f** in the swelling,
13:14 if raw **f** ever appears on him, he shall be unclean;
13:15 the raw **f** and pronounce him unclean.
13:15 Raw **f** is unclean, for it is a leprous disease.
13:16 But if the raw **f** again turns white,
13:24 the skin and the raw **f** of the burn becomes a spot,
16:27 and their **f** and their dung shall be consumed
17:11 For the life of the **f** is in the blood;
18:12 of your father's sister; she is your father's **f**.
18:13 for she is your mother's **f**.
18:17 they are your **f**; it is depravity.
19:28 You shall not make any gashes in your **f** for
20:19 for that is to lay bare one's own **f**;
21: 5 or make any gashes in their **f**.
25:49 of their own **f** may redeem them;
26:29 You shall eat the **f** of your sons, and you shall eat the **f** of your daughters.
Nu 12:12 whose **f** is half consumed when it comes out
16:22 and said, "O God, the God of the spirits of all **f**, A
18:18 but their **f** shall be yours,
Nu 19: 5 its skin, its **f**, and its blood, with its dung,
27:16 the God of the spirits of all **f**, A
Dt 5:26 For who is there of all **f** that has heard the voice A
28:53 the **f** of your own sons and daughters whom
28:55 of the **f** of his children whom he is eating,
32:42 and my sword shall devour **f**—
Jdg 8: 7 I will trample your **f** on the thorns of
9: 2 Remember also that I am your bone and your **f**."
1Sa 17:44 and I will give your **f** to the birds of the air and to
2Sa 5: 1 and said, "Look, we are your bone and **f**.
19:12 You are my kin, you are my bone and my **f**;
19:13 say to Amasa, 'Are you not my bone and my **f**?
1Ki 19:21 he boiled their **f**, and gave it to the people,
21:27 and put sackcloth over his bare **f**;
2Ki 4:34 the **f** of the child became warm.
5:10 your **f** shall be restored and you shall be clean."
5:14 his **f** was restored like the **f** of a young boy,
9:36 'In the territory of Jezreel the dogs shall eat the **f**
1Ch 11: 1 "See, we are your bone and **f**.
2Ch 32: 8 With him is an arm of **f**;
Ne 5: 5 Now our **f** is the same as that of our kindred;
Job 2: 5 now and touch his bone and his **f**,
4:15 the hair of my **f** bristled.
6:12 the strength of stones, or is my **f** bronze?
7: 5 My **f** is clothed with worms and dirt;
10: 4 Do you have eyes of **f**?
10:11 You clothed me with skin and **f**,
13:14 I will take my **f** in my teeth,
19:20 My bones cling to my skin and to my **f**,
19:22 like God, pursue me, never satisfied with my **f**?
19:26 then in my **f** I shall see God,
21: 6 and shuddering seizes my **f**.
31:31 'O that we might be sated with his **f**!'—
33:21 Their **f** is so wasted away that it cannot be seen;
33:25 let his **f** become fresh with youth;
34:15 all **f** would perish together, A
41:23 The folds of its **f** cling together;
Ps 27: 2 When evildoers assail me to devour my **f**—
38: 3 There is no soundness in my **f** because
38: 7 and there is no soundness in my **f**.
50:13 Do I eat the **f** of bulls, or drink the blood of goats?
56: 4 what can **f** do to me?
63: 1 my **f** faints for you, as in a dry and weary land
65: 2 To you all **f** shall come. A
73:26 My **f** and my heart may fail,
78:27 he rained **f** upon them like dust, winged birds like
78:39 He remembered that they were but **f**,
79: 2 **f** of your faithful to the wild animals of the earth.
84: 2 my heart and my **f** sing for joy to the living God.
119:120 My **f** trembles for fear of you,
136:25 who gives food to all **f**, A
145:21 all **f** will bless his holy name forever and ever. A
Pr 3: 8 It will be a healing for your **f** and a refreshment
4:22 and healing to all their **f**.
5:11 when your **f** and body are consumed,
14:30 A tranquil mind gives life to the **f**,
Ecc 2: 8 and delights of the **f**, and many concubines.
4: 5 Fools fold their hands and consume their own **f**.
12:12 and much study is a weariness of the **f**.
Isa 9:20 they devoured the **f** of their own kindred;
17: 4 and the fat of his **f** will grow lean.
31: 3 their horses are **f**, and not spirit.
49:26 I will make your oppressors eat their own **f**,
49:26 Then all **f** shall know that I am the LORD A
65: 4 who eat swine's **f**, with broth of abominable things
66:16 and by his sword, on all **f**; A
66:17 eating the **f** of pigs, vermin, and rodents,
66:23 all **f** shall come to worship before me, A
66:24 and they shall be an abhorrence to all **f**. A
Jer 7:21 to your sacrifices, and eat the **f**.
11:15 Can vows and sacrificial **f** avert your doom?
17: 5 in mere mortals and make mere **f** their strength,
19: 9 the **f** of their sons and the **f** of their daughters,
19: 9 all shall eat the **f** of their neighbors in the siege,
25:31 he is entering into judgment with all **f**, A
32:27 the God of all **f**; is anything too hard for me? A
45: 5 for I am going to bring disaster upon all **f**, A
51:35 May my torn **f** be avenged on Babylon,"
La 3: 4 He has made my **f** and my skin waste away,
Eze 4:14 nor has carrion **f** come into my mouth."
11:19 the heart of stone from their **f** and give them a heart of **f**,
20:48 All **f** shall see that I the LORD have kindled it; A
21: 4 of its sheath against all **f** from south to north; A
21: 5 and all **f** shall know that I the LORD have A
32: 5 I will strew your **f** on the mountains,
33:25 You eat **f** with the blood,
36:26 the heart of stone and give you a heart of **f**.
37: 6 and will cause **f** to come upon you,
37: 8 and **f** had come upon them,
39:17 and you shall eat **f** and drink blood.
39:18 You shall eat the **f** of the mighty,
40:43 on the tables the **f** of the offering was to be laid.
44: 7 uncircumcised in heart and **f**,
44: 9 No foreigner, uncircumcised in heart and **f**,
Hos 8:13 they offer choice sacrifices, though they eat **f**,
Joel 2:28 Then afterward I will pour out my spirit on all **f**; A
Mic 3: 2 and the **f** off their bones;
3: 3 who eat the **f** of my people,
3: 3 like meat in a kettle, like **f** in a cauldron.
Na 2:12 with prey and his dens with torn **f**.
Zep 1:17 be poured out like dust, and their **f** like dung.
Zec 11: 9 let those that are left devour the **f** of one another!"
11:16 but devours the **f** of the fat ones,
14:12 their **f** shall rot while they are still on their feet;
14:21 and use them to boil the **f** of the sacrifice.
Mal 2:15 Both **f** and spirit are his.
Mt 16:17 For **f** and blood has not revealed this to you,
19: 5 and the two shall become one **f**'? B
19: 6 So they are no longer two, but one **f**. B
26:41 the spirit indeed is willing, but the **f** is weak."
Mk 10: 8 and the two shall become one **f**.' B
10: 8 So they are no longer two, but one **f**. B
14:38 the spirit indeed is willing, but the **f** is weak."
Lk 3: 6 and all **f** shall see the salvation of God.' " A
24:39 for a ghost does not have **f** and bones as you see
Jn 1:13 not of blood or of the will of the **f** or of the will
1:14 And the Word became **f** and lived among us,
3: 6 What is born of the **f** is flesh,
3: 6 What is born of the flesh is **f**,
6:51 that I will give for the life of the world is my **f**."
6:52 saying, "How can this man give us his **f** to eat?"
6:53 the **f** of the Son of Man and drink his blood,
6:54 who eat my **f** and drink my blood have eternal life,
6:55 for my **f** is true food and my blood is true drink.
6:56 Those who eat my **f** and drink my blood abide
6:63 It is the spirit that gives life; the **f** is useless.
Ac 2:17 that I will pour out my Spirit upon all **f**, A
2:26 moreover my **f** will live in hope.
2:31 nor did his **f** experience corruption.'
Ro 1: 3 who was descended from David according to the **f**
4: 1 our ancestor according to the **f**?
7: 5 While we were living in the **f**, our sinful passions,
7:14 but I am of the **f**, sold into slavery under sin.
7:18 within me, that is, in my **f**.
7:25 but with my **f** I am a slave to the law of sin.
8: 3 God has done what the law, weakened by the **f**,
8: 3 by sending his own Son in the likeness of sinful **f**,
8: 3 and to deal with sin, he condemned sin in the **f**,
8: 4 not according to the **f** but according to the Spirit.
8: 5 according to the **f** set their minds on the things of the **f**,
8: 6 To set the mind on the **f** is death,
8: 7 the mind that is set on the **f** is hostile to God;
8: 8 and those who are in the **f** cannot please God.
8: 9 But you are not in the **f**;
8:12 brothers and sisters, we are debtors, not to the **f**, to live according to the **f**—
8:13 for if you live according to the **f**, you will die;
9: 3 my kindred according to the **f**.
9: 5 according to the **f**, comes the Messiah,
9: 8 the children of the **f** who are the children of God,
13:14 and make no provision for the **f**,
1Co 3: 1 but rather as people of the **f**, as infants in Christ.
3: 3 for you are still of the **f**.
3: 3 are you not of the **f**,
5: 5 over to Satan for the destruction of the **f**,
6:16 For it is said, "The two shall be one **f**." B
15:39 Not all **f** is alike, but there is one flesh A
15:39 but there is one **f** for human beings, B
15:50 **f** and blood cannot inherit the kingdom of God,
2Co 4:11 life of Jesus may be made visible in our mortal **f**.
12: 7 a thorn was given me in the **f**,
Gal 2:20 now live in the **f** I live by faith in the Son of God,
3: 3 are you now ending with the **f**?
4:23 was born according to the **f**;
4:29 the **f** persecuted the child who was born according
5:16 I say, and do not gratify the desires of the **f**.
5:17 For what the **f** desires is opposed to the Spirit, and what the Spirit desires is opposed to the **f**;
5:19 Now the works of the **f** are obvious:
5:24 to Christ Jesus have crucified the **f**
6: 8 If you sow to your own **f**, you will reap corruption from the **f**;
6:12 a good showing in the **f** that try to compel you to
6:13 so that they may boast about your **f**.
Eph 2: 3 lived among them in the passions of our **f**, following the desires of **f** and senses,
2:11 a physical circumcision made in the **f**
2:14 in his **f** he has made both groups into one
5:31 and the two will become one **f**." B
6:12 our struggle is not against enemies of blood and **f**,
Php 1:22 If I am to live in the **f**,
1:24 but to remain in the **f** is more necessary for you.
3: 2 beware of those who mutilate the **f**!
3: 3 in Christ Jesus and have no confidence in the **f**—
3: 4 too, have reason for confidence in the **f**.
3: 4 If anyone else has reason to be confident in the **f**,
Col 1:24 and in my **f** I am completing what is lacking
2:11 the body of the **f** in the circumcision of Christ;
2:13 in trespasses and the uncircumcision of your **f**,
1Ti 3:16 He was revealed in **f**, vindicated in spirit,
Phm 1:16 both in the **f** and in the Lord.
Heb 2:14 Since, therefore, the children share **f** and blood,
5: 7 In the days of his **f**,
9:13 so that their **f** is purified,
10:20 for us through the curtain (that is, through his **f**),
Jas 5: 3 and it will eat your **f** like fire.
1Pe 1:24 All **f** is like grass and all its glory like the flower A
2:11 the desires of the **f** that wage war against the soul.
3:18 He was put to death in the **f**,
4: 1 Since therefore Christ suffered in the **f**,
4: 1 (for whoever has suffered in the **f** has finished
4: 6 though they had been judged in the **f**
2Pe 2:10 —especially those who indulge their **f**
2:18 of the **f** they entice people who have just escaped
1Jn 2:16 the desire of the **f**, the desire of the eyes,
4: 2 that Jesus Christ has come in the **f** is from God,
2Jn 1: 7 not confess that Jesus Christ has come in the **f**;
Jude 1: 8 in the same way these dreamers also defile the **f**,
Rev 17:16 they will devour her **f** and burn her up with fire.
19:18 the **f** of kings, the **f** of captains, the **f** of the mighty, the **f** of horses and their riders—**f** of all,
19:21 and all the birds were gorged with their **f**.

Jdt 16:17 he will send fire and worms into their **f**;
Wis 7: 1 and in the womb of a mother I was molded into **f**,
12: 5 their sacrificial feasting on human **f** and blood.
19:21 failed to consume the **f** of perishable creatures
Sir 14:18 so are the generations of **f** and blood:
17:31 So **f** and blood devise evil.
26:13 and her skill puts **f** on his bones.
31: 1 Wakefulness over wealth wastes away one's **f**,
38:28 the breath of the fire melts his **f**,
41: 4 This is the Lord's decree for all **f**; A
44:18 that all **f** should never again be blotted out by A
44:20 he certified the covenant in his **f**,
Bar 2: 3 ate the **f** of their sons and others the **f** of their daughters.
1Mc 7:17 "The **f** of your faithful ones and their blood
2Mc 6:18 to open his mouth to eat swine's **f**.
6:19 to the rack of his own accord, spitting out the **f**,
6:21 that he was eating the **f** of the sacrificial meal
7: 1 to partake of unlawful swine's **f**.
9: 9 his **f** rotted away, and because of the stench
2Es 1:31 and new moons, and circumcisions of the **f**.
15:58 and they shall eat their own **f** in hunger for bread
4Mc 6: 6 his **f** was being torn by scourges,
7:18 to control the passions of the **f**,
9:17 Cut my limbs, burn my **f**, and twist my joints;
9:20 of **f** were falling off the axles of the machine.
9:28 flayed all his **f** up to his chin,
10: 8 he saw his own **f** torn all around and drops
15:15 She watched the **f** of her children being consumed
15:15 the **f** of the head to the chin exposed like masks.
15:20 When you saw the **f** of children burned upon
15:20 of children burned upon the **f** of other children,

FLESH (KJV) See also BODY, EARTHLY, FACE, HUMAN, HUMAN BEING, PHYSICAL

FLESHHOOK (KJV) See FORK

FLESHLY‡ (1) [FLESH]

Col 1:22 now reconciled in his **f** body through death,

FLESHPOTS (1) [FLESH, POT]

Ex 16: 3 when we sat by the **f** and ate our fill of bread;

FLEW (10) [FLY]

1Sa 14:32 so the troops **f** upon the spoil, and took sheep
2Sa 22:11 He rode on a cherub, and **f**;
Ps 18:10 He rode on a cherub, and **f**;
Isa 6: 2 two they covered their feet, and with two they **f**.
6: 6 Then one of the seraphs **f** to me,
Da 2:12 the king **f** into a violent rage and commanded
Rev 8:13 an eagle crying with a loud voice as it **f**
2Es 11: 5 Then I saw that the eagle **f** with its wings,
13: 3 I saw that this man **f** with the clouds of heaven;
13: 6 and **f** up on to it.

FLIES (15) [FLY]

Ex 8:21 I will send swarms of **f** on you, your officials,
8:21 of the Egyptians shall be filled with swarms of **f**;
8:22 so that no swarms of **f** shall be there,
8:24 and great swarms of **f** came into the house
8:24 of Egypt the land was ruined because of the **f**.
8:29 that the swarms of **f** may depart tomorrow
8:31 he removed the swarms of **f** from Pharaoh,
Dt 4:17 the likeness of any winged bird that **f** in the air,
Ps 78:45 He sent among them swarms of **f**,
91: 5 or the arrow that **f** by day,
105:31 He spoke, and there came swarms of **f**,
Ecc 10: 1 Dead **f** make the perfumer's ointment give off
Na 3:16 The locust sheds its skin and **f** away.
Wis 5:11 when a bird **f** through the air,
16: 9 For they were killed by the bites of locusts and **f**,

FLIGHT (33) [FLY]

Lev 26:36 the sound of a driven leaf shall put them to **f**,
Dt 32:30 and two put a myriad to **f**,
Jos 23:10 One of you puts to **f** a thousand,
1Ch 8:13 who put to **f** the inhabitants of Gath);
12:15 and put to **f** all those in the valleys,
Job 27:22 they flee from its power in headlong **f**.
Ps 21:12 For you will put them to **f**;
48: 5 they were in panic, they took to **f**;
104: 7 at the sound of your thunder they take to **f**.
Isa 10:31 Madmenah is in **f**, the inhabitants of Gebim flee
52:12 and you shall not go in **f**;
Jer 4:29 of horseman and archer every town takes to **f**;
25:35 **F** shall fail the shepherds,
Da 9:21 in swift **f** at the time of the evening sacrifice.
Am 2:14 **F** shall perish from the swift,
Mt 24:20 that your **f** may not be in winter or on a sabbath.
Heb 11:34 became mighty in war, put foreign armies to **f**.
Jdt 15: 3 in the hills around Bethulia also took to **f**.
Wis 5:11 of its rushing **f**, is traversed by the movement
Sir 22:22 in these cases any friend will take to **f**.
1Mc 4:20 They saw that their army had been put to **f**,
6:47 of the forces, they turned away in **f**.
10:72 for your ancestors were twice put to **f**
11:15 and met him with a strong force, and put him to **f**.
15:11 and Trypho came in his **f** to Dor,
16: 8 and Cendebeus and his army were put to **f**;
2Mc 4:42 and killed some, and put all the rest to **f**;
8: 6 He captured strategic positions and put to **f** not
2Mc 9: 2 to **f** by the inhabitants and beat a shameful retreat.
9: 4 the injury done by those who had put him to **f**;
11:12 and Lysias himself escaped by disgraceful **f**.
12:22 In their **f** they rushed headlong in every direction,
12:37 not expecting it, and put them to **f**.

FLING (4) [FLINGING, FLUNG]

2Ch 25: 8 or God will **f** you down before the enemy;
Eze 7:19 They shall **f** their silver into the streets,
29: 5 I will **f** you into the wilderness,
32: 4 on the open field I will **f** you,

FLINGING (1) [FLING]

2Sa 16:13 throwing stones and **f** dust at him.

FLINT (9) [FLINTY]

Ex 4:25 Zipporah took a **f** and cut off her son's foreskin,
Dt 8:15 He made water flow for you from **f** rock,
Jos 5: 2 "Make **f** knives and circumcise the Israelites
5: 3 So Joshua made **f** knives,
Ps 114: 8 the **f** into a spring of water.
Isa 5:28 their horses' hoofs seem like **f**,
50: 7 therefore I have set my face like **f**,
Eze 3: 9 Like the hardest stone, harder than **f**,
2Mc 10: 3 then, striking fire out of **f**, they offered sacrifices,

FLINTY (3) [FLINT]

Dt 32:13 with honey from the crags, with oil from **f** rock;
Job 28: 9 "They put their hand to the **f** rock,
Wis 11: 4 and water was given them out of **f** rock,

FLITTING (1)

Pr 26: 2 Like a sparrow in its **f**, like a swallow

FLOAT (1) [FLOATED]

2Ki 6: 6 and threw it in there, and made the iron **f**.

FLOATED (1) [FLOAT]

Ge 7:18 and the ark **f** on the face of the waters.

FLOCK (128) [FLOCKED, FLOCKS]

Ge 4: 4 Abel for his part brought of the firstlings of his **f**,
21:28 Abraham set apart seven ewe lambs of the **f**.
27: 9 Go to the **f**, and get me two choice kids,
29:10 and watered the **f** of his mother's brother Laban.
30:31 I will again feed your **f** and keep it:
30:32 let me pass through all your **f** today, removing
30:36 while Jacob was pasturing the rest of Laban's **f**.
30:40 the completely black animals in the **f** of Laban;
30:40 and did not put them with Laban's **f**.
30:41 Whenever the stronger of the **f** were breeding,
30:41 the rods in the troughs before the eyes of the **f**,
30:42 for the feebler of the **f** he did not lay them there;
31: 4 and Leah into the field where his **f** was,
31: 8 then all the **f** bore speckled;
31: 8 then all the **f** bore striped.
31:10 of the **f** I once had a dream in which I looked up
31:10 the male goats that leaped upon the **f** were striped,
31:12 the goats that leap on the **f** are striped, speckled,
31:41 for your two daughters, and six years for your **f**,
37: 2 was shepherding the **f** with his brothers;
37:12 Now his brothers went to pasture their father's **f**
37:13 not your brothers pasturing the **f** at Shechem?
37:14 see if it is well with your brothers and with the **f**;
37:16 "tell me, please, where they are pasturing the **f**."
38:17 He answered, "I will send you a kid from the **f**."
Ex 2:16 and filled the troughs to water their father's **f**.
2:17 up and came to their defense and watered their **f**.
2:19 he even drew water for us and watered the **f**."
3: 1 the **f** of his father-in-law Jethro, the priest
3: 1 he led his **f** beyond the wilderness,
Lev 1: 2 from the herd or from the **f**.
1:10 If your gift for a burnt offering is from the **f**,
3: 6 of well-being to the LORD is from the **f**,
5: 6 a female from the **f**, a sheep or a goat,
5:15 a ram without blemish from the **f**,
5:18 to the priest a ram without blemish from the **f**, or
6: 6 a ram without blemish from the **f**,
22:21 from the herd or from the **f**,
22:28 you shall not slaughter, from the herd or the **f**,
27:32 All tithes of herd and **f**,
Nu 15: 3 by fire to the LORD from the herd or from the **f**—
Dt 7:13 the increase of your cattle and the issue of your **f**,
12:21 of your herd or **f** that the LORD has given you,
14:23 as well as the firstlings of your herd and **f**,
15:14 Provide liberally out of your **f**,
15:19 of your herd and **f** you shall consecrate to
15:19 nor shear the firstling of your **f**.
16: 2 from the **f** and the herd,
28: 4 the increase of your cattle and the issue of your **f**.
28:18 the increase of your cattle and the issue of your **f**.
28:51 the increase of your cattle and the issue of your **f**,
32:14 and milk from the **f**, with fat of lambs and rams;
1Sa 17:34 and took a lamb from the **f**,
2Sa 12: 4 and he was loath to take one of his own **f** or herd
2Ch 35: 7 from the **f** to the number of thirty thousand,
Ezr 10:19 and their guilt offering was a ram of the **f**
Job 21:11 They send out their little ones like a **f**,
30: 1 to set with the dogs of my **f**.
Ps 68:10 your **f** found a dwelling in it;
77:20 You led your people like a **f** by the hand of Moses
78:52 and guided them in the wilderness like a **f**.
79:13 Then we your people, the **f** of your pasture,
Ps 80: 1 you who lead Joseph like a **f**!
SS 1: 7 where you pasture your **f**,
1: 8 follow the tracks of the **f**,
2:16 he pastures his **f** among the lilies.
4: 1 Your hair is like a **f** of goats,
4: 2 like a **f** of shorn ewes that have come up from
6: 2 to pasture his **f** in the gardens, and to gather lilies.
6: 3 he pastures his **f** among the lilies.
6: 5 Your hair is like a **f** of goats,
6: 6 Your teeth are like a **f** of ewes,
Isa 40:11 He will feed his **f** like a shepherd;
63:11 up out of the sea with the shepherds of his **f**?
Jer 10:21 and all their **f** is scattered.
13:17 because the LORD's **f** has been taken captive.
13:20 is the **f** that was given you, your beautiful **f**?
23: 2 It is you who have scattered my **f**,
23: 3 Then I myself will gather the remnant of my **f** out
25:34 roll in ashes, you lords of the **f**,
25:35 and there shall be no escape for the lords of the **f**.
25:36 and the wail of the lords of the **f**!
31:10 and will keep him as a shepherd a **f**."
31:12 and over the young of the **f** and the herd;
49:20 the little ones of the **f** shall be dragged away;
50: 8 and be like male goats leading the **f**.
50:45 the little ones of the **f** shall be dragged away;
Eze 24: 5 Take the choicest one of the **f**,
34:17 As for you, my **f**, thus says the Lord GOD:
34:22 I will save my **f**, and they shall no longer
36:37 to increase their population like a **f**.
36:38 the **f** for sacrifices, like the **f** at Jerusalem
43:23 a bull without blemish and a ram from the **f**
43:25 also a bull and a ram from the **f**, without blemish,
45:15 and one sheep from every **f** of two hundred,
Am 6: 4 and eat lambs from the **f**,
7:15 and the LORD took me from following the **f**,
Jnh 3: 7 No human being or animal, no herd or **f**,
Mic 2:12 like a **f** in its pasture; it will resound with people.
4: 8 And you, O tower of the **f**, hill of daughter Zion,
5: 4 And he shall stand and feed his **f** in the strength of
7:14 the **f** that belongs to you, which lives alone in
Hab 3:17 the **f** is cut off from the fold and there is no herd
Zec 9:16 for they are the **f** of his people;
10: 3 for the LORD of hosts cares for his **f**,
11: 4 Be a shepherd of the **f** doomed to slaughter.
11: 7 the shepherd of the **f** doomed to slaughter.
11:17 Oh, my worthless shepherd, who deserts the **f**!
Mal 1:14 in the **f** and vows to give it, and yet sacrifices to
Mt 26:31 and the sheep of the **f** will be scattered.'
Lk 2: 8 keeping watch over their **f** by night.
12:32 "Do not be afraid, little **f**,
Jn 10:16 So there will be one **f**, one shepherd.
Ac 20:28 Keep watch over yourselves and over all the **f**,
20:29 in among you, not sparing the **f**.
1Co 9: 7 Or who tends a **f** and does not get any of its milk?
1Pe 5: 2 the **f** of God that is in your charge, exercising
5: 3 but be examples to the **f**.
Tob 1: 6 of the crops and the firstlings of the **f**,
7: 9 a ram from the **f** and received them very warmly.
Sir 18:13 and turns them back, as a shepherd his **f**.
47: 3 with bears as though they were lambs of the **f**.
Bar 4:26 they were taken away like a **f** carried off by
2Es 5:18 like a shepherd who leaves the **f** in the power
15:10 my people are being led like a **f** to the slaughter;
4Mc 5: 4 leader of the **f**, was brought before the king.

FLOCKED (2) [FLOCK]

2Mc 14:14 who had fled before Judas, **f** to join Nicanor,
3Mc 1:19 in a disorderly rush **f** together in the city.

FLOCKS‡ (86) [FLOCK]

Ge 13: 5 also had **f** and herds and tents,
24:35 he has given him **f** and herds, silver and gold,
26:14 He had possessions of **f** and herds,
29: 2 the field and three **f** of sheep lying there beside it;
29: 2 for out of that well the **f** were watered.
29: 3 and when all the **f** were gathered there,
29: 8 "We cannot until all the **f** are gathered together,
30:38 He set the rods that he had peeled in front of the **f**
30:38 the watering places, where the **f** came to drink.
30:39 the **f** bred in front of the rods,
30:39 and so the **f** produced young that were striped,
30:40 and set the faces of the **f** toward the striped and
30:43 and had large **f**, and male and female slaves,
31:38 and I have not eaten the rams of your **f**.
31:43 the children are my children, the **f** are my **f**,
32: 5 donkeys, **f**, male and female slaves;
32: 7 and the **f** and herds and camels,
33:13 that the children are frail and that the **f** and herds,
33:13 they are overdriven for one day, all the **f** will die.
34:28 They took their **f** and their herds, their donkeys,
45:10 as well as your **f**, your herds,
46:32 and they have brought their **f**, and their herds,
47: 1 with their **f** and herds and all that they possess,
47: 4 for there is no pasture for your servants' **f** because
47:17 the **f**, the herds, and the donkeys.
50: 8 Only their children, their **f**,
Ex 9: 3 the donkeys, the camels, the herds, and the **f**.
10: 9 with our sons and daughters and with our **f**
10:24 Only your **f** and your herds shall remain behind.
12:32 Take your **f** and your herds, as you said,
12:38 and livestock in great numbers, both **f** and herds.
34: 3 not let **f** or herds graze in front of that mountain."
Nu 11:22 Are there enough **f** and herds to slaughter
31: 9 and they took all their cattle, their **f**,
32:16 "We will build sheepfolds here for our **f**,
32:24 for your little ones, and folds for your **f**;

Nu 32:26 Our little ones, our wives, our **f**,
Dt 8:13 and when your herds and **f** have multiplied,
12: 6 and the firstlings of your herds and **f**.
12:17 the firstlings of your herds and your **f**,
Jos 14: 4 with their pasture lands for their **f** and herds.
Jdg 5:16 to hear the piping for the **f**?
1Sa 8:17 He will take one-tenth of your **f**,
30:20 David also captured all the **f** and herds,
2Sa 12: 2 The rich man had very many **f** and herds;
1Ki 20:27 of Israel encamped opposite them like two little **f**
1Ch 4:39 to seek pasture for their **f**,
4:41 because there was pasture there for their **f**.
27:30 Over the **f** was Jaziz the Hagrite.
2Ch 32:29 and **f** and herds in abundance;
Ne 10:36 and the firstlings of our herds and of our **f**;
Job 24: 2 they seize **f** and pasture them.
Ps 65:13 the meadows clothe themselves with **f**,
78:48 and their **f** to thunderbolts.
107:41 and makes their families like **f**.
Pr 27:23 Know well the condition of your **f**,
Ecc 2: 7 I also had great possessions of herds and **f**,
SS 1: 7 be like one who is veiled beside the **f**
Isa 13:20 shepherds will not make their **f** lie down there.
17: 2 they will be places for **f**, which will lie down,
32:14 the joy of wild asses, a pasture for **f**;
60: 7 All the **f** of Kedar shall be gathered to you,
61: 5 Strangers shall stand and feed your **f**,
65:10 Sharon shall become a pasture for **f**,
Jer 3:24 for which our ancestors had labored, their **f**
5:17 they shall eat up your **f** and your herds;
6: 3 Shepherds with their **f** shall come against her.
31:24 the farmers and those who wander with their **f**.
33:12 be pasture for shepherds resting their **f**.
33:13 **f** shall again pass under the hands of
49:29 Take their tents and their **f**,
51:23 with you I smash shepherds and their **f**;
Eze 25: 5 a pasture for camels and Ammon a fold for **f**.
34:12 As shepherds seek out their **f** when they are
36:38 shall the ruined towns be filled with **f** of people.
Hos 5: 6 With their **f** and herds they shall go to seek
Joel 1:18 even the **f** of sheep are dazed.
Mic 5: 8 like a young lion among the **f** of sheep, which,
Zep 2: 6 meadows for shepherds and folds for **f**.
Jn 4:12 and with his sons and his **f** drank from it?"
Jdt 2:27 and burned all their fields and destroyed their **f**
3: 3 and all our land and all our wheat fields and our **f**
2Mc 14:23 but dismissed the **f** of people that had gathered.
2Es 5:26 the **f** that have been made you have provided
7:65 but let the cattle and the **f** rejoice.

FLOG (5) [FLOGGED, FLOGGING, FLOGGINGS]

Pr 17:26 or to **f** the noble for their integrity.
Mt 10:17 for they will hand you over to councils and **f** you
23:34 and some you will **f** in your synagogues
Mk 10:34 and spit upon him, and **f** him, and kill him;
Ac 22:25 to **f** a Roman citizen who is uncondemned?"

FLOGGED (13) [FLOG]

Dt 25: 2 If the one in the wrong deserves to be **f**,
Mt 20:19 to the Gentiles to be mocked and **f** and crucified;
Lk 18:33 After they have **f** him, they will kill him,
23:16 I will therefore have him **f** and release him."
23:22 I will therefore have him **f** and then release him."
Jn 19: 1 Then Pilate took Jesus and had him **f**.
Ac 5:40 in the apostles, they had them **f**.
Wis 16:16 were **f** by the strength of your arm,
2Mc 3:26 on either side of him and **f** him continuously,
3:34 And see that you, who have been **f** by heaven,
3:38 for you will get him back thoroughly **f**,
5:18 this man would have been **f** and turned back
4Mc 6: 3 they had tied his arms on each side they **f** him,

FLOGGING (7) [FLOG]

Pr 18: 6 and a fool's mouth invites a **f**.
19:29 and **f** for the backs of fools.
Mt 27:26 after **f** Jesus, he handed him over to be crucified.
Mk 15:15 after **f** Jesus, he handed him over to be crucified.
Ac 16:23 After they had given them a severe **f**,
22:24 and ordered him to be examined by **f**,
Heb 11:36 Others suffered mocking and **f**,

FLOGGINGS (1) [FLOG]

2Co 11:23 far more imprisonments, with countless **f**,

FLOOD (50) [FLOODED, FLOODS]

Ge 6:17 I am going to bring a **f** of waters on the earth,
7: 6 Noah was six hundred years old when the **f**
7: 7 into the ark to escape the waters of the **f**.
7:10 seven days the waters of the **f** came on the earth.
7:17 The **f** continued forty days on the earth;
9:11 be cut off by the waters of a **f**,
9:11 never again shall there be a **f** to destroy the earth."
9:15 and the waters shall never again become a **f**
9:28 After the **f** Noah lived three hundred fifty years.
10: 1 children were born to them after the **f**.
10:32 the nations spread abroad on the earth after the **f**.
11:10 the father of Arpachshad two years after the **f**;
2Sa 5:20 against my enemies before me, like a bursting **f**."
1Ch 14:11 against my enemies by my hand, like a bursting **f**."
Job 22:11 a **f** of water covers you.
22:16 their foundation was washed away by a **f**.
27:20 Terrors overtake them like a **f**;
38:34 so that a **f** of waters may cover you?
Ps 6: 6 every night I **f** my bed with tears;
29:10 The LORD sits enthroned over the **f**;
69: 2 and the **f** sweeps over me.
69:15 Do not let the **f** sweep over me,
88:17 They surround me like a **f** all day long;
124: 4 then the **f** would have swept us away,
Isa 8: 7 up against it the mighty **f** waters of the River,
8: 8 a **f**, and, pouring over, it will reach up to the neck;
Da 9:26 Its end shall come with a **f**,
11:10 which shall advance like a **f** and pass through,
11:40 against countries and pass through like a **f**.
Jnh 2: 3 and the **f** surrounded me;
Na 1: 8 even in a rushing **f**. He will make a full end of his
Mt 24:38 For as in those days before the **f** they were eating
24:39 until the **f** came and swept them all away,
Lk 6:48 when a **f** arose, the river burst against that house
17:27 and the **f** came and destroyed all of them.
2Pe 2: 5 when he brought a **f** on a world of the ungodly;
Rev 12:15 to sweep her away with the **f**.
Wis 18: 5 you destroyed them all together by a mighty **f**.
Sir 21:13 The knowledge of the wise will increase like a **f**,
39:22 and drenches it like a **f**.
40:10 and on their account the **f** came.
44:17 a remnant was left on the earth when the **f** came.
44:18 be blotted out by a **f**.
1Mc 6:11 And into what a great **f** I now am plunged!
2Mc 2:24 For considering the **f** of statistics involved and
3Mc 2: 4 by bringing on them a boundless **f**.
2Es 3: 9 in its time you brought the **f** upon the inhabitants
3:10 as death came upon Adam, so the **f** upon them.
4Mc 15:31 carrying the world in the universal **f**,
15:32 by the **f** of your emotions and the violent winds,

FLOODED (1) [FLOOD]

Wis 10: 4 When the earth was **f** because of him,

FLOODS (10) [FLOOD]

Ex 15: 5 The **f** covered them; they went down into
15: 8 the **f** stood up in a heap;
Ps 93: 3 The **f** have lifted up, O LORD, the **f** have lifted up
their voice; the **f** lift up their roaring.
98: 8 Let the **f** clap their hands;
SS 8: 7 waters cannot quench love, neither can **f** drown it.
Mt 7:25 The rain fell, the **f** came, and the winds blew
7:27 The rain fell, and the **f** came,
2Es 15:41 fire and hail and flying swords and **f** of water,

FLOOR‡ (50) [FLOORS]

Ge 50:10 When they came to the threshing **f** of Atad,
50:11 of the land saw the mourning on the threshing **f**
Nu 5:17 the dust that is on the **f** of the tabernacle and put it
15:20 as you present a donation from the threshing **f**.
18:27 the threshing **f** and the fullness of the wine press.
18:30 to the Levites as produce of the threshing **f**,
Dt 15:14 your threshing **f**, and your wine press,
16:13 from your threshing **f** and your wine press.
Jdg 3:25 There was their lord lying dead on the **f**.
6:37 to lay a fleece of wool on the threshing **f**;
Ru 3: 2 he is winnowing barley tonight at the threshing **f**.
3: 3 and go down to the threshing **f**;
3: 6 So she went down to the threshing **f** and did just
3:14 be known that the woman came to the threshing **f**."
2Sa 6: 6 When they came to the threshing **f** of Nacon,
24:16 then by the threshing **f** of Araunah the Jebusite.
24:18 and erect an altar to the LORD on the threshing **f**
24:21 "To buy the threshing **f** from you in order to build
24:24 So David bought the threshing **f** and the oxen
1Ki 6:15 the **f** of the house to the rafters of the ceiling,
6:15 and he covered the **f** of the house with boards
6:16 of the house with boards of cedar from the **f** to
6:30 The **f** of the house he overlaid with gold,
7: 7 covered with cedar from **f** to **f**.
22:10 at the threshing **f** at the entrance of the gate
2Ki 6:27 From the threshing **f** or from the wine press?"
1Ch 13: 9 When they came to the threshing **f** of Chidon,
21:15 the LORD was then standing by the threshing **f**
21:18 and erect an altar to the LORD on the threshing **f**
21:21 he went out from the threshing **f**,
21:22 of the threshing **f** that I may build on it an altar to
21:28 the LORD had answered him at the threshing **f**
2Ch 3: 1 on the threshing **f** of Ornan the Jebusite.
18: 9 at the threshing **f** at the entrance of the gate
Job 5:26 of grain comes up to the threshing **f** in its season.
39:12 and bring your grain to your threshing **f**?
Jer 51:33 Daughter Babylon is like a threshing **f** at the time
Eze 41:16 from the **f** up to the windows (now
41:20 from the **f** to the area above the door,
Hos 9: 2 Threshing **f** and wine vat shall not feed them,
13: 3 the threshing **f** or like smoke from a window.
Mic 4:12 as sheaves to the threshing **f**.
Mt 3:12 and he will clear his threshing **f**
Lk 3:17 to clear his threshing **f** and to gather the wheat
Jdt 14:15 and found him sprawled on the **f** dead,
AdE 1: 6 and silver couches were placed on a mosaic **f**
Bel 1:19 from going in. "Look at the **f**," he said,
2Es 4:32 how great a threshing **f** they will fill!"
9:17 and as is the farmer, so is the threshing **f**.

FLOORS (5) [FLOOR]

1Sa 23: 1 and are robbing the threshing **f**."
Da 2:35 like the chaff of the summer threshing **f**;
Hos 9: 1 a prostitute's pay on all threshing **f**.
Joel 2:24 The threshing **f** shall be full of grain,
Ac 20: 9 he fell to the ground three **f** below and was picked

FLOUR (62)

Ge 18: 6 "Make ready quickly three measures of choice **f**,
Ex 29: 2 You shall make them of choice wheat **f**.
29:40 of a measure of choice **f** mixed with one-fourth of
Lev 2: 1 the offering shall be of choice **f**;
2: 2 taking from it a handful of the choice **f** and oil,
2: 4 it shall be of choice **f**:
2: 5 it shall be of choice **f** mixed with oil, unleavened;
2: 7 it shall be made of choice **f** in oil.
5:11 of an ephah of choice **f** for a sin offering;
6:15 They shall take from it a handful of the choice **f**
6:20 of an ephah of choice **f** as a regular offering,
7:12 and cakes of choice **f** well soaked in oil.
14:10 of three-tenths of an ephah of choice **f** mixed
14:21 of choice **f** mixed with oil for a grain offering and
23:13 an ephah of choice **f** mixed with oil, an offering
23:17 they shall be of choice **f**, baked with leaven,
24: 5 You shall take choice **f**, and bake twelve loaves
Nu 5:15 one-tenth of an ephah of barley **f**.
6:15 cakes of choice **f** mixed with oil
7:13 both of them full of choice **f** mixed with oil for
7:19 both of them full of choice **f** mixed with oil for
7:25 both of them full of choice **f** mixed with oil for
7:31 both of them full of choice **f** mixed with oil for
7:37 both of them full of choice **f** mixed with oil for
7:43 both of them full of choice **f** mixed with oil for
7:49 both of them full of choice **f** mixed with oil for
7:55 both of them full of choice **f** mixed with oil for
7:61 both of them full of choice **f** mixed with oil for
7:67 both of them full of choice **f** mixed with oil for
7:73 both of them full of choice **f** mixed with oil for
7:79 both of them full of choice **f** mixed with oil for
8: 8 and its grain offering of choice **f** mixed with oil,
15: 4 one-tenth of an ephah of choice **f**,
15: 6 an ephah of choice **f** mixed with one-third of a hin
15: 9 three-tenths of an ephah of choice **f**,
28: 5 of an ephah of choice **f** for a grain offering,
28: 9 of an ephah of choice **f** for a grain offering, mixed
28:12 of an ephah of choice **f** for a grain offering, mixed
28:12 and two-tenths of choice **f** for a grain offering,
28:13 of choice **f** mixed with oil as a grain offering
28:20 Their grain offering shall be of choice **f** mixed
28:28 Their grain offering shall be of choice **f** mixed
29: 3 Their grain offering shall be of choice **f** mixed
29: 9 Their grain offering shall be of choice **f** mixed
29:14 Their grain offering shall be of choice **f** mixed
Jdg 6:19 and unleavened cakes from an ephah of **f**;
1Sa 1:24 along with a three-year-old bull, an ephah of **f**,
28:24 She quickly slaughtered it, and she took **f**,
1Ki 4:22 for one day was thirty cors of choice **f**,
2Ki 4:41 He said, "Then bring some **f**."
1Ch 9:29 also over the choice **f**, the wine, the oil,
23:29 the choice **f** for the grain offering,
Eze 16:13 You had choice **f** and honey and oil for food.
16:19 I fed you with choice **f** and oil and honey—
46:14 one-third of a hin of oil to moisten the choice **f**,
Mt 13:33 and mixed in with three measures of **f** until all
Lk 13:21 and mixed in with three measures of **f** until all
Rev 18:13 frankincense, wine, olive oil, choice **f** and wheat,
Sir 35: 3 The one who returns a kindness offers choice **f**,
38:11 and a memorial portion of choice **f**,
39:26 and iron and salt and wheat **f** and milk and honey,
Bel 1: 3 for it twelve bushels of choice **f** and forty sheep

FLOURISH (15) [FLOURISHES]

Job 8:11 Can reeds **f** where there is no water?
Ps 72: 7 In his days may righteousness **f**
92: 7 the wicked sprout like grass and all evildoers **f**,
92:12 The righteous **f** like the palm tree,
92:13 they **f** in the courts of our God.
103:15 they **f** like a flower of the field;
Pr 11:28 but the righteous will **f** like green leaves.
Isa 66:14 your bodies shall **f** like the grass;
Eze 17:24 I dry up the green tree and make the dry tree **f**.
Hos 13:15 Although he may **f** among rushes,
14: 7 they shall **f** as a garden;
Zec 9:17 Grain shall make the young men **f**,
Sir 1:18 making peace and perfect health to **f**.
11:22 and quickly God causes his blessing to **f**.
2Es 6:28 faithfulness shall **f**, and corruption shall

FLOURISHES (2) [FLOURISH]

Ps 90: 6 in the morning it **f** and is renewed;
Pr 14:11 but the tent of the upright **f**.

FLOUT (1)

Ps 119:85 arrogant have dug pitfalls for me; they **f** your law.

FLOW (29) [EVER-FLOWING, FLOWED, FLOWING, FLOWS, OUTFLOW]

Lev 12: 7 then she shall be clean from her **f** of blood.
20:18 laid bare her **f** and she has laid bare her **f** of blood;
Nu 24: 7 Water shall **f** from his buckets,
Dt 8:15 He made water **f** for you from flint rock,
11: 4 the Red Sea **f** over them as they pursued you,
2Ki 3:20 suddenly water began to **f** from the direction
2Ch 32: 3 with his officers and his warriors to stop the **f** of
Ps 78:16 and caused waters to **f** down like rivers.
104:10 in the valleys; they **f** between the hills,
147:18 he makes his wind blow, and the waters **f**.
Pr 4:23 for from it **f** the springs of life.
Ecc 1: 7 where the streams **f**, there they continue to **f**.
Isa 8: 6 that **f** gently, and melt in fear before Rezin and
34: 3 the mountains shall **f** with their blood.

Isa 48:21 he made water **f** for them from the rock;
Jer 9:18 and our eyelids **f** with water.
La 1:16 For these things I weep; my eyes **f** with tears;
3:48 My eyes **f** with rivers of tears because of
3:49 My eyes will **f** without ceasing, without respite,
Eze 31:4 making its rivers **f** around the place it was planted,
Joel 3:18 the hills shall **f** with milk,
3:18 all the stream beds of Judah shall **f** with water;
Am 9:13 and all the hills shall **f** with it.
Zec 14:8 that day living waters shall **f** out from Jerusalem,
Jn 7:38 'Out of the believer's heart shall **f** rivers
Wis 16:29 and **f** away like waste water.
2Es 6:24 so that for three hours they shall not **f**.

FLOWED (6) [FLOW]

1Ki 22:35 the blood from the wound had **f** into the bottom of
2Ch 32:4 the springs and the wadi that **f** through the land,
Ps 105:41 it **f** through the desert like a river.
Da 7:10 stream of fire issued and **f** out from his presence.
Rev 14:20 and blood **f** from the wine press,
2Es 1:20 not split the rock so that waters **f** in abundance?

FLOWER (18) [FLOWER-BEDS, FLOWERS]

1Ki 7:26 like the **f** of a lily; it held two thousand baths.
2Ch 4:5 like the **f** of a lily; it held three thousand baths.
Job 8:12 While yet in **f** and not cut down,
14:2 comes up like a **f** and withers,
Ps 78:31 and laid low the **f** of Israel.
103:15 they flourish like a **f** of the field;
Isa 18:5 when the blossom is over and the **f** becomes
28:1 and the fading **f** of its glorious beauty,
28:4 And the fading **f** of its glorious beauty,
40:6 their constancy is like the **f** of the field.
40:7 The grass withers, the **f** fades,
40:8 The grass withers, the **f** fades;
Jas 1:10 the rich will disappear like a **f** in the field.
1:11 its **f** falls, and its beauty perishes.
1Pe 1:24 like grass and all its glory like the **f** of grass.
1:24 The grass withers, and the **f** falls,
Wis 2:7 and let no **f** of spring pass us by.
2Es 15:50 a **f** when the heat shall rise that is sent upon you.

FLOWER-BEDS (1) [FLOWER]

Sir 24:31 I said, "I will water my garden and drench my **f**."

FLOWERS[‡] (19) [FLOWER]

Nu 8:4 From its base to its **f**, it was hammered work;
1Ki 6:18 the house had carvings of gourds and open **f**;
6:29 and open **f**, in the inner and outer rooms.
6:32 of cherubim, palm trees, and open **f**;
6:35 He carved cherubim, palm trees, and open **f**,
7:49 the **f**, the lamps, and the tongs, of gold;
2Ch 4:21 the **f**, the lamps, and the tongs, of purest gold;
SS 2:12 The **f** appear on the earth;
3Mc 7:16 crowned with all sorts of very fragrant **f**,
2Es 5:24 and from all the **f** of the world you have chosen
5:36 and make the withered **f** bloom again for me;
6:3 and before the beautiful **f** were seen,
6:44 to the taste, and **f** of inimitable color, and odors
9:17 and as are the **f**, so are the colors;
9:24 go into a field of **f** where no house has been built,
9:24 and eat only of the **f** of the field,
9:24 and drink no wine, but eat only **f**,
9:26 there I sat among the **f** and ate of the plants of
12:51 and I ate only of the **f** of the field,

FLOWING (41) [FLOW]

A. LAND FLOWING WITH MILK AND HONEY (20)

Ex 3:8 a land **f** with milk and honey, A
3:17 and the Jebusites, a land **f** with milk and honey.' A
13:5 a land **f** with milk and honey, A
33:3 Go up to a land **f** with milk and honey; A
Lev 20:24 a land **f** with milk and honey. A
Nu 16:13 up out of a land **f** with milk and honey to kill us A
16:14 not brought us into a land **f** with milk and honey, A
Dt 6:3 multiply greatly in a land **f** with milk and honey, A
8:7 a good land, a land with **f** streams, with springs
10:7 to Jotbathah, a land with **f** streams.
11:9 a land **f** with milk and honey. A
26:9 a land **f** with milk and honey. A
26:15 a land **f** with milk and honey." A
27:3 a land **f** with milk and honey, as the LORD, A
31:20 into the land **f** with milk and honey, A
Jos 3:13 waters of the Jordan **f** from above shall be cut off;
3:16 the waters **f** from above stood still,
3:16 while those **f** toward the sea of the Arabah,
5:6 a land **f** with milk and honey. A
2Ki 4:6 Then the oil stopped **f**.
Job 20:17 the streams **f** with honey and curds.
Ps 42:1 As a deer longs for **f** streams,
Pr 5:15 **f** water from your own well.
SS 4:15 and **f** streams from Lebanon.
7:5 and your **f** locks are like purple;
Isa 44:4 like willows by **f** streams.
Jer 11:5 to give them a land **f** with milk and honey, A
18:14 the mountain waters run dry, the cold **f** streams?
32:22 a land **f** with milk and honey; A
Eze 20:6 a land **f** with milk and honey, A
20:15 a land **f** with milk and honey, A
23:15 with **f** turbans on their heads,
32:6 the land with your **f** blood up to the mountains,
47:1 there, water was **f** from below the threshold of
47:1 the water was **f** down from below the south end of

Rev 22:1 **f** from the throne of God and of the Lamb
Sir 46:8 the land **f** with milk and honey. A
Bar 1:20 to give to us a land **f** with milk and honey. A
2Es 2:19 and the same number of springs **f** with milk
4Mc 6:6 his blood **f**, and his sides were being cut to pieces.
10:8 around and drops of blood **f** from his entrails.

FLOWS (10) [FLOW]

Ge 2:10 A river **f** out of Eden to water the garden,
2:11 the one that **f** around the whole land of Havilah,
2:13 it is the one that **f** around the whole land of Cush.
2:14 of the third river is Tigris, which **f** east of Assyria.
Lev 15:3 whether his member **f** with his discharge,
Nu 13:27 it **f** with milk and honey, and this is its fruit.
14:8 a land that **f** with milk and honey.
Eze 47:8 "This water **f** toward the eastern region and goes
47:12 because the water for them **f** from the sanctuary.
Jdt 7:12 of water that **f** from the foot of the mountain,

FLUENTLY (1)

Ex 4:14 I know that he can speak **f**; even now he is coming

FLUNG (5) [FLING]

Dt 9:17 of the two tablets and **f** them from my two hands,
Ps 140:10 Let them be **f** into pits, no more to rise!
La 3:53 they **f** me alive into a pit and hurled stones on me;
Am 4:3 you shall be **f** out into Harmon, says the LORD.
4Mc 12:19 he **f** himself into the braziers and

FLUSHED (2)

Tob 2:14 I became **f** with anger against her over this.
AdE 15:7 Lifting his face, **f** with splendor,

FLUTE (11) [FLUTES, FLUTISTS]

1Sa 10:5 tambourine, **f**, and lyre playing in front of them;
Isa 5:12 tambourine and **f** and wine,
30:29 of heart, as when one sets out to the sound of the **f**
Jer 48:36 Therefore my heart moans for Moab like a **f**,
48:36 and my heart moans like a **f** for the people
Mt 9:23 the **f** players and the crowd making a commotion,
11:17 'We played the **f** for you, and you did not dance;
Lk 7:32 'We played the **f** for you, and you did not dance;
1Co 14:7 such as the **f** or the harp.
Sir 40:21 The **f** and the harp make sweet melody,
1Mc 3:45 the **f** and the harp ceased to play.

FLUTES (2) [FLUTE]

Ps 5:T *To the leader: for the **f**. A Psalm of David.*
1Es 5:2 with the music of drums and **f**;

FLUTISTS (1) [FLUTE]

Rev 18:22 of **f** and trumpeters will be heard in you no more;

FLUTTERING (1)

Isa 16:2 Like **f** birds, like scattered nestlings,

FLUX (KJV) See DYSENTERY

FLY (15) [FLEW, FLIES, FLIGHT, FLYING]

Ge 1:20 and let birds **f** above the earth across the dome of
Job 5:7 to trouble just as sparks **f** upward.
20:8 They will **f** away like a dream, and not be found;
Ps 55:6 I would **f** away and be at rest;
90:10 they are soon gone, and we **f** away.
Isa 7:18 that day the LORD will whistle for the **f** that is at
60:8 Who are these that **f** like a cloud,
Hos 9:11 Ephraim's glory shall **f** away like a bird—
Na 3:17 when the sun rises, they **f** away;
Hab 1:8 they **f** like an eagle swift to devour.
Rev 12:14 she could **f** from the serpent into the wilderness,
19:17 with a loud voice he called to all the birds that **f**
Wis 5:21 Shafts of lightning will **f** with true aim,
Sir 43:14 and the clouds **f** out like birds.
2Es 5:6 and the birds shall **f** away together;

FLYING (14) [FLY]

Ps 148:10 creeping things and **f** birds!
Pr 23:5 **f** like an eagle toward heaven.
26:2 like a swallow in its **f**,
Isa 14:29 and its fruit will be a **f** fiery serpent.
29:5 and the multitude of tyrants like **f** chaff.
30:6 of lioness and roaring lion, of viper and **f** serpent,
Zec 5:1 Again I looked up and saw a **f** scroll.
5:2 I answered, "I see a **f** scroll;
Rev 4:7 and the fourth living creature like a **f** eagle.
14:6 Then I saw another angel **f** in midheaven,
Sir 11:3 The bee is small among **f** creatures,
43:17 He scatters the snow like birds **f** down,
2Es 15:41 fire and hail and **f** swords and floods of water,
4Mc 14:17 by **f** in circles around them in the anguish of love,

FOAL (3)

Ge 49:11 Binding his **f** to the vine and his donkey's colt to
Zec 9:9 on a colt, the **f** of a donkey.
Mt 21:5 and on a colt, the **f** of a donkey."

FOAM (2) [FOAMING, FOAMS]

Ps 46:3 though its waters roar and **f**,
Jude 1:13 casting up the **f** of their own shame;

FOAMING (2) [FOAM]

Ps 75:8 the hand of the LORD there is a cup with **f** wine,
Mk 9:20 on the ground and rolled about, **f** at the mouth.

FOAMS (2) [FOAM]

Mk 9:18 and he **f** and grinds his teeth and becomes rigid;
Lk 9:39 It convulses him until he **f** at the mouth;

FODDER (8)

Ge 24:25 of straw and **f** and a place to spend the night."
24:32 and gave him straw and **f** for the camels,
42:27 of them opened his sack to give his donkey **f** at
43:24 and when he had given their donkeys **f**,
Jdg 19:19 We your servants have straw and **f**
Job 6:5 or the ox low over its **f**?
Sir 33:25 **F** and a stick and burdens for a donkey;
38:26 and he is careful about **f** for the heifers.

FOE (21) [FOES]

Ex 23:22 be an enemy to your enemies and a **f** to your foes.
Est 7:6 Esther said, "A **f** and enemy,
Ps 7:4 with harm or plundered my **f** without cause,
44:10 You made us turn back from the **f**,
60:11 O grant us help against the **f**,
68:23 of your dogs may have their share from the **f**."
74:10 How long, O God, is the **f** to scoff?
78:42 or the day when he redeemed them from the **f**;
78:61 his glory to the hand of the **f**.
106:10 So he saved them from the hand of the **f**,
108:12 O grant us help against the **f**,
Jer 30:14 the punishment of a merciless **f**,
La 1:5 her children have gone away, captives before the **f**.
1:7 When her people fell into the hand of the **f**,
1:7 the **f** looked on mocking over her downfall.
2:4 with his right hand set like a **f**;
4:12 **f** or enemy could enter the gates of Jerusalem.
Zec 8:10 from the **f** for those who went out or came in,
10:5 trampling the **f** in the mud of the streets;
Sir 19:8 With friend or **f** do not report it,
1Mc 2:9 her youths by the sword of the **f**.

FOES (49) [FOE]

Ge 24:60 offspring gain possession of the gates of their **f**."
Ex 23:22 be an enemy to your enemies and a foe to your **f**.
Lev 26:17 your **f** shall rule over you,
Nu 10:35 and your **f** flee before you."
24:8 the nations that are his **f** and break their bones.
2Sa 24:13 Or will you flee three months before your **f**
1Ch 21:12 or three months of devastation by your **f**,
Est 9:1 when the Jews would gain power over their **f**,
Ps 3:1 O LORD, how many are my **f**!
6:7 they grow weak because of all my **f**.
8:2 a bulwark because of your **f**,
10:5 as for their **f**, they scoff at them.
13:4 my **f** will rejoice because I am shaken.
25:19 Consider how many are my **f**,
27:2 my adversaries and **f**—they shall stumble and fall.
30:1 and did not let my **f** rejoice over me.
38:19 Those who are my **f** without cause are mighty,
44:5 Through you we push down our **f**;
44:7 But you have saved us from our **f**,
56:1 all day long **f** oppress me;
60:12 it is he who will tread down our **f**.
69:19 my **f** are all known to you.
72:9 May his **f** bow down before him,
74:4 Your **f** have roared within your holy place;
74:23 Do not forget the clamor of your **f**,
81:14 and turn my hand against their **f**.
89:23 I will crush his **f** before him and strike
89:42 You have exalted the right hand of his **f**;
105:24 and made them stronger than their **f**,
108:13 it is he who will tread down our **f**.
110:2 Rule in the midst of your **f**.
112:8 in the end they will look in triumph on their **f**.
119:139 because my **f** forget your words.
136:24 and rescued us from our **f**,
Isa 1:24 and avenge myself on my **f**!
29:5 the multitude of your **f** shall be like small dust,
42:13 he shows himself mighty against his **f**.
Jer 30:16 and all your **f**, everyone of them,
46:10 to gain vindication from his **f**.
La 1:5 Her **f** have become the masters,
1:17 that his neighbors should become his **f**;
2:17 and exalted the might of your **f**.
Na 3:13 The gates of your land are wide open to your **f**;
Mt 10:36 one's **f** will be members of one's own household.
Rev 11:5 fire pours from their mouth and consumes their **f**;
AdE 13:15 for the eyes of our **f** are upon us to annihilate us,
Wis 5:20 with him to fight against his frenzied **f**.
11:3 withstood their enemies and fought off their **f**.
Sir 25:7 a man who lives to see the downfall of his **f**.

FOILED (2)

Jdt 16:5 But the Lord Almighty has **f** them by the hand of
3Mc 1:6 Now that he had **f** the plot,

FOLD (14) [FOLDING, FOLDS]

Ne 5:13 I also shook out the **f** of my garment and said,
Job 5:24 you shall inspect your **f** and miss nothing.
Ecc 4:5 Fools **f** their hands and consume their own flesh.
Jer 23:3 and I will bring them back to their **f**,
25:30 he will roar mightily against his **f**, and shout,
49:20 surely their **f** shall be appalled at their fate.

Jer 50: 6 they have forgotten their f.
50:45 surely their f shall be appalled at their fate.
Eze 25: 5 a pasture for camels and Ammon a f for flocks.
Mic 2:12 I will set them together like sheep in a f,
Hab 3:17 the flock is cut off from the f and there is no herd
Hag 2:12 If one carries consecrated meat in the f
2:12 and with the f touches bread, or stew, or wine,
Jn 10:16 I have other sheep that do not belong to this f.

FOLDING (4) [FOLD]

1Ki 6:34 the two leaves of the one door were f,
6:34 and the two leaves of the other door were f.
Pr 6:10 a little slumber, a little f of the hands to rest,
24:33 a little slumber, a little f of the hands to rest,

FOLDS‡ (6) [FOLD]

Nu 32:24 for your little ones, and f for your flocks;
32:36 and Beth-haran, fortified cities, and f for sheep.
Job 41:23 The f of its flesh cling together;
Ps 50: 9 a bull from your house, or goats from your f.
Jer 25:37 and the peaceful f are devastated,
Zep 2: 6 meadows for shepherds and f for flocks.

FOLIAGE (4)

Eze 17: 6 it brought forth branches, put forth f.
Da 4:12 Its f was beautiful, its fruit abundant,
4:14 strip off its f and scatter its fruit.
4:21 whose f was beautiful and its fruit abundant,

FOLK (1)

Jer 6:11 the old f and the very aged.

FOLK (KJV) See also PEOPLE

FOLLIES (1) [FOOL]

Ps 73: 7 their hearts overflow with f.

FOLLOW‡ (140) [FOLLOWED, FOLLOWER, FOLLOWERS, FOLLOWING, FOLLOWS]

Ge 24: 5 "Perhaps the woman may not be willing to f me
24: 8 But if the woman is not willing to f you,
24:39 'Perhaps the woman will not f me.'
41:31 in the land because of the famine that will f,
44: 4 Joseph said to his steward, "Go, f after the men;
Ex 11: 8 'Leave us, you and all the people who f you.'
16: 4 whether they will f my instruction or not.
23: 2 You shall not f a majority in wrongdoing;
23:24 or worship them, or f their practices,
Lev 18: 3 You shall not f their statutes.
20: 5 and all who f them in prostituting themselves
20:23 You shall not f the practices of the nation
26: 3 If you f my statutes and keep my commandments
Nu 15:39 f the lust of your own heart and your own eyes.
Dt 5:33 You must f exactly the path that
6:14 Do not f other gods, any of the gods of
8:19 the LORD your God and f other gods to serve
11:28 to f other gods that you have not known.
13: 2 "Let us f other gods" (whom you have not known)
13: 4 The LORD your God you shall f,
Jos 3: 3 then you shall set out from your place. F it,
Jdg 2:17 they did not f their example.
3:28 He said to them, "F after me;
6:34 and the Abiezrites were called out to f him.
6:35 and they too were called out to f him.
9: 3 and their hearts inclined to f Abimelech,
Ru 2: 9 the field that is being reaped, and f behind them.
1Sa 8: 3 Yet his sons did not f in his ways,
8: 5 "You are old and your sons do not f in your ways;
12:14 both you and the king who reigns over you will f
25:27 be given to the young men who f my lord.
30:21 to f David, and who had been left at
2Sa 17: 9 a slaughter among the troops who f Absalom.'
20:11 and whoever is for David, let him f Joab."
1Ki 11: 2 they will surely incline your heart to f their gods";
11: 6 and did not completely f the LORD,
11:10 that he should not f other gods;
18:21 If the LORD is God, f him;
18:21 but if Baal, then f him."
19:20 and then I will f you."
20:10 a handful for each of the people who f me."
2Ki 6:19 f me, and I will bring you to
10:31 not careful to f the law of the LORD the God
17:34 They do not worship the LORD and they do not f
23: 3 to f the LORD, keeping his commandments,
2Ch 34:31 to f the LORD, keeping his commandments,
Job 21:33 everyone will f after, and those who went
Ps 1: 1 not f the advice of the wicked, or take the path
23: 6 Surely goodness and mercy shall f me all the days
38:20 for good are my adversaries because I f
45:14 behind her the virgins, her companions, f.
81:12 to their stubborn hearts, to f their own counsels.
94:15 and all the upright in heart will f it.
Pr 5: 5 her steps f the path to Sheol.
12:11 but those who f worthless pursuits have no sense.
20: 7 happy are the children who f them!
Ecc 4:15 f that youth who replaced the king;
11: 9 F the inclination of your heart and the desire
SS 1: 8 f the tracks of the flock, and pasture your kids
Isa 45:14 over to you and be yours, they shall f you;
Jer 3:17 shall no longer stubbornly f their own evil will.
13:10 who stubbornly f their own will and have gone
18:12 We will f our own plans,
Jer 23:17 to all who stubbornly f their own stubborn hearts,
32:23 But they did not obey your voice or f your law;
42:16 that you dread shall f close after you into Egypt;
Eze 11:20 so that they may f my statutes
13: 3 for the senseless prophets who f their own spirit,
20:18 Do not f the statutes of your parents,
20:19 I the LORD am your God; f my statutes,
20:21 they did not f my statutes,
36:27 and make you f my statutes and be careful
37:24 They shall f my ordinances and be careful
43:11 so that they may observe and f the entire plan
Da 11:43 the Libyans and the Ethiopians shall f in his train.
Mt 4:19 And he said to them, "F me,
8:19 "Teacher, I will f you wherever you go."
8:22 But Jesus said to him, "F me,
9: 9 and he said to him, "F me."
10:38 not take up the cross and f me is not worthy
16:24 and take up their cross and f me.
19:21 in heaven; then come, f me."
23: 3 do whatever they teach you and f it;
Mk 1:17 "F me and I will make you fish for people."
2:14 and he said to him, "F me."
5:37 He allowed no one to f him except Peter, James,
8:34 and take up their cross and f me.
10:21 in heaven; then come, f me."
14:13 of water will meet you; f him,
15:41 to f him and provided for him when he was
Lk 5:27 and he said to him, "F me."
9:23 and take up their cross daily and f me.
9:49 because he does not f with us."
9:57 "I will f you wherever you go."
9:59 To another he said, "F me."
9:61 Another said, "I will f you, Lord;
14:27 Whoever does not carry the cross and f me cannot
18:22 in heaven; then come, f me."
21: 9 but the end will not f immediately."
22:10 f him into the house he enters
Jn 1:43 He found Philip and said to him, "F me."
10: 4 and the sheep f him because they know his voice.
10: 5 They will not f a stranger,
10:27 I know them, and they f me.
12:26 Whoever serves me must f me, and where I am,
13:36 "Where I am going, you cannot f me now;
13:36 but you will f afterward."
13:37 "Lord, why can I not f you now?
21:19 After this he said to him, "F me."
21:22 what is that to you? F me!"
Ac 5:37 at the time of the census and got people to f him;
12: 8 "Wrap your cloak around you and f me."
14:16 the nations to f their own ways;
20:30 the truth in order to entice the disciples to f them.
27:44 the rest to f, some on planks and others on pieces
Ro 4:12 not only circumcised but who also f the example
1Co 16: 1 you should f the directions I gave to the churches
Gal 6:16 As for those who will f this rule—
1Ti 5:15 For some have already turned away to f Satan.
5:24 while the sins of others f them there.
1Pe 2:21 so that you should f in his steps.
2Pe 1:16 For we did not f cleverly devised myths
2: 2 Even so, many will f their licentious ways,
Rev 14: 4 these f the Lamb wherever he goes.
14:13 from their labors, for their deeds f them."
Jdt 5: 7 not wish to f the gods of their ancestors who were
11: 6 If you f out the words of your servant,
Sir 5: 2 Do not f your inclination and strength in pursuing
5: 9 Do not winnow in every wind, or f every path.
18:30 SELF-CONTROL Do not f your base desires,
27:17 but if you betray his secrets, do not f after him.
46:10 that all the Israelites might see how good it is to f
Aza 1:17 and may we unreservedly f you,
1:18 And now with all our heart we f you;
1Mc 1:44 he directed them to f customs strange to the land,
6:23 to live by what he said, and to f his commands.
2Mc 2: 4 that the tent and the ark should f with him,
9:27 that he will f my policy and will treat you
15: 2 the Jews who were compelled to f him said,
2Es 7:35 Recompense shall f, and the reward shall

FOLLOWED‡ (129) [FOLLOW]

Ge 24:61 mounted the camels, and f the man;
32:19 the second and the third and all who f the droves,
Ex 14:28 entire army of Pharaoh that had f them into the sea;
Nu 14:24 a different spirit and has f me wholeheartedly,
16:25 the elders of Israel f him.
32:11 because they have not unreservedly f me—
32:12 for they have unreservedly f the LORD.'
Dt 4: 3 from among you everyone who f the Baal of Peor,
Jos 14: 8 yet I wholeheartedly f the LORD my God.
14: 9 you have wholeheartedly f the LORD my God.'
14:14 because he wholeheartedly f the LORD,
Jdg 2:12 they f other gods, from among the gods of
9: 4 and reckless fellows, who f him.
13:11 Manoah got up and f his wife,
1Sa 13: 7 and all the people f him trembling.
13:15 The rest of the people f Saul to join the army;
14:22 they too f closely after them in the battle.
17:13 three eldest sons of Jesse had f Saul to the battle;
17:14 David was the youngest; the three eldest f Saul,
2Sa 2:10 But the house of Judah f David.
2:19 to the right nor to the left as he f him.
3:31 And King David f the bier.
11: 8 and there f him a present from the king.
15:16 So the king left, f by all his household,
15:17 The king left, f by all the people;
15:18 the six hundred Gittites who had f him from Gath,
17:23 When Ahithophel saw that his counsel was not f,
2Sa 20: 2 of Israel withdrew from David and f Sheba son
20: 2 of Judah f their king steadfastly from the Jordan
20:14 and all the Bichrites assembled, and f him inside.
1Ki 11: 5 Solomon f Astarte the goddess of the Sidonians,
12:20 There was no one who f the house of David,
14: 8 who kept my commandments and f me
16:21 half of the people f Tibni son of Ginath,
16:21 to make him king, and half f Omri.
16:22 But the people who f Omri overcame
16:22 the people who f Tibni son of Ginath;
18:18 the commandments of the LORD and f
19:21 he set out and f Elijah, and became his servant.
20:19 and the army that f them.
2Ki 4:30 So he rose up and f her.
13: 2 and f the sins of Jeroboam son of Nebat,
17:15 they f the nations that were around them,
2Ch 22: 5 even f their advice, and went with Jehoram son
27: 2 But the people still f corrupt practices.
Ne 4:23 of the guard who f me ever took off our clothes;
12:38 and I f them with half of the people on the wall,
Job 31: 7 and my heart has f my eyes,
Jer 2: 2 how you f me in the wilderness,
8: 2 which they have f, and which they have inquired
9:14 but have stubbornly f their own hearts
Eze 5: 7 and have not f my statutes or kept my ordinances,
10:11 the others f without veering as they moved.
11:12 whose statutes you have not f,
16:47 You not only f their ways,
Mic 6:16 and you have f their counsels.
Hab 3: 5 him went pestilence, and plague f close behind.
Mt 4:20 Immediately they left their nets and f him.
4:22 the boat and their father, and f him.
4:25 And great crowds f him from Galilee,
8: 1 down from the mountain, great crowds f him;
8:10 he was amazed and said to those who f him,
8:23 when he got into the boat, his disciples f him.
9: 9 And he got up and f him.
9:19 And Jesus got up and f him, with his disciples.
9:27 Jesus went on from there, two blind men f him,
12:15 Many crowds f him, and he cured all of them,
14:13 they f him on foot from the towns.
19: 2 Large crowds f him, and he cured them there.
19:27 "Look, we have left everything and f you.
19:28 you who have f me will also sit on twelve thrones,
20:29 they were leaving Jericho, a large crowd f him.
20:34 Immediately they regained their sight and f him.
21: 9 that went ahead of him and that f were shouting,
27:55 they had f Jesus from Galilee and had provided
Mk 1:18 And immediately they left their nets and f him.
1:20 in the boat with the hired men, and f him.
2:14 And he got up and f him.
2:15 for there were many who f him.
3: 7 and a great multitude from Galilee f him;
5:24 And a large crowd f him and pressed in on him.
6: 1 to his hometown, and his disciples f him.
10:28 "Look, we have left everything and f you."
10:32 they were amazed, and those who f were afraid.
10:52 Immediately he regained his sight and f him on
11: 9 ahead and those who f were shouting,
14:54 Peter had f him at a distance,
Lk 5:11 they left everything and f him.
5:28 And he got up, left everything, and f him.
7: 9 and turning to the crowd that f him, he said,
9:11 When the crowds found out about it, they f him;
18:28 "Look, we have left our homes and f you."
18:43 Immediately he regained his sight and f him,
22:39 of Olives; and the disciples f him.
23:27 A great number of the people f him,
23:49 including the women who had f him from Galilee,
23:55 women who had come with him from Galilee f,
Jn 1:37 two disciples heard him say this, and they f Jesus.
1:40 who heard John speak and f him was Andrew,
11:31 They f her because they thought
18:15 Simon Peter and another disciple f Jesus.
Ac 5:36 all who f him were dispersed and disappeared.
5:37 and all who f him were scattered.
12: 9 Peter went out and f him;
13:43 many Jews and devout converts to Judaism f Paul
16:17 While she f Paul and us, she would cry out,
21:36 crowd that f kept shouting, "Away with him!"
1Co 10: 4 For they drank from the spiritual rock that f them,
Col 3: 7 These are the ways you also once f,
1Ti 4: 6 and of the sound teaching that you have f.
Rev 6: 8 Its rider's name was Death, and Hades f with him;
13: 3 In amazement the whole earth f the beast.
14: 8 Then another angel, a second, f, saying, "Fallen,
14: 9 Then another angel, a third, f them,
Tob 8: 3 of Egypt. But Raphael f him,
Jdt 2:24 Then he f the Euphrates and passed
9: 5 and those that went before and those that f.
15:13 while all the men of Israel f,
AdE 15: 4 while the other f, carrying her train.
Sir Pr: 1 and the Prophets and the others that f them,
51:15 from my youth I f her steps.
Bar 1:22 but all of us f the intent of our own wicked hearts
1Mc 5:43 and the whole army f him.
7:45 and as they f they kept sounding the battle call on
9:16 they turned and f close behind Judas and his men.
2Mc 2: 6 of those who f him came up intending to mark
8:36 because they f the laws ordained by him.
3Mc 2:26 themselves also f his will.
2Es 11:20 and in due time the wings that f also rose up on

FOLLOWER (1) [FOLLOW]

Sir 46: 6 for he was a devoted f of the Mighty One.

FOLLOWERS (8) [FOLLOW]

Jdg 8: 5 "Please give some loaves of bread to my **f**,
1Ki 11:24 He gathered **f** around him and became leader of
Mt 16:24 "If any want to become my **f**,
Mk 8:34 and said to them, "If any want to become my **f**,
Lk 9:23 he said to them all, "If any want to become my **f**,
Jn 18:36 my **f** would be fighting to keep me
Sir 45:18 Dathan and Abiram and their **f** and the company
2Mc 10: 1 Now Maccabeus and his **f**,

FOLLOWING (113) [FOLLOW]

Ge 45:23 To his father he sent the **f**:
47:18 that year was ended, they came to him the **f** year,
Ex 6:14 The **f** are the heads of their ancestral houses:
6:16 The **f** are the names of the sons of Levi according
Lev 11: 4 you shall not eat the **f**:
18: 4 **f** them: I am the LORD your God.
Nu 3:17 The **f** were the sons of Levi, by their names:
6:21 so they shall do, **f** the law for their consecration.
14:43 because you have turned back from **f** the LORD,
32:15 If you turn away from **f** him,
Dt 2:26 to King Sihon of Heshbon with the **f** terms
7: 4 for that would turn away your children from **f** me,
28:14 **f** other gods to serve them.
Jos 6: 8 the ark of the covenant of the LORD **f** them.
12: 7 The **f** are the kings of the land whom Joshua and
21: 3 to the Levites the **f** towns and pasture lands out
21: 9 of Simeon they gave the **f** towns mentioned
22:16 of Israel in turning away today from **f** the LORD,
22:18 that you must turn away today from **f** the LORD!
22:23 building an altar to turn away from **f** the LORD;
22:29 and turn away this day from **f** the LORD
Jdg 2:19 **f** other gods, worshiping them and bowing down
4:14 with ten thousand warriors **f** him.
5:14 From Ephraim they set out into the valley, **f** you,
9:42 On the **f** day the people went out into the fields.
9:49 and **f** Abimelech put it against the stronghold,
Ru 1:16 to leave you or to turn back from **f** you!
1Sa 12:20 yet do not turn aside from **f** the LORD,
14:13 with his armor-bearer **f** after him.
15:11 for he has turned back from **f** me,
24: 1 When Saul returned from **f** the Philistines,
2Sa 2:21 But Asahel would not turn away from **f** him.
2:22 to Asahel, "Turn away from **f** me;
7: 8 I took you from the pasture, from **f** the sheep to
24:19 **F** Gad's instructions, David went up,
1Ki 1:35 You shall go up **f** him.
1:40 And all the people went up **f** him,
9: 6 "If you turn aside from **f** me,
11:27 The **f** was the reason he rebelled against the king.
19:21 He returned from **f** him, took the yoke of oxen,
21: 1 Later the **f** events took place:
2Ki 17:21 Jeroboam drove Israel from **f** the LORD
18: 6 from **f** him but kept the commandments that
21: 2 **f** the abominable practices of the nations that
1Ch 12: 1 The **f** are those who came to David at Ziklag,
17: 7 I took you from the pasture, from **f** the sheep,
21:19 So David went up **f** Gad's instructions,
2Ch 34:33 from **f** the LORD the God of their ancestors.
35: 4 **f** the written directions of King David of Israel
36:14 **f** all the abominations of the nations;
Ezr 2:59 The **f** were those who came up from Tel-melah,
Ne 7: 5 and I found the **f** written in it:
7:61 The **f** were those who came up from Tel-melah,
Job 34:27 because they turned aside from **f** him,
Pr 20:18 wage war by **f** wise guidance.
Isa 59:13 and turning away from **f** our God,
65: 2 in a way that is not good, **f** their own devices;
66:17 **f** the one in the center, eating the flesh of pigs,
Jer 3:19 My Father, and would not turn from **f** me.
16:12 **f** your stubborn evil will, refusing to listen to me.
Eze 5: 6 rejecting my ordinances and not **f** my statutes.
Da 9:10 the voice of the LORD our God by **f** his laws,
Am 7:15 and the LORD took me from **f** the flock,
Zep 1: 6 those who have turned back from **f** the LORD,
Mt 10: 5 These twelve Jesus sent out with the **f** instructions:
26:58 But Peter was **f** him at a distance,
Mk 9:38 because he was not **f** us."
11:12 On the **f** day, when they came from Bethany,
14:51 A certain young man was **f** him,
Lk 22:54 But Peter was **f** at a distance.
Jn 1:38 When Jesus turned and saw them **f**,
6: 2 A large crowd kept **f** him,
20: 6 Simon Peter came, **f** him, and went into the tomb.
21:20 and saw the disciple whom Jesus loved **f** them;
Ac 10:24 The **f** day they came to Caesarea.
15:23 with the **f** letter: "The brothers,
16:11 a straight course to Samothrace, the **f** day
16:24 **F** these instructions, he put them in
20:15 and on the **f** day we arrived opposite Chios.
Ro 5:16 judgment **f** one trespass brought condemnation,
5:16 the free gift **f** many trespasses brings justification.
1Co 11:17 Now in the **f** instructions I do not commend you,
Eph 2: 2 **f** the course of this world,
2: 2 **f** the ruler of the power of the air,
2: 3 **f** the desires of flesh and senses,
1Ti 1:18 so that by **f** them you may fight the good fight,
2Pe 2:15 **f** the road of Balaam son of Bosor,
Rev 19:14 white and pure, were **f** him on white horses.
AdE 1: 1 the **f** things happened in the days of Artaxerxes,
13: 1 "The Great King, Artaxerxes, writes the **f** to
13: 5 perversely **f** a strange manner of life and laws,
16: 1 The **f** is a copy of this letter:
Sir 33:16 I was like a gleaner **f** the grape-pickers;
42: 1 Of the **f** things do not be ashamed,
1Mc 10:17 he wrote a letter and sent it to him, in the **f** words:
1Mc 10:25 So he sent a message to them in the **f** words:
10:51 to Ptolemy king of Egypt with the **f** message:
10:69 he sent the **f** message to the high priest Jonathan:
14:28 the **f** was proclaimed to us:
15:15 in which the **f** was written:
2Mc 9:18 for himself and wrote to the Jews the **f** letter,
1Es 2:16 the **f** letter, against those who were living in Judea
5:36 The **f** are those who came up from Tel-melah
5:38 Of the priests the **f** had assumed the priesthood
7: 1 and their associates, **f** the orders of King Darius,
8: 8 The **f** is a copy of the written commission
3Mc 5: 2 and ordered him on the **f** day to drug all
5:48 at the gate and by the **f** armed forces,
6:21 the armed forces **f** them and began trampling
6:41 and wrote the **f** letter for them to the generals in
2Es 10:59 I slept that night and the **f** one, as he had told me.
4Mc 8: 1 by **f** a philosophy in accordance
8:16 Would they not have been the **f**?

FOLLOWS (45) [FOLLOW]

Ge 50: 4 please speak to Pharaoh as **f**:
Ex 21:22 there is a miscarriage, and yet no further harm **f**,
21:23 If any harm **f**, then you shall give life for life,
Dt 1: 5 Moses undertook to expound this law as **f**:
2: 4 and charge the people as **f**:
3:18 At that time, I charged you as **f**:
27: 1 and the elders of Israel charged all the people as **f**:
27:11 The same day Moses charged the people as **f**:
32:48 that very day the LORD addressed Moses as **f**:
Jos 16: 5 of the Ephraimites by their families was as **f**:
2Sa 14: 3 Go to the king and speak to him as **f**."
2Ki 11:15 and kill with the sword anyone who **f** her."
2Ch 23:14 anyone who **f** her is to be put to the sword."
Ezr 4: 8 a letter against Jerusalem to King Artaxerxes as **f**
5: 7 in which was written as **f**:
Ne 8:15 in all their towns and in Jerusalem as **f**,
Pr 7:22 Right away he **f** her, and goes like an ox to
10: 9 but whoever **f** perverse ways will be found out.
28:18 but whoever **f** crooked ways will fall into the Pit.
28:19 but one who **f** worthless pursuits will have plenty
Eze 7:26 Disaster comes upon disaster, rumor **f** rumor;
18: 9 **f** my statutes, and is careful
18:17 observes my ordinances, and **f** my statutes;
Hos 4: 2 and adultery break out; bloodshed **f** bloodshed.
Jn 8:12 Whoever **f** me will never walk in darkness
Heb 4: 4 in one place it speaks about the seventh day as **f**,
Tob 7: 7 He also spoke to him as **f**, "Blessings on you,
1Mc 2:17 Then the king's officers spoke to Mattathias as **f**:
8:19 they entered the senate chamber and spoke as **f**:
8:31 we have written to him as **f**,
11:29 about all these things; its contents were as **f**:
13:35 and wrote him a letter as **f**,
14:22 in our public decrees, as **f**, 'Numenius son
15: 2 its contents were as **f**: "King Antiochus to Simon
2Mc 7:27 she spoke in their native language as **f**,
11:27 To the nation the king's letter was as **f**:
1Es 2:25 in Samaria and Syria and Phoenicia, wrote as **f**:
3Mc 2: 1 with calm dignity, prayed as **f**:
5:39 at his instability of mind, remonstrated as **f**:
6: 1 upon the holy God, and he prayed as **f**:
2Es 6: 7 the first age and the beginning of the age that **f**?"
6: 9 and Jacob is the beginning of the age that **f**.
4Mc 1:22 Thus desire precedes pleasure and delight **f** it.
5:15 he began to address the people as **f**:
16: 5 over them and perhaps spoken as **f**:

FOLLY‡ (48) [FOOL]

1Sa 25:25 Nabal is his name, and **f** is with him;
Job 42: 8 not to deal with you according to your **f**;
Ps 69: 5 O God, you know my **f**; the wrongs I have done
Pr 5:23 and because of their great **f** they are lost.
12:23 but the mind of a fool broadcasts **f**.
13:16 do all things intelligently, but the fool displays **f**.
14: 8 but the **f** of fools misleads.
14:18 The simple are adorned with **f**,
14:24 but **f** is the garland of fools.
14:29 but one who has a hasty temper exalts **f**.
15: 2 but the mouths of fools pour out **f**.
15:14 but the mouths of fools feed on **f**.
15:21 **F** is a joy to one who has no sense,
16:22 but **f** is the punishment of fools.
17:12 of its cubs than to confront a fool immersed in **f**.
18:13 If one gives answer before hearing, it is **f**
19: 3 One's own **f** leads to ruin,
22:15 **F** is bound up in the heart of a boy,
24: 9 The devising of **f** is sin,
26: 4 Do not answer fools according to their **f**,
26: 5 Answer fools according to their **f**,
26:11 to its vomit is a fool who reverts to his **f**.
27:22 but the **f** will not be driven out.
Ecc 1:17 to know wisdom and to know madness and **f**.
2: 3 and how to lay hold on **f**,
2:12 I turned to consider wisdom and madness and **f**;
2:13 that wisdom excels **f** as light excels darkness.
7:25 and to know that wickedness is **f** and
10: 1 so a little **f** outweighs wisdom and honor.
10: 6 **f** is set in many high places,
Isa 9:17 and every mouth spoke **f**.
32: 6 For fools speak **f**, and their minds plot iniquity:
Mk 7:22 deceit, licentiousness, envy, slander, pride, **f**.
2Ti 3: 9 their **f** will become plain to everyone.
Wis 10: 8 but also left for humankind a reminder of their **f**,
12:23 those who lived unrighteously, in a life of **f**,
Sir 8:15 and through their **f** you will perish with them.
20:31 Better are those who hide their **f** than those who
41:15 Better are those who hide their **f** than those who
Sir 47:20 and they were grieved at your **f**,
47:23 broad in **f** and lacking in sense, Rehoboam,
Bar 3:28 they perished through their **f**.
2Mc 4: 6 and that Simon would not stop his **f**.
4:40 man advanced in years and no less advanced in **f**.
14: 8 through the **f** of those whom I have mentioned
15:33 and would hang up these rewards of his **f** opposite
3Mc 3:16 who never cease from their **f**.
3:20 accommodated ourselves to their **f** and did

FOND (1)

Ge 25:28 Isaac loved Esau, because he was **f** of game;

FONDLED (3) [FONDLING]

Eze 23: 3 and their virgin bosoms were **f**.
23: 8 and **f** her virgin bosom and poured out their lust
23:21 when the Egyptians **f** your bosom

FONDLING (1) [FONDLED]

Ge 26: 8 of a window and saw him **f** his wife Rebekah.

FOOD‡ (343) [FOODS, SEAFOOD]

Ge 1:29 you shall have them for **f**.
1:30 I have given every green plant for **f**."
2: 9 that is pleasant to the sight and good for **f**,
3: 6 when the woman saw that the tree was good for **f**,
6:21 Also take with you every kind of **f** that is eaten,
6:21 and it shall serve as **f** for you and for them."
9: 3 Every moving thing that lives shall be **f** for you;
24:33 Then **f** was set before him to eat;
27: 4 Then prepare for me savory **f**, such as I like,
27: 7 and prepare for me savory **f** to eat,
27: 9 I may prepare from them savory **f** for your father,
27:14 and his mother prepared savory **f**,
27:17 Then she handed the savory **f**,
27:31 He also prepared savory **f**,
39: 6 he had no concern for anything but the **f**
40:17 all sorts of baked **f** for Pharaoh,
41:35 Let them gather all the **f** of these good years
41:35 under the authority of Pharaoh for **f** in the cities,
41:36 That **f** shall be a reserve for the land against
41:48 the **f** of the seven years when there was plenty in
41:48 and stored up **f** in the cities;
41:48 in every city the **f** from the fields around it.
42: 7 They said, "From the land of Canaan, to buy **f**."
42:10 your servants have come to buy **f**.
43: 2 "Go again, buy us a little more **f**."
43: 4 we will go down and buy you **f**;
43:20 my lord, we came down the first time to buy **f**;
43:22 down with us additional money to buy **f**.
44: 1 "Fill the men's sacks with **f**,
44:25 when our father said, 'Go again, buy us a little **f**,'
47:12 his brothers, and all his father's household with **f**,
47:13 Now there was no **f** in all the land,
47:15 to Joseph, and said, "Give us **f**!
47:16 I will give you **f** in exchange for your livestock,
47:17 Joseph gave them **f** in exchange for the horses,
47:17 That year he supplied them with **f** in exchange
47:19 Buy us and our land in exchange for **f**.
47:24 and as **f** for yourselves and your households, and
as **f** for your little ones."
49:20 Asher's **f** shall be rich,
Ex 16:22 On the sixth day they gathered twice as much **f**,
16:29 on the sixth day he gives you **f** for two days;
16:32 that they may see the **f** with which I fed you in
21:10 he shall not diminish the **f**, clothing,
29:33 the **f** by which atonement is made,
Lev 3:11 on the altar as a **f** offering by fire to the LORD.
3:16 the altar as a **f** offering by fire for a pleasing odor.
11:34 Any **f** that could be eaten shall be unclean if water
19:23 into the land and plant all kinds of trees for **f**,
21: 6 the **f** of their God; therefore they shall be holy.
21: 8 since they offer the **f** of your God;
21:17 a blemish may approach to offer the **f** of his God.
21:21 he shall not come near to offer the **f** of his God.
21:22 He may eat the **f** of his God,
22: 7 of the sacred donations, for they are his **f**.
22:11 those that are born in his house may eat of his **f**.
22:13 as in her youth, she may eat of her father's **f**.
22:25 from a foreigner to offer as **f** to your God;
25: 7 in your land all its yield shall be for **f**.
25:37 or provide them **f** at a profit.
Nu 21: 5 For there is no **f** and no water,
21: 5 and we detest this miserable **f**."
28: 2 My offering, the **f** for my offerings by fire,
28:24 for seven days, the **f** of an offering by fire,
Dt 2: 6 You shall purchase **f** from them for money,
2:28 You shall sell me **f** for money, so that I may eat,
10:18 providing them **f** and clothing.
20:19 Although you may take **f** from them,
20:20 the trees that you know do not produce **f**;
23: 4 because they did not meet you with **f** and water
28:26 Your corpses shall be **f** for every bird of the air
28:54 among you will begrudge **f** to his own brother,
28:56 the sole of her foot on the ground, will begrudge **f**
Jos 9:12 as our **f** for the journey, on the day we set out
Jdg 13:16 "If you detain me, I will not eat your **f**;
19: 5 "Fortify yourself with a bit of **f**,
Ru 1: 6 LORD had considered his people and given them **f**.
1Sa 14:24 "Cursed be anyone who eats **f** before it is evening
14:24 So none of the troops tasted **f**.
14:28 saying, 'Cursed be anyone who eats **f** this day.'
20:34 in fierce anger and ate no **f** on the second day of
2Sa 3:29 or who falls by the sword, or who lacks **f**!"
6:19 and distributed **f** among all the people,

2Sa 9:10 so that your master's grandson may have **f** to eat;
12:17 but he would not, nor did he eat **f** with them.
12:20 when he asked, they set **f** before him and he ate.
12:21 but when the child died, you rose and ate **f.**"
13: 5 and prepare the **f** in my sight,
13: 7 to your brother Amnon's house, and prepare **f**
13:10 "Bring the **f** into the chamber,
19:32 He had provided the king with **f** while he stayed
1Ki 4: 7 who provided **f** for the king and his household;
5: 9 And you shall meet my needs by providing **f**
5:11 of wheat as **f** for his household,
10: 5 the **f** of his table, the seating of his officials,
11:18 assigned him an allowance of **f,**
13: 8 nor will I eat **f** or drink water in this place.
13: 9 You shall not eat **f,** or drink water,
13:15 "Come home with me and eat some **f.**"
13:16 will I eat **f** or drink water with you in this place;
13:17 You shall not eat **f** or drink water there,
13:18 with you into your house so that he may eat **f**
13:19 and ate **f** and drank water in his house.
13:22 and have eaten **f** and drunk water in the place
13:22 'Eat no **f,** and drink no water,'
13:23 After the man of God had eaten **f** and had drunk,
19: 8 in the strength of that **f** forty days and forty nights
21: 7 Get up, eat some **f,** and be cheerful;
2Ki 4:42 bringing **f** from the first fruits to the man of God:
6:22 Set **f** and water before them so that they may eat
25: 3 in the city that there was no **f** for the people of
1Ch 12:40 came bringing **f** on donkeys, camels, mules,
2Ch 9: 4 the **f** of his table, the seating of his officials,
11:11 and put commanders in them, and stores of **f,** oil,
28:15 provided them with **f** and drink,
30:22 the people ate the **f** of the festival for seven days,
Ezr 2:63 that they were not to partake of the most holy **f,**
3: 7 to the masons and the carpenters, and **f,** drink,
Ne 5:14 neither I nor my brothers ate the **f** allowance of
5:15 and took **f** and wine from them,
5:18 yet with all this I did not demand the **f** allowance
7:65 that they were not to partake of the most holy **f,**
13:15 and I warned them at that time against selling **f.**
Est 2: 9 with her cosmetic treatments and her portion of **f,**
9:19 on which they send gifts of **f** to one another.
9:22 for sending gifts of **f** to one another and presents
Job 6: 7 they are like **f** that is loathsome to me.
12:11 Does not the ear test words as the palate tastes **f?**
20:14 yet their **f** is turned in their stomachs;
20:23 and rain it upon them as their **f.**
24: 5 scavenging in the wasteland **f** for their young.
33:20 and their appetites dainty **f.**
34: 3 for the ear tests words as the palate tastes **f.**
36:31 he governs peoples; he gives **f** in abundance.
38:41 and wander about for lack of **f?**
40:20 For the mountains yield **f** for it where all
Ps 42: 3 My tears have been my **f** day and night,
59:15 They roam about for **f,** and growl if they do
69:21 They gave me poison for **f,**
74:14 as **f** for the creatures of the wilderness.
78:18 in their heart by demanding the **f** they craved.
78:25 he sent them **f** in abundance.
78:30 while the **f** was still in their mouths,
79: 2 of your servants to the birds of the air for **f,**
104:14 to bring forth **f** from the earth,
104:21 seeking their **f** from God.
104:27 to you to give them their **f** in due season;
105:40 and gave them **f** from heaven in abundance.
107:18 they loathed any kind of **f,**
111: 5 He provides **f** for those who fear him;
136:25 who gives **f** to all flesh,
145:15 and you give them their **f** in due season.
146: 7 who gives **f** to the hungry.
147: 9 He gives to the animals their **f,**
Pr 6: 8 it prepares its **f** in summer,
12: 9 than to be self-important and lack **f.**
12:11 Those who till their land will have plenty of **f,**
13:23 The field of the poor may yield much **f,**
23: 3 the ruler's delicacies, for they are deceptive **f.**
27:27 there will be enough goats' milk for your **f,**
27:27 for the **f** of your household and nourishment
28: 3 the poor is a beating rain that leaves no **f.**
30: 8 feed me with the **f** that I need,
30:22 and a fool when glutted with **f;**
30:25 yet they provide their **f** in the summer;
31:14 she brings her **f** from far away.
31:15 She rises while it is still night and provides **f**
Isa 23:18 but her merchandise will supply abundant **f**
25: 6 of hosts will make for all peoples a feast of rich **f,**
25: 6 of rich **f** filled with marrow,
28: 1 which is on the head of those bloated with rich **f,**
28: 4 which is on the head of those bloated with rich **f,**
33:16 their **f** will be supplied, their water assured.
55: 2 and delight yourselves in rich **f.**
58:10 if you offer your **f** to the hungry and satisfy
62: 8 not again give your grain to be **f** for your enemies,
65:25 but the serpent—its **f** shall be dust!
Jer 5:17 They shall eat up your harvest and your **f;**
7:33 of this people will be **f** for the birds of the air,
16: 4 and their dead bodies shall become **f** for the birds
19: 7 for **f** to the birds of the air and to the wild animals
34:20 Their corpses shall become **f** for the birds of
40: 5 of the guard gave him an allowance of **f** and
44:17 We used to have plenty of **f,** and prospered,
52: 6 in the city that there was no **f** for the people of
La 1:11 they trade their treasures for **f**
1:19 while seeking **f** to revive their strength.
4: 4 children beg for **f,** but no one gives them anything.
4:10 became their **f** in the destruction of my people.
Eze 4:10 The **f** that you eat shall be twenty shekels a day
Eze 16:13 You had choice flour and honey and oil for **f.**
16:49 she and her daughters had pride, excess of **f,**
23:37 to them for **f** the children whom they had borne
29: 5 and to the birds of the air I have given you as **f.**
34: 5 scattered, they became **f** for all the wild animals.
34: 8 my sheep have become **f** for all the wild animals,
34:10 so that they may not be **f** for them.
44: 3 may sit in it to eat **f** before the LORD;
44: 7 profaning my temple when you offer to me my **f,**
47:12 there will grow all kinds of trees for **f.**
47:12 Their fruit will be for **f,**
48:18 Its produce shall be **f** for the workers of the city.
Da 1: 5 a daily portion of the royal rations of **f** and wine.
1: 8 not defile himself with the royal rations of **f**
1:10 he has appointed your **f** and your drink.
4:12 its fruit abundant, and it provided **f** for all.
4:21 and which provided **f** for all,
6:18 no **f** was brought to him, and sleep fled from him.
10: 3 I had eaten no rich **f,**
Hos 9: 3 and in Assyria they shall eat unclean **f.**
Joel 1:16 Is not the **f** cut off before our eyes,
Hab 1:16 for by them his portion is lavish, and his **f** is rich.
3:17 of the olive fails and the fields yield no **f;**
Hag 2:12 or oil, or any kind of **f,** does it become holy?
Mal 1: 7 By offering polluted **f** on my altar.
1:12 and the **f** for it may be despised.
3:10 so that there may be **f** in my house,
Mt 3: 4 and his **f** was locusts and wild honey.
6:25 Is not life more than **f,**
10:10 for laborers deserve their **f.**
14:15 so that they may go into the villages and buy **f**
15:26 "It is not fair to take the children's **f** and throw it
24:45 to give the other slaves their allowance of **f** at
25:35 for I was hungry and you gave me **f,**
25:37 was it that we saw you hungry and gave you **f,**
25:42 for I was hungry and you gave me no **f,**
Mk 2:25 and his companions were hungry and in need of **f?**
7:27 to take the children's **f** and throw it to the dogs."
Lk 3:11 and whoever has **f** must do likewise."
9:13 we are to go and buy **f** for all these people."
12:23 For life is more than **f,**
12:42 to give them their allowance of **f** at
Jn 4: 8 (His disciples had gone to the city to buy **f.**)
4:32 "I have **f** to eat that you do not know about."
4:34 "My **f** is to do the will of him who sent me and
6:27 Do not work for the **f** that perishes, but for the **f**
that endures for eternal life,
6:55 for my flesh is true **f** and my blood is true drink.
Ac 2:46 they broke bread at home and ate their **f** with glad
6: 1 in the daily distribution of **f.**
7:11 and our ancestors could find no **f.**
9:19 after taking some **f,** he regained his strength.
12:20 on the king's country for **f.**
14:17 and filling you with **f** and your hearts with joy."
16:34 He brought them up into the house and set **f**
23:14 by an oath to taste no **f** until we have killed Paul.
27:21 Since they had been without **f** for a long time,
27:33 Paul urged all of them to take some **f,** saying,
27:33 in suspense and remaining without **f,**
27:34 Therefore I urge you to take some **f,**
27:36 Then all of them were encouraged and took **f**
Ro 14:17 not **f** and drink but righteousness and peace
14:20 Do not, for the sake of **f,**
1Co 3: 2 I fed you with milk, not solid **f,**
3: 2 not solid food, for you were not ready for solid **f.**
6:13 **F** is meant for the stomach and the stomach for **f,**
8: 1 Now concerning **f** sacrificed to idols:
8: 4 Hence, as to the eating of **f** offered to idols,
8: 7 they still think of the **f** they eat as **f** offered to idols,
8: 8 "**F** will not bring us close to God."
8:10 be encouraged to the point of eating **f** sacrificed
8:13 Therefore, if **f** is a cause of their falling,
9: 4 Do we not have the right to our **f** and drink?
9:13 in the temple service get their **f** from the temple,
10: 3 and all ate the same spiritual **f,**
10:19 That **f** sacrificed to idols is anything,
2Co 9:10 and bread for **f** will supply and multiply your seed
11:27 hungry and thirsty, often without **f,**
Col 2:16 in matters of **f** and drink or of observing festivals,
1Ti 6: 8 but if we have **f** and clothing,
Heb 5:12 You need milk, not solid **f;**
5:14 But solid **f** is for the mature,
9:10 deal only with **f** and drink and various baptisms,
13: 9 not by regulations about **f,**
Jas 2:15 If a brother or sister is naked and lacks daily **f,**
Rev 2:14 of Israel, so that they would eat **f** sacrificed
2:20 to practice fornication and to eat **f** sacrificed
Tob 1:10 everyone of my kindred and my people ate the **f**
1:11 but I kept myself from eating the **f** of the Gentiles.
1:17 I would give my **f** to the hungry and my clothing
2: 2 for me and an abundance of **f** placed before me,
2: 5 I washed myself and ate my **f** in sorrow.
4:16 Give some of your **f** to the hungry,
Jdt 2:17 and innumerable sheep and oxen and goats for **f;**
4: 5 the villages on them and stored up **f** in preparation
5:10 to Egypt and lived there as long as they had **f.**
11:12 Since their **f** supply is exhausted
12: 9 in the tent until she ate her **f** toward evening.
13:10 who placed it in her **f** bag.
AdE 2: 9 with ointments and her portion of **f,** as well
4:16 and my maids and I will also go without **f.**
9:19 and send presents of **f** to one another,
9:22 and for sending presents of **f** to their friends and
Wis 13:12 the cast-off pieces of his work to prepare his **f,**
16: 3 that those people, when they desired **f,** might lose
16:20 of these things you gave your people **f** of angels,
19:11 when desire led them to ask for luxurious **f;**
Wis 19:21 quick-melting kind of heavenly **f.**
Sir 29:22 under their own crude roof than sumptuous **f** in
30:18 that is closed are like offerings of **f** placed upon
30:25 and merry at table will benefit from their **f.**
31:12 and do not say, "How much **f** there is here!"
31:21 If you are overstuffed with **f,** get up to vomit,
31:23 People bless the one who is liberal with **f,**
31:24 city complains of the one who is stingy with **f,**
36:23 The stomach will take any **f,** yet one **f** is better
37:20 he will be destitute of all **f,**
40:29 One loses self-respect with another person's **f,**
41: 1 and still is vigorous enough to enjoy **f!**
Bel 1:11 O king, set out the **f** and prepare the wine,
1:14 they had gone out, the king set out the **f** for Bel.
1:34 "Take the **f** that you have to Babylon, to Daniel,
1:37 Take the **f** that God has sent you."
1Mc 1:35 they stored up arms and **f,**
1:62 in their hearts not to eat unclean **f.**
1:63 to be defiled by **f** or to profane the holy covenant;
6:53 But they had no **f** in storage,
6:57 "Daily we grow weaker, our **f** supply is scant,
9:52 and in them he put troops and stores of **f.**
13:21 by way of the wilderness and to send them **f.**
13:33 and he stored **f** in the strongholds.
14:10 He supplied the towns with **f,**
2Mc 11:31 for the Jews to enjoy their own **f** and laws,
1Es 5:54 to the masons and the carpenters, and **f** and drink
8:79 and to give us **f** in the time of our servitude.
8:80 so that they have given us **f**
3Mc 6: 7 into the ground to lions as **f** for wild animals,
6:34 that the Jews would be destroyed and become **f**
2Es 1:19 and gave you manna for **f;**
9:34 or the sea a ship, or any dish **f** or drink,
12:51 and my **f** was of plants during those days.
4Mc 5: 2 and to compel them to eat pork and **f** sacrificed
5: 3 If any were not willing to eat defiling **f,**
5:19 be a petty sin if we were to eat defiling **f;**
5:25 "Therefore we do not eat defiling **f;**
6:19 an example in the eating of defiling **f.**
8: 2 any who ate defiling **f** would be freed after eating,
8:12 to persuade them out of fear to eat the defiling **f.**
8:29 to eat defiling **f,** all with one voice together,
13: 2 to their emotions and had eaten defiling **f,**

FOODS‡ (13) [FOOD]

Mk 7:19 (Thus he declared all **f** clean.)
1Ti 4: 3 and demand abstinence from **f,**
Sir 30:18 CONCERNING F Good things poured out upon a
3Mc 3: 4 they kept their separateness with respect to **f.**
3: 7 about the differences in worship and **f,**
4Mc 1:33 when we are attracted to forbidden **f** we abstain
1:34 and animals and all sorts of **f** that are forbidden
4:26 to compel everyone in the nation to eat defiling **f**
5:27 a way that you may deride us for eating defiling **f,**
7: 6 for reverence and purity, by eating defiling **f.**
8: 2 to compel an aged man to eat defiling **f,**
11:16 you intend to torture me for not eating defiling **f,**
11:25 to change our mind or to force us to eat defiling **f,**

FOOL‡ (77) [FOLLIES, FOLLY, FOOL'S, FOOLHARDY, FOOLISH, FOOLISHLY, FOOLISHNESS, FOOLS]

Nu 22:29 "Because you have made a **f** of me!
1Sa 26:21 I have been a **f,** and have made a great mistake."
2Sa 3:33 saying, "Should Abner die as a **f** dies?
Job 5: 2 vexation kills the **f,** and jealousy slays the simple.
Ps 39: 8 Do not make me the scorn of the **f.**
49:10 **f** and dolt perish together and leave their wealth
Pr 10: 8 but a babbling **f** will come to ruin.
10:14 but the babbling of a **f** brings ruin near.
10:18 and whoever utters slander is a **f.**
10:23 Doing wrong is like sport to a **f,**
11:29 and the **f** will be servant to the wise.
12:23 but the mind of a **f** broadcasts folly.
13:16 do all things intelligently, but the **f** displays folly.
14: 7 Leave the presence of a **f,**
14:16 but the **f** throws off restraint and is careless.
15: 5 A **f** despises a parent's instruction,
17: 7 Fine speech is not becoming to a **f;**
17:10 a discerning person than a hundred blows into a **f.**
17:12 of its cubs than to confront a **f** immersed in folly.
17:21 begets a **f** gets trouble; the parent of a **f** has no joy.
17:24 but the eyes of a **f** to the ends of the earth.
18: 2 A **f** takes no pleasure in understanding,
19: 1 of speech who is a **f.**
19:10 It is not fitting for a **f** to live in luxury,
20: 3 but every **f** is quick to quarrel.
21:20 in the house of the wise, but the **f** devours it.
23: 9 Do not speak in the hearing of a **f,**
26: 1 so honor is not fitting for a **f.**
26: 4 or you will be a **f** yourself.
26: 6 to send a message by a **f.**
26: 7 so does a proverb in the mouth of a **f.**
26: 8 like binding a stone in a sling to give honor to a **f.**
26: 9 of a drunkard is a proverb in the mouth of a **f.**
26:10 is one who hires a passing **f** or drunkard.
26:11 a dog that returns to its vomit is a **f** who reverts
27:22 Crush a **f** in a mortar with a pestle along
29:11 A **f** gives full vent to anger,
29:20 There is more hope for a **f** than for anyone
30:22 and a **f** when glutted with food;
Ecc 2:15 "What happens to the **f** will happen to me also;
7:17 Do not be too wicked, and do not be a **f;**
10: 2 but the heart of a **f** to the left.
Isa 32: 5 A **f** will no longer be called noble,

Hos 9: 7 “The prophet is a f, the man of the spirit is mad!”
Mt 5:22 ‘You f,’ you will be liable to the hell of fire.
Lk 12:20 But God said to him, ‘You f!
1Co 15:36 F! What you sow does
2Co 11:16 that I am a f; but if you do, then accept me as a f,
11:17 not with the Lord's authority, but as a f;
11:21 I am speaking as a f—I also dare to boast of that.
12: 6 But if I wish to boast, I will not be a f,
12:11 I have been a f!
Sir 4:27 Do not subject yourself to a f,
18:18 A f is ungracious and abusive,
19:11 the f suffers birth pangs like a woman in labor
19:12 so is gossip inside a f.
19:23 and there is a f who merely lacks wisdom.
20: 7 but a boasting f misses the right moment.
20:16 The f says, “I have no friends,
21:14 The mind of a f is like a broken jar;
21:15 when a f hears it, he laughs at it and throws it
21:18 Like a house in ruins is wisdom to a f,
21:20 A f raises his voice when he laughs,
21:22 The foot of a f rushes into a house,
22: 9 a f is like one who glues potsherds together,
22:10 a story to a f tells it to a drowsy man;
22:11 weep for the f, for he has left intelligence behind.
22:11 but the life of the f is worse than death.
22:14 And what is its name except “F”?
23:14 and behave like a f through bad habit;
25: 2 and an old f who commits adultery.
27:11 but the f changes like the moon.
31: 7 and every f will be taken captive by it.
31:30 Drunkenness increases the anger of a f
33: 5 The heart of a f is like a cart wheel,

FOOL'S (8) [FOOL]

Pr 18: 6 A f lips bring strife, and a f mouth invites a flogging.
27: 3 but a f provocation is heavier than both.
Ecc 5: 3 and a f voice with many words.
Sir 20:14 A f gift will profit you nothing,
20:20 A proverb from a f lips will be rejected,
21:16 A f chatter is like a burden on a journey,
22:18 a timid mind with a f resolve will not stand firm

FOOLHARDY (1) [FOOL]

Ps 49:13 Such is the fate of the f,

FOOLISH‡ (53) [FOOL]

Ge 31:28 What you have done is f.
Dt 32: 6 O f and senseless people?
32:21 provoke them with a f nation.
Job 2:10 “You speak as any f woman would speak.
Pr 9:13 The f woman is loud; she is ignorant
10: 1 but a f child is a mother's grief.
14: 1 but the f tears it down with her own hands.
15:20 but the f despise their mothers.
17:25 F children are a grief to their father and bitterness
30:32 If you have been f, exalting yourself,
Ecc 2:19 who knows whether they will be wise or f?
4:13 a poor but wise youth than an old but f king,
7: 7 Surely oppression makes the wise f,
Isa 19:11 The princes of Zoan are utterly f;
44:25 and makes their knowledge f;
Jer 4:22 “For my people are f, they do not know me;
5:21 O f and senseless people, who have eyes,
10: 8 They are both stupid and f;
Mt 7:26 on them will be like a f man who built his house
25: 2 Five of them were f, and five were wise.
25: 3 the f took their lamps, they took no oil with them;
25: 8 The f said to the wise, ‘Give us some of your oil,
Lk 24:25 Then he said to them, “Oh, how f you are,
Ro 1:14 both to the wise and to the f
1:31 f, faithless, heartless, ruthless.
2:20 a corrector of the f, a teacher of children, having
10:19 with a f nation I will make you angry.”
1Co 1:20 Has not God made f the wisdom of the world?
1:27 But God chose what is f in the world to shame
Gal 3: 1 You f Galatians! Who has bewitched you?
3: 3 Are you so f? Having started with the
Eph 5:17 So do not be f, but understand what the will of
Tit 3: 3 For we ourselves were once f, disobedient,
1Pe 2:15 right you should silence the ignorance of the f.
Wis 1: 3 and when his power is tested, it exposes the f;
1: 5 and will leave f thoughts behind,
3: 2 In the eyes of the f they seemed to have died,
3:12 Their wives are f, and their children evil;
11:15 In return for their f and wicked thoughts,
12:24 they were deceived like f infants.
13: 1 For all people who were ignorant of God were f
14:11 for human souls and a trap for the feet of the f.
15:14 But most f, and more miserable than an infant,
19: 3 they reached another f decision,
Sir 15: 7 f will not obtain her, and sinners will not see her.
22:12 f or the ungodly it lasts all the days of their lives.
42: 8 Do not be ashamed to correct the stupid or f or
50:26 and the f people that live in Shechem.
2Mc 2:32 be f to lengthen the preface while cutting short
12:44 it would have been superfluous and f to pray for
2Es 4:19 I answered and said, “Each made a f plan,
10: 6 “You most f of women, do you
4Mc 5:11 Will you not awaken from your f philosophy,

FOOLISHLY (8) [FOOL]

Nu 12:11 for a sin that we have so f committed.
1Sa 13:13 Samuel said to Saul, “You have done f;
2Sa 24:10 for I have done very f.”
1Ch 21: 8 for I have done very f.”
2Ch 16: 9 You have done f in this;
Pr 14:17 One who is quick-tempered acts f,
Sir 16:23 a senseless and misguided person thinks f.
3Mc 6:25 and f gathered every one of them here?

FOOLISHNESS (11) [FOOL]

2Sa 15:31 I pray you, turn the counsel of Ahithophel into f.”
Ps 38: 5 and fester because of my f;
Ecc 7:25 that wickedness is folly and that f is madness.
10:13 The words of their mouths begin in f,
1Co 1:18 about the cross is f to those who are perishing,
1:21 God decided, through the f of our proclamation,
1:23 a stumbling block to Jews and f to Gentiles,
1:25 For God's f is wiser than human wisdom,
2:14 for they are f to them,
3:19 For the wisdom of this world is f with God.
2Co 11: 1 I wish you would bear with me in a little f.

FOOLS‡ (75) [FOOL]

Ex 10: 2 how I have made f of the Egyptians
Dt 32:31 is not like our Rock; our enemies are f.
1Sa 6: 6 After he had made f of them,
Job 5: 3 I have seen f taking root,
12:17 counselors away stripped, and makes f of judges.
Ps 14: 1 F say in their hearts, “There is no God.”
53: 1 F say in their hearts, “There is no God.”
94: 8 f, when will you be wise?
Pr 1: 7 f despise wisdom and instruction.
1:22 in their scoffing and f hate knowledge?
1:32 and the complacency of f destroys them;
3:35 wise will inherit honor, but stubborn f, disgrace.
10:21 but f die for lack of sense.
12:15 F think their own way is right,
12:16 F show their anger at once,
13:19 but to turn away from evil is an abomination to f.
13:20 but the companion of f suffers harm.
14: 3 The talk of f is a rod for their backs,
14: 8 but the folly of f misleads.
14: 9 F mock at the guilt offering,
14:24 but folly is the garland of f.
14:33 but it is not known in the heart of f.
15: 2 but the mouths of f pour out folly.
15: 7 not so the minds of f.
15:14 but the mouths of f feed on folly.
16:22 but folly is the punishment of f.
17:16 Why should f have a price in hand
17:28 Even f who keep silent are considered wise;
18: 7 The mouths of f are their ruin,
19:29 and flogging for the backs of f.
24: 7 Wisdom is too high for f;
26: 3 and a rod for the back of f.
26: 4 Do not answer f according to their folly,
26: 5 Answer f according to their folly,
26:12 There is more hope for f than for them.
28:26 Those who trust in their own wits are f;
29: 9 If the wise go to law with f,
Ecc 2:14 The wise have eyes in their head, but f walk
2:16 of the wise or of f,
2:16 How can the wise die just like f?
4: 5 F fold their hands and consume their own flesh.
5: 1 to listen is better than the sacrifice offered by f;
5: 4 for he has no pleasure in f.
6: 8 For what advantage have the wise over f?
7: 4 but the heart of f is in the house of mirth.
7: 5 the rebuke of the wise than to hear the song of f.
7: 6 so is the laughter of f; this also is vanity.
7: 9 for anger lodges in the bosom of f.
9:17 to be heeded than the shouting of a ruler among f.
10: 3 Even when f walk on the road, they lack sense,
10: 3 and show to everyone that they are f.
10:12 but the lips of f consume them.
10:14 yet f talk on and on.
10:15 The toil of f wears them out,
Isa 19:13 The princes of Zoan have become f,
32: 6 For f speak folly, and their minds plot iniquity:
35: 8 no traveler, not even f, shall go astray.
44:25 the omens of liars, and makes f of diviners;
Jer 17:11 and at their end they will prove to be f.
50:36 so that they may become f!
Mt 23:17 You blind f! For which is greater,
Lk 11:40 You f! Did not the one who made the outside
Ro 1:22 Claiming to be wise, they became f;
1Co 3:18 that you are wise in this age, you should become f
4:10 We are f for the sake of Christ,
2Co 11:19 you gladly put up with f, being wise yourselves!
Wis 5: 4 and made a byword of reproach—f that we were!
15: 5 whose appearance arouses yearning in f,
Sir 6:20 f cannot remain with her.
8:17 Do not consult with f, for they cannot keep
20:13 but the courtesies of f are wasted.
21:26 The mind of f is in their mouth,
27:13 The talk of f is offensive,
34: 1 and dreams give wings to f.
Sus 1:48 “Are you such f, O Israelites,

FOOT‡ (119) [BAREFOOT, CLEFT-FOOTED, FEET, FOOT'S, FOOT-RUNNERS, FOOT-SOLDIERS, FOOTHOLD, FOOTMEN, FOOTPRINTS, FOOTSTEPS, FOOTSTOOL, FOUR-FOOTED, UNDERFOOT]

Ge 8: 9 but the dove found no place to set its f,
41:44 without your consent no one shall lift up hand or f
Ex 12:37 about six hundred thousand men on f,
19:17 They took their stand at the f of the mountain.
21:24 tooth for tooth, hand for hand, f for f,
24: 4 and built an altar at the f of the mountain,
32:19 the tablets from his hands and broke them at the f
Lev 8:23 of his right hand and on the big toe of his right f.
13:12 the skin of the diseased person from head to f,
14:14 and on the big toe of the right f.
14:17 and on the big toe of the right f.
14:25 and on the big toe of the right f.
14:28 and the big toe of the right f,
21:19 or one who has a broken f or a broken hand,
Nu 11:21 with number six hundred thousand on f;
20:19 just let us pass through on f.”
22:25 and scraped Balaam's f against the wall;
Dt 1:36 the land on which he set f,
2:28 Only allow me to pass through on f—
4:11 you approached and stood at the f of the mountain
11:10 where you sow your seed and irrigate by f like
11:24 Every place on which you set f shall be yours;
11:25 of you on all the land on which you set f,
19:21 tooth for tooth, hand for hand, f for f.
25: 9 pull his sandal off his f, spit in his face,
28:35 from the sole of your f to the crown of your head.
28:56 that she does not venture to set the sole of her f on
28:65 no resting place for the sole of your f.
32:35 for the time when their f shall slip;
33:24 and may he dip his f in oil.
Jos 1: 3 that the sole of your f will tread upon I have given
12: 3 southward to the f of the slopes of Pisgah;
14: 9 ‘Surely the land on which your f has trodden shall
Jdg 4:15 down from his chariot and fled away on f,
4:17 on f to the tent of Jael wife of Heber the Kenite;
1Sa 4:10 for there fell of Israel thirty thousand f soldiers.
15: 4 two hundred thousand f soldiers,
2Sa 2:18 Now Asahel was as swift of f as a wild gazelle.
8: 4 and twenty thousand f soldiers.
10: 6 twenty thousand f soldiers,
14:25 from the sole of his f to the crown
21:20 and six toes on each f, twenty-four in number;
1Ki 20:29 killed one hundred thousand Aramean f soldiers
2Ki 19:24 up with the sole of my f all the streams of Egypt.'
1Ch 18: 4 and twenty thousand f soldiers.
19:18 and forty thousand f soldiers,
20: 6 and six toes on each f, twenty-four in number;
Job 2: 7 from the sole of his f to the crown of his head.
23:11 My f has held fast to his steps;
31: 5 and my f has hurried to deceit—
39:15 forgetting that a f may crush them,
Ps 9:15 the net that they hid has their own f been caught.
26:12 My f stands on level ground;
36:11 Do not let the f of the arrogant tread on me,
38:16 those who boast against me when my f slips.”
66: 6 they passed through the river on f.
68:30 Trample under f those who lust after tribute;
91:12 so that you will not dash your f against a stone.
91:13 and the serpent you will trample under f.
94:18 When I thought, “My f is slipping,”
121: 3 He will not let your f be moved;
Pr 1:15 keep your f from their paths;
3:23 on your way securely and your f will not stumble.
3:26 be your confidence and will keep your f
4:27 turn your f away from evil.
25:17 Let your f be seldom in your neighbor's house,
25:19 or a lame f is trust in a faithless person in time
26: 6 It is like cutting off one's f and drinking
Ecc 10: 7 and princes walking on f like slaves.
Isa 1: 6 From the sole of the f even to the head,
11:15 and make a way to cross on f;
14:25 and on my mountains trample him under f;
26: 6 The f tramples it, the feet of the poor,
28: 3 under f will be the proud garland of the drunkards
37:25 up with the sole of my f all the streams of Egypt.'
41: 2 and tramples kings under f;
La 3:34 all the prisoners of the land are crushed under f,
Eze 1: 7 soles of their feet were like the sole of a calf's f;
6:11 Clap your hands and stamp your f, and say,
29:11 No human f shall pass through it, and no animal f
32:13 and no human f shall trouble them any more,
42: 9 At the f of these chambers ran a passage
Am 2:15 those who are swift of f shall not save themselves,
Mic 7:19 he will tread our iniquities under f.
Mt 4: 6 so that you will not dash your f against a stone.' ”
5:13 but is thrown out and trampled under f.
7: 6 before swine, or they will trample them under f
14:13 they followed him on f from the towns.
18: 8 “If your hand or your f causes you to stumble,
22:13 king said to the attendants, ‘Bind him hand and f,
Mk 6:33 on f from all the towns and arrived ahead of them.
9:45 And if your f causes you to stumble, cut it off;
Lk 4:11 so that you will not dash your f against a stone.' ”
Ac 20:18 the entire time from the first day that I set f
1Co 12:15 If the f would say, “Because I am not a hand,
Rev 10: 2 Setting his right f on the sea and his left f on
Tob 6: 3 the water and tried to swallow the young man's f,
8: 3 and at once bound him there hand and f.
Jdt 2: 5 one hundred twenty thousand f soldiers
2:19 and cavalry and picked f soldiers.
6:13 they bound Achior and left him lying at the f of
7: 2 the baggage and the f soldiers handling it,
7:12 of water that flows from the f of the mountain,
9: 7 boasting in the strength of their f soldiers,
Sir 6:36 let your f wear out his doorstep.
16:10 six hundred thousand f soldiers who assembled
21:22 The f of a fool rushes into a house,
50:15 he poured it out at the f of the altar,

Sir 51:15 my **f** walked on the straight path;
Bar 5: 6 For they went out from you on **f**,
1Mc 5:48 we will simply pass by on **f**."
6:30 of his forces was one hundred thousand **f** soldiers,
9: 4 and went to Berea with twenty thousand **f** soldiers
1Es 8:51 the king for **f** soldiers and cavalry and an escort
2Es 16:69 and shall be trampled under **f**.

FOOT'S (2) [FOOT]
Dt 2: 5 for I will not give you even so much as a **f** length
Ac 7: 5 not even a **f** length, but promised to give it to him

FOOT-RUNNERS (1) [FOOT, RUN]
Jer 12: 5 you have raced with **f** and they have wearied you,

FOOT-SOLDIERS (1) [FOOT, SOLDIER]
Jdg 20: 2 four hundred thousand **f** bearing arms.

FOOTHOLD (1) [FOOT]
Ps 69: 2 I sink in deep mire, where there is no **f**;

FOOTMEN (1) [FOOT, MAN]
2Ki 13: 7 ten chariots and ten thousand **f**;

FOOTMEN (KJV) See also FOOT-RUNNERS, FOOT SOLDIERS

FOOTPRINTS (4) [FOOT]
Ps 77:19 through the mighty waters; yet your **f** were unseen.
Jdt 6: 4 Not even their **f** will survive our attack;
Bel 1:19 he said, "and notice whose **f** these are."
1:20 "I see the **f** of men and women and children."

FOOTSTEPS (1) [FOOT, STEP]
Ps 89:51 with which they taunted the **f** of your anointed.

FOOTSTOOL‡ (14) [FOOT]
1Ch 28: 2 for the **f** of our God;
2Ch 9:18 The throne had six steps and a **f** of gold,
Ps 99: 5 Extol the LORD our God; worship at his **f**.
110: 1 until I make your enemies your **f**."
132: 7 let us worship at his **f**."
Isa 66: 1 Heaven is my throne and the earth is my **f**;
La 2: 1 not remembered his **f** in the day of his anger.
Mt 5:35 for it is his **f**, or by Jerusalem,
Lk 20:43 until I make your enemies your **f**." '
Ac 2:35 until I make your enemies your **f**." '
7:49 and the earth is my **f**.
Heb 1:13 at my right hand until I make your enemies a **f**
10:13 "until his enemies would be made a **f** for his feet."
2Es 6: 4 and before the **f** of Zion was established,

FOR (11031) See Index of Articles Etc.

FORBAD (KJV) See CHARGED, PREVENTED, REBUKED, STOP

FORBADE (1) [FORBID]
La 1:10 those whom you **f** to enter your congregation.

FORBEAR (1) [FORBEARANCE]
Job 16: 6 "If I speak, my pain is not assuaged, and if I **f**,

FORBEARANCE (6) [FORBEAR]
Jer 15:15 In your **f** do not take me away;
Ro 2: 4 Or do you despise the riches of his kindness and **f**
3:25 because in his divine **f** he had passed over
Wis 2:19 and make trial of his **f**.
12:18 and with great **f** you govern us;
2Mc 10: 4 they might be disciplined by him with **f** and not

FORBID (11) [FORBADE, FORBIDDEN, FORBIDDING, FORBIDS]
1Sa 24: 6 LORD **f** that I should do this thing to my lord,
26:11 The LORD **f** that I should raise my hand against
2Sa 23:17 "The LORD **f** that I should do this.
1Ki 21: 3 But Naboth said to Ahab, "The LORD **f**
1Ch 11:19 "My God **f** that I should do this.
Mt 16:22 and began to rebuke him, saying, "God **f** it,
Lk 20:16 When they heard this, they said, "Heaven **f**!"
Ro 2:22 You that **f** adultery, do you commit adultery?
1Co 14:39 and do not **f** speaking in tongues;
1Ti 4: 3 They **f** marriage and demand abstinence
1Mc 1:45 to **f** burnt offerings and sacrifices

FORBIDDEN (10) [FORBID]
Lev 19:23 then you shall regard their fruit as **f**;
19:23 three years it shall be **f** to you,
Dt 4:23 of anything that the LORD your God has **f** you.
17: 3 or any of the host of heaven, which I have **f**—
Ac 16: 6 having been **f** by the Holy Spirit to speak
Jdt 11:12 to use all that God by his laws has **f** them to eat.
2Mc 6: 5 with abominable offerings that were **f** by the laws.
4Mc 1:33 when we are attracted to **f** foods we abstain from
1:34 and animals and all sorts of foods that are **f** to us
5:26 but he has **f** us to eat meats that would be contrary

FORBIDDING (1) [FORBID]
Lk 23: 2 **f** us to pay taxes to the emperor,

FORBIDS (1) [FORBID]
2Mc 12:40 which the law **f** the Jews to wear.

FORCE (64) [FORCED, FORCEFUL, FORCES, FORCIBLY, FORCING]
Ge 31:31 that you would take your daughters from me by **f**.
34: 2 saw her, he seized her and lay with her by **f**.
Nu 20:20 And Edom came out against them with a large **f**,
Jos 10: 7 he and all the fighting **f** with him,
11: 7 upon them with all his fighting **f**,
Jdg 20:16 Of all this **f**, there were seven hundred picked men
1Sa 2:16 if not, I will take it by **f**."
2Sa 13:12 She answered him, "No, my brother, do not **f** me;
2Ki 11: 7 on duty in **f** on the sabbath and guard the house of
1Ch 7: 4 were units of the fighting **f**, thirty-six thousand,
Ezr 4:23 they hurried to the Jews in Jerusalem and by **f**
Est 8:11 and to annihilate any armed **f** of any people
Job 20:22 all the **f** of misery will come upon them.
36:19 or will all the **f** of your strength?
Jer 46:22 for her enemies march in **f**,
Eze 34: 4 but with **f** and harshness you have ruled them.
Da 8: 6 and it ran at it with savage **f**.
Mt 11:12 and the violent take it by **f**.
Lk 16:16 and everyone tries to enter it by **f**.
Jn 6:15 that they were about to come and take him by **f**
Ac 23:10 ordered the soldiers to go down, take him by **f**,
26:11 the synagogues I tried to **f** them to blaspheme;
27:41 stern was being broken up by the **f** of the waves.
Heb 9:17 not in **f** as long as the one who made it is alive.
Rev 1:16 and his face was like the sun shining with full **f**.
Jdt 1: 4 in **f** and his infantry to form their ranks.
9: 7 now are the Assyrians, a greatly increased **f**,
Wis 5:11 by the beat of its pinions and pierced by the **f**
18:22 not by strength of body, not by **f** of arms,
1Mc 1:17 So he invaded Egypt with a strong **f**,
1:20 and came to Jerusalem with a strong **f**.
1:29 and he came to Jerusalem with a large **f**.
3:10 and a large **f** from Samaria to fight against Israel.
3:35 to send a **f** against them to wipe out and destroy
3:40 So they set out with their entire **f**,
4: 3 and his warriors moved out to attack the king's **f**
4:16 Judas and his **f** turned back from pursuing them,
4:18 Gorgias and his **f** are near us in the hills.
5:38 it is a very large **f**.
6: 6 with a strong **f**, but had turned and fled before
6:63 but he fought against him, and took the city by **f**.
7:10 So they marched away and came with a large **f**
7:11 for they saw that they had come with a large **f**.
7:20 of the country and left with him a **f** to help him;
7:27 So Nicanor came to Jerusalem with a large **f**,
9:43 with a large **f** on the sabbath day to the banks of
9:60 He started to come with a large **f**,
10:69 and he assembled a large **f** and encamped
10:82 Then Simon brought forward his **f** and engaged
11:15 and met him with a strong **f**,
12:24 with a larger **f** than before,
16: 5 a large **f** of infantry and cavalry was coming
2Mc 1:13 When the leader reached Persia with a **f**
10:14 he maintained a **f** of mercenaries,
10:19 a **f** sufficient to besiege them;
10:24 a tremendous **f** of mercenaries and collected
10:36 the gates and let in the rest of the **f**,
13: 2 a Greek **f** of one hundred ten thousand infantry,
13:15 and with a picked **f** of the bravest young men,
3Mc 2:28 Those who object to this are to be taken by **f**
5:47 rushed out in full **f** along with the animals,
2Es 16:68 of you away and **f** you to eat what was sacrificed
4Mc 4: 5 the accursed Simon and a very strong military **f**.
11:25 to change our mind or to **f** us to eat defiling foods,

FORCED (36) [FORCE]
Ge 49:15 and became a slave at **f** labor.
Ex 1:11 over them to oppress them with **f** labor.
2:11 he went out to his people and saw their **f** labor.
Dt 20:11 then all the people in it shall serve you at **f** labor.
Jos 16:10 to this day but have been made to do **f** labor.
17:13 they put the Canaanites to **f** labor,
Jdg 1:28 they put the Canaanites to **f** labor,
1:30 and became subject to **f** labor.
1:33 of Beth-anath became subject to **f** labor for them.
1:35 and they became subject to **f** labor.
1Sa 13:12 so I **f** myself, and offered the burnt offering."
2Sa 13:14 being stronger than she, he **f** her and lay with her.
20:24 Adoram was in charge of the **f** labor;
1Ki 4: 6 of Abda was in charge of the **f** labor.
5:13 King Solomon conscripted **f** labor out
5:14 Adoniram was in charge of the **f** labor.
9:15 of the **f** labor that King Solomon conscripted
11:28 over all the **f** labor of the house of Joseph.
12:18 who was taskmaster over the **f** labor,
2Ch 8: 8 these Solomon conscripted for **f** labor,
10:18 who was taskmaster over the **f** labor,
Pr 12:24 while the lazy will be put to **f** labor.
Isa 31: 8 and his young men shall be put to **f** labor.
Ac 7:19 He dealt craftily with our race and **f** our ancestors
2Co 12:11 You **f** me to it.
Phm 1:14 be voluntary and not something **f**.
Jdt 5:11 he exploited them and **f** them to make bricks.
Wis 14:19 to please his ruler, skillfully **f** the likeness
1Mc 6:33 the king set out and took his army by a **f** march
8: 2 they had defeated them and **f** them to pay tribute,
2Mc 5: 5 When the troops on the wall had been **f** back and
6:18 was being **f** to open his mouth
8:24 and **f** them all to flee.
11:11 and **f** all the rest to flee.
3Mc 4: 5 **f** to march at a swift pace by the violence
4Mc 2: 8 one is **f** to act contrary to natural ways and to lend

FORCEFUL (1) [FORCE]
Job 6:25 How **f** are honest words!

FORCES (90) [FORCE]
Ge 14: 3 All these joined **f** in the Valley of Siddim (that is,
14:15 He divided his **f** against them by night,
Dt 33:27 He subdues the ancient gods, shatters the **f** of old;
Jos 8:13 So they stationed the **f**, the main encampment
10: 5 gathered their **f**, and went up with all their armies
11: 5 All these kings joined their **f**,
1Sa 28: 1 In those days the Philistines gathered their **f**
29: 1 Now the Philistines gathered all their **f** at Aphek,
2Sa 20:15 Joab's **f** came and besieged him in Abel
20:15 Joab's **f** were battering the wall to break it down.
2Ki 25:23 when all the captains of the **f** and their men heard
25:26 and low and the captains of the **f** set out and went
1Ch 19:17 came to them, and drew up his **f** against them.
2Ch 17: 2 He placed **f** in all the fortified cities of Judah,
32: 9 of Assyria was at Lachish with all his **f**,
Ps 110: 3 on the day you lead your **f** on the holy mountains.
Jer 40: 7 of the **f** in the open country and their troops heard
40:13 of the **f** in the open country came to Gedaliah
41:11 and all the leaders of the **f** with him heard of all
41:13 of Kareah and all the leaders of the **f** with him,
41:16 the leaders of the **f** with him took all the rest of
42: 1 Then all the commanders of the **f**,
42: 8 the commanders of the **f** who were with him,
43: 4 of Kareah and all the commanders of the **f** and all
43: 5 the commanders of the **f** took all the remnant
Da 11:10 and assemble a multitude of great **f**,
11:15 And the **f** of the south shall not stand,
11:31 **F** sent by him shall occupy and profane
Mt 5:41 and if anyone **f** you to go one mile,
Eph 6:12 the spiritual **f** of evil in the heavenly places.
Jdt 1: 6 Thus, many nations joined the **f** of the Chaldeans.
1:13 In the seventeenth year he led his **f**
1:16 he returned to Nineveh, he and all his combined **f**,
1:16 and there he and his **f** rested and feasted
6: 2 He will send his **f** and destroy them from the face
7: 2 fighting **f** numbered one hundred seventy thousand
7:12 and keep all the men in your **f** with you;
7:26 to the army of Holofernes and to all his **f**.
Wis 1:14 the generative **f** of the world are wholesome,
1Mc 3:27 and he sent and gathered all the **f** of his kingdom,
3:28 and gave a year's pay to his **f**,
3:34 And he turned over to Lysias half of his **f** and
3:37 Then the king took the remaining half of his **f**
3:41 And **f** from Syria and the land of
3:42 and that the **f** were encamped in their territory.
4: 9 when Pharaoh with his **f** pursued them.
5:11 and Timothy is leading their **f**.
5:18 a leader of the people, with the rest of the **f**,
5:32 and he said to the men of his **f**,
5:40 Timothy said to the officers of his **f**,
5:50 So the men of the **f** encamped,
5:56 and Azariah, the commanders of the **f**,
5:58 So they issued orders to the men of the **f** that were
6:28 the commanders of his **f** and those in authority.
6:29 Mercenary **f** also came to him
6:30 of his **f** was one hundred thousand foot soldiers,
6:47 the royal might and the fierce attack of the **f**,
6:56 and Media with the **f** that had gone with the king,
6:57 and said to the king, to the commanders of the **f**,
9: 6 When they saw the huge number of the enemy **f**,
9:63 Bacchides learned of this, he assembled all his **f**,
9:67 he began to attack and went into battle with his **f**;
10:36 the king's **f** to the number of thirty thousand men,
10:36 be given them that is due to all the **f** of the king.
10:48 Now King Alexander assembled large **f**
10:71 If you now have confidence in your **f**,
11: 1 Then the king of Egypt gathered great **f**,
11: 3 which Ptolemy entered the towns he stationed **f** as
11:70 commanders of the **f** of the army.
13:53 and so he made him commander of all the **f**;
14: 1 King Demetrius assembled his **f**
15:25 continually throwing his **f** against it
2Mc 3:35 he marched off with his **f** to the king.
8:16 But Maccabeus gathered his **f** together,
8:30 In encounters with the **f** of Timothy
8:32 They killed the commander of Timothy's **f**,
9: 3 to him of what had happened to Nicanor and the **f**
10:16 But Maccabeus and his **f**,
15: 6 of victory over Judas and his **f**.
1Es 3:24 since it **f** people to do these things?"
3Mc 1: 1 he gave orders to all his **f**,
4:11 with the king's **f** nor in any way claim to be inside
5:29 that the animals and the armed **f** were ready,
5:44 and they confidently posted the armed **f** at
5:48 at the gate and by the following armed **f**,
6: 5 Sennacherib exulting in his countless **f**,
6:16 with the animals and all the arrogance of his **f**.
6:19 the **f** of the enemy and filled them with confusion
6:21 the armed **f** following them and began trampling
4Mc 4:10 while Apollonius was going up with his armed **f**

FORCIBLY (3) [FORCE]
1Mc 2:46 they **f** circumcised all the uncircumcised boys
1Es 4:49 or governor or treasurer should **f** enter their doors;

3Mc 5: 7 in their bonds they were **f** confined on every side.

FORCING (3) [FORCE]

Ne 5: 5 yet we are **f** our sons and daughters to be slaves,
1Mc 2:25 the king's officer who was **f** them to sacrifice,
2Mc 14:41 about to capture the tower and were **f** the door of

FORD‡ (1) [FORDS]

Ge 32:22 and crossed the **f** of the Jabbok.

FORDS (8) [FORD]

Jos 2: 7 on the way to the Jordan as far as the **f**.
Jdg 3:28 seized the **f** of the Jordan against the Moabites,
12: 5 the Gileadites took the **f** of the Jordan against
12: 6 Then they seized him and killed him at the **f** of
2Sa 15:28 the **f** of the wilderness until word comes from you
17:16 'Do not lodge tonight at the **f** of the wilderness,
Isa 16: 2 are the daughters of Moab at the **f** of the Arnon.
Jer 51:32 the **f** have been seized, the marshes have been

FOREBEARS (3)

Ps 39:12 I am your passing guest, an alien, like all my **f**.
AdE 14: 5 and our ancestors from among all their **f**,
4Mc 9: 2 we are obviously putting our **f** to shame

FOREBODING (1)

Lk 21:26 from fear and **f** of what is coming upon the world,

FORECAST (KJV) See PLAN

FORECOURT (1) [COURT]

Mk 14:68 And he went out into the **f**.

FOREFRONT (1) [FRONT]

2Sa 11:15 "Set Uriah in the **f** of the hardest fighting,

FOREFRONT (KJV) See also ENTRANCE, FRONT, HEAD

FOREGO (2)

Ne 10:31 and we will **f** the crops of the seventh year and
2Mc 2:31 of expression and to **f** exhaustive treatment.

FOREHEAD‡ (23) [FOREHEADS]

Ex 13: 9 on your **f**, so that the teaching of the LORD may
13:16 a sign on your hand and as an emblem on your **f**
28:38 It shall be on Aaron's **f**, and Aaron shall take
28:38 it shall always be on his **f**,
Lev 13:41 If he loses the hair from his **f** and temples,
13:41 he has baldness of the **f** but he is clean.
13:42 But if there is on the bald head or the bald **f**
13:42 on his bald head or his bald **f**.
13:43 on his bald head or on his bald **f**,
Dt 6: 8 fix them as an emblem on your **f**,
11:18 and fix them as an emblem on your **f**.
1Sa 17:49 slung it, and struck the Philistine on his **f**; the stone sank into his **f**,
2Ch 26:19 the priests a leprous disease broke out on his **f**,
26:20 looked at him, he was leprous in his **f**.
Isa 48: 4 and your neck is an iron sinew and your **f** brass,
Jer 3: 3 yet you have the **f** of a whore,
48:45 it has destroyed the **f** of Moab,
Eze 3: 7 because all the house of Israel have a hard **f** and
3: 8 and your **f** hard against their foreheads.
3: 9 harder than flint, I have made your **f**;
Rev 13:16 to be marked on the right hand or the **f**,
17: 5 and on her **f** was written a name, a mystery:

FOREHEADS (8) [FOREHEAD]

Eze 3: 8 and your forehead hard against their **f**.
9: 4 on the **f** of those who sigh and groan over all
Rev 7: 3 the servants of our God with a seal on their **f**."
9: 4 not have the seal of God on their **f**.
14: 1 and his Father's name written on their **f**.
14: 9 and receive a mark on their **f** or on their hands,
20: 4 not received its mark on their **f** or their hands.
22: 4 and his name will be on their **f**.

FOREIGN‡ (60) [FOREIGNER, FOREIGNERS]

A. FOREIGN WOMEN (11)

Ge 35: 2 "Put away the **f** gods that are among you,
35: 4 So they gave to Jacob all the **f** gods that they had,
Ex 2:22 "I have been an alien residing in a **f** land."
18: 3 "I have been an alien in a **f** land"),
21: 8 he shall have no right to sell her to a **f** people,
Dt 31:16 to the **f** gods in their midst, the gods of the land
32:12 no **f** god was with him.
Jos 24:20 If you forsake the LORD and serve **f** gods,
24:23 "Then put away the **f** gods that are among you,
Jdg 10:16 So they put away the **f** gods from among them
1Sa 7: 3 then put away the **f** gods and the Astartes from
1Ki 11: 1 King Solomon loved many **f** women along with A
11: 8 He did the same for all his **f** wives,
2Ki 19:24 I dug wells and drank **f** waters,
2Ch 14: 3 He took away the **f** altars and the high places,
33:15 He took away the **f** gods and the idol from
Ezr 10: 2 and have married **f** women from the peoples of A
10:10 "You have trespassed and married **f** women, A
10:11 the peoples of the land and from the **f** wives."
10:14 in our towns who have taken **f** wives come
10:17 end of all the men who had married **f** women. A
10:18 of the priests who had married **f** women, A
10:44 All these had married **f** women, A
Ne 13: 3 they separated from Israel all those of **f** descent.
13:26 nevertheless, **f** women made even him to sin. A
13:27 against our God by marrying **f** women?" A
13:30 Thus I cleansed them from everything **f**,
Ps 81: 9 you shall not bow down to a **f** god.
137: 4 could we sing the LORD's song in a **f** land?
Jer 5:19 "As you have forsaken me and served **f** gods
8:19 to anger with their images, with their **f** idols?")
50:37 and against all the **f** troops in her midst,
Da 11:39 the strongest fortresses by the help of a **f** god.
Zep 1: 8 and all who dress themselves in **f** attire.
Mal 2:11 and has married the daughter of a **f** god.
Ac 17:18 "He seems to be a proclaimer of **f** divinities."
26:11 I pursued them even to **f** cities.
Heb 11: 9 as in a **f** land, living in tents,
11:34 became mighty in war, put **f** armies to flight.
Tob 4:12 a **f** woman, who is not of your father's tribe;
Jdt 5:18 and were led away captive to a **f** land.
6: 1 to Achior in the presence of all the **f** contingents:
Sir 29:18 and they have wandered among **f** nations.
36: 3 against **f** nations and let them see your might.
39: 4 travels in **f** lands and learns what is good and evil
49: 5 and their glory to a **f** nation,
Bar 3:10 that you are growing old in a **f** country,
1Mc 11:38 the **f** troops that he had recruited from the islands
15:33 "We have neither taken **f** land
15:33 nor seized **f** property, but only the inheritance
2Mc 4:13 and increase in the adoption of **f** ways because of
1Es 8:92 and have married **f** women from the peoples of A
8:93 that we will put away all our **f** wives,
9: 7 "You have broken the law and married **f** women, A
9: 9 the peoples of the land and from your **f** wives."
9:12 in our settlements who have **f** wives come at
9:17 the men who had **f** wives were brought to an end
9:18 in and found to have **f** wives were:
9:36 All these had married **f** women, A
3Mc 6: 3 as foreigners in a **f** land.

FOREIGNER‡ (19) [FOREIGN]

Ge 17:12 from any **f** who is not of your offspring.
17:27 the house and those bought with money from a **f**,
Ex 12:43 no **f** shall eat of it,
Lev 22:25 nor shall you accept any such animals from a **f**
Dt 14:21 or you may sell it to a **f**.
15: 3 Of a **f** you may exact it,
17:15 you are not permitted to put a **f** over you,
23:20 On loans to a **f** you may charge interest,
29:22 as well as the **f** who comes from a distant country,
Ru 2:10 of me, when I am a **f**?"
2Sa 15:19 for you are a **f**, and also an exile from your home.
1Ki 8:41 when a **f**, who is not of your people Israel, comes
8:42 when a **f** comes and prays toward this house,
8:43 and do according to all that the **f** calls to you,
Isa 56: 3 Do not let the **f** joined to the LORD say,
Eze 44: 9 No **f**, uncircumcised in heart and flesh,
Lk 17:18 to return and give praise to God except this **f**?"
1Co 14:11 a **f** to the speaker and the speaker a **f** to me.

FOREIGNERS‡ (40) [FOREIGN]

Ge 31:15 Are we not regarded by him as **f**?
Jdg 19:12 "We will not turn aside into a city of **f**,
2Sa 22:45 **F** came cringing to me;
22:46 **F** lost heart, and came trembling out
2Ch 6:32 when **f**, who are not of your people Israel, come
6:33 and do whatever the **f** ask of you,
Ne 9: 2 from all **f**, and stood and confessed their sins and
Ps 18:44 of me they obeyed me; **f** came cringing to me.
18:45 **F** lost heart, and came trembling out
Pr 20:16 seize the pledge given as surety for **f**.
27:13 seize the pledge given as surety for **f**.
Isa 1: 7 it is desolate, as overthrown by **f**.
2: 6 and they clasp hands with **f**.
56: 6 And the **f** who join themselves to the LORD,
60:10 **F** shall build up your walls,
61: 5 **f** shall till your land and dress your vines;
62: 8 to be food for your enemies, and **f** shall not drink
Eze 11: 9 of it and give you over to the hands of **f**,
28:10 the death of the uncircumcised by the hand of **f**;
30:12 the land and everything in it by the hand of **f**;
31:12 **F** from the most terrible of the nations have cut it
44: 7 in admitting **f**, uncircumcised in heart and flesh,
44: 8 but you have appointed **f** to act for you
44: 9 of all the **f** who are among the people of Israel,
Hos 7: 9 **F** devour his strength, but he does not know it;
8: 7 if it were to yield, **f** would devour it.
Ob 1:11 and **f** entered his gates and cast lots for Jerusalem,
Mt 27: 7 to buy the potter's field as a place to bury **f**.
Ac 17:21 and the **f** living there would spend their time
1Co 14:21 of strange tongues and by the lips of **f** I will speak
Heb 11:13 They confessed that they were strangers and **f** on
LtJ 6: 5 the **f** or of letting fear for these gods possess you
1Mc 4:12 **f** looked up and saw them coming against them,
4:26 the **f** who escaped went and reported to Lysias all
10:12 Then the **f** who were in the strongholds
11:68 and there in the plain the army of the **f** met him;
11:74 As many as three thousand of the **f** fell that day.
2Mc 10: 2 that had been built in the public square by the **f**,
10: 5 the sanctuary had been profaned by the **f**,
3Mc 6: 3 of your consecrated portion who are perishing as **f**

FOREKNEW (2) [KNOW]

Ro 8:29 For those whom he **f** he also predestined to
11: 2 God has not rejected his people whom he **f**.

FOREKNOW (KJV) See FOREKNEW

FOREKNOWLEDGE (4) [KNOW]

Ac 2:23 to you according to the definite plan and **f** of God,
Jdt 9: 6 and your judgment is with **f**.
11:19 For this was told me to give me **f**;
Wis 8: 8 she has **f** of signs and wonders and of

FORELOCKS (1)

Dt 14: 1 You must not lacerate yourselves or shave your **f**

FOREMOST (3)

Ge 32:17 the **f**, "When Esau my brother meets you,
1Ti 1:15 to save sinners—of whom I am the **f**.
1:16 I received mercy, so that in me, as the **f**,

FORENOON (1) [NOON]

2Sa 2:29 marching the whole **f**, they came to Mahanaim.

FOREORDAINED (1) [ORDAIN]

2Es 7:*74* their sake, but because of the times that he has **f**."

FOREORDAINED (KJV) See also DESTINED

FOREPART (KJV) See BOW, FRONT, INNER, OPPOSITE

FORERUNNER (1) [RUN]

Heb 6:20 a **f** on our behalf, has entered,

FORERUNNERS (1) [RUN]

Wis 12: 8 as **f** of your army to destroy them little by little,

FORESAIL (1) [SAIL]

Ac 27:40 then hoisting the **f** to the wind,

FORESEEING (2) [SEE]

Ac 2:31 **F** this, David spoke of the resurrection of
Gal 3: 8 **f** that God would justify the Gentiles by faith,

FORESEETH (KJV) See SEE

FORESHIP (KJV) See BOW

FORESIGHT (1) [SEE]

Ac 24: 2 for this people because of your **f**.

FORESKIN (8) [FORESKINS]

Ge 17:14 the flesh of his **f** shall be cut off from his people;
17:24 when he was circumcised in the flesh of his **f**.
17:25 when he was circumcised in the flesh of his **f**.
Ex 4:25 But Zipporah took a flint and cut off her son's **f**,
Lev 12: 3 On the eighth day the flesh of his **f** shall
Dt 10:16 Circumcise, then, the **f** of your heart,
Jer 4: 4 remove the **f** of your hearts,
9:25 to all those who are circumcised only in the **f**:

FORESKINS‡ (5) [FORESKIN]

Ge 17:11 You shall circumcise the flesh of your **f**,
17:23 he circumcised the flesh of their **f** that very day,
1Sa 18:25 a hundred **f** of the Philistines,
18:27 and David brought their **f**,
2Sa 3:14 at the price of one hundred **f** of the Philistines."

FOREST (62) [FORESTS]

Dt 19: 5 into the **f** with another to cut wood, and when one
Jos 17:15 "If you are a numerous people, go up to the **f**,
17:18 though it is a **f**, you shall clear it and possess it
1Sa 22: 5 So David left, and went into the **f** of Hereth.
2Sa 18: 6 and the battle was fought in the **f** of Ephraim.
18: 8 **f** claimed more victims that day than the sword.
18:17 threw him into a great pit in the **f**,
1Ki 7: 2 of the **F** of the Lebanon one hundred cubits long,
10:17 king put them in the House of the **F** of Lebanon.
10:21 the vessels of the House of the **F** of Lebanon were
2Ki 19:23 I entered its farthest retreat, its densest **f**.
1Ch 16:33 the trees of the **f** sing for joy before the LORD,
2Ch 9:16 king put them in the House of the **F** of Lebanon.
9:20 the vessels of the House of the **F** of Lebanon were
Ne 2: 8 the keeper of the king's **f**,
Ps 29: 9 the oaks to whirl, and strips the **f** bare;
50:10 For every wild animal of the **f** is mine,
80:13 The boar from the **f** ravages it,
83:14 As fire consumes the **f**, as the flame sets
96:12 Then shall all the trees of the **f** sing for joy
104:20 when all the animals of the **f** come creeping out.
Ecc 2: 6 I made myself pools from which to water the **f**
Isa 7: 2 of his people shook as the trees of the **f** shake
9:18 it kindled the thickets of the **f**,
10:18 The glory of his **f** and his fruitful land
10:19 The remnant of the trees of his **f** will be so few
10:34 He will hack down the thickets of the **f** with

Isa 22: 8 to the weapons of the House of the **F**,
29:17 and the fruitful field be regarded as a **f**?
32:15 and the fruitful field is deemed a **f**.
32:19 The **f** will disappear completely,
37:24 I came to its remotest height, its densest **f**.
44:14 and lets it grow strong among the trees of the **f**.
44:23 break forth into singing, O mountains, O **f**,
56: 9 all you wild animals in the **f**, come to devour!
Jer 5: 6 Therefore a lion from the **f** shall kill them,
10: 3 a tree from the **f** is cut down,
12: 8 to me like a lion in the **f**;
21:14 I will kindle a fire in its **f**,
46:23 They shall cut down her **f**, says the LORD,
Eze 15: 2 the vine branch that is among the trees of the **f**?
15: 6 the wood of the vine among the trees of the **f**,
20:46 and prophesy against the **f** land in the Negeb;
20:47 the **f** of the Negeb, Hear the word of the LORD:
31: 3 with fair branches and **f** shade,
Hos 2:12 I will make them a **f**, and the wild animals shall
Am 3: 4 Does a lion roar in the **f**, when it has no prey?
Mic 5: 8 shall be like a lion among the animals of the **f**,
7:14 lives alone in a **f** in the midst of a garden land;
Zec 11: 2 oaks of Bashan, for the thick **f** has been felled!
Jas 3: 5 How great a **f** is set ablaze by a small fire!
2Es 4:13 "I went into a **f** of trees of the plain,
4:15 up and subdue the **f** of the plain so that there
4:16 But the plan of the **f** was in vain,
4:19 for the land has been assigned to the **f**,
4:21 as the land has been assigned to the **f** and the sea
5:23 from every **f** of the earth and
9:21 and one plant out of a great **f**.
11:37 I saw what seemed to be a lion roused from the **f**,
12:31 for the lion whom you saw rousing up out of the **f**
15:30 shall go forth like wild boars from the **f**,
16: 6 Can one drive off a hungry lion in the **f**,

FORESTS (5) [FOREST]

Eze 39:10 of the field or cut down any trees in the **f**,
Hos 14: 5 he shall strike root like the **f** of Lebanon.
2Es 4:14 and so that we may make for ourselves more **f**.'
15:42 trees of the **f**, and grass of the meadows,
15:62 with fire all your **f** and your fruitful trees.

FORETOLD (10) [TELL]

2Ki 17:23 as he had **f** through all his servants the prophets.
24:13 all this as the LORD had **f**.
Isa 43: 9 and **f** to us the former things?
Ac 1:16 the Holy Spirit through David **f** concerning Judas,
3:18 In this way God fulfilled what he had **f**
7:52 They killed those who **f** the coming of
Sir 49: 6 and made its streets desolate, as Jeremiah had **f**.
2Es 6:25 be that whoever remains after all that I have **f**
7:26 the signs that I have **f** to you will come to pass,
7:27 from the evils that I have **f** shall see my wonders.

FOREVER‡ (483) [EVER]

A. FOREVER AND EVER (46)
B. STEADFAST LOVE ENDURES FOREVER (43)
C. HIS MERCY ENDURES FOREVER (17)
D. LIVE FOREVER (17)
E. NAME [BE] FOREVER (16)
F. WHO LIVES FOREVER (8)

Ge 3:22 also from the tree of life, and eat, and live **f**"— D
6: 3 "My spirit shall not abide in mortals **f**,
13:15 to you and to your offspring **f**.
43: 9 then let me bear the blame **f**.
Ex 3:15 This is my name **f**, and this my title E
15:18 The LORD will reign **f** and ever." A
31:17 It is a sign **f** between me and the people of Israel
32:13 and they shall inherit it **f**.' "
Lev 10: 9 it is a statute **f** throughout your generations.
10:15 to be your due and that of your children **f**,
16:29 This shall be a statute to you **f**:
16:31 and you shall deny yourselves; it is a statute **f**.
17: 7 a statute **f** to them throughout their generations.
23:14 it is a statute **f** throughout your generations
23:21 This is a statute **f** in all your settlements
23:31 it is a statute **f** throughout your generations
23:41 as a statute **f** throughout your generations.
24: 3 it shall be a statute **f** throughout your generations.
24: 8 of the people of Israel, as a covenant **f**.
25:32 the Levites shall **f** have the right of redemption of
Nu 18:19 it is a covenant of salt **f** before the LORD for you
24:20 but its end is to perish **f**."
24:24 and he also shall perish **f**."
Dt 5:29 with them and with their children **f**!
12:28 with you and with your children after you **f**,
15:17 and he shall be your slave **f**.
28:46 and your descendants as a sign and a portent **f**.
29:29 revealed things belong to us and to our children **f**,
32:40 to heaven, and swear: As I live **f**, D
Jos 4: 7 these stones shall be to the Israelites a memorial **f**."
4:24 and so that you may fear the LORD your God **f**."
8:28 Joshua burned Ai, and made it **f** a heap of ruins,
14: 9 be an inheritance for you and your children **f**,
1Sa 1:22 the presence of the LORD, and remain there **f**;
2:30 in and out before me **f**';
2:35 he shall go in and out before my anointed one **f**.
3:13 that I am about to punish his house **f**,
3:14 not be expiated by sacrifice or offering **f**."
13:13 would have established your kingdom over Israel **f**,
20:23 the LORD is witness between you and me **f**."
20:42 and your descendants, **f**.' "
2Sa 2:26 "Is the sword to keep devouring **f**?
2Sa 3:28 and my kingdom are **f** guiltless before the LORD
7:13 and I will establish the throne of his kingdom **f**.
7:16 and your kingdom shall be made sure **f** before me;
7:16 your throne shall be established **f**.
7:24 for yourself to be your people **f**;
7:25 confirm it **f**; do as you have promised.
7:26 Thus your name will be magnified **f** in the saying,
7:29 so that it may continue **f** before you;
7:29 the house of your servant be blessed **f**."
14:14 to keep an outcast banished **f** from his presence.
22:51 to David and his descendants **f**.
1Ki 1:31 and said, "May my lord King David live **f**!" D
2:33 of Joab and on the head of his descendants **f**;
2:45 of David shall be established before the LORD **f**."
8:13 a place for you to dwell in **f**."
9: 3 and put my name there **f**;
9: 5 I will establish your royal throne over Israel **f**,
10: 9 Because the LORD loved Israel **f**,
11:39 the descendants of David, but not **f**."
12: 7 then they will be your servants **f**."
2Ki 5:27 and to your descendants **f**."
8:19 to give a lamp to him and to his descendants **f**.
21: 7 I will put my name **f**; E
1Ch 15: 2 the ark of the LORD and to minister to him **f**.
16:15 Remember his covenant **f**,
16:34 for his steadfast love endures **f**. B
16:41 for his steadfast love endures **f**. B
17:12 and I will establish his throne **f**.
17:14 in my house and in my kingdom **f**,
17:14 and his throne shall be established **f**."
17:22 you made your people Israel to be your people **f**;
17:23 and concerning his house, let it be established **f**,
17:24 be established and magnified **f** in the saying,
17:27 that it may continue **f** before you.
17:27 you, O LORD, have blessed and are blessed **f**."
22:10 and I will establish his royal throne in Israel **f**.'
23:13 so that he and his sons **f** should make offerings
23:13 to him and pronounce blessings in his name **f**; E
23:25 and he resides in Jerusalem **f**.
28: 4 to be king over Israel **f**;
28: 7 I will establish his kingdom **f**
28: 8 for an inheritance to your children after you **f**.
28: 9 but if you forsake him, he will abandon you **f**.
29:10 the God of our ancestor Israel, **f** and ever. A
29:18 keep **f** such purposes and thoughts in the hearts
2Ch 2: 4 of the LORD our God, as ordained **f** for Israel.
5:13 For he is good, for his steadfast love endures **f**," B
6: 2 a place for you to reside in **f**."
7: 3 For he is good, for his steadfast love endures **f**." B
7: 6 for his steadfast love endures **f**— B
7:16 so that my name may be there **f**;
9: 8 your God loved Israel and would establish them **f**,
10: 7 then they will be your servants **f**."
13: 5 the kingship over Israel **f** to David and his sons by
20: 7 and give it **f** to the descendants
20:21 for his steadfast love endures **f**." B
21: 7 to give a lamp to him and to his descendants **f**.
30: 8 which he has sanctified **f**,
33: 4 "In Jerusalem shall my name be **f**." E
33: 7 I will put my name **f**; E
Ezr 3:11 for his steadfast love endures **f** toward Israel." B
9:12 and leave it for an inheritance to your children **f**.'
Ne 2: 3 I said to the king, "May the king live **f**! D
Job 4:20 they perish **f** without any regarding it.
7:16 I loathe my life; I would not live **f**. D
14:20 You prevail **f** against them, and they pass away;
19:24 and with lead they were engraved on a rock **f**!
20: 7 they will perish **f** like their own dung;
23: 7 and I should be acquitted **f** by my judge.
36: 7 but with kings on the throne he sets them **f**,
41: 4 with you to be taken as your servant **f**?
Ps 9: 5 you have blotted out their name **f** and ever. AE
9: 7 But the LORD sits enthroned **f**,
9:18 nor the hope of the poor perish **f**.
10:16 The LORD is king **f** and ever; A
12: 7 you will guard us from this generation **f**.
13: 1 Will you forget me **f**?
18:50 to David and his descendants **f**.
19: 9 the fear of the LORD is pure, enduring **f**;
21: 4 length of days **f** and ever. A
21: 6 You bestow on him blessings **f**;
22:26 May your hearts live **f**! D
28: 9 be their shepherd, and carry them **f**.
29:10 the LORD sits enthroned as king **f**.
30:12 O LORD my God, I will give thanks to you **f**.
33:11 The counsel of the LORD stands **f**,
37:18 and their heritage will abide **f**;
37:27 and do good; so you shall abide **f**.
37:28 The righteous shall be kept safe **f**,
37:29 righteous shall inherit the land, and live in it **f**.
40:11 and your faithfulness keep me safe **f**.
41:12 and set me in your presence **f**.
44: 8 and we will give thanks to your name **f**. E
44:23 Awake, do not cast us off **f**!
45: 2 therefore God has blessed you **f**.
45: 6 Your throne, O God, endures **f** and ever. A
45:17 therefore the peoples will praise you **f** and ever. A
48: 8 in the city of our God, which God establishes **f**.
48:14 that this is God, our God **f** and ever. A
48:14 He will be our guide **f**.
49: 9 that one should live on **f** and never see the grave.
49:11 Their graves are their homes **f**,
52: 5 But God will break you down **f**;
52: 8 I trust in the steadfast love of God **f** and ever. A
52: 9 I will thank you **f**, because
61: 4 Let me abide in your tent **f**,
61: 7 May he be enthroned **f** before God;
Ps 66: 7 who rules by his might **f**, whose eyes keep watch
68:16 where the LORD will reside **f**?
72:17 May his name endure **f**, his fame continue as long
72:19 Blessed be his glorious name **f**; E
73:26 God is the strength of my heart and my portion **f**.
74: 1 why do you cast us off **f**?
74:10 Is the enemy to revile your name **f**? E
74:19 do not forget the life of your poor **f**.
75: 9 But I will rejoice **f**; I will sing praises to the
77: 7 "Will the Lord spurn **f**, and never again
77: 8 Has his steadfast love ceased **f**?
78:69 like the earth, which he has founded **f**.
79: 5 Will you be angry **f**?
79:13 will give thanks to you **f**;
81:15 and their doom would last **f**.
83:17 Let them be put to shame and dismayed **f**;
85: 5 Will you be angry with us **f**?
86:12 and I will glorify your name **f**. E
89: 1 of your steadfast love, O LORD, **f**;
89: 2 I declare that your steadfast love is established **f**;
89: 4 'I will establish your descendants **f**,
89:28 **F** I will keep my steadfast love for him,
89:29 I will establish his line **f**,
89:36 His line shall continue **f**, and his throne endure
89:37 It shall be established **f** like the moon,
89:46 Will you hide yourself **f**?
89:52 Blessed be the LORD **f**. Amen and Amen.
92: 7 they are doomed to destruction **f**,
92: 8 but you, O LORD, are on high **f**.
100: 5 his steadfast love endures **f**, B
102:12 But you, O LORD, are enthroned **f**;
103: 9 nor will he keep his anger **f**.
104:31 May the glory of the LORD endure **f**;
105: 8 He is mindful of his covenant **f**,
106: 1 for his steadfast love endures **f**. B
106:31 as righteousness from generation to generation **f**.
107: 1 for his steadfast love endures **f**. B
110: 4 a priest **f** according to the order of Melchizedek."
111: 3 and his righteousness endures **f**.
111: 8 They are established **f** and ever, A
111: 9 he has commanded his covenant **f**.
111:10 have a good understanding. His praise endures **f**.
112: 3 and their righteousness endures **f**.
112: 6 they will be remembered **f**.
112: 9 their righteousness endures **f**;
117: 2 and the faithfulness of the LORD endures **f**.
118: 1 his steadfast love endures **f**! B
118: 2 Let Israel say, "His steadfast love endures **f**." B
118: 3 "His steadfast love endures **f**." B
118: 4 "His steadfast love endures **f**." B
118:29 for he is good, for his steadfast love endures **f**. B
119:44 I will keep your law continually, **f** and ever. A
119:89 The LORD exists **f**; your word is firmly fixed
119:111 Your decrees are my heritage **f**;
119:112 I incline my heart to perform your statutes **f**,
119:144 Your decrees are righteous **f**;
119:152 that you have established them **f**.
119:160 every one of your righteous ordinances endures **f**.
125: 1 which cannot be moved, but abides **f**.
132:14 "This is my resting place **f**;
135:13 Your name, O LORD, endures **f**, your renown,
136: 1 for he is good, for his steadfast love endures **f**. B
136: 2 for his steadfast love endures **f**. B
136: 3 for his steadfast love endures **f**; B
136: 4 for his steadfast love endures **f**; B
136: 5 for his steadfast love endures **f**; B
136: 6 for his steadfast love endures **f**; B
136: 7 for his steadfast love endures **f**; B
136: 8 for his steadfast love endures **f**; B
136: 9 for his steadfast love endures **f**; B
136:10 for his steadfast love endures **f**; B
136:11 for his steadfast love endures **f**; B
136:12 for his steadfast love endures **f**; B
136:13 for his steadfast love endures **f**; B
136:14 for his steadfast love endures **f**; B
136:15 for his steadfast love endures **f**; B
136:16 for his steadfast love endures **f**; B
136:17 for his steadfast love endures **f**; B
136:18 for his steadfast love endures **f**; B
136:19 for his steadfast love endures **f**; B
136:20 for his steadfast love endures **f**; B
136:21 for his steadfast love endures **f**; B
136:22 for his steadfast love endures **f**. B
136:23 for his steadfast love endures **f**; B
136:24 for his steadfast love endures **f**; B
136:25 for his steadfast love endures **f**. B
136:26 for his steadfast love endures **f**. B
138: 8 your steadfast love, O LORD, endures **f**. B
145: 1 and bless your name **f** and ever. AE
145: 2 and praise your name **f** and ever. AE
145:21 all flesh will bless his holy name **f** and ever. AE
146: 6 in them; who keeps faith **f**;
146:10 The LORD will reign **f**, your God, O Zion,
148: 6 He established them **f** and ever; A
Pr 10:25 but the righteous are established **f**.
12:19 Truthful lips endure **f**, but
27:24 for riches do not last **f**,
29:14 his throne will be established **f**.
Ecc 1: 4 and a generation comes, but the earth remains **f**.
3:14 I know that whatever God does endures **f**;
Isa 17: 2 Her towns will be deserted **f**;
25: 7 he will swallow up death **f**.
26: 4 the LORD **f**, for in the LORD GOD you have
28:28 but one does not thresh it **f**;
30: 8 that it may be for the time to come as a witness **f**.
32:14 the hill and the watchtower will become dens **f**,
32:17 the result of righteousness, quietness and trust **f**.

Isa 34:10 its smoke shall go up **f.**
34:10 no one shall pass through it **f** and ever. A
34:17 shall possess it **f,** from generation to generation
40: 8 but the word of our God will stand **f.**
47: 7 You said, "I shall be mistress **f,"**
51: 6 but my salvation will be **f,**
51: 8 but my deliverance will be **f,**
59:21 says the LORD, from now on and **f.**
60:15 I will make you majestic **f,** a joy from age to age.
60:21 they shall possess the land **f.**
64: 9 O LORD, and do not remember iniquity **f.**
65:18 But be glad and rejoice **f** in what I am creating;
Jer 3: 5 will he be angry **f,** will he be indignant to
3:12 I will not be angry **f.**
7: 7 that I gave of old to your ancestors **f** and ever. A
15:14 for in my anger a fire is kindled that shall burn **f.**
17: 4 for in my anger a fire is kindled that shall burn **f.**
17:25 and this city shall be inhabited **f.**
18:16 a thing to be hissed at **f.**
20:17 would have been my grave, and her womb **f** great.
25: 5 to you and your ancestors from of old and **f;**
31:36 of Israel would cease to be a nation before me **f.**
33:11 for his steadfast love endures **f!"** B
51:62 and it shall be desolate **f.'**
La 3:31 For the Lord will not reject **f.**
5:19 But you, O LORD, reign **f;**
Eze 27:36 to a dreadful end and shall be no more **f."**
28:19 to a dreadful end and shall be no more **f.**
37:25 and their children's children shall live there **f;**
37:25 and my servant David shall be their prince **f.**
43: 7 where I will reside among the people of Israel **f.**
43: 9 and I will reside among them **f.**
Da 2: 4 to the king (in Aramaic), "O king, live **f!** D
2:44 and bring them to an end, and it shall stand **f;**
3: 9 to King Nebuchadnezzar, "O king, live **f!** D
4:34 and praised and honored the one who lives **f.** F
5:10 The queen said, "O king, live **f!** D
6: 6 the king and said to him, "O King Darius, live **f!** D
6:21 Daniel then said to the king, "O king, live **f!** D
6:26 For he is the living God, enduring **f.**
7:18 the kingdom and possess the kingdom **f—**
7:18 and possess the kingdom forever—**f** and ever." A
12: 3 like the stars **f** and ever. A
12: 7 the one who lives **f** that it would be for a time, F
Hos 2:19 And I will take you for my wife **f;**
Joel 3:20 But Judah shall be inhabited **f,**
Am 1:11 his anger perpetually, and kept his wrath **f.**
Ob 1:10 shame shall cover you, and you shall be cut off **f.**
Jnh 2: 6 down to the land whose bars closed upon me **f;**
Mic 2: 9 young children you take away my glory **f.**
4: 5 in the name of the LORD our God **f** and ever. A
7:18 He does not retain his anger **f,**
Zep 2: 9 by nettles and salt pits, and a waste **f.**
Zec 1: 5 And the prophets, do they live **f?** D
Mal 1: 4 the people with whom the LORD is angry **f.**
Lk 1:33 He will reign over the house of Jacob **f,**
1:55 to Abraham and to his descendants **f."**
Jn 6:51 Whoever eats of this bread will live **f;** D
6:58 But the one who eats this bread will live **f."** D
8:35 the son has a place there **f.**
12:34 from the law that the Messiah remains **f.**
14:16 will give you another Advocate, to be with you **f.**
Ac 7:51 you are **f** opposing the Holy Spirit,
Ro 1:25 the Creator, who is blessed **f!**
9: 5 who is over all, God blessed **f.**
11:10 and keep their backs **f** bent."
11:36 To him be the glory **f.**
16:27 through Jesus Christ, to whom be the glory **f!**
2Co 9: 9 his righteousness endures **f."**
11:31 and Father of the Lord Jesus (blessed be he **f!**)
Gal 1: 5 to whom be the glory **f** and ever. Amen. A
Eph 3:21 in Christ Jesus to all generations, **f** and ever. A
Php 4:20 To our God and Father be glory **f** and ever. A
1Th 4:17 and so we will be with the Lord **f.**
1Ti 1:17 the only God, be honor and glory **f** and ever. A
2Ti 4:18 To him be the glory **f** and ever. A
Phm 1:15 so that you might have him back **f,**
Heb 1: 8 "Your throne, O God, is **f** and ever, A
5: 6 "You are a priest **f,** according to the order of
6:20 having become a high priest **f** according to
7: 3 the Son of God, he remains a priest **f.**
7:17 "You are a priest **f,** according to the order of
7:21 and will not change his mind, 'You are a priest **f'** "
7:24 priesthood permanently, because he continues **f.**
7:28 appoints a Son who has been made perfect **f.**
13: 8 the same yesterday and today and **f.**
13:21 to whom be the glory **f** and ever. A
1Pe 1:25 but the word of the Lord endures **f."**
4:11 him belong the glory and the power **f** and ever. A
5:11 To him be the power **f** and ever. Amen. A
1Jn 2:17 but those who do the will of God live **f.** D
2Jn 1: 2 of the truth that abides in us and will be with us **f:**
Jude 1:13 whom the deepest darkness has been reserved **f.**
1:25 and authority, before all time and now and **f.**
Rev 1: 6 to him be glory and dominion **f** and ever. A
1:18 I was dead, and see, I am alive **f** and ever; A
4: 9 seated on the throne, who lives **f** and ever, AF
4:10 and worship the one who lives **f** and ever; AF
5:13 and honor and glory and might **f** and ever!" A
7:12 and power and might be to our God **f** and ever! A
10: 6 him who lives **f** and ever, who created heaven AF
11:15 and he will reign **f** and ever." A
14:11 the smoke of their torment goes up **f** and ever. A
15: 7 of the wrath of God, who lives **f** and ever; AF
19: 3 The smoke goes up from her **f** and ever." A
20:10 they will be tormented day and night **f** and ever. A
22: 5 and they will reign **f** and ever. A

Tob 1: 4 and established for all generations **f.**
3:11 merciful God! Blessed is your name **f;** E
3:11 let all your works praise you **f.**
7:11 She is given to you from today and **f.**
8: 5 and blessed is your name in all generations **f.**
8: 5 the heavens and the whole creation bless you **f.**
8:15 Let them bless you **f.**
8:21 to you as well as to your wife now and **f.**
13: 1 Then Tobit said: "Blessed be God who lives **f,** F
13: 4 he is our Father and he is God **f.**
13:10 within you who are distressed, to all generations **f.**
13:11 the name of the chosen city will endure **f.**
13:12 But blessed **f** will be all who revere you.
13:14 with you and witness all your glory **f.**
13:17 blessed will bless the holy name **f** and ever." AE
14: 7 they will go to Jerusalem and live in safety **f** in
14:15 and he blessed the Lord God **f** and ever. A
Jdt 15:10 May the Almighty Lord bless you **f!"**
16:16 but whoever fears the Lord is great **f.**
16:17 they shall weep in pain **f.**
AdE 9:32 Esther established it by a decree **f,**
10:13 to generation **f** among his people Israel."
14:10 and to magnify **f** a mortal king.
Wis 3: 8 and the Lord will reign over them **f.**
4:18 and an outrage among the dead **f;**
5:15 righteous live **f,** and their reward is with the Lord;D
6:21 honor wisdom, so that you may reign **f.**
14:13 not exist from the beginning, nor will they last **f.**
Sir 1: 1 and with him it remains **f.**
11:33 and they may ruin your reputation **f.**
18: 1 He who lives **f** created the whole universe; F
37:26 and his name will live **f.** D
40:12 but good faith will last **f.**
40:17 and almsgiving endures **f.**
41:13 but a good name lasts **f.**
42:23 All these things live and remain **f;**
44:13 Their offspring will continue **f,**
45:24 the dignity of the priesthood **f.**
47:11 Lord took away his sins, and exalted his power **f;**
47:13 in his name and provide a sanctuary to stand **f.**
51:12 *for his mercy endures **f;*** C
51:12 *for his mercy endures **f;*** C
51:12 *for his mercy endures **f;*** C
51:12 *for his mercy endures **f;*** C
51:12 *for his mercy endures **f;*** C
51:12 *for his mercy endures **f;*** C
51:12 *for his mercy endures **f;*** C
51:12 *for his mercy endures **f;*** C
51:12 *for his mercy endures **f;*** C
51:12 *for his mercy endures **f;*** C
51:12 *for his mercy endures **f;*** C
51:12 *for his mercy endures **f;*** C
51:12 *for his mercy endures **f;*** C
51:12 *for his mercy endures **f;*** C
51:12 *for his mercy endures **f;*** C
51:12 *for his mercy endures **f;*** C
Bar 3: 3 you are enthroned **f,** and we are perishing forever.
3: 3 you are enthroned forever, and we are perishing **f.**
3:13 you would be living in peace **f.**
4: 1 of God, the law that endures **f.**
4:23 to me with joy and gladness **f.**
5: 1 and put on **f** the beauty of the glory from God.
Aza 1: 3 and glorious is your name **f!** E
1:11 For your name's sake do not give us up **f,**
1:29 and to be praised and highly exalted **f;**
1:30 and to be highly praised and highly exalted **f.**
1:31 and to be extolled and highly glorified **f.**
1:32 and to be praised and highly exalted **f.**
1:33 and to be extolled and highly exalted **f.**
1:34 and to be sung and glorified **f.**
1:35 sing praise to him and highly exalt him **f.**
1:36 sing praise to him and highly exalt him **f.**
1:37 sing praise to him and highly exalt him **f.**
1:38 sing praise to him and highly exalt him **f.**
1:39 sing praise to him and highly exalt him **f.**
1:40 sing praise to him and highly exalt him **f.**
1:41 sing praise to him and highly exalt him **f.**
1:42 sing praise to him and highly exalt him **f.**
1:43 sing praise to him and highly exalt him **f.**
1:44 sing praise to him and highly exalt him **f.**
1:45 sing praise to him and highly exalt him **f.**
1:46 sing praise to him and highly exalt him **f.**
1:47 sing praise to him and highly exalt him **f.**
1:48 sing praise to him and highly exalt him **f.**
1:49 sing praise to him and highly exalt him **f.**
1:50 sing praise to him and highly exalt him **f.**
1:51 sing praise to him and highly exalt him **f.**
1:52 sing praise to him and highly exalt him **f.**
1:53 sing praise to him and highly exalt him **f.**
1:54 sing praise to him and highly exalt him **f.**
1:55 sing praise to him and highly exalt him **f.**
1:56 sing praise to him and highly exalt him **f.**
1:57 sing praise to him and highly exalt him **f.**
1:58 sing praise to him and highly exalt him **f.**
1:59 sing praise to him and highly exalt him **f.**
1:60 sing praise to him and highly exalt him **f.**
1:61 sing praise to him and highly exalt him **f.**
1:62 sing praise to him and highly exalt him **f.**
1:63 sing praise to him and highly exalt him **f.**
1:64 sing praise to him and highly exalt him **f.**
1:65 sing praise to him and highly exalt him **f.**
1:66 sing praise to him and highly exalt him **f.**
1:67 for he is good, for his mercy endures **f.** C
1:68 give thanks to him, for his mercy endures **f."** C
1Mc 2:57 inherited the throne of the kingdom **f.**
3: 7 and his memory is blessed **f.**
4:24 "For he is good, for his mercy endures **f."** C
8:23 with the nation of the Jews at sea and on land **f,**
11:36 be canceled from this time on **f.**

1Mc 14:41 be their leader and high priest **f,**
2Mc 14:15 to him who established his own people **f**
14:36 keep undefiled **f** this house that has been
1Es 4:38 But truth endures and is strong **f,**
4:38 and lives and prevails **f** and ever. A
5:61 his goodness and his glory are **f** upon all Israel."
8:85 and leave it for an inheritance to your children **f.'**
Man 1:13 Do not be angry with me **f** or store up evil for me;
1:15 and yours is the glory **f.**
3Mc 5:43 to him would quickly render it **f** empty
2Es 8:23 and whose truth is established **f—**
9:31 and you shall be glorified through it **f.'**
4Mc 18:24 to whom be the glory **f** and ever. Amen. A

FOREVERMORE (16) [EVER]

1Ki 2:33 there shall be peace from the LORD **f."**
Ps 16:11 in your right hand are pleasures **f.**
93: 5 holiness befits your house, O LORD, **f.**
113: 2 the name of the LORD from this time on and **f.**
115:18 we will bless the LORD from this time on and **f.**
121: 8 and your coming in from this time on and **f.**
125: 2 from this time on and **f.**
131: 3 hope in the LORD from this time on and **f.**
132:12 their sons also, **f,** shall sit on your throne."
133: 3 For there the LORD ordained his blessing, life **f.**
Isa 9: 7 with righteousness from this time onward and **f.**
Eze 37:26 and will set my sanctuary among them **f.**
37:28 when my sanctuary is among them **f.**
Mic 4: 7 over them in Mount Zion now and **f.**
Tob 12:17 peace be with you. Bless God **f.**
2Es 2:35 because perpetual light will shine on you **f.**

FOREWARN (KJV) See WARN

FOREWARNED (2) [WARN]

2Pe 3:17 You therefore, beloved, since you are **f,**
Wis 18:19 for the dreams that disturbed them **f** them of this,

FORFEIT (5) [FORFEITED, FORFEITS]

2Ki 10:24 into your hands shall **f** his life."
Pr 6:31 they will **f** all the goods of their house.
Mt 16:26 if they gain the whole world but **f** their life?
Mk 8:36 to gain the whole world and **f** their life?
Lk 9:25 the whole world, but lose or **f** themselves?

FORFEITED (4) [FORFEIT]

Dt 22: 9 or the whole yield will have to be **f,**
Ezr 10: 8 and the elders all their property should be **f,**
Hab 2:10 by cutting off many peoples; you have **f** your life.
1Es 6:32 and all property **f** to the king.

FORFEITS (1) [FORFEIT]

Pr 20: 2 anyone who provokes him to anger **f** life itself.

FORGAT (KJV) See FORGETTING, FORGOT, FORGOTTEN

FORGAVE (6) [FORGIVE]

Ps 32: 5 and you **f** the guilt of my sin.
78:38 Yet he, being compassionate, **f** their iniquity,
85: 2 You **f** the iniquity of your people;
Mt 18:27 lord of that slave released him and **f** him the debt.
18:32 I **f** you all that debt because you pleaded with me.
Col 2:13 when he **f** us all our trespasses,

FORGE (1) [FORGING]

Jer 28:13 You have broken wooden bars only to **f** iron bars

FORGET‡ (67) [FORGETFUL, FORGETFULNESS, FORGETS, FORGETTING, FORGOT, FORGOTTEN]

Ge 41:51 "God has made me **f** all my hardship
Dt 4: 9 as neither to **f** the things that your eyes have seen
4:23 to **f** the covenant that the LORD your God made
4:31 he will not **f** the covenant with your ancestors
6:12 take care that you do not **f** the LORD,
8:11 Take care that you do not **f** the LORD your God,
8:19 If you do **f** the LORD your God
9: 7 not **f** how you provoked the LORD your God
24:19 in your field and **f** a sheaf in the field, you shall
25:19 of Amalek from under heaven; do not **f.**
1Sa 1:11 and remember me, and not **f** your servant,
2Ki 17:38 not **f** the covenant that I have made with you.
Job 8:13 Such are the paths of all who **f** God;
9:27 If I say, 'I will **f** my complaint;
11:16 You will **f** your misery; you will remember it
39:17 because God has made it **f** wisdom,
Ps 9:12 he does not **f** the cry of the afflicted.
9:17 all the nations that **f** God.
10:12 up your hand; do not **f** the oppressed.
13: 1 Will you **f** me forever?
44:24 Why do you **f** our affliction and oppression?
45:10 **f** your people and your father's house,
50:22 "Mark this, then, you who **f** God,
59:11 Do not kill them, or my people may **f;**
74:19 do not **f** the life of your poor forever.
74:23 Do not **f** the clamor of your foes,
78: 7 and not **f** the works of God,
103: 2 O my soul, and do not **f** all his benefits—
119:16 I will not **f** your word.
119:61 I do not **f** your law.

Ps 119:93 I will never **f** your precepts,
119:109 but I do not **f** your law.
119:139 because my foes **f** your words.
119:141 yet I do not **f** your precepts.
119:153 for I do not **f** your law.
119:176 for I do not **f** your commandments.
137: 5 If I **f** you, O Jerusalem, let my right hand wither!
Pr 3: 1 My child, do not **f** my teaching,
4: 5 Get wisdom; get insight: do not **f**,
31: 5 else they will drink and **f** what has been decreed,
31: 7 let them drink and **f** their poverty,
Isa 49:15 Can a woman **f** her nursing child,
49:15 Even these may **f**, yet I will not **f** you.
54: 4 for you will **f** the shame of your youth,
65:11 who **f** my holy mountain,
Jer 2:32 Can a girl **f** her ornaments, or a bride her attire?
23:27 to make my people **f** my name by their dreams
Eze 39:26 They shall **f** their shame, and all
Hos 4: 6 I also will **f** your children.
Am 8: 7 Surely I will never **f** any of their deeds.
Mic 6:10 Can I **f** the treasures of wickedness in the house
Jas 1:24 immediately **f** what they were like.
1:25 being not hearers who **f** but doers who act—
Wis 19: 4 and made them **f** what had happened,
Sir 7:27 and do not **f** the birth pangs of your mother.
11:27 An hour's misery makes one **f** past delights,
23:14 or you may **f** yourself in their presence,
29:15 Do not **f** the kindness of your guarantor,
37: 6 Do not **f** a friend during the battle,
38:21 Do not **f**, there is no coming back;
1Mc 1:49 so that they would **f** the law and change all
2Mc 2: 2 instructed those who were being deported not to **f**
7:23 you now **f** yourselves for the sake of his laws."
1Es 3:22 When people drink they **f** to be friendly
2Es 16:67 Cease from your sins, and **f** your iniquities,
4Mc 18:18 not **f** to teach you the song that Moses taught,

FORGETFUL (1) [FORGET]
2Pe 1: 9 and is **f** of the cleansing of past sins.

FORGETFULNESS (7) [FORGET]
Ps 88:12 or your saving help in the land of **f**?
Wis 14:26 **f** of favors, defiling of souls, sexual perversion,
16:11 not fall into deep **f** and become unresponsive
17: 3 behind a dark curtain of **f**,
3Mc 5:28 for he had implanted in the king's mind a **f** of
4Mc 1: 5 why is not sovereign over **f** and ignorance?"
2:24 it does not control **f** and ignorance?

FORGETS (5) [FORGET]
Ge 27:45 and he **f** what you have done to him;
Job 24:20 The womb **f** them; the worm finds them sweet;
Pr 2:17 of her youth and **f** her sacred covenant;
1Es 3:20 and **f** all sorrow and debt.
3:21 It makes all hearts feel rich, **f** kings and satraps,

FORGETTING (4) [FORGET]
Dt 8:14 **f** the LORD your God, who brought you out of
Jdg 3: 7 **f** the LORD their God, and worshiping the Baals
Job 39:15 **f** that a foot may crush them,
Php 3:13 **f** what lies behind and straining forward

FORGING (1) [FORGE]
Isa 44:12 and **f** it with his strong arm;

FORGIVE‡ (72) [FORGAVE, FORGIVEN, FORGIVENESS, FORGIVES, FORGIVING]
Ge 18:24 and not **f** it for the fifty righteous who are in it?
18:26 I will **f** the whole place for their sake."
50:17 I beg you, **f** the crime of your brothers and
50:17 Now therefore please **f** the crime of the servants
Ex 10:17 Do **f** my sin just this once,
32:32 But now, if you will only **f** their sin—
Nu 14:19 **F** the iniquity of this people according to
14:20 the LORD said, "I do **f**, just as you have asked;
30: 5 and the LORD will **f** her,
30: 8 and the LORD will **f** her.
30:12 and the LORD will **f** her.
Jos 24:19 he will not **f** your transgressions or your sins.
1Sa 25:28 Please **f** the trespass of your servant;
1Ki 8:30 in heaven your dwelling place; heed and **f**.
8:34 **f** the sin of your people Israel,
8:36 and **f** the sin of your servants, your people Israel,
8:39 **f**, act, and render to all whose hearts you know—
8:50 and **f** your people who have sinned against you,
2Ch 6:21 from heaven your dwelling place; hear and **f**.
6:25 and **f** the sin of your people Israel,
6:27 **f** the sin of your servants, your people Israel,
6:30 **f**, and render to all whose heart you know,
6:39 and **f** your people who have sinned against you.
7:14 and will **f** their sin and heal their land.
Ne 9:17 But you are a God ready to **f**,
Ps 25:18 and my trouble, and **f** all my sins.
65: 3 of iniquity overwhelm us, you **f** our transgressions.
79: 9 deliver us, and **f** our sins, for your name's sake.
Isa 2: 9 and everyone is brought low—do not **f** them!
Jer 18:23 Do not **f** their iniquity, do not blot out their sin
31:34 for I will **f** their iniquity,
33: 8 and I will **f** all the guilt of their sin and rebellion
36: 3 so that I may **f** their iniquity and their sin.
Eze 16:63 when I **f** you all that you have done,
Da 9:19 **f**; O Lord, listen and act and do not delay!
Hos 1: 6 on the house of Israel or **f** them.
Am 7: 2 I said, "O Lord GOD, **f**, I beg you!
Mt 6:12 And **f** us our debts, as we
6:14 For if you **f** others their trespasses, your heavenly Father will also **f** you;
6:15 but if you do not **f** others, neither will your Father **f** your trespasses.
9: 6 the Son of Man has authority on earth to **f** sins"—
18:21 the church sins against me, how often should I **f**?
18:35 not **f** your brother or sister from your heart."
Mk 2: 7 Who can **f** sins but God alone?"
2:10 the Son of Man has authority on earth to **f** sins"—
11:25 "Whenever you stand praying, **f**,
11:25 Father in heaven may also **f** you your trespasses."
Lk 5:21 Who can **f** sins but God alone?"
5:24 the Son of Man has authority on earth to **f** sins"—
6:37 **F**, and you will be forgiven;
11: 4 And **f** us our sins, for we ourselves **f** everyone indebted to us.
17: 3 and if there is repentance, you must **f**.
17: 4 and says, 'I repent,' you must **f**."
23:34 ⟦Then Jesus said, "Father, **f** them;⟧
Jn 20:23 If you **f** the sins of any, they are forgiven them;
2Co 2: 7 so now instead you should **f** and console him,
2:10 Anyone whom you **f**, I also **f**.
12:13 not burden you? **F** me this wrong!
Col 3:13 **f** each other; as the Lord has forgiven you, so you also must **f**.
1Jn 1: 9 he who is faithful and just will **f** us our sins
Sir 5: 6 he will **f** the multitude of my sins,"
16: 7 He did not **f** the ancient giants who revolted
16:11 he is mighty to **f**—but he also pours out wrath.
28: 2 **F** your neighbor the wrong he has done,
34:23 nor for a multitude of sacrifices does he **f** sins.
Man 1:13 I earnestly implore you, **f** me, O Lord,
1:13 forgive me, O Lord, **f** me!

FORGIVEN (46) [FORGIVE]
Lev 4:20 for them, and they shall be **f**.
4:26 on his behalf for his sin, and he shall be **f**.
4:31 on your behalf, and you shall be **f**.
4:35 that you have committed, and you shall be **f**.
5:10 that you have committed, and you shall be **f**.
5:13 these sins you have committed, and you shall be **f**.
5:16 the ram of the guilt offering, and you shall be **f**.
5:18 you committed unintentionally, and you shall be **f**.
6: 7 be **f** for any of the things that one may do
19:22 and the sin he committed shall be **f** him.
Nu 15:25 of the Israelites, and they shall be **f**;
15:26 All the congregation of the Israelites shall be **f**,
15:28 for the person, who then shall be **f**.
Ps 32: 1 Happy are those whose transgression is **f**,
Isa 22:14 Surely this iniquity will not be **f** you until you die,
33:24 the people who live there will be **f** their iniquity.
La 3:42 and rebelled, and you have not **f**.
Mt 6:12 as we also have **f** our debtors.
9: 2 "Take heart, son; your sins are **f**."
9: 5 For which is easier, to say, 'Your sins are **f**,'
12:31 people will be **f** for every sin and blasphemy,
12:31 but blasphemy against the Spirit will not be **f**.
12:32 a word against the Son of Man will be **f**,
12:32 against the Holy Spirit will not be **f**,
Mk 2: 5 he said to the paralytic, "Son, your sins are **f**."
2: 9 to say to the paralytic, 'Your sins are **f**,' or to say,
3:28 people will be **f** for their sins
4:12 so that they may not turn again and be **f**.' "
Lk 5:20 he said, "Friend, your sins are **f** you."
5:23 Which is easier, to say, 'Your sins are **f** you,'
6:37 Forgive, and you will be **f**;
7:47 have been **f**; hence she has shown great love.
7:47 But the one to whom little is **f**, loves little."
7:48 Then he said to her, "Your sins are **f**."
12:10 a word against the Son of Man will be **f**;
12:10 against the Holy Spirit will not be **f**.
Jn 20:23 If you forgive the sins of any, they are **f** them;
Ac 2:38 of Jesus Christ so that your sins may be **f**;
8:22 if possible, the intent of your heart may be **f** you.
Ro 4: 7 "Blessed are those whose iniquities are **f**,
2Co 2:10 What I have **f**, if I have forgiven anything,
2:10 What I have forgiven, if I have **f** anything,
Eph 4:32 forgiving one another, as God in Christ has **f** you.
Col 3:13 just as the Lord has **f** you,
Jas 5:15 and anyone who has committed sins will be **f**.
1Jn 2:12 because your sins are **f** on account of his name.

FORGIVENESS (22) [FORGIVE]
A. FORGIVENESS OF SINS (10)

Ps 130: 4 there is **f** with you, so that you may be revered.
Da 9: 9 To the Lord our God belong mercy and **f**,
Mt 26:28 which is poured out for many for the **f** of sins. A
Mk 1: 4 a baptism of repentance for the **f** of sins. A
3:29 the Holy Spirit can never have **f**, but is guilty of
Lk 1:77 of salvation to his people by the **f** of their sins.
3: 3 a baptism of repentance for the **f** of sins, A
24:47 that repentance and **f** of sins is to be proclaimed A
Ac 5:31 he might give repentance to Israel and **f** of sins. A
10:43 everyone who believes in him receives **f** of sins A
13:38 through this man **f** of sins is proclaimed to you; A
26:18 so that they may receive **f** of sins and a place A
Eph 1: 7 the **f** of our trespasses, according to the riches
Col 1:14 in whom we have redemption, the **f** of sins. A
Heb 9:22 the shedding of blood there is no **f** of sins. A
10:18 Where there is **f** of these,
Sir 5: 5 Do not be so confident of **f** that you add sin to sin.
17:29 and his **f** for those who return to him!
18:12 therefore he grants them **f** all the more.
Sir 18:20 and at the time of scrutiny you will find **f**.
21: 1 Do so no more, but ask **f** for your past sins.
Man 1: 7 and **f** to those who have sinned against you,

FORGIVES (4) [FORGIVE]
Ps 103: 3 who **f** all your iniquity, who heals all your diseases,
Pr 17: 9 One who **f** an affront fosters friendship,
Lk 7:49 "Who is this who even **f** sins?"
Sir 2:11 he **f** sins and saves in time of distress.

FORGIVING (5) [FORGIVE]
Ex 34: 7 **f** iniquity and transgression and sin,
Nu 14:18 **f** iniquity and transgression,
Ps 86: 5 For you, O Lord, are good and **f**,
99: 8 you were a **f** God to them,
Eph 4:32 **f** one another, as God in Christ has forgiven you.

FORGOT (13) [FORGET]
Ge 40:23 not remember Joseph, but **f** him.
Dt 32:18 you **f** the God who gave you birth.
1Sa 12: 9 But they **f** the LORD their God;
Ps 78:11 They **f** what he had done,
106:13 But they soon **f** his works;
106:21 They **f** God, their Savior,
Jer 23:27 just as their ancestors **f** my name for Baal.
Hos 2:13 and went after her lovers, and **f** me,
13: 6 and their heart was proud; therefore they **f** me.
Wis 16:23 be fed, even **f** its native power.
19:20 and water **f** its fire-quenching nature.
Bar 4: 8 You **f** the everlasting God, who brought you up,
3Mc 6:20 and he **f** his sullen insolence.

FORGOTTEN (49) [FORGET]
Ge 41:30 and all the plenty will be **f** in the land of Egypt;
Dt 26:13 I have neither transgressed nor **f** any
Job 19:15 the guests in my house have **f** me;
28: 4 they are **f** by travelers, they sway suspended,
Ps 9:18 For the needy shall not always be **f**,
10:11 They think in their heart, "God has **f**,
42: 9 I say to God, my rock, "Why have you **f** me?
44:17 All this has come upon us, yet we have not **f** you,
44:20 If we had **f** the name of our God,
77: 9 Has God **f** to be gracious?
119:83 yet I have not **f** your statutes.
Ecc 2:16 that in the days to come all will have been long **f**.
Isa 17:10 For you have **f** the God of your salvation,
23:15 From that day Tyre will be **f** for seventy years,
23:16 go about the city, you **f** prostitute!
44:21 O Israel, you will not be **f** by me.
49:14 "The LORD has forsaken me, my Lord has **f** me."
51:13 You have **f** the LORD, your Maker,
65:16 because the former troubles are **f** and are hidden
Jer 2:32 Yet my people have **f** me, days without number.
3:21 they have **f** the LORD their God:
13:25 because you have **f** me and trusted in lies.
18:15 But my people have **f** me,
20:11 Their eternal dishonor will never be **f**.
23:40 and perpetual shame, which shall not be **f**.
30:14 All your lovers have **f** you;
44: 9 Have you **f** the crimes of your ancestors,
50: 5 by an everlasting covenant that will never be **f**.
50: 6 to hill they have gone, they have **f** their fold.
La 3:17 I have **f** what happiness is;
5:20 Why have you **f** us completely?
Eze 22:12 and you have **f** me, says the Lord GOD.
23:35 you have **f** me and cast me behind your back,
Hos 4: 6 And since you have **f** the law of your God,
8:14 Israel has **f** his Maker, and built palaces;
Mt 16: 5 they had **f** to bring any bread.
Mk 8:14 Now the disciples had **f** to bring any bread;
Lk 12: 6 Yet not one of them is **f** in God's sight.
Heb 12: 5 And you have **f** the exhortation that addresses you
Wis 2: 4 Our name will be **f** in time,
Sir 3:14 For kindness to a father will not be **f**,
11:25 In the day of prosperity, adversity is **f**,
13:10 do not stand aloof, or you will be **f**.
35: 9 and it will never be **f**.
44:10 whose righteous deeds have not been **f**;
2Es 1: 6 for they have **f** me and have offered sacrifices
1:14 Yet you have **f** me, says the Lord.
8:53 Hades has fled and corruption has been **f**;
12:47 the Mighty One has not **f** you in your struggle.

FORK (8) [FORKS]
1Sa 2:13 with a three-pronged **f** in his hand,
2:14 the **f** brought up the priest would take for himself.
Isa 30:24 which has been winnowed with shovel and **f**.
Jer 15: 7 I have winnowed them with a winnowing **f** in
Eze 21:19 make it for a **f** in the road leading to a city;
21:21 at the **f** in the two roads, to use divination;
Mt 3:12 His winnowing **f** is in his hand,
Lk 3:17 His winnowing **f** is in his hand,

FORKS (5) [FORK]
Ex 27: 3 and shovels and basins and **f** and firepans;
38: 3 the shovels, the basins, the **f**, and the firepans:
Nu 4:14 the firepans, the **f**, the shovels, and the basins,
1Ch 28:17 and pure gold for the **f**, the basins, and the cups;
2Ch 4:16 The pots, the shovels, the **f**,

FORLORN (2)
1Sa 2: 5 but she who has many children is **f**.
Ps 35:12 They repay me evil for good; my soul is **f**.

FORM‡ (52) [FIRST-FORMED, FORMATION, FORMED, FORMING, FORMLESS, FORMS]

Ex 20: 4 whether in the **f** of anything that is in heaven
26:24 they shall **f** the two corners.
Nu 12: 8 and he beholds the **f** of the LORD.
31:51 all in the **f** of crafted articles.
Dt 4:12 You heard the sound of words but saw no **f;**
4:15 Since you saw no **f** when the LORD spoke
4:16 in the **f** of any figure—
4:23 to make for yourselves an idol in the **f** of anything
4:25 if you act corruptly by making an idol in the **f**
5: 8 whether in the **f** of anything that is in heaven
1Ki 6:25 cherubim had the same measure and the same **f.**
7:37 with the same size and the same **f.**
Job 4:16 A **f** was before my eyes; there was silence,
Ps 49:14 and their **f** shall waste away;
Isa 44:13 he makes it in human **f,** with human beauty,
45: 7 I **f** light and create darkness,
52:14 and his **f** beyond that of mortals—
53: 2 he had no **f** or majesty that we should look at him,
Eze 1: 5 This was their appearance: they were of human **f.**
1:16 and the four had the same **f,**
1:26 that seemed like a human **f.**
8: 3 It stretched out the **f** of a hand,
10: 1 like a sapphire, in **f** resembling a throne.
10: 8 to have the **f** of a human hand under their wings.
43:11 its exits and its entrances, and its whole **f—**
Da 10:16 Then one in human **f** touched my lips,
10:18 in human **f** touched me and strengthened me.
Mk 16:12 ⟦After this he appeared in another **f** to two of⟧
Lk 3:22 the Holy Spirit descended upon him in bodily **f**
Jn 5:37 You have never heard his voice or seen his **f,**
Ac 14:11 "The gods have come down to us in human **f!"**
Ro 6:17 to the **f** of teaching to which you were entrusted,
1Co 7:31 For the present **f** of this world is passing away.
Php 2: 6 though he was in the **f** of God,
2: 7 but emptied himself, taking the **f** of a slave,
2: 7 And being found in human **f,**
1Th 5:22 abstain from every **f** of evil.
2Ti 3: 5 the outward **f** of godliness but denying its power.
Heb 10: 1 of the good things to come and not the true **f**
Jdt 1: 4 in force and his infantry to **f** their ranks.
Wis 14:19 the likeness to take more beautiful **f,**
15: 5 so that they desire the lifeless **f** of a dead image.
15: 8 these workers **f** a futile god from the same clay—
15:16 for none can **f** gods that are like themselves.
18:12 by the one **f** of death,
Sir 32:16 Those who fear the Lord will **f** true judgments,
43:19 and icicles **f** like pointed thorns.
2Mc 9:18 in the **f** of a supplication.
3Mc 3:30 The letter was written in the above **f.**
2Es 10:42 (you do not now see the **f** of a woman,
4Mc 4:19 the nation's way of life and altered its **f**
15: 4 a wondrous likeness both of mind and of **f.**

FORMATION (4) [FORM]

Nu 33: 1 in military **f** under the leadership of Moses
Jdt 7:11 my lord, do not fight against them in regular **f,**
1Mc 12:26 that the enemy were being drawn up in **f** to attack
12:50 and kept marching in close **f,**

FORMED‡ (63) [FORM]

Ge 2: 7 then the LORD God **f** man from the dust of
2: 8 and there he put the man whom he had **f.**
2:19 of the ground the LORD God **f** every animal of
Ex 32: 4 He took the gold from them, **f** it in a mold,
Nu 22:36 on the boundary **f** by the Arnon,
Jos 19: 9 the tribe of Simeon **f** part of the territory of Judah;
Jdg 20:22 and again **f** the battle line in the same place where they had **f** it
1Sa 17: 2 and **f** ranks against the Philistines.
2Sa 2:25 The Benjaminites rallied around Abner and **f**
Job 1:17 "The Chaldeans **f** three columns,
33: 6 I too was **f** from a piece of clay.
Ps 90: 2 or ever you had **f** the earth and the world,
94: 9 He who **f** the eye, does he not see?
95: 5 and the dry land, which his hands have **f.**
104:26 and Leviathan that you **f** to sport in it.
139:13 For it was you who **f** my inward parts;
139:16 In your book were written all the days that were **f**
Isa 25: 1 you have done wonderful things, plans **f** of old,
27:11 he that **f** them will show them no favor.
29:16 or the thing **f** say of the one who **f** it,
43: 1 he who created you, O Jacob, he who **f** you,
43: 7 for my glory, whom I **f** and made."
43:10 Before me no god was **f,** nor shall there be any
43:21 the people whom I **f** for myself so
44: 2 who **f** you in the womb and will help you:
44:21 I **f** you, you are my servant;
44:24 your Redeemer, who **f** you in the womb:
45:18 who **f** the earth and made it (he established it; he did not create it a chaos, he **f** it to be inhabited!):
49: 5 who **f** me in the womb to be his servant,
Jer 1: 5 "Before I **f** you in the womb I knew you,
10:16 for he is the one who **f** all things,
33: 2 the LORD who **f** it to establish it—
49:20 the purposes that he has **f** against the inhabitants
49:30 a plan against you and **f** a purpose against you.
50:45 and the purposes that he has **f** against the land of
51:19 for he is the one who **f** all things,
Eze 16: 7 your breasts were **f,** and your hair had grown;
41:18 It was **f** of cherubim and palm trees,
Zec 12: 1 the heavens and founded the earth and **f**
Ac 17: 5 of some ruffians in the marketplaces they **f** a mob
17:29 an image **f** by the art and imagination of mortals.
Gal 4:19 in the pain of childbirth until Christ is **f** in you,
1Ti 2:13 For Adam was **f** first, then Eve;
2Pe 3: 5 and an earth was **f** out of water and by means
Jdt 7:18 and they **f** a vast multitude.
16:14 You sent forth your spirit, and it **f** them;
Wis 9: 2 and by your wisdom have **f** humankind
13: 4 how much more powerful is the one who **f** them.
15:11 because they failed to know the one who **f** them
15:16 and one whose spirit is borrowed **f** them;
Sir 37: 3 why were you **f** to cover the land with deceit?
51:12 *Give thanks to him who f all things,*
3Mc 6:32 they **f** choruses as a sign of peaceful joy.
2Es 6:46 to serve humankind, about to be **f.**
7:*92* to overcome the evil thought that was **f**
7:*94* they see the witness that he who **f** them bears
8:44 who have been **f** by your hands
8:44 and for whose sake you have **f** all things—
13:41 But they **f** this plan for themselves,
16:61 He **f** human beings and put a heart in the midst

FORMER (65) [FORMERLY]

Ge 26: 1 besides the **f** famine that had occurred in the days
Ex 34: 1 "Cut two tablets of stone like the **f** ones,
34: 1 on the tablets the words that were on the **f** tablets,
34: 4 So Moses cut two tablets of stone like the **f** ones;
Nu 6:12 The **f** time shall be void,
21:26 the **f** king of Moab and captured all his land as far
Dt 4:32 For ask now about **f** ages, long before your own,
10: 1 "Carve out two tablets of stone like the **f** ones,
10: 2 on the tablets the words that were on the **f** tablets,
10: 3 cut two tablets of stone like the **f** ones,
19:14 set up by **f** generations, on the property that will
Ru 4: 7 Now this was the custom in **f** times in Israel
2Ki 1:14 the two **f** captains of fifty men with their fifties;
17:34 to practice their **f** customs.
17:40 but they continued to practice their **f** custom.
1Ch 4:40 for the **f** inhabitants there belonged to Ham.
9:20 of Eleazar was chief over them in **f** times;
Ne 5:15 The **f** governors who were
Ecc 7:10 "Why were the **f** days better than these?"
Isa 9: 1 In the **f** time he brought into contempt the land
41:22 Tell us the **f** things, what they are,
42: 9 See, the **f** things have come to pass,
43: 9 and foretold to us the **f** things?
43:18 Do not remember the **f** things,
46: 9 remember the **f** things of old;
48: 3 The **f** things I declared long ago,
61: 4 they shall raise up the **f** devastations;
65:16 the **f** troubles are forgotten and are hidden
65:17 the **f** things shall not be remembered or come
Jer 36:28 Take another scroll and write on it all the **f** words
Eze 16:55 and her daughters shall return to their **f** state,
16:55 and her daughters shall return to their **f** state,
16:55 and your daughters shall return to your **f** state.
36:11 I will cause you to be inhabited as in your **f** times,
38:17 in **f** days by my servants the prophets of Israel,
Da 7:24 This one shall be different from the **f** ones,
11:13 the **f,** and after some years he shall advance with
Mic 4: 8 to you it shall come, the **f** dominion shall come,
Hag 2: 3 among you that saw this house in its **f** glory?
2: 9 be greater than the **f,** says the LORD of hosts;
Zec 1: 4 to whom the **f** prophets proclaimed,
7: 7 that the LORD proclaimed by the **f** prophets,
7:12 by his spirit through the **f** prophets.
8:11 with the remnant of this people as in the **f** days,
14:10 the Gate of Benjamin to the place of the **f** gate,
Mal 3: 4 the LORD as in the days of old and as in **f** years.
Ro 15: 4 For whatever was written in **f** days was written
Eph 3: 5 In **f** generations this mystery was
4:22 You were taught to put away your **f** way of life,
Heb 7:23 Furthermore, the **f** priests were many in number,
1Pe 3:20 who in **f** times did not obey,
Wis 19:15 the **f** for having received strangers with hostility,
1Mc 4:47 and built a new altar like the **f** one.
12: 3 to renew the **f** friendship and alliance with them."
12:16 to renew our **f** friendship and alliance with them.
2Mc 14:38 In **f** times, when there was no mingling with
15: 8 in mind the **f** times when help had come to them
1Es 5:63 old men who had seen the **f** house,
3Mc 2:29 also be reduced to their **f** limited status."
6: 4 the **f** ruler of this Egypt,
6:27 begging pardon for your **f** actions!
2Es 1:36 yet will recall their **f** state.
6:34 to think vain thoughts concerning the **f** times;
7: 1 to me on the **f** nights was sent to me again.
12:18 it shall not fall then, but shall regain its **f** power.

FORMERLY (33) [FORMER]

Dt 2:10 as the Anakim—had **f** inhabited it.
2:12 Moreover, the Horim had **f** inhabited Seir,
2:20 Rephaim **f** inhabited it,
Jos 14:15 Now the name of Hebron **f** was Kiriath-arba;
15:15 now the name of Debir **f** was Kiriath-sepher.
Jdg 1:10 (the name of Hebron was **f** Kiriath-arba);
1:11 (the name of Debir was **f** Kiriath-sepher).
1:23 to Bethel (the name of the city was **f** Luz).
18:29 but the name of the city was **f** Laish.
1Sa 9: 9 (**F** in Israel, anyone who went to inquire
9: 9 the one who is now called a prophet was **f** called
2Sa 7:10 and evildoers shall afflict them no more, as **f,**
2Ki 13: 5 and the people of Israel lived in their homes as **f.**
1Ch 17: 9 down no more, as they did **f,**
Jn 9:13 to the Pharisees the man who had **f** been blind.
Gal 1:23 "The one who **f** was persecuting us is
Gal 4: 8 **F,** when you did not know God,
1Ti 1:13 even though I was **f** a blasphemer,
Phm 1:11 **F** he was useless to you,
Heb 4: 6 and those who **f** received the good news failed
1Pe 1:14 do not be conformed to the desires that you **f** had
1Mc 3:46 because Israel **f** had a place of prayer in Mizpah.
11:27 and in as many other honors as he had **f** had,
11:34 that the king **f** received from them each year,
11:39 A certain Trypho had **f** been one
14:33 where **f** the arms of the enemy had been stored,
14:34 the borders of Azotus, where the enemy **f** lived.
15: 3 to the kingdom so that I may restore it as it **f** was,
15:27 and broke all the agreements he **f** had made
2Mc 9:16 which he had **f** plundered,
11:31 just as **f,** and none of them shall be molested
14: 3 who had **f** been high priest
2Es 5: 2 and beyond what you heard of **f.**

FORMING (7) [FORM]

Ex 14:22 the waters **f** a wall for them on their right and
14:29 the waters **f** a wall for them on their right and
Jos 17:10 with the sea **f** its boundary;
Am 7: 1 he was **f** locusts at the time
1Mc 10:23 Alexander has gotten ahead of us in **f** a friendship
3Mc 3: 8 and the crowds that suddenly were **f,**
4Mc 14: 8 **f** a chorus, encircled the sevenfold fear of tortures

FORMLESS (2) [FORM]

Ge 1: 2 the earth was a **f** void and darkness covered
Wis 11:17 which created the world out of **f** matter,

FORMS (9) [FORM]

Jos 18:14 This **f** the western side.
18:20 The Jordan **f** its boundary on the eastern side.
Am 4:13 For lo, the one who **f** the mountains,
1Co 12:28 then gifts of healing, **f** of assistance,
12:28 **f** of leadership, various kinds of tongues.
Wis 13:13 he **f** it in the likeness of a human being,
16:25 Therefore at that time also, changed into all **f,**
18: 1 but did not see their **f,**
2Mc 4:15 and putting the highest value upon Greek **f**

FORNICATION (27) [FORNICATOR, FORNICATORS]

Mt 15:19 murder, adultery, **f,** theft, false witness, slander.
Mk 7:21 that evil intentions come: **f,**
Ac 15:20 from **f** and from whatever has been strangled and
15:29 from blood and from what is strangled and from **f.**
21:25 from blood and from what is strangled and from **f."**
1Co 6:13 The body is meant not for **f** but for the Lord,
6:18 Shun **f!** Every sin that a person commits is outside
Gal 5:19 Now the works of the flesh are obvious: **f,**
Eph 5: 3 But **f** and impurity of any kind, or greed,
Col 3: 5 **f,** impurity, passion, evil desire,
1Th 4: 3 your sanctification: that you abstain from **f;**
Rev 2:14 would eat food sacrificed to idols and practice **f.**
2:20 to practice **f** and to eat food sacrificed to idols.
2:21 but she refuses to repent of her **f.**
9:21 of their murders or their sorceries or their **f**
14: 8 of the wine of the wrath of her **f."**
17: 2 the kings of the earth have committed **f,**
17: 2 and with the wine of whose **f** the inhabitants of
17: 4 of abominations and the impurities of her **f;**
18: 3 of the wine of the wrath of her **f,**
18: 3 the kings of the earth have committed **f** with her,
18: 9 who committed **f** and lived in luxury with her,
19: 2 with her **f,** and he has avenged on her the blood
Tob 4:12 "Beware, my son, of every kind of **f.**
Wis 14:12 the idea of making idols was the beginning of **f,**
Sir 23:16 one who commits **f** with his near
23:23 through her **f** she has committed adultery

FORNICATION (KJV) See also ADULTERY, PROSTITUTE, UNFAITHFULNESS, SEXUAL IMMORALITY, WHORING

FORNICATIONS See Index to Footnotes

FORNICATOR (3) [FORNICATION]

1Co 6:18 but the **f** sins against the body itself.
Eph 5: 5 Be sure of this, that no **f** or impure person,
Sir 23:17 To a **f** all bread is sweet;

FORNICATORS (5) [FORNICATION]

1Co 6: 9 **F,** idolaters, adulterers, male prostitutes,
1Ti 1:10 **f,** sodomites, slave traders, liars, perjurers,
Heb 13: 4 for God will judge **f** and adulterers.
Rev 21: 8 the murderers, the **f,** the sorcerers, the idolaters,
22:15 and sorcerers and **f** and murderers and idolaters,

FORSAKE (67) [FORSAKEN, FORSAKES, FORSAKING, FORSOOK]

Dt 31: 6 he will not fail you or **f** you."
31: 8 He will be with you; he will not fail you or **f** you.
31:16 they will **f** me, breaking my covenant
31:17 I will **f** them and hide my face from them;
Jos 1: 5 I will not fail you or **f** you.
24:16 that we should **f** the LORD to serve other gods;
24:20 If you **f** the LORD and serve foreign gods,
1Ki 6:13 and will not **f** my people Israel."
1Ch 28: 9 but if you **f** him, he will abandon you forever.

1Ch 28:20 He will not fail you or **f** you,
2Ch 7:19 and **f** my statutes and my commandments
Ezr 8:22 his power and his wrath are against all who **f** him.
Ne 9:17 and you did not **f** them.
9:19 you in your great mercies did not **f** them in
9:31 not make an end of them or **f** them,
Job 6:14 "Those who withhold kindness from a friend **f**
Ps 27: 9 Do not cast me off, do not **f** me,
27:10 If my father and mother **f** me,
37: 8 Refrain from anger, and **f** wrath.
37:28 he will not **f** his faithful ones.
38:21 Do not **f** me, O LORD;
71: 9 do not **f** me when my strength is spent.
71:18 to old age and gray hairs, O God, do not **f** me,
89:30 If his children **f** my law and do not walk
94:14 For the LORD will not **f** his people;
119: 8 I will observe your statutes; do not utterly **f** me.
119:53 because of the wicked, those who **f** your law.
138: 8 Do not **f** the work of your hands.
Pr 2:13 who **f** the paths of uprightness to walk in the ways
3: 3 Do not let loyalty and faithfulness **f** you;
4: 2 for I give you good precepts: do not **f** my teaching.
4: 6 Do not **f** her, and she will keep you;
6:20 and do not **f** your mother's teaching.
27:10 Do not **f** your friend or the friend of your parent;
28: 4 Those who **f** the law praise the wicked,
Isa 1:28 and those who **f** the LORD shall be consumed.
41:17 I the God of Israel will not **f** them.
42:16 and I will not **f** them.
55: 7 let the wicked **f** their way,
58: 2 a nation that practiced righteousness and did not **f**
65:11 But you who **f** the LORD,
Jer 2:19 Know and see that it is evil and bitter for you to **f**
14: 9 by your name; do not **f** us!
17:13 All who **f** you shall be put to shame;
51: 9 **F** her, and let each of us go to our own country;
Eze 20: 8 nor did they **f** the idols of Egypt.
Da 11:30 and pay heed to those who **f** the holy covenant.
Jnh 2: 8 Those who worship vain idols **f** their true loyalty.
Ac 21:21 the Jews living among the Gentiles to **f** Moses,
Heb 13: 5 for he has said, "I will never leave you or **f** you."
Jdt 7:30 for he will not **f** us utterly.
Sir 4:19 If they go astray she will **f** them,
10:12 The beginning of human pride is to **f** the Lord;
17:25 Turn back to the Lord and **f** your sins;
28:23 Those who **f** the Lord will fall into its power;
35: 5 and to **f** unrighteousness is an atonement.
48:15 nor did they **f** their sins,
51:10 do not **f** me in the days of trouble,
Bar 4: 1 and those who **f** her will die.
2Mc 1: 5 and may he not **f** you in time of evil.
6: 1 to compel the Jews to **f** the laws of their ancestors
6:16 he does not **f** his own people.
2Es 1:25 Because you have forsaken me, I also will **f** you.
3:15 that you would never **f** his descendants;
5:18 therefore and eat some bread, and do not **f** us,
10:34 I said, "Speak, my lord; only do not **f** me,
12:44 if you **f** us, how much better it would have been

FORSAKEN‡ (74) [FORSAKE]

Ge 24:27 not **f** his steadfast love and his faithfulness
Dt 28:20 of the evil of your deeds, because you have **f** me.
Jos 22: 3 you have not **f** your kindred these many days,
Ru 2:20 whose kindness has not **f** the living or the dead!"
1Sa 12:10 'We have sinned, because we have **f** the LORD,
1Ki 9: 9 'Because they have **f** the LORD their God,
11:33 This is because he has **f** me,
18:18 and your father's house, because you have **f**
19:10 for the Israelites have **f** your covenant,
19:14 for the Israelites have **f** your covenant,
2Ch 21:10 because he had **f** the LORD,
24:20 you have **f** the LORD, he has also **f** you."
29: 6 they have **f** him, and have turned away their faces
34:25 Because they have **f** me and have made offerings
Ezr 9: 9 yet our God has not **f** us in our slavery,
9:10 For we have **f** your commandments,
Ne 13:11 "Why is the house of God **f**?"
Job 18: 4 shall the earth be **f** because of you,
Ps 9:10 O LORD, have not **f** those who seek you.
22: 1 my God, why have you **f** me?
37:25 the righteous **f** or their children begging bread.
71:11 "Pursue and seize that person whom God has **f**,
88: 5 like those **f** among the dead,
119:87 but I have not **f** your precepts.
Isa 1: 4 have **f** the LORD, who have despised the Holy One
2: 6 For you have **f** the ways of your people,
10:14 and as one gathers eggs that have been **f**,
27:10 a habitation deserted and **f**, like the wilderness;
32:14 the palace will be **f**, the populous city deserted;
49:14 But Zion said, "The LORD has **f** me,
54: 6 For the LORD has called you like a wife **f**
60:15 Whereas you have been **f** and hated,
62: 4 You shall no more be termed **F**,
62:12 you shall be called, "Sought Out, A City Not **F**."
Jer 2:13 they have **f** me, the fountain of living water,
4:29 all the towns are **f**, and no one lives in them.
5: 7 Your children have **f** me,
5:19 "As you have **f** me and served foreign gods
7:29 the bare heights, for the LORD has rejected and **f**
9:13 they have **f** my law that I set before them,
12: 7 I have **f** my house, I have abandoned my heritage;
16:11 It is because your ancestors have **f** me,
16:11 and have **f** me and have not kept my law;
17:13 for they have **f** the fountain of living water,
19: 4 Because the people have **f** me,
49:25 How the famous city is **f**, the joyful town!
51: 5 Israel and Judah have not been **f** by their God,
La 5:20 Why have you **f** us these many days?
Eze 8:12 the LORD has **f** the land.' "
9: 9 for they say, 'The LORD has **f** the land,
Hos 4:10 they have **f** the LORD to devote themselves to
Am 5: 2 **f** on her land, with no one to raise her up.
Mt 27:46 that is, "My God, my God, why have you **f** me?"
Mk 15:34 "My God, my God, why have you **f** me?"
2Co 4: 9 but not **f**; struck down,
Jdt 9:11 protector of the **f**, savior of those without hope.
Sir 2:10 in the fear of the Lord and been **f**?
41: 8 who have **f** the law of the Most High God!
51:20 therefore I will never be **f**.
Bar 3:12 You have **f** the fountain of wisdom.
Bel 1:38 O God, and have not **f** those who love you."
1Mc 10:14 in Beth-zur did some remain who had **f** the law
2Mc 5:20 and what was **f** in the wrath of
7:16 But do not think that God has **f** our people.
1Es 8:80 Even in our bondage we were not **f** by our Lord,
2Es 1:25 Because you have **f** me, I also will forsake you.
1:27 not as though you had **f** me; you have **f** yourselves,
2: 2 'Go, my children, because I am a widow and **f**.
2: 4 For I am a widow and **f**.
12:41 that you have **f** us and sit in this place?
12:48 me, I have neither **f** you nor withdrawn from you;
13:54 because you have **f** your own ways

FORSAKES (5) [FORSAKE]

Pr 2:17 who **f** the partner of her youth
15:10 There is severe discipline for one who **f** the way,
28:13 one who confesses and **f** them will obtain mercy.
Jer 14: 5 Even the doe in the field **f** her newborn fawn
Sir 3:16 Whoever **f** a father is like a blasphemer,

FORSAKING (5) [FORSAKE]

1Sa 8: 8 **f** me and serving other gods,
Jer 1:16 for all their wickedness in **f** me;
2:17 Have you not brought this upon yourself by **f**
Hos 1: 2 land commits great whoredom by **f** the LORD."
4:12 and they have played the whore, **f** their God.

FORSOOK (4) [FORSAKE]

1Sa 31: 7 they **f** their towns and fled;
Bar 3: 8 who **f** the Lord our God.
1Mc 1:38 to her offspring, and her children **f** her.
1:52 Many of the people, everyone who **f** the law,

FORSWEAR (KJV) See SWEAR FALSELY

FORT (1) [FORTIFICATION, FORTIFICATIONS, FORTIFIED, FORTIFY, FORTIFYING, FORTRESS, FORTRESSES, FORTS, WELL-FORTIFIED]

2Mc 10:33 and they besieged the **f** for four days.

FORT (KJV) See also FORTIFICATION, FORTRESS, SIEGE TOWERS, SIEGE WALL, STRONGHOLD

FORTH‡ (182)

Ge 1:11 Then God said, "Let the earth put **f** vegetation:
1:12 The earth brought **f** vegetation:
1:20 "Let the waters bring **f** swarms of living creatures,
1:24 the earth bring **f** living creatures of every kind:
3:16 in pain you shall bring **f** children,
3:18 thorns and thistles it shall bring **f** for you;
3:23 LORD God sent him **f** from the garden of Eden,
7:11 that day all the fountains of the great deep burst **f**,
12: 5 and they set **f** to go to the land of Canaan.
14:14 he led **f** his trained men, born in his house,
Ex 32:27 and **f** from gate to gate throughout the camp,
Nu 17: 8 It put **f** buds, produced blossoms,
Dt 33: 2 he shone **f** from Mount Paran.
33:22 Dan is a lion's whelp that leaps **f** from Bashan.
1Sa 12: 8 who brought **f** your ancestors out of Egypt,
14:16 as the multitude was surging back and **f**.
17:15 and **f** from Saul to feed his father's sheep
17:20 to the encampment as the army was going **f** to
24:13 'Out of the wicked comes **f** wickedness';
2Sa 5:20 "The LORD has burst **f** against my enemies
6: 8 David was angry because the LORD had burst **f**
7:12 who shall come **f** from your body,
12:30 He also brought **f** the spoil of the city,
22: 9 glowing coals flamed **f** from him.
22:13 the brightness before him coals of fire flamed **f**.
2Ki 19: 3 and there is no strength to bring them **f**.
Ezr 6:12 or people that shall put **f** a hand to alter this,
Job 3:11 come **f** from the womb and expire?
10:18 "Why did you bring me **f** from the womb?
14: 9 at the scent of water it will bud and put **f** branches
15: 7 Were you brought **f** before the hills?
15:35 and bring **f** evil and their heart prepares deceit."
20:25 It is drawn **f** and comes out of their body,
26: 4 and whose spirit has come **f** from you?
38:27 and to make the ground put **f** grass?
38:29 From whose womb did the ice come **f**,
38:32 Can you lead **f** the Mazzaroth in their season,
38:35 Can you send **f** lightnings,
39: 4 they go **f**, and do not return to them.
41:18 Its sneezes flash **f** light, and its eyes are like
Ps 7:14 and are pregnant with mischief, and bring **f** lies.
18: 8 glowing coals flamed **f** from him.
18:14 he flashed **f** lightnings, and routed them.
19: 2 Day to day pours **f** speech,
29: 7 The voice of the LORD flashes **f** flames of fire.
50: 2 the perfection of beauty, God shines **f**.
57: 3 God will send **f** his steadfast love
80: 1 upon the cherubim, shine **f**
89:34 or alter the word that went **f** from my lips.
90: 2 Before the mountains were brought **f**,
94: 1 you God of vengeance, shine **f**!
98: 4 break **f** into joyous song and sing praises.
104:10 You make springs gush **f** in the valleys;
104:14 to bring **f** food from the earth,
104:30 When you send **f** your spirit, they are created;
119:171 My lips will pour **f** praise,
Pr 8:24 When there were no depths I was brought **f**,
8:25 before the hills, I was brought **f**—
10:31 The mouth of the righteous brings **f** wisdom,
SS 1:12 my nard gave **f** its fragrance.
2:13 The fig tree puts **f** its figs,
2:13 in blossom; they give **f** fragrance.
6:10 "Who is this that looks **f** like the dawn,
7:11 Come, my beloved, let us go **f** into the fields,
7:13 The mandrakes give **f** fragrance,
Isa 2: 3 For out of Zion shall go **f** instruction,
11:14 They shall put **f** their hand against Edom
14: 7 they break **f** into singing.
14:29 from the root of the snake will come **f** an adder,
27: 6 Israel shall blossom and put **f** shoots,
33:11 You conceive chaff, you bring **f** stubble;
35: 6 For waters shall break **f** in the wilderness,
37: 3 and there is no strength to bring them **f**.
41:21 Set **f** your case, says the LORD;
42: 1 he will bring **f** justice to the nations.
42: 3 he will faithfully bring **f** justice.
42: 9 before they spring **f**, I tell you of them.
42:13 The LORD goes **f** like a soldier,
43: 8 Bring **f** the people who are blind, yet have eyes,
43:19 now it springs **f**, do you not perceive it?
43:26 set **f** your case, so that you may be proved right.
44: 7 let them declare and set it **f** before me.
44:23 break **f** into singing, O mountains, O forest,
45:23 from my mouth has gone **f** in righteousness
48: 1 and who came **f** from the loins of Judah;
48:20 proclaim it, send it **f** to the end of the earth;
49:13 break **f**, O mountains, into singing!
52: 9 Break **f** together into singing,
55:10 making it bring **f** and sprout,
58: 8 Then your light shall break **f** like the dawn,
61:11 For as the earth brings **f** its shoots,
65: 9 I will bring **f** descendants from Jacob,
Jer 4: 4 or else my wrath will go **f** like fire,
4:31 anguish as of one bringing **f** her first child,
12: 2 they grow and bring **f** fruit;
20:18 Why did I come **f** from the womb to see toil
21:12 or else my wrath will go **f** like fire, and burn,
23:19 Wrath has gone **f**, a whirling tempest;
30:23 Wrath has gone **f**, a whirling tempest;
31: 4 and go **f** in the dance of the merrymakers.
46: 9 Let the warriors go **f**: Ethiopia and Put who carry
51:10 The LORD has brought **f** our vindication;
Eze 1: 4 around it and fire flashing **f** continually,
17: 6 it brought **f** branches, put **f** foliage.
31: 4 sending **f** its streams to all the trees of the field.
Da 12: 4 Many shall be running back and **f**,
Hos 6: 5 and my judgment goes **f** as the light.
Joel 3:18 a fountain shall come **f** from the house of
Mic 1:11 the inhabitants of Zaanan do not come **f**;
4: 2 For out of Zion shall go **f** instruction,
4:10 for now you shall go **f** from the city and camp in
5: 2 from you shall come **f** for me one who is to rule
5: 3 the time when she who is in labor has brought **f**;
Hab 1: 4 therefore judgment comes **f** perverted.
3: 4 rays came **f** from his hand,
3:10 the deep gave **f** its voice.
3:13 You came **f** to save your people,
Zec 9:14 and his arrow go **f** like lightning;
9:14 the trumpet and march **f** in the whirlwinds of
14: 3 Then the LORD will go **f** and fight
Mt 13: 8 Other seeds fell on good soil and brought **f** grain,
24:32 as its branch becomes tender and puts **f** its leaves,
Mk 4: 8 Other seed fell into good soil and brought **f** grain,
4:32 and puts **f** large branches,
5:30 Immediately aware that power had gone **f**
13:28 as its branch becomes tender and puts **f** its leaves,
Eph 1: 9 according to his good pleasure that he set **f**
1Th 1: 8 For the word of the Lord has sounded **f** from you
Jas 3:11 a spring pour **f** from the same opening both fresh
Jdt 16:14 You sent **f** your spirit, and it formed them;
Wis 3: 7 In the time of their visitation they will shine **f**,
4: 4 For even if they put **f** boughs for a while,
9:10 Send her **f** from the holy heavens,
11:18 or belch **f** a thick pall of smoke,
11:25 not called **f** by you have been preserved?
19:10 of producing animals the earth brought **f** gnats,
Sir 14:18 a spreading tree that sheds some and puts **f** others,
18:29 become wise themselves, and pour **f** apt proverbs.
23:23 and brought **f** children by another man.
24: 3 "I came **f** from the mouth of the Most High,
24:15 Like cassia and camel's thorn I gave **f** perfume,
24:17 Like the vine I bud **f** delights,
24:27 It pours **f** instruction like the Nile,
24:32 I will again make instruction shine **f** like
39: 6 he will pour **f** words of wisdom of his own
39:14 and put **f** blossoms like a lily.
40: 1 the day they come **f** from their mother's womb

Sir 44:23 From his descendants the Lord brought **f**
45: 9 to send **f** a sound as he walked,
46:12 May their bones send **f** new life from
49:10 the bones of the Twelve Prophets send **f** new life
50:27 whose mind poured **f** wisdom.
Bar 3:33 the one who sends **f** the light, and it goes;
Sus 1: 5 "Wickedness came **f** from Babylon,
1Mc 1:10 From them came **f** a sinful root,
14:36 to sally **f** and defile the environs of the sanctuary,
2Mc 2:23 which has been set **f** by Jason of Cyrene
7:10 and courageously stretched **f** his hands,
14:45 and though his blood gushed **f**
2Es 5: 8 and menstruous women shall bring **f** monsters.
5:49 For as an infant does not bring **f**,
5:49 not bring **f** any longer, so I have made
6:43 your word went **f**, and at once the work was done.
6:44 Immediately fruit came **f** in endless abundance
6:47 to bring **f** living creatures, birds, and fishes;
6:53 the sixth day you commanded the earth to bring **f**
7:62 "O earth, what have you brought **f**,
9:31 and it shall bring **f** fruit in you,
10:12 which I brought **f** in pain and bore in sorrow;
10:14 'Just as you brought **f** in sorrow,
11:42 the homes of those who brought **f** fruit,
13:10 how he sent **f** from his mouth something like
13:10 and from his tongue he shot **f** a storm of sparks.
14:40 I had drunk it, my heart poured **f** understanding,
15:23 And a fire went **f** from his wrath,
15:30 shall go **f** like wild boars from the forest,
16: 9 Fire will go **f** from his wrath,
16:14 Calamities are sent **f** and shall not return
16:32 and its roads and all its paths shall bring **f** thorns,
16:38 but when the child comes **f** from the womb,
16:67 so God will lead you **f** and deliver you

FORTHWITH (KJV) See AS SOON AS, AT ONCE, SUDDENLY, QUICKLY, RUSHED, WITHOUT DELAY

FORTIETH (3) [FORTY]

Nu 33:38 in the **f** year after the Israelites had come out of
Dt 1: 3 In the **f** year, on the first day of
1Ch 26:31 (In the **f** year of David's reign search was made,

FORTIFICATION (1) [FORT]

1Mc 10:11 squared stones, for better **f**; and they did so.

FORTIFICATIONS (3) [FORT]

Isa 25:12 The high **f** of his walls will be brought down,
1Mc 13:48 He also strengthened its **f** and built in it a house
13:52 He strengthened the **f** of the temple hill alongside

FORTIFIED (72) [FORT]

A. FORTIFIED CITIES (26)
B. FORTIFIED CITY (10)

Nu 13:19 the towns that they live in are unwalled or **f**,
13:28 and the towns are **f** and very large;
32:17 the **f** towns because of the inhabitants of the land.
32:36 and Beth-haran, **f** cities, and folds for sheep. A
Dt 1:28 the cities are large and **f** up to heaven!
9: 1 great cities, **f** to the heavens,
28:52 and **f** walls, in which you trusted, come down
Jos 10:20 when the survivors had entered into the **f** towns,
14:12 how the Anakim were there, with great **f** cities; A
19:29 reaching to the **f** city of Tyre; B
19:35 The **f** towns are Ziddim, Zer, Hammath, Rakkath,
1Sa 6:18 both **f** cities and unwalled villages. A
2Sa 20: 6 or he will find **f** cities for himself, A
1Ki 16:24 he **f** the hill, and called the city that he built,
2Ki 3:19 You shall conquer every **f** city B
10: 2 at your disposal chariots and horses, a **f** city, B
17: 9 from watchtower to **f** city; B
18: 8 from watchtower to **f** city. B
18:13 all the **f** cities of Judah and captured them. A
19:25 should make **f** cities crash into heaps of ruins, A
2Ch 8: 5 **f** cities, with walls, gates, and bars, A
11:10 **f** cities that are in Judah and in Benjamin. A
11:23 of Judah and Benjamin, in all the **f** cities; A
12: 4 **f** cities of Judah and came as far as Jerusalem. A
14: 6 He built **f** cities in Judah while the land had rest. A
17: 2 He placed forces in all the **f** cities of Judah, A
17:19 in the **f** cities throughout all Judah. A
19: 5 He appointed judges in the land in all the **f** cities A
21: 3 together with **f** cities in Judah; A
26: 9 at the Valley Gate, and at the Angle, and **f** them.
32: 1 and encamped against the **f** cities, A
33:14 put commanders of the army in all the **f** cities A
Ps 60: 9 Who will bring me to the **f** city? B
108:10 Who will bring me to the **f** city? B
Isa 2:15 against every high tower, and against every **f** wall;
25: 2 you have made the city a heap, the **f** city a ruin; B
27:10 For the **f** city is solitary, a habitation deserted B
36: 1 all the **f** cities of Judah and captured them. A
37:26 should make **f** cities crash into heaps of ruins, A
Jer 1:18 And I for my part have made you today a **f** city, B
4: 5 "Gather together, and let us go into the **f** cities!" A
5:17 with the sword your **f** cities in which you trust. A
8:14 let us go into the **f** cities and perish there; A
15:20 I will make you to this people a **f** wall of bronze;
34: 7 the only **f** cities of Judah that remained. A
Eze 21:20 the Ammonites or to Judah and to Jerusalem the **f**.
36:35 and ruined towns are now inhabited and **f**."
Hos 8:14 and Judah has multiplied **f** cities; A
Zep 1:16 the **f** cities and against the lofty battlements. A
Jdt 2:24 the **f** towns along the brook Abron,
3: 6 in the **f** towns and took picked men from them
4: 5 and **f** the villages on them and stored up food
5: 1 and **f** all the high hilltops and set up barricades in
Sir 48:17 Hezekiah **f** his city, and brought water
50: 1 and in his time **f** the temple.
50: 4 and **f** the city against siege.
1Mc 1:19 They captured the **f** cities in the land of Egypt, A
1:33 Then they **f** the city of David with
4: 7 they saw the camp of the Gentiles, strong and **f**,
4:60 At that time they **f** Mount Zion with high walls
4:61 he also **f** Beth-zur to guard it,
6:26 they have **f** both the sanctuary and Beth-zur;
9:52 He also **f** the town of Beth-zur, and Gazara,
9:62 of it that had been demolished, and they **f** it.
12:38 he **f** it and installed gates with bolts.
13:10 and he **f** it on every side.
14:33 He **f** the towns of Judea,
14:34 He also **f** Joppa, which is by the sea, and Gazara,
14:37 in it and **f** it for the safety of the country and of
2Mc 11: 5 a **f** place about five stadia from Jerusalem,
12:13 a certain town that was strongly **f** with earthworks
12:27 a **f** town where Lysias lived with multitudes

FORTIFY (5) [FORT]

Jdg 19: 5 "**F** yourself with a bit of food,
19: 8 and the girl's father said, "**F** yourself."
Isa 22:10 and you broke down the houses to **f** the wall.
Jer 51:53 and though she should **f** her strong height,
1Mc 15:39 to build up Kedron and **f** its gates,

FORTIFYING (2) [FORT]

1Mc 10:45 of rebuilding the walls of Jerusalem and **f** it all
4Mc 13: 7 by **f** the harbor of religion,

FORTITUDE (1)

4Mc 15:28 of God-fearing Abraham she remembered his **f**.

FORTRESS‡ (32) [FORT]

Dt 3: 5 All these were **f** towns with high walls,
2Sa 22: 2 The LORD is my rock, my **f**, and my deliverer,
24: 7 to the **f** of Tyre and to all the cities of the Hivites
Ne 2: 8 to make beams for the gates of the temple **f**,
9:25 And they captured **f** cities and a rich land,
Ps 18: 2 The LORD is my rock, my **f**, and my deliverer,
31: 2 Be a rock of refuge for me, a strong **f** to save me.
31: 3 You are indeed my rock and my **f**;
59: 9 for you, O God, are my **f**.
59:16 a **f** for me and a refuge in the day of my distress.
59:17 are my **f**, the God who shows me steadfast love.
62: 2 He alone is my rock and my salvation, my **f**;
62: 6 He alone is my rock and my salvation, my **f**;
71: 3 Be to me a rock of refuge, a strong **f**, to save me,
for you are my rock and my **f**.
91: 2 "My refuge and my **f**; my God, in whom I trust."
144: 2 my rock and my **f**, my stronghold
Pr 10:15 The wealth of the rich is their **f**;
Isa 17: 3 The **f** will disappear from Ephraim,
23: 1 Wail, O ships of Tarshish, for your **f** is destroyed.
23: 4 O Sidon, for the sea has spoken, the **f** of the sea,
23:14 Wail, O ships of Tarshish, for your **f** is destroyed.
Jer 48: 1 the **f** is put to shame and broken down;
Da 11: 7 He shall come against the army and enter the **f** of
11:10 and again shall carry the war as far as his **f**.
11:31 by him shall occupy and profane the temple and **f**.
Am 5: 9 so that destruction comes upon the **f**.
Hab 1:10 They laugh at every **f**, and heap up earth to take it.
1Mc 6:62 and saw what a strong **f** the place was,
9:50 the **f** in Jericho, and Emmaus, and Beth-horon,
2Mc 13:19 a strong **f** of the Jews, was turned back,
1Es 6:23 in Ecbatana, the **f** that is in the country of Media,

FORTRESSES (13) [FORT]

2Ki 8:12 you will set their **f** on fire,
2Ch 11:11 He made the **f** strong, and put commanders
17:12 He built **f** and storage cities in Judah.
Isa 23:11 concerning Canaan to destroy its **f**.
33:16 their refuge will be the **f** of rocks;
34:13 nettles and thistles in its **f**.
Da 11:19 he shall turn back toward the **f** of his own land,
11:38 He shall honor the god of **f** instead of these;
11:39 with the strongest **f** by the help of a foreign god.
Hos 10:14 and all your **f** shall be destroyed,
Mic 7:17 they shall come trembling out of their **f**;
Na 3:12 All your **f** are like fig trees with first-ripe figs—
3Mc 6:25 those who faithfully kept our country's **f**,

FORTS (2) [FORT]

2Ch 27: 4 and **f** and towers on the wooded hills.
Na 3:14 Draw water for the siege, strengthen your **f**;

FORTUNATE (4) [FORTUNE]

Ecc 4: 2 who have already died, more **f** than the living,
Isa 3:10 Tell the innocent how **f** they are,
Ac 26: 2 "I consider myself **f** that it is before you,
Sir 36:28 her husband is more **f** than other men.

FORTUNATUS (1)

1Co 16:17 and **F** and Achaicus, because they have made up

FORTUNE‡ (6) [FORTUNATE, FORTUNE-TELLING, FORTUNES]

Ge 30:11 And Leah said, "Good **f**!" so she named him Gad.
Isa 65:11 who set a table for **F** and fill cups of mixed wine
Jer 32:42 upon them all the good **f** that I now promise them.
Sir 20: 9 There may be good **f** for a person in adversity,
31: 3 The rich person toils to amass a **f**,
3Mc 3:11 Then the king, boastful of his present good **f**,

FORTUNE-TELLING (1) [FORTUNE, TELL]

Ac 16:16 a great deal of money by **f**.

FORTUNES (31) [FORTUNE]

Dt 30: 3 then the LORD your God will restore your **f**
Job 42:10 the **f** of Job when he had prayed for his friends;
Ps 14: 7 When the LORD restores the **f** of his people,
53: 6 When God restores the **f** of his people,
85: 1 you restored the **f** of Jacob.
126: 1 When the LORD restored the **f** of Zion,
126: 4 Restore our **f**, O LORD,
Jer 29:14 and I will restore your **f** and gather you from all
30: 3 when I will restore the **f** of my people,
30:18 I am going to restore the **f** of the tents of Jacob,
31:23 of Judah and in its towns when I restore their **f**:
32:44 for I will restore their **f**, says the LORD.
33: 7 I will restore the **f** of Judah and the **f** of Israel,
33:11 For I will restore the **f** of the land as at first,
33:26 For I will restore their **f**,
48:47 Yet I will restore the **f** of Moab in the latter days,
49: 6 afterward I will restore the **f** of the Ammonites,
49:39 But in the latter days I will restore the **f** of Elam,
La 2:14 not exposed your iniquity to restore your **f**,
Eze 16:53 I will restore their **f**, the **f** of Sodom and her
daughters and the **f** of Samaria
16:53 and I will restore your own **f** along with theirs,
29:14 the **f** of Egypt, and bring them back to the land
39:25 Now I will restore the **f** of Jacob,
Hos 6:11 When I would restore the **f** of my people,
Joel 3: 1 when I restore the **f** of Judah and Jerusalem,
Am 9:14 I will restore the **f** of my people Israel,
Zep 2: 7 be mindful of them and restore their **f**.
3:20 I restore your **f** before your eyes, says the LORD.

FORTY‡ (117) [FORTIETH]

A. FORTY YEARS (41)
B. FORTY DAYS (31)
C. FORTY NIGHTS (11)

Ge 5:13 the birth of Mahalalel eight hundred and **f** years,
7: 4 on the earth for **f** days and forty nights; B
7: 4 on the earth for forty days and **f** nights; C
7:12 The rain fell on the earth **f** days and forty nights. B
7:12 The rain fell on the earth forty days and **f** nights. C
7:17 The flood continued **f** days on the earth; B
8: 6 At the end of **f** days Noah opened the window of B
18:29 "Suppose **f** are found there."
18:29 He answered, "For the sake of **f** I will not do it."
25:20 Isaac was **f** years old when he married Rebekah, A
26:34 When Esau was **f** years old, A
32:15 **f** cows and ten bulls, twenty female donkeys
50: 3 they spent **f** days in doing this, B
Ex 16:35 The Israelites ate manna **f** years, A
24:18 on the mountain for **f** days and forty nights. B
24:18 on the mountain for forty days and **f** nights. C
26:19 and you shall make **f** bases of silver under
26:21 and their **f** bases of silver, two bases under
34:28 with the LORD **f** days and forty nights; B
34:28 with the LORD forty days and **f** nights; C
36:24 he made **f** bases of silver under the twenty frames,
36:26 and their **f** bases of silver,
Nu 1:33 of Ephraim were **f** thousand five hundred.
2:19 a company as enrolled of **f** thousand five hundred.
13:25 At the end of **f** days they returned from spying B
14:33 be shepherds in the wilderness for **f** years, A
14:34 **f** days, for every day a year, B
14:34 **f** years, and you shall know my displeasure." A
26:18 of those enrolled was **f** thousand five hundred.
32:13 in the wilderness for **f** years, A
Dt 2: 7 These **f** years the LORD your God has been A
8: 2 the LORD your God has led you these **f** years in A
8: 4 and your feet did not swell these **f** years. A
9: 9 on the mountain **f** days and forty nights; B
9: 9 on the mountain forty days and **f** nights; C
9:11 of **f** days and forty nights the LORD gave me B
9:11 of forty days and **f** nights the LORD gave me C
9:18 the LORD as before, **f** days and forty nights; B
9:18 the LORD as before, forty days and **f** nights; C
9:25 the **f** days and forty nights that I lay prostrate B
9:25 and **f** nights that I lay prostrate before the LORD C
10:10 I stayed on the mountain **f** days and forty nights, B
10:10 I stayed on the mountain forty days and **f** nights, C
25: 3 **F** lashes may be given but not more;
29: 5 I have led you **f** years in the wilderness. A
Jos 4:13 About **f** thousand armed for war crossed over
5: 6 the Israelites traveled **f** years in the wilderness, A
14: 7 I was **f** years old when Moses the servant of A
Jdg 3:11 So the land had rest **f** years. A
5: 8 Was shield or spear to be seen among **f** thousand
5:31 And the land had rest **f** years. A
8:28 the land had rest **f** years in the days of Gideon. A
12:14 He had **f** sons and thirty grandsons,
13: 1 into the hand of the Philistines **f** years. A
1Sa 4:18 He had judged Israel **f** years. A

1Sa 17:16 For **f** days the Philistine came forward B
2Sa 2:10 was **f** years old when he began to reign A
5:4 when he began to reign, and he reigned **f** years. A
10:18 and **f** thousand horsemen,
1Ki 2:11 time that David reigned over Israel was **f** years; A
4:26 Solomon also had **f** thousand stalls of horses
6:17 in front of the inner sanctuary, was **f** cubits long.
7:38 of bronze; each basin held **f** baths,
11:42 in Jerusalem over all Israel was **f** years. A
19:8 the strength of that food **f** days and forty nights B
19:8 the strength of that food forty days and **f** nights C
2Ki 8:9 all kinds of goods of Damascus, **f** camel loads.
12:1 he reigned **f** years in Jerusalem. A
1Ch 12:36 **f** thousand seasoned troops ready for battle.
19:18 and **f** thousand foot soldiers,
29:27 period that he reigned over Israel was **f** years; A
2Ch 9:30 in Jerusalem over all Israel **f** years. A
24:1 he reigned **f** years in Jerusalem; A
Ne 5:15 besides **f** shekels of silver.
9:21 **F** years you sustained them in the wilderness A
Job 42:16 After this Job lived one hundred and **f** years,
Ps 95:10 For **f** years I loathed that generation and said, A
Eze 4:6 **f** days I assign you, one day for each year. B
29:11 it shall be uninhabited **f** years. A
29:12 and her cities shall be a desolation **f** years A
29:13 the end of **f** years I will gather the Egyptians A
41:2 He measured the length of the nave, **f** cubits,
46:22 **f** cubits long and thirty wide;
Am 2:10 and led you **f** years in the wilderness, A
5:25 to me sacrifices and offerings the **f** years in A
Jnh 3:4 And he cried out, "**F** days more, B
Mt 4:2 He fasted **f** days and forty nights, B
4:2 He fasted forty days and **f** nights, C
Mk 1:13 He was in the wilderness **f** days, B
Lk 4:2 where for **f** days he was tempted by the devil. B
Ac 1:3 during **f** days and speaking about the kingdom B
4:22 was more than **f** years old. A
7:23 "When he was **f** years old, A
7:30 "Now when **f** years had passed, A
7:36 at the Red Sea, and in the wilderness for **f** years. A
7:42 to me slain victims and sacrifices **f** years in A
13:18 For about **f** years he put up with them in A
13:21 the tribe of Benjamin, who reigned for **f** years. A
23:13 There were more than **f** of them who joined
23:21 for more than **f** of their men are lying in ambush
2Co 11:24 from the Jews the **f** lashes minus one.
Heb 3:10 for **f** years. Therefore I was angry with that A
3:17 But with whom was he angry **f** years? A
Tob 1:21 But not **f** days passed before two B
Jdt 1:4 and **f** cubits wide to allow his armies to march out
Bel 1:3 for it twelve bushels of choice flour and **f** sheep
1Mc 3:39 and sent with them **f** thousand infantry
12:41 to meet him with **f** thousand picked warriors,
2Mc 5:2 And it happened that, for almost **f** days, B
5:14 **f** thousand in hand-to-hand fighting,
3Mc 4:15 to an end after **f** days but still uncompleted. B
6:38 of Pachon to the fourth of Epeiph, for **f** days; B
2Es 14:23 and tell them not to seek you for **f** days. B
14:36 and let no one seek me for **f** days." B
14:42 They sat **f** days; they wrote during the daytime, B
14:44 the **f** days, ninety-four books were written. B
14:45 And when the **f** days were ended, B

FORTY-EIGHT (5) [FORTY-EIGHTH]

Nu 35:7 towns that you give to the Levites shall total **f**,
Jos 21:41 the holdings of the Israelites were in all **f** towns
Ne 7:15 Of Binnui, six hundred **f**.
7:44 singers: the descendants of Asaph, one hundred **f**.
1Es 5:12 The descendants of Bani, six hundred **f**.

FORTY-EIGHTH (4) [FORTY-EIGHT]

1Mc 4:52 in the one hundred **f** year,
2Mc 11:21 one hundred **f** year, Dioscorinthius twenty-fourth."
11:33 The one hundred **f** year, Xanthicus fifteenth."
11:38 The one hundred **f** year, Xanthicus fifteenth."

FORTY FIFTH (1) [FORTY-FIVE]

1Mc 1:54 in the one hundred **f** year,

FORTY-FIRST (1) [FORTY-ONE]

2Ch 16:13 dying in the **f** year of his reign.

FORTY-FIVE‡ (19) [FORTY-FIFTH]

Ge 18:28 he said, "I will not destroy it if I find **f** there."
Nu 1:25 the tribe of Gad were **f** thousand six hundred fifty.
2:15 as enrolled of **f** thousand six hundred fifty.
26:41 of those enrolled was **f** thousand six hundred.
26:50 of those enrolled was **f** thousand four hundred.
Jos 14:10 these **f** years since the time that
1Ki 7:3 It was roofed with cedar on the **f** rafters,
Ezr 2:8 Of Zattu, nine hundred **f**.
2:34 Of Jericho, three hundred **f**.
2:66 hundred thirty-six horses, two hundred **f** mules,
Ne 7:13 Of Zattu, eight hundred **f**.
7:36 Of Jericho, three hundred **f**.
7:67 they had two hundred **f** singers, male and female.
7:68 hundred thirty-six horses, two hundred **f** mules,
Jer 52:30 into exile of the Judeans seven hundred **f** persons;
1Es 5:12 The descendants of Zattu, nine hundred **f**.
5:22 The descendants of Jerechus, three hundred **f**.
5:42 there were two hundred **f** musicians and singers.
5:43 thousand thirty-six horses, two hundred **f** mules,

FORTY-FOUR (5)

1Ch 5:18 **f** thousand seven hundred sixty, ready for service.
Rev 7:4 one hundred **f** thousand, sealed out of every tribe
14:1 were one hundred **f** thousand who had his name
14:3 one hundred **f** thousand who have been redeemed
21:17 one hundred **f** cubits by human measurement,

FORTY-NINE (2) [FORTY-NINTH]

Lev 25:8 the period of seven weeks of years gives **f** years.
Aza 1:24 the flames poured out above the furnace **f** cubits,

FORTY-NINTH (2) [FORTY-NINE]

1Mc 6:16 in the one hundred **f** year.
2Mc 13:1 In the one hundred **f** year word came to Judas

FORTY-ONE (6) [FORTY-FIRST]

Nu 1:41 the tribe of Asher were **f** thousand five hundred.
2:28 a company as enrolled of **f** thousand five hundred.
1Ki 14:21 Rehoboam was **f** years old when he began
15:10 he reigned **f** years in Jerusalem.
2Ki 14:23 in Samaria; he reigned **f** years.
2Ch 12:13 Rehoboam was **f** years old when he began

FORTY-SEVEN (4) [FORTY-SEVENTH]

Ge 47:28 the years of his life, were one hundred **f** years.
Ezr 2:38 Of Pashhur, one thousand two hundred **f**.
Ne 7:41 Of Pashhur, one thousand two hundred **f**.
1Es 5:25 one thousand two hundred **f**.

FORTY-SEVENTH (1) [FORTY-SEVEN]

1Mc 3:37 in the one hundred and **f** year.

FORTY-SIX (3) [FORTY-SIXTH]

Nu 1:21 the tribe of Reuben were **f** thousand five hundred.
2:11 a company as enrolled of **f** thousand five hundred.
Jn 2:20 under construction for **f** years,

FORTY-SIXTH (1) [FORTY-SIX]

1Mc 2:70 the one hundred **f** year and was buried in the tomb

FORTY-THIRD (1) [FORTY-THREE]

1Mc 1:20 Antiochus returned in the one hundred **f** year.

FORTY-THREE (4) [FORTY-THIRD]

Nu 26:7 enrolled was **f** thousand seven hundred thirty.
Ezr 2:25 Chephirah, and Beeroth, seven hundred **f**.
Ne 7:29 Chephirah, and Beeroth, seven hundred **f**.
1Es 5:19 from Chephirah and Beeroth, seven hundred **f**.

FORTY-TWO (16)

Nu 35:6 and in addition to them you shall give **f** towns.
Jdg 12:6 **F** thousand of the Ephraimites fell at that time.
2Ki 2:24 came out of the woods and mauled **f** of the boys.
10:14 **f** in all; he spared none of them.
2Ch 22:2 Ahaziah was **f** years old when he began to reign;
Ezr 2:10 Of Bani, six hundred **f**.
2:24 The descendants of Azmaveth, **f**.
2:64 together was **f** thousand three hundred sixty,
Ne 7:28 Of Beth-azmaveth, **f**.
7:62 of Tobiah, of Nekoda, six hundred **f**.
7:66 together was **f** thousand three hundred sixty,
11:13 heads of ancestral houses, two hundred **f**;
Rev 11:2 they will trample over the holy city for **f** months.
13:5 it was allowed to exercise authority for **f** months.
1Es 5:18 Those from Bethasmoth, **f**.
5:41 were **f** thousand three hundred sixty;

FORUM (1)

Ac 28:15 came as far as the **F** of Appius and Three Taverns

FORWARD (82) [STRAIGHTFORWARD]

Ex 14:15 Tell the Israelites to go **f**.
Lev 7:35 once they have been brought **f** to serve
8:6 Then Moses brought Aaron and his sons **f**,
8:13 And Moses brought **f** Aaron's sons,
8:14 He led **f** the bull of sin offering;
8:18 Then he brought **f** the ram of burnt offering.
8:22 Then he brought **f** the second ram,
8:24 After Aaron's sons were brought **f**,
10:4 and said to them, "Come **f**,
10:5 They came **f** and carried them by their tunics out
Nu 12:5 and Miriam; and they both came **f**.
27:1 Then the daughters of Zelophehad came **f**.
36:1 came **f** and spoke in the presence of Moses and
Dt 19:16 If a malicious witness comes **f** to accuse someone
20:2 the priest shall come **f** and speak to the troops,
21:5 Then the priests, the sons of Levi, shall come **f**,
Jos 6:7 "Go **f** and march around the city;
6:8 of rams' horns before the LORD went **f**,
7:14 In the morning therefore you shall come **f** tribe
8:19 of their place and rushed **f**.
Jdg 9:44 the company that was with him rushed **f** and stood
1Sa 16:13 upon David from that day **f**.
17:16 the Philistine came **f** and took his stand,
18:29 So Saul was David's enemy from that time **f**.
30:25 that day **f** he made it a statute and an ordinance
2Sa 2:14 "Let the young men come **f** and have a contest
2:14 Joab said, "Let them come **f**."
2:15 they came **f** and were counted as they passed by,
10:13 the people who were with him moved **f** into battle
20:8 as he went **f** it fell out.
1Ki 22:21 until a spirit came **f** and stood before the LORD,
2Ch 18:20 until a spirit came **f** and stood before the LORD,
24:13 and the repairing went **f** at their hands,
Ne 4:7 of the walls of Jerusalem was going **f** and
Job 23:8 "If I go **f**, he is not there;
Pr 4:25 Let your eyes look directly **f**,
25:6 not put yourself **f** in the king's presence or stand
Isa 48:6 From this time **f** I make you hear new things,
Jer 7:24 and looked backward rather than **f**.
Eze 39:2 I will turn you around and drive you **f**,
39:22 that I am the LORD their God, from that day **f**.
Da 3:8 at this time certain Chaldeans came **f**
Na 2:5 they stumble as they come **f**;
Hab 1:9 They all come for violence, with faces pressing **f**;
Zec 2:3 Then the angel who talked with me came **f**,
2:3 and another angel came **f** to meet him,
5:5 angel who talked with me came **f** and said to me,
5:9 Then I looked up and saw two women coming **f**.
Mt 25:20 the one who had received the five talents came **f**,
25:22 And the one with the two talents also came **f**,
25:24 one who had received the one talent also came **f**,
26:60 many false witnesses came **f**. At last two came **f**
Mk 3:3 to the man who had the withered hand, "Come **f**."
9:15 and they ran **f** to greet him.
10:35 came **f** to him and said to him, "Teacher,
Lk 2:25 looking **f** to the consolation of Israel,
7:14 Then he came **f** and touched the bier,
19:16 The first came **f** and said, 'Lord,
Jn 18:4 to happen to him, came **f** and asked them,
Ac 19:33 whom the Jews had pushed **f**.
Ro 3:25 whom God put **f** as a sacrifice of atonement
Php 3:13 forgetting what lies behind and straining **f**
Heb 11:10 For he looked **f** to the city that has foundations,
Jude 1:21 look **f** to the mercy of our Lord Jesus Christ
Jdt 7:17 So the army of the Ammonites moved **f**,
AdE 11:6 Then two great dragons came **f**,
Wis 18:21 he brought **f** the shield of his ministry,
Sir 13:10 Do not be **f**, or you may be rebuffed;
1Mc 2:23 a Jew came **f** in the sight of all to offer sacrifice
10:82 Then Simon brought **f** his force and engaged
2Mc 5:18 from his rash act as soon as he came **f**,
7:7 they brought **f** the second for their sport.
7:15 Next they brought **f** the fifth and maltreated him.
7:18 After him they brought **f** the sixth.
14:21 A chariot came **f** from each army;
15:20 When all were now looking **f** to the coming issue,
1Es 5:58 pressing **f** the work on the house of God with
2Es 7:98 for they press **f** to see the face
4Mc 8:12 to be brought **f** so as to persuade them out of fear
9:11 at his command the guards brought **f** the eldest,
12:1 the seventh and youngest of all came **f**.

FORWARDNESS (KJV) See

EAGERNESS, EARNESTNESS

FOSTER (2) [FOSTERS]

Isa 49:23 Kings shall be your **f** fathers,
AdE 2:7 And he had a **f** child,

FOSTERS (2) [FOSTER]

Pr 17:9 One who forgives an affront **f** friendship,
Sir 50:22 who **f** our growth from birth,

FOUGHT (89) [FIGHT]

Ex 17:8 Then Amalek came and **f** with Israel at Rephidim.
17:10 Joshua did as Moses told him, and **f** with Amalek,
Nu 21:1 he **f** against Israel and took some of them captive.
21:23 he came to Jahaz, and **f** against Israel.
21:26 who had **f** against the former king of Moab
Jos 10:14 for the LORD **f** for Israel.
10:29 to Libnah, and **f** against Libnah.
10:42 because the LORD God of Israel **f** for Israel.
19:47 the Danites went up and **f** against Leshem,
23:3 for it is the LORD your God who has **f** for you.
24:8 they **f** with you, and I handed them over to you,
24:11 the citizens of Jericho **f** against you,
Jdg 1:5 upon Adoni-bezek at Bezek, and **f** against him,
1:8 people of Judah **f** against Jerusalem and took it.
5:19 "The kings came, they **f**;
5:19 then **f** the kings of Canaan, at Taanach,
5:20 The stars **f** from heaven, from their
5:20 from their courses they **f** against Sisera.
9:17 for my father **f** for you, and risked his life,
9:39 of the lords of Shechem, and **f** with Abimelech.
9:45 Abimelech **f** against the city all that day;
9:52 Abimelech came to the tower, and **f** against it,
11:20 and encamped at Jahaz, and **f** with Israel.
12:4 the men of Gilead and **f** with Ephraim;
1Sa 4:10 So the Philistines **f**; Israel was defeated,
12:9 of Moab; and they **f** against them.
14:47 he **f** against all his enemies on every side—
23:5 and his men went to Keilah, **f** with the Philistines,
31:1 Now the Philistines **f** against Israel;
2Sa 8:10 and to congratulate him because he had **f**
10:17 against David and **f** with him.
11:17 The men of the city came out and **f** with Joab;
12:26 Now Joab **f** against Rabbah of the Ammonites,
12:27 and said, "I have **f** against Rabbah;
12:29 and **f** against it and took it.
14:6 and they **f** with one another in the field;
18:6 and the battle was **f** in the forest of Ephraim.
21:15 They **f** against the Philistines,
23:18 With his spear he **f** against three hundred men
2Ki 3:23 the kings must have **f** together,

2Ki 8:29 when he **f** against King Hazael of Aram.
9:15 when he **f** against King Hazael of Aram.
12:17 **f** against Gath, and took it.
13:12 the might with which he **f** against King Amaziah
14:15 and how he **f** with King Amaziah of Judah,
14:28 and all that he did, and his might, how he **f**,
1Ch 10: 1 Now the Philistines **f** against Israel;
11:20 With his spear he **f** against three hundred
18:10 he had **f** against Hadadezer and defeated him.
19:17 in array against the Arameans, they **f** with him.
2Ch 20:29 the LORD had **f** against the enemies of Israel.
22: 6 when he **f** King Hazael of Aram.
27: 5 He **f** with the king of the Ammonites
Isa 20: 1 came to Ashdod and **f** against it and took it—
63:10 he himself **f** against them.
1Co 15:32 If with merely human hopes I **f** with wild animals
2Ti 4: 7 I have **f** the good fight, I have finished the race,
Rev 12: 7 Michael and his angels **f** against the dragon.
12: 7 The dragon and his angels **f** back,
AdE 9:24 the Macedonian, **f** against them,
Wis 11: 3 They withstood their enemies and **f** off their foes.
1Mc 1: 2 He **f** many battles, conquered strongholds,
3: 2 helped him; they gladly **f** for Israel.
5:21 to Galilee and **f** many battles against the Gentiles,
5:35 and **f** against it and took it;
5:50 he **f** against the town all that day and all the night,
5:56 and of the heroic war they had **f**.
5:65 and his brothers went out and **f** the descendants
6:31 for many days they **f** and built engines of war;
6:31 and burned these with fire, and **f** courageously.
6:37 on each were four armed men who **f** from there,
6:52 also made engines of war to match theirs, and **f**
6:63 but he **f** against him, and took the city by force.
9:64 he **f** against it for many days and made machines
9:68 They **f** with Bacchides, and he was crushed
10:15 of the battles that Jonathan and his brothers had **f**,
10:76 So they **f** against it, and the people of
11:55 they **f** against Demetrius,
11:65 Simon encamped before Beth-zur and **f** against it
14:26 they have **f** and repulsed Israel's enemies
14:32 then Simon rose up and **f** for his nation.
16: 2 "My brothers and I and my father's house have **f**
2Mc 1:12 for he drove out those who **f** against the holy city.
2:21 from heaven to those who **f** bravely for Judaism,
8:20 when eight thousand Jews **f** along
10:17 and beat off all who **f** upon the wall,
11:13 because the mighty God **f** on their side.
1Es 2:26 that this city from of old has **f** against kings,
Pm 151: T *after he had f in single combat with Goliath.*

FOUL‡ (16) [FOULED]

Ex 16:20 and it bred worms and became **f**.
16:24 and it did not become **f**,
Job 31:40 and **f** weeds instead of barley."
Ps 38: 5 My wounds grow **f** and fester because
Ecc 10: 1 the perfumer's ointment give off a **f** odor;
Isa 19: 6 its canals will become **f**, and the branches
Eze 32: 2 the water with your feet, and **f** your streams.
34:18 must you **f** the rest with your feet?
Joel 2:20 its stench and **f** smell will rise up.
Rev 16: 2 and a **f** and painful sore came on those who had
16:13 And I saw three **f** spirits like frogs coming from
18: 2 a haunt of every **f** spirit, a haunt of every **f** bird, a haunt of every **f** and hateful beast.
Sir 23:13 **f** language, for it involves sinful speech.
2Mc 3:32 that some **f** play had been perpetrated by the Jews

FOUL (KJV) See also RED, STORMY, UNCLEAN

FOULED (1) [FOUL]

Eze 34:19 and drink what you have **f** with your feet?

FOUND‡ (446) [FIND]

Ge 2:20 for the man there was not **f** a helper as his partner.
6: 8 But Noah **f** favor in the sight of the LORD.
8: 9 but the dove **f** no place to set its foot,
16: 7 of the LORD **f** her by a spring of water in
18:29 "Suppose forty are **f** there."
18:30 Suppose thirty are **f** there."
18:31 Suppose twenty are **f** there."
18:32 Suppose ten are **f** there."
19:19 your servant has **f** favor with you,
26:19 in the valley and **f** there a well of spring water,
26:32 and said to him, "We have **f** water!"
27:20 "How is it that you have **f** it so quickly, my son?"
30:14 of wheat harvest Reuben went and **f** mandrakes in
30:33 if **f** with me, shall be counted stolen."
31:37 what have you **f** of all your household goods?
36:24 the Anah who **f** the springs in the wilderness,
37:15 and a man **f** him wandering in the fields;
37:17 So Joseph went after his brothers, and **f** them
37:32 and they said, "This we have **f**;
38:22 he returned to Judah, and said, "I have not **f** her;
39: 4 So Joseph **f** favor in his sight and attended him;
44: 8 Look, the money that we **f** at the top of our sacks,
44: 9 Should it be **f** with any one of your servants,
44:10 he with whom it is **f** shall become my slave,
44:12 and the cup was **f** in Benjamin's sack.
44:16 God has **f** out the guilt of your servants;
44:16 the one in whose possession the cup has been **f**."
44:17 the one in whose possession the cup was **f** shall
47:14 Joseph collected all the money to be **f** in the land
47:29 "If I have **f** favor with you,
Ge 50: 4 "If now I have **f** favor with you,
Ex 9: 7 Pharaoh inquired and **f** that not one of
12:19 seven days no leaven shall be **f** in your houses;
15:22 in the wilderness and **f** no water.
16:27 of the people went out to gather, and they **f** none.
22: 2 If a thief is **f** breaking in, and is beaten to death,
22: 4 is **f** alive in the thief's possession,
33:12 and you have also **f** favor in my sight.'
33:13 Now if I have **f** favor in your sight,
33:16 shall it be known that I have **f** favor in your sight,
33:17 for you have **f** favor in my sight,
34: 9 He said, "If now I have **f** favor in your sight,
Lev 6: 3 or have **f** something lost and lied about it—
6: 4 or the lost thing that you **f**,
Nu 11:11 Why have I not **f** favor in your sight,
11:15 if I have **f** favor in your sight—
15:32 they **f** a man gathering sticks on the sabbath day.
15:33 Those who **f** him gathering sticks brought him
31:50 what each of us **f**, articles of gold,
32: 5 They continued, "If we have **f** favor in your sight,
35:27 and is **f** by the avenger of blood outside
Dt 17: 2 If there is **f** among you,
18:10 No one shall be **f** among you who makes a son
21: 1 a body is **f** lying in open country,
22:20 of the young woman's virginity was not **f**,
22:27 Since he **f** her in the open country,
Jos 2:22 along the way and **f** nothing.
10:17 it was told Joshua, "The five kings have been **f**,
Jdg 6:17 he said to him, "If now I have **f** favor with you,
14:18 you would not have **f** out my riddle."
15:15 Then he **f** a fresh jawbone of a donkey,
21:12 And they **f** among the inhabitants
Ru 2:10 "Why have I **f** favor in your sight,
1Sa 9:20 to them, for they have been **f**.
10: 2 'The donkeys that you went to seek are **f**,
10:14 and when we saw they were not to be **f**,
10:16 "He told us that the donkeys had been **f**."
10:21 But when they sought him, he could not be **f**.
12: 5 that you have not **f** anything in my hand."
13:19 Now there was no smith to be **f** throughout all
13:22 of the battle neither sword nor spear was to be **f** in
16:22 for he has **f** favor in my sight."
20:29 So now, if I have **f** favor in your sight,
24:19 For who has ever **f** an enemy,
25:28 and evil shall not be **f** in you so long as you live.
27: 5 "If I have **f** favor in your sight,
29: 3 Since he deserted to me I have **f** no fault in him
29: 6 for I have **f** nothing wrong in you from the day
29: 8 What have you **f** in your servant from
30: 3 to the city, they **f** it burned down, and their wives
30:11 In the open country they **f** an Egyptian,
31: 3 the archers **f** him, and he was badly wounded
31: 8 they **f** Saul and his three sons fallen
2Sa 7:27 therefore your servant has **f** courage
14:22 "Today your servant knows that I have **f** favor
17:12 be **f**, and we shall light on him as the dew falls on
17:13 until not even a pebble is to be **f** there."
1Ki 1: 3 and **f** Abishag the Shunammite,
1:52 but if wickedness is **f** in him, he shall die."
11:19 Hadad **f** great favor in the sight of Pharaoh,
11:29 prophet Ahijah the Shilonite **f** him on the road.
13:14 and **f** him sitting under an oak tree.
13:28 and he went and **f** the body thrown in the road,
14:13 because in him there is **f** something pleasing to
18:10 of the kingdom or nation, that they had not **f** you.
19:19 he set out from there, and **f** Elisha son of Shaphat,
20:37 Then he **f** another man and said, "Strike me!"
21:20 Ahab said to Elijah, "Have you **f** me,
21:20 He answered, "I have **f** you.
2Ki 4:39 he **f** a wild vine and gathered from it a lapful
7: 9 until the morning light, we will be **f** guilty;
9:35 they **f** no more of her than the skull and the feet
12:10 the money that was **f** in the house of the LORD,
12:18 the gold that was **f** in the treasuries of the house
14:14 the vessels that were **f** in the house of the LORD
16: 8 Ahaz also took the silver and gold **f** in the house
17: 4 But the king of Assyria **f** treachery in Hoshea;
18:15 the silver that was **f** in the house of the LORD
19: 8 and **f** the king of Assyria fighting against Libnah;
20:13 his armory, all that was **f** in his storehouses;
22: 8 "I have **f** the book of the law in the house of
22: 9 the money that was **f** in the house,
22:13 the words of this book that has been **f**;
23: 2 of the covenant that had been **f** in the house of
23:24 the book that the priest Hilkiah had **f** in the house
25:19 and five men of the king's council who were **f** in
25:19 of the people of the land who were **f** in the city.
1Ch 4:40 where they **f** rich, good pasture,
4:41 and the Meunim who were **f** there,
10: 3 and the archers **f** him, and he was wounded by
10: 8 they **f** Saul and his sons fallen on Mount Gilboa.
17:25 your servant has **f** it possible to pray before you.
20: 2 he **f** that it weighed a talent of gold,
24: 4 Since more chief men were **f** among the sons
26:31 and men of great ability among them were **f**
28: 9 If you seek him, he will be **f** by you;
2Ch 2:17 that his father David had taken; and there were **f** to
11:23 and **f** many wives for them.
15: 2 If you seek him, he will be **f** by you,
15: 4 and sought him, he was **f** by them.
15:15 with their whole desire, and he was **f** by them,
19: 3 Nevertheless, some good is **f** in you,
20:25 they **f** livestock in great numbers, goods, clothing,
21:17 and carried away all the possessions they **f**
25: 5 ustered those twenty years old and upward, and **f**
25:24 all the vessels that were **f** in the house of God,
29:16 the unclean things that they **f** in the temple of
2Ch 34:14 the priest Hilkiah **f** the book of the law of
34:15 "I have **f** the book of the law in the house of
34:17 the money that was **f** in the house of the LORD
34:21 concerning the words of the book that has been **f**;
34:30 of the covenant that had been **f** in the house of
36: 8 and what was **f** against him,
Ezr 2:62 but they were not **f** there,
6: 2 that a scroll was **f** on which this was written:
8:15 I **f** there none of the descendants of Levi.
10:18 There were **f** of the descendants of
Ne 2: 5 and if your servant has **f** favor with you,
7: 5 And I **f** the book of the genealogy
7: 5 and I **f** the following written in it:
7:64 but it was not **f** there, so they were excluded from
8:14 And they **f** it written in the law,
9: 8 and you **f** his heart faithful before you, and made
13: 1 and in it was **f** written that no Ammonite
13:10 I also **f** out that the portions of the Levites had
Est 2:23 When the affair was investigated and **f** to be so,
4:16 gather all the Jews to be **f** in Susa,
6: 2 It was **f** written how Mordecai had told
Job 8: 8 and consider what their ancestors have **f**;
19:28 and, 'The root of the matter is **f** in him';
20: 8 They will fly away like a dream, and not be **f**;
28:12 "But where shall wisdom be **f**?
28:13 and it is not **f** in the land of the living.
32: 3 because they had **f** no answer,
32:13 Yet do not say, 'We have **f** wisdom;
33:24 into the Pit; I have **f** a ransom;
Ps 36: 2 that their iniquity cannot be **f** out and hated.
37:36 though I sought them, they could not be **f**.
68:10 your flock **f** a dwelling in it;
69:20 and for comforters, but I **f** none.
89:20 I have **f** my servant David;
109: 7 When he is tried, let him be **f** guilty;
132: 6 we **f** it in the fields of Jaar.
Pr 7:15 to seek you eagerly, and I have **f** you!
10: 9 but whoever follows perverse ways will be **f** out.
10:13 of one who has understanding wisdom is **f**,
20: 4 harvest comes, and there is nothing to be **f**.
25:16 If you have **f** honey, eat only enough for you,
30: 6 and you will be **f** a liar.
30:28 yet it is **f** in kings' palaces.
Ecc 2:10 for my heart **f** pleasure in all my toil,
7:26 I **f** more bitter than death the woman who is
7:27 See, this is what I **f**, says the Teacher,
7:28 my mind has sought repeatedly, but I have not **f**.
7:28 One man among a thousand I **f**,
7:28 but a woman among all these I have not **f**.
7:29 I **f**, that God made human beings straightforward,
9:15 Now there was **f** in it a poor wise man,
SS 3: 1 I sought him, but **f** him not;
3: 2 I sought him, but **f** him not.
3: 3 The sentinels **f** me, as they went about in the city.
3: 4 when I **f** him whom my soul loves.
5: 7 Making their rounds in the city the sentinels **f** me;
Isa 10:14 My hand has **f**, like a nest,
13:15 Whoever is **f** will be thrust through,
22: 3 All of you who were **f** were captured,
30:14 among its fragments not a sherd is **f** for taking fire
35: 9 they shall not be **f** there, but the redeemed shall
37: 8 and **f** the king of Assyria fighting against Libnah;
39: 2 all that was **f** in his storehouses.
51: 3 joy and gladness will be **f** in her,
55: 6 Seek the LORD while he may be **f**,
57:10 You **f** your desire rekindled,
65: 1 to be **f** by those who did not seek me.
65: 8 As the wine is **f** in the cluster, and they say,
Jer 2:34 Also on your skirts is **f** the lifeblood of
5:26 For scoundrels are **f** among my people;
15:16 Your words were **f**, and I ate them,
23:11 even in my house I have **f** their wickedness,
31: 2 The people who survived the sword **f** grace in
50: 7 All who **f** them have devoured them,
50:20 and the sins of Judah, and none shall be **f**;
52:25 and seven men of the king's council who were **f**
52:25 the people of the land who were **f** inside the city.
Eze 7:16 be **f** on the mountains like doves of the valleys,
22:30 not destroy it; but I **f** no one.
26:21 though sought for, you will never be **f** again,
28:15 until iniquity was **f** in you.
Da 1:19 no one was **f** to compare with Daniel, Hananiah,
1:20 he **f** them ten times better than all the magicians
2:25 "I have **f** among the exiles from Judah
2:35 so that not a trace of them could be **f**.
4:12 The animals of the field **f** shade under it,
5:11 of your father he was **f** to have enlightenment,
5:12 and solve problems were **f** in this Daniel,
5:14 understanding, and excellent wisdom are **f** in you.
5:27 on the scales and **f** wanting;
6: 4 and no negligence or corruption could be **f** in him.
6:11 The conspirators came and **f** Daniel praying
6:22 because I was **f** blameless before him;
6:23 and no kind of harm was **f** on him,
11:19 but he shall stumble and fall, and shall not be **f**.
12: 1 everyone who is **f** written in the book.
Hos 9:10 Like grapes in the wilderness, I **f** Israel.
12: 8 of my gain no offense has been **f** in me that would
Jnh 1: 3 down to Joppa and **f** a ship going to Tarshish;
Mic 1:13 for in you were **f** the transgressions of Israel.
Hab 2:12 and **f** a city on iniquity!"
Zep 3:13 nor shall a deceitful tongue be **f** in their mouths.
Mal 2: 6 and no wrong was **f** on his lips.
Mt 1:18 she was **f** to be with child from the Holy Spirit.
2: 8 and when you have **f** him,
8:10 in no one in Israel have I **f** such faith.
13:44 which someone **f** and hid;

Mt 20: 6 and **f** others standing around;
21:19 he went to it and **f** nothing at all on it but leaves.
22:10 and gathered all whom they **f**, both good and bad;
26:40 he came to the disciples and **f** them sleeping;
26:43 Again he came and **f** them sleeping,
26:60 but they **f** none, though many false witnesses came
Mk 1:37 When they **f** him, they said to him,
6:38 they had **f** out, they said, "Five, and two fish."
7:30 So she went home, **f** the child lying on the bed,
11: 4 They went away and **f** a colt tied near a door,
11:13 When he came to it, he **f** nothing but leaves,
14:16 and **f** everything as he had told them;
14:37 He came and **f** them sleeping;
14:40 And once more he came and **f** them sleeping,
14:55 to death; but they **f** none.
Lk 1:30 Mary, for you have **f** favor with God.
2:16 So they went with haste and **f** Mary and Joseph,
2:46 After three days they **f** him in the temple,
4:17 the scroll and **f** the place where it was written:
7: 9 "I tell you, not even in Israel have I **f** such faith."
7:10 they **f** the slave in good health.
8:35 they **f** the man from whom
9:11 the crowds **f** out about it, they followed him;
9:36 When the voice had spoken, Jesus was **f** alone.
13: 6 and he came looking for fruit on it and **f** none.
15: 5 he has **f** it, he lays it on his shoulders and rejoices.
15: 6 for I have **f** my sheep that was lost.'
15: 9 When she has **f** it, she calls together her friends
15: 9 for I have **f** the coin that I had lost.'
15:24 he was lost and is **f**!'
15:32 he was lost and has been **f**.' "
17:18 Was none of them **f** to return and give praise
19:32 So those who were sent departed and **f** it
22:13 they went and **f** everything as he had told them;
22:45 the disciples and **f** them sleeping because of grief,
23: 2 saying, "We **f** this man perverting our nation,
23:14 in your presence and have not **f** this man guilty
23:22 I have **f** in him no ground for the sentence
24: 2 They **f** the stone rolled away from the tomb,
24:24 to the tomb and **f** it just as the women had said;
24:33 to Jerusalem; and they **f** the eleven
Jn 1:41 He first **f** his brother Simon and said to him,
1:41 and said to him, "We have **f**
1:43 He **f** Philip and said to him, "Follow me."
1:45 Philip **f** Nathanael and said to him,
1:45 "We have **f** him about whom Moses in the law
2:14 In the temple he **f** people selling cattle, sheep,
5:14 Later Jesus **f** him in the temple and said to him,
6:25 When they **f** him on the other side of the sea,
9:35 and when he **f** him, he said,
11:17 he **f** that Lazarus had already been in
12:14 Jesus **f** a young donkey and sat on it;
Ac 5:10 When the young men came in they **f** her dead,
5:23 "We **f** the prison securely locked and
5:23 but when we opened them, we **f** no one inside."
5:39 in that case you may even be **f** fighting
7:46 who **f** favor with God and asked
8:40 But Philip **f** himself at Azotus,
9: 2 so that if he **f** any who belonged to the Way,
9:33 There he **f** a man named Aeneas,
10:27 he went in and **f** that many had assembled;
11:26 and when he had **f** him,
13:22 'I have **f** David, son of Jesse,
13:28 though they **f** no cause for a sentence of death,
17:23 I **f** among them an altar with the inscription,
18: 2 There he **f** a Jew named Aquila,
19: 1 where he **f** some disciples.
19:19 it was **f** to come to fifty thousand silver coins.
21: 2 When we **f** a ship bound for Phoenicia,
23:29 I **f** that he was accused concerning questions
24: 5 We have, in fact, **f** this man a pestilent fellow,
24:18 While I was doing this, they **f** me in the temple,
24:20 Or let these men here tell what crime they had **f**
25:25 But I **f** that he had done nothing deserving death;
27: 6 There the centurion **f** an Alexandrian ship bound
27:28 So they took soundings and **f** twenty fathoms;
27:28 they took soundings again and **f** fifteen fathoms.
28:14 There we **f** believers and were invited to stay
Ro 10:20 "I have been **f** by those who did not seek me;
1Co 4: 2 of stewards that they be **f** trustworthy.
5: 1 and of a kind that is not **f** even among pagans;
15:15 We are even **f** to be misrepresenting God,
2Co 5: 3 when we have taken it off we will not be **f** naked.
6: 3 so that no fault may be **f** with our ministry,
8:22 and **f** eager in many matters,
Gal 2:17 we ourselves have been **f** to be sinners,
Eph 5: 9 the light is **f** in all that is good and right and true.
Php 2: 7 And being **f** in human form,
3: 9 be **f** in him, not having a righteousness of my own
2Ti 1:17 he eagerly searched for me and **f** me
Heb 11: 5 and "he was not **f**, because God had taken him."
12:17 he was rejected, for he **f** no chance to repent,
1Pe 1: 7 may be **f** to result in praise and glory and honor
2:22 and no deceit was **f** in his mouth."
2Pe 3:14 strive to be **f** by him at peace,
Rev 2: 2 and have **f** them to be false.
3: 2 not **f** your works perfect in the sight of my God.
5: 4 because no one was **f** worthy to open the scroll or
14: 5 and in their mouth no lie was **f**;
16:20 and no mountains were to be **f**;
18:14 to you, never to be **f** again!"
18:21 and will be **f** no more;
18:22 an artisan of any trade will be **f** in you no more;
18:24 in you was **f** the blood of prophets and of saints,
20:11 and no place was **f** for them.
20:15 not **f** written in the book of life was thrown into
22: 3 Nothing accursed will be **f** there any more.

Tob 5: 4 and **f** the angel Raphael standing in front of him;
5: 9 "I have just **f** a man who is one
7: 1 they **f** him sitting beside the courtyard door.
8:13 and she went in and **f** them sound asleep together.
9: 6 into Raguel's house they **f** Tobias reclining
Jdt 6:14 Israelites came down from their town and **f** him;
10: 6 and **f** Uzziah standing there with the elders of
14:15 and went into the bedchamber and **f** him sprawled
AdE 2:15 Now Esther **f** favor in the eyes of all who saw her.
2:17 the king loved Esther and she **f** favor beyond all
5: 8 if I have **f** favor in the sight of the king,
6: 2 He **f** the words written about Mordecai,
7: 3 "If I have **f** favor with the king,
8: 5 "If it pleases you, and if I have **f** favor,
Wis 1: 2 he is **f** by those who do not put him to the test,
3: 5 God tested them and **f** them worthy of himself;
5:10 and when it has passed no trace can be **f**,
5:11 no evidence of its passage is **f**;
5:11 and afterward no sign of its coming is **f** there;
6:12 and is **f** by those who seek her.
6:14 for she will be **f** sitting at the gate.
7:29 Compared with the light she is **f** to be superior,
8:11 I shall be **f** keen in judgment,
16: 9 and no healing was **f** for them,
Sir Pr: 3 I **f** opportunity for no little instruction.
2: 5 gold is tested in the fire, and those **f** acceptable,
6:14 whoever finds one has **f** a treasure.
11:19 when he says, "I have **f** rest, and now I shall feast
18:17 Both are to be **f** in a gracious person.
21:16 but delight is **f** in the speech of the intelligent.
23:12 may it never be **f** in the inheritance of Jacob!
31: 8 Blessed is the rich person who is **f** blameless,
31:10 Who has been tested by it and been **f** perfect?
36:21 for you and let your prophets be **f** trustworthy.
38:33 and they are not **f** among the rulers.
44:17 Noah was **f** perfect and righteous;
44:19 and no one has been **f** like him in glory.
44:23 who **f** favor in the sight of all
51:16 and I **f** for myself much instruction.
51:20 I directed my soul to her, and in purity I **f** her.
51:26 it is to be **f** close by.
51:27 but little and **f** for myself much serenity.
Bar 3:15 Who has **f** her place?
3:30 Who has gone over the sea, and **f** her,
3:32 he **f** her by his understanding.
3:36 He **f** the whole way to knowledge,
Sus 1:63 because she was **f** innocent of a shameful deed.
1Mc 1:23 he took also the hidden treasures that he **f**.
1:56 the law that they **f** they tore to pieces and burned
1:57 Anyone **f** possessing the book of the covenant,
1:58 against those who were **f** month after month in
2:46 the uncircumcised boys that they **f** within
2:52 Was not Abraham **f** faithful when tested,
2:63 but tomorrow they will not be **f**,
4: 5 by night, he **f** no one there, so he looked for them
5: 6 where he **f** a strong band and many people,
6:53 those who had **f** safety in Judea from
6:63 He **f** Philip in control of the city,
9:34 Bacchides **f** this out on the sabbath day,
10:60 and gold and many gifts, and **f** favor with them.
12:21 It has been **f** in writing concerning the Spartans
16:22 to destroy him and killed them, for he had **f** out
2Mc 1:20 when they reported to us that they had not **f** fire
2: 5 Jeremiah came and **f** a cave-dwelling,
8: 7 He **f** the nights most advantageous
12:40 of each one of the dead they **f** sacred tokens of
14: 5 But he **f** an opportunity
1Es 2:26 and it has been **f** that this city from
4:42 for you have been **f** to be the wisest.
5:38 the priesthood but were not **f** registered:
5:39 and the genealogy of these men was not **f**,
6: 8 we **f** the elders of the Jews, who had been in exile,
6:22 if it is **f** that the building of the house of the Lord
6:23 a scroll was **f** in which this was recorded:
8: 4 for he **f** favor before the king in all his requests.
8:13 in Jerusalem all the gold and silver that may be **f**
8:42 When I **f** there none of the descendants of
8:53 and we **f** him very merciful.
9:18 in and **f** to have foreign wives were:
2Es 3:34 be **f** which way the turn of the scale will incline.
4:44 "If I have **f** favor in your sight,
5: 9 Salt waters shall be **f** in the sweet,
5:10 and it shall be sought by many but shall not be **f**,
5:56 O Lord, if I have **f** favor in your sight,
6:11 "O sovereign Lord, if I have **f** favor in your sight,
6:22 full storehouses shall suddenly be **f** to be empty;
7:75 "If I have **f** favor in your sight, O Lord,
7:*102* "If I have **f** favor in your sight,
7:*104* "Since you have **f** favor in my sight,
8:42 "If I have **f** favor in your sight, let me speak.
12: 7 "O sovereign Lord, if I have **f** favor in your sight,
13:48 who are **f** within my holy borders, shall be saved.
14:22 If then I have **f** favor with you,
4Mc 3:14 and **f** the spring, and from it boldly brought
4:23 a decree that if any of them were **f** observing

FOUNDATION (55) [FOUNDATIONS, FOUNDED, FOUNDS]

Jos 6:26 At the cost of his firstborn he shall lay its **f**,
1Ki 5:17 costly stones in order to lay the **f** of the house
6:37 the **f** of the house of the LORD was laid,
7: 9 back and front, from the **f** to the coping,
7:10 The **f** was of costly stones, huge stones,
16:34 he laid its **f** at the cost of Abiram his firstborn,
2Ch 8:16 of Solomon was accomplished from the day the **f**
23: 5 and one third at the Gate of the **F**;
Ezr 3: 3 They set up the altar on its **f**,
3: 6 the **f** of the temple of the LORD was not yet laid.
3:10 builders laid the **f** of the temple of the LORD,
3:11 because the **f** of the house of the LORD was laid.
Job 4:19 whose **f** is in the dust,
22:16 their **f** was washed away by a flood.
38: 4 "Where were you when I laid the **f** of the earth?
Ps 89:14 Righteousness and justice are the **f** of your throne;
97: 2 righteousness and justice are the **f** of his throne.
102:25 Long ago you laid the **f** of the earth,
Isa 28:16 See, I am laying in Zion a **f** stone, a tested stone,
28:16 a tested stone, a precious cornerstone, a sure **f**:
44:28 and of the temple, "Your **f** shall be laid."
48:13 My hand laid the **f** of the earth,
Jer 51:26 from you for a corner and no stone for a **f**,
Eze 13:14 so that its **f** will be laid bare;
Hab 3:13 laying it bare from **f** to roof.
Hag 2:18 day that the **f** of the LORD's temple was laid,
Zec 4: 9 hands of Zerubbabel have laid the **f** of this house;
8: 9 the **f** was laid for the rebuilding of the temple,
Mt 13:35 I will proclaim what has been hidden from the **f**
25:34 inherit the kingdom prepared for you from the **f** of
Lk 6:48 who dug deeply and laid the **f** on rock;
6:49 a house on the ground without a **f**.
11:50 with the blood of all the prophets shed since the **f**
14:29 when he has laid a **f** and is not able to finish,
Jn 17:24 because you loved me before the **f** of the world.
Ro 15:20 so that I do not build on someone else's **f**,
1Co 3:10 like a skilled master builder I laid a **f**,
3:11 For no one can lay any **f** other than the one that has been laid; that **f** is Jesus Christ.
3:12 Now if anyone builds on the **f** with gold, silver,
3:14 If what has been built on the **f** survives,
Eph 1: 4 before the **f** of the world to be holy and blameless
2:20 built upon the **f** of the apostles and prophets,
1Ti 6:19 up for themselves the treasure of a good **f** for
2Ti 2:19 But God's firm **f** stands, bearing this inscription:
Heb 4: 3 his works were finished at the **f** of the world.
6: 1 and not laying again the **f**:
9:26 to suffer again and again since the **f** of the world.
1Pe 1:20 He was destined before the **f** of the world,
Rev 13: 8 the **f** of the world in the book of life of the Lamb
17: 8 not been written in the book of life from the **f** of
Sir 1:15 She made among human beings an eternal **f**,
1Es 5:57 the **f** of the temple of God on the new moon of
3Mc 2: 9 you made it a firm **f** for the glory of your great
2Es 10:53 the field where there was no **f** of any building,

FOUNDATIONS‡ (46) [FOUNDATION]

A. FOUNDATIONS OF THE EARTH (13)

Dt 32:22 and sets on fire the **f** of the mountains.
2Sa 22: 8 the **f** of the heavens trembled and quaked,
22:16 the **f** of the world were laid bare at the rebuke of
Ezr 3:12 old people who had seen the first house on its **f**,
4:12 they are finishing the walls and repairing the **f**.
5:16 and laid the **f** of the house of God in Jerusalem;
Ps 11: 3 If the **f** are destroyed, what can the righteous do?"
18: 7 the **f** also of the mountains trembled and quaked,
18:15 the **f** of the world were laid bare at your rebuke,
82: 5 all the **f** of the earth are shaken. A
104: 5 You set the earth on its **f**,
137: 7 Tear it down! Down to its **f**!"
Pr 8:29 when he marked out the **f** of the earth, A
Isa 24:18 and the **f** of the earth tremble. A
40:21 Have you not understood from the **f** of the earth? A
51:13 the heavens and laid the **f** of the earth. A
51:16 the heavens and laying the **f** of the earth, A
54:11 and lay your **f** with sapphires.
58:12 you shall raise up the **f** of many generations;
Jer 31:37 and the **f** of the earth below can be explored, A
La 4:11 and kindled a fire in Zion that consumed its **f**.
Eze 30: 4 and its **f** are torn down.
41: 8 the **f** of the side chambers measured a full reed
Mic 1: 6 into the valley, and uncover her **f**.
6: 2 and you enduring **f** of the earth; A
Ac 16:26 so violent that the **f** of the prison were shaken;
Heb 11:10 For he looked forward to the city that has **f**,
Rev 21:14 And the wall of the city has twelve **f**,
21:19 The **f** of the wall of the city are adorned
Jdt 1: 3 and sixty cubits wide at the **f**.
16:15 For the mountains shall be shaken to their **f** with
Wis 4:19 and shake them from the **f**;
Sir 3: 9 but a mother's curse uproots their **f**.
10:16 and destroys them to the **f** of the earth. A
16:19 the **f** of the earth quiver and quake when he A
50: 2 He laid the **f** for the high double walls,
1Es 2:18 and walls and laying the **f** for a temple.
6:11 and laying the **f** of this structure?'
6:20 the **f** of the house of the Lord that is in Jerusalem.
2Es 6: 2 and before the **f** of paradise were laid,
6:15 the word concerns the end, and the **f** of the earth A
10:27 and a place of huge **f** showed itself.
15:12 Let Egypt mourn, and its **f**,
15:23 and consumed the **f** of the earth and the sinners, A
16:12 The earth and its **f** quake,
16:15 be put out until it consumes the **f** of the earth. A

FOUNDED‡ (12) [FOUNDATION]

Ex 9:18 that has ever fallen in Egypt from the day it was **f**
Ps 8: 2 of babes and infants you have **f** a bulwark because
24: 2 for he has **f** it on the seas,
78:69 like the earth, which he has **f** forever.
87: 1 On the holy mount stands the city he **f**;
89:11 that is in it—you have **f** them.
Pr 3:19 The LORD by wisdom **f** the earth;

Isa 14:32 "The LORD has f Zion, and the needy among his
Zec 12: 1 the LORD, who stretched out the heavens and f
Mt 7:25 but it did not fall, because it had been f on rock.
Heb 1:10 And, "In the beginning, Lord, you f the earth,
2Mc 2:13 and also that he f a library and collected the books

FOUNDING See Index to Footnotes

FOUNDS (1) [FOUNDATION]

Am 9: 6 and f his vault upon the earth;

FOUNTAIN‡ (26) [FOUNTAINS]

1Sa 29: 1 while the Israelites were encamped by the f that is
Ne 2:14 I went on to the F Gate and to the King's Pool;
3:15 of the district of Mizpah, repaired the F Gate;
12:37 At the F Gate, in front of them,
Ps 36: 9 with you is the f of life; in your light we see light.
68:26 the LORD, O you who are of Israel's f!"
Pr 5:18 Let your f be blessed, and rejoice in the wife
10:11 The mouth of the righteous is a f of life,
13:14 The teaching of the wise is a f of life,
14:27 The fear of the LORD is a f of life,
16:22 Wisdom is a f of life to one who has it,
18: 4 the f of wisdom is a gushing stream.
25:26 a polluted f are the righteous who give way before
Ecc 12: 6 and the pitcher is broken at the f,
SS 4:12 my bride, a garden locked, a f sealed.
4:15 a garden f, a well of living water,
Jer 2:13 they have forsaken me, the f of living water,
9: 1 and my eyes a f of tears,
17:13 for they have forsaken the f of living water,
51:36 I will dry up her sea and make her f dry;
Hos 13:15 and his f shall dry up, his spring shall be parched.
Joel 3:18 a f shall come forth from the house of the LORD
Zec 13: 1 a f shall be opened for the house of David and
Wis 11: 6 Instead of the f of an ever-flowing river,
Bar 3:12 You have forsaken the f of wisdom.
2Es 14:47 the f of wisdom, and the river of knowledge."

FOUNTAINS (6) [FOUNTAIN]

Ge 7:11 on that day all the f of the great deep burst forth,
8: 2 the f of the deep and the windows of
Pr 8:28 when he established the f of the deep,
Isa 41:18 and f in the midst of the valleys;
2Es 6:24 and the springs of the f shall stand still,
4Mc 13:21 they drank milk from the same f.

FOUR‡ (298) [FOUR-FIFTHS, FOUR-FOOTED, FOUR-SIDED, FOURFOLD, FOURS, FOURSQUARE, FOURTH, ONE-FOURTH]

Ge 2:10 and from there it divides and becomes f branches.
11:13 after the birth of Shelah f hundred three years,
11:15 after the birth of Eber f hundred three years,
11:17 after the birth of Peleg f hundred thirty years,
14: 9 and King Arioch of Ellasar, f kings against five.
15:13 and they shall be oppressed for f hundred years;
23:15 piece of land worth f hundred shekels of silver—
23:16 f hundred shekels of silver,
32: 6 and f hundred men are with him."
33: 1 and f hundred men with him.
Ex 12:40 in Egypt was f hundred thirty years.
12:41 At the end of f hundred thirty years,
22: 1 and f sheep for a sheep.
25:12 cast f rings of gold for it and put them on its f feet,
25:26 You shall make for it f rings of gold,
25:26 fasten the rings to the f corners at its f legs.
25:34 the lampstand itself there shall be f cups shaped
26: 2 and the width of each curtain f cubits;
26: 8 and the width of each curtain f cubits;
26:32 You shall hang it on f pillars of acacia overlaid
26:32 which have hooks of gold and rest on f bases
27: 2 You shall make horns for it on its f corners;
27: 4 you shall make f bronze rings at its f corners.
27:16 it shall have f pillars and with them f bases.
28:17 You shall set in it f rows of stones.
36: 9 and the width of each curtain f cubits;
36:15 and the width of each curtain f cubits;
36:36 For it he made f pillars of acacia,
36:36 and he cast for them f bases of silver.
37: 3 He cast for it f rings of gold for its f feet,
37:13 He cast for it f rings of gold,
37:13 fastened the rings to the f corners at its f legs.
37:20 On the lampstand itself there were f cups shaped
38: 2 He made horns for it on its f corners;
38: 5 He cast f rings on the four corners of
38: 5 on the f corners of the bronze grating to hold
38:19 There were f pillars; their f bases were of bronze,
38:29 and two thousand f hundred shekels;
39:10 They set in it f rows of stones.
Lev 11:23 that have f feet are detestable to you.
Nu 1:29 of Issachar were fifty-four thousand f hundred.
1:31 of Zebulun were fifty-seven thousand f hundred.
1:37 of Benjamin were thirty-five thousand f hundred.
1:43 of Naphtali were fifty-three thousand f hundred.
2: 6 as enrolled of fifty-four thousand f hundred.
2: 8 as enrolled of fifty-seven thousand f hundred.
2: 9 is one hundred eighty-six thousand f hundred.
2:16 is one hundred fifty-one thousand f hundred fifty.
2:23 as enrolled of thirty-five thousand f hundred.
2:30 as enrolled of fifty-three thousand f hundred.
7: 7 and f oxen he gave to the Gershonites,
7: 8 f wagons and eight oxen he gave to the Merarites,
Nu 7:85 of the vessels two thousand f hundred shekels
26:43 sixty-four thousand f hundred enrolled.
26:47 enrolled was fifty-three thousand f hundred.
26:50 enrolled was forty-five thousand f hundred.
Dt 3:11 it is nine cubits long and f cubits wide.)
22:12 You shall make tassels on the f corners of
Jos 19: 7 f towns with their villages;
21:18 with its pasture lands—f towns.
21:22 with its pasture lands—f towns.
21:24 with its pasture lands—f towns.
21:29 with its pasture lands—f towns;
21:31 with its pasture lands—f towns.
21:35 with its pasture lands—f towns.
21:37 with its pasture lands—f towns.
21:39 with its pasture lands—f towns in all.
Jdg 9:34 and lay in wait against Shechem in f companies.
11:40 for f days every year the daughters
19: 2 and was there some f months.
20: 2 f hundred thousand foot-soldiers bearing arms.
20:17 mustered f hundred thousand armed men,
20:47 remained at the rock of Rimmon for f months.
21:12 of Jabesh-gilead f hundred young virgins who had
1Sa 4: 2 who killed about f thousand men on the field
22: 2 with him numbered about f hundred.
25:13 and about f hundred men went up after David,
27: 7 of the Philistines was one year and f months.
30:10 on with the pursuit, he and f hundred men;
30:17 except f hundred young men,
2Sa 15: 7 At the end of f years Absalom said to the king,
21:22 These f were descended from the giants in Gath;
1Ki 6: 1 In the f hundred eightieth year after
7: 2 built on f rows of cedar pillars,
7:19 in the vestibule were of lily-work, f cubits high.
7:27 each stand was f cubits long, f cubits wide,
7:30 Each stand had f bronze wheels and axles
7:30 at the f corners were supports for a basin.
7:32 The f wheels were underneath the borders;
7:34 There were f supports at the f corners
7:38 each basin measured f cubits;
7:42 the f hundred pomegranates for
9:28 and imported from there f hundred twenty talents
18:19 with the f hundred fifty prophets of Baal and the f hundred prophets of Asherah,
18:22 but Baal's prophets number f hundred fifty.
18:33 "Fill f jars with water and pour it on
22: 6 about f hundred of them, and said to them,
2Ki 7: 3 there were f leprous men outside the city gate,
14:13 a distance of f hundred cubits.
1Ch 3: 5 Shobab, Nathan, and Solomon, f by Bath-shua,
7: 1 Tola, Puah, Jashub, and Shimron, f.
9:24 The gatekeepers were on the f sides, east, west,
9:26 for the f chief gatekeepers,
12:26 Of the Levites f thousand six hundred.
21: 5 in Judah f hundred seventy thousand who drew
21:20 his f sons who were with him hid themselves.
23: 5 f thousand gatekeepers,
23: 5 and f thousand shall offer praises to the LORD
23:10 These f were the sons of Shimei.
23:12 Amram, Izhar, Hebron, and Uzziel, f.
26:17 the north f each day, on the south f each day,
26:18 the colonnade on the west there were f at the road
2Ch 4:13 f hundred pomegranates for the two latticeworks,
8:18 and imported from there f hundred fifty talents
9:25 Solomon had f thousand stalls for horses
13: 3 f hundred thousand picked men;
18: 5 f hundred of them, and said to them,
25:23 a distance of f hundred cubits.
Ezr 1:10 other silver bowls, f hundred ten;
1:11 and silver vessels was five thousand f hundred.
2:15 Of Adin, f hundred fifty-four.
2:67 f hundred thirty-five camels,
6:17 two hundred rams, f hundred lambs,
Ne 6: 4 They sent to me f times in this way,
7:69 f hundred thirty-five camels,
11: 6 were f hundred sixty-eight valiant warriors.
Job 1:19 struck the f corners of the house,
42:16 and his children's children, f generations.
Pr 30:15 Three things are never satisfied; f never say,
30:18 for me; f I do not understand:
30:21 under f it cannot bear up:
30:24 F things on earth are small,
30:29 f are stately in their gait:
Isa 11:12 the dispersed of Judah from the f corners of
17: 6 f or five on the branches of a fruit tree,
Jer 15: 3 I will appoint over them f kinds of destroyers,
36:23 As Jehudi read three or f columns,
49:36 upon Elam the f winds from the f quarters
52:21 it was hollow and its thickness was f fingers.
52:30 all the persons were f thousand six hundred.
Eze 1: 5 of it was something like f living creatures.
1: 6 Each had f faces, and each of them had f wings.
1: 8 on their f sides they had human hands.
1: 8 And the f had their faces and their wings thus:
1:10 the f had the face of a human being,
1:15 one for each of the f of them.
1:16 and the f had the same form,
1:17 of the f directions without veering as they moved.
1:18 for the rims of all f were full of eyes all around.
7: 2 The end has come upon the f corners of the land.
10: 9 and there were f wheels beside the cherubim,
10:10 And as for their appearance, the f looked alike,
10:11 of the f directions without veering as they moved;
10:12 the wheels of the f of them—
10:14 Each one had f faces: the first face was
10:21 Each had f faces, each f wings,
14:21 upon Jerusalem my f deadly acts of judgment,
37: 9 Come from the f winds, O breath,
Eze 40:41 F tables were on the inside,
40:41 and f tables on the outside of the side of the gate,
40:42 also f tables of hewn stone for the burnt offering,
41: 5 and the width of the side chambers, f cubits,
42:20 He measured it on the f sides.
43:14 f cubits, with a width of one cubit;
43:15 and the altar hearth, f cubits;
43:15 from the altar hearth projecting upward, f horns.
43:20 and put it on the f horns of the altar,
43:20 and on the f corners of the ledge,
45:19 the f corners of the ledge of the altar,
46:21 and led me past the f corners of the court;
46:22 in the f corners of the court were small courts,
46:22 the f were of the same size.
46:23 around each of the f courts was a row of masonry,
48:16 the north side f thousand five hundred cubits,
48:16 the south side f thousand five hundred,
48:16 the east side f thousand five hundred,
48:16 and the west side f thousand and five hundred.
48:30 to be f thousand five hundred cubits by measure,
48:32 which is to be f thousand five hundred cubits,
48:33 to be f thousand five hundred cubits by measure,
48:34 which is to be f thousand five hundred cubits,
Da 1:17 To these f young men God gave knowledge
3:25 He replied, "But I see f men unbound,
7: 2 the f winds of heaven stirring up the great sea,
7: 3 and f great beasts came up out of the sea,
7: 6 The beast had f wings of a bird on its back
7: 6 of a bird on its back and f heads;
7:17 "As for these f great beasts, f kings shall arise
8: 8 came up f prominent horns toward the f winds
8:22 of which f others arose, f kingdoms shall arise
11: 4 the f winds of heaven, but not to his posterity,
Am 1: 3 For three transgressions of Damascus, and for f,
1: 6 For three transgressions of Gaza, and for f,
1: 9 For three transgressions of Tyre, and for f,
1:11 For three transgressions of Edom, and for f,
1:13 three transgressions of the Ammonites, and for f,
2: 1 For three transgressions of Moab, and for f,
2: 4 For three transgressions of Judah, and for f,
2: 6 For three transgressions of Israel, and for f,
Zec 1:18 And I looked up and saw f horns.
1:20 Then the LORD showed me f blacksmiths.
2: 6 for I have spread you abroad like the f winds
6: 1 up and saw f chariots coming out from
6: 5 "These are the f winds of heaven going out,
Mt 15:38 Those who had eaten were f thousand men,
16:10 Or the seven loaves for the f thousand,
24:31 and they will gather his elect from the f winds,
Mk 2: 3 to him a paralyzed man, carried by f of them.
8: 9 Now there were about f thousand people.
8:20 "And the seven for the f thousand,
13:27 and gather his elect from the f winds,
Lk 19: 8 I will pay back f times as much."
Jn 1:39 It was about f o'clock in the afternoon.
4:35 Do you not say, 'F months more,
6:19 When they had rowed about three or f miles,
11:17 that Lazarus had already been in the tomb f days.
11:39 a stench because he has been dead f days."
19:23 and divided them into f parts,
Ac 5:36 and a number of men, about f hundred,
7: 6 and mistreat them during f hundred years.
10:11 being lowered to the ground by its f corners.
10:30 Cornelius replied, "F days ago at this very hour,
11: 5 being lowered by its f corners;
12: 4 and handed him over to f squads of soldiers
13:20 for about f hundred fifty years.
21: 9 He had f unmarried daughters who had the gift
21:23 We have f men who are under a vow.
21:38 the f thousand assassins out into the wilderness?"
27:29 they let down f anchors from the stern and prayed
Gal 3:17 the law, which came f hundred thirty years later,
Rev 4: 6 are f living creatures, full of eyes in front
4: 8 And the f living creatures,
5: 6 between the throne and the f living creatures and
5: 8 the scroll, the f living creatures and
5:14 And the f living creatures said, "Amen!"
6: 1 and I heard one of the f living creatures call out,
6: 6 in the midst of the f living creatures saying,
7: 1 After this I saw f angels standing at the f corners of the earth, holding back the f winds of the earth
7: 2 to the f angels who had been given power
7:11 and around the elders and the f living creatures,
9:13 from the f horns of the golden altar before God,
9:14 "Release the f angels who are bound at
9:15 So the f angels were released,
14: 3 before the f living creatures and before the elders.
15: 7 Then one of the f living creatures gave
19: 4 and the f living creatures fell down
20: 8 to deceive the nations at the f corners of the earth,
Tob 2:10 For f years I remained unable to see.
8:19 and f rams and ordered them to be slaughtered.
9: 2 take f servants and two camels with you
9: 5 with the f servants and two camels went to Rages
Jdt 8: 4 as a widow for three years and f months
Wis 18:24 of the ancestors were engraved on the f rows
Sir 37:18 it sprouts f branches, good and evil, life
1Mc 6:37 on each were f armed men who fought from there,
11:57 the high priesthood and set you over the f districts
13:28 for his father and mother and f brothers.
2Mc 3:11 and that it totaled in all f hundred talents of silver
8:20 along with f thousand Macedonians;
8:21 then he divided his army into f parts.
10:33 and they besieged the fort for f days.
12:33 with three thousand infantry and f hundred cavalry.
1Es 2:13 two thousand f hundred ten silver bowls,
2:14 five thousand f hundred sixty-nine,

1Es 5: 9 of Shephatiah, f hundred seventy-two.
5:14 The descendants of Adin, f hundred fifty-four.
5:15 The descendants of Azaru, f hundred thirty-two.
5:20 and Ammidians, f hundred twenty-two.
5:43 There were f hundred thirty-five camels,
7: 7 two hundred rams, f hundred lambs,
2Es 3:19 Your glory passed through the f gates of fire
6:21 to premature children at three and f months,
7:28 those who remain shall rejoice f hundred years.
11:24 but f remained in their place.
11:39 the f beasts that I had made to reign in my world,
12:21 and f shall be kept for the time
13: 5 of people were gathered together from the f winds
16:29 as in an olive orchard three or f olives may be left
16:31 or f shall be left by those who search their houses

FOUR-FIFTHS (1) [FOUR]
Ge 47:24 and f shall be your own,

FOUR-FOOTED (4) [FOOT, FOUR]
Ac 10:12 of f creatures and reptiles and birds of the air.
11: 6 As I looked at it closely I saw f animals,
Ro 1:23 a mortal human being or birds or f animals
Bar 3:32 the earth for all time filled it with f creatures;

FOUR-SIDED (3) [FOUR, SIDE]
1Ki 6:33 to the nave doorposts of olivewood, f each,
7: 5 All the doorways and doorposts had f frames,
7:31 its borders were f, not round.

FOURFOLD (1) [FOUR]
2Sa 12: 6 he shall restore the lamb f,

FOURFOLD (KJV) See also FOUR TIMES

FOURSCORE (KJV) See EIGHTY

FOURS (4) [FOUR]
Lev 11:20 that walk upon all f are detestable to you.
11:21 on all f you may eat those that have jointed legs
11:27 among the animals that walk on all f,
11:42 and whatever moves on all f,

FOURSQUARE (1) [FOUR, SQUARE]
Rev 21:16 The city lies f, its length the same as its width;

FOURSQUARE (KJV) See also SQUARE

FOURTEEN‡ (28) [FOURTEENTH]
Ge 31:41 I served you f years for your two daughters,
46:22 to Jacob—f persons in all).
Nu 16:49 by the plague were f thousand seven hundred,
29:13 two rams, f male lambs a year old.
29:15 and one-tenth for each of the f lambs;
29:17 f male lambs a year old without blemish,
29:20 f male lambs a year old without blemish,
29:23 f male lambs a year old without blemish,
29:26 f male lambs a year old without blemish,
29:29 f male lambs a year old without blemish,
29:32 f male lambs a year old without blemish,
Jos 15:36 f towns with their villages.
18:28 f towns with their villages.
1Ki 10:26 he had f hundred chariots
1Ch 25: 5 God had given Heman f sons and three daughters.
2Ch 1:14 he had f hundred chariots
13:21 He took f wives, and became the father
Job 42:12 and he had f thousand sheep, six thousand camels,
Eze 40:48 and the width of the gate was f cubits;
43:17 f cubits long by fourteen wide,
43:17 fourteen cubits long by f wide,
Mt 1:17 from Abraham to David are f generations;
1:17 to the deportation to Babylon, f generations;
1:17 to Babylon to the Messiah, f generations.
2Co 12: 2 a person in Christ who f years ago was caught up
Gal 2: 1 Then after f years I went up again to Jerusalem
Tob 8:20 "You shall not leave here for f days,
10: 7 the f days of the wedding celebration had ended

FOURTEENTH (36) [FOURTEEN]
Ge 14: 5 the f year Chedorlaomer and the kings who were
Ex 12: 6 You shall keep it until the f day of this month;
12:18 the f day until the evening of the twenty-first day,
Lev 23: 5 In the first month, on the f day of the month,
Nu 9: 3 On the f day of this month, at twilight,
9: 5 on the f day of the month, at twilight,
9:11 In the second month on the f day, at twilight,
28:16 On the f day of the first month there shall be
Jos 5:10 the evening on the f day of the month in the plains
2Ki 18:13 In the f year of King Hezekiah,
1Ch 24:13 the thirteenth to Huppah, the f to Jeshebeab,
25:21 to the f, Mattithiah, his sons
2Ch 30:15 They slaughtered the passover lamb on the f day
35: 1 they slaughtered the passover lamb on the f day of
Ezr 6:19 On the f day of the first month
Est 9:15 in Susa gathered also on the f day of the month
9:17 and on the f day they rested and made that a day
9:18 on the thirteenth day and on the f,
9:19 hold the f day of the month of Adar as a day
9:21 that they should keep the f day of the month Adar
Isa 36: 1 In the f year of King Hezekiah,
Eze 40: 1 in the f year after the city was struck down,
45:21 In the first month, on the f day of the month,
Ac 27:27 When the f night had come,
27:33 the f day that you have been in suspense
AdE 3: 7 The lot fell on the f day of the month of Adar.
9:15 The Jews who were in Susa gathered on the f
9:17 On the f day they rested and made that same day
9:18 came together also on the f, but did not rest.
9:19 the country outside Susa keep the f of Adar as
9:21 that they should keep the f and fifteenth days
10:13 on the f and fifteenth of that month,
13: 6 on the f day of the twelfth month, Adar,
1Es 1: 1 the passover lamb on the f day of the first month,
7:10 the passover on the f day of the first month,
3Mc 6:40 the king, until the f day, on which also they made

FOURTH‡ (81) [FOUR]
Ge 1:19 and there was morning, the f day.
2:14 And the f river is the Euphrates.
15:16 they shall come back here in the f generation;
Ex 20: 5 and the f generation of those who reject me,
28:20 and the f row a beryl, an onyx, and a jasper;
34: 7 to the third and the f generation."
39:13 and the f row, a beryl, an onyx, and a jasper;
Lev 19:24 In the f year all their fruit shall be set apart
Nu 7:30 On the f day Elizur son of Shedeur,
14:18 the children to the third and the f generation.'
29:23 On the f day: ten bulls, two rams,
Dt 5: 9 the third and f generation of those who reject me,
Jos 19:17 The f lot came out for Issachar,
Jdg 14:15 On the f day they said to Samson's wife,
19: 5 On the f day they got up early in the morning,
2Sa 3: 4 the f, Adonijah son of Haggith;
1Ki 6: 1 in the f year of Solomon's reign over Israel,
6:37 In the f year the foundation of the house of
22:41 over Judah in the f year of King Ahab of Israel.
2Ki 10:30 the f generation shall sit on the throne of Israel."
15:12 on the throne of Israel to the f generation."
18: 9 In the f year of King Hezekiah,
25: 3 the ninth day of the f month the famine became
1Ch 2:14 Nethanel the f, Raddai the fifth,
3: 2 the f Adonijah, son of Haggith;
3:15 the third Zedekiah, the f Shallum.
8: 2 Nohah the f, and Rapha the fifth.
12:10 Mishmannah f, Jeremiah fifth,
23:19 Jahaziel the third, and Jekameam the f.
24: 8 the third to Harim, the f to Seorim,
24:23 Jahaziel the third, Jekameam the f.
25:11 the f to Izri, his sons and his brothers, twelve;
26: 2 Zebadiah the third, Jathniel the f,
26: 4 Joah the third, Sachar the f, Nethanel the fifth,
26:11 Tebaliah the third, Zechariah the f:
27: 7 Asahel brother of Joab was f,
27: 7 for the f month, and his son Zebadiah after him;
2Ch 3: 2 the second day of the second month of the f year
20:26 On the f day they assembled in the Valley
Ezr 8:33 On the f day, within the house of our God,
Ne 9: 3 of the law of the LORD their God for a f part of
9: 3 for another f they made confession and worshiped
Jer 25: 1 in the f year of King Jehoiakim son of Josiah
28: 1 in the fifth month of the f year,
36: 1 In the f year of King Jehoiakim son of Josiah
39: 2 in the f month, on the ninth day of the month,
45: 1 in the f year of King Jehoiakim son of Josiah
46: 2 in the f year of King Jehoiakim son of Josiah
51:59 in the f year of his reign.
52: 6 the ninth day of the f month the famine became
Eze 1: 1 In the thirtieth year, in the f month,
10:14 the third that of a lion, and the f that of an eagle.
Da 2:40 And there shall be a f kingdom, strong as iron;
3:25 and the f has the appearance of a god."
7: 7 After this I saw in the visions by night a f beast,
7:19 I desired to know the truth concerning the f beast,
7:23 "As for the f beast, there shall be a f kingdom
11: 2 The f shall be far richer than all of them,
Zec 6: 3 and the f chariot dappled gray horses.
7: 1 In the f year of King Darius,
7: 1 of the LORD came to Zechariah on the f day of
8:19 The fast of the f month, and the fast of the fifth,
Rev 4: 7 and the f living creature like a flying eagle.
6: 7 When he opened the f seal,
6: 7 I heard the voice of the f living creature call out,
6: 8 they were given authority over a f of the earth,
8:12 The f angel blew his trumpet,
16: 8 The f angel poured his bowl on the sun,
21:19 the second sapphire, the third agate, the f emerald,
Jdt 12:10 On the f day Holofernes held a banquet
AdE 11: 1 the f year of the reign of Ptolemy and Cleopatra,
Sir 26: 5 and of a f I am in great fear:
2Mc 7:13 they maltreated and tortured the f in
3Mc 6:38 the twenty-fifth of Pachon to the f of Epeiph,
2Es 6:45 "On the f day you commanded the brightness of
7:84 The f way, they shall consider the torment laid up
7:95 The f order, they understand the rest that they
11:40 You, the f that has come,
12:11 up from the sea is the f kingdom that appeared in
4Mc 10:12 they dragged in the f, saying,

FOWL (2) [FOWLER, FOWLER'S, FOWLERS, FOWLS]
1Ki 4:23 besides deer, gazelles, roebucks, and fatted f.
4Mc 1:34 when we crave seafood and f and animals

FOWLER (2) [FOWL]
Ps 91: 3 For he will deliver you from the snare of the f and
Pr 6: 5 like a bird from the hand of the f.

FOWLER'S (1) [FOWL]
Hos 9: 8 yet a f snare is on all his ways,

FOWLERS (2) [FOWL]
Ps 124: 7 like a bird from the snare of the f;
Jer 5:26 Like f they set a trap; they catch human beings.

FOWLS (1) [FOWL]
Ne 5:18 also f were prepared for me,

FOWLS (KJV) See also BIRDS

FOX (2) [FOXES]
Ne 4: 3 any f going up on it would break it down!"
Lk 13:32 He said to them, "Go and tell that f for me,

FOXES (7) [FOX]
Jdg 15: 4 So Samson went and caught three hundred f,
15: 4 and he turned the f tail to tail,
15: 5 the f go into the standing grain of the Philistines,
SS 2:15 Catch us the f, the little f, that ruin the vineyards—
Mt 8:20 And Jesus said to him, "F have holes,
Lk 9:58 And Jesus said to him, "F have holes,

FRACTURE (2)
Lev 24:20 f for f, eye for eye, tooth for tooth;

FRAGILE (2)
Wis 14: 1 of wood more f than the ship that carries him.
15:13 from earthy matter f vessels and carved images.

FRAGMENTS (3)
Isa 30:14 so ruthlessly that among its f not a sherd is found
Jn 6:12 he told his disciples, "Gather up the f left over,
6:13 and from the f of the five barley loaves,

FRAGRANCE (16) [FRAGRANT]
SS 1:12 king was on his couch, my nard gave forth its f.
2:13 in blossom; they give forth f.
4:10 and the f of your oils than any spice!
4:16 upon my garden that its f may be wafted abroad.
5:13 His cheeks are like beds of spices, yielding f.
7:13 The mandrakes give forth f,
Hos 14: 6 and his f like that of Lebanon.
14: 7 their f shall be like the wine of Lebanon.
Jn 12: 3 The house was filled with the f of the perfume.
2Co 2:14 through us spreads in every place the f that comes
2:16 to the one a f from death to death, to the other a f
from life to life.
Sir 24:15 and like choice myrrh I spread my f,
39:14 Send out f like incense, and put forth blossoms
39:14 Scatter the f, and sing a hymn of praise;
2Es 6:44 and odors of inexpressible f.

FRAGRANT (24) [FRAGRANCE]
Ex 25: 6 spices for the anointing oil and for the f incense,
30: 7 Aaron shall offer f incense on it;
31:11 anointing oil and the f incense for the holy place.
35: 8 spices for the anointing oil and for the f incense,
35:15 and the anointing oil and the f incense,
35:28 and for the anointing oil, and for the f incense.
37:29 the holy anointing oil also, and the pure f incense,
39:38 the anointing oil and the f incense,
40:27 and offered f incense on it;
Lev 4: 7 the horns of the altar of f incense that is in the tent
Nu 4:16 the f incense, the regular grain offering,
2Ch 2: 4 and dedicate it to him for offering f incense
13:11 and every evening burnt offerings and f incense,
Ps 45: 8 your robes are all f with myrrh and aloes
SS 1: 3 your anointing oils are f, your name is perfume
3: 6 with all the f powders of the merchant?
Eze 8:11 and the f cloud of incense was ascending.
Eph 5: 2 a f offering and sacrifice to God.
Php 4:18 from Epaphroditus the gifts you sent, a f offering,
Jdt 16:16 For every sacrifice as a f offering is a small thing,
Bar 5: 8 The woods and every f tree have shaded Israel
3Mc 5:45 by the very f draughts of wine mixed
7:16 crowned with all sorts of very f flowers,
2Es 2:12 The tree of life shall give them f perfume,

FRAIL (1)
Ge 33:13 "My lord knows that the children are f and that

FRAIL (KJV) See also FLEETING

FRAME (21) [FRAMED, FRAMES]
Ex 26:16 Ten cubits shall be the length of a f,
26:16 and a cubit and a half the width of each f.
26:17 be two pegs in each f to fit the frames together;
26:19 two bases under the first f for its two pegs, and
two bases under the next f for its two pegs;
26:21 under the first f, and two bases under the next f;
26:25 under the first f, and two bases under the next f.
36:21 Ten cubits was the length of a f, and a cubit and a
half the width of each f.
36:22 Each f had two pegs for fitting together;
36:24 two bases under the first f for its two pegs, and
two bases under the next f for its two pegs.
36:26 under the first f and two bases under the next f.
36:30 sixteen bases, under every f two bases.

Nu 4:10 and put it on the carrying **f.**
4:12 and put them on the carrying **f.**
Job 41:12 or its mighty strength, or its splendid **f.**
Ps 139:15 My **f** was not hidden from you,

FRAMED (1) [FRAME]
3Mc 2:26 that he **f** evil reports in the various localities;

FRAMES (43) [FRAME]
Ex 26:15 You shall make upright **f** of acacia wood for
26:17 be two pegs in each frame to fit the **f** together;
26:17 you shall make these for all the **f** of the tabernacle.
26:18 the **f** for the tabernacle: twenty **f** for the south side;
26:19 of silver under the twenty **f,** two bases under
26:20 on the north side twenty **f,**
26:22 of the tabernacle westward you shall make six **f.**
26:23 You shall make two **f** for corners of the tabernacle
26:25 And so there shall be eight **f,**
26:26 five for the **f** of the one side of the tabernacle,
26:27 for the **f** of the other side of the tabernacle,
26:27 and five bars for the **f** of the side of the tabernacle
26:28 The middle bar, halfway up the **f,**
26:29 You shall overlay the **f** with gold,
35:11 its clasps and its **f,** its bars, its pillars,
36:20 the upright **f** for the tabernacle of acacia wood.
36:22 he did this for all the **f** of the tabernacle.
36:23 The **f** for the tabernacle he made in this way: twenty **f** for the south side;
36:24 he made forty bases of silver under the twenty **f,**
36:25 on the north side, he made twenty **f**
36:27 the rear of the tabernacle westward he made six **f.**
36:28 He made two **f** for corners of the tabernacle in
36:30 There were eight **f** with their bases of silver:
36:31 five for the **f** of the one side of the tabernacle,
36:32 for the **f** of the other side of the tabernacle,
36:32 for the **f** of the tabernacle at the rear westward.
36:33 to pass through from end to end halfway up the **f.**
36:34 And he overlaid the **f** with gold,
39:33 its hooks, its **f,** its bars, its pillars, and its bases;
40:18 he laid its bases, and set up its **f,**
Nu 3:36 to be the **f** of the tabernacle, the bars, the pillars,
4:31 the **f** of the tabernacle, with its bars, pillars,
1Ki 6:4 For the house he made windows with recessed **f.**
7:4 There were window **f** in the three rows,
7:5 All the doorways and doorposts had four-sided **f,**
7:28 the borders were within the **f;**
7:29 on the borders that were set in the **f** were lions,
7:29 On the **f,** both above and below the lions
2Ki 16:17 Then King Ahaz cut off the **f** of the stands,
Ps 50:19 for evil, and your tongue **f** deceit.
Eze 41:16 all around, all three had windows with recessed **f.**

FRANKINCENSE (24) [INCENSE]
Ex 30:34 sweet spices with pure **f** (an equal part of each),
Lev 2:1 the worshiper shall pour oil on it, and put **f** on it,
2:2 a handful of the choice flour and oil, with all its **f,**
2:15 You shall add oil to it and lay **f** on it;
2:16 some of the coarse grain and oil with all its **f;**
5:11 you shall not put oil on it or lay **f** on it,
6:15 with all the **f** that is on the offering,
24:7 You shall put pure **f** with each row,
Nu 5:15 He shall pour no oil on it and put no **f** on it,
Ne 13:5 the **f,** the vessels, and the tithes of grain, wine,
13:9 with the grain offering and the **f.**
SS 3:6 perfumed with myrrh and **f,**
4:6 to the mountain of myrrh and the hill of **f.**
4:14 calamus and cinnamon, with all trees of **f,**
Isa 43:23 with offerings, or wearied you with **f.**
60:6 They shall bring gold and **f,**
66:3 whoever makes a memorial offering of **f,**
Jer 6:20 Of what use to me is **f** that comes from Sheba,
17:26 and **f,** and bringing thank offerings to the house
Mt 2:11 they offered him gifts of gold, **f,** and myrrh.
Rev 18:13 myrrh, **f,** wine, olive oil, choice flour and wheat,
3Mc 5:2 with large handfuls of **f** and plenty
5:10 a great abundance of wine and satiated with **f,**
5:45 the very fragrant draughts of wine mixed with **f**

FRANKLY (1) [FRANKNESS]
2Co 6:11 We have spoken **f** to you Corinthians;

FRANKNESS (1) [FRANKLY]
2Co 1:12 with **f** and godly sincerity, not by earthly wisdom

FRAUD (5) [FRAUDS]
Lev 6:4 or by **f** or the deposit that was committed to you,
Ps 55:11 and **f** do not depart from its marketplace.
Isa 44:20 "Is not this thing in my right hand a **f?**"
Zep 1:9 who fill their master's house with violence and **f.**
Jas 5:4 which you kept back by **f,** cry out,

FRAUDS (1) [FRAUD]
2Es 7:23 and proposed to themselves wicked **f;**

FRECKLED (KJV) See RASH

FREE‡ (132) [FREED, FREEDMEN, FREEDOM, FREELY, FREER, FREEWILL]
Ge 24:8 then you will be **f** from this oath of mine;
24:41 Then you will be **f** from my oath,
24:41 you will be **f** from my oath.'
44:10 but the rest of you shall go **f.**"
Ex 6:6 and I will **f** you from the burdens of the Egyptians
6:13 charging them to **f** the Israelites from the land
21:2 but in the seventh he shall go out a **f** person,
21:5 I will not go out a **f** person,"
21:19 then the assailant shall be **f** of liability,
21:26 the owner shall let the slave go, a **f** person,
21:27 a **f** person, to compensate for the tooth.
23:5 and you would hold back from setting it **f,**
23:5 you must help to set it **f.**
Lev 16:22 and the goat shall be set **f** in the wilderness.
16:26 the goat **f** for Azazel shall wash his clothes
25:41 Then they and their children with them shall be **f**
25:54 they and their children with them shall go **f** in
Nu 5:31 The man shall be **f** from iniquity,
32:22 and be **f** of obligation to the LORD and to Israel,
Dt 15:12 in the seventh year you shall set that person **f.**
15:13 you send a male slave out from you a **f** person,
15:18 when you send them out from you **f** persons,
21:14 you shall let her go **f** and not sell her for money.
24:5 He shall be **f** at home one year,
32:36 neither bond nor **f** remaining.
Jdg 16:20 as at other times, and shake myself **f.**"
1Sa 17:25 and make his family **f** in Israel."
1Ki 14:10 both bond and **f** in Israel,
21:21 and will cut off from Ahab every male, bond or **f,**
2Ki 9:8 I will cut off from Ahab every male, bond or **f,**
14:26 there was no one left, bond or **f,**
1Ch 9:33 the chambers of the temple **f** from other service,
Job 3:19 and the slaves are **f** from their masters.
10:1 I will give **f** utterance to my complaint;
39:5 "Who has let the wild ass go **f?**
Ps 17:1 give ear to my prayer from lips **f** of deceit.
44:2 you afflicted the peoples, but them you set **f;**
50:19 "You give your mouth **f** rein for evil,
69:18 redeem me, set me **f** because of my enemies.
102:20 to set **f** those who were doomed to die;
105:20 the ruler of the peoples set him **f.**
144:7 set me **f** and rescue me from the mighty waters,
146:7 The LORD sets the prisoners **f;**
Isa 45:13 he shall build my city and set my exiles **f,**
58:6 to let the oppressed go **f,** and to break every yoke?
Jer 2:31 Why then do my people say, "We are **f,**
34:9 that all should set **f** their Hebrew slaves,
34:10 that all would set **f** their slaves, male or female,
34:10 they obeyed and set them **f.**
34:11 the male and female slaves they had set **f,**
34:14 of you must set **f** any Hebrews who have been sold
34:14 you must set them **f** from your service."
34:16 whom you had set **f** according to their desire,
Eze 13:20 from your arms, and let the lives go **f,**
41:9 **f** space between the side chambers of the temple
41:11 The side chambers opened onto the area left **f,**
41:11 the part that was left **f** was five cubits all around.
Zec 9:11 I will set your prisoners **f** from the waterless pit.
Mt 17:26 Jesus said to him, "Then the children are **f.**
Lk 4:18 to let the oppressed go **f,**
13:12 "Woman, you are set **f** from your ailment."
13:16 be set **f** from this bondage on the sabbath day?"
Jn 8:32 and the truth will make you **f.**"
8:33 by saying, 'You will be made **f**'?"
8:36 if the Son makes you **f,** you will be **f** indeed.
Ac 13:39 by this Jesus everyone who believes is set **f**
26:32 "This man could have been set **f** if he had
Ro 5:15 But the **f** gift is not like the trespass.
5:15 of God and the **f** gift in the grace of the one man,
5:16 **f** gift is not like the effect of the one man's sin.
5:16 **f** gift following many trespasses brings justification
5:17 and the **f** gift of righteousness exercise dominion
6:18 having been set **f** from sin,
6:20 you were **f** in regard to righteousness.
6:23 but the **f** gift of God is eternal life
7:3 But if her husband dies, she is **f** from that law,
8:2 the Spirit of life in Christ Jesus has set you **f** from
8:21 be set **f** from its bondage to decay and will obtain
1Co 7:22 as whoever was **f** when called is a slave of Christ.
7:27 Do not seek to be **f.**
7:27 Are you **f** from a wife?
7:32 I want you to be **f** from anxieties.
7:39 husband dies, she is **f** to marry anyone she wishes,
9:1 Am I not **f?** Am I not an apostle?
9:18 that in my proclamation I may make the gospel **f**
9:19 For though I am **f** with respect to all,
9:21 the law (though I am not **f** from God's law but am
12:13 Jews or Greeks, slaves or **f—**
2Co 11:7 I proclaimed God's good news to you **f** of charge?
Gal 1:4 for our sins to set us **f** from the present evil age,
3:28 there is no longer slave or **f,**
4:22 by a slave woman and the other by a **f** woman.
4:23 the other, the child of the **f** woman,
4:26 she is **f,** and she is our mother.
4:30 the inheritance with the child of the **f** woman."
4:31 not of the slave but of the **f** woman.
5:1 For freedom Christ has set us **f.**
Eph 6:8 whether we are slaves or **f.**
Col 3:11 Scythian, slave and **f;** but Christ is all and in all!
Heb 2:15 and **f** those who all their lives were held
13:5 Keep your lives **f** from the love of money,
13:23 to know that our brother Timothy has been set **f;**
1Pe 2:16 As servants of God, live as **f** people,
2:24 **f** from sins, we might live for righteousness;
Rev 6:15 and everyone, slave and **f,**
13:16 both rich and poor, both **f** and slave,
19:18 flesh of all, both **f** and slave,
Tob 3:17 to Tobias son of Tobit, and by setting her **f** from
Jdt 16:23 She set her maid **f.**
Wis 1:6 not **f** blasphemers from the guilt of their words;
6:15 on her account will soon be **f** from care,
7:23 sure, **f** from anxiety, all-powerful, overseeing all,
16:14 or set **f** the imprisoned soul.
Sir 10:25 **F** citizens will serve a wise servant,
13:24 Riches are good if they are **f** from sin;
15:14 he left them in the power of their own **f** choice.
1Mc 2:11 no longer **f,** she has become a slave.
8:18 and to **f** themselves from the yoke;
10:29 now **f** you and exempt all the Jews from payment
10:31 shall be holy and **f** from tax.
10:33 of Judah into any part of my kingdom, I set **f**
11:28 Then Jonathan asked the king to **f** Judea and
2Mc 1:27 set **f** those who are slaves among the Gentiles,
9:14 he was now declaring to be **f;**
10:21 by setting their enemies **f** to fight against them.
11:25 that this nation also should be **f** from disturbance,
12:42 the people to keep themselves **f** from sin,
1Es 3:19 of the slave and the **f,** of the poor and the rich.
3Mc 7:20 they departed unharmed, **f,** and overjoyed,
2Es 12:34 in mercy he will set **f** the remnant of my people,
4Mc 14:2 more royal than kings and freer than the **f!**

FREED‡ (16) [FREE]
Ex 6:7 who has **f** you from the burdens of the Egyptians.
Lev 19:20 since she has not been **f;**
Ps 81:6 your hands were **f** from the basket.
Lk 1:64 and his tongue **f,** and he began
Ac 2:24 But God raised him up, having **f** him from death,
13:39 from all those sins from which you could not be **f**
Ro 6:7 For whoever has died is **f** from sin.
6:22 you have been **f** from sin and enslaved to God,
1Co 7:22 in the Lord as a slave is a **f** person belonging to
Rev 1:5 To him who loves us and **f** us from our sins
Wis 12:2 be **f** from wickedness and put their trust in you,
2Mc 4:47 who would have been **f** uncondemned
1Es 9:13 until we are **f** from the wrath of the Lord
2Es 11:46 so that the whole earth, **f** from your violence, may
4Mc 8:2 any who ate defiling food would be **f** after eating,
12:9 by the boy's declaration, they **f** him at once.

FREEDMEN (1) [FREE, MAN]
Ac 6:9 of those who belonged to the synagogue of the **F**

FREEDOM‡ (19) [FREE]
Lev 19:20 for another man but not ransomed or given her **f,**
Ro 8:21 from its bondage to decay and will obtain the **f** of
1Co 7:21 Even if you can gain your **f,**
2Co 3:17 and where the Spirit of the Lord is, there is **f.**
Gal 2:4 in to spy on the **f** we have in Christ Jesus,
5:1 For **f** Christ has set us free.
5:13 you were called to **f,** brothers and sisters; only do not use your **f** as an opportunity for self-indulgence
1Pe 2:16 yet do not use your **f** as a pretext for evil.
2Pe 2:19 They promise them **f,**
Sir 7:21 do not withhold from them their **f.**
30:11 Give him no **f** in his youth,
1Mc 14:26 repulsed Israel's enemies and established its **f.**"
15:7 and I grant **f** to Jerusalem and the sanctuary.
1Es 4:49 in the interest of their **f,** that no officer or satrap
4:53 to build the city should have their **f,**
3Mc 3:28 and will be awarded their **f.**
2Es 7:*101* He said to me, "They shall have **f** for seven days,
9:11 as many as scorned my law while they still had **f,**

FREELY (20) [FREE]
Ge 2:16 "You may **f** eat of every tree of the garden;
Dt 23:23 just as you have **f** vowed to the LORD your God
1Sa 14:30 How much better if today the troops had eaten **f**
2Sa 22:37 You have made me stride **f,**
1Ch 12:1 not move about **f** because of Saul son of Kish;
29:9 for with single mind they had offered **f** to
29:17 of my heart I have **f** offered all these things,
29:17 offering **f** and joyously to you.
Ezr 1:6 besides all that was **f** offered.
7:13 or Levites in my kingdom who **f** offers to go
7:15 that the king and his counselors have **f** offered to
Ps 112:9 They have distributed **f,** they have given to
Pr 11:24 Some give **f,** yet grow all the richer;
Isa 32:20 who let the ox and the donkey range **f.**
Hos 14:4 I will heal their disloyalty; I will love them **f,**
Mk 1:45 But he went out and began to proclaim it **f,**
Ac 26:26 and to him I speak **f;**
Eph 1:6 the praise of his glorious grace that he **f** bestowed
1Es 8:10 those who **f** choose to do so,
3Mc 7:12 granted them a general license so that **f,**

FREEMAN (KJV) See FREE PERSON

FREER (1) [FREE]
4Mc 14:2 more royal than kings and **f** than the free!

FREEWILL (27) [FREE, WILL]
A. FREEWILL OFFERINGS (14)
B. FREEWILL OFFERING (13)

Ex 35:29 brought it as a **f** offering to the LORD. B
36:3 and they received from Moses all the **f** offerings A
36:3 They still kept bringing him **f** offerings A
Lev 7:16 a votive offering or a **f** offering, it shall be eaten B
22:18 or as a **f** offering that is offered to the LORD B
22:21 in fulfillment of a vow or as a **f** offering, B
22:23 or too short you may present for a **f** offering; B
23:38 and apart from all your **f** offerings, A
Nu 15:3 or a sacrifice, to fulfill a vow or as a **f** offering B

Nu 29:39 to your votive offerings and your f offerings, A
Dt 12: 6 your votive gifts, your f offerings, A
12:17 your f offerings, or your donations; A
16:10 contributing a f offering in proportion to B
1Ch 29: 6 of ancestral houses made their f offerings, A
29:14 that we should be able to make this f offering? B
2Ch 31:14 was in charge of the f offerings to God, A
Ezr 1: 4 besides f offerings for the house of God A
2:68 some of the heads of families made f offerings A
3: 5 of everyone who made a f offering to the LORD. B
7:16 with the f offerings of the people and the priests, A
8:28 silver and the gold are a f offering to the LORD, B
Ps 54: 6 With a f offering I will sacrifice to you; B
Eze 46:12 When the prince provides a f offering, B
46:12 of well-being as a f offering to the LORD, B
Am 4: 5 and proclaim f offerings, publish them; A
Jdt 4:14 votive offerings, and f offerings of the people. A
16:18 their f offerings, and their gifts. A

FREEWOMAN (KJV) See FREE WOMAN

FREEZES (1) [FROZEN]
Sir 43:20 cold north wind blows, and ice f on the water;

FRENZIED (4) [FRENZY]
Wis 5:20 with him to fight against his f foes.
14:23 or hold f revels with strange customs,
4Mc 2: 4 Not only is reason proved to rule over the f urge
3:17 the emotions and quench the flames of f desires;

FRENZY (11) [FRENZIED]
1Sa 10: 5 they will be in a prophetic f.
10: 6 be in a prophetic f along with them and be turned
10:10 and he fell into a prophetic f along with them.
10:13 When his prophetic f had ended, he went home.
19:20 they saw the company of the prophets in a f,
19:20 and they also fell into a prophetic f.
19:21 and they also fell into a f.
19:21 and they also fell into a f.
19:23 As he was going, he fell into a prophetic f,
19:24 and he too fell into a f before Samuel.
4Mc 2: 3 by his reason he nullified the f of the passions.

FREQUENT (5) [FREQUENTLY]
2Co 11:26 on f journeys, in danger from rivers, danger
1Ti 5:23 for the sake of your stomach and your f ailments.
Sir 41: 5 and they f the haunts of the ungodly.
42: 5 and of f disciplining of children,
2Mc 8: 8 that he was pushing ahead with more f successes,

FREQUENTLY (4) [FREQUENT]
Lk 5:33 like the disciples of the Pharisees, f fast and pray,
Sus 1: 6 These men were f at Joakim's house,
3Mc 4:12 the Jews' compatriots from the city f went out
7: 3 f urging us with malicious intent,

FRESH‡ (33) [FRESHLY]
Ge 30:37 Jacob took f rods of poplar and almond and plane,
Lev 2:14 of your first fruits coarse new grain from f ears,
14: 5 be slaughtered over f water in an earthen vessel.
14: 6 of the bird that was slaughtered over the f water.
14:50 and shall slaughter one of the birds over f water in
14:51 the blood of the slaughtered bird and the f water,
14:52 and with the f water, and with the living bird,
15:13 and bathe his body in f water,
23:14 You shall eat no bread or parched grain or f ears
Nu 6: 3 and shall not drink any grape juice or eat grapes, f
Jdg 15:15 Then he found a f jawbone of a donkey,
16: 7 "If they bind me with seven f bowstrings that are
16: 8 of the Philistines brought her seven f bowstrings
2Ki 4:42 twenty loaves of barley and f ears of grain
Job 10:17 you bring f troops against me.
29:20 my glory was f with me,
33:25 let his flesh become f with youth;
Ps 92:10 you have poured over me f oil.
Isa 29:19 The meek shall obtain f joy in the LORD,
Jer 6: 7 keeps its water f, so she keeps f her wickedness;
Eze 17: 9 its f sprouting leaves to fade?
47: 8 of stagnant waters, the water will become f.
47: 9 once these waters reach there. It will become f;
47:11 But its swamps and marshes will not become f;
47:12 but they will bear f fruit every month,
Mt 9:17 but new wine is put into f wineskins,
Mk 2:22 but one puts new wine into f wineskins."
Lk 5:38 But new wine must be put into f wineskins.
Jas 3:11 from the same opening both f and brackish water?
3:12 No more can salt water yield f.
Tob 2:10 their f droppings fell into my eyes
2Es 15:59 you shall come and suffer f miseries.

FRESHETS (1)
Job 6:15 like a torrent-bed, like f that pass away,

FRESHLY (1) [FRESH]
Ge 8:11 and there in its beak was a f plucked olive leaf;

FRET (5) [FRETFUL]
Ps 37: 1 Do not f because of the wicked;
37: 7 do not f over those who prosper in their way,
37: 8 Do not f—it leads only to evil.
Pr 24:19 Do not f because of evildoers.
Sir 6:25 and do not f under her bonds.

FRETFUL (1) [FRET]
Pr 21:19 a desert land than with a contentious and f wife.

FRIEND‡ (95) [FRIENDLESS, FRIENDLY, FRIENDS, FRIENDSHIP, FRIENDSHIPS]
Ge 38:12 he and his f Hirah the Adullamite.
38:20 When Judah sent the kid by his f the Adullamite,
Ex 32:27 and each of you kill your brother, your f,
33:11 as one speaks to a f.
Dt 13: 6 or the wife you embrace, or your most intimate f—
Ru 4: 1 So Boaz said, "Come over, f; sit down here."
2Sa 13: 3 But Amnon had a f whose name was Jonadab,
15:37 So Hushai, David's f, came into the city,
16:16 When Hushai the Archite, David's f,
16:17 "Is this your loyalty to your f?
16:17 Why did you not go with your f?"
1Ki 4: 5 Zabud son of Nathan was priest and king's f;
5: 1 for Hiram had always been a f to David.
1Ch 27:33 and Hushai the Archite was the king's f.
2Ch 20: 7 to the descendants of your f Abraham?
Job 6:14 "Those who withhold kindness from a f forsake
6:27 over the orphan, and bargain over your f.
Ps 35:14 as though I grieved for a f or a brother;
41: 9 Even my bosom f in whom I trusted,
55:13 it is you, my equal, my companion, my familiar f,
55:20 My companion laid hands on a f and violated
88:18 You have caused f and neighbor to shun me;
Pr 7: 4 and call insight your intimate f,
17: 9 but one who dwells on disputes will alienate a f.
17:17 A f loves at all times,
18:24 but a true f sticks closer than one's nearest kin.
19: 6 and everyone is a f to a giver of gifts.
22:11 in speech will have the king as a f.
27: 6 Well meant are the wounds a f inflicts,
27:10 Do not forsake your f or the f of your parent;
SS 5:16 This is my beloved and this is my f,
Isa 41: 8 the offspring of Abraham, my f;
Jer 3: 4 "My Father, you are the f of my youth—
6:21 neighbor and f shall perish.
Mic 7: 5 in a f, have no confidence in a loved one;
Mt 11:19 a f of tax collectors and sinners!'
20:13 But he replied to one of them, 'F,
22:12 and he said to him, 'F, how did you get in here
26:50 "F, do what you are here to do."
Lk 5:20 When he saw their faith, he said, "F,
6:42 Or how can you say to your neighbor, 'F,
7:34 a f of tax collectors and sinners!'
11: 5 And he said to them, "Suppose one of you has a f,
11: 5 and you go to him at midnight and say to him, 'F,
11: 6 for a f of mine has arrived,
11: 8 up and give him anything because he is his f,
12:14 to him, "F, who set me to be a judge or arbitrator
14:10 he may say to you, 'F, move up higher';
Jn 3:29 The f of the bridegroom, who stands
11:11 he told them, "Our f Lazarus has fallen asleep,
19:12 you are no f of the emperor.
Phm 1: 1 To Philemon our dear f and co-worker,
Jas 2:23 and he was called the f of God.
4: 4 to be a f of the world becomes an enemy of God.
Wis 1:16 considering him a f, they pined away and made
Sir 6: 1 and do not become an enemy instead of a f;
7:12 or do the same to a f.
7:18 Do not exchange a f for money,
9:10 A new f is like new wine;
12: 8 A f is not known in prosperity,
12: 9 but in adversity even one's f disappears.
19: 8 With f or foe do not report it,
19:13 Question a f; perhaps he did not do it;
19:15 Question a f, for often it is slander;
20:23 Another out of shame makes promises to a f,
22:20 and one who reviles a f destroys a friendship.
22:21 Even if you draw your sword against a f,
22:22 If you open your mouth against your f,
22:22 in these cases any f will take to flight.
22:25 I am not ashamed to shelter a f,
25: 9 Happy is the one who finds a f,
27:16 and will never find a congenial f.
27:17 Love your f and keep faith with him,
29:10 Lose your silver for the sake of a brother or a f,
33: 6 A mocking f is like a stallion
33:20 To son or wife, to brother or f,
37: 1 Every f says, "I too am a f";
37: 2 for death itself when a dear f turns into an enemy?
37: 4 Some companions rejoice in the happiness of a f,
37: 5 a f for their stomachs' sake,
37: 6 Do not forget a f during the battle,
40:23 A f or companion is always welcome,
41:18 of unjust dealing, before your partner or your f;
1Mc 10:16 Come now, we will make him our f and ally."
10:19 you are a mighty warrior and worthy to be our f.
10:20 be called the king's F and you are to take our side
13:36 the high priest and f of kings,
15:32 So Athenobius, the king's F, came to Jerusalem,
2Mc 7:24 that he would take him for his F and entrust him
11:14 constraining him to be their f.
2Es 7:*104* or a master his servant, or a f his dearest f,
4Mc 12: 5 if you yield to persuasion you will be my f and

FRIENDLESS (1) [FRIEND]
Pr 19: 4 but the poor are left f.

FRIENDLY (9) [FRIEND]
Ge 34:21 "These people are f with us;
Jer 9: 8 They all speak f words to their neighbors,
12: 6 though they speak f words to you.
Ac 19:31 the province of Asia, who were f to him, sent him
Sir 6: 6 Let those who are f with you be many,
12: 9 One's enemies are f when one prospers,
1Mc 5:48 Judas sent them this f message,
1Es 3:22 When people drink they forget to be f with friends
3Mc 7: 7 into account the f and firm goodwill that they had

FRIENDS (170) [FRIEND]
Jdg 5:31 may your f be like the sun as it rises in its might."
1Sa 30:26 he sent part of the spoil to his f,
2Sa 3: 8 to his brothers, and to his f,
1Ki 16:11 not leave him a single male of his kindred or his f.
2Ki 10:11 close f, and priests, until he left him no survivor.
Est 5:10 he sent and called for his f and his wife Zeresh,
5:14 Then his wife Zeresh and all his f said to him,
6:13 and all his f everything that had happened to him,
Job 2:11 Now when Job's three f heard of all these troubles
12: 4 I am a laughingstock to my f;
16:20 My f scorn me; my eye pours out tears to God,
17: 5 Those who denounce f for reward—
19:14 My relatives and my close f have failed me;
19:19 All my intimate f abhor me,
19:21 Have pity on me, have pity on me, O you my f,
24:17 for they are f with the terrors of deep darkness.
32: 3 he was angry also at Job's three f
35: 4 I will answer you and your f with you.
42: 7 against you and against your two f;
42:10 the fortunes of Job when he had prayed for his f;
Ps 15: 3 and do no evil to their f,
38:11 My f and companions stand aloof
50:18 You make f with a thief when you see one,
122: 8 For the sake of my relatives and f I will say,
Pr 12:26 The righteous gives good advice to f,
14:20 but the rich have many f.
16:28 and a whisperer separates close f.
18:24 Some f play at friendship but
19: 4 Wealth brings many f, but
19: 7 how much more are they shunned by their f!
22:24 Make no f with those given to anger,
SS 5: 1 Eat, f, drink, and be drunk with love.
Jer 20: 4 a terror to yourself and to all your f;
20: 6 and there you shall be buried, you and all your f,
20:10 All my close f are watching for me to stumble.
34:17 by granting a release to your neighbors and f;
38:22 'Your trusted f have seduced you
La 1: 2 all her f have dealt treacherously with her,
Zec 13: 6 be "The wounds I received in the house of my f."
Mk 5:19 and said to him, "Go home to your f,
Lk 2:44 to look for him among their relatives and f.
7: 6 the centurion sent f to say to him, "Lord,
12: 4 my f, do not fear those who kill the body,
14:12 not invite your f or your brothers or your relatives
15: 6 he calls together his f and neighbors,
15: 9 she calls together her f and neighbors, saying,
15:29 a young goat so that I might celebrate with my f.
16: 9 make f for yourselves by means
21:16 even by parents and brothers, by relatives and f;
23:12 That same day Herod and Pilate became f
Jn 15:13 to lay down one's life for one's f.
15:14 You are my f if you do what I command you.
15:15 but I have called you f,
Ac 1:16 "F, the scripture had to be fulfilled, which
3:17 "And now, f, I know that you acted in ignorance,
4:23 to their f and reported what the chief priests and
6: 3 f, select from among yourselves seven men
10:24 and had called together his relatives and close f.
14:15 "F, why are you doing this?
24:23 and not to prevent any of his f from taking care
27: 3 and allowed him to go to his f to be cared for.
Ro 7: 4 my f, you have died to the law through the body
1Co 10:14 my dear f, flee from the worship of idols.
14:26 What should be done then, my f?
14:39 So, my f, be eager to prophesy,
2Co 11: 9 for my needs were supplied by the f who came
Gal 4:12 F, I beg you, become as I am,
4:28 you, my f, are children of the promise, like Isaac.
4:31 So then, f, we are children,
5:11 But my f, why am I still being persecuted
6: 1 My f, if anyone is detected in a transgression,
Php 4:21 The f who are with me greet you.
Heb 10:19 Therefore, my f, since we have confidence
3Jn 1: 3 of the f arrived and testified to your faithfulness
1: 5 you do faithfully whatever you do for the f,
1:10 he refuses to welcome the f,
1:15 The f send you their greetings.
1:15 Greet the f there, each by name.
Jdt 14: 1 Then Judith said to them, "Listen to me, my f.
AdE 1: 3 for his F and other persons of various nations,
1:13 He said to his F, "This is
2:18 a banquet lasting seven days for all his F and
3: 1 and granting him precedence over all the king's F.
5:10 and summoned his f and his wife Zosara.
5:14 His wife Zosara and his f said to him,
6: 9 let both be given to one of the king's honored F,
6:13 and his f what had befallen him.
6:13 His f and his wife said to him,
9:22 and for sending presents of food to their f and to
16: 5 the persuasion of f who have been entrusted with
Wis 7:27 into holy souls and makes them f of God,
Sir 6: 5 Pleasant speech multiplies f,
6: 7 When you gain f, gain them through testing,
6: 8 For there are f who are such when it suits them,
6: 9 And there are f who change into enemies,
6:10 And there are f who sit at your table,
6:13 and be on guard with your f.

Sir 6:14 Faithful **f** are a sturdy shelter:
6:15 Faithful **f** are beyond price;
6:16 Faithful **f** are life-saving medicine;
9:10 Do not abandon old **f**,
13:21 When the rich person totters, he is supported by **f**,
13:21 he is pushed away even by **f**.
14:13 Do good to **f** before you die,
20:16 The fool says, "I have no **f**,
30: 3 and will glory in him among his **f**.
30: 6 and one to repay the kindness of his **f**.
37: 1 but some **f** are **f** only in name.
40:20 but the love of **f** is better than either.
41:22 of abusive words, before **f**—
42: 3 and of dividing the inheritance of **f**;
Bel 1: 2 and was the most honored of all his **f**.
1Mc 2:18 and your sons will be numbered among the **F** of
2:39 When Mattathias and his **f** learned of it,
2:45 and his **f** went around and tore down the altars;
3:38 able men among the **F** of the king,
6:10 So he called all his **F** and said to them,
6:14 Then he called for Philip, one of his **F**,
6:28 He assembled all his **F**, the commanders
7: 6 "Judas and his brothers have destroyed all your **F**,
7: 8 So the king chose Bacchides, one of the king's **F**,
7:15 "We will not seek to injure you or your **F**."
8:12 but with their **f** and those who rely
8:20 so that we may be enrolled as your allies and **f**."
8:31 'Why have you made your yoke heavy on our **f**
9:26 They made inquiry and searched for the **f**
9:28 all the **f** of Judas assembled and said to Jonathan,
9:35 who were his **f**, for permission to store with them
9:39 with his **f** and his brothers to meet them
10:60 and their **F** silver and gold and many gifts,
10:65 and enrolled him among his chief **F**,
11:26 he exalted him in the presence of all his **F**.
11:27 and caused him to be reckoned among his chief **F**.
11:33 who are our **f** and fulfill their obligations to us,
11:57 and make you one of the king's **F**."
12:14 and our other allies and **f** with these wars,
12:43 with honor and commended him to all his **F**,
12:43 and commanded his **F** and his troops to obey him
14:39 made him one of his **F**, and paid him high honors.
14:40 that the Jews were addressed by the Romans as **f**
15:17 as our **f** and allies to renew our ancient friendship
15:28 He sent to him Athenobius, one of his **F**,
2Mc 1:14 Antiochus came to the place together with his **F**,
3:31 of Heliodorus's **f** quickly begged Onias to call
8: 9 one of the king's chief **F**, and sent him,
10:13 before Eupator by the king's **F**.
14:11 When he had said this, the rest of the king's **F**,
1Es 3:22 to be friendly with **f** and kindred,
8:11 the seven **F** who are my counselors have decided,
8:13 for the Lord of Israel that I and my **F** have vowed,
8:26 and his counselors and all his **F** and nobles.
3Mc 2:23 Then both **f** and bodyguards,
2:26 and many of his **f**, intently observing
3:10 and **f** and business associates had taken some
5: 3 together with those of his **F** and of
5:19 But when he, with the corroboration of his **F**,
5:26 and while the king was receiving his **F**,
5:29 Then Hermon and all the king's **F** pointed out that
5:34 The king's **F** one by one sullenly slipped away
5:44 Then the **F** and officers departed with great joy,
6:23 he wept and angrily threatened his **F**, saying,
7: 3 Certain of our **f**, frequently urging us
2Es 5: 9 and all **f** shall conquer one another;
6:24 At that time **f** shall make war on **f** like enemies,
7:*103* or **f** for those who are most dear."
4Mc 2:13 It is sovereign over the relationship of **f**,
2:13 so that one rebukes **f** when they act wickedly.
12: 8 let me speak to the king and to all his **f** that are

FRIENDSHIP (35) [FRIEND]

1Ch 12:17 "If you have come to me in **f**, to help me,
Job 29: 4 when the **f** of God was upon my tent;
Ps 25:14 The **f** of the LORD is for those who fear him,
Pr 17: 9 One who forgives an affront fosters **f**,
18:24 Some friends play at **f** but
Jas 4: 4 Do you not know that **f** with the world is enmity
Wis 7:14 those who get it obtain **f** with God,
8:18 and in **f** with her, pure delight, and in the labors
Sir 6:17 Those who fear the Lord direct their **f** aright,
22:20 and one who reviles a friend destroys a **f**.
25: 1 among brothers and sisters, **f** among neighbors,
27:18 so you have destroyed the **f** of your neighbor.
45:24 a covenant of **f** was established with him,
1Mc 8: 1 that they pledged **f** to those who came to them,
8:12 and those who rely on them they have kept **f**.
8:17 and sent them to Rome to establish **f** and alliance,
10:20 and you are to take our side and keep **f** with us."
10:23 Alexander has gotten ahead of us in forming a **f**
10:26 with us and have continued your **f** with us,
10:54 now therefore let us establish **f** with one another;
12: 1 and sent them to Rome to confirm and renew the **f**
12: 3 to renew the former **f** and alliance with them."
12: 8 a clear declaration of alliance and **f**.
12:10 to send to renew our family ties and **f** with you,
12:16 to renew our former **f** and alliance with them.
14:18 to him on bronze tablets to renew with him the **f**
14:22 have come to us to renew their **f** with us.
15:17 as our friends and allies to renew our ancient **f**
2Mc 4:11 on the mission to establish **f** and alliance with
6:22 and be treated kindly on account of his old **f**
11:26 to send word to them and give them pledges of **f**,
11:30 the thirtieth of Xanthicus will have our pledge of **f**
12:11 to grant them pledges of **f**,
14:19 and Mattathias to give and receive pledges of **f**.
4Mc 8: 5 I also exhort you to yield to me and enjoy my **f**.

FRIENDSHIPS (1) [FRIEND]

Sir 28: 9 and the sinner disrupts **f** and sows discord

FRIGHT (1) [FRIGHTEN, FRIGHTENED, FRIGHTENING, FRIGHTFUL]

Wis 11:19 but the mere sight of them could kill by **f**.

FRIGHTEN (7) [FRIGHT]

Dt 28:26 and there shall be no one to **f** them away.
2Ch 32:18 to **f** and terrify them, in order that they might take
Ne 6: 9 —for they all wanted to **f** us,
Job 13:25 Will you **f** a windblown leaf
18:11 Terrors **f** them on every side,
Jer 7:33 and no one will **f** them away.
2Co 10: 9 not want to seem as though I am trying to **f** you

FRIGHTENED (16) [FRIGHT]

Dt 18:22 do not be **f** by it.
Jos 1: 9 do not be **f** or dismayed,
10: 2 he became greatly **f**, because Gibeon was
Job 40:23 Even if the river is turbulent, it is not **f**;
Da 4: 5 I saw a dream that **f** me;
8:17 and when he came, I became **f** and fell prostrate.
Mt 2: 3 When King Herod heard this, he was **f**,
14:30 when he noticed the strong wind, he became **f**,
Lk 24:38 He said to them, "Why are you **f**,
Ac 24:25 Felix became **f** and said, "Go away for
Wis 17: 9 For even if nothing disturbing **f** them, yet,
Sir 26: 5 Of three things my heart is **f**,
1Mc 4:21 When they perceived this, they were greatly **f**,
9: 6 they were greatly **f**, and many slipped away from
2Mc 8:16 and exhorted them not to be **f** by the enemy and
2Es 10:25 so that I was too **f** to approach her,

FRIGHTENING (2) [FRIGHT]

Da 2:31 and its appearance was **f**.
2Mc 3:25 caparisoned horse, with a rider of **f** mien;

FRIGHTFUL (1) [FRIGHT]

3Mc 5:45 and had been equipped with **f** devices,

FRINGE (6) [FRINGES]

Nu 15:38 and to put a blue cord on the **f** at each corner.
15:39 You have the **f** so that, when you see it,
Mt 9:20 up behind him and touched the **f** of his cloak,
14:36 and begged him that they might touch even the **f**
Mk 6:56 and begged him that they might touch even the **f**
Lk 8:44 up behind him and touched the **f** of his clothes,

FRINGES (2) [FRINGE]

Nu 15:38 to make **f** on the corners of their garments
Mt 23: 5 they make their phylacteries broad and their **f** long.

FRISK (1)

Jer 50:11 though you **f** about like a heifer on the grass,

FRO (14)

Ge 8: 7 and it went to and **f** until the waters were dried up
2Ki 4:35 He got down, walked once to and **f** in the room,
Job 1: 7 "From going to and **f** on the earth,
2: 2 "From going to and **f** on the earth,
Jer 4:24 and all the hills moved to and **f**.
5: 1 Run to and **f** through the streets of Jerusalem,
Eze 1:13 like torches moving to and **f** among
1:14 The living creatures darted to and **f**,
Am 8:12 they shall run to and **f**,
Na 2: 4 they rush to and **f** through the squares;
Zec 7:14 so that no one went to and **f**,
9: 8 so that no one shall march to and **f**;
Eph 4:14 and **f** and blown about by every wind of doctrine,
2Es 6:29 where I was standing began to rock to and **f**.

FROGS (15)

Ex 8: 2 I will plague your whole country with **f**.
8: 3 The river shall swarm with **f**;
8: 4 The **f** shall come up on you and on your people
8: 5 and make **f** come up on the land of Egypt.' "
8: 6 and the **f** came up and covered the land of Egypt.
8: 7 and brought **f** up on the land of Egypt.
8: 8 "Pray to the LORD to take away the **f** from me
8: 9 the **f** may be removed from you and your houses
8:11 the **f** shall leave you and your houses
8:12 the LORD concerning the **f** that he had brought
8:13 **f** died in the houses, the courtyards, and the fields.
Ps 78:45 and **f**, which destroyed them.
105:30 Their land swarmed with **f**,
Rev 16:13 And I saw three foul spirits like **f** coming from
Wis 19:10 of fish the river spewed out vast numbers of **f**.

FROM (5841) See Index of Articles Etc.

FRONDS (1)

2Mc 10: 7 and beautiful branches and also **f** of palm,

FRONT (139) [FOREFRONT, FRONTED]

Ge 30:38 that he had peeled in **f** of the flocks in the troughs,
30:39 the flocks bred in **f** of the rods,
33: 2 He put the maids with their children in **f**,
41:43 and they cried out in **f** of him, "Bow the knee!"
Ex 13:21 The LORD went in **f** of them in a pillar of cloud
13:22 nor the pillar of fire by night left its place in **f** of
14: 2 and camp in **f** of Pi-hahiroth, between Migdol and the sea, in **f** of Baal-zephon;
14: 9 by Pi-hahiroth, in **f** of Baal-zephon.
14:19 from in **f** of them and took its place behind them.
17: 6 be standing there in **f** of you on the rock at Horeb.
19: 2 Israel camped there in **f** of the mountain.
23:20 I am going to send an angel in **f** of you,
23:23 When my angel goes in **f** of you,
23:27 I will send my terror in **f** of you,
23:28 And I will send the pestilence in **f** of you,
25:37 be set up so as to give light on the space in **f** of it.
26: 9 and the sixth curtain you shall double over at the **f**
27:13 the court on the **f** to the east shall be fifty cubits.
28:25 attach it in **f** to the shoulder-pieces of the ephod.
28:27 in **f** to the lower part of the two shoulder-pieces of
28:37 it shall be on the **f** of the turban.
29:10 You shall bring the bull in **f** of the tent
30: 6 You shall place it in **f** of the curtain that is above
30: 6 in **f** of the mercy seat that is over the covenant,
32:15 written on the **f** and on the back.
32:34 see, my angel shall go in **f** of you.
34: 3 and do not let flocks or herds graze in **f** of
38:13 And for the **f** to the east, fifty cubits.
39:18 in **f** to the shoulder-pieces of the ephod.
39:20 in **f** to the lower part of the two shoulder-pieces of
Lev 4: 6 of the blood seven times before the LORD in **f** of
4:17 and sprinkle it seven times before the LORD, in **f**
6:14 of Aaron shall offer it before the LORD, in **f** of
8: 9 in **f**, he set the golden ornament, the holy crown,
9: 5 They brought what Moses commanded to the **f** of
10: 4 from the **f** of the sanctuary to a place outside
16:14 with his finger on the **f** of the mercy seat,
Nu 3: 7 the whole congregation in **f** of the tent of meeting,
3:38 Those who were to camp in **f** of the tabernacle on
3:38 in **f** of the tent of meeting toward the east—
8: 2 seven lamps shall give light in **f** of the lampstand.
8: 3 up its lamps to give light in **f** of the lampstand,
14:14 and your cloud stands over them and you go in **f**
16:43 Then Moses and Aaron came to the **f** of the tent
18: 2 and your sons with you are in **f** of the tent of
19: 4 and sprinkle it seven times towards the **f** of
Dt 28:31 Your donkey shall be stolen in **f** of you,
Jos 3: 6 and pass on in **f** of the people."
3: 6 of the covenant and went in **f** of the people.
3:14 the ark of the covenant were in **f** of the people.
4: 7 that the waters of the Jordan were cut off in **f** of
4:11 and the priests, crossed over in **f** of the people.
6: 6 of rams' horns in **f** of the ark of the LORD."
8:33 in **f** of the levitical priests who carried the ark of
8:33 in **f** of Mount Gerizim and half of them in **f** of
Jdg 16: 3 and carried them to the top of the hill that is in **f**
18:21 the livestock, and the goods in **f** of them.
1Sa 10: 5 tambourine, flute, and lyre playing in **f** of them;
14: 5 One crag rose on the north in **f** of Michmash,
14: 5 and the other on the south in **f** of Geba.
17:41 with his shield-bearer in **f** of him.
2Sa 6: 4 and Ahio went in **f** of the ark.
10: 9 that the battle was set against him both in **f** and in
1Ki 6: 3 The vestibule in **f** of the nave of
6: 3 Its depth was ten cubits in **f** of the house.
6:17 house, that is, the nave in **f** of the inner sanctuary,
6:21 in **f** of the inner sanctuary,
7: 6 There was a porch in **f** with pillars,
7: 6 and a canopy in **f** of them.
7: 9 back and **f**, from the foundation to the coping,
7:49 in **f** of the inner sanctuary;
8: 8 of the poles were seen from the holy place in **f** of
8:64 the court that was in **f** of the house of the LORD;
18:46 up his loins and ran in **f** of Ahab to the entrance
2Ki 5:23 who carried them in **f** of Gehazi.
16:14 that was before the LORD he removed from the **f**
1Ch 19:10 that the line of battle was set against him both in **f**
2Ch 1: 5 was there in **f** of the tabernacle of the LORD.
3: 4 The vestibule in **f** of the nave of
3:15 In **f** of the house he made two pillars thirty-five
3:17 He set up the pillars in **f** of the temple,
5: 9 of the poles were seen from the holy place in **f** of
7: 7 the court that was in **f** of the house of the LORD;
8:12 on the altar of the LORD that he had built in **f** of
13:13 thus his troops were in **f** of Judah,
13:14 the battle was in **f** of them and behind them.
15: 8 He repaired the altar of the LORD that was in **f**
23:17 the priest of Baal, in **f** of the altars.
29:19 see, they are in **f** of the altar of the LORD."
Ne 12:36 and the scribe Ezra went in **f** of them.
12:37 At the Fountain Gate, in **f** of them,
13:21 "Why do you spend the night in **f** of the wall?
Est 2:11 Every day Mordecai would walk around in **f** of
4: 6 the open square of the city in **f** of the king's gate,
Ps 68:25 the singers in **f**, the musicians last,
Pr 8: 3 beside the gates in **f** of the town, at the entrance
Eze 2:10 it had writing on the **f** and on the back,
6: 4 I will throw down your slain in **f** of your idols.
6: 5 I will lay the corpses of the people of Israel in **f**
9: 6 So they began with the elders who were in **f** of
10:11 but in whatever direction the **f** wheel faced,
40:15 From the **f** of the gate at the entrance to the end of
40:19 Then he measured the distance from the inner **f** of
40:19 of the lower gate to the outer **f** of the inner court,
40:47 and the altar was in **f** of the temple.
41:14 the width of the east **f** of the temple and the yard,
41:21 In **f** of the holy place was something resembling
41:25 a canopy of wood in **f** of the vestibule outside.

Eze 42: 4 In f of the chambers was a passage on
42:11 with a passage in f of them;
44: 4 by way of the north gate to the f of the temple;
Joel 2: 3 Fire devours in f of them,
2:20 its f into the eastern sea, and its rear into the western sea;
Am 9: 4 though they go into captivity in f of their enemies,
Zec 14:20 of the LORD shall be as holy as the bowls in f of
Mk 2: 2 not even in f of the door;
Lk 5:19 the tiles into the middle of the crowd in f of Jesus.
14: 2 in f of him, there was a man who had dropsy.
18:39 Those who were in f sternly ordered him to
Ac 12: 6 while guards in f of the door were keeping watch
17:22 Then Paul stood in f of the Areopagus and said,
18:17 and beat him in f of the tribunal.
Rev 4: 5 and in f of the throne burn seven flaming torches,
4: 6 and in f of the throne there is something like a sea
4: 6 full of eyes in f and behind:
Tob 5: 4 and found the angel Raphael standing in f of him;
Jdt 10:22 they told him of her, he came to the f of the tent,
AdE 15: 7 on the head of the maid who went in f of her.
Sir 26:12 in f of every tent peg and open her quiver to
1Mc 1:22 and the gold decoration on the f of the temple;
4:57 the f of the temple with golden crowns
9:45 the battle is in f of us and behind us;
13:27 with polished stone at the f and back.
2Mc 3:25 at Heliodorus and struck at him with its f hoofs.
15:21 observing the masses that were in f of him and
3Mc 4:11 with a monstrous perimeter wall in f of the city,
2Es 11:36 "Look in f of you and consider what you see."

FRONTED (1) [FRONT]
Eze 40:17 thirty chambers f on the pavement.

FRONTIER (4) [FRONTIERS]
Dt 2:19 When you approach the f of the Ammonites,
Jos 22:11 of Manasseh had built an altar at the f of the land
2Ki 3:21 were called out and were drawn up at the f.
Eze 25: 9 the flank of Moab from the towns on its f,

FRONTIERS (1) [FRONTIER]
Jdt 15: 4 and to all the f of Israel,

FRONTLET See Index to Footnotes

FROST (12) [FROSTS, HOARFROST]
Ex 16:14 as fine as f on the ground.
Ps 78:47 and their sycamores with f.
147:16 He gives snow like wool; he scatters f like ashes.
148: 8 snow and f, stormy wind fulfilling his command!
Jer 36:30 be cast out to the heat by day and the f by night.
Zec 14: 6 On that day there shall not be either cold or f.
Wis 5:14 and like a light f driven away by a storm;
16:29 of an ungrateful person will melt like wintry f,
Sir 3:15 like f in fair weather, your sins will melt away.
43:19 He pours f over the earth like salt,
Bar 2:25 to the heat of day and the f of night.
2Es 7:*41* or summer or spring or heat or winter or f or cold,

FROSTS (1) [FROST]
Aza 1:50 Bless the Lord, f and snows;

FROWARD (KJV) See CROOKED, HARSH, PERVERSE

FROZEN (3) [FREEZES]
Job 37:10 and the broad waters are f fast.
38:30 and the face of the deep is f.
AdE 15: 5 as if beloved, but her heart was f with fear.

FRUIT‡ (221) [FRUITFUL, FRUITLESS, FRUITS]
Ge 1:11 and f trees of every kind on earth that bear f with
1:12 trees of every kind bearing f with the seed in it.
1:29 and every tree with seed in its f;
3: 2 "We may eat of the f of the trees in the garden;
3: 3 the f of the tree that is in the middle of the garden,
3: 6 she took of its f and ate;
3:12 she gave me f from the tree, and I ate."
4: 3 to the LORD an offering of the f of the ground,
30: 2 who has withheld from you the f of the womb?"
Ex 10:15 the plants in the land and all the f of the trees that
23:16 you gather in from the field the f of your labor.
Lev 19:23 then you shall regard their f as forbidden;
19:24 In the fourth year all their f shall be set apart
19:25 But in the fifth year you may eat of their f,
23:40 the first day you shall take the f of majestic trees,
25:19 The land will yield its f,
26: 4 and the trees of the field shall yield their f.
26:20 and the trees of the land shall not yield their f.
27:30 whether the seed from the ground or the f from
Nu 13:20 Be bold, and bring some of the f of the land."
13:26 and showed them the f of the land.
13:27 it flows with milk and honey, and this is its f.
Dt 7:13 the f of your womb and the f of your ground,
11:17 there will be no rain and the land will yield no f;
20: 6 a vineyard but not yet enjoyed its f?
20: 6 in the battle and another be first to enjoy its f.
26: 2 you shall take some of the first of all the f of
26:10 I bring the first of the f of the ground that you,
28: 4 Blessed shall be the f of your womb, the f of your ground, and the f of your livestock,
Dt 28:11 in the f of your womb, in the f of your livestock, and in the f of your ground in the land
28:18 Cursed shall be the f of your womb, the f of your
28:30 You shall plant a vineyard, but not enjoy its f.
28:33 not know shall eat up the f of your ground and
28:42 the f of your ground the cicada shall take over.
28:51 shall consume the f of your livestock and the f of
28:53 you will eat the f of your womb,
30: 9 in the f of your body, in the f of your livestock, and in the f of your soil.
Jos 24:13 the f of vineyards and oliveyards that you did
Jdg 9:11 and my delicious f, and go to sway over
2Sa 16: 2 the bread and summer f for the young men to eat,
2Ki 19:29 reap, plant vineyards, and eat their f.
19:30 shall again take root downward, and bear f upward;
Ne 9:25 olive orchards, and f trees in abundance;
9:36 to our ancestors to enjoy its f and its good gifts.
10:35 the first fruits of our soil and the first fruits of all f
10:37 and our contributions, the f of every tree,
Job 20:18 They will give back the f of their toil,
Ps 1: 3 which yield their f in its season,
72:16 may its f be like Lebanon;
78:46 and the f of their labor to the locust.
80:12 so that all who pass along the way pluck its f?
92:14 In old age they still produce f;
104:13 the earth is satisfied with the f of your work.
105:35 and ate up the f of their ground.
127: 3 the f of the womb a reward.
128: 2 You shall eat the f of the labor of your hands;
148: 9 Mountains and all hills, f trees and all cedars!
Pr 1:31 therefore they shall eat the f of their way and
8:19 My f is better than gold, even fine gold,
11:30 The f of the righteous is a tree of life,
12:12 but the root of the righteous bears f.
12:14 the f of the mouth one is filled with good things,
13: 2 the f of their words good persons eat good things,
18:20 the f of the mouth one's stomach is satisfied;
27:18 Anyone who tends a fig tree will eat its f,
31:16 with the f of her hands she plants a vineyard.
31:31 Give her a share in the f of her hands,
Ecc 2: 5 and planted in them all kinds of f trees.
SS 2: 3 and his f was sweet to my taste.
8:11 each one was to bring for its f a thousand pieces
8:12 and the keepers of the f two hundred!
Isa 3:10 for they shall eat the f of their labors.
4: 2 and the f of the land shall be the pride and glory
13:18 they will have no mercy on the f of the womb;
14:29 and its f will be a flying fiery serpent.
16: 9 for the shout over your f harvest
17: 6 four or five on the branches of a f tree,
27: 6 and fill the whole world with f.
27: 9 and this will be the full f of the removal of his sin:
32:10 the vintage will fail, the f harvest will not come.
34: 4 or f withering on a fig tree.
37:30 reap, plant vineyards, and eat their f.
37:31 shall again take root downward, and bear f upward;
57:18 creating for their mourners the f of the lips.
65:21 they shall plant vineyards and eat their f.
Jer 6:19 I am going to bring disaster on this people, the f
7:20 on the trees of the field and the f of the ground;
11:16 "A green olive tree, fair with goodly f";
11:19 saying, "Let us destroy the tree with its f,
12: 2 they grow and bring forth f;
17: 8 and it does not cease to bear f.
17:10 according to the f of their doings.
21:14 to the f of your doings, says the LORD;
31: 5 the planters shall plant, and shall enjoy the f.
32:19 according to their ways and according to the f
Eze 17: 8 so that it might produce branches and bear f
17: 9 cause its f to rot and wither,
17:23 in order that it may produce boughs and bear f,
19:12 the east wind dried it up; its f was stripped off,
19:14 has consumed its branches and f,
23:29 and take away all the f of your labor,
25: 4 in your midst; they shall eat your f,
34:27 The trees of the field shall yield their f,
36: 8 and yield your f to my people Israel;
36:30 I will make the f of the tree and the produce of
47:12 Their leaves will not wither nor their f fail,
47:12 but they will bear fresh f every month,
47:12 Their f will be for food,
Da 4:12 Its foliage was beautiful, its f abundant,
4:14 strip off its foliage and scatter its f.
4:21 whose foliage was beautiful and its f abundant,
Hos 9:10 Like the first f on the fig tree, in its first season,
9:16 their root is dried up, they shall bear no f.
10: 1 Israel is a luxuriant vine that yields its f.
10: 1 The more his f increased the more altars he built;
10:13 you have eaten the f of lies.
14: 2 and we will offer the f of our lips.
Joel 2:22 the tree bears its f, the fig tree and vine give their
Am 2: 9 I destroyed his f above, and his roots beneath.
6:12 But you have turned justice into poison and the f
8: 1 the Lord GOD showed me—a basket of summer f.
8: 2 And I said, "A basket of summer f."
9:14 and they shall make gardens and eat their f.
Mic 6: 7 the f of my body for the sin of my soul?"
7: 1 after the summer f has been gathered,
7:13 for the f of their doings.
Hab 3:17 fig tree does not blossom, and no f is on the vines;
Zec 8:12 the vine shall yield its f,
Mt 3: 8 Bear f worthy of repentance.
3:10 that does not bear good f is cut down and thrown
7:17 In the same way, every good tree bears good f, but the bad tree bears bad f.
7:18 A good tree cannot bear bad f, nor can a bad tree bear good f.
Mt 7:19 that does not bear good f is cut down and thrown
12:33 "Either make the tree good, and its f good; or make the tree bad, and its f bad; for the tree is known by its f.
13:23 who indeed bears f and yields,
21:19 "May no f ever come from you again!"
26:29 I will never again drink of this f of the vine until
Mk 4:20 they hear the word and accept it and bear f,
11:14 "May no one ever eat f from you again."
14:25 the f of the vine until that day when I drink it new
Lk 1:42 and blessed is the f of your womb.
3: 9 that does not bear good f is cut down and thrown
6:43 "No good tree bears bad f, nor again does a bad tree bear good f;
6:44 for each tree is known by its own f.
8:14 and their f does not mature.
8:15 and bear f with patient endurance.
13: 6 and he came looking for f on it and found none.
13: 7 For three years I have come looking for f
13: 9 If it bears f next year, well and good;
22:18 from now on I will not drink of the f of the vine
Jn 4:36 and is gathering f for eternal life,
12:24 but if it dies, it bears much f.
15: 2 He removes every branch in me that bears no f.
15: 2 that bears f he prunes to make it bear more f.
15: 4 the branch cannot bear f by itself unless it abides
15: 5 in me and I in them bear much f,
15: 8 that you bear much f and become my disciples.
15:16 I appointed you to go and bear f, f that will last,
Ro 7: 4 the dead in order that we may bear f for God.
7: 5 were at work in our members to bear f for death.
1Co 9: 7 a vineyard and does not eat any of its f?
Gal 5:22 By contrast, the f of the Spirit is love, joy, peace,
Eph 5: 9 for the f of the light is found in all that is good
Col 1: 6 as it is bearing f and growing in the whole world, so it has been bearing f among yourselves
1:10 as you bear f in every good work and as you grow
Heb 12:11 but later it yields the peaceful f of righteousness
13:15 that is, the f of lips that confess his name.
Jude 1:12 autumn trees without f, twice dead, uprooted;
Rev 6:13 as the fig tree drops its winter f when shaken by
18:14 f for which your soul longed has gone from you,
22: 2 the tree of life with its twelve kinds of f,
22: 2 producing its f each month;
Wis 3:13 she will have f when God examines souls.
3:15 For the f of good labors is renowned,
4: 5 and their f will be useless, not ripe enough to eat,
10: 7 plants bearing f that does not ripen,
10:10 and increased the f of his toil.
Sir 6: 3 be devoured and your f destroyed,
14:15 Will you not leave the f of your labors to another,
23:25 and her branches will not bear f.
24:17 my blossoms become glorious and abundant f.
27: 6 Its f discloses the cultivation of a tree;
28:15 and deprived them of the f of their toil.
50:10 like an olive tree laden with f,
1Mc 10:30 the half of the f of the trees that I should receive,
11:34 from the crops of the land and the f of the trees.
14: 8 and the trees of the plains their f.
2Es 3:20 so that your law might produce f in them.
3:33 not appeared and their labor has borne no f.
4:31 for yourself how much f of ungodliness a grain
6:28 and the truth, which has been so long without f,
6:44 Immediately f came forth in endless abundance
7:13 and yield the f of immortality.
7:*123* [53] whose f remains unspoiled and
8: 6 and cultivation of our understanding so that f may
8:10 from the breasts) milk, the f of the breasts,
9:31 and it shall bring forth f in you,
9:32 yet the f of the law did not perish—
10:12 for I have lost the f of my womb,
10:14 the earth also has from the beginning given her f,
11:42 the homes of those who brought forth f,
16:25 The trees shall bear f, but who will gather it?
4Mc 2:14 The f trees of the enemy are not cut down,

FRUITFUL‡ (37) [FRUIT]
Ge 1:22 "Be f and multiply and fill the waters in the seas,
1:28 and God said to them, "Be f and multiply,
8:17 and be f and multiply on the earth."
9: 1 and said to them, "Be f and multiply,
9: 7 And you, be f and multiply,
17: 6 I will make you exceedingly f;
17:20 and make him f and exceedingly numerous;
26:22 and we shall be f in the land."
28: 3 May God Almighty bless you and make you f
35:11 "I am God Almighty: be f and multiply;
41:52 "For God has made me f in the land
47:27 and were f and multiplied exceedingly.
48: 4 to make you f and increase your numbers;
49:22 Joseph is a f bough, a f bough by a spring;
Ex 1: 7 But the Israelites were f and prolific;
Lev 26: 9 I will look with favor upon you and make you f
Ps 105:24 And the LORD made his people very f,
107:34 a f land into a salty waste,
107:37 and plant vineyards, and get a f yield.
128: 3 Your wife will be like a f vine within your house;
Isa 10:18 and his f land the LORD will destroy,
16:10 Joy and gladness are taken away from the f field;
29:17 in a very little while become a f field, and the f field be regarded as a forest?
32:12 for the pleasant fields, for the f vine,
32:15 the wilderness becomes a f field, and the f field is deemed a forest.
32:16 and righteousness abide in the f field.
Jer 4:26 I looked, and lo, the f land was a desert,

Jer 23: 3 and they shall be f and multiply.
48:33 and joy have been taken away from the f land
Eze 19:10 f and full of branches from abundant water.
36:11 They shall increase and be f;
Ac 14:17 giving you rains from heaven and f seasons,
Php 1:22 I am to live in the flesh, that means f labor for me;
2Es 15:62 with fire all your forests and your f trees.

FRUITLESS (2) [FRUIT]

Wis 15: 4 nor the f toil of painters,
4Mc 16: 7 f nurturings and wretched nursings!

FRUITS‡ (63) [FRUIT]

A. FIRST FRUITS (39)

Ge 43:11 take some of the choice f of the land in your bags,
49: 3 my might and the first f of my vigor, A
Ex 23:16 of the first f of your labor, A
23:19 of the first f of your ground you shall bring into A
34:22 the first f of wheat harvest, A
34:26 of the first f of your ground you shall bring to A
Lev 2:14 you bring a grain offering of first f to the LORD, A
2:14 grain offering of your first f coarse new grain A
23:10 sheaf of the first f of your harvest to the priest. A
23:17 baked with leaven, as first f to the LORD. A
23:20 the bread of the first f as an elevation offering A
Nu 18:13 The first f of all that is in their land, A
28:26 On the day of the first f, A
Dt 18: 4 The first f of your grain, your wine, and your oil, A
33:14 with the choice f of the sun, and the rich yield of
2Sa 16: 1 one hundred of summer f, and one skin of wine.
2Ki 4:42 bringing food from the first f to the man of God: A
2Ch 31: 5 in abundance the first f of grain, wine, oil, A
Ne 10:35 first f of our soil and the first fruits of all fruit A
10:35 the first f of all fruit of every tree, year by year, A
12:44 the contributions, the first f, and the tithes, A
13:31 at appointed times, and for the first f. A
Ps 109:11 may strangers plunder the f of his toil.
Pr 3: 9 with your substance and with the first f A
18:21 and those who love it will eat its f.
SS 4:13 an orchard of pomegranates with all choicest f,
4:16 to his garden, and eat its choicest f.
7:13 and over our doors are all choice f,
Jer 2: 3 the first f of his harvest. A
2: 7 a plentiful land to eat its f and its good things.
40:10 but as for you, gather wine and summer f and oil,
40:12 and they gathered wine and summer f
48:32 upon your summer f and your vintage
Eze 44:30 The first of all the first f of all kinds, A
Mt 7:16 You will know them by their f.
7:20 Thus you will know them by their f.
21:43 to a people that produces the f of the kingdom.
Lk 3: 8 Bear f worthy of repentance.
Ro 8:23 who have the first f of the Spirit, A
11:16 If the part of the dough offered as first f is holy, A
1Co 15:20 the first f of those who have died. A
15:23 But each in his own order: Christ the first f, A
2Th 2:13 God chose you as the first f for salvation A
Jas 1:18 would become a kind of first f of his creatures. A
3:17 gentle, willing to yield, full of mercy and good f,
Rev 14: 4 from humankind as first f for God and the Lamb, A
Tob 1: 6 I would hurry off to Jerusalem with the first f of A
1: 7 of the f to the sons of Levi who ministered
Jdt 11:13 to consume the first f of the grain and the tithes A
Sir 1:16 she inebriates mortals with her f;
7:31 the first f, the guilt offering, A
7:31 and the first f of the holy things. A
24:19 you who desire me, and eat your fill of my f.
24:25 and like the Tigris at the time of the first f. A
35:10 and do not stint the first f of your hands. A
37:22 the f of his good sense will be praiseworthy.
37:23 and the f of his good sense will endure.
45:20 he allotted to him the best of the first f, A
45:20 and prepared bread of first f in abundance; A
50: 8 the days of first f, like lilies by a spring of water, A
1Mc 3:49 the vestments of the priesthood and the first f A
2Es 2:18 for you twelve trees loaded with various f,
16:46 for strangers shall gather their f,

FRUSTRATE (1) [FRUSTRATED, FRUSTRATES, FRUSTRATION]

Ezr 4: 5 and they bribed officials to f their plan throughout

FRUSTRATED (5) [FRUSTRATE]

Ne 4:15 and that God had f it, we all returned to the wall,
Jdt 11:11 not be defeated and his purpose f,
Sir 16:13 and the patience of the godly will not be f.
3Mc 5:12 in his lawless purpose and was completely f
4Mc 17: 2 the violence of the tyrant, f his evil designs,

FRUSTRATES (3) [FRUSTRATE]

Job 5:12 He f the devices of the crafty,
Ps 33:10 he f the plans of the peoples.
Isa 44:25 who f the omens of liars, and makes fools

FRUSTRATION (1) [FRUSTRATE]

Dt 28:20 panic, and f in everything you attempt to do,

FRY (1)

2Mc 7: 5 still breathing, and to f him in a pan.

FRYINGPAN (KJV) See PAN

FUEL (8)

Isa 9: 5 the garments rolled in blood shall be burned as f
9:19 and the people became like f for the fire;
40:16 Lebanon would not provide f enough,
44:15 Then it can be used as f.
Eze 15: 4 It is put in the fire for f;
15: 6 which I have given to the fire for f,
21:32 You shall be f for the fire,
Sir 28:10 In proportion to the f, so will the fire burn,

FUGITIVE (11) [FUGITIVES]

Ge 4:12 you will be a f and a wanderer on the earth."
4:14 I shall be a f and a wanderer on the earth,
Nu 35:32 the f to return to live in the land before the death
Jos 20: 4 then the f shall be taken into the city,
Pr 28:17 let that killer be a f until death;
Isa 16: 3 hide the outcasts, do not betray the f;
21:14 Bring water to the thirsty, meet the f with bread,
Eze 33:22 upon me the evening before the f came;
33:22 by the time the f came to me in the morning;
Sir 36:30 a man will become a f and a wanderer.
2Mc 4:26 was driven as a f into the land of Ammon.

FUGITIVES‡ (14) [FUGITIVE]

Nu 21:29 He has made his sons f, and his daughters captives,
Dt 7:20 until even the survivors and the f are destroyed.
Jdg 12: 4 because they said, "You are f from Ephraim,
12: 5 Whenever one of the f of Ephraim said,
Isa 15: 5 his f flee to Zoar, to Eglath-shelishiyah.
Jer 44:14 they shall not go back, except some f.
48:45 In the shadow of Heshbon f stop exhausted;
49: 5 each headlong, with no one to gather the f.
50:28 F and refugees from the land
La 4:15 So they became f and wanderers;
Ob 1:14 not have stood at the crossings to cut off his f;
Jdt 16:12 through and wounded them like the children of f;
Wis 19: 3 as f those whom they had begged and compelled
1Mc 2:43 And all who became f to escape

FULFILL (50) [FULFILLED, FULFILLING, FULFILLMENT, FULFILLS]

Ge 26: 3 and I will f the oath that I swore
Ex 23:26 I will f the number of your days.
Nu 15: 3 whether a burnt offering or a sacrifice, to f a vow
15: 8 to f a vow or as an offering of well-being to
23:19 Has he spoken, and will he not f it?
Dt 9: 5 in order to f the promise that the LORD made
1Sa 3:12 that day I will f against Eli all that I have spoken
1Ki 5: 8 I will f all your needs in the matter of cedar
12:15 about by the LORD that he might f his word,
2Ch 10:15 by God so that the LORD might f his word,
36:21 to f the word of the LORD by the mouth
36:21 it lay desolate it kept sabbath, to f seventy years.
Est 5: 8 the king to grant my petition and f my request,
Job 39: 2 Can you number the months that they f,
Ps 20: 4 grant you your heart's desire, and f all your plans.
20: 5 May the LORD f all your petitions.
119:166 O LORD, and I f your commandments.
138: 8 The LORD will f his purpose for me;
Ecc 5: 4 F what you vow.
5: 5 not vow than that you should vow and not f it.
Isa 46:10 and I will f my intention,"
Jer 28: 6 the LORD f the words that you have prophesied,
29:10 and I will f to you my promise and bring you back
33:14 when I will f the promise I made to the house
39:16 I am going to f my words against this city for evil
Eze 12:25 O rebellious house, I will speak the word and f it,
Da 11:14 up in order to f the vision,
Na 1:15 Celebrate your festivals, O Judah, f your vows,
Mt 1:22 All this took place to f what had been spoken by
2:15 This was to f what had been spoken by the Lord
3:15 for us in this way to f all righteousness."
5:17 I have come not to abolish but to f.
8:17 This was to f what had been spoken through
12:17 This was to f what had been spoken through
13:35 to f what had been spoken through the prophet:
21: 4 to f what had been spoken through the prophet,
Jn 12:38 to f the word spoken by the prophet Isaiah:
13:18 But it is to f the scripture,
15:25 It was to f the word that is written in their law,
18: 9 This was to f the word that he had spoken,
18:32 to f what Jesus had said when he indicated
19:24 This was to f what the scripture says,
19:28 he said (in order to f the scripture), "I am thirsty."
Gal 6: 2 and in this way you will f the law of Christ.
2Th 1:11 and will f by his power every good resolve
Jas 2: 8 if you really f the royal law according to
Jdt 10: 8 of our ancestors grant you favor and f your plans,
Sir 36:20 and f the prophecies spoken in your name.
1Mc 11:33 who are our friends and f their obligations to us,
1Es 4:46 that you f the vow whose fulfillment you vowed

FULFILLED‡ (62) [FULFILL]

Jos 23:15 concerning you have been f for you,
1Sa 10: 9 and all these signs were f that day.
2Sa 7:12 When your days are f and you lie down
1Ki 8:15 who with his hand has f what he promised
8:24 with your mouth and have this day f
1Ch 17:11 your days are f to go to be with your ancestors,
2Ch 1: 9 let your promise to my father David now be f,
6: 4 who with his hand has f what he promised
6:10 Now the LORD has f his promise that he made;
6:15 with your mouth and this day have f
Ne 9: 8 you have f your promise, for you are righteous.
Est 5: 6 Even to the half of my kingdom, it shall be f."
7: 2 Even to the half of my kingdom, it shall be f."
9:12 And what further is your request? It shall be f."
Pr 13:12 but a desire f is a tree of life.
Eze 12:25 the word that I speak, and it will be f.
12:28 but the word that I speak will be f,
21: 7 See, it comes and it will be f,"
Da 4:33 the sentence was f against Nebuchadnezzar.
9: 2 must be f for the devastation of Jerusalem,
Mt 2:17 Then was f what had been spoken through
2:23 through the prophets might be f,
4:14 through the prophet Isaiah might be f:
13:14 With them indeed is f the prophecy of Isaiah
26:54 But how then would the scriptures be f,
26:56 so that the scriptures of the prophets may be f."
27: 9 Then was f what had been spoken through
Mk 1:15 time is f, and the kingdom of God has come near;
14:49 But let the scriptures be f."
Lk 1: 1 an orderly account of the events that have been f
1:20 which will be f in their time,
4:21 "Today this scripture has been f in your hearing."
21:24 until the times of the Gentiles are f.
22:16 not eat it until it is f in the kingdom of God."
22:37 For I tell you, this scripture must be f in me,
22:37 and indeed what is written about me is being f."
24:44 the prophets, and the psalms must be f."
Jn 3:29 For this reason my joy has been f.
17:12 so that the scripture might be f.
19:36 so that the scripture might be f,
Ac 1:16 the scripture had to be f, which the Holy Spirit
3:18 In this way God f what he had foretold through all
13:27 they f those words by condemning him.
13:33 he has f for us, their children, by raising Jesus;
Ro 8: 4 the just requirement of the law might be f in us,
13: 8 for the one who loves another has f the law.
1Co 15:54 then the saying that is written will be f:
Jas 2:23 Thus the scripture was f that says,
Rev 10: 7 the mystery of God will be f,
17:17 until the words of God will be f.
Tob 14: 4 and believe that whatever God has said will be f
AdE 2:15 the time was f for Esther daughter of Aminadab,
10: 5 and none of them has failed to be f.
Wis 4:13 Being perfected in a short time, they f long years;
Sir 32: 2 when you have f all your duties,
34: 8 Without such deceptions the law will be f,
39:18 When he commands, his every purpose is f,
1Mc 2:55 Joshua, because he f the command,
1Es 8:21 of God be scrupulously f for the Most High God,
2Es 2:40 who have f the law of the Lord.
4:37 not move or arouse them until that measure is f.' "
4Mc 12:14 Surely they by dying nobly f their service to God,

FULFILLING (6) [FULFILL]

Dt 23:21 to the LORD your God, do not postpone f it;
1Ki 2:27 thus f the word of the LORD that he had spoken
Ps 148: 8 snow and frost, stormy wind f his command!
Ecc 5: 4 When you make a vow to God, do not delay f it;
Ro 9:31 did not succeed in f that law.
13:10 therefore, love is the f of the law.

FULFILLMENT (18) [FULFILL]

Lev 22:21 in f of a vow or as a freewill offering,
2Ch 36:22 in f of the word of the LORD spoken
Ps 119:123 and for the f of your righteous promise.
Isa 5:19 let the plan of the Holy One of Israel hasten to f,
Eze 12:23 The days are near, and the f of every vision.
13: 6 and yet they wait for the f of their word!
Lk 1:45 that there would be a f of what was spoken to her
21:22 as a f of all that is written.
Ac 7:17 near for the f of the promise that God had made
Jas 1:18 In f of his own purpose he gave us birth by
Tob 8:17 bring their lives to f in happiness and mercy."
14: 5 until the period when the times of f shall come.
Sir 19:20 and in all wisdom there is the f of the law.
21:11 and the f of the fear of the Lord is wisdom.
35: 7 for all that you offer is in f of the commandment.
1Es 1:57 in f of the word of the Lord by the mouth
4:46 that you fulfill the vow whose f you vowed to
3Mc 1:22 not tolerate the completion of his plans or the f

FULFILLS (3) [FULFILL]

Ps 57: 2 to God who f his purpose for me.
145:19 He f the desire of all who fear him;
Isa 44:26 and f the prediction of his messengers;

FULL‡ (301) [FILL]

Ge 14:10 Now the Valley of Siddim was f of bitumen pits;
23: 9 the f price let him give it to me in your presence
25: 8 an old man and f of years,
35:29 and was gathered to his people, old and f of days;
41: 7 up the seven plump and f ears.
41:22 f and good, growing on one stalk,
43:21 in the top of his sack, our money in f weight.
50:15 and pays us back in f for all the wrong that we did
Ex 21:19 and to arrange for f recovery.
22: 6 one who started the fire shall make f restitution.
22:14 f restitution shall be made.
Lev 16:12 a censer f of coals of fire from the altar before
19:29 land not become prostituted and f of depravity.
25:30 If it is not redeemed before a f year has elapsed,
26: 5 you shall eat your bread to the f,
Nu 5: 7 The person shall make f restitution for the wrong,
7:13 both of them f of choice flour mixed with oil for
7:14 one golden dish weighing ten shekels, f of incense;
7:19 both of them f of choice flour mixed with oil for

Nu 7:20 one golden dish weighing ten shekels, **f** of incense;
7:25 both of them **f** of choice flour mixed with oil for
7:26 one golden dish weighing ten shekels, **f** of incense;
7:31 both of them **f** of choice flour mixed with oil for
7:32 one golden dish weighing ten shekels, **f** of incense;
7:37 both of them **f** of choice flour mixed with oil for
7:38 one golden dish weighing ten shekels, **f** of incense;
7:43 both of them **f** of choice flour mixed with oil for
7:44 one golden dish weighing ten shekels, **f** of incense;
7:49 both of them **f** of choice flour mixed with oil for
7:50 one golden dish weighing ten shekels, **f** of incense;
7:55 both of them **f** of choice flour mixed with oil for
7:56 one golden dish weighing ten shekels, **f** of incense;
7:61 both of them **f** of choice flour mixed with oil for
7:62 one golden dish weighing ten shekels, **f** of incense;
7:67 both of them **f** of choice flour mixed with oil for
7:68 one golden dish weighing ten shekels, **f** of incense;
7:73 both of them **f** of choice flour mixed with oil for
7:74 one golden dish weighing ten shekels, **f** of incense;
7:79 both of them **f** of choice flour mixed with oil for
7:80 one golden dish weighing ten shekels, **f** of incense;
7:86 **f** of incense, weighing ten shekels apiece
14:35 in this wilderness they shall come to a **f** end,
22:18 "Although Balak were to give me his house **f**
24:13 'If Balak should give me his house **f** of silver
Dt 14:28 Every third year you shall bring out the **f** tithe
21:13 and shall remain in your house a **f** month,
25:15 You shall have only a **f** and honest weight;
25:15 you shall have only a **f** and honest measure,
31: 5 in **f** accord with the command that I have given
33:23 sated with favor, **f** of the blessing of the LORD,
34: 9 Joshua son of Nun was **f** of the spirit of wisdom,
Jdg 16:27 Now the house was **f** of men and women;
Ru 1:21 away **f**, but the LORD has brought me back empty;
2:12 and may you have a **f** reward from the LORD,
1Sa 2: 5 Those who were **f** have hired themselves out
18:27 which were given in **f** number to the king,
28:20 Immediately Saul fell **f** length on the ground,
2Sa 13:23 After two **f** years Absalom had sheepshearers
14:28 So Absalom lived two **f** years in Jerusalem,
23:11 where there was a plot of ground **f** of lentils;
1Ki 7:14 he was **f** of skill, intelligence,
2Ki 3:16 'I will make this wadi **f** of pools.'
4: 4 when each is **f**, set it aside."
4: 6 When the vessels were **f**, she said to her son,
6:17 the mountain was **f** of horses and chariots
1Ch 11:13 There was a plot of ground **f** of barley.
12:38 came to Hebron with **f** intent to make David king
21:22 give it to me at its **f** price—
21:24 I will buy them for the **f** price.
23: 1 When David was old and **f** of days,
29:28 He died in a good old age, **f** of days, riches,
2Ch 24:10 and dropped it into the chest until it was **f**.
24:15 But Jehoiada grew old and **f** of days, and died;
Ezr 6: 8 in **f** and without delay, from the royal revenue,
Est 9:29 with the Jew Mordecai, gave **f** written authority,
10: 2 and the **f** account of the high honor of Mordecai,
Job 7: 4 the night is long, and I am **f** of tossing until dawn.
11: 2 and should one **f** of talk be vindicated?
14: 1 born of woman, few of days and **f** of trouble,
15:32 It will be paid in **f** before their time,
20:11 Their bodies, once **f** of youth,
20:22 In **f** sufficiency they will be in distress;
20:23 to the **f** God will send his fierce anger into them,
21:23 One dies in **f** prosperity, being wholly at ease
21:24 his loins **f** of milk and the marrow
26: 9 He covers the face of the **f** moon,
32:18 For I am **f** of words;
36:16 and what was set on your table was **f** of fatness.
42:17 And Job died, old and **f** of days.
Ps 26:10 and whose right hands are **f** of bribes.
29: 4 the voice of the LORD is **f** of majesty.
33: 5 the earth is **f** of the steadfast love of the LORD.
65: 9 the river of God is **f** of water;
74:20 for the dark places of the land are **f** of the haunts
78:21 when the LORD heard, he was **f** of rage;
78:59 When God heard, he was **f** of wrath,
80: 5 and given them tears to drink in **f** measure.
81: 3 Blow the trumpet at the new moon, at the **f** moon,
88: 3 For my soul is **f** of troubles,
89:38 you are **f** of wrath against your anointed.
92:14 they are always green and **f** of sap,
104:24 the earth is **f** of your creatures.
111: 3 **F** of honor and majesty is his work,
119:64 The earth, O LORD, is **f** of your steadfast love;
127: 5 Happy is the man who has his quiver **f** of them.
144:12 in their youth be like plants **f** grown,
Pr 4:18 which shines brighter and brighter until **f** day.
7:20 he will not come home until **f** moon."
17: 1 a dry morsel with quiet than a house **f** of feasting
19:17 and will be repaid in **f**.
20:17 but afterward the mouth will be **f** of gravel.
29:11 A fool gives **f** vent to anger,
30: 9 or I shall be **f**, and deny you, and say, "Who is
Ecc 1: 7 All streams run to the sea, but the sea is not **f**;
2:23 For all their days are **f** of pain,
9: 3 Moreover, the hearts of all are **f** of evil;
11: 3 When clouds are **f**, they empty rain on the earth;
Isa 1:15 your hands are **f** of blood.
1:21 She that was **f** of justice, righteousness lodged
2: 6 Indeed they are **f** of diviners from the east and
6: 3 the whole earth is **f** of his glory."
10:23 For the Lord GOD of hosts will make a **f** end,
11: 9 the earth will be **f** of the knowledge of the LORD
13:21 and its houses will be **f** of howling creatures;
15: 9 For the waters of Dibon are **f** of blood;
22: 2 you that are **f** of shoutings,
Isa 22: 7 Your choicest valleys were **f** of chariots,
27: 9 this will be the **f** fruit of the removal of his sin:
30:27 his lips are **f** of indignation,
47: 9 in **f** measure, in spite of your many sorceries and
51:20 they are **f** of the wrath of the LORD,
65: 7 the hills, I will measure into their laps **f** payment
Jer 4:27 yet I will not make a **f** end.
5: 7 When I fed them to the **f**,
5:10 but do not make a **f** end;
5:18 says the LORD, I will not make a **f** end of you.
5:27 Like a cage **f** of birds, their houses are **f** of treachery;
6:11 But I am **f** of the wrath of the LORD;
12: 6 they are in **f** cry after you;
23:10 For the land is **f** of adulterers;
35: 5 I set before the Rechabites pitchers **f** of wine,
46:12 and the earth is **f** of your cry;
51: 5 though their land is **f** of guilt before the Holy One
51:56 a God of recompense, he will repay in **f**.
La 1: 1 How lonely sits the city that once was **f** of people!
4:11 The LORD gave **f** vent to his wrath;
Eze 1:18 for the rims of all four were **f** of eyes all around.
7:23 land is **f** of bloody crimes; the city is **f** of violence.
9: 9 land is **f** of bloodshed and the city **f** of perversity;
10: 4 the cloud, and the court was **f** of the brightness of
10:12 were **f** of eyes all around.
11:13 will you make a **f** end of the remnant of Israel?"
16: 7 up and became tall and arrived at **f** womanhood;
19:10 fruitful and **f** of branches from abundant water.
22: 5 you infamous one, **f** of tumult.
23:12 warriors clothed in **f** armor, mounted horsemen,
28:12 You were the signet of perfection, **f** of wisdom
37: 1 of a valley; it was **f** of bones.
38: 4 all of them clothed in **f** armor, a great company,
41: 8 of the side chambers measured a **f** reed
Da 8:23 the transgressions have reached their **f** measure,
10: 3 not anointed myself at all, for the **f** three weeks.
Joel 2:22 the fig tree and vine give their **f** yield.
2:24 The threshing floors shall be **f** of grain,
3:13 Go in, tread, for the wine press is **f**.
Am 2:13 just as a cart presses down when it is **f** of sheaves.
Mic 6:12 Your wealthy are **f** of violence;
Na 1: 8 He will make a **f** end of his adversaries,
1:12 "Though they are at **f** strength and many,
3: 1 City of bloodshed, utterly deceitful, **f** of booty—
Hab 3: 3 and the earth was **f** of his praise.
Zep 1:18 for a **f**, a terrible end he will make of all the
Zec 8: 5 of the city shall be **f** of boys and girls playing
9:15 they shall drink their blood like wine, and be **f**
Mal 3:10 Bring the **f** tithe into the storehouse,
Mt 6:22 your whole body will be **f** of light;
6:23 your whole body will be **f** of darkness.
13:48 when it was **f**, they drew it ashore, sat down,
14:20 over of the broken pieces, twelve baskets **f**.
15:37 up the broken pieces left over, seven baskets **f**.
23:25 but inside they are **f** of greed and self-indulgence.
23:27 but inside they are **f** of the bones of the dead and
23:28 but inside you are **f** of hypocrisy and lawlessness.
Mk 4:28 then the head, then the **f** grain in the head.
6:43 up twelve baskets **f** of broken pieces and of
8: 8 up the broken pieces left over, seven baskets **f**.
8:19 many baskets **f** of broken pieces did you collect?"
8:20 many baskets **f** of broken pieces did you collect?"
Lk 4: 1 Jesus, **f** of the Holy Spirit,
6:25 "Woe to you who are **f** now,
11:34 your eye is healthy, your whole body is **f** of light; but if it is not healthy, your body is **f** of darkness.
11:36 If then your whole body is **f** of light,
11:36 be as **f** of light as when a lamp gives you light
11:39 but inside you are **f** of greed and wickedness.
Jn 1:14 as of a father's only son, **f** of grace and truth.
19:29 A jar **f** of sour wine was standing there.
19:29 So they put a sponge **f** of the wine on a branch
21: 8 dragging the net **f** of fish,
21:11 **f** of large fish, a hundred fifty-three of them;
Ac 2:28 you will make me **f** of gladness
6: 3 **f** of the Spirit and of wisdom,
6: 5 a man **f** of faith and the Holy Spirit,
6: 8 Stephen, **f** of grace and power,
11:24 **f** of the Holy Spirit and of faith.
13:10 **f** of all deceit and villainy,
17:16 he was deeply distressed to see that the city was **f**
Ro 1:29 **F** of envy, murder, strife, deceit, craftiness,
3:14 "Their mouths are **f** of cursing and bitterness."
11:12 how much more will their **f** inclusion mean!
11:25 until the **f** number of the Gentiles has come in.
15:14 that you yourselves are **f** of goodness,
1Co 9:18 so as not to make **f** use of my rights in the gospel.
Eph 4:13 to the measure of the **f** stature of Christ.
Php 1: 9 and more with knowledge and **f** insight
2: 2 being in **f** accord and of one mind.
4:18 I have been paid in **f** and have more than enough;
1Th 1: 5 and in the Holy Spirit and with **f** conviction;
1Ti 1:15 The saying is sure and worthy of **f** acceptance,
2:11 Let a woman learn in silence with **f** submission.
4: 9 The saying is sure and worthy of **f** acceptance.
Heb 6:11 the same diligence so as to realize the **f** assurance
10:22 let us approach with a true heart in **f** assurance
Jas 1: 4 and let endurance have its **f** effect,
3: 8 a restless evil, **f** of deadly poison.
3:17 willing to yield, **f** of mercy and good fruits,
2Pe 2:14 They have eyes **f** of adultery, insatiable for sin.
2Jn 1: 8 but may receive a **f** reward.
Rev 1:16 and his face was like the sun shining with **f** force.
4: 6 **f** of eyes in front and behind:
4: 8 are **f** of eyes all around and inside.
5: 8 each holding a harp and golden bowls **f**
Rev 5:12 singing with **f** voice, "Worthy is the Lamb
6:12 the **f** moon became like blood,
15: 7 the seven angels seven golden bowls **f** of
17: 3 a scarlet beast that was **f** of blasphemous names,
17: 4 a golden cup **f** of abominations and the impurities
21: 9 of the seven angels who had the seven bowls **f** of
Tob 2:12 they paid her **f** wages and also gave her
11:16 along in **f** vigor and with no one leading him,
12: 9 Those who give alms will enjoy a **f** life,
Jdt 6: 4 and their fields will be **f** of their dead.
7: 6 in **f** view of the Israelites in Bethulia.
AdE 9:29 and gave **f** authority to the letter about Purim.
15: 6 clothed in the **f** array of his majesty,
15:14 my lord, and your countenance is **f** of grace."
Wis 2: 6 and make use of the creation to the **f** as in youth.
3: 4 their hope is **f** of immortality.
5:22 and hailstones **f** of wrath will be hurled as from
11:18 or newly-created unknown beasts **f** of rage,
12:21 and covenants **f** of good promises!
13:13 useful for nothing, a stick crooked and **f** of knots,
Sir 1:30 and your heart was **f** of deceit.
19:26 but inwardly he is **f** of deceit.
23:11 The one who swears many oaths is **f** of iniquity,
32:20 Do not go on a path **f** of hazards,
39:12 I am **f** like the **f** moon.
39:24 but **f** of pitfalls for the wicked.
42:16 and the work of the Lord is **f** of his glory.
50: 6 like the **f** moon at the festal season;
LtJ 6:18 Their eyes are **f** of the dust raised by the feet
Sus 1:28 **f** of their wicked plot to have Susanna put
1Mc 2:68 Pay back the Gentiles in **f**,
14: 6 and gained **f** control of the country.
2Mc 3: 6 the treasury in Jerusalem was **f** of untold sums
3:30 a little while before was **f** of fear and disturbance,
6:14 until they have reached the **f** measure
11:30 of friendship and **f** permission
13: 5 there is a tower there, fifty cubits high, **f** of ashes,
15:28 they recognized Nicanor, lying dead, in **f** armor.
1Es 1:23 for his heart was **f** of godliness.
6:28 and that **f** effort be made
3Mc 5:31 and have exhibited to an extraordinary degree a **f**
5:47 rushed out in **f** force along with the animals,
6:31 and **f** of joy they apportioned to celebrants
7:16 even to death and had received the **f** enjoyment
2Es 2:40 Take again your **f** number, O Zion,
4:27 because this age is **f** of sadness and infirmities.
4:38 all of us also are **f** of ungodliness.
4:49 And after this a cloud **f** of water passed before me
6:13 "Rise to your feet and you will hear a **f**,
6:22 and **f** storehouses shall suddenly be found to
7: 6 and it is **f** of all good things;
7:12 **f** of dangers and involved in great hardships.
7:25 and **f** things are for the **f**.
7:*68* are **f** of sins and burdened with transgressions.
7:*112* [42] the **f** glory does not remain in it;
12: 2 and their reign was brief and **f** of tumult.
12:30 this was the reign which was brief and **f** of tumult,
14:39 a **f** cup was offered to me; it was **f** of something
15:34 exceedingly threatening, **f** of wrath and storm.
15:40 Great and mighty clouds, **f** of wrath and tempest,
4Mc 7:17 "Not all have **f** command of their emotions,
13:16 Therefore let us put on the **f** armor of self-control,
14:11 that reason had **f** command over these men

FULL-TONED (1) [FILL]

Sir 50:18 with their voices in sweet and **f** melody.

FULLER See Index to Footnotes

FULLER'S (3) [FULLERS']

2Ki 18:17 which is on the highway to the **F** Field.
Isa 7: 3 of the upper pool on the highway to the **F** Field,
36: 2 of the upper pool on the highway to the **F** Field.

FULLERS' (1) [FULLER'S]

Mal 3: 2 For he is like a refiner's fire and like **f'** soap;

FULLNESS[‡] (16) [FILL]

Ex 22:29 You shall not delay to make offerings from the **f**
Nu 18:27 of the threshing floor and the **f** of the wine press.
Dt 33:16 with the choice gifts of the earth and its **f**,
Ps 16:11 In your presence there is **f** of joy;
Jn 1:16 From his **f** we have all received,
Ro 15:29 I will come in the **f** of the blessing of Christ.
1Co 10:26 for "the earth and its **f** are the Lord's."
Gal 4: 4 But when the **f** of time had come,
Eph 1:10 as a plan for the **f** of time,
1:23 which is his body, the **f** of him who fills all in all.
3:19 so that you may be filled with all the **f** of God.
Col 1:19 For in him all the **f** of God was pleased to dwell,
2: 9 For in him the whole **f** of deity dwells bodily,
2:10 and you have come to **f** in him,
Sir 1:16 To fear the Lord is **f** of wisdom;
33:11 In the **f** of his knowledge

FULLY[‡] (36) [FILL]

Dt 17:11 You must carry out **f** the law that they interpret
Ru 2:11 the death of your husband has been **f** told me,
Ecc 8:11 the human heart is **f** set to do evil.
Lk 6:40 but everyone who is **f** qualified will be like
11:21 When a strong man, **f** armed, guards his castle,
Jn 7: 8 for my time has not yet **f** come."
Ro 4:21 being **f** convinced that God was able
14: 5 Let all be **f** convinced in their own minds.

Ro 15:19 and as far around as Illyricum I have f proclaimed
1Co 13:12 I will know f, even as I have been f known.
Php 4:18 I am f satisfied, now that I have received
4:19 And my God will f satisfy every need of yours
Col 1:10 of the Lord, f pleasing to him, as you bear fruit
1:25 to make the word of God f known,
4:12 so that you may stand mature and f assured
2Ti 4:5 carry out your ministry f.
4:17 be f proclaimed and all the Gentiles might hear it.
Jas 1:15 when it is f grown, gives birth to death.
2Pe 1:19 we have the prophetic message more f confirmed.
Jude 1:5 I desire to remind you, though you are f informed,
Rev 14:15 because the harvest of the earth is f ripe."
Tob 7:10 let me explain to you the true situation more f,
Jdt 2:2 before them his secret plan and recounted f,
AdE 16:11 so f the goodwill that we have for every nation
Sir 18:5 And who can f recount his mercies?
24:28 The first man did not know wisdom f,
1Mc 9:42 they had f avenged the blood of their brother,
2Mc 4:33 When Onias became f aware of these acts,
5:2 in companies f armed with lances
14:20 When the terms had been f considered,
15:22 and he killed f one hundred eighty-five thousand
1Es 6:8 Let it be f known to our lord the king that,
3Mc 3:24 f convinced by these indications
2Es 12:8 so that you may f comfort my soul.
4Mc 3:12 respecting the king's desire, armed themselves f,

FUME (1)

Sir 20:2 How much better it is to rebuke than to f!

FUN (1)

Sir 8:4 Do not make f of one who is ill-bred,

FUNCTION (1)

Ro 12:4 and not all the members have the same f,

FUND (3) [FUNDS]

Ezr 2:69 the building f sixty-one thousand darics of gold,
Ne 7:71 into the building f twenty thousand darics of gold
1Mc 3:31 from those regions and raise a large f.

FUNDS (6) [FUND]

1Mc 3:30 He feared that he might not have such f as he had
10:41 the additional f that the government officials have
2Mc 3:6 so that the amount of the f could not be reckoned,
3:14 and went in to direct the inspection of these f.
4Mc 4:3 of thousands in private f,
4:6 with the king's authority to seize the private f in

FUNERAL (5)

Tob 14:11 and he received an honorable f.
LtJ 6:32 before their gods as some do at a f banquet.
1Mc 9:41 and the voice of their musicians into a f dirge.
2Mc 4:49 provided magnificently for their f.
5:10 he had no f of any sort and no place in the tomb

FURBISHED (KJV) See HONED, POLISHED

FURIOUS (6) [FURY]

Isa 30:30 in f anger and a flame of devouring fire,
34:2 and f against all their hoards;
Eze 5:15 and with f punishments—
Da 3:13 in f rage commanded that Shadrach, Meshach,
AdE 1:12 This offended the king and he became f.
1Mc 2:49 it is a time of ruin and f anger.

FURIOUSLY (4) [FURY]

Ac 26:11 and since I was so f enraged at them,
AdE 3:5 not doing obeisance to him, he became f angry,
2Mc 3:25 it rushed f at Heliodorus and struck at him
12:15 in the days of Joshua, rushed f upon the walls.

FURLONGS (KJV) See MILES

FURNACE (42)

Ge 19:28 of the land going up like the smoke of a f.
Ps 12:6 silver refined in a f on the ground,
21:9 You will make them like a fiery f
102:3 and my bones burn like a f.
Pr 17:3 The crucible is for silver, and the f is for gold,
27:21 The crucible is for silver, and the f is for gold,
Isa 31:9 whose fire is in Zion, and whose f is in Jerusalem.
48:10 I have tested you in the f of adversity.
Da 3:6 and worship shall immediately be thrown into a f
3:11 not fall down and worship shall be thrown into a f
3:15 you shall immediately be thrown into a f
3:17 from the f of blazing fire and out of your hand,
3:19 ordered the f heated up seven times more than
3:20 and to throw them into the f of blazing fire.
3:21 and they were thrown into the f of blazing fire.
3:22 the king's command was urgent and the f was
3:23 fell down, bound, into the f of blazing fire.
3:26 then approached the door of the f of blazing fire
Mt 13:42 and they will throw them into the f of fire,
13:50 and throw them into the f of fire,
Rev 1:15 refined as in a f, and his voice was like the sound
9:2 the shaft rose smoke like the smoke of a great f,
Wis 3:6 like gold in the f he tried them,
Sir 2:5 in the fire, and those found acceptable, in the f
Sir 22:24 The vapor and smoke of the f precede the fire;
31:26 As the f tests the work of the smith,
38:28 and he struggles with the heat of the f;
43:4 A man tending a f works in burning heat,
Aza 1:23 in kept stoking the f with naphtha,
1:24 flames poured out above the f forty-nine cubits,
1:25 those Chaldeans who were caught near the f.
1:26 But the angel of the Lord came down into the f to
1:26 and drove the fiery flame out of the f,
1:27 of the f as though a moist wind were whistling
1:28 and glorified and blessed God in the f:
1:66 from the midst of the burning fiery f;
3Mc 6:6 moistening the fiery f with dew and turning
2Es 4:48 and lo, a flaming f passed by before me,
7:*36* and the f of hell shall be disclosed,
4Mc 13:9 in Assyria who despised the same ordeal of the f.
16:3 was the raging fiery f of Mishael so intensely hot,
16:21 into the fiery f and endured it for the sake of God.

FURNISH (1) [FURNISHED, FURNISHINGS, FURNITURE]

2Es 8:8 now fashioned in the womb, and f it with members,

FURNISHED (3) [FURNISH]

Mk 14:15 a large room upstairs, f and ready.
Lk 22:12 He will show you a large room upstairs, already f.
1Mc 14:10 and f them with the means of defense,

FURNISHINGS (5) [FURNISH]

Ex 31:7 and all the f of the tent,
Nu 3:8 be in charge of all the f of the tent of meeting,
4:15 the sanctuary and all the f of the sanctuary,
7:1 and had anointed and consecrated it with all its f,
19:18 on all the f, on the persons who were there,

FURNITURE (5) [FURNISH]

Ex 25:9 the pattern of the tabernacle and of all its f,
40:9 and consecrate it and all its f,
1Ch 9:29 Others of them were appointed over the f,
Ne 13:8 and I threw all the household f of Tobiah out of
Jdt 15:11 his beds, his bowls, and all his f.

FURNITURE (KJV) See also FURNISHINGS, PRECIOUS THINGS, SADDLE, UTENSILS

FURROW (2) [FURROWS]

1Sa 14:14 an area about half a f long in an acre of land.
Job 39:10 Can you tie it in the f with ropes,

FURROWS (7) [FURROW]

Job 31:38 and its f have wept together;
Ps 65:10 You water its f abundantly, settling its ridges,
129:3 on my back; they made their f long."
Hos 10:4 up like poisonous weeds in the f of the field.
12:11 so their altars shall be like stone heaps on the f of
Sir 7:3 Do not sow in the f of injustice,
38:26 He sets his heart on plowing f,

FURTHER (38) [FURTHERED, FURTHERMORE]

Ge 45:19 You are f charged to say, 'Do this:
Ex 3:6 He said f, "I am the God of your father,
3:14 He said f, "Thus you shall say to the Israelites,
21:22 and yet no f harm follows,
27:20 You shall f command the Israelites
Lev 17:8 And say to them f: Anyone of the
20:2 Say f to the people of Israel:
1Sa 9:20 give no f thought to them,
10:3 Then you shall go on from there f and come to
2Sa 2:28 or engaged in battle any f.
19:28 What f right have I, then, to appeal to the king?"
1Ch 28:20 David said f to his son Solomon,
2Ch 34:16 and f reported to the king,
Est 9:12 And what f is your request?
Job 40:5 twice, but will proceed no f."
Ps 140:8 do not f their evil plot.
Isa 1:5 Why do you seek f beatings?
Eze 8:17 and provoke my anger still f?
23:14 But she carried her whorings f;
29:13 F, thus says the Lord GOD:
Da 10:14 For there is a f vision for those days."
Zec 1:17 Proclaim f: Thus says the LORD of hosts:
Mk 5:35 Why trouble the teacher any f?"
15:5 Jesus made no f reply, so that Pilate was amazed.
Lk 22:71 Then they said, "What f testimony do we need?
Ac 4:17 But to keep it from spreading f among the people,
15:28 on you no f burden than these essentials:
19:39 If there is anything f you want to know,
24:4 to detain you no f, I beg you to hear us briefly
28:25 as they were leaving, Paul made one f statement:
Ro 15:23 But now, with no f place for me in these regions,
2Co 5:4 we wish not to be unclothed but to be f clothed,
Heb 7:11 what f need would there have been to speak
Sir 11:23 and what f benefit can be mine?"
2Mc 2:20 and f the wars against Antiochus Epiphanes
1Es 2:29 and that such wicked proceedings go no f to
2Es 7:*102* "If I have found favor in your sight, show f to me,
4Mc 9:19 fanning the flames they tightened the wheel f.

FURTHERED (1) [FURTHER]

2Mc 14:5 that f his mad purpose when he was invited

FURTHERMORE (10) [FURTHER]

Ge 20:6 f it was I who kept you from sinning against me.
Dt 9:13 F the LORD said to me,
Jdg 18:7 F, they were far from the Sidonians
2Ch 17:6 and f he removed the high places and
Ezr 6:11 F I decree that if anyone alters this edict,
Est 1:9 F, Queen Vashti gave a banquet for the women in
8:17 F, many of the peoples of the country professed
Heb 7:23 F, the former priests were many in number,
1Es 4:10 F, he reclines, he eats and drinks and sleeps,
4Mc 14:1 F, they encouraged them to face the torture,

FURY (36) [FURIOUS, FURIOUSLY, INFURIATED]

Ge 27:44 until your brother's f turns away—
Ex 15:7 you sent out your f, it consumed them
Lev 26:28 I will continue hostile to you in f;
Dt 29:28 LORD uprooted them from their land in anger, f,
Ps 2:5 and terrify them in his f, saying,
7:6 lift yourself up against the f of my enemies;
Pr 6:34 For jealousy arouses a husband's f,
Isa 10:5 the club in their hands is my f!
42:13 like a warrior he stirs up his f;
42:25 upon him the heat of his anger and the f of war;
51:13 You fear continually all day long because of the f
51:13 But where is the f of the oppressor?
59:17 and wrapped himself in f as in a mantle.
66:15 to pay back his anger in f,
Jer 21:5 in anger, in f, and in great wrath.
La 2:4 he has poured out his f like fire.
Eze 5:13 and I will vent my f on them and satisfy myself;
5:13 when I spend my f on them.
5:15 when I execute judgments on you in anger and f,
6:12 Thus I will spend my f upon them.
16:42 So I will satisfy my f on you,
19:12 it was plucked up in f, cast down to the ground;
21:17 I too will strike hand to hand, I will satisfy my f;
23:25 in order that they may deal with you in f.
24:13 be cleansed until I have satisfied my f upon you.
Da 11:44 and he shall go out with great f to bring ruin
Hab 3:12 In f you trod the earth,
Lk 6:11 But they were filled with f and discussed
Ro 2:8 there will be wrath and f.
Heb 10:27 and a f of fire that will consume the adversaries.
Rev 16:19 and gave her the wine-cup of the f of his wrath.
19:15 he will tread the wine press of the f of the wrath
Sir 40:5 and fear of death, and f and strife.
48:10 to calm the wrath of God before it breaks out in f,
2Mc 10:35 and with savage f cut down everyone they met.
2Es 15:44 they shall pour out on it the tempest and all its f;

FUTILE (8) [FUTILITY]

Isa 1:13 bringing offerings is f; incense is an abomination
Ro 1:21 but they became f in their thinking,
1Co 3:20 the thoughts of the wise, that they are f."
15:17 your faith is f and you are still in your sins.
1Pe 1:18 that you were ransomed from the f ways inherited
Wis 15:8 these workers form a f god from the same clay—
2Es 7:14 living pass through the difficult and f experiences,
4Mc 5:11 dispel your f reasonings, adopt a mind appropriate

FUTILITY (2) [FUTILE]

Ro 8:20 for the creation was subjected to f,
Eph 4:17 as the Gentiles live, in the f of their minds.

FUTURE[‡] (26)

Ge 9:12 that is with you, for all f generations:
Ex 13:14 When in the f your child asks you,
Ps 22:30 f generations will be told about the Lord,
Pr 19:20 that you may gain wisdom for the f.
23:18 there is a f, and your hope will not be cut off.
24:14 if you find it, you will find a f,
24:20 for the evil have no f;
Ecc 3:11 he has put a sense of past and f into their minds,
10:14 and who can tell anyone what the f holds?
Isa 53:8 Who could have imagined his f?
Jer 29:11 to give you a f with hope.
31:17 there is hope for your f, says the LORD:
La 1:9 she took no thought of her f;
1Co 3:22 the world or life or death or the present or the f—
1Ti 6:19 the treasure of a good foundation for the f,
Heb 11:20 By faith Isaac invoked blessings for the f
AdE 16:8 In the f we will take care
Wis 19:1 for God knew in advance even their f actions:
Sir 3:31 Those who repay favors give thought to the f;
24:33 and leave it to all f generations.
48:24 By his dauntless spirit he saw the f,
1Mc 15:8 to the royal treasury and any such f debts shall
2Mc 11:19 in the f to help promote your welfare.
12:31 to be well disposed to their race in the f also.
3Mc 2:31 to enhance their reputation by their f association
2Es 8:46 that are f are for those who will live hereafter.

G

GAAL (9)
Jdg 9:26 When G son of Ebed moved into Shechem
9:28 G son of Ebed said, "Who is Abimelech,
9:30 of the city heard the words of G son of Ebed,
9:31 G son of Ebed and his kinsfolk have come
9:35 When G son of Ebed went out and stood in
9:36 And when G saw them, he said to Zebul, "Look,
9:37 G spoke again and said, "Look,
9:39 G went out at the head of the lords of Shechem,
9:41 and Zebul drove out G and his kinsfolk,

GAASH (4)
Jos 24:30 in the hill country of Ephraim, north of Mount G.
Jdg 2: 9 in the hill country of Ephraim, north of Mount G.
2Sa 23:30 Benaiah of Pirathon; Hiddai of the torrents of G;
1Ch 11:32 Hurai of the wadis of G, Abiel the Arbathite,

GABA (KJV) See GEBA

GABAEL (11)
Tob 1: 1 of Hananiel son of Aduel son of G son of Raphael
1:14 of silver worth ten talents in trust with G,
4: 1 the money that he had left in trust with G at Rages
4:20 that I left ten talents of silver in trust with G son
5: 3 But get back the money from G."
5: 6 with our kinsman G who lives in Rages of Media.
9: 2 Go to the home of G, give him the bond,
9: 5 to Rages in Media and stayed with G.
9: 5 G got up and counted out to him the money bags,
9: 6 He sprang up and greeted G,
10: 2 Or that G has died, and there is no one to give him

GABATHA (1)
AdE 12: 1 in the courtyard with G and Tharra,

GABBAI (1)
Ne 11: 8 his brothers G, Sallai: nine hundred twenty-eight.

GABBATHA (1)
Jn 19:13 The Stone Pavement, or in Hebrew G.

GABRI (1)
Tob 1:14 in trust with Gabael, the brother of G.

GABRIAS (1)
Tob 4:20 of silver in trust with Gabael son of G,

GABRIEL (4)
Da 8:16 calling, "G, help this man understand the vision."
9:21 the man G, whom I had seen before in a vision,
Lk 1:19 The angel replied, "I am G.
1:26 In the sixth month the angel G was sent by God to

GAD (43) [BAAL-GAD, DIBON-GAD, GAD'S, GADDING, GADITE, GADITES]
Ge 30:11 so she named him G.
35:26 The sons of Zilpah, Leah's maid: G and Asher.
46:16 The children of G: Ziphion,
49:19 G shall be raided by raiders,
Ex 1: 4 Dan and Naphtali, G and Asher.
Nu 1:14 From G, Eliasaph son of Deuel.
1:24 The descendants of G, their lineage, in their clans,
1:25 of G were forty five thousand six hundred fifty
2:14 Then the tribe of G: The leader of the
10:20 the company of the tribe of G was Eliasaph son
13:15 from the tribe of G, Geuel son of Machi.
26:15 The children of G by their clans:
Dt 27:13 Reuben, G, Asher, Zebulun, Dan, and Naphtali.
33:20 of G he said: Blessed be the enlargement of G!
33:20 G lives like a lion; he tears at arm and scalp.
Jos 18: 7 and G and Reuben and the half-tribe
20: 8 and Ramoth in Gilead, from the tribe of G,
21: 7 the tribe of G, and the tribe of Zebulun.
21:38 Out of the tribe of G:
1Sa 13: 7 Some Hebrews crossed the Jordan to the land of G
22: 5 Then the prophet G said to David,
2Sa 24: 5 toward G and on to Jazer.
24:11 the word of the LORD came to the prophet G,
24:13 So G came to David and told him;
24:14 Then David said to G, "I am in great distress;
24:18 That day G came to David and said to him,
1Ch 2: 2 Dan, Joseph, Benjamin, Naphtali, G, and Asher.
5:11 of G lived beside them in the land of Bashan as far
6:63 of the tribes of Reuben, G,
6:80 and out of the tribe of G:
21: 9 The LORD spoke to G, David's seer, saying,
21:11 So G came to David and said to him,
21:13 Then David said to G, "I am in great distress;
21:18 Then the angel of the LORD commanded G
29:29 and in the records of the seer G,
2Ch 29:25 according to the commandment of David and of G
Jer 2:36 How lightly you g about, changing your ways!
49: 1 Why then has Milcom dispossessed G,
Eze 48:27 from the east side to the west, G, one portion.
48:28 And adjoining the territory of G to the south,
48:34 three gates, the gate of G, the gate of Asher,
Rev 7: 5 from the tribe of G twelve thousand,

GAD'S (2) [GAD]
2Sa 24:19 Following G instructions, David went up,
1Ch 21:19 So David went up following G instructions,

GADARENES‡ (1)
Mt 8:28 he came to the other side, to the country of the G,

GADDI (2) [=JOHN]
Nu 13:11 from the tribe of Manasseh), G son of Susi;
1Mc 2: 2 He had five sons, John surnamed G,

GADDIEL (1)
Nu 13:10 from the tribe of Zebulun, G son of Sodi;

GADDING (1) [GAD]
1Ti 5:13 they learn to be idle, g about from house to house;

GADDEST (KJV) See GAD

GADFLY‡ (1)
Jer 46:20 a g from the north lights upon her.

GADI (2)
2Ki 15:14 of G came up from Tirzah and came to Samaria;
15:17 Menahem son of G began to reign over Israel;

GADITE (1) [GAD]
2Sa 23:36 Igal son of Nathan of Zobah; Bani the G;

GADITES (43) [GAD]
Nu 2:14 leader of the G shall be Eliasaph son of Reuel,
7:42 of Deuel, the leader of the G:
26:18 These are the clans of the G:
32: 1 and the G owned a very great number of cattle.
32: 2 G and the Reubenites came and spoke to Moses,
32: 6 But Moses said to the G and to the Reubenites,
32:25 Then the G and the Reubenites said to Moses,
32:29 Moses said to them, "If the G and the Reubenites,
32:31 The G and the Reubenites answered,
32:33 to the G and to the Reubenites and to the half-tribe
32:34 And the G rebuilt Dibon, Ataroth, Aroer,
34:14 by their ancestral houses and the tribe of the G
Dt 3:12 the Reubenites and G the territory north of Aroer,
3:16 and the G I gave the territory from Gilead as far as
4:43 Ramoth in Gilead belonging to the G,
29: 8 the G, and the half-tribe of Manasseh.
Jos 1:12 To the Reubenites, the G,
4:12 the G, and the half-tribe of Manasseh crossed
12: 6 for a possession to the Reubenites and the G and
13: 8 and the G received their inheritance,
13:24 an inheritance also to the tribe of the G,
13:28 the inheritance of the G according to their clans,
22: 1 Then Joshua summoned the Reubenites, the G,
22: 9 So the Reubenites and the G and the half-tribe
22:10 the G and the half-tribe of Manasseh built there
22:11 and the G and the half-tribe of Manasseh had built
22:13 to the Reubenites and the G and the half-tribe
22:15 They came to the Reubenites, the G,
22:21 Then the Reubenites, the G,
22:25 between us and you, you Reubenites and G;
22:30 heard the words that the Reubenites and the G and
22:31 to the Reubenites and the G and the Manassites,
22:32 the chiefs returned from the Reubenites and the G
22:33 where the Reubenites and the G were settled.
22:34 The Reubenites and the G called the altar Witness;
1Sa 10:27 had been grievously oppressing the G and
2Ki 10:33 all the land of Gilead, the G, the Reubenites,
1Ch 5:18 The Reubenites, the G, and the half-tribe
5:26 the G, and the half-tribe of Manasseh,
12: 8 the G there went over to David at the stronghold
12:14 These G were officers of the army,
12:37 and G and the half-tribe of Manasseh from beyond
26:32 to have the oversight of the Reubenites, the G,

GAHAM (1)
Ge 22:24 whose name was Reumah, bore Tebah, G,

GAHAR (2)
Ezr 2:47 Giddel, G, Reaiah,
Ne 7:49 of Hanan, of Giddel, of G,

GAI‡ (4)
AdE 2: 8 in Susa the capital in custody of G,
2: 8 Esther also was brought to G,
2:14 G the king's eunuch is in charge of the women;
2:15 she neglected none of the things that G,

GAIN‡ (81) [GAINED, GAINING, GAINS]
Ge 22:18 the nations of the earth g blessing for themselves,
24:60 may your offspring g possession of the gates
26: 4 and all the nations of the earth shall g blessing
Ex 14: 4 so that I will g glory for myself over Pharaoh
14:17 and so I will g glory for myself over Pharaoh
18:21 are trustworthy, and hate dishonest g;
1Sa 8: 3 not follow in his ways, but turned aside after g;
Est 9: 1 when the enemies of the Jews hoped to g power
9: 1 when the Jews would g power over their foes,
Job 22: 3 or is it g to him if you make your ways blameless?
30: 2 What could I g from the strength of their hands?
Ps 10: 3 those greedy for g curse and renounce the LORD.
90:12 to count our days that we may g a wise heart.
119:36 to your decrees, and not to selfish g.
Pr 1: 5 Let the wise also hear and g in learning,
1:19 Such is the end of all who are greedy for g;
4: 1 and be attentive, that you may g insight;
9: 9 teach the righteous and they will g in learning.
10:16 the g of the wicked to sin.
11:16 but the aggressive g riches.
11:18 The wicked earn no real g,
15:27 Those who are greedy for unjust g make trouble
15:32 but those who heed admonition g understanding.
19:20 that you may g wisdom for the future.
19:25 reprove the intelligent, and they will g knowledge.
28:16 but one who hates unjust g will enjoy a long life.
31:11 and he will have no lack of g.
Ecc 1: 3 What do people g from all the toil
3: 9 What g have the workers from their toil?
5:10 nor the lover of wealth, with g.
5:11 and what g has their owner but to see them
5:16 what g do they have from toiling for the wind?
Isa 33:15 who despise the g of oppression,
56:11 to their own g, one and all.
Jer 2:18 What then do you g by going to Egypt,
2:18 Or what do you g by going to Assyria,
6:13 everyone is greedy for unjust g;
8:10 to the greatest everyone is greedy for unjust g;
22:17 your eyes and heart are only on your dishonest g,
46:10 a day of retribution, to g vindication from his foes.
Eze 22:12 and make g of your neighbors by extortion;
22:13 at the dishonest g you have made,
22:27 destroying lives to get dishonest g.
28:22 O Sidon, and I will g glory in your midst.
33:31 but their heart is set on their g.
Da 2: 8 to g time, because you see I have firmly decreed:
10:12 that you set your mind to g understanding and
Hos 12: 8 in all of my g no offense has been found in me
Mic 4:13 and shall devote their g to the LORD,
Hab 2: 9 "Alas for you who get evil g for your houses,
Mt 16:26 if they g the whole world but forfeit their life?
Mk 8:36 For what will it profit them to g the whole world
Lk 9:25 What does it profit them if they g
21:19 By your endurance you will g your souls.
Ac 12:24 of God continued to advance and g adherents.
1Co 7:21 Even if you can g your freedom,
13: 3 but do not have love, I g nothing.
Php 1:21 For to me, living is Christ and dying is g.
3: 8 in order that I may g Christ
1Ti 3:13 as deacons g a good standing for themselves
6: 5 imagining that godliness is a means of g.
6: 6 there is great g in godliness combined
Tit 1: 7 or addicted to wine or violent or greedy for g;
1:11 by teaching for sordid g what it is not right
1Pe 5: 2 not for sordid g but eagerly.
Jude 1:11 to Balaam's error for the sake of g,
Wis 14: 2 For it was desire for g that planned that vessel,
Sir Pr: 3 to g learning and are disposed to live according to
6: 7 When you g friends, g them through testing,
6:33 If you love to listen you will g knowledge,
19:25 there are people who abuse favors to g a verdict.
22:23 G the trust of your neighbor in his poverty,
27: 1 Many have committed sin for g,
29:19 his pursuit of g involves him in lawsuits.
34:28 what do they g but hard work?
1Mc 2:48 and they never let the sinner g the upper hand.
2:64 for by it you will g honor.
15: 9 When we g control of our kingdom,
2Mc 5: 7 He did not, however, g control of the government;
2Es 4:15 also we may g more territory for ourselves.'

GAINED (44) [GAIN]
Ge 31: 1 he has g all this wealth from what belonged
31:18 all the property that he had g,
41:45 Thus Joseph g authority over the land of Egypt.
47:27 and they g possessions in it,
Ex 14:18 when I have g glory for myself over Pharaoh,
2Sa 11:23 "The men g an advantage over us,
Est 9:16 and g relief from their enemies,
9:22 on which the Jews g relief from their enemies,
Ps 111: 4 He has g renown by his wonderful deeds;
Pr 10: 2 Treasures g by wickedness do not profit,
16:31 it is g in a righteous life.
20:17 Bread g by deceit is sweet,
Ecc 2:11 and there was nothing to be g under the sun.
Isa 15: 7 Therefore the abundance they have g
Jer 48:36 for the riches they g have perished.
Da 7:22 when the holy ones g possession of the kingdom.
Hos 12: 8 "Ah, I am rich, I have g wealth for myself;
Lk 19:15 that he might find out what they had g by trading.
Ac 23:16 and g entrance to the barracks and told Paul.
Ro 4: 1 What then are we to say was g by Abraham,
1Co 15:32 what would I have g by it?
2Co 12: 1 It is necessary to boast; nothing is to be g by it,
Rev 18:15 merchants of these wares, who g wealth from her,
Wis 13:13 and shapes it with skill g in idleness;
Sir 34:30 and touches it again, what has been g by washing?
34:31 And what has he g by humbling himself?
51:20 With her I g understanding from the first;
51:21 therefore I have g a prize possession.
1Mc 7:22 They g control of the land of Judah

1Mc 8: 4 and how they had **g** control of the whole region
10:52 I crushed Demetrius and **g** control of our country;
10:76 and Jonathan **g** possession of Joppa.
11: 8 So King Ptolemy **g** control of the coastal cities
11:49 the city saw that the Jews had **g** control of the city
11:51 the Jews **g** glory in the sight of the king and of all
11:56 Trypho captured the elephants and **g** control
14: 6 and **g** full control of the country.
15: 3 Whereas certain scoundrels have **g** control of
2Mc 10:17 they **g** possession of the places,
13:26 convinced them, appeased them, **g** their goodwill,
3Mc 6: 5 who had already **g** control of the whole world by
2Es 3:28 Is that why it has **g** dominion over Zion?
11:32 Moreover this head **g** control of the whole earth,
4Mc 18: 4 Because of them the nation **g** peace,

GAINING (2) [GAIN]

Pr 1: 3 for **g** instruction in wise dealing,
2Mc 8: 8 When Philip saw that the man was **g** ground little

GAINS (4) [GAIN]

Jer 20: 5 I will give all the wealth of this city, all its **g**,
Php 3: 7 Yet whatever **g** I had, these I have come to regard
Wis 7:25 therefore nothing defiled **g** entrance into her.
2Mc 15:21 that he **g** the victory for those who deserve it.

GAINSAY, GAINSAYERS (KJV) See CONTRADICT, WITHSTAND

GAINSAYING (KJV) See CONTRARY, OBJECTION, REBELLION

GAIT (1)

Pr 30:29 stately in their stride; four are stately in their **g**:

GAIUS (5)

Ac 19:29 dragging with them **G** and Aristarchus,
20: 4 by **G** from Derbe, and by Timothy,
Ro 16:23 **G**, who is host to me and to the whole church,
1Co 1:14 that I baptized none of you except Crispus and **G**,
3Jn 1: 1 The elder to the beloved **G**, whom I love in truth.

GALAL‡ (3)

1Ch 9:15 **G**, and Mattaniah son of Mica, son of Zichri,
9:16 son of **G**, son of Jeduthun,
Ne 11:17 Abda son of Shammua son of **G** son of Jeduthun.

GALATIA (6) [GALATIANS]

Ac 16: 6 They went through the region of Phrygia and **G**,
18:23 to place through the region of **G** and Phrygia,
1Co 16: 1 the directions I gave to the churches of **G**.
Gal 1: 2 with me, To the churches of **G**:
2Ti 4:10 Crescens has gone to **G**, Titus to Dalmatia.
1Pe 1: 1 To the exiles of the Dispersion in Pontus, **G**,

GALATIAN See Index to Footnotes

GALATIANS‡ (3) [GALATIA]

Gal 3: 1 You foolish **G**! Who has bewitched you?
2Mc 8:20 the time of the battle against the **G** that took place
8:20 destroyed one hundred twenty thousand **G**

GALBANUM (2)

Ex 30:34 Take sweet spices, stacte, and onycha, and **g**,
Sir 24:15 like **g**, onycha, and stacte,

GALE (1)

Rev 6:13 fig tree drops its winter fruit when shaken by a **g**.

GALEED (2) [=JEGAR-SAHADUTHA]

Ge 31:47 called it Jegar-sahadutha: but Jacob called it **G**.
31:48 you and me today." Therefore he called it **G**,

GALILEAN (5) [GALILEE]

Mt 26:69 "You also were with Jesus the **G**."
Mk 14:70 you are one of them; for you are a **G**."
Lk 22:59 also was with him; for he is a **G**."
23: 6 he asked whether the man was a **G**.
Ac 5:37 After him Judas the **G** rose up at the time of

GALILEANS (5) [GALILEE]

Lk 13: 1 about the **G** whose blood Pilate had mingled
13: 2 "Do you think that because these **G** suffered
13: 2 this way they were worse sinners than all other **G**?
Jn 4:45 When he came to Galilee, the **G** welcomed him,
Ac 2: 7 "Are not all these who are speaking **G**?

GALILEE‡ (84) [GALILEAN, GALILEANS]

Jos 12:23 in Naphath-dor one the king of Goiim in **G**,
20: 7 So they set apart Kedesh in **G** in the hill country
21:32 Kedesh in **G** with its pasture lands,
1Ki 9:11 to Hiram twenty cities in the land of **G**.
2Ki 15:29 Hazor, Gilead, and **G**, all the land of Naphtali;
1Ch 6:76 Kedesh in **G** with its pasture lands,
Isa 9: 1 the land beyond the Jordan, **G** of the nations.
Mt 2:22 he went away to the district of **G**.
3:13 Then Jesus came from **G** to John at the Jordan,
4:12 that John had been arrested, he withdrew to **G**.
4:15 across the Jordan, **G** of the Gentiles—
Mt 4:18 As he walked by the Sea of **G**,
4:23 Jesus went throughout **G**,
4:25 And great crowds followed him from **G**,
15:29 he passed along the Sea of **G**,
17:22 As they were gathering in **G**, Jesus said to them,
19: 1 he left **G** and went to the region of Judea beyond
21:11 "This is the prophet Jesus from Nazareth in **G**."
26:32 after I am raised up, I will go ahead of you to **G**."
27:55 they had followed Jesus from **G** and had provided
28: 7 and indeed he is going ahead of you to **G**;
28:10 go and tell my brothers to go to **G**;
28:16 Now the eleven disciples went to **G**,
Mk 1: 9 from Nazareth of **G** and was baptized by John in
1:14 Now after John was arrested, Jesus came to **G**,
1:16 As Jesus passed along the Sea of **G**,
1:28 to spread throughout the surrounding region of **G**.
1:39 And he went throughout **G**,
3: 7 and a great multitude from **G** followed him;
6:21 and officers and for the leaders of **G**.
7:31 and went by way of Sidon towards the Sea of **G**,
9:30 They went on from there and passed through **G**.
14:28 But after I am raised up, I will go before you to **G**.
15:41 and provided for him when he was in **G**;
16: 7 and Peter that he is going ahead of you to **G**;
Lk 1:26 by God to a town in **G** called Nazareth,
2: 4 Joseph also went from the town of Nazareth in **G**
2:39 they returned to **G**, to their own town of Nazareth.
3: 1 and Herod was ruler of **G**,
4:14 filled with the power of the Spirit, returned to **G**,
4:31 He went down to Capernaum, a city in **G**,
5:17 near by (they had come from every village of **G**
8:26 the country of the Gerasenes, which is opposite **G**.
17:11 through the region between Samaria and **G**.
23: 5 from **G** where he began even to this place."
23:49 the women who had followed him from **G**,
23:55 women who had come with him from **G** followed,
24: 6 while he was still in **G**,
Jn 1:43 The next day Jesus decided to go to **G**.
2: 1 the third day there was a wedding in Cana of **G**,
2:11 Jesus did this, the first of his signs, in Cana of **G**,
4: 3 he left Judea and started back to **G**.
4:43 he went from that place to **G**
4:45 When he came to **G**, the Galileans welcomed him,
4:46 in **G** where he had changed the water into wine.
4:47 he heard that Jesus had come from Judea to **G**,
4:54 that Jesus did after coming from Judea to **G**.
6: 1 this Jesus went to the other side of the Sea of **G**,
7: 1 After this Jesus went about in **G**.
7: 9 After saying this, he remained in **G**.
7:41 "Surely the Messiah does not come from **G**,
7:52 They replied, "Surely you are not also from **G**,
7:52 that no prophet is to arise from **G**."
12:21 who was from Bethsaida in **G**, and said to him,
21: 2 Thomas called the Twin, Nathanael of Cana in **G**,
Ac 1:11 "Men of **G**, why do you stand looking up
9:31 Meanwhile the church throughout Judea, **G**,
10:37 in **G** after the baptism that John announced:
13:31 to those who came up with him from **G**
Tob 1: 2 to the south of Kedesh Naphtali in Upper **G**,
1: 5 in Dan and on all the mountains of **G**.
Jdt 1: 8 and Upper **G** and the great plain of Esdraelon,
15: 5 and in **G** outflanked them with great slaughter,
1Mc 5:14 came from **G** and made a similar report;
5:15 and all **G** of the Gentiles,
5:17 and go and rescue your kindred in **G**;
5:20 to Simon to go to **G**,
5:21 to **G** and fought many battles against the Gentiles,
5:23 Then he took the Jews of **G** and Arbatta,
5:55 in Gilead and their brother Simon was in **G**
10:30 the three districts added to it from Samaria and **G**,
11:63 of Demetrius had come to Kadesh in **G** with
12:47 two thousand of whom he left in **G**,
12:49 Then Trypho sent troops and cavalry into **G** and

GALL (13)

Job 16:13 he pours out my **g** on the ground.
20:25 and the glittering point comes out of their **g**;
La 3:19 and my homelessness is wormwood and **g**!
Mt 27:34 they offered him wine to drink, mixed with **g**;
Ac 8:23 the **g** of bitterness and the chains of wickedness."
Tob 6: 5 "Cut open the fish and take out its **g**, heart,
6: 5 For its **g**, heart, and liver are useful as medicine."
6: 6 the fish the young man gathered together the **g**,
6: 7 in the fish's heart and liver, and in the **g**?"
6: 9 And as for the **g**, anoint a person's eyes
11: 4 to him, "Have the **g** ready."
11: 8 Smear the **g** of the fish on his eyes;
11:11 with the **g** of the fish in his hand,

GALLERIES (2) [GALLERY]

Eze 41:15 together with its **g** on either side,
42: 5 for the **g** took more away from them than from

GALLERY (2) [GALLERIES]

Eze 42: 3 the chambers rose **g** by **g** in three stories.

GALLEY (1)

Isa 33:21 where no **g** with oars can go,

GALLIM (2)

1Sa 25:44 to Palti son of Laish, who was from **G**.
Isa 10:30 Cry aloud, O daughter **G**!

GALLIO (3)

Ac 18:12 But when **G** was proconsul of Achaia,
18:14 **G** said to the Jews, "If it were a matter of crime
18:17 But **G** paid no attention to any of these things.

GALLONS (1)

Jn 2: 6 each holding twenty or thirty **g**.

GALLOPING (3)

Jdg 5:22 "Then loud beat the horses' hoofs with the **g**, **g** of his steeds.
Na 3: 2 **g** horse and bounding chariot!

GALLOWS (15)

Est 2:23 both the men were hanged on the **g**.
5:14 "Let a **g** fifty cubits high be made,
5:14 and he had the **g** made.
6: 4 the king about having Mordecai hanged on the **g**
7: 9 the very **g** that Haman has prepared for Mordecai,
7:10 on the **g** that he had prepared for Mordecai.
8: 7 and they have hanged him on the **g**,
9:13 and let the ten sons of Haman be hanged on the **g**."
9:25 that he and his sons should be hanged on the **g**.
AdE 5:14 "Let a **g** be made, fifty cubits high,
5:14 and so the **g** was prepared.
6: 4 to the king about hanging Mordecai on the **g**
7: 9 Haman has even prepared a **g** for Mordecai,
7: 9 at Haman's house, a **g** fifty cubits high."
7:10 So Haman was hanged on the **g** he had prepared

GAMAD (1)

Eze 27:11 men of **G** were at your towers.

GAMAEL (1)

1Es 8:29 Of the descendants of Ithamar, **G**.

GAMALIEL (7)

Nu 1:10 from Manasseh, **G** son of Pedahzur,
2:20 of the people of Manasseh shall be **G** son
7:54 On the eighth day **G** son of Pedahzur,
7:59 This was the offering of **G** son of Pedahzur.
10:23 the company of the tribe of Manasseh was **G** son
Ac 5:34 But a Pharisee in the council named **G**,
22: 3 but brought up in this city at the feet of **G**,

GAME (11) [GAMES]

Ge 25:28 Isaac loved Esau, because he was fond of **g**;
27: 3 and go out to the field, and hunt **g** for me.
27: 5 Esau went to the field to hunt for **g** and bring it,
27: 7 'Bring me **g**, and prepare for me savory food
27:19 sit up and eat of my **g**, so that you may bless me."
27:25 that I may eat of my son's **g** and bless you."
27:31 "Let my father sit up and eat of his son's **g**,
27:33 that hunted **g** and brought it to me, and I ate it all
Pr 12:27 The lazy do not roast their **g**,
Wis 15:12 But they considered our existence an idle **g**,
Sir 36:24 As the palate tastes the kinds of **g**,

GAMES (1) [GAME]

2Mc 4:18 When the quadrennial **g** were being held at Tyre

GAMMADIMS (KJV) See GAMAD

GAMUL (1)

1Ch 24:17 the twenty-first to Jachin, the twenty-second to **G**,

GANGRENE (1)

2Ti 2:17 and their talk will spread like **g**.

GAP (2) [GAPS]

1Ki 11:27 the **g** in the wall of the city of his father David.
Ne 6: 1 the wall and that there was no **g** left in it

GAPE (1) [GAPED]

1Es 4:19 and **g** at her, and with open mouths stare at her,

GAPED (1) [GAPE]

Job 16:10 They have **g** at me with their mouths;

GAPS (1) [GAP]

Ne 4: 7 and the **g** were beginning to be closed,

GARB (1)

Dt 21:13 discard her captive's **g**, and shall remain

GARDEN (72) [GARDENER, GARDENS]

Ge 2: 8 the LORD God planted a **g** in Eden, in the east;
2: 9 the tree of life also in the midst of the **g**,
2:10 A river flows out of Eden to water the **g**,
2:15 and put him in the **g** of Eden to till it and keep it.
2:16 "You may freely eat of every tree of the **g**;
3: 1 'You shall not eat from any tree in the **g**'?"
3: 2 "We may eat of the fruit of the trees in the **g**;
3: 3 the fruit of the tree that is in the middle of the **g**,
3: 8 of the LORD God walking in the **g** at the time of
3: 8 of the LORD God among the trees of the **g**.
3:10 He said, "I heard the sound of you in the **g**,
3:23 LORD God sent him forth from the **g** of Eden,

Ge 3:24 the east of the g of Eden he placed the cherubim,
13:10 the Jordan was well watered everywhere like the g
Dt 11:10 and irrigate by foot like a vegetable g.
1Ki 21: 2 so that I may have it for a vegetable g,
2Ki 21:18 buried in the g of his house, in the g of Uzza.
21:26 He was buried in his tomb in the g of Uzza;
25: 4 of the gate between the two walls, by the king's g,
Ne 3:15 the wall of the Pool of Shelah of the king's g,
Est 1: 5 in the court of the g of the king's palace.
7: 7 from the feast in wrath and went into the palace g,
7: 8 When the king returned from the palace g to
Job 8:16 and their shoots spread over the g.
SS 4:12 A g locked is my sister, my bride, a g locked,
4:15 a g fountain, a well of living water,
4:16 Blow upon my g that its fragrance may be wafted
4:16 Let my beloved come to his g,
5: 1 I come to my g, my sister, my bride;
6: 2 My beloved has gone down to his g,
Isa 1:30 and like a g without water.
51: 3 her desert like the g of the LORD;
58:11 and you shall be like a watered g,
61:11 and as a g causes what is sown in it to spring up,
Jer 31:12 their life shall become like a watered g,
39: 4 of the city at night by way of the king's g through
52: 7 of the gate between the two walls, by the king's g,
La 2: 6 He has broken down his booth like a g,
Eze 28:13 You were in Eden, the g of God;
31: 8 The cedars in the g of God could not rival it,
31: 8 no tree in the g of God was like it in beauty.
31: 9 the envy of all the trees of Eden that were in the g
36:35 "This land that was desolate has become like the g
Hos 14: 7 they shall flourish as a g;
Joel 2: 3 Before them the land is like the g of Eden,
Mic 7:14 in a forest in the midst of a g land;
Lk 13:19 that someone took and sowed in the g;
Jn 18: 1 the Kidron valley to a place where there was a g,
18:26 asked, "Did I not see you in the g with him?"
19:41 there was a g in the place where he was crucified,
and in the g there was a new tomb
AdE 7: 7 king rose from the banquet and went into the g,
7: 8 When the king returned from the g,
Sir 24:30 like a water channel into a g.
24:31 "I will water my g and drench my flower-beds."
40:17 but kindness is like a g of blessings,
40:27 The fear of the Lord is like a g of blessing,
LtJ 6:71 a thornbush in a g on which every bird perches;
Sus 1: 4 and had a fine g adjoining his house;
1: 7 Susanna would go into her husband's g to walk.
1:15 and wished to bathe in the g, for it was a hot day.
1:17 and shut the g doors so that I can bathe."
1:18 the doors of the g and went out by the side doors
1:20 They said, "Look, the g doors are shut,
1:25 And one of them ran and opened the g doors.
1:26 people in the house heard the shouting in the g,
1:36 "While we were walking in the g alone,
1:36 shut the g doors, and dismissed the maids.
1:38 We were in a corner of the g,
2Es 3: 6 into the g that your right hand had planted before

GARDENER (2) [GARDEN]

Lk 13: 7 So he said to the g, 'See here!
Jn 20:15 Supposing him to be the g, she said to him, "Sir,

GARDENS (11) [GARDEN]

Nu 24: 6 Like palm groves that stretch far away, like g
Ecc 2: 5 I made myself g and parks,
SS 6: 2 to the beds of spices, to pasture his flock in the g,
8:13 O you who dwell in the g,
Isa 1:29 and you shall blush for the g that you have chosen.
65: 3 sacrificing in g and offering incense on bricks;
66:17 and purify themselves to go into the g,
Jer 29: 5 plant g and eat what they produce.
29:28 and plant g and eat what they produce."
Am 4: 9 I laid waste your g and your vineyards;
9:14 and they shall make g and eat their fruit.

GAREB (3)

2Sa 23:38 Ira the Ithrite; G the Ithrite;
1Ch 11:40 Ira the Ithrite, G the Ithrite,
Jer 31:39 straight to the hill G, and shall then turn to Goah.

GARLAND (9) [GARLANDS]

Pr 1: 9 for they are a fair g for your head,
4: 9 She will place on your head a fair g;
14:24 but folly is the g of fools.
Isa 28: 1 Ah, the proud g of the drunkards of Ephraim,
28: 3 under foot will be the proud g of the drunkards
28: 5 that day the LORD of hosts will be a g of glory,
61: 3 to give them a g instead of ashes,
61:10 as a bridegroom decks himself with a g,
Sir 50:12 as he stood by the hearth of the altar with a g

GARLANDS (4) [GARLAND]

Ac 14:13 brought oxen and g to the gates;
Jdt 3: 7 the countryside welcomed him with g and dances
15:13 and wearing g and singing hymns.
3Mc 4: 8 their necks encircled with ropes instead of g,

GARLIC (1)

Nu 11: 5 the melons, the leeks, the onions, and the g;

GARMENT‡ (49) [GARMENTS, UNDERGARMENTS]

Ge 9:23 Then Shem and Japheth took a g,
39:12 she caught hold of his g,
39:12 he left his g in her hand, and fled and ran outside.
39:13 When she saw that he had left his g in her hand
39:15 he left his g beside me, and fled outside."
39:16 she kept his g by her until his master came home,
39:18 he left his g beside me, and fled outside."
Lev 6:27 and when any of its blood is spattered on a g,
13:49 if the disease shows greenish or reddish in the g,
13:57 If it appears again in the g, in warp or woof,
19:19 on a g made of two different materials.
Nu 31:20 You shall purify every g, every article of skin,
Dt 22: 3 you shall do the same with a neighbor's g;
22: 5 nor shall a man put on a woman's g;
24:12 not sleep in the g given you as the pledge.
24:17 you shall not take a widow's g in pledge.
Jdg 8:25 a g, and each threw into it an earring he had taken
2Sa 20: 8 a soldier's g and over it was a belt with a sword
20:12 and threw a g over him.
1Ki 11:29 Ahijah had clothed himself with a new g.
11:30 of the new g he was wearing and tore it
Ezr 9: 3 When I heard this, I tore my g and my mantle,
Ne 5:13 I also shook out the fold of my g and said,
Job 13:28 like a g that is moth-eaten.
30:18 With violence he seizes my g;
38: 9 when I made the clouds its g,
38:14 and it is dyed like a g.
41:13 Who can strip off its outer g?
Ps 73: 6 violence covers them like a g.
102:26 they will all wear out like a g.
104: 2 wrapped in light as with a g.
104: 6 You cover it with the deep as with a g;
109:19 May it be like a g that he wraps around himself,
Pr 20:16 the g of one who has given surety for a stranger;
27:13 the g of one who has given surety for a stranger;
30: 4 Who has wrapped up the waters in a g?
SS 5: 3 I had put off my g; how could I put it on again?
Isa 50: 9 All of them will wear out like a g;
51: 6 the earth will wear out like a g,
51: 8 For the moth will eat them up like a g,
Eze 18: 7 to the hungry and covers the naked with a g,
18:16 to the hungry and covers the naked with a g,
Hag 2:12 in the fold of one's g,
Zec 8:23 grasping his g and saying, "Let us go with you,
Mal 2:16 and covering one's g with violence,
Lk 5:36 "No one tears a piece from a new g and sews it on
5:36 from a new garment and sews it on an old g;
Sir 14:17 All living beings become old like a g,
Bar 5: 1 Take off the g of your sorrow and affliction,

GARMENTS (65) [GARMENT]

Ge 3:21 And the LORD God made g of skins for the man
24:53 and g, and gave them to Rebekah;
27:15 Rebekah took the best g of her elder son Esau,
27:27 and he smelled the smell of his g,
37:34 Then Jacob tore his g, and put sackcloth
38:14 she put off her widow's g,
38:19 and taking off her veil she put on the g
41:42 he arrayed him in g of fine linen,
45:22 To each one of them he gave a set of g;
45:22 of silver and five sets of g.
49:11 he washes his g in wine and his robe in the blood
Lev 6:11 he shall take off his vestments and put on other g,
Nu 15:38 the corners of their g throughout their generations
Jos 9:13 and these g and sandals of ours are worn out from
Jdg 8:26 the pendants and the purple g worn by the kings
14:12 I will give you thirty linen g and thirty festal g.
14:13 you shall give me thirty linen g and thirty festal g."
14:19 the festal g to those who had explained the riddle.
2Sa 10: 4 cut off their g in the middle at their hips,
13:31 The king rose, tore his g, and lay on the ground;
13:31 all his servants who were standing by tore their g.
14: 2 on mourning g, do not anoint yourself with oil,
1Ki 10:25 objects of silver and gold, g, weaponry, spices,
2Ki 5: 5 six thousand shekels of gold, and ten sets of g
7:15 the whole way was littered with g and equipment
1Ch 19: 4 cut off their g in the middle at their hips,
2Ch 9:24 objects of silver and gold, g, weaponry, spices,
Ezr 9: 5 with my g and my mantle torn,
Est 4: 4 she sent g to clothe Mordecai,
Job 37:17 you whose g are hot when the earth is still because
Pr 31:24 She makes linen g and sells them;
Ecc 9: 8 Let your g always be white;
SS 4:11 the scent of your g is like the scent of Lebanon.
Isa 3:23 the g of gauze, the linen g, the turbans, and the
9: 5 and all the g rolled in blood shall be burned as fuel
52: 1 Put on your beautiful g, O Jerusalem, the holy city;
59:17 he put on g of vengeance for clothing,
61:10 for he has clothed me with the g of salvation,
63: 1 from Bozrah in g stained crimson?
63: 2 and your g like theirs who tread the wine press?"
63: 3 their juice spattered on my g,
Jer 36:24 was alarmed, nor did they tear their g.
La 4:14 with blood that no one was able to touch their g.
Eze 16:16 You took some of your g,
16:18 and you took your embroidered g to cover them,
26:16 and strip off their embroidered g.
27:24 These traded with you in choice g,
42:14 on other g before they go near to the area open to
44:19 and they shall put on other g,
Da 3:21 their trousers, their hats, and their other g,
Am 2: 8 down beside every altar on g taken in pledge;
Zec 14:14 gold, silver, and g in great abundance.
Jdt 10: 3 took off her widow's g, bathed her body
AdE 14: 2 She took off her splendid apparel and put on the g
15: 1 she took off the g in which she had worshiped,
Sir 42:13 for from g comes the moth,
LtJ 6:11 They deck their gods out with g
1Mc 5:14 other messengers, with their g torn,
10:62 The king gave orders to take off Jonathan's g and
1Es 8:71 As soon as I heard these things I tore my g
8:73 with my g and my holy mantle torn,
2Es 2:39 the shadow of this age have received glorious g

GARMITE (1)

1Ch 4:19 were the fathers of Keilah the G and Eshtemoa

GARNER (1)

Isa 62: 9 those who g it shall eat it and praise the LORD,

GARNER, GARNERS (KJV) See also BARNS, GRANARY, STOREHOUSES

GARRISON (23) [GARRISONED, GARRISONS]

1Sa 10: 5 at the place where the Philistine g is;
13: 3 Jonathan defeated the g of the Philistines that was
13: 4 When all Israel heard that Saul had defeated the g
13:23 Now a g of the Philistines had gone out to the pass
14: 1 let us go over to the Philistine g on the other side."
14: 4 over to the Philistine g, there was a rocky crag
14: 6 let us go over to the g of these uncircumcised;
14:11 So both of them showed themselves to the g of
14:12 of the g hailed Jonathan and his armor-bearer,
14:15 the g and even the raiders trembled;
2Sa 23:14 and the g of the Philistines was then at Bethlehem.
1Ch 11:16 and the g of the Philistines was then at Bethlehem.
1Mc 4:61 Judas stationed a g there to guard it;
6:18 the g in the citadel kept hemming Israel in around
6:21 of the g escaped from the siege and some of
10:75 for Apollonius had a g in Joppa.
11: 3 the towns he stationed forces as a g in each town.
11:66 took possession of the town, and set a g over it.
12:34 And he stationed a g there to guard it.
12:36 to isolate it so that its g could neither buy nor sell.
14:33 and he placed there a g of Jews.
2Mc 12:18 though in one place he had left a very strong g.
13:20 Judas sent in to the g whatever was necessary.

GARRISONED (1) [GARRISON]

2Mc 10:32 to a stronghold called Gazara, especially well g,

GARRISONS‡ (8) [GARRISON]

2Sa 8: 6 David put g among the Arameans of Damascus;
8:14 He put g in Edom; throughout all Edom he put g,
1Ch 18: 6 Then David put g in Aram of Damascus;
18:13 He put g in Edom; and all the Edomites became
2Ch 17: 2 and set g in the land of Judah,
Jdt 3: 6 to the seacoast with his army and stationed g in
1Mc 9:51 And he placed g in them to harass Israel.

GARRULOUS (2)

Sir 25:20 such is a g wife to a quiet husband.
26:27 *a loud-voiced and g wife is like a trumpet*

GAS (1)

1Es 5:34 the descendants of Masiah, the descendants of G,

GASH (2) [GASHED, GASHES, GASHING]

Jer 47: 5 How long will you g yourselves?
Hos 7:14 they g themselves for grain and wine;

GASHED (1) [GASH]

Jer 41: 5 and their bodies g, bringing grain offerings

GASHES (3) [GASH]

Lev 19:28 You shall not make any g in your flesh for
21: 5 or make any g in their flesh.
Jer 48:37 on all the hands there are g,

GASHING (1) [GASH]

Jer 16: 6 there shall be no g, no shaving of the head

GASHMU See Index to Footnotes

GASP (2) [GASPING]

Isa 42:14 now I will cry out like a woman in labor, I will g
3Mc 5:25 But the Jews, at their last g—

GASPING (3) [GASP]

Jer 4:31 the cry of daughter Zion g for breath,
4Mc 6:11 in sweat, and g heavily for breath, he amazed
11:11 g for breath and in anguish of body,

GAT (KJV) See GATHERED, GET, GOT AWAY, LAID HOLD, RETURNED, SET OUT, STOLE, TRAVELED, WENT, WON

GATAM (3)

Ge 36:11 sons of Eliphaz were Teman, Omar, Zepho, G,

Ge 36:16 **G**, and Amalek; these are the clans of Eliphaz
1Ch 1:36 The sons of Eliphaz: Teman, Omar, Zephi, **G**,

GATE‡ (287) [GATEKEEPER, GATEKEEPERS, GATES, GATEWAY, GATEWAYS]

Ge 22:17 your offspring shall possess the **g** of their enemies,
23:10 of all who went in at the **g** of his city,
23:18 the presence of all who went in at the **g** of his city.
28:17 and this is the **g** of heaven."
34:20 and his son Shechem came to the **g** of their city
34:24 of the city **g** heeded Hamor and his son Shechem;
34:24 all who went out of the **g** of his city.
Ex 27:16 For the **g** of the court there shall be
32:26 then Moses stood in the **g** of the camp,
32:27 and forth from **g** to **g** throughout the camp,
35:17 and the screen for the **g** of the court;
38:14 hangings for one side of the **g** were fifteen cubits,
38:15 the **g** of the court were hangings of fifteen cubits,
38:31 and the bases of the **g** of the court,
39:40 and its bases, and the screen for the **g** of the court,
40: 8 and hang up the screen for the **g** of the court.
40:33 and put up the screen at the **g** of the court.
Nu 4:26 for the entrance of the **g** of the court that is around
Dt 21:19 and bring him out to the elders of his town at the **g**
22:15 to the elders of the city at the **g**.
22:24 both of them to the **g** of that town and stone them
25: 7 at the **g** and say, "My husband's brother refuses
Jos 2: 5 And when it was time to close the **g** at dark,
2: 7 soon as the pursuers had gone out, the **g** was shut.
7: 5 the **g** as far as Shebarim and killing them on
8:29 threw it down at the entrance of the **g** of the city,
20: 4 the **g** of the city, and explain the case to the elders
Jdg 9:35 and stood in the entrance of the **g** of the city,
9:40 Many fell wounded, up to the entrance of the **g**.
9:44 and stood at the entrance of the **g** of the city,
16: 2 and lay in wait for him all night at the city **g**.
16: 3 of the doors of the city **g** and the two posts,
18:16 stood by the entrance of the **g**,
18:17 The priest was standing by the entrance of the **g**
Ru 4: 1 to the **g** and sat down there than the next-of-kin,
4:10 not be cut off from his kindred and from the **g**
4:11 Then all the people who were at the **g**,
1Sa 4:18 over backward from his seat by the side of the **g**;
9:18 Then Saul approached Samuel inside the **g**,
21:13 He scratched marks on the doors of the **g**,
2Sa 10: 8 up in battle array at the entrance of the **g**;
11:23 but we drove them back to the entrance of the **g**.
15: 2 to rise early and stand beside the road into the **g**;
18: 4 So the king stood at the side of the **g**,
18:24 sentinel went up to the roof of the **g** by the wall,
18:33 and went up to the chamber over the **g**, and wept;
19: 8 Then the king got up and took his seat in the **g**.
19: 8 "See, the king is sitting in the **g**";
23:15 from the well of Bethlehem that is by the **g**!"
23:16 from the well of Bethlehem that was by the **g**,
1Ki 17:10 When he came to the **g** of the town,
22:10 at the threshing floor at the entrance of the **g**
2Ki 7: 1 and two measures of barley for a shekel, at the **g**
7: 3 there were four leprous men outside the city **g**,
7:17 on whose hand he leaned to have charge of the **g**;
7:17 the people trampled him to death in the **g**,
7:18 about this time tomorrow in the **g** of Samaria,"
7:20 the people trampled him to death in the **g**.
9:31 As Jehu entered the **g**, she said, "Is it peace,
10: 8 "Lay them in two heaps at the entrance of the **g**
11: 6 (another third being at the **g** Sur and a third at the **g** behind the guards), shall guard the palace;
11:19 the LORD, marching through the **g** of the guards
14:13 Jerusalem from the Ephraim **G** to the Corner **G**,
15:35 He built the upper **g** of the house of the LORD.
23: 8 at the entrance of the **g** of Joshua the governor of
23: 8 which were on the left at the **g** of the city.
25: 4 the soldiers fled by night by the way of the **g**
1Ch 9:18 stationed previously in the king's **g** on
11:17 from the well of Bethlehem that is by the **g**!"
11:18 from the well of Bethlehem that was by the **g**,
16:42 The sons of Jeduthun were appointed to the **g**.
26:16 at the **g** of Shallecheth on the ascending road.
2Ch 18: 9 at the threshing floor at the entrance of the **g**
23: 5 and one third at the **G** of the Foundation;
23:15 the entrance of the Horse **G** of the king's house,
23:20 marching through the upper **g** to the king's house.
24: 8 and set it outside the **g** of the house of the LORD.
25:23 Jerusalem from the Ephraim **G** to the Corner **G**,
26: 9 Uzziah built towers in Jerusalem at the Corner **G**, at the Valley **G**, and at the Angle,
27: 3 He built the upper **g** of the house of the LORD,
31:14 the east **g**, was in charge of the freewill offerings
32: 6 the **g** of the city and spoke encouragingly to them,
33:14 in the valley, reaching the entrance at the Fish **G**;
35:15 The gatekeepers were at each **g**;
Ne 2:13 by the Valley **G** past the Dragon's Spring and to the Dung **G**,
2:14 on to the Fountain **G** and to the King's Pool;
2:15 Then I turned back and entered by the Valley **G**,
3: 1 with his fellow priests and rebuilt the Sheep **G**.
3: 3 The sons of Hassenaah built the Fish **G**;
3: 6 of Besodeiah repaired the Old **G**;
3:13 the inhabitants of Zanoah repaired the Valley **G**;
3:13 of the wall, as far as the Dung **G**.
3:14 of Beth-haccherem, repaired the Dung **G**;
3:15 of the district of Mizpah, repaired the Fountain **G**;
3:26 up to a point opposite the Water **G** on the east and
3:28 Above the Horse **G** the priests made repairs,
Ne 3:29 the keeper of the East **G**, made repairs.
3:31 and of the merchants, opposite the Muster **G**, and
3:32 of the corner and the Sheep **G** the goldsmiths and
8: 1 into the square before the Water **G**.
8: 3 the square before the Water **G** from early morning
8:16 the Water **G** and in the square at the **G** of Ephraim.
12:31 One went to the right on the wall to the Dung **G**;
12:37 At the Fountain **G**, in front of them,
12:37 to the Water **G** on the east.
12:39 and above the **G** of Ephraim, and by the Old **G**, and by the Fish **G** and the Tower of Hananel and the Tower of the Hundred, to the Sheep **G**; and they came to a halt at the **G** of the Guard.
Est 2:19 Mordecai was sitting at the king's **g**.
2:21 while Mordecai was sitting at the king's **g**,
3: 2 at the king's **g** bowed down and did obeisance
3: 3 the king's servants who were at the king's **g** said
4: 2 he went up to the entrance of the king's **g**,
4: 2 for no one might enter the king's **g** clothed
4: 6 the open square of the city in front of the king's **g**,
5: 9 But when Haman saw Mordecai in the king's **g**,
5:13 as I see the Jew Mordecai sitting at the king's **g**."
6:10 do so to the Jew Mordecai who sits at the king's **g**.
6:12 Then Mordecai returned to the king's **g**,
Job 5: 4 they are crushed in the **g**,
29: 7 When I went out to the **g** of the city,
31:21 because I saw I had supporters at the **g**;
Ps 69:12 the subject of gossip for those who sit in the **g**,
118:20 This is the **g** of the LORD;
127: 5 when he speaks with his enemies in the **g**.
Pr 22:22 or crush the afflicted at the **g**;
24: 7 in the **g** they do not open their mouths.
SS 7: 4 in Heshbon, by the **g** of Bath-rabbim.
Isa 14:31 O **g**; cry, O city; melt in fear,
28: 6 strength to those who turn back the battle at the **g**.
29:21 who set a trap for the arbiter in the **g**,
Jer 7: 2 Stand in the **g** of the LORD's house,
17:19 Go and stand in the People's **G**,
19: 2 the son of Hinnom at the entry of the Potsherd **G**,
20: 2 in the stocks that were in the upper Benjamin **G** of
26:10 and took their seat in the entry of the New **G** of
31:38 from the tower of Hananel to the Corner **G**.
31:40 to the corner of the Horse **G** toward the east,
36:10 at the entry of the New **G** of the LORD's house.
37:13 When he reached the Benjamin **G**,
38: 7 king happened to be sitting at the Benjamin **G**,
39: 3 the king of Babylon came and sat in the middle **g**:
39: 4 at night by way of the king's garden through the **g**
52: 7 from the city by night by the way of the **g** between
La 5:14 The old men have left the city **g**,
Eze 8: 5 and there, north of the altar **g**, in the entrance,
8:14 Then he brought me to the entrance of the north **g**
9: 2 six men came from the direction of the upper **g**,
10:19 They stopped at the entrance of the east **g** of
11: 1 up and brought me to the east **g** of the house of
40: 6 and measured the threshold of the **g**,
40: 7 the threshold of the **g** by the vestibule of the **g**
40: 9 and the vestibule of the **g** was at the inner end.
40:10 on either side of the east **g**;
40:13 the **g** from the back of the one recess to the back
40:14 **g** next to the pilaster on every side of the court.
40:15 From the front of the **g** at the entrance to the end of the inner vestibule of the **g** was fifty cubits.
40:19 of the lower **g** to the outer front of the inner court,
40:20 Then he measured the **g** of the outer court
40:21 of the same size as those of the first **g**;
40:22 the same size as those of the **g** that faced toward
40:23 the **g** on the north, as on the east, was a **g** to the
40:23 he measured from **g** to **g**, one hundred cubits.
40:24 and there was a **g** on the south;
40:27 There was a **g** on the south of the inner court;
40:27 and he measured from **g** to **g** toward the south,
40:28 he brought me to the inner court by the south **g**,
40:28 and he measured the south **g**;
40:32 on the east side, and he measured the **g**;
40:35 he brought me to the north **g**, and he measured it;
40:38 a chamber with its door in the vestibule of the **g**,
40:39 And in the vestibule of the **g** were two tables on
40:40 at the entrance of the north **g** were two tables;
40:40 of the vestibule of the **g** were two tables.
40:41 and four tables on the outside of the side of the **g**,
40:44 one at the side of the north **g** facing south,
40:44 the other at the side of the east **g** facing north.
40:48 and the width of the **g** was fourteen cubits;
40:48 sidewalls of the **g** were three cubits on either side.
42:15 he led me out by the **g** that faces east,
43: 1 Then he brought me to the **g**, the **g** facing east.
43: 4 the temple by the **g** facing east,
44: 1 to the outer **g** of the sanctuary, which faces east;
44: 2 The LORD said to me: This **g** shall remain shut;
44: 3 he shall enter by way of the vestibule of the **g**,
44: 4 by way of the north **g** to the front of the temple;
45:19 and the posts of the **g** of the inner court.
46: 1 The **g** of the inner court
46: 2 The prince shall enter by the vestibule of the **g**
46: 2 and shall take his stand by the post of the **g**.
46: 2 and he shall bow down at the threshold of the **g**.
46: 2 but the **g** shall not be closed until evening.
46: 3 of that **g** before the LORD on the sabbaths and on
46: 8 he shall come in by the vestibule of the **g**,
46: 9 the north **g** to worship shall go out by the south **g**;
46: 9 enters by the south **g** shall go out by the north **g**:
46: 9 not return by way of the **g** by which they entered,
46:12 the **g** facing east shall be opened for him;
46:12 and after he has gone out the **g** shall be closed.
46:19 which was at the side of the **g**,
47: 2 Then he brought me out by way of the north **g**,
Eze 47: 2 and led me around on the outside to the outer **g**
48:31 the **g** of Reuben, the **g** of Judah, and the **g** of Levi,
48:32 **g** of Joseph, the **g** of Benjamin, and the **g** of Dan.
48:33 the **g** of Simeon, the **g** of Issachar, and the **g** of Zebulun.
48:34 the **g** of Gad, the **g** of Asher, and the **g** of Naphtali.
Am 1: 5 I will break the **g** bars of Damascus,
5:10 They hate the one who reproves in the **g**,
5:12 and push aside the needy in the **g**.
5:15 and establish justice in the **g**;
Ob 1:13 You should not have entered the **g** of my people
Mic 1: 9 it has reached to the **g** of my people, to Jerusalem.
1:12 down from the LORD to the **g** of Jerusalem.
2:13 they will break through and pass the **g**,
Zep 1:10 a cry will be heard from the Fish **G**,
Zec 14:10 the **G** of Benjamin to the place of the former **g**, to the Corner **G**,
Mt 7:13 "Enter through the narrow **g**;
7:13 for the **g** is wide and the road is easy that leads
7:14 **g** is narrow and the road is hard that leads to life,
Lk 7:12 As he approached the **g** of the town,
16:20 And at his **g** lay a poor man named Lazarus,
Jn 5: 2 Now in Jerusalem by the Sheep **G** there is a pool,
10: 1 anyone who does not enter the sheepfold by the **g**
10: 2 The one who enters by the **g** is the shepherd of
10: 3 The gatekeeper opens the **g** for him,
10: 7 "Very truly, I tell you, I am the **g** for the sheep.
10: 9 I am the **g**. Whoever enters by me
18:16 but Peter was standing outside at the **g**.
18:16 went out, spoke to the woman who guarded the **g**,
Ac 3: 2 at the **g** of the temple called the Beautiful **G** so
3:10 and ask for alms at the Beautiful **G** of the temple;
10:17 for Simon's house and were standing by the **g**.
12:10 they came before the iron **g** leading into the city.
12:13 When he knocked at the outer **g**,
12:14 so overjoyed that, instead of opening the **g**,
12:14 and announced that Peter was standing at the **g**.
12:16 and when they opened the **g**,
16:13 the sabbath day we went outside the **g** by the river,
Heb 13:12 also suffered outside the city **g** in order to sanctify
Tob 11:15 on her way there, very near to the **g** of Nineveh.
11:16 to meet his daughter-in-law at the **g** of Nineveh.
Jdt 8:33 Stand at the town **g** tonight so that I may go out
10: 6 Then they went out to the town **g** of Bethulia
10: 9 "Order the **g** of the town to be opened for me so
10: 9 they ordered the young men to open the **g** for her,
13:11 to the sentries at the gates, "Open, open the **g**!
13:12 the town **g** and summoned the elders of the town.
13:13 They opened the **g** and welcomed them.
AdE 4: 2 He got as far as the king's **g**, and there he stopped,
16:18 at the **g** of Susa with all his household—
Wis 6:14 for she will be found sitting at the **g**.
1Mc 5:22 He pursued them to the **g** of Ptolemais;
2Mc 1: 8 and burned the **g** and shed innocent blood.
1Es 1:16 The gatekeepers were at each **g**;
5:47 a single purpose in the square before the first **g**
7: 9 and the gatekeepers were at each **g**.
9:38 in the open square before the east **g** of the temple;
9:41 He read aloud in the open square before the **g** of
3Mc 5:48 the dust raised by the elephants going out at the **g**

GATEKEEPER (3) [GATE, KEEP]

2Sa 18:26 and the sentinel called to the **g** and said, "See,
1Ch 9:21 of Meshelemiah was **g** at the entrance of the tent
Jn 10: 3 The **g** opens the gate for him,

GATEKEEPERS (42) [GATE, KEEP]

2Ki 7:10 So they came and called to the **g** of the city,
7:11 Then the **g** called out and proclaimed it to
1Ch 9:17 The **g** were: Shallum, Akkub,
9:18 These were the **g** of the camp of the Levites.
9:22 All these, who were chosen as **g** at the thresholds,
9:24 The **g** were on the four sides, east, west, north,
9:26 the four chief **g**, who were Levites, were in charge
15:18 and Mikneiah, and the **g** Obed-edom and Jeiel.
15:23 Berechiah and Elkanah were to be **g** for the ark.
15:24 Obed-edom and Jehiah also were to be **g** for
16:38 of Jeduthun and Hosah were to be **g**.
23: 5 four thousand **g**, and four thousand shall offer
26: 1 As for the divisions of the **g**:
26:12 These divisions of the **g**, corresponding
26:19 the **g** among the Korahites and the sons of Merari.
2Ch 8:14 and the **g** in their divisions for the several gates;
23: 4 who come on duty on the sabbath, shall be **g**,
23:19 the **g** at the gates of the house of the LORD so
34:13 of the Levites were scribes, and officials, and **g**.
35:15 The **g** were at each gate;
Ezr 2:42 The descendants of the **g**:
2:70 the **g**, and the temple servants lived in their towns,
7: 7 of the priests and Levites, the singers and **g**, and
10:24 Of the **g**: Shallum, Telem, and Uri.
Ne 7: 1 and I had set up the doors, and the **g**, the singers,
7: 3 while the **g** are still standing guard,
7:45 The **g**: the descendants of Shallum,
7:73 So the priests, the Levites, the **g**, the singers,
10:28 rest of the people, the priests, the Levites, the **g**,
10:39 and the **g** and the singers are.
11:19 The **g**, Akkub, Talmon and their associates,
12:25 and Akkub were **g** standing guard at
12:45 as did the singers and the **g**,
12:47 the daily portions for the singers and the **g**.
13: 5 and **g**, and the contributions for the priests.
1Es 1:16 The **g** were at each gate;
5:28 The **g**: the descendants of Shallum,
5:46 temple singers, the **g**, and all Israel in their towns.
7: 9 and the **g** were at each gate.

1Es 8: 5 of the priests and Levites and temple singers and **g**
8:22 of the priests or Levites or temple singers or **g**
9:25 Of the **g**: Shallum and Telem.

GATES‡ (147) [GATE]

Ge 24:60 may your offspring gain possession of the **g**
Dt 3: 5 double **g**, and bars, besides a great many villages.
6: 9 on the doorposts of your house and on your **g**.
11:20 on the doorposts of your house and on your **g**,
17: 5 then you shall bring out to your **g** that man or
Jos 6:26 at the cost of his youngest he shall set up its **g**!"
Jdg 5: 8 new gods were chosen, then war was in the **g**.
5:11 down to the **g** marched the people of the LORD.
1Sa 17:52 the Philistines as far as Gath and the **g** of Ekron,
23: 7 in by entering a town that has **g** and bars."
2Sa 18:24 Now David was sitting between the two **g**.
1Ki 16:34 set up its **g** at the cost of his youngest son Segub,
2Ki 23: 8 he broke down the high places of the **g** that were
1Ch 9:23 and their descendants were in charge of the **g** of the
22: 3 for nails for the doors of the **g** and for clamps,
26:13 small and great alike, for their **g**.
2Ch 8: 5 fortified cities, with walls, **g**, and bars,
8:14 gatekeepers in their divisions for the several **g**;
14: 7 and surround them with walls and towers, **g**
23:19 He stationed the gatekeepers at the **g** of the house
31: 2 to minister in the **g** of the camp of the LORD and
Ne 1: 3 and its **g** have been destroyed by fire."
2: 3 lies waste, and its **g** have been destroyed by fire?"
2: 8 to make beams for the **g** of the temple fortress,
2:13 of Jerusalem that had been broken down and its **g**
2:17 how Jerusalem lies in ruins with its **g** burned.
6: 1 up to that time I had not set up the doors in the **g**),
7: 3 "The **g** of Jerusalem are not to be opened until
11:19 who kept watch at the **g**,
12:25 at the storehouses of the **g**.
12:30 they purified the people and the **g** and the wall.
13:19 be dark at the **g** of Jerusalem before the sabbath,
13:19 And I set some of my servants over the **g**,
13:22 and come and guard the **g**,
Job 38:17 Have the **g** of death been revealed to you,
38:17 or have you seen the **g** of deep darkness?
Ps 9:13 the one who lifts me up from the **g** of death,
9:14 and, in the **g** of daughter Zion,
24: 7 Lift up your heads, O **g**!
24: 9 Lift up your heads, O **g**!
87: 2 the **g** of Zion more than all the dwellings of Jacob.
100: 4 Enter his **g** with thanksgiving,
107:18 and they drew near to the **g** of death.
118:19 Open to me the **g** of righteousness,
122: 2 Our feet are standing within your **g**, O Jerusalem.
147:13 For he strengthens the bars of your **g**;
Pr 1:21 at the entrance of the city **g** she speaks:
8: 3 beside the **g** in front of the town, at the entrance of
8:34 watching daily at my **g**, waiting beside my doors.
14:19 the wicked at the **g** of the righteous.
31:23 Her husband is known in the city **g**,
31:31 and let her works praise her in the city **g**.
Isa 3:26 And her **g** shall lament and mourn;
13: 2 the hand for them to enter the **g** of the nobles.
22: 7 and the cavalry took their stand at the **g**.
24:12 the **g** are battered into ruins.
26: 2 Open the **g**, so that the righteous nation
38:10 I am consigned to the **g** of Sheol for the rest
45: 1 and the **g** shall not be closed:
54:12 of rubies, your **g** of jewels, and all your wall
60:11 Your **g** shall always be open;
60:18 shall call your walls Salvation, and your **g** Praise.
62:10 Go through, go through the **g**,
Jer 1:15 at the entrance of the **g** of Jerusalem,
7: 2 you that enter these **g** to worship the LORD.
14: 2 Judah mourns and her **g** languish;
15: 7 with a winnowing fork in the **g** of the land;
17:19 and in all the **g** of Jerusalem,
17:20 the inhabitants of Jerusalem, who enter by these **g**.
17:21 a burden on the sabbath day or bring it in by the **g**
17:24 and bring in no burden by the **g** of this city on
17:25 by the **g** of this city kings who sit on the throne
17:27 to carry in no burden through the **g** of Jerusalem
17:27 then I will kindle a fire in its **g**;
22: 2 and your people who enter these **g**.
22: 4 the **g** of this house shall enter kings who sit on
22:19 and thrown out beyond the **g** of Jerusalem.
49:31 that has no **g** or bars, that lives alone.
51:58 and her high **g** shall be burned with fire.
La 1: 4 all her **g** are desolate, her priests groan;
2: 9 Her **g** have sunk into the ground;
4:12 that foe or enemy could enter the **g** of Jerusalem.
Eze 21:15 At all their **g** I have set the point of the sword.
21:22 to set battering rams against the **g**,
26:10 he enters your **g** like those entering a breached city.
38:11 without walls, and having no bars or **g**";
40:18 The pavement ran along the side of the **g**,
40:18 corresponding to the length of the **g**;
44:11 having oversight at the **g** of the temple,
44:17 When they enter the **g** of the inner court,
44:17 while they minister at the **g** of the inner court,
48:31 three **g**, the gate of Reuben, the gate of Judah,
48:31 **g** of the city being named after the tribes of Israel.
48:32 three **g**, the gate of Joseph, the gate of Benjamin,
48:33 three **g**, the gate of Simeon, the gate of Issachar,
48:34 three **g**, the gate of Gad, the gate of Asher,
Ob 1:11 and foreigners entered his **g** and cast lots
Na 2: 6 The river **g** are opened, the palace trembles.
3:13 The **g** of your land are wide open to your foes;
3:13 fire has devoured the bars of your **g**.
Zec 8:16 render in your **g** judgments that are true and make
Mt 16:18 and the **g** of Hades will not prevail against it.
24:33 you know that he is near, at the very **g**.
Mk 13:29 you know that he is near, at the very **g**.
Ac 9:24 the **g** day and night so that they might kill him;
14:13 brought oxen and garlands to the **g**;
Rev 21:12 It has a great, high wall with twelve **g**,
21:12 and at the **g** twelve angels,
21:12 the **g** are inscribed the names of the twelve tribes
21:13 on the east three **g**, on the north three **g**, on the
south three **g**, and on the west three **g**.
21:15 of gold to measure the city and its **g** and walls.
21:21 And the twelve **g** are twelve pearls, each of the **g**
is a single pearl,
21:25 Its **g** will never be shut by day—
22:14 to the tree of life and may enter the city by the **g**.
Tob 13:16 The **g** of Jerusalem will be built with sapphire
13:17 The **g** of Jerusalem will sing hymns of joy,
Jdt 1: 3 At its **g** he raised towers one hundred cubits high
1: 4 He made its **g** seventy cubits high
13:10 up the mountain to Bethulia, and came to its **g**.
13:11 a distance Judith called out to the sentries at the **g**,
Wis 16:13 you lead mortals down to the **g** of Hades
Sir 49:13 set up **g** and bars, and rebuilt our ruined houses.
LtJ 6:18 And just as the **g** are shut on every side
1Mc 4:38 the altar profaned, and the **g** burned.
4:57 they restored the **g** and the chambers for
5:47 of the town shut them out and blocked up the **g**
9:50 and Tephon, with high walls and **g** and bars.
10:75 but the people of the city closed its **g**,
10:76 people of the city became afraid and opened the **g**,
11: 2 and the people of the towns opened their **g** to him
12:38 he fortified it and installed **g** with bolts.
12:48 people of Ptolemais closed the **g** and seized him,
13:33 with high towers and great walls and **g** and bolts,
15:39 to build up Kedron and fortify its **g**,
2Mc 3:19 to the **g**, and some to the walls,
8:33 they burned those who had set fire to the sacred **g**,
10:36 Others broke open the **g** and let in the rest of
12: 7 Then, because the city's **g** were closed,
3Mc 5:51 as they stood now at the **g** of death.
6:18 and opened the heavenly **g**,
6:31 or rather, who stood at its **g**,
2Es 3:19 through the four **g** of fire and earthquake and wind
4Mc 3:13 Eluding the sentinels at the **g**,

GATEWAY‡ (13) [GATE, WAY]

Ge 19: 1 and Lot was sitting in the **g** of Sodom.
2Sa 3:27 Joab took him aside in the **g** to speak
Eze 8: 3 of God to Jerusalem, to the entrance of the **g** of
11: 1 There, at the entrance of the **g**,
26: 2 "Aha, broken is the **g** of the peoples;
40: 3 and he was standing in the **g**.
40: 6 Then he went into the **g** facing east,
40: 8 Then he measured the inner vestibule of the **g**,
40: 9 he measured the vestibule of the **g**, eight cubits;
40:11 he measured the width of the opening of the **g**,
40:11 and the width of the **g**, thirteen cubits.
40:16 with shutters on the inside of the **g** all around,
40:44 On the outside of the inner **g** there were chambers

GATEWAYS (2) [GATE, WAY]

Ps 65: 8 the **g** of the morning and the evening shout
Jdt 7:22 in the streets of the town and in the **g**;

GATH‡ (37) [GATH-HEPHER, GATH-RIMMON, GITTITE, GITTITES]

Jos 11:22 some remained only in Gaza, in **G**,
13: 3 Ashkelon, **G**, and Ekron), and those of the Avvim,
1Sa 5: 8 The inhabitants of **G** replied,
5: 8 So they moved the ark of the God of Israel to **G**.
5: 9 But after they had brought it to **G**,
6:17 one for Ashkelon, one for **G**, one for Ekron;
7:14 to Israel, from Ekron to **G**;
17: 4 of **G**, whose height was six cubits and a span.
17:23 the Philistine of **G**, Goliath by name,
17:52 a shout and pursued the Philistines as far as **G** and
17:52 on the way from Shaaraim as far as **G** and Ekron.
21:10 he went to King Achish of **G**.
21:12 and was very much afraid of King Achish of **G**.
27: 2 to King Achish son of Maoch of **G**.
27: 3 David stayed with Achish at **G**, he and his troops,
27: 4 When Saul was told that David had fled to **G**,
27:11 nor woman alive to be brought back to **G**,
2Sa 1:20 in **G**, proclaim it not in the streets of Ashkelon;
15:18 from **G**, passed on before the king.
21:20 There was again war at **G**,
21:22 These four were descended from the giants in **G**;
1Ki 2:39 to King Achish son of Maacah of **G**.
2:39 When it was told Shimei, "Your slaves are in **G**,"
2:40 and went to Achish in **G**, to search for his slaves;
2:40 Shimei went and brought his slaves from **G**.
2:41 that Shimei had gone from Jerusalem to **G**
2Ki 12:17 fought against **G**, and took it.
1Ch 7:21 Now the people of **G**, who were born in the land,
8:13 who put to flight the inhabitants of **G**);
18: 1 he took **G** and its villages from the Philistines.
20: 6 Again there was war at **G**,
20: 8 These were descended from the giants in **G**;
2Ch 11: 8 **G**, Mareshah, Ziph,
26: 6 the wall of **G** and the wall of Jabneh and the wall
Ps 56: T *when the Philistines seized him in* **G**.
Am 6: 2 then go down to **G** of the Philistines.
Mic 1:10 Tell it not in **G**, weep not at all;

GATH-HEPHER (2) [GATH, HEPHER]

Jos 19:13 on the east toward the sunrise to **G**, to Eth-kazin,
2Ki 14:25 the prophet, who was from **G**.

GATH-RIMMON (4) [GATH, RIMMON]

Jos 19:45 Jehud, Bene-berak, **G**,
21:24 **G** with its pasture lands—four towns.
21:25 and **G** with its pasture lands—two towns.
1Ch 6:69 with its pasture lands, **G** with its pasture lands;

GATHER‡ (152) [GATHERED, GATHERING, GATHERINGS, GATHERS, GRAPE-GATHERER, GRAPE-GATHERERS, INGATHERING]

Ge 31:46 And Jacob said to his kinsfolk, "**G** stones,"
34:30 if they **g** themselves against me and attack me,
41:35 Let them **g** all the food of these good years
49: 1 Then Jacob called his sons, and said: "**G** around,
Ex 5: 7 let them go and **g** straw for themselves.
5:12 throughout the land of Egypt, to **g** stubble
16: 4 and each day the people shall go out and **g** enough
16: 5 it will be twice as much as they **g** on other days."
16:16 '**G** as much of it as each of you needs,
16:26 Six days you shall **g** it;
16:27 the seventh day some of the people went out to **g**,
23:10 For six years you shall sow your land and **g**
23:16 you **g** in from the field the fruit of your labor.
Lev 19: 9 or **g** the gleanings of your harvest.
19:10 or **g** the fallen grapes of your vineyard;
23:22 or **g** the gleanings of your harvest;
25: 3 and six years you shall prune your vineyard, and **g**
25: 5 the aftergrowth of your harvest or **g** the grapes
25:20 if we may not sow or **g** in our crop?
Nu 11:16 "**G** for me seventy of the elders of Israel,
19: 9 Then someone who is clean shall **g** up the ashes of
21:16 the LORD said to Moses, "**G** the people together,
Dt 11:14 and you will **g** in your grain, your wine,
13:16 All of its spoil you shall **g** into its public square;
24:21 When you **g** the grapes of your vineyard,
28:38 into the field but shall **g** little in,
28:39 you shall neither drink the wine nor **g** the grapes,
30: 4 from there the LORD your God will **g** you,
Jos 2:18 not **g** into your house your father and mother,
Ru 2: 7 and **g** among the sheaves behind the reapers.'
1Sa 7: 5 Then Samuel said, "**G** all Israel at Mizpah,
2Sa 12:28 Now, then, **g** the rest of the people together,
2Ki 4:39 One of them went out into the field to **g** herbs;
22:20 Therefore, I will **g** you to your ancestors,
1Ch 16:35 and **g** and rescue us from among the nations,
22: 2 to **g** together the aliens who were residing in
2Ch 24: 5 to the cities of Judah and **g** money from all Israel
34:28 I will **g** you to your ancestors and you shall
Ne 1: 9 I will **g** them from there and bring them to
12:44 to **g** into them the portions required by the law for
Est 2: 3 of his kingdom to **g** all the beautiful young virgins
4:16 **g** all the Jews to be found in Susa,
Job 34:14 and **g** to himself his breath,
Ps 39: 6 they heap up, and do not know who will **g**.
41: 6 while their hearts **g** mischief;
47: 9 The princes of the peoples **g** as the people of
50: 5 "**G** to me my faithful ones,
102:22 when peoples **g** together, and kingdoms,
104:28 when you give to them, they **g** it up;
106:47 and **g** us from among the nations,
Pr 13:11 but those who **g** little by little will increase it.
Ecc 3: 5 and a time to **g** stones together;
SS 5: 1 I **g** my myrrh with my spice,
6: 2 to pasture his flock in the gardens, and to **g** lilies.
Isa 11:12 and **g** the dispersed of Judah from the four corners
13:14 or like sheep with no one to **g** them,
17: 5 And it shall be as when reapers **g** standing grain
34:15 there too the buzzards shall **g**,
40:11 he will **g** the lambs in his arms,
43: 5 and from the west I will **g** you;
43: 9 Let all the nations **g** together,
49:18 they all **g**, they come to you.
54: 7 but with great compassion I will **g** you.
56: 8 I will **g** others to them besides those already
60: 4 they all **g** together, they come to you;
62: 9 and those who **g** it shall drink it in my holy courts.
66:18 and I am coming to **g** all nations and tongues;
Jer 3:17 and all nations shall **g** to it,
4: 5 shout aloud and say, "**G** together,
7:18 The children **g** wood, the fathers kindle fire,
8:13 When I wanted to **g** them, says the LORD,
8:14 **G** together, let us go into the fortified cities
9:22 and no one shall **g** them."
10:17 **G** up your bundle from the ground,
23: 3 Then I myself will **g** the remnant of my flock out
29:14 and I will restore your fortunes and **g** you from all
31: 8 and **g** them from the farthest parts of the earth,
31:10 say, "He who scattered Israel will **g** him,
32:37 to **g** them from all the lands to which I drove them
40:10 but as for you, **g** wine and summer fruits and oil,
49: 5 each headlong, with no one to **g** the fugitives.
49:14 "**G** yourselves together and come against her,
Eze 11:17 I will **g** you from the peoples,
16:37 I will **g** all your lovers,
16:37 I will **g** them against you from all around,
20:34 from the peoples and **g** you out of the countries
20:41 and **g** you out of the countries
22:19 I will **g** you into the midst of Jerusalem.
22:20 so I will **g** you in my anger and in my wrath,
22:21 I will **g** you and blow upon you with the fire

Eze 28:25 When I g the house of Israel from the peoples
29:13 the end of forty years I will g the Egyptians from
34:13 I will bring them out from the peoples and g them
36:24 and g you from all the countries,
37:21 and will g them from every quarter,
39:17 and come, g from all around to the sacrificial feast
Hos 8:10 I will now g them up.
9:6 if they escape destruction, Egypt shall g them,
Joel 1:14 G the elders and all the inhabitants of the land
2:16 g the people. Sanctify the congregation;
2:16 g the children, even infants at the breast.
3:2 I will g all the nations and bring them down to
3:11 all you nations all around, g yourselves there.
Mic 2:12 I will surely g all of you, O Jacob, I will g the survivors of Israel;
4:6 the lame and g those who have been driven away,
Na 3:18 on the mountains with no one to g them.
Hab 1:9 they g captives like sand.
2:5 They g all nations for themselves,
Zep 2:1 G together, g, O shameless nation,
3:8 For my decision is to g nations,
3:19 And I will save the lame and g the outcast,
3:20 at the time when I g you;
Zec 10:8 I will signal for them and g them in,
10:10 and g them from Assyria;
14:2 I will g all the nations against Jerusalem to battle,
Mt 3:12 and will g his wheat into the granary;
6:26 they neither sow nor reap nor g into barns,
12:30 and whoever does not g with me scatters.
13:28 'Then do you want us to go and g them?'
13:30 but g the wheat into my barn.' "
23:37 to g your children together as
24:28 Wherever the corpse is, there the vultures will g.
24:31 and they will g his elect from the four winds,
25:26 and g where I did not scatter?
Mk 13:27 and g his elect from the four winds,
Lk 3:17 to clear his threshing floor and to g the wheat
5:15 many crowds would g to hear him and to be cured
11:23 and whoever does not g with me scatters.
13:34 to g your children together as
17:37 "Where the corpse is, there the vultures will g."
Jn 6:12 "G up the fragments left over,
11:52 but to g into one the dispersed children of God.
Ac 5:16 A great number of people would also g from
Eph 1:10 to g up all things in him,
Rev 14:18 "Use your sharp sickle and g the clusters of
19:17 "Come, g for the great supper of God,
20:8 Gog and Magog, in order to g them for battle;
Tob 13:5 He will g you from all the nations
AdE 4:16 "Go and g all the Jews who are in Susa and fast
Sir 36:13 G all the tribes of Jacob,
2Mc 1:27 G together our scattered people,
2:18 on us and will g us from everywhere under heaven
1Es 4:18 men g gold and silver or any other beautiful thing,
3Mc 7:3 to g together the Jews of the kingdom in a body
2Es 5:36 and g for me the scattered raindrops,
13:39 for your seeing him g to himself another multitude
14:23 He answered me and said, "Go and g the people,
16:25 The trees shall bear fruit, but who will g it?
16:43 like one who will not g the grapes;
16:46 for strangers shall g their fruits,

GATHERED (270) [GATHER]

Ge 1:9 "Let the waters under the sky be g together
1:10 and the waters that were g together he called Seas.
12:5 and all the possessions that they had g,
25:8 and was g to his people.
25:17 he breathed his last and died, and was g
29:3 and when all the flocks were g there,
29:7 it is not time for the animals to be g together.
29:8 "We cannot until all the flocks are g together,
29:22 So Laban g together all the people of the place,
35:29 he died and was g to his people,
37:7 then your sheaves g around it,
41:48 He g up all the food of the seven years
49:29 saying to them, "I am about to be g to my people.
49:33 breathed his last, and was g to his people.
Ex 8:14 they g them together in heaps, and the land stank.
16:18 those who g much had nothing over, and those who g little had no shortage; they g as much as
16:21 Morning by morning they g it,
16:22 On the sixth day they g twice as much food,
32:1 the people g around Aaron, and said to him,
32:26 And all the sons of Levi g around him.
Lev 23:39 when you have g in the produce of the land,
Nu 10:7 But when the assembly is to be g, you shall blow,
11:8 The people went around and g it,
11:24 and he g seventy elders of the people,
11:32 the least anyone g was ten homers;
14:35 to all this wicked congregation g together
16:11 and all your company have g together against
20:2 they g together against Moses and against Aaron.
20:10 Moses and Aaron g the assembly together before
20:24 "Let Aaron be g to his people.
20:26 But Aaron shall be g to his people,
21:23 Sihon g all his people together,
27:3 the company of those who g themselves together
27:13 you also shall be g to your people,
31:2 afterward you shall be g to your people."
Dt 1:25 and g some of the land's produce,
16:13 when you have g in the produce
32:50 on the mountain that you ascend and shall be g
32:50 on Mount Hor and was g to his kin;
Jos 9:2 they g together with one accord to fight Joshua
10:5 g their forces, and went up with all their armies
10:6 of the Amorites who live in the hill country are g
Jos 22:12 the whole assembly of the Israelites g at Shiloh,
24:1 Then Joshua g all the tribes of Israel to Shechem,
Jdg 2:10 that whole generation was g to their ancestors,
9:27 the field and g the grapes from their vineyards,
9:47 of the Tower of Shechem were g together.
11:20 so Sihon g all his people together,
12:4 Then Jephthah g all the men of Gilead and fought
16:23 of the Philistines g to offer a great sacrifice
20:11 So all the men of Israel g against the city,
1Sa 5:8 and g together all the lords of the Philistines,
5:11 They sent therefore and g together all the lords of
7:6 So they g at Mizpah, and drew water
7:7 the Philistines heard that the people of Israel had g
8:4 of Israel g together and came to Samuel at Ramah,
17:1 Now the Philistines g their armies for battle;
17:1 they were g at Socoh, which belongs to Judah,
17:2 and the Israelites g and encamped in the valley
20:38 So Jonathan's boy g up the arrows and came
22:2 and everyone who was discontented g to him;
28:1 In those days the Philistines g their forces for war,
28:4 Saul g all Israel, and they encamped at Gilboa.
29:1 Now the Philistines g all their forces at Aphek,
2Sa 2:30 and when he had g all the people together,
6:1 David again g all the chosen men of Israel,
10:15 they g themselves together.
10:17 When it was told David, he g all Israel together,
12:29 So David g all the people together and went
14:14 on the ground, which cannot be g up.
17:11 But my counsel is that all Israel be g to you,
21:13 they g the bones of those who had been impaled.
23:9 when they defied the Philistines who were g there
23:11 The Philistines g together at Lehi,
1Ki 10:26 Solomon g together chariots and horses;
11:24 He g followers around him and became leader of
20:1 King Ben-hadad of Aram g all his army together;
22:6 Then the king of Israel g the prophets together,
2Ki 4:39 a wild vine and g from it a lapful of wild gourds,
22:20 and you shall be g to your grave in peace;
23:1 the elders of Judah and Jerusalem should be g
1Ch 11:1 all Israel g together to David at Hebron and said,
11:13 at Pas-dammim when the Philistines were g there
15:4 Then David g together the descendants of Aaron
19:17 David was informed, he g all Israel together,
2Ch 1:14 Solomon g together chariots and horses;
12:5 who had g at Jerusalem because of Shishak,
13:7 and certain worthless scoundrels g around him
15:9 He g all Judah and Benjamin,
15:10 They were g at Jerusalem in the third month of
18:5 Then the king of Israel g the prophets together,
23:2 around through Judah and g the Levites from all
28:24 Ahaz g together the utensils of the house of God,
29:15 They g their brothers, sanctified themselves,
32:4 A great many people were g,
32:6 and g them together to him in the square at
34:28 to your ancestors and you shall be g to your grave
34:29 the king sent word and g together all the elders
Ezr 3:1 the people g together in Jerusalem.
7:28 and I g leaders from Israel to go up with me.
8:15 I g them by the river that runs to Ahava,
9:4 g around me while I sat appalled until
10:1 women, and children g to him out of Israel;
Ne 5:16 and all my servants were g there for the work.
8:1 all the people g together into the square before
12:28 The companies of the singers g together from
13:11 I g them together and set them in their stations.
Est 2:8 when many young women were g in the citadel
2:19 When the virgins were being g together,
9:2 the Jews g in their cities throughout all
9:15 in Susa g also on the fourteenth day of the month
9:16 in the king's provinces also g to defend their lives,
9:18 the Jews who were in Susa g on the thirteenth day
Job 15:27 and g fat upon their loins,
Ps 7:7 Let the assembly of the peoples be g around you,
33:7 He g the waters of the sea as in a bottle;
35:15 But at my stumbling they g in glee, they g together
107:3 and g in from the lands,
Pr 27:25 and the herbage of the mountains is g,
30:4 Who has g the wind in the hollow of the hand?
Ecc 2:8 I also g for myself silver and gold and the treasure
Isa 10:14 so I have g all the earth;
24:22 They will be g together like prisoners in a pit;
27:12 and you will be g one by one, O people of Israel.
33:4 Spoil was g as the caterpillar gathers;
34:16 and his spirit has g them.
49:5 and that Israel might be g to him,
56:8 to them besides those already g.
60:7 All the flocks of Kedar shall be g to you,
Jer 8:2 and they shall not be g or buried;
25:33 They shall not be lamented, or g, or buried;
26:9 And all the people g around Jeremiah in the house
40:12 they g wine and summer fruits in great abundance.
40:15 that all the Judeans who are g around you would
Eze 28:4 and have g gold and silver into your treasuries.
29:5 you shall fall in the open field, and not be g
38:8 a land where people were g from many nations on
38:12 and the people who were g from the nations,
39:27 the peoples and g them from their enemies' lands,
39:28 and then g them into their own land.
Da 3:27 and the king's counselors g together and saw that
Hos 1:11 of Israel shall be g together, and they shall appoint
10:10 be g against them when they are punished
Mic 1:7 for as the wages of a prostitute she g them,
4:12 he has g them as sheaves to the threshing floor.
7:1 after the summer fruit has been g,
Mt 7:16 Are grapes g from thorns, or figs from thistles?
13:2 Such great crowds g around him that he got into
16:9 and how many baskets you g?
Mt 16:10 and how many baskets you g?
18:20 For where two or three are g in my name,
22:10 the streets and g all whom they found, both good
22:34 the Sadducees, they g together,
22:41 Now while the Pharisees were g together,
25:32 All the nations will be g before him,
26:3 the chief priests and the elders of the people g in
26:57 in whose house the scribes and the elders had g.
27:17 So after they had g, Pilate said to them,
27:27 and they g the whole cohort around him.
27:62 the chief priests and the Pharisees g before Pilate
Mk 1:33 And the whole city was g around the door.
2:2 So many g around that there was no longer room
2:13 whole crowd g around him, and he taught them.
4:1 Such a very large crowd g around him that he got
5:21 a great crowd g around him;
6:30 The apostles g around Jesus,
7:1 of the scribes who had come from Jerusalem g
10:1 And crowds again g around him;
Lk 6:44 Figs are not g from thorns,
8:4 When a great crowd g and people from town
9:17 What was left over was g up,
12:1 Meanwhile, when the crowd g by the thousands,
15:13 A few days later the younger son g all he had
22:66 g together, and they brought him to their council.
23:48 And when all the crowds who had g there
24:33 the eleven and their companions g together.
Jn 6:13 So they g them up, and from the fragments of
10:24 So the Jews g around him and said to him,
15:6 such branches are g, thrown into the fire,
21:2 G there together were Simon Peter,
Ac 2:6 at this sound the crowd g and was bewildered,
4:26 and the rulers have g together against the Lord and
4:27 g together against your holy servant Jesus,
4:31 place in which they were g together was shaken;
12:12 where many had g and were praying.
13:44 The next sabbath almost the whole city g to hear
15:30 When they g the congregation together,
16:13 down and spoke to the women who had g there.
19:25 These he g together, with the workers of
28:3 Paul had g a bundle of brushwood
2Th 2:1 of our Lord Jesus Christ and our being g together
Rev 14:19 So the angel swung his sickle over the earth and g
19:19 the earth with their armies g to make war against
Tob 6:6 the young man g together the gall, heart, and liver;
13:13 for they will be g together and will praise the Lord
14:7 and are truly mindful of God will be g together;
Jdt 4:3 all the people of Judea had just now g together,
7:23 g around Uzziah and the rulers of the town
10:18 They came and g around her as she stood outside
13:13 they lit a fire to give light, and g around them.
15:12 All the women of Israel g to see her,
16:22 after her husband Manasseh died and was g
AdE 2:8 and many girls were g in Susa the capital
9:15 The Jews who were in Susa g on the fourteenth
9:16 other Jews in the kingdom g to defend themselves,
10:8 The nations are those that g to destroy the name of
Sir 25:3 If you g nothing in your youth,
47:18 you g gold like tin and amassed silver like lead.
Bar 4:37 they are coming, g from east and west,
5:5 toward the east, and see your children g from west
Sus 1:28 the people g at the house of her husband Joakim,
1Mc 1:4 He g a very strong army and ruled over countries,
2:69 Then he blessed them, and was g to his ancestors.
3:9 he g in those who were perishing.
3:10 now g together Gentiles and a large force
3:13 heard that Judas had g a large company,
3:27 and he sent and g all the forces of his kingdom,
3:46 Then they g together and went to Mizpah,
5:9 Now the Gentiles in Gilead g together against
5:10 Gentiles around us have g together to destroy us.
5:15 had g together against them "to annihilate us."
5:37 After these things Timothy g another army
5:38 "All the Gentiles around us have g to him;
5:45 Then Judas g together all the Israelites in Gilead,
5:64 People g to them and praised them.
6:20 They g together and besieged the citadel in
10:61 renegades, g together against him to accuse him;
11:1 Then the king of Egypt g great forces,
11:55 All the troops that Demetrius had discharged g
11:60 and all the army of Syria g to him as allies.
12:37 So they g together to rebuild the city;
13:6 for all the nations have g together out of hatred
14:7 He g a host of captives;
14:30 became their high priest, and was g to his people.
2Mc 4:39 the populace g against Lysimachus,
8:1 and so they g about six thousand.
8:16 But Maccabeus g his forces together,
10:21 he g the leaders of the people,
10:24 g a tremendous force of mercenaries and collected
11:2 g about eighty thousand infantry
14:23 but dismissed the flocks of people that had g.
14:30 So he g not a few of his men,
1Es 5:47 they g with a single purpose in the square before
8:27 and I g men from Israel to go up with me."
8:72 at the word of the Lord of Israel g around me,
8:91 there g around him a very great crowd of men
9:38 the whole multitude g with one accord in
3Mc 1:21 the supplications of those g there because of what
3:1 and he ordered that all should promptly be g
6:25 and foolishly g every one of them here?
2Es 1:30 I g you as a hen gathers her chicks
6:3 the innumerable hosts of angels were g together,
6:42 the waters to be g together in a seventh part of
6:47 where the water had been g together,
6:50 where the water had been g together could
7:*95* being g into their chambers and guarded by angels

2Es 7:*101* afterwards they shall be **g** in their habitations."
11: 2 and the clouds were **g** around it.
12:40 they all **g** together, from the least to the greatest,
13: 5 of people were **g** together from the four winds
13: 8 and saw that all who had **g** together against him,
13:34 and an innumerable multitude shall be **g** together,
13:47 you saw the multitude **g** together in peace.
13:49 the multitude of the nations that are **g** together,
14:27 and I **g** all the people together, and said,
16:30 or just as when a vineyard is **g**,
4Mc 18:23 with their victorious mother are **g** together into

GATHERING (18) [GATHER]

Ex 16:17 The Israelites did so, some **g** more, some less.
Nu 11:32 and night and all the next day, **g** the quails;
15:32 they found a man **g** sticks on the sabbath day.
15:33 Those who found him **g** sticks brought him
Dt 30: 3 **g** you again from all the peoples among whom
2Sa 22:12 thick clouds, a **g** of water.
1Ki 17:10 a widow was there **g** sticks;
17:12 I am now **g** a couple of sticks,
Ecc 2:26 to the sinner he gives the work of **g** and heaping,
Isa 13: 4 an uproar of kingdoms, of nations **g** together!
Mt 13:29 in **g** the weeds you would uproot the wheat along
17:22 As they were **g** in Galilee, Jesus said to them,
25:24 and **g** where you did not scatter seed;
Jn 4:36 and is **g** fruit for eternal life,
Heb 12:22 and to innumerable angels in festal **g**,
Sir 26: 5 Slander in the city, the **g** of a mob,
1Mc 13: 2 up to Jerusalem, and **g** the people together
2Mc 14:15 the Jews heard of Nicanor's coming and the **g** of

GATHERINGS (2) [GATHER]

Jer 6:11 and on the **g** of young men as well;
Sir 42:11 and put you to shame in public **g**.

GATHERS (17) [GATHER]

Nu 19:10 The one who **g** the ashes of
Ps 147: 2 he **g** the outcasts of Israel.
Pr 6: 8 and **g** its sustenance in harvest.
10: 5 A child who **g** in summer is prudent,
28: 8 by exorbitant interest **g** it for another who is kind
Isa 10:14 and as one **g** eggs that have been forsaken,
33: 4 Spoil was gathered as the caterpillar **g**;
56: 8 who **g** the outcasts of Israel,
Eze 22:20 As one **g** silver, bronze, iron, lead,
Hab 1:15 he **g** them in his seine; so he rejoices and exults.
Mt 23:37 as a hen **g** her brood under her wings,
Lk 13:34 as a hen **g** her brood under her wings,
Sir 21: 8 like one who **g** stones for his burial mound.
51:12 *Give thanks to him who g the dispersed of Israel,*
2Mc 2: 7 until God **g** his people together again
2Es 1:30 as a hen **g** her chicks under her wings.
4Mc 2: 9 so that one neither gleans the harvest nor **g**

GAUL See Index to Footnotes

GAULS (1)

1Mc 8: 2 that they were doing among the **G**,

GAUNT (1)

Ps 109:24 through fasting; my body has become **g**.

GAUNTLETS (1)

4Mc 9:26 fitting themselves with iron **g** having sharp hooks,

GAUZE (2)

Isa 3:23 the garments of **g**, the linen garments, the turbans,
AdE 1: 6 There were coverings of **g**,

GAVE‡ (718) [GIVE]

Ge 2:20 The man **g** names to all cattle,
3: 6 and she also **g** some to her husband,
3:12 "The woman whom you **g** to be with me, she **g** me
fruit from the tree, and I ate."
9: 3 and just as I **g** you the green plants,
12:20 And Pharaoh **g** his men orders concerning him;
14:20 And Abram **g** him one tenth of everything.
16: 3 and **g** her to her husband Abram as a wife.
16: 5 I **g** my slave-girl to your embrace,
18: 7 and **g** it to the servant, who hastened to prepare it.
20:14 and oxen, and male and female slaves, and **g** them
21: 3 Abraham **g** the name Isaac
21:14 and **g** it to Hagar, putting it on her shoulder,
21:19 and **g** the boy a drink.
21:27 So Abraham took sheep and oxen and **g** them
24:18 upon her hand and **g** him a drink.
24:32 and **g** him straw and fodder for the camels,
24:53 and **g** them to Rebekah; he also **g** to her brother
25: 5 Abraham **g** all he had to Isaac.
25: 6 But to the sons of his concubines Abraham **g** gifts,
25:34 Then Jacob **g** Esau bread and lentil stew,
26:18 and he **g** them the names
28: 4 land that God **g** to Abraham."
29:24 (Laban **g** his maid Zilpah to his daughter Leah to
29:28 then Laban **g** him his daughter Rachel as a wife.
29:29 (Laban **g** his maid Bilhah to his daughter Rachel
30: 4 So she **g** him her maid Bilhah as a wife;
30: 9 she took her maid Zilpah and **g** her to Jacob as
30:18 "God has given me my hire because I **g** my maid
35: 4 they **g** to Jacob all the foreign gods that they had,
35:12 The land that I **g** to Abraham and Isaac I will give
Ge 38:18 So he **g** them to her, and went in to her,
39:21 he **g** him favor in the sight of the chief jailer.
41:45 Pharaoh **g** Joseph the name Zaphenath-paneah;
41:45 and he **g** him Asenath daughter of Potiphera,
42:25 Joseph then **g** orders to fill their bags with grain,
45:21 Joseph **g** them wagons according to the instruction
45:21 and he **g** them provisions for the journey.
45:22 To each one of them he **g** a set of garments;
45:22 to Benjamin he **g** three hundred pieces of silver
46:18 whom Laban **g** to his daughter Leah;
46:25 whom Laban **g** to his daughter Rachel,
47:17 Joseph **g** them food in exchange for the horses,
47:22 and lived on the allowance that Pharaoh **g** them;
50:16 "Your father **g** this instruction before he died,
Ex 1:21 the midwives feared God, he **g** them families.
2:21 he **g** Moses his daughter Zipporah in marriage.
6:13 and **g** them orders regarding the Israelites
11: 3 The LORD **g** the people favor in the sight of
31:18 he **g** him the two tablets of the covenant,
32:24 so they **g** it to me, and I threw it into the fire,
34:32 and he **g** them in commandment all that
36: 6 So Moses **g** command, and word was proclaimed
Lev 27:34 that the LORD **g** to Moses for the people of Israel
Nu 3:51 and Moses **g** the redemption money to Aaron
7: 6 and **g** them to the Levites.
7: 7 and four oxen he **g** to the Gershonites,
7: 8 four wagons and eight oxen he **g** to the Merarites,
7: 9 But to the Kohathites he **g** none,
15:23 the LORD **g** commandment and thereafter,
17: 6 and all their leaders **g** him staffs,
22: 7 they came to Balaam, and **g** him Balak's message.
31:41 Moses **g** the tribute, the offering for the LORD,
31:47 and **g** them to the Levites who had charge of
32:28 So Moses **g** command concerning them to Eleazar
32:33 Moses **g** to them—to the Gadites
32:38 and they **g** names to the towns that they rebuilt.
32:40 so Moses **g** Gilead to Machir son of Manasseh,
Dt 2:12 the land that the LORD **g** them as a possession.)
2:33 the LORD our God **g** him over to us;
2:36 The LORD our God **g** everything to us.
3:12 I **g** to the Reubenites and Gadites
3:13 and I **g** to the half-tribe of Manasseh the rest
3:15 To Machir I **g** Gilead.
3:16 and the Gadites I **g** the territory from Gilead as far
5:22 on two stone tablets, and **g** them to me.
9:10 And the LORD **g** me the two stone tablets written
9:11 of forty days and forty nights the LORD **g** me
10: 4 and the LORD **g** them to me.
22:16 "I **g** my daughter in marriage to this man
26: 9 he brought us into this place and **g** us this land,
29: 8 We took their land and **g** it as an inheritance to
31: 9 Moses wrote down this law, and **g** it to the priests,
32:18 you forgot the God who **g** you birth.
Jos 1:14 in the land that Moses **g** you beyond the Jordan.
1:15 the LORD **g** you beyond the Jordan to the east."
6:10 To the people Joshua **g** this command:
10:12 On the day when the LORD **g** the Amorites over
10:30 The LORD **g** it also and its king into the hand
10:32 The LORD **g** Lachish into the hand of Israel,
11:23 and Joshua **g** it for an inheritance to Israel
12: 6 and Moses the servant of the LORD **g** their land
12: 7 toward Seir (and Joshua **g** their land to the tribes
13: 8 which Moses **g** them, beyond the Jordan eastward,
13: 8 as Moses the servant of the LORD **g** them:
13:14 To the tribe of Levi alone Moses **g** no inheritance;
13:15 Moses **g** an inheritance to the tribe of
13:24 Moses **g** an inheritance also to the tribe of
13:29 Moses **g** an inheritance to the half-tribe
13:33 But to the tribe of Levi Moses **g** no inheritance;
14: 3 to the Levites he **g** no inheritance among them.
14:13 and **g** Hebron to Caleb son of Jephunneh for
15:13 he **g** to Caleb son of Jephunneh a portion among
15:17 and he **g** him his daughter Achsah as wife.
15:19 So Caleb **g** her the upper springs and
17: 4 of the LORD he **g** them an inheritance among
18: 7 which Moses the servant of the LORD **g** them."
19:49 the Israelites **g** an inheritance among them
19:50 the LORD they **g** him the town that he asked for,
21: 3 the Israelites **g** to the Levites the following towns
21: 8 and their pasture lands the Israelites **g** by lot to
21: 9 of Simeon they **g** the following towns mentioned
21:11 They **g** them Kiriath-arba (Arba being the father
21:13 the descendants of Aaron the priest they **g** Hebron,
21:43 the LORD **g** to Israel all the land that he swore
21:44 And the LORD **g** them rest on every side just
22: 4 the LORD **g** you on the other side of the Jordan.
24: 3 and made his offspring many. I **g** him Isaac;
24: 4 and to Isaac I **g** Jacob and Esau.
24: 4 I **g** Esau the hill country of Seir to possess,
24:13 I **g** you a land on which you had not labored,
Jdg 1: 4 the LORD **g** the Canaanites and the Perizzites
1:13 and he **g** him his daughter Achsah as wife.
1:15 So Caleb **g** her Upper Gulloth and Lower Gulloth.
2:14 he **g** them over to plunderers who plundered them,
3: 6 and their own daughters they **g** to their sons;
3:10 to war, and the LORD **g** King Cushan-rishathaim
4:19 a skin of milk and **g** him a drink and covered him.
5:25 He asked water and she **g** him milk,
6: 1 and the LORD **g** them into the hand
6: 9 before you, and **g** you their land;
9: 4 They **g** him seventy pieces of silver out of
11:21 **g** Sihon and all his people into the hand of Israel,
11:32 and the LORD **g** them into his hand.
12: 3 and the LORD **g** them into my hand.
12: 9 **g** his thirty daughters in marriage outside his clan
13: 1 and the LORD **g** them into the hand of
14: 9 he **g** some to them, and they ate it.
Jdg 14:19 of the town, took their spoil, and **g**
15: 2 so I **g** her to your companion.
17: 4 and **g** it to the silversmith,
20:36 The Israelites **g** ground to Benjamin,
21:14 that time; and they **g** them
Ru 2:18 Then she took out and **g** her what was left over
3:17 "He **g** me these six measures of barley,
4: 7 the one took off a sandal and **g** it to the other;
4:17 The women of the neighborhood **g** him a name,
1Sa 1: 5 but to Hannah he **g** a double portion,
2:28 and I **g** to the family
4: 5 all Israel **g** a mighty shout,
4:19 and her husband were dead, she bowed and **g** birth;
9:22 and **g** them a place at the head
9:23 "Bring the portion I **g** you,
10: 9 to leave Samuel, God **g** him another heart;
14:23 So the LORD **g** Israel the victory that day.
18: 4 and **g** it to David, and his armor,
18:27 Saul **g** him his daughter Michal as a wife.
20:40 Jonathan **g** his weapons to the boy and said
21: 6 So the priest **g** him the holy bread;
22:10 **g** him provisions, and **g** him the sword of Goliath
23:13 that David had escaped from Keilah, he **g** up
24:10 how the LORD **g** you into my hand in the cave;
26:23 for the LORD **g** you into my hand today,
27: 6 So that day Achish **g** him Ziklag;
30:11 They **g** him bread and he ate, they **g** him water
30:12 also **g** him a piece of fig cake and two clusters
2Sa 4:10 this was the reward I **g** him for his news.
8: 6 The LORD **g** victory to David wherever he went.
8:14 the LORD **g** victory to David wherever he went.
12: 8 I **g** you your master's house,
12: 8 and **g** you the house of Israel and of Judah;
13:25 but he would not go but **g** him his blessing.
16:23 in those days the counsel that Ahithophel **g** was as
18: 5 And all the people heard when the king **g** orders
19:23 And the king **g** him his oath.
21: 9 he **g** them into the hands of the Gibeonites,
22:48 the God who **g** me vengeance and brought
1Ki 3:17 and I **g** birth while she was in the house.
3:18 after I **g** birth, this woman also **g** birth.
4:29 God **g** Solomon very great wisdom, discernment,
5:11 Solomon in turn **g** Hiram twenty thousand cors
5:11 Solomon **g** this to Hiram year by year.
5:12 LORD **g** Solomon wisdom, as he promised him.
8:34 and bring them again to the land that you **g**
8:40 the days that they live in the land that you **g**
8:48 which you **g** to their ancestors,
9:11 King Solomon **g** to Hiram twenty cities in the land
10:10 she **g** the king one hundred twenty talents of gold,
10:10 that which the queen of Sheba **g** to King Solomon.
10:13 Meanwhile King Solomon **g** to the queen
10:13 as what he **g** her out of Solomon's royal bounty.
11:18 to Pharaoh king of Egypt, who **g** him a house,
11:18 an allowance of food, and **g** him land.
11:19 so that he **g** him his sister-in-law for a wife,
11:20 of Tahpenes **g** birth by him to his son Genubath,
11:28 the young man was industrious he **g** him charge
12: 8 the advice that the older men **g** him,
13: 3 He **g** a sign the same day, saying,
14:15 of this good land that he **g** to their ancestors,
15: 4 for David's sake the LORD his God **g** him a lamp
15:18 and **g** them into the hands of his servants.
17:23 and **g** him to his mother;
19:21 he boiled their flesh, and **g** it to the people,
2Ki 5:23 and **g** them to two of his servants,
10:15 So he **g** him his hand.
11:12 put the crown on him, and **g** him the covenant;
13: 3 so that he **g** them repeatedly into the hand
13: 5 Therefore the LORD **g** Israel a savior,
15:12 This was the promise of the LORD that he **g**
15:19 Menahem **g** Pul a thousand talents of silver,
17:15 and the warnings that he **g** them.
17:20 he punished them and **g** them into the hand
18:15 Hezekiah **g** him all the silver that was found in
18:16 that King Hezekiah of Judah had overlaid and **g** it
21: 8 to wander any more out of the land that I **g**
22: 8 When Hilkiah **g** the book to Shaphan, he read it.
23:35 Jehoiakim **g** the silver and the gold to Pharaoh,
24:12 King Jehoiachin of Judah **g** himself up to the king
25:28 and **g** him a seat above the other seats of
1Ch 2:35 So Sheshan **g** his daughter in marriage
6:55 to them they **g** Hebron in the land of Judah
6:56 and its villages they **g** to Caleb son of Jephunneh.
6:57 To the sons of Aaron they **g** the cities of refuge:
6:64 So the people of Israel **g** the Levites the towns
6:65 They also **g** them by lot out of the tribes of Judah,
11:10 who **g** him strong support in his kingdom,
18: 6 The LORD **g** victory to David wherever he went.
18:13 the LORD **g** victory to David wherever he went.
21: 5 Joab **g** the total count of the people to David.
21:17 not I who **g** the command to count the people?
22: 2 David **g** orders to gather together
28:11 Then David **g** his son Solomon the plan of
29: 7 They **g** for the service of the house
29: 8 Whoever had precious stones **g** them to
2Ch 6:25 the land that you **g** to them and to their ancestors.
6:31 the days that they live in the land that you **g**
6:38 which you **g** to their ancestors,
7: 3 and worshiped and **g** thanks to the LORD,
9: 9 she **g** the king one hundred twenty talents of gold,
9: 9 that the queen of Sheba **g** to King Solomon.
10: 8 he rejected the advice that the older men **g** him,
11:23 he **g** them abundant provisions,
13: 5 Do you not know that the LORD God of Israel **g**
13:16 and God **g** them into their hands.
14: 6 for the LORD **g** him peace.

2Ch 15:15 and the LORD g them rest all around.
16: 8 he g them into your hand.
20:30 for his God g him rest all around.
21: 3 Their father g them many gifts, of silver, gold,
21: 3 but he g the kingdom to Jehoram,
23:11 put the crown on him, and g him the covenant;
24: 8 So the king g command, and they made a chest,
24:12 and Jehoiada g it to those who had charge of
27: 5 Ammonites g him that year one hundred talents of
28: 5 Therefore the LORD his God g him into the hand
28: 9 was angry with Judah, he g them into your hand,
28:15 they clothed them, g them sandals,
28:21 and g tribute to the king of Assyria;
30:24 For King Hezekiah of Judah g the assembly
30:24 and the officials g the assembly a thousand bulls
31: 5 the people of Israel g in abundance the first fruits
32:22 he g them rest on every side.
32:24 and he answered him and g him a sign.
33:10 to Manasseh and to his people, but they g no heed.
34:10 of the LORD g it for repairing and restoring
34:11 They g it to the carpenters and the builders
34:15 and Hilkiah g the book to Shaphan.
35: 8 the chief officers of the house of God, g to
35: 9 and Jeiel and Jozabad, the chiefs of the Levites, g
36:17 he g them all into his hand.
Ezr 2:69 According to their resources they g to
3: 7 So they g money to the masons and the carpenters,
5: 3 "Who g you a decree to build this house and
5: 9 'Who g you a decree to build this house and
5:12 he g them into the hand of King Nebuchadnezzar
7:11 the letter that King Artaxerxes g to the priest Ezra,
Ne 2: 1 I carried the wine and g it to the king.
2: 9 and g them the king's letters.
7: 2 I g my brother Hanani charge over Jerusalem,
7:70 governor g to the treasury one thousand darics
7:71 And some of the heads of ancestral houses g into
7:72 the people g was twenty thousand darics of gold,
8: 8 They g the sense, so that the people understood
9: 7 of the Chaldeans and g him the name Abraham;
9:13 and g them right ordinances and true laws,
9:14 and g them commandments and statutes and a law
9:15 For their hunger you g them bread from heaven,
9:19 nor the pillar of fire by night that g them light on
9:20 You g your good spirit to instruct them,
9:20 and g them water for their thirst.
9:22 And you g them kingdoms and peoples,
9:24 the Canaanites, and g them into their hands,
9:27 you g them into the hands of their enemies,
9:27 great mercies you g them saviors who saved them
9:34 and the warnings that you g them.
9:36 slaves in the land that you g to our ancestors
12:31 and appointed two great companies that g thanks
12:38 The other company of those who g thanks went to
12:40 So both companies of those who g thanks stood in
12:47 of Nehemiah all Israel g the daily portions for
13: 9 Then I g orders and they cleansed the chambers,
13:19 and g orders that they should not be opened until
Est 1: 3 he g a banquet for all his officials and ministers.
1: 5 the king g for all the people present in the citadel
1: 9 Queen Vashti g a banquet for the women in
2:18 Then the king g a great banquet to all his officials
2:18 and g gifts with royal liberality.
3:10 the king took his signet ring from his hand and g it
4: 8 also g him a copy of the written decree issued
4:10 to Hathach and g him a message for Mordecai,
6: 1 and he g orders to bring the book of records,
8: 1 On that day King Ahasuerus g to Queen Esther
8: 2 from Haman, and g it to Mordecai.
9:25 he g orders in writing that the wicked plot
9:29 with the Jew Mordecai, g full written authority,
Job 1:21 the LORD g, and the LORD has taken away;
28:25 When he g to the wind its weight,
32:12 I g you my attention, but there was in fact no one
34:13 Who g him charge over the earth and who laid
42:10 the LORD g Job twice as much as he had before.
42:11 of them g him a piece of money and a gold ring.
42:15 and their father g them an inheritance along
Ps 4: 1 You g me room when I was in distress.
18:36 You g me a wide place for my steps under me,
18:47 the God who g me vengeance
21: 4 you g it to him—length of days forever and ever.
69:21 They g me poison for food,
69:21 and for my thirst they g me vinegar to drink.
74:14 you g him as food for the creatures of
78:15 and g them drink abundantly as from the deep.
78:24 and g them the grain of heaven.
78:29 for he g them what they craved.
78:46 He g their crops to the caterpillar,
78:48 He g over their cattle to the hail,
78:50 but g their lives over to the plague.
78:62 He g his people to the sword,
81:12 So I g them over to their stubborn hearts,
99: 7 and the statutes that he g them.
105:32 He g them hail for rain,
105:40 and g them food from heaven in abundance.
105:44 He g them the lands of the nations,
106:15 he g them what they asked,
106:41 he g them into the hand of the nations,
135:12 and g their land as a heritage,
136:21 and g their land as a heritage,
Ecc 2:20 and g my heart up to despair concerning all
12: 7 and the breath returns to God who g it.
SS 1:12 my nard g forth its fragrance.
3: 1 I called him, but he g no answer.
5: 6 I called him, but he g no answer.
Isa 26:18 we writhed, but we g birth only to wind.
42:24 Who g up Jacob to the spoiler,
Isa 47: 6 I g them into your hand, you showed them no
50: 6 I g my back to those who struck me,
63:14 the spirit of the LORD g them rest.
66: 7 Before she was in labor she g birth;
Jer 2:27 and to a stone, "You g me birth."
3:18 of the north to the land that I g your ancestors for
7: 7 in the land that I g of old to your ancestors forever
7:14 to the place that I g to you and to your ancestors,
7:23 But this command I g them, "Obey my voice,
8:13 and what I g them has passed away from them.
16:15 to their own land that I g to their ancestors.
17: 4 the heritage that I g you,
23:39 you and the city that I g to you and your ancestors.
24:10 from the land that I g to them and their ancestors.
30: 3 and I will bring them back to the land that I g
32:12 and I g the deed of purchase to Baruch son
32:22 and you g them this land, which you swore
35:14 of Rechab g to his descendants to drink no wine;
35:15 and then you shall live in the land that I g to you
35:16 the command that their ancestor g them,
36:32 and g it to the secretary Baruch son of Neriah,
37:21 So King Zedekiah g orders,
38:16 "As the LORD lives, who g us our lives,
39:10 and g them vineyards and fields at the same time.
39:11 King Nebuchadrezzar of Babylon g command
40: 5 So the captain of the guard g him an allowance
44:30 just as I g King Zedekiah of Judah into the hand
52:32 and g him a seat above the seats of
La 4:11 The LORD g full vent to his wrath;
Eze 3: 2 I opened my mouth, and he g me the scroll to eat.
16:19 Also my bread that I g you—
16:27 and g you up to the will of your enemies,
16:33 but you g your gifts to all your lovers,
16:34 and you g payment, while no payment was given
16:36 of the blood of your children that you g to them,
17:18 because he g his hand and yet did all these things,
20:11 I g them my statutes and showed them my
20:12 Moreover I g them my sabbaths,
20:25 Moreover I g them statutes that were not good
27:10 in you; they g you splendor.
28:25 on their own soil that I g to my servant Jacob.
31: 6 the animals of the field g birth to their young;
31:11 I g it into the hand of the prince of the nations;
35: 5 and g over the people of Israel to the power of
36:28 you shall live in the land that I g to your ancestors;
37:25 in the land that I g to my servant Jacob,
39:23 and g them into the hand of their adversaries,
Da 1: 7 The palace master g them other names:
1:16 to drink, and g them vegetables.
1:17 To these four young men God g knowledge
2:48 the king promoted Daniel, g him many great gifts,
5: 6 His limbs g way, and his knees knocked together.
5:18 God g your father Nebuchadnezzar kingship,
5:19 And because of the greatness that he g him,
5:29 Then Belshazzar g the command,
6: 2 to these the satraps g account,
6:16 Then the king g the command,
6:24 The king g a command,
Hos 2: 8 She did not know that it was I who g her the grain,
13:11 I g you a king in my anger,
Am 4: 6 I g you cleanness of teeth in all your cities,
Hab 3:10 the deep g forth its voice.
Mal 2: 5 a covenant of life and well-being, which I g him;
Mt 8:18 he g orders to go over to the other side.
10: 1 and g them authority over unclean spirits,
14:19 and g them to the disciples, and the disciples g
them to the crowds.
15:36 and g them to the disciples, and the disciples g
them to the crowds.
21:23 and who g you this authority?"
22: 2 be compared to a king who g a wedding banquet
25:15 to one he g five talents,
25:35 for I was hungry and you g me food, I was thirsty
and you g me something to drink,
25:36 I was naked and you g me clothing,
25:37 was it that we saw you hungry and g you food, or
thirsty and g you something to drink?
25:38 or naked and g you clothing?
25:42 for I was hungry and you g me no food, I was
thirsty and you g me nothing to drink,
26:26 g it to the disciples, and said, "Take, eat;
26:27 and after giving thanks he g it to them, saying,
27:10 and they g them for the potter's field,
27:14 But he g him no answer,
27:48 put it on a stick, and g it to him to drink.
Mk 2:26 and he g some to his companions."
3:16 Simon (to whom he g the name Peter);
3:17 (to whom he g the name Boanerges, that is, Sons
5:13 So he g them permission.
6: 7 and g them authority over the unclean spirits.
6:21 on his birthday g a banquet for his courtiers
6:28 and g it to the girl.
6:28 Then the girl g it to her mother.
6:41 g them to his disciples to set before the people;
8: 6 and after giving thanks he broke them and g them
11:28 Who g you this authority to do them?"
14:22 g it to them, and said, "Take; this is my body."
14:23 and after giving thanks he g it to them,
14:56 For many g false testimony against him,
14:57 Some stood up and g false testimony against him,
15:36 put it on a stick, and g it to him to drink, saying,
15:37 Then Jesus g a loud cry and breathed his last.
Lk 2: 7 And she g birth to her firstborn son
4:20 he rolled up the scroll, g it back to the attendant,
5:29 Then Levi g a great banquet for him in his house;
6: 4 and g some to his companions?"
7:15 and Jesus g him to his mother.
Lk 7:44 you g me no water for my feet,
7:45 You g me no kiss, but from the time I came
8:32 So he g them permission.
9: 1 and g them power and authority over all demons
9:16 g them to the disciples to set before the crowd.
9:42 healed the boy, and g him back to his father.
10:35 g them to the innkeeper, and said,
14:16 "Someone g a great dinner and invited many.
15:16 and no one g him anything.
19:13 and g them ten pounds, and said to them,
20: 2 Who is it who g you this authority?"
22:19 he broke it and g it to them, saying,
22:43 ⟦from heaven appeared to him and g him strength⟧
23: 9 but Jesus g him no answer.
23:24 So Pilate g his verdict that their demand should
24:30 blessed and broke it, and g it to them.
24:42 They g him a piece of broiled fish,
Jn 1:12 he g power to become children of God,
2: 3 When the wine g out, the mother of Jesus said
3:16 God so loved the world that he g his only Son,
4:12 who g us the well, and with his sons
6:31 'He g them bread from heaven to eat.'"
6:32 not Moses who g you the bread from heaven,
7:22 Moses g you circumcision (it is, of course,
12: 2 There they g a dinner for him.
13:26 he g it to Judas son of Simon Iscariot.
17: 4 on earth by finishing the work that you g me
17: 6 to those whom you g me from the world.
17: 6 They were yours, and you g them to me,
17: 8 the words that you g to me I have given to them,
17: 9 but on behalf of those whom you g me,
18: 9 not lose a single one of those whom you g me."
19: 9 But Jesus g him no answer.
19:30 Then he bowed his head and g up his spirit.
19:38 of Jesus. Pilate g him permission;
21:13 Jesus came and took the bread and g it to them,
Ac 2: 4 as the Spirit g them ability.
3:25 and of the covenant that God g to your ancestors,
4:33 With great power the apostles g their testimony to
4:36 a native of Cyprus, Joseph, to whom the apostles g
5:28 "We g you strict orders not to teach in this name,
7: 8 Then he g him the covenant of circumcision.
9:41 He g her his hand and helped her up.
10: 2 he g alms generously to the people
10:23 So Peter invited them in and g them lodging.
11:17 If then God g them the same gift that he g us
13:19 he g them their land as an inheritance
13:20 After that he g them judges until the time of
13:21 and God g them Saul son of Kish,
19:33 Some of the crowd g instructions to Alexander,
25: 2 the leaders of the Jews g him a report against Paul.
25:23 Then Festus g the order and Paul was brought in.
27:15 we g way to it and were driven.
Ro 1:24 Therefore God g them up in the lusts
1:26 this reason God g them up to degrading passions.
1:28 God g them up to a debased mind and to things
4:20 he grew strong in his faith as he g glory to God,
8:32 but g him up for all of us,
11: 8 "God g them a sluggish spirit,
1Co 3: 6 I planted, Apollos watered, but God g the growth.
16: 1 the directions I g to the churches of Galatia.
2Co 8: 3 they voluntarily g according to their means,
8: 5 they g themselves first to the Lord and,
10: 8 which the Lord g for building you up and not
Gal 1: 4 who g himself for our sins to set us free from
2: 9 they g to Barnabas and me the right hand
2:20 who loved me and g himself for me.
Eph 4: 8 he g gifts to his people."
4:11 The gifts he g were that some would be apostles,
5: 2 as Christ loved us and g himself up for us,
5:25 just as Christ loved the church and g himself up
Php 2: 9 also highly exalted him and g him the name that is
1Th 4: 2 For you know what instructions we g you through
2Th 2:16 through grace g us eternal comfort and good hope,
3:10 when we were with you, we g you this command:
1Ti 2: 6 who g himself a ransom for all —this was attested
2Ti 4:17 But the Lord stood by me and g me strength,
Tit 2:14 He it is who g himself for us
Heb 7: 4 Abraham the patriarch g him a tenth of the spoils.
11:22 of the Israelites and g instructions about his burial.
Jas 1:18 In fulfillment of his own purpose he g us birth by
5:18 the heaven g rain and the earth yielded its harvest.
1Pe 1:21 who raised him from the dead and g him glory,
1Jn 5:11 God g us eternal life, and this life is in his Son.
Rev 1: 1 The revelation of Jesus Christ, which God g him
2:21 I g her time to repent,
10: 3 he g a great shout, like a lion roaring.
11:13 and the rest were terrified and g glory to the God
12: 5 And she g birth to a son, a male child,
13: 2 And the dragon g it his power and his throne
15: 7 Then one of the four living creatures g
16:19 and g her the wine-cup of the fury of his wrath.
20:13 And the sea g up the dead that were in it,
20:13 Death and Hades g up the dead that were in them,
Tob 1:13 the Most High g me favor and good standing
2:12 and also g her a young goat for a meal.
3: 4 So you g us over to plunder, exile, and death,
5: 3 "He g me his bond and I g him my bond.
7:12 to him he took her by the hand and g her
7:13 to the effect that he g her to him as wife according
9: 5 Raphael g him the bond and informed him
10:10 So Raguel promptly g Tobias his wife Sarah,
10:12 as much your parents as those who g you birth.
14: 3 and the seven sons of Tobias and g this command:
14:10 Because he g alms, Ahikar escaped the fatal trap
Jdt 6:21 the assembly to his own house and g a banquet for
7:16 and he g orders to do as they had said.

Jdt 9: 2 to whom you g a sword to take revenge
9: 3 So you g up their rulers to be killed, and their bed,
9: 4 You g up their wives for booty and their daughters
10: 5 She g her maid a skin of wine and a flask of oil,
10: 5 then she wrapped up all her dishes and g them
13: 9 and g Holofernes' head to her maid,
15:11 They g Judith the tent of Holofernes
16:19 from his bedchamber she g as a votive offering.
16:22 but she g herself to no man all the days of her life
AdE 1: 3 he g a banquet for his Friends and other persons
1: 5 the end of the festivity the king g a drinking party
1: 9 Queen Vashti g a drinking party for the women in
2:18 Then the king g a banquet lasting seven days
3:10 the king took off his signet ring and g it to Haman
4: 8 also g him a copy of what had been posted in Susa
4:15 Then Esther g the messenger this answer
6: 1 so he g orders to his secretary to bring the book
7: 9 who g information of concern to the king;
8: 2 the ring that had been taken from Haman, and g it
9:29 and g full authority to the letter about Purim.
Wis 7:17 For it is he who g me unerring knowledge
8:21 that I would not possess wisdom unless God g her
10: 2 and g him strength to rule all things.
10:10 and g him knowledge of holy things;
10:12 in his arduous contest she g him the victory,
10:14 and she g him everlasting honor.
10:17 She g to holy people the reward of their labors;
11: 7 you g them abundant water unexpectedly,
12:10 by little you g them an opportunity to repent,
12:21 to whose ancestors you g oaths and covenants full
16:20 of these things you g your people food of angels,
Sir 17: 2 He g them a fixed number of days,
17: 4 and g them dominion over beasts and birds.
17: 6 ears and a mind for thinking he g them.
17:14 And he g commandment to each of them
24: 8 "Then the Creator of all things g me a command,
24:11 Thus in the beloved city he g me a resting place,
24:15 Like cassia and camel's thorn I g forth perfume,
38: 6 And he g skill to human beings that he might
44: 3 those who g counsel because they were intelligent;
44:22 To Isaac also he g the same assurance for the sake
44:23 and g him his inheritance;
45: 3 He g him commandments for his people,
45: 5 and g him the commandments face to face,
45: 7 and g him the priesthood of the people.
45:17 In his commandments he g him authority
45:20 He added glory to Aaron and g him a heritage;
45:21 which he g to him and his descendants.
46: 9 The Lord g Caleb strength,
47: 5 and he g strength to his right arm to strike down
47: 8 In all that he did he g thanks to the Holy One,
47:10 He g beauty to the festivals,
47:11 he g him a covenant of kingship and
47:17 and the answers you g astounded the nations.
47:22 So he g a remnant to Jacob,
49: 5 They g their power to others,
51:22 The Lord g me my tongue as a reward,
Bar 2:21 and you will remain in the land that I g
3:36 and g her to his servant Jacob and to Israel,
Bel 1:22 king put them to death, and g Bel over to Daniel,
1Mc 2:24 He g vent to righteous anger;
3:28 He opened his coffers and g a year's pay
3:34 and g him orders about all that he wanted done.
3:54 they sounded the trumpets and g a loud shout.
4:30 and g the camp of the Philistines into the hands
4:50 and these g light in the temple.
5:19 and he g them this command,
5:42 the army at the stream and g them this command,
6:15 He g him the crown and his robe and the signet,
6:44 So he g his life to save his people and to win
6:57 So he quickly g orders to withdraw,
6:61 the king and the commanders g them their oath.
6:62 the oath he had sworn and g orders to tear down
8: 8 These they took from him and g to King Eumenes.
9:54 Alcimus g orders to tear down the wall of
10: 6 So Demetrius g him authority to recruit troops,
10:58 Ptolemy g him his daughter Cleopatra in marriage,
10:60 he g them and their Friends silver and gold
10:62 The king g orders to take off Jonathan's garments
10:89 He also g him Ekron and all its environs
11:10 I now regret that I g him my daughter,
11:12 So he took his daughter away from him and g her
11:23 he g orders to continue the siege.
12: 4 And the Romans g them letters to the people
12:25 for he g them no opportunity
12:43 and he g him gifts and commanded his Friends
14: 8 the ground g its increase, and the trees of
14:14 He g help to all the humble among his people;
14:48 And they g orders to inscribe this decree
15:38 and g him troops of infantry and cavalry.
16:15 he g them a great banquet, and hid men there.
2Mc 4:32 of the gold vessels of the temple and g them
4:34 and g him his right hand;
7: 3 and g orders to have pans and caldrons heated.
7:22 It was not I who g you life and breath,
8:23 and g the watchword, "The help of God";
8:28 After the sabbath they g some of the spoils
9:18 he g up all hope for himself and wrote to the Jews
12: 5 he g orders to his men
13:15 He g his troops the watchword, "God's victory,"
13:21 g secret information to the enemy;
13:22 g pledges, received theirs, withdrew,
15:15 Jeremiah stretched out his right hand and g
15:15 and as he g it he addressed him thus:
1Es 1: 7 who were present Josiah g thirty thousand lambs
1: 8 the chief officers of the temple, g to the priests for
1: 9 g the Levites for the passover five thousand sheep
1:52 because of their ungodly acts he g command
1:53 for he g them all into their hands.
2:11 he g them to Mithridates, his treasurer,
3: 1 Now King Darius g a great banquet for all
3:13 king awoke, they took the writing and g it to him,
4:15 Women g birth to the king and to every people
5:54 They g money to the masons and the carpenters,
6:15 he g them over into the hands
8: 6 by the prosperous journey that the Lord g them.
8:56 I weighed and g to them six hundred fifty talents
8:82 which you g by your servants the prophets,
8:87 and g us such a root as this;
9:41 and all the multitude g attention to the law.
3Mc 1: 1 he g orders to all his forces,
2:31 the religion of their city, readily g themselves up,
5:15 and he g him an account of the situation.
5:21 and joyfully with one accord g their approval,
6:33 g thanks to heaven unceasingly and lavishly for
2Es 1:13 I g you Moses as leader and Aaron as priest;
1:15 I g you camps for your protection,
1:19 I pitied your groanings and g you manna for food;
2: 1 and I g them commandments through my servants
3: 5 and it g you Adam, a lifeless body?
3:15 you g him Isaac, and to Isaac you g Jacob and Esau
6:51 And you g Behemoth one of the parts
6:52 but to Leviathan you g the seventh part,
7:78 the body to return again to him who g it,
9:45 and considered my distress, and g me a son.
9:45 and we g great glory to the Mighty One.
14:42 the Most High g understanding to the five men,
16:61 g each person breath and life and understanding
4Mc 2:23 To the mind he g the law;
10:17 and utterly abominable Antiochus g orders
13:13 who g us our lives, and let us use our bodies as
15:17 who alone g birth to such complete devotion!
17:12 for on that day virtue g the awards and tested them
17:15 Reverence for God was victor and g the crown
18: 3 Therefore those who g over their bodies

GAY (KJV) See FINE

GAZA‡ (25) [GAZITES]
Ge 10:19 as far as G, and in the direction of Sodom,
Dt 2:23 who had lived in settlements in the vicinity of G,
Jos 10:41 Joshua defeated them from Kadesh-barnea to G,
11:22 some remained only in G, in Gath, and in Ashdod.
13: 3 there are five rulers of the Philistines, those of G,
15:47 G, its towns and its villages;
Jdg 1:18 Judah took G with its territory,
6: 4 as far as the neighborhood of G,
16: 1 to G, where he saw a prostitute and went in
16:21 down to G and bound him with bronze shackles;
1Sa 6:17 one for Ashdod, one for G, one for Ashkelon,
1Ki 4:24 to G, over all the kings west of the Euphrates;
2Ki 18: 8 the Philistines as far as G and its territory,
Jer 25:20 Ashkelon, G, Ekron, and the remnant of Ashdod;
47: 1 before Pharaoh attacked G:
47: 5 Baldness has come upon G, Ashkelon is silenced.
Am 1: 6 For three transgressions of G, and for four,
1: 7 So I will send a fire on the wall of G,
Zep 2: 4 For G shall be deserted,
Zec 9: 5 G too, and shall writhe in anguish;
9: 5 The king shall perish from G;
Ac 8:26 to the road that goes down from Jerusalem to G."
1Mc 11:61 he went to G, but the people of G shut him out.
11:62 Then the people of G pleaded with Jonathan,

GAZARA (13)
1Mc 4:15 to G, and to the plains of Idumea, and to Azotus
7:45 from Adasa as far as G,
9:52 He also fortified the town of Beth-zur, and G,
13:43 In those days Simon encamped against G
13:53 of all the forces; and he lived at G.
14: 7 he ruled over G and Beth-zur and the citadel,
14:34 and G, which is on the borders of Azotus,
15:28 "You hold control of Joppa and G and the citadel
15:35 As for Joppa and G, which you demand,
16: 1 John went up from G and reported
16:19 He sent other troops to G to do away with John;
16:21 But someone ran ahead and reported to John at G
2Mc 10:32 Timothy himself fled to a stronghold called G,

GAZATHITES (KJV) See GAZA

GAZE (13) [GAZED, GAZING]
2Ki 8:11 He fixed his g and stared at him,
Ps 11: 4 His eyes behold, his g examines humankind.
39:13 Turn your g away from me,
Pr 4:25 and your g be straight before you.
SS 1: 6 Do not g at me because I am dark,
Isa 47:13 the heavens stand up and save you, those who g at
Mic 4:11 and let our eyes g upon Zion."
Hab 2:15 in order to g on their nakedness!"
2Co 3: 7 that the people of Israel could not g at Moses' face
Rev 11: 9 and nations will g at their dead bodies and refuse
Sir 9: 8 and do not g at beauty belonging to another;
1Es 4:31 At this the king would g at her with mouth agape.
2Es 13: 3 everything under his g trembled,

GAZED (5) [GAZE]
Ge 24:21 The man g at her in silence to learn whether or not
Jdg 5:28 the mother of Sisera g through the lattice:
SS 1: 6 because the sun has g on me.
Isa 57: 8 you have g on their nakedness.
Ac 7:55 he g into heaven and saw the glory of God

GAZELLE‡ (13) [GAZELLES]
Dt 12:15 as they would of g or deer.
12:22 Indeed, just as g or deer is eaten,
14: 5 the g, the roebuck, the wild goat, the ibex,
15:22 as you would a g or deer.
2Sa 2:18 Now Asahel was as swift of foot as a wild g.
Pr 6: 5 save yourself like a g from the hunter,
SS 2: 9 My beloved is like a g or a young stag.
2:17 be like a g or a young stag on the cleft mountains.
4: 5 Your two breasts are like two fawns, twins of a g,
7: 3 Your two breasts are like two fawns, twins of a g.
8:14 a g or a young stag upon the mountains of spices!
Isa 13:14 Like a hunted g, or like sheep with no one
Sir 27:20 and has escaped like a g from a snare.

GAZELLES (4) [GAZELLE]
1Ki 4:23 one hundred sheep, besides deer, g, roebucks,
1Ch 12: 8 and who were swift as g on the mountains:
SS 2: 7 by the g or the wild does:
3: 5 by the g or the wild does:

GAZER (KJV) See GEZER

GAZERA (1)
1Es 5:31 the descendants of Chezib, the descendants of G,

GAZEZ (2)
1Ch 2:46 and G; and Haran became the father of G.

GAZING (6) [GAZE]
SS 2: 9 g in at the windows, looking through the lattice.
Ac 1:10 he was going and they were g up toward heaven,
2Co 3:13 over his face to keep the people of Israel from g at
Wis 19: 8 after g on marvelous wonders.
Sir 41:21 and of g at another man's wife;
4Mc 15:19 at the eyes of each one in his tortures g boldly at

GAZINGSTOCK (KJV) See PUBLICLY EXPOSED, SPECTACLE

GAZITES (1) [GAZA]
Jdg 16: 2 The G were told, "Samson has come here."

GAZZAM (2)
Ezr 2:48 Rezin, Nekoda, G,
Ne 7:51 of G, of Uzza, of Paseah,

GE-HARASHIM (1)
1Ch 4:14 and Seraiah became the father of Joab father of G,

GEAR (1)
Dt 1:41 So all of you strapped on your battle g,

GEBA (20) [=GIBEAH]
Jos 18:24 Ophni, and G—twelve towns with their
21:17 with its pasture lands, G with its pasture lands,
Jdg 20:33 in ambush rushed out of their place west of G.
1Sa 13: 3 the garrison of the Philistines that was at G;
13:16 with them stayed in G of Benjamin;
14: 5 and the other on the south in front of G.
2Sa 5:25 down the Philistines from G all the way to Gezer.
1Ki 15:22 with them King Asa built G of Benjamin
2Ki 23: 8 where the priests had made offerings, from G
1Ch 6:60 of Benjamin, G with its pasture lands, Alemeth
8: 6 of the inhabitants of G, and they were carried
2Ch 16: 6 and with them he built up G and Mizpah.
Ezr 2:26 Of Ramah and G, six hundred twenty-one.
Ne 7:30 Of Ramah and G, six hundred twenty-one.
11:31 people of Benjamin also lived from G onward,
12:29 also from Beth-gilgal and from the region of G
Isa 10:29 at G they lodge for the night;
Zec 14:10 The whole land shall be turned into a plain from G
Jdt 3:10 he camped between G and Scythopolis,
1Es 5:20 Those from Kirama and G,

GEBAL (2) [GEBALITES]
Ps 83: 7 G and Ammon and Amalek, Philistia with
Eze 27: 9 The elders of G and its artisans were within you,

GEBALITES (2) [GEBAL]
Jos 13: 5 and the land of the G,
1Ki 5:18 the G did the stonecutting and prepared the timber

GEBER (1)
1Ki 4:19 G son of Uri, in the land of Gilead, the country

GEBIM (1)
Isa 10:31 the inhabitants of G flee for safety.

GECKO (1)
Lev 11:30 the g, the land crocodile, the lizard,

GEDALIAH‡ (32)
2Ki 25:22 He appointed G son of Ahikam son of Shaphan
25:23 the king of Babylon had appointed G as governor,
25:23 they came with their men to G at Mizpah, namely,

2Ki 25:24 **G** swore to them and their men, saying,
25:25 they struck down **G** so that he died,
1Ch 25: 3 Of Jeduthun, the sons of Jeduthun: **G**, Zeri,
25: 9 to **G**, to him and his brothers and his sons, twelve;
Ezr 10:18 Maaseiah, Eliezer, Jarib, and **G**.
Jer 38: 1 Now Shephatiah son of Mattan, **G** son of Pashhur,
39:14 They entrusted him to **G** son of Ahikam son
40: 5 then return to **G** son of Ahikam son of Shaphan,
40: 6 Jeremiah went to **G** son of Ahikam at Mizpah,
40: 7 that the king of Babylon had appointed **G** son
40: 8 they went to **G** at Mizpah—
40: 9 **G** son of Ahikam son of Shaphan swore to them
40:11 in Judah and had appointed **G** son of Ahikam son
40:12 and came to the land of Judah, to **G** at Mizpah;
40:13 of the forces in the open country came to **G**
40:14 But **G** son of Ahikam would not believe them.
40:15 Then Johanan son of Kareah spoke secretly to **G**
40:16 **G** son of Ahikam said to Johanan son of Kareah,
41: 1 came with ten men to **G** son of Ahikam,
41: 2 and struck down **G** son of Ahikam son of Shaphan
41: 3 also killed all the Judeans who were with **G**
41: 4 On the day after the murder of **G**,
41: 6 he said to them, "Come to **G** son of Ahikam."
41:10 had committed to **G** son of Ahikam.
41:16 after he had slain **G** son of Ahikam—
41:18 of Nethaniah had killed **G** son of Ahikam,
43: 6 of the guard had left with **G** son of Ahikam son
Zep 1: 1 that came to Zephaniah son of Cushi son of **G** son
1Es 9:22 Ishmael, and Nathanael, and **G**, and Salthas.

GEDDUR (1)

1Es 5:30 the descendants of Cathua, the descendants of **G**,

GEDEON (KJV) See GIDEON

GEDER (1) [GEDERITE]

Jos 12:13 the king of Debir one the king of **G** one

GEDERAH (3)

Jos 15:36 Adithaim, **G**, Gederothaim:
1Ch 4:23 the potters and inhabitants of Netaim and **G**;
12: 4 Jeremiah, Jahaziel, Johanan, Jozabad of **G**,

GEDERITE (1) [GEDER]

1Ch 27:28 in the Shephelah was Baal-hanan the **G**.

GEDEROTH (2)

Jos 15:41 **G**, Beth-dagon, Naamah, and Makkedah:
2Ch 28:18 and had taken Beth-shemesh, Aijalon, **G**,

GEDEROTHAIM (1)

Jos 15:36 Gederah, **G**: fourteen towns with their villages.

GEDOR (7)

Jos 15:58 Halhul, Beth-zur, **G**,
1Ch 4: 4 and Penuel was the father of **G**,
4:18 And his Judean wife bore Jered father of **G**,
4:39 They journeyed to the entrance of **G**,
8:31 **G**, Ahio, Zecher,
9:37 **G**, Ahio, Zechariah, and Mikloth;
12: 7 and Joelah and Zebadiah, sons of Jeroham of **G**.

GEHAZI (13)

2Ki 4:12 He said to his servant **G**,
4:14 **G** answered, "Well, she has no son,
4:25 he said to **G** his servant, "Look,
4:27 **G** approached to push her away.
4:29 He said to **G**, "Gird up your loins,
4:31 **G** went on ahead and laid the staff on the face of
4:36 Elisha summoned **G** and said,
5:20 **G**, the servant of Elisha the man
5:21 So **G** went after Naaman.
5:23 who carried them in front of **G**.
5:25 Elisha said to him, "Where have you been, **G**?"
8: 4 the king was talking with **G** the servant of the man
8: 5 **G** said, "My lord king, here is the woman,

GEHENNA See Index to Footnotes

GELILOTH‡ (1)

Jos 18:17 and from there goes to **G**,

GEM (1) [GEM-CUTTER, GEMS]

Wis 7: 9 Neither did I liken to her any priceless **g**,

GEM-CUTTER (1) [CUT, GEM]

Ex 28:11 As a **g** engraves signets, so you shall engrave

GEMALLI (1)

Nu 13:12 from the tribe of Dan, Ammiel son of **G**;

GEMARIAH (5)

Jer 29: 3 by the hand of Elasah son of Shaphan and **G** son
36:10 in the chamber of **G** son of Shaphan the secretary,
36:11 When Micaiah son of **G** son of Shaphan heard all
36:12 **G** son of Shaphan, Zedekiah son of Hananiah,
36:25 when Elnathan and Delaiah and **G** urged the king

GEMS (3) [GEM]

Ex 25: 7 onyx stones and **g** to be set in the ephod and for
35: 9 and onyx stones and **g** to be set in the ephod and
35:27 the leaders brought onyx stones and **g** to be set in

GENDER (KJV) See BREED

GENEALOGICAL (2) [GENEALOGY]

1Ch 4:33 And they kept a **g** record.
Ezr 2:62 These looked for their entries in the **g** records,

GENEALOGIES (13) [GENEALOGY]

Ge 10:32 according to their **g**, in their nations;
Ex 6:16 the names of the sons of Levi according to their **g**:
6:19 the families of the Levites according to their **g**.
1Ch 1:29 These are their **g**: the firstborn of Ishmael,
5:17 All of these were enrolled by **g** in the days
7: 7 by **g** was twenty-two thousand thirty-four.
7: 9 and their enrollment by **g**,
7:40 Their number enrolled by **g**, for service in war,
9: 1 So all Israel was enrolled by **g**;
9:22 They were enrolled by **g** in their villages.
Ne 7:64 among those enrolled in the **g**, but it was
1Ti 1: 4 to occupy themselves with myths and endless **g**
Tit 3: 9 But avoid stupid controversies, **g**, dissensions,

GENEALOGY (12) [GENEALOGICAL, GENEALOGIES]

1Ch 5: 1 not enrolled in the **g** according to the birthright;
5: 7 when the **g** of their generations was reckoned:
7: 5 mighty warriors, enrolled by **g**.
26:31 of David's reign search was made, of whatever **g**
2Ch 12:15 and of the seer Iddo, recorded by **g**?
31:16 except those enrolled by **g**,
Ezr 8: 1 and this is the **g** of those who went up with me
Ne 7: 5 the officials and the people to be enrolled by **g**.
7: 5 of the **g** of those who were the first to come back,
Mt 1: 1 An account of the **g** of Jesus the Messiah,
Heb 7: 3 Without father, without mother, without **g**,
1Es 5:39 the register and the **g** of these men was not found,

GENERAL (16) [GENERALS]

Jdg 4: 7 I will draw out Sisera, the **g** of Jabin's army,
Jdt 2: 4 the chief **g** of his army, second only to himself,
4: 1 Holofernes, the **g** of Nebuchadnezzar,
5: 1 Holofernes, the **g** of the Assyrian army,
7:29 and **g** lamentation arose throughout the assembly,
1Mc 8:10 a **g** against the Greeks and attacked them.
10:65 and made him **g** and governor of the province.
13:37 and we are ready to make a **g** peace with you and
14: 3 The **g** went and defeated the army of Demetrius,
2Mc 3:18 of their houses in crowds to make a **g** supplication
8: 9 a **g** and a man of experience in military service.
9:19 Antiochus their king and **g** sends hearty greetings
9:21 to take thought for the **g** security of all.
3Mc 7:12 granted them a **g** license so that freely,
2Es 9:34 Now this is the **g** rule that,
4Mc 13:22 and from both **g** education and our discipline in

GENERAL (KJV) See also COMMANDER

GENERALS (12) [GENERAL]

Rev 6:15 the kings of the earth and the magnates and the **g**
Jdt 2:14 and summoned all the commanders, **g**,
14:12 who then went to the **g** and the captains and
1Mc 14: 2 he sent one of his **g** to take him alive.
1Es 3: 2 and all the satraps and **g** and governors that were
3:14 and the satraps and **g** and governors and prefects,
4:47 for him to all the treasurers and governors and **g**
3Mc 3:12 to his **g** and soldiers in Egypt and all its districts,
4: 4 all together, by the **g** in the several cities,
4:18 the task was impossible for all the **g** in Egypt.
6:41 and wrote the following letter for them to the **g** in
7: 1 "King Ptolemy Philopator to the **g** in Egypt and

GENERATION‡ (105) [GENERATIONS]

Ge 6: 9 Noah was a righteous man, blameless in his **g**;
7: 1 that you alone are righteous before me in this **g**.
15:16 And they shall come back here in the fourth **g**;
50:23 Joseph saw Ephraim's children of the third **g**;
Ex 1: 6 Joseph died, and all his brothers, and that whole **g**.
17:16 The LORD will have war with Amalek from **g** to **g**."
20: 5 the iniquity of parents, to the third and the fourth **g**
20: 6 but showing steadfast love to the thousandth **g**
34: 7 keeping steadfast love for the thousandth **g**,
34: 7 to the third and the fourth **g**."
Nu 14:18 upon the children to the third and the fourth **g**.'
32:13 until all the **g** that had done evil in the sight of
Dt 1:35 not one of this evil **g**—
2:14 until the entire **g** of warriors had perished from
5: 9 to the third and fourth **g** of those who reject me,
5:10 but showing steadfast love to the thousandth **g**
23: 2 to the tenth **g**, none of their descendants shall
23: 3 to the tenth **g**, none of their descendants shall
23: 8 the third **g** that are born to them may be admitted
29:22 The next **g**, your children who rise up after you,
32: 5 a perverse and crooked **g**.
32:20 for they are a perverse **g**, children in whom
Jdg 2:10 that whole **g** was gathered to their ancestors, and another **g** grew up after them,
2Ki 10:30 of the fourth **g** shall sit on the throne of Israel."
15:12 on the throne of Israel to the fourth **g**."
Est 9:28 throughout every **g**, in every family, province,
Ps 12: 7 you will guard us from this **g** forever.
48:13 go through its citadels, that you may tell the next **g**
78: 4 to the coming **g** the glorious deeds of the LORD,
78: 6 that the next **g** might know them,
78: 8 a stubborn and rebellious **g**,
78: 8 a **g** whose heart was not steadfast,
79:13 from **g** to **g** we will recount your praise.
95:10 For forty years I loathed that **g** and said,
102:18 Let this be recorded for a **g** to come,
106:31 as righteousness from **g** to **g** forever.
109:13 may his name be blotted out in the second **g**.
112: 2 the **g** of the upright will be blessed.
145: 4 One **g** shall laud your works to another,
Ecc 1: 4 A **g** goes, and a **g** comes,
Isa 34:10 From **g** to **g** it shall lie waste;
34:17 from **g** to **g** they shall live in it.
Jer 2:31 And you, O **g**, behold the word of the LORD!
7:29 for the LORD has rejected and forsaken the **g**
32:18 You show steadfast love to the thousandth **g**,
Da 4: 3 and his sovereignty is from **g** to **g**.
4:34 and his kingdom endures from **g** to **g**.
Joel 1: 3 and their children another **g**.
Mt 11:16 "But to what will I compare this **g**?
12:39 "An evil and adulterous **g** asks for a sign,
12:41 of Nineveh will rise up at the judgment with this **g**
12:42 the South will rise up at the judgment with this **g**
12:45 So will it be also with this evil **g**."
16: 4 An evil and adulterous **g** asks for a sign,
17:17 Jesus answered, "You faithless and perverse **g**,
23:36 Truly I tell you, all this will come upon this **g**.
24:34 this **g** will not pass away
Mk 8:12 "Why does this **g** ask for a sign?
8:12 Truly I tell you, no sign will be given to this **g**."
8:38 and of my words in this adulterous and sinful **g**,
9:19 He answered them, "You faithless **g**,
13:30 this **g** will not pass away
Lk 1:50 for those who fear him from **g** to **g**.
7:31 "To what then will I compare the people of this **g**,
9:41 Jesus answered, "You faithless and perverse **g**,
11:29 he began to say, "This **g** is an evil **g**;
11:30 so the Son of Man will be to this **g**.
11:31 with the people of this **g** and condemn them,
11:32 of Nineveh will rise up at the judgment with this **g**
11:50 so that this **g** may be charged with the blood of all
11:51 Yes, I tell you, it will be charged against this **g**.
16: 8 in dealing with their own **g** than are the children
17:25 and be rejected by this **g**.
21:32 this **g** will not pass away
Ac 2:40 saying, "Save yourselves from this corrupt **g**."
8:33 Who can describe his **g**?
13:36 he had served the purpose of God in his own **g**,
Php 2:15 in the midst of a crooked and perverse **g**,
Heb 3:10 Therefore I was angry with that **g**, and I said,
Jude 1:14 in the seventh **g** from Adam, prophesied, saying,
Tob 13:11 **G** after **g** will give joyful praise in you,
Jdt 8:18 "For never in our **g**, nor in these present days,
AdE 9:27 Purim should be a memorial and kept from **g** to **g**,
10:13 from **g** to **g** forever among his people Israel."
Wis 3:19 For the end of an unrighteous **g** is grievous.
7:27 in every **g** she passes into holy souls
14: 6 by your hand left to the world the seed of a new **g**.
Sir 44:14 but their name lives on **g** after **g**.
1Mc 2:61 "And so observe, from **g** to **g**,

GENERATIONS (110) [GENERATION]

A. ALL ... GENERATIONS (36)

Ge 2: 4 These are the **g** of the heavens and the earth
9:12 that is with you, for all future **g**:
17: 7 and your offspring after you throughout their **g**,
17: 9 and your offspring after you throughout their **g**.
17:12 Throughout your **g** every male among you shall
Ex 3:15 and this my title for all **g**. A
12:14 throughout your **g** you shall observe it as
12:17 you shall observe this day throughout your **g** as
12:42 the LORD by all the Israelites throughout their **g**.
16:32 'Let an omer of it be kept throughout your **g**,
16:33 to be kept throughout your **g**."
27:21 to be observed throughout their **g** by the Israelites.
29:42 be a regular burnt offering throughout your **g** at
30: 8 before the LORD throughout your **g**.
30:10 Throughout your **g** he shall perform the atonement
30:21 him and for his descendants throughout their **g**.
30:31 be my holy anointing oil throughout your **g**.
31:13 a sign between me and you throughout your **g**,
31:16 observing the sabbath throughout their **g**,
40:15 a perpetual priesthood throughout all **g** to come. A
Lev 3:17 It shall be a perpetual statute throughout your **g**,
6:18 as their perpetual due throughout your **g**,
7:36 from the people of Israel throughout their **g**.
10: 9 it is a statute forever throughout your **g**.
17: 7 be a statute forever to them throughout their **g**.
21:17 of your offspring throughout their **g** who has
22: 3 among all your offspring throughout your **g** comes
23:14 throughout your **g** in all your settlements.
23:21 in all your settlements throughout your **g**.
23:31 throughout your **g** in all your settlements.
23:41 as a statute forever throughout your **g**.
23:43 so that your **g** may know that I made the people
24: 3 it shall be a statute forever throughout your **g**.
25:30 in perpetuity to the purchaser, throughout the **g**;
Nu 10: 8 a perpetual institution for you throughout your **g**.
15:15 a perpetual statute throughout your **g**;
15:21 Throughout your **g** you shall give to the LORD
15:23 and thereafter, throughout your **g**—

Nu 15:38 on the corners of their garments throughout their **g**
18:23 it shall be a perpetual statute throughout your **g.**
35:29 for you throughout your **g** wherever you live.
Dt 7: 9 and keep his commandments, to a thousand **g,**
19:14 by former **g,** on the property that will be allotted
Jos 22:27 and between the **g** after us,
Jdg 3: 2 that successive **g** of Israelites might know war,
1Ch 5: 7 when the genealogy of their **g** was reckoned:
7: 2 namely of Tola, mighty warriors of their **g,**
7: 4 by their **g,** according to their ancestral houses,
7: 9 by genealogies, according to their **g,** as heads
8:28 according to their **g,** chiefs.
9: 9 and their kindred according to their **g,**
9:34 of the Levites, according to their **g;**
16:15 the word that he commanded, for a thousand **g,**
Job 8: 8 "For inquire now of bygone **g,**
42:16 and his children's children, four **g.**
Ps 10: 6 throughout all **g** we shall not meet adversity." A
22:30 future **g** will be told about the Lord,
33:11 the thoughts of his heart to all **g.** A
45:17 I will cause your name to be celebrated in all **g;** A
49:11 their dwelling places to all **g,** A
61: 6 may his years endure to all **g!** A
71:18 until I proclaim your might to all the **g** to come. A
72: 5 and as long as the moon, throughout all **g.** A
85: 5 Will you prolong your anger to all **g?** A
89: 1 I will proclaim your faithfulness to all **g.** A
89: 4 and build your throne for all **g.'** " A
90: 1 Lord, you have been our dwelling place in all **g.** A
100: 5 and his faithfulness to all **g.** A
102:12 your name endures to all **g.** A
102:24 you whose years endure throughout all **g."** A
105: 8 the word that he commanded, for a thousand **g,**
119:90 Your faithfulness endures to all **g;** A
145:13 and your dominion endures throughout all **g.** A
146:10 your God, O Zion, for all **g.** A
Pr 27:24 nor a crown for all **g.** A
Isa 13:20 It will never be inhabited or lived in for all **g;** A
41: 4 calling the **g** from the beginning?
51: 8 be forever, and my salvation to all **g.** A
51: 9 Awake, as in days of old, the **g** of long ago!
58:12 you shall raise up the foundations of many **g;**
61: 4 the devastations of many **g.**
Jer 50:39 be peopled, or inhabited for all **g.** A
La 5:19 your throne endures to all **g.** A
Joel 3:20 be inhabited forever, and Jerusalem to all **g.** A
Mt 1:17 So all the **g** from Abraham A
1:17 from Abraham to David are fourteen **g,**
1:17 to the deportation to Babylon, fourteen **g;**
1:17 to Babylon to the Messiah, fourteen **g.**
Lk 1:48 Surely, from now on all **g** will call me blessed; A
Ac 14:16 In past **g** he allowed all the nations
15:21 For in every city, for **g** past,
Eph 3: 5 In former **g** this mystery was not made known
3:21 glory in the church and in Christ Jesus to all **g,** A
Col 1:26 that has been hidden throughout the ages and **g**
Tob 1: 4 and established for all **g** forever. A
8: 5 and blessed is your name in all **g** forever. A
13:10 within you who are distressed, to all **g** forever. A
Jdt 8:32 to do something that will go down through all **g** A
Sir 2:10 Consider the **g** of old and see:
14:18 so are the **g** of flesh and blood:
16:27 and their dominion for all **g.** A
24:33 and leave it to all future **g.**
39: 9 and his name will live through all **g.** A
44: 1 of famous men, our ancestors in their **g.**
44: 7 all these were honored in their **g,**
44:16 an example of repentance to all **g.** A
45:26 that their glory may endure through all their **g.** A
Bar 3:20 Later **g** have seen the light of day,
LtJ 6: 3 for a long time, up to seven **g;**
1Mc 2:51 which they did in their **g;**

GENERATIVE (1)
Wis 1:14 the **g** forces of the world are wholesome,

GENEROSITY (8) [GENEROUS]
Ro 12: 8 in exhortation; the giver, in **g;**
2Co 8: 2 in a wealth of **g** on their part.
9:11 for your great **g,** which will produce thanksgiving
9:13 the confession of the gospel of Christ and by the **g**
Gal 5:22 joy, peace, patience, kindness, **g,** faithfulness,
Sir 31:23 and their testimony to his **g** is trustworthy.
37:11 with a miser about **g** or with the merciless about
2Mc 13:23 the sanctuary and showed **g** to the holy place.

GENEROUS‡ (21) [GENEROSITY, GENEROUSLY]
Ex 35: 5 of a **g** heart bring the LORD's offering:
Jdg 21:22 'Be **g** and allow us to have them;
Ps 37:21 but the righteous are **g** and keep giving;
Pr 11:25 A **g** person will be enriched,
19: 6 Many seek the favor of the **g,**
22: 9 Those who are **g** are blessed,
Mt 20:15 Or are you envious because I am **g?'**
Ac 2:46 at home and ate their food with glad and **g** hearts,
Ro 10:12 of all and is **g** to all who call on him.
2Co 8: 6 so he should also complete this **g** undertaking
8: 7 so we want you to excel also in this **g** undertaking.
8: 9 For you know the **g** act of our Lord Jesus Christ,
8:19 while we are administering this **g** undertaking for
8:20 that no one should blame us about this **g** gift
1Ti 6:18 They are to do good, to be rich in good works, **g,**
Jas 1:17 Every **g** act of giving, with every perfect gift,
Tob 9: 6 of a father good and noble, upright and **g!**
AdE 16: 2 with the most **g** kindness of their benefactors,
Sir 14: 5 If one is mean to himself, to whom will he be **g?**
35:10 Be **g** when you worship the Lord,
40:14 As a **g** person has cause to rejoice,

GENEROUSLY (5) [GENEROUS]
Ps 112: 5 It is well with those who deal **g** and lend,
Ac 10: 2 he gave alms **g** to the people
Jas 1: 5 ask God, who gives to all **g** and ungrudgingly,
Sir 35:12 and as **g** as you can afford.
3Mc 7:18 for the king had **g** provided all things to them

GENITALS (1)
Dt 25:11 of his opponent by reaching out and seizing his **g,**

GENNAEUS (1)
2Mc 12: 2 Timothy and Apollonius son of **G,**

GENNESARET (4)
Mt 14:34 they had crossed over, they came to land at **G.**
Mk 6:53 they came to land at **G** and moored the boat.
Lk 5: 1 while Jesus was standing beside the lake of **G,**
1Mc 11:67 and his army encamped by the waters of **G.**

GENTILE (7) [GENTILES]
Mt 18:17 let such a one be to you as a **G** and a tax collector.
Mk 7:26 the woman was a **G,** of Syrophoenician origin.
Ac 10:28 for a Jew to associate with or to visit a **G;**
15:23 the elders, to the believers of **G** origin in Antioch
Gal 2:14 though a Jew, live like a **G** and not like a Jew,
2:15 We ourselves are Jews by birth and not **G** sinners;
1Mc 1:14 in Jerusalem, according to **G** custom,

GENTILES‡ (161) [GENTILE]
Mt 4:15 across the Jordan, Galilee of the **G**—
5:47 Do not even the **G** do the same?
6: 7 do not heap up empty phrases as the **G** do;
6:32 For it is the **G** who strive for all these things;
10: 5 "Go nowhere among the **G,**
10:18 as a testimony to them and the **G.**
12:18 and he will proclaim justice to the **G.**
12:21 And in his name the **G** will hope."
20:19 to the **G** to be mocked and flogged and crucified;
20:25 "You know that the rulers of the **G** lord it
Mk 10:33 then they will hand him over to the **G;**
10:42 that among the **G** those whom they recognize
Lk 2:32 to the **G** and for glory to your people Israel."
18:32 For he will be handed over to the **G;**
21:24 and Jerusalem will be trampled on by the **G,**
21:24 until the times of the **G** are fulfilled.
22:25 "The kings of the **G** lord it over them;
Ac 4:25 'Why did the **G** rage, and the peoples imagine
4:27 with the **G** and the peoples of Israel,
9:15 to bring my name before **G** and kings and before
10:45 the Holy Spirit had been poured out even on the **G,**
11: 1 that the **G** had also accepted the word of God.
11:18 "Then God has given even to the **G** the repentance
13:46 we are now turning to the **G.**
13:47 saying, 'I have set you to be a light for the **G,**
13:48 When the **G** heard this, they were glad and praised
14: 2 up the **G** and poisoned their minds against
14: 5 when an attempt was made by both **G** and Jews,
14:27 and how he had opened a door of faith for the **G.**
15: 3 they reported the conversion of the **G,**
15: 7 through whom the **G** would hear the message of
15:12 that God had done through them among the **G.**
15:14 how God first looked favorably on the **G,**
15:17 all the **G** over whom my name has been called.
15:19 not trouble those **G** who are turning to God,
18: 6 From now on I will go to the **G."**
21:11 and will hand him over to the **G.'** "
21:19 by one the things that God had done among the **G**
21:21 the Jews living among the **G** to forsake Moses,
21:25 But as for the **G** who have become believers,
22:21 'Go, for I will send you far away to the **G.'** "
26:17 I will rescue you from your people and from the **G**
26:20 and also to the **G,** that they should repent and turn
26:23 both to our people and to the **G."**
28:28 that this salvation of God has been sent to the **G;**
Ro 1: 5 the obedience of faith among all the **G** for the sake
1:13 among you as I have among the rest of the **G.**
2:14 When **G,** who do not possess the law,
2:24 "The name of God is blasphemed among the **G**
3:29 Is he not the God of **G** also? Yes, of **G** also,
9:24 not from the Jews only but also from the **G?**
9:30 **G,** who did not strive for righteousness,
11:11 their stumbling salvation has come to the **G,**
11:12 and if their defeat means riches for **G,**
11:13 Now I am speaking to you **G.**
11:13 Inasmuch then as I am an apostle to the **G,**
11:25 until the full number of the **G** has come in.
15: 9 that the **G** might glorify God for his mercy.
15: 9 "Therefore I will confess you among the **G,**
15:10 "Rejoice, O **G,** with his people";
15:11 all you **G,** and let all the peoples praise him";
15:12 who rises to rule the **G;** in him the **G** shall hope."
15:16 the **G** in the priestly service of the gospel of God,
15:16 so that the offering of the **G** may be acceptable,
15:18 through me to win obedience from the **G,**
15:27 **G** have come to share in their spiritual blessings,
16: 4 but also all the churches of the **G.**
16:26 the prophetic writings is made known to all the **G,**
1Co 1:23 a stumbling block to Jews and foolishness to **G,**
2Co 11:26 danger from my own people, danger from **G,**
Gal 1:16 so that I might proclaim him among the **G,**
2: 2 the gospel that I proclaim among the **G,**
2: 8 also worked through me in sending me to the **G),**
2: 9 agreeing that we should go to the **G** and they to
2:12 he used to eat with the **G.**
2:14 how can you compel the **G** to live like Jews?"
3: 8 foreseeing that God would justify the **G** by faith,
3: 8 saying, "All the **G** shall be blessed in you."
3:14 the blessing of Abraham might come to the **G,**
Eph 2:11 then, remember that at one time you **G** by birth,
3: 1 a prisoner for Christ Jesus for the sake of you **G**—
3: 6 the **G** have become fellow heirs,
3: 8 to bring to the **G** the news of the boundless riches
4:17 you must no longer live as the **G** live,
Col 1:27 how great among the **G** are the riches of the glory
1Th 2:16 from speaking to the **G** so that they may be saved.
4: 5 like the **G** who do not know God;
1Ti 2: 7 a teacher of the **G** in faith and truth.
3:16 proclaimed among **G,** believed in throughout
2Ti 4:17 be fully proclaimed and all the **G** might hear it.
1Pe 2:12 Conduct yourselves honorably among the **G,**
4: 3 in doing what the **G** like to do,
Tob 1:10 and my people ate the food of the **G,**
1:11 but I kept myself from eating the food of the **G.**
Jdt 4:12 and desecrated to the malicious joy of the **G.**
8:22 all this he will bring on our heads among the **G,**
AdE 8:17 of the **G** were circumcised and became Jews out
1Mc 1:11 and make a covenant with the **G** around us,
1:13 to observe the ordinances of the **G.**
1:15 They joined with the **G** and sold themselves
1:43 All the **G** accepted the command of the king.
2:12 the **G** have profaned them.
2:18 as all the **G** and the people of Judah and those
2:40 with the **G** for our lives and for our ordinances,
2:44 the survivors fled to the **G** for safety.
2:48 They rescued the law out of the hands of the **G**
2:68 Pay back the **G** in full,
3:10 now gathered together **G** and a large force
3:25 and terror fell on the **G** all around them.
3:26 and the **G** talked of the battles of Judas.
3:45 it was a lodging place for the **G.**
3:48 into those matters about which the **G** consulted
3:52 Here the **G** are assembled against us to destroy us;
3:58 with these **G** who have assembled against us
4: 7 And they saw the camp of the **G,**
4:11 the **G** will know that there is one who redeems
4:14 The **G** were crushed, and fled into the plain,
4:45 a lasting shame to them that the **G** had defiled it.
4:54 and on the very day that the **G** had profaned it,
4:58 and the disgrace brought by the **G** was removed.
4:60 to keep the **G** from coming and trampling them
5: 1 When the **G** all around heard that
5: 9 Now the **G** in Gilead gathered together against
5:10 **G** around us have gathered together to destroy us.
5:15 and all Galilee of the **G,**
5:19 not engage in battle with the **G** until we return."
5:21 to Galilee and fought many battles against the **G,**
5:21 and the **G** were crushed before him.
5:22 as many as three thousand of the **G** fell,
5:38 "All the **G** around us have gathered to him;
5:43 All the **G** were defeated before him,
5:57 let us go and make war on the **G** around us."
5:63 in all Israel and among all the **G,**
6:18 in every way to harm them and strengthen the **G.**
6:53 from the **G** had consumed the last of the stores.
7:23 it was more than the **G** had done.
13:41 the yoke of the **G** was removed from Israel,
14:36 so that the **G** were put out of the country,
2Mc 1:27 set free those who are slaves among the **G,**
1:27 and let the **G** know that you are our God.
6: 4 with debauchery and reveling by the **G,**
8: 5 the **G** could not withstand him,
8: 9 of no fewer than twenty thousand **G** of all nations,
8:16 of **G** who were wickedly coming against them,
8:17 that the **G** had committed against the holy place,
12:13 and inhabited by all sorts of **G.**
13:11 to revive fall into the hands of the blasphemous **G.**
14:14 And the **G** throughout Judea,
14:15 of Nicanor's coming and the gathering of the **G,**
14:30 when there was no mingling with the **G,**
15: 8 not to fear the attack of the **G,**
15:10 at the same time pointing out the perfidy of the **G**
3Mc 4: 1 a feast at public expense was arranged for the **G**
5: 6 For to the **G** it appeared that the Jews were left
5:13 of his all-powerful hand to the arrogant **G.**
6: 9 by the abominable and lawless **G.**
6:13 And let the **G** cower today in fear
6:15 Let it be shown to all the **G** that you are with us,
2Es 4:23 why Israel has been given over to the **G**

GENTLE (16) [GENTLENESS, GENTLY]
Dt 28:54 and **g** of men among you will begrudge food
28:56 She who is the most refined and **g** among you,
28:56 so **g** and refined that she does not venture to set
32: 2 like **g** rain on grass, like showers on new growth.
Pr 15: 4 A **g** tongue is a tree of life,
Jer 11:19 But I was like a **g** lamb led to the slaughter.
Mt 11:29 for I am **g** and humble in heart,
1Th 2: 7 But we were **g** among you,
1Ti 3: 3 not violent but **g,** not quarrelsome,
Tit 3: 2 to be **g,** and to show every courtesy to everyone.
Jas 3:17 **g,** willing to yield, full of mercy and good fruits,
1Pe 2:18 not only those who are kind and **g** but
3: 4 be the inner self with the lasting beauty of a **g**
Wis 2:19 so that we may find out how **g** he is,
18:14 For while **g** silence enveloped all things,

2Mc 15:12 of modest bearing and **g** manner,

GENTLEMEN (7) [MAN]

1Es 3:18 **"G,** how is wine the strongest?
3:24 **G,** is not wine the strongest,
4: 2 **"G,** are not men strongest, who rule over land
4:12 **G,** why is not the king the strongest,
4:14 **"G,** is not the king great, and are not men many,
4:32 **G,** why are not women strong,
4:34 **"G,** are not women strong?

GENTLENESS‡ (11) [GENTLE]

1Co 4:21 or with love in a spirit of **g**?
2Co 10: 1 appeal to you by the meekness and **g** of Christ—
Gal 5:23 **g,** and self-control. There is no law against such
6: 1 the Spirit should restore such a one in a spirit of **g.**
Eph 4: 2 and **g,** with patience, bearing with one another
Php 4: 5 Let your **g** be known to everyone.
1Ti 6:11 godliness, faith, love, endurance, **g.**
2Ti 2:25 correcting opponents with **g.**
Jas 3:13 that your works are done with **g** born of wisdom.
1Pe 3:16 yet do it with **g** and reverence.
AdE 15: 8 Then God changed the spirit of the king to **g,**

GENTLY (6) [GENTLE]

2Sa 18: 5 "Deal **g** for my sake with
Job 15:11 or the word that deals **g** with you?
Isa 8: 6 the waters of Shiloah that flow **g,** and melt in fear
40:11 and **g** lead the mother sheep.
Heb 5: 2 to deal **g** with the ignorant and wayward,
AdE 15: 3 on one she leaned **g** for support,

GENUBATH (2)

1Ki 11:20 sister of Tahpenes gave birth by him to his son **G,**
11:20 **G** was in Pharaoh's house among the children

GENUINE (4) [GENUINELY, GENUINENESS]

Ro 12: 9 Let love be **g;** hate what is evil,
1Co 11:19 only so will it become clear who among you are **g.**
2Co 6: 6 patience, kindness, holiness of spirit, **g** love,
1Pe 1:22 to the truth so that you have **g** mutual love,

GENUINELY (2) [GENUINE]

Php 2:20 I have no one like him who will be **g** concerned
2Mc 14: 8 first because I am **g** concerned for the interests of

GENUINENESS (2) [GENUINE]

2Co 8: 8 but I am testing the **g** of your love against
1Pe 1: 7 so that the **g** of your faith—

GER See Index to Footnotes

GERA (9)

Ge 46:21 Bela, Becher, Ashbel, **G,** Naaman, Ehi, Rosh,
Jdg 3:15 Ehud son of **G,** the Benjaminite,
2Sa 16: 5 came out whose name was Shimei son of **G;**
19:16 Shimei son of **G,** the Benjaminite, from Bahurim,
19:18 Shimei son of **G** fell down before the king,
1Ki 2: 8 There is also with you Shimei son of **G,**
1Ch 8: 3 And Bela had sons: Addar, **G,** Abihud,
8: 5 **G,** Shephuphan, and Huram.
8: 7 Ahijah, and **G,** that is, Heglam,

GERAHS (5)

Ex 30:13 of the sanctuary (the shekel is twenty **g**),
Lev 27:25 twenty **g** shall make a shekel.
Nu 3:47 the shekel of the sanctuary, a shekel of twenty **g.**
18:16 to the shekel of the sanctuary (that is, twenty **g**).
Eze 45:12 The shekel shall be twenty **g.**

GERAR (11)

Ge 10:19 in the direction of **G,** as far as Gaza,
20: 1 While residing in **G** as an alien,
20: 2 And King Abimelech of **G** sent and took Sarah.
26: 1 And Isaac went to **G,** to King Abimelech of
26: 6 So Isaac settled in **G.**
26:17 and camped in the valley of **G** and settled there.
26:20 the herders of **G** quarreled with Isaac's herders,
26:26 Then Abimelech went to him from **G,**
2Ch 14:13 the army with him pursued them as far as **G,** and
14:14 They defeated all the cities around **G,**
2Mc 13:24 as governor from Ptolemais to **G,**

GERASENES‡ (3)

Mk 5: 1 other side of the sea, to the country of the **G.**
Lk 8:26 Then they arrived at the country of the **G,**
8:37 of the surrounding country of the **G** asked Jesus

GERGESENES See Index to Footnotes

GERGESITES (1)

Jdt 5:16 the Jebusites, the Shechemites, and all the **G,**

GERIZIM (6)

Dt 11:29 on Mount **G** and the curse on Mount Ebal.
27:12 these shall stand on Mount **G** for the blessing of
Jos 8:33 half of them in front of Mount **G** and half of them
Jdg 9: 7 he went and stood on the top of Mount **G,**
2Mc 5:23 and at **G,** Andronicus;
6: 2 in **G** the temple of Zeus-the-Friend-of-Strangers,

GERON See Index to Footnotes

GERSHOM‡ (14) [GERSHOMITES]

Ex 2:22 She bore a son, and he named him **G;**
18: 3 The name of the one was **G** (for he said,
Jdg 18:30 Jonathan son of **G,** son of Moses,
1Ch 6: 1 The sons of Levi: **G,** Kohath, and Merari.
6:16 The sons of Levi: **G,** Kohath, and Merari.
6:17 These are the names of the sons of **G:**
6:20 Of **G:** Libni his son, Jahath his son,
6:43 son of Jahath, son of **G,** son of Levi.
15: 7 of **G,** Joel the chief, with one hundred thirty
23:15 The sons of Moses: **G** and Eliezer.
23:16 The sons of **G:** Shebuel the chief.
26:24 Shebuel son of **G,** son of Moses, was chief officer
Ezr 8: 2 Of the descendants of Phinehas, **G.**
1Es 8:29 Of the descendants of Phineas, **G.**

GERSHOMITES (2) [GERSHOM]

1Ch 6:62 To the **G** according to their
6:71 To the **G:** out of the half-tribe of Manasseh:

GERSHON‡ (10) [GERSHONITE, GERSHONITES]

Ge 46:11 The children of Levi: **G,** Kohath, and Merari.
Ex 6:16 **G,** Kohath, and Merari, and the length
6:17 sons of **G:** Libni and Shimei, by their families.
Nu 3:17 by their names: **G,** Kohath,
3:18 the names of the sons of **G** by their clans:
3:21 To **G** belonged the clan of the Libnites and
3:25 of the sons of **G** in the tent of meeting was to be
26:57 of **G,** the clan of the Gershonites;
1Ch 23: 6 to the sons of Levi: **G,** Kohath,
23: 7 The sons of **G** were Ladan and Shimei.

GERSHONITE‡ (2) [GERSHON]

1Ch 26:21 the heads of families belonging to Ladan the **G:**
29: 8 into the care of Jehiel the **G.**

GERSHONITES (17) [GERSHON]

Nu 3:21 these were the clans of the **G.**
3:23 of the **G** were to camp behind the tabernacle on
3:24 of Lael as head of the ancestral house of the **G.**
4:22 a census of the **G** also, by their ancestral houses
4:24 This is the service of the clans of the **G,**
4:27 All the service of the **G** shall be at the command
4:28 the service of the clans of the **G** relating to the tent
4:38 The enrollment of the **G,** by their clans
4:41 This was the enrollment of the clans of the **G,**
7: 7 Two wagons and four oxen he gave to the **G,**
10:17 and the **G** and the Merarites,
26:57 of Gershon, the clan of the **G;**
Jos 21: 6 The **G** received by lot thirteen towns from
21:27 To the **G,** one of the families of the Levites,
21:33 the several families of the **G** were in all thirteen,
1Ch 26:21 the sons of the **G** belonging to Ladan,
2Ch 29:12 and of the **G,** Joah son of Zimmah,

GERUTH (1)

Jer 41:17 and stopped at **G** Chimham near Bethlehem,

GERUTH CHIMHAM See CHIMHAM, GERUTH

GESHAN (1)

1Ch 2:47 Regem, Jotham, **G,** Pelet, Ephah, and Shaaph.

GESHAM (KJV) See GESHAN

GESHEM (4)

Ne 2:19 and **G** the Arab heard of it,
6: 1 to Sanballat and Tobiah and to **G** the Arab and to
6: 2 Sanballat and **G** sent to me,
6: 6 among the nations—and **G** also says it—

GESHUR (9) [GESHURITES]

Jos 13:13 but **G** and Maacath live within Israel to this day.
2Sa 3: 3 daughter of King Talmai of **G;**
13:37 and went to Talmai son of Ammihud, king of **G.**
13:38 Absalom, having fled to **G,**
14:23 So Joab set off, went to **G,**
14:32 'Why have I come from **G?**
15: 8 For your servant made a vow while I lived at **G**
1Ch 2:23 But **G** and Aram took from them Havvoth-jair,
3: 2 son of Maacah, daughter of King Talmai of **G;**

GESHURITES (6) [GESHUR]

Dt 3:14 the **G** and the Maacathites, and he named them—
Jos 12: 5 to the boundary of the **G** and the Maacathites,
13: 2 of the Philistines, and all those of the **G**
13:11 and the region of the **G** and Maacathites,
13:13 Yet the Israelites did not drive out the **G** or
1Sa 27: 8 and his men went up and made raids on the **G,**

GESTATION (1)

4Mc 13:21 When they were born after an equal time of **g,**

GESTURE (1)

Ac 13:16 So Paul stood up and with a **g** began to speak:

GET‡ (221) [GETS, GETTING, GOT, GOTTEN, ILL-GOTTEN]

Ge 19:14 to marry his daughters, "Up, **g** out of this place;
19:15 the angels urged Lot, saying, **"G** up,
24: 3 not **g** a wife for my son from the daughters of
24: 4 but will go to my country and to my kindred and **g**
24:38 to my kindred, and **g** a wife for my son.'
24:40 You shall **g** a wife for my son from my kindred,
27: 9 Go to the flock, and **g** me two choice kids,
27:13 only obey my word, and go, **g** them for me."
34: 4 saying, **"G** me this girl to be my wife."
34:10 live and trade in it, and **g** property in it."
40:14 and so **g** me out of this place.
Ex 2: 7 and **g** you a nurse from the Hebrew women
5: 4 from their work? **G** to your labors!"
5:11 Go and **g** straw yourselves,
10:28 Then Pharaoh said to him, **"G** away from me!
Nu 11:13 Where am I to **g** meat to give to all this people?
16:24 **G** away from the dwellings of Korah, Dathan,
16:45 **"G** away from this congregation,
17: 2 and **g** twelve staffs from them,
22:20 **g** up and go with them;
Dt 8:18 for it is he who gives you power to **g** wealth,
9:12 Then the LORD said to me, **"G** up,
10:11 The LORD said to me, **"G** up,
24:19 you shall not go back to **g** it;
25:11 If men **g** into a fight with one another,
30:12 **g** it for us so that we may hear it and observe it?"
30:13 **g** it for us so that we may hear it and observe it?"
31: 2 I am no longer able to **g** about,
Jdg 7: 9 That same night the LORD said to him, **"G** up,
7:15 he returned to the camp of Israel, and said, **"G** up;
9:33 as soon as the sun rises, **g** up and rush on the city;
14: 2 now **g** her for me as my wife."
14: 3 But Samson said to his father, **"G** her for me,
19: 9 Tomorrow you can **g** up early in the morning
19:28 **"G** up," he said to her, "we are going."
Ru 2: 9 If you **g** thirsty, go to the vessels and drink
1Sa 6: 7 **g** ready a new cart and two milch cows
9:26 **"G** up, so that I may send you on your way."
20:29 if I have found favor in your sight, let me **g** away,
23:26 David was hurrying to **g** away from Saul,
26:22 Let one of the young men come over and **g** it.
2Sa 5: 8 let him **g** up the water shaft to attack the lame and
11: 4 So David sent messengers to **g** her,
13:15 Amnon said to her, **"G** out!"
15:14 with him at Jerusalem, **"G** up!
1Ki 1: 1 with clothes, he could not **g** warm.
19: 5 an angel touched him and said to him, **"G** up
19: 7 touched him, and said, **"G** up and eat,
21: 7 **G** up, eat some food, and be cheerful;
2Ki 1: 3 the Tishbite, **"G** up, go to meet the messengers of
3:15 But **g** me a musician."
5:20 I will run after him and **g** something out of him."
7:12 we shall take them alive and **g** into the city.' "
8: 1 **"G** up and go with your household,
9: 2 go in and **g** him to leave his companions,
9:21 Joram said, **"G** ready."
2Ch 26:20 and he himself hurried to **g** out,
Ne 5: 2 we must **g** grain, so that we may eat
5: 3 our houses in order to **g** grain during the famine."
Job 9:18 he will not let me **g** my breath,
11:12 But a stupid person will **g** understanding,
20:18 of their trading they will **g** no enjoyment.
21:15 And what profit do we **g** if we pray to him?'
Ps 59:15 and growl if they do not **g** their fill.
107:37 and plant vineyards, and **g** a fruitful yield.
119:104 Through your precepts I **g** understanding;
132: 3 "I will not enter my house or **g** into my bed;
Pr 3:13 and those who **g** understanding,
4: 5 **G** wisdom; **g** insight: do not forget,
4: 7 **G** wisdom, and whatever else you **g, g** insight.
6:33 He will **g** wounds and dishonor,
11: 8 and the wicked **g** into it instead.
11:18 but those who sow righteousness **g** a true reward.
11:25 and one who gives water will **g** water.
13: 8 but the poor **g** no threats.
14:14 The perverse **g** what their ways deserve,
16:16 How much better to **g** wisdom than gold!
16:16 **g** understanding is to be chosen rather than silver.
19: 8 To **g** wisdom is to love oneself;
23: 4 Do not wear yourself out to **g** rich;
24:27 **g** everything ready for you in the field;
28:22 to **g** rich and does not know that loss is sure
28:27 but one who turns a blind eye will **g** many a curse.
Ecc 2:22 What do mortals **g** from all the toil and strain
11: 1 for after many days you will **g** it back.
Isa 40: 9 **G** you up to a high mountain, O Zion,
56:12 "Come," they say, "let us **g** wine;
Jer 8: 4 When people fall, do they not **g** up again?
25:27 Drink, **g** drunk and vomit, fall and rise no more,
32:25 "Buy the field for money and **g** witnesses"—
36:21 Then the king sent Jehudi to **g** the scroll,
49: 8 Flee, turn back, **g** down low,
La 5: 4 the wood we **g** must be bought.
5: 6 a pact with Egypt and Assyria, to **g** enough bread.
5: 9 We **g** our bread at the peril of our lives,
Eze 18:31 and **g** yourselves a new heart and a new spirit!
22:27 destroying lives to **g** dishonest gain.
Da 6:10 to **g** down on his knees three times a day to pray
Jnh 1: 6 **G** up, call on your god!
3: 2 **"G** up, go to Nineveh, that great city,

Hab 2: 9 "Alas for you who g evil gain for your houses,
Zec 6: 7 they were impatient to g off and patrol the earth.
Mt 2:13 "G up, take the child and his mother,
2:20 "G up, take the child and his mother, and go to
5:26 you will never g out until you have paid
7: 2 the measure you give will be the measure you g.
13:54 "Where did this man g this wisdom
13:56 Where then did this man g all this?"
14:22 Immediately he made the disciples g into the boat
15:33 to g enough bread in the desert to feed so great
16:23 he turned and said to Peter, "G behind me, Satan!
17: 7 saying, "G up and do not be afraid."
21:38 come, let us kill him and g his inheritance.'
22:12 how did you g in here without a wedding robe?'
24:18 the one in the field must not turn back to g a coat.
26:46 G up, let us be going.
Mk 4:24 the measure you give will be the measure you g,
5:41 "Talitha cum," which means, "Little girl, g up!"
6: 2 They said, "Where did this man g all this?
6:39 Then he ordered them to g all the people to sit
6:45 Immediately he made his disciples g into the boat
8:33 he rebuked Peter and said, "G behind me, Satan!
10:49 to him, "Take heart; g up,
13:16 the one in the field must not turn back to g a coat.
14:42 G up, let us be going.
Lk 6:38 be the measure you g back."
8:54 by the hand and called out, "Child, g up!"
9:12 to lodge and g provisions;
11: 7 I cannot g up and give you anything.'
11: 8 though he will not g up and give him anything
11: 8 at least because of his persistence he will g up
12:45 and to eat and drink and g drunk,
12:59 you will never g out until you have paid
13:31 "G away from here, for Herod wants to kill you."
15:18 I will g up and go to my father,
15:23 And g the fatted calf and kill it,
17:19 Then he said to him, "G up and go on your way;
18:30 who will not g back very much more in this age,
19:12 a distant country to g royal power for himself and
21:38 the people would g up early in the morning
22:46 G up and pray that you may not come into
Jn 1:48 "Where did you g to know me?"
4:11 Where do you g that living water?
6: 7 not buy enough bread for each of them to g
11:31 consoling her, saw Mary g up quickly and go out.
19:24 but cast lots for it to see who will g it."
Ac 8:26 "G up and go toward the south to the road
8:31 And he invited Philip to g in and sit beside him.
9: 6 But g up and enter the city,
9:11 "G up and go to the street called Straight,
9:34 g up and make your bed!"
9:40 He turned to the body and said, "Tabitha, g up."
10:13 Then he heard a voice saying, "G up, Peter;
10:20 Now g up, go down, and go with them
10:26 But Peter made him g up, saying, "Stand up;
11: 7 I also heard a voice saying to me, 'G up, Peter;
12: 7 on the side and woke him, saying, "G up quickly."
19:25 you know that we g our wealth from this business.
22:10 The Lord said to me, 'G up and go to Damascus;
22:16 now why do you delay? G up, be baptized,
22:18 'Hurry and g out of Jerusalem quickly,
22:28 a large sum of money to g my citizenship."
23:23 "G ready to leave by nine o'clock tonight
26:16 But g up and stand on your feet;
27:16 to g the ship's boat under control.
Ro 6:21 So what advantage did you then g from the things
6:22 the advantage you g is sanctification.
1Co 9: 7 who tends a flock and does not g any of its milk?
9:13 in the temple service g their food from the temple,
9:14 the gospel should g their living by the gospel.
14: 8 who will g ready for battle?
Eph 5:18 Do not g drunk with wine, for that is debauchery;
Col 3: 8 But now you must g rid of all such things—
1Th 5: 7 and those who are drunk g drunk at night.
2Ti 4:11 G Mark and bring him with you,
Jas 4: 3 in order to spend what you g on your pleasures.
Tob 2:13 I called her and said, "Where did you g this goat?
5: 2 not know the roads to Media, or how to g there."
5: 3 But g back the money from Gabael."
7:15 g the other room ready, and take her there."
8: 4 and said to Sarah, "Sister, g up, and let us pray
9: 2 give him the bond, g the money,
12:13 And that time when you did not hesitate to g up
12:20 now g up from the ground, and acknowledge God.
Jdt 7:13 where all the people of Bethulia g their water.
12: 3 where can we g you more of the same?
AdE 4:5 and ordered him to g accurate information for her
Wis 7:14 those who g it obtain friendship with God,
8:18 I went about seeking how to g her for myself.
15:12 for they say one must g money however one can,
Sir 6:27 and when you g hold of her, do not let her go.
10: 6 not g angry with your neighbor for every injury,
20:16 and I g no thanks for my good deeds.
27: 1 and those who seek to g rich will avert their eyes.
29: 6 If he can pay, his creditor will hardly g back half,
31:21 If you are overstuffed with food, g up to vomit,
Bar 3:18 those who schemed to g silver,
1Mc 3:41 and went to the camp to g the Israelites for slaves.
5:48 "Let us pass through your land to g to our land.
8: 3 to g control of the silver and gold mines there,
9: 8 "Let us g up and go against our enemies.
9:44 "Let us g up now and fight for our lives,
11: 1 to g possession of Alexander's kingdom
13:17 but he sent to g the money and the sons,
16:13 he determined to g control of the country,
2Mc 1:20 of the priests who had hidden the fire to g it.
2:15 send people to g them for you.
3:32 fearing that the king might g the notion
3:38 for you will g him back thoroughly flogged,
7:11 and from him I hope to g them back again."
7:29 that in God's mercy I may g you back again along
9: 4 "When I g there I will make Jerusalem a cemetery
13:13 and g possession of the city.
15: 7 to trust with all confidence that he would g help
2Es 7:59 the person who has what is hard to g rejoices more
4Mc 2:18 the temperate mind is able to g the better of
5:32 Therefore g your torture wheels ready and fan
6: 8 and began to kick him in the side to make him g

GETHER (2)

Ge 10:23 The descendants of Aram: Uz, Hul, G, and Mash.
1Ch 1:17 Asshur, Arpachshad, Lud, Aram, Uz, Hul, G,

GETHSEMANE (2)

Mt 26:36 Then Jesus went with them to a place called G;
Mk 14:32 They went to a place called G;

GETS (12) [GET]

Pr 9: 7 whoever rebukes the wicked g hurt.
11:16 A gracious woman g honor,
13: 4 The appetite of the lazy craves, and g nothing,
17:21 The one who begets a fool g trouble;
29:26 but it is from the LORD that one g justice.
30:23 an unloved woman when she g a husband,
2Ti 2: 4 in the army g entangled in everyday affairs;
Jdt 7:13 to keep watch to see that no one g out of the town.
Sir 13: 1 Whoever touches pitch g dirty,
29: 5 One kisses another's hands until he g a loan,
36:29 He who acquires a wife g his best possession,
40: 6 He g little or no rest;

GETTING (10) [GET]

Pr 21: 6 The g of treasures by a lying tongue is
Mt 9: 1 after g into a boat he crossed the sea and came
Mk 5:18 As he was g into the boat,
8:13 And he left them, and g into the boat again,
Lk 1: 7 and both were g on in years.
1:18 I am an old man, and my wife is g on in years."
23:41 for we are g what we deserve for our deeds,
Tob 10: 7 in and mourn and weep all night long, g no sleep
Bar 3:17 and there is no end to their g;
1Mc 5:27 the enemy are g ready to attack

GEUEL (1)

Nu 13:15 from the tribe of Gad, G son of Machi.

GEZER (15)

Jos 10:33 Then King Horam of G came up to help Lachish;
12:12 the king of Eglon one the king of G one
16: 3 then to G, and it ends at the sea.
16:10 however, drive out the Canaanites who lived in G:
21:21 of Ephraim, G with its pasture lands,
Jdg 1:29 not drive out the Canaanites who lived in G;
1:29 but the Canaanites lived among them in G.
2Sa 5:25 down the Philistines from Geba all the way to G.
1Ki 9:15 and the wall of Jerusalem, Hazor, Megiddo, G
9:16 up and captured G and burned it down, had killed
9:17 so Solomon rebuilt G), Lower Beth-horon,
1Ch 6:67 of Ephraim, G with its pasture lands,
7:28 and westward G and its towns,
14:16 down the Philistine army from Gibeon to G.
20: 4 After this, war broke out with the Philistines at G;

GEZRITES (KJV) See GIRZITES

GHOST (5) [GHOSTS]

Isa 29: 4 from the ground like the voice of a g,
Mt 14:26 they were terrified, saying, "It is a g!"
Mk 6:49 they thought it was a g and cried out;
Lk 24:37 and thought that they were seeing a g.
24:39 for a g does not have flesh and bones as you see

[GIVE UP THE] GHOST (KJV) See BREATHED HIS LAST, DIE, EXPIRE, PERISHED, SWOONED AWAY

[HOLY] GHOST (KJV) See [HOLY] SPIRIT

GHOSTS (3) [GHOST]

Dt 18:11 or who consults g or spirits,
Isa 8:19 the g and the familiar spirits that chirp and mutter;
19: 3 the idols and the spirits of the dead and the g and

GIAH (1)

2Sa 2:24 before G on the way to the wilderness of Gibeon.

GIANT (2) [GIANTS]

Sir 47: 4 In his youth did he not kill a g,
1Mc 3: 3 Like a g he put on his breastplate;

GIANT (KJV) See also WARRIOR

GIANTS (12) [GIANT]

2Sa 21:16 Ishbi-benob, one of the descendants of the g,
21:18 who was one of the descendants of the g.
21:20 he too was descended from the g.
21:22 These four were descended from the g in Gath;
1Ch 20: 4 who was one of the descendants of the g;
20: 6 he also was descended from the g.
20: 8 These were descended from the g in Gath;
Jdt 16: 6 nor did tall g set upon him;
Wis 14: 6 in the beginning, when arrogant g were perishing,
Sir 16: 7 He did not forgive the ancient g who revolted
Bar 3:26 The g were born there, who were famous of old,
3Mc 2: 4 even g who trusted in their strength and boldness,

GIBBAR (1)

Ezr 2:20 Of G, ninety-five.

GIBBETHON (6)

Jos 19:44 Eltekeh, G, Baalath,
21:23 with its pasture lands, G with its pasture lands,
1Ki 15:27 and Baasha struck him down at G,
15:27 for Nadab and all Israel were laying siege to G.
16:15 Now the troops were encamped against G,
16:17 So Omri went up from G, and all Israel with him,

GIBEA (1)

1Ch 2:49 Sheva father of Machbenah and father of G;

GIBEAH‡ (46) [=GEBA]

Jos 15:57 G, and Timnah: ten towns with their villages.
18:28 Jebus (that is, Jerusalem), G and Kiriath-jearim—
24:33 and they buried him at G,
Jdg 19:12 but we will continue on to G."
19:13 and spend the night at G or at Ramah."
19:14 and the sun went down on them near G,
19:15 to go in and spend the night at G.
19:16 and he was residing in G.
20: 4 answered, "I came to G that belongs to Benjamin,
20: 5 The lords of G rose up against me,
20: 9 But now this is what we will do to G:
20:10 who are going to repay G of Benjamin for all
20:13 Now then, hand over those scoundrels in G,
20:14 Benjaminites came together out of the towns to G,
20:15 besides the inhabitants of G.
20:19 up in the morning, and encamped against G.
20:20 up the battle line against them at G.
20:21 The Benjaminites came out of G,
20:25 Benjamin moved out against them from G
20:29 So Israel stationed men in ambush around G.
20:30 and set themselves in array against G, as before.
20:31 one of which goes up to Bethel and the other to G,
20:34 against G ten thousand picked men out
20:36 in ambush that they had stationed against G.
20:37 The troops in ambush rushed quickly upon G.
20:43 and trod them down as far as a place east of G.
1Sa 10:10 When they were going from there to G,
10:26 Saul also went to his home at G,
11: 4 When the messengers came to G of Saul,
13: 2 a thousand were with Jonathan in G of Benjamin;
13:15 they went up from Gilgal toward G of Benjamin.
14: 2 of G under the pomegranate tree that is at Migron;
14:16 Saul's lookouts in G of Benjamin were watching
15:34 and Saul went up to his house in G of Saul.
22: 6 Saul was sitting at G, under the tamarisk tree on
23:19 Then some Ziphites went up to Saul at G and said,
26: 1 Then the Ziphites came to Saul at G, saying,
2Sa 23:29 Ittai son of Ribai of G of the Benjaminites;
1Ch 11:31 Ithai son of Ribai of G of the Benjaminites,
12: 3 then Joash, both sons of Shemaah of G;
2Ch 13: 2 name was Micaiah daughter of Uriel of G.
Isa 10:29 Ramah trembles, G of Saul has fled.
Hos 5: 8 Blow the horn in G, the trumpet in Ramah.
9: 9 as in the days of G;
10: 9 Since the days of G you have sinned, O Israel;
10: 9 Shall not war overtake them in G?

GIBEATH See Index to Footnotes

GIBEATH-ELOHIM (1)

1Sa 10: 5 After that you shall come to G,

GIBEATH-HAARALOTH (1)

Jos 5: 3 and circumcised the Israelites at G.

GIBEON (38) [GIBEONITE, GIBEONITES]

Jos 9: 3 the inhabitants of G heard what Joshua had done
9:17 Now their cities were G, Chephirah, Beeroth,
10: 1 the inhabitants of G had made peace with Israel
10: 2 because G was a large city,
10: 4 up and help me, and let us attack G;
10: 5 up with all their armies and camped against G,
10:10 who inflicted a great slaughter on them at G,
10:12 "Sun, stand still at G, and Moon, in the valley of
10:41 and all the country of Goshen, as far as G.
11:19 the inhabitants of G; all were taken in battle.
18:25 G, Ramah, Beeroth,
21:17 G with its pasture lands, Geba
2Sa 2:12 went out from Mahanaim to G.
2:13 went out and met them at the pool of G.
2:16 place was called Helkath-hazzurim, which is at G.
2:24 before Giah on the way to the wilderness of G.
3:30 he had killed their brother Asahel in the battle at G.
20: 8 When they were at the large stone that is in G,
21: 6 the LORD at G on the mountain of the LORD."
1Ki 3: 4 The king went to G to sacrifice there,
3: 5 At G the LORD appeared to Solomon in a dream
9: 2 as he had appeared to him at G.

1Ch 8:29 Jeiel the father of G lived in G,
9:35 In G lived the father of G, Jeiel,
12: 4 Ishmaiah of G, a warrior among the Thirty and
14:16 and they struck down the Philistine army from G
16:39 of the LORD in the high place that was at G,
21:29 at that time in the high place at G;
2Ch 1: 3 went to the high place that was at G;
1:13 So Solomon came from the high place at G,
Ne 3: 7 the men of G and of Mizpah—
7:25 Of G, ninety-five.
Isa 28:21 he will rage as in the valley of G;
Jer 28: 1 from G, spoke to me in the house of the LORD,
41:12 They came upon him at the great pool that is in G.
41:16 whom Johanan brought back from G.

GIBEONITE (1) [GIBEON]

Ne 3: 7 Next to them repairs were made by Melatiah the G

GIBEONITES (7) [GIBEON]

Jos 10: 6 And the G sent to Joshua at the camp in Gilgal,
2Sa 21: 1 because he put the G to death."
21: 2 So the king called the G and spoke to them.
21: 2 (Now the G were not of the people of Israel,
21: 3 David said to the G, "What shall I do for you?
21: 4 The G said to him, "It is not a matter of silver
21: 9 he gave them into the hands of the G,

GIBLITES (KJV) See GEBALITES

GIDDALTI (2)

1Ch 25: 4 G, and Romamti-ezer, Joshbekashah, Mallothi,
25:29 to G, his sons and his brothers, twelve;

GIDDEL (4)

Ezr 2:47 G, Gahar, Reaiah,
2:56 Jaalah, Darkon, G,
Ne 7:49 of Hanan, of G, of Gahar,
7:58 of Jaala, of Darkon, of G,

GIDEON (43) [=JERUBBAAL]

Jdg 6:11 his son G was beating out wheat in the wine press,
6:13 G answered him, "But sir,
6:19 So G went into his house and prepared a kid,
6:22 G perceived that it was the angel of the LORD;
6:22 and G said, "Help me, Lord GOD!
6:24 Then G built an altar there to the LORD,
6:27 So G took ten of his servants,
6:29 they were told, "G son of Joash did it."
6:32 Therefore on that day G was called Jerubbaal,
6:34 But the spirit of the LORD took possession of G;
6:36 Then G said to God, "In order
6:39 Then G said to God, "Do not let your anger burn
7: 1 (that is, G) and all the troops that were with him
7: 2 to G, "The troops with you are too many for me
7: 3 let him return home.' " Thus G sifted them out;
7: 4 LORD said to G, "The troops are still too many;
7: 5 and the LORD said to G,
7: 7 Then the LORD said to G,
7:13 When G arrived, there was a man telling a dream
7:14 the sword of G son of Joash, a man of Israel;
7:15 When G heard the telling of the dream
7:18 and shout, 'For the LORD and for G!' "
7:19 So G and the hundred who were with him came to
7:20 they cried, "A sword for the LORD and for G!"
7:24 Then G sent messengers throughout all
7:25 They brought the heads of Oreb and Zeeb to G
8: 4 Then G came to the Jordan and crossed over,
8: 7 G replied, "Well then,
8:11 So G went up by the caravan route east of Nobah
8:13 When G son of Joash returned from the battle by
8:21 So G proceeded to kill Zebah and Zalmunna;
8:22 Then the Israelites said to G, "Rule over us,
8:23 G said to them, "I will not rule over you,
8:24 G said to them, "Let me make a request of you;
8:27 G made an ephod of it and put it in his town,
8:27 and it became a snare to G and to his family.
8:28 So the land had rest forty years in the days of G.
8:30 Now G had seventy sons, his own offspring,
8:32 Then G son of Joash died at a good old age,
8:33 As soon as G died, the Israelites relapsed
8:35 G) in return for all the good that he had done
Heb 11:32 For time would fail me to tell of G, Barak,
Jdt 8: 1 of Ananias son of G son of Raphain son

GIDEONI (5)

Nu 1:11 From Benjamin, Abidan son of G.
2:22 of the Benjaminites shall be Abidan son of G,
7:60 On the ninth day Abidan son of G,
7:65 This was the offering of Abidan son of G.
10:24 of the tribe of Benjamin was Abidan son of G.

GIDOM (1)

Jdg 20:45 and they were pursued as far as G,

GIER (KJV) See VULTURE

GIFT‡ (90) [GIFTED, GIFTS]

Ge 33:11 Please accept my g that is brought to you,
34:12 Put the marriage present and g as high as you like,
Lev 1:10 If your g for a burnt offering is from the flock,
7:14 as a g to the LORD;
Nu 5: 9 every g that they bring to the priest shall be his.
Nu 6:14 and they shall offer their g to the LORD,
8:19 the Levites as a g to Aaron and his sons from
18: 6 they are now yours as a g,
18: 7 I give your priesthood as a g;
18:27 It shall be reckoned to you as your g,
1Sa 2:20 by this woman for the g that she made to
2Sa 19:42 Or has he given us any g?"
1Ki 13: 7 and I will give you a g."
Job 6:22 Have I said, 'Make me a g'?
Pr 18:16 A g opens doors; it gives access to the great.
21:14 A g in secret averts anger;
25:14 without rain is one who boasts of a g never given.
Ecc 3:13 it is God's g that all should eat and drink
5:19 this is the g of God.
Isa 40:20 a g one chooses mulberry wood —wood that will
Eze 46:16 If the prince makes a g to any of his sons out
46:17 But if he makes a g out of his inheritance to one
46:17 only his sons may keep a g from his inheritance.
Mt 5:23 So when you are offering your g at the altar,
5:24 leave your g there before the altar and go;
5:24 and then come and offer your g.
8: 4 and offer the g that Moses commanded,
23:18 by the g that is on the altar is bound by the oath.'
23:19 the g or the altar that makes the g sacred?
Jn 4:10 Jesus answered her, "If you knew the g of God,
Ac 2:38 and you will receive the g of the Holy Spirit.
8:20 because you thought you could obtain God's g
10:45 the g of the Holy Spirit had been poured out even
11:17 If then God gave them the same g that he gave us
21: 9 He had four unmarried daughters who had the g
Ro 1:11 with you some spiritual g to strengthen you—
3:24 they are now justified by his grace as a g,
4: 4 not reckoned as a g but as something due.
5:15 But the free g is not like the trespass.
5:15 of God and the free g in the grace of the one man,
5:16 free g is not like the effect of the one man's sin.
5:16 g following many trespasses brings justification.
5:17 and the free g of righteousness exercise dominion
6:23 but the free g of God is eternal life
11:35 who has given a g to him, to receive a g in return?"
1Co 1: 7 in any spiritual g as you wait for the revealing
4: 7 why do you boast as if it were not a g?
7: 7 But each has a particular g from God,
16: 3 with letters to take your g to Jerusalem.
2Co 8:12 the g is acceptable according to what one has—
8:20 that no one should blame us about this generous g
9: 5 for this bountiful g that you have promised,
9: 5 so that it may be ready as a voluntary g and not as
9:15 Thanks be to God for his indescribable g!
Eph 2: 8 this is not your own doing; it is the g of God—
3: 7 to the g of God's grace that was given me by
4: 7 according to the measure of Christ's g.
Php 4:17 Not that I seek the g,
1Ti 4:14 Do not neglect the g that is in you,
2Ti 1: 6 to rekindle the g of God that is within you through
Heb 6: 4 and have tasted the heavenly g,
Jas 1:17 with every perfect g, is from above,
1Pe 3: 7 they too are also heirs of the gracious g of life—
4:10 with whatever g each of you has received.
Rev 21: 6 the thirsty I will give water as a g from the spring
22:17 the water of life as a g.
Tob 2:14 to me as a g in addition to my wages."
4: 7 not let your eye begrudge the g when you make it.
4: 8 make your g from them in proportion;
Wis 8:21 a mark of insight to know whose g she was—
Sir 1:10 upon all the living according to his g;
7:31 the guilt offering, the g of the shoulders,
11:17 The Lord's g remains with the devout,
18:15 or spoil your g by harsh words.
18:16 So a word is better than a g.
18:17 Indeed, does not a word surpass a good g?
18:18 and the g of a grudging giver makes the eyes dim.
20:10 There is the g that profits you nothing,
20:10 and the g to be paid back double.
20:14 A fool's g will profit you nothing,
26:14 A silent wife is a g from the Lord,
35:11 With every g show a cheerful face,
37:21 for the Lord has withheld the g of charm,
38: 2 for their g of healing comes from the Most High,
41:21 of taking away someone's portion or g,
41:22 and do not be insulting after making a g.
1Mc 10:39 and the land adjoining it I have given as a g to
2Mc 15:16 a g from God, with which you will strike

GIFTED (1) [GIFT]

Wis 8:19 As a child I was naturally g,

GIFTS‡ (101) [GIFT]

Ge 24:10 taking all kinds of choice g from his master;
25: 6 to the sons of his concubines Abraham gave g,
Lev 23:38 of the LORD, and apart from your g, and apart
Nu 18: 8 all the holy g of the Israelites;
18:11 the g of all the elevation offerings of the Israelites;
18:29 Out of all the g to you,
18:32 you shall not profane the holy g of the Israelites,
Dt 12: 6 your tithes and your donations, your votive g,
12:11 and your donations, and all your choice votive g
12:17 any of your votive g that you vow,
12:26 and your votive g, you shall bring to the place that
33:13 with the choice g of heaven above,
33:16 with the choice g of the earth and its fullness,
1Ki 15:15 the house of the LORD the votive g of his father
and his own votive g—
2Ki 12:18 of Judah took all the votive g that Jehoshaphat,
12:18 had dedicated, as well as his own votive g,
1Ch 26:20 of God and the treasuries of the dedicated g.
1Ch 26:26 the treasuries of the dedicated g that King David,
26:27 in battles they dedicated g for the maintenance of
26:28 all dedicated g were in the care of Shelomoth
28:12 and the treasuries for dedicated g;
2Ch 15:18 into the house of God the votive g of his father
and his own votive g—
21: 3 Their father gave them many g, of silver, gold,
32:23 Many brought g to the LORD in Jerusalem
Ezr 1: 6 with goods, with animals, and with valuable g,
Ne 9:36 to our ancestors to enjoy its fruit and its good g.
Est 2:18 and gave g with royal liberality.
9:19 on which they send g of food to one another.
9:22 for sending g of food to one another and presents
Ps 45:12 the people of Tyre will seek your favor with g,
68:18 leading captives in your train and receiving g
68:29 of your temple at Jerusalem kings bear g to you.
72:10 may the kings of Sheba and Seba bring g.
76:11 around him bring g to the one who is awesome,
Pr 19: 6 and everyone is a friend to a giver of g.
Isa 1:23 Everyone loves a bribe and runs after g.
18: 7 that time g will be brought to the LORD of hosts
Eze 16:33 G are given to all whores;
16:33 but you gave your g to all your lovers,
20:26 I defiled them through their very g,
20:31 When you offer your g
20:39 with your g and your idols.
20:40 and the choicest of your g,
Da 2: 6 you shall receive from me g and rewards
2:48 the king promoted Daniel, gave him many great g,
5:17 "Let your g be for yourself,
11:38 with precious stones and costly g.
Mic 1:14 you shall give parting g to Moresheth-gath;
Mt 2:11 they offered him g of gold, frankincense,
7:11 know how to give good g to your children,
Lk 11:13 know how to give good g to your children,
21: 1 He looked up and saw rich people putting their g
21: 5 with beautiful stones and g dedicated to God,
Ro 11:29 for the g and the calling of God are irrevocable.
12: 6 We have g that differ according to the grace given
1Co 2:12 we may understand the g bestowed on us by God.
2:14 Those who are unspiritual do not receive the g
12: 1 Now concerning spiritual g, brothers and sisters,
12: 4 Now there are varieties of g, but the same Spirit;
12: 9 to another g of healing by the one Spirit,
12:28 then deeds of power, then g of healing,
12:30 Do all possess g of healing?
12:31 But strive for the greater g.
14: 1 Pursue love and strive for the spiritual g,
14:12 since you are eager for spiritual g,
Eph 4: 8 he gave g to his people."
4:11 The g he gave were that some would be apostles,
Php 4:18 I have received from Epaphroditus the g you sent,
Heb 2: 4 and by g of the Holy Spirit,
5: 1 to offer g and sacrifices for sins.
8: 3 For every high priest is appointed to offer g
8: 4 there are priests who offer g according to the law.
9: 9 during which g and sacrifices are offered
11: 4 God himself giving approval to his g;
Tob 11:18 and many g were given to him.
13:11 bearing g in their hands for the King of heaven.
Jdt 16:18 their freewill offerings, and their g.
Wis 7:14 commended for the g that come from instruction.
Sir 7: 9 "He will consider the great number of my g,
20:29 Favors and g blind the eyes of the wise;
32:13 who fills you with his good g.
34:22 the g of the lawless are not acceptable.
LtJ 6:27 G are placed before them just as before the dead.
1Mc 2:18 be honored with silver and gold and many g."
3:30 before for his expenses and for the g that he used
10:24 of encouragement and promise them honor and g,
10:28 will grant you many immunities and give you g.
10:54 and will make g to you and to her in keeping
10:60 and their Friends silver and gold and many g,
11:24 and gold and clothing and numerous other g,
12:43 and he gave him g and commanded his Friends
16:19 so that he might give them silver and gold and g;
2Mc 1:35 the king favored he exchanged many excellent g.
1Es 2: 7 with g and with horses and cattle,
3: 5 King Darius will give rich g and great honors
8:13 to carry to Jerusalem the g for the Lord of Israel
3Mc 1: 7 and by endowing their sacred enclosures with g,
1: 8 to bring him g of welcome,
4Mc 5: 9 and wrong to spurn the g of nature.

GIHON (7)

Ge 2:13 The name of the second river is G;
1Ki 1:33 and bring him down to G.
1:38 on King David's mule, and led him to G.
1:45 the prophet Nathan have anointed him king at G;
2Ch 32:30 of G and directed them down to the west side of
33:14 an outer wall for the city of David west of G, in
Sir 24:27 like the G at the time of vintage.

GILALAI (1)

Ne 12:36 Milalai, G, Maai, Nethanel, Judah, and Hanani,

GILBOA (8)

1Sa 28: 4 Saul gathered all Israel, and they encamped at G.
31: 1 and many fell on Mount G.
31: 8 and his three sons fallen on Mount G.
2Sa 1: 6 "I happened to be on Mount G;
1:21 You mountains of G, let there be no dew or rain
21:12 on the day the Philistines killed Saul on G.
1Ch 10: 1 and fell slain on Mount G.
10: 8 they found Saul and his sons fallen on Mount G.

GILEAD‡ (109) [GILEAD'S, GILEADITE, GILEADITES, JABESH-GILEAD, RAMOTH-GILEAD]

A. LAND OF GILEAD (17)

Ge 31:21 and set his face toward the hill country of **G.**
31:23 up with him in the hill country of **G.**
31:25 with his kinsfolk camped in the hill country of **G.**
37:25 a caravan of Ishmaelites coming from **G,**
Nu 26:29 and Machir was the father of **G;**
26:29 of **G,** the clan of the Gileadites.
26:30 These are the descendants of **G:**
27: 1 Zelophehad was son of Hepher son of **G** son
32: 1 and the land of **G** was a good place for cattle, A
32:26 our livestock shall remain there in the towns of **G;**
32:29 shall give them the land of **G** for a possession; A
32:39 of Machir son of Manasseh went to **G,** captured it,
32:40 so Moses gave **G** to Machir son of Manasseh,
36: 1 of the descendants of **G** son of Machir son
Dt 2:36 the town that is in the wadi itself) as far as **G,**
3:10 the whole of **G,** and all of Bashan,
3:12 as well as half the hill country of **G** with its towns,
3:13 to the half-tribe of Manasseh the rest of **G** and all
3:15 To Machir I gave **G.**
3:16 from **G** as far as the Wadi Arnon, with the middle
4:43 Ramoth in **G** belonging to the Gadites,
34: 1 LORD showed him the whole land: **G** as far as Dan,
Jos 12: 2 the boundary of the Ammonites, that is, half of **G,**
12: 5 and over half of **G** to the boundary of King Sihon
13:11 and **G,** and the region of the Geshurites
13:25 Their territory was Jazer, and all the towns of **G,**
13:31 and half of **G,** and Ashtaroth, and Edrei, the towns
17: 1 the father of **G,** were allotted **G** and Bashan,
17: 3 of **G** son of Machir son of Manasseh had no sons,
17: 5 besides the land of **G** and Bashan, A
17: 6 The land of **G** was allotted to the rest of the A
20: 8 from the tribe of Reuben, and Ramoth in **G,**
21:38 Ramoth in **G** with its pasture lands,
22: 9 to go to the land of **G,** A
22:13 and the half-tribe of Manasseh, in the land of **G,** A
22:15 and the half-tribe of Manasseh, in the land of **G,** A
22:32 Gadites in the land of **G** to the land of Canaan, A
Jdg 5:17 **G** stayed beyond the Jordan;
10: 4 had thirty towns, which are in the land of **G,** A
10: 8 in the land of the Amorites, which is in **G.**
10:17 and they encamped in **G;**
10:18 The commanders of the people of **G** said
10:18 He shall be head over all the inhabitants of **G.**"
11: 1 **G** was the father of Jephthah.
11: 5 of **G** went to bring Jephthah from the land of Tob.
11: 7 But Jephthah said to the elders of **G,**
11: 8 The elders of **G** said to Jephthah, "Nevertheless,
11: 8 over all the inhabitants of **G.**"
11: 9 Jephthah said to the elders of **G,**
11:10 And the elders of **G** said to Jephthah,
11:11 So Jephthah went with the elders of **G,**
11:29 and he passed through **G** and Manasseh.
11:29 He passed on to Mizpah of **G,**
11:29 and from Mizpah of **G** he passed on to
12: 4 Then Jephthah gathered all the men of **G**
12: 4 and the men of **G** defeated Ephraim,
12: 5 "Let me go over," the men of **G** would say to him,
12: 7 and was buried in his town in **G.**
20: 1 Dan to Beer-sheba, including the land of **G,** A
1Sa 13: 7 the Jordan to the land of Gad and **G.**
2Sa 2: 9 He made him king over **G,** the Ashurites, Jezreel,
17:26 and Absalom encamped in the land of **G.** A
24: 6 Then they came to **G,** and to Kadesh in the land
1Ki 4:13 which are in **G,** and he had the region of Argob,
4:19 in the land of **G,** the country of King Sihon A
17: 1 Now Elijah the Tishbite, of Tishbe in **G,**
2Ki 10:33 all the land of **G,** the Gadites, the Reubenites, A
10:33 by the Wadi Arnon, that is, **G** and Bashan.
15:29 Hazor, **G,** and Galilee, all the land of Naphtali;
1Ch 2:21 of Machir father of **G,** whom he married
2:22 who had twenty-three towns in the land of **G.** A
2:23 All these were descendants of Machir, father of **G.**
5: 9 their cattle had multiplied in the land of **G.** A
5:10 in their tents throughout all the region east of **G.**
5:14 son of **G,** son of Michael, son of Jeshishai,
5:16 and they lived in **G,** in Bashan and in its towns,
6:80 Ramoth in **G** with its pasture lands,
7:14 she bore Machir the father of **G.**
7:17 These were the sons of **G** son of Machir,
26:31 among them were found at Jazer in **G.**)
27:21 for the half-tribe of Manasseh in **G,** Iddo son
Ps 60: 7 **G** is mine, and Manasseh is mine;
108: 8 **G** is mine; Manasseh is mine;
SS 4: 1 moving down the slopes of **G.**
6: 5 moving down the slopes of **G.**
Jer 8:22 Is there no balm in **G?**
22: 6 You are like **G** to me, like the summit of Lebanon;
46:11 Go up to **G,** and take balm,
50:19 of Ephraim and in **G** its hunger shall be satisfied.
Eze 47:18 along the Jordan between **G** and the land of Israel;
Hos 6: 8 **G** is a city of evildoers, tracked with blood.
12:11 In **G** there is iniquity, they shall surely come
Am 1: 3 because they have threshed **G**
1:13 in **G** in order to enlarge their territory.
Ob 1:19 and Benjamin shall possess **G.**
Mic 7:14 let them feed in Bashan and **G** as in the days
Zec 10:10 I will bring them to the land of **G** and to A
Jdt 1: 8 and those among the nations of Carmel and **G,**
15: 5 The men in **G** and in Galilee outflanked them
1Mc 5: 9 Now the Gentiles in **G** gathered together against
1Mc 5:17 Jonathan my brother and I will go to **G.**"
5:20 and eight thousand to Judas for **G.**
5:25 that had happened to their kindred in **G:**
5:27 some have been shut up in the other towns of **G;**
5:36 Maked, and Bosor, and the other towns of **G.**
5:45 Judas gathered together all the Israelites in **G,**
5:55 in **G** and their brother Simon was in Galilee
13:22 He marched off and went into the land of **G.** A

GILEAD'S (1) [GILEAD]

Jdg 11: 2 **G** wife also bore him sons;

GILEADITE (9) [GILEAD]

Jdg 10: 3 After him came Jair the **G,**
11: 1 Now Jephthah the **G,** the son of a prostitute,
11:40 to lament the daughter of Jephthah the **G.**
12: 7 Then Jephthah the **G** died,
2Sa 17:27 and Barzillai the **G** from Rogelim,
19:31 Barzillai the **G** had come down from Rogelim;
1Ki 2: 7 however, with the sons of Barzillai the **G,**
Ezr 2:61 of the daughters of Barzillai the **G,**
Ne 7:63 of the daughters of Barzillai the **G** and was called

GILEADITES (4) [GILEAD]

Nu 26:29 of Gilead, the clan of the **G.**
Jdg 12: 4 you **G**—in the heart of Ephraim and Manasseh."
12: 5 Then the **G** took the fords of the Jordan against
2Ki 15:25 conspired against him with fifty of the **G,**

GILGAL‡ (41) [BETH-GILGAL]

Dt 11:30 opposite **G,** beside the oak of Moreh.
Jos 4:19 they camped in **G** on the east border of Jericho.
4:20 of the Jordan, Joshua set up in **G,**
5: 9 And so that place is called **G** to this day.
5:10 While the Israelites were camped in **G** they kept
9: 6 They went to Joshua in the camp at **G,**
10: 6 the Gibeonites sent to Joshua at the camp in **G,**
10: 7 So Joshua went up from **G,**
10: 9 having marched up all night from **G.**
10:15 and all Israel with him, to the camp at **G.**
10:43 and all Israel with him, to the camp at **G.**
14: 6 Then the people of Judah came to Joshua at **G;**
15: 7 and so northward, turning toward **G,**
Jdg 2: 1 angel of the LORD went up from **G** to Bochim,
3:19 at the sculptured stones near **G,**
1Sa 7:16 He went on a circuit year by year to Bethel, **G,**
10: 8 And you shall go down to **G** ahead of me;
11:14 let us go to **G** and there renew the kingship."
11:15 So all the people went to **G,**
11:15 there they made Saul king before the LORD in **G.**
13: 4 the people were called out to join Saul at **G.**
13: 7 Saul was still at **G,** and all
13: 8 but Samuel did not come to **G,**
13:12 the Philistines will come down upon me at **G,**
13:15 And Samuel left and went on his way from **G.**
13:15 they went up from **G** toward Gibeah of Benjamin.
15:12 and on returning he passed on down to **G.**"
15:21 to sacrifice to the LORD your God in **G.**"
15:33 in pieces before the LORD in **G.**
2Sa 19:15 to **G** to meet the king and to bring him over
19:40 The king went on to **G,** and Chimham went on
2Ki 2: 1 Elijah and Elisha were on their way from **G.**
4:38 When Elisha returned to **G,**
Hos 4:15 Do not enter into **G,** or go up to Beth-aven,
9:15 Every evil of theirs began at **G;**
12:11 In **G** they sacrifice bulls, so their altars shall be
Am 4: 4 Come to Bethel—and transgress; to **G**—
5: 5 do not enter into **G** or cross over to Beer-sheba;
5: 5 for **G** shall surely go into exile,
Mic 6: 5 and what happened from Shittim to **G,**
1Mc 9: 2 to **G** and encamped against Mesaloth in Arbela,

GILOH (2) [GILONITE]

Jos 15:51 Holon, and **G:** eleven towns with their villages.
2Sa 15:12 David's counselor, from his city **G.**

GILONITE (2) [GILOH]

2Sa 15:12 he sent for Ahithophel the **G,** David's counselor,
23:34 Eliam son of Ahithophel the **G;**

GIMZO (1)

2Ch 28:18 Timnah with its villages, and **G** with its villages;

GIN (KJV) See TRAP

GINATH (2)

1Ki 16:21 half of the people followed Tibni son of **G,**
16:22 the people who followed Tibni son of **G;**

GINNETHOI (1)

Ne 12: 4 Iddo, **G,** Abijah,

GINNETHON (2)

Ne 10: 6 Daniel, **G,** Baruch,
12:16 of Iddo, Zechariah; of **G,** Meshullam;

GIRD‡ (13) [GIRDED, GIRDING, GIRDS]

Ex 29: 5 and **g** him with the decorated band of the ephod;
29: 9 and you shall **g** them with sashes
1Sa 2: 4 but the feeble **g** on strength.
2Ki 4:29 He said to Gehazi, "**G** up your loins,
2Ki 9: 1 of the company of prophets and said to him, "**G**
Job 38: 3 **G** up your loins like a man, I will question you,
40: 7 "**G** up your loins like a man;
Ps 45: 3 **G** your sword on your thigh, O mighty one,
65:12 the hills **g** themselves with joy,
Isa 8: 9 **g** yourselves and be dismayed; **g** yourselves and be
Jer 1:17 But you, **g** up your loins; stand up and
Na 2: 1 **g** your loins; collect all your strength.

GIRDED (11) [GIRD]

Ex 12:11 This is how you shall eat it: your loins **g,**
2Sa 6:14 David was **g** with a linen ephod.
22:33 The God who has **g** me
22:40 For you **g** me with strength for the battle;
1Ki 18:46 he **g** up his loins and ran in front of Ahab to
Ps 18:32 the God who **g** me with strength,
18:39 For you **g** me with strength for the battle;
65: 6 established the mountains; you are **g** with might.
93: 1 the LORD is robed, he is **g** with strength.
2Mc 3:19 Women, **g** with sackcloth under their breasts,
10:25 on their heads and **g** their loins with sackcloth,

GIRDED (KJV) See also CLOTHED, FASTENED, FITTED, STRAPPED, WEARING

GIRDING (1) [GIRD]

3Mc 7: 5 **g** themselves with a cruelty more savage than that

GIRDS (1) [GIRD]

Pr 31:17 She **g** herself with strength,

GIRGASHITE (1) [GIRGASHITES]

Ne 9: 8 the Perizzite, the Jebusite, and the **G;**

GIRGASHITES (6) [GIRGASHITE]

Ge 10:16 and the Jebusites, the Amorites, the **G,**
15:21 the Canaanites, the **G,** and the Jebusites."
Dt 7: 1 the Hittites, the **G,** the Amorites, the Canaanites,
Jos 3:10 Hivites, Perizzites, **G,** Amorites, and Jebusites:
24:11 the Perizzites, the Canaanites, the Hittites, the **G,**
1Ch 1:14 and the Jebusites, the Amorites, the **G,**

GIRGASITE (KJV) See GIRGASHITES

GIRL (49) [GIRL'S, GIRLS, SERVANT-GIRL, SERVANT-GIRLS, SLAVE-GIRL]

Ge 24:14 Let the **g** to whom I shall say,
24:16 The **g** was very fair to look upon, a virgin,
24:28 Then the **g** ran and told her mother's household
24:55 "Let the **g** remain with us a while,
24:57 They said, "We will call the **g,** and ask her."
34: 3 he loved the **g,** and spoke tenderly to her.
34: 4 saying, "Get me this **g** to be my wife."
34:12 only give me the **g** to be my wife."
Ex 1:16 but if it is a **g,** she shall live."
1:22 but you shall let every **g** live."
2: 8 So the **g** went and called the child's mother.
21:31 If it gores a boy or a **g,**
Jdg 5:30 A **g** or two for every man;
1Ki 1: 3 a beautiful **g** throughout all the territory of Israel,
1: 4 The **g** was very beautiful.
2Ki 5: 2 on one of their raids had taken a young **g** captive
5: 4 in and told his lord just what the **g** from the land
Est 2: 4 the **g** who pleases the king be queen instead
2: 7 the **g** was fair and beautiful,
2: 9 The **g** pleased him and won his favor,
2:12 turn came for each **g** to go in to King Ahasuerus,
2:13 When the **g** went in to
Ps 86:16 save the child of your serving **g.**
116:16 I am your servant, the child of your serving **g.**
Pr 30:19 and the way of a man with a **g.**
Jer 2:32 Can a **g** forget her ornaments, or a bride her attire?
51:22 with you I smash the young man and the **g;**
Am 2: 7 father and son go in to the same **g,**
Mt 9:24 for the **g** is not dead but sleeping."
9:25 in and took her by the hand, and the **g** got up.
14:11 head was brought on a platter and given to the **g,**
Mk 5:41 "Talitha cum," which means, "Little **g,** get up!"
5:42 And immediately the **g** got up and began to walk
6:22 and the king said to the **g,**
6:28 and gave it to the **g.**
6:28 Then the **g** gave it to her mother.
Tob 6:12 Moreover, the **g** is sensible, brave,
6:13 tonight I will speak to her father about the **g,**
6:13 concerning the **g** and arrange her engagement
Jdt 12:13 "Let this pretty **g** not hesitate to come to my lord
AdE 2: 7 The **g** was beautiful in appearance.
2: 9 The **g** pleased him and won his favor,
2:12 a **g** was to go to the king was twelve months.
Wis 9: 5 For I am your servant the son of your serving **g,**
Sir 9: 4 Do not dally with a singing **g,**
20: 4 to violate a **g** is the person who does right
30:20 as a eunuch groans when embracing a **g.**
36:26 but one **g** is preferable to another.
LtJ 6: 9 as they might for a **g** who loves ornaments.

GIRL'S (6) [GIRL]

Jdg 19: 3 **g** father saw him and came with joy to meet him.
19: 4 His father-in-law, the **g** father, made him stay,
19: 5 but the **g** father said to his son-in-law,

Jdg 19: 6 and the **g** father said to the man,
19: 8 and the **g** father said, "Fortify yourself."
19: 9 his father-in-law, the **g** father, said to him, "Look,

GIRLS (13) [GIRL]

Nu 31:18 But all the young **g** who have not known a man
1Sa 9:11 they met some **g** coming out to draw water,
Job 19:15 my serving **g** count me as a stranger;
41: 5 or will you put it on leash for your **g**?
Ps 68:25 between them **g** playing tambourines:
78:63 and their **g** had no marriage song.
La 1: 4 her young **g** grieve, and her lot is bitter.
2:10 the young **g** of Jerusalem have bowed their heads
Joel 3: 3 and sold **g** for wine, and drunk it down.
Zec 8: 5 of the city shall be full of boys and **g** playing
AdE 2: 2 "Let beautiful and virtuous **g** be sought out for
2: 8 and many **g** were gathered in Susa the capital
2Mc 5:13 and slaughter of young **g** and infants.

GIRZITES (1)

1Sa 27: 8 the **G**, and the Amalekites;

GISHPA (1)

Ne 11:21 and Ziha and **G** were over the temple servants.

GITTAH-HEPHER (KJV) See GATH-HEPHER

GITTAIM (2)

2Sa 4: 3 the people of Beeroth had fled to **G** and are there
Ne 11:33 Hazor, Ramah, **G**,

GITTITE (8) [GATH]

2Sa 6:10 to the house of Obed-edom the **G**.
6:11 in the house of Obed-edom the **G** three months;
15:19 Then the king said to Ittai the **G**,
15:22 So Ittai the **G** marched on,
18: 2 and one third under the command of Ittai the **G**.
21:19 the Bethlehemite, killed Goliath the **G**,
1Ch 13:13 to the house of Obed-edom the **G**.
20: 5 of Jair killed Lahmi the brother of Goliath the **G**,

GITTITES (1) [GATH]

2Sa 15:18 and all the six hundred **G** who had followed him

GITTITH (3)

Ps 8: T *To the leader: according to The* **G**.
81: T *To the leader: according to The* **G**.
84: T *To the leader: according to The* **G**.

GIVE‡ (1146) [GAVE, GIVEN, GIVER, GIVES, GIVING, GOD-GIVEN, LAWGIVER, LIFE-GIVING]

Ge 1:15 in the dome of the sky to **g** light upon the earth."
1:17 in the dome of the sky to **g** light upon the earth,
9: 3 as I gave you the green plants, I **g** you everything.
12: 7 and said, "To your offspring I will **g** this land."
13:15 for all the land that you see I will **g** to you and
13:17 for I will **g** it to you."
14:21 king of Sodom said to Abram, "**G** me the persons,
15: 2 Abram said, "O Lord GOD, what will you **g** me,
15: 7 to **g** you this land to possess."
15:18 saying, "To your descendants I **g** this land,
17: 8 And I will **g** to you, and to your offspring
17:16 and moreover I will **g** you a son by her.
17:16 I will bless her, and she shall **g** rise to nations;
23: 4 **g** me property among you for a burying place,
23: 9 so that he may **g** me the cave of Machpelah,
23: 9 the full price let him **g** it to me in your presence as
23:11 I **g** you the field, and I **g** you the cave that is in it;
23:11 in the presence of my people I **g** it to you;
23:13 I will **g** the price of the field;
24: 7 'To your offspring I will **g** this land,'
24:41 even if they will not **g** her to you,
24:43 "Please **g** me a little water from your jar to drink,"
25:24 When her time to **g** birth was at hand,
26: 3 and to your descendants I will **g** all these lands,
26: 4 and will **g** to your offspring all these lands;
27:28 May God **g** you of the dew of heaven,
28: 4 May he **g** to you the blessing of Abraham,
28:13 the land on which you lie I will **g** to you and
28:20 and will **g** me bread to eat and clothing to wear,
28:22 that you **g** me I will surely **g** one tenth to you."
29:19 that I **g** her to you than that I should **g** her to any
29:21 "**G** me my wife that I may go in to her,
29:27 and we will **g** you the other also in return
30: 1 she said to Jacob, "**G** me children, or I shall die!"
30:14 "Please **g** me some of your son's mandrakes."
30:26 **G** me my wives and my children
30:28 name your wages, and I will **g** it."
30:31 He said, "What shall I **g** you?"
30:31 Jacob said, "You shall not **g** me anything;
34: 8 please **g** her to him in marriage.
34: 9 Make marriages with us; **g** your daughters to us,
34:11 and whatever you say to me I will **g**.
34:12 and I will **g** whatever you ask me;
34:12 only **g** me the girl to be my wife."
34:14 to **g** our sister to one who is uncircumcised,
34:16 Then we will **g** our daughters to you,
34:21 and let us **g** them our daughters.
35:12 The land that I gave to Abraham and Isaac I will **g**
Ge 35:12 and I will **g** the land to your offspring after you."
38: 9 so that he would not **g** offspring to his brother.
38:16 She said, "What will you **g** me,
38:17 And she said, "Only if you **g** me a pledge,
38:18 He said, "What pledge shall I **g** you?"
38:26 since I did not **g** her to my son Shelah."
41:16 God will **g** Pharaoh a favorable answer."
42:25 and to **g** them provisions for their journey.
42:27 of them opened his sack to **g** his donkey fodder at
45:18 so that I may **g** you the best of the land of Egypt,
45:20 **G** no thought to your possessions,
47:15 to Joseph, and said, "**G** us food!
47:16 And Joseph answered, "**G** me your livestock,
47:16 I will **g** you food in exchange for your livestock,
47:19 just **g** us seed, so that we may live and not die,
47:24 at the harvests you shall **g** one-fifth to Pharaoh,
48: 4 and will **g** this land to your offspring after you for
48:22 I now **g** to you one portion more than
Ex 1:19 and **g** birth before the midwife comes to them."
2: 9 and I will **g** you your wages."
5: 7 "You shall no longer **g** the people straw
5:10 "Thus says Pharaoh, 'I will not **g** you straw.
6: 4 to **g** them the land of Canaan,
6: 8 into the land that I swore to **g** to Abraham, Isaac,
6: 8 I will **g** it to you for a possession.
12:25 you come to the land that the LORD will **g** you,
13: 5 which he swore to your ancestors to **g** you,
13:21 and in a pillar of fire by night, to **g** them light,
15:26 and **g** heed to his commandments
17: 2 and said, "**G** us water to drink."
18:19 I will **g** you counsel, and God be with you!
21:23 If any harm follows, then you shall **g** life for life,
22:16 he shall **g** the bride-price for her
22:17 But if her father refuses to **g** her to him,
22:29 The firstborn of your sons you shall **g** to me.
22:30 on the eighth day you shall **g** it to me.
24:12 and I will **g** you the tablets of stone,
25: 2 to **g** you shall receive the offering for me.
25:16 into the ark the covenant that I shall **g** you.
25:21 the covenant that I shall **g** you.
25:37 be set up so as to **g** light on the space in front of it.
30:12 at registration all of them shall **g** a ransom
30:13 This is what each one who is registered shall **g**:
30:14 shall **g** the LORD's offering.
30:15 The rich shall not **g** more, and the poor shall not **g** less, than the half shekel,
32:13 that I have promised I will **g** to your descendants,
33: 1 saying, 'To your descendants I will **g** it.'
33:14 and I will **g** you rest."
Lev 5:16 and shall add one-fifth to it and **g** it to the priest.
7:32 from your sacrifices of well-being you shall **g** to
14:34 which I **g** you for a possession,
15:14 the entrance of the tent of meeting and **g** them to
18:21 not **g** any of your offspring to sacrifice them
18:23 nor shall any woman **g** herself to an animal
20: 2 or of the aliens who reside in Israel, who **g** any
20: 4 when they **g** of their offspring to Molech,
20:24 and I will **g** it to you to possess,
22:14 and **g** the sacred donation to the priest.
23:38 which you **g** to the LORD.
25:38 to **g** you the land of Canaan, to be your God.
26: 4 I will **g** you your rains in their season,
26: 7 You shall **g** chase to your enemies,
26: 8 Five of you shall **g** chase to a hundred,
26: 8 a hundred of you shall **g** chase to ten thousand;
Nu 3: 9 You shall **g** the Levites to Aaron
3:48 **G** to Aaron and his sons the money by which
6:26 up his countenance upon you, and **g** you peace.
7: 5 and **g** them to the Levites,
8: 2 seven lamps shall **g** light in front of the lampstand.
8: 3 up its lamps to **g** light in front of the lampstand,
10:29 'I will **g** it to you';
11:12 Did I **g** birth to them, that you should say to me,
11:13 Where am I to get meat to **g** to all this people?
11:13 For they come weeping to me and say, '**G** us meat
11:18 the LORD will **g** you meat, and you shall eat.
11:21 and you say, 'I will **g** them meat,
14: 8 he will bring us into this land and **g** it to us,
14:16 to **g** them that he has slaughtered them in
14:23 the land that I swore to **g** to their ancestors;
15:21 Throughout your generations you shall **g** to
18: 7 I **g** your priesthood as a gift;
18:12 the choice produce that they **g** to the LORD,
18:28 and from them you shall **g** the LORD's offering
19: 3 You shall **g** it to the priest Eleazar,
20:21 to **g** Israel passage through their territory;
21: 2 "If you will indeed **g** this people into our hands,
21:16 the people together, and I will **g** them water."
22:18 "Although Balak were to **g** me his house full
24:13 'If Balak should **g** me his house full of silver
26:54 To a large tribe you shall **g** a large inheritance,
26:54 to a small tribe you shall **g** a small inheritance;
27: 4 **G** to us a possession among our father's brothers."
27: 9 then you shall **g** his inheritance to his brothers.
27:10 you shall **g** his inheritance to his father's brothers.
27:11 then you shall **g** his inheritance to
27:20 You shall **g** him some of your authority,
31:29 from their half and **g** it to Eleazar the priest as
31:30 and **g** them to the Levites who have charge of
32:11 shall see the land that I swore to **g** to Abraham,
32:29 then you shall **g** them the land of Gilead for
33:54 to a large one you shall **g** a large inheritance,
33:54 and to a small one you shall **g** a small inheritance;
34:13 the LORD has commanded to **g** to the nine tribes
35: 2 to **g**, from the inheritance that they possess, towns
35: 2 also **g** to the Levites pasture lands surrounding
35: 4 which you shall **g** to the Levites,
Nu 35: 6 that you **g** to the Levites shall include the six cities
35: 6 in addition to them you shall **g** forty-two towns.
35: 7 that you **g** to the Levites shall total forty-eight,
35: 8 for the towns that you shall **g** from the possession
35: 8 shall **g** of its towns to the Levites.
36: 2 to **g** the land for inheritance by lot to the Israelites;
36: 2 and my lord was commanded by the LORD to **g**
Dt 1: 8 to **g** to them and to their descendants after them."
1:16 "**G** the members of your community
1:35 the good land that I swore to **g** to your ancestors,
1:36 and to him and to his descendants I will **g** the land
1:39 to them I will **g** it,
2: 5 not **g** you even so much as a foot's length
2: 9 for I will not **g** you any of its land as a possession,
2:19 for I will not **g** the land of the Ammonites to you
2:31 I have begun to **g** Sihon and his land over to you.
4: 1 **g** heed to the statutes and ordinances
6:10 to Abraham, to Isaac, and to Jacob, to **g** you—
6:18 that the LORD swore to your ancestors to **g** you,
6:23 to **g** us the land that he promised on oath
7:13 the land that he swore to your ancestors to **g** you.
7:23 But the LORD your God will **g** them over to you,
10:11 the land that I swore to their ancestors to **g** them."
11: 9 that the LORD swore to your ancestors to **g** them
11:14 then he will **g** the rain for your land in its season,
11:15 he will **g** grass in your fields for your livestock,
11:21 that the LORD swore to your ancestors to **g** them,
14:21 you may **g** it to aliens residing in your towns
15: 9 with hostility and **g** nothing;
15:10 **G** liberally and be ungrudging when you do so,
16:17 all shall **g** as they are able,
18: 3 they shall **g** to the priest the shoulder,
18: 4 of the fleece of your sheep, you shall **g** him.
18:14 about to dispossess do **g** heed to soothsayers
19: 8 and he will **g** you all the land
19: 8 the land that he promised your ancestors to **g** you,
20: 4 for you against your enemies, to **g** you victory."
22:19 of silver (which they shall **g** to
22:29 the man who lay with her shall **g** fifty shekels
24:13 You shall **g** the pledge back by sunset,
26: 3 that the LORD swore to our ancestors to **g** us."
28:11 that the LORD swore to your ancestors to **g** you.
28:12 to **g** the rain of your land in its season and
28:65 There the LORD will **g** you a trembling heart,
30:20 that the LORD swore to **g** to your ancestors,
31: 5 The LORD will **g** them over to you
31: 7 the LORD has sworn to their ancestors to **g** them;
32: 1 **G** ear, O heavens, and I will speak;
32:46 **g** them as a command to your children,
33: 7 O LORD, **g** heed to Judah,
33: 8 And of Levi he said: **G** to Levi your Thummim,
34: 4 saying, 'I will **g** it to your descendants';
Jos 1: 6 the land that I swore to their ancestors to **g** them.
1:13 and will **g** you this land.'
2:12 **G** me a sign of good faith
5: 6 that he had sworn to their ancestors to **g** us,
7:19 **g** glory to the LORD God of Israel
8: 7 for the LORD your God will **g** it into your hand.
8:18 for I will **g** it into your hand."
9:24 to **g** you all the land, and to destroy all
14:12 So now **g** me this hill country of which
15:16 to him I will **g** my daughter Achsah as wife."
15:19 She said to him, "**G** me a present;
15:19 **g** me springs of water as well."
17: 4 to **g** us an inheritance along with our male kin."
20: 5 they shall not **g** up the slayer,
21:43 to their ancestors that he would **g** them;
Jdg 1: 2 I hereby **g** the land into his hand."
1:12 I will **g** him my daughter Achsah as wife."
1:15 She said to him, "**G** me a present;
1:15 **g** me also Gulloth-mayim."
4: 7 and I will **g** him into your hand.' "
4:19 he said to her, "Please **g** me a little water to drink;
5: 3 "Hear, O kings; **g** ear, O princes;
7: 2 with you are too many for me to **g** the Midianites
7: 7 and **g** the Midianites into your hand.
8: 5 "Please **g** some loaves of bread to my followers,
8: 6 that we should **g** bread to your army?"
8:15 of Zebah and Zalmunna, that we should **g** bread
8:24 of you **g** me an earring he has taken as booty."
8:25 "We will willingly **g** them," they answered.
11:30 "If you will **g** the Ammonites into my hand,
13:13 "Let the woman **g** heed to all that I said to her.
14:12 then I will **g** you thirty linen garments
14:13 then you shall **g** me thirty linen garments
15:12 we may **g** you into the hands of the Philistines."
15:13 we will only bind you and **g** you into their hands;
16: 5 and we will each **g** you eleven hundred pieces
17:10 and I will **g** you ten pieces of silver a year,
20: 7 all of you, **g** your advice and counsel here."
20:28 for tomorrow I will **g** them into your hand."
21: 1 "No one of us shall **g** his daughter in marriage
21: 7 that we will not **g** them any of our daughters
21:18 Yet we cannot **g** any of our daughters to them
Ru 4:12 that the LORD will **g** you by this young woman,
1Sa 1: 4 he would **g** portions to his wife Peninnah and
1:11 but will **g** to your servant a male child,
2:10 he will **g** strength to his king,
2:15 "**G** meat for the priest to roast;
2:16 you must **g** it now; if not, I will take it by force."
4:19 was pregnant, about to **g** birth.
4:20 But she did not answer or **g** heed.
6: 5 and **g** glory to the God of Israel;
8: 6 "**G** us a king to govern us."
8:14 and olive orchards and **g** them to his courtiers.
8:15 and of your vineyards and **g** it to his officers
9: 8 I will **g** it to the man of God, to tell us our way."

1Sa 9:20 **g** no further thought to them,
10: 4 They will greet you and **g** you two loaves
11: 3 **"G** us seven days' respite
11: 3 we will **g** ourselves up to you."
11:10 "Tomorrow we will **g** ourselves up to you,
11:12 **G** them to us so that we may put them to death."
14:37 Will you **g** them into the hand of Israel?"
14:41 O LORD God of Israel, **g** Urim;
14:41 if this guilt is in your people Israel, **g** Thummim."
17:10 **G** me a man, that we may fight together."
17:25 and will **g** him his daughter
17:44 and I will **g** your flesh to the birds of the air and to
17:46 and I will **g** the dead bodies of
17:47 the LORD's and he will **g** you into our hand."
18:17 I will **g** her to you as a wife;
18:21 "Let me **g** her to him that she may be a snare
21: 3 **G** me five loaves of bread, or whatever is here."
21: 9 David said, "There is none like it; **g** it to me."
22: 7 of Jesse **g** every one of you fields and vineyards,
23: 4 for I will **g** the Philistines into your hand."
23:14 but the LORD did not **g** him into his hand.
24: 4 'I will **g** your enemy into your hand,
24:15 and **g** sentence between me and you.
25: 8 Please **g** whatever you have at hand
25:11 **g** it to men who come from I do not know where?"
28:19 Moreover the LORD will **g** Israel along with you
28:19 the LORD will also **g** the army of Israel into
30:22 we will not **g** them any of the spoil
2Sa 3:12 and I will **g** you my support to bring all Israel over
3:14 saying, **"G** me my wife Michal,
5:19 Will you **g** them into my hand?"
5:19 I will certainly **g** the Philistines into your hand."
7:11 and I will **g** you rest from all your enemies.
12:11 and **g** them to your neighbor,
13: 5 'Let my sister Tamar come and **g** me something
14: 7 They say, '**G** up the man who struck his brother,
14: 8 and I will **g** orders concerning you."
15: 4 and I would **g** them justice."
16: 3 Israel will **g** me back my grandfather's kingdom.' "
16:20 Absalom said to Ahithophel, **"G** us your counsel;
18:11 I would have been glad to **g** you ten pieces
20:21 **g** him up alone, and I will withdraw from
23:15 "O that someone would **g** me water to drink from
1Ki 1:12 Now therefore come, let me **g** you advice,
2:17 to **g** me Abishag the Shunammite as my wife."
3: 5 and God said, "Ask what I should **g** you."
3: 9 **G** your servant therefore an understanding mind
3:12 Indeed I **g** you a wise and discerning mind;
3:13 I **g** you also what you have not asked,
3:25 then **g** half to the one, and half to the other."
3:26 "Please, my lord, **g** her the living boy;
3:27 **"G** the first woman the living boy; do not kill him.
5: 6 and I will **g** you whatever wages you set
8:46 you are angry with them and **g** them to an enemy,
11:11 I will surely tear the kingdom from you and **g** it
11:13 I will **g** one tribe to your son,
11:31 the hand of Solomon, and will **g** you ten tribes.
11:35 the kingdom away from his son and **g** it to you—
11:36 Yet to his son I will **g** one tribe,
11:38 as I built for David, and I will **g** Israel to you.
13: 7 and I will **g** you a gift."
13: 8 "If you **g** me half your kingdom,
14: 8 the kingdom away from the house of David to **g** it
14:16 He will **g** Israel up because of the sins
17:19 But he said to her, **"G** me your son."
20:13 Look, I will **g** it into your hand today;
20:28 I will **g** all this great multitude into your hand,
21: 2 And Ahab said to Naboth, **"G** me your vineyard,
21: 2 I will **g** you a better vineyard for it;
21: 2 I will **g** you its value in money."
21: 3 that I should **g** you my ancestral inheritance."
21: 4 "I will not **g** you my ancestral inheritance."
21: 6 '**G** me your vineyard for money;
21: 6 if you prefer, I will **g** you another vineyard for it';
21: 6 but he answered, 'I will not **g** you my vineyard.' "
21: 7 I will **g** you the vineyard of Naboth
21:15 which he refused to **g** you for money;
22: 6 for the LORD will **g** it into the hand of the king."
22:12 the LORD will **g** it into the hand of the king."
22:15 the LORD will **g** it into the hand of the king."
2Ki 3:14 I would **g** you neither a look nor a glance.
4:29 If you meet anyone, **g** no greeting,
4:42 Elisha said, **"G** it to the people and let them eat."
4:43 he repeated, **"G** it to the people and let them eat,
5: 7 "Am I God, to **g** death or life,
5:22 please **g** them a talent of silver and two changes
6:28 "This woman said to me, '**G** up your son;
6:29 '**G** up your son and we will eat him.'
8:19 to **g** a lamp to him and to his descendants forever.
10:15 Jehu said, "If it is, **g** me your hand."
12:11 They would **g** the money that was weighed out
14: 9 saying, '**G** your daughter to my son for a wife';
15:20 to **g** to the king of Assyria.
18:23 I will **g** you two thousand horses,
21:14 and **g** them into the hand of their enemies;
22: 5 let them **g** it to the workers who are at the house
23:35 to **g** it to Pharaoh Neco.
1Ch 11:17 "O that someone would **g** me water to drink from
12:17 the God of our ancestors see and **g** judgment."
14:10 Will you **g** them into my hand?"
14:10 "Go up, and I will **g** them into your hand."
15:13 because we did not **g** it proper care."
16: 8 O **g** thanks to the LORD, call on his name,
16:18 "To you I will **g** the land of Canaan
16:34 O **g** thanks to the LORD, for he is good;
16:35 that we may **g** thanks to your holy name,
21:22 **"G** me the site of the threshing floor
1Ch 21:22 **g** it to me at its full price—
21:23 for a grain offering. I **g** it all."
22: 9 I will **g** him peace from all his enemies
22: 9 and I will **g** peace and quiet to Israel in his days.
29: 3 of my devotion to the house of my God I **g** it to
29:12 in your hand to make great and to **g** strength to all.
29:13 we **g** thanks to you and praise your glorious name.
2Ch 1: 7 and said to him, "Ask what I should **g** you."
1:10 **G** me now wisdom and knowledge to go out
1:12 I will also **g** you riches, possessions, and honor,
6:36 you are angry with them and **g** them to an enemy,
18: 5 for God will **g** it into the hand of the king."
18:11 the LORD will **g** it into the hand of the king."
19: 8 to **g** judgment for the LORD and
20: 7 and **g** it forever to the descendants
20:21 **"G** thanks to the LORD, for his steadfast love
21: 7 to **g** a lamp to him and to his descendants forever.
25: 9 LORD is able to **g** you much more than this."
25:18 saying, '**G** your daughter to my son for a wife';
30:12 on Judah to **g** them one heart to do what the king
31: 2 of the camp of the LORD and to **g** thanks
31: 4 in Jerusalem to **g** the portion due to the priests and
Ezr 9: 9 to **g** us new life to set up the house of our God,
9: 9 and to **g** us a wall in Judea and Jerusalem.
9:12 Therefore do not **g** your daughters to their sons,
Ne 1:11 **G** success to your servant today,
2: 8 directing him to **g** me timber to make beams for
2:20 God of heaven is the one who will **g** us success,
4: 4 and **g** them over as plunder in a land of captivity.
6:13 and so they could **g** me a bad name,
9: 6 To all of them you **g** life,
9: 8 to **g** to his descendants the land of the Canaanite,
9:12 to **g** them light on the way
9:15 in to possess the land that you swore to **g** them.
10:30 We will not **g** our daughters to the peoples of
12:24 over against them, to praise and to **g** thanks,
13:25 "You shall not **g** your daughters to their sons,
Est 1:19 and let the king **g** her royal position
1:20 all women will **g** honor to their husbands,
Job 2: 4 All that people have they will **g** to save their lives.
10: 1 I will **g** free utterance to my complaint;
17: 3 who is there that will **g** surety for me?
20:10 and their hands will **g** back their wealth.
20:18 They will **g** back the fruit of their toil,
23: 6 No; but he would **g** heed to me.
31:37 I would **g** him an account of all my steps;
32:17 I also will **g** my answer;
34: 2 you wise men, and **g** ear to me, you who know;
35: 7 If you are righteous, what do you **g** to him;
39: 1 "Do you know when the mountain goats **g** birth?
39: 2 and do you know the time when they **g** birth,
39: 3 when they crouch to **g** birth to their offspring,
39:19 "Do you **g** the horse its might?
40:14 to you that your own right hand can **g** you victory.
Ps 5: 1 **G** ear to my words, O LORD;
5: 1 O LORD; **g** heed to my sighing.
6: 5 in Sheol who can **g** you praise?
7:17 I will **g** to the LORD the thanks due
9: 1 I will **g** thanks to the LORD
13: 3 **G** light to my eyes, or I will sleep the sleep
16:10 For you do not **g** me up to Sheol,
17: 1 **g** ear to my prayer from lips free of deceit.
20: 2 and **g** you support from Zion.
20: 9 **G** victory to the king, O LORD;
27:12 Do not **g** me up to the will of my adversaries,
28: 7 and with my song I **g** thanks to him.
29:11 May the LORD **g** strength to his people!
30: 4 and **g** thanks to his holy name.
30:12 O LORD my God, I will **g** thanks to you forever.
36: 8 you **g** them drink from the river of your delights.
37: 4 and he will **g** you the desires of your heart.
39:12 O LORD, and **g** ear to my cry;
41: 2 You do not **g** them up to the will of their enemies.
44: 3 nor did their own arm **g** them victory;
44: 8 and we will **g** thanks to your name forever.
49: 1 **g** ear, all inhabitants of the world,
49: 7 there is no price one can **g** to God for it.
50:19 "You **g** your mouth free rein for evil,
51:16 if I were to **g** a burnt offering,
54: 2 **g** ear to the words of my mouth
54: 6 I will **g** thanks to your name, O LORD,
55: 1 **G** ear to my prayer, O God;
57: 9 I will **g** thanks to you, O Lord, among the peoples;
60: 5 **G** victory with your right hand,
66: 2 of his name; **g** to him glorious praise.
72: 1 **G** the king your justice, O God,
72: 4 **g** deliverance to the needy,
72:11 down before him, all nations **g** him service.
75: 1 We **g** thanks to you, O God;
75: 1 we **g** thanks; your name is near.
78: 1 **G** ear, O my people, to my teaching;
78:20 he also **g** bread, or provide meat for his people?"
79:13 will **g** thanks to you forever;
80: 1 **G** ear, O Shepherd of Israel, you who lead Joseph
80:18 **g** us life, and we will call on your name.
82: 3 **G** justice to the weak and the orphan;
84: 8 O LORD God of hosts, hear my prayer; **g** ear,
85:12 The LORD will **g** what is good,
86: 6 **G** ear, O LORD, to my prayer;
86:11 **g** me an undivided heart to revere your name.
86:12 I **g** thanks to you, O Lord my God,
86:16 **g** your strength to your servant;
92: 1 to **g** thanks to the LORD, to sing praises
94: 2 **g** to the proud what they deserve!
97:12 O you righteous, and **g** thanks to his holy name!
100: 4 **G** thanks to him, bless his name.
104:27 to you to **g** them their food in due season;
Ps 104:28 when you **g** to them, they gather it up;
105: 1 O **g** thanks to the LORD, call on his name,
105:11 "To you I will **g** the land of Canaan
105:39 and fire to **g** light by night.
106: 1 O **g** thanks to the LORD, for he is good;
106:47 that we may **g** thanks to your holy name and glory
107: 1 O **g** thanks to the LORD, for he is good;
107:43 Let those who are wise **g** heed to these things,
108: 3 I will **g** thanks to you, O LORD,
108: 6 **G** victory with your right hand, and answer me,
109:30 With my mouth I will **g** great thanks to
111: 1 I will **g** thanks to the LORD
115: 1 O LORD, not to us, but to your name **g** glory,
115:14 May the LORD **g** you increase,
118: 1 O **g** thanks to the LORD, for he is good;
118:18 but he did not **g** me over to death.
118:19 that I may enter through them and **g** thanks to
118:25 O LORD, we beseech you, **g** us success!
118:28 You are my God, and I will **g** thanks to you;
118:29 O **g** thanks to the LORD, for he is good,
119:34 **G** me understanding, that I may keep your law
119:37 **g** me life in your ways.
119:40 in your righteousness **g** me life.
119:73 **g** me understanding that I may learn your
119:107 **g** me life, O LORD, according to your word.
119:125 I am your servant; **g** me understanding,
119:144 **g** me understanding that I may live.
119:154 **g** me life according to your promise.
119:156 **g** me life according to your justice.
119:169 **g** me understanding according to your word.
122: 4 to **g** thanks to the name of the LORD.
132: 4 not **g** sleep to my eyes or slumber to my eyelids,
135: 1 Praise the name of the LORD; **g** praise,
136: 1 O **g** thanks to the LORD, for he is good,
136: 2 O **g** thanks to the God of gods,
136: 3 O **g** thanks to the Lord of lords,
136:26 O **g** thanks to the God of heaven,
138: 1 I **g** you thanks, O LORD, with my whole heart;
138: 2 I bow down toward your holy temple and **g** thanks
140: 6 **g** ear, O LORD, to the voice
140:13 Surely the righteous shall **g** thanks to your name;
141: 1 **g** ear to my voice when I call to you.
142: 6 **G** heed to my cry, for I am brought very low.
142: 7 so that I may **g** thanks to your name.
143: 1 **g** ear to my supplications in your faithfulness;
145:10 All your works shall **g** thanks to you, O LORD,
145:15 and you **g** them their food in due season.
Pr 1:23 **G** heed to my reproof; I will pour out my thoughts
3: 2 of life and abundant welfare they will **g** you.
3:28 "Go, and come again, tomorrow I will **g** it"—
4: 2 for I **g** you good precepts:
5: 9 or you will **g** your honor to others,
6: 4 **G** your eyes no sleep and your eyelids no slumber;
9: 9 **G** instruction to the wise,
11:24 Some **g** freely, yet grow all the richer;
17: 8 like a magic stone in the eyes of those who **g** it;
17:18 It is senseless to **g** a pledge,
21:26 but the righteous **g** and do not hold back.
21:29 but the upright **g** thought to their ways.
22:21 you may **g** a true answer to those who sent you?
22:26 Do not be one of those who **g** pledges,
23:26 My child, **g** me your heart,
25:21 If your enemies are hungry, **g** them bread to eat;
25:21 and if they are thirsty, **g** them water to drink;
25:26 or a polluted fountain are the righteous who **g** way
26: 8 like binding a stone in a sling to **g** honor to a fool.
27:23 and **g** attention to your herds;
29:15 The rod and reproof **g** wisdom,
29:17 Discipline your children, and they will **g** you rest;
29:17 they will **g** delight to your heart.
29:19 for though they understand, they will not **g** heed.
30: 8 **g** me neither poverty nor riches;
30:15 The leech has two daughters; **"G, g,"** they cry.
31: 3 Do not **g** your strength to women,
31: 6 **G** strong drink to one who is perishing,
31:31 **G** her a share in the fruit of her hands,
Ecc 2:26 only to **g** to one who pleases God.
7:21 Do not **g** heed to everything that people say,
10: 1 Dead flies make the perfumer's ointment **g** off
SS 2:13 in blossom; they **g** forth fragrance.
7:12 There I will **g** you my love.
7:13 The mandrakes **g** forth fragrance,
8: 2 I would **g** you spiced wine to drink,
Isa 7:14 Therefore the Lord himself will **g** you a sign.
7:22 because of the abundance of milk that they **g**;
12: 1 You will say in that day: I will **g** thanks to you,
12: 4 **G** thanks to the LORD, call on his name;
13:10 and their constellations will not **g** their light;
16: 3 **"G** counsel, grant justice;
19:11 the wise counselors of Pharaoh **g** stupid counsel.
22:25 peg that was fastened in a secure place will **g** way;
24:15 Therefore in the east **g** glory to the LORD;
26:19 and the earth will **g** birth to those long dead.
28:12 "This is rest; **g** rest to the weary;
30:20 Though the Lord may **g** you the bread of adversity
30:23 He will **g** rain for the seed with which you sow
34: 1 Draw near, O nations, to hear; O peoples, **g** heed!
36: 8 I will **g** you two thousand horses,
41:27 and I **g** to Jerusalem a herald of good tidings.
42: 8 my glory I **g** to no other, nor my praise to idols.
42:12 Let them **g** glory to the LORD,
42:23 Who among you will **g** heed to this,
43: 3 I **g** Egypt as your ransom,
43: 4 and I love you, I **g** people in return for you,
43: 6 **"G** them up," and to the south, "Do not withhold;
43:20 for I **g** water in the wilderness, rivers in the desert,
43:20 to **g** drink to my chosen people,

Isa 45: 3 I will **g** you the treasures of darkness
48:11 My glory I will not **g** to another.
49: 6 I will **g** you as a light to the nations,
51: 4 Listen to me, my people, and **g** heed to me,
56: 5 I will **g**, in my house and within my walls,
56: 5 I will **g** them an everlasting name that shall not
57:11 and did not remember me or **g** me a thought?
60:19 brightness shall the moon **g** light to you by night;
61: 3 to **g** them a garland instead of ashes,
61: 8 I will faithfully **g** them their recompense,
62: 2 a new name that the mouth of the LORD will **g**.
62: 7 and **g** him no rest until he establishes Jerusalem
62: 8 I will not again **g** your grain to be food
65:15 but to his servants he will **g** a different name.
Jer 3:15 I will **g** you shepherds after my own heart,
3:19 and **g** you a pleasant land,
6:10 To whom shall I speak and **g** warning,
6:17 "**G** heed to the sound of the trumpet!"
6:17 But they said, "We will not **g** heed."
8:10 Therefore I will **g** their wives to others
11: 5 to **g** them a land flowing with milk and honey,
13:15 Hear and **g** ear; do not be haughty,
13:16 **G** glory to the LORD your God
14: 9 like a mighty warrior who cannot **g** help?
14:13 but I will **g** you true peace in this place.' "
14:22 Or can the heavens **g** showers?
15: 9 of them I will **g** to the sword before their enemies,
15:13 Your wealth and your treasures I will **g**
16: 7 nor shall anyone **g** them the cup of consolation
17: 3 and all your treasures I will **g** for spoil as the price
17:10 to **g** to all according to their ways,
18:19 **G** heed to me, O LORD,
18:21 Therefore **g** their children over to famine;
19: 7 I will **g** their dead bodies for food to the birds of
20: 4 And I will **g** all Judah into the hand of the king
20: 5 I will **g** all the wealth of this city, all its gains,
21: 7 says the LORD, I will **g** King Zedekiah of Judah,
22:13 and does not **g** them their wages;
22:25 **g** you into the hands of those who seek your life,
23:15 and **g** them poisoned water to drink;
24: 7 I will **g** them a heart to know that I am
27: 4 **G** them this charge for their masters:
27: 5 and I **g** it to whomever I please.
27:22 until the day when I **g** attention to them,
29: 6 and **g** your daughters in marriage,
29:11 to **g** you a future with hope.
31: 7 proclaim, **g** praise, and say, "Save, O LORD,
31:13 and **g** them gladness for sorrow.
31:14 I will **g** the priests their fill of fatness,
32: 3 to **g** this city into the hand of the king of Babylon,
32:22 which you swore to their ancestors to **g** them,
32:28 to **g** this city into the hands of the Chaldeans and
32:39 I will **g** them one heart and one way,
33:11 "**G** thanks to the LORD of hosts,
34: 2 to **g** this city into the hand of the king of Babylon,
38:15 And if I **g** you advice, you will not listen to me."
44:30 I am going to **g** Pharaoh Hophra, king of Egypt,
45: 5 but I will **g** you your life as a prize of war
46:17 **G** Pharaoh, king of Egypt,
50:34 that he may **g** rest to the earth,
La 2:18 **G** yourself no rest, your eyes no respite!
3:30 to **g** one's cheek to the smiter,
3:56 to my cry for help, but **g** me relief!"
3:65 **G** them anguish of heart; your curse be on them!
Eze 2: 8 open your mouth and eat what I **g** you.
3: 3 eat this scroll that I **g** you and fill your stomach
3:17 you shall **g** them warning from me.
3:18 and you **g** them no warning,
11: 2 and who **g** wicked counsel in this city;
11: 9 of it and **g** you over to the hands of foreigners,
11:17 and I will **g** you the land of Israel.
11:19 I will **g** them one heart, and put a new spirit
11:19 the heart of stone from their flesh and **g** them
15: 6 so I will **g** up the inhabitants of Jerusalem.
16:61 and **g** them to you as daughters,
17:15 that they might **g** him horses and a large army.
20:28 to **g** them, then wherever they saw any high hill
20:42 the country that I swore to **g** to your ancestors.
21:27 Until he comes whose right it is; to him I will **g** it.
23: 8 not **g** up her whorings that she had practiced
23:31 therefore I will **g** her cup into your hand.
25:10 I will **g** it along with Ammon to the people of
29:19 I will **g** the land of Egypt to King Nebuchadrezzar
32: 7 and the moon shall not **g** its light.
33: 7 you shall **g** them warning from me.
33:15 **g** back what they have taken by robbery,
33:27 in the open field I will **g** to the wild animals to
36:26 A new heart I will **g** you,
36:26 from your body the heart of stone and **g** you
39: 4 I will **g** you to birds of prey of every kind and to
39:11 that day I will **g** to Gog a place for burial in Israel,
43:19 you shall **g** to the levitical priests of the family
44:28 and you shall **g** them no holding in Israel;
44:30 also **g** to the priests the first of your dough,
46: 5 with the lambs shall be as much as he wishes to **g**,
46:11 and with the lambs as much as one wishes to **g**,
46:18 he shall **g** his sons their inheritance out
47:14 I swore to **g** it to your ancestors,
Da 2: 7 then we can **g** its interpretation."
2: 9 I shall know that you can **g** me its interpretation."
2:16 that the king **g** him time and he would tell the king
2:23 O God of my ancestors, I **g** thanks and praise,
2:24 and I will **g** the king the interpretation."
5:12 and he will **g** the interpretation."
5:15 but they were not able to **g** the interpretation of
5:16 that you can **g** interpretations and solve problems.
5:17 or **g** your rewards to someone else!
Da 9:22 I have now come out to **g** you wisdom
11:17 he shall **g** him a woman in marriage;
11:33 The wise among the people shall **g** understanding
Hos 2: 5 they **g** me my bread and my water,
2:15 From there I will **g** her her vineyards,
5: 1 **G** heed, O house of Israel!
9:14 **G** them, O LORD—what will you **g**?
9:14 **G** them a miscarrying womb and dry breasts.
9:16 Even though they **g** birth,
11: 8 How can I **g** you up, Ephraim?
13:10 of whom you said, "**G** me a king and rulers"?
Joel 1: 2 O elders, **g** ear, all inhabitants of the land!
2:22 the fig tree and vine **g** their full yield.
Jnh 4: 6 to **g** shade over his head, to save him
Mic 1:14 you shall **g** parting gifts to Moresheth-gath;
3:11 Its rulers **g** judgment for a bribe,
3:11 its prophets **g** oracles for money;
5: 3 Therefore he shall **g** them up until the time
6: 7 Shall I **g** my firstborn for my transgression,
Hag 2: 9 and in this place I will **g** prosperity,
Zec 3: 7 of my courts, and I will **g** you the right of access
8:12 the ground shall **g** its produce,
8:12 and the skies shall **g** their dew;
10: 2 tell false dreams, and **g** empty consolation.
11:12 "If it seems right to you, **g** me my wages;
12: 7 LORD will **g** victory to the tents of Judah first,
Mal 1:14 in the flock and vows to **g** it, and yet sacrifices to
2: 2 you will not lay it to heart to **g** glory to my name,
Mt 4: 9 "All these I will **g** you,
5:16 so that they may see your good works and **g** glory
5:31 let him **g** her a certificate of divorce.'
5:40 to sue you and take your coat, **g** your cloak
5:42 **G** to everyone who begs from you,
6: 2 "So whenever you **g** alms,
6: 3 when you **g** alms, do not let your left hand know
6:11 **G** us this day our daily bread.
7: 2 the measure you **g** will be the measure you get.
7: 6 "Do not **g** what is holy to dogs;
7: 9 if your child asks for bread, will **g** a stone?
7:10 Or if the child asks for a fish, will **g** a snake?
7:11 know how to **g** good gifts to your children,
7:11 in heaven **g** good things to those who ask him!
10: 8 without payment; **g** without payment.
11:28 and I will **g** you rest.
12:36 the day of judgment you will have to **g** an account
14: 8 "**G** me the head of John the Baptist here on
14:16 you **g** them something to eat."
16:19 I will **g** you the keys of the kingdom of heaven,
16:26 Or what will they **g** in return for their life?
17:27 However, so that we do not **g** offense to them,
17:27 take that and **g** it to them for you and me."
19: 7 to **g** a certificate of dismissal and to divorce her?"
19:21 and **g** the money to the poor,
20: 8 'Call the laborers and **g** them their pay,
20:14 I choose to **g** to this last the same as I **g** to you.
20:28 and to **g** his life a ransom for many."
21:41 to other tenants who will **g** him the produce at
22:21 "**G** therefore to the emperor the things that are
22:46 No one was able to **g** him an answer,
24:29 and the moon will not **g** its light;
24:45 to **g** the other slaves their allowance of food at
25: 8 foolish said to the wise, '**G** us some of your oil,
25:28 and **g** it to the one with the ten talents.
25:43 naked and you did not **g** me clothing,
26:15 "What will you **g** me if I betray him to you?"
28:12 they devised a plan to **g** a large sum of money to
Mk 4:24 the measure you **g** will be the measure you get,
5:43 and told them to **g** her something to eat.
6:22 "Ask me for whatever you wish, and I will **g** it."
6:23 I will **g** you, even half of my kingdom."
6:25 to **g** me at once the head of John the Baptist on
6:37 "You **g** them something to eat."
6:37 and **g** it to them to eat?"
8:37 Indeed, what can they **g** in return for their life?
10:21 sell what you own, and **g** the money to the poor,
10:45 and to **g** his life a ransom for many."
12: 9 He will come and destroy the tenants and **g**
12:17 "**G** to the emperor the things that are
13:24 and the moon will not **g** its light,
14:11 and promised to **g** him money.
Lk 1:32 and the Lord God will **g** to him the throne
1:57 Now the time came for Elizabeth to **g** birth,
1:62 to find out what name he wanted to **g** him.
1:77 to **g** knowledge of salvation to his people by
1:79 to **g** light to those who sit in darkness and in
4: 6 "To you I will **g** their glory and all this authority;
4: 6 and I **g** it to anyone I please.
6:30 **G** to everyone who begs from you;
6:38 **g**, and it will be given to you.
6:38 measure you **g** will be the measure you get back."
8:55 Then he directed them to **g** her something to eat.
9:13 he said to them, "You **g** them something to eat."
11: 3 **G** us each day our daily bread.
11: 7 I cannot get up and **g** you anything.'
11: 8 even though he will not get up and **g** him anything
11: 8 he will get up and **g** him whatever he needs.
11:11 will **g** a snake instead of a fish?
11:12 Or if the child asks for an egg, will **g** a scorpion?
11:13 know how to **g** good gifts to your children,
11:13 how much more will the heavenly Father **g**
11:41 So **g** for alms those things that are within;
12:32 for it is your Father's good pleasure to **g** you
12:33 Sell your possessions, and **g** alms.
12:42 to **g** them their allowance of food at
13:15 and lead it away to **g** it water?
14: 9 '**G** this person your place,'
14:12 "When you **g** a luncheon or a dinner,
Lk 14:13 But when you **g** a banquet, invite the poor,
14:33 of you can become my disciple if you do not **g**
15:12 **g** me the share of the property that will belong
16: 2 **G** me an accounting of your management,
16:12 who will **g** you what is your own?
17:18 Was none of them found to return and **g** praise
18:12 I fast twice a week; I **g** a tenth of all my income.'
19: 8 half of my possessions, Lord, I will **g** to the poor;
19:24 from him and **g** it to the one who has ten pounds.'
20:10 that they might **g** him his share of the produce of
20:16 He will come and destroy those tenants and **g**
20:25 **g** to the emperor the things that are the emperor's,
21:13 This will **g** you an opportunity to testify.
21:15 for I will **g** you words and a wisdom that none
22: 5 and agreed to **g** him money.
Jn 4: 7 and Jesus said to her, "**G** me a drink."
4:10 and who it is that is saying to you, '**G** me a drink,'
4:14 the water that I will **g** them will never be thirsty.
4:14 The water that I will **g** will become in them
4:15 The woman said to him, "Sir, **g** me this water,
6:27 which the Son of Man will **g** you.
6:30 "What sign are you going to **g** us then,
6:34 They said to him, "Sir, **g** us this bread always."
6:51 that I will **g** for the life of the world is my flesh."
6:52 saying, "How can this man **g** us his flesh to eat?"
7:19 "Did not Moses **g** you the law?
9:24 and they said to him, "**G** glory to God!
10:28 I **g** them eternal life, and they will never perish.
11:22 now I know that God will **g** you whatever you ask
13:26 "It is the one to whom I **g** this piece of bread
13:29 or, that he should **g** something to the poor.
13:34 I **g** you a new commandment,
14:16 and he will **g** you another Advocate,
14:27 Peace I leave with you; my peace I **g** to you.
14:27 I do not **g** to you as the world gives.
15:16 so that the Father will **g** you whatever you ask him
16:23 he will **g** it to you.
17: 2 to **g** eternal life to all whom you have given him.
Ac 3: 6 "I have no silver or gold, but what I have I **g** you;
5:31 as Leader and Savior that he might **g** repentance
7: 5 He did not **g** him any of it as a heritage,
7: 5 but promised to **g** it to him as his possession and
7:38 and he received living oracles to **g** to us.
8:19 "**G** me also this power so that anyone
11:14 he will **g** you a message by which you
13:15 of exhortation for the people, **g** it."
13:34 'I will **g** you the holy promises made to David.'
19:40 that we can **g** to justify this commotion."
20:32 a message that is able to build you up and to **g** you
20:35 'It is more blessed to **g** than to receive.' "
23:35 "I will **g** you a hearing
Ro 1:21 they did not honor him as God or **g** thanks to him,
2: 7 and honor and immortality, he will **g** eternal life;
8:11 from the dead will **g** life to your mortal bodies
8:32 will he not with him also **g** us everything else?
12:20 if they are thirsty, **g** them something to drink;
14: 6 since they **g** thanks to God;
14: 6 abstain in honor of the Lord and **g** thanks to God.
14:11 and every tongue shall **g** praise to God."
16: 4 to whom not only I **g** thanks,
1Co 1: 4 I **g** thanks to my God always for you because of
7: 3 husband should **g** to his wife her conjugal rights,
7:10 To the married I **g** this command—
7:25 but I **g** my opinion as one who by
10:30 because of that for which I **g** thanks?
10:32 **G** no offense to Jews or to Greeks or to the church
11:34 the other things I will **g** instructions when I come.
13: 3 If I **g** away all my possessions,
14: 7 If they do not **g** distinct notes,
14:17 For you may **g** thanks well enough,
16:18 So **g** recognition to such persons.
2Co 1:11 so that many will **g** thanks on our behalf for
4: 6 to **g** the light of the knowledge of the glory of God
9: 7 of you must **g** as you have made up your mind,
Gal 3:15 I **g** an example from daily life:
6: 9 for we will reap at harvest time, if we do not **g** up.
Eph 1:16 not cease to **g** thanks for you as I remember you
1:17 may **g** you a spirit of wisdom and revelation
4:28 Thieves must **g** up stealing;
4:29 so that your words may **g** grace to those who hear.
Php 2:30 up for those services that you could not **g** me.
Col 4:15 **G** my greetings to the brothers and sisters
1Th 1: 2 We always **g** thanks to God for all of you
2:13 We also constantly **g** thanks to God for this,
5:18 **g** thanks in all circumstances;
2Th 1: 3 We must always **g** thanks to God for you,
1: 7 and to **g** relief to the afflicted as well as to us,
2:13 But we must always **g** thanks to God for you,
3: 9 but in order to **g** you an example to imitate.
3:16 the Lord of peace himself **g** you peace at all times
1Ti 4:13 **g** attention to the public reading of scripture,
5: 7 **G** these commands as well,
5:14 so as to **g** the adversary no occasion to revile us.
2Ti 1: 7 for God did not **g** us a spirit of cowardice,
2: 7 for the Lord will **g** you understanding in all things.
4: 8 the righteous judge, will **g** me on that day,
Tit 2: 9 and to **g** satisfaction in every respect;
Heb 12:28 let us **g** thanks, by which we offer to God
13:17 over your souls and will **g** an account.
1Pe 4: 5 to **g** an accounting to him who stands ready
1Jn 5:16 you will ask, and God will **g** life to such a one—
Rev 2: 7 I will **g** permission to eat from the tree of life
2:10 and I will **g** you the crown of life.
2:17 To everyone who conquers I will **g** some of
2:17 and I will **g** a white stone,
2:23 and I will **g** to each of you as your works deserve.
2:26 I will **g** authority over the nations;

Rev 2:28 To the one who conquers I will also **g**
3:21 To the one who conquers I will **g** a place with me
4: 9 the living creatures **g** glory and honor and thanks
9:20 did not repent of the works of their hands or **g**
10: 9 to the angel and told him to **g** me the little scroll;
11:17 "We **g** you thanks, Lord God Almighty,
13:15 and it was allowed to **g** breath to the image of
14: 7 "Fear God and **g** him glory,
16: 9 and they did not repent and **g** him glory.
17:17 by agreeing to **g** their kingdom to the beast,
18: 7 so **g** her a like measure of torment and grief.
19: 7 Let us rejoice and exult and **g** him the glory,
21: 6 the thirsty I will **g** water as a gift from the spring
Tob 1: 7 I would **g** these to the priests, the sons of Aaron,
1: 8 A third tenth I would **g** to the orphans and widows
1: 8 I would bring it and **g** it to them in the third year,
1:17 I would **g** my food to the hungry and my clothing
4: 3 "My son, when I die, **g** me a proper burial.
4: 7 **g** alms from your possessions,
4: 8 not be afraid to **g** according to the little you have.
4:16 **G** some of your food to the hungry,
4:16 **G** all your surplus as alms,
4:17 the grave of the righteous, but **g** none to sinners.
4:19 but the Lord himself will **g** them good counsel;
5: 2 to **g** him so that he will recognize and trust me,
5: 2 so that he will recognize and trust me, and **g** me
7: 9 ask Raguel to **g** me my kinswoman Sarah."
7:10 at liberty to **g** her to any other man than yourself,
9: 2 Go to the home of Gabael, **g** him the bond,
10: 2 and there is no one to **g** him the money?"
12: 1 and **g** him a bonus as well."
12: 2 to **g** him half of the possessions brought back
12: 3 How much extra shall I **g** him as a bonus?"
12: 8 It is better to **g** alms than to lay up gold.
12: 9 Those who **g** alms will enjoy a full life,
13:11 Generation after generation will **g** joyful praise
14:8,9 be commanded to do what is right and to **g** alms,
Jdt 8:25 of everything let us **g** thanks to the Lord our God,
9: 9 **G** to me, a widow, the strong hand
10:13 to **g** him a true report;
11:19 For this was told me to **g** me foreknowledge;
12: 6 "Let my lord now **g** orders to allow your servant
13: 7 "**G** me strength today, O Lord God of Israel!"
13:13 they lit a fire to **g** light, and gathered around them.
14:13 so bold as to come down against us to **g** battle,
AdE 1:13 **G** therefore your ruling and judgment
1:19 but let the king **g** her royal rank to
1:20 and thus all women will **g** honor to their husbands,
5:13 But these things **g** me no pleasure as long
14:12 in this time of our affliction, and **g** me courage,
16:20 And **g** them reinforcements,
Wis 6: 2 **G** ear, you that rule over multitudes,
8: 9 knowing that she would **g** me good counsel
8:12 and when I speak they will **g** heed;
9: 4 **g** me the wisdom that sits by your throne,
12: 9 though you were not unable to **g** the ungodly into
12:19 because you **g** repentance for sins.
12:20 and opportunity to **g** up their wickedness,
13:10 are those who **g** the name "gods" to the works
16:28 that one must rise before the sun to **g** you thanks,
17: 5 And no power of fire was able to **g** light,
19:12 for, to **g** them relief, quails came up from the sea.
Sir 3:31 Those who repay favors **g** thought to the future;
4: 5 and **g** no one reason to curse you;
4: 8 **G** a hearing to the poor,
4:31 to receive and closed when it is time to **g.**
6:37 It is he who will **g** insight to your mind,
7:10 do not neglect to **g** alms.
7:25 **G** a daughter in marriage,
7:25 but **g** her to a sensible man.
7:31 **g** him his portion, as you have been commanded:
7:33 **G** graciously to all the living;
8: 9 from them you learn how to understand and to **g**
8:13 Do not **g** surety beyond your means;
8:13 but if you **g** surety, be prepared to pay.
9: 2 Do not **g** yourself to a woman and let her trample
9: 6 Do not **g** yourself to prostitutes,
10:28 and **g** yourself the esteem you deserve.
12: 3 in evil or to one who does not **g** alms.
12: 4 **G** to the devout, but do not help the sinner.
12: 5 but do not **g** to the ungodly;
12: 5 hold back their bread, and do not **g** it to them,
12: 7 **G** to the one who is good,
14:13 and reach out and **g** to them as much as you can.
14:16 **G,** and take, and indulge yourself,
15: 3 and **g** him the water of wisdom to drink.
17:27 in Hades in place of the living who **g** thanks?
18:16 Does not the dew **g** relief from the scorching heat?
23: 4 do not **g** me haughty eyes,
23: 6 and do not **g** me over to shameless passion.
26: 9 betrays an unchaste wife; her eyelids **g** her away.
26:19 *and do not **g** your strength to strangers.*
30:11 **G** him no freedom in his youth,
30:21 Do not **g** yourself over to sorrow,
31:16 and do not chew greedily, or you will **g** offense.
31:17 and do not be insatiable, or you will **g** offense.
32:22 and **g** good heed to your paths.
33: 4 draw upon your training, and **g** your answer.
33:20 to brother or friend, do not **g** power over yourself,
33:20 and do not **g** your property to another,
34: 1 and dreams **g** wings to fools.
35:12 **G** to the Most High as he has given to you,
36: 6 **G** new signs, and work other wonders;
36:16 and **g** them their inheritance, as at the beginning.
37: 7 All counselors praise the counsel they **g,**
37: 7 but some **g** counsel in their own interest.
37:11 pay no attention to any advice they **g.**
Sir 37:27 see what is bad for you and do not **g** in to it.
38:10 **G** up your faults and direct your hands rightly,
38:12 Then **g** the physician his place,
38:20 Do not **g** your heart to grief;
39: 6 of wisdom of his own and **g** thanks to the Lord
39:15 Ascribe majesty to his name and **g** thanks to him
42: 7 and when you **g** or receive, put it all in writing.
44:21 like the stars, and **g** them an inheritance from sea
46: 1 so that he might **g** Israel its inheritance.
47:22 But the Lord will never **g** up his mercy,
50:23 May he **g** us gladness of heart,
51: 1 I **g** you thanks, O Lord and King,
51: 1 I **g** thanks to your name,
51:12 ***G** thanks to the LORD, for he is good,*
51:12 ***G** thanks to the God of praises,*
51:12 ***G** thanks to the guardian of Israel,*
51:12 ***G** thanks to him who formed all things,*
51:12 ***G** thanks to redeemer of Israel,*
51:12 ***G** thanks to him who gathers the dispersed of*
51:12 ***G** thanks to him who rebuilt his city*
51:12 ***G** thanks to him who makes a horn sprout for*
51:12 ***G** thanks to him who has chosen the sons of Zadok*
51:12 ***G** thanks to the shield of Abraham,*
51:12 ***G** thanks to the rock of Isaac,*
51:12 ***G** thanks to the mighty one of Jacob,*
51:12 ***G** thanks to him who has chosen Zion,*
51:12 ***G** thanks to the King of the kings of kings,*
51:17 to him who gives wisdom I will **g** glory.
51:30 and in his own time God will **g** you your reward.
Bar 1: 6 they collected as much money as each could **g,**
1:12 The Lord will **g** us strength, and light to our eyes;
1:20 to **g** to us a land flowing with milk and honey.
2:31 I will **g** them a heart that obeys and ears that hear;
2:34 into the land that I swore to **g** to their ancestors,
3: 9 Hear the commandments of life, O Israel; **g** ear,
3:27 or **g** them the way to knowledge;
4: 3 Do not **g** your glory to another,
4:23 but God will **g** you back to me with joy
5: 4 For God will **g** you evermore the name,
LtJ 6: 1 as exiles by the king of the Babylonians, to **g** them
6:11 even **g** some of it to the prostitutes on the terrace.
6:28 but **g** none to the poor or helpless.
6:35 Likewise they are not able to **g** either wealth
6:53 up a king over a country or **g** rain to people.
6:67 or shine like the sun or **g** light like the moon.
Aza 1:11 For your name's sake do not **g** us up forever,
1:67 **G** thanks to the Lord, for he is good,
1:68 sing praise to him and **g** thanks to him,
Sus 1:20 so **g** your consent, and lie with us.
Bel 1:26 But **g** me permission, O king,
1:26 The king said, "I **g** you permission."
1Mc 1:42 and that all should **g** up their particular customs.
2:50 and **g** your lives for the covenant of our ancestors.
3:30 to **g** more lavishly than preceding kings.
8: 7 a heavy tribute and **g** hostages and surrender some
8:26 not **g** or supply grain, arms, money, or ships, just
9:55 that he could no longer say a word or **g** commands
10:28 will grant you many immunities and **g** you gifts.
10:32 also my control of the citadel in Jerusalem and **g** it
10:41 they shall **g** from now on for the service of
10:54 **g** me now your daughter as my wife,
10:89 as it is the custom to **g** to the King's Kinsmen.
11: 9 a covenant with each other, and I will **g** you
15:35 for them we will **g** you one hundred talents."
16:19 so that he might **g** them silver and gold and gifts;
2Mc 1: 3 May he **g** you all a heart to worship him and
7:23 in his mercy **g** life and breath back to you again,
7:37 **g** up body and life for the laws of our ancestors,
9:16 and all the holy vessels he would **g** back,
10:10 and will **g** a brief summary of
11:26 to them and **g** them pledges of friendship,
11:35 of the king has granted you, we also **g** consent.
12:11 to **g** him livestock and to help his people
14:19 Mattathias to **g** and receive pledges of friendship.
14:46 upon the Lord of life and spirit to **g** them back
15: 8 for the victory that the Almighty would **g** them.
1Es 3: 5 King Darius will **g** rich gifts and great honors
3: 9 they will **g** him the writing;
4:22 and bring everything and **g** it to women?
4:42 and we will **g** it to you,
4:47 that they should **g** safe conduct to him and
4:50 the Idumeans should **g** up the villages of the Jews
4:60 I **g** you thanks, O Lord of our ancestors."
5:45 and that they would **g** to the sacred treasury for
8:19 they shall take care to **g** him,
8:79 and to **g** us food in the time of our servitude.
8:81 to **g** us a stronghold in Judea and Jerusalem.
8:84 Therefore do not **g** your daughters in marriage
9: 8 and **g** glory to the Lord the God of our ancestors,
9:54 and to **g** portions to those who had none,
3Mc 1: 4 to **g** them each two minas of gold if they won
2: 2 **g** attention to us who are suffering grievously
2:20 and broken in spirit, and **g** us peace."
3:28 Any who are willing to **g** information will receive
5:17 to **g** themselves over to revelry and to make
5:31 who **g** me no ground for complaint
5:37 must I **g** you orders about these things?
2Es 1:24 to other nations and will **g** them my name,
1:35 I will **g** your houses to a people that will come,
1:39 to them I will **g** as leaders Abraham,
2:10 "Tell my people that I will **g** them the kingdom
2:10 which I was going to **g** to Israel.
2:11 will **g** to these others the everlasting habitations,
2:12 The tree of life shall **g** them fragrant perfume,
2:20 secure justice for the ward, **g** to the needy,
2:23 and I will **g** you the first place in my resurrection.
2:34 he will **g** you everlasting rest,
2Es 3:19 to **g** the law to the descendants of Jacob,
4:42 also do these places hasten to **g** back those things
5:45 to your servant that you will certainly **g** life
6:21 and pregnant women shall **g** birth
7:*32* The earth shall **g** up those who are asleep in it,
7:*32* and the chambers shall **g** up the souls
7:*99* not **g** heed shall suffer hereafter."
7:*135* [65] because he would rather **g** than take away;
7:*138* [68] because if he did not **g** out of his goodness so
8: 6 and **g** us a seed for our heart and cultivation
8: 8 And because you **g** life to the body that is
8:24 and **g** ear to the petition of your creature;
9:30 and **g** heed to my words, O descendants of Jacob.
10:24 and the Most High may **g** you rest,
10:37 Now therefore I beg you to **g** your servant
14:38 open your mouth and drink what I **g** you to drink."
14:46 in order to **g** them to the wise among your people.
4Mc 1: 6 but so that one may not **g** way to them.
8:19 and **g** up this vain opinion and this arrogance
10:13 not **g** way to the same insanity as your brothers,
11:12 because through these noble sufferings you **g** us
15: 5 that mothers are the weaker sex and **g** birth

GIVEN‡ (595) [GIVE]

Ge 1:29 I have **g** you every plant yielding seed that is upon
1:30 I have **g** every green plant for food."
15: 3 And Abram said, "You have **g** me no offspring,
16:11 for the LORD has **g** heed to your affliction.
20:16 I have **g** your brother a thousand pieces of silver;
24:35 he has **g** him flocks and herds, silver and gold,
24:36 and he has **g** him all that he has.
26:18 he gave them the names that his father had **g** them.
27:37 and I have **g** him all his brothers as servants,
29:33 he has **g** me this son also";
30: 6 and has also heard my voice and **g** me a son";
30:18 "God has **g** me my hire because I gave my maid
30:26 for you know very well the service I have **g** you."
31: 9 the livestock of your father, and **g** them to me.
31:15 and he has been using up the money **g** for us.
33: 5 children whom God has graciously **g** your servant.
38:14 yet she had not been **g** to him in marriage.
43:24 and **g** them water, and they had washed their feet,
43:24 and when he had **g** their donkeys fodder,
48: 9 "They are my sons, whom God has **g** me here."
Ex 3:16 I have **g** heed to you and to what has been done
4:31 and when they heard that the LORD had **g** heed
5:13 as when you were **g** straw."
5:16 No straw is **g** to your servants, yet they say to us,
5:18 Go now, and work; for no straw shall be **g** you,
12:36 and the LORD had **g** the people favor in the sight
13:11 and has **g** it to you,
16:15 "It is the bread that the LORD has **g** you to eat.
16:29 The LORD has **g** you the sabbath,
30:16 to the Israelites of the ransom **g** for your lives.
31: 6 and I have **g** skill to all the skillful,
31:13 **g** in order that you may know that I, the LORD,
36: 1 to whom the LORD has **g** skill and understanding
36: 2 to whom the LORD had **g** skill,
Lev 6:17 I have **g** it as their portion of my offerings by fire;
7:34 have **g** them to Aaron the priest and to his sons,
7:36 these the LORD commanded to be **g** them,
10:17 and God has **g** it to you that you may remove
17:11 and I have **g** it to you for making atonement
19:20 but not ransomed or **g** her freedom,
20: 3 because they have **g** of their offspring to Molech,
27: 9 any such that may be **g** to the LORD shall
Nu 3: 9 they are unreservedly **g** to him from among
8:16 For they are unreservedly **g** to me from among
8:19 I have **g** the Levites as a gift to Aaron and his sons
16:14 or **g** us an inheritance of fields and vineyards.
18: 8 I have **g** you charge of the offerings made to me,
18: 8 I have **g** them to you and your sons as
18:11 This also is yours: I have **g** to you,
18:12 that they give to the LORD, I have **g** to you.
18:19 that the Israelites present to the LORD I have **g**
18:21 To the Levites I have **g** every tithe in Israel for
18:24 because I have **g** to the Levites as their portion
18:26 the Israelites the tithe that I have **g** you from them
20:12 into the land that I have **g** them."
20:24 not enter the land that I have **g** to the Israelites,
21:34 for I have **g** him into your hand,
26:54 be **g** its inheritance according to its enrollment.
26:62 because there was no allotment **g** to them among
27:12 and see the land that I have **g** to the Israelites.
32: 5 let this land be **g** to your servants for a possession;
32: 7 over into the land that the LORD has **g** them?
32: 9 into the land that the LORD had **g** them.
33:53 for I have **g** you the land to possess.
Dt 1:21 See, the LORD your God has **g** the land to you;
2: 5 since I have **g** Mount Seir to Esau as a possession.
2: 9 as a possession, since I have **g** Ar as a possession
2:19 because I have **g** it to the descendants of Lot."
3:18 LORD your God has **g** you this land to occupy,
3:19 shall stay behind in the towns that I have **g** to you.
3:20 of you may return to the property that I have **g**
8:10 for the good land that he has **g** you.
9:23 "Go up and occupy the land that I have **g** you,"
12: 1 has **g** you to occupy all the days that you live on
12:15 the blessing that the LORD your God has **g** you;
12:21 of your herd or flock that the LORD has **g** you,
15:18 for six years they have **g** you services worth
16:17 of the LORD your God that he has **g** you.
20:14 which the LORD your God has **g** you.
23:15 from their owners shall not be **g** back to them.
24:12 not sleep in the garment **g** you as the pledge.
25: 3 Forty lashes may be **g** but not more;

Dt 25: 3 if more lashes than these are **g**,
25:19 when the LORD your God has **g** you rest
26:10 of the ground that you, O LORD, have **g** me."
26:11 the bounty that the LORD your God has **g** to you
26:13 and I have **g** it to the Levites, the resident aliens,
26:15 and the ground that you have **g** us, as you swore
28:31 Your sheep shall be **g** to your enemies,
28:32 and daughters shall be **g** to another people,
28:52 the land that the LORD your God has **g** you.
28:53 the LORD your God has **g** you.
29: 4 But to this day the LORD has not **g** you a mind
31: 5 in full accord with the command that I have **g**
32:30 the LORD had **g** them up?
Jos 1: 3 that the sole of your foot will tread upon I have **g**
2: 9 "I know that the LORD has **g** you the land,
2:24 the LORD has **g** all the land into our hands;
6:16 For the LORD has **g** you the city.
10:19 the LORD your God has **g** them into your hand."
14: 3 For Moses had **g** an inheritance to the two
14: 4 and no portion was **g** to the Levites in the land,
17:14 "Why have you **g** me but one lot and one portion
18: 3 the God of your ancestors, has **g** you?
20: 4 fugitive shall be taken into the city, and **g** a place,
21: 2 through Moses that we be **g** towns to live in,
21:12 the town and its villages had been **g** to Caleb son
21:21 To them were **g** Shechem,
21:27 were **g** out of the half-tribe of Manasseh,
21:34 were **g** out of the tribe of Zebulun:
21:44 LORD had **g** all their enemies into their hands.
22: 4 the LORD your God has **g** rest to your kindred,
22: 7 of the tribe of Manasseh Moses had **g** a possession
22: 7 but to the other half Joshua had **g** a possession
23: 1 when the LORD had **g** rest to Israel
23:13 that the LORD your God has **g** you.
23:15 that the LORD your God has **g** you.
23:16 from the good land that he has **g** to you."
24:33 of his son Phinehas, which had been **g** him in
Jdg 1:20 Hebron was **g** to Caleb, as Moses had said;
3:28 for the LORD has **g** your enemies the Moabites
4:14 on which the LORD has **g** Sisera into your hand.
6:10 But you have not **g** heed to my voice."
6:13 and **g** us into the hand of Midian."
7: 9 for I have **g** it into your hand.
7:14 into his hand God has **g** Midian and all the army."
7:15 LORD has **g** the army of Midian into your hand."
8: 3 God has **g** into your hands the captains of Midian,
8: 7 LORD has **g** Zebah and Zalmunna into my hand,
11:36 now that the LORD has **g** you vengeance
14:20 And Samson's wife was **g** to his companion,
15: 6 because he has taken Samson's wife and **g** her
16:23 "Our god has **g** Samson our enemy into our hand."
16:24 "Our god has **g** our enemy into our hand,
18:10 God has indeed **g** it into your hands—
Ru 1: 6 LORD had considered his people and **g** them food.
1Sa 1:28 as long as he lives, he is **g** to the LORD."
14:10 for the LORD has **g** them into our hand."
14:12 for the LORD has **g** them into the hand of Israel."
15:28 and has **g** it to a neighbor of yours,
18:19 when Saul's daughter Merab should have been **g**
18:19 she was **g** to Adriel the Meholathite as a wife.
18:27 which were **g** in full number to the king,
23: 7 And Saul said, "God has **g** him into my hand;
25:27 that your servant has brought to my lord be **g** to
25:44 Saul had **g** his daughter Michal, David's wife,
26: 8 "God has **g** your enemy into your hand today;
27: 5 let a place be **g** me in one of the country towns,
28:17 and **g** it to your neighbor, David.
30:23 my brothers, with what the LORD has **g** us;
2Sa 3: 8 and have not **g** you into the hand of David;
7: 1 the LORD had **g** him rest from all his enemies
9: 9 that belonged to Saul and to all his house I have **g**
16: 8 and the LORD has **g** the kingdom into the hand
17: 7 "This time the counsel that Ahithophel has **g** is
19:42 Or has he **g** us any gift?"
22:36 You have **g** me the shield of your salvation,
1Ki 2:21 the Shunammite be **g** to your brother Adonijah
3: 6 and have **g** him a son to sit on his throne today.
5: 4 the LORD my God has **g** me rest on every side;
5: 7 who has **g** to David a wise son to be
8:31 against a neighbor and is **g** an oath to swear,
8:36 on your land, which you have **g** to your people as
8:56 who has **g** rest to his people Israel according to all
9: 7 from the land that I have **g** them;
9:12 to see the cities that Solomon had **g** him,
9:13 "What kind of cities are these that you have **g** me,
9:16 and had **g** it as dowry to his daughter,
12:13 the advice that the older men had **g** him
13: 5 according to the sign that the man of God had **g** by
13:26 therefore the LORD has **g** him to the lion,
18:23 Let two bulls be **g** to us;
18:26 So they took the bull that was **g** them, prepared it,
20:39 if he is missing, your life shall be **g** for his life,
2Ki 5: 1 by him the LORD had **g** victory to Aram.
5:17 please let two mule-loads of earth be **g**
12:14 for that was **g** to the workers who were repairing
18:30 and this city will not be **g** into the hand of the king
19:10 by promising that Jerusalem will not be **g** into
22: 5 let it be **g** into the hand of the workers who have
22:10 "The priest Hilkiah has **g** me a book."
25:30 a regular allowance was **g** him by the king,
1Ch 5: 1 he defiled his father's bed his birthright was **g**
5:20 the Hagrites and all who were with them were **g**
6:61 To the rest of the Kohathites were **g** by lot out of
6:67 They were **g** the cities of refuge:
22:18 Has he not **g** you peace on every side?
23:25 the God of Israel, has **g** rest to his people;
25: 5 for God had **g** Heman fourteen sons

1Ch 28: 5 of all my sons, for the LORD has **g** me many,
29: 9 the people rejoiced because these had **g** willingly,
29:14 and of your own have we **g** you.
2Ch 2:12 who has **g** King David a wise son,
6:27 upon your land, which you have **g** to your people
7:20 up from the land that I have **g** you;
8: 2 Solomon rebuilt the cities that Huram had **g**
14: 7 and he has **g** us peace on every side."
18:14 they will be **g** into your hand."
20:11 of your possession that you have **g** us to inherit.
25: 9 about the hundred talents that I have **g** to the army
28: 5 He was also **g** into the hand of the king of Israel,
32:29 for God had **g** him very great possessions.
33: 8 the statutes, and the ordinances **g** through Moses."
34:14 of the law of the LORD **g** through Moses.
34:18 "The priest Hilkiah has **g** me a book."
36:23 has **g** me all the kingdoms of the earth,
Ezr 1: 2 has **g** me all the kingdoms of the earth,
6: 9 let that be **g** to them day by day without fail,
7: 6 of Moses that the LORD the God of Israel had **g**;
7:16 **g** willingly for the house of their God
7:19 The vessels that have been **g** you for the service of
9: 8 and **g** us a stake in his holy place,
9:13 and have **g** us such a remnant as this,
Ne 2: 7 let letters be **g** me to the governors of the province
8: 1 which the LORD had **g** to Israel.
10:29 which was **g** by Moses the servant of God,
13: 5 which were **g** by commandment to the Levites,
13:10 the portions of the Levites had not been **g** to them;
Est 1: 8 for the king had **g** orders to all the officials
2: 3 let their cosmetic treatments be **g** them.
2:13 the king she was **g** whatever she asked for to take
3:11 The king said to Haman, "The money is **g** to you,
5: 3 It shall be **g** you, even to the half of my kingdom."
7: 3 and if it pleases the king, let my life be **g** me—
8: 7 "See, I have **g** Esther the house of Haman,
Job 3:20 "Why is light **g** to one in misery,
3:23 Why is light **g** to one who cannot see the way,
9:24 The earth is **g** into the hand of the wicked;
15:19 to whom alone the land was **g**,
22: 7 You have **g** no water to the weary to drink,
26: 3 one who has no wisdom, and **g** much good advice!
37:10 By the breath of God ice is **g**,
38:29 and who has **g** birth to the hoarfrost of heaven?
38:36 or **g** understanding to the mind?
39: 6 to which I have **g** the steppe for its home,
39:17 and **g** it no share in understanding.
Ps 8: 6 You have **g** them dominion over the works
18:35 You have **g** me the shield of your salvation,
21: 2 You have **g** him his heart's desire,
40: 6 but you have **g** me an open ear.
60: 3 you have **g** us wine to drink that made us reel.
61: 5 you have **g** me the heritage
63:10 they shall be **g** over to the power of the sword,
66:19 he has **g** heed to the words of my prayer.
72:15 May gold of Sheba be **g** to him.
79: 2 They have **g** the bodies of your servants to
80: 5 and **g** them tears to drink in full measure.
112: 9 they have **g** to the poor;
115:16 but the earth he has **g** to human beings.
118:27 The LORD is God, and he has **g** us light.
119:93 for by them you have **g** me life.
120: 3 What shall be **g** to you?
124: 6 who has not **g** us as prey to their teeth.
141: 6 they are **g** over to those who shall condemn them,
Pr 6: 1 if you have **g** your pledge to your neighbor,
20:16 Take the garment of one who has **g** surety for
20:16 seize the pledge **g** as surety for foreigners.
22:24 Make no friends with those **g** to anger,
25:14 without rain is one who boasts of a gift never **g**.
27:13 Take the garment of one who has **g** surety for
27:13 seize the pledge **g** as surety for foreigners.
29:22 One **g** to anger stirs up strife,
Ecc 1:13 that God has **g** to human beings to be busy with.
3:10 that God has **g** to everyone to be busy with.
9: 9 all the days of your vain life that are **g** you under
12:11 the collected sayings that are **g** by one shepherd.
Isa 8:18 the children whom the LORD has **g** me are signs
9: 6 For a child has been born for us, a son **g** to us;
14: 3 When the LORD has **g** you rest from your pain
23: 4 "I have neither labored nor **g** birth,
23:11 the LORD has **g** command concerning Canaan
29:11 If it is **g** to those who can read, with the command,
29:12 And if it is **g** to those who cannot read, saying,
34: 2 has **g** them over for slaughter.
35: 2 The glory of Lebanon shall be **g** to it,
36:15 this city will not be **g** into the hand of the king
37:10 by promising that Jerusalem will not be **g** into
42: 6 I have **g** you as a covenant to the people,
49: 8 and **g** you as a covenant to the people, to establish
50: 4 The Lord GOD has **g** me the tongue of a teacher,
Jer 6:19 because they have not **g** heed to my words;
8: 6 I have **g** heed and listened,
8:14 and has **g** us poisoned water to drink,
10: 8 the instruction **g** by idols is no better than wood!
12: 7 I have **g** the beloved of my heart into the hands
12:14 the heritage that I have **g** my people Israel
13:20 is the flock that was **g** you, your beautiful flock?
21:10 it shall be **g** into the hands of the king of Babylon,
23:18 Who has **g** heed to his word so as to proclaim it?
25: 5 the LORD has **g** to you and your ancestors from
26:24 that he was not **g** over into the hands of the people
27: 6 Now I have **g** all these lands into the hand
27: 6 and I have **g** him even the wild animals of
28:14 I have even **g** him the wild animals.
32: 4 surely be **g** into the hands of the king of Babylon,
32:16 After I had **g** the deed of purchase to Baruch son

Jer 32:24 has been **g** into the hands of the Chaldeans
32:25 city has been **g** into the hands of the Chaldeans.
32:36 "It is being **g** into the hand of the king of Babylon
32:43 it has been **g** into the hands of the Chaldeans.
37:21 of bread was **g** him daily from the bakers' street,
47: 7 can it be quiet, when the LORD has **g** it an order?
51:30 The warriors of Babylon have **g** up fighting,
52:34 a regular daily allowance was **g** him by the king
La 5: 5 we are weary, we are **g** no rest.
Eze 11:15 to us this land is **g** for a possession."
15: 6 which I have **g** to the fire for fuel,
16:17 of my gold and my silver that I had **g** you,
16:33 Gifts are **g** to all whores;
16:34 while no payment was **g** to you;
20:15 not bring them into the land that I had **g** them,
21:11 The sword is **g** to be polished,
29: 5 of the earth and to the birds of the air I have **g** you
29:20 I have **g** him the land of Egypt as his payment
33:24 the land is surely **g** us to possess."
35:12 "They are laid desolate, they are **g** us to devour."
Da 1:12 Let us be **g** vegetables to eat and water to drink.
2:23 for you have **g** me wisdom and power,
2:37 to whom the God of heaven has **g** the kingdom,
2:38 into whose hand he has **g** human beings,
4:16 and let the mind of an animal be **g** to him.
4:17 the decision is **g** by order of the holy ones,
5:28 your kingdom is divided and **g** to the Medes
7: 4 and a human mind was **g** to it.
7: 6 and dominion was **g** to it.
7:11 and its body destroyed and **g** over to be burned
7:14 To him was **g** dominion and glory and kingship,
7:22 then judgment was **g** for the holy ones of
7:25 and they shall be **g** into his power for a time,
7:27 the kingdoms under the whole heaven shall be **g** to
8:12 the host was **g** over to it together with
11: 6 be **g** up, she and her attendants and her child and
Hos 2:12 "These are my pay, which my lovers have **g** me."
12:14 Ephraim has **g** bitter offense,
Joel 2:23 for he has **g** the early rain for your vindication,
Am 9:15 be plucked up out of the land that I have **g** them,
Mt 6:33 and all these things will be **g** to you as well.
7: 7 "Ask, and it will be **g** you;
9: 8 who had **g** such authority to human beings.
10:19 what you are to say will be **g** to you at that time;
12:39 be **g** to it except the sign of the prophet Jonah.
13:11 "To you it has been **g** to know the secrets of
13:11 but to them it has not been **g**.
13:12 For to those who have, more will be **g**,
14: 9 he commanded it to be **g**;
14:11 head was brought on a platter and **g** to the girl,
15: 5 from me is **g** to God,'
16: 4 no sign will be **g** to it except the sign of Jonah."
19:11 but only those to whom it is **g**.
21:43 from you and **g** to a people that produces the fruits
22:30 in the resurrection they neither marry nor are **g**
25:29 For to all those who have, more will be **g**,
26: 9 and the money **g** to the poor."
26:48 Now the betrayer had **g** them a sign, saying,
27:58 then Pilate ordered it to be **g** to him.
28:18 "All authority in heaven and on earth has been **g**
Mk 4:11 "To you has been **g** the secret of the kingdom
4:24 and still more will be **g** you.
4:25 For to those who have, more will be **g**;
6: 2 What is this wisdom that has been **g** to him?
8:12 no sign will be **g** to this generation."
12:25 they neither marry nor are **g** in marriage,
13:11 but say whatever is **g** you at that time,
14: 5 and the money **g** to the poor."
14:44 Now the betrayer had **g** them a sign, saying,
Lk 2:21 the name **g** by the angel before he was conceived
4: 6 for it has been **g** over to me,
4:17 and the scroll of the prophet Isaiah was **g** to him.
6:38 and it will be **g** to you.
7:21 and had **g** sight to many who were blind.
8:10 "To you it has been **g** to know the secrets of
8:18 for to those who have, more will be **g**;
10:19 I have **g** you authority to tread on snakes
10:28 And he said to him, "You have **g** the right answer;
11: 9 "So I say to you, Ask, and it will be **g** you;
11:29 but no sign will be **g** to it except the sign of Jonah.
12:31 and these things will be **g** to you as well.
12:48 From everyone to whom much has been **g**,
15:29 yet you have never **g** me even a young goat so
17:27 and marrying and being **g** in marriage,
19:15 to whom he had **g** the money,
19:26 'I tell you, to all those who have, more will be **g**;
20:34 "Those who belong to this age marry and are **g**
20:35 from the dead neither marry nor are **g** in marriage.
22:19 he took a loaf of bread, and when he had **g** thanks,
22:19 saying, "This is my body, which is **g** for you.
Jn 1:17 The law indeed was **g** through Moses;
1:19 This is the testimony **g** by John when
3:27 can receive anything except what has been **g**
4: 5 of ground that Jacob had **g** to his son Joseph.
4:10 and he would have **g** you living water."
5:22 The Father judges no one but has **g** all judgment
5:27 and he has **g** him authority to execute judgment,
5:36 The works that the Father has **g** me to complete,
6:11 Jesus took the loaves, and when he had **g** thanks,
6:23 the bread after the Lord had **g** thanks.
6:39 that I should lose nothing of all that he has **g** me,
10:29 What my Father has **g** me is greater than all else,
11:57 the Pharisees had **g** orders that anyone who knew
12: 5 not sold for three hundred denarii and the money **g**
12:49 but the Father who sent me has himself **g** me
13: 3 that the Father had **g** all things into his hands,
17: 2 since you have **g** him authority over all people,

Jn 17: 2 to give eternal life to all whom you have **g** him.
17: 7 Now they know that everything you have **g** me is
17: 8 the words that you gave to me I have **g** to them,
17:11 protect them in your name that you have **g** me,
17:12 I protected them in your name that you have **g** me.
17:14 I have **g** them your word,
17:22 The glory that you have **g** me I have **g** them,
17:24 I desire that those also, whom you have **g** me,
17:24 which you have **g** me because you loved me
18:11 not to drink the cup that the Father has **g** me?"
19:11 over me unless it had been **g** you from above;
Ac 3:14 and asked to have a murderer **g** to you,
3:16 that is through Jesus has **g** him this perfect health
4:12 under heaven **g** among mortals by which we must
5:32 and so is the Holy Spirit whom God has **g**
8:18 when Simon saw that the Spirit was **g** through
11:18 "Then God has **g** even to the Gentiles
12:23 because he had not **g** the glory to God,
16:23 After they had **g** them a severe flogging,
17:31 and of this he has **g** assurance to all by raising him
20: 2 and had **g** the believers much encouragement,
20:35 In all this I have **g** you an example that
21:40 When he had **g** him permission,
24:26 that money would be **g** him by Paul,
25:16 and had been **g** an opportunity to make a defense
Ro 5: 5 through the Holy Spirit that has been **g** to us.
11:35 "Or who has **g** a gift to him,
12: 3 the grace **g** to me I say to everyone among you not
12: 6 We have gifts that differ according to the grace **g**
15: 8 in order that he might confirm the promises **g** to
15:15 because of the grace **g** me by God
1Co 1: 4 because of the grace of God that has been **g** you
3:10 According to the grace of God **g** to me,
11:15 For her hair is **g** to her for a covering.
11:24 and when he had **g** thanks,
12: 7 To each is **g** the manifestation of the Spirit for
12: 8 To one is **g** through the Spirit the utterance
2Co 4:11 we are always being **g** up to death for Jesus' sake,
5: 5 who has **g** us the Spirit as a guarantee.
5:18 and has **g** us the ministry of reconciliation;
9:14 of the surpassing grace of God that he has **g** you.
12: 7 a thorn was **g** me in the flesh,
13:10 the authority that the Lord has **g** me for building
Gal 2: 9 recognized the grace that had been **g** to me,
3:21 For if a law had been **g** that could make alive,
3:22 in Jesus Christ might be **g** to those who believe.
4:15 you would have torn out your eyes and **g** them
Eph 3: 2 of the commission of God's grace that was **g** me
3: 7 according to the gift of God's grace that was **g** me
3: 8 this grace was **g** to me to bring to the Gentiles
4: 7 of us was **g** grace according to the measure
6:19 a message may be **g** to me to make known
Col 1:25 according to God's commission that was **g** to me
1Ti 4:14 which was **g** to you through prophecy with
2Ti 1: 9 This grace was **g** to us in Christ Jesus before
Heb 2:13 and the children whom God has **g** me."
4: 8 For if Joshua had **g** them rest,
6:16 oath **g** as confirmation puts an end to all dispute.
12:20 (For they could not endure the order that was **g**,
Jas 1: 5 and it will be **g** you.
1Pe 1: 3 By his great mercy he has **g** us a new birth into
2Pe 1: 3 His divine power has **g** us everything needed
1: 4 Thus he has **g** us, through these things,
3:15 to you according to the wisdom **g** him,
1Jn 3: 1 See what love the Father has **g** us,
3:24 by the Spirit that he has **g** us.
4:13 because he has **g** us of his Spirit.
5:10 the testimony that God has **g** concerning his Son.
5:20 of God has come and has **g** us understanding so
Rev 6: 2 Its rider had a bow; a crown was **g** to him,
6: 4 and he was **g** a great sword.
6: 8 they were **g** authority over a fourth of the earth,
6: 9 of God and for the testimony they had **g**;
6:11 They were each **g** a white robe and told to rest
7: 2 to the four angels who had been **g** power
8: 2 and seven trumpets were **g** to them.
8: 3 he was **g** a great quantity of incense to offer with
9: 1 he was **g** the key to the shaft of the bottomless pit;
9: 3 and they were **g** authority like the authority
11: 1 Then I was **g** a measuring rod like a staff,
11: 2 leave that out, for it is **g** over to the nations,
12:13 the woman who had **g** birth to the male child.
12:14 the woman was **g** the two wings of the great eagle,
13: 4 for he had **g** his authority to the beast,
13: 5 The beast was **g** a mouth uttering haughty
13: 7 It was **g** authority over every tribe and people
16: 6 you have **g** them blood to drink.
18:20 For God has **g** judgment for you against her."
20: 4 those seated on them were **g** authority to judge.
Tob 2:14 "It was **g** to me as a gift in addition to my wages."
5:20 life that is **g** to us by the Lord is enough for us."
6:16 I know that this very night she will be **g** to you
6:17 An odor will be **g** off;
7:11 I have **g** her to seven men of our kinsmen,
7:11 She is **g** to you in accordance with the decree in
7:11 and it has been decreed from heaven that she be **g**
7:11 She is **g** to you from today and forever.
11:18 and many gifts were **g** to him.
14: 7 and it will be **g** over to them.
Jdt 11:12 and their water has almost **g** out,
16:19 which the people had **g** her;
AdE 2: 3 and whatever else they need be **g** them.
3:13 the Jewish people on a **g** day of the twelfth month,
5: 3 It shall be **g** you, even to half of my kingdom."
6: 9 let both be **g** to one of the king's honored Friends,
8: 9 that he commanded with respect to the Jews was **g**
Wis 6: 3 For your dominion was **g** you from the Lord,
Wis 7: 7 Therefore I prayed, and understanding was **g** me;
9: 8 You have **g** command to build a temple
9:17 unless you have **g** wisdom
11: 4 and water was **g** them out of flinty rock,
14: 3 because you have **g** it a path in the sea,
18: 4 the imperishable light of the law was to be **g** to
18:22 to the oaths and covenants **g** to our ancestors.
Sir Pr: 1 Many great teachings have been **g** to us through
7:28 how can you repay what they have **g** to you?
13:22 he talks sense, but is not **g** a hearing.
14: 2 and who have not **g** up their hope.
15:17 and whichever one chooses will be **g**.
15:20 and he has not **g** anyone permission to sin.
18: 4 To none has he **g** power to proclaim his works;
26:23 *A godless wife is **g** as a portion to a lawless man,*
26:23 *a pious wife is **g** to the man who fears the Lord.*
29:15 for he has **g** his life for you.
33:13 to be **g** whatever he decides.
35:12 Give to the Most High as he has **g** to you,
43:33 and to the godly he has **g** wisdom.
47: 6 when the glorious diadem was **g** to him.
Bar 2:35 from the land that I have **g** them."
3:23 or **g** thought to her paths.
Sus 1:43 that these men have **g** false evidence against me.
1:49 for these men have **g** false evidence against her."
1:50 for God has **g** you the standing of an elder."
Bel 1:32 and every day they had been **g** two human bodies
1:32 but now they were **g** nothing,
1Mc 2: 7 and to live there when it was **g** over to the enemy,
2: 7 the sanctuary **g** over to aliens?
4:40 And when the signal was **g** with the trumpets,
5:62 of those men through whom deliverance was **g**
8:28 And to their enemies there shall not be **g** grain,
10: 8 that the king had **g** him authority to recruit troops.
10:36 and let the maintenance be **g** them that is due to all
10:39 Ptolemais and the land adjoining it I have **g** as
11:37 be **g** to Jonathan and put up in a conspicuous place
2Mc 1:18 the festival of booths and the festival of the fire **g**
3:15 and called toward heaven upon him who had **g**
4: 9 if permission were **g** to establish by his authority
4:30 of Mallus revolted because their cities had been **g**
7:30 the law that was **g** to our ancestors through Moses.
10: 7 of thanksgiving to him who had **g** success to
1Es 1: 6 to the commandment of the Lord that was **g**
1: 7 these were **g** from the king's possessions,
2:12 and by him they were **g** to Sheshbazzar,
2:27 that the people in it were **g** to rebellion and war,
3: 9 of Persia judge to be wisest the victory shall be **g**
4:51 a year should be **g** for the building of the temple
4:60 Blessed are you, who have **g** me wisdom;
4:62 because he had **g** them release and permission
6:29 and Phoenicia a portion be scrupulously **g**
8: 3 which was **g** by the God of Israel;
8:10 I have **g** orders that those of the Jewish nation and
8:14 with what is **g** by the nation for the temple
8:17 of the Lord that are **g** you for the use of the temple
8:49 whom David and the leaders had **g** for the service
8:55 and the nobles and all Israel had **g**.
8:77 and our kings and our priests were **g** over to
8:80 so that they have **g** us food
9:39 the law of Moses that had been **g** by the Lord God
3Mc 3: 2 a pretext being **g** by a report
3:25 Therefore we have **g** orders that,
4:20 the pens they used for writing had already **g** out.
5: 3 he had **g** these orders he returned to his feasting,
5:19 he had carried out completely the order **g** him,
2Es 2:26 one of the servants whom I have **g** you will perish,
4: 9 and you have **g** me no answer about them."
4:23 why Israel has been **g** over to the Gentiles
4:23 why the people whom you loved has been **g** over
5:27 you have **g** the law that is approved by all.
5:48 so I have **g** the womb of the earth to those who
5:50 "Since you have now **g** me the opportunity,
6:58 and most dear, have been **g** into their hands.
7: 9 If now the city is **g** to someone as an inheritance,
7:*100* "Will time therefore be **g** to the souls,
8: 5 for you have been **g** only a short time to live.
10:14 the earth also has from the beginning **g** her fruit,
10:23 and **g** over into the hands of those that hate us.
14:31 Then land was **g** to you for a possession in
14:32 in due time he took from you what he had **g**.
15:20 to turn and repay what they have **g** them.
16:78 It is shut off and **g** up to be consumed by fire.
4Mc 8: 3 the tyrant had **g** these orders, seven brothers—

GIVER (5) [GIVE]

Pr 19: 6 and everyone is a friend to a **g** of gifts.
Ro 12: 8 in exhortation; the **g**, in generosity;
2Co 9: 7 for God loves a cheerful **g**.
Sir 18:18 and the gift of a grudging **g** makes the eyes dim.
2Es 7:*138* [68] and he is called the **g**, because if he did

GIVES‡ (123) [GIVE]

Ex 4:11 LORD said to him, "Who **g** speech to mortals?
16: 8 the LORD **g** you meat to eat in the evening
16:29 on the sixth day he **g** you food for two days;
21: 4 If his master **g** him a wife and she bears him sons
Lev 25: 8 period of seven weeks of years **g** forty-nine years.
Nu 5:10 whatever anyone **g** to the priest shall be his.
Dt 3:20 When the LORD **g** rest to your kindred,
7: 2 when the LORD your God **g** them over to you
8:18 for it is he who **g** you power to get wealth,
12:10 when he **g** you rest from your enemies all around
19: 3 that the LORD your God **g** you as a possession,
20:13 when the LORD your God **g** it into your hand,
Jos 1:11 that the LORD your God **g** you to possess.' "
Jos 1:15 until the LORD **g** rest to your kindred as well as
2:14 and faithfully with you when the LORD **g** us
Jdg 11: 9 and the LORD **g** them over to me,
11:24 not possess what your god Chemosh **g** you
21:18 "Cursed be anyone who **g** a wife to Benjamin."
2Sa 24:23 All this, O king, Araunah **g** to the king."
1Ch 22:12 when he **g** you charge over Israel you may keep
Job 5:10 He **g** rain on the earth and sends waters on
16:11 God **g** me up to the ungodly,
19:16 I call to my servant, but he **g** me no answer;
24:23 He **g** them security, and they are supported;
33: 4 and the breath of the Almighty **g** me life.
35:10 who **g** strength in the night,
36: 6 but **g** the afflicted their right.
36:31 he governs peoples; he **g** food in abundance.
Ps 16: 7 I bless the LORD who **g** me counsel;
18:50 Great triumphs he **g** to his king,
68: 6 God **g** the desolate a home to live in;
68:11 The Lord **g** the command;
68:35 he **g** power and strength to his people.
113: 9 He **g** the barren woman a home,
119:50 that your promise **g** me life.
119:130 The unfolding of your words **g** light;
127: 2 for he **g** sleep to his beloved.
136:25 who **g** food to all flesh,
144:10 the one who **g** victory to kings,
146: 7 who **g** food to the hungry.
147: 4 he **g** to all of them their names.
147: 9 He **g** to the animals their food,
147:16 He **g** snow like wool; he scatters frost like ashes.
Pr 2: 6 For the LORD **g** wisdom;
11:25 and one who **g** water will get water.
12:17 Whoever speaks the truth **g** honest evidence,
12:26 The righteous **g** good advice to friends,
14:30 A tranquil mind **g** life to the flesh,
17: 4 and a liar **g** heed to a mischievous tongue.
18:13 one **g** answer before hearing, it is folly and shame.
18:16 A gift opens doors; it **g** access to the great.
24:26 One who **g** an honest answer **g** a kiss on the lips.
28:27 Whoever **g** to the poor will lack nothing,
29: 4 By justice a king **g** stability to the land,
29:11 A fool **g** full vent to anger,
29:13 the LORD **g** light to the eyes of both.
Ecc 2:26 For to the one who pleases him God **g** wisdom
2:26 the sinner he **g** the work of gathering and heaping,
5:18 under the sun the few days of the life God **g** us;
5:19 to whom God **g** wealth and possessions
6: 2 those to whom God **g** wealth,
7:12 the advantage of knowledge is that wisdom **g** life
7:19 Wisdom **g** strength to the wise more than ten rulers
8:15 the days of life that God **g** them under the sun.
Isa 27: 4 If it **g** me thorns and briers,
40:29 He **g** power to the faint,
41:28 when I ask, **g** an answer.
42: 5 who **g** breath to the people upon it and spirit
Jer 5:24 who **g** the rain in its season,
31:35 who **g** the sun for light by day and the fixed order
La 4: 4 children beg for food, but no one **g** them anything.
Eze 18: 7 **g** his bread to the hungry and covers the naked
18:16 but **g** his bread to the hungry and covers the naked
Da 2:21 he **g** wisdom to the wise and knowledge to those
4:17 he **g** it to whom he will and sets over it the lowliest
4:25 and **g** it to whom he will.
4:32 the kingdom of mortals and **g** it to whom he will."
Hos 4:12 and their divining rod **g** them oracles.
Zep 3:17 is in your midst, a warrior who **g** victory;
Zec 10: 1 who **g** showers of rain to you,
Mt 5:15 and it **g** light to all in the house.
10:42 and whoever **g** even a cup of cold water to one
Mk 9:41 whoever **g** you a cup of water to drink
Lk 11:36 of light as when a lamp **g** you light with its rays."
Jn 3:34 for he **g** the Spirit without measure.
5:21 just as the Father raises the dead and **g** them life,
5:21 so also the Son **g** life to whomever he wishes.
6:32 but it is my Father who **g** you the true bread
6:33 that which comes down from heaven and **g** life to
6:37 Everything that the Father **g** me will come to me,
6:63 It is the spirit that **g** life; the flesh is useless.
14:27 I do not give to you as the world **g**.
Ac 17:25 since he himself **g** to all mortals life and breath
Ro 4:17 of the God in whom he believed, who **g** life to
1Co 3: 7 but only God who **g** the growth.
9:16 this **g** me no ground for boasting,
14: 8 And if the bugle **g** an indistinct sound,
15:38 But God **g** it a body as he has chosen,
15:57 But thanks be to God, who **g** us the victory
2Co 3: 6 for the letter kills, but the Spirit **g** life.
9: 9 it is written, "He scatters abroad, he **g** to the poor;
11:20 or puts on airs, or **g** you a slap in the face.
1Th 4: 8 who also **g** his Holy Spirit to you.
1Ti 6:13 In the presence of God, who **g** life to all things,
Jas 1: 5 who **g** to all generously and ungrudgingly,
1:15 when that desire has conceived, it **g** birth to sin,
1:15 when it is fully grown, **g** birth to death.
4: 6 But he **g** all the more grace;
4: 6 but **g** grace to the humble."
1Pe 5: 5 but **g** grace to the humble."
Sir 1:12 and **g** gladness and joy and long life.
4:11 Wisdom teaches her children and **g** help
6:28 For at last you will find the rest she **g**,
20:15 He **g** little and upbraids much;
34:20 he **g** health and life and blessing.
35: 4 and one who **g** alms sacrifices a thank offering.
43:15 In his majesty he **g** the clouds their strength,
43:22 the falling dew **g** refreshment from the heat.
51:17 to him who **g** wisdom I will give glory.
2Mc 7:14 to cherish the hope God **g** of being raised again

2Mc 10:38 to Israel and **g** them the victory.
2Es 8: 9 the womb **g** up again what has been created in it,

GIVING (131) [GIVE]

Ge 24:19 When she had finished **g** him a drink, she said,
29:26 **g** the younger before the firstborn.
41:12 **g** an interpretation to each according to his dream.
Ex 20:12 in the land that the LORD your God is **g** you.
21:34 of the pit shall make restitution, **g** money
Lev 23:10 the land that I am **g** you and you reap its harvest,
25: 2 When you enter the land that I am **g** you,
Nu 5: 7 and **g** it to the one who was wronged.
13: 2 which I am **g** to the Israelites;
15: 2 into the land you are to inhabit, which I am **g** you,
Dt 1:20 which the LORD our God is **g** us.
1:25 a good land that the LORD our God is **g** us."
2:29 into the land that the LORD our God is **g** us."
3:20 the land that the LORD your God is **g** them
4: 1 the God of your ancestors, is **g** you.
4:21 that the LORD your God is **g** for your possession.
4:38 to bring you in, **g** you their land for a possession,
4:40 that the LORD your God is **g** you for all time.
5:16 in the land that the LORD your God is **g** you.
5:31 that they may do them in the land that I am **g** them
7: 3 **g** your daughters to their sons
7:16 the peoples that the LORD your God is **g** over
9: 6 the LORD your God is not **g** you this good land
11:17 the good land that the LORD is **g** you.
11:31 the land that the LORD your God is **g** you,
12: 9 the possession that the LORD your God is **g** you.
13:12 of the towns that the LORD your God is **g** you
15: 4 that the LORD your God is **g** you as a possession
15: 7 within the land that the LORD your God is **g** you,
15:14 thus **g** to him some of the bounty with which
16: 5 of your towns that the LORD your God is **g** you.
16:18 that the LORD your God is **g** you,
16:20 the land that the LORD your God is **g** you.
17: 2 of your towns that the LORD your God is **g** you,
17:14 into the land that the LORD your God is **g** you,
18: 9 into the land that the LORD your God is **g** you,
19: 1 the LORD your God is **g** you,
19: 2 that the LORD your God is **g** you to possess.
19:10 in the land that the LORD your God is **g** you as
19:14 that the LORD your God is **g** you to possess.
20:16 the LORD your God is **g** you as an inheritance,
21: 1 that the LORD your God is **g** you to possess,
21:17 **g** him a double portion of all that he has;
21:23 that the LORD your God is **g** you for possession.
24: 4 on the land that the LORD your God is **g** you as
25:15 in the land that the LORD your God is **g** you.
25:19 in the land that the LORD your God is **g** you as
26: 1 into the land that the LORD your God is **g** you as
26: 2 from the land that the LORD your God is **g** you,
26:12 **g** it to the Levites, the aliens, the orphans,
27: 2 into the land that the LORD your God is **g** you,
27: 3 the land that the LORD your God is **g** you,
28: 8 in the land that the LORD your God is **g** you.
28:55 **g** to none of them any of the flesh
32:46 "Take to heart all the words that I am **g** in witness
32:49 which I am **g** to the Israelites for a possession;
32:52 the land that I am **g** to the Israelites."
Jos 1: 2 into the land that I am **g** to them, to the Israelites.
1:15 of the land that the LORD your God is **g** them.
Jdg 21:22 by **g** your daughters to them.' "
1Sa 22:13 by **g** him bread and a sword,
2Sa 14:13 For in **g** this decision the king convicts himself,
2Ch 7: 6 that King David had made for **g** thanks to
19: 6 he is with you in **g** judgment.
30:22 sacrificing offerings of well-being and **g** thanks to
Ezr 3:11 praising and **g** thanks to the LORD,
Est 3:13 **g** orders to destroy, to kill,
8: 5 which he wrote **g** orders to destroy
9:31 and **g** orders that these days of Purim should
Ps 9: 4 you have sat on the throne **g** righteous judgment.
37:21 but the righteous are generous and keep **g**;
37:26 They are ever **g** liberally and lending,
94:13 **g** them respite from days of trouble,
104:11 **g** drink to every wild animal;
111: 6 in **g** them the heritage of the nations.
Pr 22:16 and **g** to the rich, will lead only to loss.
Isa 28: 7 they err in vision, they stumble in **g** judgment.
55:10 **g** seed to the sower and bread to the eater,
Jer 9:15 and **g** them poisonous water to drink.
43:11 **g** those who are destined for pestilence,
44:20 all the people who were **g** him this answer:
Da 8:13 **g** over of the sanctuary and host to be trampled?"
Mt 15:36 and after **g** thanks he broke them and gave them to
24:38 marrying and **g** in marriage,
26:27 and after **g** thanks he gave it to them, saying,
Mk 8: 6 the seven loaves, and after **g** thanks he broke them
14:23 and after **g** thanks he gave it to them,
Lk 22:17 Then he took a cup, and after **g** thanks he said,
Jn 7:51 not judge people without first **g** them a hearing
15:17 I am **g** you these commands so
Ac 1: 2 after **g** instructions through the Holy Spirit to
14:17 **g** you rains from heaven and fruitful seasons,
15: 8 testified to them by **g** them the Holy Spirit,
27:35 and **g** thanks to God in the presence of all,
Ro 1:27 **g** up natural intercourse with women,
9: 4 the **g** of the law, the worship, and the promises;
1Co 12:24 **g** the greater honor to the inferior member,
2Co 1:22 by putting his seal on us and **g** us his Spirit
5:12 but **g** you an opportunity to boast about us,
8:10 And in this matter I am **g** my advice:
Eph 5:20 **g** thanks to God the Father at all times and
Php 4:15 no church shared with me in the matter of **g**
Col 1:12 **g** thanks to the Father, who has enabled you
3:17 **g** thanks to God the Father through him.
1Ti 1:18 I am **g** you these instructions, Timothy, my child,
Heb 11: 4 God himself **g** approval to his gifts;
Jas 1:17 Every generous act of **g**, with every perfect gift,
Rev 12: 2 in the agony of **g** birth.
Tob 3:17 by **g** her in marriage to Tobias son of Tobit,
4:16 and do not let your eye begrudge your **g** of alms.
14: 2 **g** alms and continually blessing God
Wis 6:18 **g** heed to her laws is assurance of immortality,
13:14 **g** it a coat of red paint and coloring its surface red
17:12 but a **g** up of the helps that come from reason;
Sir 4: 3 or delay **g** to the needy.
4: 9 and do not be hesitant in **g** a verdict.
41:19 of surliness in receiving or **g**,
2Mc 2: 2 and that the prophet, after **g** them the law,
6:27 Therefore, by bravely **g** up my life now,
8:27 **g** great praise and thanks to the Lord,
8:30 **g** to those who had been tortured and to
9: 7 and **g** orders to drive even faster.
1Es 5:61 **g** thanks to the Lord, "For his goodness
3Mc 5:49 of their most miserable suspense, and **g** way
7:16 joyfully and loudly **g** thanks to the one God
2Es 2:37 **g** thanks to him who has called you to
13:57 **g** great glory and praise to the Most High for
4Mc 1:12 **g** glory to the all-wise God.
5:25 of the world in **g** us the law has shown sympathy
15:23 **g** her heart a man's courage in the very midst
16:13 and **g** rebirth for immortality to the whole number

GIZONITE (1)

1Ch 11:34 Hashem the **G**, Jonathan son of Shagee

GLAD‡ (84) [GLADDEN, GLADDENED, GLADDENS, GLADLY, GLADNESS]

Ex 4:14 and when he sees you his heart will be **g**.
2Sa 18:11 I would have been **g** to give you ten pieces
1Ch 16:31 Let the heavens be **g**, and let the earth rejoice,
Job 3:22 and are **g** when they find the grave?
22:19 The righteous see it and are **g**;
Ps 9: 2 I will be **g** and exult in you;
14: 7 Jacob will rejoice; Israel will be **g**.
16: 9 Therefore my heart is **g**, and my soul rejoices;
21: 6 you make him **g** with the joy of your presence.
32: 7 you surround me with **g** cries of deliverance.
32:11 Be **g** in the LORD and rejoice, O righteous,
33:21 Our heart is **g** in him,
34: 2 let the humble hear and be **g**.
35:27 for joy and be **g**, and say evermore, "Great is
40: 9 I have told the **g** news of deliverance in
40:16 But may all who seek you rejoice and be **g** in you;
42: 4 with **g** shouts and songs of thanksgiving,
45: 8 stringed instruments make you **g**;
46: 4 There is a river whose streams make **g** the city
48:11 be **g**, let the towns of Judah rejoice because
53: 6 Jacob will rejoice; Israel will be **g**.
67: 4 Let the nations be **g** and sing for joy,
69:32 Let the oppressed see it and be **g**;
70: 4 Let all who seek you rejoice and be **g** in you.
90:14 so that we may rejoice and be **g** all our days.
90:15 Make us **g** as many days as you have afflicted us,
92: 4 you, O LORD, have made me **g** by your work;
96:11 Let the heavens be **g**, and let the earth rejoice;
97: 1 Let the earth rejoice; let the many coastlands be **g**!
97: 8 and is **g**, and the towns of Judah rejoice,
105:38 Egypt was **g** when they departed,
107:30 Then they were **g** because they had quiet,
107:42 The upright see it and are **g**;
109:28 to shame; may your servant be **g**.
118:15 There are **g** songs of victory in the tents of
118:24 let us rejoice and be **g** in it.
122: 1 I was **g** when they said to me,
149: 2 Let Israel be **g** in its Maker;
Pr 10: 1 A wise child makes a **g** father,
15:13 A **g** heart makes a cheerful countenance,
15:20 A wise child makes a **g** father,
17: 5 those who are **g** at calamity will
23:15 if your heart is wise, my heart too will be **g**.
23:24 he who begets a wise son will be **g** in him.
23:25 Let your father and mother be **g**;
24:17 and do not let your heart be **g** when they stumble,
27: 9 Perfume and incense make the heart **g**,
27:11 Be wise, my child, and make my heart **g**,
29: 3 A child who loves wisdom makes a parent **g**,
Ecc 7: 3 for by sadness of countenance the heart is made **g**.
Isa 25: 9 let us be **g** and rejoice in his salvation.
35: 1 The wilderness and the dry land shall be **g**,
65:18 But be **g** and rejoice forever in what I am creating;
66:10 Rejoice with Jerusalem, and be **g** for her,
Jer 20:15 a son," making him very **g**.
41:13 the leaders of the forces with him, they were **g**.
La 1:21 they are **g** that you have done it.
4:21 Rejoice and be **g**, O daughter Edom,
Da 6:23 Then the king was exceedingly **g** and commanded
Hos 7: 3 By their wickedness they make the king **g**,
Joel 2:21 Do not fear, O soil; be **g** and rejoice,
2:23 be **g** and rejoice in the LORD your God;
Zec 10: 7 and their hearts shall be **g** as with wine.
Mt 5:12 and be **g**, for your reward is great in heaven,
Lk 23: 8 When Herod saw Jesus, he was very **g**,
Jn 8:56 he saw it and was **g**."
11:15 For your sake I am **g** I was not there,
Ac 2:26 therefore my heart was **g**, and my tongue rejoiced;
2:46 they broke bread at home and ate their food with **g**
13:48 they were **g** and praised the word of the Lord;
2Co 2: 2 to make me **g** but the one whom I have pained?
Php 2:17 I am **g** and rejoice with all of you—
2:18 in the same way you also must be **g** and rejoice
1Pe 4:13 be **g** and shout for joy when his glory is revealed.
Tob 8:16 Blessed are you because you have made me **g**.
AdE 5: 9 So Haman went out from the king joyful and **g**
Bar 3:34 the stars shone in their watches, and were **g**;
4:33 For just as she rejoiced at your fall and was **g**
1Mc 3: 7 but he made Jacob **g** by his deeds,
2Mc 6:30 but in my soul I am **g** to suffer these things
9:20 and your affairs are as you wish, I am **g**.
10:33 Then Maccabeus and his men were **g**,
2Es 7:*65* but let the wild animals of the field be **g**;
7:*98* and shall be **g** without fear,

GLADDEN (4) [GLAD]

Ps 86: 4 **G** the soul of your servant, for to you, O Lord,
104:15 and wine to **g** the human heart,
Sir 4:18 straight back to them again and **g** them,
40:20 Wine and music **g** the heart,

GLADDENED (1) [GLAD]

2Mc 15:27 and were greatly **g** by God's manifestation.

GLADDENS (1) [GLAD]

Ecc 10:19 wine **g** life, and money meets every need.

GLADLY (11) [GLAD]

Isa 64: 5 You meet those who **g** do right,
Lk 15:16 He would **g** have filled himself with the pods that
2Co 11:19 you **g** put up with fools, being wise yourselves!
12: 9 So, I will boast all the more **g** of my weaknesses,
12:15 I will most **g** spend and be spent for you.
Jdt 12:18 Judith said, "I will **g** drink, my lord,
1Mc 1:43 Many even from Israel **g** adopted his religion;
3: 2 helped him; they **g** fought for Israel.
2Mc 2:27 of many we will **g** endure the uncomfortable toil,
3Mc 3:15 and great benevolence, **g** treating them well.
4Mc 10:20 **G**, for the sake of God, we let our bodily members

GLADNESS‡ (67) [GLAD]

Dt 28:47 the LORD your God joyfully and with **g** of heart
2Ch 29:30 They sang praises with **g**,
30:21 of unleavened bread seven days with great **g**;
30:23 so they kept it for another seven days with **g**.
Est 8:16 For the Jews there was light and **g**, joy and honor.
8:17 there was **g** and joy among the Jews,
9:17 and made that a day of feasting and **g**.
9:18 making that a day of feasting and **g**.
9:19 of the month of Adar as a day for **g** and feasting,
9:22 that had been turned for them from sorrow into **g**
9:22 they should make them days of feasting and **g**,
Ps 4: 7 You have put **g** in my heart more than
45: 7 with the oil of **g** beyond your companions;
45:15 and **g** they are led along as they enter the palace of
51: 8 Let me hear joy and **g**;
100: 2 Worship the LORD with **g**;
106: 5 that I may rejoice in the **g** of your nation,
Pr 10:28 The hope of the righteous ends in **g**,
SS 3:11 on the day of the **g** of his heart.
Isa 16:10 Joy and **g** are taken away from the fruitful field;
24:11 the **g** of the earth is banished.
30:29 and **g** of heart, as when one sets out to the sound
35:10 they shall obtain joy and **g**,
51: 3 joy and **g** will be found in her,
51:11 they shall obtain joy and **g**,
61: 3 the oil of **g** instead of mourning,
65:14 my servants shall sing for **g** of heart,
Jer 7:34 I will bring to an end the sound of mirth and **g**,
16: 9 the voice of mirth and the voice of **g**,
25:10 from them the sound of mirth and the sound of **g**,
31: 7 Sing aloud with **g** for Jacob,
31:13 I will comfort them, and give them **g** for sorrow.
33:11 of **g**, the voice of the bridegroom and the voice of
48:33 **G** and joy have been taken away from
Joel 1:16 joy and **g** from the house of our God?
Zep 3:17 he will rejoice over you with **g**,
Zec 8:19 shall be seasons of joy and **g**,
Lk 1:14 You will have joy and **g**,
Ac 2:28 you will make me full of **g** with your presence.'
Heb 1: 9 with the oil of **g** beyond your companions."
AdE 8:16 And the Jews had light and **g**
8:17 the Jews had joy and **g**, a banquet and a holiday.
9:17 celebrating it with joy and **g**.
9:18 They celebrated the fifteenth with joy and **g**.
9:22 from sorrow into **g** and from a time of distress to
9:22 for feasting and **g** and for sending presents of food
10:13 with an assembly and joy and **g** before God,
Wis 8:16 and life with her has no pain, but **g** and joy.
Sir 1:11 and **g** and a crown of rejoicing.
1:12 and gives **g** and joy and long life.
15: 6 He will find **g** and a crown of rejoicing,
30:16 and no **g** above joy of heart.
31:28 in moderation is rejoicing of heart and **g** of soul.
35:11 and dedicate your tithe with **g**.
50:23 May he give us **g** of heart,
Bar 2:23 the voice of mirth and the voice of **g**,
3:34 They shone with **g** for him who made them.
4:23 to me with joy and **g** forever.
1Mc 4:59 of the altar should be observed with joy and **g**
5:54 So they went up to Mount Zion with joy and **g**,
7:48 and celebrated that day as a day of great **g**.
10:66 Jonathan returned to Jerusalem in peace and **g**.
2Mc 3:30 was filled with joy and **g**,

3Mc 4: 1 for the Gentiles with shouts and g,
2Es 1:37 whose children rejoice with g;
2: 3 I brought you up with g;
2:15 bring them up with g, as does a dove;

GLANCE (3) [GLANCING]
2Ki 3:14 I would give you neither a look nor a g.
SS 4: 9 you have ravished my heart with a g of your eyes,
Jdt 16:15 before your g the rocks shall melt like wax.

GLANCING (1) [GLANCE]
Isa 3:16 g wantonly with their eyes,

GLASS (6)
Job 28:17 Gold and g cannot equal it,
Rev 4: 6 of the throne there is something like a sea of g,
15: 2 And I saw what appeared to be a sea of g mixed
15: 2 standing beside the sea of g with harps of God
21:18 while the city is pure gold, clear as g.
21:21 the street of the city is pure gold, transparent as g.

GLASSES (KJV) GARMENTS OF GAUZE

GLAZE (1) [GLAZING]
Pr 26:23 the g covering an earthen vessel are smooth lips

GLAZING (1) [GLAZE]
Sir 38:30 he sets his heart to finish the g,

GLEAM (3) [GLEAMED, GLEAMING]
Ps 132:18 but on him, his crown will g."
Da 10: 6 his arms and legs like the g of burnished bronze,
Hab 3:11 at the g of your flashing spear.

GLEAMED (1) [GLEAM]
1Mc 6:39 with them and g like flaming torches.

GLEAMING (7) [GLEAM]
2Sa 23: 4 g from the rain on the grassy land.
Eze 1: 4 in the middle of the fire, something like g amber.
1:16 their appearance was like the g of beryl;
1:27 the loins I saw something like g amber, something
8: 2 like the appearance of brightness, like g amber.
10: 9 and the appearance of the wheels was like g beryl.
Sir 50: 7 like the rainbow g in splendid clouds;

GLEAN (10) [GLEANED, GLEANER, GLEANING, GLEANINGS, GLEANS]
Dt 24:21 do not g what is left;
Ru 2: 2 "Let me go to the field and g among the ears
2: 7 let me g and gather among the sheaves behind
2: 8 do not go to g in another field or leave this one,
2:15 When she got up to g,
2:15 "Let her g even among the standing sheaves,
2:16 and leave them for her to g,
2:19 to her, "Where did you g today?
Job 24: 6 a field not their own and they g in the vineyard of
Jer 6: 9 G thoroughly as a vine the remnant of Israel;

GLEANED (5) [GLEAN]
Ru 2: 3 She came and g in the field behind the reapers.
2:17 So she g in the field until evening.
2:17 Then she beat out what she had g,
2:18 and her mother-in-law saw how much she had g.
Mic 7: 1 after the vintage has been g,

GLEANER (1) [GLEAN]
Sir 33:16 I was like a g following the grape-pickers;

GLEANING (3) [GLEAN]
Jdg 8: 2 Is not the g of the grapes of Ephraim better than
Ru 2:23 g until the end of the barley and wheat harvests;
Isa 24:13 as at the g when the grape harvest is ended.

GLEANINGS (5) [GLEAN]
Lev 19: 9 or gather the g of your harvest.
23:22 or gather the g of your harvest;
Isa 17: 6 G will be left in it,
Jer 49: 9 came to you, would they not leave g?
Ob 1: 5 came to you, would they not leave g?

GLEANS (2) [GLEAN]
Isa 17: 5 one g the ears of grain in the Valley of Rephaim.
4Mc 2: 9 through reason so that one neither g the harvest

GLEDE (KJV) See KITE

GLEE (1)
Ps 35:15 But at my stumbling they gathered in g,

GLEN (1)
Zec 1: 8 He was standing among the myrtle trees in the g;

GLIDED (1) [GLIDING]
Job 4:15 spirit g past my face; the hair of my flesh bristled.

GLIDING (2) [GLIDED]
SS 7: 9 the best wine that goes down smoothly, g over lips
Jer 46:22 She makes a sound like a snake g away;

GLITTERED (1) [GLITTERING]
1Es 8:57 and twelve bronze vessels of fine bronze that g

GLITTERING (3) [GLITTERED]
Job 20:25 and the g point comes out of their gall;
Na 3: 3 Horsemen charging, flashing sword and g spear,
Sir 43: 9 a g array in the heights of the Lord.

GLOAT‡ (2) [GLOATED, GLOATING]
Ps 22:17 They stare and g over me;
Rev 11:10 and the inhabitants of the earth will g over them

GLOATED (1) [GLOAT]
Ob 1:12 But you should not have g over your brother on

GLOATING (2) [GLOAT]
Ob 1:13 not have joined in the g over Judah's disaster on
Hab 3:14 g as if ready to devour the poor who were

GLOOM (21) [GLOOMY]
Job 3: 5 Let g and deep darkness claim it.
10:21 never to return, to the land of g and deep darkness,
10:22 the land of g and chaos,
28: 3 the farthest bound the ore in g and deep darkness.
30:28 I go about in sunless g;
34:22 There is no g or deep darkness
Ps 107:10 Some sat in darkness and in g,
107:14 he brought them out of darkness and g,
Isa 8:22 but will see only distress and darkness, the g
9: 1 there will be no g for those who were in anguish.
29:18 and out of their g and darkness the eyes of
58:10 in the darkness and your g be like the noonday.
59: 9 and for brightness, but we walk in g.
Jer 13:16 he turns it into g and makes it deep darkness.
14: 2 they lie in g on the ground,
Eze 31:15 I clothed Lebanon in g for it,
Joel 2: 2 a day of darkness and g,
Am 5:20 not light, and g with no brightness in it?
Zep 1:15 a day of darkness and g,
Heb 12:18 a blazing fire, and darkness, and g, and a tempest,
AdE 11: 8 It was a day of darkness and g,

GLOOMY (2) [GLOOM]
Wis 17: 4 and dismal phantoms with g faces appeared.
Sir 25:23 g face, and wounded heart come from

GLORIES‡ (2) [GLORY]
Wis 18:24 and the g of the ancestors were engraved on
Sir 38:25 and who g in the shaft of a goad,

GLORIFIED‡ (49) [GLORY]
Lev 10: 3 and before all the people I will be g.' "
1Ch 22: 5 famous and g throughout all lands;
Isa 26:15 you have increased the nation; you are g;
44:23 and will be g in Israel.
49: 3 "You are my servant, Israel, in whom I will be g."
55: 5 the Holy One of Israel, for he has g you.
60: 9 for the Holy One of Israel, because he has g you.
60:21 the work of my hands, so that I might be g.
66: 5 the LORD be g, so that we may see your joy";
Mt 9: 8 they were filled with awe, and they g God,
Mk 2:12 so that they were all amazed and g God, saying,
Lk 5:26 and they g God and were filled with awe, saying,
7:16 Fear seized all of them; and they g God, saying,
Jn 7:39 there was no Spirit, because Jesus was not yet g.
11: 4 so that the Son of God may be g through it."
12:16 but when Jesus was g, then they remembered
12:23 "The hour has come for the Son of Man to be g.
12:28 Then a voice came from heaven, "I have g it,
13:31 Jesus said, "Now the Son of Man has been g,
13:31 and God has been g in him.
13:32 If God has been g in him,
14:13 so that the Father may be g in the Son.
15: 8 My Father is g by this,
17: 4 I g you on earth by finishing the work
17:10 and I have been g in them.
Ac 3:13 the God of our ancestors has g his servant Jesus,
Ro 8:17 with him so that we may also be g with him.
8:30 and those whom he justified he also g.
Gal 1:24 And they g God because of me.
2Th 1:10 to be g by his saints and to be marveled at on
1:12 that the name of our Lord Jesus may be g in you,
3: 1 the Lord may spread rapidly and be g everywhere,
1Pe 4:11 God may be g in all things through Jesus Christ.
Rev 18: 7 As she g herself and lived luxuriously,
AdE 14: 7 because we g their gods. You are righteous,
Wis 18: 8 you called us to yourself and g us.
19:22 O Lord, you have exalted and g your people,
Sir 3:20 but by the humble he is g.
38: 6 that he might be g in his marvelous works.
45: 3 the Lord g him in the presence of kings.
47: 6 they g him for the tens of thousands he conquered,
Aza 1:28 with one voice praised and g and blessed God in
1:31 and to be extolled and highly g forever.
1:34 and to be sung and g forever.
2Mc 3: 2 the place and g the temple with the finest presents,
1Es 8:81 and g the temple of our Lord,
3Mc 2: 9 you had g it by your magnificent manifestation,
2Es 7:98 to receive their reward when g.
9:31 and you shall be g through it forever.'

GLORIFIES (2) [GLORY]
Jn 8:54 It is my Father who g me, he of whom you say,
Wis 8: 3 She g her noble birth by living with God,

GLORIFY‡ (31) [GLORY]
Ezr 7:27 the heart of the king to g the house of the LORD
Ps 22:23 All you offspring of Jacob, g him;
50:15 I will deliver you, and you shall g me."
86: 9 O Lord, and shall g your name.
86:12 and I will g your name forever.
Isa 24:15 in the coastlands of the sea g the name of
25: 3 Therefore strong peoples will g you;
60: 7 and I will g my glorious house.
60:13 and I will g where my feet rest.
Jn 8:54 Jesus answered, "If I g myself,
12:28 Father, g your name."
12:28 "I have glorified it, and I will g it again."
13:32 also g him in himself and will g him at once.
16:14 He will g me, because he will take what is mine
17: 1 g your Son so that the Son may g you,
17: 5 g me in your own presence with the glory
21:19 the kind of death by which he would g God.)
Ro 11:13 as I am an apostle to the Gentiles, I g my ministry
15: 6 so that together you may with one voice g the God
15: 9 that the Gentiles might g God for his mercy.
1Co 6:20 therefore g God in your body.
2Co 9:13 of this ministry you g God by your obedience to
Heb 5: 5 Christ did not g himself in becoming a high priest,
1Pe 2:12 they may see your honorable deeds and g God
4:16 but g God because you bear this name.
Rev 15: 4 Lord, who will not fear and g your name?
Sir 3:10 Do not g yourself by dishonoring your father,
43:30 G the Lord and exalt him as much as you can,
1Es 8:25 to g his house that is in Jerusalem,

GLORIFYING (3) [GLORY]
Lk 2:20 g and praising God for all they had heard
5:25 and went to his home, g God.
18:43 and followed him, g God;

GLORIOUS‡ (81) [GLORY]
A. GLORIOUS NAME (8)

Ex 15: 6 Your right hand, O LORD, g in power—
28: 2 for the g adornment of your brother Aaron.
28:40 you shall make them for their g adornment.
Dt 28:58 fearing this g and awesome name,
1Ch 29:13 we give thanks to you and praise your g name. A
Ne 9: 5 Blessed be your g name, which is exalted A
Ps 66: 2 sing the glory of his name; give to him g praise.
72:19 Blessed be his g name forever; A
76: 4 G are you, more majestic than
78: 4 the coming generation the g deeds of the LORD,
87: 3 G things are spoken of you, O city of God.
90:16 and your g power to their children.
145: 5 On the g splendor of your majesty,
145:12 and the g splendor of your kingdom.
Isa 3: 8 against the LORD, defying his g presence.
4: 2 the branch of the LORD shall be beautiful and g,
9: 1 the latter time he will make g the way of the sea,
11:10 and his dwelling shall be g.
28: 1 and the fading flower of its g beauty,
28: 4 And the fading flower of its g beauty,
42:21 to magnify his teaching and make it g.
60: 7 and I will glorify my g house.
63:12 who caused his g arm to march at the right hand
63:14 to make for yourself a g name. A
63:15 from your holy and g habitation.
66:11 with delight from her g bosom.
Jer 14:21 do not dishonor your g throne;
17:12 O g throne, exalted from the beginning,
48:17 "How the mighty scepter is broken, the g staff!"
Eze 20: 6 the most g of all lands.
20:15 the most g of all lands,
Da 4:30 by my mighty power and for my g majesty?"
Zec 11: 2 for the cedar has fallen, for the g trees are ruined!
Ac 2:20 before the coming of the Lord's great and g day.
Eph 1: 6 to the praise of his g grace that he freely bestowed
1:18 the riches of his g inheritance among the saints,
Col 1:11 with all the strength that comes from his g power,
1Ti 1:11 that conforms to the g gospel of the blessed God,
Jas 2: 1 in our g Lord Jesus Christ?
1Pe 1: 8 in him and rejoice with an indescribable and g joy,
2Pe 2:10 they are not afraid to slander the g ones,
Jude 1: 8 reject authority, and slander the g ones.
Tob 3:16 both of them were heard in the g presence of God.
Jdt 9: 8 the tabernacle where your g name resides, A
16:13 O Lord, you are great and g,
Wis 5:16 a g crown and a beautiful diadem from the hand of
15: 9 they count it a g thing to mold counterfeit gods.
18: 3 and a harmless sun for their g wandering.
Sir 6:29 and her collar a g robe.
6:31 You will wear her like a g robe,
17:13 Their eyes saw his g majesty,
24:16 and my branches are g and graceful.
24:17 and my blossoms become g and abundant fruit.
27: 8 you will attain it and wear it like a g robe.
36: 7 make your hand and right arm g.
43: 1 as g to behold as the sight of the heavens.
43:12 It encircles the sky with its g arc;
45: 7 and put a g robe on him.
46: 2 How g he was when he lifted his hands

Sir 47: 6 when the g diadem was given to him.
47:11 he gave him a covenant of kingship and a g throne
48: 4 How g you were, Elijah, in your wondrous deeds!
50: 5 How g he was, surrounded by the people,
50:11 When he put on his g robe and clothed himself
50:11 he made the court of the sanctuary g.
Aza 1: 3 and g is your name forever!
1:22 the Lord God, g over the whole world."
1:30 And blessed is your g, holy name,
1Mc 2: 9 her g vessels have been carried into exile.
14:15 He made the sanctuary g,
2Mc 8:15 he had called them by his holy and g name. A
1Es 1:56 and utterly destroyed all its g things.
Man 1: 3 and sealed it with your terrible and g name; A
1: 5 for your g splendor cannot be borne, and the wrath
3Mc 2:14 holy place on earth dedicated to your g name. A
5: 8 and in a g manifestation rescue them from the fate
6:18 Then the most g, almighty,
6:18 the heavenly gates, from which two g angels
2Es 2:39 the shadow of this age have received g garments
4Mc 7: 9 to the law through your g endurance,
10: 1 When he too had endured a g death,

GLORIOUSLY (6) [GLORY]

Ex 15: 1 to the LORD, for he has triumphed g;
15:21 "Sing to the LORD, for he has triumphed g;
Isa 12: 5 Sing praises to the LORD, for he has done g;
2Mc 3:26 g beautiful and splendidly dressed,
3Mc 6:39 the Lord of all most g revealed his mercy
2Es 8:29 but regard those who have g taught your law.

GLORY‡ (468) [GLORIES, GLORIFIED, GLORIFIES, GLORIFY, GLORIFYING, GLORIOUS, GLORIOUSLY, VAINGLORY]

A. HIS GLORY (50)
B. GLORY OF THE †LORD (35)
C. YOUR GLORY (34)
D. GLORY OF ... *GOD (25)
E. MY GLORY (20)
F. GAVE/GIVE/GIVING ... GLORY (19)
G. GLORY OF THE *LORD (6)

Ex 14: 4 so that I will gain g for myself over Pharaoh
14:17 and so I will gain g for myself over Pharaoh
14:18 when I have gained g for myself over Pharaoh,
16: 7 in the morning you shall see the g of the LORD, B
16:10 and the g of the LORD appeared in the cloud. B
24:16 The g of the LORD settled on Mount Sinai, B
24:17 the g of the LORD was like a devouring fire on B
29:43 and it shall be sanctified by my g; E
33:18 Moses said, "Show me your g, I pray." C
33:22 while my g passes by I will put you in a cleft E
40:34 and the g of the LORD filled the tabernacle. B
40:35 and the g of the LORD filled the tabernacle. B
Lev 9: 6 so that the g of the LORD may appear to you." B
9:23 the g of the LORD appeared to all the people. B
26:19 I will break your proud g,
Nu 14:10 Then the g of the LORD appeared at the tent B
14:21 the earth shall be filled with the g of the LORD— B
14:22 of the people who have seen my g and the signs E
16:19 And the g of the LORD appeared to B
16:42 the cloud had covered it and the g of the LORD B
20: 6 and the g of the LORD appeared to them. B
Dt 5:24 LORD our God has shown us his g and greatness, A
Jos 7:19 give g to the LORD God of Israel F
Jdg 4: 9 on which you are going will not lead to your g, C
1Sa 4:21 meaning, "The g has departed from Israel,"
4:22 She said, "The g has departed from Israel,
6: 5 and give g to the God of Israel; F
15:29 the G of Israel will not recant or change his mind;
2Sa 1:19 Your g, O Israel, lies slain C
1Ki 8:11 g of the LORD filled the house of the LORD. B
2Ki 14:10 Be content with your g, and stay at home; C
1Ch 16:10 G in his holy name; let the hearts of those
16:24 Declare his g among the nations, A
16:28 ascribe to the LORD g and strength.
16:29 Ascribe to the LORD the g due his name;
16:35 to your holy name, and g in your praise.
29:11 are the greatness, the power, the g, the victory,
2Ch 5:14 for the g of the LORD filled the house of God. B
7: 1 and the g of the LORD filled the temple. B
7: 2 the g of the LORD filled the LORD's house. B
7: 3 the fire come down and the g of the LORD on B
Job 19: 9 He has stripped my g from me, E
29:20 my g was fresh with me, E
40:10 clothe yourself with g and splendor.
Ps 3: 3 O LORD, are a shield around me, my g, E
8: 1 You have set your g above the heavens. C
8: 5 and crowned them with g and honor.
19: 1 The heavens are telling the g of God; D
21: 5 His g is great through your help; A
24: 7 that the King of g may come in.
24: 8 Who is the King of g?
24: 9 that the King of g may come in.
24:10 Who is this King of g?
24:10 The LORD of hosts, he is the King of g.
26: 8 and the place where your g abides. C
29: 1 ascribe to the LORD g and strength.
29: 2 Ascribe to the LORD the g of his name;
29: 3 the God of g thunders, the LORD,
29: 9 and in his temple all say, "G!"
37:20 and the enemies of the LORD are like the g of
45: 3 O mighty one, in your g and majesty. C
57: 5 Let your g be over all the earth. C
57:11 Let your g be over all the earth. C
Ps 63: 2 beholding your power and g.
64:10 Let all the upright in heart g.
66: 2 sing the g of his name; give to him glorious praise.
71: 8 and with your g all day long. C
72:19 may his g fill the whole earth. A
78:61 his g to the hand of the foe. A
79: 9 O God of our salvation, for the g of your name;
85: 9 that his g may dwell in our land. A
89:17 For you are the g of their strength;
96: 3 Declare his g among the nations, A
96: 7 ascribe to the LORD g and strength.
96: 8 Ascribe to the LORD the g due his name;
97: 6 and all the peoples behold his g. A
102:15 and all the kings of the earth your g. C
102:16 LORD will build up Zion; he will appear in his g. A
104:31 May the g of the LORD endure forever; B
105: 3 G in his holy name; let the hearts of those
106: 5 that I may g in your heritage.
106:20 exchanged the g of God for the image of an ox D
106:47 to your holy name and g in your praise.
108: 5 and let your g be over all the earth. C
113: 4 and his g above the heavens. A
115: 1 O LORD, not to us, but to your name give g, F
138: 5 for great is the g of the LORD. B
145:11 They shall speak of the g of your kingdom,
148:13 his g is above earth and heaven. A
149: 5 Let the faithful exult in g;
149: 9 This is g for all his faithful ones.
Pr 14:28 The g of a king is a multitude of people;
16:31 Gray hair is a crown of g;
17: 6 and the g of children is their parents.
19:11 and it is their g to overlook an offense.
20:29 The g of youths is their strength,
25: 2 It is the g of God to conceal things, D
25: 2 but the g of kings is to search things out.
28:12 When the righteous triumph, there is great g,
Isa 2:10 and from the g of his majesty.
2:19 and from the g of his majesty,
2:21 and from the g of his majesty,
4: 2 and the fruit of the land shall be the pride and g of
4: 5 Indeed over all the g there will be a canopy.
6: 3 the whole earth is full of his g." A
8: 7 the king of Assyria and all his g; A
10:16 and under his g a burning will be kindled, A
10:18 The g of his forest and his fruitful land
13:19 And Babylon, the g of kingdoms,
14:18 All the kings of the nations lie in g,
16:14 the g of Moab will be brought into contempt,
17: 3 of Aram will be like the g of the children of Israel,
17: 4 On that day the g of Jacob will be brought low,
21:16 all the g of Kedar will come to an end;
23: 9 to defile the pride of all g,
24:15 Therefore in the east give g to the LORD; F
24:16 of g to the Righteous One.
24:23 and before his elders he will manifest his g. A
28: 5 the LORD of hosts will be a garland of g, and
35: 2 The g of Lebanon shall be given to it,
35: 2 They shall see the g of the LORD, B
40: 5 Then the g of the LORD shall be revealed, B
41:16 in the Holy One of Israel you shall g.
42: 8 my g I give to no other, nor my praise to idols. E
42:12 Let them give g to the LORD, F
43: 7 whom I created for my g, E
45:25 the offspring of Israel shall triumph and g.
46:13 I will put salvation in Zion, for Israel my g. E
48:11 My g I will not give to another. E
58: 8 the g of the LORD shall be your rear guard. B
59:19 and those in the east, his g; A
60: 1 and the g of the LORD has risen upon you. B
60: 2 and his g will appear over you. A
60:13 The g of Lebanon shall come to you, the cypress,
60:19 and your God will be your g. C
61: 3 the planting of the LORD, to display his g. A
61: 6 and in their riches you shall g.
62: 2 and all the kings your g; C
66:18 and they shall come and shall see my g, E
66:19 that have not heard of my fame or seen my g; E
66:19 and they shall declare my g among the nations. E
Jer 2:11 But my people have changed their g for something
13:11 a name, a praise, and a g.
13:16 Give g to the LORD your God F
33: 9 a praise and a g before all the nations of
48:18 Come down from g, and sit on
La 3:18 "Gone is my g, and all that I had hoped for from E
Eze 1:28 appearance of the likeness of the g of the LORD. B
3:12 and as the g of the LORD rose from its place, B
3:23 and the g of the LORD stood there, B
3:23 like the g that I had seen by the river Chebar;
8: 4 And the g of the God of Israel was there, D
9: 3 Now the g of the God of Israel had gone up from D
10: 4 Then the g of the LORD rose up from the cherub B
10: 4 full of the brightness of the g of the LORD. B
10:18 the g of the LORD went out from the threshold of B
10:19 and the g of the God of Israel was above them. D
11:22 and the g of the God of Israel was above them. D
11:23 the g of the LORD ascended from the middle of B
24:25 from them their stronghold, their joy and g,
25: 9 the g of the country, Beth-jeshimoth, Baal-meon,
28:22 O Sidon, and I will gain g in your midst.
31:18 Which among the trees of Eden was like you in g
39:13 on the day that I show my g, E
39:21 I will display my g among the nations; E
43: 2 g of the God of Israel was coming from the east; D
43: 2 and the earth shone with his g. A
43: 4 As the g of the LORD entered the temple by B
43: 5 and the g of the LORD filled the temple. B
44: 4 the g of the LORD filled the temple of the LORD; B
Da 2:37 the power, the might, and the g,
4:36 and splendor were restored to me for the g
5:18 greatness, g, and majesty.
5:20 and his g was stripped from him. A
7:14 To him was given dominion and g and kingship,
11:20 an official for the g of the kingdom;
Hos 4: 7 they changed their g into shame.
4:18 they love lewdness more than their g.
9:11 Ephraim's g shall fly away like a bird—
10: 5 over its g that has departed from it.
Mic 1:15 the g of Israel shall come to Adullam.
2: 9 young children you take away my g forever. E
Hab 2:14 filled with the knowledge of the g of the LORD, B
2:16 You will be sated with contempt instead of g.
2:16 and shame will come upon your g! C
3: 3 His g covered the heavens, A
Hag 2: 3 among you that saw this house in its former g?
Zec 2: 5 says the LORD, and I will be the g within it."
2: 8 LORD of hosts (after his g sent me) regarding A
11: 3 the wail of the shepherds, for their g is despoiled!
12: 7 that the g of the house of David and the g of the
Mal 2: 2 you will not lay it to heart to give g to my name, F
Mt 5:16 that they may see your good works and give g F
6:29 Solomon in all his g was not clothed like one A
16:27 the Son of Man is to come with his angels in the g
19:28 the Son of Man is seated on the throne of his g, A
24:30 on the clouds of heaven' with power and great g.
25:31 "When the Son of Man comes in his g, A
25:31 then he will sit on the throne of his g. A
Mk 8:38 be ashamed when he comes in the g of his Father
10:37 your right hand and one at your left, in your g." C
13:26 of Man coming in clouds' with great power and g.
Lk 2: 9 and the g of the Lord shone around them, G
2:14 "G to God in the highest heaven,
2:32 to the Gentiles and for g to your people Israel."
4: 6 "To you I will give their g and all this authority;
9:26 he comes in his g and the glory of the Father A
9:26 when he comes in his glory and the g of the Father
9:31 in g and were speaking of his departure,
9:32 since they had stayed awake, they saw his g and A
12:27 Solomon in all his g was not clothed like one A
19:38 Peace in heaven, and g in the highest heaven!"
21:27 in a cloud' with power and great g.
24:26 and then enter into his g?" A
Jn 1:14 and we have seen his g, A
1:14 the g as of a father's only son,
2:11 in Cana of Galilee, and revealed his g; A
5:41 I do not accept g from human beings.
5:44 when you accept g from one another and do not seek the g that comes from the one
7:18 Those who speak on their own seek their own g;
7:18 one who seeks the g of him who sent him is true,
8:50 Yet I do not seek my own g;
8:54 "If I glorify myself, my g is nothing. E
9:24 and they said to him, "Give g to God! F
11: 4 rather it is for God's g,
11:40 you would see the g of God?" D
12:41 Isaiah said this because he saw his g and spoke A
12:43 they loved human g more than the g that comes
17: 5 with the g that I had in your presence before
17:22 The g that you have given me I have given them,
17:24 may be with me where I am, to see my g, E
Ac 7: 2 The God of g appeared to our ancestor Abraham
7:55 the g of God and Jesus standing at the right hand D
12:23 because he had not given the g to God,
Ro 1:23 the g of the immortal God for images D
2: 7 to those who by patiently doing good seek for g
2:10 but g and honor and peace
3: 7 falsehood God's truthfulness abounds to his g, A
3:23 all have sinned and fall short of the g of God; D
4:20 he grew strong in his faith as he gave g to God, F
5: 2 we boast in our hope of sharing the g of God. D
6: 4 just as Christ was raised from the dead by the g
8:18 not worth comparing with the g about to
8:21 to decay and will obtain the freedom of the g of
9: 4 the g, the covenants, the giving of the law,
9:23 make known the riches of his g for the objects A
9:23 which he has prepared beforehand for g—
11:36 To him be the g forever.
15: 7 as Christ has welcomed you, for the g of God. D
16:27 through Jesus Christ, to whom be the g forever!
1Co 2: 7 which God decreed before the ages for our g.
2: 8 they would not have crucified the Lord of g.
10:31 do everything for the g of God. D
11:15 but if a woman has long hair, it is her g?
15:40 but the g of the heavenly is one thing,
15:41 There is one g of the sun, and another g of the moon, and another g of the stars; indeed, star differs from star in g.
15:43 It is sown in dishonor, it is raised in g.
2Co 1:20 that we say the "Amen," to the g of God. D
3: 7 in g so that the people of Israel could not gaze at Moses' face because of the g of his face, a g
3: 8 the ministry of the Spirit come in g?
3: 9 if there was g in the ministry of condemnation,
3: 9 the ministry of justification abound in g!
3:10 what once had g has lost its g because of the greater g;
3:11 for if what was set aside came through g, much more has the permanent come in g!
3:13 the people of Israel from gazing at the end of the g
3:18 the g of the Lord as though reflected in a mirror, G
3:18 the same image from one degree of g to another;
4: 4 from seeing the light of the gospel of the g
4: 6 give the light of the knowledge of the g of God D
4:15 may increase thanksgiving, to the g of God. D
4:17 for an eternal weight of g beyond all measure,

2Co 8:19 for the **g** of the Lord himself and G
8:23 of the churches, the **g** of Christ.
Gal 1: 5 to whom be the **g** forever and ever. Amen.
Eph 1:12 might live for the praise of his **g**. A
1:14 to the praise of his **g**. A
1:17 the God of our Lord Jesus Christ, the Father of **g**,
3:13 over my sufferings for you; they are your **g**. C
3:16 I pray that, according to the riches of his **g**, A
3:21 to him be **g** in the church and in Christ Jesus
Php 1:11 through Jesus Christ for the **g** and praise of God.
2:11 to the **g** of God the Father. D
3:19 and their **g** is in their shame;
3:21 that it may be conformed to the body of his **g**, A
4:19 according to his riches in **g** in Christ Jesus.
4:20 To our God and Father be **g** forever and ever.
Col 1:27 the Gentiles are the riches of the **g** of this mystery,
1:27 which is Christ in you, the hope of **g**.
3: 4 then you also will be revealed with him in **g**.
1Th 2:12 who calls you into his own kingdom and **g**.
2:20 Yes, you are our **g** and joy!
2Th 1: 9 from the presence of the Lord and from the **g**
2:14 you may obtain the **g** of our Lord Jesus Christ.
1Ti 1:17 the only God, be honor and **g** forever and ever.
3:16 believed in throughout the world, taken up in **g**.
2Ti 2:10 the salvation that is in Christ Jesus, with eternal **g**.
4:18 To him be the **g** forever and ever.
Tit 2:13 for the blessed hope and the manifestation of the **g**
Heb 1: 3 the reflection of God's **g** and the exact imprint
2: 7 you have crowned them with **g** and honor,
2: 9 now crowned with **g** and honor because of
2:10 in bringing many children to **g**,
3: 3 Yet Jesus is worthy of more **g** than Moses,
9: 5 the cherubim of **g** overshadowing the mercy seat.
13:21 to whom be the **g** forever and ever.
1Pe 1: 7 may be found to result in praise and **g** and honor
1:11 for Christ and the subsequent **g**.
1:21 who raised him from the dead and gave him **g**, F
1:24 like grass and all its **g** like the flower of grass.
4:11 To him belong the **g** and the power forever
4:13 be glad and shout for joy when his **g** is revealed. A
4:14 because the spirit of **g**, which is the Spirit of God,
5: 1 as well as one who shares in the **g** to be revealed,
5: 4 you will win the crown of **g** that never fades away.
5:10 who has called you to his eternal **g** in Christ,
2Pe 1: 3 the knowledge of him who called us by his own **g**
1:17 For he received honor and **g** from God the Father
1:17 to him by the Majestic **G**,
3:18 be the **g** both now and to the day of eternity.
Jude 1:24 without blemish in the presence of his **g** A
1:25 through Jesus Christ our Lord, be **g**, majesty,
Rev 1: 6 to him be **g** and dominion forever and ever.
4: 9 the living creatures give **g** and honor and thanks F
4:11 to receive **g** and honor and power,
5:12 and might and honor and **g** and blessing!"
5:13 be blessing and honor and **g** and might forever
7:12 and **g** and wisdom and thanksgiving and honor
11:13 and the rest were terrified and gave **g** to the God F
14: 7 "Fear God and give him **g**, F
15: 8 temple was filled with smoke from the **g** of God D
16: 9 and they did not repent and give him **g**. F
19: 1 Salvation and **g** and power to our God,
19: 7 Let us rejoice and exult and give him the **g**, F
21:11 **g** of God and a radiance like a very rare jewel, D
21:23 for the **g** of God is its light, D
21:24 and the kings of the earth will bring their **g** into it.
21:26 People will bring into it the **g** and the honor of
Tob 12:12 record of your prayer before the **g** of the Lord, G
12:15 and enter before the **g** of the Lord." G
13:14 with you and witness all your **g** forever. C
13:16 of my descendants should survive to see your **g** C
Jdt 1:14 and turned its **g** into disgrace.
10: 8 that the people of Israel may **g** and Jerusalem may
15: 9 "You are the **g** of Jerusalem,
AdE 10: 2 and the wealth and **g** of his kingdom,
13:12 or for any love of **g** that I did this, and refused
13:14 not set human **g** above the glory of God,
13:14 not set human glory above the **g** of God, D
14: 9 and to quench your altar and the **g** of your house,
15:13 and my heart was shaken with fear at your **g**. C
Wis 7:25 and a pure emanation of the **g** of the Almighty;
8:10 of her I shall have **g** among the multitudes
9:10 and from the throne of your **g** send her, C
9:11 in my actions and guard me with her **g**.
Sir 1:11 The fear of the Lord is **g** and exultation,
1:19 she heightened the **g** of those who held her fast.
3:10 for your father's dishonor is no **g** to you.
3:11 The **g** of one's father is one's own **g**,
4:13 Whoever holds her fast inherits **g**,
4:21 and there is a shame that is **g** and favor.
9:16 and let your **g** be in the fear of the Lord. C
10:22 their **g** is the fear of the Lord.
14:27 and dwells in the midst of her **g**.
17:13 and their ears heard the **g** of his voice.
20:11 There are losses for the sake of **g**,
24: 1 and tells of her **g** in the midst of her people.
24: 2 and in the presence of his hosts she tells of her **g**:
29: 6 and instead of **g** will repay him with dishonor.
30: 3 and will **g** in him among his friends.
36: 4 so use them to show your **g** to us. C
36:19 and your temple with your **g**. C
39: 8 and will **g** in the law of the Lord's covenant.
40:27 and covers a person better than any **g**.
42:16 and the work of the Lord is full of his **g**. A
42:17 so that the universe may stand firm in his **g**. A
42:25 Who could ever tire of seeing his **g**? A
43: 9 The **g** of the stars is the beauty of heaven,
44: 2 The Lord apportioned to them great **g**,
Sir 44:13 and their **g** will never be blotted out.
44:19 and no one has been found like him in **g**.
45: 2 He made him equal in **g** to the holy ones,
45: 3 and revealed to him his **g**. A
45:20 He added **g** to Aaron and gave him a heritage;
45:23 of Eleazar ranks third in **g** for being zealous in
45:26 now bless the Lord who has crowned you with **g**.
45:26 their **g** may endure through all their generations.
47: 8 the Most High, proclaiming his **g**; A
48: 4 Whose **g** is equal to yours?
49: 5 and their **g** to a foreign nation,
49: 8 It was Ezekiel who saw the vision of **g**,
49:12 destined for everlasting **g**.
50:20 and to **g** in his name;
51:17 to him who gives wisdom I will give **g**. F
Bar 2:17 will not ascribe **g** or justice to the Lord;
2:18 will declare your **g** and righteousness, O Lord. C
4: 3 Do not give your **g** to another, C
4:24 which will come to you with great **g** and with
4:37 word of the Holy One, rejoicing in the **g** of God. D
5: 1 and put on forever the beauty of the **g** from God.
5: 2 put on your head the diadem of the **g** of
5: 4 "Righteous Peace, Godly **G**."
5: 6 but God will bring them back to you, carried in **g**,
5: 7 so that Israel may walk safely in the **g** of God. D
5: 9 will lead Israel with joy, in the light of his **g**, A
Aza 1:20 and bring **g** to your name, O Lord.
1:31 Blessed are you in the temple of your holy **g**,
1Mc 1:40 Her dishonor now grew as great as her **g**;
2:12 our beauty, and our **g** have been laid waste;
3: 3 He extended the **g** of his people.
11:51 So the Jews gained **g** in the sight of the king and
12:12 And we rejoice in your **g**. C
14:21 people have told us about your **g** and honor, C
14:29 and they brought great **g** to their nation.
14:35 "The people saw Simon's faithfulness and the **g**
15: 9 your **g** will become manifest in all the earth." C
2Mc 2: 8 and the **g** of the Lord and the cloud will appear, G
5:16 that other kings had made to enhance the **g**
5:20 in all its **g** when the great Lord became reconciled.
14: 7 Therefore I have laid aside my ancestral **g**—
1Es 4:17 Women make men's clothes; they bring men **g**;
4:59 from you comes wisdom, and yours is the **g**.
5:61 goodness and his **g** are forever upon all Israel." A
9: 8 then make confession and give **g** to the Lord F
Man 1:15 and yours is the **g** forever.
3Mc 2: 9 for the **g** of your great and honored name.
2:16 But because you graciously bestowed your **g** C
2Es 2:11 Moreover, I will take back to myself their **g**,
2:36 receive the joy of your **g**; C
3:19 Your **g** passed through the four gates of fire C
7:*42* but only the splendor of the **g** of the Most High,
7:*60* it is they who have made my **g** to prevail now, E
7:*78* first of all it adores the **g** of the Most High.
7:*87* and shall wither with fear at seeing the **g** of
7:*91* with great joy the **g** of him who receives them,
7:*95* and the **g** waiting for them in the last days.
7:*112* [42] the full **g** does not remain in it;
7:*122* [52] that the **g** of the Most High will defend those
8:21 whose throne is beyond measure and whose **g** is
8:30 those who have always put their trust in your **g**. C
8:49 You will receive the greatest **g**,
8:51 concerning the **g** of those who are like yourself,
9:37 however, does not perish but survives in its **g**."
9:45 and we gave great **g** to the Mighty One.
10:23 the seal of Zion has been deprived of its **g**,
10:50 has shown you the brilliance of her **g**,
13:57 giving great **g** and praise to the Most High for
15:46 the splendor of Babylon and the **g** of her person—
15:47 for prostitution to please and **g** in your lovers,
15:50 the **g** of your strength shall wither like a flower
15:60 part of your land and abolish a portion of your **g**, C
15:63 and mar the **g** of your countenance.
16:12 at the presence of the Lord and the **g** of his power.
16:53 "I have not sinned before God and his **g**." A
16:66 before the Lord and his **g**? A
4Mc 1:12 giving **g** to the all-wise God. F
18:24 to whom be **g** forever and ever. Amen.

GLOW (3) [GLOWING]

Eze 24:11 so that it may become hot, its copper **g**,
Sir 28:12 If you blow on a spark, it will **g**;
2Mc 12: 9 so that the **g** of the light was seen in Jerusalem,

GLOWING (3) [GLOW]

2Sa 22: 9 **g** coals flamed forth from him.
Ps 18: 8 **g** coals flamed forth from him.
120: 4 with **g** coals of the broom tree!

GLUES (1)

Sir 22: 9 a fool is like one who **g** potsherds together,

GLUTTED (1) [GLUTTON]

Pr 30:22 and a fool when **g** with food;

GLUTTON (6) [GLUTTED, GLUTTONOUS, GLUTTONS, GLUTTONY]

Dt 21:20 He is a **g** and a drunkard."
Pr 23:21 for the drunkard and the **g** will come to poverty,
Mt 11:19 and they say, 'Look, a **g** and a drunkard,
Lk 7:34 and you say, 'Look, a **g** and a drunkard,
Sir 31:20 and of nausea and colic are with the **g**.
4Mc 2: 7 a **g**, or even a drunkard can learn a better way,

GLUTTONOUS (1) [GLUTTON]

Pr 23:20 or among **g** eaters of meat;

GLUTTONS (2) [GLUTTON]

Pr 28: 7 but companions of **g** shame their parents.
Tit 1:12 "Cretans are always liars, vicious brutes, lazy **g**."

GLUTTONY (6) [GLUTTON]

Sir 23: 6 Let neither **g** nor lust overcome me,
37:30 for overeating brings sickness, and **g** leads
37:31 Many have died of **g**, but the one who guards
3Mc 6:36 for drinking and **g**, but because of the deliverance
4Mc 1: 3 that hinder self-control, namely, **g** and lust,
1:27 **g**, and solitary gormandizing.

GNASH (4) [GNASHED, GNASHING]

Ps 37:12 and **g** their teeth at them;
112:10 they **g** their teeth and melt away;
La 2:16 they hiss, they **g** their teeth, they cry:
Sir 30:10 and in the end you will **g** your teeth.

GNASHED (1) [GNASH]

Job 16: 9 he has **g** his teeth at me;

GNASHING (8) [GNASH]

Ps 35:16 **g** at me with their teeth.
Mt 8:12 where there will be weeping and **g** of teeth."
13:42 where there will be weeping and **g** of teeth.
13:50 where there will be weeping and **g** of teeth.
22:13 where there will be weeping and **g** of teeth.'
24:51 where there will be weeping and **g** of teeth.
25:30 where there will be weeping and **g** of teeth.'
Lk 13:28 be weeping and **g** of teeth when you see Abraham

GNAT (1) [GNATS]

Mt 23:24 You strain out a **g** but swallow a camel!

GNATS (8) [GNAT]

Ex 8:16 so that it may become **g** throughout the whole land
8:17 and **g** came on humans and animals alike;
8:17 the earth turned into **g** throughout the whole land
8:18 magicians tried to produce **g** by their secret arts,
8:18 There were **g** on both humans and animals.
Ps 105:31 and **g** throughout their country.
Isa 51: 6 and those who live on it will die like **g**;
Wis 19:10 of producing animals the earth brought forth **g**,

GNAW (2) [GNAWED, GNAWING, GNAWS]

Job 30: 3 Through want and hard hunger they **g** the dry
Eze 23:34 and **g** its sherds, and tear out your breasts;

GNAWED (2) [GNAW]

Jer 50:17 of Babylon has **g** its bones.
Rev 16:10 people **g** their tongues in agony,

GNAWING (1) [GNAW]

Mic 6:14 and there shall be a **g** hunger within you;

GNAWS (2) [GNAW]

Job 30:17 and the pain that **g** me takes no rest.
Pr 25:20 sorrow **g** at the human heart.

GO‡ (1604) [GOES, GOING, GOINGS, GONE, WENT]

Ge 3:14 upon your belly you shall **g**,
4: 8 "Let us **g** out to the field."
7: 1 Then the LORD said to Noah, "**G** into the ark,
8:16 "**G** out of the ark, you and your wife,
11: 7 let us **g** down, and confuse their language there,
11:31 of the Chaldeans to **g** into the land of Canaan;
12: 1 "**G** from your country and your kindred
12: 5 and they set forth to **g** to the land of Canaan.
12:13 so that it may **g** well with me because of you,
13: 9 If you take the left hand, then I will **g** to the right;
13: 9 if you take the right hand, then I will **g** to the left."
15:15 yourself, you shall **g** to your ancestors in peace;
16: 2 from bearing children; **g** in to my slave-girl;
18:21 I must **g** down and see whether they have done
19: 2 then you can rise early and **g** on your way."
19:34 then you **g** in and lie with him,
22: 2 whom you love, and **g** to the land of Moriah,
22: 5 the boy and I will **g** over there;
24: 4 but will **g** to my country and to my kindred
24:11 the time when women **g** out to draw water.
24:38 but you shall **g** to my father's house,
24:51 Look, Rebekah is before you, take her and **g**,
24:55 at least ten days; after that she may **g**."
24:56 let me **g** that I may **g** to my master."
24:58 and said to her, "Will you **g** with this man?"
26: 2 "Do not **g** down to Egypt;
26:16 And Abimelech said to Isaac, "**G** away from us;
27: 3 your quiver and your bow, and **g** out to the field,
27: 9 **G** to the flock, and get me two choice kids,
27:13 only obey my word, and **g**, get them for me."
28: 2 **G** at once to Paddan-aram to the house of Bethuel,
28:15 with you and will keep you wherever you **g**,
28:20 and will keep me in this way that I **g**,
29: 7 Water the sheep, and **g**, pasture them."
29:21 "Give me my wife that I may **g** in to her,
30: 3 **g** in to her, that she may bear upon my knees and

Ge 30:25 that I may **g** to my own home and country.
30:26 for whom I have served you, and let me **g**;
31:18 to **g** to his father Isaac in the land of Canaan.
31:30 though you had to **g** because you longed greatly
32:26 Then he said, "Let me **g**, for the day is breaking."
32:26 But Jacob said, "I will not let you **g**,
33:12 and I will **g** alongside you."
35: 1 God said to Jacob, "Arise, **g** up to Bethel,
35: 3 let us **g** up to Bethel,
37:14 So he said to him, "**G** now,
37:17 for I heard them say, 'Let us **g** to Dothan.' "
37:35 and said, "No, I shall **g** down to Sheol to my son,
38: 8 "**G** in to your brother's wife and perform the duty
41:55 Pharaoh said to all the Egyptians, "**G** to Joseph;
42: 2 **g** down and buy grain for us there,
42:16 Let one of you **g** and bring your brother,
42:19 of you shall **g** and carry grain for the famine
42:33 the famine of your households, and **g** your way.
42:38 But he said, "My son shall not **g** down with you,
43: 2 "**G** again, buy us a little more food."
43: 4 we will **g** down and buy you food;
43: 5 we will not **g** down, for the man said to us,
44: 4 Joseph said to his steward, "**G**,
44:10 but the rest of you shall **g** free."
44:17 but as for you, **g** up in peace to your father."
44:25 And when our father said, '**G** again,
44:26 we said, 'We cannot **g** down.
44:26 our youngest brother goes with us, will we **g** down;
44:33 and let the boy **g** back with his brothers.
44:34 For how can I **g** back to my father if the boy is not
45: 9 Hurry and **g** up to my father and say to him,
45:17 load your animals and **g** back to the land
45:28 I must **g** and see him before I die."
46: 3 do not be afraid to **g** down to Egypt,
46: 4 I myself will **g** down with you to Egypt,
46:31 "I will **g** up and tell Pharaoh, and will say to him,
48: 7 there was still some distance to **g** to Ephrath;
50: 5 let me **g** up, so that I may bury my father;
50: 6 Pharaoh answered, "**G** up, and bury your father,
Ex 2: 7 "Shall I **g** and get you a nurse from
3:11 "Who am I that I should **g** to Pharaoh,
3:16 **G** and assemble the elders of Israel,
3:18 and the elders of Israel shall **g** to the king of Egypt
3:18 now **g** a three days' journey into the wilderness,
3:19 not let you **g** unless compelled by a mighty hand.
3:20 after that he will let you **g**.
3:21 when you **g**, you will not **g** empty-handed;
4:12 Now **g**, and I will be with your mouth
4:18 "Please let me **g** back to my kindred in Egypt
4:18 And Jethro said to Moses, "**G** in peace."
4:19 The LORD said to Moses in Midian, "**G** back
4:21 "When you **g** back to Egypt,
4:21 so that he will not let the people **g**.
4:23 "Let my son **g** that he may worship me."
4:23 But you refused to let him **g**;
4:27 "**G** into the wilderness to meet Moses."
5: 1 the God of Israel, 'Let my people **g**,
5: 2 that I should heed him and let Israel **g**?
5: 2 and I will not let Israel **g**."
5: 3 let us **g** a three days' journey into the wilderness
5: 7 let them **g** and gather straw for themselves.
5: 8 'Let us **g** and offer sacrifice to our God.'
5:11 **G** and get straw yourselves,
5:17 'Let us **g** and sacrifice to the LORD.'
5:18 **G** now, and work; for no straw shall be given
6: 1 Indeed, by a mighty hand he will let them **g**;
6:11 "**G** and tell Pharaoh king of Egypt to let the
Israelites **g** out of his land."
7: 2 to let the Israelites **g** out of his land.
7:14 he refuses to let the people **g**.
7:15 **G** to Pharaoh in the morning,
7:16 sent me to you to say, "Let my people **g**,
8: 1 "**G** to Pharaoh and say to him,
8: 1 Let my people **g**, so that they may worship me.
8: 2 If you refuse to let them **g**,
8: 8 I will let the people **g** to sacrifice to the LORD."
8:20 Let my people **g**, so that they may worship me.
8:21 For if you will not let my people **g**,
8:25 "**G**, sacrifice to your God within the land."
8:27 We must **g** a three days' journey into
8:28 "I will let you **g** to sacrifice to
8:28 provided you do not **g** very far away.
8:29 by not letting the people **g** to sacrifice to
8:32 and would not let the people **g**.
9: 1 Then the LORD said to Moses, "**G** to Pharaoh,
9: 1 Let my people **g**, so that they may worship me.
9: 2 For if you refuse to let them **g** and still hold them,
9: 7 and he would not let the people **g**.
9:13 Let my people **g**, so that they may worship me.
9:17 and will not let them **g**.
9:28 I will let you **g**; you need stay no longer."
9:35 and he would not let the Israelites **g**,
10: 1 Then the LORD said to Moses, "**G** to Pharaoh;
10: 3 Let my people **g**, so that they may worship me.
10: 4 For if you refuse to let my people **g**,
10: 7 Let the people **g**, so that they may worship
10: 8 "**G**, worship the LORD your God!
10: 8 But which ones are to **g**?"
10: 9 "We will **g** with our young and our old;
10: 9 we will **g** with our sons and daughters and
10:10 if ever I let your little ones **g** with you!
10:11 Your men may **g** and worship the LORD,
10:20 and he would not let the Israelites **g**.
10:24 Then Pharaoh summoned Moses, and said, "**G**,
10:24 Even your children may **g** with you."
10:26 Our livestock also must **g** with us;
10:27 and he was unwilling to let them **g**.

Ex 11: 1 afterwards he will let you **g** from here;
11: 1 indeed, when he lets you **g**,
11: 4 About midnight I will **g** out through Egypt.
11:10 he did not let the people of Israel **g** out of his land.
12:21 "**G**, select lambs for your families,
12:22 of you shall **g** outside the door of your house
12:31 and said, "Rise up, **g** away from my people,
12:31 **G**, worship the LORD, as you said.
13:15 When Pharaoh stubbornly refused to let us **g**,
13:17 When Pharaoh let the people **g**,
14:15 Tell the Israelites to **g** forward.
14:16 the Israelites may **g** into the sea on dry ground.
14:17 of the Egyptians so that they will **g** in after them;
16: 4 the people shall **g** out and gather enough for
17: 5 LORD said to Moses, "**G** on ahead of the people,
17: 5 the staff with which you struck the Nile, and **g**.
17: 9 "Choose some men for us and **g** out,
18:20 the way they are to **g** and the things they are to do.
18:23 and all these people will **g** to their home in peace."
19:10 "**G** to the people and consecrate them today
19:12 not to **g** up the mountain or to touch the edge of it.
19:13 they may **g** up on the mountain."
19:15 do not **g** near a woman."
19:21 "**G** down and warn the people not to break
19:24 The LORD said to him, "**G** down,
20:26 You shall not **g** up by steps to my altar,
21: 2 but in the seventh he shall **g** out a free person,
21: 3 If he comes in single, he shall **g** out single;
21: 3 then his wife shall **g** out with him.
21: 4 be her master's and he shall **g** out alone.
21: 5 I will not **g** out a free person,"
21: 7 she shall not **g** out as the male slaves do.
21:11 she shall **g** out without debt,
21:26 the owner shall let the slave **g**, a free person,
21:27 the slave shall be let **g**, a free person,
24:14 whoever has a dispute may **g** to them."
25:35 so for the six branches that **g** out of the lampstand.
28:43 Aaron and his sons shall wear them when they **g**
30:20 When they **g** into the tent of meeting,
32: 1 "Come, make gods for us, who shall **g** before us;
32: 7 The LORD said to Moses, "**G** down at once!
32:23 'Make us gods, who shall **g** before us;
32:27 **G** back and forth from gate to gate throughout
32:30 But now I will **g** up to the LORD;
32:34 But now **g**, lead the people to the place
32:34 see, my angel shall **g** in front of you.
33: 1 The LORD said to Moses, "**G**, leave this place,
33: 1 and **g** to the land of which I swore to Abraham,
33: 3 **G** up to a land flowing with milk and honey;
33: 3 but I will not **g** up among you,
33: 5 if for a single moment I should **g** up among you,
33: 7 the LORD would **g** out to the tent of meeting,
33:14 He said, "My presence will **g** with you,
33:15 And he said to him, "If your presence will not **g**,
33:16 I and your people, unless you **g** with us?
34: 9 O Lord, I pray, let the Lord **g** with us.
34:24 no one shall covet your land when you **g** up
Lev 6:12 be kept burning; it shall not **g** out.
6:13 on the altar; it shall not **g** out.
8:33 not **g** outside the entrance of the tent of meeting
10: 7 not **g** outside the entrance of the tent of meeting,
14: 3 the priest shall **g** out of the camp,
14: 7 he shall let the living bird **g** into the open field.
14:36 afterward the priest shall **g** in to inspect the house.
14:38 the priest shall **g** outside to the door of the house
14:44 the priest shall **g** and make inspection;
14:53 the living bird **g** out of the city into the open field;
16:18 Then he shall **g** out to the altar that is before
19:16 not **g** around as a slanderer among your people,
21:11 He shall not **g** where there is a dead body;
21:12 not **g** outside the sanctuary and thus profane
25:41 they shall **g** back to their own family and return
25:54 they and their children with them shall **g** free in
26: 6 and no sword shall **g** through your land.
Nu 1: 3 everyone in Israel able to **g** to war.
1:20 everyone able to **g** to war:
1:22 everyone able to **g** to war:
1:24 everyone able to **g** to war:
1:26 everyone able to **g** to war:
1:28 everyone able to **g** to war:
1:30 everyone able to **g** to war:
1:32 everyone able to **g** to war:
1:34 everyone able to **g** to war:
1:36 everyone able to **g** to war:
1:38 everyone able to **g** to war:
1:40 everyone able to **g** to war:
1:42 everyone able to **g** to war:
1:45 everyone able to **g** to war in Israel—
4: 5 Aaron and his sons shall **g** in and take down
4:19 Aaron and his sons shall **g** in and assign each to
4:20 But the Kohathites must not **g** in to look on
5: 8 the restitution for wrong shall **g** to the LORD for
6: 6 to the LORD they shall not **g** near a corpse.
8:15 Thereafter the Levites may **g** in to do service at
10: 9 When you **g** to war in your land against
10:30 But he said to him, "I will not **g**,
10:30 I will **g** back to my own land and to my kindred."
10:32 Moreover, if you **g** with us,
13:17 and said to them, "**G** up there into the Negeb,
13:17 and **g** up into the hill country,
13:30 and said, "Let us **g** up at once and occupy it,
13:31 "We are not able to **g** up against this people,
14: 3 would it not be better for us to **g** back to Egypt?"
14: 4 "Let us choose a captain, and **g** back to Egypt."
14:14 and your cloud stands over them and you **g**
14:40 We will **g** up to the place that
14:42 Do not **g** up, for the LORD is not with you;

Nu 14:44 But they presumed to **g** up to the heights of
16:30 and they **g** down alive into Sheol,
20:17 we will **g** along the King's Highway,
21: 4 to **g** around the land of Edom;
21:22 we will **g** by the King's Highway
22:12 God said to Balaam, "You shall not **g** with them;
22:13 the morning, and said to the officials of Balak, "**G**
22:13 for the LORD has refused to let me **g** with you."
22:18 I could not **g** beyond the command of
22:20 get up and **g** with them;
22:35 The angel of the LORD said to Balaam, "**G** with
23: 3 beside your burnt offerings while I **g** aside.
24: 1 so he did not **g**, as at other times,
24:11 be off with you! **G** home!
24:13 be able to **g** beyond the word of the LORD, to do
26: 2 everyone in Israel able to **g** to war."
27:12 "**G** up this mountain of the Abarim range,
27:17 who shall **g** out before them and come in
27:21 at his word they shall **g** out,
31: 3 so that they may **g** against Midian,
32: 6 "Shall your brothers **g** to war while you sit here?
32:20 if you take up arms to **g** before the LORD for
34: 4 it shall **g** on to Hazar-addar, and cross to Azmon;
34:11 and the boundary shall **g** down,
34:12 and the boundary shall **g** down to the Jordan,
35:26 the slayer shall at any time **g** outside the bounds of
Dt 1: 7 and **g** into the hill country of the Amorites as well
1: 8 **g** in and take possession of the land that I swore
1:21 **g** up, take possession, as the LORD,
1:22 to us regarding the route by which we should **g** up
1:26 But you were unwilling to **g** up.
1:41 We are ready to **g** up and fight,
1:41 and thought it easy to **g** up into the hill country.
1:42 "Say to them, 'Do not **g** up and do not fight,
3:27 **G** up to the top of Pisgah and look around you to
4:34 to **g** and take a nation for himself from the midst
5: 5 because of the fire and did not **g** up the mountain.)
5:16 be long and that it may **g** well with you in the land
5:27 **G** near, you yourself, and hear all that
5:29 so that it might **g** well with them and
5:30 **G** say to them, 'Return to your tents.'
5:33 and that it may **g** well with you,
6: 3 so that it may **g** well with you,
6:18 so that it may **g** well with you,
6:18 that you may **g** in and occupy the good land that
8: 1 and **g** in and occupy the land that
9: 1 to **g** in and dispossess nations larger
9:12 "Get up, **g** down quickly from here,
9:23 "**G** up and occupy the land that I have given you,"
10:11 **g** on your journey at the head of the people,
10:11 that they may **g** in and occupy the land
11: 8 so that you may have strength to **g** in and occupy
11:31 When you cross the Jordan to **g** in to occupy
12: 5 to put his name there. You shall **g** there,
12:25 so that all may **g** well with you and your children
12:28 that it may **g** well with you and with your children
13: 6 saying, "Let us **g** worship other gods,"
13:13 saying, "Let us **g** and worship other gods,"
14:25 With the money secure in hand, **g** to the place that
15:16 But if he says to you, "I will not **g** out from you,"
16: 7 the next morning you may **g** back to your tents.
17: 8 then you shall immediately **g** up to the place that
19:13 so that it may **g** well with you.
20: 1 When you **g** out to war against your enemies,
20: 5 He should **g** back to his house,
20: 6 He should **g** back to his house,
20: 7 He should **g** back to his house,
20: 8 He should **g** back to his house,
21:10 When you **g** out to war against your enemies,
21:13 after that you may **g** in to her and be her husband,
21:14 you shall let her **g** free and not sell her for money.
22: 7 the mother **g**, taking only the young for yourself,
22: 7 that it may **g** well with you and you may live long.
23:10 then he shall **g** outside the camp;
23:12 the camp to which you shall **g**.
23:24 If you **g** into your neighbor's vineyard,
23:25 If you **g** into your neighbor's standing grain,
24: 5 he shall not **g** out with the army or be charged
24:10 you shall not **g** into the house to take the pledge.
24:19 you shall not **g** back to get it;
25: 5 Her husband's brother shall **g** in to her,
25: 7 then his brother's widow shall **g** up to the elders at
25: 9 then his brother's wife shall **g** up to him in
26: 2 and you shall put it in a basket and **g** to the place
26: 3 You shall **g** to the priest who is in office at
28: 6 and blessed shall you be when you **g** out.
28:19 and cursed shall you be when you **g** out.
28:25 you shall **g** out against them one way and flee
28:41 for they shall **g** into captivity.
29:19 we **g** our own stubborn ways"
30:12 "Who will **g** up to heaven for us,
31: 7 the one who will **g** with this people into the land
Jos 1: 7 so that you may be successful wherever you **g**.
1: 9 the LORD your God is with you wherever you **g**."
1:11 in three days you are to cross over the Jordan, to **g**
1:16 and wherever you send us we will **g**.
2: 1 saying, "**G**, view the land, especially Jericho."
2:16 She said to them, "**G** toward the hill country,
2:16 then afterward you may **g** your way."
2:19 If any of you **g** out of the doors of your house into
3: 4 so that you may know the way you should **g**,
6: 7 "**G** forward and march around the city;
6:19 they shall **g** into the treasury of the LORD."
6:22 "**G** into the prostitute's house,
7: 2 and said to them, "**G** up and spy out the land."
7: 3 "Not all the people need **g** up;
7: 3 or three thousand men should **g** up and attack Ai.

Jos 8: 1 take all the fighting men with you, and g up now
8: 3 and all the fighting men set out to g up against Ai.
8: 4 do not g very far from the city,
8:17 not a man left in Ai or Bethel who did not g out
9:11 g to meet them, and say to them,
17:15 "If you are a numerous people, g up to the forest,
18: 4 and I will send them out that they may begin to g
18: 8 the land, saying, "G throughout the land and write
22: 4 therefore turn and g to your tents in the land
22: 8 "G back to your tents with much wealth,
22: 9 to g to the land of Gilead,
23:14 "And now I am about to g the way of all the earth,
23:16 g and serve other gods and bow down to them,
Jdg 1: 1 "Who shall g up first for us against
1: 2 The LORD said, "Judah shall g up.
1: 3 then I too will g with you into the territory allotted
1:25 but they let the man and all his family g.
4: 6 commands you, 'G, take position at Mount Tabor,
4: 8 "If you will g with me, I will g; but if you will not
g with me, I will not g."
4: 9 And she said, "I will surely g with you;
6:14 "G in this might of yours and deliver Israel from
7: 4 'This one shall g with you,' he shall g with you;
7: 4 'This one shall not g with you,' he shall not g."
7: 7 Let all the others g to their homes."
7:10 g down to the camp with your servant Purah;
8:20 So he said to Jether his firstborn, "G kill them!"
9: 9 and g to sway over the trees?'
9:11 and g to sway over the trees?'
9:13 and g to sway over the trees?'
9:32 Now therefore, g by night,
9:38 G out now and fight with them."
10:14 G and cry to the gods whom you have chosen;
11: 8 you may g with us and fight with the Ammonites,
11:25 or did he ever g to war with them?
11:37 so that I may g and wander on the mountains,
11:38 "G," he said and sent her away for two months.
11:40 the daughters of Israel would g out to lament
12: 1 and did not call us to g with you?
12: 5 of the fugitives of Ephraim said, "Let me g over,"
14: 3 that you must g to take a wife from
15: 1 He said, "I want to g into my wife's room."
15: 1 But her father would not allow him to g in.
15: 5 he let the foxes g into the standing grain of
16:20 he thought, "I will g out as at other times,
18: 2 and they said to them, "G, explore the land."
18: 6 The priest replied, "G in peace.
18: 9 They said, "Come, let us g up against them;
18: 9 Do not be slow to g,
18:10 you g, you will come to an unsuspecting people.
18:24 and the priest, and g away, and what have I left?
19: 5 up early in the morning, and he prepared to g;
19: 5 with a bit of food, and after that you may g."
19: 7 When the man got up to g,
19: 9 in the morning for your journey, and g home."
19:15 to g in and spend the night at Gibeah.
19:25 And as the dawn began to break, they let her g.
19:27 and when he went out to g on his way,
20: 8 saying, "We will not any of us g to our tents,
20: 9 we will g up against it by lot.
20:14 to g out to battle against the Israelites.
20:18 The Israelites proceeded to g up to Bethel,
20:18 "Which of us shall g up first to battle against
20:18 the LORD answered, "Judah shall g up first."
20:23 And the LORD said, "G up against them."
20:28 "Shall we g out once more to battle
20:28 The LORD answered, "G up,
21:10 and commanded them, "G, put the inhabitants
21:20 saying, "G and lie in wait in the vineyards,
21:21 and g to the land of Benjamin.
Ru 1: 7 and they went on their way to g back to the land
1: 8 "G back each of you to your mother's house.
1:11 my daughters, why will you g with me?
1:12 Turn back, my daughters, g your way,
1:16 Where you g, I will g; Where you lodge, I will
1:18 Naomi saw that she was determined to g with her,
2: 2 "Let me g to the field and glean among the ears
2: 2 She said to her, "G, my daughter."
2: 8 do not g to glean in another field or leave this one,
2: 9 g to the vessels and drink from what
2:22 that you g out with his young women,
3: 3 and put on your best clothes and g down to
3: 4 then, g and uncover his feet and lie down;
3:16 "How did things g with you, my daughter?"
3:17 of barley, for he said, 'Do not g back
1Sa 1: 3 to g up year by year from his town to worship and
1:17 Then Eli answered, "G in peace;
1:22 not g up, for she said to her husband, "As soon as
2:28 to g up to my altar, to offer incense,
2:30 the family of your ancestor should g in and out
2:35 and he shall g in and out
3: 9 Therefore Eli said to Samuel, "G, lie down;
4:16 He said, "How did it g, my son?"
6: 6 did they not let the people g, and they departed?
6: 8 Then send it off, and let it g its way.
6:20 To whom shall he g so that we may be rid
8:20 that our king may govern us and g out before us
9: 3 g and look for the donkeys."
9: 6 Let us g there now;
9: 7 Then Saul replied to the boy, "But if we g,
9: 9 "Come, let us g to the seer";
9:10 Saul said to the boy, "Good; come, let us g."
9:13 Now g up, for you will meet him immediately."
9:19 g up before me to the shrine,
9:19 in the morning I will let you g and will tell you all
9:27 "Tell the boy to g on before us,
10: 3 Then you shall g on from there further and come
1Sa 10: 8 And you shall g down to Gilgal ahead of me;
10:14 to him and to the boy, "Where did you g?"
11:14 let us g to Gilgal and there renew the kingship."
14: 1 let us g over to the Philistine garrison on
14: 4 to g over to the Philistine garrison, there was
14: 6 let us g over to the garrison
14: 9 and we will not g up to them.
14:10 if they say, 'Come up to us,' then we will g up;
14:36 "Let us g down after the Philistines by night
14:37 "Shall I g down after the Philistines?
15: 3 Now g and attack Amalek,
15: 6 Saul said to the Kenites, "G!
15:18 the LORD sent you on a mission, and said, 'G,
15:27 As Samuel turned to g away,
16: 2 Samuel said, "How can I g?
17:32 your servant will g and fight with this Philistine."
17:33 "You are not able to g against this Philistine
17:37 So Saul said to David, "G,
17:55 When Saul saw David g out against the Philistine,
19: 3 I will g out and stand beside my father in the field
19:17 and let my enemy g, so that he has escaped?"
19:17 Michal answered Saul, "He said to me, 'Let me g;
20: 5 but let me g, so that I may hide in the field until
20:11 "Come, let us g out into the field."
20:13 and send you away, so that you may g in safety.
20:19 you shall g a long way down;
20:19 g to the place where you hid yourself earlier,
20:21 I will send the boy, saying, 'G, find the arrows.'
20:22 'Look, the arrows are beyond you,' then g;
20:28 "David earnestly asked leave of me to g
20:29 'Let me g; for our family is holding a sacrifice
20:40 "G and carry them to the city."
20:42 Then Jonathan said to David, "G in peace,
21: 5 from us as always when I g on an expedition;
22: 5 leave, and g into the land of Judah."
23: 2 "Shall I g and attack these Philistines?"
23: 2 "G and attack the Philistines and save Keilah."
23: 3 how much more then if we g to Keilah against
23: 4 LORD answered him, "Yes, g down to Keilah;
23: 8 to war, to g down to Keilah, to besiege David
23:13 they wandered wherever they could g.
23:22 G and make sure once more;
23:23 Then I will g with you;
25: 5 David said to the young men, "G up to Carmel,
25: 5 and g to Nabal, and greet him in my name.
25:19 "G on ahead of me; I am coming after you."
25:35 he said to her, "G up to your house in peace;
26: 6 "Who will g down with me into the camp
26: 6 Abishai said, "I will g down with you."
26:10 or he will g down into battle and perish.
26:11 and the water jar, and let us g."
26:19 saying, 'G, serve other gods.'
28: 1 and your men are to g out with me in the army."
28: 7 so that I may g to her and inquire of her."
28:22 you may have strength when you g on your way."
29: 4 he shall not g down with us to battle,
29: 7 So g back now; and g peaceably;
29: 8 that I should not g and fight against the enemies
29: 9 'He shall not g up with us to the battle.'
29:10 and g to the place that I appointed for you.
30:22 "Because they did not g with us,
2Sa 1: 4 David said to him, "How did things g?
2: 1 "Shall I g up into any of the cities of Judah?"
2: 1 The LORD said to him, "G up."
2: 1 David said, "To which shall I g up?"
3:16 Then Abner said to him, "G back home!"
3:21 "Let me g and rally all Israel to my lord the king,
5:19 "Shall I g up against the Philistines?
5:19 The LORD said to David, "G up;
5:23 he said, "You shall not g up;
5:23 g around to their rear, and come
7: 3 Nathan said to the king, "G,
7: 5 G and tell my servant David:
11: 1 the time when kings g out to battle,
11: 8 Then David said to Uriah, "G down to your house,
11: 9 and did not g down to his house.
11:10 "Uriah did not g down to his house,"
11:10 Why did you not g down to your house?"
11:11 shall I then g to my house, to eat and to drink,
11:13 but he did not g down to his house.
11:20 'Why did you g so near the city to fight?
11:21 Why did you g so near the wall?'
12:23 I shall g to him, but he will not return to me."
13: 7 saying, "G to your brother Amnon's house,
13:24 and his servants please g with your servant?"
13:25 "No, my son, let us not all g,
13:25 but he would not g but gave him his blessing.
13:26 "If not, please let my brother Amnon g with us."
13:26 king said to him, "Why should he g with you?"
13:27 until he let Amnon and all the king's sons g
14: 3 G to the king and speak to him as follows."
14: 8 the king said to the woman, "G to your house,
14:21 g, bring back the young man Absalom."
14:24 The king said, "Let him g to his own house;
14:30 g and set it on fire."
14:32 Now let me g into the king's presence;
15: 7 "Please let me g to Hebron and pay the vow
15: 9 The king said to him, "G in peace."
15:19 G back, and stay with the king;
15:20 while I g wherever I can?
15:20 G back, and take your kinsfolk with you;
15:22 David said to Ittai, "G then, march on."
15:27 g back to the city in peace, you and Abiathar,
15:33 David said to him, "If you g on with me,
16: 9 Let me g over and take off his head."
16:17 Why did you not g with your friend?"
16:21 "G in to your father's concubines,
2Sa 17:11 and that you g to battle in person.
17:17 a servant-girl used to g and tell them,
17:17 and they would g and tell King David;
17:21 "G and cross the water quickly;
18: 2 "I myself will also g out with you."
18: 3 But the men said, "You shall not g out.
18:21 Then Joab said to a Cushite, "G,
19: 7 g out at once and speak kindly to your servants;
19: 7 for I swear by the LORD, if you do not g,
19:25 the king said to him, "Why did you not g with me,
19:26 so that I may ride on it and g with the king.'
19:34 that I should g up with the king to Jerusalem?
19:36 Your servant will g a little way over the Jordan
19:37 let him g over with my lord the king;
19:38 king answered, "Chimham shall g over with me,
20: 3 and provided for them, but did not g in to them.
21:17 "You shall not g out with us to battle any longer,
24: 1 saying, "G, count the people of Israel and Judah."
24: 2 "G through all the tribes of Israel,
24:12 "G and say to David: Thus says the LORD:
24:18 "G up and erect an altar to the LORD on
1Ki 1:13 G in at once to King David, and say to him,
1:35 You shall g up following him.
1:53 and Solomon said to him, "G home."
2: 2 "I am about to g the way of all the earth.
2: 6 do not let his gray head g down to Sheol in peace.
2:14 with you?" She said, "G on."
2:16 She said to him, "G on."
2:26 king said to the priest Abiathar, "G to Anathoth,
2:29 saying, "G, strike him down."
2:36 and do not g out from there to any place whatever.
2:37 For on the day you g out,
2:42 'Know for certain that on the day you g out and g
3: 7 I do not know how to g out or come in.
5: 9 into rafts to g by sea to the place you indicate.
8:44 "If your people g out to battle against their enemy,
9: 6 but g and serve other gods and worship them,
11:21 "Let me depart, that I may g to my own country."
11:22 "What do you lack with me that you now seek to g
11:22 And he said, "No, do let me g."
12: 5 He said to them, "G away for three days,
12:24 not g up or fight against your kindred the people
12:24 Let everyone g home, for this thing is from me."
12:27 If this people continues to g up to offer sacrifices
13: 8 I will not g in with you;
13:12 Their father said to them, "Which way did he g?"
13:16 "I cannot return with you, or g in with you;
14: 2 Jeroboam said to his wife, "G, disguise yourself,
14: 2 that you are the wife of Jeroboam, and g to Shiloh;
14: 3 some cakes, and a jar of honey, and g to him;
14: 7 G, tell Jeroboam, 'Thus says the LORD,
14:12 Therefore set out, g to your house.
15:19 g, break your alliance with King Baasha of Israel,
17: 3 "G from here and turn eastward,
17: 9 "G now to Zarephath, which belongs to Sidon,
17:12 so that I may g home and prepare it for myself
17:13 g and do as you have said;
18: 1 in the third year of the drought, saying, "G,
18: 5 "G through the land to all the springs of water and
18: 8 G, tell your lord that Elijah is here."
18:11 you say, 'G, tell your lord that Elijah is here.'
18:14 you say, 'G, tell your lord that Elijah is here';
18:21 "How long will you g limping
18:41 Elijah said to Ahab, "G up, eat and drink;
18:43 He said to his servant, "G up now,
18:43 Then he said, "G again seven times."
18:44 Then he said, "G say to Ahab,
18:44 'Harness your chariot and g down before
19:11 "G out and stand on the mountain before
19:15 Then the LORD said to him, "G,
19:20 Then Elijah said to him, "G back again;
20:31 and g out to the king of Israel;
20:33 Then he said, "G and bring him."
20:34 "I will let you g on those terms."
20:34 So he made a treaty with him and let him g.
20:42 the man g whom I had devoted to destruction,
21:15 Jezebel said to Ahab, "G,
21:16 to g down to the vineyard of Naboth the Jezreelite,
21:18 G down to meet King Ahab of Israel, who rules
22: 4 "Will you g with me to battle at Ramoth-gilead?"
22: 6 "Shall I g to battle against Ramoth-gilead,
22: 6 They said, "G up;
22:12 "G up to Ramoth-gilead and triumph;
22:15 "Micaiah, shall we g to Ramoth-gilead to battle,
22:15 He answered him, "G up and triumph;
22:17 let each one g home in peace.' "
22:20 so that he may g up and fall at Ramoth-gilead?'
22:22 'I will g out and be a lying spirit in the mouth
22:22 and you shall succeed; g out and do it.'
22:25 "You will find out on that day when you g in
22:30 "I will disguise myself and g into battle,
22:48 Jehoshaphat made ships of the Tarshish type to g
22:48 but they did not g, for the ships were wrecked
22:49 "Let my servants g with your servants in
2Ki 1: 2 so he sent messengers, telling them, "G,
1: 3 g to meet the messengers of the king of Samaria,
1: 6 'G back to the king who sent you, and say to him:
1:15 "G down with him; do not be afraid of him."
2:16 please let them g and seek your master;
2:18 he said to them, "Did I not say to you, Do not g?"
2:23 saying, "G away, baldhead! G away,
3: 7 will you g with me to battle against Moab?"
3:13 G to your father's prophets or to your mother's."
4: 3 "G outside, borrow vessels
4: 4 Then g in, and shut the door behind you
4: 7 and he said, "G sell the oil and pay your debts,
4:22 so that I may quickly g to the man of God

2Ki 4:23 He said, "Why g to him today?
4:29 and take my staff in your hand, and g.
5: 5 And the king of Aram said, "G then,
5:10 Elisha sent a messenger to him, saying, "G,
5:19 He said to him, "G in peace."
5:26 "Did I not g with you in spirit
6: 2 Let us g to the Jordan, and let us collect logs there,
6:13 He said, "G and find where he is;
6:22 and let them g to their master."
7: 5 they arose at twilight to g to the Aramean camp;
7: 9 therefore let us g and tell the king's household."
7:14 after the Aramean army, saying, "G and find out."
8: 1 "Get up and g with your household,
8: 8 a present with you and g to meet the man of God.
8:10 Elisha said to him, "G, say to him,
9: 1 of oil in your hand, and g to Ramoth-gilead.
9: 2 g in and get him to leave his companions,
9:15 then let no one slip out of the city to g and tell
11: 5 those who g off duty on the sabbath and guard
11: 9 each brought his men who were to g off duty on
12:17 Hazael set his face to g up against Jerusalem,
17:27 let him g and live there,
18:25 The LORD said to me, G up against this land,
19:31 for from Jerusalem a remnant shall g out,
20: 5 on the third day you shall g up to the house of
20: 8 and that I shall g up to the house of the LORD on
22: 4 "G up to the high priest Hilkiah,
22:13 "G, inquire of the LORD for me, for the people,
1Ch 14:10 "Shall I g up against the Philistines?
14:10 The LORD said to him, "G up,
14:14 God said to him, "You shall not g up after them;
14:14 g around and come on them opposite
14:15 in the tops of the balsam trees, then g out to battle;
17: 4 G and tell my servant David:
17:11 When your days are fulfilled to g to be
20: 1 the time when kings g out to battle,
21: 2 "G, number Israel, from Beer-sheba to Dan,
21:10 "G and say to David, 'Thus says the LORD:
21:18 to tell David that he should g up and erect an altar
21:30 but David could not g before it to inquire of God,
22:19 G and build the sanctuary of the LORD God so
2Ch 1:10 now wisdom and knowledge to g out and come in
6:34 your people g out to battle against their enemies,
6:41 O LORD God, and g to your resting place,
7:19 and g and serve other gods and worship them,
11: 4 You shall not g up or fight against your kindred.
15: 5 In those times it was not safe for anyone to g
16: 3 g, break your alliance with King Baasha of Israel,
18: 2 and induced him to g up against Ramoth-gilead.
18: 3 "Will you g with me to Ramoth-gilead?"
18: 5 "Shall we g to battle against Ramoth-gilead,
18: 5 They said, "G up;
18:11 "G up to Ramoth-gilead and triumph;
18:14 "Micaiah, shall we g to Ramoth-gilead to battle,
18:14 He answered, "G up and triumph;
18:16 let each one g home in peace.' "
18:19 so that he may g up and fall at Ramoth-gilead?'
18:21 'I will g out and be a lying spirit in the mouth
18:21 and you shall succeed; g out and do it.'
18:24 "You will find out on that day when you g in
18:29 "I will disguise myself and g into battle,
20:16 Tomorrow g down against them;
20:17 tomorrow g out against them,
20:36 He joined him in building ships to g to Tarshish;
20:37 the ships were wrecked and were not able to g
21:11 into unfaithfulness, and made Judah g astray.
23: 8 with those who were to g off duty on the sabbath;
24: 5 "G out to the cities of Judah and gather money
25: 7 "O king, do not let the army of Israel g with you,
25: 8 Rather, g by yourself and act;
25:10 letting them g home again.
25:13 not letting them g with him to battle,
26:18 to make offering. G out of the sanctuary;
34:11 for the buildings that the kings of Judah had let g
34:21 "G, inquire of the LORD for me and
36:23 may the LORD his God be with him! Let him g up."
Ezr 1: 3 are now permitted to g up to Jerusalem in Judah,
1: 5 to g up and rebuild the house of the LORD
5:15 g and put them in the temple in Jerusalem,
7:13 or Levites in my kingdom who freely offers to g
7:13 to go to Jerusalem may g with you.
7:28 and I gathered leaders from Israel to g up with me.
8:31 on the twelfth day of the first month, to g
Ne 3:15 the king's garden, as far as the stairs that g down
6:11 a man like me g into the temple to save his life?
6:11 I will not g in!"
8:10 Then he said to them, "G your way,
8:15 "G out to the hills and bring branches of olive,
9:12 on the way in which they should g.
9:15 and you told them to g in to possess the land
9:19 on the way by which they should g.
Est 1:19 let a royal order g out from him,
2:12 turn came for each girl to g in to King Ahasuerus,
2:14 she did not g in to the king again,
2:15 to g in to the king,
4: 5 to g to Mordecai to learn what was happening
4: 8 to g to the king to make supplication to him
4:16 "G, gather all the Jews to be found in Susa,
4:16 I will g to the king, though it is against the law;
5:14 g with the king to the banquet in good spirits."
Job 1: 4 to g and hold feasts in one another's houses
2:11 They met together to g and console
6:18 they g up into the waste, and perish.
7: 9 so those who g down to Sheol do not come up;
9:26 They g by like skiffs of reed,
10:21 before I g, never to return, to the land of gloom
11: 2 "Should a multitude of words g unanswered,

Job 15:13 and let such words g out of your mouth?
16:22 I shall g the way from which I shall not return.
17:16 Will it g down to the bars of Sheol?
20:13 though they are loath to let it g,
21:13 and in peace they g down to Sheol.
23: 8 "If I g forward, he is not there;
24: 5 Like wild asses in the desert they g out
24:10 They g about naked, without clothing;
27: 6 I hold fast my righteousness, and will not let it g;
27:19 They g to bed with wealth, but will do so no more;
30:28 I g about in sunless gloom;
31:34 so that I kept silence, and did not g out of doors—
34:23 not appointed a time for anyone to g before God
37: 8 animals g into their lairs and remain in their dens.
38:35 so that they may g and say to you, 'Here we are'?
39: 4 they g forth, and do not return to them.
39: 5 "Who has let the wild ass g free?
41:19 From its mouth g flaming torches;
42: 8 and g to my servant Job, and offer up
Ps 22:29 before him shall bow all who g down to the dust,
26: 6 and g around your altar, O LORD,
28: 1 I shall be like those who g down to the Pit.
30: 9 if I g down to the Pit?
31:17 let them g dumbfounded to Sheol.
32: 8 and teach you the way you should g;
38: 6 all day long I g around mourning.
40: 4 to those who g astray after false gods.
41: 6 when they g out, they tell it abroad.
43: 4 Then I will g to the altar of God,
48:12 Walk about Zion, g all around it, count its towers,
48:13 g through its citadels, that you may tell
49:17 their wealth will not g down after them.
49:19 they will g to the company of their ancestors,
50:23 to those who g the right way I will show
55:10 Day and night they g around it on its walls,
55:15 let them g down alive to Sheol;
58: 3 The wicked g astray from the womb;
60:10 You do not g out, O God, with our armies.
62: 9 in the balances they g up;
63: 9 to destroy my life shall g down into the depths of
84: 6 As they g through the valley of Baca they make it
84: 7 They g from strength to strength;
85:13 Righteousness will g before him,
88: 4 I am counted among those who g down to the Pit;
89:14 steadfast love and faithfulness g before you.
95:10 "They are a people whose hearts g astray,
104:23 People g out to their work and to their labor until
104:26 There g the ships, and Leviathan that you formed
108:11 You do not g out, O God, with our armies.
115:17 nor do any that g down into silence.
119:115 G away from me, you evildoers,
119:118 You spurn all who g astray from your statutes;
122: 1 "Let us g to the house of the LORD!"
122: 4 To it the tribes g up, the tribes of the LORD,
126: 6 Those who g out weeping,
127: 2 and g late to rest, eating the bread of anxious toil;
128: 2 you shall be happy, and it shall g well with you.
132: 7 "Let us g to his dwelling place;
132: 8 Rise up, O LORD, and g to your resting place,
139: 7 Where can I g from your spirit?
143: 7 or I shall be like those who g down to the Pit.
143: 8 Teach me the way I should g,
Pr 1:12 like those who g down to the Pit.
2:19 those who g to her never come back,
3:28 Do not say to your neighbor, "G, and come again,
4:13 do not let g; guard her, for she is your life.
4:15 do not g on it; turn away from it and pass on.
5: 5 Her feet g down to death;
5: 8 and do not g near the door of her house;
5:10 and your labors will g to the house of an alien;
6: 3 g, hurry, and plead with your neighbor.
6: 6 G to the ant, you lazybones;
6:29 no one who touches her will g unpunished.
10: 3 The LORD does not let the righteous g hungry,
11:21 Be assured, the wicked will not g unpunished,
14: 8 of the clever to understand where they g,
15:12 they will not g to the wise.
15:22 Without counsel, plans g wrong,
16: 5 be assured, they will not g unpunished.
17: 5 at calamity will not g unpunished.
18: 8 they g down into the inner parts of the body.
19: 5 A false witness will not g unpunished,
19: 9 A false witness will not g unpunished,
20:20 your lamp will g out in utter darkness.
22: 3 but the simple g on, and suffer for it.
24:11 those who g staggering to the slaughter;
24:20 the lamp of the wicked will g out.
26:22 they g down into the inner parts of the body.
27:10 do not g to the house of your kindred in the day
27:12 but the simple g on, and suffer for it.
28:12 but when the wicked prevail, people g into hiding.
28:20 in a hurry to be rich will not g unpunished.
28:28 When the wicked prevail, people g into hiding;
29: 9 If the wise g to law with fools,
31:18 Her lamp does not g out at night.
Ecc 3:20 All g to one place; all are from the
5: 1 Guard your steps when you g to the house of God;
5:15 so they shall g again, naked as they came;
5:16 just as they came, so shall they g;
6: 6 do not all g to one place?
7: 2 It is better to g to the house of mourning than to g
to the house of feasting;
7:18 without letting g of the other;
8: 3 Do not be terrified; g from his presence,
8:10 they used to g in and out of the holy place,
8:15 for this will g with them in their toil through
9: 3 and after that they g to the dead.

Ecc 9: 7 G, eat your bread with enjoyment,
12: 5 because all must g to their eternal home,
12: 5 and the mourners will g about the streets;
SS 3: 2 "I will rise now and g about the city,
3: 4 and would not let him g until I brought him
7:11 Come, my beloved, let us g forth into the fields,
7:12 let us g out early to the vineyards,
Isa 2: 3 "Come, let us g up to the mountain of the LORD,
2: 3 For out of Zion shall g forth instruction,
3:16 mincing along as they g, tinkling with their feet;
5:13 my people g into exile without knowledge;
5:14 nobility of Jerusalem and her multitude g down,
5:24 and their blossom g up like dust;
6: 8 "Whom shall I send, and who will g for us?"
6: 9 And he said, "G and say to this people:
7: 3 the LORD said to Isaiah, G out to meet Ahaz,
7: 6 Let us g up against Judah and cut off Jerusalem
7:24 With bow and arrows one will g there,
7:25 you will not g there for fear of briers and thorns;
14:17 who would not let his prisoners g home?"
14:19 who g down to the stones of the Pit,
15: 5 For at the ascent of Luhith they g up weeping;
18: 2 G, you swift messengers,
20: 2 of Amoz, saying, "G, and loose the sackcloth
21: 2 G up, O Elam, lay siege, O Media;
21: 6 "G, post a lookout, let him announce what he sees.
22:15 Come, g to this steward, to Shebna,
23:16 g about the city, you forgotten prostitute!
28:13 in order that they may g, and fall backward,
30: 2 who set out to g down to Egypt without asking
30: 8 G now, write it before them on a tablet,
30:29 as when one sets out to the sound of the flute to g
31: 1 Alas for those who g down to Egypt for help
33:21 where no galley with oars can g,
34:10 its smoke shall g up forever.
35: 8 no traveler, not even fools, shall g astray.
36:10 The LORD said to me, G up against this land,
37:32 for from Jerusalem a remnant shall g out,
38: 5 "G and say to Hezekiah, Thus says the LORD,
38:18 those who g down to the Pit cannot hope
38:22 "What is the sign that I shall g up to the house of
43:26 Accuse me, let us g to trial;
45: 2 I will g before you and level the mountains,
45:16 the makers of idols g in confusion together.
46: 2 but themselves g into captivity.
47: 5 Sit in silence, and g into darkness,
48:17 who leads you in the way you should g.
48:20 G out from Babylon, flee from Chaldea,
49:17 and those who laid you waste g away from you.
51: 4 for a teaching will g out from me,
51:14 they shall not die and g down to the Pit,
52:11 Depart, depart, g out from there!
52:11 Touch no unclean thing; g out from the midst of it,
52:12 For you shall not g out in haste,
52:12 and you shall not g in flight;
52:12 for the LORD will g before you,
54: 9 that the waters of Noah would never again g over
55:12 you shall g out in joy, and be led back in peace;
58: 6 to let the oppressed g free,
58: 8 your vindicator shall g before you,
60:20 Your sun shall no more g down,
62:10 G through, g through the gates,
63:14 Like cattle that g down into the valley,
66:17 Those who sanctify and purify themselves to g
66:24 And they shall g out and look at the dead bodies
Jer 1: 7 for you shall g to all to whom I send you,
2: 2 G and proclaim in the hearing of Jerusalem,
2:25 for I have loved strangers, and after them I will g."
3:12 G, and proclaim these words toward the north,
4: 4 or else my wrath will g forth like fire,
4: 5 and let us g into the fortified cities!"
5: 5 Let me g to the rich and speak to them;
5:10 G up through her vine-rows and destroy,
6:25 Do not g out into the field, or walk on the road;
7: 6 if you do not g after other gods to your own hurt,
7: 9 and g after other gods that you have not known,
7:10 only to g on doing all these abominations?
7:12 G now to my place that was in Shiloh,
7:31 And they g on building the high place of Topheth,
8: 4 If they g astray, do they not turn back?
8:14 let us g into the fortified cities and perish there;
9: 2 I might leave my people and g away from them!
11:12 and the inhabitants of Jerusalem will g and cry out
12: 9 G, assemble all the wild animals;
13: 1 "G and buy yourself a linen loincloth,
13: 4 and g now to the Euphrates,
13: 6 after many days the LORD said to me, "G now to
14:18 If I g out into the field, look—
15: 1 Send them out of my sight, and let them g!
15: 2 And when they say to you, "Where shall we g?"
16: 5 or g to lament, or bemoan them;
16: 8 not g into the house of feasting to sit with them,
17:19 G and stand in the People's Gate,
17:19 the kings of Judah enter and by which they g out,
18: 2 g down to the potter's house,
19: 1 G and buy a potter's earthenware jug.
19: 2 and g out to the valley of the son of Hinnom at
19:10 the jug in the sight of those who g with you,
20: 6 shall g into captivity, and to Babylon you shall g;
21: 9 but those who g out and surrender to
21:12 or else my wrath will g forth like fire, and burn,
22: 1 G down to the house of the king of Judah,
22:20 G up to Lebanon, and cry out,
22:22 and your lovers shall g into captivity;
25: 6 not g after other gods to serve and worship them,
25:16 and stagger and g out of their minds because of
25:29 You shall not g unpunished,

Jer 27:18 and in Jerusalem may not **g** to Babylon.
28:13 **G,** tell Hananiah, Thus says the LORD:
29:16 your kinsfolk who did not **g** out with you
30:16 everyone of them, shall **g** into captivity;
31: 4 and **g** forth in the dance of the merrymakers.
31: 6 "Come, let us **g** up to Zion,
31:39 And the measuring line shall **g** out farther,
34: 2 **G** and speak to King Zedekiah of Judah and say
34: 3 and you shall **g** to Babylon.
35: 2 **G** to the house of the Rechabites, and speak
35:11 and let us **g** to Jerusalem for fear of the army of
35:13 **G** and say to the people of Judah and
35:15 and do not **g** after other gods to serve them,
36: 6 so you **g** yourself, and on a fast day in the hearing
36:19 Then the officials said to Baruch, "**G** and hide,
37: 9 "The Chaldeans will surely **g** away from us," for they will not **g** away.
37:12 Jeremiah set out from Jerusalem to **g** to the land
38: 2 but those who **g** out to the Chaldeans shall live;
38:20 and it shall **g** well with you,
39:16 **G** and say to Ebed-melech the Ethiopian:
40: 1 of the guard had let him **g** from Ramah,
40: 4 **g** wherever you think it good and right to **g.**
40: 5 or **g** wherever you think it right to **g."**
40: 5 an allowance of food and a present, and let him **g.**
40: 9 and it shall **g** well with you.
40:15 "Please let me **g** and kill Ishmael son
41:17 near Bethlehem, intending to **g** to Egypt
42: 3 the LORD your God show us where we should **g**
42: 6 that it may **g** well with us when we obey the voice
42:14 'No, we will **g** to the land of Egypt,
42:15 If you are determined to enter Egypt and **g**
42:17 to **g** to Egypt to settle there shall die by the sword,
42:18 be poured out on you when you **g** to Egypt.
42:19 O remnant of Judah, Do not **g** to Egypt.
42:22 by pestilence in the place where you desire to **g**
43: 2 'Do not **g** to Egypt to settle there';
44:14 Although they long to **g** back to live there,
44:14 they shall not **g** back, except some fugitives.
44:19 "Indeed we will **g** on making offerings to
45: 5 a prize of war in every place to which you may **g."**
46: 9 Let the warriors **g** forth: Ethiopia and Put
46:11 **G** up to Gilead, and take balm,
46:16 let us **g** back to our own people and to the land
48: 5 at the ascent of Luhith they **g** up weeping bitterly;
48: 7 Chemosh shall **g** out into exile,
49: 3 For Milcom shall **g** into exile,
49:12 shall you be the one to **g** unpunished?
49:12 You shall not **g** unpunished; you must drink it.
49:29 and a cry shall **g** up: "Terror is all around!"
50: 8 and **g** out of the land of the Chaldeans,
50:21 **G** up to the land of Merathaim; **g** up against her,
50:27 Kill all her bulls, let them **g** down to the slaughter.
50:33 and refuse to let them **g.**
50:38 it is a land of images, and they **g** mad over idols.
51: 9 and let each of us **g** to our own country;
51:50 You survivors of the sword, **g,** do not linger!
Eze 1:12 wherever the spirit would **g,** they went,
1:20 Wherever the spirit would **g,** they went,
3: 1 eat this scroll, and **g,** speak to the house of Israel.
3: 4 **g** to the house of Israel and speak my very words
3:11 then **g** to the exiles, to your people, and speak
3:22 and he said to me, Rise up, **g** out into the valley,
3:24 **G,** shut yourself inside your house.
3:25 so that you cannot **g** out among the people;
8: 9 to me, "**G** in, and see the vile abominations
9: 4 "**G** through the city, through Jerusalem,
9: 7 and fill the courts with the slain. **G!"**
10: 2 "**G** within the wheelwork underneath
12: 3 and **g** into exile by day in their sight;
12: 3 you shall **g** like an exile from your place
12: 4 you shall **g** out yourself at evening in their sight,
12: 4 as those do who **g** into exile.
12:11 they shall **g** into exile, into captivity."
12:12 on his shoulder in the dark, and shall **g** out;
12:16 among the nations where they **g;**
13:20 from your arms, and let the lives **g** free,
14:11 house of Israel may no longer **g** astray from me,
20:29 What is the high place to which you **g?**
20:30 after the manner of your ancestors and **g** astray
20:39 **G** serve your idols, everyone of you now
21: 4 therefore my sword shall **g** out of its sheath
26:20 with those who **g** down to the Pit,
30: 9 messengers shall **g** out from me in ships to terrify
30:17 and the cities themselves shall **g** into captivity.
30:18 and its daughter-towns shall **g** into captivity.
31:14 with those who **g** down to the Pit.
31:16 down to Sheol with those who **g** down to the Pit;
32:18 with those who **g** down to the Pit.
32:19 "Whom do you surpass in beauty? **G** down!
32:24 They bear their shame with those who **g** down to
32:25 and they bear their shame with those who **g** down
32:29 with those who **g** down to the Pit.
32:30 bear their shame with those who **g** down to the Pit.
35: 7 and I will cut off from it all who come and **g.**
36:20 and yet they had to **g** out of his land."
38: 8 the latter years you shall **g** against a land restored
38:11 "I will **g** up against the land of unwalled villages;
39: 9 of Israel will **g** out and make fires of the weapons
42:14 they shall not **g** out of it into the outer court
42:14 before they **g** near to the area open to the people."
44: 3 and shall **g** out by the same way.
44:19 When they **g** out into the outer court to the people,
46: 2 Then he shall **g** out, but the gate shall not
46: 8 and he shall **g** out by the same way.
46: 9 by the north gate to worship shall **g** out by
46: 9 and whoever enters by the south gate shall **g** out
Eze 46: 9 but shall **g** out straight ahead.
46:10 and when they **g** out, he shall **g** out.
46:12 Then he shall **g** out, and after he has gone out
48:11 not **g** astray when the people of Israel went astray,
Da 6:10 he continued to **g** to his house,
11: 4 be uprooted and **g** to others besides these.
11:11 the south shall **g** out and do battle against the king
11:44 and he shall **g** out with great fury to bring ruin
12: 9 He said, "**G** your way, Daniel,
12:13 But you, **g** your way, and rest;
Hos 1: 2 the LORD said to Hosea, "**G,**
2: 5 For she said, "I will **g** after my lovers;
2: 7 "I will **g** and return to my first husband,
3: 1 The LORD said to me again, "**G,**
4:14 for the men themselves **g** aside with whores,
4:15 Do not enter into Gilgal, or **g** up to Beth-aven,
5: 6 With their flocks and herds they shall **g** to seek
5:11 because he was determined to **g** after vanity.
5:14 I myself will tear and **g** away;
7:11 they call upon Egypt, they **g** to Assyria.
7:12 As they **g,** I will cast my net over them;
11:10 They shall **g** after the LORD,
Joel 3:13 **G** in, tread, for the wine press is full.
Am 1: 5 and the people of Aram shall **g** into exile to Kir,
1:15 then their king shall **g** into exile,
2: 7 father and son **g** in to the same girl,
4:10 the stench of your camp **g** up into your nostrils;
5: 5 for Gilgal shall surely **g** into exile,
6: 2 from there **g** to Hamath the great;
6: 2 then **g** down to Gath of the Philistines.
6: 7 they shall now be the first to **g** into exile,
7:11 and Israel must **g** into exile away from his land.' "
7:12 And Amaziah said to Amos, "O seer, **g,**
7:15 '**G,** prophesy to my people Israel.'
7:17 in an unclean land, and Israel shall surely **g**
8: 9 I will make the sun **g** down at noon,
9: 4 they **g** into captivity in front of their enemies,
Ob 1:21 Those who have been saved shall **g** up
Jnh 1: 2 "**G** at once to Nineveh, that great city, and cry out
1: 3 to **g** with them to Tarshish,
3: 2 **g** to Nineveh, that great city,
3: 4 Jonah began to **g** into the city, going a day's walk.
Mic 1: 8 I will **g** barefoot and naked;
2:10 Arise and **g;** for this is no place to rest,
2:11 to **g** about uttering empty falsehoods,
2:13 The one who breaks out will **g** up before them;
3: 6 The sun shall **g** down upon the prophets,
4: 2 "Come, let us **g** up to the mountain of the LORD,
4: 2 For out of Zion shall **g** forth instruction,
4:10 for now you shall **g** forth from the city and camp
4:10 in the open country; you shall **g** to Babylon.
Na 3:11 You also will be drunken, you will **g** into hiding;
Hag 1: 8 **G** up to the hills and bring wood and build
Zec 6: 6 the white ones **g** toward the west country,
6: 6 and the dappled ones **g** toward the south country."
6: 7 And he said, "**G,** patrol the earth."
6: 8 Then he cried out to me, "Lo, those who **g** toward
6:10 and **g** the same day to the house of Josiah son
8:21 the inhabitants of one city shall **g** to another,
8:21 "Come, let us **g** to entreat the favor of the LORD,
8:23 a Jew, grasping his garment and saying, "Let us **g**
9:14 and his arrow **g** forth like lightning;
11: 5 Those who buy them kill them and **g** unpunished;
14: 2 half the city shall **g** into exile,
14: 3 Then the LORD will **g** forth and fight
14:16 that have come against Jerusalem shall **g** up year
14:17 the families of the earth do not **g** up to Jerusalem
14:18 of Egypt do not **g** up and present themselves,
14:18 the LORD inflicts on the nations that do not **g** up
14:19 and the punishment of all the nations that do not **g**
Mal 4: 2 You shall **g** out leaping like calves from the stall.
Mt 2: 8 saying, "**G** and search diligently for the child;
2: 8 so that I may also **g** and pay him homage."
2:20 and **g** to the land of Israel,
2:22 he was afraid to **g** there.
5:24 leave your gift there before the altar and **g;**
5:30 of your members than for your whole body to **g**
5:41 anyone forces you to **g** one mile, **g** also the second
6: 6 **g** into your room and shut the door and pray
7:23 **g** away from me, you evildoers.'
8: 4 but **g,** show yourself to the priest,
8: 9 and I say to one, '**G,**' and he goes, and to another,
8:13 And to the centurion Jesus said, "**G;**
8:18 he gave orders to **g** over to the other side.
8:19 "Teacher, I will follow you wherever you **g."**
8:21 "Lord, first let me **g** and bury my father."
8:32 And he said to them, "**G!"**
9: 6 "Stand up, take your bed and **g** to your home."
9:13 **G** and learn what this means, 'I desire mercy,
9:24 "**G** away; for the girl is not dead but sleeping."
10: 5 "**G** nowhere among the Gentiles,
10: 6 but **g** rather to the lost sheep of the house of Israel.
10: 7 As you **g,** proclaim the good news,
11: 4 "**G** and tell John what you hear and see:
11: 7 "What did you **g** out into the wilderness
11: 8 What then did you **g** out to see?
11: 9 What then did you **g** out to see?
13:28 'Then do you want us to **g** and gather them?'
14:15 so that they may **g** into the villages and buy food
14:16 Jesus said to them, "They need not **g** away;
14:22 the disciples get into the boat and **g** on ahead to
16:21 to show his disciples that he must **g** to Jerusalem
17:27 **g** to the sea and cast a hook;
18:12 not leave the ninety-nine on the mountains and **g**
18:15 **g** and point out the fault when the two
19:21 Jesus said to him, "If you wish to be perfect, **g,**
19:24 for a camel to **g** through the eye of a needle than
Mt 20: 4 'You also **g** into the vineyard,
20: 7 He said to them, 'You also **g** into the vineyard.'
20:14 Take what belongs to you and **g;**
21: 2 "**G** into the village ahead of you,
21:28 'Son, **g** and work in the vineyard today.'
21:30 and he answered, 'I **g,** sir'; but he did not **g.**
22: 9 **G** therefore into the main streets,
23:13 For you do not **g** in yourselves,
24:17 on the housetop must not **g** down to take what is
24:26 He is in the wilderness,' do not **g** out.
25: 9 you had better **g** to the dealers and buy some
25:46 And these will **g** away into eternal punishment,
26:18 He said, "**G** into the city to a certain man,
26:32 I am raised up, I will **g** ahead of you to Galilee."
26:36 "Sit here while I **g** over there and pray."
27:64 otherwise his disciples may **g** and steal him away,
27:65 **g,** make it as secure as you can."
28: 7 Then **g** quickly and tell his disciples,
28:10 **g** and tell my brothers to **g** to Galilee;
28:19 **G** therefore and make disciples of all nations,
Mk 1:38 "Let us **g** on to the neighboring towns,
1:44 but **g,** show yourself to the priest,
1:45 so that Jesus could no longer **g** into a town openly,
2:11 stand up, take your mat and **g** to your home."
4:35 "Let us **g** across to the other side."
5:19 and said to him, "**G** home to your friends,
5:34 **g** in peace, and be healed of your disease."
6:36 so that they may **g** into the surrounding country
6:37 to **g** and buy two hundred denarii worth of bread,
6:38 "How many loaves have you? **G** and see."
6:45 into the boat and **g** on ahead to the other side,
7:29 Then he said to her, "For saying that, you may **g—**
8:26 saying, "Do not even **g** into the village."
9:12 to **g** through many sufferings and be treated
9:43 to have two hands and to **g** to hell,
10:21 **g,** sell what you own, and give the money to
10:25 for a camel to **g** through the eye of a needle than
10:52 "**G;** your faith has made you well."
11: 2 "**G** into the village ahead of you,
13:15 the one on the housetop must not **g** down or enter
14:12 to **g** and make the preparations for you to eat
14:13 saying to them, "**G** into the city,
14:28 I am raised up, I will **g** before you to Galilee."
16: 1 so that they might **g** and anoint him.
16: 7 But **g,** tell his disciples and Peter that he is going
16:15 ⟦**G** into all the world and proclaim the good news⟧
Lk 1:17 the spirit and power of Elijah he will **g** before him,
1:76 for you will **g** before the Lord to prepare his ways,
2:15 "Let us **g** now to Bethlehem and see this thing
4:18 to let the oppressed **g** free,
5: 8 "**G** away from me, Lord, for I am a sinful man!"
5:14 "**G,**" he said, "and show yourself to the priest, and,
5:24 stand up and take your bed and **g** to your home."
7: 8 and I say to one, '**G,**' and he goes, and to another,
7:22 "**G** and tell John what you have seen and heard:
7:24 "What did you **g** out into the wilderness
7:25 What then did you **g** out to see?
7:26 What then did you **g** out to see?
7:50 "Your faith has saved you; **g** in peace."
8:14 but as they **g** on their way,
8:22 "Let us **g** across to the other side of the lake."
8:31 They begged him not to order them to **g** back into
8:48 your faith has made you well; **g** in peace."
9:12 so that they may **g** into the surrounding villages
9:13 we are to **g** and buy food for all these people."
9:51 he set his face to **g** to Jerusalem.
9:57 "I will follow you wherever you **g."**
9:59 he said, "Lord, first let me **g** and bury my father."
9:60 as for you, **g** and proclaim the kingdom of God."
10: 1 and place where he himself intended to **g.**
10: 3 **G** on your way. See, I am sending you out like
10:10 **g** out into its streets and say,
10:37 Jesus said to him, "**G** and do likewise."
11: 5 and you **g** to him at midnight and say to him,
12:58 when you **g** with your accuser before a magistrate,
13:27 **g** away from me, all you evildoers!'
13:32 He said to them, "**G** and tell that fox for me,
14:10 you are invited, **g** and sit down at the lowest place,
14:18 and I must **g** out and see it;
14:21 '**G** out at once into the streets and lanes of
14:23 '**G** out into the roads and lanes,
15: 4 not leave the ninety-nine in the wilderness and **g**
15:18 I will get up and **g** to my father,
15:28 Then he became angry and refused to **g** in.
17:14 "**G** and show yourselves to the priests."
17:19 Then he said to him, "Get up and **g** on your way;
17:23 Do not **g,** do not set off in pursuit.
18:25 for a camel to **g** through the eye of a needle than
19:30 "**G** into the village ahead of you,
21: 8 Do not **g** after them.
21:37 and at night he would **g** out and spend the night on
22: 8 "**G** and prepare the Passover meal for us
22:33 I am ready to **g** with you to prison and to death!"
Jn 1:43 The next day Jesus decided to **g** to Galilee.
4: 4 But he had to **g** through Samaria.
4:16 Jesus said to her, "**G,** call your husband,
4:50 Jesus said to him, "**G;** your son will live."
6:67 "Do you also wish to **g** away?"
6:68 "Lord, to whom can we **g?**
7: 1 to **g** about in Judea because the Jews were looking
7: 3 and **g** to Judea so that your disciples also may see
7: 8 **G** to the festival yourselves.
7:35 "Where does this man intend to **g** that we will
7:35 to **g** to the Dispersion among the Greeks and teach
8:11 ⟦**G** your way, and from now on do not sin again."⟧
9: 7 to him, "**G,** wash in the pool
9:11 and said to me, '**G** to Siloam and wash.'

Jn 10: 9 and will come in and **g** out and find pasture.
11: 7 "Let us **g** to Judea again."
11:15 But let us **g** to him."
11:16 "Let us also **g**, that we may die with him."
11:31 consoling her, saw Mary get up quickly and **g** out.
11:44 Jesus said to them, "Unbind him, and let him **g**."
11:48 If we let him **g** on like this,
13: 1 to depart from this world and **g** to the Father.
14: 2 would I have told you that I **g** to prepare a place
14: 3 And if I **g** and prepare a place for you,
15:16 And I appointed you to **g** and bear fruit,
16: 7 it is to your advantage that I **g** away,
16: 7 for if I do not **g** away,
16: 7 but if I **g**, I will send him to you.
18: 8 So if you are looking for me, let these men **g**."
20: 5 but he did not **g** in.
20:17 But **g** to my brothers and say to them,
21: 3 They said to him, "We will **g** with you."
21:18 and to **g** wherever you wished.
21:18 and take you where you do not wish to **g**."
Ac 1:11 in the same way as you saw him **g** into heaven."
1:25 from which Judas turned aside to **g**
3: 3 he saw Peter and John about to **g** into the temple,
4:21 After threatening them again, they let them **g**,
5:20 "**G**, stand in the temple and tell the people
5:40 not to speak in the name of Jesus, and let them **g**.
7: 3 'Leave your country and your relatives and **g** to
8:26 and **g** toward the south to the road that goes down
8:29 "**G** over to this chariot and join it."
9:11 "Get up and **g** to the street called Straight,
9:15 But the Lord said to him, "**G**,
10:20 **g** down, and **g** with them without hesitation;
11: 3 "Why did you **g** to uncircumcised men and eat
11:12 The Spirit told me to **g** with them and not to make
15: 2 of the others were appointed to **g** up to Jerusalem
16: 7 they attempted to **g** into Bithynia,
16:35 saying, "Let those men **g**."
16:36 saying, "The magistrates sent word to let you **g**;
16:36 therefore come out now and **g** in peace."
17: 9 from Jason and the others, they let them **g**.
18: 6 From now on I will **g** to the Gentiles."
19:21 Paul resolved in the Spirit to **g** through Macedonia
19:21 and then to **g** on to Jerusalem.
19:30 Paul wished to **g** into the crowd,
20:13 intending to **g** by land himself.
21: 4 the Spirit they told Paul not to **g** on to Jerusalem.
21:12 we and the people there urged him not to **g** up
21:15 After these days we got ready and started to **g** up
21:24 **g** through the rite of purification with them,
22:10 The Lord said to me, 'Get up and **g** to Damascus;
22:21 '**G**, for I will send you far away to the Gentiles.' "
23:10 ordered the soldiers to **g** down, take him by force,
23:32 The next day they let the horsemen **g** on with him,
24:25 and said, "**G** away for the present;
25: 4 and that he himself intended to **g** there shortly.
25: 9 to **g** up to Jerusalem and be tried there before me
25:12 to the emperor you will **g**."
25:20 I asked whether he wished to **g** to Jerusalem and
27: 3 and allowed him to **g** to his friends to be cared for.
28:26 '**G** to this people and say,
Ro 6: 2 How can we who died to sin **g** on living in it?
15:24 when I **g** to Spain. For I do hope to see
1Co 5:10 since you would then need to **g** out of the world.
10:27 to a meal and you are disposed to **g**,
16: 4 If it seems advisable that I should **g** also,
16: 6 that you may send me on my way, wherever I **g**.
2Co 9: 5 So I thought it necessary to urge the brothers to **g**
12: 1 I will **g** on to visions and revelations of the Lord.
12:18 I urged Titus to **g**, and sent the brother with him.
Gal 1:17 nor did I **g** up to Jerusalem
1:18 Then after three years I did **g** up to Jerusalem
2: 9 agreeing that we should **g** to the Gentiles and they
Eph 4:26 do not let the sun **g** down on your anger,
Php 2:23 to send him as soon as I see how things **g** with me;
2Th 3: 4 and will **g** on doing the things that we command.
2Ti 3:13 But wicked people and impostors will **g** from bad
Heb 3:10 and I said, 'They always **g** astray in their hearts,
6: 1 Therefore let us **g** on toward perfection,
9: 6 the priests **g** continually into the first tent
13:13 Let us then **g** to him outside the camp and bear
Jas 2:16 and one of you says to them, "**G** in peace;
4:13 "Today or tomorrow we will **g** to such and such
1Jn 2:11 and does not know the way to **g**,
3Jn 1: 2 that all may **g** well with you and that you may be
Jude 1:11 For they **g** the way of Cain,
Rev 3:12 you will never **g** out of it.
10: 8 from heaven spoke to me again, saying, "**G**, take
13:10 to be taken captive, into captivity you **g**;
16: 1 "**G** and pour out on the earth the seven bowls of
16:14 who **g** abroad to the kings of the whole world,
17: 8 about to ascend from the bottomless pit and **g**
Tob 1: 7 up a second tenth in money and **g** and distribute it
1:14 Until his death I used to **g** into Media,
1:15 and I could no longer **g** there.
2: 2 I said to my son Tobias, "**G**, my child,
3: 6 release me to **g** to the eternal home, and do not,
3: 9 Because your husbands are dead? **G** with them!
4:15 Do not drink wine to excess or let drunkenness **g**
5: 3 find yourself a trustworthy man to **g** with you,
5: 4 So Tobias went out to look for a man to **g**
5: 5 "Do you know the way to **g** to Media?"
5: 7 young man, until I **g** in and tell my father;
5: 8 whether he is trustworthy enough to **g** with you."
5:10 "My son Tobias wishes to **g** to Media.
5:10 "I can **g** with him and I know all the roads,
5:14 to **g** with me to Jerusalem and worshiped
5:15 and my son. So **g** with my son,
Tob 5:16 Raphael answered, "I will **g** with him;
6:18 Now when you are about to **g** to bed with her,
6:18 You will save her, and she will **g** with you.
8:12 of the maids and have her **g** in to see if he is alive.
9: 2 **G** to the home of Gabael, give him the bond,
10: 7 When the sun had set she would **g** in and mourn
10: 7 to let me **g** so that I may return to my own father.
10:12 **G** in peace, daughter, and may I hear
10:12 Then he bade them farewell and let them **g**.
10:12 **G** in peace, my child.
12:13 up and leave your dinner to **g** and bury the dead,
13:13 **G**, then, and rejoice over the children of
14: 7 they will **g** to Jerusalem and live in safety forever
Jdt 2:10 You shall **g** and seize all their territory for me
2:19 to **g** ahead of King Nebuchadnezzar and to cover
5: 9 the place where they were living and **g** to the land
5:20 then we can **g** up and defeat them.
5:24 Therefore let us **g** ahead, Lord Holofernes,
7:13 we and our people will **g** up to the tops of
8:32 I am about to do something that will **g** down
8:33 Stand at the town gate tonight so that I may **g** out
8:35 Uzziah and the rulers said to her, "**G** in peace,
8:35 and may the Lord God **g** before you,
10: 9 the town to be opened for me so that I may **g** out
10:13 by which he can **g** and capture all the hill country
10:15 **G** at once to his tent;
10:19 for if we let them **g** they will be able to beguile
11:17 but every night your servant will **g** out into
11:18 so that you may **g** out with your whole army,
12: 6 now give orders to allow your servant to **g** out
12:11 "**G** and persuade the Hebrew woman who is
12:12 a woman **g** without having intercourse with her.
14: 2 and let every able-bodied man **g** out of the town;
14: 2 against the Assyrian outpost; only do not **g** down.
14: 3 and **g** into the camp and rouse the officers of
AdE 2:12 a girl was to **g** to the king was twelve months.
2:14 not **g** in to the king again unless she is summoned
2:15 to **g** in to the king,
4: 8 to **g** in to the king and plead for his favor in behalf
4:10 And she said to him, "**G** to Mordecai and say,
4:11 and it is now thirty days since I was called to **g** to
4:13 Mordecai told him to **g** back and say to her,
4:16 "**G** and gather all the Jews who are in Susa
4:16 and my maids and I will also **g** without food.
4:16 After that I will **g** to the king, contrary to the law,
5:14 Then, **g** merrily with the king to the dinner."
13: 7 in a single day **g** down in violence to Hades,
Wis 1:10 and the sound of grumbling does not **g** unheard.
10: 8 so that their failures could never **g** unnoticed.
13: 6 for perhaps they **g** astray while seeking God
15: 8 a short time before and after a little while **g** to
Sir 4:19 If they **g** astray she will forsake them,
6:27 and when you get hold of her, do not let her **g**.
7: 8 not even for one will you **g** unpunished.
8:14 Do not **g** to law against a judge,
8:15 Do not **g** traveling with the reckless,
9: 3 Do not **g** near a loose woman,
12:13 or all those who **g** near wild animals?
25:26 If she does not **g** as you direct,
27:19 so you have let your neighbor **g**,
27:20 Do not **g** after him, for he is too far off,
29:24 It is a miserable life to **g** from house to house;
31: 8 and who does not **g** after gold.
32:11 **g** home quickly and do not linger.
32:20 Do not **g** on a path full of hazards,
33:33 which way will you **g** to seek him?
38:32 and wherever they live, they will not **g** hungry.
41:10 so the ungodly **g** from curse to destruction.
42:10 or having a husband, for fear she may **g** astray, or,
Bar 4:19 **G**, my children, **g**; for I have been left desolate.
4:28 just as you were disposed to **g** astray from God,
LtJ 6:58 and **g** off with this booty,
6:62 When God commands the clouds to **g** over
Sus 1: 7 Susanna would **g** into her husband's garden
1:13 One day they said to each other, "Let us **g** home,
Bel 1:13 to **g** in regularly and consume the provisions.
1Mc 1:11 "Let us **g** and make a covenant with the Gentiles
3:31 then he determined to **g** to Persia and collect
3:39 and seven thousand cavalry to **g** into the land
3:56 he told to **g** home again, according to the law.
4:36 let us **g** up to cleanse the sanctuary
5:17 "Choose your men and **g** and rescue your kindred
5:17 Jonathan my brother and I will **g** to Gilead."
5:20 to Simon to **g** to Galilee,
5:45 a very large company, to **g** to the land of Judah.
5:46 and they could not **g** around it to the right or to
5:46 they had to **g** through it.
5:57 let us **g** and make war on the Gentiles around us."
5:66 he marched off to **g** into the land of the Philistines,
7: 7 let him **g** and see all the ruin
8:23 "May all **g** well with the Romans and with
9: 8 "Let us get up and **g** against our enemies.
9:29 like him to **g** against our enemies and Bacchides,
9:69 Then he decided to **g** back to his own land.
10:63 to his officers, "**G** out with him into the middle of
12:17 We have commanded them to **g** also to you
12:45 and will turn around and **g** home.
13:22 So Trypho got all his cavalry ready to **g**,
13:22 and he did not **g** because of the snow.
15:41 so that they might **g** out and make raids along
16: 3 and **g** out and fight for our nation,
2Mc 5: 9 having embarked to **g** to the Lacedaemonians
6:17 we must **g** on briefly with the story.
6:20 to **g** who have the courage to refuse things
7:19 that you will **g** unpunished for having tried to fight
11:26 be of good cheer and **g** on happily in the conduct
11:30 Therefore those who **g** home by the thirtieth
2Mc 12:24 With great guile he begged them to let him **g**
12:25 to restore them unharmed, they let him **g**, for
15:36 by public vote never to let this day **g** unobserved,
1Es 2: 5 **g** up to Jerusalem, which is in Judea,
2: 8 and all whose spirit the Lord had stirred to **g** up
2:29 and that such wicked proceedings **g** no further to
4: 4 if he sends them out against the enemy, they **g**,
4:11 no one may **g** away to attend to his own affairs,
4:19 they let all those things **g**,
4:63 to **g** up and build Jerusalem and the temple
5: 1 the heads of ancestral houses were chosen to **g** up,
5: 3 And he made them **g** up with them.
8:10 may **g** with you to Jerusalem.
8:27 and I gathered men from Israel to **g** up with me."
8:45 I told them to **g** to Iddo,
9:51 "so **g** your way, eat the fat and drink the sweet,
2Es 1: 5 "**G**, declare to my people their evil deeds,
2: 2 The mother who bore them says to them, '**G**,
2: 4 **G**, my children, and ask for mercy from the Lord.'
2:13 **G** and you will receive; pray
2:33 a command from the Lord on Mount Horeb to **g**
2:48 Then the angel said to me, "**G**,
4: 5 "**G**, weigh for me the weight of fire,
4:14 'Come, let us **g** and make war against the sea,
4:15 let us **g** up and subdue the forest of the plain so
4:40 "**G** and ask a pregnant woman whether,
5:19 "**G** away from me and do not come near me
9:24 but **g** into a field of flowers
10:10 and, lo, almost all **g** to perdition,
10:17 Therefore **g** into the town to your husband."
10:18 I will not **g** into the city, but I will die here."
10:53 to **g** into the field where there was no foundation
10:55 but **g** in and see the splendor or the vastness of
12:49 Now **g** to your homes, every one of you,
13:41 of the nations and **g** to a more distant region,
13:45 Through that region there was a long way to **g**,
14:18 Truth shall **g** farther away,
14:20 For I will **g**, as you have commanded me,
14:23 "**G** and gather the people,
15:17 For a person will desire to **g** into a city,
15:30 shall **g** forth like wild boars from the forest,
15:43 They shall **g** on steadily to Babylon and blot it out.
16: 9 Fire will **g** forth from his wrath,
16:32 because no sheep will **g** along them.
4Mc 11:16 for not eating defiling foods, **g** on torturing!"
12:12 and these throughout all time will never let you **g**.
14: 6 agreed to **g** to death for its sake.
18: 7 and did not **g** outside my father's house;
18:14 which says, 'Even though you **g** through the fire,

GOAD (1) [GOADS]

Sir 38:25 and who glories in the shaft of a **g**,

GOAD (KJV) See also OXGOAD

GOADS (3) [GOAD]

1Sa 13:21 for sharpening the axes and for setting the **g**.
Ecc 12:11 The sayings of the wise are like **g**,
Ac 26:14 It hurts you to kick against the **g**.'

GOAH (1)

Jer 31:39 straight to the hill Gareb, and shall then turn to **G**.

GOAL (4)

Php 3:12 or have already reached the **g**;
3:14 on toward the **g** for the prize of the heavenly call
Sir 35:21 and it will not rest until it reaches its **g**;
2Es 5:40 **g** of the love that I have promised to my people."

GOAT (66) [GOAT-DEMONS, GOATS, GOATS', HE-GOAT]

Ge 15: 9 a female **g** three years old, a ram three years old,
37:31 Then they took Joseph's robe, slaughtered a **g**,
Lev 3:12 If your offering is a **g**,
4:23 as his offering a male **g** without blemish.
4:24 He shall lay his hand on the head of the **g**;
4:28 a female **g** without blemish as your offering,
5: 6 a female from the flock, a sheep or a **g**,
7:23 You shall eat no fat of ox or sheep or **g**.
9: 3 'Take a male **g** for a sin offering;
9:15 the **g** of the sin offering that was for the people,
10:16 Then Moses made inquiry about the **g** of
16: 9 Aaron shall present the **g** on which the lot fell for
16:10 but the **g** on which the lot fell for Azazel shall
16:15 He shall slaughter the **g** of the sin offering that is
16:18 of the blood of the bull and of the blood of the **g**,
16:20 he shall present the live **g**.
16:21 both his hands on the head of the live **g**,
16:21 all their sins, putting them on the head of the **g**,
16:22 The **g** shall bear on itself all their iniquities to
16:22 and the **g** shall be set free in the wilderness.
16:26 the **g** free for Azazel shall wash his clothes
16:27 the **g** of the sin offering, whose blood was brought
17: 3 of Israel slaughters an ox or a lamb or a **g** in
22:27 When an ox or a sheep or a **g** is born,
23:19 You shall also offer one male **g** for a sin offering,
Nu 7:16 one male **g** for a sin offering;
7:22 one male **g** as a sin offering;
7:28 one male **g** for a sin offering;
7:34 one male **g** for a sin offering;
7:40 one male **g** for a sin offering;
7:46 one male **g** for a sin offering;
7:52 one male **g** for a sin offering;

Nu 7:58 one male g for a sin offering;
7:64 one male g for a sin offering;
7:70 one male g for a sin offering;
7:76 one male g for a sin offering;
7:82 one male g for a sin offering;
15:24 and one male g for a sin offering.
15:27 a female g a year old for a sin offering.
18:17 or the firstborn of a sheep, or the firstborn of a g,
28:15 And there shall be one male g for a sin offering to
28:22 also one male g for a sin offering,
28:30 with one male g, to make atonement for you.
29: 5 with one male g for a sin offering,
29:11 with one male g for a sin offering,
29:16 also one male g for a sin offering,
29:19 also one male g for a sin offering,
29:22 also one male g for a sin offering,
29:25 also one male g for a sin offering,
29:28 also one male g for a sin offering,
29:31 also one male g for a sin offering,
29:34 also one male g for a sin offering,
29:38 also one male g for a sin offering,
Dt 14: 4 the ox, the sheep, the g,
14: 5 the roebuck, the wild g, the ibex, the antelope,
Eze 43:22 a male g without blemish for a sin offering;
43:25 For seven days you shall provide daily a g for
45:23 and a male g daily for a sin offering.
Da 8: 5 I was watching, a male g appeared from the west,
8: 5 The g had a horn between its eyes.
8: 8 Then the male g grew exceedingly great;
8:21 The male g is the king of Greece,
Lk 15:29 yet you have never given me even a young g so
Tob 2:12 and also gave her a young g for a meal.
2:13 When she returned to me, the g began to bleat.
2:13 I called her and said, "Where did you get this g?

GOAT-DEMONS (4) [DEMON, GOAT]

Lev 17: 7 that they may no longer offer their sacrifices for g,
2Ch 11:15 and for the g, and for the calves that he had made.
Isa 13:21 there ostriches will live, and there g will dance.
34:14 g shall call to each other;

GOATH (KJV) See GOAH

GOATS‡ (70) [GOAT]

Ge 30:32 and the spotted and speckled among the g;
30:33 not speckled and spotted among the g and black
30:35 the male g that were striped and spotted, and all
30:35 all the female g that were speckled and spotted,
31:10 the male g that leaped upon the flock were striped,
31:12 the g that leap on the flock are striped, speckled,
31:38 your ewes and your female g have not miscarried,
32:14 two hundred female g and twenty male g,
Ex 12: 5 you may take it from the sheep or from the g.
Lev 1:10 from the sheep or g, your offering shall be a male
16: 5 the people of Israel two male g for a sin offering,
16: 7 the two g and set them before the LORD at
16: 8 and Aaron shall cast lots on the two g,
22:19 of the cattle or the sheep or the g.
Nu 7:17 five male g, and five male lambs a year old.
7:23 five male g, and five male lambs a year old.
7:29 five male g, and five male lambs a year old.
7:35 five male g, and five male lambs a year old.
7:41 five male g, and five male lambs a year old.
7:47 five male g, and five male lambs a year old.
7:53 five male g, and five male lambs a year old.
7:59 five male g, and five male lambs a year old.
7:65 five male g, and five male lambs a year old.
7:71 five male g, and five male lambs a year old.
7:77 five male g, and five male lambs a year old.
7:83 five male g, and five male lambs a year old.
7:87 and twelve male g for a sin offering;
7:88 the male g sixty, the male lambs a year old sixty.
31:28 whether persons, oxen, donkeys, sheep, or g.
31:30 whether persons, oxen, donkeys, sheep, or g—
31:36 thirty-seven thousand five hundred sheep and g,
31:37 of sheep and g was six hundred seventy-five.
31:43 thirty-seven thousand five hundred sheep and g,
Dt 32:14 Bashan bulls and g, together with the choicest
1Sa 24: 2 in the direction of the Rocks of the Wild G.
25: 2 he had three thousand sheep and a thousand g.
1Ki 20:27 like two little flocks of g,
2Ch 14:15 and carried away sheep and g in abundance,
17:11 and seven thousand seven hundred male g.
29:21 and seven male g for a sin offering for
29:23 Then the male g for the sin offering were brought
Ezr 6:17 and as a sin offering for all Israel, twelve male g,
8:35 and as a sin offering twelve male g;
Job 39: 1 "Do you know when the mountain g give birth?
Ps 50: 9 a bull from your house, or g from your folds.
50:13 or drink the blood of g?
66:15 I will make an offering of bulls and g.
104:18 The high mountains are for the wild g;
Pr 27:26 and the g the price of a field;
SS 4: 1 Your hair is like a flock of g,
6: 5 Your hair is like a flock of g,
Isa 1:11 in the blood of bulls, or of lambs, or of g.
34: 6 with the blood of lambs and g,
Jer 50: 8 and be like male g leading the flock.
51:40 down like lambs to the slaughter, like rams and g.
Eze 27:21 rams, and g; in these they did business with you.
34:17 between sheep and sheep, between rams and g:
39:18 of rams, of lambs, and of g, of bulls,
Mt 25:32 as a shepherd separates the sheep from the g,
25:33 the sheep at his right hand and the g at the left.
Heb 9:12 not with the blood of g and calves,
9:13 For if the blood of g and bulls,
9:19 he took the blood of calves and g,
10: 4 For it is impossible for the blood of bulls and g
11:37 they went about in skins of sheep and g, destitute,
Jdt 2:17 and innumerable sheep and oxen and g for food;
Sir 47: 3 with lions as though they were young g,
1Es 7: 8 and twelve male g for the sin of all Israel,
8:66 and as a thank offering twelve male g—

GOATS' (11) [GOAT]

Ex 25: 4 purple, and crimson yarns and fine linen, g hair,
26: 7 You shall also make curtains of g hair for a tent
35: 6 and crimson yarns, and fine linen; g hair,
35:23 or purple or crimson yarn or fine linen or g hair
35:26 to use their skill spun the g hair.
36:14 He also made curtains of g hair for a tent over
Nu 31:20 every article of skin, everything made of g hair,
1Sa 19:13 she put a net of g hair on its head,
19:16 with the covering of g hair on its head.
Pr 27:27 there will be enough g milk for your food,
2Es 16: 2 Bind on sackcloth and cloth of g hair,

GOB (2)

2Sa 21:18 this a battle took place with the Philistines, at G;
21:19 there was another battle with the Philistines at G;

GOBLETS (2)

Est 1: 7 Drinks were served in golden g, g of different

*GOD‡ (4500) [GOD'S, GOD-FEARING, GOD-GIVEN, GOD-HATERS, GODDESS, GODLESS, GODLINESS, GODLY, GODS, GODS', STAR-GOD]

A. †LORD MY/HIS/OUR/THEIR/YOUR *GOD (642)
B. *GOD OF ISRAEL (226)
C. HOUSE OF ... *GOD (120)
D. MAN OF *GOD (81)
E. KINGDOM OF *GOD (68)
F. *GOD OF ... ANCESTORS (61)
G. †LORD *GOD (61)
H. BEFORE *GOD (55)
I. *LORD MY/HIS/THEIR/OUR/YOUR *GOD (47)
J. ARK OF [THE] *GOD (44)
K. *LORD *GOD (44)
L. WORD OF *GOD (42)
M. SON OF ... *GOD (40)
N. LIVING *GOD (36)
O. *GOD OF HEAVEN (31)
P. LAW OF ... *GOD (26)
Q. *GOD OF HOSTS (25)
R. GLORY OF ... *GOD (25)
S. HAND OF ... *GOD (24)
T. POWER OF *GOD (23)
U. SPIRIT OF *GOD (23)
V. *GOD OF JACOB (22)
W. GRACE OF *GOD (21)
X. WILL OF ... *GOD (21)
Y. FEAR [YOUR] *GOD (20)
Z. ANGEL OF *GOD (19)
*GOD OF ABRAHAM (18) See ABRAHAM
MOST HIGH *GOD (18) See HIGH, MOST
BLESSED [BE] ... *GOD (15) See BLESSED
CHILDREN OF *GOD (15) See CHILDREN
*GOD THE FATHER (15) See FATHER
FEAR OF *GOD (13) See FEAR
*GOD AND FATHER (13) See FATHER
TEMPLE OF *GOD (12) See TEMPLE
*GOD OUR FATHER (11) See FATHER
LOVE OF *GOD (9) See LOVE
*GOD ... APPEARED (8) See APPEARED
*GOD MOST HIGH (8) See HIGH, MOST
SERVANT OF *GOD (8) See SERVANT
WORDS OF *GOD (8) See WORDS
*GOD BLESSED (7) See BLESSED
GREAT *GOD (7) See GREAT

Ge 1: 1 In the beginning when G created the heavens and
1: 2 a wind from G swept over the face of the waters.
1: 3 G said, "Let there be light"; and there was light.
1: 4 And G saw that the light was good;
1: 4 and G separated the light from the darkness.
1: 5 G called the light Day,
1: 6 And G said, "Let there be a dome in the midst of
1: 7 So G made the dome and separated the waters
1: 8 G called the dome Sky.
1: 9 And G said, "Let the waters under the sky
1:10 G called the dry land Earth,
1:10 And G saw that it was good.
1:11 Then G said, "Let the earth put forth vegetation:
1:12 And G saw that it was good.
1:14 And G said, "Let there be lights in the dome of
1:16 G made the two great lights—
1:17 G set them in the dome of the sky to give light
1:18 And G saw that it was good.
1:20 And G said, "Let the waters bring forth swarms
1:21 So G created the great sea monsters
1:21 And G saw that it was good.
1:22 G blessed them, saying, "Be fruitful and multiply
1:24 G said, "Let the earth bring forth living creatures
1:25 G made the wild animals of the earth
1:25 And G saw that it was good.
1:26 Then G said, "Let us make humankind
1:27 So G created humankind in his image,
1:27 in the image of G he created them;
1:28 G blessed them, and G said to them,
1:29 G said, "See, I have given you every plant
1:31 G saw everything that he had made, and indeed,
2: 2 And on the seventh day G finished the work
2: 3 So G blessed the seventh day and hallowed it,
2: 3 on it G rested from all the work that he had done
2: 4 that the LORD G made the earth and the heavens, G
2: 5 LORD G had not caused it to rain upon the earth, G
2: 7 then the LORD G formed man from the dust of G
2: 8 LORD G planted a garden in Eden, in the east; G
2: 9 the ground the LORD G made to grow every tree G
2:15 The LORD G took the man and put him in G
2:16 And the LORD G commanded the man, G
2:18 Then the LORD G said, "It is not good that G
2:19 the ground the LORD G formed every animal of G
2:21 So the LORD G caused a deep sleep to fall upon G
2:22 the LORD G had taken from the man he made G
3: 1 that the LORD G had made. G
3: 1 He said to the woman, "Did G say,
3: 3 but G said, 'You shall not eat of the fruit of
3: 5 for G knows that when you eat of it your eyes will
3: 5 and you will be like G, knowing good and evil."
3: 8 the LORD G walking in the garden at the time of G
3: 8 the presence of the LORD G among the trees of G
3: 9 But the LORD G called to the man, G
3:13 Then the LORD G said to the woman, G
3:14 The LORD G said to the serpent, G
3:21 the LORD G made garments of skins for the man G
3:22 Then the LORD G said, "See, G
3:23 LORD G sent him forth from the garden of Eden, G
4:25 "G has appointed for me another child instead
5: 1 When G created humankind,
5: 1 he made them in the likeness of G.
5:22 Enoch walked with G after the birth
5:24 Enoch walked with G;
5:24 then he was no more, because G took him.
6: 2 the sons of G saw that they were fair;
6: 4 the sons of G went in to the daughters of humans,
6: 9 in his generation; Noah walked with G.
6:12 And G saw that the earth was corrupt;
6:13 And G said to Noah, "I have determined to make
6:22 Noah did this; he did all that G commanded him.
7: 9 as G had commanded Noah.
7:16 went in as G had commanded him;
8: 1 But G remembered Noah and all the wild animals
8: 1 And G made a wind blow over the earth,
8:15 Then G said to Noah,
9: 1 G blessed Noah and his sons, and said to them,
9: 6 for in his own image G made humankind.
9: 8 Then G said to Noah and to his sons with him,
9:12 G said, "This is the sign of the covenant
9:16 remember the everlasting covenant between G
9:17 G said to Noah, "This is the sign of the covenant
9:26 "Blessed by the LORD my G be Shem; A
9:27 May G make space for Japheth,
14:18 he was priest of G Most High.
14:19 "Blessed be Abram by G Most High,
14:20 and blessed be G Most High,
14:22 "I have sworn to the LORD, G Most High,
16:13 "Have I really seen G and remained alive
17: 1 and said to him, "I am G Almighty;
17: 3 Then Abram fell on his face; and G said to him,
17: 7 to be G to you and to your offspring after you.
17: 8 and I will be their G."
17: 9 G said to Abraham, "As for you,
17:15 G said to Abraham, "As for Sarai your wife,
17:18 to G, "O that Ishmael might live
17:19 G said, "No, but your wife Sarah shall bear you
17:22 G went up from Abraham.
17:23 as G had said to him.
19:29 when G destroyed the cities of the Plain,
19:29 G remembered Abraham,
20: 3 But G came to Abimelech in a dream by night,
20: 6 Then G said to him in the dream, "Yes,
20:11 There is no fear of G at all in this place,
20:13 G caused me to wander from my father's house,
20:17 Then Abraham prayed to G;
20:17 and G healed Abimelech,
21: 2 at the time of which G had spoken to him.
21: 4 as G had commanded him.
21: 6 Now Sarah said, "G has brought laughter for me,
21:12 But G said to Abraham, "Do not be distressed
21:17 And G heard the voice of the boy;
21:17 and the angel of G called to Hagar from heaven, Z
21:17 for G has heard the voice of the boy where he is.
21:19 G opened her eyes and she saw a well of water.
21:20 G was with the boy, and he grew up;
21:22 said to Abraham, "G is with you in all that you do;
21:23 now therefore swear to me here by G that you will
21:33 on the name of the LORD, the Everlasting G.
22: 1 After these things G tested Abraham.
22: 3 to the place in the distance that G had shown him.
22: 8 "G himself will provide the lamb for
22: 9 they came to the place that G had shown him,
22:12 for now I know that you fear G, Y
24: 3 the G of heaven and earth, O
24: 7 The LORD, the G of heaven, O
24:12 he said, "O LORD, G of my master Abraham,
24:27 the G of my master Abraham,
24:42 'O LORD, the G of my master Abraham,
24:48 the G of my master Abraham,
25:11 the death of Abraham G blessed his son Isaac.
26:24 "I am the G of your father Abraham;
27:20 "Because the LORD your G granted me success." A
27:28 May G give you of the dew of heaven,
28: 3 May G Almighty bless you and make you fruitful
28: 4 land that G gave to Abraham."

*GOD distinguishes the words translated "God" and "god" from the compound name "Lord GOD," where GOD represents the name *Yahweh*. For this name see the heading †GOD on pages 541-42.

Ge 28:12 angels of G were ascending and descending on it.
28:13 G of Abraham your father and the G of Isaac;
28:17 This is none other than the house of G, C
28:20 Jacob made a vow, saying, "If G will be with me,
28:21 then the LORD shall be my G,
30: 2 "Am I in the place of G,
30: 6 Then Rachel said, "G has judged me,
30:17 And G heeded Leah, and she conceived
30:18 "G has given me my hire because I gave my maid
30:20 "G has endowed me with a good dowry;
30:22 Then G remembered Rachel,
30:22 and G heeded her and opened her womb.
30:23 and said, "G has taken away my reproach";
31: 5 But the G of my father has been with me.
31: 7 but G did not permit him to harm me.
31: 9 Thus G has taken away the livestock
31:11 Then the angel of G said to me in the dream, Z
31:13 I am the G of Bethel,
31:16 that G has taken away from our father belongs
31:16 now then, do whatever G has said to you."
31:24 But G came to Laban the Aramean in a dream
31:29 but the G of your father spoke to me last night,
31:42 If the G of my father, the G of Abraham and the
31:42 G saw my affliction and the labor of my hands,
31:50 remember that G is witness between you and me."
31:53 May the G of Abraham and the G of Nahor"—
31:53 the G of their father—"judge between us."
32: 1 on his way and the angels of G met him;
32: 9 "O G of my father Abraham and God
32: 9 of my father Abraham and G of my father Isaac,
32:28 for you have striven with G and with humans,
32:30 saying, "For I have seen G face to face,
33: 5 whom G has graciously given your servant."
33:10 truly to see your face is like seeing the face of G—
33:11 because G has dealt graciously with me,
35: 1 G said to Jacob, "Arise, go up to Bethel,
35: 1 Make an altar there to the G who appeared to you
35: 3 the G who answered me in the day of my distress
35: 5 terror from G fell upon the cities all around them,
35: 7 because it was there that G had revealed himself
35: 9 G appeared to Jacob again when he came
35:10 G said to him, "Your name is Jacob;
35:11 G said to him, "I am G Almighty:
35:13 Then G went up from him at the place
35:15 the place where G had spoken with him Bethel.
39: 9 do this great wickedness, and sin against G?"
40: 8 "Do not interpretations belong to G?
41:16 G will give Pharaoh a favorable answer."
41:25 G has revealed to Pharaoh what he is about to do.
41:28 G has shown to Pharaoh what he is about to do.
41:32 that the thing is fixed by G,
41:32 and G will shortly bring it about.
41:38 one in whom is the spirit of G?" U
41:39 "Since G has shown you all this,
41:51 "G has made me forget all my hardship
41:52 "For G has made me fruitful in the land
42:18 "Do this and you will live, for I fear G: Y
42:28 saying, "What is this that G has done to us?"
43:14 may G Almighty grant you mercy before the man,
43:23 G and the G of your father must have put treasure
43:29 G be gracious to you, my son!"
44:16 G has found out the guilt of your servants;
45: 5 for G sent me before you to preserve life.
45: 7 G sent me before you to preserve for you
45: 8 So it was not you who sent me here, but G;
45: 9 G has made me lord of all Egypt;
46: 1 he offered sacrifices to the G of his father Isaac.
46: 2 G spoke to Israel in visions of the night, and said,
46: 3 Then he said, "I am G, the G of your father;
48: 3 "G Almighty appeared to me at Luz in the land
48: 9 "They are my sons, whom G has given me here."
48:11 and here G has let me see your children also."
48:15 "The G before whom my ancestors Abraham
48:15 the G who has been my shepherd all my life
48:20 'G make you like Ephraim and like Manasseh.' "
48:21 but G will be with you and will bring you again to
49:25 by the G of your father,
50:17 the crime of the servants of the G of your father."
50:19 Am I in the place of G?
50:20 to me, G intended it for good, in order to preserve
50:24 but G will surely come to you,
50:25 saying, "When G comes to you,
Ex 1:17 But the midwives feared G;
1:20 So G dealt well with the midwives;
1:21 the midwives feared G, he gave them families.
2:23 Out of the slavery their cry for help rose up to G.
2:24 G heard their groaning,
2:24 and G remembered his covenant with Abraham,
2:25 G looked upon the Israelites,
2:25 and G took notice of them.
3: 1 and came to Horeb, the mountain of G.
3: 4 G called to him out of the bush, "Moses, Moses!"
3: 6 "I am the G of your father, the G of Abraham,
3: 6 the G of Isaac, and the God of Jacob."
3: 6 the God of Isaac, and the G of Jacob." V
3: 6 Moses hid his face, for he was afraid to look at G.
3:11 But Moses said to G, "Who am I that I should go
3:12 you shall worship G on this mountain."
3:13 to G, "If I come to the Israelites and say to them,
3:13 'The G of your ancestors has sent me to you,' F
3:14 G said to Moses, "I AM WHO I AM."
3:15 G also said to Moses, "Thus you shall say to
3:15 the G of your ancestors, the God of Abraham, F
3:15 the G of Abraham, the G of Isaac,
3:15 and the G of Jacob, has sent me to you': V
3:16 the G of your ancestors, the God of Abraham, F
3:16 the God of your ancestors, the G of Abraham,

Ex 3:18 the G of the Hebrews, has met with us;
3:18 so that we may sacrifice to the LORD our G.' A
4: 5 the G of their ancestors, the God of Abraham, F
4: 5 the G of Abraham, the G of Isaac,
4: 5 and the G of Jacob, has appeared to you." V
4: 7 G said, "Put your hand back into your cloak"—
4:16 and you shall serve as G for him.
4:20 and Moses carried the staff of G in his hand.
4:27 he met him at the mountain of G and kissed him.
5: 1 "Thus says the LORD, the G of Israel, B
5: 3 "The G of the Hebrews has revealed himself to us;
5: 3 the wilderness to sacrifice to the LORD our G, A
5: 8 'Let us go and offer sacrifice to our G.'
6: 2 G also spoke to Moses and said to him:
6: 3 Isaac, and Jacob as G Almighty,
6: 7 I will take you as my people, and I will be your G.
6: 7 You shall know that I am the LORD your G, A
7: 1 "See, I have made you like G to Pharaoh,
7:16 Say to him, 'The LORD, the G of the Hebrews,
8:10 that there is no one like the LORD our G, A
8:19 "This is the finger of G!"
8:25 "Go, sacrifice to your G within the land."
8:26 that we offer to the LORD our G are offensive to A
8:27 the wilderness and sacrifice to the LORD our G A
8:28 to the LORD your G in the wilderness, A
9: 1 'Thus says the LORD, the G of the Hebrews:
9:13 'Thus says the LORD, the G of the Hebrews:
9:30 I know that you do not yet fear the LORD G." G
10: 3 "Thus says the LORD, the G of the Hebrews,
10: 7 so that they may worship the LORD their G; A
10: 8 "Go, worship the LORD your G! A
10:16 "I have sinned against the LORD your G, A
10:17 and pray to the LORD your G that at A
10:25 to sacrifice to the LORD our G. A
10:26 of them for the worship of the LORD our G, A
13:17 G did not lead them by way of the land of
13:17 for G thought, "If the people face war,
13:18 So G led the people by the roundabout way of
13:19 saying, "G will surely take notice of you,
14:19 The angel of G who was going before Z
15: 2 this is my G, and I will praise him,
15: 2 and I will praise him, my father's G,
15:26 of the LORD your G, and do what is right A
16:12 you shall know that I am the LORD your G.' " A
17: 9 the top of the hill with the staff of G in my hand."
18: 1 heard of all that G had done for Moses and
18: 4 "The G of my father was my help,
18: 5 where Moses was encamped at the mountain of G,
18:12 brought a burnt offering and sacrifices to G;
18:12 with Moses' father-in-law in the presence of G.
18:15 "Because the people come to me to inquire of G.
18:16 to them the statutes and instructions of G."
18:19 I will give you counsel, and G be with you!
18:19 You should represent the people before G, H
18:19 and you should bring their cases before G; H
18:21 men who fear G, are trustworthy, Y
18:23 If you do this, and G so commands you,
19: 3 Then Moses went up to G;
19:17 the people out of the camp to meet G.
19:19 Moses would speak and G would answer him
20: 1 Then G spoke all these words:
20: 2 I am the LORD your G, who brought you out of A
20: 5 for I the LORD your G am a jealous God, A
20: 5 for I the LORD your God am a jealous G,
20: 7 of the name of the LORD your G, A
20:10 seventh day is a sabbath to the LORD your G; A
20:12 in the land that the LORD your G is giving you. A
20:19 but do not let G speak to us, or we will die."
20:20 for G has come only to test you and to put the fear
20:21 near to the thick darkness where G was.
21: 6 then his master shall bring him before G. H
21:13 but came about by an act of G,
22: 8 owner of the house shall be brought before G, H
22: 9 the case of both parties shall come before G; H
22: 9 the one whom G condemns shall pay double to
22:20 Whoever sacrifices to any g,
22:28 You shall not revile G, or curse a leader
23:19 into the house of the LORD your G. A
23:25 You shall worship the LORD your G, A
24:10 and they saw the G of Israel. B
24:11 G did not lay his hand on the chief men of
24:11 also they beheld G, and they ate and drank.
24:13 and Moses went up into the mountain of G.
29:45 and I will be their G.
29:46 And they shall know that I am the LORD their G, A
29:46 I am the LORD their G. A
31:18 G finished speaking with Moses on Mount Sinai,
31:18 tablets of stone, written with the finger of G.
32:11 But Moses implored the LORD his G, and said, A
32:16 The tablets were the work of G,
32:16 and the writing was the writing of G,
32:27 the G of Israel, 'Put your sword on your side, B
34: 6 a G merciful and gracious, slow to anger,
34:14 (for you shall worship no other g,
34:14 whose name is Jealous, is a jealous G).
34:23 before the LORD G, the God G
34:23 before the LORD God, the G of Israel. B
34:24 up to appear before the LORD your G three times A
34:26 to the house of the LORD your G. A
34:29 because he had been talking with G.
Lev 2:13 the salt of the covenant with your G;
4:22 that by commandments of the LORD his G ought A
10:17 and G has given it to you that you may remove
11:44 For I am the LORD your G; A
11:45 to be your G; you shall be holy, for I am holy.
18: 2 I am the LORD your G. A
18: 4 I am the LORD your G. A

Lev 18:21 and so profane the name of your G:
18:30 I am the LORD your G. A
19: 2 for I the LORD your G am holy. A
19: 3 I am the LORD your G. A
19: 4 I am the LORD your G. A
19:10 I am the LORD your G. A
19:12 profaning the name of your G: I am the LORD.
19:14 you shall fear your G: I am the LORD. Y
19:25 I am the LORD your G. A
19:31 I am the LORD your G. A
19:32 and you shall fear your G: I am the LORD. Y
19:34 I am the LORD your G. A
19:36 I am the LORD your G, A
20: 7 for I am the LORD your G. A
20:24 I am the LORD your G; A
21: 6 They shall be holy to their G,
21: 6 and not profane the name of their G;
21: 6 the food of their G; therefore they shall be holy.
21: 7 For they are holy to their G,
21: 8 since they offer the food of your G;
21:12 and thus profane the sanctuary of his G;
21:12 for the consecration of the anointing oil of his G is
21:17 a blemish may approach to offer the food of his G.
21:21 he shall not come near to offer the food of his G.
21:22 He may eat the food of his G,
22:25 from a foreigner to offer as food to your G;
22:33 of the land of Egypt to be your G:
23:14 until you have brought the offering of your G:
23:22 I am the LORD your G. A
23:28 on your behalf before the LORD your G. A
23:40 and you shall rejoice before the LORD your G A
23:43 I am the LORD your G. A
24:15 Anyone who curses G shall bear the sin.
24:22 for I am the LORD your G. A
25:17 but you shall fear your G; Y
25:17 for I am the LORD your G. A
25:36 but fear your G; let them live with you. Y
25:38 I am the LORD your G, A
25:38 to give you the land of Canaan, to be your G.
25:43 over them with harshness, but shall fear your G. Y
25:55 I am the LORD your G. A
26: 1 for I am the LORD your G. A
26:12 And I will walk among you, and will be your G,
26:13 I am the LORD your G who brought you out of A
26:44 for I am the LORD their G; A
26:45 to be their G: I am the LORD.
Nu 6: 7 because their consecration to G is upon the head.
10: 9 be remembered before the LORD your G and A
10:10 on your behalf before the LORD your G: A
10:10 I am the LORD your G. A
12:13 And Moses cried to the LORD, "O G,
15:40 and you shall be holy to your G.
15:41 I am the LORD your G, who brought you out of A
15:41 to be your G: I am the LORD your God.
15:41 I am the LORD your G. A
16: 9 that the G of Israel has separated you from B
16:22 They fell on their faces, and said, "O G,
16:22 and said, "O God, the G of the spirits of all flesh,
21: 5 The people spoke against G and against Moses,
22: 9 G came to Balaam and said,
22:10 Balaam said to G, "King Balak son of Zippor
22:12 G said to Balaam, "You shall not go with them;
22:18 not go beyond the command of the LORD my G, A
22:20 That night G came to Balaam and said to him,
22:38 The word G puts in my mouth,
23: 4 Then G met Balaam; and Balaam said to him,
23: 8 How can I curse whom G has not cursed?
23:19 G is not a human being,
23:21 The LORD their G is with them, A
23:22 G, who brings them out of Egypt,
23:23 of Jacob and Israel, 'See what G has done!'
23:27 perhaps it will please G that you may curse them
24: 2 Then the spirit of G came upon him, U
24: 4 the oracle of one who hears the words of G,
24: 8 G who brings him out of Egypt,
24:16 the words of G, and knows the knowledge of
24:23 "Alas, who shall live when G does this?
25:13 because he was zealous for his G,
27:16 the G of the spirits of all flesh,
Dt 1: 6 The LORD our G spoke to us at Horeb, A
1:10 The LORD your G has multiplied you, A
1:11 May the LORD, the G of your ancestors, F
1:19 Then, just as the LORD our G had ordered us, A
1:20 which the LORD our G is giving us. A
1:21 See, the LORD your G has given the land to you; A
1:21 the G of your ancestors, has promised you; F
1:25 a good land that the LORD our G is giving us." A
1:26 against the command of the LORD your G; A
1:30 The LORD your G, who goes before you, A
1:31 you saw how the LORD your G carried you, A
1:32 you have no trust in the LORD your G, A
1:41 just as the LORD our G commanded us." A
2: 7 Surely the LORD your G has blessed you A
2: 7 These forty years the LORD your G has been A
2:29 into the land that the LORD our G is giving us." A
2:30 for the LORD your G had hardened his spirit A
2:33 the LORD our G gave him over to us; A
2:36 The LORD our G gave everything to us. A
2:37 just as the LORD our G had charged. A
3: 3 the LORD our G also handed over to us King Og A
3:18 LORD your G has given you this land to occupy, A
3:20 the land that the LORD your G is giving them A
3:21 the LORD your G has done to these two kings; A
3:22 for it is the LORD your G who fights for you." A
3:24 what g in heaven or on earth can perform deeds
4: 1 the G of your ancestors, is giving you. F
4: 2 the LORD your G with which I am charging you. A

***GOD** distinguishes the words translated "God" and "god" from the compound name "Lord GOD," where GOD represents the name *Yahweh.* For this name see the heading **†GOD** on pages 541-42.

Dt 4: 3 how the LORD your G destroyed from A
4: 4 to the LORD your G are all alive today. A
4: 5 See, just as the LORD my G has charged me, A
4: 7 For what other great nation has a g so near to it as
4: 7 near to it as the LORD our G is whenever we call A
4:10 how you once stood before the LORD your G A
4:19 things that the LORD your G has allotted to all A
4:21 the LORD your G is giving for your possession. A
4:23 the covenant that the LORD your G made A
4:23 that the LORD your G has forbidden you. A
4:24 LORD your G is a devouring fire, a jealous God. A
4:24 LORD your God is a devouring fire, a jealous G.
4:25 in the sight of the LORD your G, A
4:29 From there you will seek the LORD your G, A
4:30 you will return to the LORD your G A
4:31 Because the LORD your G is a merciful God, A
4:31 Because the LORD your God is a merciful G,
4:32 ever since the day that G created human beings on
4:33 the voice of a g speaking out of a fire,
4:34 Or has any g ever attempted to go and take
4:34 as the LORD your G did for you in Egypt A
4:35 that you would acknowledge that the LORD is G;
4:39 to heart that the LORD is G in heaven above and
4:40 that the LORD your G is giving you for all time. A
5: 2 LORD our G made a covenant with us at Horeb. A
5: 6 I am the LORD your G, who brought you out of A
5: 9 for I the LORD your G am a jealous God, A
5: 9 for I the LORD your God am a jealous G,
5:11 of the name of the LORD your G, A
5:12 as the LORD your G commanded you. A
5:14 seventh day is a sabbath to the LORD your G; A
5:15 the LORD your G brought you out from there A
5:15 therefore the LORD your G commanded you A
5:16 as the LORD your G commanded you, A
5:16 in the land that the LORD your G is giving you. A
5:24 the LORD our G has shown us his glory A
5:24 Today we have seen that G may speak to someone
5:25 we hear the voice of the LORD our G any longer, A
5:26 the voice of the living G speaking out of fire, N
5:27 and hear all that the LORD our G will say. A
5:27 tell us everything that the LORD our G tells you, A
5:32 to do as the LORD your G has commanded you; A
5:33 that the LORD your G has commanded you, A
6: 1 that the LORD your G charged me to teach you A
6: 2 the LORD your G all the days of your life, A
6: 3 the G of your ancestors, has promised you. F
6: 4 The LORD is our G, the LORD alone.
6: 5 the LORD your G with all your heart, A
6:10 the LORD your G has brought you into the land A
6:13 The LORD your G you shall fear; A
6:15 because the LORD your G, A
6:15 who is present with you, is a jealous G.
6:15 The anger of the LORD your G would be kindled A
6:16 Do not put the LORD your G to the test, A
6:17 the commandments of the LORD your G, A
6:20 that the LORD our G has commanded you?" A
6:24 to fear the LORD our G, for our lasting good, A
6:25 before the LORD our G, A
7: 1 When the LORD your G brings you into the land A
7: 2 when the LORD your G gives them over to you A
7: 6 For you are a people holy to the LORD your G; A
7: 6 the LORD your G has chosen you out of all A
7: 9 Know therefore that the LORD your G is God, A
7: 9 Know therefore that the LORD your God is G,
7: 9 the faithful G who maintains covenant loyalty
7:12 the LORD your G will maintain with you A
7:16 the peoples that the LORD your G is giving over A
7:18 Just remember what the LORD your G did A
7:19 by which the LORD your G brought you out. A
7:19 The LORD your G will do the same to all A
7:20 the LORD your G will send the pestilence A
7:21 Have no dread of them, for the LORD your G, A
7:21 is a great and awesome G.
7:22 The LORD your G will clear away these nations A
7:23 the LORD your G will give them over to you, A
7:25 for it is abhorrent to the LORD your G. A
8: 2 the LORD your G has led you these forty years A
8: 5 a child so the LORD your G disciplines you. A
8: 6 keep the commandments of the LORD your G, A
8: 7 LORD your G is bringing you into a good land, A
8:10 and bless the LORD your G for the good land A
8:11 that you do not forget the LORD your G, A
8:14 forgetting the LORD your G, A
8:18 But remember the LORD your G, A
8:19 the LORD your G and follow other gods to serve A
8:20 not obey the voice of the LORD your G. A
9: 3 the LORD your G is the one who crosses over A
9: 4 the LORD your G thrusts them out before you, A
9: 5 the LORD your G is dispossessing them A
9: 6 that the LORD your G is A
9: 7 how you provoked the LORD your G to wrath in A
9:10 the two stone tablets written with the finger of G;
9:16 the LORD your G, by casting for yourselves A
9:23 against the command of the LORD your G, A
10: 9 as the LORD your G promised him.) A
10:12 what does the LORD your G require of you? A
10:12 Only to fear the LORD your G, A
10:12 to serve the LORD your G with all your heart A
10:13 to keep the commandments of the LORD your G A
10:14 of heavens belong to the LORD your G, A
10:17 LORD your G is God of gods and Lord of lords, A
10:17 LORD your God is G of gods and Lord of lords,
10:17 the great G, mighty and awesome,
10:20 You shall fear the LORD your G; A
10:21 He is your praise; he is your G,
10:22 the LORD your G has made you as numerous as A
11: 1 You shall love the LORD your G, therefore, A

Dt 11: 2 or seen the discipline of the LORD your G), A
11:12 a land that the LORD your G looks after. A
11:12 The eyes of the LORD your G are always on it, A
11:13 loving the LORD your G, A
11:22 loving the LORD your G, A
11:25 the LORD your G will put the fear and dread A
11:27 the commandments of the LORD your G A
11:28 the commandments of the LORD your G, A
11:29 the LORD your G has brought you into the land A
11:31 the land that the LORD your G is giving you, A
12: 1 the land that the LORD, the G of your ancestors, F
12: 4 not worship the LORD your G in such ways. A
12: 5 the place that the LORD your G will choose out A
12: 7 in the presence of the LORD your G, A
12: 7 in which the LORD your G has blessed you. A
12: 9 that the LORD your G is giving you. A
12:10 in the land that the LORD your G is allotting A
12:11 to the place that the LORD your G will choose as A
12:12 And you shall rejoice before the LORD your G, A
12:15 that the LORD your G has given you; A
12:18 in the presence of the LORD your G at the place A
12:18 at the place that the LORD your G will choose, A
12:18 rejoicing in the presence of the LORD your G A
12:20 When the LORD your G enlarges your territory, A
12:21 If the place where the LORD your G will choose A
12:27 on the altar of the LORD your G; A
12:27 beside the altar of the LORD your G, A
12:28 and right in the sight of the LORD your G. A
12:29 When the LORD your G has cut off before you A
12:31 You must not do the same for the LORD your G, A
13: 3 for the LORD your G is testing you, A
13: 3 the LORD your G with all your heart and soul. A
13: 4 The LORD your G you shall follow, A
13: 5 against the LORD your G— A
13: 5 in which the LORD your G commanded you A
13:10 to turn you away from the LORD your G, A
13:12 of the towns that the LORD your G is giving you A
13:16 as a whole burnt offering to the LORD your G. A
13:18 if you obey the voice of the LORD your G A
13:18 in the sight of the LORD your G. A
14: 1 You are children of the LORD your G. A
14: 2 For you are a people holy to the LORD your G; A
14:21 For you are a people holy to the LORD your G. A
14:23 In the presence of the LORD your G, A
14:23 you may learn to fear the LORD your G always. A
14:24 But if, when the LORD your G has blessed you, A
14:24 the place where the LORD your G will choose A
14:25 to the place that the LORD your G will choose; A
14:26 in the presence of the LORD your G, A
14:29 the LORD your G may bless you in all the work A
15: 4 the LORD your G is giving you as a possession A
15: 5 if only you will obey the LORD your G A
15: 6 When the LORD your G has blessed you, A
15: 7 the land that the LORD your G is giving you, A
15:10 the LORD your G will bless you in all your work A
15:14 with which the LORD your G has blessed you. A
15:15 and the LORD your G redeemed you; A
15:18 LORD your G will bless you in all that you do. A
15:19 flock you shall consecrate to the LORD your G; A
15:20 in the presence of the LORD your G year by year A
15:21 you shall not sacrifice it to the LORD your G; A
16: 1 by keeping the passover for the LORD your G, A
16: 1 the LORD your G brought you out of Egypt A
16: 2 the passover sacrifice for the LORD your G, A
16: 5 that the LORD your G is giving you. A
16: 6 at the place that the LORD your G will choose as A
16: 7 at the place that the LORD your G will choose; A
16: 8 be a solemn assembly for the LORD your G, A
16:10 the festival of weeks for the LORD your G, A
16:10 that you have received from the LORD your G. A
16:11 Rejoice before the LORD your G— A
16:11 at the place that the LORD your G will choose A
16:15 the festival for the LORD your G at the place A
16:15 for the LORD your G will bless you A
16:16 before the LORD your G at the place A
16:17 according to the blessing of the LORD your G A
16:18 that the LORD your G is giving you, A
16:20 the land that the LORD your G is giving you. A
16:21 the altar that you make for the LORD your G; A
16:22 things that the LORD your G hates. A
17: 1 to the LORD your G an ox or a sheep that has A
17: 1 for that is abhorrent to the LORD your G. A
17: 2 that the LORD your G is giving you, A
17: 2 in the sight of the LORD your G, A
17: 8 to the place that the LORD your G will choose, A
17:12 to minister there to the LORD your G, A
17:14 the land that the LORD your G is giving you, A
17:15 a king whom the LORD your G will choose. A
17:19 so that he may learn to fear the LORD his G, A
18: 5 For the LORD your G has chosen Levi out A
18: 7 he may minister in the name of the LORD his G, A
18: 9 the land that the LORD your G is giving you, A
18:12 the LORD your G is driving them out before you. A
18:13 remain completely loyal to the LORD your G. A
18:14 the LORD your G does not permit you to do so. A
18:15 The LORD your G will raise up for you a prophet A
18:16 This is what you requested of the LORD your G A
18:16 "If I hear the voice of the LORD my G any more, A
19: 1 When the LORD your G has cut off A
19: 1 the LORD your G is giving you, A
19: 2 that the LORD your G is giving you to possess. A
19: 3 that the LORD your G gives you as a possession, A
19: 8 If the LORD your G enlarges your territory, A
19: 9 by loving the LORD your G and walking always A
19:10 the LORD your G is giving you as an inheritance, A
19:14 that the LORD your G is giving you to possess. A
20: 1 for the LORD your G is with you, A

Dt 20: 4 for it is the LORD your G who goes with you, A
20:13 when the LORD your G gives it into your hand, A
20:14 which the LORD your G has given you. A
20:16 the LORD your G is giving you as an inheritance, A
20:17 just as the LORD your G has commanded, A
20:18 and you thus sin against the LORD your G. A
21: 1 that the LORD your G is giving you to possess, A
21: 5 the LORD your G has chosen them to minister A
21:10 and the LORD your G hands them over to you A
21:23 the LORD your G is giving you for possession. A
22: 5 such things is abhorrent to the LORD your G. A
23: 5 (Yet the LORD your G refused to heed Balaam; A
23: 5 the LORD your G turned the curse into a blessing A
23: 5 because the LORD your G loved you.) A
23:14 the LORD your G travels along with your camp, A
23:18 into the house of the LORD your G in payment A
23:18 both of these are abhorrent to the LORD your G. A
23:20 so that the LORD your G may bless you A
23:21 If you make a vow to the LORD your G, A
23:21 the LORD your G will surely require it of you, A
23:23 as you have freely vowed to the LORD your G A
24: 4 the LORD your G is giving you as a possession. A
24: 9 Remember what the LORD your G did to Miriam A
24:13 it will be to your credit before the LORD your G. A
24:18 and the LORD your G redeemed you from there; A
24:19 so that the LORD your G may bless you A
25:15 in the land that the LORD your G is giving you. A
25:16 are abhorrent to the LORD your G. A
25:18 behind you; he did not fear G.
25:19 when the LORD your G has given you rest A
25:19 the LORD your G is giving you as an inheritance A
26: 1 into the land that the LORD your G is giving you A
26: 2 the land that the LORD your G is giving you, A
26: 2 to the place that the LORD your G will choose as A
26: 3 the LORD your G that I have come into the land A
26: 4 down before the altar of the LORD your G, A
26: 5 before the LORD your G: A
26: 7 to the LORD, the G of our ancestors; F
26:10 before the LORD your G and bow down before A
26:10 and bow down before the LORD your G. A
26:11 the bounty that the LORD your G has given A
26:13 then you shall say before the LORD your G: A
26:14 I have obeyed the LORD my G, A
26:16 the LORD your G is commanding you A
26:17 obtained the LORD's agreement: to be your G;
26:19 for you to be a people holy to the LORD your G, A
27: 2 the land that the LORD your G is giving you, A
27: 3 the land that the LORD your G is giving you, A
27: 3 as the LORD, the G of your ancestors, F
27: 5 an altar there to the LORD your G, A
27: 6 the altar of the LORD your G of unhewn stones. A
27: 6 up burnt offerings on it to the LORD your G, A
27: 7 rejoicing before the LORD your G. A
27: 9 the people of the LORD your G. A
27:10 Therefore obey the LORD your G, A
28: 1 If you will only obey the LORD your G, A
28: 1 the LORD your G will set you high above all A
28: 2 if you obey the LORD your G: A
28: 8 in the land that the LORD your G is giving you. A
28: 9 of the LORD your G and walk in his ways. A
28:13 the commandments of the LORD your G, A
28:15 But if you will not obey the LORD your G A
28:45 because you did not obey the LORD your G, A
28:47 the LORD your G joyfully and with gladness A
28:52 the land that the LORD your G has given you. A
28:53 the LORD your G has given you. A
28:58 and awesome name, the LORD your G, A
28:62 because you did not obey the LORD your G. A
29: 6 that you may know that I am the LORD your G. A
29:10 all of you, before the LORD your G— A
29:12 into the covenant of the LORD your G, sworn by A
29:12 the LORD your G is making with you today; A
29:13 and that he may be your G,
29:14 with us today before the LORD our G, A
29:18 from the LORD our G to serve the gods A
29:25 covenant of the LORD, the G of their ancestors, F
29:29 The secret things belong to the LORD our G, A
30: 1 where the LORD your G has driven you, A
30: 2 and return to the LORD your G, A
30: 3 then the LORD your G will restore your fortunes A
30: 3 the LORD your G has scattered you. A
30: 4 from there the LORD your G will gather you, A
30: 5 The LORD your G will bring you into the land A
30: 6 the LORD your G will circumcise your heart and A
30: 6 the LORD your G with all your heart and A
30: 7 The LORD your G will put all these curses A
30: 9 the LORD your G will make you abundantly A
30:10 when you obey the LORD your G A
30:10 to the LORD your G with all your heart and A
30:16 the commandments of the LORD your G A
30:16 by loving the LORD your G, A
30:16 and the LORD your G will bless you in the land A
30:20 the LORD your G, obeying him, and holding fast A
31: 3 The LORD your G himself will cross over A
31: 6 it is the LORD your G who goes with you; A
31:11 to appear before the LORD your G at the place A
31:12 the LORD your G and to observe diligently all A
31:13 may hear and learn to fear the LORD your G, A
31:17 not these troubles come upon us because our G is
31:26 the ark of the covenant of the LORD your G; A
32: 3 ascribe greatness to our G!
32: 4 faithful G, without deceit, just and upright is he;
32:12 no foreign g was with him.
32:15 He abandoned G who made him,
32:17 They sacrificed to demons, not G,
32:18 you forgot the G who gave you birth.
32:21 They made me jealous with what is no g,

*GOD distinguishes the words translated "God" and "god" from the compound name "Lord GOD," where GOD represents the name *Yahweh*. For this name see the heading †GOD on pages 541-42.

Dt 32:39 there is no g besides me.
33: 1 the blessing with which Moses, the man of G, D
33:12 the High G surrounds him all day long—
33:26 There is none like G, O Jeshurun,
Jos 1: 9 the LORD your G is with you wherever you go." A
1:11 that the LORD your G gives you to possess.' " A
1:13 LORD your G is providing you a place of rest, A
1:15 of the land that the LORD your G is giving them. A
1:17 Only may the LORD your G be with you, A
2:11 The LORD your G is indeed God in heaven A
2:11 The LORD your God is indeed G in heaven
3: 3 the covenant of the LORD your G being carried A
3: 9 near and hear the words of the LORD your G." A
3:10 the living G who without fail will drive out from N
4: 5 "Pass on before the ark of the LORD your G into A
4:23 For the LORD your G dried up the waters of A
4:23 as the LORD your G did to the Red Sea, A
4:24 so that you may fear the LORD your G forever." A
7:13 for thus says the LORD, the G of Israel, B
7:19 to the LORD G of Israel and make confession BG
7:20 who sinned against the LORD G of Israel. BG
8: 7 for the LORD your G will give it into your hand. A
8:30 Mount Ebal an altar to the LORD, the G of Israel, B
9: 9 because of the name of the LORD your G; A
9:18 to them by the LORD, the G of Israel. B
9:19 G of Israel, and now we must not touch them. B
9:23 and drawers of water for the house of my G." C
9:24 LORD your G had commanded his servant Moses A
10:19 LORD your G has given them into your hand." A
10:40 as the LORD G of Israel commanded. BG
10:42 because the LORD G of Israel fought for Israel. BG
13:14 to the LORD G of Israel are their inheritance, BG
13:33 the LORD G of Israel is their inheritance, BG
14: 6 the man of G in Kadesh-barnea concerning you D
14: 8 yet I wholeheartedly followed the LORD my G. A
14: 9 wholeheartedly followed the LORD my G.' A
14:14 the LORD, the G of Israel. B
18: 3 the G of your ancestors, has given you? F
18: 6 for you here before the LORD our G. A
22: 3 to keep the charge of the LORD your G. A
22: 4 the LORD your G has given rest to your kindred, A
22: 5 to love the LORD your G, A
22:16 that you have committed against the G of Israel B
22:19 an altar other than the altar of the LORD our G. A
22:22 "The LORD, G of gods! The LORD, G of gods!
22:24 to do with the LORD, the G of Israel? B
22:29 the altar of the LORD our G that stands A
22:33 and the Israelites blessed G and spoke no more
22:34 "it is a witness between us that the LORD is G."
23: 3 the LORD your G has done to all these nations A
23: 3 it is the LORD your G who has fought for you. A
23: 5 LORD your G will push them back before you, A
23: 5 as the LORD your G promised you. A
23: 8 but hold fast to the LORD your G, A
23:10 since it is the LORD your G who fights for you, A
23:11 therefore, to love the LORD your G. A
23:13 know assuredly that the LORD your G will A
23:13 that the LORD your G has given you. A
23:14 that the LORD your G promised concerning you; A
23:15 the good things that the LORD your G promised A
23:15 that the LORD your G has given you. A
23:16 the covenant of the LORD your G, A
24: 1 and they presented themselves before G. H
24: 2 "Thus says the LORD, the G of Israel: B
24:17 for it is the LORD our G who brought us A
24:18 we also will serve the LORD, for he is our G."
24:19 "You cannot serve the LORD, for he is a holy G.
24:19 for he is a holy God. He is a jealous G;
24:23 incline your hearts to the LORD, the G of Israel." B
24:24 "The LORD our G we will serve, A
24:26 in the book of the law of G; P
24:27 if you deal falsely with your G."
Jdg 1: 7 as I have done, so G has paid me back."
2:12 abandoned the LORD, the G of their ancestors, F
3: 7 forgetting the LORD their G, A
3:20 and said, "I have a message from G for you."
4: 6 and said to him, "The LORD, the G of Israel, B
4:23 that day G subdued King Jabin of Canaan before
5: 3 I will make melody to the LORD, the G of Israel. B
5: 5 before the LORD, the G of Israel. B
6: 8 "Thus says the LORD, the G of Israel: B
6:10 'I am the LORD your G; A
6:20 The angel of G said to him, Z
6:26 and build an altar to the LORD your G on the top A
6:31 If he is a g, let him contend for himself,
6:36 Then Gideon said to G, "In order
6:39 to G, "Do not let your anger burn
6:40 And G did so that night.
7:14 into his hand G has given Midian and all
8: 3 G has given into your hands the captains
8:33 making Baal-berith their g.
8:34 Israelites did not remember the LORD their G, A
9: 7 you lords of Shechem, so that G may listen to you.
9:23 But G sent an evil spirit between Abimelech and
9:27 Then they went into the temple of their g,
9:56 Thus G repaid Abimelech for
9:57 and G also made all the wickedness of the people
10:10 because we have abandoned our G
11:21 Then the LORD, the G of Israel, B
11:23 So now the LORD, the G of Israel, B
11:24 not possess what your g Chemosh gives you
11:24 the LORD our G has conquered for our benefit? A
13: 5 for the boy shall be a nazirite to G from birth.
13: 6 "A man of G came to me, D
13: 6 his appearance was like that of an angel of G, Z
13: 7 for the boy shall be a nazirite to G from birth to
13: 8 let the man of G whom you sent come to us D

Jdg 13: 9 G listened to Manoah, and the angel
13: 9 the angel of G came again to the woman Z
13:22 "We shall surely die, for we have seen G."
15:19 So G split open the hollow place that is at Lehi,
16:17 a nazirite to G from my mother's womb.
16:23 a great sacrifice to their g Dagon, and to rejoice;
16:23 for they said, "Our g has given Samson our enemy
16:24 When the people saw him, they praised their g;
16:24 "Our g has given our enemy into our hand,
16:28 and strengthen me only this once, O G, so that
18: 5 "Inquire of G that we may know whether
18:10 G has indeed given it into your hands—
18:31 as long as the house of G was at Shiloh. C
20: 2 in the assembly of the people of G,
20:18 where they inquired of G,
20:27 of the covenant of G was there in those days,
21: 2 and sat there until evening before G, H
21: 3 They said, "O LORD, the G of Israel, B
Ru 1:16 be my people, and your G my G.
2:12 the G of Israel, under whose wings you have B
1Sa 1:17 the G of Israel grant the petition you have made B
2: 1 my strength is exalted in my G.
2: 2 there is no Rock like our G.
2: 3 for the LORD is a G of knowledge,
2:27 A man of G came to Eli and said to him, D
2:30 Therefore the LORD the G of Israel declares: B
3: 3 the lamp of G had not yet gone out,
3: 3 where the ark of G was. J
3:13 because his sons were blaspheming G,
3:17 May G do so to you and more also,
4: 4 were there with the ark of the covenant of G.
4:11 The ark of G was captured; J
4:13 for his heart trembled for the ark of G. J
4:17 are dead, and the ark of G has been captured." J
4:18 When he mentioned the ark of G, J
4:19 heard the news that the ark of G was captured, J
4:21 because the ark of G had been captured and J
4:22 for the ark of G has been captured." J
5: 1 When the Philistines captured the ark of G, J
5: 2 the Philistines took the ark of G and brought it J
5: 7 ark of the G of Israel must not remain with us; BJ
5: 7 for his hand is heavy on us and on our g Dagon."
5: 8 shall we do with the ark of the G of Israel?" BJ
5: 8 "Let the ark of G be moved on to us." J
5: 8 they moved the ark of the G of Israel to Gath. BJ
5:10 they sent the ark of the G of Israel to Ekron. BJ
5:10 But when the ark of G came to Ekron, J
5:10 around to us the ark of the G of Israel to kill us BJ
5:11 and said, "Send away the ark of the G of Israel, BJ
5:11 The hand of G was very heavy there; S
6: 3 "If you send away the ark of the G of Israel, BJ
6: 5 and give glory to the G of Israel; B
6:20 to stand before the LORD, this holy G?
7: 8 not cease to cry out to the LORD our G for us, A
9: 6 said to him, "There is a man of G in this town; D
9: 7 and there is no present to bring to the man of G. D
9: 8 I will give it to the man of G, to tell us our way." D
9: 9 anyone who went to inquire of G would say,
9:10 So they went to the town where the man of G D
9:27 that I may make known to you the word of G." L
10: 3 up to G at Bethel will meet you there,
10: 7 do whatever you see fit to do, for G is with you.
10: 9 G gave him another heart;
10:10 and the spirit of G possessed him, U
10:18 the G of Israel, 'I brought up Israel out of Egypt, B
10:19 But today you have rejected your G,
10:26 went warriors whose hearts G had touched.
11: 6 And the spirit of G came upon Saul in power U
12: 9 But they forgot the LORD their G; A
12:12 though the LORD your G was your king. A
12:14 over you will follow the LORD your G, it will A
12:19 "Pray to the LORD your G for your servants, A
13:13 not kept the commandment of the LORD your G, A
14:18 Saul said to Ahijah, "Bring the ark of G here." J
14:18 at that time the ark of G went with the Israelites. J
14:36 But the priest said, "Let us draw near to G here."
14:37 So Saul inquired of G, "Shall I go down after
14:41 Then Saul said, "O LORD G of Israel, BG
14:41 O LORD G of Israel, give Urim; BG
14:44 Saul said, "G do so to me and more also;
14:45 for he has worked with G today."
15:15 to sacrifice to the LORD your G; A
15:21 to sacrifice to the LORD your G in Gilgal." A
15:30 so that I may worship the LORD your G." A
16:15 "See now, an evil spirit from G is tormenting you.
16:16 and when the evil spirit from G is upon you,
16:23 whenever the evil spirit from G came upon Saul,
17:26 that he should defy the armies of the living G?" N
17:36 since he has defied the armies of the living G." N
17:45 the G of the armies of Israel,
17:46 all the earth may know that there is a G in Israel,
18:10 next day an evil spirit from G rushed upon Saul,
19:20 spirit of G came upon the messengers of Saul, U
19:23 and the spirit of G came upon him. U
20:12 "By the LORD, the G of Israel! B
22: 3 until I know what G will do for me."
22:13 and by inquiring of G for him,
22:15 the first time that I have inquired of G for him?
23: 7 And Saul said, "G has given him into my hand;
23:10 David said, "O LORD, the G of Israel, B
23:11 O LORD, the G of Israel, I beseech you, B
25:22 G do so to David and more also,
25:29 of the living under the care of the LORD your G; A
25:32 the G of Israel, who sent you to meet me today! B
25:34 For as surely as the LORD the G of Israel lives, B
26: 8 "G has given your enemy into your hand today;
28:15 and G has turned away from me

1Sa 29: 9 as blameless in my sight as an angel of G; Z
30: 6 David strengthened himself in the LORD his G. A
30:15 "Swear to me by G that you will not kill me,
2Sa 2:27 Joab said, "As G lives, if you had not spoken,
3: 9 So may G do to Abner and so may he add to it!
3:35 but David swore, saying, "So may G do to me,
5:10 for the LORD, the G of hosts, was with him. Q
6: 2 to bring up from there the ark of G, J
6: 3 They carried the ark of G on a new cart, J
6: 4 with the ark of G; and Ahio went in front J
6: 6 Uzzah reached out his hand to the ark of G J
6: 7 against Uzzah; and G struck him there
6: 7 and he died there beside the ark of G. J
6:12 because of the ark of G." J
6:12 So David went and brought up the ark of G from J
7: 2 but the ark of G stays in a tent." J
7:22 Therefore you are great, O LORD G; G
7:22 and there is no G besides you,
7:23 on earth whose G went to redeem it as a people,
7:24 and you, O LORD, became their G.
7:25 O LORD G, as for the word G
7:26 'The LORD of hosts is G over Israel';
7:27 For you, O LORD of hosts, the G of Israel, B
7:28 And now, O Lord GOD, you are G,
9: 3 of Saul to whom I may show the kindness of G?"
10:12 and for the cities of our G;
12: 7 Thus says the LORD, the G of Israel: B
12:16 David therefore pleaded with G for the child;
14:11 may the king keep the LORD your G in mind, A
14:13 a thing against the people of G?
14:14 But G will not take away a life;
14:16 both me and my son off from the heritage of G.'
14:17 for my lord the king is like the angel of G, Z
14:17 The LORD your G be with you!" A
14:20 the wisdom of the angel of G to know all things Z
15:24 carrying the ark of the covenant of G.
15:24 They set down the ark of G, J
15:25 "Carry the ark of G back into the city. J
15:29 So Zadok and Abiathar carried the ark of G back J
15:32 where G was worshiped, Hushai the Archite came
16:23 as if one consulted the oracle of G;
18:28 and said, "Blessed be the LORD your G, A
19:13 So may G do to me, and more,
19:27 But my lord the king is like the angel of G; Z
21:14 After that, G heeded supplications for the land.
22: 3 my G, my rock, in whom I take refuge, my shield
22: 7 upon the LORD; to my G I called.
22:22 and have not wickedly departed from my G.
22:30 and by my G I can leap over a wall.
22:31 This G—his way is perfect;
22:32 For who is G, but the LORD?
22:32 And who is a rock, except our G?
22:33 The G who has girded me
22:47 Blessed be my rock, and exalted be my G,
22:48 the G who gave me vengeance and brought
23: 1 the oracle of the man whom G exalted,
23: 1 the anointed of the G of Jacob, V
23: 3 The G of Israel has spoken, B
23: 3 over people justly, ruling in the fear of G,
23: 5 Is not my house like this with G?
24: 3 "May the LORD your G increase the number of A
24:23 the LORD your G respond favorably to you." A
24:24 not offer burnt offerings to the LORD my G A
1Ki 1:17 you swore to your servant by the LORD your G, A
1:30 as I swore to you by the LORD, the G of Israel, B
1:36 May the LORD, the G of my lord the king,
1:47 saying, 'May G make the name
1:48 'Blessed be the LORD, the G of Israel, B
2: 3 and keep the charge of the LORD your G, A
2:23 "So may G do to me, and more also,
3: 5 and G said, "Ask what I should give you."
3: 7 And now, O LORD my G, A
3:11 G said to him, "Because you have asked this,
3:28 they perceived that the wisdom of G was in him,
4:29 G gave Solomon very great wisdom, discernment,
5: 3 a house for the name of the LORD his G A
5: 4 the LORD my G has given me rest on every side; A
5: 5 a house for the name of the LORD my G, A
8:15 He said, "Blessed be the LORD, the G of Israel, B
8:17 house for the name of the LORD, the G of Israel. B
8:20 house for the name of the LORD, the G of Israel. B
8:23 He said, "O LORD, G of Israel, B
8:23 there is no G like you in heaven above or
8:25 Therefore, O LORD, G of Israel, B
8:26 O G of Israel, let your word be confirmed, B
8:27 "But will G indeed dwell on the earth?
8:28 O LORD my G, heeding the cry and the prayer A
8:57 The LORD our G be with us, A
8:59 be near to the LORD our G day and night, A
8:60 of the earth may know that the LORD is G;
8:61 to the LORD our G, walking in his statutes A
8:65 before the LORD our G, seven days. A
9: 9 'Because they have forsaken the LORD their G, A
10: 9 Blessed be the LORD your G, A
10:24 which G had put into his mind.
11: 4 and his heart was not true to the LORD his G, A
11: 9 the G of Israel, who had appeared to him twice, B
11:23 G raised up another adversary against Solomon,
11:31 for thus says the LORD, the G of Israel, "See, B
11:33 Chemosh the g of Moab, and Milcom the god of
11:33 and Milcom the g of the Ammonites,
12:22 word of G came to Shemaiah the man of God: L
12:22 word of God came to Shemaiah the man of G: D
13: 1 a man of G came out of Judah by the word of D
13: 4 the king heard what the man of G cried out D
13: 5 according to the sign that the man of G had D
13: 6 The king said to the man of G, D

*GOD distinguishes the words translated "God" and "god" from the compound name "Lord GOD," where GOD represents the name *Yahweh*. For this name see the heading †GOD on pages 541-42.

1Ki 13: 6 "Entreat now the favor of the LORD your **G**, A
13: 6 So the man of **G** entreated the LORD; D
13: 7 Then the king said to the man of **G**, D
13: 8 But the man of **G** said to the king, D
13:11 that the man of **G** had done that day in Bethel; D
13:12 the man of **G** who came from Judah had gone. D
13:14 He went after the man of **G**, D
13:14 "Are you the man of **G** who came from Judah?" D
13:19 Then the man of **G** went back with him, D
13:21 to the man of **G** who came from Judah, D
13:21 that the LORD your **G** commanded you, A
13:23 After the man of **G** had eaten food and D
13:26 "It is the man of **G** who disobeyed the word of D
13:29 The prophet took up the body of the man of **G**, D
13:31 in the grave in which the man of **G** is buried; D
14: 7 'Thus says the LORD, the **G** of Israel: B
14:13 the **G** of Israel, in the house of Jeroboam. B
15: 3 his heart was not true to the LORD his **G**, A
15: 4 the LORD his **G** gave him a lamp in Jerusalem, A
15:30 he provoked the LORD, the **G** of Israel. B
16:13 thus the LORD **G** of Israel to anger with their idols. BG
16:26 provoking the LORD, the **G** of Israel, B
16:33 the LORD, the **G** of Israel, than had all the kings B
17: 1 said to Ahab, "As the LORD the **G** of Israel lives, B
17:12 But she said, "As the LORD your **G** lives, A
17:14 For thus says the LORD the **G** of Israel: B
17:18 "What have you against me, O man of **G**? D
17:20 He cried out to the LORD, "O LORD my **G**, A
17:21 and cried out to the LORD, "O LORD my **G**, A
17:24 "Now I know that you are a man of **G**, D
18:10 As the LORD your **G** lives, A
18:21 If the LORD is **G**, follow him;
18:24 on the name of your **g** and I will call on the name
18:24 the **g** who answers by fire is indeed **G**."
18:25 call on the name of your **g**, but put no fire to it."
18:27 "Cry aloud! Surely he is a **g**;
18:36 "O LORD, **G** of Abraham, Isaac, and Israel,
18:36 let it be known this day that you are **G** in Israel,
18:37 are **G**, and that you have turned their hearts back."
18:39 "The LORD indeed is **G**; the LORD indeed is **G**."
19: 8 and forty nights to Horeb the mount of **G**.
19:10 for the LORD, the **G** of hosts; Q
19:14 for the LORD, the **G** of hosts; Q
20:28 A man of **G** approached and said to the king D
20:28 'The LORD is a **g** of the hills but he is not a **g**
21:10 saying, 'You have cursed **G** and the king.'
21:13 saying, "Naboth cursed **G** and the king."
22:53 he provoked the LORD, the **G** of Israel, to anger, B
2Ki 1: 2 "Go, inquire of Baal-zebub, the **g** of Ekron,
1: 3 because there is no **G** in Israel that you are going
1: 3 that you are going to inquire of Baal-zebub, the **g**
1: 6 Is it because there is no **G** in Israel
1: 6 to inquire of Baal-zebub, the **g** of Ekron?
1: 9 "O man of **G**, the king says, 'Come down.' " D
1:10 "If I am a man of **G**, D
1:11 He went up and said to him, "O man of **G**, D
1:12 But Elijah answered them, "If I am a man of **G**, D
1:12 fire of **G** came down from heaven and consumed
1:13 and entreated him, "O man of **G**, D
1:16 to inquire of Baal-zebub, the **g** of Ekron,—
1:16 is it because there is no **G** in Israel to inquire
2:14 saying, "Where is the LORD, the **G** of Elijah?"
4: 7 She came and told the man of **G**, and he said, D
4: 9 regularly passes our way is a holy man of **G**. D
4:16 She replied, "No, my lord, O man of **G**; D
4:21 up and laid him on the bed of the man of **G**, D
4:22 so that I may quickly go to the man of **G** D
4:25 and came to the man of **G** at Mount Carmel. D
4:25 When the man of **G** saw her coming, D
4:27 When she came to the man of **G** at the mountain, D
4:27 But the man of **G** said, "Let her alone, D
4:40 "O man of **G**, there is death in the pot!" D
4:42 food from the first fruits to the man of **G**: D
5: 7 he tore his clothes and said, "Am I **G**,
5: 8 when Elisha the man of **G** heard that the king D
5:11 stand and call on the name of the LORD his **G**, A
5:14 according to the word of the man of **G**; D
5:15 Then he returned to the man of **G**, D
5:15 that there is no **G** in all the earth except in Israel;
5:17 or sacrifice to any **g** except the LORD.
5:20 the servant of Elisha the man of **G**, thought, D
6: 6 Then the man of **G** said, "Where did it fall?" D
6: 9 But the man of **G** sent word to the king of Israel, D
6:10 to the place of which the man of **G** spoke. D
6:15 When an attendant of the man of **G** rose early D
6:31 "So may **G** do to me, and more,
7: 2 the king leaned said to the man of **G**, D
7:17 as the man of **G** had said when the king came D
7:18 For when the man of **G** had said to the king, D
7:19 the captain had answered the man of **G**, D
8: 2 and did according to the word of the man of **G**; D
8: 4 with Gehazi the servant of the man of **G**, D
8: 7 it was told him, "The man of **G** has come here," D
8: 8 a present with you and go to meet the man of **G**. D
8:11 Then the man of **G** wept. D
9: 6 "Thus says the LORD the **G** of Israel: B
10:31 to follow the law of the LORD the **G** of Israel B
13:19 Then the man of **G** was angry with him, D
14:25 of the LORD, the **G** of Israel, which he spoke B
16: 2 in the sight of the LORD his **G**, A
17: 7 of Israel had sinned against the LORD their **G**, A
17: 9 that were not right against the LORD their **G**. A
17:14 who did not believe in the LORD their **G**. A
17:16 the commandments of the LORD their **G** A
17:19 of the LORD their **G** but walked in the customs A
17:26 do not know the law of the **g** of the land; P
17:26 they do not know the law of the **g** of the land." P
2Ki 17:27 and teach them the law of the **g** of the land." P
17:39 but you shall worship the LORD your **G**; A
18: 5 He trusted in the LORD the **G** of Israel; B
18:12 not obey the voice of the LORD their **G** A
18:22 if you say to me, 'We rely on the LORD our **G**,' A
19: 4 be that the LORD your **G** heard all the words of A
19: 4 king of Assyria has sent to mock the living **G**, N
19: 4 the words that the LORD your **G** has heard; A
19:10 Do not let your **G** on whom you rely deceive you
19:15 "O LORD the **G** of Israel, B
19:15 above the cherubim, you are **G**, you alone, of all
19:16 which he has sent to mock the living **G**. N
19:19 So now, O LORD our **G**, save us, I pray you, A
19:19 that you, O LORD, are **G** alone."
19:20 saying, "Thus says the LORD, the **G** of Israel: B
19:37 he was worshiping in the house of his **g** Nisroch, C
20: 5 the **G** of your ancestor David:
21:12 therefore thus says the LORD, the **G** of Israel, B
21:22 **G** of his ancestors, and did not walk in the way F
22:15 "Thus says the LORD, the **G** of Israel: B
22:18 Thus says the LORD, the **G** of Israel: B
23:16 the man of **G** proclaimed, when Jeroboam stood D
23:16 of the man of **G** who had predicted these things. D
23:17 the tomb of the man of **G** who came from Judah D
23:21 to the LORD your **G** as prescribed in this book A
1Ch 4:10 Jabez called on the **G** of Israel, saying, B
4:10 And **G** granted what he asked.
5:20 for they cried to **G** in the battle,
5:22 Many fell slain, because the war was of **G**.
5:25 transgressed against the **G** of their ancestors, F
5:25 whom **G** had destroyed before them.
5:26 the **G** of Israel stirred up the spirit of King Pul B
6:48 the service of the tabernacle of the house of **G**. C
6:49 that Moses the servant of **G** had commanded.
9:11 of Ahitub, the chief officer of the house of **G**; C
9:13 for the work of the service of the house of **G**. C
9:26 chambers and the treasures of the house of **G**. C
9:27 they would spend the night near the house of **G**; C
11: 2 The LORD your **G** said to you: A
11:19 "My **G** forbid that I should do this.
12:17 the **G** of our ancestors see and give judgment." F
12:18 For your **G** is the one who helps you."
12:22 until there was a great army, like an army of **G**.
13: 2 and if it is the will of the LORD our **G**, A
13: 3 Then let us bring again the ark of our **G** to us; J
13: 5 to bring the ark of **G** from Kiriath-jearim. J
13: 6 to bring up from there the ark of **G**, the LORD, J
13: 7 They carried the ark of **G** on a new cart, J
13: 8 David and all Israel were dancing before **G** H
13:10 and he died there before **G**. H
13:12 David was afraid of **G** that day;
13:12 "How can I bring the ark of **G** into my care?" J
13:14 The ark of **G** remained with the household of J
14:10 David inquired of **G**, "Shall I go up against
14:11 "**G** has burst out against my enemies by my hand,
14:14 When David again inquired of **G**, **G** said to him,
14:15 for **G** has gone out before you to strike down
14:16 David did as **G** had commanded him,
15: 1 a place for the ark of **G** and pitched a tent for it. J
15: 2 but the Levites were to carry the ark of **G**, J
15:12 up the ark of the LORD, the **G** of Israel, B
15:13 the LORD our **G** burst out against us, A
15:14 to bring up the ark of the LORD, the **G** of Israel. B
15:15 Levites carried the ark of **G** on their shoulders J
15:24 were to blow the trumpets before the ark of **G**. J
15:26 because **G** helped the Levites who were carrying
16: 1 They brought in the ark of **G**, J
16: 1 and offerings of well-being before **G**. H
16: 4 to thank, and to praise the LORD, the **G** of Israel. B
16: 6 before the ark of the covenant of **G**.
16:14 He is the LORD our **G**; A
16:35 Say also: "Save us, O **G** of our salvation,
16:36 Blessed be the LORD, the **G** of Israel, B
17: 2 "Do all that you have in mind, for **G** is with you."
17:16 "Who am I, O LORD **G**, and what is my house, G
17:17 even this was a small thing in your sight, O **G**;
17:17 as someone of high rank, O LORD **G**! G
17:20 O LORD, and there is no **G** besides you,
17:21 one nation on the earth whom **G** went to redeem
17:22 and you, O LORD, became their **G**.
17:24 'The LORD of hosts, the **G** of Israel, B
17:24 the God of Israel, is Israel's **G**';
17:25 my **G**, have revealed to your servant
17:26 And now, O LORD, you are **G**,
19:13 for our people and for the cities of our **G**;
21: 7 But **G** was displeased with this thing,
21: 8 David said to **G**, "I have sinned greatly in
21:15 And **G** sent an angel to Jerusalem to destroy it;
21:17 And David said to **G**, "Was it not I who gave
21:17 Let your hand, I pray, O LORD my **G**, A
21:30 but David could not go before it to inquire of **G**,
22: 1 "Here shall be the house of the LORD **G** G
22: 2 for building the house of **G**. C
22: 6 to build a house for the LORD, the **G** of Israel. B
22: 7 to build a house to the name of the LORD my **G**. A
22:11 in building the house of the LORD your **G**, A
22:12 the law of the LORD your **G**. A
22:18 "Is not the LORD your **G** with you? A
22:19 and heart to seek the LORD your **G**. A
22:19 of the LORD **G** so that the ark of the covenant G
22:19 and the holy vessels of **G** may be brought into
23:14 but as for Moses the man of **G**, D
23:25 For David said, "The LORD, the **G** of Israel, B
23:28 and any work for the service of the house of **G**; C
24: 5 of **G** among both the sons of Eleazar and the sons
24:19 as the LORD **G** of Israel had commanded him. BG
25: 5 according to the promise of **G** to exalt him;
1Ch 25: 5 for **G** had given Heman fourteen sons
25: 6 and lyres for the service of the house of **G**. C
26: 5 Peullethai the eighth; for **G** blessed him.
26:20 the treasuries of the house of **G** C
26:32 the Manassites for everything pertaining to **G**
28: 2 for the footstool of our **G**;
28: 3 But **G** said to me, 'You shall not build a house
28: 4 Yet the LORD **G** of Israel chose me BG
28: 8 and in the hearing of our **G**,
28: 8 the commandments of the LORD your **G**; A
28: 9 you, my son Solomon, know the **G** of your father,
28:12 the treasuries of the house of **G**, C
28:20 for the LORD **G**, my God, is with you. G
28:20 for the LORD God, my **G**, is with you.
28:21 the Levites for all the service of the house of **G**; C
29: 1 "My son Solomon, whom alone **G** has chosen,
29: 1 not be for mortals but for the LORD **G**. G
29: 2 So I have provided for the house of my **G**, C
29: 3 of my devotion to the house of my **G** I give it C
29: 3 of my God I give it to the house of my **G**: C
29: 7 service of the house of **G** five thousand talents C
29:10 the **G** of our ancestor Israel, forever and ever.
29:13 And now, our **G**, we give thanks to you
29:16 O LORD our **G**, all this abundance A
29:17 I know, my **G**, that you search the heart,
29:18 O LORD, the **G** of Abraham, Isaac, and Israel,
29:20 "Bless the LORD your **G**." A
29:20 blessed the LORD, the **G** of their ancestors, F
2Ch 1: 1 the LORD his **G** was with him A
1: 4 the ark of **G** up from Kiriath-jearim to the place J
1: 7 That night **G** appeared to Solomon,
1: 8 to **G**, "You have shown great and steadfast love
1: 9 O LORD **G**, let your promise to my father David G
1:11 **G** answered Solomon, "Because this was
2: 4 to build a house for the name of the LORD my **G** A
2: 4 and the appointed festivals of the LORD our **G**, A
2: 5 for our **G** is greater than other gods.
2:12 "Blessed be the LORD **G** of Israel, BG
3: 3 for building the house of **G**: C
4:11 that he did for King Solomon on the house of **G**: C
4:19 the things that were in the house of **G**: C
5: 1 all the vessels in the treasuries of the house of **G**. C
5:14 for the glory of the LORD filled the house of **G**. C
6: 4 he said, "Blessed be the LORD, the **G** of Israel, B
6: 7 house for the name of the LORD, the **G** of Israel. B
6:10 house for the name of the LORD, the **G** of Israel. B
6:14 He said, "O LORD, **G** of Israel, B
6:14 "O LORD, God of Israel, there is no **G** like you,
6:16 Therefore, O LORD, **G** of Israel, B
6:17 Therefore, O LORD, **G** of Israel, B
6:18 "But will **G** indeed reside with mortals on earth?
6:19 and his plea, O LORD my **G**, heeding the cry and A
6:40 Now, O my **G**, let your eyes be open
6:41 "Now rise up, O LORD **G**, G
6:41 Let your priests, O LORD **G**, G
6:42 O LORD **G**, do not reject your anointed one. G
7: 5 king and all the people dedicated the house of **G**. C
7:22 the **G** of their ancestors who brought them out F
8:14 for so David the man of **G** had commanded. D
9: 8 Blessed be the LORD your **G**, A
9: 8 on his throne as king for the LORD your **G**. A
9: 8 Because your **G** loved Israel
9:23 which **G** had put into his mind.
10:15 it was a turn of affairs brought about by **G**
11: 2 of the LORD came to Shemaiah the man of **G**: D
11:16 the LORD **G** of Israel came after them from all BG
11:16 to sacrifice to the LORD, the **G** of their ancestors. F
13: 5 Do you not know that the LORD **G** of Israel BG
13:10 But as for us, the LORD is our **G**,
13:11 for we keep the charge of the LORD our **G**, A
13:12 See, **G** is with us at our head,
13:12 the **G** of your ancestors; for you cannot succeed. F
13:15 **G** defeated Jeroboam and all Israel before Abijah
13:16 and **G** gave them into their hands.
13:18 they relied on the LORD, the **G** of their ancestors. F
14: 2 and right in the sight of the LORD his **G**. A
14: 4 Judah to seek the LORD, the **G** of their ancestors, F
14: 7 because we have sought the LORD our **G**; A
14:11 Asa cried to the LORD his **G**, "O LORD, A
14:11 Help us, O LORD our **G**, for we rely on you, A
14:11 O LORD, you are our **G**;
15: 1 The spirit of **G** came upon Azariah son of Oded. U
15: 3 For a long time Israel was without the true **G**,
15: 4 the **G** of Israel, and sought him, B
15: 6 for **G** troubled them with every sort of distress.
15: 9 when they saw that the LORD his **G** was A
15:12 the **G** of their ancestors, with all their heart and F
15:13 the **G** of Israel, should be put to death, B
15:18 into the house of **G** the votive gifts of his father C
16: 7 and did not rely on the LORD your **G**, A
17: 4 but sought the **G** of his father and walked
18: 5 for **G** will give it into the hand of the king."
18:13 "As the LORD lives, whatever my **G** says,
18:31 **G** drew them away from him,
19: 3 and have set your heart to seek **G**."
19: 4 back to the LORD, the **G** of their ancestors. F
19: 7 of justice with the LORD our **G**, A
20: 6 **G** of our ancestors, are you not God in heaven? F
20: 6 God of our ancestors, are you not **G** in heaven?
20: 7 not, O our **G**, drive out the inhabitants of this land
20:12 O our **G**, will you not execute judgment
20:19 stood up to praise the LORD, the **G** of Israel, B
20:20 in the LORD your **G** and you will be established; A
20:29 of **G** came on all the kingdoms of the countries
20:30 for his **G** gave him rest all around.
20:33 set their hearts upon the **G** of their ancestors. F
21:10 forsaken the LORD, the **G** of his ancestors. F

***GOD** distinguishes the words translated "God" and "god" from the compound name "Lord GOD," where GOD represents the name *Yahweh*. For this name see the heading †**GOD** on pages 541-42.

2Ch 21:12 the G of your father David:
22: 7 by G that the downfall of Ahaziah should come
22:12 hidden in the house of G, C
23: 3 a covenant with the king in the house of G. C
23: 9 which were in the house of G; C
24: 5 from all Israel to repair the house of your G, C
24: 7 had broken into the house of G, C
24: 9 the tax that Moses the servant of G laid on Israel
24:13 restored the house of G to its proper condition C
24:16 and for G and his house.
24:18 of the LORD, the G of their ancestors, and served F
24:20 the spirit of G took possession of Zechariah U
24:20 above the people and said to them, "Thus says G:
24:24 abandoned the LORD, the G of their ancestors. F
24:27 of the rebuilding of the house of G are written C
25: 7 But a man of G came to him and said, "O king, D
25: 8 or G will fling you down before the enemy;
25: 8 for G has power to help or to overthrow."
25: 9 Amaziah said to the man of G, D
25: 9 The man of G answered, "The LORD is able D
25:16 "I know that G has determined to destroy you,
25:24 all the vessels that were found in the house of G, C
26: 5 He set himself to seek G in the days of Zechariah,
26: 5 who instructed him in the fear of G;
26: 5 as he sought the LORD, G made him prosper.
26: 7 G helped him against the Philistines,
26:16 For he was false to the LORD his G, A
26:18 it will bring you no honor from the LORD G." G
27: 6 he ordered his ways before the LORD his G. A
28: 5 the LORD his G gave him into the hand of A
28: 6 abandoned the LORD, the G of their ancestors. F
28: 9 the G of your ancestors, was angry with Judah, F
28:10 against the LORD your G? A
28:24 the utensils of the house of G, C
28:24 and cut in pieces the utensils of the house of G. C
28:25 to anger the LORD, the G of his ancestors. F
29: 5 the LORD, the G of your ancestors, and carry out F
29: 6 in the sight of the LORD our G; A
29: 7 offerings in the holy place to the G of Israel. B
29:10 a covenant with the LORD, the G of Israel, B
29:36 the people rejoiced because of what G had done
30: 1 to keep the passover to the LORD the G of Israel. B
30: 5 to the LORD the G of Israel, at Jerusalem; B
30: 6 return to the LORD, the G of Abraham, Isaac,
30: 7 faithless to the LORD G of their ancestors, FG
30: 8 and serve the LORD your G, A
30: 9 For the LORD your G is gracious and merciful, A
30:12 The hand of G was also on Judah to give them S
30:16 according to the law of Moses the man of G; D
30:19 who set their hearts to seek G,
30:19 the LORD the G of their ancestors, F
30:22 to the LORD the G of their ancestors. F
31: 6 that had been consecrated to the LORD their G, A
31:13 of Azariah the chief officer of the house of G. C
31:14 was in charge of the freewill offerings to G,
31:20 and right and faithful before the LORD his G. A
31:21 he undertook in the service of the house of G, C
31:21 to seek his G, he did with all his heart;
32: 8 but with us is the LORD our G, A
32:11 'The LORD our G will save us from the hand of A
32:14 your G should be able to save you from my hand?
32:15 for no g of any nation or kingdom has been able
32:15 much less will your G save you out of my hand!"
32:17 to throw contempt on the LORD the G of Israel B
32:17 so the G of Hezekiah will not rescue his people
32:19 the G of Jerusalem as if he were like the gods of
32:21 When he came into the house of his g, C
32:29 for G had given him very great possessions.
32:31 the land, G left him to himself, in order to test him
33: 7 in the house of G, of which God said to David C
33: 7 of which G said to David and to his son Solomon,
33:12 of the LORD his G and humbled himself greatly A
33:12 greatly before the G of his ancestors. F
33:13 He prayed to him, and G received his entreaty,
33:13 Manasseh knew that the LORD indeed was G.
33:16 to serve the LORD the G of Israel. B
33:17 but only to the LORD their G. A
33:18 rest of the acts of Manasseh, his prayer to his G,
33:18 to him in the name of the LORD G of Israel, BG
33:19 His prayer, and how G received his entreaty,
34: 3 he began to seek the G of his ancestor David,
34: 8 to repair the house of the LORD his G. A
34: 9 that had been brought into the house of G, C
34:23 "Thus says the LORD, the G of Israel: B
34:26 Thus says the LORD, the G of Israel: B
34:27 before G when you heard his words H
34:32 according to the covenant of G,
34:32 to the covenant of God, the G of their ancestors. F
34:33 in Israel worship the LORD their G. A
34:33 following the LORD the G of their ancestors. F
35: 3 serve the LORD your G and his people Israel. A
35: 8 and Jehiel, the chief officers of the house of G, C
35:21 and G has commanded me to hurry.
35:21 Cease opposing G, who is with me,
35:22 to the words of Neco from the mouth of G,
36: 5 in the sight of the LORD his G. A
36:12 in the sight of the LORD his G. A
36:13 who had made him swear by G;
36:13 against turning to the LORD, the G of Israel. B
36:15 The LORD, the G of their ancestors, F
36:16 but they kept mocking the messengers of G,
36:18 All the vessels of the house of G, large and C
36:19 They burned the house of G, C
36:23 The LORD, the G of heaven, O
36:23 may the LORD his G be with him! A
Ezr 1: 2 The LORD, the G of heaven, O
1: 3 may their G be with them!—
Ezr 1: 3 and rebuild the house of the LORD, the G B
1: 3 he is the G who is in Jerusalem;
1: 4 besides freewill offerings for the house of G C
1: 5 everyone whose spirit G had stirred—
2:68 for the house of G, to erect it C
3: 2 set out to build the altar of the G of Israel, B
3: 2 as prescribed in the law of Moses the man of G. D
3: 8 after their arrival at the house of G at Jerusalem, C
3: 9 of the workers in the house of G. C
4: 1 a temple to the LORD, the G of Israel, B
4: 2 for we worship your G as you do,
4: 3 with us in building a house to our G;
4: 3 we alone will build to the LORD, the G of Israel, B
4:24 the work on the house of G in Jerusalem stopped C
5: 1 the name of the G of Israel who was over them. B
5: 2 of Jozadak set out to rebuild the house of G C
5: 2 with them were the prophets of G, helping them.
5: 5 the eye of their G was upon the elders of the Jews,
5: 8 to the house of the great G,
5:11 the servants of the G of heaven and earth, O
5:12 our ancestors had angered the G of heaven, O
5:13 a decree that this house of G should be rebuilt. C
5:14 the gold and silver vessels of the house of G, C
5:15 and let the house of G be rebuilt on its site." C
5:16 the foundations of the house of G in Jerusalem; C
5:17 the rebuilding of this house of G in Jerusalem. C
6: 3 Concerning the house of G at Jerusalem, C
6: 5 let the gold and silver vessels of the house of G, C
6: 5 you shall put them in the house of G." C
6: 7 let the work on this house of G alone; C
6: 7 the elders of the Jews rebuild this house of G C
6: 8 of the Jews for the rebuilding of this house of G: C
6: 9 or sheep for burnt offerings to the G of heaven, O
6:10 offer pleasing sacrifices to the G of heaven, O
6:12 G who has established his name there overthrow
6:12 or to destroy this house of G in Jerusalem. C
6:14 their building by command of the G of Israel B
6:16 celebrated the dedication of this house of G C
6:17 of this house of G one hundred bulls, C
6:18 in their courses for the service of G at Jerusalem,
6:21 of the land to worship the LORD, the G of Israel. B
6:22 he aided them in the work on the house of G, C
6:22 in the work on the house of God, the G of Israel. B
7: 6 the law of Moses that the LORD the G of Israel B
7: 6 for the hand of the LORD his G was upon him. A
7: 9 for the gracious hand of his G was upon him. S
7:12 the scribe of the law of the G of heaven: OP
7:14 and Jerusalem according to the law of your G, P
7:15 have freely offered to the G of Israel, B
7:16 given willingly for the house of their G C
7:17 on the altar of the house of your G in Jerusalem. C
7:18 you may do, according to the will of your G. X
7:19 for the service of the house of your G, C
7:19 you shall deliver before the G of Jerusalem.
7:20 else is required for the house of your G, C
7:21 the scribe of the law of the G of heaven, OP
7:23 Whatever is commanded by the G of heaven, O
7:23 with zeal for the house of the G of heaven, CO
7:24 or other servants of this house of G. C
7:25 Beyond the River who know the laws of your G;
7:26 All who will not obey the law of your G and P
7:27 Blessed be the LORD, the G of our ancestors, F
7:28 for the hand of the LORD my G was upon me, A
8:17 to send us ministers for the house of our G. C
8:18 Since the gracious hand of our G was upon us, S
8:21 that we might deny ourselves before our G,
8:22 hand of our G is gracious to all who seek him, S
8:23 So we fasted and petitioned our G for this,
8:25 the offering for the house of our G that the king, C
8:28 offering to the LORD, the G of your ancestors. F
8:30 bring them to Jerusalem, to the house of our G. C
8:31 the hand of our G was upon us, S
8:33 On the fourth day, within the house of our G, C
8:35 offered burnt offerings to the G of Israel, B
8:36 they supported the people and the house of G. C
9: 4 all who trembled at the words of the G of Israel, B
9: 5 spread out my hands to the LORD my G, A
9: 6 "O my G, I am too ashamed and embarrassed to
9: 6 lift my face to you, my G,
9: 8 by the LORD our G, who has left us a remnant, A
9: 9 yet our G has not forsaken us in our slavery,
9: 9 to give us new life to set up the house of our G, C
9:10 "And now, our G, what shall we say after this?
9:13 and for our great guilt, seeing that you, our G,
9:15 O LORD, G of Israel, you are just, B
10: 1 throwing himself down before the house of G, C
10: 2 with our G and have married foreign women
10: 3 So now let us make a covenant with our G
10: 3 at the commandment of our G;
10: 6 Then Ezra withdrew from before the house of G, C
10: 9 in the open square before the house of G, C
10:11 confession to the LORD the G of your ancestors, F
10:14 of our G on this account is averted from us."
Ne 1: 4 fasting and praying before the G of heaven. O
1: 5 I said, "O LORD G of heaven, GO
1: 5 the great and awesome G who keeps covenant
2: 4 So I prayed to the G of heaven. O
2: 8 for the gracious hand of my G was upon me. S
2:12 I told no one what my G had put into my heart
2:18 the hand of my G had been gracious upon me, S
2:20 G of heaven is the one who will give us success, O
4: 4 Hear, O our G, for we are despised;
4: 9 So we prayed to our G,
4:15 and that G had frustrated it,
4:20 Our G will fight for us."
5: 9 Should you not walk in the fear of our G,
5:13 "So may G shake out everyone from house and
Ne 5:15 But I did not do so, because of the fear of G.
5:19 Remember for my good, O my G,
6: 9 But now, O G, strengthen my hands.
6:10 he said, "Let us meet together in the house of G, C
6:12 I perceived and saw that G had not sent him at all,
6:14 Remember Tobiah and Sanballat, O my G,
6:16 with the help of our G.
7: 2 a faithful man and feared G more than many.
7: 5 Then my G put it into my mind to assemble
8: 6 Then Ezra blessed the LORD, the great G,
8: 8 So they read from the book, from the law of G, P
8: 9 "This day is holy to the LORD your G; A
8:16 their courts and in the courts of the house of G, C
8:18 he read from the book of the law of G. P
9: 3 from the book of the law of the LORD their G A
9: 3 and worshiped the LORD their G. A
9: 4 with a loud voice to the LORD their G. A
9: 5 up and bless the LORD your G from everlasting A
9: 7 the G who chose Abram and brought him out
9:17 But you are a G ready to forgive,
9:18 'This is your G who brought you up out of Egypt,'
9:31 for you are a gracious and merciful G.
9:32 our G—the great and mighty and awesome G,
10:28 peoples of the lands to adhere to the law of G, P
10:29 which was given by Moses the servant of G,
10:32 of a shekel for the service of the house of our G: C
10:33 and for all the work of the house of our G. C
10:34 to bring it into the house of our G, C
10:34 to burn on the altar of the LORD our G, A
10:36 the house of our G, to the priests who minister C
10:36 the priests who minister in the house of our G, C
10:37 to the chambers of the house of our G; C
10:38 up a tithe of the tithes to the house of our G, C
10:39 We will not neglect the house of our G. C
11:11 officer of the house of G, C
11:16 over the outside work of the house of G; C
11:22 in charge of the work of the house of G. C
12:24 to the commandment of David the man of G, D
12:36 the musical instruments of David the man of G; D
12:40 those who gave thanks stood in the house of G, C
12:43 for G had made them rejoice with great joy;
12:45 They performed the service of their G and
12:46 there were songs of praise and thanksgiving to G.
13: 1 or Moabite should ever enter the assembly of G,
13: 2 yet our G turned the curse into a blessing.
13: 4 over the chambers of the house of our G, C
13: 7 a room for him in the courts of the house of G. C
13: 9 I brought back the vessels of the house of G, C
13:11 "Why is the house of G forsaken?" C
13:14 Remember me, O my G, concerning this,
13:14 that I have done for the house of my G and C
13:18 and did not our G bring all this disaster on us and
13:22 Remember this also in my favor, O my G,
13:25 and I made them take an oath in the name of G,
13:26 he was beloved by his G, and G made him king
13:27 against our G by marrying foreign women?"
13:29 Remember them, O my G,
13:31 Remember me, O my G, for good.
Job 1: 1 one who feared G and turned away from evil.
1: 5 and cursed G in their hearts."
1: 8 and upright man who fears G and turns away
1: 9 "Does Job fear G for nothing? Y
1:16 of G fell from heaven and burned up the sheep
1:22 not sin or charge G with wrongdoing.
2: 3 and upright man who fears G and turns away
2: 9 persist in your integrity? Curse G, and die."
2:10 Shall we receive the good at the hand of G, S
3: 4 May G above not seek it, or light shine on it.
3:23 the way, whom G has fenced in?
4: 6 Is not your fear of G your confidence,
4: 9 By the breath of G they perish,
4:17 'Can mortals be righteous before G? H
5: 8 "As for me, I would seek G,
5: 8 and to G I would commit my cause.
5:17 "How happy is the one whom G reproves;
6: 4 the terrors of G are arrayed against me.
6: 8 and that G would grant my desire;
6: 9 that it would please G to crush me,
8: 3 Does G pervert justice?
8: 5 If you will seek G and make supplication to
8:13 Such are the paths of all who forget G;
8:20 "See, G will not reject a blameless person,
9: 2 but how can a mortal be just before G? H
9:13 "G will not turn back his anger;
10: 2 I will say to G, Do not condemn me;
11: 5 But oh, that G would speak,
11: 6 that G exacts of you less than your guilt deserves.
11: 7 "Can you find out the deep things of G?
12: 4 I, who called upon G and he answered me,
12: 6 and those who provoke G are secure,
12: 6 who bring their g in their hands.
12:13 "With G are wisdom and strength;
13: 3 and I desire to argue my case with G.
13: 7 Will you speak falsely for G,
13: 8 will you plead the case for G?
15: 4 But you are doing away with the fear of G,
15: 4 and hindering meditation before G. H
15: 8 Have you listened in the council of G?
15:11 Are the consolations of G too small for you,
15:13 so that you turn your spirit against G,
15:15 G puts no trust even in his holy ones,
15:25 Because they stretched out their hands against G,
16: 7 Surely now G has worn me out;
16:11 G gives me up to the ungodly,
16:20 My friends scorn me; my eye pours out tears to G,
16:21 he would maintain the right of a mortal with G,
18:21 such is the place of those who do not know G."

*GOD distinguishes the words translated "God" and "god" from the compound name "Lord GOD," where GOD represents the name *Yahweh*. For this name see the heading †GOD on pages 541-42.

Job 19: 6 know then that G has put me in the wrong,
19:21 for the hand of G has touched me! S
19:22 Why do you, like G, pursue me,
19:26 then in my flesh I shall see G,
20:15 G casts them out of their bellies.
20:23 to the full G will send his fierce anger into them,
20:29 This is the portion of the wicked from G,
20:29 the heritage decreed for them by G."
21: 9 and no rod of G is upon them.
21:14 They say to G, 'Leave us alone!
21:17 How often does G distribute pains in his anger?
21:19 'G stores up their iniquity for their children.'
21:22 Will any teach G knowledge,
22: 2 "Can a mortal be of use to G?
22:12 "Is not G high in the heavens?
22:13 Therefore you say, 'What does G know?
22:17 They said to G, 'Leave us alone,'
22:21 "Agree with G, and be at peace;
22:26 and lift up your face to G.
23:16 G has made my heart faint;
24:12 yet G pays no attention to their prayer.
24:22 G prolongs the life of the mighty by his power;
25: 2 "Dominion and fear are with G;
25: 4 How then can a mortal be righteous before G? H
26: 6 Sheol is naked before G, H
27: 2 "As G lives, who has taken away my right,
27: 3 as long as my breath is in me and the spirit of G U
27: 8 the hope of the godless when G cuts them off,
27: 8 when G takes away their lives?
27: 9 Will G hear their cry when trouble comes
27:10 Will they call upon G at all times?
27:11 I will teach you concerning the hand of G; S
27:13 "This is the portion of the wicked with G,
28:23 "G understands the way to it,
29: 2 as in the days when G watched over me;
29: 4 when the friendship of G was upon my tent;
30:11 G has loosed my bowstring and humbled me,
31: 2 What would be my portion from G above,
31: 6 and let G know my integrity!—
31:14 what then shall I do when G rises up?
31:23 For I was in terror of calamity from G,
31:28 for I should have been false to G above.
32: 2 at Job because he justified himself rather than G;
32:13 G may vanquish him, not a human.'
33: 4 The spirit of G has made me, U
33: 6 See, before G I am as you are; H
33:12 I will answer you: G is greater than any mortal.
33:14 For G speaks in one way, and in two,
33:26 Then he prays to G, and is accepted by him,
33:26 and G repays him for his righteousness.
33:29 "G indeed does all these things, twice, three times,
34: 5 'I am innocent, and G has taken away my right;
34: 9 'It profits one nothing to take delight in G.'
34:10 far be it from G that he should do wickedness,
34:12 Of a truth, G will not do wickedly,
34:23 not appointed a time for anyone to go before G H
34:31 "For has anyone said to G,
34:37 and multiplies his words against G."
35: 2 You say, 'I am in the right before G.' H
35:10 But no one says, 'Where is G my Maker,
35:13 Surely G does not hear an empty cry,
36: 5 "Surely G is mighty and does not despise any;
36:22 See, G is exalted in his power;
36:26 Surely G is great, and we do not know him;
37: 5 G thunders wondrously with his voice;
37:10 By the breath of G ice is given,
37:14 stop and consider the wondrous works of G.
37:15 Do you know how G lays his command
37:22 around G is awesome majesty.
38:41 when its young ones cry to G,
39:17 because G has made it forget wisdom,
40: 2 Anyone who argues with G must respond."
40: 9 Have you an arm like G,
40:19 "It is the first of the great acts of G—
Ps 3: 2 "There is no help for you in G."
3: 7 Deliver me, O my G!
4: 1 when I call, O G of my right!
5: 2 my King and my G, for to you I pray.
5: 4 For you are not a G who delights in wickedness;
5:10 Make them bear their guilt, O G;
7: 1 O LORD my G, in you I take refuge; A
7: 3 O LORD my G, if I have done this, A
7: 6 awake, O my G; you have appointed a judgment.
7: 9 you who test the minds and hearts, O righteous G.
7:10 G is my shield, who saves the upright in heart.
7:11 G is a righteous judge, and a G who has indignation every day.
7:12 If one does not repent, G will whet his sword;
8: 5 Yet you have made them a little lower than G,
9:17 all the nations that forget G.
10: 4 "G will not seek it out";
10: 4 all their thoughts are, "There is no G."
10:11 They think in their heart, "G has forgotten,
10:12 Rise up, O LORD; O G, lift up your hand;
10:13 Why do the wicked renounce G,
13: 3 Consider and answer me, O LORD my G! A
14: 1 in their hearts, "There is no G."
14: 2 if there are any who are wise, who seek after G.
14: 5 for G is with the company of the righteous.
16: 1 Protect me, O G, for in you I take refuge.
16: 4 who choose another g multiply their sorrows;
17: 6 I call upon you, for you will answer me, O G;
18: 2 my G, my rock in whom I take refuge, my shield,
18: 6 to my G I cried for help.
18:21 and have not wickedly departed from my G.
18:28 the LORD, my G, lights up my darkness. A
18:29 and by my G I can leap over a wall.
Ps 18:30 This G— his way is perfect;
18:31 For who is G except the LORD?
18:31 And who is a rock besides our G?—
18:32 the G who girded me with strength,
18:46 and exalted be the G of my salvation,
18:47 the G who gave me vengeance
19: 1 The heavens are telling the glory of G; R
20: 1 The name of the G of Jacob protect you! V
20: 5 and in the name of our G set up our banners.
20: 7 but our pride is in the name of the LORD our G. A
22: 1 My G, my G, why have you forsaken me?
22: 2 O my G, I cry by day, but you do not answer;
22:10 since my mother bore me you have been my G.
24: 5 and vindication from the G of their salvation.
24: 6 who seek the face of the G of Jacob. V
25: 2 O my G, in you I trust;
25: 5 and teach me, for you are the G of my salvation;
25:22 Redeem Israel, O G, out of all its troubles.
27: 9 do not forsake me, O G of my salvation!
29: 3 the G of glory thunders, the LORD,
30: 2 O LORD my G, I cried to you for help, A
30:12 O LORD my G, I will give thanks to you forever. A
31: 5 you have redeemed me, O LORD, faithful G.
31:14 I trust in you, O LORD; I say, "You are my G."
33:12 Happy is the nation whose G is the LORD,
35:23 for my cause, my G and my Lord!
35:24 Vindicate me, O LORD, my G, A
36: 1 there is no fear of G before their eyes.
36: 7 How precious is your steadfast love, O G!
37:31 The law of their G is in their hearts; P
38:15 it is you, O LORD my G, who will answer. A
38:21 O my G, do not be far from me;
40: 3 a song of praise to our G.
40: 5 You have multiplied, O LORD my G, A
40: 8 I delight to do your will, O my G;
40:17 do not delay, O my G.
41:13 Blessed be the LORD, the G of Israel, B
42: 1 so my soul longs for you, O G.
42: 2 My soul thirsts for G, for the living God.
42: 2 My soul thirsts for God, for the living G. N
42: 2 When shall I come and behold the face of G?
42: 3 to me continually, "Where is your G?"
42: 4 and led them in procession to the house of G, C
42: 5 Hope in G; for I shall again praise him,
42: 6 and my G. My soul is cast down within
42: 8 a prayer to the G of my life.
42: 9 I say to G, my rock, "Why have you forgotten me?
42:10 to me continually, "Where is your G?"
42:11 Hope in G; for I shall again praise him, my help and my G.
43: 1 O G, and defend my cause against
43: 2 For you are the G in whom I take refuge;
43: 4 Then I will go to the altar of G, to G my exceeding joy;
43: 4 and I will praise you with the harp, O G, my G.
43: 5 Hope in G; for I shall again praise him, my help and my G.
44: 1 O G, our ancestors have told us,
44: 4 You are my King and my G;
44: 8 In G we have boasted continually,
44:20 If we had forgotten the name of our G,
44:20 or spread out our hands to a strange g,
44:21 would not G discover this?
45: 2 therefore G has blessed you forever.
45: 6 Your throne, O G, endures forever and ever.
45: 7 Therefore G, your G, has anointed you with the oil of gladness
46: 1 G is our refuge and strength,
46: 4 a river whose streams make glad the city of G,
46: 5 G is in the midst of the city;
46: 5 G will help it when the morning dawns.
46: 7 the G of Jacob is our refuge. V
46:10 "Be still, and know that I am G!
46:11 the G of Jacob is our refuge. V
47: 1 shout to G with loud songs of joy.
47: 5 G has gone up with a shout,
47: 6 Sing praises to G, sing praises;
47: 7 For G is the king of all the earth;
47: 8 G is king over the nations;
47: 8 G sits on his holy throne.
47: 9 of the peoples gather as the people of the G
47: 9 For the shields of the earth belong to G;
48: 1 and greatly to be praised in the city of our G.
48: 3 Within its citadels G has shown himself
48: 8 in the city of our G, which G establishes forever.
48: 9 O G, in the midst of your temple.
48:10 Your name, O G, like your praise,
48:14 that this is G, our G forever and ever.
49: 7 there is no price one can give to G for it.
49:15 G will ransom my soul from the power of Sheol,
50: 1 G the LORD, speaks and summons the earth
50: 2 the perfection of beauty, G shines forth.
50: 3 Our G comes and does not keep silence,
50: 6 declare his righteousness, for G himself is judge.
50: 7 I am G, your G.
50:14 Offer to G a sacrifice of thanksgiving,
50:16 But to the wicked G says:
50:22 "Mark this, then, you who forget G,
50:23 the right way I will show the salvation of G."
51: 1 O G, according to your steadfast love;
51:10 Create in me a clean heart, O G,
51:14 Deliver me from bloodshed, O G, O G of my salvation,
51:17 The sacrifice acceptable to G is a broken spirit;
51:17 a broken and contrite heart, O G,
52: 5 But G will break you down forever;
52: 7 "See the one who would not take refuge in G,
Ps 52: 8 I am like a green olive tree in the house of G. C
52: 8 I trust in the steadfast love of G forever and ever.
53: 1 in their hearts, "There is no G."
53: 2 G looks down from heaven on humankind to see
53: 2 if there are any who are wise, who seek after G.
53: 4 and do not call upon G?
53: 5 For G will scatter the bones of the ungodly;
53: 5 they will be put to shame, for G has rejected them.
53: 6 When G restores the fortunes of his people,
54: 1 O G, by your name, and vindicate me
54: 2 O G; give ear to the words of my mouth.
54: 3 they do not set G before them.
54: 4 But surely, G is my helper;
55: 1 O G; do not hide yourself from my supplication.
55:14 we walked in the house of G with the throng. C
55:16 But I call upon G, and the LORD will save me.
55:19 G, who is enthroned from of old,
55:19 because they do not change, and do not fear G.
55:23 you, O G, will cast them down into the lowest pit;
56: 1 O G, for people trample on me;
56: 4 In G, whose word I praise, in G I trust;
56: 7 in wrath cast down the peoples, O G!
56: 9 This I know, that G is for me.
56:10 In G, whose word I praise, in the LORD,
56:11 in G I trust; I am
56:12 My vows to you I must perform, O G;
56:13 so that I may walk before G in the light of life. H
57: 1 O G, be merciful to me,
57: 2 I cry to G Most High, to G who fulfills his purpose
57: 3 G will send forth his steadfast love
57: 5 Be exalted, O G, above the heavens.
57: 7 O G, my heart is steadfast.
57:11 Be exalted, O G, above the heavens.
58: 6 O G, break the teeth in their mouths;
58:11 surely there is a G who judges on earth."
59: 1 from my enemies, O my G;
59: 5 You, LORD G of hosts, are God of Israel. GQ
59: 5 You, LORD God of hosts, are G of Israel. B
59: 9 for you, O G, are my fortress.
59:10 My G in his steadfast love will meet me;
59:10 my G will let me look in triumph on my enemies.
59:13 to the ends of the earth that G rules over Jacob.
59:17 I will sing praises to you, for you, O G,
59:17 the G who shows me steadfast love.
60: 1 O G, you have rejected us, broken our defenses;
60: 6 G has promised in his sanctuary:
60:10 Have you not rejected us, O G?
60:10 You do not go out, O G, with our armies.
60:12 With G we shall do valiantly;
61: 1 Hear my cry, O G; listen to my prayer.
61: 5 O G, have heard my vows;
61: 7 May he be enthroned forever before G; H
62: 1 For G alone my soul waits in silence;
62: 5 For G alone my soul waits in silence,
62: 7 On G rests my deliverance and my honor;
62: 7 my mighty rock, my refuge is in G.
62: 8 G is a refuge for us.
62:11 Once G has spoken; twice have I heard this: that power belongs to G,
63: 1 O G, you are my G, I seek you, my soul thirsts
63:11 But the king shall rejoice in G;
64: 1 Hear my voice, O G, in my complaint;
64: 7 But G will shoot his arrow at them;
64: 9 they will tell what G has brought about,
65: 1 Praise is due to you, O G, in Zion;
65: 5 with deliverance, O G of our salvation;
65: 9 the river of G is full of water;
66: 1 Make a joyful noise to G, all the earth;
66: 3 Say to G, "How awesome are your deeds!
66: 5 Come and see what G has done:
66: 8 Bless our G, O peoples, let the sound of his praise
66:10 For you, O G, have tested us;
66:16 and hear, all you who fear G, Y
66:19 But truly G has listened; he has given heed to the
66:20 be G, because he has not rejected my prayer
67: 1 May G be gracious to us and bless us
67: 3 Let the peoples praise you, O G;
67: 5 O G; let all the peoples praise you.
67: 6 G, our G, has blessed us.
67: 7 May G continue to bless us;
68: 1 Let G rise up, let his enemies be scattered;
68: 2 let the wicked perish before G. H
68: 3 be joyful; let them exult before G; H
68: 4 Sing to G, sing praises to his name;
68: 5 Father of orphans and protector of widows is G
68: 6 G gives the desolate a home to live in;
68: 7 O G, when you went out before your people,
68: 8 heavens poured down rain at the presence of G,
68: 8 the G of Sinai, at the presence of G,
68: 8 at the presence of God, the G of Israel. B
68: 9 Rain in abundance, O G, you showered abroad;
68:10 O G, you provided for the needy.
68:16 at the mount that G desired for his abode,
68:19 who daily bears us up; G is our salvation.
68:20 Our G is a G of salvation,
68:21 But G will shatter the heads of his enemies,
68:24 Your solemn processions are seen, O G,
68:24 O God, the processions of my G, my King,
68:26 "Bless G in the great congregation,
68:28 Summon your might, O G;
68:28 show your strength, O G,
68:31 let Ethiopia hasten to stretch out its hands to G.
68:32 Sing to G, O kingdoms of the earth;
68:34 Ascribe power to G, whose majesty is over Israel;
68:35 Awesome is G in his sanctuary, the God of Israel;
68:35 God in his sanctuary, the G of Israel; B
68:35 and strength to his people. Blessed be G!

***GOD** distinguishes the words translated "God" and "god" from the compound name "Lord GOD," where GOD represents the name *Yahweh*. For this name see the heading †GOD on pages 541-42.

Ps 69: 1 O **G,** for the waters have come up to my neck.
69: 3 My eyes grow dim with waiting for my **G.**
69: 5 O **G,** you know my folly;
69: 6 be dishonored because of me, O **G** of Israel. B
69:13 At an acceptable time, O **G,**
69:29 let your salvation, O **G,** protect me.
69:30 I will praise the name of **G** with a song;
69:32 you who seek **G,** let your hearts revive.
69:35 **G** will save Zion and rebuild the cities of Judah;
70: 1 Be pleased, O **G,** to deliver
70: 4 love your salvation say evermore, "**G** is great!"
70: 5 But I am poor and needy; hasten to me, O **G!**
71: 4 Rescue me, O my **G,** from the hand of the wicked,
71:11 and seize that person whom **G** has forsaken,
71:12 O **G,** do not be far from me;
71:12 O my **G,** make haste to help me!
71:17 O **G,** from my youth you have taught me,
71:18 So even to old age and gray hairs, O **G,**
71:19 O **G,** reach the high heavens.
71:19 You who have done great things, O **G,**
71:22 with the harp for your faithfulness, O my **G;**
72: 1 O **G,** and your righteousness to a king's son.
72:18 Blessed be the LORD, the **G** of Israel, B
73: 1 Truly **G** is good to the upright,
73:11 And they say, "How can **G** know?
73:17 until I went into the sanctuary of **G;**
73:26 but **G** is the strength of my heart
73:28 But for me it is good to be near **G;**
74: 1 O **G,** why do you cast us off forever?
74: 8 they burned all the meeting places of **G** in
74:10 How long, O **G,** is the foe to scoff?
74:12 Yet **G** my King is from of old,
74:22 Rise up, O **G,** plead your cause;
75: 1 O **G;** we give thanks; your name is near.
75: 7 but it is **G** who executes judgment,
75: 9 I will sing praises to the **G** of Jacob. V
76: 1 In Judah **G** is known, his name is great in Israel.
76: 6 At your rebuke, O **G** of Jacob, V
76: 9 when **G** rose up to establish judgment,
76:11 Make vows to the LORD your **G,** A
77: 1 I cry aloud to **G,** aloud to God,
77: 1 aloud to **G,** that he may hear me.
77: 3 I think of **G,** and I moan;
77: 9 Has **G** forgotten to be gracious?
77:13 Your way, O **G,** is holy.
77:13 What **g** is so great as our **G?**
77:14 You are the **G** who works wonders;
77:16 O **G,** when the waters saw you, they were afraid;
78: 7 that they should set their hope in **G,** and not forget
78: 7 and not forget the works of **G,**
78: 8 whose spirit was not faithful to **G.**
78:18 They tested **G** in their heart by demanding
78:19 They spoke against **G,** saying,
78:19 saying, "Can **G** spread a table in the wilderness?
78:22 because they had no faith in **G,**
78:31 the anger of **G** rose against them and he killed
78:34 they repented and sought **G** earnestly.
78:35 They remembered that **G** was their rock,
78:35 the Most High **G** their redeemer.
78:41 They tested **G** again and again,
78:56 Yet they tested the Most High **G,**
78:59 When **G** heard, he was full of wrath,
79: 1 O **G,** the nations have come into your inheritance;
79: 9 Help us, O **G** of our salvation,
79:10 Why should the nations say, "Where is their **G?**"
80: 3 O **G;** let your face shine, that we may be saved.
80: 4 LORD **G** of hosts, how long will you be angry GQ
80: 7 Restore us, O **G** of hosts; let your face shine, Q
80:14 Turn again, O **G** of hosts; Q
80:19 Restore us, O LORD **G** of hosts; GQ
81: 1 Sing aloud to **G** our strength;
81: 1 shout for joy to the **G** of Jacob. V
81: 4 an ordinance of the **G** of Jacob. V
81: 9 There shall be no strange **g** among you;
81: 9 you shall not bow down to a foreign **g.**
81:10 I am the LORD your **G,** A
82: 1 **G** has taken his place in the divine council;
82: 8 Rise up, O **G,** judge the earth;
83: 1 O **G,** do not keep silence;
83: 1 do not hold your peace or be still, O **G!**
83:12 the pastures of **G** for our own possession."
83:13 O my **G,** make them like whirling dust,
84: 2 heart and my flesh sing for joy to the living **G.** N
84: 3 O LORD of hosts, my King and my **G.**
84: 7 the **G** of gods will be seen in Zion.
84: 8 O LORD **G** of hosts, hear my prayer; GQ
84: 8 give ear, O **G** of Jacob! V
84: 9 O **G;** look on the face of your anointed.
84:10 a doorkeeper in the house of my **G** than live in C
84:11 For the LORD **G** is a sun and shield; G
85: 4 Restore us again, O **G** of our salvation,
85: 8 Let me hear what **G** the LORD will speak,
86: 2 your servant who trusts in you. You are my **G;**
86:10 and do wondrous things; you alone are **G.**
86:12 I give thanks to you, O Lord my **G,** I
86:14 O **G,** the insolent rise up against me;
86:15 But you, O Lord, are a **G** merciful and gracious,
87: 3 Glorious things are spoken of you, O city of **G.**
88: 1 **G** of my salvation, when, at night,
89: 7 a **G** feared in the council of the holy ones,
89: 8 O LORD **G** of hosts, who is as mighty as you, GQ
89:26 He shall cry to me, 'You are my Father, my **G,**
90: T *A Prayer of Moses, the man of* ***G.*** D
90: 2 from everlasting to everlasting you are **G.**
90:17 Let the favor of the Lord our **G** be upon us, I
91: 2 "My refuge and my fortress; my **G,**
92:13 they flourish in the courts of our **G.**

Ps 94: 1 LORD, you **G** of vengeance, you **G** of vengeance,
94: 7 the **G** of Jacob does not perceive." V
94:22 and my **G** the rock of my refuge.
94:23 the LORD our **G** will wipe them out. A
95: 3 For the LORD is a great **G,**
95: 7 For he is our **G,** and we are the people
97: 8 because of your judgments, O **G.**
98: 3 of the earth have seen the victory of our **G.**
99: 5 Extol the LORD our **G;** worship at his footstool. A
99: 8 O LORD our **G,** you answered them; A
99: 8 you were a forgiving **G** to them,
99: 9 Extol the LORD our **G,** and worship A
99: 9 for the LORD our **G** is holy. A
100: 3 Know that the LORD is **G.**
102:24 "O my **G,**" I say, "do not take me away at
104: 1 O LORD my **G,** you are very great. A
104:21 seeking their food from **G.**
104:33 I will sing praise to my **G** while I have being.
105: 7 He is the LORD our **G;** A
106:14 and put **G** to the test in the desert;
106:20 They exchanged the glory of **G** for the image of R
106:21 They forgot **G,** their Savior,
106:47 Save us, O LORD our **G,** A
106:48 Blessed be the LORD, the **G** of Israel, B
107:11 for they had rebelled against the words of **G,**
108: 1 O **G,** my heart is steadfast;
108: 5 Be exalted, O **G,** above the heavens,
108: 7 **G** has promised in his sanctuary:
108:11 Have you not rejected us, O **G?**
108:11 You do not go out, O **G,** with our armies.
108:13 With **G** we shall do valiantly;
109: 1 Do not be silent, O **G** of my praise.
109:26 Help me, O LORD my **G!** A
113: 5 Who is like the LORD our **G,** A
114: 7 at the presence of the **G** of Jacob, V
115: 2 Why should the nations say, "Where is their **G?**"
115: 3 Our **G** is in the heavens;
116: 5 and righteous; our **G** is merciful.
118:27 The LORD is **G,** and he has given us light.
118:28 You are my **G,** and I will give thanks to you;
118:28 you are my **G,** I will extol you.
119:115 that I may keep the commandments of my **G.**
122: 9 For the sake of the house of the LORD our **G,** A
123: 2 so our eyes look to the LORD our **G,** A
135: 2 in the courts of the house of our **G.** C
136: 2 O give thanks to the **G** of gods,
136:26 O give thanks to the **G** of heaven, O
139:17 How weighty to me are your thoughts, O **G!**
139:19 O that you would kill the wicked, O **G,**
139:23 Search me, O **G,** and know my heart;
140: 6 to the LORD, "You are my **G;**
143:10 Teach me to do your will, for you are my **G.**
144: 9 I will sing a new song to you, O **G;**
144:15 happy are the people whose **G** is the LORD.
145: 1 my **G** and King, and bless your name forever
146: 2 I will sing praises to my **G** all my life long.
146: 5 Happy are those whose help is the **G** of Jacob, V
146: 5 whose hope is in the LORD their **G,** A
146:10 The LORD will reign forever, your **G,** O Zion,
147: 1 How good it is to sing praises to our **G;**
147: 7 make melody to our **G** on the lyre.
147:12 Praise your **G,** O Zion!
149: 6 of **G** be in their throats and two-edged swords
150: 1 Praise **G** in his sanctuary;
Pr 2: 5 of the LORD and find the knowledge of **G.**
3: 4 and good repute in the sight of **G** and of people.
25: 2 It is the glory of **G** to conceal things, R
30: 1 I am weary, O **G,** I am weary, O **G.**
30: 5 Every word of **G** proves true; L
30: 9 and steal, and profane the name of my **G.**
Ecc 1:13 that **G** has given to human beings to be busy with.
2:24 This also, I saw, is from the hand of **G;** S
2:26 For to the one who pleases him **G** gives wisdom
2:26 only to give to one who pleases **G.**
3:10 that **G** has given to everyone to be busy with.
3:11 yet they cannot find out what **G** has done from
3:14 I know that whatever **G** does endures forever;
3:14 **G** has done this, so that all should stand in awe
3:15 and **G** seeks out what has gone by.
3:17 **G** will judge the righteous and the wicked,
3:18 with regard to human beings that **G** is testing them
5: 1 your steps when you go to the house of **G;** C
5: 2 let your heart be quick to utter a word before **G,** H
5: 2 for **G** is in heaven, and you upon earth;
5: 4 you make a vow to **G,** do not delay fulfilling it;
5: 6 why should **G** be angry at your words,
5: 7 and a multitude of words; but fear **G.** Y
5:18 under the sun the few days of the life **G** gives us;
5:19 to whom **G** gives wealth and possessions
5:19 find enjoyment in their toil—this is the gift of **G.**
5:20 because **G** keeps them occupied with the joy
6: 2 those to whom **G** gives wealth,
6: 2 yet **G** does not enable them to enjoy these things,
7:13 Consider the work of **G;** who can make straight
7:14 **G** has made the one as well as the other,
7:18 for the one who fears **G** shall succeed with both.
7:26 one who pleases **G** escapes her,
7:29 that **G** made human beings straightforward,
8:12 know that it will be well with those who fear **G,** Y
8:13 because they do not stand in fear before **G.** H
8:15 the days of life that **G** gives them under the sun.
8:17 then I saw all the work of **G,**
9: 1 the wise and their deeds are in the hand of **G;** S
9: 7 for **G** has long ago approved what you do.
11: 5 so you do not know the work of **G,**
11: 9 but know that for all these things **G** will bring you
12: 7 and the breath returns to **G** who gave it.

Ecc 12:13 Fear **G,** and keep his commandments; Y
12:14 For **G** will bring every deed into judgment,
Isa 1:10 Listen to the teaching of our **G,**
2: 3 to the house of the **G** of Jacob; CV
5:16 the Holy **G** shows himself holy by righteousness.
7:11 Ask a sign of the LORD your **G;** A
7:13 that you weary my **G** also?
8:10 but it will not stand, for **G** is with us.
9: 6 and he is named Wonderful Counselor, Mighty **G,**
10:21 the remnant of Jacob, to the mighty **G.**
12: 2 Surely **G** is my salvation;
13:19 and Gomorrah when **G** overthrew them.
14:13 I will raise my throne above the stars of **G;**
17: 6 says the LORD **G** of Israel. BG
17:10 For you have forgotten the **G** of your salvation,
17:10 and set out slips of an alien **g,**
21:10 the **G** of Israel, I announce to you. B
21:17 for the LORD, the **G** of Israel, has spoken. B
24:15 glorify the name of the LORD, the **G** of Israel. B
25: 1 O LORD, you are my **G;**
25: 9 It will be said on that day, Lo, this is our **G;**
26:13 LORD our **G,** other lords besides you have ruled A
28:26 For they are well instructed; their **G** teaches them.
29:23 and will stand in awe of the **G** of Israel. B
30:18 For the LORD is a **G** of justice;
31: 3 The Egyptians are human, and not **G;**
35: 2 the glory of the LORD, the majesty of our **G.**
35: 4 Here is your **G.** He will come with vengeance,
36: 7 if you say to me, 'We rely on the LORD our **G,**' A
37: 4 It may be that the LORD your **G** heard the words A
37: 4 king of Assyria has sent to mock the living **G,** N
37: 4 the words that the LORD your **G** has heard; A
37:10 Do not let your **G** on whom you rely deceive you
37:16 **G** of Israel, who are enthroned above B
37:16 you are **G,** you alone, of all the kingdoms of
37:17 which he has sent to mock the living **G.** N
37:20 So now, O LORD our **G,** save us from his hand, A
37:21 "Thus says the LORD, the **G** of Israel: B
37:38 he was worshiping in the house of his **g** Nisroch, C
38: 5 the **G** of your ancestor David:
40: 1 Comfort, O comfort my people, says your **G.**
40: 3 make straight in the desert a highway for our **G.**
40: 8 but the word of our **G** will stand forever.
40: 9 say to the cities of Judah, "Here is your **G!**"
40:18 To whom then will you liken **G,**
40:27 and my right is disregarded by my **G**"?
40:28 The LORD is the everlasting **G,**
41:10 do not be afraid, for I am your **G;**
41:13 For I, the LORD your **G,** hold your right hand; A
41:17 I the **G** of Israel will not forsake them. B
42: 5 Thus says **G,** the LORD,
43: 3 For I am the LORD your **G,** A
43:10 Before me no **g** was formed,
43:12 when there was no strange **g** among you;
43:13 I am **G,** and also henceforth I am He;
44: 6 besides me there is no **g.**
44: 8 Is there any **g** besides me?
44:10 a **g** or cast an image that can do no good?
44:15 Then he makes a **g** and worships it,
44:17 The rest of it he makes into a **g,** his idol,
44:17 "Save me, for you are my **g!**"
45: 3 the **G** of Israel, who call you by your name. B
45: 5 besides me there is no **g.**
45:14 "**G** is with you alone, and there is no other;
45:14 there is no **g** besides him."
45:15 Truly, you are a **G** who hides himself,
45:15 you are a God who hides himself, O **G** of Israel, B
45:18 who created the heavens (he is **G!**),
45:20 and keep on praying to a **g** that cannot save.
45:21 There is no other **g** besides me, a righteous **G** and a Savior;
45:22 For I am **G,** and there is no other.
46: 6 they hire a goldsmith, who makes it into a **g;**
46: 9 for I am **G,** and there is no other;
46: 9 I am **G,** and there is no one like me,
48: 1 and invoke the **G** of Israel, B
48: 2 and lean on the **G** of Israel; B
48:17 I am the LORD your **G,** who teaches you A
49: 4 and my reward with my **G.**"
49: 5 and my **G** has become my strength—
50:10 in the name of the LORD and relies upon his **G?**
51:15 For I am the LORD your **G,** A
51:20 of the wrath of the LORD, the rebuke of your **G.**
51:22 your **G** who pleads the cause of his people:
52: 7 who says to Zion, "Your **G** reigns."
52:10 of the earth shall see the salvation of our **G.**
52:12 and the **G** of Israel will be your rear guard. B
53: 4 yet we accounted him stricken, struck down by **G,**
54: 5 the **G** of the whole earth he is called.
54: 6 a man's youth when she is cast off, says your **G.**
55: 5 because of the LORD your **G,** A
55: 7 that he may have mercy on them, and to our **G,**
57:21 There is no peace, says my **G,** for the wicked.
58: 2 and did not forsake the ordinance of their **G;**
58: 2 they delight to draw near to **G.**
59: 2 between you and your **G,**
59:13 and turning away from following our **G,**
60: 9 for the name of the LORD your **G,** A
60:19 and your **G** will be your glory.
61: 2 and the day of vengeance of our **G;**
61: 6 you shall be named ministers of our **G;**
61:10 my whole being shall exult in my **G;**
62: 3 and a royal diadem in the hand of your **G.** S
62: 5 so shall your **G** rejoice over you.
64: 4 no eye has seen any **G** besides you,
65:16 the **G** of faithfulness, and whoever takes an oath
65:16 in the land shall swear by the **G** of faithfulness;

***GOD** distinguishes the words translated "God" and "god" from the compound name "Lord GOD," where GOD represents the name *Yahweh.* For this name see the heading **†GOD** on pages 541-42.

Isa 66: 9 shut the womb? says your **G**.
Jer 2:17 upon yourself by forsaking the LORD your **G**, A
2:19 and bitter for you to forsake the LORD your **G**; A
3:13 that you have rebelled against the LORD your **G**, A
3:21 they have forgotten the LORD their **G**: A
3:22 for you are the LORD our **G**. A
3:23 in the LORD our **G** is the salvation of Israel. A
3:25 for we have sinned against the LORD our **G**, A
3:25 not obeyed the voice of the LORD our **G**." A
5: 4 the way of the LORD, the law of their **G**. P
5: 5 the way of the LORD, the law of their **G**." P
5:14 Therefore thus says the LORD, the **G** of hosts: Q
5:19 "Why has the LORD our **G** done all these things A
5:24 "Let us fear the LORD our **G**, A
7: 3 Thus says the LORD of hosts, the **G** of Israel: B
7:21 Thus says the LORD of hosts, the **G** of Israel: B
7:23 and I will be your **G**, and you shall be my people;
7:28 that did not obey the voice of the LORD their **G**, A
8:14 for the LORD our **G** has doomed us to perish, A
9:15 thus says the LORD of hosts, the **G** of Israel: B
10:10 But the LORD is the true **G**;
10:10 he is the living **G** and the everlasting King. N
11: 3 Thus says the LORD, the **G** of Israel: B
11: 4 So shall you be my people, and I will be your **G**,
13:12 Thus says the LORD, the **G** of Israel: B
13:16 the LORD your **G** before he brings darkness, A
14:22 Is it not you, O LORD our **G**? A
15:16 I am called by your name, O LORD, **G** of hosts. Q
16: 9 For thus says the LORD of hosts, the **G** of Israel: B
16:10 against the LORD our **G**?" A
19: 3 Thus says the LORD of hosts, the **G** of Israel: B
19:15 the LORD of hosts, the **G** of Israel: B
21: 4 Thus says the LORD, the **G** of Israel: B
22: 9 the covenant of the LORD their **G**, A
23: 2 Therefore thus says the LORD, the **G** of Israel, B
23:23 Am I a **G** near by, says the LORD,
23:23 says the LORD, and not a **G** far off?
23:36 and so you pervert the words of the living **G**, N
23:36 the LORD of hosts, our **G**.
24: 5 the LORD, the **G** of Israel: B
24: 7 and they shall be my people and I will be their **G**,
25:15 For thus the LORD, the **G** of Israel, said to me: B
25:27 Thus says the LORD of hosts, the **G** of Israel: B
26:13 and obey the voice of the LORD your **G**, A
26:16 to us in the name of the LORD our **G**." A
27: 4 Thus says the LORD of hosts, the **G** of Israel: B
27:21 the **G** of Israel, concerning the vessels left in B
28: 2 the LORD of hosts, the **G** of Israel: B
28:14 For thus says the LORD of hosts, the **G** of Israel: B
29: 4 **G** of Israel, to all the exiles whom I have sent B
29: 8 For thus says the LORD of hosts, the **G** of Israel: B
29:21 the **G** of Israel, concerning Ahab son of Kolaiah B
29:25 the LORD of hosts, the **G** of Israel: B
30: 2 the LORD, the **G** of Israel: B
30: 9 the LORD their **G** and David their king, A
30:22 you shall be my people, and I will be your **G**.
31: 1 I will be the **G** of all the families of Israel,
31: 6 "Come, let us go up to Zion, to the LORD our **G**." A
31:18 let me come back, for you are the LORD my **G**. A
31:23 Thus says the LORD of hosts, the **G** of Israel: B
31:33 and I will be their **G**, and they shall be my people.
32:14 the LORD of hosts, the **G** of Israel: B
32:15 For thus says the LORD of hosts, the **G** of Israel: B
32:18 and mighty **G** whose name is the LORD of hosts,
32:27 the **G** of all flesh; is anything too hard for me?
32:36 therefore thus says the LORD, the **G** of Israel, B
32:38 They shall be my people, and I will be their **G**.
33: 4 For thus says the LORD, the **G** of Israel, B
34: 2 the LORD, the **G** of Israel: B
34:13 the LORD, the **G** of Israel: B
35: 4 Hanan son of Igdaliah, the man of **G**, D
35:13 the LORD of hosts, the **G** of Israel: B
35:17 Therefore, thus says the LORD, the **G** of hosts, Q
35:17 the God of hosts, the **G** of Israel: B
35:18 Thus says the LORD of hosts, the **G** of Israel: B
35:19 thus says the LORD of hosts, the **G** of Israel: B
37: 3 "Please pray for us to the LORD our **G**." A
37: 7 Thus says the LORD, **G** of Israel: B
38:17 "Thus says the LORD, the **G** of hosts, Q
38:17 the God of hosts, the **G** of Israel, B
39:16 Thus says the LORD of hosts, the **G** of Israel: B
40: 2 "The LORD your **G** threatened this place A
42: 2 and pray to the LORD your **G** for us— A
42: 3 the LORD your **G** show us where we should go A
42: 4 the LORD your **G** as you request, and whatever A
42: 5 to everything that the LORD your **G** sends us A
42: 6 of the LORD our **G** to whom we are sending you, A
42: 6 when we obey the voice of the LORD our **G**." A
42: 9 "Thus says the LORD, the **G** of Israel, B
42:13 thus disobeying the voice of the LORD your **G** A
42:15 Thus says the LORD of hosts, the **G** of Israel: B
42:18 thus says the LORD of hosts, the **G** of Israel: B
42:20 For you yourselves sent me to the LORD your **G**, A
42:20 saying, 'Pray for us to the LORD our **G**, A
42:20 and whatever the LORD our **G** says, A
42:21 of the LORD your **G** in anything that he sent me A
43: 1 the people all these words of the LORD their **G**, A
43: 1 with which the LORD their **G** had sent him A
43: 2 The LORD our **G** did not send you to say, A
43:10 Thus says the LORD of hosts, the **G** of Israel: B
44: 2 the LORD of hosts, the **G** of Israel: B
44: 7 And now thus says the LORD **G** of hosts, GQ
44: 7 the LORD God of hosts, the **G** of Israel: B
44:11 thus says the LORD of hosts, the **G** of Israel: B
44:25 the LORD of hosts, the **G** of Israel: B
45: 2 the **G** of Israel, to you, O Baruch: B
46:25 The LORD of hosts, the **G** of Israel, said: B
Jer 48: 1 Thus says the LORD of hosts, the **G** of Israel: B
50: 4 as they seek the LORD their **G**. A
50:18 thus says the LORD of hosts, the **G** of Israel: B
50:28 in Zion the vengeance of the LORD our **G**, A
50:40 As when **G** overthrew Sodom and Gomorrah
51: 5 and Judah have not been forsaken by their **G**,
51:10 in Zion the work of the LORD our **G**. A
51:33 For thus says the LORD of hosts, the **G** of Israel: B
51:56 for the LORD is a **G** of recompense,
La 3:41 up our hearts as well as our hands to **G** in heaven.
Eze 1: 1 the heavens were opened, and I saw visions of **G**.
8: 3 and brought me in visions of **G** to Jerusalem,
8: 4 And the glory of the **G** of Israel was there, BR
8: 5 Then **G** said to me, "O mortal,
9: 3 Now the glory of the **G** of Israel had gone up BR
10: 5 like the voice of **G** Almighty when he speaks.
10:19 the glory of the **G** of Israel was above them. BR
10:20 creatures that I saw underneath the **G** of Israel B
11:20 they shall be my people, and I will be their **G**.
11:22 the glory of the **G** of Israel was above them. BR
11:24 and brought me in a vision by the spirit of **G** U
14:11 they shall be my people, and I will be their **G**,
20: 5 I swore to them, saying, I am the LORD your **G**. A
20: 7 I am the LORD your **G**. A
20:19 I the LORD am your **G**;
20:20 that you may know that I the LORD am your **G**.
28: 2 your heart is proud and you have said, "I am a **g**;
28: 2 yet you are but a mortal, and no **g**,
28: 2 you compare your mind with the mind of a **g**.
28: 6 you compare your mind with the mind of a **g**,
28: 9 Will you still say, "I am a **g**,"
28: 9 and no **g**, in the hands of those who wound you?
28:13 in Eden, the garden of **G**;
28:14 you were on the holy mountain of **G**;
28:16 as a profane thing from the mountain of **G**,
28:26 And they shall know that I am the LORD their **G**. A
31: 8 The cedars in the garden of **G** could not rival it,
31: 8 no tree in the garden of **G** was like it in beauty.
31: 9 the trees of Eden that were in the garden of **G**.
34:24 And I, the LORD, will be their **G**,
34:30 They shall know that I, the LORD their **G**, A
34:31 the sheep of my pasture and I am your **G**,
36:28 and you shall be my people, and I will be your **G**.
37:27 and I will be their **G**, and they shall be my people.
39:22 of Israel shall know that I am the LORD their **G**, A
39:28 Then they shall know that I am the LORD their **G** A
40: 2 He brought me, in visions of **G**,
43: 2 glory of the **G** of Israel was coming from BR
44: 2 for the LORD, the **G** of Israel, has entered by it; B
Da 1: 2 as well as some of the vessels of the house of **G**. C
1: 9 Now **G** allowed Daniel to receive favor
1:17 To these four young men **G** gave knowledge
2:18 told them to seek mercy from the **G** of heaven O
2:19 and Daniel blessed the **G** of heaven. O
2:20 "Blessed be the name of **G** from age to age,
2:23 To you, O **G** of my ancestors, F
2:28 but there is a **G** in heaven who reveals mysteries,
2:37 whom the **G** of heaven has given the kingdom, O
2:44 days of those kings the **G** of heaven will set up O
2:45 The great **G** has informed the king what shall
2:47 your **G** is **G** of gods and Lord of kings and
3:15 the **g** that will deliver you out of my hands?"
3:17 If our **G** whom we serve is able to deliver us from
3:25 and the fourth has the appearance of a **g**."
3:26 and Abednego, servants of the Most High **G**,
3:28 "Blessed be the **G** of Shadrach, Meshach,
3:28 and worship any **g** except their own **G**.
3:29 the **G** of Shadrach, Meshach, and Abednego shall
3:29 for there is no other **g** who is able to deliver
4: 2 the Most High **G** has worked for me I am pleased
4: 8 after the name of my **g**, and who is endowed with
5: 3 the house of **G** in Jerusalem, C
5:18 Most High **G** gave your father Nebuchadnezzar
5:21 the Most High **G** has sovereignty over the kingdom
5:23 but the **G** in whose power is your very breath,
5:26 **G** has numbered the days of your kingdom
6: 5 in connection with the law of his **G**." P
6:10 on his knees three times a day to pray to his **G**
6:11 and seeking mercy before his **G**.
6:16 The king said to Daniel, "May your **G**,
6:20 "O Daniel, servant of the living **G**, N
6:20 has your **G** whom you faithfully serve been able
6:22 My **G** sent his angel and shut the lions' mouths so
6:23 because he had trusted in his **G**.
6:26 and fear before the **G** of Daniel:
6:26 For he is the living **G**, enduring forever. N
9: 3 Then I turned to the Lord **G**, K
9: 4 to the LORD my **G** and made confession, A
9: 4 saying, "Ah, Lord, great and awesome **G**,
9: 9 To the Lord our **G** belong mercy and forgiveness, I
9:10 of the LORD our **G** by following his laws, A
9:11 the servant of **G**, have been poured out upon us,
9:13 We did not entreat the favor of the LORD our **G**, A
9:14 the LORD our **G** is right in all that he has done; A
9:15 "And now, O Lord our **G**, I
9:17 O our **G**, listen to the prayer of your servant and
9:18 Incline your ear, O my **G**, and hear.
9:19 For your own sake, O my **G**,
9:20 the LORD my **G** on behalf of the holy mountain A
9:20 on behalf of the holy mountain of my **G**—
10:12 and to humble yourself before your **G**,
11:32 to their **G** shall stand firm and take action.
11:36 and consider himself greater than any **g**,
11:36 and shall speak horrendous things against the **G**
11:37 he shall pay no respect to any other **g**,
11:38 He shall honor the **g** of fortresses instead of these;
11:38 a **g** whom his ancestors did not know
Da 11:39 the strongest fortresses by the help of a foreign **g**.
Hos 1: 7 and I will save them by the LORD their **G**; A
1: 9 for you are not my people and I am not your **G**."
1:10 be said to them, "Children of the living **G**." N
2:23 and he shall say, "You are my **G**."
3: 5 the LORD their **G**, and David their king; A
4: 1 and no knowledge of **G** in the land.
4: 6 And since you have forgotten the law of your **G**, P
4:12 and they have played the whore, forsaking their **G**.
5: 4 not permit them to return to their **G**.
6: 6 the knowledge of **G** rather than burnt offerings.
7:10 yet they do not return to the LORD their **G**, A
8: 2 Israel cries to me, "My **G**, we—
8: 6 For it is from Israel, an artisan made it; it is not **G**.
9: 1 the whore, departing from your **G**.
9: 8 The prophet is a sentinel for my **G** over Ephraim,
9: 8 and hostility in the house of his **G**. C
9:17 not listened to him, my **G** will reject them;
11: 9 for I am **G** and no mortal,
11:12 but Judah still walks with **G**,
12: 3 and in his manhood he strove with **G**.
12: 5 LORD the **G** of hosts, the LORD is his name! Q
12: 6 But as for you, return to your **G**,
12: 6 and wait continually for your **G**.
12: 9 I am the LORD your **G** from the land of Egypt; A
13: 4 the LORD your **G** ever since the land of Egypt; A
13: 4 no **G** but me, and besides me there is no savior.
13:16 because she has rebelled against her **G**;
14: 1 Return, O Israel, to the LORD your **G**, A
14: 3 we will say no more, 'Our **G**,'
Joel 1:13 the night in sackcloth, you ministers of my **G**!
1:13 from the house of your **G**. C
1:14 of the land to the house of the LORD your **G**, A
1:16 joy and gladness from the house of our **G**? C
2:13 Return to the LORD, your **G**, A
2:14 and a drink offering for the LORD, your **G**? A
2:17 be said among the peoples, 'Where is their **G**?' "
2:23 be glad and rejoice in the LORD your **G**; A
2:26 and praise the name of the LORD your **G**, A
2:27 the LORD, am your **G** and there is no other.
3:17 So you shall know that I, the LORD your **G**, A
Am 2: 8 and in the house of their **G** they drink wine bought
3:13 says the Lord GOD, the **G** of hosts: Q
4:11 as when **G** overthrew Sodom and Gomorrah,
4:12 I will do this to you, prepare to meet your **G**,
4:13 the LORD, the **G** of hosts, is his name! Q
5:14 and so the LORD, the **G** of hosts, Q
5:15 it may be that the LORD, the **G** of hosts, Q
5:16 thus says the LORD, the **G** of hosts, the Lord: Q
5:27 says the LORD, whose name is the **G** of hosts. Q
6: 8 by himself (says the LORD, the **G** of hosts): Q
6:14 O house of Israel, says the LORD, the **G** of hosts, Q
8:14 and say, "As your **g** lives, O Dan," and,
9:15 that I have given them, says the LORD your **G**. A
Jnh 1: 5 the mariners were afraid, and each cried to his **g**.
1: 6 Get up, call on your **g**!
1: 6 Perhaps the **g** will spare us a thought so that we
1: 9 "I worship the LORD, the **G** of heaven, O
2: 1 to the LORD his **G** from the belly of the fish, A
2: 6 up my life from the Pit, O LORD my **G**. A
3: 5 And the people of Nineveh believed **G**;
3: 8 and they shall cry mightily to **G**.
3: 9 **G** may relent and change his mind;
3:10 When **G** saw what they did,
3:10 **G** changed his mind about the calamity
4: 2 for I knew that you are a gracious **G** and merciful,
4: 6 The LORD **G** appointed a bush, G
4: 7 **G** appointed a worm that attacked the bush,
4: 8 When the sun rose, **G** prepared a sultry east wind,
4: 9 But **G** said to Jonah, "Is it right for you to
Mic 3: 7 for there is no answer from **G**.
4: 2 to the house of the **G** of Jacob; CV
4: 5 all the peoples walk, each in the name of its **g**,
4: 5 in the name of the LORD our **G** forever and ever. A
5: 4 in the majesty of the name of the LORD his **G**. A
6: 6 and bow myself before **G** on high? H
6: 8 and to walk humbly with your **G**?
7: 7 wait for the **G** of my salvation; my **G** will hear me.
7:10 "Where is the LORD your **G**?" A
7:17 they shall turn in dread to the LORD our **G**, A
7:18 Who is a **G** like you,
Na 1: 2 A jealous and avenging **G** is the LORD,
Hab 1:11 their own might is their **g**!
1:12 Are you not from of old, O LORD my **G**, A
3: 3 **G** came from Teman, the Holy One
3:18 I will exult in the **G** of my salvation.
Zep 2: 7 For the LORD their **G** will be mindful of them A
2: 9 as I live, says the LORD of hosts, the **G** of Israel, B
3: 2 it has not drawn near to its **G**.
3:17 The LORD, your **G**, is in your midst, A
Hag 1:12 obeyed the voice of the LORD their **G**, A
1:12 as the LORD their **G** had sent him; A
1:14 on the house of the LORD of hosts, their **G**,
Zec 6:15 the voice of the LORD your **G**. A
8: 8 They shall be my people and I will be their **G**,
8:23 for we have heard that **G** is with you."
9: 7 it too shall be a remnant for our **G**;
9:16 On that day the LORD their **G** will save them A
10: 6 I am the LORD their **G** and I will answer them. A
11: 4 Thus said the LORD my **G**: A
12: 5 through the LORD of hosts, their **G**."
12: 8 and the house of David shall be like **G**,
13: 9 and they will say, "The LORD is our **G**."
14: 5 Then the LORD my **G** will come, A
Mal 1: 9 And now implore the favor of **G**,
2:10 Has not one **G** created us?
2:11 and has married the daughter of a foreign **g**.

***GOD** distinguishes the words translated "God" and "god" from the compound name "Lord GOD," where GOD represents the name *Yahweh*. For this name see the heading †**GOD** on pages 541-42.

Mal 2:15 Did not one G make her?
2:15 And what does the one G desire?
2:16 I hate divorce, says the LORD, the G of Israel, B
2:17 Or by asking, "Where is the G of justice?"
3: 8 Will anyone rob G? Yet you are robbing me!
3:14 You have said, "It is vain to serve G.
3:15 but when they put G to the test they escape."
3:18 between one who serves G and one who does
Mt 1:23 which means, "G is with us."
3: 9 for I tell you, G is able from these stones to raise
3:16 he saw the Spirit of G descending like a dove U
4: 3 "If you are the Son of G, M
4: 4 every word that comes from the mouth of G.' "
4: 6 "If you are the Son of G, throw yourself down; M
4: 7 'Do not put the Lord your G to the test.' " I
4:10 for it is written, 'Worship the Lord your G, I
5: 8 "Blessed are the pure in heart, for they will see G.
5: 9 for they will be called children of G.
5:34 either by heaven, for it is the throne of G,
6:24 You cannot serve G and wealth.
6:30 But if G so clothes the grass of the field,
6:33 for the kingdom of G and his righteousness, E
8:29 "What have you to do with us, Son of G? M
9: 8 they were filled with awe, and they glorified G,
12: 4 the house of G and ate the bread of the Presence, C
12:28 if it is by the Spirit of G that I cast out demons, U
12:28 then the kingdom of G has come to you. E
14:33 saying, "Truly you are the Son of G." M
15: 3 "And why do you break the commandment of G
15: 4 For G said, 'Honor your father and your mother,'
15: 5 you might have had from me is given to G,'
15: 6 you make void the word of G. L
15:31 And they praised the G of Israel. B
16:16 "You are the Messiah, the Son of the living G." N
16:22 saying, "G forbid it, Lord!
19: 6 what G has joined together, let no one separate."
19:24 to enter the kingdom of G." E
19:26 but for G all things are possible."
21:31 the prostitutes are going into the kingdom of G E
21:43 the kingdom of G will be taken away from you E
22:16 and teach the way of G in accordance with truth,
22:21 and to G the things that are God's."
22:29 the scriptures nor the power of G. T
22:31 have you not read what was said to you by G,
22:32 'I am the G of Abraham, the G of Isaac,
22:32 the God of Isaac, and the G of Jacob'? V
22:32 He is G not of the dead, but of the living."
22:37 the Lord your G with all your heart, I
23:22 by the throne of G and by the one who is seated
26:61 the temple of G and to build it in three days.' "
26:63 "I put you under oath before the living G, N
26:63 tell us if you are the Messiah, the Son of G." M
27:40 are the Son of G, come down from the cross." M
27:43 He trusts in G; let G deliver him now, if he wants
27:46 is, "My G, my G, why have you forsaken me?"
Mk 1: 1 of the good news of Jesus Christ, the Son of G. M
1:14 proclaiming the good news of G,
1:15 and the kingdom of G has come near; E
1:24 I know who you are, the Holy One of G."
2: 7 Who can forgive sins but G alone?"
2:12 so that they were all amazed and glorified G,
2:26 He entered the house of G, C
3:11 "You are the Son of G!" M
3:35 the will of G is my brother and sister and X
4:11 has been given the secret of the kingdom of G, E
4:26 "The kingdom of G is as if someone would E
4:30 "With what can we compare the kingdom of G, E
5: 7 Jesus, Son of the Most High G?
5: 7 I adjure you by G, do not torment me."
7: 8 You abandon the commandment of G and hold
7: 9 a fine way of rejecting the commandment of G
7:11 from me is Corban' (that is, an offering to G)—
7:13 the word of G through your tradition L
9: 1 until they see that the kingdom of G has come E
9:47 the kingdom of G with one eye than to have E
10: 6 'G made them male and female.'
10: 9 what G has joined together, let no one separate."
10:14 to such as these that the kingdom of G belongs. E
10:15 whoever does not receive the kingdom of G as E
10:18 No one is good but G alone.
10:23 to enter the kingdom of G!" E
10:24 how hard it is to enter the kingdom of G! E
10:25 to enter the kingdom of G." E
10:27 but not for G; for G all things are possible."
11:22 Jesus answered them, "Have faith in G.
12:14 but teach the way of G in accordance with truth.
12:17 and to G the things that are God's."
12:24 the scriptures nor the power of G? T
12:26 how G said to him, 'I am the G of Abraham, the G of Isaac,
12:26 the God of Isaac, and the G of Jacob'? V
12:27 He is G not of the dead, but of the living;
12:29 the Lord our G, the Lord is one; I
12:30 shall love the Lord your G with all your heart, I
12:34 "You are not far from the kingdom of G." E
13:19 from the beginning of the creation that G created
14:25 day when I drink it new in the kingdom of G." E
15:34 "My G, my G, why have you forsaken me?"
15:43 for the kingdom of G, went boldly to Pilate E
16:19 ⟦heaven and sat down at the right hand of G.⟧ S
Lk 1: 6 Both of them were righteous before G, H
1: 8 as priest before G and his section was on duty, H
1:16 of the people of Israel to the Lord their G. I
1:19 I stand in the presence of G,
1:26 the sixth month the angel Gabriel was sent by G
1:30 Mary, for you have found favor with G.
1:32 and the Lord G will give to him the throne K

Lk 1:35 he will be called Son of G. M
1:37 For nothing will be impossible with G."
1:47 and my spirit rejoices in G my Savior,
1:64 and he began to speak, praising G.
1:68 "Blessed be the Lord G of Israel, BK
1:78 By the tender mercy of our G,
2:13 of the heavenly host, praising G and saying,
2:14 "Glory to G in the highest heaven,
2:20 glorifying and praising G for all they had heard
2:28 Simeon took him in his arms and praised G,
2:38 and began to praise G and to speak about the child
2:40 and the favor of G was upon him.
3: 2 the word of G came to John son of Zechariah L
3: 6 and all flesh shall see the salvation of G.' "
3: 8 for I tell you, G is able from these stones to raise
3:38 of Enos, son of Seth, son of Adam, son of G. M
4: 3 The devil said to him, "If you are the Son of G, M
4: 8 'Worship the Lord your G, and serve only him.' I
4: 9 saying to him, "If you are the Son of G, M
4:12 'Do not put the Lord your G to the test.' " I
4:34 I know who you are, the Holy One of G."
4:41 shouting, "You are the Son of G!" M
4:43 of the kingdom of G to the other cities also; E
5: 1 in on him to hear the word of G, L
5:21 Who can forgive sins but G alone?"
5:25 and went to his home, glorifying G.
5:26 and they glorified G and were filled with awe,
6: 4 the house of G and took and ate the bread of C
6:12 and he spent the night in prayer to G.
6:20 for yours is the kingdom of G. E
7:16 Fear seized all of them; and they glorified G,
7:16 and "G has looked favorably on his people!"
7:28 the least in the kingdom of G is greater than he." E
7:29 acknowledged the justice of G,
8: 1 bringing the good news of the kingdom of G. E
8:10 to know the secrets of the kingdom of G; E
8:11 the parable is this: The seed is the word of G. L
8:21 my brothers are those who hear the word of G L
8:28 Jesus, Son of the Most High G?
8:39 and declare how much G has done for you."
9: 2 to proclaim the kingdom of G and to heal. E
9:11 and spoke to them about the kingdom of G, E
9:20 Peter answered, "The Messiah of G."
9:27 taste death before they see the kingdom of G." E
9:43 And all were astounded at the greatness of G.
9:60 go and proclaim the kingdom of G." E
9:62 and looks back is fit for the kingdom of G." E
10: 9 'The kingdom of G has come near to you.' E
10:11 know this: the kingdom of G has come near.' E
10:27 love the Lord your G with all your heart, I
11:20 it is by the finger of G that I cast out the demons,
11:20 then the kingdom of G has come to you. E
11:28 Blessed rather are those who hear the word of G L
11:42 and neglect justice and the love of G;
11:49 Therefore also the Wisdom of G said,
12: 8 also will acknowledge before the angels of G;
12: 9 be denied before the angels of G.
12:20 But G said to him, 'You fool!
12:21 for themselves but are not rich toward G."
12:24 nor barn, and yet G feeds them.
12:28 But if G so clothes the grass of the field,
13:13 up straight and began praising G.
13:18 "What is the kingdom of G like? E
13:20 "To what should I compare the kingdom of G? E
13:28 and all the prophets in the kingdom of G, E
13:29 and will eat in the kingdom of G. E
14:15 who will eat bread in the kingdom of G!" E
15:10 of the angels of G over one sinner who repents."
16:13 You cannot serve G and wealth."
16:15 in the sight of others; but G knows your hearts;
16:15 an abomination in the sight of G.
16:16 good news of the kingdom of G is proclaimed, E
17:15 turned back, praising G with a loud voice.
17:18 and give praise to G except this foreigner?"
17:20 Pharisees when the kingdom of G was coming, E
17:20 "The kingdom of G is not coming with things E
17:21 For, in fact, the kingdom of G is among you." E
18: 2 a judge who neither feared G nor had respect
18: 4 I have no fear of G and no respect for anyone,
18: 7 not G grant justice to his chosen ones who cry
18:11 'G, I thank you that I am not like other people:
18:13 but was beating his breast and saying, 'G,
18:16 to such as these that the kingdom of G belongs. E
18:17 whoever does not receive the kingdom of G as E
18:19 No one is good but G alone.
18:24 to enter the kingdom of G! E
18:25 to enter the kingdom of G." E
18:27 What is impossible for mortals is possible for G."
18:29 for the sake of the kingdom of G, E
18:43 and followed him, glorifying G;
18:43 and all the people, when they saw it, praised G.
19:11 the kingdom of G was to appear immediately. E
19:37 of the disciples began to praise G joyfully with
19:44 not recognize the time of your visitation from G."
20:21 but teach the way of G in accordance with truth.
20:25 and to G the things that are God's."
20:36 because they are like angels and are children of G,
20:37 as the G of Abraham, the G of Isaac,
20:37 the God of Isaac, and the G of Jacob. V
20:38 Now he is G not of the dead, but of the living;
21: 5 with beautiful stones and gifts dedicated to G,
21:31 you know that the kingdom of G is near. E
22:16 eat it until it is fulfilled in the kingdom of G." E
22:18 of the vine until the kingdom of G comes." E
22:69 be seated at the right hand of the power of G." T
22:70 of them asked, "Are you, then, the Son of G?" M
23:35 let him save himself if he is the Messiah of G,

Lk 23:40 other rebuked him, saying, "Do you not fear G,
23:47 centurion saw what had taken place, he praised G
23:51 was waiting expectantly for the kingdom of G. E
24:19 in deed and word before G and all the people, H
24:53 they were continually in the temple blessing G.
Jn 1: 1 and the Word was with G, and the Word was G.
1: 2 He was in the beginning with G.
1: 6 There was a man sent from G,
1:12 he gave power to become children of G,
1:13 of the flesh or of the will of man, but of G.
1:18 No one has ever seen G.
1:18 It is G the only Son, who is close to the Father's
1:29 "Here is the Lamb of G who takes away the sin of
1:34 and have testified that this is the Son of G." M
1:36 he exclaimed, "Look, here is the Lamb of G!"
1:49 replied, "Rabbi, you are the Son of G! M
1:51 the angels of G ascending and descending upon
3: 2 that you are a teacher who has come from G;
3: 2 that you do apart from the presence of G."
3: 3 kingdom of G without being born from above." E
3: 5 the kingdom of G without being born of water E
3:16 G so loved the world that he gave his only Son,
3:17 G did not send the Son into the world to condemn
3:18 not believed in the name of the only Son of G. M
3:21 that their deeds have been done in G."
3:33 his testimony has certified this, that G is true.
3:34 He whom G has sent speaks the words of G,
4:10 Jesus answered her, "If you knew the gift of G,
4:24 G is spirit, and those who worship him must
5:18 but was also calling G his own Father,
5:18 thereby making himself equal to G.
5:25 the dead will hear the voice of the Son of G, M
5:42 I know that you do not have the love of G in you.
5:44 that comes from the one who alone is G?
6:27 For it is on him that G the Father has set his seal."
6:28 "What must we do to perform the works of G?"
6:29 Jesus answered them, "This is the work of G,
6:33 For the bread of G is that which comes down
6:45 'And they shall all be taught by G.'
6:46 the Father except the one who is from G;
6:69 and know that you are the Holy One of G."
7:17 Anyone who resolves to do the will of G X
7:17 will know whether the teaching is from G
8:40 the truth that I heard from G.
8:41 we have one father, G himself."
8:42 Jesus said to them, "If G were your Father,
8:42 for I came from G and now I am here.
8:47 Whoever is from G hears the words of G.
8:47 not hear them is that you are not from G."
8:54 he of whom you say, 'He is our G,'
9:16 "This man is not from G,
9:24 and they said to him, "Give glory to G!
9:29 We know that G has spoken to Moses,
9:31 We know that G does not listen to sinners,
9:33 this man were not from G, he could do nothing."
10:33 a human being, are making yourself G."
10:35 the word of G came were called 'gods'— L
11: 4 that the Son of G may be glorified through it." M
11:22 I know that G will give you whatever you ask
11:27 I believe that you are the Messiah, the Son of G, M
11:40 you would see the glory of G?" R
11:52 but to gather into one the dispersed children of G.
12:43 the glory that comes from G.
13: 3 that he had come from G and was going to G,
13:31 and G has been glorified in him.
13:32 If G has been glorified in him, G will also glorify
14: 1 Believe in G, believe also in me.
16: 2 that by doing so they are offering worship to G.
16:27 and have believed that I came from G.
16:30 by this we believe that you came from G."
17: 3 that they may know you, the only true G,
19: 7 die because he has claimed to be the Son of G." M
20:17 and your Father, to my G and your G.' "
20:28 Thomas answered him, "My Lord and my G!"
20:31 believe that Jesus is the Messiah, the Son of G, M
21:19 the kind of death by which he would glorify G.)
Ac 1: 3 and speaking about the kingdom of G. E
2:17 be, G declares, that I will pour out my Spirit
2:22 a man attested to you by G with deeds of power,
2:22 and signs that G did through him among you,
2:23 to the definite plan and foreknowledge of G,
2:24 But G raised him up, having freed him from death,
2:30 he knew that G had sworn with an oath to him
2:32 This Jesus G raised up, and of that all
2:33 Being therefore exalted at the right hand of G, S
2:36 with certainty that G has made him both Lord
2:39 everyone whom the Lord our G calls to him." I
2:47 praising G and having the goodwill of all
3: 8 walking and leaping and praising G.
3: 9 All the people saw him walking and praising G,
3:13 The G of Abraham, the G of Isaac,
3:13 the God of Isaac, and the G of Jacob, V
3:13 G of our ancestors has glorified his servant Jesus F
3:15 whom G raised from the dead.
3:18 In this way G fulfilled what he had foretold
3:19 and turn to G so that your sins may be wiped out,
3:21 universal restoration that G announced long ago
3:22 'The Lord your G will raise up for you I
3:25 and of the covenant that G gave to your ancestors,
3:26 When G raised up his servant,
4:10 whom G raised from the dead.
4:19 to listen to you rather than to G, you must judge;
4:21 for all of them praised G for what had happened.
4:24 they raised their voices together to G and said,
4:31 with the Holy Spirit and spoke the word of G L
5: 4 You did not lie to us but to G!"
5:29 "We must obey G rather than any human authority.

***GOD** distinguishes the words translated "God" and "god" from the compound name "Lord GOD," where GOD represents the name *Yahweh*. For this name see the heading †**GOD** on pages 541-42.

Ac 5:30 The G of our ancestors raised up Jesus, F
5:31 G exalted him at his right hand as Leader
5:32 and so is the Holy Spirit whom G has given
5:39 of G, you will not be able to overthrow them—
5:39 even be found fighting against G!"
6: 2 not right that we should neglect the word of G L
6: 7 The word of G continued to spread; L
6:11 speak blasphemous words against Moses and G."
7: 2 The G of glory appeared to our ancestor Abraham
7: 4 G had him move from there to this country
7: 6 And G spoke in these terms,
7: 7 I will judge the nation that they serve,' said G,
7: 9 sold him into Egypt; but G was with him,
7:17 for the fulfillment of the promise that G had made
7:20 and he was beautiful before G. H
7:25 that his kinsfolk would understand that G
7:32 'I am the G of your ancestors, F
7:32 the G of Abraham, Isaac, and Jacob.'
7:35 and whom G now sent as both ruler and liberator
7:37 'G will raise up a prophet for you
7:42 But G turned away from them and handed them
7:43 and the star of your g Rephan,
7:44 as G directed when he spoke to Moses,
7:45 the nations that G drove out before our ancestors.
7:46 with G and asked that he might find
7:55 glory of G and Jesus standing at the right hand R
7:55 and Jesus standing at the right hand of G. S
7:56 the Son of Man standing at the right hand of G!" S
8:10 This man is the power of G that is called Great." T
8:12 the kingdom of G and the name of Jesus Christ, E
8:14 that Samaria had accepted the word of G, L
8:21 for your heart is not right before G. H
9:20 saying, "He is the Son of G." M
10: 2 He was a devout man who feared G
10: 2 to the people and prayed constantly to G.
10: 3 in which he clearly saw an angel of G coming Z
10: 4 alms have ascended as a memorial before G. H
10:15 a second time, "What G has made clean,
10:28 but G has shown me that I should
10:31 and your alms have been remembered before G. H
10:33 of us are here in the presence of G to listen to all
10:34 "I truly understand that G shows no partiality,
10:38 how G anointed Jesus of Nazareth with the Holy
10:38 were oppressed by the devil, for G was with him.
10:40 but G raised him on the third day and allowed him
10:41 to all the people but to us who were chosen by G
10:42 to testify that he is the one ordained by G as judge
10:46 in tongues and extolling G.
11: 1 the Gentiles had also accepted the word of G. L
11: 9 from heaven, 'What G has made clean, you must
11:17 If then G gave them the same gift that he gave us
11:17 who was I that I could hinder G?"
11:18 And they praised G, saying,
11:18 "Then G has given even to the Gentiles
11:23 When he came and saw the grace of G, W
12: 5 the church prayed fervently to G for him.
12:22 The people kept shouting, "The voice of a g,
12:23 because he had not given the glory to G,
12:24 the word of G continued to advance and gain L
13: 5 proclaimed the word of G in the synagogues L
13: 7 and Saul and wanted to hear the word of G. L
13:16 "You Israelites, and others who fear G, listen. Y
13:17 The G of this people Israel chose our ancestors
13:21 and G gave them Saul son of Kish,
13:23 Of this man's posterity G has brought to Israel
13:26 of Abraham's family, and others who fear G, Y
13:30 But G raised him from the dead;
13:32 that what G promised to our ancestors
13:36 of G in his own generation, died, was laid
13:37 he whom G raised up experienced no corruption.
13:43 and urged them to continue in the grace of G. W
13:46 that the word of G should be spoken first to you. L
14:15 from these worthless things to the living G, N
14:22 that we must enter the kingdom of G." E
14:26 the grace of G for the work that they had W
14:27 the church together and related all that G had done
15: 4 and they reported all that G had done with them.
15: 7 that in the early days G made a choice among you,
15: 8 And G, who knows the human heart,
15:10 Now therefore why are you putting G to the test
15:12 and wonders that G had done through them among
15:14 Simeon has related how G first looked favorably
15:19 not trouble those Gentiles who are turning to G,
16:10 being convinced that G had called us to proclaim
16:14 A certain woman named Lydia, a worshiper of G,
16:17 "These men are slaves of the Most High G,
16:25 and Silas were praying and singing hymns to G,
16:34 that he had become a believer in G.
17:13 that the word of G had been proclaimed by Paul L
17:23 an altar with the inscription, 'To an unknown g.'
17:24 The G who made the world and everything in it,
17:27 so that they would search for G and perhaps grope
17:30 G has overlooked the times of human ignorance,
18: 7 of a man named Titius Justus, a worshiper of G;
18:11 teaching the word of G among them. L
18:13 to worship G in ways that are contrary to the law."
18:21 he said, "I will return to you, if G wills."
18:26 they took him aside and explained the Way of G
19: 8 argued persuasively about the kingdom of G. E
19:11 G did extraordinary miracles through Paul,
20:21 both Jews and Greeks about repentance toward G
20:27 from declaring to you the whole purpose of G.
20:28 to shepherd the church of G that he obtained with
20:32 And now I commend you to G and to the message
21:19 he related one by one the things that G had done
21:20 When they heard it, they praised G.
22: 3 being zealous for G, just as all of you are today.

Ac 22:14 'The G of our ancestors has chosen you F
23: 1 with a clear conscience before G." H
23: 3 At this Paul said to him, "G will strike you,
24:14 I worship the G of our ancestors, F
24:15 I have a hope in G—a hope that they themselves
24:16 a clear conscience toward G and all people.
26: 6 on account of my hope in the promise made by G
26: 8 by any of you that G raises the dead?
26:18 to light and from the power of Satan to G,
26:20 to G and do deeds consistent with repentance.
26:22 To this day I have had help from G,
26:29 I pray to G that not only you but
27:23 last night there stood by me an angel of the G Z
27:24 G has granted safety to all those who are sailing
27:25 in G that it will be exactly as I have been told.
27:35 and giving thanks to G in the presence of all,
28: 6 and began to say that he was a g.
28:15 Paul thanked G and took courage.
28:23 the kingdom of G and trying to convince them E
28:28 to you then that this salvation of G has been sent
28:31 proclaiming the kingdom of G and teaching E
Ro 1: 1 set apart for the gospel of G,
1: 4 Son of G with power according to the spirit of M
1: 7 Grace to you and peace from G our Father and
1: 8 I thank my G through Jesus Christ for all of you,
1: 9 For G, whom I serve with my spirit
1:16 the power of G for salvation to everyone who T
1:17 the righteousness of G is revealed through faith
1:18 For the wrath of G is revealed from heaven
1:19 For what can be known about G is plain to them,
1:19 because G has shown it to them.
1:21 for though they knew G, they did not honor him as
G or give thanks to him,
1:23 exchanged the glory of the immortal G for R
1:24 Therefore G gave them up in the lusts
1:25 because they exchanged the truth about G for a lie
1:26 this reason G gave them up to degrading passions.
1:28 And since they did not see fit to acknowledge G,
1:28 G gave them up to a debased mind and to things
2: 3 you will escape the judgment of G?
2:11 For G shows no partiality.
2:16 according to my gospel, G, through Jesus Christ,
2:17 and rely on the law and boast of your relation to G
2:23 do you dishonor G by breaking the law?
2:24 of G is blasphemed among the Gentiles because
2:29 not from others but from G.
3: 2 the Jews were entrusted with the oracles of G.
3: 3 their faithlessness nullify the faithfulness of G?
3: 4 Although everyone is a liar, let G be proved true,
3: 5 if our injustice serves to confirm the justice of G,
3: 5 That G is unjust to inflict wrath on us?
3: 6 For then how could G judge the world?
3:11 there is no one who seeks G.
3:18 "There is no fear of G before their eyes."
3:19 the whole world may be held accountable to G.
3:21 the righteousness of G has been disclosed,
3:22 the righteousness of G through faith
3:23 all have sinned and fall short of the glory of G; R
3:25 whom G put forward as a sacrifice of atonement
3:29 Or is G the G of Jews only? Is he not the G of
Gentiles also?
3:30 since G is one; and he will justify the circumcised
4: 2 has something to boast about, but not before G. H
4: 3 "Abraham believed G, and it was reckoned to him
4: 6 of those to whom G reckons righteousness apart
4:17 in the presence of the G in whom he believed,
4:20 concerning the promise of G,
4:20 he grew strong in his faith as he gave glory to G,
4:21 that G was able to do what he had promised.
5: 1 with G through our Lord Jesus Christ,
5: 2 we boast in our hope of sharing the glory of G. R
5: 8 But G proves his love for us in that
5: 9 be saved through him from the wrath of G.
5:10 we were reconciled to G through the death
5:11 we even boast in G through our Lord Jesus Christ,
5:15 grace of G and the free gift in the grace of the W
6:10 but the life he lives, he lives to G.
6:11 to sin and alive to G in Christ Jesus.
6:13 to G as those who have been brought from death
6:13 and present your members to G as instruments
6:17 But thanks be to G that you,
6:22 you have been freed from sin and enslaved to G,
6:23 of G is eternal life in Christ Jesus our Lord.
7: 4 the dead in order that we may bear fruit for G.
7:22 For I delight in the law of G in my inmost self, P
7:25 Thanks be to G through Jesus Christ our Lord!
7:25 then, with my mind I am a slave to the law of G, P
8: 3 For G has done what the law,
8: 7 the mind that is set on the flesh is hostile to G;
8: 8 and those who are in the flesh cannot please G.
8: 9 since the Spirit of G dwells in you. U
8:14 For all who are led by the Spirit of G are U
8:14 who are led by the Spirit of God are children of G.
8:16 with our spirit that we are children of G,
8:17 then heirs, heirs of G and joint heirs with Christ—
8:19 for the revealing of the children of G;
8:21 the freedom of the glory of the children of G.
8:27 And G, who searches the heart,
8:27 for the saints according to the will of G. X
8:28 for good for those who love G,
8:31 If G is for us, who is against us?
8:33 It is G who justifies.
8:34 who was raised, who is at the right hand of G, S
8:39 will be able to separate us from the love of G
9: 5 who is over all, G blessed forever.
9: 6 It is not as though the word of G had failed. L
9: 8 of the flesh who are the children of G,

Ro 9:16 but on G who shows mercy.
9:20 a human being, to argue with G?
9:22 What if G, desiring to show his wrath and
9:26 they shall be called children of the living G." N
10: 1 my heart's desire and prayer to G for them is
10: 2 I can testify that they have a zeal for G,
10: 3 of the righteousness that comes from G,
10: 9 and believe in your heart that G raised him from
11: 1 I ask, then, has G rejected his people?
11: 2 G has not rejected his people whom he foreknew.
11: 2 how he pleads with G against Israel?
11: 8 "G gave them a sluggish spirit,
11:21 For if G did not spare the natural branches,
11:22 Note then the kindness and the severity of G:
11:23 for G has the power to graft them in again.
11:28 the gospel they are enemies of G for your sake;
11:29 for the gifts and the calling of G are irrevocable.
11:30 Just as you were once disobedient to G but have
11:32 For G has imprisoned all in disobedience so
11:33 of the riches and wisdom and knowledge of G!
12: 1 brothers and sisters, by the mercies of G,
12: 1 holy and acceptable to G,
12: 2 so that you may discern what is the will of G— X
12: 3 to the measure of faith that G has assigned.
12:19 but leave room for the wrath of G;
13: 1 for there is no authority except from G,
13: 1 that exist have been instituted by G.
13: 2 resists authority resists what G has appointed,
13: 4 It is the servant of G to execute wrath on
14: 3 for G has welcomed them.
14: 6 since they give thanks to G;
14: 6 abstain in honor of the Lord and give thanks to G.
14:10 we will all stand before the judgment seat of G.
14:11 and every tongue shall give praise to G."
14:12 So then, each of us will be accountable to G.
14:17 the kingdom of G is not food and drink but E
14:18 The one who thus serves Christ is acceptable to G
14:20 for the sake of food, destroy the work of G.
14:22 have as your own conviction before G. H
15: 5 May the G of steadfastness
15: 6 that together you may with one voice glorify the G
15: 7 as Christ has welcomed you, for the glory of G. R
15: 8 of the truth of G in order that he might confirm
15: 9 that the Gentiles might glorify G for his mercy.
15:13 May the G of hope fill you with all joy and peace
15:15 because of the grace given me by G
15:16 in the priestly service of the gospel of G,
15:17 then, I have reason to boast of my work for G.
15:19 by the power of the Spirit of G, U
15:30 to join me in earnest prayer to G on my behalf,
15:33 The G of peace be with all of you. Amen.
16:20 The G of peace will shortly crush Satan
16:25 Now to G who is able to strengthen you according
16:26 according to the command of the eternal G,
16:27 the only wise G, through Jesus Christ, to whom
1Co 1: 1 to be an apostle of Christ Jesus by the will of G, X
1: 2 of G that is in Corinth, to those who are sanctified
1: 3 Grace to you and peace from G our Father and
1: 4 I give thanks to my G always for you because of
1: 4 the grace of G that has been given you W
1: 9 G is faithful; by him you were called into the
1:14 I thank G that I baptized none
1:18 to us who are being saved it is the power of G. T
1:20 Has not G made foolish the wisdom of the world?
1:21 For since, in the wisdom of G, the world did not
know G through wisdom, G decided,
1:24 Christ the power of G and the wisdom of God. T
1:24 Christ the power of God and the wisdom of G.
1:27 But G chose what is foolish in the world to shame
1:27 G chose what is weak in the world to shame
1:28 G chose what is low and despised in the world,
1:29 so that no one might boast in the presence of G.
1:30 who became for us wisdom from G,
2: 1 the mystery of G to you in lofty words or wisdom.
2: 5 not on human wisdom but on the power of G. T
2: 7 which G decreed before the ages for our glory.
2: 9 what G has prepared for those who love him"—
2:10 these things G has revealed to us through
2:10 Spirit searches everything, even the depths of G.
2:11 what is truly God's except the Spirit of G. U
2:12 but the Spirit that is from G,
2:12 we may understand the gifts bestowed on us by G.
3: 6 I planted, Apollos watered, but G gave the growth.
3: 7 but only G who gives the growth.
3:10 According to the grace of G given to me, W
3:17 G will destroy that person.
3:19 the wisdom of this world is foolishness with G.
3:23 and you belong to Christ, and Christ belongs to G.
4: 5 each one will receive commendation from G.
4: 9 For I think that G has exhibited us apostles as last
4:20 kingdom of G depends not on talk but on power. E
5:13 G will judge those outside.
6: 9 not inherit the kingdom of G? E
6:10 none of these will inherit the kingdom of G. E
6:11 of the Lord Jesus Christ and in the Spirit of our G.
6:13 and G will destroy both one and the other.
6:14 And G raised the Lord and will also raise us
6:19 which you have from G, and that you are
6:20 therefore glorify G in your body.
7: 7 But each has a particular gift from G,
7:15 It is to peace that G has called you.
7:17 that the Lord has assigned, to which G called you.
7:19 obeying the commandments of G is everything.
7:24 brothers and sisters, there remain with G.
7:40 And I think that I too have the Spirit of G. U
8: 3 but anyone who loves G is known by him.
8: 4 and that "there is no G but one."

*GOD distinguishes the words translated "God" and "god" from the compound name "Lord GOD," where GOD represents the name *Yahweh*. For this name see the heading †GOD on pages 541-42.

1Co 8: 6 yet for us there is one G,
8: 8 "Food will not bring us close to G."
9: 9 Is it for oxen that G is concerned?
10: 5 G was not pleased with most of them,
10:13 G is faithful, and he will not let you be tested
10:20 they sacrifice to demons and not to G.
10:31 do everything for the glory of G. R
10:32 to Jews or to Greeks or to the church of G,
11: 3 and G is the head of Christ.
11: 7 since he is the image and reflection of G;
11:12 but all things come from G.
11:13 for a woman to pray to G with her head unveiled?
11:16 nor do the churches of G.
11:22 Or do you show contempt for the church of G
12: 3 the Spirit of G ever says "Let Jesus be cursed!" U
12: 6 the same G who activates all of them in everyone.
12:18 But as it is, G arranged the members in the body,
12:24 But G has so arranged the body,
12:28 And G has appointed in the church first apostles,
14: 2 in a tongue do not speak to other people but to G;
14:18 I thank G that I speak in tongues more than all
14:25 will bow down before G and worship him, H
14:25 declaring, "G is really among you."
14:28 in church and speak to themselves and to G.
14:33 for G is a G not of disorder but of peace.
14:36 Or did the word of G originate with you? L
15: 9 because I persecuted the church of G.
15:10 But by the grace of G I am what I am, W
15:10 it was not I, but the grace of G that is with me. W
15:15 We are even found to be misrepresenting G,
15:15 because we testified of G that he raised Christ—
15:24 when he hands over the kingdom to G the Father,
15:27 "G has put all things in subjection under his feet."
15:28 so that G may be all in all.
15:34 for some people have no knowledge of G.
15:38 But G gives it a body as he has chosen,
15:50 flesh and blood cannot inherit the kingdom of G, E
15:57 But thanks be to G, who gives us the victory
2Co 1: 1 Paul, an apostle of Christ Jesus by the will of G, X
1: 1 To the church of G that is in Corinth,
1: 2 Grace to you and peace from G our Father and
1: 3 be the G and Father of our Lord Jesus Christ,
1: 3 the Father of mercies and the G of all consolation,
1: 4 with which we ourselves are consoled by G.
1: 9 not on ourselves but on G who raises the dead.
1:12 not by earthly wisdom but by the grace of G— W
1:18 As surely as G is faithful,
1:19 For the Son of G, Jesus Christ, M
1:20 that we say the "Amen," to the glory of G. R
1:21 But it is G who establishes us with you in Christ
1:23 But I call on G as witness against me:
2:14 But thanks be to G, who in Christ always leads us
2:15 of Christ to G among those who are being saved
2:17 persons sent from G and standing in his presence.
3: 3 not with ink but with the Spirit of the living G, N
3: 4 that we have through Christ toward G.
3: 5 our competence is from G,
4: 2 to the conscience of everyone in the sight of G.
4: 4 the g of this world has blinded the minds of
4: 4 who is the image of G.
4: 6 For it is the G who said,
4: 6 the light of the knowledge of the glory of G R
4: 7 that this extraordinary power belongs to G
4:15 may increase thanksgiving, to the glory of G. R
5: 1 we have a building from G,
5: 5 He who has prepared us for this very thing is G,
5:11 but we ourselves are well known to G,
5:13 For if we are beside ourselves, it is for G;
5:18 All this is from G, who reconciled us to himself
5:19 in Christ G was reconciling the world to himself,
5:20 since G is making his appeal through us;
5:20 on behalf of Christ, be reconciled to G.
5:21 in him we might become the righteousness of G.
6: 1 we urge you also not to accept the grace of G W
6: 4 as servants of G we have commended ourselves
6: 7 truthful speech, and the power of G; T
6:16 What agreement has the temple of G with idols?
6:16 For we are the temple of the living G; N
6:16 For we are the temple of the living God; as G said,
6:16 and I will be their G, and they shall be my people.
7: 1 making holiness perfect in the fear of G.
7: 6 But G, who consoles the downcast,
7:12 for us might be made known to you before G. H
8: 1 about the grace of G that has been granted to W
8: 5 first to the Lord and, by the will of G, to us, X
8:16 But thanks be to G who put in the heart of Titus
9: 7 for G loves a cheerful giver.
9: 8 And G is able to provide you with every blessing
9:11 which will produce thanksgiving to G through us;
9:12 but also overflows with many thanksgivings to G.
9:13 Through the testing of this ministry you glorify G
9:14 the surpassing grace of G that he has given you. W
9:15 Thanks be to G for his indescribable gift!
10: 5 up against the knowledge of G,
10:13 but will keep within the field that G has assigned
11:11 Because I do not love you? G knows I do!
11:31 The G and Father of the Lord Jesus (blessed be he
12: 2 or out of the body I do not know; G knows.
12: 3 or out of the body I do not know; G knows—
12:19 We are speaking in Christ before G. H
12:21 my G may humble me before you,
13: 4 but lives by the power of G. T
13: 4 we will live with him by the power of G. T
13: 7 to G that you may not do anything wrong—
13:11 and the G of love and peace will be with you.
13:13 The grace of the Lord Jesus Christ, the love of G,
Gal 1: 1 but through Jesus Christ and G the Father,
Gal 1: 3 Grace to you and peace from G our Father and
1: 4 according to the will of our G and Father, X
1:13 the church of G and was trying to destroy it.
1:15 when G, who had set me apart before I was born
1:20 what I am writing to you, before G, I do not lie! H
1:24 And they glorified G because of me.
2: 6 to me; G shows no partiality)—
2:19 the law I died to the law, so that I might live to G.
2:20 in the flesh I live by faith in the Son of G, M
2:21 I do not nullify the grace of G; W
3: 5 does G supply you with the Spirit
3: 6 Just as Abraham "believed G,
3: 8 foreseeing that G would justify the Gentiles
3:11 it is evident that no one is justified before G H
3:17 not annul a covenant previously ratified by G,
3:18 but G granted it to Abraham through the promise.
3:20 involves more than one party; but G is one.
3:21 Is the law then opposed to the promises of G?
3:26 for in Christ Jesus you are all children of G
4: 4 the fullness of time had come, G sent his Son,
4: 6 G has sent the Spirit of his Son into our hearts,
4: 7 and if a child then also an heir, through G.
4: 8 Formerly, when you did not know G,
4: 9 Now, however, that you have come to know G,
4: 9 or rather to be known by G,
4:14 but welcomed me as an angel of G, Z
5:21 not inherit the kingdom of G. E
6: 7 G is not mocked, for you reap whatever you sow.
6:16 and mercy, and upon the Israel of G.
Eph 1: 1 Paul, an apostle of Christ Jesus by the will of G, X
1: 2 Grace to you and peace from G our Father and
1: 3 be the G and Father of our Lord Jesus Christ,
1:17 I pray that the G of our Lord Jesus Christ,
1:20 G put this power to work in Christ
2: 4 But G, who is rich in mercy,
2: 8 not your own doing; it is the gift of G—
2:10 which G prepared beforehand to be our way
2:12 having no hope and without G in the world.
2:16 and might reconcile both groups to G in one body
2:19 and also members of the household of G,
2:22 into a dwelling place for G.
3: 9 for ages in G who created all things;
3:10 of G in its rich variety might now be made known
3:12 to G in boldness and confidence through faith
3:19 that you may be filled with all the fullness of G.
4: 6 one G and Father of all,
4:13 the faith and of the knowledge of the Son of G, M
4:18 of G because of their ignorance and hardness
4:24 to the likeness of G in true righteousness
4:30 And do not grieve the Holy Spirit of G, U
4:32 as G in Christ has forgiven you.
5: 1 Therefore be imitators of G, as beloved children,
5: 2 a fragrant offering and sacrifice to G.
5: 5 in the kingdom of Christ and of G.
5: 6 for because of these things the wrath of G comes
5:20 to G the Father at all times and for everything in
6: 6 doing the will of G from the heart. X
6:11 Put on the whole armor of G,
6:13 Therefore take up the whole armor of G,
6:17 which is the word of G. L
6:23 from G the Father and the Lord Jesus Christ.
Php 1: 2 Grace to you and peace from G our Father and
1: 3 I thank my G every time I remember you,
1: 8 For G is my witness, how I long for all of you
1:11 through Jesus Christ for the glory and praise of G.
2: 6 though he was in the form of G,
2: 6 did not regard equality with G as something to
2: 9 Therefore G also highly exalted him and gave him
2:11 to the glory of G the Father. R
2:13 for it is G who is at work in you,
2:15 of G without blemish in the midst of a crooked
2:27 But G had mercy on him,
3: 3 in the Spirit of G and boast in Christ Jesus U
3: 9 the righteousness from G based on faith.
3:14 the prize of the heavenly call of G in Christ Jesus.
3:15 this too G will reveal to you.
3:19 Their end is destruction; their g is the belly;
4: 6 let your requests be made known to G.
4: 7 the peace of G, which surpasses all understanding,
4: 9 and the G of peace will be with you.
4:18 a sacrifice acceptable and pleasing to G.
4:19 And my G will fully satisfy every need of yours
4:20 To our G and Father be glory forever and ever.
Col 1: 1 Paul, an apostle of Christ Jesus by the will of G, X
1: 2 Grace to you and peace from G our Father.
1: 3 In our prayers for you we always thank G,
1: 6 and truly comprehended the grace of G. W
1:10 and as you grow in the knowledge of G.
1:15 He is the image of the invisible G,
1:19 in him all the fullness of G was pleased to dwell,
1:20 and through him G was pleased to reconcile
1:25 to make the word of G fully known, L
1:27 To them G chose to make known how great
2:12 with him through faith in the power of G, T
2:13 G made you alive together with him,
2:19 grows with a growth that is from G.
3: 1 where Christ is, seated at the right hand of G. S
3: 3 and your life is hidden with Christ in G.
3: 6 On account of these the wrath of G is coming
3:16 hymns, and spiritual songs to G.
3:17 giving thanks to G the Father through him.
4: 3 as well that G will open to us a door for the word,
4:11 among my co-workers for the kingdom of G, E
4:12 and fully assured in everything that G wills.
1Th 1: 1 To the church of the Thessalonians in G the Father
1: 2 to G for all of you and mention you in your prayers,
1: 3 remembering before our G and Father your work
1Th 1: 4 For we know, brothers and sisters beloved by G,
1: 8 in every place your faith in G has become known,
1: 9 and how you turned to G from idols, to serve a
living and true G,
2: 2 courage in our G to declare to you the gospel of G
2: 4 as we have been approved by G to be entrusted
2: 4 but to please G who tests our hearts.
2: 5 As you know and as G is our witness,
2: 8 not only the gospel of G but also our own selves,
2: 9 while we proclaimed to you the gospel of G.
2:10 You are witnesses, and G also, how pure, upright,
2:12 and pleading that you lead a life worthy of G,
2:13 We also constantly give thanks to G for this,
2:13 when you received the word of G that you heard L
2:14 the churches of G in Christ Jesus that are in Judea,
2:15 they displease G and oppose everyone
3: 2 our brother and co-worker for G in proclaiming
3: 9 How can we thank G enough for you in return
3: 9 the joy that we feel before our G because of you?
3:11 Now may our G and Father himself
3:13 that you may be blameless before our G
4: 1 from us how you ought to live and to please G
4: 3 For this is the will of G, your sanctification: X
4: 5 like the Gentiles who do not know G;
4: 7 For G did not call us to impurity but in holiness.
4: 8 not human authority but G,
4: 9 for you yourselves have been taught by G
4:14 G will bring with him those who have died.
5: 9 For G has destined us not for wrath but
5:18 for this is the will of G in Christ Jesus for you. X
5:23 May the G of peace himself sanctify you entirely;
2Th 1: 1 the church of the Thessalonians in G our Father
1: 2 Grace to you and peace from G our Father and
1: 3 We must always give thanks to G for you,
1: 4 the churches of G for your steadfastness and faith
1: 5 This is evidence of the righteous judgment of G,
1: 5 to make you worthy of the kingdom of G, E
1: 6 of G to repay with affliction those who afflict you,
1: 8 on those who do not know G and on those who do
1:11 asking that our G will make you worthy of his call
1:12 to the grace of our G and the Lord Jesus Christ. W
2: 4 above every so-called g or object of worship, so
that he takes his seat in the temple of G, declaring
himself to be G.
2:11 For this reason G sends them a powerful delusion,
2:13 But we must always give thanks to G for you,
2:13 because G chose you as the first fruits
2:16 and G our Father, who loved us and
3: 5 to the love of G and to the steadfastness of Christ.
1Ti 1: 1 of Christ Jesus by the command of G our Savior
1: 2 from G the Father and Christ Jesus our Lord.
1:11 conforms to the glorious gospel of the blessed G,
1:17 the only G, be honor and glory forever and ever.
2: 3 and is acceptable in the sight of G our Savior,
2: 5 there is one G; there is also one mediator between
G and humankind,
2:10 is proper for women who profess reverence for G.
3:15 how one ought to behave in the household of G,
3:15 which is the church of the living G, N
4: 3 which G created to be received with thanksgiving
4: 4 For everything created by G is good,
4:10 because we have our hope set on the living G, N
5: 5 has set her hope on G and continues
5:21 of G and of Christ Jesus and of the elect angels,
6: 1 so that the name of G and the teaching may not
6:11 But as for you, man of G, shun all this; D
6:13 In the presence of G, who gives life to all things,
6:17 on G who richly provides us with everything
2Ti 1: 1 Paul, an apostle of Christ Jesus by the will of G, X
1: 2 from G the Father and Christ Jesus our Lord.
1: 3 I am grateful to G— whom I worship with a
1: 6 to rekindle the gift of G that is within you through
1: 7 for G did not give us a spirit of cowardice,
1: 8 relying on the power of G, T
2: 9 But the word of G is not chained. L
2:14 before G that they are to avoid wrangling H
2:15 to present yourself to G as one approved by him,
2:25 G may perhaps grant that they will repent
3: 4 lovers of pleasure rather than lovers of G,
3:16 All scripture is inspired by G and is useful
3:17 that everyone who belongs to G may be proficient,
4: 1 In the presence of G and of Christ Jesus,
Tit 1: 1 Paul, a servant of G and an apostle of Jesus Christ,
1: 2 of eternal life that G, who never lies, promised
1: 3 by the command of G our Savior,
1: 4 from G the Father and Christ Jesus our Savior.
1:16 They profess to know G, but they deny him
2: 5 so that the word of G may not be discredited. L
2:10 be an ornament to the doctrine of G our Savior.
2:11 For the grace of G has appeared, W
2:13 the glory of our great G and Savior, Jesus Christ.
3: 4 and loving kindness of G our Savior appeared,
3: 8 so that those who have come to believe in G may
Phm 1: 3 Grace to you and peace from G our Father and
1: 4 in my prayers, I always thank my G
Heb 1: 1 Long ago G spoke to our ancestors in many
1: 5 For to which of the angels did G ever say,
1: 8 But of the Son he says, "Your throne, O G,
1: 9 therefore G, your G, has anointed you
2: 4 while G added his testimony by signs
2: 5 Now G did not subject the coming world,
2: 8 G left nothing outside their control.
2: 9 grace of G he might taste death for everyone. W
2:10 It was fitting that G, for whom and
2:13 and the children whom G has given me."
2:17 and faithful high priest in the service of G,
3: 4 but the builder of all things is G.)

***GOD** distinguishes the words translated "God" and "god" from the compound name "Lord GOD," where GOD represents the name *Yahweh*. For this name see the heading †**GOD** on pages 541-42.

Heb 3:12 that turns away from the living G. N
4: 3 just as G has said, "As in my anger I swore,
4: 4 G rested on the seventh day from all his works."
4: 8 G would not speak later about another day.
4: 9 a sabbath rest still remains for the people of G;
4:10 also cease from their labors as G did from his.
4:12 Indeed, the word of G is living and active, L
4:14 the Son of G, let us hold fast to our confession. M
5: 1 in charge of things pertaining to G on their behalf,
5: 4 but takes it only when called by G,
5:10 having been designated by G a high priest
5:12 the basic elements of the oracles of G.
6: 1 repentance from dead works and faith toward G,
6: 3 And we will do this, if G permits.
6: 5 and have tasted the goodness of the word of G L
6: 6 Son of G and are holding him up to contempt. M
6: 7 receives a blessing from G.
6:10 For G is not unjust; he will not overlook your work
6:13 When G made a promise to Abraham,
6:17 when G desired to show even more clearly to
6:18 in which it is impossible that G would prove false,
7: 1 priest of the Most High G,
7: 3 but resembling the Son of G, M
7:19 through which we approach G.
7:25 to save those who approach G through him,
8: 8 G finds fault with them when he says:
8:10 and I will be their G, and they shall be my people.
9:14 to G, purify our conscience from dead works
9:14 from dead works to worship the living G! N
9:20 the blood of the covenant that G has ordained
9:24 now to appear in the presence of G on our behalf.
10: 7 'See, G, I have come to do your will, O G'
10:12 "he sat down at the right hand of G," S
10:21 since we have a great priest over the house of G, C
10:29 by those who have spurned the Son of G, M
10:31 to fall into the hands of the living G. N
10:36 so that when you have done the will of G, X
11: 3 that the worlds were prepared by the word of G, L
11: 4 to G a more acceptable sacrifice than Cain's.
11: 4 G himself giving approval to his gifts;
11: 5 and "he was not found, because G had taken him."
11: 5 before he was taken away that "he had pleased G."
11: 6 And without faith it is impossible to please G,
11: 7 warned by G about events as yet unseen,
11:10 whose architect and builder is G.
11:16 Therefore G is not ashamed to be called their G;
11:19 the fact that G is able even to raise someone from
11:25 of G than to enjoy the fleeting pleasures of sin.
11:40 since G had provided something better so
12: 2 at the right hand of the throne of G.
12: 7 G is treating you as children;
12:15 that no one fails to obtain the grace of G; W
12:22 to Mount Zion and to the city of the living G, N
12:23 and to G the judge of all,
12:28 by which we offer to G an acceptable worship
12:29 for indeed our G is a consuming fire.
13: 4 for G will judge fornicators and adulterers.
13: 7 those who spoke the word of G to you; L
13:15 let us continually offer a sacrifice of praise to G,
13:16 for such sacrifices are pleasing to G.
13:20 Now may the G of peace,
Jas 1: 1 a servant of G and of the Lord Jesus Christ,
1: 5 If any of you is lacking in wisdom, ask G,
1:13 should say, "I am being tempted by G";
1:13 for G cannot be tempted by evil
1:27 Religion that is pure and undefiled before G, H
2: 5 Has not G chosen the poor in the world to be rich
2:19 You believe that G is one; you do well.
2:23 "Abraham believed G, and it was reckoned to him
2:23 and he was called the friend of G.
3: 9 we curse those who are made in the likeness of G.
4: 4 that friendship with the world is enmity with G?
4: 4 be a friend of the world becomes an enemy of G.
4: 5 "G yearns jealously for the spirit that he has made
4: 6 "G opposes the proud, but gives grace to the
4: 7 Submit yourselves therefore to G.
4: 8 Draw near to G, and he will draw near to you.
1Pe 1: 2 and destined by G the Father and sanctified by
1: 3 be the G and Father of our Lord Jesus Christ!
1: 5 the power of G through faith for a salvation I
1:21 Through him you have come to trust in G,
1:21 so that your faith and hope are set on G.
1:23 through the living and enduring word of G. L
2: 5 to offer spiritual sacrifices acceptable to G
2:12 they may see your honorable deeds and glorify G
2:16 As servants of G, live as free people,
2:17 Love the family of believers. Fear G. Y
2:19 For it is a credit to you if, being aware of G,
3: 5 in G used to adorn themselves by accepting
3:18 in order to bring you to G.
3:20 when G waited patiently in the days of Noah,
3:21 but as an appeal to G for a good conscience,
3:22 into heaven and is at the right hand of G, S
4: 2 by human desires but by the will of G. X
4: 6 they might live in the spirit as G does.
4:10 Like good stewards of the manifold grace of G, W
4:11 so as one speaking the very words of G;
4:11 so with the strength that G supplies, so that G may
4:14 which is the Spirit of G, is resting on you. U
4:16 but glorify G because you bear this name.
4:17 for judgment to begin with the household of G;
4:17 for those who do not obey the gospel of G?
5: 2 the flock of G that is in your charge, exercising
5: 2 as G would have you do it—
5: 5 "G opposes the proud, but gives grace to the
5: 6 therefore under the mighty hand of G, S
5:10 after you have suffered for a little while, the G
1Pe 5:12 and to testify that this is the true grace of G. W
2Pe 1: 1 as ours through the righteousness of our G
1: 2 be yours in abundance in the knowledge of G and
1:17 For he received honor and glory from G the Father
1:21 by the Holy Spirit spoke from G.
2: 4 if G did not spare the angels when they sinned,
3: 5 that by the word of G heavens existed long ago L
3:12 for and hastening the coming of the day of G,
1Jn 1: 5 G is light and in him there is no darkness at all.
2: 5 the love of G has reached perfection.
2:14 you are strong and the word of G abides in you, L
2:17 but those who do the will of G live forever. X
3: 1 that we should be called children of G;
3: 8 The Son of G was revealed for this purpose, M
3: 9 Those who have been born of G do not sin,
3: 9 because they have been born of G.
3:10 of G and the children of the devil are revealed
3:10 all who do not do what is right are not from G,
3:20 for G is greater than our hearts,
3:21 we have boldness before G; H
4: 1 but test the spirits to see whether they are from G;
4: 2 By this you know the Spirit of G: U
4: 2 that Jesus Christ has come in the flesh is from G,
4: 3 that does not confess Jesus is not from G.
4: 4 Little children, you are from G,
4: 6 We are from G. Whoever knows G listens to us,
4: 6 and whoever is not from G does not listen to us.
4: 7 let us love one another, because love is from G;
4: 7 everyone who loves is born of G and knows G.
4: 8 does not love does not know G, for G is love.
4: 9 G sent his only Son into the world so
4:10 not that we loved G but that he loved us
4:11 Beloved, since G loved us so much,
4:12 No one has ever seen G;
4:12 if we love one another, G lives in us,
4:15 G abides in those who confess that Jesus is
4:15 in those who confess that Jesus is the Son of G, M
4:15 that Jesus is the Son of God, and they abide in G.
4:16 So we have known and believe the love that G has
4:16 G is love, and those who abide in love abide in G,
and G abides in them.
4:20 Those who say, "I love G,"
4:20 cannot love G whom they have not seen.
4:21 those who love G must love their brothers
5: 1 that Jesus is the Christ has been born of G,
5: 2 By this we know that we love the children of G,
when we love G and obey his commandments.
5: 3 love of G is this, that we obey his commandments.
5: 4 for whatever is born of G conquers the world.
5: 5 the one who believes that Jesus is the Son of G? M
5: 9 the testimony of G is greater;
5: 9 the testimony of G that he has testified to his Son.
5:10 the Son of G have the testimony in their hearts. M
5:10 Those who do not believe in G have made him
5:10 by not believing in the testimony that G has given
5:11 G gave us eternal life, and this life is in his Son.
5:12 whoever does not have the Son of G does M
5:13 you who believe in the name of the Son of G, M
5:16 you will ask, and G will give life to such a one—
5:18 We know that those who are born of G do not sin,
5:18 but the one who was born of G protects them,
5:20 the Son of G has come and has given us M
5:20 He is the true G and eternal life.
2Jn 1: 3 with us from G the Father and from Jesus Christ,
1: 9 but goes beyond it, does not have G;
3Jn 1: 6 to send them on in a manner worthy of G;
1:11 Whoever does good is from G; whoever does evil
has not seen G.
Jude 1: 1 who are beloved in G the Father and kept safe
1: 4 pervert the grace of our G into licentiousness W
1:21 keep yourselves in the love of G;
1:25 to the only G our Savior,
Rev 1: 1 The revelation of Jesus Christ, which G gave him
1: 2 word of G and to the testimony of Jesus Christ, L
1: 6 priests serving his G and Father,
1: 8 says the Lord G, who is and who was and K
1: 9 island called Patmos because of the word of G L
2: 7 from the tree of life that is in the paradise of G.
2:18 These are the words of the Son of G, M
3: 1 the words of him who has the seven spirits of G
3: 2 not found your works perfect in the sight of my G.
3:12 I will make you a pillar in the temple of my G;
3:12 I will write on you the name of my G, and the
name of the city of my G,
3:12 that comes down from my G out of heaven,
4: 5 which are the seven spirits of G;
4: 8 "Holy, holy, holy, the Lord G the Almighty, K
4:11 and G, to receive glory and honor and power,
5: 6 which are the seven spirits of G sent out into all
5: 9 and by your blood you ransomed for G saints
5:10 to be a kingdom and priests serving our G,
6: 9 the word of G and for the testimony they had L
7: 2 having the seal of the living G, N
7: 3 until we have marked the servants of our G with
7:10 "Salvation belongs to our G who is seated on
7:11 on their faces before the throne and worshiped G,
7:12 and power and might be to our G forever
7:15 For this reason they are before the throne of G,
7:17 and G will wipe away every tear from their eyes."
8: 2 And I saw the seven angels who stand before G, H
8: 4 rose before G from the hand of the angel. H
9: 4 not have the seal of G on their foreheads.
9:13 from the four horns of the golden altar before G, H
10: 7 the mystery of G will be fulfilled,
11: 1 "Come and measure the temple of G and the altar
11:11 the breath of life from G entered them,
11:13 terrified and gave glory to the G of heaven. O
Rev 11:16 sit on their thrones before G fell on their faces H
11:16 before God fell on their faces and worshiped G,
11:17 Lord G Almighty, who are and who were, K
12: 5 But her child was snatched away and taken to G
12: 6 where she has a place prepared by G,
12:10 and the power and the kingdom of our G and
12:10 who accuses them day and night before our G.
12:17 those who keep the commandments of G and hold
13: 6 to utter blasphemies against G,
14: 4 from humankind as first fruits for G and
14: 7 "Fear G and give him glory, Y
14:12 the commandments of G and hold fast to the faith
14:19 into the great wine press of the wrath of G.
15: 1 for with them the wrath of G is ended.
15: 2 standing beside the sea of glass with harps of G
15: 3 they sing the song of Moses, the servant of G,
15: 3 "Great and amazing are your deeds, Lord G K
15: 7 of the wrath of G, who lives forever and ever;
15: 8 from the glory of G and from his power, R
16: 1 on the earth the seven bowls of the wrath of G."
16: 7 And I heard the altar respond, "Yes, O Lord G, K
16: 9 but they cursed the name of G,
16:11 cursed the G of heaven because of their pains O
16:14 to assemble them for battle on the great day of G
16:19 G remembered great Babylon and gave her
16:21 until they cursed G for the plague of the hail,
17:17 For G has put it into their hearts
17:17 until the words of G will be fulfilled.
18: 5 and G has remembered her iniquities.
18: 8 for mighty is the Lord G who judges her." K
18:20 For G has given judgment for you against her."
19: 1 Salvation and glory and power to our G,
19: 4 and worshiped G who is seated on the throne,
19: 5 "Praise our G, all you his servants,
19: 6 For the Lord our G the Almighty reigns. I
19: 9 And he said to me, "These are true words of G."
19:10 who hold the testimony of Jesus. Worship G!
19:13 and his name is called The Word of G. L
19:15 the wine press of the fury of the wrath of G
19:17 "Come, gather for the great supper of G,
20: 4 their testimony to Jesus and for the word of G. L
20: 6 but they will be priests of G and of Christ,
21: 2 coming down out of heaven from G,
21: 3 "See, the home of G is among mortals.
21: 3 He will dwell with them as their G;
21: 3 and G himself will be with them;
21: 7 and I will be their G and they will be my children.
21:10 down out of heaven from G.
21:11 glory of G and a radiance like a very rare jewel, R
21:22 for its temple is the Lord G the Almighty and K
21:23 for the glory of G is its light, R
22: 1 flowing from the throne of G and of the Lamb
22: 3 But the throne of G and of the Lamb will be in it,
22: 5 for the Lord G will be their light, K
22: 6 for the Lord, the G of the spirits of the prophets,
22: 9 who keep the words of this book. Worship G!"
22:18 if anyone adds to them, G will add to that person
22:19 G will take away that person's share in the tree
Tob 1: 4 of G, had been consecrated and established
1:12 Because I was mindful of G with all my heart,
2: 2 who is wholeheartedly mindful of G,
3:11 "Blessed are you, merciful G!
3:16 of them were heard in the glorious presence of G.
4: 7 the face of G will not be turned away from you.
4:14 If you serve G you will receive payment.
4:19 At all times bless the Lord G, K
4:21 You have great wealth if you fear G and flee Y
4:21 in the sight of the Lord your G." I
5: 4 he did not perceive that he was an angel of G. Z
5:10 the time is near for G to heal you; take courage."
5:14 to him, "Welcome! G save you,
5:17 May G in heaven bring you safely there
7:12 And may the G of heaven prosper your journey O
8: 5 "Blessed are you, O G of our ancestors, F
8:15 they blessed the G of heaven, and Raguel said, O
8:15 "Blessed are you, O G, with every pure blessing;
9: 6 Blessed be G, for I see in Tobias the very image
11:14 "Blessed be G, and blessed be his great name,
11:15 in rejoicing and praising G at the top of his voice.
11:16 Then Tobit, rejoicing and praising G,
11:17 Tobit acknowledged that G had been merciful
11:17 Blessed be your G who has brought you to us,
12: 6 "Bless G and acknowledge him in the presence
12: 6 to all people the deeds of G.
12: 7 but to acknowledge and reveal the works of G,
12:11 but to reveal with due honor the works of G.'
12:14 And at the same time G sent me to heal you
12:17 Bless G forevermore.
12:18 but by the will of G. X
12:20 now get up from the ground, and acknowledge G.
12:22 They kept blessing G and singing his praises,
12:22 and they acknowledged G
12:22 when an angel of G had appeared to them. Z
13: 1 Then Tobit said: "Blessed be G who lives forever,
13: 4 because he is our Lord and he is our G;
13: 4 he is our Father and he is G forever.
13: 7 As for me, I exalt my G,
13:17 Blessed be the G of Israel!' B
14: 2 giving alms and continually blessing G
14: 4 the word of G that Nahum spoke about Nineveh, L
14: 4 by the prophets of Israel, whom G sent,
14: 4 and believe that whatever G has said will
14: 4 the temple of G in it will be burned to the ground,
14: 5 "But G will again have mercy on them,
14: 5 and G will bring them back into the land of Israel;
14: 5 and they will rebuild the temple of G,
14: 5 and in it the temple of G will be rebuilt,

*GOD distinguishes the words translated "God" and "god" from the compound name "Lord GOD," where GOD represents the name *Yahweh*. For this name see the heading †GOD on pages 541-42.

Tob 14: 6 be converted and worship G in truth.
14: 7 and in righteousness they will praise the eternal G.
14: 7 in those days and are truly mindful of G will
14: 7 Those who sincerely love G will rejoice,
14:8,9 serve G faithfully and do what is pleasing
14:8,9 be mindful of G and to bless his name at all times
14:10 For G repaid him to his face
14:15 Tobias praised G for all he had done to the people
14:15 and he blessed the Lord G forever and ever. K
Jdt 3: 8 and tribes should call upon him as a g.
4: 2 and for the temple of the Lord their G. I
4: 9 of Israel cried out to G with great fervor,
4:12 to the G of Israel not to allow their infants to B
5: 8 and worshiped the G of heaven, O
5: 8 the G they had come to know,
5: 9 Then their G commanded them to leave the place
5:12 They cried out to their G,
5:13 Then G dried up the Red Sea before them,
5:17 as they did not sin against their G they prospered,
5:17 for the G who hates iniquity is with them.
5:18 The temple of their G was razed to the ground,
5:19 But now they have returned to their G,
5:20 against their G and we find out their offense,
5:21 for their Lord and G will defend them,
6: 2 of Israel because their G will defend them?
6: 2 What g is there except Nebuchadnezzar?
6: 2 Their G will not save them;
6:18 people fell down and worshiped G, and cried out:
6:19 "O Lord G of heaven, see their arrogance, KO
6:21 that night they called on the G of Israel for help. B
7:19 The Israelites then cried out to the Lord their G, I
7:24 "Let G judge between you and us!
7:25 G has sold us into their hands,
7:28 against you heaven and earth and our G, the Lord
7:29 they cried out to the Lord G with a loud voice. K
7:30 by that time the Lord our G will turn his mercy I
8: 8 for she feared G with great devotion.
8:11 even sworn and pronounced this oath between G
8:12 Who are you to put G to the test today,
8:12 and to set yourselves up in the place of G
8:14 how do you expect to search out G,
8:14 No, my brothers, do not anger the Lord our G. I
8:16 not try to bind the purposes of the Lord our G; I
8:16 for G is not like a human being, to be threatened,
8:20 But we know no other g but him,
8:23 but the Lord our G will turn it to dishonor. I
8:25 everything let us give thanks to the Lord our G, I
8:35 "Go in peace, and may the Lord G go before K
9: 1 in the house of G in Jerusalem, C
9: 2 "O Lord G of my ancestor Simeon, K
9: 4 O G, my G, hear me also—a widow.
9:11 But you are the G of the lowly,
9:12 please, G of my father, G of the heritage of Israel,
9:14 and understand that you are G, the G of all power
10: 1 Judith had stopped crying out to the G of Israel, B
10: 8 "May the G of our ancestors grant you favor F
10: 8 She bowed down to G.
11: 6 G will accomplish something through you,
11:10 unless they sin against their G.
11:11 by which they are about to provoke their G
11:12 to use all that G by his laws has forbidden them
11:13 the priests who minister in the presence of our G
11:16 G has sent me to accomplish with you things
11:17 and serves the G of heaven night and day. O
11:17 into the valley and pray to G.
11:22 "G has done well to send you ahead of the people,
11:23 you do as you have said, your G shall be my G,
12: 8 prayed the Lord G of Israel to direct her way BK
13: 4 said in her heart, "O Lord G of all might, K
13: 7 "Give me strength today, O Lord G of Israel!" BK
13:11 G, our G, is with us, still showing his power
13:14 she said to them with a loud voice, "Praise G,
13:14 Praise G, who has not withdrawn his mercy from
13:17 They bowed down and worshiped G,
13:17 and said with one accord, "Blessed are you our G,
13:18 the Most High G above all other women on earth;
13:18 and blessed be the Lord G, K
13:19 hearts of those who remember the power of G. T
13:20 May G grant this to be a perpetual honor to you,
13:20 walking in the straight path before our G."
14:10 Achior saw all that the G of Israel had done, B
14:10 God of Israel had done, he believed firmly in G.
15:10 and G is well pleased with it.
16: 1 Begin a song to my G with tambourines,
16: 2 For the Lord is a G who crushes wars;
16:13 I will sing to my G a new song:
16:18 they arrived at Jerusalem, they worshiped G.
16:19 dedicated to G all the possessions of Holofernes,
AdE 2:20 but she was to fear G and keep his laws, Y
6:13 because the living G is with him." N
10: 4 Mordecai said, "These things have come from G;
10: 9 this is Israel, who cried out to G and were saved.
10: 9 G has done great signs and wonders,
10:10 one for the people of G and one for all the nations,
10:11 of decision before G and among all the nations. H
10:12 And G remembered his people
10:13 with an assembly and joy and gladness before G, H
11:10 Then they cried out to G;
11:12 in this dream what G had determined to do,
13:14 glory of G, and I will not bow down to anyone R
13:15 And now, O Lord G and King, God of Abraham, K
13:15 And now, O Lord God and King, G of Abraham,
14: 3 She prayed to the Lord G of Israel, and said: BK
14:18 except in you, O Lord G of Abraham. K
14:19 O G, whose might is over all,
15: 2 invoking the aid of the all-seeing G and Savior,
15: 8 G changed the spirit of the king to gentleness,
AdE 15:13 "I saw you, my lord, like an angel of G, Z
16: 4 that they will escape the evil-hating justice of G,
16:16 and are children of the living G, N
16:18 for G, who rules over all things,
16:21 For G, who rules over all things,
Wis 1: 3 For perverse thoughts separate people from G,
1: 6 because G is witness of their inmost feelings,
1:13 because G did not make death,
2:13 He professes to have knowledge of G,
2:16 and boasts that G is his father.
2:22 the secret purposes of G, nor hoped for the wages
2:23 for G created us for incorruption,
3: 1 the souls of the righteous are in the hand of G, S
3: 5 G tested them and found them worthy of himself;
3:13 she will have fruit when G examines souls.
4: 1 because it is known both by G and by mortals.
4: 6 against their parents when G examines them.
4:10 There were some who pleased G and were loved
5: 5 among the children of G?
6: 4 or walk according to the purpose of G,
6:19 and immortality brings one near to G;
7: 7 I called on G, and the spirit of wisdom came
7:14 those who get it obtain friendship with G,
7:15 May G grant me to speak with judgment,
7:25 For she is a breath of the power of G, T
7:26 a spotless mirror of the working of G,
7:27 into holy souls and makes them friends of G,
7:28 for G loves nothing so much as
8: 3 She glorifies her noble birth by living with G,
8: 4 For she is an initiate in the knowledge of G,
8:21 not possess wisdom unless G gave her to me—
9: 1 "O G of my ancestors and Lord of mercy, F
9:13 For who can learn the counsel of G?
10: 5 and preserved him blameless before G, H
10:10 she showed him the kingdom of G, E
12: 7 a worthy colony of the servants of G.
12:13 For neither is there any g besides you,
12:26 the deserved judgment of G.
12:27 the true G the one whom they had before refused
13: 1 of G were foolish by nature;
13: 6 for perhaps they go astray while seeking G
14: 8 and the perishable thing because it was named a g.
14: 9 to G are the ungodly and their ungodliness;
14:11 because, though part of what G created,
14:15 as a g what was once a dead human being,
14:22 for them to err about the knowledge of G,
14:30 about G in devoting themselves to idols,
15: 1 But you, our G, are kind and true, patient,
15: 8 these workers form a futile g from
15:19 but they have escaped both the praise of G
16:18 they were being pursued by the judgment of G;
19: 1 for G knew in advance even their future actions:
Sir 3:17 then you will be loved by those whom G accepts.
4:28 and the Lord G will fight for you. K
7: 9 and when I make an offering to the Most High G,
11:22 and quickly G causes his blessing to flourish.
20:15 such a one is hateful to G and humans.
21: 5 of the poor goes from their lips to the ears of G,
23: 4 O Lord, Father and G of my life,
24:23 the book of the covenant of the Most High G,
25: 1 they are beautiful in the sight of G and of mortals:
32:14 The one who seeks G will accept his discipline,
36: 1 Have mercy upon us, O G of all,
36: 5 as we have known that there is no G but you,
36:22 will know that you are the Lord, the G of the ages.
41: 8 who have forsaken the law of the Most High G!
45: 1 and was beloved by G and people,
47:13 because G made all his borders tranquil,
47:18 In the name of the Lord G, K
47:18 who is called the G of Israel, B
48:10 to calm the wrath of G before it breaks out in fury,
49: 8 which G showed him above the chariot of
49: 9 For G also mentioned Job who held fast to all
50:17 the Almighty, G Most High.
50:22 And now bless the G of all,
51: 1 O Lord and King, and praise you, O G my Savior.
51:12 *Give thanks to the G of praises,*
51:30 and in his own time G will give you your reward.
Bar 1:10 and offer them on the altar of the Lord our G; I
1:13 Pray also for us to the Lord our G, I
1:13 for we have sinned against the Lord our G, I
1:15 And you shall say: The Lord our G is in the right, I
1:18 and have not heeded the voice of the Lord our G, I
1:19 we have been disobedient to the Lord our G, I
1:21 to the voice of the Lord our G in all the words of I
1:22 in the sight of the Lord our G. I
2: 5 because our nation sinned against the Lord our G, I
2: 6 The Lord our G is in the right, I
2:11 And now, O Lord G of Israel, BK
2:12 O Lord our G, against all your ordinances. I
2:15 the earth may know that you are the Lord our G, I
2:19 before you our prayer for mercy, O Lord our G. I
2:27 Yet you have dealt with us, O Lord our G, I
2:31 and know that I am the Lord their G. I
2:35 an everlasting covenant with them to be their G
3: 1 O Lord Almighty, G of Israel, B
3: 4 O Lord Almighty, G of Israel, B
3: 4 who did not heed the voice of the Lord their G, I
3: 6 you are the Lord our G, and it is you, O Lord, I
3: 8 who forsook the Lord our G. I
3:13 If you had walked in the way of G,
3:24 O Israel, how great is the house of G, C
3:27 G did not choose them, or give them the way
3:35 This is our G; no other can be compared to him.
4: 1 She is the book of the commandments of G,
4: 4 O Israel, for we know what is pleasing to G.
4: 6 over to your enemies because you angered G.
Bar 4: 7 by sacrificing to demons and not to G.
4: 8 You forgot the everlasting G,
4: 9 she saw the wrath that came upon you from G,
4: 9 G has brought great sorrow upon me;
4:12 because they turned away from the law of G. P
4:21 Take courage, my children, cry to G,
4:23 but G will give you back to me with joy
4:24 so they soon will see your salvation by G,
4:25 the wrath that has come upon you from G.
4:27 Take courage, my children, and cry to G,
4:28 For just as you were disposed to go astray from G,
4:36 and see the joy that is coming to you from G.
4:37 rejoicing in the glory of G. R
5: 1 and put on forever the beauty of the glory from G.
5: 2 the robe of the righteousness that comes from G;
5: 3 for G will show your splendor everywhere
5: 4 For G will give you evermore the name,
5: 5 rejoicing that G has remembered them.
5: 6 but G will bring them back to you,
5: 7 For G has ordered that every high mountain and
5: 7 so that Israel may walk safely in the glory of G. R
5: 9 For G will lead Israel with joy,
LtJ 6: 1 the message that G had commanded him.
6: 2 of the sins that you have committed before G, H
6:51 and that there is no work of G in them.
6:62 When G commands the clouds to go over
Aza 1: 1 singing hymns to G and blessing the Lord.
1: 3 Lord, G of our ancestors, and worthy of praise; F
1:22 Let them know that you alone are the Lord G, K
1:28 one voice praised and glorified and blessed G
1:29 O Lord, G of our ancestors, F
1:68 All who worship the Lord, bless the G of gods,
Sus 1:42 "O eternal G, you know what is secret
1:45 G stirred up the holy spirit of
1:50 for G has given you the standing of an elder."
1:55 the angel of G has received the sentence from Z
1:55 angel of God has received the sentence from G
1:59 angel of G is waiting with his sword to split you Z
1:60 a great shout and blessed G,
1:63 and his wife praised G for their daughter Susanna,
Bel 1: 4 But Daniel worshiped his own G.
1: 5 but the living G, who created heaven N
1: 6 "Do you not think that Bel is a living g? N
1:24 "You cannot deny that this is a living g; N
1:25 Daniel said, "I worship the Lord my G, I
1:25 for he is the living G. N
1:37 Take the food that G has sent you."
1:38 Daniel said, "You have remembered me, O G,
1:39 the angel of G immediately returned Habakkuk Z
1:41 "You are great, O Lord, the G of Daniel,
2Mc 1: 2 May G do good to you,
1:11 by G out of grave dangers we thank him greatly
1:17 Blessed in every way be our G,
1:20 after many years had passed, when it pleased G,
1:24 The prayer was to this effect: "O Lord, Lord G, K
1:27 and let the Gentiles know that you are our G.
2: 4 up and had seen the inheritance of G.
2: 7 until G gathers his people together again
2:17 It is G who has saved all his people,
2:18 We have hope in G that he will soon have mercy
3:24 by the power of G, and became faint T
3:28 the sovereign power of G. T
3:34 report to all people the majestic power of G." T
3:36 to all concerning the deeds of the supreme G,
3:38 for there is certainly some power of G about T
6: 1 and no longer to live by the laws of G;
7: 6 "The Lord G is watching over us and K
7:14 to cherish the hope G gives of being raised again
7:16 But do not think that G has forsaken our people.
7:18 because of our sins against our own G.
7:19 for having tried to fight against G!"
7:28 and recognize that G did not make them out
7:31 will certainly not escape the hands of G.
7:35 the judgment of the almighty, all-seeing G.
7:36 but you, by the judgment of G,
7:37 appealing to G to show mercy soon to our nation
7:37 to make you confess that he alone is G,
8:18 he said, "but we trust in the Almighty G,
8:23 and gave the watchword, "The help of G";
9: 5 But the all-seeing Lord, the G of Israel, B
9: 8 making the power of G manifest to all. T
9:11 and to come to his senses under the scourge of G,
9:12 "It is right to be subject to G;
9:12 mortals should not think that they are equal to G."
9:17 to proclaim the power of G. T
9:18 for the judgment of G had justly come upon him,
10:16 after making solemn supplication and imploring G
10:25 with sackcloth, in supplication to G.
11: 4 He took no account whatever of the power of G, T
11: 9 And together they all praised the merciful G,
11:13 because the mighty G fought on their side.
12: 6 calling upon G, the righteous judge,
12:16 They took the town by the will of G, X
13:13 of G before the king's army could enter Judea
14:33 I will level this shrine of G to the ground
15:14 Jeremiah, the prophet of G."
15:16 a gift from G, with which you will strike
15:26 in battle with invocations to G and prayers.
15:27 with their hands and praying to G in their hearts,
1Es 1: 4 the Lord your G and serve his people Israel; I
1:27 I was not sent against you by the Lord G, K
1:48 the laws of the Lord, the G of Israel. B
1:49 the temple that G had made holy.
1:50 The G of their ancestors sent his messenger F
4:40 Blessed be the G of truth!"
4:62 And they praised the G of their ancestors, F
5:44 they came to the temple of G that is in Jerusalem,

*GOD distinguishes the words translated "God" and "god" from the compound name "Lord GOD," where GOD represents the name *Yahweh*. For this name see the heading †GOD on pages 541-42.

1Es 5:48 and prepared the altar of the G of Israel, B
5:49 directions in the book of Moses the man of G. D
5:53 made any vow to G began to offer sacrifices to G,
5:53 though the temple of G was not yet built.
5:56 after their coming to the temple of G in Jerusalem,
5:57 and they laid the foundation of the temple of G
5:58 work on the house of G with a single purpose. C
5:67 the temple for the Lord G of Israel. BK
5:70 with us in building the house for the Lord our G, I
6: 1 to them in the name of the Lord G of Israel. BK
6:31 libations may be made to the Most High G for
7: 4 by the command of the Lord G of Israel. BK
7: 9 services of the Lord G of Israel in accordance BK
7:15 for the service of the Lord G of Israel. BK
8: 3 which was given by the G of Israel; B
8:16 in accordance with the will of your G; X
8:17 of the temple of your G that is in Jerusalem.
8:18 to you as necessary for the temple of your G,
8:19 and reader of the law of the Most High G sends
8:21 in the law of G be scrupulously fulfilled for P
8:21 be scrupulously fulfilled for the Most High G,
8:23 "And you, Ezra, according to the wisdom of G,
8:23 to judge all those who know the law of your G, P
8:24 All who transgress the law of your G or the law P
8:27 I was encouraged by the help of the Lord my G, I
8:65 the G of Israel, twelve bulls for all Israel, B
8:79 a light for us in the house of the Lord our G, I
9: 8 give glory to the Lord the G of our ancestors, F
9:39 that had been given by the Lord G of Israel. BK
9:46 And Ezra blessed the Lord G Most High, K
9:46 the G of hosts, the Almighty, Q
Man 1: 1 O Lord Almighty, G of our ancestors, F
1: 8 Therefore you, O Lord, G of the righteous,
1:13 For you, O Lord, are the G of those who repent,
3Mc 1: 9 to the supreme G and made thank offerings
1:16 the supreme G to aid in the present situation and
2:21 Thereupon G, who oversees all things,
3: 4 but because they worshiped G
3:11 and not considering the might of the supreme G,
4:16 uttering improper words against the supreme G.
5: 7 their merciful G and Father,
5:13 the appointed hour, praised their holy G
5:25 and mournful dirges implored the supreme G
5:28 This was the act of G who rules over all things,
5:30 of G his whole mind had been deranged
5:35 praised the manifest Lord G, King of kings, K
6: 1 to stop calling upon the holy G, and he prayed
6: 2 Almighty G Most High, governing all creation
6:11 saying, 'Not even their g has rescued them.'
6:18 and true G revealed his holy face and opened
6:28 of the almighty and living G of heaven, NO
6:29 praised their holy G and Savior,
6:32 praising G, their Savior and worker of wonders.
6:36 the deliverance that had come to them through G.
7: 2 the great G guiding our affairs according
7: 6 to realize that the G of heaven surely defends O
7: 9 over every power, the Most High G, in everything
7:10 the holy G and the law of God should receive
7:10 and the law of G should receive the punishment P
7:12 his kingdom who had transgressed the law of G. P
7:16 But those who had held fast to G even to death
7:16 giving thanks to the one G of their ancestors, F
7:22 the supreme G perfectly performed great deeds
2Es 1:29 you should be my people and I should be your G,
2: 3 Lord G and have done what is evil in my sight. K
2:45 and have confessed the name of G.
2:47 answered and said to me, "He is the Son of G, M
2:48 the wonders of the Lord G that you have seen." K
7:20 law of G that is set before them be disregarded! P
7:48 which has alienated us from G,
7:79 and hated those who fear G— Y
8:58 and said in their hearts that there is no G—
9:45 And after thirty years G heard your servant,
10:16 For if you acknowledge the decree of G to be just,
15:20 says G, from the rising sun and from the south,
15:21 into their bosom. Thus says the Lord G: K
15:26 For G knows all who sin against him;
15:27 G will not deliver you, because you have sinned
15:48 and devices. Therefore G says,
15:56 says the Lord, so G will do to you
16: 8 The Lord G sends calamities, K
16:53 for G will burn coals of fire on the head
16:53 "I have not sinned before G and his glory." H
16:62 and the spirit of Almighty G,
16:67 Indeed, G is the judge; fear him!
16:67 so G will lead you forth and deliver you
16:75 Do not fear or doubt, for G is your guide.
16:76 says the Lord G, must not let your sins weigh K
4Mc 1:12 giving glory to the all-wise G.
2:21 Now when G fashioned human beings,
3:16 he poured out the drink as an offering to G.
4: 9 with women and children were imploring G in
5:24 proper reverence we worship the only living G. N
5:25 we believe that the law was established by G,
6:26 he lifted up his eyes to G and said,
6:27 O G, that though I might have saved myself,
7:19 do not die to G, but live to G.
7:21 by the whole rule of philosophy, and trusts in G,
9: 8 shall have the prize of virtue and shall be with G,
10:18 G hears also those who are mute.
10:20 Gladly, for the sake of G,
10:21 G will visit you swiftly, for you are cutting out
12:11 and also your kingdom from G,
12:14 they by dying nobly fulfilled their service to G,
12:17 I call on the G of our ancestors to be merciful F
13: 3 Instead, by reason, which is praised before G, H
13:13 with all our hearts consecrate ourselves to G,
4Mc 13:15 those who transgress the commandment of G.
13:22 and our discipline in the law of G. P
15: 8 of the fear of G she disdained the temporary safety
15:24 mother disregarded all these because of faith in G.
16:14 O mother, soldier of G in the cause of religion,
16:18 through G that you have had a share in the world
16:19 to endure any suffering for the sake of G.
16:21 the fiery furnace and endured it for the sake of G.
16:22 You too must have the same faith in G and not
16:25 that those who die for the sake of G live to God,
16:25 that those who die for the sake of God live to G,
17: 4 maintaining firm an enduring hope in G.
17: 5 before G and are firmly set in heaven with them. H
17:10 looking to G and enduring torture even to death."
17:15 Reverence for G was victor and gave the crown
17:20 who have been consecrated for the sake of G,
18:23 have received pure and immortal souls from G,

†GOD (307) [†LORD]

A. THUS SAYS THE *LORD †GOD (134)
B. SAYS THE *LORD †GOD (93)
C. *LORD †GOD OF HOSTS (16)

Ge 15: 2 But Abram said, "O Lord G,
15: 8 But he said, "O Lord G,
Ex 23:17 year all your males shall appear before the Lord G.
Dt 3:24 "O Lord G, you have only begun
9:26 to the LORD and said, "Lord G, do not destroy
Jos 7: 7 Joshua said, "Ah, Lord G!
Jdg 6:22 and Gideon said, "Help me, Lord G!
16:28 Samson called to the LORD and said, "Lord G,
2Sa 7:18 "Who am I, O Lord G, and what is my house,
7:19 this was a small thing in your eyes, O Lord G;
7:19 be instruction for the people, O Lord G!
7:20 For you know your servant, O Lord G!
7:28 And now, O Lord G, you are God,
7:29 for you, O Lord G, have spoken,
1Ki 2:26 the ark of the Lord G before my father David,
8:53 brought our ancestors out of Egypt, O Lord G."
2Ch 32:16 His servants said still more against the Lord G
Ps 68:20 and to G, the Lord, belongs escape from death.
69: 6 put to shame because of me, O Lord G of hosts; C
71:16 the mighty deeds of the Lord G,
73:28 I have made the Lord G my refuge,
141: 8 my eyes are turned toward you, O G, my Lord;
Isa 3:15 says the Lord G of hosts. BC
7: 7 therefore thus says the Lord G: A
10:23 For the Lord G of hosts will make a full end, C
10:24 Therefore thus says the Lord G of hosts: AC
12: 2 for the LORD G is my strength and my might;
22: 5 For the Lord G of hosts has a day of tumult C
22:12 In that day the Lord G of hosts called to C
22:14 says the Lord G of hosts. BC
22:15 Thus says the Lord G of hosts: AC
25: 8 Lord G will wipe away the tears from all faces,
26: 4 in the LORD G you have an everlasting rock.
28:16 therefore thus says the Lord G, See, I am laying A
28:22 a decree of destruction from the Lord G of hosts C
30:15 For thus said the Lord G, the Holy One of Israel:
40:10 See, the Lord G comes with might,
48:16 And now the Lord G has sent me and his spirit.
49:22 Thus says the Lord G: I will soon lift up my A
50: 4 Lord G has given me the tongue of a teacher,
50: 5 The Lord G has opened my ear,
50: 7 The Lord G helps me;
50: 9 It is the Lord G who helps me;
52: 4 For thus says the Lord G: A
56: 8 Thus says the Lord G, who gathers the outcasts A
61: 1 The spirit of the Lord G is upon me,
61:11 the Lord G will cause righteousness and praise
65:13 Therefore thus says the Lord G: A
65:15 and the Lord G will put you to death;
Jer 1: 6 Then I said, "Ah, Lord G!
2:19 says the Lord G of hosts. BC
2:22 of your guilt is still before me, says the Lord G. B
4:10 Then I said, "Ah, Lord G,
7:20 Therefore thus says the Lord G: A
14:13 Then I said: "Ah, Lord G!
32:17 Ah Lord G! It is you who made the heavens
32:25 Yet you, O Lord G, have said to me,
44:26 saying, 'As the Lord G lives.'
46:10 That day is the day of the Lord G of hosts, C
46:10 the Lord G of hosts holds a sacrifice in the land C
49: 5 says the Lord G of hosts, BC
50:25 the Lord G of hosts has a task to do in the land C
50:31 O arrogant one, says the Lord G of hosts; BC
Eze 2: 4 to them, "Thus says the Lord G." A
3:11 Say to them, "Thus says the Lord G"; A
3:27 "Thus says the Lord G"; A
4:14 Then I said, "Ah Lord G!
5: 5 Thus says the Lord G: This is Jerusalem; A
5: 7 Therefore thus says the Lord G: A
5: 8 therefore thus says the Lord G: A
5:11 Therefore, as I live, says the Lord G, surely, B
6: 3 hear the word of the Lord G!
6: 3 Thus says the Lord G to the mountains and A
6:11 Thus says the Lord G: Clap your hands A
7: 2 thus says the Lord G to the land of Israel: A
7: 5 Thus says the Lord G: Disaster after disaster! A
8: 1 the hand of the Lord G fell upon me there.
9: 8 on my face and cried out, "Ah Lord G!
11: 7 Therefore thus says the Lord G: A
11: 8 the sword upon you, says the Lord G. B
11:13 cried with a loud voice, and said, "Ah Lord G!
11:16 Therefore say: Thus says the Lord G: A
11:17 Therefore say: Thus says the Lord G: A
Eze 11:21 upon their own heads, says the Lord G. B
12:10 Say to them, "Thus says the Lord G: A
12:19 Thus says the Lord G concerning the inhabitants A
12:23 Tell them therefore, "Thus says the Lord G: A
12:25 the word and fulfill it, says the Lord G. B
12:28 Therefore say to them, Thus says the Lord G: A
12:28 that I speak will be fulfilled, says the Lord G. B
13: 3 Thus says the Lord G, Alas for the senseless A
13: 8 Therefore thus says the Lord G: A
13: 8 I am against you, says the Lord G. B
13: 9 and you shall know that I am the Lord G.
13:13 Therefore thus says the Lord G: A
13:16 when there was no peace, says the Lord G. B
13:18 and say, Thus says the Lord G: A
13:20 Therefore thus says the Lord G: A
14: 4 and say to them, Thus says the Lord G: A
14: 6 say to the house of Israel, Thus says the Lord G: A
14:11 and I will be their God, says the Lord G. B
14:14 by their righteousness, says the Lord G. B
14:16 as I live, says the Lord G, B
14:18 as I live, says the Lord G, B
14:20 and Job were in it, as I live, says the Lord G, B
14:21 For thus says the Lord G: A
14:23 that I have done in it, says the Lord G. B
15: 6 Therefore thus says the Lord G: A
15: 8 they have acted faithlessly, says the Lord G. B
16: 3 Thus says the Lord G to Jerusalem: A
16: 8 says the Lord G, and you became mine. B
16:14 that I had bestowed on you, says the Lord G. B
16:19 and so it was, says the Lord G. B
16:23 to you! says the Lord G), B
16:30 How sick is your heart, says the Lord G, B
16:36 Thus says the Lord G, Because your lust was A
16:43 upon your head, says the Lord G. B
16:48 As I live, says the Lord G, B
16:59 Yes, thus says the Lord G: A
16:63 that you have done, says the Lord G. B
17: 3 Say: Thus says the Lord G: A
17: 9 Say: Thus says the Lord G: Will it prosper? A
17:16 As I live, says the Lord G, B
17:19 Therefore thus says the Lord G: A
17:22 Thus says the Lord G: I myself will take a sprig A
18: 3 As I live, says the Lord G, B
18: 9 he shall surely live, says the Lord G. B
18:23 in the death of the wicked, says the Lord G, and B
18:30 of you according to your ways, says the Lord G. B
18:32 in the death of anyone, says the Lord G. B
20: 3 Thus says the Lord G: Why are you coming? A
20: 3 As I live, says the Lord G, B
20: 5 to them: Thus says the Lord G: A
20:27 and say to them, Thus says the Lord G: A
20:30 to the house of Israel, Thus says the Lord G: A
20:31 As I live, says the Lord G, B
20:33 As I live, says the Lord G, B
20:36 into judgment with you, says the Lord G. B
20:39 O house of Israel, thus says the Lord G: A
20:40 the mountain height of Israel, says the Lord G, B
20:44 O house of Israel, says the Lord G. B
20:47 Thus says the Lord G, I will kindle a fire in you, A
20:49 Then I said, "Ah Lord G!
21: 7 and it will be fulfilled," says the Lord G. B
21:13 not happen? says the Lord G. B
21:24 Therefore thus says the Lord G: A
21:26 thus says the Lord G: Remove the turban, A
21:28 Thus says the Lord G concerning the A
22: 3 You shall say, Thus says the Lord G: A city! A
22:12 and you have forgotten me, says the Lord G. B
22:19 Therefore thus says the Lord G: A
22:28 saying, "Thus says the Lord G," A
22:31 upon their heads, says the Lord G. B
23:22 Therefore, O Oholibah, thus says the Lord G: A
23:28 For thus says the Lord G: A
23:32 Thus says the Lord G: You shall drink your A
23:34 for I have spoken, says the Lord G. B
23:35 Therefore thus says the Lord G: A
23:46 For thus says the Lord G: A
23:49 and you shall know that I am the Lord G.
24: 3 and say to them, Thus says the Lord G: A
24: 6 Therefore thus says the Lord G: A
24: 9 thus says the Lord G: Woe to the bloody city! A
24:14 your doings I will judge you, says the Lord G. B
24:21 to the house of Israel, Thus says the Lord G: A
24:24 then you shall know that I am the Lord G.
25: 3 Hear the word of the Lord G:
25: 3 Thus says the Lord G, Because you said, "Aha!" A
25: 6 For thus says the Lord G: A
25: 8 Thus says the Lord G: A
25:12 Thus says the Lord G: A
25:13 thus says the Lord G, I will stretch out my hand A
25:14 they shall know my vengeance, says the Lord G. B
25:15 Thus says the Lord G: A
25:16 therefore thus says the Lord G, A
26: 3 Therefore, thus says the Lord G: A
26: 5 I have spoken, says the Lord G. B
26: 7 For thus says the Lord G: A
26:14 for I the LORD have spoken, says the Lord G. B
26:15 Thus says the Lord G to Tyre: A
26:19 For thus says the Lord G: A
26:21 you will never be found again, says the Lord G. B
27: 3 on many coastlands, Thus says the Lord G: A
28: 2 say to the prince of Tyre, Thus says the Lord G: A
28: 6 Therefore thus says the Lord G: A
28:10 for I have spoken, says the Lord G. B
28:12 and say to him, Thus says the Lord G: A
28:22 and say, Thus says the Lord G: A
28:24 And they shall know that I am the Lord G.
28:25 Thus says the Lord G: A

*GOD distinguishes the words translated "God" and "god" from the compound name "Lord GOD," where GOD represents the name *Yahweh*. For this name see the heading †GOD on pages 541-42.
†GOD represents the proper name of God, *Yahweh*, in the compound name Lord GOD. Words translated "God" and "god" are indexed under the heading *GOD on pages 527-41.

Eze 29: 3 and say, Thus says the Lord G: A
29: 8 Therefore, thus says the Lord G: A
29:13 Further, thus says the Lord G: A
29:16 Then they shall know that I am the Lord G.
29:19 Therefore thus says the Lord G: A
29:20 because they worked for me, says the Lord G. B
30: 2 Thus says the Lord G: Wail, "Alas for the day!" A
30: 6 within it by the sword, says the Lord G. B
30:10 Thus says the Lord G: I will put an end to the A
30:13 Thus says the Lord G: I will destroy the idols A
30:22 Therefore thus says the Lord G: A
31:10 Therefore thus says the Lord G: A
31:15 Thus says the Lord G: On the A
31:18 and all his horde, says the Lord G. B
32: 3 Thus says the Lord G: In an A
32: 8 and put darkness on your land, says the Lord G. B
32:11 For thus says the Lord G: A
32:14 to run like oil, says the Lord G. B
32:16 its hordes they shall chant it, says the Lord G. B
32:31 killed by the sword, says the Lord G. B
32:32 Pharaoh and all his multitude, says the Lord G. B
33:11 Say to them, As I live, says the Lord G, B
33:25 Therefore say to them, Thus says the Lord G: A
33:27 Say this to them, Thus says the Lord G: A
34: 2 to the shepherds: Thus says the Lord G: A
34: 8 says the Lord G, because my sheep have B
34:10 Thus says the Lord G, I am against the A
34:11 For thus says the Lord G: A
34:15 I will make them lie down, says the Lord G. B
34:17 As for you, my flock, thus says the Lord G: A
34:20 Therefore, thus says the Lord G to them: A
34:30 are my people, says the Lord G. B
34:31 and I am your God, says the Lord G. B
35: 3 and say to it, Thus says the Lord G: A
35: 6 says the Lord G, I will prepare you for blood, B
35:11 as I live, says the Lord G, B
35:14 Thus says the Lord G: A
36: 2 Thus says the Lord G: A
36: 3 and say: Thus says the Lord G: A
36: 4 hear the word of the Lord G:
36: 4 Thus says the Lord G to the mountains and A
36: 5 therefore thus says the Lord G: A
36: 6 and valleys, Thus says the Lord G: A
36: 7 therefore thus says the Lord G: A
36:13 Thus says the Lord G: A
36:14 of children, says the Lord G; B
36:15 to stumble, says the Lord G. B
36:22 to the house of Israel, Thus says the Lord G: A
36:23 that I am the LORD, says the Lord G, B
36:32 says the Lord G; let that be known to you. B
36:33 Thus says the Lord G: On the A
36:37 Thus says the Lord G: I will A
37: 3 I answered, "O Lord G, you know."
37: 5 Thus says the Lord G to these bones: A
37: 9 to the breath: Thus says the Lord G: A
37:12 and say to them, Thus says the Lord G: A
37:19 say to them, Thus says the Lord G: A
37:21 then say to them, Thus says the Lord G: A
37:23 they shall be my people, and I will be their G.
38: 3 and say: Thus says the Lord G: A
38:10 Thus says the Lord G: On that A
38:14 to Gog: Thus says the Lord G: A
38:17 Thus says the Lord G: Are you he of whom A
38:18 says the Lord G, my wrath shall be aroused. B
38:21 in all my mountains, says the Lord G; B
39: 1 and say: Thus says the Lord G: A
39: 5 for I have spoken, says the Lord G. B
39: 8 It has happened, says the Lord G. B
39:10 those who plundered them, says the Lord G. B
39:13 the day that I show my glory, says the Lord G. B
39:17 As for you, mortal, thus says the Lord G: A
39:20 and all kinds of soldiers, says the Lord G. B
39:25 Therefore thus says the Lord G: A
39:29 upon the house of Israel, says the Lord G. B
43:18 Mortal, thus says the Lord G: A
43:19 says the Lord G, a bull for a sin offering. B
43:27 and I will accept you, says the Lord G. B
44: 6 to the house of Israel, Thus says the Lord G: A
44: 9 Thus says the Lord G: No foreigner, A
44:12 concerning them, says the Lord G, B
44:15 the fat and the blood, says the Lord G. B
44:27 he shall offer his sin offering, says the Lord G. B
45: 9 Thus says the Lord G: Enough, A
45: 9 of my people, says the Lord G. B
45:15 to make atonement for them, says the Lord G. B
45:18 Thus says the Lord G: In the A
46: 1 Thus says the Lord G: The gate of the A
46:16 Thus says the Lord G: A
47:13 Thus says the Lord G: These are the boundaries A
47:23 assign them their inheritance, says the Lord G. B
48:29 and these are their portions, says the Lord G. B
Am 1: 8 of the Philistines shall perish, says the Lord G. B
3: 7 Surely the Lord G does nothing,
3: 8 The Lord G has spoken; who can but prophesy?
3:11 Therefore thus says the Lord G: A
3:13 says the Lord G, the God of hosts: B
4: 2 The Lord G has sworn by his holiness:
4: 5 O people of Israel! says the Lord G. B
5: 3 For thus says the Lord G: A
6: 8 The Lord G has sworn by himself
7: 1 This is what the Lord G showed me:
7: 2 I said, "O Lord G, forgive, I beg you!
7: 4 This is what the Lord G showed me:
7: 4 the Lord G was calling for a shower of fire,
7: 5 Then I said, "O Lord G, cease, I beg you!
7: 6 "This also shall not be," said the Lord G.
8: 1 This is what the Lord G showed me—

Am 8: 3 in that day," says the Lord G; B
8: 9 On that day, says the Lord G, B
8:11 The time is surely coming, says the Lord G, B
9: 5 The Lord, G of hosts, he who touches the earth C
9: 8 eyes of the Lord G are upon the sinful kingdom,
Ob 1: 1 Thus says the Lord G concerning Edom: A
Mic 1: 2 and let the Lord G be a witness against you,
Hab 3:19 G, the Lord, is my strength;
Zep 1: 7 Be silent before the Lord G!
Zec 9:14 the Lord G will sound the trumpet

GOD'S‡ (141) [*GOD]

A. GOD'S WILL (7)
B. GOD'S SON (4)

Ge 6:11 Now the earth was corrupt in G sight,
28:22 which I have set up for a pillar, shall be G house;
32: 2 when Jacob saw them he said, "This is G camp!"
Ex 9:28 Enough of G thunder and hail!
Nu 22:22 G anger was kindled because he was going,
Dt 1:17 be intimidated by anyone, for the judgment is G.
21:23 for anyone hung on a tree is under G curse.
2Ch 1: 3 for G tent of meeting, which Moses the servant of
20:15 for the battle is not yours but G.
25:20 But Amaziah would not listen—it was G doing,
Ne 10:29 enter into a curse and an oath to walk in G law,
Job 11: 4 'My conduct is pure, and I am clean in G sight.'
20:28 dragged off in the day of G wrath.
36: 2 for I have yet something to say on G behalf.
Ps 68:18 against the LORD G abiding there.
78:10 They did not keep G covenant,
114: 2 Judah became G sanctuary, Israel his dominion.
Pr 14: 9 but the upright enjoy G favor.
Ecc 3:13 it is G gift that all should eat and drink
Isa 35: 8 but it shall be for G people;
La 3: 1 under the rod of G wrath;
Mt 22:21 and to God the things that are G."
27:43 for he said, 'I am G Son.'" B
27:54 "Truly this man was G Son!" B
Mk 12:17 and to God the things that are G."
15:39 he said, "Truly this man was G Son!" B
Lk 7:30 the Pharisees and the lawyers rejected G purpose
12: 6 Yet not one of them is forgotten in G sight.
20:25 and to God the things that are G."
Jn 3:36 but must endure G wrath.
9: 3 so that G works might be revealed in him.
10:36 because I said, 'I am G Son'? B
11: 4 rather it is for G glory,
Ac 2:11 about G deeds of power."
4:19 in G sight to listen to you rather than to God,
8:20 you thought you could obtain G gift with money!
17:29 Since we are G offspring,
20:24 to testify to the good news of G grace.
23: 4 "Do you dare to insult G high priest?"
Ro 1: 7 To all G beloved in Rome, who are called to
1:10 that by G will I may somehow at last succeed A
1:32 They know G decree,
2: 2 that G judgment on those who do such things is
2: 4 not realize that G kindness is meant to lead you
2: 5 when G righteous judgment will be revealed.
2:13 of the law who are righteous in G sight,
3: 7 my falsehood G truthfulness abounds to his glory,
5: 5 because G love has been poured into our hearts
8: 7 it does not submit to G law—
8:33 Who will bring any charge against G elect?
9:11 (so that G purpose of election might continue,
9:14 Is there injustice on G part?
10: 3 they have not submitted to G righteousness.
11:22 but G kindness toward you,
13: 4 for it is G servant for your good.
13: 6 for the authorities are G servants,
15:32 so that by G will I may come to you with joy A
1Co 1:25 For G foolishness is wiser than human wisdom,
and G weakness is stronger than human strength.
2: 7 But we speak G wisdom, secret and hidden,
2:11 also no one comprehends what is truly G except
2:14 not receive the gifts of G Spirit,
3: 9 For we are G servants, working together; you are
G field, G building.
3:16 you are G temple and that G Spirit dwells in you?
3:17 If anyone destroys G temple,
3:17 For G temple is holy, and you are that temple.
4: 1 as servants of Christ and stewards of G mysteries.
9:21 not free from G law but am under Christ's law)
2Co 1:20 For in him every one of G promises is a "Yes."
2:17 For we are not peddlers of G word like so many;
4: 1 by G mercy that we are engaged in this ministry,
4: 2 we refuse to practice cunning or to falsify G word;
11: 7 I proclaimed G good news to you free of charge?
Gal 1: 2 and all the members of G family who are with me,
1:10 now seeking human approval, or G approval?
Eph 1:14 toward redemption as G own people,
3: 2 of the commission of G grace that was given me
3: 7 according to the gift of G grace that was given me
Php 1: 7 for all of you share in G grace with me,
1:28 And this is G doing.
Col 1: 9 the knowledge of G will in all spiritual wisdom A
1:25 according to G commission that was given to me
2: 2 and have the knowledge of G mystery,
3:12 As G chosen ones, holy and beloved,
1Th 2:13 G word, which is also at work in you believers.
2:16 but G wrath has overtaken them at last.
4:16 and with the sound of G trumpet,
1Ti 3: 5 how can he take care of G church?
4: 5 for it is sanctified by G word and by prayer.
5: 4 for this is pleasing in G sight.

2Ti 2:19 G firm foundation stands, bearing this inscription:
Tit 1: 1 the faith of G elect and the knowledge of the truth
1: 7 For a bishop, as G steward, must be blameless;
Heb 1: 3 the reflection of G glory and the exact imprint of
G very being,
1: 6 he says, "Let all G angels worship him."
3: 2 just as Moses also "was faithful in all G house."
3: 5 Moses was faithful in all G house as a servant,
3: 6 however, was faithful over G house as a son,
4:10 for those who enter G rest also cease
10:10 And it is by G will that we have been sanctified A
Jas 1:20 for your anger does not produce G righteousness.
1Pe 2: 4 by mortals yet chosen and precious in G sight,
2: 9 a royal priesthood, a holy nation, G own people,
2:10 but now you are G people;
2:15 For it is G will that by doing right A
2:20 and suffer for it, you have G approval.
3: 4 which is very precious in G sight.
3:17 if suffering should be G will, A
4:19 in accordance with G will entrust themselves to A
1Jn 3: 2 Beloved, we are G children now;
3: 9 because G seed abides in them;
3:17 How does G love abide in anyone who has
4: 9 G love was revealed among us in this way:
5:19 We know that we are G children,
Rev 3:14 and true witness, the origin of G creation:
11:19 Then G temple in heaven was opened,
14:10 they will also drink the wine of G wrath,
Tob 3:17 so that he might see G light with his eyes;
14: 2 and acknowledging G majesty.
Wis 2:18 for if the righteous man is G child,
4:15 that G grace and mercy are with his elect,
18:13 they acknowledged your people to be G child.
Sir 38: 8 G works will never be finished;
46: 1 as his name implies, a great savior of G elect,
47:10 while they praised G holy name,
51:29 May your soul rejoice in G mercy,
Bar 4:13 not walk in the ways of G commandments,
5: 8 fragrant tree have shaded Israel at G command.
2Mc 7:29 so that in G mercy I may get you back again along
7:36 of ever-flowing life, under G covenant;
8:13 and distrustful of G justice ran off and got away.
12:11 hard fight, Judas and his companions, with G help,
13:15 He gave his troops the watchword, "G victory,"
15:27 and were greatly gladdened by G manifestation.
1Es 4:36 All G works quake and tremble,
4Mc 15: 3 for eternal life according to G promise.
16:24 to die rather than violate G commandment.

GOD-FEARING (6) [FEAR, *GOD]

Ac 10:22 "Cornelius, a centurion, an upright and G man,
Jdt 8:31 Now since you are a G woman, pray for us,
11:17 Your servant is indeed G and serves the God
Sir 19:24 Better are the G who lack understanding than
4Mc 15:28 of G Abraham she remembered his fortitude.
16:12 Yet that holy and G mother did not wail with such

GOD-GIVEN (2) [GIVE, *GOD]

Ezr 7:25 Ezra, according to the G wisdom you possess,
2Mc 6:23 and moreover according to the holy G law,

GOD-HATED See Index to Footnotes

GOD-HATERS (1) [*GOD, HATE]

Ro 1:30 G, insolent, haughty, boastful, inventors of evil,

GOD-WARD (KJV) See BEFORE *GOD, IN *GOD, TOWARD *GOD

GODDESS‡ (5) [*GOD]

1Ki 11: 5 Solomon followed Astarte the g of the Sidonians,
11:33 worshiped Astarte the g of the Sidonians,
Ac 19:27 but also that the temple of the great g Artemis will
19:37 nor blasphemers of our g.
2Mc 1:13 by the priests of the g Nanea.

GODHEAD (KJV) See DEITY, DIVINE NATURE

GODLESS (25) [*GOD]

2Sa 23: 6 But the g are all like thorns that are thrown away;
Job 8:13 the hope of the g shall perish.
13:16 that the g shall not come before him.
15:34 For the company of the g is barren,
17: 8 and the innocent stir themselves up against the g.
20: 5 and the joy of the g is but for a moment?
27: 8 what is the hope of the g when God cuts them off,
34:30 so that the g should not reign,
36:13 "The g in heart cherish anger;
Ps 119:122 do not let the g oppress me.
Pr 11: 7 and the expectation of the g comes to nothing.
11: 9 the g would destroy their neighbors,
Isa 9:17 for everyone was g and an evildoer,
10: 6 Against a g nation I send him,
33:14 trembling has seized the g:
1Ti 1: 9 for the g and sinful, for the unholy and profane,
Heb 12:16 an immoral and g person,
2Pe 3: 7 until the day of judgment and destruction of the g.
Sir 26:23 *A g wife is given as a portion to a lawless man,*
1Mc 3:15 Once again a strong army of g men went up
7: 5 to him all the renegade and g men of Israel;
9:25 Bacchides chose the g and put them in charge of

†GOD represents the proper name of God, *Yahweh*, in the compound name Lord GOD. Words translated "God" and "god" are indexed under the heading ***GOD** on pages 527-41.

1Mc 9:73 and he destroyed the g out of Israel.
2Mc 8: 2 on the temple that had been profaned by the g;
2Es 4:23 over to g tribes, and the law

GODLINESS (19) [*GOD]

1Ti 2: 2 that we may lead a quiet and peaceable life in all g
4: 7 and old wives' tales. Train yourself in g,
4: 8 g is valuable in every way,
6: 3 and the teaching that is in accordance with g,
6: 5 imagining that g is a means of gain.
6: 6 in g combined with contentment;
6:11 pursue righteousness, g, faith, love, endurance,
2Ti 3: 5 to the outward form of g but denying its power.
Tit 1: 1 of the truth that is in accordance with g,
2Pe 1: 3 for life and g, through the knowledge
1: 6 with endurance, and endurance with g,
1: 7 and g with mutual affection,
3:11 to be in leading lives of holiness and g,
Wis 10:12 that g is more powerful than anything else.
Sir 1:25 but g is an abomination to a sinner.
49: 3 in lawless times he made g prevail.
2Mc 12:45 that is laid up for those who fall asleep in g,
1Es 1:23 for his heart was full of g.
4Mc 7:22 not be able to overcome the emotions through g?

GODLY (24) [*GOD]

Ps 12: 1 O LORD, for there is no longer anyone who is g;
52: 1 O mighty one, of mischief done against the g?
Mal 2:15 And what does the one God desire? G offspring.
2Co 1:12 in the world with frankness and g sincerity,
7: 9 for you felt a g grief,
7:10 For g grief produces a repentance that leads
7:11 For see what earnestness this g grief has produced
2Ti 3:12 to live a g life in Christ Jesus will be persecuted.
Tit 2:12 that are self-controlled, upright, and g,
2Pe 2: 9 the Lord knows how to rescue the g from trial,
Sir 6:35 Be ready to listen to every g discourse,
16:13 and the patience of the g will not be frustrated.
23:12 Such conduct will be far from the g,
27:11 The conversation of the g is always wise,
27:29 in the fall of the g will be caught in a snare,
28:22 It has no power over the g;
33:14 so the sinner is the opposite of the g.
37:12 with a g person whom you know to be a keeper of
39:27 All these are good for the g,
43:33 and to the g he has given wisdom.
44:10 But these also were g men,
44:23 the Lord brought forth a g man,
Bar 5: 4 "Righteous Peace, G Glory."
4Mc 10:10 are suffering because of our g training and virtue,

GODS‡ (312) [*GOD]

A. OTHER GODS (65)
B. THEIR GODS (49)

Ge 31:19 and Rachel stole her father's household g.
31:30 why did you steal my g?"
31:32 anyone with whom you find your g shall not live.
31:32 Jacob did not know that Rachel had stolen the g.
31:34 Now Rachel had taken the household g
31:35 So he searched, but did not find the household g.
35: 2 "Put away the foreign g that are among you,
35: 4 they gave to Jacob all the foreign g that they had,
Ex 12:12 on all the g of Egypt I will execute judgments:
15:11 "Who is like you, O LORD, among the g?
18:11 Now I know that the LORD is greater than all g,
20: 3 you shall have no other g before me. A
20:23 You shall not make g of silver alongside me,
20:23 nor shall you make for yourselves g of gold.
23:13 Do not invoke the names of other g; A
23:24 you shall not bow down to their g, B
23:32 shall make no covenant with them and their g. B
23:33 for if you worship their g, B
32: 1 "Come, make g for us, who shall go before us;
32: 4 and they said, "These are your g, O Israel,
32: 8 and said, 'These are your g, O Israel,
32:23 They said to me, 'Make us g,
32:31 they have made for themselves g of gold.
34:15 for when they prostitute themselves to their g B
34:15 to their gods and sacrifice to their g, B
34:16 to their g will make your sons B
34:16 also prostitute themselves to their g. B
Nu 25: 2 the people to the sacrifices of their g, B
25: 2 and the people ate and bowed down to their g. B
33: 4 LORD executed judgments even against their g. B
Dt 4:28 There you will serve other g made A
5: 7 you shall have no other g before me. A
6:14 Do not follow other g, any of the gods of A
6:14 of the g of the peoples who are all around you,
7: 4 from following me, to serve other g. A
7:16 you shall not serve their g, B
7:25 The images of their g you shall burn with fire. B
8:19 the LORD your God and follow other g to serve A
10:17 LORD your God is God of g and Lord of lords,
11:16 serving other g and worshiping them, A
11:28 to follow other g that you have not known. A
12: 2 about to dispossess served their g, B
12: 3 and hew down the idols of their g, B
12:30 do not inquire concerning their g, saying, B
12:30 saying, "How did these nations worship their g? B
12:31 that the LORD hates they have done for their g. B
12:31 and their daughters in the fire to their g. B
13: 2 "Let us follow other g" (whom you have A
13: 6 saying, "Let us go worship other g," A
13: 7 any of the g of the peoples that are around you,
Dt 13:13 saying, "Let us go and worship other g," A
17: 3 by going to serve other g and worshiping them— A
18:20 any prophet who speaks in the name of other g, A
20:18 the abhorrent things that they do for their g, B
28:14 following other g to serve them. A
28:36 where you shall serve other g, of wood and stone. A
28:64 and there you shall serve other g, A
29:18 from the LORD our God to serve the g
29:26 turned and served other g, worshiping them, A
29:26 g whom they had not known and whom he had
30:17 but are led astray to bow down to other g A
31:16 to the foreign g in their midst, the g of the land
31:18 the evil they have done by turning to other g. A
31:20 they will turn to other g and serve them, A
32: 8 of the peoples according to the number of the g;
32:16 They made him jealous with strange g,
32:37 Then he will say: Where are their g, B
32:43 O heavens, his people, worship him, all you g!
33:27 He subdues the ancient g,
Jos 22:22 "The LORD, God of g! The LORD, God of g!
23: 7 or make mention of the names of their g, B
23:16 and go and serve other g and bow down to them, A
24: 2 lived beyond the Euphrates and served other g. A
24:14 the g that your ancestors served beyond the River
24:15 whether the g your ancestors served in the region
24:15 beyond the River or the g of the Amorites
24:16 the LORD to serve other g; A
24:20 If you forsake the LORD and serve foreign g,
24:23 "Then put away the foreign g that are among you,
Jdg 2: 3 and their g shall be a snare to you." B
2:12 they followed other g, from among the gods of A
2:12 the g of the peoples who were all around them,
2:17 lusted after other g and bowed down to them. A
2:19 following other g, worshiping them and bowing A
3: 6 and they worshiped their g. B
5: 8 new g were chosen, then war was in the gates.
6:10 not pay reverence to the g of the Amorites,
9: 9 'Shall I stop producing my rich oil by which g
9:13 'Shall I stop producing my wine that cheers g
10: 6 the g of Aram, the g of Sidon, the g of Moab, the g
of the Ammonites, and the g of the Philistines.
10:13 you have abandoned me and worshiped other g; A
10:14 Go and cry to the g whom you have chosen;
10:16 So they put away the foreign g from among them
18:24 He replied, "You take my g that I made,
Ru 1:15 to her people and to her g;
1Sa 4: 7 for they said, "G have come into the camp."
4: 8 from the power of these mighty g?
4: 8 the g who struck the Egyptians with every sort
6: 5 perhaps he will lighten his hand on you and your g
7: 3 then put away the foreign g and the Astartes from
8: 8 forsaking me and serving other g, A
17:43 And the Philistine cursed David by his g.
26:19 saying, 'Go, serve other g.' A
2Sa 7:23 before his people nations and their g? B
1Ki 9: 6 but go and serve other g and worship them, A
9: 9 and embraced other g, worshiping them A
11: 2 surely incline your heart to follow their g"; B
11: 4 his wives turned away his heart after other g; A
11: 8 who offered incense and sacrificed to their g. B
11:10 that he should not follow other g; A
12:28 Here are your g, O Israel,
14: 9 and have gone and made for yourself other g, A
19: 2 saying, "So may the g do to me, and more also,
20:10 "The g do so to me, and more also,
20:23 "Their g are g of the hills,
2Ki 17: 7 They had worshiped other g A
17:29 But every nation still made g of its own
17:31 the fire to Adrammelech and Anammelech, the g
17:33 the LORD but also served their own g,
17:35 "You shall not worship other g or bow A
17:37 You shall not worship other g; A
17:38 You shall not worship other g, A
18:33 the g of the nations ever delivered its land out of
18:34 Where are the g of Hamath and Arpad?
18:34 Where are the g of Sepharvaim, Hena, and Ivvah?
18:35 Who among all the g of the countries have
19:12 Have the g of the nations delivered them,
19:18 and have hurled their g into the fire, B
19:18 they were no g but the work of human hands
22:17 and have made offerings to other g, A
1Ch 5:25 and prostituted themselves to the g of the peoples
10:10 They put his armor in the temple of their g, B
14:12 They abandoned their g there, B
16:25 he is to be revered above all g.
16:26 For all the g of the peoples are idols,
2Ch 2: 5 for our God is greater than other g. A
7:19 and go and serve other g and worship them, A
7:22 and they adopted other g, A
13: 8 the golden calves that Jeroboam made as g
13: 9 or seven rams becomes a priest of what are no g.
25:14 he brought the g of the people of Seir,
25:14 set them up as his g, and worshiped them,
25:15 "Why have you resorted to a people's g who could
25:20 because they had sought the g of Edom.
28:23 For he sacrificed to the g of Damascus,
28:23 "Because the g of the kings of Aram helped them,
28:25 to make offerings to other g, A
32:13 Were the g of the nations of those lands at all able
32:14 Who among all the g of those nations
32:17 "Just as the g of the nations in other lands did
32:19 of Jerusalem as if he were like the g of the peoples
33:15 He took away the foreign g and the idol from
34:25 and have made offerings to other g, A
Ezr 1: 7 from Jerusalem and placed in the house of his g.
Job 41: 9 not even the g overwhelmed at the sight of it?
41:25 When it raises itself up the g are afraid;
Ps 40: 4 to those who go astray after false g.
58: 1 Do you indeed decree what is right, you g?
82: 1 in the midst of the g he holds judgment:
82: 6 I say, "You are g, children of the Most High,
84: 7 the God of g will be seen in Zion.
86: 8 There is none like you among the g, O Lord,
95: 3 and a great King above all g.
96: 4 he is to be revered above all g.
96: 5 For all the g of the peoples are idols,
97: 7 all g bow down before him.
97: 9 you are exalted far above all g.
135: 5 our Lord is above all g.
136: 2 O give thanks to the God of g,
138: 1 before the g I sing your praise;
Isa 8:19 should not a people consult their g, B
8:21 be enraged and will curse their king and their g. B
21: 9 the images of her g lie shattered on the ground."
36:18 of the g of the nations saved their land out of
36:19 Where are the g of Hamath and Arpad?
36:19 Where are the g of Sepharvaim?
36:20 Who among all the g of these
37:12 Have the g of the nations delivered them,
37:19 and have hurled their g into the fire, B
37:19 they were no g, but the work of human hands—
41:23 that we may know that you are g;
42:17 who say to cast images, "You are our g."
Jer 1:16 they have made offerings to other g, A
2:11 Has a nation changed its g,
2:11 even though they are no g?
2:28 But where are your g that you made for yourself?
2:28 you have as many g as you have towns, O Judah.
5: 7 and have sworn by those who are no g.
5:19 "As you have forsaken me and served foreign g
7: 6 if you do not go after other g to your own hurt, A
7: 9 and go after other g that you have not known, A
7:18 and they pour out drink offerings to other g, A
10:11 The g who did not make the heavens and
11:10 they have gone after other g to serve them; A
11:12 and cry out to the g to whom they make offerings,
11:13 For your g have become as many as your towns,
13:10 after other g to serve them and worship them, A
16:11 after other g and have served and worshiped A
16:13 and there you shall serve other g day and night, A
16:20 mortals make for themselves g? Such are no g!
19: 4 to other g whom neither they nor their ancestors A
19:13 and libations have been poured out to other g. A
22: 9 and worshiped other g and served them." A
25: 6 not go after other g to serve and worship them, A
32:29 and libations have been poured out to other g, A
35:15 and do not go after other g to serve them, A
43:12 He shall kindle a fire in the temples of the g
43:13 temples of the g of Egypt he shall burn with fire.
44: 3 they went to make offerings and serve other g A
44: 5 and make no offerings to other g. A
44: 8 making offerings to other g in the land of Egypt A
44:15 to other g, and all the women who stood by, A
46:25 and Pharaoh, and Egypt and her g and her kings,
48:35 at a high place and make offerings to their g. B
Eze 28: 2 I sit in the seat of the g, in the heart of the seas,"
Da 1: 2 and placed the vessels in the treasury of his g,
2:11 and no one can reveal it to the king except the g,
2:47 is God of g and Lord of kings and a revealer
3:12 They do not serve your g and they do not worship
3:14 not serve my g and you do not worship
3:18 not serve your g and we will not worship
4: 8 and who is endowed with a spirit of the holy g—
4: 9 of the holy g and that no mystery is too difficult
4:18 for you are endowed with a spirit of the holy g."
5: 4 They drank the wine and praised the g of gold
5:11 with a spirit of the holy g.
5:11 and wisdom like the wisdom of the g.
5:14 I have heard of you that a spirit of the g is in you,
5:23 You have praised the g of silver and gold,
11: 8 Even their g, with their idols and B
11:36 shall speak horrendous things against the God of g.
11:37 He shall pay no respect to the g of his ancestors,
Hos 3: 1 they turn to other g and love raisin cakes." A
Na 1:14 the house of your g I will cut off the carved image
Zep 2:11 he will shrivel all the g of the earth,
Jn 10:34 "Is it not written in your law, 'I said, you are g'?
10:35 to whom the word of God came were called 'g'—
Ac 7:40 'Make g for us who will lead the way for us;
14:11 "The g have come down to us in human form!"
19:26 by saying that g made with hands are not g.
1Co 8: 5 there may be so-called g in heaven or on earth—as
in fact there are many g and many lords—
Gal 4: 8 to beings that by nature are not g.
Jdt 3: 8 for he had been commissioned to destroy all the g
5: 7 the g of their ancestors who were in Chaldea.
5: 8 from the presence of their g. B
8:18 or town of ours that worships g made with hands,
AdE 14: 7 because we glorified their g. B
14:12 O King of the g and Master of all dominion!
Wis 12:24 accepting as g those animals that
12:27 at those creatures that they had thought to be g,
13: 2 or the luminaries of heaven were the g that rule
13: 3 of these things people assumed them to be g,
13:10 are those who give the name "g" to the works
15: 9 a glorious thing to mold counterfeit g.
15:15 they thought that all their heathen idols were g,
15:16 for none can form g that are like themselves.
Bar 1:22 of our own wicked hearts by serving other g A
LtJ 6: 4 in Babylon you will see g made of silver and gold
6: 5 or of letting fear for these g possess you
6: 9 and make crowns for the heads of their g, B
6:10 silver from their g and spend it on themselves, B
6:11 They deck their g out with garments B

LtJ 6:11 these g of silver and gold and wood
6:16 From this it is evident that they are not g;
6:18 so are their g when they have been set up in B
6:19 though their g can see none of them. B
6:23 From this you will know that they are not g;
6:27 if any of these g falls to the ground,
6:28 the sacrifices that are offered to these g and use
6:29 you know by these things that they are not g,
6:30 For how can they be called g?
6:30 Women serve meals for g of silver and gold
6:32 They howl and shout before their g as some do B
6:33 The priests take some of the clothing of their g B
6:40 must anyone think that they are g, or call them g?
6:44 must anyone think that they are g, or call them g?
6:47 then can the things that are made by them be g?
6:48 as to where they can hide themselves and their g. B
6:49 How then can one fail to see that these are not g,
6:51 to all the nations and kings that they are not g but
6:52 Who then can fail to know that they are not g?
6:55 a temple of wooden g overlaid with gold or silver,
6:55 but the g will be burned up like timbers.
6:56 then must anyone admit or think that they are g?
6:57 G made of wood and overlaid with silver
6:59 than to be these false g;
6:59 that protects its contents, than these false g;
6:59 also a wooden pillar in a palace, than these false g.
6:64 one must not think that they are g, nor call them g,
6:65 Since you know then that they are not g,
6:69 So we have no evidence whatever that they are g;
6:70 which guards nothing, so are their g of wood, B
6:71 In the same way, their g of wood, B
6:72 upon them you will know that they are not g;
Aza 1:68 All who worship the Lord, bless the God of g,
1Mc 3:48 the Gentiles consulted the likenesses of their g. B
5:68 the carved images of their g he burned with fire; B
2Mc 11:23 Now that our father has gone on to the g,
2Es 1:6 and have offered sacrifices to strange g.

GODS' (1) [*GOD]

3Mc 3:14 by the g deliberate alliance with us in battle,

GOES‡ (153) [GO]

Ge 32:20 "I may appease him with the present that g ahead
44:26 Only if our youngest brother g with us,
Ex 8:20 as he g out to the water, and say to him,
22:26 you shall restore it before the sun g down;
23:23 When my angel g in front of you,
28:29 on his heart when he g into the holy place,
28:30 on Aaron's heart when he g in before the LORD;
28:35 when he g into the holy place before the LORD,
Lev 14:36 the priest g to examine the disease, or all that is in
Nu 5:12 any man's wife g astray and is unfaithful to him,
5:29 g astray and defiles herself,
Dt 1:30 The LORD your God, who g before you,
1:33 who g before you on the way to seek out a place
19:5 Suppose someone g into the forest with another
20:4 for it is the LORD your God who g with you,
24:2 and g off to become another man's wife.
31:6 it is the LORD your God who g with you;
31:8 It is the LORD who g before you.
Jos 15:3 it g out southward of the ascent of Akrabbim,
15:3 and g up south of Kadesh-barnea,
15:4 g out by the Wadi of Egypt,
15:6 and the boundary g up to Beth-hoglah, and passes
15:6 and the boundary g up to the Stone of Bohan,
15:7 and the boundary g up to Debir from the Valley
15:8 then the boundary g up by the valley of the son
15:8 and the boundary g up to the top of the mountain
15:10 Chesalon), and g down to Beth-shemesh,
15:11 the boundary g out to the slope of the hill north
15:11 along to Mount Baalah, and g out to Jabneel;
16:3 then it g down westward to the territory of
16:6 and the boundary g from there to the sea;
16:7 it g down from Janoah to Ataroth and to Naarah,
16:8 the boundary g westward to the Wadi Kanah,
17:7 the boundary g along southward to the inhabitants
17:9 the boundary of Manasseh g along the north side
18:12 boundary g up to the slope of Jericho on the north,
18:13 then the boundary g down to Ataroth-addar,
18:14 Then the boundary g in another direction,
18:15 and the boundary g from there to Ephron,
18:16 then the boundary g down to the border of
18:16 and it then g down the valley of Hinnom,
18:17 and from there g to Geliloth,
18:17 it g down to the Stone of Bohan, Reuben's son;
18:18 the slope of Beth-arabah it g down to the Arabah;
19:11 then its boundary g up westward,
19:12 from Sarid it g in the other direction eastward
19:12 from there it g to Daberath, then up to Japhia;
19:27 g to Beth-dagon, and touches Zebulun and
19:34 and g from there to Hukkok,
Jdg 5:9 My heart g out to the commanders
20:31 of which g up to Bethel and the other to Gibeah,
21:19 of the highway that g up from Bethel to Shechem,
1Sa 6:9 And watch; if it g up on the way to its own land,
9:13 before he g up to the shrine to eat.
30:24 of the one who g down into the battle shall be
2Sa 3:35 or anything else before the sun g down!"
2Ki 5:18 when my master g into the house of Rimmon
12:20 on the way that g down to Silla.
Ne 9:37 Its rich yield g to the kings whom you have set
Est 4:11 that if any man or woman g to the king inside
Job 14:21 they are brought low, and it g unnoticed.
34:8 who g in company with evildoers and walks with
39:21 it g out to meet the weapons.
Ps 19:4 yet their voice g out through all the earth,
39:6 Surely everyone g about like a shadow.
74:23 uproar of your adversaries that g up continually.
97:3 Fire g before him, and consumes his adversaries
Pr 6:12 and a villain g around with crooked speech,
7:22 and g like an ox to the slaughter,
10:17 but one who rejects a rebuke g astray.
11:10 it g well with the righteous, the city rejoices;
11:13 A gossip g about telling secrets,
13:9 but the lamp of the wicked g out.
15:33 and humility g before honor.
16:18 Pride g before destruction,
18:12 but humility g before honor.
20:14 bad," says the buyer, then g away and boasts.
22:10 Drive out a scoffer, and strife g out;
23:31 when it sparkles in the cup and g down smoothly.
26:2 an undeserved curse g nowhere.
26:20 For lack of wood the fire g out,
Ecc 1:4 A generation g, and a generation comes,
1:5 The sun rises and the sun g down,
1:6 g around to the north; round and round g the wind,
3:21 Who knows whether the human spirit g upward
3:21 and the spirit of animals g downward to the earth?
6:4 For it comes into vanity and g into darkness,
SS 7:9 like the best wine that g down smoothly,
Isa 42:13 The LORD g forth like a soldier,
55:11 so shall my word be that g out from my mouth;
59:4 no one g to law honestly;
Jer 3:1 If a man divorces his wife and she g from him
5:6 everyone who g out of them shall be torn
6:29 the refining g on, for the wicked are not removed.
9:4 and every neighbor g around like a slanderer.
14:2 and the cry of Jerusalem g up.
22:10 weep rather for him who g away,
Eze 7:14 but no one g to battle,
11:21 But as for those whose heart g
23:44 they have gone in to her, as one g in to a whore.
26:15 when slaughter g on within you?
44:27 On the day that he g into the holy place,
47:8 "This water flows toward the eastern region and g
47:9 Wherever the river g, every living creature
47:9 and everything will live where the river g.
Hos 6:4 like the dew that g away early.
6:5 and my judgment g forth as the light.
13:3 or like the dew that g away early,
Mic 5:8 when it g through, treads down and tears in pieces,
Na 2:11 where the lion g, and the lion's cubs,
Zec 5:3 "This is the curse that g out over the face of
6:6 with the black horses g toward the north country,
Mt 8:9 and I say to one, 'Go,' and he g, and to another,
12:45 Then it g and brings along seven
13:44 in his joy he g and sells all that he has and buys
15:11 not what g into the mouth that defiles a person,
15:17 that whatever g into the mouth enters the stomach,
and g out into the sewer?
26:24 The Son of Man g as it is written of him,
Mk 4:29 the grain is ripe, at once he g in with his sickle,
7:18 Do you not see that whatever g into a person
7:19 and g out into the sewer?"
14:21 For the Son of Man g as it is written of him,
Lk 7:8 and I say to one, 'Go,' and he g, and to another,
11:26 Then it g and brings seven other spirits more evil
16:30 but if someone g to them from the dead,
Jn 3:8 not know where it comes from or where it g.
10:4 When he has brought out all his own, he g ahead
Ac 8:26 "Get up and go toward the south to the road that g
1Co 6:6 but a believer g to court against a believer—
11:21 each of you g ahead with your own supper,
11:21 and one g hungry and another becomes drunk.
2Co 7:15 And his heart g out all the more to you,
Heb 9:7 but only the high priest g into the second,
2Jn 1:9 but g beyond it, does not have God;
Rev 14:4 these follow the Lamb wherever he g.
14:11 the smoke of their torment g up forever and ever.
17:11 but it belongs to the seven, and it g to destruction.
19:3 The smoke g up from her forever and ever."
Tob 5:18 the staff of our hand as he g in and out before us?
AdE 2:13 Then she g in to the king;
2:13 g with him from the harem to the king's palace.
4:11 of the empire know that if any man or woman g to
Wis 6:16 because she g about seeking those worthy of her,
Sir 21:5 The prayer of the poor g from their lips to the ears
32:10 and approval g before one who is modest.
34:31 and g again and does the same things,
39:11 and if he g to rest, it is enough for him.
Bar 3:33 the one who sends forth the light, and it g;
1Es 4:23 and g out to travel and rob and steal and to sail
8:14 and rams and lambs and what g with them,
2Es 10:13 the multitude that is now in it g as it came';

GOG‡ (12) [HAMON-GOG]

1Ch 5:4 The sons of Joel: Shemaiah his son, G his son,
Eze 38:2 set your face toward G, of the land of Magog,
38:3 O G, chief prince of Meshech and Tubal;
38:14 Therefore, mortal, prophesy, and say to G:
38:16 O G, I display my holiness before their eyes.
38:18 when G comes against the land of Israel,
38:21 the sword against G in all my mountains, says
39:1 And you, mortal, prophesy against G, and say:
39:1 O G, chief prince of Meshech and Tubal!
39:11 On that day I will give to G a place for burial
39:11 for there G and all his horde will be buried;
Rev 20:8 G and Magog, in order to gather them for battle;

GOIIM (3)

Ge 14:1 of Elam, and King Tidal of G,
14:9 King Tidal of G, King Amraphel of Shinar,
Jos 12:23 the king of Dor in Naphath-dor one the king of G

GOING‡ (286) [GO]

Ge 6:13 now I am g to destroy them along with the earth.
6:17 I am g to bring a flood of waters on the earth,
15:12 As the sun was g down,
16:8 where have you come from and where are you g?"
19:28 and saw the smoke of the land g up like the smoke
24:42 you will only make successful the way I am g!
32:17 'To whom do you belong? Where are you g?
38:13 "Your father-in-law is g up to Timnah
48:4 'I am g to make you fruitful
Ex 7:15 as he is g out to the water;
13:4 Today, in the month of Abib, you are g out.
14:8 the Israelites, who were g out boldly.
14:19 The angel of God who was g before
16:4 "I am g to rain bread from heaven for you,
19:9 "I am g to come to you in a dense cloud,
23:4 upon your enemy's ox or donkey g astray,
23:20 I am g to send an angel in front of you,
25:32 and there shall be six branches g out of its sides,
25:33 so for the six branches g out of the lampstand.
34:12 the inhabitants of the land to which you are g,
37:18 There were six branches g out of its sides,
37:19 so for the six branches g out of the lampstand.
Nu 10:33 of the LORD g before them three days' journey,
11:15 If this is the way you are g to treat me,
22:22 God's anger was kindled because he was g,
24:14 So now, I am g to my people;
32:7 of the Israelites from g over into the land that
32:9 they discouraged the hearts of the Israelites from g
Dt 2:7 he knows your g through this great wilderness.
2:18 "Today you are g to cross the boundary of Moab
4:22 For I am g to die in this land without crossing over
4:22 but you are g to cross over to take possession of
9:5 or the uprightness of your heart that you are g in
12:20 and you say, "I am g to eat some meat,"
17:3 by g to serve other gods and worshiping them—
22:13 but after g in to her,
31:16 the gods of the land into which they are g;
33:18 Rejoice, Zebulun, in your g out;
Jos 3:11 of the Lord of all the earth is g to pass before you
10:11 while they were g down the slope of Beth-horon,
14:11 for war, and for g and coming.
16:1 g up from Jericho into the hill country to Bethel;
16:2 then g from Bethel to Luz, it passes along
18:3 about g in and taking possession of the land that
18:17 in a northerly direction g on to En-shemesh,
19:13 and g on to Rimmon it bends toward Neah;
Jdg 4:9 on which you are g will not lead to your glory,
4:14 The LORD is indeed g out before you."
6:37 I am g to lay a fleece of wool on
9:21 Then Jotham ran away and fled, g to Beer,
17:9 and I am g to live wherever I can find a place."
19:17 "Where are you g and where do you come from?"
19:18 and I am g to my home.
19:28 "Get up," he said to her, "we are g."
20:10 who are g to repay Gibeah of Benjamin for all
20:40 the whole city g up in smoke toward the sky!
1Sa 9:27 As they were g down to the outskirts of the town,
10:3 three men g up to God
10:10 When they were g from there to Gibeah,
17:20 to the encampment as the army was g forth to
19:23 As he was g, he fell into a prophetic frenzy,
2Sa 2:24 sun was g down they came to the hill of Ammah,
11:7 and how the war was g.
1Ki 15:17 from g out or coming in to King Asa of Judah.
17:11 As she was g to bring it, he called to her and said,
21:26 He acted most abominably in g after idols,
2Ki 1:3 in Israel that you are g to inquire of Baal-zebub,
2:23 and while he was g up on the way,
3:26 When the king of Moab saw that the battle was g
6:9 because the Arameans are g down there."
19:27 your g out and coming in,
2Ch 16:1 to prevent anyone from g out or coming into
22:7 of Ahaziah should come about through his g
Ne 2:20 and we his servants are g to start building;
4:3 any fox g up on it would break it down!"
4:7 of the walls of Jerusalem was g forward and
Job 1:7 "From g to and fro on the earth,
2:2 "From g to and fro on the earth,
33:24 and says, 'Deliver him from g down into the Pit;
33:28 He has redeemed my soul from g down to the Pit,
Ps 121:8 The LORD will keep your g out and your coming
Pr 7:27 g down to the chambers of death.
9:15 who are g straight on their way,
Ecc 9:10 or wisdom in Sheol, to which you are g.
Isa 37:28 your g out and coming in,
58:13 if you honor it, not g your own ways,
Jer 2:18 What then do you gain by g to Egypt,
2:18 Or what do you gain by g to Assyria,
2:25 Keep your feet from g unshod and your throat
5:15 I am g to bring upon you a nation from far away,
6:19 I am g to bring disaster on this people,
6:28 all stubbornly rebellious, g about with slanders;
10:18 I am g to sling out the inhabitants of the land
11:11 assuredly I am g to bring disaster upon them
11:22 I am g to punish them;
15:6 says the LORD, you are g backward;
16:9 I am g to banish from this place,
16:21 "Therefore I am surely g to teach them,
16:21 this time I am g to teach them my power
19:3 I am g to bring such disaster upon this place that
21:4 I am g to turn back the weapons of war that are
23:15 "I am g to make them eat wormwood,
25:9 I am g to send for all the tribes of the north, says

Jer 28:16 I am **g** to send you off the face of the earth.
29:17 I am **g** to let loose on them sword, famine,
29:21 I am **g** to deliver them into the hand
29:32 I am **g** to punish Shemaiah of Nehelam
29:32 to see the good that I am **g** to do to my people,
30:10 for I am **g** to save you from far away,
30:18 I am **g** to restore the fortunes of the tents of Jacob,
31: 8 I am **g** to bring them from the land of the north,
32: 3 I am **g** to give this city into the hand of the king
32: 7 Hanamel son of your uncle Shallum is **g** to come
32:28 I am **g** to give this city into the hands of
32:37 I am **g** to gather them from all the lands
33: 6 I am **g** to bring it recovery and healing;
34: 2 I am **g** to give this city into the hand of the king
34:17 I am **g** to grant a release to you,
34:22 I am **g** to command, says the LORD,
35:17 I am **g** to bring on Judah and on all the inhabitants
37: 4 Jeremiah was still **g** in and out among the people,
37: 7 is **g** to return to its own land, to Egypt.
39: 4 **g** out of the city at night by way of
39:16 I am **g** to fulfill my words against this city for evil
42: 4 I am **g** to pray to the LORD your God
43:10 I am **g** to send and take my servant King
44:16 we are not **g** to listen to you.
44:27 I am **g** to watch over them for harm and not
44:29 that I am **g** to punish you in this place,
44:30 I am **g** to give Pharaoh Hophra, king of Egypt,
45: 4 I am **g** to break down what I have built,
45: 5 for I am **g** to bring disaster upon all flesh,
46:27 for I am **g** to save you from far away,
49: 5 I am **g** to bring terror upon you,
49:35 I am **g** to break the bow of Elam,
50: 9 For I am **g** to stir up and bring against Babylon
50:18 I am **g** to punish the king of Babylon and his land,
51: 1 I am **g** to stir up a destructive wind
51:36 I am **g** to defend your cause and take vengeance
Eze 4:16 I am **g** to break the staff of bread in Jerusalem;
37:12 I am **g** to open your graves,
40: 6 Then he went into the gateway facing east, **g**
44:10 **g** astray from me after their idols
44:25 not defile themselves by **g** near to a dead person;
47: 3 **G** on eastward with a cord in his hand,
Da 10:11 pay attention to the words that I am **g** to speak
Jnh 1: 3 down to Joppa and found a ship **g** to Tarshish;
3: 4 Jonah began to go into the city, **g** a day's walk.
Mic 2:13 they will break through and pass the gate, **g** out
Zec 2: 2 Then I asked, "Where are you **g?**"
2: 9 See now, I am **g** to raise my hand against them,
3: 8 I am **g** to bring my servant the Branch.
6: 5 "These are the four winds of heaven **g** out,
8:21 to seek the LORD of hosts; I myself am **g.**"
Mal 3:14 or by **g** about as mourners before the LORD
Mt 3: 5 the people of Jerusalem and all Judea were **g** out
8:33 The swineherds ran off, and on **g** into the town,
17:22 Son of Man is **g** to be betrayed into human hands,
20: 8 beginning with the last and then **g** to the first.'
20:17 While Jesus was **g** up to Jerusalem,
20:18 we are **g** up to Jerusalem,
21:31 and the prostitutes are **g** into the kingdom of God
23:13 and when others are **g** in, you stop them.
24: 1 As Jesus came out of the temple and was **g** away,
25: 8 for our lamps are **g** out.'
25:14 "For it is as if a man, **g** on a journey,
26:39 And **g** a little farther, he threw himself on
26:46 Get up, let us be **g.** See, my betrayer is at hand."
26:58 and **g** inside, he sat with the guards in order to see
28: 7 and indeed he is **g** ahead of you to Galilee;
28:11 While they were **g,** some of the guard went into
Mk 1: 5 and all the people of Jerusalem were **g** out to him,
2:23 One sabbath he was **g** through the grainfields;
6:31 For many were coming and **g,**
6:33 Now many saw them **g** and recognized them,
7:15 there is nothing outside a person that by **g**
10:32 They were on the road, **g** up to Jerusalem,
10:33 "See, we are **g** up to Jerusalem,
13:34 It is like a man **g** on a journey,
14:35 And **g** a little farther, he threw himself on
14:42 Get up, let us be **g.** See, my betrayer is at hand."
16: 7 and Peter that he is **g** ahead of you to Galilee;
Lk 1:59 and they were **g** to name him Zechariah
6: 1 while Jesus was **g** through the grainfields,
9:44 of Man is **g** to be betrayed into human hands."
9:57 As they were **g** along the road,
10:30 "A man was **g** down from Jerusalem to Jericho,
10:31 Now by chance a priest was **g** down that road;
12:54 you immediately say, 'It is **g** to rain';
14: 1 On one occasion when Jesus was **g** to the house of
14:19 and I am **g** to try them out;
14:31 what king, **g** out to wage war against another king,
15:26 of the slaves and asked what was **g** on.
17:11 On the way to Jerusalem Jesus was **g** through
18:31 "See, we are **g** up to Jerusalem,
18:36 When he heard a crowd **g** by,
19: 4 because he was **g** to pass that way.
19:28 he went on ahead, **g** up to Jerusalem.
22:22 For the Son of Man is **g** as it has been determined,
24:13 Now on that same day two of them were **g** to
24:28 they came near the village to which they were **g,**
24:28 he walked ahead as if he were **g** on.
Jn 3:26 here he is baptizing, and all are **g** to him."
4:51 As he was **g** down, his slaves met him
6: 6 for he himself knew what he was **g** to do.
6:21 the land toward which they were **g.**
6:30 "What sign are you **g** to give us then,
6:71 though one of the twelve, was **g** to betray him.
7: 8 I am not **g** to this festival,
7:33 and then I am **g** to him who sent me.
Jn 8:14 where I have come from and where I am **g,**
8:14 not know where I come from or where I am **g.**
8:21 Again he said to them, "I am **g** away,
8:21 Where I am **g,** you cannot come."
8:22 Then the Jews said, "Is he **g** to kill himself?
8:22 Is that what he means by saying, 'Where I am **g,**
10:32 For which of these are you **g** to stone me?"
10:33 not for a good work that we are **g** to stone you,
11: 8 and are you **g** there again?"
11:11 but I am **g** there to awaken him."
11:31 because they thought that she was **g** to the tomb
12:35 you do not know where you are **g.**
13: 3 and that he had come from God and was **g** to God,
13: 6 "Lord, are you **g** to wash my feet?"
13:27 "Do quickly what you are **g** to do."
13:33 'Where I am **g,** you cannot come.'
13:36 "Lord, where are you **g?**"
13:36 Jesus answered, "Where I am **g,**
14: 4 And you know the way to the place where I am **g.**"
14: 5 "Lord, we do not know where you are **g.**
14:12 because I am **g** to the Father.
14:28 You heard me say to you, 'I am **g** away,
14:28 you would rejoice that I am **g** to the Father,
16: 5 But now I am **g** to him who sent me;
16: 5 yet none of you asks me, 'Where are you **g?'**
16:10 because I am **g** to the Father
16:17 and 'Because I am **g** to the Father'?"
16:28 I am leaving the world and am **g** to the Father."
21: 3 Simon Peter said to them, "I am **g** fishing."
21:20 "Lord, who is it that is **g** to betray you?"
Ac 1:10 he was **g** and they were gazing up toward heaven,
3: 1 One day Peter and John were **g** up to the temple at
5:24 wondering what might be **g** on.
8:36 As they were **g** along the road,
9: 3 as he was **g** along and approaching Damascus,
12: 6 very night before Herod was **g** to bring him out,
13:42 As Paul and Barnabas were **g** out,
16:16 One day, as we were **g** to the place of prayer,
16:37 and now are they **g** to discharge us in secret?
23:20 as though they were **g** to inquire more thoroughly
Ro 15:25 I am **g** to Jerusalem in a ministry to the saints;
2Co 8:17 he is **g** to you of his own accord.
Php 4:12 the secret of being well-fed and of **g** hungry,
Heb 11: 8 and he set out, not knowing where he was **g.**
Jas 1:24 for they look at themselves and, on **g** away,
1Pe 2:25 For you were **g** astray like sheep,
1Jn 2:19 But by **g** out they made it plain that none
Rev 16:15 not **g** about naked and exposed to shame.")
Tob 4:10 and keeps you from **g** into the Darkness.
10: 1 how many days Tobias would need for **g** and
Jdt 6: 7 Now my slaves are **g** to take you back into
7:21 their cisterns were **g** dry,
10:11 the women were **g** straight on through the valley,
10:12 from, and where are you **g?**"
13: 3 for she said she would be **g** out for her prayers.
14: 2 set a captain over them, as if you were **g** down to
Wis 3: 3 and their **g** from us to be their destruction;
Sus 1: 8 to see her, **g** in and walking about, and they began
Bel 1:11 priests of Bel said, "See, we are now **g** outside;
1:19 Daniel laughed and restrained the king from **g** in.
1:29 **G** to the king, they said, "Hand Daniel over to us,
1:33 and was **g** into the field to take it to the reapers.
1Mc 6: 1 King Antiochus was **g** through
7:24 and preventing those in the city from **g** out into
10:77 and went to Azotus as though he were **g** farther.
13:49 the citadel at Jerusalem were prevented from **g** in
15:25 he shut Trypho up and kept him from **g** out or in.
1Es 2:20 Since the building of the temple is now **g** on,
4:47 to all who were **g** up with him to build Jerusalem.
4:49 He wrote in behalf of all the Jews who were **g** up
6:10 These operations are **g** on rapidly,
3Mc 4:11 into the city and to those from the city **g** out into
5:18 After the party had been **g** on for some time,
5:48 the Jews saw the dust raised by the elephants **g** out
2Es 2:10 which I was **g** to give to Israel.
4Mc 4:10 while Apollonius was **g** up with his armed forces

GOINGS (3) [GO]

2Sa 3:25 and to learn your comings and **g** and to learn all
2Ki 11: 8 Be with the king in his comings and **g.**"
2Ch 23: 7 Stay with the king in his comings and **g.**"

GOLAN (4)

Dt 4:43 and **G** in Bashan belonging to the Manassites.
Jos 20: 8 and **G** in Bashan, from the tribe of Manasseh.
21:27 **G** in Bashan with its pasture lands,
1Ch 6:71 **G** in Bashan with its pasture lands and Ashtaroth

GOLD‡ (524) [GOLD-PLATED, GOLD-WOVEN, GOLDEN, GOLDEN-CLAD, GOLDSMITH, GOLDSMITHS]

A. SILVER ... GOLD (96)
B. GOLD ... SILVER (71)
C. PURE GOLD (44)
D. FINE GOLD (11)

Ge 2:11 the whole land of Havilah, where there is **g;**
2:12 and the **g** of that land is good;
13: 2 in livestock, in silver, and in **g.** A
24:22 the man took a **g** nose-ring weighing a half shekel,
24:22 two bracelets for her arms weighing ten **g** shekels,
24:35 he has given him flocks and herds, silver and **g,** A
24:53 servant brought out jewelry of silver and of **g,** A
Ge 41:42 and put a **g** chain around his neck.
44: 8 why then would we steal silver or **g** A
Ex 3:22 for jewelry of silver and of **g,** and clothing, A
11: 2 to ask her neighbor for objects of silver and **g.**" A
12:35 the Egyptians for jewelry of silver and **g,** A
20:23 nor shall you make for yourselves gods of **g.**
25: 3 that you shall receive from them: **g,** silver, B
25:11 You shall overlay it with pure **g,** C
25:11 you shall make a molding of **g** upon it all around.
25:12 You shall cast four rings of **g** for it and put them
25:13 of acacia wood, and overlay them with **g.**
25:17 Then you shall make a mercy seat of pure **g;** C
25:18 You shall make two cherubim of **g;**
25:24 You shall overlay it with pure **g,** C
25:24 and make a molding of **g** around it.
25:25 and a molding of **g** around the rim.
25:26 You shall make for it four rings of **g,**
25:28 of acacia wood, and overlay them with **g,** and
25:29 you shall make them of pure **g.** C
25:31 You shall make a lampstand of pure **g.** C
25:36 the whole of it one hammered piece of pure **g.** C
25:38 Its snuffers and trays shall be of pure **g.** C
25:39 shall be made from a talent of pure **g.** C
26: 6 You shall make fifty clasps of **g,**
26:29 You shall overlay the frames with **g,**
26:29 and shall make their rings of **g** to hold the bars;
26:29 and you shall overlay the bars with **g.**
26:32 on four pillars of acacia overlaid with **g,**
26:32 which have hooks of **g** and rest on four bases
26:37 and overlay them with **g;**
26:37 their hooks shall be of **g,**
28: 5 they shall use **g,** blue, purple, and crimson yarns,
28: 6 They shall make the ephod of **g,** of blue, purple,
28: 8 of **g,** of blue, purple, and crimson yarns,
28:11 you shall mount them in settings of **g** filigree.
28:13 You shall make settings of **g** filigree,
28:14 and two chains of pure **g,** twisted like cords; C
28:15 of **g,** of blue and purple and crimson yarns,
28:20 they shall be set in **g** filigree.
28:22 for the breastpiece chains of pure **g,** twisted C
28:23 you shall make for the breastpiece two rings of **g,**
28:24 the two cords of **g** in the two rings at the edges of
28:26 You shall make two rings of **g,**
28:27 You shall make two rings of **g,**
28:33 with bells of **g** between them all around—
28:36 You shall make a rosette of pure **g,** C
30: 3 You shall overlay it with pure **g,** its top, C
30: 3 you shall make for it a molding of **g** all around.
30: 5 of acacia wood, and overlay them with **g.**
31: 4 to work in **g,** silver, and bronze, B
32: 2 the **g** rings that are on the ears of your wives,
32: 3 all the people took off the **g** rings from their ears,
32: 4 He took the **g** from them, formed it in a mold,
32:24 So I said to them, 'Whoever has **g,** take it off';
32:31 they have made for themselves gods of **g.**
35: 5 bring the LORD's offering: **g,** silver, B
35:22 and pendants, all sorts of **g** objects,
35:22 everyone bringing an offering of **g** to the LORD.
35:32 to work in **g,** silver, and bronze, B
36:13 And he made fifty clasps of **g,**
36:34 And he overlaid the frames with **g,**
36:34 and made rings of **g** for them to hold the bars,
36:34 and overlaid the bars with **g.**
36:36 and overlaid them with **g;**
36:36 of **g,** and he cast for them four bases
36:38 He overlaid their capitals and their bases with **g,**
37: 2 He overlaid it with pure **g** inside and outside, C
37: 2 and made a molding of **g** around it.
37: 3 He cast for it four rings of **g** for its four feet,
37: 4 and overlaid them with **g,**
37: 6 He made a mercy seat of pure **g;** C
37: 7 He made two cherubim of hammered **g;**
37:11 He overlaid it with pure **g,** C
37:11 and made a molding of **g** around it.
37:12 and made a molding of **g** around the rim.
37:13 He cast for it four rings of **g,**
37:15 and overlaid them with **g.**
37:16 And he made the vessels of pure **g** that were to C
37:17 He also made the lampstand of pure **g.** C
37:22 the whole of it one hammered piece of pure **g.** C
37:23 and its snuffers and its trays of pure **g.** C
37:24 made it and all its utensils of a talent of pure **g.** C
37:26 He overlaid it with pure **g,** its top, C
37:26 and he made for it a molding of **g** all around,
37:28 and overlaid them with **g.**
38:24 All the **g** that was used for the work,
38:24 in all the construction of the sanctuary, the **g** from
39: 2 He made the ephod of **g,** of blue, purple,
39: 3 **G** leaf was hammered out and cut into threads
39: 5 of **g,** of blue, purple, and crimson yarns,
39: 6 enclosed in settings of **g** filigree and engraved like
39: 8 in skilled work, like the work of the ephod, of **g,**
39:13 they were enclosed in settings of **g** filigree.
39:15 They made on the breastpiece chains of pure **g,** C
39:16 of **g** filigree and two **g** rings, and put the two rings
39:17 and they put the two cords of **g** in the two rings at
39:19 Then they made two rings of **g,**
39:20 They made two rings of **g,**
39:25 They also made bells of pure **g,** C
39:30 the rosette of the holy diadem of pure **g,** C
Lev 24: 4 up the lamps on the lampstand of pure **g** before C
24: 6 six in a row, on the table of pure **g.** C
Nu 7:86 according to the shekel of the sanctuary, all the **g**
8: 4 out of hammered work of **g.**
22:18 to give me his house full of silver and **g,** A
24:13 give me his house full of silver and **g,** A
31:22 **g,** silver, bronze, iron, tin, and lead— B

Nu 31:50 articles of g, armlets and bracelets, signet rings,
31:51 and Eleazar the priest received the g from them,
31:52 And all the g of the offering that they offered to
31:54 So Moses and Eleazar the priest received the g
Dt 7:25 the silver or the g that is on them and take it A
8:13 and your silver and g is multiplied, A
17:17 silver and g he must not acquire in great quantity A
29:17 filthy idols of wood and stone, of silver and g, A
Jos 6:19 silver and g, and vessels of bronze and iron, A
6:24 silver and g, and the vessels of bronze and iron, A
7:21 and a bar of g weighing fifty shekels,
7:24 and the bar of g, with his sons and daughters,
22: 8 and with very much livestock, with silver, g, A
Jdg 8:26 of g (apart from the crescents and the pendants
1Sa 6: 4 "Five g tumors and five g mice,
6: 8 and put in a box at its side the figures of g,
6:11 with the g mice and the images of their tumors.
6:15 in which were the g objects,
6:17 the g tumors, which the Philistines returned as
6:18 also the g mice, according to the number of all
2Sa 1:24 who put ornaments of g on your apparel.
8: 7 the g shields that were carried by the servants
8:10 Joram brought with him articles of silver, g, A
8:11 together with the silver and g that he dedicated A
12:30 the weight of it was a talent of g,
21: 4 of silver or g between us and Saul or his house; A
1Ki 6:20 he overlaid it with pure g. C
6:21 the inside of the house with pure g, C
6:21 then he drew chains of g across,
6:21 of the inner sanctuary, and overlaid it with g.
6:22 Next he overlaid the whole house with g,
6:22 to the inner sanctuary he overlaid with g.
6:28 He also overlaid the cherubim with g.
6:30 The floor of the house he overlaid with g,
6:32 overlaid them with g, and spread g on the cherubim
6:35 with g evenly applied upon the carved work.
7:49 the lampstands of pure g, five on the south side C
7:49 the flowers, the lamps, and the tongs, of g;
7:50 dishes for incense, and firepans, of pure g; C
7:50 and for the doors of the nave of the temple, of g.
7:51 the silver, the g, and the vessels, A
9:11 with cedar and cypress timber and g,
9:14 to the king one hundred twenty talents of g.
9:28 from there four hundred twenty talents of g,
10: 2 with camels bearing spices, and very much g,
10:10 she gave the king one hundred twenty talents of g,
10:11 the fleet of Hiram, which carried g from Ophir,
10:14 The weight of g that came to Solomon
10:14 in one year was six hundred sixty-six talents of g,
10:16 made two hundred large shields of beaten g;
10:16 of g went into each large shield.
10:17 He made three hundred shields of beaten g;
10:17 three minas of g went into each shield;
10:18 and overlaid it with the finest g.
10:21 All King Solomon's drinking vessels were of g,
10:21 of the Forest of Lebanon were of pure g; C
10:22 ships of Tarshish used to come bringing g, silver, B
10:25 objects of silver and g, garments, weaponry, A
12:28 the king took counsel, and made two calves of g.
14:26 the shields of g that Solomon had made;
15:15 and his own votive gifts—silver, g, A
15:18 the silver and the g that were left in the treasures A
15:19 I am sending you a present of silver and g; A
20: 3 Your silver and g are mine; A
20: 5 saying, 'Deliver to me your silver and g, A
20: 7 my silver, and my g; and I did not refuse him." A
22:48 of the Tarshish type to go to Ophir for g;
2Ki 5: 5 six thousand shekels of g,
7: 8 ate and drank, carried off silver, g, and clothing, A
12:13 trumpets, or any vessels of g, or of silver, B
12:18 the g that was found in the treasuries of the house
14:14 He seized all the g and silver, B
16: 8 Ahaz also took the silver and g found in the A
18:14 of silver and thirty talents of g.
18:16 the g from the doors of the temple of the LORD,
20:13 the silver, the g, the spices, the precious oil, A
23:33 of one hundred talents of silver and a talent of g.
23:35 Jehoiakim gave the silver and the g to Pharaoh, A
23:35 He exacted the silver and the g from the people A
24:13 he cut in pieces all the vessels of g in the temple
25:15 of g the captain of the guard took away for
25:15 the captain of the guard took away for the g,
1Ch 18: 7 the g shields that were carried by the servants
18:10 He sent all sorts of articles of g, of silver, B
18:11 silver and g that he had carried off from all A
20: 2 he found that it weighed a talent of g,
21:25 So David paid Ornan six hundred shekels of g
22:14 of the LORD one hundred thousand talents of g,
22:16 g, silver, bronze, and iron. B
28:14 weight of g for all golden vessels for each service,
28:15 the weight of g for each lampstand and its lamps,
28:16 weight of g for each table for the rows of bread,
28:17 and pure g for the forks, the basins, and the cups; C
28:18 altar of incense made of refined g, and its weight;
29: 2 so far as I was able, the g for the things of g,
29: 3 I have a treasure of my own of g and silver, B
29: 4 three thousand talents of g,
29: 4 of the g of Ophir, and seven thousand talents
29: 5 g for the things of g and silver for the things of
29: 7 and ten thousand darics of g,
2Ch 1:15 silver and g as common in Jerusalem as stone, A
2: 7 send me an artisan skilled to work in g, silver B
2:14 He is trained to work in g, silver, bronze, iron, B
3: 4 He overlaid it on the inside with pure g. C
3: 5 he lined with cypress, covered it with fine g, D
3: 6 The g was g from Parvaim.
3: 7 So he lined the house with g—

2Ch 3: 8 he overlaid it with six hundred talents of fine g. D
3: 9 The weight of the nails was fifty shekels of g.
3: 9 He overlaid the upper chambers with g.
3:10 and overlaid them with g.
4: 8 And he made one hundred basins of g.
4:20 the lampstands and their lamps of pure g to burn C
4:21 the flowers, the lamps, and the tongs, of purest g;
4:22 basins, ladles, and firepans, of pure g. C
4:22 and the doors of the nave of the temple were of g.
5: 1 and stored the silver, the g, A
8:18 from there four hundred fifty talents of g
9: 1 and camels bearing spices and very much g
9: 9 she gave the king one hundred twenty talents of g,
9:10 and the servants of Solomon who brought g
9:13 The weight of g that came to Solomon
9:13 in one year was six hundred sixty-six talents of g,
9:14 the governors of the land brought g and silver B
9:15 made two hundred large shields of beaten g;
9:15 of beaten g went into each large shield.
9:16 He made three hundred shields of beaten g;
9:16 three hundred shekels of g went into each shield;
9:17 and overlaid it with pure g. C
9:18 The throne had six steps and a footstool of g,
9:20 Solomon's drinking vessels were of g,
9:20 of the Forest of Lebanon were of pure g; C
9:21 of Tarshish used to come bringing g, silver, B
9:24 objects of silver and g, garments, weaponry, A
12: 9 the shields of g that Solomon had made;
13:11 set out the rows of bread on the table of pure g, C
15:18 and his own votive gifts—silver, g, A
16: 2 Then Asa took silver and g from the treasures of A
16: 3 I am sending to you silver and g; A
21: 3 Their father gave them many gifts, of silver, g, A
24:14 and ladles, and vessels of g and silver. B
25:24 He seized all the g and silver, B
32:27 he made for himself treasuries for silver, for g, A
36: 3 of silver and one talent of g.
Ezr 1: 4 by the people of their place with silver and g, A
1: 6 with g, with goods, with animals,
1: 9 And this was the inventory: g basins, thirty;
1:10 g bowls, thirty; other silver bowls,
1:11 the total of the g and silver vessels was B
2:69 the building fund sixty-one thousand darics of g,
5:14 the g and silver vessels of the house of God, B
6: 5 let the g and silver vessels of the house of God, B
7:15 and also to convey the silver and g that the king A
7:16 silver and g that you shall find in the whole A
7:18 to do with the rest of the silver and g, A
8:25 And I weighed out to them the silver and the g A
8:26 talents, and one hundred talents of g,
8:27 twenty g bowls worth a thousand darics,
8:27 of fine polished bronze as precious as g.
8:28 and the silver and the g are a freewill offering A
8:30 and the Levites took over the silver, the g, A
8:33 within the house of our God, the silver, the g, A
Ne 7:70 to the treasury one thousand darics of g,
7:71 into the building fund twenty thousand darics of g
7:72 the people gave was twenty thousand darics of g,
Est 1: 6 g and silver on a mosaic pavement of porphyry, B
Job 3:15 or with princes who have g,
22:24 if you treat g like dust,
22:24 and g of Ophir like the stones of the torrent-bed,
22:25 if the Almighty is your g and your precious silver,
23:10 when he has tested me, I shall come out like g.
28: 1 and a place for g to be refined.
28: 6 the place of sapphires, and its dust contains g.
28:15 It cannot be gotten for g,
28:16 It cannot be valued in the g of Ophir,
28:17 G and glass cannot equal it,
28:17 nor can it be exchanged for jewels of fine g. D
28:19 nor can it be valued in pure g. C
31:24 "If I have made g my trust,
31:24 or called fine g my confidence; D
42:11 of them gave him a piece of money and a g ring.
Ps 19:10 More to be desired are they than g,
19:10 desired are they than gold, even much fine g; D
21: 3 you set a crown of fine g on his head. D
45: 9 at your right hand stands the queen in g of Ophir.
68:13 with silver, its pinions with green g.
72:15 May g of Sheba be given to him.
105:37 Then he brought Israel out with silver and g, A
115: 4 Their idols are silver and g, A
119:72 to me than thousands of g and silver pieces. B
119:127 Truly I love your commandments more than g,
119:127 more than gold, more than fine g. D
135:15 The idols of the nations are silver and g, A
Pr 3:14 and her revenue better than g.
8:10 and knowledge rather than choice g;
8:19 My fruit is better than g, even fine gold,
8:19 My fruit is better than gold, even fine g, D
11:22 Like a g ring in a pig's snout is a beautiful woman
16:16 How much better to get wisdom than g!
17: 3 The crucible is for silver, and the furnace is for g,
20:15 There is g, and abundance of costly stones;
22: 1 and favor is better than silver or g. A
25:11 A word fitly spoken is like apples of g in a setting
25:12 a g ring or an ornament of g is a wise rebuke to
27:21 The crucible is for silver, and the furnace is for g,
Ecc 2: 8 for myself silver and g and the treasure of kings A
SS 1:11 We will make you ornaments of g,
3:10 He made its posts of silver, its back of g,
5:11 His head is the finest g;
5:14 His arms are rounded g, set with jewels.
5:15 His legs are alabaster columns, set upon bases of g.
Isa 2: 7 Their land is filled with silver and g, A
2:20 their idols of silver and their idols of g,
13:12 I will make mortals more rare than fine g, D

Isa 13:12 and humans than the g of Ophir.
13:17 for silver and do not delight in g.
31: 7 throw away your idols of silver and idols of g,
39: 2 the silver, the g, the spices, the precious oil, A
40:19 and a goldsmith overlays it with g,
46: 6 Those who lavish g from the purse,
60: 6 They shall bring g and frankincense,
60: 9 their silver and g with them, A
60:17 Instead of bronze I will bring g,
Jer 4:30 that you deck yourself with ornaments of g,
10: 4 people deck it with silver and g; A
10: 9 from Tarshish, and g from Uphaz.
52:19 both those of g and those of silver. B
La 4: 1 g has grown dim, how the pure gold is changed!
4: 1 gold has grown dim, how the pure g is changed! C
4: 2 worth their weight in fine g— D
Eze 7:19 their g shall be treated as unclean.
7:19 silver and g cannot save them on the day of A
16:13 You were adorned with g and silver, B
16:17 took your beautiful jewels of my g and my silver B
27:22 and all precious stones, and g.
28: 4 have gathered g and silver into your treasuries. B
28:13 in g were your settings and your engravings.
38:13 to carry away silver and g, A
Da 2:32 The head of that statue was of fine g, D
2:35 iron, the clay, the bronze, the silver, and the g, A
2:38 you are the head of g.
2:45 the bronze, the clay, the silver, and the g. A
5: 2 that they bring in the vessels of g and silver B
5: 3 the vessels of g and silver that had been taken B
5: 4 the wine and praised the gods of g and silver, B
5: 7 have a chain of g around his neck,
5:16 have a chain of g around your neck,
5:23 You have praised the gods of silver and g, A
5:29 a chain of g was put around his neck,
10: 5 with a belt of g from Uphaz around his waist.
11: 8 and with their precious vessels of silver and g, A
11:38 not know he shall honor with g and silver, B
11:43 the treasures of g and of silver, and all the riches B
Hos 2: 8 upon her silver and g that they used for Baal. A
8: 4 silver and g they made idols for their own A
Joel 3: 5 For you have taken my silver and my g, A
Na 2: 9 "Plunder the silver, plunder the g!
Hab 2:19 See, it is g and silver plated, B
Zep 1:18 silver nor their g will be able to save them A
Hag 2: 8 The silver is mine, and the g is mine,
Zec 4: 2 And I said, "I see a lampstand all of g,
6:10 Collect silver and g from the exiles— A
6:11 Take the silver and g and make a crown, A
9: 3 and g like the dirt of the streets.
13: 9 and test them as g is tested.
14:14 g, silver, and garments in great abundance. B
Mal 3: 3 of Levi and refine them like g and silver, B
Mt 2:11 they offered him gifts of g, frankincense,
10: 9 Take no g, or silver, or copper in your belts, B
23:16 by the g of the sanctuary is bound by the oath.'
23:17 the g or the sanctuary that has made the g sacred?
Ac 3: 6 But Peter said, "I have no silver or g, A
17:29 not to think that the deity is like g, or silver, B
20:33 I coveted no one's silver or g or clothing. A
1Co 3:12 builds on the foundation with g, silver, B
1Ti 2: 9 not with their hair braided, or with g, pearls,
2Ti 2:20 not only of g and silver but also of wood and B
Heb 9: 4 with g, in which there were a golden urn holding
Jas 2: 2 if a person with g rings and in fine clothes comes
5: 3 Your g and silver have rusted, B
1Pe 1: 7 being more precious than g that,
1:18 not with perishable things like silver or g, A
3: 3 and by wearing g ornaments or fine clothing;
Rev 3:18 from me g refined by fire so that you may be rich;
9: 7 On their heads were what looked like crowns of g;
9:20 up worshiping demons and idols of g and silver B
17: 4 and adorned with g and jewels and pearls,
18:12 cargo of g, silver, jewels B
18:16 in purple and scarlet, adorned with g, with jewels,
21:15 to me had a measuring rod of g to measure the city
21:18 wall is built of jasper, while the city is pure g, C
21:21 and the street of the city is pure g, C
Tob 12: 8 It is better to give alms than to lay up g.
13:16 The towers of Jerusalem will be built with g,
13:16 and their battlements with pure g. C
Jdt 2:18 amount of g and silver from the royal palace. B
5: 9 and grew very prosperous in g and silver B
8: 7 Her husband Manasseh had left her g and silver, B
10:21 under a canopy that was woven with purple and g,
AdE 1: 6 of purple linen attached to g and silver blocks B
1: 6 G and silver couches were placed on B
1: 7 The cups were of g and silver, B
8:15 the royal robe and wearing a g crown and a turban
15: 6 all covered with g and precious stones.
Wis 3: 6 like g in the furnace he tried them,
7: 9 because all g is but a little sand in her sight,
13:10 g and silver fashioned with skill, B
15: 9 but they compete with workers in g and silver, B
Sir 2: 5 For g is tested in the fire,
7:18 or a real brother for the g of Ophir.
7:19 for her charm is worth more than g.
8: 2 for g has ruined many, and has perverted the minds
28:24 As you lock up your silver and g, A
29:11 and it will profit you more than g.
30:15 Health and fitness are better than any g,
31: 5 One who loves g will not be justified;
31: 6 Many have come to ruin because of g,
31: 8 and who does not go after g.
32: 5 in a setting of g is a concert of music at a banquet
32: 6 of emerald in a rich setting of g is the melody
40:25 G and silver make one stand firm, B

Sir 41:12 outlive you longer than a thousand hoards of **g.**
45:10 of **g** and violet and purple,
45:11 in a setting of **g,** the work of a jeweler,
45:12 with a **g** crown upon his turban,
47:18 gathered **g** like tin and amassed silver like lead.
50: 9 like a vessel of hammered **g** studded with all kinds
51:28 and through me you will acquire silver and **g.** A
Bar 3:17 hoarded up silver and **g** in which people trust, A
3:30 and found her, and will buy her for pure **g?** C
LtJ 6: 4 Babylon you will see gods made of silver and **g** A
6: 8 they themselves are overlaid with **g** and silver; B
6: 9 People take **g** and make crowns for the heads
6:10 Sometimes the priests secretly take **g** and silver B
6:11 these gods of silver and **g** and wood A
6:24 As for the **g** that they wear for beauty—
6:30 Women serve meals for gods of silver and **g** A
6:39 and overlaid with **g** and silver are like stones B
6:50 made of wood and overlaid with **g** and silver, B
6:55 temple of wooden gods overlaid with **g** or silver, B
6:57 wood and overlaid with silver and **g** are unable A
6:58 of their **g** and silver and of the robes they wear, B
6:70 gods of wood, overlaid with **g** and silver. B
6:71 their gods of wood, overlaid with **g** and silver, B
1Mc 1:22 and the **g** decoration on the front of the temple;
1:23 He took the silver and the **g,** A
2:18 and your sons will be honored with silver and **g** A
3:41 they took silver and **g** in immense amounts, A
4:23 and they seized a great amount of **g** and silver, B
6: 1 a city famed for its wealth in silver and **g.** A
6:12 I seized all its vessels of silver and **g,** A
6:39 When the sun shone on the shields of **g** and brass,
8: 3 to get control of the silver and **g** mines there, A
10:60 and their Friends silver and **g** and many gifts, A
11:24 silver and **g** and clothing and numerous other A
11:58 He also sent him **g** plate and a table service,
11:58 to drink from **g** cups and dress in purple and wear a **g** buckle.
13:37 the **g** crown and the palm branch that you sent,
14:24 a large **g** shield weighing one thousand minas,
14:43 that he should be clothed in purple and wear **g.**
14:44 or to be clothed in purple or put on a **g** buckle.
15:18 a **g** shield weighing one thousand minas.
15:26 silver and **g** and a large amount of military A
15:32 and the sideboard with its **g** and silver plate, B
16:11 he had a large store of silver and **g,** A
16:19 that he might give them silver and **g** and gifts; A
2Mc 2: 2 on seeing the **g** and silver statues B
3:11 of silver and two hundred of **g.**
3:25 to have armor and weapons of **g.**
4:32 of the **g** vessels of the temple and gave them
4:39 many of the **g** vessels had already been stolen.
11: 8 clothed in white and brandishing weapons of **g.**
14: 4 presenting to him a crown of **g** and a palm,
1Es 1:36 of silver and one talent of **g.**
2: 6 by the people of your place with **g** and silver, B
2: 9 with silver and **g,** with horses and cattle, A
2:13 The number of these was: one thousand **g** cups,
2:13 twenty-nine silver censers, thirty **g** bowls,
2:14 All the vessels were handed over, **g** and silver, B
3: 6 and drink from **g** cups, and sleep on a **g** bed,
3: 6 and have a chariot with **g** bridles,
4:18 If men gather **g** and silver B
4:19 to **g** or silver or any other beautiful thing. B
5:45 for the work a thousand minas of **g,**
6:18 And the holy vessels of **g** and of silver, B
6:26 both of **g** and of silver, B
8:13 Jerusalem all the **g** and silver that may be found B
8:14 both **g** and silver for bulls and rams and lambs B
8:16 the **g** and silver, perform it in accordance with B
8:55 to them the silver and the **g** and the holy vessels A
8:56 and a hundred talents of **g,**
8:57 of fine bronze that glittered like **g.**
8:58 and the silver and the **g** are vowed to the Lord, A
8:60 and the Levites who took the silver and the **g** A
8:62 the silver and the **g** were weighed and delivered A
3Mc 1: 4 to give them each two minas of **g** if they won
2Es 7:55 Say to her, 'You produce **g** and silver and B
7:56 but silver is more abundant than **g,**
8: 2 but only a little dust from which **g** comes,
16:73 like **g** that is tested by fire.

GOLD-PLATED (1) [GOLD, PLATED]

Isa 30:22 defile your silver-covered idols and your **g** images.

GOLD-WOVEN (1) [GOLD, WEAVE]

Ps 45:13 princess is decked in her chamber with **g** robes;

GOLDEN (83) [GOLD]

Ex 28:34 a **g** bell and a pomegranate alternating all around
30: 4 And you shall make two **g** rings for it;
37:27 and made two **g** rings for it under its molding,
39:38 the **g** altar, the anointing oil and
40: 5 You shall put the **g** altar for incense before the ark
40:26 He put the **g** altar in the tent of meeting before
Lev 8: 9 and on the turban, in front, he set the **g** ornament,
Nu 4:11 Over the **g** altar they shall spread a blue cloth,
7:14 one **g** dish weighing ten shekels, full of incense;
7:20 one **g** dish weighing ten shekels, full of incense;
7:26 one **g** dish weighing ten shekels, full of incense;
7:32 one **g** dish weighing ten shekels, full of incense;
7:38 one **g** dish weighing ten shekels, full of incense;
7:44 one **g** dish weighing ten shekels, full of incense;
7:50 one **g** dish weighing ten shekels, full of incense;
7:56 one **g** dish weighing ten shekels, full of incense;
7:62 one **g** dish weighing ten shekels, full of incense;
Nu 7:68 one **g** dish weighing ten shekels, full of incense;
7:74 one **g** dish weighing ten shekels, full of incense;
7:80 one **g** dish weighing ten shekels, full of incense;
7:84 twelve silver basins, twelve **g** dishes,
7:86 the twelve **g** dishes, full of incense,
Jdg 8:24 (For the enemy had **g** earrings,
8:26 The weight of the **g** earrings
1Ki 7:48 the **g** altar, the **g** table for the bread of the Presence,
2Ki 10:29 the **g** calves that were in Bethel and in Dan.
1Ch 28:14 weight of gold for all **g** vessels for each service,
28:15 the weight of the **g** lampstands and their lamps,
28:17 for the **g** bowls and the weight of each;
28:18 also his plan for the **g** chariot of the cherubim
2Ch 4: 7 He made ten **g** lampstands as prescribed,
4:19 the **g** altar, the tables for the bread of the Presence,
13: 8 with you the **g** calves that Jeroboam made as gods
13:11 and care for the **g** lampstand so
Est 1: 7 Drinks were served in **g** goblets,
4:11 if the king holds out the **g** scepter to someone,
5: 2 and he held out to her the **g** scepter that was
8: 4 The king held out the **g** scepter to Esther,
8:15 with a great **g** crown and a mantle of fine linen
Job 37:22 Out of the north comes **g** splendor;
Ecc 12: 6 and the **g** bowl is broken,
Jer 51: 7 Babylon was a **g** cup in the LORD's hand,
Da 3: 1 a **g** statue whose height was sixty cubits
3: 5 the **g** statue that King Nebuchadnezzar has set up.
3: 7 the **g** statue that King Nebuchadnezzar had set up.
3:10 shall fall down and worship the **g** statue,
3:12 not worship the **g** statue that you have set up."
3:14 not worship the **g** statue that I have set up?
3:18 not worship the **g** statue that you have set up."
Zec 4:12 which pour out the oil through the two **g** pipes?"
Heb 9: 4 In it stood the **g** altar of incense and the ark of
9: 4 in which there were a **g** urn holding the manna,
Rev 1:12 and on turning I saw seven **g** lampstands,
1:13 a long robe and with a **g** sash across his chest.
1:20 and the seven **g** lampstands:
2: 1 who walks among the seven **g** lampstands:
4: 4 with **g** crowns on their heads.
5: 8 each holding a harp and **g** bowls full of incense,
8: 3 Another angel with a **g** censer came and stood at
8: 3 the saints on the **g** altar that is before the throne.
9:13 from the four horns of the **g** altar before God,
14:14 with a **g** crown on his head,
15: 6 with **g** sashes across their chests.
15: 7 the seven angels seven **g** bowls full of the wrath
17: 4 holding in her hand a **g** cup full of abominations
AdE 4:11 the king stretches out the **g** scepter is safe—
8: 4 The king extended his **g** scepter to Esther,
15:11 Then he raised the **g** scepter and touched her neck
Sir 6:30 Her yoke is a **g** ornament,
21:21 the sensible person education is like a **g** ornament,
26:18 Like **g** pillars on silver bases,
45: 9 with many **g** bells all around,
1Mc 1:21 the sanctuary and took the **g** altar,
1:22 the bowls, the **g** censers, the curtain, the crowns,
4:57 of the temple with **g** crowns and small shields;
6: 2 Its temple was very rich, containing **g** shields,
10:20 He also sent him a purple robe and a **g** crown.
10:89 and he sent to him a **g** buckle,
2Mc 5: 3 the flash of **g** trappings, and armor of all kinds.
10:29 on horses with **g** bridles, and they were leading
15:15 and gave to Judas a **g** sword,
1Es 8:57 and twenty **g** bowls, and twelve bronze vessels

GOLDEN-CLAD (1) [GOLD]

2Mc 5: 2 there appeared over all the city **g** cavalry charging

GOLDSMITH (4) [GOLD, SMITH]

Isa 40:19 workman casts it, and a **g** overlays it with gold,
41: 7 The artisan encourages the **g,**
46: 6 they hire a **g,** who makes it into a god;
Jer 10: 9 the work of the artisan and of the hands of the **g;**

GOLDSMITHS (6) [GOLD, SMITH]

Ne 3: 8 Next to them Uzziel son of Harhaiah, one of the **g,**
3:31 After him Malchijah, one of the **g,**
3:32 of the corner and the Sheep Gate the **g** and
Jer 10:14 **g** are all put to shame by their idols;
51:17 **g** are all put to shame by their idols;
LtJ 6:45 They are made by carpenters and **g;**

GOLGOTHA (3)

Mt 27:33 a place called **G** (which means Place of a Skull),
Mk 15:22 place called **G** (which means the place of a skull)
Jn 19:17 Place of the Skull, which in Hebrew is called **G.**

GOLIATH (8)

1Sa 17: 4 the camp of the Philistines a champion named **G,**
17:23 the champion, the Philistine of Gath, **G** by name,
21: 9 The priest said, "The sword of **G** the Philistine,
22:10 and gave him the sword of **G** the Philistine."
2Sa 21:19 the Bethlehemite, killed **G** the Gittite,
1Ch 20: 5 of Jair killed Lahmi the brother of **G** the Gittite,
Sir 47: 4 in the sling and struck down the boasting **G?**
Pm 151: T *after he had fought in single combat with* **G.**

GOMER (6)

Ge 10: 2 The descendants of Japheth: **G,** Magog, Madai,
10: 3 The descendants of **G:** Ashkenaz,
1Ch 1: 5 The descendants of Japheth: **G,** Magog, Madai,
1: 6 The descendants of **G:** Ashkenaz,
Eze 38: 6 **G** and all its troops; Beth-togarmah from the
Hos 1: 3 So he went and took **G** daughter of Diblaim,

GOMORRAH (24)

Ge 10:19 as far as Gaza, and in the direction of Sodom, **G,**
13:10 before the LORD had destroyed Sodom and **G.**
14: 2 King Birsha of **G,** King Shinab of Admah,
14: 8 Then the king of Sodom, the king of **G,**
14:10 and as the kings of Sodom and **G** fled,
14:11 So the enemy took all the goods of Sodom and **G,**
18:20 "How great is the outcry against Sodom and **G**
19:24 the LORD rained on Sodom and **G** sulfur and fire
19:28 and **G** and toward all the land of the Plain and saw
Dt 29:23 like the destruction of Sodom and **G,**
32:32 from the vineyards of **G;**
Isa 1: 9 like Sodom, and become like **G.**
1:10 to the teaching of our God, you people of **G!**
13:19 be like Sodom and **G** when God overthrew them.
Jer 23:14 and its inhabitants like **G.**
49:18 and **G** and their neighbors were overthrown,
50:40 God overthrew Sodom and **G** and their neighbors,
Am 4:11 as when God overthrew Sodom and **G,**
Zep 2: 9 like Sodom and the Ammonites like **G,**
Mt 10:15 be more tolerable for the land of Sodom and **G** on
Ro 9:29 like Sodom and been made like **G.**"
2Pe 2: 6 and **G** to ashes he condemned them to extinction
Jude 1: 7 Sodom and **G** and the surrounding cities, which,
2Es 2: 8 remember what I did to Sodom and **G,**

GONE (245) [GO]

Ge 12:19 Now then, here is your wife, take her, and be **g.**"
15:17 When the sun had **g** down and it was dark,
21:15 When the water in the skin was **g,**
27:30 when Jacob had scarcely **g** out from the presence
28: 7 and his mother and **g** to Paddan-aram.
31:19 Now Laban had **g** to shear his sheep,
34:17 then we will take our daughter and be **g.**"
35: 3 and has been with me wherever I have **g.**"
37:17 The man said, "They have **g** away,
37:30 and said, "The boy is **g;** and I, where can I turn?"
44: 4 they had **g** only a short distance from the city,
47:15 For our money is **g.**"
47:16 exchange for your livestock, if your money is **g.**"
49: 9 from the prey, my son, you have **g** up.
50:14 and all who had **g** up with him to bury his father.
Ex 9:29 "As soon as I have **g** out of the city,
12:32 and your herds, as you said, and be **g.**
19: 1 the third new moon after the Israelites had **g** out of
33: 8 of their tents and watch Moses until he had **g** into
Nu 5:20 But if you have **g** astray while
11:26 but they had not **g** out to the tent,
13:31 Then the men who had **g** up with him said,
13:32 "The land that we have **g** through as spies is a land
16: 3 and said to them, "You have **g** too far!
16: 7 You Levites have **g** too far!"
16:46 For wrath has **g** out from the LORD;
31:21 the priest said to the troops who had **g** to battle:
31:36 the portion of those who had **g** out to war,
Dt 13:13 among you have **g** out and led the inhabitants of
32:36 when he sees that their power is **g,**
Jos 2: 7 soon as the pursuers had **g** out, the gate was shut.
10:24 to the chiefs of the warriors who had **g** with him,
Jdg 3:24 After he had **g,** the servants came.
4:12 of Abinoam had **g** up to Mount Tabor,
11:36 to me according to what has **g** out of your mouth,
18:14 the five men who had **g** to spy out the land (that is,
18:17 the five men who had **g** to spy out
20: 3 that the people of Israel had **g** up to Mizpah.)
Ru 1:15 your sister-in-law has **g** back to her people and
3:10 you have not **g** after young men,
4: 1 No sooner had Boaz **g** up to the gate and sat
1Sa 3: 3 the lamp of God had not yet **g** out,
9: 7 For the bread in our sacks is **g,**
13:23 the Philistines had **g** out to the pass of Michmash.
14: 3 Now the people did not know that Jonathan had **g.**
14:17 "Call the roll and see who has **g** from us."
14:21 with the Philistines and had **g** up with them into
14:22 when all the Israelites who had **g** into hiding in
15:20 I have **g** on the mission on which
20:41 As soon as the boy had **g,**
25:37 In the morning, when the wine had **g** out of Nabal,
30:22 and worthless fellows among the men who had **g**
2Sa 3: 7 "Why have you **g** in to my father's concubine?"
3:22 and he had **g** away in peace.
3:23 and he has **g** away in peace."
5:24 for then the LORD has **g** out before you to strike
6:13 the ark of the LORD had **g** six paces,
15:13 hearts of the Israelites have **g** after Absalom."
17:21 After they had **g,** the men came up out of the well,
24: 8 So when they had **g** through all the land,
1Ki 1:25 For today he has **g** down and has sacrificed oxen,
1:45 and they have **g** up from there rejoicing,
2:41 When Solomon was told that Shimei had **g**
9:16 of Egypt had **g** up and captured Gezer
12:28 "You have **g** up to Jerusalem long enough.
13:12 that the man of God who came from Judah had **g.**
14: 9 above all those who were before you and have **g**
14:10 just as one burns up dung until it is all **g.**
18:12 As soon as I have **g** from you,
20:40 your servant was busy here and there, he was **g.**"
21:18 where he has **g** to take possession.
22:13 The messenger who had **g**
2Ki 1: 4 'You shall not leave the bed to which you have **g,**
1: 6 you shall not leave the bed to which you have **g,**
1:16 you shall not leave the bed to which you have **g,**
5:19 when Naaman had **g** from him a short distance,
5:25 "Your servant has not **g** anywhere at all."

2Ki 19:23 ‘With my many chariots I have g up the heights of
20: 4 Before Isaiah had g out of the middle court,
1Ch 14:15 for God has g out before you to strike down
2Ch 18:12 The messenger who had g
19: 2 wrath has g out against you from the LORD.
Ezr 4:12 that the Jews who came up from you to us have g
Ne 2: 6 “How long will you be g,
2:16 not know where I had g or what I was doing;
13:10 had g back to their fields.
Job 6:24 make me understand how I have g wrong.
7: 8 while your eyes are upon me, I shall be g.
19:10 He breaks me down on every side, and I am g,
24:24 They are exalted a little while, and then are g;
27:19 they open their eyes, and it is g.
27:21 The east wind lifts them up and they are g;
30: 2 All their vigor is g.
Ps 14: 3 They have all g astray, they are all alike perverse;
30: 3 restored me to life from among those g down to
38: 4 For my iniquities have g over my head;
38:10 it also has g from me.
42: 7 all your waves and your billows have g over me.
44: 9 and have not g out with our armies.
47: 5 God has g up with a shout,
51: T *came to him, after he had g in to Bathsheba.*
90:10 they are soon g, and we fly away.
103:16 and it is g, and its place knows it no more.
109:23 I am g like a shadow at evening;
119:176 I have g astray like a lost sheep;
124: 4 the torrent would have g over us;
124: 5 then over us would have g the raging waters.
Pr 7:19 he has g on a long journey.
23: 5 When your eyes light upon it, it is g;
27:25 When the grass is g, and new growth appears,
Ecc 3:15 and God seeks out what has g by.
SS 2:11 for now the winter is past, the rain is over and g.
5: 6 but my beloved had turned and was g.
6: 1 has your beloved g, O fairest among women?
6: 2 My beloved has g down to his garden,
Isa 10:27 He has g up from Rimmon,
15: 2 Dibon has g up to the temple,
15: 8 For a cry has g around the land of Moab;
22: 1 What do you mean that you have g up, all of you,
37:24 ‘With my many chariots I have g up the heights of
45:23 from my mouth has g forth in righteousness
51: 5 my salvation has g out and my arms will rule
53: 6 All we like sheep have g astray;
57: 8 you have uncovered your bed, you have g up to it,
Jer 2:23 “I am not defiled, I have not g after the Baals”?
4: 7 A lion has g up from its thicket,
4: 7 he has g out from his place to make your land
5:23 they have turned aside and g away.
8:18 My joy is g, grief is upon me, my heart is sick.
9:10 of the air and the animals have fled and are g.
9:14 and have g after the Baals,
10:20 my children have g from me,
11:10 they have g after other gods to serve them;
13:10 who stubbornly follow their own will and have g
16:11 and have g after other gods and have served
18:15 and have g into bypaths, not the highway,
19: 5 and g on building the high places of Baal
23:19 Wrath has g forth, a whirling tempest;
30:23 Wrath has g forth, a whirling tempest;
37:21 until all the bread of the city was g.
48:11 from vessel to vessel, nor has he g into exile;
48:15 and the choicest of his young men have g down
48:45 for a fire has g out from Heshbon,
50: 6 from mountain to hill they have g,
La 1: 3 Judah has g into exile with suffering
1: 5 her children have g away, captives before the foe.
1:18 my young women and young men have g
3:18 “G is my glory, and all that I had hoped for from
Eze 7:10 Your doom has g out.
9: 3 Now the glory of the God of Israel had g up from
11:15 “They have g far from the LORD;
11:16 a little while in the countries where they have g.
13: 5 You have not g up into the breaches,
19:14 And fire has g out from its stem,
23:31 You have g the way of your sister;
23:44 they have g in to her, as one goes in to a whore.
24: 6 whose rust has not g out of it!
32:30 who have g down in shame with the slain,
37:21 from the nations among which they have g,
46:12 and after he has g out the gate shall be closed.
Da 2:14 who had g out to execute the wise men
Hos 8: 9 For they have g up to Assyria,
Jnh 1: 5 had g down into the hold of the ship and had lain
Mic 1:16 for they have g from you into exile.
Na 1:11 From you one has g out who plots evil against
3:17 no one knows where they have g.
Mt 9:32 After they had g away, a demoniac who was mute
10:23 for truly I tell you, you will not have g through all
12:43 “When the unclean spirit has g out of a person,
18:12 and one of them has g astray,
Mk 3:21 “He has g out of his mind.”
5:30 Immediately aware that power had g forth
7:30 found the child lying on the bed, and the demon g.
Lk 2:15 When the angels had left them and g into heaven,
5: 2 the fishermen had g out of them
7:24 When John’s messengers had g,
8: 2 from whom seven demons had g out,
8:35 the man from whom the demons had g sitting at
8:38 The man from whom the demons had g begged
8:46 for I noticed that power had g out from me.”
11:14 when the demon had g out,
11:24 “When the unclean spirit has g out of a person,
16: 9 by means of dishonest wealth so that when it is g,
19: 7 “He has g to be the guest of one who is a sinner.”
Jn 4: 8 (His disciples had g to the city to buy food.)
4:45 for they too had g to the festival.
6:22 but that his disciples had g away alone.
7:10 But after his brothers had g to the festival,
7:50 Nicodemus, who had g to Jesus before,
12:19 Look, the world has g after him!”
13:31 When he had g out, Jesus said,
21: 9 When they had g ashore, they saw
Ac 13: 6 When they had g through the whole island as far
15:24 that certain persons who have g out from us,
16:19 that their hope of making money was g,
19:21 He said, “After I have g there,
20: 2 When he had g through those regions
20:25 among whom I have g about proclaiming
20:29 I know that after I have g,
25: 7 the Jews who had g down
27: 9 because even the Fast had already g by,
Ro 10:18 for “Their voice has g out to all the earth,
13:12 the night is far g, the day is near.
2Ti 4:10 and g to Thessalonica; Crescens has g to Galatia,
1Pe 3:22 who has g into heaven and is at the right hand
2Pe 2:15 They have left the straight road and have g astray,
1Jn 4: 1 for many false prophets have g out into the world.
2Jn 1: 7 Many deceivers have g out into the world,
Rev 18:14 fruit for which your soul longed has g from you,
Tob 1: 3 for my kindred and my people who had g with me
3:10 When she had g up to her father’s upper room,
5:10 for I have often g to Media
8: 4 parents had g out and shut the door of the room,
Jdt 8:18 as was done in days g by.
10:10 The men of the town watched her until she had g
AdE 15: 6 When she had g through all the doors,
Wis 4: 2 and they long for it when it has g;
17: 1 therefore uninstructed souls have g astray.
18:14 and night in its swift course was now half g,
Bar 3:19 They have vanished and g down to Hades,
3:29 Who has g up into heaven, and taken her,
3:30 Who has g over the sea, and found her,
Sus 1:19 When the maids had g out,
Bel 1:14 they had g out, the king set out the food for Bel.
1Mc 2:31 the king’s command had g down to
6: 5 that had g into the land of Judah had been routed;
6: 6 that Lysias had g first with a strong force,
6:56 from Persia and Media with the forces that had g
2Mc 2: 4 the mountain where Moses had g up and had seen
6:24 that Eleazar in his ninetieth year had g over to
10:13 and had g over to Antiochus Epiphanes.
11:23 Now that our father has g on to the gods,
12:10 When they had g more than a mile from there,
12:17 When they had g ninety-five miles from there,
1Es 2:18 that the Jews who came up from you to us have g
2Es 4:45 or whether for us the greater part has g by.
4:46 For I know what has g by,
4:48 and when the flame had g by I looked, and lo,
7:*78* the decisive decree has g out from the Most High
7:*136* [66] now living and to those who are g and
10:22 our Levites have g into exile,
11:32 the world than all the wings that had g before.
11:40 have conquered all the beasts that have g before;
12: 2 that had g over to it rose up and set themselves up

GONG (1)

1Co 13: 1 not have love, I am a noisy g or a clanging cymbal.

GOOD‡ (827) [BEST, BETTER, GOOD-LOOKING, GOODLY, GOODNESS, GOODNESS', GOODS, GOODWILL]

A. GOOD NEWS (61)
B. DO GOOD (37)
C. GOOD THINGS (33)
D. WHAT IS GOOD (27)
E. SEEMS GOOD (23)
F. GOOD ... EVIL (22)
G. NOT ... GOOD (19)
H. GOOD HEALTH (17)
I. GOOD LAND (17)
J. EVIL ... GOOD (17)
K. FOR HE IS GOOD (13)
L. GOOD WORKS (12)
M. GOOD DEEDS (9)
N. GOOD WORK (9)

Ge 1: 4 And God saw that the light was g;
1:10 And God saw that it was g.
1:12 And God saw that it was g.
1:18 And God saw that it was g.
1:21 And God saw that it was g.
1:25 And God saw that it was g.
1:31 and indeed, it was very g.
2: 9 that is pleasant to the sight and g for food,
2: 9 and the tree of the knowledge of g and evil. F
2:12 and the gold of that land is g;
2:17 the tree of the knowledge of g and evil you shall F
2:18 “It is not g that the man should be alone; G
3: 5 and you will be like God, knowing g and evil.” F
3: 6 when the woman saw that the tree was g for food,
3:22 has become like one of us, knowing g and evil; F
15:15 you shall be buried in a g old age.
18: 7 tender and g, and gave it to the servant,
21:16 she went and sat down opposite him a g way off,
24:50 we cannot speak to you anything bad or g.
25: 8 Abraham breathed his last and died in a g old age,
26:29 to you nothing but g and have sent you away
27:46 what g will my life be to me?”
30:11 And Leah said, “G fortune!”
30:20 Leah said, “God has endowed me with a g dowry;
30:34 Laban said, “G! Let it be as you have said.”
31:24 that you say not a word to Jacob, either g or bad.”
31:29 ‘Take heed that you speak to Jacob neither g
32: 9 and I will do you g,’
32:12 Yet you have said, ‘I will surely do you g,
41: 5 seven ears of grain, plump and g,
41:22 full and g, growing on one stalk,
41:24 and the thin ears swallowed up the seven g ears.
41:26 The seven g cows are seven years,
41:26 and the seven g ears are seven years;
41:35 Let them gather all the food of these g years
44: 4 say to them, ‘Why have you returned evil for g? J
45:23 ten donkeys loaded with the g things of Egypt, C
46:29 fell on his neck, and wept on his neck a g while.
49:15 he saw that a resting place was g, and that
50:20 to me, God intended it for g, in order to preserve
Ex 3: 8 and to bring them up out of that land to a g
18: 9 for all the g that the LORD had done to Israel,
18:17 “What you are doing is not g. G
Lev 5: 4 a rash oath for a bad or a g purpose,
27:10 either g for bad or bad for g;
27:12 The priest shall assess it: whether g or bad,
27:14 whether g or bad, as the priest assesses it,
27:33 Let no one inquire whether it is g or bad,
Nu 10:29 for the LORD has promised g to Israel.”
10:32 whatever g the LORD does for us,
13:19 and whether the land they live in is g or bad,
14: 7 through as spies is an exceedingly g land. I
24:13 to do either g or bad of my own will;
32: 1 and the land of Gilead was a g place for cattle,
Dt 1:14 “The plan you have proposed is a g one.”
1:23 The plan seemed g to me,
1:25 a g land that the LORD our God is giving us.” I
1:35 the g land that I swore to give to your ancestors, I
3:25 Let me cross over to see the g land beyond I
3:25 that g hill country and the Lebanon.”
4:21 the Jordan and that I should not enter the g land I
4:22 to cross over to take possession of that g land. I
6:18 Do what is right and g in the sight of the LORD,
6:18 the g land that the LORD swore to your ancestors I
6:24 to fear the LORD our God, for our lasting g,
8: 7 LORD your God is bringing you into a g land, I
8:10 and bless the LORD your God for the g land I
8:16 and in the end to do you g.
9: 6 the LORD your God is not giving you this g land I
11:17 then you will perish quickly off the g land that I
12:28 because you will be doing what is g and right in D
Jos 2:12 Give me a sign of g faith
9:25 as it seems g and right in your sight to do to us.” E
21:45 of all the g promises that the LORD had made to
22: 5 Take g care to observe the commandment
23:13 until you perish from this g land that I
23:14 not one thing has failed of all the g things that C
23:15 the g things that the LORD your God promised C
23:15 until he has destroyed you from this g land that I
23:16 and you shall perish quickly from the g land I
24:20 and consume you, after having done you g.”
Jdg 8:32 Then Gideon son of Joash died at a g old age,
8:35 in return for all the g that he had done to Israel.
9:15 ‘If in g faith you are anointing me king over you,
9:16 if you acted in g faith and honor
9:19 you have acted in g faith and honor with Jerubbaal
10:15 do to us whatever seems g to you; E
18: 9 for we have seen the land, and it is very g.
Ru 3:13 if he will act as next-of-kin for you, g;
1Sa 2:24 it is not a g report that I hear the people of
3:18 let him do what seems g to him.” E
9:10 Saul said to the boy, “G; come, let us go.”
11:10 and you may do to us whatever seems g to you.” E
12:23 and I will instruct you in the g and the right way.
14:36 They said, “Do whatever seems g to you.” E
14:40 people said to Saul, “Do what seems g to you.” E
16:18 prudent in speech, and a man of g presence;
19: 4 because his deeds have been of g service to you;
20: 7 If he says, ‘G!’ it will be well
24: 4 and you shall do to him as it seems g to you.’ ” E
24:17 for you have repaid me g,
24:19 with g for what you have done to me this day.
25:15 Yet the men were very g to us,
25:21 but he has returned me evil for g. J
25:30 to all the g that he has spoken concerning you,
25:33 Blessed be your g sense, and blessed be you,
26:16 This thing that you have done is not g. G
31: 9 to carry the g news to the houses of their idols A
2Sa 3:13 He said, “G; I will make a covenant with you.
4:10 Saul is dead,’ thought he was bringing g news, A
7:28 you have promised this g thing to your servant;
10:12 and may the LORD do what seems g to him.” E
13:22 But Absalom spoke to Amnon neither g nor bad;
14:17 is like the angel of God, discerning g and evil. F
15: 3 “See, your claims are g and right;
15:26 let him do to me what seems g to him.” E
16:12 the LORD will repay me with g for this cursing
17: 7 the counsel that Ahithophel has given is not g.” G
17:14 the LORD had ordained to defeat the g counsel
18:27 The king said, “He is a g man,
18:27 “He is a good man, and comes with g tidings.”
18:31 the Cushite said, “G tidings for my lord the king!
19:27 do therefore what seems g to you. E
19:37 and do for him whatever seems g to you.” E
19:38 and I will do for him whatever seems g to you; E
24:22 the king take and offer up what seems g to him; E
1Ki 1:42 a worthy man and surely you bring g news.” A
3: 9 able to discern between g and evil; F
8:36 the g way in which they should walk;
8:56 not one word has failed of all his g promise,

1Ki 8:66 to their tents, joyful and in g spirits because of all
12: 7 speak g words to them when you answer them,
14:15 of this g land that he gave to their ancestors, I
21: 2 or, if it seems g to you, E
2Ki 2:19 "The location of this city is g, as my lord sees;
3:19 every g tree you shall fell,
3:19 every g piece of land you shall ruin with stones."
3:25 on every g piece of land everyone threw a stone,
3:25 and every g tree they felled.
7: 9 This is a day of g news; A
20: 3 and have done what is g in your sight." D
20:19 word of the LORD that you have spoken is g."
1Ch 4:40 g pasture, and the land was very broad, quiet,
10: 9 carry the g news to their idols and to the people. A
13: 2 "If it seems g to you, E
16:34 O give thanks to the LORD, for he is g; K
17:26 you have promised this g thing to your servant;
19:13 and may the LORD do what seems g to him." E
21:23 and let my lord the king do what seems g to him; E
22:13 Be strong and of g courage.
28: 8 that you may possess this g land, I
28:20 "Be strong and of g courage, and act.
29:28 He died in a g old age, full of days, riches,
2Ch 5:13 "For he is g, for his steadfast love endures K
6:27 the g way in which they should walk;
7: 3 "For he is g, for his steadfast love endures K
7:10 joyful and in g spirits because of the goodness that
10: 7 and speak g words to them,
12:12 moreover, conditions were g in Judah.
14: 2 Asa did what was g and right in the sight of
19: 3 Nevertheless, some g is found in you,
19:11 and may the LORD be with the g!"
24:16 because he had done g in Israel,
30:18 "The g LORD pardon all
30:22 to all the Levites who showed g skill in the service
31:20 he did what was g and right and faithful before
32: 7 "Be strong and of g courage.
32:32 the rest of the acts of Hezekiah, and his g deeds, M
Ezr 3:11 "For he is g, for his steadfast love endures K
5:17 And now, if it seems g to the king, E
7:18 Whatever seems g to you and your colleagues E
9:12 so that you may be strong and eat the g of the land
Ne 2:18 So they committed themselves to the common g.
5: 9 So I said, "The thing that you are doing is not g. G
5:19 Remember for my g, O my God,
6:19 Also they spoke of his g deeds in my presence, M
9:13 g statutes and commandments,
9:20 You gave your g spirit to instruct them,
9:36 to our ancestors to enjoy its fruit and its g gifts.
13:14 do not wipe out my g deeds that I have done M
13:31 Remember me, O my God, for g.
Est 3:11 to do with them as it seems g to you." E
5: 9 Haman went out that day happy and in g spirits.
5:13 Yet all this does me no g so long as I see
5:14 then go with the king to the banquet in g spirits."
10: 3 the g of his people and interceded for the welfare
Job 2:10 Shall we receive the g at the hand of God,
7: 7 my eye will never again see g.
9:25 they flee away, they see no g.
9:27 will put off my sad countenance and be of g cheer,'
10: 3 Does it seem g to you to oppress,
15: 3 or in words with which they can do no g?
21:25 in bitterness of soul, never having tasted of g.
22:18 Yet he filled their houses with g things— C
22:21 in this way g will come to you.
24:21 and do no g to the widow.
26: 3 and given much g advice!
30:26 But when I looked for g, evil came; F
34: 4 let us determine among ourselves what is g. D
Ps 4: 6 "O that we might see some g!
14: 1 there is no one who does g.
14: 3 there is no one who does g, no, not one.
16: 2 I have no g apart from you."
25: 8 G and upright is the LORD;
34: 8 O taste and see that the LORD is g;
34:10 but those who seek the LORD lack no g thing.
34:12 and covets many days to enjoy g?
34:14 Depart from evil, and do g; BJ
35:12 They repay me evil for g; my soul is forlorn. J
36: 3 they have ceased to act wisely and do g. B
36: 4 they are set on a way that is not g; G
37: 3 Trust in the LORD, and do g; B
37:27 Depart from evil, and do g; BJ
38:20 who render me evil for g are my adversaries J
38:20 my adversaries because I follow after g.
51:18 Do g to Zion in your good pleasure; B
51:18 Do good to Zion in your g pleasure;
52: 3 You love evil more than g,
52: 9 the faithful I will proclaim your name, for it is g.
53: 1 there is no one who does g.
53: 3 there is no one who does g, no, not one.
54: 6 to your name, O LORD, for it is g.
69:16 O LORD, for your steadfast love is g;
73: 1 Truly God is g to the upright,
73:28 But for me it is g to be near God;
84:11 No g thing does the LORD withhold
85:12 The LORD will give what is g, D
86: 5 For you, O Lord, are g and forgiving,
92: 1 It is g to give thanks to the LORD, to sing praises
100: 5 For the LORD is g; his steadfast love endures
103: 5 who satisfies you with g as long as you live so
104:28 open your hand, they are filled with g things. C
106: 1 O give thanks to the LORD, for he is g; K
107: 1 O give thanks to the LORD, for he is g; K
107: 9 and the hungry he fills with g things. C
109: 5 reward me evil for g, and hatred for my love. J
109:21 because your steadfast love is g, deliver me.

Ps 111:10 all those who practice it have a g understanding.
118: 1 O give thanks to the LORD, for he is g; K
118:29 O give thanks to the LORD, for he is g, K
119:39 for your ordinances are g.
119:66 Teach me g judgment and knowledge,
119:68 You are g and do good; teach me your statutes.
119:68 You are good and do g; teach me your statutes. B
119:71 It is g for me that I was humbled,
122: 9 of the LORD our God, I will seek your g.
125: 4 Do g, O LORD, to those who are good, B
125: 4 Do good, O LORD, to those who are g,
133: 1 How very g and pleasant it is
135: 3 Praise the LORD, for the LORD is g;
136: 1 O give thanks to the LORD, for he is g, K
143:10 Let your g spirit lead me on a level path.
145: 9 The LORD is g to all,
147: 1 How g it is to sing praises to our God;
Pr 2: 9 and justice and equity, every g path;
2:20 Therefore walk in the way of the g,
3: 4 So you will find favor and g repute in the sight
3:27 Do not withhold g from those to whom it is due,
4: 2 for I give you g precepts:
8:14 I have g advice and sound wisdom;
11:22 a beautiful woman without g sense.
11:23 The desire of the righteous ends only in g;
11:27 Whoever diligently seeks g seeks favor,
12: 2 The g obtain favor from the LORD,
12: 4 A g wife is the crown of her husband,
12: 8 One is commended for g sense,
12:14 the fruit of the mouth one is filled with g things, C
12:25 but a g word cheers it up.
12:26 The righteous gives g advice to friends,
13: 2 the fruit of their words g persons eat good things,
13: 2 the fruit of their words good persons eat g things, C
13:15 G sense wins favor, but the way of
13:22 g leave an inheritance to their children's children,
14:14 perverse get what their ways deserve, and the g,
14:19 The evil bow down before the g, J
14:22 Those who plan g find loyalty and faithfulness.
15: 3 keeping watch on the evil and the g. J
15:23 and a word in season, how g it is!
15:30 and g news refreshes the body. A
16:29 and lead them in a way that is not g. G
17:13 from the house of one who returns evil for g. J
17:22 A cheerful heart is a g medicine,
18:22 He who finds a wife finds a g thing,
19: 2 Desire without knowledge is not g, G
19:11 Those with g sense are slow to anger,
20:23 and false scales are not g. G
21:28 but a g listener will testify successfully.
22: 1 A g name is to be chosen rather than great riches,
24:13 My child, eat honey, for it is g,
24:23 Partiality in judging is not g. G
24:25 and a g blessing will come upon them.
25:25 so is g news from a far country. A
25:27 It is not g to eat much honey, G
28:21 To show partiality is not g— G
31:12 She does him g, and not harm,
Ecc 2: 3 on folly, until I might see what was g for mortals
4: 9 because they have a g reward for their toil.
5:18 This is what I have seen to be g:
6: 3 if he does not enjoy life's g things, C
6: 6 yet enjoy no g—do not all go to one place?
6:12 For who knows what is g for mortals D
7: 1 A g name is better than precious ointment,
7:11 Wisdom is as g as an inheritance,
7:18 It is g that you should take hold of the one,
7:20 so righteous as to do g without ever sinning. B
9: 2 the g and the evil, to the clean and the unclean, F
9: 2 As are the g, so are the sinners;
9:18 but one bungler destroys much g.
11: 6 this or that, or whether both alike will be g.
12:14 including every secret thing, whether g or evil. F
Isa 1:17 learn to do g; seek justice, B
1:19 you shall eat the g of the land;
5:20 Ah, you who call evil g and good evil, J
5:20 Ah, you who call evil good and g evil, F
7:15 how to refuse the evil and choose the g.
7:16 how to refuse the evil and choose the g,
32: 4 The minds of the rash will have g judgment,
38: 3 and have done what is g in your sight." D
39: 8 word of the LORD that you have spoken is g."
40: 9 O Zion, herald of g tidings;
40: 9 O Jerusalem, herald of g tidings, lift it up,
41: 7 saying of the soldering, "It is g";
41:23 do g, or do harm, that we may be afraid B
41:27 and I give to Jerusalem a herald of g tidings.
44:10 a god or cast an image that can do no g?
48:17 who teaches you for your own g,
52: 7 who brings g news, who announces salvation, A
55: 2 Listen carefully to me, and eat what is g, D
61: 1 he has sent me to bring g news to the oppressed, A
65: 2 who walk in a way that is not g, G
Jer 2: 7 a plentiful land to eat its fruits and its g things. C
4:22 but do not know how to do g." B
5:25 and your sins have deprived you of g.
6:16 for the ancient paths, where the g way lies;
8:15 We look for peace, but find no g,
10: 5 for they cannot do evil, nor is it in them to do g. B
13: 7 now the loincloth was ruined; it was g for nothing.
13:10 shall be like this loincloth, which is g for nothing.
13:23 you can do g who are accustomed to do evil. B
14:19 We look for peace, but find no g;
15:11 Surely I have intervened in your life for g,
18: 4 into another vessel, as seemed g to him.
18:10 about the g that I had intended to do to it.
18:20 Is evil a recompense for g?

Jer 18:20 Remember how I stood before you to speak g
21:10 against this city for evil and not for g, says
24: 2 One basket had very g figs, like first-ripe figs,
24: 3 I said, "Figs, the g figs very g,
24: 5 Like these g figs, so I will regard as g the exiles
24: 6 I will set my eyes upon them for g,
26:14 Do with me as seems g and right to you. E
29:32 to see the g that I am going to do to my people,
32:39 for their own g and the g of their children
32:40 never to draw back from doing g to them;
32:41 I will rejoice in doing g to them,
32:42 so I will bring upon them all the g fortune that I
33: 9 the nations of the earth who shall hear of all the g
33: 9 of all the g and all the prosperity I provide for it.
33:11 to the LORD of hosts, for the LORD is g,
37:20 be g enough to listen to my plea,
39:16 against this city for evil and not for g,
40: 4 come, and I will take g care of you;
40: 4 go wherever you think it g and right to go.
42: 2 "Be g enough to listen to our plea,
42: 6 Whether it is g or bad,
44:27 to watch over them for harm and not for g;
La 3:25 The LORD is g to those who wait for him,
3:26 It is g that one should wait quietly for
3:27 It is g for one to bear the yoke in youth,
3:38 the mouth of the Most High that g and bad come?
Eze 17: 8 it was transplanted to g soil by abundant waters,
18:18 and did what is not g among his people, G
20:25 not g and ordinances by which they could not G
24: 4 all the g pieces, the thigh and the shoulder;
34:14 I will feed them with g pasture,
34:14 there they shall lie down in g grazing land,
34:18 Is it not enough for you to feed on the g pasture,
36:11 and will do more g to you than ever before.
36:31 and your dealings that were not g; G
Da 3:15 the statue that I have made, well and g.
Hos 4:13 poplar, and terebinth, because their shade is g.
8: 3 Israel has spurned the g; the enemy shall pursue
14: 2 accept that which is g, and we will offer
Am 5:14 Seek g and not evil, that you may live; F
5:15 Hate evil and love g, and establish justice in J
9: 4 I will fix my eyes on them for harm and not for g.
Mic 1:12 the inhabitants of Maroth wait anxiously for g,
2: 7 not my words do g to one who walks uprightly? B
3: 2 you who hate the g and love the evil, who tear
6: 8 He has told you, O mortal, what is g; D
Na 1: 7 The LORD is g, a stronghold in a day of trouble;
1:15 the feet of one who brings g tidings,
Zep 1:12 "The LORD will not do g, nor will he do harm." B
Zec 8:15 to do g to Jerusalem and to the house of Judah; B
Mal 2:17 "All who do evil are g in the sight of the LORD, J
Mt 3:10 every tree therefore that does not bear g fruit is cut
4:23 in their synagogues and proclaiming the g news A
5:13 It is no longer g for anything,
5:16 that they may see your g works and give glory L
5:45 for he makes his sun rise on the evil and on the g,
7:11 know how to give g gifts to your children,
7:11 in heaven give g things to those who ask him! C
7:17 In the same way, every g tree bears g fruit,
7:18 A g tree cannot bear bad fruit, nor can a bad tree
bear g fruit.
7:19 that does not bear g fruit is cut down and thrown
9:35 and proclaiming the g news of the kingdom, A
10: 7 As you go, proclaim the g news, A
11: 5 and the poor have g news brought to them. A
12:12 So it is lawful to do g on the sabbath." B
12:33 "Either make the tree g, and its fruit g;
12:34 How can you speak g things, when you are evil? C
12:35 The g person brings good things out of
12:35 The good person brings g things out of C
12:35 good person brings good things out of a g treasure,
13: 8 Other seeds fell on g soil and brought forth grain,
13:23 But as for what was sown on g soil,
13:24 be compared to someone who sowed g seed
13:27 'Master, did you not sow g seed in your field?
13:37 "The one who sows the g seed is the Son of Man;
13:38 and the g seed are the children of the kingdom;
13:48 and put the g into baskets but threw out the bad.
17: 4 Peter said to Jesus, "Lord, it is g for us to be here;
19:16 what g deed must I do to have eternal life?"
19:17 "Why do you ask me about what is g? D
19:17 There is only one who is g.
22:10 and gathered all whom they found, both g
24:14 And this g news of the kingdom will A
25:21 'Well done, g and trustworthy slave;
25:23 'Well done, g and trustworthy slave;
26:10 She has performed a g service for me.
26:13 wherever this g news is proclaimed in A
Mk 1: 1 The beginning of the g news of Jesus Christ, A
1:14 proclaiming the g news of God, A
1:15 repent, and believe in the g news." A
3: 4 Is it lawful to do g or to do harm on the sabbath, B
4: 8 Other seed fell into g soil and brought forth grain,
4:20 And these are the ones sown on the g soil:
9: 5 "Rabbi, it is g for us to be here;
9:50 Salt is g; but if salt has lost its saltiness,
10:17 and asked him, "G Teacher,
10:18 Jesus said to him, "Why do you call me g?
10:18 No one is g but God alone.
10:29 for my sake and for the sake of the g news, A
13:10 g news must first be proclaimed to all nations. A
14: 6 She has performed a g service for me.
14: 9 the g news is proclaimed in the whole world, A
16:15 ⟦Go into all the world and proclaim the g news⟧ A
16:20 ⟦and proclaimed the g news everywhere.⟧ A
Lk 1:19 to speak to you and to bring you this g news. A
1:53 he has filled the hungry with g things, C

Lk 2:10 I am bringing you **g** news of great joy for all A
3: 9 every tree therefore that does not bear **g** fruit is cut
3:18 he proclaimed the **g** news to the people. A
4:18 he has anointed me to bring **g** news to the poor. A
4:43 "I must proclaim the **g** news of the kingdom A
5:39 desires new wine, but says, 'The old is **g.'** "
6: 9 is it lawful to do **g** or to do harm on the sabbath, B
6:27 Love your enemies, do **g** to those who hate you, B
6:33 If you do **g** to those who do good to you, B
6:33 If you do good to those who do **g** to you, B
6:35 But love your enemies, do **g**, and lend, B
6:38 A **g** measure, pressed down, shaken together,
6:43 "No **g** tree bears bad fruit,
6:43 nor again does a bad tree bear **g** fruit;
6:45 The **g** person out of the **g** treasure of the heart produces **g**,
7:10 they found the slave in **g** health. H
7:22 the poor have **g** news brought to them. A
8: 1 and bringing the **g** news of the kingdom of God. A
8: 8 Some fell into **g** soil, and when it grew,
8:15 But as for that in the **g** soil,
8:15 hold it fast in an honest and **g** heart,
9: 6 the **g** news and curing diseases everywhere. A
9:33 "Master, it is **g** for us to be here;
11:13 know how to give **g** gifts to your children,
12:32 for it is your Father's **g** pleasure to give you
13: 9 If it bears fruit next year, well and **g**;
14:34 "Salt is **g**; but if salt has lost its taste,
16:16 the **g** news of the kingdom of God is proclaimed, A
16:25 during your lifetime you received your **g** things, C
18:18 A certain ruler asked him, **"G** Teacher,
18:19 Jesus said to him, "Why do you call me **g?**
18:19 No one is **g** but God alone.
19:17 He said to him, 'Well done, **g** slave!
20: 1 the people in the temple and telling the **g** news, A
23:50 there was a **g** and righteous man named Joseph,
Jn 1:46 "Can anything **g** come out of Nazareth?"
2:10 "Everyone serves the **g** wine first,
2:10 But you have kept the **g** wine until now."
5:29 those who have done **g**, to the resurrection of life,
7:12 While some were saying, "He is a **g** man,"
10:11 "I am the **g** shepherd.
10:11 The **g** shepherd lays down his life for the sheep.
10:14 I am the **g** shepherd.
10:32 have shown you many **g** works from the Father. L
10:33 not for a **g** work that we are going to stone you, N
Ac 4: 9 of a **g** deed done to someone who was sick
4:10 before you in **g** health by the name of Jesus H
6: 3 from among yourselves seven men of **g** standing,
8:12 the **g** news about the kingdom of God and A
8:25 the **g** news to many villages of the Samaritans. A
8:35 he proclaimed to him the **g** news about Jesus. A
8:40 he proclaimed the **g** news to all the towns A
9:36 She was devoted to **g** works and acts of charity. L
10:38 about doing **g** and healing all who were oppressed
11:24 for he was a **g** man,
13:32 the **g** news that what God promised A
14: 7 there they continued proclaiming the **g** news. A
14:15 and we bring you **g** news, A
14:17 not left himself without a witness in doing **g—**
14:21 After they had proclaimed the **g** news to that city A
15: 7 Gentiles would hear the message of the **g** news A
15:28 For it has seemed **g** to the Holy Spirit and to us
16:10 that God had called us to proclaim the **g** news A
17:18 because he was telling the **g** news about Jesus A
20:24 to testify to the **g** news of God's grace. A
Ro 2: 7 to those who by patiently doing **g** seek for glory
2:10 and honor and peace for everyone who does **g**,
3: 8 "Let us do evil so that **g** may come"? J
4:19 which was already as **g** as dead (for he was about
5: 7 for a **g** person someone might actually dare to die.
7:12 and the commandment is holy and just and **g.**
7:13 Did what is **g**, then, bring death to me? D
7:13 sin, working death in me through what is **g**, D
7:16 if I do what I do not want, I agree that the law is **g.**
7:18 For I know that nothing **g** dwells within me,
7:19 For I do not do the **g** I want,
7:21 when I want to do what is **g**, evil lies close DF
8:28 We know that all things work together for **g**
9:11 before they had been born or had done anything **g**
10:15 beautiful are the feet of those who bring **g** news! A
10:16 But not all have obeyed the **g** news; A
12: 2 what is **g** and acceptable and perfect. D
12: 9 hate what is evil, hold fast to what is **g;** D
12:21 but overcome evil with **g.** J
13: 3 For rulers are not a terror to **g** conduct, but to bad.
13: 3 do what is **g**, and you will receive its approval; D
13: 4 for it is God's servant for your **g.**
14:16 So do not let your **g** be spoken of as evil.
14:21 it is **g** not to eat meat or drink wine or do anything
15: 2 of us must please our neighbor for the **g** purpose
15:19 as Illyricum I have fully proclaimed the **g** news A
15:20 to proclaim the **g** news, A
16:19 be wise in what is **g** and guileless in what is evil. D
1Co 5: 6 Your boasting is not a **g** thing. G
7:35 but to promote **g** order and unhindered devotion to
9:11 If we have sown spiritual **g** among you,
12: 7 the manifestation of the Spirit for the common **g.**
15: 1 of the **g** news that I proclaimed to you, A
15:33 "Bad company ruins **g** morals."
2Co 2:12 came to Troas to proclaim the **g** news of Christ, A
5:10 has been done in the body, whether **g** or evil. F
6: 8 in ill repute and **g** repute.
8:18 the churches for his proclaiming the **g** news; A
9: 8 you may share abundantly in every **g** work. N
10:12 they do not show **g** sense.
10:14 to come all the way to you with the **g** news A

2Co 10:16 may proclaim the **g** news in lands beyond you, A
11: 7 proclaimed God's **g** news to you free of charge? A
Gal 4:17 They make much of you, but for no **g** purpose;
4:18 It is **g** to be made much of for a good purpose
4:18 to be made much of for a **g** purpose at all times,
6: 6 the word must share in all **g** things C
6:10 let us work for the **g** of all,
6:12 a **g** showing in the flesh that try to compel you to
Eph 1: 5 according to the **g** pleasure of his will,
1: 9 according to his **g** pleasure that he set forth
2:10 created in Christ Jesus for **g** works, L
5: 9 the light is found in all that is **g** and right and true.
6: 8 knowing that whatever **g** we do,
Php 1: 6 a **g** work among you will bring it to completion N
2:13 both to will and to work for his **g** pleasure.
Col 1:10 every **g** work and as you grow in the knowledge N
1Th 3: 6 brought us the **g** news of your faith and love. A
5:15 always seek to do **g** to one another and to all. B
5:21 but test everything; hold fast to what is **g;** D
2Th 1:11 by his power every **g** resolve and work of faith,
2:14 through our proclamation of the **g** news, A
2:16 through grace gave us eternal comfort and **g** hope,
2:17 and strengthen them in every **g** work and word. N
1Ti 1: 5 a **g** conscience, and sincere faith.
1: 8 Now we know that the law is **g**,
1:18 that by following them you may fight the **g** fight,
1:19 having faith and a **g** conscience.
2:10 but with **g** works, as is proper L
3:13 a **g** standing for themselves and great boldness in
4: 4 For everything created by God is **g**,
4: 6 you will be a **g** servant of Christ Jesus,
5:10 she must be well attested for her **g** works, L
5:10 and devoted herself to doing **g** in every way.
5:25 So also **g** works are conspicuous; L
6:12 Fight the **g** fight of the faith;
6:12 and for which you made the **g** confession in
6:13 before Pontius Pilate made the **g** confession,
6:18 They are to do **g**, to be rich in good works, B
6:18 They are to do good, to be rich in **g** works, L
6:19 for themselves the treasure of a **g** foundation for
2Ti 1:14 Guard the **g** treasure entrusted to you,
2: 3 Share in suffering like a **g** soldier of Christ Jesus.
2:14 to avoid wrangling over words, which does no **g**
2:21 the owner of the house, ready for every **g** work. N
3: 3 slanderers, profligates, brutes, haters of **g**,
3:17 equipped for every **g** work. N
4: 7 I have fought the **g** fight, I have finished the race,
Tit 1:16 disobedient, unfit for any **g** work. N
2: 3 they are to teach what is **g**, D
2: 5 chaste, **g** managers of the household, kind,
2: 7 yourself in all respects a model of **g** works, L
2:14 people of his own who are zealous for **g** deeds. M
3: 1 to be obedient, to be ready for every **g** work, N
3: 8 be careful to devote themselves to **g** works; L
3:14 to **g** works in order to meet urgent needs, L
Phm 1: 6 when you perceive all the **g** that we may do
1:14 in order that your **g** deed might be voluntary and
Heb 4: 2 indeed the **g** news came to us just as to them; A
4: 6 **g** news failed to enter because of disobedience, A
5:14 by practice to distinguish **g** from evil. F
9:11 Christ came as a high priest of the **g** things C
10: 1 law has only a shadow of the **g** things to come C
10:24 to provoke one another to love and **g** deeds, M
11:12 from one person, and this one as **g** as dead,
12:10 but he disciplines us for our **g**,
13:16 not neglect to do **g** and to share what you have, B
13:21 in everything **g** so that you may do his will,
Jas 2:14 What **g** is it, my brothers and sisters,
2:16 not supply their bodily needs, what is the **g**
3:13 Show by your **g** life that your works are done
3:17 gentle, willing to yield, full of mercy and **g** fruits,
1Pe 1:12 to you through those who brought you **g** news A
1:25 word is the **g** news that was announced to you. A
2: 3 if indeed you have tasted that the Lord is **g.**
3: 6 you do what is **g** and never let fears alarm you. D
3:10 "Those who desire life and desire to see **g** days,
3:11 let them turn away from evil and do **g;** BJ
3:13 if you are eager to do what is **g?** D
3:16 for your **g** conduct in Christ may be put to shame.
3:17 For it is better to suffer for doing **g**,
3:21 but as an appeal to God for a **g** conscience,
4:10 Like **g** stewards of the manifold grace of God,
4:19 to a faithful Creator, while continuing to do **g.** B
3Jn 1: 2 with you and that you may be in **g** health, H
1:11 do not imitate what is evil but imitate what is **g.** D
1:11 Whoever does **g** is from God;
Tob 1:13 the Most High gave me favor and **g** standing
2: 1 **g** dinner was prepared for me and I reclined to eat.
4: 9 So you will be laying up a **g** treasure for yourself
4:19 but the Lord himself will give them **g** counsel;
4:21 from every sin and do what is **g** in the sight of D
5:14 and of **g** and noble lineage.
5:14 Your kindred are **g** people; you come of **g** stock.
5:16 in **g** health and return to you in good health, H
5:16 in good health and return to you in **g** health, H
5:17 and return you in **g** health to me; H
5:21 our child will leave in **g** health and return to us H
5:21 in good health and return to us in **g** health. H
5:21 on the day when he returns to you in **g** health. H
5:22 For a **g** angel will accompany him;
5:22 and he will come back in **g** health." H
6:12 and very beautiful, and her father is a **g** man."
7: 1 brothers; welcome and **g** health!" H
7: 4 Then she asked them, "Is he in **g** health?" H
7: 5 They replied, "He is alive and in **g** health." H
7: 7 my child, son of a **g** and noble father!"
8: 6 said, 'It is not **g** that the man should be alone; G

Tob 9: 6 **"G** and noble son of a father **g** and noble,
10:12 may I hear a **g** report about you as long as I live."
12: 6 the living for the **g** things he has done for you. C
12: 7 It is **g** to conceal the secret of a king,
12: 7 Do **g** and evil will not overtake you. BF
12: 8 Prayer with fasting is **g**, but better than
12:11 'It is **g** to conceal the secret of a king,
13:10 Acknowledge the Lord, for he is **g**, K
14: 4 scattered and taken as captives from the **g** land; I
Jdt 15: 8 in Jerusalem came to witness the **g** things that C
15:10 you have done great **g** to Israel,
AdE 1:10 when the king was in **g** humor, he told Haman,
16:22 "Therefore you shall observe this with all **g** cheer
Wis 2: 6 therefore, let us enjoy the **g** things that exist, C
3: 5 they will receive great **g**, because God tested them
3:15 For the fruit of **g** labors is renowned,
4: 5 not ripe enough to eat, and **g** for nothing.
4:12 fascination of wickedness obscures what is **g**, D
5: 8 And what **g** has our boasted wealth brought us?
7:11 All **g** things came to me along with her, C
7:22 unpolluted, distinct, invulnerable, loving the **g**,
8: 9 knowing that she would give me **g** counsel
8:19 and a **g** soul fell to my lot;
8:20 or rather, being **g**, I entered an undefiled body.
10: 8 not only were hindered from recognizing the **g**,
12:19 and you have filled your children with **g** hope,
12:21 and covenants full of **g** promises!
13: 1 and they were unable from the **g** things C
14:26 confusion over what is **g**, D
18: 9 the holy children of **g** people offered sacrifices,
Sir 1:24 then the lips of many tell of their **g** sense.
2: 9 You who fear the Lord, hope for **g** things, C
6:19 and wait for her **g** harvest.
7:13 for it is a habit that results in no **g.**
7:19 Do not dismiss a wise and **g** wife,
11: 2 Do not praise individuals for their **g** looks,
11:14 **G** things and bad, life and death, C
11:31 for they lie in wait, turning **g** into evil, F
12: 1 If you do **g**, know to whom you do it, B
12: 1 and you will be thanked for your **g** deeds. M
12: 2 Do **g** to the devout, and you will be repaid— B
12: 3 No **g** comes to one who persists in evil or
12: 5 Do **g** to the humble, but do not give to B
12: 5 as much evil for all the **g** you have done to them.
12: 7 Give to the one who is **g**,
13:24 Riches are **g** if they are free from sin;
13:25 either for **g** or for evil. F
14: 7 If ever he does **g**, it is by mistake;
14:13 Do **g** to friends before you die, B
14:14 do not let your share of desired **g** pass by you.
16:29 and filled it with his **g** things. C
17: 7 and showed them **g** and evil. F
18: 8 What is **g** in them, and what is evil? DF
18:15 child, do not mix reproach with your **g** deeds, M
18:17 Indeed, does not a word surpass a **g** gift?
20: 9 There may be **g** fortune for a person in adversity,
20:16 and I get no thanks for my **g** deeds. M
25: 4 and for the aged to possess **g** counsel!
26: 1 Happy is the husband of a **g** wife;
26: 3 A **g** wife is a great blessing;
26:16 is the beauty of a **g** wife in her well-ordered home.
26:21 *confidence in their **g** descent, will grow great.*
26:26 *Happy is the husband of a **g** wife;*
29:14 A **g** person will be surety for his neighbor,
30:18 **G** things poured out upon a mouth that is closed C
31:17 Be the first to stop, as befits **g** manners,
32: 6 of gold is the melody of music with **g** wine.
32:11 Leave in **g** time and do not be the last;
32:13 who fills you with his **g** gifts.
32:22 and give **g** heed to your paths.
33:14 **G** is the opposite of evil, and life the opposite F
37: 9 tell you, "Your way is **g,"** and then stand aside
37:18 **g** and evil, life and death; F
37:22 the fruits of his **g** sense will be praiseworthy.
37:23 and the fruits of his **g** sense will endure.
37:28 For not everything is **g** for everyone,
38:21 you do the dead no **g**, and you injure yourself.
39: 4 and learns what is **g** and evil in the human lot. DF
39:16 "All the works of the Lord are very **g**,
39:25 the beginning **g** things were created for the good, C
39:25 the beginning good things were created for the **g**,
39:25 but for sinners **g** things and bad. C
39:27 All these are **g** for the godly,
39:33 All the works of the Lord are **g**,
39:34 No one can say, "This is not as **g** as that,"
39:34 for everything proves **g** in its appointed time.
40:12 but **g** faith will last forever.
40:25 but **g** counsel is esteemed more than either.
41:13 The days of a **g** life are numbered,
41:13 but a **g** name lasts forever.
41:16 it is not **g** to feel shame in every circumstance, G
42: 6 there is an untrustworthy wife, a seal is a **g** thing;
42:14 of a man than a woman who does **g**;
46:10 so that all the Israelites might see how **g** it is
51:12 *Give thanks to the LORD, for he is **g**,* K
51:18 and I was zealous for the **g**,
51:30 Do your work in **g** time,
LtJ 6:34 Whether one does evil to them or **g**,
6:38 They cannot take pity on a widow or do **g** to B
6:64 either to decide a case or to do **g** to anyone. B
Aza 1: 7 done what you have commanded us for our own **g.**
1:67 Give thanks to the Lord, for he is **g**, K
1Mc 4:24 "For he is **g**, for his mercy endures forever." K
6:12 the inhabitants of Judah without **g** reason.
6:40 and they advanced steadily and in **g** order.
10:27 we will repay you with **g** for what you do for us.
11:33 We have determined to do **g** to the nation of B

1Mc 14: 4 He sought the g of his nation;
14: 9 they all talked together of g things, C
15:20 And it has seemed g to us to accept the shield
16:17 an act of great treachery and returned evil for g. J
2Mc 1: 2 May God do g to you, B
1:10 and to the Jews in Egypt, Greetings and g health. H
4:37 wept because of the moderation and g conduct
4:45 But Menelaus, already as g as beaten,
5: 4 the apparition might prove to have been a g omen.
6:28 a noble example of how to die a g death willingly
7:20 she bore it with g courage because of her hope in
9:19 and general sends hearty greetings and g wishes
9:22 for I have g hope of recovering from my illness,
11: 6 prayed the Lord to send a g angel to save Israel.
11:15 Maccabeus, having regard for the common g,
11:26 and be of g cheer and go on happily in the conduct
11:28 We also are in g health. H
15:12 who had been high priest, a noble and g man,
15:23 a g angel to spread terror and trembling before us.
1Es 2:21 in order that, if it seems g to you, E
8:85 so that you may be strong and eat the g things C
8:94 as seems g to you and to all who obey the law of E
3Mc 1:10 he marveled at the g order of the temple,
3: 5 of life with the g deeds of upright people, M
3: 5 they were established in g repute with everyone.
3: 6 of other races paid no heed to their g service
3:11 Then the king, boastful of his present g fortune,
3:12 and all its districts, greetings and g health: H
3:22 in a contrary spirit, and disdained what is g. D
3:26 be established for ourselves in g order and in
4: 8 in lamentations instead of g cheer
7: 1 in his government, greetings and g health: H
2Es 2:14 I set aside evil and created g;
2:25 "G nurse, nourish your children;
3:22 but what was g departed, and the evil remained.
4:29 the field where the g has been sown will not come.
7: 6 and it is full of all g things; C
7:*82* because they cannot now make a g repentance so
7:*117* [47] For what g is it to all that they live in sorrow
7:*119* [49] For what g is it to us,
7:*120* [50] And what g is it that
8:36 to those who have no store of g works." L
4Mc 2:23 a kingdom that is temperate, just, g,
4: 1 a political opponent of the noble and g man,
12:11 since you have received g things and C
18: 9 who lived out his life with g children,

GOOD-LOOKING (1) [GOOD]

Ge 39: 6 Now Joseph was handsome and g.

GOODLIER, GOODLIEST, GOODLY (KJV) See also BEAUTIFUL, BEST, FAIR, FINE, HANDSOME, LOVELY, MAJESTIC, PRECIOUS, NOBLE

GOODLY (4) [GOOD]

Ps 16: 6 in pleasant places; I have a g heritage.
45: 1 My heart overflows with a g theme;
Pr 28:10 but the blameless will have a g inheritance.
Jer 11:16 "A green olive tree, fair with g fruit";

GOODMAN (KJV) See HUSBAND, LANDOWNER, OWNER

GOODNESS (33) [GOOD]

Ex 33:19 he said, "I will make all my g pass before you,
1Ki 8:66 joyful and in good spirits because of all the g that
2Ch 6:41 and let your faithful rejoice in your g.
7:10 of the g that the LORD had shown to David and
Ne 9:25 and delighted themselves in your great g.
9:35 and in the great g you bestowed on them,
Ps 23: 6 Surely g and mercy shall follow me all the days
27:13 that I shall see the g of the LORD in the land of
31:19 O how abundant is your g that you have laid up
65: 4 We shall be satisfied with the g of your house,
68:10 in your g, O God, you provided for the needy.
145: 7 They shall celebrate the fame of your abundant g,
Jer 31:12 and they shall be radiant over the g of the LORD,
Hos 3: 5 they shall come in awe to the LORD and to his g
Zec 9:17 For what g and beauty are his!
Ro 15:14 that you yourselves are full of g,
Tit 1: 8 a lover of g, prudent, upright, devout,
3: 4 But when the g and loving kindness
Heb 6: 5 and have tasted the g of the word of God and
2Pe 1: 3 of him who called us by his own glory and g.
1: 5 support your faith with g, and g with knowledge,
AdE 16: 4 by the boasts of those who know nothing of g,
Wis 1: 1 the Lord in g and seek him with sincerity of heart;
7:26 and an image of his g.
12:22 when we judge, we may meditate upon your g,
1Es 5:61 his g and his glory are forever upon all Israel."
Man 1: 7 to your great g you have promised repentance
1:14 and in me you will manifest your g;
2Es 7:*138* [68] because if he did not give out of his g so
8:36 O Lord, your righteousness and g will be declared,
8:52 g is established and wisdom perfected beforehand.
4Mc 1:10 died for the sake of nobility and g,

GOODNESS' (1) [GOOD]

Ps 25: 7 for your g sake, O LORD!

GOODS (50) [GOOD]

Ge 14:11 the enemy took all the g of Sodom and Gomorrah,
14:12 who lived in Sodom, and his g, and departed.
14:16 Then he brought back all the g,
14:16 and also brought back his nephew Lot with his g,
14:21 "Give me the persons, but take the g for yourself."
31:37 Although you have felt about through all my g,
31:37 what have you found of all your household g?
46: 6 the g that they had acquired in the land of Canaan,
Ex 22: 7 When someone delivers to a neighbor money or g
22: 8 not the owner had laid hands on the neighbor's g.
Nu 16:32 everyone who belonged to Korah and all their g.
31: 9 their flocks, and all their g as booty.
Dt 6:11 houses filled with all sorts of g that you did
Jdg 18:21 the livestock, and the g in front of them.
2Ki 8: 9 all kinds of g of Damascus, forty camel loads.
2Ch 20:25 they found livestock in great numbers, g, clothing,
Ezr 1: 4 with g and with animals, besides freewill offerings
1: 6 with g, with animals, and with valuable gifts,
7:26 or for confiscation of their g or for imprisonment."
Ne 9:25 took possession of houses filled with all sorts of g,
Est 3:13 the month of Adar, and to plunder their g.
8:11 and women, and to plunder their g
Pr 6:31 they will forfeit all the g of their house.
Ecc 5:11 When g increase, those who eat them increase;
Jer 5:26 they take over the g of others.
49:29 their curtains and all their g;
Eze 27:16 with you because of your abundant g;
27:18 Damascus traded with you for your abundant g—
38:12 who are acquiring cattle and g,
38:13 to take away cattle and g,
Ob 1:13 not have looted his g on the day of his calamity.
Hab 2: 6 How long will you load yourselves with g taken
Lk 6:30 and if anyone takes away your g,
12:18 and there I will store all my grain and my g.
12:19 'Soul, you have ample g laid up for many years;
Ac 2:45 and g and distribute the proceeds to all,
1Jn 3:17 the world's g and sees a brother or sister in need
Tob 10:10 clothing, money, and household g.
AdE 3:13 which is Adar, and to plunder their g.
Sir 1:17 she fills their whole house with desirable g,
10:27 Better is the worker who has g in plenty than
11:19 "I have found rest, and now I shall feast on my g!"
14: 4 and others will live in luxury on his g.
34:21 If one sacrifices ill-gotten g,
1Mc 5:13 and children and g, and have destroyed about
5:45 with their wives and children and g,
9:40 and the Jews took all their g.
2Es 15:19 the sword, and plunder their g, because of hunger
16:46 and plunder their g, overthrow their houses,
16:72 For they shall destroy and plunder their g,

GOODWILL‡ (25) [GOOD, WILL]

Ac 2:47 praising God and having the g of all the people.
2Co 8:19 the glory of the Lord himself and to show our g.
Gal 4:15 What has become of the g you felt?
Php 1:15 from envy and rivalry, but others from g.
AdE 2:23 in the royal library in praise of the g shown
6: 4 While the king was inquiring about the g shown
13: 3 for his unchanging g and steadfast fidelity,
16: 6 of their evil natures beguile the sincere g
16:11 so fully the g that we have for every nation
Sir Pr: 2 You are invited therefore to read it with g
36:22 according to your g toward your people,
1Mc 11:33 because of the g they show toward us.
2Mc 6:29 before had acted toward him with g now changed
9:21 I remember with affection your esteem and g.
9:26 to you and to maintain your present g,
11:19 you will maintain your g toward the government,
12:30 the Jews who lived there bore witness to the g that
13:26 convinced them, appeased them, gained their g,
14:26 But when Alcimus noticed their g for one another,
14:37 of and for his g was called father of the Jews.
15:30 the man who maintained his youthful g
3Mc 3: 3 continued to maintain g and unswerving loyalty
6:26 the beginning differed from all nations in their g
7: 7 into account the friendly and firm g that they had
4Mc 13:25 A common zeal for nobility strengthened their g

GOPHER (KJV) See CYPRESS

GORE (5) [GORES]

Ex 21:29 If the ox has been accustomed to g in the past,
21:36 if it was known that the ox was accustomed to g in
1Ki 22:11 With these you shall g the Arameans
2Ch 18:10 With these you shall g the Arameans
4Mc 9:20 of g, and pieces of flesh were falling off the axles

GORES (4) [GORE]

Ex 21:28 When an ox g a man or a woman to death,
21:31 If it g a boy or a girl,
21:32 If the ox g a male or female slave,
Dt 33:17 with them he g the peoples,

GORGE (2) [GORGED]

Jer 48:28 that nests on the sides of the mouth of a g.
Eze 32: 4 the wild animals of the whole earth g themselves

GORGED (4) [GORGE]

Dt 32:15 You grew fat, bloated, and g!
Isa 9:20 They g on the right, but still were hungry,
34: 6 it is sated with blood, it is g with fat,
Rev 19:21 and all the birds were g with their flesh.

GORGEOUS (KJV) See ELEGANT

GORGIAS (10) [GORGIAS'S]

1Mc 3:38 and Nicanor and G, able men among the Friends
4: 1 Now G took five thousand infantry
4: 5 When G entered the camp of Judas by night,
4:18 G and his force are near us in the hills.
5:59 G and his men came out of the town to meet them
2Mc 8: 9 He associated with him G,
10:14 When G became governor of the region,
12:32 festival called Pentecost, they hurried against G,
12:35 of G, and grasping his cloak was dragging him off
12:35 so G escaped and reached Marisa.

GORGIAS'S (1) [GORGIAS]

2Mc 12:37 against G troops when they were not expecting it,

GORMANDIZER (1) [GORMANDIZING]

4Mc 2: 7 be that someone who is habitually a solitary g,

GORMANDIZING (1) [GORMANDIZER]

4Mc 1:27 indiscriminate eating, gluttony, and solitary g.

GORTYNA (1)

1Mc 15:23 and to Aradus and G and Cnidus and Cyprus

GOSHEN (16)

Ge 45:10 You shall settle in the land of G,
46:28 to Joseph to lead the way before him into G.
46:28 When they came to the land of G,
46:29 and went up to meet his father Israel in G.
46:34 in order that you may settle in the land of G,
47: 1 they are now in the land of G."
47: 4 let your servants settle in the land of G."
47: 6 let them live in the land of G;
47:27 in the land of Egypt, in the region of G;
50: 8 and their herds were left in the land of G.
Ex 8:22 But on that day I will set apart the land of G,
9:26 Only in the land of G, where the Israelites were,
Jos 10:41 and all the country of G, as far as Gibeon.
11:16 the land of G and the lowland and the Arabah and
15:51 G, Holon, and Giloh: eleven towns with their
Jdt 1: 9 Tahpanhes and Raamses and the whole land of G,

GOSPEL‡ (70)

Mk 8:35 and for the sake of the g, will save it.
Ro 1: 1 called to be an apostle, set apart for the g of God,
1: 3 the g concerning his Son, who was descended
1: 9 whom I serve with my spirit by announcing the g
1:15 —hence my eagerness to proclaim the g to you
1:16 For I am not ashamed of the g;
2:16 according to my g, God, through Jesus Christ,
11:28 the g they are enemies of God for your sake;
15:16 the Gentiles in the priestly service of the g of God,
16:25 to my g and the proclamation of Jesus Christ,
1Co 1:17 not send me to baptize but to proclaim the g,
4:15 in Christ Jesus I became your father through the g.
9:12 an obstacle in the way of the g of Christ.
9:14 who proclaim the g should get their living by the g.
9:16 the g, this gives me no ground for boasting,
9:16 and woe to me if I do not proclaim the g!
9:18 that in my proclamation I may make the g free
9:18 so as not to make full use of my rights in the g.
9:23 I do it all for the sake of the g,
2Co 4: 3 And even if our g is veiled,
4: 4 to keep them from seeing the light of the g of
9:13 by your obedience to the confession of the g
11: 4 or a different g from the one you accepted,
Gal 1: 6 grace of Christ and are turning to a different g—
1: 7 not that there is another g,
1: 7 and want to pervert the g of Christ.
1: 8 to you a g contrary to what we proclaimed to you,
1: 9 to you a g contrary to what you received,
1:11 that the g that was proclaimed by me is not
2: 2 the acknowledged leaders) the g that I proclaim
2: 5 the truth of the g might always remain with you.
2: 7 when they saw that I had been entrusted with the g
2: 7 just as Peter had been entrusted with the g for
2:14 not acting consistently with the truth of the g,
3: 8 declared the g beforehand to Abraham, saying,
4:13 of a physical infirmity that I first announced the g
Eph 1:13 the g of your salvation, and had believed in him,
3: 6 in the promise in Christ Jesus through the g.
3: 7 Of this g I have become a servant according to
6:15 to proclaim the g of peace.
6:19 with boldness the mystery of the g,
Php 1: 5 because of your sharing in the g from the first day
1: 7 and in the defense and confirmation of the g.
1:12 to me has actually helped to spread the g,
1:16 that I have been put here for the defense of the g;
1:27 live your life in a manner worthy of the g
1:27 by side with one mind for the faith of the g,
2:22 with me in the work of the g.
4: 3 beside me in the work of the g,
4:15 that in the early days of the g,
Col 1: 5 of this hope before in the word of the truth, the g
1:23 without shifting from the hope promised by the g
1:23 I, Paul, became a servant of this g.
1Th 1: 5 of the g came to you not in word only,
2: 2 we had courage in our God to declare to you the g
2: 4 by God to be entrusted with the message of the g,
2: 8 not only the g of God but also our own selves,
2: 9 of you while we proclaimed to you the g of God.

1Th 3: 2 and co-worker for God in proclaiming the g
2Th 1: 8 not know God and on those who do not obey the g
1Ti 1:11 that conforms to the glorious g of the blessed God,
2Ti 1: 8 but join with me in suffering for the g,
1:10 and immortality to light through the g.
1:11 For this g I was appointed a herald and an apostle
2: 8 a descendant of David—that is my g,
Phm 1:13 in your place during my imprisonment for the g;
1Pe 4: 6 For this is the reason the g was proclaimed even to
4:17 the end for those who do not obey the g of God?
Rev 14: 6 with an eternal g to proclaim to those who live on

GOSSAMER (1)

Job 8:14 Their confidence is g, a spider's house their trust.

GOSSIP (7) [GOSSIPED, GOSSIPS]

Ps 69:12 I am the subject of g for those who sit in the gate,
Pr 11:13 A g goes about telling secrets,
20:19 A g reveals secrets;
Eze 36: 3 and you became an object of g and slander among
2Co 12:20 jealousy, anger, selfishness, slander, g, conceit,
Sir 19: 6 but one who hates g has less evil.
19:12 so is g inside a fool.

GOSSIPED (1) [GOSSIP]

3Mc 3: 7 instead they g about the differences in worship

GOSSIPS (3) [GOSSIP]

Ro 1:29 murder, strife, deceit, craftiness, they are g,
1Ti 5:13 but also g and busybodies,
Sir 28:13 Curse the g and the double-tongued,

GOT (145) [GET]

Ge 21:21 and his mother g a wife for him from the land
27:14 and g them and brought them to his mother;
32:22 The same night he g up and took his two wives,
38:19 Then she g up and went away,
Ex 2: 3 When she could hide him no longer she g
2:17 Moses g up and came to their defense
Nu 16:25 So Moses g up and went to Dathan and Abiram;
16:27 So they g away from the dwellings of Korah,
22:21 So Balaam g up in the morning,
24:25 Then Balaam g up and went back to his place,
25: 7 saw it, he g up and left the congregation.
Jdg 4: 9 Deborah g up and went with Barak to Kedesh.
4:15 Sisera g down from his chariot and fled away
5:19 they g no spoils of silver.
9:34 the troops with him g up by night and lay in wait
13:11 Manoah g up and followed his wife,
19: 5 On the fourth day they g up early in the morning,
19: 7 When the man g up to go,
19: 8 the fifth day he g up early in the morning to leave;
19: 9 with his concubine and his servant g up to leave,
19:10 he g up and departed, and arrived opposite Jebus
19:27 In the morning her master g up,
20: 8 All the people g up as one, saying,
20:19 Then the Israelites g up in the morning,
21: 4 On the next day, the people g up early,
Ru 2:15 When she g up to glean,
3:14 g up before one person could recognize another;
1Sa 3: 6 Samuel g up and went to Eli, and said,
3: 8 And he g up and went to Eli, and said, "Here I am,
9:26 Saul g up, and both he and Samuel went out into
20:42 He g up and left; and Jonathan went into the city.
24: 7 Saul g up and left the cave, and went on his way.
25: 1 Then David g up and went down to the wilderness
25:42 Abigail g up hurriedly and rode away on
28:23 So he g up from the ground and sat on the bed.
2Sa 3:24 why did you dismiss him, so that he g away?
15: 1 After this Absalom g himself a chariot and horses,
15: 9 So he g up, and went to Hebron.
19: 8 Then the king g up and took his seat in the gate.
1Ki 1:49 Then all the guests of Adonijah g up trembling
1:50 g up and went to grasp the horns of the altar.
3:20 She g up in the middle of the night
14:17 Then Jeroboam's wife g up and went away,
19: 3 Then he was afraid; he g up and fled for his life,
19: 8 He g up, and ate and drank;
2Ki 4:34 Then he g up on the bed and lay upon the child,
4:35 He g down, walked once to and fro in the room,
4:35 then g up again and bent over him;
7:12 The king g up in the night,
8: 2 So the woman g up and did according to the word
9: 6 So Jehu g up and went inside;
9:21 And they g his chariot ready.
1Ch 10:12 the valiant warriors g up and took away the body
2Ch 24: 3 Jehoiada g two wives for him,
28:15 Then those who were mentioned by name g up
Ezr 1: 5 g ready to go up and rebuild the house of
9: 5 At the evening sacrifice I g up from my fasting,
Ne 2:12 I g up during the night, I and a few men with me;
Ecc 2: 8 I g singers, both men and women,
Jer 32:10 I signed the deed, sealed it, g witnesses,
41: 2 with him g up and struck down Gedaliah son
Eze 29:18 yet neither he nor his army g anything from Tyre
33:24 yet he g possession of the land;
Da 6:19 the king g up and hurried to the den of lions.
Mt 2:14 Then Joseph g up, took the child and his mother
2:21 Then Joseph g up, took the child and his mother,
8:15 and she g up and began to serve him.
8:23 he g into the boat, his disciples followed him.
8:26 Then he g up and rebuked the winds and the sea;
9: 9 And he g up and followed him.
9:19 Jesus g up and followed him, with his disciples.
Mt 9:25 in and took her by the hand, and the girl g up.
13: 2 Such great crowds gathered around him that he g
14:29 So Peter g out of the boat,
14:32 When they g into the boat, the wind ceased.
15:39 he g into the boat and went to the region
25: 7 Then all those bridesmaids g up
27:48 At once one of them ran and g a sponge,
Mk 1:35 he g up and went out to a deserted place,
2:14 And he g up and followed him.
4: 1 a very large crowd gathered around him that he g
5:42 And immediately the girl g up and began to walk
6:51 he g into the boat with them and the wind ceased.
6:54 When they g out of the boat,
8:10 And immediately he g into the boat
Lk 4:29 They g up, drove him out of the town,
4:39 Immediately she g up and began to serve them.
5: 3 He g into one of the boats,
5:28 And he g up, left everything, and followed him.
6: 8 He g up and stood there.
8:22 One day he g into a boat with his disciples,
8:37 So he g into the boat and returned.
8:55 Her spirit returned, and she g up at once.
13:25 the owner of the house has g up and shut the door,
15:27 because he has g him back safe and sound.'
22:45 When he g up from prayer,
24:12 But Peter g up and ran to the tomb;
24:33 same hour they g up and returned to Jerusalem;
Jn 6:17 g into a boat, and started across the sea
6:22 They also saw that Jesus had not g into the boat
6:24 they themselves g into the boats and went
11:29 she heard it, she g up quickly and went to him.
13: 4 g up from the table, took off his outer robe,
21: 3 They went out and g into the boat,
Ac 5:37 the time of the census and g people to follow him;
8:27 So he g up and went.
9: 8 Saul g up from the ground,
9:18 Then he g up and was baptized,
9:34 And immediately he g up.
9:39 So Peter g up and went with them;
10:23 The next day he g up and went with them,
14:20 he g up and went into the city.
21:15 After these days we g ready and started to go up
26:30 Then the king g up, and with him the governor
Tob 8: 4 Tobias g out of bed and said to Sarah, "Sister,
8: 5 So she g up, and they began to pray and implore
9: 5 So Gabael g up and counted out to him
9: 6 In the morning they both g up early and went to
11:10 Then Tobit g up and came stumbling out through
Jdt 12: 5 Toward the morning watch she g up
15: 7 the hill country and in the plain g a great amount
AdE 4: 2 He g as far as the king's gate,
6:11 So Haman g the robe and the horse;
9:16 and g relief from their enemies.
9:22 on these days the Jews g relief from their enemies.
Sus 1:19 the two elders g up and ran to her.
1:39 and he opened the doors and g away.
Bel 1:39 So Daniel g up and ate.
1Mc 6:46 He g under the elephant, stabbed it from beneath,
13:22 So Trypho g all his cavalry ready to go,
2Mc 5: 7 in the end he g only disgrace from his conspiracy,
5:27 with about nine others, g away to the wilderness,
7:11 and said nobly, "I g these from Heaven,
8: 5 As soon as Maccabeus g his army organized,
8:13 of God's justice ran off and g away.
8:30 and g possession of some exceedingly high
11: 6 and his men g word that Lysias was besieging
11:12 Most of them g away stripped and wounded,
12:28 and they g the town into their hands,
13:23 he g word that Philip, who had been left in charge
1Es 1:31 He g into his second chariot;
4:47 Then King Darius g up and kissed him,
2Es 6:17 When I heard this, I g to my feet and listened;
10: 3 I g up in the night and fled,
13:57 Then I g up and walked in the field,

GOTHOLIAH (1)

1Es 8:33 Of the descendants of Elam, Jeshaiah son of G,

GOTHONIEL (1)

Jdt 6:15 of the tribe of Simeon, and Chabris son of G,

GOTTEN (8) [GET]

Dt 8:17 the might of my own hand have g me this wealth."
Job 28:15 It cannot be g for gold,
31:25 or because my hand had g much;
Ps 44:10 and our enemies have g spoil.
98: 1 and his holy arm have g him victory.
Pr 13:11 Wealth hastily g will dwindle,
1Mc 10:23 Alexander has g ahead of us in forming
2Es 5:27 and from all the multitude of peoples you have g

GOUGE (3) [GOUGED]

1Sa 10:27 He would g out the right eye of each of them
11: 2 namely that I g out everyone's right eye,
4Mc 5:30 even if you g out my eyes and burn my entrails.

GOUGED (2) [GOUGE]

Jdg 16:21 So the Philistines seized him and g out his eyes.
1Sa 10:27 king of the Ammonites, had not g out.

GOURD (KJV) See BUSH

GOURDS (2)

1Ki 6:18 the house had carvings of g and open flowers;
2Ki 4:39 a wild vine and gathered from it a lapful of wild g,

GOVERN (15) [GOVERNED, GOVERNING, GOVERNMENT, GOVERNOR, GOVERNOR'S, GOVERNORS, GOVERNS]

1Sa 8: 5 appoint for us, then, a king to g us,
8: 6 "Give us a king to g us."
8:20 and that our king may g us and go out before us
1Ki 3: 9 therefore an understanding mind to g your people,
3: 9 for who can g this your great people?"
21: 7 to him, "Do you now g Israel?
Job 34:17 Shall one who hates justice g?
Pr 8:16 by me rulers rule, and nobles, all who g rightly.
Wis 3: 8 They will g nations and rule over peoples,
8:14 I shall g peoples, and nations will be subject
12:18 and with great forbearance you g us;
Sus 1: 5 who were supposed to g the people."
1Mc 8:15 concerning the people, to g them well.
4Mc 5:16 who have been persuaded to g our lives by
6:33 we properly attribute to it the power to g.

GOVERNED (1) [GOVERN]

AdE 16:15 but are g by most righteous laws

GOVERNING (5) [GOVERN]

2Ki 15: 5 g the people of the land.
2Ch 26:21 g the people of the land.
Ro 13: 1 Let every person be subject to the g authorities;
Sir 43: 6 g the times, their everlasting sign.
3Mc 6: 2 g all creation with mercy,

GOVERNMENT (30) [GOVERN]

AdE 13: 5 and is ill-disposed to our g,
13: 7 and leave our g completely secure
16: 1 and to those who are loyal to our g, greetings.
Sir 10: 4 The g of the earth is in the hand of the Lord,
1Mc 6:56 and that he was trying to seize control of the g.
10:41 that the g officials have not paid as they did in
2Mc 3:38 "If you have any enemy or plotter against your g,
4: 2 the g the man who was the benefactor of the city,
4:21 that Philometor had become hostile to his g,
5: 7 He did not, however, gain control of the g;
8: 8 to come to the aid of the king's g.
9:24 for they would know to whom the g was left.
10:11 appointed one Lysias to have charge of the g and
11: 1 who was in charge of the g,
11:19 If you will maintain your goodwill toward the g,
13: 2 his guardian, who had charge of the g.
13:23 who had been left in charge of the g,
14:10 it is impossible for the g to find peace."
14:26 He told him that Nicanor was disloyal to the g,
3Mc 3: 7 but were hostile and greatly opposed to his g.
3:13 "I myself and our g are faring well.
3:26 we are sure that for the remaining time the g will
6:28 an unimpeded and notable stability to our g."
7: 1 the generals in Egypt and all in authority in his g,
7: 4 that our g would never be firmly established
7:11 be favorably disposed toward the king's g.
4Mc 4: 3 because I am loyal to the king's g,
4:19 and altered its form of g in complete violation of
8: 7 in my g if you will renounce the ancestral tradition
12: 5 and a leader in the g of the kingdom."

GOVERNMENTS (KJV) See AUTHORITY

GOVERNOR‡ (80) [GOVERN]

Ge 42: 6 Now Joseph was g over the land;
1Ki 22:26 and return him to Amon the g of the city and
2Ki 10: 5 So the steward of the palace, and the g of the city,
23: 8 the entrance of the gate of Joshua the g of the city,
25:22 of Shaphan as g over the people who remained in
25:23 the king of Babylon had appointed Gedaliah as g,
2Ch 18:25 and return him to Amon the g of the city and
19:11 the g of the house of Judah,
34: 8 Maaseiah the g of the city,
Ezr 2:63 the g told them that they were not to partake of
5: 3 At the same time Tattenai the g of the province
5: 6 of the letter that Tattenai the g of the province
5:14 a man named Sheshbazzar, whom he had made g.
6: 6 you, Tattenai, g of the province Beyond the River,
6: 7 let the g of the Jews and the elders of
6:13 Tattenai, the g of the province Beyond the River,
Ne 3: 7 the jurisdiction of the g of the province Beyond
5:14 from the time that I was appointed to be their g in
5:14 nor my brothers ate the food allowance of the g.
5:18 not demand the food allowance of the g,
7:65 the g told them that they were not to partake of
7:70 g gave to the treasury one thousand darics of gold,
8: 9 And Nehemiah, who was the g,
10: 1 the names of Nehemiah the g, son of Hacaliah,
12:26 the days of the g Nehemiah and of the priest Ezra,
Jer 40: 5 of Babylon appointed g of the towns of Judah,
40: 7 of Ahikam g in the land,
40:11 of Ahikam son of Shaphan as g over them,
41: 2 king of Babylon had appointed him g in the land.
41:18 the king of Babylon had made g over the land.
Hag 1: 1 g of Judah, and to Joshua son of Jehozadak,
1:14 g of Judah, and the spirit of Joshua son
2: 2 g of Judah, and to Joshua son of Jehozadak,
2:21 to Zerubbabel, g of Judah, saying, I am about
Mal 1: 8 Try presenting that to your g;

Mt 27: 2 and handed him over to Pilate the **g**.
27:11 Now Jesus stood before the **g**;
27:11 the **g** asked him, "Are you the King of the Jews?"
27:14 so that the **g** was greatly amazed.
27:15 at the festival the **g** was accustomed to release
27:21 The **g** again said to them,
27:27 the **g** took Jesus into the governor's headquarters,
Lk 2: 2 and was taken while Quirinius was **g** of Syria.
3: 1 when Pontius Pilate was **g** of Judea,
20:20 over to the jurisdiction and authority of the **g**.
Ac 23:24 and take him safely to Felix the **g**."
23:26 "Claudius Lysias to his Excellency the **g** Felix,
23:33 to Caesarea and delivered the letter to the **g**,
24: 1 and they reported their case against Paul to the **g**.
24:10 the **g** motioned to him to speak, Paul replied:
26:30 the **g** and Bernice and those who had been seated
2Co 11:32 the **g** under King Aretas guarded the city
1Mc 7: 8 **g** of the province Beyond the River;
10:65 and made him general and **g** of the province.
10:69 And Demetrius appointed Apollonius the **g**
11:59 He appointed Jonathan's brother Simon **g** from
14:42 be **g** over them and that he should take charge of
16:11 of Abubus had been appointed **g** over the plain
2Mc 3: 5 at that time was **g** of Coelesyria and Phoenicia,
4: 4 and **g** of Coelesyria and Phoenicia,
8: 8 the **g** of Coelesyria and Phoenicia,
10:11 of the government and to be chief **g** of Coelesyria
10:14 When Gorgias became **g** of the region,
12: 2 and in addition to these Nicanor the **g** of Cyprus,
12:32 they hurried against Gorgias, the **g** of Idumea,
13:24 left Hegemonides as **g** from Ptolemais to Gerar,
14:12 appointed him **g** of Judea,
1Es 2:12 and by him they were given to Sheshbazzar, the **g**
4:49 or **g** or treasurer should forcibly enter their doors;
6: 3 the **g** of Syria and Phoenicia and Sathrabuzanes
6: 7 the **g** of Syria and Phoenicia, and Sathrabuzanes,
6:18 to Zerubbabel and Sheshbazzar the **g**
6:27 So Darius commanded Sisinnes the **g** of Syria
6:27 the servant of the Lord and **g** of Judea,
6:29 to Zerubbabel the **g**, for sacrifices to the Lord,
7: 1 Then Sisinnes the **g** of Coelesyria and Phoenicia,
3Mc 2: 3 For you, the creator of all things and the **g** of all,
4Mc 2:22 among the senses as a sacred **g** over them all.
4: 2 So he came to Apollonius, **g** of Syria, Phoenicia,
7:16 most certainly devout reason is **g** of the emotions.

GOVERNOR'S (3) [GOVERN]

Mt 27:27 of the governor took Jesus into the **g** headquarters,
28:14 If this comes to the **g** ears,
Mk 15:16 of the palace (that is, the **g** headquarters);

GOVERNORS (50) [GOVERN]

1Ki 10:15 from all the kings of Arabia and the **g** of the land.
20:14 By the young men who serve the district **g**."
20:15 the young men who serve the district **g**,
20:17 young men who serve the district **g** went out first.
20:19 the young men who serve the district **g**,
2Ch 9:14 and the **g** of the land brought gold and silver
23:20 the **g** of the people, and all the people of the land,
Ezr 8:36 to the king's satraps and to the **g** of the province
Ne 2: 7 let letters be given me to the **g** of the province
2: 9 I came to the **g** of the province Beyond the River,
5:15 The former **g** who were before me laid heavy
Est 1: 3 the nobles and **g** of the provinces were present,
3:12 to the **g** over all the provinces and to the officials
8: 9 the **g** and the officials of the provinces from India
9: 3 and the **g**, and the royal officials were supporting
Jer 51:23 with you I smash **g** and deputies.
51:28 the kings of the Medes, with their **g** and deputies,
51:57 also her **g**, her deputies, and her warriors;
Eze 23: 6 in blue, **g** and commanders, all
23:12 She lusted after the Assyrians, **g** and commanders,
23:23 **g** and commanders all of them,
Da 3: 2 and the **g**, the counselors, the treasurers,
3: 3 So the satraps, the prefects, and the **g**,
3:27 And the satraps, the prefects, the **g**,
6: 7 and the **g** are agreed that the king should establish
Mt 10:18 be dragged before **g** and kings because of me,
Mk 13: 9 you will stand before **g** and kings because of me,
Lk 21:12 and you will be brought before kings and **g**
1Pe 2:14 of **g**, as sent by him to punish those who do wrong
Jdt 5: 2 and the commanders of Ammon and all the **g** of
AdE 1: 3 and the **g** of the provinces.
1:11 and to have her display her beauty to all the **g** and
1:14 the **g** of the Persians and Medes who were closest
1:16 Then Muchaeus said to the king and the **g**,
1:16 the king but also all the king's **g** and officials"
1:18 of the Persian and Median **g**,
1:21 This speech pleased the king and the **g**,
3:12 of King Artaxerxes to the magistrates and the **g**
3:12 the **g** were addressed each in his own language.
8: 9 and **g** of the provinces from Media to Ethiopia,
9: 3 The chief provincial **g**, the princes,
13: 1 to the **g** of the hundred twenty-seven provinces
16: 1 to the **g** of the provinces from India to Ethiopia,
2Mc 5:22 He left **g** to oppress the people:
12: 2 But some of the **g** in various places,
1Es 3: 2 the satraps and generals and **g** that were under him
3:14 and the satraps and generals and **g** and prefects,
4:47 and wrote letters for him to all the treasurers and **g**
4:48 the **g** in Coelesyria and Phoenicia and to those
8:67 the king's orders to the royal stewards and to the **g**

GOVERNS (2) [GOVERN]

Job 36:31 by these he **g** peoples; he gives food in abundance.
2Es 13:58 because he **g** the times and whatever things come

GOWN (1)

Jdt 16: 8 with a tiara and put on a linen **g** to beguile him.

GOZAN (5)

2Ki 17: 6 the river of **G**, and in the cities of the Medes.
18:11 the river of **G**, and in the cities of the Medes,
19:12 the nations that my predecessors destroyed, **G**,
1Ch 5:26 Habor, Hara, and the river **G**, to this day.
Isa 37:12 the nations that my predecessors destroyed, **G**,

GRACE‡ (127) [GRACIOUS, GRACIOUSLY, GRACIOUSNESS]

Ps 45: 2 **g** is poured upon your lips;
Jer 31: 2 The people who survived the sword found **g** in
Zec 4: 7 bring out the top stone amid shouts of '**G**, **g** to it!'
Jn 1:14 as of a father's only son, full of **g** and truth.
1:16 From his fullness we have all received, **g** upon **g**.
1:17 **g** and truth came through Jesus Christ.
Ac 4:33 and great **g** was upon them all.
6: 8 Stephen, full of **g** and power,
11:23 When he came and saw the **g** of God, he rejoiced,
13:43 and urged them to continue in the **g** of God.
14: 3 the word of his **g** by granting signs and wonders to
14:26 the **g** of God for the work that they had completed.
15:11 we believe that we will be saved through the **g** of
15:40 believers commending him to the **g** of the Lord.
18:27 through **g** had become believers,
20:24 to testify to the good news of God's **g**.
20:32 to God and to the message of his **g**,
Ro 1: 5 through whom we have received **g** and apostleship
1: 7 **G** to you and peace from God our Father and
3:24 they are now justified by his **g** as a gift,
4:16 that the promise may rest on **g** and be guaranteed
5: 2 through whom we have obtained access to this **g**
5:15 **g** of God and the free gift in the **g** of the one man,
5:17 surely will those who receive the abundance of **g**
5:20 but where sin increased, **g** abounded all the more,
5:21 so **g** might also exercise dominion
6: 1 in sin in order that **g** may abound?
6:14 since you are not under law but under **g**.
6:15 because we are not under law but under **g**?
11: 5 at the present time there is a remnant, chosen by **g**.
11: 6 But if it is by **g**, it is no longer on the basis of
works, otherwise **g** would no longer be **g**.
12: 3 the **g** given to me I say to everyone among you not
12: 6 We have gifts that differ according to the **g** given
15:15 because of the **g** given me by God
16:20 The **g** of our Lord Jesus Christ be with you.
1Co 1: 3 **G** to you and peace from God our Father and
1: 4 to my God always for you because of the **g** of God
3:10 According to the **g** of God given to me,
15:10 But by the **g** of God I am what I am,
15:10 and his **g** toward me has not been in vain.
15:10 it was not I, but the **g** of God that is with me.
16:23 The **g** of the Lord Jesus be with you.
2Co 1: 2 **G** to you and peace from God our Father and
1:12 not by earthly wisdom but by the **g** of God—
4:15 Yes, everything is for your sake, so that **g**,
6: 1 we urge you also not to accept the **g** of God
8: 1 the **g** of God that has been granted to the churches
9:14 of the surpassing **g** of God that he has given you.
12: 9 "My **g** is sufficient for you,
13:13 The **g** of the Lord Jesus Christ, the love of God,
Gal 1: 3 **G** to you and peace from God our Father and
1: 6 the one who called you in the **g** of Christ
1:15 before I was born and called me through his **g**,
2: 9 recognized the **g** that had been given to me,
2:21 I do not nullify the **g** of God;
5: 4 you have fallen away from **g**.
6:18 the **g** of our Lord Jesus Christ be with your spirit,
Eph 1: 2 **G** to you and peace from God our Father and
1: 6 the praise of his glorious **g** that he freely bestowed
1: 7 according to the riches of his **g**
2: 5 by **g** you have been saved—
2: 7 of his **g** in kindness toward us in Christ Jesus.
2: 8 For by **g** you have been saved through faith,
3: 2 of the commission of God's **g** that was given me
3: 7 according to the gift of God's **g** that was given me
3: 8 this **g** was given to me to bring to the Gentiles
4: 7 of us was given **g** according to the measure
4:29 so that your words may give **g** to those who hear.
6:24 **G** be with all who have an undying love
Php 1: 2 **G** to you and peace from God our Father and
1: 7 for all of you share in God's **g** with me,
4:23 The **g** of the Lord Jesus Christ be with your spirit.
Col 1: 2 **G** to you and peace from God our Father.
1: 6 the day you heard it and truly comprehended the **g**
4:18 Remember my chains. **G** be with you.
1Th 1: 1 and the Lord Jesus Christ: **G** to you and peace.
5:28 The **g** of our Lord Jesus Christ be with you.
2Th 1: 2 **G** to you and peace from God our Father and
1:12 to the **g** of our God and the Lord Jesus Christ.
2:16 through **g** gave us eternal comfort and good hope,
3:18 The **g** of our Lord Jesus Christ be with all of you.
1Ti 1: 2 **G**, mercy, and peace from God the Father
1:14 the **g** of our Lord overflowed for me with the faith
6:21 as regards the faith. **G** be with you.
2Ti 1: 2 **G**, mercy, and peace from God the Father
1: 9 but according to his own purpose and **g**.
1: 9 This **g** was given to us in Christ Jesus before
2: 1 my child, be strong in the **g** that is in Christ Jesus;
4:22 The Lord be with your spirit. **G** be with you.
Tit 1: 4 **G** and peace from God the Father
2:11 For the **g** of God has appeared,
3: 7 having been justified by his **g**,
3:15 **G** be with all of you.
Phm 1: 3 **G** to you and peace from God our Father and
1:25 The **g** of the Lord Jesus Christ be with your spirit.
Heb 2: 9 by the **g** of God he might taste death for everyone.
4:16 therefore approach the throne of **g** with boldness,
4:16 so that we may receive mercy and find **g** to help
10:29 and outraged the Spirit of **g**?
12:15 See to it that no one fails to obtain the **g** of God;
13: 9 for it is well for the heart to be strengthened by **g**,
13:25 **G** be with all of you.
Jas 4: 6 But he gives all the more **g**;
4: 6 God opposes the proud, but gives **g** to the humble.
1Pe 1: 2 May **g** and peace be yours in abundance.
1:10 of the **g** that was to be yours made careful search
1:13 on the **g** that Jesus Christ will bring you
4:10 Like good stewards of the manifold **g** of God,
5: 5 God opposes the proud, but gives **g** to the humble.
5:10 a little while, the God of all **g**, who has called you
5:12 and to testify that this is the true **g** of God.
2Pe 1: 2 May **g** and peace be yours in abundance in
3:18 But grow in the **g** and knowledge of our Lord
2Jn 1: 3 **G**, mercy, and peace will be with us from God
Jude 1: 4 who pervert the **g** of our God into licentiousness
Rev 1: 4 **G** to you and peace from him who is and who was
22:21 The **g** of the Lord Jesus be with all the saints.
AdE 15:14 my lord, and your countenance is full of **g**."
Wis 3: 9 because **g** and mercy are upon his holy ones,
4:15 that God's **g** and mercy are with his elect,
Sir 40:22 The eye desires **g** and beauty,
2Es 2:32 my springs run over, and my **g** will not fail."

GRACEFUL (4) [GRACEFULLY, GRACEFULNESS]

Ge 29:17 and Rachel was **g** and beautiful.
Pr 5:19 a lovely deer, a **g** doe.
SS 7: 1 **g** are your feet in sandals, O queenly maiden!
Sir 24:16 and my branches are glorious and **g**.

GRACEFULLY (1) [GRACEFUL]

Na 3: 4 **g** alluring, mistress of sorcery,

GRACEFULNESS (1) [GRACEFUL]

4Mc 6: 2 he remained adorned with the **g** of his piety.

GRACIOUS‡ (67) [GRACE]

Ge 43:29 God be **g** to you, my son!"
Ex 33:19 and I will be **g** to whom I will be **g**,
34: 6 the LORD, a God merciful and **g**, slow to anger,
Nu 6:25 to shine upon you, and be **g** to you;
2Sa 12:22 LORD may be **g** to me, and the child may live.'
2Ki 13:23 the LORD was **g** to them and had compassion
2Ch 30: 9 For the LORD your God is **g** and merciful,
Ezr 7: 9 for the **g** hand of his God was upon him.
8:18 Since the **g** hand of our God was upon us,
8:22 that the hand of our God is **g** to all who seek him,
Ne 2: 8 for the **g** hand of my God was upon me.
2:18 I told them that the hand of my God had been **g**
9:17 you are a God ready to forgive, **g** and merciful,
9:31 for you are a **g** and merciful God.
Job 33:24 and he is **g** to that person, and says, 'Deliver him
Ps 4: 1 Be **g** to me, and hear my prayer.
6: 2 Be **g** to me, O LORD, for I am languishing;
9:13 Be **g** to me, O LORD.
25:16 Turn to me and be **g** to me,
26:11 redeem me, and be **g** to me.
27: 7 when I cry aloud, be **g** to me and answer me!
30:10 Hear, O LORD, and be **g** to me!
31: 9 Be **g** to me, O LORD, for I am in distress;
41: 4 As for me, I said, "O LORD, be **g** to me;
41:10 But you, O LORD, be **g** to me, and raise me up,
56: 1 Be **g** to me, O God, for people trample on me;
67: 1 be **g** to us and bless us and make his face to shine
77: 9 Has God forgotten to be **g**?
86: 3 be **g** to me, O Lord,
86:15 But you, O Lord, are a God merciful and **g**,
86:16 Turn to me and be **g** to me;
103: 8 The LORD is merciful and **g**,
111: 4 the LORD is **g** and merciful.
112: 4 they are **g**, merciful, and righteous.
116: 5 **G** is the LORD, and righteous;
119:58 be **g** to me according to your promise.
119:132 Turn to me and be **g** to me,
135: 3 sing to his name, for he is **g**.
145: 8 The LORD is **g** and merciful,
145:13 and **g** in all his deeds.
147: 1 for he is **g**, and a song of praise is fitting.
Pr 11:16 A **g** woman gets honor,
15:26 to the LORD, but **g** words are pure.
22:11 a pure heart and are **g** in speech will have the king
Isa 30:18 Therefore the LORD waits to be **g** to you;
30:19 surely be **g** to you at the sound of your cry;
33: 2 O LORD, be **g** to us; we wait for you.
63: 7 I will recount the **g** deeds of the LORD,
Joel 2:13 your God, for he is **g** and merciful, slow to anger,
Am 5:15 will be **g** to the remnant of Joseph.
Jnh 4: 2 for I knew that you are a **g** God and merciful,
Zec 1:13 the LORD replied with **g** and comforting words
Mal 1: 9 implore the favor of God, that he may be **g** to us.
Mt 11:26 yes, Father, for such was your **g** will.
Lk 4:22 of him and were amazed at the **g** words that came
10:21 yes, Father, for such was your **g** will.
Col 4: 6 Let your speech always be **g**, seasoned with salt,

1Pe 3: 7 since they too are also heirs of the g gift of life—
Sir 5: 5 and a g tongue multiplies courtesies.
18:17 Both are to be found in a g person.
2Mc 2:22 the Lord with great kindness became g to them—
10:26 be g to them and to be an enemy to their enemies
14: 9 and our hard-pressed nation with the g kindness
1Es 8:10 In accordance with my g decision,
2Es 7:*133* [63] and g, because he is g to those who turn

GRACIOUSLY (8) [GRACE]

Ge 33: 5 children whom God has g given your servant."
33:11 because God has dealt g with me,
Ps 119:29 and g teach me your law.
Pr 26:25 when an enemy speaks g, do not believe it,
Php 1:29 For he has g granted you the privilege not only
Wis 6:16 and she g appears to them in their paths,
Sir 7:33 Give g to all the living;
3Mc 2:16 you g bestowed your glory on your people Israel,

GRACIOUSNESS (1) [GRACE]

Ac 24: 4 to hear us briefly with your customary g.

GRADUALLY (1)

Ge 8: 3 and the waters g receded from the earth.

GRAFF, GRAFFED (KJV) See GRAFTED

GRAFT (1) [GRAFTED]

Ro 11:23 for God has the power to g them in again.

GRAFTED (5) [GRAFT]

Ro 11:17 were g in their place to share the rich root of
11:19 so that I might be g in."
11:23 if they do not persist in unbelief, will be g in,
11:24 from what is by nature a wild olive tree and g,
11:24 be g back into their own olive tree.

GRAIN‡ (271) [GRAINFIELDS, GRAINS, GRANARIES, GRANARY]

A. GRAIN OFFERING (125)
B. GRAIN OFFERINGS (15)

Ge 27:28 and plenty of g and wine.
27:37 and with g and wine I have sustained him.
41: 5 seven ears of g, plump and good,
41:22 and I saw in my dream seven ears of g,
41:35 up g under the authority of Pharaoh for food in
41:49 So Joseph stored up g in such abundance—
41:57 all the world came to Joseph in Egypt to buy g,
42: 1 When Jacob learned that there was g in Egypt,
42: 2 I have heard," he said, "that there is g in Egypt;
42: 2 go down and buy g for us there,
42: 3 of Joseph's brothers went down to buy g in Egypt.
42: 5 among the other people who came to buy g,
42:19 The rest of you shall go and carry g for the famine
42:25 Joseph then gave orders to fill their bags with g,
42:26 They loaded their donkeys with their g,
42:33 take g for the famine of your households,
43: 2 up the g that they had brought from Egypt,
44: 2 with his money for the g."
45:23 and ten female donkeys loaded with g, bread,
47:14 in exchange for the g that they bought;
Ex 22: 6 in thorns so that the stacked g or the standing g
29:41 with it a g offering and its drink offering, A
30: 9 or a burnt offering, or a g offering; A
40:29 on it the burnt offering and the g offering as A
Lev 2: 1 When anyone presents a g offering to the LORD, A
2: 3 of the g offering shall be for Aaron and his sons, A
2: 4 you present a g offering baked in the oven, A
2: 5 If your offering is g prepared on a griddle,
2: 6 on it; it is a g offering. A
2: 7 If your offering is g prepared in a pan,
2: 8 the LORD the g offering that is prepared in any A
2: 9 from the g offering its token portion and turn A
2:10 the g offering shall be for Aaron and his sons; A
2:11 No g offering that you bring to the LORD shall A
2:13 You shall not omit from your g offerings the salt B
2:14 you bring a g offering of first fruits to the LORD, A
2:14 bring as the g offering of your first fruits A
2:14 of your first fruits coarse new g from fresh ears,
2:15 lay frankincense on it; it is a g offering. A
2:16 of the coarse g and oil with all its frankincense;
5:13 the g offering, the rest shall be for the priest. A
6:14 This is the ritual of the g offering: A
6:15 of the choice flour and oil of the g offering, A
6:21 as a g offering of baked pieces, A
6:23 Every g offering of a priest shall A
7: 9 And every g offering baked in the oven, A
7:10 every other g offering, mixed with oil or dry, A
7:37 the g offering, the sin offering, the guilt offering, A
9: 4 and a g offering mixed with oil. A
9:17 He presented the g offering, and, A
10:12 Take the g offering that is left from A
14:10 and a g offering of three-tenths of an ephah A
14:20 the burnt offering and the g offering on the altar. A
14:21 of choice flour mixed with oil for a g offering A
14:31 for a burnt offering, along with a g offering; A
23:13 And the g offering with it shall be two-tenths of A
23:14 You shall eat no bread or parched g or fresh ears
23:16 then you shall present an offering of new g to
23:18 with their g offering and their drink offerings, A
23:37 burnt offerings and g offerings, B
26:10 You shall eat old g long stored,
Nu 4:16 the regular g offering, and the anointing oil, A
5:15 for it is a g offering of jealousy, A
5:15 a g offering of remembrance, A
5:18 in her hands the g offering of remembrance, A
5:18 which is the g offering of jealousy. A
5:25 The priest shall take the g offering of jealousy A
5:25 and shall elevate the g offering before the LORD A
5:26 the priest shall take a handful of the g offering, A
6:15 with their g offering and their drink offerings. A
6:17 the accompanying g offering and drink offering. A
7:13 of choice flour mixed with oil for a g offering; A
7:19 of choice flour mixed with oil for a g offering; A
7:25 of choice flour mixed with oil for a g offering; A
7:31 of choice flour mixed with oil for a g offering; A
7:37 of choice flour mixed with oil for a g offering; A
7:43 of choice flour mixed with oil for a g offering; A
7:49 of choice flour mixed with oil for a g offering; A
7:55 of choice flour mixed with oil for a g offering; A
7:61 of choice flour mixed with oil for a g offering; A
7:67 of choice flour mixed with oil for a g offering; A
7:73 of choice flour mixed with oil for a g offering; A
7:79 of choice flour mixed with oil for a g offering; A
7:87 a year old, with their g offering; A
8: 8 let them take a young bull and its g offering A
15: 4 to the LORD shall present also a g offering, A
15: 6 For a ram, you shall offer a g offering, A
15: 9 then you shall present with the bull a g offering, A
15:24 with its g offering and its drink offering, A
18: 9 g offering, sin offering, or guilt offering, A
18:12 of the oil and all the best of the wine and of the g,
18:27 as the g of the threshing floor and the fullness of
20: 5 It is no place for g, or figs, or vines,
28: 5 of an ephah of choice flour for a g offering, A
28: 8 a g offering and a drink offering like the one A
28: 9 of an ephah of choice flour for a g offering, A
28:12 of an ephah of choice flour for a g offering, A
28:12 and two-tenths of choice flour for a g offering, A
28:13 of choice flour mixed with oil as a g offering A
28:20 Their g offering shall be of choice flour mixed A
28:26 when you offer a g offering of new grain to A
28:26 of new g to the LORD at your festival of weeks,
28:28 Their g offering shall be of choice flour mixed A
28:31 to the regular burnt offering with its g offering, A
29: 3 Their g offering shall be of choice flour mixed A
29: 6 of the new moon and its g offering, A
29: 6 and the regular burnt offering and its g offering, A
29: 9 Their g offering shall be of choice flour mixed A
29:11 and the regular burnt offering and its g offering, A
29:14 Their g offering shall be of choice flour mixed A
29:16 its g offering and its drink offering. A
29:18 g offering and the drink offerings for the bulls, A
29:19 to the regular burnt offering and its g offering, A
29:21 g offering and the drink offerings for the bulls, A
29:22 to the regular burnt offering and its g offering A
29:24 g offering and the drink offerings for the bulls, A
29:25 its g offering and its drink offering. A
29:27 g offering and the drink offerings for the bulls, A
29:28 to the regular burnt offering and its g offering A
29:30 g offering and the drink offerings for the bulls, A
29:31 its g offering, and its drink offerings. A
29:33 g offering and the drink offerings for the bulls, A
29:34 besides the regular burnt offering, its g offering, A
29:37 g offering and the drink offerings for the bull, A
29:38 to the regular burnt offering and its g offering A
29:39 as your burnt offerings, your g offerings, B
Dt 7:13 your g and your wine and your oil,
11:14 and you will gather in your g, your wine,
12:17 may you eat within your towns the tithe of your g,
14:23 you shall eat the tithe of your g, your wine,
16: 9 the time the sickle is first put to the standing g.
18: 4 The first fruits of your g, your wine, and your oil,
23:25 If you go into your neighbor's standing g,
23:25 not put a sickle to your neighbor's standing g.
25: 4 not muzzle an ox while it is treading out the g.
28:51 leaving you neither g, wine, and oil,
33:28 in a land of g and wine, where the heavens drop
Jos 5:11 unleavened cakes and parched g.
22:23 we did so to offer burnt offerings or g offerings B
22:29 building an altar for burnt offering, g offering, A
Jdg 13:19 So Manoah took the kid with the g offering, A
13:23 have accepted a burnt offering and a g offering A
15: 5 the foxes go into the standing g of the Philistines,
15: 5 and burned up the shocks and the standing g,
Ru 2: 2 to the field and glean among the ears of g,
2:14 and he heaped up for her some parched g.
3: 7 he went to lie down at the end of the heap of g.
1Sa 8:15 of your g and of your vineyards and give it
17:17 "Take for your brothers an ephah of this parched g
25:18 five measures of parched g,
2Sa 17:19 and spread out g on it;
17:28 wheat, barley, meal, parched g, beans and lentils,
1Ki 8:64 g offerings and the fat pieces of the sacrifices B
8:64 g offerings and the fat pieces of the sacrifices B
2Ki 4:42 twenty loaves of barley and fresh ears of g
16:13 and offered his burnt offering and his g offering, A
16:15 and the evening g offering, A
16:15 the king's burnt offering, and his g offering, A
16:15 their g offering, and their drink offering; A
18:32 a land of g and wine,
1Ch 21:23 and the wheat for a g offering. A
23:29 the choice flour for the g offering, A
2Ch 7: 7 not hold the burnt offering and the g offering A
31: 5 in abundance the first fruits of g, wine, oil, honey,
32:28 storehouses also for the yield of g, wine, and oil;
Ezr 7:17 and their g offerings and their drink offerings, B
Ne 5: 2 we must get g, so that we may eat and stay alive."
5: 3 our houses in order to get g during the famine."
Ne 5:10 and my servants are lending them money and g.
5:11 and their houses, and the interest on money, g,
10:31 in merchandise or any g on the sabbath day to sell,
10:33 the regular g offering, the regular burnt offering, A
10:39 the sons of Levi shall bring the contribution of g,
13: 5 where they had previously put the g offering, A
13: 5 the frankincense, the vessels, and the tithes of g,
13: 9 with the g offering and the frankincense. A
13:12 Then all Judah brought the tithe of the g, wine,
13:15 and bringing in heaps of g and loading them
Job 5:26 of g comes up to the threshing floor in its season.
24:24 they are cut off like the heads of g.
39:12 and bring your g to your threshing floor?
Ps 4: 7 in my heart more than when their g
65: 9 you provide the people with g,
65:13 the valleys deck themselves with g,
72:16 May there be abundance of g in the land;
78:24 and gave them the g of heaven.
Pr 11:26 The people curse those who hold back g,
14: 4 Where there are no oxen, there is no g;
27:22 in a mortar with a pestle along with crushed g,
Isa 16: 9 and your g harvest has ceased.
17: 5 And it shall be as when reapers gather standing g
17: 5 one gleans the ears of g in the Valley of Rephaim.
23: 3 your revenue was the g of Shihor,
28:28 G is crushed for bread, but one does
30:23 and g, the produce of the ground,
36:17 a land of g and wine,
57: 6 you have brought a g offering. A
62: 8 not again give your g to be food for your enemies,
66: 3 whoever presents a g offering, A
66:20 the Israelites bring a g offering in a clean vessel A
Jer 14:12 they offer burnt offering and g offering, A
17:26 g offerings and frankincense, B
31:12 over the g, the wine, and the oil,
33:18 to offer burnt offerings, to make g offerings, B
41: 5 bringing g offerings and incense to present at B
50:26 pile her up like heaps of g, and destroy her utterly;
Eze 36:29 and I will summon the g and make it abundant
42:13 the g offering, the sin offering, A
44:29 They shall eat the g offering, the sin offering, A
45:15 This is the offering for g offerings, B
45:17 g offerings, and drink offerings, at the festivals, B
45:17 he shall provide the sin offerings, g offerings, B
45:24 He shall provide as a g offering an ephah A
45:25 burnt offerings, and g offerings, and for the oil. B
46: 5 the g offering with the ram shall be an ephah, A
46: 5 the g offering with the lambs shall be as much A
46: 7 as a g offering he shall provide an ephah with A
46:11 g offering with a young bull shall be an ephah, A
46:14 g offering with it morning by morning regularly, A
46:14 as a g offering to the LORD; A
46:15 Thus the lamb and the g offering and the oil A
46:20 and where they shall bake the g offering, A
Da 2:46 that a g offering and incense be offered to him. A
Hos 2: 8 She did not know that it was I who gave her the g,
2: 9 Therefore I will take back my g in its time,
2:22 the earth shall answer the g, the wine, and the oil,
7:14 they gash themselves for g and wine;
8: 7 standing g has no heads, it shall yield no meal;
Joel 1: 9 The g offering and the drink offering are cut off A
1:10 for the g is destroyed, the wine dries up,
1:13 G offering and drink offering are withheld from A
1:17 the granaries are ruined because the g has failed.
2:14 a g offering and a drink offering for the LORD, A
2:19 I am sending you g, wine, and oil,
2:24 The threshing floors shall be full of g,
Am 5:11 from them levies of g, you have built houses
5:22 offer me your burnt offerings and g offerings, B
8: 5 will the new moon be over so that we may sell g;
Hag 1:11 on the g, the new wine, the oil,
Zec 9:17 G shall make the young men flourish,
Mt 12: 1 and they began to pluck heads of g and to eat.
13: 8 Other seeds fell on good soil and brought forth g,
13:26 So when the plants came up and bore g,
Mk 2:23 his disciples began to pluck heads of g.
4: 7 up and choked it, and it yielded no g.
4: 8 Other seed fell into good soil and brought forth g,
4:28 then the head, then the full g in the head.
4:29 But when the g is ripe,
Lk 6: 1 his disciples plucked some heads of g,
12:18 and there I will store all my g and my goods.
Jn 12:24 unless a g of wheat falls into the earth and dies, it remains just a single g;
Ac 7:12 But when Jacob heard that there was g in Egypt,
1Co 9: 9 not muzzle an ox while it is treading out the g."
15:37 perhaps of wheat or of some other g.
1Ti 5:18 not muzzle an ox while it is treading out the g,"
Tob 1: 7 likewise the tenth of the g, wine, olive oil,
Jdt 10: 5 and filled a bag with roasted g, dried fig cakes,
11:13 to consume the first fruits of the g and the tithes of
Sir 18:10 Like a drop of water from the sea and a g of sand,
40:22 but the green shoots of g more than either.
Bar 1:10 and prepare a g offering, and offer them on A
1Mc 8:26 not give or supply g, arms, money, or ships, just
8:28 And to their enemies there shall not be given g,
10:30 and instead of collecting the third of the g and
2Mc 1: 8 and we offered sacrifice and g offering, A
2Es 4:30 a g of evil seed was sown in Adam's heart from
4:31 for yourself how much fruit of ungodliness a g
4:32 When heads of g without number are sown,
15:42 and grass of the meadows, and their g.

GRAINFIELDS (3) [FIELD, GRAIN]

Mt 12: 1 that time Jesus went through the g on the sabbath;
Mk 2:23 One sabbath he was going through the g;

Lk 6: 1 One sabbath while Jesus was going through the g,

GRAINS (2) [GRAIN]
Isa 48:19 and your descendants like its g;
Heb 11:12 and as the innumerable g of sand by the seashore."

GRANARIES (2) [GRAIN]
Jer 50:26 Come against her from every quarter; open her g;
Joel 1:17 the g are ruined because the grain has failed.

GRANARY (2) [GRAIN]
Mt 3:12 and will gather his wheat into the g;
Lk 3:17 and to gather the wheat into his g;

GRANDCHILDREN (5) [CHILD]
Ge 31:55 kissed his g and his daughters and blessed them;
Ex 10: 2 and g how I have made fools of the Egyptians
1Ch 8:40 having many children and g, one hundred fifty.
Pr 17: 6 G are the crown of the aged,
1Ti 5: 4 If a widow has children or g,

GRANDDAUGHTER (2) [DAUGHTER]
2Ki 8:26 Athaliah, a g of King Omri of Israel.
2Ch 22: 2 His mother's name was Athaliah, a g of Omri.

GRANDEUR (1)
Sir 17: 9 to proclaim the g of his works.

GRANDFATHER (2) [FATHER]
2Sa 9: 7 I will restore to you all the land of your g Saul,
Sir Pr: 1 to help the outsiders. So my g Jesus,

GRANDFATHER'S (1) [FATHER]
2Sa 16: 3 of Israel will give me back my g kingdom.' "

GRANDMOTHER (2) [MOTHER]
2Ti 1: 5 in your g Lois and your mother Eunice and now,
4Mc 16: 9 or have the happiness of being called g.

GRANDPARENTS (1) [PARENT]
Ex 10: 6 that neither your parents nor your g have seen,

GRANDSON (8) [SON]
Ge 11:31 Terah took his son Abram and his g Lot son
Jdg 8:22 "Rule over us, you and your son and your g also;
2Sa 9: 9 to all his house I have given to your master's g.
9:10 so that your master's g may have food to eat;
9:10 but your master's g Mephibosheth shall always eat
19:24 Mephibosheth g of Saul came down to meet
2Ch 22: 9 for they said, "He is the g of Jehoshaphat,
Jer 27: 7 the nations shall serve him and his son and his g,

GRANDSONS (1) [SON]
Jdg 12:14 He had forty sons and thirty g,

GRANT (72) [GRANTED, GRANTING, GRANTS]
Ge 19:21 He said to him, "Very well, I g you this favor too,
24:12 please g me success today and show steadfast love
43:14 may God Almighty g you mercy before the man,
Lev 26: 6 And I will g peace in the land,
Nu 25:12 say, 'I hereby g him my covenant of peace.
Dt 15: 1 Every seventh year you shall g a remission
Jdg 11:37 G me two months, so that I may go and wander on
Ru 1: 9 The LORD g that you may find security,
1Sa 1:17 of Israel g the petition you have made to him."
10:27 of each of them and would not g Israel a deliverer.
2Sa 14:21 Then the king said to Joab, "Very well, I g this;
1Ki 8:36 and g rain on your land,
8:50 g them compassion in the sight of their captors,
1Ch 22:12 the LORD g you discretion and understanding,
29:19 G to my son Solomon that
2Ch 12: 7 but I will g them some deliverance,
Ezr 3: 7 according to the g that they had from King Cyrus
9: 8 in order that he may brighten our eyes and g us
Ne 1:11 and g him mercy in the sight of this man!"
2: 7 that they may g me passage until I arrive in Judah;
Est 5: 8 the king to g my petition and fulfill my request,
Job 6: 8 and that God would g my desire;
13:20 Only g two things to me, then I will
Ps 20: 4 May he g you your heart's desire,
60:11 O g us help against the foe,
85: 7 O LORD, and g us your salvation.
108:12 O g us help against the foe,
140: 8 Do not g, O LORD, the desires of the wicked;
Isa 16: 3 Give counsel, g justice; make your shade like night
Jer 34:17 I am going to g a release to you,
42:12 I will g you mercy, and he will have mercy on you
Mt 14: 7 on oath to g her whatever she might ask.
20:23 this is not mine to g,
Mk 10:37 And they said to him, "G us to sit,
10:40 at my right hand or at my left is not mine to g,
Lk 1:73 that he swore to our ancestor Abraham, to g us
18: 3 'G me justice against my opponent.'
18: 5 I will g her justice, so that she may
18: 7 not God g justice to his chosen ones who cry
18: 8 I tell you, he will quickly g justice to them.
Ac 4:29 and g to your servants to speak your word
24:27 and since he wanted to g the Jews a favor,
Ro 15: 5 the God of steadfastness and encouragement g you
Eph 3:16 he may g that you may be strengthened
2Ti 1:16 May the Lord g mercy to the household
1:18 the Lord g that he will find mercy from the Lord
2:25 God may perhaps g that they will repent and come
Rev 11: 3 And I will g my two witnesses authority
Tob 7:11 and prosper you both this night and g you mercy
7:16 Lord of heaven g you joy in place of your sorrow.
8: 4 and implore our Lord that he g us mercy
8: 7 G that she and I may find mercy and
9: 6 May the Lord g the blessing of heaven to you
Jdt 10: 8 of our ancestors g you favor and fulfill your plans,
13:20 May God g this to be a perpetual honor to you,
Wis 7:15 May God g me to speak with judgment,
Sir 38:14 that he g them success in diagnosis and in healing,
45:26 May the Lord g you wisdom of mind
Bar 2:14 and g us favor in the sight
1Mc 10:28 We will g you many immunities
10:40 also g fifteen thousand shekels of silver yearly out
11:35 from all these we shall g them release.
11:50 "G us peace, and make the Jews stop fighting
11:66 Then they asked him to g them terms of peace,
13:34 to King Demetrius with a request to g relief to
13:37 to our officials to g you release from tribute.
14:46 All the people agreed to g Simon the right to act
15: 7 and I g freedom to Jerusalem and the sanctuary.
2Mc 3:31 the Most High to g life to one who was lying quite
12:11 to g them pledges of friendship,
2Es 8: 6 g to your servant that we may pray before you,
4Mc 11:12 they are splendid favors that you g us

GRANTED (52) [GRANT]
Ge 25:21 and the LORD g his prayer,
27:20 "Because the LORD your God g me success."
47:11 and g them a holding in the land of Egypt,
Jdg 15:18 "You have g this great victory by the hand
1Sa 1:27 LORD has g me the petition that I made to him.
25:35 and I have g your petition."
2Sa 14:22 in that the king has g the request of his servant."
1Ki 1:48 who today has g one of my offspring to sit
2Ki 2:10 it will be g you; if not, it will not."
1Ch 4:10 And God g what he asked.
5:20 he g their entreaty because they trusted in him.
2Ch 1:12 wisdom and knowledge are g to you.
9:12 Meanwhile King Solomon g the queen
Ezr 7: 6 and the king g him all that he asked,
Ne 2: 8 And the king g me what I asked,
Est 2:18 He also g a holiday to the provinces,
5: 6 It shall be g you.
7: 2 It shall be g you.
9:12 It shall be g you.
Job 10:12 You have g me life and steadfast love,
Pr 10:24 but the desire of the righteous will be g.
Mk 15:45 he g the body to Joseph.
Lk 23:24 that their demand should be g.
Jn 5:26 so he has g the Son also to have life in himself;
6:65 that no one can come to me unless it is g by
Ac 27:24 God has g safety to all those who are sailing
2Co 1:11 for the blessing g us through the prayers of many.
8: 1 the grace of God that has been g to the churches
Gal 3:18 but God g it to Abraham through the promise.
Php 1:29 For he has graciously g you the privilege not only
Rev 19: 8 to her it has been g to be clothed with fine linen,
Tob 6:18 of heaven that mercy and safety may be g to you.
AdE 2:18 and he g a remission of taxes to those who were
5: 6 It shall be g you."
7: 2 It shall be g to you, even to half of my kingdom."
7: 3 let my life be g me at my petition,
8: 1 On that very day King Artaxerxes g to Esther all
8: 7 "Now that I have g all of Haman's property to you
Sir 6:37 and your desire for wisdom will be g.
17: 2 but g them authority over everything on the earth.
26: 3 be g among the blessings of the man who fears
1Mc 11:34 in Jerusalem we have g release from
11:58 and g him the right to drink from gold cups
15: 5 that the kings before me have g you,
2Mc 3:33 since for his sake the Lord has g you your life.
11:15 For the king g every request in behalf of
11:35 to what Lysias the kinsman of the king has g you,
3Mc 3:16 when we had g very great revenues to the temple
6:28 of our ancestors until now has g an unimpeded
6:41 The king g their request at once and wrote
7:12 g them a general license so that freely,
4Mc 5: 8 When nature has g it to us,

GRANTING (4) [GRANT]
Jer 34:17 not obeyed me by g a release to your neighbors
Ac 14: 3 to the word of his grace by g signs and wonders to
AdE 3: 1 and g him precedence over all the king's Friends.
Wis 12:20 g them time and opportunity to give

GRANTS‡ (7) [GRANT]
Ps 147:14 He g peace within your borders;
Sir 17:24 Yet to those who repent he g a return,
18:12 therefore he g them forgiveness all the more.
1Mc 11:36 not one of these g shall be canceled from this time
13:38 All the g that we have made to you remain valid,
3Mc 5:11 by him who g it to whomever he wishes.
2Es 5: 4 But if the Most High g that you live,

GRAPE (10) [GRAPE-GATHERER, GRAPE-GATHERERS, GRAPE-PICKER, GRAPE-PICKERS, GRAPES, GRAPEVINE]
Nu 6: 3 and shall not drink any g juice or eat grapes,
Job 15:33 They will shake off their unripe g, like the vine,
SS 7:12 whether the g blossoms have opened and
Isa 18: 5 over and the flower becomes a ripening g,
24:13 as at the gleaning when the g harvest is ended.
Sir 39:26 the blood of the g and oil and clothing.
50:15 and poured a drink offering of the blood of the g;
51:15 to the ripening g my heart delighted in her;
2Es 9:21 and saved for myself one g out of a cluster,
9:22 but let my g and my plant be saved,

GRAPE-GATHERER (1) [GATHER, GRAPE]
Jer 6: 9 like a g, pass your hand again over its branches.

GRAPE-GATHERERS (2) [GATHER, GRAPE]
Jer 49: 9 If g came to you, would they not leave gleanings?
Ob 1: 5 If g came to you, would they not leave gleanings?

GRAPE-PICKER (1) [GRAPE, PICK]
Sir 33:17 and like a g I filled my wine press.

GRAPE-PICKERS (1) [GRAPE, PICK]
Sir 33:16 I was like a gleaner following the g;

GRAPES (37) [GRAPE]
Ge 40:10 and the clusters ripened into g.
40:11 I took the g and pressed them into Pharaoh's cup,
49:11 in wine and his robe in the blood of g;
Lev 19:10 or gather the fallen g of your vineyard;
25: 5 the aftergrowth of your harvest or gather the g
Nu 6: 3 and shall not drink any grape juice or eat g,
13:20 Now it was the season of the first ripe g.
13:23 from there a branch with a single cluster of g,
Dt 23:24 you may eat your fill of g, as many as you wish,
24:21 When you gather the g of your vineyard,
28:39 you shall neither drink the wine nor gather the g,
32:14 you drank fine wine from the blood of g.
32:32 their g are g of poison,
Jdg 8: 2 Is not the gleaning of the g of Ephraim better than
9:27 the field and gathered the g from their vineyards,
Ne 13:15 and also wine, g, figs, and all kinds of burdens,
Isa 5: 2 he expected it to yield g, but it yielded wild g.
5: 4 I expected it to yield g, why did it yield wild g?
Jer 8:13 there are no g on the vine, nor figs on the fig tree;
25:30 and shout, like those who tread g,
31:29 "The parents have eaten sour g,
31:30 the teeth of everyone who eats sour g shall be set
Eze 18: 2 "The parents have eaten sour g,
Hos 9:10 Like g in the wilderness, I found Israel.
Am 9:13 and the treader of g the one who sows the seed;
Mic 6:15 you shall tread g, but not drink wine.
Mt 7:16 Are g gathered from thorns, or figs from thistles?
Lk 6:44 nor are g picked from a bramble bush.
Rev 14:18 of the vine of the earth, for its g are ripe."
1Mc 6:34 the elephants the juice of g and mulberries,
2Es 12:42 like a cluster of g from the vintage,
16:26 The g shall ripen, but who will tread them?
16:43 like one who will not gather the g;
4Mc 2: 9 nor gathers the last g from the vineyard.

GRAPEVINE (2) [GRAPE, VINE]
Nu 6: 4 that is produced by the g,
Jas 3:12 my brothers and sisters, yield olives, or a g figs?

GRAPPLED (1)
Sir 51:19 My soul g with wisdom,

GRASP‡ (8) [GRASPED, GRASPING, GRASPS]
1Ki 1:50 got up and went to g the horns of the altar.
Ps 71: 4 from the g of the unjust and cruel.
Pr 27:16 to restrain her is to restrain the wind or to g oil in
Jer 6:23 They g the bow and the javelin,
15:21 and redeem you from the g of the ruthless.
Lk 18:34 and they did not g what was said.
Tit 1: 9 a firm g of the word that is trustworthy
Sir 16:20 But no human mind can g this,

GRASPED (12) [GRASP]
Ex 4: 4 so he reached out his hand and g it,
Jdg 16:29 And Samson g the two middle pillars on which
1Sa 17:51 he g his sword, drew it out of its sheath,
2Sa 2:16 Each g his opponent by the head,
1Ki 2:28 Joab fled to the tent of the LORD and g the horns
2Ki 2:12 he g his own clothes and tore them in two pieces.
Pr 30:28 the lizard can be g in the hand,
Isa 45: 1 whose right hand I have g to subdue nations
Eze 21:11 sword is given to be polished, to be g in the hand;
29: 7 when they g you with the hand, you broke,
Tob 6: 4 young man g the fish and drew it up on the land.
2Es 10:30 he g my right hand and strengthened me

GRASPING (4) [GRASP]
Jdg 19:29 and g his concubine he cut her into twelve pieces,
Zec 8:23 g his garment and saying, "Let us go with you,
Sir 26: 7 taking hold of her is like g a scorpion.
2Mc 12:35 and g his cloak was dragging him off

GRASPS (1) [GRASP]
Job 30:18 he g me by the collar of my tunic.

GRASS (64) [GRASSY]

Ge 41: 2 and they grazed in the reed **g.**
41:18 came up out of the Nile and fed in the reed **g.**
Nu 22: 4 as an ox licks up the **g** of the field."
Dt 11:15 he will give **g** in your fields for your livestock,
32: 2 like gentle rain on **g,** like showers on new growth.
1Ki 18: 5 perhaps we may find **g** to keep the horses
2Ki 19:26 like plants of the field and like tender **g,**
19:26 like **g** on the housetops, blighted before it is grown.
Job 5:25 and your offspring like the **g** of the earth.
6: 5 Does the wild ass bray over its **g,**
38:27 and to make the ground put forth **g?**
40:15 it eats **g** like an ox.
Ps 37: 2 for they will soon fade like the **g,**
58: 7 like **g** let them be trodden down and wither.
72: 6 May he be like rain that falls on the mown **g,**
72:16 and may people blossom in the cities like the **g** of
90: 5 like **g** that is renewed in the morning;
92: 7 the wicked sprout like **g** and all evildoers flourish,
102: 4 My heart is stricken and withered like **g;**
102:11 like an evening shadow; I wither away like **g.**
103:15 As for mortals, their days are like **g;**
104:14 You cause the **g** to grow for the cattle,
106:20 of God for the image of an ox that eats **g.**
129: 6 the **g** on the housetops that withers before it grows
147: 8 makes **g** grow on the hills.
Pr 19:12 but his favor is like dew on the **g.**
27:25 When the **g** is gone, and new growth appears,
Isa 5:24 and as dry **g** sinks down in the flame,
15: 6 the **g** is withered, the new growth fails,
35: 7 the **g** shall become reeds and rushes.
37:27 like plants of the field and like tender **g,**
37:27 like **g** on the housetops, blighted before it is grown.
40: 6 All people are **g,** their constancy is like the flower
40: 7 The **g** withers, the flower fades,
40: 7 blows upon it; surely the people are **g.**
40: 8 The **g** withers, the flower fades;
51:12 a human being who fades like **g?**
66:14 your bodies shall flourish like the **g;**
Jer 12: 4 and the **g** of every field wither?
14: 5 forsakes her newborn fawn because there is no **g.**
50:11 though you frisk about like a heifer on the **g,**
Da 4:15 in the tender **g** of the field.
4:15 with the animals of the field in the **g** of the earth.
4:23 in the **g** of the field;
4:25 You shall be made to eat **g** like oxen,
4:32 You shall be made to eat **g** like oxen,
4:33 ate **g** like oxen, and his body was bathed with
5:21 he was fed **g** like oxen,
Am 7: 2 When they had finished eating the **g** of the land,
Mic 5: 7 from the LORD, like showers on the **g,** which do
Mt 6:30 But if God so clothes the **g** of the field,
14:19 Then he ordered the crowds to sit down on the **g.**
Mk 6:39 the people to sit down in groups on the green **g.**
Lk 12:28 But if God so clothes the **g** of the field,
Jn 6:10 Now there was a great deal of **g** in the place;
1Pe 1:24 "All flesh is like **g** and all its glory like the flower
of **g.** The **g** withers, and the flower falls,
Rev 8: 7 and all green **g** was burned up.
9: 4 the **g** of the earth or any green growth or any tree,
Sir 40:16 or river bank are plucked up before any **g;**
43:21 and withers the tender **g** like fire.
2Es 9:27 After seven days, while I lay on the **g,**
15:42 trees of the forests, and **g** of the meadows,

GRASSHOPPER (3) [GRASSHOPPERS]

Lev 11:22 and the **g** according to its kind.
Ecc 12: 5 the **g** drags itself along and desire fails;
Na 3:15 like the locust, multiply like the **g!**

GRASSHOPPERS (3) [GRASSHOPPER]

Nu 13:33 and to ourselves we seemed like **g,**
Isa 40:22 and its inhabitants are like **g;**
Na 3:17 like **g,** your scribes like swarms of locusts settling

GRASSY (2) [GRASS]

2Sa 23: 4 gleaming from the rain on the **g** land.
Wis 19: 7 and a **g** plain out of the raging waves,

GRATEFUL (3) [GRATITUDE]

1Ti 1:12 I am **g** to Christ Jesus our Lord,
2Ti 1: 3 I am **g** to God—whom I worship with a
2Mc 3:33 "Be very **g** to the high priest Onias,

GRATIFY‡ (2)

Ro 13:14 for the flesh, to **g** its desires.
Gal 5:16 I say, and do not **g** the desires of the flesh.

GRATING (6)

Ex 27: 4 You shall also make for it a **g,**
35:16 with its **g** of bronze, its poles, and all its utensils,
38: 4 He made for the altar a **g,** a network of bronze,
38: 5 the four corners of the bronze **g** to hold the poles;
38:30 the bronze **g** for it and all the utensils of the altar,
39:39 and its **g** of bronze, its poles, and all its utensils;

GRATITUDE‡ (4) [GRATEFUL]

Ac 24: 3 in every way and everywhere with utmost **g.**
Col 3:16 and with **g** in your hearts sing psalms, hymns,
2Mc 2:27 to secure the **g** of many we will gladly endure
2Es 1:37 to witness the **g** of the people that is to come,

GRAVE (38) [GRAVES]

Ge 18:20 and Gomorrah and how very **g** their sin!
35:20 and Jacob set up a pillar at her **g;**
Nu 19:16 or a **g,** shall be unclean seven days.
19:18 the slain, the corpse, or the **g.**
2Sa 3:32 The king lifted up his voice and wept at the **g**
1Ki 13:30 He laid the body in his own **g;**
13:31 in the **g** in which the man of God is buried;
14:13 he alone of Jeroboam's family shall come to the **g,**
2Ki 13:21 and the man was thrown into the **g** of Elisha;
22:20 and you shall be gathered to your **g** in peace;
2Ch 34:28 and you shall be gathered to your **g** in peace;
Job 3:22 and are glad when they find the **g?**
5:26 You shall come to your **g** in ripe old age,
10:19 carried from the womb to the **g.**
17: 1 my days are extinct, the **g** is ready for me.
21:32 When they are carried to the **g,**
Ps 49: 9 one should live on forever and never see the **g.**
49:14 straight to the **g** they descend,
88: 5 like the slain that lie in the **g,**
88:11 Is your steadfast love declared in the **g,**
SS 8: 6 for love is strong as death, passion fierce as the **g.**
Isa 14:19 away from your **g,** like loathsome carrion,
53: 9 They made his **g** with the wicked and his tomb
Jer 20:17 so my mother would have been my **g,**
Eze 32:23 Its company is all around its **g,** all of them killed,
32:24 Elam is there, and all its hordes around its **g;**
Na 1:14 I will make your **g,** for you are worthless."
Tob 2: 7 sun had set, I went and dug a **g** and buried him.
4: 4 when she dies, bury her beside me in the same **g.**
4:17 Place your bread on the **g** of the righteous,
6:15 and mother's life down to their **g,** grieving
8: 9 and they went and dug a **g,**
8:11 When they had finished digging the **g,**
8:18 Then he ordered his servants to fill in the **g**
Sir 30:18 like offerings of food placed upon a **g.**
2Mc 1:11 by God out of **g** dangers we thank him greatly
2Es 2:23 commit them to the **g** and mark it,
5:35 Or why did not my mother's womb become my **g,**

GRAVECLOTHES (KJV) See STRIPS OF CLOTH

GRAVED, GRAVEN (KJV) See CARVED, ENGRAVED, IDOL, IMAGE

GRAVEL (2)

Pr 20:17 but afterward the mouth will be full of **g.**
La 3:16 He has made my teeth grind on **g,**

GRAVES‡ (22) [GRAVE]

Ex 14:11 "Was it because there were no **g** in Egypt
2Sa 19:37 near the **g** of my father and my mother.
2Ki 23: 6 beat it to dust and threw the dust of it upon the **g**
2Ch 34: 4 he made dust of them and scattered it over the **g**
Ne 2: 3 when the city, the place of my ancestors' **g,**
2: 5 to the city of my ancestors' **g,**
3:16 repaired from a point opposite the **g** of David,
Ps 5: 9 throats are open **g;** they flatter with their tongues.
49:11 Their **g** are their homes forever,
Eze 32:22 and all its company, their **g** all around it,
32:23 Their **g** are set in the uttermost parts of the Pit.
32:25 their **g** all around it, all of them uncircumcised,
32:26 their **g** all around them, all of them uncircumcised,
37:12 I am going to open your **g,**
37:12 and bring you up from your **g,** O my people;
37:13 when I open your **g,** and bring you up from your **g,**
Mt 23:29 the prophets and decorate the **g** of the righteous,
Lk 11:44 For you are like unmarked **g,**
Jn 5:28 when all who are in their **g** will hear his voice
Ro 3:13 "Their throats are opened **g;**
Wis 19: 3 and were lamenting at the **g** of their dead,

GRAVING See Index to Footnotes

GRAVITY (1)

Tit 2: 7 and in your teaching show integrity, **g,**

GRAVITY (KJV) See also RESPECTFUL

GRAY (20) [GRAY-HAIRED, GRAY-HEADED]

Ge 42:38 you would bring down my **g** hairs with sorrow
44:29 you will bring down my **g** hairs in sorrow
44:31 the **g** hairs of your servant our father with sorrow
Dt 32:25 nursing child and old **g** head.
1Sa 12: 2 I am old and **g,** but my sons are with you.
1Ki 2: 6 do not let his **g** head go down to Sheol in peace.
2: 9 to do to him, and you must bring his **g** head down
Ps 71:18 So even to old age and **g** hairs, O God,
Pr 16:31 **G** hair is a crown of glory;
20:29 but the beauty of the aged is their **g** hair.
Isa 46: 4 even when you turn **g** I will carry you.
Hos 7: 9 **g** hairs are sprinkled upon him,
Zec 6: 3 and the fourth chariot dappled **g** horses.
Wis 2:10 let us not spare the widow or regard the **g** hairs of
4: 9 but understanding is **g** hair for anyone,
Sir 6:18 when you have **g** hair you will still find wisdom.
2Mc 6:23 of his old age and the **g** hairs that he had reached
15:13 distinguished by his **g** hair and dignity,
4Mc 5: 7 for I respect your age and your **g** hairs.
7:15 O man of blessed age and of venerable **g** hair and

GRAY-HAIRED (2) [GRAY, HAIR]

Job 15:10 The **g** and the aged are on our side,
Sir 25: 4 How attractive is sound judgment in the **g,**

GRAY-HEADED (1) [GRAY, HEAD]

3Mc 4: 5 For a multitude of **g** old men,

GRAYHEADED (KJV) See GRAY, GRAY-HAIRED

GRAZE (7) [GRAZED, GRAZING]

Ex 22: 5 or lets livestock loose to **g** in someone else's field,
34: 3 not let flocks or herds **g** in front of that mountain."
Isa 5:17 Then the lambs shall **g** as in their pasture,
11: 7 The cow and the bear shall **g,**
14:30 The firstborn of the poor will **g,**
27:10 the calves **g** there, there they lie down,
30:23 On that day your cattle will **g** in broad pastures;

GRAZED (2) [GRAZE]

Ge 41: 2 and they **g** in the reed grass.
Ex 22: 5 someone causes a field or vineyard to be **g** over,

GRAZING (1) [GRAZE]

Eze 34:14 there they shall lie down in good **g** land,

GREASE (KJV) See GROSS

GREAT‡ (1097) [GREATER, GREATEST, GREATLY, GREATNESS]

A. GREAT MULTITUDE (20)
B. GREAT POWER (20)
C. GREAT KING (18)
D. GREAT THINGS (15)
E. GREAT CITY (14)
F. GREAT JOY (13)
G. GREAT SEA (12)
H. GREAT CROWD (11)
I. GREAT DISTRESS (9)
J. GREAT *GOD (7)

Ge 1:16 God made the two **g** lights—
1:21 the **g** sea monsters and every living creature
6: 5 the wickedness of humankind was **g** in the earth,
7:11 that day all the fountains of the **g** deep burst forth,
10:12 Nineveh and Calah; that is the **g** city. E
12: 2 I will make of you a **g** nation, and I will bless you,
and make your name **g,**
12:17 and his house with **g** plagues because of Sarai,
13: 6 for their possessions were so **g** that they could
13:13 **g** sinners against the LORD.
15: 1 your reward shall be very **g.**"
15:14 afterward they shall come out with **g** possessions.
15:18 from the river of Egypt to the **g** river,
17:20 and I will make him a **g** nation.
18:18 that Abraham shall become a **g** and mighty nation,
18:20 "How **g** is the outcry against Sodom
19:11 both small and **g,** so that they were unable to find
19:13 the outcry against its people has become **g** before
19:19 you have shown me **g** kindness in saving my life;
20: 9 that you have brought such **g** guilt on me
21: 8 a **g** feast on the day that Isaac was weaned.
21:18 for I will make a **g** nation of him."
26:14 of flocks and herds, and a **g** household,
27:34 he cried out with an exceedingly **g** and bitter cry,
36: 7 For their possessions were too **g** for them
39: 9 How then could I do this **g** wickedness,
41:29 of **g** plenty throughout all the land of Egypt.
46: 3 for I will make of you a **g** nation there.
48:19 also shall become a people, and he also shall be **g.**
50: 9 It was a very **g** company.
50:10 a very **g** and sorrowful lamentation;
Ex 3: 3 "I must turn aside and look at this **g** sight,
7: 4 out of the land of Egypt by **g** acts of judgment.
8:24 and **g** swarms of flies came into the house
11: 3 Moses himself was a man of **g** importance in
12:38 and livestock in **g** numbers, both flocks and herds.
14:10 In **g** fear the Israelites cried out to the LORD.
14:31 Israel saw the **g** work that the LORD did against
32:10 and of you I will make a **g** nation."
32:11 of Egypt with **g** power and with a mighty hand? B
32:21 that you have brought so **g** a sin upon them?"
32:30 "You have sinned a **g** sin.
32:31 "Alas, this people has sinned a **g** sin;
Lev 11:17 the little owl, the cormorant, the **g** owl,
11:29 the mouse, the **g** lizard according to its kind,
19:15 not be partial to the poor or defer to the **g:**
Nu 11:33 the LORD struck the people with a very **g** plague.
13:32 and all the people that we saw in it are of **g** size.
14:17 of the LORD be **g** in the way that you promised
22: 3 Moab was in **g** dread of the people,
22:17 surely do you **g** honor, and whatever you say
32: 1 and the Gadites owned a very **g** number of cattle.
34: 6 you shall have the **G** Sea and its coast; G
34: 7 from the **G** Sea you shall mark out your line G
Dt 1: 7 as far as the **g** river, the river Euphrates.
1:17 hear out the small and the **g** alike;
1:19 and went through all that **g** and terrible wilderness
2: 7 he knows your going through this **g** wilderness.
3: 5 double gates, and bars, besides a **g** many villages.
4: 6 this **g** nation is a wise and discerning people!"
4: 7 For what other **g** nation has a god so near to it as

Dt 4: 8 And what other g nation has statutes
4:32 has anything so g as this ever happened or has its
4:36 On earth he showed you his g fire,
4:37 of Egypt with his own presence, by his g power, B
5:25 For this g fire will consume us;
6:22 before our eyes g and awesome signs and wonders
7:19 the g trials that your eyes saw,
7:21 who is present with you, is a g and awesome God.
7:23 and throw them into g panic,
8:15 who led you through the g and terrible wilderness,
9: 1 g cities, fortified to the heavens,
9:29 by your g power and by your outstretched arm." B
10:17 the g God, mighty and awesome, J
10:21 who has done for you these g and awesome things
11: 7 for it is your own eyes that have seen every g deed
14:16 the little owl and the g owl, the water hen
14:24 distance is so g that you are unable to transport it,
16: 3 you came out of the land of Egypt in g haste,
17:17 and gold he must not acquire in g quantity
18:16 or ever again see this g fire, I will die."
19: 6 But if the distance is too g,
26: 5 few in number, and there he became a g nation,
29: 3 the g trials that your eyes saw, the signs, and those g wonders.
29:24 What caused this g display of anger?"
29:28 fury, and g wrath, and cast them into another land,
Jos 1: 4 and the Lebanon as far as the g river,
1: 4 to the G Sea in the west shall be your territory. G
6: 5 then all the people shall shout with a g shout;
6:20 they raised a g shout, and the wall fell down flat;
7: 9 Then what will you do for your g name?"
7:26 a g heap of stones that remains to this day.
8:29 and raised over it a g heap of stones,
9: 1 in the lowland all along the coast of the G Sea G
9:24 so we were in g fear for our lives because of you,
10:10 who inflicted a g slaughter on them at Gibeon,
10:20 a very g slaughter on them,
11: 4 They came out, with all their troops, a g army,
11: 8 as far as G Sidon and Misrephoth-maim,
14:12 how the Anakim were there, with g fortified cities;
15:47 the Wadi of Egypt, and the G Sea with its coast. G
17:17 a numerous people, and have g power; B
19:28 Rehob, Hammon, Kanah, as far as G Sidon;
22: 8 and iron, and with a g quantity of clothing;
22:10 an altar by the Jordan, an altar of g size.
23: 4 from the Jordan to the G Sea in the west. G
23: 9 For the LORD has driven out before you g
24:17 and who did those g signs in our sight.
Jdg 2: 7 the g work that the LORD had done for Israel.
2:15 and they were in g distress. I
5:15 the clans of Reuben there were g searchings
5:16 the clans of Reuben there were g searchings
11:35 you have become the cause of g trouble to me.
15: 8 down hip and thigh with g slaughter;
15:18 "You have granted this g victory by the hand
16: 5 and find out what makes his strength so g,
16: 6 "Please tell me what makes your strength so g,
16:15 not told me what makes your strength so g."
16:23 a g sacrifice to their god Dagon, and to rejoice;
1Sa 1:16 for I have been speaking out of my g anxiety
2:17 the sin of the young men was very g in the sight of
4: 6 "What does this g shouting in the camp of
4:10 There was a very g slaughter,
4:17 and there has also been a g slaughter among
5: 9 against the city, causing a very g panic;
6: 9 then it is he who has done us this g harm;
6:18 The g stone, beside which they set down the ark of
6:19 because the LORD had made a g slaughter
12:16 Now therefore take your stand and see this g thing
12:17 that you have done in the sight of the LORD is g
12:22 not cast away his people, for his g name's sake,
12:24 for consider what g things he has done for you. D
14:15 and it became a very g panic.
14:20 so that there was very g confusion.
14:30 slaughter among the Philistines has not been g."
14:45 who has accomplished this g victory in Israel?
15:22 "Has the LORD as g delight in burnt offerings
18:15 When Saul saw that he had g success,
18:30 so that his fame became very g.
19: 1 But Saul's son Jonathan took g delight in David.
19: 5 the LORD brought about a g victory for all Israel.
19:22 He came to the g well that is in Secu;
20: 2 either g or small without disclosing it to me;
26:13 with a g distance between them.
26:21 I have been a fool, and have made a g mistake."
28:15 Saul answered, "I am in g distress, I
30: 2 and all who were in it, both small and g;
30: 6 David was in g danger;
30:16 the g amount of spoil they had taken from the land
30:19 Nothing was missing, whether small or g,
2Sa 3:38 a prince and a g man has fallen this day in Israel?
7: 9 and I will make for you a g name, like the name of the g ones of the earth.
7:19 also of your servant's house for a g while to come.
7:22 Therefore you are g, O LORD God;
7:23 doing g and awesome things for them,
8: 8 King David took a g amount of bronze.
12:30 the spoil of the city, a very g amount.
13:15 Amnon was seized with a very g loathing for her;
18: 7 and the slaughter there was g on that day,
18: 9 the mule went under the thick branches of a g oak.
18:17 threw him into a g pit in the forest, and raised over him a very g heap of stones.
18:29 I saw a g tumult, but I do not know what it was."
21:20 where there was a man of g size,
22:36 and your help has made me g.
23:10 The LORD brought about a g victory that day.
2Sa 23:12 and the LORD brought about a g victory.
23:20 a valiant warrior from Kabzeel, a doer of g deeds;
24:14 Then David said to Gad, "I am in g distress; I
24:14 into the hand of the LORD, for his mercy is g;
1Ki 1:40 playing on pipes and rejoicing with g joy, F
3: 6 "You have shown g and steadfast love
3: 6 you have kept for him this g and steadfast love,
3: 8 a g people, so numerous they cannot be numbered
3: 9 for who can govern this your g people?"
4:13 sixty g cities with walls and bronze bars);
4:29 God gave Solomon very g wisdom, discernment,
5: 7 to David a wise son to be over this g people."
5:17 At the king's command, they quarried out g,
7: 9 and from outside to the g court.
7:12 The g court had three courses of dressed stone
8:42 —for they shall hear of your g name,
8:65 a g assembly, people from Lebo-hamath to
10: 2 She came to Jerusalem with a very g retinue,
10:10 a g quantity of spices, and precious stones;
10:11 a g quantity of almug wood and precious stones.
10:18 The king also made a g ivory throne,
11:19 Hadad found g favor in the sight of Pharaoh,
19:11 a g wind, so strong that it was splitting mountains
20:13 Have you seen all this g multitude? A
20:21 and defeated the Arameans with a g slaughter.
20:28 I will give all this g multitude into your hand, A
22:31 "Fight with no one small or g,
2Ki 3:27 And g wrath came upon Israel,
5: 1 was a g man and in high favor with his master,
6:14 So he sent horses and chariots there and a g army;
6:23 So he prepared for them a g feast;
6:25 famine in Samaria became so g that
7: 6 and of horses, the sound of a g army,
8: 4 "Tell me all the g things that Elisha has done." D
8:13 that he should do this g thing?"
10:19 for I have a g sacrifice to offer to Baal;
12:10 that there was a g deal of money in the chest,
16:15 "Upon the g altar offer the morning burnt offering,
17:21 the LORD and made them commit g sin.
17:36 with g power and with an outstretched arm; B
18:17 and the Rabshakeh with a g army from Lachish
18:19 Thus says the g king, the king of Assyria: C
18:28 Hear the word of the g king, the king of Assyria! C
22:13 for g is the wrath of the LORD that is kindled
23: 2 the prophets, and all the people, both small and g;
23:26 not turn from the fierceness of his g wrath,
25: 9 every g house he burned down.
1Ch 11:14 and the LORD saved them by a g victory.
11:22 a valiant man of Kabzeel, a doer of g deeds;
11:23 And he killed an Egyptian, a man of g stature,
12:22 until there was a g army, like an army of God.
16:25 For g is the LORD, and greatly to be praised;
17: 8 like the name of the g ones of the earth.
17:17 also spoken of your servant's house for a g while
17:19 you have done all these g deeds,
17:19 making known all these g things. D
17:21 for yourself a name for g and terrible things,
20: 2 the booty of the city, a very g amount.
20: 6 where there was a man of g size,
21:13 Then David said to Gad, "I am in g distress; I
21:13 the hand of the LORD, for his mercy is very g;
22: 3 David also provided g stores of iron for nails for
22: 4 for the Sidonians and Tyrians brought g quantities
22: 5 So David provided materials in g quantity
22: 8 have shed much blood and have waged g wars;
22:14 With g pains I have provided for the house of
25: 8 And they cast lots for their duties, small and g,
26: 6 for they were men of g ability.
26:13 small and g alike, for their gates.
26:31 and men of g ability among them were found
29: 1 is young and inexperienced, and the work is g;
29: 2 besides g quantities of onyx and stones for setting,
29:12 in your hand to make g and to give strength to all.
29:22 before the LORD on that day with g joy. F
2Ch 1: 1 with him and made him exceedingly g.
1: 8 "You have shown g and steadfast love
1:10 for who can rule this g people of yours?"
2: 5 The house that I am about to build will be g,
2: 9 house I am about to build will be g and wonderful.
4: 9 He made the court of the priests, and the g court,
4:18 Solomon made all these things in g quantities,
6:32 come from a distant land because of your g name,
7: 8 and all Israel with him, a very g congregation,
9: 1 having a very g retinue and camels bearing spices
9: 9 a very g quantity of spices, and precious stones:
9:17 The king also made a g ivory throne,
13: 8 a g multitude and have with you the golden calves A
13:17 and his army defeated them with g slaughter;
14:13 The people of Judah carried away a g quantity
15: 5 for g disturbances afflicted all the inhabitants of
15: 9 for g numbers had deserted to him from Israel
16:14 and they made a very g fire in his honor.
17: 5 and he had g riches and honor.
17:13 He carried out g works in the cities of Judah.
18: 1 Now Jehoshaphat had g riches and honor;
18:30 "Fight with no one small or g,
20: 2 A g multitude is coming against you from Edom, A
20:12 this g multitude that is coming against us. A
20:15 'Do not fear or be dismayed at this g multitude; A
20:25 they found livestock in g numbers, goods,
21:14 the LORD will bring a g plague on your people,
21:19 and he died in g agony.
24:24 LORD delivered into their hand a very g army,
28: 5 who defeated him and took captive a g number
28: 5 who defeated him with g slaughter.
28:13 For our guilt is already g,
29:35 Besides the g number of burnt offerings there was
2Ch 30: 5 they had not kept it in g numbers as prescribed.
30:21 of unleavened bread seven days with g gladness;
30:24 The priests sanctified themselves in g numbers.
30:26 There was g joy in Jerusalem, F
31:10 so that we have this g supply left over."
32: 4 A g many people were gathered,
32:27 Hezekiah had very g riches and honor;
32:29 for God had given him very g possessions.
33:14 and raised it to a very g height.
34:21 wrath of the LORD that is poured out on us is g,
34:30 all the people both g and small;
36:16 of the LORD against his people became so g
Ezr 3:11 with a g shout when they praised the LORD,
4:10 the g and noble Osnappar deported and settled in
5: 8 to the house of the g God. J
5:11 which a g king of Israel built and finished. C
9:13 upon us for our evil deeds and for our g guilt,
10: 1 a very g assembly of men, women,
Ne 1: 3 who escaped captivity are in g trouble and shame;
1: 5 the g and awesome God who keeps covenant
1:10 by your g power and your strong hand. B
3:27 the g projecting tower as far as the wall of Ophel.
4:14 Remember the LORD, who is g and awesome,
4:19 "The work is g and widely spread out,
5: 1 Now there was a g outcry of the people and
5: 7 And I called a g assembly to deal with them,
6: 3 "I am doing a g work and I cannot come down.
8: 6 Then Ezra blessed the LORD, the g God, J
8:12 and to send portions and to make g rejoicing,
8:17 And there was very g rejoicing.
9:18 and had committed g blasphemies,
9:19 you in your g mercies did not forsake them in
9:25 and delighted themselves in your g goodness.
9:26 and they committed g blasphemies.
9:27 your g mercies you gave them saviors who saved
9:31 in your g mercies you did not make an end
9:32 the g and mighty and awesome God,
9:35 and in the g goodness you bestowed on them,
9:37 at their pleasure, and we are in g distress." I
12:31 and appointed two g companies that gave thanks
12:43 They offered g sacrifices that day and rejoiced,
12:43 for God had made them rejoice with g joy; F
13:27 to you and do all this g evil and act treacherously
Est 1: 4 while he displayed the g wealth of his kingdom
1: 5 both g and small, a banquet lasting for seven days,
2:18 Then the king gave a g banquet to all his officials
4: 3 there was g mourning among the Jews,
8:15 with a g golden crown and a mantle of fine linen
Job 1:19 and suddenly a g wind came across the desert,
2:13 for they saw that his suffering was very g.
3:19 The small and the g are there,
5: 9 He does g things and unsearchable, D
8: 2 and the words of your mouth be a g wind?
8: 7 your latter days will be very g.
9:10 who does g things beyond understanding, D
12:23 He makes nations g, then destroys them;
22: 5 Is not your wickedness g?
31:25 if I have rejoiced because my wealth was g,
31:34 because I stood in g fear of the multitude,
36:26 Surely God is g, and we do not know him;
37: 5 he does g things that we cannot comprehend. D
37:23 he is g in power and justice,
38:21 and the number of your days is g!
39:11 Will you depend on it because its strength is g,
40:19 "It is the first of the g acts of God—
Ps 12: 3 the tongue that makes g boasts,
14: 5 There they shall be in g terror,
18:35 your help has made me g.
18:50 G triumphs he gives to his king,
19:11 in keeping them there is g reward.
19:13 and innocent of g transgression.
21: 5 His glory is g through your help;
22:25 From you comes my praise in the g congregation;
25:11 O LORD, pardon my guilt, for it is g.
26:12 in the g congregation I will bless the LORD.
33:16 A king is not saved by his g army;
33:16 a warrior is not delivered by his g strength.
33:17 and by its g might it cannot save.
35:18 Then I will thank you in the g congregation;
35:27 "G is the LORD, who delights in the welfare of his
36: 6 your judgments are like the g deep;
40: 9 of deliverance in the g congregation;
40:10 and your faithfulness from the g congregation.
40:16 say continually, "G is the LORD!"
47: 2 is awesome, a g king over all the earth. C
48: 1 G is the LORD and greatly to be praised in
48: 2 in the far north, the city of the g King. C
53: 5 There they shall be in g terror,
66: 3 your g power, your enemies cringe before you. B
68:11 g is the company of those who bore the tidings:
68:26 "Bless God in the g congregation,
70: 4 who love your salvation say evermore, "God is g!"
71:19 You who have done g things, O God, D
76: 1 In Judah God is known, his name is g in Israel.
77:13 What god is so g as our God?
79:11 to your g power preserve those doomed B
86:10 For you are g and do wondrous things;
86:13 For g is your steadfast love toward me;
89: 7 g and awesome above all that are around him?
90:11 Your wrath is as g as the fear that is due you.
92: 5 How g are your works, O LORD!
95: 3 For the LORD is a g God, J
95: 3 and a g King above all gods. C
96: 4 For g is the LORD, and greatly to be praised;
99: 2 The LORD is g in Zion;
99: 3 Let them praise your g and awesome name.
103:11 g is his steadfast love toward those who fear him;

Ps 104: 1 O LORD my God, you are very g.
104:25 Yonder is the sea, g and wide,
104:25 living things both small and g.
106:21 their Savior, who had done g things in Egypt, D
109:30 With my mouth I will give g thanks to
111: 2 G are the works of the LORD,
115:13 the LORD, both small and g.
117: 2 For g is his steadfast love toward us,
119:156 G is your mercy, O LORD;
119:162 I rejoice at your word like one who finds g spoil.
119:165 G peace have those who love your law;
126: 2 "The LORD has done g things for them." D
126: 3 LORD has done g things for us, and we rejoiced. D
130: 7 and with him is g power to redeem. B
131: 1 with things too g and too marvelous for me.
135: 5 For I know that the LORD is g;
136: 4 who alone does g wonders,
136: 7 the g lights, for his steadfast love endures forever;
136:17 who struck down g kings,
138: 5 for g is the glory of the LORD.
145: 3 G is the LORD, and greatly to be praised;
147: 5 G is our Lord, and abundant in power;
Pr 5:23 and because of their g folly they are lost.
6:35 and refuses a bribe no matter how g.
13: 7 others pretend to be poor, yet have g wealth.
14:29 Whoever is slow to anger has g understanding,
15:16 a little with the fear of the LORD than g treasure
18:16 A gift opens doors; it gives access to the g.
22: 1 A good name is to be chosen rather than g riches,
25: 6 the king's presence or stand in the place of the g;
28:12 When the righteous triumph, there is g glory,
Ecc 1:16 I said to myself, "I have acquired g wisdom,
1:16 and my mind has had g experience of wisdom
2: 4 I made g works; I built houses
2: 7 I also had g possessions of herds and flocks,
2: 9 So I became g and surpassed all who were
2:21 This also is vanity and a g evil.
9:13 and it seemed g to me.
9:14 A g king came against it and besieged it, C
9:14 building g siegeworks against it.
10: 4 for calmness will undo g offenses.
10: 5 as g an error as if it proceeded from the ruler:
SS 2: 3 With g delight I sat in his shadow,
Isa 9: 2 in darkness have seen a g light;
12: 6 for g in your midst is the Holy One of Israel.
13: 4 a tumult on the mountains as of a g multitude! A
16:14 in spite of all its g multitude; A
27: 1 and g and strong sword will punish Leviathan
27:13 And on that day a g trumpet will be blown,
29: 6 of hosts with thunder and earthquake and g noise,
30:25 on a day of the g slaughter, when the towers fall.
32: 2 like the shade of a g rock in a weary land.
34: 6 a g slaughter in the land of Edom.
36: 2 to King Hezekiah at Jerusalem, with a g army.
36: 4 Thus says the g king, the king of Assyria: C
36:13 "Hear the words of the g king, C
38:17 it was for my welfare that I had g bitterness;
40:26 because he is g in strength, mighty in power,
47: 9 in spite of your many sorceries and the g power B
51:10 the waters of the g deep;
53:12 Therefore I will allot him a portion with the g,
54: 7 but with g compassion I will gather you.
54:13 and g shall be the prosperity of your children.
56:12 tomorrow will be like today, g beyond measure."
63: 1 marching in his g might?"
63: 7 and the g favor to the house of Israel
Jer 4: 6 from the north, and a g destruction.
5: 6 transgressions are many, their apostasies are g.
5:27 therefore they have become g and rich,
6: 1 for evil looms out of the north, and g destruction.
6:22 the land of the north, a g nation is stirring from
10: 6 you are g, and your name is g in might.
10:22 a g commotion from the land of the north to make
11:16 with the roar of a g tempest he will set fire to it,
13: 9 the pride of Judah and the g pride of Jerusalem.
16: 6 Both g and small shall die in this land;
16:10 the LORD pronounced all this g evil against us?
20:17 been my grave, and her womb forever g.
21: 5 in anger, in fury, and in g wrath.
21: 6 they shall die of a g pestilence.
22: 8 the LORD dealt in this way with that g city?" E
25:14 For many nations and g kings shall make slaves
25:32 and a g tempest is stirring from the farthest parts
26:19 But we are about to bring g disaster on ourselves!"
27: 5 It is I who by my g power B
27: 7 and g kings shall make him their slave.
28: 8 against many countries and g kingdoms.
30: 7 that day is so g there is none like it;
30:14 your guilt is g, because your sins are so numerous.
30:15 your guilt is g, because your sins are so numerous,
31: 8 a g company, they shall return here.
32:17 by your g power and by your outstretched arm! B
32:18 O g and mighty God whose name is the LORD
32:19 g in counsel and mighty in deed;
32:21 and outstretched arm, and with g terror;
32:37 in my anger and my wrath and in g indignation;
32:42 Just as I have brought all this g disaster
33: 3 and will tell you g and hidden things that you have
36: 7 for g is the anger and wrath that
40:12 and summer fruits in g abundance.
41:12 They came upon him at the g pool that is
44: 7 Why are you doing such g harm to yourselves,
44:15 and all the women who stood by, a g assembly,
44:26 Lo, I swear by my g name, says the LORD,
45: 5 And you, do you seek g things for yourself? D
48: 3 "Desolation and g destruction!"
50: 9 a company of g nations from the land of the north;
Jer 50:22 noise of battle is in the land, and g destruction!
51:54 A g crashing from the land of the Chaldeans!
52:13 every g house he burned down.
La 1: 1 she that was g among the nations!
3:23 they are new every morning; g is your faithfulness.
Eze 1: 4 a g cloud with brightness around it
8: 6 the g abominations that the house
9: 9 of the house of Israel and Judah is exceedingly g;
13:11 be a deluge of rain, g hailstones will fall,
17: 3 A g eagle, with g wings and long pinions,
17: 7 another g eagle, with g wings and much plumage.
17:17 Pharaoh with his mighty army and g company will
21:14 A sword for g slaughter—
24: 9 I will even make the pile g.
25:17 I will execute g vengeance on them
26: 7 chariots, cavalry, and a g and powerful army.
26:19 and the g waters cover you,
27:12 with you out of the abundance of your g wealth;
27:18 because of your g wealth of every kind—
28: 5 By your g wisdom in trade
29: 3 the g dragon sprawling in the midst of its channels,
30:16 Pelusium shall be in g agony;
31: 3 and of g height, its top among the clouds.
31: 6 and in its shade all g nations lived.
36:23 I will sanctify my g name,
38: 4 a g company, all of them with shield and buckler,
38:13 to seize a g amount of booty?"
38:15 all of them riding on horses, a g horde,
38:19 On that day there shall be a g shaking in the land
39:17 a g sacrificial feast on the mountains of Israel,
47: 7 of the river a g many trees on the one side and on
47:10 its fish will be of a g many kinds,
47:10 like the fish of the G Sea. G
47:15 from the G Sea by way of Hethlon G
47:19 there along the Wadi of Egypt to the G Sea. G
47:20 the G Sea shall be the boundary to G
48:28 there along the Wadi of Egypt to the G Sea. G
Da 2: 6 from me gifts and rewards and g honor.
2:10 In fact no king, however g and powerful,
2:31 there was a g statue.
2:35 that struck the statue became a g mountain
2:45 The g God has informed the king what shall J
2:48 the king promoted Daniel, gave him many g gifts,
4: 3 How g are his signs, how mighty his wonders!
4:10 at the center of the earth, and its height was g.
4:11 The tree grew g and strong,
4:20 The tree that you saw, which grew g and strong,
4:22 You have grown g and strong.
5: 1 King Belshazzar made a g festival for a thousand
7: 2 the four winds of heaven stirring up the g sea, G
7: 3 and four g beasts came up out of the sea,
7: 7 It had g iron teeth and was devouring,
7:17 "As for these four g beasts,
8: 8 Then the male goat grew exceedingly g;
8: 8 at the height of its power, the g horn was broken,
8: 9 which grew exceedingly g toward the south,
8:21 and the g horn between its eyes is the first king.
8:25 and in his own mind he shall be g.
9: 4 saying, "Ah, Lord, g and awesome God,
9:12 upon us a calamity so g that what has been done
9:18 but on the ground of your g mercies.
10: 1 The word was true, and it concerned a g conflict.
10: 4 I was standing on the bank of the g river (that is,
10: 7 though a g trembling fell upon them,
10: 8 So I was left alone to see this g vision.
11: 3 who shall rule with g dominion and take action
11:10 and assemble a multitude of g forces,
11:11 who shall muster a g multitude, which shall, A
11:13 after some years he shall advance with a g army
11:25 against the king of the south with a g army,
11:28 He shall return to his land with g wealth,
11:44 with g fury to bring ruin and complete destruction
12: 1 "At that time Michael, the g prince,
Hos 1: 2 for the land commits g whoredom by forsaking
1:11 for g shall be the day of Jezreel.
5:13 and sent to the g king. C
9: 7 Because of your g iniquity, your hostility is g.
10: 6 be carried to Assyria as tribute to the g king. C
10:15 O Bethel, because of your g wickedness.
Joel 2: 2 upon the mountains a g and powerful army comes;
2:11 Truly the day of the LORD is g;
2:20 Surely he has done g things! D
2:21 for the LORD has done g things! D
2:25 the destroyer, and the cutter, my g army,
2:31 before the g and terrible day of the LORD comes.
3:13 The vats overflow, for their wickedness is g.
Am 3: 9 and see what g tumults are within it,
3:15 and the g houses shall come to an end,
5:12 and how g are your sins—
6: 2 from there go to Hamath the g;
6:11 and the g house shall be shattered to bits,
7: 4 it devoured the g deep and was eating up the land.
8: 5 We will make the ephah small and the shekel g,
Jnh 1: 2 that g city, and cry out against it; E
1: 4 But the LORD hurled a g wind upon the sea,
1:12 of me that this g storm has come upon you."
3: 2 go to Nineveh, that g city, E
3: 5 they proclaimed a fast, and everyone, g and small,
4:11 be concerned about Nineveh, that g city, E
Mic 5: 4 for now he shall be g to the ends of the earth;
Na 1: 3 The LORD is slow to anger but g in power,
Zep 1:14 The g day of the LORD is near,
Zec 4: 7 What are you, O g mountain?
7:12 Therefore g wrath came from the LORD of hosts.
8: 2 I am jealous for Zion with g jealousy,
8: 2 and I am jealous for her with g wrath.
8: 4 each with staff in hand because of their g age.
Zec 12:11 that day the mourning in Jerusalem will be as g as
14:13 On that day a g panic from the LORD shall fall
14:14 gold, silver, and garments in g abundance.
Mal 1: 5 "G is the LORD beyond the borders of Israel!"
1:11 to its setting my name is g among the nations,
1:11 for my name is g among the nations,
1:14 for I am a g King, says the LORD of hosts, C
4: 5 before the g and terrible day of the LORD comes.
Mt 4:16 the people who sat in darkness have seen a g light,
4:25 And g crowds followed him from Galilee,
5:12 for your reward is g in heaven,
5:19 and teaches them will be called g in the kingdom
5:35 or by Jerusalem, for it is the city of the g King. C
6:23 the light in you is darkness, how g is the darkness!
7:27 and it fell—and g was its fall!"
8: 1 down from the mountain, g crowds followed him;
8:18 Now when Jesus saw g crowds around him,
8:24 g that the boat was being swamped by the waves;
13: 2 Such g crowds gathered around him that he got
13:46 on finding one pearl of g value,
14:14 When he went ashore, he saw a g crowd; H
15:28 Jesus answered her, "Woman, g is your faith!
15:30 G crowds came to him, bringing with them
15:33 to get enough bread in the desert to feed so g
16:21 to Jerusalem and undergo g suffering at the hands
18: 6 if a g millstone were fastened around your neck
20:25 and their g ones are tyrants over them.
20:26 but whoever wishes to be g among you must
24:21 For at that time there will be g suffering,
24:24 and false prophets will appear and produce g signs
24:30 on the clouds of heaven' with power and g glory.
27:19 for today I have suffered a g deal because of
27:60 a g stone to the door of the tomb and went away.
28: 2 And suddenly there was a g earthquake;
28: 8 they left the tomb quickly with fear and g joy, F
Mk 3: 7 and a g multitude from Galilee followed him; A
3: 8 they came to him in g numbers from Judea,
4:37 A g windstorm arose, and the waves beat into
4:41 And they were filled with g awe and said
5:11 on the hillside a g herd of swine was feeding;
5:21 a g crowd gathered around him; H
6:34 As he went ashore, he saw a g crowd; H
8: 1 again a g crowd without anything to eat, H
8: 3 and some of them have come from a g distance."
8:31 that the Son of Man must undergo g suffering,
9:14 they saw a g crowd around them, H
9:42 if a g millstone were hung around your neck
10:42 and their g ones are tyrants over them.
10:43 but whoever wishes to become g among you must
13: 2 Jesus asked him, "Do you see these g buildings?
13:26 'the Son of Man coming in clouds' with g power B
Lk 1:15 for he will be g in the sight of the Lord.
1:32 be g, and will be called the Son of the Most High,
1:49 for the Mighty One has done g things for me, D
1:58 that the Lord had shown his g mercy to her,
2:10 I am bringing you good news of g joy for all F
2:36 She was of a g age,
2:48 and I have been searching for you in g anxiety."
5:29 Then Levi gave a g banquet for him in his house;
6:17 a g crowd of his disciples and a great multitude H
6:17 a great crowd of his disciples and a g multitude A
6:23 for surely your reward is g in heaven;
6:35 Your reward will be g, and you will be children of
6:49 and g was the ruin of that house."
7:16 saying, "A g prophet has risen among us!"
7:47 hence she has shown g love.
8: 4 When a g crowd gathered and people from town H
8:37 for they were seized with g fear.
9:22 "The Son of Man must undergo g suffering,
9:37 down from the mountain, a g crowd met him. H
14:16 "Someone gave a g dinner and invited many.
16:26 between you and us a g chasm has been fixed,
21:11 be g earthquakes, and in various places famines
21:11 and there will be dreadful portents and g signs
21:23 For there will be g distress on the earth and I
21:27 in a cloud' with power and g glory.
22:44 ⟦his sweat became like g drops of blood falling⟧
23:27 A g number of the people followed him,
24:52 and returned to Jerusalem with g joy; F
Jn 6:10 Now there was a g deal of grass in the place;
7:37 On the last day of the festival, the g day,
12: 9 g crowd of the Jews learned that he was there, H
12:12 the g crowd that had come to the festival heard H
19:31 because that sabbath was a day of g solemnity.
Ac 2:20 the coming of the Lord's g and glorious day.
4:33 With g power the apostles gave their testimony B
4:33 and g grace was upon them all.
5: 5 And g fear seized all who heard of it.
5:11 And g fear seized the whole church
5:14 g numbers of both men and women,
5:16 A g number of people would also gather from
6: 7 g many of the priests became obedient to the faith.
6: 8 did g wonders and signs among the people.
7:11 throughout Egypt and Canaan, and g suffering,
8: 8 So there was g joy in that city. F
8: 9 saying that he was someone g.
8:10 "This man is the power of God that is called G."
8:13 the signs and g miracles that took place.
11:21 and a g number became believers and turned to
11:24 And a g many people were brought to the Lord.
11:26 with the church and taught a g many people,
13:17 and made the people g during their stay in the land
14: 1 and spoke in such a way that a g number of
15: 3 and brought g joy to all the believers. F
16:16 of divination and brought her owners a g deal
17: 4 a g many of the devout Greeks and not a few of
19:27 also that the temple of the g goddess Artemis will

Ac 19:28 "**G** is Artemis of the Ephesians!"
19:34 "**G** is Artemis of the Ephesians!"
19:35 of the **g** Artemis and of the statue that fell
21:35 of the mob was so **g** that he had to be carried by
21:40 and when there was a **g** hush,
22: 6 about noon a **g** light from heaven suddenly shone
23: 9 Then a **g** clamor arose, and certain scribes of
25:23 and Bernice came with **g** pomp,
26:22 and so I stand here, testifying to both small and **g**,
28:23 they came to him at his lodgings in **g** numbers.
Ro 9: 2 I have **g** sorrow and unceasing anguish
2Co 3:12 we have such a hope, we act with **g** boldness,
6: 4 through **g** endurance, in afflictions, hardships,
7: 4 I often boast about you; I have **g** pride in you;
8:22 because of his **g** confidence in you.
9:11 be enriched in every way for your **g** generosity,
Eph 1:19 according to the working of his **g** power. B
2: 4 out of the **g** love with which he loved us
5:32 This is a **g** mystery, and I am applying it to Christ
Col 1:27 To them God chose to make known how **g** among
1Th 2: 2 to you the gospel of God in spite of **g** opposition.
2:17 we longed with **g** eagerness to see you face
1Ti 3:13 a good standing for themselves and **g** boldness in
3:16 the mystery of our religion is **g**:
6: 6 there is **g** gain in godliness combined
2Ti 4:14 Alexander the coppersmith did me **g** harm;
Tit 2:13 and the manifestation of the glory of our **g** God J
Heb 2: 3 how can we escape if we neglect so **g** a salvation?
4:14 we have a **g** high priest who has passed through
7: 4 See how **g** he is!
10:21 since we have a **g** priest over the house of God,
10:35 of yours; it brings a **g** reward.
12: 1 we are surrounded by so **g** a cloud of witnesses,
13:20 the **g** shepherd of the sheep,
Jas 3: 5 yet it boasts of **g** exploits.
3: 5 How **g** a forest is set ablaze by a small fire!
1Pe 1: 3 By his **g** mercy he has given us a new birth into
2Pe 1: 4 his precious and very **g** promises,
Jude 1: 6 in deepest darkness for the judgment of the **g** Day.
Rev 2:22 into **g** distress, unless they repent of her doings; I
6: 4 and he was given a **g** sword.
6:12 I looked, and there came a **g** earthquake;
6:17 for the **g** day of their wrath has come,
7: 9 there was a **g** multitude that no one could count, A
7:14 These are they who have come out of the **g** ordeal;
8: 3 he was given a **g** quantity of incense to offer with
8: 8 and something like a **g** mountain,
8:10 and a **g** star fell from heaven, blazing like a torch,
9: 2 the shaft rose smoke like the smoke of a **g** furnace,
9:14 angels who are bound at the **g** river Euphrates."
10: 3 he gave a **g** shout, like a lion roaring.
11: 8 of the **g** city that is prophetically called Sodom E
11:13 At that moment there was a **g** earthquake,
11:17 you have taken your **g** power and begun to reign. B
11:18 and all who fear your name, both small and **g**,
12: 1 A **g** portent appeared in heaven:
12: 3 a **g** red dragon, with seven heads and ten horns,
12: 9 The **g** dragon was thrown down,
12:12 the devil has come down to you, with **g** wrath,
12:14 woman was given the two wings of the **g** eagle,
13: 2 and his throne and **g** authority.
13:13 It performs **g** signs, even making fire come down
13:16 Also it causes all, both small and **g**,
14: 8 followed, saying, "Fallen, fallen is Babylon the **g**!
14:19 and he threw it into the **g** wine press of the wrath
15: 1 I saw another portent in heaven, **g** and amazing:
15: 3 "**G** and amazing are your deeds,
16:12 the **g** river Euphrates, and its water was dried up
16:14 to assemble them for battle on the **g** day of God
16:19 The **g** city was split into three parts, E
16:19 God remembered **g** Babylon and gave her
17: 1 of the **g** whore who is seated on many waters,
17: 5 "Babylon the **g**, mother of whores and
17:18 The woman you saw is the **g** city that rules over E
18: 1 down from heaven, having **g** authority;
18: 2 "Fallen, fallen is Babylon the **g**!
18:10 "Alas, alas, the **g** city, Babylon, the mighty city! E
18:16 alas, the **g** city, clothed in fine linen, E
18:18 "What city was like the **g** city?" E
18:19 "Alas, alas, the **g** city, where all who had ships E
18:21 like a **g** millstone and threw it into the sea, saying,
18:21 "With such violence Babylon the **g** city will E
19: 1 to be the loud voice of a **g** multitude in heaven, A
19: 2 he has judged the **g** whore who corrupted the earth
19: 5 and all who fear him, small and **g**."
19: 6 to be the voice of a **g** multitude, A
19:17 "Come, gather for the **g** supper of God,
19:18 flesh of all, both free and slave, both small and **g**."
20: 1 the key to the bottomless pit and a **g** chain.
20:11 I saw a **g** white throne and the one who sat on it;
20:12 And I saw the dead, **g** and small,
21:10 And in the spirit he carried me away to a **g**,
21:12 It has a **g**, high wall with twelve gates,
Tob 3: 6 and **g** is the sorrow within me.
4:13 For in pride there is ruin and **g** confusion.
4:21 You have **g** wealth if you fear God and flee
5:13 the son of the **g** Hananiah, one of your relatives."
8:16 you have dealt with us according to your **g** mercy.
11:14 "Blessed be God, and blessed be his **g** name,
13: 2 and he brings up from the **g** abyss,
13:15 My soul blesses the Lord, the **g** King! C
14: 2 and was buried with **g** honor in Nineveh.
14:13 He treated his parents-in-law with **g** respect
Jdt 1: 1 over the Assyrians in the **g** city of Nineveh. E
1: 5 against King Arphaxad in the **g** plain that is on
1: 8 and Upper Galilee and the **g** plain of Esdraelon,
2: 5 the **G** King, the lord of the whole earth: C
Jdt 2:16 and he organized them as a **g** army is marshaled
3: 2 the servants of Nebuchadnezzar, the **G** King, C
3: 9 near Dothan, facing the **g** ridge of Judea;
4: 9 every man of Israel cried out to God with **g** fervor,
5: 2 In **g** anger he called together all the princes
5:10 so **g** a multitude that their race could not
7: 2 the foot soldiers handling it, a very **g** multitude. A
7:18 and supply trains spread out in **g** number,
7:24 a **g** injury in not making peace with the Assyrians.
7:29 Then **g** and general lamentation arose throughout
7:32 In the town they were in **g** misery.
8: 8 for she feared God with **g** devotion.
8:19 they suffered a **g** catastrophe before our enemies.
10:18 There was **g** excitement in the whole camp,
12:20 and drank a **g** quantity of wine,
13: 4 everyone went out, and no one, either small or **g**,
13:13 They all ran together, both small and **g**,
14: 9 a **g** shout and made a joyful noise in their town.
15: 5 and in Galilee outflanked them with **g** slaughter,
15: 6 and plundered it, acquiring **g** riches.
15: 7 in the hill country and in the plain got a **g** amount
15: 9 you are the **g** boast of Israel,
15: 9 you are the **g** pride of our nation!
15:10 you have done **g** good to Israel,
16:13 O Lord, you are **g** and glorious,
16:16 but whoever fears the Lord is **g** forever.
AdE 10: 3 of King Artaxerxes and was **g** in the kingdom,
10: 9 God has done **g** signs and wonders,
11: 2 the second year of the reign of Artaxerxes the **G**,
11: 3 He was a Jew living in the city of Susa, a **g** man,
11: 6 Then two **g** dragons came forward,
11: 8 affliction and **g** tumult on the earth!
11:10 as though from a tiny spring, there came a **g** river,
12: 6 a Bougean, who was in **g** honor with the king,
13: 1 This is a copy of the letter: "The **G** King, C
16: 1 "The **G** King, Artaxerxes, C
Wis 3: 5 they will receive **g** good, because God tested them
3:14 and a place of **g** delight in the temple of the Lord.
5: 1 Then the righteous will stand with **g** confidence in
6: 7 because he himself made both small and **g**,
11:21 For it is always in your power to show **g** strength,
12:18 and with **g** forbearance you govern us;
12:20 if you punished with such **g** care and indulgence
14:22 but though living in **g** strife due to ignorance,
14:22 they call such **g** evils peace.
17: 1 **G** are your judgments and hard to describe;
18: 1 But for your holy ones there was very **g** light.
Sir Pr: 1 Many **g** teachings have been given to us through
3:20 For **g** is the might of the Lord;
4: 7 bow your head low to the **g**.
5: 6 Do not say, "His mercy is **g**,
5:15 In **g** and small matters cause no harm,
7: 9 "He will consider the **g** number of my gifts,
7:25 and you complete a **g** task;
11: 1 and seats them among the **g**.
15:18 For **g** is the wisdom of the Lord;
16:12 **G** as his mercy, so also is his chastisement;
17:29 How **g** is the mercy of the Lord,
18: 9 in their life is **g** if they reach one hundred years.
18:32 Do not revel in **g** luxury,
20:27 and one who is sensible pleases the **g**.
20:28 and those who please the **g** atone for injustice.
23:14 among the **g**, or you may forget yourself
24:29 and her counsel deeper than the **g** abyss.
25:10 How **g** is the one who finds wisdom!
25:22 and **g** disgrace when a wife supports her husband.
26: 3 A good wife is a **g** blessing;
26: 5 and of a fourth I am in **g** fear:
26: 8 A drunken wife arouses **g** anger;
26:21 *confidence in their good descent, will grow* **g**.
28:14 and overturned the houses of the **g**.
31:12 Are you seated at the table of the **g**?
32: 9 Among the **g** do not act as their equal;
33:19 Hear me, you who are **g** among the people,
38: 3 and in the presence of the **g** they are admired.
38:16 and as one in **g** pain begin the lament.
38:27 each is diligent in making a **g** variety;
39: 4 He serves among the **g** and appears before rulers;
39: 6 If the **g** Lord is willing, he will be filled with
43: 5 **G** is the Lord who made it;
43:29 Awesome is the Lord and very **g**,
44: 2 The Lord apportioned to them **g** glory,
44:19 Abraham was the **g** father of a multitude
45: 2 and made him **g**, to the terror of his enemies.
46: 1 as his name implies, a **g** savior of God's elect,
46: 5 and the **g** Lord answered him with hailstones
48:18 and made **g** boasts in his arrogance.
48:22 who was **g** and trustworthy in his visions.
49: 4 all of them were **g** sinners,
50:22 who everywhere works **g** wonders,
51:24 and why do you endure such **g** thirst?
Bar 1: 4 and to all the people, small and **g**,
2:11 and with signs and wonders and with **g** power B
2:25 They perished in **g** misery,
2:27 in all your kindness and in all your **g** compassion,
2:29 this very **g** multitude will surely turn into A
3:24 O Israel, how **g** is the house of God,
3:25 It is **g** and has no bounds;
3:26 who were famous of old, **g** in stature,
4: 9 God has brought **g** sorrow upon me;
4:24 which will come to you with **g** glory and with
4:34 I will take away her pride in her **g** population,
Sus 1:31 of **g** refinement and beautiful in appearance.
1:60 whole assembly raised a **g** shout and blessed God,
1:64 that day onward Daniel had a **g** reputation among
Bel 1:18 and shouted in a loud voice, "You are **g**, O Bel,
1:23 Now in that place there was a **g** dragon,
Bel 1:41 The king shouted with a loud voice, "You are **g**,
1Mc 1:24 He shed much blood, and spoke with **g** arrogance.
1:33 of David with a **g** strong wall and strong towers,
1:35 they stored them there, and became a **g** menace,
1:40 Her dishonor now grew as **g** as her glory;
1:64 Very **g** wrath came upon Israel.
2:17 "You are a leader, honored and **g** in this town,
2:51 you will receive **g** honor and an everlasting name.
2:58 Elijah, because of **g** zeal for the law,
2:70 all Israel mourned for him with **g** lamentation.
3:17 fight against so **g** and so strong a multitude?
3:20 in **g** insolence and lawlessness to destroy us
4:23 and they seized a **g** amount of gold and silver,
4:23 and cloth dyed blue and sea purple, and **g** riches.
4:25 Thus Israel had a **g** deliverance that day.
4:39 and mourned with **g** lamentation;
4:58 There was very **g** joy among the people, F
5:16 heard these messages, a **g** assembly was called
5:23 and led them to Judea with **g** rejoicing.
5:45 the small and the **g**, with their wives and children
5:61 Thus the people suffered a **g** rout because,
6: 4 So he fled and in **g** disappointment left there
6:11 And into what a **g** flood I now am plunged!
7: 8 he was a **g** man in the kingdom and was faithful to
7:19 and killed them and threw them into a **g** pit.
7:22 of the land of Judah and did **g** damage in Israel.
7:35 And he went out in **g** anger.
7:48 and celebrated that day as a day of **g** gladness.
8: 4 until they crushed them and inflicted **g** disaster
8: 6 They also had defeated Antiochus the **G**,
9:20 All Israel made **g** lamentation for him;
9:24 In those days a very **g** famine occurred,
9:27 So there was **g** distress in Israel, I
9:35 with them the **g** amount of baggage that they had.
9:37 family of Jambri are celebrating a **g** wedding,
9:37 a daughter of one of the **g** nobles of Canaan,
9:39 and saw a tumultuous procession with a **g** amount
9:56 And Alcimus died at that time in **g** agony.
10:37 Let some of them be stationed in the **g** strongholds
10:46 the **g** wrongs that Demetrius had done in Israel
10:58 celebrated her wedding at Ptolemais with **g** pomp,
10:86 of the city came out to meet him with **g** pomp.
11: 1 Then the king of Egypt gathered **g** forces,
11:42 but I will confer **g** honor on you and your nation,
12:49 and the **G** Plain to destroy all Jonathan's soldiers.
12:52 and his companions and were in **g** fear;
13: 3 yourselves know what **g** things my brothers D
13:17 he would not arouse **g** hostility among the people,
13:26 All Israel bewailed him with **g** lamentation,
13:29 erecting about them **g** columns,
13:32 and he brought **g** calamity on the land.
13:33 with high towers and **g** walls and gates and bolts,
13:42 the **g** high priest and commander and leader of
13:44 and a **g** tumult arose in the city.
13:51 because a **g** enemy had been crushed and removed
14:11 and Israel rejoiced with **g** joy. F
14:27 which is the third year of the **g** high priest Simon,
14:28 in the **g** assembly of the priests and the people and
14:29 and they brought **g** glory to their nation.
14:32 He spent **g** sums of his own money;
14:36 doing **g** damage to its purity.
15: 9 we will bestow **g** honor on you and your nation
15:29 you have done **g** damage in the land,
15:32 and his **g** magnificence, he was amazed.
15:35 they were causing **g** damage among the people
16:15 he gave them a **g** banquet, and hid men there.
16:17 an act of **g** treachery and returned evil for good.
2Mc 1:22 shone out, a **g** fire blazed up, so that all marveled.
2:18 for he has rescued us from **g** evils and has purified
2:19 and the purification of the **g** temple,
2:22 Lord with **g** kindness became gracious to them—
3:21 and the anxiety of the high priest in his **g** anguish.
3:24 so **g** a manifestation that all who had been so bold
3:28 with a **g** retinue and all his bodyguard but was
3:35 to the Lord and made very **g** vows to the Savior
5:20 when the **g** Lord became reconciled.
5:26 with his armed warriors and killed **g** numbers
6:13 of **g** kindness not to let the impious alone for long,
6:31 only to the young but to the **g** body of his nation.
8:16 by the enemy and not to fear the **g** multitude A
8:20 and took a **g** amount of booty.
8:27 giving **g** praise and thanks to the Lord,
10:38 the Lord who shows **g** kindness to Israel
12:15 calling against the **g** Sovereign of the world,
12:24 With **g** guile he begged them to let him go
12:27 **g** stores of war engines and missiles were there.
13: 1 that Antiochus Eupator was coming with a **g** army
14:13 to install Alcimus as high priest of the **g** temple.
14:31 he went to the **g** and holy temple while
1Es 1:54 **g** and small, the treasure chests of the Lord,
2: 9 and with a very **g** number of votive offerings
3: 1 Now King Darius gave a **g** banquet for all
3: 5 King Darius will give rich gifts and **g** honors
4:14 is not the king **g**, and are not men many,
4:28 "Is not the king **g** in his power?
4:35 Is not the one who does these things **g**?
4:35 But truth is **g**, and stronger than all things.
4:41 all the people shouted and said, "**G** is truth,
5:62 and shouted with a **g** shout,
6: 9 building in the city of Jerusalem a **g** new house for
6:14 by a king of Israel who was **g** and strong,
7: 2 supervised the holy work with very **g** care,
8: 7 For Ezra possessed **g** knowledge,
8:76 and we are in **g** sin to this day.
8:86 about because of our evil deeds and our **g** sins.
8:91 gathered around him a very **g** crowd of men H
8:91 for there was **g** weeping among the multitude.

1Es 9: 2 for he was mourning over the **g** iniquities of
9: 11 But the multitude is **g** and it is winter,
9: 54 to those who had none, and to make **g** rejoicing;
Man 1: 7 of **g** compassion, long-suffering,
1: 7 to your **g** goodness you have promised repentance
1: 14 you will save me according to your **g** mercy,
3Mc 2: 9 for the glory of your **g** and honored name.
2: 12 and rescued them from **g** evils,
2: 13 because of our many and **g** sins we are crushed
2: 23 panic-stricken in their exceedingly **g** fear.
3: 9 for such a **g** community ought not be left to its fate
3: 15 with clemency and **g** benevolence,
3: 16 And when we had granted very **g** revenues to
5: 10 until they had been filled with a **g** abundance
5: 23 began to move them along in the **g** colonnade.
5: 44 the Friends and officers departed with **g** joy, F
6: 2 "King of **g** power, Almighty God Most High, B
6: 17 when the Jews observed this they raised **g** cries
6: 33 convening a **g** banquet to celebrate these events,
7: 2 **g** God guiding our affairs according to our desire. J
7: 22 So the supreme God perfectly performed **g** deeds
2Es 1: 9 on whom I have bestowed such **g** benefits?
1: 14 and did **g** wonders among you.
2: 42 saw on Mount Zion a **g** multitude that I could A
2: 43 In their midst was a young man of **g** stature,
2: 48 how **g** and how many are the wonders of
3: 16 and Jacob became a **g** multitude. A
4: 32 how **g** a threshing floor they will fill!"
5: 1 the earth shall be seized with **g** terror,
7: 12 full of dangers and involved in **g** hardships.
7: *61* not grieve over the **g** number of those who perish;
7: *91* with **g** joy the glory of him who receives them, F
7: *92* with **g** effort to overcome the evil thought
8: 14 with so **g** labor was fashioned by your command,
8: 50 because they have walked in **g** pride.
8: 55 not ask any more questions about the **g** number
8: 63 you have already shown me a **g** number of
9: 21 And I saw and spared some with **g** difficulty,
9: 21 and one plant out of a **g** forest.
9: 45 and we gave **g** glory to the Mighty One.
10: 7 mother of us all, is in deep grief and **g** distress. I
10: 11 she who lost so **g** a multitude,
10: 24 Therefore shake off your **g** sadness
11: 40 you have held sway over the world with **g** terror,
12: 3 I woke up in **g** perplexity of mind and **g** fear,
12: 5 the **g** fear with which I have been terrified tonight.
12: 18 that kingdom **g** struggles shall arise, and it shall be
13: 6 that he carved out for himself a **g** mountain,
13: 11 of fire and the flaming breath and the **g** storm,
13: 13 Then I woke up in **g** terror,
13: 19 For they shall see **g** dangers and much distress,
13: 57 giving **g** glory and praise to the Most High for
15: 19 of hunger for bread and because of **g** tribulation.
15: 30 with **g** power they shall come and engage them B
15: 31 combine in **g** power and turn to pursue them, B
15: 37 there shall be fear and **g** trembling on the earth;
15: 40 **G** and mighty clouds, full of wrath and tempest,
16: 21 the sword, famine, and **g** confusion.
16: 26 For in all places there shall be **g** solitude;
16: 38 has **g** pains around her womb for two
16: 68 The burning wrath of a **g** multitude is kindled A
16: 70 be a **g** uprising against those who fear the Lord.
4Mc 4: 10 instilling in them **g** fear and trembling.
5: 20 in matters either small or **g** is of equal seriousness,
11: 23 and I myself will bring a **g** avenger upon you,
13: 15 for **g** is the struggle of the soul and the danger
15: 22 How **g** and how many torments the mother
16: 4 so many and such **g** emotions by devout reason.

GREATER‡ (105) [GREAT]

Ge 1: 16 the **g** light to rule the day and the lesser light
4: 13 "My punishment is **g** than I can bear!
39: 9 He is not **g** in this house than I am,
41: 40 with regard to the throne will I be **g** than you."
48: 19 his younger brother shall be **g** than he,
Ex 18: 11 Now I know that the LORD is **g** than all gods,
Nu 14: 12 of you a nation **g** and mightier than they."
Dt 4: 38 before you nations **g** and mightier than yourselves,
2Sa 5: 10 And David became **g** and **g**, for the LORD,
13: 15 his loathing was even **g** than the lust he had felt
13: 16 for this wrong in sending me away is **g** than
1Ki 1: 37 and make his throne **g** than the throne
1: 47 and make his throne **g** than your throne.'
1Ch 11: 9 And David became **g** and **g**,
2Ch 2: 5 for our God is **g** than other gods.
17: 12 Jehoshaphat grew steadily **g**.
32: 7 for there is one **g** with us than with him.
Job 33: 12 I will answer you: God is **g** than any mortal.
Isa 10: 10 of the idols whose images were **g** than those
La 4: 6 For the chastisement of my people has been **g** than
Eze 8: 6 Yet you will see still **g** abominations."
8: 13 "You will see still **g** abominations
8: 15 You will see still **g** abominations than these."
Da 7: 20 and that seemed **g** than the others.
11: 5 and shall rule a realm **g** than his own realm.
11: 25 of the south shall wage war with a much **g**
11: 36 and consider himself **g** than any god,
11: 37 for he shall consider himself **g** than all.
Am 6: 2 Or is your territory **g** than their territory,
Hag 2: 9 The latter splendor of this house shall be **g** than
Mt 11: 11 of women no one has arisen **g** than John
11: 11 the least in the kingdom of heaven is **g** than he.
12: 6 I tell you, something **g** than the temple is here.
12: 41 and see, something **g** than Jonah is here!
12: 42 and see, something **g** than Solomon is here!
23: 17 For which is **g**, the gold or the sanctuary
23: 19 For which is **g**, the gift or the altar that makes
Mk 12: 31 There is no other commandment **g** than these."
12: 40 They will receive the **g** condemnation."
Lk 7: 28 of women no one is **g** than John;
7: 28 yet the least in the kingdom of God is **g** than he."
7: 43 the one for whom he canceled the **g** debt."
11: 31 and see, something **g** than Solomon is here!
11: 32 and see, something **g** than Jonah is here!
20: 47 They will receive the **g** condemnation."
22: 27 For who is **g**, the one who is at the table or
Jn 1: 50 You will see **g** things than these."
4: 12 Are you **g** than our ancestor Jacob,
5: 20 and he will show him **g** works than these,
5: 36 But I have a testimony **g** than John's.
8: 53 Are you **g** than our father Abraham, who died?
10: 29 What my Father has given me is **g** than all else,
13: 16 I tell you, servants are not **g** than their master,
13: 16 nor are messengers **g** than the one who sent them.
14: 12 in fact, will do **g** works than these,
14: 28 because the Father is **g** than I.
15: 13 No one has **g** love than this,
15: 20 'Servants are not **g** than their master.'
19: 11 over to you is guilty of a **g** sin."
Ro 6: 19 as slaves to impurity and to **g** and **g** iniquity,
1Co 12: 23 we think less honorable we clothe with **g** honor,
12: 23 less respectable members are treated with **g** respect
12: 24 giving the **g** honor to the inferior member,
12: 31 But strive for the **g** gifts.
14: 5 One who prophesies is **g** than one who speaks
2Co 3: 10 had glory has lost its glory because of the **g** glory;
11: 23 with far **g** labors, far more imprisonments,
Php 1: 14 dare to speak the word with **g** boldness and
Heb 2: 1 we must pay **g** attention to what we have heard,
6: 13 because he had no one **g** by whom to swear,
6: 16 of course, swear by someone **g** than themselves,
9: 11 the **g** and perfect tent (not made with hands,
11: 26 for the Christ to be **g** wealth than the treasures
Jas 3: 1 that we who teach will be judged with **g** strictness.
2Pe 2: 11 though **g** in might and power,
1Jn 3: 20 for God is **g** than our hearts,
4: 4 for the one who is in you is **g** than the one who is
5: 9 the testimony of God is **g**;
3Jn 1: 4 I have no **g** joy than this,
Rev 2: 19 I know that your last works are **g** than the first.
Wis 8: 12 if I speak at **g** length,
16: 17 the fire had still **g** effect,
Sir Pr: 1 even **g** progress in living according to the law.
3: 18 **g** you are, the more you must humble yourself;
10: 24 none of them is **g** than the one who fears the Lord.
39: 11 he will leave a name **g** than a thousand,
43: 28 For he is **g** than all his works.
43: 32 Many things **g** than these lie hidden,
1Mc 6: 27 they will do still **g** things,
3Mc 7: 21 also possessed **g** prestige among their enemies,
2Es 4: 34 "Do not be in a **g** hurry than the Most High.
4: 45 or whether for us the **g** part has gone by.
4: 50 and the fire is **g** than the smoke,
4: 50 so the quantity that passed was far **g**;
5: 13 you shall hear yet **g** things than these."
6: 31 I will again declare to you **g** things than these,
7: 13 the entrances of the **g** world are broad and safe,
7: *98* which is **g** than all that have been mentioned,
9: 16 as a wave is **g** than a drop of water."
11: 29 it was **g** than the other two heads.
11: 32 it had **g** power over the world than all the wings
4Mc 15: 9 she felt a **g** tenderness toward them.

GREATEST‡ (29) [GREAT]

Jos 14: 15 this Arba was the **g** man among the Anakim.
1Ch 12: 14 least equal to a hundred and the **g** to a thousand.
Job 1: 3 this man was the **g** of all the people of the east.
Jer 6: 13 For from the least to the **g** of them,
8: 10 because from the least to the **g** everyone is greedy
31: 34 from the least of them to the **g**, says the LORD;
42: 1 and all the people from the least to the **g**,
42: 8 and all the people from the least to the **g**,
44: 12 from the least to the **g**, they shall die by the sword
Mt 13: 32 but when it has grown it is the **g** of shrubs
18: 1 "Who is the **g** in the kingdom of heaven?"
18: 4 Whoever becomes humble like this child is the **g**
22: 36 which commandment in the law is the **g**?"
22: 38 This is the **g** and first commandment.
23: 11 The **g** among you will be your servant.
Mk 4: 32 yet when it is sown it grows up and becomes the **g**
9: 34 with one another who was the **g**.
Lk 9: 46 among them as to which one of them was the **g**.
9: 48 for the least among all of you is the **g**."
22: 24 to which one of them was to be regarded as the **g**.
22: 26 the **g** among you must become like the youngest,
Ac 8: 10 All of them, from the least to the **g**,
1Co 13: 13 and the **g** of these is love.
Heb 8: 11 from the least of them to the **g**.
Jdt 12: 18 because today is the **g** day in my whole life."
2Mc 5: 6 at the cost of one's kindred is the **g** misfortune,
15: 18 their **g** and first fear was for
2Es 8: 49 You will receive the **g** glory,
12: 40 they all gathered together, from the least to the **g**,

GREATLY‡ (110) [GREAT]

Ge 3: 16 "I will **g** increase your pangs in childbearing;
7: 18 The waters swelled and increased **g** on the earth;
16: 10 so **g** multiply your offspring that they cannot
24: 35 The LORD has **g** blessed my master,
31: 30 Even though you had to go because you longed **g**
32: 7 Then Jacob was **g** afraid and distressed;
45: 13 You must tell my father how **g** I am honored
Nu 14: 39 to all the Israelites, the people mourned **g**.
Dt 6: 3 and so that you may multiply **g** in a land flowing
Jos 10: 2 he became **g** frightened, because Gibeon was
Jdg 6: 6 Thus Israel was **g** impoverished because
10: 9 so that Israel was **g** distressed.
1Sa 11: 6 and his anger was **g** kindled.
11: 15 and there Saul and all the Israelites rejoiced **g**.
12: 18 all the people **g** feared the LORD and Samuel.
16: 21 and entered his service. Saul loved him **g**,
17: 11 they were dismayed and **g** afraid.
17: 25 The king will **g** enrich the man who kills him,
28: 5 he was afraid, and his heart trembled **g**.
2Sa 1: 26 **g** beloved were you to me;
10: 5 for the men were **g** ashamed.
12: 5 David's anger was **g** kindled against the man.
24: 10 "I have sinned **g** in what I have done.
1Ki 5: 7 Hiram heard the words of Solomon, he rejoiced **g**,
18: 3 (Now Obadiah revered the LORD **g**;
2Ki 6: 11 the king of Aram was **g** perturbed because of this;
1Ch 4: 38 and their clans increased **g**.
16: 25 For great is the LORD, and **g** to be praised;
19: 5 for they felt **g** humiliated.
21: 8 "I have sinned **g** in that I have done this thing.
29: 9 King David also rejoiced **g**.
2Ch 33: 12 the LORD his God and humbled himself **g** before
Ne 2: 10 it displeased them **g** that someone had come
4: 1 he was angry and **g** enraged,
6: 16 all the nations around us were afraid and fell **g**
Job 35: 15 and he does not **g** heed transgression,
Ps 21: 1 O LORD, and in your help how **g** he exults!
48: 1 Great is the LORD and **g** to be praised in the city
65: 9 You visit the earth and water it, you **g** enrich it;
96: 4 For great is the LORD, and **g** to be praised;
107: 38 By his blessing they multiply **g**,
112: 1 who **g** delight in his commandments.
116: 10 even when I said, "I am **g** afflicted";
145: 3 Great is the LORD, and **g** to be praised;
Pr 23: 24 The father of the righteous will **g** rejoice;
Isa 8: 21 through the land, **g** distressed and hungry;
61: 10 I will **g** rejoice in the LORD,
Jer 3: 1 Would not such a land be **g** polluted?
20: 11 They will be **g** shamed, for they will not succeed.
Eze 20: 13 and my sabbaths they **g** profaned.
Da 5: 9 Then King Belshazzar became **g** terrified
7: 28 As for me, Daniel, my thoughts **g** terrified me,
9: 23 to declare it, for you are **g** beloved.
10: 11 He said to me, "Daniel, **g** beloved,
10: 19 He said, "Do not fear, **g** beloved, you are safe.
Zec 9: 9 Rejoice **g**, O daughter Zion!
Mt 17: 23 And they were **g** distressed.
18: 31 they were **g** distressed, and they went and reported
19: 25 they were **g** astounded and said,
26: 22 And they became **g** distressed and began to say
27: 14 so that the governor was **g** amazed.
Mk 6: 20 When he heard him, he was **g** perplexed;
10: 26 They were **g** astounded and said to one another,
14: 11 When they heard it, they were **g** pleased,
Lk 22: 5 They were **g** pleased and agreed
Jn 3: 29 rejoices **g** at the bridegroom's voice.
11: 33 he was **g** disturbed in spirit and deeply moved.
11: 38 Then Jesus, again **g** disturbed, came to the tomb.
Ac 6: 7 number of the disciples increased **g** in Jerusalem,
10: 17 while Peter was **g** puzzled about what to make of
18: 27 On his arrival he **g** helped those who
2Co 10: 15 of action among you may be **g** enlarged,
Php 4: 10 I rejoice in the Lord **g** that now
2Pe 2: 7 a righteous man **g** distressed by the licentiousness
Rev 17: 6 When I saw her, I was **g** amazed.
Jdt 2: 28 in Azotus and Ascalon feared him **g**.
4: 2 they were therefore **g** terrified at his approach;
7: 4 they were **g** terrified and said to one another,
9: 7 "Here now are the Assyrians, a **g** increased force,
10: 7 they were very **g** astounded at her beauty and said
12: 20 Holofernes was **g** pleased with her,
13: 17 All the people were **g** astonished.
14: 19 they tore their tunics and were **g** dismayed,
Wis 18: 17 in dreadful dreams **g** troubled them,
Sir 1: 8 There is but one who is wise, **g** to be feared,
1Mc 2: 14 put on sackcloth, and mourned **g**.
3: 27 Antiochus heard these reports, he was **g** angered;
3: 31 He was **g** perplexed in mind;
4: 21 When they perceived this, they were **g** frightened,
5: 63 and his brothers were **g** honored in all Israel and
7: 48 The people rejoiced **g** and celebrated that day as
8: 13 and they have been **g** exalted.
9: 6 they were **g** frightened, and many slipped away
10: 8 They were **g** alarmed when they heard that
10: 68 he was **g** distressed and returned to Antioch.
16: 22 When he heard this, he was **g** shocked;
2Mc 1: 11 by God out of grave dangers we thank him **g**
8: 32 and one who had **g** troubled the Jews.
15: 27 and were **g** gladdened by God's manifestation.
3Mc 3: 7 but were hostile and **g** opposed to his government.
4: 16 The king was **g** and continually filled with joy,
2Es 3: 3 My spirit was **g** agitated, and I began
5: 33 "Are you **g** disturbed in mind over Israel?
6: 14 if the place where you are standing is **g** shaken
6: 37 My spirit was **g** aroused, and my soul was
9: 41 I am **g** embittered in spirit and deeply distressed."
9: 45 I rejoiced **g** over him, I and my husband
10: 39 for your people and mourned **g** over Zion.
4Mc 4: 22 and that the people of Jerusalem had rejoiced **g**.
8: 5 and **g** respect the beauty and the number

GREATNESS (34) [GREAT]

Ex 15: 7 In the **g** of your majesty you overthrew your

Nu 14:19 the iniquity of this people according to the **g**
Dt 3:24 you have only begun to show your servant your **g**
5:24 the LORD our God has shown us his glory and **g,**
9:26 whom you redeemed in your **g,**
11: 2 but it is you who must acknowledge his **g,**
32: 3 of the LORD; ascribe **g** to our God!
2Sa 7:21 you have wrought all this **g,**
1Ch 29:11 Yours, O LORD, are the **g,** the power, the glory,
2Ch 9: 6 half of the **g** of your wisdom had been told to me;
Ne 13:22 spare me according to the **g** of your steadfast love.
Job 23: 6 Would he contend with me in the **g** of his power?
36:18 and do not let the **g** of the ransom turn you aside.
Ps 145: 3 be praised; his **g** is unsearchable.
145: 6 and I will declare your **g.**
150: 2 praise him according to his surpassing **g!**
Jer 13:22 the **g** of your iniquity that your skirts are lifted up,
Eze 31: 2 Whom are you like in your **g?**
31: 7 It was beautiful in its **g,** in the length
31:18 the trees of Eden was like you in glory and in **g?**
38:23 So I will display my **g** and my holiness
Da 4:22 Your **g** has increased and reaches to heaven,
4:36 and still more **g** was added to me.
5:18 God gave your father Nebuchadnezzar kingship, **g,**
5:19 And because of the **g** that he gave him,
7:27 and dominion and the **g** of the kingdoms under
Lk 9:43 And all were astounded at the **g** of God.
Eph 1:19 and what is the immeasurable **g** of his power
Tob 13: 4 He has shown you his **g** even there.
Wis 6: 7 in awe of anyone, or show deference to **g;**
13: 5 For from the **g** and beauty of created things comes
Sir 51: 3 in the **g** of your mercy and of your name,
1Mc 9:22 and his **g,** have not been recorded,
1Es 4:46 and request of you, and this befits your **g.**

GREAVES (1)
1Sa 17: 6 He had **g** of bronze on his legs and a javelin

GRECIA, GRECIANS (KJV) See GREECE, GREEKS, HELLENISTS

GREECE (6) [GREEK, GREEKS]
Da 8:21 The male goat is the king of **G,**
10:20 the prince of **G** will come.
11: 2 he shall stir up all against the kingdom of **G.**
Zec 9:13 O **G,** and wield you like a warrior's sword.
Ac 20: 2 the believers much encouragement, he came to **G,**
1Mc 1: 1 (He had previously become king of **G.**)

GREED (10) [GREEDILY, GREEDY]
Job 20:20 in their **g** they let nothing escape.
Mt 23:25 but inside they are full of **g** and self-indulgence.
Lk 11:39 but inside you are full of **g** and wickedness.
12:15 Be on your guard against all kinds of **g;**
Eph 5: 3 But fornication and impurity of any kind, or **g,**
Col 3: 5 passion, evil desire, and **g** (which is idolatry).
1Th 2: 5 with words of flattery or with a pretext for **g;**
2Pe 2: 3 And in their **g** they will exploit you
2:14 They have hearts trained in **g.**
2Mc 4:50 But Menelaus, because of the **g** of those in power,

GREEDILY (2) [GREED]
Ps 57: 4 I lie down among lions that **g** devour human prey;
Sir 31:16 and do not chew **g,** or you will give offense.

GREEDY (25) [GREED]
1Sa 2:29 with **g** eye at my sacrifices and my offerings
2:32 Then in distress you will look with **g** eye on all
Ps 10: 3 those **g** for gain curse and renounce the LORD.
Pr 1:19 Such is the end of all who are **g** for gain;
15:27 Those who are **g** for unjust gain make trouble
28:25 The **g** person stirs up strife,
Jer 6:13 everyone is **g** for unjust gain;
8:10 to the greatest everyone is **g** for unjust gain;
12: 9 Is the hyena **g** for my heritage at my command?
Hos 4: 8 they are **g** for their iniquity
1Co 5:10 or the **g** and robbers, or idolaters,
5:11 of brother or sister who is sexually immoral or **g,**
6:10 the **g,** drunkards, revilers, robbers—
Eph 4:19 **g** to practice every kind of impurity.
5: 5 or one who is **g** (that is, an idolater),
1Ti 3: 8 not indulging in much wine, not **g** for money;
Tit 1: 7 or addicted to wine or violent or **g** for gain;
Sir 14: 9 eye of the **g** person is not satisfied with his share;
14: 9 **g** injustice withers the soul.
31:12 Do not be **g** at it, and do not say,
31:13 Remember that a **g** eye is a bad thing.
31:13 What has been created more **g** than the eye?
37:29 Do not be **g** for every delicacy,
1Mc 4:17 not be **g** for plunder, for there is a battle before us;
4Mc 2: 9 If one is **g,** one is ruled by the law through reason

GREEK‡ (22) [GREECE]
Jn 19:20 and it was written in Hebrew, in Latin, and in **G.**
Ac 9:36 whose name was Tabitha, which in **G** is Dorcas.
16: 1 but his father was a **G.**
16: 3 for they all knew that his father was a **G.**
17:12 not a few **G** women and men of high standing.
21:37 The tribune replied, "Do you know **G?**
Ro 1:16 to the Jew first and also to the **G.**
2: 9 the Jew first and also the **G,**
2:10 the Jew first and also the **G.**
10:12 For there is no distinction between Jew and **G;**
Gal 2: 3 to be circumcised, though he was a **G.**
Gal 3:28 There is no longer Jew or **G,**
Col 3:11 In that renewal there is no longer **G** and Jew,
Rev 9:11 and in **G** he is called Apollyon.
2Mc 4:10 at once shifted his compatriots over to the **G** way
4:12 the noblest of the young men to wear the **G** hat.
4:15 and putting the highest value upon **G** forms
6: 8 to the neighboring **G** cities that they should adopt
6: 9 not choose to change over to **G** customs.
11:24 not consent to our father's change to **G** customs,
13: 2 a **G** force of one hundred ten thousand infantry,
4Mc 8: 8 Enjoy your youth by adopting the **G** way of life

GREEKS‡ (26) [GREECE]
Joel 3: 6 the people of Judah and Jerusalem to the **G,**
Jn 7:35 the Dispersion among the **G** and teach the **G?**
12:20 up to worship at the festival were some **G.**
Ac 14: 1 of both Jews and **G** became believers.
17: 4 the devout **G** and not a few of the leading women.
18: 4 and would try to convince Jews and **G.**
19:10 so that all the residents of Asia, both Jews and **G,**
19:17 both Jews and **G,** everyone was awestruck;
20:21 as I testified to both Jews and **G** about repentance
21:28 that, he has actually brought **G** into the temple
Ro 1:14 I am a debtor both to **G** and to barbarians,
3: 9 both Jews and **G,** are under the power of sin,
1Co 1:22 For Jews demand signs and **G** desire wisdom,
1:24 but to those who are the called, both Jews and **G,**
10:32 Give no offense to Jews or to **G** or to the church
12:13 Jews or **G,** slaves or free—
1Mc 1:10 of the kingdom of the **G.**
6: 2 the Macedonian king who first reigned over the **G.**
8: 9 The **G** planned to come and destroy them,
8:10 a general against the **G** and attacked them.
8:18 of the **G** was enslaving Israel completely.
2Mc 4:36 and the **G** shared their hatred of the crime.
11: 2 He intended to make the city a home for **G,**
3Mc 3: 8 The **G** in the city, though wronged in no way,
4Mc 18:20 the **G** quenched fire with fire in his cruel caldrons,

GREEN (36) [EVERGREEN, GREENISH]
Ge 1:30 I have given every **g** plant for food."
9: 3 and just as I gave you the **g** plants,
Ex 10:15 nothing **g** was left, no tree, no plant in the field,
1Ki 14:23 on every high hill and under every **g** tree;
2Ki 16: 4 on the hills, and under every **g** tree.
17:10 on every high hill and under every **g** tree;
2Ch 28: 4 on the hills, and under every **g** tree.
Job 15:32 and their branch will not be **g.**
39: 8 and it searches after every **g** thing.
Ps 23: 2 He makes me lie down in **g** pastures;
37: 2 and wither like the **g** herb.
52: 8 But I am like a **g** olive tree in the house of God.
58: 9 whether **g** or ablaze, may he sweep them away!
68:13 a dove covered with silver, its pinions with **g** gold.
92:14 they are always **g** and full of sap,
Pr 11:28 but the righteous will flourish like **g** leaves.
SS 1:16 truly lovely. Our couch is **g;**
Isa 44: 4 They shall spring up like a **g** tamarisk,
57: 5 with lust among the oaks, under every **g** tree;
Jer 2:20 and under every **g** tree you sprawled and played
3: 6 up on every high hill and under every **g** tree,
3:13 among strangers under every **g** tree,
11:16 The LORD once called you, "A **g** olive tree,
17: 2 beside every **g** tree, and on the high hills,
17: 8 and its leaves shall stay **g;**
Eze 6:13 under every **g** tree, and under every leafy oak,
17:24 I dry up the **g** tree and make the dry tree flourish.
20:47 in you, and it shall devour every **g** tree in you
Joel 2:22 for the pastures of the wilderness are **g;**
Mk 6:39 the people to sit down in groups on the **g** grass.
Lk 23:31 For if they do this when the wood is **g,**
Rev 6: 8 I looked and there was a pale **g** horse!
8: 7 and all **g** grass was burned up.
9: 4 the grass of the earth or any **g** growth or any tree,
Sir 40:22 but the **g** shoots of grain more than either.
50: 8 like a **g** shoot on Lebanon on a summer day;

GREENISH (2) [GREEN]
Lev 13:49 if the disease shows **g** or reddish in the garment,
14:37 in the walls of the house with **g** or reddish spots,

GREET (48) [GREETED, GREETING, GREETINGS, GREETS]
1Sa 10: 4 They will **g** you and give you two loaves of bread,
25: 5 and go to Nabal, and **g** him in my name.
2Sa 8:10 to **g** him and to congratulate him
1Ch 18:10 to **g** him and to congratulate him,
Isa 14: 9 it rouses the shades to **g** you,
Mt 5:47 And if you **g** only your brothers and sisters,
10:12 As you enter the house, **g** it.
Mk 9:15 and they ran forward to **g** him.
Lk 10: 4 and **g** no one on the road.
Ro 16: 3 **G** Prisca and Aquila, who work with me
16: 5 **G** also the church in their house.
16: 5 **G** my beloved Epaenetus,
16: 6 **G** Mary, who has worked very hard among you.
16: 7 **G** Andronicus and Junia, my relatives who were
16: 8 **G** Ampliatus, my beloved in the Lord.
16: 9 **G** Urbanus, our co-worker in Christ,
16:10 **G** Apelles, who is approved in Christ.
16:10 **G** those who belong to the family of Aristobulus.
16:11 **G** my relative Herodion. Greet those in the
16:11 **G** those in the Lord who belong to the family
16:12 **G** those workers in the Lord,
Ro 16:12 **G** the beloved Persis, who has worked hard in
16:13 **G** Rufus, chosen in the Lord;
16:13 and **g** his mother—a mother to me also.
16:14 **G** Asyncritus, Phlegon, Hermes, Patrobas,
16:15 **G** Philologus, Julia, Nereus and his sister,
16:16 **G** one another with a holy kiss.
16:16 All the churches of Christ **g** you.
16:22 the writer of this letter, **g** you in the Lord.
16:23 the city treasurer, and our brother Quartus, **g** you.
1Co 16:19 **g** you warmly in the Lord.
16:20 **G** one another with a holy kiss.
2Co 13:12 **G** one another with a holy kiss.
13:12 All the saints **g** you.
Php 4:21 **G** every saint in Christ Jesus.
4:21 The friends who are with me **g** you.
4:22 All the saints **g** you, especially those of
Col 4:14 Luke, the beloved physician, and Demas **g** you.
1Th 5:26 **G** all the brothers and sisters with a holy kiss.
2Ti 4:19 **G** Prisca and Aquila, and the household
Tit 3:15 **G** those who love us in the faith.
Heb 13:24 **G** all your leaders and all the saints.
1Pe 5:14 **G** one another with a kiss of love.
3Jn 1:15 **G** the friends there, each by name.
Sir 41:20 and of silence, before those who **g** you;
1Mc 7:33 of the people came out to **g** him peaceably and
12:17 also to you and **g** you and deliver to you this letter
3Mc 1: 8 of their council and elders to **g** him,

GREETED (17) [GREET]
Jdg 18:15 at the home of Micah, and **g** him.
1Sa 6:19 the people of Beth-shemesh when they **g** the ark
17:22 ran to the ranks, and went and **g** his brothers.
2Ki 10:15 he **g** him, and said to him,
Mt 23: 7 and to be **g** with respect in the marketplaces,
Mk 12:38 and to be **g** with respect in the marketplaces,
Lk 1:40 the house of Zechariah and **g** Elizabeth.
11:43 the seat of honor in the synagogues and to be **g**
20:46 and love to be **g** with respect in the marketplaces,
Ac 18:22 he went up to Jerusalem and **g** the church,
21: 7 and we **g** the believers and stayed with them
Heb 11:13 but from a distance they saw and **g** them.
Tob 5:10 So he went in to him, and Tobit **g** him first.
7: 1 They **g** him first, and he replied,
9: 6 He sprang up and **g** Gabael,
1Mc 7:29 and they **g** one another peaceably;
11: 6 and they **g** one another and spent the night there.

GREETING (12) [GREET]
2Ki 4:29 If you meet anyone, give no **g,**
Ezr 4:11 of the province Beyond the River, send **g.**
4:17 in the rest of the province Beyond the River, **g.**
Lk 1:29 and pondered what sort of **g** this might be.
1:41 When Elizabeth heard Mary's **g,**
1:44 For as soon as I heard the sound of your **g,**
Ac 21:19 After **g** them, he related one by one the things
1Co 16:21 I, Paul, write this **g** with my own hand.
Col 4:18 I, Paul, write this **g** with my own hand.
2Th 3:17 I, Paul, write this **g** with my own hand.
Sir 4: 8 and return their **g** politely.
1Es 8: 9 the priest and reader of the law of the Lord, **g.**

GREETINGS (39) [GREET]
Mt 26:49 At once he came up to Jesus and said, **"G,** Rabbi!"
28: 9 Suddenly Jesus met them and said, **"G!"**
Lk 1:28 And he came to her and said, **"G,** favored one!
Ac 15:23 in Antioch and Syria and Cilicia, **g.**
23:26 to his Excellency the governor Felix, **g.**
1Co 16:19 The churches of Asia send **g.**
16:20 All the brothers and sisters send **g.**
Col 4:15 Give my **g** to the brothers and sisters in Laodicea,
2Ti 4:21 Eubulus sends **g** to you, as do Pudens and Linus
Tit 3:15 All who are with me send **g** to you.
Phm 1:23 my fellow prisoner in Christ Jesus, sends **g** to you,
Heb 13:24 Those from Italy send you **g.**
Jas 1: 1 To the twelve tribes in the Dispersion: **G.**
1Pe 5:13 sends you **g;** and so does my son Mark.
2Jn 1:13 The children of your elect sister send you their **g.**
3Jn 1:15 The friends send you their **g.**
Tob 5:10 He replied, "Joyous **g** to you!"
7: 1 They greeted him first, and he replied, "Joyous **g,**
AdE 16: 1 and to those who are loyal to our government, **g.**
1Mc 10:18 "King Alexander to his brother Jonathan, **g.**
10:25 "King Demetrius to the nation of the Jews, **g.**
11:30 and to the nation of the Jews, **g.**
11:32 'King Demetrius to his father Lasthenes, **g.**
12: 6 the Jewish people to their brothers the Spartans, **g.**
12:20 to the high priest Onias, **g.**
13:36 and to the elders and nation of the Jews, **g.**
14:20 and the rest of the Jewish people, our brothers, **g.**
15: 2 and ethnarch and to the nation of the Jews, **g.**
15:16 consul of the Romans, to King Ptolemy, **g.**
2Mc 1: 1 of Judea, To their Jewish kindred in Egypt, **G**
1:10 and to the Jews in Egypt, **G** and good health.
9:19 Antiochus their king and general sends hearty **g**
11:16 "Lysias to the people of the Jews, **g.**
11:22 "King Antiochus to his brother Lysias, **g.**
11:27 to the senate of the Jews and to the other Jews, **g.**
11:34 to the people of the Jews, **g.**
1Es 6: 8 "To King Darius, **g.** Let it be fully
3Mc 3:12 in Egypt and all its districts, **g** and good health:
7: 1 in authority in his government, **g** and good health:

GREETS (6) [GREET]
2Ki 4:29 give no greeting, and if anyone **g** you,
Ro 16:21 Timothy, my co-worker, **g** you;

Ro 16:23 who is host to me and to the whole church, g you.
Col 4:10 Aristarchus my fellow prisoner g you,
4:11 And Jesus who is called Justus g you.
4:12 a servant of Christ Jesus, g you.

GREW‡ (72) [GROW]

Ge 19:25 and what g on the ground.
21: 8 The child g, and was weaned;
21:20 God was with the boy, and he g up;
25:27 When the boys g up, Esau was a skillful hunter,
30:43 Thus the man g exceedingly rich,
Ex 1: 7 they multiplied and g exceedingly strong,
2:10 When the child g up, she brought him
16:21 but when the sun g hot, it melted.
17:12 But Moses' hands g weary;
19:19 As the blast of the trumpet g louder and louder,
Dt 32:15 Jacob ate his fill; Jeshurun g fat, and kicked.
32:15 You g fat, bloated, and gorged!
Jos 17:13 But when the Israelites g strong,
Jdg 1:28 When Israel g strong, they put the Canaanites
2:10 and another generation g up after them,
5: 7 they g fat on plunder, because you arose, Deborah,
11: 2 and when his wife's sons g up,
13:24 The boy g, and the LORD blessed him.
1Sa 2:21 boy Samuel g up in the presence of the LORD.
3:19 As Samuel g up, the LORD was with him
2Sa 3: 1 David g stronger and stronger,
12: 3 and it g up with him and with his children;
15:12 The conspiracy g in strength,
21:15 against the Philistines, and David g weary.
23:10 down the Philistines until his arm g weary,
1Ki 18:45 while the heavens g black with clouds and wind;
22:35 The battle g hot that day,
2Ch 12: 1 of Rehoboam was established and he g strong,
13:21 But Abijah g strong. He took fourteen wives,
17:12 Jehoshaphat g steadily greater.
18:34 The battle g hot that day, and the king
24:15 But Jehoiada g old and full of days, and died;
26:16 But when he had become strong he g proud,
Est 9: 4 as the man Mordecai g more and more powerful.
Ps 39: 2 to no avail; my distress g worse,
Isa 53: 2 For he g up before him like a young plant,
57:10 You g weary from your many wanderings,
Eze 16: 7 You g up and became tall and arrived
16:13 You g exceedingly beautiful, fit to be a queen.
17:10 wither on the bed where it g?
31: 5 its boughs g large and its branches long,
Da 4:11 The tree g great and strong,
4:20 The tree that you saw, which g great and strong,
4:33 until his hair g as long as eagles' feathers
8: 8 Then the male goat g exceedingly great;
8: 9 which g exceedingly great toward the south,
8:10 It g as high as the host of heaven.
10: 8 and my complexion g deathly pale,
Jnh 1:13 for the sea g more and more stormy against them.
Mt 13: 7 and the thorns g up and choked them.
Mk 4: 7 and the thorns g up and choked it,
5:26 and she was no better, but rather g worse.
6:35 When it g late, his disciples came to him and said,
Lk 1:80 The child g and became strong in spirit,
2:40 child g and became strong, filled with wisdom;
8: 6 and as it g up, it withered for lack of moisture.
8: 7 and the thorns g with it and choked it.
8: 8 Some fell into good soil, and when it g,
13:19 it g and became a tree,
Ac 19:20 So the word of the Lord g mightily and prevailed.
Ro 4:20 he g strong in his faith as he gave glory to God,
Rev 18:19 all who had ships at sea g rich by her wealth!
Jdt 5: 9 and g very prosperous in gold and silver
16:23 and g old in her husband's house,
Sir 24:13 "I g tall like a cedar in Lebanon,
24:14 I g tall like a palm tree in En-gedi,
24:14 and like a plane tree beside water I g tall.
1Mc 1:40 Her dishonor now g as great as her glory;
10:81 and the enemy's horses g tired.
2Mc 5:27 they continued to live on what g wild,
2Es 9:47 when he g up and I came to take a wife for him,
11: 3 I saw that out of its wings there g opposing wings;

GREY, GREYHEADED (KJV) See GRAY

GREYHOUND (KJV) See ROOSTER

GRIDDLE (3)

Lev 2: 5 If your offering is grain prepared on a g,
6:21 It shall be made with oil on a g;
7: 9 and all that is prepared in a pan or on a g,

GRIEF‡ (40) [GRIEF-STRICKEN, GRIEVANCE, GRIEVE, GRIEVED, GRIEVING, GRIEVOUS, GRIEVOUSLY]

1Sa 25:31 my lord shall have no cause of g,
Job 17: 7 My eye has grown dim from g,
Ps 6: 7 My eyes waste away because of g;
10:14 Indeed you note trouble and g,
31: 9 my eye wastes away from g,
77:10 "It is my g that the right hand of
Pr 10: 1 but a foolish child is a mother's g.
14:13 in laughter the heart is sad, and the end of joy is g.
17:25 Foolish children are a g to their father
Isa 17:11 yet the harvest will flee away in a day of g
Jer 8:18 My joy is gone, g is upon me, my heart is sick.
La 3:32 Although he causes g, he will have compassion
3:51 My eyes cause me g at the fate of all
Eze 21: 6 with breaking heart and bitter g before their eyes.
Lk 22:45 and found them sleeping because of g,
2Co 7: 9 but because your g led to repentance;
7: 9 for you felt a godly g,
7:10 For godly g produces a repentance that leads
7:10 but worldly g produces death.
7:11 see what earnestness this godly g has produced
Rev 18: 7 so give her a like measure of torment and g.
18: 7 I am no widow, and I will never see g,'
Tob 3: 1 Then with much g and anguish of heart I wept,
Wis 8: 9 and encouragement in cares and g.
11:12 for a twofold g possessed them,
14:15 consumed with g at an untimely bereavement,
Sir 22: 4 but one who acts shamefully is a g to her father.
29:19 The sinner comes to g through surety;
30: 5 upon with joy and at death, without g.
36:25 A perverse mind will cause g,
38:17 then be comforted for your g.
38:18 For g may result in death,
38:20 Do not give your heart to g;
Bar 4:34 and her insolence will be turned to g.
1Es 8:71 and sat down in anxiety and g.
3Mc 7: 9 against them or cause them any g at all,
2Es 5:34 "No, my lord, but because of my g I have spoken;
7:*131* [61] there shall not be g at their destruction,
10: 7 the mother of us all, is in deep g and great distress.
4Mc 18: 9 and did not have the g of bereavement.

GRIEF-STRICKEN (1) [GRIEF]

1Es 8:72 and I sat g until the evening sacrifice.

GRIEVANCE (1) [GRIEF]

1Co 6: 1 When any of you has a g against another,

GRIEVE‡ (18) [GRIEF]

1Sa 2:33 be spared to weep out his eyes and g his heart;
16: 1 "How long will you g over Saul?
Isa 51:19 These two things have befallen you—who will g
La 1: 4 her young girls g, and her lot is bitter.
3:33 for he does not willingly afflict or g anyone.
Eph 4:30 And do not g the Holy Spirit of God,
1Th 4:13 you may not g as others do who have no hope.
Tob 4: 3 and do not g her in anything.
10: 6 Do not g for him, my dear; he will soon be here."
10:12 do nothing to g her all the days of your life.
13:14 Happy also are all people who g with you because
Wis 14:24 or g one another by adultery,
Sir 3:12 and do not g him as long as he lives;
4: 2 Do not g the hungry, or anger one in need.
30: 9 play with him, and he will g you.
37:12 and who will g with you if you fail.
2Es 7:*61* not g over the great number of those who perish;
4Mc 16:12 nor did she g as they were dying.

GRIEVED‡ (39) [GRIEF]

Ge 6: 6 and it g him to his heart.
1Sa 15:35 until the day of his death, but Samuel g over Saul.
20: 3 'Do not let Jonathan know this, or he will be g.'
20:34 for he was g for David,
Ne 8:10 and do not be g, for the joy of
8:11 for this day is holy; do not be g."
Job 30:25 Was not my soul g for the poor?
Ps 35:14 as though I g for a friend or a brother;
78:40 against him in the wilderness and g him in
Isa 19:10 and all who work for wages will be g.
54: 6 like a wife forsaken and g in spirit,
63:10 But they rebelled and g his holy spirit;
Am 6: 6 but are not g over the ruin of Joseph!
Mt 14: 9 The king was g, yet out of regard for his oaths and
26:37 and began to be g and agitated.
26:38 he said to them, "I am deeply g, even to death;
Mk 3: 5 he was g at their hardness of heart and said to
6:26 The king was deeply g;
14:34 he said to them, "I am deeply g, even to death;
2Co 7: 8 for I see that I g you with that letter,
7: 9 Now I rejoice, not because you were g,
Tob 3:10 On that day she was g in spirit and wept.
Sir 21:24 the discreet would be g by the disgrace.
26:28 At two things my heart is g, and because of
47:20 and they were g at your folly,
Bar 2:18 but the person who is deeply g,
4: 8 who brought you up, and you g Jerusalem,
4:33 so she will be g at her own desolation.
1Mc 14:16 that Jonathan had died, and they were deeply g.
2Mc 4:35 were g and displeased at the unjust murder of
4:37 Antiochus was g at heart and filled with pity,
14:28 and g that he had to annul their agreement when
1Es 1:24 and how they g the Lord deeply,
3Mc 3: 8 being g at the situation, and expected
2Es 8:15 I will speak about your people, for whom I am g,
9:38 and was deeply g at heart;
9:40 and why are you g at heart?"
10:50 that you are sincerely g and profoundly distressed
4Mc 16:22 the same faith in God and not be g.

GRIEVING (7) [GRIEF]

2Sa 19: 2 troops heard that day, "The king is g for his son."
Mt 19:22 the young man heard this word, he went away g,
Mk 10:22 he heard this, he was shocked and went away g,
Ac 20:38 g especially because of what he had said,
Tob 6:15 and mother's life down to their grave, g for me—
2Es 7:*80* always g and sad, in seven ways.
10:11 or you who are g for one alone?

GRIEVOUS (21) [GRIEF]

Ge 41:31 for it will be very g.
50:11 a g mourning on the part of the Egyptians."
Dt 28:35 and on the legs with g boils of which you cannot
28:59 and lasting afflictions and g and lasting maladies.
Ecc 2:17 because what is done under the sun was g to me;
5:13 There is a g ill that I have seen under the sun:
5:16 This also is a g ill:
6: 2 This is vanity; it is a g ill.
Jer 14:17 down with a crushing blow, with a very g wound.
30:12 Your hurt is incurable, your wound is g.
Mic 2:10 of uncleanness that destroys with a g destruction.
Wis 3:19 For the end of an unrighteous generation is g.
Sir 27:15 and their abuse is g to hear.
2Mc 6: 3 Harsh and utterly g was the onslaught of evil.
3Mc 5:47 the g and pitiful destruction of
6: 5 speaking g words with boasting and insolence,
2Es 5:21 the thoughts of my heart were very g to me again.
11:40 and over all the earth with g oppression;
14:15 lay to one side the thoughts that are most g to you,
4Mc 9: 4 to be more g than death itself.
16: 8 and the more g anxieties of your upbringing.

GRIEVOUSLY (6) [GRIEF]

1Sa 10:27 had been g oppressing the Gadites and
La 1: 8 Jerusalem sinned g, so she has become
Eze 25:12 of Judah and has g offended in taking vengeance
Zec 12: 3 all who lift it shall g hurt themselves.
Aza 1: 6 in all matters we have sinned g.
3Mc 2: 2 give attention to us who are suffering g from

GRIM-FACED (1) [FACE]

Dt 28:50 a g nation showing no respect to the old or favor

GRIND (5) [GRINDING, GRINDS]

Job 31:10 then let my wife g for another,
Ecc 12: 3 and the women who g cease working
Isa 47: 2 Take the millstones and g meal, remove your veil,
La 3:16 He has made my teeth g on gravel,
5:13 Young men are compelled to g,

GRINDING (6) [GRIND]

Dt 9:21 g it thoroughly, until it was reduced to dust;
Ecc 12: 4 and the sound of the g is low,
Isa 3:15 by g the face of the poor?
Mt 24:41 Two women will be g meal together;
Lk 17:35 There will be two women g meal together;
Sir 51: 3 from g teeth about to devour me,

GRINDS (1) [GRIND]

Mk 9:18 and he foams and g his teeth and becomes rigid;

GRIP (2) [GRIPPED, GRIPPING]

Dt 25:11 of one intervenes to rescue her husband from the g
Sir 6: 2 Do not fall into the g of passion,

GRIPPED (1) [GRIP]

1Mc 6: 9 because deep disappointment continually g him,

GRIPPING (1) [GRIP]

Ge 25:26 with his hand g Esau's heel;

GRISLED (KJV) See DAPPLED, MOTTLED

GROAN‡ (21) [GROANED, GROANING, GROANINGS, GROANS]

Job 24:12 From the city the dying g,
Ps 12: 5 the poor are despoiled, because the needy g,
38: 8 I g because of the tumult of my heart.
Pr 5:11 and at the end of your life you will g,
29: 2 but when the wicked rule, the people g.
Jer 22:23 how you will g when pangs come upon you,
51:52 and through all her land the wounded shall g.
La 1: 4 all her gates are desolate, her priests g;
1:11 All her people g as they search for bread;
Eze 9: 4 of those who sigh and g over all the abominations
24:23 but you shall pine away in your iniquities and g
26:15 at the sound of your fall, when the wounded g,
30:24 but I will break the arms of Pharaoh, and he will g
Joel 1:18 How the animals g! The herds of cattle
Mic 4:10 Writhe and g, O daughter Zion,
Ro 8:23 g inwardly while we wait for adoption,
2Co 5: 2 For in this tent we g, longing to be clothed
5: 4 we are still in this tent, we g under our burden,
Wis 5: 3 and in anguish of spirit they will g, and say,
2Es 16:39 in coming upon the earth, and the world will g,
4Mc 9:21 worthy of Abraham, did not g,

GROANED (7) [GROAN]

Ex 2:23 The Israelites g under their slavery, and cried out.
Jdt 14:16 with a loud voice and wept and g and shouted,
Sus 1:22 Susanna g and said, "I am completely trapped.
1Mc 1:26 rulers and elders g, young women
2Mc 6:30 about to die under the blows, he g aloud and said:
3Mc 4: 2 and they g because of the unexpected destruction
6:34 g as they themselves were overcome by disgrace,

GROANING (15) [GROAN]

Ex 2:24 God heard their g, and God remembered his
6: 5 I have also heard the g of the Israelites whom

Jdg 2:18 to pity by their **g** because of those who persecuted
Job 23: 2 his hand is heavy despite my **g**.
Ps 22: 1 from the words of my **g?**
32: 3 my body wasted away through my **g** all day long.
102: 5 Because of my loud **g** my bones cling to my skin.
Jer 45: 3 I am weary with my **g**, and I find no rest."
La 1:21 They heard how I was **g**,
Mal 2:13 the LORD's altar with tears, with weeping and **g**
Ac 7:34 in Egypt and have heard their **g**,
Ro 8:22 that the whole creation has been **g** in labor pains
Tob 3: 1 and with **g** began to pray:
Wis 11:12 and a **g** at the memory of what had occurred.
Sir 41: 9 you will beget them only for **g**.

GROANINGS (2) [GROAN]

Job 3:24 and my **g** are poured out like water.
2Es 1:19 I pitied your **g** and gave you manna for food;

GROANS (9) [GROAN]

Ps 79:11 Let the **g** of the prisoners come before you;
102:20 to hear the **g** of the prisoners,
La 1: 8 she herself **g**, and turns her face away.
1:22 for my **g** are many and my heart is faint.
Eze 30:24 before him with the **g** of one mortally wounded.
Sir 30:20 and **g** as a eunuch **g** when embracing a girl.
3Mc 1:18 and filled the streets with **g** and lamentations.
5:49 and **g** they kissed each other, embracing relatives

GROPE (6) [GROPING]

Dt 28:29 you shall **g** about at noon as blind people **g**
Job 5:14 and **g** at noonday as in the night.
12:25 They **g** in the dark without light;
Isa 59:10 We **g** like the blind along a wall,
Ac 17:27 so that they would search for God and perhaps **g**

GROPING (2) [GROPE]

Isa 59:10 **g** like those who have no eyes;
Ac 13:11 and he went about **g** for someone to lead him by

GROSS (1)

Ps 119:70 Their hearts are fat and **g**,

GROSS (KJV) See also DEEP, DULL, THICK

GROUND‡ (322) [GROUNDED, GROUNDLESS, GROUNDS, UNDERGROUND]

Ge 1:25 everything that creeps upon the **g** of every kind.
2: 5 and there was no one to till the **g**;
2: 6 and water the whole face of the **g**—
2: 7 of the **g**, and breathed into his nostrils the breath
2: 9 of the **g** the LORD God made to grow every tree
2:19 of the **g** the LORD God formed every animal of
3:17 cursed is the **g** because of you;
3:19 you return to the **g**, for out of it you were taken;
3:23 to till the **g** from which he was taken.
4: 2 and Cain a tiller of the **g**.
4: 3 to the LORD an offering of the fruit of the **g**,
4:10 brother's blood is crying out to me from the **g!**
4:11 And now you are cursed from the **g**,
4:12 till the **g**, it will no longer yield to you its strength;
5:29 he named him Noah, saying, "Out of the **g** that
6: 1 people began to multiply on the face of the **g**,
6:20 of every creeping thing of the **g** according
7: 4 from the face of the **g**."
7: 8 and of everything that creeps on the **g**,
7:23 on the face of the **g**, human beings and animals
8: 8 if the waters had subsided from the face of the **g**;
8:13 and saw that the face of the **g** was drying.
8:21 the **g** because of humankind, for the inclination of
9: 2 on everything that creeps on the **g**,
18: 2 and bowed down to the **g**.
19: 1 and bowed down with his face to the **g**.
19:25 and what grew on the **g**.
23: 6 none of us will withhold from you any burial **g**
24:52 he bowed himself to the **g** before the LORD.
33: 3 bowing himself to the **g** seven times,
37:10 and bow to the **g** before you?"
38: 9 he spilled his semen on the **g** whenever he went in
42: 6 before him with their faces to the **g**.
43:26 and bowed to the **g** before him.
44:11 Then each one quickly lowered his sack to the **g**,
44:14 and they fell to the **g** before him.
Ex 3: 5 for the place on which you are standing is holy **g**."
4: 3 And he said, "Throw it on the **g**."
4: 3 he threw the staff on the **g**, and it became a snake;
4: 9 from the Nile and pour it on the dry **g**;
4: 9 from the Nile will become blood on the dry **g**."
14:16 that the Israelites may go into the sea on dry **g**.
14:22 The Israelites went into the sea on dry **g**,
14:29 But the Israelites walked on dry **g** through the sea,
15:19 but the Israelites walked through the sea on dry **g**.
16:14 as fine as frost on the **g**.
23:19 of the first fruits of your **g** you shall bring into
32:20 **g** it to powder, scattered it on the water,
34:26 of the first fruits of your **g** you shall bring to
Lev 11:21 with which to leap on the **g**.
20:25 or by bird or by anything with which the **g** teems,
27:30 the **g** or the fruit from the tree, are the LORD's;
Nu 11: 8 **g** it in mills or beat it in mortars,
11:31 about two cubits deep on the **g**.
16:30 and the **g** opens its mouth and swallows them up,
16:31 the **g** under them was split apart.
Dt 4:18 the likeness of anything that creeps on the **g**,
7:13 the fruit of your womb and the fruit of your **g**,
12:16 you shall pour it out on the **g** like water.
12:24 you shall pour it out on the **g** like water.
15:23 you shall pour it out on the **g** like water.
22: 6 you come on a bird's nest, in any tree or on the **g**,
26: 2 of the first of all the fruit of the **g**,
26:10 now I bring the first of the fruit of the **g** that you,
26:15 and the **g** that you have given us, as you swore
28: 4 the fruit of your **g**, and the fruit of your livestock,
28:11 of your **g** in the land that the LORD swore
28:18 of your **g**, the increase of your cattle and the issue
28:33 not know shall eat up the fruit of your **g** and
28:42 and the fruit of your **g** the cicada shall take over.
28:51 the fruit of your livestock and the fruit of your **g**
28:56 not venture to set the sole of her foot on the **g**,
Jos 3:17 While all Israel were crossing over on dry **g**,
3:17 of the covenant of the LORD stood on dry **g** in
4:18 and the soles of the priests' feet touched dry **g**,
4:22 'Israel crossed over the Jordan here on dry **g**.'
7: 6 to the **g** on his face before the ark of the LORD
7:21 They now lie hidden in the **g** inside my tent,
17:15 and clear **g** there for yourselves in the land of
24:32 in the portion of **g** that Jacob had bought from
Jdg 4:21 until it went down into the **g**—
6:37 and it is dry on all the **g**,
6:39 and on all the **g** let there be dew."
6:40 and on all the **g** there was dew.
13:20 and they fell on their faces to the **g**.
16:21 and he **g** at the mill in the prison.
20:36 The Israelites gave **g** to Benjamin,
Ru 2:10 Then she fell prostrate, with her face to the **g**,
1Sa 3:19 with him and let none of his words fall to the **g**.
5: 3 on his face to the **g** before the ark of the LORD.
5: 4 to the **g** before the ark of the LORD, and the head
8:12 and some to plow his **g** and to reap his harvest,
14:25 and there was honey on the **g**.
14:32 and slaughtered them on the **g**;
14:45 not one hair of his head shall fall to the **g**;
17:49 and he fell face down on the **g**.
20:41 and prostrated himself with his face to the **g**.
24: 8 David bowed with his face to the **g**,
25:23 fell before David on her face, bowing to the **g**.
25:41 She rose and bowed down, with her face to the **g**,
26: 7 with his spear stuck in the **g** at his head;
26: 8 therefore let me pin him to the **g** with one stroke
26:20 Now therefore, do not let my blood fall to the **g**,
28:13 "I see a divine being coming up out of the **g**."
28:14 and he bowed with his face to the **g**,
28:20 Immediately Saul fell full length on the **g**,
28:23 So he got up from the **g** and sat on the bed.
30:16 they were spread out all over the **g**,
2Sa 1: 2 he fell to the **g** and did obeisance.
2:22 why should I strike you to the **g?**
8: 2 making them lie down on the **g**,
12:16 and went in and lay all night on the **g**.
12:17 urging him to rise from the **g**;
12:20 Then David rose from the **g**, washed,
13:31 king rose, tore his garments, and lay on the **g**;
14: 4 she fell on her face to the **g** and did obeisance,
14:11 not one hair of your son shall fall to the **g**."
14:14 we are like water spilled on the **g**,
14:22 to the **g** and did obeisance, and blessed the king;
14:33 and prostrated himself with his face to the **g**
17:12 we shall light on him as the dew falls on the **g**;
18:11 Why then did you not strike him there to the **g?**
18:28 before the king with his face to the **g**,
20:10 the belly so that his entrails poured out on the **g**,
23:10 but he stood his **g**. He struck down the Philistines
23:11 where there was a plot of **g** full of lentils;
24:20 before the king with his face to the **g**.
1Ki 1:23 to the king, with his face to the **g**.
1:31 Then Bathsheba bowed with her face to the **g**,
1:52 not one of his hairs shall fall to the **g**;
7:46 in the clay **g** between Succoth and Zarethan.
2Ki 2: 8 until the two of them crossed on dry **g**.
2:15 to meet him and bowed to the **g** before him.
4:37 She came and fell at his feet, bowing to the **g**;
9:25 the plot of **g** belonging to Naboth the Jezreelite;
9:26 I swear I will repay you on this very plot of **g**.'
9:26 lift him out and throw him on the plot of **g**,
13:18 to the king of Israel, "Strike the **g** with them";
1Ch 11:13 There was a plot of **g** full of barley.
21:21 and did obeisance to David with his face to the **g**.
2Ch 4:17 in the clay **g** between Succoth and Zeredah.
7: 3 down on the pavement with their faces to the **g**,
20:18 Jehoshaphat bowed down with his face to the **g**,
20:24 there were corpses lying on the **g**;
Ne 8: 6 the LORD with their faces to the **g**.
Job 1:20 shaved his head, and fell on the **g** and worshiped.
2:13 with him on the **g** seven days and seven nights,
5: 6 nor does trouble sprout from the **g**;
14: 8 and its stump dies in the **g**,
16:13 he pours out my gall on the **g**.
18:10 A rope is hid for them in the **g**,
30: 3 and hard hunger they gnaw the dry and desolate **g**,
30: 6 in holes in the **g**, and in the rocks.
38:27 and to make the **g** put forth grass?
39:14 and lets them be warmed on the **g**,
39:24 With fierceness and rage it swallows the **g**;
Ps 7: 5 trample my life to the **g**,
12: 6 silver refined in a furnace on the **g**,
17:11 they set their eyes to cast me to the **g**.
26:12 My foot stands on level **g**;
44:25 our bodies cling to the **g**.
74: 7 of your name, bringing it to the **g**.
80: 9 You cleared the **g** for it;
Ps 83:10 who became dung for the **g**.
85:11 Faithfulness will spring up from the **g**,
89:44 and hurled his throne to the **g**.
104:30 and you renew the face of the **g**.
105:35 and ate up the fruit of their **g**.
107:33 springs of water into thirsty **g**,
143: 3 enemy has pursued me, crushing my life to the **g**,
147: 6 he casts the wicked to the **g**.
Pr 24:31 the **g** was covered with nettles,
Isa 2:19 Enter the caves of the rocks and the holes of the **g**,
3:26 ravaged, she shall sit upon the **g**.
14:12 How you are cut down to the **g**,
21: 9 all the images of her gods lie shattered on the **g**."
25:12 laid low, cast to the **g**, even to the dust.
26: 5 He lays it low to the **g**, casts it to the dust.
28:24 Do they continually open and harrow their **g?**
29: 4 your voice shall come from the **g** like the voice of
30:23 for the seed with which you sow the **g**,
30:23 and grain, the produce of the **g**,
30:24 the oxen and donkeys that till the **g** will eat silage,
35: 7 and the thirsty **g** springs of water;
40: 4 the uneven **g** shall become level,
42:16 the rough places into level **g**.
44: 3 and streams on the dry **g**;
47: 1 Sit on the **g** without a throne, daughter Chaldea!
49:23 With their faces to the **g** they shall bow down
51:23 like the **g** and like the street for them to walk on.
53: 2 and like a root out of dry **g**;
Jer 4: 3 Break up your fallow **g**, and do not sow among
7:20 on the trees of the field and the fruit of the **g**;
8: 2 they shall be like dung on the surface of the **g**.
10:17 Gather up your bundle from the **g**,
14: 2 they lie in gloom on the **g**,
14: 4 because the **g** is cracked.
16: 4 like dung on the surface of the **g**.
25:33 they shall become dung on the surface of the **g**.
48:18 Come down from glory, and sit on the parched **g**,
51:58 broad wall of Babylon shall be leveled to the **g**,
La 2: 2 to the **g** in dishonor the kingdom and its rulers.
2: 9 Her gates have sunk into the **g**;
2:10 The elders of daughter Zion sit on the **g** in silence;
2:10 of Jerusalem have bowed their heads to the **g**.
2:11 on the **g** because of the destruction of my people,
2:21 young and the old are lying on the **g** in the streets;
Eze 13:14 to the **g**, so that its foundation will be laid bare;
19:12 But it was plucked up in fury, cast down to the **g**;
24: 7 she did not pour it out on the **g**,
26:11 and your strong pillars shall fall to the **g**.
26:16 and shall sit on the **g**;
28:17 I cast you to the **g**; I exposed you before kings,
32: 4 I will throw you on the **g**,
38:20 and all creeping things that creep on the **g**,
38:20 and every wall shall tumble to the **g**.
42: 6 the **g** more than the lower and the middle ones.
43:14 the **g** to the lower ledge, two cubits, with a width
Da 4:15 But leave its stump and roots in the **g**,
4:23 but leave its stump and roots in the **g**,
6: 5 not find any **g** for complaint against this Daniel
7: 4 and it was lifted up from the **g** and made to stand
8: 5 the face of the whole earth without touching the **g**.
8: 7 it threw the ram down to the **g** and trampled
8:12 it cast truth to the **g**,
8:18 I fell into a trance, face to the **g**;
9:18 not present our supplication before you on the **g**
9:18 but on the **g** of your great mercies.
10: 9 I fell into a trance, face to the **g**.
10:15 I turned my face toward the **g** and was speechless.
Hos 2:18 and the creeping things of the **g**;
10:11 but I will make Ephraim break the **g**;
10:12 reap steadfast love; break up your fallow **g**;
Joel 1:10 The fields are devastated, the **g** mourns;
Am 3: 5 Does a snare spring up from the **g**,
3:14 horns of the altar shall be cut off and fall to the **g**.
5: 7 and bring righteousness to the **g!**
9: 9 but no pebble shall fall to the **g**.
Ob 1: 3 "Who will bring me down to the **g?**"
Zec 8:12 the **g** shall give its produce,
Mt 5:32 except on the **g** of unchastity,
10:29 of them will fall to the **g** apart from your Father
13: 5 Other seeds fell on rocky **g**,
13:20 As for what was sown on rocky **g**,
15:35 Then ordering the crowd to sit down on the **g**,
17: 6 they fell to the **g** and were overcome by fear.
25:18 the one talent went off and dug a hole in the **g**
25:25 and I went and hid your talent in the **g**.
26:39 he threw himself on the **g** and prayed, "My Father,
Mk 4: 5 Other seed fell on rocky **g**,
4:16 And these are the ones sown on rocky **g**:
4:26 as if someone would scatter seed on the **g**,
4:31 which, when sown upon the **g**,
8: 6 Then he ordered the crowd to sit down on the **g**;
9:20 and he fell on the **g** and rolled about,
14:35 he threw himself on the **g** and prayed that,
Lk 5:12 he bowed with his face to the **g** and begged him,
6:49 not act is like a man who built a house on the **g**
9:42 the demon dashed him to the **g** in convulsions.
19:44 They will crush you to the **g**,
22:44 ⟦his sweat became like great drops of blood falling down on the **g**.⟧
23:22 I have found in him no **g** for the sentence of death;
24: 5 and bowed their faces to the **g**,
Jn 4: 5 of **g** that Jacob had given to his son Joseph.
8: 6 ⟦down and wrote with his finger on the **g**.⟧
8: 8 ⟦once again he bent down and wrote on the **g**.⟧
9: 6 on the **g** and made mud with the saliva and spread
18: 6 "I am he," they stepped back and fell to the **g**.
Ac 7:33 for the place where you are standing is holy **g**.

Ac 7:54 they became enraged and g their teeth at Stephen.
9: 4 He fell to the g and heard a voice saying to him,
9: 8 Saul got up from the g, and
10:11 being lowered to the g by its four corners.
20: 9 he fell to the g three floors below and was picked
22: 7 I fell to the g and heard a voice saying to me,
26:14 When we had all fallen to the g,
Ro 3:30 he will justify the uncircumcised on the g of faith
1Co 9:15 no one will deprive me of my g for boasting!
9:16 this gives me no g for boasting,
10:25 without raising any question on the g
10:27 before you without raising any question on the g
1Ti 6: 2 on the g that they are members of the church;
Heb 6: 7 G that drinks up the rain falling on it repeatedly,
11:38 and in caves and holes in the g.
Tob 12:20 So now get up from the g, and acknowledge God.
14: 4 the temple of God in it will be burned to the g,
Jdt 5:18 The temple of their God was razed to the g,
12:15 Her maid went ahead and spread for her on the g
14:18 Look, Holofernes is lying on the g,
16: 4 and dash my infants to the g,
Wis 4:19 to the g, and shake them from the foundations;
11:22 and like a drop of morning dew that falls on the g.
Sir 11: 5 Many kings have had to sit on the g,
31:10 Let it be for him a g for boasting.
33:10 All human beings come from the g,
46:20 and lifted up his voice from the g in prophecy,
50:17 Then all the people together quickly fell to the g
Bar 5: 7 up, to make level g, so that Israel may walk safely
LtJ 6:27 if any of these gods falls to the g,
Aza 1:54 Bless the Lord, all that grows in the g;
1Mc 4:40 and fell face down on the g.
6:46 but it fell to the g upon him and he died.
14: 8 the g gave its increase, and the trees of
2Mc 2:30 the duty of the original historian to occupy the g,
3:27 to the g and deep darkness came over him,
8: 3 and about to be leveled to the g;
8: 8 When Philip saw that the man was gaining g little
9:14 to level to the g and to make a cemetery, he was
14:33 a prisoner, I will level this shrine of God to the g
1Es 8:91 weeping and lying on the g before the temple,
9:47 and fell to the g and worshiped the Lord.
3Mc 2:22 so that he lay helpless on the g and,
5:31 who give me no g for complaint
5:43 against Judea and rapidly level it to the g with fire
5:43 and by burning to the g the temple inaccessible
5:50 with one accord on the g,
6: 7 down into the g to lions as food for wild animals,
2Es 8:41 as the farmer sows many seeds in the g and plants
9:34 when the g has received seed, or the sea a ship,
15:13 Let the farmers that till the g mourn,
4Mc 6: 7 Although he fell to the g because his body could
15:15 their toes and fingers scattered on the g,

GROUNDED (1) [GROUND]
Eph 3:17 as you are being rooted and g in love.

GROUNDLESS (1) [GROUND]
Sir 40: 7 astonished that his fears were g.

GROUNDS (4) [GROUND]
Isa 29:21 and without g deny justice to the one in the right.
Da 6: 4 So the presidents and the satraps tried to find g
6: 4 But they could find no g for complaint
Sir 13:19 likewise the poor are feeding g for the rich.

GROUP (9) [GROUPED, GROUPING, GROUPINGS, GROUPS]
2Sa 2:13 One g sat on one side of the pool,
Lk 2:44 Assuming that he was in the g of travelers,
24:22 Moreover, some women of our g astounded us.
Ac 4:32 Now the whole g of those who believed were
20:30 Some even from your own g will come distorting
23: 9 and certain scribes of the Pharisees' g stood up
1Mc 7:12 a g of scribes appeared in a body before Alcimus
10:61 A g of malcontents from Israel, renegades,
3Mc 6:35 arranged the aforementioned choral g and passed

GROUPED (1) [GROUP]
4Mc 8: 4 g about their mother as though a chorus,

GROUPING (1) [GROUP]
1Es 1:11 the g of the ancestral houses, before the people,

GROUPINGS (3) [GROUP]
2Ch 35: 5 Take position in the holy place according to the g
35:12 that they might distribute them according to the g
1Es 1: 5 Stand in order in the temple according to the g of

GROUPS (8) [GROUP]
2Sa 18: 2 And David divided the army into three g:
Mk 6:39 the people to sit down in g on the green grass.
6:40 So they sat down in g of hundreds and of fifties.
Lk 9:14 "Make them sit down in g of about fifty each."
Eph 2:14 in his flesh he has made both g into one
2:16 and might reconcile both g to God in one body
1Es 5: 4 to their ancestral houses in the tribes, over their g:
8:28 according to their ancestral houses and their g,

GROVELS (1)
Sir 40: 3 on a splendid throne to the one who g in dust

GROVES (5)
Nu 24: 6 Like palm g that stretch far away,
Dt 6:11 vineyards and olive g that you did not plant—
Jdg 15: 5 as well as the vineyards and olive g.
Jdt 3: 8 and cut down their sacred g;
2Es 16:28 those who have hidden themselves in thick g

GROW‡ (73) [AFTERGROWTH, GREW, GROWING, GROWN, GROWS, GROWTH, OVERGROWN, VINEGROWER]
Ge 2: 9 the ground the LORD God made to g every tree
48:16 and let them g into a multitude on the earth."
Nu 6: 5 they shall let the locks of the head g long.
Jdg 16:22 But the hair of his head began to g again
1Sa 2:26 the boy Samuel continued to g both in stature and
3: 2 to g dim so that he could not see, was lying down
Ezr 4:22 why should damage g to the hurt of the king?"
Job 8:11 "Can papyrus g where there is no marsh?
17: 9 they that have clean hands g stronger and stronger.
21: 7 reach old age, and g mighty in power?
31:40 let thorns g instead of wheat,
39: 4 they g up in the open;
Ps 6: 7 they g weak because of all my foes.
38: 5 My wounds g foul and fester because
69: 3 My eyes g dim with waiting for my God.
92:12 and g like a cedar in Lebanon.
104:14 You cause the grass to g for the cattle,
147: 8 makes grass g on the hills.
Pr 11:24 Some give freely, yet g all the richer;
Isa 9: 7 His authority shall g continually,
11: 1 and a branch shall g out of his roots.
17: 4 and the fat of his flesh will g lean.
17:11 though you make them g on the day
19: 9 and the carders and those at the loom will g pale.
29:22 no longer shall his face g pale.
34:13 Thorns shall g over its strongholds,
40:28 He does not faint or g weary;
42: 4 He will not g faint or be crushed
44:14 and lets it g strong among the trees of the forest.
57:16 for then the spirits would g faint before me,
Jer 4:28 and the heavens above g black;
12: 2 they g and bring forth fruit;
Eze 7:17 All hands shall g feeble, all knees turn to water.
16: 7 and g up like a plant of the field."
31: 4 The waters nourished it, the deep made it g tall,
31:14 the waters may g to lofty height or set their tops
44:20 not shave their heads or let their locks g long;
47:12 there will g all kinds of trees for food.
Da 5:10 let your thoughts terrify you or your face g pale.
8:24 He shall g strong in power,
11: 5 "Then the king of the south shall g strong,
11: 5 but one of his officers shall g stronger than he
Hos 10: 8 Thorn and thistle shall g up on their altars.
Joel 2: 6 them peoples are in anguish, all faces g pale.
Jnh 4:10 which you did not labor and which you did not g;
Na 2:10 all loins quake, all faces g pale!
Zep 3:16 do not let your hands g weak.
Mt 6:28 Consider the lilies of the field, how they g;
13:30 Let both of them g together until the harvest;
24:12 the love of many will g cold.
Mk 4:27 and the seed would sprout and g,
Lk 12:27 Consider the lilies, how they g:
Jn 21:18 when you g old, you will stretch out your hands,
1Co 4:12 and we g weary from the work of our own hands.
Gal 6: 9 So let us not g weary in doing what is right,
Eph 4:15 we must g up in every way into him who is
Col 1:10 in every good work and as you g in the knowledge
Heb 12: 3 so that you may not g weary or lose heart.
1Pe 2: 2 so that by it you may g into salvation—
2Pe 3:18 But g in the grace and knowledge of our Lord
Tob 8: 7 and that we may g old together."
Sir 7:10 Do not g weary when you pray;
11:20 and g old in your work.
16:27 They neither hunger nor g weary,
26:21 *confidence in their good descent, will g great.*
43:30 summon all your strength, and do not g weary,
1Mc 2:64 be courageous and g strong in the law,
6:57 "Daily we g weaker, our food supply is scant,
2Es 2:19 on which roses and lilies g;
7:*34* truth shall stand, and faithfulness shall g strong.
14:10 age has lost its youth, and the times begin to g old.
15:13 to g and their trees shall be ruined by blight
4Mc 13:22 and they g stronger from this common nurture

GROWING (16) [GROW]
Ge 41: 5 plump and good, were g on one stalk.
41:22 full and good, g on one stalk,
Ecc 2: 6 from which to water the forest of g trees.
Isa 32:13 for the soil of my people g up in thorns and briers;
Jnh 1:11 For the sea was g more and more tempestuous.
Mk 4: 8 g up and increasing and yielding thirty and sixty
Col 1: 6 Just as it is bearing fruit and g in the whole world,
2Th 1: 3 as is right, because your faith is g abundantly,
Heb 8:13 what is obsolete and g old will soon disappear.
Sir 8: 6 for some of us are also g old.
39:13 and blossom like a rose g by a stream of water.
Bar 3:10 that you are g old in a foreign country,
2Mc 4:50 remained in office, g in wickedness,
2Es 15:16 g strong against one another,
4Mc 1:28 Just as pleasure and pain are two plants g from
13:20 g from the same blood and through the same life,

GROWL (6) [GROWLING, GROWLS]
Ex 11: 7 But not a dog shall g at any of the Israelites—
Ps 59:15 and g if they do not get their fill.
Isa 5:29 they g and seize their prey, they carry it off,
59:11 We all g like bears; like doves
Jer 51:38 they shall g like lions' whelps.
Jdt 11:19 and no dog will so much as g at you.

GROWLING (2) [GROWL]
Pr 19:12 A king's anger is like the g of a lion,
20: 2 The dread anger of a king is like the g of a lion;

GROWLS (1) [GROWL]
Isa 31: 4 As a lion or a young lion g over its prey, and—

GROWN‡ (40) [GROW]
Ge 18:12 "After I have g old, and my husband is old,
38:14 She saw that Shelah was g up,
Ex 2:11 One day, after Moses had g up,
Lev 13:37 and black hair has g in it, the itch is healed,
Dt 31:20 and they have eaten their fill and g fat,
Ru 1:13 would you then wait until they were g?
2Sa 10: 5 "Remain at Jericho until your beards have g,
1Ki 12: 8 and consulted with the young men who had g up
12:10 young men who had g up with him said to him,
2Ki 19:26 like grass on the housetops, blighted before it is g.
1Ch 19: 5 "Remain at Jericho until your beards have g,
2Ch 10: 8 and consulted the young men who had g up
10:10 young men who had g up with him said to him,
Job 17: 7 My eye has g dim from grief,
Ps 144:12 May our sons in their youth be like plants full g,
Isa 37:27 like grass on the housetops, blighted before it is g.
Jer 5:28 they have g fat and sleek.
9: 3 they have g strong in the land for falsehood,
La 4: 1 the gold has g dim, how the pure gold is changed!
5:17 because of these things our eyes have g dim:
Eze 7:11 Violence has g into a rod of wickedness.
16: 7 your breasts were formed, and your hair had g;
Da 4:22 You have g great and strong.
Mt 13:15 For this people's heart has g dull,
13:32 but when it has g it is the greatest of shrubs
Jn 3: 4 "How can anyone be born after having g old?
Ac 28:27 For this people's heart has g dull,
1Co 7:29 the appointed time has g short;
Heb 11:24 By faith Moses, when he was g up,
Jas 1:15 it gives birth to sin, and that sin, when it is fully g,
Rev 2: 3 and that you have not g weary.
18: 3 and the merchants of the earth have g rich from
Wis 14:16 Then the ungodly custom, g strong with time,
1Mc 6: 6 that the Jews had g strong from the arms, supplies,
7:25 that Judas and those with him had g strong,
16: 3 But now I have g old,
2Mc 5:24 and commanded him to kill all the g men and
2Es 4:10 the things with which you have g up;
7:*48* For an evil heart has g up in us,
4Mc 18: 9 and when these sons had g up their father died.

GROWS‡ (17) [GROW]
Ge 38:11 until my son Shelah g up"—
Ex 10: 5 and they shall devour every tree of yours that g in
1Ki 4:33 in the Lebanon to the hyssop that g in the wall;
2Ki 19:29 This year you shall eat what g of itself,
Job 14: 8 Though its root g old in the earth,
31: 8 and let what g for me be rooted out.
Ps 88: 9 my eye g dim through sorrow.
129: 6 the grass on the housetops that withers before it g
Isa 5:30 and the light g dark with clouds.
37:30 This year eat what g of itself,
Hos 11: 8 my compassion g warm and tender.
Mk 4:32 when it is sown it g up and becomes the greatest
Eph 2:21 In him the whole structure is joined together and g
Col 2:19 g with a growth that is from God.
Aza 1:54 Bless the Lord, all that g in the ground;
2Es 7:*64* But now the mind g with us,
7:*71* for you have said that the mind g with us.

GROWTH (14) [GROW]
Dt 29:18 a root sprouting poisonous and bitter g.
32: 2 like gentle rain on grass, like showers on new g.
Ps 65:10 softening it with showers, and blessing its g.
Pr 27:25 When the grass is gone, and new g appears,
Isa 15: 6 the grass is withered, the new g fails,
Am 7: 1 at the time the latter g began to sprout (it was the latter g after the king's mowings).
1Co 3: 6 I planted, Apollos watered, but God gave the g.
3: 7 but only God who gives the g.
Eph 4:16 promotes the body's g in building itself up in love.
Col 2:19 grows with a g that is from God.
Jas 1:21 of all sordidness and rank g of wickedness,
Rev 9: 4 not to damage the grass of the earth or any green g
Sir 50:22 who fosters our g from birth,

GRUDGE (3) [GRUDGING]
Ge 50:15 a g against us and pays us back in full for all
Lev 19:18 not take vengeance or bear a g against any
Mk 6:19 And Herodias had a g against him,

GRUDGING (3) [GRUDGE]
Wis 7:13 I learned without guile and I impart without g;
Sir 14: 6 No one is worse than one who is g to himself;
18:18 and the gift of a g giver makes the eyes dim.

GRUMBLE (3) [GRUMBLED, GRUMBLERS, GRUMBLING]
Isa 29:24 and those who g will accept instruction.

Lk 19: 7 All who saw it began to g and said,
Jas 5: 9 Beloved, do not g against one another,

GRUMBLED (3) [GRUMBLE]

Dt 1:27 you g in your tents and said,
Ps 106:25 They g in their tents, and did not obey the voice of
Mt 20:11 they received it, they g against the landowner,

GRUMBLERS (1) [GRUMBLE]

Jude 1:16 These are g and malcontents;

GRUMBLING (5) [GRUMBLE]

Lk 15: 2 the Pharisees and the scribes were g and saying,
Wis 1:10 and the sound of g does not go unheard.
1:11 Beware then of useless g,
Sir 46: 7 and stilled their wicked g.
1Mc 11:39 that all the troops were g against Demetrius.

GUARANTEE (4) [GUARANTEED, GUARANTEEING, GUARANTOR]

Ps 119:122 G your servant's well-being;
Pr 11:15 To g loans for a stranger brings trouble,
2Co 5: 5 who has given us the Spirit as a g.
Heb 7:22 Jesus has also become the g of a better covenant.

GUARANTEED (2) [GUARANTEE]

Ro 4:16 that the promise may rest on grace and be g
Heb 6:17 he g it by an oath,

GUARANTEEING (1) [GUARANTEE]

Jos 9:15 g their lives by a treaty;

GUARANTOR (2) [GUARANTEE]

Sir 29:15 Do not forget the kindness of your g,
29:16 A sinner wastes the property of his g,

GUARD (147) [BODYGUARD, BODYGUARDS, GUARDED, GUARDIAN, GUARDIANS, GUARDING, GUARDROOM, GUARDS, SAFEGUARD]

Ge 3:24 and a sword flaming and turning to g the way to
37:36 one of Pharaoh's officials, the captain of the g.
39: 1 an officer of Pharaoh, the captain of the g,
40: 3 in custody in the house of the captain of the g,
40: 4 The captain of the g charged Joseph with them,
41:10 in custody in the house of the captain of the g.
41:12 a servant of the captain of the g.
Ex 23:20 to g you on the way and to bring you to the place
Nu 1:53 the g duty of the tabernacle of the covenant.
10:25 acting as the rear g of all the camps, set out,
Dt 23: 9 against your enemies you shall g
24: 8 G against an outbreak of a leprous skin disease
Jos 6: 9 the rear g came after the ark,
6:13 and the rear g came after the ark of the LORD,
8:13 that was north of the city and its rear g west of
10:18 and set men by it to g them;
Jdg 8:11 for the army was off its g.
1Sa 2: 9 "He will g the feet of his faithful ones,
19: 2 therefore be on g tomorrow morning;
22:17 The king said to the g who stood around him,
2Sa 20: 3 and put them in a house under g,
1Ki 14:27 to the hands of the officers of the g,
14:28 the g carried them and brought them back to
20:39 and brought a man to me, and said, 'G this man;
2Ki 9:14 with all Israel had been on g at Ramoth-gilead
11: 5 those who go off duty on the sabbath and g
11: 6 at the gate behind the guards), shall g the palace;
11: 7 on duty in force on the sabbath and g the house of
11:11 to g the king on every side.
11:13 the g and of the people, she went into the house of
25:10 of the g broke down the walls around Jerusalem.
25:11 Nebuzaradan the captain of the g carried into exile
25:12 the captain of the g left some of the poorest people
25:15 the captain of the g took away for the gold,
25:18 The captain of the g took the chief priest Seraiah,
25:20 Nebuzaradan the captain of the g took them,
1Ch 26:16 G corresponded to g.
2Ch 12:10 to the hands of the officers of the g,
12:11 the g would come along bearing them,
23:10 and he set all the people as a g for the king,
Ezr 8:29 G them and keep them until you weigh them
Ne 3:25 the upper house of the king at the court of the g.
4: 9 set a g as a protection against them day and night.
4:22 that they may be a g for us by night and may labor
4:23 the g who followed me ever took off our clothes;
7: 3 while the gatekeepers are still standing g,
12:25 and Akkub were gatekeepers standing g at
12:39 and they came to a halt at the Gate of the G.
13:22 and come and g the gates,
Job 7:12 or the Dragon, that you set a g over me?
Ps 12: 7 you will g us from this generation forever.
17: 8 G me as the apple of the eye;
25:20 O g my life, and deliver me;
39: 1 "I will g my ways that I may not sin
91:11 concerning you to g you in all your ways.
127: 1 LORD guards the city, the g keeps watch in vain.
140: 4 G me, O LORD, from the hands of the wicked;
141: 3 Set a g over my mouth, O LORD;
Pr 2:11 and understanding will g you.
4: 6 love her, and she will g you.
4:13 g her, for she is your life.
5: 2 and your lips may g knowledge.
13: 3 Those who g their mouths preserve their lives;
16:17 those who g their way preserve their lives.
Ecc 5: 1 G your steps when you go to the house of God;
Isa 27: 3 I g it night and day so that no one can harm it;
52:12 and the God of Israel will be your rear g.
58: 8 the glory of the LORD shall be your rear g.
Jer 32: 2 the court of the g that was in the palace of the king
32: 8 the g, in accordance with the word of the LORD,
32:12 the Judeans who were sitting in the court of the g.
33: 1 while he was still confined in the court of the g:
37:21 they committed Jeremiah to the court of the g;
37:21 So Jeremiah remained in the court of the g.
38: 6 the king's son, which was in the court of the g,
38:13 And Jeremiah remained in the court of the g.
38:28 And Jeremiah remained in the court of the g until
39: 9 the captain of the g exiled to Babylon the rest of
39:10 the captain of the g left in the land of Judah some
39:11 the captain of the g, saying,
39:13 So Nebuzaradan the captain of the g,
39:14 and took Jeremiah from the court of the g.
39:15 while he was confined in the court of the g:
40: 1 the captain of the g had let him go from Ramah,
40: 2 captain of the g took Jeremiah and said to him,
40: 5 the captain of the g gave him an allowance of food
41:10 whom Nebuzaradan, the captain of the g,
43: 6 of the g had left with Gedaliah son of Ahikam son
52:14 who were with the captain of the g,
52:15 of the g carried into exile some of the poorest of
52:16 the captain of the g left some of the poorest people
52:19 captain of the g took away the small bowls also,
52:24 The captain of the g took the chief priest Seraiah,
52:26 Then Nebuzaradan the captain of the g took them,
52:30 Nebuzaradan the captain of the g took into exile of
Da 1:11 the g whom the palace master had appointed
1:16 the g continued to withdraw their royal rations and
Mic 7: 5 g the doors of your mouth from her who lies
Na 2: 1 against you. G the ramparts;
Zec 9: 8 Then I will encamp at my house as a g,
Mal 2: 7 For the lips of a priest should g knowledge,
Mt 5:25 and the judge to the g,
27:65 Pilate said to them, "You have a g of soldiers;
27:66 So they went with the g and made the tomb secure
28:11 some of the g went into the city and told
Mk 6:27 a soldier of the g with orders to bring John's head.
14:44 arrest him and lead him away under g."
Lk 8:29 under g and bound with chains and shackles,
12:15 Be on your g against all kinds of greed;
17: 3 Be on your g! If another disciple sins,
21:34 "Be on g so that your hearts are not weighed down
Ac 12: 4 over to four squads of soldiers to g him,
12:10 After they had passed the first and the second g,
21:24 but that you yourself observe and g the law.
23:27 I came with the g and rescued him.
23:35 that he be kept under g in Herod's headquarters.
Php 1:13 the whole imperial g and to everyone else
4: 7 will g your hearts and your minds in Christ Jesus.
2Th 3: 3 he will strengthen you and g you from
1Ti 6:20 Timothy, g what has been entrusted to you.
2Ti 1:12 to g until that day what I have entrusted to him.
1:14 G the good treasure entrusted to you,
2Jn 1: 8 Be on your g, so that you do
Jdt 7: 5 they remained on g all that night.
AdE 6: 2 on g and sought to lay hands on King Artaxerxes.
Wis 9:11 in my actions and g me with her glory.
Sir 6:13 and be on g with your friends.
12:11 take care to be on your g against him.
13:13 Be on your g and very careful,
22:27 Who will set a g over my mouth,
26:11 Be on g against her impudent eye,
32:23 G yourself in every act, for this is the keeping of
34:19 a g against stumbling and a help against falling.
1Mc 4:61 Judas stationed a garrison there to g it;
4:61 he also fortified Beth-zur to g it,
5:18 with the rest of the forces, in Judea to g it;
6:50 So the king took Beth-zur and stationed a g there
9:53 and put them under g in the citadel at Jerusalem.
10:32 he may station in it men of his own choice to g it.
12:34 And he stationed a garrison there to g it.
13:12 and Jonathan was with him under g.
14: 3 and took him to Arsaces, who put him under g.
1Es 3: 4 who kept g over the person of the king,
8:59 and on g until you deliver them to the leaders of
3Mc 5:44 the places in the city most favorable for keeping g.
2Es 2:20 "G the rights of the widow,

GUARDED (14) [GUARD]

Dt 32:10 cared for him, g him as the apple of his eye.
2Ki 12: 9 the priests who g the threshold put in it all
Est 2:21 two of the king's eunuchs, who g the threshold,
6: 2 two of the king's eunuchs, who g the threshold,
Hos 12:12 and for a wife he g sheep.
12:13 and by a prophet he was g.
Jn 17:12 I g them, and not one of them was lost except
18:16 went out, spoke to the woman who g the gate,
2Co 11:32 under King Aretas g the city of Damascus in order
Gal 3:23 and g under the law until faith would be revealed.
1Es 4:56 and wages should be provided for all who g
2Es 7:85 how the habitations of the others are g by angels
7:95 being gathered into their chambers and g
4Mc 18: 7 but I g the rib from which woman was made.

GUARDIAN (8) [GUARD]

Eze 28:14 With an anointed cherub as g I placed you;
28:16 the g cherub drove you out from among the stones
1Pe 2:25 but now you have returned to the shepherd and g
Sir 51:12 *Give thanks to the g of Israel,*
2Mc 11: 1 Lysias, the king's g and kinsman,
13: 2 his g, who had charge of the government.
14: 2 with Antiochus and his g Lysias.
4Mc 15:32 O g of the law, overwhelmed from every side by

GUARDIANS (9) [GUARD]

2Ki 10: 1 to the elders, and to the g of the sons of Ahab,
10: 5 along with the elders and the g, sent word to Jehu:
23: 4 and the g of the threshold,
25:18 and the three g of the threshold;
1Ch 9:19 g of the thresholds of the tent,
9:19 of the camp of the LORD, g of the entrance.
Jer 52:24 and the three g of the threshold;
1Co 4:15 though you might have ten thousand g in Christ,
Gal 4: 2 but they remain under g and trustees until

GUARDING (3) [GUARD]

Ps 119: 9 By g it according to your word.
Pr 2: 8 g the paths of justice and preserving the way
Ac 28:16 with the soldier who was g him.

GUARDROOM (2) [GUARD, ROOM]

1Ki 14:28 and brought them back to the g.
2Ch 12:11 and would then bring them back to the g.

GUARDS (44) [GUARD]

2Ki 10:25 Jehu said to the g and to the officers,
10:25 The g and the officers threw them out,
11: 4 the Carites and of the g and had them come to him
11: 6 the gate Sur and a third at the gate behind the g),
11:11 the g stood, every man with his weapons
11:18 The priest posted g over the house of the LORD.
11:19 He took the captains, the Carites, the g,
11:19 of the LORD, marching through the gate of the g
1Ch 9:23 that is, the house of the tent, as g.
Ne 7: 3 Appoint g from among the inhabitants
Ps 97:10 he g the lives of his faithful;
127: 1 LORD g the city, the guard keeps watch in vain.
Pr 13: 6 Righteousness g one whose way is upright,
Ecc 12: 3 in the day when the g of the house tremble,
Da 3:20 and ordered some of the strongest g in his army
Na 3:17 Your g are like grasshoppers,
Mt 26:58 and going inside, he sat with the g in order to see
28: 4 of him the g shook and became like dead men.
Mk 14:54 and he was sitting with the g,
14:65 The g also took him over and beat him.
Lk 11:21 When a strong man, fully armed, g his castle,
Ac 5:23 the prison securely locked and the g standing at
12: 6 while g in front of the door were keeping watch
12:19 he examined the g and ordered them to be put
Jdt 7: 7 he seized them and set g of soldiers over them,
10:20 the g of Holofernes and all his servants came out
12: 7 So Holofernes commanded his g not to hinder her.
Sir 18:27 when sin is all around, one g against wrongdoing.
37:31 but the one who g against it prolongs his life.
40:29 but one who is intelligent and well instructed g
LtJ 6:70 which g nothing, so are their gods of wood,
4Mc 3:12 When his g complained bitterly because of
5: 2 ordered the g to seize each and every Hebrew and
6: 1 the g who were standing by dragged him violently
6: 8 of the cruel g rushed at him and began to kick him
6:23 And you, g of the tyrant, why do you delay?"
6:24 the g brought him to the fire.
8:13 When the g had placed before them wheels
9:11 at his command the g brought forward the eldest,
9:16 when the g said, "Agree to eat so that you may
9:26 the g brought in the next eldest,
11: 9 the g bound him and dragged him to the catapult;
11:27 not the g of the tyrant but those of the divine law
17: 1 Some of the g said that when she also was about

GUDGODAH (2)

Dt 10: 7 they journeyed to G, and from G to Jotbathah,

GUESS (1)

Wis 9:16 We can hardly g at what is on earth,

GUEST (12) [GUEST-ROOM, GUESTS]

Jdg 19:23 Since this man is my g, do not do this vile thing.
2Sa 12: 4 and prepared that for the g who had come to him."
Ps 39:12 I am your passing g, an alien, like all my forebears.
Mk 14:14 Where is my g room where I may eat the Passover
Lk 19: 7 "He has gone to be the g of one who is a sinner."
22:11 'The teacher asks you, "Where is the g room,
Phm 1:22 One thing more—prepare a g room for me,
AdE 16:10 of our kindliness), having become our g,
Wis 5:14 like the remembrance of a g who stays but a day.
Sir 29:23 and you will hear no reproach for being a g.
29:24 as a g you should not open your mouth;
29:27 "Be off, stranger, for an honored g is here;

GUEST-ROOM (1) [GUEST, ROOM]

Sir 29:27 my brother has come for a visit, and I need the g."

GUESTCHAMBER (KJV) See GUEST ROOM

GUESTS[‡] (23) [GUEST]

1Sa 9:24 so that you might eat with the g."
2Sa 15:11 they were invited g, and they went
1Ki 1:41 Adonijah and all the g who were with him heard it

1Ki 1:49 Then all the **g** of Adonijah got up trembling
Job 19:15 the **g** in my house have forgotten me;
Pr 9:18 that her **g** are in the depths of Sheol.
Zep 1: 7 a sacrifice, he has consecrated his **g**.
Mt 9:15 "The wedding **g** cannot mourn as long as
14: 9 yet out of regard for his oaths and for the **g**,
22:10 so the wedding hall was filled with **g**.
22:11 "But when the king came in to see the **g**,
Mk 2:19 "The wedding **g** cannot fast while
6:22 she pleased Herod and his **g**;
6:26 yet out of regard for his oaths and for the **g**,
Lk 5:34 "You cannot make wedding **g** fast while
14: 7 he noticed how the **g** chose the places of honor,
14:15 One of the dinner **g**, on hearing this, said to him,
Jn 2:10 the inferior wine after the **g** have become drunk.
Ac 17: 7 and Jason has entertained them as **g**.
AdE 1: 8 to comply with his pleasure and with that of the **g**.
Wis 19:14 of **g** who were their benefactors.
3Mc 5:14 seeing that the **g** were assembled,
5:36 the party in the same manner and urged the **g**

GUIDANCE (8) [GUIDE]

1Ch 10:13 moreover, he had consulted a medium, seeking **g**,
10:14 and did not seek **g** from the LORD.
Job 37:12 They turn round and round by his **g**,
Pr 11:14 Where there is no **g**, a nation falls,
20:18 wage war by following wise **g**.
24: 6 for by wise **g** you can wage your war,
La 2: 9 **g** is no more, and her prophets obtain no vision
4Mc 14: 6 and feet are moved in harmony with the **g** of

GUIDE (25) [GUIDANCE, GUIDED, GUIDEPOSTS, GUIDES, GUIDING]

Job 38:32 or can you **g** the Bear with its children?
Ps 31: 3 for your name's sake lead me and **g** me,
48:14 He will be our **g** forever.
67: 4 for you judge the peoples with equity and **g**
73:24 You **g** me with your counsel,
Isa 42:16 by paths they have not known I will **g** them.
49:10 and by springs of water will **g** them.
51:18 to **g** her among all the children she has borne;
58:11 The LORD will **g** you continually,
Lk 1:79 to **g** our feet into the way of peace."
6:39 "Can a blind person **g** a blind person?
Jn 16:13 he will **g** you into all the truth;
Ac 1:16 who became a **g** for those who arrested Jesus—
Ro 2:19 and if you are sure that you are a **g** to the blind,
Jas 3: 3 to make them obey us, we **g** their whole bodies.
Rev 7:17 and he will **g** them to springs of the water of life,
Tob 5:10 Can you accompany him and **g** him?
7:11 **g** and prosper you both this night
Wis 7:15 for he is the **g** even of wisdom and the corrector of
9:11 and she will **g** me wisely in my actions
18: 3 of fire as a **g** for your people's unknown journey,
1Mc 6:15 that he might **g** his son Antiochus and bring him
2Es 8:11 and afterwards you will still **g** it in your mercy.
16:75 Do not fear or doubt, for God is your **g**.
4Mc 1:30 For reason is the **g** of the virtues,

GUIDED[‡] (13) [GUIDE]

Ex 15:13 you **g** them by your strength to your holy abode.
Dt 32:12 LORD alone **g** him; no foreign god was with him.
Job 31:18 and from my mother's womb I **g** the widow—
Ps 78:52 and **g** them in the wilderness like a flock.
78:72 and **g** them with skillful hand.
Lk 2:27 **G** by the Spirit, Simeon came into the temple;
Gal 5:25 we live by the Spirit, let us also be **g** by the Spirit.
Jas 3: 4 yet they are **g** by a very small rudder wherever
Jdt 13:18 and the earth, who has **g** you to cut off the head of
Wis 10:10 she **g** him on straight paths;
10:17 she **g** them along a marvelous way,
14: 6 and **g** by your hand left to the world the seed of
2Mc 5:15 in all the world, **g** by Menelaus, who had become

GUIDEPOSTS (1) [GUIDE, POST]

Jer 31:21 up road markers for yourself, make yourself **g**;

GUIDES (7) [GUIDE]

Pr 11: 3 The integrity of the upright **g** them,
Mt 15:14 Let them alone; they are blind **g** of the blind.
15:14 And if one blind person **g** another,
23:16 "Woe to you, blind **g**, who say,
23:24 You blind **g**! You strain out a gnat
Ac 8:31 He replied, "How can I, unless someone **g** me?"
1Mc 4: 2 Men from the citadel were his **g**.

GUIDING (2) [GUIDE]

Ecc 2: 3 my mind still **g** me with wisdom—
3Mc 7: 2 the great God **g** our affairs according to our desire.

GUILD (1)

1Ch 4:21 families of the **g** of linen workers at Beth-ashbea;

GUILE (6) [GUILELESS]

Ps 119:78 because they have subverted me with **g**;
Pr 26:26 though hatred is covered with **g**,
1Pe 2: 1 Rid yourselves, therefore, of all malice, and all **g**,
Wis 4:11 change their understanding or **g** deceive their souls.
7:13 I learned without **g** and I impart without grudging;
2Mc 12:24 With great **g** he begged them to let him go

GUILE (KJV) See also DECEIT, FRAUD, TREACHERY, TRICKERY

GUILELESS (1) [GUILE]

Ro 16:19 to be wise in what is good and **g** in what is evil.

GUILT (137) [BLOODGUILT, GUILTLESS, GUILTY]

A. GUILT OFFERING (39)

Ge 20: 9 that you have brought such great **g** on me
26:10 and you would have brought **g** upon us."
44:16 God has found out the **g** of your servants;
Ex 28:38 on himself any **g** incurred in the holy offering that
28:43 or they will bring **g** on themselves and die.
Lev 4: 3 thus bringing **g** on the people,
4:13 not to be done and incur **g**;
4:22 not to be done and incurs **g**,
4:27 not to be done and incurs **g**,
5: 5 When you realize your **g** in any of these,
5:15 you shall bring, as your **g** offering to the LORD, A
5:15 by the sanctuary shekel; it is a **g** offering. A
5:16 on your behalf with the ram of the **g** offering, A
5:17 to be done, you have incurred **g**, and are subject
5:18 or the equivalent, as a **g** offering; A
5:19 It is a **g** offering; you have incurred guilt A
5:19 you have incurred **g** before the LORD.
6: 4 when you have sinned and realize your **g**,
6: 5 to its owner when you realize your **g**.
6: 6 as your **g** offering to the LORD, A
6: 6 or its equivalent, for a **g** offering. A
6: 7 of the things that one may do and incur **g** thereby.
6:17 like the sin offering and the **g** offering. A
7: 1 This is the ritual of the **g** offering. A
7: 2 they shall slaughter the **g** offering, A
7: 5 to the LORD; it is a **g** offering. A
7: 7 The **g** offering is like the sin offering, A
7:18 and the one who eats of it shall incur **g**.
7:37 grain offering, the sin offering, the **g** offering, A
10:17 that you may remove the **g** of the congregation,
14:12 and offer it as a **g** offering, A
14:13 for the **g** offering, like the sin offering, A
14:14 the blood of the **g** offering and put it on the lobe A
14:17 on top of the blood of the **g** offering. A
14:21 a **g** offering to be elevated, to make atonement A
14:24 the priest shall take the lamb of the **g** offering A
14:25 the **g** offering and shall take some of the blood A
14:25 shall take some of the blood of the **g** offering, A
14:28 where the blood of the **g** offering was placed. A
17:16 or bathe their body, they shall bear their **g**.
19:17 or you will incur **g** yourself.
19:21 but he shall bring a **g** offering for himself to A
19:21 of the tent of meeting, a ram as **g** offering. A
19:22 the ram of **g** offering before the LORD for his sin A
22: 9 that they may not incur **g** and die in the sanctuary
22:16 causing them to bear **g** requiring a guilt offering,
22:16 causing them to bear guilt requiring a **g** offering, A
Nu 5: 6 with the LORD, that person incurs **g**
6:11 because they incurred **g** by reason of the corpse.
6:12 bring a male lamb a year old as a **g** offering. A
15:31 a person shall be utterly cut off and bear the **g**.
18: 9 grain offering, sin offering, or **g** offering, A
18:22 or else they will incur **g** and die.
18:32 You shall incur no **g** by reason of it,
30:15 then he shall bear her **g**.
Dt 15: 9 to the LORD against you, and you would incur **g**.
19:13 you shall purge the **g** of innocent blood
21: 8 not let the **g** of innocent blood remain in the midst
21: 9 So you shall purge the **g** of innocent blood
23:21 surely require it of you, and you would incur **g**.
23:22 if you refrain from vowing, you will not incur **g**.
24: 4 the LORD, and you shall not bring **g** on the land
24:15 to the LORD against you, and you would incur **g**.
Jdg 21:22 But neither did you incur **g**
1Sa 6: 3 but by all means return him a **g** offering. A
6: 4 "What is the **g** offering that we shall return A
6: 8 which you are returning to him as a **g** offering. A
6:17 which the Philistines returned as a **g** offering to A
14:41 If this **g** is in me or in my son Jonathan,
14:41 if this **g** is in your people Israel, give Thummim."
20: 1 "What have I done? What is my **g**?
20: 8 But if there is **g** in me, kill me yourself;
25:24 "Upon me alone, my lord, be the **g**;
26:18 What **g** is on my hands?
2Sa 3:29 May the **g** fall on the head of Joab,
14: 9 "On me be the **g**, my lord the king,
14:32 if there is **g** in me, let him kill me!"
22:24 and I kept myself from **g**.
24:10 I pray you, take away the **g** of your servant;
1Ki 2:31 the **g** for the blood that Joab shed without cause.
2Ki 12:16 The money from the **g** offerings and the money
1Ch 21: 3 Why should he bring **g** on Israel?"
21: 8 now, I pray you, take away the **g** of your servant;
2Ch 19:10 so that they may not incur **g** before the LORD
19:10 Do so, and you will not incur **g**.
24:18 upon Judah and Jerusalem for this **g** of theirs.
28:13 to bring on us **g** against the LORD in addition to our present sins and **g**.
28:13 For our **g** is already great,
33:23 but this Amon incurred more and more **g**.
Ezr 9: 6 and our **g** has mounted up to the heavens.
9: 7 to this day we have been deep in **g**,
9:13 upon us for our evil deeds and for our great **g**,
9:15 Here we are before you in our **g**,
Ezr 10:10 and so increased the **g** of Israel.
10:19 and their **g** offering was a ram of the flock A
10:19 a ram of the flock for their **g**;
Ne 4: 5 Do not cover their **g**, and do not let their sin
Job 11: 6 that God exacts of you less than your **g** deserves.
Ps 5:10 Make them bear their **g**, O God;
18:23 and I kept myself from **g**.
25:11 For your name's sake, O LORD, pardon my **g**,
32: 5 and you forgave the **g** of my sin.
69:27 Add **g** to their **g**; may they have no acquittal
Pr 14: 9 Fools mock at the **g** offering, A
Isa 6: 7 your **g** has departed and your sin is blotted out."
14:21 Prepare slaughter for his sons because of the **g**
24: 6 and its inhabitants suffer for their **g**;
27: 9 Therefore by this the **g** of Jacob will be expiated,
Jer 2:22 the stain of your **g** is still before me,
3:13 Only acknowledge your **g**,
30:14 your **g** is great, because your sins are so numerous.
30:15 your **g** is great, because your sins are so numerous,
32:18 the **g** of parents into the laps of their children
33: 8 I will cleanse them from all the **g** of their sin
33: 8 the **g** of their sin and rebellion against me.
51: 5 though their land is full of **g** before the Holy One
51: 6 Do not perish because of her **g**,
Eze 9: 9 "The **g** of the house of Israel
16:49 This was the **g** of your sister Sodom:
21:23 but he brings their **g** to remembrance,
21:24 you have brought your **g** to remembrance,
40:39 and the sin offering and the **g** offering were to A
42:13 the sin offering, and the **g** offering, A
44:29 the sin offering, and the **g** offering; A
46:20 place where the priests shall boil the **g** offering A
Hos 5: 5 Ephraim stumbles in his **g**;
5:15 until they acknowledge their **g** and seek my face.
10: 2 Their heart is false; now they must bear their **g**.
13: 1 but he incurred **g** through Baal and died.
13:16 Samaria shall bear her **g**, because she has rebelled
14: 2 say to him, "Take away all **g**;
Zec 3: 4 "See, I have taken your **g** away from you,
3: 9 I will remove the **g** of this land in a single day.
Wis 1: 6 not free blasphemers from the **g** of their words;
Sir 7:31 the first fruits, the **g** offering, A

GUILTLESS (8) [GUILT]

1Sa 26: 9 against the LORD's anointed, and be **g**?"
2Sa 3:28 and my kingdom are forever **g** before the LORD
14: 9 let the king and his throne be **g**."
1Ki 2: 9 do not hold him **g**, for you are a wise man;
Mt 12: 5 in the temple break the sabbath and yet are **g**?
12: 7 you would not have condemned the **g**.
2Co 7:11 At every point you have proved yourselves **g** in
Sir 9:12 that they will not be held **g** all their lives.

GUILTY[‡] (44) [GUILT]

Ex 23: 7 for I will not acquit the **g**.
34: 7 yet by no means clearing the **g**,
Lev 5: 2 you have become unclean, and are **g**.
5: 3 when you come to know it, you shall be **g**.
5: 4 you shall in any of these be **g**.
17: 4 he shall be held **g** of bloodshed;
Nu 5: 8 with which atonement is made for the **g** party.
14:18 but by no means clearing the **g**,
2Sa 19:19 "May my lord not hold me **g** or remember
1Ki 8:32 the **g** by bringing their conduct on their own head,
2Ki 7: 9 until the morning light, we will be found **g**;
2Ch 6:23 the **g** by bringing their conduct on their own head,
Job 10: 7 although you know that I am not **g**,
22:30 He will deliver even those who are **g**;
Ps 51: 5 I was born **g**, a sinner
68:21 the hairy crown of those who walk in their **g** ways.
109: 7 When he is tried, let him be found **g**;
Pr 18: 5 It is not right to be partial to the **g**,
21: 8 The way of the **g** is crooked,
30:10 and you will be held **g**.
Isa 3:11 Woe to the **g**! How unfortunate they are,
5:23 who acquit the **g** for a bribe,
50: 9 Lord GOD who helps me; who will declare me **g**?
Jer 2: 3 All who ate of it were held **g**;
3:11 Faithless Israel has shown herself less **g** than false Judah.
12: 1 Why does the way of the **g** prosper?
25:31 and the **g** he will put to the sword,
50: 7 and their enemies have said, "We are not **g**,
Eze 18:24 for the treachery of which they are **g** and
22: 4 You have become **g** by the blood
23:45 But righteous judges shall declare them **g**
Hos 4:15 O Israel, do not let Judah become **g**.
Joel 3:21 and I will not clear the **g**,
Jnh 1:14 Do not make us **g** of innocent blood;
Na 1: 3 and the LORD will by no means clear the **g**.
Hab 1:11 they transgress and become **g**;
Mk 3:29 but is **g** of an eternal sin"—
Lk 23:14 in your presence and have not found this man **g**
Jn 19:11 therefore the one who handed me over to you is **g**
1Jn 3: 4 Everyone who commits sin is **g** of lawlessness;
Jdt 5:21 But if they are not a **g** nation,
Sir 42: 8 or the aged who are **g** of sexual immorality.
Sus 1:53 condemning the innocent and acquitting the **g**,
2Mc 13: 6 to destruction anyone **g** of sacrilege or notorious

GULL (2)

Lev 11:16 the nighthawk, the sea **g**, the hawk of any kind;
Dt 14:15 the nighthawk, the sea **g**, the hawk, of any kind;

GULLIES (2)
Job 30: 6 In the **g** of wadis they must live,
Jdt 2: 8 Their wounded shall fill their ravines and **g,**

GULLOTH (2) [GULLOTH-MAYIM]
Jdg 1:15 So Caleb gave her Upper **G** and Lower **G.**

GULLOTH-MAYIM (1) [GULLOTH]
Jdg 1:15 in the land of the Negeb, give me also **G."**

GULP (1)
Ob 1:16 they shall drink and **g** down,

GUM (3)
Ge 37:25 with their camels carrying **g,** balm, and resin,
43:11 a little balm and a little honey, **g,** resin,
Nu 11: 7 and its color was like the color of **g** resin.

GUNI (4) [GUNITES]
Ge 46:24 The children of Naphtali: Jahzeel, **G,** Jezer,
Nu 26:48 of **G,** the clan of the Gunites;
1Ch 5:15 son of **G,** was chief in their clan;
7:13 The descendants of Naphtali: Jahziel, **G,** Jezer,

GUNITES (1) [GUNI]
Nu 26:48 of Guni, the clan of the **G;**

GUR (1)
2Ki 9:27 they shot him in the chariot at the ascent to **G,**

GUR-BAAL (1) [BAAL]
2Ch 26: 7 against the Arabs who lived in **G,**

GUSH (1) [GUSHED, GUSHING]
Ps 104:10 You make springs **g** forth in the valleys;

GUSHED (6) [GUSH]
1Ki 18:28 with swords and lances until the blood **g** out
Ps 78:20 Even though he struck the rock so that water **g** out
105:41 He opened the rock, and water **g** out;
Isa 48:21 he split open the rock and the water **g** out.
Ac 1:18 in the middle and all his bowels **g** out.
2Mc 14:45 and though his blood **g** forth

GUSHING (2) [GUSH]
Pr 18: 4 the fountain of wisdom is a **g** stream.
Jn 4:14 in them a spring of water **g** up to eternal life."

GYMNASIUM (4)
1Mc 1:14 So they built a **g** in Jerusalem,
2Mc 4: 9 by his authority a **g** and a body of youth for it,
4:12 He took delight in establishing a **g** right under
4Mc 4:20 not only was a **g** constructed at the very citadel

---

H

HA (1)
Isa 29:15 **H!** You who hide a plan too deep

HA-SATAN See Index to Footnotes

HAAHASHTARI (1)
1Ch 4: 6 bore him Ahuzzam, Hepher, Temeni, and **H.**

HABAIAH (2) [=HOBAIAH]
Ezr 2:61 the descendants of **H,** Hakkoz,
1Es 5:38 the descendants of **H,** the descendants of Hakkoz,

HABAKKUK (8)
Hab 1: 1 The oracle that the prophet **H** saw.
3: 1 A prayer of the prophet **H** according to Shigionoth.
Bel 1:33 Now the prophet **H** was in Judea;
1:34 But the angel of the Lord said to **H,**
1:35 **H** said, "Sir, I have never seen Babylon,
1:37 Then **H** shouted, "Daniel, Daniel!
1:39 of God immediately returned **H** to his own place.
2Es 1:40 and Nahum and **H,** Zephaniah, Haggai, Zechariah

HABAZZINIAH (1)
Jer 35: 3 So I took Jaazaniah son of Jeremiah son of **H,**

HABERGEONS (KJV) See COAT OF MAIL, BODY-ARMOR

HABIT (4) [HABITS, HABITUAL, HABITUALLY]
Nu 22:30 Have I been in the **h** of treating you this way?"
Heb 10:25 as is the **h** of some, but encouraging one another,
Sir 7:13 for it is a **h** that results in no good.
23:14 and behave like a fool through bad **h;**

HABITABLE (3) [INHABIT]
Ex 16:35 until they came to a **h** land;
Job 37:12 that he commands them on the face of the **h** world.
3Mc 4: 3 What district or city, or what **h** place at all,

HABITATION (17) [INHABIT]
Dt 12: 5 of all your tribes as his **h** to put his name there.
26:15 Look down from your holy **h,** from heaven,
Job 28: 4 They open shafts in a valley away from human **h;**
Ps 46: 4 the holy **h** of the Most High.
68: 5 and protector of widows is God in his holy **h.**
79: 7 For they have devoured Jacob and laid waste his **h.**
104:12 By the streams the birds of the air have their **h;**
132:13 he has desired it for his **h:**
Isa 22:16 and carving a **h** for yourself in the rock?
27:10 fortified city is solitary, a **h** deserted and forsaken,
32:18 My people will abide in a peaceful **h,**
33:20 Your eyes will see Jerusalem, a quiet **h,**
63:15 from your holy and glorious **h.**
Jer 10:25 and consumed him, and have laid waste his **h.**
25:30 and from his holy **h** utter his voice;
Wis 9: 8 and an altar in the city of your **h,**
2Mc 14:35 that there should be a temple for your **h** among us;

HABITATION (KJV) See also ABODE, ANCESTORS, CAMP, DWELLING, FOLD, LIVE, PLACE, REFUGE, RESIDE, STONGHOLD, THRONE, TOWN

HABITATIONS (7) [INHABIT]
Job 18:15 sulfur is scattered upon their **h.**
Isa 54: 2 and let the curtains of your **h** be stretched out;
2Es 2:11 and will give to these others the everlasting **h,**
7:*80* such spirits shall not enter into **h,**
7:*85* they shall see how the **h** of the others are guarded
7:*101* and afterwards they shall be gathered in their **h."**
7:*121* [51] safe and healthful **h** have been reserved for us,

HABITS (2) [HABIT]
4Mc 1:29 and so tames the jungle of **h** and emotions.
13:27 and companionship and virtuous **h** had augmented

HABITUAL‡ (1) [HABIT]
Sir 20:25 A thief is preferable to a **h** liar,

HABITUALLY (2) [HABIT]
Sir 23: 9 nor **h** utter the name of the Holy One;
4Mc 2: 7 Otherwise how could it be that someone who is **h**

HABOR (3)
2Ki 17: 6 He placed them in Halah, on the **H,**
18:11 settled them in Halah, on the **H,** the river of Gozan,
1Ch 5:26 **H,** Hara, and the river Gozan, to this day.

HACALIAH (2)
Ne 1: 1 The words of Nehemiah son of **H.**
10: 1 the names of Nehemiah the governor, son of **H,**

HACHILAH (3)
1Sa 23:19 on the hill of **H,** which is south of Jeshimon.
26: 1 saying, "David is in hiding on the hill of **H,**
26: 3 Saul encamped on the hill of **H,**

HACHMONI (2)
1Ch 11:11 Jashobeam, son of **H,** was chief of the Three;
27:32 Jehiel son of **H** attended the king's sons.

HACHMONITE (KJV) See HACHMONI; See also Index to Footnotes

HACHRATHEUS‡ (3)
AdE 4: 5 Then Esther summoned **H,**
4: 9 **H** went in and told Esther all these things.
4:12 When **H** delivered her entire message to Mordecai,

HACK (1) [HACKED]
Isa 10:34 He will **h** down the thickets of the forest with

HACKED (1) [HACK]
Ps 74: 5 At the upper entrance they **h** the wooden trellis

HAD‡ (607 of 3470) [HAVE] See Index of Articles Etc. for an Exhaustive Listing (See Introduction, page xi)
Ge 4: 4 And the LORD **h** regard for Abel and his offering,
4: 5 but for Cain and his offering he **h** no regard.
5: 4 and he **h** other sons and daughters.
5: 7 and **h** other sons and daughters.
5:10 and **h** other sons and daughters.
5:13 and **h** other sons and daughters.
5:16 and **h** other sons and daughters.
5:19 and **h** other sons and daughters.
5:22 and **h** other sons and daughters.
5:26 and **h** other sons and daughters.
5:30 and **h** other sons and daughters.
6:10 And Noah **h** three sons, Shem, Ham, and Japheth.
11: 1 Now the whole earth **h** one language
11: 3 And they **h** brick for stone, and bitumen for mortar
11:11 and **h** other sons and daughters.
11:13 and **h** other sons and daughters.
11:15 and **h** other sons and daughters.
11:17 and **h** other sons and daughters.
11:19 and **h** other sons and daughters.
11:21 and **h** other sons and daughters.
11:23 and **h** other sons and daughters.
11:25 and **h** other sons and daughters.
11:30 Now Sarai was barren; she **h** no child.
12:16 he dealt well with Abram; and he **h** sheep, oxen,
12:20 with his wife and all that he **h.**
13: 1 he and his wife, and all that he **h,** and Lot
13: 5 Now Lot, who went with Abram, also **h** flocks
16: 1 **h** an Egyptian slave-girl whose name was Hagar,
24: 2 who **h** charge of all that he **h,**
24:29 Rebekah **h** a brother whose name was Laban;
25: 5 Abraham gave all he **h** to Isaac.
26:14 He **h** possessions of flocks and herds,
28: 9 to be his wife in addition to the wives he **h.**
29:16 Now Laban **h** two daughters;
29:20 because of the love he **h** for her.
30:30 For you **h** little before I came,
30:35 speckled and spotted, every one that **h** white on it,
30:43 the man grew exceedingly rich, and **h** large flocks,
31:10 During the mating of the flock I once **h** a dream
31:21 So he fled with all that he **h;**
31:30 Even though you **h** to go because you longed
32:13 and from what he **h** with him he took a present
32:23 and likewise everything that he **h.**
35: 4 they gave to Jacob all the foreign gods that they **h,**
35:16 Rachel was in childbirth, and she **h** hard labor.
37: 5 Once Joseph **h** a dream, and when he told it
37: 9 He **h** another dream, and told it to his brothers,
37: 9 saying, "Look, I have **h** another dream:
37:10 "What kind of dream is this that you have **h?**
37:32 **h** the long robe with sleeves taken to their father,
39: 4 and put him in charge of all that he **h.**
39: 5 overseer in his house and over all that he **h,**
39: 5 the blessing of the LORD was on all that he **h,**
39: 6 So he left all that he **h** in Joseph's charge; and with him there, he **h** no concern for anything
40: 8 They said to him, "We have **h** dreams,
40:16 he said to Joseph, "I also **h** a dream:
41:15 Pharaoh said to Joseph, "I have **h** a dream,
41:43 He **h** him ride in the chariot of his second-in-command;
41:50 Joseph **h** two sons,
42:24 And he picked out Simeon and **h** him bound
43: 6 to tell the man that you **h** another brother?"
46: 1 Israel set out on his journey with all that he **h**
47:22 for the priests **h** a fixed allowance from Pharaoh,
Ex 2:16 The priest of Midian **h** seven daughters.
7:24 all the Egyptians **h** to dig along the Nile for water
10:23 but all the Israelites **h** light where they lived.
14: 6 So he **h** his chariot made ready,
16:18 and those who gathered little **h** no shortage;
36:22 Each frame **h** two pegs for fitting together;
Lev 21: 3 close to him because she has **h** no husband,
22: 4 or a man who has **h** an emission of semen,
Nu 3: 4 in the wilderness of Sinai, and they **h** no children.
3:32 oversight of those who **h** charge of the sanctuary.
3:38 whatever **h** to be done for the Israelites;
5:13 if a man has **h** intercourse with her but it is hidden
5:20 some man other than your husband has **h** intercourse with you,"
7: 9 holy things that **h** to be carried on the shoulders.
11: 4 The rabble among them **h** a strong craving;
11: 4 wept again, and said, "If only we **h** meat to eat!
11:18 saying, 'If only we **h** meat to eat!
11:34 there they buried the people who **h** the craving.
22:29 I wish I **h** a sword in my hand!
26:33 Now Zelophehad son of Hepher **h** no sons,
27: 3 but died for his own sin; and he **h** no sons.
27: 4 taken away from his clan because he **h** no son?"
27:22 He took Joshua and **h** him stand before Eleazar
31:47 the Levites who **h** charge of the tabernacle
Dt 4:25 When you have **h** children and children's children,
5:29 If only they **h** such a mind as this, to fear me
Jos 5:12 and the Israelites no longer **h** manna;
7:24 donkeys, and sheep, and his tent and all that he **h;**
8:20 They **h** no power to flee this way or that,
11:23 And the land **h** rest from war.
14:15 And the land **h** rest from war.
17: 3 son of Machir son of Manasseh **h** no sons,
17:11 Manasseh **h** Beth-shean and its villages, Ibleam
19: 2 It **h** for its inheritance Beer-sheba, Sheba,
21:42 Each of these towns **h** its pasture lands around it;
22:17 Have we not **h** enough of the sin at Peor
Jdg 1:19 because they **h** chariots of iron.
3: 1 who **h** no experience of any war in Canaan
3: 2 to teach those who **h** no experience of it before):
3:11 So the land **h** rest forty years.
3:30 And the land **h** rest eighty years.
4: 3 for he **h** nine hundred chariots of iron,
5:31 And the land **h** rest forty years.
7:13 and he said, "I **h** a dream, and in it a cake of barley
8:24 (For the enemy **h** golden earrings,
8:28 the land **h** rest forty years in the days of Gideon.

Jdg 8:30 Now Gideon **h** seventy sons, his own offspring,
for he **h** many wives.
10: 4 He **h** thirty sons who rode on thirty donkeys;
10: 4 and they **h** thirty towns, which are in the land
11:34 he **h** no son or daughter except her.
12: 9 He **h** thirty sons.
12:14 He **h** forty sons and thirty grandsons,
14: 4 At that time the Philistines **h** dominion over Israel.
16:19 and **h** him shave off the seven locks of his head.
17: 5 This man Micah **h** a shrine, and he made an ephod
18: 7 and **h** no dealings with Aram.
18:28 and they **h** no dealings with Aram.
19: 3 He **h** with him his servant and a couple of donkeys
19:10 He **h** with him a couple of saddled donkeys,
21: 6 But the Israelites **h** compassion for Benjamin
21:15 The people **h** compassion on Benjamin because
Ru 2: 1 Now Naomi **h** a kinsman on her husband's side,
2:14 ate until she was satisfied, and she **h** some left
1Sa 1: 2 He **h** two wives; the name of the one was Hannah,
1: 2 Peninnah **h** children, but Hannah **h** no children.
2:12 they **h** no regard for the LORD
9: 2 He **h** a son whose name was Saul,
13:22 but Saul and his son Jonathan **h** them.
16:12 Now he was ruddy, and **h** beautiful eyes,
17: 5 He **h** a helmet of bronze on his head,
17: 6 He **h** greaves of bronze on his legs
17:12 named Jesse, who **h** eight sons.
18:10 Saul **h** his spear in his hand;
18:14 David **h** success in all his undertakings;
18:15 When Saul saw that he **h** great success,
18:30 David **h** more success than all the servants of Saul,
25: 2 The man was very rich; he **h** three thousand sheep
28:24 Now the woman **h** a fatted calf in the house.
30: 4 and wept, until they **h** no more strength to weep.
2Sa 3: 7 Now Saul **h** a concubine whose name was Rizpah
3:37 the king **h** no part in the killing of Abner
4: 2 Saul's son **h** two captains of raiding bands;
4: 4 Jonathan **h** a son who was crippled in his feet.
6:23 And Michal the daughter of Saul **h** no child
9:10 Now Ziba **h** fifteen sons and twenty servants.
9:12 Mephibosheth **h** a young son whose name was
12: 2 The rich man **h** very many flocks and herds;
12: 6 he did this thing, and because he **h** no pity."
13: 1 David's son Absalom **h** a beautiful sister
13: 3 But Amnon **h** a friend whose name was Jonadab,
13:23 Absalom **h** sheepshearers at Baal-hazor,
14: 6 Your servant **h** two sons, and they fought
15: 4 Then all who **h** a suit or cause might come to me,
17:18 a man at Bahurim, who **h** a well in his courtyard;
21:20 man of great size, who **h** six fingers on each hand,
23: 8 the names of the warriors whom David **h:**
23:21 The Egyptian **h** a spear in his hand;
1Ki 1:38 and **h** Solomon ride on King David's mule,
1:44 and they **h** him ride on the king's mule;
2:19 and **h** a throne brought for the king's mother,
4: 7 Solomon **h** twelve officials over all Israel,
4: 7 each one **h** to make provision for one month
4:11 (he **h** Taphath, Solomon's daughter, as his wife);
4:13 (he **h** the villages of Jair son of Manasseh,
4:13 and he **h** the region of Argob, which is in Bashan,
4:24 For he **h** dominion over all the region west
4:24 and he **h** peace on all sides.
4:26 Solomon also **h** forty thousand stalls of horses
5:15 Solomon also **h** seventy thousand laborers
6:18 The cedar within the house **h** carvings of gourds
6:25 both cherubim **h** the same measure
7: 5 the doorways and doorposts **h** four-sided frames,
7:12 The great court **h** three courses of dressed stone
7:12 so **h** the inner court of the house of the LORD,
7:28 the construction of the stands: they **h** borders;
7:30 Each stand **h** four bronze wheels and axles
7:36 lions, and palm trees, where each **h** space,
8:17 My father David **h** it in mind to build a house
9:23 five hundred fifty, who **h** charge of the people
10:19 The throne **h** six steps.
10:22 For the king **h** a fleet of ships of Tarshish at sea
10:26 he **h** fourteen hundred chariots and
16:33 than **h** all the kings of Israel who were before him.
20:33 and he **h** him come up into the chariot.
21: 1 Naboth the Jezreelite **h** a vineyard in Jezreel,
2Ki 1:17 because Ahaziah **h** no son.
4:44 He set it before them, they ate, and **h** some left,
6:30 the people could see that he **h** sackcloth on
10: 1 Now Ahab **h** seventy sons in Samaria.
10:16 So he **h** him ride in his chariot.
11: 4 and **h** them come to him in the house of the LORD.
12:11 the workers who **h** the oversight of the house
13:23 was gracious to them and **h** compassion on them;
25:17 The second pillar **h** the same, with the latticework.
1Ch 2: 4 Judah **h** five sons in all.
2:18 Caleb son of Hezron **h** children by his wife
2:22 who **h** twenty-three towns in the land of Gilead.
2:26 Jerahmeel also **h** another wife,
2:34 Now Sheshan **h** no sons, only daughters;
2:34 but Sheshan **h** an Egyptian slave,
2:52 Shobal father of Kiriath-jearim **h** other sons:
4: 5 Ashhur father of Tekoa **h** two wives,
4:27 Shimei **h** sixteen sons and six daughters;
5:18 and the half-tribe of Manasseh **h** valiant warriors,
6:66 the families of the sons of Kohath **h** towns
7: 4 for they **h** many wives and sons.
7:15 and Zelophehad **h** daughters.
8: 3 And Bela **h** sons: Addar, Gera, Abihud,
8: 8 And Shaharaim **h** sons in the country of Moab
8: 9 He **h** sons by his wife Hodesh: Jobab, Zibia,
8:11 He also **h** sons by Hushim: Abitub and Elpaal.
8:38 Azel **h** six sons, and these are their names:

1Ch 9:27 and they **h** charge of opening it every morning.
9:28 Some of them **h** charge of the utensils of service,
9:32 the Kohathites **h** charge of the rows of bread,
9:44 Azel **h** six sons, and these are their names:
11:23 The Egyptian **h** in his hand a spear
12:32 those who **h** understanding of the times,
13:14 the household of Obed-edom and all that he **h.**
14: 4 the names of the children whom he **h** in Jerusalem:
16:42 Heman and Jeduthun **h** with them trumpets
20: 6 man of great size, who **h** six fingers on each hand,
23:17 Eliezer **h** no other sons,
24: 2 and Abihu died before their father, and **h** no sons;
24:19 These **h** as their appointed duty in their service
24:28 Of Mahli: Eleazar, who **h** no sons.
26: 2 Meshelemiah **h** sons: Zechariah the firstborn,
26: 4 Obed-edom **h** sons: Shemaiah the firstborn,
26: 9 Meshelemiah **h** sons and brothers, able men,
26:10 Hosah, of the sons of Merari, **h** sons: Shimri
26:12 **h** duties, just as their kindred did, ministering
26:20 Ahijah **h** charge of the treasuries of the house
26:30 **h** the oversight of Israel west of the Jordan
28:12 and the plan of all that he **h** in mind:
29: 8 Whoever **h** precious stones gave them to the
2Ch 1:12 such as none of the kings **h** who were before you,
1:14 he **h** fourteen hundred chariots and
6: 7 My father David **h** it in mind to build a house
9:18 The throne **h** six steps and a footstool of gold,
9:25 Solomon **h** four thousand stalls for horses
14: 1 In his days the land **h** rest for ten years.
14: 5 And the kingdom **h** rest under him.
14: 6 built fortified cities in Judah while the land **h** rest.
14: 6 He **h** no war in those years,
14: 8 Asa **h** an army of three hundred thousand
14:15 also attacked the tents of those who **h** livestock,
17: 5 to Jehoshaphat, and he **h** great riches and honor.
17:13 He **h** soldiers, mighty warriors, in Jerusalem
18: 1 Now Jehoshaphat **h** great riches and honor;
19: 8 They **h** their seat at Jerusalem.
21: 2 He **h** brothers, the sons of Jehoshaphat:
22: 9 And the house of Ahaziah **h** no one able to rule
24:12 Jehoiada gave it to those who **h** charge of the work
26:10 for he **h** large herds, both in the Shephelah and
26:10 and he **h** farmers and vinedressers in the hills
26:11 Moreover Uzziah **h** an army of soldiers, fit for war
26:19 Now he **h** a censer in his hand to make offering,
30:17 the Levites **h** to slaughter the passover lamb
31:10 we have **h** enough to eat and have plenty to spare;
32:27 Hezekiah **h** very great riches and honor;
34:10 who **h** the oversight of the house of the LORD
36:15 because he **h** compassion on his people
36:17 **h** no compassion on young man or young woman,
Ezr 1: 8 King Cyrus of Persia **h** them released
2:65 and they **h** two hundred male and female singers.
2:66 They **h** seven hundred thirty-six horses,
3: 7 the grant that they **h** from King Cyrus of Persia.
4:20 Jerusalem has **h** mighty kings who ruled
Ne 4: 6 for the people **h** a mind to work.
4:18 the builders **h** his sword strapped at his side
7:67 and they **h** two hundred forty-five singers,
7:68 They **h** seven hundred thirty-six horses,
9:28 after they **h** rest, they again did evil before you,
9:28 so that they **h** dominion over them;
Est 1:14 who **h** access to the king,
2: 7 his cousin, for she **h** neither father nor mother;
2: 8 Hegai, who **h** charge of the women.
2:15 the king's eunuch, who **h** charge of the women,
5:14 and he **h** the gallows made.
Job 1: 3 He **h** seven thousand sheep, three thousand camels
29:12 poor who cried, and the orphan who **h** no helper.
29:24 I smiled on them when they **h** no confidence;
31:21 because I saw I **h** supporters at the gate;
31:35 Oh, that I **h** one to hear me!
31:35 that I **h** the indictment written by my adversary!
34:27 and **h** no regard for any of his ways,
42:10 the LORD gave Job twice as much as he **h** before.
42:12 he **h** fourteen thousand sheep, six thousand camels
42:13 He also **h** seven sons and three daughters.
Ps 55: 6 And I say, "O that I **h** wings like a dove!
78:22 because they **h** no faith in God,
78:63 and their girls **h** no marriage song.
106:14 But they **h** a wanton craving in the wilderness,
107:30 Then they were glad because they **h** quiet,
120: 6 have I **h** my dwelling among those who hate peace
123: 3 for we have **h** more than enough of contempt.
123: 4 Our soul has **h** more than its fill of the scorn
Pr 7:14 "I **h** to offer sacrifices, and today I have paid
Ecc 1:16 and my mind has **h** great experience of wisdom
2: 7 and **h** slaves who were born in my house;
2: 7 I also **h** great possessions of herds and flocks,
SS 8:11 Solomon **h** a vineyard at Baal-hamon;
Isa 1:11 I have **h** enough of burnt offerings of rams
5: 1 My beloved **h** a vineyard on a very fertile hill.
6: 2 in attendance above him; each **h** six wings:
38:17 it was for my welfare that I **h** great bitterness;
53: 2 he **h** no form or majesty that we should look
60:10 but in my favor I have **h** mercy on you.
Jer 4:23 and to the heavens, and they **h** no light.
9: 2 O that I **h** in the desert a traveler's lodging
24: 2 One basket **h** very good figs, like first-ripe figs,
24: 2 but the other basket **h** very bad figs,
52:22 And the second pillar **h** the same,
Eze 1: 6 Each **h** four faces, and each of them **h** four wings.
1: 8 on their four sides they **h** human hands.
1: 8 And the four **h** their faces and their wings thus:
1:10 the four **h** the face of a human being,
1:11 each creature **h** two wings, each of which touched
1:16 and the four **h** the same form,

Eze 1:23 and each of the creatures **h** two wings covering
2:10 it **h** writing on the front and on the back,
8:11 Each **h** his censer in his hand, and the fragrant
9: 3 the man clothed in linen, who **h** the writing case
10:14 Each one **h** four faces: the first face was
10:21 Each **h** four faces, each four wings,
16:13 You **h** choice flour and honey and oil for food
16:49 she and her daughters **h** pride, excess of food,
36:20 and yet they **h** to go out of his land.
36:21 But I **h** concern for my holy name,
40:16 The recesses and their pilasters **h** windows,
40:16 and the vestibules also **h** windows on the inside
40:24 they **h** the same dimensions as the others.
40:26 It **h** palm trees on its pilasters, one on either side.
40:31 on its pilasters, and its stairway **h** eight steps.
40:34 and it **h** palm trees on its pilasters, on either side;
40:34 and its stairway **h** eight steps.
40:35 it **h** the same dimensions as the others.
40:36 size as the others; and it **h** windows all around.
40:37 and it **h** palm trees on its pilasters, on either side;
40:37 and its stairway **h** eight steps.
41: 8 I saw also that the temple **h** a raised platform
41:16 all three **h** windows with recessed frames.
41:18 Each cherub **h** two faces:
41:23 The nave and the holy place **h** each a double door.
41:24 The doors **h** two leaves apiece,
42: 6 they **h** no pillars like the pillars of the outer court;
42:20 It **h** a wall around it, five hundred cubits long
Da 1:17 Daniel also **h** insight into all visions and dreams.
2: 3 "I have **h** such a dream that my spirit is troubled
3:27 that the fire had not **h** any power over the bodies
4:21 in whose branches the birds of the air **h** nests—
6:10 which **h** windows in its upper room open toward
7: 1 Daniel **h** a dream and visions of his head
7: 4 The first was like a lion and **h** eagles' wings.
7: 5 **h** three tusks in its mouth among its teeth
7: 6 The beast **h** four wings of a bird on its back and
7: 7 It **h** great iron teeth and was devouring,
7: 7 all the beasts that preceded it, and it **h** ten horns.
7:20 the horn that **h** eyes and a mouth that spoke
8: 3 a ram standing beside the river. It **h** two horns.
8: 5 The goat **h** a horn between its eyes.
Joel 2:18 jealous for his land, and **h** pity on his people.
Jnh 3: 7 Then he **h** a proclamation made in Nineveh:
Zec 5: 9 they **h** wings like the wings of a stork,
6: 2 The first chariot **h** red horses, the second chariot
Mt 1:25 but **h** no marital relations with her until
9:36 he saw the crowds, he **h** compassion for them,
13: 5 sprang up quickly, since they **h** no depth of soil.
13: 6 and since they **h** no root, they withered away.
13:46 he went and sold all that he **h** and bought it.
14:10 he sent and **h** John beheaded in the prison.
14:14 he **h** compassion for them and cured their sick.
15: 5 'Whatever support you might have **h** from me
18:33 Should you not have **h** mercy on your fellow
slave, as I **h** mercy on you?'
19:22 he went away grieving, for he **h** many possessions.
21:28 A man **h** two sons; he went to the first and said
25:17 one who **h** the two talents made two more talents.
27:16 they **h** a notorious prisoner, called Jesus Barabbas.
Mk 3: 1 and a man was there who **h** a withered hand.
3: 3 And he said to the man who **h** the withered hand,
3:10 all who **h** diseases pressed upon him to touch him.
4: 5 it sprang up quickly, since it **h** no depth of soil.
4: 6 and since it **h** no root, it withered away.
5: 4 and no one **h** the strength to subdue him.
5:15 the very man who had **h** the legion;
5:26 many physicians, and had spent all that she **h;**
6:19 And Herodias **h** a grudge against him,
6:31 and they **h** no leisure even to eat.
6:34 a great crowd; and he **h** compassion for them,
7:11 'Whatever support you might have **h** from me
7:25 a woman whose little daughter **h** an unclean spirit
7:32 a deaf man who **h** an impediment in his speech;
8:14 and they **h** only one loaf with them in the boat.
10:22 went away grieving, for he **h** many possessions.
12:44 put in everything she **h,** all she **h** to live on.
Lk 1: 7 they **h** no children, because Elizabeth was barren,
4:33 a man who **h** the spirit of an unclean demon,
4:40 all those who **h** any who were sick with various
6: 8 he said to the man who **h** the withered hand,
7: 2 centurion there **h** a slave whom he valued highly,
7:13 When the Lord saw her, he **h** compassion for her
7:41 "A certain creditor **h** two debtors; one owed
8:27 a man of the city who **h** demons met him.
8:42 for he **h** an only daughter, about twelve years old,
8:43 and though she had spent all she **h** on physicians,
10:39 She **h** a sister named Mary, who sat at the Lord's
13: 6 "A man **h** a fig tree planted in his vineyard;
14: 2 in front of him, there was a man who **h** dropsy.
15:11 Jesus said, "There was a man who **h** two sons.
15:13 the younger son gathered all he **h** and traveled
15:32 But we **h** to celebrate and rejoice,
16: 1 "There was a rich man who **h** a manager,
17: 6 "If you **h** faith the size of a mustard seed,
18: 2 who neither feared God nor **h** respect for people.
21: 4 out of her poverty has put in all she **h** to live on.
22: 7 on which the Passover lamb **h** to be sacrificed.
Jn 4: 4 But he **h** to go through Samaria.
4:18 for you have **h** five husbands,
13:29 because Judas **h** the common purse,
17: 5 glory that I **h** in your presence before the world
18:10 Then Simon Peter, who **h** a sword, drew it,
19: 1 Then Pilate took Jesus and **h** him flogged.
19:19 Pilate also **h** an inscription written and put on
Ac 1:16 "Friends, the scripture **h** to be fulfilled,
2:44 believed were together and **h** all things in common;

Ac 2:45 distribute the proceeds to all, as any **h** need.
4:35 and it was distributed to each as any **h** need.
5:27 they **h** them stand before the council.
5:40 called in the apostles, they **h** them flogged.
6:6 They **h** these men stand before the apostles,
7:4 God **h** him move from there to this country
7:5 descendants after him, even though he **h** no child.
7:44 "Our ancestors **h** the tent of testimony
10:3 One afternoon at about three o'clock he **h** a vision
11:15 the Holy Spirit fell upon them just as it **h** upon us
12:2 He **h** James, the brother of John, killed
13:5 And they **h** John also to assist them.
14:9 and seeing that he **h** faith to be healed,
15:2 after Paul and Barnabas **h** no small dissension
15:21 Moses has **h** those who proclaim him,
16:3 and **h** him circumcised because of the Jews
16:9 During the night Paul **h** a vision:
16:16 we met a slave girl who **h** a spirit of divination
16:22 the magistrates **h** them stripped of their clothing
18:18 he **h** his hair cut, for he was under a vow.
18:19 and **h** a discussion with the Jews.
19:13 over those who **h** evil spirits,
21:9 He **h** four unmarried daughters who **h** the gift of
21:35 that he **h** to be carried by the soldiers.
22:30 brought Paul down and **h** him stand before them.
23:28 I **h** him brought to their council.
25:19 they **h** certain points of disagreement with him
26:22 To this day I have **h** help from God,
28:9 the people on the island who **h** diseases also came
28:19 though I **h** no charge to bring against my nation.
Ro 4:11 as a seal of the righteousness that he **h** by faith
4:12 the faith that our ancestor Abraham **h**
1Co 2:8 if they **h**, they would not have crucified the Lord
7:29 those who have wives be as though they **h** none,
7:30 those who buy as though they **h** no possessions,
7:31 deal with the world as though they **h** no dealings
2Co 3:10 Indeed, what once **h** glory has lost its glory
7:5 our bodies **h** no rest, but we were afflicted
8:15 "The one who **h** much did not have too much, and the one who **h** little did not have too little."
Gal 4:22 For it is written that Abraham **h** two sons,
Php 1:30 you are having the same struggle that you saw I **h**
2:27 But God **h** mercy on him, and not only on him
3:7 gains I **h**, these I have come to regard as loss
4:10 concerned for me, but **h** no opportunity to show it.
1Th 1:9 what kind of welcome we **h** among you,
2:2 at Philippi, as you know, we **h** courage in our God
Heb 2:17 he **h** to become like his brothers and sisters
6:13 because he **h** no one greater by whom to swear,
8:9 and so I **h** no concern for them, says the Lord.
9:1 even the first covenant **h** regulations for worship
9:26 for then he would have **h** to suffer again and again
10:34 you **h** compassion for those who were in prison
11:15 they would have **h** opportunity to return.
12:9 Moreover, we **h** human parents to discipline us,
1Pe 1:6 for a little while you have **h** to suffer various trials,
1:14 to the desires that you formerly **h** in ignorance.
1Jn 2:7 that you have **h** from the beginning;
2Jn 1:5 but one we have **h** from the beginning, let us love
Rev 2:4 that you have abandoned the love you **h** at first.
6:2 Its rider **h** a bow; a crown was given to him,
8:6 Now the seven angels who **h** the seven trumpets
9:9 they **h** scales like iron breastplates,
9:14 saying to the sixth angel who **h** the trumpet,
13:11 it **h** two horns like a lamb and it spoke like a
14:1 one hundred forty-four thousand who **h** his name
14:17 and he too **h** a sharp sickle.
14:18 with a loud voice to him who **h** the sharp sickle,
16:2 who **h** the mark of the beast and who worshiped
16:9 God, who **h** authority over these plagues,
17:1 one of the seven angels who **h** the seven bowls
17:3 and it **h** seven heads and ten horns.
18:19 where all who **h** ships at sea grew rich by her
21:9 one of the seven angels who **h** the seven bowls
21:15 The angel who talked to me **h** a measuring rod
Tob 1:21 and he **h** authority over the entire administration.
3:6 because I have **h** to listen to undeserved insults,
3:10 saying to him, 'You **h** only one beloved daughter
8:2 liver and heart out of the bag where he **h** them
8:17 Blessed are you because you **h** compassion
11:15 Though he afflicted me, he has **h** mercy upon me.
Jdt 4:13 heard their prayers and **h** regard for their distress;
5:10 to Egypt and lived there as long as they **h** food.
7:22 they no longer **h** any strength.
9:5 What you **h** in mind has happened;
12:11 the eunuch who **h** charge of his personal affairs,
AdE 2:7 he **h** a foster-child, the daughter of his father's
2:8 brought to Gai, who **h** custody of the women.
8:16 And the Jews **h** light and gladness
8:17 the Jews **h** joy and gladness, a banquet
10:5 the dream that I **h** concerning these matters,
11:2 son of Kish, of the tribe of Benjamin, **h** a dream.
11:12 and after he awoke he **h** it on his mind,
14:18 Your servant has **h** no joy since the day
Wis 5:13 and we **h** no sign of virtue to show,
7:5 no king has **h** a different beginning of existence;
13:9 for if they **h** the power to know so much that they
15:17 they have life, but the idols never **h**.
16:17 the fire **h** still greater effect,
16:25 according to the desire of those who **h** need,
18:12 **h** corpses too many to count.
Sir 11:5 Many kings have **h** to sit on the ground,
25:24 From a woman sin **h** its beginning,
31:10 Who has **h** the power to transgress
Bar 3:28 so they perished because they **h** no wisdom,
4:13 They **h** no regard for his statutes;
4:15 which **h** no respect for the aged
Sus 1:4 Joakim was very rich, and **h** a fine garden
1:6 all who **h** a case to be tried came to them there.
1:64 Daniel **h** a great reputation among the people.
Bel 1:3 Now the Babylonians **h** an idol called Bel,
1Mc 1:53 hiding in every place of refuge they **h**.
1:60 the women who **h** their children circumcised,
2:2 He **h** five sons, John surnamed Gaddi,
2:28 to the hills and left all that they **h** in the town.
3:30 he might not have such funds as he **h** before
3:46 Israel formerly **h** a place of prayer in Mizpah.
4:25 Thus Israel **h** a great deliverance that day.
5:46 to the right or to the left; they **h** to go through it.
6:49 they **h** no provisions there to withstand a siege,
6:53 But they **h** no food in storage,
7:50 So the land of Judah **h** rest for a few days.
9:7 for he **h** no time to assemble them.
9:35 the great amount of baggage that they **h**.
9:36 seized John and all that he **h**, and left with it.
9:57 and the land of Judah **h** rest for two years.
10:75 for Apollonius **h** a garrison in Joppa.
10:77 into the plain, for he **h** a large troop of cavalry
11:27 as many other honors as he had formerly **h**,
11:40 the hatred that the troops of Demetrius **h** for him;
14:4 The land **h** rest all the days of Simon.
16:11 he **h** a large store of silver and gold,
2Mc 3:4 **h** a disagreement with the high priest
3:13 because of the orders he **h** from the king,
5:10 **h** no one to mourn for him; he **h** no funeral
6:4 and **h** intercourse with women within the sacred
8:36 proclaimed that the Jews **h** a Defender,
10:15 Idumeans, who **h** control of important strongholds,
11:10 their heavenly ally, for the Lord **h** mercy on them.
12:20 who **h** with him one hundred twenty thousand
13:2 his guardian, who **h** charge of the government.
13:2 Each of them **h** a Greek force of
13:18 king, having **h** a taste of the daring of the Jews,
14:28 and grieved that he **h** to annul their agreement
14:39 to exhibit the enmity that he **h** for the Jews,
15:19 And those who **h** to remain in the city
1Es 1:17 things that **h** to do with the sacrifices to the Lord
5:55 the decree that they **h** in writing from King Cyrus
9:17 And the cases of the men who **h** foreign wives
9:45 for he **h** the place of honor in the presence of all.
9:54 and to give portions to those who **h** none,
3Mc 4:9 others **h** their feet secured by unbreakable fetters,
7:4 the ill-will that these people **h** toward all nations.
7:7 friendly and firm goodwill that they **h** toward us
2Es 3:26 for they also **h** the evil heart.
7:72 because though they **h** understanding,
8:56 For when they **h** opportunity to choose,
9:11 scorned my law while they still **h** freedom,
9:43 "Your servant was barren and **h** no child,
11:1 On the second night I **h** a dream:
11:1 an eagle that **h** twelve feathered wings
11:32 it **h** greater power over the world than all
4Mc 1:33 we abstain from the pleasure to be **h** from them?
4:13 although otherwise he **h** scruples about doing so,
5:7 Although you have **h** them for so long a time,
7:6 which **h** room only for reverence and purity,
14:11 that reason **h** full command over these men
15:7 she **h** sympathy for them;
16:10 Alas, I who **h** so many and beautiful children
16:18 through God that you have **h** a share in the world

HADAD (14) [HADAD-RIMMON]

Ge 25:15 **H**, Tema, Jetur, Naphish, and Kedemah.
36:35 Husham died, and **H** son of Bedad,
36:36 **H** died, and Samlah of Masrekah succeeded him
1Ki 11:14 **H** the Edomite; he was of the royal house in Edom.
11:17 but **H** fled to Egypt with some
11:19 **H** found great favor in the sight of Pharaoh,
11:21 When **H** heard in Egypt that David slept
11:21 **H** said to Pharaoh, "Let me depart,
11:25 the days of Solomon, making trouble as **H** did;
1Ch 1:30 Mishma, Dumah, Massa, **H**, Tema,
1:46 When Husham died, **H** son of Bedad,
1:47 When **H** died, Samlah of Masrekah succeeded him.
1:50 When Baal-hanan died, **H** succeeded him;
1:51 And **H** died. The clans of Edom

HADAD-RIMMON (1) [HADAD, RIMMON]

Zec 12:11 in Jerusalem will be as great as the mourning for **H**

HADADEZER (21)

2Sa 8:3 also struck down King **H** son of Rehob of Zobah,
8:5 the Arameans of Damascus came to help King **H**
8:7 that were carried by the servants of **H**,
8:8 From Betah and from Berothai, towns of **H**,
8:9 that David had defeated the whole army of **H**,
8:10 because he had fought against **H** and defeated him.
8:10 Now **H** had often been at war with Toi.
8:12 from the spoil of King **H** son of Rehob of Zobah.
10:16 **H** sent and brought out the Arameans who were
10:16 with Shobach the commander of the army of **H**
10:19 When all the kings who were servants of **H** saw
1Ki 11:23 who had fled from his master, King **H** of Zobah.
1Ch 18:3 David also struck down King **H** of Zobah,
18:5 the Arameans of Damascus came to help King **H**
18:7 that were carried by the servants of **H**,
18:8 From Tibhath and from Cun, cities of **H**,
18:9 that David had defeated the whole army of King **H**
18:10 because he had fought against **H** and defeated him.
18:10 Now **H** had often been at war with Tou.
19:16 with Shophach the commander of the army of **H**
19:19 the servants of **H** saw that they had been defeated

HADAR (1)

Ge 36:39 and **H** succeeded him as king,

HADASHAH (1)

Jos 15:37 Zenan, **H**, Migdal-gad,

HADASSAH (1)

Est 2:7 Mordecai had brought up **H**, that is Esther,

HADES‡ (36)

Mt 11:23 No, you will be brought down to **H**.
16:18 and the gates of **H** will not prevail against it.
Lk 10:15 No, you will be brought down to **H**.
16:23 In **H**, where he was being tormented,
Ac 2:27 For you will not abandon my soul to **H**,
2:31 saying, 'He was not abandoned to **H**,
Rev 1:18 and I have the keys of Death and of **H**.
6:8 Its rider's name was Death, and **H** followed with
20:13 Death and **H** gave up the dead that were in them,
20:14 Death and **H** were thrown into the lake of fire.
Tob 3:10 in his old age down in sorrow to **H**.
4:19 he chooses otherwise, he casts down to deepest **H**.
13:2 down to **H** in the lowest regions of the earth,
AdE 13:7 so may in a single day go down in violence to **H**,
Wis 1:14 and the dominion of **H** is not on earth.
2:1 and no one has been known to return from **H**.
16:13 you lead mortals down to the gates of **H**
17:14 upon them from the recesses of powerless **H**,
Sir 14:12 and the decree of **H** has not been shown to you.
14:16 because in **H** one cannot look for luxury.
17:27 Who will sing praises to the Most High in **H**
21:10 but at its end is the pit of **H**.
28:21 its death is an evil death, and **H** is preferable to it.
41:4 there are no questions asked in **H**.
48:5 You raised a corpse from death and from **H**,
51:5 from the deep belly of **H**, from an unclean tongue
51:6 and my life was on the brink of **H** below.
Bar 2:17 O Lord, and see, for the dead who are in **H**,
3:11 that you are counted among those in **H**?
3:19 They have vanished and gone down to **H**,
Aza 1:66 For he has rescued us from **H** and saved us from
2Mc 6:23 telling them to send him to **H**.
2Es 4:7 or which are the exits of **H**,
4:8 nor as yet into **H**, neither did I ever ascend
4:41 "In **H** the chambers of the souls are like the womb.
8:53 **H** has fled and corruption has been forgotten;

HADID (3)

Ezr 2:33 Of Lod, **H**, and Ono, seven hundred twenty-five.
Ne 7:37 Of Lod, **H**, and Ono, seven hundred twenty-one.
11:34 **H**, Zeboim, Neballat,

HADLAI (1)

2Ch 28:12 Jehizkiah son of Shallum, and Amasa son of **H**,

HADORAM (4) [=ADORAM, =JORAM]

Ge 10:27 **H**, Uzal, Diklah,
1Ch 1:21 **H**, Uzal, Diklah,
18:10 he sent his son **H** to King David,
2Ch 10:18 When King Rehoboam sent **H**,

HADRACH (1)

Zec 9:1 against the land of **H** and will rest upon Damascus.

HAELEPH (1)

Jos 18:28 **H**, Jebus (that is, Jerusalem),

HAFT (KJV) See HILT

HAGAB (2)

Ezr 2:46 **H**, Shamlai, Hanan,
1Es 5:30 the descendants of Ketab, the descendants of **H**,

HAGABA (1)

Ne 7:48 of Lebana, of **H**, of Shalmai,

HAGABAH (2)

Ezr 2:45 Lebanah, **H**, Akkub,
1Es 5:29 the descendants of Lebanah, the descendants of **H**,

HAGAR (15)

Ge 16:1 She had an Egyptian slave-girl whose name was **H**,
16:3 Abram's wife, took **H** the Egyptian, her slave-girl,
16:4 He went in to **H**, and she conceived;
16:8 And he said, "**H**, slave-girl of Sarai,
16:15 **H** bore Abram a son; and Abram named his son, whom **H** bore, Ishmael.
16:16 when **H** bore him Ishmael.
21:9 But Sarah saw the son of **H** the Egyptian,
21:14 and gave it to **H**, putting it on her shoulder,
21:17 and the angel of God called to **H** from heaven,
21:17 and said to her, "What troubles you, **H**?
25:12 whom **H** the Egyptian, Sarah's slave-girl,
Gal 4:24 One woman, in fact, is **H**, from Mount Sinai,
4:25 Now **H** is Mount Sinai in Arabia and corresponds
Bar 3:23 the descendants of **H**, who seek for understanding

HAGARENES, HAGARITE, HAGERITES (KJV) See HAGRITES

HAGGAI (14)

Ezr 5: 1 Now the prophets, **H** and Zechariah son of Iddo,
6:14 of the prophet **H** and Zechariah son of Iddo.
Hag 1: 1 by the prophet **H** to Zerubbabel son of Shealtiel,
1: 3 the word of the LORD came by the prophet **H,**
1:12 and the words of the prophet **H,**
1:13 Then **H,** the messenger of the LORD,
2: 1 the word of the LORD came by the prophet **H,**
2:10 the word of the LORD came by the prophet **H,**
2:13 Then **H** said, "If one who is unclean by contact
2:14 **H** then said, So is it with this people,
2:20 The word of the LORD came a second time to **H**
1Es 6: 1 the prophets **H** and Zechariah son
7: 3 while the prophets **H** and Zechariah prophesied;
2Es 1:40 Zephaniah, **H,** Zechariah and Malachi,

HAGGARD (1)

2Sa 13: 4 why are you so **h** morning after morning?

HAGGEDOLIM (1)

Ne 11:14 their overseer was Zabdiel son of **H.**

HAGGERI (KJV) See HAGRI

HAGGI (2) [HAGGITES]

Ge 46:16 Ziphion, **H,** Shuni, Ezbon, Eri, Arodi, and Areli.
Nu 26:15 of **H,** the clan of the Haggites;

HAGGIAH (1)

1Ch 6:30 Shimea his son, **H** his son, and Asaiah his son.

HAGGITES (1) [HAGGI]

Nu 26:15 of Haggi, the clan of the **H;**

HAGGITH (5)

2Sa 3: 4 the fourth, Adonijah son of **H;**
1Ki 1: 5 Now Adonijah son of **H** exalted himself, saying,
1:11 not heard that Adonijah son of **H** has become king
2:13 Then Adonijah son of **H** came to Bathsheba,
1Ch 3: 2 the fourth Adonijah, son of **H;**

HAGRI (1) [HAGRITE, HAGRITES]

1Ch 11:38 Joel the brother of Nathan, Mibhar son of **H,**

HAGRITE (1) [HAGRI]

1Ch 27:30 Over the flocks was Jaziz the **H.**

HAGRITES (4) [HAGRI]

1Ch 5:10 And in the days of Saul they made war on the **H,**
5:19 They made war on the **H,** Jetur, Naphish,
5:20 the **H** and all who were with them were given
Ps 83: 6 of Edom and the Ishmaelites, Moab and the **H,**

HAI (KJV) See AI

HAIL‡ (38) [HAILED, HAILSTONES]

Ex 9:18 the heaviest **h** to fall that has ever fallen in Egypt
9:19 under shelter will die when the **h** comes down
9:22 toward heaven so that **h** may fall on the whole land
9:23 and the LORD sent thunder and **h,**
9:23 And the LORD rained **h** on the land of Egypt;
9:24 there was **h** with fire flashing continually in
9:24 such heavy **h** as had never fallen in all the land
9:25 The **h** struck down everything that was in
9:25 the **h** also struck down all the plants of the field,
9:26 where the Israelites were, there was no **h.**
9:28 Enough of God's thunder and **h!**
9:29 thunder will cease, and there will be no more **h,**
9:33 then the thunder and the **h** ceased,
9:34 that the rain and the **h** and the thunder had ceased,
10: 5 the last remnant left you after the **h,**
10:12 all that the **h** has left."
10:15 and all the fruit of the trees that the **h** had left;
Job 38:22 or have you seen the storehouses of the **h,**
Ps 78:47 He destroyed their vines with **h,**
78:48 He gave over their cattle to the **h,**
105:32 He gave them **h** for rain,
147:17 He hurls down **h** like crumbs—
148: 8 fire and **h,** snow and frost,
Isa 28: 2 like a storm of **h,** a destroying tempest,
28:17 **h** will sweep away the refuge of lies,
Hag 2:17 of your toil with blight and mildew and **h;**
Mt 27:29 saying, **"H,** King of the Jews!"
Mk 15:18 They began saluting him, **"H,** King of the Jews!"
Jn 19: 3 They kept coming up to him, saying, **"H,**
Rev 8: 7 and there came **h** and fire, mixed with blood,
11:19 peals of thunder, an earthquake, and heavy **h.**
16:21 until they cursed God for the plague of the **h,**
Wis 16:16 by unusual rains and **h** and relentless storms,
16:22 that blazed in the **h** and flashed in the showers
Sir 39:29 Fire and **h** and famine and pestilence,
2Es 7:*41* or **h** or rain or dew,
15:13 be ruined by blight and **h** and by a terrible tempest.
15:41 fire and **h** and flying swords and floods of water,

HAILED (1) [HAIL]

1Sa 14:12 of the garrison **h** Jonathan and his armor-bearer,

HAILSTONES‡ (10) [HAIL]

Jos 10:11 of the **h** than the Israelites killed with the sword.
Ps 18:12 before him there broke through his clouds **h**
Isa 30:30 with a cloudburst and tempest and **h.**
Eze 13:11 There will be a deluge of rain, great **h** will fall,
13:13 and **h** in wrath to destroy it.
38:22 and I will pour down torrential rains and **h,**
Rev 16:21 huge **h,** each weighing about a hundred pounds,
Wis 5:22 **h** full of wrath will be hurled as from a catapult;
Sir 43:15 and the **h** are broken in pieces.
46: 5 great Lord answered him with **h** of mighty power.

HAIR‡ (96) [GRAY-HAIRED, HAIRS, HAIRY, LONG-HAIRED, WHITE-HAIRED]

Ex 25: 4 purple, and crimson yarns and fine linen, goats' **h,**
26: 7 You shall also make curtains of goats' **h** for a tent
35: 6 and crimson yarns, and fine linen; goats' **h,**
35:23 or purple or crimson yarn or fine linen or goats' **h**
35:26 to use their skill spun the goats' **h.**
36:14 He also made curtains of goats' **h** for a tent over
Lev 10: 6 "Do not dishevel your **h,** and do
13: 3 and if the **h** in the diseased area has turned white
13: 4 and the **h** in it has not turned white,
13:10 in the skin that has turned the **h** white,
13:20 the skin and its **h** has turned white,
13:21 if the priest examines it and the **h** on it is not white,
13:25 If the **h** in the spot has turned white
13:26 But if the priest examines it and the **h** in the spot is
13:30 If it appears deeper than the skin and the **h**
13:31 the skin and there is no black **h** in it,
13:32 itch has not spread, and there is no yellow **h** in it,
13:36 the priest need not seek for the yellow **h;**
13:37 and black **h** has grown in it, the itch is healed,
13:40 If anyone loses the **h** from his head,
13:41 If he loses the **h** from his forehead and temples,
13:45 and let the **h** of his head be disheveled;
14: 8 and shave off all his **h,** and bathe himself in water,
14: 9 On the seventh day he shall shave all his **h:**
14: 9 he shall shave all his **h.**
19:27 You shall not round off the **h** on your temples
21:10 shall not dishevel his **h,** nor tear his vestments.
Nu 5:18 dishevel the woman's **h,** and place in her hands
6:18 and shall take the **h** from the consecrated head
31:20 every article of skin, everything made of goats' **h,**
Jdg 16:22 But the **h** of his head began to grow again
20:16 every one could sling a stone at a **h,** and not miss.
1Sa 14:45 not one **h** of his head shall fall to the ground;
19:13 she put a net of goats' **h** on its head,
19:16 with the covering of goats' **h** on its head.
2Sa 14:11 not one **h** of your son shall fall to the ground."
14:26 When he cut the **h** of his head (for at the end
14:26 he cut it), he weighed the **h** of his head,
Ezr 9: 3 and pulled **h** from my head and beard,
Ne 13:25 and beat some of them and pulled out their **h;**
Job 4:15 the **h** of my flesh bristled.
Pr 16:31 Gray **h** is a crown of glory;
20:29 but the beauty of the aged is their gray **h.**
23: 7 for like a **h** in the throat,
SS 4: 1 Your **h** is like a flock of goats,
6: 5 Your **h** is like a flock of goats,
Isa 3:24 and instead of well-set **h,** baldness;
7:20 the head and the **h** of the feet,
Jer 7:29 Cut off your **h** and throw it away;
La 4: 7 their bodies were more ruddy than coral, their **h**
Eze 5: 1 then take balances for weighing, and divide the **h.**
5: 2 One third of the **h** you shall burn in the fire inside
16: 7 your breasts were formed, and your **h** had grown;
44:20 they shall only trim the **h** of their heads.
Da 3:27 the **h** of their heads was not singed,
4:33 until his **h** grew as long as eagles' feathers
7: 9 and the **h** of his head like pure wool;
Mic 1:16 and cut off your **h** for your pampered children;
Mt 3: 4 of camel's **h** with a leather belt around his waist,
5:36 for you cannot make one **h** white or black.
Mk 1: 6 Now John was clothed with camel's **h,**
Lk 7:38 with her tears and to dry them with her **h.**
7:44 with her tears and dried them with her **h.**
21:18 But not a **h** of your head will perish.
Jn 11: 2 with perfume and wiped his feet with her **h;**
12: 3 anointed Jesus' feet, and wiped them with her **h.**
Ac 18:18 At Cenchreae he had his **h** cut,
27:34 for none of you will lose a **h** from your heads."
1Co 11: 6 not veil herself, then she should cut off her **h;**
11: 6 for a woman to have her **h** cut off or to be shaved,
11:14 that if a man wears long **h,** it is degrading to him,
11:15 but if a woman has long **h,** it is her glory?
11:15 For her **h** is given to her for a covering.
1Ti 2: 9 not with their **h** braided, or with gold, pearls,
1Pe 3: 3 outwardly by braiding your **h,**
Rev 1:14 His head and his **h** were white as white wool,
9: 8 their **h** like women's hair, and their teeth
9: 8 like women's **h,** and their teeth like lions' teeth;
Jdt 10: 3 She combed her **h,** put on a tiara,
13: 7 took hold of the **h** of his head, and said,
16: 8 she fastened her **h** with a tiara and put on
AdE 14: 2 to adorn she covered with her tangled **h.**
Wis 4: 9 but understanding is gray **h** for anyone,
Sir 6:18 when you have gray **h** you will still find wisdom.
27:14 Their cursing and swearing make one's **h** stand
Bel 1:27 Then Daniel took pitch, fat, and **h,**
1:36 by the crown of his head and carried him by his **h;**
2Mc 7: 7 They tore off the skin of his head with the **h,**
15:13 distinguished by his gray **h** and dignity,
1Es 8:71 and pulled out **h** from my head and beard,
3Mc 1:18 sprinkled their **h** with dust,
4: 6 their myrrh-perfumed **h** sprinkled with ashes,
6: 6 you rescued unharmed, even to a **h,**
2Es 1: 8 the **h** of your head and hurl all evils upon them,
16: 2 Bind on sackcloth and cloth of goats' **h,**
4Mc 7:15 O man of blessed age and of venerable gray **h** and

HAIRS (13) [HAIR]

Ge 42:38 you would bring down my gray **h** with sorrow
44:29 you will bring down my gray **h** in sorrow
44:31 the gray **h** of your servant our father with sorrow
1Ki 1:52 not one of his **h** shall fall to the ground;
Ps 40:12 they are more than the **h** of my head,
69: 4 the **h** of my head are those who hate me
71:18 So even to old age and gray **h,** O God,
Hos 7: 9 gray **h** are sprinkled upon him,
Mt 10:30 And even the **h** of your head are all counted.
Lk 12: 7 But even the **h** of your head are all counted.
Wis 2:10 let us not spare the widow or regard the gray **h** of
2Mc 6:23 and the gray **h** that he had reached with distinction
4Mc 5: 7 for I respect your age and your gray **h.**

HAIRY (6) [HAIR]

Ge 25:25 The first came out red, all his body like a **h** mantle;
27:11 "Look, my brother Esau is a **h** man,
27:23 his hands were **h** like his brother Esau's hands;
2Ki 1: 8 They answered him, "A **h** man,
Ps 68:21 **h** crown of those who walk in their guilty ways.
Zec 13: 4 they will not put on a **h** mantle in order to deceive,

HAKELDAMA (1)

Ac 1:19 so that the field was called in their language **H,**

HAKKATAN (2)

Ezr 8:12 Of the descendants of Azgad, Johanan son of **H,**
1Es 8:38 Of the descendants of Azgad, Johanan son of **H,**

HAKKOZ (6)

1Ch 24:10 the seventh to **H,** the eighth to Abijah,
Ezr 2:61 the descendants of Habaiah, **H,**
Ne 3: 4 of Uriah son of **H** made repairs.
3:21 of Uriah son of **H** repaired another section from
7:63 the descendants of Hobaiah, of **H,**
1Es 5:38 the descendants of Habaiah, the descendants of **H,**

HAKUPHA (3)

Ezr 2:51 Bakbuk, **H,** Harhur,
Ne 7:53 of Bakbuk, of **H,** of Harhur,
1Es 5:31 the descendants of Acuph, the descendants of **H,**

HALAH (4)

2Ki 17: 6 He placed them in **H,** on the Habor,
18:11 settled them in **H,** on the Habor,
1Ch 5:26 and brought them to **H,** Habor, Hara,
Ob 1:20 the Israelites who are in **H** shall possess Phoenicia

HALAK (2)

Jos 11:17 from Mount **H,** which rises toward Seir, as far
12: 7 in the valley of Lebanon to Mount **H,**

HALE (KJV) See DRAGGED

HALF‡ (121) [HALF-SHARE, HALF-TRIBE, HALFWAY, HALVES, ONE-HALF]

Ge 15:10 laying each **h** over against the other;
24:22 the man took a gold nose-ring weighing a **h** shekel,
Ex 24: 6 Moses took **h** of the blood and put it in basins,
24: 6 and **h** of the blood he dashed against the altar.
25:10 it shall be two and a **h** cubits long, a cubit and a **h**
wide, and a cubit and a **h** high.
25:17 two cubits and a **h** shall be its length, and a cubit
and a **h** its width.
25:23 one cubit wide, and a cubit and a **h** high.
26:12 the **h** curtain that remains,
26:16 and a cubit and a **h** the width of each frame.
30:13 **h** a shekel according to the shekel of the sanctuary
30:13 **h** a shekel as an offering to the LORD.
30:15 and the poor shall not give less, than the **h** shekel,
30:23 and of sweet-smelling cinnamon **h** as much, that is,
36:21 and a cubit and a **h** the width of each frame.
37: 1 it was two and a **h** cubits long, a cubit and a **h**
wide, and a cubit and a **h** high.
37: 6 two cubits and a **h** was its length, and a cubit and a
h its width.
37:10 one cubit wide, and a cubit and a **h** high.
38:26 a **h** a shekel, measured by the sanctuary shekel),
Lev 6:20 **h** of it in the morning and **h** in the evening.
Nu 12:12 whose flesh is **h** consumed when it comes out
15: 9 mixed with **h** a hin of oil,
15:10 and you shall present as a drink offering **h** a hin
28:14 Their drink offerings shall be **h** a hin of wine for
31:29 Take it from their **h** and give it to Eleazar the priest
31:30 But from the Israelites' **h** you shall take one out
31:42 the Israelites' **h,** which Moses separated from that
31:43 congregation's **h** was three hundred thirty-seven
31:47 the Israelites' **h** Moses took one of every fifty,
Dt 3:12 well as **h** the hill country of Gilead with its towns,
Jos 8:33 **h** of them in front of Mount Gerizim and **h** of them
12: 2 the boundary of the Ammonites, that is, **h**
12: 5 over **h** of Gilead to the boundary of King Sihon
13:25 and **h** the land of the Ammonites, to Aroer,
13:31 and **h** of Gilead, and Ashtaroth, and Edrei,
13:31 to their clans—for **h** the Machirites.
22: 7 Now to the one **h** of the tribe
22: 7 but to the other **h** Joshua had given a possession
1Sa 14:14 an area about **h** a furrow long in an acre of land.

2Sa 10: 4 shaved off **h** the beard of each,
18: 3 If **h** of us die, they will not care about us.
19:40 and also **h** the people of Israel,
1Ki 3:25 then give **h** to the one, and **h** to the other."
7:31 it was a cubit and a **h** wide.
7:32 and the height of a wheel was a cubit and a **h.**
7:35 of the stand there was a round band **h** a cubit high;
10: 7 Not even **h** had been told me;
13: 8 "If you give me **h** your kingdom,
16: 9 his servant Zimri, commander of **h** his chariots,
16:21 **h** of the people followed Tibni son of Ginath, to make him king, and **h** followed Omri.
1Ch 2:52 Haroeh, **h** of the Menuhoth.
2:54 Atroth-beth-joab, and **h** of the Manahathites,
6:61 out of the half-tribe, the **h** of Manasseh, ten towns.
2Ch 9: 6 Not even **h** of the greatness
Ne 3: 9 ruler of **h** the district of Jerusalem, made repairs.
3:12 ruler of **h** the district of Jerusalem, made repairs,
3:16 ruler of **h** the district of Beth-zur,
3:17 ruler of **h** the district of Keilah,
3:18 son of Henadad, ruler of **h** the district of Keilah;
4: 6 and all the wall was joined together to **h** its height;
4:16 **h** of my servants worked on construction,
4:16 and **h** held the spears, shields, bows,
4:21 and **h** of them held the spears from break of dawn
12:32 them went Hoshaiah and **h** the officials of Judah,
12:38 I followed them with **h** of the people on the wall,
12:40 and I and **h** of the officials with me;
13:24 **h** of their children spoke the language of Ashdod,
Est 5: 3 even to the **h** of my kingdom."
5: 6 Even to the **h** of my kingdom, it shall be fulfilled."
7: 2 Even to the **h** of my kingdom, it shall be fulfilled."
Ps 55:23 and treacherous shall not live out **h** their days.
Isa 44:16 **H** of it he burns in the fire;
44:16 over this **h** he roasts meat, eats it and is satisfied.
44:19 "**H** of it I burned in the fire;
Eze 16:51 Samaria has not committed **h** your sins;
40:42 a cubit and a **h** long, and one cubit and a **h** wide,
43:17 with a rim around it a **h** a cubit wide,
Da 7:25 into his power for a time, two times, and **h** a time.
9:27 and for **h** of the week he shall make sacrifice
12: 7 that it would be for a time, two times, and **h** a time,
Zec 14: 2 **h** the city shall go into exile,
14: 4 that one **h** of the Mount shall withdraw northward, and the other **h** southward.
14: 8 **h** of them to the eastern sea and **h** of them to the
Mk 6:23 I will give you, even **h** of my kingdom."
Lk 10:30 beat him, and went away, leaving him **h** dead.
19: 8 **h** of my possessions, Lord, I will give to the poor;
Rev 8: 1 there was silence in heaven for about **h** an hour.
11: 9 and a **h** days members of the peoples and tribes
11:11 But after the three and a **h** days,
12:14 where she is nourished for a time, and times, and **h**
Tob 8:21 Take at once **h** of what I own and return in safety
8:21 the other **h** will be yours when my wife and I die.
10:10 as well as **h** of all his property:
12: 2 to give him **h** of the possessions brought back
12: 4 my child, to receive **h** of all that he brought back."
12: 5 for your wages **h** of all that you brought back,
AdE 5: 3 It shall be given you, even to **h** of my kingdom."
7: 2 even to **h** of my kingdom."
Wis 18:14 and night in its swift course was now **h** gone,
18:18 down **h** dead, made known why they were dying;
Sir 29: 6 If he can pay, his creditor will hardly get back **h,**
1Mc 3:34 And he turned over to Lysias **h** of his forces and
3:37 Then the king took the remaining **h** of his forces
10:30 the **h** of the fruit of the trees that I should receive,
2Es 11:17 as long as you have ruled, not even **h** as long."
13:45 a journey of a year and a **h;**
14:12 as well as **h** of the tenth part;
14:12 two of its parts remain, besides **h** of the tenth part.
4Mc 4:11 down **h** dead in the temple area that was open

HALF-SHARE (1) [HALF, SHARE]

Nu 31:36 The **h,** the portion of those who had gone out

HALF-TRIBE (36) [HALF, TRIBE]

Nu 32:33 to the Gadites and to the Reubenites and to the **h**
34:13 to give to the nine tribes and to the **h;**
34:14 and also the **h** of Manasseh;
34:15 and the **h** have taken their inheritance beyond
Dt 3:13 and I gave to the **h** of Manasseh the rest of Gilead
29: 8 the Gadites, and the **h** of Manasseh.
Jos 1:12 the Gadites, and the **h** of Manasseh Joshua said,
4:12 and the **h** of Manasseh crossed over armed before
12: 6 to the Reubenites and the Gadites and the **h**
13: 7 for an inheritance to the nine tribes and the **h**
13: 8 With the other **h** of Manasseh the Reubenites and
13:29 Moses gave an inheritance to the **h** of Manasseh;
13:29 it was allotted to the **h** of the Manassites according
18: 7 the **h** of Manasseh have received their inheritance
21: 5 from the tribe of Dan, and the **h** of Manasseh.
21: 6 and from the **h** of Manasseh in Bashan.
21:25 Out of the **h** of Manasseh:
21:27 were given out of the **h** of Manasseh,
22: 1 the Gadites, and the **h** of Manasseh,
22: 9 the Gadites and the **h** of Manasseh returned home,
22:10 and the Gadites and the **h** of Manasseh built there
22:11 the **h** of Manasseh had built an altar at the frontier
22:13 to the Reubenites and the Gadites and the **h**
22:15 and the **h** of Manasseh, in the land of Gilead,
22:21 and the **h** of Manasseh said in answer to the heads
1Ch 5:18 and the **h** of Manasseh had valiant warriors,
5:23 members of the **h** of Manasseh lived in the land;
5:26 and the **h** of Manasseh, and brought them to Halah,
6:61 out of the **h,** the half of Manasseh, ten towns.
1Ch 6:70 and out of the **h** of Manasseh,
6:71 To the Gershomites: out of the **h** of Manasseh:
12:31 Of the **h** of Manasseh, eighteen thousand,
12:37 the Reubenites and Gadites and the **h** of Manasseh
26:32 the **h** of the Manassites for everything pertaining
27:20 for the **h** of Manasseh, Joel son of Pedaiah;
27:21 **h** of Manasseh in Gilead, Iddo son of Zechariah;

HALFWAY (4) [HALF]

Ex 26:28 The middle bar, **h** up the frames,
27: 5 the ledge of the altar so that the net shall extend **h**
36:33 the middle bar to pass through from end to end **h**
38: 4 under its ledge, extending **h** down.

HALHUL (1)

Jos 15:58 **H,** Beth-zur, Gedor,

HALI (1)

Jos 19:25 Its boundary included Helkath, **H,** Beten,

HALICARNASSUS (1)

1Mc 15:23 and to Pamphylia, and to Lycia, and to **H,**

HALL (13)

1Sa 9:22 and his servant-boy and brought them into the **h,**
1Ki 7: 6 He made the **H** of Pillars fifty cubits long
7: 7 He made the **H** of the Throne where he was
7: 7 to pronounce judgment, the **H** of Justice, covered
7: 8 in the other court back of the **h,**
7: 8 a house like this **h** for Pharaoh's daughter,
Est 5: 1 of the king's palace, opposite the king's **h.**
7: 8 to the banquet **h,** Haman had thrown himself on
Da 5:10 came into the banqueting **h.**
Mt 22:10 so the wedding **h** was filled with guests.
Ac 19: 9 and argued daily in the lecture **h** of Tyrannus.
25:23 the audience **h** with the military tribunes and
1Mc 16:16 in the banquet **h** and killed him and his two sons,

HALLELUJAH (6)

Rev 19: 1 of a great multitude in heaven, saying, "**H!**
19: 3 Once more they said, "**H!**
19: 4 on the throne, saying, "Amen. **H!**"
19: 6 the sound of mighty thunderpeals, crying out, "**H!**
Tob 13:17 and all her houses will cry, '**H!**
3Mc 7:13 their priests and the whole multitude shouted the **H**

HALLOHESH (2)

Ne 3:12 Next to him Shallum son of **H,**
10:24 **H,** Pilha, Shobek,

HALLOW (3) [HALLOWED]

Lev 16:19 and cleanse it and **h** it from the uncleannesses of
25:10 And you shall **h** the fiftieth year
Eze 20:20 and **h** my sabbaths that they may be a sign

HALLOW, HALLOWED (KJV) See also CONSECRATE, DEDICATE, HOLY, SANCTIFY

HALLOWED (5) [HALLOW]

Ge 2: 3 So God blessed the seventh day and **h** it,
Mt 6: 9 Our Father in heaven, **h** be your name.
Lk 11: 2 Father, **h** be your name. Your kingdom come.
Sir 33: 9 Some days he exalted and **h,**
2Mc 15: 2 that he who sees all things has honored and **h**

HALOHESH (KJV) See HALLOHESH

HALT (4) [HALTED, HALTINGLY]

Ne 12:39 and they came to a **h** at the Gate of the Guard.
Isa 10:32 This very day he will **h** at Nob,
Na 2: 8 "**H! H!**"—but no one turns back.

HALTED (3) [HALT]

2Ki 5: 9 and **h** at the entrance of Elisha's house.
Joel 2: 8 they burst through the weapons and are not **h.**
2Mc 10:27 and when they came near the enemy they **h.**

HALTINGLY (1) [HALT]

1Sa 15:32 And Agag came to him **h.**

HALVES (2) [HALF]

SS 4: 3 like **h** of a pomegranate behind your veil.
6: 7 like **h** of a pomegranate behind your veil.

HAM (17)

Ge 5:32 Noah became the father of Shem, **H,** and Japheth.
6:10 And Noah had three sons, Shem, **H,** and Japheth.
7:13 the very same day Noah with his sons, Shem and **H**
9:18 of Noah who went out of the ark were Shem, **H,**
9:18 **H** was the father of Canaan.
9:22 And **H,** the father of Canaan,
10: 1 the descendants of Noah's sons, Shem, **H,**
10: 6 descendants of **H:** Cush, Egypt, Put, and Canaan.
10:20 These are the descendants of **H,** by their families,
14: 5 the Zuzim in **H,** the Emim in Shaveh-kiriathaim,
1Ch 1: 4 Noah, Shem, **H,** and Japheth.
1: 8 descendants of **H:** Cush, Egypt, Put, and Canaan.
4:40 for the former inhabitants there belonged to **H.**
Ps 78:51 the first issue of their strength in the tents of **H.**
105:23 Jacob lived as an alien in the land of **H.**
105:27 and miracles in the land of **H.**
106:22 wondrous works in the land of **H,**

HAMAN (101) [HAMAN'S]

Est 3: 1 After these things King Ahasuerus promoted **H** son
3: 2 down and did obeisance to **H;**
3: 4 and he would not listen to them, they told **H,**
3: 5 When **H** saw that Mordecai did not bow down or do obeisance to him, **H** was infuriated.
3: 6 **H** plotted to destroy all the Jews,
3: 7 before **H** for the day and for the month,
3: 8 Then **H** said to King Ahasuerus,
3:10 from his hand and gave it to **H** son of Hammedatha
3:11 The king said to **H,** "The money is given to you,
3:12 and an edict, according to all that **H** commanded,
3:15 The king and **H** sat down to drink;
4: 7 exact sum of money that **H** had promised to pay
5: 4 **H** come today to a banquet that I have prepared
5: 5 Then the king said, "Bring **H** quickly,
5: 5 So the king and **H** came to the banquet
5: 8 let the king and **H** come tomorrow to the banquet
5: 9 **H** went out that day happy and in good spirits.
5: 9 But when **H** saw Mordecai in the king's gate,
5:10 nevertheless **H** restrained himself and went home.
5:11 and **H** recounted to them the splendor of his riches,
5:12 **H** added, "Even Queen Esther let no one
5:14 This advice pleased **H,** and he had
6: 4 Now **H** had just entered the outer court of
6: 5 So the king's servants told him, "**H** is there,
6: 6 So **H** came in, and the king said to him,
6: 6 **H** said to himself, "Whom would the king wish
6: 7 So **H** said to the king,
6:10 Then the king said to **H,** "Quickly,
6:11 So **H** took the robes and the horse
6:12 but **H** hurried to his house,
6:13 When **H** told his wife Zeresh
6:14 the king's eunuchs arrived and hurried **H** off to
7: 1 the king and **H** went in to feast with Queen Esther.
7: 6 Esther said, "A foe and enemy, this wicked **H!**"
7: 6 **H** was terrified before the king and the queen.
7: 7 but **H** stayed to beg his life from Queen Esther,
7: 8 **H** had thrown himself on the couch
7: 9 the very gallows that **H** has prepared for Mordecai,
7:10 So they hanged **H** on the gallows
8: 1 to Queen Esther the house of **H,** the enemy of
8: 2 which he had taken from **H,**
8: 2 So Esther set Mordecai over the house of **H.**
8: 3 and pleading with him to avert the evil design of **H**
8: 5 be written to revoke the letters devised by **H** son
8: 7 "See, I have given Esther the house of **H,**
9:10 of **H** son of Hammedatha, the enemy of the Jews;
9:12 and also the ten sons of **H.**
9:13 let the ten sons of **H** be hanged on the gallows."
9:14 and the ten sons of **H** were hanged.
9:24 **H** son of Hammedatha the Agagite,
AdE 1:10 when the king was in good humor, he told **H,**
3: 1 these events King Artaxerxes promoted **H** son
3: 2 So all who were at court used to do obeisance to **H,**
3: 4 Then they informed **H** that Mordecai was resisting
3: 5 So when **H** learned that Mordecai was
3: 7 In the twelfth year of King Artaxerxes **H** came to
3: 8 Then **H** said to King Artaxerxes,
3:10 So the king took off his signet ring and gave it to **H**
3:11 The king told **H,** "Keep the money,
3:15 And while the king and **H** caroused together,
4: 7 how **H** had promised to pay ten thousand talents
4: 8 for **H,** who stands next to the king,
5: 4 let him and **H** come to the dinner
5: 5 Then the king said, "Bring **H** quickly,
5: 8 and **H** come to the dinner that I shall prepare them,
5: 9 **H** went out from the king joyful and glad of heart.
5:12 And **H** said, "The queen did not invite anyone to
5:14 This advice pleased **H,** and so
6: 4 about the goodwill shown by Mordecai, **H** was in
6: 4 Now **H** had come to speak to the king
6: 5 "**H** is standing in the courtyard."
6: 6 Then the king said to **H,**
6: 6 And **H** said to himself, "Whom would
6:10 Then the king said to **H,**
6:11 So **H** got the robe and the horse;
6:12 and **H** hurried back to his house,
6:13 **H** told his wife Zosara
6:14 the eunuchs arrived and hurriedly brought **H** to
7: 1 So the king and **H** went in to drink with the queen.
7: 6 Esther said, "Our enemy is this evil man **H!**"
7: 6 **H** was terrified in the presence of the king
7: 7 and **H** began to beg for his life from the queen,
7: 8 **H** had thrown himself on the couch,
7: 8 **H,** when he heard, turned away his face.
7: 9 **H** has even prepared a gallows for Mordecai,
7: 9 So the king said, "Let **H** be hanged on that."
7:10 So **H** was hanged on the gallows he had prepared
8: 1 to Esther all the property of the persecutor **H.**
8: 2 The king took the ring that had been taken from **H,**
8: 3 to avert all the evil that **H** had planned against
8: 5 letters that **H** wrote and sent to destroy the Jews
9:10 of **H** son of Hammedatha, the Bougean, the enemy
9:24 —how **H** son of Hammedatha,
10: 7 The two dragons are **H** and myself.
12: 6 But **H** son of Hammedatha, a Bougean,
13: 3 how this might be accomplished, **H—**
13: 6 the letters written by **H,** who is in charge of affairs
13:12 and refused to bow down to this proud **H;**
16:10 For **H** son of Hammedatha,

AdE 16:17 not to put in execution the letters sent by **H** son

HAMAN'S (9) [HAMAN]
Est 7: 8 the mouth of the king, they covered **H** face.
7: 9 whose word saved the king, stands at **H** house,
AdE 3:12 and in accordance with **H** instructions they wrote
7: 9 it is standing at **H** house,
8: 2 over everything that had been **H.**
8: 7 **H** property to you and have hanged him on a tree
9:13 Also, hang up the bodies of **H** ten sons."
9:14 over to the Jews of the city the bodies of **H** sons
14:17 And your servant has not eaten at **H** table,

HAMATH‡ (25) [HAMATH-ZOBAH, HAMATHITES, LEBO-HAMATH]
2Sa 8: 9 When King Toi of **H** heard that David had defeated
2Ki 14:28 and how he recovered for Israel Damascus and **H,**
17:24 Cuthah, Avva, **H,** and Sepharvaim,
17:30 the people of **H** made Ashima;
18:34 Where are the gods of **H** and Arpad?
19:13 Where is the king of **H,** the king of Arpad,
23:33 at Riblah in the land of **H,**
25:21 and put them to death at Riblah in the land of **H.**
1Ch 18: 3 toward **H,** as he went to set up a monument at
18: 9 of **H** heard that David had defeated the whole army
2Ch 8: 4 and all the storage towns that he built in **H.**
Isa 10: 9 Is not **H** like Arpad?
11:11 from Ethiopia, from Elam, from Shinar, from **H,**
36:19 Where are the gods of **H** and Arpad?
37:13 Where is the king of **H,** the king of Arpad,
Jer 39: 5 in the land of **H;** and he passed sentence on him.
49:23 **H** and Arpad are confounded,
52: 9 to the king of Babylon at Riblah in the land of **H,**
52:27 and put them to death at Riblah in the land of **H.**
Eze 47:16 the border of Damascus and the border of **H),**
47:17 with the border of **H** to the north.
48: 1 on the border of Damascus, with **H** to the north),
Am 6: 2 from there go to **H** the great;
Zec 9: 2 **H** also, which borders on it, Tyre and Sidon,
1Mc 12:25 from Jerusalem and met them in the region of **H,**

HAMATH-ZOBAH (1) [HAMATH, ZOBAH]
2Ch 8: 3 Solomon went to **H,** and captured it.

HAMATHITES (2) [HAMATH]
Ge 10:18 the Arvadites, the Zemarites, and the **H.**
1Ch 1:16 the Arvadites, the Zemarites, and the **H.**

HAMMATH (2)
Jos 19:35 The fortified towns are Ziddim, Zer, **H,** Rakkath,
1Ch 2:55 These are the Kenites who came from **H,**

HAMMEDATHA (11)
Est 3: 1 of **H** the Agagite, and advanced him
3:10 from his hand and gave it to Haman son of **H**
8: 5 the letters devised by Haman son of **H** the Agagite,
9:10 the ten sons of Haman son of **H,** the enemy of
9:24 Haman son of **H** the Agagite,
AdE 3: 1 of **H,** a Bougean, advancing him
9:10 of Haman son of **H,** the Bougean, the enemy of
9:24 —how Haman son of **H,** the Macedonian, fought
12: 6 But Haman son of **H,** a Bougean,
16:10 Haman son of **H,** a Macedonian (really an alien
16:17 in execution the letters sent by Haman son of **H,**

HAMMELECH (KJV) See THE KING

HAMMER (7) [HAMMERED, HAMMERS]
Jdg 4:21 and took a **h** in her hand,
1Ki 6: 7 that neither **h** nor ax nor any tool of iron was heard
Isa 41: 7 and the one who smooths with the **h** encourages
Jer 10: 4 with **h** and nails so that it cannot move.
23:29 and like a **h** that breaks a rock in pieces?
50:23 the **h** of the whole earth is cut down and broken!
Sir 38:28 the sound of the **h** deafens his ears,

HAMMERED (14) [HAMMER]
Ex 25:18 you shall make them of **h** work,
25:31 the shaft of the lampstand shall be made of **h** work;
25:36 the whole of it one **h** piece of pure gold.
37: 7 He made two cherubim of **h** gold;
37:17 the shaft of the lampstand were made of **h** work;
37:22 the whole of it one **h** piece of pure gold.
39: 3 Gold leaf was **h** out and cut into threads to work
Nu 8: 4 out of **h** work of gold.
8: 4 From its base to its flowers, it was **h** work;
10: 2 you shall make them of **h** work;
16:38 Make them into **h** plates as a covering for the altar,
16:39 and they were **h** out as a covering for the altar—
Sir 50: 9 of **h** gold studded with all kinds of precious stones;
50:16 they blew their trumpets of **h** metal;

HAMMERS (2) [HAMMER]
Ps 74: 6 And then, with hatchets and **h,**
Isa 44:12 with **h,** and forging it with his strong arm;

HAMMIPHKAD See Index to Footnotes

HAMMOLECHETH (1)
1Ch 7:18 his sister **H** bore Ishhod, Abiezer, and Mahlah.

HAMMON (2)
Jos 19:28 Ebron, Rehob, **H,** Kanah, as far as Great Sidon;
1Ch 6:76 with its pasture lands, **H** with its pasture lands,

HAMMOTH-DOR (1)
Jos 21:32 for the slayer, **H** with its pasture lands, and Kartan

HAMMUEL (1)
1Ch 4:26 **H** his son, Zaccur his son, Shimei his son.

HAMON-GOG (2) [BAAL-HAMON, GOG]
Eze 39:11 it shall be called the Valley of **H.**
39:15 until the buriers have buried it in the Valley of **H.**

HAMONAH (1)
Eze 39:16 (A city **H** is there also.)

HAMOR (13) [HAMOR'S]
Ge 33:19 And from the sons of **H,** Shechem's father,
34: 2 When Shechem son of **H** the Hivite,
34: 4 So Shechem spoke to his father **H,** saying,
34: 6 And **H** the father of Shechem went out to Jacob
34: 8 But **H** spoke with them, saying,
34:13 and his father **H** deceitfully,
34:18 Their words pleased **H** and Hamor's son Shechem.
34:20 So **H** and his son Shechem came to the gate
34:24 of the city gate heeded **H** and his son Shechem;
34:26 killed **H** and his son Shechem with the sword,
Jos 24:32 from the children of **H,** the father of Shechem,
Jdg 9:28 and Zebul his officer serve the men of **H** father
Ac 7:16 for a sum of silver from the sons of **H** in Shechem.

HAMOR'S (1) [HAMOR]
Ge 34:18 Their words pleased Hamor and **H** son Shechem.

HAMPERED (1)
Pr 4:12 When you walk, your step will not be **h;**

HAMRAN (1)
1Ch 1:41 sons of Dishon: **H,** Eshban, Ithran, and Cheran.

HAMSTRING (1) [HAMSTRUNG]
Jos 11: 6 you shall **h** their horses, and burn their chariots

HAMSTRUNG (4) [HAMSTRING]
Ge 49: 6 and at their whim they **h** oxen.
Jos 11: 9 he **h** their horses, and burned their chariots
2Sa 8: 4 David **h** all the chariot horses,
1Ch 18: 4 David **h** all the chariot horses,

HAMUEL (KJV) See HAMMUEL

HAMUL (3) [HAMULITES]
Ge 46:12 and the children of Perez were Hezron and **H.**
Nu 26:21 of **H,** the clan of the Hamulites.
1Ch 2: 5 The sons of Perez: Hezron and **H.**

HAMULITES (1) [HAMUL]
Nu 26:21 of Hamul, the clan of the **H.**

HAMUTAL (3)
2Ki 23:31 His mother's name was **H** daughter of Jeremiah
24:18 His mother's name was **H** daughter of Jeremiah
Jer 52: 1 His mother's name was **H** daughter of Jeremiah

HANA (1)
1Es 5:30 the descendants of **H,** the descendants of Cathua,

HANAEL (1)
Tob 1:21 the son of my brother **H** over all the accounts

HANAMEL (4)
Jer 32: 7 **H** son of your uncle Shallum is going to come
32: 8 my cousin **H** came to me in the court of the guard,
32: 9 I bought the field at Anathoth from my cousin **H,**
32:12 in the presence of my cousin **H,**

HANAN (13)
1Ch 8:23 Abdon, Zichri, **H,**
8:38 Obadiah, and **H;** all these were the sons of Azel.
9:44 Bocheru, Ishmael, Sheariah, Obadiah, and **H;**
11:43 **H** son of Maacah, and Joshaphat the Mithnite,
Ezr 2:46 Hagab, Shamlai, **H,**
Ne 7:49 of **H,** of Giddel, of Gahar,
8: 7 Kelita, Azariah, Jozabad, **H,** Pelaiah, the Levites,
10:10 Shebaniah, Hodiah, Kelita, Pelaiah, **H,**
10:22 Pelatiah, **H,** Anaiah,
10:26 Ahiah, **H,** Anan,
13:13 as their assistant **H** son of Zaccur son of Mattaniah,
Jer 35: 4 into the chamber of the sons of **H** son of Igdaliah,
1Es 9:48 **H,** Pelaiah, the Levites, taught the law of the Lord,

HANANAEL See Index to Footnotes

HANANEL (4)
Ne 3: 1 of the Hundred and as far as the Tower of **H.**
12:39 by the Fish Gate and the Tower of **H** and the
Jer 31:38 be rebuilt for the LORD from the tower of **H** to
Zec 14:10 from the Tower of **H** to the king's wine presses.

HANANI (12)
1Ki 16: 1 the LORD came to Jehu son of **H** against Baasha,
16: 7 of the LORD came by the prophet Jehu son of **H**
1Ch 25: 4 and Jerimoth, Hananiah, **H,** Eliathah, Giddalti,
25:25 to **H,** his sons and his brothers, twelve;
2Ch 16: 7 At that time the seer **H** came to King Asa of Judah,
19: 2 Jehu son of **H** the seer went out to meet him
20:34 are written in the Annals of Jehu son of **H,**
Ezr 10:20 Of the descendants of Immer: **H** and Zebadiah.
Ne 1: 2 **H,** came with certain men from Judah;
7: 2 I gave my brother **H** charge over Jerusalem,
12:36 Milalai, Gilalai, Maai, Nethanel, Judah, and **H,**
1Es 9:21 **H** and Zebadiah and Maaseiah and Shemaiah

HANANIAH (37) [=SHADRACH]
1Ch 3:19 Meshullam and **H,** and Shelomith was their sister;
3:21 The sons of **H:** Pelatiah
8:24 **H,** Elam, Anthothijah,
25: 4 **H,** Hanani, Eliathah, Giddalti, and Romamti-ezer,
25:23 to **H,** his sons and his brothers, twelve;
2Ch 26:11 the officer Maaseiah, under the direction of **H,** one
Ezr 10:28 Jehohanan, **H,** Zabbai, and Athlai.
Ne 3: 8 Next to him **H,** one of the perfumers, made repairs;
3:30 After him **H** son of Shelemiah and Hanun sixth son
7: 2 along with **H** the commander of the citadel—
10:23 Hoshea, **H,** Hasshub,
12:12 of Seraiah, Meraiah; of Jeremiah, **H;**
12:41 Miniamin, Micaiah, Elioenai, Zechariah, and **H,**
Jer 28: 1 the prophet **H** son of Azzur, from Gibeon,
28: 5 the prophet **H** in the presence of the priests and all
28:10 Then the prophet **H** took the yoke from the neck of
28:11 And **H** spoke in the presence of all the people,
28:12 Sometime after the prophet **H** had broken the yoke
28:13 tell **H,** Thus says the LORD:
28:15 And the prophet Jeremiah said to the prophet **H,**
28:15 "Listen, **H,** the LORD has not sent you,
28:17 in the seventh month, the prophet **H** died.
36:12 Gemariah son of Shaphan, Zedekiah son of **H,**
37:13 of **H** arrested the prophet Jeremiah saying,
Da 1: 6 Among them were Daniel, **H,** Mishael,
1: 7 **H** he called Shadrach, Mishael he called Meshach,
1:11 the palace master had appointed over Daniel, **H,**
1:19 no one was found to compare with Daniel, **H,**
2:17 to his home and informed his companions, **H,**
Tob 5:13 He replied, "I am Azariah, the son of the great **H,**
5:14 For I knew **H** and Nathan,
Aza 1:66 "Bless the Lord, **H,** Azariah, and Mishael;
1Mc 2:59 **H,** Azariah, and Mishael believed and were saved
1Es 8:48 of the descendants of **H,** and their descendants,
9:29 Jehohanan and **H** and Zabbai and Emathis.
4Mc 16:21 the lions, and **H,** Azariah, and Mishael were hurled
18:12 and he taught you about **H,** Azariah,

HANANIEL‡ (1)
Tob 1: 1 of **H** son of Aduel son of Gabael son of Raphael of

HAND‡ (1176) [BAREHANDED, EMPTY-HANDED, HAND-TO-HAND, HANDBREADTH, HANDBREADTHS, HANDED, HANDFUL, HANDFULS, HANDING, HANDIWORK, HANDS, HIGH-HANDEDLY, LEFT-HANDED, SINGLE-HANDED]
A. RIGHT HAND (137)
B. INTO ... HAND (120)
C. FROM ... HAND (114)
D. HAND OF THE †LORD (32)
E. AT HAND (25)
F. HAND OF ... *GOD (24)
G. MIGHTY HAND (22)
H. LEFT HAND (18)
I. HAND OF THE *LORD (7)

Ge 3:22 he might reach out his **h** and take also from the tree
4:11 to receive your brother's blood from your **h.** C
8: 9 So he put out his **h** and took it and brought it into
9: 2 into your **h** they are delivered. B
13: 9 If you take the left **h,** then I will go to the right; H
13: 9 if you take the right **h,** then I will go to the left." A
14:20 who has delivered your enemies into your **h!"** B
16:12 with his **h** against everyone,
16:12 and everyone's **h** against him;
19:16 and his wife and his two daughters by the **h,**
21:18 lift up the boy and hold him fast with your **h,**
21:30 from my **h,** in order that you may be a witness C
22:10 Then Abraham reached out his **h** and took
22:12 not lay your **h** on the boy or do anything to him;
24: 2 "Put your **h** under my thigh
24: 9 So the servant put his **h** under the thigh
24:18 and quickly lowered her jar upon her **h**
24:49 I may turn either to the right **h** or to the left." A
25:24 When her time to give birth was at **h,** E
25:26 with his **h** gripping Esau's heel;
31:39 of my **h** you required it,
32:11 Deliver me, please, from the **h** of my brother, C
32:11 from the hand of my brother, from the **h** of Esau, C
32:16 These he delivered into the **h** of his servants, B
33:10 then accept my present from my **h;** C
37:22 into this pit here in the wilderness, but lay no **h**

Ge 37:22 of their **h** and restore him to his father.
38:18 and the staff that is in your **h.**"
38:28 While she was in labor, one put out a **h;**
38:28 midwife took and bound on his **h** a crimson thread,
38:29 But just then he drew back his **h,**
38:30 with the crimson thread on his **h;**
39: 8 and he has put everything that he has in my **h.**
39:12 But he left his garment in her **h,**
39:13 When she saw that he had left his garment in her **h**
40:11 Pharaoh's cup was in my **h;**
40:11 and placed the cup in Pharaoh's **h.**"
40:13 and you shall place Pharaoh's cup in his **h,**
40:21 and he placed the cup in Pharaoh's **h;**
41:42 Removing his signet ring from his **h,** C
41:42 Pharaoh put it on Joseph's **h;**
41:44 without your consent no one shall lift up **h** or foot
46: 4 and Joseph's own **h** shall close your eyes."
47:29 put your **h** under my thigh and promise
48:13 Ephraim in his right **h** toward Israel's left, A
48:13 and Manasseh in his left **h** toward Israel's right, H
48:14 But Israel stretched out his right **h** and laid it on A
48:14 and his left **h** on the head of Manasseh, H
48:17 Joseph saw that his father laid his right **h** on A
48:17 so he took his father's **h,**
48:18 put your right **h** on his head." A
48:22 portion that I took from the **h** of the Amorites C
49: 8 your **h** shall be on the neck of your enemies;
Ex 3:19 not let you go unless compelled by a mighty **h.** G
3:20 So I will stretch out my **h** and strike Egypt
4: 2 The LORD said to him, "What is that in your **h?**"
4: 4 the LORD said to Moses, "Reach out your **h,**
4: 4 so he reached out his **h** and grasped it,
4: 4 and it became a staff in his **h—**
4: 6 "Put your **h** inside your cloak."
4: 6 He put his **h** into his cloak;
4: 6 he took it out, his **h** was leprous, as white as snow.
4: 7 God said, "Put your **h** back into your cloak"—
4: 7 so he put his **h** back into his cloak,
4:17 Take in your **h** this staff,
4:20 and Moses carried the staff of God in his **h.**
5:21 and have put a sword in their **h** to kill us."
6: 1 Indeed, by a mighty **h** he will let them go; G
6: 1 a mighty **h** he will drive them out of his land." G
7: 4 I will lay my **h** upon Egypt and bring my people
7: 5 when I stretch out my **h** against Egypt and bring
7:15 by at the river bank to meet him, and take in your **h**
7:17 with the staff that is in my **h** I will strike the water
7:19 and stretch out your **h** over the waters of Egypt—
8: 5 'Stretch out your **h** with your staff over the rivers,
8: 6 Aaron stretched out his **h** over the waters of Egypt;
8:17 Aaron stretched out his **h** with his staff and struck
9: 3 the **h** of the LORD will strike with D
9:15 For by now I could have stretched out my **h**
9:22 "Stretch out your **h** toward heaven so
10:12 "Stretch out your **h** over the land of Egypt,
10:21 "Stretch out your **h** toward heaven so
10:22 So Moses stretched out his **h** toward heaven,
12:11 on your feet, and your staff in your **h;**
13: 3 from there by strength of **h;**
13: 9 on your **h** and as a reminder on your forehead,
13: 9 a strong **h** the LORD brought you out of Egypt.
13:14 'By strength of **h** the LORD brought us out
13:16 It shall serve as a sign on your **h** and as an emblem
13:16 an emblem on your forehead that by strength of **h**
14:16 and stretch out your **h** over the sea and divide it,
14:21 Then Moses stretched out his **h** over the sea.
14:26 "Stretch out your **h** over the sea,
14:27 So Moses stretched out his **h** over the sea,
15: 6 Your right **h,** O LORD, glorious in power— A
15: 6 your right **h,** O LORD, shattered the enemy. A
15: 9 I will draw my sword, my **h** shall destroy them.'
15:12 You stretched out your right **h,** A
15:20 Aaron's sister, took a tambourine in her **h;**
16: 3 "If only we had died by the **h** of the LORD in D
17: 5 in your **h** the staff with which you struck the Nile,
17: 9 the top of the hill with the staff of God in my **h.**"
17:11 Whenever Moses held up his **h,** Israel prevailed;
17:11 and whenever he lowered his **h,** Amalek prevailed.
17:16 He said, "A **h** upon the banner of the LORD!
19:13 No **h** shall touch them, but they shall be stoned
21:24 tooth for tooth, **h** for **h,** foot for foot,
23:31 for I will **h** over to you the inhabitants of the land,
24:11 not lay his **h** on the chief men of the people
32:11 of Egypt with great power and with a mighty **h?** G
33:22 I will cover you with my **h** until I have passed by;
33:23 I will take away my **h,** and you shall see my back;
34: 4 and took in his **h** the two tablets of stone.
34:29 with the two tablets of the covenant in his **h,**
Lev 1: 4 You shall lay your **h** on the head of
3: 2 You shall lay your **h** on the head of the offering
3: 8 and lay your **h** on the head of the offering.
3:13 and lay your **h** on its head;
4: 4 the tent of meeting before the LORD and lay his **h**
4:24 He shall lay his **h** on the head of the goat;
4:29 You shall lay your **h** on the head of
4:33 You shall lay your **h** on the head of
8:23 right ear and on the thumb of his right **h** A
14:14 and on the thumb of the right **h,** A
14:15 of oil and pour it into the palm of his own left **h,** H
14:16 dip his right finger in the oil that is in his left **h** H
14:17 that remains in his **h** the priest shall put on the lobe
14:17 and on the thumb of the right **h,** A
14:18 the priest's **h** he shall put on the head of the one to
14:25 and on the thumb of the right **h,** A
14:26 of the oil into the palm of his own left **h,** H
14:27 that is in his left **h** seven times before the LORD. H
14:28 the oil that is in his **h** on the lobe of the right ear of

Lev 14:28 and on the thumb of the right **h,** A
14:29 the priest's **h** he shall put on the head of the one to
21:19 or one who has a broken foot or a broken **h,**
Nu 4:33 under the **h** of Ithamar son of Aaron the priest.
5:18 In his own **h** the priest shall have the water
5:25 of jealousy out of the woman's **h,** and shall elevate
20:11 up his **h** and struck the rock twice with his staff;
20:17 to the right **h** or to the left until we have passed A
21:34 for I have given him into your **h,** B
22: 7 with the fees for divination in their **h;**
22:23 with a drawn sword in his **h;**
22:29 I wish I had a sword in my **h!**
22:31 with his drawn sword in his **h;**
25: 7 Taking a spear in his **h,**
27:18 and lay your **h** upon him;
31: 6 and the trumpets for sounding the alarm in his **h.**
35:17 Or anyone who strikes another with a stone in **h**
35:18 with a weapon of wood in **h** that could cause death,
35:21 the **h,** and death ensues, then the one who struck
Dt 1:27 to **h** us over to the Amorites to destroy us.
2:15 Indeed, the LORD's own **h** was against them,
2:30 and made his heart defiant in order to **h** him over
4:34 by war, by a mighty **h** and an outstretched arm, G
5:15 with a mighty **h** and an outstretched arm; G
6: 8 Bind them as a sign on your **h,**
6:21 LORD brought us out of Egypt with a mighty **h.** G
7: 8 the LORD has brought you out with a mighty **h,** G
7: 8 from the **h** of Pharaoh king of Egypt. C
7:19 the mighty **h** and the outstretched arm by which G
7:24 He will **h** their kings over to you
8:17 of my own **h** have gotten me this wealth."
9:26 you brought out of Egypt with a mighty **h.** G
10: 3 up the mountain with the two tablets in my **h.**
11: 2 his mighty **h** and his outstretched arm, G
11:18 and you shall bind them as a sign on your **h,**
13: 9 your own **h** shall be first against them
13: 9 and afterwards the **h** of all the people.
13:17 to destruction stick to your **h,**
14:25 With the money secure in **h,**
15: 8 You should rather open your **h,**
15:11 "Open your **h** to the poor and needy neighbor
19:21 life for life, eye for eye, tooth for tooth, **h** for **h,**
20:13 when the LORD your God gives it into your **h,** B
23:14 to save you and to **h** over your enemies to you,
23:25 you may pluck the ears with your **h,**
24: 1 puts it in her **h,** and sends her out of his house;
24: 3 writes her a bill of divorce, puts it in her **h,**
25:12 you shall cut off her **h;** show no pity.
25:19 from all your enemies on every **h,** in the land that
26: 4 priest takes the basket from your **h** and sets it C
26: 8 of Egypt with a mighty **h** and an outstretched G
32:27 and say, "Our **h** is triumphant;
32:35 because the day of their calamity is at **h,** E
32:39 and no one can deliver from my **h.** C
32:40 For I lift up my **h** to heaven, and swear:
32:41 and my **h** takes hold on judgment;
Jos 1: 7 do not turn from it to the right **h** or to the left, A
2:19 a **h** is laid upon any who are with you in the house,
4:24 the earth may know that the **h** of the LORD D
5:13 before him with a drawn sword in his **h.**
7: 7 to **h** us over to the Amorites so as to destroy us?
8: 7 for the LORD your God will give it into your **h.** B
8:18 "Stretch out the sword that is in your **h** toward Ai;
8:18 for I will give it into your **h.**" B
8:18 the sword that was in his **h** toward the city.
8:19 As soon as he stretched out his **h,**
8:26 For Joshua did not draw back his **h,**
9:11 'Take provisions in your **h** for the journey;
9:25 And now we are in your **h:**
10:19 the LORD your God has given them into your **h.**" B
10:30 The LORD gave it also and its king into the **h** B
10:32 The LORD gave Lachish into the **h** of Israel, B
11: 6 for tomorrow at this time I will **h** over all of them,
20: 9 so as not to die by the **h** of the avenger of blood,
22:31 saved the Israelites from the **h** of the LORD." CD
24:10 so I rescued you out of his **h.**
Jdg 1: 2 I hereby give the land into his **h.**" B
1: 4 the Canaanites and the Perizzites into their **h;** B
1:35 **h** of the house of Joseph rested heavily on them,
2:15 the **h** of the LORD was against them D
2:18 from the **h** of their enemies all the days of the C
3: 8 into the **h** of King Cushan-rishathaim B
3:10 King Cushan-rishathaim of Aram into his **h;** B
3:10 and his **h** prevailed over Cushan-rishathaim.
3:21 Then Ehud reached with his left **h,** H
3:28 given your enemies the Moabites into your **h.**" B
3:30 Moab was subdued that day under the **h** of Israel.
4: 2 So the LORD sold them into the **h** of King Jabin B
4: 7 and I will give him into your **h.'** " B
4: 9 the LORD will sell Sisera into the **h** of a woman." B
4:14 on which the LORD has given Sisera into your **h.** B
4:21 and took a hammer in her **h,**
4:24 Then the **h** of the Israelites bore harder and harder
5:26 She put her **h** to the tent peg and her right hand to
5:26 She put her hand to the tent peg and her right **h** A
6: 1 and the LORD gave them into the **h** B
6: 2 The **h** of Midian prevailed over Israel;
6: 9 and I delivered you from the **h** of the Egyptians, C
6: 9 and from the **h** of all who oppressed you, C
6:13 and given us into the **h** of Midian." B
6:14 this might of yours and deliver Israel from the **h** C
6:21 of the staff that was in his **h,** and touched the meat
6:36 to see whether you will deliver Israel by my **h,**
6:37 I shall know that you will deliver Israel by my **h,**
7: 2 for me to give the Midianites into their **h.** B
7: 2 saying, 'My own **h** has delivered me.'
7: 7 and give the Midianites into your **h.** B

Jdg 7: 9 for I have given it into your **h.** B
7:14 into his **h** God has given Midian and all the B
7:15 LORD has given the army of Midian into your **h.** B
8: 7 LORD has given Zebah and Zalmunna into my **h,** B
8:22 for you have delivered us out of the **h** of Midian."
8:34 from the **h** of all their enemies on every side; C
9:17 and rescued you from the **h** of Midian; C
9:48 Abimelech took an ax in his **h,**
10: 7 and he sold them into the **h** of the Philistines B
10: 7 the Philistines and into the **h** of the Ammonites, B
10:12 you cried to me, and I delivered you out of their **h.**
11:21 gave Sihon and all his people into the **h** of Israel, B
11:30 "If you will give the Ammonites into my **h,** B
11:32 and the LORD gave them into his **h.** B
12: 2 I called you, you did not deliver me from their **h.** C
12: 3 I took my life in my **h,**
12: 3 and the LORD gave them into my **h.** B
13: 1 the LORD gave them into the **h** of the Philistines B
13: 5 he who shall begin to deliver Israel from the **h** C
15:18 "You have granted this great victory by the **h**
16:23 god has given Samson our enemy into our **h.**" B
16:24 "Our god has given our enemy into our **h,** B
16:26 to the attendant who held him by the **h,**
16:29 his right **h** on the one and his left hand on A
16:29 his right hand on the one and his left **h** on H
17: 3 "I consecrate the silver to the LORD from my **h** C
18:19 Put your **h** over your mouth, and come with us,
20:13 Now then, **h** over those scoundrels in Gibeah,
20:28 for tomorrow I will give them into your **h.**" B
Ru 1:13 the **h** of the LORD has turned against me." D
4: 5 day you acquire the field from the **h** of Naomi, C
4: 9 from the **h** of Naomi all that belonged to C
1Sa 2:13 with a three-pronged fork in his **h,**
5: 6 The **h** of the LORD was heavy upon the people D
5: 7 for his **h** is heavy on us and on our god Dagon."
5: 9 the **h** of the LORD was against the city, D
5:11 The **h** of God was very heavy there; F
6: 3 will not his **h** then turn from you?"
6: 5 perhaps he will lighten his **h** on you and your gods
6: 9 we shall know that it is not his **h** that struck us;
7: 3 he will deliver you out of the **h** of the Philistines."
7: 8 he may save us from the **h** of the Philistines." C
7:13 the **h** of the LORD was against the Philistines D
7:14 and Israel recovered their territory from the **h** of C
9:16 He shall save my people from the **h** of C
10: 1 of the LORD and you will save them from the **h** C
10:18 and I rescued you from the **h** of the Egyptians C
10:18 Egyptians and from the **h** of all the kingdoms C
12: 3 from whose **h** have I taken a bribe to blind my C
12: 4 or oppressed us or taken anything from the **h** C
12: 5 that you have not found anything in my **h.**"
12: 9 and he sold them into the **h** of Sisera, B
12: 9 and into the **h** of the Philistines, B
12: 9 and into the **h** of the king of Moab; B
12:10 but now rescue us out of the **h** of our enemies,
12:11 and rescued you out of the **h** of your enemies
12:15 **h** of the LORD will be against you and your king. D
14:10 for the LORD has given them into our **h.** B
14:12 the LORD has given them into the **h** of Israel." B
14:19 and Saul said to the priest, "Withdraw your **h.**"
14:27 so he extended the staff that was in his **h,**
14:27 and put his **h** to his mouth;
14:37 Will you give them into the **h** of Israel?" B
14:43 with the tip of the staff that was in my **h;**
16:23 David took the lyre and played it with his **h,**
17:37 will save me from the **h** of this Philistine." C
17:40 Then he took his staff in his **h,**
17:40 his sling was in his **h,**
17:46 the LORD will deliver you into my **h,** B
17:47 the LORD's and he will give you into our **h.**" B
17:49 David put his **h** in his bag, took out a stone,
17:50 there was no sword in David's **h.**
17:57 with the head of the Philistine in his **h.**
18:10 Saul had his spear in his **h;**
18:17 For Saul thought, "I will not raise a **h** against him;
18:21 that the **h** of the Philistines may be against him."
18:25 Now Saul planned to make David fall by the **h** of
19: 5 for he took his life in his **h** when he attacked
19: 9 as he sat in his house with his spear in his **h,**
21: 3 Now then, what have you at **h?** E
21: 4 "I have no ordinary bread at **h,** only holy bread E
22: 6 with his spear in his **h,**
22:17 because their **h** also is with David;
22:17 the king would not raise their **h** to attack the priests
23: 4 for I will give the Philistines into your **h.**" B
23: 6 he came down with an ephod in his **h.**
23: 7 And Saul said, "God has given him into my **h;** B
23:12 of Keilah surrender me and my men into the **h** B
23:14 but the LORD did not give him into his **h.** B
23:16 there he strengthened his **h** through the LORD.
23:17 for the **h** of my father Saul shall not find you;
23:20 our part will be to surrender him into the king's **h.**"
24: 4 'I will give your enemy into your **h,** B
24: 6 the LORD's anointed, to raise my **h** against him;
24:10 how the LORD gave you into my **h** in the cave; B
24:10 I said, 'I will not raise my **h** against my lord;
24:11 my father, see the corner of your cloak in my **h;**
24:12 but my **h** shall not be against you.
24:13 but my **h** shall not be against you.
24:20 kingdom of Israel shall be established in your **h.**
25: 8 at **h** to your servants and to your son David.' E
25:26 and from taking vengeance with your own **h,**
25:33 and from avenging myself by my own **h!**
25:35 from her **h** what she had brought him; C
26: 8 "God has given your enemy into your **h** today; B
26: 9 who can raise his **h** against the LORD's anointed,
26:11 The LORD forbid that I should raise my **h** against

1Sa 26:23 for the LORD gave you into my **h** today, B
26:23 into my hand today, but I would not raise my **h**
27: 1 "I shall now perish one day by the **h** of Saul;
27: 1 and I shall escape out of his **h."**
28:17 for the LORD has torn the kingdom out of your **h,**
28:21 I have taken my life in my **h,**
30:15 or **h** me over to my master,
2Sa 1:14 to lift your **h** to destroy the LORD's anointed?"
3: 8 and have not given you into the **h** of David; B
3:18 from the **h** of the Philistines, C
4:11 And now shall I not require his blood at your **h,**
5:19 Will you give them into my **h?"** B
5:19 I will certainly give the Philistines into your **h."** B
6: 6 Uzzah reached out his **h** to the ark of God
6: 7 because he reached out his **h** to the ark;
8: 1 David took Metheg-ammah out of the **h** of
11:14 and sent it by the **h** of Uriah.
12: 7 and I rescued you from the **h** of Saul; C
13: 5 so that I may see it and eat it from her **h.'"** C
13: 6 so that I may eat from her **h."** C
13:10 so that I may eat from your **h."** C
13:19 she put her **h** on her head, and went away,
14:16 from the **h** of the man who would cut both me C
14:19 king said, "Is the **h** of Joab with you in all this?"
15: 5 he would put out his **h** and take hold of them,
16: 8 and the LORD has given the kingdom into the **h** B
18:12 in my **h** the weight of a thousand pieces of silver,
18:12 I would not raise my **h** against the king's son;
18:13 On the other **h,** if I had dealt treacherously
18:14 He took three spears in his **h,**
18:28 who has delivered up the men who raised their **h**
19: 9 The king delivered us from the **h** of our enemies, C
19: 9 and saved us from the **h** of the Philistines; C
20: 9 Joab took Amasa by the beard with his right **h** A
20:10 But Amasa did not notice the sword in Joab's **h;**
20:21 has lifted up his **h** against King David;
21: 6 The king said, "I will **h** them over."
21:20 who had six fingers on each **h,**
22: 1 the LORD delivered him from the **h** of all his C
22: 1 and from the **h** of Saul. C
23: 6 for they cannot be picked up with the **h;**
23:10 though his **h** clung to the sword.
23:21 The Egyptian had a spear in his **h;**
23:21 snatched the spear out of the Egyptian's **h,**
24:14 let us fall into the **h** of the LORD, BD
24:16 the angel stretched out his **h** toward Jerusalem
24:16 "It is enough; now stay your **h."**
24:17 Let your **h,** I pray, be against me and
1Ki 2:46 the kingdom was established in the **h** of Solomon.
8:15 who with his **h** has fulfilled what he promised
8:24 and have this day fulfilled with your **h.**
8:42 your mighty **h,** and your outstretched arm— G
11:12 I will tear it out of the **h** of your son.
11:31 to tear the kingdom from the **h** of Solomon, C
13: 4 Jeroboam stretched out his **h** from the altar, saying,
13: 4 the **h** that he stretched out against him withered so
13: 6 so that my **h** may be restored to me."
13: 6 and the king's **h** was restored to him,
17:11 "Bring me a morsel of bread in your **h."**
18: 9 that you would **h** your servant over to Ahab,
18:44 a person's **h** is rising out of the sea."
18:46 But the **h** of the LORD was on Elijah; D
20:13 Look, I will give it into your **h** today; B
20:28 I will give all this great multitude into your **h,** B
22: 3 yet we are doing nothing to take it out of the **h** of
22: 6 for the LORD will give it into the **h** of the king." B
22:12 the LORD will give it into the **h** of the king." B
22:15 the LORD will give it into the **h** of the king." B
2Ki 3:18 for he will also **h** Moab over to you.
4:29 "Gird up your loins, and take my staff in your **h,**
5:11 and would wave his **h** over the spot,
6: 7 So he reached out his **h** and took it.
7: 2 Then the captain on whose **h** the king leaned said
7:17 the captain on whose **h** he leaned to have charge of
9: 1 take this flask of oil in your **h,**
10:15 Jehu said, "If it is, give me your **h."**
10:15 So he gave him his **h.**
11: 8 the king, each with weapons in **h;**
11:11 every man with his weapons in his **h,**
12: 7 from your donors but **h** it over for the repair of
12:15 those into whose **h** they delivered the money B
13: 3 so that he gave them repeatedly into the **h** B
13: 3 then into the **h** of Ben-hadad son of Hazael. B
13: 5 so that they escaped from the **h** of the Arameans; C
14: 5 in his **h** he killed his servants who had murdered
14:27 he saved them by the **h** of Jeroboam son of Joash.
16: 7 and rescue me from the **h** of the king of Aram C
16: 7 the king of Aram and from the **h** of the king of C
17: 7 the land of Egypt from under the **h** of Pharaoh king
17:20 he punished them and gave them into the **h** B
17:39 he will deliver you out of the **h**
18:21 which will pierce the **h** of anyone who leans on it.
18:29 for he will not be able to deliver you out of my **h.**
18:30 this city will not be given into the **h** of the king B
18:33 the nations ever delivered its land out of the **h** of
18:34 Have they delivered Samaria out of my **h?**
18:35 have delivered their countries out of my **h,**
18:35 LORD should deliver Jerusalem out of my **h?'"**
19:10 not be given into the **h** of the king of Assyria. B
19:14 letter from the **h** of the messengers and read it; C
19:19 save us, I pray you, from his **h,** C
20: 6 and this city out of the **h** of the king of Assyria;
21:14 and give them into the **h** of their enemies; B
22: 5 into the **h** of the workers who have the oversight B
22: 7 for the money that is delivered into their **h,** B
22: 9 into the **h** of the workers who have oversight of B
1Ch 4:10 and that your **h** might be with me,
5:10 on the Hagrites, who fell by their **h;**
6:15 into exile by the **h** of Nebuchadnezzar.
11:23 The Egyptian had in his **h** a spear like
11:23 snatched the spear out of the Egyptian's **h,**
12: 2 and sling stones with either the right **h** or the left; A
13: 9 Uzzah put out his **h** to hold the ark,
13:10 he struck him down because he put out his **h** to
14:10 Will you give them into my **h?"** B
14:10 "Go up, and I will give them into your **h."** B
14:11 "God has burst out against my enemies by my **h,**
20: 6 who had six fingers on each **h,**
20: 8 they fell by the **h** of David and his servants.
21:13 let me fall into the **h** of the LORD, BD
21:15 to the destroying angel, "Enough! Stay your **h."**
21:16 and in his **h** a drawn sword stretched out
21:17 Let your **h,** I pray, O LORD my God,
22:18 the inhabitants of the land into my **h;** B
29:12 In your **h** are power and might;
29:12 in your **h** to make great and to give strength to all.
29:16 a house for your holy name comes from your **h** C
2Ch 6: 4 who with his **h** has fulfilled what he promised
6:15 and this day have fulfilled with your **h.**
6:32 and your mighty **h,** and your outstretched arm, G
12: 5 so I have abandoned you to the **h** of Shishak."
12: 7 be poured out on Jerusalem by the **h** of Shishak.
13: 8 the kingdom of the LORD in the **h** of the sons
16: 8 he gave them into your **h.** B
17: 5 the LORD established the kingdom in his **h.**
18: 5 for God will give it into the **h** of the king." B
18:11 the LORD will give it into the **h** of the king." B
18:14 they will be given into your **h."** B
20: 6 In your **h** are power and might,
23: 7 each with his weapons in his **h;**
23:10 everyone with weapon in **h,**
24:24 LORD delivered into their **h** a very great army, B
25: 3 in his **h** he killed his servants who had murdered
25:15 not deliver their own people from your **h?"** C
25:20 it was God's doing, in order to **h** them over,
26:19 Now he had a censer in his **h** to make offering,
28: 5 LORD his God gave him into the **h** of the king B
28: 5 was also given into the **h** of the king of Israel, B
28: 9 was angry with Judah, he gave them into your **h,** B
30: 6 remnant of you who have escaped from the **h** C
30:12 The **h** of God was also on Judah F
32:11 'The LORD our God will save us from the **h** of C
32:13 at all able to save their lands out of my **h?**
32:14 to save his people from my **h,** C
32:14 God should be able to save you from my **h?** C
32:15 to save his people from my **h** or from the hand C
32:15 to save his people from my hand or from the **h** C
32:15 much less will your God save you out of my **h!"**
32:17 Hezekiah will not rescue his people from my **h."** C
32:22 from the **h** of King Sennacherib of Assyria C
32:22 Assyria and from the **h** of all his enemies; C
34:17 of the LORD and have delivered it into the **h** of B
36:17 he gave them all into his **h.** B
Ezr 5:12 gave them into the **h** of King Nebuchadnezzar B
6:12 or people that shall put forth a **h** to alter this,
7: 6 for the **h** of the LORD his God was upon him. D
7: 9 for the gracious **h** of his God was upon him. F
7:14 to the law of your God, which is in your **h,**
7:28 for the **h** of the LORD my God was upon me, D
8:18 Since the gracious **h** of our God was upon us, F
8:22 the **h** of our God is gracious to all who seek him, F
8:26 weighed out into their **h** six hundred fifty talents B
8:31 the **h** of our God was upon us, F
8:31 from the **h** of the enemy and from ambushes C
Ne 1:10 by your great power and your strong **h.**
2: 8 for the gracious **h** of my God was upon me. F
2:18 that the **h** of my God had been gracious F
4:17 that each labored on the work with one **h** and
4:23 each kept his weapon in his right **h.** A
6: 5 to me with an open letter in his **h.**
8: 4 Uriah, Hilkiah, and Maaseiah on his right **h;** A
8: 4 Zechariah, and Meshullam on his left **h.** H
11:24 at the king's **h** in all matters concerning the people.
Est 3:10 the king took his signet ring from his **h** and C
5: 2 to her the golden scepter that was in his **h.**
Job 1:11 But stretch out your **h** now,
1:12 only do not stretch out your **h** against him!"
2: 5 But stretch out your **h** now and touch his bone
2:10 Shall we receive the good at the **h** of God, F
5:15 from the **h** of the mighty. C
6: 9 that he would let loose his **h** and cut me off!
6:23 Or, 'Save me from an opponent's **h'?** C
6:23 Or, 'Ransom me from the **h** of oppressors'? C
8:20 nor take the **h** of evildoers.
9:24 The earth is given into the **h** of the wicked; B
9:33 who might lay his **h** on us both.
10: 7 and there is no one to deliver out of your **h?**
11:14 If iniquity is in your **h,** put it far away,
12: 9 does not know that the **h** of God has done this? D
12:10 In his **h** is the life of every living thing and
13:14 and put my life in my **h.**
13:21 withdraw your **h** far from me,
15:23 They know that a day of darkness is ready at **h;** E
19:21 for the **h** of God has touched me! F
21: 5 and be appalled, and lay your **h** upon your mouth.
23: 2 his **h** is heavy despite my groaning.
26:13 his **h** pierced the fleeing serpent.
27:11 I will teach you concerning the **h** of God; F
28: 9 "They put their **h** to the flinty rock,
29:20 and my bow ever new in my **h.'**
30:12 On my right **h** the rabble rise up; A
30:21 with the might of your **h** you persecute me.
31:21 if I have raised my **h** against the orphan,
31:25 or because my **h** had gotten much;
Job 31:27 and my mouth has kissed my **h;**
34:20 and the mighty are taken away by no human **h.**
35: 7 or what does he receive from your **h?** C
37: 7 serves as a sign on everyone's **h,**
39:11 and will you **h** over your labor to it?
40: 4 I lay my **h** on my mouth.
40:14 that your own right **h** can give you victory. A
Ps 10:12 O God, lift up your **h;** do not forget the oppressed.
16: 8 he is at my right **h,** I shall not be moved. A
16:11 in your right **h** are pleasures forevermore. A
17: 7 from their adversaries at your right **h.** A
17:14 from mortals—by your **h,** O LORD—
18: T *LORD delivered from the* **h** *of all his enemies,* C
18: T *and from the* **h** *of Saul.* C
18:35 and your right **h** has supported me; A
20: 6 with mighty victories by his right **h.** A
21: 8 Your **h** will find out all your enemies;
21: 8 your right **h** will find out those who hate you. A
31: 5 Into your **h** I commit my spirit; B
31: 8 have not delivered me into the **h** of the enemy; B
31:15 My times are in your **h;**
31:15 from the **h** of my enemies and persecutors. C
32: 4 For day and night your **h** was heavy upon me;
36:11 or the **h** of the wicked drive me away.
37:24 for the LORD holds us by the **h.**
38: 2 and your **h** has come down on me.
39:10 I am worn down by the blows of your **h.**
44: 2 you with your own **h** drove out the nations,
44: 3 but your right **h,** and your arm, A
45: 4 let your right **h** teach you dread deeds. A
45: 9 at your right **h** stands the queen in gold of Ophir. A
48:10 Your right **h** is filled with victory. A
60: 5 Give victory with your right **h,** A
63: 8 My soul clings to you; your right **h** upholds me. A
71: 4 Rescue me, O my God, from the **h** of the wicked, C
73:23 I am continually with you; you hold my right **h.** A
74:11 Why do you hold back your **h;**
74:11 why do you keep your **h** in your bosom?
75: 8 For in the **h** of the LORD there is a cup D
76: 5 none of the troops was able to lift a **h.**
77: 2 the night my **h** is stretched out without wearying;
77:10 that the right **h** of the Most High has changed." A
77:20 You led your people like a flock by the **h** of Moses
78:54 to the mountain that his right **h** had won. A
78:61 his glory to the **h** of the foe.
78:72 and guided them with skillful **h.**
80:15 the stock that your right **h** planted. A
80:17 But let your **h** be upon the one at your right hand,
80:17 let your hand be upon the one at your right **h,** A
81:14 and turn my **h** against their foes.
82: 4 deliver them from the **h** of the wicked." C
85: 9 his salvation is at **h** for those who fear him, E
88: 5 for they are cut off from your **h.** C
89:13 strong is your **h,** high your right hand.
89:13 strong is your hand, high your right **h.** A
89:21 my **h** shall always remain with him;
89:25 I will set his **h** on the sea and his right hand on
89:25 I will set his hand on the sea and his right **h** on A
89:42 You have exalted the right **h** of his foes; A
89:44 You have removed the scepter from his **h,** C
91: 7 ten thousand at your right **h,** A
95: 4 In his **h** are the depths of the earth;
95: 7 and the sheep of his **h.**
97:10 he rescues them from the **h** of the wicked. C
98: 1 right **h** and his holy arm have gotten him A
104:28 you open your **h,** they are filled with good things.
106:10 So he saved them from the **h** of the foe, C
106:10 and delivered them from the **h** of the enemy. C
106:26 Therefore he raised his **h** and swore to them
106:41 he gave them into the **h** of the nations, B
108: 6 Give victory with your right **h,** and answer me, A
109:27 Let them know that this is your **h;**
109:31 For he stands at the right **h** of the needy, A
110: 1 The LORD says to my lord, "Sit at my right **h** A
110: 5 The Lord is at your right **h;** A
118:15 "The right **h** of the LORD does valiantly; AD
118:16 the right **h** of the LORD is exalted; AD
118:16 the right **h** of the LORD does valiantly." AD
119:109 I hold my life in my **h** continually,
119:173 Let your **h** be ready to help me,
121: 5 the LORD is your shade at your right **h.** A
123: 2 the eyes of servants look to the **h** of their master,
123: 2 as the eyes of a maid to the **h** of her mistress,
127: 4 in the **h** of a warrior are the sons of one's youth.
136:12 with a strong **h** and an outstretched arm,
137: 5 forget you, O Jerusalem, let my right **h** wither! A
138: 7 you stretch out your **h,** and your right hand
138: 7 and your right **h** delivers me. A
139: 5 behind and before, and lay your **h** upon me.
139:10 even there your **h** shall lead me,
139:10 and your right **h** shall hold me fast. A
142: 4 Look on my right **h** and see— A
144: 7 Stretch out your **h** from on high;
144: 7 rescue me from the mighty waters, from the **h** C
144:11 and deliver me from the **h** of aliens, C
145:16 You open your **h,** satisfying the desire
Pr 1:24 have stretched out my **h** and no one heeded,
3:16 Long life is in her right **h;** A
3:16 in her left **h** are riches and honor. H
6: 5 like a bird from the **h** of the fowler. C
10: 4 A slack **h** causes poverty, but the hand of
10: 4 but the **h** of the diligent makes rich.
12:24 The **h** of the diligent will rule,
17:16 Why should fools have a price in **h** to buy wisdom,
19:24 The lazy person buries a **h** in the dish,
21: 1 heart is a stream of water in the **h** of the LORD; D
26: 9 by the **h** of a drunkard is a proverb in the mouth

Pr 26:15 The lazy person buries a **h** in the dish,
27:16 to restrain the wind or to grasp oil in the right **h.** A
30: 4 the wind in the hollow of the **h?**
30:28 the lizard can be grasped in the **h,**
30:32 put your **h** on your mouth.
31:20 She opens her **h** to the poor,
Ecc 2:24 This also, I saw, is from the **h** of God; CF
9: 1 the wise and their deeds are in the **h** of God; F
9:10 Whatever your **h** finds to do, do with your might;
SS 2: 6 O that his left **h** were under my head, H
2: 6 and that his right **h** embraced me! A
5: 4 My beloved thrust his **h** into the opening,
7: 1 the work of a master **h.**
8: 3 O that his left **h** were under my head, H
8: 3 and that his right **h** embraced me! A
Isa 1:12 who asked this from your **h?** C
1:25 I will turn my **h** against you;
5:25 and he stretched out his **h** against them
5:25 and his **h** is stretched out still.
8:11 while his **h** was strong upon me, and warned me
9:12 his **h** is stretched out still.
9:17 his **h** is stretched out still.
9:21 his **h** is stretched out still.
10: 4 his **h** is stretched out still.
10:10 As my **h** has reached to the kingdoms of
10:13 "By the strength of my **h** I have done it,
10:14 My **h** has found, like a nest,
11: 8 the weaned child shall put its **h** on the adder's den.
11:11 the Lord will extend his **h** yet a second time
11:14 They shall put forth their **h** against Edom
11:15 and will wave his **h** over the River
13: 2 the **h** for them to enter the gates of the nobles.
13:22 its time is close at **h,** and its days will not be E
14:26 the **h** that is stretched out over all the nations.
14:27 His **h** is stretched out, and who will turn it back?
19: 4 the Egyptians into the **h** of a hard master; B
19:16 and tremble with fear before the **h** that the LORD
22:21 I will commit your authority to his **h,**
23:11 He has stretched out his **h** over the sea,
25:10 For the **h** of the LORD will rest on this mountain. D
26:11 O LORD, your **h** is lifted up,
28: 2 with his **h** he will hurl them down to the earth.
28: 4 whoever sees it, eats it up as soon as it comes to **h.**
31: 3 When the LORD stretches out his **h,**
34:17 his **h** has portioned it out to them with the line;
36: 6 which will pierce the **h** of anyone who leans on it.
36:15 this city will not be given into the **h** of the king B
36:18 the gods of the nations saved their land out of the **h**
36:19 Have they delivered Samaria out of my **h?**
36:20 countries have saved their countries out of my **h,**
36:20 the LORD should save Jerusalem out of my **h?'** "
37:10 not be given into the **h** of the king of Assyria. B
37:14 letter from the **h** of the messengers and read it; C
37:20 So now, O LORD our God, save us from his **h,** C
38: 6 and this city out of the **h** of the king of Assyria,
40: 2 that she has received from the LORD's **h** double C
40:12 in the hollow of his **h** and marked off the heavens
41:10 I will uphold you with my victorious right **h.** A
41:13 For I, the LORD your God, hold your right **h;** A
41:20 that the **h** of the LORD has done this, D
42: 6 I have taken you by the **h** and kept you;
43:13 there is no one who can deliver from my **h;** C
44: 5 yet another will write on the **h,** "The LORD's,"
44:20 "Is not this thing in my right **h** a fraud?" A
45: 1 whose right **h** I have grasped to subdue nations A
47: 6 I gave them into your **h,** you showed them no B
48:13 My **h** laid the foundation of the earth,
48:13 and my right **h** spread out the heavens; A
49: 2 in the shadow of his **h** he hid me;
49:22 I will soon lift up my **h** to the nations,
50: 2 Is my **h** shortened, that it cannot redeem?
50:11 This is what you shall have from my **h:** C
51:16 and hidden you in the shadow of my **h,**
51:17 who have drunk at the **h** of the LORD the cup D
51:18 by the **h** among all the children she has brought up.
51:22 I have taken from your **h** the cup of staggering; C
51:23 And I will put it into the **h** of your tormentors, B
59: 1 See, the LORD's **h** is not too short to save,
62: 3 be a crown of beauty in the **h** of the LORD, D
62: 3 and a royal diadem in the **h** of your God. F
62: 8 The LORD has sworn by his right **h** and A
63:12 to march at the right **h** of Moses, A
64: 7 and have delivered us into the **h** of our iniquity. B
64: 8 we are all the work of your **h.**
66: 2 All these things my **h** has made,
66:14 and it shall be known that the **h** of the LORD is D
Jer 1: 9 the LORD put out his **h** and touched my mouth;
6: 9 pass your **h** again over its branches.
6:12 for I will stretch out my **h** against the inhabitants
11:21 or you will die by our **h"—**
15: 6 so I have stretched out my **h** against you
15:17 under the weight of your **h** I sat alone,
15:21 I will deliver you out of the **h** of the wicked,
18: 4 of clay was spoiled in the potter's **h,**
18: 6 Just like the clay in the potter's **h,**
18: 6 so are you in my **h,** O house of Israel.
19: 7 and by the **h** of those who seek their life.
20: 4 And I will give all Judah into the **h** of the king B
20: 5 of the kings of Judah into the **h** of their enemies, B
21: 5 I myself will fight against you with outstretched **h**
21:12 in the morning, and deliver from the **h** of C
22: 3 and righteousness, and deliver from the **h** of C
22:24 of Judah were the signet ring on my right **h,** A
25:15 Take from my **h** this cup of the wine of wrath, C
25:17 So I took the cup from the LORD's **h,**
25:28 refuse to accept the cup from your **h** to drink, C
26:24 But the **h** of Ahikam son of Shaphan was

Jer 27: 3 the **h** of the envoys who have come to Jerusalem
27: 6 into the **h** of King Nebuchadnezzar of Babylon, B
27: 8 until I have completed its destruction by his **h.**
29: 3 the **h** of Elasah son of Shaphan and Gemariah son
29:21 deliver them into the **h** of King Nebuchadrezzar B
31:32 by the **h** to bring them out of the land of Egypt—
32: 3 give this city into the **h** of the king of Babylon, B
32:21 with a strong **h** and outstretched arm,
32:28 into the **h** of King Nebuchadrezzar of Babylon, B
32:36 being given into the **h** of the king of Babylon B
34: 2 give this city into the **h** of the king of Babylon, B
34: 3 And you yourself shall not escape from his **h,** C
34:21 I will **h** them over to their enemies and
36:14 So Baruch son of Neriah took the scroll in his **h**
38:16 or **h** you over to these men who seek your life." C
38:18 and you yourself shall not escape from their **h."** C
38:23 and you yourself shall not escape from their **h,** C
42:11 to save you and to rescue you from his **h.** C
43: 3 to **h** us over to the Chaldeans,
44:30 just as I gave King Zedekiah of Judah into the **h** B
46:26 I will **h** them over to those who seek their life,
48:16 near at **h** and his doom approaches swiftly. E
51: 7 Babylon was a golden cup in the LORD's **h,**
51:25 I will stretch out my **h** against you,
La 1: 7 When her people fell into the **h** of the foe, B
1:14 by his **h** they were fastened together;
2: 3 he has withdrawn his right **h** from them A
2: 4 with his right **h** set like a foe; A
2: 7 has delivered into the **h** of the enemy the walls B
2: 8 he did not withhold his **h** from destroying;
3: 3 against me alone he turns his **h,**
4: 6 though no **h** was laid on it.
5: 8 there is no one to deliver us from their **h.** C
Eze 1: 3 and the **h** of the LORD was on him there. D
2: 9 I looked, and a **h** was stretched out to me,
3:14 the **h** of the LORD being strong upon me. D
3:18 but their blood I will require at your **h.**
3:20 but their blood I will require at your **h.**
3:22 Then the **h** of the LORD was upon me there; D
6:14 I will stretch out my **h** against them,
7:21 I will **h** it over to strangers as booty,
8: 1 the **h** of the Lord GOD fell upon me there. I
8: 3 It stretched out the form of a **h,**
8:11 Each had his censer in his **h,**
9: 1 each with his destroying weapon in his **h."**
9: 2 each with his weapon for slaughter in his **h;**
10: 7 And a cherub stretched out his **h** from among
10: 8 to have the form of a human **h** under their wings.
13: 9 My **h** will be against the prophets who see false
13:23 I will save my people from your **h.** C
14: 9 and I will stretch out my **h** against him,
14:13 and I stretch out my **h** against it,
16:27 Therefore I stretched out my **h** against you,
17:18 because he gave his **h** and yet did all these things,
18: 8 withholds his **h** from iniquity,
18:17 withholds his **h** from iniquity, takes no advance
20:22 But I withheld my **h,** and acted for the sake
20:33 surely with a mighty **h** and an outstretched arm, G
20:34 with a mighty **h** and an outstretched arm, G
21:11 to be grasped in the **h;**
21:11 to be placed in the slayer's **h.**
21:14 And you, mortal, prophesy; Strike **h** to **h.**
21:17 I too will strike **h** to **h,** I will satisfy my fury;
21:22 Into his right **h** comes the lot for Jerusalem, AB
21:24 to remembrance, you shall be taken in **h.**
23:31 therefore I will give her cup into your **h.** B
25: 7 therefore I have stretched out my **h** against you,
25: 7 and will **h** you over as plunder to the nations.
25:13 I will stretch out my **h** against Edom,
25:14 I will lay my vengeance upon Edom by the **h**
25:16 I will stretch out my **h** against the Philistines,
28:10 of the uncircumcised by the **h** of foreigners;
29: 7 with the **h,** you broke, and tore all their shoulders;
30:10 by the **h** of King Nebuchadrezzar of Babylon.
30:12 and will sell the land into the **h** of evildoers; B
30:12 the land and everything in it by the **h** of foreigners;
30:22 and I will make the sword fall from his **h.** C
30:24 and put my sword in his **h;**
30:25 put my sword into the **h** of the king of Babylon. B
31:11 I gave it into the **h** of the prince of the nations; B
33: 6 but their blood I will require at the sentinel's **h.**
33: 8 but their blood I will require at your **h.**
33:22 the **h** of the LORD had been upon me the evening D
34:10 and I will demand my sheep at their **h,**
35: 3 I stretch out my **h** against you to make you
37: 1 The **h** of the LORD came upon me, D
37:17 so that they may become one in your **h.**
37:19 about to take the stick of Joseph (which is in the **h**
37:19 in order that they may be one in my **h.**
37:20 which you write are in your **h** before their eyes,
39: 3 I will strike your bow from your left **h,** H
39: 3 will make your arrows drop out of your right **h.** A
39:21 and my **h** that I have laid on them.
39:23 and gave them into the **h** of their adversaries, B
40: 1 the **h** of the LORD was upon me, D
40: 3 with a linen cord and a measuring reed in his **h;**
40: 5 the man's **h** was six long cubits, each being a cubit
47: 3 Going on eastward with a cord in his **h,**
Da 2:38 into whose **h** he has given human beings, B
3:17 from the furnace of blazing fire and out of your **h,**
4:35 There is no one who can stay his **h** or say to him,
5: 5 Immediately the fingers of a human **h** appeared
5: 5 The king was watching the **h** as it wrote.
5:24 the **h** was sent and this writing was inscribed.
8:25 under his **h,** and in his own mind he shall
9:15 a mighty **h** and made your name renowned even G
10:10 then a **h** touched me and roused me to my hands

Da 11:42 He shall stretch out his **h** against the countries,
12: 7 his right **h** and his left hand toward heaven. A
12: 7 his right hand and his left **h** toward heaven. H
Hos 2:10 and no one shall rescue her out of my **h.**
7: 5 he stretched out his **h** with mockers.
11: 8 How can I **h** you over, O Israel?
Joel 3: 8 will sell your sons and your daughters into the **h** B
Am 1: 6 into exile entire communities, to **h** them over
1: 8 I will turn my **h** against Ekron,
5:19 went into the house and rested a **h** against the wall,
7: 7 with a plumb line in his **h.**
9: 2 from there shall my **h** take them;
Jnh 4:11 not know their right **h** from their left, A
Mic 5: 9 Your **h** shall be lifted up over your adversaries,
5:12 and I will cut off sorceries from your **h,** C
6:14 and what you save, I will **h** over to the sword.
7: 4 now their confusion is at **h.** E
Hab 2:16 The cup in the LORD's right **h** will come around A
3: 4 rays came forth from his **h,** C
Zep 1: 4 I will stretch out my **h** against Judah,
1: 7 For the day of the LORD is at **h;** E
2:13 And he will stretch out his **h** against the north,
Zec 2: 1 up and saw a man with a measuring line in his **h.**
2: 9 See now, I am going to raise my **h** against them,
3: 1 and Satan standing at his right **h** to accuse him. A
4:10 and shall see the plummet in the **h** of Zerubbabel.
8: 4 each with staff in **h** because of their great age.
11: 6 every one, to fall each into the **h** of a neighbor, B
11: 6 and each into the **h** of the king; B
11: 6 and I will deliver no one from their **h.** C
13: 7 I will turn my **h** against the little ones.
14:13 so that each will seize the **h** of a neighbor,
14:13 and the **h** of the one will be raised against the **h**
Mal 1:13 Shall I accept that from your **h?** C
2:13 the offering or accepts it with favor at your **h.**
Mt 3:12 His winnowing fork is in his **h,**
5:25 or your accuser may **h** you over to the judge,
5:30 And if your right **h** causes you to sin, A
6: 3 your left **h** know what your right hand is doing, H
6: 3 your left hand know what your right **h** is doing, A
8: 3 He stretched out his **h** and touched him, saying,
8:15 he touched her **h,** and the fever left her,
9:18 but come and lay your **h** on her, and she will live."
9:25 he went in and took her by the **h,**
10:17 for they will **h** you over to councils and flog you
10:19 When they **h** you over, do not worry about
12:10 a man was there with a withered **h,**
12:13 Then he said to the man, "Stretch out your **h."**
14:31 Jesus immediately reached out his **h**
18: 8 "If your **h** or your foot causes you to stumble,
20:19 then they will **h** him over to the Gentiles to
20:21 one at your right **h** and one at your left, A
20:23 but to sit at my right **h** and at my left, A
22:13 king said to the attendants, 'Bind him **h** and foot,
22:44 "Sit at my right **h,** until I put your enemies A
24: 9 "Then they will **h** you over to be tortured
25:33 the sheep at his right **h** and the goats at the left. A
25:34 Then the king will say to those at his right **h,** A
25:41 Then he will say to those at his left **h,** H
26:23 "The one who has dipped his **h** into the bowl
26:45 See, the hour is at **h,** and the Son of Man E
26:46 let us be going. See, my betrayer is at **h."** E
26:51 one of those with Jesus put his **h** on his sword,
26:64 Son of Man seated at the right **h** of Power A
27:29 They put a reed in his right **h** and A
Mk 1:31 He came and took her by the **h** and lifted her up.
1:41 Jesus stretched out his **h** and touched him,
3: 1 and a man was there who had a withered **h.**
3: 3 And he said to the man who had the withered **h,**
3: 5 of heart and said to the man, "Stretch out your **h."**
3: 5 He stretched it out, and his **h** was restored.
5:41 He took her by the **h** and said to her,
7:32 and they begged him to lay his **h** on him.
8:23 He took the blind man by the **h** and led him out of
9:27 But Jesus took him by the **h** and lifted him up,
9:43 If your **h** causes you to stumble, cut it off;
10:33 then they will **h** him over to the Gentiles;
10:37 one at your right **h** and one at your left, A
10:40 but to sit at my right **h** or at my left is not mine A
12:36 'Sit at my right **h,** until I put your enemies A
13: 9 for they will **h** you over to councils;
13:11 When they bring you to trial and **h** you over,
14:42 Get up, let us be going. See, my betrayer is at **h.** E
14:62 Son of Man seated at the right **h** of the Power,' A
16:19 ⟦heaven and sat down at the right **h** of God.⟧ AF
Lk 1:66 For, indeed, the **h** of the Lord was with him. I
1:71 be saved from our enemies and from the **h** C
3:17 His winnowing fork is in his **h,**
5:13 Then Jesus stretched out his **h,** touched him,
6: 6 a man there whose right **h** was withered. A
6: 8 he said to the man who had the withered **h,**
6:10 he said to him, "Stretch out your **h."**
6:10 He did so, and his **h** was restored.
8:54 But he took her by the **h** and called out, "Child,
9:62 a **h** to the plow and looks back is fit for
12:58 and the judge **h** you over to the officer,
20:20 so as to **h** him over to the jurisdiction and authority
20:42 'The Lord said to my Lord, "Sit at my right **h,** A
21:12 they will **h** you over to synagogues and prisons,
22:21 and his **h** is on the table.
22:69 the Son of Man will be seated at the right **h** A
Jn 10:12 The hired **h,** who is not the shepherd and does
10:13 The hired **h** runs away because a hired **h** does not
10:28 No one will snatch them out of my **h.**
10:29 and no one can snatch it out of the Father's **h.**
20:25 in the mark of the nails and my **h** in his side,
20:27 Reach out your **h** and put it in my side.

Ac 2:25 he is at my right **h** so that I will not be shaken; A
2:33 Being therefore exalted at the right **h** of God, AF
2:34 'The Lord said to my Lord, "Sit at my right **h**, A
3: 7 he took him by the right **h** and raised him up; A
4:28 to do whatever your **h**
4:30 while you stretch out your **h** to heal,
5:31 God exalted him at his right **h** as Leader A
7:50 Did not my **h** make all these things?'
7:55 and Jesus standing at the right **h** of God. AF
7:56 Son of Man standing at the right **h** of God!" AF
9: 8 by the **h** and brought him into Damascus.
9:41 He gave her his **h** and helped her up.
11:21 The **h** of the Lord was with them, I
12:17 He motioned to them with his **h** to be silent,
13:11 now listen—the **h** of the Lord is against you, I
13:11 about groping for someone to lead him by the **h**.
18:10 and no one will lay a **h** on you to harm you,
21:11 the man who owns this belt and will **h** him over to
22:11 those who were with me took my **h** and led me
23:19 The tribune took him by the **h**,
25:16 the custom of the Romans to **h** over anyone before
26: 1 Then Paul stretched out his **h** and began
28: 3 driven out by the heat, fastened itself on his **h**.
28: 4 the natives saw the creature hanging from his **h**, C
Ro 7:21 I want to do what is good, evil lies close at **h**. E
8:34 who was raised, who is at the right **h** of God, AF
1Co 5: 5 to **h** this man over to Satan for the destruction of
12:15 If the foot would say, "Because I am not a **h**,
12:21 The eye cannot say to the **h**,
13: 3 and if I **h** over my body so that I may boast,
14: 3 On the other **h**, those who prophesy speak
16:21 I, Paul, write this greeting with my own **h**.
2Co 6: 7 the weapons of righteousness for the right **h** A
Gal 2: 9 to Barnabas and me the right **h** of fellowship, A
6:11 when I am writing in my own **h**!
Eph 1:20 from the dead and seated him at his right **h** in A
Col 3: 1 where Christ is, seated at the right **h** of God. AF
4:18 I, Paul, write this greeting with my own **h**.
2Th 3:17 I, Paul, write this greeting with my own **h**.
Phm 1:19 I, Paul, am writing this with my own **h**:
Heb 1: 3 sat down at the right **h** of the Majesty on high, A
1:13 "Sit at my right **h** until I make your enemies A
7:18 on the one **h**, the abrogation of
7:19 on the other **h**, the introduction of a better hope,
8: 1 a high priest, one who is seated at the right **h** of A
8: 9 the day when I took them by the **h** to lead them
10:12 "he sat down at the right **h** of God," AF
12: 2 and has taken his seat at the right **h** of the throne A
1Pe 3:22 gone into heaven and is at the right **h** of God, AF
5: 6 under the mighty **h** of God, FG
Rev 1:16 In his right **h** he held seven stars, A
1:17 But he placed his right **h** on me, saying, A
1:20 of the seven stars that you saw in my right **h**, A
2: 1 the seven stars in his right **h**, who walks among A
5: 1 Then I saw in the right **h** of the one seated on A
5: 7 and took the scroll from the right **h** of the one AC
6: 5 Its rider held a pair of scales in his **h**,
8: 4 rose before God from the **h** of the angel. C
10: 2 He held a little scroll open in his **h**.
10: 5 and the land raised his right **h** to heaven A
10: 8 in the **h** of the angel who is standing on the sea
10:10 the little scroll from the **h** of the angel and ate it; C
13:16 to be marked on the right **h** or the forehead, A
14:14 and a sharp sickle in his **h**!
17: 4 holding in her **h** a golden cup full of abominations
20: 1 holding in his **h** the key to the bottomless pit and
Tob 5:18 the staff of our **h** as he goes in and out before us?
7:12 to him he took her by the **h** and gave her to Tobias,
8: 3 and at once bound him there **h** and foot.
11:11 with the gall of the fish in his **h**,
13: 2 and there is nothing that can escape his **h**.
Jdt 2: 7 to whom I will **h** them over to be plundered.
2:11 but **h** them over to slaughter and plunder
2:12 I have spoken I will accomplish by my own **h**.
6:10 and take him away to Bethulia and **h** him over to
8:33 the Lord will deliver Israel by my **h**.
9: 9 a widow, the strong **h** to do what I plan.
9:10 crush their arrogance by the **h** of a woman.
10:15 some of us will escort you and **h** you over to him.
12: 4 by my **h** what he has determined."
13:14 by my **h** this very night!"
13:15 Lord has struck him down by the **h** of a woman.
14: 6 and saw the head of Holofernes in the **h** of one of
15:10 You have done all this with your own **h**;
16: 5 But the Lord Almighty has foiled them by the **h** of
AdE 14: 4 for my danger is in my **h**.
14:14 But save us by your **h**, and help me,
16: 7 much from the more ancient records that we **h** on,
16: 7 as from investigation of matters close at **h**. E
Wis 2:18 will deliver him from the **h** of his adversaries. C
3: 1 the souls of the righteous are in the **h** of God, F
5:16 a beautiful diadem from the **h** of the Lord, CI
5:16 because with his right **h** he will cover them, A
7:16 For both we and our words are in his **h**,
9:16 and what is at **h** we find with labor; E
10:20 and praised with one accord your defending **h**;
11: 1 Wisdom prospered their works by the **h** of
11:17 For your all-powerful **h**, which created
13:10 or a useless stone, the work of an ancient **h**.
14: 6 and guided by your **h** left to the world the seed of
16:15 To escape from your **h** is impossible; C
19: 8 where those protected by your **h** passed through
Sir 4:19 and **h** them over to their ruin.
4:31 Do not let your **h** be stretched out to receive
5:12 but if not, put your **h** over your mouth.
7:32 Stretch out your **h** to the poor,
8:16 and where no help is at **h**, E

Sir 10: 4 government of the earth is in the **h** of the Lord, I
10: 5 Human success is in the **h** of the Lord, I
12:12 Do not let him sit at your right **h**, A
15:16 stretch out your **h** for whichever you choose.
21:19 and like manacles on his right **h**. A
22: 2 anyone that picks it up will shake it off his **h**.
27:19 And as you allow a bird to escape from your **h**, C
29: 1 a helping **h** they keep the commandments.
31:14 Do not reach out your **h** for everything you see,
33:13 Like clay in the **h** of the potter,
33:13 so all are in the **h** of their Maker,
33:22 that you should look to the **h** of your children.
36: 3 Lift up your **h** against foreign nations
36: 7 make your **h** and right arm glorious.
49:11 He was like a signet ring on the right **h**, A
50:15 he held out his **h** for the cup and poured
51: 3 from the **h** of those seeking my life, C
51: 8 and save them from the **h** of their enemies. C
Bar 2:11 land of Egypt with a mighty **h** and with signs G
4:18 upon you will deliver you from the **h** C
4:21 and he will deliver you from the power and **h** of
LtJ 6:15 Another has a dagger in its right **h**, and an ax, A
Bel 1:29 Going to the king, they said, "**H** Daniel over to us,
1Mc 2:22 by turning aside from our religion to the right **h** A
2:48 and they never let the sinner gain the upper **h**.
3: 6 and deliverance prospered by his **h**.
4:30 the mighty warrior by the **h** of your servant David,
4:31 Hem in this army by the **h** of your people Israel,
7:47 right **h** that he had so arrogantly stretched out, A
9:47 Jonathan stretched out his **h** to strike Bacchides,
11:40 insistently urged him to **h** Antiochus over to him,
12:27 to keep their arms at **h** so as to be ready all night E
12:34 for he had heard that they were ready to **h** over
12:39 and to raise his **h** against King Antiochus.
12:42 he was afraid to raise his **h** against him.
12:45 I will **h** it over to you as well as
15:21 **h** them over to the high priest Simon,
15:30 **h** over the cities that you have seized and
2Mc 4:34 and gave him his right **h**; A
7:34 you raise your **h** against the children of heaven.
8:11 and promising to **h** over ninety slaves for a talent,
12:31 as the festival of weeks was close at **h**. E
14:31 and commanded them to **h** the man over.
14:33 he stretched out his right **h** toward the sanctuary, A
14:33 "If you do not **h** Judas over to me as a prisoner,
15:15 Jeremiah stretched out his right **h** and gave A
15:17 the matter by fighting **h** to **h** with all courage,
15:20 at **h** with their army drawn up for battle, E
1Es 4:29 she would sit at the king's right **h** A
4:30 and slap the king with her left **h**. H
8:47 And by the mighty **h** of our G
8:61 the mighty **h** of our Lord, which was upon us; G
3Mc 5:13 of his all-powerful **h** to the arrogant Gentiles.
5:46 and urged the king on to the matter at **h**. E
6:10 from the **h** of the enemy, and destroy us, C
2Es 2:34 at the end of the age is close at **h**. E
3: 6 into the garden that your right **h** had planted A
6: 8 for Jacob's **h** held Esau's heel from the beginning.
6:10 The beginning of a person is the **h**,
6:10 Ezra, between the heel and the **h**, Ezra!"
7: 7 that there is fire on the right **h** and deep water A
10:30 he grasped my right **h** and strengthened me A
13: 9 he neither lifted his **h** nor held a spear
15:11 but I will bring them out with a mighty **h** and G
15:22 My right **h** will not spare the sinners, A
15:26 he will **h** them over to death and slaughter.
15:56 and will **h** you over to adversities.
16: 2 for your destruction is at **h**. E
16:13 For his right **h** that bends the bow is strong, A
16:74 the days of tribulation are at **h**, E
4Mc 8:16 Let us consider, on the other **h**,
13:12 the father by whose **h** Isaac would have submitted
16:20 and when Isaac saw his father's **h** wielding a knife

HAND-TO-HAND (1) [HAND]

2Mc 5:14 forty thousand in **h** fighting,

HANDBAGS (1) [BAG]

Isa 3:22 the festal robes, the mantles, the cloaks, and the **h**;

HANDBREADTH (7) [HAND]

Ex 25:25 You shall make around it a rim a **h** wide,
37:12 He made around it a rim a **h** wide,
1Ki 7:26 Its thickness was a **h**; its brim was made like the
2Ch 4: 5 Its thickness was a **h**; its rim was made like the
Eze 40: 5 each being a cubit and a **h** in length;
40:43 There were pegs, one **h** long,
43:13 by cubits (the cubit being one cubit and a **h**):

HANDBREADTHS (1) [HAND]

Ps 39: 5 You have made my days a few **h**,

HANDED‡ (82) [HAND]

Ge 27:17 Then she **h** the savory food,
Nu 21: 3 and **h** over the Canaanites;
Dt 2:24 I have **h** over to you King Sihon the Amorite
3: 2 "Do not fear him, for I have **h** him over to you,
3: 3 So the LORD our God also **h** over to us King Og
19:12 to have the culprit taken from there and **h** over to
Jos 6: 2 "See, I have **h** Jericho over to you,
8: 1 I have **h** over to you the king of Ai with his people,
10: 8 "Do not fear them, for I have **h** them over to you;
11: 8 And the LORD **h** them over to Israel,
24: 8 they fought with you, and I **h** them over to you,

Jos 24:11 and I **h** them over to you.
Jdg 2:23 and had not **h** them over to Joshua.
1Sa 30:23 and **h** over to us the raiding party that attacked us.
2Sa 21: 6 let seven of his sons be **h** over to us,
2Ki 3:10 three kings, only to be **h** over to Moab."
3:13 three kings, only to be **h** over to Moab."
Ezr 9: 7 and our priests have been **h** over to the kings of
Ne 9:30 you **h** them over to the peoples of the lands.
Est 6: 9 be **h** over to one of the king's most noble officials;
Jer 34: 3 but shall surely be captured and **h** over to him;
34:20 shall be **h** over to their enemies and
37:17 "You shall be **h** over to the king of Babylon."
38: 3 surely be **h** over to the army of the king of Babylon
38:18 then this city shall be **h** over to the Chaldeans,
38:19 be **h** over to them and they would abuse me."
39:17 you shall not be **h** over to those whom you dread.
46:24 she shall be **h** over to a people from the north.
La 1:14 Lord **h** me over to those whom I cannot withstand.
Eze 31:14 all of them are **h** over to death, to the world below;
32:20 Egypt has been **h** over to the sword;
Ob 1:14 you should not have **h** over his survivors on
Mt 11:27 All things have been **h** over to me by my Father;
18:34 And in anger his lord **h** him over to be tortured
20:18 the Son of Man will be **h** over to the chief priests
25:20 saying, 'Master, you **h** over to me five talents;
25:22 saying, 'Master, you **h** over to me two talents;
26: 2 and the Son of Man will be **h** over to be crucified."
27: 2 and **h** him over to Pilate the governor.
27:18 of jealousy that they had **h** him over.
27:26 after flogging Jesus, he **h** him over to be crucified.
Mk 7:13 of God through your tradition that you have **h** on.
10:33 the Son of Man will be **h** over to the chief priests
15: 1 led him away, and **h** him over to Pilate.
15:10 of jealousy that the chief priests had **h** him over.
15:15 after flogging Jesus, he **h** him over to be crucified.
Lk 1: 2 just as they were **h** on to us by those who from
10:22 All things have been **h** over to me by my Father;
18:32 For he will be **h** over to the Gentiles;
23:25 and he **h** Jesus over as they wished.
24: 7 that the Son of Man must be **h** over to sinners,
24:20 and how our chief priests and leaders **h** him over to
Jn 18:30 we would not have **h** him over to you."
18:35 Your own nation and the chief priests have **h** you
18:36 be fighting to keep me from being **h** over to
19:11 therefore the one who **h** me over to you is guilty of
19:16 Then he **h** him over to them to be crucified.
Ac 2:23 **h** over to you according to the definite plan
3:13 whom you **h** over and rejected in the presence
6:14 and will change the customs that Moses **h** on
7:42 But God turned away from them and **h** them over
12: 4 he put him in prison and **h** him over to four squads
28:17 yet I was arrested in Jerusalem and **h** over to
Ro 4:25 who was **h** over to death for our trespasses
1Co 11: 2 and maintain the traditions just as I **h** them on
11:23 I received from the Lord what I also **h** on to you,
15: 3 For I **h** on to you as of first importance what I
Jdt 8:19 That was why our ancestors were **h** over to
10:12 they are about to be **h** over to you to be devoured.
11:15 on that very day they will be **h** over to you to
AdE 2:13 she is **h** to the person appointed,
9:14 and **h** over to the Jews of the city the bodies
14: 6 and you have **h** us over to our enemies
Wis 14:15 **h** on to his dependents secret rites and initiations.
Sir 11: 6 and the honored have been **h** over to others.
Bar 4: 6 but you were **h** over to your enemies
Aza 1: 9 You have **h** us over to our enemies,
Bel 1:30 and under compulsion he **h** Daniel over to them.
2Mc 10: 4 with forbearance and not be **h** over to blasphemous
1Es 2:14 All the vessels were **h** over, gold and silver,
2Es 3:27 So you **h** over your city to your enemies.
5:28 O Lord, why have you **h** the one over to the many,

HANDFUL (8) [HAND]

Lev 2: 2 After taking from it a **h** of the choice flour and oil,
5:12 up a **h** of it as its memorial portion, and turn this
6:15 a **h** of the choice flour and oil of the grain offering,
9:17 the grain offering, and, taking a **h** of it, he turned it
Nu 5:26 and the priest shall take a **h** of the grain offering,
1Ki 17:12 only a **h** of meal in a jar, and a little oil in a jug;
20:10 if the dust of Samaria will provide a **h** for each of
Ecc 4: 6 Better is a **h** with quiet than two handfuls with toil,

HANDFULS (7) [HAND]

Ex 9: 8 "Take **h** of soot from the kiln,
Lev 16:12 and two **h** of crushed sweet incense,
Ru 2:16 also pull out some **h** for her from the bundles,
Ecc 4: 6 Better is a handful with quiet than two **h** with toil,
Eze 13:19 among my people for **h** of barley and for pieces
2Mc 4:41 others took **h** of the ashes that were lying around,
3Mc 5: 2 with large **h** of frankincense and plenty

HANDING (2) [HAND]

2Ch 32:11 **h** you over to die by famine and by thirst,
Eze 25: 4 therefore I am **h** you over to the people of the east

HANDIWORK (2) [HAND]

Ps 19: 1 and the firmament proclaims his **h**.
Sir 38:28 He sets his heart on finishing his **h**,

HANDKERCHIEFS (1)

Ac 19:12 so that when the **h** or aprons

HANDLE (7) [HANDLED, HANDLES, HANDLING]

Dt 19: 5 the **h** and strikes the other person who then dies;
2Ch 25: 5 able to **h** spear and shield.
Jer 2: 8 Those who **h** the law did not know me;
Eze 27:29 and down from their ships come all that **h** the oar.
Am 2:15 those who **h** the bow shall not stand,
Col 2:21 "Do not **h,** Do not taste, Do not touch"?
Wis 13:11 a tree easy to **h** and skillfully strip off all its bark,

HANDLED (1) [HANDLE]

2Mc 7:39 and **h** him worse than the others,

HANDLES (4) [HANDLE]

SS 5: 5 upon the **h** of the bolt.
Isa 10:15 or the saw magnify itself against the one who **h** it?
45: 9 or "Your work has no **h**"?
Sir 38:25 How can one become wise who **h** the plow,

HANDLING (2) [HANDLE]

Nu 35:23 while **h** any stone that could cause death,
Jdt 7: 2 not counting the baggage and the foot soldiers **h** it,

HANDMAID (KJV) See MAID, SERVANT, SLAVE, SLAVE-GIRL

HANDMILL (1) [MILL]

Ex 11: 5 of the female slave who is behind the **h,**

HANDPIKES (1)

Eze 39: 9 bows and arrows, **h** and spears—

HANDS‡ (584) [HAND]

A. INTO ... HANDS (78)
B. HANDS ON (60)
C. FROM ... HANDS (24)
D. HUMAN HANDS (22)

Ge 5:29 from our work and from the toil of our **h."**
19:10 the men inside reached out their **h** and brought Lot
20: 5 of my heart and the innocence of my **h."**
27:16 and she put the skins of the kids on his **h** and on
27:22 but the **h** are the **h** of Esau."
27:23 his **h** were hairy like his brother Esau's **h;**
31:42 God saw my affliction and the labor of my **h,**
37:21 Reuben heard it, he delivered him out of their **h,**
37:27 and not lay our **h** on him, for he is our brother, B
39: 3 LORD caused all that he did to prosper in his **h.**
42:37 Put him in my **h,** and I will bring him back
48:14 crossing his **h,** for Manasseh was the firstborn.
49:24 and his arms were made agile by the **h** of
Ex 9:29 I will stretch out my **h** to the LORD;
9:33 and stretched out his **h** to the LORD;
15:17 O LORD, that your **h** have established.
17:12 But Moses' **h** grew weary;
17:12 Aaron and Hur held up his **h,** one on one side,
17:12 so his **h** were steady until the sun set.
22: 8 the owner had laid **h** on the neighbor's goods. B
22:11 the two of them that the one has not laid **h** on B
23: 1 You shall not join **h** with the wicked to act as
29:10 Aaron and his sons shall lay their **h** on the head B
29:15 and his sons shall lay their **h** on the head of B
29:19 and his sons shall lay their **h** on the head of B
29:20 and on the thumbs of their right **h,**
29:25 Then you shall take them from their **h,** C
30:19 the water Aaron and his sons shall wash their **h**
30:21 They shall wash their **h** and their feet,
32:15 carrying the two tablets of the covenant in his **h,**
32:19 he threw the tablets from his **h** and broke them C
35:25 All the skillful women spun with their **h,**
40:31 and his sons washed their **h** and their feet.
Lev 4:15 of the congregation shall lay their **h** on the head B
7:30 Your own **h** shall bring the LORD's offering
8:14 and Aaron and his sons laid their **h** upon the head
8:18 and his sons laid their **h** on the head of the ram, B
8:22 and his sons laid their **h** on the head of the ram, B
8:24 on the thumbs of their right **h** and on the big toes
8:28 from their **h** and turned them into smoke on C
9:22 Aaron lifted his **h** toward the people
15:11 without his having rinsed his **h**
16:21 Then Aaron shall lay both his **h** on the head of B
24:14 let all who were within hearing lay their **h** on B
26:25 and you shall be delivered into enemy **h.** A
Nu 5:18 place in her **h** the grain offering of remembrance,
8:10 the Israelites shall lay their **h** on the Levites, B
8:12 shall lay their **h** on the heads of the bulls, B
21: 2 "If you will indeed give this people into our **h,** A
24:10 and he struck his **h** together.
27:23 he laid his **h** on him and commissioned him— B
Dt 4:28 you will serve other gods made by human **h,** D
9:15 the two tablets of the covenant were in my two **h.**
9:17 of the two tablets and flung them from my two **h,** C
17: 7 The **h** of the witnesses shall be the first raised
17: 7 and afterward the **h** of all the people.
21: 6 that town nearest the body shall wash their **h** over
21: 7 "Our **h** did not shed this blood,
21:10 and the LORD your God **h** them over to you
31:29 to anger through the work of your **h."**
33: 7 strengthen his **h** for him, and be a help against
33:11 his substance, and accept the work of his **h;**
34: 9 because Moses had laid his **h** on him; B
Jos 2:24 the LORD has given all the land into our **h;** A
21:44 LORD had given all their enemies into their **h.** A
Jdg 7: 5 putting their **h** to their mouths,
7: 8 So he took the jars of the troops from their **h,** C
7:11 and afterward your **h** shall be strengthened
7:16 and put trumpets into the **h** of all of them, A
7:19 and smashed the jars that were in their **h.**
7:20 holding in their left **h** the torches,
7:20 and in their right **h** the trumpets to blow;
8: 3 has given into your **h** the captains of Midian, A
8: 6 in your possession the **h** of Zebah and Zalmunna,
8:15 in your possession the **h** of Zebah and Zalmunna,
9:24 who strengthened his **h** to kill his brothers.
13:23 a burnt offering and a grain offering at our **h,**
14: 9 He scraped it out into his **h,** and went on, A
15:12 we may give you into the **h** of the Philistines." A
15:13 we will only bind you and give you into their **h;** A
15:14 and his bonds melted off his **h.**
15:18 and fall into the **h** of the uncircumcised?" A
16:18 and brought the money in their **h.**
18:10 God has indeed given it into your **h**— A
19:27 with her **h** on the threshold. B
1Sa 5: 4 both his **h** were lying cut off upon the threshold;
14:13 Then Jonathan climbed up on his **h** and feet,
14:26 but they did not put their **h** to their mouths,
14:48 of the **h** of those who plundered them.
24:11 that there is no wrong or treason in my **h.**
24:18 not kill me when the LORD put me into your **h.** A
26:18 What guilt is on my **h?**
28:19 along with you into the **h** of the Philistines; A
28:19 the army of Israel into the **h** of the Philistines." A
2Sa 2: 7 Therefore let your **h** be strong, and be valiant;
3:34 Your **h** were not bound, your feet were
4:12 they cut off their **h** and feet,
16:21 **h** of all who are with you will be strengthened."
21: 9 he gave them into the **h** of the Gibeonites, A
21:22 they fell by the **h** of David and his servants.
22:21 to the cleanness of my **h** he recompensed me.
22:35 He trains my **h** for war,
24:14 but let me not fall into human **h."** AD
1Ki 8:22 and spread out his **h** to heaven.
8:38 of their own hearts so that they stretch out their **h**
8:54 he had knelt with **h** outstretched toward heaven;
14:27 and committed them to the **h** of the officers of
15:18 and gave them into the **h** of his servants. A
16: 7 provoking him to anger with the work of his **h,**
20: 6 and lay **h** on whatever pleases them, B
2Ki 3:11 who used to pour water on the **h** of Elijah, is here."
4:34 his eyes upon his eyes, and his **h** upon his **h;**
9:35 the skull and the feet and the palms of her **h.**
10:24 into your **h** shall forfeit his life." A
11:12 they clapped their **h** and shouted,
11:16 So they laid **h** on her; B
12:11 into the **h** of the workers who had the oversight A
13:16 Elisha laid his **h** on the king's hands. B
13:16 Elisha laid his hands on the king's **h.**
19:18 they were no gods but the work of human **h**— D
22:17 to anger with all the work of their **h,**
1Ch 5:20 with them were given into their **h,** A
12:17 though my **h** have done no wrong,
21:13 but let me not fall into human **h."** AD
2Ch 6:12 the whole assembly of Israel, and spread out his **h.**
6:13 and spread out his **h** toward heaven.
6:29 so that they stretch out their **h** toward this house;
12:10 and committed them to the **h** of the officers of
13:16 and God gave them into their **h.** A
15: 7 Do not let your **h** be weak,
23:15 So they laid **h** on her; B
24:13 and the repairing went forward at their **h,**
29:23 they laid their **h** on them, B
30:16 that they received from the **h** of the Levites. C
32:17 not rescue their people from my **h,** C
32:19 which are the work of human **h.** D
34:25 to anger with all the works of their **h,**
Ezr 5: 8 is being done diligently and prospers in their **h.**
8:33 into the **h** of the priest Meremoth son of Uriah, A
9: 5 spread out my **h** to the LORD my God,
Ne 6: 9 thinking, "Their **h** will drop from the work,
6: 9 But now, O God, strengthen my **h.**
8: 6 "Amen, Amen," lifting up their **h.**
9:24 the Canaanites, and gave them into their **h,** A
9:27 you gave them into the **h** of their enemies, A
9:27 from the **h** of their enemies. C
9:28 you abandoned them to the **h** of their enemies,
13:21 If you do so again, I will lay **h** on you." B
Est 3: 6 But he thought it beneath him to lay **h** on B
3: 9 of silver into the **h** of those who have charge of A
8: 7 because he plotted to lay **h** on the Jews. B
9: 2 to lay **h** on those who had sought their ruin; B
9:16 but they laid no **h** on the plunder. B
Job 1:10 You have blessed the work of his **h,**
4: 3 you have strengthened the weak **h.**
5:12 so that their **h** achieve no success.
5:18 he strikes, but his **h** heal.
9:30 If I wash myself with soap and cleanse my **h**
10: 3 of your **h** and favor the schemes of the wicked?
10: 8 Your **h** fashioned and made me;
11:13 you will stretch out your **h** toward him.
12: 6 who bring their god in their **h.**
14:15 you would long for the work of your **h.**
15:25 Because they stretched out their **h** against God,
16:11 and casts me into the **h** of the wicked. A
16:17 though there is no violence in my **h,**
17: 9 they that have clean **h** grow stronger and stronger.
20:10 and their **h** will give back their wealth.
22:30 because of the cleanness of your **h."**
27:23 It claps its **h** at them,
29: 9 and laid their **h** on their mouths; B
30: 2 What could I gain from the strength of their **h?**
31: 7 and if any spot has clung to my **h;**
34:19 for they are all the work of his **h?**
34:37 he claps his **h** among us,
36:32 He covers his **h** with the lightning,
41: 8 Lay **h** on it; think of the B
Ps 7: 3 if I have done this, if there is wrong in my **h,**
8: 6 over the works of your **h;**
9:16 the wicked are snared in the work of their own **h.**
10:14 that you may take it into your **h;** A
18:20 to the cleanness of my **h** he recompensed me.
18:24 according to the cleanness of my **h** in his sight.
18:34 He trains my **h** for war,
22:16 My **h** and feet have shriveled;
24: 4 Those who have clean **h** and pure hearts,
26: 6 I wash my **h** in innocence,
26:10 those in whose **h** are evil devices,
26:10 and whose right **h** are full of bribes.
28: 2 as I lift up my **h** toward your most holy sanctuary.
28: 4 repay them according to the work of their **h;**
28: 5 or the work of his **h,**
44:20 or spread out our **h** to a strange god,
47: 1 Clap your **h,** all you peoples;
55:20 My companion laid **h** on a friend and violated B
58: 2 your **h** deal out violence on earth.
63: 4 I will lift up my **h** and call on your name.
68:31 let Ethiopia hasten to stretch out its **h** to God.
73:13 and washed my **h** in innocence.
81: 6 your **h** were freed from the basket.
88: 9 I spread out my **h** to you.
90:17 and prosper for us the work of our **h**—
90:17 O prosper the work of our **h!**
91:12 On their **h** they will bear you up,
92: 4 at the works of your **h** I sing for joy.
95: 5 and the dry land, which his **h** have formed.
98: 8 Let the floods clap their **h;**
102:25 and the heavens are the work of your **h.**
111: 7 The works of his **h** are faithful and just;
115: 4 and gold, the work of human **h.** D
115: 7 They have **h,** but do not feel;
119:73 Your **h** have made and fashioned me;
125: 3 righteous might not stretch out their **h** to do wrong.
128: 2 You shall eat the fruit of the labor of your **h;**
129: 7 with which reapers do not fill their **h** or binders
134: 2 Lift up your **h** to the holy place,
135:15 and gold, the work of human **h.** D
138: 8 Do not forsake the work of your **h.**
140: 4 O LORD, from the **h** of the wicked; C
141: 2 and the lifting up of my **h** as an evening sacrifice.
143: 5 I meditate on the works of your **h.**
143: 6 I stretch out my **h** to you;
144: 1 who trains my **h** for war, and my fingers for battle;
144: 8 and whose right **h** are false.
144:11 and whose right **h** are false.
149: 6 be in their throats and two-edged swords in their **h,**
Pr 6:10 a little slumber, a little folding of the **h** to rest,
6:17 a lying tongue, and **h** that shed innocent blood,
14: 1 but the foolish tears it down with her own **h.**
21:25 for lazy **h** refuse to labor.
24:33 a little slumber, a little folding of the **h** to rest,
31:13 She seeks wool and flax, and works with willing **h.**
31:16 with the fruit of her **h** she plants a vineyard.
31:19 She puts her **h** to the distaff,
31:19 and her **h** hold the spindle.
31:20 and reaches out her **h** to the needy.
31:31 Give her a share in the fruit of her **h,**
Ecc 2:11 Then I considered all that my **h** had done and
4: 5 Fools fold their **h** and consume their own flesh.
5: 6 and destroy the work of your **h?**
5:14 they have nothing in their **h.**
5:15 which they may carry away with their **h.**
7:26 whose heart is snares and nets, whose **h** are fetters;
11: 6 and at evening do not let your **h** be idle;
SS 5: 5 and my **h** dripped with myrrh,
Isa 1:15 When you stretch out your **h,**
1:15 your **h** are full of blood.
2: 6 and they clasp **h** with foreigners.
2: 8 they bow down to the work of their **h,**
3:11 for what their **h** have done shall be done to them.
5:12 or see the work of his **h!**
10: 5 the club in their **h** is my fury!
13: 7 Therefore all **h** will be feeble,
17: 8 not have regard for the altars, the work of their **h,**
19:25 and Assyria the work of my **h,**
25:11 Though they spread out their **h** in the midst of it,
25:11 as swimmers spread out their **h** to swim,
25:11 be laid low despite the struggle of their **h.**
29:23 For when he sees his children, the work of my **h,**
31: 7 which your **h** have sinfully made for you.
35: 3 Strengthen the weak **h,** and make firm
37:19 but the work of human **h**— D
45:11 or command me concerning the work of my **h?**
45:12 it was my **h** that stretched out the heavens,
49:16 See, I have inscribed you on the palms of my **h;**
55:12 and all the trees of the field shall clap their **h.**
59: 3 For your **h** are defiled with blood,
59: 6 and deeds of violence are in their **h.**
60:21 the work of my **h,** so that I might be glorified.
65: 2 I held out my **h** all day long to a rebellious people,
65:22 my chosen shall long enjoy the work of their **h.**
Jer 1:16 and worshiped the works of their own **h.**
2:37 you will come away with your **h** on your head; B
4:31 stretching out her **h,** "Woe is me!
6:24 "We have heard news of them, our **h** fall helpless;
10: 3 and worked with an ax by the **h** of an artisan;
10: 9 They are the work of the artisan and of the **h** of
12: 7 beloved of my heart into the **h** of her enemies. A

Jer 20:13 the life of the needy from the **h** of evildoers. C
21: 4 to turn back the weapons of war that are in your **h**
21: 7 into the **h** of King Nebuchadrezzar of Babylon, A
21: 7 into the **h** of their enemies, A
21: 7 into the **h** of those who seek their lives. A
21:10 shall be given into the **h** of the king of Babylon, A
22:25 give you into the **h** of those who seek your life, A
22:25 into the **h** of those of whom you are afraid, A
22:25 into the **h** of King Nebuchadrezzar of Babylon A
22:25 of Babylon and into the **h** of the Chaldeans. A
23:14 they strengthen the **h** of evildoers,
25: 6 not provoke me to anger with the work of your **h.**
25: 7 with the work of your **h** to your own harm.
25:14 according to their deeds and the work of their **h.**
26:14 But as for me, here I am in your **h.**
26:24 he was not given over into the **h** of the people A
30: 6 do I see every man with his **h** on his loins like B
31:11 has redeemed him from **h** too strong for him. C
32: 4 of the **h** of the Chaldeans, but shall surely be
32: 4 given into the **h** of the king of Babylon, A
32:24 into the **h** of the Chaldeans who are fighting A
32:25 city has been given into the **h** of the Chaldeans. A
32:28 to give this city into the **h** of the Chaldeans and A
32:30 but provoke me to anger by the work of their **h,**
32:43 it has been given into the **h** of the Chaldeans. A
33:13 under the **h** of the one who counts them,
38: 5 King Zedekiah said, "Here he is; he is in your **h;**
40: 4 from the fetters on your **h.**
43: 9 Take some large stones in your **h,**
44: 8 to anger with the works of your **h,**
44:30 into the **h** of his enemies, those who seek his A
47: 3 not turn back for children, so feeble are their **h,**
48:37 on all the **h** there are gashes,
50:43 of them, and his **h** fell helpless;
La 1:10 Enemies have stretched out their **h**
1:17 Zion stretches out her **h,** but there is no one
2:15 All who pass along the way clap their **h** at you;
2:19 Lift your **h** to him for the lives of your children,
3:41 up our hearts as well as our **h** to God in heaven.
3:64 O LORD, according to the work of their **h!**
4: 2 as earthen pots, the work of a potter's **h!**
4:10 The **h** of compassionate women have boiled their
5:12 Princes are hung up by their **h;**
Eze 1: 8 on their four sides they had human **h.** D
6:11 Clap your **h** and stamp your foot, and say,
7:17 All **h** shall grow feeble, all knees turn to water.
7:27 and the **h** of the people of the land shall tremble.
10: 2 fill your **h** with burning coals from among
10: 7 and put it into the **h** of the man clothed in linen, A
10:21 underneath their wings something like human **h.** D
11: 9 I will take you out of it and give you over to the **h**
12: 7 through the wall with my own **h;**
13:21 and save my people from your **h;** C
13:21 they shall no longer be prey in your **h;**
16:39 I will deliver you into their **h,** A
21: 7 Every heart will melt and all **h** will be feeble,
21:31 I will deliver you into brutish **h,** A
22:13 I strike my **h** together at
22:14 or can your **h** remain strong in the days
23: 9 I delivered her into the **h** of her lovers, A
23: 9 into the **h** of the Assyrians, for whom she lusted. A
23:28 into the **h** of those whom you hate, A
23:28 into the **h** of those from whom you turned A
23:37 and blood is on their **h;**
23:45 they are adulteresses and blood is on their **h.**
25: 6 Because you have clapped your **h**
28: 9 and no god, in the **h** of those who wound you?
34:27 from the **h** of those who enslaved them. C
Da 2:34 a stone was cut out, not by human **h,** D
2:45 that a stone was cut from the mountain not by **h,**
3:15 who is the god that will deliver you out of my **h?"**
8:25 But he shall be broken, and not by human **h.** D
10:10 then a hand touched me and roused me to my **h**
Hos 12: 7 A trader, in whose **h** are false balances,
14: 3 'Our God,' to the work of our **h.**
Jnh 3: 8 and from the violence that is in their **h.**
Mic 4:10 there the LORD will redeem you from the **h** C
5:13 down no more to the work of your **h;**
7: 3 Their **h** are skilled to do evil;
7:16 they shall lay their **h** on their mouths; B
Na 3:19 All who hear the news about you clap their **h**
Hab 3:10 The sun raised high its **h;**
Zep 3:16 do not let your **h** grow weak.
Hag 2:14 and so with every work of their **h;**
Zec 4: 9 "The **h** of Zerubbabel have laid the foundation
4: 9 his **h** shall also complete it.
8: 9 of hosts: Let your **h** be strong—
8:13 Do not be afraid, but let your **h** be strong.
Mal 1:10 and I will not accept an offering from your **h.** C
Mt 4: 6 and 'On their **h** they will bear you up,
15: 2 For they do not wash their **h** before they eat."
15:20 but to eat with unwashed **h** does not defile."
16:21 at the **h** of the elders and chief priests and scribes,
17:12 the Son of Man is about to suffer at their **h."**
17:22 of Man is going to be betrayed into human **h,** AD
18: 8 to enter life maimed or lame than to have two **h**
19:13 that he might lay his **h** on them and pray. B
19:15 And he laid his **h** on them and went on his way. B
26:45 the Son of Man is betrayed into the **h** of sinners. A
26:50 they came and laid **h** on Jesus and arrested him. B
27:24 he took some water and washed his **h** before
Mk 5:23 Come and lay your **h** on her, B
6: 2 What deeds of power are being done by his **h!**
6: 5 except that he laid his **h** on a few sick people B
7: 2 of his disciples were eating with defiled **h,**
7: 3 do not eat unless they thoroughly wash their **h,**
7: 5 the tradition of the elders, but eat with defiled **h?"**
Mk 8:23 put saliva on his eyes and laid his **h** on him, B
8:25 Then Jesus laid his **h** on his eyes again; B
9:31 Son of Man is to be betrayed into human **h,** AD
9:43 to enter life maimed than to have two **h** and to go
10:16 he took them up in his arms, laid his **h** on them, B
14:41 the Son of Man is betrayed into the **h** of sinners. A
14:46 Then they laid **h** on him and arrested him. B
14:58 'I will destroy this temple that is made with **h,**
14:58 three days I will build another, not made with **h.' "**
16:18 ⟦they will pick up snakes in their **h,**⟧
16:18 ⟦they will lay their **h** on the sick,⟧ B
Lk 1:74 being rescued from the **h** of our enemies, C
4:11 and 'On their **h** they will bear you up,
4:40 he laid his **h** on each of them and cured them. B
6: 1 rubbed them in their **h,** and ate them.
9:44 of Man is going to be betrayed into human **h."** AD
10:30 and fell into the **h** of robbers, who stripped him, A
10:36 was a neighbor to the man who fell into the **h** of A
13:13 When he laid his **h** on her, B
15:17 of my father's hired **h** have bread enough and
15:19 treat me like one of your hired **h." '**
20:19 they wanted to lay **h** on him at that very hour, B
22:53 you did not lay **h** on me. B
23:46 said, "Father, into your **h** I commend my spirit." A
24:39 Look at my **h** and my feet; see that it is I myself.
24:40 he had said this, he showed them his **h** and his feet.
24:50 and, lifting up his **h,** he blessed them.
Jn 3:35 the Son and has placed all things in his **h.**
7:30 tried to arrest him, but no one laid **h** on him, B
7:44 but no one laid **h** on him. B
10:39 but he escaped from their **h.** C
11:44 his **h** and feet bound with strips of cloth,
13: 3 that the Father had given all things into his **h,** A
13: 9 not my feet only but also my **h** and my head!"
20:20 he said this, he showed them his **h** and his side.
20:25 "Unless I see the mark of the nails in his **h,**
20:27 "Put your finger here and see my **h.**
21:18 when you grow old, you will stretch out your **h,**
Ac 2:23 you crucified and killed by the **h** of those outside
6: 6 who prayed and laid their **h** on them. B
7:41 and reveled in the works of their **h.**
7:48 not dwell in houses made with human **h;** D
8:17 Then Peter and John laid their **h** on them, B
8:18 through the laying on of the apostles' **h,**
8:19 on whom I lay my **h** may receive the Holy Spirit."
9:12 a man named Ananias come in and lay his **h** on B
9:17 He laid his **h** on Saul and said, "Brother Saul, B
12: 1 About that time King Herod laid violent **h**
12:11 and rescued me from the **h** of Herod and from C
13: 3 fasting and praying they laid their **h** on them B
17:24 does not live in shrines made by human **h,** D
17:25 nor is he served by human **h,** D
19: 6 When Paul had laid his **h** on them, B
19:26 of people by saying that gods made with **h** are
20:34 that I worked with my own **h** to support myself
21:11 bound his own feet and **h** with it, and said,
27:19 and on the third day with their own **h** they threw
28: 8 cured him by praying and putting his **h** on him. B
Ro 10:21 "All day long I have held out my **h** to a disobedient
1Co 4:12 and we grow weary from the work of our own **h.**
15:24 when he **h** over the kingdom to God the Father,
2Co 5: 1 a house not made with **h,** eternal in the heavens.
11:33 a window in the wall, and escaped from his **h.** C
Eph 2:11 in the flesh by human **h—** D
4:28 and work honestly with their own **h,**
1Th 4:11 to mind your own affairs, and to work with your **h,**
1Ti 2: 8 lifting up holy **h** without anger or argument;
4:14 to you through prophecy with the laying on of **h** by
2Ti 1: 6 that is within you through the laying on of my **h;**
Heb 1:10 and the heavens are the work of your **h;**
6: 2 laying on of **h,** resurrection of the dead,
9:11 the greater and perfect tent (not made with **h,**
9:24 did not enter a sanctuary made by human **h,** D
10:31 fearful thing to fall into the **h** of the living God. A
12:12 Therefore lift your drooping **h**
Jas 4: 8 Cleanse your **h,** you sinners,
1Jn 1: 1 what we have looked at and touched with our **h,**
Rev 7: 9 robed in white, with palm branches in their **h.**
9:20 the works of their **h** or give up worshiping demons
14: 9 receive a mark on their foreheads or on their **h,**
15: 2 beside the sea of glass with harps of God in their **h.**
20: 4 not received its mark on their foreheads or their **h.**
Tob 3:11 with **h** outstretched toward the window,
11:13 with both his **h** he peeled off the white films from
13: 9 he afflicted you for the deeds of your **h,**
13:11 bearing gifts in their **h** for the King of heaven.
Jdt 7:25 God has sold us into their **h,** A
8:18 or town of ours that worships gods made with **h,**
11:13 for any of the people even to touch with their **h.**
11:22 to strengthen our **h** and bring destruction
13: 4 in this hour on the work of my **h** for the exaltation
15:12 She took ivy-wreathed wands in her **h**
16: 2 he delivered me from the **h** of my pursuers. C
16: 6 not fall by the **h** of the young men, nor did the sons
AdE 6: 2 and sought to lay **h** on King Artaxerxes. B
12: 2 and learned that they were preparing to lay **h** on B
14:19 and save us from the **h** of evildoers. C
Wis 1:12 or bring on destruction by the works of your **h;**
3:14 the eunuch whose **h** have done no lawless deed,
7:11 and in her **h** uncounted wealth.
8:12 they will put their **h** on their mouths. B
8:18 and in the labors of her **h,** unfailing wealth,
12: 6 you willed to destroy by the **h** of our ancestors,
12: 9 the ungodly into the **h** of the righteous in battle, A
13:10 the name "gods" to the works of human **h,** D
13:19 and work and success with his **h** he asks strength
of a thing whose **h** have no strength.
Wis 14: 8 But the idol made with **h** is accursed,
15:17 and what they make with lawless **h** is dead;
Sir 2:12 Woe to timid hearts and to slack **h,**
2:17 Let us fall into the **h** of the Lord, A
2:17 but not into the **h** of mortals; A
8: 1 or you may fall into their **h.** A
12:18 Then he will shake his head, and clap his **h,**
25:23 Drooping **h** and weak knees come from
29: 5 One kisses another's **h** until he gets a loan,
33:26 leave his **h** idle, and he will seek liberty.
35:10 and do not stint the first fruits of your **h.**
38:10 Give up your faults and direct your **h** rightly,
38:13 There may come a time when recovery lies in the **h**
38:31 All these rely on their **h,**
42: 6 and where there are many **h,** lock things up.
43:12 the **h** of the Most High have stretched it out.
46: 2 when he lifted his **h** and brandished his sword
48:19 their hearts were shaken and their **h** trembled,
48:20 spreading out their **h** toward him.
50:12 received the portions from the **h** of the priests, C
50:13 in their splendor held the Lord's offering in their **h**
50:20 down and raised his **h** over the whole congregation
51:19 I spread out my **h** to the heavens,
LtJ 6:51 that they are not gods but the work of human **h,** D
Sus 1:22 if I do not, I cannot escape your **h.**
1:23 I choose not to do it; I will fall into your **h,** A
1:34 before the people and laid their **h** on her head. B
Bel 1: 5 "Because I do not revere idols made with **h,**
1Mc 2:47 and the work prospered in their **h.**
2:48 They rescued the law out of the **h** of the Gentiles
4:30 Philistines into the **h** of Jonathan son of Saul, A
5:12 Now then, come and rescue us from their **h,** C
5:50 and the town was delivered into his **h.** A
6:25 that they have stretched out their **h;**
7:35 and his army are delivered into my **h** this time, A
9:46 to Heaven that you may be delivered from the **h** C
12: 9 encouragement the holy books that are in our **h,**
14:31 to invade their country and lay **h** on their B
14:36 In his days things prospered in his **h,**
16: 2 until this day, and things have prospered in our **h**
2Mc 3:20 And holding up their **h** to heaven,
5:16 He took the holy vessels with his polluted **h,**
5:16 with profane **h** the votive offerings
6:26 yet whether I live or die I shall not escape the **h** of
7: 4 be cut out and that they scalp him and cut off his **h**
7:10 and courageously stretched forth his **h,**
7:14 but choose to die at the **h** of mortals and to cherish
7:31 will certainly not escape the **h** of God.
12:24 into the **h** of Dositheus and Sosipater and their A
12:28 and they got the town into their **h,** A
13:11 into the **h** of the blasphemous Gentiles. A
14:34 the priests stretched out their **h** toward heaven
14:42 to die nobly rather than to fall into the **h** A
14:46 took them in both **h** and hurled them at the crowd,
15:12 with outstretched **h** for the whole body of the Jews.
15:21 stretched out his **h** toward heaven and called upon
15:27 with their **h** and praying to God in their hearts,
1Es 1:53 man or child, for he gave them all into their **h.** A
6:10 in their **h** and being completed with all splendor
6:15 into the **h** of King Nebuchadnezzar of Babylon, A
6:33 and nation that shall stretch out their **h** to hinder
7:15 to strengthen their **h** for the service of
8:73 kneeling down and stretching out my **h** to the Lord
9:47 up their **h,** and fell to the ground and worshiped
Pm 151: 2 My **h** made a harp; my fingers fashioned a lyre.
3Mc 2: 1 and extending his **h** with calm dignity, prayed
2: 8 And when they had seen works of your **h,**
5: 5 the Jews went out in the evening and bound the **h**
5:25 stretched their **h** toward heaven and
7:10 of the king that at their own **h** those of
2Es 1:26 for you have defiled your **h** with blood,
2:46 on them and putting palms in their **h?"**
3: 5 Yet he was the creation of your **h,**
5:30 they should be punished at your own **h."**
6:58 and most dear, have been given into their **h.** A
8: 7 For you alone exist, and we are a work of your **h,**
8:44 by your **h** and are called your own image
10:23 and given over into the **h** of those that hate us. A
13:36 as you saw the mountain carved out without **h.**
15:15 up to fight against nation, with swords in their **h.**
15:53 and clapping your **h** and talking about their death
4Mc 4:11 stretched out his **h** toward heaven,
9:11 they bound his **h** and arms with thongs
9:28 with the iron **h,** flayed all his flesh up to his chin,
10: 5 they disjointed his **h** and feet
14: 6 Just as the **h** and feet are moved in harmony with
15:20 severed **h** upon **h,** scalped heads upon heads,
17:19 "All who are consecrated are under your **h."**

HANDSOME (15)

Ge 39: 6 Now Joseph was **h** and good-looking.
1Sa 9: 2 a son whose name was Saul, a **h** young man.
9: 2 a man among the people of Israel more **h** than he;
16:12 he was ruddy, and had beautiful eyes, and was **h.**
17:42 ruddy and **h** in appearance.
2Sa 23:21 And he killed an Egyptian, a **h** man.
1Ki 1: 6 He was also a very **h** man,
Ps 45: 2 You are the most **h** of men;
Eze 23: 6 all of them **h** young men, mounted horsemen.
23:12 mounted horsemen, all of them **h** young men.
23:23 and all the Assyrians with them, **h** young men,
Da 1: 4 and **h,** versed in every branch of wisdom, endowed
Pm 151: 5 My brothers were **h** and tall,
4Mc 8: 3 **h,** modest, noble, and accomplished
8:10 have compassion for your youth and **h** appearance.

HANDSTAVES (KJV) See HANDPIKES

HANDYWORK (KJV) See HANDIWORK

HANES (1)
Isa 30: 4 his officials are at Zoan and his envoys reach **H,**

HANG (22) [HANGED, HANGING, HANGINGS, HANGS, HUNG]
Ge 40:19 and **h** you on a pole;
Ex 26:12 shall **h** over the back of the tabernacle.
26:13 shall **h** over the sides of the tabernacle,
26:32 You shall **h** it on four pillars of acacia overlaid
26:33 You shall **h** the curtain under the clasps,
40: 8 and **h** up the screen for the gate of the court.
Dt 21:22 and you **h** him on a tree,
28:66 Your life shall **h** in doubt before you;
Est 7: 9 And the king said, **"H** him on that."
Pr 26: 7 The legs of a disabled person **h** limp;
SS 4: 4 on it **h** a thousand bucklers,
Isa 22:24 And they will **h** on him the whole weight
Eze 15: 3 a peg from it on which to **h** any object?
Mt 22:40 On these two commandments **h** all the law and
Tob 3:10 her father's upper room, she intended to **h** herself.
3:10 It is better for me not to **h** myself,
6: 4 "Catch hold of the fish and **h** on to it!"
Jdt 14: 1 Take this head and **h** it upon the parapet
AdE 9:13 Also, **h** up the bodies of Haman's ten sons."
9:14 of the city the bodies of Haman's sons to **h** up.
9:25 telling him to **h** Mordecai;
2Mc 15:33 and would **h** up these rewards of his folly opposite

HANGED (22) [HANG]
Ge 40:22 but the chief baker he **h,**
41:13 I was restored to my office, and the baker was **h."**
Jos 8:29 And he **h** the king of Ai on a tree until evening;
2Sa 17:23 He set his house in order, and **h** himself;
Est 2:23 both the men were **h** on the gallows.
5:14 the morning tell the king to have Mordecai **h** on it;
6: 4 the king about having Mordecai **h** on the gallows
7:10 So they **h** Haman on the gallows
8: 7 and they have **h** him on the gallows,
9:13 let the ten sons of Haman be **h** on the gallows."
9:14 and the ten sons of Haman were **h.**
9:25 that he and his sons should be **h** on the gallows.
Mt 27: 5 and he went and **h** himself.
Lk 23:39 the criminals who were **h** there kept deriding him
Tob 3:10 but she **h** herself because of her distress.'
AdE 2:23 He investigated the two eunuchs and **h** them.
5:14 the morning tell the king to have Mordecai **h** on it.
7: 9 So the king said, "Let Haman be **h** on that."
7:10 So Haman was **h** on the gallows he had prepared
8: 7 and have **h** him on a tree because he acted against
9:25 and he and his sons were **h.**
16:18 has been **h** at the gate of Susa

HANGING‡ (7) [HANG]
2Sa 18: 9 and he was left **h** between heaven and earth,
18:10 and told Joab, "I saw Absalom **h** in an oak."
Ac 5:30 whom you had killed by **h** him on a tree.
10:39 They put him to death by **h** him on a tree;
28: 4 When the natives saw the creature **h** from his hand,
AdE 6: 4 to the king about **h** Mordecai on the gallows
2Mc 6:10 with their babies **h** at their breasts,

HANGINGS (18) [HANG]
Ex 27: 9 On the south side the court shall have **h**
27:11 be **h** one hundred cubits long,
27:12 on the west side there shall be fifty cubits of **h,**
27:14 There shall be fifteen cubits of **h** on the one side,
27:15 There shall be fifteen cubits of **h** on the other side,
27:18 with **h** of fine twisted linen and bases of bronze.
35:17 the **h** of the court, its pillars and its bases,
38: 9 the **h** of the court were of fine twisted linen,
38:11 north side there were **h** one hundred cubits long;
38:12 For the west side there were **h** fifty cubits long,
38:14 The **h** for one side of the gate were fifteen cubits,
38:15 of the gate of the court were **h** of fifteen cubits,
38:16 the **h** around the court were of fine twisted linen.
38:18 corresponding to the **h** of the court.
39:40 the **h** of the court, its pillars, and its bases,
Nu 3:26 the **h** of the court, the screen for the entrance of
4:26 the **h** of the court, and the screen for the entrance
Est 1: 6 and blue **h** tied with cords of fine linen and purple

HANGS (3) [HANG]
Job 26: 7 and **h** the earth upon nothing.
Isa 33:23 Your rigging **h** loose; it cannot hold the mast firm
Gal 3:13 "Cursed is everyone who **h** on a tree"—

HANIEL (KJV) See HANNIEL

HANNA See Index to Footnotes

HANNAH (13)
1Sa 1: 2 He had two wives; the name of the one was **H,**
1: 2 Peninnah had children, but **H** had no children.
1: 5 but to **H** he gave a double portion,
1: 7 Therefore **H** wept and would not eat.
1: 8 Her husband Elkanah said to her, **"H,**
1: 9 **H** rose and presented herself before the LORD.
1Sa 1:13 **H** was praying silently; only her lips moved,
1:15 But **H** answered, "No, my lord,
1:19 Elkanah knew his wife **H,** and
1:20 In due time **H** conceived and bore a son.
1:22 But **H** did not go up, for she said to her husband,
2: 1 **H** prayed and said, "My heart exults in the LORD;
2:21 And the LORD took note of **H;**

HANNATHON (1)
Jos 19:14 then on the north the boundary makes a turn to **H,**

HANNIEL (2)
Nu 34:23 of the tribe of the Manassites a leader, **H** son
1Ch 7:39 The sons of Ulla: Arah, **H,** and Rizia.

HANOCH (6) [HANOCHITES]
Ge 25: 4 The sons of Midian were Ephah, Epher, **H,** Abida,
46: 9 **H,** Pallu, Hezron, and Carmi.
Ex 6:14 **H,** Pallu, Hezron, and Carmi;
Nu 26: 5 of **H,** the clan of the Hanochites;
1Ch 1:33 Ephah, Epher, **H,** Abida, and Eldaah.
5: 3 **H,** Pallu, Hezron, and Carmi.

HANOCHITES (1) [HANOCH]
Nu 26: 5 of Hanoch, the clan of the **H;**

HANUN (11)
2Sa 10: 1 and his son **H** succeeded him.
10: 2 "I will deal loyally with **H** son of Nahash,
10: 3 the princes of the Ammonites said to their lord **H,**
10: 4 So **H** seized David's envoys,
1Ch 19: 2 "I will deal loyally with **H** son of Nahash,
19: 2 When David's servants came to **H** in the land of
19: 3 the officials of the Ammonites said to **H,**
19: 4 So **H** seized David's servants, shaved them,
19: 6 **H** and the Ammonites sent a thousand talents
Ne 3:13 **H** and the inhabitants of Zanoah repaired
3:30 and **H** sixth son of Zalaph repaired another section.

HAP (KJV) See HAPPENED

HAPHARAIM (1)
Jos 19:19 **H,** Shion, Anaharath,

HAPLY (KJV) See BETTER, IN THAT CASE, OTHERWISE, PERHAPS

HAPPEN (34) [HAPPENED, HAPPENING, HAPPENS]
Ge 49: 1 I may tell you what will **h** to you in days to come.
Ex 2: 4 to see what would **h** to him.
Dt 12:13 not offer your burnt offerings at any place you **h**
1Ki 14: 3 he will tell you what shall **h** to the child."
2Ki 7: 2 in the sky, could such a thing **h?"**
7:19 in the sky, could such a thing **h?"**
7:20 It did indeed **h** to him;
Job 37:13 or for his land, or for love, he causes it to **h.**
Ecc 2:15 "What happens to the fool will **h** to me also;
9:11 but time and chance **h** to them all.
10:14 No one knows what is to **h,**
11: 2 for you do not know what disaster may **h** on earth.
Isa 23:15 it will **h** to Tyre as in the song about the prostitute:
41:22 Let them bring them, and tell us what is to **h.**
Jer 6:18 and know, O congregation, what will **h** to them.
38:20 Jeremiah said, "That will not **h.**
Eze 20:32 What is in your mind shall never **h—**
21:13 If you despise the rod, will it not **h?**
Da 2:28 to King Nebuchadnezzar what will **h** at the end
10:14 and have come to help you understand what is to **h**
Zec 6:15 This will **h** if you diligently obey the voice of
Mt 16:22 This must never **h** to you."
26:54 which say it must **h** in this way?"
Mk 10:32 and began to tell them what was to **h** to him,
Lk 23:31 what will **h** when it is dry?"
Jn 18: 4 Then Jesus, knowing all that was to **h** to him,
Ac 8:24 that nothing of what you have said may **h** to me."
13:40 that what the prophets said does not **h** to you:
20:22 not knowing what will **h** to me there,
AdE 2:11 to see what would **h** to Esther.
Wis 2:17 and let us test what will **h** at the end of his life;
2Mc 9:25 for opportunities and waiting to see what will **h.**
2Es 13:20 and not to see what will **h** in the last days."
14:16 now seen **h** shall take place hereafter.

HAPPENED (110) [HAPPEN]
Ge 38: 1 It **h** at that time that Judah went down
42:29 they told him all that had **h** to them, saying,
42:36 All this has **h** to me!"
Dt 4:30 all these things have **h** to you in time to come,
4:32 as this ever **h** or has its like ever been heard of?
30: 1 When all these things have **h** to you,
Jos 2:23 and told him all that had **h** to them.
Jdg 6:13 why then has all this **h** to us?
9:24 This **h** so that the violence done to
19:30 a thing ever **h** since the day that the Israelites came
Ru 2: 3 As it **h,** she came to the part of the field belonging
1Sa 4: 7 For nothing like this has **h** before.
6: 9 it **h** to us by chance."
2Sa 1: 6 "I **h** to be on Mount Gilboa;
4: 4 it **h** that he fell and became lame.
11: 2 It **h,** late one afternoon, when David rose
2Sa 18: 9 Absalom **h** to meet the servants of David.
20: 1 a Benjaminite, **h** to be there.
1Ki 2:39 But it **h** at the end of three years that two
2Ki 15:12 to the fourth generation." And so it **h.**
Est 1: 1 This **h** in the days of Ahasuerus,
4: 7 and Mordecai told him all that had **h** to him,
6:13 and all his friends everything that had **h** to him,
9:26 and of what had **h** to them,
Isa 20: 6 this is what has **h** to those in whom we hoped and
Jer 5:30 An appalling and horrible thing has **h** in the land:
32:24 What you spoke has **h,** as you yourself can see.
38: 7 The king **h** to be sitting at the Benjamin Gate,
41: 3 and the Chaldean soldiers who **h** to be there.
48:19 and the woman escaping; say, "What has **h?"**
Eze 39: 8 It has **h,** says the Lord GOD.
Joel 1: 2 Has such a thing **h** in your days,
Mic 6: 5 and what **h** from Shittim to Gilgal,
Mt 8:33 they told the whole story about what had **h** to
18:31 When his fellow slaves saw what had **h,**
28:11 and told the chief priests everything that had **h.**
Mk 5:14 Then people came to see what it was that had **h.**
5:16 Those who had seen what had **h** to the demoniac
5:33 But the woman, knowing what had **h** to her,
Lk 1:43 And why has this **h** to me,
8:34 When the swineherds saw what had **h,**
8:35 Then people came out to see what had **h,**
8:56 but he ordered them to tell no one what had **h.**
24:12 then he went home, amazed at what had **h.**
24:14 with each other about all these things that had **h.**
24:35 Then they told what had **h** on the road,
Ac 3:10 with wonder and amazement at what had **h** to him.
4:21 for all of them praised God for what had **h.**
5: 7 in, not knowing what had **h.**
7:40 we do not know what has **h** to him.'
10:16 This **h** three times, and the thing was suddenly
11:10 This **h** three times; then everything was pulled up
13:12 When the proconsul saw what had **h,** he believed,
17:17 also in the marketplace every day with those who **h**
28: 6 a long time and saw that nothing unusual had **h**
28: 8 It so **h** that the father of Publius lay sick in bed
28: 9 After this **h,** the rest of the people on
Ro 9:10 something similar **h** to Rebecca
1Co 10:11 These things **h** to them to serve as an example,
Php 1:12 that what has **h** to me has actually helped to spread
2Ti 3:11 and suffering the things that **h** to me in Antioch,
2Pe 2:22 It has **h** to them according to the true proverb,
Tob 3: 7 it also **h** that Sarah, the daughter of Raguel,
10: 6 Probably something unexpected has **h** there.
12:20 Write down all these things that have **h** to you."
Jdt 6:16 and Uzziah questioned him about what had **h.**
8:26 and what **h** to Jacob in Syrian Mesopotamia,
9: 5 What you had in mind has **h;**
15: 1 they were amazed at what had **h.**
15: 5 for they were told what had **h** in the camp of
AdE 1: 1 the following things **h** in the days of Artaxerxes,
4: 4 she was deeply troubled by what she heard had **h,**
4: 7 So Mordecai told him what had **h** and
10: 9 wonders that have never **h** among the nations.
Wis 19: 4 and made them forget what had **h,**
Sir 5: 4 Do not say, "I sinned, yet what has **h** to me?"
48:25 and the hidden things before they **h.**
Sus 1:26 they rushed in at the side door to see what had **h**
1Mc 4:20 for the smoke that was seen showed what had **h.**
4:26 and reported to Lysias all that had **h.**
4:27 for things had not **h** to Israel as he had intended,
5:25 and told them all that had **h** to their kindred
2Mc 4:30 it **h** that the people of Tarsus and
4:32 other vessels, as it **h,** he had sold to Tyre and
5: 2 And it **h** that, for almost forty days,
5:11 When news of what had **h** reached the king,
5:18 it had not **h** that they were involved in many sins,
7: 1 It **h** also that seven brothers
7:18 Therefore astounding things have **h.**
9: 1 About that time, as it **h,** Antiochus had retreated
9: 3 news came to him of what had **h** to Nicanor and
9:24 so that, if anything unexpected **h**
10: 5 It **h** that on the same day on which
10:21 When word of what had **h** came to Maccabeus,
11: 1 being vexed at what had **h,**
12:31 they joined battle, it **h** that a few of the Jews fell.
12:42 for they had seen with their own eyes what had **h**
13:17 This **h,** just as day was dawning,
1Es 1:25 After all these acts of Josiah, it **h** that Pharaoh,
8:86 And all that has **h** to us has come about because
3Mc 1: 8 and to congratulate him on what had **h,**
1:15 "But since this has **h,"** the king said,
4:12 And when this had **h,** the king,
7: 8 for the irrational things that have **h.**
2Es 9:42 I said to her, "What has **h** to you? Tell me."
10: 1 "But it **h** that when my son entered his wedding
10: 6 and what has **h** to us?
10:49 and you began to console her for what had **h.**
14:22 and I will write everything that has **h** in the world
4Mc 4:14 went away to report to the king what had **h** to him.

HAPPENING (7) [HAPPEN]
Est 4: 5 to go to Mordecai to learn what was **h** and why.
Ecc 8:17 that no one can find out what is **h** under the sun.
Mk 9:21 "How long has this been **h** to him?"
Lk 18:36 he heard a crowd going by, he asked what was **h.**
Ac 12: 9 that what was **h** with the angel's help was real;
1Pe 4:12 as though something strange were **h** to you.
4Mc 14: 9 they not only saw what was **h,**

HAPPENS (9) [HAPPEN]
Ex 22: 3 but if it **h** after sunrise, bloodguilt is incurred.

Pr 12:21 No harm **h** to the righteous,
Ecc 2:15 "What **h** to the fool will happen to me also;
9:3 This is an evil in all that **h** under the sun,
9:6 never again will they have any share in all that **h**
Lk 12:54 'It is going to rain'; and so it **h.**
12:55 be scorching heat'; and it **h.**
Jn 5:14 so that nothing worse **h** to you."
Sir 37:9 and then stand aside to see what **h** to you.

HAPPIER (1) [HAPPY]
La 4:9 **H** were those pierced by the sword than those

HAPPILY (1) [HAPPY]
2Mc 11:26 and be of good cheer and go on **h** in the conduct

HAPPINESS (6) [HAPPY]
La 3:17 I have forgotten what **h** is;
Tob 8:17 bring their lives to fulfillment in **h** and mercy."
10:13 Tobias parted from Raguel with **h** and joy,
Sir 8:19 or you may drive away your **h.**
37:4 Some companions rejoice in the **h** of a friend,
4Mc 16:9 or have the **h** of being called grandmother.

HAPPIZZEZ (1)
1Ch 24:15 the seventeenth to Hezir, the eighteenth to **H,**

HAPPY‡ (90) [HAPPIER, HAPPILY, HAPPINESS]
Ge 30:13 And Leah said, **"H** am I!
30:13 women will call me **h";** so she named him Asher.
Dt 24:5 to be **h** with the wife whom he has married.
33:29 **H** are you, O Israel!
1Ki 4:20 they ate and drank and were **h.**
10:8 **H** are your wives! **H** are these your servants,
2Ch 9:7 **H** are your people! **H** are these your servants,
Est 5:9 Haman went out that day **h** and in good spirits.
Job 5:17 "How **h** is the one whom God reproves;
8:19 See, these are their **h** ways,
Ps 1:1 **H** are those who do not follow the advice of
2:12 **H** are all who take refuge in him.
32:1 **H** are those whose transgression is forgiven,
32:2 **H** are those to whom the LORD imputes no iniquity,
33:12 **H** is the nation whose God is the LORD,
34:8 **h** are those who take refuge in him.
40:4 **H** are those who make the LORD their trust,
41:1 **H** are those who consider the poor;
41:2 they are called **h** in the land.
49:18 Though in their lifetime they count themselves **h**
65:4 **H** are those whom you choose and bring near
72:17 may they pronounce him **h.**
84:4 **H** are those who live in your house,
84:5 **H** are those whose strength is in you,
84:12 **h** is everyone who trusts in you.
89:15 **H** are the people who know the festal shout,
94:12 **H** are those whom you discipline, O LORD,
106:3 **H** are those who observe justice,
112:1 **H** are those who fear the LORD,
119:1 **H** are those whose way is blameless,
119:2 **H** are those who keep his decrees,
127:5 **H** is the man who has his quiver full of them.
128:1 **H** is everyone who fears the LORD,
128:2 you shall be **h,** and it shall go well with you.
137:8 **H** shall they be who pay you back what you have
137:9 **H** shall they be who take your little ones
144:15 **H** are the people to whom such blessings fall;
144:15 **h** are the people whose God is the LORD.
146:5 **H** are those whose help is the God of Jacob,
Pr 3:13 **H** are those who find wisdom,
3:18 those who hold her fast are called **h.**
8:32 **h** are those who keep my ways.
8:34 **H** is the one who listens to me,
14:21 but **h** are those who are kind to the poor.
16:20 and **h** are those who trust in the LORD.
20:7 **h** are the children who follow them!
28:14 **H** is the one who is never without fear,
29:18 but **h** are those who keep the law.
31:28 Her children rise up and call her **h;**
Ecc 3:12 for them than to be **h** and enjoy themselves as long
10:17 **H** are you, O land, when your king is a nobleman,
SS 6:9 The maidens saw her and called her **h;**
Isa 32:20 **H** will you be who sow beside every stream,
56:2 **H** is the mortal who does this,
Da 12:12 **H** are those who persevere and attain
Jnh 4:6 so Jonah was very **h** about the bush.
Mal 3:12 Then all nations will count you **h,**
3:15 Now we count the arrogant **h;**
Lk 19:6 So he hurried down and was **h** to welcome him.
Tob 13:14 **H** are those who love you, and **h** are those who rejoice in your prosperity.
13:14 **H** also are all people who grieve with you because
13:16 How **h** I will be if a remnant
AdE 15:5 and she looked **h,** as if beloved,
Wis 2:16 he calls the last end of the righteous **h,**
18:1 and counted them **h** for not having suffered,
Sir 1:13 Those who fear the Lord will have a **h** end;
11:28 Call no one **h** before his death;
13:26 The sign of a **h** heart is a cheerful face,
14:1 **H** are those who do not blunder with their lips,
14:2 **H** are those whose hearts do not condemn them,
14:20 **H** is the person who meditates on wisdom
25:8 **H** the man who lives with a sensible wife,
25:8 **H** is the one who does not sin with the tongue,
25:9 **H** is the one who finds a friend,
25:23 from the wife who does not make her husband **h.**
Sir 26:1 **H** is the husband of a good wife;
26:26 ***H** is the husband of a good wife;*
28:19 **H** is the one who is protected from it,
31:27 It has been created to make people **h.**
34:17 **H** is the soul that fears the Lord!
37:24 and all who see him will call him **h.**
48:11 **H** are those who saw you and were adorned
50:28 **H** are those who concern themselves
Bar 4:4 **H** are we, O Israel, for we know what is pleasing
1Mc 6:23 We were **h** to serve your father,
10:55 **"H** was the day on which you returned to the land
4Mc 18:9 A **h** man was he, who lived out his life

HAR-HERES (1)
Jdg 1:35 The Amorites continued to live in **H,** in Aijalon,

HARA (1)
1Ch 5:26 Habor, **H,** and the river Gozan, to this day.

HARADAH (2)
Nu 33:24 from Mount Shepher and camped at **H.**
33:25 They set out from **H** and camped at Makheloth.

HARAN (21) [BETH-HARAN]
Ge 11:26 he became the father of Abram, Nahor, and **H.**
11:27 Terah was the father of Abram, Nahor, and **H;**
11:27 and **H** was the father of Lot.
11:28 **H** died before his father Terah in the land
11:29 the daughter of **H** the father of Milcah and Iscah.
11:31 and his grandson Lot son of **H,**
11:31 but when they came to **H,** they settled there.
11:32 two hundred five years; and Terah died in **H.**
12:4 seventy-five years old when he departed from **H.**
12:5 and the persons whom they had acquired in **H;**
27:43 flee at once to my brother Laban in **H,**
28:10 Jacob left Beer-sheba and went toward **H.**
29:4 They said, "We are from **H."**
2Ki 19:12 my predecessors destroyed, Gozan, **H,** Rezeph,
1Ch 2:46 Ephah also, Caleb's concubine, bore **H,** Moza,
2:46 and **H** became the father of Gazez.
23:9 sons of Shimei: Shelomoth, Haziel, and **H,** three.
Isa 37:12 my predecessors destroyed, Gozan, **H,** Rezeph,
Eze 27:23 **H,** Canneh, Eden, the merchants of Sheba, Asshur,
Ac 7:2 in Mesopotamia, before he lived in **H,**
7:4 the country of the Chaldeans and settled in **H.**

HARARITE (5)
2Sa 23:11 Next to him was Shammah son of Agee, the **H.**
23:33 son of Shammah the **H;** Ahiam son of Sharar
23:33 Ahiam son of Sharar the **H;**
1Ch 11:34 Jonathan son of Shagee the **H,**
11:35 Ahiam son of Sachar the **H,** Eliphal son of Ur,

HARASS (5) [HARASSED, HARASSING]
Nu 25:17 **"H** the Midianites, and defeat them;
Dt 2:9 "Do not **h** Moab or engage them in battle,
2:19 do not **h** them or engage them in battle,
1Mc 6:38 to **h** the enemy while being themselves protected
9:51 And he placed garrisons in them to **h** Israel.

HARASSED (2) [HARASS]
Nu 25:18 for they have **h** you by the trickery
Mt 9:36 because they were **h** and helpless,

HARASSING (1) [HARASS]
2Mc 10:15 of important strongholds, were **h** the Jews;

HARBONA (2)
Est 1:10 Biztha, **H,** Bigtha and Abagtha, Zethar and Carkas,
7:9 Then **H,** one of the eunuchs in attendance on

HARBOR (10) [HARBORING, HARBORS]
Isa 23:10 this is a **h** no more.
Ac 27:12 the **h** was not suitable for spending the winter,
27:12 It was a **h** of Crete,
Sir 28:3 Does anyone **h** anger against another,
1Mc 14:5 To crown all his honors he took Joppa for a **h,**
2Mc 12:6 He set fire to the **h** by night, burned the boats,
12:9 the Jamnites by night and set fire to the **h** and
14:1 of Seleucus had sailed into the **h** of Tripolis with
1Es 5:55 from Lebanon and convey them in rafts to the **h**
4Mc 13:7 by fortifying the **h** of religion,

HARBORING (1) [HARBOR]
Pr 26:24 in speaking while **h** deceit within;

HARBORS (2) [HARBOR]
Sir 28:5 If a mere mortal **h** wrath,
4Mc 13:6 For just as towers jutting out over **h** hold back

HARD‡ (78) [HARD-HEARTED, HARD-PRESSED, HARDEN, HARDENED, HARDENING, HARDENS, HARDER, HARDEST, HARDNESS, HARDSHIP, HARDSHIPS]
Ge 19:9 Then they pressed **h** against the man Lot,
35:16 Rachel was in childbirth, and she had **h** labor.
35:17 When she was in her **h** labor,
47:9 few and **h** have been the years of my life.
Ge 49:23 they shot at him and pressed him **h.**
Ex 1:14 and made their lives bitter with **h** service in mortar
18:26 **h** cases they brought to Moses,
Dt 1:17 Any case that is too **h** for you, bring to me,
26:6 by imposing **h** labor on us,
30:11 that I am commanding you today is not too **h**
1Sa 13:6 in distress (for the troops were **h** pressed),
14:52 There was **h** fighting against the Philistines all
31:3 The battle pressed **h** upon Saul;
1Ki 10:1 she came to test him with **h** questions.
12:4 Now therefore lighten the **h** service of your father
2Ki 2:10 He responded, "You have asked a **h** thing;
1Ch 10:3 The battle pressed **h** on Saul;
2Ch 9:1 she came to Jerusalem to test him with **h** questions,
10:4 Now therefore lighten the **h** service of your father
Job 7:1 "Do not human beings have a **h** service on earth,
30:3 Through want and **h** hunger they gnaw the dry
30:25 Did I not weep for those whose day was **h?**
37:18 spread out the skies, **h** as a molten mirror?
38:30 The waters become **h** like stone,
41:24 heart is as **h** as stone, as **h** as the lower millstone.
Ps 60:3 You have made your people suffer **h** things;
107:12 Their hearts were bowed down with **h** labor;
118:13 I was pushed **h,** so that I was falling,
Pr 15:15 All the days of the poor are **h,**
Isa 14:3 the **h** service with which you were made to serve,
19:4 the Egyptians into the hand of a **h** master;
Jer 32:17 Nothing is too **h** for you.
32:27 is anything too **h** for me?
La 1:3 into exile with suffering and **h** servitude;
5:5 With a yoke on our necks we are **h** driven;
Eze 3:7 because all the house of Israel have a **h** forehead
3:8 See, I have made your face **h** against their faces,
3:8 and your forehead **h** against their foreheads.
29:18 of Babylon made his army labor **h** against Tyre;
Jnh 1:13 the men rowed **h** to bring the ship back to land,
Mt 7:14 gate is narrow and the road is **h** that leads to life,
13:15 and their ears are **h** of hearing,
19:23 it will be **h** for a rich person to enter the kingdom
23:4 They tie up heavy burdens, **h** to bear,
Mk 10:23 "How **h** it will be for those who have wealth
10:24 how **h** it is to enter the kingdom of God!
Lk 11:46 For you load people with burdens **h** to bear,
18:24 "How **h** it is for those who have wealth to enter
Ac 28:27 and their ears are **h** of hearing,
Ro 2:5 But by your **h** and impenitent heart you are storing
16:6 Greet Mary, who has worked very **h** among you.
16:12 who has worked **h** in the Lord.
Php 1:23 I am **h** pressed between the two:
Col 4:13 for him that he has worked **h** for you and for those
Heb 5:11 About this we have much to say that is **h**
10:32 you endured a **h** struggle with sufferings,
1Pe 4:18 And "If it is **h** for the righteous to be saved,
2Pe 3:16 There are some things in them **h** to understand,
Wis 11:4 and from **h** stone a remedy for their thirst.
17:1 Great are your judgments and **h** to describe;
Sir 7:15 Do not hate **h** labor or farm work,
29:28 It is **h** for a sensible person to bear scolding
34:28 what do they gain but **h** work?
40:1 **H** work was created for everyone,
48:13 Nothing was too **h** for him, and when he was dead,
Bel 1:30 The king saw that they were pressing him **h,**
1Mc 9:68 They pressed him very **h,** for his plan
15:14 he pressed the town **h** from land and sea,
2Mc 8:20 yet when the Macedonians were **h** pressed,
9:7 fall was so **h** as to torture every limb of his body.
11:5 about five stadia from Jerusalem, and pressed it **h.**
12:11 After a **h** fight, Judas and his companions,
12:21 that place was **h** to besiege and difficult of access
1Es 5:72 peoples of the land pressed **h** upon those in Judea,
3Mc 4:14 the **h** labor that has been briefly mentioned before,
5:7 with tears and a voice **h** to silence they all called
2Es 7:59 for the person who has what is **h**

HARD-HEARTED‡ (3) [HARD, HEART]
Dt 15:7 be **h** or tight-fisted toward your needy neighbor.
Pr 28:14 but one who is **h** will fall into calamity.
Mt 19:8 because you were so **h** that Moses allowed you

HARD-PRESSED (1) [HARD, PRESS]
2Mc 14:9 to take thought for our country and our **h** nation

HARDEN (11) [HARD]
Ex 4:21 but I will **h** his heart,
7:3 But I will **h** Pharaoh's heart,
14:4 I will **h** Pharaoh's heart, and he will pursue them,
14:17 Then I will **h** the hearts of the Egyptians so
Jos 11:20 For it was the LORD's doing to **h** their hearts so
1Sa 6:6 Why should you **h** your hearts as the Egyptians
Ps 95:8 Do not **h** your hearts, as at Meribah,
Isa 63:17 from your ways and **h** our heart,
Heb 3:8 do not **h** your hearts as in the rebellion,
3:15 do not **h** your hearts as in the rebellion."
4:7 if you hear his voice, do not **h** your hearts."

HARDENED‡ (26) [HARD]
Ex 7:13 Still Pharaoh's heart was **h,**
7:14 the LORD said to Moses, "Pharaoh's heart is **h;**
7:22 so Pharaoh's heart remained **h,**
8:15 he **h** his heart, and would not listen to them,
8:19 But Pharaoh's heart was **h,**
8:32 But Pharaoh **h** his heart this time also,
9:7 But the heart of Pharaoh was **h,**
9:12 But the LORD **h** the heart of Pharaoh,
9:34 he sinned once more and **h** his heart,

Ex 9:35 So the heart of Pharaoh was h,
10: 1 for I have h his heart and the heart of his officials,
10:20 But the LORD h Pharaoh's heart,
10:27 But the LORD h Pharaoh's heart,
11:10 but the LORD h Pharaoh's heart,
14: 8 The LORD h the heart of Pharaoh king of Egypt
Dt 2:30 for the LORD your God had h his spirit
1Sa 6: 6 as the Egyptians and Pharaoh h their hearts?
2Ch 36:13 and h his heart against turning to the LORD,
Da 5:20 when his heart was lifted up and his spirit was h so
Mk 6:52 about the loaves, but their hearts were h.
8:17 not perceive or understand? Are your hearts h?
Jn 12:40 "He has blinded their eyes and h their heart,
Ro 11: 7 The elect obtained it, but the rest were h,
2Co 3:14 But their minds were h.
Heb 3:13 none of you may be h by the deceitfulness of sin.
1Es 1:48 and h his heart and transgressed the laws of

HARDENING‡ (1) [HARD]
Ro 11:25 a h has come upon part of Israel,

HARDENS (2) [HARD]
Job 7: 5 my skin h, then breaks out again.
Ro 9:18 and he h the heart of whomever he chooses.

HARDER (5) [HARD]
Jdg 4:24 Then the hand of the Israelites bore h and h
Jer 5: 3 They have made their faces h than rock;
Eze 3: 9 Like the hardest stone, h than flint,
1Co 15:10 On the contrary, I worked h than any of them—

HARDEST (2) [HARD]
2Sa 11:15 "Set Uriah in the forefront of the h fighting,
Eze 3: 9 Like the h stone, harder than flint,

HARDLY (3)
Wis 9:16 We can h guess at what is on earth,
Sir 26:29 A merchant can h keep from wrongdoing,
29: 6 If he can pay, his creditor will h get back half,

HARDNESS (4) [HARD]
Ecc 8: 1 and the h of one's countenance is changed.
Mk 3: 5 he was grieved at their h of heart and said to
10: 5 of your h of heart he wrote this commandment
Eph 4:18 of God because of their ignorance and h of heart.

HARDSHIP (7) [HARD]
Ge 41:51 "God has made me forget all my h
Ex 18: 8 all the h that had beset them on the way,
Dt 15:18 a h when you send them out from you free persons,
Ne 9:32 do not treat lightly all the h that has come upon us,
Ro 8:35 Will h, or distress, or persecution, or famine,
2Co 11:27 and h, through many a sleepless night, hungry
2Ti 2: 9 for which I suffer h, even to the point

HARDSHIPS (5) [HARD]
1Ki 2:26 you shared in all the h my father endured."
Ps 132: 1 remember in David's favor all the h he endured;
2Co 6: 4 through great endurance, in afflictions, h,
12:10 I am content with weaknesses, insults, h,
2Es 7:12 full of dangers and involved in great h.

HARE (2)
Lev 11: 6 The h, for even though it chews the cud,
Dt 14: 7 the camel, the h, and the rock badger,

HAREM (10)
Est 2: 3 the h in the citadel of Susa under custody of Hegai,
2: 9 and her maids to the best place in the h.
2:11 around in front of the court of the h,
2:13 for to take with her from the h to the king's palace.
2:14 then in the morning she came back to the second h
AdE 2: 3 to be brought to the h in Susa,
2: 9 and her maids with special favor in the h.
2:11 in the courtyard of the h,
2:13 and goes with him from the h to the king's palace.
2:14 to the second h, where Gai the king's eunuch is

HAREPH (1)
1Ch 2:51 and H father of Beth-gader.

HARETH (KJV) See HERETH

HARHAIAH (1)
Ne 3: 8 Next to them Uzziel son of H,

HARHAS (1)
2Ki 22:14 son of H, keeper of the wardrobe;

HARHUR (2)
Ezr 2:51 Bakbuk, Hakupha, H,
Ne 7:53 of Bakbuk, of Hakupha, of H,

HARIM (11)
1Ch 24: 8 the third to H, the fourth to Seorim,
Ezr 2:32 Of H, three hundred twenty.
2:39 Of H, one thousand seventeen.
10:21 Of the descendants of H: Maaseiah,
10:31 Of the descendants of H: Eliezer,
Ne 3:11 Malchijah son of H and Hasshub son
7:35 Of H, three hundred twenty.
7:42 Of H, one thousand seventeen.
10: 5 H, Meremoth, Obadiah,
10:27 Malluch, H, and Baanah.
12:15 of H, Adna; of Meraioth, Helkai;

HARIPH (2)
Ne 7:24 Of H, one hundred twelve.
10:19 H, Anathoth, Nebai,

HARK (3)
Jer 8:19 H, the cry of my poor people from far and wide in
25:36 H! the cry of the shepherds,
48: 3 H! a cry from Horonaim, "Desolation

HARLOT (KJV) See FAITHLESS ONE, PROSTITUTE, WHORE; See also Index to Footnotes

HARM (85) [HARMED, HARMFUL, HARMING, HARMLESS]
Ge 26:29 so that you will do us no h,
31: 7 but God did not permit him to h me.
31:29 It is in my power to do you h;
31:52 beyond this heap and this pillar to me, for h.
42: 4 for he feared that h might come to him.
42:38 If h should come to him on the journey
44:29 also from me, and h comes to him, you will bring
48:16 the angel who has redeemed me from all h, bless
50:20 Even though you intended to do h to me,
Ex 21:22 and yet no further h follows,
21:23 If any h follows, then you shall give life for life,
Nu 35:23 not enemies, and no h was intended,
Jos 24:20 then he will turn and do you h, and consume you,
1Sa 6: 9 then it is he who has done us this great h;
20:13 But if my father intends to do you h,
24: 9 'David seeks to do you h'?
25: 7 and we did them no h, and they missed nothing,
25:15 men were very good to us, and we suffered no h,
26:21 my son David, for I will never h you again,
2Sa 12:18 He may do himself some h."
18:32 and all who rise up to do you h,
20: 6 of Bichri will do us more h than Absalom;
1Ch 4:10 and that you would keep me from hurt and h!"
16:22 not touch my anointed ones; do my prophets no h."
Ne 6: 2 But they intended to do me h.
Job 5:19 in seven no h shall touch you.
24:21 "They h the childless woman,
Ps 7: 4 if I have repaid my ally with h or plundered my foe
71:24 for those who tried to do me h have been put
105:15 not touch my anointed ones; do my prophets no h."
Pr 3:29 Do not plan h against your
3:30 when no h has been done to you.
11:17 but the cruel do themselves h.
12:21 No h happens to the righteous,
13:20 but the companion of fools suffers h.
19:23 filled with it one rests secure and suffers no h.
31:12 She does him good, and not h,
Ecc 8: 5 Whoever obeys a command will meet no h,
Isa 27: 3 I guard it night and day so that no one can h it;
41:23 do good, or do h, that we may be afraid
Jer 25: 6 Then I will do you no h."
25: 7 with the work of your hands to your own h.
29:11 plans for your welfare and not for h,
38: 4 not seeking the welfare of this people, but their h."
39:12 look after him well and do him no h,
44: 7 Why are you doing such great h to yourselves,
44:27 I am going to watch over them for h and not
Da 6:23 and no kind of h was found on him,
Am 9: 4 I will fix my eyes on them for h and not for good.
Mic 3:11 No h shall come upon us."
Hab 2: 9 on high to be safe from the reach of h!"
Zep 1:12 "The LORD will not do good, nor will he do h."
Mk 3: 4 "Is it lawful to do good or to do h on the sabbath,
Lk 4:35 of him without having done him any h.
6: 9 is it lawful to do good or to do h on the sabbath,
Ac 16:28 Paul shouted in a loud voice, "Do not h yourself,
18:10 and no one will lay a hand on you to h you,
28: 5 the creature into the fire and suffered no h.
2Ti 4:14 Alexander the coppersmith did me great h;
1Pe 3:13 Now who will h you if you are eager
Rev 9:10 and in their tails is their power to h people
9:19 and with them they inflict h.
11: 5 And if anyone wants to h them,
11: 5 anyone who wants to h them must be killed
Tob 6:15 It does not h her, but it kills anyone who desires
12: 2 It would do no h to give him half of
AdE 13: 5 doing all the h they can so that our kingdom may
Wis 11:19 not only could the h they did destroy people,
14:29 and expect to suffer no h.
Sir 4:22 Do not show partiality, to your own h,
5:15 In great and small matters cause no h,
11:24 "I have enough, and what h can come to me now?"
13:12 they will not spare you h or imprisonment.
22:26 But if h should come to me because of him,
36:11 may those who h your people meet destruction.
Aza 1:21 Let all who do h to your servants be put to shame;
1Mc 5:48 No one will do you h;
6:18 They were trying in every way to h them
7:14 and he will not h us."
9:71 to Jonathan that he would not try to h him as long
15:19 and countries that they should not seek their h
3Mc 7: 8 with no one in any place doing them h at all
2Es 7:115 [45] or to h someone who is victorious."
11:42 have laid low the walls of those who did you no h.
12:41 and what h have we done you,

HARMAGEDON (1)
Rev 16:16 at the place that in Hebrew is called H.

HARMED (4) [HARM]
Nu 16:15 and I have not h any one of them."
Da 3:27 not singed, their tunics were not h,
2Co 7: 9 so that you were not h in any way by us.
Rev 2:11 Whoever conquers will not be h by

HARMFUL (5) [HARM]
2Ki 4:41 And there was nothing h in the pot.
1Ti 6: 9 by many senseless and h desires that plunge people
Heb 13:17 for that would be h to you.
2Mc 15:39 For just as it is h to drink wine alone, or, again,
2Es 15: 6 and their h doings have reached their limit.

HARMING (1) [HARM]
Ge 50:17 of your brothers and the wrong they did in h you.'

HARMLESS (1) [HARM]
Wis 18: 3 and a h sun for their glorious wandering.

HARMON (1)
Am 4: 3 and you shall be flung out into H, says the LORD.

HARMONIOUS (1) [HARMONY]
4Mc 14: 3 and h concord of the seven brothers on behalf

HARMONY (8) [HARMONIOUS]
Ro 12:16 Live in h with one another;
15: 5 and encouragement grant you to live in h
Col 3:14 which binds everything together in perfect h.
Sir 25: 1 and a wife and a husband who live in h.
4Mc 3:21 a revolution against the public h and caused many
7: 7 in h with the law and philosopher of divine life!
14: 6 Just as the hands and feet are moved in h with
14: 7 O most holy seven, brothers in h!

HARNEPHER (1)
1Ch 7:36 The sons of Zophah: Suah, H, Shual, Beri, Imrah,

HARNESS (4)
1Ki 18:44 'H your chariot and go down before
Jer 46: 4 H the horses; mount the steeds!
Mic 1:13 H the steeds to the chariots, inhabitants of Lachish;
1Mc 6:37 they were fastened on each animal by special h,

HAROD (4)
Jdg 7: 1 and encamped beside the spring of H;
2Sa 23:25 Shammah of H; Elika of H;
1Ch 11:27 Shammoth of H, Helez the Pelonite,

HAROEH (1)
1Ch 2:52 Shobal father of Kiriath-jearim had other sons: H,

HARORITE See Index to Footnotes

HAROSHETH-HA-GOIIM (3)
Jdg 4: 2 of his army was Sisera, who lived in H.
4:13 from H to the Wadi Kishon.
4:16 Barak pursued the chariots and the army to H.

HARP (26) [HARPISTS, HARPS]
1Sa 10: 5 with h, tambourine, flute, and lyre playing in front
Ps 33: 2 make melody to him with the h of ten strings.
43: 4 and I will praise you with the h, O God, my God.
49: 4 I will solve my riddle to the music of the h.
57: 8 Awake, O h and lyre! I will awake the dawn.
71:22 also praise you with the h for your faithfulness,
81: 2 sound the tambourine, the sweet lyre with the h.
92: 3 to the music of the lute and the h,
108: 2 Awake, O h and lyre! I will awake the dawn.
144: 9 upon a ten-stringed h I will play to you,
150: 3 praise him with lute and h!
Isa 5:12 whose feasts consist of lyre and h,
16:11 Therefore my heart throbs like a h for Moab,
23:16 Take a h, go about the city,
Da 3: 5 lyre, trigon, h, drum, and entire musical ensemble,
3: 7 lyre, trigon, h, drum, and entire musical ensemble,
3:10 lyre, trigon, h, drum, and entire musical ensemble,
3:15 lyre, trigon, h, drum, and entire musical ensemble
Am 6: 5 of the h, and like David improvise on instruments
1Co 14: 7 such as the flute or the h.
Rev 5: 8 each holding a h and golden bowls full of incense,
Wis 19:18 as on a h the notes vary the nature of the rhythm,
Sir 40:21 The flute and the h make sweet melody,
1Mc 3:45 the flute and the h ceased to play.
Pm 151: 2 My hands made a h; my fingers fashioned a lyre.
2Es 10:22 our h has been laid low,

HARPISTS (2) [HARP]
Rev 14: 2 the voice I heard was like the sound of h playing
18:22 and the sound of h and minstrels and of flutists

HARPOONS (1)

Job 41: 7 Can you fill its skin with **h**,

HARPS (22) [HARP]

2Sa 6: 5 and **h** and tambourines and castanets and cymbals.
1Ki 10:12 lyres also and **h** for the singers;
1Ch 13: 8 and **h** and tambourines and cymbals and trumpets.
15:16 on **h** and lyres and cymbals,
15:20 and Benaiah were to play **h** according to Alamoth;
15:28 and cymbals, and made loud music on **h** and lyres.
16: 5 Benaiah, Obed-edom, and Jeiel, with **h** and lyres;
25: 1 who should prophesy with lyres, **h**, and cymbals.
25: 6 **h**, and lyres for the service of the house of God.
2Ch 5:12 arrayed in fine linen, with cymbals, **h**, and lyres,
9:11 lyres also and **h** for the singers;
20:28 with **h** and lyres and trumpets,
29:25 the LORD with cymbals, **h**, and lyres,
Ne 12:27 with cymbals, **h**, and lyres.
Ps 137: 2 On the willows there we hung up our **h**.
Isa 14:11 and the sound of your **h**;
Am 5:23 I will not listen to the melody of your **h**.
Rev 14: 2 like the sound of harpists playing on their **h**,
15: 2 standing beside the sea of glass with **h** of God
Sir 39:15 with songs on your lips, and with **h**;
1Mc 4:54 it was dedicated with songs and **h** and lutes
13:51 and with **h** and cymbals and stringed instruments,

HARROW (3)

Job 39:10 or will it **h** the valleys after you?
Isa 28:24 Do they continually open and **h** their ground?
Hos 10:11 Judah must plow; Jacob must **h** for himself.

HARSH (18) [HARSHLY, HARSHNESS]

Ex 33: 4 When the people heard these **h** words,
Pr 15: 1 but a **h** word stirs up anger.
Mal 3:13 You have spoken **h** words against me,
Mt 25:24 saying, 'Master, I knew that you were a **h** man,
Lk 19:21 because you are a **h** man;
19:22 You knew, did you, that I was a **h** man,
1Pe 2:18 and gentle but also those who are **h**.
Jude 1:15 the **h** things that ungodly sinners have spoken
Tob 13:12 Cursed are all who speak a **h** word against you;
Jdt 8: 9 the **h** words spoken by the people against the ruler,
Wis 17:19 or the **h** crash of rocks hurled down,
Sir 6:20 She seems very **h** to the undisciplined;
18:15 or spoil your gift by **h** words.
2Mc 6: 3 **H** and utterly grievous was the onslaught of evil.
3Mc 3:25 with insulting and **h** treatment,
4: 4 a **h** and ruthless spirit were they being sent off,
4: 6 as they were torn by the **h** treatment of the heathen.
7: 5 They also led them out with **h** treatment as slaves,

HARSHA (2)

Ezr 2:52 Bazluth, Mehida, **H**,
Ne 7:54 of Bazlith, of Mehida, of **H**,

HARSHLY (11) [HARSH]

Ge 16: 6 Sarai dealt **h** with her, and she ran away from her.
42: 7 he treated them like strangers and spoke **h** to them.
42:30 the lord of the land, spoke **h** to us,
Dt 26: 6 When the Egyptians treated us **h** and afflicted us,
Ru 1:21 why call me Naomi when the LORD has dealt **h**
1Sa 20:10 "Who will tell me if your father answers you **h**?"
1Ki 12:13 The king answered the people **h**.
2Ch 10:13 The king answered them **h**.
Col 3:19 Husbands, love your wives and never treat them **h**.
1Ti 5: 1 Do not speak **h** to an older man,
1Mc 11:53 that Jonathan had done him, but treated him very **h**.

HARSHNESS (4) [HARSH]

Lev 25:43 You shall not rule over them with **h**,
25:46 no one shall rule over the other with **h**.
25:53 however, rule with **h** over them in your sight.
Eze 34: 4 but with force and **h** you have ruled them.

HART (KJV) See DEER, STAG

HARUM (1)

1Ch 4: 8 Zobebah, and the families of Aharhel son of **H**.

HARUMAPH (1)

Ne 3:10 of **H** made repairs opposite his house;

HARUPHITE (1)

1Ch 12: 5 Jerimoth, Bealiah, Shemariah, Shephatiah the **H**;

HARUZ (1)

2Ki 21:19 mother's name was Meshullemeth daughter of **H**

HARVEST (82) [HARVESTED, HARVESTERS, HARVESTING, HARVESTS]

Ge 8:22 As long as the earth endures, seedtime and **h**,
30:14 of wheat **h** Reuben went and found mandrakes in
45: 6 in which there will be neither plowing nor **h**.
Ex 22:29 to make offerings from the fullness of your **h** and
23:16 You shall observe the festival of **h**,
34:21 even in plowing time and in **h** time you shall rest.
34:22 the first fruits of wheat **h**,
Lev 19: 9 When you reap the **h** of your land,
Lev 19: 9 or gather the gleanings of your **h**.
23:10 the land that I am giving you and you reap its **h**,
23:10 you shall bring the sheaf of the first fruits of your **h**
23:22 When you reap the **h** of your land,
23:22 or gather the gleanings of your **h**;
25: 5 the aftergrowth of your **h** or gather the grapes
25:11 or reap the aftergrowth, or **h** the unpruned vines.
Dt 24:19 When you reap your **h** in your field and forget
26: 2 which you **h** from the land that
Jos 3:15 overflows all its banks throughout the time of **h**.
Jdg 15: 1 After a while, at the time of the wheat **h**,
Ru 1:22 to Bethlehem at the beginning of the barley **h**.
2:21 until they have finished all my **h**.' "
1Sa 6:13 of Beth-shemesh were reaping their wheat **h** in
8:12 and some to plow his ground and to reap his **h**,
12:17 Is it not the wheat **h** today?
2Sa 21: 9 They were put to death in the first days of **h**,
21: 9 at the beginning of barley **h**.
21:10 from the beginning of **h** until rain fell on them
23:13 the beginning of **h** three of the thirty chiefs went
Job 5: 5 The hungry eat their **h**, and they take it even out of
31:12 and it would burn to the root all my **h**.
Pr 6: 8 and gathers its sustenance in **h**.
10: 5 but a child who sleeps in **h** brings shame.
20: 4 **h** comes, and there is nothing to be found.
25:13 of snow in the time of **h** are faithful messengers
26: 1 Like snow in summer or rain in **h**,
Isa 9: 3 they rejoice before you as with joy at the **h**,
16: 9 for the shout over your fruit **h**
16: 9 and your grain **h** has ceased.
17: 5 and their arms **h** the ears,
17:11 yet the **h** will flee away in a day of grief and
18: 4 like a cloud of dew in the heat of **h**.
18: 5 For before the **h**, when the blossom is over and
23: 3 your revenue was the grain of Shihor, the **h** of
24:13 as at the gleaning when the grape **h** is ended.
32:10 for the vintage will fail, the fruit **h** will not come.
Jer 2: 3 the first fruits of his **h**.
5:17 They shall eat up your **h** and your food;
5:24 and keeps for us the weeks appointed for the **h**."
8:20 "The **h** is past, the summer is ended,
50:16 and the wielder of the sickle in time of **h**;
51:33 yet a little while and the time of her **h** will come.
Hos 6:11 For you also, O Judah, a **h** is appointed.
Joel 3:13 Put in the sickle, for the **h** is ripe.
Am 4: 7 when there were still three months to the **h**;
Mt 9:37 Then he said to his disciples, "The **h** is plentiful,
9:38 the Lord of the **h** to send out laborers into his **h**."
13:30 Let both of them grow together until the **h**; and at
h time I will tell the reapers,
13:39 **h** is the end of the age, and the reapers are angels.
21:34 When the **h** time had come,
21:41 the produce at the **h** time."
Mk 4:29 in with his sickle, because the **h** has come."
Lk 10: 2 He said to them, "The **h** is plentiful,
10: 2 the Lord of the **h** to send out laborers into his **h**.
Jn 4:35 'Four months more, then comes the **h**'?
Ro 1:13 that I may reap some **h** among you as I have
2Co 9:10 and increase the **h** of your righteousness.
Gal 6: 9 for we will reap at **h** time, if we do not give up.
Php 1:11 having produced the **h** of righteousness that comes
Jas 3:18 And a **h** of righteousness is sown in peace
5:18 the heaven gave rain and the earth yielded its **h**.
Rev 14:15 because the **h** of the earth is fully ripe."
Jdt 2:27 into the plain of Damascus during the wheat **h**,
8: 2 had died during the barley **h**.
Sir 6:19 and wait for her good **h**.
20:28 Those who cultivate the soil heap up their **h**,
24:26 with understanding, and like the Jordan at **h** time.
2Es 4:28 but the **h** of it has not yet come.
4:35 And when will the **h** of our reward come?
4Mc 2: 9 the **h** nor gathers the last grapes from the vineyard.

HARVESTED (2) [HARVEST]

Hag 1: 6 You have sown much, and **h** little;
Jdt 4: 5 since their fields had recently been **h**.

HARVESTERS (1) [HARVEST]

Jas 5: 4 of the **h** have reached the ears of the Lord of hosts.

HARVESTING (1) [HARVEST]

Jn 4:35 and see how the fields are ripe for **h**.

HARVESTS (4) [HARVEST]

Ge 47:24 And at the **h** you shall give one-fifth to Pharaoh,
Lev 25:16 for it is a certain number of **h** that are being sold
Ru 2:23 gleaning until the end of the barley and wheat **h**;
Jer 12:13 be ashamed of their **h** because of the fierce anger

HAS‡ (332 of 2937) [HAVE] See Index of Articles Etc. for an Exhaustive Listing (See Introduction, page xi)

Ge 1:30 everything that **h** the breath of life,
24:36 and he has given him all that he **h**.
39: 8 master **h** no concern about anything in the house,
39: 8 and he has put everything that he **h** in my hand.
Ex 24:14 whoever **h** a dispute may go to them.
32:24 So I said to them, 'Whoever **h** gold, take it off';
Lev 11: 3 animal that **h** divided hoofs and is cleft-footed
11: 7 The pig, for even though it **h** divided hoofs
11: 9 Everything in the waters that **h** fins and scales,
11:26 animal that **h** divided hoofs but is not cleft-footed
11:42 whatever **h** many feet, all the creatures that swarm
13: 2 a person **h** on the skin of his body a swelling
Lev 13:24 Or, when the body **h** a burn on the skin
13:29 When a man or woman **h** a disease on the head
13:38 When a man or a woman **h** spots on the skin
13:41 he **h** baldness of the forehead but he is clean.
13:45 The person who **h** the leprous disease
13:46 shall remain unclean as long as he **h** the disease;
14:32 the ritual for the one who **h** a leprous disease,
15: 2 When any man **h** a discharge from his member,
15:16 If a man **h** an emission of semen, he shall bathe
15:18 If a man lies with a woman and **h** an emission
15:19 When a woman **h** a discharge of blood
15:25 If a woman **h** a discharge of blood for many days,
15:25 or if she **h** a discharge beyond the time
15:32 for him who **h** an emission of semen,
15:33 for anyone, male or female, who **h** a discharge,
19:20 If a man **h** sexual relations with a woman
20:15 If a man **h** sexual relations with an animal,
20:16 If a woman approaches any animal and **h** sexual
relations with it,
21:17 who **h** a blemish may approach to offer the food
21:18 For no one who **h** a blemish shall draw near,
21:18 or one who **h** a mutilated face or a limb too long,
21:19 or one who **h** a broken foot or a broken hand,
21:21 who **h** a blemish shall come near to offer
21:21 since he **h** a blemish, he shall not come near
21:23 because he **h** a blemish, that he may not profane
22: 4 one of Aaron's offspring who **h** a leprous disease
22:20 You shall not offer anything that **h** a blemish,
22:23 An ox or a lamb that **h** a limb too long or too short
22:24 Any animal that **h** its testicles bruised or crushed
25:26 If the person **h** no one to redeem it,
Nu 5: 2 everyone who is leprous, or **h** a discharge,
5: 8 If the injured party **h** no next of kin
14:24 my servant Caleb, because he **h** a different spirit
27: 8 "If a man dies, and **h** no son, then you shall pass
27: 9 If he **h** no daughter, then you shall give his
27:10 If he **h** no brothers, then you shall give his
27:11 if his father **h** no brothers, then you shall give his
Dt 4: 7 For what other great nation **h** a god so near to it
4: 8 what other great nation **h** statutes and ordinances
10: 9 Therefore Levi **h** no allotment or inheritance
14: 6 animal that divides the hoof and **h** the hoof cleft
14: 9 whatever **h** fins and scales you may eat.
15:21 But if it **h** any defect—any serious defect,
17: 1 an ox or a sheep that **h** a defect,
21:15 If a man **h** two wives, one of them loved
21:17 giving him a double portion of all that he **h**;
21:18 If someone **h** a stubborn and rebellious son
25: 5 and one of them dies and **h** no son,
25: 7 the man **h** no desire to marry his brother's widow,
Jos 7:15 burned with fire, together with all that he **h**,
1Sa 2: 5 but she who **h** many children is forlorn.
23: 7 by entering a town that **h** gates and bars.
25:21 I protected all that this fellow **h** in the wilderness,
2Sa 3:29 Joab never be without one who **h** a discharge,
13:24 and said, "Your servant **h** sheepshearers;
14:20 my lord **h** wisdom like the wisdom of the angel
14:30 Joab's field is next to mine, and he **h** barley there;
17: 5 and let us hear too what he **h** to say.
2Ki 4:14 "Well, she **h** no son, and her husband is old."
1Ch 28:21 volunteer who **h** skill for any kind of service;
2Ch 25: 8 for God **h** power to help or to overthrow.
Job 1:10 a fence around him and his house and all that he **h**,
1:11 and touch all that he **h**, and he will curse you
1:12 "Very well, all that he **h** is in your power;
12:13 he **h** counsel and understanding.
26: 2 "How you have helped one who **h** no power!
26: 2 How you have assisted the arm that **h** no strength!
26: 3 How you have counseled one who **h** no wisdom,
26: 6 naked before God, and Abaddon **h** no covering.
32:19 My heart is indeed like wine that **h** no vent;
38:28 "**H** the rain a father,
38:37 Who **h** the wisdom to number the clouds?
39:16 though its labor should be in vain, yet it **h** no fear;
41:33 On earth it **h** no equal, a creature without fear.
42: 7 spoken of me what is right, as my servant Job **h**.
Ps 2: 4 the LORD **h** them in derision.
7:11 and a God who **h** indignation every day.
37:16 Better is a little that the righteous person **h** than
72:13 He **h** pity on the weak and the needy,
103:13 As a father **h** compassion for his children,
103:13 so the LORD **h** compassion for those who fear him.
104:17 the stork **h** its home in the fir trees.
109:11 May the creditor seize all that he **h**;
123: 2 to the LORD our God, until he **h** mercy upon us.
127: 5 Happy is the man who **h** his quiver full of them.
Pr 6:32 But he who commits adultery **h** no sense;
10:13 On the lips of one who **h** understanding
12:14 and manual labor **h** its reward.
14:26 In the fear of the LORD one **h** strong confidence,
14:29 Whoever is slow to anger **h** great understanding,
14:29 but one who **h** a hasty temper exalts folly.
14:33 at home in the mind of one who **h** understanding,
14:35 A servant who deals wisely **h** the king's favor,
15:14 one who **h** understanding seeks knowledge,
15:15 but a cheerful heart **h** a continual feast.
15:21 Folly is a joy to one who **h** no sense,
16:22 Wisdom is a fountain of life to one who **h** it,
17:21 the parent of a fool **h** no joy.
17:27 one who is cool in spirit **h** understanding.
23:29 Who **h** woe? Who **h** sorrow? Who **h** strife?
23:29 Who **h** complaining? Who **h** wounds without
cause? Who **h** redness of eyes?
25: 4 and the smith **h** material for a vessel;
28: 2 When a land rebels it **h** many rulers;
30:15 The leech **h** two daughters; "Give, give,"
Ecc 5: 4 for he **h** no pleasure in fools.

Ecc 5:11 and what gain **h** their owner but to see them
6: 3 does not enjoy life's good things, or **h** no burial,
8: 6 For every matter **h** its time and way,
8: 8 No one **h** power over the wind to restrain the wind
9: 4 whoever is joined with all the living **h** hope,
SS 8: 8 We have a little sister, and she **h** no breasts.
Isa 2:12 the LORD of hosts **h** a day against all that is proud
22: 5 For the Lord GOD of hosts **h** a day of tumult
28: 2 See, the Lord **h** one who is mighty and strong;
29:16 the one who formed it, "He **h** no understanding"?
34: 6 The LORD **h** a sword; it is sated with blood,
34: 6 For the LORD **h** a sacrifice in Bozrah,
34: 8 For the LORD **h** a day of vengeance,
45: 9 or "Your work **h** no handles"?
49:10 for he who **h** pity on them will lead them,
50:10 who walks in darkness and **h** no light,
54:10 says the LORD, who **h** compassion on you.
Jer 5:23 But this people **h** a stubborn and rebellious heart;
6:25 for the enemy **h** a sword, terror is on every side.
11:15 What right **h** my beloved in my house,
23:28 Let the prophet who **h** a dream tell the dream,
23:28 the one who **h** my word speak my word faithfully.
25:31 for the LORD **h** an indictment against the nations;
49: 1 **H** Israel no sons? **H** he no heir?
49:31 that **h** no gates or bars, that lives alone.
50:25 for the Lord GOD of hosts **h** a task to do
La 1: 2 among all her lovers she **h** no one to comfort her;
Eze 9: 6 but touch no one who **h** the mark.
18:10 If he **h** a son who is violent, a shedder of blood,
18:14 But if this man **h** a son who sees all the sins
33:32 a singer of love songs, one who **h** a beautiful voice
Da 3:25 and the fourth **h** the appearance of a god.
4:25 the Most High **h** sovereignty over the kingdom
4:32 the Most High **h** sovereignty over the kingdom
5:21 Most High God **h** sovereignty over the kingdom
6:26 never be destroyed, and his dominion **h** no end.
Hos 3: 1 love a woman who **h** a lover and is an adulteress,
4: 1 the LORD **h** an indictment against the inhabitants
8: 7 The standing grain **h** no heads,
12: 2 The LORD **h** an indictment against Judah,
Joel 1: 6 and it **h** the fangs of a lioness.
Am 3: 4 Does a lion roar in the forest, when it **h** no prey?
Mic 6: 2 for the LORD **h** a controversy with his people,
Mal 1:14 Cursed be the cheat who **h** a male in the flock
Mt 5:23 your brother or sister **h** something against you,
8:20 but the Son of Man **h** nowhere to lay his head.
9: 6 the Son of Man **h** authority on earth to forgive sins
11:18 and they say, 'He **h** a demon';
12:11 "Suppose one of you **h** only one sheep and it falls
13:21 a person **h** no root, but endures only for a while,
13:44 he goes and sells all that he **h** and buys that field.
18:12 If a shepherd **h** a hundred sheep,
Mk 2:10 the Son of Man **h** authority on earth to forgive sins
3:22 "He **h** Beelzebul, and by the ruler of the demons
3:30 for they had said, "He **h** an unclean spirit.
9:17 he **h** a spirit that makes him unable to speak;
Lk 1:61 said to her, "None of your relatives **h** this name.
3:11 "Whoever **h** two coats must share with anyone
who **h** none; and whoever **h** food must do likewise.
5:24 the Son of Man **h** authority on earth to forgive sins
7:33 drinking no wine, and you say, 'He **h** a demon';
9:58 but the Son of Man **h** nowhere to lay his head.
11: 5 "Suppose one of you **h** a friend, and you go to him
12: 5 after he has killed, **h** authority to cast into hell.
14: 5 "If one of you **h** a child or an ox that has fallen
14:28 to see whether he **h** enough to complete it?
17:31 anyone on the housetop who **h** belongings
19:24 and give it to the one who **h** ten pounds.
19:25 (And they said to him, 'Lord, he **h** ten pounds!')
22:36 "But now, the one who **h** a purse must take it,
22:36 And the one who **h** no sword must sell his cloak
23:15 Neither **h** Herod, for he sent him back to us.
Jn 3:29 He who **h** the bride is the bridegroom.
3:36 Whoever believes in the Son **h** eternal life;
4:44 a prophet **h** no honor in the prophet's own country
5: 2 in Hebrew Beth-zatha, which **h** five porticoes.
5:24 and believes him who sent me **h** eternal life,
5:26 For just as the Father **h** life in himself,
6: 9 a boy here who **h** five barley loaves and two fish.
6:47 truly, I tell you, whoever believes **h** eternal life.
8:35 the son **h** a place there forever.
10:20 saying, "He **h** a demon and is out of his mind.
10:21 "These are not the words of one who **h** a demon.
12:48 and does not receive my word **h** a judge;
14:30 He **h** no power over me;
15:13 No one **h** greater love than this,
16:15 All that the Father **h** is mine.
16:21 When a woman is in labor, she **h** pain,
Ac 9:14 he **h** authority from the chief priests to bind all
23:17 to the tribune, for he **h** something to report to him.
23:18 he **h** something to tell you."
Ro 1:16 for salvation to everyone who **h** faith,
3: 1 Then what advantage **h** the Jew?
3:11 there is no one who **h** understanding,
3:26 and that he justifies the one who **h** faith in Jesus.
4: 2 he **h** something to boast about, but not before God.
6: 9 death no longer **h** dominion over him.
9:18 So then he **h** mercy on whomever he chooses,
9:21 **H** the potter no right over the clay, to make
11:23 for God **h** the power to graft them in again.
14:18 acceptable to God and **h** human approval.
1Co 6: 1 When any of you **h** a grievance against another,
7: 7 But each **h** a particular gift from God,
7:12 that if any believer **h** a wife who is an unbeliever,
7:13 if any woman **h** a husband who is an unbeliever,
7:36 if his passions are strong, and so it **h** to be,
8: 7 not everyone, however, who **h** this knowledge.
1Co 11:15 but if a woman **h** long hair, it is her glory?
12:12 For just as the body is one and **h** many members,
14:26 When you come together, each one **h** a hymn,
16:12 He will come when he **h** the opportunity.
16:22 anyone be accursed who **h** no love for the Lord.
2Co 3:11 much more **h** the permanent come in glory!
6:16 What agreement **h** the temple of God with idols?
8:12 the gift is acceptable according to what one **h**—
Eph 5: 5 **h** any inheritance in the kingdom of Christ
Php 3: 4 If anyone else **h** reason to be confident in the flesh
Col 3:13 if anyone **h** a complaint against another, forgive
1Ti 5: 4 If a widow **h** children or grandchildren,
5:16 If any believing woman **h** relatives
6: 4 and **h** a morbid craving for controversy
6:16 It is he alone who **h** immortality and dwells in
2Ti 2:15 a worker who **h** no need to be ashamed,
Heb 2:14 destroy the one who **h** the power of death,
3: 3 the builder of a house **h** more honor than the house
7:27 he **h** no need to offer sacrifices day after day,
10: 1 Since the law **h** only a shadow of the good things
Jas 1:21 word that **h** the power to save your souls.
2:17 So faith by itself, if it **h** no works, is dead.
1Jn 2:23 No one who denies the Son **h** the Father;
2:23 everyone who confesses the Son **h** the Father also.
3:17 who **h** the world's goods and sees a brother
4:16 known and believe the love that God **h** for us.
4:18 for fear **h** to do with punishment,
5:12 Whoever **h** the Son **h** life; whoever does not have
2Jn 1: 9 whoever abides in the teaching **h** both the Father
3Jn 1:12 and so **h** the truth itself.
Rev 2: 7 Let anyone who **h** an ear listen to what the Spirit is
2:11 Let anyone who **h** an ear listen to what the Spirit is
2:12 words of him who **h** the sharp two-edged sword:
2:17 Let anyone who **h** an ear listen to what the Spirit is
2:18 the Son of God, who **h** eyes like a flame of fire,
2:29 Let anyone who **h** an ear listen to what the Spirit is
3: 1 the words of him who **h** the seven spirits of God
3: 6 Let anyone who **h** an ear listen to what the Spirit is
3: 7 the holy one, the true one, who **h** the key of David,
3:13 Let anyone who **h** an ear listen to what the Spirit is
3:22 Let anyone who **h** an ear listen to what the Spirit is
12: 6 wilderness, where she **h** a place prepared by God,
13: 9 Let anyone who **h** an ear listen:
14:18 the angel who **h** authority over fire,
17: 9 "This calls for a mind that **h** wisdom:
19:12 and he **h** a name inscribed that no one knows but
19:16 On his robe and on his thigh he **h** a name inscribed
20: 6 Over these the second death **h** no power,
21:11 It **h** the glory of God and a radiance
21:12 It **h** a great, high wall with twelve gates,
21:14 And the wall of the city **h** twelve foundations,
21:23 the city **h** no need of sun or moon to shine on it,
Tob 3:15 only child; he **h** no other child to be his heir;
3:15 and he **h** no close relative or other kindred
4:19 For none of the nations **h** understanding,
6:11 and he **h** a daughter named Sarah.
6:12 He **h** no male heir and no daughter except Sarah
6:15 now, since I am the only son my father **h**,
7:10 brother, **h** the right to marry my daughter Sarah.
Jdt 8:15 he **h** power to protect us within any time
AdE 14:11 do not surrender your scepter to what **h** no being;
Wis 8: 8 she **h** foreknowledge of signs and wonders
8:16 for companionship with her **h** no bitterness,
8:16 and life with her **h** no pain, but gladness and joy.
13:16 for it is only an image and **h** need of help.
Sir 10:27 Better is the worker who **h** goods in plenty than
13:17 No more **h** a sinner with the devout.
15:12 for he **h** no need of the sinful.
16:17 and who from on high **h** me in mind?
18:14 **h** compassion on those who accept his discipline
19: 4 who trusts others too quickly **h** a shallow mind,
19: 6 but one who hates gossip **h** less evil.
21:18 knowledge is talk that **h** no meaning.
25:11 to whom can we compare the one who **h** it?
26:25 *but one who **h** a sense of shame will fear the Lord.*
28: 4 If one **h** no mercy toward another like himself,
28:22 It **h** no power over the godly;
34: 5 and like a woman in labor, the mind **h** fantasies.
36:31 So who will trust a man that **h** no nest,
38:24 the one who **h** little business can become wise.
40:14 As a generous person **h** cause to rejoice,
45:22 But in the land of the people he **h** no inheritance,
45:22 and he **h** no portion among the people;
Bar 3:25 It is great and **h** no bounds; it is high
LtJ 6:15 Another **h** a dagger in its right hand, and an ax,
6:73 therefore, is someone upright who **h** no idols;
Bel 1: 5 and **h** dominion over all living creatures.
2Mc 2:29 **h** to consider only what is suitable for its
3:39 For he who **h** his dwelling in heaven watches over
7: 6 and in truth **h** compassion on us,
13: 5 and it **h** a rim running around it that on all sides
1Es 4:14 that rules them, or **h** the mastery over them?
8:22 that no one **h** authority to impose any tax on them.
3Mc 1:27 to call upon him who **h** all power to defend them
2Es 7: 4 but it **h** an entrance set in a narrow place, so
7:39 a day that **h** no sun or moon or stars,
7:*59* the person who **h** what is hard to get rejoices more
than the person who **h** what is plentiful.
7:*132* [62] he **h** mercy on those who have not yet come
10:14 the earth also **h** from the beginning given her fruit,
12:47 for the Most High **h** you in remembrance,
16:38 **h** great pains around her womb for two or three

HASADIAH (2)

1Ch 3:20 Ohel, Berechiah, **H**, and Jushab-hesed, five.
Bar 1: 1 of Mahseiah son of Zedekiah son of **H** son

HASENUAH (KJV) See HASSENUAH

HASH-BADDANAH (1)

Ne 8: 4 and Pedaiah, Mishael, Malchijah, Hashum, **H**,

HASHABIAH (19)

1Ch 6:45 son of **H**, son of Amaziah, son of Hilkiah,
9:14 son of Azrikam, son of **H**, of the sons of Merari;
25: 3 Gedaliah, Zeri, Jeshaiah, Shimei, **H**,
25:19 the twelfth to **H**, his sons and his brothers, twelve;
26:30 Of the Hebronites, **H** and his brothers,
27:17 for Levi, **H** son of Kemuel; for Aaron, Zadok;
2Ch 35: 9 and **H** and Jeiel and Jozabad,
Ezr 8:19 also **H** and with him Jeshaiah of the descendants
8:24 Sherebiah, **H**, and ten of their kin with them.
10:25 Ramiah, Izziah, Malchijah, Mijamin, Eleazar, **H**,
Ne 3:17 next to him **H**, ruler of half the district of Keilah,
10:11 Mica, Rehob, **H**,
11:15 of Hasshub son of Azrikam son of **H** son of Bunni;
11:22 in Jerusalem was Uzzi son of Bani son of **H** son
12:21 of Hilkiah, **H**; of Jedaiah, Nethanel.
12:24 And the leaders of the Levites: **H**, Sherebiah,
1Es 1: 9 and **H** and Ochiel and Joram,
8:48 also **H** and Annunus and his brother Jeshaiah,
8:54 and **H**, and ten of their kinsmen with them;

HASHABNAH (1)

Ne 10:25 Rehum, **H**, Maaseiah,

HASHABNEIAH (2)

Ne 3:10 and next to him Hattush son of **H** made repairs.
9: 5 Then the Levites, Jeshua, Kadmiel, Bani, **H**,

HASHBADANA (KJV) See HASH-BADDANAH

HASHEM (1)

1Ch 11:34 **H** the Gizonite, Jonathan son of Shagee

HASHMONAH (2)

Nu 33:29 They set out from Mithkah and camped at **H**.
33:30 They set out from **H** and camped at Moseroth.

HASHUB (KJV) See HASSHUB

HASHUBAH (1)

1Ch 3:20 and **H**, Ohel, Berechiah, Hasadiah,

HASHUM (7)

Ge 46:23 The children of Dan: **H**.
Ezr 2:19 Of **H**, two hundred twenty-three.
10:33 Of the descendants of **H**: Mattenai,
Ne 7:22 Of **H**, three hundred twenty-eight.
8: 4 and Pedaiah, Mishael, Malchijah, **H**,
10:18 Hodiah, **H**, Bezai,
1Es 9:33 Of the descendants of **H**: Mattenai

HASHUPHA (KJV) See HASUPHA

HASIDEANS (3)

1Mc 2:42 Then there united with them a company of **H**,
7:13 The **H** were first among the Israelites to seek peace
2Mc 14: 6 "Those of the Jews who are called **H**,

HASRAH (2)

2Ch 34:22 the wife of Shallum son of Tokhath son of **H**,
1Es 5:31 the descendants of **H**, the descendants of Basthai,

HASSENAAH (1)

Ne 3: 3 The sons of **H** built the Fish Gate;

HASSENUAH (2)

1Ch 9: 7 son of Hodaviah, son of **H**,
Ne 11: 9 Judah son of **H** was second in charge of the city.

HASSHUB (5)

1Ch 9:14 Shemaiah son of **H**, son of Azrikam,
Ne 3:11 and **H** son of Pahath-moab repaired another section
3:23 and **H** made repairs opposite their house.
10:23 Hoshea, Hananiah, **H**,
11:15 of **H** son of Azrikam son of Hashabiah son

HASSOPHERETH (1)

Ezr 2:55 The descendants of Solomon's servants: Sotai, **H**,

HASTE (22) [HASTEN, HASTENED, HASTENING, HASTENS, HASTILY, HASTY]

Dt 16: 3 you came out of the land of Egypt in great **h**,
Jos 4:10 The people crossed over in **h**.
1Sa 21: 8 because the king's business required **h**."
2Sa 4: 4 and, in her **h** to flee,
2Ki 7:15 that the Arameans had thrown away in their **h**.
Ps 38:22 make **h** to help me, O Lord, my salvation.
40:13 O LORD, make **h** to help me.
69:17 in distress—make **h** to answer me.
70: 1 O LORD, make **h** to help me!

Ps 71:12 O my God, make **h** to help me!
SS 1: 4 Draw me after you, let us make **h.**
8:14 Make **h,** my beloved, and be like a gazelle or
Isa 5:19 "Let him make **h,** let him speed his work
52:12 For you shall not go out in **h,**
Jer 46: 5 their warriors are beaten down, and have fled in **h.**
Lk 1:39 In those days Mary set out and went with **h** to
2:16 So they went with **h** and found Mary and Joseph,
1Mc 6:63 Then he set off in **h** and returned to Antioch.
2Mc 11:37 Therefore make **h** and send messengers so
3Mc 4:15 with bitter **h** and zealous intensity from the rising
2Es 4:42 as a woman who is in labor makes **h** to escape
5:42 so for those who are first there is no **h."**

HASTEN (8) [HASTE]
Ex 12:33 the people to **h** their departure from the land,
Ps 68:31 let Ethiopia **h** to stretch out its hands to God.
70: 5 But I am poor and needy; **h** to me, O God!
SS 4: 6 I will **h** to the mountain of myrrh and the hill
Isa 5:19 the plan of the Holy One of Israel **h** to fulfillment,
Na 2: 5 they **h** to the wall, and the mantelet is set up.
Sir 36:10 **H** the day, and remember the appointed time,
2Es 4:42 so also do these places **h** to give back those things

HASTEN (KJV) See also CHOOSE, ENJOYMENT, HASTE, HURRY, QUICKLY, WATCHING

HASTENED (4) [HASTE]
Ge 18: 6 And Abraham **h** into the tent to Sarah, and said,
18: 7 and gave it to the servant, who **h** to prepare it.
2Mc 12:29 Setting out from there, they **h** to Scythopolis,
4Mc 14: 5 though running the course toward immortality, **h**

HASTENING (2) [HASTE]
Zep 1:14 great day of the LORD is near, near and **h** fast;
2Pe 3:12 waiting for and **h** the coming of the day of God,

HASTENS‡ (1) [HASTE]
Wis 6:13 She **h** to make herself known

HASTILY (6) [HASTE]
Pr 13:11 Wealth **h** gotten will dwindle,
25: 8 do not **h** bring into court;
1Ti 5:22 Do not ordain anyone **h,** and do not participate in
Wis 19: 2 to depart and **h** sent them out,
Sir 6: 7 gain them through testing, and do not trust them **h.**
2Es 6:34 then you will not act **h** in the last times.' "

HASTY (5) [HASTE]
Pr 14:29 but one who has a **h** temper exalts folly.
21: 5 but everyone who is **h** comes only to want.
29:20 Do you see someone who is **h** in speech?
Sir 28:11 A **h** quarrel kindles a fire, and a **h** dispute sheds blood.

HASUPHA (3)
Ezr 2:43 The temple servants: the descendants of Ziha, **H,**
Ne 7:46 temple servants: the descendants of Ziha, of **H,**
1Es 5:29 the descendants of Esau, the descendants of **H,**

HAT (1) [HATS]
2Mc 4:12 the noblest of the young men to wear the Greek **h.**

HATACH (KJV) See HATHACH

HATCH (3) [HATCHES, HATCHING]
Isa 34:15 the owl nest and lay and **h** and brood in its shadow;
59: 5 They **h** adders' eggs, and weave the spider's web;
4Mc 14:16 **h** the nestlings and ward off the intruder.

HATCHES (1) [HATCH]
Isa 59: 5 and the crushed egg **h** out a viper.

HATCHETS (1)
Ps 74: 6 And then, with **h** and hammers,

HATCHING (1) [HATCH]
Jer 17:11 Like the partridge **h** what it did not lay,

HATE‡ (108) [EVIL-HATING, GOD-HATERS, HATED, HATEFUL, HATER, HATERS, HATES, HATING, HATRED]
Ge 26:27 that you **h** me and have sent me away from you?"
Ex 18:21 are trustworthy, and **h** dishonest gain;
Lev 19:17 You shall not **h** in your heart anyone of your kin;
Dt 7:15 but he will lay them on all who **h** you.
32:41 and will repay those who **h** me.
32:43 he will repay those who **h** him,
33:11 of those that **h** him, so that they do not rise again.
Jdg 14:16 saying, "You **h** me; you do not really love me.
2Sa 19: 6 for love of those who **h** you and for hatred
1Ki 22: 8 Micaiah son of Imlah; but I **h** him,
2Ch 1:11 wealth, honor, or the life of those who **h** you,
18: 7 Micaiah son of Imlah; but I **h** him,
19: 2 "Should you help the wicked and love those who **h**
Job 8:22 Those who **h** you will be clothed with shame,
Ps 5: 5 before your eyes; you **h** all evildoers.
9:13 See what I suffer from those who **h** me;
21: 8 your right hand will find out those who **h** you.
25:19 and with what violent hatred they **h** me.
26: 5 I **h** the company of evildoers,
31: 6 You **h** those who pay regard to worthless idols,
34:21 and those who **h** the righteous will be condemned.
35:19 or those who **h** me without cause wink the eye.
38:19 and many are those who **h** me wrongfully.
41: 7 All who **h** me whisper together about me;
44: 7 and have put to confusion those who **h** us.
45: 7 you love righteousness and **h** wickedness.
50:17 For you **h** discipline, and you cast my words
68: 1 let those who **h** him flee before him.
69: 4 of my head are those who **h** me without cause;
81:15 Those who **h** the LORD would cringe before him,
83: 2 those who **h** you have raised their heads.
86:17 those who **h** me may see it and be put to shame,
89:23 before him and strike down those who **h** him.
97:10 The LORD loves those who **h** evil;
101: 3 I **h** the work of those who fall away;
105:25 whose hearts he then turned to **h** his people,
109: 3 They beset me with words of **h,**
118: 7 I shall look in triumph on those who **h** me.
119:104 therefore I **h** every false way.
119:113 I **h** the double-minded, but I love your law.
119:128 by all your precepts; I **h** every false way.
119:163 I **h** and abhor falsehood, but I love your law.
120: 6 among those who **h** peace.
129: 5 May all who **h** Zion be put to shame
139:21 Do I not **h** those who **h** you, O LORD?
139:22 I **h** them with perfect hatred;
Pr 1:22 in their scoffing and fools **h** knowledge?
8:13 and the way of evil and perverted speech I **h.**
8:36 all who **h** me love death."
9: 8 A scoffer who is rebuked will only **h** you;
12: 1 but those who **h** to be rebuked are stupid.
13: 5 The righteous **h** falsehood,
13:24 Those who spare the rod **h** their children,
15:27 but those who **h** bribes will live.
25:17 the neighbor will become weary of you and **h** you.
29:10 The bloodthirsty **h** the blameless,
29:24 To be a partner of a thief is to **h** one's own life;
Ecc 3: 8 a time to love, and a time to **h;**
9: 1 whether it is love or **h** one does not know.
9: 6 and their **h** and their envy have already perished;
Isa 61: 8 I **h** robbery and wrongdoing;
66: 5 Your own people who **h** you and reject you
Jer 12: 8 against me—therefore I **h** her.
44: 4 I beg you not to do this abominable thing that I **h!"**
Eze 23:28 into the hands of those whom you **h,** into the hands
35: 6 since you did not **h** bloodshed,
Da 4:19 "My lord, may the dream be for those who **h** you,
Hos 9:15 there I came to **h** them.
Am 5:10 They **h** the one who reproves in the gate,
5:15 **H** evil and love good, and establish justice in
5:21 I **h,** I despise your festivals,
6: 8 I abhor the pride of Jacob and **h** his strongholds;
Mic 3: 2 you who **h** the good and love the evil, who tear
Zec 8:17 for all these are things that I **h,** says the LORD.
Mal 2:16 For I **h** divorce, says the LORD, the God of Israel,
Mt 5:43 'You shall love your neighbor and **h** your enemy.'
6:24 for a slave will either **h** the one and love the other,
24:10 they will betray one another and **h** one another.
Lk 1:71 and from the hand of all who **h** us.
6:22 "Blessed are you when people **h** you,
6:27 Love your enemies, do good to those who **h** you,
14:26 "Whoever comes to me and does not **h** father
16:13 for a slave will either **h** the one and love the other,
Jn 3:20 For all who do evil **h** the light and do not come to
7: 7 The world cannot **h** you, but it hates me
12:25 and those who **h** their life in this world will keep it
Ro 7:15 I do not do what I want, but I do the very thing I **h.**
12: 9 **h** what is evil, hold fast to what is good;
1Jn 3:15 All who **h** a brother or sister are murderers,
4:20 "I love God," and **h** their brothers or sisters,
Rev 2: 6 you **h** the works of the Nicolaitans, which I also **h.**
17:16 they and the beast will **h** the whore;
Tob 4:15 And what you **h,** do not do to anyone.
AdE 14:13 and turn his heart to **h** the man who is fighting
14:15 and you know that I **h** the splendor of the wicked
Sir 7:15 Do not **h** hard labor or farm work,
17:26 and **h** intensely what he abhors.
19: 9 and in time will **h** you.
21: 6 Those who **h** reproof walk in the sinner's steps,
25: 2 I **h** three kinds of people, and I loathe their manner
25:14 Any suffering, but not suffering from those who **h!**
33: 2 The wise will not **h** the law,
1Mc 9:29 and to deal with those of our nation who **h** us.
3Mc 6: 9 And now, you who **h** insolence,
2Es 5:30 If you really **h** your people,
10:23 and given over into the hands of those that **h** us.

HATED‡ (51) [HATE]
Ge 27:41 Now Esau **h** Jacob because of the blessing
29:33 "Because the LORD has heard that I am **h,**
37: 4 they **h** him, and could not speak peaceably to him.
37: 5 and when he told it to his brothers, they **h** him
37: 8 So they **h** him even more because of his dreams
Dt 9:28 and because he **h** them, he has brought them out
2Sa 13:22 nor bad; for Absalom **h** Amnon,
22:18 from my strong enemy, from those who **h** me;
22:41 those who **h** me, and I destroyed them.
Est 9: 5 and did as they pleased to those who **h** them.
9:16 killed seventy-five thousand of those who **h** them;
Job 16: 9 He has torn me in his wrath, and **h** me;
31:29 "If I have rejoiced at the ruin of those who **h** me,
Ps 18:17 and from those who **h** me;
18:40 and those who **h** me I destroyed.
36: 2 that their iniquity cannot be found out and **h.**
106:41 so that those who **h** them ruled over them.
Pr 1:29 Because they **h** knowledge and did not choose
5:12 how I **h** discipline, and my heart despised reproof!
14:17 acts foolishly, and the schemer is **h.**
19: 7 If the poor are **h** even by their kin,
Ecc 2:17 So I **h** life, because what is done under
2:18 I **h** all my toil in which I had toiled under the sun,
Isa 60:15 Whereas you have been forsaken and **h,**
Eze 16:37 all those you loved and all those you **h;**
Mal 1: 3 but I have **h** Esau; I have made his hill country
Mt 10:22 and you will be **h** by all because of my name.
24: 9 you will be **h** by all nations because of my name.
Mk 13:13 and you will be **h** by all because of my name.
Lk 19:14 But the citizens of his country **h** him and sent
21:17 You will be **h** by all because of my name.
Jn 15:18 be aware that it **h** me before it **h** you.
15:24 now they have seen and **h** both me and my Father.
15:25 'They **h** me without a cause.'
17:14 the world has **h** them because they do not belong
Ro 9:13 "I have loved Jacob, but I have **h** Esau."
Heb 1: 9 You have loved righteousness and **h** wickedness;
Wis 11:24 you would not have made anything if you had **h** it.
12: 4 you **h** for their detestable practices,
Sir 9:18 and the one who is reckless in speech is **h.**
20: 8 and whoever pretends to authority is **h.**
21:28 A whisperer degrades himself and is **h**
27:24 I have **h** many things, but him above all;
37:20 A skillful speaker may be **h;**
1Mc 7:26 who **h** and detested Israel,
11:21 But certain renegades who **h** their nation went to
11:38 under his predecessors **h** him.
2Mc 5: 8 pursued by everyone, **h** as a rebel against the laws,
2Es 7:79 and **h** those who fear God—
11:42 you have **h** those who tell the truth,

HATEFUL‡ (13) [HATE]
Rev 18: 2 a haunt of every foul and **h** beast.
AdE 16:24 also most **h** to wild animals and birds for all time.
Wis 14: 9 For equally **h** to God are the ungodly
15:18 Moreover, they worship even the most **h** animals,
17: 5 of the stars avail to illumine that **h** night.
Sir 10: 7 Arrogance is **h** to the Lord and to mortals,
20:15 such a one is **h** to God and humans.
Aza 1: 9 lawless and **h** rebels, and to an unjust king,
3Mc 3: 4 For this reason they appeared **h** to some;
3:27 will be tortured to death with the most **h** torments,
2Es 15:48 You have imitated that **h** one in all her deeds
15:60 As they pass by they shall crush the **h** city,
4Mc 5:27 which are most **h** to us.

HATEFUL (KJV) See also DESPICABLE, HATED

HATER (2) [HATE]
4Mc 11: 4 **H** of virtue, **h** of humankind,

HATERS (1) [HATE]
2Ti 3: 3 slanderers, profligates, brutes, **h** of good,

HATES‡ (27) [HATE]
Ex 23: 5 When you see the donkey of one who **h** you lying
Dt 1:27 because the LORD **h** us that he has brought us out
12:31 that the LORD **h** they have done for their gods.
16:22 things that the LORD your God **h.**
2Sa 5: 8 the lame and the blind, those whom David **h."**
Job 34:17 Shall one who **h** justice govern?
Ps 11: 5 and his soul **h** the lover of violence.
Pr 6:16 There are six things that the LORD **h,**
11:16 but she who **h** virtue is covered with shame.
15:10 but one who **h** a rebuke will die.
26:28 A lying tongue **h** its victims,
28:16 but one who **h** unjust gain will enjoy a long life.
Isa 1:14 and your appointed festivals my soul **h;**
Jn 7: 7 but it **h** me because I testify against it
15:18 "If the world **h** you, be aware that it hated me
15:19 therefore the world **h** you.
15:23 Whoever **h** me **h** my Father also.
Eph 5:29 For no one ever **h** his own body,
1Jn 2:11 But whoever **h** another believer is in the darkness,
3:13 brothers and sisters, that the world **h** you.
Jdt 5:17 for the God who **h** iniquity is with them.
Sir 12: 6 also **h** sinners and will inflict punishment on
15:11 for he does not do what he **h.**
15:13 The Lord **h** all abominations;
19: 6 but one who **h** gossip has less evil.
27:24 above all; even the Lord **h** him.

HATHACH (4)
Est 4: 5 Esther called for **H,** one of the king's eunuchs,
4: 6 **H** went out to Mordecai in the open square of
4: 9 **H** went and told Esther what Mordecai had said.
4:10 Then Esther spoke to **H** and gave him a message

HATHATH (1)
1Ch 4:13 of Othniel: **H** and Meonothai.

HATING (3) [HATE]
Tit 3: 3 despicable, **h** one another.
1Jn 2: 9 while **h** a brother or sister, is still in the darkness.
Jude 1:23 **h** even the tunic defiled by their bodies.

HATIPHA (3)
Ezr 2:54 Neziah, and **H.**
Ne 7:56 of Neziah, of **H.**
1Es 5:32 the descendants of Neziah, the descendants of **H.**

HATITA (3)
Ezr 2:42 of Shallum, of Ater, of Talmon, of Akkub, of **H,**
Ne 7:45 of Ater, of Talmon, of Akkub, of **H,** of Shobai,
1Es 5:28 the descendants of **H,** the descendants of Shobai,

HATRED (21) [HATE]
Nu 35:20 Likewise, if someone pushes another from **h,**
2Sa 19:6 for love of those who hate you and for **h**
Ps 25:19 and with what violent **h** they hate me.
109:5 they reward me evil for good, and **h** for my love.
139:22 I hate them with perfect **h;**
Pr 8:13 The fear of the LORD is **h** of evil.
10:12 **H** stirs up strife, but love covers all offenses.
10:18 Lying lips conceal **h,** and whoever utters slander is
15:17 of vegetables where love is than a fatted ox and **h**
26:26 though **h** is covered with guile,
Eze 23:29 and they shall deal with you in **h,**
35:11 that you showed because of your **h** against them;
Wis 19:13 for they practiced a more bitter **h** of strangers.
1Mc 11:40 and told of the **h** that the troops of Demetrius had
13:6 for all the nations have gathered together out of **h**
2Mc 3:1 of the high priest Onias and his **h** of wickedness,
4:3 When his **h** progressed to such a degree that
4:36 and the Greeks shared their **h** of the crime.
4:49 even the Tyrians, showing their **h** of the crime,
8:4 and to show his **h** of evil.
4Mc 9:3 in your **h** for us do not pity us

HATS (1) [HAT]
Da 3:21 their trousers, their **h,** and their other garments,

HATTIL (2)
Ezr 2:57 Shephatiah, **H,** Pochereth-hazzebaim, and Ami.
Ne 7:59 of **H,** of Pochereth-hazzebaim, of Amon.

HATTUSH (6)
1Ch 3:22 **H,** Igal, Bariah, Neariah, and Shaphat, six.
Ezr 8:2 Of Ithamar, Daniel. Of David, **H,**
Ne 3:10 next to him **H** son of Hashabneiah made repairs.
10:4 **H,** Shebaniah, Malluch,
12:2 Amariah, Malluch, **H,**
1Es 8:29 Of the descendants of David, **H** son of Shecaniah.

HAUGHTILY (4) [HAUGHTY]
2Ki 19:22 you raised your voice and **h** lifted your eyes?
Ps 31:23 but abundantly repays the one who acts **h.**
Isa 37:23 you raised your voice and **h** lifted your eyes?
Mic 2:3 and you shall not walk **h,** for it will be an evil time.

HAUGHTINESS (2) [HAUGHTY]
Isa 2:17 The **h** of people shall be humbled,
Jer 48:29 his pride, and his arrogance, and the **h** of his heart.

HAUGHTY‡ (23) [HAUGHTILY, HAUGHTINESS]
2Sa 22:28 but your eyes are upon the **h** to bring them down.
Ps 18:27 but the **h** eyes you bring down.
101:5 A **h** look and an arrogant heart I will not tolerate.
138:6 but the **h** he perceives from far away.
Pr 6:17 **h** eyes, a lying tongue, and hands
16:18 and a **h** spirit before a fall.
18:12 Before destruction one's heart is **h,**
21:4 **H** eyes and a proud heart—
21:24 The proud, **h** person, named "Scoffer,"
Isa 2:11 The **h** eyes of people shall be brought low,
3:16 of Zion are **h** and walk with outstretched necks,
5:15 and the eyes of the **h** are humbled.
10:12 of the king of Assyria and his **h** pride.
Jer 13:15 do not be **h,** for the LORD has spoken
Eze 16:50 They were **h,** and did abominable things
Zep 3:11 and you shall no longer be **h** in my holy mountain.
Ro 1:30 God-haters, insolent, **h,** boastful, inventors of evil,
12:16 do not be **h,** but associate with the lowly;
1Ti 6:17 command them not to be **h,**
Rev 13:5 a mouth uttering **h** and blasphemous words,
Sir 23:4 Father and God of my life, do not give me **h** eyes,
26:9 The **h** stare betrays an unchaste wife;
3Mc 1:27 and not to overlook this unlawful and **h** deed.

HAUL (2) [HAULED]
Eze 32:3 and I will **h** you up in my dragnet.
Jn 21:6 not able to **h** it in because there were so many fish.

HAULED (1) [HAUL]
Jn 21:11 So Simon Peter went aboard and **h** the net ashore,

HAUNT‡ (6) [HAUNTED, HAUNTS]
Ps 44:19 yet you have broken us in the **h** of jackals,
Isa 34:13 It shall be the **h** of jackals, an abode for ostriches.
35:7 the **h** of jackals shall become a swamp,
Rev 18:2 a **h** of every foul spirit, a **h** of every foul bird, a **h** of every foul and hateful beast.

HAUNTED (1) [HAUNT]
Sir 9:13 and you will not be **h** by the fear of death.

HAUNTS (3) [HAUNT]
Ps 74:20 dark places of the land are full of the **h** of violence.
Sir 41:5 and they frequent the **h** of the ungodly.
2Es 5:8 the wild animals shall roam beyond their **h,**

HAURAN (2)
Eze 47:16 which is on the border of **H.**
47:18 On the east side, between **H** and Damascus;

HAVE‡ (1180 of 5723) [HAD, HAS, HAVING]
See Index of Articles Etc. for an Exhaustive Listing (See Introduction, page xi)

Ge 1:26 and let them **h** dominion over the fish of the sea,
1:28 and **h** dominion over the fish of the sea and
1:29 with seed in its fruit; you shall **h** them for food.
4:20 ancestor of those who live in tents and **h** livestock.
11:6 they are one people, and they **h** all one language;
18:10 in due season, and your wife Sarah shall **h** a son.
18:14 in due season, and Sarah shall **h** a son.
19:8 I **h** two daughters who have not known a man;
19:12 the men said to Lot, **"H** you anyone else here?
19:12 sons, daughters, or anyone you **h** in the city—
24:25 She added, "We **h** plenty of straw and fodder
27:38 Esau said to his father, **"H** you only one blessing,
30:3 and that I too may **h** children through her."
31:32 point out what I **h** that is yours, and take it."
32:5 I **h** oxen, donkeys, flocks, male and female slaves;
33:9 But Esau said, "I **h** enough, my brother; keep what you **h** for yourself."
33:11 and because I **h** everything I want."
35:17 "Do not be afraid; for now you will **h** another son.
37:8 Are you indeed to **h** dominion over us?"
43:7 'Is your father still alive? **H** you another brother?'
43:18 so that he may **h** an opportunity to fall upon us,
44:19 saying, **'H** you a father or a brother?'
44:20 we said to my lord, 'We **h** a father, an old man,
45:10 your flocks, your herds, and all that you **h.**
45:11 and all that you **h,** will not come to poverty.'
46:32 and their herds, and all that they **h.'**
47:26 to this day, that Pharaoh should **h** the fifth.
50:21 So **h** no fear; I myself will provide for you
Ex 9:19 Send, therefore, and **h** your livestock and everything that you **h** in the open field brought
10:9 because we **h** the LORD's festival to celebrate."
10:10 Plainly, you **h** some evil purpose in mind.
10:25 Moses said, "You must also let us **h** sacrifices
12:36 so that they let them **h** what they asked.
14:14 The LORD will fight for you, and you **h** only to keep still."
15:9 divide the spoil, my desire shall **h** its fill of them.
16:12 and in the morning you shall **h** your fill of bread;
17:16 LORD will **h** war with Amalek from generation
18:16 When they **h** a dispute, they come to me
19:10 **H** them wash their clothes
20:3 you shall **h** no other gods before me.
21:8 he shall **h** no right to sell her to a foreign people,
23:12 so that your ox and your donkey may **h** relief,
25:8 And **h** them make me a sanctuary,
26:32 which **h** hooks of gold and rest on four bases
27:9 the court shall **h** hangings of fine twisted linen
27:16 it shall **h** four pillars and with them four bases.
28:3 And you shall speak to all who **h** ability,
28:7 It shall **h** two shoulder-pieces attached to its two
28:32 It shall **h** an opening for the head in the middle
35:2 but on the seventh day you shall **h** a holy sabbath
Lev 7:7 the priest who makes atonement with it shall **h** it.
7:33 shall **h** the right thigh for a portion.
11:4 or **h** divided hoofs, you shall not eat the following:
11:4 it does not **h** divided hoofs; it is unclean for you.
11:5 it does not **h** divided hoofs; it is unclean for you.
11:6 it does not **h** divided hoofs; it is unclean for you.
11:10 or the streams that does not **h** fins and scales,
11:12 that does not **h** fins and scales is detestable to you.
11:21 may eat those that **h** jointed legs above their feet,
11:23 other winged insects that **h** four feet are detestable
14:41 He shall **h** the inside of the house scraped
14:45 He shall **h** the house torn down, its stones and
15:32 This is the ritual for those who **h** a discharge:
16:4 shall **h** the linen undergarments next to his body,
18:20 not **h** sexual relations with your kinsman's wife,
18:23 You shall not **h** sexual relations with any animal
18:23 give herself to an animal to **h** sexual relations
19:36 You shall **h** honest balances, honest weights,
23:7 On the first day you shall **h** a holy convocation;
24:22 shall **h** one law for the alien and for the citizen:
25:9 Then you shall **h** the trumpet sounded loud;
25:9 you shall **h** the trumpet sounded throughout all
25:31 But houses in villages that **h** no walls around them
25:32 the Levites shall forever **h** the right of redemption
25:44 for the male and female slaves whom you may **h,**
25:48 they shall **h** the right of redemption;
26:10 and you shall **h** to clear out the old to make way
26:35 it shall **h** the rest it did not **h** on your sabbaths
26:37 shall **h** no power to stand against your enemies.
Nu 3:32 the leaders of the Levites, and to **h** oversight
4:16 Eleazar son of Aaron the priest shall **h** charge
4:27 and in all that they **h** to do; and you shall assign
5:18 the priest shall **h** the water of bitterness
8:7 **h** them shave their whole body with a razor
8:13 Then you shall **h** the Levites stand before Aaron
9:14 you shall **h** one statute for both the resident alien
11:16 and **h** them take their place there with you.
15:16 alien who resides with you shall **h** the same law
15:29 shall **h** the same law for anyone who acts in error.
15:39 You **h** the fringe so that, when you see it,
18:20 You shall **h** no allotment in their land, nor shall you **h** any share among them; I am your share
18:23 But among the Israelites they shall **h** no allotment,
18:24 that they shall **h** no allotment among the Israelites.
22:38 but do I **h** power to say just anything?
24:7 and his seed shall **h** abundant water,
25:1 to **h** sexual relations with the women of Moab
27:19 **h** him stand before Eleazar the priest and all
28:25 the seventh day you shall **h** a holy convocation;
28:26 festival of weeks, you shall **h** a holy convocation;
29:1 the seventh month you shall **h** a holy convocation;
29:7 this seventh month you shall **h** a holy convocation,
29:12 the seventh month you shall **h** a holy convocation;
29:35 On the eighth day you shall **h** a solemn assembly;
31:30 to the Levites who **h** charge of the tabernacle
32:4 a land for cattle; and your servants **h** cattle.
32:30 they shall **h** possessions among you in the land
34:6 the western boundary, you shall **h** the Great Sea
Dt 1:29 I said to you, **"H** no dread or fear of them.
1:32 But in spite of this, you **h** no trust in the LORD
3:19 I know that you **h** much livestock—
5:7 you shall **h** no other gods before me.
5:26 the living God speaking out of fire, as we **h,**
7:21 **H** no dread of them, for the LORD your God,
8:13 gold is multiplied, and all that you **h** is multiplied,
11:8 you may **h** strength to go in and occupy the land
12:12 (since they **h** no allotment or inheritance with you)
12:20 you may eat meat whenever you **h** the desire.
14:7 Yet of those that chew the cud or **h** the hoof cleft
14:10 does not **h** fins and scales you shall not eat;
14:27 they **h** no allotment or inheritance with you.
14:29 they **h** no allotment or inheritance with you,
17:18 he shall **h** a copy of this law written for him
18:1 tribe of Levi, shall **h** no allotment or inheritance
18:2 shall **h** no inheritance among the other members
18:8 They shall **h** equal portions to eat, even though they **h** income from the sale of family possessions.
19:12 to **h** the culprit taken from there and handed over
22:8 otherwise you might **h** bloodguilt on your house,
22:9 or the whole yield will **h** to be forfeited,
23:12 You shall **h** a designated area outside the camp
23:13 With your utensils you shall **h** a trowel;
25:1 two persons **h** a dispute and enter into litigation,
25:8 If he persists, saying, "I **h** no desire to marry her,"
25:13 You shall not **h** in your bag two kinds of weights,
25:14 shall not **h** in your house two kinds of measures,
25:15 You shall **h** only a full and honest weight; you shall **h** only a full and honest measure,
28:40 shall **h** olive trees throughout all your territory,
28:41 You shall **h** sons and daughters, but they shall not
30:3 God will restore your fortunes and **h** compassion
31:6 Be strong and bold; **h** no fear or dread of them,
32:36 the LORD will vindicate his people, **h** compassion
Jos 6:6 and **h** seven priests carry seven trumpets of rams'
6:7 **h** the armed men pass on before the ark
17:16 Canaanites who live in the plain **h** chariots of iron,
17:17 and **h** great power; you shall not **h** one lot only,
17:18 the Canaanites, though they **h** chariots of iron,
18:7 The Levites **h** no portion among you,
22:24 'What **h** you to do with the LORD, the God of
22:25 you **h** no portion in the LORD.
22:27 "You **h** no portion in the LORD." '
Jdg 3:19 and said, "I **h** a secret message for you, O king."
3:20 and said, "I **h** a message from God for you."
4:18 "Turn aside, my lord, turn aside to me; **h** no fear."
8:6 "Do you already **h** in your possession the hands
8:15 'Do you already **h** in your possession the hands
18:24 and the priest, and go away, and what **h** I left?
19:19 your servants **h** straw and fodder for our donkeys,
19:22 so that we may **h** intercourse with him."
21:22 say to them, 'Be generous and allow us to **h** them;
Ru 1:11 Do I still **h** sons in my womb that they may
1:12 go your way, for I am too old to **h** a husband.
1:12 even if I should **h** a husband tonight and bear sons,
2:12 and may you **h** a full reward from the LORD,
1Sa 7:1 Eleazar, to **h** charge of the ark of the LORD.
8:19 "No! but we are determined to **h** a king over us,
9:7 present to bring to the man of God. What **h** we?"
9:8 "Here, I **h** with me a quarter shekel of silver;
9:12 the people **h** a sacrifice today at the shrine.
11:9 by the time the sun is hot, you shall **h** deliverance.
15:3 attack Amalek, and utterly destroy all that they **h;**
18:8 what more can he **h** but the kingdom?"
21:3 Now then, what **h** you at hand?
21:4 answered David, "I **h** no ordinary bread at hand,
25:6 to your house, and peace be to all that you **h.**
25:7 I hear that you **h** shearers; now your shepherds
25:8 give whatever you **h** at hand to your servants
25:31 my lord shall **h** no cause of grief, or pangs
28:13 king said to her, **"H** no fear; what do you see?"
28:22 Eat, that you may **h** strength when you go on
29:10 in the morning, and leave as soon as you **h** light."
2Sa 2:14 "Let the young men come forward and **h** a contest
7:3 said to the king, "Go, do all that you **h** in mind;
9:10 so that your master's grandson may **h** food to eat;
16:10 "What **h** I to do with you, you sons of Zeruiah?
18:18 "I **h** no son to keep my name in remembrance
18:22 seeing that you **h** no reward for the tidings?"
19:22 "What **h** I to do with you, you sons of Zeruiah,
19:28 What further right **h** I, then, to appeal to the king?
19:34 said to the king, "How many years **h** I still to live
19:43 "We **h** ten shares in the king, and in David also we **h** more than you.
20:1 "We **h** no portion in David, no share in the son
21:5 we should **h** no place in all the territory of Israel
1Ki 1:33 and **h** my son Solomon ride on my own mule,

1Ki 1:53 Then King Solomon sent to **h** him brought down
2:14 Then he said, "May I **h** a word with you?"
2:16 And now I **h** one request to make of you;
2:20 she said, "I **h** one small request to make of you;
8:50 so that they may **h** compassion on them
11:36 my servant David may always **h** a lamp before me
12:16 "What share do we **h** in David? We **h** no inheritance in the son of Jesse.
17:18 She then said to Elijah, "What **h** you against me,
18:18 "I have not troubled Israel; but you **h**,
18:19 Now therefore **h** all Israel assemble for me
20:4 O king, I am yours, and all that I **h**."
20:22 and consider well what you **h** to do;
21:2 so that I may **h** it for a vegetable garden,
21:10 and **h** them bring a charge against him, saying
22:17 on the mountains, like sheep that **h** no shepherd;
22:17 LORD said, 'These **h** no master; let each one go
2Ki 2:16 we **h** fifty strong men among your servants;
3:13 to the king of Israel, "What **h** I to do with you?
3:14 were it not that I **h** regard for King Jehoshaphat
4:2 Tell me, what do you **h** in the house?"
4:8 wealthy woman lived, who urged him to **h** a meal.
4:13 Would you **h** a word spoken on your behalf
4:43 says the LORD, 'They shall eat and **h** some left.' "
7:17 the captain on whose hand he leaned to **h** charge
9:5 announced, "I **h** a message for you, commander.
9:18 Jehu responded, "What **h** you to do with peace?
9:19 Jehu answered, "What **h** you to do with peace?
10:2 and you **h** at your disposal chariots and horses,
10:19 for I **h** a great sacrifice to offer to Baal;
22:4 and **h** him count the entire sum of the money
22:5 who **h** the oversight of the house of the LORD;
22:9 workers who **h** oversight of the house of the LORD.
1Ch 4:27 but his brothers did not **h** many children, nor did
13:2 priests and Levites in the cities that **h** pasture lands
17:2 said to David, "Do all that you **h** in mind,
22:15 You **h** an abundance of workers: stonecutters,
23:4 **h** charge of the work in the house of the LORD,
23:11 but Jeush and Beriah did not **h** many sons,
26:32 to **h** the oversight of the Reubenites, the Gadites,
29:3 I **h** a treasure of my own of gold and silver,
2Ch 1:12 before you, and none after you shall **h** the like.
10:16 "What share do we **h** in David? We **h** no inheritance in the son of Jesse.
13:8 a great multitude and **h** with you the golden calves
13:10 We **h** priests ministering to the LORD
13:12 his priests **h** their battle trumpets to sound the call
16:9 for from now on you will **h** wars.
18:16 LORD said, 'These **h** no master; let each one go
21:15 yourself will **h** a severe sickness with a disease
28:10 But what **h** you except sins against the LORD
31:10 we have had enough to eat and **h** plenty to spare;
31:10 so that we **h** this great supply left over.
34:12 the sons of the Kohathites, to **h** oversight.
35:21 saying, "What **h** I to do with you, king of Judah?
Ezr 3:8 to **h** the oversight of the work on the house
4:3 "You shall **h** no part with us in building a house
4:16 you will then **h** no possession in the province
5:17 **h** a search made in the royal archives there
Ne 2:20 but you **h** no share or claim or historic right
9:37 they **h** power also over our bodies and
10:28 all who **h** knowledge and understanding,
Est 3:9 those who **h** charge of the king's business,
5:14 in the morning tell the king to **h** Mordecai hanged
8:5 seems right before the king, and I **h** his approval,
Job 2:4 All that people **h** they will give to save their lives.
3:9 let it hope for light, but **h** none;
3:15 or with princes who **h** gold,
3:26 I **h** no rest; but trouble comes.
5:16 So the poor **h** hope, and injustice shuts its mouth
6:8 "O that I might **h** my request, and that God would
6:13 In truth I **h** no help in me, and any resource
7:1 "Do not human beings **h** a hard service on earth,
10:4 Do you **h** eyes of flesh? Do you see as humans
11:18 And you will **h** confidence, because there is hope;
12:3 But I **h** understanding as well as you;
12:5 Those at ease **h** contempt for misfortune,
13:13 "Let me **h** silence, and I will speak,
13:15 See, he will kill me; I **h** no hope;
16:3 **H** windy words no limit? Or what provokes you
17:9 that **h** clean hands grow stronger and stronger.
18:17 and they **h** no name in the street.
18:19 They **h** no offspring or descendant
19:21 **H** pity on me, **h** pity on me, O you my friends,
24:7 without clothing, and **h** no covering in the cold.
33:32 If you **h** anything to say, answer me;
34:10 "Therefore, hear me, you who **h** sense,
34:16 "If you **h** understanding, hear this;
34:34 Those who **h** sense will say to me,
35:3 If you ask, 'What advantage **h** I? How am I better
36:2 for I **h** yet something to say on God's behalf.
38:4 Tell me, if you **h** understanding.
39:12 Do you **h** faith in it that it will return,
40:9 **H** you an arm like God, and can you thunder
Ps 13:2 and **h** sorrow in my heart all day long?
14:4 **H** they no knowledge, all the evildoers
16:2 "You are my Lord; I **h** no good apart from you."
16:6 in pleasant places; I **h** a goodly heritage.
17:14 may their children **h** more than enough;
19:13 do not let them **h** dominion over me.
24:4 Those who **h** clean hands and pure hearts,
34:9 for those who fear him **h** no want.
35:25 say to themselves, "Aha, we **h** our heart's desire."
37:19 in the days of famine they **h** abundance.
45:16 you, O king, shall **h** sons;
50:16 "What right **h** you to recite my statutes,
51:1 **H** mercy on me, O God, according to your

Ps 51:16 For you **h** no delight in sacrifice;
53:4 **H** they no knowledge, those evildoers,
56:6 As they hoped to **h** my life,
58:4 They **h** venom like the venom of a serpent,
68:23 your dogs may **h** their share from the foe.
69:27 Add guilt to their guilt; may they **h** no acquittal
72:8 May he **h** dominion from sea to sea,
72:12 the poor and those who **h** no helper.
73:4 For they **h** no pain; their bodies are sound
73:25 Whom **h** I in heaven but you?
74:20 **H** regard for your covenant,
80:14 **h** regard for this vine,
82:5 They **h** neither knowledge nor understanding,
88:4 I am like those who **h** no help,
89:13 You **h** a mighty arm; strong is your hand,
90:13 How long? **H** compassion on your servants!
102:13 You will rise up and **h** compassion on Zion,
102:14 servants hold its stones dear, and **h** pity on its dust.
102:27 but you are the same, and your years **h** no end.
104:12 the birds of the air **h** their habitation;
104:33 I will sing praise to my God while I **h** being.
111:10 all those who practice it **h** a good understanding.
115:5 They **h** mouths, but do not speak;
115:6 They **h** ears, but do not hear;
115:7 They **h** hands, but do not feel;
119:42 Then I shall **h** an answer for those who taunt me,
119:99 I **h** more understanding than all my teachers
119:117 and **h** regard for your statutes continually.
119:133 and never let iniquity **h** dominion over me.
119:165 Great peace **h** those who love your law;
123:3 **H** mercy upon us, O LORD, **h** mercy upon us,
135:14 and **h** compassion on his servants.
135:16 They **h** mouths, but they do not speak;
135:16 they **h** eyes, but they do not see;
135:17 they **h** ears, but they do not hear,
Pr 1:14 your lot among us; we will all **h** one purse"—
1:25 and would **h** none of my reproof,
1:30 would **h** none of my counsel,
3:28 tomorrow I will give it"—when you **h** it with you.
8:14 I **h** good advice and sound wisdom;
8:14 I **h** insight, I **h** strength.
12:9 Better to be despised and **h** a servant,
12:11 Those who till their land will **h** plenty of food,
12:11 those who follow worthless pursuits **h** no sense.
12:20 but those who counsel peace **h** joy.
13:7 others pretend to be poor, yet **h** great wealth.
13:25 The righteous **h** enough to satisfy their appetite,
14:20 by their neighbors, but the rich **h** many friends.
14:26 and one's children will **h** a refuge.
17:16 Why should fools **h** a price in hand to buy wisdom, when they **h** no mind to learn?
18:1 showing contempt for all who **h** sound judgment.
19:19 you effect a rescue, you will only **h** to do it again.
20:13 open your eyes, and you will **h** plenty of bread.
22:2 The rich and the poor **h** this in common:
22:11 are gracious in speech will **h** the king as a friend.
23:2 put a knife to your throat if you **h** a big appetite.
24:5 those who **h** knowledge than those who **h** strength;
24:20 for the evil **h** no future;
24:25 but those who rebuke the wicked will **h** delight,
25:10 and your ill repute will **h** no end.
28:10 but the blameless will **h** a goodly inheritance.
28:19 Anyone who tills the land will **h** plenty of bread,
28:19 worthless pursuits will **h** plenty of poverty.
29:7 the wicked **h** no such understanding.
29:13 The poor and the oppressor **h** this in common:
30:2 I do not **h** human understanding.
30:3 nor **h** I knowledge of the holy ones.
30:27 locusts **h** no king, yet all of them march in rank;
31:11 and he will **h** no lack of gain.
Ecc 2:14 The wise **h** eyes in their head, but fools walk
2:25 who can eat or who can **h** enjoyment?
3:9 What gain **h** the workers from their toil?
3:19 They all **h** the same breath, and humans **h** no advantage over the animals;
4:9 because they **h** a good reward for their toil.
4:10 alone and falls and does not **h** another to help.
5:16 what gain do they **h** from toiling for the wind?
6:8 For what advantage **h** the wise over fools?
6:8 what do the poor **h** who know how to conduct
9:5 the dead know nothing; they **h** no more reward,
9:6 again will they **h** any share in all that happens
12:1 when you will say, "I **h** no pleasure in them";
SS 8:8 We **h** a little sister, and she has no breasts.
8:12 you, O Solomon, may **h** the thousand,
Isa 2:22 mortals, who **h** only breath in their nostrils,
3:6 "You **h** a cloak; you shall be our leader,
8:20 Surely, those who speak like this will **h** no dawn!
9:17 why the Lord did not **h** pity on their young people,
10:7 not what he intends, nor does he **h** this in mind;
10:13 and by my wisdom, for I **h** understanding;
13:17 Medes against them, who **h** no regard for silver
13:18 they will **h** no mercy on the fruit of the womb;
14:1 But the LORD will **h** compassion on Jacob
17:8 they will not **h** regard for the altars,
22:11 or **h** regard for him who planned it long ago.
22:16 What right do you **h** here? Who are your relatives
23:12 to Cyprus—even there you will **h** no rest.
26:1 We **h** a strong city; he sets up victory
26:4 for in the LORD GOD you **h** an everlasting rock.
27:4 I **h** no wrath.
27:11 he that made them will not **h** compassion on them,
28:15 and with Sheol we **h** an agreement;
30:29 You shall **h** a song as in the night
32:3 the eyes of those who **h** sight will not be closed, and the ears of those who **h** hearing will listen.
32:4 The minds of the rash will **h** good judgment,

Isa 43:8 Bring forth the people who are blind, yet **h** eyes, who are deaf, yet **h** ears!
45:20 They **h** no knowledge—those who carry about
49:13 and will **h** compassion on his suffering ones.
50:2 Or **h** I no power to deliver?
50:11 This is what you shall **h** from my hand:
51:7 you people who **h** my teaching in your hearts;
54:8 with everlasting love I will **h** compassion on you,
55:1 and you that **h** no money, come, buy and eat!
55:7 return to the LORD, that he may **h** mercy on them,
56:11 dogs **h** a mighty appetite; they never **h** enough.
56:11 The shepherds also **h** no understanding;
59:10 groping like those who **h** no eyes;
Jer 2:28 for you **h** as many gods as you **h** towns, O Judah.
3:3 yet you **h** the forehead of a whore,
4:22 they are stupid children, they **h** no understanding.
5:4 "These are only the poor, they **h** no sense;
5:21 foolish and senseless people, who **h** eyes, but do not see, who **h** ears, but do not hear.
5:31 my people love to **h** it so, but what will you do
6:23 they are cruel and **h** no mercy,
10:5 they **h** to be carried, for they cannot walk.
12:15 I will again **h** compassion on them,
13:14 I will not pity or spare or **h** compassion
14:13 shall not see the sword, nor shall you **h** famine,
14:18 trade throughout the land, and **h** no knowledge.
15:5 Who will **h** pity on you, O Jerusalem,
16:2 nor shall you **h** sons or daughters in this place.
21:7 not pity them, or spare them, or **h** compassion.
21:9 shall live and shall **h** their lives as a prize of war.
29:6 Take wives and **h** sons and daughters;
29:11 For surely I know the plans I **h** for you,
29:32 he shall not **h** anyone living among this people
30:10 But as for you, **h** no fear, my servant Jacob,
30:10 Jacob shall return and **h** quiet and ease,
30:18 and **h** compassion on his dwellings;
31:20 I will surely **h** mercy on him, says the LORD.
33:21 that he would not **h** a son to reign on his throne,
33:26 restore their fortunes, and will **h** mercy upon them.
35:5 and I said to them, "**H** some wine."
35:9 We **h** no vineyard or field or seed;
36:30 He shall **h** no one to sit upon the throne of David,
38:2 they shall **h** their lives as a prize of war, and live
38:14 king said to Jeremiah, "I **h** something to ask you;
39:18 but you shall **h** your life as a prize of war,
41:8 "Do not kill us, for we **h** stores of wheat, barley,
42:12 will grant you mercy, and he will **h** mercy on you
42:17 shall **h** no remnant or survivor from the disaster
44:17 We used to **h** plenty of food, and prospered,
46:27 But as for you, **h** no fear, my servant Jacob,
46:27 Jacob shall return and **h** quiet and ease,
46:28 As for you, **h** no fear, my servant Jacob,
49:12 do not deserve to drink the cup still **h** to drink it,
49:32 scatter to every wind those who **h** shaven temples,
50:42 they are cruel and **h** no mercy.
La 3:21 But this I call to mind, and therefore I **h** hope:
3:32 Although he causes grief, he will **h** compassion
3:37 Who can command and **h** it done,
Eze 3:7 because all the house of Israel **h** a hard forehead
4:15 will let you **h** cow's dung instead of human dung,
5:11 my eye will not spare, and I will **h** no pity.
7:4 My eye will not spare you, I will **h** no pity.
7:9 My eye will not spare; I will **h** no pity.
8:18 my eye will not spare, nor will I **h** pity;
9:10 my eye will not spare, nor will I **h** pity,
10:8 cherubim appeared to **h** the form of a human hand
12:2 who **h** eyes to see but do not see, who **h** ears to hear but do not hear;
18:23 **H** I any pleasure in the death of the wicked,
18:32 For I **h** no pleasure in the death of anyone,
26:20 or **h** a place in the land of the living.
33:11 I **h** no pleasure in the death of the wicked,
37:24 king over them; and they shall all **h** one shepherd.
39:25 and **h** mercy on the whole house of Israel;
40:45 for the priests who **h** charge of the temple,
40:46 for the priests who **h** charge of the altar;
44:18 They shall **h** linen turbans on their heads,
45:8 but they shall let the house of Israel **h** the land
45:10 You shall **h** honest balances, an honest ephah,
47:13 Joseph shall **h** two portions.
48:10 the priests shall **h** an allotment measuring
48:13 the Levites shall **h** an allotment
48:17 The city shall **h** open land:
Da 2:21 and knowledge to those who **h** understanding.
2:30 wisdom that I **h** more than any other living being,
3:16 we **h** no need to present a defense to you in this
4:1 May you **h** abundant prosperity!
5:7 **h** a chain of gold around his neck, and rank third
5:11 he was found to **h** enlightenment, understanding,
5:16 **h** a chain of gold around your neck, and rank third
6:25 the whole world: "May you **h** abundant prosperity!
8:7 The ram did not **h** power to withstand it;
Hos 1:2 a wife of whoredom and **h** children of whoredom,
1:6 for I will no longer **h** pity on the house of Israel
1:7 But I will **h** pity on the house of Judah,
2:4 Upon her children also I will **h** no pity,
2:23 And I will **h** pity on Lo-ruhamah, and I will say
3:3 you shall not **h** intercourse with a man,
10:3 "We **h** no king, for we do not fear the LORD,
14:8 O Ephraim, what **h** I to do with idols?
Joel 2:4 They **h** the appearance of horses,
Am 5:3 that marched out a thousand shall **h** a hundred left,
5:3 which marched out a hundred shall **h** ten left.
Mic 2:5 Therefore you will **h** no one to cast the line by lot
3:5 who cry "Peace" when they **h** something to eat,
5:12 and you shall **h** no more soothsayers;
7:5 no trust in a friend, **h** no confidence in a loved one

Mic 7:19 He will again **h** compassion upon us;
Hab 1:14 like crawling things that **h** no ruler.
2: 5 like Death they never **h** enough.
Hag 1: 6 you eat, but you never **h** enough; you drink, but you never **h** your fill;
Zec 3: 7 you shall rule my house and **h** charge of my courts
10: 6 bring them back because I **h** compassion on them,
11: 5 and their own shepherds **h** no pity on them.
11: 6 no longer **h** pity on the inhabitants of the earth,
12: 5 "The inhabitants of Jerusalem **h** strength
Mal 1:10 I **h** no pleasure in you, says the LORD of hosts,
2:10 **H** we not all one father?
Mt 3: 9 'We **h** Abraham as our ancestor';
5:46 love those who love you, what reward do you **h?**
6: 1 then you **h** no reward from your Father in heaven.
7:12 do to others as you would **h** them do to you;
8: 8 I am not worthy to **h** you come under my roof;
8:20 "Foxes **h** holes, and birds of the air **h** nests;
8:29 "What **h** you to do with us, Son of God?
9:12 "Those who are well **h** no need of a physician,
9:27 crying loudly, "**H** mercy on us, Son of David!"
10:21 against parents and **h** them put to death;
10:26 "So **h** no fear of them; for nothing is covered up
12:36 the day of judgment you will **h** to give an account
13: 5 on rocky ground, where they did not **h** much soil,
13:12 For to those who **h**, more will be given, and they will **h** an abundance; but from those who **h** nothing, even what they **h** will be taken away.
14: 4 telling him, "It is not lawful for you to **h** her."
15:22 shouting, "**H** mercy on me, Lord, Son of David;
15:32 and said, "I **h** compassion for the crowd,
15:34 Jesus asked them, "How many loaves **h** you?"
17:15 "Lord, **h** mercy on my son, for he is an epileptic
17:20 I tell you, if you **h** faith the size of a mustard seed,
18: 8 than to **h** two hands or two feet and to be thrown
18: 9 than to **h** two eyes and to be thrown into the hell
18:26 saying, '**H** patience with me, and I will pay you
18:29 '**H** patience with me, and I will pay you.'
19:16 what good deed must I do to **h** eternal life?"
19:21 and you will **h** treasure in heaven;
19:27 and followed you. What then will we **h?"**
20:30 shouted, "Lord, **h** mercy on us, Son of David!"
20:31 loudly, "**H** mercy on us, Lord, Son of David!"
21:21 "Truly I tell you, if you **h** faith and do not doubt,
23: 6 They love to **h** the place of honor at banquets
23: 7 and to **h** people call them rabbi.
23: 8 for you **h** one teacher, and you are all students.
23: 9 for you **h** one Father—the one in heaven.
23:10 for you **h** one instructor, the Messiah.
25:25 Here you **h** what is yours.'
25:29 For to all those who **h**, more will be given, and they will **h** an abundance; but from those who **h** nothing, even what they **h** will be taken away.
26:11 For you always **h** the poor with you, but you will not always **h** me.
26:62 high priest stood up and said, "**H** you no answer?
27:20 to ask for Barabbas and to **h** Jesus killed.
27:65 Pilate said to them, "You **h** a guard of soldiers;
Mk 1:24 "What **h** you to do with us, Jesus of Nazareth?
2:17 "Those who are well **h** no need of a physician,
2:19 As long as they **h** the bridegroom with them,
3: 9 He told his disciples to **h** a boat ready for him
3:15 and to **h** authority to cast out demons.
3:29 against the Holy Spirit can never **h** forgiveness,
4: 5 fell on rocky ground, where it did not **h** much soil,
4:17 But they **h** no root, and endure only for a while;
4:25 those who **h**, more will be given; and from those who **h** nothing, even what they **h** will be taken
4:40 "Why are you afraid? **H** you still no faith?"
5: 7 "What **h** you to do with me, Jesus,
6:18 "It is not lawful for you to **h** your brother's wife."
6:38 "How many loaves **h** you? Go and see."
7: 9 "You **h** a fine way of rejecting the commandment
8: 2 "I **h** compassion for the crowd,
8: 5 He asked them, "How many loaves do you **h?"**
8:16 to one another, "It is because we **h** no bread."
8:18 Do you **h** eyes, and fail to see? Do you **h** ears, and fail to hear?
9:22 but if you are able to do anything, **h** pity on us
9:43 maimed than to **h** two hands and to go to hell,
9:45 lame than to **h** two feet and to be thrown into hell.
9:47 than to **h** two eyes and to be thrown into hell,
9:50 **H** salt in yourselves, and be at peace
10:21 and you will **h** treasure in heaven;
10:23 "How hard it will be for those who **h** wealth to enter the kingdom of God!"
10:47 and say, "Jesus, Son of David, **h** mercy on me!"
10:48 more loudly, "Son of David, **h** mercy on me!"
11:22 Jesus answered them, "**H** faith in God.
11:25 forgive, if you **h** anything against anyone;
12:39 and to **h** the best seats in the synagogues
13:12 will rise against parents and **h** them put to death;
14: 7 For you always **h** the poor with you,
14: 7 but you will not always **h** me.
14:60 and asked Jesus, "**H** you no answer?
15: 4 Pilate asked him again, "**H** you no answer?
15:11 to **h** him release Barabbas for them instead.
Lk 1:14 You will **h** joy and gladness,
3: 8 'We **h** Abraham as our ancestor';
4:34 What **h** you to do with us, Jesus of Nazareth?
5:31 "Those who are well **h** no need of a physician,
6:31 Do to others as you would **h** them do to you.
7:40 said to him, "Simon, I **h** something to say to you."
8:13 But these **h** no root; they believe only for a while
8:18 who **h**, more will be given; and from those who do not **h**, even what they seem to **h** will be taken
8:28 "What **h** you to do with me, Jesus,
Lk 9:13 "We **h** no more than five loaves and two fish—
9:58 "Foxes **h** holes, and birds of the air **h** nests;
11:43 you love to **h** the seat of honor in the synagogues
12:17 for I **h** no place to store my crops?'
12:19 'Soul, you **h** ample goods laid up for many years;
12:24 they **h** neither storehouse nor barn,
12:35 "Be dressed for action and **h** your lamps lit;
12:37 he will fasten his belt and **h** them sit down to eat,
12:50 I **h** a baptism with which to be baptized,
15:17 'How many of my father's hired hands **h** bread
16:24 He called out, 'Father Abraham, **h** mercy on me,
16:28 for I **h** five brothers—that he may warn them,
16:29 replied, 'They **h** Moses and the prophets;
17:13 out, saying, "Jesus, Master, **h** mercy on us!"
18: 4 'Though I **h** no fear of God and no respect for
18:22 and you will **h** treasure in heaven;
18:24 "How hard it is for those who **h** wealth to enter the kingdom of God!
18:38 shouted, "Jesus, Son of David, **h** mercy on me!"
18:39 more loudly, "Son of David, **h** mercy on me!"
19:26 'I tell you, to all those who **h**, more will be given; but from those who **h** nothing, even what they **h** will be taken away.
20:46 and to **h** the best seats in the synagogues
21:36 praying that you may **h** the strength to escape
23:16 I will therefore **h** him flogged and release him."
23:22 therefore **h** him flogged and then release him."
24:39 Touch me and see; for a ghost does not **h** flesh and bones as you see that I **h."**
24:41 he said to them, "**H** you anything here to eat?"
Jn 1:22 Let us **h** an answer for those who sent us.
2: 3 mother of Jesus said to him, "They **h** no wine."
3:15 that whoever believes in him may **h** eternal life.
3:16 in him may not perish but may **h** eternal life.
4:11 "Sir, you **h** no bucket, and the well is deep.
4:15 or **h** to keep coming here to draw water.
4:17 The woman answered him, "I **h** no husband."
4:17 "You are right in saying, 'I **h** no husband';
4:18 and the one you **h** now is not your husband.
4:32 "I **h** food to eat that you do not know about."
5: 7 "Sir, I **h** no one to put me into the pool
5:26 so he has granted the Son also to **h** life in himself;
5:36 But I **h** a testimony greater than John's.
5:38 and you do not **h** his word abiding in you,
5:39 because you think that in them you **h** eternal life;
5:40 Yet you refuse to come to me to **h** life.
5:42 I know that you do not **h** the love of God in you.
6:40 see the Son and believe in him may **h** eternal life;
6:53 and drink his blood, you **h** no life in you.
6:54 eat my flesh and drink my blood **h** eternal life,
6:68 You **h** the words of eternal life.
7:15 saying, "How does this man **h** such learning,
7:20 The crowd answered, "You **h** a demon!
8: 6 they might **h** some charge to bring against him.
8:12 but will **h** the light of life.
8:26 I **h** much to say about you and much to condemn;
8:35 The slave does not **h** a permanent place
8:41 "We are not illegitimate children; we **h** one father,
8:48 saying that you are a Samaritan and **h** a demon?"
8:49 Jesus answered, "I do not **h** a demon;
8:52 said to him, "Now we know that you **h** a demon.
9:41 "If you were blind, you would not **h** sin.
10:10 I came that they may **h** life, and **h** it abundantly.
10:16 I **h** other sheep that do not belong to this fold.
10:18 I **h** power to lay it down, and I **h** power to take it
11:50 better for you to **h** one man die for the people than to **h** the whole nation destroyed."
12: 8 You always **h** the poor with you, but you do not always **h** me."
12:35 Walk while you **h** the light,
12:36 While you **h** the light, believe in the light,
13: 8 "Unless I wash you, you **h** no share with me."
13:35 my disciples, if you **h** love for one another."
14:21 They who **h** my commandments and keep them
15:22 they would not **h** sin; but now they **h** no excuse
15:24 works that no one else did, they would not **h** sin.
16:12 "I still **h** many things to say to you,
16:20 you will **h** pain, but your pain will turn into joy.
16:22 So you **h** pain now; but I will see you again,
16:30 and do not need to **h** anyone question you;
16:33 said this to you, so that in me you may **h** peace.
17:13 they may **h** my joy made complete in themselves.
18:14 it was better to **h** one person die for the people.
18:39 But you **h** a custom that I release someone for you
19: 7 The Jews answered him, "We **h** a law,
19:10 Do you not know that I **h** power to release you,
19:11 "You would **h** no power over me unless
19:15 priests answered, "We **h** no king but the emperor."
19:31 to **h** the legs of the crucified men broken
20:31 that through believing you may **h** life in his name.
21: 5 said to them, "Children, you **h** no fish, **h** you?"
21:12 Jesus said to them, "Come and **h** breakfast."
Ac 2:22 listen to what I **h** to say: Jesus of Nazareth,
3: 6 "I **h** no silver or gold, but what I **h** I give you;
3:14 and asked to **h** a murderer given to you,
5:21 and sent to the prison to **h** them brought.
8:21 You **h** no part or share in this,
10:22 come to his house and to hear what you **h** to say."
10:47 who have received the Holy Spirit just as we **h?"**
13:15 if you **h** any word of exhortation for the people,
13:28 they asked Pilate to **h** him killed.
17:15 instructions to **h** Silas and Timothy join him
17:28 For 'In him we live and move and **h** our being';
17:31 he will **h** the world judged in righteousness
19:38 Demetrius and the artisans with him **h** a complaint
20:16 so that he might not **h** to spend time in Asia;
21:23 We **h** four men who are under a vow.
Ac 22:16 Get up, be baptized, and **h** your sins washed away,
23:19 and asked, "What is it that you **h** to report to me?"
23:30 also to state before you what they **h** against him."
24:15 I **h** a hope in God—a hope that they themselves
24:16 I do my best always to **h** a clear conscience
24:19 make an accusation, if they **h** anything against me.
24:23 keep him in custody, but to let him **h** some liberty
24:25 when I **h** an opportunity, I will send for you."
25: 3 to **h** him transferred to Jerusalem.
25: 5 "let those of you who **h** the authority come down
25:26 examined him, I may **h** something to write—
26: 1 to Paul, "You **h** permission to speak for yourself."
27:25 keep up your courage, men, for I **h** faith in God
27:26 But we will **h** to run aground on some island."
Ro 1:13 as I **h** among the rest of the Gentiles.
2: 1 Therefore you **h** no excuse, whoever you are,
2:27 will condemn you that **h** the written code
4:11 and who thus **h** righteousness reckoned to them,
5: 1 we **h** peace with God through our Lord Jesus
5:15 more surely **h** the grace of God and the free gift
6:14 For sin will **h** no dominion over you,
8: 9 Anyone who does not **h** the Spirit of Christ
8:23 we ourselves, who **h** the first fruits of the Spirit,
9: 2 I **h** great sorrow and unceasing anguish
9: 9 this time I will return and Sarah shall **h** a son."
9:15 "I will **h** mercy on whom I **h** mercy, and I will **h** compassion on whom I **h** compassion."
10: 2 I can testify that they **h** a zeal for God, but it is not
10:18 have they not heard? Indeed they **h;**
12: 4 For as in one body we **h** many members, and not all the members **h** the same function,
12: 6 We **h** gifts that differ according to the grace given
13: 3 Do you wish to **h** no fear of the authority?
14:22 The faith that you **h**, **h** as your own conviction before God.
14:22 Blessed are those who **h** no reason to condemn
14:23 But those who **h** doubts are condemned if they eat,
15: 4 encouragement of the scriptures we might **h** hope.
15:17 In Christ Jesus, then, I **h** reason to boast
15:23 I desire, as I **h** for many years, to come to you
1Co 2:16 But we **h** the mind of Christ.
3: 8 and the one who waters **h** a common purpose,
4: 7 What do you **h** that you did not receive?
4: 8 Already you **h** all you want!
4:15 For though you might **h** ten thousand guardians in Christ, you do not **h** many fathers.
5:12 For what **h** I to do with judging those outside?
6: 4 If you **h** ordinary cases, then, do you appoint as judges those who **h** no standing in the church?
6: 7 to **h** lawsuits at all with one another is already
6:19 the Holy Spirit within you, which you **h** from God,
7: 2 each man should **h** his own wife and each woman
7: 4 the wife does not **h** authority over her own body,
7: 4 husband does not **h** authority over his own body,
7:25 concerning virgins, I **h** no command of the Lord,
7:29 those who **h** wives be as though they had none,
7:40 And I think that I too **h** the Spirit of God.
8: 2 does not yet **h** the necessary knowledge;
9: 4 Do we not **h** the right to our food and drink?
9: 5 Do we not **h** the right to be accompanied by a
9: 6 is it only Barnabas and I who **h** no right to refrain
9:17 For if I do this of my own will, I **h** a reward;
11: 6 disgraceful for a woman to **h** her hair cut off or
11: 7 For a man ought not to **h** his head veiled,
11:10 a woman ought to **h** a symbol of authority
11:16 we **h** no such custom, nor do the churches of God.
11:19 Indeed, there **h** to be factions among you,
11:22 What! Do you not **h** homes to eat and drink in?
12:21 eye cannot say to the hand, "I **h** no need of you," nor again the head to the feet, "I **h** no need of you."
12:25 the members may **h** the same care for one another.
13: 1 but do not **h** love, I am a noisy gong or a clanging
13: 2 And if I **h** prophetic powers, and understand all
13: 2 and if I **h** all faith, so as to remove mountains, but do not **h** love, I am nothing.
13: 3 but do not **h** love, I gain nothing.
14:37 claims to be a prophet, or to **h** spiritual powers,
15:34 for some people **h** no knowledge of God.
2Co 1:15 so that you might **h** a double favor;
2: 4 let you know the abundant love that I **h** for you.
3: 4 confidence that we **h** through Christ toward God.
3:12 we **h** such a hope, we act with great boldness
4: 7 But we **h** this treasure in clay jars,
4:13 But just as we **h** the same spirit of faith that is in
5: 1 we **h** a building from God, a house not made
5: 8 we do **h** confidence, and we would rather be away
6:15 What agreement does Christ **h** with Beliar?
7: 1 Since we **h** these promises, beloved, let us cleanse
7: 4 I often boast about you; I **h** great pride in you;
7:16 I rejoice, because I **h** complete confidence in you.
8:12 not according to what one does not **h.**
8:15 "The one who had much did not **h** too much, and the one who had little did not **h** too little."
8:16 the same eagerness for you that I myself **h.**
10: 4 but they **h** divine power to destroy strongholds.
12:21 may **h** to mourn over many who previously sinned
13:10 I may not **h** to be severe in using the authority
Gal 2: 4 to spy on the freedom we **h** in Christ Jesus,
6:10 whenever we **h** an opportunity, let us work for the
Eph 1: 7 In him we **h** redemption through his blood,
2:18 both of us **h** access in one Spirit to the Father.
3:12 in whom we **h** access to God in boldness
3:18 I pray that you may **h** the power to comprehend,
4:28 so as to **h** something to share with the needy.
6: 9 that both of you **h** the same Master in heaven,
6:24 who **h** an undying love for our Lord Jesus Christ.
Php 1:30 that you saw I had and now hear that I still **h.**

Php 2:20 I **h** no one like him who will be genuinely
2:27 so that I would not **h** one sorrow after another.
3:3 and **h** no confidence in the flesh—
3:4 though I, too, **h** reason for confidence in the flesh.
3:4 has reason to be confident in the flesh, I **h** more:
3:17 who live according to the example you **h** in us.
4:11 I have learned to be content with whatever I **h**.
4:12 it is to **h** little, and I know what it is to **h** plenty.
4:18 I have been paid in full and **h** more than enough;
Col 1:4 and of the love that you **h** for all the saints,
1:14 in whom we **h** redemption, the forgiveness of sins.
1:18 that he might come to **h** first place in everything.
2:2 they may **h** all the riches of assured understanding
and **h** the knowledge of God's mystery,
2:23 These **h** indeed an appearance of wisdom
4:1 for you know that you also **h** a Master in heaven.
4:16 **h** it read also in the church of the Laodiceans;
1Th 1:8 so that we **h** no need to speak about it.
4:9 you do not need to **h** anyone write to you,
4:13 you may not grieve as others do who **h** no hope.
5:1 you do not need to **h** anything written to you.
5:12 labor among you, and **h** charge of you in the Lord
2Th 3:2 from wicked and evil people; for not all **h** faith.
3:4 And we **h** confidence in the Lord concerning you,
3:9 This was not because we do not **h** that right,
1Ti 2:12 no woman to teach or to **h** authority over a man;
4:10 because we **h** our hope set on the living God,
5:14 I would **h** younger widows marry, bear children,
6:2 who **h** believing masters must not be disrespectful
6:8 but if we **h** food and clothing, we will be content
2Ti 2:6 who ought to **h** the first share of the crops.
Tit 1:9 He must **h** a firm grasp of the word
Phm 1:15 for a while, so that you might **h** him back forever,
1:20 brother, let me **h** this benefit from you in the Lord!
Heb 2:11 and those who are sanctified all **h** one Father.
3:12 that none of you may **h** an evil, unbelieving heart
4:14 Since, then, we **h** a great high priest
4:15 For we do not **h** a high priest who is unable to
4:15 but we **h** one who in every respect has been tested
5:11 About this we **h** much to say that is hard to explain
6:19 We **h** this hope, a sure and steadfast anchor
7:5 who receive the priestly office **h** a commandment
7:26 fitting that we should **h** such a high priest, holy,
8:1 we **h** such a high priest, one who is seated
8:3 for this priest also to **h** something to offer.
10:2 would no longer **h** any consciousness of sin?
10:19 since we **h** confidence to enter the Most Holy Place
10:21 since we **h** a great priest over the house of God,
10:39 but among those who **h** faith and so are saved.
12:8 If you do not **h** that discipline in which all children
13:5 and be content with what you **h**;
13:10 We **h** an altar from which those who officiate
13:10 those who officiate in the tent **h** no right to eat.
13:14 For here we **h** no lasting city, but we are looking
13:16 Do not neglect to do good and to share what you **h**,
13:18 we are sure that we **h** a clear conscience,
Jas 1:4 and let endurance **h** its full effect,
2:3 and say, "**H** a seat here, please,"
2:14 if you say you **h** faith but do not **h** works?
2:18 someone will say, "You **h** faith and I **h** works."
3:14 But if you **h** bitter envy and selfish ambition
4:2 You want something and do not **h** it;
4:2 You do not **h**, because you do not ask.
5:14 elders of the church and **h** them pray over them,
1Pe 1:22 so that you **h** genuine mutual love,
2:20 do right and suffer for it, you **h** God's approval.
3:8 all of you, **h** unity of spirit, sympathy, love for one
4:5 But they will **h** to give an accounting to him
5:2 but willingly, as God would **h** you do it—
2Pe 1:19 we **h** the prophetic message more fully confirmed.
2:14 They **h** eyes full of adultery, insatiable for sin.
2:14 They **h** hearts trained in greed.
1Jn 1:3 so that you also may **h** fellowship with us;
1:6 If we say that we **h** fellowship with him
1:7 we **h** fellowship with one another,
1:8 If we say that we **h** no sin, we deceive ourselves,
2:1 But if anyone does sin, we **h** an advocate
2:20 by the Holy One, and all of you **h** knowledge.
2:28 so that when he is revealed we may **h** confidence
3:3 And all who **h** this hope in him purify themselves,
3:15 and you know that murderers do not **h** eternal life
3:21 if our hearts do not condemn us, we **h** boldness
4:17 that we may **h** boldness on the day of judgment,
4:21 The commandment we **h** from him is this:
5:10 who believe in the Son of God **h** the testimony
5:12 whoever does not **h** the Son of God does not **h** life
5:13 so that you may know that you **h** eternal life.
5:14 And this is the boldness we **h** in him,
2Jn 1:9 but goes beyond it, does not **h** God;
1:12 Although I **h** much to write to you,
3Jn 1:4 I **h** no greater joy than this, to hear that
1:13 I **h** much to write to you, but I would rather not
Jude 1:22 And **h** mercy on some who are wavering;
1:23 and **h** mercy on still others with fear,
Rev 1:18 and I **h** the keys of Death and of Hades.
2:4 But I **h** this against you, that you have abandoned
2:10 be tested, and for ten days you will **h** affliction.
2:14 But I **h** a few things against you: you **h** some there
2:15 So you also **h** some who hold to the teaching of
2:20 But I **h** this against you: you tolerate that woman
2:25 only hold fast to what you **h** until I come.
3:1 you **h** a name of being alive, but you are dead.
3:4 Yet you **h** still a few persons in Sardis
3:8 I know that you **h** but little power,
3:11 I am coming soon; hold fast to what you **h**,
9:4 only those people who do not **h** the seal of God
9:10 They **h** tails like scorpions, with stingers,
Rev 9:11 They **h** as king over them the angel of
11:6 They **h** authority to shut the sky,
11:6 and they **h** authority over the waters to turn them
13:17 no one can buy or sell who does not **h** the mark,
22:14 so that they will **h** the right to the tree of life
Tob 2:13 for we **h** no right to eat anything stolen.
3:17 For Tobias was entitled to **h** her before all others
4:8 If you **h** many possessions, make your gift from
4:8 not be afraid to give according to the little you **h**.
4:21 You **h** great wealth if you fear God and flee from
5:17 Tobit then said to him, "**H** a safe journey."
6:12 **h** before all other men a hereditary claim on her.
6:13 "You **h** every right to take her in marriage.
6:15 and they **h** no other son to bury them."
6:18 I presume that you will **h** children by her,
8:12 "Send one of the maids and **h** her go in to see
10:11 and said, "Farewell, my child; **h** a safe journey.
13:9 again **h** mercy on the children of the righteous.
14:5 "But God will again **h** mercy on them,
Jdt 6:19 and **h** pity on our people in their humiliation,
7:9 "Listen to what we **h** to say, my lord,
7:21 and on no day did they **h** enough water to drink,
7:25 For now we **h** no one to help us;
10:16 you stand before him, **h** no fear in your heart,
10:19 these people, who **h** women like this among them?
11:19 You will drive them like sheep that **h** no shepherd,
12:2 I will **h** enough with the things I brought with me.
12:4 will not use up the supplies I **h** with me
12:17 "**H** a drink and be merry with us!"
AdE 1:8 but the king wished to **h** it so, and he commanded
1:11 and to **h** her display her beauty to all the governors
5:14 in the morning tell the king to **h** Mordecai hanged
13:4 who **h** laws contrary to those of every nation
13:17 and **h** mercy upon your inheritance;
14:3 help me, who am alone and **h** no helper but you,
14:14 help me, who am alone and **h** no helper but you,
14:15 You **h** knowledge of all things, and you know
16:11 the goodwill that we **h** for every nation
Wis 2:13 He professes to **h** knowledge of God,
3:13 she will **h** fruit when God examines souls.
3:18 If they die young, they will **h** no hope
4:18 unrighteous will see, and will **h** contempt for them
6:14 who rises early to seek her will **h** no difficulty,
7:10 and I chose to **h** her rather than light,
7:15 and to **h** thoughts worthy of what I have received
8:10 I shall **h** glory among the multitudes
8:13 Because of her I shall **h** immortality,
9:2 humankind to **h** dominion over the creatures
12:18 for you **h** power to act whenever you choose.
13:19 asks strength of a thing whose hands **h** no strength
15:15 though these **h** neither the use of their eyes to see
15:17 since they **h** life, but the idols never had.
16:13 For you **h** power over life and death;
Sir Pr:2 does not **h** exactly the same sense when translated
1:13 Those who fear the Lord will **h** a happy end;
2:13 Woe to the faint-hearted who **h** no trust!
2:13 Therefore they will **h** no shelter.
3:5 honor their father will **h** joy in their own children,
3:6 Those who respect their father will **h** long life,
3:13 because you **h** all your faculties do not despise
5:1 Do not rely on your wealth, or say, "I **h** enough."
5:3 Do not say, "Who can **h** power over me?"
6:4 Evil passion destroys those who **h** it,
6:18 when you **h** gray hair you will still find wisdom.
7:22 Do you **h** cattle? Look after them;
7:23 Do you **h** children? Discipline them,
7:24 you **h** daughters? Be concerned for their chastity,
7:26 Do you **h** a wife who pleases you? Do not divorce
9:13 Keep far from those who **h** power to kill,
11:24 Do not say, "I **h** enough, and what harm can come
12:16 an enemy may **h** tears in his eyes, but if he finds
12:16 he will never **h** enough of your blood.
13:17 What does a wolf **h** in common with a lamb?
16:3 to die childless better than to **h** ungodly children.
20:16 The fool says, "I **h** no friends, and I get no thanks
22:13 Stay clear of him, or you may **h** trouble,
29:26 prepare the table; let me eat what you **h** there."
30:10 not laugh with him, or you will **h** sorrow with him,
30:12 and you will **h** sorrow of soul from him.
31:21 get up to vomit, and you will **h** relief.
33:21 While you are still alive and **h** breath in you,
33:31 If you **h** but one slave, treat him like yourself,
33:31 If you **h** but one slave, treat him like a brother
34:1 The senseless **h** vain and false hopes,
36:1 **H** mercy upon us, O God of all,
36:17 **H** mercy, O Lord, on the people called by
36:18 **H** pity on the city of your sanctuary,
37:24 A wise person will **h** praise heaped upon him,
39:12 I **h** more on my mind to express;
41:9 If you **h** children, calamity will be theirs;
41:12 **H** regard for your name, since it will outlive you
43:12 the hands of the Most High **h** stretched it out.
45:24 descendants should **h** the dignity of the priesthood
Bar 3:2 Lord, and **h** mercy, for we have sinned before you.
LtJ 6:41 and abandon them, for they **h** no sense.
6:54 deliver one who is wronged, for they **h** no power;
6:69 So we **h** no evidence whatever that they are gods
Aza 1:15 In our day we **h** no ruler, or prophet, or leader,
Sus 1:28 full of their wicked plot to **h** Susanna put to death.
Bel 1:34 "Take the food that you **h** to Babylon, to Daniel,
1Mc 3:30 He feared that he might not **h** such funds as he had
4:6 did not **h** armor and swords such as they desired.
4:61 so that the people might **h** a stronghold
9:8 We may **h** the strength to fight them."
9:9 dissuade him, saying, "We do not **h** the strength.
10:24 honor and gifts, so that I may **h** their help.
10:35 No one shall **h** authority to exact anything
1Mc 10:71 If you now **h** confidence in your forces,
10:71 for I **h** with me the power of the cities.
12:9 Therefore, though we **h** no need of these things,
since we **h** as encouragement the holy books
12:15 for we **h** the help that comes from Heaven
12:53 for they said, "They **h** no leader or helper.
14:23 the people of the Spartans may **h** a record of them.
14:49 so that Simon and his sons might **h** them.
15:34 Now that we **h** the opportunity, we are firmly
2Mc 2:15 So if you **h** need of them, send people to get them
2:18 We **h** hope in God that he will soon **h** mercy on us
3:25 Its rider was seen to **h** armor and weapons of gold.
3:38 "If you **h** any enemy or plotter against your
6:20 as all ought to go who **h** the courage to refuse
7:3 and gave orders to **h** pans and caldrons heated.
7:6 said, 'And he will **h** compassion on his servants.' "
7:7 "Will you eat rather than **h** your body punished
7:16 said, "Because you **h** authority among mortals,
7:27 deriding the cruel tyrant: "My son, **h** pity on me.
8:2 to **h** pity on the temple that had been profaned
8:3 to **h** mercy on the city that was being destroyed
9:13 who would no longer **h** mercy on him,
9:22 for I **h** good hope of recovering from my illness,
10:11 Lysias to **h** charge of the government
11:30 will **h** our pledge of friendship and full permission
11:37 send messengers so that we may **h** your judgment.
14:3 to be safe or to **h** access again to the holy altar,
14:25 He urged him to marry and **h** children;
14:35 "O Lord of all, though you **h** need of nothing,
1Es 1:26 "What **h** we to do with each other, O king of Judea
2:24 no longer **h** access to Coelesyria and Phoenicia."
3:6 and **h** a chariot with gold bridles,
4:27 Many **h** perished, or stumbled, or sinned
4:53 to build the city should **h** their freedom,
5:58 to **h** charge of the work of the Lord.
8:82 Lord, what shall we say, when we **h** these things?
8:85 do not seek ever to **h** peace with them,
9:12 all those in our settlements who **h** foreign wives
9:18 who were brought in and found to **h** foreign wives
9:51 and send portions to those who **h** none;
Man 1:10 and I **h** no relief; for I have provoked your wrath
3Mc 2:9 though you **h** no need of anything;
2:10 you promised that if we should **h** reverses
2:30 shall **h** equal citizenship with the Alexandrians
3:18 because of the benevolence that we **h** toward all.
3:24 shall not **h** these impious people behind our backs
6:12 O Eternal One, who **h** all might and all power,
watch over us now and **h** mercy on us
6:13 who **h** power to save the nation of Jacob.
7:6 the clemency that we **h** toward all people
2Es 1:34 and your sons will **h** no children,
2:6 so that they may **h** no offspring.
2:21 and let the blind **h** a vision of my splendor.
2:27 but you shall rejoice and **h** abundance.
5:41 "Yet, O Lord, you **h** charge of those who are alive
7:*52* "If you **h** just a few precious stones,
7:*73* What, then, will they **h** to say in the judgment,
7:*77* For you **h** a treasure of works stored up
7:*91* for they shall **h** rest in seven orders.
7:*101* "They shall **h** freedom for seven days,
7:*115* [45] no one will then be able to **h** mercy
7:*137* [67] those who inhabit it would not **h** life—
7:*138* [68] one ten-thousandth of humankind could **h** life;
8:25 and as long as I **h** understanding I will answer.
8:29 the destruction of those who **h** the ways of cattle,
8:32 For if you have desired to **h** pity on us, who **h** no
works of righteousness,
8:33 the righteous, who **h** many works laid up with you,
8:36 merciful to those who **h** no store of good works.
8:45 and **h** mercy on your inheritance, for you **h** mercy
13:14 deemed me worthy to **h** my prayer heard by you;
13:23 who **h** works and faith toward the Almighty.
13:33 and the warfare that they **h** against one another;
15:16 they shall in their might **h** no respect for their king
15:19 People shall **h** no pity for their neighbors,
16:33 Virgins shall mourn because they **h** no
16:33 women shall mourn because they **h** no husbands;
16:33 daughters shall mourn, because they **h** no help.
16:44 like those who will **h** no children;
16:47 conduct business, do so only to **h** it plundered;
4Mc 1:12 I shall shortly **h** an opportunity to speak of this;
1:21 both pleasure and pain **h** many consequences.
5:12 and **h** compassion on your old age by honoring
5:14 to eat meat unlawfully, Eleazar asked to **h** a word.
5:28 But you shall **h** no such occasion to laugh at me,
7:17 "Not all **h** full command of their emotions,
because not all **h** prudent reason."
8:7 will **h** positions of authority in my government
8:10 Even I, your enemy, **h** compassion for your youth
8:20 and **h** compassion on our mother's age;
9:8 shall **h** the prize of virtue and shall be with God,
10:14 "You do not **h** a fire hot enough to make me
12:13 to cut out the tongues of men who **h** feelings like
14:14 animals, as well as human beings, **h** a sympathy
15:4 because of their birthpangs **h** a deeper sympathy
16:9 or **h** the happiness of being called grandmother.
16:11 when I die, I shall **h** none of my sons to bury me."
16:22 You too must **h** the same faith in God
16:23 who **h** religious knowledge not to withstand pain."
18:9 and did not **h** the grief of bereavement.

HAVEN (4)

Ge 49:13 he shall be a **h** for ships,
Ps 107:30 and he brought them to their desired **h**.
2Es 12:42 and like a **h** for a ship saved from a storm.
4Mc 7:3 the rudder of religion until he sailed into the **h**

HAVENS (1)
Ac 27: 8 we came to a place called Fair **H**,

HAVILAH (7)
Ge 2:11 it is the one that flows around the whole land of **H**,
10: 7 Seba, **H**, Sabtah, Raamah, and Sabteca.
10:29 **H**, and Jobab; all these were the descendants of
25:18 They settled from **H** to Shur,
1Sa 15: 7 from **H** as far as Shur, which is east of Egypt.
1Ch 1: 9 Seba, **H**, Sabta, Raama, and Sabteca.
1:23 **H**, and Jobab; all these were the descendants of

HAVING (64 of 172) [HAVE] See Index of Articles Etc. for an Exhaustive Listing (See Introduction, page xi)
Ge 41:11 he and I, each **h** a dream with its own meaning.
Lev 20:18 If a man lies with a woman **h** her sickness
22:22 or maimed, or **h** a discharge or an itch or scabs—
Nu 3:38 **h** charge of the rites within the sanctuary,
9:15 over the tabernacle, **h** the appearance of fire.
Jos 7:15 And the one who is taken as **h** the devoted things
Jdg 3:27 from the hill country, **h** him at their head.
1Ki 5:16 **h** charge of the people who did the work.
1Ch 4:42 went to Mount Seir, **h** as their leaders Pelatiah,
8:40 mighty warriors, archers, **h** many children
23:22 Eleazar died **h** no sons, but only daughters;
23:28 **h** the care of the courts and the chambers,
2Ch 9: 1 **h** a very great retinue and camels bearing spices
13: 3 engaged in battle, **h** an army of valiant warriors,
17: 9 taught in Judah, **h** the book of the law of the LORD
Ne 5: 3 "We are **h** to pledge our fields, our vineyards,
5: 4 "We are **h** to borrow money on our fields
Est 6: 4 to speak to the king about **h** Mordecai hanged
Ps 106:24 **h** no faith in his promise.
Pr 6: 7 Without **h** any chief or officer or ruler,
25:16 or else, **h** too much, you will vomit it.
Isa 41:15 a threshing sledge, sharp, new, and **h** teeth;
Eze 38:11 living without walls, and **h** no bars or gates";
44:11 **h** oversight at the gates of the temple,
Da 8:15 standing before me, **h** the appearance of a man,
Mt 7:29 for he taught them as one **h** authority,
16: 8 why are you talking about **h** no bread?
Mk 1:22 for he taught them as one **h** authority,
8:17 "Why are you talking about **h** no bread?
Lk 7: 4 saying, "He is worthy of **h** you do this for him,
15: 4 **h** a hundred sheep and losing one of them,
15: 8 what woman **h** ten silver coins, if she loses one
Ac 2:47 praising God and **h** the goodwill of all the people.
Ro 2:14 though not **h** the law, are a law to themselves.
2:20 **h** in the law the embodiment of knowledge
1Co 7: 7 one **h** one kind and another a different kind.
11: 5 it is one and the same thing as **h** her head shaved.
2Co 9: 8 so that by always **h** enough of everything,
Eph 2:12 strangers to the covenants of promise, **h** no hope
Php 1:30 you are **h** the same struggle that you saw I had
2: 2 be of the same mind, **h** the same love,
3: 9 be found in him, not **h** a righteousness of my own
4:12 of going hungry, of **h** plenty and of being in need.
1Ti 1:19 **h** faith and a good conscience.
2Ti 4: 3 not put up with sound doctrine, but **h** itching ears,
Heb 7: 3 **h** neither beginning of days nor end of life,
Rev 5: 6 **h** seven horns and seven eyes, which are the seven
7: 2 **h** the seal of the living God, and he called
9:19 their tails are like serpents, **h** heads;
13: 1 I saw a beast rising out of the sea **h** ten horns
18: 1 angel coming down from heaven, **h** great authority
Jdt 12:12 if we let such a woman go without **h** intercourse
Sir 26:21 *and, **h** confidence in their good descent,*
42:10 or **h** a husband, for fear she may go astray,
47:15 and you filled it with proverbs **h** deep meaning.
LtJ 26:26 **H** no feet, they are carried on the shoulders
2Mc 4: 5 but **h** in view the welfare, both public and private,
4:25 but **h** the hot temper of a cruel tyrant
10:23 **H** success at arms in everything he undertook,
10:28 the one **h** as pledge of success and victory
11:10 advanced in battle order, **h** their heavenly ally,
11:15 Maccabeus, **h** regard for the common good,
1Es 1:10 priests and the Levites, **h** the unleavened bread,
4Mc 9:26 with iron gauntlets **h** sharp hooks,
16:13 On the contrary, as though **h** a mind like adamant

HAVOC (1)
Ac 9:21 "Is not this the man who made **h** in Jerusalem

HAVOCK (KJV) See RAVAGING

HAVVOTH-JAIR (4) [JAIR]
Nu 32:41 and captured their villages, and renamed them **H**.
Dt 3:14 after himself, **H**, as it is to this day.)
Jdg 10: 4 and are called **H** to this day.
1Ch 2:23 But Geshur and Aram took from them **H**,

HAWK (4)
Lev 11:16 the nighthawk, the sea gull, the **h** of any kind;
Dt 14:15 the nighthawk, the sea gull, the **h**, of any kind;
Job 39:26 "Is it by your wisdom that the **h** soars,
Isa 34:11 But the **h** and the hedgehog shall possess it;

HAY (1)
1Co 3:12 silver, precious stones, wood, **h**, straw—

HAYAH See Index to Footnotes

HAZAEL (24)
1Ki 19:15 you arrive, you shall anoint **H** as king over Aram.
19:17 Whoever escapes from the sword of **H**,
2Ki 8: 8 the king said to **H**, "Take a present with you
8: 9 So **H** went to meet him, taking a present with him,
8:12 **H** asked, "Why does my lord weep?"
8:13 **H** said, "What is your servant, who is a mere dog,
8:15 until he died. And **H** succeeded him.
8:28 of Ahab to wage war against King **H** of Aram
8:29 when he fought against King **H** of Aram.
9:14 at Ramoth-gilead against King **H** of Aram;
9:15 when he fought against King **H** of Aram.
10:32 **H** defeated them throughout the territory of Israel:
12:17 At that time King **H** of Aram went up,
12:17 when **H** set his face to go up against Jerusalem,
12:18 and sent these to King **H** of Aram.
12:18 Then **H** withdrew from Jerusalem.
13: 3 into the hand of King **H** of Aram,
13: 3 then into the hand of Ben-hadad son of **H**.
13:22 Now King **H** of Aram oppressed Israel all the days
13:24 When King **H** of Aram died,
13:25 of Jehoahaz took again from Ben-hadad son of **H**
2Ch 22: 5 of King Ahab of Israel to make war against King **H**
22: 6 when he fought King **H** of Aram.
Am 1: 4 So I will send a fire on the house of **H**,

HAZAIAH (1)
Ne 11: 5 of Col-hozeh son of **H** son of Adaiah son

HAZAR-ADDAR (1) [ADDAR]
Nu 34: 4 then it shall go on to **H**, and cross to Azmon;

HAZAR-ENAN (2)
Nu 34: 9 and its end shall be at **H**;
34:10 You shall mark out your eastern boundary from **H**

HAZAR-ENON (2)
Eze 47:17 So the boundary shall run from the sea to **H**,
48: 1 as far as **H** (which is on the border of Damascus,

HAZAR-GADDAH (1)
Jos 15:27 **H**, Heshmon, Beth-pelet,

HAZAR-SHUAL (4) [SHUAL]
Jos 15:28 **H**, Beer-sheba, Biziothiah,
19: 3 **H**, Balah, Ezem,
1Ch 4:28 They lived in Beer-sheba, Moladah, **H**,
Ne 11:27 in **H**, in Beer-sheba and its villages,

HAZAR-SUSAH (1)
Jos 19: 5 Ziklag, Beth-marcaboth, **H**,

HAZAR-SUSIM (1)
1Ch 4:31 **H**, Beth-biri, and Shaaraim.

HAZARDED (KJV) See RISKED

HAZARDS (1)
Sir 32:20 Do not go on a path full of **h**,

HAZARHATTICON (KJV) See HAZER-HATTICON

HAZARMAVETH (2)
Ge 10:26 Joktan became the father of Almodad, Sheleph, **H**,
1Ch 1:20 Joktan became the father of Almodad, Sheleph, **H**,

HAZAZON-TAMAR (2) [=EN-GEDI]
Ge 14: 7 and also the Amorites who lived in **H**.
2Ch 20: 2 already they are at **H**" (that is, En-gedi).

HAZEL (KJV) See ALMOND

HAZER-HATTICON (1)
Eze 47:16 as far as **H**, which is on the border of Hauran.

HAZERIM (KJV) See SETTLEMENTS

HAZEROTH (6)
Nu 11:35 From Kibroth-hattaavah the people journeyed to **H**.
12: 1 While they were at **H**, Miriam and Aaron spoke
12:16 After that the people set out from **H**,
33:17 from Kibroth-hattaavah and camped at **H**.
33:18 They set out from **H** and camped at Rithmah.
Dt 1: 1 between Paran and Tophel, Laban, **H**,

HAZIEL (1)
1Ch 23: 9 sons of Shimei: Shelomoth, **H**, and Haran, three.

HAZO (1)
Ge 22:22 Chesed, **H**, Pildash, Jidlaph, and Bethuel."

HAZOR (19) [BAAL-HAZOR, KERIOTH-HEZRON]
Jos 11: 1 When King Jabin of **H** heard of this,
11:10 Joshua turned back at that time, and took **H**,
11:10 that time **H** was the head of all those kingdoms.
11:11 and he burned **H** with fire.
11:13 of the towns that stood on mounds except **H**,
12:19 the king of Madon one the king of **H** one
15:23 Kedesh, **H**, Ithnan,
15:25 Hazor-hadattah, Kerioth-hezron (that is, **H**),
19:36 Adamah, Ramah, **H**,
Jdg 4: 2 of King Jabin of Canaan, who reigned in **H**;
4:17 for there was peace between King Jabin of **H** and
1Sa 12: 9 commander of the army of King Jabin of **H**,
1Ki 9:15 the Millo and the wall of Jerusalem, **H**, Megiddo,
2Ki 15:29 **H**, Gilead, and Galilee, all the land of Naphtali;
Ne 11:33 **H**, Ramah, Gittaim,
Jer 49:28 and the kingdoms of **H** that King Nebuchadrezzar
49:30 hide in deep places, O inhabitants of **H**!
49:33 **H** shall become a lair of jackals,
1Mc 11:67 in the morning they marched to the plain of **H**,

HAZOR-HADATTAH (1)
Jos 15:25 **H**, Kerioth-hezron (that is, Hazor),

HAZZELELPONI (1)
1Ch 4: 3 and the name of their sister was **H**,

HE (10591) [HIM, HIMSELF, HIS] See Index of Articles Etc.

HE-GOAT (1) [GOAT]
Pr 30:31 the **h**, and a king striding before his people.

HEAD‡ (407) [BALD-HEAD, BEHEADED, FIGUREHEAD, GRAY-HEADED, HEAD-ON, HEADBANDS, HEADDRESSES, HEADED, HEADLONG, HEADQUARTERS, HEADS, HEADSTRONG, HOTHEAD, HOTHEADS, MANY-HEADED]
Ge 3:15 he will strike your **h**, and you will strike his heel."
24:26 The man bowed his **h** and worshiped the LORD
24:48 Then I bowed my **h** and worshiped the LORD,
28:11 he put it under his **h** and lay down in that place.
28:18 that he had put under his **h** and set it up for a pillar
40:13 within three days Pharaoh will lift up your **h**
40:16 there were three cake baskets on my **h**,
40:17 the birds were eating it out of the basket on my **h**."
40:19 within three days Pharaoh will lift up your **h**—
40:20 the **h** of the chief cupbearer and the **h** of the chief
47:31 Then Israel bowed himself on the **h** of his bed.
48:14 and laid it on the **h** of Ephraim,
48:14 and his left hand on the **h** of Manasseh,
48:17 that his father laid his right hand on the **h**
48:17 from Ephraim's **h** to Manasseh's **h**.
48:18 put your right hand on his **h**."
49:26 may they be on the **h** of Joseph,
Ex 12: 9 but roasted over the fire, with its **h**, legs,
28:32 It shall have an opening for the **h** in the middle
29: 6 and you shall set the turban on his **h**,
29: 7 and pour it on his **h** and anoint him.
29:10 Aaron and his sons shall lay their hands on the **h** of
29:15 and his sons shall lay their hands on the **h** of
29:17 and put them with its parts and its **h**,
29:19 and his sons shall lay their hands on the **h** of
34: 8 And Moses quickly bowed his **h** toward the earth,
38:26 a beka a **h** (that is, half a shekel, measured by
Lev 1: 4 You shall lay your hand on the **h** of
1: 8 the **h** and the suet, on the wood that is on the fire
1:12 with its **h** and its suet,
1:15 priest shall bring it to the altar and wring off its **h**,
3: 2 the **h** of the offering and slaughter it at the entrance
3: 8 and lay your hand on the **h** of the offering.
3:13 and lay your hand on its **h**;
4: 4 the LORD and lay his hand on the **h** of the bull;
4:11 the skin of the bull and all its flesh, as well as its **h**,
4:15 the congregation shall lay their hands on the **h** of
4:24 He shall lay his hand on the **h** of the goat;
4:29 You shall lay your hand on the **h** of
4:33 You shall lay your hand on the **h** of
5: 8 wringing its **h** at the nape without severing it.
8: 9 And he set the turban on his **h**, and on the turban,
8:12 He poured some of the anointing oil on Aaron's **h**
8:14 and Aaron and his sons laid their hands upon the **h**
8:18 and his sons laid their hands on the **h** of the ram,
8:20 and Moses turned into smoke the **h** and the parts
8:22 and his sons laid their hands on the **h** of the ram,
9:13 and the **h**, which he turned into smoke on the altar.
13:12 the skin of the diseased person from **h** to foot,
13:29 When a man or woman has a disease on the **h** or in
13:30 it is an itch, a leprous disease of the **h** or the beard.
13:40 If anyone loses the hair from his **h**,
13:42 But if there is on the bald **h** or the bald forehead
13:42 it is a leprous disease breaking out on his bald **h**
13:43 on his bald **h** or on his bald forehead,
13:44 the disease is on his **h**.
13:45 and let the hair of his **h** be disheveled;
14: 9 of **h**, beard, eyebrows; he shall shave all his hair.
14:18 the priest's hand he shall put on the **h** of the one to
14:29 the priest's hand he shall put on the **h** of the one to
16:21 Then Aaron shall lay both his hands on the **h** of
16:21 all their sins, putting them on the **h** of the goat,
21:10 on whose **h** the anointing oil has been poured
24:14 within hearing lay their hands on his **h**,
Nu 1: 4 each man the **h** of his ancestral house.

Nu 3:24 as **h** of the ancestral house of the Gershonites.
3:30 of Uzziel as **h** of the ancestral house of the clans of
3:35 The **h** of the ancestral house of the clans
6: 5 their nazirite vow no razor shall come upon the **h**;
6: 5 they shall let the locks of the **h** grow long.
6: 7 because their consecration to God is upon the **h**.
6: 9 defiling the consecrated **h**,
6: 9 they shall shave the **h** on the day of their cleansing;
6:11 They shall sanctify the **h** that same day,
6:12 because the consecrated **h** was defiled.
6:18 Then the nazirites shall shave the consecrated **h** at
6:18 from the consecrated **h** and put it on the fire under
6:19 after they have shaved the consecrated **h**.
17: 3 be one staff for the **h** of each ancestral house.
25:14 **h** of an ancestral house belonging to
25:15 who was the **h** of a clan,
Dt 2: 3 skirting this hill country long enough. **H** north,
3:28 because it is he who shall cross over at the **h**
10:11 "Get up, go on your journey at the **h** of the people,
19: 5 the **h** slips from the handle and strikes
21:12 she shall shave her **h**, pare her nails,
28:13 The LORD will make you the **h**, and not the tail;
28:23 The sky over your **h** shall be bronze,
28:35 from the sole of your foot to the crown of your **h**.
28:44 they shall be the **h** and you shall be the tail.
32:25 nursing child and old gray **h**.
33:16 Let these come on the **h** of Joseph,
33:21 he came at the **h** of the people,
Jos 11:10 that time Hazor was the **h** of all those kingdoms.
22:14 of them the **h** of a family among the clans of Israel.
Jdg 3:27 from the hill country, having him at their **h**.
5:26 she struck Sisera a blow, she crushed his **h**,
9:39 So Gaal went out at the **h** of the lords of Shechem,
9:53 an upper millstone on Abimelech's **h**,
10:18 He shall be **h** over all the inhabitants of Gilead."
11: 8 the Ammonites, and become **h** over us, over all
11: 9 over to me, I will be your **h**."
11:11 the people made him **h** and commander over them;
13: 5 No razor is to come on his **h**,
16:13 of my **h** with the web and make it tight with
16:14 the seven locks of his **h** and wove them into
16:17 "A razor has never come upon my **h**;
16:17 If my **h** were shaved, then my strength would leave
16:19 and had him shave off the seven locks of his **h**.
16:22 But the hair of his **h** began to grow again
1Sa 1:11 and no razor shall touch his **h**."
4:12 with his clothes torn and with earth upon his **h**.
5: 4 and the **h** of Dagon and
9: 2 he stood **h** and shoulders above everyone else.
9:22 a place at the **h** of those who had been invited,
10: 1 Samuel took a vial of oil and poured it on his **h**,
10:23 he was **h** and shoulders taller than any of them.
14:45 not one hair of his **h** shall fall to the ground;
15:17 are you not the **h** of the tribes of Israel?
17: 5 He had a helmet of bronze on his **h**,
17: 7 his spear's **h** weighed six hundred shekels of iron;
17:38 he put a bronze helmet on his **h** and clothed him
17:46 and I will strike you down and cut off your **h**;
17:51 then he cut off his **h** with it.
17:54 the **h** of the Philistine and brought it to Jerusalem;
17:57 with the **h** of the Philistine in his hand.
19:13 she put a net of goats' hair on its **h**,
19:16 with the covering of goats' hair on its **h**.
25:39 the evildoing of Nabal upon his own **h**."
26: 7 with his spear stuck in the ground at his **h**;
26:11 but now take the spear that is at his **h**,
26:12 So David took the spear that was at Saul's **h** and
26:16 or the water jar that was at his **h**?"
31: 9 They cut off his **h**, stripped off his armor,
2Sa 1: 2 with his clothes torn and dirt on his **h**.
1:10 the crown that was on his **h** and the armlet that was
1:16 David said to him, "Your blood be on your **h**;
2:16 Each grasped his opponent by the **h**,
3: 8 he said, "Am I a dog's **h** for Judah?
3:29 May the guilt fall on the **h** of Joab,
4: 7 Then they took his **h** and traveled by way of
4: 8 They brought the **h** of Ishbaal to David at Hebron
4: 8 "Here is the **h** of Ishbaal, son of Saul, your enemy,
4:12 the **h** of Ishbaal they took and buried in the tomb
10:16 of the army of Hadadezer at their **h**.
12:30 He took the crown of Milcom from his **h**;
12:30 and it was placed on David's **h**.
13:19 But Tamar put ashes on her **h**,
13:19 she put her hand on her **h**, and went away,
14:25 to the crown of his **h** there was no blemish in him.
14:26 When he cut the hair of his **h**
14:26 he cut it), he weighed the hair of his **h**,
15:30 with his **h** covered and walking barefoot;
15:32 to meet him with his coat torn and earth on his **h**.
16: 9 Let me go over and take off his **h**."
18: 9 His **h** caught fast in the oak,
20:21 "His **h** shall be thrown over the wall to you."
20:22 And they cut off the **h** of Sheba son of Bichri,
22:44 you kept me as the **h** of the nations;
1Ki 2: 6 do not let his gray **h** go down to Sheol in peace.
2: 9 to do to him, and you must bring his gray **h** down
2:32 on his own **h**, because, without the knowledge
2:33 So shall their blood come back on the **h** of Joab
and on the **h** of his descendants forever;
2:37 your blood shall be on your own **h**."
2:44 LORD will bring back your evil on your own **h**.
8:32 by bringing their conduct on their own **h**,
19: 6 and there at his **h** was a cake baked on hot stones,
21: 9 and seat Naboth at the **h** of the assembly;
21:12 a fast and seated Naboth at the **h** of the assembly.
2Ki 4:19 He complained to his father, "Oh, my **h**, my **h**!"
6: 5 one was felling a log, his ax **h** fell into the water;

2Ki 6:25 a donkey's **h** was sold for eighty shekels of silver,
6:31 if the **h** of Elisha son of Shaphat stays
6:32 this murderer has sent someone to take off my **h**?
9: 3 Then take the flask of oil, pour it on his **h**, and say,
9: 6 the young man poured the oil on his **h**,
9:30 she painted her eyes, and adorned her **h**,
19:21 virgin daughter Zion; she tosses her **h**—
1Ch 10: 9 They stripped him and took his **h** and his armor,
10:10 and fastened his **h** in the temple of Dagon.
19:16 of the army of Hadadezer at their **h**.
20: 2 David took the crown of Milcom from his **h**;
20: 2 and it was placed on David's **h**.
29:11 O LORD, and you are exalted as **h** above all.
2Ch 6:23 by bringing their conduct on their own **h**,
13:12 See, God is with us at our **h**,
20:27 with Jehoshaphat at their **h**,
Ezr 5:10 down the names of the men at their **h**.
9: 3 and pulled hair from my **h** and beard,
Est 2:17 on her **h** and made her queen instead of Vashti.
6: 8 with a royal crown on its **h**.
6:12 mourning and with his **h** covered.
9:25 against the Jews should come upon his own **h**,
Job 1:20 Then Job arose, tore his robe, shaved his **h**,
2: 7 from the sole of his foot to the crown of his **h**.
10:15 If I am righteous, I cannot lift up my **h**,
16: 4 against you, and shake my **h** at you.
19: 9 and taken the crown from my **h**.
20: 6 and their **h** reaches to the clouds,
29: 3 when his lamp shone over my **h**, and
41: 7 or its **h** with fishing spears?
Ps 3: 3 my glory, and the one who lifts up my **h**.
18:43 you made me **h** of the nations;
21: 3 you set a crown of fine gold on his **h**.
23: 5 you anoint my **h** with oil; my cup overflows.
27: 6 my **h** is lifted up above my enemies all around me,
35:13 I prayed with **h** bowed on my bosom,
38: 4 For my iniquities have gone over my **h**;
40:12 they are more than the hairs of my **h**,
69: 4 of my **h** are those who hate me without cause;
110: 7 therefore he will lift up his **h**.
133: 2 It is like the precious oil on the **h**,
140: 7 you have covered my **h** in the day of battle.
141: 5 Never let the oil of the wicked anoint my **h**,
Pr 1: 9 for they are a fair garland for your **h**,
4: 9 She will place on your **h** a fair garland;
10: 6 Blessings are on the **h** of the righteous,
11:26 but a blessing is on the **h** of those who sell it.
Ecc 2:14 The wise have eyes in their **h**,
9: 8 do not let oil be lacking on your **h**.
SS 2: 6 O that his left hand were under my **h**,
5: 2 for my **h** is wet with dew, my locks with the drops
5:11 His **h** is the finest gold;
7: 5 Your **h** crowns you like Carmel,
8: 3 O that his left hand were under my **h**,
Isa 1: 5 The whole **h** is sick, and the whole heart faint.
1: 6 From the sole of the foot even to the **h**,
7: 8 For the **h** of Aram is Damascus, and the **h** of
Damascus is Rezin.
7: 9 The **h** of Ephraim is Samaria, and the **h** of
Samaria is the son of Remaliah.
7:20 the **h** and the hair of the feet,
9:14 So the LORD cut off from Israel **h** and tail,
9:15 the **h**, and prophets who teach lies are the tail;
15: 2 On every **h** is baldness, every beard is shorn;
19:15 Neither **h** nor tail, palm branch or reed,
28: 1 which is on the **h** of those bloated with rich food,
28: 4 which is on the **h** of those bloated with rich food,
37:22 virgin daughter Zion; she tosses her **h**—
51:20 they lie at the **h** of every street like an antelope in
58: 5 Is it to bow down the **h** like a bulrush,
59:17 and a helmet of salvation on his **h**;
Jer 2:16 and Tahpanhes have broken the crown of your **h**.
2:37 with your hands on your **h**;
9: 1 O that my **h** were a spring of water,
13:18 beautiful crown has come down from your **h**."
13:21 as **h** over you those whom you have trained to
16: 6 no shaving of the **h** for them.
23:19 it will burst upon the **h** of the wicked.
30:23 it will burst upon the **h** of the wicked.
48:27 but whenever you spoke of him you shook your **h**!
48:37 For every **h** is shaved and every beard cut off;
La 2:19 who faint for hunger at the **h** of every street.
3:54 water closed over my **h**; I said, "I am lost."
4: 1 sacred stones lie scattered at the **h** of every street.
5:16 The crown has fallen from our **h**;
Eze 5: 1 use it as a barber's razor and run it over your **h**
8: 3 and took me by a lock of my **h**;
16:12 and a beautiful crown upon your **h**.
16:25 at the **h** of every street you built your lofty place
16:31 building your platform at the **h** of every street,
16:43 therefore, I have returned your deeds upon your **h**,
17:19 surely return upon his **h** my oath that he despised,
29:18 **h** was made bald and every shoulder was rubbed
42:12 the entrance at the **h** of the corresponding passage,
Da 1:10 you would endanger my **h** with the king."
2:28 the visions of your **h** as you lay in bed were these:
2:32 The **h** of that statue was of fine gold,
2:38 you are the **h** of gold.
4: 5 in bed and the visions of my **h** terrified me.
4:13 in the visions of my **h** as I lay in bed,
7: 1 Daniel had a dream and visions of his **h** as he lay
7: 9 and the hair of his **h** like pure wool;
7:15 and the visions of my **h** terrified me.
7:20 and concerning the ten horns that were on its **h**,
Hos 1:11 and they shall appoint for themselves one **h**;
Joel 2:11 The LORD utters his voice at the **h** of his army;
Am 2: 7 they who trample the **h** of the poor into the dust of

Am 8:10 on all loins, and baldness on every **h**;
Ob 1:15 your deeds shall return on your own **h**.
Jnh 2: 5 weeds were wrapped around my **h**
4: 6 over his **h**, to save him from his discomfort;
4: 8 on the **h** of Jonah so that he was faint and asked
Mic 2:13 on before them, the LORD at their **h**.
Na 3:10 even her infants were dashed in pieces at the **h**
Hab 3:13 You crushed the **h** of the wicked house,
3:14 with his own arrows the **h** of his warriors,
Zec 1:21 so that no **h** could be raised;
3: 5 And I said, "Let them put a clean turban on his **h**."
3: 5 So they put a clean turban on his **h** and clothed him
6:11 the **h** of the high priest Joshua son of Jehozadak;
12: 8 like the angel of the LORD, at their **h**.
Mt 5:36 And do not swear by your **h**,
6:17 you fast, put oil on your **h** and wash your face,
8:20 but the Son of Man has nowhere to lay his **h**."
10:30 And even the hairs of your **h** are all counted.
14: 8 the **h** of John the Baptist here on a platter."
14:11 **h** was brought on a platter and given to the girl,
22:20 Then he said to them, "Whose **h** is this,
26: 7 and she poured it on his **h** as he sat at the table.
27:29 they put it on his **h**.
27:30 and took the reed and struck him on the **h**.
27:37 Over his **h** they put the charge against him,
Mk 4:28 the stalk, then the **h**, then the full grain in the **h**.
6:24 She replied, "The **h** of John the baptizer."
6:25 to give me at once the **h** of John the Baptist on
6:27 of the guard with orders to bring John's **h**.
6:28 brought his **h** on a platter,
12: 4 this one they beat over the **h** and insulted.
12:16 Then he said to them, "Whose **h** is this,
14: 3 the jar and poured the ointment on his **h**.
15:19 They struck his **h** with a reed, spat upon him,
Lk 7:46 You did not anoint my **h** with oil,
9:58 but the Son of Man has nowhere to lay his **h**."
12: 7 But even the hairs of your **h** are all counted.
20:24 Whose **h** and whose title does it bear?"
21:18 But not a hair of your **h** will perish.
Jn 13: 9 not my feet only but also my hands and my **h**!"
19: 2 a crown of thorns and put it on his **h**,
19:30 Then he bowed his **h** and gave up his spirit.
20: 7 and the cloth that had been on Jesus' **h**,
20:12 one at the **h** and the other at the feet.
1Co 11: 3 But I want you to understand that Christ is the **h** of
every man, and the husband is the **h** of his wife,
and God is the **h** of Christ.
11: 4 with something on his **h** disgraces his **h**,
11: 5 with her **h** unveiled disgraces her **h**—
11: 5 and the same thing as having her **h** shaved.
11: 7 For a man ought not to have his **h** veiled,
11:10 to have a symbol of authority on her **h**,
11:13 for a woman to pray to God with her **h** unveiled?
12:21 nor again the **h** to the feet,
Eph 1:22 and has made him the **h** over all things for
4:15 up in every way into him who is the **h**,
5:23 the husband is the **h** of the wife just as Christ is
the **h** of the church,
Col 1:18 He is the **h** of the body, the church;
2:10 who is the **h** of every ruler and authority.
2:19 and not holding fast to the **h**,
1Pe 2: 7 that the builders rejected has become the very **h** of
Rev 1:14 His **h** and his hair were white as white wool,
10: 1 wrapped in a cloud, with a rainbow over his **h**;
12: 1 and on her **h** a crown of twelve stars.
14:14 with a golden crown on his **h**,
19:12 and on his **h** are many diadems;
Jdt 9: 1 Then Judith prostrated herself, put ashes on her **h**,
13: 6 She went up to the bedpost near Holofernes' **h**,
13: 7 took hold of the hair of his **h**, and said,
13: 8 with all her might, and cut off his **h**.
13: 9 and gave Holofernes' **h** to her maid,
13:15 Then she pulled the **h** out of the bag and showed it
13:15 and said, "See here, the **h** of Holofernes,
13:18 and the earth, who has guided you to cut off the **h**
14: 1 Take this **h** and hang it upon the parapet
14: 6 and saw the **h** of Holofernes in the hand of one of
14:11 as it was dawn they hung the **h** of Holofernes on
14:15 on the floor dead, with his **h** missing.
14:18 on the ground, and his **h** is missing!"
AdE 1:11 as queen and to place the diadem on her **h**,
6:12 mourning and with his **h** covered.
14: 2 and instead of costly perfumes she covered her **h**
14:16 the sign of my proud position, which is upon my **h**
15: 7 on the **h** of the maid who went in front of her.
Wis 18:24 and your majesty was on the diadem upon his **h**.
Sir 4: 7 bow your **h** low to the great.
12:18 Then he will shake his **h**, and clap his hands,
13: 7 he will pass you by and shake his **h** at you.
27:25 a stone straight up throws it on his own **h**,
44:23 he made to rest on the **h** of Jacob;
Bar 5: 2 put on your **h** the diadem of the glory of
Sus 1:34 up before the people and laid their hands on her **h**.
1:55 This lie has cost you your **h**,
1:59 This lie has cost you also your **h**,
Bel 1:36 by the crown of his **h** and carried him by his hair;
1Mc 7:47 they cut off Nicanor's **h** and the right hand
11:13 Thus he put two crowns on his **h**,
11:17 the Arab cut off the **h** of Alexander and sent it
11:71 Jonathan tore his clothes, put dust on his **h**,
2Mc 7: 7 They tore off the skin of his **h** with the hair,
11: 8 a horseman appeared at their **h**,
15:30 to cut off Nicanor's **h** and arm and carry them
15:32 the vile Nicanor's **h** and that profane man's arm,
15:35 Judas hung Nicanor's **h** from the citadel,
1Es 4:30 the crown from the king's **h** and put it on her own,
6:12 for a list of the names of those who are at their **h**.

1Es 8:71 and pulled out hair from my **h** and beard,
2Es 1: 8 the hair of your **h** and hurl all evils upon them,
2:43 and on the **h** of each of them he placed a crown,
9:38 and there were ashes on her **h.**
11: 4 the middle **h** was larger than the other heads,
11:24 from the six and remained under the **h** that was on
11:31 and how the **h** turned with those that were with it
11:32 Moreover this **h** gained control of the whole earth,
11:33 and saw the **h** in the middle suddenly disappear,
11:35 the **h** on the right side devour the one on the left.
12: 2 and saw that the remaining **h** had disappeared.
12:26 As for your seeing that the large **h** disappeared,
12:29 over to the **h** which was on the right side,
16:53 for God will burn coals of fire on the **h**
4Mc 15:15 the flesh of the **h** to the chin exposed like masks.

HEAD-ON (1) [HEAD]

Ac 27:15 the ship was caught and could not be turned **h** into

HEADBANDS (1) [HEAD]

Isa 3:18 the finery of the anklets, the **h,** and the crescents;

HEADDRESSES (5) [HEAD]

Ex 28:40 you shall make tunics and sashes and **h;**
29: 9 you shall gird them with sashes and tie **h** on them;
39:28 and the **h** of fine linen,
Lev 8:13 and fastened sashes around them, and tied **h**
Isa 3:20 the **h,** the armlets, the sashes, the perfume boxes,

HEADED (3) [HEAD]

Dt 1:28 Where are we **h?** Our kindred have made
2: 8 When we had **h** out along the route of
3: 1 When we **h** up the road to Bashan,

HEADLONG (9) [HEAD]

Job 27:22 they flee from its power in **h** flight.
Ps 37:24 we shall not fall **h,** for the LORD holds us by
Jer 8: 6 like a horse plunging **h** into battle.
49: 5 each **h,** with no one to gather the fugitives.
Ac 1:18 and falling **h,** he burst open in the middle
2Mc 6:10 and then hurled them down **h** from the wall.
12:22 In their flight they rushed **h** in every direction,
3Mc 6:23 and saw them all fallen **h** to destruction,
4Mc 4:25 were thrown **h** from heights along

HEADQUARTERS (7) [HEAD, QUARTER]

Mt 27:27 of the governor took Jesus into the governor's **h,**
Mk 15:16 of the palace (that is, the governor's **h);**
Jn 18:28 Then they took Jesus from Caiaphas to Pilate's **h.**
18:28 They themselves did not enter the **h,**
18:33 Then Pilate entered the **h** again, summoned Jesus,
19: 9 He entered his **h** again and asked Jesus,
Ac 23:35 that he be kept under guard in Herod's **h.**

HEADS (205) [HEAD]

Ge 43:28 And they bowed their **h** and did obeisance.
Ex 6:14 The following are the **h** of their ancestral houses:
6:25 the **h** of the ancestral houses of the Levites
18:25 from all Israel and appointed them as **h** over
Lev 21: 5 They shall not make bald spots upon their **h,**
Nu 1:16 the **h** of the divisions of Israel.
7: 2 **h** of their ancestral houses, the leaders of the tribes,
8:12 Levites shall lay their hands on the **h** of the bulls,
10: 4 then the leaders, the **h** of the tribes of Israel,
30: 1 Moses said to the **h** of the tribes of the Israelites:
31:26 the priest and the **h** of the ancestral houses of
32:28 the **h** of the ancestral houses of the Israelite tribes.
36: 1 The **h** of the ancestral houses of the clans of
36: 1 the **h** of the ancestral houses of the Israelites;
Dt 5:23 all the **h** of your tribes and your elders;
Jos 7: 6 and they put dust on their **h.**
14: 1 and the **h** of the families of the tribes of
19:51 the priest Eleazar and Joshua son of Nun and the **h**
21: 1 Then the **h** of the families of the Levites came to
21: 1 to Joshua son of Nun and to the **h** of the families of
22:21 of Manasseh said in answer to the **h** of the families
22:30 the **h** of the families of Israel who were with him,
23: 2 their elders and **h,** their judges and officers,
24: 1 and summoned the elders, the **h,** the judges,
Jdg 7:25 They brought the **h** of Oreb and Zeeb to Gideon
8:28 and they lifted up their **h** no more.
9:57 of the people of Shechem fall back on their **h,**
1Sa 29: 4 Would it not be with the **h** of the men here?
2Sa 15:30 the people who were with him covered their **h**
1Ki 8: 1 the elders of Israel and all the **h** of the tribes,
20:31 around our waists and ropes on our **h,** and go out
20:32 put ropes on their **h,** went to the king of Israel,
2Ki 10: 6 take the **h** of your master's sons and come to me
10: 7 they put their **h** in baskets and sent them to him
10: 8 "They have brought the **h** of the king's sons,"
1Ch 5:24 These were the **h** of their clans:
5:24 mighty warriors, famous men, **h** of their clans.
7: 2 Ibsam, and Shemuel, **h** of their ancestral houses,
7: 7 Jerimoth, and Iri, five, **h** of ancestral houses,
7: 9 as **h** of their ancestral houses, mighty warriors,
7:11 according to the **h** of their ancestral houses,
7:40 **h** of ancestral houses, select mighty warriors,
8: 6 the sons of Ehud (they were **h** of ancestral houses
8:10 These were his sons, **h** of ancestral houses.
8:13 and Shema (they were **h** of ancestral houses of
8:28 These were the **h** of ancestral houses,
9: 9 All these were **h** of families according
9:13 **h** of their ancestral houses,
1Ch 9:33 the **h** of ancestral houses of the Levites,
9:34 These were **h** of ancestral houses of the Levites,
12:19 to his master Saul at the cost of our **h.")**
15:12 "You are the **h** of families of the Levites;
23: 9 These were the **h** of families of Ladan.
23:24 the **h** of families as they were enrolled according to
24: 4 under sixteen **h** of ancestral houses of the sons
24: 6 and the **h** of ancestral houses of the priests and of
24:31 and the **h** of ancestral houses of the priests and of
26:21 **h** of families belonging to Ladan the Gershonite:
26:26 the **h** of families, and the officers of the thousands
26:32 of ability, **h** of families, to have the oversight of
27: 1 the **h** of families, the commanders of the thousands
29:20 and bowed their **h** and prostrated themselves
2Ch 1: 2 and all the leaders of all Israel, the **h** of families.
5: 2 the elders of Israel and all the **h** of the tribes,
19: 8 and priests and **h** of families of Israel,
23: 2 and the **h** of families of Israel,
26:12 The whole number of the **h** of ancestral houses
Ezr 1: 5 The **h** of the families of Judah and Benjamin,
2:68 some of the **h** of families made freewill offerings
3:12 many of the priests and Levites and **h** of families,
4: 2 they approached Zerubbabel and the **h** of families
4: 3 the rest of the **h** of families in Israel said to them,
8: 1 These are their family **h,** and this is the genealogy
8:29 before the chief priests and the Levites and the **h**
9: 6 for our iniquities have risen higher than our **h,**
10:16 Ezra the priest selected men, **h** of families,
Ne 4: 4 turn their taunt back on their own **h,**
7:70 Now some of the **h** of ancestral houses contributed
7:71 And some of the **h** of ancestral houses gave into
8: 6 Then they bowed their **h** and worshiped
8:13 On the second day the **h** of ancestral houses of all
9: 1 and with earth on their **h.**
11:13 **h** of ancestral houses, two hundred forty-two;
12:12 **h** of ancestral houses, were:
12:22 there were recorded the **h** of ancestral houses;
12:23 The Levites, **h** of ancestral houses,
Job 2:12 and threw dust in the air upon their **h.**
24:24 they are cut off like the **h** of grain.
Ps 7:16 Their mischief returns upon their own **h,**
7:16 and on their own **h** their violence descends.
22: 7 they make mouths at me, they shake their **h;**
24: 7 Lift up your **h,** O gates!
24: 9 Lift up your **h,** O gates!
66:12 you let people ride over our **h;**
68:21 But God will shatter the **h** of his enemies,
74:13 you broke the **h** of the dragons in the waters.
74:14 You crushed the **h** of Leviathan;
83: 2 those who hate you have raised their **h.**
109:25 when they see me, they shake their **h.**
110: 6 he will shatter **h** over the wide earth.
140: 9 Those who surround me lift up their **h;**
Pr 25:22 for you will heap coals of fire on their **h,**
Isa 3:17 with scabs the **h** of the daughters of Zion,
29:10 you prophets, and covered your **h,** you seers.
35:10 everlasting joy shall be upon their **h;**
51:11 everlasting joy shall be upon their **h;**
Jer 14: 3 They are ashamed and dismayed and cover their **h,**
14: 4 the farmers are dismayed; they cover their **h.**
18:16 All who pass by it are horrified and shake their **h.**
La 2:10 they have thrown dust on their **h** and put
2:10 the young girls of Jerusalem have bowed their **h** to
2:15 they hiss and wag their **h** at daughter Jerusalem;
Eze 1:22 the **h** of the living creatures there was something
1:22 shining like crystal, spread out above their **h.**
1:25 a voice from above the dome over their **h;**
1:26 above the dome over their **h** there was something
7:18 Shame shall be on all faces, baldness on all their **h.**
9:10 but I will bring down their deeds upon their **h."**
10: 1 that was over the **h** of the cherubim there appeared
11:21 I will bring their deeds upon their own **h,**
13:18 make veils for the **h** of persons of every height,
22:31 I have returned their conduct upon their **h,**
23:15 with flowing turbans on their **h,**
23:42 and beautiful crowns upon their **h.**
24:23 Your turbans shall be on your **h** and your sandals
27:30 They throw dust on their **h** and wallow in ashes;
32:27 whose swords were laid under their **h,**
33: 4 their blood shall be upon their own **h.**
44:18 They shall have linen turbans on their **h,**
44:20 not shave their **h** or let their locks grow long;
44:20 they shall only trim the hair of their **h.**
Da 3:27 the hair of their **h** was not singed,
7: 6 of a bird on its back and four **h;**
Hos 8: 7 The standing grain has no **h,** it shall yield no meal;
Joel 3: 4 upon your own **h** swiftly and speedily.
3: 7 and I will turn your deeds back upon your own **h.**
Am 9: 1 and shatter them on the **h** of all the people;
Mic 3: 1 you **h** of Jacob and rulers of the house of Israel!
Mt 12: 1 and they began to pluck **h** of grain and to eat.
27:39 Those who passed by derided him, shaking their **h**
Mk 2:23 his disciples began to pluck **h** of grain.
15:29 shaking their **h** and saying, "Aha!
Lk 6: 1 his disciples plucked some **h** of grain,
21:28 stand up and raise your **h,**
Ac 18: 6 "Your blood be on your own **h!**
21:24 and pay for the shaving of their **h.**
27:34 for none of you will lose a hair from your **h."**
Ro 12:20 doing this you will heap burning coals on their **h."**
Rev 4: 4 with golden crowns on their **h.**
9: 7 On their **h** were what looked like crowns of gold;
9:17 the **h** of the horses were like lions' **h,**
9:19 their tails are like serpents, having **h;**
12: 3 a great red dragon, with seven **h** and ten horns,
12: 3 and seven diadems on his **h.**
13: 1 of the sea having ten horns and seven **h;**
Rev 13: 1 and on its **h** were blasphemous names.
13: 3 One of its **h** seemed to have received a death-blow,
17: 3 and it had seven **h** and ten horns.
17: 7 and of the beast with seven **h** and ten horns
17: 9 the seven **h** are seven mountains on which
18:19 And they threw dust on their **h,**
Jdt 4:11 on their **h** and spread out their sackcloth before
8:22 all this he will bring on our **h** among the Gentiles,
9: 9 and send your wrath upon their **h.**
Sir 11: 1 The wisdom of the humble lifts their **h** high,
11:13 raises up their **h** to the amazement of the many.
17:23 and he will bring their recompense on their **h.**
20:11 and there are some who have raised their **h**
36:12 Crush the **h** of hostile rulers who say,
LtJ 6: 9 People take gold and make crowns for the **h**
6:22 swallows, and birds alight on their bodies and **h;**
6:31 their **h** and beards shaved, and their **h** uncovered.
1Mc 3:47 put on sackcloth and sprinkled ashes on their **h,**
6:35 and with brass helmets on their **h;**
2Mc 1:16 they dismembered them and cut off their **h**
10:25 Maccabeus and his men sprinkled dust on their **h**
14:15 they sprinkled dust on their **h** and prayed
1Es 2: 8 Then arose the **h** of families of the tribes of Judah
5: 1 this the **h** of ancestral houses were chosen to go up,
5:44 Some of the **h** of families,
5:63 of the levitical priests and **h** of ancestral houses,
5:68 and the **h** of the ancestral houses and said to them,
5:70 the **h** of the ancestral houses in Israel said to them,
8:59 and to the **h** of the ancestral houses of Israel,
8:75 For our sins have risen higher than our **h,**
3Mc 3:19 among all nations who hold their **h** high
2Es 4:32 When **h** of grain without number are sown,
11: 1 that had twelve feathered wings and three **h.**
11: 4 But its **h** were at rest;
11: 4 the middle head was larger than the other **h,**
11: 9 but let the **h** be reserved for the last."
11:10 and saw that the voice did not come from its **h,**
11:23 the eagle's body except the three **h** that were at rest
11:29 one of the **h** that were at rest (the one that was in
11:29 it was greater than the other two **h.**
11:30 And I saw how it allied the two **h** with itself,
11:34 But the two **h** remained, which also in
11:45 your most evil little wings, your malicious **h,**
12:17 the eagle's **h** but from the midst of its body, this is
12:22 "As for your seeing three **h** at rest,
12:24 Therefore they are called the **h** of the eagle,
4Mc 15:20 severed hands upon hands, scalped **h** upon **h,**

HEADSTONE (KJV) See TOP STONE

HEADSTRONG (4) [HEAD]

Sir 26:10 Keep strict watch over a **h** daughter, or else,
26:25 *A **h** wife is regarded as a dog,*
30: 8 and an unchecked son turns out **h.**
42:11 Keep strict watch over a **h** daughter,

HEADY (KJV) See RECKLESS

HEAL (36) [HEALED, HEALER, HEALING, HEALS, HEALTH, HEALTHFUL, HEALTHY]

Nu 12:13 Moses cried to the LORD, "O God, please **h** her."
Dt 32:39 I kill and I make alive; I wound and I **h;**
2Ki 20: 5 I have seen your tears; indeed, I will **h** you;
20: 8 "What shall be the sign that the LORD will **h** me,
2Ch 7:14 and will forgive their sin and **h** their land.
Job 5:18 he strikes, but his hands **h.**
Ps 6: 2 **h** me, for my bones are shaking with terror.
41: 3 in their illness you **h** all their infirmities.
41: 4 **h** me, for I have sinned against you."
Ecc 3: 3 a time to kill, and a time to **h;**
Isa 19:22 and he will listen to their supplications and **h** them.
57:18 I have seen their ways, but I will **h** them;
57:19 says the LORD; and I will **h** them.
Jer 3:22 O faithless children, I will **h** your faithlessness.
17:14 **H** me, O LORD, and I shall be healed;
30:17 and your wounds I will **h,** says the LORD,
33: 6 I will **h** them and reveal to them abundance
51: 9 We tried to **h** Babylon, but she could not
La 2:13 For vast as the sea is your ruin; who can **h** you?
Hos 5:13 But he is not able to cure you or **h** your wound.
6: 1 for it is he who has torn, and he will **h** us;
7: 1 when I would **h** Israel, the corruption
14: 4 I will **h** their disloyalty; I will love them freely,
Zec 11:16 or seek the wandering, or **h** the maimed,
Mt 13:15 and turn—and I would **h** them.'
Lk 5:17 and the power of the Lord was with him to **h.**
7: 3 asking him to come and **h** his slave.
9: 2 to proclaim the kingdom of God and to **h.**
Jn 4:47 and begged him to come down and **h** his son,
12:40 and turn—and I would **h** them."
Ac 4:30 while you stretch out your hand to **h,**
28:27 and turn—and I would **h** them.'
Tob 3:17 So Raphael was sent to **h** both of them:
5:10 the time is near for God to **h** you; take courage."
12:14 And at the same time God sent me to **h** you
Sir 38: 9 but pray to the Lord, and he will **h** you.

HEALED (55) [HEAL]

Ge 20:17 and God **h** Abimelech, and also **h** his wife
Lev 13:18 there is on the skin of one's body a boil that has **h,**
13:37 and black hair has grown in it, the itch is **h,**
14: 3 If the disease is **h** in the leprous person,
14:48 shall pronounce the house clean; the disease is **h.**
Dt 28:27 scurvy, and itch, of which you cannot be **h.**

Dt 28:35 with grievous boils of which you cannot be **h**,
Jos 5: 8 in their places in the camp until they were **h**.
1Sa 6: 3 Then you will be **h** and will be ransomed;
2Ki 8:29 King Joram returned to be **h** in Jezreel of
9:15 but King Joram had returned to be **h** in Jezreel of
2Ch 22: 6 be **h** in Jezreel of the wounds that he had received
30:20 The LORD heard Hezekiah, and **h** the people.
Ps 30: 2 I cried to you for help, and you have **h** me.
107:20 he sent out his word and **h** them,
Isa 6:10 with their minds, and turn and be **h**."
53: 5 and by his bruises we are **h**.
Jer 15:18 my wound incurable, refusing to be **h?**
17:14 Heal me, O LORD, and I shall be **h**;
51: 8 Bring balm for her wound; perhaps she may be **h**.
51: 9 We tried to heal Babylon, but she could not be **h**.
Eze 34: 4 you have not **h** the sick,
Hos 11: 3 but they did not know that I **h** them.
Mt 8: 8 but only speak the word, and my servant will be **h**.
8:13 And the servant was **h** in that hour.
14:36 and all who touched it were **h**.
15:28 And her daughter was **h** instantly.
Mk 5:29 she felt in her body that she was **h** of her disease.
5:34 go in peace, and be **h** of your disease."
6:56 and all who touched it were **h**.
Lk 6:18 to hear him and to be **h** of their diseases;
6:19 for power came out from him and **h** all of them.
7: 7 But only speak the word, and let my servant be **h**.
8:36 who had been possessed by demons had been **h**.
8:47 and how she had been immediately **h**.
9:11 and **h** those who needed to be cured.
9:42 But Jesus rebuked the unclean spirit, **h** the boy,
14: 4 So Jesus took him and **h** him, and sent him away.
17:15 Then one of them, when he saw that he was **h**,
22:51 And he touched his ear and **h** him.
Jn 5:13 the man who had been **h** did not know who it was,
7:23 because I **h** a man's whole body on the sabbath?
Ac 4: 9 and are asked how this man has been **h**,
14: 9 at him intently and seeing that he had faith to be **h**,
Heb 12:13 not be put out of joint, but rather be **h**.
Jas 5:16 and pray for one another, so that you may be **h**.
1Pe 2:24 by his wounds you have been **h**.
Rev 13: 3 but its mortal wound had been **h**.
13:12 whose mortal wound had been **h**.
Tob 2:10 I went to physicians to be **h**,
6: 9 upon the white films, and the eyes will be **h**."
12: 3 he brought the money back with me, and he **h** you.
Wis 16:10 for your mercy came to their help and **h** them.
2Es 7:*104* to be ill or sleep or eat or be **h** in his place,

HEALER (1) [HEAL]

Isa 3: 7 "I will not be a **h**; in my house there is neither

HEALING‡ (29) [HEAL]

Pr 3: 8 a **h** for your flesh and a refreshment for your body.
4:22 and **h** to all their flesh.
12:18 but the tongue of the wise brings **h**.
13:17 messenger brings trouble, but a faithful envoy, **h**.
29: 1 will suddenly be broken beyond **h**.
Isa 19:22 The LORD will strike Egypt, striking and **h**;
58: 8 and your **h** shall spring up quickly;
Jer 8:15 for a time of **h**, but there is terror instead.
14:19 Why have you struck us down so that there is no **h**
14:19 for a time of **h**, but there is terror instead.
30:13 no medicine for your wound, no **h** for you.
33: 6 I am going to bring it recovery and **h**;
46:11 there is no **h** for you.
Eze 30:21 it has not been bound up for **h** or wrapped with
47:12 Their fruit will be for food, and their leaves for **h**."
Mal 4: 2 of righteousness shall rise, with **h** in its wings.
Ac 4:22 sign of **h** had been performed was more than forty
10:38 about doing good and **h** all who were oppressed by
1Co 12: 9 to another gifts of **h** by the one Spirit,
12:28 then deeds of power, then gifts of **h**,
12:30 Do all possess gifts of **h?**
Rev 22: 2 the leaves of the tree are for the **h** of the nations.
Wis 16: 9 and no **h** was found for them,
Sir 3:28 When calamity befalls the proud, there is no **h**,
21: 3 there is no **h** for the wound it inflicts.
28: 3 and expect **h** from the Lord?
38: 2 for their gift of **h** comes from the Most High,
38:14 that he grant them success in diagnosis and in **h**,
2Es 7:*123* [53] and in which are abundance and **h**,

HEALS (8) [HEAL]

Ex 15:26 for I am the LORD who **h** you."
Ps 103: 3 forgives all your iniquity, who **h** all your diseases,
147: 3 He **h** the brokenhearted, and binds
Isa 30:26 and **h** the wounds inflicted by his blow.
Ac 9:34 Peter said to him, "Aeneas, Jesus Christ **h** you;
Wis 16:12 but it was your word, O Lord, that **h** all people.
Sir 38: 7 By them the physician **h** and takes away pain;
43:22 A mist quickly **h** all things;

HEALTH‡ (32) [HEAL]

Ps 38: 3 there is no **h** in my bones because of my sin.
Pr 16:24 sweetness to the soul and **h** to the body.
Isa 38:16 Oh, restore me to **h** and make me live!
Jer 8:22 the **h** of my poor people not been restored?
30:17 For I will restore **h** to you,
Lk 7:10 they found the slave in good **h**.
Ac 3:16 that is through Jesus has given him this perfect **h**
4:10 in good **h** by the name of Jesus Christ of Nazareth,
3Jn 1: 2 with you and that you may be in good **h**,
Tob 5:16 in good **h** and return to you in good **h**,
5:17 and return you in good **h** to me;
Tob 5:21 will leave in good **h** and return to us in good **h**.
5:21 on the day when he returns to you in good **h**.
5:22 and he will come back in good **h**."
7: 1 brothers; welcome and good **h!**"
7: 4 Then she asked them, "Is he in good **h?**"
7: 5 They replied, "He is alive and in good **h**."
Wis 7:10 I loved her more than **h** and beauty,
13:18 For **h** he appeals to a thing that is weak;
Sir 1:18 making peace and perfect **h** to flourish.
18:19 and before you fall ill, take care of your **h**.
30:15 **H** and fitness are better than any gold,
30:16 There is no wealth better than **h** of body,
34:20 he gives **h** and life and blessing.
38: 8 and from him **h** spreads over all the earth.
2Mc 1:10 and to the Jews in Egypt, Greetings and good **h**.
9:19 and good wishes for their **h** and prosperity.
11:28 We also are in good **h**.
3Mc 3:12 in Egypt and all its districts, greetings and good **h:**
7: 1 in his government, greetings and good **h:**

HEALTHFUL (1) [HEAL]

2Es 7:*121* [51] and **h** habitations have been reserved for us,

HEALTHY (6) [HEAL]

Zec 11:16 or heal the maimed, or nourish the **h**,
Mt 6:22 if your eye is **h**, your whole body will be full
Lk 11:34 If your eye is **h**, your whole body is full of light;
but if it is not **h**, your body is full of darkness.
Sir 30:14 **h**, and fit than rich and afflicted in body.
31:20 **H** sleep depends on moderate eating;

HEAP‡ (47) [HEAPED, HEAPING, HEAPS, STONEHEAP]

Ge 31:46 and made a **h**; and they ate there by the **h**.
31:48 "This **h** is a witness between you and me today."
31:51 Laban said to Jacob, "See this **h** and see the pillar,
31:52 This **h** is a witness, and the pillar is a witness,
31:52 that I will not pass beyond this **h** to you,
31:52 and you will not pass beyond this **h** and this pillar
Ex 15: 8 the floods stood up in a **h**;
Lev 4:12 to the ash **h**, and shall burn it on a wood fire;
4:12 at the ash **h** it shall be burned.
26:30 I will **h** your carcasses on the carcasses
Dt 32:23 I will **h** disasters upon them,
Jos 3:13 they shall stand in a single **h**."
3:16 rising up in a single **h** far off at Adam,
7:26 a great **h** of stones that remains to this day.
8:28 Joshua burned Ai, and made it forever a **h** of ruins,
8:29 and raised over it a great **h** of stones,
Ru 3: 7 he went to lie down at the end of the **h** of grain.
1Sa 2: 8 he lifts the needy from the ash **h**,
20:41 the stone **h** and prostrated himself with his face to
2Sa 18:17 and raised over him a very great **h** of stones.
1Ki 9: 8 This house will become a **h** of ruins;
Job 27:16 Though they **h** up silver like dust,
Ps 39: 6 they **h** up, and do not know who will gather.
78:13 and made the waters stand like a **h**.
113: 7 and lifts the needy from the ash **h**,
Pr 25:22 for you will **h** coals of fire on their heads,
SS 7: 2 Your belly is a **h** of wheat, encircled with lilies.
Isa 3: 6 and this **h** of ruins shall be under your rule."
17: 1 and will become a **h** of ruins.
25: 2 For you have made the city a **h**,
Jer 9:11 I will make Jerusalem a **h** of ruins, a lair of jackals;
26:18 Jerusalem shall become a **h** of ruins,
51:37 and Babylon shall become a **h** of ruins,
Eze 24:10 **H** up the logs, kindle the fire;
Mic 1: 6 I will make Samaria a **h** in the open country,
3:12 Jerusalem shall become a **h** of ruins,
Hab 1:10 and **h** up earth to take it.
2: 6 "Alas for you who **h** up what is not your own!"
Hag 2:16 When one came to a **h** of twenty measures,
Mt 6: 7 do not **h** up empty phrases as the Gentiles do;
Ro 12:20 for by doing this you will **h** burning coals
Tob 5:19 Do not **h** money upon money,
Sir 8: 3 and do not **h** wood on their fire.
20:28 Those who cultivate the soil **h** up their harvest,
39:17 At his word the waters stood in a **h**,
4Mc 9:20 the **h** of coals was being quenched by the drippings

HEAPED (4) [HEAP]

Ru 2:14 and he **h** up for her some parched grain.
Zec 9: 3 and **h** up silver like dust,
Rev 18: 5 for her sins are **h** high as heaven,
Sir 37:24 A wise person will have praise **h** upon him,

HEAPING (2) [HEAP]

Ecc 2:26 to the sinner he gives the work of gathering and **h**,
Lk 22:65 They kept **h** many other insults on him.

HEAPS (20) [HEAP]

Ex 8:14 And they gathered them together in **h**,
Jdg 15:16 "With the jawbone of a donkey, **h** upon **h**,
2Ki 10: 8 "Lay them in two **h** at the entrance of the gate until
19:25 that you should make fortified cities crash into **h**
2Ch 31: 6 to the LORD their God, and laid them in **h**.
31: 7 In the third month they began to pile up the **h**,
31: 8 Hezekiah and the officials came and saw the **h**,
31: 9 the priests and the Levites about the **h**.
Ne 4: 2 Will they revive the stones out of the **h**
13:15 and bringing in **h** of grain and loading them
Job 15:28 houses destined to become **h** of ruins;
Isa 37:26 that you should make fortified cities crash into **h**
Jer 50:26 pile her up like **h** of grain, and destroy her utterly;
La 4: 5 up in purple cling to ash **h**.
Hos 12:11 so their altars shall be like stone **h** on the furrows
Na 3: 3 **h** of corpses, dead bodies without end—
Wis 18:23 the dead had already fallen on one another in **h**,
1Mc 11: 4 for they had piled them in **h** along his route.
2Es 2: 9 whose land lies in lumps of pitch and **h** of ashes.

HEAR‡ (462) [HEARD, HEARER, HEARERS, HEARING, HEARS, OVERHEARD, OVERHEARING]

Ge 4:23 "Adah and Zillah, **h** my voice;
23: 6 "**H** us, my lord; you are a mighty prince among us.
23: 8 **h** me, and entreat for me Ephron son of Zohar,
23:11 my lord, **h** me; I give you the field,
41:15 that when you **h** a dream you can interpret it."
49: 2 Assemble and **h**, O sons of Jacob;
Ex 19: 9 that the people may **h** when I speak with you and
32:18 it is the sound of revelers that I **h**."
Nu 7:89 he would **h** the voice speaking to him from above
9: 8 so that I may **h** what the LORD will command
12: 6 And he said, "**H** my words:
14:13 "Then the Egyptians will **h** of it,
16: 8 Then Moses said to Korah, "**H** now, you Levites!
23:18 "Rise, Balak, and **h**; listen to me, O son of Zippor:
Dt 1:17 **h** out the small and the great alike;
1:17 bring to me, and I will **h** it."
2:25 when they **h** report of you,
4: 6 who, when they **h** all these statutes, will say,
4:10 and I will let them **h** my words,
4:28 objects of wood and stone that neither see, nor **h**,
4:36 From heaven he made you **h** his voice
5: 1 Moses convened all Israel, and said to them: **H**,
5:25 we **h** the voice of the LORD our God any longer,
5:27 and **h** all that the LORD our God will say.
6: 3 **H** therefore, O Israel, and observe them diligently,
6: 4 **H**, O Israel: The LORD is our God,
9: 1 **H**, O Israel! You are about to cross the Jordan
13:11 Then all Israel shall **h** and be afraid,
13:12 If you **h** it said about one of the towns that
17: 4 and if it is reported to you or you **h** of it,
17:13 All the people will **h** and be afraid,
18:16 "If I **h** the voice of the LORD my God any more,
19:20 The rest shall **h** and be afraid,
20: 3 and shall say to them: "**H**, O Israel!
21:21 and all Israel will **h**, and be afraid.
27: 9 Keep silence and **h**, O Israel!
29: 4 or eyes to see, or ears to **h**.
29:19 All who **h** the words of this oath
30:12 get it for us so that we may **h** it and observe it?"
30:13 get it for us so that we may **h** it and observe it?"
30:17 But if your heart turns away and you do not **h**,
31:12 so that they may **h** and learn to fear
31:13 may **h** and learn to fear the LORD your God,
32: 1 let the earth **h** the words of my mouth.
Jos 3: 9 near and **h** the words of the LORD your God."
6: 5 as soon as you **h** the sound of the trumpet,
7: 9 and all the inhabitants of the land will **h** of it,
Jdg 5: 3 "**H**, O kings; give ear, O princes;
5:16 to **h** the piping for the flocks?
7:11 and you shall **h** what they say,
14:13 So they said to him, "Ask your riddle; let us **h** it."
1Sa 2:23 For I **h** of your evil dealings from all these people.
2:24 that I **h** the people of the LORD spreading abroad.
13: 3 saying, "Let the Hebrews **h!**"
15:14 and the lowing of cattle that I **h?**"
22: 7 "**H** now, you Benjaminites;
25: 7 I **h** that you have shearers;
25:24 and **h** the words of your servant.
26:19 let my lord the king **h** the words of his servant.
2Sa 5:24 When you **h** the sound of marching in the tops of
14:16 For the king will **h**, and deliver his servant from
15: 3 but there is no one deputed by the king to **h** you."
15:10 "As soon as you **h** the sound of the trumpet,
15:35 So whatever you **h** from the king's house,
15:36 by them you shall report to me everything you **h**."
16:21 after the house; and all Israel will **h**
17: 5 and let us **h** too what he has to say."
1Ki 4:34 People came from all the nations to **h** the wisdom
8:30 **H** the plea of your servant and of your people
8:30 O **h** in heaven your dwelling place;
8:32 then **h** in heaven, and act,
8:34 then **h** in heaven, forgive the sin
8:36 then **h** in heaven, and forgive the sin
8:39 then **h** in heaven your dwelling place, forgive, act,
8:42 —for they shall **h** of your great name,
8:43 then **h** in heaven your dwelling place,
8:45 then **h** in heaven their prayer and their plea,
8:49 then **h** in heaven your dwelling place their prayer
10: 8 who continually attend you and **h** your wisdom!
10:24 the presence of Solomon to **h** his wisdom,
22:19 "Therefore **h** the word of the LORD:
22:28 And he said, "**H**, you peoples, all of you!"
2Ki 7: 1 But Elisha said, "**H** the word of the LORD:
7: 6 For the Lord had caused the Aramean army to **h**
18:28 "**H** the word of the great king, the king of Assyria!
19: 7 that he shall **h** a rumor and return to his own land;
19:16 Incline your ear, O LORD, and **h**;
19:16 **h** the words of Sennacherib,
20:16 "**H** the word of the LORD:
1Ch 14:15 When you **h** the sound of marching in the tops of
28: 2 "**H** me, my brothers and my people.
2Ch 6:21 And **h** the plea of your servant and
6:21 may you **h** from heaven your dwelling place;
6:21 from heaven your dwelling place; **h** and forgive.

2Ch 6:23 may you **h** from heaven, and act,
6:25 may you **h** from heaven, and forgive the sin
6:27 may you **h** in heaven, forgive the sin
6:30 may you **h** from heaven, your dwelling place,
6:33 may you **h** from heaven your dwelling place,
6:35 then **h** from heaven their prayer and their plea,
6:39 **h** from heaven your dwelling place their prayer
7:14 then I will **h** from heaven,
9:7 who continually attend you and **h** your wisdom!
9:23 the presence of Solomon to **h** his wisdom,
15:2 He went out to meet Asa and said to him, **"H** me,
18:18 "Therefore **h** the word of the LORD:
18:27 And he said, **"H,** you peoples, all of you!"
20:9 and you will **h** and save.'
28:11 Now **h** me, and send back the captives whom you
Ne 1:6 and your eyes open to **h** the prayer of your servant
4:4 **H,** O our God, for we are despised;
4:20 to us wherever you **h** the sound of the trumpet.
8:2 both men and women and all who could **h**
Job 3:18 they do not **h** the voice of the taskmaster.
5:27 **H,** and know it for yourself."
13:6 **H** now my reasoning, and listen to the pleadings
20:3 I **h** censure that insults me,
22:27 You will pray to him, and he will **h** you,
26:14 and how small a whisper do we **h** of him!
27:9 Will God **h** their cry when trouble comes
31:35 that I had one to **h** me!
33:1 **h** my speech, O Job, and listen to all my words.
34:2 **"H** my words, you wise men, and give ear
34:10 "Therefore, **h** me, you who have sense,
34:16 "If you have understanding, **h** this;
34:34 and the wise who **h** me will say,
35:13 Surely God does not **h** an empty cry,
37:14 **"H** this, O Job; stop and consider the wondrous
39:7 it does not **h** the shouts of the driver.
42:4 **'H,** and I will speak; I will question you,
Ps 4:1 Be gracious to me, and **h** my prayer.
5:3 O LORD, in the morning you **h** my voice;
10:17 O LORD, you will **h** the desire of the meek;
17:1 **H** a just cause, O LORD;
17:6 incline your ear to me, **h** my words.
27:7 **H,** O LORD, when I cry aloud,
28:1 my rock, do not refuse to **h** me,
28:2 **H** the voice of my supplication,
30:10 **H,** O LORD, and be gracious to me!
31:13 For I **h** the whispering of many—
34:2 let the humble **h** and be glad.
38:13 But I am like the deaf, I do not **h;**
38:14 Truly, I am like one who does not **h,**
39:12 **"H** my prayer, O LORD, and give ear to my cry;
45:10 **H,** O daughter, consider and incline your ear;
49:1 **H** this, all you peoples; give ear,
50:7 **"H,** O my people, and I will speak,
51:8 Let me **h** joy and gladness;
54:2 **H** my prayer, O God; give ear to the
55:17 and he will **h** my voice.
55:19 will **h,** and will humble them—
58:5 so that it does not **h** the voice of charmers or of
59:7 for "Who," they think, "will **h** us?"
61:1 **H** my cry, O God; listen to my prayer.
64:1 **H** my voice, O God, in my complaint;
66:16 Come and **h,** all you who fear God,
77:1 aloud to God, that he may **h** me.
81:5 I **h** a voice I had not known:
81:8 **H,** O my people, while I admonish you;
84:8 O LORD God of hosts, **h** my prayer;
85:8 Let me **h** what God the LORD will speak,
94:9 He who planted the ear, does he not **h?**
102:1 **H** my prayer, O LORD; let my cry come to you.
102:20 to **h** the groans of the prisoners,
115:6 They have ears, but do not **h;**
119:149 In your steadfast love **h** my voice;
130:2 **h** my voice! Let your ears be attentive
135:17 but they do not **h,** and there is no breath
143:1 **H** my prayer, O LORD; give ear to my
143:8 Let me **h** of your steadfast love in the morning,
Pr 1:5 Let the wise also **h** and gain in learning,
1:8 **H,** my child, your father's instruction,
4:10 **H,** my child, and accept my words,
8:6 **H,** for I will speak noble things
8:33 **H** instruction and be wise, and do not neglect it.
19:27 in order that you may **h** instruction.
22:17 Incline your ear and **h** my words,
23:19 **H,** my child, and be wise, and direct your mind in
Ecc 7:5 It is better to **h** the rebuke of the wise than to **h**
7:21 or you may **h** your servant cursing you;
SS 2:14 let me see your face, let me **h** your voice;
8:13 for your voice; let me **h** it.
Isa 1:2 **H,** O heavens, and listen, O earth;
1:10 **H** the word of the LORD, you rulers of Sodom!
7:13 Then Isaiah said: **"H** then, O house of David!
11:3 or decide by what his ears **h;**
21:3 I am bowed down so that I cannot **h,**
24:16 From the ends of the earth we **h** songs of praise,
28:12 and this is repose"; yet they would not **h.**
28:14 Therefore **h** the word of the LORD,
28:23 and **h** my voice; Pay attention, and **h** my speech.
29:18 On that day the deaf shall **h** the words of a scroll,
30:9 who will not **h** the instruction of the LORD;
30:11 let us **h** no more about the Holy One of Israel."
30:21 your ears shall **h** a word behind you, saying,
32:9 Rise up, you women who are at ease, **h** my voice;
33:13 **H,** you who are far away, what I have done;
34:1 Draw near, O nations, to **h;** O peoples, give heed!
34:1 Let the earth **h,** and all that fills it;
36:13 **H** the words of the great king, the king of Assyria!
37:7 so that he shall **h** a rumor,

Isa 37:17 Incline your ear, O LORD, and **h;**
37:17 **h** all the words of Sennacherib,
39:5 **"H** the word of the LORD of hosts:
42:20 his ears are open, but he does not **h.**
43:9 and let them **h** and say, "It is true."
44:1 But now **h,** O Jacob my servant,
47:8 Now therefore **h** this, you lover of pleasures,
48:1 **H** this, O house of Jacob, who are called by
48:6 From this time forward I make you **h** new things,
48:14 Assemble, all of you, and **h!**
48:16 Draw near to me, **h** this!
51:21 Therefore **h** this, you who are wounded,
59:1 nor his ear too dull to **h.**
59:2 from you so that he does not **h.**
65:24 while they are yet speaking I will **h.**
66:5 **H** the word of the LORD,
Jer 2:4 **H** the word of the LORD, O house of Jacob,
4:19 for I **h** the sound of the trumpet, the alarm of war.
4:21 and **h** the sound of the trumpet?
5:21 **H** this, O foolish and senseless people,
5:21 but do not see, who have ears, but do not **h.**
6:10 and give warning, that they may **h?**
6:18 Therefore **h,** O nations, and know, O congregation,
6:19 **H,** O earth; I am going to bring
7:2 **H** the word of the LORD, all you people of Judah,
7:16 and do not intercede with me, for I will not **h** you.
9:20 **H,** O women, the word of the LORD,
10:1 **H** the word that the LORD speaks to you,
10:22 **H,** a noise! Listen, it is coming—
11:2 **H** the words of this covenant,
11:6 **H** the words of this covenant and do them.
13:10 This evil people, who refuse to **h** my words,
13:15 **H** and give ear; do not be haughty,
14:12 Although they fast, I do not **h** their cry,
17:20 **H** the word of the LORD, you kings of Judah,
17:23 they stiffened their necks and would not **h**
18:2 and there I will let you **h** my words."
19:3 You shall say: **H** the word of the LORD,
19:15 stiffened their necks, refusing to **h** my words.
20:10 For I **h** many whispering: "Terror is all around!
20:16 let him **h** a cry in the morning and an alarm
21:11 **H** the word of the LORD,
22:2 **H** the word of the LORD,
22:29 O land, land, land, **h** the word of the LORD!
23:18 of the LORD so as to see and to **h** his word?
25:4 nor inclined your ears to **h**
29:12 upon me and come and pray to me, I will **h** you.
29:20 **h** the word of the LORD:
31:10 **H** the word of the LORD, O nations,
33:9 before all the nations of the earth who shall **h** of all
34:4 Yet **h** the word of the LORD,
37:20 Now please **h** me, my lord king:
38:25 the officials should **h** that I have spoken with you,
42:14 or **h** the sound of the trumpet,
42:15 then **h** the word of the LORD,
44:24 **"H** the word of the LORD,
44:26 Therefore **h** the word of the LORD,
49:20 Therefore **h** the plan that the LORD has made
50:45 Therefore **h** the plan that the LORD has made
La 1:18 but **h,** all you peoples, and behold my suffering;
Eze 2:5 Whether they **h** or refuse to **h** (for they are a
2:7 whether they **h** or refuse to **h;**
2:8 But you, mortal, **h** what I say to you;
3:10 that I shall speak to you receive in your heart and **h**
3:11 whether they **h** or refuse to **h.**
3:17 whenever you **h** a word from my mouth,
3:27 let those who will **h, h;** and let those who refuse to **h,** refuse;
6:3 **h** the word of the Lord GOD!
12:2 who have ears to **h** but do not **h;**
13:2 **"H** the word of the LORD!"
16:35 Therefore, O whore, **h** the word of the LORD:
18:25 **H** now, O house of Israel: Is my way unfair?
20:47 **H** the word of the LORD:
25:3 **H** the word of the Lord GOD:
33:4 then if any who **h** the sound of the trumpet do
33:7 whenever you **h** a word from my mouth,
33:30 "Come and **h** what the word is that comes from
33:31 as my people, and they **h** your words, but they will
33:32 they **h** what you say, but they will not do it.
34:7 you shepherds, **h** the word of the LORD:
34:9 you shepherds, **h** the word of the LORD:
36:1 O mountains of Israel, **h** the word of the LORD.
36:4 **h** the word of the Lord GOD:
36:15 and no longer will I let you **h** the insults of
37:4 O dry bones, **h** the word of the LORD.
Da 3:5 that when you **h** the sound of the horn,
3:15 if you are ready when you **h** the sound of the horn,
4:9 **H** the dream that I saw; tell me its interpretation.
5:23 wood, and stone, which do not see or **h** or know;
9:18 Incline your ear, O my God, and **h.**
9:19 O Lord, **h;** O Lord, forgive;
Hos 4:1 **H** the word of the LORD, O people of Israel;
5:1 **H** this, O priests! Give heed,
Joel 1:2 **H** this, O elders, give ear, all inhabitants of
Am 3:1 **H** this word that the LORD has spoken
3:13 **H,** and testify against the house of Jacob,
4:1 **H** this word, you cows of Bashan who are
5:1 **H** this word that I take up over you in lamentation,
7:16 "Now therefore **h** the word of the LORD.
8:4 **H** this, you that trample on the needy,
Mic 1:2 **H,** you peoples, all of you;
3:9 **H** this, you rulers of the house of Jacob and chiefs
6:1 **H** what the LORD says: Rise,
6:1 and let the hills **h** your voice.
6:2 **H,** you mountains, the controversy of the LORD,
6:9 **H,** O tribe and assembly of the city!

Mic 7:7 of my salvation; my God will **h** me.
Na 3:19 All who **h** the news about you clap their hands
Hab 3:16 I **h,** and I tremble within;
Zec 1:4 But they did not **h** or heed me, says the LORD.
7:11 and stopped their ears in order not to **h.**
7:12 They made their hearts adamant in order not to **h**
7:13 Just as, when I called, they would not **h,** so,
7:13 I would not **h,** says the LORD of hosts,
Mt 10:27 and what you **h** whispered,
11:4 "Go and tell John what you **h** and see:
11:5 the lame walk, the lepers are cleansed, the deaf **h,**
12:19 nor will anyone **h** his voice in the streets.
13:16 for they see, and your ears, for they **h.**
13:17 and to **h** what you **h,** but did not **h** it.
13:18 **"H** then the parable of the sower.
21:16 "Do you **h** what these are saying?"
24:6 And you will **h** of wars and rumors of wars;
27:13 "Do you not **h** how many accusations they make
Mk 4:9 And he said, "Let anyone with ears to **h** listen!"
4:15 when they **h,** Satan immediately comes
4:16 when they **h** the word, they immediately receive it
4:18 these are the ones who **h** the word,
4:20 they **h** the word and accept it and bear fruit,
4:23 Let anyone with ears to **h** listen!"
4:24 And he said to them, "Pay attention to what you **h;**
4:33 as they were able to **h** it;
6:11 not welcome you and they refuse to **h** you,
7:37 even makes the deaf to **h** and the mute to speak."
8:18 Do you have ears, and fail to **h?**
12:29 Jesus answered, "The first is, **'H,** O Israel:
13:7 When you **h** of wars and rumors of wars,
Lk 5:1 the crowd was pressing in on him to **h** the word
5:15 many crowds would gather to **h** him and to
6:18 to **h** him and to be healed of their diseases;
7:22 the lame walk, the lepers are cleansed, the deaf **h,**
8:8 he called out, "Let anyone with ears to **h** listen!"
8:13 when they **h** the word, receive it with joy.
8:14 these are the ones who **h;**
8:15 these are the ones who, when they **h** the word,
8:21 and my brothers are those who **h** the word of God
9:9 but who is this about whom I **h** such things?"
10:24 and to **h** what you **h,** but did not **h** it."
11:28 "Blessed rather are those who **h** the word of God
14:35 Let anyone with ears to **h** listen!"
16:2 'What is this that I **h** about you?
21:9 "When you **h** of wars and insurrections,
Jn 3:8 and you **h** the sound of it,
5:25 when the dead will **h** the voice of the Son of God,
5:25 and those who **h** will live.
5:28 when all who are in their graves will **h** his voice
5:30 on my own. As I **h,** I judge;
8:47 The reason you do not **h** them is that you are not
9:27 Why do you want to **h** it again?
10:3 and the sheep **h** his voice.
10:27 My sheep **h** my voice.
11:42 I knew that you always **h** me,
14:24 and the word that you **h** is not mine,
Ac 2:8 And how is it that we **h,** each of us,
2:11 in our own languages we **h** them speaking
2:33 he has poured out this that you both see and **h.**
10:22 to come to his house and to **h** what you have
13:7 and Saul and wanted to **h** the word of God.
13:44 the whole city gathered to **h** the word of the Lord.
15:7 the Gentiles would **h** the message of the good news
17:32 but others said, "We will **h** you again about this."
19:26 You also see and **h** that not only in Ephesus but
21:22 They will certainly **h** that you have come.
22:9 not **h** the voice of the one who was speaking to me.
22:14 to see the Righteous One and to **h** his own voice;
24:4 to **h** us briefly with your customary graciousness.
25:22 "I would like to **h** the man myself."
25:22 "Tomorrow," he said, "you will **h** him."
28:22 But we would like to **h** from you what you think,
Ro 10:14 are they to **h** without someone to proclaim him?
11:8 eyes that would not see and ears that would not **h,**
1Co 11:18 I **h** that there are divisions among you;
2Co 3:14 when they **h** the reading of the old covenant,
Eph 4:29 so that your words may give grace to those who **h.**
Php 1:27 whether I come and see you or am absent and **h**
1:30 the same struggle that you saw I had and now **h**
2Th 3:11 For we **h** that some of you are living in idleness,
2Ti 4:17 be fully proclaimed and all the Gentiles might **h** it.
Phm 1:5 because I **h** of your love for all the saints
Heb 3:7 as the Holy Spirit says, "Today, if you **h** his voice,
3:15 As it is said, "Today, if you **h** his voice,
4:7 if you **h** his voice, do not harden your hearts."
3Jn 1:4 to **h** that my children are walking in the truth.
Rev 1:3 and blessed are those who **h**
3:20 if you **h** my voice and open the door,
9:20 which cannot see or **h** or walk.
Tob 3:15 O Lord, to take my life, **h** me in my disgrace."
5:10 I **h** people but I cannot see them."
10:12 may I **h** a good report about you as long as I live."
Jdt 8:17 and he will **h** our voice, if it pleases him.
9:4 O God, my God, **h** me also—a widow.
9:12 King of all your creation, **h** my prayer!
11:16 the whole world wherever people shall **h**
14:7 In every nation those who **h** your name will
AdE 13:17 **H** my prayer, and have mercy
14:19 **h** the voice of the despairing,
Wis 8:15 dread monarchs will be afraid of me when they **h**
15:15 nor ears with which to **h,** nor fingers to feel with,
Sir 4:6 their Creator will **h** their prayer.
5:11 Be quick to **h,** but deliberate in answering.
19:15 so do not believe everything you **h.**
19:27 He hides his face and pretends not to **h,**
27:15 and their abuse is grievous to **h.**

Sir 29:23 and you will **h** no reproach for being a guest.
29:25 and besides this you will **h** rude words like these:
33:19 **H** me, you who are great among the people,
36:22 **H,** O Lord, the prayer of your servants,
42: 1 Be ashamed of repeating what you **h,**
43:24 and we marvel at what we **h.**
45: 5 He allowed him to **h** his voice,
51:28 **H** but a little of my instruction,
Bar 1: 3 and to all the people who came to **h** the book,
2:14 **H,** O Lord, our prayer and our supplication,
2:16 Incline your ear, O Lord, and **h;**
2:31 I will give them a heart that obeys and ears that **h;**
3: 2 **H,** O Lord, and have mercy,
3: 4 **h** now the prayer of the people of Israel,
3: 9 **H** the commandments of life, O Israel;
2Mc 1: 5 May he **h** your prayers and be reconciled to you,
1Es 5:65 so that the people could not **h** the trumpets because
9:40 men and women, and all the priests to **h** the law,
2Es 2:34 I say to you, O nations that **h** and understand,
5: 7 by night, and all shall **h** his voice.
5:13 you shall **h** yet greater things than these."
6:13 "Rise to your feet and you will **h** a full,
6:23 and when all **h** it, they shall suddenly be terrified.
7:*51* not many but few, while the ungodly abound, **h**
8:19 Therefore **h** my voice and understand my words,
8:24 **h,** O Lord, the prayer of your servant, and give ear
9:30 '**H** me, O Israel, and give heed to my words,
10:35 and I **h** what I do not understand
10:56 afterward you will **h** as much as your ears can **h.**
13:33 "Then, when all the nations **h** his voice,
14:28 "**H** these words, O Israel.
15:29 so that all who **h** them will fear and tremble.
16:27 or even to **h** a human voice.
16:40 **H** my words, O my people;
4Mc 14: 9 we ourselves shudder as we **h** of the suffering

HEARD[‡] (733) [HEAR]

Ge 3: 8 They **h** the sound of the LORD God walking in
3:10 He said, "I **h** the sound of you in the garden,
14:14 Abram **h** that his nephew had been taken captive,
17:20 As for Ishmael, I have **h** you;
21:17 And God **h** the voice of the boy;
21:17 for God has **h** the voice of the boy where he is.
21:26 and I have not **h** of it until today."
24:30 and when he **h** the words of his sister Rebekah,
24:52 When Abraham's servant **h** their words,
27: 6 "I **h** your father say to your brother Esau,
27:34 When Esau **h** his father's words,
29:13 Laban **h** the news about his sister's son Jacob,
29:33 "Because the LORD has **h** that I am hated,
30: 6 and has also **h** my voice and given me a son";
31: 1 Now Jacob **h** that the sons of Laban were saying,
34: 5 Jacob **h** that Shechem had defiled his daughter
34: 7 When they **h** of it, the men were indignant
35:22 Bilhah his father's concubine; and Israel **h** of it.
37:17 man said, "They have gone away, for I **h** them say,
37:21 But when Reuben **h** it, he delivered him out
39:15 and when he **h** me raise my voice and cry out,
39:19 his master **h** the words that his wife spoke to him,
41:15 I have **h** it said of you that when you hear
42: 2 I have **h,**" he said, "that there is grain in Egypt;
43:25 for they had **h** that they would dine there.
45: 2 And he wept so loudly that the Egyptians **h** it,
45: 2 and the household of Pharaoh **h** it.
45:16 When the report was **h** in Pharaoh's house,
Ex 2:15 When Pharaoh **h** of it, he sought to kill Moses.
2:24 God **h** their groaning, and God remembered his
3: 7 I have **h** their cry on account of their taskmasters.
4:31 and when they **h** that the LORD had given heed to
6: 5 I have also **h** the groaning of the Israelites whom
15:14 The peoples **h,** they trembled;
16: 7 he has **h** your complaining against the LORD.
16: 8 the LORD has **h** the complaining that you utter
16: 9 for he has **h** your complaining.' "
16:12 "I have **h** the complaining of the Israelites;
18: 1 **h** of all that God had done for Moses and
23:13 do not let them be **h** on your lips.
28:35 be **h** when he goes into the holy place before
32:17 Joshua **h** the noise of the people as they shouted,
33: 4 When the people **h** these harsh words,
Lev 5: 1 that you have **h** a public adjuration to testify and—
10:20 And when Moses **h** that, he agreed.
Nu 11: 1 the LORD **h** it and his anger was kindled.
11:10 Moses **h** the people weeping
12: 2 And the LORD **h** it.
14:14 They have **h** that you, O LORD,
14:15 then the nations who have **h** about you will say,
14:27 I have **h** the complaints of the Israelites,
14:28 "I will do to you the very things I **h** you say:
16: 4 When Moses **h** it, he fell on his face.
20:16 he **h** our voice, and sent an angel
21: 1 **h** that Israel was coming by the way of Atharim,
22:36 When Balak **h** that Balaam had come,
30:11 and her husband **h** it and said nothing to her,
30:14 he said nothing to her at the time that he **h** of them.
30:15 he nullifies them some time after he has **h** of them,
33:40 **h** of the coming of the Israelites.
Dt 1:34 LORD **h** your words, he was wrathful and swore:
4:12 You **h** the sound of words but saw no form;
4:32 or has its like ever been **h** of?
4:33 Has any people ever **h** the voice of a god speaking out of a fire, as you have **h,**
4:36 while you **h** his words coming out of the fire.
5:23 When you **h** the voice out of the darkness,
5:24 and we have **h** his voice out of the fire.
5:26 that has **h** the voice of the living God speaking out
Dt 5:28 The LORD **h** your words when you spoke to me,
5:28 "I have **h** the words of this people,
9: 2 You have **h** it said of them,
26: 7 the LORD **h** our voice and saw our affliction,
Jos 2:10 For we have **h** how the LORD dried up the water
2:11 As soon as we **h** it, our hearts melted,
5: 1 **h** that the LORD had dried up the waters of
6:10 "You shall not shout or let your voice be **h,**
6:20 As soon as the people **h** the sound of the trumpets,
9: 1 and the Jebusites—**h** of this,
9: 3 the inhabitants of Gibeon **h** what Joshua had done
9: 9 for we have **h** a report of him,
9:16 they **h** that they were their neighbors
10: 1 of Jerusalem **h** how Joshua had taken Ai,
11: 1 When King Jabin of Hazor **h** of this,
14:12 for you **h** on that day how the Anakim were there,
22:11 The Israelites **h** that the Reubenites and
22:12 And when the people of Israel **h** of it,
22:30 **h** the words that the Reubenites and the Gadites
24:27 for it has **h** all the words of the LORD
Jdg 7:15 When Gideon **h** the telling of the dream
9:30 When Zebul the ruler of the city **h** the words
9:46 all the lords of the Tower of Shechem **h** of it,
18:25 "You had better not let your voice be **h** among us
20: 3 (Now the Benjaminites **h** that the people
Ru 1: 6 for she had **h** in the country of Moab that
1Sa 1:13 only her lips moved, but her voice was not **h;**
2:22 He **h** all that his sons were doing to all Israel,
4: 6 When the Philistines **h** the noise of the shouting,
4:14 When Eli **h** the sound of the outcry, he said,
4:19 she **h** the news that the ark of God was captured,
7: 7 When the Philistines **h** that the people
7: 7 of Israel **h** of it they were afraid of the Philistines.
8:21 When Samuel had **h** all the words of the people,
11: 6 upon Saul in power when he **h** these words,
13: 3 and the Philistines **h** of it.
13: 4 When all Israel **h** that Saul had defeated
14:22 into hiding in the hill country of Ephraim **h** that
14:27 But Jonathan had not **h** his father charge the troops
17:11 Saul and all Israel **h** these words of the Philistine,
17:23 as before. And David **h** him.
17:28 His eldest brother Eliab **h** him talking to the men;
17:31 When the words that David spoke were **h,**
22: 1 when his brothers and all his father's house **h** of it,
22: 6 Saul **h** that David and those who were
23:10 your servant has **h** that Saul seeks to come
23:11 now, will Saul come down as your servant has **h?**
23:25 When Saul **h** that, he pursued David into
25: 4 David **h** in the wilderness
25:39 When David **h** that Nabal was dead, he said,
31:11 But when the inhabitants of Jabesh-gilead **h** what
2Sa 3:28 Afterward, when David **h** of it, he said,
4: 1 When Saul's son Ishbaal **h** that Abner had died
5:17 the Philistines **h** that David had been anointed king
5:17 David **h** about it and went down to the stronghold.
7:22 according to all that we have **h** with our ears.
8: 9 of Hamath **h** that David had defeated
10: 7 When David **h** of it, he sent Joab and all the army
11:26 the wife of Uriah **h** that her husband was dead,
13:21 When King David **h** of all these things,
18: 5 And all the people **h** when the king gave orders
19: 2 for the troops **h** that day,
22: 7 From his temple he **h** my voice,
22:45 as soon as they **h** of me, they obeyed me.
1Ki 1:11 "Have you not **h** that Adonijah son
1:41 Adonijah and all the guests who were with him **h** it
1:41 When Joab **h** the sound of the trumpet, he said,
1:45 This is the noise that you **h.**
3:28 All Israel **h** of the judgment that
4:34 the kings of the earth who had **h** of his wisdom.
5: 1 when he **h** that they had anointed him king in place
5: 7 When Hiram **h** the words of Solomon,
5: 8 "I have **h** the message that you have sent to me;
6: 7 nor ax nor any tool of iron was **h** in the temple
9: 3 "I have **h** your prayer and your plea,
10: 1 the queen of Sheba **h** of the fame of Solomon,
10: 6 that I **h** in my own land of your accomplishments
10: 7 and prosperity far surpass the report that I had **h.**
11:21 When Hadad **h** in Egypt that David slept
12: 2 of Nebat **h** of it (for he was still in Egypt,
12:20 When all Israel **h** that Jeroboam had returned,
13: 4 the king **h** what the man of God cried out against
13:26 from the way **h** of it, he said, "It is the man
14: 6 But when Ahijah **h** the sound of her feet,
15:21 When Baasha **h** of it, he stopped building Ramah
16:16 and the troops who were encamped **h** it said,
19:13 When Elijah **h** it, he wrapped his face in his mantle
20:12 When Ben-hadad **h** this message—
20:31 we have **h** that the kings of the house
21:15 As soon as Jezebel **h** that Naboth had been stoned
21:16 As soon as Ahab **h** that Naboth was dead,
21:27 When Ahab **h** those words,
2Ki 3:21 the Moabites **h** that the kings had come up to fight
5: 8 But when Elisha the man of God **h** that the king
6:30 When the king **h** the words of
7:10 but there was no one to be seen or **h** there,
9:30 When Jehu came to Jezreel, Jezebel **h** of it;
11:13 Athaliah **h** the noise of the guard and of the people,
19: 1 When King Hezekiah **h** it, he tore his clothes,
19: 4 be that the LORD your God **h** all the words of
19: 4 the words that the LORD your God has **h;**
19: 6 not be afraid because of the words that you have **h,**
19: 8 for he had **h** that the king had left Lachish.
19: 9 the king **h** concerning King Tirhakah of Ethiopia,
19:11 you have **h** what the kings of Assyria have done
19:20 I have **h** your prayer to me about King Sennacherib
19:25 Have you not **h** that I determined it long ago?
2Ki 20: 5 I have **h** your prayer, I have seen your tears;
20:12 for he had **h** that Hezekiah had been sick.
22:11 When the king **h** the words of the book of the law,
22:18 Regarding the words that you have **h,**
22:19 when you **h** how I spoke against this place,
22:19 I also have **h** you, says the LORD.
25:23 when all the captains of the forces and their men **h**
1Ch 10:11 But when all Jabesh-gilead **h** everything that
14: 8 the Philistines **h** that David had been anointed king
14: 8 and David **h** of it and went out against them.
17:20 according to all that we have **h** with our ears.
18: 9 of Hamath **h** that David had defeated
19: 8 When David **h** of it, he sent Joab and all the army
2Ch 5:13 of the trumpeters and singers to make themselves **h**
7:12 "I have **h** your prayer, and have chosen this place
9: 1 the queen of Sheba **h** of the fame of Solomon,
9: 5 that I **h** in my own land of your accomplishments
9: 6 you far surpass the report that I had **h.**
10: 2 When Jeroboam son of Nebat **h** of it (for he was
15: 8 When Asa **h** these words, the prophecy
16: 5 When Baasha **h** of it, he stopped building Ramah,
20:29 on all the kingdoms of the countries when they **h**
23:12 When Athaliah **h** the noise of the people running
30:20 The LORD **h** Hezekiah, and healed the people.
30:27 up and blessed the people, and their voice was **h;**
33:13 and God received his entreaty, **h** his plea,
34:19 the king **h** the words of the law he tore his clothes.
34:26 Regarding the words that you have **h,**
34:27 when you **h** his words against this place
34:27 I also have **h** you, says the LORD.
Ezr 3:13 so loudly that the sound was **h** far away.
4: 1 When the adversaries of Judah and Benjamin **h**
9: 3 When I **h** this, I tore my garment and my mantle,
Ne 1: 4 When I **h** these words I sat down and wept,
2:10 and Tobiah the Ammonite official **h** this,
2:19 and Geshem the Arab **h** of it,
4: 1 when Sanballat **h** that we were building the wall,
4: 7 and the Ashdodites **h** that the repairing of the walls
4:15 our enemies **h** that their plot was known to us,
5: 6 when I **h** their outcry and these complaints.
6:16 And when all our enemies **h** of it,
8: 9 the people wept when they **h** the words of the law.
9: 9 of our ancestors in Egypt and **h** their cry at
9:27 to you and you **h** them from heaven,
9:28 they turned and cried to you, you **h** from heaven,
12:43 The joy of Jerusalem was **h** far away.
13: 3 When the people **h** the law,
Est 1:18 the noble ladies of Persia and Media who have **h** of
Job 2:11 when Job's three friends **h** of all these troubles
3: 7 let no joyful cry be **h** in it.
4:16 there was silence, then I **h** a voice:
13: 1 my ear has **h** and understood it.
16: 2 "I have **h** many such things;
28:22 'We have **h** a rumor of it with our ears.'
29:11 When the ear **h,** it commended me,
33: 8 and I have **h** the sound of your words.
34:28 and he **h** the cry of the afflicted—
37: 4 not restrain the lightnings when his voice is **h.**
42: 5 I had **h** of you by the hearing of the ear,
Ps 6: 8 for the LORD has **h** the sound of my weeping.
6: 9 The LORD has **h** my supplication;
18: 6 From his temple he **h** my voice,
18:44 As soon as they **h** of me they obeyed me;
19: 3 nor are there words; their voice is not **h;**
22:24 but **h** when I cried to him.
28: 6 for he has **h** the sound of my pleadings.
31:22 But you **h** my supplications when I cried out
34: 6 This poor soul cried, and was **h** by the LORD,
40: 1 he inclined to me and **h** my cry.
44: 1 We have **h** with our ears,
48: 8 As we have **h,** so have we seen in the city of
61: 5 For you, O God, have **h** my vows;
62:11 Once God has spoken; twice have I **h** this:
66: 8 O peoples, let the sound of his praise be **h,**
78: 3 things that we have **h** and known,
78:21 Therefore, when the LORD **h,** he was full of rage;
78:59 When God **h,** he was full of wrath,
92:11 my ears have **h** the doom of my evil assailants.
106:44 he regarded their distress when he **h** their cry.
116: 1 because he has **h** my voice and my supplications.
132: 6 We **h** of it in Ephrathah;
138: 4 for they have **h** the words of your mouth.
Pr 21:13 you will cry out and not be **h.**
Ecc 12:13 The end of the matter; all has been **h.**
SS 2:12 and the voice of the turtledove is **h** in our land.
Isa 5: 7 righteousness, but **h** a cry!
6: 8 Then I **h** the voice of the Lord saying,
7: 2 the house of David **h** that Aram had allied itself
15: 4 their voices are **h** as far as Jahaz;
16: 6 We have **h** of the pride of Moab
21:10 what I have **h** from the LORD of hosts,
28:22 for I have **h** a decree of destruction from
30:30 the LORD will cause his majestic voice to be **h**
37: 1 When King Hezekiah **h** it, he tore his clothes,
37: 4 It may be that the LORD your God **h** the words of
37: 4 the words that the LORD your God has **h;**
37: 6 not be afraid because of the words that you have **h,**
37: 8 for he had **h** that the king had left Lachish.
37: 9 the king **h** concerning King Tirhakah of Ethiopia,
37: 9 When he **h** it, he sent messengers to Hezekiah,
37:11 you have **h** what the kings of Assyria have done
37:26 Have you not **h** that I determined it long ago?
38: 5 I have **h** your prayer, I have seen your tears;
39: 1 for he **h** that he had been sick and had recovered.
40:21 Have you not known? Have you not **h?**
40:28 Have you not known? Have you not **h?**
41:26 none who proclaimed, none who **h** your words.

Isa 42: 2 or make it **h** in the street;
48: 6 You have **h;** now see all this;
48: 7 before today you have never **h** of them,
48: 8 You have never **h,** you have never known,
52:15 that which they had not **h** they shall contemplate.
53: 1 Who has believed what we have **h?**
58: 4 as you do today will not make your voice **h**
60:18 Violence shall no more be **h** in your land,
64: 4 From ages past no one has **h,** no ear has perceived,
65:19 no more shall the sound of weeping be **h** in it,
66: 8 Who has **h** of such a thing?
66:19 the coastlands far away that have not **h** of my fame
Jer 3:21 A voice on the bare heights is **h,**
4:31 For I **h** a cry as of a woman in labor,
6: 7 violence and destruction are **h** within her;
6:24 "We have **h** news of them, our hands fall helpless;
8:16 The snorting of their horses is **h** from Dan;
9:10 and the lowing of cattle is not **h;**
9:19 For a sound of wailing is **h** from Zion:
18:13 Who has **h** the like of this?
18:22 May a cry be **h** from their houses,
20: 1 **h** Jeremiah prophesying these things.
23:25 I have **h** what the prophets have said who prophesy
26: 7 and all the people **h** Jeremiah speaking these words
26:10 When the officials of Judah **h** these things,
26:11 as you have **h** with your own ears."
26:12 and this city all the words you have **h.**
26:21 **h** his words, the king sought to put him to death;
26:21 but when Uriah **h** of it,
30: 5 We have **h** a cry of panic, of terror, and no peace.
31:15 A voice is **h** in Ramah, lamentation and bitter
31:18 Indeed I **h** Ephraim pleading:
33:10 or animal, there shall once more be **h**
36:11 of Shaphan **h** all the words of the LORD from
36:13 And Micaiah told them all the words that he had **h,**
36:16 When they **h** all the words,
36:24 nor any of his servants who **h** all these words,
37: 5 Chaldeans who were besieging Jerusalem **h** news
38: 1 of Malchiah **h** the words that Jeremiah was saying
38: 7 **h** that they had put Jeremiah into the cistern.
40: 7 in the open country and their troops **h** that the king
40:11 the Ammonites and in Edom and in other lands **h**
41:11 and all the leaders of the forces with him **h** of all
46:12 The nations have **h** of your shame,
48: 5 of Horonaim they have **h** the distressing cry
48:29 We have **h** of the pride of Moab—
49:14 I have **h** tidings from the LORD,
49:21 the sound of their cry shall be **h** at the Red Sea.
49:23 for they have **h** bad news;
50:43 The king of Babylon **h** news of them,
50:46 and her cry shall be **h** among the nations.
51:46 Do not be fainthearted or fearful at the rumors **h** in
51:51 to shame, for we have **h** insults;
La 1:21 They **h** how I was groaning,
1:21 All my enemies **h** of my trouble;
3:56 you **h** my plea, "Do not close your ear to my cry
3:61 You have **h** their taunts, O LORD,
Eze 1:24 I **h** the sound of their wings like the sound
1:28 and I **h** the voice of someone speaking.
2: 2 and I **h** him speaking to me.
3:12 I **h** behind me the sound of loud rumbling;
10: 5 of the cherubim was **h** as far as the outer court,
19: 9 into custody, so that his voice should be **h** no more
26:13 the sound of your lyres shall be **h** no more.
33: 5 They **h** the sound of the trumpet and did
35:12 have **h** all the abusive speech that you uttered
35:13 and multiplied your words against me; I **h** it.
43: 6 I **h** someone speaking to me out of the temple.
Da 3: 7 as soon as all the peoples **h** the sound of the horn,
5:10 she **h** the discussion of the king and his lords,
5:14 I have **h** of you that a spirit of the gods is in you,
5:16 But I have **h** that you can give interpretations
6:14 king **h** the charge, he was very much distressed.
8:13 Then I **h** a holy one speaking,
8:16 and I **h** a human voice by the Ulai,
10: 9 Then I **h** the sound of his words;
10: 9 and when I **h** the sound of his words,
10:12 your words have been **h,** and I have come because
12: 7 And I **h** him swear by the one who lives forever
12: 8 I **h** but could not understand;
Ob 1: 1 We have **h** a report from the LORD,
Jnh 2: 2 of the belly of Sheol I cried, and you **h** my voice.
Na 2:13 the voice of your messengers shall be **h** no more.
Hab 3: 2 O LORD, I have **h** of your renown,
Zep 1:10 a cry will be **h** from the Fish Gate,
2: 8 I have **h** the taunts of Moab and the revilings of
Zec 8:23 for we have **h** that God is with you."
Mt 2: 3 When King Herod **h** this, he was frightened,
2: 9 When they had **h** the king, they set out;
2:18 "A voice was **h** in Ramah, wailing
2:22 when he **h** that Archelaus was ruling over Judea
4:12 Now when Jesus **h** that John had been arrested,
5:21 "You have **h** that it was said to those
5:27 "You have **h** that it was said,
5:33 you have **h** that it was said to those
5:38 "You have **h** that it was said,
5:43 "You have **h** that it was said,
6: 7 that they will be **h** because of their many words.
8:10 When Jesus **h** him, he was amazed and said
9:12 But when he **h** this, he said,
11: 2 John **h** in prison what the Messiah was doing,
12:24 But when the Pharisees **h** it, they said,
14: 1 At that time Herod the ruler **h** reports about Jesus;
14:13 Now when Jesus **h** this, he withdrew from there in
14:13 But when the crowds **h** it,
15:12 when they **h** what you said?"
17: 6 When the disciples **h** this, they fell to the ground
Mt 19:22 When the young man **h** this word,
19:25 the disciples **h** this, they were greatly astounded
20:24 the ten **h** it, they were angry with the two brothers.
20:30 When they **h** that Jesus was passing by,
21:15 and **h** the children crying out in the temple,
21:45 the chief priests and the Pharisees **h** his parables,
22:22 When they **h** this, they were amazed;
22:33 the crowd **h** it, they were astounded at his teaching.
22:34 the Pharisees **h** that he had silenced the Sadducees,
26:65 You have now **h** his blasphemy.
27:47 When some of the bystanders **h** it, they said,
Mk 2:17 When Jesus **h** this, he said to them,
3:21 When his family **h** it, they went out to restrain him,
5:27 She had **h** about Jesus, and came up behind him in
6: 2 and many who **h** him were astounded.
6:14 Herod **h** of it, for Jesus' name had become known.
6:16 But when Herod **h** of it, he said, "John,
6:20 When he **h** him, he was greatly perplexed;
6:29 When his disciples **h** about it,
6:55 the sick on mats to wherever they **h** he was.
7:25 an unclean spirit immediately **h** about him,
10:22 When he **h** this, he was shocked
10:41 the ten **h** this, they began to be angry with James
10:47 When he **h** that it was Jesus of Nazareth,
11:14 And his disciples **h** it.
11:18 And when the chief priests and the scribes **h** it,
12:28 One of the scribes came near and **h** them disputing
14:11 When they **h** it, they were greatly pleased,
14:58 "We **h** him say, 'I will destroy this temple
14:64 You have **h** his blasphemy!
15:35 When some of the bystanders **h** it, they said,
16:11 ⟦**h** that he was alive and had been seen by her,⟧
Lk 1:13 Zechariah, for your prayer has been **h.**
1:41 When Elizabeth **h** Mary's greeting,
1:44 For as soon as I **h** the sound of your greeting,
1:58 Her neighbors and relatives **h** that
1:66 All who **h** them pondered them and said,
2:18 and all who **h** it were amazed at what
2:20 glorifying and praising God for all they had **h**
2:47 And all who **h** him were amazed
4:23 the things that we have **h** you did at Capernaum.' "
4:28 When they **h** this, all in the synagogue were filled
7: 3 When he **h** about Jesus, he sent some Jewish elders
7: 9 When Jesus **h** this he was amazed at him,
7:22 "Go and tell John what you have seen and **h:**
7:29 (And all the people who **h** this,
8:12 The ones on the path are those who have **h;**
8:50 When Jesus **h** this, he replied, "Do not fear.
9: 7 Herod the ruler **h** about all that had taken place,
12: 3 in the dark will be **h** in the light,
15:25 and approached the house, he **h** music
16:14 Pharisees, who were lovers of money, **h** all this,
18:22 When Jesus **h** this, he said to him,
18:23 he **h** this, he became sad; for he was very rich.
18:26 Those who **h** it said, "Then who can be saved?"
18:36 When he **h** a crowd going by,
19:48 for all the people were spellbound by what they **h.**
20:16 When they **h** this, they said, "Heaven forbid!"
22:71 We have **h** it ourselves from his own lips!"
23: 6 When Pilate **h** this, he asked whether the man was
23: 8 because he had **h** about him and was hoping
Jn 1:37 The two disciples **h** him say this,
1:40 One of the two who **h** John speak
3:32 He testifies to what he has seen and **h,**
4: 1 Now when Jesus learned that the Pharisees had **h,**
4:42 for we have **h** for ourselves,
4:47 he **h** that Jesus had come from Judea to Galilee,
5:37 You have never **h** his voice or seen his form,
6:45 Everyone who has **h** and learned from
6:60 When many of his disciples **h** it, they said,
7:32 The Pharisees **h** the crowd muttering such things
7:40 When they **h** these words, some in the crowd said,
8: 9 ⟦When they **h** it, they went away, one by one,⟧
8:26 I declare to the world what I have **h** from him."
8:38 you should do what you have **h** from the Father."
8:40 man who has told you the truth that I **h** from God.
9:32 the world began has it been **h** that anyone opened
9:35 Jesus **h** that they had driven him out,
9:40 of the Pharisees near him **h** this and said to him,
11: 4 But when Jesus **h** it, he said,
11: 6 after having **h** that Lazarus was ill,
11:20 When Martha **h** that Jesus was coming,
11:29 when she **h** it, she got up quickly and went to him.
11:41 "Father, I thank you for having **h** me.
12:12 the festival **h** that Jesus was coming to Jerusalem.
12:18 also because they **h** that he had performed this sign
12:29 The crowd standing there **h** it and said
12:34 "We have **h** from the law that
14:28 You **h** me say to you, 'I am going away,
15:15 to you everything that I have **h** from my Father.
18:21 Ask those who **h** what I said to them;
19: 8 when Pilate **h** this, he was more afraid than ever.
19:13 When Pilate **h** these words,
21: 7 When Simon Peter **h** that it was the Lord,
Ac 1: 4 "This," he said, "is what you have **h** from me;
2: 6 because each one **h** them speaking in
2:37 Now when they **h** this, they were cut to the heart
4: 4 But many of those who **h** the word believed;
4:20 from speaking about what we have seen and **h."**
4:24 When they **h** it, they raised their voices together
5: 5 Ananias **h** these words, he fell down and died.
5: 5 And great fear seized all who **h** of it.
5:11 the whole church and all who **h** of these things.
5:21 When they **h** this, they entered the temple
5:24 of the temple and the chief priests **h** these words,
5:33 When they **h** this, they were enraged and wanted
6:11 "We have **h** him speak blasphemous words
Ac 6:14 for we have **h** him say that this Jesus
7:12 But when Jacob **h** that there was grain in Egypt,
7:29 When he **h** this, Moses fled and became
7:34 in Egypt and have **h** their groaning,
7:54 When they **h** these things, they became enraged
8:14 at Jerusalem **h** that Samaria had accepted the word
8:30 up to it and **h** him reading the prophet Isaiah.
9: 4 He fell to the ground and **h** a voice saying to him,
9: 7 with him stood speechless because they **h** the voice
9:13 "Lord, I have **h** from many about this man,
9:21 All who **h** him were amazed and said,
9:38 the disciples, who **h** that Peter was there,
10:13 he **h** a voice saying, "Get up, Peter; kill and eat."
10:31 'Cornelius, your prayer has been **h**
10:44 the Holy Spirit fell upon all who **h** the word.
10:46 for they **h** them speaking in tongues
11: 1 the apostles and the believers who were in Judea **h**
11: 7 I also **h** a voice saying to me, 'Get up, Peter;
11:18 When they **h** this, they were silenced.
13:48 the Gentiles **h** this, they were glad and praised
14:14 When the apostles Barnabas and Paul **h** of it,
15:24 Since we have **h** that certain persons who
16:38 when they **h** that they were Roman citizens;
17: 8 the city officials were disturbed when they **h** this,
17:32 When they **h** of the resurrection of the dead,
18: 8 of the Corinthians who **h** Paul became believers
18:26 but when Priscilla and Aquila **h** him,
19: 2 we have not even **h** that there is a Holy Spirit."
19:10 both Jews and Greeks, **h** the word of the Lord.
19:28 When they **h** this, they were enraged and shouted,
21:12 When we **h** this, we and the people there urged him
21:20 When they **h** it, they praised God.
22: 2 When they **h** him addressing them in Hebrew,
22: 7 I fell to the ground and **h** a voice saying to me,
22:15 to all the world of what you have seen and **h.**
22:26 When the centurion **h** that,
23:16 Now the son of Paul's sister **h** about the ambush;
24:24 he sent for Paul and **h** him speak concerning faith
26:14 I **h** a voice saying to me in the Hebrew language,
28:15 The believers from there, when they **h** of us,
Ro 10:14 to believe in one of whom they have never **h?**
10:17 So faith comes from what is **h,** and what is **h**
comes through the word of Christ.
10:18 But I ask, have they not **h?**
15:21 those who have never **h** of him shall understand."
1Co 2: 9 as it is written, "What no eye has seen, nor ear **h,**
2Co 12: 4 was caught up into Paradise and **h** things that are
12: 6 of me than what is seen in me or **h** from me,
Gal 1:13 You have **h,** no doubt, of my earlier life
1:23 they only **h** it said, "The one who formerly was
3: 2 the works of the law or by believing what you **h?**
3: 5 or by your believing what you **h?**
Eph 1:13 In him you also, when you had **h** the word of truth,
1:15 I have **h** of your faith in the Lord Jesus
3: 2 for surely you have already **h** of the commission
4:21 you have **h** about him and were taught in him,
Php 2:26 has been distressed because you **h** that he was ill.
4: 9 the things that you have learned and received and **h**
Col 1: 4 for we have **h** of your faith in Christ Jesus and of
1: 5 You have **h** of this hope before in the word of
1: 6 the day you **h** it and truly comprehended the grace
1: 9 For this reason, since the day we **h** it,
1:23 from the hope promised by the gospel that you **h,**
1Th 2:13 you received the word of God that you **h** from us,
2Ti 1:13 to the standard of sound teaching that you have **h**
2: 2 and what you have **h** from me
Heb 2: 1 we must pay greater attention to what we have **h,**
2: 3 and it was attested to us by those who **h** him,
3:16 who were they who **h** and yet were rebellious?
4: 2 but the message they **h** did not benefit them,
5: 7 and he was **h** because of his reverent submission.
Jas 5:11 You have **h** of the endurance of Job,
2Pe 1:18 We ourselves **h** this voice come from heaven,
2: 8 by their lawless deeds that he saw and **h),**
1Jn 1: 1 what we have **h,** what we have seen with our eyes,
1: 3 we declare to you what we have seen and **h** so
1: 5 the message we have **h** from him and proclaim
2: 7 the old commandment is the word that you have **h.**
2:18 As you have **h** that antichrist is coming,
2:24 Let what you **h** from the beginning abide in you.
2:24 If what you **h** from the beginning abides in you,
3:11 this is the message you have **h** from the beginning,
4: 3 of which you have **h** that it is coming;
2Jn 1: 6 this is the commandment just as you have **h** it from
Rev 1:10 and I **h** behind me a loud voice like a trumpet
3: 3 Remember then what you received and **h;**
4: 1 which I had **h** speaking to me like a trumpet, said,
5:11 and I **h** the voice of many angels surrounding
5:13 Then I **h** every creature in heaven and on earth and
6: 1 and I **h** one of the four living creatures call out,
6: 3 I **h** the second living creature call out, "Come!"
6: 5 I **h** the third living creature call out, "Come!"
6: 6 and I **h** what seemed to be a voice in the midst of
6: 7 I **h** the voice of the fourth living creature call out,
7: 4 And I **h** the number of those who were sealed,
8:13 and I **h** an eagle crying with a loud voice as it flew
9:13 and I **h** a voice from the four horns of
9:16 cavalry was two hundred million; I **h** their number.
10: 4 but I **h** a voice from heaven saying,
10: 8 voice that I had **h** from heaven spoke to me again,
11:12 they **h** a loud voice from heaven saying to them,
12:10 Then I **h** a loud voice in heaven, proclaiming,
14: 2 And I **h** a voice from heaven like the sound
14: 2 the voice I **h** was like the sound of harpists playing
14:13 And I **h** a voice from heaven saying, "Write this:
16: 1 Then I **h** a loud voice from the temple telling
16: 5 And I **h** the angel of the waters say, "You are just,

Rev 16: 7 And I **h** the altar respond, "Yes, O Lord God,
18: 4 Then I **h** another voice from heaven saying,
18:22 of flutists and trumpeters will be **h** in you no more;
18:22 sound of the millstone will be **h** in you no more;
18:23 of bridegroom and bride will be **h** in you no more;
19: 1 After this I **h** what seemed to be the loud voice of
19: 6 Then I **h** what seemed to be the voice of
21: 3 And I **h** a loud voice from the throne saying, "See,
22: 8 I, John, am the one who **h** and saw these things.
22: 8 And when I **h** and saw them,
Tob 3:16 of them were **h** in the glorious presence of God.
6:14 I have **h** that she already has been married
6:14 I have **h** people saying that it was a demon
6:18 When Tobias **h** the words of Raphael and learned
14:15 Before he died he **h** of the destruction of Nineveh,
Jdt 4: 1 When the Israelites living in Judea **h** of everything
4:13 The Lord **h** their prayers and had regard
8: 1 Now in those days Judith **h** about these things:
8: 9 When Judith **h** the harsh words spoken by
8: 9 and when she **h** all that Uzziah said to them,
10:14 the men **h** her words, and observed her face—
11: 8 For we have **h** of your wisdom and skill,
11: 9 in your council, we have **h** his words,
13:12 When the people of her town **h** her voice,
14:19 When the leaders of the Assyrian army **h** this,
15: 1 When the men in the tents **h** it,
15: 5 When the Israelites **h** it, with one accord they fell
AdE 4: 4 by what she **h** had happened,
7: 8 Haman, when he **h**, turned away his face.
14: 5 since I was born I have **h** in the tribe of my family
Wis 11:13 when they **h** that through their own punishments
18: 1 Their enemies **h** their voices but did
Sir 3: 5 and when they pray they will be **h.**
16: 5 and my ear has **h** things more striking than these.
17:13 and their ears **h** the glory of his voice.
19: 9 for someone may have **h** you and watched you,
19:10 Have you **h** something? Let it die with you.
19:11 Having **h** something, the fool suffers birth pangs
45: 9 to make their ringing **h** in the temple as a reminder
46:17 and made his voice **h** with a mighty sound;
48: 7 You **h** rebuke at Sinai and judgments of vengeance
48:20 The Holy One quickly **h** them from heaven,
51:11 of thanksgiving." My prayer was **h,**
Bar 3:22 She has not been **h** of in Canaan,
Sus 1:26 people in the house **h** the shouting in the garden,
1:44 The Lord **h** her cry.
Bel 1:28 When the Babylonians **h** about it,
1Mc 3:13 **h** that Judas had gathered a large company,
3:27 When King Antiochus **h** these reports,
3:41 the traders of the region **h** what was said to them,
4: 3 But Judas **h** of it, and he
4:27 When he **h** it, he was perplexed and discouraged,
5: 1 around **h** that the altar had been rebuilt and
5:16 When Judas and the people **h** these messages,
5:56 **h** of their brave deeds and of
5:63 wherever their name was **h.**
6: 1 when he **h** that Elymais in Persia was a city famed
6: 8 When the king **h** this news,
6:28 The king was enraged when he **h** this.
6:41 All who **h** the noise made by their multitude,
6:55 Then Lysias **h** that Philip, whom King Antiochus
8: 1 Now Judas **h** of the fame of the Romans,
8:12 as many as have **h** of their fame have feared them.
9: 1 When Demetrius **h** that Nicanor
9:33 and all who were with him **h** of it,
9:43 When Bacchides **h** of this,
10: 2 When King Demetrius **h** of it,
10: 8 when they **h** that the king had given him authority
10:15 Now King Alexander **h** of all the promises
10:15 and he **h** of the battles that Jonathan
10:19 We have **h** about you, that you are
10:22 When Demetrius **h** of these
10:26 we have **h** of it and rejoiced.
10:46 When Jonathan and the people **h** these words,
10:68 When King Alexander **h** of it,
10:74 When Jonathan **h** the words of Apollonius,
10:77 When Apollonius **h** of it, he mustered
10:88 When King Alexander **h** of these things,
11:15 Alexander **h** of it, he came against him in battle.
11:22 When he **h** this he was angry,
11:22 as soon as he **h** it he set out and came to Ptolemais;
11:23 When Jonathan **h** this, he gave orders to continue
11:63 Then Jonathan **h** that the officers
12:24 Now Jonathan **h** that the commanders
12:28 When the enemy **h** that Jonathan
12:34 for he had **h** that they were ready to hand over
13: 1 Simon **h** that Trypho had assembled a large army
13: 7 the people was rekindled when they **h** these words,
14: 2 When King Arsaces of Persia and Media **h**
14:16 It was **h** in Rome, and as far away as Sparta,
14:17 they **h** that his brother Simon had become high
14:25 When the people **h** these things they said,
14:40 For he had **h** that the Jews were addressed by
16:22 When he **h** this, he was greatly shocked;
2Mc 1: 8 We prayed to the Lord and were **h,**
10:13 He **h** himself called a traitor at every turn,
11:24 We have **h** that the Jews do not consent
12: 5 Judas **h** of the cruelty visited on his compatriots,
13:10 But when Judas **h** of this,
14:15 the Jews **h** of Nicanor's coming and the gathering
15: 1 When Nicanor **h** that Judas and his troops were in
1Es 5:65 so that the sound was **h** far away;
5:66 enemies of the tribe of Judah and Benjamin **h** it,
8:71 As soon as I **h** these things I tore my garments
9:50 now they were all weeping as they **h** the law—
3Mc 2:21 having **h** the lawful supplication,
5:48 and **h** the loud and tumultuous noise,
3Mc 6:23 For when he **h** the shouting
2Es 1:35 who without having **h** me will believe.
4:11 When I **h** this, I fell on my face
5: 2 and beyond what you **h** of formerly.
5: 7 the many do not know shall make his voice **h**
5:19 He **h** what I said and left me.
6:17 When I **h** this, I got to my feet and listened;
6:32 your voice has surely been **h** by the Most High;
8:18 now also I have **h** of the swiftness of the judgment
9:45 And after thirty years God **h** your servant,
11:36 Then I **h** a voice saying to me,
11:37 and I **h** how it uttered a human voice to the eagle,
12:31 and as for all his words that you have **h,**
12:40 When all the people **h** that the seven days were
13: 4 all who **h** his voice melted as wax melts
13:14 and have deemed me worthy to have my prayer **h**
14: 8 and the interpretations that you have **h;**
4Mc 4:22 he **h** that a rumor of his death had spread and that
8:15 But when they had **h** the inducements and saw
9:27 and they **h** his noble decision.
10:17 When he **h** this, the bloodthirsty, murderous,
14: 9 not only **h** the direct word of threat,

HEARER (1) [HEAR]

Wis 1: 6 and a true observer of their hearts, and a **h**

HEARERS (7) [HEAR]

Ro 2:13 the **h** of the law who are righteous in God's sight,
1Ti 4:16 doing this you will save both yourself and your **h.**
Heb 12:19 the **h** beg that not another word be spoken to them.
Jas 1:22 and not merely **h** who deceive themselves.
1:23 For if any are **h** of the word and not doers,
1:25 being not **h** who forget but doers who act—
4Mc 15:21 the songs of swans attract the attention of their **h**

HEARING‡ (75) [HEAR]

Ge 23:10 and Ephron the Hittite answered Abraham in the **h**
23:13 to Ephron in the **h** of the people of the land,
23:16 the silver that he had named in the **h** of the Hittites,
Ex 17:14 as a reminder in a book and recite it in the **h**
24: 7 and read it in the **h** of the people;
Lev 24:14 and let all who were within **h** lay their hands
Nu 11: 1 in the **h** of the LORD about their misfortunes,
11:18 for you have wailed in the **h** of the LORD, saying,
Dt 1:16 "Give the members of your community a fair **h,**
31:11 you shall read this law before all Israel in their **h.**
31:28 in their **h** and call heaven and earth to witness
31:30 in the **h** of the whole assembly of Israel:
32:44 and recited all the words of this song in the **h** of
Jdg 7: 3 Now therefore proclaim this in the **h** of the troops,
9: 2 "Say in the **h** of all the lords of Shechem,
9: 3 on his behalf in the **h** of all the lords of Shechem;
17: 2 and even spoke it in my **h,—**
1Sa 11: 4 they reported the matter in the **h** of the people;
2Sa 18:12 for in our **h** the king commanded you and Abishai
2Ki 18:26 within the **h** of the people who are on the wall."
23: 2 in their **h** all the words of the book of the covenant
1Ch 28: 8 and in the **h** of our God,
2Ch 34:30 in their **h** all the words of the book of the covenant
Ne 13: 1 that day they read from the book of Moses in the **h**
Job 33: 8 "Surely, you have spoken in my **h,**
42: 5 I had heard of you by the **h** of the ear,
Pr 18:13 If one gives answer before **h,** it is folly and shame.
20:12 The **h** ear and the seeing eye—
23: 9 Do not speak in the **h** of a fool,
Ecc 1: 8 not satisfied with seeing, or the ear filled with **h.**
Isa 5: 9 The LORD of hosts has sworn in my **h:**
32: 3 and the ears of those who have **h** will listen.
33:15 who stop their ears from **h** of bloodshed
36:11 within the **h** of the people who are on the wall."
49:20 of your bereavement will yet say in your **h:**
Jer 2: 2 Go and proclaim in the **h** of Jerusalem,
28: 7 this word that I speak in your **h** and in the **h** of all
29:29 The priest Zephaniah read this letter in the **h** of
36: 6 and on a fast day in the **h** of the people in
36: 6 You shall read them also in the **h** of all the people
36:10 Then, in the **h** of all the people,
36:13 when Baruch read the scroll in the **h** of the people.
36:14 the scroll that you read in the **h** of the people,
Eze 8:18 and though they cry in my **h** with a loud voice,
9: 1 Then he cried in my **h** with a loud voice, saying,
9: 5 To the others he said in my **h,**
10:13 wheels, they were called in my **h** "the wheelwork."
Am 8:11 but of **h** the words of the LORD.
Zec 8: 9 you that have recently been **h** these words from
Mt 13:13 and **h** they do not listen, nor do they understand.'
13:15 and their ears are hard of **h,**
Mk 3: 8 **h** all that he was doing,
9:25 that keeps this boy from speaking and **h,**
Lk 4:21 "Today this scripture has been fulfilled in your **h."**
7: 1 After Jesus had finished all his sayings in the **h** of
14:15 One of the dinner guests, on **h** this, said to him,
20:45 In the **h** of all the people he said to the disciples,
Jn 7:51 not judge people without first giving them a **h**
Ac 8: 6 **h** and seeing the signs that he did,
17:21 in nothing but telling or **h** something new.
19: 5 On **h** this, they were baptized in the name of
23:35 "I will give you a **h** when your accusers arrive."
24:22 adjourned the **h** with the comment,
28:27 and their ears are hard of **h,**
1Co 12:17 whole body were an eye, where would the **h** be?
12:17 If the whole body were **h,** where would the sense
AdE 1:18 on **h** what she has said to the king,
Sir 4: 8 Give a **h** to the poor,
13:22 he talks sense, but is not given a **h.**
1Mc 10: 7 in the **h** of all the people and of those in the citadel.
2Mc 14:18 **h** of the valor of Judas and his troops
3Mc 4:12 **h** that the Jews' compatriots from
5:35 Then the Jews, on **h** what the king had said,
2Es 12:17 "As for your **h** a voice that spoke,

HEARKEN (1)

2Mc 8: 3 to **h** to the blood that cried out to him;

HEARKEN, HEARKENED, HEARKENETH, HEARKENING (KJV)

See also AGREED, CONSENT, HEAR, HEED[ED], LISTEN[ED]

HEARS‡ (48) [HEAR]

Ge 21: 6 everyone who **h** will laugh with me."
Nu 24: 4 the oracle of one who **h** the words of God,
24:16 of one who **h** the words of God, and knows
30: 4 and her father **h** of her vow or her pledge
30: 5 to her at the time that he **h** of it, no vow of hers,
30: 7 her husband **h** of it and says nothing to her at the time that he **h,**
30: 8 But if, at the time that her husband **h** of it,
30:12 at the time that he **h** them,
1Sa 3:11 in Israel that will make both ears of anyone who **h**
16: 2 If Saul **h** of it, he will kill me."
2Sa 17: 9 whoever **h** it will say, 'There has been a slaughter
2Ki 21:12 that the ears of everyone who **h** of it will tingle.
Ps 4: 3 the LORD **h** when I call to him.
34:17 When the righteous cry for help, the LORD **h,**
69:33 For the LORD **h** the needy,
97: 8 Zion **h** and is glad, and the towns of Judah rejoice,
145:19 he also **h** their cry, and saves them.
Pr 15:29 but he **h** the prayer of the righteous.
25:10 or else someone who **h** you will bring shame
29:24 one **h** the victim's curse, but discloses nothing.
Isa 30:19 when he **h** it, he will answer you.
Jer 19: 3 that the ears of everyone who **h** of it will tingle.
36: 3 that when the house of Judah **h** of all the disasters
Da 3:10 that everyone who **h** the sound of the horn, pipe,
Mt 7:24 "Everyone then who **h** these words of mine
7:26 And everyone who **h** these words of mine and does
13:19 When anyone **h** the word of the kingdom and does
13:20 this is the one who **h** the word
13:22 this is the one who **h** the word,
13:23 this is the one who **h** the word and understands it,
Lk 6:47 **h** my words, and acts on them.
6:49 But the one who **h** and does not act is like
Jn 3:29 friend of the bridegroom, who stands and **h** him,
5:24 I tell you, anyone who **h** my word
8:47 Whoever is from God **h** the words of God.
12:47 I do not judge anyone who **h** my words and does
16:13 but will speak whatever he **h,**
1Jn 5:14 if we ask anything according to his will, he **h** us.
5:15 And if we know that he **h** us in whatever we ask,
Rev 22:17 And let everyone who **h** say, "Come."
22:18 I warn everyone who **h** the words of the prophecy
Wis 1:10 because a jealous ear **h** all things,
Sir 21:15 When an intelligent person **h** a wise saying,
21:15 when a fool **h** it, he laughs at it and throws it
22:26 whoever **h** of it will beware of him.
Pm 151: 3 The Lord himself; it is he who **h.**
4Mc 10:18 God **h** also those who are mute.

HEART‡ (718) [BROKENHEARTED, DISHEARTENED, DOWNHEARTED, FAINTHEARTED, HARD-HEARTED, HEART'S, HEARTACHE, HEARTED, HEARTLESS, HEARTS, MERRY-HEARTED, STOUTHEARTED, TENDERHEARTED, WHOLEHEARTED, WHOLEHEARTEDLY]

A. ALL ... HEART (44)
B. WHOLE HEART (17)
C. HUMAN HEART (16)
D. HARDEN/HARDENED ... HEART (16)

Ge 6: 6 and it grieved him to his **h.**
8:21 the LORD said in his **h,** "I will never again curse
8:21 inclination of the human **h** is evil from youth; C
20: 5 I did this in the integrity of my **h** and the innocence
20: 6 I know that you did this in the integrity of your **h;**
24:45 "Before I had finished speaking in my **h,**
34: 8 **h** of my son Shechem longs for your daughter;
42:28 At this they lost **h** and turned trembling
Ex 4:14 and when he sees you his **h** will be glad.
4:21 but I will harden his **h,** D
7: 3 But I will harden Pharaoh's **h,** D
7:13 Still Pharaoh's **h** was hardened,
7:14 LORD said to Moses, "Pharaoh's **h** is hardened;
7:22 so Pharaoh's **h** remained hardened,
7:23 and he did not take even this to **h.**
8:15 he hardened his **h,** and would not listen to them, D
8:19 But Pharaoh's **h** was hardened,
8:32 But Pharaoh hardened his **h** this time also, D
9: 7 But the **h** of Pharaoh was hardened,
9:12 But the LORD hardened the **h** of Pharaoh, D
9:34 he sinned once more and hardened his **h,** D
9:35 So the **h** of Pharaoh was hardened,
10: 1 I have hardened his **h** and the heart of his D
10: 1 hardened his heart and the **h** of his officials,

Ex 10:20 But the LORD hardened Pharaoh's **h**, D
10:27 But the LORD hardened Pharaoh's **h**, D
11:10 but the LORD hardened Pharaoh's **h**, D
14: 4 I will harden Pharaoh's **h**, D
14: 8 LORD hardened the **h** of Pharaoh king of Egypt D
15: 8 the deeps congealed in the **h** of the sea.
23: 9 you know the **h** of an alien,
28:29 the breastpiece of judgment on his **h** when he goes
28:30 on Aaron's **h** when he goes in before the LORD;
28:30 the judgment of the Israelites on his **h** before
35: 5 of a generous **h** bring the LORD's offering:
35:21 And they came, everyone whose **h** was stirred,
35:22 all who were of a willing **h** brought brooches
36: 2 everyone whose **h** was stirred to come to do
Lev 19:17 You shall not hate in your **h** anyone of your kin;
26:41 if then their uncircumcised **h** is humbled
Nu 15:39 follow the lust of your own **h** and your own eyes.
Dt 2:30 and made his **h** defiant in order to hand him over
4:29 if you search after him with all your **h** and soul. A
4:39 to **h** that the LORD is God in heaven above and
6: 5 love the LORD your God with all your **h**, A
6: 6 that I am commanding you today in your **h**.
7: 7 that the LORD set his **h** on you and chose you—
8: 2 testing you to know what was in your **h**,
8: 5 then in your **h** that as a parent disciplines a child
9: 5 your righteousness or the uprightness of your **h**
10:12 to serve the LORD your God with all your **h** and A
10:15 yet the LORD set his **h** in love
10:16 Circumcise, then, the foreskin of your **h**,
11:13 with all your **h** and with all your soul— A
11:18 You shall put these words of mine in your **h**
13: 3 love the LORD your God with all your **h** and A
17:17 or else his **h** will turn away;
20: 3 Do not lose **h**, or be afraid, or panic,
20: 8 or he might cause the **h** of his comrades to melt
26:16 so observe them diligently with all your **h** and A
28:47 and with gladness of **h** for the abundance
28:65 There the LORD will give you a trembling **h**,
28:67 of the dread that your **h** shall feel and the sights
29:18 whose **h** is already turning away from
30: 2 and your children obey him with all your **h** and A
30: 6 the LORD your God will circumcise your **h** and the
h of your descendants,
30: 6 love the LORD your God with all your **h** and A
30:10 turn to the LORD your God with all your **h** and A
30:14 in your mouth and in your **h** for you to observe.
30:17 But if your **h** turns away and you do not hear,
32:46 "Take to **h** all the words that I am giving in witness
Jos 14: 8 up with me made the **h** of the people melt;
22: 5 serve him with all your **h** and with all your A
Jdg 5: 9 My **h** goes out to the commanders
5:15 of Reuben there were great searchings of **h**.
5:16 of Reuben there were great searchings of **h**.
12: 4 in the **h** of Ephraim and Manasseh."
16:15 'I love you,' when your **h** is not with me?
1Sa 1: 8 Why is your **h** sad?
2: 1 "My **h** exults in the LORD;
2:33 be spared to weep out his eyes and grieve his **h**;
2:35 who shall do according to what is in my **h** and
4:13 for his **h** trembled for the ark of God.
7: 3 If you are returning to the LORD with all your **h**, A
7: 3 Direct your **h** to the LORD, and serve him only,
10: 9 to leave Samuel, God gave him another **h**;
12:20 but serve the LORD with all your **h**; A
12:24 and serve him faithfully with all your **h**; A
13:14 the LORD has sought out a man after his own **h**;
16: 7 but the LORD looks on the **h**."
17:28 I know your presumption and the evil of your **h**;
17:32 "Let no one's **h** fail because of him;
21:12 to **h** and was very much afraid of King Achish
24: 5 to the **h** because he had cut off a corner
25:36 Nabal's **h** was merry within him,
25:37 and his **h** died within him; he became like a stone.
27: 1 David said in his **h**, "I shall now perish one day by
28: 5 he was afraid, and his **h** trembled greatly.
29:10 As for the evil report, do not take it to **h**,
2Sa 3:21 that you may reign over all that your **h** desires."
6:16 and she despised him in her **h**.
7:21 of your promise, and according to your own **h**,
13:20 do not take this to **h**."
13:28 "Watch when Amnon's **h** is merry with wine,
13:33 therefore, do not let my lord the king take it to **h**,
13:39 the **h** of the king went out, yearning for Absalom;
17:10 valiant warrior, whose **h** is like the **h** of a lion,
18:14 and thrust them into the **h** of Absalom,
22:46 Foreigners lost **h**, and came trembling out
24:10 to the **h** because he had numbered the people.
1Ki 2: 4 to walk before me in faithfulness with all their **h** A
2:44 "You know in your own **h** all the evil that you did
3: 6 and in uprightness of **h** toward you;
8:23 before you with all their **h**, A
8:39 for only you know what is in every human **h**— C
8:48 if they repent with all their **h** and soul A
9: 3 my eyes and my **h** will be there for all time.
9: 4 with integrity of **h** and uprightness,
11: 2 surely incline your **h** to follow their gods";
11: 3 and his wives turned away his **h**.
11: 4 his wives turned away his **h** after other gods; and
his **h** was not true to the LORD his God, as was the
h of his father David.
11: 9 because his **h** had turned away from the LORD,
12:27 the **h** of this people will turn again to their master,
14: 8 and followed me with all his **h**, A
15: 3 his **h** was not true to the LORD his God, like the **h**
of his father David.
15:14 the **h** of Asa was true to the LORD all his days.
2Ki 9:24 so that the arrow pierced his **h**;
2Ki 10:15 "Is your **h** as true to mine as mine is to yours?"
10:30 with all that was in my **h** have dealt with the house
10:31 of the LORD the God of Israel with all his **h**; A
14:10 and your **h** has lifted you up.
20: 3 before you in faithfulness with a whole **h**, B
22:19 because your **h** was penitent,
23: 3 and his statutes, with all his **h** and all his soul, A
23:25 who turned to the LORD with all his **h**, A
1Ch 12:17 to help me, then my **h** will be knit to you;
15:29 and she despised him in her **h**.
17:19 O LORD, and according to your own **h**,
22:19 set your mind and **h** to seek the LORD your God.
28: 9 and serve him with single mind and willing **h**;
29:17 I know, my God, that you search the **h**,
29:17 of my **h** I have freely offered all these things,
2Ch 1:11 "Because this was in your **h**,
6:14 before you with all their **h**— A
6:30 forgive, and render to all whose **h** you know, A
6:30 for only you know the human **h**. C
6:38 if they repent with all their **h** and soul A
7:16 my eyes and my **h** will be there for all time.
12:14 for he did not set his **h** to seek the LORD.
15:12 with all their **h** and with all their soul. A
15:15 for they had sworn with all their **h**, A
15:17 Nevertheless the **h** of Asa was true all his days.
16: 9 to strengthen those whose **h** is true to him.
17: 6 His **h** was courageous in the ways of the LORD;
19: 3 and have set your **h** to seek God."
19: 9 in faithfulness, and with your whole **h**; B
22: 9 who sought the LORD with all his **h**." A
25: 2 yet not with a true **h**.
25:19 and your **h** has lifted you up in boastfulness.
29:10 it is in my **h** to make a covenant with the LORD,
29:31 of a willing **h** brought burnt offerings.
30:12 on Judah to give them one **h** to do what the king
31:21 he did with all his **h**; and he prospered. A
32:25 to the benefit done to him, for his **h** was proud.
32:26 Hezekiah humbled himself for the pride of his **h**,
32:31 to test him and to know all that was in his **h**.
34:27 because your **h** was penitent
34:31 and his statutes, with all his **h** and all his soul, A
36:13 and hardened his **h** against turning to the LORD, D
Ezr 6:22 had turned the **h** of the king of Assyria to them,
7:10 Ezra had set his **h** to study the law of the LORD,
7:27 the **h** of the king to glorify the house of the LORD
Ne 2: 2 This can only be sadness of the **h**."
2:12 I told no one what my God had put into my **h** to do
9: 8 and you found his **h** faithful before you, and made
Job 9: 4 He is wise in **h**, and mighty
10:13 Yet these things you hid in your **h**;
11:13 "If you direct your **h** rightly,
15:12 Why does your **h** carry you away,
15:35 and bring forth evil and their **h** prepares deceit."
17:11 my plans are broken off, the desires of my **h**.
19:27 My **h** faints within me!
22:22 and lay up his words in your **h**.
23:16 God has made my **h** faint;
27: 6 my **h** does not reproach me for any of my days.
29:13 and I caused the widow's **h** to sing for joy.
31: 7 and my **h** has followed my eyes,
31: 9 "If my **h** has been enticed by a woman,
31:27 and my **h** has been secretly enticed,
32:19 My **h** is indeed like wine that has no vent;
33: 3 My words declare the uprightness of my **h**,
36:13 "The godless in **h** cherish anger;
37: 1 "At this also my **h** trembles,
41:24 Its **h** is as hard as stone,
Ps 4: 7 You have put gladness in my **h** more than
7:10 God is my shield, who saves the upright in **h**.
9: 1 I will give thanks to the LORD with my whole **h**; B
10: 3 For the wicked boast of the desires of their **h**,
10: 6 They think in their **h**, "We shall not be moved;
10:11 They think in their **h**, "God has forgotten,
10:17 you will strengthen their **h**,
11: 2 to shoot in the dark at the upright in **h**.
12: 2 with flattering lips and a double **h** they speak.
13: 2 and have sorrow in my **h** all day long?
13: 5 my **h** shall rejoice in your salvation.
15: 2 and speak the truth from their **h**;
16: 7 in the night also my **h** instructs me.
16: 9 Therefore my **h** is glad, and my soul rejoices;
17: 3 If you try my **h**, if you visit me by night,
18:45 Foreigners lost **h**, and came trembling out
19: 8 precepts of the LORD are right, rejoicing the **h**;
19:14 the words of my mouth and the meditation of my **h**
22:14 my **h** is like wax; it is melted within my breast;
25:17 Relieve the troubles of my **h**,
26: 2 and try me; test my **h** and mind.
27: 3 an army encamp against me, my **h** shall not fear;
27: 8 "Come," my **h** says, "seek his face!"
27:14 be strong, and let your **h** take courage;
28: 7 and my shield; in him my **h** trusts;
28: 7 so I am helped, and my **h** exults,
31:24 Be strong, and let your **h** take courage,
32:11 O righteous, and shout for joy, all you upright in **h**.
33:11 the thoughts of his **h** to all generations.
33:21 Our **h** is glad in him,
36:10 and your salvation to the upright of **h**!
37: 4 and he will give you the desires of your **h**.
37:15 their sword shall enter their own **h**,
38: 8 I groan because of the tumult of my **h**.
38:10 My **h** throbs, my strength fails me;
39: 3 my **h** became hot within me.
40: 8 your law is within my **h**."
40:10 I have not hidden your saving help within my **h**,
40:12 the hairs of my head, and my **h** fails me.
44:18 Our **h** has not turned back,
Ps 44:21 For he knows the secrets of the **h**.
45: 1 My **h** overflows with a goodly theme;
45: 5 Your arrows are sharp in the **h** of
46: 2 though the mountains shake in the **h** of the sea;
49: 3 the meditation of my **h** shall be understanding.
51: 6 therefore teach me wisdom in my secret **h**.
51:10 Create in me a clean **h**, O God,
51:17 a broken and contrite **h**, O God,
55: 4 My **h** is in anguish within me,
55:21 but with a **h** set on war;
57: 7 My **h** is steadfast, O God,
57: 7 O God, my **h** is steadfast.
61: 2 of the earth I call to you, when my **h** is faint.
62: 8 pour out your **h** before him; God is a refuge for us.
62:10 if riches increase, do not set your **h** on them.
64: 6 For the human **h** and mind are deep. C
64:10 Let all the upright in **h** glory.
66:18 If I had cherished iniquity in my **h**,
69:20 Insults have broken my **h**, so that I am in despair.
73: 1 to those who are pure in **h**.
73:13 All in vain I have kept my **h** clean
73:21 my soul was embittered, when I was pricked in **h**,
73:26 My flesh and my **h** may fail,
73:26 the strength of my **h** and my portion forever.
77: 6 I commune with my **h** in the night;
78: 8 a generation whose **h** was not steadfast,
78:18 in their **h** by demanding the food they craved.
78:37 Their **h** was not steadfast toward him;
78:72 With upright **h** he tended them,
84: 2 my **h** and my flesh sing for joy to the living God.
84: 5 in whose **h** are the highways to Zion.
86:11 give me an undivided **h** to revere your name.
86:12 O Lord my God, with my whole **h**, B
90:12 to count our days that we may gain a wise **h**.
94:15 and all the upright in **h** will follow it.
94:19 When the cares of my **h** are many,
97:11 and joy for the upright in **h**.
101: 2 I will walk with integrity of **h** within my house;
101: 4 Perverseness of **h** shall be far from me;
101: 5 haughty look and an arrogant **h** I will not tolerate.
102: 4 My **h** is stricken and withered like grass;
104:15 and wine to gladden the human **h**, C
104:15 and bread to strengthen the human **h**. C
108: 1 My **h** is steadfast, O God, my heart is steadfast;
108: 1 my **h** is steadfast; I will sing and make melody.
109:22 and my **h** is pierced within me.
111: 1 I will give thanks to the LORD with my whole **h**, B
119: 2 who seek him with their whole **h**, B
119: 7 I will praise you with an upright **h**,
119:10 With my whole **h** I seek you; B
119:11 I treasure your word in my **h**,
119:34 and observe it with my whole **h**. B
119:36 Turn my **h** to your decrees, and not to selfish gain.
119:58 I implore your favor with all my **h**; A
119:69 but with my whole **h** I keep your precepts. B
119:80 May my **h** be blameless in your statutes,
119:111 they are the joy of my **h**.
119:112 I incline my **h** to perform your statutes forever,
119:145 With my whole **h** I cry; answer me, O LORD. B
119:161 but my **h** stands in awe of your words.
131: 1 my **h** is not lifted up, my eyes are
138: 1 O LORD, with my whole **h**; B
139:23 Search me, O God, and know my **h**;
141: 4 Do not turn my **h** to any evil,
143: 4 my **h** within me is appalled.
Pr 2: 2 to wisdom and inclining your **h** to understanding;
2:10 into your **h**, and knowledge will be pleasant
3: 1 but let your **h** keep my commandments;
3: 3 write them on the tablet of your **h**.
3: 5 Trust in the LORD with all your **h**, A
4: 4 and said to me, "Let your **h** hold fast my words;
4:21 from your sight; keep them within your **h**.
4:23 Keep your **h** with all vigilance,
5:12 how I hated discipline, and my **h** despised reproof!
6:18 a **h** that devises wicked plans,
6:21 Bind them upon your **h** always;
6:25 Do not desire her beauty in your **h**,
7: 3 write them on the tablet of your **h**.
7:10 decked out like a prostitute, wily of **h**.
10: 8 The wise of **h** will heed commandments,
12:25 Anxiety weighs down the human **h**, C
13:12 Hope deferred makes the **h** sick,
14:10 The **h** knows its own bitterness,
14:13 in laughter the **h** is sad, and the end of joy is grief.
14:33 but it is not known in the **h** of fools.
15:13 A glad **h** makes a cheerful countenance,
15:13 but by sorrow of **h** the spirit is broken.
15:15 but a cheerful **h** has a continual feast.
15:30 The light of the eyes rejoices the **h**,
16:21 The wise of **h** is called perceptive,
17: 3 but the LORD tests the **h**.
17:22 A cheerful **h** is a good medicine,
18:12 Before destruction one's **h** is haughty,
19: 3 yet the **h** rages against the LORD.
19:18 do not set your **h** on their destruction.
20: 9 Who can say, "I have made my **h** clean;
21: 1 The king's **h** is a stream of water in the hand of
21: 2 but the LORD weighs the **h**.
21: 4 Haughty eyes and a proud **h**—
22:11 a pure **h** and are gracious in speech will have
22:15 Folly is bound up in the **h** of a boy,
23:15 My child, if your **h** is wise, my **h** too will be glad.
23:17 Do not let your **h** envy sinners,
23:26 My child, give me your **h**,
24:12 does not he who weighs the **h** perceive it?
24:17 and do not let your **h** be glad when they stumble,
25:20 on a wound is one who sings songs to a heavy **h**.

Pr 25:20 sorrow gnaws at the human **h.** C
26:23 an earthen vessel are smooth lips with an evil **h.**
27: 9 Perfume and incense make the **h** glad,
27:11 Be wise, my child, and make my **h** glad,
27:19 so one human **h** reflects another. C
29:17 they will give delight to your **h.**
31:11 The **h** of her husband trusts in her,
Ecc 2:10 I kept my **h** from no pleasure,
2:10 for my **h** found pleasure in all my toil,
2:20 and gave my **h** up to despair concerning all the toil
3:17 I said in my **h,** God will judge the righteous and
3:18 I said in my **h** with regard to human beings
5: 2 nor let your **h** be quick to utter a word before God,
7: 2 and the living will lay it to **h.**
7: 3 for by sadness of countenance the **h** is made glad.
7: 4 The **h** of the wise is in the house of mourning;
7: 4 but the **h** of fools is in the house of mirth.
7: 7 and a bribe corrupts the **h.**
7:22 **h** knows that many times you have yourself cursed
7:26 whose **h** is snares and nets,
8:11 the human **h** is fully set to do evil. C
9: 1 All this I laid to **h,** examining it all,
9: 7 and drink your wine with a merry **h;**
10: 2 The **h** of the wise inclines to the right,
10: 2 but the **h** of a fool to the left.
11: 9 and let your **h** cheer you in the days of your youth.
11: 9 Follow the inclination of your **h** and the desire
SS 3:11 on the day of the gladness of his **h.**
4: 9 You have ravished my **h,** my sister, my bride,
4: 9 you have ravished my **h** with a glance
5: 2 I slept, but my **h** was awake.
8: 6 Set me as a seal upon your **h,**
Isa 1: 5 The whole head is sick, and the whole **h** faint. B
7: 2 the **h** of Ahaz and the **h** of his people shook as
7: 4 and do not let your **h** be faint because
9: 9 but in pride and arrogance of **h** they said:
10: 7 but it is in his **h** to destroy,
13: 7 and every human **h** will melt, C
14:13 You said in your **h,** "I will ascend to heaven;
15: 5 My **h** cries out for Moab;
16:11 Therefore my **h** throbs like a harp for Moab,
19: 1 and the **h** of the Egyptians will melt within them.
30:29 of **h,** as when one sets out to the sound of the flute
35: 4 Say to those who are of a fearful **h,** "Be strong,
38: 3 before you in faithfulness with a whole **h,** B
42:25 it burned him, but he did not take it to **h.**
46:12 Listen to me, you stubborn of **h,**
47: 7 not lay these things to **h** or remember their end.
47: 8 who say in your **h,** "I am, and there is no one
47:10 and you said in your **h,** "I am, and there is no one
49:21 you will say in your **h,** "Who has borne me these?
57: 1 The righteous perish, and no one takes it to **h;**
57:15 and to revive the **h** of the contrite.
59:13 and uttering them from the **h.**
60: 5 your **h** shall thrill and rejoice,
63: 4 For the day of vengeance was in my **h,**
63:15 The yearning of your **h** and your compassion?
63:17 from your ways and harden our **h,** D
65:14 my servants shall sing for gladness of **h,**
65:14 but you shall cry out for pain of **h,**
66:14 You shall see, and your **h** shall rejoice;
Jer 3:10 not return to me with her whole **h,** B
3:15 I will give you shepherds after my own **h,**
4:14 wash your **h** clean of wickedness so that you may
4:18 It has reached your very **h."**
4:19 Oh, the walls of my **h!**
4:19 My **h** is beating wildly; I cannot keep silent;
5:23 But this people has a stubborn and rebellious **h;**
8:18 My joy is gone, grief is upon me, my **h** is sick.
9:26 and all the house of Israel is uncircumcised in **h.**
11:20 who judge righteously, who try the **h** and the mind,
12: 3 and test me—my **h** is with you.
12: 7 the beloved of my **h** into the hands of her enemies.
12:11 but no one lays it to **h.**
13:22 And if you say in your **h,**
14:19 Does your **h** loathe Zion?
15: 1 yet my **h** would not turn toward this people.
15:16 to me a joy and the delight of my **h;**
17: 9 The **h** is devious above all else;
17:10 I the LORD test the mind and search the **h,**
20:12 you test the righteous, you see the **h** and the mind;
22:17 your eyes and **h** are only on your dishonest gain,
23: 9 My **h** is crushed within me, all my bones shake;
23:26 and who prophesy the deceit of their own **h?**
24: 7 I will give them a **h** to know that I am the LORD;
24: 7 for they shall return to me with their whole **h.** B
29:13 if you seek me with all your **h,** A
32:39 I will give them one **h** and one way,
32:41 with all my **h** and all my soul. A
48:29 and his arrogance, and the haughtiness of his **h.**
48:36 Therefore my **h** moans for Moab like a flute,
48:36 and my **h** moans like a flute for the people
48:41 shall be like the **h** of a woman in labor.
49:16 and the pride of your **h** have deceived you,
49:22 and the **h** of the warriors of Edom in that day shall
be like the **h** of a woman in labor.
La 1:20 my **h** is wrung within me, because I have been
1:22 for my groans are many and my **h** is faint.
2:19 Pour out your **h** like water before the presence of
3:65 Give them anguish of **h;** your curse be on them!
Eze 3: 7 of Israel have a hard forehead and a stubborn **h.**
3:10 that I shall speak to you receive in your **h** and hear
6: 9 by their wanton **h** that turned away from me,
11:19 I will give them one **h,** and put a new spirit
11:19 remove the **h** of stone from their flesh and give
them a **h** of flesh,
11:21 for those whose **h** goes after their detestable things

Eze 16:30 How sick is your **h,** says the Lord GOD,
18:31 and get yourselves a new **h** and a new spirit!
20:16 for their **h** went after their idols.
21: 6 with breaking **h** and bitter grief before their eyes.
21: 7 Every **h** will melt and all hands will be feeble,
25:15 and with malice of **h** took revenge in destruction;
27: 4 Your borders are in the **h** of the seas;
27:25 So you were filled and heavily laden in the **h** of
27:26 east wind has wrecked you in the **h** of the seas.
27:27 sink into the **h** of the seas on the day of your ruin.
28: 2 your **h** is proud and you have said, "I am a god;
28: 2 I sit in the seat of the gods, in the **h** of the seas,"
28: 5 and your **h** has become proud in your wealth.
28: 8 you shall die a violent death in the **h** of the seas.
28:17 Your **h** was proud because of your beauty;
31:10 and its **h** was proud of its height,
33:31 but their **h** is set on their gain.
36:26 A new **h** I will give you,
36:26 remove from your body the **h** of stone and give
you a **h** of flesh.
44: 7 uncircumcised in **h** and flesh,
44: 9 No foreigner, uncircumcised in **h** and flesh,
Da 5:20 But when his **h** was lifted up
5:22 you, Belshazzar his son, have not humbled your **h,**
11:12 his **h** shall be exalted, and he shall overthrow tens
11:28 but his **h** shall be set against the holy covenant.
11:30 and he shall lose **h** and withdraw.
Hos 7: 6 their **h** burns within them;
7:14 They do not cry to me from the **h,**
10: 2 Their **h** is false; now they must bear their guilt.
11: 8 My **h** recoils within me; my compassion grows
13: 6 they were satisfied, and their **h** was proud;
13: 8 and will tear open the covering of their **h;**
Joel 2:12 says the LORD, return to me with all your **h,** A
Am 2:16 of **h** among the mighty shall flee away naked in
Ob 1: 3 Your proud **h** has deceived you,
1: 3 You say in your **h,** "Who will bring me down
Jnh 2: 3 You cast me into the deep, into the **h** of the seas,
Zep 3:14 Rejoice and exult with all your **h,** A
Mal 2: 2 if you will not lay it to **h** to give glory to my name,
2: 2 because you do not lay it to **h.**
Mt 5: 8 "Blessed are the pure in **h,** for they will see God.
5:28 has already committed adultery with her in his **h.**
6:21 where your treasure is, there your **h** will be also.
9: 2 "Take **h,** son; your sins are forgiven."
9:22 Jesus turned, and seeing her he said, "Take **h,**
11:29 for I am gentle and humble in **h,**
12:34 out of the abundance of the **h** the mouth speaks.
12:40 and three nights the Son of Man will be in the **h** of
13:15 For this people's **h** has grown dull,
13:15 and understand with their **h** and turn—
13:19 and snatches away what is sown in the **h;**
14:27 "Take **h,** it is I; do not be afraid."
15:18 what comes out of the mouth proceeds from the **h,**
15:19 For out of the **h** come evil intentions, murder,
18:35 not forgive your brother or sister from your **h."**
22:37 love the Lord your God with all your **h,** A
Mk 3: 5 he was grieved at their hardness of **h** and said to
6:50 immediately he spoke to them and said, "Take **h,**
7:19 not the **h** but the stomach,
7:21 For it is from within, from the human **h,** C
10: 5 of your hardness of **h** he wrote this commandment
10:49 they called the blind man, saying to him, "Take **h;**
11:23 and if you do not doubt in your **h,**
12:30 shall love the Lord your God with all your **h,** A
12:33 and 'to love him with all the **h,** and with all A
Lk 2:19 and pondered them in her **h.**
2:51 His mother treasured all these things in her **h.**
6:45 of the good treasure of the **h** produces good,
6:45 of the abundance of the **h** that the mouth speaks.
8:15 hold it fast in an honest and good **h,**
10:27 shall love the Lord your God with all your **h,** A
12:34 where your treasure is, there your **h** will be also.
18: 1 about their need to pray always and not to lose **h.**
24:25 of **h** to believe all that the prophets have declared!
Jn 1:18 who is close to the Father's **h,**
7:38 the believer's **h** shall flow rivers of living water.' "
12:40 "He has blinded their eyes and hardened their **h,**
12:40 and understand with their **h** and turn—
13: 2 The devil had already put it into the **h** of Judas son
Ac 1:24 "Lord, you know everyone's **h.**
2:26 therefore my **h** was glad, and my tongue rejoiced;
2:37 to the **h** and said to Peter and to the other apostles,
4:32 of those who believed were of one **h** and soul,
5: 3 "why has Satan filled your **h** to lie to
5: 4 is it that you have contrived this deed in your **h?**
7:23 it came into his **h** to visit his relatives,
7:51 uncircumcised in **h** and ears,
8:21 for your **h** is not right before God.
8:22 the intent of your **h** may be forgiven you.
13:22 son of Jesse, to be a man after my **h,**
15: 8 And God, who knows the human **h,** C
16:14 The Lord opened her **h** to listen eagerly
21:13 weeping and breaking my **h?**
28:27 For this people's **h** has grown dull,
28:27 and understand with their **h** and turn—
Ro 2: 5 But by your hard and impenitent **h** you are storing
2:29 and real circumcision is a matter of the **h**—
6:17 have become obedient from the **h** to the form
8:27 And God, who searches the **h,**
9: 2 and unceasing anguish in my **h.**
9:18 and he hardens the **h** of whomever he chooses. D
10: 6 "Do not say in your **h,** 'Who will ascend
10: 8 "The word is near you, on your lips and in your **h"**
10: 9 and believe in your **h** that God raised him from
10:10 For one believes with the **h** and so is justified,
1Co 2: 9 nor ear heard, nor the human **h** conceived, C

1Co 4: 5 in darkness and will disclose the purposes of the **h.**
14:25 the secrets of the unbeliever's **h** are disclosed,
2Co 2: 4 and anguish of **h** and with many tears,
4: 1 in this ministry, we do not lose **h.**
4:16 So we do not lose **h.**
5:12 in outward appearance and not in the **h.**
6:11 our **h** is wide open to you.
7:15 And his **h** goes out all the more to you,
8:16 But thanks be to God who put in the **h** of Titus
Eph 1:18 with the eyes of your **h** enlightened,
3:13 that you may not lose **h** over my sufferings
4:18 because of their ignorance and hardness of **h.**
6: 5 in singleness of **h,** as you obey Christ;
6: 6 doing the will of God from the **h.**
Php 1: 7 because you hold me in your **h,**
Col 3:21 do not provoke your children, or they may lose **h.**
1Th 2:17 separated from you—in person, not in **h**—
1Ti 1: 5 that comes from a pure **h,**
2Ti 2:22 with those who call on the Lord from a pure **h.**
Phm 1:12 I am sending him, that is, my own **h,** back to you.
1:20 Refresh my **h** in Christ.
Heb 3:12 unbelieving **h** that turns away from the living God.
4:12 to judge the thoughts and intentions of the **h.**
10:22 let us approach with a true **h** in full assurance
12: 3 so that you may not grow weary or lose **h.**
12: 5 or lose **h** when you are punished by him;
13: 9 for it is well for the **h** to be strengthened by grace,
1Pe 1:22 love one another deeply from the **h.**
3: 8 sympathy, love for one another, a tender **h,**
Rev 18: 7 Since in her **h** she says, 'I rule as a queen;
Tob 1:12 Because I was mindful of God with all my **h,** A
3: 1 Then with much grief and anguish of **h** I wept,
4:13 and in your **h** do not disdain your kindred,
4:19 and do not let them be erased from your **h.**
6: 5 "Cut open the fish and take out its gall, **h,**
6: 5 For its gall, **h,** and liver are useful as medicine."
6: 6 the young man gathered together the gall, **h,**
6: 7 what medicinal value is there in the fish's **h**
6: 8 He replied, "As for the fish's **h** and liver,
6:17 take some of the fish's liver and **h,**
6:18 and his **h** was drawn to her.
8: 2 and he took the fish's liver and **h** out of the bag
13: 6 to him with all your **h** and with all your soul, A
Jdt 6: 9 If you really hope in your **h** that they will not
8:14 of the human **h** or understand the workings of C
8:28 "All that you have said was spoken out of a true **h,**
10:16 you stand before him, have no fear in your **h,**
11: 1 woman, and do not be afraid in your **h,**
12:16 Holofernes' **h** was ravished with her
13: 4 Then Judith, standing beside his bed, said in her **h,**
AdE 5: 9 from the king joyful and glad of **h.**
14:13 and turn his **h** to hate the man who is fighting
15: 5 as if beloved, but her **h** was frozen with fear.
15:13 and my **h** was shaken with fear at your glory.
Wis 1: 1 in goodness and seek him with sincerity of **h;**
4:15 or take such a thing to **h,**
8:17 and pondered in my **h** that in kinship
8:21 and with my whole **h** I said: B
15:10 Their **h** is ashes, their hope is cheaper than dirt,
Sir 1:12 The fear of the Lord delights the **h,**
1:30 and your **h** was full of deceit.
2: 2 Set your **h** right and be steadfast,
5: 2 and strength in pursuing the desires of your **h.**
7:27 With all your **h** honor your father, A
9: 9 or your **h** may turn aside to her,
10:12 the **h** has withdrawn from its Maker.
12:16 but in his **h** he plans to throw you into a pit;
13:25 The **h** changes the countenance,
13:26 The sign of a happy **h** is a cheerful face,
14:21 in his **h** on her ways and ponders her secrets,
21: 6 but those who fear the Lord repent in their **h.**
22:19 and one who pricks the **h** makes clear its feelings.
25:13 Any wound, but not a wound of the **h!**
25:23 and wounded **h** come from an evil wife.
26: 4 Whether rich or poor, his **h** is content,
26: 5 Of three things my **h** is frightened,
26:28 At two things my **h** is grieved,
30:16 and no gladness above joy of **h.**
30:22 A joyful **h** is life itself,
31:28 the proper time and in moderation is rejoicing of **h**
33: 5 The **h** of a fool is like a cart wheel,
37:13 And heed the counsel of your own **h,**
38:10 and cleanse your **h** from all sin.
38:18 and a sorrowful **h** saps one's strength.
38:19 but the life of the poor weighs down the **h.**
38:20 Do not give your **h** to grief;
38:26 He sets his **h** on plowing furrows,
38:27 they set their **h** on painting a lifelike image,
38:28 He sets his **h** on finishing his handiwork,
38:30 he sets his **h** to finish the glazing,
39: 5 He sets his **h** to rise early to seek
39:35 So now sing praise with all your **h** and voice, A
40: 2 Perplexities and fear of **h** are theirs,
40:20 Wine and music gladden the **h,**
42:18 He searches out the abyss and the human **h;** C
47: 8 he sang praise with all his **h,** A
49: 3 He kept his **h** fixed on the Lord;
50:23 May he give us gladness of **h,**
50:28 and those who lay them to **h** will become wise.
51:15 to the ripening grape my **h** delighted in her;
51:21 My **h** was stirred to seek her;
Bar 2:31 I will give them a **h** that obeys and ears that hear;
LtJ 6: 6 But say in your **h,** "It is you, O Lord,
Aza 1:16 Yet with a contrite **h** and a humble spirit may we
1:18 And now with all our **h** we follow you; A
1:65 you who are holy and humble in **h;**
Sus 1:35 for her **h** trusted in the Lord.

Sus 1:56 and lust has perverted your **h**.
1Mc 1: 3 he was exalted, and his **h** was lifted up.
2:24 he burned with zeal and his **h** was stirred.
12:28 they were afraid and were terrified at **h**;
16:13 His **h** was lifted up; he determined to get
2Mc 1: 3 May he give you all a **h** to worship him and
1: 3 to do his will with a strong **h** and a willing spirit.
1: 4 May he open your **h** to his law
3:16 of the high priest was to be wounded at **h**,
3:17 at him the pain lodged in his **h**.
4:37 Antiochus was grieved at **h** and filled with pity,
11: 9 and were strengthened in **h**,
1Es 1:23 for his **h** was full of godliness.
1:48 and hardened his **h** and transgressed the laws D
8:25 who put this into the **h** of the king,
Man 1:11 And now I bend the knee of my **h**,
3Mc 5:47 with invulnerable **h** and with his own eyes,
2Es 3: 1 and my thoughts welled up in my **h**,
3:20 "Yet you did not take away their evil **h** from them,
3:21 For the first Adam, burdened with an evil **h**,
3:26 for they also had the evil **h**.
3:28 "Then I said in my **h**,
3:29 during these thirty years. And my **h** failed me,
4: 4 and will teach you why the **h** is evil."
4: 7 'How many dwellings are in the **h** of the sea,
4:30 a grain of evil seed was sown in Adam's **h** from
5:21 the thoughts of my **h** were very grievous
5:34 for every hour I suffer agonies of **h**,
6:26 the **h** of the earth's inhabitants shall be changed
6:36 Then on the eighth night my **h** was troubled
7:*48* For an evil **h** has grown up in us,
8: 4 O my soul, and drink wisdom, O my **h**.
8: 6 for our **h** and cultivation of our understanding so
9:27 my **h** was troubled again as it was before.
9:38 When I said these things in my **h**, I looked around,
9:38 and was deeply grieved at **h**;
9:40 and why are you grieved at **h**?"
10:25 to approach her, and my **h** was terrified.
10:55 do not be afraid, and do not let your **h** be terrified;
13: 3 the figure of a man come up out of the **h** of the sea.
13:25 your seeing a man come up from the **h** of the sea,
13:51 Why did I see the man coming up from the **h** of
14: 8 Lay up in your **h** the signs that I have shown you,
14:25 I will light in your **h** the lamp of understanding,
14:40 I had drunk it, my **h** poured forth understanding,
16:61 He formed human beings and put a **h** in the midst
4Mc 7:18 as many as attend to religion with a whole **h**, B
15:23 giving her **h** a man's courage in the very midst
15:29 the prize of the contest in your **h**!

HEART'S (8) [HEART]

Ps 20: 4 May he grant you your **h** desire,
21: 2 You have given him his **h** desire,
35:25 "Aha, we have our **h** desire."
Eze 24:21 the delight of your eyes, and your **h** desire;
24:25 the delight of their eyes and their **h** affection,
Ro 10: 1 my **h** desire and prayer to God for them is
Jdt 8:29 for your **h** disposition is right.
Sir 32:12 Amuse yourself there to your **h** content,

HEARTACHE (2) [HEART]

Sir 26: 6 it is **h** and sorrow when a wife is jealous of a rival,
30: 7 and will suffer **h** at every cry.

HEARTED (1) [HEART]

1Th 5:14 to admonish the idlers, encourage the faint **h**,

HEARTH‡ (6) [HEARTHS]

Lev 6: 9 The burnt offering itself shall remain on the **h** upon
Isa 30:14 not a sherd is found for taking fire from the **h**,
Eze 43:15 and the altar **h**, four cubits;
43:15 and from the altar **h** projecting upward, four horns.
43:16 The altar **h** shall be square,
Sir 50:12 as he stood by the **h** of the altar with a garland

HEARTHS (1) [HEARTH]

Eze 46:23 with **h** made at the bottom of the rows all around.

HEARTLESS (1) [HEART]

Ro 1:31 foolish, faithless, **h**, ruthless.

HEARTS‡ (202) [HEART]

Ge 6: 5 of the thoughts of their **h** was only evil continually.
Ex 14:17 the **h** of the Egyptians so that they will go in
25: 2 from all whose **h** prompt them
35:26 all the women whose **h** moved them
35:29 and women whose **h** made them willing
Lev 26:36 I will send faintness into their **h** in the lands
Nu 32: 7 the **h** of the Israelites from going over into the land
32: 9 they discouraged the **h** of the Israelites from going
Dt 1:28 Our kindred have made our **h** melt by reporting,
29:19 thinking in their **h**, "We are safe even
Jos 2:11 As soon as we heard it, our **h** melted,
5: 1 their **h** melted, and there was no longer any spirit
7: 5 The **h** of the people melted and turned to water.
11:20 For it was the LORD's doing to harden their **h** so
23:14 and you know in your **h** and souls, all of you,
24:23 and incline your **h** to the LORD,
Jdg 9: 3 and their **h** inclined to follow Abimelech,
16:25 And when their **h** were merry, they said,
1Sa 6: 6 Why should you harden your **h** as the Egyptians
6: 6 as the Egyptians and Pharaoh hardened their **h**?
10:26 with him went warriors whose **h** God had touched.
2Sa 15: 6 so Absalom stole the **h** of the people of Israel.
15:13 "The **h** of the Israelites have gone after Absalom."
19:14 Amasa swayed the **h** of all the people of Judah
1Ki 8:38 of their own **h** so that they stretch out their hands
8:39 forgive, act, and render to all whose **h** you know—
8:58 but incline our **h** to him,
18:37 are God, and that you have turned their **h** back."
1Ch 16:10 let the **h** of those who seek the LORD rejoice.
29:18 keep forever such purposes and thoughts in the **h**
29:18 and direct their **h** toward you.
2Ch 11:16 Those who had set their **h** to seek the LORD God
20:33 not yet set their **h** upon the God of their ancestors.
30:19 who set their **h** to seek God,
Job 1: 5 and cursed God in their **h**."
Ps 5: 9 in their mouths; their **h** are destruction;
7: 9 you who test the minds and **h**, O righteous God.
10:13 the wicked renounce God, and say in their **h**,
14: 1 Fools say in their **h**, "There is no God."
17:10 They close their **h** to pity;
22:26 May your **h** live forever!
24: 4 Those who have clean hands and pure **h**,
28: 3 while mischief is in their **h**.
33:15 he who fashions the **h** of them all,
36: 1 to the wicked deep in their **h**;
37:31 The law of their God is in their **h**;
41: 6 while their **h** gather mischief;
53: 1 Fools say in their **h**, "There is no God."
55:15 for evil is in their homes and in their **h**.
58: 2 No, in your **h** you devise wrongs;
69:32 you who seek God, let your **h** revive.
73: 7 their **h** overflow with follies.
81:12 So I gave them over to their stubborn **h**,
85: 8 to his faithful, to those who turn to him in their **h**.
95: 8 Do not harden your **h**, as at Meribah,
95:10 "They are a people whose **h** go astray,
105: 3 let the **h** of those who seek the LORD rejoice.
105:25 whose **h** he then turned to hate his people,
107:12 Their **h** were bowed down with hard labor;
112: 7 their **h** are firm, secure in the LORD.
112: 8 Their **h** are steady, they will not be afraid;
119:70 Their **h** are fat and gross, but I delight in your law.
125: 4 and to those who are upright in their **h**.
Pr 7:25 Do not let your **h** turn aside to her ways;
15:11 how much more human **h**!
Ecc 5:20 God keeps them occupied with the joy of their **h**.
9: 3 Moreover, the **h** of all are full of evil;
9: 3 madness is in their **h** while they live,
Isa 29:13 while their **h** are far from me,
51: 7 you people who have my teaching in your **h**;
Jer 4: 4 remove the foreskin of your **h**,
5:24 They do not say in their **h**,
9:14 but have stubbornly followed their own **h**
12: 2 you are near in their mouths yet far from their **h**.
17: 1 on the tablet of their **h**,
17: 5 whose **h** turn away from the LORD.
23:17 to all who stubbornly follow their own stubborn **h**,
23:26 Will the **h** of the prophets ever turn back—
31:33 and I will write it on their **h**;
32:40 and I will put the fear of me in their **h**,
48:41 The **h** of the warriors of Moab, on that day,
La 3:41 up our **h** as well as our hands to God in heaven.
5:15 The joy of our **h** has ceased;
5:17 Because of this our **h** are sick,
Eze 14: 3 these men have taken their idols into their **h**,
14: 4 the house of Israel who take their idols into their **h**
14: 5 that I may take hold of the **h** of the house of Israel,
14: 7 into their **h** and placing their iniquity as
21:15 therefore **h** melt and many stumble.
32: 9 I will trouble the **h** of many peoples,
Joel 2:13 rend your **h** and not your clothing.
Na 2:10 **H** faint and knees tremble, all loins quake,
Zep 1:12 those who say in their **h**,
Zec 7:10 do not devise evil in your **h** against one another.
7:12 They made their **h** adamant in order not to hear
8:17 do not devise evil in your **h** against one another,
10: 7 and their **h** shall be glad as with wine.
10: 7 their **h** shall exult in the LORD.
Mal 4: 6 He will turn the **h** of parents to their children and
the **h** of children to their parents,
Mt 9: 4 said, "Why do you think evil in your **h**?
15: 8 but their **h** are far from me;
Mk 2: 6 scribes were sitting there, questioning in their **h**,
2: 8 "Why do you raise such questions in your **h**?
6:52 but their **h** were hardened.
7: 6 but their **h** are far from me;
8:17 not perceive or understand? Are your **h** hardened?
Lk 1:17 to turn the **h** of parents to their children,
1:51 the proud in the thoughts of their **h**.
3:15 all were questioning in their **h** concerning John,
5:22 "Why do you raise such questions in your **h**?
8:12 devil comes and takes away the word from their **h**,
16:15 of others; but God knows your **h**;
21:34 "Be on guard so that your **h** are not weighed down
24:32 not our **h** burning within us while he was talking
24:38 and why do doubts arise in your **h**?
Jn 14: 1 "Do not let your **h** be troubled.
14:27 Do not let your **h** be troubled,
16: 6 to you, sorrow has filled your **h**.
16:22 but I will see you again, and your **h** will rejoice,
Ac 2:46 and ate their food with glad and generous **h**,
7:39 and in their **h** they turned back to Egypt,
14:17 and filling you with food and your **h** with joy."
15: 9 and in cleansing their **h** by faith
Ro 1:24 Therefore God gave them up in the lusts of their **h**
2:15 that what the law requires is written on their **h**,
5: 5 because God's love has been poured into our **h**
16:18 and by smooth talk and flattery they deceive the **h**
2Co 1:22 on us and giving us his Spirit in our **h** as
3: 2 You yourselves are our letter, written on our **h**,
3: 3 not on tablets of stone but on tablets of human **h**.
4: 6 in our **h** to give the light of the knowledge of
6:13 to children—open wide your **h** also.
7: 2 Make room in your **h** for us;
7: 3 for I said before that you are in our **h**,
Gal 4: 6 God has sent the Spirit of his Son into our **h**,
Eph 3:17 and that Christ may dwell in your **h** through faith,
5:19 singing and making melody to the Lord in your **h**,
6:22 how we are, and to encourage your **h**.
Php 4: 7 will guard your **h** and your minds in Christ Jesus.
Col 2: 2 I want their **h** to be encouraged and united in love,
3:15 And let the peace of Christ rule in your **h**,
3:16 and with gratitude in your **h** sing psalms, hymns,
4: 8 how we are and that he may encourage your **h**;
1Th 2: 4 but to please God who tests our **h**.
3:13 so strengthen your **h** in holiness that you may
2Th 2:17 comfort your **h** and strengthen them
3: 5 May the Lord direct your **h** to the love of God and
Phm 1: 7 **h** of the saints have been refreshed through you,
Heb 3: 8 do not harden your **h** as in the rebellion,
3:10 and I said, 'They always go astray in their **h**,
3:15 do not harden your **h** as in the rebellion."
4: 7 if you hear his voice, do not harden your **h**."
8:10 and write them on their **h**, and I will be their God,
10:16 I will put my laws in their **h**,
10:22 with our **h** sprinkled clean from an evil conscience
Jas 1:26 and do not bridle their tongues but deceive their **h**,
3:14 and selfish ambition in your **h**,
4: 8 and purify your **h**, you double-minded.
5: 5 you have fattened your **h** in a day of slaughter.
5: 8 Strengthen your **h**, for the coming of
1Pe 3:15 but in your **h** sanctify Christ as Lord.
2Pe 1:19 the day dawns and the morning star rises in your **h**.
2:14 They have **h** trained in greed.
1Jn 3:19 that we are from the truth and will reassure our **h**
3:20 whenever our **h** condemn us;
3:20 for God is greater than our **h**,
3:21 Beloved, if our **h** do not condemn us,
5:10 in the Son of God have the testimony in their **h**.
Rev 2:23 that I am the one who searches minds and **h**,
17:17 into their **h** to carry out his purpose by agreeing
Jdt 8:27 as he did them, to search their **h**,
13:19 the **h** of those who remember the power of God.
Wis 1: 6 and a true observer of their **h**,
2: 2 reason is a spark kindled by the beating of our **h**;
Sir 2:12 Woe to timid **h** and to slack hands,
2:17 Those who fear the Lord prepare their **h**,
14: 2 Happy are those whose **h** do not condemn them,
17: 8 into their **h** to show them the majesty of his works.
31:26 so wine tests **h** when the insolent quarrel.
46:11 whose **h** did not fall into idolatry and who did
48:10 to turn the **h** of parents to their children,
48:19 Then their **h** were shaken and their hands trembled,
Bar 1:22 of us followed the intent of our own wicked **h**
2: 8 each of us, from the thoughts of our wicked **h**.
3: 7 in our **h** so that we would call upon your name;
3: 7 in our exile, for we have put away from our **h** all
LtJ 6:20 of the temple, but their **h**, it is said, are eaten away
1Mc 1:62 in Israel stood firm and were resolved in their **h**
2Mc 2: 3 that the law should not depart from their **h**.
15:27 with their hands and praying to God in their **h**,
1Es 2: 9 from many whose **h** were stirred.
3:21 It makes all **h** feel rich, forgets kings and satraps,
3Mc 4: 2 everywhere their **h** were burning,
2Es 3:22 in the **h** of the people along with the evil root;
8:58 and said in their **h** that there is no God—
9:36 as well as our **h** that received it;
12:38 whose **h** you know are able to comprehend
14:34 will rule over your minds and discipline your **h**,
16:54 and their thoughts and their **h**.
16:63 and what you think in your **h**!
4Mc 13:13 "Let us with all our **h** consecrate ourselves to God,

HEARTY (3)

Tob 5:14 you come of good stock. **H** welcome!"
Sir 19:30 A person's attire and **h** laughter,
2Mc 9:19 Antiochus their king and general sends **h** greetings

HEAT (50) [HEATED, OVERHEATED]

Ge 8:22 cold and **h**, summer and winter, day and night,
18: 1 he sat at the entrance of his tent in the **h** of the day.
31:40 by day the **h** consumed me, and the cold by night,
Dt 28:22 fever, inflammation, with fiery **h** and drought,
1Sa 11:11 the camp and cut down the Ammonites until the **h**
2Sa 4: 5 the **h** of the day they came to the house of Ishbaal,
Job 6:17 In time of **h** they disappear;
24:19 Drought and **h** snatch away the snow waters;
30:30 and my bones burn with **h**.
Ps 19: 6 and nothing is hid from its **h**.
32: 4 my strength was dried up as by the **h** of summer.
58: 9 Sooner than your pots can feel the **h** of thorns,
Isa 4: 6 a shade by day from the **h**,
18: 4 I will quietly look from my dwelling like clear **h**
18: 4 like a cloud of dew in the **h** of harvest.
25: 4 shelter from the rainstorm and a shade from the **h**.
25: 5 like **h** in a dry place, you subdued the **h** with
42:25 upon him the **h** of his anger and the fury of war;
Jer 2:24 in her **h** sniffing the wind!
17: 8 It shall not fear when **h** comes,
36:30 and his dead body shall be cast out to the **h** by day
La 5:10 Our skin is black as an oven from the scorching **h**
Eze 3:14 I went in bitterness in the **h** of my spirit,
Hos 7: 5 of our king the officials became sick with the **h**
Na 1: 6 Who can endure the **h** of his anger?

Zep 3: 8 all the **h** of my anger;
Mt 20:12 the burden of the day and the scorching **h.'**
Lk 12:55 'There will be scorching **h'**; and it happens.
Ac 28: 3 driven out by the **h,** fastened itself on his hand.
Jas 1:11 sun rises with its scorching **h** and withers the field;
Rev 7:16 the sun will not strike them, nor any scorching **h;**
16: 9 they were scorched by the fierce **h,**
Tob 2: 9 and my face was uncovered because of the **h.**
Jdt 8: 3 he was overcome by the burning **h,**
Wis 2: 4 by the rays of the sun and overcome by its **h.**
Sir 14:27 who is sheltered by her from the **h,**
18:16 not the dew give relief from the scorching **h?**
38:28 and he struggles with the **h** of the furnace;
43: 3 and who can withstand its burning **h?**
43: 4 A man tending a furnace works in burning **h,**
43:22 the falling dew gives refreshment from the **h.**
45:19 and in the **h** of his anger they were destroyed;
Bar 2:25 and indeed they have been thrown out to the **h**
Aza 1:44 Bless the Lord, fire and **h;**
1:45 Bless the Lord, winter cold and summer **h;**
2Mc 14:43 But in the **h** of the struggle he did not hit exactly,
2Es 1:20 of the **h** I clothed you with the leaves of trees.
7:*41* or summer or spring or **h** or winter or frost or cold,
15:50 like a flower when the **h** shall rise that is sent

HEATED (5) [HEAT]

Da 3:19 ordered the furnace **h** up seven times more than
Hos 7: 4 They are all adulterers; they are like a **h** oven,
2Mc 7: 3 and gave orders to have pans and caldrons **h.**
7: 4 These were **h** immediately,
4Mc 11:19 sharp spits that had been **h** in the fire,

HEATH (KJV) See SHRUB, WILD ASS

HEATHEN (5)

Wis 12: 5 These initiates from the midst of a **h** cult,
14:11 there will be a visitation also upon the **h** idols,
15:15 For they thought that all their **h** idols were gods,
LtJ 6: 4 and which cause the **h** to fear.
3Mc 4: 6 as they were torn by the harsh treatment of the **h.**

HEAVE [OFFERING] (KJV) See ELEVATION [OFFERING]

HEAVEN‡ (609) [HEAVEN'S, HEAVENLY, HEAVENS, MIDHEAVEN]

A. HEAVEN ... EARTH (64)
B. KINGDOM OF HEAVEN (32)
C. *GOD OF HEAVEN (31)
D. DOWN FROM HEAVEN (30)
E. HOST OF HEAVEN (20)
F. UNDER HEAVEN (19)
G. FATHER IN HEAVEN (14)
H. *LORD OF HEAVEN (11)
I. STARS OF HEAVEN (11)
J. EARTH ... HEAVEN (8)

Ge 6:17 under **h** all flesh in which is the breath of life; F
7:19 under the whole **h** were covered;
14:19 by God Most High, maker of **h** and earth; A
14:22 God Most High, maker of **h** and earth, A
15: 5 "Look toward **h** and count the stars,
19:24 and fire from the LORD out of **h;**
21:17 and the angel of God called to Hagar from **h,**
22:11 But the angel of the LORD called to him from **h,**
22:15 to Abraham a second time from **h,**
22:17 as numerous as the stars of **h** and as the sand I
24: 3 the God of **h** and earth, AC
24: 7 The LORD, the God of **h,** C
26: 4 as numerous as the stars of **h,** and will give I
27:28 May God give you of the dew of **h,**
27:39 and away from the dew of **h** on high.
28:12 the top of it reaching to **h;**
28:17 and this is the gate of **h."**
49:25 with blessings of **h** above,
Ex 9:22 toward **h** so that hail may fall on the whole land
9:23 Then Moses stretched out his staff toward **h,**
10:21 "Stretch out your hand toward **h** so that there may
10:22 So Moses stretched out his hand toward **h,**
16: 4 "I am going to rain bread from **h** for you,
17:14 the remembrance of Amalek from under **h."** F
20: 4 whether in the form of anything that is in **h** above,
20:11 For in six days the LORD made **h** and earth, A
20:22 for yourselves that I spoke with you from **h.**
24:10 like the very **h** for clearness.
31:17 that in six days the LORD made **h** and earth, A
32:13 like the stars of **h,** and all this land I
Dt 1:10 that today you are as numerous as the stars of **h.** I
1:28 the cities are large and fortified up to **h!**
2:25 of you upon the peoples everywhere under **h;** F
3:24 in **h** or on earth can perform deeds and mighty A
4:19 the moon, and the stars, all the host of **h,** E
4:19 to all the peoples everywhere under **h.** F
4:26 I call **h** and earth to witness against you today A
4:32 ask from one end of **h** to the other:
4:36 From **h** he made you hear his voice
4:39 the LORD is God in **h** above and on the earth A
5: 8 in the form of anything that is in **h** above,
7:24 and you shall blot out their name from under **h;** F
9:14 and blot out their name from under **h;** F
10:14 Although **h** and the **h** of heavens belong to the LORD your God,
10:22 as numerous as the stars in **h.**
17: 3 or any of the host of **h,** which I have forbidden— E

Dt 25:19 the remembrance of Amalek from under **h;** F
26:15 Look down from your holy habitation, from **h,**
28:62 once you were as numerous as the stars in **h,**
29:20 the LORD will blot out their names from under **h.** F
30:12 It is not in **h,** that you should say,
30:12 that you should say, "Who will go up to **h** for us,
30:19 I call **h** and earth to witness against you today A
31:28 in their hearing and call **h** and earth to witness A
32:40 For I lift up my hand to **h,** and swear:
33:13 with the choice gifts of **h** above,
Jos 2:11 The LORD your God is indeed God in **h** above
10:11 from **h** on them as far as Azekah, and they died;
Jdg 5:20 from **h,** from their courses they fought
13:20 When the flame went up toward **h** from the altar,
1Sa 2:10 the Most High will thunder in **h.**
5:12 and the cry of the city went up to **h.**
2Sa 18: 9 and he was left hanging between **h** and earth, A
22:14 The LORD thundered from **h;**
1Ki 8:22 and spread out his hands to **h.**
8:23 like you in **h** above or on earth beneath, A
8:27 Even **h** and the highest **h** cannot contain you,
8:30 O hear in **h** your dwelling place; heed and forgive.
8:32 in **h,** and act, and judge your servants, condemning
8:34 in **h,** forgive the sin of your people Israel,
8:35 "When **h** is shut up and there is no rain
8:36 then hear in **h,** and forgive the sin
8:39 in **h** your dwelling place, forgive, act, and render
8:43 then hear in **h** your dwelling place,
8:45 then hear in **h** their prayer and their plea,
8:49 then hear in **h** your dwelling place their prayer
8:54 he had knelt with hands outstretched toward **h;**
22:19 the host of **h** standing beside him to the right E
2Ki 1:10 down from **h** and consume you and your fifty." D
1:10 Then fire came down from **h,** D
1:12 down from **h** and consume you and your fifty." D
1:12 of God came down from **h** and consumed him D
1:14 down from **h** and consumed the two former D
2: 1 when the LORD was about to take Elijah up to **h**
2:11 and Elijah ascended in a whirlwind into **h.**
14:27 the name of Israel from under **h,** F
17:16 worshiped all the host of **h,** and served Baal. E
19:15 you have made **h** and earth. A
21: 3 worshiped all the host of **h,** and served them. E
21: 5 He built altars for all the host of **h** in the E
23: 4 for Asherah, and for all the host of **h;** E
1Ch 21:16 of the LORD standing between earth and **h,** J
21:26 and he answered him with fire from **h** on the altar
27:23 to make Israel as numerous as the stars of **h.** I
2Ch 2: 6 But who is able to build him a house, since **h,** even highest **h,** cannot contain him?
2:12 made **h** and earth, who has given King David A
6:13 and spread out his hands toward **h.**
6:14 there is no God like you, in **h** or on earth, A
6:18 Even **h** and the highest **h** cannot contain you,
6:21 may you hear from **h** your dwelling place;
6:23 from **h,** and act, and judge your servants, repaying
6:25 from **h,** and forgive the sin of your people Israel,
6:26 "When **h** is shut up and there is no rain
6:27 may you hear in **h,** forgive the sin
6:30 from **h,** your dwelling place, forgive, and render
6:33 may you hear from **h** your dwelling place,
6:35 then hear from **h** their prayer and their plea,
6:39 then hear from **h** your dwelling place their prayer
7: 1 down from **h** and consumed the burnt offering D
7:14 then I will hear from **h,**
18:18 with all the host of **h** standing to the right and to E
20: 6 God of our ancestors, are you not God in **h?**
28: 9 in a rage that has reached up to **h.**
30:27 their prayer came to his holy dwelling in **h.**
32:20 of Amoz prayed because of this and cried to **h.**
33: 3 made sacred poles, worshiped all the host of **h,** E
33: 5 He built altars for all the host of **h** in the E
36:23 The LORD, the God of **h,** C
Ezr 1: 2 The LORD, the God of **h,** C
5:11 We are the servants of the God of **h** and earth, AC
5:12 our ancestors had angered the God of **h,** C
6: 9 or sheep for burnt offerings to the God of **h,** C
6:10 may offer pleasing sacrifices to the God of **h,** C
7:12 the scribe of the law of the God of **h:** Peace. C
7:21 the scribe of the law of the God of **h,** C
7:23 Whatever is commanded by the God of **h,** C
7:23 be done with zeal for the house of the God of **h,** C
Ne 1: 4 fasting and praying before the God of **h.** C
1: 5 I said, "O LORD God of **h,** C
2: 4 So I prayed to the God of **h.** C
2:20 God of **h** is the one who will give us success, C
9: 6 you have made **h,** the **h** of heavens,
9: 6 and the host of **h** worships you. E
9:13 and spoke with them from **h,**
9:15 For their hunger you gave them bread from **h,**
9:23 the stars of **h,** and brought them into the land I
9:27 to you and you heard them from **h,**
9:28 they turned and cried to you, you heard from **h,**
Job 1:16 from **h** and burned up the sheep and the servants,
11: 8 It is higher than **h**—what can you do?
16:19 Even now, in fact, my witness is in **h,**
22:14 and he walks on the dome of **h.'**
25: 2 he makes peace in his high **h.**
26:11 The pillars of **h** tremble, and are astounded
37: 3 Under the whole **h** he lets it loose,
38:29 and who has given birth to the hoarfrost of **h?**
41:11 under the whole **h,** who?
Ps 11: 4 the LORD's throne is in **h.**
14: 2 The LORD looks down from **h** on humankind D
20: 6 from his holy **h** with mighty victories
33:13 The LORD looks down from **h;** D
53: 2 God looks down from **h** on humankind to see D

Ps 57: 3 He will send from **h** and save me,
69:34 Let **h** and earth praise him, A
73: 9 They set their mouths against **h,**
73:25 Whom have I in **h** but you?
78:23 and opened the doors of **h;**
78:24 and gave them the grain of **h.**
80:14 look down from **h,** and see; D
102:19 from **h** the LORD looked at the earth, A
105:40 and gave them food from **h** in abundance.
107:26 They mounted up to **h,** they went down to
115:15 be blessed by the LORD, who made **h** and earth. A
119:89 your word is firmly fixed in **h.**
121: 2 from the LORD, who made **h** and earth. A
124: 8 the name of the LORD, who made **h** and earth. A
134: 3 May the LORD, maker of **h** and earth, A
135: 6 in **h** and on earth, in the seas and all deeps. A
136:26 O give thanks to the God of **h,** C
139: 8 If I ascend to **h,** you are there;
146: 6 who made **h** and earth, the sea, and all that is A
148:13 his glory is above earth and **h.** J
Pr 23: 5 flying like an eagle toward **h.**
30: 4 Who has ascended to **h** and come down?
Ecc 1:13 search out by wisdom all that is done under **h;** F
2: 3 to do under **h** during the few days of their life. F
3: 1 and a time for every matter under **h:** F
5: 2 for God is in **h,** and you upon earth;
Isa 7:11 let it be deep as Sheol or high as **h.**
14:12 you are fallen from **h,** O Day Star, son of Dawn!
14:13 You said in your heart, "I will ascend to **h;**
24:18 For the windows of **h** are opened,
24:21 On that day the LORD will punish the host of **h** E
24:21 the LORD will punish the host of heaven in **h,**
34: 4 All the host of **h** shall rot away, E
37:16 you have made **h** and earth. A
55:10 For as the rain and the snow come down from **h,** D
63:15 Look down from **h** and see, D
66: 1 **H** is my throne and the earth is my footstool;
Jer 7:18 to make cakes for the queen of **h;**
8: 2 the sun and the moon and all the host of **h,** E
19:13 to the whole host of **h,** E
23:24 Do I not fill **h** and earth? A
33:22 the host of **h** cannot be numbered and the sands E
33:25 and night and the ordinances of **h** and earth, A
44:17 to the queen of **h** and pour out libations to her,
44:18 to the queen of **h** and pouring out libations to her,
44:19 to the queen of **h** and pouring out libations to her;
44:25 to the queen of **h** and to pour out libations to her.'
49:36 the four winds from the four quarters of **h;**
51: 9 up to **h** and has been lifted up even to the skies.
51:53 Though Babylon should mount up to **h,**
La 2: 1 He has thrown down from **h** to earth the AD
3:41 up our hearts as well as our hands to God in **h.**
3:50 until the LORD from **h** looks down and sees.
Eze 8: 3 and the spirit lifted me up between earth and **h,** J
Da 2:18 and told them to seek mercy from the God of **h** C
2:19 and Daniel blessed the God of **h.** C
2:28 but there is a God in **h** who reveals mysteries,
2:37 to whom the God of **h** has given the kingdom, C
2:44 God of **h** will set up a kingdom that shall never C
4:11 tree grew great and strong, its top reached to **h,**
4:13 a holy watcher, coming down from **h.** D
4:15 Let him be bathed with the dew of **h.**
4:20 that its top reached to **h** and was visible to the end
4:22 Your greatness has increased and reaches to **h,**
4:23 king saw a holy watcher coming down from **h** D
4:23 and let him be bathed with the dew of **h,**
4:25 you shall be bathed with the dew of **h,**
4:26 from the time that you learn that **H** is sovereign.
4:31 in the king's mouth, a voice came from **h:**
4:33 and his body was bathed with the dew of **h,**
4:34 lifted my eyes to **h,** and my reason returned to me.
4:35 the host of **h** and the inhabitants of the earth. E
4:37 praise and extol and honor the King of **h,**
5:21 and his body was bathed with the dew of **h,**
5:23 You have exalted yourself against the Lord of **h!** H
6:27 he works signs and wonders in **h** and on earth; A
7: 2 in my vision by night the four winds of **h** stirring
7:13 like a human being coming with the clouds of **h.**
7:27 of the kingdoms under the whole **h** shall be given
8: 8 toward the four winds of **h.**
8:10 It grew as high as the host of **h.** E
9:12 before been done under the whole **h.**
11: 4 toward the four winds of **h,** but not to his posterity,
12: 7 raised his right hand and his left hand toward **h.**
Am 9: 2 though they climb up to **h,**
Jnh 1: 9 "I worship the LORD, the God of **h,** C
Zec 2: 6 I have spread you abroad like the four winds of **h,**
6: 5 "These are the four winds of **h** going out,
Mal 3:10 not open the windows of **h** for you and pour down
Mt 3: 2 "Repent, for the kingdom of **h** has come near." B
3:17 And a voice from **h** said, "This is my Son,
4:17 "Repent, for the kingdom of **h** has come near." B
5: 3 for theirs is the kingdom of **h.** B
5:10 for theirs is the kingdom of **h.** B
5:12 Rejoice and be glad, for your reward is great in **h,**
5:16 and give glory to your Father in **h.** G
5:18 For truly I tell you, until **h** and earth pass away, A
5:19 will be called least in the kingdom of **h;** B
5:19 be called great in the kingdom of **h.** B
5:20 you will never enter the kingdom of **h.** B
5:34 But I say to you, Do not swear at all, either by **h,**
5:45 so that you may be children of your Father in **h;** G
6: 1 then you have no reward from your Father in **h.** G
6: 9 Our Father in **h,** hallowed be your name. G
6:10 Your will be done, on earth as it is in **h.** J
6:20 but store up for yourselves treasures in **h,**
7:11 Father in **h** give good things to those who G

Mt 7:21 'Lord, Lord,' will enter the kingdom of **h**, B
7:21 the one who does the will of my Father in **h**. G
8:11 and Isaac and Jacob in the kingdom of **h**, B
10: 7 'The kingdom of **h** has come near.' B
10:32 I also will acknowledge before my Father in **h**; G
10:33 I also will deny before my Father in **h**. G
11:11 the least in the kingdom of **h** is greater than he. B
11:12 the kingdom of **h** has suffered violence, B
11:23 And you, Capernaum, will you be exalted to **h**?
11:25 "I thank you, Father, Lord of **h** and earth, AH
12:50 whoever does the will of my Father in **h** G
13:11 to know the secrets of the kingdom of **h**, B
13:24 "The kingdom of **h** may be compared B
13:31 "The kingdom of **h** is like a mustard seed that B
13:33 "The kingdom of **h** is like yeast that a woman B
13:44 kingdom of **h** is like treasure hidden in a field, B
13:45 kingdom of **h** is like a merchant in search of B
13:47 the kingdom of **h** is like a net that was thrown B
13:52 for the kingdom of **h** is like the master of B
14:19 five loaves and the two fish, he looked up to **h**,
16: 1 to show them a sign from **h**.
16:17 not revealed this to you, but my Father in **h**. G
16:19 I will give you the keys of the kingdom of **h**, B
16:19 whatever you bind on earth will be bound in **h**,
16:19 whatever you loose on earth will be loosed in **h**."
18: 1 "Who is the greatest in the kingdom of **h**?" B
18: 3 you will never enter the kingdom of **h**. B
18: 4 is the greatest in the kingdom of **h**. B
18:10 for, I tell you, in **h** their angels continually see
18:10 the face of my Father in **h**. G
18:14 So it is not the will of your Father in **h** that one G
18:18 whatever you bind on earth will be bound in **h**,
18:18 whatever you loose on earth will be loosed in **h**.
18:19 it will be done for you by my Father in **h**. G
18:23 kingdom of **h** may be compared to a king who B
19:12 for the sake of the kingdom of **h**. B
19:14 to such as these that the kingdom of **h** belongs." B
19:21 and you will have treasure in **h**;
19:23 hard for a rich person to enter the kingdom of **h**. B
20: 1 kingdom of **h** is like a landowner who went out B
21: 9 Hosanna in the highest **h**!"
21:25 Did the baptism of John come from **h**,
21:25 "If we say, 'From **h**,' he will say to us,
22: 2 kingdom of **h** may be compared to a king who B
22:30 but are like angels in **h**.
23: 9 for you have one Father—the one in **h**.
23:13 For you lock people out of the kingdom of **h**. B
23:22 and whoever swears by **h**,
24:29 the stars will fall from **h**, and the powers of **h** will be shaken.
24:30 Then the sign of the Son of Man will appear in **h**,
24:30 'the Son of Man coming on the clouds of **h**'
24:31 from one end of **h** to the other.
24:35 **H** and earth will pass away, A
24:36 neither the angels of **h**, nor the Son,
25: 1 "Then the kingdom of **h** will be like this. B
26:64 of Power and coming on the clouds of **h**."
28: 2 for an angel of the Lord, descending from **h**,
28:18 "All authority in **h** and on earth has been given A
Mk 1:11 And a voice came from **h**, "You are my Son,
6:41 looked up to **h**, and blessed and broke the loaves,
7:34 Then looking up to **h**, he sighed and said to him,
8:11 asking him for a sign from **h**, to test him.
10:21 and you will have treasure in **h**;
11:10 Hosanna in the highest **h**!"
11:25 your Father in **h** may also forgive you your G
11:30 Did the baptism of John come from **h**,
11:31 "If we say, 'From **h**,' he will say,
12:25 but are like angels in **h**.
13:25 and the stars will be falling from **h**,
13:27 from the ends of the earth to the ends of **h**.
13:31 **H** and earth will pass away, A
13:32 neither the angels in **h**, nor the Son,
14:62 and 'coming with the clouds of **h**.' "
16:19 ⟦taken up into **h** and sat down at the right hand⟧
Lk 2:14 "Glory to God in the highest **h**,
2:15 When the angels had left them and gone into **h**,
3:21 and was praying, the **h** was opened,
3:22 And a voice came from **h**, "You are my Son,
4:25 when the **h** was shut up three years and six months,
6:23 for surely your reward is great in **h**;
9:16 he looked up to **h**, and blessed and broke them,
9:54 to come down from **h** and consume them?" D
10:15 And you, Capernaum, will you be exalted to **h**?
10:18 "I watched Satan fall from **h** like a flash
10:20 but rejoice that your names are written in **h**."
10:21 "I thank you, Father, Lord of **h** and earth, AH
11:16 kept demanding from him a sign from **h**.
12:33 an unfailing treasure in **h**, where no thief comes
15: 7 be more joy in **h** over one sinner who repents than
15:18 "Father, I have sinned against **h** and before you;
15:21 'Father, I have sinned against **h** and before you;
16:17 But it is easier for **h** and earth to pass away, A
17:29 it rained fire and sulfur from **h** and destroyed all
18:13 standing far off, would not even look up to **h**,
18:22 and you will have treasure in **h**;
19:38 Peace in **h**, and glory in the highest **h**!"
20: 4 Did the baptism of John come from **h**,
20: 5 saying, "If we say, 'From **h**,' he will say,
20:16 When they heard this, they said, "**H** forbid!"
21:11 be dreadful portents and great signs from **h**.
21:33 **H** and earth will pass away, A
22:43 ⟦from **h** appeared to him and gave him strength.⟧
24:51 he withdrew from them and was carried up into **h**.
Jn 1:32 "I saw the Spirit descending from **h** like a dove,
1:51 you will see **h** opened and the angels
3:13 into **h** except the one who descended from **h**,
Jn 3:27 anything except what has been given from **h**.
3:31 The one who comes from **h** is above all.
6:31 it is written, 'He gave them bread from **h** to eat.' "
6:32 it was not Moses who gave you the bread from **h**,
6:32 my Father who gives you the true bread from **h**.
6:33 bread of God is that which comes down from **h** D
6:38 for I have come down from **h**, D
6:41 "I am the bread that came down from **h**." D
6:42 can he now say, 'I have come down from **h**'?" D
6:50 This is the bread that comes down from **h**, D
6:51 I am the living bread that came down from **h**. D
6:58 This is the bread that came down from **h**, D
12:28 Then a voice came from **h**, "I have glorified it,
17: 1 he looked up to **h** and said, "Father,
Ac 1: 2 until the day when he was taken up to **h**,
1:10 he was going and they were gazing up toward **h**,
1:11 why do you stand looking up toward **h**?
1:11 who has been taken up from you into **h**,
1:11 in the same way as you saw him go into **h**."
2: 2 And suddenly from **h** there came a sound like
2: 5 from every nation under **h** living in Jerusalem. F
2:19 And I will show portents in the **h** above and signs
3:21 in **h** until the time of universal restoration
4:12 under **h** given among mortals by which we must F
4:24 "Sovereign Lord, who made the **h** and the earth, A
7:42 worship the host of **h**, as it is written in the book E
7:49 '**H** is my throne, and the earth is my footstool.
7:55 into **h** and saw the glory of God and Jesus standing
9: 3 suddenly a light from **h** flashed around him.
10:11 He saw the **h** opened and something like
10:16 and the thing was suddenly taken up to **h**.
11: 5 a large sheet coming down from **h**, D
11: 9 But a second time the voice answered from **h**,
11:10 then everything was pulled up again to **h**.
14:15 who made the **h** and the earth and the sea A
14:17 giving you rains from **h** and fruitful seasons,
17:24 he who is Lord of **h** and earth, AH
19:35 and of the statue that fell from **h**?
22: 6 about noon a great light from **h** suddenly shone
26:13 I saw a light from **h**, brighter than the sun,
Ro 1:18 of God is revealed from **h** against all ungodliness
10: 6 'Who will ascend into **h**?' "
1Co 8: 5 there may be so-called gods in **h** or on earth— A
15:47 the second man is from **h**.
15:48 as is the man of **h**, so are those who are of **h**.
15:49 we will also bear the image of the man of **h**.
2Co 12: 2 fourteen years ago was caught up to the third **h**—
Gal 1: 8 or an angel from **h** should proclaim to you a gospel
Eph 1:10 things in **h** and things on earth.
3:15 from whom every family in **h** and on earth A
6: 9 that both of you have the same Master in **h**,
Php 2:10 in **h** and on earth and under the earth, A
3:20 But our citizenship is in **h**,
Col 1: 5 because of the hope laid up for you in **h**.
1:16 in him all things in **h** and on earth were created, A
1:20 whether on earth or in **h**, J
1:23 has been proclaimed to every creature under **h**. F
4: 1 for you know that you also have a Master in **h**.
1Th 1:10 to wait for his Son from **h**, whom he raised from
4:16 the sound of God's trumpet, will descend from **h**,
2Th 1: 7 when the Lord Jesus is revealed from **h**
Heb 9:24 but he entered into **h** itself,
11:12 the stars of **h** and as the innumerable grains of sand
12:23 the assembly of the firstborn who are enrolled in **h**,
12:25 if we reject the one who warns from **h**!
12:26 not only the earth but also the **h**." J
Jas 5:12 either by **h** or by earth or by any other oath, A
5:18 the **h** gave rain and the earth yielded its harvest.
1Pe 1: 4 undefiled, and unfading, kept in **h** for you,
1:12 by the Holy Spirit sent from **h**—
3:22 who has gone into **h** and is at the right hand
2Pe 1:18 We ourselves heard this voice come from **h**,
Rev 3:12 that comes down from my God out of **h**,
4: 1 this I looked, and there in **h** a door stood open!
4: 2 and there in **h** stood a throne,
5: 3 in **h** or on earth or under the earth was able A
5:13 Then I heard every creature in **h** and on earth A
8: 1 there was silence in **h** for about half an hour.
8:10 and a great star fell from **h**, blazing like a torch,
9: 1 and I saw a star that had fallen from **h** to earth, A
10: 1 saw another mighty angel coming down from **h**, D
10: 4 but I heard a voice from **h** saying,
10: 5 on the sea and the land raised his right hand to **h**
10: 6 who created **h** and what is in it,
10: 8 voice that I had heard from **h** spoke to me again,
11:12 they heard a loud voice from **h** saying to them,
11:12 to **h** in a cloud while their enemies watched them.
11:13 were terrified and gave glory to the God of **h**. C
11:15 and there were loud voices in **h**, saying,
11:19 Then God's temple in **h** was opened,
12: 1 A great portent appeared in **h**:
12: 3 Then another portent appeared in **h**:
12: 4 third of the stars of **h** and threw them to the earth. I
12: 7 And war broke out in **h**;
12: 8 and there was no longer any place for them in **h**.
12:10 Then I heard a loud voice in **h**, proclaiming,
13: 6 that is, those who dwell in **h**.
13:13 even making fire come down from **h** to earth AD
14: 2 a voice from **h** like the sound of many waters and
14: 7 and worship him who made **h** and earth, A
14:13 And I heard a voice from **h** saying, "Write this:
14:17 Then another angel came out of the temple in **h**,
15: 1 I saw another portent in **h**, great and amazing:
15: 5 the temple of the tent of witness in **h** was opened,
16:11 and cursed the God of **h** because of their pains C
16:21 dropped from **h** on people, until they cursed God
18: 1 this I saw another angel coming down from **h**, D
Rev 18: 4 Then I heard another voice from **h** saying,
18: 5 for her sins are heaped high as **h**,
18:20 O **h**, you saints and apostles and prophets!
19: 1 to be the loud voice of a great multitude in **h**,
19:11 Then I saw **h** opened, and there was a white horse!
19:14 And the armies of **h**, wearing fine linen,
20: 1 Then I saw an angel coming down from **h**, D
20: 9 fire came down from **h** and consumed them. D
20:11 the earth and the **h** fled from his presence, J
21: 1 Then I saw a new **h** and a new earth; A
21: 1 the first **h** and the first earth had passed away, A
21: 2 coming down out of **h** from God,
21:10 the holy city Jerusalem coming down out of **h**
Tob 1:18 of judgment that the king of **h** executed upon him
5:10 I cannot see the light of **h**,
5:17 in **h** bring you safely there and return you
6:18 Lord of **h** that mercy and safety may be granted H
7:11 and it has been decreed from **h** that she be given
7:11 May the Lord of **h**, my child, guide H
7:12 God of **h** prosper your journey with his peace." C
7:16 Lord of **h** grant you joy in place of your sorrow. H
8:15 So they blessed the God of **h**, and Raguel said, C
9: 6 May the Lord grant the blessing of **h** to you
10:11 The Lord of **h** prosper you and your wife Sarah. H
10:12 the Lord of **h** bring you back safely, H
10:13 praising the Lord of **h** and earth, King over all, AH
13: 7 and my soul rejoices in the King of **h**.
13:11 bearing gifts in their hands for the King of **h**.
13:16 to see your glory and acknowledge the King of **h**.
Jdt 5: 8 and worshiped the God of **h**, C
6:19 God of **h**, see their arrogance, and have pity C
7:28 to witness against you **h** and earth and our God, A
9:12 of the heritage of Israel, Lord of **h** and earth, AH
11:17 and serves the God of **h** night and day. C
AdE 13:10 for you have made **h** and earth A
13:10 and earth and every wonderful thing under **h**. F
Wis 13: 2 luminaries of **h** were the gods that rule the world.
16:20 and without their toil you supplied them from **h**
18:15 your all-powerful word leaped from **h**,
18:16 and touched **h** while standing on the earth.
Sir 1: 3 The height of **h**, the breadth of the earth, the abyss,
16:18 Lo, **h** and the highest **h**,
17:32 He marshals the host of the height of **h**;
24: 5 the vault of **h** and traversed the depths of the abyss.
43: 9 The glory of the stars is the beauty of **h**,
46:17 Then the Lord thundered from **h**,
48:20 The Holy One quickly heard them from **h**,
Bar 1:11 that their days on earth may be like the days of **h**.
2: 2 Under the whole **h** there has not been done the like
3:29 Who has gone up into **h**, and taken her,
5: 3 will show your splendor everywhere under **h**. F
LtJ 6:55 they are like crows between **h** and earth. A
Aza 1:13 to multiply their descendants like the stars of **h** I
1:34 Blessed are you in the firmament of **h**,
1:41 Bless the Lord, stars of **h**; I
Sus 1: 9 and turned away their eyes from looking to **H**
1:35 Through her tears she looked up toward **H**,
Bel 1: 5 who created **h** and earth and has dominion A
1Mc 2:37 **h** and earth testify for us A
2:58 of great zeal for the law, was taken up into **h**.
3:18 in the sight of **H** there is no difference
3:19 but strength comes from **H**.
3:50 and they cried aloud to **H**,
3:60 But as his will in **h** may be, so shall he do."
4:10 And now, let us cry to **H**,
4:24 On their return they sang hymns and praises to **H**
4:40 with the trumpets, they cried out to **H**.
4:55 on their faces and worshiped and blessed **H**,
5:31 and that the cry of the town went up to **H**,
9:46 to **H** that you may be delivered from the hands
12:15 we have the help that comes from **H** for our aid,
16: 3 and may the help that comes from **H** be with you."
2Mc 2:10 down from **h** and consumed the sacrifices, D
2:18 and will gather us from everywhere under **h** F
2:21 from **h** to those who fought bravely for Judaism,
3:15 in their priestly vestments and called toward **h**
3:20 And holding up their hands to **h**,
3:34 And see that you, who have been flogged by **h**,
3:39 For he who has his dwelling in **h** watches over
7:11 and said nobly, "I got these from **H**, and because
7:28 to look at the **h** and the earth and see everything A
7:34 you raise your hand against the children of **h**.
8:20 by the help that came to them from **h**,
9: 4 But the judgment of **h** rode with him!
9:10 that he could touch the stars of **h**. I
9:20 As my hope is in **h**,
10:29 the enemy from **h** five resplendent men on horses
14:34 Then the priests stretched out their hands toward **h**
15: 3 if there were a sovereign in **h** who had commanded
15: 4 "It is the living Lord himself, the Sovereign in **h**,
15: 8 when help had come to them from **h**,
15:21 stretched out his hands toward **h** and called upon
15:34 And they all, looking to **h**,
1Es 4:34 The earth is vast, and **h** is high, J
4:36 The whole earth calls upon truth, and **h** blesses her.
4:46 to the King of **h** with your own lips."
4:58 he lifted up his face to **h** toward Jerusalem,
4:58 and praised the King of **h**, saying,
6:13 the Lord who created the **h** and the earth. A
6:15 in **h**, and provoked him, he gave them over into
8:75 and our mistakes have mounted up to **h**
Man 1: 2 you who made **h** and earth with all their order; A
1: 9 up and see the height of **h** because of the multitude
1:15 For all the host of **h** sings your praise, E
3Mc 2:15 For your dwelling is the **h** of heavens,
4:21 of him who was aiding the Jews from **h**.
5: 9 So their entreaty ascended fervently to **h**.

3Mc 5:25 toward **h** and with most tearful supplication
5:50 the help that they had received before from **h,**
6:17 the Jews observed this they raised great cries to **h**
6:28 the children of the almighty and living God of **h,** C
6:33 gave thanks to **h** unceasingly and lavishly for
7: 6 Since we have come to realize that the God of **h** C
2Es 2:14 Call, O call **h** and earth to witness: A
4: 8 neither did I ever ascend into **h.'**
6:38 'Let **h** and earth be made,' A
11: 2 and all the winds of **h** blew upon it,
11: 6 I saw how all things under **h** were subjected to it, F
13: 3 And I saw that this man flew with the clouds of **h;**
13: 5 of **h** to make war against the man who came up out
16:55 and "Let the **h** be made," and it was made.
16:59 the **h** like a dome and made it secure upon
4Mc 4:10 from their weapons appeared from **h,**
4:11 stretched out his hands toward **h,**
6: 6 yet while the old man's eyes were raised to **h,**
17: 5 The moon in **h,** with the stars,
17: 5 stand in honor before God and are firmly set in **h**

HEAVEN'S (1) [HEAVEN]

1Mc 16: 3 and you by **H** mercy are mature in years.

HEAVENLY (38) [HEAVEN]

A. HEAVENLY FATHER (7)

Job 1: 6 One day the **h** beings came to present themselves
2: 1 One day the **h** beings came to present themselves
38: 7 and all the **h** beings shouted for joy?
Ps 29: 1 O **h** beings, ascribe to the LORD glory
89: 6 Who among the **h** beings is like the LORD,
Mt 5:48 Be perfect, therefore, as your **h** Father is perfect. A
6:14 your **h** Father will also forgive you; A
6:26 and yet your **h** Father feeds them. A
6:32 and indeed your **h** Father knows A
15:13 "Every plant that my **h** Father has not planted A
18:35 So my **h** Father will also do to every one of you, A
Lk 2:13 with the angel a multitude of the **h** host,
11:13 how much more will the **h** Father give A
Jn 3:12 how can you believe if I tell you about **h** things?
Ac 26:19 I was not disobedient to the **h** vision,
1Co 15:40 There are both **h** bodies and earthly bodies,
15:40 but the glory of the **h** is one thing,
2Co 5: 2 longing to be clothed with our **h** dwelling—
Eph 1: 3 with every spiritual blessing in the **h** places,
1:20 and seated him at his right hand in the **h** places,
2: 6 up with him and seated us with him in the **h** places
3:10 to the rulers and authorities in the **h** places.
6:12 against the spiritual forces of evil in the **h** places.
Php 3:14 I press on toward the goal for the prize of the **h** call
2Ti 4:18 and save me for his **h** kingdom.
Heb 3: 1 brothers and sisters, holy partners in a **h** calling,
6: 4 and have tasted the **h** gift,
8: 5 that is a sketch and shadow of the **h** one;
9:23 of the **h** things to be purified with these rites,
9:23 **h** things themselves need better sacrifices than
11:16 as it is, they desire a better country, that is, a **h** one.
12:22 to the city of the living God, the **h** Jerusalem,
Wis 19:21 quick-melting kind of **h** food.
2Mc 11:10 They advanced in battle order, having their **h** ally,
3Mc 6:18 the **h** gates, from which two glorious angels
4Mc 4:11 for him and propitiate the wrath of the **h** army.
9:15 enemy of **h** justice, savage of mind,
11: 3 from the **h** justice for even more crimes.

HEAVENS‡ (188) [HEAVEN]

A. HEAVENS AND ... EARTH (17)

Ge 1: 1 beginning when God created the **h** and the earth, A
2: 1 Thus the **h** and the earth were finished, A
2: 4 These are the generations of the **h** and the earth A
2: 4 that the LORD God made the earth and the **h,**
7:11 and the windows of the **h** were opened.
8: 2 of the deep and the windows of the **h** were closed,
8: 2 the rain from the **h** was restrained,
11: 4 and a tower with its top in the **h,**
Dt 4:11 while the mountain was blazing up to the very **h,**
4:19 And when you look up to the **h** and see the sun,
9: 1 great cities, fortified to the **h,**
10:14 the heaven of **h** belong to the LORD your God,
11:17 be kindled against you and he will shut up the **h,**
11:21 as long as the **h** are above the earth.
28:12 for you his rich storehouse, the **h,** to give the rain
32: 1 O **h,** and I will speak;
32:43 Praise, O **h,** his people, worship him, all you gods!
33:26 O Jeshurun, who rides through the **h** to your help,
33:28 where the **h** drop down dew.
Jdg 5: 4 and the **h** poured, the clouds indeed poured water.
2Sa 21:10 of harvest until rain fell on them from the **h;**
22: 8 the foundations of the **h** trembled and quaked,
22:10 He bowed the **h,** and came down;
1Ki 18:45 while the **h** grew black with clouds and wind;
2Ki 23: 5 the constellations, and all the host of the **h.**
1Ch 16:26 but the LORD made the **h.**
16:31 Let the **h** be glad, and let the earth rejoice,
29:11 for all that is in the **h** and on the earth is yours; A
2Ch 7:13 When I shut up the **h** so that there is no rain,
Ezr 9: 6 and our guilt has mounted up to the **h.**
Ne 9: 6 you have made heaven, the heaven of **h,**
Job 9: 8 who alone stretched out the **h** and trampled
14:12 until the **h** are no more,
15:15 and the **h** are not clean in his sight;
20: 6 Even though they mount up high as the **h,**
20:27 The **h** will reveal their iniquity,
Job 22:12 "Is not God high in the **h?**
26:13 By his wind the **h** were made fair;
28:24 and sees everything under the **h.**
35: 5 Look at the **h** and see;
38:33 Do you know the ordinances of the **h?**
38:37 Or who can tilt the waterskins of the **h,**
Ps 2: 4 He who sits in the **h** laughs;
8: 1 You have set your glory above the **h.**
8: 3 When I look at your **h,** the work of your fingers,
18: 9 He bowed the **h,** and came down;
18:13 The LORD also thundered in the **h,**
19: 1 The **h** are telling the glory of God;
19: 4 In the **h** he has set a tent for the sun,
19: 6 Its rising is from the end of the **h,**
33: 6 By the word of the LORD the **h** were made,
36: 5 Your steadfast love, O LORD, extends to the **h,**
50: 4 He calls to the **h** above and to the earth,
50: 6 The **h** declare his righteousness,
57: 5 Be exalted, O God, above the **h.**
57:10 For your steadfast love is as high as the **h;**
57:11 Be exalted, O God, above the **h.**
68: 8 the **h** poured down rain at the presence of God,
68:33 O rider in the **h,** the ancient **h;**
71:19 and your righteousness, O God, reach the high **h.**
76: 8 From the **h** you uttered judgment;
78:26 He caused the east wind to blow in the **h,**
78:69 He built his sanctuary like the high **h,**
89: 2 your faithfulness is as firm as the **h.**
89: 5 Let the **h** praise your wonders,
89:11 The **h** are yours, the earth also is yours;
89:29 and his throne as long as the **h** endure.
96: 5 but the LORD made the **h.**
96:11 Let the **h** be glad, and let the earth rejoice;
97: 6 The **h** proclaim his righteousness;
102:25 and the **h** are the work of your hands.
103:11 For as the **h** are high above the earth,
103:19 The LORD has established his throne in the **h,**
104: 2 You stretch out the **h** like a tent,
108: 4 For your steadfast love is higher than the **h,**
108: 5 Be exalted, O God, above the **h,**
113: 4 and his glory above the **h.**
113: 6 who looks far down on the **h** and the earth? A
115: 3 Our God is in the **h;** he does whatever he pleases.
115:16 The **h** are the LORD's **h,**
123: 1 O you who are enthroned in the **h!**
136: 5 the **h,** for his steadfast love endures forever;
144: 5 Bow your **h,** O LORD, and come down;
147: 8 He covers the **h** with clouds,
148: 1 Praise the LORD from the **h;**
148: 4 Praise him, you highest **h,** and you waters above the **h!**
Pr 3:19 by understanding he established the **h;**
8:27 When he established the **h,** I was there,
25: 3 Like the **h** for height, like the earth for depth,
Isa 1: 2 Hear, O **h,** and listen, O earth;
13: 5 from the end of the **h,**
13:10 For the stars of the **h** and their constellations will
13:13 Therefore I will make the **h** tremble,
24: 4 the **h** languish together with the earth.
34: 5 When my sword has drunk its fill in the **h,** lo,
40:12 the hollow of his hand and marked off the **h** with
40:22 who stretches out the **h** like a curtain,
42: 5 who created the **h** and stretched them out,
44:23 Sing, O **h,** for the LORD has done it;
44:24 who alone stretched out the **h,**
45: 8 Shower, O **h,** from above,
45:12 it was my hands that stretched out the **h,**
45:18 who created the **h** (he is God!),
47:13 let those who study the **h** stand up and save you,
48:13 and my right hand spread out the **h;**
49:13 Sing for joy, O **h,** and exult, O earth;
50: 3 I clothe the **h** with blackness,
51: 6 Lift up your eyes to the **h,**
51: 6 for the **h** will vanish like smoke,
51:13 who stretched out the **h** and laid the foundations of
51:16 stretching out the **h** and laying the foundations of
55: 9 For as the **h** are higher than the earth,
64: 1 O that you would tear open the **h** and come down,
65:17 For I am about to create new **h** and a new earth; A
66:22 For as the new **h** and the new earth, A
Jer 2:12 Be appalled, O **h,** at this, be shocked,
4:23 and to the **h,** and they had no light.
4:28 and the **h** above grow black;
8: 7 Even the stork in the **h** knows its times;
10: 2 or be dismayed at the signs of the **h;**
10:11 the **h** and the earth shall perish from the earth A
10:11 from the earth and from under the **h.**
10:12 and by his understanding stretched out the **h.**
10:13 there is a tumult of waters in the **h,**
14:22 Or can the **h** give showers?
31:37 If the **h** above can be measured,
32:17 the **h** and the earth by your great power and A
51:15 and by his understanding stretched out the **h.**
51:16 a tumult of waters in the **h,**
51:48 Then the **h** and the earth, and all that is in them, A
La 3:66 and destroy them from under the LORD's **h.**
4:19 Our pursuers were swifter than the eagles in the **h;**
Eze 1: 1 the **h** were opened, and I saw visions of God.
32: 7 When I blot you out, I will cover the **h,**
32: 8 the shining lights of the **h** I will darken above you,
Hos 2:21 I will answer the **h** and they shall answer the earth;
Joel 2:10 The earth quakes before them, the **h** tremble.
2:30 I will show portents in the **h** and on the earth, A
3:16 and the **h** and the earth shake. A
Am 9: 6 in the **h,** and founds his vault upon the earth;
Na 3:16 your merchants more than the stars of the **h.**
Hab 3: 3 His glory covered the **h,** and the earth was full of
Zep 1: 5 down on the roofs to the host of the **h;**
Hag 1:10 Therefore the **h** above you have withheld the dew,
2: 6 in a little while, I will shake the **h** and the earth A
2:21 saying, I am about to shake the **h** and the earth, A
Zec 12: 1 the LORD, who stretched out the **h** and founded
Mt 3:16 the **h** were opened to him and he saw the Spirit
Mk 1:10 he saw the **h** torn apart and the Spirit descending
13:25 and the powers in the **h** will be shaken.
Lk 21:26 for the powers of the **h** will be shaken.
Ac 2:34 For David did not ascend into the **h,**
7:56 "I see the **h** opened and the Son of Man standing at
2Co 5: 1 a house not made with hands, eternal in the **h.**
Eph 4:10 the same one who ascended far above all the **h,**
Heb 1:10 and the **h** are the work of your hands;
4:14 a great high priest who has passed through the **h,**
7:26 separated from sinners, and exalted above the **h.**
8: 1 the right hand of the throne of the Majesty in the **h,**
2Pe 3: 5 that by the word of God **h** existed long ago and
3: 7 present **h** and earth have been reserved for fire, A
3:10 and then the **h** will pass away with a loud noise,
3:12 of which the **h** will be set ablaze and dissolved,
3:13 we wait for new **h** and a new earth, A
Rev 12:12 Rejoice then, you **h** and those who dwell in them!
Tob 8: 5 Let the **h** and the whole creation bless you forever.
Jdt 13:18 who created the **h** and the earth, A
Wis 9:10 Send her forth from the holy **h,**
9:16 but who has traced out what is in the **h?**
Sir 24: 4 I dwelt in the highest **h,**
43: 1 as glorious to behold as the sight of the **h.**
43: 8 shining in the vault of the **h!**
45:15 and for his descendants as long as the **h** endure,
48: 3 By the word of the Lord he shut up the **h,**
51:19 I spread out my hands to the **h,**
LtJ 6:67 they cannot show signs in the **h** for the nations,
Aza 1:36 Bless the Lord, you **h;** sing praise to him
1:38 Bless the Lord, all you waters above the **h;**
2Mc 15:23 So now, O Sovereign of the **h,**
1Es 4:34 for it makes the circuit of the **h** and returns
3Mc 2: 2 Lord, king of the **h,** and sovereign of all creation,
2:15 For your dwelling is the heaven of **h,**
2Es 3:18 You bent down the **h** and shook the earth,
4:21 and he who is above the **h** can understand what is above the height of the **h."**

HEAVES (1)

Na 1: 5 the earth **h** before him, the world and all who live

HEAVIER (5) [HEAVY]

Ex 5: 9 Let **h** work be laid on them;
Job 6: 3 For then it would be **h** than the sand of the sea;
Pr 27: 3 but a fool's provocation is **h** than both.
Wis 17:21 but still **h** than darkness were they to themselves.
Sir 22:14 What is **h** than lead?

HEAVIEST (1) [HEAVY]

Ex 9:18 Tomorrow at this time I will cause the **h** hail to fall

HEAVILY (7) [HEAVY]

Nu 20:20 against them with a large force, **h** armed.
Jdg 1:35 the hand of the house of Joseph rested **h** on them,
Eze 27:25 you were filled and **h** laden in the heart of the seas.
Sir 31:19 He does not breathe **h** when in bed.
1Mc 2:30 because troubles pressed **h** upon them.
2Mc 15:18 and sisters and relatives, lay upon them less **h;**
4Mc 6:11 bathed in sweat, and gasping **h** for breath,

HEAVY (64) [HEAVIER, HEAVIEST, HEAVILY]

Ex 9:24 such **h** hail as had never fallen in all the land
18:18 the task is too **h** for you; you cannot do it alone.
Nu 11:14 for they are too **h** for me.
Dt 1:12 how can I bear the **h** burden of your disputes all
1Sa 4:18 for he was an old man, and **h.**
5: 6 of the LORD was **h** upon the people of Ashdod,
5: 7 for his hand is **h** on us and on our god Dagon."
5:11 The hand of God was very **h** there;
19: 8 He launched a **h** attack on them,
23: 5 and dealt them a **h** defeat.
2Sa 14:26 when it was **h** on him, he cut it),
1Ki 12: 4 "Your father made our yoke **h.**
12: 4 of your father and his **h** yoke that he placed on us,
12:10 'Your father made our yoke **h,**
12:11 Now, whereas my father laid on you a **h** yoke,
12:14 "My father made your yoke **h,**
14: 6 For I am charged with **h** tidings for you.
18:45 and wind; there was a **h** rain.
2Ch 10: 4 "Your father made our yoke **h.**
10: 4 of your father and his **h** yoke that he placed on us,
10:10 'Your father made our yoke **h,**
10:11 Now, whereas my father laid on you a **h** yoke,
10:14 "My father made your yoke **h,** but I will add to it;
Ezr 10: 9 because of this matter and because of the **h** rain.
10:13 But the people are many, and it is a time of **h** rain;
Ne 5:15 before me laid **h** burdens on the people,
5:18 because of the **h** burden of labor on the people.
Job 23: 2 his hand is **h** despite my groaning.
33: 7 my pressure will not be **h** on you.
37: 6 and the shower of rain, his **h** shower of rain,
Ps 32: 4 For day and night your hand was **h** upon me;
38: 4 they weigh like a burden too **h** for me.
88: 7 Your wrath lies **h** upon me,
144:14 and may our cattle be **h** with young.
Pr 25:20 on a wound is one who sings songs to a **h** heart.
27: 3 A stone is **h,** and sand is weighty,

Pr 29: 4 but one who makes **h** exactions ruins it.
Ecc 6: 1 and it lies **h** upon humankind:
8: 6 although the troubles of mortals lie **h** upon them.
Isa 24:20 its transgression lies **h** upon it, and it falls,
47: 6 on the aged you made your yoke exceedingly **h.**
La 3: 7 he has put **h** chains on me;
Zec 12: 3 On that day I will make Jerusalem a **h** stone for all
Mt 11:28 all you that are weary and are carrying **h** burdens,
23: 4 They tie up **h** burdens, hard to bear,
26:43 and found them sleeping, for their eyes were **h.**
Mk 14:40 for their eyes were very **h;**
Ac 27:10 the voyage will be with danger and much **h** loss,
Rev 11:19 peals of thunder, an earthquake, and **h** hail.
Wis 17:21 while over those people alone **h** night was spread,
Sir 6:21 She will be like a **h** stone to test them,
13: 2 Do not lift a weight too **h** for you,
30:13 Discipline your son and make his yoke **h,**
33:30 and if he does not obey, make his fetters **h.**
40: 1 and a **h** yoke is laid on the children of Adam,
1Mc 5: 3 a **h** blow and humbled them and despoiled them.
5:34 they fled before him, and he dealt them a **h** blow.
8: 7 after him should pay a **h** tribute and give hostages
8:31 'Why have you made your yoke **h** on our friends
13:22 but that night a very **h** snow fell,
2Mc 4:16 For this reason **h** disaster overtook them,
2Es 4:49 before me and poured down a **h** and violent rain,
15:35 against one another and shall pour out a **h** tempest
15:38 **h** storm clouds shall be stirred up from the south,

HEBER (11) [HEBERITES]

Ge 46:17 The children of Beriah: **H** and Malchiel
Nu 26:45 of **H,** the clan of the Heberites;
Jdg 4:11 **H** the Kenite had separated from the other Kenites,
4:17 on foot to the tent of Jael wife of **H** the Kenite;
4:17 between King Jabin of Hazor and the clan of **H**
4:21 But Jael wife of **H** took a tent peg,
5:24 the wife of **H** the Kenite,
1Ch 4:18 **H** father of Soco, and Jekuthiel father of Zanoah.
7:31 **H** and Malchiel, who was the father of Birzaith.
7:32 **H** became the father of Japhlet, Shomer, Hotham,
8:17 Zebadiah, Meshullam, Hizki, **H,**

HEBERITES (1) [HEBER]

Nu 26:45 of Heber, the clan of the **H;**

HEBREW‡ (33) [HEBREWS, HEBREWS']

Ge 14:13 one who had escaped came and told Abram the **H,**
39:14 my husband has brought among us a **H** to insult us!
39:17 "The **H** servant, whom you have brought
41:12 A young **H** was there with us,
Ex 1:15 The king of Egypt said to the **H** midwives,
1:16 to the **H** women, and see them on the birthstool,
1:19 the **H** women are not like the Egyptian women;
2: 7 "Shall I go and get you a nurse from the **H** women
2:11 He saw an Egyptian beating a **H,**
2:13 "Why do you strike your fellow **H?"**
21: 2 When you buy a male **H** slave,
Dt 15:12 whether a **H** man or a **H** woman,
Jer 34: 9 that all should set free their **H** slaves,
Jnh 1: 9 "I am a **H,"** he replied.
Jn 5: 2 called in **H** Beth-zatha, which has five porticoes.
19:13 The Stone Pavement, or in **H** Gabbatha.
19:17 which in **H** is called Golgotha.
19:20 and it was written in **H,** in Latin, and in Greek.
20:16 She turned and said to him in **H,** "Rabbouni!"
Ac 21:40 he addressed them in the **H** language, saying:
22: 2 When they heard him addressing them in **H,**
26:14 I heard a voice saying to me in the **H** language,
Php 3: 5 of the tribe of Benjamin, a **H** born of Hebrews;
Rev 9:11 his name in **H** is Abaddon,
16:16 at the place that in **H** is called Harmagedon.
Jdt 12:11 the **H** woman who is in your care to join us and
14:18 One **H** woman has brought disgrace on the house
Sir Pr: 2 For what was originally expressed in **H** does
4Mc 5: 2 ordered the guards to seize each and every **H** and
8: 2 that others of the **H** captives be brought,
12: 7 his mother had exhorted him in the **H** language,
16:15 and said to your sons in the **H** language,

HEBREWS‡ (30) [HEBREW]

Ge 40:15 For in fact I was stolen out of the land of the **H;**
43:32 because the Egyptians could not eat with the **H,**
Ex 1:22 that is born to the **H** you shall throw into the Nile,
2:13 he went out the next day, he saw two **H** fighting;
3:18 'The LORD, the God of the **H,** has met with us;
5: 3 "The God of the **H** has revealed himself to us;
7:16 Say to him, 'The LORD, the God of the **H,**
9: 1 'Thus says the LORD, the God of the **H:**
9:13 'Thus says the LORD, the God of the **H:**
10: 3 "Thus says the LORD, the God of the **H,**
1Sa 4: 6 great shouting in the camp of the **H** mean?"
4: 9 become slaves to the **H** as they have been to you;
13: 3 throughout all the land, saying, "Let the **H** hear!"
13: 7 Some **H** crossed the Jordan to the land of Gad
13:19 **H** must not make swords or spears for themselves"
14:11 and the Philistines said, "Look, **H** are coming out
14:21 the **H** who previously had been with the Philistines
29: 3 "What are these **H** doing here?"
Jer 34:14 of you must set free any **H** who have been sold
Ac 6: 1 the **H** because their widows were being neglected
2Co 11:22 Are they **H?** So am I. Are they Israelites?
Php 3: 5 of the tribe of Benjamin, a Hebrew born of **H;**
Jdt 10:12 She replied, "I am a daughter of the **H,**
2Mc 7:31 who have contrived all sorts of evil against the **H,**
11:13 and realized that the **H** were invincible because
15:37 the city has been in the possession of the **H.**
4Mc 4:11 the **H** to pray for him and propitiate the wrath of
9: 6 of the **H** because of their religion lived piously
9:18 that children of the **H** alone are invincible
17: 9 to destroy the way of life of the **H.**

HEBREWS' (1) [HEBREW]

Ex 2: 6 "This must be one of the **H'** children," she said.

HEBRON‡ (75) [HEBRONITES, =KIRIATH-ARBA, =MAMRE]

Ge 13:18 and settled by the oaks of Mamre, which are at **H;**
23: 2 Kiriath-arba (that is, **H)** in the land of Canaan;
23:19 Mamre, (that is, **H)** in the land of Canaan.
35:27 at Mamre, or Kiriath-arba (that is, **H),**
37:14 So he sent him from the valley of **H.**
Ex 6:18 The sons of Kohath: Amram, Izhar, **H,** and Uzziel,
Nu 3:19 Amram, Izhar, **H,** and Uzziel.
13:22 They went up into the Negeb, and came to **H;**
13:22 (**H** was built seven years before Zoan in Egypt.)
Jos 10: 3 of Jerusalem sent a message to King Hoham of **H,**
10: 5 the king of Jerusalem, the king of **H,**
10:23 the king of Jerusalem, the king of **H,**
10:36 Joshua went up with all Israel from Eglon to **H;**
10:39 just as he had done to **H,** and,
11:21 from **H,** from Debir, from Anab,
12:10 the king of Jerusalem one the king of **H** one
14:13 and gave **H** to Caleb son of Jephunneh for
14:14 So **H** became the inheritance of Caleb son
14:15 Now the name of **H** formerly was Kiriath-arba;
15:13 that is, **H** (Arba was the father of Anak).
15:54 (that is, **H),** and Zior: nine towns with their
20: 7 (that is, **H)** in the hill country of Judah.
21:11 that is **H,** in the hill country of Judah,
21:13 the descendants of Aaron the priest they gave **H,**
Jdg 1:10 Judah went against the Canaanites who lived in **H**
1:10 (the name of **H** was formerly Kiriath-arba);
1:20 **H** was given to Caleb, as Moses had said;
16: 3 to the top of the hill that is in front of **H.**
1Sa 30:31 in **H,** all the places where David
2Sa 2: 1 "To which shall I go up?" He said, "To **H."**
2: 3 and they settled in the towns of **H.**
2:11 The time that David was king in **H** over the house
2:32 and the day broke upon them at **H.**
3: 2 Sons were born to David at **H:**
3: 5 These were born to David in **H.**
3:12 Abner sent messengers to David at **H,** saying,
3:19 then Abner went to tell David at **H** all that Israel
3:20 When Abner came with twenty men to David at **H,**
3:22 But Abner was not with David at **H,**
3:27 When Abner returned to **H,**
3:32 They buried Abner at **H.**
4: 1 Saul's son Ishbaal heard that Abner had died at **H,**
4: 8 They brought the head of Ishbaal to David at **H**
4:12 and hung their bodies beside the pool at **H.**
4:12 and buried in the tomb of Abner at **H.**
5: 1 Then all the tribes of Israel came to David at **H,**
5: 3 So all the elders of Israel came to the king at **H;**
5: 3 and King David made a covenant with them at **H**
5: 5 At **H** he reigned over Judah seven years
5:13 In Jerusalem, after he came from **H,**
15: 7 to **H** and pay the vow that I have made to
15: 8 then I will worship the LORD in **H."**
15: 9 So he got up, and went to **H.**
15:10 Absalom has become king at **H!"**
1Ki 2:11 he reigned seven years in **H,**
1Ch 2:42 The sons of Mareshah father of **H.**
2:43 sons of **H:** Korah, Tappuah, Rekem, and Shema.
3: 1 the sons of David who were born to him in **H:**
3: 4 six were born to him in **H,**
6: 2 The sons of Kohath: Amram, Izhar, **H,** and Uzziel.
6:18 The sons of Kohath: Amram, Izhar, **H,** and Uzziel.
6:55 to them they gave **H** in the land of Judah
6:57 **H,** Libnah with its pasture lands, Jattir,
11: 1 all Israel gathered together to David at **H** and said,
11: 3 So all the elders of Israel came to the king at **H,**
11: 3 and David made a covenant with them at **H** before
12:23 the armed troops who came to David in **H** to turn
12:38 came to **H** with full intent to make David king
15: 9 of **H,** Eliel the chief, with eighty of his kindred;
23:12 Amram, Izhar, **H,** and Uzziel, four.
23:19 The sons of **H:** Jeriah the chief,
24:23 The sons of **H:** Jeriah the chief,
29:27 he reigned seven years in **H,**
2Ch 11:10 and **H,** fortified cities that are in Judah and
1Mc 5:65 He struck **H** and its villages and tore

HEBRONITES (6) [HEBRON]

Nu 3:27 the clan of the **H,** and the clan of the Uzzielites;
26:58 the clan of the Libnites, the clan of the **H,**
1Ch 26:23 Of the Amramites, the Izharites, the **H,**
26:30 Of the **H,** Hashabiah and his brothers,
26:31 Of the **H,** Jerijah was chief of the Hebronites.
26:31 Of the Hebronites, Jerijah was chief of the **H.**

HEDGE (3)

Isa 5: 5 I will remove its **h,** and it shall be devoured;
Hos 2: 6 Therefore I will **h** up her way with thorns;
Mic 7: 4 the most upright of them a thorn **h.**

HEDGEHOG (2)

Isa 14:23 And I will make it a possession of the **h,**
34:11 But the hawk and the **h** shall possess it;

HEED‡ (90) [HEEDED, HEEDING, HEEDLESS, HEEDS]

Ge 16:11 for the LORD has given **h** to your affliction.
31:24 "Take **h** that you say not a word to Jacob,
31:29 to me last night, saying, 'Take **h** that you speak
39:23 The chief jailer paid no **h** to anything that was
Ex 3:16 I have given **h** to you and to what has been done
4: 8 "If they will not believe you or **h** the first sign,
4: 9 they will not believe even these two signs or **h** you,
4:31 and when they heard that the LORD had given **h**
5: 2 that I should **h** him and let Israel go?
15:26 and give **h** to his commandments
22:23 when they cry out to me, I will surely **h** their cry;
Dt 1:45 the LORD would neither **h** your voice
3:26 with me on your account and would not **h** me.
4: 1 give **h** to the statutes and ordinances
4:30 you will return to the LORD your God and **h** him.
7:12 If you **h** these ordinances, by diligently
11:13 If you will only **h** his every commandment
13: 3 you must not **h** the words of those prophets
13: 8 you must not yield to or **h** any such persons.
18:14 to dispossess do give **h** to soothsayers and diviners,
18:15 you shall **h** such a prophet.
18:19 not **h** the words that the prophet shall speak
21:18 who does not **h** them when they discipline him,
23: 5 (Yet the LORD your God refused to **h** Balaam;
33: 7 O LORD, give **h** to Judah,
Jdg 6:10 But you have not given **h** to my voice."
11:28 the king of the Ammonites did not **h** the message
13:13 "Let the woman give **h** to all that I said to her.
1Sa 4:20 But she did not answer or give **h.**
12:14 and serve him and **h** his voice and not rebel against
12:15 but if you will not **h** the voice of the LORD,
15:22 and to **h** than the fat of rams.
1Ki 2: 4 'If your heirs take **h** to their way,
8:29 that you may **h** the prayer that your servant prays
8:30 in heaven your dwelling place; **h** and forgive.
1Ch 28:10 Take **h** now, for the LORD has chosen you
2Ch 6:20 and may you **h** the prayer that your servant prays
33:10 to Manasseh and to his people, but they gave no **h.**
Job 23: 6 No; but he would give **h** to me.
33:31 Pay **h,** Job, listen to me; be silent, and I will speak.
35:15 and he does not greatly **h** transgression,
Ps 5: 1 O LORD; give **h** to my sighing.
31: 7 you have taken **h** of my adversities,
66:19 he has given **h** to the words of my prayer.
107:43 Let those who are wise give **h** to these things,
142: 6 Give **h** to my cry, for I am brought very low.
Pr 1:23 Give **h** to my reproof; I will pour out my thoughts
10: 8 The wise of heart will **h** commandments,
15:32 but those who **h** admonition gain understanding.
17: 4 and a liar gives **h** to a mischievous tongue.
29:19 for though they understand, they will not give **h.**
Ecc 7:21 Do not give **h** to everything that people say,
Isa 7: 4 Take **h,** be quiet, do not fear,
34: 1 Draw near, O nations, to hear; O peoples, give **h!**
42:23 Who among you will give **h** to this,
51: 4 Listen to me, my people, and give **h** to me,
Jer 6:17 "Give **h** to the sound of the trumpet!"
6:17 But they said, "We will not give **h."**
6:19 because they have not given **h** to my words;
8: 6 I have given **h** and listened,
11: 3 Cursed be anyone who does not **h** the words
11:10 who refused to **h** my words;
18:18 and let us not **h** any of his words."
18:19 Give **h** to me, O LORD, and listen
22: 5 But if you will not **h** these words,
23:18 Who has given **h** to his word so as to proclaim it?
26: 5 and to **h** the words of my servants
29:19 because they did not **h** my words,
Da 3:12 These pay no **h** to you, O King.
11:30 and pay **h** to those who forsake the holy covenant.
Hos 5: 1 Give **h,** O house of Israel!
Zec 1: 4 But they did not hear or **h** me, says the LORD.
Mal 2:16 So take **h** to yourselves and do not be faithless.
Tob 10: 7 the road her son had taken, and would **h** no one.
Wis 6:18 giving **h** to her laws is assurance of immortality,
8:12 and when I speak they will give **h;**
13: 1 nor did they recognize the artisan while paying **h**
Sir 23:27 and nothing sweeter than to **h** the commandments
28:16 Those who pay **h** to slander will not find rest,
32:22 and give good **h** to your paths.
33:19 and you leaders of the congregation, pay **h!**
37:13 And **h** the counsel of your own heart,
Bar 3: 4 who did not **h** the voice of the Lord their God,
1Mc 8:16 they all **h** the one man,
1Es 1:28 and did not **h** the words of the prophet Jeremiah
1:47 and did not **h** the words that were spoken by
3Mc 1:26 But he, in his arrogance, took **h** of nothing,
3: 6 of other races paid no **h** to their good service
2Es 7:99 not give **h** shall suffer hereafter."
9:30 and give **h** to my words, O descendants of Jacob.

HEEDED (18) [HEED]

Ge 30:17 And God **h** Leah, and she conceived
30:22 and God **h** her and opened her womb.
34:24 of the city gate **h** Hamor and his son Shechem;
Jos 10:14 when the LORD **h** a human voice;
1Sa 19: 6 Saul **h** the voice of Jonathan;
25:35 see, I have **h** your voice,
2Sa 21:14 After that, God **h** supplications for the land.
1Ki 12:24 So they **h** the word of the LORD
20:25 He **h** their voice, and did so.
2Ki 13: 4 the LORD, and the LORD **h** him;
2Ch 11: 4 So they **h** the word of the LORD and turned back

Ne 9:34 not kept your law or **h** the commandments and
Pr 1:24 have stretched out my hand and no one **h,**
Ecc 9:16 and his words are not **h.**"
9:17 The quiet words of the wise are more to be **h** than
Jer 26: 5 to you urgently—though you have not **h—**
Wis 12:26 not **h** the warning of mild rebukes will experience
Bar 1:18 and have not **h** the voice of the Lord our God,

HEEDING (4) [HEED]

1Ki 8:28 **h** the cry and the prayer that your servant prays
2Ch 6:19 **h** the cry and the prayer that your servant prays
Bar 1:19 and we have been negligent, in not **h** his voice.
2: 5 against the Lord our God, in not **h** his voice.

HEEDLESS (2) [HEED]

Pr 13:10 By insolence the **h** make strife,
19:16 those who are **h** of their ways will die.

HEEDS‡ (5) [HEED]

Pr 10:17 Whoever **h** instruction is on the path to life,
13:18 but one who **h** reproof is honored.
15: 5 but the one who **h** admonition is prudent.
15:31 The ear that **h** wholesome admonition will lodge
Sir 35: 2 one who **h** the commandments makes an offering

HEEL‡ (8) [HEELS]

Ge 3:15 he will strike your head, and you will strike his **h.**"
25:26 with his hand gripping Esau's **h;**
Job 18: 9 A trap seizes them by the **h;**
Ps 41: 9 who ate of my bread, has lifted the **h** against me.
Jn 13:18 one who ate my bread has lifted his **h** against me.'
2Es 6: 8 for Jacob's hand held Esau's **h** from the beginning.
6:10 and the end of a person is the **h;**
6:10 Ezra, between the **h** and the hand, Ezra!"

HEELS (5) [HEEL]

Ge 49:17 bites the horse's **h** so that its rider falls backward.
49:19 but he shall raid at their **h.**
Dt 33: 3 marched at your **h,** accepted direction from you.
Jdg 5:15 into the valley they rushed out at his **h.**
Job 18:11 and chase them at their **h.**

HEGAI (4)

Est 2: 3 under custody of **H,** the king's eunuch, who is
2: 8 in the citadel of Susa in custody of **H,**
2: 8 into the king's palace and put in custody of **H,**
2:15 for nothing except what **H** the king's eunuch,

HEGEMONIDES (1)

2Mc 13:24 left **H** as governor from Ptolemais to Gerar,

HEGLAM (1)

1Ch 8: 7 **H,** who became the father of Uzza and Ahihud.

HEIFER‡ (17) [HEIFER'S, HEIFERS]

Ge 15: 9 He said to him, "Bring me a **h** three years old,
Nu 19: 2 the Israelites to bring you a red **h** without defect,
19: 5 Then the **h** shall be burned in his sight;
19: 6 throw them into the fire in which the **h** is burning.
19: 8 The one who burns the **h** shall wash his clothes
19: 9 up the ashes of the **h,** and deposit them outside
19:10 of the **h** shall wash his clothes and be unclean
Dt 21: 3 the body shall take a **h** that has never been worked,
21: 4 the elders of that town shall bring the **h** down to
21: 6 over the **h** whose neck was broken in the wadi,
Jdg 14:18 he said to them, "If you had not plowed with my **h,**
1Sa 16: 2 And the LORD said, "Take a **h** with you, and say,
Jer 46:20 A beautiful **h** is Egypt—a gadfly from the
50:11 though you frisk about like a **h** on the grass,
Hos 4:16 Like a stubborn **h,** Israel is stubborn;
10:11 Ephraim was a trained **h** that loved to thresh,
Heb 9:13 with the sprinkling of the ashes of a **h,**

HEIFER'S (1) [HEIFER]

Dt 21: 4 and shall break the **h** neck there in the wadi.

HEIFERS (1) [HEIFER]

Sir 38:26 and he is careful about fodder for the **h.**

HEIGHT‡ (58) [HIGH]

Ge 6:15 its width fifty cubits, and its **h** thirty cubits.
31:54 on the **h** and called his kinsfolk to eat bread;
Ex 27:18 the width fifty, and the **h** five cubits,
Nu 23: 3 And he went to a bare **h.**
1Sa 16: 7 on the **h** of his stature, because I have rejected him;
17: 4 of Gath, whose **h** was six cubits and a span.
22: 6 under the tamarisk tree on the **h,**
1Ki 6:26 The **h** of one cherub was ten cubits,
7:15 Eighteen cubits was the **h** of the one,
7:16 the **h** of the one capital was five cubits,
7:16 and the **h** of the other capital was five cubits.
7:31 within the crown whose **h** was one cubit;
7:32 and the **h** of a wheel was a cubit and a half.
2Ki 25:17 The **h** of the one pillar was eighteen cubits,
25:17 the **h** of the capital was three cubits;
2Ch 3: 4 and its **h** was one hundred twenty cubits.
33:14 and raised it to a very great **h.**
Ezr 6: 3 its **h** shall be sixty cubits and its width sixty cubits,
Ne 4: 6 and all the wall was joined together to half its **h;**
Ps 102:19 that he looked down from his holy **h,**
Pr 25: 3 Like the heavens for **h,** like the earth for depth,
Isa 16: 3 make your shade like night at the **h** of noon;
22:16 cutting a tomb on the **h,**
26: 5 For he has brought low the inhabitants of the **h;**
37:24 I came to its remotest **h,** its densest forest.
Jer 26:18 and the mountain of the house a wooded **h.'**
31:12 They shall come and sing aloud on the **h** of Zion,
49:16 who hold the **h** of the hill.
51:53 and though she should fortify her strong **h,**
52:21 pillars, the **h** of the one pillar was eighteen cubits,
52:22 the **h** of the one capital was five cubits;
Eze 13:18 and make veils for the heads of persons of every **h,**
17:23 On the mountain **h** of Israel I will plant it,
19:11 it stood out in its **h** with its mass of branches.
20:40 For on my holy mountain, the mountain **h** of Israel,
31: 3 with fair branches and forest shade, and of great **h,**
31:10 and its heart was proud of its **h,**
31:14 by the waters may grow to lofty **h** or set their tops
31:14 that drink water may reach up to them in **h.**
40: 5 of the wall, one reed; and the **h,**
43:13 This shall be the **h** of the altar:
Da 3: 1 a golden statue whose **h** was sixty cubits
4:10 a tree at the center of the earth, and its **h** was great.
8: 8 but at the **h** of its power,
Am 2: 9 whose **h** was like the **h** of cedars,
Mic 3:12 and the mountain of the house a wooded **h.**
Ro 8:39 nor **h,** nor depth, nor anything else
Eph 3:18 what is the breadth and length and **h** and depth,
Rev 21:16 its length and width and **h** are equal.
Jdt 7:10 but on the **h** of the mountains where they live,
Sir 1: 3 The **h** of heaven, the breadth of the earth,
17:32 He marshals the host of the **h** of heaven;
Bar 5: 5 Arise, O Jerusalem, stand upon the **h;**
2Mc 6:15 when our sins have reached their **h.**
1Es 6:25 its **h** to be sixty cubits and its width sixty cubits,
Man 1: 9 I am not worthy to look up and see the **h** of heaven
2Es 4:21 can understand what is above the **h** of the heavens.

HEIGHTENED (1) [HIGH]

Sir 1:19 and she **h** the glory of those who held her fast.

HEIGHTS‡ (36) [HIGH]

Nu 14:40 and went up to the **h** of the hill country,
14:44 they presumed to go up to the **h** of the hill country,
21:28 and swallowed up the **h** of the Arnon.
Dt 12: 2 on the mountain **h,** on the hills,
32:13 He set him atop the **h** of the land,
Jdg 5:18 Naphtali too, on the **h** of the field.
2Sa 22:34 and set me secure on the **h.**
2Ki 19:23 'With my many chariots I have gone up the **h** of
Ps 18:33 and set me secure on the **h.**
95: 4 the **h** of the mountains are his also.
148: 1 from the heavens; praise him in the **h!**
Pr 8: 2 On the **h,** beside the way,
Ecc 12: 5 when one is afraid of **h,** and terrors are in the road;
Isa 14:13 on the mount of assembly on the **h** of Zaphon;
33:16 they will live on the **h;**
37:24 'With my many chariots I have gone up the **h** of
41:18 I will open rivers on the bare **h,**
49: 9 on all the bare **h** shall be their pasture;
58:14 and I will make you ride upon the **h** of the earth;
Jer 3: 2 Look up to the bare **h,** and see!
3:21 A voice on the bare **h** is heard,
4:11 the bare **h** in the desert toward my poor people,
7:29 raise a lamentation on the bare **h,**
12:12 the bare **h** in the desert spoilers have come;
14: 6 The wild asses stand on the bare **h,**
Eze 34:14 and the mountain **h** of Israel shall be their pasture;
36: 2 and, "The ancient **h** have become our possession,"
Am 4:13 and treads on the **h** of the earth—
Ob 1: 3 whose dwelling is in the **h.**
Hab 3:19 and makes me tread upon the **h.**
Sir 24:13 and like a cypress on the **h** of Hermon.
26:16 Like the sun rising in the **h** of the Lord,
43: 9 a glittering array in the **h** of the Lord.
2Es 6: 4 and before the **h** of the air were lifted up,
16:60 so as to send rivers from the **h** to water the earth.
4Mc 4:25 were thrown headlong from **h** along

HEINOUS (1)

Job 31:11 For that would be a **h** crime;

HEIR (16) [HEIRS]

Ge 15: 2 and the **h** of my house is Eliezer of Damascus?"
15: 3 and so a slave born in my house is to be my **h.**"
15: 4 "This man shall not be your **h;** no one but your
very own issue shall be your **h.**"
2Sa 14: 7 even if we destroy the **h** as well.'
Jer 49: 1 Has Israel no sons? Has he no **h?**
Mt 21:38 they said to themselves, 'This is the **h;**
Mk 12: 7 those tenants said to one another, 'This is the **h;**
Lk 20:14 among themselves and said, 'This is the **h;**
Gal 4: 7 and if a child then also an **h,** through God.
Heb 1: 2 whom he appointed **h** of all things,
11: 7 by this he condemned the world and became an **h**
Tob 3:15 he has no other child to be his **h;**
6:12 He has no male **h** and no daughter except Sarah
Sir 23:22 and presents him with an **h** by another man.
2Es 7: 9 the **h** receive the inheritance unless by passing

HEIRS (16) [HEIR]

Jdg 21:17 "There must be **h** for the survivors of Benjamin,
1Ki 2: 4 'If your **h** take heed to their way,
Ezr 7:23 upon the realm of the king and his **h.**
Mt 8:12 while the **h** of the kingdom will be thrown into
Ro 4:14 If it is the adherents of the law who are to be the **h,**
8:17 then **h,** **h** of God and joint **h** with Christ—
Gal 3:29 **h** according to the promise.
4: 1 My point is this: **h,** as long as they are minors,
Eph 3: 6 the Gentiles have become fellow **h,**
Tit 3: 7 we might become **h** according to the hope
Heb 6:17 to the **h** of the promise the unchangeable character
11: 9 who were **h** with him of the same promise.
Jas 2: 5 the poor in the world to be rich in faith and to be **h**
1Pe 3: 7 they too are also **h** of the gracious gift of life—

HELAH (2)

1Ch 4: 5 of Tekoa had two wives, **H** and Naarah;
4: 7 The sons of **H:** Zereth, Izhar, and Ethnan.

HELAM (2)

2Sa 10:16 and they came to **H,** with Shobach the commander
10:17 and crossed the Jordan, and came to **H.**

HELBAH (1)

Jdg 1:31 or of Achzib, or of **H,** or of Aphik, or of Rehob;

HELBON (1)

Eze 27:18 wine of **H,** and white wool.

HELD‡ (104) [HOLD]

Ge 34: 5 so Jacob **h** his peace until they came.
36:43 to their settlements in the land that they **h.**
50:10 they **h** there a very great and sorrowful
Ex 17:11 Whenever Moses **h** up his hand, Israel prevailed;
17:12 Aaron and Hur **h** up his hands, one on one side,
21:16 that person has been sold or is still **h** in possession,
37:14 The rings that **h** the poles used for carrying
Lev 17: 4 he shall be **h** guilty of bloodshed;
19:20 or given her freedom, an inquiry shall be **h.**
Dt 4: 4 while those of you who **h** fast to the LORD
15: 2 every creditor shall remit the claim that is **h** against
Jdg 16:26 and Samson said to the attendant who **h** him by
Ru 3:15 So she **h** it, and he measured out six measures
1Sa 9: 6 he is a man **h** in honor.
10:27 But he **h** his peace.
2Sa 6:22 by them I shall be **h** in honor."
1Ki 7:26 like the flower of a lily; it **h** two thousand baths.
7:38 of bronze; each basin **h** forty baths,
8:65 So Solomon **h** the festival at that time,
2Ki 18: 6 For he **h** fast to the LORD;
2Ch 4: 5 like the flower of a lily; it **h** three thousand baths.
7: 8 At that time Solomon **h** the festival for seven days,
7: 9 On the eighth day they **h** a solemn assembly;
11:12 So he **h** Judah and Benjamin.
Ne 4:16 and half **h** the spears, shields, bows,
4:17 on the work with one hand and with the other **h**
4:21 and half of them **h** the spears from break of dawn
Est 5: 2 and he **h** out to her the golden scepter that was
7: 4 men and women, I would have **h** my peace;
8: 4 The king **h** out the golden scepter to Esther,
Job 23:11 My foot has **h** fast to his steps;
Ps 17: 5 My steps have **h** fast to your paths;
39: 2 I was silent and still; I **h** my peace to no avail;
94:18 your steadfast love, O LORD, **h** me up.
106:46 to be pitied by all who **h** them captive.
Pr 30:10 and you will be **h** guilty.
SS 3: 4 I **h** him, and would not let him go
7: 5 a king is **h** captive in the tresses.
Isa 38:17 but you have **h** back my life from the pit
42:14 For a long time I have **h** my peace,
53: 3 and we **h** him of no account.
65: 2 I **h** out my hands all day long to
Jer 2: 3 All who ate of it were **h** guilty;
8: 5 They have **h** fast to deceit,
50:33 all their captors have **h** them fast and refuse
Mk 15: 1 the chief priests **h** a consultation with the elders
Jn 19:29 on a branch of hyssop and **h** it to his mouth.
Ac 2:24 it was impossible for him to be **h** in its power.
4:32 but everything they owned was **h** in common.
5:13 but the people **h** them in high esteem.
25:21 to be **h** until I could send him to the emperor."
Ro 3:19 and the whole world may be **h** accountable to God.
7: 6 dead to that which **h** us captive,
10:21 "All day long I have **h** out my hands to
1Co 4:10 You are **h** in honor, but we in disrepute.
Col 2:19 and **h** together by its ligaments and sinews,
2Ti 2:26 having been **h** captive by him to do his will.
Heb 2:15 and free those who all their lives were **h** in slavery
13: 4 Let marriage be **h** in honor by all,
Rev 1:16 In his right hand he **h** seven stars,
6: 5 Its rider **h** a pair of scales in his hand,
9:15 who had been **h** ready for the hour, the day,
10: 2 He **h** a little scroll open in his hand.
Jdt 12:10 On the fourth day Holofernes **h** a banquet
AdE 1: 5 This was **h** for six days in the courtyard of
1: 6 **h** by cords of purple linen attached to gold
9: 4 that Mordecai's name be **h** in honor throughout
11:11 lowly were exalted and devoured those **h** in honor.
Wis 3:17 Even if they live long they will be **h** of no account,
5: 4 "These are persons whom we once **h** in derision
15:12 and life a festival **h** for profit,
17: 2 For when lawless people supposed that they **h**
17: 4 even the inner chamber that **h** them protected them
18:23 he intervened and **h** back the wrath,
Sir 1:19 she heightened the glory of those who **h** her fast.
9:12 that they will not be **h** guiltless all their lives.
11:10 you will not be **h** blameless.
24: 6 and over every people and nation I have **h** sway.

Sir 49: 9 also mentioned Job who **h** fast to all the ways
50:13 of Aaron in their splendor **h** the Lord's offering
50:15 he **h** out his hand for the cup and poured
1Mc 3:45 The sanctuary was trampled down, and aliens **h**
13:15 in connection with the offices he **h**,
2Mc 4:18 When the quadrennial games were being **h** at Tyre
12:24 because he **h** the parents of most of them,
14:22 so they duly **h** the consultation.
1Es 4:50 up the villages of the Jews that they **h**;
3Mc 7:16 But those who had **h** fast to God even to death
7:21 being **h** in honor and awe;
7:22 so that those who **h** any of it restored it to them
2Es 2:43 And I was **h** spellbound.
5:15 the angel who had come and talked with me **h** me
6: 8 for Jacob's hand **h** Esau's heel from the beginning.
9:35 but the things that **h** them remain;
11:18 and **h** the rule as the earlier ones had done,
11:40 you have **h** sway over the world with great terror,
13: 9 he neither lifted his hand nor **h** a spear
16:69 And those who consent to eat shall be **h** in derision
4Mc 1:10 for the honor in which they are **h**.
4: 1 Onias, who then **h** the high priesthood for life.
5:18 not truly divine and we had wrongly **h** it to
7: 4 with many ingenious war machines has ever **h** out
15:26 this mother **h** two ballots, one bearing death and
17: 3 you **h** firm and unswerving against the earthquake

HELDAI (3)

1Ch 27:15 for the twelfth month, was **H** the Netophathite,
Zec 6:10 from **H,** Tobijah, and Jedaiah—
6:14 And the crown shall be in the care of **H,** Tobijah,

HELEB (1) [=HELED]

2Sa 23:29 **H** son of Baanah of Netophah;

HELECH (1)

Eze 27:11 of Arvad and **H** were on your walls all around;

HELED (1) [=HELEB]

1Ch 11:30 **H** son of Baanah of Netophah,

HELEK (2) [HELEKITES]

Nu 26:30 of **H,** the clan of the Helekites;
Jos 17: 2 by their families, Abiezer, **H,** Asriel, Shechem,

HELEKITES (1) [HELEK]

Nu 26:30 of Helek, the clan of the **H;**

HELEM[‡] (1)

1Ch 7:35 The sons of **H** his brother:

HELEPH (1)

Jos 19:33 And its boundary ran from **H,**

HELEZ (5)

2Sa 23:26 **H** the Paltite; Ira son of Ikkesh of Tekoa;
1Ch 2:39 Azariah became the father of **H,** and **H** of Eleasah.
11:27 Shammoth of Harod, **H** the Pelonite,
27:10 for the seventh month, was **H** the Pelonite,

HELI (1)

Lk 3:23 the son (as was thought) of Joseph son of **H,**

HELIODORUS (12) [HELIODORUS'S]

2Mc 3: 7 king chose **H,** who was in charge of his affairs,
3: 8 **H** at once set out on his journey,
3:13 But **H,** because of the orders he had from the king,
3:23 **H** went on with what had been decided.
3:25 at **H** and struck at him with its front hoofs.
3:32 by the Jews with regard to **H,**
3:33 the same young men appeared again to **H** dressed
3:35 Then **H** offered sacrifice to the Lord
3:37 When the king asked **H** what sort of person would
3:40 the episode of **H** and the protection of the treasury,
4: 1 that it was he who had incited **H** and had been
5:18 **H** had been, whom King Seleucus sent to inspect

HELIODORUS'S (1) [HELIODORUS]

2Mc 3:31 Some of **H** friends quickly begged Onias to call

HELIOPOLIS (1) [=ON]

Jer 43:13 He shall break the obelisks of **H,**

HELKAI (1)

Ne 12:15 of Harim, Adna; of Meraioth, **H;**

HELKATH (2)

Jos 19:25 Its boundary included **H,** Hali, Beten, Achshaph,
21:31 **H** with its pasture lands, and Rehob

HELKATH-HAZZURIM (1)

2Sa 2:16 that place was called **H,** which is at Gibeon.

HELL[‡] (15)

Mt 5:22 'You fool,' you will be liable to the **h** of fire.
5:29 for your whole body to be thrown into **h.**
5:30 for your whole body to go into **h.**
10:28 both soul and body in **h.**
18: 9 to have two eyes and to be thrown into the **h**
Mt 23:15 the new convert twice as much a child of **h**
23:33 How can you escape being sentenced to **h?**
Mk 9:43 to have two hands and to go to **h,**
9:45 to have two feet and to be thrown into **h.**
9:47 to have two eyes and to be thrown into **h,**
Lk 12: 5 after he has killed, has authority to cast into **h.**
Jas 3: 6 and is itself set on fire by **h.**
2Pe 2: 4 but cast them into **h** and committed them to chains
2Es 2:29 so that your children may not see **h.**
7:*36* and the furnace of **h** shall be disclosed,

HELLENISTS (3) [HELLENIZATION]

Ac 6: 1 the **H** complained against the Hebrews
9:29 He spoke and argued with the **H;**
11:20 spoke to the **H** also, proclaiming the Lord Jesus.

HELLENIZATION (1) [HELLENISTS]

2Mc 4:13 of **H** and increase in the adoption of foreign ways

HELMET (11) [HELMETS]

1Sa 17: 5 He had a **h** of bronze on his head,
17:38 he put a bronze **h** on his head and clothed him with
Ps 60: 7 Ephraim is my **h;** Judah is my scepter.
108: 8 Ephraim is my **h;** Judah is my scepter.
Isa 59:17 and a **h** of salvation on his head;
Eze 23:24 and **h,** and I will commit the judgment to them,
27:10 they hung shield and **h** in you;
38: 5 all of them with buckler and **h;**
Eph 6:17 Take the **h** of salvation, and the sword of
1Th 5: 8 and for a **h** the hope of salvation.
Wis 5:18 and wear impartial justice as a **h;**

HELMETS (3) [HELMET]

2Ch 26:14 **h,** coats of mail, bows, and stones for slinging.
Jer 46: 4 Take your stations with your **h,** whet your lances,
1Mc 6:35 and with brass **h** on their heads;

HELON (5)

Nu 1: 9 From Zebulun, Eliab son of **H.**
2: 7 leader of the Zebulunites shall be Eliab son of **H,**
7:24 On the third day Eliab son of **H,**
7:29 This was the offering of Eliab son of **H.**
10:16 of the tribe of Zebulun was Eliab son of **H.**

HELP[‡] (260) [HELPED, HELPER, HELPERS, HELPFUL, HELPING, HELPLESS, HELPLESSNESS, HELPS]

Ge 4: 1 "I have produced a man with the **h** of the LORD."
49:25 by the God of your father, who will **h** you,
Ex 2:23 Out of the slavery their cry for **h** rose up to God.
18: 4 "The God of my father was my **h,**
21:19 but recovers and walks around outside with the **h**
23: 5 you must **h** to set it free.
Nu 1:44 whom Moses and Aaron enrolled with the **h** of
Dt 22: 3 You may not withhold your **h.**
22: 4 you shall **h** to lift it up.
22:24 the young woman because she did not cry for **h** in
22:27 the engaged woman may have cried for **h,**
28:29 and robbed, without anyone to **h.**
28:31 be given to your enemies, without anyone to **h** you.
32:38 Let them rise up and **h** you,
33: 7 and be a **h** against his adversaries.
33:26 who rides through the heavens to your **h,**
33:29 shield of your **h,** and the sword of your triumph!
Jos 1:14 over armed before your kindred and shall **h** them,
10: 4 "Come up and **h** me, and let us attack Gibeon;
10: 6 come up to us quickly, and save us, and **h** us;
10:33 Then King Horam of Gezer came up to **h** Lachish;
Jdg 4: 3 Then the Israelites cried out to the LORD for **h;**
5:23 because they did not come to the **h** of the LORD, to
the **h** of the LORD against the mighty.
6: 6 and the Israelites cried out to the LORD for **h.**
6:22 and Gideon said, **"H** me, Lord GOD!
2Sa 8: 5 of Damascus came to **h** King Hadadezer of Zobah,
10:11 too strong for me, then you shall **h** me;
10:11 then I will come and **h** you.
10:19 So the Arameans were afraid to **h**
14: 4 to the ground and did obeisance, and said, **"H,**
18: 3 it is better that you send us **h** from the city."
22:36 and your **h** has made me great.
23: 5 not cause to prosper all my **h** and my desire?
2Ki 6:26 a woman cried out to him, **"H,** my lord king!"
6:27 Let the LORD **h** you.
6:27 How can I **h** you?
14:26 bond or free, and no one to **h** Israel.
15:19 of silver, so that he might **h** him confirm his hold
1Ch 5:20 and when they received **h** against them,
12:17 "If you have come to me in friendship, to **h** me,
12:19 (Yet he did not **h** them,
12:22 to day people kept coming to David to **h** him,
12:33 to **h** David with singleness of purpose.
18: 5 of Damascus came to **h** King Hadadezer of Zobah,
19:12 for me, then you shall **h** me;
19:12 for you, then I will **h** you.
19:19 not willing to **h** the Ammonites any more.
22:17 the leaders of Israel to **h** his son Solomon,
2Ch 14:11 **H** us, O LORD our God, for we rely on you,
16:12 but sought **h** from physicians.
19: 2 "Should you **h** the wicked and love those who hate
20: 4 Judah assembled to seek **h** from the LORD;
25: 8 for God has power to **h** or to overthrow."
26:13 to **h** the king against the enemy.
28:16 to the king of Assyria for **h.**
2Ch 28:21 but it did not **h** him.
28:23 I will sacrifice to them so that they may **h** me."
32: 8 to **h** us and to fight our battles."
Ne 6:16 that this work had been accomplished with the **h**
Job 6:13 In truth I have no **h** in me,
24:12 and the throat of the wounded cries for **h;**
26: 4 With whose **h** have you uttered words,
30:24 when in disaster they cry for **h.**
30:28 I stand up in the assembly and cry for **h.**
35: 9 they call for **h** because of the arm of the mighty.
36:13 they do not cry for **h** when he binds them.
Ps 3: 2 "There is no **h** for you in God."
12: 1 **H,** O LORD, for there is no longer anyone who is
18: 6 to my God I cried for **h.**
18:35 your **h** has made me great.
18:41 for **h,** but there was no one to save them;
20: 2 May he send you **h** from the sanctuary,
20: 6 Now I know that the LORD will **h** his anointed;
21: 1 O LORD, and in your **h** how greatly he exults!
21: 5 His glory is great through your **h;**
22:11 for trouble is near and there is no one to **h.**
22:19 O my **h,** come quickly to my aid!
27: 9 you who have been my **h.**
28: 2 as I cry to you for **h,**
30: 2 O LORD my God, I cried to you for **h,**
31:22 when I cried out to you for **h.**
33:20 he is our **h** and shield.
34:17 When the righteous cry for **h,** the LORD hears,
35: 2 and rise up to **h** me!
38:22 make haste to **h** me, O Lord, my salvation.
40:10 I have not hidden your saving **h** within my heart,
40:13 O LORD, make haste to **h** me.
40:17 You are my **h** and my deliverer;
42: 5 for I shall again praise him, my **h**
42:11 for I shall again praise him, my **h** and my God.
43: 5 for I shall again praise him, my **h** and my God.
44:26 Rise up, come to our **h.**
46: 1 a very present **h** in trouble.
46: 5 God will **h** it when the morning dawns.
59: 4 Rouse yourself, come to my **h** and see!
60:11 O grant us **h** against the foe, for human **h** is
worthless.
63: 7 for you have been my **h,**
69:13 answer me. With your faithful **h**
70: 1 O LORD, make haste to **h** me!
70: 5 You are my **h** and my deliverer;
71:12 O my God, make haste to **h** me!
71:24 of your righteous **h,** for those who tried
79: 9 **H** us, O God of our salvation,
88: 4 I am like those who have no **h,**
88:12 or your saving **h** in the land of forgetfulness?
94:17 If the LORD had not been my **h,**
106: 4 **h** me when you deliver them;
107:12 they fell down, with no one to **h.**
108:12 O grant us **h** against the foe, for human **h** is
worthless.
109:26 **H** me, O LORD my God!
115: 9 He is their **h** and their shield.
115:10 He is their **h** and their shield.
115:11 He is their **h** and their shield.
118: 7 The LORD is on my side to **h** me;
119:86 I am persecuted without cause; **h** me!
119:147 I rise before dawn and cry for **h;**
119:173 Let your hand be ready to **h** me,
119:175 and let your ordinances **h** me.
121: 1 from where will my **h** come?
121: 2 My **h** comes from the LORD,
124: 8 Our **h** is in the name of the LORD,
146: 3 in mortals, in whom there is no **h.**
146: 5 Happy are those whose **h** is the God of Jacob,
Pr 20:22 wait for the LORD, and he will **h** you.
Ecc 4:10 and falls and does not have another to **h.**
Isa 10: 3 To whom will you flee for **h,**
20: 6 and to whom we fled for **h** and deliverance from
22: 5 down of walls and a cry for **h** to the mountains.
30: 5 that brings neither **h** nor profit,
30: 7 For Egypt's **h** is worthless and empty,
31: 1 for those who go down to Egypt for **h** and who rely
38:13 I cry for **h** until morning;
41:10 I will strengthen you, I will **h** you,
41:13 it is I who say to you, "Do not fear, I will **h** you."
41:14 I will **h** you, says the LORD;
44: 2 who formed you in the womb and will **h** you:
57:12 but they will not **h** you.
58: 9 you shall cry for **h,** and he will say, Here I am.
Jer 14: 9 like a mighty warrior who cannot give **h?**
37: 7 Pharaoh's army, which set out to **h** you,
La 1: 7 and there was no one to **h** her,
3: 8 though I call and cry for **h,** he shuts out my prayer;
3:56 "Do not close your ear to my cry for **h,**
4:17 Our eyes failed, ever watching vainly for **h;**
Eze 17:17 and great company will not **h** him in war,
30: 8 and all who **h** it are broken.
Da 8:16 "Gabriel, **h** this man understand the vision."
10:13 Michael, one of the chief princes, came to **h** me,
10:14 and have come to **h** you understand what is
11:34 When they fall victim, they shall receive a little **h,**
11:39 He shall deal with the strongest fortresses by the **h**
11:45 Yet he shall come to his end, with no one to **h** him.
Hos 13: 9 I will destroy you, O Israel; who can **h** you?
Hab 1: 2 O LORD, how long shall I cry for **h,**
Zec 6:15 Those who are far off shall come and **h** to build
Mt 15:25 and knelt before him, saying, "Lord, **h** me."
Mk 9:22 have pity on us and **h** us."
9:24 "I believe; **h** my unbelief!"
Lk 5: 7 in the other boat to come and **h** them.
10:40 Tell her then to **h** me."

Ac 12: 9 with the angel's **h** was real;
16: 9 "Come over to Macedonia and **h** us."
17: 5 and with the **h** of some ruffians in
21:28 "Fellow Israelites, **h!** This is the man
26:22 To this day I have had **h** from God,
27:34 for it will **h** you survive;
Ro 16: 2 and **h** her in whatever she may require from you,
Php 1:10 to **h** you to determine what is best,
1:19 the **h** of the Spirit of Jesus Christ this will turn out
4: 3 my loyal companion, **h** these women,
4:16 you sent me **h** for my needs more than once.
1Th 5:14 encourage the faint hearted, **h** the weak,
2Ti 1:14 with the **h** of the Holy Spirit living in us.
Heb 2:16 For it is clear that he did not come to **h** angels,
2:18 he is able to **h** those who are being tested.
4:16 so that we may receive mercy and find grace to **h**
1Jn 3:17 a brother or sister in need and yet refuses **h?**
Rev 12:16 But the earth came to the **h** of the woman;
Jdt 6:21 all that night they called on the God of Israel for **h.**
7:25 For now we have no one to **h** us;
7:31 But if these days pass by, and no **h** comes for us,
8:15 he does not choose to **h** us within these five days,
8:17 let us call upon him to **h** us,
9: 4 pollution of their blood and called on you for **h—**
13: 5 Now indeed is the time to **h** your heritage and
AdE 4:14 **h** and protection will come to the Jews
14: 3 **h** me, who am alone and have no helper but you,
14:14 But save us by your hand, and **h** me,
Wis 2:18 if the righteous man is God's child, he will **h** him,
13:16 because he knows that it cannot **h** itself,
13:16 for it is only an image and has need of **h.**
16:10 for your mercy came to their **h** and healed them.
19:22 and you have not neglected to **h** them at all times
Sir Pr: 1 be able through the spoken and written word to **h**
2: 6 Trust in him, and he will **h** you;
3:12 My child, **h** your father in his old age,
4:11 Wisdom teaches her children and gives **h**
8:16 and where no **h** is at hand,
11:12 There are others who are slow and need **h,**
12: 4 Give to the devout, but do not **h** the sinner.
12: 7 but do not **h** the sinner.
12:17 pretending to **h,** he will trip you up.
25:18 and he cannot **h** sighing bitterly.
29: 4 and cause trouble to those who **h** them.
29: 9 **H** the poor for the commandment's sake,
31:18 do not **h** yourself before they do.
34:19 a guard against stumbling and a **h** against falling.
37: 5 Some companions **h** a friend
40:26 and with it there is no need to seek for **h.**
51: 7 and there was no one to **h** me;
51:10 when there is no **h** against the proud.
Bar 4:17 But I, how can I **h** you?
LtJ 6:58 and they will not be able to **h** themselves.
6:68 for they can flee to shelter and **h** themselves.
1Mc 3:15 of godless men went up with him to **h** him,
3:53 if you do not **h** us?"
5:39 They also have hired Arabs to **h** them,
7: 7 and let him punish them and all who **h** them."
7:20 of the country and left with him a force to **h** him;
8:13 Those whom they wish to **h** and to make kings,
8:32 If now they appeal again for **h** against you,
10:24 so that I may have their **h."**
10:74 and his brother Simon met him to **h** him.
11:43 you will do well to send me men who will **h** me,
12:15 we have the **h** that comes from Heaven for our aid,
14: 1 and marched into Media to obtain **h,**
14:14 He gave **h** to all the humble among his people;
16: 3 may the **h** that comes from Heaven be with you."
2Mc 3:28 but was now unable to **h** himself.
8:19 of the occasions when **h** came to their ancestors;
8:20 by the **h** that came to them from heaven,
8:23 and gave the watchword, "The **h** of God";
8:35 the **h** of the Lord by opponents whom he regarded
11:19 in the future to **h** promote your welfare.
12:11 Judas and his companions, with God's **h,**
12:11 promising to give him livestock and to **h** his people
13:10 to **h** those who were on the point of being deprived
13:13 to march out and decide the matter by the **h** of God
13:17 because the Lord's **h** protected him.
15: 7 to trust with all confidence that he would get **h**
15: 8 in mind the former times when **h** had come to them
15:35 a clear and conspicuous sign to everyone of the **h**
1Es 4:48 and to **h** him build the city.
6: 2 with the **h** of the prophets of the Lord who were
6:28 to **h** those who have returned from the exile
8:27 I was encouraged by the **h** of the Lord my God,
3Mc 2:33 They remained resolutely hopeful of obtaining **h,**
2:33 depriving them of companionship and mutual **h.**
3: 8 were not strong enough to **h** them,
4:16 even to communicate or to come to one's **h,**
5:25 the supreme God to **h** them again at once.
5:50 when they considered the **h** that they had received
2Es 2:18 I will send you **h,** my servants Isaiah
3: 4 when you planted the earth—and that without **h—**
16:33 daughters shall mourn, because they have no **h.**
4Mc 3: 3 but reason can **h** to deal with anger.
14:17 to **h** their young by flying in circles around them in

HELPED (29) [HELP]

Ex 2:19 "An Egyptian **h** us against the shepherds;
1Sa 7:12 for he said, "Thus far the LORD has **h** us."
1Ch 12: 1 they were among the mighty warriors who **h** him
12:21 They **h** David against the band of raiders,
15:26 And because God **h** the Levites who were carrying
2Ch 18:31 and Jehoshaphat cried out, and the LORD **h** him.
20:23 they all **h** to destroy one another.
2Ch 26: 7 God **h** him against the Philistines,
26:15 for he was marvelously **h** until he became strong.
28:23 "Because the gods of the kings of Aram **h** them,
29:34 the Levites, **h** them until the work was finished—
32: 3 that were outside the city; and they **h** him.
Ne 8: 7 the Levites, **h** the people to understand the law,
Job 26: 2 "How you have **h** one who has no power!
Ps 28: 7 so I am **h,** and my heart exults,
86:17 LORD, have **h** me and comforted me.
118:13 so that I was falling, but the LORD **h** me.
Isa 31: 3 the helper will stumble, and the one **h** will fall,
49: 8 on a day of salvation I have **h** you;
Lk 1:54 He has **h** his servant Israel,
Ac 9:41 He gave her his hand and **h** her up.
18:27 On his arrival he greatly **h** those who
2Co 6: 2 and on a day of salvation I have **h** you."
Php 1:12 that what has happened to me has actually **h**
1Ti 5:10 washed the saints' feet, **h** the afflicted,
1Mc 3: 2 and all who had joined his father **h** him;
1Es 2: 6 be **h** by the people of your place with gold
2: 9 their neighbors **h** them with everything,
3Mc 2:12 when our fathers were oppressed you **h** them

HELPER‡ (21) [HELP]

Ge 2:18 I will make him a **h** as his partner."
2:20 for the man there was not found a **h** as his partner.
37: 2 he was a **h** to the sons of Bilhah and Zilpah,
Job 29:12 and the orphan who had no **h.**
Ps 10:14 you have been the **h** of the orphan.
30:10 O LORD, be my **h!"**
54: 4 God is my **h;** the Lord is the upholder of my life.
72:12 the poor and those who have no **h.**
Isa 31: 3 LORD stretches out his hand, the **h** will stumble,
63: 5 I looked, but there was no **h;**
Jer 47: 4 from Tyre and Sidon every **h** that remains.
Heb 13: 6 "The Lord is my **h;** I will not be afraid.
Tob 8: 6 for him you made his wife Eve as a **h** and support.
8: 6 let us make a **h** for him like himself.'
Jdt 9:11 you are the God of the lowly, **h** of the oppressed,
AdE 14: 3 help me, who am alone and have no **h** but you,
14:14 and help me, who am alone and have no **h** but you,
Sir 36:29 a **h** fit for him and a pillar of support.
51: 2 and **h** and have delivered me from destruction and
51: 2 In the face of my adversaries you have been my **h**
1Mc 12:53 for they said, "They have no leader or **h.**

HELPERS‡ (7) [HELP]

Job 9:13 the **h** of Rahab bowed beneath him.
Isa 31: 2 and against the **h** of those who work iniquity.
Eze 12:14 his **h** and all his troops;
32:21 mighty chiefs shall speak of them, with their **h,**
Na 3: 9 Put and the Libyans were her **h.**
Ac 19:22 So he sent two of his **h,** Timothy and Erastus,
Sir 40:24 Kindred and **h** are for a time of trouble,

HELPFUL (1) [HELP]

Ac 20:20 I did not shrink from doing anything **h,**

HELPING (7) [HELP]

2Ch 14:11 there is no difference for you between **h** the mighty
Ezr 5: 2 and with them were the prophets of God, **h** them.
Ps 22: 1 Why are you so far from **h** me,
Lk 18: 7 Will he delay long in **h** them?
2Co 1:11 as you also join in **h** us by your prayers,
Sir 29: 1 a **h** hand they keep the commandments.
1Mc 10:72 and who the others are that are **h** us.

HELPLESS (10) [HELP]

Ps 10: 8 Their eyes stealthily watch for the **h;**
10:10 they crouch, and the **h** fall by their might.
10:14 the **h** commit themselves to you;
Jer 6:24 "We have heard news of them, our hands fall **h;**
50:43 of them, and his hands fell **h;**
Mt 9:36 because they were harassed and **h,**
Wis 12: 6 these parents who murder **h** lives,
LtJ 6:28 but give none to the poor or **h.**
2Mc 7: 5 When he was utterly **h,** the king ordered them
3Mc 2:22 so that he lay **h** on the ground and,

HELPLESSNESS (1) [HELP]

3Mc 2:13 subjected to our enemies, and overtaken by **h.**

HELPS‡ (11) [HELP]

1Ch 12:18 peace to you, and peace to the one who **h** you!
12:18 For your God is the one who **h** you."
Ps 37:40 The LORD **h** them and rescues them;
Ecc 10:10 but wisdom **h** one to succeed.
Isa 41: 6 Each one **h** the other, saying to one another,
50: 7 The Lord GOD **h** me;
50: 9 It is the Lord GOD who **h** me;
Ro 8:26 Likewise the Spirit **h** us in our weakness;
Jdt 8:11 to our enemies unless the Lord turns and **h** us
Wis 17:12 but a giving up of the **h** that come from reason;
4Mc 2:14 from marauders and **h** raise up what has fallen.

HEM (11) [HEMMED, HEMMING]

Ex 28:33 On its lower **h** you shall make pomegranates
28:33 purple, and crimson yarns, all around the lower **h,**
28:34 a pomegranate alternating all around the lower **h** of
39:24 the lower **h** of the robe they made pomegranates
39:25 the bells between the pomegranates on the lower **h**
39:26 a bell and a pomegranate all around on the lower **h**
1Sa 15:27 Saul caught hold of the **h** of his robe, and it tore.
Ps 139: 5 You **h** me in, behind and before,
Isa 6: 1 and the **h** of his robe filled the temple.
Lk 19:43 and **h** you in on every side.
1Mc 4:31 **H** in this army by the hand of your people Israel,

HEMAN (18)

Ge 36:22 The sons of Lotan were Hori and **H;**
1Ki 4:31 and **H,** Calcol, and Darda, children of Mahol;
1Ch 2: 6 Zimri, Ethan, **H,** Calcol, and Dara, five in all.
6:33 **H,** the singer, son of Joel, son of Samuel,
15:17 So the Levites appointed **H** son of Joel;
15:19 The singers **H,** Asaph, and Ethan were
16:41 With them were **H** and Jeduthun,
16:42 **H** and Jeduthun had with them trumpets
25: 1 and of **H,** and of Jeduthun,
25: 4 Of **H,** the sons of **H:** Bukkiah,
25: 5 All these were the sons of **H** the king's seer,
25: 5 for God had given **H** fourteen sons
25: 6 Jeduthun, and **H** were under the order of the king.
2Ch 5:12 Asaph, **H,** and Jeduthun, their sons and kindred,
29:14 and of the sons of **H,** Jehuel and Shimei;
35:15 and Asaph, and **H,** and the king's seer Jeduthun.
Ps 88: T *A Maskil of **H** the Ezrahite.*

HEMATH (KJV) See HAMMATH, LEBO-HAMATH

HEMDAN (1)

Ge 36:26 **H,** Eshban, Ithran, and Cheran.

HEMLOCK (KJV) See POISON, POISONOUS

HEMMED (2) [HEM]

1Mc 3:18 "It is easy for many to be **h** in by few,
11:65 and fought against it for many days and **h** it in.

HEMMING (1) [HEM]

1Mc 6:18 in the citadel kept **h** Israel in around the sanctuary.

HEMORRHAGE (2) [HEMORRHAGES]

Mk 5:29 Immediately her **h** stopped;
Lk 8:44 and immediately her **h** stopped.

HEMORRHAGES (3) [HEMORRHAGE]

Mt 9:20 a woman who had been suffering from **h**
Mk 5:25 a woman who had been suffering from **h**
Lk 8:43 a woman who had been suffering from **h**

HEN‡ (5)

Lev 11:18 the water **h,** the desert owl, the carrion vulture,
Dt 14:16 the little owl and the great owl, the water **h**
Mt 23:37 as a **h** gathers her brood under her wings,
Lk 13:34 as a **h** gathers her brood under her wings,
2Es 1:30 as a **h** gathers her chicks under her wings.

HENA (3)

2Ki 18:34 Where are the gods of Sepharvaim, **H,** and Ivvah?
19:13 the king of the city of Sepharvaim, the king of **H,**
Isa 37:13 the king of the city of Sepharvaim, the king of **H,**

HENADAD (4)

Ezr 3: 9 Binnui and Hodaviah along with the sons of **H,**
Ne 3:18 After him their kin made repairs: Binnui, son of **H,**
3:24 Binnui son of **H** repaired another section,
10: 9 Jeshua son of Azaniah, Binnui of the sons of **H,**

HENCE (5) [HENCEFORTH]

Lk 7:47 **h** she has shown great love.
Ro 1:15 **—h** my eagerness to proclaim the gospel to you
1Co 8: 4 **H,** as to the eating of food offered to idols,
Heb 8: 3 **h** it is necessary for this priest also
9:18 **H** not even the first covenant was inaugurated

HENCE (KJV) See also AWAY, FROM HERE, LEAVE, PLACE

HENCEFORTH (6) [HENCE]

Isa 43:13 I am God, and also **h** I am He;
1Mc 10:30 I release them from this day and **h.**
11:35 And the other payments **h** due to us of the tithes,
15: 8 be canceled for you from **h** and for all time.
2Es 7:99 of the souls of the righteous, as **h** is announced;
14: 9 and **h** you shall live with my Son and

HENNA (2)

SS 1:14 My beloved is to me a cluster of **h** blossoms in
4:13 of pomegranates with all choicest fruits, **h**

HENOCH (KJV) See HANOCH

HEPHER (9) [GATH-HEPHER, HEPHERITES]

Nu 26:32 and of **H,** the clan of the Hepherites.
26:33 Zelophehad son of **H** had no sons, but daughters:
27: 1 Zelophehad was son of **H** son of Gilead son
Jos 12:17 the king of Tappuah one the king of **H** one

Jos 17: 2 Abiezer, Helek, Asriel, Shechem, **H,** and Shemida;
17: 3 Now Zelophehad son of **H** son of Gilead son
1Ki 4: 10 (to him belonged Socoh and all the land of **H);**
1Ch 4: 6 **H,** Temeni, and Haahashtari.
11: 36 **H** the Mecherathite, Ahijah the Pelonite,

HEPHERITES (1) [HEPHER]

Nu 26: 32 and of Hepher, the clan of the **H.**

HEPHZIBAH‡ (1)

2Ki 21: 1 His mother's name was **H.**

HER (2182) [SHE] See Index of Articles Etc.

HERALD (10)

2Ch 36: 22 a **h** throughout all his kingdom and also declared in
Ezr 1: 1 so that he sent a **h** throughout all his kingdom,
Isa 40: 9 O Zion, **h** of good tidings;
40: 9 O Jerusalem, **h** of good tidings, lift it up,
41: 27 and I give to Jerusalem a **h** of good tidings.
Da 3: 4 the **h** proclaimed aloud, "You are commanded,
1Ti 2: 7 a **h** and an apostle (I am telling the truth,
2Ti 1: 11 For this gospel I was appointed a **h** and an apostle
2Pe 2: 5 even though he saved Noah, a **h** of righteousness,
4Mc 6: 4 while a **h** who faced him cried out,

HERB (3) [HERBAGE, HERBS]

Ge 2: 5 the earth and no **h** of the field had yet sprung up—
Ps 37: 2 and wither like the green **h.**
Wis 16: 12 For neither **h** nor poultice cured them,

HERBAGE (3) [HERB]

Pr 27: 25 and the **h** of the mountains is gathered,
Isa 42: 15 and dry up all their **h;**
Jer 14: 6 their eyes fail because there is no **h.**

HERBS (4) [HERB]

Ex 12: 8 over the fire with unleavened bread and bitter **h.**
Nu 9: 11 they shall eat it with unleavened bread and bitter **h.**
2Ki 4: 39 One of them went out into the field to gather **h;**
Lk 11: 42 For you tithe mint and rue and **h** of all kinds,

HERCULES (2)

2Mc 4: 19 silver drachmas for the sacrifice to **H.**
4: 20 by the sender for the sacrifice to **H,**

HERD (30) [HERDERS, HERDS, HERDSMAN]

Ge 18: 7 Abraham ran to the **h,** and took a calf,
Lev 1: 2 you shall bring your offering from the **h** or from
1: 3 If the offering is a burnt offering from the **h,**
3: 1 if you offer an animal of the **h,**
4: 3 a bull of the **h** without blemish as a sin offering to
4: 14 a bull of the **h** for a sin offering and bring it before
22: 21 from the **h** or from the flock,
22: 28 you shall not slaughter, from the **h** or the flock,
27: 32 All tithes of **h** and flock,
Nu 15: 3 an offering by fire to the LORD from the **h** or
Dt 12: 21 of your **h** or flock that the LORD has given you,
14: 23 as well as the firstlings of your **h** and flock,
15: 19 of your **h** and flock you shall consecrate to
16: 2 from the flock and the **h,**
32: 14 curds from the **h,** and milk from the flock, with fat
2Sa 12: 4 and he was loath to take one of his own flock or **h**
17: 29 sheep, and cheese from the **h,**
Est 8: 10 on fast steeds bred from the royal **h.**
Ps 68: 30 the **h** of bulls with the calves of the peoples.
Jer 31: 12 and over the young of the flock and the **h;**
Jnh 3: 7 No human being or animal, no **h** or flock,
Hab 3: 17 the flock is cut off from the fold and there is no **h**
Mt 8: 30 a large **h** of swine was feeding at some distance
8: 31 "If you cast us out, send us into the **h** of swine."
8: 32 the whole **h** rushed down the steep bank into
Mk 5: 11 on the hillside a great **h** of swine was feeding;
5: 13 and the **h,** numbering about two thousand,
Lk 8: 32 on the hillside a large **h** of swine was feeding;
8: 33 and the **h** rushed down the steep bank into the lake
Tob 8: 19 and he went out to the **h** and brought two steers

HERDERS (6) [HERD]

Ge 13: 7 the **h** of Abram's livestock and the **h** of Lot's
13: 8 and between your **h** and my **h;**
26: 20 the **h** of Gerar quarreled with Isaac's **h,**

HERDS (42) [HERD]

Ge 13: 5 also had flocks and **h** and tents,
24: 35 he has given him flocks and **h,** silver and gold,
26: 14 He had possessions of flocks and **h,**
32: 7 and the flocks and **h** and camels,
33: 13 that the children are frail and that the flocks and **h,**
34: 28 They took their flocks and their **h,** their donkeys,
45: 10 as well as your flocks, your **h,**
46: 32 and they have brought their flocks, and their **h,**
47: 1 with their flocks and **h** and all that they possess,
47: 17 the flocks, the **h,** and the donkeys.
47: 18 and the **h** of cattle are my lord's.
50: 8 and their **h** were left in the land of Goshen.
Ex 9: 3 the horses, the donkeys, the camels, the **h,**
10: 9 and daughters and with our flocks and **h,**
10: 24 Only your flocks and your **h** shall remain behind.
12: 32 Take your flocks and your **h,** as you said,
Ex 12: 38 and livestock in great numbers, both flocks and **h.**
34: 3 not let flocks or **h** graze in front of that mountain."
Nu 11: 22 Are there enough flocks and **h** to slaughter
Dt 8: 13 and when your **h** and flocks have multiplied,
12: 6 and the firstlings of your **h** and flocks.
12: 17 the firstlings of your **h** and your flocks,
Jos 14: 4 with their pasture lands for their flocks and **h.**
1Sa 30: 20 David also captured all the flocks and **h,**
2Sa 12: 2 The rich man had very many flocks and **h;**
1Ch 27: 29 Over the **h** that pastured in Sharon was Shitrai
27: 29 Over the **h** in the valleys was Shaphat son of Adlai.
2Ch 26: 10 and hewed out many cisterns, for he had large **h,**
32: 29 and flocks and **h** in abundance;
Ne 10: 36 and the firstlings of our **h** and of our flocks;
Pr 27: 23 and give attention to your **h;**
Ecc 2: 7 I also had great possessions of **h** and flocks,
Isa 65: 10 and the Valley of Achor a place for **h** to lie down,
Jer 3: 24 their flocks and their **h,** their sons
5: 17 they shall eat up your flocks and your **h;**
49: 32 their **h** of cattle a spoil.
Hos 5: 6 With their flocks and **h** they shall go to seek
12: 1 Ephraim **h** the wind, and pursues
Joel 1: 18 The **h** of cattle wander about
Zep 2: 14 **H** shall lie down in it, every wild animal;
Jdt 2: 27 and destroyed their flocks and **h**
3: 3 and our flocks and **h** and all our encampments lie

HERDSMAN (1) [HERD, MAN]

Am 7: 14 but I am a **h,** and a dresser of sycamore trees,

HERE‡ (392) [HEREAFTER, HEREBY, HEREIN]

Ge 12: 19 Now then, **h** is your wife, take her, and be gone."
15: 16 they shall come back **h** in the fourth generation;
19: 9 And they said, "This fellow came **h** as an alien,
19: 12 the men said to Lot, "Have you anyone else **h?**
19: 15 take your wife and your two daughters who are **h,**
21: 23 now therefore swear to me **h** by God that you will
22: 1 And he said, **"H** I am."
22: 5 Then Abraham said to his young men, "Stay **h**
22: 7 And he said, **"H** I am, my son."
22: 7 He said, "The fire and the wood are **h,**
22: 11 And he said, **"H** I am."
24: 13 I am standing **h** by the spring of water,
24: 43 I am standing **h** by the spring of water;
27: 1 and he answered, **"H** I am."
27: 18 and he said, **"H** I am; who are you, my son?"
29: 6 "Yes," they replied, "and **h** is his daughter Rachel,
30: 3 Then she said, **"H** is my maid Bilhah;
31: 11 'Jacob,' and I said, **'H** I am!'
31: 37 Set it **h** before my kinsfolk and your kinsfolk,
37: 13 He answered, **"H** I am."
37: 19 They said to one another, **"H** comes this dreamer.
37: 22 throw him into this pit **h** in the wilderness,
38: 21 But they said, "No prostitute has been **h."**
38: 22 the townspeople said, 'No prostitute has been **h.'** "
39: 8 and said to his master's wife, "Look, with me **h,**
40: 15 and **h** also I have done nothing
42: 15 **H** is how you shall be tested:
42: 15 unless your youngest brother comes **h!**
42: 19 of your brothers stay **h** where you are imprisoned.
42: 28 **h** it is in my sack!"
44: 16 **h** we are then, my lord's slaves,
45: 5 or angry with yourselves, because you sold me **h;**
45: 8 So it was not you who sent me **h,** but God;
45: 13 Hurry and bring my father down **h."**
46: 2 And he said, **"H** I am."
47: 23 **h** is seed for you; sow the land.
48: 9 "They are my sons, whom God has given me **h."**
48: 11 and **h** God has let me see your children also."
50: 18 and said, "We are **h** as your slaves."
50: 25 you shall carry up my bones from **h."**
Ex 3: 4 And he said, **"H** I am."
11: 1 afterwards he will let you go from **h;**
13: 19 then you must carry my bones with you from **h."**
24: 14 To the elders he had said, "Wait **h** for us,
33: 15 do not carry us up from **h.**
Nu 14: 40 the heights of the hill country, saying, "**H** we are.
20: 4 for us and our livestock to die **h?**
20: 16 and **h** we are in Kadesh,
22: 8 He said to them, "Stay **h** tonight,
22: 19 You remain **h,** as the others did,
23: 1 Balaam said to Balak, "Build me seven altars **h,**
23: 3 "Stay **h** beside your burnt offerings
23: 9 **H** is a people living alone, and not reckoning itself
23: 15 "Stand **h** beside your burnt offerings,
23: 29 Balaam said to Balak, "Build me seven altars **h,**
31: 16 These women **h,** on Balaam's advice,
32: 6 "Shall your brothers go to war while you sit **h?**
32: 16 "We will build sheepfolds **h** for our flocks,
Dt 5: 3 but with us, who are all of us **h** alive today.
5: 31 But you, stand **h** by me, and I will tell you all
9: 12 "Get up, go down quickly from **h,**
12: 8 You shall not act as we are acting **h** today,
20: 15 which are not towns of the nations **h.**
22: 17 But **h** is the evidence of my daughter's virginity."
29: 14 not only with you who stand **h** with us today
29: 15 but also with those who are not **h** with us today.
Jos 2: 2 "Some Israelites have come **h** tonight to search out
4: 3 'Take twelve stones from **h** out of the middle of
4: 22 'Israel crossed over the Jordan **h** on dry ground.'
9: 12 **H** is our bread; it was still warm
14: 10 and **h** I am today, eighty-five years old.
17: 9 The towns **h,** to the south of the wadi,
18: 6 in seven divisions and bring the description **h**
Jos 18: 6 for you **h** before the LORD our God.
18: 8 and I will cast lots for you **h** before the LORD
23: 7 that you may not be mixed with these nations left **h**
23: 12 the survivors of these nations left **h** among you,
Jdg 4: 20 if anybody comes and asks you, 'Is anyone **h?'**
6: 18 Do not depart from **h** until I come to you,
6: 26 on the top of the stronghold **h,** in proper order;
8: 15 and said, **"H** are Zebah and Zalmunna,
14: 15 Have you invited us **h** to impoverish us?"
16: 2 The Gazites were told, "Samson has come **h."**
18: 3 over and asked him, "Who brought you **h?**
18: 3 What is your business **h?"**
19: 9 Spend the night **h** and enjoy yourself.
19: 24 **H** are my virgin daughter and his concubine;
20: 7 all of you, give your advice and counsel **h."**
Ru 2: 14 At mealtime Boaz said to her, "Come **h,**
3: 2 Now **h** is our kinsman Boaz,
4: 1 So Boaz said, "Come over, friend; sit down **h."**
4: 2 and said, "Sit down **h";** so they sat down.
4: 4 Buy it in the presence of those sitting **h,**
1Sa 1: 26 the woman who was standing **h** in your presence,
3: 4 and he said, **"H** I am!"
3: 5 ran to Eli, and said, **"H** I am, for you called me."
3: 6 Samuel got up and went to Eli, and said, **"H** I am,
3: 8 And he got up and went to Eli, and said, **"H** I am,
3: 16 He said, **"H** I am."
4: 3 of the covenant of the LORD **h** from Shiloh,
9: 8 The boy answered Saul again, **"H,**
9: 11 and said to them, "Is the seer **h?"**
9: 17 **"H** is the man of whom I spoke to you.
9: 27 stop **h** yourself for a while,
10: 22 of the LORD, "Did the man come **h?"**
12: 3 **H** I am; testify against me
12: 13 See, **h** is the king whom you have chosen,
13: 9 So Saul said, "Bring the burnt offering **h** to me,
14: 18 Saul said to Ahijah, "Bring the ark of God **h."**
14: 33 roll a large stone before me **h."**
14: 34 and slaughter them **h,** and eat;
14: 36 But the priest said, "Let us draw near to God **h."**
14: 38 Saul said, "Come **h,** all you leaders of the people;
14: 43 that was in my hand; **h** I am,
15: 32 "Bring Agag king of the Amalekites **h** to me."
16: 11 Samuel said to Jesse, "Are all your sons **h?"**
16: 11 for we will not sit down until he comes **h."**
18: 17 Saul said to David, **"H** is my elder daughter Merab
21: 3 Give me five loaves of bread, or whatever is **h."**
21: 8 "Is there no spear or sword **h** with you?
21: 9 is **h** wrapped in a cloth behind the ephod;
21: 9 take it, for there is none **h** except that one."
22: 12 He answered, **"H** I am, my lord."
23: 3 "Look, we are afraid **h** in Judah;
23: 9 he said to the priest Abiathar, "Bring the ephod **h."**
24: 4 **"H** is the day of which the LORD said to you,
26: 22 David replied, **"H** is the spear, O king!
29: 3 "What are these Hebrews doing **h?"**
29: 4 Would it not be with the heads of the men **h?**
30: 26 **"H** is a present for you from the spoil of
2Sa 1: 7 to me. I answered, **'H** sir.'
1: 10 and I have brought them **h** to my lord."
1: 15 "Come **h** and strike him down."
4: 8 **"H** is the head of Ishbaal, son of Saul, your enemy,
5: 6 who said to David, "You will not come in **h,**
5: 6 thinking, "David cannot come in **h."**
11: 12 Then David said to Uriah, "Remain **h** today also,
14: 32 Come **h,** that I may send you to the king with
15: 26 But if he says, 'I take no pleasure in you,' **h** I am,
18: 30 The king said, "Turn aside, and stand **h."**
19: 37 But **h** is your servant Chimham;
20: 4 to me within three days, and be **h** yourself."
20: 16 Tell Joab, 'Come **h,** I want to speak to you.' "
24: 22 **h** are the oxen for the burnt offering,
1Ki 1: 23 The king was told, **"H** is the prophet Nathan."
2: 30 But he said, "No, I will die **h."**
12: 28 **H** are your gods, O Israel, who brought you up out
17: 3 "Go from **h** and turn eastward,
18: 8 Go, tell your lord that Elijah is **h."**
18: 10 and when they would say, 'He is not **h,'**
18: 11 now you say, 'Go, tell your lord that Elijah is **h.'**
18: 14 now you say, 'Go, tell your lord that Elijah is **h';**
19: 9 saying, "What are you doing **h,** Elijah?"
19: 13 "What are you doing **h,** Elijah?"
20: 40 your servant was busy **h** and there, he was gone."
22: 7 of the LORD **h** of whom we may inquire?"
2Ki 2: 2 Elijah said to Elisha, "Stay **h;**
2: 4 Elijah said to him, "Elisha, stay **h;**
2: 6 Then Elijah said to him, "Stay **h;**
3: 11 "Is there no prophet of the LORD **h,**
3: 11 to pour water on the hands of Elijah, is **h."**
7: 3 "Why should we sit **h** until we die?
7: 4 but if we sit **h,** we shall also die.
7: 13 since those left **h** will suffer the fate of
8: 5 Gehazi said, "My lord king, **h** is the woman,
8: 5 and **h** is her son whom Elisha restored to life."
8: 7 it was told him, "The man of God has come **h,"**
10: 23 and see that there is no worshiper of the LORD **h**
1Ch 11: 5 "You will not come in **h."**
22: 1 **"H** shall be the house of the LORD God and here
22: 1 of the LORD God and **h** the altar of burnt offering
28: 21 **H** are the divisions of the priests and the Levites
29: 17 now I have seen your people, who are present **h,**
2Ch 18: 6 of the LORD **h** of whom we may inquire?"
23: 3 Jehoiada said to them, **"H** is the king's son!
28: 13 "You shall not bring the captives in **h,**
Ezr 4: 2 King Esar-haddon of Assyria who brought us **h."**
9: 15 **H** we are before you in our guilt,
Ne 9: 36 **H** we are, slaves to this day—
Job 31: 35 to hear me! **(H** is my signature!

Job 38:11 and **h** shall your proud waves be stopped'?
38:35 so that they may go and say to you, '**H** we are'?
Ps 40: 7 Then I said, "**H** I am;
132:14 **h** I will reside, for I have desired it.
Pr 9: 4 that are simple, turn in **h**!" To those
9:16 "You who are simple, turn in **h**!"
25: 7 "Come up **h**," than to be put lower in the presence
Isa 5:26 **H** they come, swiftly, speedily!
6: 8 And I said, "**H** am I; send me!"
22:16 What right do you have **h**?
22:16 Who are your relatives **h**, that you have cut out a tomb **h** for yourself,
28:10 line upon line, line upon line, **h** a little,
28:13 line upon line, line upon line, **h** a little,
35: 4 **H** is your God. He will come with vengeance,
40: 9 say to the cities of Judah, "**H** is your God!"
42: 1 **H** is my servant, whom I uphold, my chosen,
52: 5 Now therefore what am I doing **h**,
52: 6 that it is I who speak; **h** am I.
57: 3 come **h**, you children of a sorceress,
58: 9 you shall cry for help, and he will say, **H** I am.
65: 1 I said, "**H** I am, **h** I am,"
Jer 3:22 "**H** we come to you; for you are the LORD our God.
4:16 Tell the nations, "**H** they are!"
7: 8 **H** you are, trusting in deceptive words to no avail.
14:13 **H** are the prophets saying to them,
16:12 for **h** you are, every one of you,
22:11 He shall return **h** no more,
26:14 But as for me, **h** I am in your hands.
31: 8 a great company, they shall return **h**.
38: 5 King Zedekiah said, "**H** he is;
38:10 "Take three men with you from **h**,
La 4:15 "They shall stay **h** no longer."
Eze 8: 6 that the house of Israel are committing **h**,
8: 9 the vile abominations that they are committing **h**."
8:17 of Judah commits the abominations done **h**?
40: 4 for you were brought **h** in order
Da 3:26 of the Most High God, come out! Come **h**!"
7:28 **H** the account ends.
Zec 3: 7 of access among those who are standing **h**.
6:12 **H** is a man whose name is Branch:
Mt 8:29 Have you come **h** to torment us before the time?"
12: 6 I tell you, something greater than the temple is **h**.
12:18 "**H** is my servant, whom I have chosen,
12:41 and see, something greater than Jonah is **h**!
12:42 and see, something greater than Solomon is **h**!
12:49 he said, "**H** are my mother and my brothers!
14: 8 the head of John the Baptist **h** on a platter."
14:17 "We have nothing **h** but five loaves and two fish."
14:18 And he said, "Bring them **h** to me."
16:28 there are some standing **h** who will not taste death
17: 4 Peter said to Jesus, "Lord, it is good for us to be **h**;
17: 4 if you wish, I will make three dwellings **h**,
17:17 Bring him **h** to me."
17:20 'Move from **h** to there,' and it will move;
20: 6 'Why are you standing **h** idle all day?'
22:12 how did you get in **h** without a wedding robe?'
24: 2 not one stone will be left **h** upon another;
24:23 to you, 'Look! **H** is the Messiah!'
25: 6 'Look! **H** is the bridegroom!
25:25 **H** you have what is yours.'
26:36 "Sit **h** while I go over there and pray."
26:38 remain **h**, and stay awake with me."
26:50 "Friend, do what you are **h** to do."
28: 6 He is not **h**; for he has been raised, as he said.
Mk 3:34 he said, "**H** are my mother and my brothers!
6: 3 and are not his sisters **h** with us?"
8: 4 "How can one feed these people with bread **h** in
9: 1 there are some standing **h** who will not taste death
9: 5 "Rabbi, it is good for us to be **h**;
10:49 Jesus stood still and said, "Call him **h**."
11: 3 and will send it back **h** immediately.' "
13: 2 Not one stone will be left **h** upon another;
13:21 that time, 'Look! **H** is the Messiah!'
14:32 and he said to his disciples, "Sit **h** while I pray."
14:34 remain **h**, and keep awake."
16: 6 He has been raised; he is not **h**.
Lk 1:38 Then Mary said, "**H** am I, the servant of the Lord;
4: 9 throw yourself down from **h**,
4:23 'Do **h** also in your hometown the things
6: 8 the withered hand, "Come and stand **h**."
9:12 for we are **h** in a deserted place."
9:27 there are some standing **h** who will not taste death
9:33 "Master, it is good for us to be **h**;
9:41 with you? Bring your son **h**."
11:31 and see, something greater than Solomon is **h**!
11:32 and see, something greater than Jonah is **h**!
13: 7 So he said to the gardener, 'See **h**!
13:31 "Get away from **h**, for Herod wants to kill you."
15:17 but **h** I am dying of hunger!
16:25 but now he is comforted **h**, and you are in agony.
16:26 so that those who might want to pass from **h**
17: 7 'Come **h** at once and take your place at the table'?
17:21 nor will they say, 'Look, **h** it is!'
17:23 'Look there!' or 'Look **h**!'
19:20 the other came, saying, 'Lord, **h** is your pound.
19:27 bring them **h** and slaughter them
19:30 Untie it and bring it **h**.
22:38 They said, "Lord, look, **h** are two swords."
23:14 and **h** I have examined him in your presence
24: 5 He is not **h**, but has risen.
24:41 he said to them, "Have you anything **h** to eat?"
24:49 so stay **h** in the city until you have been clothed
Jn 1:29 "**H** is the Lamb of God who takes away the sin of
1:36 he exclaimed, "Look, **h** is the Lamb of God!"
1:47 "**H** is truly an Israelite in whom there is no deceit!"
2:16 "Take these things out of **h**!
Jn 3:26 **h** he is baptizing, and all are going to him."
4:15 or have to keep coming **h** to draw water."
4:23 But the hour is coming, and is now **h**,
4:37 For **h** the saying holds true,
5:25 I tell you, the hour is coming, and is now **h**,
6: 9 a boy **h** who has five barley loaves and two fish.
6:25 they said to him, "Rabbi, when did you come **h**?"
7: 3 "Leave **h** and go to Judea so that your disciples
7: 6 but your time is always **h**.
7:26 And **h** he is, speaking openly,
8:42 for I came from God and now I am **h**.
9:30 The man answered, "**H** is an astonishing thing!
11:21 Martha said to Jesus, "Lord, if you had been **h**,
11:28 "The Teacher is **h** and is calling for you."
11:32 and said to him, "Lord, if you had been **h**,
11:42 for the sake of the crowd standing **h**,
18:36 But as it is, my kingdom is not from **h**."
19: 5 Pilate said to them, "**H** is the man!"
19:14 He said to the Jews, "**H** is your King!"
19:26 he said to his mother, "Woman, **h** is your son."
19:27 Then he said to the disciple, "**H** is your mother."
20:27 "Put your finger **h** and see my hands.
Ac 5:28 yet **h** you have filled Jerusalem with your teaching
8:36 and the eunuch said, "Look, **h** is water!
9:10 He answered, "**H** I am, Lord."
9:14 and **h** he has authority from the chief priests
9:17 who appeared to you on your way **h**,
9:21 not come **h** for the purpose of bringing them bound
9:32 as Peter went **h** and there among all the believers,
10:33 now all of us are **h** in the presence of God to listen
16:28 "Do not harm yourself, for we are all **h**."
17: 6 the world upside down have come **h** also,
19:37 these men **h** who are neither temple robbers
24:19 to be **h** before you to make an accusation,
24:20 Or let these men **h** tell what crime they had found
25:14 "There is a man **h** who was left in prison by Felix.
25:17 So when they met **h**, I lost no time,
25:24 "King Agrippa and all **h** present with us,
25:24 both in Jerusalem and **h**, shouting that he ought not
26: 6 And now I stand **h** on trial on account of my hope
26:22 and so I stand **h**, testifying to both small and great,
28:21 and none of the brothers coming **h** has reported
2Co 12:14 **H** I am, ready to come to you this third time.
Php 1:16 that I have been put **h** for the defense of the gospel;
Col 4: 9 They will tell you about everything **h**.
2Th 2: 2 to the effect that the day of the Lord is already **h**.
Heb 2:13 in him." And again, "**H** am I and
13:14 For **h** we have no lasting city,
Jas 2: 3 the fine clothes and say, "Have a seat **h**, please,"
Rev 4: 1 up **h**, and I will show you what must take place
11:12 from heaven saying to them, "Come up **h**!"
13:10 **H** is a call for the endurance and faith of the saints.
14:12 **H** is a call for the endurance of the saints,
Tob 2: 3 And I replied, "**H** I am, my child."
2: 8 yet **h** he is again burying the dead!"
5: 5 he replied, "and I have come **h** to work."
6:11 "**H** I am," he answered.
8:20 "You shall not leave **h** for fourteen days,
8:20 but shall stay **h** eating and drinking with me;
10: 6 Do not grieve for him, my dear; he will soon be **h**."
14:8,9 So now, my son, leave Nineveh; do not remain **h**.
Jdt 9: 6 on presented themselves and said, '**H** we are!'
9: 7 "**H** now are the Assyrians, a greatly increased
12: 3 For none of your people are **h** with us."
13:15 and said, "See **h**, the head of Holofernes,
13:15 and **h** is the canopy beneath which he lay
AdE 14:18 since the day that I was brought **h** until now,
Wis 18:18 and one **h** and another there, hurled
Sir 29:26 "Come **h**, stranger, prepare the table;
29:27 "Be off, stranger, for an honored guest is **h**;
31:12 and do not say, "How much food there is **h**!"
Bar 1:10 They said: **H** we send you money;
3:34 he called them, and they said, "**H** we are!"
1Mc 2:65 "**H** is your brother Simeon who, I know,
3:52 **H** the Gentiles are assembled against us
6:13 **h** I am, perishing of bitter disappointment in
12:45 For that is why I am **h**."
2Mc 1: 6 We are now praying for you **h**.
9:25 and I have written to him what is written **h**.
14: 7 mean the high priesthood—and have now come **h**,
14:33 and build **h** a splendid temple to Dionysus."
15:37 So I will **h** end my story.
15:39 And **h** will be the end.
1Es 5:69 of the Assyrians, who brought us **h**."
6:20 Then this Sheshbazzar, after coming **h**,
6:34 that it be done with all diligence as **h** prescribed."
3Mc 1:20 and nurses abandoned even newborn children **h**
3:21 to all our amnesty toward their compatriots **h**, both
4:16 and foolishly gathered every one of them **h**?
2Es 3:29 I came **h** I saw ungodly deeds without number,
4:12 to be **h** than to come **h** and live in ungodliness,
4:35 saying, 'How long are we to remain **h**?
7:*38* **h** are delight and rest, and there are fire
10: 4 I intend not to return to the town, but to stay **h**;
10:18 I will not go into the city, but I will die **h**."
10:58 But tomorrow night you shall remain **h**,
12:39 But as for you, wait **h** seven days more,
14: 2 I answered, "**H** I am, Lord," and I rose to my feet.
14:25 and you shall come **h**, and I will light in your heart
14:33 And now you are **h**, and your people are farther in
4Mc 4: 3 "I have come **h** because I am loyal to
10:19 **h** is my tongue; cut it off,
17: 9 "**H** lie buried an aged priest and an aged woman

HEREAFTER (11) [HERE]

Isa 41:23 Tell us what is to come **h**,
Eze 20:39 Go serve your idols, everyone of you now and **h**,
Da 2:29 came thoughts of what would be **h**,
2:45 great God has informed the king what shall be **h**.
AdE 13: 7 government completely secure and untroubled **h**."
16:23 that both now and **h** it may represent deliverance
Wis 2: 2 and **h** we shall be as though we had never been,
2Es 7:*99* that those who would not give heed shall suffer **h**."
8:46 things that are future are for those who will live **h**.
14:16 that you have now seen happen shall take place **h**.
14:20 but who will warn those who will be born **h**?

HEREAFTER (KJV) See also AFTER, AGAIN, FROM NOW ON, LATER, LONGER, TO COME

HEREBY (6) [HERE]

Ex 34:10 He said: I **h** make a covenant.
Nu 3:12 I **h** accept the Levites from among the Israelites
25:12 say, 'I **h** grant him my covenant of peace.
Jos 1: 9 I **h** command you: Be strong
Jdg 1: 2 I **h** give the land into his hand."
6:14 from the hand of Midian; I **h** commission you."

HEREDITARY (1)

Tob 6:12 have before all other men a **h** claim on her.

HEREIN (1) [HERE]

1Es 6:32 or nullify any of the things **h** written,

HEREIN (KJV) See also HERE, THIS

HERES (1)

Jdg 8:13 from the battle by the ascent of **H**,

HERESH (1)

1Ch 9:15 **H**, Galal, and Mattaniah son of Mica, son of Zichri,

HERETH (1)

1Sa 22: 5 So David left, and went into the forest of **H**.

HERETICK (KJV) See CAUSES DIVISIONS

HERETOFORE (KJV) See BEFORE, IN THE PAST, PREVIOUSLY

HERITAGE‡ (59) [HERITAGES]

Jos 18: 7 for the priesthood of the LORD is their **h**;
1Sa 10: 1 that the LORD has anointed you ruler over his **h**:
26:19 from my share in the **h** of the LORD,
2Sa 14:16 both me and my son off from the **h** of God.'
20:19 why will you swallow up the **h** of the LORD?"
21: 3 that you may bless the **h** of the LORD?"
1Ki 8:51 (for they are your people and **h**,
8:53 to be your **h**, just as you promised through Moses,
2Ki 21:14 I will cast off the remnant of my **h**,
Job 20:29 the **h** decreed for them by God."
27:13 the **h** that oppressors receive from the Almighty:
31: 2 and my **h** from the Almighty on high?
Ps 2: 8 Ask of me, and I will make the nations your **h**,
16: 6 in pleasant places; I have a goodly **h**.
28: 9 O save your people, and bless your **h**;
33:12 the people whom he has chosen as his **h**.
37:18 and their **h** will abide forever;
47: 4 He chose our **h** for us,
61: 5 the **h** of those who fear your name.
68: 9 you restored your **h** when it languished;
74: 2 which you redeemed to be the tribe of your **h**.
78:62 and vented his wrath on his **h**.
94: 5 O LORD, and afflict your **h**.
94:14 he will not abandon his **h**;
106: 5 that I may glory in your **h**.
106:40 against his people, and he abhorred his **h**;
111: 6 in giving them the **h** of the nations.
119:111 Your decrees are my **h** forever;
127: 3 Sons are indeed a **h** from the LORD,
135:12 and gave their land as a **h**, a **h** to his people Israel.
136:21 as a **h**, for his steadfast love endures forever;
136:22 a **h** to his servant Israel,
Isa 19:25 the work of my hands, and Israel my **h**."
47: 6 I was angry with my people, I profaned my **h**;
54:17 This is the **h** of the servants of the LORD
58:14 I will feed you with the **h** of your ancestor Jacob,
63:17 for the sake of the tribes that are your **h**.
Jer 2: 7 and made my **h** an abomination.
3:18 to the land that I gave your ancestors for a **h**.
3:19 the most beautiful **h** of all the nations.
12: 7 I have forsaken my house, I have abandoned my **h**;
12: 8 My **h** has become to me like a lion in the forest;
12: 9 Is the hyena greedy for my **h** at my command?
12:14 the **h** that I have given my people Israel to inherit:
12:15 I will bring them again to their **h** and to their land,
17: 4 By your own act you shall lose the **h**
50:11 though you exult, O plunderers of my **h**,
Joel 2:17 O LORD, and do not make your **h** a mockery,
3: 2 on account of my people and my **h** Israel,
Mal 1: 3 I have made his hill country a desolation and his **h**
Ac 7: 5 He did not give him any of it as a **h**,
Jdt 9:12 God of the **h** of Israel, Lord of heaven and earth,
13: 5 the time to help your **h** and to carry out my design
Sir 24:12 in the portion of the Lord, his **h**.

Sir 45:20 He added glory to Aaron and gave him a **h;**
45:25 that the king's **h** passes only from son to son, so the **h** of Aaron is for his descendants alone.
2Mc 14:15 and always upholds his own **h**

HERITAGES (1) [HERITAGE]

Isa 49: 8 to establish the land, to apportion the desolate **h;**

HERMAS (1)

Ro 16:14 Greet Asyncritus, Phlegon, Hermes, Patrobas, **H,**

HERMES (2)

Ac 14:12 Barnabas they called Zeus, and Paul they called **H,**
Ro 16:14 Greet Asyncritus, Phlegon, **H,** Patrobas, Hermas,

HERMOGENES (1)

2Ti 1:15 including Phygelus and **H.**

HERMON (24) [BAAL-HERMON, =SENIR, =SIRION]

Dt 3: 8 from the Wadi Arnon to Mount **H**
3: 9 (the Sidonians call **H** Sirion,
4:48 as far as Mount Sirion (that is, **H**),
Jos 11: 3 and the Hivites under **H** in the land of Mizpah.
11:17 in the valley of Lebanon below Mount **H.**
12: 1 from the Wadi Arnon to Mount **H,**
12: 5 over Mount **H** and Salecah and all Bashan to
13: 5 from Baal-gad below Mount **H** to Lebo-hamath,
13:11 and all Mount **H,** and all Bashan to Salecah;
1Ch 5:23 from Bashan to Baal-hermon, Senir, and Mount **H.**
Ps 42: 6 I remember you from the land of Jordan and of **H,**
89:12 Tabor and **H** joyously praise your name.
133: 3 It is like the dew of **H,**
SS 4: 8 from the peak of Senir and **H,**
Sir 24:13 and like a cypress on the heights of **H.**
3Mc 5: 1 so he summoned **H,** keeper of the elephants,
5: 4 And **H,** keeper of the elephants,
5:10 **H,** however, when he had drugged
5:18 the king summoned **H** and
5:23 **H,** having equipped the animals,
5:26 **H** arrived and invited him to come out,
5:29 Then **H** and all the king's Friends pointed out that
5:33 So **H** suffered an unexpected and dangerous threat,
5:37 After summoning **H** he said in a threatening tone,

HEROD (42) [HEROD'S, HERODIANS]

Mt 2: 1 In the time of King **H,**
2: 3 When King **H** heard this, he was frightened,
2: 7 Then **H** secretly called for the wise men
2:12 having been warned in a dream not to return to **H,**
2:13 **H** is about to search for the child, to destroy him."
2:15 and remained there until the death of **H.**
2:16 **H** saw that he had been tricked by the wise men,
2:19 When **H** died, an angel of the Lord suddenly
2:22 over Judea in place of his father **H,**
14: 1 At that time **H** the ruler heard reports about Jesus;
14: 3 For **H** had arrested John, bound him,
14: 5 Though **H** wanted to put him to death,
14: 6 before the company, and she pleased **H**
Mk 6:14 **H** heard of it, for Jesus' name had become known.
6:16 But when **H** heard of it, he said, "John,
6:17 For **H** himself had sent men who arrested John,
6:17 because **H** had married her.
6:18 For John had been telling **H,**
6:20 for **H** feared John, knowing that he was a righteous
6:21 an opportunity came when **H** on his birthday gave
6:22 she pleased **H** and his guests;
8:15 of the yeast of the Pharisees and the yeast of **H.**"
Lk 1: 5 In the days of King **H** of Judea,
3: 1 and **H** was ruler of Galilee,
3:19 But **H** the ruler, who had been rebuked by him
3:19 and because of all the evil things that **H** had done,
9: 7 **H** the ruler heard about all that had taken place,
9: 9 **H** said, "John I beheaded;
13:31 "Get away from here, for **H** wants to kill you."
23: 7 he sent him off to **H,**
23: 8 When **H** saw Jesus, he was very glad,
23:11 **H** with his soldiers treated him with contempt
23:12 That same day **H** and Pilate became friends
23:15 Neither has **H,** for he sent him back to us.
Ac 4:27 For in this city, in fact, both **H** and Pontius Pilate,
12: 1 About that time King **H** laid violent hands
12: 6 very night before **H** was going to bring him out,
12:11 and rescued me from the hands of **H** and from all
12:19 **H** had searched for him and could not find him,
12:20 **H** was angry with the people of Tyre and Sidon.
12:21 On an appointed day **H** put on his royal robes,
13: 1 Manaen a member of the court of **H** the ruler,

HEROD'S (4) [HEROD]

Mt 14: 6 But when **H** birthday came,
Lk 8: 3 the wife of **H** steward Chuza, and Susanna,
23: 7 when he learned that he was under **H** jurisdiction,
Ac 23:35 that he be kept under guard in **H** headquarters.

HERODIANS‡ (3) [HEROD]

Mt 22:16 they sent their disciples to him, along with the **H,**
Mk 3: 6 and immediately conspired with the **H** against him,
12:13 Then they sent to him some Pharisees and some **H**

HERODIAS (6)

Mt 14: 3 bound him, and put him in prison on account of **H,**
14: 6 the daughter of **H** danced before the company,
Mk 6:17 bound him, and put him in prison on account of **H,**
6:19 And **H** had a grudge against him,
6:22 When his daughter **H** came in and danced,
Lk 3:19 who had been rebuked by him because of **H,**

HERODION (1)

Ro 16:11 Greet my relative **H.** Greet those in the Lord

HEROES‡ (3) [HEROIC]

Ge 6: 4 These were the **h** that were of old,
Isa 5:22 you who are **h** in drinking wine and valiant
Jer 48:14 can you say, "We are **h** and mighty warriors"?

HEROIC (1) [HEROES]

1Mc 5:56 and of the **h** war they had fought.

HERON (2)

Lev 11:19 the **h** of any kind, the hoopoe, and the bat.
Dt 14:18 the **h,** of any kind; the hoopoe and the bat.

HERS (4) [SHE]

Ge 3:15 and between your offspring and **h;**
Nu 30: 5 no vow of **h,** and no pledge
2Ki 8: 6 saying, "Restore all that was **h,**
La 1: 7 all the precious things that were **h** in days of old.

HERSELF (72) [SHE] See Index of Articles Etc.

HESED (KJV) See BEN-HESED

HESHBON (39)

Nu 21:25 in **H,** and in all its villages.
21:26 For **H** was the city of King Sihon of the Amorites,
21:27 the ballad singers say, "Come to **H,** let it be built;
21:28 fire came out from **H,** flame from the city of Sihon.
21:30 So their posterity perished from **H** to Dibon,
21:34 to King Sihon of the Amorites, who ruled in **H.**"
32: 3 Dibon, Jazer, Nimrah, **H,** Elealeh, Sebam, Nebo,
32:37 And the Reubenites rebuilt **H,** Elealeh, Kiriathaim,
Dt 1: 4 who reigned in **H,** and King Og of Bashan,
2:24 over to you King Sihon the Amorite of **H,**
2:26 the wilderness of Kedemoth to King Sihon of **H**
2:30 But King Sihon of **H** was not willing to let us pass
3: 2 to King Sihon of the Amorites, who reigned in **H.**"
3: 6 as we had done to King Sihon of **H,**
4:46 the Amorites, who reigned at **H,** whom Moses and
29: 7 King Sihon of **H** and King Og of Bashan came out
Jos 9:10 beyond the Jordan, King Sihon of **H,** and King Og
12: 2 King Sihon of the Amorites who lived at **H,**
12: 5 of Gilead to the boundary of King Sihon of **H.**
13:10 in **H,** as far as the boundary of the Ammonites;
13:17 with **H,** and all its towns that are in the tableland;
13:21 of King Sihon of the Amorites, who reigned in **H,**
13:26 and from **H** to Ramath-mizpeh and Betonim,
13:27 the rest of the kingdom of King Sihon of **H,**
21:39 **H** with its pasture lands, Jazer
Jdg 11:19 to King Sihon of the Amorites, king of **H;**
11:26 While Israel lived in **H** and its villages,
1Ch 6:81 **H** with its pasture lands, and Jazer
Ne 9:22 of King Sihon of **H** and the land of King Og
SS 7: 4 Your eyes are pools in **H,** by the gate of
Isa 15: 4 **H** and Elealeh cry out, their voices are heard as far
16: 8 For the fields of **H** languish,
16: 9 I drench you with my tears, O **H** and Elealeh;
Jer 48: 2 In **H** they planned evil against her:
48:34 **H** and Elealeh cry out; as far
48:45 In the shadow of **H** fugitives stop exhausted;
48:45 for a fire has gone out from **H,**
49: 3 Wail, O **H,** for Ai is laid waste!
Jdt 5:15 by their might destroyed all the inhabitants of **H;**

HESHMON (1)

Jos 15:27 Hazar-gaddah, **H,** Beth-pelet,

HESITANT (1) [HESITATE]

Sir 4: 9 and do not be **h** in giving a verdict.

HESITATE‡ (4) [HESITANT, HESITATION]

Job 30:10 they do not **h** to spit at the sight of me.
Tob 12:13 when you did not **h** to get up and leave your dinner
Jdt 12:13 "Let this pretty girl not **h** to come to my lord to
Sir 7:35 Do not **h** to visit the sick,

HESITATION (1) [HESITATE]

Ac 10:20 get up, go down, and go with them without **h;**

HETH (2) [HITTITE, HITTITES]

Ge 10:15 the father of Sidon his firstborn, and **H,**
1Ch 1:13 the father of Sidon his firstborn, and **H,**

HETHLON (2)

Eze 47:15 from the Great Sea by way of **H** to Lebo-hamath,
48: 1 Beginning at the northern border, on the **H** road,

HEW (4) [HEWED, HEWERS, HEWN, ROCK-HEWN]

Dt 6:11 hewn cisterns that you did not **h,**
7: 5 smash their pillars, **h** down their sacred poles,
12: 3 and **h** down the idols of their gods,
Isa 18: 5 and the spreading branches he will **h** away.

HEW (KJV) See also CARVE, CUT, PREPARED

HEWED (6) [HEW]

Ge 50: 5 In the tomb that I **h** out for myself in the land
1Sa 15:33 And Samuel **h** Agag in pieces before the LORD
2Ch 14: 3 broke down the pillars, **h** down the sacred poles,
26:10 in the wilderness and **h** out many cisterns,
31: 1 to the cities of Judah and broke down the pillars, **h**
Isa 5: 2 and **h** out a wine vat in it;

HEWER[S] (KJV) See also CUT, STONECUTTERS

HEWERS (3) [HEW]

Jos 9:21 So they became **h** of wood and drawers of water
9:23 **h** of wood and drawers of water for the house
9:27 that day Joshua made them **h** of wood and drawers

HEWN (17) [HEW]

Ex 20:25 do not build it of **h** stones;
Dt 6:11 **h** cisterns that you did not hew,
2Ch 16:14 in the tomb that he had **h** out for himself in the city
Ezr 5: 8 It is being built of **h** stone,
6: 4 with three courses of **h** stones and one course
Ne 9:25 **h** cisterns, vineyards, olive orchards,
Pr 9: 1 she has **h** her seven pillars.
Isa 51: 1 Look to the rock from which you were **h,**
La 3: 9 he has blocked my ways with **h** stones,
Eze 40:42 also four tables of **h** stone for the burnt offering,
Hos 6: 5 Therefore I have **h** them by the prophets,
Am 5:11 you have built houses of **h** stone,
Mt 27:60 which he had **h** in the rock.
Mk 15:46 laid it in a tomb that had been **h** out of the rock.
Jdt 1: 2 with **h** stones three cubits thick and six cubits long;
1Es 6: 9 of **h** stone, with costly timber laid in the walls.
6:25 of **h** stone and one course of new native timber;

HEZEKI (KJV) See HIZKI

HEZEKIAH (140)

2Ki 16:20 of David; his son **H** succeeded him.
18: 1 **H** son of King Ahaz of Judah began to reign.
18: 9 In the fourth year of King **H,**
18:10 In the sixth year of **H,**
18:13 In the fourteenth year of King **H,**
18:14 King **H** of Judah sent to the king of Assyria
18:14 of King **H** of Judah three hundred talents of silver
18:15 **H** gave him all the silver that was found in
18:16 At that time **H** stripped the gold from the doors of
18:16 that King **H** of Judah had overlaid and gave it to
18:17 a great army from Lachish to King **H** at Jerusalem.
18:19 The Rabshakeh said to them, "Say to **H:**
18:22 and altars **H** has removed, saying to Judah and
18:29 Thus says the king: 'Do not let **H** deceive you,
18:30 not let **H** make you rely on the LORD by saying,
18:31 not listen to **H;** for thus says the king of Assyria:
18:32 not listen to **H** when he misleads you by saying,
18:37 to **H** with their clothes torn and told him the words
19: 1 When King **H** heard it, he tore his clothes,
19: 3 They said to him, "Thus says **H,**
19: 5 When the servants of King **H** came to Isaiah,
19: 9 he sent messengers again to **H,** saying,
19:10 "Thus shall you speak to King **H** of Judah:
19:14 **H** received the letter from the hand of
19:14 then **H** went up to the house of the LORD
19:15 And **H** prayed before the LORD, and said:
19:20 Then Isaiah son of Amoz sent to **H,** saying,
20: 1 In those days **H** became sick and was at the point
20: 2 Then **H** turned his face to the wall and prayed to
20: 3 in your sight." **H** wept bitterly.
20: 5 and say to **H** prince of my people
20: 8 **H** said to Isaiah, "What shall be the sign that
20:10 **H** answered, "It is normal for the shadow
20:12 with letters and a present to **H,**
20:12 for he had heard that **H** had been sick.
20:13 **H** welcomed them; he showed them all his treasure
20:13 or in all his realm that **H** did not show them.
20:14 Then the prophet Isaiah came to King **H,**
20:14 **H** answered, "They have come from a far country,
20:15 **H** answered, "They have seen all that is
20:16 Isaiah said to **H,** "Hear the word of the LORD:
20:19 Then **H** said to Isaiah, "The word of the LORD
20:20 The rest of the deeds of **H,** all his power,
20:21 **H** slept with his ancestors;
21: 3 the high places that his father **H** had destroyed;
1Ch 3:13 Ahaz his son, **H** his son, Manasseh his son,
4:41 came in the days of King **H** of Judah,
2Ch 28:27 His son **H** succeeded him.
29: 1 **H** began to reign when he was twenty-five years
29:18 Then they went inside to King **H** and said,
29:20 Then King **H** rose early, assembled the officials of
29:27 Then **H** commanded that the burnt offering
29:30 King **H** and the officials commanded the Levites
29:31 Then **H** said, "You have
29:36 And **H** and all the people rejoiced because
30: 1 **H** sent word to all Israel and Judah,
30:18 But **H** prayed for them, saying,
30:20 The LORD heard **H,** and healed the people.

2Ch 30:22 **H** spoke encouragingly to all
30:24 For King **H** of Judah gave the assembly
31: 2 **H** appointed the divisions of the priests and of
31: 8 When **H** and the officials came and saw the heaps,
31: 9 **H** questioned the priests and the Levites about
31:11 Then **H** commanded them to prepare
31:13 by the appointment of King **H** and of Azariah
31:20 **H** did this throughout all Judah;
32: 2 When **H** saw that Sennacherib had come
32: 5 **H** set to work resolutely and built up the entire
32: 8 by the words of King **H** of Judah.
32: 9 to King **H** of Judah and to all the people of Judah
32:11 Is not **H** misleading you, handing you over to die
32:12 not this same **H** who took away his high places
32:15 therefore do not let **H** deceive you or mislead you
32:16 against the Lord GOD and against his servant **H**.
32:17 of **H** will not rescue his people from my hand."
32:20 Then King **H** and the prophet Isaiah son
32:22 So the LORD saved **H** and the inhabitants
32:23 in Jerusalem and precious things to King **H**
32:24 In those days **H** became sick and was at the point
32:25 But **H** did not respond according to
32:26 Then **H** humbled himself for the pride of his heart,
32:26 not come upon them in the days of **H**.
32:27 **H** had very great riches and honor;
32:30 This same **H** closed the upper outlet of the waters
32:30 **H** prospered in all his works.
32:32 Now the rest of the acts of **H**, and his good deeds,
32:33 **H** slept with his ancestors, and they buried him on
33: 3 the high places that his father **H** had pulled down,
Ezr 2:16 Of Ater, namely of **H**, ninety-eight.
Ne 7:21 Of Ater, namely of **H**, ninety-eight.
10:17 Ater, **H**, Azzur,
Pr 25: 1 that the officials of King **H** of Judah copied.
Isa 1: 1 Jotham, Ahaz, and **H**, kings of Judah.
36: 1 In the fourteenth year of King **H**,
36: 2 the Rabshakeh from Lachish to King **H**
36: 4 The Rabshakeh said to them, "Say to **H**:
36: 7 and altars **H** has removed, saying to Judah and
36:14 Thus says the king: 'Do not let **H** deceive you,
36:15 not let **H** make you rely on the LORD by saying,
36:16 not listen to **H**; for thus says the king of Assyria:
36:18 Do not let **H** mislead you by saying,
36:22 the recorder, came to **H** with their clothes torn,
37: 1 When King **H** heard it, he tore his clothes,
37: 3 They said to him, "Thus says **H**,
37: 5 When the servants of King **H** came to Isaiah,
37: 9 When he heard it, he sent messengers to **H**, saying,
37:10 "Thus shall you speak to King **H** of Judah:
37:14 **H** received the letter from the hand of
37:14 then **H** went up to the house of the LORD
37:15 And **H** prayed to the LORD, saying:
37:21 Then Isaiah son of Amoz sent to **H**, saying:
38: 1 In those days **H** became sick and was at the point
38: 2 Then **H** turned his face to the wall,
38: 3 in your sight." And **H** wept bitterly.
38: 5 "Go and say to **H**, Thus says the LORD, the God
38: 9 A writing of King **H** of Judah,
38:22 **H** also had said, "What is the sign that I shall go up
39: 1 with letters and a present to **H**,
39: 2 **H** welcomed them; he showed them his treasure
39: 2 or in all his realm that **H** did not show them.
39: 3 the prophet Isaiah came to King **H** and said to him,
39: 3 **H** answered, "They have come to me from
39: 4 **H** answered, "They have seen all that is
39: 5 to **H**, "Hear the word of the LORD of hosts:
39: 8 Then **H** said to Isaiah, "The word of the LORD
Jer 15: 4 the earth because of what King Manasseh son of **H**
26:18 of King **H** of Judah, said to all the people of Judah:
26:19 Did King **H** of Judah and all Judah actually put
Hos 1: 1 Jotham, Ahaz, and **H** of Judah,
Mic 1: 1 the days of Kings Jotham, Ahaz, and **H** of Judah,
Zep 1: 1 of Cushi son of Gedaliah son of Amariah son of **H**,
Mt 1: 9 and Ahaz the father of **H**,
1:10 and **H** the father of Manasseh,
Sir 48:17 **H** fortified his city, and brought water
48:22 For **H** did what was pleasing to the Lord,
49: 4 Except for David and **H** and Josiah,
2Mc 15:22 you sent your angel in the time of King **H** of Judea,
1Es 5:15 The descendants of Ater, namely of **H**, ninety-two.
9:43 Azariah, Uriah, **H**, and Baalsamus on his right,
2Es 7:*110* [40] **H** for the people in the days of Sennacherib,

HEZION (1)

1Ki 15:18 to King Ben-hadad son of Tabrimmon son of **H**

HEZIR (2)

1Ch 24:15 the seventeenth to **H**, the eighteenth to Happizzez,
Ne 10:20 Magpiash, Meshullam, **H**,

HEZRAI (KJV) See HEZRO; See also Index to Footnotes

HEZRO (2)

2Sa 23:35 **H** of Carmel; Paarai the Arbite;
1Ch 11:37 **H** of Carmel, Naarai son of Ezbai,

HEZRON (20) [HEZRONITES]

Ge 46: 9 Hanoch, Pallu, **H**, and Carmi.
46:12 and the children of Perez were **H** and Hamul.
Ex 6:14 Hanoch, Pallu, **H**, and Carmi;
Nu 26: 6 of **H**, the clan of the Hezronites;
26:21 of **H**, the clan of the Hezronites;
Jos 15: 3 and goes up south of Kadesh-barnea, along by **H**,
Ru 4:18 Perez became the father of **H**,
4:19 **H** of Ram, Ram of Amminadab,
1Ch 2: 5 The sons of Perez: **H** and Hamul.
2: 9 The sons of **H**, who were born to him:
2:18 Caleb son of **H** had children by his wife Azubah,
2:21 Afterward **H** went in to the daughter
2:24 After the death of **H**, in Caleb-ephrathah,
2:24 Abijah wife of **H** bore him Ashhur,
2:25 The sons of Jerahmeel, the firstborn of **H**:
4: 1 sons of Judah: Perez, **H**, Carmi, Hur, and Shobal.
5: 3 Hanoch, Pallu, **H**, and Carmi.
Mt 1: 3 Perez the father of **H**, and **H** the father of Aram,
Lk 3:33 son of Admin, son of Arni, son of **H**, son of Perez,

HEZRONITES (2) [HEZRON]

Nu 26: 6 of Hezron, the clan of the **H**;
26:21 of Hezron, the clan of the **H**;

HID‡ (51) [HIDE]

Ge 3: 8 and his wife **h** themselves from the presence of
3:10 because I was naked; and I **h** myself."
35: 4 and Jacob **h** them under the oak that was
Ex 2: 2 that he was a fine baby, she **h** him three months.
2:12 and seeing no one he killed the Egyptian and **h** him
3: 6 Moses **h** his face, for he was afraid to look at God.
Jos 2: 4 But the woman took the two men and **h** them.
6:17 with her in her house shall live because she **h**
6:25 For she **h** the messengers whom Joshua sent
10:16 these five kings fled and **h** themselves in the cave
Jdg 9: 5 survived, for he **h** himself.
1Sa 3:18 So Samuel told him everything and **h** nothing
13: 6 the people **h** themselves in caves and in holes and
20:19 go to the place where you **h** yourself earlier,
20:24 So David **h** himself in the field.
1Ki 18: 4 **h** them fifty to a cave,
18:13 how I **h** a hundred of the LORD's prophets fifty
2Ki 7: 8 gold, and clothing, and went and **h** them.
7: 8 carried off things from it, and went and **h** them.
11: 2 Thus she **h** him from Athaliah,
1Ch 21:20 his four sons who were with him **h** themselves,
2Ch 22:11 **h** him from Athaliah, so that she did not kill him;
Job 10:13 Yet these things you **h** in your heart;
18:10 A rope is **h** for them in the ground,
Ps 9:15 the net that they **h** has their own foot been caught.
19: 6 and nothing is **h** from its heat.
30: 7 you **h** your face; I was dismayed.
35: 7 For without cause they **h** their net for me;
35: 8 And let the net that they **h** ensnare them;
Isa 49: 2 in the shadow of his hand he **h** me;
49: 2 in his quiver he **h** me away.
54: 8 In overflowing wrath for a moment I **h** my face
57:17 I struck them, I **h** and was angry;
64: 5 because you **h** yourself we transgressed.
Jer 13: 5 So I went, and **h** it by the Euphrates,
36:26 But the LORD **h** them.
Eze 39:23 So I **h** my face from them and gave them into
39:24 and **h** my face from them.
Da 10: 7 and they fled and **h** themselves.
Mt 5:14 A city built on a hill cannot be **h**.
13:44 which someone found and **h**;
25:18 a hole in the ground and **h** his master's money.
25:25 and I went and **h** your talent in the ground.
Jn 8:59 but Jesus **h** himself and went out of the temple.
12:36 Jesus had said this, he departed and **h** from them.
Rev 6:15 **h** in the caves and among the rocks of
Tob 1:19 that I was burying them; so I **h** myself.
Sir 17:15 they will not be **h** from his eyes.
1Mc 9:38 they went up and **h** under cover of the mountain.
16:15 he gave them a great banquet, and **h** men there.
2Mc 1:19 the fire of the altar and secretly **h** it in the hollow

HIDDAI (1)

2Sa 23:30 Benaiah of Pirathon; **H** of the torrents of Gaash;

HIDDEKEL (KJV) See TIGRIS

HIDDEN‡ (100) [HIDE]

Ge 4:14 and I shall be **h** from your face;
Nu 5:13 if a man has had intercourse with her but it is **h**
Dt 33:19 the affluence of the seas and the **h** treasures of
Jos 2: 6 up to the roof and **h** them with the stalks of flax
7:21 They now lie **h** in the ground inside my tent,
7:22 **h** in his tent with the silver underneath.
10:17 **h** in the cave at Makkedah."
10:27 into the cave where they had **h** themselves;
1Sa 10:22 "See, he has **h** himself among the baggage."
14:11 of the holes where they have **h** themselves."
2Sa 17: 9 Even now he has **h** himself in one of the pits,
18:13 against his life (and there is nothing **h** from
1Ki 10: 3 there was nothing **h** from the king that he could
2Ki 4:27 the LORD has **h** it from me and has not told me."
6:29 But she has **h** her son."
11: 3 **h** in the house of the LORD,
2Ch 9: 2 there was nothing **h** from Solomon that he could
22:12 **h** in the house of God,
Job 3:21 and dig for it more than for **h** treasures;
5:21 You shall be **h** from the scourge of the tongue,
15:18 and their ancestors have not **h**,
28:11 **h** things they bring to light.
28:21 It is **h** from the eyes of all living,
Ps 10:11 he has **h** his face, he will never see it."
19:12 Clear me from **h** faults.
31: 4 take me out of the net that is **h** for me,
38: 9 my sighing is not **h** from you.
Ps 40:10 I have not **h** your saving help within my heart,
69: 5 the wrongs I have done are not **h** from you.
139:15 My frame was not **h** from you,
140: 5 The arrogant have **h** a trap for me,
142: 3 In the path where I walk they have **h** a trap for me.
Pr 2: 4 and search for it as for **h** treasures—
27: 5 Better is open rebuke than **h** love.
Isa 29:14 and the discernment of the discerning shall be **h**.
40:27 O Israel, "My way is **h** from the LORD,
42:22 all of them are trapped in holes and **h** in prisons;
45: 3 of darkness and riches **h** in secret places,
48: 6 **h** things that you have not known.
51:16 and **h** you in the shadow of my hand,
59: 2 and your sins have **h** his face from you so
64: 7 for you have **h** your face from us,
65:16 because the former troubles are forgotten and are **h**
Jer 13: 7 I took the loincloth from the place where I had **h** it.
16:17 they are not **h** from my presence,
33: 3 and will tell you great and **h** things that you have
33: 5 for I have **h** my face from this city because
41: 8 barley, oil, and honey **h** in the fields."
Eze 28: 3 no secret is **h** from you;
Da 2:22 He reveals deep and **h** things;
Hos 5: 3 I know Ephraim, and Israel is not **h** from me;
13:14 Compassion is **h** from my eyes.
Hab 3: 4 from his hand, where his power lay **h**.
Zep 2: 3 be **h** on the day of the LORD's wrath.
Mt 11:25 because you have **h** these things from the wise and
13:35 I will proclaim what has been **h** from
13:44 kingdom of heaven is like treasure **h** in a field,
Mk 4:22 For there is nothing **h**, except to be disclosed;
Lk 8:17 For nothing is **h** that will not be disclosed,
8:47 When the woman saw that she could not remain **h**,
10:21 because you have **h** these things from the wise and
18:34 in fact, what he said was **h** from them,
19:42 But now they are **h** from your eyes.
1Co 2: 7 But we speak God's wisdom, secret and **h**,
4: 5 now **h** in darkness and will disclose the purposes
Eph 3: 9 the plan of the mystery **h** for ages
Col 1:26 the mystery that has been **h** throughout the ages
2: 3 in whom are **h** all the treasures of wisdom
3: 3 and your life is **h** with Christ in God.
1Ti 5:25 and even when they are not, they cannot remain **h**.
Heb 4:13 And before him no creature is **h**,
11:23 By faith Moses was **h** by his parents
Rev 2:17 the **h** manna, and I will give a white stone,
Wis 14:21 And this became a **h** trap for humankind,
Sir 3:22 for what is **h** is not your concern.
12: 8 nor is an enemy **h** in adversity.
16:17 Do not say, "I am **h** from the Lord,
17:20 Their iniquities are not **h** from him,
20:30 **H** wisdom and unseen treasure,
23:19 of human behavior and see into **h** corners.
39: 3 the **h** meanings of proverbs and is at home with
39:19 and nothing can be **h** from his eyes.
41:14 **h** wisdom and unseen treasure—
42:19 and he reveals the traces of **h** things.
42:20 and nothing is **h** from him.
43:32 Many things greater than these lie **h**,
48:25 and the **h** things before they happened.
Sus 1:16 who had **h** themselves and were watching her.
Bel 1:13 for beneath the table they had made a **h** entrance,
1Mc 1:23 he took also the **h** treasures that he found.
2Mc 1:20 the descendants of the priests who had **h** the fire
1:33 in the place where the exiled priests had **h** the fire,
12:41 who reveals the things that are **h**;
2Es 5: 1 and the way of truth shall be **h**,
7:26 and the land that now is **h** shall be disclosed.
8:53 illness is banished from you, and death is **h**;
12:37 put it in a **h** place;
16:28 those who have **h** themselves in thick groves
16:62 and searches out **h** things in **h** places.

HIDE‡ (88) [HID, HIDDEN, HIDES, HIDING]

Ge 18:17 "Shall I **h** from Abraham what I am about to do,
47:18 not **h** from my lord that our money is all spent;
Ex 2: 3 When she could **h** him no longer she got
Dt 31:17 I will forsake them and **h** my face from them;
31:18 that day I will surely **h** my face on account of all
32:20 He said: I will **h** my face from them,
Jos 2:16 **H** yourselves there three days,
7:19 do not **h** it from me."
Jdg 6:11 to **h** it from the Midianites.
1Sa 3:17 Do not **h** it from me.
3:17 if you **h** anything from me of all that he told you."
19: 2 stay in a secret place and **h** yourself.
20: 2 and why should my father **h** this from me?
20: 5 so that I may **h** in the field until the third evening.
1Ki 17: 3 and **h** yourself by the Wadi Cherith,
20:30 Ben-hadad also fled, and entered the city to **h**.
22:25 that day when you go in to **h** in an inner chamber."
2Ki 7:12 the camp to **h** themselves in the open country,
2Ch 18:24 that day when you go in to **h** in an inner chamber."
Job 3:10 and **h** trouble from my eyes.
13:20 then I will not **h** myself from your face:
13:24 Why do you **h** your face,
14:13 Oh that you would **h** me in Sheol,
20:12 though they **h** it under their tongues,
24: 4 the poor of the earth all **h** themselves.
34:22 where evildoers may **h** themselves.
40:13 **H** them all in the dust together;
Ps 10: 1 Why do you **h** yourself in times of trouble?
13: 1 How long will you **h** your face from me?
17: 8 **h** me in the shadow of your wings,
22:24 he did not **h** his face from me,
27: 5 he will **h** me in his shelter in the day of trouble;

Ps 27: 9 Do not **h** your face from me.
31:20 of your presence you **h** them from human plots;
32: 5 and I did not **h** my iniquity;
44:24 Why do you **h** your face?
51: 9 **H** your face from my sins,
55: 1 do not **h** yourself from my supplication.
55:12 who deal insolently with me—I could **h** from them.
64: 2 **H** me from the secret plots of the wicked,
69:17 Do not **h** your face from your servant,
78: 4 We will not **h** them from their children;
88:14 Why do you **h** your face from me?
89:46 Will you **h** yourself forever?
102: 2 not **h** your face from me in the day of my distress.
104:29 When you **h** your face, they are dismayed;
119:19 do not **h** your commandments from me.
143: 7 Do not **h** your face from me,
Pr 22: 3 The clever see danger and **h;**
27:12 The clever see danger and **h;**
Isa 1:15 I will **h** my eyes from you;
2:10 and **h** in the dust from the terror of the LORD,
3: 9 like Sodom, they do not **h** it.
16: 3 **h** the outcasts, do not betray the fugitive;
26:20 **h** yourselves for a little while until
29:15 You who **h** a plan too deep for the LORD,
30:20 yet your Teacher will not **h** himself any more,
50: 6 I did not **h** my face from insult and spitting.
53: 3 from whom others **h** their faces he was despised,
58: 7 and not to **h** yourself from your own kin?
Jer 13: 4 and **h** it there in a cleft of the rock."
13: 6 the loincloth that I commanded you to **h** there."
23:24 Who can **h** in secret places so
36:19 Then the officials said to Baruch, "Go and **h,**
38:14 do not **h** anything from me."
49:30 Flee, wander far away, **h** in deep places,
Eze 39:29 and I will never again **h** my face from them,
Am 9: 3 Though they **h** themselves on the top of Carmel,
9: 3 they **h** from my sight at the bottom of the sea,
Mic 3: 4 he will **h** his face from them at that time,
Rev 6:16 on us and **h** us from the face of the one seated on
Tob 13: 6 to you and will no longer **h** his face from you.
Wis 6:22 and I will **h** no secrets from you,
7:13 I do not **h** her wealth,
Sir 4:23 and do not **h** your wisdom.
6:12 they turn against you, and **h** themselves from you.
20:31 Better are those who **h** their folly than those who **h** their wisdom.
22:25 and I will not **h** from him.
23:18 Darkness surrounds me, the walls **h** me,
26: 8 arouses great anger; she cannot **h** her shame.
37:10 **h** your intentions from those who are jealous
41:15 Better are those who **h** their folly than those who **h** their wisdom.
LtJ 6:48 as to where they can **h** themselves and their gods.
2Es 5: 9 conquer one another; then shall reason **h** itself,
16:63 Woe to those who sin and want to **h** their sins!
16:66 will you **h** your sins before the Lord and his glory?

HIDES (7) [HIDE]

Job 23: 9 on the left he **h,** and I cannot behold him;
34:29 When he **h** his face, who can behold him,
42: 3 'Who is this that **h** counsel without knowledge?'
Isa 45:15 Truly, you are a God who **h** himself,
Lk 8:16 "No one after lighting a lamp **h** it under a jar,
2Co 4: 2 the shameful things that one **h;**
Sir 19:27 He **h** his face and pretends not to hear,

HIDING (28) [HIDE]

Jdg 6: 2 the Israelites provided for themselves **h** places in
1Sa 14:22 into **h** in the hill country of Ephraim heard that
23:19 "David is **h** among us in the strongholds
23:23 around and learn all the **h** places where he lurks,
26: 1 saying, "David is in **h** on the hill of Hachilah,
2Ch 22: 9 while **h** in Samaria and was brought to Jehu,
Job 31:33 by **h** my iniquity in my bosom,
Ps 10: 8 in **h** places they murder the innocent.
32: 7 You are a **h** place for me;
54: T *and told Saul, "David is in **h** among us."*
119:114 You are my **h** place and my shield;
Pr 28:12 but when the wicked prevail, people go into **h.**
28:28 When the wicked prevail, people go into **h;**
Isa 8:17 who is **h** his face from the house of Jacob,
32: 2 Each will be like a **h** place from the wind,
Jer 49:10 I have uncovered his **h** places,
La 3:10 He is a bear lying in wait for me, a lion in **h;**
Na 3:11 You also will be drunken, you will go into **h;**
Hab 3:14 as if ready to devour the poor who were in **h.**
Sus 1:18 they did not see the elders, because they were **h.**
1:37 Then a young man, who was **h** there,
1Mc 1:53 into **h** in every place of refuge they had.
2:31 the king's command had gone down to the **h** places
2:36 or hurl a stone at them or block up their **h** places,
2:41 not all die as our kindred died in their **h** places."
2Mc 10:37 They killed Timothy, who was **h** in a cistern,
14:30 and went into **h** from Nicanor.
2Es 2:31 I will bring them out of the **h** places of the earth,

HIEL (1)

1Ki 16:34 In his days **H** of Bethel built Jericho;

HIERAPOLIS (1)

Col 4:13 for you and for those in Laodicea and in **H.**

HIERONYMUS (1)

2Mc 12: 2 as well as **H** and Demophon,

HIGGAION (1)

Ps 9:16 snared in the work of their own hands. ***H.** Selah*

HIGH‡ (589) [HEIGHT, HEIGHTENED, HEIGHTS, HIGH-HANDEDLY, HIGH-PRIESTLY, HIGHER, HIGHEST, HIGHLANDS, HIGHLY, HIGHWAY, HIGHWAYS]

A. MOST HIGH (187)
B. HIGH PRIEST (126)
C. HIGH PLACES (68)
D. ON HIGH (30)
E. MOST HIGH *GOD (18)
F. HIGH PLACE (16)
G. *GOD MOST HIGH (8)

Ge 7:17 and bore up the ark, and it rose **h** above the earth.
7:19 so mightily on the earth that all the **h** mountains
14:18 he was priest of God Most **H.** AG
14:19 "Blessed be Abram by God Most **H,** AG
14:20 and blessed be God Most **H,** AG
14:22 "I have sworn to the LORD, God Most **H,** AG
27:39 and away from the dew of heaven on **h.** D
34:12 Put the marriage present and gift as **h** as you like,
Ex 25:10 a cubit and a half wide, and a cubit and a half **h.**
25:23 one cubit wide, and a cubit and a half **h.**
27: 1 altar shall be square, and it shall be three cubits **h.**
30: 2 it shall be square, and shall be two cubits **h;**
37: 1 a cubit and a half wide, and a cubit and a half **h.**
37:10 one cubit wide, and a cubit and a half **h.**
37:25 it was square, and was two cubits **h;**
38: 1 it was square, and three cubits **h.**
38:18 along the width of it, five cubits **h,**
Lev 26:30 I will destroy your **h** places and cut C
Nu 24:16 and knows the knowledge of the Most **H,** A
33:52 and demolish all their **h** places. C
35:25 the **h** priest who was anointed with the holy oil. B
35:28 the city of refuge until the death of the **h** priest; B
35:28 death of the **h** priest the slayer may return home. B
35:32 live in the land before the death of the **h** priest. B
Dt 2:36 there was no citadel too **h** for us.
3: 5 All these were fortress towns with **h** walls,
26:19 to set you **h** above all nations that he has made,
28: 1 the LORD your God will set you **h** above all
28:52 It shall besiege you in all your towns until your **h**
32: 8 When the Most **H** apportioned the nations, A
33:12 the **H** God surrounds him all day long—
Jos 20: 6 the death of the one who is **h** priest at the time: B
1Sa 2:10 the Most **H** will thunder in heaven. A
2Sa 1:19 O Israel, lies slain upon your **h** places! C
1:25 Jonathan lies slain upon your **h** places. C
22:14 the Most **H** uttered his voice. A
22:17 He reached from on **h,** he took me, D
1Ki 3: 2 The people were sacrificing at the **h** places, C
3: 3 he sacrificed and offered incense at the **h** places. C
3: 4 for that was the principal **h** place; F
4: 2 and these were his **h** officials:
6: 2 twenty cubits wide, and thirty cubits **h.**
6:10 against the whole house, each story five cubits **h,**
6:20 and twenty cubits **h;** he overlaid it with pure gold.
6:23 of olivewood, each ten cubits **h.**
7: 2 fifty cubits wide, and thirty cubits **h,**
7:19 in the vestibule were of lily-work, four cubits **h.**
7:23 ten cubits from brim to brim, and five cubits **h.**
7:27 four cubits wide, and three cubits **h.**
7:35 of the stand there was a round band half a cubit **h;**
11: 7 **h** place for Chemosh the abomination of Moab, F
12:31 He also made houses on **h** places, C
12:32 he placed in Bethel the priests of the **h** places C
13: 2 the priests of the **h** places who offer incense C
13:32 against all the houses of the **h** places that are in C
13:33 the **h** places again from among all the people; C
13:33 to be priests he consecrated for the **h** places. C
14:23 they also built for themselves **h** places, pillars, C
14:23 on every **h** hill and under every green tree;
15:14 But the **h** places were not taken away. C
22:43 yet the **h** places were not taken away, C
22:43 and offered incense on the **h** places. C
2Ki 5: 1 was a great man and in **h** favor with his master,
12: 3 Nevertheless the **h** places were not taken away; C
12: 3 to sacrifice and make offerings on the **h** places. C
12:10 the king's secretary and the **h** priest went up, B
14: 4 But the **h** places were not removed; C
14: 4 and made offerings on the **h** places. C
15: 4 Nevertheless the **h** places were not taken away; C
15: 4 and made offerings on the **h** places. C
15:35 Nevertheless the **h** places were not removed; C
15:35 and made offerings on the **h** places. C
16: 4 sacrificed and made offerings on the **h** places, C
17: 9 for themselves **h** places at all their towns, C
17:10 on every **h** hill and under every green tree;
17:11 there they made offerings on all the **h** places, C
17:29 **h** places that the people of Samaria had made, C
17:32 of people as priests of the **h** places, C
17:32 for them in the shrines of the **h** places. C
18: 4 removed the **h** places, broke down the pillars, C
18:22 is it not he whose **h** places C
21: 3 For he rebuilt the **h** places C
22: 4 "Go up to the **h** priest Hilkiah, and have him B
22: 8 **h** priest Hilkiah said to Shaphan the secretary, B
23: 4 The king commanded the **h** priest Hilkiah, B
23: 5 to make offerings in the **h** places at the cities C
23: 8 **h** places where the priests had made offerings, C
23: 8 broke down the **h** places of the gates that were C
2Ki 23: 9 The priests of the **h** places, however, C
23:13 The king defiled the **h** places that were east C
23:15 the **h** place erected by Jeroboam son of Nebat, F
23:15 he pulled down that altar along with the **h** place. F
23:15 He burned the **h** place, crushing it to dust; F
23:19 the **h** places that were in the towns of Samaria, C
23:20 the priests of the **h** places who were there, C
25:26 **h** and low and the captains of the forces set out
1Ch 16:39 before the tabernacle of the LORD in the **h** place F
17:17 You regard me as someone of **h** rank,
21:29 of burnt offering were at that time in the **h** place F
2Ch 1: 3 went to the **h** place that was at Gibeon; F
1:13 So Solomon came from the **h** place at Gibeon, F
3:15 the house he made two pillars thirty-five cubits **h,**
4: 1 twenty cubits wide, and ten cubits **h.**
4: 2 ten cubits from rim to rim, and five cubits **h.**
6:13 and three cubits **h,** and had set it in the court;
11:15 had appointed his own priests for the **h** places, C
14: 3 He took away the foreign altars and the **h** places, C
14: 5 of Judah the **h** places and the incense altars. C
15:17 But the **h** places were not taken out of Israel. C
17: 6 the **h** places and the sacred poles from Judah. C
20:33 Yet the **h** places were not removed; C
21:11 he made **h** places in the hill country of Judah, C
28: 4 sacrificed and made offerings on the **h** places, C
28:25 of Judah he made **h** places to make offerings C
31: 1 the **h** places and the altars throughout all Judah C
32:12 this same Hezekiah who took away his **h** places C
33: 3 the **h** places that his father Hezekiah had pulled C
33:17 people, however, still sacrificed at the **h** places, C
33:19 the sites on which he built **h** places and set up C
34: 3 to purge Judah and Jerusalem of the **h** places, C
34: 9 They came to the **h** priest Hilkiah and delivered B
Ne 3: 1 Then the **h** priest Eliashib set to work B
3:20 to the door of the house of the **h** priest Eliashib. B
13:28 son of the **h** priest Eliashib, B
Est 1:20 to their husbands, **h** and low alike."
5:14 "Let a gallows fifty cubits **h** be made,
7: 9 stands at Haman's house, fifty cubits **h."**
10: 2 and the full account of the **h** honor of Mordecai,
Job 5:11 he sets on **h** those who are lowly, D
16:19 and he that vouches for me is on **h.** D
20: 6 Even though they mount up **h** as the heavens,
21:22 seeing that he judges those that are on **h?** D
22:12 "Is not God **h** in the heavens?
25: 2 he makes peace in his **h** heaven.
31: 2 and my heritage from the Almighty on **h?** D
39:27 the eagle mounts up and makes its nest on **h?** D
Ps 7: 7 and over it take your seat on **h.** D
7:17 to the name of the LORD, the Most **H.** A
9: 2 I will sing praise to your name, O Most **H.** A
10: 5 your judgments are on **h,** out of their sight; D
18:13 and the Most **H** uttered his voice. A
18:16 He reached down from on **h,** he took me; D
21: 7 love of the Most **H** he shall not be moved. A
27: 5 he will set me **h** on a rock.
44:12 demanding no **h** price for them.
46: 4 the holy habitation of the Most **H.** A
47: 2 For the LORD, the Most **H,** is awesome, A
49: 2 both low and **h,** rich and poor together.
50:14 and pay your vows to the Most **H.** A
56: 2 for many fight against me. O Most **H,** A
57: 2 I cry to God Most **H,** AG
57:10 For your steadfast love is as **h** as the heavens;
62: 9 those of **h** estate are a delusion;
68:18 You ascended the **h** mount,
71:19 O God, reach the **h** heavens.
73:11 Is there knowledge in the Most **H?"** A
75: 5 do not lift up your horn on **h,** D
77:10 that the right hand of the Most **H** has changed." A
78:17 rebelling against the Most **H** in the desert. A
78:35 the Most **H** God their redeemer. AE
78:56 Yet they tested the Most **H** God, AE
78:58 they provoked him to anger with their **h** places; C
78:69 He built his sanctuary like the **h** heavens,
82: 6 I say, "You are gods, children of the Most **H,** A
83:18 are the Most **H** over all the earth. A
87: 5 for the Most **H** himself will establish it. A
89:13 strong is your hand, **h** your right hand.
91: 1 You who live in the shelter of the Most **H,** A
91: 9 the Most **H** your dwelling place, A
92: 1 to sing praises to your name, O Most **H;** A
92: 8 but you, O LORD, are on **h** forever. D
93: 4 majestic on **h** is the LORD! D
97: 9 For you, O LORD, are most **h** over all the earth; A
103:11 For as the heavens are **h** above the earth,
104:18 The **h** mountains are for the wild goats;
106: 7 but rebelled against the Most **H** at the Red Sea. A
107:11 and spurned the counsel of the Most **H.** A
113: 4 The LORD is **h** above all nations,
113: 5 like the LORD our God, who is seated on **h,** D
131: 1 my eyes are not raised too **h;**
138: 6 For though the LORD is **h,** he regards the lowly;
139: 6 it is so **h** that I cannot attain it.
144: 7 Stretch out your hand from on **h;** D
149: 6 Let the **h** praises of God be in their throats
Pr 9:14 on a seat at the **h** places of the town, C
17:19 one who builds a **h** threshold invites broken bones.
18:11 in their imagination it is like a **h** wall.
24: 7 Wisdom is too **h** for fools;
30:13 how lofty are their eyes, how **h** their eyelids lift!
30:19 the way of a ship on the **h** seas,
Ecc 5: 8 for the **h** official is watched by a higher,
10: 6 folly is set in many **h** places, C
Isa 2:12 against all that is lifted up and **h;**
2:14 the **h** mountains, and against all the lofty hills;
2:15 against every **h** tower,

Isa 6: 1 I saw the Lord sitting on a throne, **h** and lofty;
7:11 let it be deep as Sheol or **h** as heaven.
14:14 I will make myself like the Most **H."** A
15: 2 to the **h** places to weep; C
16:12 when he wearies himself upon the **h** place, F
25:12 **h** fortifications of his walls will be brought down,
30:13 for you like a break in a **h** wall, bulging out,
30:25 On every lofty mountain and every **h** hill
32:15 until a spirit from on **h** is poured out on us, D
33: 5 The LORD is exalted, he dwells on **h;** D
36: 7 is it not he whose **h** places C
40: 9 Get you up to a **h** mountain, O Zion,
40:26 Lift up your eyes on **h** and see: Who created D
52:13 be exalted and lifted up, and shall be very **h.**
57: 7 a **h** and lofty mountain you have set your bed,
57:15 thus says the **h** and lofty one who inhabits eternity,
57:15 I dwell in the **h** and holy place,
58: 4 not make your voice heard on **h.** D
Jer 2:20 On every **h** hill and under every green tree
3: 6 up on every **h** hill and under every green tree,
7:31 And they go on building the **h** place of Topheth, F
17: 2 beside every green tree, and on the **h** hills,
19: 5 the **h** places of Baal to burn their children in C
25:30 The LORD will roar from on **h,** D
32:35 They built the **h** places of Baal in the valley of C
48:35 at a **h** place and make offerings to their gods. F
49:16 Although you make your nest as **h** as the eagle's,
51:58 and her **h** gates shall be burned with fire.
La 1:13 From on **h** he sent fire; D
3:35 in the presence of the Most **H,** A
3:38 mouth of the Most **H** that good and bad come? A
Eze 6: 3 and I will destroy your **h** places. C
6: 6 be waste and your **h** places ruined, C
6:13 on every **h** hill, on all the mountain tops,
17:22 I myself will plant it on a **h** and lofty mountain.
17:24 I bring low the **h** tree, I make **h** the low tree;
20:28 then wherever they saw any **h** hill or any leafy tree,
20:29 What is the **h** place to which you go? F
21:26 Exalt that which is low, abase that which is **h.**
27:26 Your rowers have brought you into the **h** seas.
31: 5 So it towered **h** above all the trees of the field;
31:10 it towered **h** and set its top among the clouds,
34: 6 over all the mountains and on every **h** hill;
40: 2 and set me down upon a very **h** mountain,
40:42 and one cubit and a half wide, and one cubit **h,**
41:22 three cubits **h,** two cubits long,
43:13 its base shall be one cubit **h,** and one cubit wide,
Da 3:26 and Abednego, servants of the Most **H** God, AE
4: 2 the Most **H** God has worked for me AE
4:17 that the Most **H** is sovereign over the kingdom A
4:24 of the Most **H** that has come upon my lord A
4:25 the Most **H** has sovereignty over the kingdom A
4:32 the Most **H** has sovereignty over the kingdom A
4:34 I blessed the Most **H,** and praised and honored A
5:18 Most **H** God gave your father Nebuchadnezzar AE
5:21 Most **H** God has sovereignty over the kingdom AE
7:18 Most **H** shall receive the kingdom and possess A
7:22 for the holy ones of the Most **H,** A
7:25 He shall speak words against the Most **H,** A
7:25 shall wear out the holy ones of the Most **H,** A
7:27 to the people of the holy ones of the Most **H;** A
8:10 It grew as **h** as the host of heaven.
Hos 10: 8 The **h** places of Aven, the sin of Israel, C
11: 7 To the Most **H** they call, A
Am 7: 9 the **h** places of Isaac shall be made desolate, C
Mic 1: 3 will come down and tread upon the **h** places of C
1: 5 And what is the **h** place of Judah? F
6: 6 and bow myself before God on **h?** D
Hab 2: 9 setting your nest on **h** to be safe from the reach D
3:10 The sun raised **h** its hands;
Hag 1: 1 and to Joshua son of Jehozadak, the **h** priest: B
1:12 the **h** priest, with all the remnant of the people, B
1:14 the **h** priest, and the spirit of all the remnant of B
2: 2 the **h** priest, and to the remnant of the people, B
2: 4 O Joshua, son of Jehozadak, the **h** priest; B
Zec 3: 1 Then he showed me the **h** priest Joshua standing B
3: 8 Now listen, Joshua, **h** priest, B
6:11 the head of the **h** priest Joshua son of Jehozadak; B
Mt 4: 8 to a very **h** mountain and showed him all
17: 1 his brother John and led them up a **h** mountain,
26: 3 the people gathered in the palace of the **h** priest, B
26:51 drew it, and struck the slave of the **h** priest, B
26:57 the **h** priest, in whose house the scribes and B
26:58 as far as the courtyard of the **h** priest; B
26:62 **h** priest stood up and said, "Have you no B
26:63 Then the **h** priest said to him, B
26:65 Then the **h** priest tore his clothes and said, B
Mk 2:26 when Abiathar was **h** priest, B
5: 7 Jesus, Son of the Most **H** God? AE
9: 2 and led them up a **h** mountain apart,
14:47 and struck the slave of the **h** priest, B
14:53 They took Jesus to the **h** priest; B
14:54 right into the courtyard of the **h** priest; B
14:60 **h** priest stood up before them and asked Jesus, B
14:61 Again the **h** priest asked him, B
14:63 Then the **h** priest tore his clothes and said, B
14:66 one of the servant-girls of the **h** priest came by. B
Lk 1:32 and will be called the Son of the Most **H,** A
1:35 the power of the Most **H** will overshadow you; A
1:76 child, will be called the prophet of the Most **H;** A
1:78 the dawn from on **h** will break upon us, D
3: 2 during the **h** priesthood of Annas and Caiaphas,
4:38 from a **h** fever, and they asked him
6:35 and you will be children of the Most **H;** A
8:28 Jesus, Son of the Most **H** God? AE
22:50 Then one of them struck the slave of the **h** priest B
22:54 bringing him into the **h** priest's house.

Lk 24:49 you have been clothed with power from on **h."** D
Jn 11:49 of them, Caiaphas, who was **h** priest that year, B
11:51 but being **h** priest that year he prophesied B
18:10 struck the **h** priest's slave, and cut off his right ear.
18:13 the father-in-law of Caiaphas, the **h** priest B
18:15 Since that disciple was known to the **h** priest, B
18:15 with Jesus into the courtyard of the **h** priest, B
18:16 other disciple, who was known to the **h** priest, B
18:19 the **h** priest questioned Jesus about his disciples B
18:22 saying, "Is that how you answer the **h** priest?" B
18:24 Annas sent him bound to Caiaphas the **h** priest. B
18:26 One of the slaves of the **h** priest, B
Ac 4: 6 the **h** priest, Caiaphas, John, and Alexander, B
5:13 but the people held them in **h** esteem.
5:17 Then the **h** priest took action; B
5:21 When the **h** priest and those with him arrived, B
5:27 The **h** priest questioned them, B
7: 1 the **h** priest asked him, "Are these things so?" B
7:48 Yet the Most **H** does not dwell in houses made A
9: 1 the disciples of the Lord, went to the **h** priest B
13:50 the Jews incited the devout women of **h** standing
16:17 "These men are slaves of the Most **H** God, AE
17:12 not a few Greek women and men of **h** standing.
19:14 a Jewish **h** priest named Sceva were doing this. B
22: 5 as the **h** priest and the whole council B
23: 2 the **h** priest Ananias ordered those standing B
23: 4 "Do you dare to insult God's **h** priest?" B
23: 5 "I did not realize, brothers, that he was **h** priest; B
24: 1 **h** priest Ananias came down with some elders B
Eph 4: 8 "When he ascended on **h** he made captivity D
1Ti 2: 2 for kings and all who are in **h** positions,
Heb 1: 3 sat down at the right hand of the Majesty on **h,** D
2:17 that he might be a merciful and faithful **h** priest B
3: 1 the apostle and **h** priest of our confession, B
4:14 we have a great **h** priest who has passed through B
4:15 not have a **h** priest who is unable to sympathize B
5: 1 Every **h** priest chosen from among mortals is B
5: 5 a **h** priest, but was appointed by the one who B
5:10 **h** priest according to the order of Melchizedek. B
6:20 having become a **h** priest forever according to B
7: 1 the Most **H** God, met Abraham as he was AE
7:26 was fitting that we should have such a **h** priest, B
7:27 Unlike the other **h** priests, he has no need
7:28 the law appoints as **h** priests those who are subject
8: 1 we have such a **h** priest, B
8: 3 For every **h** priest is appointed to offer gifts B
9: 7 but only the **h** priest goes into the second, B
9:11 Christ came as a **h** priest of the good things B
9:25 the **h** priest enters the Holy Place year after year B
13:11 the **h** priest as a sacrifice for sin are burned B
Rev 14:20 as **h** as a horse's bridle,
18: 5 for her sins are heaped **h** as heaven,
21:10 **h** mountain and showed me
21:12 It has a great, **h** wall with twelve gates,
Tob 1:13 the Most **H** gave me favor and good standing A
4:11 excellent offering in the presence of the Most **H.** A
Jdt 1: 2 the walls seventy cubits **h** and fifty cubits wide.
1: 3 At its gates he raised towers one hundred cubits **h**
1: 4 He made its gates seventy cubits **h**
4: 5 the **h** hilltops and fortified the villages on them
4: 6 The **h** priest, Joakim, who was in Jerusalem at B
4: 8 as they had been ordered by the **h** priest Joakim B
4:14 The **h** priest Joakim and all the priests who B
5: 1 and fortified all the **h** hilltops and set up barricades
7: 4 neither the **h** mountains nor the valleys nor
13:18 by the Most **H** God above all other women AE
15: 8 Then the **h** priest Joakim and the elders of B
AdE 5:14 "Let a gallows be made, fifty cubits **h,**
7: 9 at Haman's house, a gallows fifty cubits **h."**
16:16 and are children of the living God, most **h,** A
Wis 5:15 and the Most **H** takes care of them. A
6: 3 and your sovereignty from the Most **H;** A
6: 5 severe judgment falls on those in **h** places. C
9:17 and sent your holy spirit from on **h?** D
Sir 4:10 you will then be like a son of the Most **H,** A
7: 4 Do not seek from the Lord **h** office,
7: 9 when I make an offering to the Most **H** God, AE
7:15 which was created by the Most **H.** A
9:15 be about the law of the Most **H.** A
11: 1 The wisdom of the humble lifts their heads **h,**
12: 2 if not by them, certainly by the Most **H.** A
12: 6 For the Most **H** also hates sinners A
16:17 and who from on **h** has me in mind? D
17:26 Return to the Most **H** and turn away from A
17:27 Who will sing praises to the Most **H** in Hades A
19:17 and let the law of the Most **H** take its course. A
22:18 Fences set on a **h** place will not stand firm F
23:18 The Most **H** will not remember sins." A
23:23 she has disobeyed the law of the Most **H;** A
24: 2 assembly of the Most **H** she opens her mouth, A
24: 3 "I came forth from the mouth of the Most **H,** A
24:23 the book of the covenant of the Most **H** God, AE
28: 7 remember the covenant of the Most **H,** A
29:11 according to the commandments of the Most **H,** A
33:15 Look at all the works of the Most **H;** A
34: 6 they are sent by intervention from the Most **H,** A
34:23 The Most **H** is not pleased with the offerings of A
35: 8 and its pleasing odor rises before the Most **H.** A
35:12 Give to the Most **H** as he has given to you, A
35:21 it will not desist until the Most **H** responds A
37:14 better informed than seven sentinels sitting **h**
37:15 the Most **H** that he may direct your way in truth. A
38: 2 for their gift of healing comes from the Most **H,** A
38:34 to the study of the law of the Most **H!** A
39: 5 and to petition the Most **H;** A
41: 4 then should you reject the will of the Most **H?** A
41: 8 have forsaken the law of the Most **H** God! AE

Sir 42: 2 of the law of the Most **H** and his covenant, A
42:18 For the Most **H** knows all that may be known; A
43: 2 the work of the Most **H.** A
43: 8 a beacon to the hosts on **h,** D
43:12 the hands of the Most **H** have stretched it out. A
44:20 He kept the law of the Most **H,** A
46: 5 He called upon the Most **H,** the Mighty One, A
47: 5 For he called on the Lord, the Most **H,** A
47: 8 the Most **H,** proclaiming his glory; A
48: 5 by the word of the Most **H.** A
49: 4 for they abandoned the law of the Most **H;** A
50: 1 and the pride of his people was the **h** priest, B
50: 2 He laid the foundations for the **h** double walls,
50: 2 the **h** retaining walls for the temple enclosure.
50: 7 the sun shining on the temple of the Most **H,** A
50:14 and arranging the offering to the Most **H,** A
50:15 a pleasing odor to the Most **H,** the king of all. A
50:16 mighty fanfare as a reminder before the Most **H.** A
50:17 the Almighty, God Most **H.** AG
50:19 people of the Lord Most **H** offered their prayers A
50:21 to receive the blessing from the Most **H.** A
Bar 1: 7 to the **h** priest Jehoiakim son of Hilkiah son B
3:25 and has no bounds; it is **h** and immeasurable.
5: 7 For God has ordered that every **h** mountain and
1Mc 4:60 At that time they fortified Mount Zion with **h** walls
6: 7 the sanctuary with **h** walls as before,
6:40 of the king's army was spread out on the **h** hills,
7: 5 who wanted to be **h** priest. B
7: 9 the ungodly Alcimus, whom he made **h** priest; B
7:21 Alcimus struggled to maintain his **h** priesthood,
9:50 and Tephon, with **h** walls and gates and bars.
10:20 we have appointed you today to be the **h** priest B
10:32 citadel in Jerusalem and give it to the **h** priest, B
10:38 and obey no other authority than the **h** priest. B
10:69 the following message to the **h** priest Jonathan: B
11:27 in the **h** priesthood and in as many other honors
11:57 "I confirm you in the **h** priesthood and set you over
12: 3 "The **h** priest Jonathan and B
12: 6 "The **h** priest Jonathan, the senate of the nation, B
12: 7 time past a letter was sent to the **h** priest Onias B
12:20 to the **h** priest Onias, greetings. B
12:36 to erect a **h** barrier between the citadel and the city
13:27 he made it **h** so that it might be seen,
13:33 with **h** towers and great walls and gates and bolts,
13:36 the **h** priest and friend of kings, B
13:42 the great **h** priest and commander and leader of B
14:17 that his brother Simon had become **h** priest B
14:20 the city of the Spartans to the **h** priest Simon B
14:23 a copy of this to the **h** priest Simon.' " B
14:27 the third year of the great **h** priest Simon, B
14:30 rallied the nation, became their **h** priest, B
14:35 and they made him their leader and **h** priest, B
14:38 King Demetrius confirmed him in the **h** priesthood,
14:39 of his Friends, and paid him **h** honors.
14:41 be their leader and **h** priest forever, B
14:47 So Simon accepted and agreed to be **h** priest, B
15: 2 the **h** priest and ethnarch and to the nation of B
15:17 They had been sent by the **h** priest Simon and B
15:21 hand them over to the **h** priest Simon, B
15:24 a copy of these things to the **h** priest Simon. B
16:12 for he was son-in-law of the **h** priest. B
16:24 are written in the annals of his **h** priesthood,
16:24 the time that he became **h** priest after his father. B
2Mc 3: 1 the **h** priest Onias and his hatred of wickedness, B
3: 4 with the **h** priest about the administration of B
3: 9 and had been kindly welcomed by the **h** priest B
3:10 The **h** priest explained B
3:16 appearance of the **h** priest was to be wounded B
3:21 the anxiety of the **h** priest in his great anguish. B
3:31 the Most **H** to grant life to one who was lying A
3:32 So the **h** priest, fearing that the king might get B
3:33 While the **h** priest was making an atonement, B
3:33 "Be very grateful to the **h** priest Onias, B
4: 7 of Onias obtained the **h** priesthood by corruption,
4:13 who was ungodly and no true **h** priest, B
4:24 and secured the **h** priesthood for himself,
4:25 possessing no qualification for the **h** priesthood,
4:29 as deputy in the **h** priesthood,
4:31 leaving Andronicus, a man of **h** rank,
6:18 Eleazar, one of the scribes in **h** position,
6:23 But making a **h** resolve, worthy of his years and
8:30 of some exceedingly **h** strongholds,
9: 8 that he could weigh the **h** mountains in a balance,
11: 3 and to put up the **h** priesthood for sale every year.
13: 5 For there is a tower there, fifty cubits **h,**
14: 3 who had formerly been **h** priest B
14: 7 I mean the **h** priesthood—
14:13 install Alcimus as **h** priest of the great temple. B
15:12 Onias, who had been **h** priest, B
1Es 2: 3 The Lord of Israel, the Lord Most **H,** A
4:34 The earth is vast, and heaven is **h,**
5:40 until a **h** priest should appear wearing Urim B
6:31 libations may be made to the Most **H** God AE
8: 2 of Eleazar son of Aaron the **h** priest. B
8:19 reader of the law of the Most **H** God sends for, AE
8:21 be scrupulously fulfilled for the Most **H** God, AE
9:46 And Ezra blessed the Lord God Most **H,** AG
Man 1: 7 for you are the Lord Most **H,** A
3Mc 1:11 only the **h** priest who was pre-eminent over all— B
1:20 they crowded together at the most **h** temple. A
2: 1 Then the **h** priest Simon, facing the sanctuary, B
3:19 among all nations who hold their heads **h**
6: 2 Almighty God Most **H,** governing all creation AG
7: 9 the Most **H** God, in everything and AE
2Es 3: 3 I began to speak anxious words to the Most **H,** A
4: 2 the way of the Most **H?"** A
4:11 the way of the Most **H?** A

2Es 4:34 "Do not be in a greater hurry than the Most **H.** A
5: 4 But if the Most **H** grants that you live, A
5:22 to speak words in the presence of the Most **H.** A
5:34 the way of the Most **H** and to search out A
6:32 voice has surely been heard by the Most **H;** A
6:36 I began to speak in the presence of the Most **H.** A
7:19 or wiser than the Most **H!** A
7:23 even declared that the Most **H** does not exist, A
7:*33* Most **H** shall be revealed on the seat of A
7:*37* Then the Most **H** will say to the nations A
7:*42* only the splendor of the glory of the Most **H,** A
7:*50* this reason the Most **H** has made not one world A
7:*70* "When the Most **H** made the world and Adam A
7:*74* Most **H** has been patient with those who inhabit A
7:*77* a treasure of works stored up with the Most **H,** A
7:*78* decisive decree has gone out from the Most **H** A
7:*78* first of all it adores the glory of the Most **H.** A
7:*79* way of the Most **H,** who have despised his law A
7:*81* they have scorned the law of the Most **H.** A
7:*83* the covenants of the Most **H.** A
7:*87* of the Most **H** in whose presence they sinned A
7:*88* of those who have kept the ways of the Most **H,** A
7:*89* they laboriously served the Most **H,** A
7:*102* the ungodly or to entreat the Most **H** for them— A
7:*122* [52] the Most **H** will defend those who have led A
7:*132* [62] that the Most **H** is now called merciful, A
8: 1 "The Most **H** made this world for the sake of A
8:48 be praiseworthy before the Most **H,** A
8:56 despised the Most **H,** and were contemptuous A
8:59 For the Most **H** did not intend that anyone A
9: 2 that it is the very time when the Most **H** is about A
9: 4 Most **H** spoke from the days that were of old, A
9: 6 so also are the times of the Most **H:** A
9:25 and pray to the Most **H** continually. A
9:28 I began to speak before the Most **H,** and said, A
9:44 during those thirty years I prayed to the Most **H,** A
10:24 and the Most **H** may give you rest, A
10:38 the Most **H** has revealed many secrets to you. A
10:50 Most **H,** seeing that you are sincerely grieved A
10:52 the Most **H** would reveal these things to you. A
10:54 where the city of the Most **H** was to be revealed. A
10:57 and you have been called to be with the Most **H** A
10:59 and the Most **H** will show you A
10:59 Most **H** will do to those who inhabit the earth A
11:38 The Most **H** says to you, A
11:43 Your insolence has come up before the Most **H,** A
11:44 The Most **H** has looked at his times; A
12: 4 because you search out the ways of the Most **H.** A
12: 6 entreat the Most **H** that he may strengthen me A
12:23 last days the Most **H** will raise up three kings, A
12:30 It is these whom the Most **H** has kept for A
12:32 the Messiah whom the Most **H** has kept until A
12:36 to learn this secret of the Most **H.** A
12:39 be shown whatever it pleases the Most **H** A
12:47 for the Most **H** has you in remembrance, A
13:13 and prayed to the Most **H,** and said, A
13:26 this is he whom the Most **H** has been keeping A
13:29 Most **H** will deliver those who are on the earth. A
13:44 that time the Most **H** performed signs for them, A
13:47 Most **H** will stop the channels of the river again, A
13:56 for there is a reward laid up with the Most **H.** A
13:57 the Most **H** for the wonders that he does A
14:31 the ways that the Most **H** commanded you. A
14:42 the Most **H** gave understanding to the five men, A
14:45 forty days were ended, the Most **H** spoke to me, A
15:35 and there shall be blood from the sword as **h** as
15:40 and shall pour out upon every **h** and lofty place
4Mc 4: 1 Onias, who then held the **h** priesthood for life.
4:13 Moved by these words, the **h** priest Onias, B
4:16 and appointed Onias's brother Jason as **h** priest. B
4:18 appointed him **h** priest and ruler of the nation. B
5: 1 in state with his counselors on a certain **h** place, F

HIGH-HANDEDLY (1) [HAND, HIGH]

Nu 15:30 But whoever acts **h,** whether a native or an alien,

HIGH-PRIESTLY (1) [HIGH, PRIEST]

Ac 4: 6 and Alexander, and all who were of the **h** family.

HIGHER (17) [HIGH]

Nu 24: 7 his king shall be **h** than Agag,
Dt 28:43 among you shall ascend above you **h** and **h,**
Ezr 9: 6 for our iniquities have risen **h** than our heads,
Job 11: 8 It is **h** than heaven—what can you do?
35: 5 observe the clouds, which are **h** than you.
Ps 61: 2 Lead me to the rock that is **h** than I;
108: 4 For your steadfast love is **h** than the heavens,
Ecc 5: 8 for the high official is watched by a **h,**
5: 8 and there are yet **h** ones over them.
Isa 55: 9 For as the heavens are **h** than the earth,
55: 9 so are my ways **h** than your ways
Lk 14:10 he may say to you, 'Friend, move up **h**';
Sir 43: 1 pride of the **h** realms is the clear vault of the sky,
1Mc 12:36 to build the walls of Jerusalem still **h,**
14:37 and built the walls of Jerusalem **h.**
1Es 8:75 For our sins have risen **h** than our heads,

HIGHEST‡ (20) [HIGH]

1Ki 8:27 Even heaven and the **h** heaven cannot contain you,
2Ch 2: 6 since heaven, even **h** heaven, cannot contain him?
6:18 Even heaven and the **h** heaven cannot contain you,
Job 22:12 See the **h** stars, how lofty they are!
Ps 89:27 the **h** of the kings of the earth.
137: 6 if I do not set Jerusalem above my **h** joy.
148: 4 Praise him, you **h** heavens,
Pr 9: 3 she calls from the **h** places in the town,
Isa 2: 2 the LORD's house shall be established as the **h** of
17: 6 two or three berries in the top of the **h** bough,
Mic 4: 1 the LORD's house shall be established as the **h** of
Mt 21: 9 Hosanna in the **h** heaven!"
Mk 11:10 Hosanna in the **h** heaven!"
Lk 2:14 "Glory to God in the **h** heaven,
19:38 Peace in heaven, and glory in the **h** heaven!"
Sir 16:18 Lo, heaven and the **h** heaven,
24: 4 I dwelt in the **h** heavens,
2Mc 4:15 and putting the **h** value upon Greek forms
2Es 4:34 but the **H** is in a hurry on behalf of many.
4Mc 1: 2 in addition it includes the praise of the **h** virtue—

HIGHLANDS‡ (1) [HIGH, LAND]

2Es 15:58 Those who are in the mountains and **h** shall perish

HIGHLY (50) [HIGH]

1Ch 14: 2 and that his kingdom was **h** exalted for the sake
29:25 The LORD **h** exalted Solomon in the sight
Ps 47: 9 shields of the earth belong to God; he is **h** exalted.
Pr 4: 8 Prize her **h,** and she will exalt you;
Lk 7: 2 A centurion there had a slave whom he valued **h,**
Ro 12: 3 not to think of yourself more **h** than you ought
Php 2: 9 also **h** exalted him and gave him the name that is
1Th 5:13 esteem them very **h** in love because of their work.
Tob 14:14 He died **h** respected at the age
Jdt 6:20 Then they reassured Achior, and praised him **h.**
Sir Pr: 3 seemed **h** necessary that I should myself devote
19:24 the **h** intelligent who transgress the law.
Aza 1:29 and to be praised and **h** exalted forever;
1:30 and to be **h** praised and **h** exalted forever.
1:31 and to be extolled and **h** glorified forever.
1:32 and to be praised and **h** exalted forever.
1:33 and to be extolled and **h** exalted forever.
1:35 sing praise to him and **h** exalt him forever.
1:36 sing praise to him and **h** exalt him forever.
1:37 sing praise to him and **h** exalt him forever.
1:38 sing praise to him and **h** exalt him forever.
1:39 sing praise to him and **h** exalt him forever.
1:40 sing praise to him and **h** exalt him forever.
1:41 sing praise to him and **h** exalt him forever.
1:42 sing praise to him and **h** exalt him forever.
1:43 sing praise to him and **h** exalt him forever.
1:44 sing praise to him and **h** exalt him forever.
1:45 sing praise to him and **h** exalt him forever.
1:46 sing praise to him and **h** exalt him forever.
1:47 sing praise to him and **h** exalt him forever.
1:48 sing praise to him and **h** exalt him forever.
1:49 sing praise to him and **h** exalt him forever.
1:50 sing praise to him and **h** exalt him forever.
1:51 sing praise to him and **h** exalt him forever.
1:52 sing praise to him and **h** exalt him forever.
1:53 sing praise to him and **h** exalt him forever.
1:54 sing praise to him and **h** exalt him forever.
1:55 sing praise to him and **h** exalt him forever.
1:56 sing praise to him and **h** exalt him forever.
1:57 sing praise to him and **h** exalt him forever.
1:58 sing praise to him and **h** exalt him forever.
1:59 sing praise to him and **h** exalt him forever.
1:60 sing praise to him and **h** exalt him forever.
1:61 sing praise to him and **h** exalt him forever.
1:62 sing praise to him and **h** exalt him forever.
1:63 sing praise to him and **h** exalt him forever.
1:64 sing praise to him and **h** exalt him forever.
1:65 sing praise to him and **h** exalt him forever.
1:66 sing praise to him and **h** exalt him forever.

HIGHMINDED (KJV) See CONCEITED, HAUGHTY, PROUD

HIGHWAY‡ (20) [HIGH, WAY]

Nu 20:17 we will go along the King's **H,**
20:19 The Israelites said to him, "We will stay on the **h;**
21:22 we will go by the King's **H** until we have passed
Jdg 21:19 of the **h** that goes up from Bethel to Shechem,
1Sa 6:12 the direction of Beth-shemesh along one **h,** lowing
2Sa 20:12 Amasa lay wallowing in his blood on the **h,**
20:12 he carried Amasa from the **h** into a field,
20:13 Once he was removed from the **h,**
2Ki 18:17 which is on the **h** to the Fuller's Field.
Pr 15:19 but the path of the upright is a level **h.**
16:17 The **h** of the upright avoids evil;
Isa 7: 3 the end of the conduit of the upper pool on the **h** to
11:16 so there shall be a **h** from Assyria for the remnant
19:23 that day there will be a **h** from Egypt to Assyria,
35: 8 A **h** shall be there, and it shall be called
36: 2 He stood by the conduit of the upper pool on the **h**
40: 3 make straight in the desert a **h** for our God.
62:10 build up, build up the **h,** clear it of stones,
Jer 18:15 and have gone into bypaths, not the **h,**
31:21 consider well the **h,** the road by which you went.

HIGHWAYS (8) [HIGH, WAY]

Ps 84: 5 in whose heart are the **h** to Zion.
Isa 33: 8 The **h** are deserted, travelers have quit the road.
49:11 and my **h** shall be raised up.
59: 7 desolation and destruction are in their **h.**
Tob 1:15 the **h** into Media became unsafe
1Mc 5: 4 a snare to the people and ambushed them on the **h.**
15:41 that they might go out and make raids along the **h**
2Es 1:13 and made safe **h** for you where there was no road;

HILEN (1)

1Ch 6:58 **H** with its pasture lands, Debir

HILEZ See Index to Footnotes

HILKIAH (43)

2Ki 18:18 there came out to them Eliakim son of **H,**
18:26 Then Eliakim son of **H,** and Shebnah,
18:37 of **H,** who was in charge of the palace, and Shebna
22: 4 "Go up to the high priest **H,** and have him count
22: 8 The high priest **H** said to Shaphan the secretary,
22: 8 When **H** gave the book to Shaphan, he read it.
22:10 "The priest **H** has given me a book."
22:12 Then the king commanded the priest **H,**
22:14 So the priest **H,** Ahikam, Achbor, Shaphan,
23: 4 The king commanded the high priest **H,**
23:24 the book that the priest **H** had found in the house of
1Ch 6:13 Shallum of **H, H** of Azariah,
6:45 son of Hashabiah, son of Amaziah, son of **H,**
9:11 and Azariah son of **H,** son of Meshullam, son
26:11 **H** the second, Tebaliah the third, Zechariah
2Ch 34: 9 They came to the high priest **H** and delivered
34:14 the priest **H** found the book of the law of
34:15 **H** said to the secretary Shaphan,
34:15 and **H** gave the book to Shaphan.
34:18 "The priest **H** has given me a book."
34:20 Then the king commanded **H,**
34:22 So **H** and those whom the king had sent went to
35: 8 **H,** Zechariah, and Jehiel, the chief officers of
Ezr 7: 1 Ezra son of Seraiah, son of Azariah, son of **H,**
Ne 8: 4 Anaiah, Uriah, **H,** and Maaseiah on his right hand;
11:11 of **H** son of Meshullam son of Zadok son
12: 7 Amok, **H,** Jedaiah. These were the leaders of the
12:21 of **H,** Hashabiah; of Jedaiah, Nethanel.
Isa 22:20 that day I will call my servant Eliakim son of **H,**
36: 3 And there came out to him Eliakim son of **H,**
36:22 of **H,** who was in charge of the palace, and Shebna
Jer 1: 1 The words of Jeremiah son of **H,**
29: 3 of Elasah son of Shaphan and Gemariah son of **H,**
Jdt 8: 1 of Ahitub son of Elijah son of **H** son of Eliab son
Bar 1: 1 of Zedekiah son of Hasadiah son of **H** wrote
1: 7 the high priest Jehoiakim son of **H** son of Shallum,
Sus 1: 2 He married the daughter of **H,** named Susanna,
1:29 "Send for Susanna daughter of **H,**
1:63 **H** and his wife praised God
1Es 1: 8 **H,** Zechariah, and Jehiel, the chief officers of
8: 1 of Seraiah son of Azariah son of **H** son of Shallum
2Es 1: 1 of **H** son of Shallum son of Zadok son of Ahitub

HILL‡ (175) [DUNGHILL, DUNGHILLS, HILLS, HILLSIDE, HILLTOPS]

A. HILL COUNTRY (118)

Ge 10:30 the **h** country of the east. A
12: 8 From there he moved on to the **h** country on A
14: 6 the **h** country of Seir as far as El-paran A
14:10 and the rest fled to the **h** country. A
31:21 and set his face toward the **h** country of Gilead. A
31:23 until he caught up with him in the **h** country A
31:25 Now Jacob had pitched his tent in the **h** country, A
31:25 with his kinsfolk camped in the **h** country A
31:54 ate bread and tarried all night in the **h** country. A
36: 8 So Esau settled in the **h** country of Seir; A
36: 9 of the Edomites, in the **h** country of Seir. A
Ex 17: 9 the top of the **h** with the staff of God in my hand."
17:10 Aaron, and Hur went up to the top of the **h.**
Nu 13:17 and go up into the **h** country, A
13:29 and the Amorites live in the **h** country; A
14:40 and went up to the heights of the **h** country, A
14:44 to go up to the heights of the **h** country, A
14:45 the Canaanites who lived in that **h** country came A
Dt 1: 7 go into the **h** country of the Amorites as well A
1: 7 the Arabah, the **h** country, the Shephelah, A
1:19 on the way to the **h** country of the Amorites, A
1:20 have reached the **h** country of the Amorites, A
1:24 They set out and went up into the **h** country, A
1:41 and thought it easy to go up into the **h** country A
1:43 and presumptuously went up into the **h** country. A
1:44 in that **h** country then came out against you A
2: 3 "You have been skirting this **h** country long A
2:37 as well as the towns of the **h** country, A
3:12 half the **h** country of Gilead with its towns, A
3:25 that good **h** country and the Lebanon." A
Jos 2:16 She said to them, "Go toward the **h** country, A
2:22 into the **h** country and stayed there three days, A
2:23 two men came down again from the **h** country. A
9: 1 the **h** country and in the lowland all along A
10: 6 in the **h** country are gathered against us." A
10:40 the **h** country and the Negeb and the lowland A
11: 2 to the kings who were in the northern **h** country, A
11: 3 the Perizzites, and the Jebusites in the **h** country, A
11:16 the **h** country and all the Negeb and all the land A
11:16 the lowland and the Arabah and the **h** country A
11:21 and wiped out the Anakim from the **h** country, A
11:21 from Anab, and from all the **h** country of Judah, A
11:21 and from all the **h** country of Israel; A
12: 8 in the **h** country, in the lowland, in the Arabah, A
13: 6 **h** country from Lebanon to Misrephoth-maim, A
13:19 and Zereth-shahar on the **h** of the valley,
14:12 So now give me this **h** country of which A
15:11 of the **h** north of Ekron, then the boundary bends
15:48 And in the **h** country, Shamir, Jattir, Socoh, A
16: 1 from Jericho into the **h** country to Bethel; A
17:15 the **h** country of Ephraim is too narrow for you." A

Jos 17:16 "The **h** country is not enough for us; A
17:18 but the **h** country shall be yours, for though it is A
18:12 then up through the **h** country westward; A
19:50 Timnath-serah in the **h** country of Ephraim; A
20: 7 in Galilee in the **h** country of Naphtali, A
20: 7 and Shechem in the **h** country of Ephraim, A
20: 7 Hebron) in the **h** country of Judah. A
21:11 that is Hebron, in the **h** country of Judah, A
21:21 its pasture lands in the **h** country of Ephraim, A
24: 4 I gave Esau the **h** country of Seir to possess, A
24:30 which is in the **h** country of Ephraim, A
24:33 which had been given him in the **h** country A
Jdg 1: 9 the Canaanites who lived in the **h** country, A
1:19 and he took possession of the **h** country, A
1:34 the Danites back into the **h** country; A
2: 9 in the **h** country of Ephraim, A
3:27 the trumpet in the **h** country of Ephraim; A
3:27 went down with him from the **h** country, A
4: 5 between Ramah and Bethel in the **h** country A
7: 1 below the **h** of Moreh, in the valley.
7:24 throughout all the **h** country of Ephraim, A
10: 1 lived at Shamir in the **h** country of Ephraim, A
12:15 in the **h** country of the Amalekites. A
16: 3 and carried them to the top of the **h** that is in front
17: 1 **h** country of Ephraim whose name was Micah. A
17: 8 the house of Micah in the **h** country of Ephraim A
18: 2 When they came to the **h** country of Ephraim, A
18:13 From there they passed on to the **h** country A
19: 1 in the remote parts of the **h** country of Ephraim, A
19:16 The man was from the **h** country of Ephraim, A
19:18 to the remote parts of the **h** country of Ephraim, A
1Sa 1: 1 a Zuphite from the **h** country of Ephraim, A
7: 1 and brought it to the house of Abinadab on the **h.**
9: 4 the **h** country of Ephraim and passed through A
9:11 As they went up the **h** to the town,
13: 2 and the **h** country of Bethel, and a thousand A
14:22 into hiding in the **h** country of Ephraim heard A
14:23 battle spread out over the **h** country of Ephraim. A
23:14 in the **h** country of the Wilderness of Ziph. A
23:19 on the **h** of Hachilah, which is south of Jeshimon.
26: 1 saying, "David is in hiding on the **h** of Hachilah,
26: 3 Saul encamped on the **h** of Hachilah,
26:13 and stood on top of a **h** far away,
2Sa 2:24 As the sun was going down they came to the **h**
2:25 they took their stand on the top of a **h.**
6: 3 of the house of Abinadab, which was on the **h.**
20:21 But a man of the **h** country of Ephraim, A
1Ki 4: 8 Ben-hur, in the **h** country of Ephraim; A
5:15 eighty thousand stonecutters in the **h** country, A
12:25 Then Jeroboam built Shechem in the **h** country A
14:23 on every high **h** and under every green tree;
16:24 the **h** of Samaria from Shemer for two talents
16:24 he fortified the **h,** and called the city that he built,
16:24 after the name of Shemer, the owner of the **h.**
2Ki 1: 9 who was sitting on the top of a **h,** and said to him,
5:22 to me from the **h** country of Ephraim; A
17:10 on every high **h** and under every green tree;
1Ch 6:67 its pasture lands in the **h** country of Ephraim, A
2Ch 2: 2 eighty thousand stonecutters in the **h** country, A
2:18 eighty thousand as stonecutters in the **h** country, A
13: 4 of Mount Zemaraim that is in the **h** country A
15: 8 the towns that he had taken in the **h** country A
19: 4 from Beer-sheba to the **h** country of Ephraim, A
21:11 he made high places in the **h** country of Judah, A
27: 4 he built cities in the **h** country of Judah, A
Ps 2: 6 "I have set my king on Zion, my holy **h.**"
3: 4 and he answers me from his holy **h.**
15: 1 Who may dwell on your holy **h?**
24: 3 Who shall ascend the **h** of the LORD?
43: 3 let them bring me to your holy **h** and
78:54 And he brought them to his holy **h,**
SS 4: 6 the mountain of myrrh and the **h** of frankincense.
Isa 5: 1 My beloved had a vineyard on a very fertile **h.**
10:32 at the mount of daughter Zion, the **h** of Jerusalem.
13: 2 On a bare **h** raise a signal, cry aloud to them;
30:17 like a signal on a **h.**
30:25 and every high **h** there will be brooks running
31: 4 down to fight upon Mount Zion and upon its **h.**
32:14 the **h** and the watchtower will become dens
40: 4 and every mountain and **h** be made low;
Jer 2:20 On every high **h** and under every green tree
3: 6 up on every high **h** and under every green tree,
16:16 from every mountain and every **h,**
17:26 from the **h** country, and from the Negeb, A
31: 6 a day when sentinels will call in the **h** country A
31:23 O abode of righteousness, O holy **h!**"
31:39 straight to the **h** Gareb, and shall then turn
32:44 and in the cities of Judah, of the **h** country, A
33:13 In the towns of the **h** country, of the Shephelah, A
49:16 who hold the height of the **h.**
50: 6 from mountain to **h** they have gone,
Eze 6:13 on every high **h,** on all the mountain tops,
20:28 wherever they saw any high **h** or any leafy tree,
34: 6 over all the mountains and on every high **h;**
34:26 I will make them and the region around my **h**
Mic 4: 8 And you, O tower of the flock, **h** of daughter Zion,
Mal 1: 3 I have made his **h** country a desolation A
Mt 5:14 A city built on a **h** cannot be hid.
Lk 1:39 with haste to a Judean town in the **h** country, A
1:65 about throughout the entire **h** country of Judea. A
3: 5 and every mountain and **h** shall be made low,
4:29 to the brow of the **h** on which their town was built,
Jdt 1: 6 people of the **h** country and all those who lived A
2:22 and chariots, and went up into the **h** country. A
5: 3 what people is this that lives in the **h** country? A
5:15 they took possession of all the **h** country. A
5:19 and have settled in the **h** country, A
Jdt 6: 7 the **h** country and put you in one of the towns A
6:11 they went up into the **h** country and came A
6:12 and ran out of the town to the top of the **h,**
6:13 So having taken shelter below the **h,**
6:13 and left him lying at the foot of the **h,**
7: 1 the **h** country and make war on the Israelites. A
7:18 encamped in the **h** country opposite Dothan; A
10:13 by which he can go and capture all the **h** country A
11: 2 if your people who live in the **h** country had A
15: 2 across the plain and through the **h** country. A
15: 5 in Jerusalem and all the **h** country also came, A
15: 7 Even the villages and towns in the **h** country A
Sir 46: 9 so that he went up to the **h** country, A
1Mc 4:46 the stones in a convenient place on the temple **h**
10:70 against us in the **h** country? A
13:52 the fortifications of the temple **h** alongside
16:20 to take possession of Jerusalem and the temple **h.**

HILLEL (2)

Jdg 12:13 him Abdon son of **H** the Pirathonite judged Israel.
12:15 Then Abdon son of **H** the Pirathonite died,

HILLS (72) [HILL]

Ge 19:17 flee to the **h,** or else you will be consumed."
19:19 but I cannot flee to the **h,**
19:30 of Zoar and settled in the **h** with his two daughters,
49:26 the bounties of the everlasting **h;**
Nu 23: 9 from the **h** I behold him;
Dt 8: 7 underground waters welling up in valleys and **h,**
8: 9 and from whose **h** you may mine copper.
11:11 that you are crossing over to occupy is a land of **h**
12: 2 on the **h,** and under every leafy tree.
33:15 and the abundance of the everlasting **h;**
1Ki 20:23 "Their gods are gods of the **h,**
20:28 'The LORD is a god of the **h** but he is not a god
2Ki 16: 4 on the **h,** and under every green tree.
2Ch 26:10 and he had farmers and vinedressers in the **h** and
27: 4 and forts and towers on the wooded **h.**
28: 4 on the **h,** and under every green tree.
Ne 8:15 "Go out to the **h** and bring branches of olive,
Job 15: 7 Were you brought forth before the **h?**
Ps 50:10 the cattle on a thousand **h.**
65:12 the **h** gird themselves with joy,
72: 3 and the **h,** in righteousness.
98: 8 let the **h** sing together for joy
104:10 in the valleys; they flow between the **h,**
114: 4 The mountains skipped like rams, the **h** like lambs.
114: 6 that you skip like rams? O **h,**
121: 1 I lift up my eyes to the **h**—
147: 8 makes grass grow on the **h.**
148: 9 Mountains and all **h,** fruit trees and all cedars!
Pr 8:25 the mountains had been shaped, before the **h,**
SS 2: 8 leaping upon the mountains, bounding over the **h.**
Isa 2: 2 and shall be raised above the **h;**
2:14 and against all the lofty **h;**
7:25 and as for all the **h** that used to be hoed with a hoe,
40:12 and weighed the mountains in scales and the **h** in
41:15 and you shall make the **h** like chaff.
42:15 I will lay waste mountains and **h,**
54:10 the mountains may depart and the **h** be removed,
55:12 the mountains and the **h** before you shall burst
65: 7 on the mountains and reviled me on the **h,**
Jer 3:23 Truly the **h** are a delusion,
4:24 they were quaking, and all the **h** moved to and fro.
13:27 your shameless prostitutions on the **h** of
17: 2 beside every green tree, and on the high **h,**
50:19 on the **h** of Ephraim and in Gilead its hunger shall
Eze 6: 3 the Lord GOD to the mountains and the **h,** to
35: 8 on your **h** and in your valleys and
36: 4 to the mountains and the **h,** the watercourses and
36: 6 and say to the mountains and **h,**
Hos 4:13 and make offerings upon the **h,** under oak, poplar,
10: 8 Cover us, and to the **h,** Fall on us.
Joel 3:18 the **h** shall flow with milk,
Am 9:13 and all the **h** shall flow with it.
Mic 4: 1 and shall be raised up above the **h.**
6: 1 and let the **h** hear your voice.
Na 1: 5 The mountains quake before him, and the **h** melt;
Hab 3: 6 the everlasting **h** sank low.
Zep 1:10 a loud crash from the **h.**
Hag 1: 8 up to the **h** and bring wood and build the house,
1:11 I have called for a drought on the land and the **h,**
Lk 23:30 'Fall on us'; and to the **h,**
Jdt 7: 4 nor the valleys nor the **h** will bear their weight."
15: 3 Those who had camped in the **h** around Bethulia
16: 3 and their cavalry covered the **h.**
Bar 5: 7 that every high mountain and the everlasting **h**
Aza 1:53 Bless the Lord, mountains and **h;**
1Mc 2:28 and his sons fled to the **h** and left all that they had
4: 5 so he looked for them in the **h,** because he said,
4:18 Gorgias and his force are near us in the **h.**
4:19 a detachment appeared, coming out of the **h.**
6:39 the **h** were ablaze with them and gleamed
6:40 of the king's army was spread out on the high **h,**
2Es 15:42 mountains and **h,** trees of the forests,

HILLSIDE (3) [HILL]

2Sa 16:13 along on the **h** opposite him and cursed as he went,
Mk 5:11 there on the **h** a great herd of swine was feeding;
Lk 8:32 there on the **h** a large herd of swine was feeding;

HILLTOPS (2) [HILL]

Jdt 4: 5 the high **h** and fortified the villages on them
5: 1 and fortified all the high **h** and set up barricades in

HILT (1)

Jdg 3:22 the **h** also went in after the blade,

HIM (6317) [HE] See Index of Articles Etc.

HIMSELF (447) [HE] See Index of Articles Etc.

HIN (22)

Ex 29:40 of choice flour mixed with one-fourth of a **h**
29:40 and one-fourth of a **h** of wine for a drink offering.
30:24 and a **h** of olive oil;
Lev 19:36 honest weights, an honest ephah, and an honest **h:**
23:13 with it shall be of wine, one-fourth of a **h.**
Nu 15: 4 mixed with one-fourth of a **h** of oil.
15: 5 you shall offer one-fourth of a **h** of wine as
15: 6 of choice flour mixed with one-third of a **h** of oil;
15: 7 as a drink offering you shall offer one-third of a **h**
15: 9 mixed with half a **h** of oil,
15:10 and you shall present as a drink offering half a **h**
28: 5 mixed with one-fourth of a **h** of beaten oil.
28: 7 Its drink offering shall be one-fourth of a **h**
28:14 Their drink offerings shall be half a **h** of wine for
28:14 one-third of a **h** for a ram,
28:14 and one-fourth of a **h** for a lamb.
Eze 4:11 one-sixth of a **h;** at fixed times you shall drink.
45:24 and a **h** of oil to each ephah.
46: 5 together with a **h** of oil to each ephah.
46: 7 together with a **h** of oil to each ephah.
46:11 together with a **h** of oil to an ephah.
46:14 one-third of a **h** of oil to moisten the choice flour,

HIND (KJV) See DEER, DOE

HINDER (14) [HINDERED, HINDERING, HINDRANCE]

Nu 22:16 'Do not let anything **h** you from coming to me;
1Sa 14: 6 for nothing can **h** the LORD from saving by many
Job 11:10 and assembles for judgment, who can **h** him?
Isa 43:13 I work and who can **h** it?
Ac 11:17 who was I that I could **h** God?"
1Pe 3: 7 so that nothing may **h** your prayers.
Jdt 12: 7 So Holofernes commanded his guards not to **h** her.
Sir 18:22 Let nothing **h** you from paying a vow promptly,
1Es 2:30 and began to **h** the builders.
6:33 and nation that shall stretch out their hands to **h**
2Es 3: 8 and you did not **h** them.
4Mc 1: 3 over those emotions that **h** self-control,
1: 4 that it masters the emotions that **h** one from justice,
2: 6 so it is with the emotions that **h** one from justice.

HINDERED (6) [HINDER]

Lk 11:52 and you **h** those who were entering."
Ro 15:22 the reason that I have so often been **h** from coming
Wis 10: 8 they not only were **h** from recognizing the good,
1Mc 9:55 Alcimus was stricken and his work was **h;**
1Es 5:72 cut off their supplies, and **h** their building;
3Mc 3: 2 a pretext being given by a report that they **h** others

HINDERING (2) [HINDER]

Job 15: 4 and **h** meditation before God.
1Th 2:16 by **h** us from speaking to the Gentiles so

HINDERMOST, HINDMOST (KJV) See LAST, LAGGING BEHIND, REAR

HINDQUARTERS (2)

1Ki 7:25 The **h** of each were toward the inside.
2Ch 4: 4 The **h** of each were toward the inside.

HINDRANCE (2) [HINDER]

Ac 28:31 with all boldness and without **h.**
Ro 14:13 a stumbling block or **h** in the way of another.

HINGES (1)

Pr 26:14 a door turns on its **h,** so does a lazy person in bed.

HINNOM (12) [BEN-HINNOM]

Jos 15: 8 the boundary goes up by the valley of the son of **H**
15: 8 the mountain that lies over against the valley of **H,**
18:16 the son of **H,** which is at the north end of the valley
18:16 and it then goes down the valley of **H,**
2Ch 28: 3 he made offerings in the valley of the son of **H,**
33: 6 through fire in the valley of the son of **H,**
Ne 11:30 they camped from Beer-sheba to the valley of **H.**
Jer 7:31 which is in the valley of the son of **H,**
7:32 or the valley of the son of **H,**
19: 2 and go out to the valley of the son of **H** at the entry
19: 6 or the valley of the son of **H,**
32:35 of Baal in the valley of the son of **H,**

HIP (6) [HIPS]

Ge 32:25 he struck him on the **h** socket;
32:25 and Jacob's **h** was put out of joint as he wrestled
32:31 as he passed Penuel, limping because of his **h.**
32:32 not eat the thigh muscle that is on the **h** socket,
32:32 he struck Jacob on the **h** socket at the thigh muscle.
Jdg 15: 8 down **h** and thigh with great slaughter;

HIPPODROME (3)
3Mc 4:11 be enclosed in the **h** that had been built with
5:46 of people crowding their way into the **h**—
6:16 the king arrived at the **h** with the animals and all

HIPS (3) [HIP]
Ex 28:42 they shall reach from the **h** to the thighs;
2Sa 10: 4 cut off their garments in the middle at their **h,**
1Ch 19: 4 cut off their garments in the middle at their **h,**

HIRAH (2)
Ge 38: 1 near a certain Adullamite whose name was **H.**
38:12 he and his friend **H** the Adullamite.

HIRAM (22) [HIRAM'S, =HURAM, =HURAM-ABI]
2Sa 5:11 King **H** of Tyre sent messengers to David,
1Ki 5: 1 Now King **H** of Tyre sent his servants to Solomon,
5: 1 for **H** had always been a friend to David.
5: 2 Solomon sent word to **H,** saying,
5: 7 When **H** heard the words of Solomon,
5: 8 **H** sent word to Solomon, "I have heard
5:10 So **H** supplied Solomon's every need for timber
5:11 Solomon in turn gave **H** twenty thousand cors
5:11 Solomon gave this to **H** year by year.
5:12 There was peace between **H** and Solomon;
7:13 King Solomon invited and received **H** from Tyre.
7:40 **H** also made the pots, the shovels, and the basins.
7:40 So **H** finished all the work that he did
7:45 all these vessels that **H** made for King Solomon for
9:11 King **H** of Tyre having supplied Solomon
9:11 King Solomon gave to **H** twenty cities in the land
9:12 But when **H** came from Tyre to see the cities
9:14 **H** had sent to the king one hundred twenty talents
9:27 **H** sent his servants with the fleet,
10:11 the fleet of **H,** which carried gold from Ophir,
10:22 of ships of Tarshish at sea with the fleet of **H.**
1Ch 14: 1 King **H** of Tyre sent messengers to David,

HIRAM'S (1) [HIRAM]
1Ki 5:18 So Solomon's builders and **H** builders and

HIRE (4) [HIRED, HIRES, HIRING]
Ge 30:18 "God has given me my **h** because I gave my maid
1Ch 19: 6 to **h** chariots and cavalry from Mesopotamia,
Isa 46: 6 they **h** a goldsmith, who makes it into a god;
Mt 20: 1 in the morning to **h** laborers for his vineyard.

HIRED‡ (37) [HIRE]
Ge 30:16 for I have **h** you with my son's mandrakes."
Ex 12:45 no bound or **h** servant may eat of it.
22:15 if it was **h,** only the hiring fee is due.
Lev 22:10 No bound or **h** servant of the priest shall eat of
25: 6 your **h** and your bound laborers who live with you;
25:40 They shall remain with you as **h** or bound laborers.
25:50 the owner shall be rated as the time of a **h** laborer.
25:53 As a laborer **h** by the year they shall be under
Dt 15:18 services worth the wages of **h** laborers;
23: 4 because they **h** against you Balaam son of Beor,
Jdg 9: 4 of Baal-berith with which Abimelech **h** worthless
18: 4 "Micah did such and such for me, and he **h** me,
1Sa 2: 5 Those who were full have **h** themselves out
2Sa 10: 6 the Ammonites sent and **h** the Arameans
2Ki 7: 6 "The king of Israel has **h** the kings of the Hittites
1Ch 19: 7 They **h** thirty-two thousand chariots and the king
2Ch 24:12 and they **h** masons and carpenters to restore
25: 6 He also **h** one hundred thousand mighty warriors
Ne 6:12 because Tobiah and Sanballat had **h** him.
6:13 He was **h** for this purpose,
13: 2 but **h** Balaam against them to curse them—
Isa 7:20 that day the Lord will shave with a razor **h** beyond
16:14 In three years, like the years of a **h** worker,
21:16 according to the years of a **h** worker,
Mal 3: 5 against those who oppress the **h** workers
Mt 20: 7 They said to him, 'Because no one has **h** us.
20: 9 When those **h** about five o'clock came,
Mk 1:20 in the boat with the **h** men,
Lk 15:15 So he went and **h** himself out to one of the citizens
15:17 of my father's **h** hands have bread enough and
15:19 treat me like one of your **h** hands." '
Jn 10:12 The **h** hand, who is not the shepherd and does
10:13 The **h** hand runs away because a **h** hand does
Jdt 4:10 and every resident alien and **h** laborer
Sir 7:20 or **h** laborers who devote themselves to their task.
1Mc 5:39 They also have **h** Arabs to help them,

HIRELING (KJV) See HIRED HAND, HIRED WORKERS, LABORERS

HIRES (1) [HIRE]
Pr 26:10 wounds everybody is one who **h** a passing fool

HIRING (1) [HIRE]
Ex 22:15 if it was hired, only the **h** fee is due.

HIS (7714) [HE] See Index of Articles Etc.

HISS (7) [HISSED, HISSES, HISSING]
1Ki 9: 8 by it will be astonished, and will **h;**
Jer 19: 8 be horrified and will **h** because of all its disasters.
Jer 49:17 be horrified and will **h** because of all its disasters.
50:13 be appalled and **h** because of all her wounds.
La 2:15 they **h** and wag their heads at daughter Jerusalem;
2:16 they **h,** they gnash their teeth, they cry:
Eze 27:36 The merchants among the peoples **h** at you;

HISSED (2) [HISS]
Jer 18:16 a thing to be **h** at forever.
19: 8 I will make this city a horror, a thing to be **h** at;

HISSES (3) [HISS]
Job 27:23 and **h** at them from its place.
Zep 2:15 Everyone who passes by it **h** and shakes the fist.
Sir 22: 1 and every one **h** at his disgrace.

HISSING (8) [HISS]
2Ch 29: 8 and of **h,** as you see with your own eyes.
Jer 25: 9 and make them an object of horror and of **h,**
25:18 an object of **h** and of cursing, as they are today;
29:18 to be an object of cursing, and horror, and **h,**
51:37 an object of horror and of **h,** without inhabitant.
Mic 6:16 and your inhabitants an object of **h;**
Wis 17: 9 by the passing of wild animals and the **h** of snakes
2Es 15:29 their **h** shall spread over the earth,

HISTORIAN (1) [HISTORY]
2Mc 2:30 the duty of the original **h** to occupy the ground,

HISTORIC (1) [HISTORY]
Ne 2:20 but you have no share or claim or **h** right

HISTORIES (1) [HISTORY]
1Es 1:33 These things are written in the book of the **h** of

HISTORY (4) [HISTORIAN, HISTORIC, HISTORIES]
2Ch 9:29 are they not written in the **h** of the prophet Nathan,
2Mc 2:24 the narratives of **h** because of the mass of material,
2:32 the preface while cutting short the **h** itself.
4Mc 17: 7 to paint the **h** of your religion as an artist might,

HIT (2)
1Ki 20:37 So the man **h** him, striking and wounding him.
2Mc 14:43 But in the heat of the struggle he did not **h** exactly,

HITCHED (1)
Jdt 15:11 and loaded her mules and **h** up her carts and piled

HITHER (KJV) See BACK, BRING, CLOSER, GET, HERE

HITHERTO (KJV) See AT THAT TIME, IN TIME PAST, PREVIOUSLY, SINCE, STILL, THUS FAR, UNTIL NOW

HITTITE (25) [HETH]
Ge 23:10 the **H** answered Abraham in the hearing of
25: 9 in the field of Ephron son of Zohar the **H,**
26:34 he married Judith daughter of Beeri the **H,**
26:34 and Basemath daughter of Elon the **H;**
27:46 "I am weary of my life because of the **H** women.
27:46 If Jacob marries one of the **H** women such as these,
36: 2 Adah daughter of Elon the **H,**
49:29 in the cave in the field of Ephron the **H,**
49:30 the field that Abraham bought from Ephron the **H**
50:13 as a burial site from Ephron the **H.**
1Sa 26: 6 Then David said to Ahimelech the **H,**
2Sa 11: 3 the wife of Uriah the **H."**
11: 6 David sent word to Joab, "Send me Uriah the **H."**
11:17 Uriah the **H** was killed as well.
11:21 'Your servant Uriah the **H** is dead too.' "
11:24 and your servant Uriah the **H** is dead also."
12: 9 You have struck down Uriah the **H** with the sword,
12:10 have taken the wife of Uriah the **H** to be your wife.
23:39 Uriah the **H**—thirty-seven in all.
1Ki 11: 1 Ammonite, Edomite, Sidonian, and **H** women,
15: 5 except in the matter of Uriah the **H.**
1Ch 11:41 Uriah the **H,** Zabad son of Ahlai,
Ne 9: 8 the **H,** the Amorite, the Perizzite, the Jebusite,
Eze 16: 3 your father was an Amorite, and your mother a **H.**
16:45 Your mother was a **H** and your father an Amorite.

HITTITES (37) [HETH]
Ge 15:20 the **H,** the Perizzites, the Rephaim,
23: 3 up from beside his dead, and said to the **H,**
23: 5 The **H** answered Abraham,
23: 7 Abraham rose and bowed to the **H,**
23:10 Now Ephron was sitting among the **H;**
23:10 in the hearing of the **H,**
23:16 that he had named in the hearing of the **H,**
23:18 as a possession in the presence of the **H,**
23:20 in it passed from the **H** into Abraham's possession
25:10 the field that Abraham purchased from the **H.**
49:32 the cave that is in it were purchased from the **H."**
Ex 3: 8 the **H,** the Amorites, the Perizzites, the Hivites,
3:17 to the land of the Canaanites, the **H,** the Amorites,
13: 5 the **H,** the Amorites, the Hivites, and the Jebusites,
23:23 the **H,** the Perizzites, the Canaanites, the Hivites,
23:28 the Canaanites, and the **H** from before you.
Ex 33: 2 the **H,** the Perizzites, the Hivites, and the Jebusites.
34:11 the **H,** the Perizzites, the Hivites, and the Jebusites.
Nu 13:29 the **H,** the Jebusites, and the Amorites live in
Dt 7: 1 the **H,** the Girgashites, the Amorites,
20:17 the **H** and the Amorites, the Canaanites and
Jos 1: 4 the river Euphrates, all the land of the **H,**
3:10 **H,** Hivites, Perizzites, Girgashites, Amorites,
9: 1 the **H,** the Amorites, the Canaanites, the Perizzites,
11: 3 the Amorites, the **H,** the Perizzites,
12: 8 the land of the **H,** Amorites, Canaanites, Perizzites,
24:11 the Canaanites, the **H,** the Girgashites, the Hivites,
Jdg 1:26 the man went to the land of the **H** and built a city,
3: 5 the Israelites lived among the Canaanites, the **H,**
2Sa 24: 6 and to Kadesh in the land of the **H;**
1Ki 9:20 the **H,** the Perizzites, the Hivites, and the Jebusites,
10:29 to all the kings of the **H** and the kings of Aram.
2Ki 7: 6 the **H** and the kings of Egypt to fight against us."
2Ch 1:17 to all the kings of the **H** and the kings of Aram.
8: 7 All the people who were left of the **H,**
Ezr 9: 1 the **H,** the Perizzites, the Jebusites, the Ammonites,
1Es 8:69 the Canaanites, the **H,** the Perizzites, the Jebusites,

HIVE (1)
4Mc 14:19 sting those who approach their **h** and defend it

HIVITE (2) [HIVITES]
Ge 34: 2 When Shechem son of Hamor the **H,**
36: 2 of Anah son of Zibeon the **H,**

HIVITES (24) [HIVITE]
Ge 10:17 the **H,** the Arkites, the Sinites,
Ex 3: 8 the Hittites, the Amorites, the Perizzites, the **H,**
3:17 the Hittites, the Amorites, the Perizzites, the **H,**
13: 5 the Hittites, the Amorites, the **H,** and the Jebusites,
23:23 the Hittites, the Perizzites, the Canaanites, the **H,**
23:28 which shall drive out the **H,** the Canaanites,
33: 2 the Hittites, the Perizzites, the **H,** and the Jebusites.
34:11 the Hittites, the Perizzites, the **H,** and the Jebusites.
Dt 7: 1 the Amorites, the Canaanites, the Perizzites, the **H,**
20:17 and the Perizzites, the **H** and the Jebusites—
Jos 3:10 **H,** Perizzites, Girgashites, Amorites, and Jebusites:
9: 1 the Amorites, the Canaanites, the Perizzites, the **H,**
9: 7 But the Israelites said to the **H,**
11: 3 and the **H** under Hermon in the land of Mizpah.
11:19 except the **H,** the inhabitants of Gibeon;
12: 8 Canaanites, Perizzites, **H,** and Jebusites):
24:11 the Canaanites, the Hittites, the Girgashites, the **H,**
Jdg 3: 3 and the **H** who lived on Mount Lebanon,
3: 5 the Hittites, the Amorites, the Perizzites, the **H,**
2Sa 24: 7 to the fortress of Tyre and to all the cities of the **H**
1Ki 9:20 the Hittites, the Perizzites, the **H,** and the Jebusites,
1Ch 1:15 the **H,** the Arkites, the Sinites,
2Ch 8: 7 the **H,** and the Jebusites, who were not of Israel,
Isa 17: 9 like the deserted places of the **H** and the Amorites,

HIZKI (1)
1Ch 8:17 Zebadiah, Meshullam, **H,** Heber,

HIZKIAH (1)
1Ch 3:23 sons of Neariah: Elioenai, **H,** and Azrikam, three.

HO (1)
Isa 55: 1 **H,** everyone who thirsts, come to the waters;

HO (KJV) See also COME, UP

HOARDED (2) [HOARDS]
Isa 23:18 her profits will not be stored or **h,**
Bar 3:17 and who **h** up silver and gold in which people trust,

HOARDS (2) [HOARDED]
Isa 34: 2 and furious against all their **h;**
Sir 41:12 since it will outlive you longer than a thousand **h**

HOARFROST (1) [FROST]
Job 38:29 and who has given birth to the **h** of heaven?

HOAR (KJV) See GRAY, FINE FLAKES

HOARY (KJV) See AGED, HOARFROST, GRAY HAIR, WHITE-HAIRED

HOBAB‡ (3)
Nu 10:29 Moses said to **H** son of Reuel the Midianite,
Jdg 1:16 The descendants of **H** the Kenite,
4:11 the descendants of **H** the father-in-law of Moses,

HOBAH (1)
Ge 14:15 and routed them and pursued them to **H,**

HOBAIAH (1) [=HABAIAH]
Ne 7:63 Also, of the priests: the descendants of **H,**

HOCK (1)
2Es 15:36 and a man's thigh and a camel's **h.**

HOD (1)
1Ch 7:37 Bezer, **H,** Shamma, Shilshah, Ithran, and Beera.

HODAH See Index to Footnotes

HODAIAH (KJV) See HODIAH

HODAVIAH (5)

1Ch 3:24 The sons of Elioenai: **H,** Eliashib, Pelaiah, Akkub,
5:24 Epher, Ishi, Eliel, Azriel, Jeremiah, **H,** and Jahdiel,
9: 7 Sallu son of Meshullam, son of **H,**
Ezr 2:40 of the descendants of **H,** seventy-four.
3: 9 Binnui and **H** along with the sons of Henadad,

HODESH (1)

1Ch 8: 9 He had sons by his wife **H:**

HODEVAH (1)

Ne 7:43 namely of Kadmiel of the descendants of **H,**

HODIAH (7)

1Ch 4:19 The sons of the wife of **H,** the sister of Naham,
Ne 8: 7 Shabbethai, **H,** Maaseiah, Kelita, Azariah, Jozabad,
9: 5 Sherebiah, **H,** Shebaniah, and Pethahiah, said,
10:10 Shebaniah, **H,** Kelita, Pelaiah, Hanan,
10:13 **H,** Bani, Beninu.
10:18 **H,** Hashum, Bezai,
1Es 9:48 **H,** Maiannas and Kelita, Azariah and Jozabad,

HODIJAH (KJV) See HODIAH

HOE (1) [HOED]

Isa 7:25 that used to be hoed with a **h,** you will not go there

HOED (2) [HOE]

Isa 5: 6 I will make it a waste; it shall not be pruned or **h,**
7:25 and as for all the hills that used to be **h** with a hoe,

HOGLAH (4)

Nu 26:33 Noah, **H,** Milcah, and Tirzah.
27: 1 Mahlah, Noah, **H,** Milcah, and Tirzah.
36:11 Mahlah, Tirzah, **H,** Milcah, and Noah,
Jos 17: 3 Mahlah, Noah, **H,** Milcah, and Tirzah.

HOHAM (1)

Jos 10: 3 of Jerusalem sent a message to King **H** of Hebron,

HOISED (KJV) See HOISTING

HOISTING (2)

Ac 27:17 **h** it up they took measures to undergird the ship;
27:40 **h** the foresail to the wind, they made for the beach.

HOLD‡ (167) [HELD, HOLDING, HOLDINGS, HOLDS]

Ge 21:18 lift up the boy and **h** him fast with your hand,
39:12 she caught **h** of his garment,
43: 9 you can **h** me accountable for him.
Ex 9: 2 For if you refuse to let them go and still **h** them,
12:16 On the first day you shall **h** a solemn assembly,
23: 5 and you would **h** back from setting it free,
23:14 Three times in the year you shall **h** a festival
25:27 that **h** the poles used for carrying the table shall
26:29 and shall make their rings of gold to **h** the bars;
30: 4 and they shall **h** the poles with which to carry it.
36:34 and made rings of gold for them to **h** the bars,
37:27 to **h** the poles with which to carry it.
38: 5 on the four corners of the bronze grating to **h**
Lev 20:25 which I have set apart for you to **h** unclean.
23:21 you shall **h** a holy convocation;
25:24 Throughout the land that you **h,**
Dt 9:17 So I took **h** of the two tablets and flung them
10:20 to him you shall **h** fast,
13: 4 him you shall serve, and to him you shall **h** fast.
18:19 I myself will **h** accountable.
21:19 then his father and his mother shall take **h** of him
32:41 and my hand takes **h** on judgment;
Jos 22: 5 to keep his commandments, and to **h** fast to him,
23: 8 but **h** fast to the LORD your God,
Jdg 16: 3 took **h** of the doors of the city gate and
Ru 3:15 "Bring the cloak you are wearing and **h** it out."
1Sa 15:27 Saul caught **h** of the hem of his robe, and it tore.
2Sa 1:11 Then David took **h** of his clothes and tore them;
6: 6 to the ark of God and took **h** of it,
13:11 she brought them near him to eat, he took **h** of her,
15: 5 he would put out his hand and take **h** of them,
19:19 "May my lord not **h** me guilty or remember
1Ki 1:51 see, he has laid **h** of the horns of the altar, saying,
2: 9 do not **h** him guiltless, for you are a wise man;
11:30 Ahijah laid **h** of the new garment he was wearing
2Ki 4:24 do not **h** back for me unless I tell you."
4:27 she caught **h** of his feet.
6:32 that you shut the door and **h** it closed against him.
15:19 of silver, so that he might help him confirm his **h**
1Ch 13: 9 Uzzah put out his hand to **h** the ark,
2Ch 7: 7 not **h** the burnt offering and the grain offering and
Est 4:16 and **h** a fast on my behalf,
9:19 **h** the fourteenth day of the month of Adar as a day
Job 1: 4 to go and **h** feasts in one another's houses in turn;
8:15 if one lays **h** of it, it will not endure.
9:28 for I know you will not **h** me innocent.
17: 9 Yet the righteous **h** to their way,
18: 9 a snare lays **h** of them.
Job 20:13 and **h** it in their mouths,
27: 6 I **h** fast my righteousness, and will not let it go;
30:16 days of affliction have taken **h** of me.
38:13 so that it might take **h** of the skirts of the earth,
Ps 16: 5 and my cup; you **h** my lot.
31:20 you **h** them safe under your shelter
35: 2 Take **h** of shield and buckler,
39:12 do not **h** your peace at my tears.
48: 6 trembling took **h** of them there,
59: 8 you **h** all the nations in derision.
64: 5 They **h** fast to their evil purpose;
73:23 I am continually with you; you **h** my right hand.
74:11 Why do you **h** back your hand;
83: 1 do not **h** your peace or be still, O God!
102:14 For your servants **h** its stones dear,
116: 3 the pangs of Sheol laid **h** on me;
119:101 I **h** back my feet from every evil way,
119:109 I **h** my life in my hand continually,
119:117 **H** me up, that I may be safe and have regard
139:10 and your right hand shall **h** me fast.
Pr 3:18 She is a tree of life to those who lay **h** of her;
3:18 those who **h** her fast are called happy.
4: 4 and said to me, "Let your heart **h** fast my words;
4:13 Keep **h** of instruction;
5: 2 so that you may **h** on to prudence,
11:26 The people curse those who **h** back grain,
21:26 but the righteous give and do not **h** back.
24:11 if you **h** back from rescuing those taken away
31:19 and her hands **h** the spindle.
Ecc 2: 3 and how to lay **h** on folly,
7:18 It is good that you should take **h** of the one,
SS 7: 8 I say I will climb the palm tree and lay **h**
Isa 4: 1 Seven women shall take **h** of one man in that day,
22:17 He will seize firm **h** on you,
33:23 it cannot **h** the mast firm in its place,
41:13 For I, the LORD your God, **h** your right hand;
54: 2 be stretched out; do not **h** back;
56: 4 the things that please me and **h** fast my covenant,
56: 6 and do not profane it, and **h** fast my covenant—
58: 1 Shout out, do not **h** back!
64: 7 or attempts to take **h** of you;
Jer 2:13 cracked cisterns that can **h** no water.
6:24 anguish has taken **h** of us, pain as of a woman in
8:21 I mourn, and dismay has taken **h** of me.
13:21 Will not pangs take **h** of you,
26: 2 do not **h** back a word.
26: 8 and the prophets and all the people laid **h** of him,
33:24 and how they **h** my people in such contempt
34: 9 so that no one should **h** another Judean in slavery.
49:16 who **h** the height of the hill.
49:24 anguish and sorrows have taken **h** of her,
Eze 14: 5 in order that I may take **h** of the hearts of the house
38: 7 and **h** yourselves in reserve for them.
Da 2:43 but they will not **h** together,
Hos 12: 6 you, return to your God, **h** fast to love and justice,
Jnh 1: 5 had gone down into the **h** of the ship and had lain
Na 3:14 tread the mortar, take **h** of the brick mold!
Zec 8:23 from nations of every language shall take **h** of
Mal 2: 4 that my covenant with Levi may **h,**
Mt 12:11 will you not lay **h** of it and lift it out?
28: 9 And they came to him, took **h** of his feet,
Mk 7: 8 You abandon the commandment of God and **h**
14:51 but a linen cloth. They caught **h** of him,
Lk 8:15 **h** it fast in an honest and good heart,
Jn 20:17 Jesus said to her, "Do not **h** on to me,
Ac 7:60 "Lord, do not **h** this sin against them."
Ro 3:28 For we **h** that a person is justified by faith apart
12: 9 hate what is evil, **h** fast to what is good;
1Co 15: 2 if you **h** firmly to the message that I proclaimed
Php 1: 7 because you **h** me in your heart,
3:16 Only let us **h** fast to what we have attained.
Col 1:17 and in him all things **h** together.
1Th 5:21 but test everything; **h** fast to what is good;
2Th 2:15 and **h** fast to the traditions that you were taught
1Ti 3: 9 they must **h** fast to the mystery of the faith with
6:12 take **h** of the eternal life,
6:19 so that they may take **h** of the life that really is life.
2Ti 1:13 **H** to the standard of sound teaching
Heb 3: 6 and we are his house if we **h** firm the confidence
3:14 if only we **h** our first confidence firm to the end.
4:14 the Son of God, let us **h** fast to our confession.
10:23 Let us **h** fast to the confession of our hope
Rev 2:14 you have some there who **h** to the teaching
2:15 So you also have some who **h** to the teaching of
2:24 who do not **h** this teaching,
2:25 only **h** fast to what you have until I come.
3:11 I am coming soon; **h** fast to what you have,
12:17 those who keep the commandments of God and **h**
14:12 the commandments of God and **h** fast to the faith
19:10 with you and your comrades who **h** the testimony
Tob 6: 4 "Catch **h** of the fish and hang on to it!"
Jdt 2:10 and you shall **h** them for me until the day
7:30 Let us **h** out for five days more;
13: 7 took **h** of the hair of his head, and said,
Wis 4: 3 a deep root or take a firm **h.**
14:23 or **h** frenzied revels with strange customs,
Sir 1:24 They **h** back their words until the right moment;
6:27 and when you get **h** of her, do not let her go.
12: 5 **h** back their bread, and do not give it to them,
21:14 like a broken jar; it can **h** no knowledge.
26: 7 taking **h** of her is like grasping a scorpion.
32: 8 be as one who knows and can still **h** his tongue.
43:26 and by his word all things **h** together.
Bar 3:20 nor understood her paths, nor laid **h** of her.
4: 1 All who **h** her fast will live,
Sus 1:39 we saw them embracing, we could not **h** the man,
1Mc 6:50 and stationed a guard there to **h** it.
1Mc 15: 7 that you have built and now **h** shall remain yours.
15:28 "You **h** control of Joppa and Gazara and the citadel
2Mc 4:27 Although Menelaus continued to **h** the office,
12:35 on horseback and was a strong man, caught **h**
3Mc 3:19 among all nations who **h** their heads high
2Es 5:44 the Creator, nor can the world **h**
6:50 water had been gathered together could not **h** them
11:21 and others of them rose up, but did not **h** the rule.
11:25 to set themselves up and **h** the rule.
12:15 But the second that is to reign shall **h** sway for
4Mc 11:27 therefore, unconquered, we **h** fast to reason."
13: 6 For just as towers jutting out over harbors **h** back

HOLDING (46) [HOLD]

Ge 17: 8 for a perpetual **h;** and I will be their God."
47:11 and granted them a **h** in the land of Egypt,
48: 4 to your offspring after you for a perpetual **h.'**
Ex 6: 5 the Israelites whom the Egyptians are **h** as slaves,
Lev 11:36 But a spring or a cistern **h** water shall be clean,
27:21 as a devoted field; it becomes the priest's **h.**
27:24 from whom it was bought, whose **h** the land is.
Dt 11:22 walking in all his ways, and **h** fast to him,
30:20 obeying him, and **h** fast to him;
Jos 21:12 to Caleb son of Jephunneh as his **h.**
Jdg 7:20 **h** in their left hands the torches,
1Sa 20:29 for our family is **h** a sacrifice in the city,
25:36 he was **h** a feast in his house,
Isa 6: 6 **h** a live coal that had been taken from the altar
Jer 6:11 I am weary of **h** it in.
20: 9 I am weary with **h** it in, and I cannot.
Eze 44:28 and you shall give them no **h** in Israel; I am their **h.**
45: 5 as their **h** for cities to live in.
45: 6 the holy district you shall assign as a **h** for the city
45: 7 and the **h** of the city, alongside the holy district
and the **h** of the city,
46:16 it is their **h** by inheritance.
46:18 thrusting them out of their **h;**
46:18 inheritance out of his own **h,** so that none of my
people shall be dispossessed of their **h.**
Lk 22:63 the men who were **h** Jesus began to mock him
Jn 2: 6 each **h** twenty or thirty gallons.
Ac 20: 7 Paul was **h** a discussion with them;
Php 2:16 by your **h** fast to the word of life that I can boast
Col 2:19 and not **h** fast to the head,
1Ti 4: 8 **h** promise for both the present life and the life
2Ti 3: 5 **h** to the outward form of godliness
Heb 6: 6 the Son of God and are **h** him up to contempt.
9: 4 in which there were a golden urn **h** the manna,
Rev 2:13 Yet you are **h** fast to my name,
5: 8 each **h** a harp and golden bowls full of incense,
7: 1 **h** back the four winds of the earth so
17: 4 **h** in her hand a golden cup full of abominations
20: 1 **h** in his hand the key to the bottomless pit and
Tob 11:11 and **h** him firmly, he blew into his eyes, saying,
Sir 29: 1 by **h** out a helping hand they keep
1Mc 15:34 we are firmly **h** the inheritance of our ancestors.
2Mc 3:20 And **h** up their hands to heaven,
2Es 13:28 not **h** a spear or weapon of war, yet destroying
4Mc 5:10 by **h** a vain opinion concerning the truth,

HOLDINGS (2) [HOLD]

Jos 21:41 the **h** of the Israelites were in all forty-eight towns
2Ch 11:14 and their **h** and had come to Judah and Jerusalem,

HOLDS (19) [HOLD]

2Sa 3:29 or who **h** a spindle, or who falls by the sword,
Est 4:11 if the king **h** out the golden scepter to someone,
Ps 37:24 for the LORD **h** us by the hand.
82: 1 in the midst of the gods he **h** judgment:
Pr 29:11 but the wise quietly **h** it back.
Ecc 10:14 and who can tell anyone what the future **h?**
Isa 56: 2 the one who **h** it fast, who keeps the sabbath,
Jer 46:10 the Lord GOD of hosts **h** a sacrifice in the land of
Eze 23:32 you shall be scorned and derided, it **h** so much.
Am 1: 5 and the one who **h** the scepter from Beth-eden;
1: 8 and the one who **h** the scepter from Ashkelon;
Jn 4:37 For here the saying **h** true,
Heb 7:24 but he **h** his priesthood permanently,
Rev 2: 1 These are the words of him who **h** the seven stars
Wis 1: 7 that which **h** all things together knows what is said,
Sir 4:13 Whoever **h** her fast inherits glory,
15: 1 and whoever **h** to the law will obtain wisdom.
27:30 yet a sinner **h** on to them.
LtJ 6:14 One of them **h** a scepter, like a district judge,

HOLE (6) [HOLES]

Dt 23:13 a **h** with it and then cover up your excrement.
2Ki 12: 9 the priest Jehoiada took a chest, made a **h** in its lid,
Ps 7:15 and fall into the **h** that they have made.
Isa 11: 8 The nursing child shall play over the **h** of the asp,
Eze 8: 7 I looked, and there was a **h** in the wall.
Mt 25:18 the one talent went off and dug a **h** in the ground

HOLES (10) [HOLE]

1Sa 13: 6 and in **h** and in rocks and in tombs and in cisterns.
14:11 of the **h** where they have hidden themselves."
Job 30: 6 in **h** in the ground, and in the rocks.
Isa 2:19 the caves of the rocks and the **h** of the ground,
42:22 all of them are trapped in **h** and hidden in prisons;
Hag 1: 6 to put them into a bag with **h.**
Mt 8:20 And Jesus said to him, "Foxes have **h,**
Lk 9:58 And Jesus said to him, "Foxes have **h,**
Heb 11:38 and in caves and **h** in the ground.
4Mc 14:16 in precipitous chasms and in **h** and tops of trees,

HOLIDAY (8)

Est 2:18 He also granted a **h** to the provinces,
8:17 and joy among the Jews, a festival and a **h.**
9:19 **h** on which they send gifts of food to one another.
9:22 into gladness and from mourning into a **h;**
AdE 8:17 the Jews had joy and gladness, a banquet and a **h.**
9:19 the fourteenth of Adar as a joyful **h,**
9:19 the fifteenth day of Adar as their joyful **h,**
9:22 into gladness and from a time of distress to a **h,**

HOLIES (1) [HOLY]

Heb 9:3 the second curtain was a tent called the Holy of **H.**

HOLILY (KJV) See PURE

HOLINESS‡ (40) [HOLY]

Ex 15:11 Who is like you, majestic in **h,**
Nu 20:12 to show my **h** before the eyes of the Israelites,
20:13 and by which he showed his **h.**
27:14 not show my **h** before their eyes at the waters."
Dt 32:51 by failing to maintain my **h** among the Israelites.
Ps 89:35 Once and for all I have sworn by my **h;**
93:5 **h** befits your house, O LORD, forevermore.
Eze 20:41 and I will manifest my **h** among you in the sight of
28:22 and manifest my **h** in it;
28:25 manifest my **h** in them in the sight of the nations,
36:23 when through you I display my **h** before their eyes.
38:16 O Gog, I display my **h** before their eyes.
38:23 and my **h** and make myself known in the eyes
39:27 and through them have displayed my **h** in the sight
44:19 so that they may not communicate **h** to the people
46:20 into the outer court and so communicate **h** to
Am 4:2 The Lord GOD has sworn by his **h:**
Lk 1:75 in **h** and righteousness before him all our days.
Ro 1:4 according to the spirit of **h** by resurrection from
2Co 6:6 patience, kindness, **h** of spirit, genuine love,
7:1 making **h** perfect in the fear of God.
Eph 4:24 to the likeness of God in true righteousness and **h.**
1Th 3:13 in **h** that you may be blameless before our God
4:4 of you know how to control your own body in **h**
4:7 For God did not call us to impurity but in **h.**
1Ti 2:15 provided they continue in faith and love and **h,**
Heb 12:10 in order that we may share his **h.**
12:14 and the **h** without which no one will see the Lord.
2Pe 3:11 of persons ought you to be in leading lives of **h**
Wis 2:22 nor hoped for the wages of **h,**
5:19 he will take **h** as an invincible shield,
6:10 be made holy who observe holy things in **h,**
9:3 and rule the world in **h** and righteousness,
14:30 they swore unrighteously through contempt for **h.**
Sir 36:4 As you have used us to show your **h** to them,
45:12 inscribed like a seal with **"H,"**
2Mc 3:12 be done to those people who had trusted in the **h** of
14:36 O holy One, Lord of all **h,**
4Mc 7:9 and you did not abandon the **h** that you praised,
11:20 being tortured he said, "O contest befitting **h,**

HOLLOW (10)

Ex 27:8 You shall make it **h,** with boards.
38:7 he made it **h,** with boards.
Jdg 15:19 So God split open the **h** place that is at Lehi,
1Sa 25:29 of your enemies he shall sling out as from the **h** of
Pr 30:4 Who has gathered the wind in the **h** of the hand?
Isa 40:12 the **h** of his hand and marked off the heavens with
Jer 52:21 it was **h** and its thickness was four fingers.
Wis 17:19 or an echo thrown back from a **h** of the mountains,
2Mc 1:19 the altar and secretly hid it in the **h** of a dry cistern,
4Mc 8:24 against compulsion or take **h** pride in being put to

HOLM (1)

Isa 44:14 He cuts down cedars or chooses a **h** tree or an oak

HOLOFERNES (41) [HOLOFERNES']

Jdt 2:4 Nebuchadnezzar, king of the Assyrians, called **H,**
2:14 So **H** left the presence of his lord,
2:22 From there **H** took his whole army, the infantry,
3:5 The men came to **H** and told him all this.
4:1 in Judea heard of everything that **H,**
5:1 to **H,** the general of the Assyrian army,
5:24 Therefore let us go ahead, Lord **H,**
6:1 **H,** the commander of the Assyrian army,
6:10 Then **H** ordered his slaves,
6:17 of **H,** and all that he had said in the presence of
6:17 that **H** had boasted he would do against the house
7:1 The next day **H** ordered his whole army,
7:6 second day **H** led out all his cavalry in full view
7:16 These words pleased **H** and all his attendants,
7:26 as booty to the army of **H** and to all his forces.
10:13 to see **H** the commander of your army, to give him
10:17 and they brought them to the tent of **H.**
10:18 around her as she stood outside the tent of **H,**
10:20 Then the guards of **H** and all his servants came out
10:21 **H** was resting on his bed under a canopy
10:23 When Judith came into the presence of **H**
11:1 Then **H** said to her, "Take courage, woman,
11:20 Her words pleased **H** and all his servants.
11:22 Then **H** said to her, "God has done well
12:3 **H** said to her, "If your supply runs out,
12:5 Then the servants of **H** brought her into the tent,
12:6 and sent this message to **H:**
12:7 So **H** commanded his guards not to hinder her.
12:10 On the fourth day **H** held a banquet
12:13 So Bagoas left the presence of **H,**
Jdt 12:15 ahead and spread for her on the ground before **H**
12:17 So **H** said to her, "Have a drink and be merry
12:20 **H** was greatly pleased with her,
13:2 with **H** stretched out on his bed,
13:15 and said, "See here, the head of **H,**
14:3 They will rush into the tent of **H** and will
14:6 of **H** in the hand of one of the men in the assembly
14:11 it was dawn they hung the head of **H** on the wall.
14:18 Look, **H** is lying on the ground,
15:11 the tent of **H** and all his silver dinnerware,
16:19 also dedicated to God all the possessions of **H,**

HOLOFERNES' (5) [HOLOFERNES]

Jdt 5:22 **H** officers and all the inhabitants of the seacoast
12:16 **H** heart was ravished with her
13:6 She went up to the bedpost near **H** head,
13:9 Soon afterward she went out and gave **H** head
14:13 They came to **H** tent and said to the steward

HOLON‡ (3)

Jos 15:51 **H,** and Giloh: eleven towns with their villages.
21:15 **H** with its pasture lands, Debir
Jer 48:21 Judgment has come upon the tableland, upon **H,**

HOLPEN (KJV) See HELP, HELPED, STRONG ARM

HOLY‡ (779) [HOLIES, HOLINESS, HOLY-MINDED]

A. HOLY SPIRIT (95)
B. HOLY PLACE (78)
C. HOLY ONE (66)
D. MOST HOLY (50)
E. HOLY NAME (30)
F. HOLY ONES (28)
G. HOLY MOUNTAIN (22)
H. HOLY CITY (19)
I. HOLY THINGS (16)
J. HOLY CONVOCATION (15)
K. HOLY VESSELS (15)
L. HOLY TEMPLE (14)
M. MOST HOLY PLACE (13)
N. HOLY PEOPLE (8)

Ex 3:5 the place on which you are standing is **h** ground."
15:13 you guided them by your strength to your **h** abode.
16:23 a **h** sabbath to the LORD;
19:6 be for me a priestly kingdom and a **h** nation.
19:23 'Set limits around the mountain and keep it **h.'** "
20:8 Remember the sabbath day, and keep it **h.**
26:33 the curtain shall separate for you the **h** place B
26:33 for you the holy place from the most **h.** D
26:34 the ark of the covenant in the most **h** place. BDM
28:29 on his heart when he goes into the **h** place, B
28:35 when he goes into the **h** place before the LORD, B
28:36 like the engraving of a signet, **"H** to the LORD."
28:38 on himself any guilt incurred in the **h** offering that
28:43 come near the altar to minister in the **h** place; B
29:6 and put the **h** diadem on the turban.
29:21 then he and his vestments shall be **h,**
29:30 the tent of meeting to minister in the **h** place. B
29:31 and boil its flesh in a **h** place; B
29:33 of them, because they are **h.**
29:34 it shall not be eaten, because it is **h.**
29:37 and consecrate it, and the altar shall be most **h;** D
29:37 whatever touches the altar shall become **h.**
30:10 It is most **h** to the LORD. D
30:25 it shall be a **h** anointing oil.
30:29 so that they may be most **h;** D
30:29 whatever touches them will become **h.**
30:31 be my **h** anointing oil throughout your generations.
30:32 it is **h,** and it shall be **h** to you.
30:35 seasoned with salt, pure and **h;**
30:36 it shall be for you most **h.** D
30:37 it shall be regarded by you as **h** to the LORD.
31:10 the **h** vestments for the priest Aaron and
31:11 and the fragrant incense for the **h** place. B
31:14 You shall keep the sabbath, because it is **h** for you;
31:15 but the seventh day is a sabbath of solemn rest, **h**
35:2 but on the seventh day you shall have a **h** sabbath
35:19 for ministering in the **h** place, B
35:19 the **h** vestments for the priest Aaron,
37:29 He made the **h** anointing oil also,
39:1 for ministering in the **h** place; B
39:30 the rosette of the **h** diadem of pure gold,
39:30 like the engraving of a signet, **"H** to the LORD."
39:41 for ministering in the **h** place, B
40:9 so that it shall become **h.**
40:10 so that the altar shall be most **h.** D
Lev 2:3 most **h** part of the offerings by fire to the LORD. D
2:10 it is a most **h** part of the offerings by fire to D
5:15 and sins unintentionally in any of the **h** things of I
5:16 And you shall make restitution for the **h** thing
6:16 shall be eaten as unleavened cakes in a **h** place; B
6:17 it is most **h,** like the sin offering and D
6:18 anything that touches them shall become **h.**
6:25 the burnt offering is slaughtered; it is most **h.** D
6:26 it shall be eaten in a **h** place, B
6:27 Whatever touches its flesh shall become **h;**
6:27 you shall wash the bespattered part in a **h** place. B
6:29 among the priests shall eat of it; it is most **h.** D
6:30 the tent of meeting for atonement in the **h** place; B
7:1 the ritual of the guilt offering. It is most **h;** D
7:6 it shall be eaten in a **h** place; it is most holy. B
Lev 7:6 in a holy place; it is most **h.** D
8:9 in front, he set the golden ornament, the **h** crown,
10:3 those who are near me I will show myself **h,**
10:10 to distinguish between the **h** and the common,
10:12 beside the altar, for it is most **h;** D
10:13 shall eat it in a **h** place, because it is your due B
10:17 For it is most **h,** and God has given it to you D
11:44 sanctify yourselves therefore, and be **h,** for I am **h.**
11:45 you shall be **h,** for I am **h.**
12:4 she shall not touch any **h** thing,
14:13 burnt offering are slaughtered in the **h** place; B
14:13 to the priest: it is most **h.** D
16:3 Thus shall Aaron come into the **h** place: B
16:4 He shall put on the **h** linen tunic,
16:4 wear the linen turban; these are the **h** vestments.
16:20 When he has finished atoning for the **h** place B
16:23 that he put on when he went into the **h** place, B
16:24 He shall bathe his body in water in a **h** place, B
16:27 in the **h** place, shall be taken outside the camp; B
16:32 wearing the linen vestments, the **h** vestments.
19:2 shall be **h,** for I the LORD your God am **h.**
19:8 they have profaned what is **h** to the LORD;
20:3 defiling my sanctuary and profaning my **h** name. E
20:7 Consecrate yourselves therefore, and be **h;**
20:26 You shall be **h** to me; for I the LORD am **h,**
21:6 They shall be **h** to their God,
21:6 of their God; therefore they shall be **h.**
21:7 For they are **h** to their God,
21:8 and you shall treat them as **h,** since they offer
21:8 they shall be **h** to you, for I the LORD, I who sanctify you, am **h.**
21:22 of the most **h** as well as of the holy. D
21:22 of the most holy as well as of the **h.**
22:2 so that they may not profane my **h** name; E
22:32 You shall not profane my **h** name, E
23:2 that you shall proclaim as **h** convocations,
23:3 a sabbath of complete rest, a **h** convocation; J
23:4 the **h** convocations, which you shall celebrate at
23:7 On the first day you shall have a **h** convocation; J
23:8 the seventh day there shall be a **h** convocation: J
23:20 they shall be **h** to the LORD for the priest.
23:21 you shall hold a **h** convocation; J
23:24 **h** convocation commemorated with trumpet J
23:27 it shall be a **h** convocation for you: J
23:35 The first day shall be a **h** convocation; J
23:36 the eighth day you shall observe a **h** convocation J
23:37 as times of **h** convocation, for presenting to J
24:9 who shall eat them in a **h** place, B
24:9 for they are most **h** portions for him from D
25:12 For it is a jubilee; it shall be **h** to you:
27:9 that may be given to the LORD shall be **h.**
27:10 both that one and its substitute shall be **h.**
27:21 it shall be **h** to the LORD as a devoted field;
27:28 every devoted thing is most **h** to the LORD. D
27:30 they are **h** to the LORD.
27:32 shall be **h** to the LORD.
27:33 then both it and the substitute shall be **h** and
Nu 4:4 the tent of meeting concerns the most **h** things. DI
4:15 but they must not touch the **h** things, I
4:19 die when they come near to the most **h** things: DI
4:20 in to look on the **h** things even for a moment; I
5:17 the priest shall take **h** water in an earthen vessel,
6:5 to the LORD, they shall be **h;**
6:8 All their days as nazirites they are **h** to the LORD.
6:20 they are a **h** portion for the priest,
7:9 **h** things that had to be carried on the shoulders. I
10:21 the Kohathites, who carried the **h** things, set out; I
15:40 and you shall be **h** to your God.
16:3 All the congregation are **h,** everyone of them,
16:5 and who is **h,** and who will be allowed
16:7 man whom the LORD chooses shall be the **h** one. C
16:38 For the censers of these sinners have become **h** at
16:38 before the LORD and they became **h.**
18:8 all the **h** gifts of the Israelites;
18:9 This shall be yours from the most **h** things, DI
18:9 that they render to me as a most **h** thing, D
18:10 As a most **h** thing you shall eat it; D
18:10 it shall be **h** to you.
18:17 you shall not redeem; they are **h.**
18:19 All the **h** offerings that the Israelites present to
18:32 you shall not profane the **h** gifts of the Israelites,
28:18 On the first day there shall be a **h** convocation. J
28:25 the seventh day you shall have a **h** convocation; J
28:26 you shall have a **h** convocation; J
29:1 seventh month you shall have a **h** convocation; J
29:7 a **h** convocation, and deny yourselves; J
29:12 seventh month you shall have a **h** convocation; J
35:25 of the high priest who was anointed with the **h** oil.
Dt 5:12 Observe the sabbath day and keep it **h,**
7:6 For you are a people **h** to the LORD your God;
14:2 For you are a people **h** to the LORD your God;
14:21 For you are a people **h** to the LORD your God.
23:14 therefore your camp must be **h,**
26:15 Look down from your **h** habitation, from heaven,
26:19 for you to be a people **h** to the LORD your God,
28:9 The LORD will establish you as his **h** people, N
33:2 With him were myriads of **h** ones; F
33:3 all his **h** ones were in your charge; F
Jos 5:15 for the place where you stand is **h."**
24:19 "You cannot serve the LORD, for he is a **h** God.
1Sa 2:2 "There is no **H** One like the LORD, C
6:20 to stand before the LORD, this **h** God?
21:4 "I have no ordinary bread at hand, only **h** bread—
21:5 the vessels of the young men are **h** even when it is
21:5 how much more today will their vessels be **h?"**
21:6 So the priest gave him the **h** bread;
1Ki 6:16 as an inner sanctuary, as the most **h** place. BDM

1Ki 7:50 part of the house, the most **h** place, BDM
8: 4 and all the **h** vessels that were in the tent; K
8: 6 of the house, in the most **h** place, BDM
8: 8 the poles were seen from the **h** place in front of B
8:10 And when the priests came out of the **h** place, B
2Ki 4: 9 who regularly passes our way is a **h** man of God.
19:22 Against the **H** One of Israel! C
1Ch 6:49 doing all the work of the most **h** place, BDM
9:29 and over all the **h** utensils,
16:10 Glory in his **h** name; let the hearts of those E
16:29 Worship the LORD in **h** splendor;
16:35 that we may give thanks to your **h** name, E
22:19 of the covenant of the LORD and the **h** vessels K
23:13 to consecrate the most **h** things, so that he DI
23:28 the cleansing of all that is **h**,
29: 3 to all that I have provided for the **h** house,
29:16 for building you a house for your **h** name comes E
2Ch 3: 8 He made the most **h** place; BDM
3:10 In the most **h** place he made two carved BDM
4:22 the inner doors to the most **h** place and BDM
5: 5 and all the **h** vessels that were in the tent; K
5: 7 of the house, in the most **h** place, BDM
5: 9 the poles were seen from the **h** place in front of B
5:11 when the priests came out of the **h** place B
8:11 to which the ark of the LORD has come are **h**."
20:21 to sing to the LORD and praise him in **h** splendor,
23: 6 they may enter, for they are **h**,
29: 5 and carry out the filth from the **h** place. B
29: 7 or made burnt offerings in the **h** place to the God B
30:17 to make it **h** to the LORD.
30:27 their prayer came to his **h** dwelling in heaven.
31:14 for the LORD and the most **h** offerings. D
31:18 for they were faithful in keeping themselves **h**.
35: 3 were **h** to the LORD, "Put the **h** ark in the house
35: 5 in the **h** place according to the groupings of B
35:13 they boiled the **h** offerings in pots, in caldrons,
Ezr 2:63 that they were not to partake of the most **h** food, D
8:28 And I said to them, "You are **h** to the LORD,
8:28 to the LORD, and the vessels are **h**;
9: 2 Thus the **h** seed has mixed itself with the peoples
9: 8 and given us a stake in his **h** place, B
Ne 7:65 that they were not to partake of the most **h** food, D
8: 9 "This day is **h** to the LORD your God;
8:10 for this day is **h** to our LORD;
8:11 "Be quiet, for this day is **h**; do not be grieved."
9:14 and you made known your **h** sabbath to them
10:31 not buy it from them on the sabbath or on a **h** day;
11: 1 of ten to live in the **h** city Jerusalem, H
11:18 in the **h** city were two hundred eighty-four. H
13:22 to keep the sabbath day **h**.
Job 5: 1 To which of the **h** ones will you turn? F
6:10 for I have not denied the words of the **H** One. C
15:15 God puts no trust even in his **h** ones, F
Ps 2: 6 "I have set my king on Zion, my **h** hill."
3: 4 and he answers me from his **h** hill.
5: 7 I will bow down toward your **h** temple in awe L
11: 4 The LORD is in his **h** temple; L
15: 1 Who may dwell on your **h** hill?
16: 3 As for the **h** ones in the land, they are the noble, F
20: 6 from his **h** heaven with mighty victories
22: 3 Yet you are **h**, enthroned on the praises of Israel.
24: 3 And who shall stand in his **h** place? B
28: 2 I lift up my hands toward your most **h** sanctuary. D
29: 2 worship the LORD in **h** splendor.
30: 4 and give thanks to his **h** name. E
33:21 because we trust in his **h** name. E
34: 9 O fear the LORD, you his **h** ones, F
43: 3 let them bring me to your **h** hill and
46: 4 the **h** habitation of the Most High.
47: 8 God sits on his **h** throne.
48: 1 of our God. His **h** mountain, G
51:11 and do not take your **h** spirit from me. A
65: 4 with the goodness of your house, your **h** temple. L
68: 5 and protector of widows is God in his **h** habitation.
68:17 the Lord came from Sinai into the **h** place. B
71:22 I will sing praises to you with the lyre, O **H** One C
74: 4 Your foes have roared within your **h** place; B
77:13 Your way, O God, is **h**.
78:41 and provoked the **H** One of Israel. C
78:54 And he brought them to his **h** hill,
79: 1 they have defiled your **h** temple; L
87: 1 On the **h** mount stands the city he founded;
89: 5 your faithfulness in the assembly of the **h** ones. F
89: 7 a God feared in the council of the **h** ones, F
89:18 our king to the **H** One of Israel. C
89:20 with my **h** oil I have anointed him;
96: 9 Worship the LORD in **h** splendor;
97:12 O you righteous, and give thanks to his **h** name! E
98: 1 and his **h** arm have gotten him victory.
99: 3 and awesome name. **H** is he!
99: 5 worship at his footstool. **H** is he!
99: 9 and worship at his **h** mountain; G
99: 9 for the LORD our God is **h**.
102:19 that he looked down from his **h** height,
103: 1 and all that is within me, bless his **h** name. E
105: 3 Glory in his **h** name; let the hearts of those E
105:42 For he remembered his **h** promise, and Abraham,
106:16 and of Aaron, the **h** one of the LORD. C
106:47 we may give thanks to your **h** name and glory E
110: 3 the day you lead your forces on the **h** mountains.
111: 9 **H** and awesome is his name.
134: 2 Lift up your hands to the **h** place, B
138: 2 I bow down toward your **h** temple and give L
145:21 all flesh will bless his **h** name forever and ever. E
Pr 9:10 and the knowledge of the **H** One is insight. C
20:25 It is a snare for one to say rashly, "It is **h**,"
30: 3 nor have I knowledge of the **h** ones. F

Ecc 8:10 they used to go in and out of the **h** place, B
Isa 1: 4 who have despised the **H** One of Israel, C
4: 3 in Zion and remains in Jerusalem will be called **h**,
5:16 the **H** God shows himself **h** by righteousness.
5:19 of the **H** One of Israel hasten to fulfillment, C
5:24 have despised the word of the **H** One of Israel. C
6: 3 "**H, h, h** is the LORD of hosts;
6:13 The **h** seed is its stump.
8:13 the LORD of hosts, him you shall regard as **h**;
10:17 and his **H** One a flame; C
10:20 but will lean on the LORD, the **H** One of Israel, C
11: 9 not hurt or destroy on all my **h** mountain; G
12: 6 for great in your midst is the **H** One of Israel. C
17: 7 and their eyes will look to the **H** One of Israel; C
27:13 the LORD on the **h** mountain at Jerusalem. G
29:19 people shall exult in the **H** One of Israel. C
29:23 they will sanctify the **H** One of Jacob, C
30:11 let us hear no more about the **H** One of Israel." C
30:12 Therefore thus says the **H** One of Israel: C
30:15 For thus said the Lord GOD, the **H** One of Israel: C
30:29 a song as in the night when a **h** festival is kept;
31: 1 but do not look to the **H** One of Israel or consult C
35: 8 and it shall be called the **H** Way;
37:23 Against the **H** One of Israel! C
40:25 or who is my equal? says the **H** One. C
41:14 your Redeemer is the **H** One of Israel. C
41:16 in the **H** One of Israel you shall glory. C
41:20 the **H** One of Israel has created it. C
43: 3 I am the LORD your God, the **H** One of Israel, C
43:14 your Redeemer, the **H** One of Israel: C
43:15 the LORD, your **H** One, the Creator of Israel, C
45:11 Thus says the LORD, the **H** One of Israel, C
47: 4 is the **H** One of Israel. C
48: 2 For they call themselves after the **h** city, H
48:17 your Redeemer, the **H** One of Israel: C
49: 7 the Redeemer of Israel and his **H** One, C
49: 7 the **H** One of Israel, who has chosen you." C
52: 1 beautiful garments, O Jerusalem, the **h** city; H
52:10 The LORD has bared his **h** arm before the eyes
54: 5 the **H** One of Israel is your Redeemer, C
55: 5 the **H** One of Israel, for he has glorified you. C
56: 7 to my **h** mountain, and make them joyful G
57:13 the land and inherit my **h** mountain. G
57:15 lofty one who inhabits eternity, whose name is **H**:
57:15 I dwell in the high and **h** place, B
58:13 from pursuing your own interests on my **h** day;
58:13 a delight and the **h** day of the LORD honorable;
60: 9 and for the **H** One of Israel, C
60:14 the Zion of the **H** One of Israel. C
62: 9 those who gather it shall drink it in my **h** courts.
62:12 They shall be called, "The **H** People, N
63:10 But they rebelled and grieved his **h** spirit; A
63:11 the one who put within them his **h** spirit, A
63:15 from your **h** and glorious habitation.
63:18 Your **h** people took possession for a little while; N
64:10 Your **h** cities have become a wilderness,
64:11 Our **h** and beautiful house,
65: 5 do not come near me, for I am too **h** for you."
65:11 who forget my **h** mountain, G
65:25 not hurt or destroy on all my **h** mountain, G
66:20 on dromedaries, to my **h** mountain Jerusalem, G
Jer 2: 3 Israel was **h** to the LORD,
17:22 but keep the sabbath day **h**,
17:24 but keep the sabbath day **h** and do no work on it,
17:27 you do not listen to me, to keep the sabbath day **h**,
23: 9 because of the LORD and because of his **h** words.
25:30 and from his **h** habitation utter his voice;
31:23 O abode of righteousness, O **h** hill!"
50:29 the LORD, the **H** One of Israel. C
51: 5 land is full of guilt before the **H** One of Israel. C
51:51 for aliens have come into the **h** places of
Eze 7:24 and their **h** places shall be profaned.
20:39 but my **h** name you shall no more profane E
20:40 For on my **h** mountain, the mountain height G
22: 8 You have despised my **h** things, I
22:26 to my teaching and have profaned my **h** things; I
22:26 they have made no distinction between the **h** and
28:14 you were on the **h** mountain of God; G
36:20 wherever they came, they profaned my **h** name, E
36:21 But I had concern for my **h** name, E
36:22 but for the sake of my **h** name, E
39: 7 My **h** name I will make known E
39: 7 I will not let my **h** name be profaned any more; E
39: 7 that I am the LORD, the **H** One in Israel. C
39:25 and I will be jealous for my **h** name. E
41: 4 And he said to me, This is the most **h** place. BDM
41:21 front of the **h** place was something resembling B
41:23 nave and the **h** place had each a double door. B
42:13 the **h** chambers, where the priests who approach
42:13 the LORD shall eat the most **h** offerings; D
42:13 there they shall deposit the most **h** offerings— D
42:13 and the guilt offering, for the place is **h**.
42:14 When the priests enter the **h** place, B
42:14 in which they minister, for these are **h**;
42:20 a separation between the **h** and the common.
43: 7 house of Israel shall no more defile my **h** name, E
43: 8 they were defiling my **h** name E
43:12 top of the mountain all around shall be most **h**. D
44:19 and lay them in the **h** chambers;
44:23 the difference between the **h** and the common,
44:24 and they shall keep my sabbaths **h**.
44:27 On the day that he goes into the **h** place, B
44:27 into the inner court, to minister in the **h** place, B
45: 1 for the LORD a portion of the land as a **h** district,
45: 1 it shall be **h** throughout its entire extent.
45: 3 In the **h** district you shall measure off
45: 3 shall be the sanctuary, the most **h** place. BDM

Eze 45: 4 It shall be a **h** portion of the land;
45: 4 be both a place for their houses and a **h** place B
45: 6 as the **h** district you shall assign as a holding for
45: 7 on both sides of the **h** district and the holding of
45: 7 alongside the **h** district and the holding of the city,
46:19 to the north row of the **h** chambers for the priests;
48:10 These shall be the allotments of the **h** portion:
48:12 as a special portion from the **h** portion of the land,
48:12 a most **h** place, adjoining the territory of BDM
48:14 for it is **h** to the LORD.
48:18 the **h** portion shall be ten thousand cubits to
48:18 and it shall be alongside the **h** portion.
48:20 the **h** portion together with the property of the city.
48:21 What remains on both sides of the **h** portion and
48:21 the twenty-five thousand cubits of the **h** portion to
48:21 The **h** portion with the sanctuary of the temple in
Da 4: 8 and who is endowed with a spirit of the **h** gods—
4: 9 of the **h** gods and that no mystery is too difficult
4:13 and there was a **h** watcher,
4:17 the decision is given by order of the **h** ones, F
4:18 for you are endowed with a spirit of the **h** gods."
4:23 a **h** watcher coming down from heaven and saying,
5:11 with a spirit of the **h** gods.
7:18 But the **h** ones of the Most High shall receive F
7:21 with the **h** ones and was prevailing over them, F
7:22 then judgment was given for the **h** ones of F
7:22 the **h** ones gained possession of the kingdom. F
7:25 shall wear out the **h** ones of the Most High, F
7:27 to the people of the **h** ones of the Most High; F
8:13 Then I heard a **h** one speaking, C
8:13 and another **h** one said to the one that spoke, C
8:24 the powerful and the people of the **h** ones. F
9:16 from your city Jerusalem, your **h** mountain; G
9:20 the LORD my God on behalf of the **h** mountain G
9:24 for your people and your **h** city: H
9:24 and to anoint a most **h** place. BDM
11:28 but his heart shall be set against the **h** covenant.
11:30 be enraged and take action against the **h** covenant.
11:30 and pay heed to those who forsake the **h** covenant.
11:45 between the sea and the beautiful **h** mountain. G
12: 7 the shattering of the power of the **h** people N
Hos 11: 9 I am God and no mortal, the **H** One in your C
11:12 and is faithful to the **H** One. C
Joel 2: 1 sound the alarm on my **h** mountain! G
3:17 dwell in Zion, my **h** mountain. G
3:17 And Jerusalem shall be **h**,
Am 2: 7 so that my **h** name is profaned; E
Ob 1:16 For as you have drunk on my **h** mountain, G
1:17 be those that escape, and it shall be **h**;
Jnh 2: 4 how shall I look again upon your **h** temple?' L
2: 7 and my prayer came to you, into your **h** temple. L
Mic 1: 2 the Lord from his **h** temple. L
Hab 1:12 O LORD my God, my **H** One? C
2:20 But the LORD is in his **h** temple; L
3: 3 the **H** One from Mount Paran. C
Zep 3:11 shall no longer be haughty in my **h** mountain. G
Hag 2:12 or oil, or any kind of food, does it become **h**?
Zec 2:12 as his portion in the **h** land,
2:13 for he has roused himself from his **h** dwelling.
8: 3 LORD of hosts shall be called the **h** mountain. G
14: 5 and all the **h** ones with him. F
14:20 on the bells of the horses, "**H** to the LORD."
14:20 of the LORD shall be as **h** as the bowls in front of
Mt 1:18 she was found to be with child from the **H** Spirit. A
1:20 the child conceived in her is from the **H** Spirit. A
3:11 He will baptize you with the **H** Spirit and fire. A
4: 5 the devil took him to the **h** city and placed him H
7: 6 "Do not give what is **h** to dogs;
12:32 whoever speaks against the **H** Spirit will not A
24:15 the desolating sacrilege standing in the **h** place, B
27:53 the tombs and entered the **h** city and appeared H
28:19 of the Father and of the Son and of the **H** Spirit, A
Mk 1: 8 but he will baptize you with the **H** Spirit." A
1:24 I know who you are, the **H** One of God." C
3:29 against the **H** Spirit can never have forgiveness, A
6:20 knowing that he was a righteous and **h** man,
8:38 in the glory of his Father with the **h** angels."
12:36 David himself, by the **H** Spirit, declared, A
13:11 for it is not you who speak, but the **H** Spirit. A
Lk 1:15 his birth he will be filled with the **H** Spirit. A
1:35 "The **H** Spirit will come upon you, A
1:35 therefore the child to be born will be **h**;
1:41 And Elizabeth was filled with the **H** Spirit A
1:49 for me, and **h** is his name.
1:67 with the **H** Spirit and spoke this prophecy: A
1:70 through the mouth of his **h** prophets from of old,
1:72 and has remembered his **h** covenant,
2:23 "Every firstborn male shall be designated as **h** to
2:25 and the **H** Spirit rested on him. A
2:26 by the **H** Spirit that he would not see death A
3:16 He will baptize you with the **H** Spirit and fire. A
3:22 the **H** Spirit descended upon him in bodily form A
4: 1 the **H** Spirit, returned from the Jordan and A
4:34 I know who you are, the **H** One of God." C
9:26 and the glory of the Father and of the **h** angels.
10:21 in the **H** Spirit and said, "I thank you, Father, A
11:13 the heavenly Father give the **H** Spirit A
12:10 but whoever blasphemes against the **H** Spirit A
12:12 for the **H** Spirit will teach you at A
Jn 1:33 the one who baptizes with the **H** Spirit.' A
6:69 to believe and know that you are the **H** One C
11:48 and destroy both our **h** place and our nation." B
14:26 But the Advocate, the **H** Spirit, A
17:11 **H** Father, protect them in your name
20:22 and said to them, "Receive the **H** Spirit. A
Ac 1: 2 the **H** Spirit to the apostles whom he had chosen. A
1: 5 with the **H** Spirit not many days from now." A

Ac 1: 8 when the **H** Spirit has come upon you; A
1:16 which the **H** Spirit through David foretold A
2: 4 All of them were filled with the **H** Spirit and A
2:27 or let your **H** One experience corruption. C
2:33 from the Father the promise of the **H** Spirit, A
2:38 and you will receive the gift of the **H** Spirit. A
3:14 the **H** and Righteous One and asked to have
3:21 God announced long ago through his **h** prophets.
4: 8 Peter, filled with the **H** Spirit, said to them, A
4:25 by the **H** Spirit through our ancestor David, A
4:27 gathered together against your **h** servant Jesus,
4:30 through the name of your **h** servant Jesus."
4:31 and they were all filled with the **H** Spirit and A
5: 3 Satan filled your heart to lie to the **H** Spirit and A
5:32 and so is the **H** Spirit whom God has given A
6: 5 a man full of faith and the **H** Spirit, A
6:13 against this **h** place and the law; B
7:33 for the place where you are standing is **h** ground.
7:51 you are forever opposing the **H** Spirit, A
7:55 But filled with the **H** Spirit, A
8:15 for them that they might receive the **H** Spirit A
8:17 and they received the **H** Spirit. A
8:19 whom I lay my hands may receive the **H** Spirit." A
9:17 and be filled with the **H** Spirit." A
9:31 of the Lord and in the comfort of the **H** Spirit, A
10:22 a **h** angel to send for you to come to his house
10:38 of Nazareth with the **H** Spirit and with power; A
10:44 the **H** Spirit fell upon all who heard the word. A
10:45 the gift of the **H** Spirit had been poured out A
10:47 the **H** Spirit just as we have?" A
11:15 the **H** Spirit fell upon them just as it had upon us A
11:16 but you will be baptized with the **H** Spirit.' A
11:24 full of the **H** Spirit and of faith. A
13: 2 and fasting, the **H** Spirit said, "Set apart A
13: 4 So, being sent out by the **H** Spirit, A
13: 9 also known as Paul, filled with the **H** Spirit, A
13:34 'I will give you the **h** promises made to David.'
13:35 not let your **H** One experience corruption.' C
13:52 were filled with joy and with the **H** Spirit. A
15: 8 testified to them by giving them the **H** Spirit, A
15:28 For it has seemed good to the **H** Spirit and to us A
16: 6 having been forbidden by the **H** Spirit to speak A
19: 2 the **H** Spirit when you became believers?" A
19: 2 we have not even heard that there is a **H** Spirit." A
19: 6 the **H** Spirit came upon them, A
20:23 that the **H** Spirit testifies to me in every city A
20:28 of which the **H** Spirit has made you overseers, A
21:11 and said, "Thus says the **H** Spirit, A
21:28 into the temple and has defiled this **h** place." B
28:25 **H** Spirit was right in saying to your ancestors A
Ro 1: 2 through his prophets in the **h** scriptures,
5: 5 through the **H** Spirit that has been given to us. A
7:12 So the law is **h**, and the commandment is holy
7:12 and the commandment is **h** and just and good.
9: 1 my conscience confirms it by the **H** Spirit— A
11:16 If the part of the dough offered as first fruits is **h**,
11:16 then the whole batch is **h**;
11:16 and if the root is **h**, then the branches also are holy.
11:16 and if the root is holy, then the branches also are **h**.
12: 1 as a living sacrifice, **h** and acceptable to God,
14:17 righteousness and peace and joy in the **H** Spirit. A
15:13 in hope by the power of the **H** Spirit. A
15:16 be acceptable, sanctified by the **H** Spirit. A
16:16 Greet one another with a **h** kiss.
1Co 3:17 For God's temple is **h**, and you are that temple.
6:19 know that your body is a temple of the **H** Spirit A
7:14 unbelieving husband is made **h** through his wife,
7:14 unbelieving wife is made **h** through her husband.
7:14 but as it is, they are **h**.
7:34 so that they may be **h** in body and spirit;
12: 3 can say "Jesus is Lord" except by the **H** Spirit. A
16:20 Greet one another with a **h** kiss.
2Co 13:12 Greet one another with a **h** kiss.
13:13 communion of the **H** Spirit be with all of you. A
Eph 1: 4 the world to be **h** and blameless before him in love.
1:13 with the seal of the promised **H** Spirit; A
2:21 and grows into a **h** temple in the Lord; L
3: 5 now been revealed to his **h** apostles and prophets
4:30 And do not grieve the **H** Spirit of God, A
5:26 to make her **h** by cleansing her with the washing
5:27 yes, so that she may be **h** and without blemish.
Col 1:22 to present you **h** and blameless and irreproachable
3:12 As God's chosen ones, **h** and beloved,
1Th 1: 5 and in the **H** Spirit and with full conviction; A
1: 6 the word with joy inspired by the **H** Spirit, A
4: 8 who also gives his **H** Spirit to you. A
5:26 Greet all the brothers and sisters with a **h** kiss.
1Ti 2: 8 lifting up **h** hands without anger or argument;
2Ti 1: 9 who saved us and called us with a **h** calling,
1:14 with the help of the **H** Spirit living in us. A
Tit 3: 5 the water of rebirth and renewal by the **H** Spirit. A
Heb 2: 4 and by gifts of the **H** Spirit, A
3: 1 **h** partners in a heavenly calling,
3: 7 Therefore, as the **H** Spirit says, "Today, A
6: 4 and have shared in the **H** Spirit, A
7:26 **h**, blameless, undefiled, separated from sinners,
9: 2 this is called the **H** Place. B
9: 3 Behind the second curtain was a tent called the **H**
9: 8 By this the **H** Spirit indicates that the way into A
9:12 he entered once for all into the **H** Place, B
9:25 the high priest enters the **H** Place year after year B
10:15 And the **H** Spirit also testifies to us, A
1Pe 1:12 by the **H** Spirit sent from heaven— A
1:15 Instead, as he who called you is **h**, be **h** yourselves
1:16 for it is written, "You shall be **h**, for I am **h**."
2: 5 be built into a spiritual house, to be a **h** priesthood,
2: 9 a royal priesthood, a **h** nation, God's own people,
1Pe 3: 5 in this way long ago that the **h** women who hoped
2Pe 1:18 while we were with him on the **h** mountain. G
1:21 men and women moved by the **H** Spirit spoke A
2:21 the **h** commandment that was passed on to them.
3: 2 the words spoken in the past by the **h** prophets,
1Jn 2:20 But you have been anointed by the **H** One, C
Jude 1:14 Lord is coming with ten thousands of his **h** ones, F
1:20 build yourselves up on your most **h** faith; D
1:20 on your most holy faith; pray in the **H** Spirit; A
Rev 3: 7 These are the words of the **h** one, the true one, C
4: 8 they sing, **"H, h, h,** the Lord God the Almighty,
6:10 "Sovereign Lord, **h** and true,
11: 2 and they will trample over the **h** city H
14:10 the presence of the **h** angels and in the presence
15: 4 For you alone are **h**. All nations will come
16: 5 "You are just, O **H** One, who are and were, C
20: 6 and **h** are those who share in the first resurrection.
21: 2 And I saw the **h** city, the new Jerusalem, H
21:10 the **h** city Jerusalem coming down out of heaven H
22:11 and the **h** still be **h**."
22:19 in the tree of life and in the **h** city, H
Tob 11:14 and blessed be all his **h** angels.
11:14 his **h** name be blessed throughout all the ages. E
13: 9 the **h** city, he afflicted you for the deeds H
13:11 of the remotest parts of the earth to your **h** name, E
13:17 blessed will bless the **h** name forever and ever." E
Wis 1: 5 For a **h** and disciplined spirit will flee from deceit,
3: 9 because grace and mercy are upon his **h** ones, F
4:15 and that he watches over his **h** ones. F
6:10 For they will be made **h** who observe holy things
6:10 For they will be made holy who observe **h** things I
7:22 There is in her a spirit that is intelligent, **h**, unique,
7:27 into **h** souls and makes them friends of God,
9: 8 to build a temple on your **h** mountain, G
9: 8 of the **h** tent that you prepared from the beginning.
9:10 Send her forth from the **h** heavens,
9:17 and sent your **h** spirit from on high? A
10:10 and gave him knowledge of **h** things; I
10:15 A **h** people and blameless race wisdom N
10:17 She gave to **h** people the reward of their labors; N
10:20 they sang hymns, O Lord, to your **h** name, E
11: 1 by the hand of a **h** prophet.
12: 3 Those who lived long ago in your **h** land
17: 2 that they held the **h** nation in their power,
18: 1 But for your **h** ones there was very great light. F
18: 2 and were thankful that your **h** ones, F
18: 5 had resolved to kill the infants of your **h** ones, F
18: 9 the **h** children of good people offered sacrifices,
Sir 4:14 Those who serve her minister to the **H** One; C
7:31 and the first fruits of the **h** things. I
17:10 And they will praise his **h** name, E
23: 9 nor habitually utter the name of the **H** One; C
24:10 In the **h** tent I ministered before him,
26:17 Like the shining lamp on the **h** lampstand,
33:12 and some he made **h** and brought near to himself;
42:17 his **h** ones to recount all his marvelous works, F
43:10 the **H** One they stand in their appointed places; C
45: 2 He made him equal in glory to the **h** ones, F
45: 6 a **h** man like Moses who was his brother,
45:15 Moses ordained him, and anointed him with **h** oil;
47: 8 In all that he did he gave thanks to the **H** One, C
47:10 while they praised God's **h** name, E
48:20 The **H** One quickly heard them from heaven, C
49:12 the house and raised a temple **h** to the Lord,
50:11 when he went up to the **h** altar,
Bar 2:16 O Lord, look down from your **h** dwelling,
4:22 and joy has come to me from the **H** One, C
4:37 of the **H** One, rejoicing in the glory of God. C
5: 5 from west and east at the word of the **H** One, C
Aza 1: 5 the **h** city of our ancestors; H
1:12 of your servant Isaac and Israel your **h** one, C
1:30 And blessed is your glorious, **h** name, E
1:31 Blessed are you in the temple of your **h** glory,
1:65 Bless the Lord, you who are **h** and humble in heart;
Sus 1:45 up the **h** spirit of a young lad named Daniel, A
1Mc 1:15 and abandoned the **h** covenant.
1:63 to be defiled by food or to profane the **h** covenant;
2: 7 the ruin of my people, the ruin of the **h** city, H
2:12 And see, our **h** place, our beauty, B
4:49 They made new **h** vessels, K
10:31 shall be **h** and free from tax.
11:37 up in a conspicuous place on the **h** mountain.' " G
12: 9 since we have as encouragement the **h** books
2Mc 1: 7 and his company revolted from the **h** land and
1:12 he drove out those who fought against the **h** city. H
1:26 and preserve your portion and make it **h**.
1:29 Plant your people in your **h** place, B
2:18 from everywhere under heaven into his **h** place, B
3: 1 the **h** city was inhabited in unbroken peace H
3:18 **h** place was about to be brought into dishonor. B
4:48 the villages and the **h** vessels quickly suffered K
5:15 Antiochus dared to enter the most **h** temple DL
5:16 He took the **h** vessels with his polluted hands, K
5:17 the reason he was disregarding the **h** place. B
5:19 not choose the nation for the sake of the **h** place, B
5:25 and waited until the **h** sabbath day;
6:11 in view of their regard for that most **h** day. D
6:23 and moreover according to the **h** God-given law,
6:28 and nobly for the revered and **h** laws."
6:30 "It is clear to the Lord in his **h** knowledge that,
8:15 he had called them by his **h** and glorious name.
8:17 the Gentiles had committed against the **h** place, B
8:23 the **h** book, and gave the watchword, "The help
9:14 that the **h** city, which he was hurrying to level H
9:16 the **h** sanctuary, which he had formerly plundered,
9:16 and all the **h** vessels he would give back, K
10: 7 to the purifying of his own **h** place. B
2Mc 12:45 it was a **h** and pious thought.
13: 8 against the altar whose fire and ashes were **h**,
13:10 of the law and their country and the **h** temple, L
13:23 and showed generosity to the **h** place. B
14: 3 to be safe or to have access again to the **h** altar,
14:31 and **h** temple while the priests were offering L
14:36 O **h** One, Lord of all holiness, C
15:14 and prays much for the people and the **h** city— H
15:16 "Take this **h** sword, a gift from God,
15:24 against your **h** people be struck down." N
15:32 against the **h** house of the Almighty.
1Es 1: 3 the Lord and put the **h** ark of the Lord in the house
1:41 Nebuchadnezzar also took some **h** vessels of K
1:45 with the **h** vessels of the Lord, K
1:49 the temple that God had made **h**.
1:53 with the sword around their **h** temple, L
1:54 They took all the **h** vessels of the Lord, K
2:10 King Cyrus also brought out the **h** vessels of K
5:40 Attharias told them not to share in the **h** things I
6:18 And the **h** vessels of gold and of silver, K
6:26 and that the **h** vessels of the house of the Lord, K
7: 2 supervised the **h** work with very great care,
7: 3 The **h** work prospered, while the prophets Haggai
7: 5 the **h** house was finished by the twenty-third day
8:17 the **h** vessels of the Lord that are given you K
8:55 gold and the **h** vessels of the house of our Lord, K
8:58 "You are **h** to the Lord, and the vessels are **h**,
8:70 the **h** race has been mixed with the alien peoples
8:71 and my **h** mantle, and pulled out hair
8:73 with my garments and my **h** mantle torn,
8:78 to leave to us a root and a name in your **h** place, B
9:50 "This day is **h** to the Lord"—
9:52 for the day is **h** to the Lord;
9:53 saying, "This day is **h**; do not be sorrowful."
3Mc 1: 9 and did what was fitting for the **h** place. B
1:23 a considerable disturbance in the **h** place; B
2: 2 **h** among the holy ones, the only ruler, almighty,
2: 2 holy among the **h** ones, the only ruler, almighty, F
2: 6 Pharaoh who had enslaved your **h** people Israel. N
2:13 now, O **h** King, that because of our many
2:14 profane man undertakes to violate the **h** place B
2:21 the first Father of all, **h** among the holy ones,
2:21 the first Father of all, holy among the **h** ones, F
5:13 the appointed hour, praised their **h** God
6: 1 to stop calling upon the **h** God, and he prayed
6: 5 the spear and was lifted up against your **h** city, H
6:18 and true God revealed his **h** face and opened
6:29 praised their **h** God and Savior,
7:10 the **h** God and the law of God should receive
7:20 as **h** on a pillar and dedicating a place of prayer at
2Es 2:41 from the beginning, may be made **h**."
10:22 our **h** things have been polluted, I
13:48 who are found within my **h** borders, shall be saved.
14:22 send the **h** spirit into me, A
4Mc 4: 9 to shield the **h** place that was being treated B
4:12 the blessedness of the **h** place before all people. B
6:30 he said this, the **h** man died nobly in his tortures;
7: 4 as did that most **h** man. D
13: 8 a **h** chorus of religion and encouraged one another,
14: 6 with the guidance of the mind, so those **h** youths,
14: 7 O most **h** seven, brothers in harmony! D
16:12 Yet that **h** and God-fearing mother did not wail

HOLY-MINDED (1) [HOLY, MIND]

4Mc 17: 4 Take courage, therefore, O **h** mother,

HOLYDAY (KJV) See FESTIVALS

HOMAGE (4)

Mt 2: 2 and have come to pay him **h**."
2: 8 so that I may also go and pay him **h**."
2:11 and they knelt down and paid him **h**.
Mk 15:19 spat upon him, and knelt down in **h** to him.

HOMAM (1)

1Ch 1:39 Hori and **H**; and Lotan's sister was Timna.

HOME[‡] (168) [HOMEBORN, HOMELAND, HOMELESS, HOMELESSNESS, HOMES, HOMESTEAD, HOMETOWN]

Ge 27:39 away from the fatness of the earth shall your **h** be,
30:25 that I may go to my own **h** and country.
31:55 then he departed and returned **h**.
39:16 by her until his master came **h**,
43:26 When Joseph came **h**, they brought him
Ex 18:23 and all these people will go to their **h** in peace."
Lev 18: 9 whether born at **h** or born abroad.
Nu 22:34 if it is displeasing to you, I will return **h**."
24:11 be off with you! Go **h**! I said,
35:28 the death of the high priest the slayer may return **h**.
Dt 6: 7 when you are at **h** and when you are away,
11:19 when you are at **h** and when you are away,
21:12 and so you bring her **h** to your house:
24: 5 He shall be free at **h** one year,
Jos 20: 6 then the slayer may return **h**,
22: 9 and the half-tribe of Manasseh returned **h**,
Jdg 7: 3 and trembling, let him return **h**.' "
9:55 that Abimelech was dead, they all went **h**.
11: 9 you bring me **h** again to fight with the Ammonites,
11:34 Then Jephthah came to his **h** at Mizpah;
18:15 at the **h** of Micah, and greeted him.
18:22 they were some distance from the **h** of Micah,
18:26 he turned and went back to his **h**.
19: 9 early in the morning for your journey, and go **h**."

Jdg 19:18 and I am going to my **h.**
19:28 and the man set out for his **h.**
1Sa 2:11 Then Elkanah went **h** to Ramah,
2:20 and then they would return to their **h.**
4:10 and they fled, everyone to his **h.**
6: 7 but take their calves **h,** away from them.
6:10 and shut up their calves at **h.**
7:17 he would come back to Ramah, for his **h** was there;
8:22 to the people of Israel, "Each of you return **h.**"
10:13 When his prophetic frenzy had ended, he went **h.**
10:26 Saul also went to his **h** at Gibeah,
13: 2 the rest of the people he sent **h** to their tents.
18: 6 As they were coming **h,** when David returned
23:18 David remained at Horesh, and Jonathan went **h.**
24:22 Then Saul went **h;**
25: 1 They buried him at his **h** in Ramah.
2Sa 3:16 Then Abner said to him, "Go back **h!**"
13: 7 Then David sent **h** to Tamar, saying,
14:13 the king does not bring his banished one **h** again.
15:19 you are a foreigner, and also an exile from your **h.**
17: 3 the people back to you as a bride comes **h**
17:23 he saddled his donkey and went off **h**
19:30 since my lord the king has arrived **h** safely."
19:39 and he returned to his own **h.**
1Ki 1:53 and Solomon said to him, "Go **h.**"
5:14 be a month in the Lebanon and two months at **h;**
12:24 Let everyone go **h,** for this thing is from me."
12:24 the word of the LORD and went **h** again,
13: 7 "Come **h** with me and dine,
13:15 "Come **h** with me and eat some food."
17:12 I may go **h** and prepare it for myself and my son,
20:43 The king of Israel set out toward **h,**
21: 4 Ahab went **h** resentful and sullen because
22:17 let each one go **h** in peace.' "
2Ki 8:21 who had surrounded him; but his army fled **h.**
14:10 Be content with your glory, and stay at **h;**
14:12 Judah was defeated by Israel; everyone fled **h.**
19:36 Then King Sennacherib of Assyria left, went **h,**
1Ch 16:43 and David went **h** to bless his household.
2Ch 11: 4 Let everyone return **h,** for this thing is from me."
18:16 let each one go **h** in peace.' "
25:10 to him from Ephraim, letting them go **h** again.
25:10 and returned **h** in fierce anger.
25:19 in boastfulness. Now stay at **h;**
25:22 Judah was defeated by Israel; everyone fled **h.**
Est 5:10 nevertheless Haman restrained himself and went **h.**
Job 2:11 each of them set out from his **h—**
38:20 and that you may discern the paths to its **h?**
39: 6 to which I have given the steppe for its **h,**
39:28 It lives on the rock and makes its **h** in the fastness
Ps 49:14 their form shall waste away; Sheol shall be their **h.**
68: 6 God gives the desolate a **h** to live in;
68:12 The women at **h** divide the spoil,
84: 3 Even the sparrow finds a **h,**
104:17 the stork has its **h** in the fir trees.
113: 9 He gives the barren woman a **h,**
119:54 have been my songs wherever I make my **h.**
126: 6 shall come **h** with shouts of joy,
Pr 7:11 She is loud and wayward; her feet do not stay at **h;**
7:19 For my husband is not at **h;**
7:20 he will not come **h** until full moon."
14:33 at **h** in the mind of one who has understanding,
24:15 Do not lie in wait like an outlaw against the **h** of
27: 8 that strays from its nest is one who strays from **h.**
Ecc 12: 5 because all must go to their eternal **h,**
Isa 14:17 who would not let his prisoners go **h?**"
37:37 Then King Sennacherib of Assyria left, went **h,**
Jer 2:24 a wild ass at **h** in the wilderness,
39:14 of Ahikam son of Shaphan to be brought **h.**
Eze 36: 8 for they shall soon come **h.**
Da 2:17 Daniel went to his **h** and informed his companions,
4: 4 at ease in my **h** and prospering in my palace.
Zep 3:20 At that time I will bring you **h,**
Hag 1: 9 and when you brought it **h,** I blew it away.
Zec 10:10 I will bring them **h** from the land of Egypt,
Mt 2:23 There he made his **h** in a town called Nazareth,
4:13 He left Nazareth and made his **h** in Capernaum by
8: 6 "Lord, my servant is lying at **h** paralyzed,
9: 6 "Stand up, take your bed and go to your **h.**"
9: 7 And he stood up and went to his **h.**
17:25 And when he came **h,** Jesus spoke of it first,
Mk 2: 1 it was reported that he was at **h.**
2:11 stand up, take your mat and go to your **h.**"
3:19 who betrayed him. Then he went **h;**
5:19 and said to him, "Go **h** to your friends,
7:30 So she went **h,** found the child lying on the bed,
8:26 Then he sent him away to his **h,** saying,
13:34 when he leaves **h** and puts his slaves in charge,
Lk 1:23 his time of service was ended, he went to his **h.**
1:56 about three months and then returned to her **h.**
5:24 stand up and take your bed and go to your **h.**"
5:25 took what he had been lying on, and went to his **h,**
8:39 to your **h,** and declare how much God has done
9:61 but let me first say farewell to those at my **h.**"
10:38 a woman named Martha welcomed him into her **h.**
15: 6 And when he comes **h,** he calls together his friends
18:14 this man went down to his **h** justified rather than
23:48 they returned **h,** beating their breasts.
24:12 then he went **h,** amazed at what had happened.
Jn 7:53 ⟦Then each of them went **h,**⟧
11:20 she went and met him, while Mary stayed at **h.**
12: 1 to Bethany, the **h** of Lazarus, whom he had raised
14:23 we will come to them and make our **h** with them.
16:32 each one to his **h,** and you will leave me alone.
19:27 from that hour the disciple took her into his own **h.**
Ac 2:46 they broke bread at **h** and ate their food with glad
5:42 at **h** they did not cease to teach and proclaim Jesus
8:28 and was returning **h;** seated in his
10:32 he is staying in the **h** of Simon, a tanner,
16:15 come and stay at my **h.**"
16:40 After leaving the prison they went to Lydia's **h;**
21: 6 we went on board the ship, and they returned **h.**
1Co 11:34 If you are hungry, eat at **h,**
14:35 let them ask their husbands at **h.**
2Co 5: 6 while we are at **h** in the body we are away from
5: 8 be away from the body and at **h** with the Lord.
5: 9 So whether we are at **h** or away,
2Pe 3:13 where righteousness is at **h.**
Rev 21: 3 "See, the **h** of God is among mortals.
Tob 2: 1 Then during the reign of Esar-haddon I returned **h,**
3: 6 release me to go to the eternal **h,** and do not,
6:11 "We must stay this night in the **h** of Raguel.
9: 2 Go to the **h** of Gabael, give him the bond,
11:17 Come in now to your **h,** and welcome,
Jdt 7:32 The women and children he sent **h.**
8: 5 at **h** where she set up a tent for herself on the roof
16:21 this they all returned **h** to their own inheritances.
AdE 5:10 he went **h** and summoned his friends
Sir 4:30 Do not be like a lion in your **h,**
11:29 Do not invite everyone into your **h,**
11:34 into your **h** and they will stir up trouble for you,
26:16 is the beauty of a good wife in her well-ordered **h.**
27: 9 so honesty comes **h** to those who practice it.
32:11 go **h** quickly and do not linger.
39: 3 the hidden meanings of proverbs and is at **h** with
Sus 1:13 One day they said to each other, "Let us go **h,**
1:52 your sins have now come **h,**
1Mc 3:56 he told to go **h** again, according to the law.
12:45 and will turn around and go **h.**
2Mc 9:29 And Philip, one of his courtiers, took his body **h;**
11: 2 He intended to make the city a **h** for Greeks,
11:29 to return **h** and look after your own affairs.
11:30 Therefore those who go **h** by the thirtieth
2Es 16:72 and drive them out of house and **h.**

HOMEBORN (2) [BEAR, HOME]
Ex 23:12 and your **h** slave and the resident alien may
Jer 2:14 Is he a **h** servant?

HOMEBORN (KJV) See also NATIVE

HOMELAND (3) [HOME, LAND]
Heb 11:14 in this way make it clear that they are seeking a **h.**
4Mc 17:21 the tyrant was punished, and the **h** purified—
18: 4 of the law in the **h** they ravaged the enemy.

HOMELESS (2) [HOME]
Isa 58: 7 and bring the **h** poor into your house;
1Co 4:11 we are poorly clothed and beaten and **h,**

HOMELESSNESS (1) [HOME]
La 3:19 of my affliction and my **h** is wormwood and gall!

HOMER‡ (9) [HOMERS]
Lev 27:16 fifty shekels of silver to a **h** of barley seed.
Isa 5:10 and a **h** of seed shall yield a mere ephah.
Eze 45:11 the bath containing one-tenth of a **h,**
45:11 and the ephah one-tenth of a **h;**
45:11 the **h** shall be the standard measure.
45:13 one-sixth of an ephah from each **h** of wheat,
45:13 and one-sixth of an ephah from each **h** of barley,
45:14 like the **h,** contains ten baths);
Hos 3: 2 So I bought her for fifteen shekels of silver and a **h**

HOMERS (1) [HOMER]
Nu 11:32 the least anyone gathered was ten **h;**

HOMES (38) [HOME]
Nu 32:18 We will not return to our **h** until all
Jdg 7: 7 Let all the others go to their **h.**"
1Sa 10:25 Then Samuel sent all the people back to their **h.**
2Sa 6:19 Then all the people went back to their **h.**
18:17 Meanwhile all the Israelites fled to their **h.**
19: 8 Meanwhile, all the Israelites had fled to their **h.**
20:22 and all went to their **h,**
2Ki 13: 5 the people of Israel lived in their **h** as formerly.
1Ch 16:43 Then all the people departed to their **h,**
2Ch 7:10 the people away to their **h,**
Ne 4:14 sons, your daughters, your wives, and your **h.**"
Ps 49:11 Their graves are their **h** forever,
55:15 for evil is in their **h** and in their hearts.
Pr 30:26 yet they make their **h** in the rocks;
La 5: 2 over to strangers, our **h** to aliens.
Hos 11:11 and I will return them to their **h,** says the LORD.
Mk 8: 3 If I send them away hungry to their **h,**
Lk 16: 4 people may welcome me into their **h.'**
16: 9 they may welcome you into the eternal **h.**
18:28 "Look, we have left our **h** and followed you."
Jn 20:10 Then the disciples returned to their **h.**
1Co 11:22 Do you not have **h** to eat and drink in?
Tob 13:12 all who overthrow your towers and set your **h**
Sir 28:15 Slander has driven virtuous women from their **h,**
44: 6 living peacefully in their **h—**
1Mc 6:54 the rest scattered to their own **h,**
11:38 all of them to their own **h,**
12:45 now to their **h** and choose for yourself a few men
1Es 5:47 and the Israelites were all in their own **h,**
3Mc 4:18 some still residing in their **h,**
5:21 and all went to their own **h.**
6:25 has driven from their **h** those who faithfully kept
6:27 Send them back to their **h** in peace,
6:37 asking for dismissal to their **h.**
7: 8 to return to their own **h,**
7:20 by land and sea and river to their own **h.**
2Es 11:42 the **h** of those who brought forth fruit,
12:49 Now go to your **h,** every one of you,

HOMESTEAD (1) [HOME]
Ac 1:20 'Let his **h** become desolate,

HOMETOWN (5) [HOME, TOWN]
Mt 13:54 He came to his **h** and began to teach the people
Mk 6: 1 He left that place and came to his **h,**
6: 4 "Prophets are not without honor, except in their **h,**
Lk 4:23 in your **h** the things that we have heard you did
4:24 no prophet is accepted in the prophet's **h.**

HOMICIDE (4)
Dt 4:42 to which a **h** could flee,
4:42 the **h** could flee to one of these cities and live:
19: 3 so that any **h** can flee to one of them.
19: 4 Now this is the case of a **h** who might flee there

HONED (1)
Eze 21:10 for slaughter, **h** to flash like lightning!

HONEST (23) [HONESTLY, HONESTY]
Ge 42:11 We are all sons of one man; we are **h** men;
42:19 if you are **h** men, let one of your brothers stay here
42:31 we said to him, 'We are **h** men, we are not spies.
42:33 'By this I shall know that you are **h** men:
42:34 and I shall know that you are not spies but **h** men.
Lev 19:36 You shall have **h** balances, **h** weights, an **h** ephah, and an **h** hin:
Dt 25:15 You shall have only a full and **h** weight;
25:15 you shall have only a full and **h** measure,
Jos 14: 7 and I brought him an **h** report.
1Sa 29: 6 "As the LORD lives, you have been **h,**
Job 6:25 How forceful are **h** words!
Pr 12:17 Whoever speaks the truth gives **h** evidence,
16:11 **H** balances and scales are the LORD's;
24:26 One who gives an **h** answer gives a kiss on
Eze 45:10 shall have **h** balances, an **h** ephah, and an **h** bath.
Lk 8:15 hold it fast in an **h** and good heart,
20:20 and sent spies who pretended to be **h,**
Sir 29: 3 Keep your promise and be **h** with him,

HONESTLY‡ (5) [HONEST]
2Ki 12:15 to pay out to the workers, for they dealt **h.**
22: 7 that is delivered into their hand, for they deal **h.**"
Isa 59: 4 No one brings suit justly, no one goes to law **h;**
Jer 8: 6 but they do not speak **h;**
Eph 4:28 and work **h** with their own hands,

HONESTY (2) [HONEST]
Ge 30:33 So my **h** will answer for me later,
Sir 27: 9 so **h** comes home to those who practice it.

HONEY (64) [HONEYCOMB, HONEYCOMBS]
A. LAND FLOWING WITH MILK AND HONEY (20)

Ge 43:11 a little balm and a little **h,** gum, resin,
Ex 3: 8 a land flowing with milk and **h,** A
3:17 the Jebusites, a land flowing with milk and **h.'** A
13: 5 a land flowing with milk and **h,** A
16:31 and the taste of it was like wafers made with **h.**
33: 3 Go up to a land flowing with milk and **h;** A
Lev 2:11 not turn any leaven or **h** into smoke as an offering
20:24 a land flowing with milk and **h.** A
Nu 13:27 it flows with milk and **h,** and this is its fruit.
14: 8 a land that flows with milk and **h.**
16:13 out of a land flowing with milk and **h** to kill us A
16:14 brought us into a land flowing with milk and **h,** A
Dt 6: 3 in a land flowing with milk and **h,** A
8: 8 a land of olive trees and **h,**
11: 9 a land flowing with milk and **h.** A
26: 9 a land flowing with milk and **h.** A
26:15 a land flowing with milk and **h.**" A
27: 3 a land flowing with milk and **h,** as the LORD, A
31:20 into the land flowing with milk and **h,** A
32:13 he nursed him with **h** from the crags,
Jos 5: 6 a land flowing with milk and **h.** A
Jdg 14: 8 a swarm of bees in the body of the lion, and **h.**
14: 9 that he had taken the **h** from the carcass of the lion.
14:18 "What is sweeter than **h?**
1Sa 14:25 and there was **h** on the ground.
14:26 upon the honeycomb, the **h** was dripping out;
14:29 because I tasted a little of this **h.**
14:43 "I tasted a little **h** with the tip of the staff that was
2Sa 17:29 **h** and curds, sheep, and cheese from the herd,
1Ki 14: 3 some cakes, and a jar of **h,** and go to him;
2Ki 18:32 a land of olive oil and **h,**
2Ch 31: 5 wine, oil, **h,** and of all the produce of the field;
Job 20:17 the streams flowing with **h** and curds.
Ps 19:10 sweeter also than **h,** and drippings of the
81:16 and with **h** from the rock I would satisfy you."
119:103 sweeter than **h** to my mouth!
Pr 5: 3 For the lips of a loose woman drip **h,**
24:13 My child, eat **h,** for it is good,
25:16 If you have found **h,** eat only enough for you,
25:27 It is not good to eat much **h,**
27: 7 The sated appetite spurns **h,**

SS 4:11 **h** and milk are under your tongue;
5: 1 I eat my honeycomb with my **h**,
Isa 7:15 He shall eat curds and **h** by the time he knows how
7:22 that is left in the land shall eat curds and **h**.
Jer 11: 5 to give them a land flowing with milk and **h**, A
32:22 a land flowing with milk and **h**; A
41: 8 barley, oil, and **h** hidden in the fields."
Eze 3: 3 Then I ate it; and in my mouth it was as sweet as **h**.
16:13 You had choice flour and **h** and oil for food.
16:19 I fed you with choice flour and oil and **h**—
20: 6 a land flowing with milk and **h**, A
20:15 a land flowing with milk and **h**, A
27:17 from Minnith, millet, **h**, oil,
Mt 3: 4 and his food was locusts and wild **h**.
Mk 1: 6 and he ate locusts and wild **h**.
Rev 10: 9 but sweet as **h** in your mouth."
10:10 it was sweet as **h** in my mouth,
Sir 24:20 For the memory of me is sweeter than **h**,
39:26 and iron and salt and wheat flour and milk and **h**,
46: 8 the land flowing with milk and **h**. A
49: 1 his memory is as sweet as **h** to every mouth,
Bar 1:20 to give to us a land flowing with milk and **h**. A
2Es 2:19 number of springs flowing with milk and **h**,

HONEYCOMB (8) [HONEY]

1Sa 14:25 All the troops came upon a **h**;
14:26 When the troops came upon the **h**,
14:27 and dipped the tip of it in the **h**,
Ps 19:10 sweeter also than honey, and drippings of the **h**.
Pr 16:24 Pleasant words are like a **h**,
24:13 and the drippings of the **h** are sweet to your taste.
SS 5: 1 I eat my **h** with my honey,
Sir 24:20 and the possession of me sweeter than the **h**.

HONEYCOMBS (1) [HONEY]

4Mc 14:19 for making **h** defend themselves against intruders

HONOR‡ (227) [HONORABLE, HONORABLY, HONORED, HONORING, HONORS]

Ge 30:20 now my husband will **h** me,
Ex 20:12 **H** your father and your mother,
Nu 22:17 surely do you great **h**, and whatever you say
22:37 Am I not able to **h** you?"
Dt 5:16 **H** your father and your mother,
26:19 in praise and in fame and in **h**;
Jdg 9:16 and **h** when you made Abimelech king,
9:19 you have acted in good faith and **h** with Jerubbaal
13:17 that we may **h** you when your words come true?"
1Sa 2: 8 with princes and inherit a seat of **h**.
2:29 and **h** your sons more than me
2:30 for those who **h** me I will **h**,
9: 6 he is a man held in **h**.
15:30 yet **h** me now before the elders of my people and
2Sa 6:22 by them I shall be held in **h**."
1Ki 3:13 both riches and **h** all your life;
1Ch 16:27 **H** and majesty are before him;
29:12 Riches and **h** come from you,
29:28 and **h**; and his son Solomon succeeded him.
2Ch 1:11 and you have not asked for possessions, wealth, **h**,
1:12 I will also give you riches, possessions, and **h**,
16:14 and they made a very great fire in his **h**.
17: 5 and he had great riches and **h**.
18: 1 Now Jehoshaphat had great riches and **h**;
21:19 His people made no fire in his **h**,
26:18 and it will bring you no **h** from the LORD God."
32:27 Hezekiah had very great riches and **h**;
32:33 the inhabitants of Jerusalem did him **h** at his death.
Est 1:20 all women will give **h** to their husbands,
6: 3 "What **h** or distinction has been bestowed
6: 6 be done for the man whom the king wishes to **h**?"
6: 6 "Whom would the king wish to **h** more than me?"
6: 7 "For the man whom the king wishes to **h**,
6: 9 let him robe the man whom the king wishes to **h**,
6: 9 be done for the man whom the king wishes to **h**.' "
6:11 be done for the man whom the king wishes to **h**."
8:16 the Jews there was light and gladness, joy and **h**.
10: 2 and the full account of the high **h** of Mordecai,
Job 14:21 Their children come to **h**, and they do not know it;
30:15 my **h** is pursued as by the wind,
Ps 4: 2 How long, you people, shall my **h** suffer shame?
8: 5 and crowned them with glory and **h**.
15: 4 but who **h** those who fear the LORD;
45: 9 daughters of kings are among your ladies of **h**;
50:23 who bring thanksgiving as their sacrifice **h** me;
62: 7 On God rests my deliverance and my **h**;
71:21 You will increase my **h**,
73:24 and afterward you will receive me with **h**.
84:11 and shield; he bestows favor and **h**.
91:15 I will rescue them and **h** them.
96: 6 **H** and majesty are before him;
104: 1 You are clothed with **h** and majesty,
111: 3 Full of **h** and majesty is his work,
112: 9 their horn is exalted in **h**.
Pr 3: 9 **H** the LORD with your substance and with
3:16 in her left hand are riches and **h**.
3:35 wise will inherit **h**, but stubborn fools, disgrace.
4: 8 she will **h** you if you embrace her.
5: 9 or you will give your **h** to others,
8:18 Riches and **h** are with me,
11:16 A gracious woman gets **h**,
14:31 but those who are kind to the needy **h** him.
15:33 and humility goes before **h**.
18:12 but humility goes before **h**.
Pr 21:21 and kindness will find life and **h**.
22: 4 for humility and fear of the LORD is riches and **h**
25:27 or to seek **h** on top of **h**.
26: 1 so **h** is not fitting for a fool.
26: 8 like binding a stone in a sling to give **h** to a fool.
29:23 but one who is lowly in spirit will obtain **h**.
Ecc 6: 2 to whom God gives wealth, possessions, and **h**, so
10: 1 so a little folly outweighs wisdom and **h**.
Isa 22:23 he will become a throne of **h** to his ancestral house.
29:13 and **h** me with their lips, while their hearts are far
43:20 The wild animals will **h** me,
58:13 if you **h** it, not going your own ways,
La 4:16 no **h** was shown to the priests,
Eze 39:13 and it will bring them **h** on the day
Da 2: 6 from me gifts and rewards and great **h**.
4:37 praise and extol and **h** the King of heaven,
5:19 honored those he wanted to **h**,
11:38 He shall **h** the god of fortresses instead of these;
11:38 a god whom his ancestors did not know he shall **h**
Zec 6:13 he shall bear royal **h**, and shall sit and rule
Mal 1: 6 If then I am a father, where is the **h** due me?
Mt 13:57 not without **h** except in their own country and
15: 4 For God said, '**H** your father and your mother,'
15: 5 then that person need not **h** the father.
19:19 **H** your father and mother; also,
23: 6 They love to have the place of **h** at banquets and
Mk 6: 4 Jesus said to them, "Prophets are not without **h**,
7:10 For Moses said, '**H** your father and your mother';
10:19 **H** your father and mother.' "
12:39 the best seats in the synagogues and places of **h**
Lk 11:43 the seat of **h** in the synagogues and to be greeted
14: 7 he noticed how the guests chose the places of **h**,
14: 8 do not sit down at the place of **h**,
18:20 **H** your father and mother.' "
20:46 the best seats in the synagogues and places of **h**
Jn 4:44 a prophet has no **h** in the prophet's own country).
5:23 all may **h** the Son just as they **h** the Father.
5:23 Anyone who does not **h** the Son does not **h**
8:49 but I **h** my Father, and you dishonor me.
12:26 Whoever serves me, the Father will **h**.
Ro 1:21 they did not **h** him as God or give thanks to him,
2: 7 and **h** and immortality, he will give eternal life;
2:10 and **h** and peace for everyone who does good,
12:10 outdo one another in showing **h**.
13: 7 to whom respect is due, **h** to whom **h** is due.
14: 6 observe it in **h** of the Lord.
14: 6 Also those who eat, eat in **h** of the Lord,
14: 6 abstain in **h** of the Lord and give thanks to God.
1Co 4:10 You are held in **h**, but we in disrepute.
12:23 we think less honorable we clothe with greater **h**,
12:24 giving the greater **h** to the inferior member,
2Co 6: 8 in **h** and dishonor, in ill repute
Eph 6: 2 "**H** your father and mother"—
Php 2:29 then in the Lord with all joy, and **h** such people,
1Th 4: 4 how to control your own body in holiness and **h**,
1Ti 1:17 the only God, be **h** and glory forever and ever.
5: 3 **H** widows who are really widows.
5:17 of double **h**, especially those who labor
6: 1 of slavery regard their masters as worthy of all **h**,
6:16 to him be **h** and eternal dominion.
Heb 2: 7 you have crowned them with glory and **h**,
2: 9 with glory and **h** because of the suffering of death,
3: 3 just as the builder of a house has more **h** than
5: 4 And one does not presume to take this **h**,
13: 4 Let marriage be held in **h** by all,
1Pe 1: 7 may be found to result in praise and glory and **h**
2:17 **H** everyone. Love the family of believers. Fear God. **H** the emperor.
3: 7 paying **h** to the woman as the weaker sex,
2Pe 1:17 For he received **h** and glory from God the Father
Rev 4: 9 the living creatures give glory and **h** and thanks to
4:11 to receive glory and **h** and power,
5:12 and wealth and wisdom and might and **h** and glory
5:13 on the throne and to the Lamb be blessing and **h**
7:12 and **h** and power and might be to our God forever
21:26 People will bring into it the glory and the **h** of
Tob 4: 3 **H** your mother and do not abandon her all the days
10:12 **H** your father-in-law and your mother-in-law,
10:13 "I have been commanded by the Lord to **h** you all
12: 6 With fitting **h** declare to all people the deeds
12: 7 and with fitting **h** to acknowledge him.
12:11 but to reveal with due **h** the works of God.'
14: 2 and was buried with great **h** in Nineveh.
Jdt 13:20 May God grant this to be a perpetual **h** to you,
15:12 and some of them performed a dance in her **h**.
AdE 1:20 and thus all women will give **h** to their husbands,
5:11 And he told them about his riches and the **h** that
6: 3 "What **h** or dignity did we bestow
6: 6 for the person whom I wish to **h**?"
6: 6 "Whom would the king wish to **h** more than me?"
6: 7 "For a person whom the king wishes to **h**,
6:11 be done to everyone whom the king wishes to **h**."
9: 3 the royal secretaries were paying **h** to the Jews,
9: 4 that Mordecai's name be held in **h** throughout
11:11 lowly were exalted and devoured those held in **h**.
12: 6 a Bougean, who was in great **h** with the king,
Wis 3:17 and finally their old age will be without **h**.
5: 4 and that their end was without **h**.
6:21 **h** wisdom, so that you may reign forever.
8:10 the multitudes and **h** in the presence of the elders,
10:14 and she gave him everlasting **h**.
14:17 people could not **h** monarchs in their presence,
Sir 3: 3 Those who **h** their father atone for sins,
3: 5 Those who **h** their father will have joy
3: 6 and those who **h** their mother obey the Lord;
3: 8 **H** your father by word and deed,
5:13 **H** and dishonor come from speaking,
Sir 7: 4 or the seat of **h** from the king.
7:27 With all your heart **h** your father,
7:31 Fear the Lord and **h** the priest,
10: 5 and it is he who confers **h** upon the lawgiver.
10:19 Whose offspring are worthy of **h**?
10:19 Whose offspring are worthy of **h**?
10:19 Whose offspring are unworthy of **h**?
10:19 Whose offspring are unworthy of **h**?
10:20 of **h**, but those who fear the Lord are worthy
10:20 but those who fear the Lord are worthy of **h**
10:23 and it is not proper to **h** one who is sinful.
10:28 My child, **h** yourself with humility,
10:29 And who will **h** those who dishonor themselves?
33:23 bring no stain upon your **h**.
37:26 One who is wise among his people will inherit **h**,
38: 1 **H** physicians for their services,
44: 1 HYMN IN **H** OF OUR ANCESTORS
47:20 You stained your **h**, and defiled your family line,
1Mc 1:39 her sabbaths into a reproach, her **h** into contempt.
2: 8 Her temple has become like a person without **h**;
2:51 you will receive great **h** and an everlasting name.
2:64 for by it you will gain **h**.
3:14 a name for myself and win **h** in the kingdom.
9:10 and leave no cause to question our **h**."
10: 3 a letter in peaceable words to **h** him;
10:24 of encouragement and promise them **h** and gifts,
10:64 When his accusers saw the **h** that was paid him,
11:42 but I will confer great **h** on you and your nation,
11:60 the people of the city met him and paid him **h**.
12: 8 Onias welcomed the envoy with **h**,
12:43 So he received him with **h** and commended him
14: 4 as was the **h** shown him, all his days.
14:21 to our people have told us about your glory and **h**,
14:23 to receive these men with **h** and to put a copy
14:40 Romans had received the envoys of Simon with **h**.
15: 9 we will bestow great **h** on you and your nation and
2Mc 5:16 to enhance the glory and **h** of the place.
6: 7 and to walk in the procession in **h** of Dionysus.
6:19 welcoming death with **h** rather than life
14:21 seats of **h** were set in place;
1Es 8: 4 and the king showed him **h**,
9:45 for he had the place of **h** in the presence of all.
3Mc 1:12 saying, "Even if those men are deprived of this **h**,
3:16 went up to **h** the temple of those wicked people,
3:17 to enter their inner temple and **h** it
4:16 organizing feasts in **h** of all his idols,
7:21 being held in **h** and awe;
4Mc 1:10 but I would also call them blessed for the **h**
1:26 covetousness, thirst for **h**, rivalry, and malice;
17: 5 stand in **h** before God and are firmly set in heaven
17:20 are honored, not only with this **h**,

HONORABLE (10) [HONOR]

Pr 20: 3 It is **h** to refrain from strife,
Isa 3: 5 be insolent to the elder, and the base to the **h**.
32: 5 nor a villain said to be **h**.
58:13 a delight and the holy day of the LORD **h**;
1Co 12:23 that we think less **h** we clothe with greater honor,
Php 4: 8 Finally, beloved, whatever is true, whatever is **h**,
1Pe 2:12 they may see your **h** deeds and glorify God
Tob 14:11 and he received an **h** funeral.
2Mc 7:20 was especially admirable and worthy of **h** memory.
4Mc 5:36 O king, shall not defile the **h** mouth of my old age,

HONORABLY (5) [HONOR]

Ro 13:13 let us live **h** as in the day,
Heb 13:18 desiring to act **h** in all things.
1Pe 2:12 Conduct yourselves **h** among the Gentiles, so that,
AdE 13: 4 that we **h** intend cannot be brought about.
2Mc 12:43 In doing this he acted very well and **h**,

HONORED (63) [HONOR]

Ge 34:19 Now he was the most **h** of all his family.
45:13 You must tell my father how greatly I am **h**
Jdg 9: 9 by which gods and mortals are **h**,
1Sa 22:14 and is **h** in your house.
2Sa 6:20 and said, "How the king of Israel **h** himself today,
1Ch 4: 9 Jabez was **h** more than his brothers;
Est 5:11 all the promotions with which the king had **h** him,
Pr 13:18 but one who heeds reproof is **h**.
27:18 and anyone who takes care of a master will be **h**.
Isa 23: 8 whose traders were the **h** of the earth?
23: 9 to shame all the **h** of the earth.
43: 4 Because you are precious in my sight, and **h**,
43:23 or **h** me with your sacrifices.
49: 5 for I am **h** in the sight of the LORD,
Jer 30:19 I will make them **h**, and they shall not
La 1: 8 all who **h** her despise her, for they have seen her
Da 4:34 and praised and **h** the one who lives forever.
5:19 **h** those he wanted to honor,
5:23 and to whom belong all your ways, you have not **h**.
Hag 1: 8 so that I may take pleasure in it and be **h**,
Lk 14:10 then you will be **h** in the presence of all who sit at
1Co 12:26 if one member is **h**, all rejoice together with it.
Jdt 12:13 to come to my lord to be **h** in his presence,
16:21 of her life she was **h** throughout the whole country.
AdE 6: 9 let both be given to one of the king's **h** Friends,
10: 3 as well as **h** by the Jews.
14:17 and I have not **h** the king's feast or drunk the wine
16: 2 the more they are **h** with
Wis 4: 8 For old age is not **h** for length of time,
14:15 he now **h** as a god what was once
14:17 made a visible image of the king whom they **h**,
14:20 of worship the one whom shortly before they had **h**
Sir 10:24 The prince and the judge and the ruler are **h**,

Sir 10:30 The poor are **h** for their knowledge,
10:30 while the rich are **h** for their wealth.
10:31 One who is **h** in poverty,
11: 4 and do not exalt yourself when you are **h;**
11: 6 and the **h** have been handed over to others.
24:12 I took root in an **h** people,
29:27 "Be off, stranger, for an **h** guest is here;
44: 7 all these were **h** in their generations,
46:12 the names of those who have been **h** live again
49:16 Shem and Seth and Enosh were **h,**
Sus 1: 4 to him because he was the most **h** of them all.
Bel 1: 2 and was the most **h** of all his friends.
1Mc 1: 6 So he summoned his most **h** officers,
2:17 "You are a leader, **h** and great in this town,
2:18 and your sons will be **h** with silver and gold
5:63 and his brothers were greatly **h** in all Israel and
7:26 Then the king sent Nicanor, one of his **h** princes,
10:65 Thus the king **h** him and enrolled him
10:88 of these things, he **h** Jonathan still more;
2Mc 3: 2 it came about that the kings themselves **h** the place
3:12 the sanctity and inviolability of the temple that is **h**
13:23 with them and offered sacrifice, **h** the sanctuary
15: 2 that he who sees all things has **h** and hallowed
1Es 8:26 and who **h** me in the sight of the king
8:67 and these officials **h** the people and the temple of
3Mc 2: 9 for the glory of your great and **h** name.
6:13 O **h** One, who have power to save the nation
2Es 7:*60* and through them my name has now been **h.**
4Mc 5:35 **h** priesthood and knowledge of the law.
17:20 are **h,** not only with this honor,

HONORING (5) [HONOR]

2Sa 10: 3 that David is **h** your father just
1Ch 17:18 to you for **h** your servant?
19: 3 that he is **h** your father?
Sir 26:26 *A wife* **h** *her husband will seem wise to all,*
4Mc 5:12 on your old age by **h** my humane advice?

HONORS (12) [HONOR]

Mal 1: 6 A son **h** his father, and servants their master.
Mt 15: 8 'This people **h** me with their lips,
Mk 7: 6 as it is written, 'This people **h** me with their lips,
Ac 28:10 They bestowed many **h** on us,
AdE 6: 9 be done to everyone whom the king **h.'"**
Sir 3: 2 For the Lord **h** a father above his children,
1Mc 11:27 and in as many other **h** as he had formerly had,
14: 5 To crown all his **h** he took Joppa for a harbor,
14:39 made him one of his Friends, and paid him high **h.**
2Mc 4:15 the **h** prized by their ancestors and putting
1Es 3: 5 King Darius will give rich gifts and great **h**
4Mc 11: 6 But these deeds deserve **h,** not tortures."

HOOF (6) [HOOFBEATS, HOOFS]

Ex 10:26 not a **h** shall be left behind,
Dt 14: 6 that divides the **h** and has the **h** cleft in two,
14: 7 the cud or have the **h** cleft you shall not eat these:
14: 7 because they chew the cud but do not divide the **h;**
14: 8 because it divides the **h** but does not chew the cud,

HOOFBEATS (1) [HOOF]

Jdg 5:28 Why tarry the **h** of his chariots?'

HOOFS (16) [HOOF]

Lev 11: 3 Any animal that has divided **h** and is cleft-footed
11: 4 among those that chew the cud or have divided **h,**
11: 4 it does not have divided **h;** it is unclean for you.
11: 5 it does not have divided **h;** it is unclean for you.
11: 6 it does not have divided **h;** it is unclean for you.
11: 7 for even though it has divided **h** and is cleft-footed,
11:26 that has divided **h** but is not cleft-footed or does
Jdg 5:22 "Then loud beat the horses' **h** with the galloping,
Ps 69:31 an ox or a bull with horns and **h.**
Isa 5:28 all their bows bent, their horses' **h** seem like flint,
Jer 47: 3 the noise of the stamping of the **h** of his stallions,
Eze 26:11 the **h** of his horses he shall trample all your streets.
32:13 nor shall the **h** of cattle trouble them.
Mic 4:13 for I will make your horn iron and your **h** bronze;
Zec 11:16 the flesh of the fat ones, tearing off even their **h.**
2Mc 3:25 at Heliodorus and struck at him with its front **h.**

HOOK (5) [FISHHOOK, FISHHOOKS, HOOKS]

2Ki 19:28 I will put my **h** in your nose and my bit
Job 41: 2 or pierce its jaw with a **h?**
Isa 37:29 I will put my **h** in your nose and my bit
Hab 1:15 The enemy brings all of them up with a **h;**
Mt 17:27 go to the sea and cast a **h;**

HOOKS (27) [HOOK]

Ex 26:32 which have **h** of gold and rest on four bases
26:37 their **h** shall be of gold,
27:10 **h** of the pillars and their bands shall be of silver.
27:11 **h** of the pillars and their bands shall be of silver.
27:17 their **h** shall be of silver, and their bases of bronze.
36:36 their **h** were of gold, and he cast
36:38 and its five pillars with their **h.**
38:10 the **h** of the pillars and their bands were of silver.
38:11 the **h** of the pillars and their bands were of silver.
38:12 the **h** of the pillars and their bands were of silver.
38:17 the **h** of the pillars and their bands were of silver;
38:19 their four bases were of bronze, their **h** of silver,
38:28 he made **h** for the pillars,
39:33 its **h,** its frames, its bars, its pillars, and its bases;
Job 40:24 Can one take it with **h** or pierce its nose with
Isa 2: 4 and their spears into pruning **h;**
18: 5 he will cut off the shoots with pruning **h,**
19: 8 all who cast **h** in the Nile will lament,
Eze 19: 4 and they brought him with **h** to the land of Egypt.
19: 9 With **h** they put him in a cage,
29: 4 I will put **h** in your jaws,
38: 4 I will turn you around and put **h** into your jaws,
Joel 3:10 and your pruning **h** into spears;
Am 4: 2 when they shall take you away with **h,**
Mic 4: 3 and their spears into pruning **h;**
4Mc 8:13 rack and **h** and catapults and caldrons,
9:26 with iron gauntlets having sharp **h,**

HOOPOE (2)

Lev 11:19 the stork, the heron of any kind, the **h,** and the bat.
Dt 14:18 the stork, the heron, of any kind; the **h** and the bat.

HOOT (1)

Zep 2:14 the owl shall **h** at the window,

HOPE‡ (187) [HOPED, HOPEFUL, HOPELESS, HOPES, HOPING]

Ru 1:12 Even if I thought there was **h** for me,
2Ki 6:33 Why should I **h** in the LORD any longer?"
1Ch 29:15 on the earth are like a shadow, and there is no **h.**
Ezr 10: 2 but even now there is **h** for Israel in spite of this.
Job 3: 9 let it **h** for light, but have none;
4: 6 and the integrity of your ways your **h?**
5:16 So the poor have **h,** and injustice shuts its mouth.
6:19 caravans of Tema look, the travelers of Sheba **h.**
7: 6 and come to their end without **h.**
8:13 the **h** of the godless shall perish.
11:18 And you will have confidence, because there is **h;**
11:20 and their **h** is to breathe their last."
13:15 I have no **h;** but I will defend my ways to his face.
14: 7 "For there is **h** for a tree, if it is cut down,
14:19 so you destroy the **h** of mortals.
17:15 where then is my **h?** Who will see my **h?**
19:10 and I am gone, he has uprooted my **h** like a tree.
27: 8 the **h** of the godless when God cuts them off,
41: 9 Any **h** of capturing it will be disappointed;
Ps 9:18 nor the **h** of the poor perish forever.
33:17 The war horse is a vain **h** for victory,
33:18 on those who **h** in his steadfast love,
33:22 O LORD, be upon us, even as we **h** in you.
39: 7 My **h** is in you.
42: 5 and why are you disquieted within me? **H** in God;
42:11 and why are you disquieted within me? **H** in God;
43: 5 and why are you disquieted within me? **H** in God;
62: 5 for my **h** is from him.
65: 5 you are the **h** of all the ends of the earth and of
69: 6 not let those who **h** in you be put to shame because
71: 5 For you, O Lord, are my **h,** my trust, O LORD,
71:14 But I will **h** continually, and will praise you
78: 7 that they should set their **h** in God, and not forget
119:43 for my **h** is in your ordinances.
119:49 in which you have made me **h.**
119:81 for your salvation; I **h** in your word.
119:114 and my shield; I **h** in your word.
119:116 and let me not be put to shame in my **h.**
119:147 I put my **h** in your words.
119:166 I **h** for your salvation, O LORD,
130: 5 my soul waits, and in his word I **h;**
130: 7 O Israel, **h** in the LORD!
131: 3 **h** in the LORD from this time on
146: 5 whose **h** is in the LORD their God,
147:11 in those who **h** in his steadfast love.
Pr 10:28 The **h** of the righteous ends in gladness,
11: 7 When the wicked die, their **h** perishes,
13:12 **H** deferred makes the heart sick,
19:18 Discipline your children while there is **h;**
23:18 there is a future, and your **h** will not be cut off.
24:14 and your **h** will not be cut off.
26:12 There is more **h** for fools than for them.
29:20 There is more **h** for a fool than for anyone
Ecc 9: 4 But whoever is joined with all the living has **h,**
Isa 8:17 and I will **h** in him.
20: 5 and confounded because of Ethiopia their **h** and
38:18 down to the Pit cannot **h** for your faithfulness.
51: 5 the coastlands wait for me, and for my arm they **h.**
Jer 14: 8 O **h** of Israel, its savior in time of trouble,
14:22 We set our **h** on you, for it is you who do all this.
17:13 O **h** of Israel! O LORD! All who forsake you
29:11 to give you a future with **h.**
31:17 there is **h** for your future, says the LORD:
50: 7 the LORD, the **h** of their ancestors."
La 3:21 But this I call to mind, and therefore I have **h:**
3:24 says my soul, "therefore I will **h** in him."
3:29 to the dust (there may yet be **h**),
Eze 19: 5 she saw that she was thwarted, that her **h** was lost,
37:11 and our **h** is lost; we are cut off completely.'
Hos 2:15 and make the Valley of Achor a door of **h.**
Zec 9:12 Return to your stronghold, O prisoners of **h;**
Mt 12:21 And in his name the Gentiles will **h."**
Lk 6:34 If you lend to those from whom you **h** to receive,
Jn 5:45 on whom you have set your **h.**
Ac 2:26 moreover my flesh will live in **h.**
16:19 that their **h** of making money was gone,
23: 6 I am on trial concerning the **h** of the resurrection of
24:15 I have a **h** in God—
24:15 a **h** that they themselves also accept—
26: 6 And now I stand here on trial on account of my **h**
26: 7 a promise that our twelve tribes **h** to attain,
26: 7 It is for this **h,** your Excellency,
Ac 27:20 all **h** of our being saved was at last abandoned.
28:20 of the **h** of Israel that I am bound with this chain."
Ro 4:18 against **h,** he believed that he would become
5: 2 and we boast in our **h** of sharing the glory of God.
5: 4 and character produces **h,**
5: 5 and **h** does not disappoint us,
8:20 but by the will of the one who subjected it, in **h**
8:24 For in **h** we were saved.
8:24 Now **h** that is seen is not **h.**
8:25 But if we **h** for what we do not see,
12:12 Rejoice in **h,** be patient in suffering,
15: 4 of the scriptures we might have **h.**
15:12 in him the Gentiles shall **h."**
15:13 May the God of **h** fill you with all joy and peace
15:13 so that you may abound in **h** by the power of
15:24 For I do **h** to see you on my journey and to be sent
1Co 9:10 in **h** and whoever threshes should thresh in **h** of
13:13 And now faith, **h,** and love abide, these three;
16: 7 for I **h** to spend some time with you,
2Co 1: 7 Our **h** for you is unshaken;
1:10 on him we have set our **h**
1:13 I **h** you will understand until the end—
3:12 Since, then, we have such a **h,**
5:11 but we ourselves are well known to God, and I **h**
10:15 but our **h** is that, as your faith increases,
13: 6 I **h** you will find out that we have not failed.
Gal 5: 5 we eagerly wait for the **h** of righteousness.
Eph 1:12 who were the first to set our **h** on Christ,
1:18 the **h** to which he has called you,
2:12 having no **h** and without God in the world.
4: 4 just as you were called to the one **h** of your calling,
Php 1:20 and **h** that I will not be put to shame in any way,
2:19 I **h** in the Lord Jesus to send Timothy to you soon,
2:23 I **h** therefore to send him as soon as I see
Col 1: 5 because of the **h** laid up for you in heaven.
1: 5 You have heard of this **h** before in the word of
1:23 without shifting from the **h** promised by the gospel
1:27 which is Christ in you, the **h** of glory.
1Th 1: 3 of faith and labor of love and steadfastness of **h**
2:19 For what is our **h** or joy or crown of boasting
4:13 you may not grieve as others do who have no **h.**
5: 8 and for a helmet the **h** of salvation.
2Th 2:16 through grace gave us eternal comfort and good **h,**
1Ti 1: 1 of God our Savior and of Christ Jesus our **h,**
3:14 I **h** to come to you soon,
4:10 because we have our **h** set on the living God,
5: 5 has set her **h** on God and continues in supplications
Tit 1: 2 in the **h** of eternal life that God,
2:13 for the blessed **h** and the manifestation of the glory
3: 7 we might become heirs according to the **h**
Heb 3: 6 the confidence and the pride that belong to **h.**
6:11 as to realize the full assurance of **h** to the very end,
6:18 be strongly encouraged to seize the **h** set before us.
6:19 We have this **h,** a sure and steadfast anchor of
6:19 a **h** that enters the inner shrine behind the curtain,
7:19 on the other hand, the introduction of a better **h,**
10:23 to the confession of our **h** without wavering,
1Pe 1: 3 a new birth into a living **h** through the resurrection
1:13 set all your **h** on the grace
1:21 so that your faith and **h** are set on God.
3:15 from you an accounting for the **h** that is in you;
1Jn 3: 3 And all who have this **h** in him purify themselves,
2Jn 1:12 instead I **h** to come to you and talk with you face
3Jn 1:14 instead I **h** to see you soon,
Jdt 6: 9 If you really **h** in your heart that they will not
8:20 and so we **h** that he will not disdain us or any
9:11 of the forsaken, savior of those without **h.**
Wis 3: 4 their **h** is full of immortality.
3:11 Their **h** is vain, their labors are unprofitable,
3:18 they will have no **h** and no consolation on the day
5:14 the **h** of the ungodly is like thistledown carried by
12:19 and you have filled your children with good **h,**
14: 6 the **h** of the world took refuge on a raft,
15: 6 for such objects of **h** are those who either make
15:10 Their heart is ashes, their **h** is cheaper than dirt,
16:29 for the **h** of an ungrateful person will melt
17:13 and **h,** defeated by this inward weakness,
Sir 2: 6 make your ways straight, and **h** in him.
2: 9 You who fear the Lord, **h** for good things,
14: 2 and who have not given up their **h.**
17:24 and he encourages those who are losing **h.**
27:21 but whoever has betrayed secrets is without **h.**
34: 7 and those who put their **h** in them have perished.
34:15 for their **h** is in him who saves them.
34:16 or play the coward, for he is their **h.**
49:10 of Jacob and delivered them with confident **h.**
Bar 4:22 For I have put my **h** in the Everlasting to save you,
Sus 1:60 who saves those who **h** in him.
2Mc 2:18 We have **h** in God that he will soon have mercy
3:29 of the divine intervention and deprived of any **h**
5: 9 having embarked to go to the Lacedaemonians in **h**
7:11 and from him I **h** to get them back again."
7:14 to cherish the **h** God gives of being raised again
7:20 she bore it with good courage because of her **h** in
9:18 he gave up all **h** for himself and wrote to the Jews
9:20 As my **h** is in heaven,
9:22 for I have good **h** of recovering from my illness,
1Es 8:92 but even now there is **h** for Israel.
2Es 5:12 At that time people shall **h** but not obtain;
7:*120* [50] that an everlasting **h** has been promised to us,
11:46 and may **h** for the judgment and mercy
4Mc 17: 4 maintaining firm an enduring **h** in God.

HOPED (11) [HOPE]

Est 9: 1 the enemies of the Jews **h** to gain power over them,
Ps 56: 6 As they **h** to have my life,

Ps 119:74 because I have **h** in your word.
Isa 20: 6 this is what has happened to those in whom we **h**
La 3:18 and all that I had **h** for from the LORD."
Lk 24:21 But we had **h** that he was the one to redeem Israel.
Ac 24:26 the same time he **h** that money would be given him
1Co 15:19 If for this life only we have **h** in Christ,
Heb 11: 1 Now faith is the assurance of things **h** for,
1Pe 3: 5 in this way long ago that the holy women who **h**
Wis 2:22 nor **h** for the wages of holiness,

HOPEFUL (1) [HOPE]

3Mc 2:33 They remained resolutely **h** of obtaining help,

HOPELESS (1) [HOPE]

Jer 2:25 But you said, "It is **h**, for I have loved strangers,

HOPES‡ (9) [HOPE]

Ps 62:10 and set no vain **h** on robbery;
Zec 9: 5 Ekron also, because its **h** are withered.
Ro 8:24 For who **h** for what is seen?
1Co 13: 7 It bears all things, believes all things, **h** all things,
15:32 If with merely human **h** I fought with wild animals
1Ti 6:17 or to set their **h** on the uncertainty of riches,
Wis 13:10 But miserable, with their **h** set on dead things,
Sir 34: 1 The senseless have vain and false **h**,
2Mc 7:34 not be elated in vain and puffed up by uncertain **h**,

HOPHNI (5)

1Sa 1: 3 **H** and Phinehas, were priests of the LORD.
2:34 The fate of your two sons, **H** and Phinehas,
4: 4 The two sons of Eli, **H** and Phinehas,
4:11 and the two sons of Eli, **H** and Phinehas, died.
4:17 your two sons also, **H** and Phinehas, are dead,

HOPHRA (1)

Jer 44:30 I am going to give Pharaoh **H**, king of Egypt,

HOPING (4) [HOPE]

Lk 23: 8 and was **h** to see him perform some sign.
Ro 4:18 **H** against hope, he believed that he would become
Phm 1:22 I am **h** through your prayers to be restored to you.
2Es 7:18 can endure difficult circumstances while **h**

HOPPER (1) [HOPPING]

Joel 2:25 the **h**, the destroyer, and the cutter, my great army,

HOPPING (2) [HOPPER]

Joel 1: 4 the **h** locust has eaten, and what the **h** locust left,

HOR (12)

Nu 20:22 the whole congregation, came to Mount **H**.
20:23 the LORD said to Moses and Aaron at Mount **H**,
20:25 and bring them up Mount **H**;
20:27 up Mount **H** in the sight of the whole congregation.
21: 4 From Mount **H** they set out by the way to
33:37 They set out from Kadesh and camped at Mount **H**,
33:38 Aaron the priest went up Mount **H** at the command
33:39 when he died on Mount **H**.
33:41 from Mount **H** and camped at Zalmonah.
34: 7 you shall mark out your line to Mount **H**;
34: 8 from Mount **H** you shall mark it out
Dt 32:50 on Mount **H** and was gathered to his kin;

HOR-HAGGIDGAD (2)

Nu 33:32 They set out from Bene-jaakan and camped at **H**.
33:33 They set out from **H** and camped at Jotbathah.

HORAM (1)

Jos 10:33 Then King **H** of Gezer came up to help Lachish;

HORDE‡ (6) [HORDES]

Nu 22: 4 "This **h** will now lick up all that is around us,
2Ch 32: 7 the king of Assyria and all the **h** that is with him,
Eze 31:18 This is Pharaoh and all his **h**, says the Lord GOD.
38:13 Have you assembled your **h** to carry off plunder,
38:15 all of them riding on horses, a great **h**,
39:11 for there Gog and all his **h** will be buried;

HORDES (12) [HORDE]

Eze 30:10 I will put an end to the **h** of Egypt,
30:15 and cut off the **h** of Thebes.
31: 2 say to Pharaoh king of Egypt and to his **h**:
32:12 I will cause your **h** to fall by the swords
32:12 and all its **h** shall perish.
32:16 Over Egypt and all its **h** they shall chant it,
32:18 wail over the **h** of Egypt, and send them down,
32:20 carry away both it and its **h**.
32:24 Elam is there, and all its **h** around its grave;
32:25 a bed among the slain with all its **h**, their graves all
32:31 he will be consoled for all his **h**—
2Mc 2:21 the whole land and pursued the barbarian **h**,

HOREB (19) [=SINAI]

Ex 3: 1 and came to **H**, the mountain of God.
17: 6 be standing there in front of you on the rock at **H**.
33: 6 of their ornaments, from Mount **H** onward.
Dt 1: 2 eleven days to reach Kadesh-barnea from **H**.)
1: 6 The LORD our God spoke to us at **H**,
1:19 we set out from **H** and went through all that great
4:10 the LORD your God at **H**, when the LORD said
4:15 when the LORD spoke to you at **H** out of the fire,
5: 2 LORD our God made a covenant with us at **H**.
9: 8 Even at **H** you provoked the LORD to wrath,
18:16 at **H** on the day of the assembly when you said:
29: 1 to the covenant that he had made with them at **H**.
1Ki 8: 9 of stone that Moses had placed there at **H**,
19: 8 of that food forty days and forty nights to **H**
2Ch 5:10 the two tablets that Moses put there at **H**,
Ps 106:19 They made a calf at **H** and worshiped a cast image.
Mal 4: 4 and ordinances that I commanded him at **H**
Sir 48: 7 at Sinai and judgments of vengeance at **H**.
2Es 2:33 received a command from the Lord on Mount **H**

HOREM (1)

Jos 19:38 Migdal-el, **H**, Beth-anath, and Beth-shemesh—

HORESH (4)

1Sa 23:15 in the Wilderness of Ziph at **H** when he learned
23:16 and came to David at **H**;
23:18 David remained at **H**, and Jonathan went home.
23:19 "David is hiding among us in the strongholds of **H**,

HORI (3) [HORITE, HORITES]

Ge 36:22 The sons of Lotan were **H** and Heman;
Nu 13: 5 from the tribe of Simeon, Shaphat son of **H**;
1Ch 1:39 **H** and Homam; and Lotan's sister was Timna.

HORIM (2)

Dt 2:12 Moreover, the **H** had formerly inhabited Seir,
2:22 by destroying the **H** before them so

HORITE (1) [HORI]

Ge 36:20 These are the sons of Seir the **H**,

HORITES (4) [HORI]

Ge 14: 6 the **H** in the hill country of Seir as far as El-paran
36:21 these are the clans of the **H**,
36:29 These are the clans of the **H**:
36:30 these are the clans of the **H**,

HORMAH (9)

Nu 14:45 pursuing them as far as **H**.
21: 3 so the place was called **H**.
Dt 1:44 They beat you down in Seir as far as **H**.
Jos 12:14 the king of **H** one the king of Arad one
15:30 Eltolad, Chesil, **H**,
19: 4 Eltolad, Bethul, **H**,
Jdg 1:17 So the city was called **H**.
1Sa 30:30 in **H**, in Bor-ashan, in Athach,
1Ch 4:30 Bethuel, **H**, Ziklag,

HORN‡ (38) [HORNS]

Jos 6: 5 When they make a long blast with the ram's **h**,
1Sa 16: 1 Fill your **h** with oil and set out;
16:13 Then Samuel took the **h** of oil,
2Sa 22: 3 my shield and the **h** of my salvation,
1Ki 1:39 the **h** of oil from the tent and anointed Solomon.
1Ch 15:28 to the sound of the **h**, trumpets, and cymbals,
Ps 18: 2 and the **h** of my salvation, my stronghold.
75: 4 and to the wicked, "Do not lift up your **h**;
75: 5 do not lift up your **h** on high,
89:17 by your favor our **h** is exalted.
89:24 and in my name his **h** shall be exalted.
92:10 But you have exalted my **h** like that of the wild ox;
98: 6 and the sound of the **h** make a joyful noise before
112: 9 their **h** is exalted in honor.
132:17 There I will cause a **h** to sprout up for David;
148:14 He has raised up a **h** for his people,
Jer 48:25 The **h** of Moab is cut off, and his arm is broken,
Eze 7:14 the **h** and made everything ready;
29:21 that day I will cause a **h** to sprout up for the house
Da 3: 5 that when you hear the sound of the **h**,
3: 7 as soon as all the peoples heard the sound of the **h**,
3:10 that everyone who hears the sound of the **h**, pipe,
3:15 if you are ready when you hear the sound of the **h**,
7: 8 when another **h** appeared, a little one coming up
7: 8 There were eyes like human eyes in this **h**,
7:11 of the arrogant words that the **h** was speaking.
7:20 and concerning the other **h**,
7:20 **h** that had eyes and a mouth that spoke arrogantly,
7:21 this **h** made war with the holy ones
8: 5 The goat had a **h** between its eyes.
8: 8 at the height of its power, the great **h** was broken,
8: 9 Out of one of them came another **h**, a little one,
8:21 and the great **h** between its eyes is the first king.
8:22 As for the **h** that was broken,
Hos 5: 8 Blow the **h** in Gibeah, the trumpet in Ramah.
Mic 4:13 for I will make your **h** iron and your hoofs bronze;
Sir 51:12 *who makes a **h** to sprout for the house of David,*
51:12 *He has raised up a **h** for his people,*

HORNET (1)

Jos 24:12 I sent the **h** ahead of you,

HORNETS See Index to Footnotes

HORNS‡ (70) [HORN]

Ge 22:13 caught in a thicket by its **h**.
Ex 27: 2 You shall make **h** for it on its four corners;
27: 2 its **h** shall be of one piece with it,
29:12 the blood of the bull and put it on the **h** of the altar
30: 2 its **h** shall be of one piece with it.
30: 3 its top, and its sides all around and its **h**;
30:10 the rite of atonement on its **h**.
37:25 its **h** were of one piece with it.
37:26 its top, and its sides all around, and its **h**;
38: 2 He made **h** for it on its four corners;
38: 2 its **h** were of one piece with it,
Lev 4: 7 The priest shall put some of the blood on the **h** of
4:18 He shall put some of the blood on the **h** of the altar
4:25 the sin offering with his finger and put it on the **h**
4:30 of its blood with his finger and put it on the **h** of
4:34 the sin offering with his finger and put it on the **h**
8:15 and with his finger put some on each of the **h** of
9: 9 in the blood and put it on the **h** of the altar;
16:18 and put it on each of the **h** of the altar.
Nu 23:22 is like the **h** of a wild ox for them.
24: 8 is like the **h** of a wild ox for him;
Dt 33:17 His **h** are the **h** of a wild ox;
Jos 6: 4 of rams' **h** before the ark.
6: 6 of rams' **h** in front of the ark of the LORD."
6: 8 of rams' **h** before the LORD went forward,
6:13 of rams' **h** before the ark of the LORD passed on,
1Ki 1:50 got up and went to grasp the **h** of the altar.
1:51 see, he has laid hold of the **h** of the altar, saying,
2:28 to the tent of the LORD and grasped the **h** of
22:11 Zedekiah son of Chenaanah made for himself **h**
2Ch 15:14 and with shouting, and with trumpets, and with **h**.
18:10 Zedekiah son of Chenaanah made for himself **h**
Ps 22:21 From the **h** of the wild oxen you have rescued me.
69:31 the LORD more than an ox or a bull with **h**
75:10 All the **h** of the wicked I will cut off,
75:10 but the **h** of the righteous shall be exalted.
118:27 up to the **h** of the altar.
Jer 17: 1 and on the **h** of their altars,
Eze 34:21 with your **h** until you scattered them far and wide,
43:15 from the altar hearth projecting upward, four **h**.
43:20 and put it on the four **h** of the altar,
Da 7: 7 the beasts that preceded it, and it had ten **h**.
7: 8 the **h**, when another horn appeared,
7: 8 three of the earlier **h** were plucked up by the roots.
7:20 and concerning the ten **h** that were on its head,
7:24 the ten **h**, out of this kingdom ten kings shall arise,
8: 3 a ram standing beside the river. It had two **h**.
8: 3 Both **h** were long, but one was longer than
8: 6 the two **h** that I had seen standing beside the river,
8: 7 against it and struck the ram, breaking its two **h**.
8: 8 in its place there came up four prominent **h** toward
8:20 As for the ram that you saw with the two **h**,
Am 3:14 **h** of the altar shall be cut off and fall to the ground.
Zec 1:18 And I looked up and saw four **h**.
1:19 "These are the **h** that have scattered Judah, Israel,
1:21 "These are the **h** that scattered Judah,
1:21 down the **h** of the nations that lifted up their horns
1:21 of the nations that lifted up their **h** against the land
Rev 5: 6 having seven **h** and seven eyes,
9:13 from the four **h** of the golden altar before God,
12: 3 a great red dragon, with seven heads and ten **h**,
13: 1 And I saw a beast rising out of the sea having ten **h**
13: 1 and on its **h** were ten diadems,
13:11 it had two **h** like a lamb and it spoke like a dragon.
17: 3 and it had seven heads and ten **h**.
17: 7 and of the beast with seven heads and ten **h**
17:12 And the ten **h** that you saw are ten kings who have
17:16 And the ten **h** that you saw,
Jdt 9: 8 and to break off the **h** of your altar with the sword.

HORONAIM (5)

2Sa 13:34 he saw many people coming from the **H** road by
Isa 15: 5 on the road to **H** they raise a cry of destruction;
Jer 48: 3 a cry from **H**, "Desolation and great destruction!"
48: 5 at the descent of **H** they have heard the distressing
48:34 from Zoar to **H** and Eglath-shelishiyah.

HORONITE (3) [BETH-HORON]

Ne 2:10 the **H** and Tobiah the Ammonite official heard this,
2:19 Sanballat the **H** and Tobiah the Ammonite official,
13:28 was the son-in-law of Sanballat the **H**;

HORRENDOUS (1)

Da 11:36 and shall speak **h** things against the God of gods.

HORRIBLE (3) [HORROR]

Jer 5:30 An appalling and **h** thing has happened in the land:
18:13 The virgin Israel has done a most **h** thing.
Hos 6:10 In the house of Israel I have seen a **h** thing;

HORRIBLY (1) [HORROR]

Eze 27:35 their kings are **h** afraid, their faces are convulsed.

HORRIFIED (3) [HORROR]

Jer 18:16 All who pass by it are **h** and shake their heads.
19: 8 everyone who passes by it will be **h** and will hiss
49:17 everyone who passes by it will be **h** and will hiss

HORRIFY (1) [HORROR]

Eze 20:26 in order that I might **h** them,

HORROR (29) [HORRIBLE, HORRIBLY, HORRIFIED, HORRIFY, HORROR-STRICKEN]

Dt 28:25 an object of **h** to all the kingdoms of the earth.
28:37 You shall become an object of **h**, a proverb,
2Ch 29: 8 and he has made them an object of **h**,

Job 18:20 and **h** seizes those of the east.
Ps 31:11 a **h** to my neighbors, an object of dread
55: 5 upon me, and **h** overwhelms me.
64: 8 all who see them will shake with **h.**
88: 8 you have made me a thing of **h** to them.
Isa 21: 4 My mind reels, **h** has appalled me;
Jer 15: 4 a **h** to all the kingdoms of the earth because
18:16 making their land a **h,** a thing to be hissed
19: 8 I will make this city a **h,** a thing to be hissed at;
24: 9 I will make them a **h,** an evil thing,
25: 9 and make them an object of **h** and of hissing,
29:18 and will make them a **h** to all the kingdoms of
29:18 to be an object of cursing, and **h,** and hissing,
34:17 I will make you a **h** to all the kingdoms of
42:18 You shall become an object of execration and **h,**
44:12 they shall become an object of execration and **h,**
48:39 So Moab has become a derision and a **h**
49:13 Bozrah shall become an object of **h** and ridicule,
49:17 Edom shall become an object of **h;**
50:23 How Babylon has become a **h** among the nations!
51:37 an object of **h** and of hissing, without inhabitant.
51:41 How Babylon has become an object of **h** among
51:43 Her cities have become an object of **h,**
Eze 5:15 a warning and a **h,** to the nations around you,
7:18 They shall put on sackcloth, **h** shall cover them.
23:33 A cup of **h** and desolation is the cup of your sister

HORROR-STRICKEN (1) [HORROR, STRIKE]

2Es 15:37 those who see that wrath shall be **h,**

HORSE (44) [HORSE'S, HORSEBACK, HORSEMAN, HORSEMEN, HORSES, HORSES', WAR-HORSES]

Ex 15: 1 **h** and rider he has thrown into the sea.
15:21 **h** and rider he has thrown into the sea."
1Ki 10:29 and a **h** for one hundred fifty;
20:20 but King Ben-hadad of Aram escaped on a **h** with
20:25 **h** for **h,** and chariot for chariot;
2Ch 1:17 and a **h** for one hundred fifty;
23:15 into the entrance of the **H** Gate of the king's house,
Ne 3:28 Above the **H** Gate the priests made repairs,
Est 6: 8 and a **h** that the king has ridden,
6: 9 Let the robes and the **h** be handed over to one of
6:10 take the robes and the **h,** as you have said,
6:11 and the **h** and robed Mordecai and led him riding
Job 39:18 it laughs at the **h** and its rider.
39:19 "Do you give the **h** its might?
Ps 32: 9 Do not be like a **h** or a mule,
33:17 The war **h** is a vain hope for victory,
76: 6 O God of Jacob, both rider and **h** lay stunned.
147:10 His delight is not in the strength of the **h,**
Pr 21:31 The **h** is made ready for the day of battle,
26: 3 A whip for the **h,** a bridle for the donkey,
Isa 43:17 who brings out chariot and **h,** army and warrior;
63:13 Like a **h** in the desert, they did not stumble.
Jer 8: 6 like a **h** plunging headlong into battle.
31:40 to the corner of the **H** Gate toward the east,
51:21 with you I smash the **h** and its rider;
Na 3: 2 galloping **h** and bounding chariot!
Zec 1: 8 In the night I saw a man riding on a red **h!**
9:10 from Ephraim and the war **h** from Jerusalem;
10: 3 and will make them like his proud war **h.**
12: 4 says the LORD, I will strike every **h** with panic,
12: 4 I strike every **h** of the peoples with blindness.
Rev 6: 2 I looked, and there was a white **h!**
6: 4 And out came another **h,** bright red;
6: 5 I looked, and there was a black **h!**
6: 8 I looked and there was a pale green **h!**
19:11 I saw heaven opened, and there was a white **h!**
19:19 against the rider on the **h** and against his army.
19:21 rest were killed by the sword of the rider on the **h,**
AdE 6: 8 and the **h** on which the king rides,
6: 9 the king loves and mount him on the **h,**
6:11 So Haman got the robe and the **h;**
Sir 30: 8 An unbroken **h** turns out stubborn,
2Mc 3:25 to them a magnificently caparisoned **h,** with a rider

HORSE'S (3) [HORSE]

Ge 49:17 bites the **h** heels so that its rider falls backward.
Rev 14:20 as high as a **h** bridle,
2Es 15:35 be blood from the sword as high as a **h** belly

HORSEBACK (6) [HORSE]

Est 6: 9 the man on **h** through the open square of the city,
Ecc 10: 7 I have seen slaves on **h,**
Jdt 2:15 together with twelve thousand archers on **h,**
AdE 8:14 So the messengers on **h** set out with all speed
2Mc 12:35 who was on **h** and was a strong man,
4Mc 4:10 angels on **h** with lightning flashing

HORSELEACH (KJV) See LEECH

HORSEMAN (5) [HORSE, MAN]

2Ki 9:17 "I see a company." Joram said, "Take a **h;**
9:18 So the **h** went to meet him;
9:19 Then he sent out a second **h,**
Jer 4:29 At the noise of **h** and archer every town takes
2Mc 11: 8 a **h** appeared at their head,

HORSEMEN (28) [HORSE, MAN]

Jos 24: 6 with chariots and **h** to the Red Sea.
1Sa 8:11 and appoint them to his chariots and to be his **h,**
13: 5 thirty thousand chariots, and six thousand **h,**
2Sa 1: 6 while the chariots and the **h** drew close to him.
8: 4 from him one thousand seven hundred **h,**
10:18 and forty thousand **h,** and wounded Shobach
1Ki 1: 5 he prepared for himself chariots and **h,**
4:26 of horses for his chariots, and twelve thousand **h.**
2Ki 2:12 The chariots of Israel and its **h!"**
13: 7 with an army of not more than fifty **h,** ten chariots
13:14 The chariots of Israel and its **h!"**
18:24 when you rely on Egypt for chariots and for **h?**
Isa 21: 7 When he sees riders, **h** in pairs, riders on donkeys,
21: 9 Look, there they come, riders, **h** in pairs!"
31: 1 in chariots because they are many and in **h**
36: 9 when you rely on Egypt for chariots and for **h?**
Eze 23: 6 all of them handsome young men, mounted **h.**
23:12 mounted **h,** all of them handsome young men.
38: 4 horses and **h,** all of them clothed in full armor,
Da 11:40 with chariots and **h,** and with many ships.
Hos 1: 7 or by sword, or by war, or by horses, or by **h."**
Na 3: 3 **H** charging, flashing sword and glittering spear,
Hab 1: 8 Their **h** come from far away;
Ac 23:23 seventy **h,** and two hundred spearmen.
23:32 The next day they let the **h** go on with him,
1Mc 6:30 hundred thousand foot soldiers, twenty thousand **h,**
6:35 five hundred picked **h** were assigned to each beast.
15:41 up Kedron and stationed **h** and troops there,

HORSES (119) [HORSE]

Ge 47:17 and Joseph gave them food in exchange for the **h,**
Ex 9: 3 the **h,** the donkeys, the camels, the herds,
14: 9 all Pharaoh's **h** and chariots,
14:23 all of Pharaoh's **h,** chariots, and chariot drivers.
15:19 When the **h** of Pharaoh with his chariots
Dt 11: 4 to their **h** and chariots, how he made the water of
17:16 Even so, he must not acquire many **h** for himself,
17:16 the people to Egypt in order to acquire more **h,**
20: 1 against your enemies, and see **h** and chariots,
Jos 11: 4 with very many **h** and chariots.
11: 6 you shall hamstring their **h,**
11: 9 he hamstrung their **h,** and burned their chariots
2Sa 8: 4 David hamstrung all the chariot **h,**
15: 1 After this Absalom got himself a chariot and **h,**
1Ki 4:26 also had forty thousand stalls of **h** for his chariots,
4:28 to the required place barley and straw for the **h**
10:25 spices, **h,** and mules, so much year by year.
10:26 Solomon gathered together chariots and **h;**
10:26 and twelve thousand **h,** which he stationed in
10:28 Solomon's import of **h** was from Egypt and Kue,
18: 5 perhaps we may find grass to keep the **h**
20: 1 thirty-two kings were with him, along with **h**
20:21 king of Israel went out, attacked the **h** and chariots,
22: 4 my people are your people, my **h** are your **h."**
2Ki 2:11 a chariot of fire and **h** of fire separated the two
3: 7 my people are your people, my **h** are your **h."**
5: 9 So Naaman came with his **h** and chariots,
6:14 So he sent **h** and chariots there and a great army;
6:15 army with **h** and chariots was all around the city.
6:17 the mountain was full of **h** and chariots of fire all
7: 6 and of **h,** the sound of a great army,
7: 7 in the twilight and abandoned their tents, their **h,**
7:10 nothing but the **h** tied, the donkeys tied,
7:13 "Let some men take five of the remaining **h,**
9:33 of her blood spattered on the wall and on the **h,**
10: 2 and you have at your disposal chariots and **h,**
14:20 brought him on **h;** he was buried in Jerusalem
18:23 I will give you two thousand **h,**
23:11 the **h** that the kings of Judah had dedicated to
1Ch 18: 4 David hamstrung all the chariot **h,**
2Ch 1:14 Solomon gathered together chariots and **h;**
1:14 and twelve thousand **h,** which he stationed in
1:16 Solomon's **h** were imported from Egypt and Kue;
9:24 spices, **h,** and mules, so much year by year.
9:25 Solomon had four thousand stalls for **h** and
chariots, and twelve thousand **h,**
9:28 **H** were imported for Solomon from Egypt and
25:28 They brought him back on **h;**
Ezr 2:66 They had seven hundred thirty-six **h,**
Ne 7:68 They had seven hundred thirty-six **h,**
Ps 20: 7 Some take pride in chariots, and some in **h,**
Isa 2: 7 their land is filled with **h,** and there is no end to
28:28 one drives the cart wheel and **h** over it,
30:16 We will flee upon **h"**—therefore you shall flee!
31: 1 down to Egypt for help and who rely on **h,**
31: 3 their **h** are flesh, and not spirit.
36: 8 I will give you two thousand **h,**
66:20 on **h,** and in chariots, and in litters, and on mules,
Jer 4:13 his **h** are swifter than eagles—
6:23 they ride on **h,** equipped like a warrior for battle,
8:16 The snorting of their **h** is heard from Dan;
12: 5 how will you compete with **h?**
17:25 riding in chariots and on **h,** they and their officials,
22: 4 riding in chariots and on **h,** they,
46: 4 Harness the **h;** mount the steeds!
46: 9 Advance, O **h,** and dash madly, O chariots!
50:37 A sword against her **h** and against her chariots,
50:42 upon **h,** set in array as a warrior for battle,
51:27 bring up **h** like bristling locusts.
Eze 17:15 that they might give him **h** and a large army.
23:23 officers and warriors, all of them riding on **h.**
26: 7 king of kings, together with **h,** chariots, cavalry,
26:10 His **h** shall be so many
26:11 the hoofs of his **h** he shall trample all your streets.
27:14 Beth-togarmah exchanged for your wares **h,**
27:14 for your wares horses, war **h,**
38: 4 **h** and horsemen, all of them clothed in full armor,
38:15 all of them riding on **h,** a great horde,
39:20 be filled at my table with **h** and charioteers,
Hos 1: 7 or by sword, or by war, or by **h,** or by horsemen."
14: 3 Assyria shall not save us; we will not ride upon **h;**
Joel 2: 4 They have the appearance of **h,**
Am 2:15 nor shall those who ride **h** save their lives;
4:10 I carried away your **h;** and I made the stench of
6:12 Do **h** run on rocks?
Mic 5:10 I will cut off your **h** from among you
Hab 1: 8 Their **h** are swifter than leopards,
1: 8 menacing than wolves at dusk; their **h** charge.
3: 8 when you drove your **h,** your chariots to victory?
3:15 You trampled the sea with your **h,**
Hag 2:22 and the **h** and their riders shall fall,
Zec 1: 8 and behind him were red, sorrel, and white **h.**
6: 2 The first chariot had red **h,** the second chariot
black **h,**
6: 3 the third chariot white **h,** and the fourth chariot
dappled gray **h.**
6: 6 with the black **h** goes toward the north country,
10: 5 and they shall put to shame the riders on **h.**
14:15 And a plague like this plague shall fall on the **h,**
14:20 be inscribed on the bells of the **h,**
Jas 3: 3 into the mouths of **h** to make them obey us,
Rev 9: 7 In appearance the locusts were like **h** equipped
9: 9 like the noise of many chariots with **h** rushing
9:17 And this was how I saw the **h** in my vision:
9:17 the heads of the **h** were like lions' heads,
9:19 power of the **h** is in their mouths and in their tails;
18:13 **h** and chariots, slaves—and human lives.
19:14 white and pure, were following him on white **h.**
19:18 the flesh of **h** and their riders—
Jdt 9: 7 priding themselves in their **h** and riders,
Wis 19: 9 For they ranged like **h,** and leaped like lambs,
Sir 48: 9 in a chariot with **h** of fire.
1Mc 10:81 and the enemy's **h** grew tired.
2Mc 10:29 the enemy from heaven five resplendent men on **h**
1Es 2: 7 with gifts and with **h** and cattle,
2: 9 with silver and gold, with **h** and cattle,
5:43 and seven thousand thirty-six **h,**

HORSES' (3) [HORSE]

Jdg 5:22 "Then loud beat the **h** hoofs with the galloping,
2Ki 11:16 through the **h** entrance to the king's house,
Isa 5:28 all their bows bent, their **h** hoofs seem like flint,

HOSAH (5)

Jos 19:29 then the boundary turns to **H,** and it ends at the sea;
1Ch 16:38 while Obed-edom son of Jeduthun and **H** were to
26:10 **H,** of the sons of Merari, had sons:
26:11 all the sons and brothers of **H** totaled thirteen.
26:16 For Shuppim and **H** it came out for the west,

HOSANNA (6)

Mt 21: 9 **"H** to the Son of David! Blessed is the one who
21: 9 **H** in the highest heaven!"
21:15 **"H** to the Son of David,"
Mk 11: 9 ahead and those who followed were shouting, **"H!**
11:10 **H** in the highest heaven!"
Jn 12:13 and went out to meet him, shouting, **"H!**

HOSEA (5)

Hos 1: 1 word of the LORD that came to **H** son of Beeri,
1: 2 LORD first spoke through **H,** the LORD said to **H,**
Ro 9:25 As indeed he says in **H,**
2Es 1:39 and **H** and Amos and Micah and Joel and Obadiah

HOSEN (KJV) See TROUSERS

HOSHAIAH (3)

Ne 12:32 after them went **H** and half the officials of Judah,
Jer 42: 1 and Johanan son of Kareah and Azariah son of **H,**
43: 2 Azariah son of **H** and Johanan son of Kareah

HOSHAMA (1)

1Ch 3:18 Pedaiah, Shenazzar, Jekamiah, **H,** and Nedabiah;

HOSHEA‡ (13) [=JOSHUA]

Nu 13: 8 from the tribe of Ephraim, **H** son of Nun;
13:16 And Moses changed the name of **H** son of Nun
2Ki 15:30 Then **H** son of Elah made a conspiracy
17: 1 **H** son of Elah began to reign in Samaria
17: 3 **H** became his vassal, and paid him tribute.
17: 4 But the king of Assyria found treachery in **H;**
17: 6 of **H** the king of Assyria captured Samaria;
18: 1 In the third year of King **H** son of Elah of Israel,
18: 9 which was the seventh year of King **H** son of Elah
18:10 which was the ninth year of King **H** of Israel,
1Ch 27:20 for the Ephraimites, **H** son of Azaziah;
Ne 10:23 **H,** Hananiah, Hasshub,
2Es 13:40 in the days of King **H,** whom Shalmaneser, king of

HOSPITABLE (3) [HOSPITABLY, HOSPITALITY]

1Ti 3: 2 temperate, sensible, respectable, **h,** an apt teacher,
Tit 1: 8 be **h,** a lover of goodness, prudent, upright, devout,
1Pe 4: 9 Be **h** to one another without complaining.

HOSPITABLY (1) [HOSPITABLE]

Ac 28: 7 who received us and entertained us **h**

HOSPITALITY (3) [HOSPITABLE]

Ro 12:13 of the saints; extend **h** to strangers.
1Ti 5:10 as one who has brought up children, shown **h**,
Heb 13: 2 Do not neglect to show **h** to strangers,

HOST (44) [HOSTS]

A. HOST OF HEAVEN (20)

Dt 4:19 the moon, and the stars, all the **h** of heaven, A
17: 3 the sun or the moon or any of the **h** of heaven, A
33: 2 at his right, a **h** of his own.
1Ki 22:19 the **h** of heaven standing beside him to the right A
2Ki 17:16 worshiped all the **h** of heaven, and served Baal. A
21: 3 worshiped all the **h** of heaven, and served them. A
21: 5 the **h** of heaven in the two courts of the house A
23: 4 for Asherah, and for all the **h** of heaven; A
23: 5 the constellations, and all the **h** of the heavens.
2Ch 18:18 with all the **h** of heaven standing to the right A
33: 3 sacred poles, worshiped all the **h** of heaven, A
33: 5 the **h** of heaven in the two courts of the house A
Ne 9: 6 with all their **h**, the earth and all that is on it,
9: 6 and the **h** of heaven worships you. A
Ps 33: 6 and all their **h** by the breath of his mouth.
148: 2 Praise him, all his angels; praise him, all his **h!**
Isa 24:21 the LORD will punish the **h** of heaven in heaven, A
34: 4 All the **h** of heaven shall rot away, A
34: 4 their **h** shall wither like a leaf withering on a vine,
40:26 He who brings out their **h** and numbers them,
45:12 and I commanded all their **h**.
Jer 8: 2 and all the **h** of heaven, which they have loved A
19:13 to the whole **h** of heaven, A
33:22 the **h** of heaven cannot be numbered and A
Eze 23:24 from the north with chariots and wagons and a **h**
Da 4:35 and he does what he wills with the **h** of heaven A
8:10 It grew as high as the **h** of heaven. A
8:10 It threw down to the earth some of the **h** and some
8:11 Even against the prince of the **h** it acted arrogantly;
8:12 the **h** was given over to it together with
8:13 and the giving over of the sanctuary and **h** to
Joel 2:11 how vast is his **h!** Numberless are those who obey
Zep 1: 5 those who bow down on the roofs to the **h** of
Lk 2:13 with the angel a multitude of the heavenly **h**,
14: 8 distinguished than you has been invited by your **h**;
14: 9 the **h** who invited both of you may come and say
14:10 so that when your **h** comes, he may say to you,
Ac 7:42 handed them over to worship the **h** of heaven, A
Ro 16:23 Gaius, who is **h** to me and to the whole church,
Sir 17:32 He marshals the **h** of the height of heaven;
29:25 the **h** and provide drink without being thanked,
1Mc 14: 7 He gathered a **h** of captives;
15: 3 and have recruited a **h** of mercenary troops
Man 1:15 For all the **h** of heaven sings your praise, A

HOSTAGE (1) [HOSTAGES]

1Mc 1:10 he had been a **h** in Rome.

HOSTAGES (8) [HOSTAGE]

2Ki 14:14 as well as **h**; then he returned to Samaria.
2Ch 25:24 also **h**; then he returned to Samaria.
1Mc 8: 7 after him should pay a heavy tribute and give **h**
9:53 of the leading men of the land as **h** and put them
10: 6 and he commanded that the **h** in the citadel should
10: 9 But those in the citadel released the **h** to Jonathan,
11:62 and took the sons of their rulers as **h** and sent them
13:16 of silver and two of his sons as **h**,

HOSTILE (23) [HOSTILITIES, HOSTILITY]

Lev 26:21 If you continue **h** to me, and will not obey me,
26:23 not turned back to me, but continue **h** to me,
26:24 then I too will continue **h** to you:
26:27 despite this, you disobey me, and continue **h** to me,
26:28 I will continue **h** to you in fury;
26:40 moreover, that they continued **h** to me—
26:41 continued **h** to them and brought them into the land
Isa 11:13 and Judah shall not be **h** towards Ephraim.
Lk 11:53 to be very **h** toward him and to cross-examine him
Ro 8: 7 For this reason the mind that is set on the flesh is **h**
Col 1:21 And you who were once estranged and **h** in mind,
Jdt 5:11 So the king of Egypt became **h** to them;
AdE 13: 4 in the world there is scattered a certain **h** people,
13: 7 so that those who have long been **h** and remain
Sir 36:12 Crush the heads of **h** rulers who say,
1Mc 6:24 of our people besieged the citadel and became **h**
2Mc 4:21 that Philometor had become **h** to his government,
14:11 the rest of the king's Friends, who were **h** to Judas,
1Es 5:50 for all the peoples of the land were **h** to them
3Mc 3: 1 but was still more bitterly **h** toward those in
3: 2 a **h** rumor was circulated against the Jewish nation
3: 7 but were **h** and greatly opposed to his government.
5: 3 the army who were especially **h** toward the Jews.

HOSTILITIES (1) [HOSTILE]

Eze 25:15 with unending **h** the Philistines acted in vengeance,

HOSTILITY‡ (10) [HOSTILE]

Dt 15: 9 view your needy neighbor with **h** and give nothing;
Jdg 9:25 out of **h** to him, the lords of Shechem set ambushes
Isa 11:13 the **h** of Judah shall be cut off;
Hos 9: 7 Because of your great iniquity, your **h** is great.
9: 8 and **h** in the house of his God.
Eph 2:14 down the dividing wall, that is, the **h** between us.
2:16 thus putting to death that **h** through it.
Heb 12: 3 Consider him who endured such **h** against himself
Wis 19:15 the former for having received strangers with **h**,
1Mc 13:17 that he would not arouse great **h** among the people,

HOSTS (293) [HOST]

A. †LORD OF HOSTS (245)
B. *GOD OF HOSTS (25)
C. *LORD †GOD OF HOSTS (16)

1Sa 1: 3 to worship and to sacrifice to the LORD of **h** A
1:11 She made this vow: "O LORD of **h**, A
4: 4 the ark of the covenant of the LORD of **h**, A
15: 2 Thus says the LORD of **h**, A
17:45 but I come to you in the name of the LORD of **h**, A
2Sa 5:10 for the LORD, the God of **h**, was with him. B
6: 2 LORD of **h** who is enthroned on the cherubim. A
6:18 the people in the name of the LORD of **h**, A
7: 8 Thus says the LORD of **h**: A
7:26 'The LORD of **h** is God over Israel'; A
7:27 For you, O LORD of **h**, the God of Israel, A
1Ki 18:15 Elijah said, "As the LORD of **h** lives, A
19:10 for the LORD, the God of **h**; B
19:14 for the LORD, the God of **h**; B
2Ki 3:14 Elisha said, "As the LORD of **h** lives, A
19:31 The zeal of the LORD of **h** will do this. A
1Ch 11: 9 for the LORD of **h** was with him. A
17: 7 Thus says the LORD of **h**: A
17:24 'The LORD of **h**, the God of Israel, A
Ps 24:10 The LORD of **h**, he is the King of glory. A
46: 7 The LORD of **h** is with us; A
46:11 The LORD of **h** is with us; A
48: 8 so have we seen in the city of the LORD of **h**, A
59: 5 You, LORD God of **h**, are God of Israel. B
69: 6 to shame because of me, O Lord GOD of **h**; C
80: 4 O LORD God of **h**, how long will you be angry B
80: 7 Restore us, O God of **h**; let your face shine, B
80:14 Turn again, O God of **h**; look down from B
80:19 Restore us, O LORD God of **h**; B
84: 1 lovely is your dwelling place, O LORD of **h!** A
84: 3 O LORD of **h**, my King and my God. A
84: 8 O LORD God of **h**, hear my prayer; B
84:12 O LORD of **h**, happy is everyone who trusts A
89: 8 O LORD God of **h**, who is as mighty as you, B
103:21 Bless the LORD, all his **h**,
Isa 1: 9 If the LORD of **h** had not left us a few survivors, A
1:24 Therefore says the Sovereign, the LORD of **h**, A
2:12 the LORD of **h** has a day against all that is proud A
3: 1 For now the Sovereign, the LORD of **h**, A
3:15 says the Lord GOD of **h**. C
5: 7 vineyard of the LORD of **h** is the house of Israel, A
5: 9 The LORD of **h** has sworn in my hearing: A
5:16 But the LORD of **h** is exalted by justice, A
5:24 the instruction of the LORD of **h**, A
6: 3 "Holy, holy, holy is the LORD of **h**; A
6: 5 yet my eyes have seen the King, the LORD of **h!**" A
8:13 But the LORD of **h**, him you shall regard as holy; A
8:18 and portents in Israel from the LORD of **h**, A
9: 7 The zeal of the LORD of **h** will do this. A
9:13 or seek the LORD of **h**. A
9:19 the wrath of the LORD of **h** the land was burned, A
10:16 Therefore the Sovereign, the LORD of **h**, A
10:23 For the Lord GOD of **h** will make a full end, C
10:24 Therefore thus says the Lord GOD of **h**: C
10:26 The LORD of **h** will wield a whip against them, A
10:33 Look, the Sovereign, the LORD of **h**, A
13: 4 The LORD of **h** is mustering an army for battle. A
13:13 of the LORD of **h** in the day of his fierce anger. A
14:22 I will rise up against them, says the LORD of **h**, A
14:23 the broom of destruction, says the LORD of **h**. A
14:24 The LORD of **h** has sworn: A
14:27 LORD of **h** has planned, and who will annul it? A
17: 3 of the children of Israel, says the LORD of **h**. A
18: 7 to the LORD of **h** from a people tall and smooth, A
18: 7 the place of the name of the LORD of **h**. A
19: 4 says the Sovereign, the LORD of **h**. A
19:12 the LORD of **h** has planned against Egypt. A
19:16 the hand that the LORD of **h** raises against them. A
19:17 that the LORD of **h** is planning against them. A
19:18 and swear allegiance to the LORD of **h**. A
19:20 a sign and a witness to the LORD of **h** in the land A
19:25 whom the LORD of **h** has blessed, A
21:10 what I have heard from the LORD of **h**, A
22: 5 For the Lord GOD of **h** has a day of tumult C
22:12 In that day the Lord GOD of **h** called to weeping C
22:14 The LORD of **h** has revealed himself in my ears: A
22:14 says the Lord GOD of **h**. C
22:15 Thus says the Lord GOD of **h**: C
22:25 On that day, says the LORD of **h**, A
23: 9 The LORD of **h** has planned it— A
24:23 for the LORD of **h** will reign on Mount Zion and A
25: 6 the LORD of **h** will make for all peoples A
28: 5 the LORD of **h** will be a garland of glory, A
28:22 a decree of destruction from the Lord GOD of **h** C
28:29 This also comes from the LORD of **h**; A
29: 6 the LORD of **h** with thunder and earthquake A
31: 4 so the LORD of **h** will come down to fight upon A
31: 5 so the LORD of **h** will protect Jerusalem; A
37:16 "O LORD of **h**, God of Israel, who are enthroned A
37:32 The zeal of the LORD of **h** will do this. A
39: 5 "Hear the word of the LORD of **h**: A
44: 6 and his Redeemer, the LORD of **h**: A
45:13 not for price or reward, says the LORD of **h**. A
47: 4 Our Redeemer—the LORD of **h** is his name— A
48: 2 the LORD of **h** is his name. A
51:15 the LORD of **h** is his name. A
54: 5 the LORD of **h** is his name; A
Jer 2:19 fear of me is not in you, says the Lord GOD of **h**. C
Jer 5:14 Therefore thus says the LORD, the God of **h**: B
6: 6 For thus says the LORD of **h**: A
6: 9 Thus says the LORD of **h**: A
7: 3 Thus says the LORD of **h**, the God of Israel: A
7:21 Thus says the LORD of **h**, the God of Israel: A
8: 3 where I have driven them, says the LORD of **h**. A
9: 7 Therefore thus says the LORD of **h**: A
9:15 thus says the LORD of **h**, the God of Israel: A
9:17 Thus says the LORD of **h**: A
10:16 the LORD of **h** is his name. A
11:17 The LORD of **h**, who planted you, A
11:20 But you, O LORD of **h**, who judge righteously, A
11:22 therefore thus says the LORD of **h**: A
15:16 I am called by your name, O LORD, God of **h**. B
16: 9 For thus says the LORD of **h**, the God of Israel: A
19: 3 Thus says the LORD of **h**, the God of Israel: A
19:11 Thus says the LORD of **h**: A
19:15 Thus says the LORD of **h**, the God of Israel: A
20:12 O LORD of **h**, you test the righteous, A
23:15 thus says the LORD of **h** concerning the prophets: A
23:16 Thus says the LORD of **h**: A
23:36 the LORD of **h**, our God. A
25: 8 Therefore thus says the LORD of **h**: A
25:27 you shall say to them, Thus says the LORD of **h**, A
25:28 Thus says the LORD of **h**: You must drink! A
25:29 the inhabitants of the earth, says the LORD of **h**. A
25:32 Thus says the LORD of **h**: A
26:18 'Thus says the LORD of **h**, A
27: 4 Thus says the LORD of **h**, the God of Israel: A
27:18 then let them intercede with the LORD of **h**, A
27:19 thus says the LORD of **h** concerning the pillars, A
27:21 thus says the LORD of **h**, the God of Israel, A
28: 2 "Thus says the LORD of **h**, the God of Israel: A
28:14 For thus says the LORD of **h**, the God of Israel: A
29: 4 Thus says the LORD of **h**, the God of Israel, A
29: 8 For thus says the LORD of **h**, the God of Israel: A
29:17 Thus says the LORD of **h**, A
29:21 Thus says the LORD of **h**, the God of Israel, A
29:25 Thus says the LORD of **h**, the God of Israel: A
30: 8 On that day, says the LORD of **h**, A
31:23 Thus says the LORD of **h**, the God of Israel: A
31:35 the LORD of **h** is his name: A
32:14 Thus says the LORD of **h**, the God of Israel: A
32:15 For thus says the LORD of **h**, the God of Israel: A
32:18 and mighty God whose name is the LORD of **h**, A
33:11 "Give thanks to the LORD of **h**, A
33:12 Thus says the LORD of **h**: A
35:13 Thus says the LORD of **h**, the God of Israel: A
35:17 Therefore, thus says the LORD, the God of **h**, B
35:18 Thus says the LORD of **h**, the God of Israel: A
35:19 thus says the LORD of **h**, the God of Israel: A
38:17 "Thus says the LORD, the God of **h**, B
39:16 Thus says the LORD of **h**, the God of Israel: A
42:15 Thus says the LORD of **h**, the God of Israel: A
42:18 "For thus says the LORD of **h**, the God of Israel: A
43:10 Thus says the LORD of **h**, the God of Israel: A
44: 2 Thus says the LORD of **h**, the God of Israel: A
44: 7 thus says the LORD God of **h**, the God of Israel: B
44:11 thus says the LORD of **h**, the God of Israel: A
44:25 Thus says the LORD of **h**, the God of Israel: A
46:10 That day is the day of the Lord GOD of **h**, C
46:10 the Lord GOD of **h** holds a sacrifice in the land C
46:18 says the King, whose name is the LORD of **h**, A
46:25 The LORD of **h**, the God of Israel, said: A
48: 1 Thus says the LORD of **h**, the God of Israel: A
48:15 says the King, whose name is the LORD of **h**. A
49: 5 says the Lord GOD of **h**, from all your neighbors, C
49: 7 Thus says the LORD of **h**: A
49:26 be destroyed in that day, says the LORD of **h**. A
49:35 Thus says the LORD of **h**: A
50:18 thus says the LORD of **h**, the God of Israel: A
50:25 for the Lord GOD of **h** has a task to do in the land C
50:31 O arrogant one, says the Lord GOD of **h**; C
50:33 Thus says the LORD of **h**: A
50:34 the LORD of **h** is his name. A
51: 5 not been forsaken by their God, the LORD of **h**, A
51:14 The LORD of **h** has sworn by himself: A
51:19 the LORD of **h** is his name. A
51:33 For thus says the LORD of **h**, the God of Israel: A
51:57 says the King, whose name is the LORD of **h**. A
51:58 Thus says the LORD of **h**: A
Hos 12: 5 The LORD the God of **h**, the LORD is his name! B
Am 3:13 says the Lord GOD, the God of **h**: B
4:13 the LORD, the God of **h**, is his name! B
5:14 and so the LORD, the God of **h**, will be with you, B
5:15 it may be that the LORD, the God of **h**, B
5:16 thus says the LORD, the God of **h**, the Lord: B
5:27 says the LORD, whose name is the God of **h**. B
6: 8 by himself (says the LORD, the God of **h**): B
6:14 O house of Israel, says the LORD, the God of **h**, B
9: 5 The Lord, GOD of **h**, he who touches the earth C
Mic 4: 4 for the mouth of the LORD of **h** has spoken. A
Na 2:13 See, I am against you, says the LORD of **h**, A
3: 5 says the LORD of **h**, and will lift up your skirts A
Hab 2:13 not from the LORD of **h** that peoples labor only A
Zep 2: 9 Therefore, as I live, says the LORD of **h**, A
2:10 and boasted against the people of the LORD of **h**. A
Hag 1: 2 Thus says the LORD of **h**: A
1: 5 Now therefore thus says the LORD of **h**: A
1: 7 Thus says the LORD of **h**: A
1: 9 says the LORD of **h**. A
1:14 and worked on the house of the LORD of **h**, A
2: 4 work, for I am with you, says the LORD of **h**, A
2: 6 For thus says the LORD of **h**: A
2: 7 with splendor, says the LORD of **h**. A
2: 8 and the gold is mine, says the LORD of **h**. A
2: 9 be greater than the former, says the LORD of **h**; A

Hag 2: 9 I will give prosperity, says the LORD of **h.** A
2:11 Thus says the LORD of **h:** A
2:23 On that day, says the LORD of **h,** I will take you, A
2:23 for I have chosen you, says the LORD of **h.** A
Zec 1: 3 Therefore say to them, Thus says the LORD of **h:** A
1: 3 Return to me, says the LORD of **h,** A
1: 3 and I will return to you, says the LORD of **h.** A
1: 4 "Thus says the LORD of **h,** A
1: 6 "The LORD of **h** has dealt with us according A
1:12 the angel of the LORD said, "O LORD of **h,** A
1:14 Thus says the LORD of **h;** A
1:16 my house shall be built in it, says the LORD of **h,** A
1:17 Proclaim further: Thus says the LORD of **h:** A
2: 8 said the LORD of **h** (after his glory sent me) A
2: 9 you will know that the LORD of **h** has sent me. A
2:11 that the LORD of **h** has sent me to you. A
3: 7 "Thus says the LORD of **h:** A
3: 9 I will engrave its inscription, says the LORD of **h,** A
3:10 On that day, says the LORD of **h,** A
4: 6 but by my spirit, says the LORD of **h.** A
4: 9 that the LORD of **h** has sent me to you. A
5: 4 I have sent it out, says the LORD of **h,** A
6:12 Thus says the LORD of **h:** A
6:15 that the LORD of **h** has sent me to you. A
7: 3 of the house of the LORD of **h** and the prophets, A
7: 4 Then the word of the LORD of **h** came to me: A
7: 9 Thus says the LORD of **h:** A
7:12 that the LORD of **h** had sent by his spirit through A
7:12 Therefore great wrath came from the LORD of **h.** A
7:13 I would not hear, says the LORD of **h,** A
8: 1 The word of the LORD of **h** came to me, saying: A
8: 2 Thus says the LORD of **h:** A
8: 3 the LORD of **h** shall be called the holy mountain. A
8: 4 Thus says the LORD of **h:** A
8: 6 Thus says the LORD of **h:** A
8: 6 to me, says the LORD of **h?** A
8: 7 Thus says the LORD of **h:** A
8: 9 Thus says the LORD of **h:** A
8: 9 the house of the LORD of **h.** A
8:11 as in the former days, says the LORD of **h.** A
8:14 For thus says the LORD of **h:** A
8:14 and I did not relent, says the LORD of **h,** A
8:18 The word of the LORD of **h** came to me, saying: A
8:19 Thus says the LORD of **h:** A
8:20 Thus says the LORD of **h:** A
8:21 and to seek the LORD of **h;** I myself am going." A
8:22 to seek the LORD of **h** in Jerusalem, A
8:23 Thus says the LORD of **h:** A
9:15 The LORD of **h** will protect them, A
10: 3 for the LORD of **h** cares for his flock, A
12: 5 Jerusalem have strength through the LORD of **h,** A
13: 2 On that day, says the LORD of **h,** A
13: 7 man who is my associate," says the LORD of **h.** A
14:16 LORD of **h,** and to keep the festival of booths. A
14:17 the LORD of **h,** there will be no rain upon them. A
14:21 and Judah shall be sacred to the LORD of **h,** A
14:21 be traders in the house of the LORD of **h** A
Mal 1: 4 the ruins," the LORD of **h** says: A
1: 6 says the LORD of **h** to you, O priests, A
1: 8 says the LORD of **h.** A
1: 9 says the LORD of **h.** A
1:10 I have no pleasure in you, says the LORD of **h,** A
1:11 among the nations, says the LORD of **h.** A
1:13 you say, and you sniff at me, says the LORD of **h.** A
1:14 for I am a great King, says the LORD of **h,** A
2: 2 the LORD of **h,** then I will send the curse on you A
2: 4 with Levi may hold, says the LORD of **h.** A
2: 7 for he is the messenger of the LORD of **h.** A
2: 8 the covenant of Levi, says the LORD of **h,** A
2:12 or to bring an offering to the LORD of **h.** A
2:16 with violence, says the LORD of **h.** A
3: 1 indeed, he is coming, says the LORD of **h.** A
3: 5 and do not fear me, says the LORD of **h.** A
3: 7 and I will return to you, says the LORD of **h.** A
3:10 and thus put me to the test, says the LORD of **h;** A
3:11 the field shall not be barren, says the LORD of **h.** A
3:12 be a land of delight, says the LORD of **h.** A
3:14 about as mourners before the LORD of **h?** A
3:17 They shall be mine, says the LORD of **h,** A
4: 1 up, says the LORD of **h,** A
4: 3 on the day when I act, says the LORD of **h.** A
Ro 9:29 "If the Lord of **h** had not left survivors to us,
Jas 5: 4 the ears of the Lord of **h.**
Sir 24: 2 and in the presence of his **h** she tells of her glory:
43: 8 a beacon to the **h** on high, shining in the vault of
1Es 9:46 the God of **h,** the Almighty, B
2Es 6: 3 innumerable **h** of angels were gathered together,
8:21 before whom the **h** of angels stand trembling

HOT (38) [HOT-TEMPERED, HOTHEAD, HOTHEADS, HOTLY]

Ex 11: 8 And in **h** anger he left Pharaoh.
16:21 but when the sun grew **h,** it melted.
32:10 so that my wrath may burn **h** against them
32:11 why does your wrath burn **h** against your people,
32:19 the dancing, Moses' anger burned **h,** and he threw
32:22 "Do not let the anger of my lord burn **h;**
Dt 19: 6 of blood in **h** anger might pursue and overtake
Jdg 14:19 In **h** anger he went back to his father's house.
1Sa 11: 9 'Tomorrow, by the time the sun is **h,**
21: 6 be replaced by **h** bread on the day it is taken away.
1Ki 19: 6 and there at his head was a cake baked on **h** stones,
22:35 The battle grew **h** that day,
2Ch 18:34 The battle grew **h** that day,
Ne 7: 3 not to be opened until the sun is **h;**
Job 6:17 when it is **h,** they vanish from their place.
Job 37:17 you whose garments are **h** when the earth is still
Ps 39: 3 my heart became **h** within me.
85: 3 you turned from your **h** anger.
119:53 **H** indignation seizes me because of the wicked,
Pr 6:28 Or can one walk on **h** coals without scorching
26:21 As charcoal is to **h** embers and wood to fire,
Jer 4:11 A **h** wind comes from me out of the bare heights in
La 4:11 he poured out his **h** anger,
Eze 24:11 so that it may become **h,** its copper glow,
36: 5 I am speaking in my **h** jealousy against the rest of
Hos 7: 7 All of them are **h** as an oven,
Zec 10: 3 My anger is **h** against the shepherds,
1Ti 4: 2 of liars whose consciences are seared with a **h** iron.
Rev 3:15 you are neither cold nor **h.**
3:15 I wish that you were either cold or **h.**
3:16 because you are lukewarm, and neither cold nor **h,**
Sir 23:16 **H** passion that blazes like a fire will not
43: 4 but three times as **h** is the sun scorching
Sus 1:15 for it was a **h** day.
2Mc 4:25 the **h** temper of a cruel tyrant and the rage of
4Mc 10:14 "You do not have a fire **h** enough to make me play
15:22 on the wheel and with the **h** irons!
16: 3 the raging fiery furnace of Mishael so intensely **h,**

HOT-TEMPERED (3) [HOT, TEMPER]

Jdg 18:25 among us or else **h** fellows will attack you,
Pr 15:18 Those who are **h** stir up strife,
Sir 28: 8 be fewer; for the **h** kindle strife,

HOTHAM‡ (2)

1Ch 7:32 Heber became the father of Japhlet, Shomer, **H,**
11:44 Shama and Jeiel sons of **H** the Aroerite,

HOTHAN (KJV) See HOTHAM

HOTHEAD (1) [HEAD, HOT]

Pr 29:22 and the **h** causes much transgression.

HOTHEADS (1) [HEAD, HOT]

Pr 22:24 and do not associate with **h,**

HOTHIR (2)

1Ch 25: 4 and Romamti-ezer, Joshbekashah, Mallothi, **H,**
25:28 to **H,** his sons and his brothers, twelve;

HOTLY (2) [HOT]

Ge 31:36 What is my sin, that you have **h** pursued me?
2Es 7:*61* they are set on fire and burn **h,**

HOUGH, HOUGHED (KJV) See HAMSTRING, HAMSTRUNG

HOUR‡ (79) [HOUR'S, HOURS]

Mt 6:27 by worrying add a single **h** to your span of life?
8:13 And the servant was healed in that **h.**
14:15 "This is a deserted place, and the **h** is now late;
20:12 'These last worked only one **h,**
24:36 "But about that day and **h** no one knows,
24:44 for the Son of Man is coming at an unexpected **h.**
24:50 on a day when he does not expect him and at an **h**
25:13 for you know neither the day nor the **h.**
26:40 "So, could you not stay awake with me one **h?**
26:45 the **h** is at hand, and the Son of Man is betrayed
26:55 At that **h** Jesus said to the crowds,
Mk 6:35 and the **h** is now very late;
13:32 "But about that day or **h** no one knows,
14:35 if it were possible, the **h** might pass from him.
14:37 Could you not keep awake one **h?**
14:41 and taking your rest? Enough! The **h** has come;
Lk 10:21 At that same **h** Jesus rejoiced in the Holy Spirit
12:12 at that very **h** what you ought to say."
12:25 by worrying add a single **h** to your span of life?
12:39 if the owner of the house had known at what **h**
12:40 for the Son of Man is coming at an unexpected **h."**
12:46 on a day when he does not expect him and at an **h**
13:31 that very **h** some Pharisees came and said to him,
20:19 they wanted to lay hands on him at that very **h,**
22:14 When the **h** came, he took his place at the table,
22:53 But this is your **h,** and the power of darkness!"
22:59 Then about an **h** later still another kept insisting,
24:33 That same **h** they got up and returned to Jerusalem;
Jn 2: 4 My **h** has not yet come."
4:21 the **h** is coming when you will worship
4:23 But the **h** is coming, and is now here,
4:52 So he asked them the **h** when he began to recover,
4:53 that this was the **h** when Jesus had said to him,
5:25 "Very truly, I tell you, the **h** is coming,
5:28 for the **h** is coming when all who are
7:30 because his **h** had not yet come.
8:20 because his **h** had not yet come.
12:23 **h** has come for the Son of Man to be glorified.
12:27 'Father, save me from this **h'?**
12:27 No, it is for this reason that I have come to this **h.**
13: 1 that his **h** had come to depart from this world
16: 2 an **h** is coming when those who kill you will think
16: 4 so that when their **h** comes you may remember
16:21 she has pain, because her **h** has come.
16:25 The **h** is coming when I will no longer speak
16:32 The **h** is coming, indeed it has come,
17: 1 up to heaven and said, "Father, the **h** has come;
19:27 that **h** the disciple took her into his own home.
Ac 3: 1 and John were going up to the temple at the **h**
Ac 10:30 Cornelius replied, "Four days ago at this very **h,**
16:18 And it came out that very **h.**
16:33 At the same **h** of the night he took them
22:13 In that very **h** I regained my sight and saw him.
1Co 4:11 To the present **h** we are hungry and thirsty,
15:30 why are we putting ourselves in danger every **h?**
1Jn 2:18 Children, it is the last **h!**
2:18 From this we know that it is the last **h.**
Rev 3: 3 you will not know at what **h** I will come to you.
3:10 I will keep you from the **h** of trial that is coming
8: 1 there was silence in heaven for about half an **h.**
9:15 who had been held ready for the **h,** the day,
14: 7 for the **h** of his judgment has come;
14:15 for the **h** to reap has come,
17:12 but they are to receive authority as kings for one **h,**
18:10 For in one **h** your judgment has come."
18:17 For in one **h** all this wealth has been laid waste!"
18:19 For in one **h** she has been laid waste.
Jdt 13: 4 in this **h** on the work of my hands for the exaltation
AdE 10:11 the **h** and moment and day of decision before God
Sir 33:24 in the **h** of death, distribute your inheritance.
2Mc 8:25 they were obliged to return because the **h** was late.
3Mc 2:19 and reveal your mercy at this **h.**
5:13 the Jews, since they had escaped the appointed **h,**
5:14 now, since it was nearly the middle of the tenth **h,**
5:15 that the **h** of the banquet was already slipping by,
2Es 5:34 for every **h** I suffer agonies of heart,
7:*89* and withstood danger every **h** so
9:44 Every **h** and every day during those
14:26 tomorrow at this **h** you shall begin to write."

HOUR'S (1) [HOUR]

Sir 11:27 An **h** misery makes one forget past delights,

HOURS (5) [HOUR]

Jn 11: 9 "Are there not twelve **h** of daylight?
Ac 5: 7 After an interval of about three **h** his wife came in,
19:34 for about two **h** all of them shouted in unison,
2Es 6:24 so that for three **h** they shall not flow.
16:38 around her womb for two or three **h** beforehand,

HOUSE‡ (1824) [HOUSEHOLD, HOUSEHOLDER, HOUSEHOLDS, HOUSES, HOUSETOP, HOUSETOPS, STOREHOUSE, STOREHOUSES]

A. HOUSE OF THE †LORD (240)
B. HOUSE OF ISRAEL (160)
C. HOUSE OF ... *GOD (120)
D. THIS HOUSE (62)
E. FATHER'S HOUSE (52)
F. MY HOUSE (47)
G. HOUSE OF JUDAH (41)
H. KING'S HOUSE (39)
I. HOUSE OF DAVID (27)
J. HOUSE OF JACOB (25)
K. WHOLE HOUSE (17)
L. REBELLIOUS HOUSE (15)
M. HOUSE OF THE *LORD (14)
N. HOUSE OF SLAVERY (13)
O. †LORD'S HOUSE (13)

Ge 12: 1 and your kindred and your father's **h** to the land E
12:15 And the woman was taken into Pharaoh's **h.**
12:17 and his **h** with great plagues because of Sarai,
14:14 born in his **h,** three hundred eighteen of them,
15: 2 and the heir of my **h** is Eliezer of Damascus?" F
15: 3 and so a slave born in my **h** is to be my heir." F
17:12 in your **h** and the one bought with your money
17:13 Both the slave born in your **h** and the one bought
17:23 the slaves born in his **h** or bought with his money,
17:23 every male among the men of Abraham's **h,**
17:27 and all the men of his **h,**
17:27 slaves born in the **h** and those bought with money
19: 2 turn aside to your servant's **h** and spend the night,
19: 3 so they turned aside to him and entered his **h;**
19: 4 all the people to the last man, surrounded the **h;**
19:10 and brought Lot into the **h** with them,
19:11 the men who were at the door of the **h,**
20:13 God caused me to wander from my father's **h,** E
20:18 the LORD had closed fast all the wombs of the **h**
24: 2 Abraham said to his servant, the oldest of his **h,**
24: 7 who took me from my father's **h** and from E
24:23 Is there room in your father's **h** for us to spend E
24:27 the LORD has led me on the way to the **h**
24:31 when I have prepared the **h** and a place for
24:32 So the man came into the **h;**
24:38 but you shall go to my father's **h,** E
24:40 for my son from my kindred, from my father's **h.** E
27:15 which were with her in the **h,**
28: 2 Go at once to Paddan-aram to the **h** of Bethuel,
28:17 This is none other than the **h** of God, C
28:21 so that I come again to my father's **h** in peace, E
28:22 which I have set up for a pillar, shall be God's **h;**
29:13 and kissed him, and brought him to his **h.**
31:14 or inheritance left to us in our father's **h?** E
31:30 because you longed greatly for your father's **h,** E
31:41 These twenty years I have been in your **h;**
33:17 Jacob journeyed to Succoth, and built himself a **h,**
34:26 and took Dinah out of Shechem's **h,**
38:11 in your father's **h** until my son Shelah grows up" E
38:11 So Tamar went to live in her father's **h.** E
39: 2 he was in the **h** of his Egyptian master.
39: 4 of his **h** and put him in charge of all that he had.
39: 5 From the time that he made him overseer in his **h**

Ge 39: 5 LORD blessed the Egyptian's **h** for Joseph's sake;
39: 5 the LORD was on all that he had, in **h** and field.
39: 8 my master has no concern about anything in the **h,**
39: 9 He is not greater in this **h** than I am, D
39:11 however, when he went into the **h** to do his work,
39:11 and while no one else was in the **h,**
40: 3 and he put them in custody in the **h** of the captain
40: 7 who were with him in custody in his master's **h,**
41:10 the chief baker in custody in the **h** of the captain
41:40 You shall be over my **h,** F
41:51 forget all my hardship and all my father's **h."** E
43:16 he said to the steward of his **h,**
43:16 "Bring the men into the **h,**
43:17 and brought the men to Joseph's **h.**
43:18 because they were brought to Joseph's **h,**
43:19 up to the steward of Joseph's **h** and spoke with him
43:19 and spoke with him at the entrance to the **h.**
43:24 the steward had brought the men into Joseph's **h,**
43:26 the present that they had carried into the **h,**
44: 1 Then he commanded the steward of his **h,**
44: 8 or gold from your lord's **h?**
44:14 Judah and his brothers came to Joseph's **h**
45: 8 to Pharaoh, and lord of all his **h** and ruler over all
45:16 When the report was heard in Pharaoh's **h,**
46:27 **h** of Jacob who came into Egypt were seventy. J
47:14 and Joseph brought the money into Pharaoh's **h.**
Ex 2: 1 Now a man from the **h** of Levi went and married
3:22 the neighbor's **h** for jewelry of silver and of gold,
7:23 Pharaoh turned and went into his **h,**
8:24 into the **h** of Pharaoh and into his officials' houses;
12:22 None of you shall go outside the door of your **h**
12:30 for there was not a **h** without someone dead.
12:46 It shall be eaten in one **h;**
12:46 you shall not take any of the animal outside the **h,**
13: 3 out of the **h** of slavery, N
13:14 brought us out of Egypt, from the **h** of slavery. N
16:31 The **h** of Israel called it manna; B
19: 3 saying, "Thus you shall say to the **h** of Jacob, J
20: 2 out of the **h** of slavery; N
20:17 You shall not covet your neighbor's **h;**
22: 7 and they are stolen from the neighbor's **h,**
22: 8 the owner of the **h** shall be brought before God,
23:19 you shall bring into the **h** of the LORD A
34:26 you shall bring to the **h** of the LORD A
40:38 all the **h** of Israel at each stage of their journey. B
Lev 10: 6 but your kindred, the whole **h** of Israel, BK
14:34 and I put a leprous disease in a **h** in the land
14:35 the owner of the **h** shall come and tell the priest,
14:35 to me to be some sort of disease in my **h."** F
14:36 the **h** before the priest goes to examine the disease,
14:36 or all that is in the **h** will become unclean;
14:36 and afterward the priest shall go in to inspect the **h.**
14:37 in the walls of the **h** with greenish or reddish spots,
14:38 the door of the **h** and shut up the **h** seven days.
14:39 if the disease has spread in the walls of the **h,**
14:41 the inside of the **h** scraped thoroughly,
14:42 and take other plaster and plaster the **h.**
14:43 If the disease breaks out again in the **h,**
14:43 after he has taken out the stones and scraped the **h**
14:44 if the disease has spread in the **h,**
14:44 it is a spreading leprous disease in the **h;**
14:45 He shall have the **h** torn down,
14:45 its stones and timber and all the plaster of the **h,**
14:46 the **h** while it is shut up shall be unclean until
14:47 and all who sleep in the **h** shall wash their clothes;
14:47 and all who eat in the **h** shall wash their clothes.
14:48 not spread in the **h** after the **h** was plastered, the
priest shall pronounce the **h** clean;
14:49 For the cleansing of the **h** he shall take two birds,
14:51 and sprinkle the **h** seven times.
14:52 Thus he shall cleanse the **h** with the blood of
14:53 so he shall make atonement for the **h,**
16: 6 shall make atonement for himself and for his **h.**
16:11 shall make atonement for himself and for his **h;**
16:17 and has made atonement for himself and for his **h**
17: 3 the **h** of Israel slaughters an ox or a lamb or B
17: 8 of the **h** of Israel or of the aliens who reside B
17:10 of the **h** of Israel or of the aliens who reside B
22:11 those that are born in his **h** may eat of his food.
22:13 without offspring, and returns to her father's **h,** E
22:18 of the **h** of Israel or of the aliens residing B
25:29 If anyone sells a dwelling **h** in a walled city,
25:30 a **h** that is in a walled city shall pass in perpetuity
27:14 If a person consecrates a **h** to the LORD,
27:15 the one who consecrates the **h** wishes to redeem it,
Nu 1: 4 each man the head of his ancestral **h.**
1:44 twelve men, each representing his ancestral **h.**
3:24 as head of the ancestral **h** of the Gershonites.
3:30 of Uzziel as head of the ancestral **h** of the clans of
3:35 The head of the ancestral **h** of the clans
12: 7 he is entrusted with all my **h.** F
17: 2 from them, one for each ancestral **h,** from all
17: 3 be one staff for the head of each ancestral **h.**
17: 8 the staff of Aaron for the **h** of Levi had sprouted.
18: 1 You and your sons and your ancestral **h**
18:11 everyone who is clean in your **h** may eat them.
18:13 everyone who is clean in your **h** may eat of it.
20:29 all the **h** of Israel mourned for Aaron thirty days. B
22:18 Balak were to give me his **h** full of silver and gold,
24:13 'If Balak should give me his **h** full of silver
25:14 head of an ancestral **h** belonging to the Simeonites.
25:15 Zur, who was the head of a clan, an ancestral **h**
30: 3 while within her father's **h,** in her youth, E
30:10 And if she made a vow in her husband's **h,**
30:16 while she is still young and in her father's **h.** E
Dt 5: 6 out of the **h** of slavery; N
5:21 Neither shall you desire your neighbor's **h,**

Dt 6: 9 and write them on the doorposts of your **h** and
6:12 out of the **h** of slavery. N
7: 8 and redeemed you from the **h** of slavery, N
7:26 Do not bring an abhorrent thing into your **h,**
8:14 out of the **h** of slavery, N
11:20 on the doorposts of your **h** and on your gates,
13: 5 Egypt and redeemed you from the **h** of slavery N
13:10 Egypt, out of the **h** of slavery. N
20: 5 "Has anyone built a new **h** but not dedicated it?
20: 5 He should go back to his **h,**
20: 6 He should go back to his **h,**
20: 7 He should go back to his **h,**
20: 8 He should go back to his **h,**
21:12 and so you bring her home to your **h:**
21:13 and shall remain in your **h** a full month,
22: 2 you shall bring it to your own **h,**
22: 8 When you build a new **h,** you shall make a parapet
22: 8 otherwise you might have bloodguilt on your **h,**
22:21 to the entrance of her father's **h** and the men E
22:21 in Israel by prostituting herself in her father's **h.** E
23:18 into the **h** of the LORD your God in payment A
24: 1 puts it in her hand, and sends her out of his **h;**
24: 1 house; she then leaves his **h**
24: 3 of his **h** (or the second man who married her dies);
24:10 you shall not go into the **h** to take the pledge.
25: 9 to the man who does not build up his brother's **h."**
25:10 as "the **h** of him whose sandal was pulled off."
25:14 not have in your **h** two kinds of measures,
26:11 to you and to your **h.**
26:13 "I have removed the sacred portion from the **h,**
28:30 You shall build a **h,** but not live in it.
Jos 2: 1 the **h** of a prostitute whose name was Rahab,
2: 3 who entered your **h,** for they have come only
2:15 for her **h** was on the outer side of the city wall
2:18 not gather into your **h** your father and mother,
2:19 of you go out of the doors of your **h** into the street,
2:19 a hand is laid upon any who are with you in the **h,**
6:17 with her in her **h** shall live because she hid
6:22 "Go into the prostitute's **h,**
6:24 they put into the treasury of the **h** of the LORD. A
9:23 and drawers of water for the **h** of my God." C
17:17 Then Joshua said to the **h** of Joseph,
18: 5 and the **h** of Joseph in their territory on the north.
21:45 the LORD had made to the **h** of Israel had failed; B
24:17 out of the **h** of slavery, N
Jdg 1:22 The **h** of Joseph also went up against Bethel;
1:23 The **h** of Joseph sent out spies to Bethel (the name
1:35 the hand of the **h** of Joseph rested heavily on them,
6: 8 and brought you out of the **h** of slavery; N
6:19 So Gideon went into his **h** and prepared a kid,
8:29 Jerubbaal son of Joash went to live in his own **h.**
8:35 not exhibit loyalty to the **h** of Jerubbaal (that is,
9: 5 He went to his father's **h** at Ophrah, E
9:16 if you have dealt well with Jerubbaal and his **h,**
9:18 up against my father's **h** this day, E
9:19 with Jerubbaal and with his **h** this day, then rejoice
10: 9 against Benjamin and against the **h** of Ephraim;
11: 2 "You shall not inherit anything in our father's **h;** E
11: 7 and drove me out of my father's **h?** E
11:31 then whoever comes out of the doors of my **h** F
12: 1 We will burn your **h** down over you!"
14:15 we will burn you and your father's **h** with fire. E
14:19 In hot anger he went back to his father's **h.** E
16:26 "Let me feel the pillars on which the **h** rests,
16:27 Now the **h** was full of men and women;
16:29 the two middle pillars on which the **h** rested,
16:30 the **h** fell on the lords and all the people who were
17: 4 and it was in the **h** of Micah.
17: 8 to the **h** of Micah in the hill country of Ephraim
17:12 and was in the **h** of Micah.
18: 2 to the **h** of Micah, they stayed there.
18: 3 While they were at Micah's **h,**
18:13 and came to the **h** of Micah.
18:15 So they turned in that direction and came to the **h**
18:18 the men went into Micah's **h** and took the idol
18:19 for you to be priest to the **h** of one person,
18:22 in the houses near Micah's **h** were called out,
18:31 as long as the **h** of God was at Shiloh. C
19: 2 to her father's **h** at Bethlehem in Judah, E
19: 3 When he reached her father's **h,** E
19:21 So he brought him into his **h,** and fed the donkeys;
19:22 a perverse lot, surrounded the **h,**
19:22 They said to the old man, the master of the **h,**
19:22 "Bring out the man who came into your **h,**
19:23 And the man, the master of the **h,**
19:26 at the door of the man's **h** where her master was,
19:27 opened the doors of the **h,**
19:27 there was his concubine lying at the door of the **h,**
19:29 When he had entered his **h,** he took a knife,
20: 5 and surrounded the **h** at night.
Ru 1: 8 "Go back each of you to your mother's **h.**
1: 9 each of you in the **h** of your husband."
4:11 the woman who is coming into your **h** like Rachel
4:11 who together built up the **h** of Israel. B
4:12 may your **h** be like the **h** of Perez,
1Sa 1: 7 as often as she went up to the **h** of the LORD, A
1:19 then they went back to their **h** at Ramah.
1:24 She brought him to the **h** of the LORD at Shiloh; A
2:27 when they were slaves to the **h** of Pharaoh.
2:35 I will build him a sure **h,**
3:12 against Eli all that I have spoken concerning his **h,**
3:13 that I am about to punish his **h** forever,
3:14 the **h** of Eli that the iniquity of Eli's **h** shall not
3:15 then he opened the doors of the **h** of the LORD. A
5: 2 the ark of God and brought it into the **h** of Dagon
5: 5 and all who enter the **h** of Dagon do not step on
7: 1 and brought it to the **h** of Abinadab on the hill.

1Sa 7: 2 and all the **h** of Israel lamented after the LORD. B
7: 3 Then Samuel said to all the **h** of Israel, B
9:18 "Tell me, please, where is the **h** of the seer?"
9:20 if not on you and on all your ancestral **h?"**
15:34 and Saul went up to his **h** in Gibeah of Saul.
18: 2 and would not let him return to his father's **h.** E
18:10 and he raved within his **h,**
19: 9 as he sat in his **h** with his spear in his hand,
19:11 Saul sent messengers to David's **h** to keep watch
20:15 never cut off your faithful love from my **h,** F
20:16 Jonathan made a covenant with the **h** of David, I
21:15 Shall this fellow come into my **h?"** F
22: 1 his brothers and all his father's **h** heard of it, E
22:11 all his father's **h,** the priests who were at Nob; E
22:14 and is honored in your **h.**
22:15 his servant or to any member of my father's **h;** E
22:16 Ahimelech, you and all your father's **h."** E
22:22 responsible for the lives of all your father's **h.** E
24:21 not wipe out my name from my father's **h."** E
25: 6 'Peace be to you, and peace be to your **h,**
25:17 against our master and against all his **h;**
25:28 the LORD will certainly make my lord a sure **h,**
25:35 he said to her, "Go up to your **h** in peace;
25:36 he was holding a feast in his **h,**
28:24 Now the woman had a fatted calf in the **h.**
2Sa 1:12 for the army of the LORD and for the **h** of Israel, B
2: 4 they anointed David king over the **h** of Judah. G
2: 7 the **h** of Judah has anointed me king over them." G
2:10 But the **h** of Judah followed David. G
2:11 David was king in Hebron over the **h** of Judah G
3: 1 There was a long war between the **h** of Saul and
3: 1 between the house of Saul and the **h** of David; I
3: 1 while the **h** of Saul became weaker and weaker.
3: 6 While there was war between the **h** of Saul and
3: 6 between the house of Saul and the **h** of David, I
3: 6 Abner was making himself strong in the **h** of Saul.
3: 8 to the **h** of your father Saul, to his brothers,
3:10 to transfer the kingdom from the **h** of Saul,
3:19 Israel and the whole **h** of Benjamin were ready K
3:29 and on all his father's **h;** E
3:29 the **h** of Joab never be without one who has
4: 5 the heat of the day they came to the **h** of Ishbaal,
4: 6 They came inside the **h** as though to take wheat,
4: 7 Now they had come into the **h** while he was lying
4:11 a righteous man on his bed in his own **h!**
5: 8 "The blind and the lame shall not come into the **h."**
5:11 and carpenters and masons who built David a **h.**
6: 3 and brought it out of the **h** of Abinadab,
6: 5 David and all the **h** of Israel were dancing B
6:10 instead David took it to the **h** of Obed-edom
6:11 in the **h** of Obed-edom the Gittite three months;
6:12 the ark of God from the **h** of Obed-edom to the city
6:15 David and all the **h** of Israel brought up the ark B
7: 1 Now when the king was settled in his **h,**
7: 2 "See now, I am living in a **h** of cedar,
7: 5 Are you the one to build me a **h** to live in?
7: 6 a **h** since the day I brought up the people of Israel
7: 7 saying, "Why have you not built me a **h** of cedar?"
7:11 to you that the LORD will make you a **h.**
7:13 He shall build a **h** for my name,
7:16 Your **h** and your kingdom shall
7:18 "Who am I, O Lord GOD, and what is my **h,** F
7:19 also of your servant's **h** for a great while to come.
7:25 concerning your servant and concerning his **h,**
7:26 and the **h** of your servant David will be established
7:27 saying, 'I will build you a **h';**
7:29 now therefore may it please you to bless the **h**
7:29 and with your blessing shall the **h** of your servant
9: 1 of the **h** of Saul to whom I may show kindness
9: 2 a servant of the **h** of Saul whose name was Ziba,
9: 3 of the **h** of Saul to whom I may show the kindness
9: 4 "He is in the **h** of Machir son of Ammiel,
9: 5 Then King David sent and brought him from the **h**
9: 9 to all his **h** I have given to your master's grandson.
9:12 in Ziba's **h** became Mephibosheth's servants.
11: 2 was walking about on the roof of the king's **h,** H
11: 4 Then she returned to her **h.**
11: 8 Then David said to Uriah, "Go down to your **h,**
11: 8 Uriah went out of the king's **h,** H
11: 9 the entrance of the king's **h** with all the servants H
11: 9 and did not go down to his **h.**
11:10 they told David, "Uriah did not go down to his **h,"**
11:10 Why did you not go down to your **h?"**
11:11 shall I then go to my **h,** to eat and to drink, F
11:13 but he did not go down to his **h.**
11:27 David sent and brought her to his **h,**
12: 8 I gave you your master's **h,**
12: 8 and gave you the **h** of Israel and of Judah; B
12:10 therefore the sword shall never depart from your **h,**
12:11 up trouble against you from within your own **h;**
12:15 Then Nathan went to his **h.**
12:17 The elders of his **h** stood beside him,
12:20 He went into the **h** of the LORD, and worshiped; A
12:20 he then went to his own **h;**
13: 7 saying, "Go to your brother Amnon's **h,**
13: 8 So Tamar went to her brother Amnon's **h,**
13:20 a desolate woman, in her brother Absalom's **h.**
14: 8 Then the king said to the woman, "Go to your **h,**
14: 9 my lord the king, and on my father's **h;** E
14:24 The king said, "Let him go to his own **h;**
14:24 So Absalom went to his own **h,**
14:31 Then Joab rose and went to Absalom at his **h,**
15:16 behind to look after the **h.**
15:17 and they stopped at the last **h.**
15:35 So whatever you hear from the king's **h,** H
16: 3 for he said, 'Today the **h** of Israel will give me B
16: 5 a man of the family of the **h** of Saul

2Sa 16: 8 of the **h** of Saul, in whose place you have reigned;
16:21 the ones he has left to look after the **h;**
17:18 and came to the **h** of a man at Bahurim,
17:20 Absalom's servants came to the woman at the **h,**
17:23 He set his **h** in order, and hanged himself;
19: 5 Then Joab came into the **h** to the king, and said,
19:11 be the last to bring the king back to his **h?**
19:17 And Ziba, the servant of the **h** of Saul,
19:20 the **h** of Joseph to come down to meet my lord
19:28 For all my father's **h** were doomed to death E
20: 3 David came to his **h** at Jerusalem;
20: 3 after the **h,** and put them in a house under guard,
20: 3 and put them in a **h** under guard,
21: 1 "There is bloodguilt on Saul and on his **h,**
21: 4 of silver or gold between us and Saul or his **h;**
23: 5 Is not my **h** like this with God? F
24:17 I pray, be against me and against my father's **h."** E
1Ki 2:24 and who has made me a **h** as he promised,
2:27 of the LORD that he had spoken concerning the **h**
2:31 and from my father's **h** the guilt for the blood E
2:33 but to David, and to his descendants, and to his **h,**
2:34 he was buried at his own **h** near the wilderness.
2:36 and said to him, "Build yourself a **h** in Jerusalem,
3: 1 of David, until he had finished building his own **h**
3: 1 **h** of the LORD and the wall around Jerusalem. A
3: 2 because no **h** had yet been built for the name of
3:17 my lord, this woman and I live in the same **h;**
3:17 and I gave birth while she was in the **h.**
3:18 there was no one else with us in the **h,**
3:18 only the two of us were in the **h.**
5: 3 a **h** for the name of the LORD his God because of
5: 5 to build a **h** for the name of the LORD my God,
5: 5 shall build the **h** for my name.'
5:17 costly stones in order to lay the foundation of the **h**
5:18 the timber and the stone to build the **h.**
6: 1 he began to build the **h** of the LORD. A
6: 2 The **h** that King Solomon built for
6: 3 of the nave of the **h** was twenty cubits wide,
6: 3 across the width of the **h.**
6: 3 Its depth was ten cubits in front of the **h.**
6: 4 For the **h** he made windows with recessed frames.
6: 5 He also built a structure against the wall of the **h,**
6: 5 running around the walls of the **h,**
6: 6 for around the outside of the **h** he made offsets on
6: 6 not be inserted into the walls of the **h.**
6: 7 The **h** was built with stone finished at the quarry,
6: 8 for the middle story was on the south side of the **h:**
6: 9 So he built the **h,** and finished it;
6: 9 he roofed the **h** with beams and planks of cedar.
6:10 He built the structure against the whole **h,** K
6:10 and it was joined to the **h** with timbers of cedar.
6:12 "Concerning this **h** that you are building, D
6:14 So Solomon built the **h,** and finished it.
6:15 the walls of the **h** on the inside with boards
6:15 from the floor of the **h** to the rafters of the ceiling,
6:15 and he covered the floor of the **h** with boards
6:16 of the **h** with boards of cedar from the floor to
6:17 The **h,** that is, the nave in front of
6:18 the **h** had carvings of gourds and open flowers;
6:19 in the innermost part of the **h,**
6:21 Solomon overlaid the inside of the **h**
6:22 Next he overlaid the whole **h** with gold, K
6:22 in order that the whole **h** might be perfect; K
6:27 the cherubim in the innermost part of the **h;**
6:27 the center of the **h** were touching wing to wing.
6:29 of the **h** all around about with carved engravings
6:30 The floor of the **h** he overlaid with gold,
6:37 the foundation of the **h** of the LORD was laid, A
6:38 the **h** was finished in all its parts,
7: 1 Solomon was building his own **h** thirteen years,
7: 1 and he finished his entire **h.**
7: 2 He built the **H** of the Forest of
7: 8 His own **h** where he would reside,
7: 8 also made a **h** like this hall for Pharaoh's daughter,
7:12 so had the inner court of the **h** of the LORD, A
7:12 of the LORD, and the vestibule of the **h.**
7:39 He set five of the stands on the south side of the **h,**
7:39 and five on the north side of the **h;**
7:39 he set the sea on the southeast corner of the **h.**
7:40 he did for King Solomon on the **h** of the LORD: A
7:45 for the **h** of the LORD were of burnished bronze. A
7:48 all the vessels that were in the **h** of the LORD: A
7:50 for the doors of the innermost part of the **h,**
7:51 that King Solomon did on the **h** of the LORD A
7:51 in the treasuries of the **h** of the LORD. A
8: 6 in the inner sanctuary of the **h,**
8:10 a cloud filled the **h** of the LORD, A
8:11 the glory of the LORD filled the **h** of the LORD. A
8:13 I have built you an exalted **h,**
8:16 of Israel in which to build a **h,** that my name might
8:17 in mind to build a **h** for the name of the LORD,
8:18 'You did well to consider building a **h**
8:19 nevertheless you shall not build the **h,**
8:19 be born to you shall build the **h** for my name.'
8:20 and have built the **h** for the name of the LORD,
8:27 much less this **h** that I have built! D
8:29 be open night and day toward this **h,** D
8:31 comes and swears before your altar in this **h,** D
8:33 pray and plead with you in this **h,** D
8:38 so that they stretch out their hands toward this **h;** D
8:42 when a foreigner comes and prays toward this **h,** D
8:43 that your name has been invoked on this **h** D
8:44 that you have chosen and the **h** that I have built
8:48 and the **h** that I have built for your name;
8:63 people of Israel dedicated the **h** of the LORD. A
8:64 the court that was in front of the **h** of the LORD; A
9: 1 the **h** of the LORD and the king's house and all A

1Ki 9: 1 king's **h** and all that Solomon desired to build, H
9: 3 I have consecrated this **h** that you have built, D
9: 7 and the **h** that I have consecrated
9: 8 This **h** will become a heap of ruins; D
9: 8 a thing to this land and to this **h?'** D
9:10 the **h** of the LORD and the king's house, A
9:10 the house of the LORD and the king's **h,** H
9:15 to build the **h** of the LORD and his own house, A
9:15 to build the house of the LORD and his own **h,**
9:24 of David to her own **h** that Solomon had built
9:25 So he completed the **h.**
10: 4 the **h** that he had built,
10: 5 offerings that he offered at the **h** of the LORD, A
10:12 the **h** of the LORD, and for the king's house, A
10:12 the king's **h,** lyres also and harps for the singers; H
10:17 king put them in the **H** of the Forest of Lebanon.
10:21 the vessels of the **H** of the Forest of Lebanon were
11:14 he was of the royal **h** in Edom.
11:18 to Pharaoh king of Egypt, who gave him a **h,**
11:20 whom Tahpenes weaned in Pharaoh's **h;**
11:20 Genubath was in Pharaoh's **h** among the children
11:28 over all the forced labor of the **h** of Joseph.
11:38 and will build you an enduring **h,**
12:16 Look now to your own **h,** O David."
12:19 in rebellion against the **h** of David to this day. I
12:20 There was no one who followed the **h** of David, I
12:21 he assembled all the **h** of Judah and the tribe G
12:21 to fight against the **h** of Israel, B
12:23 and to all the **h** of Judah and Benjamin, G
12:26 the kingdom may well revert to the **h** of David. I
12:27 to go up to offer sacrifices in the **h** of the LORD A
13: 2 'A son shall be born to the **h** of David, I
13:18 with you into your **h** so that he may eat food
13:19 and ate food and drank water in his **h.**
13:34 This matter became sin to the **h** of Jeroboam,
14: 4 and came to the **h** of Ahijah.
14: 8 the kingdom away from the **h** of David to give it I
14:10 I will bring evil upon the **h** of Jeroboam.
14:10 and will consume the **h** of Jeroboam,
14:12 Therefore set out, go to your **h.**
14:13 the God of Israel, in the **h** of Jeroboam.
14:14 who shall cut off the **h** of Jeroboam today,
14:17 she came to the threshold of the **h,** the child died.
14:26 he took away the treasures of the **h** of the LORD A
14:26 of the LORD and the treasures of the king's **h;** H
14:27 who kept the door of the king's **h.** H
14:28 As often as the king went into the **h** of the LORD, A
15:15 the **h** of the LORD the votive gifts of his father A
15:18 were left in the treasures of the **h** of the LORD A
15:18 of the LORD and the treasures of the king's **h,** H
15:27 Baasha son of Ahijah, of the **h** of Issachar,
15:29 he killed all the **h** of Jeroboam;
15:29 he left to the **h** of Jeroboam not one that breathed,
16: 3 I will consume Baasha and his **h,** and I will make
your **h** like the **h** of Jeroboam
16: 7 of Hanani against Baasha and his **h,**
16: 7 in being like the **h** of Jeroboam,
16: 9 drinking himself drunk in the **h** of Arza,
16:11 he killed all the **h** of Baasha;
16:12 Thus Zimri destroyed all the **h** of Baasha,
16:18 he went into the citadel of the king's **h;** H
16:18 the king's **h** over himself with fire, and died— H
16:32 He erected an altar for Baal in the **h** of Baal,
17:17 this the son of the woman, the mistress of the **h,**
17:23 from the upper chamber into the **h,** and gave him
18:18 but you have, and your father's **h,** E
20: 6 and they shall search your **h** and the houses
20:31 the kings of the **h** of Israel are merciful kings; B
21: 2 because it is near my **h;** F
21:22 and I will make your **h** like the **h** of Jeroboam
21:22 and like the **h** of Baasha son of Ahijah,
21:29 in his son's days I will bring the disaster on his **h."**
22:39 and all that he did, and the ivory **h** that he built,
2Ki 4: 2 Tell me, what do you have in the **h?"**
4: 2 She answered, "Your servant has nothing in the **h,**
4:32 When Elisha came into the **h,**
5: 9 and halted at the entrance of Elisha's **h.**
5:18 when my master goes into the **h** of Rimmon
5:18 and I bow down in the **h** of Rimmon,
5:18 when I do bow down in the **h** of Rimmon,
6:32 Now Elisha was sitting in his **h,**
8: 3 to appeal to the king for her **h** and her land.
8: 5 to life appealed to the king for her **h** and her land.
8:18 as the **h** of Ahab had done,
8:27 He also walked in the way of the **h** of Ahab,
8:27 as the **h** of Ahab had done,
8:27 for he was son-in-law to the **h** of Ahab.
9: 7 You shall strike down the **h** of your master Ahab,
9: 8 For the whole **h** of Ahab shall perish; K
9: 9 the **h** of Ahab like the **h** of Jeroboam son of
9: 9 and like the **h** of Baasha son of Ahijah.
10: 3 and fight for your master's **h."**
10:10 which the LORD spoke concerning the **h** of Ahab;
10:11 So Jehu killed all who were left of the **h** of Ahab
10:30 that was in my heart have dealt with the **h** of Ahab,
11: 3 hidden in the **h** of the LORD, A
11: 4 and had them come to him in the **h** of the LORD. A
11: 4 and put them under oath in the **h** of the LORD; A
11: 5 on the sabbath and guard the king's **h** H
11: 7 on the sabbath and guard the **h** of the LORD A
11:10 which were in the **h** of the LORD; A
11:11 from the south side of the **h** to the north side of
11:11 of the house to the north side of the **h,**
11:11 around the altar and the **h,**
11:13 she went into the **h** of the LORD to the people; A
11:15 "Let her not be killed in the **h** of the LORD." A
11:16 through the horses' entrance to the king's **h,** H

2Ki 11:18 all the people of the land went to the **h** of Baal,
11:18 The priest posted guards over the **h** of the LORD. A
11:19 brought the king down from the **h** of the LORD, A
11:19 through the gate of the guards to the king's **h.** H
11:20 with the sword at the king's **h.** H
12: 4 that is brought into the **h** of the LORD, A
12: 4 offerings brought into the **h** of the LORD A
12: 5 the **h** wherever any need of repairs is discovered."
12: 6 the priests had made no repairs on the **h.**
12: 7 "Why are you not repairing the **h?**
12: 7 but hand it over for the repair of the **h."**
12: 8 from the people nor repair the **h.**
12: 9 the right side as one entered the **h** of the LORD; A
12: 9 money that was brought into the **h** of the LORD. A
12:10 the money that was found in the **h** of the LORD, A
12:11 who had the oversight of the **h** of the LORD; A
12:11 the builders who worked on the **h** of the LORD, A
12:12 stone for making repairs on the **h** of the LORD, A
12:12 as well as for any outlay for repairs of the **h.**
12:13 But for the **h** of the LORD no basins of silver, A
12:13 money that was brought into the **h** of the LORD, A
12:14 who were repairing the **h** of the LORD A
12:16 was not brought into the **h** of the LORD; A
12:18 found in the treasuries of the **h** of the LORD A
12:18 of the house of the LORD and of the king's **h,** H
12:20 and killed Joash in the **h** of Millo,
13: 6 the **h** of Jeroboam, which he caused Israel to sin,
14:14 the vessels that were found in the **h** of the LORD A
14:14 of the LORD and in the treasuries of the king's **h,** H
15: 5 and lived in a separate **h.**
15:35 He built the upper gate of the **h** of the LORD. A
16: 8 silver and gold found in the **h** of the LORD A
16: 8 of the LORD and in the treasures of the king's **h,** H
16:14 the LORD he removed from the front of the **h,**
16:14 place between his altar and the **h** of the LORD, A
16:18 for the king he removed from the **h** of the LORD. A
17:21 When he had torn Israel from the **h** of David, I
18:15 the silver that was found in the **h** of the LORD A
18:15 the LORD and in the treasuries of the king's **h.** H
19: 1 and went into the **h** of the LORD. A
19:14 then Hezekiah went up to the **h** of the LORD A
19:30 the **h** of Judah shall again take root downward, G
19:37 he was worshiping in the **h** of his god Nisroch, C
20: 1 Set your **h** in order, for you shall die;
20: 5 you shall go up to the **h** of the LORD. A
20: 8 and that I shall go up to the **h** of the LORD on A
20:13 he showed them all his treasure **h,** the silver,
20:13 there was nothing in his **h** or in all his realm
20:15 He said, "What have they seen in your **h?"**
20:15 "They have seen all that is in my **h;** F
20:17 Days are coming when all that is in your **h,** and
21: 4 He built altars in the **h** of the LORD, A
21: 5 of heaven in the two courts of the **h** of the LORD. A
21: 7 in the **h** of which the LORD said to David and
21: 7 "In this **h,** and in Jerusalem, D
21:13 and the plummet for the **h** of Ahab;
21:18 and was buried in the garden of his **h,**
21:23 and killed the king in his **h.**
22: 3 the secretary, to the **h** of the LORD, saying, A
22: 4 that has been brought into the **h** of the LORD, A
22: 5 who have the oversight of the **h** of the LORD; A
22: 5 to the workers who are at the **h** of the LORD, A
22: 5 at the house of the LORD, repairing the **h,**
22: 6 to buy timber and quarried stone to repair the **h.**
22: 8 found the book of the law in the **h** of the LORD." A
22: 9 the money that was found in the **h,**
22: 9 who have oversight of the **h** of the LORD." A
23: 2 The king went up to the **h** of the LORD, A
23: 2 that had been found in the **h** of the LORD. A
23: 6 the image of Asherah from the **h** of the LORD, A
23: 7 prostitutes that were in the **h** of the LORD, A
23:11 at the entrance to the **h** of the LORD, A
23:12 made in the two courts of the **h** of the LORD, A
23:24 priest Hilkiah had found in the **h** of the LORD. A
23:27 and the **h** of which I said, My name shall be there."
24:13 of the **h** of the LORD, and the treasures of A
24:13 and the treasures of the king's **h;** H
25: 9 He burned the **h** of the LORD, the king's house, A
25: 9 He burned the house of the LORD, the king's **h,** H
25: 9 every great **h** he burned down.
25:13 bronze pillars that were in the **h** of the LORD, A
25:13 the bronze sea that were in the **h** of the LORD, A
25:16 which Solomon had made for the **h** of the LORD, A
1Ch 2:55 father of the **h** of Rechab.
6:10 as priest in the **h** that Solomon built in Jerusalem).
6:31 of the service of song in the **h** of the LORD, A
6:32 until Solomon had built the **h** of the LORD A
6:48 all the service of the tabernacle of the **h** of God. C
7:23 because disaster had befallen his **h.**
9:11 son of Ahitub, the chief officer of the **h** of God; C
9:13 the work of the service of the **h** of God. C
9:19 and his kindred of his ancestral **h,** the Korahites,
9:23 in charge of the gates of the **h** of the LORD, A
9:23 that is, the **h** of the tent, as guards.
9:26 the chambers and the treasures of the **h** of God. C
9:27 they would spend the night near the **h** of God; C
10: 6 he and his three sons and all his **h** died together.
12:27 Jehoiada, leader of the **h** of Aaron,
12:28 twenty-two commanders from his own ancestral **h.**
12:29 to keep their allegiance to the **h** of Saul.
13: 7 on a new cart, from the **h** of Abinadab, and Uzzah
13:13 he took it instead to the **h** of Obed-edom
13:14 the household of Obed-edom in his **h** three months,
14: 1 and masons and carpenters to build a **h** for him.
15:25 the ark of the covenant of the LORD from the **h**
17: 1 Now when David settled in his **h,**
17: 1 "I am living in a **h** of cedar,

1Ch 17: 4 You shall not build me a **h** to live in.
17: 5 not lived in a **h** since the day I brought out Israel
17: 6 saying, Why have you not built me a **h** of cedar?
17:10 I declare to you that the LORD will build you a **h.**
17:12 He shall build a **h** for me,
17:14 in my **h** and in my kingdom forever, F
17:16 "Who am I, O LORD God, and what is my **h,** F
17:17 also spoken of your servant's **h** for a great while
17:23 concerning your servant and concerning his **h,**
17:24 and the **h** of your servant David will be established
17:25 to your servant that you will build a **h** for him;
17:27 may it please you to bless the **h** of your servant,
21:17 be against me and against my father's **h;** E
22: 1 "Here shall be the **h** of the LORD God and here A
22: 2 prepare dressed stones for building the **h** of God. C
22: 5 and the **h** that is to be built for the LORD must
22: 6 for his son Solomon and charged him to build a **h**
22: 7 to build a **h** to the name of the LORD my God.
22: 8 you shall not build a **h** to my name,
22:10 He shall build a **h** for my name.
22:11 you may succeed in building the **h** of the LORD A
22:14 the **h** of the LORD one hundred thousand talents A
22:19 of God may be brought into a **h** built for the name
23: 4 have charge of the work in the **h** of the LORD, A
23:24 the work for the service of the **h** of the LORD. A
23:28 of Aaron for the service of the **h** of the LORD, A
23:28 and any work for the service of the **h** of God; C
23:32 for the service of the **h** of the LORD." A
24: 6 one ancestral **h** being chosen for Eleazar
24:19 in their service to enter the **h** of the LORD A
25: 6 for the music in the **h** of the LORD with cymbals, A
25: 6 harps, and lyres for the service of the **h** of God. C
26:12 ministering in the **h** of the LORD; A
26:20 had charge of the treasuries of the **h** of God C
26:22 in charge of the treasuries of the **h** of the LORD. A
26:27 for the maintenance of the **h** of the LORD. A
28: 2 to build a **h** of rest for the ark of the covenant of
28: 3 'You shall not build a **h** for my name,
28: 4 of Israel chose me from all my ancestral **h** to
28: 4 and in the **h** of Judah my father's house, G
28: 4 and in the house of Judah my father's **h,** E
28: 6 'It is your son Solomon who shall build my **h** F
28:10 for the LORD has chosen you to build a **h** as
28:12 for the courts of the **h** of the LORD, A
28:12 the treasuries of the **h** of God, C
28:13 all the work of the service in the **h** of the LORD; A
28:13 the vessels for the service in the **h** of the LORD, A
28:20 for the service of the **h** of the LORD is finished. A
28:21 the Levites for all the service of the **h** of God; C
29: 2 So I have provided for the **h** of my God, C
29: 3 for the holy **h,** I have a treasure of my own of gold
29: 3 because of my devotion to the **h** of my God C
29: 3 of my God I give it to the **h** of my God: C
29: 4 for overlaying the walls of the **h,**
29: 7 the service of the **h** of God five thousand talents C
29: 8 to the treasury of the **h** of the LORD, A
29:16 for building you a **h** for your holy name comes
2Ch 2: 3 and sent him cedar to build himself a **h** to live in.
2: 4 to build a **h** for the name of the LORD my God
2: 5 The **h** that I am about to build will be great,
2: 6 But who is able to build him a **h,** since heaven,
2: 6 Who am I to build a **h** for him,
2: 9 **h** I am about to build will be great and wonderful.
3: 1 Solomon began to build the **h** of the LORD A
3: 3 for building the **h** of God: C
3: 4 of the nave of the **h** was twenty cubits long,
3: 4 across the width of the **h;**
3: 6 He adorned the **h** with settings of precious stones.
3: 7 So he lined the **h** with gold—
3: 8 its length, corresponding to the width of the **h,**
3:11 touched the wall of the **h,** and its other wing,
3:12 touched the wall of the **h,** and the other wing,
3:15 of the **h** he made two pillars thirty-five cubits high,
4:10 He set the sea at the southeast corner of the **h.**
4:11 that he did for King Solomon for the **h** of God: C
4:16 bronze for King Solomon for the **h** of the LORD. A
4:19 made all the things that were in the **h** of God: C
5: 1 work that Solomon did for the **h** of the LORD A
5: 1 all the vessels in the treasuries of the **h** of God, C
5: 7 in the inner sanctuary of the **h,**
5:13 for his steadfast love endures forever," the **h,**
5:13 the **h** of the LORD, was filled with a cloud, A
5:14 for the glory of the LORD filled the **h** of God. C
6: 2 I have built you an exalted **h,**
6: 5 of the tribes of Israel in which to build a **h,**
6: 7 in mind to build a **h** for the name of the LORD,
6: 8 'You did well to consider building a **h**
6: 9 nevertheless you shall not build the **h,**
6: 9 be born to you shall build the **h** for my name.'
6:10 and have built the **h** for the name of the LORD,
6:18 how much less this **h** that I have built! D
6:20 be open day and night toward this **h,** D
6:22 comes and swears before your altar in this **h,** D
6:24 pray and plead with you in this **h,** D
6:29 that they stretch out their hands toward this **h;** D
6:32 when they come and pray toward this **h,** D
6:33 that your name has been invoked on this **h** D
6:34 that you have chosen and the **h** that I have built
6:38 and the **h** that I have built for your name,
7: 2 The priests could not enter the **h** of the LORD, A
7: 2 the glory of the LORD filled the LORD's **h.** O
7: 5 king and all the people dedicated the **h** of God. C
7: 7 the court that was in front of the **h** of the LORD; A
7:11 Thus Solomon finished the **h** of the LORD and A
7:11 the house of the LORD and the king's **h;** H
7:11 Solomon had planned to do in the **h** of the LORD A
7:11 and in his own **h** he successfully accomplished.

2Ch 7:12 and have chosen this place for myself as a **h**
7:16 For now I have chosen and consecrated this **h** D
7:20 this **h,** which I have consecrated for my name, D
7:21 And regarding this **h,** now exalted, D
7:21 a thing to this land and to this **h?'** D
8: 1 which Solomon had built the **h** of the LORD A
8: 1 built the house of the LORD and his own **h,**
8:11 the city of David to the **h** that he had built for her,
8:11 "My wife shall not live in the **h** of King David
8:16 the foundation of the **h** of the LORD was laid A
8:16 until the **h** of the LORD was finished completely. A
9: 3 the **h** that he had built,
9: 4 offerings that he offered at the **h** of the LORD, A
9:11 the **h** of the LORD and for the king's house, A
9:11 the house of the LORD and for the king's **h,** H
9:16 king put them in the **H** of the Forest of Lebanon.
9:20 the vessels of the **H** of the Forest of Lebanon were
10:16 Look now to your own **h,** O David."
10:19 in rebellion against the **h** of David to this day. I
11: 1 **h** of Judah and Benjamin to fight against Israel, G
12: 9 he took away the treasures of the **h** of the LORD A
12: 9 of the LORD and the treasures of the king's **h;** H
12:10 who kept the door of the king's **h.** H
12:11 Whenever the king went into the **h** of the LORD, A
15: 8 in front of the vestibule of the **h** of the LORD. A
15:18 into the **h** of God the votive gifts of his father C
16: 2 and gold from the treasures of the **h** of the LORD A
16: 2 of the house of the LORD and the king's **h,** H
19: 1 of Judah returned in safety to his **h** in Jerusalem.
19:11 the governor of the **h** of Judah, G
20: 5 in the **h** of the LORD, before the new court, A
20: 9 we will stand before this **h,** and before you, D
20: 9 and before you, for your name is in this **h,** D
20:28 to the **h** of the LORD. A
21: 6 as the **h** of Ahab had done;
21: 7 would not destroy the **h** of David because of I
21:13 as the **h** of Ahab led Israel into unfaithfulness,
21:13 members of your father's **h,** E
21:17 that belonged to the king's **h,** H
22: 3 He also walked in the ways of the **h** of Ahab,
22: 4 as the **h** of Ahab had done;
22: 7 the LORD had anointed to destroy the **h** of Ahab.
22: 8 Jehu was executing judgment on the **h** of Ahab,
22: 9 **h** of Ahaziah had no one able to rule the kingdom.
22:10 to destroy all the royal family of the **h** of Judah. G
22:12 hidden in the **h** of God, C
23: 3 a covenant with the king in the **h** of God. C
23: 5 one third shall be at the king's **h,** H
23: 5 shall be in the courts of the **h** of the LORD. A
23: 6 Do not let anyone enter the **h** of the LORD A
23: 7 and whoever enters the **h** shall be killed.
23: 9 which were in the **h** of God; C
23:10 from the south side of the **h** to the north side of
23:10 of the house to the north side of the **h,**
23:10 around the altar and the **h.**
23:12 she went into the **h** of the LORD to the people; A
23:14 "Do not put her to death in the **h** of the LORD." A
23:15 the entrance of the Horse Gate of the king's **h,** H
23:17 Then all the people went to the **h** of Baal,
23:18 Jehoiada assigned the care of the **h** of the LORD A
23:18 to be in charge of the **h** of the LORD, A
23:19 the gatekeepers at the gates of the **h** of the LORD A
23:20 brought the king down from the **h** of the LORD, A
23:20 marching through the upper gate to the king's **h.** H
24: 4 Joash decided to restore the **h** of the LORD. A
24: 5 from all Israel to repair the **h** of your God, C
24: 7 wicked woman, had broken into the **h** of God, C
24: 7 all the dedicated things of the **h** of the LORD A
24: 8 and set it outside the gate of the **h** of the LORD. A
24:12 had charge of the work of the **h** of the LORD, A
24:12 and carpenters to restore the **h** of the LORD, A
24:12 in iron and bronze to repair the **h** of the LORD. A
24:13 restored the **h** of God to its proper condition C
24:14 with it were made utensils for the **h** of the LORD, A
24:14 in the **h** of the LORD regularly all the days A
24:16 and for God and his **h.**
24:18 They abandoned the **h** of the LORD, A
24:21 to death in the court of the **h** of the LORD. A
24:27 of the rebuilding of the **h** of God are written in C
25:24 all the vessels that were found in the **h** of God, C
25:24 he seized also the treasures of the king's **h,** H
26:19 the presence of the priests in the **h** of the LORD, A
26:21 and being leprous lived in a separate **h,**
26:21 for he was excluded from the **h** of the LORD. A
27: 3 He built the upper gate of the **h** of the LORD, A
28:21 the **h** of the LORD and the houses of the king A
28:24 gathered together the utensils of the **h** of God, C
28:24 and cut in pieces the utensils of the **h** of God. C
28:24 of the **h** of the LORD and made himself altars A
29: 3 he opened the doors of the **h** of the LORD A
29: 5 and sanctify the **h** of the LORD, A
29:15 to cleanse the **h** of the LORD. A
29:16 the inner part of the **h** of the LORD to cleanse it, A
29:16 of the LORD into the court of the **h** of the LORD; A
29:17 for eight days they sanctified the **h** of the LORD, A
29:18 "We have cleansed all the **h** of the LORD, A
29:20 and went up to the **h** of the LORD. A
29:25 the Levites in the **h** of the LORD with cymbals, A
29:31 and thank offerings to the **h** of the LORD." A
29:35 the service of the **h** of the LORD was restored. A
30: 1 that they should come to the **h** of the LORD A
30:15 brought burnt offerings into the **h** of the LORD. A
31:10 chief priest Azariah, who was of the **h** of Zadok,
31:10 to bring the contributions into the **h** of the LORD, A
31:11 to prepare store-chambers in the **h** of the LORD; A
31:13 and of Azariah the chief officer of the **h** of God. C
31:16 all who entered the **h** of the LORD as the duty A

2Ch 31:21 the service of the **h** of God, and in accordance C
32:21 When he came into the **h** of his god, C
33: 4 He built altars in the **h** of the LORD, A
33: 5 of heaven in the two courts of the **h** of the LORD. A
33: 7 the idol that he had made he set in the **h** of God, C
33: 7 "In this **h,** and in Jerusalem, D
33:15 gods and the idol from the **h** of the LORD, A
33:15 built on the mountain of the **h** of the LORD A
33:20 and they buried him in his **h.**
33:24 against him and killed him in his **h.**
34: 8 when he had purged the land and the **h,**
34: 8 recorder, to repair the **h** of the LORD his God. A
34: 9 money that had been brought into the **h** of God, C
34:10 who had the oversight of the **h** of the LORD, A
34:10 who were working in the **h** of the LORD A
34:10 for repairing and restoring the **h.**
34:14 that had been brought into the **h** of the LORD, A
34:15 found the book of the law in the **h** of the LORD"; A
34:17 the money that was found in the **h** of the LORD A
34:30 The king went up to the **h** of the LORD, A
34:30 that had been found in the **h** of the LORD. A
35: 2 in the service of the **h** of the LORD. A
35: 3 the holy ark in the **h** that Solomon son of David,
35: 5 be Levites for each division of an ancestral **h.**
35: 8 and Jehiel, the chief officers of the **h** of God, C
35:21 but against the **h** with which I am at war;
36: 7 of the vessels of the **h** of the LORD to Babylon A
36:10 with the precious vessels of the **h** of the LORD, A
36:14 the **h** of the LORD that he had consecrated A
36:17 in the **h** of their sanctuary, and had no compassion
36:18 All the vessels of the **h** of God, large and small, C
36:18 and the treasures of the **h** of the LORD, A
36:19 They burned the **h** of God, C
36:23 he has charged me to build him a **h** at Jerusalem,
Ezr 1: 2 and he has charged me to build him a **h**
1: 3 and rebuild the **h** of the LORD, A
1: 4 besides freewill offerings for the **h** of God C
1: 5 got ready to go up and rebuild the **h** of the LORD A
1: 7 the vessels of the **h** of the LORD A
1: 7 from Jerusalem and placed in the **h** of his gods.
2:36 the descendants of Jedaiah, of the **h** of Jeshua,
2:68 as they came to the **h** of the LORD in Jerusalem, A
2:68 made freewill offerings for the **h** of God, C
3: 8 the second year after their arrival at the **h** of God C
3: 8 the oversight of the work on the **h** of the LORD. A
3: 9 took charge of the workers in the **h** of God. C
3:11 the foundation of the **h** of the LORD was laid. A
3:12 old people who had seen the first **h**
3:12 wept with a loud voice when they saw this **h,** D
4: 3 "You shall have no part with us in building a **h**
4:24 the work on the **h** of God in Jerusalem stopped C
5: 2 son of Jozadak set out to rebuild the **h** of God C
5: 3 "Who gave you a decree to build this **h** and D
5: 8 to the **h** of the great God. C
5: 9 'Who gave you a decree to build this **h** and D
5:11 of heaven and earth, and we are rebuilding the **h**
5:12 destroyed this **h** and carried away the people D
5:13 a decree that this **h** of God should be rebuilt. CD
5:14 the gold and silver vessels of the **h** of God, C
5:15 and let the **h** of God be rebuilt on its site." C
5:16 the foundations of the **h** of God in Jerusalem; C
5:17 King Cyrus for the rebuilding of this **h** of God CD
6: 3 Concerning the **h** of God at Jerusalem, C
6: 3 the house of God at Jerusalem, let the **h** be rebuilt,
6: 5 let the gold and silver vessels of the **h** of God, C
6: 5 you shall put them in the **h** of God." C
6: 7 let the work on this **h** of God alone; CD
6: 7 the elders of the Jews rebuild this **h** of God CD
6: 8 of the Jews for the rebuilding of this **h** of God: CD
6:11 beam shall be pulled out of the **h** of the perpetrator,
6:11 The **h** shall be made a dunghill.
6:12 or to destroy this **h** of God in Jerusalem. CD
6:15 and this **h** was finished on the third day of D
6:16 the dedication of this **h** of God with joy. CD
6:17 dedication of this **h** of God one hundred bulls, CD
6:22 that he aided them in the work on the **h** of God, C
7:16 willingly for the **h** of their God in Jerusalem. C
7:17 on the altar of the **h** of your God in Jerusalem. C
7:19 given you for the service of the **h** of your God, C
7:20 whatever else is required for the **h** of your God, C
7:23 be done with zeal for the **h** of the God of heaven, C
7:24 or other servants of this **h** of God. CD
7:27 the heart of the king to glorify the **h** of the LORD A
8:17 to send us ministers for the **h** of our God. C
8:25 the offering for the **h** of our God that the king, C
8:29 within the chambers of the **h** of the LORD." A
8:30 to bring them to Jerusalem, to the **h** of our God. C
8:33 On the fourth day, within the **h** of our God, C
8:36 and they supported the people and the **h** of God. C
9: 9 to give us new life to set up the **h** of our God, C
10: 1 throwing himself down before the **h** of God, C
10: 6 Then Ezra withdrew from before the **h** of God, C
10: 9 sat in the open square before the **h** of God, C
Ne 2: 8 and for the **h** that I shall occupy."
3:10 of Harumaph made repairs opposite his **h;**
3:16 far as the artificial pool and the **h** of the warriors.
3:20 to the door of the **h** of the high priest Eliashib.
3:21 from the door of the **h** of Eliashib to the end of
3:21 of the house of Eliashib to the end of the **h**
3:23 and Hasshub made repairs opposite their **h.**
3:23 of Ananiah made repairs beside his own **h.**
3:24 the **h** of Azariah to the Angle and to the corner.
3:25 the tower projecting from the upper **h** of the king
3:28 each one opposite his own **h.**
3:29 of Immer made repairs opposite his own **h.**
3:31 made repairs as far as the **h** of the temple servants
4:16 themselves behind the whole **h** of Judah, GK

Ne 5:13 “So may God shake out everyone from **h** and
6:10 One day when I went into the **h** of Shemaiah son
6:10 who was confined to his **h**, he said,
6:10 he said, “Let us meet together in the **h** of God, C
7:39 descendants of Jedaiah, namely the **h** of Jeshua,
8:16 in their courts and in the courts of the **h** of God, C
10:32 of a shekel for the service of the **h** of our God: C
10:33 and for all the work of the **h** of our God. C
10:34 to bring it into the **h** of our God, C
10:35 year by year, to the **h** of the LORD; A
10:36 to the **h** of our God, to the priests who minister C
10:36 to the priests who minister in the **h** of our God, C
10:37 the priests, to the chambers of the **h** of our God; C
10:38 up a tithe of the tithes to the **h** of our God, C
10:39 We will not neglect the **h** of our God. C
11:11 officer of the **h** of God, C
11:12 and their associates who did the work of the **h**,
11:16 were over the outside work of the **h** of God; C
11:22 singers, in charge of the work of the **h** of God. C
12:37 at the ascent of the wall, above the **h** of David, I
12:40 of those who gave thanks stood in the **h** of God, C
13:4 over the chambers of the **h** of our God, C
13:7 a room for him in the courts of the **h** of God. C
13:9 and I brought back the vessels of the **h** of God, C
13:11 “Why is the **h** of God forsaken?” C
13:14 that I have done for the **h** of my God C
Est 1:22 that every man should be master in his own **h**.
6:12 but Haman hurried to his **h**,
7:8 the queen in my presence, in my own **h**?”
7:9 whose word saved the king, stands at Haman’s **h**,
8:1 to Queen Esther the **h** of Haman, the enemy of
8:2 So Esther set Mordecai over the **h** of Haman.
8:7 “See, I have given Esther the **h** of Haman,
9:4 For Mordecai was powerful in the king’s **h**, H
Job 1:10 a fence around him and his **h** and all that he has,
1:13 and drinking wine in the eldest brother’s **h**,
1:18 and drinking wine in their eldest brother’s **h**,
1:19 struck the four corners of the **h**,
8:14 confidence is gossamer, a spider’s **h** their trust.
8:15 If one leans against its **h**, it will not stand;
17:13 If I look for Sheol as my **h**, F
19:15 the guests in my **h** have forgotten me; F
20:19 they have seized a **h** that they did not build.
20:28 The possessions of their **h** will be carried away,
21:28 For you say, ‘Where is the **h** of the prince?
30:23 and to the **h** appointed for all living.
42:11 and they ate bread with him in his **h**;
Ps 5:7 of your steadfast love, will enter your **h**, I will bow
23:6 in the **h** of the LORD my whole life long. A
26:8 O LORD, I love the **h** in which you dwell,
27:4 in the **h** of the LORD all the days of my life, A
36:8 They feast on the abundance of your **h**,
42:4 and led them in procession to the **h** of God, C
45:10 forget your people and your father’s **h**, E
50:9 I will not accept a bull from your **h**,
52:T *“David has come to the h of Ahimelech.”*
52:8 But I am like a green olive tree in the **h** of God. C
55:14 we walked in the **h** of God with the throng. C
59:T *Saul ordered his h watched in order to kill him.*
65:4 We shall be satisfied with the goodness of your **h**,
66:13 I will come into your **h** with burnt offerings;
69:9 It is zeal for your **h** that has consumed me;
84:4 Happy are those who live in your **h**,
84:10 be a doorkeeper in the **h** of my God than live in C
92:13 They are planted in the **h** of the LORD; A
93:5 holiness befits your **h**, O LORD, forevermore.
98:3 and faithfulness to the **h** of Israel. B
101:2 I will walk with integrity of heart within my **h**; F
101:7 who practices deceit shall remain in my **h**; F
105:21 He made him lord of his **h**,
114:1 the **h** of Jacob from a people of strange language, J
115:10 O **h** of Aaron, trust in the LORD!
115:12 he will bless the **h** of Israel; B
115:12 he will bless the **h** of Aaron;
116:19 in the courts of the **h** of the LORD, A
118:3 Let the **h** of Aaron say,
118:26 We bless you from the **h** of the LORD. A
122:1 “Let us go to the **h** of the LORD!” A
122:5 the thrones of the **h** of David. I
122:9 For the sake of the **h** of the LORD our God, A
127:1 Unless the LORD builds the **h**,
128:3 be like a fruitful vine within your **h**;
132:3 “I will not enter my **h** or get into my bed; F
134:1 who stand by night in the **h** of the LORD! A
135:2 you that stand in the **h** of the LORD, A
135:2 in the courts of the **h** of our God. C
135:19 O **h** of Israel, bless the LORD! B
135:19 O **h** of Aaron, bless the LORD!
135:20 O **h** of Levi, bless the LORD!
Pr 3:33 The LORD’s curse is on the **h** of the wicked,
5:8 and do not go near the door of her **h**;
5:10 and your labors will go to the **h** of an alien;
6:31 they will forfeit all the goods of their **h**.
7:6 window of my **h** I looked out through my lattice, F
7:8 taking the road to her **h**
7:27 Her **h** is the way to Sheol,
9:1 Wisdom has built her **h**, she has hewn her seven
9:14 She sits at the door of her **h**,
12:7 but the **h** of the righteous will stand.
14:1 The wise woman builds her **h**,
14:11 The **h** of the wicked is destroyed,
15:6 In the **h** of the righteous there is much treasure,
15:25 The LORD tears down the **h** of the proud,
17:1 a dry morsel with quiet than a **h** full of feasting
17:13 not depart from the **h** of one who returns evil
19:14 **H** and wealth are inherited from parents,
21:9 in a corner of the housetop than in a **h** shared with

Pr 21:12 The Righteous One observes the **h** of the wicked;
21:20 Precious treasure remains in the **h** of the wise,
24:3 a **h** is built, and by understanding it is established;
24:27 and after that build your **h**.
25:17 Let your foot be seldom in your neighbor’s **h**,
25:24 in a corner of the housetop than in a **h** shared with
27:10 the **h** of your kindred in the day of your calamity.
Ecc 2:7 and had slaves who were born in my **h**; F
5:1 Guard your steps when you go to the **h** of God; C
7:2 It is better to go to the **h** of mourning than to go to
the **h** of feasting;
7:4 The heart of the wise is in the **h** of mourning;
7:4 but the heart of fools is in the **h** of mirth.
10:18 and through indolence the **h** leaks.
12:3 of the **h** tremble, and the strong men are bent,
SS 1:17 the beams of our **h** are cedar, our rafters are pine.
2:4 He brought me to the banqueting **h**,
3:4 until I brought him into my mother’s **h**,
8:2 I would lead you and bring you into the **h**
8:7 If one offered for love all the wealth of his **h**,
Isa 2:2 the LORD’s **h** shall be established as the highest O
2:3 to the **h** of the God of Jacob; C
2:5 O **h** of Jacob, come, let us walk in the light of J
2:6 the ways of your people, O **h** of Jacob. J
3:7 in my **h** there is neither bread nor cloak; F
5:7 vineyard of the LORD of hosts is the **h** of Israel, B
5:8 Ah, you who join **h** to **h**,
6:4 and the **h** filled with smoke.
7:2 the **h** of David heard that Aram had allied itself I
7:13 Then Isaiah said: “Hear then, O **h** of David! I
7:17 on your people and on your ancestral **h** such days
8:17 who is hiding his face from the **h** of Jacob, J
10:20 the survivors of the **h** of Jacob will no more lean J
14:1 and attach themselves to the **h** of Jacob. J
14:2 and the **h** of Israel will possess the nations B
22:8 you looked to the weapons of the **H** of the Forest,
22:18 O you disgrace to your master’s **h**!
22:21 inhabitants of Jerusalem and to the **h** of Judah. G
22:22 place on his shoulder the key of the **h** of David; I
22:23 a throne of honor to his ancestral **h**.
22:24 on him the whole weight of his ancestral **h**,
24:10 every **h** is shut up so that no one can enter.
29:22 concerning the **h** of Jacob: J
31:2 but will rise against the **h** of the evildoers,
37:1 and went into the **h** of the LORD. A
37:14 then Hezekiah went up to the **h** of the LORD A
37:31 the **h** of Judah shall again take root downward, G
37:38 he was worshiping in the **h** of his god Nisroch, C
38:1 Set your **h** in order, for you shall die;
38:20 all the days of our lives, at the **h** of the LORD. A
38:22 the sign that I shall go up to the **h** of the LORD?” A
39:2 he showed them his treasure **h**, the silver, the gold,
39:2 There was nothing in his **h** or in all his realm
39:4 He said, “What have they seen in your **h**?”
39:4 “They have seen all that is in my **h**; F
39:6 Days are coming when all that is in your **h**, and
46:3 Listen to me, O **h** of Jacob, J
46:3 all the remnant of the **h** of Israel, B
48:1 O **h** of Jacob, who are called by the name of J
56:5 in my **h** and within my walls, F
56:7 and make them joyful in my **h** of prayer; F
56:7 for my **h** shall be called a house of prayer F
56:7 for my house shall be called a **h** of prayer
58:1 to the **h** of Jacob their sins. J
58:7 and bring the homeless poor into your **h**;
60:7 and I will glorify my glorious **h**.
63:7 and the great favor to the **h** of Israel B
64:11 Our holy and beautiful **h**,
66:1 what is the **h** that you would build for me,
66:20 in a clean vessel to the **h** of the LORD. A
Jer 2:4 Hear the word of the LORD, O **h** of Jacob, J
2:4 and all the families of the **h** of Israel. B
2:26 so the **h** of Israel shall be shamed— B
3:18 In those days the **h** of Judah shall join the house G
3:18 the house of Judah shall join the **h** of Israel, B
3:20 so you have been faithless to me, O **h** of Israel, B
5:11 For the **h** of Israel and the house B
5:11 the **h** of Judah have been utterly faithless to me, G
5:15 O **h** of Israel, says the LORD. B
5:20 Declare this in the **h** of Jacob, proclaim it in J
7:2 Stand in the gate of the LORD’s **h**, O
7:10 before me in this **h**, which is called by my name, D
7:11 Has this **h**, which is called by my name, D
7:14 I will do to the **h** that is called by my name,
7:30 they have set their abominations in the **h**
9:26 and all the **h** of Israel is uncircumcised in heart. B
10:1 that the LORD speaks to you, O **h** of Israel. B
11:10 **h** of Israel and the house of Judah have broken B
11:10 and the **h** of Judah have broken the covenant G
11:15 What right has my beloved in my **h**, F
11:17 the **h** of Israel and the house of Judah have done, B
11:17 the house of Israel and the **h** of Judah have done, G
12:7 I have forsaken my **h**, I have abandoned my F
12:14 I will pluck up the **h** of Judah from among them. G
13:11 the whole **h** of Israel and the whole house BK
13:11 of Israel and the whole **h** of Judah cling to me, GK
16:5 Do not enter the **h** of mourning, or go to lament,
16:8 not go into the **h** of feasting to sit with them,
17:26 bringing thank offerings to the **h** of the LORD. A
18:2 go down to the potter’s **h**,
18:3 So I went down to the potter’s **h**,
18:6 O **h** of Israel, just as this potter has done? B
18:6 so are you in my hand, O **h** of Israel. B
19:14 he stood in the court of the LORD’s **h** and said O
20:1 who was chief officer in the **h** of the LORD, A
20:2 the upper Benjamin Gate of the **h** of the LORD. A
20:6 And you, Pashhur, and all who live in your **h**,

Jer 21:11 To the **h** of the king of Judah say:
21:12 O **h** of David! Thus says the LORD: I
22:1 Go down to the **h** of the king of Judah,
22:4 through the gates of this **h** shall enter kings D
22:5 that this **h** shall become a desolation. D
22:6 the LORD concerning the **h** of the king of Judah:
22:13 Woe to him who builds his **h** by unrighteousness,
22:14 a spacious **h** with large upper rooms,”
23:8 the **h** of Israel out of the land of the north and B
23:11 even in my **h** I have found their wickedness, F
26:2 Stand in the court of the LORD’s **h**, O
26:2 that come to worship in the **h** of the LORD; A
26:6 then I will make this **h** like Shiloh, D
26:7 in the **h** of the LORD. A
26:9 saying, ‘This **h** shall be like Shiloh, D
26:9 gathered around Jeremiah in the **h** of the LORD. A
26:10 up from the king’s **h** to the house of the LORD H
26:10 the **h** of the LORD and took their seat in the entry A
26:10 the entry of the New Gate of the **h** of the LORD. A
26:12 the LORD who sent me to prophesy against this **h** D
26:18 and the mountain of the **h** a wooded height.’
27:16 of the LORD’s **h** will soon be brought back O
27:18 that the vessels left in the **h** of the LORD, A
27:18 in the **h** of the king of Judah,
27:21 concerning the vessels left in the **h** of the LORD, A
27:21 in the **h** of the king of Judah, and in Jerusalem:
28:1 from Gibeon, spoke to me in the **h** of the LORD, A
28:3 to this place all the vessels of the LORD’s **h**, O
28:5 people who were standing in the **h** of the LORD; A
28:6 from Babylon the vessels of the **h** of the LORD, A
29:26 that there may be officers in the **h** of the LORD A
31:27 the **h** of Israel and the house of Judah B
31:27 the house of Israel and the **h** of Judah G
31:31 a new covenant with the **h** of Israel and B
31:31 with the house of Israel and the **h** of Judah. G
31:33 covenant that I will make with the **h** of Israel B
32:34 up their abominations in the **h** that bears my name,
33:11 they bring thank offerings to the **h** of the LORD: A
33:14 the promise I made to the **h** of Israel and B
33:14 to the house of Israel and the **h** of Judah. G
33:17 a man to sit on the throne of the **h** of Israel, B
34:13 out of the **h** of slavery, saying, N
34:15 before me in the **h** that is called by my name;
35:2 to the **h** of the Rechabites, and speak with them,
35:2 and bring them to the **h** of the LORD, A
35:3 all his sons, and the whole **h** of the Rechabites. K
35:4 to the **h** of the LORD into the chamber of the A
35:7 nor shall you ever build a **h**, or sow seed;
35:18 But to the **h** of the Rechabites Jeremiah said:
36:3 when the **h** of Judah hears of all the disasters G
36:5 I am prevented from entering the **h** of the LORD; A
36:6 of the people in the LORD’s **h** you shall read O
36:8 the words of the LORD in the LORD’s **h**. O
36:10 in the **h** of the LORD, A
36:10 at the entry of the New Gate of the LORD’s **h**. O
36:12 to the king’s **h**, into the secretary’s chamber; H
37:15 and they beat him and imprisoned him in the **h** of
37:16 Thus Jeremiah was put in the cistern **h**, in the cells,
37:17 The king questioned him secretly in his **h**,
37:20 not send me back to the **h** of the secretary Jonathan
38:7 a eunuch in the king’s **h**, H
38:8 So Ebed-melech left the king’s **h** and spoke to H
38:11 the men with him and went to the **h** of the king,
38:17 and you and your **h** shall live.
38:22 of all the women remaining in the **h** of the king
38:26 the king not to send me back to the **h** of Jonathan
39:8 The Chaldeans burned the king’s **h** and H
48:13 as the **h** of Israel was ashamed of Bethel, B
48:45 a flame from the **h** of Sihon;
51:51 into the holy places of the LORD’s **h**. O
52:13 He burned the **h** of the LORD, the king’s house, A
52:13 He burned the house of the LORD, the king’s **h**, H
52:13 every great **h** he burned down.
52:17 pillars of bronze that were in the **h** of the LORD, A
52:17 the bronze sea that were in the **h** of the LORD, A
52:20 Solomon had made for the **h** of the LORD, A
La 1:20 in the **h** it is like death.
2:7 a clamor was raised in the **h** of the LORD as on A
Eze 2:5 or refuse to hear (for they are a rebellious **h**), L
2:6 for they are a rebellious **h**. L
2:7 for they are a rebellious **h**. L
2:8 do not be rebellious like that rebellious **h**; L
3:1 eat this scroll, and go, speak to the **h** of Israel. B
3:4 the **h** of Israel and speak my very words to them. B
3:5 but to the **h** of Israel— B
3:7 But the **h** of Israel will not listen to you, B
3:7 because all the **h** of Israel have a hard forehead B
3:9 for they are a rebellious **h**. L
3:17 I have made you a sentinel for the **h** of Israel; B
3:24 Go, shut yourself inside your **h**.
3:26 for they are a rebellious **h**. L
3:27 for they are a rebellious **h**. L
4:3 This is a sign for the **h** of Israel. B
4:4 place the punishment of the **h** of Israel upon it; B
4:5 you shall bear the punishment of the **h** of Israel. B
4:6 and bear the punishment of the **h** of Judah; G
5:4 a fire will come out against all the **h** of Israel. B
6:11 all the vile abominations of the **h** of Israel! B
8:1 on the fifth day of the month, as I sat in my **h**, F
8:6 that the **h** of Israel are committing here, B
8:10 and all the idols of the **h** of Israel. B
8:11 stood seventy of the elders of the **h** of Israel, B
8:12 the elders of the **h** of Israel are doing in the dark, B
8:14 entrance of the north gate of the **h** of the LORD; A
8:16 into the inner court of the **h** of the LORD; A
8:17 Is it not bad enough that the **h** of Judah commits G
9:3 on which it rested to the threshold of the **h**.

Eze 9: 6 with the elders who were in front of the **h**.
9: 7 Then he said to them, "Defile the **h**,
9: 9 of the **h** of Israel and Judah is exceedingly great; B
10: 3 on the south side of the **h** when the man went in;
10: 4 up from the cherub to the threshold of the **h**;
10: 4 the **h** was filled with the cloud,
10: 18 of the LORD went out from the threshold of the **h**
10: 19 entrance of the east gate of the **h** of the LORD; A
11: 1 brought me to the east gate of the **h** of the LORD, A
11: 5 This is what you think, O **h** of Israel; B
11: 15 your fellow exiles, the whole **h** of Israel, BK
12: 2 you are living in the midst of a rebellious **h**, L
12: 3 for they are a rebellious **h**. L
12: 3 though they are a rebellious **h**. L
12: 6 for I have made you a sign for the **h** of Israel. B
12: 9 has not the **h** of Israel, the rebellious house, B
12: 9 has not the house of Israel, the rebellious **h**, L
12: 10 prince in Jerusalem and all the **h** of Israel in it." B
12: 24 or flattering divination within the **h** of Israel. B
12: 25 but in your days, O rebellious **h**, L
12: 27 the **h** of Israel is saying, "The vision that he sees B
13: 5 or repaired a wall for the **h** of Israel, B
13: 9 nor be enrolled in the register of the **h** of Israel, B
14: 4 **h** of Israel who take their idols into their hearts B
14: 5 I may take hold of the hearts of the **h** of Israel, B
14: 6 say to the **h** of Israel, Thus says the Lord GOD: B
14: 7 For any of those of the **h** of Israel, B
14: 11 the **h** of Israel may no longer go astray from me, B
17: 2 and speak an allegory to the **h** of Israel. B
17: 12 Say now to the rebellious **h**: L
18: 6 or lift up his eyes to the idols of the **h** of Israel, B
18: 15 or lift up his eyes to the idols of the **h** of Israel, B
18: 25 Hear now, O **h** of Israel: Is my way unfair? B
18: 29 **h** of Israel says, "The way of the Lord is unfair." B
18: 29 O **h** of Israel, are my ways unfair? B
18: 30 Therefore I will judge you, O **h** of Israel, B
18: 31 Why will you die, O **h** of Israel? B
20: 5 I swore to the offspring of the **h** of Jacob— J
20: 13 **h** of Israel rebelled against me in the wilderness; B
20: 27 mortal, speak to the **h** of Israel and say to them, B
20: 30 say to the **h** of Israel, Thus says the Lord GOD: B
20: 31 And shall I be consulted by you, O **h** of Israel? B
20: 39 for you, O **h** of Israel, thus says the Lord GOD: B
20: 40 says the Lord GOD, there all the **h** of Israel, B
20: 44 O **h** of Israel, says the Lord GOD. B
22: 18 the **h** of Israel has become dross to me; B
23: 39 This is what they did in my **h**. F
24: 3 And utter an allegory to the rebellious **h** and say L
24: 21 Say to the **h** of Israel, Thus says the Lord GOD: B
25: 3 and over the **h** of Judah when it went into exile; G
25: 8 The **h** of Judah is like all the other nations, G
25: 12 the **h** of Judah and has grievously offended G
28: 24 **h** of Israel shall no longer find a pricking brier B
28: 25 When I gather the **h** of Israel from the peoples B
29: 6 you were a staff of reed to the **h** of Israel; B
29: 16 be the reliance of the **h** of Israel; B
29: 21 cause a horn to sprout up for the **h** of Israel, B
33: 7 mortal, I have made a sentinel for the **h** of Israel; B
33: 10 Now you, mortal, say to the **h** of Israel, B
33: 11 for why will you die, O **h** of Israel? B
33: 20 O **h** of Israel, I will judge all of you according B
34: 30 and that they, the **h** of Israel, are my people, B
35: 15 rejoiced over the inheritance of the **h** of Israel, B
36: 10 the whole **h** of Israel, all of it; BK
36: 17 when the **h** of Israel lived on their own soil, B
36: 21 the **h** of Israel had profaned among the nations B
36: 22 say to the **h** of Israel, Thus says the Lord GOD: B
36: 22 It is not for your sake, O **h** of Israel, B
36: 32 and dismayed for your ways, O **h** of Israel. B
36: 37 let the **h** of Israel ask me to do this for them: B
37: 11 "Mortal, these bones are the whole **h** of Israel. BK
37: 16 (the stick of Ephraim) and all the **h** of Israel B
39: 12 the **h** of Israel shall spend burying them, B
39: 22 The **h** of Israel shall know that I am B
39: 23 **h** of Israel went into captivity for their iniquity, B
39: 25 and have mercy on the whole **h** of Israel; BK
39: 29 when I pour out my spirit upon the **h** of Israel, B
40: 4 declare all that you see to the **h** of Israel." B
43: 7 **h** of Israel shall no more defile my holy name, B
43: 10 mortal, describe the temple to the **h** of Israel, B
44: 6 Say to the rebellious **h**, to the house of Israel, L
44: 6 Say to the rebellious house, to the **h** of Israel, B
44: 6 O **h** of Israel, let there be an end B
44: 12 their idols and made the **h** of Israel stumble B
44: 22 but only a virgin of the stock of the **h** of Israel, B
44: 30 in order that a blessing may rest on your **h**.
45: 6 it shall belong to the whole **h** of Israel. BK
45: 8 but they shall let the **h** of Israel have the land B
45: 17 all the appointed festivals of the **h** of Israel: B
45: 17 to make atonement for the **h** of Israel. B
Da 1: 2 as well as some of the vessels of the **h** of God. C
5: 3 the **h** of God in Jerusalem, C
6: 10 he continued to go to his **h**,
Hos 1: 4 for in a little while I will punish the **h** of Jehu for
1: 4 will put an end to the kingdom of the **h** of Israel. B
1: 6 for I will no longer have pity on the **h** of Israel B
1: 7 But I will have pity on the **h** of Judah, G
5: 1 Give heed, O **h** of Israel! B
5: 1 Listen, O **h** of the king! For the judgment pertains
5: 12 and like rottenness to the **h** of Judah. G
5: 14 and like a young lion to the **h** of Judah. G
6: 10 In the **h** of Israel I have seen a horrible thing; B
8: 1 One like a vulture is over the **h** of the LORD, A
9: 4 it shall not come to the **h** of the LORD. A
9: 8 and hostility in the **h** of his God. C
9: 15 of their deeds I will drive them out of my **h**. F
11: 12 and the **h** of Israel with deceit; B

Joel 1: 9 drink offering are cut off from the **h** of the LORD. A
1: 13 offering are withheld from the **h** of your God. C
1: 14 of the land to the **h** of the LORD your God, A
1: 16 joy and gladness from the **h** of our God? C
3: 18 the **h** of the LORD and water the Wadi Shittim. A
Am 1: 4 So I will send a fire on the **h** of Hazael,
2: 8 and in the **h** of their God they drink wine bought
3: 13 Hear, and testify against the **h** of Jacob, J
3: 15 down the winter **h** as well as the summer house;
3: 15 down the winter house as well as the summer **h**;
5: 1 I take up over you in lamentation, O **h** of Israel: B
5: 4 For thus says the LORD to the **h** of Israel: B
5: 6 he will break out against the **h** of Joseph like fire,
5: 19 went into the **h** and rested a hand against the wall,
5: 25 the forty years in the wilderness, O **h** of Israel? B
6: 1 to whom the **h** of Israel resorts! B
6: 9 If ten people remain in one **h**, they shall die.
6: 10 shall take up the body to bring it out of the **h**,
6: 10 to someone in the innermost parts of the **h**,
6: 11 and the great **h** shall be shattered to bits,
6: 11 and the little **h** to pieces.
6: 14 raising up against you a nation, O **h** of Israel, B
7: 9 and I will rise against the **h** of Jeroboam with
7: 10 against you in the very center of the **h** of Israel; B
7: 16 and do not preach against the **h** of Isaac.'
9: 8 that I will not utterly destroy the **h** of Jacob, J
9: 9 and shake the **h** of Israel among all the nations B
Ob 1: 17 and the **h** of Jacob shall take possession J
1: 18 The **h** of Jacob shall be a fire, J
1: 18 **h** of Joseph a flame, and the **h** of Esau stubble;
1: 18 and there shall be no survivor of the **h** of Esau;
Mic 1: 5 and for the sins of the **h** of Israel. B
2: 2 they oppress householder and **h**,
2: 7 Should this be said, O **h** of Jacob? J
3: 1 you heads of Jacob and rulers of the **h** of Israel! B
3: 9 rulers of the **h** of Jacob and chiefs of the house J
3: 9 house of Jacob and chiefs of the **h** of Israel, B
3: 12 and the mountain of the **h** a wooded height.
4: 1 the LORD's **h** shall be established as the highest O
4: 2 to the **h** of the God of Jacob; C
6: 4 and redeemed you from the **h** of slavery; N
6: 10 treasures of wickedness in the **h** of the wicked,
6: 16 of Omri and all the works of the **h** of Ahab,
Na 1: 14 the **h** of your gods I will cut off the carved image
Hab 2: 10 for your **h** by cutting off many peoples;
3: 13 You crushed the head of the wicked **h**,
Zep 1: 9 who fill their master's **h** with violence and fraud.
2: 7 the possession of the remnant of the **h** of Judah, G
Hag 1: 2 not yet come to rebuild the LORD's **h**. O
1: 4 while this **h** lies in ruins? D
1: 8 Go up to the hills and bring wood and build the **h**,
1: 9 Because my **h** lies in ruins, F
1: 14 and they came and worked on the **h** of the LORD A
2: 3 among you that saw this **h** in its former glory? D
2: 7 and I will fill this **h** with splendor, D
2: 9 The latter splendor of this **h** shall be greater than D
Zec 1: 16 my **h** shall be built in it, says the LORD of hosts, F
3: 7 shall rule my **h** and have charge of my courts, F
4: 9 of Zerubbabel have laid the foundation of this **h**; D
5: 4 and it shall enter the **h** of the thief,
5: 4 the **h** of anyone who swears falsely by my name;
5: 4 and it shall abide in that **h** and consume it,
5: 11 "To the land of Shinar, to build a **h** for it;
6: 10 the same day to the **h** of Josiah son of Zephaniah.
7: 3 of the **h** of the LORD of hosts and the prophets, A
8: 9 the **h** of the LORD of hosts. A
8: 13 O **h** of Judah and house of Israel, G
8: 13 O house of Judah and **h** of Israel, B
8: 15 to do good to Jerusalem and to the **h** of Judah; G
8: 19 and cheerful festivals for the **h** of Judah: G
9: 8 Then I will encamp at my **h** as a guard, F
10: 3 LORD of hosts cares for his flock, the **h** of Judah, G
10: 6 I will strengthen the **h** of Judah, G
10: 6 and I will save the **h** of Joseph.
11: 13 into the treasury in the **h** of the LORD. A
12: 4 But on the **h** of Judah I will keep a watchful eye, G
12: 7 of the **h** of David and the glory of the inhabitants I
12: 8 and the **h** of David shall be like God, I
12: 10 the **h** of David and the inhabitants of Jerusalem, I
12: 12 the family of the **h** of David by itself, I
12: 12 the family of the **h** of Nathan by itself,
12: 13 of the **h** of Levi by itself, and their wives
13: 1 a fountain shall be opened for the **h** of David I
13: 6 "The wounds I received in the **h** of my friends."
14: 20 the **h** of the LORD shall be as holy as the bowls A
14: 21 shall no longer be traders in the **h** of the LORD A
Mal 3: 10 so that there may be food in my **h**, F
Mt 2: 11 the **h**, they saw the child with Mary his mother;
5: 15 and it gives light to all in the **h**.
7: 24 on them will be like a wise man who built his **h**
7: 25 and the winds blew and beat on that **h**,
7: 26 on them will be like a foolish man who built his **h**
7: 27 and the winds blew and beat against that **h**,
8: 14 When Jesus entered Peter's **h**,
9: 10 And as he sat at dinner in the **h**,
9: 23 to the leader's **h** and saw the flute players and
9: 28 he entered the **h**, the blind men came to him;
10: 6 but go rather to the lost sheep of the **h** of Israel. B
10: 12 As you enter the **h**, greet it.
10: 13 If the **h** is worthy, let your peace come upon it;
10: 14 the dust from your feet as you leave that **h** or town.
10: 25 If they have called the master of the **h** Beelzebul,
12: 4 the **h** of God and ate the bread of the Presence, C
12: 25 and no city or **h** divided against itself will stand.
12: 29 a strong man's **h** and plunder his property,
12: 29 Then indeed the **h** can be plundered.
12: 44 says, 'I will return to my **h** from which I came.' F

Mt 13: 1 That same day Jesus went out of the **h** and sat
13: 36 Then he left the crowds and went into the **h**.
13: 57 in their own country and in their own **h**."
15: 24 sent only to the lost sheep of the **h** of Israel." B
21: 13 'My **h** shall be called a house of prayer'; F
21: 13 'My house shall be called a **h** of prayer';
23: 38 See, your **h** is left to you, desolate.
24: 17 not go down to take what is in the **h**;
24: 43 if the owner of the **h** had known in what part of
24: 43 and would not have let his **h** be broken into.
26: 6 Jesus was at Bethany in the **h** of Simon the leper,
26: 18 the Passover at your **h** with my disciples.' "
26: 57 in whose **h** the scribes and the elders had gathered.
Mk 1: 29 they entered the **h** of Simon and Andrew,
2: 15 And as he sat at dinner in Levi's **h**,
2: 26 He entered the **h** of God, C
3: 25 And if a **h** is divided against itself, that **h** will not be able to stand.
3: 27 a strong man's **h** and plunder his property
3: 27 then indeed the **h** can be plundered.
5: 35 some people came from the leader's **h** to say,
5: 38 they came to the **h** of the leader of the synagogue,
6: 4 and among their own kin, and in their own **h**."
6: 10 He said to them, "Wherever you enter a **h**,
7: 17 When he had left the crowd and entered the **h**,
7: 24 a **h** and did not want anyone to know he was there.
9: 28 When he had entered the **h**,
9: 33 and when he was in the **h** he asked them,
10: 10 Then in the **h** the disciples asked him again
10: 29 there is no one who has left **h** or brothers or sisters
11: 17 'My **h** shall be called a house of prayer for all F
11: 17 'My house shall be called a **h** of prayer for all
13: 15 not go down or enter the **h** to take anything away;
13: 35 not know when the master of the **h** will come,
14: 3 he was at Bethany in the **h** of Simon the leper,
14: 14 say to the owner of the **h**, 'The Teacher asks,
Lk 1: 27 a man whose name was Joseph, of the **h** of David. I
1: 33 He will reign over the **h** of Jacob forever, J
1: 40 the **h** of Zechariah and greeted Elizabeth.
1: 69 He has raised up a mighty savior for us in the **h**
2: 4 he was descended from the **h** and family of David.
2: 49 not know that I must be in my Father's **h**?" E
4: 38 After leaving the synagogue he entered Simon's **h**.
5: 29 Then Levi gave a great banquet for him in his **h**;
6: 4 entered the **h** of God and took and ate the bread C
6: 48 That one is like a man building a **h**,
6: 48 the river burst against that **h** but could not shake it,
6: 49 not act is like a man who built a **h** on the ground
6: 49 and great was the ruin of that **h**."
7: 6 but when he was not far from the **h**,
7: 10 When those who had been sent returned to the **h**,
7: 36 into the Pharisee's **h** and took his place at the table.
7: 37 that he was eating in the Pharisee's **h**,
7: 44 "Do you see this woman? I entered your **h**;
8: 27 and he did not live in a **h** but in the tombs.
8: 41 at Jesus' feet and begged him to come to his **h**,
8: 49 someone came from the leader's **h** to say,
8: 51 When he came to the **h**,
9: 4 Whatever **h** you enter, stay there,
10: 5 Whatever **h** you enter, first say,
10: 5 first say, 'Peace to this **h**!' D
10: 7 Remain in the same **h**, eating
10: 7 Do not move about from **h** to **h**.
11: 17 against itself becomes a desert, and **h** falls on **h**.
11: 24 says, 'I will return to my **h** from which I came.' F
12: 39 if the owner of the **h** had known at what hour
12: 39 he would not have let his **h** be broken into.
13: 25 When once the owner of the **h** has got up and shut
13: 35 See, your **h** is left to you.
14: 1 On one occasion when Jesus was going to the **h** of
14: 21 owner of the **h** became angry and said to his slave,
14: 23 so that my **h** may be filled. F
15: 8 sweep the **h**, and search carefully until she finds it?
15: 25 and when he came and approached the **h**,
16: 27 father, I beg you to send him to my father's **h**— E
17: 31 on the housetop who has belongings in the **h** must
18: 29 there is no one who has left **h** or wife or brothers
19: 5 for I must stay at your **h** today."
19: 9 "Today salvation has come to this **h**, D
19: 46 "It is written, 'My **h** shall be a house of prayer'; F
19: 46 "It is written, 'My house shall be a **h** of prayer';
22: 10 follow him into the **h** he enters
22: 11 and say to the owner of the **h**,
22: 54 bringing him into the high priest's **h**.
Jn 2: 16 Stop making my Father's **h** a marketplace!" E
2: 17 "Zeal for your **h** will consume me."
11: 31 The Jews who were with her in the **h**,
12: 3 The **h** was filled with the fragrance of the perfume.
14: 2 In my Father's **h** there are many dwelling places. E
20: 19 of the **h** where the disciples had met were locked
20: 26 A week later his disciples were again in the **h**,
Ac 2: 2 and it filled the entire **h** where they were sitting.
2: 36 the entire **h** of Israel know with certainty B
7: 20 three months he was brought up in his father's **h**; E
7: 42 forty years in the wilderness, O **h** of Israel? B
7: 46 might find a dwelling place for the **h** of Jacob. J
7: 47 But it was Solomon who built a **h** for him.
7: 49 What kind of **h** will you build for me,
8: 3 But Saul was ravaging the church by entering **h**
8: 3 the church by entering house after **h**;
9: 11 and at the **h** of Judas look for a man
9: 17 So Ananias went and entered the **h**.
10: 6 a tanner, whose **h** is by the seaside."
10: 17 They were asking for Simon's **h** and were standing
10: 22 to come to his **h** and to hear what you have to say."
10: 30 I was praying in my **h** when suddenly a man F
11: 11 arrived at the **h** where we were.

Ac 11:12 and we entered the man's **h.**
11:13 the angel standing in his **h** and saying, 'Send
12:12 soon as he realized this, he went to the **h** of Mary,
16:32 of the Lord to him and to all who were in his **h.**
16:34 He brought them up into the **h** and set food
17: 5 to the assembly, they attacked Jason's **h.**
18: 7 to the **h** of a man named Titius Justus, a worshiper
18: 7 his **h** was next door to the synagogue.
19:16 that they fled out of the **h** naked and wounded.
20:20 and teaching you publicly and from **h** to **h,**
21: 8 and we went into the **h** of Philip the evangelist,
21:16 also came along and brought us to the **h** of Mnason
Ro 16: 5 Greet also the church in their **h.**
1Co 16:19 together with the church in their **h,**
2Co 5: 1 a **h** not made with hands, eternal in the heavens.
Col 4:15 and to Nympha and the church in her **h.**
1Ti 5:13 gadding about from **h** to house;
5:13 gadding about from house to **h;**
2Ti 2:20 In a large **h** there are utensils not only of gold
2:21 dedicated and useful to the owner of the **h,**
Phm 1: 2 and to the church in your **h:**
Heb 3: 2 just as Moses also "was faithful in all God's **h.**"
3: 3 the builder of a **h** has more honor than the **h** itself.
3: 4 (For every **h** is built by someone,
3: 5 Moses was faithful in all God's **h** as a servant,
3: 6 however, was faithful over God's **h** as a son,
3: 6 and we are his **h** if we hold firm the confidence
8: 8 with the **h** of Israel and with the house of Judah; B
8: 8 with the house of Israel and with the **h** of Judah; G
8:10 I will make with the **h** of Israel after those days, B
10:21 since we have a great priest over the **h** of God, C
1Pe 2: 5 let yourselves be built into a spiritual **h,**
2Jn 1:10 into the **h** or welcome anyone who comes to you
Tob 1: 4 of my ancestor Naphtali deserted the **h** of David I
1: 5 and our ancestral **h** of Naphtali sacrificed to
3:17 that Tobit returned from the courtyard into his **h,**
6:13 and bring her back with us to your **h.**"
6:16 to take a wife from your father's **h?** E
7: 1 So he took him to Raguel's **h,**
7: 1 Then he brought them into his **h.**
8:11 Raguel went into his **h** and called his wife,
9: 6 into Raguel's **h** they found Tobias reclining
11: 3 and prepare the **h** while they are still on the way."
13:16 For Jerusalem will be built as his **h** for all ages.
Jdt 4:15 to look with favor on the whole **h** of Israel. BK
6:17 had boasted he would do against the **h** of Israel. B
6:21 from the assembly to his own **h** and gave a banquet
8: 5 up a tent for herself on the roof of her **h.**
8: 6 festivals and days of rejoicing of the **h** of Israel. B
9: 1 incense was being offered in the **h** of God C
9:13 and against your sacred **h,**
9:13 and against the **h** your children possess.
10: 2 down into the **h** where she lived on sabbaths and
11: 7 under Nebuchadnezzar and all his **h.**
13:14 not withdrawn his mercy from the **h** of Israel, B
14: 5 recognize the man who despised the **h** of Israel B
14: 6 So they summoned Achior from the **h** of Uzziah.
14:10 he was circumcised, and joined the **h** of Israel, B
14:18 One Hebrew woman has brought disgrace on the **h**
16:23 and grew old in her husband's **h,**
16:24 and the **h** of Israel mourned her for seven days. B
AdE 1:22 so that in every **h** respect would be shown
6:12 and Haman hurried back to his **h,**
7: 8 "Will he dare even assault my wife in my own **h?"**
7: 9 it is standing at Haman's **h,**
14: 9 and to quench your altar and the glory of your **h,**
Wis 8:16 When I enter my **h,** I shall find rest with her; F
Sir 1:17 she fills their whole **h** with desirable goods, K
14:24 near her **h** and fastens his tent peg to her walls;
21: 4 thus the **h** of the proud will be laid waste.
21: 8 Whoever builds his **h** with other people's money is
21:18 Like a **h** in ruins is wisdom to a fool,
21:22 The foot of a fool rushes into a **h,**
23: 11 and the scourge will not leave his **h.**
23:11 for his **h** will be filled with calamities.
27: 3 his **h** will be quickly overthrown.
29:21 bread, and clothing, and also a **h** to assure privacy.
29:22 than sumptuous food in the **h** of others.
29:24 It is a miserable life to go from **h** to **h;**
42:10 seduced and become pregnant in her father's **h;** E
42:11 no spot that overlooks the approaches to the **h.**
47:13 so that he might build a **h** in his name and provide
48:15 but with a ruler from the **h** of David. I
49:12 the **h** and raised a temple holy to the Lord,
50: 1 Simon son of Onias, who in his life repaired the **h,**
50: 5 as he came out of the **h** of the curtain.
51:12 *who makes a horn to sprout for the **h** of David,* I
51:23 and lodge in the **h** of instruction.
Bar 1: 8 Baruch took the vessels of the **h** of the Lord, M
1:14 in the **h** of the Lord on the days of the festivals M
2:26 the **h** that is called by your name you have made
2:26 because of the wickedness of the **h** of Israel B
2:26 of the house of Israel and the **h** of Judah. G
3:24 O Israel, how great is the **h** of God, C
LtJ 6:59 a **h** that protects its contents, than these false gods;
Sus 1: 4 and had a fine garden adjoining his **h;**
1: 6 These men were frequently at Joakim's **h,**
1:26 people in the **h** heard the shouting in the garden,
1:28 people gathered at the **h** of her husband Joakim,
1Mc 1:28 and all the **h** of Jacob was clothed with shame. J
7:35 then if I return safely I will burn up this **h.**" D
7:37 "You chose this **h** to be called by your name, D
7:37 be for your people a **h** of prayer and supplication.
9:55 a word or give commands concerning his **h.**
13: 3 and I and the **h** of my father have done for the laws
13:48 and built in it a **h** for himself.
1Mc 14:26 and the **h** of his father have stood firm;
16: 2 brothers and I and my father's **h** have fought E
2Mc 2:29 as the master builder of a new **h** must be concerned
8:33 who had fled into one little **h;**
14:36 keep undefiled forever this **h** that has been D
15:32 against the holy **h** of the Almighty.
1Es 1: 3 the **h** that King Solomon, son of David, had built;
1:55 They burned the **h** of the Lord, M
2: 4 and he has commanded me to build him a **h**
2: 5 and build the **h** of the Lord of Israel— M
2: 8 to go up to build the **h** in Jerusalem for the Lord;
3: 1 all that were born in his **h,**
5: 5 of the **h** of David, of the lineage of Phares, I
5:44 they would erect the **h** on its site,
5:58 the work on the **h** of God with a single purpose. C
5:62 the Lord for the erection of the **h** of the Lord. M
5:63 old men who had seen the former **h,**
5:70 "You have nothing to do with us in building the **h**
6: 2 son of Jozadak began to build the **h** of the Lord M
6: 4 "By whose order are you building this **h** D
6: 9 in the city of Jerusalem a great new **h** for the Lord,
6:11 'At whose command are you building this **h** D
6:14 The **h** was built many years ago by a king
6:16 and they pulled down the **h,**
6:17 King Cyrus wrote that this **h** should be rebuilt. D
6:18 of the **h** in Jerusalem and stored in his own temple,
6:20 laid the foundations of the **h** of the Lord M
6:22 it is found that the building of the **h** of the Lord M
6:24 the building of the **h** of the Lord in Jerusalem, M
6:26 and that the holy vessels of the **h** of the Lord, M
6:26 of the **h** in Jerusalem and carried away to Babylon,
6:26 should be restored to the **h** in Jerusalem,
6:27 the Jews to build this **h** of the Lord on its site. DM
6:28 until the **h** of the Lord is finished; M
6:32 be taken out of the **h** of the perpetrator,
6:33 or damage that **h** of the Lord in Jerusalem. M
7: 5 the holy **h** was finished by the twenty-third day
8:25 to glorify his **h** that is in Jerusalem,
8:46 to send us men to serve as priests in the **h**
8:55 silver and the gold and the holy vessels of the **h**
8:59 in the chambers of the **h** of our Lord."
8:62 and the gold were weighed and delivered in the **h**
8:79 a light for us in the **h** of the Lord our God, M
Pm 151: 1 and the youngest in my father's **h;** E
3Mc 2:10 And because you love the **h** of Israel, B
2:18 'We have trampled down the **h** of the sanctuary as
2Es 1: 7 out of the **h** of bondage?
1:33 "Thus says the Lord Almighty: Your **h** is desolate;
9:24 into a field of flowers where no **h** has been built,
10:51 to remain in the field where no **h** had been built,
12:46 and do not be sorrowful, O **h** of Jacob; J
14:13 set your **h** in order, and reprove your people;
16:42 and let the one who builds a **h** be like one who will
16:72 and drive them out of **h** and home.
4Mc 18: 7 pure virgin and did not go outside my father's **h;** E

HOUSEHOLD‡ (97) [HOUSE]

Ge 7: 1 "Go into the ark, you and all your **h,**
18:19 that he may charge his children and his **h** after him
24:28 girl ran and told her mother's **h** about these things.
26:14 and a great **h,** so that the Philistines envied him.
30:30 But now when shall I provide for my own **h** also?"
31:19 and Rachel stole her father's **h** gods.
31:34 Now Rachel had taken the **h** gods and put them in
31:35 So he searched, but did not find the **h** gods.
31:37 what have you found of all your **h** goods?
34:30 I shall be destroyed, both I and my **h.**"
35: 2 Jacob said to his **h** and to all who were with him,
36: 6 his daughters, and all the members of his **h,**
39:14 she called out to the members of her **h** and said
45: 2 and the **h** of Pharaoh heard it.
45:11 so that you and your **h,** and all that you have,
46:31 Joseph said to his brothers and to his father's **h,**
46:31 'My brothers and my father's **h,**
47:12 his brothers, and all his father's **h** with food,
50: 4 Joseph addressed the **h** of Pharaoh,
50: 7 of Pharaoh, the elders of his **h,** and all the elders of
50: 8 all the **h** of Joseph, his brothers, and his father's **h.**
50:22 Joseph remained in Egypt, he and his father's **h;**
Ex 1: 1 to Egypt with Jacob, each with his **h:**
12: 3 to take a lamb for each family, a lamb for each **h.**
12: 4 If a **h** is too small for a whole lamb,
Dt 6:22 against Pharaoh and all his **h.**
14:26 you and your **h** rejoicing together.
15:16 because he loves you and your **h,**
15:20 You shall eat it, you together with your **h,**
Jos 7:14 the **h** that the LORD takes shall come near one
7:18 And he brought near his **h** one by one,
24:15 as for me and my **h,** we will serve the LORD."
Jdg 18:25 and you will lose your life and the lives of your **h.**"
1Sa 1:21 The man Elkanah and all his **h** went up to offer to
2:33 all the members of your **h** shall die by the sword.
27: 3 he and his troops, every man with his **h,**
2Sa 2: 3 the men who were with him, every one with his **h;**
6:11 and the LORD blessed Obed-edom and all his **h.**
6:12 the **h** of Obed-edom and all that belongs to him,
6:20 David returned to bless his **h.**
6:21 who chose me in place of your father and all his **h,**
15:16 So the king left, followed by all his **h,**
16: 2 "The donkeys are for the king's **h** to ride,
19:18 to bring over the king's **h,** and to do his pleasure.
19:41 and brought the king and his **h** over the Jordan,
1Ki 4: 7 who provided food for the king and his **h;**
5: 9 by providing food for my **h.**"
5:11 of wheat as food for his **h,**
17:15 that she as well as he and her **h** ate for many days.
2Ki 7: 9 therefore let us go and tell the king's **h.**"
7:11 and proclaimed it to the king's **h.**
8: 1 "Get up and go with your **h,**
8: 2 she went with her **h** and settled in the land of
1Ch 13:14 The ark of God remained with the **h** of Obed-edom
13:14 the LORD blessed the **h** of Obed-edom and all
16:43 and David went home to bless his **h.**
Ne 13: 8 and I threw all the **h** furniture of Tobiah out of
Job 21:21 For what do they care for their **h** after them,
Pr 27:27 of your **h** and nourishment for your servant-girls.
31:15 while it is still night and provides food for her **h**
31:21 She is not afraid for her **h** when it snows,
31:21 for all her **h** are clothed in crimson.
31:27 She looks well to the ways of her **h,**
Isa 22:15 to Shebna, who is master of the **h,** and say to him:
Mic 7: 6 your enemies are members of your own **h.**
Mt 10:25 how much more will they malign those of his **h!**
10:36 and one's foes will be members of one's own **h.**
13:52 of heaven is like the master of a **h** who brings out
24:45 whom his master has put in charge of his **h,**
Lk 12:52 From now on five in one **h** will be divided,
Jn 4:53 So he himself believed, along with his whole **h.**
8:35 slave does not have a permanent place in the **h;**
Ac 7:10 over Egypt and over all his **h.**
10: 2 a devout man who feared God with all his **h;**
11:14 a message by which you and your entire **h** will
16:15 When she and her **h** were baptized, she urged us,
16:31 and you will be saved, you and your **h.**"
16:34 and he and his entire **h** rejoiced that he had become
18: 8 a believer in the Lord, together with all his **h;**
1Co 1:16 (I did baptize also the **h** of Stephanas;
16:15 you know that members of the **h** of Stephanas were
Eph 2:19 with the saints and also members of the **h** of God,
Php 4:22 especially those of the emperor's **h.**
1Ti 3: 4 He must manage his own **h** well,
3: 5 someone does not know how to manage his own **h,**
3:15 you may know how one ought to behave in the **h**
2Ti 1:16 May the Lord grant mercy to the **h** of Onesiphorus,
4:19 Greet Prisca and Aquila, and the **h** of Onesiphorus.
Tit 2: 5 chaste, good managers of the **h,** kind,
Heb 11: 7 the warning and built an ark to save his **h;**
1Pe 4:17 the time has come for judgment to begin with the **h**
Tob 10:10 clothing, money, and **h** goods.
AdE 16:18 hanged at the gate of Susa with all his **h—**
LtJ 6:59 or a **h** utensil that serves its owner's need,
Bel 1:29 or else we will kill you and your **h.**"
2Es 3:11 But you left one of them, Noah with his **h,**

HOUSEHOLDER (2) [HOUSE]

Mic 2: 2 they oppress **h** and house, people and
Mt 13:27 And the slaves of the **h** came and said to him,

HOUSEHOLDS (16) [HOUSE]

Ge 42:19 and carry grain for the famine of your **h,**
42:33 take grain for the famine of your **h,**
45:18 Take your father and your **h** and come to me,
47:24 for the field and as food for yourselves and your **h,**
Nu 16:32 and swallowed them up, along with their **h—**
18:31 You may eat it in any place, you and your **h;**
Dt 11: 6 along with their **h,** their tents,
12: 7 of the LORD your God, you and your **h** together,
Jos 7:14 clan that the LORD takes shall come near by **h,**
Pr 11:29 Those who trouble their **h** will inherit wind,
15:27 for unjust gain make trouble for their **h,**
Jer 23:34 I will punish them and their **h.**
1Ti 3:12 let them manage their children and their **h** well;
5:14 bear children, and manage their **h,**
2Ti 3: 6 among them are those who make their way into **h**
4Mc 2:19 censure the **h** of Simeon and Levi

HOUSES‡ (228) [HOUSE]

Ge 34:29 all that was in the **h.**
Ex 6:14 The following are the heads of their ancestral **h:**
6:25 of the ancestral **h** of the Levites by their families.
8: 3 and into the **h** of your officials and of your people,
8: 9 from you and your **h** and be left only in the Nile."
8:11 and your **h** and your officials and your people;
8:13 frogs died in the **h,** the courtyards, and the fields.
8:21 your officials, and your people, and into your **h;**
8:21 the **h** of the Egyptians shall be filled with swarms
8:24 into the house of Pharaoh and into his officials' **h;**
10: 6 shall fill your **h,** and the **h** of all your officials
12: 7 on the two doorposts and the lintel of the **h**
12:13 The blood shall be a sign for you on the **h**
12:15 the first day you shall remove leaven from your **h,**
12:19 For seven days no leaven shall be found in your **h;**
12:23 the destroyer to enter your **h** to strike you down.
12:27 for he passed over the **h** of the Israelites in Egypt,
12:27 he struck down the Egyptians but spared our **h.**' "
Lev 14:55 for leprous diseases in clothing and **h,**
25:31 But **h** in villages that have no walls
25:32 of redemption of the **h** in the cities belonging
25:33 **h** sold in a city belonging to them—
25:33 because the **h** in the cities of the Levites
Nu 1: 2 by ancestral **h,** according to the number of names,
1:18 in their clans, by their ancestral **h,** according to
1:20 their lineage, in their clans, by their ancestral **h,**
1:22 their lineage, in their clans, by their ancestral **h,**
1:24 their lineage, in their clans, by their ancestral **h,**
1:26 their lineage, in their clans, by their ancestral **h,**
1:28 their lineage, in their clans, by their ancestral **h,**
1:30 their lineage, in their clans, by their ancestral **h,**
1:32 their lineage, in their clans, by their ancestral **h,**
1:34 their lineage, in their clans, by their ancestral **h,**
1:36 their lineage, in their clans, by their ancestral **h,**

Nu 1:38 their lineage, in their clans, by their ancestral **h,**
1:40 their lineage, in their clans, by their ancestral **h,**
1:42 their lineage, in their clans, by their ancestral **h,**
1:45 by their ancestral **h,** from twenty years old
2: 2 under ensigns by their ancestral **h;**
2:32 of the Israelites by their ancestral **h;**
2:34 everyone by clans, according to ancestral **h.**
3:15 Enroll the Levites by ancestral **h** and by clans.
3:20 the clans of the Levites, by their ancestral **h.**
4: 2 by their clans and their ancestral **h,**
4:22 by their ancestral **h** and by their clans;
4:29 by their clans and their ancestral **h;**
4:34 by their clans and their ancestral **h,**
4:38 by their clans and their ancestral **h,**
4:40 ancestral **h** was two thousand six hundred thirty.
4:42 by their clans and their ancestral **h,**
4:46 by their clans and their ancestral **h,**
7: 2 heads of their ancestral **h,** the leaders of the tribes,
17: 2 from all the leaders of their ancestral **h.**
17: 6 one for each leader, according to their ancestral **h,**
26: 2 by their ancestral **h,** everyone in Israel able to go
31:26 the priest and the heads of the ancestral **h** of
32:28 the heads of the ancestral **h** of the Israelite tribes.
34:14 the Reubenites by their ancestral **h** and the tribe of
34:14 by their ancestral **h** have taken their inheritance,
36: 1 of the ancestral **h** of the clans of the descendants
36: 1 the heads of the ancestral **h** of the Israelites;
Dt 6:11 **h** filled with all sorts of goods that you did not fill,
8:12 and have built fine **h** and live in them,
19: 1 and settled in their towns and in their **h,**
Jos 9:12 it was still warm when we took it from our **h**
Jdg 18:22 in the **h** near Micah's house were called out,
20: 8 nor will any of us return to our **h.**
1Sa 31: 9 to carry the good news to the **h** of their idols and to
1Ki 8: 1 the leaders of the ancestral **h** of the Israelites,
9:10 in which Solomon had built the two **h,**
12:31 He also made **h** on high places,
13:32 and against all the **h** of the high places that are in
20: 6 and they shall search your house and the **h**
2Ki 23: 7 He broke down the **h** of the male temple prostitutes
25: 9 the king's house, and all the **h** of Jerusalem;
1Ch 7: 2 Ibsam, and Shemuel, heads of their ancestral **h,**
7: 4 by their generations, according to their ancestral **h,**
7: 7 and Iri, five, heads of ancestral **h,** mighty warriors;
7: 9 as heads of their ancestral **h,** mighty warriors,
7:11 according to the heads of their ancestral **h,**
7:40 heads of ancestral **h,** select mighty warriors,
8: 6 the sons of Ehud (they were heads of ancestral **h** of
8:10 These were his sons, heads of ancestral **h.**
8:13 and Shema (they were heads of ancestral **h** of
8:28 These were the heads of ancestral **h,**
9: 9 of families according to their ancestral **h.**
9:13 besides their kindred, heads of their ancestral **h,**
9:33 the heads of ancestral **h** of the Levites,
9:34 These were heads of ancestral **h** of the Levites,
12:30 mighty warriors, notables in their ancestral **h.**
15: 1 David built **h** for himself in the city of David,
23:24 These were the sons of Levi by their ancestral **h,**
24: 4 under sixteen heads of ancestral **h** of the sons
24: 6 and the heads of ancestral **h** of the priests and of
24:30 of the Levites according to their ancestral **h.**
24:31 and the heads of ancestral **h** of the priests and of
26: 6 in their ancestral **h,** for they were men
26:13 and they cast lots by ancestral **h,**
28:11 and of its **h,** its treasuries, its upper rooms,
29: 6 leaders of ancestral **h** made their freewill offerings,
2Ch 5: 2 leaders of the ancestral **h** of the people of Israel,
17:14 This was the muster of them by ancestral **h:**
25: 5 by ancestral **h** under commanders of the thousands
26:12 The whole number of the heads of ancestral **h**
28:21 the house of the LORD and the **h** of the king and
31:17 of the priests was according to their ancestral **h;**
35: 4 Make preparations by your ancestral **h**
35: 5 to the groupings of the ancestral **h** of your kindred
35:12 to the groupings of the ancestral **h** of the people,
Ne 5: 3 and our **h** in order to get grain during the famine."
5:11 and their **h,** and the interest on money, grain, wine,
7: 3 and others before their own **h."**
7: 4 people within it were few and no **h** had been built.
7:61 not prove their ancestral **h** or their descent,
7:70 of the heads of ancestral **h** contributed to the work.
7:71 And some of the heads of ancestral **h** gave into
8:13 On the second day the heads of ancestral **h** of all
8:16 each on the roofs of their **h,**
9:25 took possession of **h** filled with all sorts of goods,
10:34 by ancestral **h,** at appointed times, year by year,
11:13 heads of ancestral **h,** two hundred forty-two;
12:12 heads of ancestral **h,** were:
12:22 there were recorded the heads of ancestral **h;**
12:23 The Levites, heads of ancestral **h,**
Job 1: 4 to go and hold feasts in one another's **h** in turn;
3:15 who fill their **h** with silver.
4:19 how much more those who live in **h** of clay,
7:10 they return no more to their **h,**
15:28 in **h** that no one should inhabit,
15:28 **h** destined to become heaps of ruins;
21: 9 Their **h** are safe from fear,
22:18 Yet he filled their **h** with good things—
24:16 In the dark they dig through **h;**
27:18 They build their **h** like nests,
Ps 49:16 when the wealth of their **h** increases.
112: 3 Wealth and riches are in their **h,**
Pr 1:13 we shall fill our **h** with booty.
Ecc 2: 4 I built **h** and planted vineyards for myself;
Isa 3:14 the spoil of the poor is in your **h.**
5: 9 Surely many **h** shall be desolate,
5: 9 large and beautiful **h,** without inhabitant.
Isa 6:11 **h** without people, and the land is utterly desolate;
8:14 for both **h** of Israel he will become
13:16 their **h** will be plundered, and their wives ravished.
13:21 and its **h** will be full of howling creatures;
22:10 You counted the **h** of Jerusalem,
22:10 and you broke down the **h** to fortify the wall.
32:13 yes, for all the joyous **h** in the jubilant city.
65:21 They shall build **h** and inhabit them;
Jer 5: 7 they committed adultery and trooped to the **h**
5:27 their **h** are full of treachery;
6:12 Their **h** shall be turned over to others,
17:22 not carry a burden out of your **h** on the sabbath
18:22 May a cry be heard from their **h,**
19:13 the **h** of Jerusalem and the **h** of the kings of Judah
19:13 the **h** upon whose roofs offerings have been made
29: 5 Build **h** and live in them;
29:28 build **h** and live in them,
32:15 **H** and fields and vineyards shall again be bought
32:29 the **h** on whose roofs offerings have been made
33: 4 the **h** of this city and the **h** of the kings of Judah
35: 9 and not to build **h** to live in.
39: 8 The Chaldeans burned the king's house and the **h**
52:13 the king's house, and all the **h** of Jerusalem;
Eze 7:24 of the nations to take possession of their **h.**
11: 3 'The time is not near to build **h;**
16:41 They shall burn your **h** and execute judgments
23:47 and their daughters, and burn up their **h.**
26:12 down your walls and destroy your fine **h.**
28:26 and shall build **h** and plant vineyards.
33:30 and at the doors of the **h,** say to one another,
45: 4 be both a place for their **h** and a holy place for
Da 2: 5 and your **h** shall be laid in ruins.
3:29 be torn limb from limb, and their **h** laid in ruins;
Joel 2: 9 They climb up into the **h,** they enter through the
Am 3:15 and the **h** of ivory shall perish,
3:15 and the great **h** shall come to an end,
5:11 you have built **h** of hewn stone,
Mic 1:14 the **h** of Achzib shall be a deception to the kings
2: 2 They covet fields, and seize them; **h,**
2: 9 of my people you drive out from their pleasant **h;**
Hab 2: 9 "Alas for you who get evil gain for your **h,**
Zep 1:13 be plundered, and their **h** laid waste.
1:13 Though they build **h,** they shall not inhabit them;
2: 7 and in the **h** of Ashkelon they shall lie down
Hag 1: 4 a time for you yourselves to live in your paneled **h,**
1: 9 while all of you hurry off to your own **h.**
Zec 14: 2 be taken and the **h** looted and the women raped;
Mt 19:29 And everyone who has left **h** or brothers or sisters
Mk 10:30 **h,** brothers and sisters, mothers and children,
12:40 They devour widows' **h** and for the sake
Lk 20:47 They devour widows' **h** and for the sake
Ac 4:34 as owned lands or **h** sold them and brought
7:48 Yet the Most High does not dwell in **h** made
Tob 13:17 and all her **h** will cry, 'Hallelujah!
Sir 3: 9 father's blessing strengthens the **h** of the children,
28:14 and overturned the **h** of the great.
49:13 and set up gates and bars, and rebuilt our ruined **h.**
1Mc 1:31 and tore down its **h** and its surrounding walls.
1:55 and offered incense at the doors of the **h** and in
3:56 Those who were building **h,**
13:47 and cleansed the **h** in which the idols were located,
2Mc 3:18 of their **h** in crowds to make a general supplication
5:12 and to kill those who went into their **h.**
1Es 1: 5 to the groupings of the ancestral **h** of you Levites,
1:11 the grouping of the ancestral **h,** before the people,
5: 1 this the heads of ancestral **h** were chosen to go up,
5: 4 according to their ancestral **h** in the tribes,
5:37 by their ancestral **h** or lineage that they belonged
5:63 of the levitical priests and heads of ancestral **h,**
5:68 and the heads of the ancestral **h** and said to them,
5:70 the heads of the ancestral **h** in Israel said to them,
8:28 according to their ancestral **h** and their groups,
8:59 and to the heads of the ancestral **h** of Israel,
9:16 for himself the leading men of their ancestral **h,** all
3Mc 1:20 some in **h** and some in the streets,
2:18 as the **h** of the abominations are trampled down.'
7:18 until all of them arrived at their own **h.**
2Es 1:35 I will give your **h** to a people that will come,
15:18 the **h** shall be destroyed, and people shall be afraid.
15:19 shall make an assault upon their **h** with the sword,
15:49 sword, and pestilence, bringing ruin to your **h,**
16:31 be left by those who search their **h** with the sword.
16:46 overthrow their **h,** and take their children captive;
16:47 their **h** and possessions, and their persons,

HOUSETOP (6) [HOUSE]

Ps 102: 7 I lie awake; I am like a lonely bird on the **h.**
Pr 21: 9 to live in a corner of the **h** than in a house shared
25:24 to live in a corner of the **h** than in a house shared
Mt 24:17 the one on the **h** must not go down to take what is
Mk 13:15 on the **h** must not go down or enter the house
Lk 17:31 on the **h** who has belongings in the house must

HOUSETOPS (9) [HOUSE]

2Ki 19:26 like grass on the **h,** blighted before it is grown.
Ps 129: 6 like the grass on the **h** that withers before it grows
Isa 15: 3 the **h** and in the squares everyone wails and melts
22: 1 that you have gone up, all of you, to the **h,**
37:27 like grass on the **h,** blighted before it is grown.
Jer 48:38 the **h** of Moab and in the squares there is nothing
Mt 10:27 and what you hear whispered, proclaim from the **h.**
Lk 12: 3 behind closed doors will be proclaimed from the **h.**
4Mc 14:15 protect their young by building on the **h,**

HOVERING (1) [HOVERS]

Isa 31: 5 Like birds **h** overhead, so the LORD

HOVERS (1) [HOVERING]

Dt 32:11 As an eagle stirs up its nest, and **h** over its young;

HOW‡ (761)

Ge 6:15 This is **h** you are to make it:
15: 8 **h** am I to know that I shall possess it?"
18:20 **"H** great is the outcry against Sodom and
Gomorrah and **h** very grave their sin!
20: 9 **H** have I sinned against you,
27:20 **"H** is it that you have found it so quickly,
28:17 he was afraid, and said, **"H** awesome is this place!
30:29 "You yourself know **h** I have served you,
30:29 and **h** your cattle have fared with me.
39: 9 **H** then could I do this great wickedness,
42:15 Here is **h** you shall be tested:
44:16 **H** can we clear ourselves?
44:34 For **h** can I go back to my father if the boy is not
45:13 You must tell my father **h** greatly I am honored
47: 8 **"H** many are the years of your life?"
Ex 2:18 **"H** is it that you have come back so soon today?"
3: 9 I have also seen **h** the Egyptians oppress them.
5:16 Look **h** your servants are beaten!
6:12 **h** then shall Pharaoh listen to me,
10: 2 and grandchildren **h** I have made fools of
10: 3 **'H** long will you refuse to humble yourself
10: 7 **"H** long shall this fellow be a snare to us?
12:11 This is **h** you shall eat it:
16:28 The LORD said to Moses, **"H** long will you refuse
18: 1 **h** the LORD had brought Israel out of Egypt.
18: 8 and **h** the LORD had delivered them.
19: 4 and **h** I bore you on eagles' wings and brought you
32: 9 "I have seen this people, **h** stiff-necked they are.
32:13 **h** you swore to them by your own self,
33:16 For **h** shall it be known that I have found favor
36: 1 to know **h** to do any work in the construction of
Nu 4:19 This is **h** you must deal with them in order
8: 4 Now this was **h** the lampstand was made,
14:11 **"H** long will this people despise me?
14:11 And **h** long will they refuse to believe in me,
14:27 **H** long shall this wicked congregation complain
16:28 "This is **h** you shall know that
20:15 **h** our ancestors went down to Egypt, and we lived
23: 8 **H** can I curse whom God has not cursed?
23: 8 **H** can I denounce those whom the LORD has not
24: 5 **h** fair are your tents, O Jacob,
24:22 **H** long shall Asshur take you away captive?"
Dt 1:12 But **h** can I bear the heavy burden
1:31 you saw **h** the LORD your God carried you,
4: 3 **h** the LORD your God destroyed from
4:10 **h** you once stood before the LORD your God
7: 5 But this is **h** you must deal with them:
7:17 more numerous than I; **h** can I dispossess them?"
9: 7 not forget **h** you provoked the LORD your God
11: 4 **h** he made the water of the Red Sea flow over them
11: 6 **h** in the midst of all Israel
12:30 saying, **"H** did these nations worship their gods?
18:21 **"H** can we recognize a word that the LORD has
25:18 **h** he attacked you on the way, when you were faint
29:16 You know **h** we lived in the land of Egypt,
29:16 and **h** we came through the midst of the nations
31:27 For I know well **h** rebellious and stubborn you are.
31:27 **h** much more after my death!
32:30 **H** could one have routed a thousand,
Jos 2:10 For we have heard **h** the LORD dried up the water
9: 7 then **h** can we make a treaty with you?"
10: 1 When King Adoni-zedek of Jerusalem heard **h**
10: 1 and **h** the inhabitants of Gibeon had made peace
14:12 for you heard on that day **h** the Anakim were there,
18: 3 **"H** long will you be slack about going in
Jdg 6:15 He responded, "But sir, **h** can I deliver Israel?
16: 5 and **h** we may overpower him,
16: 6 and **h** you could be bound,
16:10 please tell me **h** you could be bound."
16:13 tell me **h** you could be bound."
16:15 Then she said to him, **"H** can you say, 'I love you,'
18:24 **H** then can you ask me, 'What is the matter?' "
20: 3 "Tell us, **h** did this criminal act come about?"
Ru 2:11 and **h** you left your father and mother
2:18 her mother-in-law saw **h** much she had gleaned.
3:16 **"H** did things go with you, my daughter?"
3:18 my daughter, until you learn **h** the matter turns out,
1Sa 1:14 **"H** long will you make a drunken spectacle
2:22 and **h** they lay with the women who served at
4:16 He said, **"H** did it go, my son?"
5: 7 when the inhabitants of Ashdod saw **h** things were,
10:11 before saw **h** he prophesied with the prophets,
10:27 **"H** can this man save us?"
14:29 see **h** my eyes have brightened because I tasted
14:30 **H** much better if today the troops had eaten freely
14:38 and let us find out **h** this sin has arisen today.
16: 1 **"H** long will you grieve over Saul?
16: 2 Samuel said, **"H** can I go?
17:18 See **h** your brothers fare, and bring some token
21: 5 **h** much more today will their vessels be holy?"
23: 3 **h** much more then if we go to Keilah against
24:10 This very day your eyes have seen **h**
24:18 Today you have explained **h** you have dealt well
28: 9 **h** he has cut off the mediums and the wizards from
29: 4 **h** could this fellow reconcile himself to his lord?
2Sa 1: 4 David said to him, **"H** did things go?
1: 5 **"H** do you know that Saul and his son
1:19 **H** the mighty have fallen!

2Sa 1:25 **H** the mighty have fallen in the midst of the battle!
1:27 **H** the mighty have fallen, and the weapons
2:22 **H** then could I show my face
2:26 **H** long will it be before you order your people
4:11 **H** much more then, when wicked men have killed
6:9 **"H** can the ark of the LORD come into my care?"
6:20 **"H** the king of Israel honored himself today,
11:7 David asked **h** Joab and the people fared,
11:7 and **h** the war was going.
12:18 **h** then can we tell him the child is dead?
13:18 for this is **h** the virgin daughters of
16:11 **h** much more now may this Benjaminite!
19:19 "May my lord not hold me guilty or remember **h**
19:34 **"H** many years have I still to live,
21:3 **H** shall I make expiation, that you may bless
24:2 so that I may know **h** many there are."
1Ki 2:5 **h** he dealt with the two commanders of the armies
3:7 I do not know **h** to go out or come in.
5:6 that there is no one among us who knows **h**
12:6 **"H** do you advise me to answer this people?"
14:19 **h** he warred and **h** he reigned,
18:9 And he said, **"H** have I sinned,
18:13 **h** I hid a hundred of the LORD's prophets fifty to
18:21 **"H** long will you go limping
19:1 and **h** he had killed all the prophets with the sword.
20:7 See **h** this man is seeking trouble;
21:29 "Have you seen **h** Ahab has humbled himself
22:16 **"H** many times must I make you swear
22:22 **'H?'** the LORD asked him.
22:45 that he showed, and **h** he waged war, are they
2Ki 4:43 **"H** can I set this before a hundred people?"
5:7 and see **h** he is trying to pick a quarrel with me."
5:13 **H** much more, when all he said to you was, 'Wash,
6:27 **H** can I help you?
8:5 the king **h** Elisha had restored a dead person to life,
9:11 "You know the sort and **h** they babble."
9:25 and I rode side by side behind his father Ahab **h**
10:4 not withstand him; **h** then can we stand?"
13:4 **h** the king of Aram oppressed them.
14:15 and **h** he fought with King Amaziah of Judah,
14:28 and all that he did, and his might, **h** he fought,
14:28 **h** he recovered for Israel Damascus and Hamath,
17:28 he taught them **h** they should worship the LORD.
18:24 **H** then can you repulse a single captain among
20:3 **h** I have walked before you in faithfulness with
20:20 **h** he made the pool and the conduit
22:19 when you heard **h** I spoke against this place,
1Ch 13:12 **"H** can I bring the ark of God into my care?"
2Ch 6:18 **h** much less this house that I have built!
10:6 **"H** do you advise me to answer this people?"
18:15 **"H** many times must I make you swear
18:20 The LORD asked him, **'H?'**
19:9 He charged them: "This is **h** you shall act:
32:15 **H** much less will your God save you out
33:19 His prayer, and **h** God received his entreaty,
Ne 2:6 **"H** long will you be gone,
2:17 **h** Jerusalem lies in ruins with its gates burned.
Est 2:11 to learn **h** Esther was and **h** she fared.
5:11 and **h** he had advanced him above the officials and
6:2 It was found written **h** Mordecai had told
8:6 For **h** can I bear to see the calamity that is coming
8:6 **h** can I bear to see the destruction of my kindred?"
Job 4:19 **h** much more those who live in houses of clay,
5:17 **"H** happy is the one whom God reproves;
6:24 make me understand **h** I have gone wrong.
6:25 **H** forceful are honest words!
8:2 **"H** long will you say these things,
9:2 but **h** can a mortal be just before God?
9:14 **H** then can I answer him,
13:23 **H** many are my iniquities and my sins?
15:16 **h** much less one who is abominable and corrupt,
16:6 and if I forbear, **h** much of it leaves me?
18:2 **"H** long will you hunt for words?
19:2 **"H** long will you torment me,
19:28 If you say, **'H** we will persecute him!'
21:17 **"H** often is the lamp of the wicked put out?
21:17 **H** often does calamity come upon them?
21:17 **H** often does God distribute pains in his anger?
21:18 **H** often are they like straw before the wind,
21:34 **H** then will you comfort me with empty nothings?
22:12 See the highest stars, **h** lofty they are!
25:4 **H** then can a mortal be righteous before God?
25:4 **H** can one born of woman be pure?
25:6 **h** much less a mortal, who is a maggot,
26:2 **"H** you have helped one who has no power!
26:2 **H** you have assisted the arm that has no strength!
26:3 **H** you have counseled one who has no wisdom,
26:14 and **h** small a whisper do we hear of him!
31:1 **h** then could I look upon a virgin?
32:22 For I do not know **h** to flatter—
35:3 **H** am I better off than if I had sinned?'
35:14 **H** much less when you say that you do not see him,
37:15 Do you know **h** God lays his command upon them,
Ps 3:1 O LORD, **h** many are my foes!
4:2 **H** long, you people, shall my honor suffer shame?
4:2 **H** long will you love vain words,
6:3 while you, O LORD—**h** long?
7:14 See **h** they conceive evil, and are pregnant
8:1 **h** majestic is your name in all the earth!
8:9 **h** majestic is your name in all the earth!
11:1 **h** can you say to me, "Flee like a bird to
13:1 **H** long, O LORD? Will you forget me forever?
13:1 **H** long will you hide your face from me?
13:2 **H** long must I bear pain in my soul,
13:2 **H** long shall my enemy be exalted over me?
21:1 O LORD, and in your help **h** greatly he exults!
25:19 Consider **h** many are my foes,
Ps 31:19 O **h** abundant is your goodness that you have laid
35:17 **H** long, O LORD, will you look on?
36:7 **H** precious is your steadfast love, O God!
39:4 let me know **h** fleeting my life is.
42:4 **h** I went with the throng, and led them in
62:3 **H** long will you assail a person,
66:3 Say to God, **"H** awesome are your deeds!
73:11 And they say, **"H** can God know?
73:16 But when I thought **h** to understand this,
73:19 **H** they are destroyed in a moment,
74:9 and there is no one among us who knows **h** long.
74:10 **H** long, O God, is the foe to scoff?
74:18 Remember this, O LORD, **h** the enemy scoffs,
74:22 remember **h** the impious scoff at you all day long.
78:40 **H** often they rebelled against him in the wilderness
79:5 **H** long, O LORD? Will you be angry
80:4 **h** long will you be angry
82:2 **H** long will you judge unjustly and show partiality
84:1 **H** lovely is your dwelling place,
89:46 **H** long, O LORD? Will you hide yourself forever?
89:46 **H** long will your wrath burn like fire?
89:47 Remember **h** short my time is—
89:50 Remember, O Lord, **h** your servant is taunted;
89:50 **h** I bear in my bosom the insults of the peoples,
90:13 O LORD! **H** long? Have compassion on your
92:5 **H** great are your works, O LORD!
94:3 O LORD, **h** long shall the wicked,
94:3 **h** long shall the wicked exult?
103:14 For he knows **h** we were made;
104:24 O LORD, **h** manifold are your works!
119:9 **H** can young people keep their way pure?
119:84 **H** long must your servant endure?
119:97 Oh, **h** I love your law!
119:103 **H** sweet are your words to my taste,
119:159 Consider **h** I love your precepts;
132:2 **h** he swore to the LORD and vowed to
133:1 **H** very good and pleasant it is
137:4 **H** could we sing the LORD's song in
137:7 **h** they said, "Tear it down!
139:17 **H** weighty to me are your thoughts, O God!
139:17 **H** vast is the sum of them!
147:1 **H** good it is to sing praises to our God;
Pr 1:22 **H** long, O simple ones, will you love being simple?
1:22 **H** long will scoffers delight in their scoffing
5:12 and you say, "Oh, **h** I hated discipline,
6:9 **H** long will you lie there, O lazybones?
6:35 and refuses a bribe no matter **h** great.
11:31 **h** much more the wicked and the sinner!
15:11 **h** much more human hearts!
15:23 and a word in season, **h** good it is!
15:28 The mind of the righteous ponders **h** to answer,
16:16 **H** much better to get wisdom than gold!
19:7 **h** much more are they shunned by their friends!
20:24 **h** then can we understand our own ways?
21:27 **h** much more when brought with evil intent.
30:1 I am weary, O God. **H** can I prevail?
30:13 **h** lofty are their eyes, **h** high their eyelids lift!
Ecc 2:3 with my mind **h** to cheer my body with wine—
2:3 and **h** to lay hold on folly,
2:16 **H** can the wise die just like fools?
4:11 but **h** can one keep warm alone?
5:1 for they do not know **h** to keep from doing evil.
6:8 the poor have who know **h** to conduct themselves
6:11 the more vanity, so **h** is one the better?
8:7 for who can tell them **h** it will be?
8:16 **h** one's eyes see sleep neither day nor night,
9:1 **h** the righteous and the wise and their deeds are in
11:5 Just as you do not know **h** the breath comes to
SS 4:1 **H** beautiful you are, my love, **h** very beautiful!
4:10 **H** sweet is your love, my sister, my bride!
4:10 **h** much better is your love than wine,
5:3 **h** could I put it on again?
5:3 I had bathed my feet; **h** could I soil them?
7:1 **H** graceful are your feet in sandals,
7:6 **H** fair and pleasant you are, O loved one,
Isa 1:21 **H** the faithful city has become a whore!
3:10 Tell the innocent **h** fortunate they are,
3:11 to the guilty! **H** unfortunate they are,
6:11 Then I said, **"H** long, O Lord?"
7:15 the time he knows **h** to refuse the evil and choose
7:16 the child knows **h** to refuse the evil and choose
8:4 child knows **h** to call "My father" or "My mother,"
14:4 **H** the oppressor has ceased!
14:4 **H** his insolence has ceased!
14:12 **H** you are fallen from heaven, O Day Star,
14:12 **H** you are cut down to the ground,
16:6 heard of the pride of Moab—**h** proud he is!—
19:11 **H** can you say to Pharaoh, "I am one of the sages,
20:6 And we, **h** shall we escape?' "
36:9 **H** then can you repulse a single captain among
38:3 **h** I have walked before you in faithfulness with
50:4 I may know **h** to sustain the weary with a word.
52:7 **H** beautiful upon the mountains are the feet of
Jer 1:6 Truly I do not know **h** to speak,
2:2 **h** you followed me in the wilderness,
2:21 **H** then did you turn degenerate and become
2:23 **H** can you say, "I am not defiled,
2:33 **H** well you direct your course to seek lovers!
2:36 **H** lightly you gad about, changing your ways!
3:5 This is **h** you have spoken,
3:6 that faithless one, Israel, **h** she went up
3:19 I thought **h** I would set you among my children,
4:10 **h** utterly you have deceived this people
4:14 **H** long shall your evil schemes lodge within you?
4:18 This is your doom; **h** bitter it is!
4:21 **H** long must I see the standard,
4:22 but do not know **h** to do good."
Jer 5:7 **H** can I pardon you?
6:15 they did not know **h** to blush.
8:8 **H** can you say, "We are wise,
8:12 they did not know **h** to blush.
9:19 from Zion: **"H** we are ruined!
12:4 **H** long will the land mourn,
12:5 **h** will you compete with horses?
12:5 **h** will you fare in the thickets of the Jordan?
13:27 **H** long will it be before you are made clean?
17:15 See **h** they say to me,
18:20 Remember **h** I stood before you to speak good
22:23 **h** you will groan when pangs come upon you,
23:26 **H** long? Will the hearts of the
25:29 and **h** can you possibly avoid punishment?
28:11 This is **h** I will break the yoke
31:22 **H** long will you waver, O faithless daughter?
33:24 Have you not observed **h** these people say,
33:24 and **h** they hold my people in such contempt
36:17 "Tell us now, **h** did you write all these words?
47:5 **H** long will you gash yourselves?
47:6 **H** long until you are quiet?
47:7 **H** can it be quiet, when the LORD has given it
48:14 **H** can you say, "We are heroes
48:17 say, **"H** the mighty scepter is broken,
48:39 **H** it is broken! **H** they wail!
48:39 **H** Moab has turned his back in shame!
49:25 **H** the famous city is forsaken, the joyful town!
50:23 **H** the hammer of the whole earth is cut down
50:23 **H** Babylon has become a horror among the
51:41 **H** Sheshach is taken, the pride of the whole earth
51:41 **H** Babylon has become an object of horror among
La 1:1 **H** lonely sits the city that once was full of people!
1:1 **H** like a widow she has become,
1:11 O LORD, and see **h** worthless I have become.
1:20 See, O LORD, **h** distressed I am;
1:21 They heard **h** I was groaning,
2:1 **H** the Lord in his anger has humiliated daughter
4:1 **H** the gold has grown dim, **h** the pure gold is changed!
4:2 **h** they are reckoned as earthen pots,
Eze 6:9 **h** I was crushed by their wanton heart
14:21 **H** much more when I send
15:2 O mortal, **h** does the wood of
15:5 for nothing; **h** much less—
16:30 **H** sick is your heart, says the Lord GOD,
21:10 **H** can we make merry? You have despised the rod,
26:17 **H** you have vanished from the seas,
33:10 of them; **h** then can we live?"
44:23 and show them **h** to distinguish between
Da 4:3 **H** great are his signs, **h** mighty his wonders!
8:13 "For **h** long is this vision concerning
10:17 **H** can my lord's servant talk with my lord?
12:6 **"H** long shall it be until the end of these wonders?"
Hos 8:5 **H** long will they be incapable of innocence?
11:8 **H** can I give you up, Ephraim?
11:8 **H** can I hand you over, O Israel?
11:8 **H** can I make you like Admah?
11:8 **H** can I treat you like Zeboiim?
Joel 1:18 **H** the animals groan! The herds of cattle
2:11 **h** vast is his host! Numberless are those who obey
Am 3:10 They do not know **h** to do right, says the LORD,
5:12 For I know **h** many are your transgressions,
5:12 and **h** great are your sins—
7:2 I beg you! **H** can Jacob stand?
7:5 I beg you! **H** can Jacob stand?
Ob 1:5 plunderers by night —**h** you have been destroyed!
1:6 **H** Esau has been pillaged, his treasures searched
Jnh 2:4 **h** shall I look again upon your holy temple?'
3:10 **h** they turned from their evil ways,
Mic 2:4 **h** he removes it from me
Hab 1:2 O LORD, **h** long shall I cry for help,
2:6 **H** long will you load yourselves with goods taken
Zep 2:8 **h** they have taunted my people and made boasts
Hag 1:5 Consider **h** you have fared.
1:7 Consider **h** you have fared.
2:3 **H** does it look to you now?
2:16 **h** did you fare? When one came to a
Zec 1:12 **h** long will you withhold mercy from Jerusalem
Mal 1:2 But you say, **"H** have you loved us?"
1:6 You say, **"H** have we despised your name?"
1:7 And you say, **"H** have we polluted it?"
2:17 Yet you say, **"H** have we wearied him?"
3:7 But you say, **"H** shall we return?"
3:8 But you say, **"H** are we robbing you?"
3:13 Yet you say, **"H** have we spoken against you?"
Mt 5:13 salt has lost its taste, **h** can its saltiness be restored?
6:23 the light in you is darkness, **h** great is the darkness!
6:28 Consider the lilies of the field, **h** they grow;
7:4 Or **h** can you say to your neighbor,
7:11 know **h** to give good gifts to your children,
7:11 **h** much more will your Father
10:19 not worry about **h** you are to speak or what you are
10:25 **h** much more will they malign those
12:12 **H** much more valuable is a human being than
12:14 and conspired against him, **h** to destroy him.
12:26 **h** then will his kingdom stand?
12:29 Or **h** can one enter a strong man's house
12:34 **H** can you speak good things, when you are evil?
15:34 Jesus asked them, **"H** many loaves have you?"
16:3 You know **h** to interpret the appearance of the sky,
16:9 and **h** many baskets you gathered?
16:10 and **h** many baskets you gathered?
16:11 **H** could you fail to perceive that I was not
17:17 **H** much longer must I be with you?
17:17 **H** much longer must I put up with you?
18:21 sins against me, **h** often should I forgive?
21:20 saying, **"H** did the fig tree wither at once?"

Mt 22:12 **h** did you get in here without a wedding robe?'
22:43 "**H** is it then that David by
22:45 If David thus calls him Lord, **h** can he be his son?"
23:19 **H** blind you are! For which is greater,
23:33 **H** can you escape being sentenced to hell?
23:37 **H** often have I desired to gather your children
26:54 But **h** then would the scriptures be fulfilled,
26:58 with the guards in order to see **h** this would end.
27:13 "Do you not hear **h** many accusations they make
Mk 3: 6 with the Herodians against him, **h** to destroy him.
3:23 "**H** can Satan cast out Satan?
4:13 Then **h** will you understand all the parables?
4:27 and grow, he does not know **h.**
5:19 and tell them **h** much the Lord has done for you,
5:20 in the Decapolis **h** much Jesus had done for him;
5:31 **h** can you say, 'Who touched me?' "
6:38 And he said to them, "**H** many loaves have you?
8: 4 "**H** can one feed these people with bread here in
8: 5 He asked them, "**H** many loaves do you have?"
8:19 for the five thousand, **h** many baskets full
8:20 for the four thousand, **h** many baskets full
9:12 **H** then is it written about the Son of Man,
9:19 **h** much longer must I be among you?
9:19 **H** much longer must I put up with you?
9:21 "**H** long has this been happening to him?"
9:50 but if salt has lost its saltiness, **h** can you season it?
10:23 "**H** hard it will be for those who have wealth
10:24 **h** hard it is to enter the kingdom of God!
12:26 **h** God said to him, 'I am the God of Abraham,
12:35 "**H** can the scribes say that the Messiah is the son
12:37 so **h** can he be his son?"
15: 4 See **h** many charges they bring against you."
Lk 1:18 "**H** will I know that this is so?
1:34 Mary said to the angel, "**H** can this be,
6:42 Or **h** can you say to your neighbor, 'Friend,
8:18 Then pay attention to **h** you listen;
8:36 Those who had seen it told them **h**
8:39 and declare **h** much God has done for you."
8:39 throughout the city **h** much Jesus had done
8:47 and **h** she had been immediately healed.
9:41 **h** much longer must I be with you and bear
11:13 know **h** to give good gifts to your children,
11:13 **h** much more will the heavenly Father give
11:18 against himself, **h** will his kingdom stand?
12:11 do not worry about **h** you are to defend yourselves
12:24 Of **h** much more value are you than the birds!
12:27 Consider the lilies, **h** they grow:
12:28 **h** much more will he clothe you—
12:49 and **h** I wish it were already kindled!
12:56 You know **h** to interpret the appearance of earth
12:56 not know **h** to interpret the present time?
13:34 **H** often have I desired to gather your children
14: 7 he noticed **h** the guests chose the places of honor,
14:34 salt has lost its taste, **h** can its saltiness be restored?
15:17 But when he came to himself he said, '**H** many
16: 5 '**H** much do you owe my master?'
16: 7 Then he asked another, 'And **h** much do you owe?'
18:24 "**H** hard it is for those who have wealth to enter
20:41 "**H** can they say that the Messiah is David's son?
20:44 so **h** can he be his son?"
21: 5 **h** it was adorned with beautiful stones
22: 4 of the temple police about **h** he might betray him
22:61 **h** he had said to him,
23:55 and they saw the tomb and **h** his body was laid.
24: 6 Remember **h** he told you, while he was still
24:20 and **h** our chief priests and leaders handed him
24:25 "Oh, **h** foolish you are, and **h** slow of heart to
24:35 and **h** he had been made known to them in
Jn 3: 4 "**H** can anyone be born after having grown old?
3: 9 Nicodemus said to him, "**H** can these things be?"
3:12 **h** can you believe if I tell you
4: 9 Samaritan woman said to him, "**H** is it that you,
4:35 and see **h** the fields are ripe for harvesting.
5:44 **H** can you believe when you accept glory
5:47 **h** will you believe what I say?"
6:42 **H** can he now say, 'I have come down
6:52 saying, "**H** can this man give us his flesh to eat?"
7:15 saying, "**H** does this man have such learning,
9:10 "Then **h** were your eyes opened?"
9:15 also began to ask him **h** he had received his sight
9:16 "**H** can a man who is a sinner perform such signs?"
9:19 **H** then does he now see?"
9:21 but we do not know **h** it is that now he sees,
9:26 **H** did he open your eyes?"
10:24 "**H** long will you keep us in suspense?
11:36 So the Jews said, "See **h** he loved him!"
12:34 **H** can you say that the Son of Man must
14: 5 **H** can we know the way?"
14: 9 **H** can you say, 'Show us the Father'?
14:22 "Lord, **h** is it that you will reveal yourself to us,
18:22 saying, "Is that **h** you answer the high priest?"
Ac 2: 8 And **h** is it that we hear, each of us,
4: 9 and are asked **h** this man has been healed,
5: 4 **H** is it that you have contrived this deed
5: 9 "**H** is it that you have agreed together to put
8:31 He replied, "**H** can I, unless someone guides me?"
9:13 **h** much evil he has done to your saints
9:16 I myself will show him **h** much he must suffer for
9:27 and described for them **h** on the road he had seen
9:27 and **h** in Damascus he had spoken boldly in
10:38 **h** God anointed Jesus of Nazareth with the Holy
10:38 **h** he went about doing good
11:13 He told us **h** he had seen the angel standing
11:16 I remembered the word of the Lord, **h** he had said,
12:17 for them **h** the Lord had brought him out of
14:27 **h** he had opened a door of faith for the Gentiles.
15:14 Simeon has related **h** God first looked favorably on
Ac 15:36 the word of the Lord and see **h** they are doing."
17:22 I see **h** extremely religious you are in every way.
20:18 "You yourselves know **h** I lived among you
21:20 **h** many thousands of believers there are among
25:20 I was at a loss **h** to investigate these questions,
Ro 3: 6 For then **h** could God judge the world?
4:10 **H** then was it reckoned to him?
6: 2 **H** can we who died to sin go on living in it?
8:26 for we do not know **h** to pray as we ought,
10:14 But **h** are they to call on one in whom they have
10:14 And **h** are they to believe in one
10:14 And **h** are they to hear without someone
10:15 **h** are they to proclaim him unless they are sent?
10:15 As it is written, "**H** beautiful are the feet
11: 2 **h** he pleads with God against Israel?
11:12 **h** much more will their full inclusion mean!
11:24 **h** much more will these natural branches
11:33 **H** unsearchable are his judgments and **h**
inscrutable his ways!
13:11 **h** it is now the moment for you to wake from sleep.
1Co 3:10 Each builder must choose with care **h** to build
7:32 about the affairs of the Lord, **h** to please the Lord;
7:33 about the affairs of the world, **h** to please his wife,
7:34 the affairs of the world, **h** to please her husband.
14: 6 **h** will I benefit you unless I speak to you
14: 7 **h** will anyone know what is being played?
14: 9 **h** will anyone know what is being said?
14:16 **h** can anyone in the position of an outsider say
15:12 **h** can some of you say there is no resurrection of
15:35 But someone will ask, "**H** are the dead raised?
2Co 3: 8 **h** much more will the ministry of the Spirit come
7:15 and **h** you welcomed him with fear and trembling.
12:13 **H** have you been worse off than the other churches
Gal 2:14 **h** can you compel the Gentiles to live like Jews?"
4: 9 **h** can you turn back again to the weak
4: 9 **H** can you want to be enslaved to them again?
Eph 3: 3 and **h** the mystery was made known to me
5:15 Be careful then **h** you live,
6:21 you also may know **h** I am and what I am doing,
6:22 to let you know **h** we are,
Php 1: 8 **h** I long for all of you with the compassion
2:22 **h** like a son with a father he has served with me in
2:23 therefore to send him as soon as I see **h** things go
Col 1:27 To them God chose to make known **h** great among
2: 1 For I want you to know **h** much I am struggling
4: 6 you may know **h** you ought to answer everyone.
4: 8 so that you may know **h** we are and
1Th 1: 9 and **h** you turned to God from idols,
2:10 You are witnesses, and God also, **h** pure, upright,
3: 9 **H** can we thank God enough for you in return
4: 1 from us **h** you ought to live and to please God (as,
4: 4 of you know **h** to control your own body
2Th 3: 7 you yourselves know **h** you ought to imitate us;
1Ti 3: 5 not know **h** to manage his own household,
3: 5 **h** can he take care of God's church?
3:15 you may know **h** one ought to behave in
2Ti 1:18 And you know very well **h**
3:15 and **h** from childhood you have known
Phm 1:16 especially to me but **h** much more to you,
Heb 2: 3 **h** can we escape if we neglect so great a salvation?
7: 4 See **h** great he is!
9:14 **h** much more will the blood of Christ,
10:24 And let us consider **h** to provoke one another
10:29 **H** much worse punishment do you think will
12:25 on earth, **h** much less will we escape if we reject
Jas 3: 5 **H** great a forest is set ablaze by a small fire!
5:11 **h** the Lord is compassionate and merciful.
2Pe 2: 9 the Lord knows **h** to rescue the godly from trial,
1Jn 3:17 **H** does God's love abide in anyone who has
3Jn 1: 3 namely **h** you walk in the truth.
Rev 6:10 **h** long will it be before you judge
9:17 And this was **h** I saw the horses in my vision:
Tob 2: 6 the prophecy of Amos, **h** he said against Bethel,
5: 2 but **h** can I obtain the money from him,
5: 2 not know the roads to Media, or **h** to get there."
7: 2 to his wife Edna, "**H** much
10: 1 Now, day by day, Tobit kept counting **h**
10: 7 I have already explained to you **h** I left him."
11: 2 "You are aware of **h** we left your father.
12: 2 He replied, "Father, **h** much shall I pay him?
12: 3 **H** much extra shall I give him as a bonus?"
13:16 **H** happy I will be if a remnant
Jdt 4: 1 **h** he had plundered and destroyed all their temples,
5: 3 **H** large is their army, and in what does their power
8: 9 and **h** he promised them under oath to surrender
8:14 **h** do you expect to search out God,
8:26 and **h** he tested Isaac, and what happened to Jacob
AdE 1:13 "This is **h** Vashti has answered me.
1:17 the queen had said and **h** she had defied the king).
2: 1 or remembered what he had said and **h**
4: 7 So Mordecai told him what had happened and **h**
5:11 and **h** he had advanced him to be the first in
6: 2 **h** he had told the king about
8: 6 **H** can I look on the ruin of my people?
8: 6 **H** can I be safe if my ancestral nation is
9:24 —**h** Haman son of Hammedatha,
9:24 **h** he made a decree and cast lots to destroy them,
9:25 and **h** he went in to the king, telling him
13: 3 "When I asked my counselors **h** this might
Wis 2:19 so that we may find out **h** gentle he is,
6:22 I will tell you what wisdom is and **h** she came to
8:18 I went about seeking **h** to get her for myself.
11: 8 at that time **h** you punished their enemies.
11: 9 they learned **h** the ungodly were tormented
11:25 **H** would anything have endured if you had
11:25 Or **h** would anything not called forth
13: 3 them know **h** much better than these is their Lord,
Wis 13: 4 from them **h** much more powerful is the one who
13: 9 **h** did they fail to find sooner the Lord
16: 4 while to these others it was merely shown **h**
19: 2 **h,** though they themselves had permitted your
19:10 **h** instead of producing animals
Sir 7:28 **h** can you repay what they have given to you?
8: 8 because from them you will learn discipline and **h**
8: 9 from them you learn **h** to understand and to give
10: 9 **H** can dust and ashes be proud?
10:31 honored in poverty, **h** much more in wealth!
10:31 one dishonored in wealth, **h** much more in poverty!
11:19 not know **h** long it will be until he leaves them
11:28 by **h** he ends, a person becomes known.
13: 2 **H** can the clay pot associate with the iron kettle?
17:29 **H** great is the mercy of the Lord,
20: 2 **H** much better it is to rebuke than to fume!
20:17 **H** many will ridicule him, and **h** often!
25: 3 **h** can you find anything in your old age?
25: 4 **H** attractive is sound judgment in the gray-haired,
25: 5 **H** attractive is wisdom in the aged,
25:10 **H** great is the one who finds wisdom!
31:12 and do not say, "**H** much food there is here!"
31:19 **H** ample a little is for a well-disciplined person!
38:25 **H** can one become wise who handles the plow,
38:34 **H** different the one who devotes himself to
41: 1 **h** bitter is the thought of you to the one at peace
41: 2 **h** welcome is your sentence to one who is needy
42:22 **H** desirable are all his works, and **h** sparkling they
43: 8 **h** marvelous it is in this change,
46: 2 **H** glorious he was when he lifted his hands
46:10 so that all the Israelites might see **h** good it is
47:14 **H** wise you were when you were young!
48: 4 **H** glorious you were, Elijah,
49:11 **H** shall we magnify Zerubbabel?
50: 4 He considered **h** to save his people from ruin,
50: 5 **H** glorious he was, surrounded by the people,
Bar 3:24 O Israel, **h** great is the house of God,
3:24 **h** vast the territory that he possesses!
4:17 But I, **h** can I help you?
LtJ 6:30 For **h** can they be called gods?
6:47 **h** then can the things that are made by them
6:49 **H** then can one fail to see that these are not gods,
Sus 1:57 This is **h** you have been treating the daughters
Bel 1: 6 not see **h** much he eats and drinks every day?"
1Mc 3:17 they said to Judas, "**H** can we, few as we are,
3:53 **H** will we be able to withstand them,
4: 9 Remember **h** our ancestors were saved at
4:35 and **h** ready they were either to live or to die nobly,
6:22 "**H** long will you fail to do justice and
8: 2 **h** they had defeated them and forced them
8: 4 and **h** they had gained control of the whole region
9:21 "**H** is the mighty fallen, the savior of Israel!"
9:38 Remembering **h** their brother John had been killed,
10:46 in Israel and **h** much he had oppressed them.
14:25 "**H** shall we thank Simon and his sons?
2Mc 6:28 and leave to the young a noble example of **h** to die
7:17 and see **h** his mighty power will torture you
7:22 not know **h** you came into being in my womb.
8:19 **h,** in the time of Sennacherib,
9:25 I understand **h** the princes along the borders and
10: 6 remembering **h** not long before,
13:26 This is **h** the king's attack
15:37 This, then, is **h** matters turned out with Nicanor,
1Es 1:24 and **h** they grieved the Lord deeply,
3:18 **h** is wine the strongest? It leads astray the minds
3Mc 5:37 "**H** many times, you poor wretch,
5:40 **h** long will you put us to the test,
2Es 1: 9 **H** long shall I endure them,
2:48 tell my people **h** great and how many are
2:48 and **h** many are the wonders of the Lord God
3:30 because I have seen **h** you endure those who sin,
3:31 and have not shown to anyone **h** your way may
4: 7 '**H** many dwellings are in the heart of the sea,
4: 7 or **h** many streams are at the source of the deep,
4: 7 or **h** many streams are above the firmament,
4:11 **h** then can your mind comprehend the way of
4:11 And **h** can one who is already worn out by
4:30 **h** much ungodliness it has produced until now—
4:31 for yourself **h** much fruit of ungodliness a grain
4:32 **h** great a threshing floor they will fill!"
4:33 Then I answered and said, "**H** long?
4:35 saying, '**H** long are we to remain here?
5:39 and **h** can I speak concerning the things
5:45 "**H** have you said to your servant
6:59 **H** long will this be so?"
7: 5 **h** can they come to the broad part unless they pass
7: 9 **h** will the heir receive the inheritance unless
7:*53* I said, "Lord, **h** could that be?"
7:*73* or **h** will they answer in the last times?
7:*74* **H** long the Most High has been patient
7:*85* they shall see **h** the habitations of
7:*86* they shall see **h** some of them will cross over
7:97 when it is shown them **h** their face is to shine like
7:97 and **h** they are to be made like the light of the stars,
7:*106* [36] "**H** then do we find that first Abraham prayed
9:13 to be curious about **h** the ungodly will be punished;
9:13 but inquire **h** the righteous will be saved,
10:20 for **h** many are the adversities of Zion?—
10:21 For you see **h** our sanctuary has been laid waste,
10:49 you saw her likeness, **h** she mourned for her son,
11: 6 And I saw **h** all things
11:30 And I saw **h** it allied the two heads with itself,
11:31 and **h** the head turned with those that were with it
11:37 and I heard **h** it uttered a human voice to the eagle,
12:41 "**H** have we offended you,
12:44 **h** much better it would have been for us if we
13:10 but I saw only **h** he sent forth

2Es 15:20 See **h** I am calling together all the kings of
16:66 Or **h** will you hide your sins before the Lord
4Mc 1:14 **h** many kinds of emotions there are,
1:33 **h** is it that when we are attracted
2: 7 Otherwise **h** could it be
2:24 **H** is it then, one might say,
9:29 "**H** sweet is any kind of death for the religion
13: 5 **H** then can one fail to confess the sovereignty
14:13 Observe **h** complex is a mother's love
15:22 **H** great and **h** many torments the mother then suffered
16: 6 "O **h** wretched am I and many times unhappy!

HOWBEIT (KJV) See BUT, FORMERLY, HOWEVER, NEVERTHELESS, RATHER, SINCE, THOUGH, YET

HOWEVER‡ (56)
Ge 39:11 **h,** when he went into the house to do his work,
42:13 the youngest, **h,** is now with our father,
Ex 3:19 **h,** that the king of Egypt will not let you go
Lev 25:53 **h,** rule with harshness over them in your sight.
27:26 **h,** which as a firstling belongs to the LORD,
Nu 1:47 **h,** were not numbered by their ancestral tribe along
16:41 **h,** the whole congregation of the Israelites rebelled
Dt 2:37 **h,** on the land of the Ammonites,
12:16 The blood, **h,** you must not eat;
15: 4 There will, **h,** be no one in need among you,
15:23 Its blood, **h,** you must not eat;
20:14 You may, **h,** take as your booty the women,
22:20 If, **h,** this charge is true, that evidence of
Jos 2: 6 **h,** brought them up to the roof and hidden them
16:10 **h,** drive out the Canaanites who lived in Gezer:
1Ki 2: 7 **h,** with the sons of Barzillai the Gileadite,
2:15 **h,** the kingdom has turned about
3: 2 The people were sacrificing at the high places, **h,**
11:13 I will not, **h,** tear away the entire kingdom;
2Ki 17:40 not listen, **h,** but they continued
23: 9 The priests of the high places, **h,**
2Ch 33:17 The people, **h,** still sacrificed at the high places,
Ezr 5:13 **H,** King Cyrus of Babylon,
Ecc 6: 3 but **h** many are the days of his years,
8:17 **H** much they may toil in seeking,
Eze 3:21 If, **h,** you warn the righteous not to sin,
44:25 for father or mother, **h,** and for son or daughter,
Da 2:10 In fact no king, **h** great and powerful,
4:18 **h,** for you are endowed with a spirit of
11:11 who shall muster a great multitude, which shall, **h,**
11:33 **h,** they shall fall by sword and flame,
Mt 17:27 **H,** so that we do not give offense to them,
Jn 11:13 Jesus, **h,** had been speaking about his death,
Ac 13:13 John, **h,** left them and returned to Jerusalem;
28: 5 **h,** shook off the creature into the fire
Ro 15:25 **h,** I am going to Jerusalem in a ministry to
1Co 7:17 **H** that may be, let each of you lead the life that
8: 7 It is not everyone, **h,** who has this knowledge.
2Co 10:13 We, **h,** will not boast beyond limits,
Gal 4: 9 Now, **h,** that you have come to know God,
5:15 If, **h,** you bite and devour one another,
Eph 5:33 Each of you, **h,** should love his wife as himself,
Heb 3: 6 Christ, **h,** was faithful over God's house as a son,
2Pe 2:12 These people, **h,** are like irrational animals,
AdE 3: 2 Mordecai, **h,** did not do obeisance.
Wis 15:12 for they say one must get money **h** one can,
Sus 1:40 **h,** seize this woman and asked who
2Mc 4:19 Those who carried the money, **h,**
5: 7 He did not, **h,** gain control of the government;
1Es 1:28 Josiah, **h,** did not turn back to his chariot,
3Mc 2:31 Now some, **h,** with an obvious abhorrence of
3: 3 **h,** continued to maintain goodwill
5:10 **h,** when he had drugged the pitiless elephants
5:36 **h,** reconvened the party in the same manner
2Es 9:23 do not, **h,** fast during them,
9:37 **h,** does not perish but survives in its glory."

HOWL (2) [HOWLING]
Isa 52: 5 Their rulers **h,** says the LORD, and continually,
LtJ 6:32 They **h** and shout before their gods as some do at

HOWLING (5) [HOWL]
Dt 32:10 in a desert land, in a **h** wilderness waste;
Ps 59: 6 **h** like dogs and prowling about the city.
59:14 **h** like dogs and prowling about the city.
Isa 13:21 and its houses will be full of **h** creatures;
Mk 5: 5 the tombs and on the mountains he was always **h**

HOWSOEVER (KJV) See COME WHAT MAY

HOZAI See Index to Footnotes

HU See Index to Footnotes

HUBBAH (1)
1Ch 7:34 The sons of Shemer: Ahi, Rohgah, **H,** and Aram.

HUBS (1)
1Ki 7:33 their rims, their spokes, and their **h** were all cast.

HUDDLE (1)
Job 30: 7 under the nettles they **h** together.

HUGE (10)
Jos 10:11 the LORD threw down **h** stones from heaven
1Ki 7:10 The foundation was of costly stones, **h** stones,
2Ch 16: 8 Were not the Ethiopians and the Libyans a **h** army
Da 2:31 This statue was **h,** its brilliance extraordinary;
Rev 16:21 and **h** hailstones, each weighing about
Jdt 2:18 **h** amount of gold and silver from the royal palace.
Sir 43:25 all kinds of living things, and **h** sea-monsters.
1Mc 9: 6 When they saw the **h** number of the enemy forces,
3Mc 6: 8 And Jonah, wasting away in the belly of a **h,**
2Es 10:27 and a place of **h** foundations showed itself.

HUKKOK (1)
Jos 19:34 and goes from there to **H,**

HUKOK (1)
1Ch 6:75 **H** with its pasture lands, and Rehob

HUL (2)
Ge 10:23 descendants of Aram: Uz, **H,** Gether, and Mash.
1Ch 1:17 Elam, Asshur, Arpachshad, Lud, Aram, Uz, **H,**

HULDAH (2)
2Ki 22:14 and Asaiah went to the prophetess **H** the wife
2Ch 34:22 the king had sent went to the prophet **H,**

HUMAN‡ (339) [HUMANITY, HUMANKIND, HUMANS, SUPERHUMAN]
A. HUMAN BEINGS (73)
B. HUMAN BEING (37)
C. HUMAN HANDS (22)
D. HUMAN HEART (16)

Ge 6: 7 from the earth the **h** beings I have created— A
7:21 that swarm on the earth, and all **h** beings; A
7:23 **h** beings and animals and creeping things and A
8:21 the inclination of the **h** heart is evil from youth; D
9: 5 and from **h** beings, each one for the blood A
9: 5 I will require a reckoning for **h** life.
9: 6 Whoever sheds the blood of a **h,**
9: 6 by a **h** shall that person's blood be shed;
Ex 9:19 every **h** or animal that is in the open field and is
9:25 throughout all the land of Egypt, both **h**
12:12 both **h** beings and animals; A
13: 2 of **h** beings and animals, is mine. A
13:15 from **h** firstborn to the firstborn of animals.
19:13 whether animal or **h** being, they shall not live.' B
Lev 5: 3 Or when you touch **h** uncleanness—
7:21 **h** uncleanness or an unclean animal
22: 5 made unclean or any **h** being by whom he may B
24:17 Anyone who kills a **h** being shall be put to death. B
24:21 but one who kills a **h** being shall be put to death. B
27: 2 concerning the equivalent for a **h** being, B
27:28 be it **h** or animal, or inherited landholding,
27:29 No **h** beings who have been devoted A
Nu 3:13 both **h** and animal; they shall be mine.
8:17 the firstborn among the Israelites are mine, both **h**
18:15 **h** and animal, which is offered to the LORD,
18:15 but the firstborn of **h** beings you shall redeem, A
19:11 of any **h** being shall be unclean seven days. B
19:13 the body of a **h** being who has died, B
19:16 or who has died naturally, or a **h** bone, or a grave,
23:19 God is not a **h** being, B
31:26 an inventory of the booty captured, both **h**
Dt 4:28 you will serve other gods made by **h** hands, C
4:32 ever since the day that God created **h** beings on A
20:19 in the field **h** beings that they should come A
Jos 10:14 when the LORD heeded a **h** voice;
2Sa 7:14 with blows inflicted by **h** beings. A
24:14 but let me not fall into **h** hands." C
1Ki 8:39 for only you know what is in every **h** heart— D
13: 2 and **h** bones shall be burned on you.' "
2Ki 19:18 they were no gods but the work of **h** hands— C
23:14 and covered the sites with **h** bones.
23:20 and burned **h** bones on them.
1Ch 21:13 but let me not fall into **h** hands." C
2Ch 6:30 for only you know the **h** heart. D
19: 6 on behalf of **h** beings but on the LORD's behalf; A
32:19 which are the work of **h** hands. C
Job 4:17 Can **h** beings be pure before their Maker? A
5: 7 but **h** beings are born to trouble just A
7: 1 "Do not **h** beings have a hard service on earth, A
7:17 What are **h** beings, that you make so much A
10: 5 or your years like **h** years,
11:12 when a wild ass is born **h.**
12:10 and the breath of every **h** being. B
15: 7 "Are you the firstborn of the **h** race?
25: 6 who is a maggot, and a **h** being, who is a worm!" B
28: 4 in a valley away from **h** habitation;
32:13 God may vanquish him, not a **h.'**
34:20 and the mighty are taken away by no **h** hand.
35: 8 and your righteousness, other **h** beings. A
38:26 on the desert, which is empty of **h** life,
Ps 8: 4 what are **h** beings that you are mindful of them, A
9:20 let the nations know that they are only **h.**
22: 6 But I am a worm, and not **h;**
31:20 of your presence you hide them from **h** plots;
57: 4 down among lions that greedily devour **h** prey;
60:11 against the foe, for **h** help is worthless.
64: 6 For the **h** heart and mind are deep. D
76:10 **H** wrath serves only to praise you,
104:15 and wine to gladden the **h** heart, D
104:15 and bread to strengthen the **h** heart. D
108:12 against the foe, for **h** help is worthless.
115: 4 and gold, the work of **h** hands. C
115:16 but the earth he has given to **h** beings. A
119:134 Redeem me from **h** oppression,
135: 8 both **h** beings and animals; A
135:15 and gold, the work of **h** hands. C
144: 3 LORD, what are **h** beings that you regard them, A
Pr 5:21 For **h** ways are under the eyes of the LORD,
8:31 in his inhabited world and delighting in the **h** race.
12:25 Anxiety weighs down the **h** heart, D
15:11 before the LORD, how much more **h** hearts!
16: 9 The **h** mind plans the way,
18:14 The **h** spirit will endure sickness;
19:21 The **h** mind may devise many plans,
20: 5 The purposes in the **h** mind are like deep water,
20:27 The **h** spirit is the lamp of the LORD,
25:20 sorrow gnaws at the **h** heart. D
27:19 so one **h** heart reflects another. D
27:20 and **h** eyes are never satisfied.
30: 2 Surely I am too stupid to be **h;**
30: 2 I do not have **h** understanding.
Ecc 1:13 that God has given to **h** beings to be busy with. A
3:18 with regard to **h** beings that God is testing them A
3:21 Who knows whether the **h** spirit goes upward and
6: 7 All **h** toil is for the mouth,
6:10 and it is known what **h** beings are, A
7:29 that God made **h** beings straightforward, A
8:11 the **h** heart is fully set to do evil. D
Isa 13: 7 and every **h** heart will melt, D
29:13 of me is a **h** commandment learned by rote;
31: 3 The Egyptians are **h,** and not God;
37:19 but the work of **h** hands— C
44:11 the artisans too are merely **h.**
44:13 he makes it in **h** form, with **h** beauty,
51:12 a **h** being who fades like grass? B
52:14 beyond **h** semblance, and his form beyond that
66: 3 an ox is like one who kills a **h** being; B
Jer 5:26 Like fowlers they set a trap; they catch **h** beings. A
7:20 on **h** beings and animals, on the trees A
9:22 "**H** corpses shall fall like dung upon the open field,
10:23 that the way of **h** beings is not in their control, A
21: 6 both **h** beings and animals; A
32:43 It is a desolation, without **h** beings or animals; A
33:10 "It is a waste without **h** beings or animals," A
33:10 without inhabitants, **h** or animal,
33:12 without **h** beings or animals, A
36:29 and will cut off from it **h** beings and animals? A
50: 3 both **h** beings and animals shall flee away. A
51:62 that neither **h** beings nor animals shall live in it, A
La 3:35 when **h** rights are perverted in the presence of
Eze 1: 5 This was their appearance: they were of **h** form.
1: 8 on their four sides they had **h** hands. C
1:10 the four had the face of a **h** being, B
1:26 a throne was something that seemed like a **h** form.
4:12 baking it in their sight on **h** dung.
4:15 I will let you have cow's dung instead of **h** dung,
8: 2 there was a figure that looked like a **h** being; B
10: 8 to have the form of a **h** hand under their wings.
10:14 the second face was that of a **h** being, B
10:21 underneath their wings something like **h** hands. C
13:18 of persons of every height, in the hunt for **h** lives!
14:13 and cut off from it **h** beings and animals, A
14:17 and I cut off **h** beings and animals from it; A
22:25 they have devoured **h** lives;
27:13 they exchanged **h** beings and vessels of bronze A
29: 8 and will cut off from you **h** being and animal; B
29:11 No **h** foot shall pass through it,
32:13 and no **h** foot shall trouble them any more,
36:11 I will multiply **h** beings and animals upon you. A
38:20 and all **h** beings that are on the face of the earth, A
39:15 anyone who sees a **h** bone shall set up a sign by it,
41:19 **h** face turned toward the palm tree on the one side,
Da 2:34 a stone was cut out, not by **h** hands, C
2:38 into whose hand he has given **h** beings, A
4:16 Let his mind be changed from that of a **h,**
4:17 and sets over it the lowliest of **h** beings.' A
4:25 You shall be driven away from **h** society,
4:32 You shall be driven away from **h** society,
4:33 He was driven away from **h** society,
5: 5 a **h** hand appeared and began writing on the plaster
5:21 He was driven from **h** society,
6: 7 divine or **h,** for thirty days, except to you, O king,
6:12 that anyone who prays to anyone, divine or **h,**
7: 4 and made to stand on two feet like a **h** being; B
7: 4 and a **h** mind was given to it.
7: 8 There were eyes like **h** eyes in this horn,
7:13 like a **h** being coming with the clouds of heaven. B
8:16 and I heard a **h** voice by the Ulai,
8:25 But he shall be broken, and not by **h** hands. C
10:16 Then one in **h** form touched my lips,
10:18 in **h** form touched me and strengthened me.
Hos 11: 4 I led them with cords of **h** kindness,
Jnh 3: 7 No **h** being or animal, no herd or flock, B
3: 8 **H** beings and animals shall be covered A
Hab 2: 8 because of **h** bloodshed, and violence to the earth,
2:17 because of **h** bloodshed and violence to the earth,
Hag 1:11 on **h** beings and animals, and on all their labors. A
Zec 12: 1 the earth and formed the **h** spirit within:
Mt 9: 8 who had given such authority to **h** beings. A
12:12 much more valuable is a **h** being than a sheep! B
15: 9 teaching **h** precepts as doctrines.' "
16:23 not on divine things but on **h** things."
17:22 Son of Man is going to be betrayed into **h** hands, C
21:25 or was it of **h** origin?"
21:26 if we say, 'Of **h** origin,' we are afraid of the crowd;
Mk 7: 7 teaching **h** precepts as doctrines.'
7: 8 the commandment of God and hold to **h** tradition."

Mk 7:21 For it is from within, from the **h** heart, D
8:33 not on divine things but on **h** things."
9:31 "The Son of Man is to be betrayed into **h** hands, C
11:30 or was it of **h** origin?
11:32 But shall we say, 'Of **h** origin'?"—
Lk 2:52 and in divine and **h** favor.
9:44 Son of Man is going to be betrayed into **h** hands. C
16:15 for what is prized by **h** beings is an abomination A
20: 4 or was it of **h** origin?"
20: 6 we say, 'Of **h** origin,' all the people will stone us;
Jn 5:34 Not that I accept such **h** testimony,
5:41 I do not accept glory from **h** beings. A
8:15 You judge by **h** standards; I judge no one.
10:33 only a **h** being, are making yourself God." B
12:43 for they loved **h** glory more than the glory
16:21 because of the joy of having brought a **h** being B
Ac 5:29 "We must obey God rather than any **h** authority.
5:38 if this plan or this undertaking is of **h** origin,
7:48 not dwell in houses made with **h** hands; C
14:11 "The gods have come down to us in **h** form!"
15: 8 And God, who knows the **h** heart, D
17:24 does not live in shrines made by **h** hands, C
17:25 nor is he served by **h** hands, C
17:30 God has overlooked the times of **h** ignorance,
Ro 1:23 a mortal **h** being or birds or four-footed animals B
3: 5 (I speak in a **h** way.)
3:20 For "no **h** being will be justified in his sight" B
6:19 in **h** terms because of your natural limitations.
9:16 So it depends not on **h** will or exertion,
9:20 indeed are you, a **h** being, to argue with God? B
14:18 to God and has **h** approval.
1Co 1:25 For God's foolishness is wiser than **h** wisdom,
1:25 and God's weakness is stronger than **h** strength.
1:26 not many of you were wise by **h** standards,
2: 5 that your faith might rest not on **h** wisdom but on
2: 9 nor ear heard, nor the **h** heart conceived, D
2:11 what **h** being knows what is truly human except B
2:11 what is truly **h** except the **h** spirit that is within?
2:13 of these things in words not taught by **h** wisdom
3: 3 and behaving according to **h** inclinations?
3: 4 "I belong to Apollos," are you not merely **h?**
3:21 So let no one boast about **h** leaders.
4: 3 that I should be judged by you or by any **h** court.
7:23 do not become slaves of **h** masters.
9: 8 Do I say this on **h** authority?
15:21 For since death came through a **h** being, B
15:21 of the dead has also come through a **h** being; B
15:32 If with merely **h** hopes I fought with wild animals
15:39 flesh is alike, but there is one flesh for **h** beings, A
2Co 1:17 according to ordinary **h** standards,
3: 3 not on tablets of stone but on tablets of **h** hearts.
5:16 therefore, we regard no one from a **h** point of view;
5:16 we once knew Christ from a **h** point of view,
10: 2 who think we are acting according to **h** standards.
10: 3 Indeed, we live as **h** beings, A
10: 3 but we do not wage war according to **h** standards;
10: 4 for the weapons of our warfare are not merely **h,**
11:18 since many boast according to **h** standards,
Gal 1: 1 neither by **h** commission nor from **h** authorities,
1:10 Am I now seeking **h** approval, or God's approval?
1:11 that was proclaimed by me is not of **h** origin;
1:12 for I did not receive it from a **h** source,
1:16 I did not confer with any **h** being, B
Eph 2:11 circumcision made in the flesh by **h** hands— C
Php 2: 7 the form of a slave, being born in **h** likeness.
2: 7 And being found in **h** form,
Col 2: 8 to **h** tradition, according to the elemental spirits of
2:18 puffed up without cause by a **h** way of thinking,
2:22 they are simply **h** commands and teachings.
1Th 2:13 not as a **h** word but as what it really is,
4: 8 not **h** authority but God, who
1Ti 2: 5 and humankind, Christ Jesus, himself **h,**
Heb 2: 6 What are **h** beings that you are mindful of them, A
6:16 **H** beings, of course, swear by someone A
9:24 did not enter a sanctuary made by **h** hands, C
12: 9 Moreover, we had **h** parents to discipline us,
Jas 3: 7 can be tamed and has been tamed by the **h** species,
5:17 Elijah was a **h** being like us, B
1Pe 2:13 the authority of every **h** institution,
4: 2 the rest of your earthly life no longer by **h** desires
2Pe 1:21 because no prophecy ever came by **h** will,
2:16 a **h** voice and restrained the prophet's madness.
1Jn 5: 9 If we receive **h** testimony,
Rev 4: 7 the third living creature with a face like a **h** face,
9: 7 their faces were like **h** faces,
18:13 and chariots, slaves—and **h** lives.
21:17 one hundred forty-four cubits by **h** measurement,
Tob 8: 6 From the two of them the **h** race has sprung.
Jdt 8:12 up in the place of God in **h** affairs?
8:14 of the **h** heart or understand the workings of D
8:14 or understand the workings of the **h** mind;
8:16 for God is not like a **h** being, to be threatened, B
11: 7 Not only do **h** beings serve him because of you, A
AdE 13:14 that I might not set **h** glory above the glory of God,
16:24 shall be made not only impassable for **h** beings, A
Wis 7:20 powers of spirits and the thoughts of **h** beings, A
9: 6 for even one who is perfect among **h** beings A
12: 5 and their sacrificial feasting on **h** flesh and blood.
13:10 the name "gods" to the works of **h** hands, C
13:13 he forms it in the likeness of a **h** being, B
14:11 for **h** souls and a trap for the feet of the foolish.
14:14 For through **h** vanity they entered the world,
14:15 as a god what was once a dead **h** being, B
14:20 before they had honored as a **h** being. B
15: 4 For neither has the evil intent of **h** art misled us,
15:16 For a **h** being made them, B
Sir 1:15 She made among **h** beings an eternal foundation, A
Sir 10: 5 **H** success is in the hand of the Lord,
10: 9 Even in life the **h** body decays.
10:12 The beginning of **h** pride is to forsake the Lord;
10:18 Pride was not created for **h** beings, A
10:19 Whose offspring are worthy of honor? **H** offspring.
10:19 offspring are unworthy of honor? **H** offspring.
15:19 and he knows every **h** action.
16:20 But no **h** mind can grasp this,
17: 1 The Lord created **h** beings out of earth, A
17:30 For not everything is within **h** capability,
17:30 since **h** beings are not immortal. A
17:32 but all **h** beings are dust and ashes. A
18: 7 When **h** beings have finished, A
18: 8 What are **h** beings, and of what use are they? A
18:13 compassion of **h** beings is for their neighbors, A
20:22 or lose it because of **h** respect.
21: 2 Its teeth are lion's teeth, and can destroy **h** lives.
23:19 to **h** eyes and he does not realize that the eyes of
23:19 they look upon every aspect of **h** behavior and see
31:27 Wine is very life to **h** beings if taken A
33:10 All **h** beings come from the ground, A
38: 6 And he gave skill to **h** beings that he might A
39: 4 and learns what is good and evil in the **h** lot.
39:26 The basic necessities of **h** life are water and fire
40: 8 To all creatures, **h** and animal,
41:11 The **h** body is a fleeting thing,
42:18 He searches out the abyss and the **h** heart; D
51: 7 I looked for **h** assistance, and there was none.
LtJ 6:11 with garments like **h** beings— A
6:51 that they are not gods but the work of **h** hands, C
Bel 1:32 and every day they had been given two **h** bodies
2Mc 7:28 And in the same way the **h** race came into being.
1Es 4:37 all **h** beings are unrighteous, A
Man 1: 7 and very merciful, and you relent at **h** suffering.
3Mc 2:15 unapproachable by **h** beings. A
6:26 have accepted willingly the worst of **h** dangers?
2Es 6:39 the sound of **h** voices was not yet there.
7:29 and all who draw **h** breath.
7:*65* Let the **h** race lament, but let the wild animals of
8: 6 the likeness of a **h** being may be able to live. B
10:54 because no work of **h** construction could endure
11:37 and I heard how it uttered a **h** voice to the eagle,
13:41 where no **h** beings had ever lived, A
16:27 a person will long to see another **h** being, B
16:27 or even to hear a **h** voice.
16:61 He formed **h** beings and put a heart in the midst A
4Mc 1:16 of divine and **h** matters and the causes of these.
1:17 and **h** affairs to our advantage.
2:21 Now when God fashioned **h** beings, A
4:13 that Apollonius had been overcome by **h** treachery
14:14 Even unreasoning animals, as well as **h** beings, A
17:14 and the world and the **h** race were the spectators.

HUMANE (2)

Wis 7:23 **h,** steadfast, sure, free from anxiety, all-powerful,
4Mc 5:12 on your old age by honoring my **h** advice?

HUMANITY (3) [HUMAN]

Job 7:20 If I sin, what do I do to you, you watcher of **h?**
Zep 1: 3 I will cut off **h** from the face of the earth,
Eph 2:15 that he might create in himself one new **h** in place

HUMANKIND‡ (55) [HUMAN]

Ge 1:26 Then God said, "Let us make **h** in our image,
1:27 So God created **h** in his image,
5: 1 When God created **h,** he made them in the likeness
5: 2 and named them **"H"** when they were created.
6: 5 that the wickedness of **h** was great in the earth,
6: 6 LORD was sorry that he had made **h** on the earth,
8:21 "I will never again curse the ground because of **h,**
9: 6 for in his own image God made **h.**
Dt 32: 8 when he divided **h,** he fixed the boundaries of
32:26 and blot out the memory of them from **h;**
Job 28:28 And he said to **h,** 'Truly, the fear of the Lord,
Ps 11: 4 His eyes behold, his gaze examines **h.**
12: 1 the faithful have disappeared from **h.**
12: 8 as vileness is exalted among **h.**
14: 2 The LORD looks down from heaven on **h** to see
21:10 and their children from among **h.**
33:13 LORD looks down from heaven; he sees all **h.**
53: 2 God looks down from heaven on **h** to see
94:10 he who teaches knowledge to **h,**
107: 8 for his wonderful works to **h.**
107:15 for his wonderful works to **h.**
107:21 for his wonderful works to **h.**
107:31 for his wonderful works to **h.**
Ecc 6: 1 and it lies heavy upon **h:**
Isa 45:12 I made the earth, and created **h** upon it;
Jer 32:20 and to this day in Israel and among all **h,**
49:15 among the nations, despised by **h.**
Mk 2:27 he said to them, "The sabbath was made for **h,** and not **h** for the sabbath;
Eph 3: 5 not made known to **h,** as it has now been revealed
1Ti 2: 5 there is also one mediator between God and **h,**
Rev 9:15 the month, and the year, to kill a third of **h.**
9:18 By these three plagues a third of **h** was killed,
9:20 rest of **h,** who were not killed by these plagues,
14: 4 They have been redeemed from **h** as first fruits
Wis 9: 2 by your wisdom have formed **h** to have dominion
10: 8 but also left for **h** a reminder of their folly,
14:21 And this became a hidden trap for **h,**
16:26 that it is not the production of crops that feeds **h**
Sir 11: 4 and his works are concealed from **h.**
15:14 It was he who created **h** in the beginning,
33:10 and **h** was created out of the dust.
Sir 45: 4 choosing him out of all **h.**
Bar 3:37 Afterward she appeared on earth and lived with **h.**
LtJ 6:26 revealing to **h** their worthlessness.
1Mc 12:53 on them and blot out the memory of them from **h."**
2Mc 7:23 who shaped the beginning of **h** and devised
2Es 6:46 and you commanded them to serve **h,**
7:*138* [68] not one ten-thousandth of **h** could have life;
8:15 About all **h** you know best;
10:14 that is, **h,** to him who made her.'
14: 9 for you shall be taken up from among **h,**
14:14 cast away from you the burdens of **h,**
16:19 as scourges for the correction of **h.**
4Mc 11: 4 Hater of virtue, hater of **h,**

HUMANS‡ (22) [HUMAN]

Ge 6: 4 the sons of God went in to the daughters of **h,**
32:28 for you have striven with God and with **h,**
Ex 8:17 and gnats came on **h** and animals alike;
8:18 There were gnats on both **h** and animals.
9: 9 and shall cause festering boils on **h** and animals
9:10 and it caused festering boils on **h** and animals.
9:22 on **h** and animals and all the plants of the field in
Job 10: 4 Do you have eyes of flesh? Do you see as **h** see?
14:10 **h** expire, and where are they?
Ps 36: 6 you save **h** and animals alike, O LORD.
Ecc 3:19 the fate of **h** and the fate of animals is the same;
3:19 and **h** have no advantage over the animals;
Isa 13:12 and **h** than the gold of Ophir.
31: 8 and a sword, not of **h,** shall devour him;
Jer 31:27 of Israel and the house of Judah with the seed of **h**
Eze 14:19 to cut off **h** and animals from it;
14:21 and pestilence, to cut off **h** and animals from it!
19: 3 to catch prey; he devoured **h.**
25:13 and cut off from it **h** and animals,
Zep 1: 3 I will sweep away **h** and animals;
Sir 20:15 such a one is hateful to God and **h.**
2Mc 11: 9 to assail not only **h** but the wildest animals or walls

HUMBLE‡ (57) [HUMBLED, HUMBLES, HUMBLEST, HUMBLING, HUMBLY]

Ex 10: 3 long will you refuse to **h** yourself before me?
Nu 12: 3 Now the man Moses was very **h,**
Dt 8: 2 in order to **h** you, testing you to know what was
8:16 to **h** you and to test you,
2Sa 22:28 You deliver a **h** people, but your eyes are upon
2Ch 7:14 by my name **h** themselves,
33:23 He did not **h** himself before the LORD,
36:12 He did not **h** himself before
Job 22:29 you say it is pride; for he saves the **h.**
Ps 18:27 For you deliver a **h** people,
25: 9 He leads the **h** in what is right,
25: 9 and teaches the **h** his way.
34: 2 let the **h** hear and be glad.
55:19 will hear, and will **h** them—
89:22 the wicked shall not **h** him.
149: 4 he adorns the **h** with victory.
Pr 3:34 but to the **h** he shows favor.
11: 2 but wisdom is with the **h.**
Isa 57:15 and also with those who are contrite and **h** in spirit,
57:15 to revive the spirit of the **h,**
58: 3 Why **h** ourselves, but you do not notice?"
58: 5 Is such the fast that I choose, a day to **h** oneself?
66: 2 to the **h** and contrite in spirit,
Eze 17:14 that the kingdom might be **h** and not lift itself up,
Da 10:12 to gain understanding and to **h** yourself
Zep 2: 3 Seek the LORD, all you **h** of the land,
3:12 For I will leave in the midst of you a people **h**
Zec 9: 9 **h** and riding on a donkey, on a colt,
Mt 11:29 for I am gentle and **h** in heart,
18: 4 Whoever becomes **h** like this child is the greatest
21: 5 **h,** and mounted on a donkey, and on a colt,
23:12 and all who **h** themselves will be exalted.
Lk 14:11 and those who **h** themselves will be exalted."
18:14 but all who **h** themselves will be exalted."
2Co 10: 1 I who am **h** when face to face with you,
12:21 my God may **h** me before you,
Jas 4: 6 "God opposes the proud, but gives grace to the **h."**
4:10 **H** yourselves before the Lord,
1Pe 3: 8 love for one another, a tender heart, and a **h** mind.
5: 5 but gives grace to the **h."**
5: 6 **H** yourselves therefore under the mighty hand
Sir 2:17 and **h** themselves before him.
3:18 The greater you are, the more you must **h** yourself;
3:20 but by the **h** he is glorified.
7:17 **H** yourself to the utmost, for the punishment of
10:15 and plants the **h** in their place.
11: 1 The wisdom of the **h** lifts their heads high,
12: 5 Do good to the **h,** but do not give to the ungodly;
13:21 he is supported by friends, but when the **h** falls,
13:22 If the **h** person slips, they even criticize him;
18:21 Before falling ill, **h** yourself;
20:11 who have raised their heads from **h** circumstances.
29: 8 be patient with someone in **h** circumstances,
35:21 The prayer of the **h** pierces the clouds,
Aza 1:16 a contrite heart and a **h** spirit may we be accepted,
1:65 Bless the Lord, you who are holy and **h** in heart;
1Mc 14:14 He gave help to all the **h** among his people;

HUMBLED‡ (37) [HUMBLE]

Lev 26:41 if then their uncircumcised heart is **h**
Dt 8: 3 He **h** you by letting you hunger,
1Ki 21:29 "Have you seen how Ahab has **h** himself
21:29 Because he has **h** himself before me,
2Ki 22:19 and you **h** yourself before the LORD,
2Ch 12: 6 the officers of Israel and the king **h** themselves

2Ch 12: 7 When the LORD saw that they **h** themselves,
12: 7 saying: "They have **h** themselves;
12:12 Because he **h** himself the wrath of
30:11 and Zebulun **h** themselves and came to Jerusalem.
32:26 Then Hezekiah **h** himself for the pride of his heart,
33:12 the LORD his God and **h** himself greatly before
33:19 the images, before he **h** himself, these are written
33:23 as his father Manasseh had **h** himself,
34:27 because your heart was penitent and you **h** yourself
34:27 and you have **h** yourself before me,
Job 30:11 Because God has loosed my bowstring and **h** me,
Ps 69:10 When I **h** my soul with fasting,
119:67 I was **h** I went astray, but now I keep your word.
119:71 It is good for me that I was **h,**
119:75 and that in faithfulness you have **h** me.
Isa 2: 9 so people are **h,** and everyone is brought low—
2:11 and the pride of everyone shall be **h;**
2:17 The haughtiness of people shall be **h,**
5:15 and the eyes of the haughty are **h.**
Da 5:22 you, Belshazzar his son, have not **h** your heart,
Mt 23:12 All who exalt themselves will be **h,**
Lk 14:11 For all who exalt themselves will be **h,**
18:14 for all who exalt themselves will be **h,**
Php 2: 8 he **h** himself and became obedient to the point
Jdt 4: 9 and they **h** themselves with much fasting.
AdE 14: 2 and she utterly **h** her body;
Wis 17: 7 The delusions of their magic art lay **h,**
1Mc 5: 3 a heavy blow and **h** them and despoiled them.
12:15 from our enemies, and our enemies were **h.**
2Mc 8:35 having been **h** with the help of the Lord
2Es 8:49 because you have **h** yourself,

HUMBLES‡ (2) [HUMBLE]

Sir 7:11 for there is One who **h** and exalts.
12:11 Even if he **h** himself and walks bowed down,

HUMBLEST (1) [HUMBLE]

1Sa 9:21 the **h** of all the families of the tribe of Benjamin.

HUMBLING (2) [HUMBLE]

2Co 11: 7 Did I commit a sin by **h** myself so that you might
Sir 34:31 And what has he gained by **h** himself?

HUMBLY (1) [HUMBLE]

Mic 6: 8 and to walk **h** with your God?

HUMILIATE (1) [HUMILIATED, HUMILIATION, HUMILITY]

1Co 11:22 the church of God and **h** those who have nothing?

HUMILIATED (7) [HUMILIATE]

1Ch 19: 5 he sent messengers to them, for they felt greatly **h.**
Job 22:29 When others are **h,** you say it is pride;
La 2: 1 How the Lord in his anger has **h** daughter Zion!
2Co 9: 4 and find that you are not ready, we would be **h—**
Jdt 13:17 who have this day **h** the enemies of your people."
AdE 6:13 and you have begun to be **h** before him,
Sir 13: 8 and **h** when you are enjoying yourself.

HUMILIATION‡ (12) [HUMILIATE]

Job 19: 5 and make my **h** an argument against me,
Pr 29:23 A person's pride will bring **h,**
Isa 30: 3 and the shelter in the shadow of Egypt your **h.**
Ac 8:33 In his **h** justice was denied him.
Php 3:21 He will transform the body of our **h** that it may
Jdt 6:19 and have pity on our people in their **h,**
Sir 2: 4 and in times of **h** be patient.
2: 5 and those found acceptable, in the furnace of **h.**
1Mc 3:51 and your priests mourn in **h.**
3Mc 2:12 in their **h,** and rescued them
2Es 6:19 and when the **h** of Zion is complete.
12:48 to seek mercy on account of the **h** of our sanctuary.

HUMILITY (15) [HUMILIATE]

Pr 15:33 of the LORD is instruction in wisdom, and **h** goes
18:12 Before destruction one's heart is haughty, but **h** goes before honor.
22: 4 The reward for **h** and fear of the LORD is riches
Zep 2: 3 seek righteousness, seek **h;**
Ac 20:19 serving the Lord with all **h** and with tears,
Eph 4: 2 with all **h** and gentleness, with patience, bearing
Php 2: 3 but in **h** regard others as better than yourselves.
Col 2:23 **h,** and severe treatment of the body,
3:12 clothe yourselves with compassion, kindness, **h,**
1Pe 5: 5 And all of you must clothe yourselves with **h**
Sir 1:27 fidelity and **h** are his delight.
3:17 My child, perform your tasks with **h;**
10:28 My child, honor yourself with **h,**
13:20 **H** is an abomination to the proud;
36:28 If kindness and **h** mark her speech,

HUMOR (1)

AdE 1:10 On the seventh day, when the king was in good **h,**

HUMPS (1)

Isa 30: 6 and their treasures on the **h** of camels,

HUMTAH (1)

Jos 15:54 **H,** Kiriath-arba (that is, Hebron), and Zior:

HUNCHBACK (1)

Lev 21:20 a **h,** or a dwarf, or a man with a blemish in his eyes

HUNDRED‡ (752) [HUNDREDFOLD, HUNDREDS, HUNDREDTH]

Ge 5: 3 When Adam had lived one **h** thirty years,
5: 4 the father of Seth were eight **h** years;
5: 5 the days that Adam lived were nine **h** thirty years;
5: 6 When Seth had lived one **h** five years,
5: 7 after the birth of Enosh eight **h** seven years,
5: 8 Thus all the days of Seth were nine **h** twelve years;
5:10 after the birth of Kenan eight **h** fifteen years,
5:11 Thus all the days of Enosh were nine **h** five years;
5:13 after the birth of Mahalalel eight **h** and forty years,
5:14 the days of Kenan were nine **h** and ten years;
5:16 after the birth of Jared eight **h** thirty years,
5:17 of Mahalalel were eight **h** ninety-five years;
5:18 Jared had lived one **h** sixty-two years he became
5:19 Jared lived after the birth of Enoch eight **h** years,
5:20 the days of Jared were nine **h** sixty-two years;
5:22 after the birth of Methuselah three **h** years,
5:23 the days of Enoch were three **h** sixty-five years.
5:25 Methuselah had lived one **h** eighty-seven years,
5:26 after the birth of Lamech seven **h** eighty-two years,
5:27 of Methuselah were nine **h** sixty-nine years;
5:28 When Lamech had lived one **h** eighty-two years,
5:30 after the birth of Noah five **h** ninety-five years,
5:31 of Lamech were seven **h** seventy-seven years;
5:32 After Noah was five **h** years old,
6: 3 their days shall be one **h** twenty years."
6:15 the length of the ark three **h** cubits,
7: 6 Noah was six **h** years old when the flood
7:24 the waters swelled on the earth for one **h** fifty days.
8: 3 the end of one **h** fifty days the waters had abated;
8:13 In the six **h** first year, in the first month,
9:28 After the flood Noah lived three **h** fifty years.
9:29 All the days of Noah were nine **h** fifty years;
11:10 When Shem was one **h** years old,
11:11 after the birth of Arpachshad five **h** years,
11:13 after the birth of Shelah four **h** three years,
11:15 after the birth of Eber four **h** three years,
11:17 after the birth of Peleg four **h** thirty years,
11:19 Peleg lived after the birth of Reu two **h** nine years,
11:21 after the birth of Serug two **h** seven years,
11:23 Serug lived after the birth of Nahor two **h** years,
11:25 after the birth of Terah one **h** nineteen years,
11:32 The days of Terah were two **h** five years;
14:14 born in his house, three **h** eighteen of them,
15:13 and they shall be oppressed for four **h** years;
17:17 a child be born to a man who is a **h** years old?
21: 5 a **h** years old when his son Isaac was born to him.
23: 1 Sarah lived one **h** twenty-seven years;
23:15 a piece of land worth four **h** shekels of silver—
23:16 the hearing of the Hittites, four **h** shekels of silver,
25: 7 of Abraham's life, one **h** seventy-five years.
25:17 of the life of Ishmael, one **h** thirty-seven years;
32: 6 and four **h** men are with him."
32:14 two **h** female goats and twenty male goats,
32:14 two **h** ewes and twenty rams,
33: 1 and four **h** men with him.
33:19 he bought for one **h** pieces of money the plot
35:28 Now the days of Isaac were one **h** eighty years.
45:22 but to Benjamin he gave three **h** pieces of silver
47: 9 "The years of my earthly sojourn are one **h** thirty;
47:28 the years of his life, were one **h** forty-seven years.
50:22 and Joseph lived one **h** ten years.
50:26 And Joseph died, being one **h** ten years old;
Ex 6:16 length of Levi's life was one **h** thirty-seven years.
6:18 of Kohath's life was one **h** thirty-three years.
6:20 of Amram's life was one **h** thirty-seven years.
12:37 about six **h** thousand men on foot,
12:40 in Egypt was four **h** thirty years.
12:41 At the end of four **h** thirty years, on that very day,
14: 7 he took six **h** picked chariots and all
27: 9 of fine twisted linen one **h** cubits long for that side;
27:11 be hangings one **h** cubits long,
27:18 The length of the court shall be one **h** cubits,
30:23 of liquid myrrh five **h** shekels,
30:23 as much, that is, two **h** fifty,
30:23 and two **h** fifty of aromatic cane,
30:24 and five **h** of cassia—measured by the
38: 9 of fine twisted linen, one **h** cubits long;
38:11 north side there were hangings one **h** cubits long;
38:24 was twenty-nine talents and seven **h** thirty shekels,
38:25 congregation who were counted was one **h** talents
38:25 and one thousand seven **h** seventy-five shekels,
38:26 for six **h** three thousand, five **h** fifty men.
38:27 The **h** talents of silver were for casting the bases of
38:27 one **h** bases for the **h** talents,
38:28 Of the thousand seven **h** seventy-five shekels
38:29 and two thousand four **h** shekels;
Lev 26: 8 Five of you shall give chase to a **h,**
26: 8 and a **h** of you shall give chase to ten thousand;
Nu 1:21 the tribe of Reuben were forty-six thousand five **h.**
1:23 of Simeon were fifty-nine thousand three **h.**
1:25 of Gad were forty-five thousand six **h** fifty.
1:27 of Judah were seventy-four thousand six **h.**
1:29 of Issachar were fifty-four thousand four **h.**
1:31 of Zebulun were fifty-seven thousand four **h.**
1:33 of the tribe of Ephraim were forty thousand five **h.**
1:35 of Manasseh were thirty-two thousand two **h.**
1:37 of Benjamin were thirty-five thousand four **h.**
1:39 the tribe of Dan were sixty-two thousand seven **h.**
1:41 the tribe of Asher were forty-one thousand five **h.**
1:43 of Naphtali were fifty-three thousand four **h.**
Nu 1:46 was six **h** three thousand five **h** fifty.
2: 4 as enrolled of seventy-four thousand six **h.**
2: 6 as enrolled of fifty-four thousand four **h.**
2: 8 as enrolled of fifty-seven thousand four **h.**
2: 9 is one **h** eighty-six thousand four **h.**
2:11 a company as enrolled of forty-six thousand five **h.**
2:13 as enrolled of fifty-nine thousand three **h.**
2:15 as enrolled of forty-five thousand six **h** fifty.
2:16 is one **h** fifty-one thousand four **h** fifty.
2:19 a company as enrolled of forty thousand five **h.**
2:21 as enrolled of thirty-two thousand two **h.**
2:23 as enrolled of thirty-five thousand four **h.**
2:24 is one **h** eight thousand one **h.**
2:26 as enrolled of sixty-two thousand seven **h.**
2:28 as enrolled of forty-one thousand five **h.**
2:30 as enrolled of fifty-three thousand four **h.**
2:31 of Dan is one **h** fifty-seven thousand six **h.**
2:32 companies was six **h** three thousand five **h** fifty.
3:22 was seven thousand five **h.**
3:28 there were eight thousand six **h,**
3:34 a month old and upward, was six thousand two **h.**
3:43 was twenty-two thousand two **h** seventy-three.
3:46 the price of redemption of the two **h** seventy-three
3:50 one thousand three **h** sixty-five shekels,
4:36 by clans was two thousand seven **h** fifty.
4:40 ancestral houses was two thousand six **h** thirty.
4:44 by their clans was three thousand two **h.**
4:48 their enrollment was eight thousand five **h** eighty.
7:13 was one silver plate weighing one **h** thirty shekels,
7:19 one silver plate weighing one **h** thirty shekels,
7:25 was one silver plate weighing one **h** thirty shekels,
7:31 was one silver plate weighing one **h** thirty shekels,
7:37 was one silver plate weighing one **h** thirty shekels,
7:43 was one silver plate weighing one **h** thirty shekels,
7:49 was one silver plate weighing one **h** thirty shekels,
7:55 was one silver plate weighing one **h** thirty shekels,
7:61 was one silver plate weighing one **h** thirty shekels,
7:67 was one silver plate weighing one **h** thirty shekels,
7:73 was one silver plate weighing one **h** thirty shekels,
7:79 was one silver plate weighing one **h** thirty shekels,
7:85 each silver plate weighing one **h** thirty shekels
7:85 the vessels two thousand four **h** shekels according
7:86 the gold of the dishes being one **h** twenty shekels;
11:21 people I am with number six **h** thousand on foot;
16: 2 two **h** fifty Israelite men, leaders of
16:17 before the LORD, two **h** fifty censers;
16:35 and consumed the two **h** fifty men offering
16:49 by the plague were fourteen thousand seven **h,**
26: 7 enrolled was forty-three thousand seven **h** thirty.
26:10 when the fire devoured two **h** fifty men;
26:14 twenty-two thousand two **h.**
26:18 of those enrolled was forty thousand five **h.**
26:22 of those enrolled was seventy-six thousand five **h.**
26:25 sixty-four thousand three **h** enrolled.
26:27 of those enrolled was sixty thousand five **h.**
26:34 of those enrolled was fifty-two thousand seven **h.**
26:37 of those enrolled was thirty-two thousand five **h.**
26:41 of those enrolled was forty-five thousand six **h.**
26:43 sixty-four thousand four **h** enrolled.
26:47 of those enrolled was fifty-three thousand four **h.**
26:50 of those enrolled was forty-five thousand four **h.**
26:51 six **h** and one thousand seven **h** thirty.
31:28 one item out of every five **h,** whether persons,
31:32 totaled six **h** seventy-five thousand sheep,
31:36 three **h** thirty-seven thousand five **h** sheep
31:37 of sheep and goats was six **h** seventy-five.
31:39 The donkeys were thirty thousand five **h,**
31:43 three **h** thirty-seven thousand five **h** sheep
31:45 thirty thousand five **h** donkeys,
31:52 was sixteen thousand seven **h** fifty shekels.
33:39 Aaron was one **h** twenty-three years old
Dt 22:19 they shall fine him one **h** shekels
31: 2 "I am now one **h** twenty years old.
34: 7 Moses was one **h** twenty years old when he died;
Jos 7:21 and two **h** shekels of silver,
24:29 died, being one **h** ten years old.
24:32 the father of Shechem, for one **h** pieces of money;
Jdg 2: 8 died at the age of one **h** ten years.
3:31 who killed six **h** of the Philistines with an oxgoad.
4: 3 for he had nine **h** chariots of iron,
4:13 nine **h** chariots of iron, and all the troops who were
7: 6 The number of those that lapped was three **h;**
7: 7 "With the three **h** that lapped I will deliver you,
7: 8 to their own tents, but retained the three **h.**
7:16 he divided the three **h** men into three companies,
7:19 and the **h** who were with him came to the outskirts
7:22 When they blew the three **h** trumpets,
8: 4 he and the three **h** who were with him,
8:10 **h** twenty thousand men bearing arms had fallen.
8:26 he requested was one thousand seven **h** shekels
11:26 three **h** years, why did you not recover them within
15: 4 So Samson went and caught three **h** foxes,
16: 5 we will each give you eleven **h** pieces of silver."
17: 2 eleven **h** pieces of silver that were taken from you,
17: 3 Then he returned the eleven **h** pieces of silver
17: 4 his mother took two **h** pieces of silver,
18:11 Six **h** men of the Danite clan,
18:16 While the six **h** men of the Danites,
18:17 of the gate with the six **h** men armed with weapons
20: 2 four **h** thousand foot-soldiers bearing arms.
20:10 We will take ten men of a **h** throughout all
20:10 and a **h** of a thousand,
20:16 seven **h** picked men who were left-handed;
20:17 mustered four **h** thousand armed men,
20:35 destroyed twenty-five thousand one **h** men
20:47 But six **h** turned and fled toward the wilderness to
21:12 four **h** young virgins who had never slept with a

1Sa 11: 8 those from Israel were three **h** thousand,
13:15 with him, about six **h** men.
14: 2 troops that were with him were about six **h** men,
15: 4 two **h** thousand foot soldiers,
17: 7 and his spear's head weighed six **h** shekels of iron;
18:25 a **h** foreskins of the Philistines,
18:27 and killed one **h** of the Philistines;
22: 2 Those who were with him numbered about four **h.**
23:13 Then David and his men, who were about six **h,**
25:13 and about four **h** men went up after David,
25:13 while two **h** remained with the baggage.
25:18 Then Abigail hurried and took two **h** loaves,
25:18 one **h** clusters of raisins, and two **h** cakes of figs.
27: 2 he and the six **h** men who were with him,
30: 9 he and the six **h** men who were with him.
30:10 David went on with the pursuit, he and four **h** men;
30:10 two **h** stayed behind, too exhausted to cross
30:17 one of them escaped, except four **h** young men,
30:21 to the two **h** men who had been too exhausted
2Sa 2:31 of David had killed of Benjamin three **h** sixty
3:14 at the price of one **h** foreskins of the Philistines."
8: 4 from him one thousand seven **h** horsemen,
8: 4 but left enough for a **h** chariots.
10:18 of the Arameans seven **h** chariot teams,
14:26 two **h** shekels by the king's weight.
15:11 Two **h** men from Jerusalem went with Absalom;
15:18 the six **h** Gittites who had followed him from Gath,
16: 1 carrying two **h** loaves of bread, one **h** bunches of raisins, one **h** of summer fruits,
21:16 whose spear weighed three **h** shekels of bronze,
23: 8 against eight **h** whom he killed at one time.
23:18 With his spear he fought against three **h** men
24: 9 in Israel there were eight **h** thousand soldiers able
24: 9 and those of Judah were five **h** thousand.
1Ki 4:23 one **h** sheep, besides deer, gazelles, roebucks,
5:16 Solomon's three thousand three **h** supervisors who
6: 1 In the four **h** eightieth year after the Israelites came
7: 2 of the Forest of the Lebanon one **h** cubits long,
7:20 there were two **h** pomegranates in rows all around;
7:42 the four **h** pomegranates for the two latticeworks,
8:63 and one **h** twenty thousand sheep.
9:14 to the king one **h** twenty talents of gold.
9:23 five **h** fifty, who had charge of
9:28 imported from there four **h** twenty talents of gold,
10:10 she gave the king one **h** twenty talents of gold,
10:14 to Solomon in one year was six **h** sixty-six talents
10:16 King Solomon made two **h** large shields
10:16 six **h** shekels of gold went into each large shield.
10:17 He made three **h** shields of beaten gold;
10:26 he had fourteen **h** chariots
10:29 be imported from Egypt for six **h** shekels of silver,
10:29 and a horse for one **h** fifty;
11: 3 Among his wives were seven **h** princesses and three **h** concubines;
12:21 one **h** eighty thousand chosen troops to fight
18: 4 Obadiah took a **h** prophets,
18:13 I hid a **h** of the LORD's prophets fifty to a cave,
18:19 with the four **h** fifty prophets of Baal and the four **h** prophets of Asherah,
18:22 but Baal's prophets number four **h** fifty.
20:15 the district governors, two **h** thirty-two;
20:29 killed one **h** thousand Aramean foot soldiers
22: 6 about four **h** of them, and said to them,
2Ki 3: 4 to the king of Israel one **h** thousand lambs,
3: 4 and the wool of one **h** thousand rams.
3:26 with him seven **h** swordsmen to break through,
4:43 "How can I set this before a **h** people?"
14:13 a distance of four **h** cubits.
18:14 of King Hezekiah of Judah three **h** talents of silver
19:35 down one **h** eighty-five thousand in the camp of
23:33 on the land of one **h** talents of silver and a talent
1Ch 4:42 And some of them, five **h** men of the Simeonites,
5:18 expert in war, forty-four thousand seven **h** sixty,
5:21 two **h** fifty thousand sheep, two thousand donkeys,
5:21 and one **h** thousand captives.
7: 2 of David being twenty-two thousand six **h.**
7: 9 mighty warriors, was twenty thousand two **h.**
7:11 mighty warriors, seventeen thousand two **h,**
8:40 and grandchildren, one **h** fifty.
9: 6 Jeuel and their kin, six **h** ninety.
9: 9 according to their generations, nine **h** fifty-six.
9:13 one thousand seven **h** sixty,
9:22 at the thresholds, were two **h** twelve.
11:11 against three **h** whom he killed at one time.
11:20 With his spear he fought against three **h**
12:14 least equal to a **h** and the greatest to a thousand.
12:24 spear numbered six thousand eight **h** armed troops.
12:25 mighty warriors, seven thousand one **h.**
12:26 Of the Levites four thousand six **h.**
12:27 and with him three thousand seven **h.**
12:30 Of the Ephraimites, twenty thousand eight **h,**
12:32 to know what Israel ought to do, two **h** chiefs,
12:35 twenty-eight thousand six **h** equipped for battle.
12:37 one **h** twenty thousand armed with all the weapons
15: 5 Uriel the chief, with one **h** twenty of his kindred;
15: 6 Asaiah the chief, with two **h** twenty of his kindred;
15: 7 Joel the chief, with one **h** thirty of his kindred;
15: 8 Shemaiah the chief, with two **h** of his kindred;
15:10 with one **h** twelve of his kindred.
18: 4 but left one **h** of them.
21: 5 In all Israel there were one million one **h** thousand
21: 5 and in Judah four **h** seventy thousand who drew
21:25 So David paid Ornan six **h** shekels of gold
22:14 for the house of the LORD one **h** thousand talents
25: 7 numbered two **h** eighty-eight.
26:30 one thousand seven **h** men of ability,
26:32 two thousand seven **h** men of ability,
1Ch 29: 7 and one **h** thousand talents of iron.
2Ch 1:14 he had fourteen **h** chariots
1:17 a chariot for six **h** shekels of silver,
1:17 and a horse for one **h** fifty;
2: 2 with three thousand six **h** to oversee them.
2:17 to be one **h** fifty-three thousand six **h.**
2:18 and three thousand six **h** as overseers to make
3: 4 and its height was one **h** twenty cubits.
3: 8 he overlaid it with six **h** talents of fine gold.
3:16 and he made one **h** pomegranates,
4: 8 And he made one **h** basins of gold.
4:13 the four **h** pomegranates for the two latticeworks,
5:12 with one **h** twenty priests who were trumpeters).
7: 5 and one **h** twenty thousand sheep.
8:10 two **h** fifty of them, who exercised authority over
8:18 and imported from there four **h** fifty talents of gold
9: 9 she gave the king one **h** twenty talents of gold,
9:13 to Solomon in one year was six **h** sixty-six talents
9:15 King Solomon made two **h** large shields
9:15 six **h** shekels of beaten gold went
9:16 He made three **h** shields of beaten gold;
9:16 three **h** shekels of gold went into each shield;
11: 1 he assembled one **h** eighty thousand chosen troops
12: 3 with twelve **h** chariots and sixty thousand cavalry.
13: 3 four **h** thousand picked men;
13: 3 with eight **h** thousand picked mighty warriors.
13:17 five **h** thousand picked men of Israel fell slain.
14: 8 Asa had an army of three **h** thousand from Judah,
14: 8 and two **h** eighty thousand troops
14: 9 with an army of a million men and three **h** chariots,
15:11 seven **h** oxen and seven thousand sheep.
17:11 also brought him seven thousand seven **h** rams
17:11 and seven thousand seven **h** male goats.
17:14 with three **h** thousand mighty warriors,
17:15 with two **h** eighty thousand,
17:16 with two **h** thousand mighty warriors.
17:17 with two **h** thousand armed with bow and shield,
17:18 with one **h** eighty thousand armed for war.
18: 5 four **h** of them, and said to them,
24:15 he was one **h** thirty years old at his death.
25: 5 that they were three **h** thousand picked troops fit
25: 6 He also hired one **h** thousand mighty warriors from Israel for one **h** talents of silver.
25: 9 about the **h** talents that I have given to the army
25:23 a distance of four **h** cubits.
26:12 of mighty warriors was two thousand six **h.**
26:13 an army of three **h** seven thousand five **h,**
27: 5 The Ammonites gave him that year one **h** talents
28: 6 of Remaliah killed one **h** twenty thousand in Judah
28: 8 of Israel took captive two **h** thousand of their kin,
29:32 one **h** rams, and two **h** lambs;
29:33 The consecrated offerings were six **h** bulls
35: 8 the passover offerings two thousand six **h** lambs
35: 8 and kids and three **h** bulls.
35: 9 and kids and five **h** bulls.
36: 3 a tribute of one **h** talents of silver and one talent
Ezr 1:10 other silver bowls, four **h** ten;
1:11 and silver vessels was five thousand four **h.**
2: 3 two thousand one **h** seventy-two.
2: 4 Of Shephatiah, three **h** seventy-two.
2: 5 Of Arah, seven **h** seventy-five.
2: 6 two thousand eight **h** twelve.
2: 7 Of Elam, one thousand two **h** fifty-four.
2: 8 Of Zattu, nine **h** forty-five.
2: 9 Of Zaccai, seven **h** sixty.
2:10 Of Bani, six **h** forty-two.
2:11 Of Bebai, six **h** twenty-three.
2:12 Of Azgad, one thousand two **h** twenty-two.
2:13 Of Adonikam, six **h** sixty-six.
2:15 Of Adin, four **h** fifty-four.
2:17 Of Bezai, three **h** twenty-three.
2:18 Of Jorah, one **h** twelve.
2:19 Of Hashum, two **h** twenty-three.
2:21 Of Bethlehem, one **h** twenty-three.
2:23 Of Anathoth, one **h** twenty-eight.
2:25 Chephirah, and Beeroth, seven **h** forty-three.
2:26 Of Ramah and Geba, six **h** twenty-one.
2:27 The people of Michmas, one **h** twenty-two.
2:28 Of Bethel and Ai, two **h** twenty-three.
2:30 Of Magbish, one **h** fifty-six.
2:31 Of the other Elam, one thousand two **h** fifty-four.
2:32 Of Harim, three **h** twenty.
2:33 Of Lod, Hadid, and Ono, seven **h** twenty-five.
2:34 Of Jericho, three **h** forty-five.
2:35 Of Senaah, three thousand six **h** thirty.
2:36 of the house of Jeshua, nine **h** seventy-three.
2:38 Of Pashhur, one thousand two **h** forty-seven.
2:41 the descendants of Asaph, one **h** twenty-eight.
2:42 of Hatita, and of Shobai, in all one **h** thirty-nine.
2:58 of Solomon's servants were three **h** ninety-two.
2:60 Tobiah, and Nekoda, six **h** fifty-two.
2:64 together was forty-two thousand three **h** sixty,
2:65 there were seven thousand three **h** thirty-seven;
2:65 and they had two **h** male and female singers.
2:66 seven **h** thirty-six horses, two **h** forty-five mules,
2:67 four **h** thirty-five camels, and six thousand seven **h** twenty donkeys.
2:69 of silver, and one **h** priestly robes.
6:17 at the dedication of this house of God one **h** bulls, two **h** rams, four **h** lambs,
7:22 up to one **h** talents of silver, one **h** cors of wheat, one **h** baths of wine, one **h** baths of oil,
8: 3 with whom were registered one **h** fifty males.
8: 4 and with him two **h** males.
8: 5 and with him three **h** males.
8: 9 and with him two **h** eighteen males.
8:10 and with him one **h** sixty males.
Ezr 8:12 and with him one **h** ten males.
8:20 besides two **h** twenty of the temple servants,
8:26 I weighed out into their hand six **h** fifty talents
8:26 one **h** silver vessels worth . . . talents, and one **h** talents of gold,
Ne 3: 1 far as the Tower of the **H** and as far as the Tower
5:17 there were at my table one **h** fifty people,
7: 8 two thousand one **h** seventy-two.
7: 9 Of Shephatiah, three **h** seventy-two.
7:10 Of Arah, six **h** fifty-two.
7:11 two thousand eight **h** eighteen.
7:12 Of Elam, one thousand two **h** fifty-four.
7:13 Of Zattu, eight **h** forty-five.
7:14 Of Zaccai, seven **h** sixty.
7:15 Of Binnui, six **h** forty-eight.
7:16 Of Bebai, six **h** twenty-eight.
7:17 Of Azgad, two thousand three **h** twenty-two.
7:18 Of Adonikam, six **h** sixty-seven.
7:20 Of Adin, six **h** fifty-five.
7:22 Of Hashum, three **h** twenty-eight.
7:23 Of Bezai, three **h** twenty-four.
7:24 Of Hariph, one **h** twelve.
7:26 of Bethlehem and Netophah, one **h** eighty-eight.
7:27 Of Anathoth, one **h** twenty-eight.
7:29 Chephirah, and Beeroth, seven **h** forty-three.
7:30 Of Ramah and Geba, six **h** twenty-one.
7:31 Of Michmas, one **h** twenty-two.
7:32 Of Bethel and Ai, one **h** twenty-three.
7:34 one thousand two **h** fifty-four.
7:35 Of Harim, three **h** twenty.
7:36 Of Jericho, three **h** forty-five.
7:37 Of Lod, Hadid, and Ono, seven **h** twenty-one.
7:38 Of Senaah, three thousand nine **h** thirty.
7:39 namely the house of Jeshua, nine **h** seventy-three.
7:41 Of Pashhur, one thousand two **h** forty-seven.
7:44 the descendants of Asaph, one **h** forty-eight.
7:45 of Akkub, of Hatita, of Shobai, one **h** thirty-eight.
7:60 of Solomon's servants were three **h** ninety-two.
7:62 of Tobiah, of Nekoda, six **h** forty-two.
7:66 together was forty-two thousand three **h** sixty,
7:67 there were seven thousand three **h** thirty-seven;
7:67 they had two **h** forty-five singers, male and female.
7:68 seven **h** thirty-six horses, two **h** forty-five mules,
7:69 four **h** thirty-five camels, and six thousand seven **h** twenty donkeys.
7:70 fifty basins, and five **h** thirty priestly robes.
7:71 of gold and two thousand two **h** minas of silver.
11: 6 Jerusalem were four **h** sixty-eight valiant warriors.
11: 8 his brothers Gabbai, Sallai: nine **h** twenty-eight.
11:12 the work of the house, eight **h** twenty-two;
11:13 heads of ancestral houses, two **h** forty-two;
11:14 valiant warriors, one **h** twenty-eight;
11:18 the Levites in the holy city were two **h** eighty-four.
11:19 at the gates, were one **h** seventy-two.
12:39 and the Tower of Hananel and the Tower of the **H,**
Est 1: 1 over one **h** twenty-seven provinces from India
1: 4 one **h** eighty days in all.
8: 9 one **h** twenty-seven provinces,
9: 6 the Jews killed and destroyed five **h** people.
9:12 of Susa the Jews have killed five **h** people and also
9:15 the month of Adar and they killed three **h** persons
9:30 the one **h** twenty-seven provinces of the kingdom
Job 1: 3 camels, five **h** yoke of oxen, five **h** donkeys,
42:16 After this Job lived one **h** and forty years,
Pr 17:10 into a discerning person than a **h** blows into a fool.
Ecc 6: 3 man may beget a **h** children, and live many years;
8:12 sinners do evil a **h** times and prolong their lives,
SS 8:12 and the keepers of the fruit two **h!**
Isa 37:36 down one **h** eighty-five thousand in the camp of
65:20 for one who dies at a **h** years will be considered a youth, and one who falls short of a **h** will
Jer 52:23 the latticework numbered one **h.**
52:29 from Jerusalem eight **h** thirty-two persons;
52:30 of the Judeans seven **h** forty-five persons;
52:30 all the persons were four thousand six **h.**
Eze 4: 5 three **h** ninety days, equal to the number of
4: 9 three **h** ninety days, you shall eat it.
40:19 to the outer front of the inner court, one **h** cubits.
40:23 he measured from gate to gate, one **h** cubits.
40:27 from gate to gate toward the south, one **h** cubits.
40:47 the court, one **h** cubits deep, and one **h** cubits wide,
41:13 Then he measured the temple, one **h** cubits deep;
41:13 and the building with its walls, one **h** cubits deep;
41:14 of the temple and the yard, one **h** cubits.
41:15 with its galleries on either side, one **h** cubits.
42: 2 that was on the north side was one **h** cubits,
42: 4 ten cubits wide and one **h** cubits deep,
42: 8 those opposite the temple were one **h** cubits long.
42:16 five **h** cubits by the measuring reed.
42:17 five **h** cubits by the measuring reed.
42:18 five **h** cubits by the measuring reed.
42:19 five **h** cubits by the measuring reed.
42:20 five **h** cubits long and five **h** cubits wide,
45: 2 a square plot of five **h** by five **h** cubits shall
45:15 and one sheep from every flock of two **h,**
48:16 the north side four thousand five **h** cubits,
48:16 the south side four thousand five **h,**
48:16 the east side four thousand five **h,**
48:16 and the west side four thousand and five **h.**
48:17 north two **h** fifty cubits, on the south two **h** fifty, on the east two **h** fifty, on the west two **h** fifty.
48:30 to be four thousand five **h** cubits by measure,
48:32 which is to be four thousand five **h** cubits,
48:33 to be four thousand five **h** cubits by measure,
48:34 which is to be four thousand five **h** cubits,
Da 6: 1 to set over the kingdom one **h** twenty satraps,
8:14 "For two thousand three **h** evenings and mornings;

Da 12:11 there shall be one thousand two **h** ninety days.
12:12 and attain the thousand three **h** thirty-five days.
Am 5: 3 that marched out a thousand shall have a **h** left,
5: 3 and that which marched out a **h** shall have ten left.
Jnh 4:11 a **h** and twenty thousand persons who do
Mt 18:12 If a shepherd has a **h** sheep,
18:28 of his fellow slaves who owed him a **h** denarii;
Mk 6:37 to go and buy two **h** denarii worth of bread,
14: 5 for more than three **h** denarii,
Lk 7:41 one owed five **h** denarii, and the other fifty.
15: 4 having a **h** sheep and losing one of them,
16: 6 He answered, 'A **h** jugs of olive oil.'
16: 7 He replied, 'A **h** containers of wheat.'
Jn 12: 5 "Why was this perfume not sold for three **h** denarii
19:39 weighing about a **h** pounds.
21: 8 only about a **h** yards off.
21:11 full of large fish, a **h** fifty-three of them;
Ac 1:15 the crowd numbered about one **h** twenty persons)
5:36 and a number of men, about four **h**, joined him;
7: 6 and mistreat them during four **h** years.
13:20 for about four **h** fifty years.
23:23 for Caesarea with two **h** soldiers,
23:23 seventy horsemen, and two **h** spearmen.
27:37 (We were in all two **h** seventy-six persons in
Ro 4:19 as good as dead (for he was about a **h** years old),
1Co 15: 6 to more than five **h** brothers and sisters at one time,
Gal 3:17 the law, which came four **h** thirty years later,
Rev 7: 4 one **h** forty-four thousand,
9:16 number of the troops of cavalry was two **h** million;
11: 3 to prophesy for one thousand two **h** sixty days,
12: 6 be nourished for one thousand two **h** sixty days.
13:18 Its number is six **h** sixty-six.
14: 1 were one **h** forty-four thousand who had his name
14: 3 **h** forty-four thousand who have been redeemed
14:20 for a distance of about two **h** miles.
16:21 each weighing about a **h** pounds,
21:16 he measured the city with his rod, fifteen **h** miles;
21:17 one **h** forty-four cubits by human measurement,
Tob 14: 2 in peace when he was one **h** twelve years old,
14:14 at the age of one **h** seventeen years.
Jdt 1: 3 At its gates he raised towers one **h** cubits high
1:16 and feasted for one **h** twenty days.
2: 5 one **h** twenty thousand foot soldiers
2:15 one **h** twenty thousand of them,
7: 2 fighting forces numbered one **h** seventy thousand
10:17 from their number a **h** men to accompany her
16:23 reaching the age of one **h** five.
AdE 1: 1 over one **h** twenty-seven provinces from India
1: 4 during the course of one **h** eighty days,
3:12 There were one **h** twenty-seven provinces in all,
8: 9 one **h** twenty-seven provinces,
9: 6 in the city of Susa the Jews killed five **h** people,
9:12 the capital, the Jews have destroyed five **h** people.
9:15 on the fourteenth and killed three **h** people,
13: 1 to the governors of the **h** twenty-seven provinces
16: 1 one **h** twenty-seven provinces,
Sir 16:10 on the six **h** thousand foot soldiers who assembled
18: 9 in their life is great if they reach one **h** years.
41: 4 Whether life lasts for ten years or a **h** or
46: 8 of six **h** thousand infantry,
1Mc 1:10 in the one **h** thirty-seventh year of the kingdom of
1:20 Antiochus returned in the one **h** forty-third year.
1:54 in the one **h** forty-fifth year,
2:70 in the one **h** forty-sixth year and was buried in
3:24 eight **h** of them fell, and the rest fled into the land
3:37 and left Antioch his capital in the one **h**
4:52 in the one **h** forty-eighth year,
6:16 in the one **h** forty-ninth year.
6:20 and besieged the citadel in the one **h** fiftieth year;
6:30 of his forces was one **h** thousand foot soldiers,
6:35 and five **h** picked horsemen were assigned
6:42 and six **h** of the king's army fell.
7: 1 In the one **h** fifty-first year Demetrius son
7:32 About five **h** of the army of Nicanor fell,
7:41 down one **h** eighty-five thousand of the Assyrians.
8: 6 to fight against them with one **h** twenty elephants
8:15 three **h** twenty senators constantly deliberate
9: 3 of the one **h** fifty-second year they encamped
9: 6 until no more than eight **h** of them were left.
9:54 In the one **h** and fifty-third year,
10: 1 In the one **h** sixtieth year Alexander Epiphanes,
10:21 in the seventh month of the one **h** sixtieth year,
10:57 came to Ptolemais in the one **h** sixty-second year.
10:67 In the one **h** sixty-fifth year Demetrius son
11:19 in the one **h** sixty-seventh year.
11:28 and promised him three **h** talents.
11:45 to the number of a **h** and twenty thousand,
11:47 and they killed on that day about one **h** thousand.
13:16 now one **h** talents of silver and two of his sons
13:19 So he sent the sons and the **h** talents,
13:41 In the one **h** seventieth year the yoke of
13:51 in the one **h** seventy-first year,
14: 1 one **h** seventy-second year King Demetrius
14:27 in the one **h** seventy-second year,
15:10 In the one **h** seventy-fourth year Antiochus set out
15:13 and with him were one **h** twenty thousand warriors
15:31 or else pay me five **h** talents of silver for
15:31 that you have caused and five **h** talents more for
15:35 for them we will give you one **h** talents."
16:14 in the one **h** seventy-seventh year,
2Mc 1: 7 in the one **h** sixty-ninth year,
1: 9 in the one **h** eighty-eighth year.
3:11 in all four **h** talents of silver and two **h** of gold.
4: 8 at an interview three **h** sixty talents of silver,
4: 9 to pay one **h** fifty more if permission were given
4:19 to carry three **h** silver drachmas for the sacrifice
4:24 outbidding Jason by three **h** talents of silver.
2Mc 5:21 So Antiochus carried off eighteen **h** talents from
8:19 when one **h** eighty-five thousand perished,
8:20 destroyed one **h** twenty thousand Galatians
8:22 putting fifteen **h** men under each.
10:31 Twenty thousand five **h** were slaughtered, besides six **h** cavalry.
11:11 of them and sixteen **h** cavalry,
11:21 The one **h** forty-eighth year,
11:33 The one **h** forty-eighth year, Xanthicus fifteenth."
11:38 The one **h** forty-eighth year, Xanthicus fifteenth."
12: 4 to sea and drowned them, at least two **h**.
12:10 with five **h** cavalry attacked them.
12:20 who had with him one **h** twenty thousand infantry and two thousand five **h** cavalry.
12:33 with three thousand infantry and four **h** cavalry.
13: 1 In the one **h** forty-ninth year word came to Judas
13: 2 a Greek force of one **h** ten thousand infantry, five thousand three **h** cavalry,
13: 2 and three **h** chariots armed with scythes.
14: 4 in about the one **h** fifty-first year,
14:39 sent more than five **h** soldiers to arrest him;
15:22 and he killed fully one **h** eighty-five thousand in
1Es 1: 8 for the passover two thousand six **h** sheep and three **h** calves.
1: 9 passover five thousand sheep and seven **h** calves.
1:36 the nation one **h** talents of silver and one talent
2:13 two thousand four **h** ten silver bowls,
2:14 gold and silver, five thousand four **h** sixty-nine,
3: 2 in the **h** twenty-seven satrapies from India
5: 9 two thousand one **h** seventy-two.
5: 9 descendants of Shephatiah, four **h** seventy-two.
5:10 The descendants of Arah, seven **h** fifty-six.
5:11 two thousand eight **h** twelve.
5:12 one thousand two **h** fifty-four.
5:12 The descendants of Zattu, nine **h** forty-five.
5:12 The descendants of Chorbe, seven **h** five.
5:12 The descendants of Bani, six **h** forty-eight.
5:13 The descendants of Bebai, six **h** twenty-three.
5:13 one thousand three **h** twenty-two.
5:14 The descendants of Adonikam, six **h** sixty-seven.
5:14 The descendants of Adin, four **h** fifty-four.
5:15 The descendants of Azaru, four **h** thirty-two.
5:16 The descendants of Annias, one **h** one.
5:16 The descendants of Bezai, three **h** twenty-three.
5:16 The descendants of Arsiphurith, one **h** twelve.
5:17 descendants of Bethlomon, one **h** twenty-three.
5:18 Those from Anathoth, one **h** fifty-eight.
5:19 from Chephirah and Beeroth, seven **h** forty-three.
5:20 Chadiasans and Ammidians, four **h** twenty-two.
5:20 Those from Kirama and Geba, six **h** twenty-one.
5:21 Those from Macalon, one **h** twenty-two.
5:21 The descendants of Niphish, one **h** fifty-six.
5:22 and Ono, seven **h** twenty-five.
5:22 The descendants of Jerechus, three **h** forty-five.
5:23 three thousand three **h** thirty.
5:24 of the descendants of Anasib, nine **h** seventy-two.
5:25 one thousand two **h** forty-seven.
5:27 the descendants of Asaph, one **h** twenty-eight.
5:28 the descendants of Shobai, in all one **h** thirty-nine.
5:35 of Solomon's servants were three **h** seventy-two.
5:37 and the descendants of Nekoda, six **h** fifty-two.
5:41 were forty-two thousand three **h** sixty;
5:42 servants were seven thousand three **h** thirty-seven;
5:42 there were two **h** forty-five musicians and singers.
5:43 There were four **h** thirty-five camels,
5:43 two **h** forty-five mules, and five thousand five **h** twenty-five donkeys.
5:45 and one **h** priests' vestments.
7: 7 of the temple of the Lord one **h** bulls, two **h** rams, four **h** lambs,
8:20 up to a **h** talents of silver, and likewise up to a **h** cors of wheat, a **h** baths of wine,
8:30 Zechariah, and with him a **h** fifty men enrolled.
8:31 and with him two **h** men.
8:32 and with him three **h** men.
8:32 and with him two **h** fifty men.
8:35 and with him two **h** twelve men.
8:36 and with him a **h** sixty men.
8:38 and with him a **h** ten men.
8:49 two **h** twenty temple servants;
8:56 six **h** fifty talents of silver, and silver vessels worth a **h** talents, and a **h** talents of gold,
3Mc 5: 2 to drug all the elephants—five **h** in number—
7:15 that day they put to death more than three **h** men;
2Es 7:28 and those who remain shall rejoice four **h** years.
4Mc 4:17 the king three thousand six **h** sixty talents annually.

HUNDREDFOLD (10) [HUNDRED]

Ge 26:12 and in the same year reaped a **h**.
2Sa 24: 3 the number of the people a **h**,
1Ch 21: 3 the LORD increase the number of his people a **h**!
Mt 13: 8 some a **h**, some sixty, some thirty.
13:23 who indeed bears fruit and yields, in one case a **h**,
19:29 will receive a **h**, and will inherit eternal life.
Mk 4: 8 and yielding thirty and sixty and a **h**."
4:20 and bear fruit, thirty and sixty and a **h**."
10:30 who will not receive a **h** now in this age—
Lk 8: 8 and when it grew, it produced a **h**."

HUNDREDS (21) [HUNDRED]

Ex 18:21 over them as officers over thousands, **h**,
18:25 as officers over thousands, **h**, fifties, and tens.
Nu 31:14 of thousands and the commanders of **h**,
31:48 of thousands and the commanders of **h**,
31:52 of thousands and the commanders of **h**,
31:54 from the commanders of thousands and of **h**,
Dt 1:15 commanders of thousands, commanders of **h**,
1Sa 22: 7 of thousands and commanders of **h**?
29: 2 As the lords of the Philistines were passing on by **h**
2Sa 18: 1 of thousands and commanders of **h**.
18: 4 all the army marched out by **h** and by thousands.
1Ch 13: 1 the commanders of the thousands and of the **h**,
26:26 and the officers of the thousands and the **h**,
27: 1 the commanders of the thousands and the **h**,
28: 1 the **h**, the stewards of all the property and cattle of
29: 6 the commanders of the thousands and of the **h**,
2Ch 1: 2 the commanders of the thousands and of the **h**,
23: 1 into a compact with the commanders of the **h**,
25: 5 under commanders of the thousands and of the **h**
Mk 6:40 So they sat down in groups of **h** and of fifties.
1Mc 3:55 in charge of thousands and **h** and fifties and tens.

HUNDREDTH (1) [HUNDRED]

Ge 7:11 In the six **h** year of Noah's life,

HUNG (16) [HANG]

Dt 21:23 for anyone **h** on a tree is under God's curse.
Jos 10:26 and he **h** them on five trees.
10:26 And they **h** on the trees until evening.
2Sa 4:12 and **h** their bodies beside the pool at Hebron.
21:12 where the Philistines had **h** them up,
Ps 137: 2 On the willows there we **h** up our harps.
La 5:12 Princes are **h** up by their hands;
Eze 27:10 they **h** shield and helmet in you;
27:11 They **h** their quivers all around your walls;
Mk 9:42 if a great millstone were **h** around your neck
Lk 17: 2 It would be better for you if a millstone were **h**
Jdt 13: 6 and took down his sword that **h** there.
14:11 as it was dawn they **h** the head of Holofernes on
1Mc 1:61 and they **h** the infants from their mothers' necks.
4:51 They placed the bread on the table and **h** up
2Mc 15:35 Judas **h** Nicanor's head from the citadel,

HUNGER (34) [HUNGRY]

Ex 16: 3 to kill this whole assembly with **h**."
Dt 8: 3 He humbled you by letting you **h**,
28:48 against you, in **h** and thirst, in nakedness and lack
32:24 wasting **h**, burning consumption,
Ne 9:15 For their **h** you gave them bread from heaven,
Job 18:12 Their strength is consumed by **h**,
30: 3 and hard **h** they gnaw the dry and desolate ground,
Ps 34:10 The young lions suffer want and **h**,
Pr 16:26 for them; their **h** urges them on.
19:15 an idle person will suffer **h**.
Isa 5:13 their nobles are dying of **h**,
49:10 they shall not **h** or thirst,
Jer 38: 9 by throwing him into the cistern to die there of **h**,
50:19 of Ephraim and in Gilead its **h** shall be satisfied.
La 2:19 who faint for **h** at the head of every street.
4: 9 by the sword than those pierced by **h**,
Eze 7:19 They shall not satisfy their **h** or fill their stomachs
34:29 so that they shall no more be consumed with **h** in
Hos 9: 4 for their bread shall be for their **h** only;
Mic 6:14 and there shall be a gnawing **h** within you;
7: 1 there is no first-ripe fig for which I **h**.
Mt 5: 6 "Blessed are those who **h** and thirst
Lk 15:17 but here I am dying of **h**!
16:21 who longed to satisfy his **h** with what fell from
Ac 27:38 After they had satisfied their **h**,
2Co 6: 5 imprisonments, riots, labors, sleepless nights, **h**;
Rev 7:16 They will **h** no more, and thirst no more;
Sir 16:27 They neither **h** nor grow weary,
18:25 In the time of plenty think of the time of **h**;
24:21 Those who eat of me will **h** for more,
2Es 15:19 of **h** for bread and because of great tribulation.
15:57 Your children shall die of **h**,
15:58 in the mountains and highlands shall perish of **h**,
15:58 in **h** for bread and drink their own blood in thirst

HUNGRY‡ (56) [HUNGER, MONEY-HUNGRY]

1Sa 2: 5 but those who were **h** are fat with spoil.
2Sa 17:29 "The troops are **h** and weary and thirsty in
Job 5: 5 The **h** eat their harvest, and they take it even out of
22: 7 and you have withheld bread from the **h**.
24:10 though **h**, they carry the sheaves;
Ps 50:12 "If I were **h**, I would not tell you,
107: 5 **h** and thirsty, their soul fainted within them.
107: 9 and the **h** he fills with good things.
107:36 And there he lets the **h** live,
146: 7 who gives food to the **h**.
Pr 6:30 to satisfy their appetite when they are **h**.
10: 3 The LORD does not let the righteous go **h**,
25:21 If your enemies are **h**, give them bread to eat;
Isa 8:21 through the land, greatly distressed and **h**;
8:21 when they are **h**, they will be enraged
9:20 They gorged on the right, but still were **h**,
29: 8 a **h** person dreams of eating and wakes up still **h**,
32: 6 to leave the craving of the **h** unsatisfied,
44:12 he becomes **h** and his strength fails,
58: 7 Is it not to share your bread with the **h**,
58:10 if you offer your food to the **h** and satisfy the needs
65:13 My servants shall eat, but you shall be **h**;
Jer 42:14 or hear the sound of the trumpet, or be **h** for bread,
Eze 18: 7 gives his bread to the **h** and covers the naked with
18:16 but gives his bread to the **h** and covers the naked
Mt 12: 1 his disciples were **h**, and they began to pluck heads
12: 3 when he and his companions were **h**?
15:32 and I do not want to send them away **h**,
21:18 when he returned to the city, he was **h**.

Mt 25:35 for I was **h** and you gave me food,
25:37 when was it that we saw you **h** and gave you food,
25:42 for I was **h** and you gave me no food,
25:44 that we saw you **h** or thirsty or a stranger or naked
Mk 2:25 and his companions were **h** and in need of food?
8:3 If I send them away **h** to their homes,
11:12 when they came from Bethany, he was **h.**
Lk 1:53 he has filled the **h** with good things,
6:3 when he and his companions were **h?**
6:21 "Blessed are you who are **h** now,
6:25 "Woe to you who are full now, for you will be **h.**
Jn 6:35 Whoever comes to me will never be **h,**
Ac 10:10 He became **h** and wanted something to eat;
Ro 12:20 No, "if your enemies are **h,** feed them;
1Co 4:11 To the present hour we are **h** and thirsty,
11:21 and one goes **h** and another becomes drunk.
11:34 If you are **h,** eat at home,
2Co 11:27 **h** and thirsty, often without food, cold and naked.
Php 4:12 the secret of being well-fed and of going **h,**
Tob 1:17 I would give my food to the **h** and my clothing to
4:16 Give some of your food to the **h,**
Sir 4:2 Do not grieve the **h,** or anger one in need.
38:32 and wherever they live, they will not go **h.**
1Mc 13:49 So they were very **h,** and many of them perished
2Es 1:17 When you were **h** and thirsty in the wilderness,
16:6 Can one drive off a **h** lion in the forest,

HUNT (12) [HUNTED, HUNTER, HUNTERS, HUNTING, HUNTS]

Ge 27:3 and go out to the field, and **h** game for me.
27:5 Esau went to the field to **h** for game and bring it,
Job 10:16 Bold as a lion you **h** me;
18:2 "How long will you **h** for words?
38:39 "Can you **h** the prey for the lion,
Ps 140:11 let evil speedily **h** down the violent!
Jer 16:16 and they shall **h** them from every mountain
Eze 13:18 for the heads of persons of every height, in the **h**
13:18 Will you **h** down lives among my people,
13:20 I am against your bands with which you **h** lives;
13:20 the lives that you **h** down like birds.
Mic 7:2 and they **h** each other with nets.

HUNTED (7) [HUNT]

Ge 27:33 "Who was it then that **h** game and brought it to me,
Isa 13:14 Like a **h** gazelle, or like sheep with no one
Jer 50:17 Israel is a **h** sheep driven away by lions.
La 3:52 without cause have **h** me like a bird;
Mk 1:36 And Simon and his companions **h** for him.
Tob 2:8 He has already been **h** down to be put to death
1Mc 2:47 They **h** down the arrogant,

HUNTER (5) [HUNT]

Ge 10:9 He was a mighty **h** before the LORD;
10:9 "Like Nimrod a mighty **h** before the LORD."
25:27 When the boys grew up, Esau was a skillful **h,**
Pr 6:5 save yourself like a gazelle from the **h,**
Sir 14:22 like a **h,** and lying in wait on her paths;

HUNTERS (1) [HUNT]

Jer 16:16 and afterward I will send for many **h,**

HUNTING (2) [HUNT]

Ge 27:30 his brother Esau came in from his **h.**
1Sa 24:11 though you are **h** me to take my life.

HUNTS (2) [HUNT]

Lev 17:13 who **h** down an animal or bird that may
1Sa 26:20 like one who **h** a partridge in the mountains."

HUPHAM (1) [HUPHAMITES]

Nu 26:39 of **H,** the clan of the Huphamites.

HUPHAMITES (1) [HUPHAM]

Nu 26:39 of Hupham, the clan of the **H.**

HUPPAH (1)

1Ch 24:13 the thirteenth to **H,** the fourteenth to Jeshebeab,

HUPPIM (3)

Ge 46:21 Ashbel, Gera, Naaman, Ehi, Rosh, Muppim, **H,**
1Ch 7:12 And Shuppim and **H** were the sons of Ir,
7:15 And Machir took a wife for **H** and for Shuppim.

HUR (15)

Ex 17:10 Aaron, and **H** went up to the top of the hill.
17:12 Aaron and **H** held up his hands, one on one side,
24:14 for Aaron and **H** are with you;
31:2 I have called by name Bezalel son of Uri son of **H,**
35:30 by name Bezalel son of Uri son of **H,** of the tribe
38:22 Bezalel son of Uri son of **H,** of the tribe of Judah,
Nu 31:8 Evi, Rekem, Zur, **H,** and Reba,
Jos 13:21 Evi and Rekem and Zur and **H** and Reba,
1Ch 2:19 Caleb married Ephrath, who bore him **H.**
2:20 **H** became the father of Uri,
2:50 The sons of **H** the firstborn of Ephrathah:
4:1 Perez, Hezron, Carmi, **H,** and Shobal.
4:4 These were the sons of **H,**
2Ch 1:5 the bronze altar that Bezalel son of Uri, son of **H,**
Ne 3:9 Next to them Rephaiah son of **H,**

HURAI (1)

1Ch 11:32 **H** of the wadis of Gaash, Abiel the Arbathite,

HURAM (10) [=HIRAM]

1Ch 8:5 Gera, Shephuphan, and **H.**
2Ch 2:3 Solomon sent word to King **H** of Tyre:
2:11 Then King **H** of Tyre answered in a letter
2:12 **H** also said, "Blessed be the LORD God of Israel,
4:11 And **H** made the pots, the shovels, and the basins.
4:11 Thus **H** finished the work that he did
8:2 Solomon rebuilt the cities that **H** had given to him,
8:18 **H** sent him, in the care of his servants,
9:10 Moreover the servants of **H** and the servants
9:21 to Tarshish with the servants of **H;**

HURAM-ABI (2) [=HIRAM]

2Ch 2:13 "I have dispatched **H,** a skilled artisan,
4:16 and all the equipment for these **H** made

HURI (1)

1Ch 5:14 These were the sons of Abihail son of **H,**

HURL (12) [HURLED, HURLING, HURLS]

Ps 60:8 Moab is my washbasin; on Edom I **h** my shoe;
108:9 Moab is my washbasin; on Edom I **h** my shoe;
Isa 22:17 The LORD is about to **h** you away violently,
28:2 with his hand he will **h** them down to the earth.
Jer 16:13 Therefore I will **h** you out of this land into a land
18:21 **h** them out to the power of the sword,
22:26 I will **h** you and the mother who bore you
Eze 26:3 I will **h** many nations against you,
Zec 9:4 of its possessions and **h** its wealth into the sea,
Lk 4:29 so that they might **h** him off the cliff.
1Mc 2:36 But they did not answer them or **h** a stone at them
2Es 1:8 the hair of your head and **h** all evils upon them,

HURLED (15) [HURL]

2Ki 19:18 and have **h** their gods into the fire,
Ne 4:5 for they have **h** insults in the face of the builders.
Ps 89:44 and **h** his throne to the ground.
Isa 37:19 and have **h** their gods into the fire,
Jer 22:28 Why are he and his offspring **h** out and cast away
La 3:53 they flung me alive into a pit and **h** stones on me;
Jnh 1:4 But the LORD **h** a great wind upon the sea,
Rev 8:7 mixed with blood, and they were **h** to the earth;
Wis 5:22 and hailstones full of wrath will be **h** as from
17:19 or the harsh crash of rocks **h** down,
18:18 and one here and another there, **h** down half dead,
2Mc 6:10 and then **h** them down headlong from the wall.
11:11 They **h** themselves like lions against the enemy,
14:46 took them in both hands and **h** them at the crowd,
4Mc 16:21 and Mishael were **h** into the fiery furnace

HURLING (1) [HURL]

2Mc 5:3 **h** of missiles, the flash of golden trappings,

HURLS (5) [HURL]

Nu 35:20 or **h** something at another, lying in wait,
35:22 or **h** any object without lying in wait,
Job 27:22 It **h** at them without pity;
Ps 147:17 He **h** down hail like crumbs—
Eze 26:3 as the sea **h** its waves.

HURRICANE (1)

Ps 83:15 with your tempest and terrify them with your **h.**

HURRIED[‡] (28) [HURRY]

Ge 43:30 With that, Joseph **h** out, because he was overcome
Ex 9:20 of the LORD **h** their slaves and livestock off to
Jos 8:14 **h** out early in the morning to
1Sa 25:18 Then Abigail **h** and took two hundred loaves,
25:23 she **h** and alighted from the donkey,
25:34 unless you had **h** and come to meet me,
2Sa 19:16 **h** to come down with the people of Judah
2Ch 26:20 They **h** him out, and he himself **h** to get out,
Ezr 4:23 they **h** to the Jews in Jerusalem and by force
Est 6:12 but Haman **h** to his house,
6:14 the king's eunuchs arrived and **h** Haman off to
8:14 mounted on their swift royal steeds, **h** out,
Job 31:5 and my foot has **h** to deceit—
Da 6:19 the king got up and **h** to the den of lions.
Mk 6:33 and they **h** there on foot from all the towns
Lk 19:6 So he **h** down and was happy to welcome him.
Jdt 13:12 they **h** down to the town gate and summoned
AdE 6:12 and Haman **h** back to his house,
Sus 1:50 So all the people **h** back.
1Mc 13:10 So he assembled all the warriors and **h** to complete
2Mc 3:18 also **h** out of their houses in crowds to make
4:14 they **h** to take part in the unlawful proceedings in
5:21 from the temple, and **h** away to Antioch, thinking
9:25 to most of you when I **h** off to the upper provinces;
12:20 in command of the divisions, and **h** after Timothy,
12:32 festival called Pentecost, they **h** against Gorgias,
3Mc 1:17 behind in the city were agitated and **h** out,

HURRIEDLY (10) [HURRY]

Ge 41:14 and he was **h** brought out of the dungeon.
Ex 10:16 Pharaoh **h** summoned Moses and Aaron and said,
12:11 your staff in your hand; and you shall eat it **h.**
1Sa 25:42 Abigail got up **h** and rode away on a donkey;
1Ki 12:18 King Rehoboam then **h** mounted his chariot to flee
2Ki 9:13 Then **h** they all took their cloaks and spread them
2Ch 10:18 King Rehoboam **h** mounted his chariot to flee
Pr 19:2 and one who moves too **h** misses the way.
AdE 6:14 the eunuchs arrived and **h** brought Haman to
2Mc 4:31 So the king went **h** to settle the trouble,

HURRIES (2) [HURRY]

Ecc 1:5 and **h** to the place where it rises.
Sir 43:5 at his orders it **h** on its course.

HURRY (27) [HURRIED, HURRIEDLY, HURRIES, HURRYING]

Ge 19:22 **H,** escape there, for I can do nothing
45:9 **H** and go up to my father and say to him,
45:13 **H** and bring my father down here."
Jos 10:13 and did not **h** to set for about a whole day.
1Sa 9:12 there he is just ahead of you. **H;**
20:38 Jonathan called after the boy, **"H,** be quick,
23:27 a messenger came to Saul, saying, **"H** and come;
2Sa 15:14 **H,** or he will soon overtake us,
2Ch 35:21 and God has commanded me to **h.**
Ps 55:8 I would **h** to find a shelter for myself from
119:60 I **h** and do not delay to keep your commandments.
Pr 1:16 for their feet run to evil, and they **h** to shed blood.
6:3 go, **h,** and plead with your neighbor.
6:18 feet that **h** to run to evil,
28:20 one who is in a **h** to be rich will not go unpunished.
28:22 a **h** to get rich and does not know that loss is sure
Hag 1:9 while all of you **h** off to your own houses.
Lk 19:5 "Zacchaeus, **h** and come down;
Ac 22:18 **'H** and get out of Jerusalem quickly,
Tob 1:6 I would **h** off to Jerusalem with the first fruits of
14:4 and **h** off to Media, for I believe the word of God
Sir 11:11 There are those who work and struggle and **h,**
3Mc 7:10 not immediately **h** to make their departure,
2Es 4:34 "Do not be in a greater **h** than the Most High.
4:34 You, indeed, are in a **h** for yourself,
4:34 but the Highest is in a **h** on behalf of many.
14:15 and **h** to escape from these times.

HURRYING[‡] (5) [HURRY]

1Sa 23:26 David was **h** to get away from Saul,
Jdt 10:15 "You have saved your life by **h** down
2Mc 9:14 which he was **h** to level to the ground and to make
2Es 4:26 because the age is **h** swiftly to its end.
14:18 that you saw in the vision is already **h** to come."

HURT (34) [HURTFUL, HURTING, HURTS]

1Ch 4:10 and that you would keep me from **h** and harm!"
Ezr 4:22 why should damage grow to the **h** of the king?"
Ps 15:4 who stand by their oath even to their **h;**
38:12 those who seek to **h** me speak of ruin,
40:14 and brought to dishonor who desire my **h.**
70:2 and brought to dishonor who desire to **h** me.
71:13 let those who seek to **h** me be covered with scorn
105:18 His feet were **h** with fetters,
Pr 9:7 whoever rebukes the wicked gets **h.**
23:35 "They struck me," you will say, "but I was not **h;**
Ecc 5:13 riches were kept by their owners to their **h,**
8:9 over another to the other's **h.**
10:9 Whoever quarries stones will be **h** by them;
Isa 11:9 not **h** or destroy on all my holy mountain;
65:25 not **h** or destroy on all my holy mountain,
Jer 7:6 if you do not go after other gods to your own **h,**
7:19 Is it not themselves, to their own **h?**
8:21 For the **h** of my poor people I am **h,** I mourn,
10:19 Woe is me because of my **h!**
30:12 Your **h** is incurable, your wound is grievous.
30:15 Why do you cry out over your **h?**
Da 3:25 in the middle of the fire, and they are not **h;**
6:22 the lions' mouths so that they would not **h** me,
Na 3:19 There is no assuaging your **h,**
Zec 12:3 all who lift it shall grievously **h** themselves.
Mk 16:18 ⟦if they drink any deadly thing, it will not **h** them;⟧
Lk 10:19 of the enemy; and nothing will **h** you.
Jn 21:17 Peter felt **h** because he said to him the third time,
Jdt 11:1 for I have never **h** anyone who chose
11:4 No one will **h** you.
Sir 9:1 or you will teach her an evil lesson to your own **h.**
31:30 the anger of a fool to his own **h,**
4Mc 5:10 you continue to despise me to your own **h.**

HURTFUL[‡] (1) [HURT]

Ezr 4:15 in the annals that this is a rebellious city, **h** to kings

HURTING (1) [HURT]

1Sa 25:34 who has restrained me from **h** you,

HURTS (2) [HURT]

Ex 21:35 If someone's ox **h** the ox of another, so that it dies,
Ac 26:14 It **h** you to kick against the goads.'

HUSBAND[‡] (149) [HUSBAND'S, HUSBANDS, HUSBANDS']

Ge 3:6 and she also gave some to her **h,**
3:16 yet your desire shall be for your **h,**
16:3 and gave her to her **h** Abram as a wife.
18:12 saying, "After I have grown old, and my **h** is old,
29:32 surely now my **h** will love me."
29:34 "Now this time my **h** will be joined to me,
30:15 a small matter that you have taken away my **h?**
30:18 because I gave my maid to my **h";**

Ge 30:20 now my **h** will honor me,
39:14 my **h** has brought among us a Hebrew to insult us!
Ex 21:22 be fined what the woman's **h** demands,
Lev 21: 3 close to him because she has had no **h**,
21: 4 as a **h** among his people and so profane himself.
21: 7 a woman divorced from her **h**.
Nu 5:13 with her but it is hidden from her **h**, so
5:20 some man other than your **h** has had intercourse
5:27 and has been unfaithful to her **h**,
30: 7 and her **h** hears of it and says nothing to her at
30: 8 But if, at the time that her **h** hears of it,
30:11 and her **h** heard it and said nothing to her,
30:12 her **h** nullifies them at the time that he hears them,
30:12 Her **h** has nullified them,
30:13 her **h** may allow to stand, or her **h** may nullify.
30:14 But if her **h** says nothing to her from day to day,
30:16 that the LORD commanded Moses concerning a **h**
Dt 21:13 after that you may go in to her and be her **h**,
24: 4 her first **h**, who sent her away, is not permitted
25:11 and the wife of one intervenes to rescue her **h** from
28:56 will begrudge food to the **h** whom she embraces,
Jdg 13: 6 Then the woman came and told her **h**,
13: 9 but her **h** Manoah was not with her.
13:10 So the woman ran quickly and told her **h**,
14:15 "Coax your **h** to explain the riddle to us,
19: 3 Then her **h** set out after her,
20: 4 Levite, the **h** of the woman who was murdered,
Ru 1: 3 But Elimelech, the **h** of Naomi, died,
1: 5 woman was left without her two sons and her **h**.
1: 9 each of you in the house of your **h**."
1:12 go your way, for I am too old to have a **h**.
1:12 even if I should have a **h** tonight and bear sons,
2:11 since the death of your **h** has been fully told me,
1Sa 1: 8 Her **h** Elkanah said to her, "Hannah,
1:18 ate and drank with her **h**,
1:22 But Hannah did not go up, for she said to her **h**,
1:23 Her **h** Elkanah said to her,
2:19 she went up with her **h** to offer the yearly sacrifice.
4:19 and that her father-in-law and her **h** were dead,
4:21 and because of her father-in-law and her **h**.
25:19 But she did not tell her **h** Nabal.
2Sa 3:15 Ishbaal sent and took her from her **h** Paltiel the son
3:16 But her **h** went with her,
11:26 When the wife of Uriah heard that her **h** was dead,
14: 5 She answered, "Alas, I am a widow; my **h** is dead.
14: 7 to my **h** neither name nor remnant on the face of
17: 3 to you as a bride comes home to her **h**.
2Ki 4: 1 "Your servant my **h** is dead;
4: 9 She said to her **h**, "Look, I am sure
4:14 "Well, she has no son, and her **h** is old."
4:22 Then she called to her **h**, and said,
4:26 Is your **h** all right?
Pr 7:19 For my **h** is not at home;
12: 4 A good wife is the crown of her **h**,
30:23 an unloved woman when she gets a **h**,
31:11 The heart of her **h** trusts in her,
31:23 Her **h** is known in the city gates,
31:28 her **h** too, and he praises her:
Isa 54: 5 For your Maker is your **h**,
Jer 3:20 Instead, as a faithless wife leaves her **h**,
6:11 both **h** and wife shall be taken,
31:32 a covenant that they broke, though I was their **h**,
Eze 16:32 who receives strangers instead of her **h**!
16:45 who loathed her **h** and her children;
Hos 2: 2 for she is not my wife, and I am not her **h**—
2: 7 she shall say, "I will go and return to my first **h**,
2:16 "My **h**," and no longer will you call me, "My
Baal."
Joel 1: 8 a virgin dressed in sackcloth for the **h** of her youth.
Mt 1:16 and Jacob the father of Joseph the **h** of Mary,
1:19 Her **h** Joseph, being a righteous man and unwilling
Mk 10:12 and if she divorces her **h** and marries another,
Lk 2:36 with her **h** seven years after her marriage,
16:18 a woman divorced from her **h** commits adultery.
Jn 4:16 Jesus said to her, "Go, call your **h**,
4:17 The woman answered him, "I have no **h**."
4:17 "You are right in saying, 'I have no **h**';
4:18 and the one you have now is not your **h**.
Ac 5: 8 "Tell me whether you and your **h** sold the land
5: 9 of those who have buried your **h** are at the door,
5:10 so they carried her out and buried her beside her **h**.
Ro 7: 2 a married woman is bound by the law to her **h**
7: 2 but if her **h** dies, she is discharged from the law
concerning the **h**.
7: 3 if she lives with another man while her **h** is alive.
7: 3 But if her **h** dies, she is free from that law,
9:10 when she had conceived children by one **h**,
1Co 7: 2 and each woman her own **h**.
7: 3 The **h** should give to his wife her conjugal rights,
and likewise the wife to her **h**.
7: 4 have authority over her own body, but the **h** does;
7: 4 the **h** does not have authority over his own body,
7:10 that the wife should not separate from her **h**
7:11 or else be reconciled to her **h**),
7:11 and that the **h** should not divorce his wife.
7:13 And if any woman has a **h** who is an unbeliever,
7:14 the unbelieving **h** is made holy through his wife,
7:14 the unbelieving wife is made holy through her **h**.
7:16 Wife, for all you know, you might save your **h**.
7:16 **H**, for all you know, you might save your wife.
7:34 about the affairs of the world, how to please her **h**.
7:39 A wife is bound as long as her **h** lives.
7:39 But if the **h** dies, she is free to marry
11: 3 and the **h** is the head of his wife,
2Co 11: 2 for I promised you in marriage to one **h**,
Eph 5:23 For the **h** is the head of the wife just as Christ is
5:33 and a wife should respect her **h**.
Rev 21: 2 prepared as a bride adorned for her **h**.
Jdt 8: 2 Her **h** Manasseh, who belonged to her tribe
8: 7 Her **h** Manasseh had left her gold and silver,
10: 3 to wear while her **h** Manasseh was living.
16:22 the days of her life after her **h** Manasseh died
16:23 and they buried her in the cave of her **h** Manasseh;
16:24 of kin to her **h** Manasseh,
AdE 1:22 in every house respect would be shown to every **h**.
15: 9 "What is it, Esther? I am your **h**. Take courage;
Sir 4:10 and be like a **h** to their mother;
22: 4 A sensible daughter obtains a **h** of her own,
22: 5 An impudent daughter disgraces father and **h**,
23:22 a woman who leaves her **h** and presents him with
23:23 she has committed an offense against her **h**;
25: 1 and a wife and a **h** who live in harmony.
25:18 Her **h** sits among the neighbors,
25:20 such is a garrulous wife to a quiet **h**.
25:22 and great disgrace when a wife supports her **h**.
25:23 from the wife who does not make her **h** happy.
26: 1 Happy is the **h** of a good wife;
26: 2 A loyal wife brings joy to her **h**,
26:13 A wife's charm delights her **h**,
26:24 *daughter will even be embarrassed before her* **h**.
26:26 *A wife honoring her* **h** *will seem wise to all,*
26:26 *Happy is the* **h** *of a good wife;*
36:26 A woman will accept any man as a **h**,
36:28 her **h** is more fortunate than other men.
42:10 or having a **h**, for fear she may go astray, or,
Sus 1:28 the people gathered at the house of her **h** Joakim,
1:63 and so did her **h** Joakim and all her relatives,
2Es 9:43 though I lived with my **h** for thirty years.
9:45 I and my **h** and all my neighbors;
10:17 Therefore go into the town to your **h**."
4Mc 18: 9 In the time of my maturity I remained with my **h**,

HUSBAND'S (12) [HUSBAND]

Nu 5:19 to uncleanness while under your **h** authority,
5:20 you have gone astray while under your **h** authority,
5:29 when a wife, while under her **h** authority,
30:10 And if she made a vow in her **h** house,
Dt 25: 5 Her **h** brother shall go in to her,
25: 5 and performing the duty of a **h** brother to her,
25: 7 at the gate and say, "My **h** brother refuses
25: 7 he will not perform the duty of a **h** brother to me."
Ru 2: 1 Now Naomi had a kinsman on her **h** side,
Pr 6:34 For jealousy arouses a **h** fury,
Jdt 16:23 and grew old in her **h** house,
Sus 1: 7 Susanna would go into her **h** garden to walk.

HUSBANDMAN (KJV) See FARMER, MAN OF THE SOIL, TILLER OF THE SOIL, VINE GROWER

HUSBANDS‡ (29) [HUSBAND]

Ru 1:11 in my womb that they may become your **h**?
Est 1:17 causing them to look with contempt on their **h**,
1:20 vast as it is, all women will give honor to their **h**,
Eze 16:45 who loathed their **h** and their children.
Am 4: 1 who say to their **h**, "Bring something to drink!"
Jn 4:18 for you have had five **h**,
1Co 14:35 let them ask their **h** at home.
Eph 5:22 Wives, be subject to your **h** as you are to the Lord.
5:24 so also wives ought to be, in everything, to their **h**.
5:25 **H**, love your wives, just as Christ loved the church
5:28 In the same way, **h** should love their wives
Col 3:18 Wives, be subject to your **h**,
3:19 **H**, love your wives and never treat them harshly.
Tit 2: 4 the young women to love their **h**,
2: 5 kind, being submissive to their **h**,
1Pe 3: 1 in the same way, accept the authority of your **h**,
3: 5 by accepting the authority of their **h**.
3: 7 **H**, in the same way, show consideration
Tob 3: 8 For she had been married to seven **h**,
3: 8 "You are the one who kills your **h**!
3: 8 you have already been married to seven **h** and have
3: 9 Because your **h** are dead?
3:15 Already seven **h** of mine have died.
6:14 to seven **h** and that they died in the bridal chamber.
AdE 1:18 will likewise dare to insult their **h**.
1:20 and thus all women will give honor to their **h**,
3Mc 4: 8 Their **h**, in the prime of youth,
2Es 16:33 women shall mourn because they have no **h**;
16:34 and their **h** shall perish of famine.

HUSBANDS' (1) [HUSBAND]

Jer 44:19 libations to her without our **h** being involved?"

HUSH (2) [HUSHED]

Am 6:10 Then the relative shall say, "**H**!
Ac 21:40 and when there was a great **h**,

HUSHAH (1)

1Ch 4: 4 and Ezer the father of **H**.

HUSHAI (14)

2Sa 15:32 **H** the Archite came to meet him with his coat torn
15:37 So **H**, David's friend, came into the city,
16:16 When **H** the Archite, David's friend,
16:16 **H** said to Absalom, "Long live the king!
16:17 Absalom said to **H**, "Is this your loyalty
16:18 **H** said to Absalom, "No;
17: 5 Then Absalom said, "Call **H** the Archite also,
17: 6 When **H** came to Absalom, Absalom said to him,
2Sa 17: 7 Then **H** said to Absalom, "This time the counsel
17: 8 **H** continued, "You know that your father
17:14 "The counsel of **H** the Archite is better than
17:15 Then **H** said to the priests Zadok and Abiathar,
1Ki 4:16 Baana son of **H**, in Asher and Bealoth;
1Ch 27:33 and **H** the Archite was the king's friend.

HUSHAM (4)

Ge 36:34 and **H** of the land of the Temanites succeeded him
36:35 **H** died, and Hadad son of Bedad,
1Ch 1:45 **H** of the land of the Temanites succeeded him.
1:46 When **H** died, Hadad son of Bedad,

HUSHATHITE (5)

2Sa 21:18 then Sibbecai the **H** killed Saph,
23:27 Abiezer of Anathoth; Mebunnai the **H**;
1Ch 11:29 Sibbecai the **H**, Ilai the Ahohite,
20: 4 then Sibbecai the **H** killed Sippai,
27:11 Eighth, for the eighth month, was Sibbecai the **H**,

HUSHED (3) [HUSH]

Job 29:10 the voices of princes were **h**,
Ps 107:29 and the waves of the sea were **h**.
Isa 16:10 in the presses; the vintage-shout is **h**.

HUSHIM‡ (3)

1Ch 7:12 and Huppim were the sons of Ir, **H** the son of Aher.
8: 8 after he had sent away his wives **H** and Baara.
8:11 He also had sons by **H**: Abitub and Elpaal.

HUSK (KJV) See GRAIN, SKINS

HUT (1)

Isa 24:20 earth staggers like a drunkard, it sways like a **h**;

HUZ (KJV) See UZ

HUZZAB (KJV) See DECREED

HYACINTH See Index to Footnotes

HYDASPES (1)

Jdt 1: 6 the Tigris, and the **H**, and, on the plain, Arioch,

HYENA (2) [HYENAS]

Jer 12: 9 Is the **h** greedy for my heritage at my command?
Sir 13:18 What peace is there between a **h** and a dog?

HYENAS (3) [HYENA]

Isa 13:22 **H** will cry in its towers, and jackals in
34:14 Wildcats shall meet with **h**,
Jer 50:39 wild animals shall live with **h** in Babylon,

HYMENAEUS (2)

1Ti 1:20 among them are **H** and Alexander,
2Ti 2:17 Among them are **H** and Philetus,

HYMN (5) [HYMNS]

Mt 26:30 When they had sung the **h**,
Mk 14:26 When they had sung the **h**,
1Co 14:26 When you come together, each one has a **h**,
Sir 39:14 Scatter the fragrance, and sing a **h** of praise;
44: 1 **H** IN HONOR OF OUR ANCESTORS

HYMNS (18) [HYMN]

Ac 16:25 and Silas were praying and singing **h** to God,
Eph 5:19 as you sing psalms and **h** and spiritual songs
Col 3:16 and with gratitude in your hearts sing psalms, **h**,
Tob 13:17 The gates of Jerusalem will sing **h** of joy,
Jdt 15:13 and wearing garlands and singing **h**.
Wis 10:20 they sang **h**, O Lord, to your holy name,
Sir 51:11 and will sing **h** of thanksgiving."
Aza 1: 1 singing **h** to God and blessing the Lord.
1Mc 4:24 On their return they sang **h** and praises
4:33 let all who know your name praise you with **h**."
13:47 and then entered it with **h** and praise.
13:51 and cymbals and stringed instruments, and with **h**
2Mc 1:30 Then the priests sang the **h**.
10: 7 they offered **h** of thanksgiving
10:38 with **h** and thanksgivings they blessed
12:37 of their ancestors he raised the battle cry, with **h**;
1Es 5:61 they sang **h**, giving thanks to the Lord,
4Mc 10:21 a tongue that has been melodious with divine **h**."

HYPOCRISY (8) [HYPOCRITE, HYPOCRITES, HYPOCRITICAL]

Mt 23:28 but inside you are full of **h** and lawlessness.
Mk 12:15 But knowing their **h**, he said to them,
Lk 12: 1 of the yeast of the Pharisees, that is, their **h**.
Gal 2:13 And the other Jews joined him in this **h**,
2:13 so that even Barnabas was led astray by their **h**.
1Ti 4: 2 through the **h** of liars whose consciences are seared
Jas 3:17 without a trace of partiality or **h**.
2Mc 13: 3 also joined them and with utter **h** urged Antiochus

HYPOCRITE (4) [HYPOCRISY]

Mt 7: 5 You **h**, first take the log out of your own eye,
Lk 6:42 You **h**, first take the log out of your own eye,

Sir 1:29 Do not be a **h** before others,
32:15 but the **h** will stumble at it.

HYPOCRITES‡ (16) [HYPOCRISY]

Ps 26: 4 nor do I consort with **h;**
Mt 6: 2 as the **h** do in the synagogues and in the streets,
6: 5 "And whenever you pray, do not be like the **h;**
6:16 whenever you fast, do not look dismal, like the **h,**
15: 7 You **h!** Isaiah prophesied rightly about you
22:18 said, "Why are you putting me to the test, you **h?**
23:13 "But woe to you, scribes and Pharisees, **h!**
23:15 Woe to you, scribes and Pharisees, **h!**
23:23 "Woe to you, scribes and Pharisees, **h!**
23:25 "Woe to you, scribes and Pharisees, **h!**
23:27 "Woe to you, scribes and Pharisees, **h!**
23:29 "Woe to you, scribes and Pharisees, **h!**
24:51 He will cut him in pieces and put him with the **h,**
Mk 7: 6 "Isaiah prophesied rightly about you **h,**
Lk 12:56 You **h!** You know how to interpret
13:15 But the Lord answered him and said, "You **h!**

HYPOCRITICAL (1) [HYPOCRISY]

Sir 33: 2 the one who is **h** about it is like a boat in a storm.

HYRCANUS (1)

2Mc 3:11 and also some money of **H** son of Tobias,

HYSSOP (12)

Ex 12:22 a bunch of **h,** dip it in the blood that is in the basin,
Lev 14: 4 and **h** be brought for the one who is to be cleansed.
14: 6 the cedarwood and the crimson yarn and the **h,**
14:49 with cedarwood and crimson yarn and **h,**
14:51 the cedarwood and the **h** and the crimson yarn,
14:52 and with the cedarwood and **h** and crimson yarn;
Nu 19: 6 The priest shall take cedarwood, **h,**
19:18 then a clean person shall take **h,**
1Ki 4:33 the cedar that is in the Lebanon to the **h** that grows
Ps 51: 7 Purge me with **h,** and I shall be clean;
Jn 19:29 the wine on a branch of **h** and held it to his mouth.
Heb 9:19 with water and scarlet wool and **h,**

I

I (9803) [ME, MY, MYSELF] See Index of Articles Etc.

I AM (61 of 1036) See Index of Articles Etc. for Exhaustive Listings of I and AM (See Introduction, page xi). See also †LORD, phrase H. I AM THE †LORD.

Ge 15: 1 "Do not be afraid, Abram, **I am** your shield;
17: 1 **"I am** God Almighty; walk before me, and be blameless.
Ex 3:14 God said to Moses, **"I AM WHO I AM."** He said further, "Thus you shall say to the Israelites, **'I AM** has sent me to you.' "
Ps 46:10 "Be still, and know that **I am** God!
Isa 41:10 do not fear, for **I am** with you, do not be afraid, for **I am** your God;
43: 3 For **I am** the LORD your God, the Holy One of Israel, your Savior.
43:11 I, **I am** the LORD, and besides me there is no savior.
43:15 **I am** the LORD, your Holy One, the Creator of Israel, your King.
44: 6 **I am** the first and **I am** the last; besides me there is no god.
48:12 **I am** He; **I am** the first, and **I am** the last.
Jer 3:14 Return, O faithless children, says the LORD, for **I am** your master;
32:27 See, **I am** the LORD, the God of all flesh; is anything too hard for me?
Mt 16:15 He said to them, "But who do you say that **I am?"**
28:20 **I am** with you always, to the end of the age."
Mk 8:29 He asked them, "But who do you say that **I am?"**
14:62 Jesus said, **"I am;** and 'you will see the Son of Man seated at the right hand of the Power,'
Jn 6:35 Jesus said to them, **"I am** the bread of life.
6:41 **"I am** the bread that came down from heaven."
6:48 **I am** the bread of life.
6:51 **I am** the living bread that came down from heaven.
8:12 saying, **"I am** the light of the world.
8:24 die in your sins unless you believe that **I am** he."
8:28 So Jesus said, "When you have lifted up the Son of Man, then you will realize that **I am** he,
8:58 Very truly, I tell you, before Abraham was, **I am."**
9: 5 as I am in the world, **I am** the light of the world."
10: 7 "Very truly, I tell you, **I am** the gate for the sheep.
10: 9 **I am** the gate. Whoever enters by me will be saved
10:11 **"I am** the good shepherd. The good shepherd lays down his life for the sheep.
10:14 **I am** the good shepherd.
Jn 10:36 blaspheming because I said, **'I am** God's Son'?
11:25 **"I am** the resurrection and the life.
13:19 when it does occur, you may believe that **I am** he.
14: 6 **"I am** the way, and the truth, and the life.
14:10 Do you not believe that **I am** in the Father and the Father is in me?
14:11 Believe me that **I am** in the Father and the Father is in me;
14:20 On that day you will know that **I am** in my Father, and you in me, and I in you.
15: 1 **"I am** the true vine, and my Father is the vinegrower.
15: 5 **I am** the vine, you are the branches.
18: 5 Jesus replied, **"I am** he."
18: 6 When Jesus said to them, **"I am** he," they stepped back and fell to the ground.
18: 8 Jesus answered, "I told you that **I am** he.
Ac 9: 5 **"I am** Jesus, whom you are persecuting.
18:10 **I am** with you, and no one will lay a hand on you
22: 8 **I am** Jesus of Nazareth whom you are persecuting.
26:15 **'I am** Jesus whom you are persecuting.
Rev 1: 8 **"I am** the Alpha and the Omega," says the Lord God, who is and who was and who is to come,
1:17 "Do not be afraid; **I am** the first and the last,
1:18 I was dead, and see, **I am** alive forever and ever;
3:11 **I am** coming soon; hold fast to what you have,
21: 6 Then he said to me, "It is done! **I am** the Alpha and the Omega, the beginning and the end.
22: 7 "See, **I am** coming soon!
22:12 "See, **I am** coming soon; my reward is with me,
22:13 **I am** the Alpha and the Omega, the first and the last, the beginning and the end."
22:16 **I am** the root and the descendant of David, the bright morning star."
22:20 "Surely **I am** coming soon."

IBEX (1)

Dt 14: 5 the roebuck, the wild goat, the **i,** the antelope,

IBHAR (3)

2Sa 5:15 **I,** Elishua, Nepheg, Japhia,
1Ch 3: 6 then **I,** Elishama, Eliphelet,
14: 5 **I,** Elishua, and Elpelet;

IBLEAM (3)

Jos 17:11 and its villages, **I** and its villages, the inhabitants
Jdg 1:27 or the inhabitants of **I** and its villages,
2Ki 9:27 in the chariot at the ascent to Gur, which is by **I.**

IBNEIAH (1)

1Ch 9: 8 **I** son of Jeroham, Elah son of Uzzi, son of Michri,

IBNIJAH (1)

1Ch 9: 8 of Shephatiah, son of Reuel, son of **I;**

IBRI (1)

1Ch 24:27 of Jaaziah, Beno, Shoham, Zaccur, and **I.**

IBSAM (1)

1Ch 7: 2 Uzzi, Rephaiah, Jeriel, Jahmai, **I,** and Shemuel,

IBZAN (2)

Jdg 12: 8 After him **I** of Bethlehem judged Israel.
12:10 Then **I** died, and was buried at Bethlehem.

ICE (7) [ICICLES]

Job 6:16 that run dark with **i,** turbid with melting snow.
37:10 By the breath of God **i** is given,
38:29 From whose womb did the **i** come forth,
Wis 16:22 Snow and **i** withstood fire without melting,
Sir 43:20 cold north wind blows, and **i** freezes on the water;
Aza 1:49 Bless the Lord, **i** and cold;
2Es 3:19 of fire and earthquake and wind and **i,**

ICHABOD (1) [ICHABOD'S]

1Sa 4:21 She named the child **I,** meaning,

ICHABOD'S (1) [ICHABOD]

1Sa 14: 3 **I** brother, son of Phinehas son of Eli,

ICICLES (1) [ICE]

Sir 43:19 and **i** form like pointed thorns.

ICONIUM (6)

Ac 13:51 in protest against them, and went to **I.**
14: 1 The same thing occurred in **I,**
14:19 But Jews came there from Antioch and **I** and won
14:21 they returned to Lystra, then on to **I** and Antioch.
16: 2 of by the believers in Lystra and **I.**
2Ti 3:11 the things that happened to me in Antioch, **I,**

IDALAH (1)

Jos 19:15 Nahalal, Shimron, **I,** and Bethlehem—

IDBASH (1)

1Ch 4: 3 of Etam: Jezreel, Ishma, and **I;**

IDDO (18)

1Ki 4:14 Ahinadab son of **I,** in Mahanaim;
1Ch 6:21 **I** his son, Zerah his son, Jeatherai his son.
27:21 for the half-tribe of Manasseh in Gilead, **I** son
2Ch 9:29 the visions of the seer **I** concerning Jeroboam son
12:15 of the prophet Shemaiah and of the seer **I,**
13:22 are written in the story of the prophet **I.**
Ezr 5: 1 Now the prophets, Haggai and Zechariah son of **I,**
6:14 of the prophet Haggai and Zechariah son of **I.**
8:17 and sent them to **I,** the leader at
8:17 to say to **I** and his colleagues the temple servants
Ne 12: 4 **I,** Ginnethoi, Abijah,
12:16 of **I,** Zechariah; of Ginnethon, Meshullam;
Zec 1: 1 the prophet Zechariah son of Berechiah son of **I,**
1: 7 the prophet Zechariah son of Berechiah son of **I;**
1Es 6: 1 of **I** prophesied to the Jews who were in Judea
8:45 I told them to go to **I,**
8:46 and ordered them to tell **I** and his kindred and
9:35 Mazitias, Zabad, **I,** Joel, Benaiah.

IDEA (2)

Wis 14:12 **i** of making idols was the beginning of fornication,
2Mc 9: 4 the **i** of turning upon the Jews the injury done

IDIOTS (1)

3Mc 5:40 as though we are **i,** ordering now for a third time

IDLE‡ (14) [IDLENESS, IDLER, IDLERS]

Pr 19:15 an **i** person will suffer hunger.
Ecc 11: 6 and at evening do not let your hands be **i;**
Am 6: 5 who sing **i** songs to the sound of the harp,
Mt 20: 3 he saw others standing **i** in the marketplace;
20: 6 'Why are you standing here **i** all day?'
Lk 24:11 But these words seemed to them an **i** tale,
2Th 3: 7 we were not **i** when we were with you,
1Ti 5:13 Besides that, they learn to be **i,**
5:13 and they are not merely **i,**
Tit 1:10 **i** talkers and deceivers, especially those of
2Pe 2: 3 pronounced against them long ago, has not been **i,**
Wis 15:12 But they considered our existence an **i** game,
Sir 33:26 leave his hands **i,** and he will seek liberty.
33:28 Put him to work, in order that he may not be **i,**

IDLENESS (7) [IDLE]

Pr 31:27 and does not eat the bread of **i.**
2Th 3: 6 to keep away from believers who are living in **i**
3:11 For we hear that some of you are living in **i,**
Tob 4:13 And in **i** there is loss and dire poverty,
4:13 because **i** is the mother of famine.
Wis 13:13 and shapes it with skill gained in **i;**
Sir 33:29 for **i** teaches much evil.

IDLER (3) [IDLE]

Sir 22: 1 The **i** is like a filthy stone,
22: 2 The **i** is like the filth of dunghills;
37:11 with an **i** about any work or with a seasonal laborer

IDLERS (1) [IDLE]

1Th 5:14 And we urge you, beloved, to admonish the **i,**

IDOL (34) [IDOLATER, IDOLATERS, IDOLATROUS, IDOLATRY, IDOLS]

Ex 20: 4 You shall not make for yourself an **i,**
Dt 4:16 not act corruptly by making an **i** for yourselves,
4:23 and not to make for yourselves an **i** in the form
4:25 if you act corruptly by making an **i** in the form
5: 8 You shall not make for yourself an **i,**
27:15 be anyone who makes an **i** or casts an image,
Jdg 17: 3 to make an **i** of cast metal."
17: 4 who made it into an **i** of cast metal;
18:14 teraphim, and an **i** of cast metal?
18:17 the land proceeded to enter and take the **i**
18:18 the men went into Micah's house and took the **i**
18:20 He took the ephod, the teraphim, and the **i,**
18:30 Then the Danites set up the **i** for themselves.
18:31 So they maintained as their own Micah's **i**
1Sa 19:13 Michal took an **i** and laid it on the bed;
19:16 the messengers came in, the **i** was in the bed,
2Ch 33: 7 The carved image of the **i** that he had made he set
33:15 He took away the foreign gods and the **i** from
Isa 40:19 An **i?**—A workman casts it,
44:17 The rest of it he makes into a god, his **i,**
48: 5 so that you would not say, "My **i** did them,
66: 3 like one who blesses an **i.**
Hos 10: 6 and Israel shall be ashamed of his **i.**
Hab 2:18 What use is an **i** once its maker has shaped it—
2:18 though the product is only an **i** that cannot speak!
Ac 7:41 offered a sacrifice to the **i,**
1Co 8: 4 we know that "no **i** in the world really exists,"
8: 7 of the food they eat as food offered to an **i;**
8:10 eating in the temple of an **i,** might they not,
10:19 or that an **i** is anything?
Wis 14: 8 But the **i** made with hands is accursed,
Sir 30:19 Of what use to an **i** is a sacrifice?
Bel 1: 3 Now the Babylonians had an **i** called Bel,
1Mc 10:83 the temple of their **i,** for safety.

IDOLATER (2) [IDOL]

1Co 5:11 or is an **i,** reviler, drunkard, or robber.
Eph 5: 5 or one who is greedy (that is, an **i),**

IDOLATERS (5) [IDOL]

1Co 5:10 or the greedy and robbers, or **i,**
6: 9 Fornicators, **i,** adulterers, male prostitutes,

1Co 10: 7 Do not become **i** as some of them did;
Rev 21: 8 the murderers, the fornicators, the sorcerers, the **i**,
22:15 and sorcerers and fornicators and murderers and **i**,

IDOLATROUS (3) [IDOL]

2Ki 23: 5 He deposed the **i** priests whom the kings
Hos 10: 5 and its **i** priests shall wail over it,
Zep 1: 4 of Baal and the name of the **i** priests;

IDOLATRY (7) [IDOL]

1Sa 15:23 and stubbornness is like iniquity and **i.**
Eze 23:49 and you shall bear the penalty for your sinful **i;**
43: 9 Now let them put away their **i** and the corpses
Gal 5:20 **i**, sorcery, enmities, strife,
Col 3: 5 passion, evil desire, and greed (which is **i**).
1Pe 4: 3 drunkenness, revels, carousing, and lawless **i.**
Sir 46:11 into **i** and who did not turn away from the Lord—

IDOLS (146) [IDOL]

Ex 34:17 You shall not make cast **i.**
Lev 19: 4 not turn to **i** or make cast images for yourselves:
26: 1 for yourselves no **i** and erect no carved images
26:30 on the carcasses of your **i.**
Dt 7: 5 down their sacred poles, and burn their **i** with fire.
12: 3 and hew down the **i** of their gods,
29:17 the filthy **i** of wood and stone, of silver and gold,
32:21 provoked me with their **i.**
1Sa 31: 9 to carry the good news to the houses of their **i** and
2Sa 5:21 The Philistines abandoned their **i** there,
1Ki 15:12 and removed all the **i** that his ancestors had made.
16:13 the LORD God of Israel to anger with their **i.**
16:26 the God of Israel, to anger by their **i.**
21:26 He acted most abominably in going after **i**,
2Ki 17:12 they served **i**, of which the LORD had said
17:15 They went after false **i** and became false;
21:11 and has caused Judah also to sin with his **i;**
21:21 served the **i** that his father served,
23:24 **i**, and all the abominations that were seen in
1Ch 10: 9 to carry the good news to their **i** and to the people.
16:26 For all the gods of the peoples are **i**,
2Ch 15: 8 and put away the abominable **i** from all the land
24:18 and served the sacred poles and the **i.**
Ps 31: 6 You hate those who pay regard to worthless **i**,
78:58 they moved him to jealousy with their **i.**
96: 5 For all the gods of the peoples are **i**,
97: 7 those who make their boast in worthless **i;**
106:36 They served their **i**, which became a snare
106:38 whom they sacrificed to the **i** of Canaan;
115: 4 Their **i** are silver and gold,
135:15 The **i** of the nations are silver and gold,
Isa 2: 8 Their land is filled with **i;**
2:18 The **i** shall utterly pass away.
2:20 to the bats their **i** of silver and their **i** of gold,
10:10 of the **i** whose images were greater than those
10:11 not do to Jerusalem and her **i** what I have done
19: 1 the **i** of Egypt will tremble at his presence,
19: 3 the **i** and the spirits of the dead and the ghosts and
30:22 Then you will defile your silver-covered **i**
31: 7 you shall throw away your **i** of silver and **i** of gold,
42: 8 my glory I give to no other, nor my praise to **i.**
44: 9 All who make **i** are nothing,
45:16 the makers of **i** go in confusion together.
45:20 those who carry about their wooden **i**,
46: 1 Nebo stoops, their **i** are on beasts and cattle;
57:13 you cry out, let your collection of **i** deliver you!
Jer 8:19 to anger with their images, with their foreign **i**?")
10: 5 Their **i** are like scarecrows in a cucumber field,
10: 8 the instruction given by **i** is no better than wood!
10:14 goldsmiths are all put to shame by their **i;**
14:22 Can any **i** of the nations bring rain?
16:18 with the carcasses of their detestable **i**,
50: 2 Her images are put to shame, her **i** are dismayed.
50:38 For it is a land of images, and they go mad over **i.**
51:17 goldsmiths are all put to shame by their **i;**
51:52 says the LORD, when I will punish her **i**,
Eze 6: 4 and I will throw down your slain in front of your **i.**
6: 5 of the people of Israel in front of their **i;**
6: 6 your **i** broken and destroyed,
6: 9 and their wanton eyes that turned after their **i.**
6:13 their slain lie among their **i** around their altars,
6:13 wherever they offered pleasing odor to all their **i.**
8:10 and all the **i** of the house of Israel.
14: 3 these men have taken their **i** into their hearts,
14: 4 of those of the house of Israel who take their **i**
14: 4 with the multitude of their **i**,
14: 5 all of whom are estranged from me through their **i.**
14: 6 Repent and turn away from your **i;**
14: 7 taking their **i** into their hearts
16:36 and because of all your abominable **i**,
18: 6 upon the mountains or lift up his eyes to the **i** of
18:12 lifts up his eyes to the **i**, commits abomination,
18:15 upon the mountains or lift up his eyes to the **i** of
20: 7 and do not defile yourselves with the **i** of Egypt;
20: 8 nor did they forsake the **i** of Egypt.
20:16 for their heart went after their **i.**
20:18 nor defile yourselves with their **i.**
20:24 and their eyes were set on their ancestors' **i.**
20:31 you defile yourselves with all your **i** to this day.
20:39 Go serve your **i**, everyone of you now
20:39 with your gifts and your **i.**
22: 3 making its **i**, defiling itself.
22: 4 and defiled by the **i** that you have made;
23: 7 and she defiled herself with all the **i** of everyone
23:30 and polluted yourself with their **i.**
23:37 with their **i** they have committed adultery;
Eze 23:39 they had slaughtered their children for their **i**,
30:13 I will destroy the **i** and put an end to the images
33:25 and lift up your eyes to your **i**, and shed blood;
36:18 and for the **i** with which they had defiled it.
36:25 and from all your **i** I will cleanse you.
37:23 with their **i** and their detestable things,
44:10 from me after their **i** when Israel went astray,
44:12 before their **i** and made the house of Israel stumble
Da 11: 8 with their **i** and with their precious vessels
Hos 4:17 Ephraim is joined to **i**—let him alone.
8: 4 and gold they made **i** for their own destruction.
11: 2 to the Baals, and offering incense to **i.**
13: 2 **i** of silver made according to their understanding,
14: 8 O Ephraim, what have I to do with **i**?
Jnh 2: 8 who worship vain **i** forsake their true loyalty.
Mic 1: 7 and all her **i** I will lay waste;
Zec 13: 2 I will cut off the names of the **i** from the land,
Ac 15:20 from things polluted by **i** and from fornication and
15:29 that you abstain from what has been sacrificed to **i**
17:16 to see that the city was full of **i.**
21:25 from what has been sacrificed to **i** and from blood
Ro 2:22 You that abhor **i**, do you rob temples?
1Co 8: 1 Now concerning food sacrificed to **i:**
8: 4 Hence, as to the eating of food offered to **i**,
8: 7 some have become so accustomed to **i** until now,
8:10 to the point of eating food sacrificed to **i**?
10:14 my dear friends, flee from the worship of **i.**
10:19 That food sacrificed to **i** is anything,
12: 2 you were enticed and led astray to **i** that could
2Co 6:16 What agreement has the temple of God with **i**?
1Th 1: 9 and how you turned to God from **i**,
1Jn 5:21 Little children, keep yourselves from **i.**
Rev 2:14 so that they would eat food sacrificed to **i**
2:20 and to eat food sacrificed to **i.**
9:20 of their hands or give up worshiping demons and **i**
Tob 14: 6 They will all abandon their **i**,
AdE 14: 8 but they have covenanted with their **i**
14:10 the mouths of the nations for the praise of vain **i**,
Wis 14:11 there will be a visitation also upon the heathen **i**,
14:12 idea of making **i** was the beginning of fornication,
14:27 the worship of **i** not to be named is the beginning
14:29 in lifeless **i** they swear wicked oaths and expect
14:30 about God in devoting themselves to **i**,
15:15 For they thought that all their heathen **i** were gods,
15:17 since they have life, but the **i** never had.
LtJ 6:44 Whatever is done for these **i** is false.
6:63 But these **i** are not to be compared with them
6:73 therefore, is someone upright who has no **i;**
Bel 1: 5 "Because I do not revere **i** made with hands,
1Mc 1:43 they sacrificed to **i** and profaned the sabbath.
1:47 and sacred precincts and shrines for **i**,
13:47 the houses in which the **i** were located,
2Mc 12:40 of the dead they found sacred tokens of the **i**
1Es 2:10 from Jerusalem and stored in his temple of **i.**
Pm 151: 6 and he cursed me by his **i.**
3Mc 4:16 organizing feasts in honor of all his **i**,
2Es 16:68 and force you to eat what was sacrificed to **i.**
4Mc 5: 2 to eat pork and food sacrificed to **i.**

IDUEL (1)

1Es 8:43 I sent word to Eliezar, **I**, Maasmas,

IDUMEA (7) [IDUMEANS]

Mk 3: 8 Jerusalem, **I**, beyond the Jordan,
1Mc 4:15 and to the plains of **I**, and to Azotus and Jamnia;
4:29 They came into **I** and encamped at Beth-zur,
4:61 the people might have a stronghold that faced **I.**
5: 3 Judas made war on the descendants of Esau in **I**,
6:31 through **I** and encamped against Beth-zur,
2Mc 12:32 they hurried against Gorgias, the governor of **I**,

IDUMEANS (3) [IDUMEA]

2Mc 10:15 the **I**, who had control of important strongholds,
10:16 rushed to the strongholds of the **I.**
1Es 4:50 that the **I** should give up the villages of the Jews

IEZER (1) [IEZERITES]

Nu 26:30 of **I**, the clan of the Iezerites;

IEZERITES (1) [IEZER]

Nu 26:30 of Iezer, the clan of the **I;**

IF‡ (1938)

Ge 4: 7 **I** you do well, will you not be accepted?
4: 7 **i** you do not do well, sin is lurking at the door;
4:24 **I** Cain is avenged sevenfold,
8: 8 to see **i** the waters had subsided from the face of
13: 9 **I** you take the left hand, then I will go to the right;
13: 9 or **i** you take the right hand,
13:16 so that **i** one can count the dust of the earth,
15: 5 **i** you are able to count them."
18: 3 He said, "My lord, **i** I find favor with you,
18:21 that has come to me; and **i** not,
18:26 "**I** I find at Sodom fifty righteous in the city,
18:28 "I will not destroy it **i** I find forty-five there."
18:30 he said, "Oh do not let the Lord be angry **i** I speak.
18:30 "I will not do it, **i** I find thirty there."
18:32 not let the Lord be angry **i** I speak just once more.
20: 7 But **i** you do not restore her,
23: 8 "**I** you are willing that I should bury my dead out
23:13 "**I** you only will listen to me!
24: 8 But **i** the woman is not willing to follow you,
24:41 even **i** they will not give her to you,
24:42 **i** now you will only make successful
Ge 24:49 **i** you will deal loyally and truly with my master,
24:49 and **i** not, tell me, so that I may turn either to
25:22 she said, "**I** it is to be this way, why do I live?"
27:46 **I** Jacob marries one of the Hittite women such
28:20 saying, "**I** God will be with me,
30:27 Laban said to him, "**I** you will allow me to say so,
30:31 **i** you will do this for me,
30:33 **i** found with me, shall be counted stolen."
31: 8 **I** he said, 'The speckled shall be your wages,'
31: 8 and **i** he said, 'The striped shall be your wages,'
31:42 **I** the God of my father,
31:50 **I** you ill-treat my daughters,
31:50 or **i** you take wives in addition to my daughters,
32: 8 "**I** Esau comes to the one company and destroys it,
33:10 Jacob said, "No, please; **i** I find favor with you,
33:13 and **i** they are overdriven for one day,
34:17 But **i** you will not listen to us and be circumcised,
34:30 **i** they gather themselves against me and attack me,
37:14 see **i** it is well with your brothers and with
37:26 "What profit is it **i** we kill our brother
38:17 And she said, "Only **i** you give me a pledge,
42:19 **i** you are honest men, let one
42:37 "You may kill my two sons **i** I do
42:38 **I** harm should come to him on the journey
43: 4 **I** you will send our brother with us,
43: 5 but **i** you will not send him,
43: 9 **I** I do not bring him back to you and set him
43:10 **I** we had not delayed, we would
43:11 their father Israel said to them, "**I** it must be so,
43:14 As for me, **i** I am bereaved of my children,
44:22 for **i** he should leave his father,
44:26 Only **i** our youngest brother goes with us,
44:29 **I** you take this one also from me,
44:32 saying, '**I** I do not bring him back to you,
44:34 For how can I go back to my father **i** the boy is not
47: 6 and **i** you know that there are capable men
47:16 for your livestock, **i** your money is gone."
47:29 "**I** I have found favor with you,
50: 4 "**I** now I have found favor with you,
50:15 "What **i** Joseph still bears a grudge against us
Ex 1:16 and see them on the birthstool, **i** it is a boy,
1:16 but **i** it is a girl, she shall live."
3:13 "**I** I come to the Israelites and say to them,
4: 8 "**I** they will not believe you or heed the first sign,
4: 9 **I** they will not believe even these two signs
8: 2 **I** you refuse to let them go,
8:21 For **i** you will not let my people go,
8:26 **I** we offer in the sight of the Egyptians sacrifices
9: 2 For **i** you refuse to let them go and still hold them,
10: 4 For **i** you refuse to let my people go,
10:10 **i** ever I let your little ones go with you!
12: 4 **I** a household is too small for a whole lamb,
12:48 **I** an alien who resides with you wants to celebrate
13:13 **i** you do not redeem it, you must break its neck.
13:17 for God thought, "**I** the people face war,
15:26 "**I** you will listen carefully to the voice of
16: 3 "**I** only we had died by the hand of the LORD in
18:23 **I** you do this, and God so commands you,
19: 5 **i** you obey my voice and keep my covenant,
20:25 But **i** you make for me an altar of stone,
20:25 for **i** you use a chisel upon it you profane it.
21: 3 **I** he comes in single, he shall go out single;
21: 3 **i** he comes in married, then his wife shall go out
21: 4 **I** his master gives him a wife
21: 5 But **i** the slave declares, "I love my master,
21: 8 **I** she does not please her master,
21: 9 **I** he designates her for his son,
21:10 **I** he takes another wife to himself,
21:11 And **i** he does not do these three things for her,
21:13 **I** it was not premeditated,
21:14 But **i** someone willfully attacks and kills another
21:21 But **i** the slave survives a day or two,
21:23 **I** any harm follows, then you shall give life
21:27 **I** the owner knocks out a tooth of a male
21:29 **I** the ox has been accustomed to gore in the past,
21:30 **I** a ransom is imposed on the owner,
21:31 **I** it gores a boy or a girl,
21:32 **I** the ox gores a male or female slave,
21:33 **I** someone leaves a pit open,
21:35 **I** someone's ox hurts the ox of another,
21:36 But **i** it was known that the ox was accustomed
22: 1 thief shall make restitution, but **i** unable to do so,
22: 2 **I** a thief is found breaking in,
22: 3 but **i** it happens after sunrise,
22: 7 then the thief, **i** caught, shall pay double.
22: 8 **I** the thief is not caught,
22:12 But **i** it was stolen, restitution shall be made
22:13 **I** it was mangled by beasts,
22:15 **I** the owner was present, there shall
22:15 **i** it was hired, only the hiring fee is due.
22:17 But **i** her father refuses to give her to him,
22:23 **I** you do abuse them, when they cry out to me,
22:25 **I** you lend money to my people,
22:26 **I** you take your neighbor's cloak in pawn,
22:27 And **i** your neighbor cries out to me, I will listen,
23:22 But **i** you listen attentively to his voice and do all
23:33 for **i** you worship their gods,
29:34 **I** any of the flesh for the ordination,
32:32 But now, **i** you will only forgive their sin—
32:32 but **i** not, blot me out of the book
33: 5 **i** for a single moment I should go up among you,
33:13 Now **i** I have found favor in your sight,
33:15 And he said to him, "**I** your presence will not go,
34: 9 He said, "**I** now I have found favor in your sight,
34:20 **i** you will not redeem it you shall break its neck.
40:37 but **i** the cloud was not taken up,
Lev 1: 3 **I** the offering is a burnt offering from the herd,

Lev 1:10 **I** your gift for a burnt offering is from the flock,
1:14 **I** your offering to the LORD is a burnt offering
2: 5 **I** your offering is grain prepared on a griddle,
2: 7 **I** your offering is grain prepared in a pan,
2:14 **I** you bring a grain offering of first fruits to
3: 1 **I** the offering is a sacrifice of well-being,
3: 1 **i** you offer an animal of the herd,
3: 6 **I** your offering for a sacrifice of well-being to
3: 7 **I** you present a sheep as your offering,
3:12 **I** your offering is a goat,
4: 3 **I** it is the anointed priest who sins,
4:13 **I** the whole congregation of Israel
4:27 **I** anyone of the ordinary people
4:32 **I** the offering you bring as a sin offering is
5: 7 But **i** you cannot afford a sheep,
5:11 But **i** you cannot afford two turtledoves
5:17 **I** any of you sin without knowing it,
6: 2 or by robbery, or **i** you have defrauded a neighbor,
6: 3 **i** you swear falsely regarding any of
6:28 but **i** it is boiled in a bronze vessel,
7:12 **I** you offer it for thanksgiving,
7:16 But **i** the sacrifice you offer is a votive offering or
7:18 **I** any of the flesh of your sacrifice
7:25 **I** any one of you eats the fat from an animal
10:19 **I** I had eaten the sin offering today,
11:33 And **i** any of them falls into any earthen vessel,
11:34 food that could be eaten shall be unclean **i** water
11:34 that could be drunk shall be unclean **i** it was
11:37 **I** any part of their carcass falls
11:38 but **i** water is put on the seed and any part
11:39 **I** an animal of which you may eat dies,
12: 2 **I** a woman conceives and bears a male child,
12: 5 **I** she bears a female child,
12: 8 **I** she cannot afford a sheep,
13: 3 and **i** the hair in the diseased area has turned white
13: 4 But **i** the spot is white in the skin of his body,
13: 5 and **i** he sees that the disease is checked and
13: 6 and **i** the disease has abated and the disease has
13: 7 But **i** the eruption spreads in the skin
13: 8 and **i** the eruption has spread in the skin,
13:10 and **i** there is a white swelling in the skin
13:12 But **i** the disease breaks out in the skin,
13:13 and **i** the disease has covered all his body,
13:14 But **i** raw flesh ever appears on him,
13:16 But **i** the raw flesh again turns white,
13:17 and **i** the disease has turned white,
13:20 and **i** it appears deeper than the skin
13:21 But **i** the priest examines it and the hair on it is
13:22 **I** it spreads in the skin,
13:23 But **i** the spot remains in one place and does
13:25 **I** the hair in the spot has turned white
13:26 But **i** the priest examines it and the hair in
13:27 **i** it is spreading in the skin,
13:28 But **i** the spot remains in one place and does
13:30 **I** it appears deeper than the skin and the hair
13:31 **I** the priest examines the itching disease,
13:32 **i** the itch has not spread,
13:34 **i** the itch has not spread in the skin and it appears
13:35 But **i** the itch spreads in the skin
13:36 **I** the itch has spread in the skin,
13:37 But **i** in his eyes the itch is checked,
13:39 and **i** the spots on the skin of the body are of
13:40 **I** anyone loses the hair from his head,
13:41 **I** he loses the hair from his forehead and temples,
13:42 But **i** there is on the bald head or the bald forehead
13:43 **i** the diseased swelling is reddish-white
13:49 **i** the disease shows greenish or reddish in
13:51 **I** the disease has spread in the cloth,
13:53 **I** the priest makes an examination,
13:55 **I** the diseased spot has not changed color,
13:56 **I** the priest makes an examination,
13:57 **I** it appears again in the garment, in warp or woof,
14: 3 **I** the disease is healed in the leprous person,
14:21 But **i** he is poor and cannot afford so much,
14:37 **i** the disease is in the walls of the house
14:37 and **i** it appears to be deeper than the surface,
14:39 **i** the disease has spread in the walls of the house,
14:43 **I** the disease breaks out again in the house,
14:44 **i** the disease has spread in the house,
14:48 **I** the priest comes and makes an inspection,
15: 8 **I** the one with the discharge spits
15:16 **I** a man has an emission of semen,
15:18 **I** a man lies with a woman and has an emission
15:24 **I** any man lies with her, and her impurity falls
15:25 **I** a woman has a discharge of blood
15:25 or **i** she has a discharge beyond the time
15:28 **I** she is cleansed of her discharge,
17: 3 **I** anyone of the house of Israel slaughters an ox or
17:10 **I** anyone of the house of Israel or of
17:16 **i** they do not wash themselves or bathe their body,
19: 7 **I** it is eaten at all on the third day,
19:20 **I** a man has sexual relations with a woman who is
20: 4 And **i** the people of the land should ever close
20: 6 **I** any turn to mediums and wizards,
20:10 **I** a man commits adultery with the wife
20:12 **I** a man lies with his daughter-in-law,
20:13 **I** a man lies with a male as with a woman,
20:14 **I** a man takes a wife and her mother also,
20:15 **I** a man has sexual relations with an animal,
20:16 **I** a woman approaches any animal
20:17 **I** a man takes his sister, a daughter of his father or
20:18 **I** a man lies with a woman having her sickness
20:20 **I** a man lies with his uncle's wife,
20:21 **I** a man takes his brother's wife, it is impurity;
22: 3 **I** anyone among all your offspring
22:11 but **i** a priest acquires anyone by purchase,
22:12 **I** a priest's daughter marries a layman,

Lev 22:13 but **i** a priest's daughter is widowed or divorced,
22:14 **I** a man eats of the sacred donation unintentionally,
25:16 **I** the years are more, you shall increase the price,
25:16 **i** the years are fewer, you shall diminish the price;
25:20 **i** we may not sow or gather in our crop?
25:25 **I** anyone of your kin falls into difficulty and sells
25:26 **I** the person has no one to redeem it,
25:28 But **i** there is not sufficient means to recover it,
25:29 **I** anyone sells a dwelling house in a walled city,
25:30 **I** it is not redeemed before a full year has elapsed,
25:35 **I** any of your kin fall into difficulty
25:39 **I** any who are dependent on you become
25:47 **I** resident aliens among you prosper,
25:47 and **i** any of your kin fall into difficulty with one
25:49 or **i** they prosper they may redeem themselves.
25:51 **I** many years remain, they shall pay
25:52 and **i** few years remain until the jubilee year,
25:54 And **i** they have not been redeemed in any
26: 3 **I** you follow my statutes
26:14 But **i** you will not obey me,
26:15 **i** you spurn my statutes, and abhor my ordinances,
26:18 And **i** in spite of this you will not obey me,
26:21 **I** you continue hostile to me,
26:23 **I** in spite of these punishments you have
26:25 and **i** you withdraw within your cities,
26:27 But **i**, despite this, you disobey me,
26:37 as **i** to escape a sword, though no one pursues;
26:40 But **i** they confess their iniquity and the iniquity
26:41 **i** then their uncircumcised heart is humbled
27: 4 **I** the person is a female,
27: 5 **I** the age is from five to twenty years of age,
27: 6 **I** the age is from one month to five years,
27: 7 And **i** the person is sixty years old or over,
27: 8 **I** any cannot afford the equivalent,
27: 9 **I** it concerns an animal that may be brought as
27:10 and **i** one animal is substituted for another,
27:11 **I** it concerns any unclean animal that may not
27:13 But **i** it is to be redeemed,
27:14 **I** a person consecrates a house to the LORD,
27:15 And **i** the one who consecrates the house wishes
27:16 **I** a person consecrates to the LORD any inherited
27:17 **I** the person consecrates the field as of the year
27:18 but **i** the field is consecrated after the jubilee,
27:19 And **i** the one who consecrates the field wishes
27:20 but **i** the field is not redeemed,
27:20 or **i** it has been sold to someone else,
27:22 **I** someone consecrates to the LORD a field
27:27 **I** it is an unclean animal, it shall be ransomed
27:27 **i** it is not redeemed, it shall be sold
27:31 **I** persons wish to redeem any of their tithes,
27:33 **i** one makes substitution for it,
Nu 5: 8 **I** the injured party has no next of kin
5:12 **I** any man's wife goes astray and is unfaithful
5:13 **i** a man has had intercourse with her
5:14 **i** a spirit of jealousy comes on him,
5:14 or **i** a spirit of jealousy comes on him,
5:19 saying, "**I** no man has lain with you,
5:19 **i** you have not turned aside to uncleanness while
5:20 But **i** you have gone astray while
5:20 **i** you have defiled yourself
5:27 **i** she has defiled herself and has been unfaithful
5:28 **i** the woman has not defiled herself and is clean,
6: 7 Even **i** their father or mother, brother or sister,
6: 9 **I** someone dies very suddenly nearby,
9:21 or **i** it continued for a day and a night,
10: 4 But **i** only one is blown, then the leaders,
10:32 Moreover, **i** you go with us,
11: 4 and said, "**I** only we had meat to eat!
11:15 **I** this is the way you are going to treat me,
11:15 **i** I have found favor in your sight—
11:18 saying, '**I** only we had meat to eat!
12:14 "**I** her father had but spit in her face,
14: 8 **I** the LORD is pleased with us,
14:15 Now **i** you kill this people all at one time,
15:22 But **i** you unintentionally fail
15:24 then **i** it was done unintentionally without
16:29 **I** these people die a natural death,
16:29 or **i** a natural fate comes on them,
16:30 But **i** the LORD creates something new,
19:12 but **i** they do not purify themselves on
20:19 and **I** we drink of your water,
21: 2 "**I** you will indeed give this people into our hands,
22:20 "**I** the men have come to summon you,
22:33 **I** it had not turned away from me,
22:34 **i** it is displeasing to you, I will return home."
24:13 '**I** Balak should give me his house full of silver
27: 8 You shall also say to the Israelites, "**I** a man dies,
27: 9 **I** he has no daughter,
27:10 **I** he has no brothers,
27:11 And **i** his father has no brothers,
30: 5 But **i** her father expresses disapproval to her at
30: 6 **I** she marries, while obligated by her vows
30: 8 But **i**, at the time that her husband hears of it,
30:10 And **i** she made a vow in her husband's house,
30:12 But **i** her husband nullifies them at the time
30:14 **i** her husband says nothing to her from day to day,
30:15 But **i** he nullifies them some time
32: 5 "**I** we have found favor in your sight,
32:15 **I** you turn away from following him,
32:20 So Moses said to them, "**I** you do this—
32:20 **i** you take up arms to go before the LORD for
32:23 But **i** you do not do this,
32:29 "**I** the Gadites and the Reubenites,
32:30 but **i** they will not cross over with you armed,
33:55 But **i** you do not drive out the inhabitants of
35:20 Likewise, **i** someone pushes another from hatred,
35:22 But **i** someone pushes another suddenly

Nu 35:26 But **i** the slayer shall at any time go outside
35:30 **I** anyone kills another, the murderer shall be put
36: 3 But **i** they are married into another Israelite tribe,
Dt 2:27 "**I** you let me pass through your land,
4:25 **i** you act corruptly by making an idol in the form
4:29 and you will find him **i** you search after him
5:25 **i** we hear the voice of the LORD
5:29 **I** only they had such a mind as this,
6:25 **I** we diligently observe this entire commandment
7:12 **I** you heed these ordinances,
7:17 **I** you say to yourself, "These nations are more
8:19 **I** you do forget the LORD your God
11:13 **I** you will only heed his every commandment
11:22 **I** you will diligently observe this entire
11:27 **i** you obey the commandments of the LORD
11:28 **i** you do not obey the commandments of the LORD
12:21 **I** the place where the LORD your God will choose
13: 1 **I** prophets or those who divine by dreams appear
13: 6 **I** anyone secretly entices you—
13: 6 even **i** it is your brother, your father's son
13:12 **I** you hear it said about one of the towns that
13:14 **I** the charge is established that such
13:18 **i** you obey the voice of the LORD your God
14:24 But **i**, when the LORD your God has blessed you,
15: 5 **i** only you will obey the LORD your God
15: 7 **I** there is among you anyone in need,
15:12 **I** a member of your community,
15:16 But **i** he says to you, "I will not go out from you,"
15:21 But **i** it has any defect—
17: 2 **I** there is found among you,
17: 4 and **i** it is reported to you or you hear of it,
17: 8 **I** a judicial decision is too difficult for you
18: 6 **I** a Levite leaves any of your towns,
18:16 "**I** I hear the voice of the LORD
18:22 **I** a prophet speaks in the name of the LORD but
19: 6 But **i** the distance is too great,
19: 8 **I** the LORD your God enlarges your territory,
19:11 But **i** someone at enmity with another lies in wait
19:16 **I** a malicious witness comes forward
19:18 **I** the witness is a false witness,
20:11 **I** it accepts your terms of peace and surrenders
20:12 **I** it does not submit to you peacefully,
20:19 **I** you besiege a town for a long time,
21: 1 **I**, in the land that the LORD your God is giving you
21:14 But **i** you are not satisfied with her,
21:15 **I** a man has two wives,
21:15 and **i** both the loved and the disliked
21:18 **I** someone has a stubborn and rebellious son
22: 2 **I** the owner does not reside near you or you do
22: 6 **I** you come on a bird's nest,
22: 8 **i** anyone should fall from it.
22:20 **I**, however, this charge is true,
22:22 **I** a man is caught lying with the wife
22:23 **I** there is a young woman,
22:25 But **i** the man meets the engaged woman in
22:28 **I** a man meets a virgin who is not engaged,
23:10 **I** one of you becomes unclean because of
23:21 **I** you make a vow to the LORD your God,
23:22 But **i** you refrain from vowing,
23:24 **I** you go into your neighbor's vineyard,
23:25 **I** you go into your neighbor's standing grain,
24: 7 **I** someone is caught kidnaping another Israelite,
24:12 **I** the person is poor, you shall not sleep in
25: 2 **I** the one in the wrong deserves to be flogged,
25: 3 **i** more lashes than these are given,
25: 7 But **i** the man has no desire
25: 8 **I** he persists, saying, "I have no desire
25:11 **I** men get into a fight with one another,
28: 1 **I** you will only obey the LORD your God,
28: 2 **i** you obey the LORD your God:
28: 9 **i** you keep the commandments of the LORD
28:13 **i** you obey the commandments of the LORD
28:14 and **i** you do not turn aside from any of the words
28:15 But **i** you will not obey the LORD your God
28:58 **I** you do not diligently observe all the words
28:67 morning you shall say, "**I** only it were evening!"
28:67 "**I** only it were morning!"—
30: 1 **i** you call them to mind among all the nations
30: 4 Even **i** you are exiled to the ends of the world,
30:16 **I** you obey the commandments of the LORD
30:17 But **i** your heart turns away and you do not hear,
31:27 **I** you already have been so rebellious toward
32:29 **I** they were wise, they would understand this;
Jos 2:14 **I** you do not tell this business of ours,
2:18 **i** we invade the land and you do
2:19 **I** any of you go out of the doors of your house into
2:19 but **i** a hand is laid upon any who are with you in
2:20 But **i** you tell this business of ours,
17:15 "**I** you are a numerous people, go up to the forest,
20: 5 And **i** the avenger of blood is in pursuit,
22:18 **I** you rebel against the LORD today,
22:19 But now, **i** your land is unclean,
22:22 **I** it was in rebellion or in breach of faith toward
22:23 or **i** we did so to offer burnt offerings
22:28 **I** this should be said to us or to our descendants
23:12 For **i** you turn back, and join the survivors
23:16 **I** you transgress the covenant of the LORD
24:15 Now **i** you are unwilling to serve the LORD,
24:20 **I** you forsake the LORD and serve foreign gods,
24:27 **i** you deal falsely with your God."
Jdg 4: 8 Barak said to her, "**I** you will go with me,
4: 8 but **i** you will not go with me, I will not go."
4:20 and **i** anybody comes and asks you,
6:13 "But sir, **i** the LORD is with us,
6:17 "**I** now I have found favor with you,
6:31 **I** he is a god, let him contend for himself,
6:37 **i** there is dew on the fleece alone,

Jdg 7:10 But **i** you fear to attack, go down to the camp
8:19 as the LORD lives, **i** you had saved them alive,
9:15 '**I** in good faith you are anointing me king
9:15 but **i** not, let fire come out of the bramble
9:16 **i** you acted in good faith and honor
9:16 and **i** you have dealt well with Jerubbaal
9:19 **i**, I say, you have acted in good faith and honor
9:20 but **i** not, let fire come out from Abimelech,
9:29 **I** only this people were under my command!
11: 9 "**I** you bring me home again to fight with
11:30 "**I** you will give the Ammonites into my hand,
11:36 **i** you have opened your mouth to the LORD,
13:16 "**I** you detain me, I will not eat your food;
13:16 but **i** you want to prepare a burnt offering,
13:23 "**I** the LORD had meant to kill us,
14:12 **I** you can explain it to me within the seven days of
14:13 But **i** you cannot explain it to me,
14:18 "**I** you had not plowed with my heifer,
15: 7 Samson said to them, "**I** this is what you do,
16: 7 "**I** they bind me with seven fresh bowstrings
16:11 "**I** they bind me with new ropes that have
16:13 "**I** you weave the seven locks of my head with
16:17 **I** my head were shaved, then my strength would
21:22 Then **i** their fathers or their brothers come
Ru 1:12 Even **i** I thought there was hope for me,
1:12 **i** I should have a husband tonight and bear sons,
1:17 **i** even death parts me from you!"
2: 9 **I** you get thirsty, go to the vessels and drink
3:13 **i** he will act as next-of-kin for you, good;
3:13 **I** he is not willing to act as next-of-kin for you,
4: 4 **I** you will redeem it, redeem it;
4: 4 but **i** you will not, tell me, so that I may know;
1Sa 1:11 **i** only you will look on the misery of your servant,
2:16 And **i** the man said to him,
2:16 **i** not, I will take it by force."
2:25 **I** one person sins against another,
2:25 but **i** someone sins against the LORD,
3: 9 and **i** he calls you, you shall say, 'Speak, LORD,
3:17 **i** you hide anything from me of all
6: 3 "**I** you send away the ark of the God of Israel,
6: 9 **i** it goes up on the way to its own land,
6: 9 but **i** not, then we shall know that it is not his hand
7: 3 "**I** you are returning to the LORD
9: 7 Then Saul replied to the boy, "But **i** we go,
9:20 **i** not on you and on all your ancestral house?"
11: 3 Then, **i** there is no one to save us,
12:14 **I** you will fear the LORD and serve him
12:14 and **i** both you and the king who reigns
12:15 but **i** you will not heed the voice of the LORD,
12:25 But **i** you still do wickedly,
14: 9 **I** they say to us, 'Wait until we come to you,'
14:10 **i** they say, 'Come up to us,' then we will go up;
14:30 How much better **i** today the troops had eaten
14:39 even **i** it is in my son Jonathan,
14:41 **I** this guilt is in me or in my son Jonathan,
14:41 but **i** this guilt is in your people Israel,
16: 2 **I** Saul hears of it, he will kill me."
17: 9 **I** he is able to fight with me and kill me,
17: 9 but **i** I prevail against him and kill him,
17:35 and **i** it turned against me,
19: 3 **i** I learn anything I will tell you."
19:11 "**I** you do not save your life tonight,
20: 6 **I** your father misses me at all, then say,
20: 7 **I** he says, 'Good!' it will be well
20: 7 it will be well with your servant; but **i** he is angry,
20: 8 But **i** there is guilt in me, kill me yourself;
20: 9 **I** I knew that it was decided by my father
20:10 Then David said to Jonathan, "Who will tell me **i**
20:12 **i** he is well disposed toward David,
20:13 But **i** my father intends to do you harm,
20:13 **i** I do not disclose it to you, and send you away,
20:14 **I** I am still alive, show me the faithful love of
20:14 of the LORD; but **i** I die,
20:15 even **i** the LORD were to cut off every one of
20:21 **I** I say to the boy, 'Look,
20:22 But **i** I say to the young man, 'Look,
20:29 So now, **i** I have found favor in your sight,
21: 9 **i** you will take that, take it,
23: 3 how much more then **i** we go to Keilah against
23:23 Then I will go with you; and **i** he is in the land,
25:22 **i** by morning I leave so much as one male
25:29 **I** anyone should rise up to pursue you and
26:19 **I** it is the LORD who has stirred you up
26:19 but **i** it is mortals, may they be cursed before
27: 5 "**I** I have found favor in your sight,
2Sa 2:27 Joab said, "As God lives, **i** you had not spoken,
3:35 "So may God do to me, and more, **i** I taste bread
10:11 He said, "**I** the Arameans are too strong for me,
10:11 but **i** the Ammonites are too strong for you,
11:20 **i** the king's anger rises, and **i** he says to you,
12: 8 and **i** that had been too little,
13:26 Then Absalom said, "**I** not,
13:33 as **i** all the king's sons were dead;
14: 7 even **i** we destroy the heir as well.'
14:10 The king said, "**I** anyone says anything to you,
14:32 **i** there is guilt in me, let him kill me!"
15: 4 "**I** only I were judge in the land!
15: 8 **I** the LORD will indeed bring me back
15:25 **I** I find favor in the eyes of the LORD,
15:26 But **i** he says, 'I take no pleasure in you,'
15:33 David said to him, "**I** you go on with me,
15:34 But **i** you return to the city and say to Absalom,
16:10 **I** he is cursing because the LORD has said
16:23 that Ahithophel gave was as **i** one consulted
17: 6 **I** not, you tell us."
17:13 **I** he withdraws into a city,
18: 3 For **i** we flee, they will not care about us.
2Sa 18: 3 **I** half of us die, they will not care about us.
18:12 "Even **i** I felt in my hand the weight of
18:13 **i** I had dealt treacherously against his life
18:25 The king said, "**I** he is alone,
19: 6 for I perceive that **i** Absalom were alive and all
19: 7 for I swear by the LORD, **i** you do not go,
19:13 **i** you are not the commander of my army from
20: 3 living as **i** in widowhood.
1Ki 1:52 "**I** he proves to be a worthy man,
1:52 but **i** wickedness is found in him, he shall die."
2: 4 '**I** your heirs take heed to their way,
3:14 **I** you will walk in my ways,
6:12 **i** you will walk in my statutes,
8:25 **i** only your children look to their way,
8:31 "**I** someone sins against a neighbor and is given
8:37 "**I** there is famine in the land, **i** there is plague,
8:37 **i** their enemy besieges them in any of their cities;
8:44 "**I** your people go out to battle
8:46 "**I** they sin against you—
8:47 yet **i** they come to their senses in the land
8:48 **i** they repent with all their heart and soul in
9: 4 As for you, **i** you will walk before me,
9: 6 **I** you turn aside from following me,
11:38 **I** you will listen to all that I command you,
12: 7 "**I** you will be a servant to this people today
12:27 **I** this people continues to go up to offer sacrifices
13: 8 "**I** you give me half your kingdom,
16:31 And as **i** it had been a light thing for him to walk
18:21 **I** the LORD is God, follow him;
18:21 but **i** Baal, then follow him."
19: 2 **i** I do not make your life like the life of one
20:10 **i** the dust of Samaria will provide a handful
20:18 He said, "**I** they have come out for peace,
20:18 **i** they have come out for war, take them alive."
20:39 **i** he is missing, your life shall be given for his life,
21: 2 or, **i** it seems good to you,
21: 6 **i** you prefer, I will give you another vineyard
22:28 Micaiah said, "**I** you return in peace,
2Ki 1:10 "**I** I am a man of God,
1:12 But Elijah answered them, "**I** I am a man of God,
2:10 yet, **i** you see me as I am being taken from you,
2:10 it will be granted you; **i** not,
4:29 **I** you meet anyone, give no greeting,
4:29 give no greeting, and **i** anyone greets you,
5: 3 "**I** only my lord were with the prophet who is
5:13 **i** the prophet had commanded you
5:17 Then Naaman said, "**I** not,
6:31 **i** the head of Elisha son of Shaphat stays
7: 2 **i** the LORD were to make windows in the sky,
7: 4 **I** we say, 'Let us enter the city,'
7: 4 but **i** we sit here, we shall also die.
7: 4 **i** they spare our lives, we shall live;
7: 4 and **i** they kill us, we shall but die."
7: 9 **i** we are silent and wait until the morning light,
7:19 **i** the LORD were to make windows in the sky,
9:15 So Jehu said, "**I** this is your wish,
10: 6 saying, "**I** you are on my side,
10: 6 and **i** you are ready to obey me,
10:15 Jehu said, "**I** it is, give me your hand."
18:22 But **i** you say to me,
18:23 **i** you are able on your part to set riders on them.
20:19 **i** there will be peace and security in my days?"
21: 8 **i** only they will be careful to do according to all
1Ch 12:17 "**I** you have come to me in friendship, to help me,
12:17 **i** you have come to betray me to my adversaries,
13: 2 "**I** it seems good to you,
13: 2 and **i** it is the will of the LORD our God,
19:12 He said, "**I** the Arameans are too strong for me,
19:12 but **i** the Ammonites are too strong for you,
22:13 Then you will prosper **i** you are careful to observe
28: 7 I will establish his kingdom forever **i**
28: 9 **I** you seek him, he will be found by you;
28: 9 **i** you forsake him, he will abandon you forever.
2Ch 6:16 **i** only your children keep to their way,
6:22 "**I** someone sins against another and is required
6:28 "**I** there is famine in the land, **i** there is plague,
6:28 **i** their enemies besiege them in any of
6:34 "**I** your people go out to battle
6:36 "**I** they sin against you—
6:37 then **i** they come to their senses in the land
6:38 **i** they repent with all their heart and soul in
7:14 **i** my people who are called
7:17 As for you, **i** you walk before me,
7:19 "But **i** you turn aside and forsake my statutes
10: 7 "**I** you will be kind to this people and please them,
15: 2 **I** you seek him, he will be found by you,
15: 2 he will be found by you, but **i** you abandon him,
18:27 Micaiah said, "**I** you return in peace,
20: 9 '**I** disaster comes upon us,
30: 9 not turn away his face from you, **i** you return
32:19 the God of Jerusalem as **i** he were like the gods of
33: 8 **i** only they will be careful to do all
Ezr 4:13 **i** this city is rebuilt and the walls finished,
4:16 **i** this city is rebuilt and its walls finished,
5:17 And now, **i** it seems good to the king,
6:11 that **i** anyone alters this edict,
10: 8 and that **i** any did not come within three days,
Ne 1: 8 '**I** you are unfaithful, I will scatter you among
1: 9 but **i** you return to me
2: 5 Then I said to the king, "**I** it pleases the king,
2: 5 and **i** your servant has found favor with you,
2: 7 Then I said to the king, "**I** it pleases the king,
10:31 and **i** the peoples of the land bring in merchandise
13:21 **I** you do so again, I will lay hands on you."
Est 1:19 **I** it pleases the king, let a royal order go out
3: 9 **I** it pleases the king, let a decree be issued
4:11 and the people of the king's provinces know that **i**
Est 4:11 Only **i** the king holds out the golden scepter
4:14 For **i** you keep silence at such a time as this,
4:16 against the law; and **i** I perish,
5: 4 Then Esther said, "**I** it pleases the king,
5: 8 **I** I have won the king's favor,
5: 8 and **i** it pleases the king to grant my petition
6:13 and his wife Zeresh said to him, "**I** Mordecai,
7: 3 Queen Esther answered, "**I** I have won your favor,
7: 3 and **i** it pleases the king, let my life be given me—
7: 4 **I** we had been sold merely as slaves,
8: 5 "**I** it pleases the king, and **i** I have won his favor,
8: 5 and **i** the thing seems right before the king,
9:13 Esther said, "**I** it pleases the king,
Job 4: 2 "**I** one ventures a word with you,
6:26 as **i** the speech of the desperate were wind?
7:20 **I** I sin, what do I do to you,
8: 4 **I** your children sinned against him,
8: 5 **I** you will seek God and make supplication to
8: 6 **i** you are pure and upright,
8:15 **I** one leans against its house, it will not stand;
8:15 **i** one lays hold of it, it will not endure.
8:18 **I** they are destroyed from their place,
9: 3 **I** one wished to contend with him,
9:16 **I** I summoned him and he answered me,
9:19 **I** it is a contest of strength, he is the strong one!
9:19 **I** it is a matter of justice, who can summon him?
9:24 **i** it is not he, who then is it?
9:27 **I** I say, 'I will forget my complaint;
9:30 **I** I wash myself with soap and cleanse my hands
9:34 **I** he would take his rod away from me,
10:14 **I** I sin, you watch me, and do not acquit me
10:15 **I** I am wicked, woe to me!
10:15 **I** I am righteous, I cannot lift up my head,
11:10 **I** he passes through, and imprisons,
11:13 "**I** you direct your heart rightly,
11:14 **I** iniquity is in your hand, put it far away,
12:14 **I** he tears down, no one can rebuild;
12:14 **i** he shuts someone in, no one can open up.
12:15 **I** he withholds the waters, they dry up;
12:15 **i** he sends them out, they overwhelm the land.
13: 5 **I** you would only keep silent,
13:10 surely rebuke you **i** in secret you show partiality.
14: 7 "For there is hope for a tree, **i** it is cut down,
14:14 **I** mortals die, will they live again?
16: 4 **i** you were in my place;
16: 6 "**I** I speak, my pain is not assuaged, and **i** I forbear,
17:13 **I** I look for Sheol as my house,
17:13 **i** I spread my couch in darkness,
17:14 **i** I say to the Pit,
19: 4 And even **i** it is true that I have erred,
19: 5 **I** indeed you magnify yourselves against me,
19:28 **I** you say, 'How we will persecute him!'
21:15 And what profit do we get **i** we pray to him?'
22: 3 to the Almighty **i** you are righteous,
22: 3 is it gain to him **i** you make your ways blameless?
22:23 **I** you return to the Almighty, you will be restored,
22:23 **i** you remove unrighteousness from your tents,
22:24 **i** you treat gold like dust,
22:25 and **i** the Almighty is your gold
23: 8 "**I** I go forward, he is not there;
23:17 **I** only I could vanish in darkness,
24:25 **I** it is not so, who will prove me a liar,
25: 5 **I** even the moon is not bright and the stars are
27:14 **I** their children are multiplied, it is for the sword;
31: 5 "**I** I have walked with falsehood,
31: 7 **i** my step has turned aside from the way,
31: 7 and **i** any spot has clung to my hands;
31: 9 "**I** my heart has been enticed by a woman,
31:13 "**I** I have rejected the cause of my male
31:16 "**I** I have withheld anything that the poor desired,
31:19 **i** I have seen anyone perish for lack of clothing,
31:21 **i** I have raised my hand against the orphan,
31:24 "**I** I have made gold my trust,
31:25 **i** I have rejoiced because my wealth was great,
31:26 **i** I have looked at the sun when it shone,
31:29 "**I** I have rejoiced at the ruin
31:31 **i** those of my tent ever said, 'O that we might
31:33 **i** I have concealed my transgressions as others do,
31:38 "**I** my land has cried out against me,
31:39 **i** I have eaten its yield without payment,
33: 5 Answer me, **i** you can; set your words in order
33:23 Then, **i** there should be for one of them an angel,
33:32 **I** you have anything to say, answer me;
33:33 **I** not, listen to me; be silent,
34:14 **I** he should take back his spirit to himself,
34:16 "**I** you have understanding, hear this;
34:32 **i** I have done iniquity, I will do it no more'?
35: 3 **I** you ask, 'What advantage have I?
35: 3 How am I better off than **i** I had sinned?'
35: 6 **I** you have sinned, what do you accomplish
35: 6 And **i** your transgressions are multiplied,
35: 7 **I** you are righteous, what do you give to him;
36: 8 And **i** they are bound in fetters and caught in
36:11 **I** they listen, and serve him,
36:12 But **i** they do not listen,
38: 4 Tell me, **i** you have understanding.
38:18 Declare, **i** you know all this.
39:16 as **i** they were not its own;
40:23 Even **i** the river is turbulent, it is not frightened;
Ps 7: 3 **i** I have done this, **i** there is wrong in my hands,
7: 4 **i** I have repaid my ally with harm
7:12 **I** one does not repent, God will whet his sword;
11: 3 **I** the foundations are destroyed,
14: 2 on humankind to see **i** there are any who are wise,
17: 3 **I** you try my heart, **i** you visit me by night,
17: 3 **i** you test me, you will find no wickedness in me;
21:11 **I** they plan evil against you,

Ps 21:11 they plan evil against you, **i** they devise mischief,
27:10 **I** my father and mother forsake me,
28: 1 for **i** you are silent to me, I shall be like those who
30: 9 **i** I go down to the Pit?
44:20 **I** we had forgotten the name of our God,
50:12 "**I** I were hungry, I would not tell you,
51:16 **i** I were to give a burnt offering,
53: 2 on humankind to see **i** there are any who are wise,
59:15 and growl **i** they do not get their fill.
62:10 **i** riches increase, do not set your heart on them.
66:18 **I** I had cherished iniquity in my heart,
73:15 **I** I had said, "I will talk on in this way,"
81: 8 O Israel, **i** you would but listen to me!
89:30 **I** his children forsake my law and do not walk
89:31 **i** they violate my statutes and do
90:10 or perhaps eighty, **i** we are strong;
94:17 **I** the LORD had not been my help,
119:92 **I** your law had not been my delight,
124: 1 **I** it had not been the LORD who was
124: 2 **i** it had not been the LORD who was on our side,
130: 3 **I** you, O LORD, should mark iniquities, Lord,
132:12 **I** your sons keep my covenant and my decrees
137: 5 **I** I forget you, O Jerusalem,
137: 6 **i** I do not remember you,
137: 6 **i** I do not set Jerusalem above my highest joy.
139: 8 **I** I ascend to heaven, you are there;
139: 8 **i** I make my bed in Sheol, you are there.
139: 9 **I** I take the wings of the morning and settle at
139:11 **I** I say, "Surely the darkness shall cover me,
139:24 See **i** there is any wicked way in me,
Pr 1:10 My child, **i** sinners entice you, do not consent.
1:11 **I** they say, "Come with us,
2: 1 **i** you accept my words and treasure
2: 3 **i** you indeed cry out for insight,
2: 4 **i** you seek it like silver, and search for it as
3:24 **I** you sit down, you will not be afraid;
4: 8 she will honor you **i** you embrace her.
4:12 and **i** you run, you will not stumble.
6: 1 **i** you have given your pledge to your neighbor,
6: 1 **i** you have bound yourself to another,
6:31 Yet **i** they are caught, they will pay sevenfold;
9:12 **I** you are wise, you are wise for yourself;
9:12 **i** you scoff, you alone will bear it.
11:31 **I** the righteous are repaid on earth,
18:13 **I** one gives answer before hearing,
19: 7 **I** the poor are hated even by their kin,
19:19 **i** you effect a rescue, you will only have
20:20 **I** you curse father or mother,
21:13 **I** you close your ear to the cry of the poor,
22:18 for it will be pleasant **i** you keep them within you,
22:18 **i** all of them are ready on your lips.
22:27 **I** you have nothing with which to pay,
23: 2 put a knife to your throat **i** you have a big appetite.
23:13 **i** you beat them with a rod, they will not die.
23:14 **I** you beat them with the rod,
23:15 My child, **i** your heart is wise,
24:10 **I** you faint in the day of adversity,
24:11 **i** you hold back from rescuing those taken away
24:12 **i** you say, "Look, we did not know this"—
24:14 **i** you find it, you will find a future,
25:16 **I** you have found honey, eat only enough for you,
25:21 **I** your enemies are hungry, give them bread to eat;
25:21 and **i** they are thirsty, give them water to drink;
28:17 **I** someone is burdened with the blood of another,
29: 9 **I** the wise go to law with fools,
29:12 **I** a ruler listens to falsehood,
29:14 **I** a king judges the poor with equity,
30:32 **I** you have been foolish, exalting yourself,
30:32 exalting yourself, or **i** you have been devising evil,
Ecc 4:10 For **i** they fall, one will lift up the other;
4:11 Again, **i** two lie together, they keep warm;
5: 8 **I** you see in a province the oppression of the poor
6: 3 **i** he does not enjoy life's good things,
10: 4 **I** the anger of the ruler rises against you,
10: 5 as great an error as **i** it proceeded from the ruler:
10:10 **I** the iron is blunt, and one does not whet the edge,
10:11 **I** the snake bites before it is charmed,
SS 1: 8 **I** you do not know, O fairest among women,
5: 8 O daughters of Jerusalem, **i** you find my beloved,
8: 1 **I** I met you outside, I would kiss you,
8: 7 **I** one offered for love all the wealth of his house,
8: 9 **I** she is a wall, we will build upon her a battlement
8: 9 but **i** she is a door, we will enclose her with boards
Isa 1: 9 **I** the LORD of hosts had not left us a few
1:19 **I** you are willing and obedient,
1:20 but **i** you refuse and rebel, you shall be devoured
5:30 And **i** one look to the land—
6:13 Even **i** a tenth part remain in it,
7: 9 **I** you do not stand firm in faith,
8:19 Now **i** people say to you, "Consult the ghosts and
10:15 As **i** a rod should raise the one who lifts it up,
10:15 or as **i** a staff should lift the one who is not wood!
21:12 **I** you will inquire, inquire; come back again."
26:10 **I** favor is shown to the wicked,
27: 4 **I** it gives me thorns and briers,
29:11 **I** it is given to those who can read,
29:12 And **i** it is given to those who cannot read, saying,
33:12 And the peoples will be as **i** burned to lime,
36: 7 But **i** you say to me,
36: 8 **i** you are able on your part to set riders on them.
46: 7 **I** one cries out to it,
54:15 **I** anyone stirs up strife, it is not from me;
58: 2 as **i** they were a nation
58: 9 **I** you remove the yoke from among you,
58:10 **i** you offer your food to the hungry and satisfy
58:13 **I** you refrain from trampling the sabbath,
58:13 **i** you call the sabbath a delight and the holy day of
Isa 58:13 **i** you honor it, not going your own ways,
Jer 2:10 see **i** there has ever been such a thing.
2:28 Let them come, **i** they can save you,
3: 1 **I** a man divorces his wife and she goes from him
4: 1 **I** you return, O Israel, says the LORD,
4: 1 O Israel, says the LORD, **i** you return to me,
4: 1 **i** you remove your abominations
4: 2 and **i** you swear, "As the LORD lives!"
5: 1 and see **i** you can find one person who acts justly
7: 5 For **i** you truly amend your ways and your doings,
7: 5 **i** you truly act justly one with another,
7: 6 **i** you do not oppress the alien,
7: 6 **i** you do not go after other gods to your own hurt,
8: 4 **I** they go astray, do they not turn back?
12: 5 **I** you have raced with foot-runners
12: 5 And **i** in a safe land you fall down,
12:16 **i** they will diligently learn the ways of my people,
12:17 But **i** any nation will not listen,
13:17 But **i** you will not listen, my soul will weep
13:22 And **i** you say in your heart,
14:18 **I** I go out into the field, look—
14:18 And **i** I enter the city, look—
15:19 Therefore thus says the LORD: **I** you turn back,
15:19 **I** you utter what is precious,
17:24 But **i** you listen to me, says the LORD,
17:27 But **i** you do not listen to me,
18: 8 but **i** that nation, concerning which
18:10 but **i** it does evil in my sight,
20: 9 **I** I say, "I will not mention him,
22: 4 For **i** you will indeed obey this word,
22: 5 But **i** you will not heed these words,
22:24 even **i** King Coniah son of Jehoiakim
23:22 But **i** they had stood in my council,
23:38 But **i** you say, "the burden of the LORD,"
25:28 And **i** they refuse to accept the cup
26: 4 **I** you will not listen to me,
26:15 Only know for certain that **i** you put me to death,
27: 8 **i** any nation or kingdom will not serve this king,
27:18 **I** indeed they are prophets,
27:18 and **i** the word of the LORD is with them,
29:13 **i** you seek me with all your heart,
31:36 **I** this fixed order were ever to cease
31:37 **I** the heavens above can be measured,
33:20 **I** any of you could break my covenant with
33:25 Only **i** I had not established my covenant with day
37:10 Even **i** you defeated the whole army
38:15 Jeremiah said to Zedekiah, "**I** I tell you,
38:15 **i** I give you advice, you will not listen to me."
38:17 **I** you will only surrender to the officials of
38:18 But **i** you do not surrender to the officials of
38:21 But **i** you are determined not to surrender,
38:25 **I** the officials should hear that I have spoken
40: 4 **I** you wish to come with me to Babylon, come,
40: 4 **i** you do not wish to come with me to Babylon,
40: 5 **I** you remain, then return to Gedaliah son
42: 5 against us **i** we do not act according to everything
42:10 **I** you will only remain in this land,
42:13 But **i** you continue to say,
42:15 **I** you are determined to enter Egypt and go
49: 9 **I** grape-gatherers came to you,
49: 9 **I** thieves came by night, even they would pillage
49:12 **I** those who do not deserve to drink
La 1:12 Look and see **i** there is any sorrow like my sorrow,
2:22 You invited my enemies from all around as **i** for
3:37 **i** the Lord has not ordained it?
Eze 3: 6 **i** I sent you to them, they would listen to you.
3:18 **I** I say to the wicked, "You shall surely die,"
3:19 But **i** you warn the wicked,
3:20 **i** the righteous turn from their righteousness
3:21 **I**, however, you warn the righteous not to sin,
7:16 **I** any survivors escape, they shall be found on
14: 9 **I** a prophet is deceived and speaks a word, I,
14:14 even **i** Noah, Daniel, and Job, these three, were
14:15 **I** I send wild animals through the land to ravage it,
14:16 even **i** these three men were in it, as I live, says
14:17 Or **i** I bring a sword upon that land and say,
14:19 Or **i** I send a pestilence into that land,
14:20 even **i** Noah, Daniel, and Job were in it,
16:20 As **i** your whorings were not enough!
18: 5 **I** a man is righteous and does what is lawful
18: 6 **i** he does not eat upon the mountains or lift
18:10 **I** he has a son who is violent, a shedder of blood,
18:14 But **i** this man has a son who sees all the sins
18:21 But **i** the wicked turn away from all their sins
20:39 **i** you will not listen to me;
21:13 **I** you despise the rod, will it not happen?
33: 2 **I** I bring the sword upon a land,
33: 3 and **i** the sentinel sees the sword coming upon
33: 4 then **i** any who hear the sound of the trumpet do
33: 5 But **i** they had taken warning,
33: 6 But **i** the sentinel sees the sword coming and does
33: 8 **I** I say to the wicked, "O wicked ones,
33: 9 But **i** you warn the wicked to turn from their ways,
33:13 yet **i** they trust in their righteousness
33:14 yet **i** they turn from their sin and do what is lawful
33:15 **i** the wicked restore the pledge,
46:16 **I** the prince makes a gift to any of his sons out
46:17 But **i** he makes a gift out of his inheritance to one
Da 1:10 **I** he should see you in poorer condition than
2: 5 **i** you do not tell me both the dream
2: 6 **i** you do tell me the dream and its interpretation,
2: 9 **i** you do not tell me the dream,
3:15 Now **i** you are ready when you hear the sound of
3:15 But **i** you do not worship,
3:17 **I** our God whom we serve is able to deliver us
3:18 But **i** not, be it known to you, O king,
5:16 Now **i** you are able to read the writing
Hos 8: 7 **i** it were to yield, foreigners would devour it.
9: 6 For even **i** they escape destruction,
9:12 Even **i** they bring up children,
Joel 3: 4 **I** you are paying me back,
Am 3: 4 from its den, **i** it has caught nothing?
5:19 **i** someone fled from a lion, and was met by a bear;
6: 9 **I** ten people remain in one house, they shall die.
6:10 And **i** a relative, one who burns the dead,
Ob 1: 5 **I** thieves came to you, **i** plunderers by night
1: 5 **I** grape-gatherers came to you,
Mic 2:11 **I** someone were to go about uttering
5: 5 **I** the Assyrians come into our land and tread
5: 6 the Assyrians **i** they come into our land or tread
Na 3:12 **i** shaken they fall into the mouth of the eater.
Hab 1: 5 that you would not believe **i** you were told.
2: 3 **I** it seems to tarry, wait for it;
3:14 as **i** ready to devour the poor who were in hiding.
Hag 2:12 **I** one carries consecrated meat in the fold
2:13 "**I** one who is unclean by contact with
Zec 3: 7 **I** you will walk in my ways
6:15 This will happen **i** you diligently obey the voice of
11:12 I then said to them, "**I** it seems right to you,
11:12 give me my wages; but **i** not,
13: 3 And **i** any prophets appear again,
13: 6 And **i** anyone asks them, "What are these wounds
14:17 **I** any of the families of the earth do not go up
14:18 And **i** the family of Egypt do not go up
Mal 1: 4 **I** Edom says, "We are shattered
1: 6 **I** then I am a father, where is the honor due me?
1: 6 And **i** I am a master, where is the respect due me?
2: 2 **I** you will not listen, **i** you will not lay it to heart
3:10 see **i** I will not open the windows of heaven
Mt 4: 3 "**I** you are the Son of God,
4: 6 "**I** you are the Son of God, throw yourself down;
4: 9 **i** you will fall down and worship me."
5:13 but **i** salt has lost its taste,
5:22 But I say to you that **i** you are angry with a brother
5:22 and **i** you insult a brother or sister,
5:22 and **i** you say, 'You fool,'
5:23 **i** you remember that your brother
5:29 **I** your right eye causes you to sin,
5:30 And **i** your right hand causes you to sin,
5:39 But **i** anyone strikes you on the right cheek,
5:40 and **i** anyone wants to sue you and take your coat,
5:41 and **i** anyone forces you to go one mile,
5:46 For **i** you love those who love you,
5:47 And **i** you greet only your brothers and sisters,
6:14 For **i** you forgive others their trespasses,
6:15 but **i** you do not forgive others,
6:22 **i** your eye is healthy, your whole body will be full
6:23 but **i** your eye is unhealthy,
6:23 **I** then the light in you is darkness,
6:30 But **i** God so clothes the grass of the field,
7: 9 **i** your child asks for bread, will give a stone?
7:10 Or **i** the child asks for a fish, will give a snake?
7:11 **I** you then, who are evil, know how
8: 2 "Lord, **i** you choose, you can make me clean."
8:31 The demons begged him, "**I** you cast us out,
9:21 "**I** I only touch his cloak, I will be made well."
10:13 **I** the house is worthy, let your peace come upon it;
10:13 but **i** it is not worthy, let your peace return to you.
10:14 **I** anyone will not welcome you or listen
10:25 **I** they have called the master of
11:14 and **i** you are willing to accept it,
11:21 For **i** the deeds of power done
11:23 For **i** the deeds of power done
12: 7 But **i** you had known what this means,
12:26 **I** Satan casts out Satan, he is divided
12:27 **I** I cast out demons by Beelzebul,
12:28 **i** it is by the Spirit of God that I cast out demons,
14:28 Peter answered him, "Lord, **i** it is you,
15:14 And **i** one blind person guides another,
16:24 "**I** any want to become my followers,
16:26 For what will it profit them **i** they gain
17: 4 **i** you wish, I will make three dwellings here,
17:20 **i** you have faith the size of a mustard seed,
18: 6 "**I** any of you put a stumbling block before one
18: 6 be better for you **i** a great millstone were fastened
18: 8 "**I** your hand or your foot causes you to stumble,
18: 9 And **i** your eye causes you to stumble,
18:12 **I** a shepherd has a hundred sheep,
18:13 And **i** he finds it, truly I tell you,
18:15 "**I** another member of the church sins against you,
18:15 **I** the member listens to you,
18:16 But **i** you are not listened to,
18:17 **I** the member refuses to listen to them,
18:17 **i** the offender refuses to listen even to the church,
18:19 **i** two of you agree on earth
18:21 **i** another member of the church sins against me,
18:35 **i** you do not forgive your brother or sister
19:10 "**I** such is the case of a man with his wife,
19:17 **I** you wish to enter into life,
19:21 Jesus said to him, "**I** you wish to be perfect, go,
21: 3 **I** anyone says anything to you, just say this,
21:21 **i** you have faith and do not doubt,
21:21 but even **i** you say to this mountain,
21:24 **i** you tell me the answer,
21:25 And they argued with one another, "**I** we say,
21:26 But **i** we say, 'Of human origin,'
22:24 Moses said, '**I** a man dies childless,
22:45 **I** David thus calls him Lord,
23:30 '**I** we had lived in the days of our ancestors,
24:22 And **i** those days had not been cut short,
24:23 Then **i** anyone says to you, 'Look!
24:24 to lead astray, **i** possible, even the elect.
24:26 So, **i** they say to you, 'Look!
24:26 **I** they say, 'Look! He is in the inner rooms,'

Mt 24:43 i the owner of the house had known in what part
24:48 But i that wicked slave says to himself,
25:14 "For it is as i a man, going on a journey,
26:15 "What will you give me i I betray him to you?"
26:39 i it is possible, let this cup pass from me;
26:42 "My Father, i this cannot pass unless I drink it,
26:63 tell us i you are the Messiah, the Son of God."
27:40 I you are the Son of God,
27:43 let God deliver him now, i he wants to;
28:14 I this comes to the governor's ears,
Mk 1:40 and kneeling he said to him, "I you choose,
3:24 I a kingdom is divided against itself,
3:25 And i a house is divided against itself,
3:26 i Satan has risen up against himself and is divided,
4:26 as i someone would scatter seed on the ground,
5:28 "I I but touch his clothes, I will be made well."
6:11 I any place will not welcome you and they refuse
7:11 But you say that i anyone tells father or mother,
8:3 I I send them away hungry to their homes,
8:34 "I any want to become my followers,
9:22 but i you are able to do anything,
9:23 Jesus said to him, "I you are able!—
9:42 "I any of you put a stumbling block before one
9:42 be better for you i a great millstone were hung
9:43 I your hand causes you to stumble, cut it off;
9:45 And i your foot causes you to stumble, cut it off;
9:47 And i your eye causes you to stumble, tear it out;
9:50 i salt has lost its saltiness, how can you season it?
10:12 i she divorces her husband and marries another,
11:3 I anyone says to you, 'Why are you doing this?'
11:23 Truly I tell you, i you say to this mountain,
11:23 and i you do not doubt in your heart,
11:25 forgive, i you have anything against anyone;
11:31 They argued with one another, "I we say,
12:19 Moses wrote for us that 'i a man's brother dies,
13:20 And i the Lord had not cut short those days,
13:21 And i anyone says to you at that time, 'Look!
13:22 to lead astray, i possible, the elect.
14:35 i it were possible, the hour might pass from him.
15:44 Then Pilate wondered i he were already dead;
16:18 [[and i they drink any deadly thing, it will not hurt]]
Lk 4:3 The devil said to him, "I you are the Son of God,
4:7 I you, then, will worship me, it will all be yours."
4:9 saying to him, "I you are the Son of God,
5:5 Yet i you say so, I will let down the nets."
5:12 "Lord, i you choose, you can make me clean."
6:29 I anyone strikes you on the cheek,
6:30 and i anyone takes away your goods,
6:32 "I you love those who love you,
6:33 I you do good to those who do good to you,
6:34 I you lend to those from whom you hope
7:39 he said to himself, "I this man were a prophet,
9:23 "I any want to become my followers,
9:25 What does it profit them i they gain
10:6 And i anyone is there who shares in peace,
10:6 but i not, it will return to you.
10:13 For i the deeds of power done
11:11 i your child asks for a fish,
11:12 i the child asks for an egg, will give a scorpion?
11:13 I you then, who are evil, know how
11:18 I Satan also is divided against himself,
11:19 Now i I cast out the demons by Beelzebul,
11:20 But i it is by the finger of God that I cast out
11:34 I your eye is healthy, your whole body is full
11:34 i it is not healthy, your body is full of darkness.
11:36 I then your whole body is full of light,
12:26 I then you are not able to do so small a thing as
12:28 But i God so clothes the grass of the field,
12:38 I he comes during the middle of the night,
12:39 i the owner of the house had known at what hour
12:45 But i that slave says to himself,
12:45 and i he begins to beat the other slaves,
13:9 I it bears fruit next year, well and good;
13:9 but i not, you can cut it down.' "
14:5 "I one of you has a child or an ox that has fallen
14:32 I he cannot, then, while the other is still far away,
14:33 of you can become my disciple i you do not give
14:34 "Salt is good; but i salt has lost its taste,
15:8 i she loses one of them, does not light a lamp,
16:11 I then you have not been faithful with
16:12 And i you have not been faithful
16:30 but i someone goes to them from the dead,
16:31 'I they do not listen to Moses and the prophets,
16:31 be convinced even i someone rises from
17:2 It would be better for you i a millstone were hung
17:3 I another disciple sins, you must rebuke
17:3 and i there is repentance, you must forgive.
17:4 And i the same person sins
17:6 "I you had faith the size of a mustard seed,
19:8 and i I have defrauded anyone of anything,
19:31 I anyone asks you, 'Why are you untying it?'
19:40 He answered, "I tell you, i these were silent,
19:42 "I you, even you, had only recognized on this day
20:5 saying, "I we say, 'From heaven,' he will say,
20:6 But i we say, 'Of human origin,'
20:28 Moses wrote for us that i a man's brother dies,
22:42 i you are willing, remove this cup from me;
22:52 "Have you come out with swords and clubs as i
22:67 They said, "I you are the Messiah, tell us."
22:67 He replied, "I I tell you, you will not believe;
22:68 and i I question you, you will not answer.
23:31 For i they do this when the wood is green,
23:35 let him save himself i he is the Messiah of God,
23:37 "I you are the King of the Jews, save yourself!"
24:28 he walked ahead as i he were going on.
Jn 1:25 "Why then are you baptizing i you are neither
3:12 I I have told you about earthly things and you do
Jn 3:12 can you believe i I tell you about heavenly things?
4:10 Jesus answered her, "I you knew the gift of God,
5:31 "I I testify about myself, my testimony is not true.
5:43 i another comes in his own name,
5:46 I you believed Moses, you would believe me,
5:47 But i you do not believe what he wrote,
6:62 Then what i you were to see the Son
7:4 I you do these things, show yourself to the world."
7:23 I a man receives circumcision on the sabbath
8:14 "Even i I testify on my own behalf,
8:16 Yet even i I do judge, my judgment is valid;
8:19 I you knew me, you would know my Father also."
8:31 "I you continue in my word,
8:36 i the Son makes you free, you will be free indeed.
8:39 "I you were Abraham's children,
8:42 Jesus said to them, "I God were your Father,
8:46 I I tell the truth, why do you not believe me?
8:54 Jesus answered, "I I glorify myself,
8:55 i I would say that I do not know him,
9:33 I this man were not from God,
9:41 Jesus said to them, "I you were blind,
10:24 I you are the Messiah, tell us plainly."
10:35 I those to whom the word
10:37 I I am not doing the works of my Father,
10:38 But i I do them, even though you do
11:12 disciples said to him, "Lord, i he has fallen asleep,
11:21 Martha said to Jesus, "Lord, i you had been here,
11:32 "Lord, i you had been here,
11:40 "Did I not tell you that i you believed,
11:48 I we let him go on like this,
12:24 but i it dies, it bears much fruit.
12:35 I you walk in the darkness,
13:14 So i I, your Lord and Teacher,
13:17 I you know these things, you are blessed
13:17 you are blessed i you do them.
13:32 I God has been glorified in him,
13:35 i you have love for one another."
14:2 I it were not so, would I have told you that I go
14:3 And i I go and prepare a place for you,
14:7 I you know me, you will know my Father also.
14:11 but i you do not, then believe me because of
14:14 I in my name you ask me for anything, I will do it.
14:15 "I you love me, you will keep my commandments.
14:28 I you loved me, you would rejoice that I am going
15:7 I you abide in me, and my words abide in you,
15:10 I you keep my commandments,
15:14 You are my friends i you do what I command you.
15:18 "I the world hates you, be aware that it hated me
15:19 I you belonged to the world,
15:20 I they persecuted me, they will persecute you;
15:20 i they kept my word, they will keep yours also.
15:22 I I had not come and spoken to them,
15:24 I I had not done among them the works
16:7 for i I do not go away,
16:7 but i I go, I will send him to you.
16:23 i you ask anything of the Father in my name,
18:8 So i you are looking for me, let these men go."
18:23 Jesus answered, "I I have spoken wrongly,
18:23 i I have spoken rightly, why do you strike me?"
18:30 They answered, "I this man were not a criminal,
18:36 I my kingdom were from this world,
19:12 but the Jews cried out, "I you release this man,
20:15 she said to him, "Sir, i you have carried him away,
20:23 I you forgive the sins of any,
20:23 i you retain the sins of any, they are retained."
21:22 "I it is my will that he remain until I come,
21:23 but, "I it is my will that he remain until I come,
21:25 i every one of them were written down,
Ac 4:9 i we are questioned today because of
5:38 i this plan or this undertaking is of human origin,
5:39 but i it is of God, you will not be able
8:22 and pray to the Lord that, i possible,
9:2 so that i he found any who belonged to the Way,
11:17 I then God gave them the same gift
13:15 i you have any word of exhortation for the people,
13:41 even i someone tells you.' "
15:29 I you keep yourselves from these,
16:15 "I you have judged me to be faithful to the Lord,
18:14 "I it were a matter of crime or serious villainy,
18:21 he said, "I will return to you, i God wills."
19:38 I therefore Demetrius and the artisans
19:39 I there is anything further you want to know,
20:16 he was eager to be in Jerusalem, i possible,
20:24 i only I may finish my course and the ministry
23:9 What i a spirit or an angel has spoken to him?"
24:19 i they have anything against me.
25:5 and i there is anything wrong about the man,
25:11 Now i I am in the wrong
25:11 but i there is nothing to their charges against me,
26:5 i they are willing to testify,
26:32 "This man could have been set free i he had
27:39 on which they planned to run the ship ashore, i
Ro 2:17 But i you call yourself a Jew and rely on the law
2:19 and i you are sure that you are a guide to the blind,
2:25 Circumcision indeed is of value i you obey
2:25 but i you break the law,
2:26 i those who are uncircumcised keep
3:3 What i some were unfaithful?
3:5 But i our injustice serves to confirm the justice
3:7 But i through my falsehood God's truthfulness
4:2 For i Abraham was justified by works,
4:14 I it is the adherents of the law who are to be
5:10 For i while we were enemies,
5:15 i the many died through the one man's trespass,
5:17 I, because of the one man's trespass,
6:5 i we have been united with him in a death like his,
6:8 But i we have died with Christ,
Ro 6:16 not know that i you present yourselves to anyone
7:2 but i her husband dies, she is discharged from
7:3 an adulteress i she lives with another man
7:3 But i her husband dies, she is free from that law,
7:3 and i she marries another man,
7:7 Yet, i it had not been for the law,
7:7 not have known what it is to covet i the law had
7:16 Now i I do what I do not want,
7:20 Now i I do what I do not want,
8:10 But i Christ is in you,
8:11 I the Spirit of him who raised Jesus from
8:13 for i you live according to the flesh, you will die;
8:13 but i by the Spirit you put to death the deeds of
8:17 and i children, then heirs, heirs of God
8:17 i, in fact, we suffer with him so that we may also
8:25 But i we hope for what we do not see,
8:31 I God is for us, who is against us?
9:22 What i God, desiring to show his wrath and
9:23 and what i he has done so in order to make known
9:29 "I the Lord of hosts had not left survivors to us,
9:32 but as i it were based on works.
10:9 because i you confess with your lips
11:6 But i it is by grace,
11:12 Now i their stumbling means riches for the world,
11:12 and i their defeat means riches for Gentiles,
11:15 i their rejection is the reconciliation of the world,
11:16 I the part of the dough offered
11:16 i the root is holy, then the branches also are holy.
11:17 But i some of the branches were broken off,
11:18 I you do boast, remember that it is not you
11:21 For i God did not spare the natural branches,
11:23 those of Israel, i they do not persist in unbelief,
11:24 For i you have been cut from what is by nature
12:18 I it is possible, so far as it depends on you,
12:20 No, "i your enemies are hungry, feed them;
12:20 i they are thirsty, give them something to drink;
13:4 But i you do what is wrong, you should be afraid,
14:8 I we live, we live to the Lord, and i we die,
14:15 I your brother or sister is being injured
14:23 those who have doubts are condemned i they eat,
15:27 for i the Gentiles have come to share
1Co 2:8 for i they had, they would not have crucified
3:12 Now i anyone builds on the foundation with gold,
3:14 I what has been built on the foundation survives,
3:15 I the work is burned up,
3:17 I anyone destroys God's temple,
3:18 I you think that you are wise in this age,
4:7 And i you received it, why do you boast as i it
were not a gift?
4:19 But I will come to you soon, i the Lord wills,
5:3 as i present I have already pronounced judgment
6:2 And i the world is to be judged by you,
6:4 I you have ordinary cases, then,
7:9 But i they are not practicing self-control,
7:11 (but i she does separate, let her remain unmarried
7:12 that i any believer has a wife who is an unbeliever,
7:13 i any woman has a husband who is an unbeliever,
7:15 i the unbelieving partner separates, let it be so;
7:21 Even i you can gain your freedom,
7:28 But i you marry, you do not sin, and i a virgin
marries, she does not sin.
7:36 I anyone thinks that he is not behaving properly
7:36 i his passions are strong, and so it has to be,
7:37 But i someone stands firm in his resolve,
7:39 But i the husband dies, she is free
7:40 in my judgment she is more blessed i she remains
8:8 We are no worse off i we do not eat,
8:8 and no better off i we do.
8:10 For i others see you, who possess knowledge,
8:13 Therefore, i food is a cause of their falling,
9:2 I I am not an apostle to others,
9:11 I we have sown spiritual good among you,
9:11 is it too much i we reap your material benefits?
9:12 I others share this rightful claim on you,
9:16 I I proclaim the gospel, this gives me no ground
9:16 and woe to me i I do not proclaim the gospel!
9:17 For i I do this of my own will, I have a reward;
9:17 but i not of my own will,
10:12 So i you think you are standing,
10:27 I an unbeliever invites you to a meal
10:28 But i someone says to you,
10:30 I I partake with thankfulness,
11:6 For i a woman will not veil herself,
11:6 but i it is disgraceful for a woman
11:14 Does not nature itself teach you that i
11:15 but i a woman has long hair,
11:16 But i anyone is disposed to be contentious—
11:31 i we judged ourselves, we would not be judged.
11:34 I you are hungry, eat at home,
12:15 I the foot would say, "Because I am not a hand,
12:16 And i the ear would say,
12:17 I the whole body were an eye,
12:17 I the whole body were hearing,
12:19 I all were a single member,
12:26 I one member suffers, all suffer together with it;
12:26 i one member is honored,
13:1 I I speak in the tongues of mortals and of angels,
13:2 And i I have prophetic powers,
13:2 and i I have all faith, so as to remove mountains,
13:3 I I give away all my possessions,
13:3 and i I hand over my body so that I may boast,
14:6 i I come to you speaking in tongues,
14:7 I they do not give distinct notes,
14:8 And i the bugle gives an indistinct sound,
14:9 i in a tongue you utter speech that is
14:11 I then I do not know the meaning of a sound,
14:14 For i I pray in a tongue,

1Co 14:16 Otherwise, i you say a blessing with the spirit,
14:23 I, therefore, the whole church comes together
14:24 But i all prophesy, an unbeliever
14:27 I anyone speaks in a tongue,
14:28 But i there is no one to interpret,
14:30 I a revelation is made to someone
14:35 I there is anything they desire to know,
15: 2 i you hold firmly to the message that I proclaimed
15:12 i Christ is proclaimed as raised from the dead,
15:13 I there is no resurrection of the dead,
15:14 and i Christ has not been raised,
15:15 whom he did not raise i it is true that the dead are
15:16 For i the dead are not raised,
15:17 I Christ has not been raised,
15:19 I for this life only we have hoped in Christ,
15:29 I the dead are not raised at all,
15:32 I with merely human hopes I fought
15:32 I the dead are not raised, "Let us eat and drink,
15:44 I there is a physical body,
16: 4 I it seems advisable that I should go also,
16: 7 to spend some time with you, i the Lord permits.
16:10 I Timothy comes, see that he has nothing to fear
2Co 1: 6 I we are being afflicted, it is for your consolation
1: 6 i we are being consoled, it is for your consolation,
2: 2 For i I cause you pain,
2: 5 But i anyone has caused pain,
2:10 What I have forgiven, i I have forgiven anything,
3: 7 Now i the ministry of death,
3: 9 i there was glory in the ministry of condemnation,
3:11 for i what was set aside came through glory,
4: 3 And even i our gospel is veiled,
5: 1 that i the earthly tent we live in is destroyed,
5: 3 i indeed, when we have taken it off we will not
5:13 For i we are beside ourselves, it is for God;
5:13 i we are in our right mind, it is for you.
5:17 So i anyone is in Christ, there is a new creation:
7: 8 For even i I made you sorry with my letter,
7:14 i I have been somewhat boastful about you to him,
8:12 For i the eagerness is there,
9: 4 i some Macedonians come with me and find
10: 7 I you are confident that you belong to Christ,
10: 8 even i I boast a little too much of our authority,
11: 4 For i someone comes
11: 4 or i you receive a different spirit from
11:15 So it is not strange i his ministers
11:16 but i you do, then accept me as a fool,
11:30 I I must boast, I will boast of the things
12: 6 But i I wish to boast, I will not be a fool,
12:15 I I love you more, am I to be loved less?
13: 2 that i I come again, I will not be lenient—
Gal 1: 8 But even i we or an angel
1: 9 i anyone proclaims to you a gospel contrary
1:10 I I were still pleasing people,
2:14 I said to Cephas before them all, "I you,
2:17 But i, in our effort to be justified in Christ,
2:18 But i I build up again the very things
2:21 for i justification comes through the law,
3: 4 i it really was for nothing.
3:18 For i the inheritance comes from the law,
3:21 For i a law had been given that could make alive,
3:29 And i you belong to Christ,
4: 7 and i a child then also an heir, through God.
5: 2 that i you let yourselves be circumcised,
5:11 why am I still being persecuted i
5:15 I, however, you bite and devour one another,
5:18 But i you are led by the Spirit,
5:25 I we live by the Spirit,
6: 1 i anyone is detected in a transgression,
6: 3 i those who are nothing think they are something,
6: 8 I you sow to your own flesh,
6: 8 but i you sow to the Spirit,
6: 9 i we do not give up.
Php 1:22 I I am to live in the flesh,
2: 1 I then there is any encouragement in Christ,
2:17 But even i I am being poured out as a libation over
3: 4 I anyone else has reason to be confident in
3:11 i somehow I may attain the resurrection from
3:15 and i you think differently about anything,
4: 8 i there is any excellence and
4: 8 and i there is anything worthy of praise,
Col 2:20 I with Christ you died to the elemental spirits of
2:20 why do you live as i you still belonged to
3: 1 So i you have been raised with Christ,
3:13 i anyone has a complaint against another,
4:10 i he comes to you, welcome him.
1Th 3: 8 i you continue to stand firm in the Lord.
1Ti 1: 8 that the law is good, i one uses it legitimately.
3: 5 for i someone does not know how
3:10 then, i they prove themselves blameless,
3:15 i I am delayed, you may know how one ought
4: 6 I you put these instructions before the brothers
5: 4 I a widow has children or grandchildren,
5: 9 on the list i she is not less than sixty years old
5:16 I any believing woman has relatives who are
6: 8 but i we have food and clothing,
2Ti 2:11 The saying is sure: I we have died with him,
2:12 i we endure, we will also reign with him;
2:12 i we deny him, he will also deny us;
2:13 i we are faithless, he remains faithful—
Phm 1:17 So i you consider me your partner,
1:18 I he has wronged you in any way,
Heb 2: 2 i the message declared through angels was valid,
2: 3 can we escape i we neglect so great a salvation?
3: 6 and we are his house i we hold firm
3: 7 the Holy Spirit says, "Today, i you hear his voice,
3:14 i only we hold our first confidence firm to the end.
3:15 As it is said, "Today, i you hear his voice,

Heb 3:18 i not to those who were disobedient?
4: 7 i you hear his voice, do not harden your hearts."
4: 8 For i Joshua had given them rest,
6: 3 And we will do this, i God permits.
6: 8 But i it produces thorns and thistles,
7:11 Now i perfection had been attainable through
8: 4 Now i he were on earth,
8: 7 For i that first covenant had been faultless,
9:13 For i the blood of goats and bulls,
10:26 For i we willfully persist in sin
11:15 I they had been thinking of the land
11:29 the people passed through the Red Sea as i
12: 8 I you do not have that discipline
12:20 "I even an animal touches the mountain,
12:25 for i they did not escape when they refused
12:25 on earth, how much less will we escape i we reject
13:23 and i he comes in time,
Jas 1: 5 I any of you is lacking in wisdom, ask God,
1:23 For i any are hearers of the word and not doers,
1:26 I any think they are religious,
2: 2 For i a person with gold rings and
2: 2 and i a poor person in dirty clothes also comes in,
2: 3 and i you take notice of the one wearing
2: 8 You do well i you really fulfill the royal law
2: 9 But i you show partiality,
2:11 i you do not commit adultery but i you murder,
2:14 i you say you have faith but do not have works?
2:15 I a brother or sister is naked and lacks daily food,
2:17 So faith by itself, i it has no works, is dead.
3: 3 I we put bits into the mouths of horses
3:14 But i you have bitter envy and selfish ambition
4:11 but i you judge the law,
4:15 Instead you ought to say, "I the Lord wishes,
5:19 i anyone among you wanders from the truth
1Pe 1: 6 even i now for a little while you have had
1:17 I you invoke as Father the one who judges all
2: 3 i indeed you have tasted that the Lord is good.
2:19 For it is a credit to you i, being aware of God,
2:20 I you endure when you are beaten
2:20 i you endure when you do right and suffer for it,
3: 1 so that, even i some of them do not obey the word,
3:13 Now who will harm you i you are eager
3:14 But even i you do suffer for doing what is right,
3:17 i suffering should be God's will,
4:14 I you are reviled for the name of Christ,
4:16 Yet i any of you suffers as a Christian,
4:17 i it begins with us, what will be the end
4:18 And "I it is hard for the righteous to be saved,
2Pe 1: 8 For i these things are yours and are increasing
1:10 for i you do this, you will never stumble.
2: 4 i God did not spare the angels when they sinned,
2: 5 and i he did not spare the ancient world,
2: 6 and i by turning the cities of Sodom
2: 7 and i he rescued Lot, a righteous man
2:20 For i, after they have escaped the defilements of
1Jn 1: 6 I we say that we have fellowship with him
1: 7 i we walk in the light as he himself is in the light,
1: 8 I we say that we have no sin,
1: 9 I we confess our sins, he who is faithful
1:10 I we say that we have not sinned,
2: 1 But i anyone does sin, we have an advocate with
2: 3 i we obey his commandments.
2:19 for i they had belonged to us,
2:24 I what you heard from the beginning abides
2:29 I you know that he is righteous,
3:21 Beloved, i our hearts do not condemn us,
4:12 No one has ever seen God; i we love one another,
5: 9 I we receive human testimony,
5:14 that i we ask anything according to his will,
5:15 i we know that he hears us in whatever we ask,
5:16 I you see your brother or sister committing what is
3Jn 1:10 So i I come, I will call attention
Rev 2: 5 I not, I will come to you
2:16 I not, I will come to you soon and make war
3: 3 I you do not wake up, I will come like a thief,
3: 5 I you conquer, you will be clothed like them
3:12 I you conquer, I will make you a pillar in
3:20 i you hear my voice and open the door,
5: 6 a Lamb standing as i it had been slaughtered,
11: 5 And i anyone wants to harm them,
13:10 I you are to be taken captive,
13:10 i you kill with the sword, with the sword you must
22:18 i anyone adds to them, God will add to that person
22:19 i anyone takes away from the words of the book
Tob 1:17 and i I saw the dead body of any
3:15 But i it is not pleasing to you, O Lord,
4: 8 I you have many possessions,
4: 8 i few, do not be afraid to give according to
4:14 I you serve God you will receive payment.
4:19 but i he chooses otherwise,
4:21 You have great wealth i you fear God and flee
8:12 of the maids and have her go in to see i he is alive.
8:12 But i he is dead, let us bury him
9: 4 i I delay even one day I will upset him very much.
13: 6 I you turn to him with all your heart and
13:16 be i a remnant of my descendants should survive
Jdt 5:20 i there is any oversight in this people and they sin
5:21 But i they are not a guilty nation,
6: 9 I you really hope in your heart that they will not
7:31 But i these days pass by,
8:15 For i he does not choose to help us
8:17 and he will hear our voice, i it pleases him.
8:21 For i we are captured, all Judea will be captured
10:19 for i we let them go they will be able to beguile
11: 2 i your people who live in the hill country had
11: 6 I you follow out the words of your servant,
11:23 I you do as you have said,

Jdt 12: 3 Holofernes said to her, "I your supply runs out,
12:12 For it would be a disgrace i we let such
12:12 I we do not seduce her, she will laugh at us."
14: 2 set a captain over them, as i you were going down
14:15 of Israel and sent him to us as i to his death."
AdE 1:19 I therefore it pleases the king,
3: 9 I it pleases the king, let it be decreed that they are
4:11 of the empire know that i any man or woman goes
4:14 For i you keep quiet at such a time as this,
4:16 contrary to the law, even i I must die."
5: 4 I it pleases the king, let him and Haman come to
5: 8 i I have found favor in the sight of the king,
6:13 "I Mordecai is of the Jewish people,
7: 3 "I I have found favor with the king,
8: 5 "I it pleases you, and i I have found favor,
8: 6 can I be safe i my ancestral nation is destroyed?"
15: 5 as i beloved, but her heart was frozen with fear.
Wis 2:17 Let us see i his words are true,
2:18 for i the righteous man is God's child,
3:17 i they live long they will be held of no account,
3:18 I they die young, they will have no hope
4: 4 For even i they put forth boughs for a while,
6:21 Therefore i you delight in thrones and scepters,
8: 5 I riches are a desirable possession in life,
8: 6 And i understanding is effective,
8: 7 And i anyone loves righteousness,
8: 8 And i anyone longs for wide experience,
8:12 i I speak at greater length,
11:24 not have made anything i you had hated it.
11:25 How would anything have endured i you had
12:20 For i you punished with such great care
13: 3 I through delight in the beauty
13: 4 i people were amazed at their power and working,
13: 9 for i they had the power to know so much
15: 2 even i we sin we are yours, knowing your power;
17: 9 For even i nothing disturbing frightened them, yet,
Sir 1:26 I you desire wisdom, keep the commandments,
3:13 even i his mind fails, be patient with him;
4: 6 for i in bitterness of soul some should curse you,
4:16 I they remain faithful, they will inherit her;
4:19 I they go astray she will forsake them,
5:12 I you know what to say, answer your neighbor;
5:12 but i not, put your hand over your mouth.
6:12 but i you are brought low,
6:32 I you are willing, my child,
6:32 and i you apply yourself you will become clever.
6:33 I you love to listen you will gain knowledge,
6:33 and i you pay attention you will become wise.
6:36 I you see an intelligent person,
7:22 i they are profitable to you, keep them.
8:12 but i you do lend anything, count it as a loss.
8:13 but i you give surety, be prepared to pay.
9:13 But i you approach them, make no misstep,
11:10 i you multiply activities, you will not
11:10 I you pursue, you will not overtake,
12: 1 I you do good, know to whom you do it,
12: 2 i not by them, certainly by the Most High.
12:11 i he humbles himself and walks bowed down,
12:15 He stands by you for a while, but i you falter,
12:16 an enemy may have tears in his eyes, but i
12:17 I evil comes upon you, you will find him there
13: 4 A rich person will exploit you i you can be of use
13: 4 but i you are in need he will abandon you.
13: 5 I you own something, he will live with you;
13:22 I the rich person slips, many come to the rescue;
13:22 I the humble person slips, they even criticize him;
13:24 Riches are good i they are free from sin;
14: 5 I one is mean to himself,
14: 7 I ever he does good, it is by mistake;
15:15 I you choose, you can keep the commandments,
16: 2 I they multiply, do not rejoice in them,
16:11 Even i there were only one stiff-necked person,
16:11 it would be a wonder i he remained unpunished.
18: 9 The number of days in their life is great i
18:31 I you allow your soul to take pleasure
19:13 or i he did, so that he may not do it again.
19:14 or i he said it, so that he may not repeat it.
19:28 Even i lack of strength keeps him from sinning,
21: 2 for i you approach sin, it will bite you.
22:21 Even i you draw your sword against a friend,
22:22 I you open your mouth against your friend,
22:26 But i harm should come to me because of him,
23:11 I he swears in error, his sin remains on him, and i he disregards it, he sins doubly; i he swears a false oath, he will not be justified,
25: 3 I you gathered nothing in your youth,
25:26 I she does not go as you direct,
26:11 and do not be surprised i she sins against you.
26:26 *but i she dishonors him in her pride*
27: 3 I a person is not steadfast in the fear of the Lord,
27: 8 I you pursue justice, you will attain it and wear it
27:17 i you betray his secrets, do not follow after him.
27:27 I a person does evil, it will roll back upon him,
28: 4 I one has no mercy toward another like himself,
28: 5 I a mere mortal harbors wrath,
28:12 I you blow on a spark, it will glow;
28:12 i you spit on it, it will be put out;
29: 6 I he can pay, his creditor will hardly get back half,
29: 6 I he cannot pay, the borrower has robbed the other
31: 4 and i ever he rests he becomes needy.
31:18 I you are seated among many persons,
31:21 I you are overstuffed with food, get up to vomit,
31:27 Wine is very life to human beings i taken
32: 1 I they make you master of the feast,
32: 7 Speak, you who are young, i you are obliged to,
32: 7 but no more than twice, and only i asked.
33:30 and i he does not obey, make his fetters heavy.

Sir 33:31 I you have but one slave, treat him like yourself,
33:31 I you have but one slave, treat him like a brother,
33:32 I you ill-treat him, and he leaves you
34:21 I one sacrifices ill-gotten goods,
34:30 I one washes after touching a corpse,
34:31 So i one fasts for his sins,
36:28 I kindness and humility mark her speech,
37:12 and who will grieve with you i you fail.
37:22 I a person is wise to his own advantage,
39: 6 I the great Lord is willing,
39:11 I he lives long, he will leave a name greater than
39:11 and i he goes to rest, it is enough for him.
41: 9 I you have children, calamity will be theirs;
42: 9 or i married, for fear she may be disliked;
50:29 For i they put them into practice,
Bar 2:22 But i you will not obey the voice of the Lord
2:29 "I you will not obey my voice,
3:13 I you had walked in the way of God,
LtJ 6:27 i any of these gods falls to the ground,
6:27 I anyone sets it upright, it cannot move itself;
6:27 and i it is tipped over, it cannot straighten itself.
6:35 i one makes a vow to them and does not keep it,
Sus 1:21 I you refuse, we will testify against you that
1:22 For i I do this, it will mean death for me;
1:22 i I do not, I cannot escape your hands.
1:54 then, i you really saw this woman, tell me this:
Bel 1: 8 I you do not tell me who is eating these provisions,
1: 9 But i you prove that Bel is eating them,
1:12 i you do not find that Bel has eaten it all,
1Mc 2:19 "Even i all the nations that live under the rule of
2:40 "I we all do as our kindred have done and refuse
3:53 i you do not help us?"
5:40 "I he crosses over to us first,
5:41 But i he shows fear and camps on the other side of
7:35 then i I return safely I will burn up this house."
8:24 I war comes first to Rome or to any of their allies
8:27 i war comes first to the nation of the Jews,
8:30 I after these terms are in effect
8:32 I now they appeal again for help against you,
9:10 I our time has come, let us die bravely
10:71 I you now have confidence in your forces,
11:42 on you and your nation, i I find an opportunity.
13:40 And i any of you are qualified to be enrolled
15:21 Therefore i any scoundrels have fled to you
2Mc 2:15 So i you have need of them,
3:38 "I you have any enemy or plotter
3:38 for you will get him back thoroughly flogged, i
4: 9 to pay one hundred fifty more i
4:46 taking the king aside into a colonnade as i
4:47 who would have been freed uncondemned i
5:18 But i it had not happened that they were involved
6:26 Even i for the present I would avoid
7:24 and enviable i he would turn from the ways
7:33 And i our living Lord is angry for a little while,
8:15 i not for their own sake,
8:18 and even, i necessary, the whole world."
9:20 I you and your children are well
9:24 i anything unexpected happened
10: 4 but that, i they should ever sin,
11:19 I you will maintain your goodwill toward
11:28 I you are well, it is as we desire.
12:44 For i he were not expecting
12:45 But i he was looking to the splendid reward
13:10 now i ever to help those who were on the point
14:33 "I you do not hand Judas over to me as a prisoner,
15: 3 the thrice-accursed wretch asked i there were
15:38 I it is well told and to the point,
15:38 i it is poorly done and mediocre,
1Es 2: 5 I any of you, therefore, are of his people,
2:19 Now i this city is built and the walls finished,
2:21 in order that, i it seems good to you,
2:24 that i this city is built and its walls finished,
4: 4 I he tells them to make war on one another,
4: 4 and i he sends them out against the enemy,
4: 5 i they win the victory, they bring everything to
4: 7 I he tells them to kill, they kill;
4: 7 i he tells them to release, they release;
4: 8 i he tells them to attack, they attack;
4: 8 i he tells them to lay waste, they lay waste;
4: 8 i he tells them to build, they build;
4: 9 i he tells them to cut down, they cut down;
4: 9 i he tells them to plant, they plant.
4:18 I men gather gold and silver
4:31 I she smiles at him, he laughs;
4:31 i she loses her temper with him, he flatters her,
6:21 Now therefore, O king, i it seems wise to do so,
6:22 i it is found that the building of the house of
6:22 and i it is approved by our lord the king,
6:32 that i anyone should transgress or nullify any of
9: 4 i any did not meet there within two or three days,
3Mc 1: 4 promising to give them each two minas of gold i
1:12 "Even i those men are deprived of this honor,
2:10 you promised that i we should have reverses
2:30 "But i any of them prefer
3:24 i a sudden disorder later arises against us,
5:31 "I your parents or children were present,
5:32 i it were not for an affection arising
6:10 "Even i our lives have become entangled
7: 9 For you should know that i we devise any evil
2Es 4: 4 I you can solve one of them for me,
4: 7 And he said to me, "I I had asked you,
4:18 I now you were a judge between them,
4:26 "I you are alive, you will see, and i you live long,
4:29 I therefore that which has been sown is
4:29 and i the place where the evil has been sown does
4:44 "I I have found favor in your sight,
4:44 and i it is possible, and i I am worthy,
2Es 5: 4 But i the Most High grants that you live,
5:13 and i you pray again, and weep as you do now,
5:30 I you really hate your people,
5:45 I therefore all creatures will live at one time and
5:46 'I you bear ten children, why one after another?'
5:56 O Lord, i I have found favor in your sight,
6:11 i I have found favor in your sight,
6:14 And i the place where you are
6:31 I therefore you will pray again and fast again
6:59 I the world has indeed been created for us,
7: 5 I there are those who wish to reach the sea,
7: 9 I now the city is given to someone as
7:*52* "I you have just a few precious stones,
7:*62* i the mind is made out of the dust like
7:*63* For it would have been better i the dust itself had
7:*69* i after death we were not to come into judgment,
7:*75* "I I have found favor in your sight, O Lord,
7:*79* I it is one of those who have shown scorn
7:*102* "I I have found favor in your sight,
7:*111* [41] So i now, when corruption has increased
7:*116* [46] it would have been better i the earth had
7:*119* [49] i an immortal time has been promised to us,
7:*128* [58] i they are defeated they shall suffer what you have said, but i they are victorious they shall
7:*137* [67] for i he did not make them abound, the world
7:*138* [68] because i he did not give out of his goodness
7:*139* [69] and the judge, because i he did not pardon
8:14 I then you will suddenly and quickly destroy what
8:32 For i you have desired to have pity on us,
8:42 "I I have found favor in your sight, let me speak.
8:43 I the farmer's seed does not come up,
8:43 or i it has been ruined by too much rain,
9:23 "Now, i you will let seven days more pass—
10:12 But i you say to me, 'My lamentation is not like
10:16 i you acknowledge the decree of God to be just,
12: 7 i I have found favor in your sight,
12: 7 and i I have been accounted righteous before you
12: 7 i my prayer has indeed come up before your face,
12:44 Therefore i you forsake us,
12:44 for us i we also had been consumed in the burning
14:22 I then I have found favor with you,
14:34 I you, then, will rule over your minds
15:31 and i they combine in great power and turn
15:53 i you had not killed my chosen people continually,
4Mc 1: 3 I, then, it is evident that reason rules
1: 5 "I reason rules the emotions,
2: 9 I one is greedy, one is ruled by the law
2:20 For i reason could not control anger,
2:24 that i reason is master of the emotions,
4:12 and that i he were spared he would praise
4:17 Jason agreed that i the office were conferred
4:23 a decree that i any of them were found observing
5: 3 I any were not willing to eat defiling food,
5:10 that you will do something even more senseless i,
5:13 i there is some power watching over this religion
5:18 Even i, as you suppose, our law were
5:19 not suppose that it would be a petty sin i we were
5:30 i you gouge out my eyes and burn my entrails.
6:18 be irrational i having lived in accordance
6:20 be shameful i we should survive for a little while
6:32 For i the emotions had prevailed over reason,
7:16 I, therefore, because of piety
8: 2 but i any were to refuse,
8: 7 of authority in my government i you will renounce
8: 9 But i by disobedience you rouse my anger,
8:11 Will you not consider this, that i you disobey,
8:16 what arguments might have been used i some
8:17 and exhorted us to accept kind treatment i
8:21 and let us seriously consider that i
8:26 when we can live in peace i we obey the king?"
9: 6 And i the aged men of the Hebrews because
9: 7 and i you take our lives because of our religion,
9:27 they inquired i he were willing to eat,
10:18 he said, "Even i you remove my organ of speech,
11:16 So i you intend to torture me for
12: 4 You too, i you do not obey,
12: 5 but i you yield to persuasion you will be my friend
13: 2 For i they had been slaves to their emotions
13: 7 For i we so die, Abraham and Isaac
14:17 I they are not able to keep the intruder away,
16: 1 I, then, a woman, advanced in years and mother
16: 5 Consider this also: I this woman, though a mother,
16:17 For it would be shameful i,
17: 7 I it were possible for us to paint the history

IGAL (3)

Nu 13: 7 from the tribe of Issachar, I son of Joseph;
2Sa 23:36 I son of Nathan of Zobah; Bani the Gadite;
1Ch 3:22 Hattush, I, Bariah, Neariah, and Shaphat, six.

IGDALIAH (1)

Jer 35: 4 into the chamber of the sons of Hanan son of I,

IGEAL (KJV) See IGAL

IGNOBLE (1)

3Mc 4:12 to lament bitterly the i misfortune of their kindred,

IGNOMINIOUSLY (1)

3Mc 6:34 and their fire-breathing boldness was i quenched.

IGNOMINY (KJV) See DISHONOR

IGNORANCE (13) [IGNORE]

Eze 45:20 for anyone who has sinned through error or i;
Ac 3:17 "And now, friends, I know that you acted in i,
17:30 While God has overlooked the times of human i,
Eph 4:18 alienated from the life of God because of their i
1Pe 1:14 to the desires that you formerly had in i.
2:15 that by doing right you should silence the i of
Wis 14:22 but though living in great strife due to i,
17:13 prefers i of what causes the torment.
Sir 4:25 but be ashamed of your i.
51:19 and lamented my i of her.
2Mc 11:31 in any way for what may have been done in i.
4Mc 1: 5 why is it not sovereign over forgetfulness and i?"
2:24 it does not control forgetfulness and i?

IGNORANT‡ (11) [IGNORE]

Ps 73:22 I was stupid and i; I was like a
Pr 9:13 she is i and knows nothing.
Ro 10: 3 being i of the righteousness that comes from God,
2Co 2:11 for we are not i of his designs.
Heb 5: 2 He is able to deal gently with the i and wayward,
2Pe 3:16 the i and unstable twist to their own destruction,
Wis 13: 1 For all people who were i of God were foolish
Sir 20:19 continually on the lips of the i.
20:24 it is continually on the lips of the i.
21:18 a house in ruins is wisdom to a fool, and to the i,
4Mc 13:19 You are not i of the affection of family ties,

IGNORANTLY (1) [IGNORE]

1Ti 1:13 I received mercy because I had acted i in unbelief,

IGNORE (9) [IGNORANCE, IGNORANT, IGNORANTLY, IGNORED, IGNORES]

Dt 22: 1 or sheep straying away and i them;
22: 4 or ox fallen on the road and i it;
Pr 12:16 but the prudent i an insult.
15:32 Those who i instruction despise themselves,
2Pe 3: 5 They deliberately i this fact,
3: 8 But do not i this one fact, beloved,
Sir 8: 9 Do not i the discourse of the aged,
30:11 and do not i his errors.
35:17 He will not i the supplication of the orphan,

IGNORED (3) [IGNORE]

Dt 33: 9 he i his kin, and did not acknowledge his children.
Pr 1:25 and because you have i all my counsel
2Es 7:23 the Most High does not exist, and they i his ways.

IGNORES (1) [IGNORE]

Pr 13:18 and disgrace are for the one who i instruction,

IGNORING See Index to Footnotes

IIM (1)

Jos 15:29 Baalah, I, Ezem,

IJE-ABARIM (KJV) See IYE-ABARIM

IJON (3)

1Ki 15:20 He conquered I, Dan, Abel-beth-maacah,
2Ki 15:29 of Assyria came and captured I,
2Ch 16: 4 They conquered I, Dan, Abel-maim,

IKKESH (3)

2Sa 23:26 Helez the Paltite; Ira son of I of Tekoa;
1Ch 11:28 Ira son of I of Tekoa, Abiezer of Anathoth,
27: 9 for the sixth month, was Ira son of I the Tekoite;

ILAI (1)

1Ch 11:29 Sibbecai the Hushathite, I the Ahohite,

ILIADUN (1)

1Es 5:58 and the sons of Joda son of I,

ILL (34) [ILLNESS]

Ge 48: 1 After this Joseph was told, "Your father is i."
2Sa 12:15 wife bore to David, and it became very i.
13: 2 that he made himself i because of his sister Tamar,
13: 5 "Lie down on your bed, and pretend to be i;
13: 6 So Amnon lay down, and pretended to be i;
1Ki 17:17 the mistress of the house, became i;
2Ki 8: 7 while King Ben-hadad of Aram was i.
9:16 and went to Jezreel, where Joram was lying i.
Ps 106:32 and it went i with Moses on their account;
Pr 25:10 and your i repute will have no end.
Ecc 5:13 There is a grievous i that I have seen under
5:16 This also is a grievous i:
6: 2 This is vanity; it is a grievous i.
Lk 7: 2 and who was i and close to death.
Jn 4:46 Now there was a royal official whose son lay i
5: 5 One man was there who had been i
11: 1 Now a certain man was i, Lazarus of Bethany,
11: 2 her brother Lazarus was i.
11: 3 "Lord, he whom you love is i."
11: 6 after having heard that Lazarus was i,
Ac 9:37 At that time she became i and died.
1Co 11:30 For this reason many of you are weak and i,
2Co 6: 8 in i repute and good repute.
Php 2:26 because you heard that he was i.
2:27 He was indeed so i that he nearly died.

2Ti 4:20 Trophimus I left i in Miletus.
Jdt 8: 8 No one spoke i of her,
Sir 18:19 and before you fall i, take care of your health.
18:21 Before falling i, humble yourself;
38: 9 My child, when you are i, do not delay,
2Mc 6:29 toward him with goodwill now changed to i will,
12: 3 as though there were no i will to the Jews;
3Mc 3: 2 by some who conspired to do them i,
2Es 7:*104* to be i or sleep or eat or be healed in his place,

ILL-BRED (1) [BREED]
Sir 8: 4 Do not make fun of one who is i,

ILL-DISPOSED (2) [DISPOSED]
AdE 13: 5 and is i to our government,
3Mc 3:24 fully convinced by these indications that they are i

ILL-GOTTEN (1) [GET]
Sir 34:21 If one sacrifices i goods, the offering is blemished;

ILL-MANNERED (1) [MANNER]
Sir 21:24 It is i for a person to listen at a door;

ILL-NATURED (2) [NATURE]
1Sa 25:17 he is so i that no one can speak to him."
25:25 My lord, do not take seriously this i fellow, Nabal;

ILL-TIMED (1) [TIME]
Sir 22: 6 Like music in time of mourning is i conversation,

ILL-TREAT (2) [TREAT]
Ge 31:50 If you i my daughters, or if you take wives
Sir 33:32 If you i him, and he leaves you and runs away,

ILL-TREATMENT (1) [TREAT]
Heb 11:25 to share i with the people of God than to enjoy

ILL-WILL (2) [WILL]
3Mc 3:19 By maintaining their manifest i toward us,
7: 4 of the i that these people had toward all nations.

ILLEGITIMATE (4)
Hos 5: 7 for they have borne i children.
Jn 8:41 They said to him, "We are not i children;
Heb 12: 8 then you are i and not his children.
Wis 4: 3 and none of their i seedlings will strike a deep root

ILLICIT (3)
Nu 3: 4 before the LORD when they offered i fire before
26:61 and Abihu died when they offered i fire before
Dt 23: 2 an i union shall not be admitted to the assembly of

ILLNESS (12) [ILL]
Dt 7:15 The LORD will turn away from you every i;
1Ki 17:17 his i was so severe that there was no breath left
2Ki 8: 8 whether I shall recover from this i."
8: 9 saying, 'Shall I recover from this i?' "
13:14 Now when Elisha had fallen sick with the i
Ps 41: 3 in their i you heal all their infirmities.
Jn 11: 4 he said, "This i does not lead to death;
Sir 10:10 A long i baffles the physician;
31: 2 and a severe i carries off sleep.
2Mc 9:21 from the region of Persia I suffered an annoying i,
9:22 for I have good hope of recovering from my i,
2Es 8:53 i is banished from you, and death is hidden;

ILLUMINE (1) [ILLUMINED]
Wis 17: 5 nor did the brilliant flames of the stars avail to i

ILLUMINED (1) [ILLUMINE]
Wis 17:20 For the whole world was i with brilliant light,

ILLUSIONS (1)
Isa 30:10 speak to us smooth things, prophesy i,

ILLUSTRIOUS (1)
1Es 4:29 the daughter of the i Bartacus;

ILLYRICUM (1)
Ro 15:19 around as I I have fully proclaimed the good news

IMAGE‡ (62) [IMAGES]
Ge 1:26 Then God said, "Let us make humankind in our i,
1:27 So God created humankind in his i, in the i of God
5: 3 according to his i, and named him Seth.
9: 6 for in his own i God made humankind.
Ex 32: 4 formed it in a mold, and cast an i of a calf;
32: 8 they have cast for themselves an i of a calf,
Dt 9:12 they have cast an i for themselves."
9:16 by casting for yourselves an i of a calf;
27:15 be anyone who makes an idol or casts an i,
1Ki 15:13 she had made an abominable i for Asherah;
15:13 down her i and burned it at the Wadi Kidron.
2Ki 21: 7 The carved i of Asherah that he had made he set in
23: 6 He brought out the i of Asherah from the house of
2Ch 15:16 because she had made an abominable i
15:16 Asa cut down her i, crushed it,
33: 7 The carved i of the idol that he had made he set in
Ne 9:18 when they had cast an i of a calf for themselves
Ps 106:19 They made a calf at Horeb and worshiped a cast i.
106:20 the glory of God for the i of an ox that eats grass.
Isa 40:20 a skilled artisan to set up an i that will not topple.
44:10 a god or cast an i that can do no good?
44:15 makes it a carved i and bows down before it.
48: 5 my carved i and my cast i commanded them."
Jer 44:19 that we made cakes for her, marked with her i,
Eze 8: 3 to the seat of the i of jealousy,
8: 5 in the entrance, was this i of jealousy.
Hos 13: 2 And now they keep on sinning and make a cast i
Na 1:14 I will cut off the carved i and the cast i.
Hab 2:18 a cast i, a teacher of lies?
Ac 17:29 an i formed by the art and imagination of mortals.
Ro 8:29 also predestined to be conformed to the i
1Co 11: 7 since he is the i and reflection of God;
15:49 Just as we have borne the i of the man of dust,
15:49 we will also bear the i of the man of heaven.
2Co 3:18 the same i from one degree of glory to another;
4: 4 the glory of Christ, who is the i of God.
Col 1:15 He is the i of the invisible God,
3:10 in knowledge according to the i of its creator.
Rev 13:14 to make an i for the beast that had been wounded
13:15 and it was allowed to give breath to the i of
13:15 of the beast so that the i of the beast could
13:15 and cause those who would not worship the i of
14: 9 "Those who worship the beast and its i,
14:11 or night for those who worship the beast and its i
15: 2 and those who had conquered the beast and its i
16: 2 the mark of the beast and who worshiped its i.
19:20 of the beast and those who worshiped its i.
20: 4 They had not worshiped the beast or its i and had
Tob 9: 6 for I see in Tobias the very i of my cousin Tobit."
Wis 2:23 and made us in the i of his own eternity,
7:26 and an i of his goodness.
13:16 for it is only an i and has need of help.
14:15 an i of his child, who had been suddenly taken
14:17 made a visible i of the king whom they honored,
15: 5 so that they desire the lifeless form of a dead i.
17:21 an i of the darkness that was destined
Sir 17: 3 and made them in his own i.
38:27 they set their heart on painting a lifelike i,
2Es 8:44 and are called your own i because they are made

IMAGES (45) [IMAGE]
Lev 19: 4 Do not turn to idols or make cast i for yourselves:
26: 1 and erect no carved i or pillars, and you shall
Nu 33:52 all their figured stones, destroy all their cast i,
Dt 7:25 The i of their gods you shall burn with fire.
1Sa 6: 5 you must make i of your tumors and i of your mice
6:11 box with the gold mice and the i of their tumors.
1Ki 14: 9 and cast i, provoking me to anger,
2Ki 11:18 his altars and his i they broke in pieces,
17:16 and made for themselves cast i of two calves;
17:41 but also served their carved i;
2Ch 23:17 his altars and his i they broke in pieces,
28: 2 He even made cast i for the Baals;
33:19 and set up the sacred poles and the i,
33:22 to all the i that his father Manasseh had made,
34: 3 the sacred poles, and the carved and the cast i.
34: 4 the sacred poles and the carved and the cast i;
34: 7 beat the sacred poles and the i into powder,
Ps 97: 7 All worshipers of i are put to shame,
Isa 10:10 of the idols whose i were greater than those
10:11 what I have done to Samaria and her i?"
21: 9 all the i of her gods lie shattered on the ground."
30:22 your silver-covered idols and your gold-plated i.
41:29 their works are nothing; their i are empty wind.
42:17 those who trust in carved i,
42:17 who say to cast i, "You are our gods."
Jer 8:19 "Why have they provoked me to anger with their i,
10:14 for their i are false, and there is no breath in them.
50: 2 Her i are put to shame, her idols are dismayed.
50:38 For it is a land of i, and they go mad over idols.
51:17 for their i are false, and there is no breath in them.
51:47 the days are coming when I will punish the i
Eze 7:20 they made their abominable i,
8:12 each in his room of i?
16:17 and made for yourself male i,
23:14 i of the Chaldeans portrayed in vermilion,
30:13 I will destroy the idols and put an end to the i
Am 5:26 your i, which you made for yourselves;
Mic 1: 7 All her i shall be beaten to pieces,
5:13 and I will cut off your i and your pillars from
Ac 7:43 the i that you made to worship;
Ro 1:23 for i resembling a mortal human being or birds
Wis 14:16 of monarchs carved i were worshiped.
15:13 from earthy matter fragile vessels and carved i.
1Mc 5:68 and the carved i of their gods he burned with fire;

IMAGINATION (4) [IMAGINE]
Pr 18:11 in their i it is like a high wall.
Eze 13: 2 say to those who prophesy out of their own i:
13:17 who prophesy out of their own i;
Ac 17:29 an image formed by the art and i of mortals.

IMAGINATIONS (3) [IMAGINE]
2Es 6: 5 before the i of those who now sin were estranged,
16:54 he knows their i and their thoughts
16:63 He knows your i and what you think

IMAGINE (5) [IMAGINATION, IMAGINATIONS, IMAGINED, IMAGINING]
Ps 41: 7 they i the worst for me.
Ac 4:25 and the peoples i vain things?
Ro 2: 3 Do you i, whoever you are,
Eph 3:20 abundantly far more than all we can ask or i,
2Es 16:21 upon earth that people will i that peace is assured

IMAGINED (3) [IMAGINE]
Isa 53: 8 Who could have i his future?
Wis 14:17 they i their appearance far away,
2Mc 9: 8 and had i that he could weigh the high mountains

IMAGINING (2) [IMAGINE]
1Ti 6: 5 i that godliness is a means of gain.
2Mc 5: 6 but i that he was setting up trophies of victory

IMALKUE (2)
1Mc 11:39 So he went to I the Arab,
11:40 He also reported to I what Demetrius had done

IMITATE (11) [IMITATED, IMITATING, IMITATORS]
Dt 18: 9 you must not learn to i the abhorrent practices
2Th 3: 7 For you yourselves know how you ought to i us;
3: 9 but in order to give you an example to i.
Heb 13: 7 the outcome of their way of life, and i their faith.
3Jn 1:11 do not i what is evil but i what is good.
Wis 4: 2 When it is present, people i it,
15: 9 with workers in gold and silver, and i workers
2Mc 4:16 and wished to i completely became their enemies
4Mc 9:23 "I me, brothers," he said.
13: 9 let us i the three youths in Assyria who despised

IMITATED (1) [IMITATE]
2Es 15:48 You have i that hateful one in all her deeds

IMITATING (2) [IMITATE]
Dt 12:30 take care that you are not snared into i them,
Php 3:17 Brothers and sisters, join in i me,

IMITATORS (6) [IMITATE]
1Co 4:16 I appeal to you, then, be i of me.
11: 1 Be i of me, as I am of Christ.
Eph 5: 1 Therefore be i of God, as beloved children,
1Th 1: 6 And you became i of us and of the Lord,
2:14 became i of the churches of God in Christ Jesus
Heb 6:12 but i of those who through faith

IMLAH (4)
1Ki 22: 8 inquire of the LORD, Micaiah son of I;
22: 9 "Bring quickly Micaiah son of I."
2Ch 18: 7 inquire of the LORD, Micaiah son of I;
18: 8 "Bring quickly Micaiah son of I."

IMMANU See Index to Footnotes

IMMANUEL (2) [=EMMANUEL]
Isa 7:14 and shall bear a son, and shall name him I.
8: 8 the breadth of your land, O I.

IMMATURITY (1)
Pr 9: 6 Lay aside i, and live, and walk in the way

IMMEASURABLE (5)
Eph 1:19 the i greatness of his power for us who believe,
2: 7 that in the ages to come he might show the i riches
Bar 3:25 It is great and has no bounds; it is high and i.
Man 1: 6 yet i and unsearchable is your promised mercy,
3Mc 2: 9 when you had created the boundless and i earth,

IMMEDIATELY (97)
Ex 21:20 or female slave with a rod and the slave dies i,
Dt 17: 8 then you shall i go up to the place that
Jdg 9:54 I he called to the young man who carried his armor
1Sa 9:13 Now go up, for you will meet him i."
28:20 I Saul fell full length on the ground,
Da 3: 6 down and worship shall i be thrown into a furnace
3:15 you shall i be thrown into a furnace
4:33 I the sentence was fulfilled
5: 5 I the fingers of a human hand appeared
Mt 4:20 I they left their nets and followed him.
4:22 I they left the boat and their father,
8: 3 I his leprosy was cleansed.
13:20 this is the one who hears the word and i receives it
13:21 on account of the word, that person i falls away.
14:22 I he made the disciples get into the boat and go on
14:27 i Jesus spoke to them and said, "Take heart, it is I;
14:31 Jesus i reached out his hand and caught him,
20:34 I they regained their sight and followed him.
21: 2 and i you will find a donkey tied,
21: 3 And he will send them i."
24:29 "I after the suffering of those days the sun will
Mk 1:12 And the Spirit i drove him out into the wilderness.
1:18 And i they left their nets and followed him.
1:20 I he called them; and they left their father Zebedee
1:42 I the leprosy left him, and he was made clean.
2:12 and i took the mat and went out before all of them;
3: 6 and i conspired with the Herodians against him,
4:15 when they hear, Satan i comes and takes away
4:16 they hear the word, they i receive it with joy.
4:17 on account of the word, i they fall away.
5: 2 i a man out of the tombs with

Mk 5:29 **I** her hemorrhage stopped;
5:30 **I** aware that power had gone forth from him,
5:42 And **i** the girl got up and began to walk
6:25 **I** she rushed back to the king and requested,
6:27 **I** the king sent a soldier of the guard with orders
6:45 **I** he made his disciples get into the boat and go on
6:50 **i** he spoke to them and said, "Take heart, it is I;
7:25 an unclean spirit **i** heard about him,
7:35 And **i** his ears were opened,
8:10 And **i** he got into the boat with his disciples
9:15 they were **i** overcome with awe,
9:20 When the spirit saw him, **i** it convulsed the boy,
9:24 **I** the father of the child cried out, "I believe;
10:52 **I** he regained his sight and followed him on
11: 2 and **i** as you enter it, you will find tied there a colt
11: 3 'The Lord needs it and will send it back here **i**.' "
14:43 **I**, while he was still speaking, Judas,
Lk 1:64 **I** his mouth was opened and his tongue freed,
4:39 **I** she got up and began to serve them.
5:13 **I** the leprosy left him.
5:25 **I** he stood up before them,
6:49 When the river burst against it, **i** it fell,
8:44 and **i** her hemorrhage stopped.
8:47 and how she had been **i** healed.
12:54 you **i** say, 'It is going to rain'; and so it happens.
13:13 **i** she stood up straight and began praising God.
14: 5 will you not **i** pull it out on a sabbath day?"
18:43 **I** he regained his sight and followed him,
19:11 that the kingdom of God was to appear **i**.
21: 9 but the end will not follow **i**."
Jn 6:21 and **i** the boat reached the land
13:30 after receiving the piece of bread, he **i** went out.
Ac 3: 7 and **i** his feet and ankles were made strong.
5:10 **I** she fell down at his feet and died.
9:18 And **i** something like scales fell from his eyes,
9:20 **i** he began to proclaim Jesus in the synagogues,
9:34 And **i** he got up.
10:33 Therefore I sent for you **i**,
12:23 And **i**, because he had not given the glory to God,
13:11 **I** mist and darkness came over him,
16:10 we **i** tried to cross over to Macedonia,
16:26 and **i** all the doors were opened
17:14 Then the believers **i** sent Paul away to the coast,
21:30 and **i** the doors were shut.
21:32 **I** he took soldiers and centurions and ran down
22:29 **I** those who were about to examine him drew back
Jas 1:24 on going away, **i** forget what they were like.
Jdt 4: 5 They **i** seized all the high hilltops and fortified
Sus 1:55 the sentence from God and will **i** cut you in two."
Bel 1:39 of God **i** returned Habakkuk to his own place.
2Mc 4:34 he **i** put him out of the way.
4:38 he **i** stripped off the purple robe from Andronicus,
6:13 the impious alone for long, but to punish them **i**.
7: 4 These were heated **i**, and he commanded that
8:11 So he **i** sent to the towns on the seacoast,
10:22 and **i** captured the two towers.
14:12 He **i** chose Nicanor, who had been in command of
14:16 they set out from there **i** and engaged them
1Es 1:30 **i** his servants took him out of the line of battle.
3Mc 4: 8 seeing death **i** before them.
6:29 **i** released, praised their holy God and Savior,
7:10 the Jews did not **i** hurry to make their departure,
2Es 3: 7 but he transgressed it, and **i** you appointed death
6:44 **I** fruit came forth in endless abundance and
7:*80* but shall **i** wander about in torments,
4Mc 10: 8 They **i** brought him to the wheel,

IMMENSE (3)

1Mc 3:41 they took silver and gold in **i** amounts, and fetters,
3Mc 1:28 of the crowds resulted in an **i** uproar;
4:17 the census of the Jews because of their **i** number,

IMMER (13)

1Ch 9:12 son of Meshullam, son of Meshillemith, son of **I**;
24:14 the fifteenth to Bilgah, the sixteenth to **I**,
Ezr 2:37 Of **I**, one thousand fifty-two.
2:59 Tel-harsha, Cherub, Addan, and **I**,
10:20 Of the descendants of **I**: Hanani and Zebadiah.
Ne 3:29 of **I** made repairs opposite his own house.
7:40 Of **I**, one thousand fifty-two.
7:61 Tel-harsha, Cherub, Addon, and **I**,
11:13 of Ahzai son of Meshillemoth son of **I**,
Jer 20: 1 Now the priest Pashhur son of **I**,
1Es 5:24 The descendants of **I**, one thousand and fifty-two.
5:36 under the leadership of Cherub, Addan, and **I**,
9:21 Of the descendants of **I**: Hanani

IMMERSED (2)

2Ki 5:14 and **i** himself seven times in the Jordan,
Pr 17:12 of its cubs than to confront a fool **i** in folly.

IMMINENT (1)

1Mc 9: 7 and the battle was **i**, he was crushed in spirit,

IMMORAL (4) [IMMORALITY]

1Co 5: 9 not to associate with sexually **i** persons—
5:10 not at all meaning the **i** of this world,
5:11 of brother or sister who is sexually **i** or greedy,
Heb 12:16 an **i** and godless person, who sold his birthright

IMMORALITY (7) [IMMORAL]

1Co 5: 1 that there is sexual **i** among you, and of a kind
7: 2 But because of cases of sexual **i**,
10: 8 not indulge in sexual **i** as some of them did,
2Co 12:21 and have not repented of the impurity, sexual **i**,
Jude 1: 7 indulged in sexual **i** and pursued unnatural lust,
Sir 41:17 Be ashamed of sexual **i**, before your father
42: 8 or foolish or the aged who are guilty of sexual **i**.

IMMORTAL (11) [IMMORTALITY]

Ro 1:23 the glory of the **i** God for images resembling
1Ti 1:17 To the King of the ages, **i**, invisible, the only God,
Wis 1:15 For righteousness is **i**.
12: 1 For your **i** spirit is in all things.
Sir 17:30 since human beings are not **i**.
2Es 2:45 and have put on the **i**,
7:*113* [43] and the beginning of the **i** age to come,
7:*119* [49] if an **i** time has been promised to us,
4Mc 7: 3 until he sailed into the haven of **i** victory.
14: 6 as though moved by an **i** spirit of devotion,
18:23 and have received pure and **i** souls from God,

IMMORTALITY‡ (19) [IMMORTAL]

Ro 2: 7 for glory and honor and **i**, he will give eternal life;
1Co 15:53 and this mortal body must put on **i**.
15:54 and this mortal body puts on **i**,
1Ti 6:16 It is he alone who has **i** and dwells
2Ti 1:10 who abolished death and brought life and **i** to light
Wis 3: 4 their hope is full of **i**.
4: 1 for in the memory of virtue is **i**,
6:18 and giving heed to her laws is assurance of **i**,
6:19 and **i** brings one near to God;
8:13 Because of her I shall have **i**,
8:17 in my heart that in kinship with wisdom there is **i**,
15: 3 and to know your power is the root of **i**.
2Es 7:13 and yield the fruit of **i**.
7:*96* that they are to receive and enjoy in **i**.
8:54 and in the end the treasure of **i** is made manifest.
4Mc 9:22 but as though transformed by fire into **i**,
14: 5 as though running the course toward **i**,
16:13 a mind like adamant and giving rebirth for **i** to
17:12 The prize was **i** in endless life.

IMMOVABLE (5)

Job 41:23 of its flesh cling together; it is firmly cast and **i**.
Isa 33:20 an **i** tent, whose stakes will never be pulled up,
Ac 27:41 the bow stuck and remained **i**,
1Co 15:58 Therefore, my beloved, be steadfast, **i**,
3Mc 6:19 binding them with **i** shackles.

IMMUNE (2) [IMMUNITIES, IMMUNITY]

Nu 5:19 be **i** to this water of bitterness that brings
5:28 she shall be **i** and be able to conceive children.

IMMUNITIES (1) [IMMUNE]

1Mc 10:28 We will grant you many **i** and give you gifts.

IMMUNITY (1) [IMMUNE]

1Mc 10:34 be days of **i** and release for all the Jews who are

IMMUTABILITY, IMMUTABLE (KJV) See UNCHANGEABLE

IMNA (1)

1Ch 7:35 Zophah, **I**, Shelesh, and Amal.

IMNAH (4) [IMNITES]

Ge 46:17 **I**, Ishvah, Ishvi, Beriah, and their sister Serah.
Nu 26:44 of **I**, the clan of the Imnites;
1Ch 7:30 **I**, Ishvah, Ishvi, Beriah, and their sister Serah.
2Ch 31:14 Kore son of **I** the Levite, keeper of the east gate,

IMNITES (1) [IMNAH]

Nu 26:44 of Imnah, the clan of the **I**;

IMPAIRED (1)

Sir 3:24 and wrong opinion has **i** their judgment.

IMPALE (2) [IMPALED]

Nu 25: 4 and **i** them in the sun before the LORD,
2Sa 21: 6 and we will **i** them before the LORD at Gibeon

IMPALED (4) [IMPALE]

2Sa 21: 9 they **i** them on the mountain before the LORD.
21:13 they gathered the bones of those who had been **i**.
Ezr 6:11 who then shall be **i** on it.
1Es 6:32 who then shall be **i** upon it,

IMPART (2) [IMPARTS]

Wis 7:13 I learned without guile and I **i** without grudging;
Sir 16:25 I will **i** discipline precisely

IMPARTIAL (1) [IMPARTIALLY]

Wis 5:18 and wear **i** justice as a helmet;

IMPARTIALLY (2) [IMPARTIAL]

1Pe 1:17 the one who judges all people **i** according
4Mc 5:24 so that in all our dealings we act **i**,

IMPARTS (1) [IMPART]

Ps 119:130 it **i** understanding to the simple.

IMPASSABLE (1)

AdE 16:24 It shall be made not only **i** for human beings,

IMPATIENT (5)

Nu 21: 4 but the people became **i** on the way.
Job 4: 5 But now it has come to you, and you are **i**;
21: 4 Why should I not be **i**?
Zec 6: 7 they were **i** to get off and patrol the earth.
11: 8 for I had become **i** with them,

IMPEDIMENT (1)

Mk 7:32 to him a deaf man who had an **i** in his speech;

IMPELLED (1)

Wis 14:18 the artisan **i** even those who did not know the king

IMPENDING (1)

1Co 7:26 I think that, in view of the **i** crisis,

IMPENETRABLE (1)

Jer 46:23 says the LORD, though it is **i**,

IMPENITENT (1)

Ro 2: 5 by your hard and **i** heart you are storing up wrath

IMPERFECTLY (1)

Sir Pr: 2 we may seem to have rendered some phrases **i**.

IMPERIAL (3) [EMPIRE]

Ac 25:21 in custody for the decision of his **I** Majesty,
25:25 and when he appealed to his **I** Majesty,
Php 1:13 throughout the whole **i** guard and to everyone else

IMPERISHABILITY (2) [IMPERISHABLE]

1Co 15:53 For this perishable body must put on **i**,
15:54 When this perishable body puts on **i**,

IMPERISHABLE‡ (8) [IMPERISHABILITY]

Mk 16: S ⟦sacred and **i** proclamation of eternal salvation.⟧
1Co 9:25 to receive a perishable wreath, but we an **i** one.
15:42 What is sown is perishable, what is raised is **i**.
15:50 nor does the perishable inherit the **i**.
15:52 trumpet will sound, and the dead will be raised **i**,
1Pe 1: 4 and into an inheritance that is **i**,
1:23 not of perishable but of **i** seed,
Wis 18: 4 the **i** light of the law was to be given to the world.

IMPETUOUS (2)

Hab 1: 6 the Chaldeans, that fierce and **i** nation, who march
Sir 2: 2 and do not be **i** in time of calamity.

IMPIETIES (1) [IMPIOUS]

3Mc 6:10 our lives have become entangled in **i** in our exile,

IMPIETY (7) [IMPIOUS]

2Ti 2:16 for it will lead people into more and more **i**,
Tit 2:12 training us to renounce **i** and worldly passions,
2Mc 8:33 so these received the proper reward for their **i**.
1Es 1:42 and his uncleanness and **i**,
4Mc 6:19 and ourselves become a pattern of **i** to the young
9:32 you suffer torture by the threats that come from **i**.
10:11 because of your **i** and bloodthirstiness,

IMPIOUS (9) [IMPIETIES, IMPIETY, IMPIOUSLY]

Ps 74:18 and an **i** people reviles your name.
74:22 remember how the **i** scoff at you all day long.
2Mc 3:11 To such an extent the **i** Simon had misrepresented
6:13 it is a sign of great kindness not to let the **i** alone
3Mc 2: 2 to us who are suffering grievously from an **i**
3: 1 When the **i** king comprehended this situation,
3:24 we shall not have these **i** people behind our backs
5:47 he, when he had filled his **i** mind with a deep rage,
4Mc 12:11 "You profane tyrant, most **i** of all the wicked,

IMPIOUSLY (4) [IMPIOUS]

Ps 35:16 they **i** mocked more and more,
2Mc 1:17 on those who have behaved **i**.
2Es 15: 8 concerning their ungodly acts that they **i** commit,
4Mc 9:15 not because I am a murderer, or as one who acts **i**,

IMPLACABLE (1)

2Ti 3: 3 **i**, slanderers, profligates, brutes, haters of good,

IMPLACABLE (KJV) See also RUTHLESS

IMPLANTED (4) [PLANT]

Jas 1:21 the **i** word that has the power to save your souls.
3Mc 5:28 for he had **i** in the king's mind a forgetfulness of
4Mc 13:19 the fathers to their descendants and which was **i** in
15: 6 In seven pregnancies she had **i**

IMPLEAD (KJV) See BRING CHARGES

IMPLEMENTS (2)

1Sa 8:12 and to make his **i** of war and the equipment
Zec 11:15 Take once more the **i** of a worthless shepherd.

IMPLIES (1) [IMPLY]
Sir 46: 1 He became, as his name **i**,

IMPLORE (11) [IMPLORED, IMPLORING]
1Sa 2:36 to **i** him for a piece of silver or a loaf of bread,
2Ki 20: 3 now, O LORD, I **i** you, how I have walked
Ps 119:58 I **i** your favor with all my heart;
Isa 38: 3 now, O LORD, I **i** you, how I have walked
Mal 1: 9 **i** the favor of God, that he may be gracious to us.
Tob 8: 4 and **i** our Lord that he grant us mercy and safety."
8: 5 and they began to pray and **i** that they might
Man 1:13 I earnestly **i** you, forgive me, O Lord, forgive me!
2Es 2:41 **i** the Lord's authority that your people,
4:22 Then I answered and said, "I **i** you, my lord,
5:56 I said, "I **i** you, O Lord,

IMPLORED (11) [IMPLORE]
Ex 32:11 But Moses **i** the LORD his God, and said,
Wis 8:21 so I appealed to the Lord and **i** him,
2Mc 8: 2 They **i** the Lord to look upon
8:14 and at the same time **i** the Lord
8:29 and **i** the merciful Lord to be wholly reconciled
10: 4 and **i** the Lord that they might never again fall
10:26 they **i** him to be gracious to them and to be
13:12 in the same petition and had **i** the merciful Lord
3Mc 5:13 and again **i** him who is easily reconciled to show
5:25 and mournful dirges **i** the supreme God
4Mc 16:13 she **i** them and urged them on to death for the sake

IMPLORING (5) [IMPLORE]
Tob 6:18 **i** the Lord of heaven that mercy and safety may
2Mc 10:16 after making solemn supplication and **i** God
Man 1:11 the knee of my heart, **i** you for your kindness.
3Mc 5:51 **i** the Ruler over every power to manifest himself
4Mc 4: 9 and children were **i** God in the temple to shield

IMPLY (3) [IMPLIES]
1Co 10:19 What do I **i** then?
10:20 No, I **i** that what pagans sacrifice,
2Co 1:24 I do not mean to **i** that we lord it over your faith;

IMPORT (1) [IMPORTED]
1Ki 10:28 Solomon's **i** of horses was from Egypt and Kue,

IMPORTANCE (2) [IMPORTANT]
Ex 11: 3 Moses himself was a man of great **i** in the land
1Co 15: 3 on to you as of first **i** what I in turn had received:

IMPORTANT (5) [IMPORTANCE, SELF-IMPORTANT]
Ex 18:22 let them bring every **i** case to you,
Mk 12:33 this is much more **i** than all whole burnt offerings
Ac 21:39 from Tarsus in Cilicia, a citizen of an **i** city;
Sir 33: 7 Why is one day more **i** than another,
2Mc 10:15 the Idumeans, who had control of **i** strongholds,

IMPORTED (6) [IMPORT]
1Ki 9:28 **i** from there four hundred twenty talents of gold,
10:29 be **i** from Egypt for six hundred shekels of silver,
2Ch 1:16 Solomon's horses were **i** from Egypt and Kue;
1:17 They **i** from Egypt, and then exported,
8:18 and **i** from there four hundred fifty talents of gold
9:28 Horses were **i** for Solomon from Egypt and

IMPORTUNITY (KJV) See PERSISTENCE

IMPOSE (5) [IMPOSED, IMPOSING, SELF-IMPOSED]
2Ki 18:14 whatever you **i** on me I will bear."
Ezr 7:24 that it shall not be lawful to **i** tribute,
Pr 17:26 To **i** a fine on the innocent is not right,
Ac 15:28 to **i** on you no further burden than these essentials:
1Es 8:22 and that no one has authority to **i** any tax on them

IMPOSED (10) [IMPOSE]
Ex 1:14 They were ruthless in all the tasks that they **i**
21:30 If a ransom is **i** on the owner,
21:30 then the owner shall pay whatever is **i** for
Jos 7:11 they have transgressed my covenant that I **i**
2Ki 23:33 and **i** tribute on the land of one hundred talents
Jer 15:11 surely I have **i** enemies on you in a time of trouble
La 3:28 to sit alone in silence when the Lord has **i** it,
Eze 26:17 who **i** your terror on all the mainland!
Am 2: 8 they drink wine bought with fines they **i**.
Heb 9:10 the body **i** until the time comes to set things right.

IMPOSING (2) [IMPOSE]
Ex 1:13 The Egyptians became ruthless in **i** tasks on
Dt 26: 6 and afflicted us, by **i** hard labor on us,

IMPOSSIBLE (19)
Ge 11: 6 that they propose to do will now be **i** for them.
2Sa 13: 2 a virgin and it seemed **i** to Amnon to do anything
Zec 8: 6 though it seems **i** to the remnant of this people
8: 6 should it also seem **i** to me,
Mt 17:20 and nothing will be **i** for you."
19:26 Jesus looked at them and said, "For mortals it is **i**,
Mk 10:27 Jesus looked at them and said, "For mortals it is **i**,
Lk 1:37 For nothing will be **i** with God."
13:33 because it is **i** for a prophet to be killed outside
18:27 "What is **i** for mortals is possible for God."
Ac 2:24 because it was **i** for him to be held in its power.
Heb 6: 4 For it is **i** to restore again
6:18 in which it is **i** that God would prove false,
10: 4 For it is **i** for the blood of bulls and goats
11: 6 And without faith it is **i** to please God,
Wis 16:15 To escape from your hand is **i**;
2Mc 3:12 And he said that it was utterly **i** that wrong should
14:10 it is **i** for the government to find peace."
3Mc 4:18 the task was **i** for all the generals in Egypt.

IMPOSTOR (1) [IMPOSTORS]
Mt 27:63 that **i** said while he was still alive,

IMPOSTORS (2) [IMPOSTOR]
2Co 6: 8 We are treated as **i**, and yet are true;
2Ti 3:13 wicked people and **i** will go from bad to worse,

IMPOTENT (KJV) See CRIPPLED, INVALID, SICK

IMPOVERISH (1) [POOR]
Jdg 14:15 Have you invited us here to **i** us?"

IMPOVERISHED (3) [POOR]
Lev 25:39 If any who are dependent on you become so **i**
Jdg 6: 6 Thus Israel was greatly **i** because of Midian;
Sir 18:32 or you may become **i** by its expense.

IMPRECATIONS (1)
4Mc 12:19 After he had uttered these **i**,

IMPRESS (1) [IMPRESSED]
4Mc 15: 4 We **i** upon the character of a small child

IMPRESSED (1) [IMPRESS]
3Mc 1: 9 and being **i** by its excellence and its beauty,

IMPRINT (1)
Heb 1: 3 He is the reflection of God's glory and the exact **i**

IMPRISONED‡ (10) [PRISON]
Ge 42:19 let one of your brothers stay here where you are **i**.
2Ki 17: 4 the king of Assyria confined him and **i** him.
Jer 37:15 and **i** him in the house of the secretary Jonathan,
Ac 22:19 they themselves know that in every synagogue I **i**
Ro 11:32 For God has **i** all in disobedience so that he may
Gal 3:22 scripture has **i** all things under the power of sin,
3:23 we were **i** and guarded under the law
Wis 16:14 or set free the **i** soul.
18: 4 to be deprived of light and **i** in darkness,
18: 4 those who had kept your children **i**,

IMPRISONMENT (13) [PRISON]
Ezr 7:26 or for confiscation of their goods or for **i**."
Ac 20:23 the Holy Spirit testifies to me in every city that **i**
23:29 but was charged with nothing deserving death or **i**.
26:31 "This man is doing nothing to deserve death or **i**."
Php 1: 7 both in my **i** and in the defense and confirmation
1:13 and to everyone else that my **i** is for Christ;
1:14 having been made confident in the Lord by my **i**,
1:17 but intending to increase my suffering in my **i**.
Phm 1:10 whose father I have become during my **i**.
1:13 be of service to me in your place during my **i** for
Heb 11:36 and flogging, and even chains and **i**.
Sir 13:12 they will not spare you harm or **i**.
1Es 8:24 or some other punishment, either fine or **i**."

IMPRISONMENTS (2) [PRISON]
2Co 6: 5 beatings, **i**, riots, labors, sleepless nights, hunger;
11:23 with far greater labors, far more **i**,

IMPRISONS (1) [PRISON]
Job 11:10 If he passes through, and **i**,

IMPROPER (1) [IMPROPRIETY]
3Mc 4:16 and uttering **i** words against the supreme God.

IMPROPRIETY (1) [IMPROPER]
Dt 23: 9 against your enemies you shall guard against any **i**.

IMPROVED (2)
Hos 10: 1 as his country **i**, he **i** his pillars.

IMPROVISE (1)
Am 6: 5 and like David **i** on instruments of music;

IMPUDENCE (1) [IMPUDENT]
Sir 25:22 There is wrath and **i** and great disgrace when

IMPUDENT (4) [IMPUDENCE]
Pr 7:13 and with **i** face she says to him:
Eze 2: 4 The descendants are **i** and stubborn.
Sir 22: 5 An **i** daughter disgraces father and husband,
26:11 Be on guard against her **i** eye,

IMPUDENT (KJV) See also STUBBORN

IMPULSE (1) [IMPULSES]
Jdt 15: 2 with one **i** all rushed out and fled by every path

IMPULSES (1) [IMPULSE]
4Mc 1:35 and all the **i** of the body are bridled by reason.

IMPURE (2) [IMPURITIES, IMPURITY]
Eph 5: 5 Be sure of this, that no fornicator or **i** person,
1Th 2: 3 not spring from deceit or **i** motives or trickery,

IMPURITIES (1) [IMPURE]
Rev 17: 4 of abominations and the **i** of her fornication;

IMPURITY (18) [IMPURE]
Lev 15:19 she shall be in her **i** for seven days,
15:20 upon which she lies during her **i** shall be unclean;
15:24 If any man lies with her, and her **i** falls on him,
15:25 not at the time of her **i**,
15:25 or if she has a discharge beyond the time of her **i**,
15:25 as in the days of her **i**, she shall be unclean.
15:26 be treated as the bed of her **i**;
15:26 as in the uncleanness of her **i**.
20:21 If a man takes his brother's wife, it is **i**;
Zec 13: 1 to cleanse them from sin and **i**.
Ro 1:24 God gave them up in the lusts of their hearts to **i**,
6:19 as you once presented your members as slaves to **i**
2Co 12:21 and have not repented of the **i**,
Gal 5:19 fornication, **i**, licentiousness,
Eph 4:19 greedy to practice every kind of **i**.
5: 3 But fornication and **i** of any kind, or greed,
Col 3: 5 fornication, **i**, passion, evil desire,
1Th 4: 7 For God did not call us to **i** but in holiness.

IMPUTE (1) [IMPUTES]
1Sa 22:15 Do not let the king **i** anything to his servant or

IMPUTE, IMPUTED, IMPUTETH, IMPUTING (KJV) See also COUNTING, CREDITED, HOLD GUILTY, RECKON, RECKONED, RECKONS, TAKEN INTO ACCOUNT

IMPUTES (1) [IMPUTE]
Ps 32: 2 to whom the LORD **i** no iniquity,

IMRAH (1)
1Ch 7:36 Suah, Harnepher, Shual, Beri, **I**,

IMRI (2)
1Ch 9: 4 son of Omri, son of **I**, son of Bani,
Ne 3: 2 And next to them Zaccur son of **I** built.

IN (14450) [INMOST, INNER, INNERMOST, WITHIN] See Index of Articles Etc.

INABILITY (1)
AdE 16: 3 but in their **i** to stand prosperity,

INACCESSIBLE (1)
3Mc 5:43 and by burning to the ground the temple **i**

INAPPROPRIATE (3)
Sir 14: 3 Riches are **i** for a small-minded person;
20:19 A coarse person is like an **i** story,
2Mc 4:19 for sacrifice, because that was **i**, but to expend it

INASMUCH (4)
2Sa 14:13 In giving this decision the king convicts himself, **i**
Mal 2: 9 **i** as you have not kept my ways
Ro 11:13 **I** then as I am an apostle to the Gentiles,
2Es 7:*51* **I** as you have said that the righteous are not many

INAUGURATED (1)
Heb 9:18 not even the first covenant was **i** without blood.

INBORN (1) [BEAR]
Wis 12:10 that their origin was evil and their wickedness **i**,

INCAPABLE (1)
Hos 8: 5 How long will they be **i** of innocence?

INCENSE (114) [FRANKINCENSE]
Ex 25: 6 spices for the anointing oil and for the fragrant **i**,
25:29 You shall make its plates and dishes for **i**,
30: 1 You shall make an altar on which to offer **i**;
30: 7 Aaron shall offer fragrant **i** on it;
30: 8 a regular **i** offering before the LORD
30: 9 You shall not offer unholy **i** on it,
30:27 the lampstand and its utensils, and the altar of **i**,
30:35 and make an **i** blended as by the perfumer,
30:37 When you make **i** according to this composition,
31: 8 with all its utensils, and the altar of **i**,
31:11 anointing oil and the fragrant **i** for the holy place.

Ex 35: 8 spices for the anointing oil and for the fragrant **i**,
35:15 the altar of **i**, with its poles, and the anointing oil and the fragrant **i**,
35:28 and for the anointing oil, and for the fragrant **i**.
37:16 its plates and dishes for **i**,
37:25 He made the altar of **i** of acacia wood,
37:29 the holy anointing oil also, and the pure fragrant **i**,
39:38 the anointing oil and the fragrant **i**,
40: 5 You shall put the golden altar for **i** before the ark
40:27 and offered fragrant **i** on it;
Lev 4: 7 the horns of the altar of fragrant **i** that is in the tent
10: 1 each took his censer, put fire in it, and laid **i** on it;
16:12 and two handfuls of crushed sweet **i**,
16:13 and put the **i** on the fire before the LORD,
16:13 the cloud of the **i** may cover the mercy seat that is
26:30 and cut down your **i** altars;
Nu 4: 7 and put on it the plates, the dishes for **i**, the bowls,
4:16 the fragrant **i**, the regular grain offering,
7:14 one golden dish weighing ten shekels, full of **i**;
7:20 one golden dish weighing ten shekels, full of **i**;
7:26 one golden dish weighing ten shekels, full of **i**;
7:32 one golden dish weighing ten shekels, full of **i**;
7:38 one golden dish weighing ten shekels, full of **i**;
7:44 one golden dish weighing ten shekels, full of **i**;
7:50 one golden dish weighing ten shekels, full of **i**;
7:56 one golden dish weighing ten shekels, full of **i**;
7:62 one golden dish weighing ten shekels, full of **i**;
7:68 one golden dish weighing ten shekels, full of **i**;
7:74 one golden dish weighing ten shekels, full of **i**;
7:80 one golden dish weighing ten shekels, full of **i**;
7:86 full of **i**, weighing ten shekels apiece according to
16: 7 and lay **i** on them before the LORD;
16:17 and put **i** on it, and each one
16:18 and they put fire in the censers and laid **i** on them,
16:35 the two hundred fifty men offering the **i**.
16:40 shall approach to offer **i** before the LORD,
16:46 put fire on it from the altar and lay **i** on it,
16:47 He put on the **i**, and made atonement for
Dt 33:10 they place **i** before you, and whole burnt offerings
1Sa 2:28 to offer **i**, to wear an ephod before me;
1Ki 3: 3 only, he sacrificed and offered **i** at the high places.
7:50 basins, dishes for **i**, and firepans, of pure gold;
9:25 offering **i** before the LORD.
11: 8 who offered **i** and sacrificed to their gods.
12:33 and he went up to the altar to offer **i**.
13: 1 Jeroboam was standing by the altar to offer **i**,
13: 2 the priests of the high places who offer **i** on you,
22:43 and the people still sacrificed and offered **i** on
2Ki 25:14 the shovels, the snuffers, the dishes for **i**,
1Ch 6:49 on the altar of burnt offering and on the altar of **i**,
9:29 also over the choice flour, the wine, the oil, the **i**,
28:18 the altar of **i** made of refined gold, and its weight;
2Ch 2: 4 and dedicate it to him for offering fragrant **i**
13:11 and every evening burnt offerings and fragrant **i**,
14: 5 the cities of Judah the high places and the **i** altars.
26:16 of the LORD to make offering on the altar of **i**.
26:19 in the house of the LORD, by the altar of **i**.
29: 7 and have not offered **i** or made burnt offerings in
30:14 the altars for offering **i** they took away and threw
34: 4 he demolished the **i** altars that stood above them.
34: 7 and demolished all the **i** altars throughout all
Ps 141: 2 Let my prayer be counted as **i** before you,
Pr 27: 9 Perfume and **i** make the heart glad,
Isa 1:13 **i** is an abomination to me.
17: 8 either the sacred poles or the altars of **i**.
27: 9 no sacred poles or **i** altars will remain standing.
65: 3 sacrificing in gardens and offering **i** on bricks;
65: 7 because they offered **i** on the mountains
Jer 41: 5 and **i** to present at the temple of the LORD.
Eze 6: 4 and your **i** stands shall be broken;
6: 6 your **i** stands cut down, and your works wiped out.
8:11 and the fragrant cloud of **i** was ascending.
16:18 and set my oil and my **i** before them.
23:41 on which you had placed my **i** and my oil.
Da 2:46 that a grain offering and **i** be offered to him.
Hos 2:13 when she offered **i** to them and decked herself
11: 2 they kept sacrificing to the Baals, and offering **i**
Mal 1:11 and in every place **i** is offered to my name,
Lk 1: 9 to enter the sanctuary of the Lord and offer **i**.
1:10 Now at the time of the **i** offering,
1:11 standing at the right side of the altar of **i**.
Heb 9: 4 In it stood the golden altar of **i** and the ark of
Rev 5: 8 each holding a harp and golden bowls full of **i**,
8: 3 a great quantity of **i** to offer with the prayers of all
8: 4 And the smoke of the **i**,
18:13 spice, **i**, myrrh, frankincense, wine, olive oil,
Tob 6:17 and put them on the embers of the **i**.
8: 2 and put them on the embers of the **i**.
Jdt 9: 1 when the evening **i** was being offered in the house
Wis 18:21 prayer and propitiation by **i**;
Sir 24:15 and stacte, and like the odor of **i** in the tent.
39:14 Send out fragrance like **i**,
45:16 **i** and a pleasing odor as a memorial portion,
49: 1 of Josiah is like blended **i** prepared by the skill of
50: 9 like fire and **i** in the censer, like a vessel
Bar 1:10 and **i**, and prepare a grain offering, and offer them
LtJ 6:42 sit along the passageways, burning bran for **i**.
Aza 1:15 no burnt offering, or sacrifice, or oblation, or **i**,
1Mc 1:55 and offered **i** at the doors of the houses and in
4:49 the altar of **i**, and the table into the temple.
4:50 Then they offered **i** on the altar and lit the lamps
2Mc 2: 5 the tent and the ark and the altar of **i**;
10: 3 of two years, and they offered **i** and lighted lamps

INCENSED (3)

Isa 41:11 all who are **i** against you shall be ashamed
45:24 all who were **i** against him shall come to him and
Wis 12:27 in their suffering they became **i** at those creatures
AdE 13: 6 all—wives and children **i**—be utterly destroyed

INCESSANT (1)

3Mc 4: 2 But among the Jews there was **i** mourning,

INCIDENT (1)

2Mc 4:43 against Menelaus about this **i**.

INCITE (1) [INCITED, INCITING]

Ac 17:13 they came there too, to stir up and **i** the crowds.

INCITED (5) [INCITE]

2Sa 24: 1 and he **i** David against them, saying, "Go,
1Ch 21: 1 and **i** David to count the people of Israel.
Job 2: 3 although you **i** me against him,
Ac 13:50 But the Jews **i** the devout women of high standing
2Mc 4: 1 that it was he who had **i** Heliodorus and had been

INCITING (1) [INCITE]

Jer 43: 3 but Baruch son of Neriah is **i** you against us,

INCLINATION (5) [INCLINE]

Ge 6: 5 and that every **i** of the thoughts
8:21 for the **i** of the human heart is evil from youth;
Ecc 11: 9 the **i** of your heart and the desire of your eyes,
Sir 5: 2 Do not follow your **i** and strength in pursuing
37: 3 O **i** to evil, why were you formed to cover the land

INCLINATIONS‡ (2) [INCLINE]

1Co 3: 3 and behaving according to human **i**?
4Mc 2:21 he planted in them emotions and **i**,

INCLINE (31) [INCLINATION, INCLINATIONS, INCLINED, INCLINES, INCLINING]

Jos 24:23 and **i** your hearts to the LORD,
1Ki 8:58 but **i** our hearts to him,
11: 2 they will surely **i** your heart to follow their gods";
2Ki 19:16 **I** your ear, O LORD, and hear;
Ps 10:17 you will strengthen their heart, you will **i** your ear
17: 6 **i** your ear to me, hear my words.
31: 2 **I** your ear to me; rescue me speedily.
45:10 Hear, O daughter, consider and **i** your ear;
49: 4 I will **i** my ear to a proverb;
71: 2 **i** your ear to me and save me.
78: 1 **i** your ears to the words of my mouth.
86: 1 **I** your ear, O LORD, and answer me,
88: 2 **i** your ear to my cry.
102: 2 **I** your ear to me; answer me speedily in the day
119:112 I **i** my heart to perform your statutes forever,
Pr 4:20 **i** your ear to my sayings.
5: 1 **i** your ear to my understanding,
5:13 or **i** my ear to my instructors.
22:17 **I** your ear and hear my words,
Isa 37:17 **I** your ear, O LORD, and hear;
55: 3 **I** your ear, and come to me;
Jer 7:24 Yet they did not obey or **i** their ear, but,
11: 8 Yet they did not obey or **i** their ear,
17:23 Yet they did not listen or **i** their ear;
34:14 not listen to me or **i** their ears to me.
35:15 But you did not **i** your ear or obey me.
44: 5 But they did not listen or **i** their ear,
Da 9:18 **I** your ear, O my God, and hear.
Bar 2:16 **I** your ear, O Lord, and hear;
3Mc 3:22 Since they **i** constantly to evil,
2Es 3:34 be found which way the turn of the scale will **i**.

INCLINED (7) [INCLINE]

Dt 31:21 For I know what they are **i** to do even now,
Jdg 9: 3 and their hearts **i** to follow Abimelech,
Ps 40: 1 he **i** to me and heard my cry.
116: 2 Because he **i** his ear to me,
Jer 25: 4 you have neither listened nor **i** your ears to hear
Sir 51:16 I **i** my ear a little and received her,
2Mc 2:25 to make it easy for those who are **i** to memorize,

INCLINES (3) [INCLINE]

1Sa 14: 7 "Do all that your mind **i** to.
Ecc 10: 2 The heart of the wise **i** to the right,
2Mc 13: 5 that on all sides **i** precipitously into the ashes.

INCLINING (1) [INCLINE]

Pr 2: 2 to wisdom and **i** your heart to understanding;

INCLOSE (KJV) See ENCLOSE

INCLUDE (4) [INCLUDED, INCLUDES, INCLUDING, INCLUSION]

Nu 35: 6 that you give to the Levites shall **i** the six cities
1Ch 21: 6 he did not **i** Levi and Benjamin in the numbering,
1Co 15:27 that this does not **i** the one who put all things
2Es 7:76 not **i** yourself with those who have shown scorn,

INCLUDED (5) [INCLUDE]

Nu 14:29 and of all your number, **i** in the census,
Jos 19:18 Its territory **i** Jezreel, Chesulloth, Shunem,
19:25 Its boundary **i** Helkath, Hali, Beten, Achshaph,
19:41 The territory of its inheritance **i** Zorah, Eshtaol,

INCLUDES (1) [INCLUDE]

4Mc 1: 2 in addition it **i** the praise of the highest virtue—

INCLUDING (21) [INCLUDE]

Ge 17:12 **i** the slave born in your house and the one bought
46:26 not **i** the wives of his sons,
Dt 2:36 on the edge of the Wadi Arnon (**i** the town that is
Jdg 20: 1 from Dan to Beer-sheba, **i** the land of Gilead,
21:10 **i** the women and the little ones.
2Ki 13: 8 and all that he did, **i** his might, are they not written
15:15 **i** the conspiracy that he made,
1Ch 13: 2 **i** the priests and Levites in the cities
Ecc 12:14 **i** every secret thing, whether good or evil.
Da 6: 2 and over them three presidents, **i** Daniel;
Lk 7:29 all the people who heard this, **i** the tax collectors,
23:49 **i** the women who had followed him from Galilee,
Ac 1:14 **i** Mary the mother of Jesus, as well as his brothers.
17:12 **i** not a few Greek women and men
17:34 **i** Dionysius the Areopagite and
Ro 1: 6 **i** yourselves who are called to belong
9:24 **i** us whom he has called,
2Co 1: 1 **i** all the saints throughout Achaia:
2Ti 1:15 **i** Phygelus and Hermogenes.
AdE 9: 7 **i** Pharsannestain, Delphon, Phasga,
1Mc 3:13 **i** a body of faithful soldiers who stayed with him

INCLUSION (1) [INCLUDE]

Ro 11:12 how much more will their full **i** mean!

INCOME (6)

Dt 18: 8 they have **i** from the sale of family possessions.
Pr 3:14 for her **i** is better than silver,
15: 6 but trouble befalls the **i** of the wicked.
16: 8 Better is a little with righteousness than large **i**
Lk 18:12 I fast twice a week; I give a tenth of all my **i**.'
1Mc 10:42 from the **i** of the services of the temple,

INCOMPETENT (1)

1Co 6: 2 are you **i** to try trivial cases?

INCOMPLETE (1)

Sir 42:24 one opposite the other, and he has made nothing **i**.

INCOMPREHENSION (1)

3Mc 5:27 since he had been completely overcome by **i**—

INCONTINENCY (KJV) See LACK OF SELF-CONTROL

INCONVENIENT (1)

Wis 2:12 because he is **i** to us and opposes our actions;

INCORRUPTIBLE‡ (1) [INCORRUPTION]

2Es 7:97 like the light of the stars, being **i** from then on.

INCORRUPTIBLE, INCORRUPTION (KJV) See also IMPERISHABLE

INCORRUPTION (2) [INCORRUPTIBLE]

Wis 2:23 for God created us for **i**,
2Es 4:11 by the corrupt world understand **i**?"

INCREASE (50) [INCREASED, INCREASES, INCREASING, INCREASINGLY]

Ge 3:16 "I will greatly **i** your pangs in childbearing;
48: 4 to make you fruitful and **i** your numbers;
Ex 1:10 let us deal shrewdly with them, or they will **i** and,
Lev 25:16 If the years are more, you shall **i** the price,
Nu 32:14 to **i** the LORD's fierce anger against Israel!
Dt 1:11 **i** you a thousand times more and bless you,
7:13 the **i** of your cattle and the issue of your flock,
8: 1 so that you may live and **i**,
28: 4 the **i** of your cattle and the issue of your flock.
28:18 the **i** of your cattle and the issue of your flock.
28:51 nor the **i** of your cattle and the issue of your flock,
32:22 it devours the earth and its **i**,
Jdg 9:29 I would say to him, '**I** your army,
2Sa 24: 3 the LORD your God **i** the number of the people
1Ch 21: 3 "May the LORD **i** the number of his people
Job 10:17 and **i** your vexation toward me;
Ps 62:10 if riches **i**, do not set your heart on them.
67: 6 The earth has yielded its **i**;
71:21 You will **i** my honor, and comfort me once again.
73:12 always at ease, they **i** in riches.
85:12 and our land will yield its **i**.
115:14 May the LORD give you **i**,
144:13 may our sheep **i** by thousands,
Pr 13:11 but those who gather little by little will **i** it.
21:11 when the wise are instructed, they **i** in knowledge.
28:28 but when they perish, the righteous **i**.
Ecc 1:18 and those who **i** knowledge **i** sorrow.
5:11 When goods **i**, those who eat them **i**;
Jer 33:22 so I will **i** the offspring of my servant David,
Eze 34:27 and the earth shall yield its **i**.
36:11 They shall **i** and be fruitful;
36:37 to **i** their population like a flock.

Da 12: 4 be running back and forth, and evil shall **i.**"
Mt 24:12 And because of the **i** of lawlessness,
Lk 17: 5 The apostles said to the Lord, "**I** our faith!"
Jn 3:30 He must **i,** but I must decrease."
2Co 4:15 may **i** thanksgiving, to the glory of God.
9:10 for sowing and **i** the harvest of your righteousness.
Php 1:17 not sincerely but intending to **i** my suffering
1Th 3:12 And may the Lord make you **i** and abound in love
Sir 18: 6 It is not possible to diminish or **i** them,
21:13 The knowledge of the wise will **i** like a flood,
28:10 and in proportion to the obstinacy, so will strife **i;**
28:10 and in proportion to his wealth he will **i** his wrath.
Bar 2:34 and I will **i** them, and they will not be diminished.
1Mc 14: 8 the ground gave its **i,** and the trees of
2Mc 4:13 and **i** in the adoption of foreign ways
2Es 5:10 unrighteousness and unrestraint shall **i** on earth.

INCREASED (38) [INCREASE]

Ge 7:17 and the waters **i,** and bore up the ark,
7:18 The waters swelled and **i** greatly on the earth;
30:30 before I came, and it has **i** abundantly;
Ex 23:30 until you have **i** and possess the land.
Lev 19:25 that their yield may be **i** for you:
1Sa 14:19 the tumult in the camp of the Philistines **i** more
1Ch 4:38 in their families, and their clans **i** greatly.
Ezr 10:10 and so **i** the guilt of Israel.
Job 1:10 and his possessions have **i** in the land.
Ps 138: 3 you answered me, you **i** my strength of soul.
Isa 9: 3 You have multiplied the nation, you have **i** its joy;
26:15 have **i** the nation, O LORD, you have **i** the nation;
Jer 3:16 And when you have multiplied and **i** in the land,
Eze 23:19 Yet she **i** her whorings, remembering the days
28: 5 in trade you have **i** your wealth,
Da 4:22 Your greatness has **i** and reaches to heaven,
Hos 4: 7 The more they **i,** the more they sinned against me;
10: 1 The more his fruit **i** the more altars he built;
Na 3:16 You **i** your merchants more than the stars of
Lk 2:52 And Jesus **i** in wisdom and in years,
Ac 6: 7 the number of the disciples **i** greatly in Jerusalem,
7:17 our people in Egypt **i** and multiplied
9:31 in the comfort of the Holy Spirit, it **i** in numbers.
16: 5 the churches were strengthened in the faith and **i**
Ro 5:20 but where sin **i,** grace abounded all the more,
Jdt 9: 7 "Here now are the Assyrians, a greatly **i** force,
Wis 10:10 and **i** the fruit of his toil.
Sir 47:24 Their sins **i** more and more,
1Mc 3:42 and his brothers saw that misfortunes had **i** and
1Es 9: 7 and so have **i** the sin of Israel.
3Mc 2:25 he arrived in Egypt, he **i** in his deeds of malice,
2Es 1: 6 that the sins of their parents have **i** in them,
5: 2 be **i** beyond what you yourself see,
7:*111* [41] So if now, when corruption has **i**
7:*114* [44] righteousness has **i** and truth has appeared.
14:17 the more shall evils be **i** upon its inhabitants.
14:40 and wisdom **i** in my breast,

INCREASES (7) [INCREASE]

Ps 49:16 when the wealth of their houses **i.**
Pr 16:21 and pleasant speech **i** persuasiveness.
23:28 She lies in wait like a robber and **i** the number of
29:16 When the wicked are in authority, transgression **i,**
2Co 10:15 but our hope is that, as your faith **i,**
Sir 21:12 but there is a cleverness that **i** bitterness.
31:30 Drunkenness **i** the anger of a fool to his own hurt,

INCREASING (6) [INCREASE]

2Sa 15:12 and the people with Absalom kept **i.**
Mk 4: 8 growing up and **i** and yielding thirty and sixty and
Lk 11:29 When the crowds were **i,** he began to say,
Ac 6: 1 when the disciples were **i** in number,
2Th 1: 3 the love of everyone of you for one another is **i.**
2Pe 1: 8 For if these things are yours and are **i** among you,

INCREASINGLY (1) [INCREASE]

Ac 9:22 Saul became **i** more powerful and confounded

INCREDIBLE (3)

Ac 26: 8 Why is it thought **i** by any of you that God raises
Wis 16:17 most **i** of all—in water, which quenches all things,
19: 5 that your people might experience an **i** journey,

INCUR (19) [INCURRED, INCURRING, INCURS]

Lev 4:13 not to be done and **i** guilt;
6: 7 of the things that one may do and **i** guilt thereby.
7:18 and the one who eats of it shall **i** guilt.
19:17 or you will **i** guilt yourself.
22: 9 that they may not **i** guilt and die in the sanctuary
Nu 18:22 or else they will **i** guilt and die.
18:32 You shall **i** no guilt by reason of it,
Dt 15: 9 to the LORD against you, and you would **i** guilt.
23:21 surely require it of you, and you would **i** guilt.
23:22 if you refrain from vowing, you will not **i** guilt.
24:15 to the LORD against you, and you would **i** guilt.
Jdg 21:22 But neither did you **i** guilt
2Ch 19:10 so that they may not **i** guilt before the LORD
19:10 Do so, and you will not **i** guilt.
Ro 13: 2 and those who resist will **i** judgment.
1Ti 5:12 and so they **i** condemnation
Sir 9: 5 or you may stumble and **i** penalties for her.
3Mc 3:28 the property of those who **i** the punishment,
4Mc 11: 3 that by murdering me you will **i** punishment from

INCURABLE (9)

2Ch 21:18 in his bowels with an **i** disease.
Job 34: 6 my wound is **i,** though I am
Isa 17:11 harvest will flee away in a day of grief and **i** pain.
Jer 15:18 Why is my pain unceasing, my wound **i,**
30:12 Your hurt is **i,** your wound is grievous.
30:15 cry out over your hurt? Your pain is **i.**
Mic 1: 9 For her wound is **i.**
Jdt 5:12 the whole land of Egypt with **i** plagues.
2Mc 9: 5 struck him with an **i** and invisible blow.

INCURRED (11) [INCUR]

Ex 22: 2 and is beaten to death, no bloodguilt is **i;**
22: 3 but if it happens after sunrise, bloodguilt is **i.**
28:38 on himself any guilt **i** in the holy offering that
Lev 5:17 you have **i** guilt, and are subject to punishment.
5:19 you have **i** guilt before the LORD.
Nu 6:11 because they **i** guilt by reason of the corpse.
35:27 by the avenger, no bloodguilt shall be **i.**
2Ch 33:23 but this Amon **i** more and more guilt.
Hos 13: 1 but he **i** guilt through Baal and died.
2Mc 9:16 the expenses **i** for the sacrifices he would provide
3Mc 1: 3 that this man **i** the vengeance meant for the king.

INCURRING (2) [INCUR]

Tob 6:13 or promise her to another man without **i** the penalty
2Es 13:20 into these things, though **i** peril, than to pass from

INCURS (5) [INCUR]

Lev 4:22 not to be done and **i** guilt,
4:27 not to be done and **i** guilt,
Nu 5: 6 with the LORD, that person **i** guilt
Sir 6: 1 for a bad name **i** shame and reproach;
23:16 of individuals multiply sins, and a third **i** wrath.

INDEBTED (1) [DEBT]

Lk 11: 4 for we ourselves forgive everyone **i** to us.

INDECENT (1)

Dt 23:14 so that he may not see anything **i** among you

INDECISION (1)

2Es 15:33 and trembling shall come upon their army, and **i**

INDEED (219)

Ge 1:31 God saw everything that he had made, and **i,**
18:13 and say, 'Shall I **i** bear a child, now that I am old?'
18:23 "Will you **i** sweep away the righteous with
20:12 Besides, she is **i** my sister,
22:17 I will **i** bless you, and I will make your offspring
37: 8 "Are you **i** to reign over us?
37: 8 Are you **i** to have dominion over us?"
37:10 Shall we **i** come, I and your mother
44: 5 Does he not **i** use it for divination?
Ex 3: 7 **I,** I know their sufferings,
4:16 He **i** shall speak for you to the people;
6: 1 **I,** by a mighty hand he will let them go;
10:10 He said to them, "The LORD **i** will be with you,
11: 1 **i,** when he lets you go, he will drive you away.
19: 5 **I,** the whole earth is mine,
Nu 12: 1 (for he had **i** married a Cushite woman);
21: 2 "If you will **i** give this people into our hands,
27: 7 you shall **i** let them possess an inheritance
Dt 2:15 **I,** the LORD's own hand was against them,
9:13 that this people is **i** a stubborn people.
9:16 Then I saw that you had **i** sinned against
12:22 **I,** just as gazelle or deer is eaten,
13: 3 to know whether you **i** love the LORD your God
17:15 you may **i** set over you a king whom
29:24 they and **i** all the nations will wonder,
32:31 **I** their rock is not like our Rock;
32:36 **I** the LORD will vindicate his people,
33: 3 **I,** O favorite among peoples,
Jos 2:11 The LORD your God is **i** God in heaven above
17:17 "You are **i** a numerous people,
Jdg 4:14 The LORD is **i** going out before you."
5: 4 and the heavens poured, the clouds **i** poured water.
5:29 Her wisest ladies make answer, **i,**
18:10 God has **i** given it into your hands—
1Sa 21: 5 "**I** women have been kept from us as always
26: 4 and learned that Saul had **i** arrived.
2Sa 13:15 **i,** his loathing was even greater than
15: 8 If the LORD will **i** bring me back to Jerusalem,
22:29 **I,** you are my lamp, O LORD,
1Ki 3:12 **I** I give you a wise and discerning mind;
8:27 "But will God **i** dwell on the earth?
18:24 the god who answers by fire is **i** God."
18:39 "The LORD **i** is God; the LORD **i** is God."
21:25 (**I,** there was no one like Ahab,
2Ki 7:20 It did **i** happen to him;
14:10 You have **i** defeated Edom,
20: 5 I have seen your tears; **i,** I will heal you;
22:16 I will **i** bring disaster on this place and
24:20 **I,** Jerusalem and Judah so angered the LORD
1Ch 12:22 **I** from day to day people kept coming to David
2Ch 6:15 **I,** you promised with your mouth
6:18 "But will God **i** reside with mortals on earth?
33:13 Then Manasseh knew that the LORD **i** was God.
34:24 I will **i** bring disaster upon this place and
Ne 5:16 **I,** I devoted myself to the work on this wall,
6:10 **i,** tonight they are coming to kill you."
Job 9: 2 "**I** I know that this is so;
13:18 I have **i** prepared my case;
19: 5 If **i** you magnify yourselves against me,
21:16 Is not their prosperity **i** their own achievement?
26:14 These are **i** but the outskirts of his ways;
32:19 My heart is **i** like wine that has no vent;
33:29 "God **i** does all these things, twice, three times,
Ps 10:14 **I** you note trouble and grief,
18:48 **i,** you exalted me above my adversaries;
22:29 **i,** shall all who sleep in the earth bow down;
31: 3 You are **i** my rock and my fortress;
51: 5 **I,** I was born guilty, a sinner
58: 1 Do you **i** decree what is right,
73:27 **I,** those who are far from you will perish;
76: 7 But you **i** are awesome!
84: 2 **i** it faints for the courts of the LORD;
127: 3 Sons are **i** a heritage from the LORD,
Pr 2: 3 if you **i** cry out for insight, and raise your voice
19:23 The fear of the LORD is life **i;**
Ecc 4:14 One can **i** come out of prison to reign,
8: 7 **I,** they do not know what is to be,
Isa 2: 6 **I** they are full of diviners from the east and
4: 5 **I** over all the glory there will be a canopy.
26:12 O LORD, you will ordain peace for us, for **i,**
41:24 **i,** are nothing and your work is nothing at all;
59:12 Our transgressions **i** are with us,
65: 6 I will **i** repay into their laps
Jer 14: 7 our apostasies **i** are many,
22: 4 For if you will **i** obey this word,
27:18 If **i** they are prophets, and if the word of
28:14 and they shall **i** serve him;
31:18 **I** I heard Ephraim pleading:
44:19 "**I** we will go on making offerings to the queen
52: 3 **I,** Jerusalem and Judah so angered the LORD
Eze 28: 3 You are **i** wiser than Daniel;
36: 3 Because they made you desolate **i,**
Da 9:14 **I,** the LORD our God is right in all
11:18 **i,** he shall turn his insolence back upon him.
Hos 9:12 Woe to them **i** when I depart from them!
Joel 2:11 Truly the day of the LORD is great; terrible **i**—
Am 2:11 Is it not **i** so, O people of Israel?
6:14 **I,** I am raising up against you a nation,
Mal 2: 2 **i** I have already cursed them,
3: 1 **i,** he is coming, says the LORD of hosts.
Mt 6:32 and **i** your heavenly Father knows
12:29 Then **i** the house can be plundered.
13:14 With them **i** is fulfilled the prophecy of Isaiah
13:14 'You will **i** listen, but never understand, and you will **i** look, but never perceive.
13:23 who **i** bears fruit and yields,
17:11 "Elijah **i** is coming and will restore all things;
20:23 He said to them, "You will **i** drink my cup,
26:41 the spirit **i** is willing, but the flesh is weak."
28: 7 and **i** he is going ahead of you to Galilee;
Mk 3:27 then **i** the house can be plundered.
4:12 in order that 'they may **i** look, but not perceive, and may **i** listen, but not understand;
8:37 **I,** what can they give in return for their life?
9:12 "Elijah is **i** coming first to restore all things.
14:38 the spirit **i** is willing, but the flesh is weak."
Lk 1:66 For, **i,** the hand of the Lord was with him.
13:30 **I,** some are last who will be first,
18:25 **I,** it is easier for a camel to go through the eye of
19:43 **I,** the days will come upon you,
20:36 **I** they cannot die anymore,
22:37 and **i** what is written about me is being fulfilled."
23:15 **I,** he has done nothing to deserve death.
23:41 And we **i** have been condemned justly,
24:23 that they had **i** seen a vision of angels who said
24:34 They were saying, "The Lord has risen **i,**
Jn 1:17 The law **i** was given through Moses;
3:17 "**I,** God did not send the Son into the world
5:21 **I,** just as the Father raises the dead
6:14 "This is **i** the prophet who is to come into
6:40 This is **i** the will of my Father,
8:36 So if the Son makes you free, you will be free **i.**
8:41 You are **i** doing what your father does."
16: 2 **I,** an hour is coming when those who kill you
16:32 The hour is coming, **i** it has come,
Ac 2:15 **I,** these are not drunk, as you suppose,
17:27 though **i** he is not far from each one of us.
26: 9 "**I,** I myself was convinced that I ought
26:26 **I** the king knows about these things,
27:24 and **i,** God has granted safety
28:26 You will **i** listen, but never understand, and you will **i** look, but never perceive.
Ro 2:25 Circumcision **i** is of value if you obey the law;
5: 7 **I,** rarely will anyone die for a righteous person—
5:13 sin was **i** in the world before the law,
8: 7 to God's law—**i** it cannot,
8:34 at the right hand of God, who **i** intercedes for us.
9:20 who **i** are you, a human being, to argue with God?
9:25 As **i** he says in Hosea,
10:18 have they not heard? **I** they have;
14:20 Everything is **i** clean, but it is wrong for you
15:27 and **i** they owe it to them;
1Co 4: 8 **I,** I wish that you had become kings,
4:15 **I,** in Christ Jesus I became your father through
8: 5 **I,** even though there may be so-called gods
9:10 It was **i** written for our sake,
9:15 **I,** I would rather die than that—
11: 8 **I,** man was not made from woman,
11:19 **I,** there have to be factions among you,
12:14 **I,** the body does not consist of one member but
15:41 **i,** star differs from star in glory.
2Co 1: 9 **I,** we felt that we had received the sentence
1:12 **I,** this is our boast, the testimony
3:10 **I,** what once had glory has lost its glory because
3:14 **I,** to this very day, when they hear the reading of

2Co 3:15 **I,** to this very day whenever Moses is read,
5: 3 if **i,** when we have taken it off we will not
10: 3 **I,** we live as human beings,
12:11 **I** you should have been the ones commending me,
13: 5 unless, **i,** you fail to meet the test!
Gal 3:21 then righteousness would **i** come through the law.
Php 2:27 He was **i** so ill that he nearly died.
4:10 **i,** you were concerned for me,
4:15 You Philippians **i** know that in the early days of
Col 2:23 These have **i** an appearance of wisdom
3:15 to which **i** you were called in the one body.
1Th 3: 3 **I,** you yourselves know
4:10 and **i** you do love all the brothers and sisters
5:11 and build up each other, as **i** you are doing.
2Th 1: 6 For it is **i** just of God to repay
2Ti 3:12 **I,** all who want to live a godly life
Phm 1: 7 I have **i** received much joy and encouragement
1:11 but now he is **i** useful both to you and to me.
Heb 4: 2 For **i** the good news came to us just as to them;
4:12 **I,** the word of God is living and active,
9:22 **I,** under the law almost everything is purified
11: 2 **I,** by faith our ancestors received approval.
11:16 **i,** he has prepared a city for them.
12:21 **I,** so terrifying was the sight that Moses said,
12:29 for **i** our God is a consuming fire.
Jas 5:11 **I** we call blessed those who showed endurance.
1Pe 2: 3 if **i** you have tasted that the Lord is good.
2Pe 1:14 as **i** our Lord Jesus Christ has made clear to me.
Tob 4:11 **I,** almsgiving, for all who practice it,
6:13 **I** he knows that you, rather than any other man,
11:15 and that she was, **i,** on her way there,
14: 4 **I,** everything that was spoken by the prophets
Jdt 7:27 We shall **i** become slaves,
11:10 **I** our nation cannot be punished,
11:17 Your servant is **i** God-fearing and serves the God
13: 5 Now **i** is the time to help your heritage and
AdE 1:11 for she was **i** a beautiful woman.
Sir 18:17 **I,** does not a word surpass a good gift?
35:22 **I,** the Lord will not delay,
Bar 2:25 and **i** they have been thrown out to the heat of day
2Mc 12:12 realizing that they might **i** be useful in many ways,
3Mc 1:29 because **i** all at that time preferred death to
2:11 And **i** you are faithful and true.
2Es 3:36 You may **i** find individuals who have kept
4:34 You, **i,** are in a hurry for yourself,
6:59 If the world has **i** been created for us,
7:26 "For **i** the time will come,
8:38 For **i** I will not concern myself about
12: 7 and if my prayer has **i** come up before your face,
16:21 **I,** provisions will be so cheap upon earth
16:67 **I,** God is the judge; fear him!
4Mc 7:13 Most amazing, **i,** though he was an old man,
17: 8 **I** it would be proper to inscribe

INDEPENDENT (2)
1Co 11:11 woman is not **i** of man or man **i** of woman.

INDESCRIBABLE (2)
2Co 9:15 Thanks be to God for his **i** gift!
1Pe 1: 8 now, you believe in him and rejoice with an **i**

INDESTRUCTIBLE (1)
Heb 7:16 but through the power of an **i** life.

INDIA (8) [INDIAN]
Est 1: 1 over one hundred twenty-seven provinces from **I**
8: 9 the officials of the provinces from **I** to Ethiopia,
AdE 1: 1 over one hundred twenty-seven provinces from **I**
3:12 and the governors in every province from **I**
13: 1 from **I** to Ethiopia and to the officials under them:
16: 1 the governors of the provinces from **I** to Ethiopia,
1Mc 8: 8 the countries of **I,** Media,
1Es 3: 2 in the hundred twenty-seven satrapies from **I**

INDIAN (1) [INDIA]
1Mc 6:37 from there, and also its **I** driver.

INDICATE (6) [INDICATED, INDICATES, INDICATING, INDICATIONS]
1Ki 5: 9 into rafts to go by sea to the place you **i.**
Jn 12:33 He said this to **i** the kind of death he was to die.
21:19 (He said this to **i** the kind of death
1Mc 8:25 as the occasion may **i** to them.
8:27 as the occasion may **i** to them.
1Es 6:30 for daily use as the priests in Jerusalem may **i,**

INDICATED (5) [INDICATE]
1Sa 14:41 And Jonathan and Saul were **i** by the lot,
Jn 18:32 (This was to fulfill what Jesus had said when he **i**
1Pe 1:11 the Spirit of Christ within them **i** when it testified
AdE 13: 6 that those **i** to you in the letters written by Haman,
2Mc 11:17 and have asked about the matters **i** in it.

INDICATES (2) [INDICATE]
Heb 9: 8 By this the Holy Spirit **i** that the way into
12:27 **i** the removal of what is shaken—

INDICATING (2) [INDICATE]
Ac 25:27 to me unreasonable to send a prisoner without **i**
3Mc 5:26 **i** that what the king desired was ready for action.

INDICATIONS (1) [INDICATE]
3Mc 3:24 by these **i** that they are ill-disposed toward us

INDICTMENT (4)
Job 31:35 Oh, that I had the **i** written by my adversary!
Jer 25:31 for the LORD has an **i** against the nations;
Hos 4: 1 for the LORD has an **i** against the inhabitants of
12: 2 The LORD has an **i** against Judah,

INDIGNANT (8) [INDIGNANTLY, INDIGNATION]
Ge 34: 7 they heard of it, the men were **i** and very angry,
Jer 3: 5 will he be **i** to the end?"
Mk 10:14 when Jesus saw this, he was **i** and said to them,
Lk 13:14 **i** because Jesus had cured on the sabbath,
2Co 11:29 Who is made to stumble, and I am not **i?**
Bel 1:28 they were very **i** and conspired against the king,
2Mc 13:25 The people of Ptolemais were **i** over the treaty;
4Mc 9:10 the tyrant was not only **i,**

INDIGNANTLY (1) [INDIGNANT]
4Mc 4: 7 The people **i** protested his words,

INDIGNATION (24) [INDIGNANT]
Ps 7:11 and a God who has **i** every day.
38: 3 in my flesh because of your **i;**
69:24 Pour out your **i** upon them,
78:49 He let loose on them his fierce anger, wrath, **i,**
85: 4 and put away your **i** toward us.
102:10 because of your **i** and anger;
119:53 Hot **i** seizes me because of the wicked,
Isa 10:25 For in a very little while my **i** will come to an end,
13: 5 the LORD and the weapons of his **i,**
30:27 his lips are full of **i,** and his tongue is like a
66:14 and his **i** is against his enemies.
Jer 10:10 and the nations cannot endure his **i.**
15:17 for you had filled me with **i.**
32:37 in my anger and my wrath and in great **i;**
La 2: 6 and in his fierce **i** has spurned king and priest.
Eze 21:31 I will pour out my **i** upon you,
22:24 not rained upon in the day of **i.**
22:31 Therefore I have poured out my **i** upon them;
23:25 I will direct my **i** against you,
Mic 7: 9 I must bear the **i** of the LORD,
Na 1: 6 Who can stand before his **i?**
Zep 3: 8 to pour out upon them my **i,**
2Co 7:11 what **i,** what alarm, what longing, what zeal,
2Es 8:23 and whose **i** makes the mountains melt away,

INDISCRIMINATE (1)
4Mc 1:27 **i** eating, gluttony, and solitary gormandizing.

INDISPENSABLE (1)
1Co 12:22 members of the body that seem to be weaker are **i,**

INDISTINCT (1)
1Co 14: 8 And if the bugle gives an **i** sound,

INDIVIDUAL (5) [INDIVIDUALLY, INDIVIDUALS]
Nu 15:27 An **i** who sins unintentionally shall present
1Ki 8:38 from any **i** or from all your people Israel,
2Ch 6:29 from any **i** or from all your people Israel,
31: 1 to their cities, all to their **i** properties.
Job 34:29 whether it be a nation or an **i?**—

INDIVIDUALLY (8) [INDIVIDUAL]
Nu 1: 2 according to the number of names, every male **i;**
1:18 of names from twenty years old and upward, **i,**
1:20 **i,** every male from twenty years old and upward,
1:22 **i,** every male from twenty years old and upward,
Ro 12: 5 and **i** we are members one of another.
1Co 12:11 who allots to each one **i** just as the Spirit chooses.
12:27 you are the body of Christ and **i** members of it.
3Mc 4:14 The entire race was to be registered **i,**

INDIVIDUALS (10) [INDIVIDUAL]
Ex 21:18 When **i** quarrel and one strikes the other with
Dt 1:13 Choose for each of your tribes **i** who are wise,
1:15 wise and reputable **i,** and installed them as leaders
1Ch 23:24 the **i** from twenty years old and upward who were
Ecc 4: 8 the case of solitary **i,** without sons or brothers;
Ac 15: 1 Then certain **i** came down from Judea
Sir 11: 2 Do not praise **i** for their good looks,
11:26 the Lord on the day of death to reward **i** according
23:16 Two kinds of **i** multiply sins,
2Es 3:36 indeed find **i** who have kept your commandments,

INDOLENCE (1)
Ecc 10:18 and through **i** the house leaks.

INDOMITABLE (1)
4Mc 15:13 nurture and **i** suffering by mothers!

INDOORS (1)
2Mc 3:19 of the young women who were kept **i** ran together

INDUCED (3) [INDUCEMENTS]
2Ch 18: 2 and **i** him to go up against Ramoth-gilead.
2Mc 4:12 and he **i** the noblest of the young men to wear
4:46 **i** the king to change his mind.

INDUCEMENTS (1) [INDUCED]
4Mc 8:15 they had heard the **i** and saw the dreadful devices,

INDULGE[‡] (6) [INDULGED, INDULGENCE, INDULGENT, INDULGING, SELF-INDULGENCE, SELF-INDULGENT]
Hos 4:18 their drinking is ended, they **i** in sexual orgies;
1Co 10: 8 not **i** in sexual immorality as some of them did,
2Pe 2:10 —especially those who **i** their flesh
Jude 1:16 and malcontents; they **i** their own lusts;
Sir 14:16 Give, and take, and **i** yourself,
30:23 **I** yourself and take comfort,

INDULGED (2) [INDULGE]
Jude 1: 7 **i** in sexual immorality and pursued unnatural lust,
AdE 9:10 and they **i** themselves in plunder.

INDULGENCE[‡] (2) [INDULGE]
Wis 12:20 For if you punished with such great care and **i**
2Es 7:*114* [44] sinful **i** has come to an end,

INDULGENT (2) [INDULGE]
Sir Pr: 2 and to be **i** in cases where,
7:24 and do not show yourself too **i** with them.

INDULGING (3) [INDULGE]
1Ti 3: 8 not **i** in much wine, not greedy for money;
2Pe 3: 3 scoffing and **i** their own lusts
Jude 1:18 **i** their own ungodly lusts."

INDUSTRIOUS[‡] (1)
1Ki 11:28 the young man was **i** he gave him charge over all

INEBRIATES (1)
Sir 1:16 she **i** mortals with her fruits;

INEFFECTIVE (2) [INEFFECTUAL]
2Pe 1: 8 from being **i** and unfruitful in the knowledge
4Mc 7:14 that of Isaac he rendered the many-headed rack **i.**

INEFFECTUAL (1) [INEFFECTIVE]
Heb 7:18 earlier commandment because it was weak and **i**

INESCAPABLE (2) [INESCAPABLY]
Wis 16: 4 that upon those oppressors **i** want should come,
17:17 they were seized, and endured the **i** fate;

INESCAPABLY (1) [INESCAPABLE]
3Mc 7: 9 and **i** as an antagonist to avenge such acts.

INEXCUSABLE (KJV) See NO EXCUSE

INEXHAUSTIBLE (1)
2Es 9:19 both with an unfailing table and an **i** pasture,

INEXPERIENCED (4)
1Ch 22: 5 For David said, "My son Solomon is young and **i,**
29: 1 whom alone God has chosen, is young and **i,**
Wis 13:18 for aid he entreats a thing that is utterly **i;**
Sir 34:10 An **i** person knows few things,

INEXPRESSIBLE (1)
2Es 6:44 of inimitable color, and odors of **i** fragrance.

INFALLIBLE (KJV) See CONVINCING

INFAMOUS (2)
Eze 22: 5 from you will mock you, you **i** one, full of tumult.
3Mc 3:23 in accordance with their **i** way of life,

INFANT (9) [INFANTS]
1Sa 15: 3 child and **i,** ox and sheep, camel and donkey.' "
Job 3:16 like an **i** that never sees the light?
24: 9 and take as a pledge the **i** of the poor.
Isa 65:20 No more shall there be in it an **i** that lives but
Jer 44: 7 to cut off man and woman, child and **i,**
La 4: 4 The tongue of the **i** sticks to the roof of its mouth
Heb 5:13 on milk, being still an **i,** is unskilled in the word
Wis 15:14 But most foolish, and more miserable than an **i,**
2Es 5:49 For as an **i** does not bring forth,

INFANTRY (18)
Jdt 1: 4 to march out in force and his **i** to form their ranks.
2:22 From there Holofernes took his whole army, the **i,**
7: 2 forces numbered one hundred seventy thousand **i**
7:20 The whole Assyrian army, their **i,** chariots,
Sir 46: 8 of six hundred thousand **i,**
1Mc 3:39 and sent with them forty thousand **i**
4: 1 Now Gorgias took five thousand **i**
4:28 the next year he mustered sixty thousand picked **i**
15:38 and gave him troops of **i** and cavalry.
16: 5 where a large force of **i** and cavalry was coming
16: 7 and placed the cavalry in the center of the **i,**
2Mc 11: 2 about eighty thousand **i** and all his cavalry

2Mc 11: 4 but was elated with his ten thousands of **i**,
12:20 who had with him one hundred twenty thousand **i**
12:33 with three thousand **i** and four hundred cavalry.
13: 2 a Greek force of one hundred ten thousand **i**,
3Mc 1: 1 both **i** and cavalry, took with him his sister Arsinoë
4Mc 17:24 and courageous for **i** battle and siege,

INFANTS‡ (30) [INFANT]

1Sa 22:19 men and women, children and **i**, oxen, donkeys,
Ps 8: 2 of the mouths of babes and **i** you have founded
Isa 13:16 Their **i** will be dashed to pieces before their eyes;
La 2:11 because **i** and babes faint in the streets of the city.
Hos 11: 4 I was to them like those who lift **i** to their cheeks.
Joel 2:16 gather the children, even **i** at the breast.
Na 3:10 even her **i** were dashed in pieces at the head
Mt 11:25 and the intelligent and have revealed them to **i**;
21:16 of **i** and nursing babies you have prepared praise
24:19 and to those who are nursing **i** in those days!
Mk 13:17 and to those who are nursing **i** in those days!
Lk 10:21 and the intelligent and have revealed them to **i**;
18:15 even **i** to him that he might touch them;
21:23 and to those who are nursing **i** in those days!
Ac 7:19 and forced our ancestors to abandon their **i** so
1Co 3: 1 but rather as people of the flesh, as **i** in Christ.
14:20 rather, be **i** in evil, but in thinking be adults.
1Pe 2: 2 Like newborn **i**, long for the pure, spiritual milk,
Jdt 4:12 to allow their **i** to be carried off and their wives to
16: 4 and dash my **i** to the ground,
Wis 10:21 and made the tongues of **i** speak clearly.
11: 7 in rebuke for the decree to kill the **i**,
12:24 they were deceived like foolish **i**.
18: 5 they had resolved to kill the **i** of your holy ones,
1Mc 1:61 and they hung the **i** from their mothers' necks.
2: 9 Her **i** have been killed in her streets,
2Mc 5:13 and children, and slaughter of young girls and **i**.
3Mc 3:27 whether old people or children or even **i**,
6:14 of **i** and their parents entreat you with tears.
4Mc 4:25 with their **i**, though they had known beforehand

INFERIOR (9)

Job 12: 3 I am not **i** to you.
13: 2 What you know, I also know; I am not **i** to you.
Da 2:39 After you shall arise another kingdom **i** to yours,
Jn 2:10 the **i** wine after the guests have become drunk.
1Co 12:24 giving the greater honor to the **i** member,
2Co 11: 5 that I am not in the least **i** to these super-apostles.
12:11 for I am not at all **i** to these super-apostles.
Heb 7: 7 It is beyond dispute that the **i** is blessed by
Sir 25: 8 and the one who has not served an **i**.

INFERRED (1) [INFERS]

Wis 19:18 be clearly **i** from the sight of what took place.

INFERS (1) [INFERRED]

Wis 8: 8 and **i** the things to come;

INFIDEL (KJV) See UNBELIEVER

INFINITE (KJV) See BEYOND MEASURE, NO END, WITHOUT LIMIT

INFIRMITIES (5) [INFIRMITY]

Ps 41: 3 in their illness you heal all their **i**.
Isa 53: 4 Surely he has borne our **i** and carried our diseases;
Mt 8:17 "He took our **i** and bore our diseases."
Lk 8: 2 women who had been cured of evil spirits and **i**:
2Es 4:27 because this age is full of sadness and **i**.

INFIRMITY (3) [INFIRMITIES]

Lev 15:33 for her who is in the **i** of her period,
Isa 53: 3 a man of suffering and acquainted with **i**;
Gal 4:13 of a physical **i** that I first announced the gospel

INFLAMED (6) [INFLAMMATION]

Isa 5:11 who linger in the evening to be **i** by wine,
Jer 51:39 When they are **i**, I will set out their drink
2Mc 4:38 **I** with anger, he immediately stripped off
14:11 quickly **i** Demetrius still more.
4Mc 3:11 in the enemy's territory tormented and **i** him,
16: 3 **i** as she saw her seven sons tortured

INFLAMMATION (1) [INFLAMED]

Dt 28:22 fever, **i**, with fiery heat and drought,

INFLEXIBLE (2)

3Mc 5: 1 Then the king, completely **i**,
5:12 and was completely frustrated in his **i** plan.

INFLICT (9) [INFLICTED, INFLICTING, INFLICTIONS, INFLICTS]

Dt 7:15 Egypt that you experienced, he will not **i** on you,
28:61 the LORD will **i** on you until you are destroyed.
Jdg 20:31 As before they began to **i** casualties on the troops,
20:39 to **i** casualties on the Israelites, killing about thirty
Ro 3: 5 That God is unjust to **i** wrath on us?
Rev 9:19 and with them they **i** harm.
Sir 12: 6 also hates sinners and will **i** punishment on
48: 8 You anointed kings to **i** retribution,
3Mc 2:27 to **i** public disgrace on the Jewish community,

INFLICTED (13) [INFLICT]

Lev 24:20 the injury **i** is the injury to be suffered.
Jos 10:10 who **i** a great slaughter on them at Gibeon,
Jdg 11:33 He **i** a massive defeat on them from Aroer to
2Sa 7:14 with blows **i** by human beings.
2Ki 8:29 in Jezreel of the wounds that the Arameans had **i**
9:15 in Jezreel of the wounds that the Arameans had **i**
2Ch 16:10 And Asa **i** cruelties on some of the people at
Job 2: 7 and **i** loathsome sores on Job from the sole
Isa 30:26 and heals the wounds **i** by his blow.
La 1:12 which the LORD **i** on the day of his fierce anger.
AdE 16:18 for God, who rules over all things, has speedily **i**
1Mc 8: 4 until they crushed them and **i** great disaster
2Mc 9:28 such as he had **i** on others,

INFLICTING (4) [INFLICT]

Jos 10:20 the Israelites had finished **i** a very great slaughter
2Th 1: 8 **i** vengeance on those who do not know God and
2Mc 3:26 and flogged him continuously, **i** many blows
3Mc 2: 6 You made known your mighty power by **i** many

INFLICTIONS (1) [INFLICT]

2Mc 9: 6 the bowels of others with many and strange **i**.

INFLICTS (3) [INFLICT]

Pr 27: 6 Well meant are the wounds a friend **i**,
Zec 14:18 the plague that the LORD **i** on the nations that do
Sir 21: 3 there is no healing for the wound it **i**.

INFLUENCE (3) [INFLUENCED, INFLUENTIAL]

Da 5: 2 Under the **i** of the wine,
Sir 47:15 Your **i** spread throughout the earth,
4Mc 12: 6 and to **i** her to persuade the surviving son to obey

INFLUENCED (1) [INFLUENCE]

4Mc 15:11 though so many factors **i** the mother to suffer

INFLUENTIAL (2) [INFLUENCE]

Sir 13: 9 When an **i** person invites you, be reserved,
29:18 it has driven the **i** into exile,

INFORM (7) [INFORMATION, INFORMED]

Dt 32: 7 ask your father, and he will **i** you;
2Sa 15:28 until word comes from you to **i** me."
Ezr 4:14 therefore we send and **i** the king,
Tob 10: 8 to your father Tobit and they will **i** him
Sus 1:50 "Come, sit among us and **i** us,
1Es 6:12 that we might **i** you in writing who the leaders are,
4Mc 4: 4 to the king and went up to Seleucus to **i** him of

INFORMATION (6) [INFORM]

1Sa 23:23 and come back to me with sure **i**.
Ezr 5:10 We also asked them their names, for your **i**,
AdE 4: 5 and ordered him to get accurate **i** for her
7: 9 who gave **i** of concern to the king;
2Mc 13:21 gave secret **i** to the enemy;
3Mc 3:28 Any who are willing to give **i** will receive

INFORMED (27) [INFORM]

1Ki 1:51 Solomon was **i**, "Adonijah is afraid
2Ki 22:10 Shaphan the secretary **i** the king,
1Ch 19:17 When David was **i**, he gathered all Israel together,
2Ch 34:18 The secretary Shaphan **i** the king,
Pr 20:15 but the lips **i** by knowledge are a precious jewel.
Da 2:17 Daniel went to his home and **i** his companions,
2:45 great God has **i** the king what shall be hereafter.
Ac 23:22 "Tell no one that you have **i** me of this."
23:30 I was **i** that there would be a plot against the man,
24:22 But Felix, who was rather well **i** about the Way,
25:15 the Jews **i** me about him and asked for a sentence
1Co 10:28 out of consideration for the one who **i** you,
Jude 1: 5 I desire to remind you, though you are fully **i**,
Tob 1:19 one of the Ninevites went and **i** the king about me,
8:14 the maid came out and **i** them that he was alive
9: 5 and **i** him that Tobit's son Tobias had married
Jdt 11: 8 the most **i** and the most astounding
AdE 3: 4 Then they **i** Haman that Mordecai was resisting
12: 2 and he **i** the king concerning them.
Sir 37:14 our own mind sometimes keeps us better **i** than
2Mc 3: 7 of the money about which he had been **i**.
4: 1 who had **i** about the money
11:18 I have **i** the king of everything that needed to
11:29 Menelaus has **i** us that you wish to return home
13: 4 and when Lysias **i** him that this man was to blame
14:20 and the leader had **i** the people,
1Es 8:22 You are also **i** that no tribute or any other tax is to

INFURIATED (5) [FURY]

Est 3: 5 down or do obeisance to him, Haman was **i**.
5: 9 nor trembled before him, he was **i** with Mordecai;
Mt 2:16 he was **i**, and he sent and killed all the children in
3Mc 3: 1 he became so **i** that not only was he enraged
4Mc 9:10 as at those who are disobedient, but also **i**,

INGATHERING (2) [GATHER]

Ex 23:16 You shall observe the festival of **i** at the end of
34:22 and the festival of **i** at the turn of the year.

INGENIOUS (2)

4Mc 7: 4 with many **i** war machines has ever held out as did
15:24 of seven children and the **i** and various rackings,

INHABIT (25) [HABITABLE, HABITATION, HABITATIONS, INHABITANT, INHABITANTS, INHABITED, INHABITING, INHABITS]

Nu 15: 2 When you come into the land you are to **i**,
Job 15:28 in houses that no one should **i**,
Ps 109:10 may they be driven out of the ruins they **i**.
Isa 26:18 and no one is born to **i** the world.
65:21 They shall build houses and **i** them;
65:22 They shall not build and another **i**;
Jer 50:39 with hyenas in Babylon, and ostriches shall **i** her;
Am 9:14 and they shall rebuild the ruined cities and **i** them;
Zep 1:13 Though they build houses, they shall not **i** them;
Ac 17:26 From one ancestor he made all nations to **i**
Jdt 5: 3 What towns do they **i**?
2Es 3:28 Are the deeds of those who **i** Babylon any better?
4:21 and the sea to its waves, so also those who **i**
4:39 on account of the sins of those who **i** the earth."
5: 1 when those who **i** the earth shall be seized
5: 6 And one shall reign whom those who **i**
6:24 the earth and those who **i** it shall be terrified,
7:*74* the Most High has been patient with those who **i**
7:*137* [67] world with those who **i** it would not have life
8:17 for I see the failings of us who **i** the earth;
8:20 you who **i** eternity, whose eyes are exalted
8:50 for many miseries will affect those who **i**
10:59 the Most High will do to those who **i** the earth in
11: 5 it reigned over the earth and over those who **i** it.
13:30 of mind shall come over those who **i** the earth.

INHABITANT‡ (21) [INHABIT]

Isa 5: 9 large and beautiful houses, without **i**.
6:11 And he said: "Until cities lie waste without **i**,
24:17 and the snare are upon you, O **i** of the earth!
33:24 And no **i** will say, "I am sick";
Jer 2:15 his cities are in ruins, without **i**.
4: 7 your cities will be ruins without **i**.
9:11 the towns of Judah a desolation, without **i**.
21:13 See, I am against you, O **i** of the valley,
22:23 O **i** of Lebanon, nested among the cedars,
26: 9 and this city shall be desolate, without **i**'?"
34:22 towns of Judah I will make a desolation without **i**.
44: 2 today they are a desolation, without an **i** in them,
44:22 without **i**, as it is to this day.
46:19 Memphis shall become a waste, a ruin, without **i**.
48: 9 her towns shall become a desolation, with no **i**
48:19 Stand by the road and watch, you **i** of Aroer!
51:29 the land of Babylon a desolation, without **i**.
51:37 an object of horror and of hissing, without **i**.
Eze 7: 7 Your doom has come to you, O **i** of the land.
Zep 2: 5 and I will destroy you until no **i** is left.
Jdt 7:20 until all the water containers of every **i**

INHABITANTS‡ (259) [INHABIT]

A. INHABITANTS OF JERUSALEM (49)
B. ALL THE INHABITANTS (38)
C. INHABITANTS OF THE EARTH (19)

Ge 19:25 and all the Plain, and all the **i** of the cities, B
34:30 the **i** of the land, the Canaanites and the Perizzites;
36:20 the sons of Seir the Horite, the **i** of the land:
50:11 the Canaanite **i** of the land saw the mourning on
Ex 15:14 pangs seized the **i** of Philistia.
15:15 all the **i** of Canaan melted away. B
23:31 for I will hand over to you the **i** of the land,
34:12 Take care not to make a covenant with the **i** of
34:15 You shall not make a covenant with the **i** of
Lev 18:25 and the land vomited out its **i**.
18:27 (for the **i** of the land, who were
25:10 throughout the land to all its **i**.
Nu 13:32 through as spies is a land that devours its **i**;
14:14 and they will tell the **i** of this land.
32:17 in the fortified towns because of the **i** of the land.
33:52 you shall drive out all the **i** of the land from B
33:55 But if you do not drive out the **i** of the land from
Dt 13:13 from among you have gone out and led the **i** of
13:15 you shall put the **i** of that town to the sword,
Jos 2: 9 that all the **i** of the land melt in fear before you. B
2:24 all the **i** of the land melt in fear before us." B
7: 9 Canaanites and all the **i** of the land will hear of B
8:14 he and all his people, the **i** of the city,
8:24 When Israel had finished slaughtering all the **i** B
8:26 until he had utterly destroyed all the **i** of Ai. B
9: 3 when the **i** of Gibeon heard what Joshua had done
9:11 our elders and all the **i** of our country said to us, B
9:24 and to destroy all the **i** of the land before you; B
10: 1 how the **i** of Gibeon had made peace with Israel
11:19 the **i** of Gibeon; all were taken in battle.
13: 6 all the **i** of the hill country from Lebanon B
15:15 From there he went up against the **i** of Debir;
15:63 not drive out the Jebusites, the **i** of Jerusalem; A
17: 7 then the boundary goes along southward to the **i**
17:11 the **i** of Dor and its villages,
17:11 the **i** of En-dor and its villages,
17:11 the **i** of Taanach and its villages,
17:11 and the **i** of Megiddo and its villages
Jdg 1:11 From there they went against the **i** of Debir
1:19 but could not drive out the **i** of the plain,
1:27 not drive out the **i** of Beth-shean and its villages,
1:27 or the **i** of Dor and its villages,

Jdg 1:27 or the **i** of Ibleam and its villages,
1:27 or the **i** of Megiddo and its villages;
1:30 Zebulun did not drive out the **i** of Kitron,
1:30 not drive out the inhabitants of Kitron, or the **i**
1:31 Asher did not drive out the **i** of Acco,
1:31 or the **i** of Sidon, or of Ahlab, or of Achzib,
1:32 the **i** of the land; for they did not drive them out.
1:33 Naphtali did not drive out the **i** of Beth-shemesh,
1:33 or the **i** of Beth-anath, but lived among
1:33 but lived among the Canaanites, the **i** of the land;
1:33 nevertheless the **i** of Beth-shemesh and
2:2 do not make a covenant with the **i** of this land;
5:23 says the angel of the LORD, curse bitterly its **i**,
10:18 He shall be head over all the **i** of Gilead." B
11:8 over all the **i** of Gilead." B
20:15 from their towns, besides the **i** of Gibeah.
21:9 not one of the **i** of Jabesh-gilead was there.
21:10 "Go, put the **i** of Jabesh-gilead to the sword,
21:12 And they found among the **i**
1Sa 5:7 And when the **i** of Ashdod saw how things were,
5:8 The **i** of Gath replied, "Let the ark of God
5:9 he struck the **i** of the city, both young and old,
6:21 So they sent messengers to the **i** of Kiriath-jearim,
11:5 So they told him the message from the **i** of Jabesh.
11:9 "Thus shall you say to the **i** of Jabesh-gilead:
11:9 the messengers came and told the **i** of Jabesh,
11:10 So the **i** of Jabesh said,
23:5 Thus David rescued the **i** of Keilah.
31:11 But when the **i** of Jabesh-gilead heard what
2Sa 5:6 the **i** of the land, who said to David,
2Ki 19:26 while their **i**, shorn of strength, are dismayed
22:16 on this place and on its **i**—
22:19 against its **i**, that they should become a desolation
23:2 all the **i** of Jerusalem, the priests, the prophets, AB
1Ch 4:23 the potters and **i** of Netaim and Gederah;
4:40 for the former **i** there belonged to Ham.
8:6 of the **i** of Geba, and they were carried into exile
8:13 the **i** of Aijalon, who put to flight the **i** of Gath);
11:4 where the Jebusites were, the **i** of the land.
11:5 The **i** of Jebus said to David,
22:18 he has delivered the **i** of the land into my hand;
2Ch 15:5 great disturbances afflicted all the **i** of the lands. B
20:7 the **i** of this land before your people Israel,
20:15 He said, "Listen, all Judah and **i** of Jerusalem, A
20:18 the **i** of Jerusalem fell down before the LORD, A
20:20 "Listen to me, O Judah and **i** of Jerusalem! A
20:23 the **i** of Mount Seir, destroying them utterly;
20:23 and when they had made an end of the **i** of Seir,
21:11 and led the **i** of Jerusalem into unfaithfulness, A
21:13 and the **i** of Jerusalem into unfaithfulness, A
22:1 The **i** of Jerusalem made his youngest son A
32:22 the LORD saved Hezekiah and the **i** of Jerusalem A
32:26 both he and the **i** of Jerusalem, A
32:33 all Judah and the **i** of Jerusalem did him honor A
33:9 Manasseh misled Judah and the **i** of Jerusalem, A
34:9 and Benjamin and from the **i** of Jerusalem. A
34:24 upon this place and upon its **i**,
34:27 against this place and its **i**,
34:28 the disaster that I will bring on this place and its **i**."
34:30 with all the people of Judah, the **i** of Jerusalem, A
34:32 **i** of Jerusalem acted according to the covenant A
35:18 and by the **i** of Jerusalem. A
Ezr 4:6 they wrote an accusation against the **i** of Judah
Ne 3:13 and the **i** of Zanoah repaired the Valley Gate;
7:3 Appoint guards from among the **i** of Jerusalem, A
9:24 and you subdued before them the **i** of the land,
Job 26:5 The shades below tremble, the waters and their **i**.
Ps 33:8 let all the **i** of the world stand in awe of him. B
33:14 he watches all the **i** of the earth— BC
49:1 give ear, all **i** of the world,
75:3 When the earth totters, with all its **i**,
83:7 Philistia with the **i** of Tyre;
107:34 because of the wickedness of its **i**.
Isa 5:3 And now, **i** of Jerusalem and people of Judah, A
8:14 a trap and a snare for the **i** of Jerusalem. A
9:9 Ephraim and the **i** of Samaria—
10:31 the **i** of Gebim flee for safety.
18:3 All you **i** of the world, you who live on the earth,
20:6 In that day the **i** of this coastland will say, 'See,
21:14 O **i** of the land of Tema.
22:21 be a father to the **i** of Jerusalem and to the house A
23:2 Be still, O **i** of the coast, O merchants of Sidon,
23:6 Cross over to Tarshish—wail, O **i** of the coast!
24:1 and he will twist its surface and scatter its **i**.
24:5 The earth lies polluted under its **i**;
24:6 and its **i** suffer for their guilt;
24:6 **i** of the earth dwindled, and few people are left. C
26:5 For he has brought low the **i** of the height;
26:9 the **i** of the world learn righteousness.
26:21 to punish the **i** of the earth for their iniquity; C
30:19 Truly, O people in Zion, **i** of Jerusalem, A
37:27 while their **i**, shorn of strength, are dismayed
38:11 I shall look upon mortals no more among the **i** of
40:22 and its **i** are like grasshoppers;
42:10 the coastlands and their **i**.
42:11 let the **i** of Sela sing for joy,
49:19 surely now you will be too crowded for your **i**,
Jer 1:14 disaster shall break out on all the **i** of the land. B
4:3 to the people of Judah and to the **i** of Jerusalem: A
4:4 O people of Judah and **i** of Jerusalem, A
6:12 I will stretch out my hand against the **i** of the land,
8:1 of the **i** of Jerusalem shall be brought out A
10:18 to sling out the **i** of the land at this time,
11:2 to the people of Judah and the **i** of Jerusalem. A
11:9 the people of Judah and the **i** of Jerusalem. A
11:12 of Judah and the **i** of Jerusalem will go and cry A
13:13 I am about to fill all the **i** of this land— B
Jer 13:13 and all the **i** of Jerusalem—with drunkenness. AB
17:20 and all Judah, and all the **i** of Jerusalem, AB
17:25 the people of Judah and the **i** of Jerusalem; A
18:11 to the people of Judah and the **i** of Jerusalem: A
19:3 O kings of Judah and **i** of Jerusalem. A
19:12 and to its **i**, making this city like Topheth.
21:6 And I will strike down the **i** of this city,
23:14 of them have become like Sodom to me, and its **i**
25:2 the people of Judah and all the **i** of Jerusalem: AB
25:9 and I will bring them against this land and its **i**,
25:29 a sword against all the **i** of the earth, BC
25:30 against all the **i** of the earth. BC
26:15 upon yourselves and upon this city and its **i**,
32:32 the citizens of Judah and the **i** of Jerusalem. A
33:10 without **i**, human or animal,
35:13 to the people of Judah and the **i** of Jerusalem, A
35:17 on Judah and on all the **i** of Jerusalem AB
36:31 I will bring on them, and on the **i** of Jerusalem, A
42:18 wrath were poured out on the **i** of Jerusalem, A
46:8 let me destroy cities and their **i**.
47:2 and all the **i** of the land shall wail. B
48:28 and live on the rock, O **i** of Moab!
48:43 Terror, pit, and trap are before you, O **i** of Moab!
49:8 Flee, turn back, get down low, **i** of Dedan!
49:20 and the purposes that he has formed against the **i**
49:30 hide in deep places, O **i** of Hazor!
50:21 and attack the **i** of Pekod and utterly destroy
50:34 but unrest to the **i** of Babylon.
50:35 says the LORD, and against the **i** of Babylon,
51:1 against Babylon and against the **i** of Leb-qamai;
51:12 and done what he spoke concerning the **i**
51:24 and all the **i** of Chaldea before your very eyes B
51:35 the **i** of Zion shall say.
51:35 "May my blood be avenged on the **i** of Chaldea,"
La 4:12 nor did any of the **i** of the world,
Eze 11:15 are those of whom the **i** of Jerusalem have said, A
12:19 the **i** of Jerusalem in the land of Israel: A
15:6 so I will give up the **i** of Jerusalem. A
26:17 once mighty on the sea, you and your **i**,
27:8 The **i** of Sidon and Arvad were your rowers;
27:35 All the **i** of the coastlands are appalled at you; B
29:6 all the **i** of Egypt shall know that I am the LORD B
33:24 the **i** of these waste places in the land
Da 4:35 All the **i** of the earth are accounted as nothing, BC
4:35 with the host of heaven and the **i** of the earth. C
9:7 on us, the people of Judah, the **i** of Jerusalem, A
Hos 4:1 LORD has an indictment against the **i** of the land.
10:5 **i** of Samaria tremble for the calf of Beth-aven.
Joel 1:2 O elders, give ear, all **i** of the land!
1:14 the elders and all the **i** of the land to the house B
2:1 Let all the **i** of the land tremble, B
Am 1:5 and cut off the **i** from the Valley of Aven,
1:8 I will cut off the **i** from Ashdod,
Mic 1:11 Pass on your way, **i** of Shaphir,
1:11 the **i** of Zaanan do not come forth;
1:12 For the **i** of Maroth wait anxiously for good,
1:13 Harness the steeds to the chariots, **i** of Lachish;
1:15 a conqueror upon you, **i** of Mareshah;
6:12 your **i** speak lies, with tongues of deceit
6:16 and your **i** an object of hissing;
7:13 But the earth will be desolate because of its **i**,
Zep 1:4 and against all the **i** of Jerusalem; AB
1:11 The **i** of the Mortar wail, for all
1:18 end he will make of all the **i** of the earth. BC
2:5 **i** of the seacoast, you nation of the Cherethites!
3:6 without people, without **i**.
Zec 8:20 Peoples shall yet come, the **i** of many cities;
8:21 the **i** of one city shall go to another,
11:6 I will no longer have pity on the **i** of the earth, C
12:5 "The **i** of Jerusalem have strength through A
12:7 glory of the **i** of Jerusalem may not be exalted A
12:8 the LORD will shield the **i** of Jerusalem A
12:10 on the house of David and the **i** of Jerusalem, A
13:1 for the house of David and the **i** of Jerusalem, A
Rev 3:10 on the whole world to test the **i** of the earth. C
6:10 and avenge our blood on the **i** of the earth?" C
8:13 "Woe, woe, woe to the **i** of the earth, C
11:10 and the **i** of the earth will gloat over them C
11:10 a torment to the **i** of the earth. C
13:8 and all the **i** of the earth will worship it, BC
13:12 it makes the earth and its **i** worship the first beast,
13:14 the **i** of earth, telling them to make an image for
17:2 the wine of whose fornication the **i** of the earth C
17:8 And the **i** of the earth, C
Tob 13:11 to you from far away, the **i** of the remotest parts
14:4 All of our kindred, **i** of the land of Israel,
Jdt 1:12 with his sword also all the **i** of the land of Moab, B
3:4 Our towns and their **i** are also your slaves;
5:15 by their might destroyed all the **i** of Heshbon; B
5:22 Holofernes' officers and all the **i** of the seacoast B
Sir 10:2 as the ruler of the city is, so are all its **i**.
Bar 1:15 on the people of Judah, on the **i** of Jerusalem, A
2:23 and the whole land will be a desolation without **i**.
1Mc 1:28 Even the land trembled for its **i**,
6:12 to destroy the **i** of Judah without good reason.
11:18 in the strongholds were killed by the **i** of
2Mc 9:2 the result that Antiochus was put to flight by the **i**
2Es 3:9 in its time you brought the flood upon the **i** of
3:25 but the **i** of the city transgressed,
3:34 in a balance our iniquities and those of the **i** of
3:35 have the **i** of the earth not sinned in your sight? C
6:18 when I draw near to visit the **i** of the earth, C
6:26 of the earth's **i** shall be changed and converted to
11:32 and with much oppression dominated its **i**;
11:34 also in like manner ruled over the earth and its **i**.
12:24 and its **i** more oppressively than all who were
14:17 the more shall evils be increased upon its **i**.
2Es 14:20 world lies in darkness, and its **i** are without light.
15:40 shall rise and destroy all the earth and its **i**,

INHABITED‡ (36) [INHABIT]

Dt 2:10 as the Anakim—had formerly **i** it.
2:12 Moreover, the Horim had formerly **i** Seir,
2:20 Rephaim formerly **i** it,
Jdg 1:17 and they defeated the Canaanites who **i** Zephath,
11:21 the land of the Amorites, who **i** that country.
Ps 107:4 finding no way to an **i** town;
107:7 until they reached an **i** town.
Pr 8:31 in his **i** world and delighting in the human race.
Isa 13:20 It will never be **i** or lived in for all generations;
44:26 who says of Jerusalem, "It shall be **i**,"
45:18 he did not create it a chaos, he formed it to be **i**!):
Jer 17:25 and this city shall be **i** forever.
46:26 Afterward Egypt shall be **i** as in the days of old,
50:13 of the wrath of the LORD she shall not be **i**,
50:39 she shall never again be peopled, or **i**
Eze 12:20 The **i** cities shall be laid waste,
26:19 a city laid waste, like cities that are not **i**,
26:20 so that you will not be **i** or have a place in the land
34:13 and in all the **i** parts of the land.
35:9 and your cities shall never be **i**.
36:10 the towns shall be **i** and the waste places rebuilt;
36:11 I will cause you to be **i** as in your former times,
36:33 I will cause the towns to be **i**,
36:35 the waste and desolate and ruined towns are now **i**
38:12 to assail the waste places that are now **i**,
Joel 3:20 But Judah shall be **i** forever,
Zec 2:4 Jerusalem shall be **i** like villages without walls,
7:7 when Jerusalem was **i** and in prosperity,
7:7 and when the Negeb and the Shephelah were **i**?
12:6 while Jerusalem shall again be **i** in its place,
14:11 And it shall be **i**, for never again shall it
Sir 38:32 Without them no city can be **i**,
Bar 4:35 and for a long time she will be **i** by demons.
2Mc 3:1 While the holy city was **i** in unbroken peace and
9:17 a Jew and would visit every **i** place to proclaim
12:13 and **i** by all sorts of Gentiles.

INHABITING (1) [INHABIT]

3Mc 3:15 not rule the nations **i** Coelesyria and Phoenicia by

INHABITS (2) [INHABIT]

Isa 42:11 up their voice, the villages that Kedar **i**;
57:15 thus says the high and lofty one who **i** eternity,

INHERIT‡ (48) [INHERITANCE, INHERITANCES, INHERITED, INHERITORS, INHERITS]

Ge 21:10 for the son of this slave woman shall not **i** along
Ex 32:13 and they shall **i** it forever.' "
Lev 20:24 But I have said to you: You shall **i** their land,
25:46 for them to **i** as property.
Nu 26:55 to the names of their ancestral tribes they shall **i**.
32:19 not **i** with them on the other side of the Jordan and
33:54 according to your ancestral tribes you shall **i**.
34:13 This is the land that you shall **i** by lot,
Jdg 11:2 "You shall not **i** anything in our father's house;
1Sa 2:8 the ash heap, to make them sit with princes and **i**
2Ki 2:9 "Please let me **i** a double share of your spirit."
2Ch 20:11 of your possession that you have given us to **i**.
Ps 37:9 but those who wait for the LORD shall **i** the land.
37:11 But the meek shall **i** the land,
37:22 for those blessed by the LORD shall **i** the land,
37:29 righteous shall **i** the land, and live in it forever.
37:34 and he will exalt you to **i** the land;
69:36 the children of his servants shall **i** it,
Pr 3:35 wise will **i** honor, but stubborn fools, disgrace.
11:29 Those who trouble their households will **i** wind,
Isa 57:13 the land and **i** my holy mountain.
65:9 my chosen shall **i** it, and my servants shall settle
Jer 12:14 that I have given my people Israel to **i**:
Zec 2:12 The LORD will **i** Judah as his portion in
Mt 5:5 "Blessed are the meek, for they will **i** the earth.
19:29 will receive a hundredfold, and will **i** eternal life.
25:34 **i** the kingdom prepared for you from
Mk 10:17 "Good Teacher, what must I do to **i** eternal life?"
Lk 10:25 he said, "what must I do to **i** eternal life?"
18:18 "Good Teacher, what must I do to **i** eternal life?"
Ro 4:13 For the promise that he would **i** the world did
1Co 6:9 not know that wrongdoers will not **i** the kingdom
6:10 none of these will **i** the kingdom of God.
15:50 flesh and blood cannot **i** the kingdom of God, nor
does the perishable **i** the imperishable.
Gal 5:21 those who do such things will not **i** the kingdom
Heb 1:14 for the sake of those who are to **i** salvation?
6:12 through faith and patience **i** the promises.
12:17 when he wanted to **i** the blessing, he was rejected,
1Pe 3:9 that you might **i** a blessing.
Rev 21:7 Those who conquer will **i** these things,
Tob 4:12 and their posterity will **i** the land.
6:12 it is right for you to **i** her father's possessions.
Sir 4:16 If they remain faithful, they will **i** her;
15:6 and will **i** an everlasting name.
37:26 One who is wise among his people will **i** honor,
2Es 7:17 in your law that the righteous shall **i** these things,
7:*96* and shall **i** what is to come;

INHERITANCE (207) [INHERIT]

Ge 31:14 or **i** left to us in our father's house?
48:6 the names of their brothers with regard to their **i**.
Ex 34:9 and take us for your **i**."

Nu 16:14 or given us an **i** of fields and vineyards.
26:53 the land shall be apportioned for **i** according to
26:54 To a large tribe you shall give a large **i,** and to a small tribe you shall give a small **i;**
26:54 be given its **i** according to its enrollment.
26:56 Their **i** shall be apportioned according to lot
27: 7 an **i** among their father's brothers and pass the **i**
27: 8 then you shall pass his **i** on to his daughter.
27: 9 then you shall give his **i** to his brothers.
27:10 then you shall give his **i** to his father's brothers.
27:11 then you shall give his **i** to the nearest kinsman
32:18 until all the Israelites have obtained their **i.**
32:19 because our **i** has come to us on this side of
32:32 but the possession of our **i** shall remain with us
33:54 to a large one you shall give a large **i,** and to a small one you shall give a small **i;**
33:54 **i** shall belong to the person on whom the lot falls;
34: 2 the land that shall fall to you for an **i,**
34:14 by their ancestral houses have taken their **i,** and
34:15 the half-tribe have taken their **i** beyond the Jordan
34:17 the men who shall apportion the land to you for **i:**
34:18 of every tribe to apportion the land for **i.**
34:29 the LORD commanded to apportion the **i** for
35: 2 from the **i** that they possess,
35: 8 each, in proportion to the **i** that it obtains,
36: 2 to give the land for **i** by lot to the Israelites;
36: 2 the **i** of our brother Zelophehad to his daughters.
36: 3 then their **i** will be taken from the **i** of our ancestors and added to the **i** of the tribe
36: 3 be taken away from the allotted portion of our **i.**
36: 4 then their **i** will be added to the **i** of the tribe into which they have married; and their **i** will be taken from the **i** of our ancestral tribe."
36: 7 so that no **i** of the Israelites shall be transferred
36: 7 for all Israelites shall retain the **i** of their ancestral
36: 8 Every daughter who possesses an **i** in any tribe of
36: 8 may continue to possess their ancestral **i.**
36: 9 No **i** shall be transferred from one tribe to another;
36: 9 the tribes of the Israelites shall retain its own **i.'** "
36:12 their **i** remained in the tribe of their father's clan.
Dt 10: 9 Levi has no allotment or **i** with his kindred; the LORD is his **i,** as the LORD your God promised
12:12 in your towns (since they have no allotment or **i**
14:27 because they have no allotment or **i** with you.
14:29 because they have no allotment or **i** with you,
18: 1 shall have no allotment or **i** within Israel.
18: 2 but they shall have no **i** among the other members
18: 2 the LORD is their **i,** as he promised them.
19:10 that the LORD your God is giving you as an **i,**
20:16 that the LORD your God is giving you as an **i,**
25:19 that the LORD your God is giving you as an **i**
26: 1 that the LORD your God is giving you as an **i**
29: 8 We took their land and gave it as an **i** to
Jos 11:23 an **i** to Israel according to their tribal allotments.
13: 6 only allot the land to Israel for an **i,**
13: 7 therefore divide this land for an **i** to the nine tribes
13: 8 the Reubenites and the Gadites received their **i,**
13:14 To the tribe of Levi alone Moses gave no **i;**
13:14 by fire to the LORD God of Israel are their **i,**
13:15 Moses gave an **i** to the tribe of the Reubenites
13:23 This was the **i** of the Reubenites,
13:24 Moses gave an **i** also to the tribe of the Gadites,
13:28 the **i** of the Gadites according to their clans,
13:29 Moses gave an **i** to the half-tribe of Manasseh;
13:33 But to the tribe of Levi Moses gave no **i;**
13:33 LORD God of Israel is their **i,** as he said to them.
14: 2 Their **i** was by lot, as the LORD had commanded
14: 3 an **i** to the two and one-half tribes beyond
14: 3 but to the Levites he gave no **i** among them.
14: 9 on which your foot has trodden shall be an **i**
14:13 gave Hebron to Caleb son of Jephunneh for an **i.**
14:14 the **i** of Caleb son of Jephunneh the Kenizzite
15:20 the **i** of the tribe of the people of Judah according
16: 4 and Ephraim—received their **i.**
16: 5 of their **i** on the east was Ataroth-addar as far
16: 8 Such is the **i** of the tribe of the Ephraimites
16: 9 that were set apart for the Ephraimites within the **i**
17: 4 "The LORD commanded Moses to give us an **i**
17: 4 the LORD he gave them an **i** among the kinsmen
17: 6 because the daughters of Manasseh received an **i**
17:14 but one lot and one portion as an **i,**
18: 2 among the Israelites seven tribes whose **i** had not
18: 7 the half-tribe of Manasseh have received their **i**
18:20 This is the **i** of the tribe of Benjamin,
18:28 This is the **i** of the tribe of Benjamin according
19: 1 its **i** lay within the **i** of the tribe of Judah.
19: 2 It had for its **i** Beer-sheba, Sheba, Moladah,
19: 8 This was the **i** of the tribe of Simeon according
19: 9 The **i** of the tribe of Simeon formed part of
19: 9 the tribe of Simeon obtained an **i** within their **i.**
19:10 The boundary of its **i** reached as far as Sarid;
19:16 This is the **i** of the tribe of Zebulun,
19:23 This is the **i** of the tribe of Issachar,
19:31 This is the **i** of the tribe of Asher according
19:39 This is the **i** of the tribe of Naphtali according
19:41 The territory of its **i** included Zorah, Eshtaol,
19:48 This is the **i** of the tribe of Dan,
19:49 the Israelites gave an **i** among them to Joshua son
21: 3 and pasture lands out of their **i.**
23: 4 as an **i** for your tribes those nations that remain,
24:30 They buried him in his own **i** at Timnath-serah,
24:32 it became an **i** of the descendants of Joseph.
Jdg 2: 9 So they buried him within the bounds of his **i**
Ru 4: 5 to maintain the dead man's name on his **i."**
4: 6 for myself without damaging my own **i.**
4:10 to maintain the dead man's name on his **i,**
1Ki 8:36 which you have given to your people as an **i.**
12:16 We have no **i** in the son of Jesse.
21: 3 that I should give you my ancestral **i."**
21: 4 he had said, "I will not give you my ancestral **i."**
1Ch 16:18 the land of Canaan as your portion for an **i."**
28: 8 leave it for an **i** to your children after you forever.
2Ch 6:27 which you have given to your people as an **i.**
10:16 We have no **i** in the son of Jesse.
Ezr 9:12 and eat the good of the land and leave it for an **i**
Ne 11:20 all of them in their **i.**
Job 42:15 and their father gave them an **i** along
Ps 78:71 the shepherd of his people Jacob, of Israel, his **i.**
79: 1 the nations have come into your **i;**
105:11 the land of Canaan as your portion for an **i."**
Pr 13:22 The good leave an **i** to their children's children,
17: 2 and will share the **i** as one of the family.
28:10 but the blameless will have a goodly **i.**
Ecc 7:11 Wisdom is as good as an **i,**
Jer 10:16 and Israel is the tribe of his **i;**
16:18 and have filled my **i** with their abominations.
51:19 and Israel is the tribe of his **i;**
La 5: 2 Our **i** has been turned over to strangers,
Eze 35:15 As you rejoiced over the **i** of the house of Israel,
36:12 they shall possess you, and you shall be their **i.**
44:28 This shall be their **i:** I am their **i;**
45: 1 When you allot the land as an **i,**
46:16 prince makes a gift to any of his sons out of his **i,**
46:16 it shall belong to his sons, it is their holding by **i.**
46:17 he makes a gift out of his **i** to one of his servants,
46:17 only his sons may keep a gift from his **i.**
46:18 prince shall not take any of the **i** of the people,
46:18 he shall give his sons their **i** out
47:13 the land for **i** among the twelve tribes of Israel.
47:14 and this land shall fall to you as your **i.**
47:22 as an **i** for yourselves and for the aliens who reside
47:22 with you they shall be allotted an **i** among
47:23 there you shall assign them their **i,**
48:29 This is the land that you shall allot as an **i** among
Mic 2: 2 and house, people and their **i.**
2: 4 the LORD alters the **i** of my people;
Mt 21:38 come, let us kill him and get his **i.'**
Mk 12: 7 come, let us kill him, and the **i** will be ours.'
Lk 12:13 tell my brother to divide the family **i** with me."
20:14 let us kill him so that the **i** may be ours.'
Ac 13:19 he gave them their land as an **i**
20:32 and to give you the **i** among all who are sanctified.
Gal 3:18 For if the **i** comes from the law,
4:30 not share the **i** with the child of the free woman."
Eph 1:11 In Christ we have also obtained an **i,**
1:14 of our **i** toward redemption as God's own people,
1:18 the riches of his glorious **i** among the saints,
5: 5 has any **i** in the kingdom of Christ and of God.
Col 1:12 who has enabled you to share in the **i** of the saints
3:24 the Lord you will receive the **i** as your reward;
Heb 9:15 the promised eternal **i,** because
11: 8 for a place that he was to receive as an **i;**
1Pe 1: 4 and into an **i** that is imperishable,
Jdt 8:22 captivity of the land and the desolation of our **i—**
AdE 10:12 God remembered his people and vindicated his **i.**
13:15 and they desire to destroy the **i** that has been yours
13:17 Hear my prayer, and have mercy upon your **i;**
14: 5 among all their forebears, for an everlasting **i,** and
14: 9 and to destroy your **i,** to stop the mouths
Sir 9: 6 or you may lose your **i.**
22:23 so that you may share with him in his **i.**
23:12 may it never be found in the **i** of Jacob!
24: 8 and in Israel receive your **i.'**
24:23 the law that Moses commanded us as an **i** for
33:24 in the hour of death, distribute your **i.**
36:16 and give them their **i,** as at the beginning.
41: 6 The **i** of the children of sinners will perish,
42: 3 and of dividing the **i** of friends;
44:11 and their **i** with their children's children.
44:21 like the stars, and give them an **i** from sea to sea
44:23 with his blessings, and gave him his **i;**
45:22 But in the land of the people he has no **i,**
45:22 for the Lord himself is his portion and **i.**
46: 1 so that he might give Israel its **i.**
46: 8 to lead the people into their **i,**
46: 9 and his children obtained it for an **i,**
1Mc 2:56 received an **i** in the land.
15:33 but only the **i** of our ancestors,
15:34 we are firmly holding the **i** of our ancestors.
2Mc 2: 4 where Moses had gone up and had seen the **i**
2:17 and has returned the **i** to all,
1Es 8:85 the good things of the land and leave it for an **i**
2Es 6:59 why do we not possess our world as an **i?**
7: 9 If now the city is given to someone as an **i,**
7: 9 how will the heir receive the **i** unless by passing
8:16 about your **i,** for whom I lament, and about Israel,
8:45 But spare your people and have mercy on your **i,**
4Mc 18: 3 also were deemed worthy to share in a divine **i.**

INHERITANCES (9) [INHERIT]

Jos 13:32 These are the **i** that Moses distributed in the plains
14: 1 These are the **i** that the Israelites received in
18: 4 writing a description of it with a view to their **i.**
19:49 the several territories of the land as **i,**
19:51 the **i** that the priest Eleazar and Joshua son of Nun
24:28 So Joshua sent the people away to their **i.**
Jdg 2: 6 to their own **i** to take possession of the land.
Jdt 16:21 After this they all returned home to their own **i.**
1Mc 6:24 and they have seized our **i.**

INHERITED (11) [INHERIT]

Lev 27:16 the LORD any **i** landholding, its assessment shall
27:22 which is not a part of the **i** landholding,
27:28 or **i** landholding, may be sold or redeemed;
Pr 19:14 House and wealth are **i** from parents,
Jer 16:19 Our ancestors have **i** nothing but lies,
Heb 1: 4 as the name he has **i** is more excellent than theirs.
1Pe 1:18 that you were ransomed from the futile ways **i**
Tob 14:13 He **i** both the property of Raguel and that
Jdt 4:12 and the towns they had **i** to be destroyed,
1Mc 2:10 not **i** her palaces and has not seized her spoils?
2:57 **i** the throne of the kingdom forever.

INHERITOR See Index to Footnotes

INHERITORS (1) [INHERIT]

Isa 65: 9 and from Judah **i** of my mountains;

INHERITS (2) [INHERIT]

Sir 4:13 Whoever holds her fast **i** glory,
10:11 one is dead he **i** maggots and vermin and worms.

INHUMAN (1)

2Ti 3: 3 **i,** implacable, slanderers, profligates,

INIMITABLE (1)

2Es 6:44 to the taste, and flowers of **i** color, and odors

INIQUITIES‡ (63) [INIQUITY]

Lev 16:21 and confess over it all the **i** of the people of Israel,
16:22 The goat shall bear on itself all their **i** to
26:39 in the land of your enemies because of their **i;**
26:39 also they shall languish because of the **i**
Ezr 9: 6 for our **i** have risen higher than our heads,
9: 7 and for our **i** we, our kings,
9:13 have punished us less than our **i** deserved
Ne 9: 2 and stood and confessed their sins and the **i** of their
Job 13:23 How many are my **i** and my sins?
13:26 and make me reap the **i** of my youth.
22: 5 There is no end to your **i.**
Ps 38: 4 For my **i** have gone over my head;
40:12 my **i** have overtaken me, until I cannot see;
51: 9 and blot out all my **i.**
79: 8 Do not remember against us the **i** of our ancestors;
90: 8 You have set our **i** before you,
103:10 nor repay us according to our **i.**
107:17 and because of their **i** endured affliction;
130: 3 If you, O LORD, should mark **i,** Lord,
130: 8 It is he who will redeem Israel from all its **i.**
Pr 5:22 The **i** of the wicked ensnare them,
Isa 43:24 you have wearied me with your **i.**
53: 5 for our transgressions, crushed for our **i;**
53:11 and he shall bear their **i.**
59: 2 your **i** have been barriers between you
59:12 with us, and we know our **i:**
64: 6 We all fade like a leaf, and our **i,** like the wind,
65: 7 their **i** and their ancestors' **i** together,
Jer 5:25 Your **i** have turned these away,
11:10 They have turned back to the **i** of their ancestors
14: 7 Although our **i** testify against us, act, O LORD,
La 4:13 for the sins of her prophets and the **i** of her priests,
5: 7 they are no more, and we bear their **i.**
Eze 24:23 but you shall pine away in your **i** and groan
28:18 By the multitude of your **i,**
36:31 and you shall loathe yourselves for your **i**
36:33 On the day that I cleanse you from all your **i,**
43:10 and let them be ashamed of their **i.**
Da 4:27 and your **i** with mercy to the oppressed,
9:13 turning from our **i** and reflecting on his fidelity.
9:16 because of our sins and the **i** of our ancestors,
Am 3: 2 therefore I will punish you for all your **i.**
Mic 7:19 he will tread our **i** under foot.
Ro 4: 7 "Blessed are those whose **i** are forgiven,
Heb 8:12 For I will be merciful toward their **i,**
Rev 18: 5 and God has remembered her **i.**
Tob 13: 5 He will afflict you for your **i,**
Sir 17:20 Their **i** are not hidden from him,
Bar 3: 5 Do not remember the **i** of our ancestors,
3: 8 and punished for all the **i** of our ancestors,
1Es 8:90 See, we are now before you in our **i,**
9: 2 he was mourning over the great **i** of the multitude.
Man 1: 9 of heaven because of the multitude of my **i.**
2Es 1: 5 to their children the **i** that they have committed
3:34 Now therefore weigh in a balance our **i** and those
7:*68* For all who have been born are entangled in **i,**
7:*138* [68] those who have committed **i** might be relieved
16:20 Yet for all this they will not turn from their **i,**
16:65 and your own **i** shall stand as your accusers on
16:67 Cease from your sins, and forget your **i,**
16:76 or your **i** prevail over you.
16:77 by their sins and overwhelmed by their **i!**

INIQUITOUS (1) [INIQUITY]

Isa 10: 1 Ah, you who make **i** decrees,

INIQUITY‡ (162) [INIQUITIES, INIQUITOUS]

Ge 15:16 for the **i** of the Amorites is not yet complete."
Ex 20: 5 punishing children for the **i** of parents,
34: 7 forgiving **i** and transgression and sin,
34: 7 but visiting the **i** of the parents upon the children
34: 9 pardon our **i** and our sin,
Lev 18:25 and I punished it for its **i,**
26:40 But if they confess their **i** and the **i** of their
26:41 and they make amends for their **i,**
26:43 while they shall make amends for their **i,**
Nu 5:15 bringing **i** to remembrance.

Nu 5:31 The man shall be free from i,
5:31 but the woman shall bear her i.
14:18 forgiving i and transgression,
14:18 the i of the parents upon the children to the third
14:19 the i of this people according to the greatness
14:34 for every day a year, you shall bear your i,
Dt 5: 9 punishing children for the i of parents,
Jos 22:20 And he did not perish alone for his i!' "
1Sa 3:13 for the i that he knew,
3:14 of Eli that the i of Eli's house shall not be expiated
15:23 and stubbornness is like i and idolatry.
2Sa 7:14 When he commits i, I will punish him with
Job 4: 8 those who plow i and sow trouble reap the same.
7:21 not pardon my transgression and take away my i?
10: 6 that you seek out my i and search for my sin,
10:14 I sin, you watch me, and do not acquit me of my i.
11:11 when he sees i, will he not consider it?
11:14 If i is in your hand, put it far away,
14:17 and you would cover over my i.
15: 5 For your i teaches your mouth,
15:16 one who drinks i like water!
20:27 The heavens will reveal their i,
21:19 You say, 'God stores up their i for their children.'
31: 3 and disaster the workers of i?
31:28 also would be an i to be punished by the judges,
31:33 by hiding my i in my bosom,
33: 9 I am pure, and there is no i in me.
34:32 if I have done i, I will do it no more'?
36:10 and commands that they return from i.
36:21 Do not turn to i; because of that
36:33 he is jealous with anger against i.
Ps 10: 7 under their tongues are mischief and i.
32: 2 to whom the LORD imputes no i,
32: 5 and I did not hide my i;
36: 2 in their own eyes that their i cannot be found out
38:18 I confess my i; I am sorry for my sin.
49: 5 when the i of my persecutors surrounds me,
51: 2 Wash me thoroughly from my i,
55:10 and i and trouble are within it;
65: 3 When deeds of i overwhelm us,
66:18 If I had cherished i in my heart,
78:38 Yet he, being compassionate, forgave their i,
85: 2 You forgave the i of your people;
89:32 with the rod and their i with scourges;
94:23 for their i and wipe them out for their wickedness;
103: 3 forgives all your i, who heals all your diseases,
106: 6 we have committed i, have done wickedly.
106:43 and were brought low through their i.
109:14 May the i of his father be remembered before
119:133 and never let i have dominion over me.
141: 4 in company with those who work i;
Pr 16: 6 By loyalty and faithfulness i is atoned for,
19:28 and the mouth of the wicked devours i.
Isa 1: 4 Ah, sinful nation, people laden with i,
1:13 I cannot endure solemn assemblies with i.
5:18 Ah, you who drag i along with cords of falsehood,
13:11 and the wicked for their i;
22:14 Surely this i will not be forgiven you until you die,
26:21 to punish the inhabitants of the earth for their i;
30:13 therefore this i shall become for you like a break
31: 2 and against the helpers of those who work i.
32: 6 For fools speak folly, and their minds plot i:
33:24 the people who live there will be forgiven their i.
53: 6 and the LORD has laid on him the i of us all.
59: 3 with blood, and your fingers with i;
59: 4 conceiving mischief and begetting i.
59: 6 Their works are works of i,
59: 7 their thoughts are thoughts of i,
64: 7 and have delivered us into the hand of our i.
64: 9 O LORD, and do not remember i forever.
Jer 9: 5 they commit i and are too weary to repent.
13:22 the greatness of your i that your skirts are lifted
14:10 he will remember their i and punish their sins.
14:20 O LORD, the i of our ancestors,
16:10 against us? What is our i?
16:17 nor is their i concealed from my sight.
16:18 And I will doubly repay their i and their sin,
18:23 Do not forgive their i, do not blot out their sin
25:12 the land of the Chaldeans, for their i,
31:34 for I will forgive their i,
36: 3 so that I may forgive their i and their sin.
36:31 and his offspring and his servants for their i;
50:20 says the LORD, the i of Israel shall be sought,
La 2:14 not exposed your i to restore your fortunes,
4:22 The punishment of your i, O daughter Zion,
4:22 but your i, O daughter Edom, he will punish,
Eze 3:18 those wicked persons shall die for their i;
3:19 they shall die for their i;
3:20 turn from their righteousness and commit i,
7:13 of their i, they cannot maintain their lives.
7:16 all of them moaning over their i.
7:19 For it was the stumbling block of their i.
11: 2 these are the men who devise i
14: 3 placed their i as a stumbling block before them;
14: 4 and place their i as a stumbling block before them,
14: 7 and placing their i as a stumbling block
18: 8 withholds his hand from i,
18:17 withholds his hand from i, takes no advance
18:17 he shall not die for his father's i;
18:18 not good among his people, he dies for his i.
18:19 "Why should not the son suffer for the i of
18:20 A child shall not suffer for the i of a parent,
18:20 nor a parent suffer for the i of a child;
18:24 and commit i and do the same abominable things
18:26 from their righteousness and commit i,
18:26 for the i that they have committed they shall die.
18:30 otherwise i will be your ruin.
Eze 28:15 until i was found in you.
29:16 they will recall their i, when they turned to them
33: 6 they are taken away in their i,
33: 8 the wicked shall die in their i,
33: 9 the wicked shall die in their i,
33:13 if they trust in their righteousness and commit i,
33:13 in the i that they have committed they shall die.
33:15 and walk in the statutes of life, committing no i—
33:18 and commit i, they shall die for it.
39:23 the house of Israel went into captivity for their i,
44:12 and made the house of Israel stumble into i,
Da 9:24 to put an end to sin, and to atone for i,
Hos 4: 8 they are greedy for their i.
8:13 he will remember their i, and punish their sins;
9: 7 Because of your great i, your hostility is great.
9: 9 he will remember their i, he will punish their sins.
10:10 when they are punished for their double i.
12:11 In Gilead there is i, they shall surely come
13:12 Ephraim's i is bound up; his sin is kept in store.
14: 1 for you have stumbled because of your i.
Mic 7:18 pardoning i and passing over the transgression of
Hab 2:12 and found a city on i!"
Zec 5: 6 And he said, "This is their i in all the land."
Mal 2: 6 and he turned many from i.
Ro 6:19 as slaves to impurity and to greater and greater i,
Tit 2:14 that he might redeem us from all i and purify
Jas 3: 6 among our members as a world of i;
Jdt 5:17 for the God who hates i is with them.
Sir 17:26 Return to the Most High and turn away from i,
23:11 The one who swears many oaths is full of i,
25:19 Any i is small compared to a woman's i;
Bar 3: 7 the i of our ancestors who sinned against you.
1Es 8:70 and the nobles have been sharing in this i."
8:72 as I mourned over this i,
2Es 3:13 And when they were committing i in your sight,
6:19 and when I require from the doers of i the penalty
6:19 from the doers of iniquity the penalty of their i,
7:72 though they had understanding, they committed i;
7:126 [56] For while we lived and committed i we did
14:31 and your ancestors committed i and did not keep
15: 6 because i has spread throughout every land,
16:50 so righteousness shall abhor i,
16:52 a very short time i will be removed from the earth,

INITIATE (1) [INITIATED, INITIATES, INITIATIONS]

Wis 8: 4 For she is an i in the knowledge of God,

INITIATED (1) [INITIATE]

3Mc 2:30 if any of them prefer to join those who have been i

INITIATES (1) [INITIATE]

Wis 12: 5 These i from the midst of a heathen cult,

INITIATIONS (2) [INITIATE]

Wis 14:15 and handed on to his dependents secret rites and i.
14:23 For whether they kill children in their i,

INJURE (9) [INJURED, INJURIES, INJURY]

Ex 21:22 When people who are fighting i
Ps 56: 5 All day long they seek to i my cause;
Pr 8:36 but those who miss me i themselves;
AdE 12: 6 determined to i Mordecai and his people because
16: 3 and not only seek to i our subjects,
Sir 38:21 you do the dead no good, and you i yourself.
1Mc 7:15 "We will not seek to i you or your Friends."
4Mc 4: 1 of slander he was unable to i Onias in the eyes of
9: 7 do not suppose that you can i us by torturing us.

INJURED (12) [INJURE]

Ex 21:18 the other with a stone or fist so that the i party,
22:10 and it dies or is i or is carried off,
22:14 an animal from another and it is i or dies,
Lev 22:22 Anything blind, or i, or maimed,
Nu 5: 8 If the i party has no next of kin
2Ki 1: 2 in his upper chamber in Samaria, and lay i;
Eze 34: 4 you have not bound up the i,
34:16 and I will bind up the i,
Ro 14:15 If your brother or sister is being i by what you eat,
2Mc 12:22 so that often they were i by their own men
2Es 2:21 care for the i and the weak,
11:42 you have oppressed the meek and i the peaceable;

INJURIES (1) [INJURE]

Isa 30:26 when the LORD binds up the i of his people,

INJURY (10) [INJURE]

Lev 24:19 maims another shall suffer the same i in return:
24:20 the i inflicted is the i to be suffered.
2Ki 1: 2 whether I shall recover from this i."
Jdt 7:24 a great i in not making peace with the Assyrians.
Wis 18: 2 though previously wronged, were doing them no i;
Sir 10: 6 Do not get angry with your neighbor for every i,
2Mc 3:39 he strikes and destroys those who come to do it i."
9: 4 the i done by those who had put him to flight;
14:40 that by arresting him he would do them an i.

INJUSTICE‡ (19)

Job 5:16 So the poor have hope, and i shuts its mouth.
Pr 13:23 but it is swept away through i.
16: 8 with righteousness than large income with i.
22: 8 Whoever sows i will reap calamity,
Isa 58: 6 to loose the bonds of i,
Jer 22:13 and his upper rooms by i;
Hos 10:13 You have plowed wickedness, you have reaped i,
Ro 3: 5 But if our i serves to confirm the justice of God,
9:14 Is there i on God's part?
Tob 14: 7 but those who commit sin and i will vanish
14:11 and what i does—it brings death!
Sir 7: 3 Do not sow in the furrows of i,
7: 6 or you may be unable to root out i;
10: 7 and i is outrageous to both.
10: 8 on account of i and insolence and wealth.
14: 9 with his share; greedy i withers the soul.
20:28 and those who please the great atone for i.
40:12 All bribery and i will be blotted out,
3Mc 2: 4 You destroyed those who in the past committed i,

INK (4)

Jer 36:18 and I wrote them with i on the scroll."
2Co 3: 3 not with i but with the Spirit of the living God,
2Jn 1:12 I would rather not use paper and i;
3Jn 1:13 but I would rather not write with pen and i;

INKHORN (KJV) See WRITING CASE

INLAID (2)

SS 3:10 its interior was i with love.
Eze 27: 6 of pines from the coasts of Cyprus, i with ivory.

INMOST (5) [IN]

Pr 20:27 the lamp of the LORD, searching every i part.
SS 5: 4 and my i being yearned for him.
Ro 7:22 For I delight in the law of God in my i self,
Wis 1: 6 because God is witness of their i feelings,
4Mc 14:13 toward an emotion felt in her i parts.

INN (2) [INNKEEPER]

Lk 2: 7 because there was no place for them in the i.
10:34 brought him to an i, and took care of him.

INNATE (2)

3Mc 3:22 in their i malice they took this in a contrary spirit,
4Mc 16: 3 as was her i parental love,

INNER‡ (73) [IN]

Ex 12: 9 with its head, legs, and i organs.
Lev 10:18 not brought into the i part of the sanctuary.
Jdg 16: 9 While men were lying in wait in an i chamber,
16:12 (The men lying in wait were in an i chamber.)
1Ki 6: 5 both the nave and the i sanctuary;
6:16 and he built this within as an i sanctuary,
6:17 house, that is, the nave in front of the i sanctuary,
6:19 The i sanctuary he prepared in the innermost part
6:20 interior of the i sanctuary was twenty cubits long,
6:21 in front of the i sanctuary,
6:22 that belonged to the i sanctuary he overlaid
6:23 In the i sanctuary he made two cherubim
6:29 and open flowers, in the i and outer rooms.
6:30 in the i and outer rooms.
6:31 For the entrance to the i sanctuary he made doors
6:36 the i court with three courses of dressed stone
7:12 so had the i court of the house of the LORD,
7:49 in front of the i sanctuary;
8: 6 in the i sanctuary of the house,
8: 8 from the holy place in front of the i sanctuary;
22:25 that day when you go in to hide in an i chamber."
2Ki 9: 2 and take him into an i chamber.
1Ch 28:11 its treasuries, its upper rooms, and its i chambers,
2Ch 4:20 to burn before the i sanctuary, as prescribed;
4:22 the i doors to the most holy place and the doors of
5: 7 in the i sanctuary of the house,
5: 9 from the holy place in front of the i sanctuary;
18:24 that day when you go in to hide in an i chamber."
29:16 the i part of the house of the LORD to cleanse it,
Est 4:11 to the king inside the i court without being called,
5: 1 on her royal robes and stood in the i court of
Pr 18: 8 they go down into the i parts of the body.
26:22 they go down into the i parts of the body.
Eze 8: 3 of the gateway of the i court that faces north,
8:16 And he brought me into the i court of the house of
10: 3 and a cloud filled the i court.
40: 7 of the gate at the i end was one reed deep.
40: 8 Then he measured the i vestibule of the gateway,
40: 9 and the vestibule of the gate was at the i end.
40:15 at the entrance to the end of the i vestibule of
40:19 from the i front of the lower gate to the outer front of the i court,
40:23 as on the east, was a gate to the i court;
40:27 There was a gate on the south of the i court;
40:28 he brought me to the i court by the south gate,
40:32 Then he brought me to the i court on the east side,
40:44 the i gateway there were chambers for the singers in the i court,
41: 3 into the i room and measured the pilasters of
41:15 the temple and the i room and the outer vestibule
41:17 even to the i room, and on the outside.
41:17 And on all the walls all around in the i room and
42: 3 the twenty cubits that belonged to the i court,
42: 4 of the chambers was a passage on the i side,
43: 5 and brought me into the i court;
44:17 When they enter the gates of the i court,
44:17 while they minister at the gates of the i court,
44:21 when he enters the i court.
44:27 into the i court, to minister in the holy place,

Eze 45:19 and the posts of the gate of the **i** court.
46: 1 of the **i** court that faces east shall remain closed on
Mt 24:26 He is in the **i** rooms,' do not believe it.
Lk 2:35 so that the **i** thoughts of many will be revealed—
9:47 But Jesus, aware of their **i** thoughts,
2Co 4:16 our **i** nature is being renewed day by day.
Eph 3:16 in your **i** being with power through his Spirit,
Heb 6:19 a hope that enters the **i** shrine behind the curtain,
1Pe 3: 4 be the **i** self with the lasting beauty of a gentle
AdE 4:11 to the king inside the **i** court without being called,
Wis 17: 4 even the **i** chamber that held them protected them
1Mc 9:54 down the wall of the **i** court of the sanctuary.
3Mc 3:17 because when we proposed to enter their **i** temple
4Mc 13: 6 for those who sail into the **i** basin,

INNERMOST‡ (8) [IN]

1Sa 24: 3 Now David and his men were sitting in the **i** parts
1Ki 6:19 The inner sanctuary he prepared in the **i** part of
6:27 He put the cherubim in the **i** part of the house;
7:50 the sockets for the doors of the **i** part of the house,
Pr 20:30 beatings make clean the **i** parts.
Am 6:10 shall say to someone in the **i** parts of the house,
Ac 16:24 he put them in the **i** cell and fastened their feet in
Sir 42:18 he understands their **i** secrets.

INNKEEPER (1) [INN, KEEP]

Lk 10:35 gave them to the **i**, and said, 'Take care of him;

INNOCENCE (7) [INNOCENT]

Ge 20: 5 the integrity of my heart and the **i** of my hands."
2Sa 15:11 they were invited guests, and they went in their **i**,
Ps 26: 6 I wash my hands in **i**, and go around your altar,
73:13 and washed my hands in **i**.
Hos 8: 5 How long will they be incapable of **i**?
1Mc 2:37 "Let us all die in our **i**;
2:60 because of his **i**, was delivered from the mouth of

INNOCENT‡ (68) [INNOCENCE]

Ge 20: 4 so he said, "Lord, will you destroy an **i** people?
Ex 23: 7 and do not kill the **i** and those in the right,
Dt 19:10 so that the blood of an **i** person may not be shed in
19:13 you shall purge the guilt of **i** blood from Israel,
21: 8 do not let the guilt of **i** blood remain in the midst
21: 9 So you shall purge the guilt of **i** blood
27:25 be anyone who takes a bribe to shed **i** blood."
Jos 2:19 for their own death, and we shall be **i**;
1Sa 19: 5 an **i** person by killing David without cause?"
2Ki 10: 9 he stood and said to all the people, "You are **i**.
21:16 Moreover Manasseh shed very much **i** blood,
24: 4 and also for the **i** blood that he had shed;
24: 4 for he filled Jerusalem with **i** blood,
Job 4: 7 "Think now, who that was **i** ever perished?
9:15 Though I am **i**, I cannot answer him;
9:20 I am **i**, my own mouth would condemn me;
9:23 he mocks at the calamity of the **i**.
9:28 for I know you will not hold me **i**.
17: 8 and the **i** stir themselves up against the godless.
22:19 the **i** laugh them to scorn,
27:17 and the **i** will divide the silver.
34: 5 For Job has said, 'I am **i**,
Ps 10: 8 in hiding places they murder the **i**.
15: 5 and do not take a bribe against the **i**.
19:13 I shall be blameless, and **i** of great transgression.
94:21 and condemn the **i** to death.
106:38 they poured out **i** blood, the blood of their sons
Pr 1:11 let us wantonly ambush the **i**;
2:21 and the **i** will remain in it;
6:17 a lying tongue, and hands that shed **i** blood,
17:26 To impose a fine on the **i** is not right,
18: 5 or to subvert the **i** in judgment.
24:24 Whoever says to the wicked, "You are **i**,"
Isa 3:10 Tell the **i** how fortunate they are,
5:23 and deprive the **i** of their rights!
59: 7 and they rush to shed **i** blood;
Jer 2:34 on your skirts is found the lifeblood of the **i** poor,
2:35 "I am **i**; surely his anger has turned from me."
7: 6 and the widow, or shed **i** blood in this place,
19: 4 they have filled this place with the blood of the **i**,
22: 3 and the widow, or shed **i** blood in this place.
22:17 for shedding **i** blood, and for practicing oppression
26:15 you will be bringing **i** blood upon yourselves and
Joel 3:19 in whose land they have shed **i** blood.
Jnh 1:14 Do not make us guilty of **i** blood;
Mt 10:16 so be wise as serpents and **i** as doves.
27: 4 He said, "I have sinned by betraying **i** blood."
27:19 "Have nothing to do with that **i** man,
27:24 "I am **i** of this man's blood; see to it yourselves."
Lk 23:47 "Certainly this man was **i**."
Ac 18: 6 on your own heads! I am **i**.
Php 2:15 so that you may be blameless and **i**,
1Ti 1: 9 not for the **i** but for the lawless and disobedient,
Tob 3:14 that I am **i** of any defilement with a man,
AdE 4: 1 "An **i** nation is being destroyed!"
16: 5 in part responsible for the shedding of **i** blood,
Wis 4:12 and roving desire perverts the **i** mind.
Sir 26:29 nor is a tradesman **i** of sin.
Sus 1:53 condemning the **i** and acquitting the guilty,
1:53 'You shall not put an **i** and righteous person
1:62 Thus **i** blood was spared that day.
1:63 because she was found **i** of a shameful deed.
1Mc 1:37 On every side of the sanctuary they shed **i** blood;
2Mc 1: 8 and burned the gate and shed **i** blood.
8: 4 also the lawless destruction of the **i** babies and
2Es 15: 8 I and righteous blood cries out to me,
15: 9 and will receive to myself all the **i** blood from
15:22 not cease from those who shed **i** blood on earth.

INNUMERABLE (11)

Job 21:33 and those who went before are **i**.
Ps 104:25 great and wide, creeping things **i** are there,
Joel 1: 6 For a nation has invaded my land, powerful and **i**;
Heb 11:12 "as many as the stars of heaven and as the **i** grains
12:22 and to **i** angels in festal gathering,
Jdt 2:17 and **i** sheep and oxen and goats for food;
2Es 6: 3 the **i** hosts of angels were gathered together,
7:*140* [70] be left only very few of the **i** multitude."
13: 5 an **i** multitude of people were gathered together
13:11 that suddenly nothing was seen of the **i** multitude
13:34 and an **i** multitude shall be gathered together,

INORDINATE (KJV) See LUSTING, PASSION

INQUIRE (48) [INQUIRED, INQUIRER, INQUIRIES, INQUIRING, INQUIRY]

Ge 25:22 So she went to **i** of the LORD.
Ex 18:15 "Because the people come to me to **i** of God.
Lev 27:33 Let no one **i** whether it is good or bad,
Nu 27:21 who shall **i** for him by the decision of the Urim
Dt 12:30 do not **i** concerning their gods, saying,
13:14 you shall **i** and make a thorough investigation.
Jdg 18: 5 "**I** of God that we may know whether
1Sa 9: 9 anyone who went to **i** of God would say, "Come,
17:56 The king said, "**I** whose son the stripling is."
28: 7 so that I may go to her and **i** of her."
2Sa 11: 3 David sent someone to **i** about the woman.
20:18 to say in the old days, 'Let them **i** at Abel';
1Ki 14: 5 "The wife of Jeroboam is coming to **i** of you
22: 5 "**I** first for the word of the LORD."
22: 7 of the LORD here of whom we may **i**?"
22: 8 by whom we may **i** of the LORD, Micaiah son
2Ki 1: 2 "Go, **i** of Baal-zebub, the god of Ekron,
1: 3 in Israel that you are going to **i** of Baal-zebub,
1: 6 in Israel that you are sending to **i** of Baal-zebub,
1:16 you have sent messengers to **i** of Baal-zebub,
1:16 is it because there is no God in Israel to **i**
3:11 through whom we may **i** of the LORD?"
8: 8 **I** of the LORD through him,
16:15 but the bronze altar shall be for me to **i** by."
22:13 **i** of the LORD for me, for the people,
22:18 who sent you to **i** of the LORD,
1Ch 21:30 but David could not go before it to **i** of God,
2Ch 18: 4 "**I** first for the word of the LORD."
18: 6 of the LORD here of whom we may **i**?"
18: 7 by whom we may **i** of the LORD, Micaiah son
32:31 to **i** about the sign that had been done in the land,
34:21 **i** of the LORD for me and for those who are left
34:26 who sent you to **i** of the LORD,
Job 8: 8 "For **i** now of bygone generations,
Ps 27: 4 the beauty of the LORD, and to **i** in his temple.
Isa 11:10 the nations shall **i** of him,
21:12 If you will **i**, **i**; come back again."
Jer 10:21 shepherds are stupid, and do not **i** of the LORD;
21: 2 "Please **i** of the LORD on our behalf,
37: 7 who sent you to me to **i** of me, Pharaoh's army,
Eze 14: 7 and yet come to a prophet to **i** of me by him,
Ac 23:20 as though they were going to **i** more thoroughly
Wis 6: 3 he will search out your works and **i**
1Mc 3:48 of the law to **i** into those matters about which
2Es 4:23 For I did not wish to **i** about the ways above,
8:51 and **i** concerning the glory of those who are
9:13 but **i** how the righteous will be saved,

INQUIRED (34) [INQUIRE]

Ge 43:27 He **i** about their welfare, and said,
Ex 9: 7 Pharaoh **i** and found that not one of the livestock
Jdg 1: 1 the death of Joshua, the Israelites **i** of the LORD,
20:18 to go up to Bethel, where they **i** of God, "Which
20:23 and they **i** of the LORD,
20:27 And the Israelites **i** of the LORD (for the ark of
1Sa 10:22 So they **i** again of the LORD,
14:37 So Saul **i** of God, "Shall I go down after
22:10 he **i** of the LORD for him,
22:15 Is today the first time that I have **i** of God for him?
23: 2 David **i** of the LORD, "Shall I go
23: 4 Then David **i** of the LORD again.
28: 6 When Saul **i** of the LORD,
30: 8 David **i** of the LORD, "Shall I pursue this band?
2Sa 2: 1 After this David **i** of the LORD,
5:19 David **i** of the LORD, "Shall I go up against
5:23 When David **i** of the LORD, he said,
21: 1 and David **i** of the LORD.
1Ch 14:10 David **i** of God, "Shall I go up against
14:14 When David again **i** of God, God said to him,
2Ch 1: 5 And Solomon and the assembly **i** at it.
Jer 8: 2 and which they have **i** of and worshiped;
Da 1:20 and understanding concerning which the king **i**
Zep 1: 6 who have not sought the LORD or **i** of him.
Mt 2: 4 he **i** of them where the Messiah was to be born.
Ac 4: 7 in their midst, they **i**, "By what power or
21:33 he **i** who he was and what he had done.
AdE 12: 2 He overheard their conversation and **i**
2Mc 3: 9 and he **i** whether this really was the situation.
3Mc 1:13 And he **i** why, when he entered every other temple,
5:27 **i** what the matter was for which this had been
2Es 5:50 Then I **i** and said, "Since you have now given me
4Mc 9:27 torturing him, they **i** if he were willing to eat,
11:13 When the tyrant **i** whether he was willing to eat

INQUIRER (1) [INQUIRE]

Eze 14:10 of the **i** and the punishment of the prophet shall be

INQUIRIES (1) [INQUIRE]

Ezr 7:14 to make **i** about Judah and Jerusalem according to

INQUIRING (4) [INQUIRE]

Jdg 6:29 After searching and **i**, they were told,
1Sa 22:13 and by **i** of God for him,
1Pe 1:11 **i** about the person or time that the Spirit of Christ
AdE 6: 4 king was **i** about the goodwill shown by Mordecai,

INQUIRY (11) [INQUIRE]

Lev 10:16 Moses made **i** about the goat of the sin offering,
19:20 but not ransomed or given her freedom, an **i** shall
Dt 17: 4 and you make a thorough **i**,
19:18 and the judges shall make a thorough **i**.
Job 31:14 When he makes **i**, what shall I answer him?
1Pe 1:10 that was to be yours made careful search and **i**,
Wis 1: 9 **i** will be made into the counsels of the ungodly,
6: 8 But a strict **i** is in store for the mighty.
1Mc 9:26 They made **i** and searched for the friends of Judas,
3Mc 7: 5 without any **i** or examination to put them to death.
4Mc 1:13 Our **i**, accordingly, is whether reason is sovereign

INQUISITION (KJV) See AVENGES, INQUIRY, INVESTIGATED

INSANE (1) [INSANITY]

Ac 26:24 Too much learning is driving you **i**!"

INSANITY (1) [INSANE]

4Mc 10:13 do not give way to the same **i** as your brothers,

INSATIABLE (3)

Eze 16:28 with the Assyrians, because you were **i**;
2Pe 2:14 They have eyes full of adultery, **i** for sin.
Sir 31:17 and do not be **i**, or you will give offense.

INSCRIBE (3) [INSCRIBED, INSCRIBING, INSCRIPTION]

Isa 30: 8 write it before them on a tablet, and **i** it in a book,
1Mc 14:48 they gave orders to **i** this decree on bronze tablets,
4Mc 17: 8 to **i** on their tomb these words as a reminder to

INSCRIBED (13) [INSCRIBE]

Ne 9:38 and on that sealed document are **i** the names
Job 19:23 O that they were **i** in a book!
Isa 49:16 See, I have **i** you on the palms of my hands;
Da 5:24 the hand was sent and this writing was **i**.
5:25 And this is the writing that was **i**:
10:21 But I am to tell you what is **i** in the book of truth.
Zec 14:20 that day there shall be **i** on the bells of the horses,
Rev 19:12 he has a name **i** that no one knows but himself.
19:16 On his robe and on his thigh he has a name **i**,
21:12 on the gates are **i** the names of the twelve tribes of
AdE 1:19 **i** in accordance with the laws of the Medes
Sir 45:12 **i** like a seal with "Holiness,"
3Mc 2:30 not appear to be an enemy of all, he **i** below:

INSCRIBING (1) [INSCRIBE]

3Mc 7:20 after **i** them as holy on a pillar and dedicating

INSCRIPTION (9) [INSCRIBE]

Ex 39:30 and wrote on it an **i**, like the engraving of a signet,
Zec 3: 9 I will engrave its **i**, says the LORD of hosts,
Mk 15:26 The **i** of the charge against him read,
Lk 23:38 There was also an **i** over him,
Jn 19:19 Pilate also had an **i** written and put on the cross.
19:20 Many of the Jews read this **i**,
Ac 17:23 I found among them an altar with the **i**,
2Ti 2:19 But God's firm foundation stands, bearing this **i**:
3Mc 2:27 a stone on the tower in the courtyard with this **i**:

INSCRUTABLE (1)

Ro 11:33 are his judgments and how **i** his ways!

INSECT (1) [INSECTS]

Isa 41:14 Do not fear, you worm Jacob, you **i** Israel!

INSECTS (4) [INSECT]

Lev 11:20 All winged **i** that walk upon all
11:21 But among the winged **i** that walk
11:23 But all other winged **i**
Dt 14:19 And all winged **i** are unclean for you;

INSECURELY (1)

Wis 4: 4 standing **i** they will be shaken by the wind,

INSERTED (1)

1Ki 6: 6 in order that the supporting beams should not be **i**

INSIDE (67)

Ge 6:14 and cover it **i** and out with pitch.
19:10 the men **i** reached out their hands and brought Lot
Ex 4: 6 "Put your hand **i** your cloak."
25:11 **i** and outside you shall overlay it,
28:26 on its **i** edge next to the ephod.

Ex 37: 2 He overlaid it with pure gold i and outside,
39:19 on its i edge next to the ephod.
Lev 13:55 in fire, whether the leprous spot is on the i or on
14:41 the i of the house scraped thoroughly,
16: 2 at any time into the sanctuary i the curtain before
16:12 and he shall bring it i the curtain
16:15 for the people and bring its blood i the curtain,
Jos 6: 1 Now Jericho was shut up i and out because of
7:21 They now lie hidden in the ground i my tent,
Jdg 7:16 and empty jars, with torches i the jars,
1Sa 9:18 Then Saul approached Samuel i the gate, and said,
2Sa 4: 6 They came i the house as though to take wheat,
6:17 i the tent that David had pitched for it;
20:14 all the Bichrites assembled, and followed him i.
1Ki 6:15 the walls of the house on the i with boards
6:15 he covered them on the i with wood;
6:21 Solomon overlaid the i of the house
7:25 The hindquarters of each were toward the i.
2Ki 5:24 he took the bags from them, and stored them i;
6:20 and they saw that they were i Samaria.
9: 6 So Jehu got up and went i;
16:18 on the sabbath that had been built i the palace,
1Ch 16: 1 and set it i the tent that David had pitched for it;
2Ch 3: 4 He overlaid it on the i with pure gold.
4: 4 The hindquarters of each were toward the i.
29:18 Then they went i to King Hezekiah and said,
Ne 4:22 "Let every man and his servant pass the night i
Est 4:11 to the king i the inner court without being called,
5: 1 The king was sitting on his royal throne i
Isa 65: 4 who sit i tombs, and spend the night
Jer 52:25 the people of the land who were found i the city.
Eze 3:24 Go, shut yourself i your house.
5: 2 the hair you shall burn in the fire i the city,
7:15 The sword is outside, pestilence and famine are i;
11:11 and you shall not be the meat i it;
24: 7 For the blood she shed is i it;
40:16 with shutters on the i of the gateway all around,
40:16 vestibules also had windows on the i all around;
40:22 and its vestibule was on the i.
40:26 its vestibule was on the i.
40:41 Four tables were on the i,
40:43 one handbreadth long, fastened all around the i.
46:23 On the i, around each of the four courts was a row
Mt 23:25 but i they are full of greed and self-indulgence.
23:26 First clean the i of the cup,
23:27 but i they are full of the bones of the dead and
23:28 but i you are full of hypocrisy and lawlessness.
26:58 and going i, he sat with the guards in order to see
Lk 11:39 but i you are full of greed and wickedness.
11:40 not the one who made the outside make the i also?
21:21 and those i the city must leave it,
Ac 5:23 but when we opened them, we found no one i."
1Co 5:12 Is it not those who are i that you are to judge?
Rev 4: 8 are full of eyes all around and i.
5: 1 on the i and on the back, sealed with seven seals;
AdE 4:11 to the king i the inner court without being called,
Sir 19:12 so is gossip i a fool.
40:30 but it kindles a fire i him.
Aza 1:27 and made the i of the furnace as though
Bel 1: 7 for this thing is only clay i and bronze outside,
2Mc 1:15 with a few men i the wall of the sacred precinct,
3Mc 4:11 with the king's forces nor in any way claim to be i

INSIGHT (17)

Job 34:35 without knowledge, his words are without i.'
Pr 1: 2 for understanding words of i,
2: 3 if you indeed cry out for i, and raise your voice
3: 5 and do not rely on your own i.
4: 1 and be attentive, that you may gain i;
4: 5 Get wisdom; get i: do not forget, nor turn away
4: 7 Get wisdom, and whatever else you get, get i.
7: 4 and call i your intimate friend,
8:14 I have good advice and sound wisdom; I have i,
9: 6 and live, and walk in the way of i."
9:10 and the knowledge of the Holy One is i.
Da 1: 4 endowed with knowledge and i,
1:17 Daniel also had i into all visions and dreams.
Eph 1: 8 that he lavished on us. With all wisdom and i
Php 1: 9 and more with knowledge and full i
Wis 8:21 it was a mark of i to know whose gift she was—
Sir 6:37 It is he who will give i to your mind,

INSIGNIFICANT (1)

3Mc 1: 3 and arranged that a certain i man should sleep in

INSINCERELY (2) [INSINCERITY]

Da 11:34 and many shall join them i.
3Mc 3:17 but i by deed, because when we proposed

INSINCERITY (1) [INSINCERELY]

1Pe 2: 1 therefore, of all malice, and all guile, i, envy,

INSIST (4) [INSISTED, INSISTENT, INSISTENTLY, INSISTING]

1Co 13: 5 It does not i on its own way;
Eph 4:17 Now this I affirm and i on in the Lord:
1Ti 4:11 These are the things you must i on and teach.
Tit 3: 8 I desire that you i on these things,

INSISTED (2) [INSIST]

Ac 12:15 But she i that it was so.
Jdt 5:22 and all the inhabitants of the seacoast and Moab i

INSISTENT (1) [INSIST]

Lk 23: 5 But they were i and said,

INSISTENTLY (2) [INSIST]

Sir 13: 9 be reserved, and he will invite you more i.
1Mc 11:40 and i urged him to hand Antiochus over to him,

INSISTING (2) [INSIST]

Lk 22:59 Then about an hour later still another kept i,
Col 2:18 i on self-abasement and worship of angels,

INSOFAR (1)

1Pe 4:13 rejoice i as you are sharing Christ's sufferings,

INSOLENCE (23) [INSOLENT]

Pr 13:10 By i the heedless make strife,
Isa 13:11 and lay low the i of tyrants.
14: 4 How his i has ceased!
16: 6 of his arrogance, his pride, and his i;
Jer 48:30 I myself know his i, says the LORD;
Da 11:18 But a commander shall put an end to his i;
11:18 indeed, he shall turn his i back upon him.
AdE 13:12 that it was not in i or pride or for any love of glory
Wis 12:17 and you rebuke any i among those who know it.
Sir 10: 6 and do not resort to acts of i.
10: 8 from nation to nation on account of injustice and i
21: 4 Panic and i will waste away riches;
Bar 4:34 and her i will be turned to grief.
1Mc 3:20 against us in great i and lawlessness to destroy us
2Mc 9: 7 Yet he did not in any way stop his i,
3Mc 2: 3 and you judge those who have done anything in i
2:21 scourged him who had exalted himself in i
6: 4 exalted with lawless i and boastful tongue,
6: 5 speaking grievous words with boasting and i, you,
6: 9 And now, you who hate i,
6:12 now and have mercy on us who by the senseless i
6:20 and he forgot his sullen i.
2Es 11:43 Your i has come up before the Most High,

INSOLENT (14) [INSOLENCE, INSOLENTLY]

Ps 19:13 Keep back your servant also from the i;
54: 3 i have risen against me, the ruthless seek my life;
75: 5 up your horn on high, or speak with i neck."
86:14 O God, the i rise up against me;
119:21 You rebuke the i, accursed ones,
Isa 3: 5 the youth will be i to the elder,
33:19 No longer will you see the i people,
Jer 43: 2 of Kareah and all the other i men said to Jeremiah,
Ro 1:30 God-haters, i, haughty, boastful, inventors of evil,
Sir 8:11 Do not let the i bring you to your feet,
31:26 so wine tests hearts when the i quarrel.
32:18 an i and proud person will not be deterred by fear.
35:23 until he destroys the multitude of the i,
2Mc 1:28 Punish those who oppress and are i with pride.

INSOLENTLY (5) [INSOLENT]

Ne 9:10 you knew that they acted i against our ancestors.
Job 16:10 they have struck me i on the cheek;
Ps 31:18 Let the lying lips be stilled that speak i against
55:12 it is not adversaries who deal i with me—
2Mc 12:14 behaved most i toward Judas and his men,

INSOMUCH (KJV) See AS A RESULT, BECAUSE, IF POSSIBLE, SO MUCH

INSPECT (3) [INSPECTED, INSPECTION, INSPECTORS, INSPECTS]

Lev 14:36 and afterward the priest shall go in to i the house.
Job 5:24 you shall i your fold and miss nothing.
2Mc 5:18 whom King Seleucus sent to i the treasury.

INSPECTED (3) [INSPECT]

Ne 2:13 and I i the walls of Jerusalem
2:15 So I went up by way of the valley by night and i
1Es 8:41 and we encamped there three days, and I i them.

INSPECTION (5) [INSPECT]

Lev 14:39 on the seventh day and make an i;
14:44 the priest shall go and make i;
14:48 If the priest comes and makes an i,
2Mc 3: 8 of i of the cities of Coelesyria and Phoenicia,
3:14 a day and went in to direct the i of these funds.

INSPECTORS (1) [INSPECT]

1Mc 1:51 He appointed i over all the people

INSPECTS (1) [INSPECT]

Eze 21:21 he consults the teraphim, he i the liver.

INSPIRATION (1) [INSPIRE]

2Mc 15:11 with confidence in shields and spears as with the i

INSPIRE (2) [AWE-INSPIRING, INSPIRATION, INSPIRED, INSPIRES]

Isa 47:12 be able to succeed, perhaps you may i terror.
Jer 49:16 The terror you i and the pride

INSPIRED (7) [INSPIRE]

Ex 35:34 And he has i him to teach,
Pr 16:10 I decisions are on the lips of a king;
1Th 1: 6 of persecution you received the word with joy i by
2Ti 3:16 All scripture is i by God and is useful for teaching,
Wis 15:11 to know the one who formed them and i them
1Mc 4:35 and observed the boldness that i those of Judas,
1Es 9:55 were i by the words which they had been taught.

INSPIRES (2) [INSPIRE]

Ps 76:12 who i fear in the kings of the earth.
Col 1:29 with all the energy that he powerfully i within me.

INSTABILITY (1)

3Mc 5:39 wondering at his i of mind,

INSTALL (1) [INSTALLED, INSTALLMENT]

2Mc 14:13 and to i Alcimus as high priest of the great temple.

INSTALLED (5) [INSTALL]

Dt 1:15 and i them as leaders over you,
Jdg 17: 5 and i one of his sons, who became his priest.
17:12 So Micah i the Levite,
Mic 5: 5 against them seven shepherds and eight i as rulers.
1Mc 12:38 he fortified it and i gates with bolts.

INSTALLMENT (1) [INSTALL]

2Co 1:22 and giving us his Spirit in our hearts as a first i.

INSTANCE (1)

Ru 3:10 this last i of your loyalty is better than the first;

INSTANT (5) [INSTANTLY]

Isa 29: 5 And in an i, suddenly,
30:13 whose crash comes suddenly, in an i;
Lk 4: 5 the devil led him up and showed him in an i all
Wis 18:12 since in one i their most valued children had been destroyed.
Sir 11:21 the Lord to make the poor rich suddenly, in an i.

INSTANTLY (4) [INSTANT]

Mt 9:22 And i the woman was made well.
15:28 And her daughter was healed i.
17:18 and it came out of him, and the boy was cured i.
Bel 1:42 and they were i eaten before his eyes.

INSTEAD‡ (79)

Ge 4:25 "God has appointed for me another child i
22:13 and offered it up as a burnt offering i of his son.
Nu 24:10 but i you have blessed them these three times.
Jdg 15: 2 Why not take her i?"
2Sa 6:10 i David took it to the house of Obed-edom
18:33 Would I had died i of you, O Absalom, my son,
1Ki 14:27 so King Rehoboam made shields of bronze i,
1Ch 13:13 he took it i to the house of Obed-edom the Gittite.
2Ch 28:20 and oppressed him i of strengthening him.
Est 2: 4 And let the girl who pleases the king be queen i
2:17 the royal crown on her head and made her queen i
Job 31:40 let thorns grow i of wheat,
31:40 and foul weeds i of barley."
Pr 8:10 Take my instruction i of silver,
11: 8 and the wicked get into it i.
Isa 3:24 I of perfume there will be a stench; and i of a sash, a rope; and i of well-set hair, baldness; and i of a rich robe, a binding of sackcloth; i of beauty,
22:13 but i there was joy and festivity,
33:15 who wave away a bribe i of accepting it,
55:13 I of the thorn shall come up the cypress;
55:13 i of the brier shall come up the myrtle;
60:17 I of bronze I will bring gold, i of iron I will bring silver; i of wood, bronze, i of stones, iron.
61: 3 a garland i of ashes, the oil of gladness i of mourning, the mantle of praise i of a faint spirit.
Jer 3:20 I, as a faithless wife leaves her husband,
8:15 for a time of healing, but there is terror i.
14:19 for a time of healing, but there is terror i.
29:26 The LORD himself has made you priest i of
44:17 I, we will do everything that we have vowed,
Eze 4:15 I will let you have cow's dung i of human dung,
16:32 who receives strangers i of her husband!
36:34 i of being the desolation that it was in the sight
Da 11:38 He shall honor the god of fortresses i of these;
Hab 2:16 You will be sated with contempt i of glory.
Mk 15:11 to have him release Barabbas for them i.
Lk 11:11 will give a snake i of a fish?
12:31 I, strive for his kingdom, and these things will
Jn 19:34 I, one of the soldiers pierced his side with a spear,
Ac 7:39 Our ancestors were unwilling to obey him; i,
12:14 she was so overjoyed that, i of opening the gate,
25:19 I they had certain points of disagreement with him
Ro 13:14 I, put on the Lord Jesus Christ,
14:13 but resolve i never to put a stumbling block
1Co 6: 1 i of taking it before the saints?
2Co 2: 7 so now i you should forgive and console him,
Eph 5: 4 but i, let there be thanksgiving.
5:11 of darkness, but i expose them.
Jas 4:15 I you ought to say, "If the Lord wishes,
1Pe 1:15 I, as he who called you is holy,
2Jn 1:12 i I hope to come to you and talk with you face
3Jn 1:14 i I hope to see you soon,
AdE 2: 4 the woman who pleases the king shall be queen i
4: 4 and sent some clothes to Mordecai to put on i

AdE 14: 2 and **i** of costly perfumes she covered her head
16:21 for his chosen people **i** of a day of destruction
Wis 11: 6 **I** of the fountain of an ever-flowing river,
16: 2 **I** of this punishment you showed kindness
16:20 **I** of these things you gave your people food
19:10 how **i** of producing animals
19:10 and **i** of fish the river spewed out vast numbers
Sir 6: 1 and do not become an enemy **i** of a friend;
29: 6 and **i** of glory will repay him with dishonor.
1Mc 10:30 and **i** of collecting the third of the grain and
1Es 4:39 but it does what is righteous **i** of anything
3Mc 3: 7 **i** they gossiped about the differences in worship
4: 6 all together raising a lament **i** of a wedding song,
4: 8 their necks encircled with ropes **i** of garlands,
4: 8 of their marriage festival in lamentations **i**
5:31 a rich feast for the savage animals **i** of the Jews,
5:32 In fact you would have been deprived of life **i**
6:31 arranged for a banquet of deliverance **i** of a bitter
4Mc 13: 3 **I,** by reason, which is praised before God,

INSTIGATED (1)
Ac 6:11 Then they secretly **i** some men to say,

INSTILLING (1)
4Mc 4:10 **i** in them great fear and trembling.

INSTINCT (2) [INSTINCTIVELY]
2Pe 2:12 mere creatures of **i**, born to be caught and killed.
Jude 1:10 like irrational animals, they know by **i.**

INSTINCTIVELY (1) [INSTINCT]
Ro 2:14 do **i** what the law requires, these,

INSTITUTED (2) [INSTITUTION]
Ro 13: 1 those authorities that exist have been **i** by God.
3Mc 6:36 they **i** the observance of the aforesaid days as

INSTITUTION (2) [INSTITUTED]
Nu 10: 8 a perpetual **i** for you throughout your generations.
1Pe 2:13 Lord's sake accept the authority of every human **i,**

INSTRUCT (17) [INSTRUCTED, INSTRUCTING, INSTRUCTION, INSTRUCTIONS, INSTRUCTOR, INSTRUCTORS, INSTRUCTS]
Dt 17:10 diligently observing everything they **i** you.
24: 8 the levitical priests **i** you, just
1Sa 12:23 and I will **i** you in the good and the right way.
2Ch 19:10 statutes or ordinances, then you shall **i** them,
Ne 9:20 You gave your good spirit to **i** them,
Ps 32: 8 I will **i** you and teach you the way you should go;
105:22 to **i** his officials at his pleasure,
Ro 15:14 and able to **i** one another.
1Co 2:16 the mind of the Lord so as to **i** him?"
10:11 and they were written down to **i** us,
14:19 in order to **i** others also,
1Ti 1: 3 in Ephesus so that you may **i** certain people not
2Ti 3:15 to **i** you for salvation through faith in Christ Jesus.
2Es 5:32 He said to me, "Listen to me, and I will **i** you;
7:*49* "Listen to me, Ezra, and I will **i** you,
10:33 "Stand up like a man, and I will **i** you."
14:13 the lowly among them, and **i** those that are wise.

INSTRUCTED (25) [INSTRUCT]
Ge 32:17 He **i** the foremost,
32:19 He likewise **i** the second and the third
47:11 in the land of Rameses, as Pharaoh had **i.**
50:12 Thus his sons did for him as he had **i** them.
Jdg 21:20 And they **i** the Benjaminites, saying,
Ru 2:15 When she got up to glean, Boaz **i** his young men,
3: 6 and did just as her mother-in-law had **i** her.
2Sa 11:19 and he **i** the messenger,
2Ki 12: 2 because the priest Jehoiada **i** him.
2Ch 26: 5 who **i** him in the fear of God;
Job 4: 3 you have **i** many; you have strengthened the weak
Pr 21:11 when the wise are **i**, they increase in knowledge.
Isa 28:26 For they are well **i**; their God teaches them.
40:13 or as his counselor has **i** him?
Lk 1: 4 the things about which you have been **i.**
Jn 8:28 but I speak these things as the Father **i** me.
Ac 7:22 So Moses was **i** in all the wisdom of the Egyptians
18:25 He had been **i** in the Way of the Lord;
Ro 2:18 and determine what is best because you are **i** in
2Ti 3: 7 who are always being **i** and can never arrive at
Wis 6:11 long for them, and you will be **i.**
6:25 Therefore be **i** by my words, and you will profit.
Sir 40:29 but one who is intelligent and well **i** guards
2Mc 2: 2 **i** those who were being deported not to forget
2Es 8:12 and **i** it in your law,

INSTRUCTING (2) [INSTRUCT]
Ge 32: 4 **i** them, "Thus you shall say to my lord Esau:
Mt 11: 1 when Jesus had finished **i** his twelve disciples,

INSTRUCTION‡ (63) [INSTRUCT]
Ge 45:21 Joseph gave them wagons according to the **i**
50:16 saying, "Your father gave this **i** before he died,
Ex 16: 4 whether they will follow my **i** or not.
24:12 which I have written for their **i.**"
Jos 22: 5 the commandment and **i** that Moses the servant of
2Sa 7:19 May this be **i** for the people, O Lord GOD!
Job 22:22 Receive **i** from his mouth,
36:10 He opens their ears to **i,**
Ps 60: T *A Miktam of David; for **i;***
Pr 1: 2 For learning about wisdom and **i,**
1: 3 for gaining **i** in wise dealing,
1: 7 fools despise wisdom and **i.**
1: 8 Hear, my child, your father's **i,**
4: 1 Listen, children, to a father's **i**, and be attentive,
4:13 Keep hold of **i**; do not let go;
8:10 Take my **i** instead of silver,
8:33 Hear **i** and be wise, and do not neglect it.
9: 9 Give **i** to the wise, and they will become wiser still;
10:17 Whoever heeds **i** is on the path to life,
13:18 and disgrace are for the one who ignores **i,**
15: 5 A fool despises a parent's **i,**
15:32 Those who ignore **i** despise themselves,
15:33 The fear of the LORD is **i** in wisdom,
19:20 Listen to advice and accept **i,**
19:27 in order that you may hear **i.**
23:12 Apply your mind to **i** and your ear to words
23:23 buy wisdom, **i,** and understanding.
24:32 I saw and considered it; I looked and received **i.**
Isa 2: 3 For out of Zion shall go forth **i,**
5:24 for they have rejected the **i** of the LORD of hosts,
8:20 for teaching and for **i?**"
29:24 and those who grumble will accept **i.**
30: 9 children who will not hear the **i** of the LORD;
Jer 10: 8 the **i** given by idols is no better than wood!
17:23 and would not hear or receive **i.**
18:18 for **i** shall not perish from the priest,
Eze 7:26 **i** shall perish from the priest,
Mic 4: 2 For out of Zion shall go forth **i,**
Mal 2: 6 True **i** was in his mouth,
2: 7 and people should seek **i** from his mouth,
2: 8 you have caused many to stumble by your **i;**
2: 9 but have shown partiality in your **i.**
Ro 15: 4 in former days was written for our **i,**
Eph 6: 4 bring them up in the discipline and **i** of the Lord.
1Ti 1: 5 aim of such **i** is love that comes from a pure heart,
Heb 6: 2 **i** about baptisms, laying on of hands, resurrection
Wis 3:11 for those who despise wisdom and **i** are miserable.
6:17 of wisdom is the most sincere desire for **i,**
6:17 and concern for **i** is love of her,
7:14 commended for the gifts that come from **i.**
Sir Pr: 1 for these we should praise Israel for **i** and wisdom.
Pr: 1 to write something pertaining to **i** and wisdom,
Pr: 3 I found opportunity for no little **i.**
23: 7 my children, to **i** concerning the mouth;
24:27 It pours forth **i** like the Nile,
24:32 I will again make **i** shine forth like the dawn,
33:18 but for all who seek **i.**
44: 4 they were wise in their words of **i;**
50:27 **I** in understanding and knowledge I have written
51:16 and I found for myself much **i.**
51:23 and lodge in the house of **i.**
51:26 and let your souls receive **i;**
51:28 Hear but a little of my **i,**

INSTRUCTIONS (27) [INSTRUCT]
Ex 16:28 to keep my commandments and **i?**
18:16 I make known to them the statutes and **i** of God."
18:20 and **i** and make known to them the way they are
2Sa 24:19 Following Gad's **i**, David went up,
1Ch 21:19 So David went up following Gad's **i,**
2Ch 23: 6 the other people shall observe the **i** of the LORD.
Hos 8:12 Though I write for him the multitude of my **i,**
Mt 10: 5 These twelve Jesus sent out with the following **i:**
Ac 1: 2 after giving **i** through the Holy Spirit to
15:24 though with no **i** from us,
16:24 Following these **i**, he put them in
17:15 and after receiving **i** to have Silas
19:33 Some of the crowd gave **i** to Alexander,
23:31 So the soldiers, according to their **i,**
1Co 11:17 Now in the following **i** I do not commend you,
11:34 About the other things I will give **i** when I come.
Col 4:10 concerning whom you have received **i**—
1Th 4: 2 For you know what **i** we gave you through
1Ti 1:18 I am giving you these **i**, Timothy, my child,
3:14 but I am writing these **i** to you so that,
4: 6 If you put these **i** before the brothers and sisters,
5:21 I warn you to keep these **i** without prejudice,
Heb 11:22 of the Israelites and gave **i** about his burial.
Tob 1: 8 of Moses and according to the **i** of Deborah,
AdE 2:20 such were the **i** of Mordecai;
3:12 and in accordance with Haman's **i** they wrote in
3:13 **I** were sent by couriers throughout all the empire

INSTRUCTOR (2) [INSTRUCT]
Mt 23:10 for you have one **i**, the Messiah.
4Mc 9: 6 which our aged **i** also overcame.

INSTRUCTORS (2) [INSTRUCT]
Pr 5:13 the voice of my teachers or incline my ear to my **i.**
Mt 23:10 Nor are you to be called **i,**

INSTRUCTS (4) [INSTRUCT]
Ps 16: 7 in the night also my heart **i** me.
25: 8 therefore he **i** sinners in the way.
Sir 37:23 A wise person **i** his own people,
4Mc 5:24 it **i** us in justice, so that in all our dealings

INSTRUMENT‡ (3) [INSTRUMENTS]
Eze 33:32 a beautiful voice and plays well on an **i;**
Ac 9:15 an **i** whom I have chosen to bring my name
Sir 43: 2 proclaims as it rises what a marvelous **i** it is,

INSTRUMENTS (37) [INSTRUMENT]
1Sa 18: 6 with songs of joy, and with musical **i.**
1Ch 15:16 as the singers to play on musical **i,**
16:42 and cymbals for the music, and **i** for sacred song.
23: 5 the LORD with the **i** that I have made for praise."
2Ch 5:13 with trumpets and cymbals and other musical **i,**
7: 6 also, with the **i** for music to the LORD
23:13 with their musical **i** leading in the celebration.
29:26 The Levites stood with the **i** of David,
29:27 accompanied by the **i** of King David of Israel.
30:21 accompanied by loud **i** for the LORD.
34:12 Other Levites, all skillful with **i** of music,
Ne 12:36 with the musical **i** of David the man of God;
Ps 4: T *To the leader: with stringed **i.***
6: T *To the leader: with stringed **i;***
45: 8 From ivory palaces stringed **i** make you glad;
54: T *To the leader: with stringed **i.***
55: T *To the leader: with stringed **i.***
61: T *To the leader: with stringed **i.***
67: T *To the leader: with stringed **i.***
76: T *To the leader: with stringed **i.***
Isa 38:20 we will sing to stringed **i** all the days of our lives,
Eze 40:42 on which the **i** were to be laid with which
Am 6: 5 and like David improvise on **i** of music;
Hab 3:19 To the leader: with stringed **i.**
Ro 6:13 No longer present your members to sin as **i**
6:13 and present your members to God as **i**
1Co 14: 7 the same way with lifeless **i** that produce sound,
1Mc 13:51 and with harps and cymbals and stringed **i,**
1Es 5:59 with musical **i** and trumpets, and the Levites,
4Mc 6: 1 by dragged him violently to the **i** of torture.
6:25 with maliciously contrived **i,**
8: 1 have prevailed over the most painful **i** of torture.
8:12 he ordered the **i** of torture to be brought forward
8:19 not fear the **i** of torture and consider the threats
8:25 to death for fearing the **i** of torture.
10: 5 they disjointed his hands and feet with their **i,**
10: 7 the **i** and scalped him with their fingernails in

INSULT (15) [INSULTED, INSULTING, INSULTS]
Ge 39:14 husband has brought among us a Hebrew to **i** us!
39:17 came in to me to **i** me;
1Sa 25:39 the LORD who has judged the case of Nabal's **i**
Ps 69: 9 the insults of those who **i** you have fallen on me.
Pr 12:16 but the prudent ignore an **i.**
14:31 Those who oppress the poor **i** their Maker,
17: 5 Those who mock the poor **i** their Maker;
Isa 50: 6 I did not hide my face from **i** and spitting.
Jer 15:15 know that on your account I suffer **i.**
Mt 5:22 and if you **i** a brother or sister,
Lk 11:45 when you say these things, you **i** us too."
Ac 23: 4 "Do you dare to **i** God's high priest?"
Ro 15: 3 insults of those who **i** you have fallen on me."
AdE 1:18 will likewise dare to **i** their husbands.
Wis 2:19 Let us test him with **i** and torture,

INSULTED (6) [INSULT]
Ps 69:10 they **i** me for doing so.
Mk 12: 4 this one they beat over the head and **i.**
Lk 18:32 and he will be mocked and **i** and spat upon.
20:11 also they beat and **i** and sent away empty-handed.
AdE 1:16 "Queen Vashti has **i** not only the king but also all
Sir 8: 4 or your ancestors may be **i.**

INSULTING (2) [INSULT]
Sir 41:22 and do not be **i** after making a gift.
3Mc 3:25 with **i** and harsh treatment,

INSULTS (23) [INSULT]
1Sa 25:14 and he shouted **i** at them.
Ne 4: 5 for they have hurled **i** in the face of the builders.
Job 20: 3 I hear censure that **i** me,
Ps 69: 9 the **i** of those who insult you have fallen on me.
69:10 You know the **i** I receive,
69:20 **I** have broken my heart, so that I am in despair.
89:50 how I bear in my bosom the **i** of the peoples,
Jer 51:51 to shame, for we have heard **i;**
La 3:30 to the smiter, and be filled with **i.**
Eze 34:29 and no longer suffer the **i** of the nations.
36: 6 because you have suffered the **i** of the nations;
36: 7 that are all around you shall themselves suffer **i.**
36:15 the **i** of the nations, no longer shall you bear
Hos 12:14 down on him and pay him back for his **i.**
Lk 22:65 They kept heaping many other **i** on him.
Ro 15: 3 "The **i** of those who insult you have fallen on me."
2Co 12:10 Therefore I am content with weaknesses, **i,**
Tob 3: 6 because I have had to listen to undeserved **i,**
3: 6 see so much distress in my life and to listen to **i.**"
Sir 13: 3 A rich person does wrong, and even adds **i;**
22:24 furnace precede the fire; so **i** precede bloodshed.
29:28 about lodging and the **i** of the moneylender.
3Mc 5:22 as in devising all sorts of **i** for those they thought

INSURES (1)
4Mc 9: 4 which **i** our safety through transgression of

INSURRECTION (3) [INSURRECTIONS]
Mk 15: 7 rebels who had committed murder during the **i.**
Lk 23:19 in prison for an **i** that had taken place in the city,
23:25 one who had been put in prison for **i** and murder,

INSURRECTIONS (1) [INSURRECTION]

Lk 21: 9 "When you hear of wars and **i**, do not be terrified;

INTACT (1)

Tob 9: 5 to him the money bags, with their seals **i**;

INTEGRITY (26)

Ge 20: 5 the **i** of my heart and the innocence of my hands."
20: 6 I know that you did this in the **i** of your heart;
1Ki 9: 4 with **i** of heart and uprightness,
Job 2: 3 He still persists in his **i**,
2: 9 "Do you still persist in your **i**?
4: 6 and the **i** of your ways your hope?
27: 5 until I die I will not put away my **i** from me.
31: 6 and let God know my **i**!—
Ps 7: 8 to my righteousness and according to the **i** that is
25:21 May **i** and uprightness preserve me,
26: 1 O LORD, for I have walked in my **i**,
26:11 But as for me, I walk in my **i**;
41:12 But you have upheld me because of my **i**,
101: 2 I will walk with **i** of heart within my house;
Pr 10: 9 Whoever walks in **i** walks securely,
11: 3 The **i** of the upright guides them,
14:32 but the righteous find a refuge in their **i**.
17:26 or to flog the noble for their **i**.
19: 1 in **i** than one perverse of speech who is a fool.
20: 7 The righteous walk in **i**—happy are the children
28: 6 Better to be poor and walk in **i** than to be crooked
28:18 One who walks in **i** will be safe,
Mal 2: 6 He walked with me in **i** and uprightness,
Tit 2: 7 and in your teaching show **i**, gravity,
Sir 7: 6 be partial to the powerful, and so mar your **i**.
2Mc 7:40 So he died in his **i**,

INTELLIGENCE (7) [INTELLIGENT]

Ex 31: 3 **i**, and knowledge in every kind of craft,
35:31 with skill, **i**, and knowledge in every kind of craft,
1Ki 7:14 **i**, and knowledge in working bronze.
Pr 8: 5 acquire **i**, you who lack it.
Wis 15:18 when judged by their lack of **i**;
Sir 22:11 and weep for the fool, for he has left **i** behind.
2Mc 11:13 As he was not without **i**,

INTELLIGENT‡ (31) [INTELLIGENCE, INTELLIGENTLY]

Pr 11:12 but an **i** person remains silent.
17:28 when they close their lips, they are deemed **i**.
18:15 An **i** mind acquires knowledge,
19:25 reprove the **i**, and they will gain knowledge.
20: 5 but the **i** will draw them out.
28: 2 but with an **i** ruler there is lasting order.
28:11 but an **i** poor person sees through the pose.
Ecc 9:11 nor riches to the **i**, nor favor to the skillful;
Mt 11:25 from the wise and the **i** and have revealed them
Lk 10:21 from the wise and the **i** and have revealed them
Ac 13: 7 with the proconsul, Sergius Paulus, an **i** man,
Wis 7:22 There is in her a spirit that is **i**, holy, unique,
7:23 and penetrating through all spirits that are **i**, pure,
Sir 3:29 The mind of the **i** appreciates proverbs,
6:36 If you see an **i** person, rise early to visit him;
7:21 Let your soul love **i** slaves;
9:15 Let your conversation be with **i** people,
10: 1 and the rule of an **i** person is well ordered.
10:23 It is not right to despise one who is **i** but poor,
10:25 and an **i** person will not complain.
16: 4 one **i** person a city can be filled with people,
18:28 Every **i** person knows wisdom,
19: 2 Wine and women lead **i** men astray,
19:24 the highly **i** who transgress the law.
21:15 When an **i** person hears a wise saying,
21:16 but delight is found in the speech of the **i**.
22:17 an **i** thought is like stucco decoration that makes
26:28 **i** men who are treated contemptuously,
36:24 so an **i** mind detects false words.
40:29 but one who is **i** and well instructed guards
44: 3 those who gave counsel because they were **i**;

INTELLIGENTLY (2) [INTELLIGENT]

Pr 13:16 clever do all things **i**, but the fool displays folly.
Sir 14:20 who meditates on wisdom and reasons **i**,

INTELLIGIBLE (1)

1Co 14: 9 if in a tongue you utter speech that is not **i**,

INTEND (20) [INTENDED, INTENDING, INTENDS, INTENT, INTENTION, INTENTIONS, INTENTLY, INTENTS]

Jdg 11:23 Do you **i** to take their place?
1Ki 5: 5 So I **i** to build a house for the name of
2Ch 28:10 Now you **i** to subjugate the people of Judah
Ne 6: 6 that you and the Jews **i** to rebel;
Jer 26: 3 about the disaster that I **i** to bring on them because
36: 3 the house of Judah hears of all the disasters that I **i**
Jn 7:35 does this man **i** to go that we will not find him?
7:35 Does he **i** to go to the Dispersion among
1Co 16: 5 for I **i** to pass through Macedonia—
2Co 8:20 We **i** that no one should blame us
8:21 for we **i** to do what is right not only in
2Pe 1:12 I **i** to keep on reminding you of these things,
Jdt 9: 8 for they **i** to defile your sanctuary,
AdE 13: 4 that we honorably **i** cannot be brought about.
1Mc 15: 3 and I **i** to lay claim to the kingdom so
1Mc 15: 4 and **i** to make a landing in the country so
2Mc 7: 2 said, "What do you **i** to ask and learn from us?
2Es 8:59 For the Most High did not **i** that anyone should
10: 4 now I **i** not to return to the town, but to stay here;
4Mc 11:16 if you **i** to torture me for not eating defiling foods,

INTENDED (22) [INTEND]

Ge 31:20 in that he did not tell him that he **i** to flee.
50:20 though you **i** to do harm to me, God **i** it for good,
Nu 35:23 though they were not enemies, and no harm was **i**,
Dt 9:25 the LORD when the LORD **i** to destroy you,
Jdg 20: 5 They **i** to kill me, and they raped my concubine
2Ch 11:22 for he **i** to make him king.
32: 2 that Sennacherib had come and **i** to fight
Ne 6: 2 But they **i** to do me harm.
Jer 18: 8 I will change my mind about the disaster that I **i**
18:10 about the good that I had **i** to do to it.
Mk 6:48 He **i** to pass them by.
Lk 10: 1 to every town and place where he himself **i** to go.
Ac 20: 7 since he **i** to leave the next day,
25: 4 and that he himself **i** to go there shortly.
Ro 1:13 that I have often **i** to come to you
2Th 1: 5 is **i** to make you worthy of the kingdom of God,
Tob 3:10 to her father's upper room, she **i** to hang herself.
1Mc 4:27 for things had not happened to Israel as he had **i**,
2Mc 4:20 So this money was **i** by the sender for the sacrifice
11: 2 He **i** to make the city a home for Greeks,
3Mc 1:22 of his plans or the fulfillment of his **i** purpose.

INTENDING (13) [INTEND]

Jer 41:17 at Geruth Chimham near Bethlehem, **i** to go
Lk 14:28 For which of you, **i** to build a tower,
Ac 12: 4 **i** to bring him out to the people after the Passover.
20:13 **i** to take Paul on board there;
20:13 for he had made this arrangement, **i** to go
Php 1:17 not sincerely but **i** to increase my suffering
Sir 19:16 A person may make a slip without **i** it.
1Mc 11:63 **i** to remove him from office.
2Mc 1:14 On the pretext of **i** to marry her,
2: 6 of those who followed him came up **i** to mark
10:24 He came on, **i** to take Judea by storm.
12: 7 **i** to come again and root out the whole community
3Mc 1: 2 **i** single-handed to kill him and thereby end

INTENDS (2) [INTEND]

1Sa 20:13 But if my father **i** to do you harm,
Isa 10: 7 But this is not what he **i**,

INTENSE (3) [INTENSELY, INTENSIFY, INTENSIFYING, INTENSITY]

2Mc 9:28 having endured the more **i** suffering,
4Mc 12:12 justice has laid up for you **i** and eternal fire
14:10 For the power of fire is **i** and swift,

INTENSELY (3) [INTENSE]

Wis 16:19 in the midst of water it burned more **i** than fire,
Sir 17:26 and hate **i** what he abhors.
4Mc 16: 3 was the raging fiery furnace of Mishael so **i** hot,

INTENSIFY (1) [INTENSE]

Wis 14:18 not know the king to **i** their worship.

INTENSIFYING (1) [INTENSE]

2Mc 4: 4 was **i** the malice of Simon.

INTENSITY (1) [INTENSE]

3Mc 4:15 therefore conducted with bitter haste and zealous **i**

INTENT (14) [INTEND]

Ex 32:12 with evil **i** that he brought them out to kill them in
Nu 35:11 slayer who kills a person without **i** may flee there.
35:15 who kills a person without **i** may flee there.
Jos 20: 3 who kills a person without **i** or by mistake may flee
20: 9 who killed a person without **i** could flee there,
1Ch 12:38 came to Hebron with full **i** to make David king
Pr 21:27 how much more when brought with evil **i**.
Ac 8:22 the **i** of your heart may be forgiven you.
Wis 15: 4 For neither has the evil **i** of human art misled us,
Sir 38:28 sitting by the anvil, **i** on his iron-work;
Bar 1:22 of us followed the **i** of our own wicked hearts
1Mc 7:30 that Nicanor had come to him with treacherous **i**,
2Mc 4:14 that the priests were no longer **i** upon their service
3Mc 7: 3 frequently urging us with malicious **i**,

INTENTION (4) [INTEND]

SS 2: 4 and his **i** toward me was love.
Isa 46:10 "My purpose shall stand, and I will fulfill my **i**,"
1Pe 4: 1 also with the same **i** (for whoever has suffered in
2Pe 3: 1 in them I am trying to arouse your sincere **i**

INTENTIONS (5) [INTEND]

Mt 15:19 For out of the heart come evil **i**, murder, adultery,
Mk 7:21 from the human heart, that evil **i** come:
Heb 4:12 it is able to judge the thoughts and **i** of the heart.
Sir 37:10 hide your **i** from those who are jealous of you.
2Mc 14: 5 and was asked about the attitude and **i** of the Jews.

INTENTLY (9) [INTEND]

Mk 8:25 and he looked **i** and his sight was restored,
Ac 3: 4 Peter looked **i** at him, as did John, and said,
6:15 And all who sat in the council looked **i** at him,
Ac 13: 9 as Paul, filled with the Holy Spirit, looked **i** at him
14: 9 at him **i** and seeing that he had faith to be healed,
23: 1 While Paul was looking **i** at the council he said,
Tob 11: 5 Meanwhile Anna sat looking **i** down the road
Sir 9: 5 Do not look **i** at a virgin,
3Mc 2:26 **i** observing the king's purpose,

INTENTS (2) [INTEND]

Jer 23:20 until he has executed and accomplished the **i**
30:24 until he has executed and accomplished the **i**

INTERCEDE (4) [INTERCEDED, INTERCEDES, INTERCESSION, INTERCESSIONS]

1Sa 2:25 someone can **i** for the sinner with the LORD;
Jer 7:16 and do not **i** with me, for I will not hear you.
27:18 then let them **i** with the LORD of hosts,
2Es 7:*102* the day of judgment the righteous will be able to **i**

INTERCEDED (4) [INTERCEDE]

Dt 9:20 but I **i** also on behalf of Aaron at that same time.
Est 10: 3 for he sought the good of his people and **i** for
Ps 106:30 Then Phinehas stood up and **i**,
Tob 1:22 Ahikar **i** for me, and I returned to Nineveh.

INTERCEDES (3) [INTERCEDE]

Ro 8:26 that very Spirit **i** with sighs too deep for words.
8:27 Spirit **i** for the saints according to the will of God.
8:34 at the right hand of God, who indeed **i** for us.

INTERCESSION (3) [INTERCEDE]

1Sa 2:25 against the LORD, who can make **i**?"
Isa 53:12 and made **i** for the transgressors.
Heb 7:25 since he always lives to make **i** for them.

INTERCESSIONS (1) [INTERCEDE]

1Ti 2: 1 prayers, **i**, and thanksgivings be made for everyone

INTERCOURSE (9)

Nu 5:13 if a man has had **i** with her but it is hidden
5:20 and some man other than your husband has had **i**
Jdg 19:22 so that we may have **i** with him."
Hos 3: 3 you shall not have **i** with a man, nor I with you."
Ro 1:26 Their women exchanged natural **i** for unnatural,
1:27 giving up natural **i** with women,
Jdt 12:12 if we let such a woman go without having **i**
2Mc 6: 4 who dallied with prostitutes and had **i** with women
4Mc 2: 3 For when he was young and in his prime for **i**,

INTERDICT (7)

Da 6: 7 an ordinance and enforce an **i**,
6: 8 O king, establish the **i** and sign the document,
6: 9 Therefore King Darius signed the document and **i**.
6:12 the king and said concerning the **i**,
6:12 Did you not sign an **i**,
6:13 O king, or to the **i** you have signed,
6:15 that no **i** or ordinance that the king establishes can

INTEREST (26) [INTERESTS]

Ex 22:25 you shall not exact **i** from them.
Lev 25:36 not take **i** in advance or otherwise make a profit
25:37 not lend them your money at **i** taken in advance,
Dt 23:19 not charge **i** on loans to another Israelite, **i** on money, **i** on provisions, **i** on anything that is lent.
23:20 On loans to a foreigner you may charge **i**, but on loans to another Israelite you may not charge **i**,
Ne 5: 7 "You are all taking **i** from your own people."
5:10 Let us stop this taking of **i**.
5:11 and their houses, and the **i** on money, grain, wine,
Ps 15: 5 who do not lend money at **i**,
Pr 28: 8 by exorbitant **i** gathers it for another who is kind
Isa 58: 3 Look, you serve your own **i** on your fast day,
Eze 18: 8 does not take advance or accrued **i**,
18:13 takes advance or accrued **i**; shall he then live?
18:17 takes no advance or accrued **i**,
22:12 you take both advance **i** and accrued **i**,
Mt 25:27 I would have received what was my own with **i**.
Lk 19:23 when I returned, I could have collected it with **i**.'
Sir 37: 7 but some give counsel in their own **i**.
37: 8 and learn first what is his **i**,
1Es 4:49 in the **i** of their freedom, that no officer or satrap
4Mc 2: 8 without **i** to the needy and to cancel the debt when

INTERESTS‡ (7) [INTEREST]

Isa 58:13 from pursuing your own **i** on my holy day;
58:13 serving your own **i**, or pursuing your own affairs;
1Co 7:34 and his **i** are divided.
Php 2: 4 Let each of you look not to your own **i**, but to the **i** of others.
2:21 All of them are seeking their own **i**,
2Mc 14: 8 first because I am genuinely concerned for the **i** of

INTERIOR (6)

1Ki 6:20 **i** of the inner sanctuary was twenty cubits long,
SS 3:10 its **i** was inlaid with love. Daughters of Jerusalem,
Eze 42:15 he had finished measuring the **i** of the temple area,
Ac 19: 1 Paul passed through the **i** regions and came
1Mc 4:48 also rebuilt the sanctuary and the **i** of the temple,
2Es 14:33 you are here, and your people are farther in the **i**.

INTERLACING (1)
Jer 2:23 a restive young camel **i** her tracks,

INTERMARRY (3) [MARRY]
Dt 7: 3 Do not **i** with them, giving your daughters
Jos 23:12 and **i** with them, so that you marry their women
Ezr 9:14 shall we break your commandments again and **i**

INTERMEDDLE (KJV) See SHARES

INTERNAL (1)
2Mc 9: 5 and with sharp **i** tortures—

INTERPRET (14) [INTERPRETATION, INTERPRETATIONS, INTERPRETED, INTERPRETER, INTERPRETERS, INTERPRETING, INTERPRETS]
Ge 40: 8 and there is no one to **i** them."
41: 8 but there was no one who could **i** them to Pharaoh.
41:15 and there is no one who can **i** it.
41:15 that when you hear a dream you can **i** it."
Dt 17:11 that they **i** for you or the ruling that they announce
Da 5:12 and understanding to **i** dreams, explain riddles,
Mt 16: 3 You know how to **i** the appearance of the sky,
16: 3 but you cannot **i** the signs of the times.
Lk 12:56 You know how to **i** the appearance of earth
12:56 why do you not know how to **i** the present time?
1Co 12:30 Do all speak in tongues? Do all **i**?
14:13 in a tongue should pray for the power to **i**.
14:27 and each in turn; and let one **i**.
14:28 But if there is no one to **i**,

INTERPRETATION (56) [INTERPRET]
Ge 40:12 Then Joseph said to him, "This is its **i**:
40:16 When the chief baker saw that the **i** was favorable,
40:18 And Joseph answered, "This is its **i**:
41:12 giving an **i** to each according to his dream.
Jdg 7:15 Gideon heard the telling of the dream and its **i**,
Ne 8: 8 from the law of God, with **i**.
Ecc 8: 1 And who knows the **i** of a thing?
Da 2: 4 and we will reveal the **i**."
2: 5 if you do not tell me both the dream and its **i**,
2: 6 But if you do tell me the dream and its **i**,
2: 6 Therefore tell me the dream and its **i**."
2: 7 then we can give its **i**."
2: 9 and I shall know that you can give me its **i**."
2:16 and he would tell the king the **i**.
2:24 and I will give the king the **i**."
2:25 from Judah a man who can tell the king the **i**."
2:26 to tell me the dream that I have seen and its **i**?"
2:30 in order that the **i** may be known to the king and
2:36 now we will tell the king its **i**.
2:45 The dream is certain, and its **i** trustworthy."
4: 6 in order that they might tell me the **i** of the dream.
4: 7 but they could not tell me its **i**.
4: 9 Hear the dream that I saw; tell me its **i**.
4:18 Now you, Belteshazzar, declare the **i**,
4:18 of my kingdom are unable to tell me the **i**.
4:19 do not let the dream or the **i** terrify you."
4:19 and its **i** for your enemies!
4:24 the **i**, O king, and it is a decree of the Most High
5: 7 and tell me its **i** shall be clothed in purple,
5: 8 not read the writing or tell the king the **i**.
5:12 Now let Daniel be called, and he will give the **i**."
5:15 in before me to read this writing and tell me its **i**,
5:15 but they were not able to give the **i** of the matter.
5:16 if you are able to read the writing and tell me its **i**,
5:17 the writing to the king and let him know the **i**.
5:26 This is the **i** of the matter:
7:16 that he would disclose to me the **i** of the matter:
1Co 12:10 to another the **i** of tongues.
14:26 a lesson, a revelation, a tongue, or an **i**.
2Pe 1:20 of scripture is a matter of one's own **i**,
2Es 4:47 and I will show you the **i** of a parable.
10:43 misfortune of her son—this is the **i**:
12: 8 the **i** and meaning of this terrifying vision so
12:10 "This is the **i** of this vision that you have seen:
12:16 This is the **i** of the twelve wings that you saw.
12:17 but from the midst of its body, this is the **i**:
12:19 to its wings, this is the **i**:
12:22 for your seeing three heads at rest, this is the **i**:
12:30 this is the **i**: It is these whom the Most High has
12:35 This is the dream that you saw, and this is its **i**.
13:15 now show me the **i** of this dream also.
13:21 "I will tell you the **i** of the vision,
13:22 concerning those who do not survive, this is the **i**:
13:25 "This is the **i** of the vision:
13:28 that came to conquer him, this is the **i**:
13:53 This is the **i** of the dream that you saw.

INTERPRETATIONS (3) [INTERPRET]
Ge 40: 8 Joseph said to them, "Do not **i** belong to God?
Da 5:16 that you can give **i** and solve problems.
2Es 14: 8 and the **i** that you have heard;

INTERPRETED (4) [INTERPRET]
Ge 40:22 just as Joseph had **i** to them.
41:12 When we told him, he **i** our dreams to us,
41:13 As he **i** to us, so it turned out;
Lk 24:27 he **i** to them the things about himself in all

INTERPRETER‡ (1) [INTERPRET]
Ge 42:23 since he spoke with them through an **i**.

INTERPRETERS (1) [INTERPRET]
Isa 43:27 and your **i** transgressed against me.

INTERPRETING (1) [INTERPRET]
1Co 2:13 **i** spiritual things to those who are spiritual.

INTERPRETS (1) [INTERPRET]
1Co 14: 5 unless someone **i**, so that the church may be built up.

INTERRUPT (4)
2Ch 35:15 they did not need to **i** their service,
Sir 11: 8 and do not **i** when another is speaking.
32: 3 and do not **i** the music.
1Es 1:16 no one needed to **i** his daily duties,

INTERVAL (3) [INTERVALS]
Da 11:35 for there is still an **i** until the time appointed.
Ac 5: 7 After an **i** of about three hours his wife came in,
3Mc 4:17 But after the previously mentioned **i** of time

INTERVALS (5) [INTERVAL]
2Ki 20: 9 the shadow has now advanced ten **i**; shall it retreat ten **i**?"
20:10 "It is normal for the shadow to lengthen ten **i**; rather let the shadow retreat ten **i**."
20:11 and he brought the shadow back the ten **i**,

INTERVENE (1) [INTERVENED, INTERVENES, INTERVENTION]
Isa 59:16 and was appalled that there was no one to **i**;

INTERVENED (2) [INTERVENE]
Jer 15:11 Surely I have **i** in your life for good,
Wis 18:23 he **i** and held back the wrath,

INTERVENES (1) [INTERVENE]
Dt 25:11 and the wife of one **i** to rescue her husband from

INTERVENTION (2) [INTERVENE]
Sir 34: 6 Unless they are sent by **i** from the Most High,
2Mc 3:29 the divine **i** and deprived of any hope of recovery,

INTERVIEW (1)
2Mc 4: 8 at an **i** three hundred sixty talents of silver,

INTESTINES (1)
Tob 6: 5 Keep them with you, but throw away the **i**.

INTIMATE (6)
Dt 13: 6 or the wife you embrace, or your most **i** friend—
Job 19:19 All my **i** friends abhor me,
Pr 7: 4 "You are my sister," and call insight your **i** friend,
Sus 1:54 Under what tree did you see them being **i**
1:57 and they were **i** with you through fear;
1:58 Under what tree did you catch them being **i**

INTIMIDATE (3) [INTIMIDATED]
Ne 6:13 to **i** me and make me sin by acting in this way,
6:19 And Tobiah sent letters to **i** me.
Sir 48:12 nor could anyone **i** him at all.

INTIMIDATED (3) [INTIMIDATE]
Dt 1:17 you shall not be **i** by anyone,
Php 1:28 and are in no way **i** by your opponents.
1Pe 3:14 Do not fear what they fear, and do not be **i**,

INTO (1736) See Index of Articles Etc.

INTOLERABLE (1)
2Mc 9:10 Because of his **i** stench no one was able to carry

INTONED (1)
2Sa 1:17 David **i** this lamentation over Saul and his son

INTOXICANTS (1) [INTOXICATED]
1Sa 1:11 He shall drink neither wine nor **i**,

INTOXICATED (2) [INTOXICANTS]
Pr 5:19 may you be **i** always by her love.
5:20 Why should you be **i**, my son,

INTREAT, INTREATED, INTREATIES, INTREATY (KJV) See DEALT WELL WITH, IMPLORE, INSULTED, INTERCESSION, MISTREATED, PRAY, PRAYED, SEEK, SUPPLICATIONS

INTRICATE (1) [INTRICATELY]
AdE 16:13 with **i** craft and deceit asked for the destruction

INTRICATELY (1) [INTRICATE]
Ps 139:15 **i** woven in the depths of the earth.

INTRIGUE (3) [INTRIGUES]
Da 8:23 a king of bold countenance shall arise, skilled in **i**.
11:21 and obtain the kingdom through **i**.
11:32 He shall seduce with **i** those who violate

INTRIGUES (1) [INTRIGUE]
2Es 9: 3 **i** of nations, wavering of leaders,

INTRODUCED (3) [INTRODUCTION]
2Ki 17: 8 and in the customs that the kings of Israel had **i**.
17:19 but walked in the customs that Israel had **i**.
2Mc 4:11 of living and **i** new customs contrary to the law.

INTRODUCTION (1) [INTRODUCED]
Heb 7:19 there is, on the other hand, the **i** of a better hope,

INTRUDER (2) [INTRUDERS]
4Mc 14:16 hatch the nestlings and ward off the **i**.
14:17 If they are not able to keep the **i** away,

INTRUDERS (2) [INTRUDER]
Jude 1: 4 For certain **i** have stolen in among you,
4Mc 14:19 making honeycombs defend themselves against **i**

INVADE (14) [INVADED, INVADERS, INVADING, INVASION]
Jos 2:18 if we **i** the land and you do not tie this crimson
2Ki 13:20 of Moabites used to **i** the land in the spring of
2Ch 20:10 whom you would not let Israel **i** when they came
27: 2 only he did not **i** the temple of the LORD.
La 1:10 she has even seen the nations **i** her sanctuary,
Da 11: 9 the latter shall **i** the realm of the king of the south,
Na 1:15 for never again shall the wicked **i** you;
1Mc 4:35 in order to **i** Judea again with an even larger army.
12:25 he gave them no opportunity to **i** his own country.
13: 1 a large army to **i** the land of Judah and destroy it,
13:12 Then Trypho left Ptolemais with a large army to **i**
13:20 this Trypho came to **i** the country and destroy it,
14:31 to **i** their country and lay hands on their sanctuary,
15:40 the people and **i** Judea and take the people captive

INVADED (10) [INVADE]
2Ki 17: 5 king of Assyria **i** all the land and came to Samaria;
2Ch 21:17 They came up against Judah, **i** it,
28:17 For the Edomites had again **i** and defeated Judah,
32: 1 King Sennacherib of Assyria came and **i** Judah
Joel 1: 6 a nation has **i** my land, powerful and innumerable;
Jdt 4: 7 since by them Judea could be **i**;
Sir 48:18 In his days Sennacherib **i** the country;
1Mc 1:17 So he **i** Egypt with a strong force,
14: 2 and Media heard that Demetrius had **i** his territory,
15:10 and **i** the land of his ancestors.

INVADERS (1) [INVADE]
Eze 39:14 and bury any **i** who remain on the face of the land,

INVADING (1) [INVADE]
2Mc 11: 5 **I** Judea, he approached Beth-zur,

INVALID (1) [INVALIDS]
Isa 10:18 and it will be as when an **i** wastes away.

INVALIDATE (1)
4Mc 5:18 even so would it be right for us to **i** our reputation

INVALIDS (1) [INVALID]
Jn 5: 3 In these lay many **i**—blind, lame, and paralyzed.

INVASION (2) [INVADE]
2Mc 5: 1 About this time Antiochus made his second **i**
8:12 Word came to Judas concerning Nicanor's **i**;

INVENTED (1) [INVENTING, INVENTION, INVENTOR, INVENTORS]
2Ch 26:15 **i** by skilled workers, on the towers and the corners

INVENTING (1) [INVENTED]
Ne 6: 8 you are **i** them out of your own mind"

INVENTION (1) [INVENTED]
Wis 14:12 and the **i** of them was the corruption of life;

INVENTOR (1) [INVENTED]
4Mc 11:23 you **i** of tortures and enemy of those who are truly

INVENTORS (1) [INVENTED]
Ro 1:30 God-haters, insolent, haughty, boastful, **i** of evil,

INVENTORY (2)
Nu 31:26 the ancestral houses of the congregation make an **i**
Ezr 1: 9 And this was the **i**: gold basins,

INVESTED (1)
Mt 25:27 you ought to have **i** my money with the bankers,

INVESTIGATE (5) [INVESTIGATED, INVESTIGATING, INVESTIGATION]
Ac 25:20 Since I was at a loss how to **i** these questions,
Wis 13: 9 to know so much that they could **i** the world,
Sir 3:21 nor **i** what is beyond your power.
11: 7 Do not find fault before you **i;**
1Es 9:16 of the tenth month they began their sessions to **i**

INVESTIGATED (3) [INVESTIGATE]
Est 2:23 When the affair was **i** and found to be so,
AdE 2:23 He **i** the two eunuchs and hanged them.
2Mc 1:34 the king **i** the matter, and enclosed the place

INVESTIGATING (1) [INVESTIGATE]
Lk 1: 3 after **i** everything carefully from the very first,

INVESTIGATION (3) [INVESTIGATE]
Dt 13:14 then you shall inquire and make a thorough **i.**
Job 34:24 He shatters the mighty without **i,**
AdE 16: 7 as from **i** of matters close at hand.

INVETERATE (1)
3Mc 4: 1 for the **i** enmity that had long ago been

INVINCIBLE (7)
Jdt 16:13 and glorious, wonderful in strength, **i.**
Wis 5:19 he will take holiness as an **i** shield,
2Mc 11:13 and realized that the Hebrews were **i** because
3Mc 4:21 an act of the **i** providence of him who was aiding
6:13 the Gentiles cower today in fear of your **i** might,
4Mc 9:18 that children of the Hebrews alone are **i**
11:21 For religious knowledge, O tyrant, is **i.**

INVIOLABILITY (1)
2Mc 3:12 of the place and in the sanctity and **i** of the temple

INVISIBLE (7)
Job 33:21 and their bones, once **i,** now stick out.
Ro 1:20 of the world his eternal power and divine nature, **i**
Col 1:15 He is the image of the **i** God,
1:16 things visible and **i,** whether thrones or dominions
1Ti 1:17 To the King of the ages, immortal, **i,**
Heb 11:27 for he persevered as though he saw him who is **i.**
2Mc 9: 5 struck him with an incurable and **i** blow.

INVITATION (1) [INVITE]
3Mc 5:27 and being struck by the unusual **i** to come out—

INVITATIONS (1) [INVITE]
3Mc 5:14 the person who was in charge of the **i,**

INVITE (16) [INVITATION, INVITATIONS, INVITED, INVITES, INVITING]
Ex 2:20 **I** him to break bread."
34:15 someone among them will **i** you,
1Sa 16: 3 **I** Jesse to the sacrifice,
1Ki 1:10 but he did not **i** the prophet Nathan or Benaiah or
1:26 But he did not **i** me, your servant,
Job 1: 4 and **i** their three sisters to eat and drink with them.
Zec 3:10 you shall **i** each other to come under your vine
Mt 22: 9 and **i** everyone you find to the wedding banquet.'
Lk 14:12 do not **i** your friends or your brothers
14:12 in case they may **i** you in return,
14:13 But when you give a banquet, **i** the poor,
Jdt 12:10 and did not **i** any of his officers.
AdE 5:12 "The queen did not **i** anyone to the dinner with
Wis 1:12 Do not **i** death by the error of your life,
Sir 11:29 Do not **i** everyone into your home,
13: 9 be reserved, and he will **i** you more insistently.

INVITED‡ (41) [INVITE]
Nu 25: 2 These **i** the people to the sacrifices of their gods,
Jos 24: 9 He sent and **i** Balaam son of Beor to curse you,
Jdg 14:15 Have you **i** us here to impoverish us?"
1Sa 9:13 afterward those eat who are **i.**
9:22 a place at the head of those who had been **i,**
16: 5 And he sanctified Jesse and his sons and **i** them to
2Sa 11:13 David **i** him to eat and drink in his presence
13:23 and Absalom **i** all the king's sons.
15:11 they were **i** guests, and they went
1Ki 1: 9 which is beside En-rogel, and he **i** all his brothers,
1:19 and has **i** all the children of the king,
1:19 but your servant Solomon he has not **i.**
1:25 and has **i** all the king's children,
7:13 King Solomon **i** and received Hiram from Tyre.
Est 5:12 Tomorrow also I am **i** by her,
La 2:22 You **i** my enemies from all around as if for a day
Mt 22: 3 He sent his slaves to call those who had been **i** to
22: 4 saying, 'Tell those who have been **i:**
22: 8 but those **i** were not worthy.
Lk 7:39 Now when the Pharisee who had **i** him saw it,
11:37 a Pharisee **i** him to dine with him;
14: 8 you are **i** by someone to a wedding banquet,
14: 8 someone more distinguished than you has been **i**
14: 9 host who **i** both of you may come and say to you,
14:10 But when you are **i,** go and sit down at
14:12 He said also to the one who had **i** him,
Lk 14:16 "Someone gave a great dinner and **i** many.
14:17 to say to those who had been **i,** 'Come;
14:24 none of those who were **i** will taste my dinner.'"
Jn 2: 2 and his disciples had also been **i** to the wedding.
Ac 7:14 and **i** his father Jacob and all his relatives to come
8:31 And he **i** Philip to get in and sit beside him.
10:23 So Peter **i** them in and gave them lodging.
10:48 Then they **i** him to stay for several days.
28:14 and were **i** to stay with them for seven days.
Rev 19: 9 Blessed are those who are **i** to the marriage supper
AdE 5:12 and I am **i** again tomorrow.
Sir Pr: 2 You are **i** therefore to read it with goodwill
2Mc 12: 3 they **i** the Jews who lived among them to embark,
14: 5 that furthered his mad purpose when he was **i**
3Mc 5:26 Hermon arrived and **i** him to come out,

INVITES (5) [INVITE]
Pr 17:19 one who builds a high threshold **i** broken bones.
18: 6 and a fool's mouth **i** a flogging.
1Co 10:27 an unbeliever **i** you to a meal and you are disposed
Sir 13: 9 When an influential person **i** you, be reserved,
4Mc 3:19 now **i** us to a narrative demonstration

INVITING (2) [INVITE]
Tob 9: 5 that Tobit's son Tobias had married and was **i** him
2Mc 8:11 **i** them to buy Jewish slaves and promising to hand

INVOCATIONS (1) [INVOKE]
2Mc 15:26 the enemy in battle with **i** to God and prayers.

INVOKE (7) [INVOCATIONS, INVOKED, INVOKES, INVOKING]
Ge 4:26 At that time people began to **i** the name of
48:20 saying, "By you Israel will **i** blessings, saying,
Ex 23:13 Do not **i** the names of other gods;
1Ch 16: 4 to **i,** to thank, and to praise the LORD,
Isa 48: 1 and **i** the God of Israel, but not in truth or right.
Ac 9:14 the chief priests to bind all who **i** your name."
1Pe 1:17 If you **i** as Father the one who judges all people

INVOKED (8) [INVOKE]
Ge 12: 8 and there he built an altar to the LORD and **i**
1Ki 8:43 so that they may know that your name has been **i**
2Ch 6:33 and that they may know that your name has been **i**
Ps 72:15 and blessings **i** for him all day long.
Ac 9:21 in Jerusalem among those who **i** this name?
Heb 11:20 By faith Isaac **i** blessings for the future on Jacob
Jas 2: 7 the excellent name that was **i** over you?
2Es 4:25 But what will he do for his name that is **i** over us?

INVOKES (1) [INVOKE]
Isa 65:16 Then whoever **i** a blessing in the land shall bless

INVOKING (1) [INVOKE]
AdE 15: 2 after **i** the aid of the all-seeing God and Savior,

INVOLVED (9) [INVOLVES, INVOLVING]
Lev 25:52 according to the years **i** they shall make payment
Nu 15:26 because the whole people was **i** in the error.
Jer 44:19 to her without our husbands' being **i?"**
Heb 9:16 a will is **i,** the death of the one who made it must
AdE 16: 5 and have been **i** in irremediable calamities,
Sir 12:14 with a sinner and becomes **i** in the other's sins.
2Mc 2:24 the flood of statistics **i** and the difficulty there is
5:18 it had not happened that they were **i** in many sins,
2Es 7:12 full of dangers and **i** in great hardships.

INVOLVES (3) [INVOLVED]
Gal 3:20 a mediator **i** more than one party; but God is one.
Sir 23:13 foul language, for it **i** sinful speech.
29:19 his pursuit of gain **i** him in lawsuits.

INVOLVING (2) [INVOLVED]
Ex 22: 9 In any case of disputed ownership **i** ox, donkey,
3Mc 2:28 a registration **i** poll tax and to the status of slaves.

INVULNERABLE (3)
Wis 7:22 clear, unpolluted, distinct, **i,** loving the good,
2Mc 8:36 and that therefore the Jews were **i,**
3Mc 5:47 with **i** heart and with his own eyes,

INWARD‡ (6) [INWARDLY]
2Sa 5: 9 David built the city all around from the Millo **i.**
Job 30:27 My **i** parts are in turmoil, and are never still;
38:36 Who has put wisdom in the **i** parts,
Ps 51: 6 You desire truth in the **i** being;
139:13 For it was you who formed my **i** parts;
Wis 17:13 defeated by this **i** weakness,

INWARDLY (8) [INWARD]
Ps 62: 4 they bless with their mouths, but **i** they curse.
Jer 9: 8 but **i** are planning to lay an ambush.
Mt 7:15 in sheep's clothing but **i** are ravenous wolves.
Ro 2:29 Rather, a person is a Jew who is one **i,**
8:23 groan **i** while we wait for adoption,
Wis 8:17 When I considered these things **i,**
Sir 19:26 but **i** he is full of deceit.
2Mc 5:11 raging **i,** he left Egypt and took the city by storm.

INWARDS (KJV) See ENTRAILS

IOB See Index to Footnotes

IOTA See Index to Footnotes

IPHDEIAH (1)
1Ch 8:25 **I,** and Penuel were the sons of Shashak.

IPHTAH (1)
Jos 15:43 **I,** Ashnah, Nezib,

IPHTAH-EL (2)
Jos 19:14 and it ends at the valley of **I;**
19:27 and touches Zebulun and the valley of **I** northward

IR (2)
Nu 24:19 and destroy the survivors of **I."**
1Ch 7:12 And Shuppim and Huppim were the sons of **I,**

IR-MOAB (1)
Nu 22:36 he went out to meet him at **I,**

IR-NAHASH (1)
1Ch 4:12 Paseah, and Tehinnah the father of **I.**

IR-SHEMESH (1) [=BETH-SHEMESH]
Jos 19:41 of its inheritance included Zorah, Eshtaol, **I,**

IRA (6)
2Sa 20:26 and **I** the Jairite was also David's priest.
23:26 Helez the Paltite; **I** son of Ikkesh of Tekoa;
23:38 **I** the Ithrite; Gareb the Ithrite;
1Ch 11:28 **I** son of Ikkesh of Tekoa, Abiezer of Anathoth,
11:40 **I** the Ithrite, Gareb the Ithrite,
27: 9 was **I** son of Ikkesh the Tekoite;

IRAD (2)
Ge 4:18 To Enoch was born **I;** and **I** was the father of Mehujael,

IRAM (2)
Ge 36:43 Magdiel, and **I;** these are the clans of Edom
1Ch 1:54 Magdiel, and **I;** these are the clans of Edom.

IRI (1)
1Ch 7: 7 Ezbon, Uzzi, Uzziel, Jerimoth, and **I,** five,

IRIJAH (2)
Jer 37:13 a sentinel there named **I** son of Shelemiah son
37:14 But **I** would not listen to him,

IRON‡ (114) [IRON-SMELTER, IRON-WORK, IRONS, IRONSMITH]
Ge 4:22 who made all kinds of bronze and **i** tools.
Lev 26:19 and I will make your sky like **i** and your earth
Nu 31:22 gold, silver, bronze, **i,** tin, and lead—
35:16 But anyone who strikes another with an **i** object,
Dt 3:11 In fact his bed, an **i** bed,
8: 9 a land whose stones are **i** and
27: 5 of stones on which you have not used an **i** tool.
28:23 and the earth under you **i.**
28:48 an **i** yoke on your neck until he has destroyed you.
33:25 Your bars are **i** and bronze;
Jos 6:19 all silver and gold, and vessels of bronze and **i,**
6:24 and the vessels of bronze and **i,**
8:31 on which no **i** tool has been used";
17:16 in the plain have chariots of **i,**
17:18 though they have chariots of **i,**
19:38 **I,** Migdal-el, Horem, Beth-anath,
22: 8 and **i,** and with a great quantity of clothing;
Jdg 1:19 because they had chariots of **i.**
4: 3 for he had nine hundred chariots of **i,**
4:13 nine hundred chariots of **i,**
1Sa 17: 7 his spear's head weighed six hundred shekels of **i;**
2Sa 12:31 to work with saws and **i** picks and **i** axes,
23: 7 to touch them one uses an **i** bar or the shaft of
1Ki 6: 7 nor ax nor any tool of **i** was heard in the temple
22:11 for himself horns of **i,** and he said, "Thus says
2Ki 6: 6 and threw it in there, and made the **i** float.
1Ch 20: 3 set them to work with saws and **i** picks and axes.
22: 3 David also provided great stores of **i** for nails for
22:14 and bronze and **i** beyond weighing,
22:16 gold, silver, bronze, and **i.**
29: 2 the **i** for the things of **i,**
29: 7 and one hundred thousand talents of **i.**
2Ch 2: 7 and **i,** and in purple, crimson, and blue fabrics,
2:14 He is trained to work in gold, silver, bronze, **i,**
18:10 for himself horns of **i,** and he said, "Thus says
24:12 also workers in **i** and bronze to repair the house of
Job 19:24 with an **i** pen and with lead they were engraved on
20:24 They will flee from an **i** weapon;
28: 2 **I** is taken out of the earth,
40:18 its limbs like bars of **i.**
41:27 It counts **i** as straw, and bronze as rotten wood.
Ps 2: 9 You shall break them with a rod of **i,**
105:18 his neck was put in a collar of **i;**
107:16 and cuts in two the bars of **i.**
149: 8 with fetters and their nobles with chains of **i,**
Pr 27:17 **I** sharpens **i,** and one person sharpens the wits of
Ecc 10:10 If the **i** is blunt, and one does not whet the edge,

Isa 45: 2 the doors of bronze and cut through the bars of **i**,
48: 4 your neck is an **i** sinew and your forehead brass,
60:17 instead of **i** I will bring silver;
60:17 instead of wood, bronze, instead of stones, **i**.
Jer 1:18 an **i** pillar, and a bronze wall,
6:28 they are bronze and **i**, all of them act corruptly.
15:12 Can **i** and bronze break **i** from the north?
17: 1 The sin of Judah is written with an **i** pen;
28:13 You have broken wooden bars only to forge **i** bars
28:14 an **i** yoke on the neck of all these nations so
Eze 4: 3 an **i** plate and place it as an **i** wall between you
22:18 all of them, silver, bronze, tin, **i**, and lead.
22:20 As one gathers silver, bronze, **i**, lead,
27:12 **i**, tin, and lead they exchanged for your wares.
27:19 wrought **i**, cassia, and sweet cane were bartered
Da 2:33 its legs of **i**, its feet partly of **i** and partly of clay.
2:34 the statue on its feet of **i** and clay and broke them
2:35 Then the **i**, the clay, the bronze, the silver,
2:40 And there shall be a fourth kingdom, strong as **i**;
just as **i** crushes and smashes everything,
2:41 and toes partly of potter's clay and partly of **i**,
2:41 but some of the strength of **i** shall be in it, as you
saw the **i** mixed with the clay.
2:42 As the toes of the feet were part **i** and part clay,
2:43 As you saw the **i** mixed with clay,
2:43 just as **i** does not mix with clay.
2:45 and that it crushed the **i**, the bronze, the clay,
4:15 with a band of **i** and bronze,
4:23 with a band of **i** and bronze,
5: 4 gods of gold and silver, bronze, **i**, wood, and stone.
5:23 gods of gold and silver, of bronze, **i**, wood,
7: 7 It had great **i** teeth and was devouring,
7:19 with its teeth of **i** and claws of bronze,
Am 1: 3 with threshing sledges of **i**.
Mic 4:13 for I will make your horn **i** and your hoofs bronze;
Ac 12:10 they came before the **i** gate leading into the city.
1Ti 4: 2 of liars whose consciences are seared with a hot **i**.
Rev 2:27 with an **i** rod, as when clay pots are shattered—
9: 9 they had scales like **i** breastplates,
12: 5 who is to rule all the nations with a rod of **i**.
18:12 all articles of costly wood, bronze, **i**, and marble,
19:15 and he will rule them with a rod of **i**;
Wis 13:15 and sets it in the wall, and fastens it there with **i**.
17:16 thus was kept shut up in a prison not made of **i**;
Sir 13: 2 How can the clay pot associate with the **i** kettle?
22:15 a piece of **i** are easier to bear than a stupid person.
28:20 For its yoke is a yoke of **i**,
39:26 and **i** and salt and wheat flour and milk and honey,
48:17 he tunneled the rock with **i** tools,
2Mc 11: 9 but the wildest animals or walls of **i**.
Man 1:10 I am weighted down with many an **i** fetter,
3Mc 3:25 and bound securely with **i** fetters,
4: 9 driven under the constraint of **i** bonds;
2Es 7:*55* and also **i** and lead and clay;
7:*56* and **i** than bronze, and lead than **i**,
4Mc 8:13 braziers and thumbscrews and **i** claws and wedges
9:26 with **i** gauntlets having sharp hooks,
9:28 with the **i** hands, flayed all his flesh up to his chin,
11:10 and fitting **i** clamps on them,
14:19 as though with an **i** dart,

IRON-SMELTER (3) [IRON, SMELT]

Dt 4:20 and brought you out of the **i**, out of Egypt,
1Ki 8:51 out of Egypt, from the midst of the **i**).
Jer 11: 4 out of the land of Egypt, from the **i**, saying,

IRON-WORK (1) [IRON]

Sir 38:28 sitting by the anvil, intent on his **i**;

IRONS (2) [IRON]

Ps 107:10 prisoners in misery and in **i**,
4Mc 15:22 on the wheel and with the hot **i**!

IRONSMITH (1) [IRON, SMITH]

Isa 44:12 The **i** fashions it and works it over the coals,

IRPEEL (1)

Jos 18:27 Rekem, **I**, Taralah,

IRRATIONAL (9) [IRRATIONALLY]

2Pe 2:12 These people, however, are like **i** animals,
Jude 1:10 like **i** animals, they know by instinct.
Wis 11:15 to worship **i** serpents and worthless animals,
11:15 you sent upon them a multitude of **i** creatures
3Mc 7: 8 at all or reproaching them for the **i** things
4Mc 2:19 and Levi for their **i** slaughter of the entire tribe of
3:11 But a certain **i** desire for the water in
5:22 at our philosophy as though living by it were **i**,
6:18 be **i** if having lived in accordance with truth up

IRRATIONALLY (1) [IRRATIONAL]

4Mc 6:14 so **i** destroying yourself through these evil things?

IRREMEDIABLE (1)

AdE 16: 5 and have been involved in **i** calamities,

IRREPROACHABLE (1)

Col 1:22 so as to present you holy and blameless and **i**

IRRESISTIBLE (2)

Wis 7:22 distinct, invulnerable, loving the good, keen, **i**,
2Mc 1:13 leader reached Persia with a force that seemed **i**,

IRRESOLUTE (1)

2Ch 13: 7 when Rehoboam was young and **i** and could

IRREVERENCE (1)

2Mc 4:17 It is no light thing to show **i** to the divine laws—

IRREVOCABLE (2)

Ro 11:29 for the gifts and the calling of God are **i**.
3Mc 5:42 an **i** oath that he would send them to death

IRRIGATE (1) [IRRIGATES]

Dt 11:10 where you sow your seed and **i** by foot like

IRRIGATES (1) [IRRIGATE]

4Mc 1:29 and ties up and waters and thoroughly **i**,

IRRITABLE (1) [IRRITATE]

1Co 13: 5 it is not **i** or resentful;

IRRITATE (1) [IRRITABLE]

1Sa 1: 6 Her rival used to provoke her severely, to **i** her,

IRU (1)

1Ch 4:15 **I**, Elah, and Naam; and the son of Elah: Kenaz.

IS (8219) [BE] See Index of Articles Etc.

ISAAC‡ (151) [ISAAC'S]

Ge 17:19 and you shall name him **I**.
17:21 But my covenant I will establish with **I**,
21: 3 the name **I** to his son whom Sarah bore him.
21: 4 And Abraham circumcised his son **I**
21: 5 a hundred years old when his son **I** was born
21: 8 a great feast on the day that **I** was weaned.
21: 9 to Abraham, playing with her son **I**.
21:10 not inherit along with my son **I**."
21:12 through **I** that offspring shall be named for you.
22: 2 He said, "Take your son, your only son **I**,
22: 3 of his young men with him, and his son **I**;
22: 6 of the burnt offering and laid it on his son **I**,
22: 7 **I** said to his father Abraham, "Father!"
22: 9 He bound his son **I**, and laid him on the altar,
24: 4 and to my kindred and get a wife for my son **I**."
24:14 one whom you have appointed for your servant **I**.
24:62 Now **I** had come from Beer-lahai-roi,
24:63 **I** went out in the evening to walk in the field;
24:64 And Rebekah looked up, and when she saw **I**,
24:66 the servant told **I** all the things that he had done.
24:67 Then **I** brought her into his mother Sarah's tent.
24:67 So **I** was comforted after his mother's death.
25: 5 Abraham gave all he had to **I**.
25: 6 and he sent them away from his son **I**,
25: 9 His sons **I** and Ishmael buried him in the cave
25:11 After the death of Abraham God blessed his son **I**.
25:11 And **I** settled at Beer-lahai-roi.
25:19 These are the descendants of **I**, Abraham's son:
25:19 Abraham was the father of **I**,
25:20 **I** was forty years old when he married Rebekah,
25:21 **I** prayed to the LORD for his wife,
25:26 **I** was sixty years old when she bore them.
25:28 **I** loved Esau, because he was fond of game;
26: 1 And **I** went to Gerar, to King Abimelech of
26: 2 The LORD appeared to **I** and said,
26: 6 So **I** settled in Gerar.
26: 8 When **I** had been there a long time,
26: 9 So Abimelech called for **I**, and said,
26: 9 **I** said to him, "Because I thought I might die
26:12 **I** sowed seed in that land,
26:16 And Abimelech said to **I**, "Go away from us;
26:17 So **I** departed from there and camped in the valley
26:18 **I** dug again the wells of water that had been dug in
26:27 **I** said to them, "Why have you come to me,
26:31 and **I** set them on their way,
26:35 and they made life bitter for **I** and Rebekah.
27: 1 When **I** was old and his eyes were dim so
27: 5 Now Rebekah was listening when **I** spoke
27:20 But **I** said to his son,
27:21 Then **I** said to Jacob, "Come near,
27:22 So Jacob went up to his father **I**,
27:26 Then his father **I** said to him,
27:30 As soon as **I** had finished blessing Jacob,
27:30 from the presence of his father **I**,
27:32 His father **I** said to him, "Who are you?"
27:33 Then **I** trembled violently, and said,
27:37 **I** answered Esau, "I have already made him your
lord,
27:39 Then his father **I** answered him:
27:46 Then Rebekah said to **I**, "I am weary of my life
28: 1 Then **I** called Jacob and blessed him,
28: 5 Thus **I** sent Jacob away;
28: 6 that **I** had blessed Jacob and sent him away
28: 8 the Canaanite women did not please his father **I**,
28:13 God of Abraham your father and the God of **I**;
31:18 to go to his father **I** in the land of Canaan.
31:42 the God of Abraham and the Fear of **I**,
31:53 So Jacob swore by the Fear of his father **I**,
32: 9 of my father Abraham and God of my father **I**,
35:12 The land that I gave to Abraham and **I** I will give
35:27 Jacob came to his father **I** at Mamre,
35:27 where Abraham and **I** had resided as aliens.
35:28 Now the days of **I** were one hundred eighty years.
35:29 And **I** breathed his last; he died
46: 1 he offered sacrifices to the God of his father **I**.
48:15 before whom my ancestors Abraham and **I** walked,
48:16 and the name of my ancestors Abraham and **I**;
49:31 there **I** and his wife Rebekah were buried;
50:24 to the land that he swore to Abraham, to **I**,
Ex 2:24 God remembered his covenant with Abraham, **I**,
3: 6 the God of **I**, and the God of Jacob."
3:15 the God of **I**, and the God of Jacob,
3:16 of **I**, and of Jacob, has appeared to me, saying:
4: 5 the God of **I**, and the God of Jacob,
6: 3 I appeared to Abraham, **I**,
6: 8 **I**, and Jacob; I will give it to you for a possession.
32:13 Remember Abraham, **I**, and Israel, your servants,
33: 1 to the land of which I swore to Abraham, **I**,
Lev 26:42 also my covenant with **I** and also my covenant
Nu 32:11 to **I**, and to Jacob, because they have
Dt 1: 8 to Abraham, to **I**, and to Jacob,
6:10 to Abraham, to **I**, and to Jacob, to give you—
9: 5 to Abraham, to **I**, and to Jacob.
9:27 Remember your servants, Abraham, **I**, and Jacob;
29:13 to Abraham, to **I**, and to Jacob.
30:20 to Abraham, to **I**, and to Jacob.
34: 4 to **I**, and to Jacob, saying,
Jos 24: 3 and made his offspring many. I gave him **I**;
24: 4 and to **I** I gave Jacob and Esau.
1Ki 18:36 "O LORD, God of Abraham, **I**, and Israel,
2Ki 13:23 **I**, and Jacob, and would not destroy them;
1Ch 1:28 The sons of Abraham: **I** and Ishmael.
1:34 Abraham became the father of **I**.
1:34 The sons of **I**: Esau and Israel.
16:16 with Abraham, his sworn promise to **I**,
29:18 O LORD, the God of Abraham, **I**, and Israel,
2Ch 30: 6 return to the LORD, the God of Abraham, **I**,
Ps 105: 9 with Abraham, his sworn promise to **I**,
Jer 33:26 as rulers over the offspring of Abraham, **I**,
Am 7: 9 the high places of **I** shall be made desolate,
7:16 and do not preach against the house of **I**.'
Mt 1: 2 Abraham was the father of **I**, and **I** the father of
Jacob,
8:11 with Abraham and **I** and Jacob in the kingdom
22:32 the God of **I**, and the God of Jacob'?
Mk 12:26 'I am the God of Abraham, the God of **I**,
Lk 3:34 son of **I**, son of Abraham, son of Terah,
13:28 of teeth when you see Abraham and **I** and Jacob
20:37 the God of **I**, and the God of Jacob.
Ac 3:13 The God of Abraham, the God of **I**,
7: 8 of **I** and circumcised him on the eighth day;
7: 8 and **I** became the father of Jacob,
7:32 the God of Abraham, **I**, and Jacob.'
Ro 9: 7 through **I** that descendants shall be named
9:10 by one husband, our ancestor **I**.
Gal 4:28 my friends, are children of the promise, like **I**.
Heb 11: 9 living in tents, as did **I** and Jacob,
11:17 when put to the test, offered up **I**.
11:18 "It is through **I** that descendants shall be named
11:20 By faith **I** invoked blessings for the future
Jas 2:21 by works when he offered his son **I** on the altar?
Tob 4:12 Remember, my son, that Noah, Abraham, **I**,
Jdt 8:26 and how he tested **I**, and what happened to Jacob
Sir 44:22 To **I** also he gave the same assurance for the sake
51:12 *Give thanks to the rock of* ***I***,
Bar 2:34 **I**, and Jacob, and they will rule over it;
Aza 1:12 of your servant **I** and Israel your holy one,
2Mc 1: 2 with Abraham and **I** and Jacob.
Man 1: 1 and **I** and Jacob and of their righteous offspring;
1: 8 for Abraham and **I** and Jacob,
2Es 1:39 **I**, and Jacob, and Hosea and Amos and Micah
3:15 you gave him **I**, and to **I** you gave Jacob and Esau.
6: 8 He said to me, "From Abraham to **I**,
4Mc 7:14 of **I** he rendered the many-headed rack ineffective.
7:19 like our patriarchs Abraham and **I** and Jacob,
13:12 the father by whose hand **I** would have submitted
13:17 Abraham and **I** and Jacob will welcome us,
16:20 to sacrifice his son **I**, the ancestor of our nation;
16:20 and when **I** saw his father's hand wielding a knife
16:25 as do Abraham and **I** and Jacob and all
18:11 and **I** who was offered as a burnt offering,

ISAAC'S (4) [ISAAC]

Ge 26:19 which **I** servants dug in the valley and found there
26:20 the herders of Gerar quarreled with **I** herders,
26:25 And there **I** servants dug a well.
26:32 That same day **I** servants came and told him about

ISAIAH‡ (59) [ISAIAH'S]

2Ki 19: 2 to the prophet **I** son of Amoz.
19: 5 When the servants of King Hezekiah came to **I**,
19: 6 **I** said to them, "Say to your master, 'Thus says
19:20 Then **I** son of Amoz sent to Hezekiah, saying,
20: 1 The prophet **I** son of Amoz came to him,
20: 4 Before **I** had gone out of the middle court,
20: 7 Then **I** said, "Bring a lump of figs.
20: 8 Hezekiah said to **I**, "What shall be the sign that
20: 9 **I** said, "This is the sign to you from the LORD,
20:11 The prophet **I** cried to the LORD;
20:14 Then the prophet **I** came to King Hezekiah,
20:16 **I** said to Hezekiah, "Hear the word of the LORD:
20:19 Then Hezekiah said to **I**, "The word of
2Ch 26:22 the prophet **I** son of Amoz wrote.
32:20 the prophet **I** son of Amoz prayed because of this
32:32 in the vision of the prophet **I** son of Amoz in
Isa 1: 1 The vision of **I** son of Amoz,
2: 1 that **I** son of Amoz saw concerning Judah
7: 3 Then the LORD said to **I**, Go out to meet Ahaz,
7:13 Then **I** said: "Hear then, O house of David!
13: 1 concerning Babylon that **I** son of Amoz saw.

Isa 20: 2 at that time the LORD had spoken to I son
20: 3 as my servant I has walked naked and barefoot
37: 2 to the prophet I son of Amoz.
37: 5 When the servants of King Hezekiah came to I,
37: 6 I said to them, "Say to your master, 'Thus says
37:21 Then I son of Amoz sent to Hezekiah, saying:
38: 1 The prophet I son of Amoz came to him,
38: 4 Then the word of the LORD came to I:
38:21 Now I had said, "Let them take a lump of figs,
39: 3 prophet I came to King Hezekiah and said to him,
39: 5 Then I said to Hezekiah, "Hear the word of
39: 8 Then Hezekiah said to I, "The word of
Mt 3: 3 the prophet I spoke when he said, "The voice
4:14 through the prophet I might be fulfilled:
8:17 fulfill what had been spoken through the prophet I,
12:17 fulfill what had been spoken through the prophet I:
13:14 With them indeed is fulfilled the prophecy of I
15: 7 I prophesied rightly about you when he said:
Mk 1: 2 As it is written in the prophet I, "See,
7: 6 "I prophesied rightly about you hypocrites,
Lk 3: 4 the book of the words of the prophet I, "The voice
4:17 and the scroll of the prophet I was given to him.
Jn 1:23 the way of the Lord,' " as the prophet I said.
12:38 to fulfill the word spoken by the prophet I:
12:39 And so they could not believe, because I also said,
12:41 I said this because he saw his glory and spoke
Ac 8:28 seated in his chariot, he was reading the prophet I.
8:30 up to it and heard him reading the prophet I.
28:25 in saying to your ancestors through the prophet I,
Ro 9:27 And I cries out concerning Israel,
9:29 And as I predicted, "If the Lord of hosts had
10:16 for I says, "Lord, who has believed our message?"
10:20 Then I is so bold as to say,
15:12 and again I says, "The root of Jesse shall come,
Sir 48:20 and delivered them through I.
48:22 as he was commanded by the prophet I,
2Es 2:18 I will send you help, my servants I and Jeremiah.
4Mc 18:14 He reminded you of the scripture of I, which says,

ISAIAH'S (1) [ISAIAH]

Sir 48:23 In I days the sun went backward,

ISCAH (1)

Ge 11:29 the daughter of Haran the father of Milcah and I.

ISCARIOT (11) [JUDAS]

Mt 10: 4 and Judas I, the one who betrayed him.
26:14 Then one of the twelve, who was called Judas I,
Mk 3:19 and Judas I, who betrayed him.
14:10 Then Judas I, who was one of the twelve,
Lk 6:16 and Judas I, who became a traitor.
22: 3 Then Satan entered into Judas called I,
Jn 6:71 He was speaking of Judas son of Simon I, for he,
12: 4 But Judas I, one of his disciples (the one who was
13: 2 the heart of Judas son of Simon I to betray him.
13:26 he gave it to Judas son of Simon I.
14:22 Judas (not I) said to him, "Lord,

ISDAEL (1)

1Es 5:33 the descendants of Lozon, the descendants of I,

ISH See Index to Footnotes

ISH-BOSHETH (KJV) See ISHBAAL; See also Index to Footnotes

ISH-HAI See Index to Footnotes

ISHBAAL‡ (14) [=ESH-BAAL]

2Sa 2: 8 had taken I son of Saul,
2:10 I, Saul's son, was forty years old when he began
2:12 and the servants of I son of Saul,
2:15 twelve for Benjamin and I son of Saul,
3: 7 And I said to Abner, "Why have you gone in
3: 8 The words of I made Abner very angry;
3:11 And I could not answer Abner another word,
3:14 Then David sent messengers to Saul's son I,
3:15 I sent and took her from her husband Paltiel
4: 1 Saul's son I heard that Abner had died at Hebron,
4: 5 the heat of the day they came to the house of I,
4: 8 They brought the head of I to David at Hebron
4: 8 "Here is the head of I, son of Saul, your enemy,
4:12 But the head of I they took and buried in the tomb

ISHBAH (1)

1Ch 4:17 Shammai, and I father of Eshtemoa.

ISHBAK (2)

Ge 25: 2 She bore him Zimran, Jokshan, Medan, Midian, I,
1Ch 1:32 she bore Zimran, Jokshan, Medan, Midian, I,

ISHBI-BENOB (1)

2Sa 21:16 I, one of the descendants of the giants,

ISHHOD (1)

1Ch 7:18 And his sister Hammolecheth bore I, Abiezer,

ISHI (5)

1Ch 2:31 The son of Appaim: I. The son of I: Sheshan.
4:20 The sons of I: Zoheth and Ben-zoheth.
4:42 Neariah, Rephaiah, and Uzziel, sons of I;
5:24 These were the heads of their clans: Epher, I,

ISHIAH (KJV) See ISSHIAH

ISHMA (1)

1Ch 4: 3 These were the sons of Etam: Jezreel, I,

ISHMAEL (48) [ISHMAEL'S, ISHMAELITE, ISHMAELITES]

Ge 16:11 you shall call him I, for the LORD has given heed
16:15 and Abram named his son, whom Hagar bore, I.
16:16 Abram was eighty-six years old when Hagar bore him I.
17:18 "O that I might live in your sight!"
17:20 As for I, I have heard you;
17:23 Then Abraham took his son I and all
17:25 And his son I was thirteen years old
17:26 and his son I were circumcised;
25: 9 and I buried him in the cave of Machpelah,
25:12 These are the descendants of I, Abraham's son,
25:13 These are the names of the sons of I,
25:13 Nebaioth, the firstborn of I;
25:16 These are the sons of I and these are their names,
25:17 (This is the length of the life of I,
28: 9 Esau went to I and took Mahalath daughter of Abraham's son I,
2Ki 25:23 I son of Nethaniah, Johanan son of Kareah,
25:25 I son of Nethaniah son of Elishama,
1Ch 1:28 The sons of Abraham: Isaac and I.
1:29 the firstborn of I, Nebaioth;
1:31 These are the sons of I.
8:38 Azrikam, Bocheru, I, Sheariah, Obadiah,
9:44 Azrikam, Bocheru, I, Sheariah, Obadiah,
2Ch 19:11 and Zebadiah son of I, the governor of the house
23: 1 Azariah son of Jeroham, I son of Jehohanan,
Ezr 10:22 Elioenai, Maaseiah, I, Nethanel, Jozabad,
Jer 40: 8 I son of Nethaniah, Johanan son of Kareah,
40:14 that Baalis king of the Ammonites has sent I son
40:15 "Please let me go and kill I son of Nethaniah,
40:16 for you are telling a lie about I."
41: 1 I son of Nethaniah son of Elishama,
41: 2 I son of Nethaniah and the ten men with him got
41: 3 I also killed all the Judeans who were
41: 6 And I son of Nethaniah came out from Mizpah
41: 7 I son of Nethaniah and the men
41: 8 there were ten men among them who said to I,
41: 9 the cistern into which I had thrown all the bodies
41: 9 I son of Nethaniah filled that cistern
41:10 Then I took captive all the rest of
41:10 I son of Nethaniah took them captive and set out
41:11 of all the crimes that I son of Nethaniah had done,
41:12 and went to fight against I son of Nethaniah.
41:13 the people who were with I saw Johanan son
41:14 So all the people whom I had carried away captive
41:15 But I son of Nethaniah escaped from Johanan
41:16 the rest of the people whom I son
41:18 for they were afraid of them, because I son
1Es 9:22 Elioenai, Maaseiah, I, and Nathanael,

ISHMAEL'S (1) [ISHMAEL]

Ge 36: 3 and Basemath, I daughter, sister of Nebaioth.

ISHMAELITE (3) [ISHMAEL]

2Sa 17:25 Amasa was the son of a man named Ithra the I,
1Ch 2:17 and the father of Amasa was Jether the I.
27:30 Over the camels was Obil the I.

ISHMAELITES (7) [ISHMAEL]

Ge 37:25 up they saw a caravan of I coming from Gilead,
37:27 Come, let us sell him to the I,
37:28 and sold him to the I for twenty pieces of silver.
39: 1 from the I who had brought him down there.
Jdg 8:24 enemy had golden earrings, because they were I.)
Ps 83: 6 the tents of Edom and the I,
Jdt 2:23 the Rassisites and the I on the border of the desert,

ISHMAIAH (2)

1Ch 12: 4 I of Gibeon, a warrior among the Thirty and
27:19 for Zebulun, I son of Obadiah;

ISHMEELITE, ISHMEELITES (KJV) See ISHMAELITE, ISHMAELITES

ISHMERAI (1)

1Ch 8:18 I, Izliah, and Jobab were the sons of Elpaal.

ISHOD (KJV) See ISHHOD

ISHPAH (1)

1Ch 8:16 Michael, I, and Joha were sons of Beriah.

ISHPAN (1)

1Ch 8:22 I, Eber, Eliel,

ISHSHAH See Index to Footnotes

ISHTOB (KJV) See MEN OF TOB

ISHUAH (KJV) See ISHVAH

ISHUAI, ISHUI (KJV) See ISHVI

ISHVAH (2)

Ge 46:17 Imnah, I, Ishvi, Beriah, and their sister Serah.
1Ch 7:30 Imnah, I, Ishvi, Beriah, and their sister Serah.

ISHVI (4) [ISHVITES]

Ge 46:17 Imnah, Ishvah, I, Beriah, and their sister Serah.
Nu 26:44 of I, the clan of the Ishvites;
1Sa 14:49 sons of Saul were Jonathan, I, and Malchishua;
1Ch 7:30 Imnah, Ishvah, I, Beriah, and their sister Serah.

ISHVITES (1) [ISHVI]

Nu 26:44 of Ishvi, the clan of the I;

ISLAND (10) [ISLANDS, ISLES]

Ac 13: 6 When they had gone through the whole i as far
27:16 of a small i called Cauda we were scarcely able
27:26 But we will have to run aground on some i."
28: 1 we then learned that the i was called Malta.
28: 7 to the leading man of the i,
28: 9 of the people on the i who had diseases also came
28:11 on a ship that had wintered at the i,
Rev 1: 9 on the i called Patmos because of the word of God
6:14 every mountain and i was removed from its place.
16:20 And every i fled away, and no mountains were to

ISLANDS (9) [ISLAND]

Est 10: 1 on the land and on the i of the sea.
Isa 42:15 I will turn the rivers into i, and dry up the pools.
Zep 2:11 each in its place, all the coasts and i of the nations.
Sir 43:23 By his plan he stilled the deep and planted i in it.
47:16 Your fame reached to far-off i,
1Mc 6:29 also came to him from other kingdoms and from i
8:11 The remaining kingdoms and i,
11:38 the foreign troops that he had recruited from the i
15: 1 sent a letter from the i of the sea to Simon,

ISLES (3) [ISLAND]

Ps 72:10 of Tarshish and of the i render him tribute,
Isa 40:15 see, he takes up the i like fine dust.
1Mc 14: 5 and opened a way to the i of the sea.

ISMACHIAH (1)

2Ch 31:13 Asahel, Jerimoth, Jozabad, Eliel, I, Mahath,

ISMAIAH (KJV) See ISHMAIAH

ISOLATE (1)

1Mc 12:36 to i it so that its garrison could neither buy

ISPAH (KJV) See ISHPAH

ISRAEL‡ (2290) [EL-ELOHE-ISRAEL, ISRAEL'S, ISRAELITE, ISRAELITES, ISRAELITES', =JACOB]

A. *GOD OF ISRAEL (226)
B. PEOPLE OF ISRAEL (209)
C. ALL ISRAEL (166)
D. HOUSE OF ISRAEL (160)
E. PEOPLE ISRAEL (85)
F. KING OF ISRAEL (82)
G. TRIBES OF ISRAEL (53)
H. KINGS OF ISRAEL (42)
I. LAND OF ISRAEL (35)
J. ELDERS OF ISRAEL (33)
K. KING OVER [ALL] ISRAEL (29)
L. MEN OF ISRAEL (24)
M. ISRAEL AND JUDAH (21)
N. MOUNTAINS OF ISRAEL (16)
O. ASSEMBLY OF ISRAEL (14)
P. SONS OF ISRAEL (14)
Q. CONGREGATION OF ISRAEL (13)
R. JUDAH AND ISRAEL (8)

Ge 32:28 "You shall no longer be called Jacob, but I,
34: 7 because he had committed an outrage in I by lying
35:10 but I shall be your name."
35:10 So he was called I.
35:21 I journeyed on, and pitched his tent beyond
35:22 While I lived in that land,
35:22 Bilhah his father's concubine; and I heard of it.
37: 3 Now I loved Joseph more than any other
37:13 And I said to Joseph, "Are
42: 5 the sons of I were among the other people P
43: 6 I said, "Why did you treat me so badly as to tell
43: 8 Then Judah said to his father I,
43:11 Then their father I said to them, "If it must be so,
45:21 The sons of I did so. P
45:28 I said, "Enough! My son Joseph is still alive.
46: 1 When I set out on his journey with all that he had
46: 2 God spoke to I in visions of the night, and said,
46: 5 and the sons of I carried their father Jacob, P
46:28 I sent Judah ahead to Joseph to lead the way
46:29 and went up to meet his father I in Goshen.
46:30 I said to Joseph, "I can die now,
47:27 Thus I settled in the land of Egypt,
47:31 Then I bowed himself on the head of his bed.

Ge 48: 8 **I** saw Joseph's sons, he said, "Who are these?"
48:10 Now the eyes of **I** were dim with age,
48:11 **I** said to Joseph, "I did not expect to see your face;
48:14 But **I** stretched out his right hand and laid it on
48:20 saying, "By you **I** will invoke blessings, saying,
48:21 Then **I** said to Joseph, "I am about to die,
49: 2 of Jacob; listen to **I** your father.
49: 7 I will divide them in Jacob, and scatter them in **I.**
49:16 as one of the tribes of **I.** G
49:24 by the name of the Shepherd, the Rock of **I,**
49:28 All these are the twelve tribes of **I,** G
50: 2 So the physicians embalmed **I;**
Ex 1: 1 the sons of **I** who came to Egypt with Jacob, P
3:16 Go and assemble the elders of **I,** and say to them, J
3:18 elders of **I** shall go to the king of Egypt and say J
4:22 'Thus says the LORD: **I** is my firstborn son.
5: 1 "Thus says the LORD, the God of **I,** A
5: 2 that I should heed him and let **I** go?
5: 2 I do not know the LORD, and I will not let **I** go."
6:14 the sons of Reuben, the firstborn of **I:**
9: 4 the livestock of **I** and the livestock of Egypt,
11: 7 a distinction between Egypt and **I.**
11:10 he did not let the people of **I** go out of his land. B
12: 3 congregation of **I** that on the tenth of this month Q
12: 6 congregation of **I** shall slaughter it at twilight. Q
12:15 until the seventh day shall be cut off from **I.**
12:19 be cut off from the congregation of **I,** Q
12:21 Moses called all the elders of **I** and said to them, J
12:47 The whole congregation of **I** shall celebrate it. Q
14: 5 "What have we done, letting **I** leave our service?"
14:20 between the army of Egypt and the army of **I.**
14:30 the LORD saved **I** that day from the Egyptians;
14:30 and **I** saw the Egyptians dead on the seashore.
14:31 **I** saw the great work that the LORD did against
15:22 Then Moses ordered **I** to set out from the Red Sea,
16: 1 and **I** came to the wilderness of Sin,
16:31 The house of **I** called it manna; D
17: 5 and take some of the elders of **I** with you; J
17: 6 Moses did so, in the sight of the elders of **I.** J
17: 8 Amalek came and fought with **I** at Rephidim.
17:11 Whenever Moses held up his hand, **I** prevailed;
18: 1 God had done for Moses and for his people **I,** E
18: 1 how the LORD had brought **I** out of Egypt.
18: 9 for all the good that the LORD had done to **I,**
18:12 elders of **I** to eat bread with Moses' father-in-law J
18:25 from all **I** and appointed them as heads over C
19: 2 **I** camped there in front of the mountain.
24: 1 and Abihu, and seventy of the elders of **I,** J
24: 4 corresponding to the twelve tribes of **I.** G
24: 5 He sent young men of the people of **I,** B
24: 9 Abihu, and seventy of the elders of **I** went up, J
24:10 and they saw the God of **I.** A
24:11 on the chief men of the people of **I;** B
24:17 of the mountain in the sight of the people of **I.** B
28: 9 and engrave on them the names of the sons of **I,** P
28:11 the two stones with the names of the sons of **I;** P
28:12 as stones of remembrance for the sons of **I;** P
28:21 to the names of the sons of **I;** P
28:29 So Aaron shall bear the names of the sons of **I** P
31:17 a sign forever between me and the people of **I** B
32: 4 and they said, "These are your gods, O **I,**
32: 8 and said, 'These are your gods, O **I,**
32:13 Remember Abraham, Isaac, and **I,** your servants,
32:27 the God of **I,** 'Put your sword on your side, A
34:23 before the LORD God, the God of **I.** A
34:27 a covenant with you and with **I.**
39: 6 according to the names of the sons of **I.** P
39: 7 to be stones of remembrance for the sons of **I;** P
39:14 to the names of the sons of **I;** P
40:38 all the house of **I** at each stage of their journey. D
Lev 1: 2 Speak to the people of **I** and say to them: B
4: 2 Speak to the people of **I,** saying: B
4:13 the whole congregation of **I** errs unintentionally Q
7:23 Speak to the people of **I,** saying: B
7:29 Speak to the people of **I,** saying: B
7:34 the thigh that is offered, from the people of **I,** B
7:34 as a perpetual due from the people of **I.** B
7:36 the people of **I** throughout their generations. B
7:38 people of **I** to bring their offerings to the LORD, B
9: 1 and his sons and the elders of **I.** J
9: 3 And say to the people of **I,** B
10: 6 but your kindred, the whole house of **I,** D
10:11 you are to teach the people of **I** all the statutes B
10:14 of the offerings of well-being of the people of **I.** B
11: 2 Speak to the people of **I,** saying: B
12: 2 Speak to the people of **I,** saying: B
15: 2 Speak to the people of **I** and say to them: B
15:31 the people of **I** separate from their uncleanness, B
16: 5 congregation of the people of **I** two male goats B
16:16 because of the uncleannesses of the people of **I,** B
16:17 and for his house and for all the assembly of **I.** O
16:19 from the uncleannesses of the people of **I.** B
16:21 over it all the iniquities of the people of **I,** B
16:34 the people of **I** once in the year for all their sins. B
17: 2 to Aaron and his sons and to all the people of **I** B
17: 3 house of **I** slaughters an ox or a lamb or a goat D
17: 5 the people of **I** may bring their sacrifices that B
17: 8 of the house of **I** or of the aliens who reside D
17:10 of the house of **I** or of the aliens who reside D
17:12 Therefore I have said to the people of **I:** B
17:13 And anyone of the people of **I,** B
17:14 therefore I have said to the people of **I:** B
18: 2 Speak to the people of **I** and say to them: B
19: 2 all the congregation of the people of **I** and say B
20: 2 Say further to the people of **I:** B
20: 2 Any of the people of **I,** or of the aliens who B
20: 2 or of the aliens who reside in **I,**

Lev 21:24 Aaron and to his sons and to all the people of **I.** B
22: 2 the people of **I,** which they dedicate to me, B
22: 3 which the people of **I** dedicate to the LORD, B
22:15 the sacred donations of the people of **I,** B
22:18 to Aaron and his sons and all the people of **I** B
22:18 the house of **I** or of the aliens residing in Israel D
22:18 or of the aliens residing in **I** presents an offering,
22:32 that I may be sanctified among the people of **I:** B
23: 2 Speak to the people of **I** and say to them: B
23:10 Speak to the people of **I** and say to them: B
23:24 Speak to the people of **I,** saying: B
23:34 Speak to the people of **I,** saying: B
23:42 all that are citizens in **I** shall live in booths,
23:43 people of **I** live in booths when I brought them B
23:44 to the people of **I** the appointed festivals of B
24: 2 Command the people of **I** to bring you pure oil B
24: 8 as a commitment of the people of **I,** B
24:10 an Egyptian came out among the people of **I;** B
24:15 And speak to the people of **I,** saying: B
24:23 Moses spoke thus to the people of **I;** B
24:23 people of **I** did as the LORD had commanded B
25: 2 Speak to the people of **I** and say to them: B
25:33 are their possession among the people of **I.** B
25:55 For to me the people of **I** are servants; B
26:46 the people of **I** on Mount Sinai through Moses. B
27: 2 Speak to the people of **I** and say to them: B
27:34 that the LORD gave to Moses for the people of **I** B
Nu 1: 3 everyone in **I** able to go to war.
1:16 the heads of the divisions of **I.**
1:44 with the help of the leaders of **I,**
1:45 everyone able to go to war in **I**—
3:13 I consecrated for my own all the firstborn in **I,**
4:46 and Aaron and the leaders of **I** enrolled,
7: 2 the leaders of **I,** heads of their ancestral houses,
7:84 when it was anointed, from the leaders of **I:**
10: 4 then the leaders, the heads of the tribes of **I,** G
10:29 for the LORD has promised good to **I.**"
10:36 O LORD of the ten thousand thousands of **I.**"
11:16 "Gather for me seventy of the elders of **I,** J
11:30 Moses and the elders of **I** returned to the camp. J
16: 9 that the God of **I** has separated you from A
16: 9 from the congregation of **I,** Q
16:25 the elders of **I** followed him. J
16:34 All **I** around them fled at their outcry, C
18:14 Every devoted thing in **I** shall be yours.
18:21 To the Levites I have given every tithe in **I** for
19:13 such persons shall be cut off from **I.**
20:13 where the people of **I** quarreled with the LORD, B
20:14 "Thus says your brother **I:**
20:21 to give **I** passage through their territory;
20:21 so **I** turned away from them.
20:29 all the house of **I** mourned for Aaron thirty days. D
21: 1 heard that **I** was coming by the way of Atharim,
21: 1 against **I** and took some of them captive.
21: 2 Then **I** made a vow to the LORD and said,
21: 3 The LORD listened to the voice of **I,**
21:17 Then **I** sang this song: "Spring up,
21:21 **I** sent messengers to King Sihon of the Amorites,
21:23 not allow **I** to pass through his territory.
21:23 and went out against **I** to the wilderness;
21:23 he came to Jahaz, and fought against **I.**
21:24 **I** put him to the sword, and took possession
21:25 **I** took all these towns, and Israel settled in all
21:25 and **I** settled in all the towns of the Amorites,
21:31 Thus **I** settled in the land of the Amorites.
22: 2 of Zippor saw all that **I** had done to the Amorites.
22: 3 Moab was overcome with fear of the people of **I.** B
22:41 from there he could see part of the people of **I.** B
23: 7 for me; Come, denounce **I!**'
23:10 or number the dust-cloud of **I?**
23:21 nor has he seen trouble in **I.**
23:23 against Jacob, no divination against **I;**
23:23 now it shall be said of Jacob and **I,**
24: 1 Balaam saw that it pleased the LORD to bless **I,**
24: 2 Balaam looked up and saw **I** camping tribe
24: 5 O Jacob, your encampments, O **I!**
24:17 and a scepter shall rise out of **I;**
24:18 a possession of its enemies, while **I** does valiantly.
25: 1 While **I** was staying at Shittim,
25: 3 Thus **I** yoked itself to the Baal of Peor,
25: 3 and the LORD's anger was kindled against **I.**
25: 4 of the LORD may turn away from **I.**"
25: 5 And Moses said to the judges of **I,**
25: 8 the plague was stopped among the people of **I.** B
26: 2 everyone in **I** able to go to war."
26: 5 Reuben, the firstborn of **I.**
31: 4 thousand from each of the tribes of **I** to the war." G
31: 5 So out of the thousands of **I,**
32: 4 the LORD subdued before the congregation of **I** Q
32:13 And the LORD's anger was kindled against **I,**
32:14 to increase the LORD's fierce anger against **I!**
32:22 and be free of obligation to the LORD and to **I,**
Dt 1: 1 that Moses spoke to all **I** beyond the Jordan— C
2:12 as **I** has done in the land that
4: 1 now, **I,** give heed to the statutes and ordinances
5: 1 Moses convened all **I,** and said to them: C
5: 1 Hear, O **I,** the statutes and ordinances
6: 3 Hear therefore, O **I,** and observe them diligently,
6: 4 O **I:** The LORD is our God, the LORD alone.
9: 1 O **I!** You are about to cross
10:12 now, O **I,** what does the LORD your God require
11: 6 in the midst of all **I** the earth opened its mouth C
13:11 Then all **I** shall hear and be afraid, C
17: 4 that such an abhorrent thing has occurred in **I,**
17:12 So you shall purge the evil from **I.**
17:20 descendants may reign long over his kingdom in **I.**
18: 1 shall have no allotment or inheritance within **I.**

Dt 18: 6 from wherever he has been residing in **I,**
19:13 you shall purge the guilt of innocent blood from **I,**
20: 3 and shall say to them: "Hear, O **I!**
21: 8 Absolve, O LORD, your people **I,** E
21: 8 in the midst of your people **I.**" E
21:21 and all **I** will hear, and be afraid. C
22:19 because he has slandered a virgin of **I.**
22:21 in **I** by prostituting herself in her father's house.
22:22 So you shall purge the evil from **I.**
23:17 of the daughters of **I** shall be a temple prostitute;
23:17 none of the sons of **I** shall be a temple prostitute. P
25: 6 so that his name may not be blotted out of **I.**
25: 7 to perpetuate his brother's name in **I;**
25:10 Throughout **I** his family shall be known as
26:15 and bless your people **I** and the ground E
27: 1 the elders of **I** charged all the people as follows: J
27: 9 Moses and the levitical priests spoke to all **I,** C
27: 9 Keep silence and hear, O **I!**
29: 2 Moses summoned all **I** and said to them: C
29:10 your elders, and your officials, all the men of **I,** L
29:21 from all the tribes of **I** for calamity, G
31: 1 had finished speaking all these words to all **I,** C
31: 7 and said to him in the sight of all **I:** C
31: 9 and to all the elders of **I.** J
31:11 when all **I** comes to appear before C
31:11 shall read this law before all **I** in their hearing. C
31:30 in the hearing of the whole assembly of **I:** O
32:45 had finished reciting all these words to all **I,** C
33: 5 of the people assembled—the united tribes of **I.** G
33:10 They teach Jacob your ordinances, and **I** your law;
33:21 the justice of the LORD, and his ordinances for **I.**
33:28 So **I** lives in safety, untroubled is Jacob's abode in
33:29 Happy are you, O **I!**
34:10 since has there arisen a prophet in **I** like Moses,
34:12 that Moses performed in the sight of all **I.** C
Jos 3: 7 to exalt you in the sight of all **I,** C
3:12 So now select twelve men from the tribes of **I,** G
3:17 While all **I** were crossing over on dry ground, C
4:14 the LORD exalted Joshua in the sight of all **I;** C
4:22 '**I** crossed over the Jordan here on dry ground.'
6:18 and make the camp of **I** an object for destruction,
6:23 and set them outside the camp of **I.**
6:25 Her family has lived in **I** ever since.
7: 6 he and the elders of **I;** J
7: 8 now that **I** has turned their backs to their enemies!
7:11 **I** has sinned; they have transgressed my covenant
7:13 for thus says the LORD, the God of **I,** A
7:13 "There are devoted things among you, O **I;**
7:15 and for having done an outrageous thing in **I.**' "
7:16 and brought **I** near tribe by tribe,
7:19 the LORD God of **I** and make confession to him. A
7:20 the one who sinned against the LORD God of **I.** A
7:24 and all **I** with him took Achan son of Zerah, C
7:25 And all **I** stoned him to death; C
8:10 with the elders of **I,** before the people to Ai. J
8:14 to the meeting place facing the Arabah to meet **I**
8:15 and all **I** made a pretense of being beaten C
8:17 in Ai or Bethel who did not go out after **I;**
8:17 they left the city open, and pursued **I.**
8:21 and all **I** saw that the ambush had taken the city C
8:22 on the other; and **I** struck them down
8:24 When **I** had finished slaughtering all
8:24 all **I** returned to Ai, and attacked it with C
8:27 Only the livestock and the spoil of that city **I** took
8:30 an altar to the LORD, the God of **I,** A
8:33 All **I,** alien as well as citizen, C
8:33 that they should bless the people of **I.** B
8:35 not read before all the assembly of **I,** O
9: 2 with one accord to fight Joshua and **I.**
9:18 to them by the LORD, the God of **I.** A
9:19 the God of **I,** and now we must not touch them. A
10: 1 the inhabitants of Gibeon had made peace with **I**
10:10 And the LORD threw them into a panic before **I,**
10:11 As they fled before **I,** while they were going down
10:12 and he said in the sight of **I,** "Sun,
10:14 for the LORD fought for **I.**
10:15 Then Joshua returned, and all **I** with him, C
10:29 and all **I** with him, to Libnah, C
10:30 also and its king into the hand of **I;**
10:31 all **I** with him, to Lachish, and laid siege to it, C
10:32 The LORD gave Lachish into the hand of **I,**
10:34 From Lachish Joshua passed on with all **I** C
10:36 Joshua went up with all **I** from Eglon to Hebron; C
10:38 with all **I,** turned back to Debir and assaulted it, C
10:40 as the LORD God of **I** commanded. A
10:42 because the LORD God of **I** fought for Israel. A
10:42 because the LORD God of Israel fought for **I.**
10:43 Then Joshua returned, and all **I** with him, C
11: 5 at the waters of Merom, to fight with **I.**
11: 6 over all of them, slain, to **I;**
11: 8 And the LORD handed them over to **I,**
11:13 But **I** burned none of the towns that stood
11:16 and the hill country of **I** and its lowland,
11:20 so that they would come against **I** in battle,
11:21 and from all the hill country of **I;**
11:23 and Joshua gave it for an inheritance to **I**
12: 7 to the tribes of **I** as a possession according to G
13: 6 only allot the land to **I** for an inheritance,
13:13 but Geshur and Maacath live within **I** to this day.
13:14 to the LORD God of **I** are their inheritance, A
13:33 the LORD God of **I** is their inheritance, A
14:10 while **I** was journeying through the wilderness;
14:14 the LORD, the God of **I.** A
21:43 to **I** all the land that he swore to their ancestors
21:45 the LORD had made to the house of **I** had failed; D
22:12 And when the people of **I** heard of it, B
22:14 one from each of the tribal families of **I,**

Jos 22:14 of them the head of a family among the clans of I.
22:16 against the God of I in turning away today A
22:18 with the whole congregation of I tomorrow. Q
22:20 and wrath fell upon all the congregation of I? Q
22:21 in answer to the heads of the families of I,
22:22 He knows; and let I itself know!
22:24 to do with the LORD, the God of I? A
22:30 the heads of the families of I who were with him,
23: 1 to I from all their enemies all around,
23: 2 Joshua summoned all I, their elders C
24: 1 Joshua gathered all the tribes of I to Shechem, G
24: 1 the heads, the judges, and the officers of I;
24: 2 "Thus says the LORD, the God of I: A
24: 9 set out to fight against I.
24:23 to the LORD, the God of I." A
24:31 I served the LORD all the days of Joshua,
24:31 the work that the LORD did for I.
Jdg 1:28 When I grew strong, they put the Canaanites
2: 7 the great work that the LORD had done for I.
2:10 the LORD or the work that he had done for I.
2:14 So the anger of the LORD was kindled against I,
2:20 So the anger of the LORD was kindled against I;
2:22 to test I, whether or not they would take care
3: 1 in I who had no experience of any war in Canaan
3: 4 for the testing of I, to know whether I would obey
3: 8 the anger of the LORD was kindled against I,
3:10 of the LORD came upon him, and he judged I;
3:12 against I, because they had done what was evil in
3:13 and the Amalekites, he went and defeated I;
3:30 Moab was subdued that day under the hand of I.
3:31 with an oxgoad. He too delivered I.
4: 4 a prophetess, wife of Lappidoth, was judging I.
4: 6 "The LORD, the God of I, commands you, 'Go, A
5: 2 in I, when the people offer themselves willingly—
5: 3 I will make melody to the LORD, the God of I. A
5: 5 the One of Sinai, before the LORD, the God of I. A
5: 7 The peasantry prospered in I,
5: 7 Deborah, arose as a mother in I.
5: 8 or spear to be seen among forty thousand in I?
5: 9 of I who offered themselves willingly among
5:11 the triumphs of his peasantry in I.
6: 2 The hand of Midian prevailed over I;
6: 4 and leave no sustenance in I,
6: 6 Thus I was greatly impoverished because
6: 8 "Thus says the LORD, the God of I: A
6:14 in this might of yours and deliver I from the hand
6:15 He responded, "But sir, how can I deliver I?
6:36 to see whether you will deliver I by my hand,
6:37 I shall know that you will deliver I by my hand,
7: 2 I would only take the credit away from me,
7: 8 and he sent all the rest of I back to their own tents,
7:14 the sword of Gideon son of Joash, a man of I;
7:15 he returned to the camp of I, and said, "Get up;
7:23 the men of I were called out from Naphtali L
8:27 and all I prostituted themselves to it there, C
8:35 in return for all the good that he had done to I.
9:22 Abimelech ruled over I three years.
10: 1 in the hill country of Ephraim, rose to deliver I.
10: 2 He judged I twenty-three years.
10: 3 who judged I twenty-two years.
10: 7 So the anger of the LORD was kindled against I,
10: 9 so that I was greatly distressed.
10:16 and he could no longer bear to see I suffer.
11: 4 After a time the Ammonites made war against I.
11: 5 And when the Ammonites made war against I,
11:13 "Because I, on coming from Egypt,
11:15 I did not take away the land of Moab or the land
11:16 I went through the wilderness to the Red Sea
11:17 I then sent messengers to the king of Edom,
11:17 So I remained at Kadesh.
11:19 I then sent messengers to King Sihon of
11:19 and I said to him, 'Let us pass through your land
11:20 Sihon did not trust I to pass through his territory;
11:20 and encamped at Jahaz, and fought with I.
11:21 Then the LORD, the God of I, A
11:21 gave Sihon and all his people into the hand of I,
11:21 so I occupied all the land of the Amorites,
11:23 So now the LORD, the God of I, A
11:23 the Amorites for the benefit of his people I. E
11:25 Did he ever enter into conflict with I,
11:26 While I lived in Heshbon and its villages,
11:33 Ammonites were subdued before the people of I. B
11:40 the daughters of I would go out to lament
12: 7 Jephthah judged I six years.
12: 8 After him Ibzan of Bethlehem judged I.
12: 9 He judged I seven years.
12:11 After him Elon the Zebulunite judged I;
12:11 and he judged I ten years.
12:13 him Abdon son of Hillel the Pirathonite judged I.
12:14 on seventy donkeys; he judged I eight years.
13: 5 It is he who shall begin to deliver I from the hand
14: 4 At that time the Philistines had dominion over I.
15:20 And he judged I in the days of the Philistines
16:31 He had judged I twenty years.
17: 6 In those days there was no king in I;
18: 1 In those days there was no king in I.
18: 1 among the tribes of I had been allotted to them. G
18:19 or to be priest to a tribe and clan in I?"
18:29 after their ancestor Dan, who was born to I;
19: 1 In those days, when there was no king in I,
19:12 who do not belong to the people of I; B
19:29 and sent her throughout all the territory of I.
20: 2 The chiefs of all the people, of all the tribes of I, G
20: 3 that the people of I had gone up to Mizpah.) B
20: 6 for they have committed a vile outrage in I.
20:10 of a hundred throughout all the tribes of I, G
20:10 for all the disgrace that they have done in I."
Jdg 20:11 So all the men of I gathered against the city, L
20:12 The tribes of I sent men through all the tribe of G
20:13 and purge the evil from I."
20:29 So I stationed men in ambush around Gibeah.
20:31 killing about thirty men of I. L
20:34 ten thousand picked men out of all I, C
20:35 The LORD defeated Benjamin before I;
20:38 Now the agreement between the main body of I
20:39 the main body of I should turn in battle.
20:41 Then the main body of I turned,
21: 3 They said, "O LORD, the God of I, A
21: 3 that today there should be one tribe lacking in I?"
21: 5 the tribes of I did not come up in the assembly G
21: 6 and said, "One tribe is cut off from I this day.
21: 8 the tribes of I who did not come up to the LORD G
21:15 the LORD had made a breach in the tribes of I. G
21:17 in order that a tribe may not be blotted out from I.
21:25 In those days there was no king in I;
Ru 2:12 God of I, under whose wings you have come A
4: 7 Now this was the custom in former times in I
4: 7 this was the manner of attesting in I.
4:11 who together built up the house of I. D
4:14 and may his name be renowned in I!
1Sa 1:17 the God of I grant the petition you have made A
2:22 He heard all that his sons were doing to all I, C
2:28 tribes of I to be my priest, to go up to my altar, G
2:28 by fire from the people of I. B
2:29 of every offering of my people I?' E
2:30 Therefore the LORD the God of I declares: A
2:32 the prosperity that shall be bestowed upon I;
3:11 in I that will make both ears of anyone who hears
3:20 And all I from Dan to Beer-sheba knew C
4: 1 And the word of Samuel came to all I. C
4: 1 for war against I, and Israel went out to battle
4: 1 and I went out to battle against them;
4: 2 The Philistines drew up in line against I,
4: 2 I was defeated by the Philistines,
4: 3 the troops came to the camp, the elders of I said, J
4: 5 all I gave a mighty shout, C
4:10 So the Philistines fought; I was defeated,
4:10 for there fell of I thirty thousand foot soldiers.
4:17 "I has fled before the Philistines,
4:18 He had judged I forty years.
4:21 meaning, "The glory has departed from I,"
4:22 She said, "The glory has departed from I,
5: 7 The ark of the God of I must not remain with us; A
5: 8 What shall we do with the ark of the God of I?" A
5: 8 So they moved the ark of the God of I to Gath. A
5:10 So they sent the ark of the God of I to Ekron. A
5:10 ark of the God of I to kill us and our people?" A
5:11 and said, "Send away the ark of the God of I, A
6: 3 "If you send away the ark of the God of I, A
6: 5 and give glory to the God of I; A
7: 2 and all the house of I lamented after the LORD. D
7: 3 Then Samuel said to all the house of I, D
7: 4 So I put away the Baals and the Astartes,
7: 5 Then Samuel said, "Gather all I at Mizpah, C
7: 6 And Samuel judged the people of I at Mizpah. B
7: 7 that the people of I had gathered at Mizpah, B
7: 7 the lords of the Philistines went up against I.
7: 7 the people of I heard of it they were afraid B
7: 8 The people of I said to Samuel, B
7: 9 Samuel cried out to the LORD for I,
7:10 the Philistines drew near to attack I;
7:10 and they were routed before I.
7:11 the men of I went out of Mizpah and pursued L
7:13 and did not again enter the territory of I;
7:14 that the Philistines had taken from I were restored
7:14 from Israel were restored to I, from Ekron
7:14 and I recovered their territory from the hand of
7:14 There was peace also between I and the Amorites.
7:15 Samuel judged I all the days of his life.
7:16 and he judged I in all these places.
7:17 he administered justice there to I,
8: 1 he made his sons judges over I.
8: 4 elders of I gathered together and came to Samuel J
8:22 Samuel then said to the people of I, B
9: 2 among the people of I more handsome than he; B
9: 9 (Formerly in I, anyone who went to inquire
9:16 shall anoint him to be ruler over my people I. E
9:21 from the least of the tribes of I, G
10: 1 LORD has anointed you ruler over his people I. E
10:18 the God of I, 'I brought up Israel out of Egypt, A
10:18 the God of Israel, 'I brought up I out of Egypt,
10:20 Then Samuel brought all the tribes of I near, G
10:27 of each of them and would not grant I a deliverer.
11: 2 and thus put disgrace upon all I." C
11: 3 through all the territory of I.
11: 7 throughout all the territory of I by messengers,
11: 8 those from I were three hundred thousand,
11:13 for today the LORD has brought deliverance to I."
12: 1 Samuel said to all I, "I have listened to you C
13: 1 and he reigned . . . and two years over I.
13: 2 Saul chose three thousand out of I;
13: 4 When all I heard that Saul had defeated C
13: 4 also that I had become odious to the Philistines,
13: 5 The Philistines mustered to fight with I,
13:13 established your kingdom over I forever,
13:19 to be found throughout all the land of I; I
14:12 for the LORD has given them into the hand of I."
14:23 So the LORD gave I the victory that day.
14:37 Will you give them into the hand of I?"
14:39 For as the LORD lives who saves I,
14:40 He said to all I, "You shall be on one side, C
14:41 Then Saul said, "O LORD God of I, A
14:41 O LORD God of I, give Urim; A
14:41 if this guilt is in your people I, give Thummim." E
1Sa 14:45 who has accomplished this great victory in I?
14:47 When Saul had taken the kingship over I,
14:48 and rescued I out of the hands
15: 1 to anoint you king over his people I; E
15: 6 people of I when they came up out of Egypt." B
15:17 are you not the head of the tribes of I? G
15:17 The LORD anointed you king over I. K
15:26 LORD has rejected you from being king over I." K
15:28 the kingdom of I from you this very day,
15:29 the Glory of I will not recant or change his mind;
15:30 now before the elders of my people and before I,
15:35 that he had made Saul king over I. K
16: 1 I have rejected him from being king over I. K
17: 3 and I stood on the mountain on the other side,
17: 8 He stood and shouted to the ranks of I,
17:10 the Philistine said, "Today I defy the ranks of I!
17:11 Saul and all I heard these words of the Philistine, C
17:19 Now Saul, and they, and all the men of I, L
17:21 I and the Philistines drew up for battle,
17:25 Surely he has come up to defy I.
17:25 and make his family free in I."
17:26 and takes away the reproach from I?
17:45 the God of the armies of I,
17:46 all the earth may know that there is a God in I,
17:52 troops of I and Judah rose up with a shout and M
18: 6 the women came out of all the towns of I,
18:16 But all I and Judah loved David; CM
18:18 and who are my kinsfolk, my father's family in I,
19: 5 the LORD brought about a great victory for all I. C
20:12 "By the LORD, the God of I! A
23:10 David said, "O LORD, the God of I, A
23:11 O LORD, the God of I, I beseech you, A
23:17 you shall be king over I, and I shall be second K
24: 2 Saul took three thousand chosen men out of all I, C
24:14 Against whom has the king of I come out? F
24:20 kingdom of I shall be established in your hand.
25: 1 and all I assembled and mourned for him. C
25:30 and has appointed you prince over I,
25:32 the God of I, who sent you to meet me today! A
25:34 For as surely as the LORD the God of I lives, A
26: 2 with three thousand chosen men of I, L
26:15 Who is like you in I?
26:20 the king of I has come out to seek a single flea, F
27: 1 seeking me any longer within the borders of I,
27:12 made himself utterly abhorrent to his people I; E
28: 1 gathered their forces for war, to fight against I.
28: 3 and all I had mourned for him and buried him C
28: 4 Saul gathered all I, and they encamped at Gilboa. C
28:19 Moreover the LORD will give I along with you
28:19 the army of I into the hands of the Philistines."
29: 3 "Is this not David, the servant of King Saul of I,
30:25 a statute and an ordinance for I;
31: 1 Now the Philistines fought against I;
31: 1 and the men of I fled before the Philistines, L
31: 7 When the men of I who were on the other side L
31: 7 the men of I had fled and that Saul and his sons L
2Sa 1: 3 "I have escaped from the camp of I."
1:12 for the army of the LORD and for the house of I, D
1:19 O I, lies slain upon your high places!
1:24 O daughters of I, weep over Saul,
2: 9 Jezreel, Ephraim, Benjamin, and over all I. C
2:10 was forty years old when he began to reign over I,
2:17 men of I were beaten by the servants of David. L
2:28 they no longer pursued I or engaged
3:10 set up the throne of David over I and over Judah,
3:12 I will give you my support to bring all I over C
3:17 Abner sent word to the elders of I, saying, J
3:18 my servant David I will save my people I E
3:19 then Abner went to tell David at Hebron all that I
3:21 "Let me go and rally all I to my lord the king, C
3:37 So all the people and all I understood that day C
3:38 a prince and a great man has fallen this day in I?
4: 1 his courage failed, and all I was dismayed. C
5: 1 Then all the tribes of I came to David at Hebron, G
5: 2 it was you who led out I and brought it in.
5: 2 It is you who shall be shepherd of my people I, E
5: 2 you who shall be ruler over I."
5: 3 So all the elders of I came to the king at Hebron; J
5: 3 and they anointed David king over I. K
5: 5 over all I and Judah thirty-three years. CM
5:12 that the LORD had established him king over I, K
5:12 for the sake of his people I. E
5:17 that David had been anointed king over I, K
6: 1 David again gathered all the chosen men of I, L
6: 5 David and all the house of I were dancing D
6:15 David and all the house of I brought up the ark D
6:19 the whole multitude of I, both men and women,
6:20 "How the king of I honored himself today, F
6:21 to appoint me as prince over I,
7: 6 house since the day I brought up the people of I B
7: 7 about among all the people of I, B
7: 7 a word with any of the tribal leaders of I,
7: 7 whom I commanded to shepherd my people I, E
7: 8 the sheep to be prince over my people I; E
7:10 a place for my people I and will plant them, E
7:11 time that I appointed judges over my people I; E
7:23 Who is like your people, like I?
7:24 And you established your people I for yourself E
7:26 'The LORD of hosts is God over I';
7:27 For you, O LORD of hosts, the God of I, A
8:15 So David reigned over all I; C
10: 9 he chose some of the picked men of I, L
10:15 Arameans saw that they had been defeated by I,
10:17 it was told David, he gathered all I together, C
10:18 The Arameans fled before I;
10:19 that they had been defeated by I,
10:19 they made peace with I, and became subject

2Sa 11: 1 David sent Joab with his officers and all I C
11:11 "The ark and I and Judah remain in booths; M
12: 7 Thus says the LORD, the God of I: A
12: 7 I anointed you king over I, K
12: 8 and gave you the house of I and of Judah; D
12:12 but I will do this thing before all I, C
13:12 for such a thing is not done in I;
13:13 you, you would be as one of the scoundrels in I.
14:25 in all I there was no one to be praised so much C
15: 2 "Your servant is of such and such a tribe in I,"
15: 6 so Absalom stole the hearts of the people of I. B
15:10 the tribes of I, saying, "As soon as you hear G
16: 3 house of I will give me back my grandfather's D
16:21 and all I will hear that you have made C
16:22 in to his father's concubines in the sight of all I. C
17: 4 advice pleased Absalom and all the elders of I. J
17:10 for all I knows that your father is a warrior, C
17:11 But my counsel is that all I be gathered to you, C
17:13 then all I will bring ropes to that city, C
17:14 Absalom and all the men of I said, L
17:15 counsel Absalom and the elders of I; J
17:24 crossed the Jordan with all the men of I. L
18: 6 So the army went out into the field against I;
18: 7 men of I were defeated there by the servants of L
18:16 and the troops came back from pursuing I,
19: 9 the tribes of I, saying, "The king delivered us G
19:11 The talk of all I has come to the king. C
19:22 Shall anyone be put to death in I this day?
19:22 do I not know that I am this day king over I?" K
19:40 and also half the people of I, B
19:41 Then all the people of I came to the king, B
19:42 the people of Judah answered the people of I, B
19:43 the people of I answered the people of Judah, B
19:43 the words of the people of I. B
20: 1 Everyone to your tents, O I!"
20: 2 So all the people of I withdrew from David B
20:14 all the tribes of I to Abel of Beth-maacah; G
20:19 of those who are peaceable and faithful in I;
20:19 you seek to destroy a city that is a mother in I;
20:23 Now Joab was in command of all the army of I;
21: 2 Now the Gibeonites were not of the people of I, B
21: 2 the people of I had sworn to spare them, B
21: 2 in his zeal for the people of I and Judah.) BM
21: 4 neither is it for us to put anyone to death in I."
21: 5 we should have no place in all the territory of I—
21:15 The Philistines went to war again with I,
21:17 so that you do not quench the lamp of I."
21:21 When he taunted I, Jonathan son
23: 1 the favorite of the Strong One of I:
23: 3 The God of I has spoken, A
23: 3 the Rock of I has said to me:
24: 1 the anger of the LORD was kindled against I,
24: 1 saying, "Go, count the people of I and Judah." BM
24: 2 "Go through all the tribes of I, G
24: 4 of the king to take a census of the people of I. B
24: 9 in I there were eight hundred thousand soldiers
24:15 on I from that morning until the appointed time;
24:25 and the plague was averted from I.
1Ki 1: 3 for a beautiful girl throughout all the territory of I,
1:20 eyes of all I are on you to tell them who shall sit C
1:30 as I swore to you by the LORD, the God of I, A
1:34 and the prophet Nathan anoint him king over I; K
1:35 for I have appointed him to be ruler over I and
1:48 'Blessed be the LORD, the God of I, A
2: 4 not fail you a successor on the throne of I.'
2: 5 with the two commanders of the armies of I,
2:11 time that David reigned over I was forty years;
2:15 and that all I expected me to reign; C
2:32 Abner son of Ner, commander of the army of I,
3:28 All I heard of the judgment that C
4: 1 King Solomon was king over all I, CK
4: 7 Solomon had twelve officials over all I, C
4:20 Judah and I were as numerous as the sand by R
4:25 During Solomon's lifetime Judah and I lived R
5:13 Solomon conscripted forced labor out of all I; C
6: 1 in the fourth year of Solomon's reign over I,
6:13 I will dwell among the children of I,
6:13 and will not forsake my people I." E
8: 1 Then Solomon assembled the elders of I and all J
8: 2 All the people of I assembled to King Solomon B
8: 3 And all the elders of I came, J
8: 5 King Solomon and all the congregation of I, Q
8:14 around and blessed all the assembly of I, O
8:14 while all the assembly of I stood. O
8:15 He said, "Blessed be the LORD, the God of I, A
8:16 the day that I brought my people I out of Egypt, E
8:16 not chosen a city from any of the tribes of I G
8:16 but I chose David to be over my people I.' E
8:17 a house for the name of the LORD, the God of I. A
8:20 I sit on the throne of I, as the LORD promised,
8:20 for the name of the LORD, the God of I. A
8:22 in the presence of all the assembly of I, O
8:23 He said, "O LORD, God of I, A
8:25 Therefore, O LORD, God of I, A
8:25 a successor before me to sit on the throne of I,
8:26 O God of I, let your word be confirmed, A
8:30 your people I when they pray toward this place; E
8:33 "When your people I, having sinned against you, E
8:34 forgive the sin of your people I, E
8:36 your people I, when you teach them the good E
8:38 all your people I, all knowing the afflictions E
8:41 who is not of your people I, E
8:43 as do your people I, and so that they may know E
8:52 and to the plea of your people I, E
8:55 he stood and blessed all the assembly of I with O
8:56 has given rest to his people I according to all E
8:59 the cause of his people I, as each day requires; E

1Ki 8:62 Then the king, and all I with him, C
8:63 the people of I dedicated the house of the LORD. B
8:65 Solomon held the festival at that time, and all I C
8:66 to his servant David and to his people I. E
9: 5 I will establish your royal throne over I forever,
9: 5 not fail you a successor on the throne of I.'
9: 7 then I will cut I off from the land
9: 7 and I will become a proverb and a taunt
9:20 the Jebusites, who were not of the people of I— B
10: 9 in you and set you on the throne of I!
10: 9 Because the LORD loved I forever,
11: 9 the God of I, who had appeared to him twice, A
11:16 (for Joab and all I remained there six months, C
11:25 He was an adversary of I all the days of Solomon,
11:25 he despised I and reigned over Aram.
11:31 for thus says the LORD, the God of I, "See, A
11:32 city that I have chosen out of all the tribes of I. G
11:37 you shall be king over I. K
11:38 as I built for David, and I will give I to you.
11:42 in Jerusalem over all I was forty years. C
12: 1 all I had come to Shechem to make him king. C
12: 3 the assembly of I came and said to Rehoboam, O
12:16 all I saw that the king would not listen to them, C
12:16 To your tents, O I! Look now to your own house,
12:16 So I went away to their tents.
12:18 all I stoned him to death. C
12:19 So I has been in rebellion against the house
12:20 When all I heard that Jeroboam had returned, C
12:20 to the assembly and made him king over all I. CK
12:21 to fight against the house of I, D
12:24 up or fight against your kindred the people of I. B
12:28 O I, who brought you up out of the land
12:33 he appointed a festival for the people of I, B
14: 7 'Thus says the LORD, the God of I: A
14: 7 made you leader over my people I, E
14:10 both bond and free in I,
14:13 All I shall mourn for him and bury him; C
14:13 the God of I, in the house of Jeroboam. A
14:14 the LORD will raise up for himself a king over I, K
14:15 "The LORD will strike I,
14:15 he will root up I out of this good land that he gave
14:16 He will give I up because of the sins of Jeroboam,
14:16 which he sinned and which he caused I to commit.
14:18 All I buried him and mourned for him, C
14:19 in the Book of the Annals of the Kings of I. H
14:21 the LORD had chosen out of all the tribes of I, G
14:24 that the LORD drove out before the people of I. B
15: 9 In the twentieth year of King Jeroboam of I,
15:16 between Asa and King Baasha of I all their days.
15:17 King Baasha of I went up against Judah,
15:19 go, break your alliance with King Baasha of I,
15:20 of his armies against the cities of I.
15:25 Nadab son of Jeroboam began to reign over I in
15:25 he reigned over I two years.
15:26 of his ancestor and in the sin that he caused I
15:27 Nadab and all I were laying siege to Gibbethon. C
15:30 that he committed and that he caused I to commit,
15:30 to which he provoked the LORD, the God of I. A
15:31 in the Book of the Annals of the Kings of I? H
15:32 between Asa and King Baasha of I all their days.
15:33 Baasha son of Ahijah began to reign over all I C
15:34 of Jeroboam and in the sin that he caused I
16: 2 the dust and made you leader over my people I, E
16: 2 and have caused my people I to sin, E
16: 5 in the Book of the Annals of the Kings of I? H
16: 8 of Baasha began to reign over I in Tirzah;
16:13 and that they caused I to commit,
16:13 the LORD God of I to anger with their idols. A
16:14 in the Book of the Annals of the Kings of I? H
16:16 therefore all I made Omri, C
16:16 king over I that day in the camp. K
16:17 Omri went up from Gibbethon, and all I with C
16:19 and for the sin that he committed, causing I to sin.
16:20 in the Book of the Annals of the Kings of I? H
16:21 Then the people of I were divided into two parts; B
16:23 Omri began to reign over I;
16:26 and in the sins that he caused I to commit,
16:26 provoking the LORD, the God of I, A
16:27 in the Book of the Annals of the Kings of I? H
16:29 Ahab son of Omri began to reign over I;
16:29 over I in Samaria twenty-two years.
16:33 the anger of the LORD, the God of I, A
16:33 than had all the kings of I who were before him. H
17: 1 said to Ahab, "As the LORD the God of I lives, A
17:14 For thus says the LORD the God of I: A
18:17 Ahab said to him, "Is it you, you troubler of I?"
18:18 He answered, "I have not troubled I;
18:19 have all I assemble for me at Mount Carmel, C
18:31 saying, "I shall be your name";
18:36 "O LORD, God of Abraham, Isaac, and I,
18:36 let it be known this day that you are God in I,
19:16 of Nimshi as king over I; K
19:18 Yet I will leave seven thousand in I,
20: 2 into the city to King Ahab of I, and said to him:
20: 4 The king of I answered, "As you say, my lord, F
20: 7 the king of I called all the elders of the land, F
20:11 The king of I answered, "Tell him: F
20:13 Then a certain prophet came up to King Ahab of I
20:15 after them he mustered all the people of I, B
20:20 the Arameans fled and I pursued them,
20:21 The king of I went out, F
20:22 prophet approached the king of I and said to him, F
20:26 and went up to Aphek to fight against I.
20:27 people of I encamped opposite them like two B
20:28 man of God approached and said to the king of I, F
20:31 the kings of the house of I are merciful kings; D
20:31 and go out to the king of I; F

1Ki 20:32 put ropes on their heads, went to the king of I, F
20:34 The king of I responded, "I will let you go F
20:40 king of I said to him, "So shall your judgment F
20:41 king of I recognized him as one of the prophets. F
20:43 The king of I set out toward home, F
21: 7 to him, "Do you now govern I?
21:18 to meet King Ahab of I, who rules in Samaria;
21:21 from Ahab every male, bond or free, in I;
21:22 to anger and have caused I to sin.
22: 1 three years Aram and I continued without war.
22: 2 of Judah came down to the king of I. F
22: 3 The king of I said to his servants, F
22: 4 Jehoshaphat replied to the king of I, F
22: 5 But Jehoshaphat also said to the king of I, F
22: 6 the king of I gathered the prophets together, F
22: 8 The king of I said to Jehoshaphat, F
22: 9 the king of I summoned an officer and said, F
22:10 king of I and King Jehoshaphat of Judah were F
22:17 "I saw all I scattered on the mountains, C
22:18 The king of I said to Jehoshaphat, F
22:26 The king of I then ordered, "Take Micaiah, F
22:29 king of I and King Jehoshaphat of Judah went F
22:30 The king of I said to Jehoshaphat, F
22:30 king of I disguised himself and went into battle. F
22:31 but only with the king of I." F
22:32 they said, "It is surely the king of I." F
22:33 of the chariots saw that it was not the king of I, F
22:34 struck the king of I between the scale armor and F
22:39 in the Book of the Annals of the Kings of I? H
22:41 over Judah in the fourth year of King Ahab of I.
22:44 Jehoshaphat also made peace with the king of I. F
22:51 to reign over I in Samaria in the seventeenth year
22:51 he reigned two years over I.
22:52 the way of Jeroboam son of Nebat, who caused I
22:53 he provoked the LORD, the God of I, to anger, A
2Ki 1: 1 After the death of Ahab, Moab rebelled against I.
1: 3 in I that you are going to inquire of Baal-zebub,
1: 6 in I that you are sending to inquire of Baal-zebub,
1:16 is it because there is no God in I to inquire
1:18 in the Book of the Annals of the Kings of I? H
2:12 The chariots of I and its horsemen!"
3: 1 Jehoram son of Ahab became king over I K
3: 3 which he caused I to commit;
3: 4 to the king of I one hundred thousand lambs, F
3: 5 the king of Moab rebelled against the king of I. F
3: 6 of Samaria at that time and mustered all I. C
3: 9 So the king of I, the king of Judah, F
3:10 Then the king of I said, "Alas! F
3:11 one of the servants of the king of I answered, F
3:12 king of I and Jehoshaphat and the king of Edom F
3:13 Elisha said to the king of I, F
3:13 But the king of I said to him, "No; F
3:24 But when they came to the camp of I,
3:27 And great wrath came upon I,
5: 2 a young girl captive from the land of I, I
5: 4 the girl from the land of I had said. I
5: 5 and I will send along a letter to the king of I." F
5: 6 He brought the letter to the king of I, which read, F
5: 7 When the king of I read the letter, F
5: 8 that the king of I had torn his clothes, F
5: 8 that he may learn that there is a prophet in I."
5:12 better than all the waters of I?
5:15 that there is no God in all the earth except in I;
6: 8 Once when the king of Aram was at war with I,
6: 9 But the man of God sent word to the king of I, F
6:10 The king of I sent word to the place of which F
6:11 tell me who among us sides with the king of I?" F
6:12 It is Elisha, the prophet in I,
6:12 who tells the king of I the words that you speak F
6:21 When the king of I saw them he said to Elisha, F
6:23 no longer came raiding into the land of I. I
6:26 as the king of I was walking on the city wall, F
7: 6 "The king of I has hired the kings of the Hittites F
7:13 the fate of the whole multitude of I
8:12 know the evil that you will do to the people of I; B
8:16 In the fifth year of King Joram son of Ahab of I,
8:18 He walked in the way of the kings of I, H
8:25 the twelfth year of King Joram son of Ahab of I,
8:26 a granddaughter of King Omri of I.
9: 3 I anoint you king over I.' K
9: 6 "Thus says the LORD the God of I: A
9: 6 over the people of the LORD, over I.
9: 8 cut off from Ahab every male, bond or free, in I.
9:12 'Thus says the LORD, I anoint you king over I.' K
9:14 with all I had been on guard at Ramoth-gilead C
9:21 Joram of I and King Ahaziah of Judah set out,
10:21 Jehu sent word throughout all I; C
10:28 Thus Jehu wiped out Baal from I.
10:29 which he caused I to commit—
10:30 the fourth generation shall sit on the throne of I."
10:31 of the LORD the God of I with all his heart; A
10:31 which he caused I to commit.
10:32 the LORD began to trim off parts of I.
10:32 Hazael defeated them throughout the territory of I:
10:34 in the Book of the Annals of the Kings of I? H
10:36 reigned over I in Samaria was twenty-eight years.
13: 1 Jehoahaz son of Jehu began to reign over I
13: 2 which he caused I to sin;
13: 3 The anger of the LORD was kindled against I,
13: 4 for he saw the oppression of I,
13: 5 Therefore the LORD gave I a savior,
13: 5 the people of I lived in their homes as formerly. B
13: 6 which he caused I to sin, but walked in them;
13: 8 in the Book of the Annals of the Kings of I? H
13:10 Jehoash son of Jehoahaz began to reign over I
13:11 which he caused I to sin, but he walked in them.
13:12 in the Book of the Annals of the Kings of I? H

2Ki 13:13 Joash was buried in Samaria with the kings of I. H
13:14 King Joash of I went down to him,
13:14 The chariots of I and its horsemen!"
13:16 Then he said to the king of I, "Draw the bow"; F
13:18 He said to the king of I, F
13:22 of Aram oppressed I all the days of Jehoahaz.
13:25 and recovered the towns of I.
14: 1 the second year of King Joash son of Joahaz of I,
14: 8 son of Jehu, of I, saying, "Come,
14: 9 King Jehoash of I sent word to King Amaziah
14:11 So King Jehoash of I went up;
14:12 Judah was defeated by I; everyone fled home.
14:13 King Jehoash of I captured King Amaziah
14:15 in the Book of the Annals of the Kings of I? H
14:16 and was buried in Samaria with the kings of I; H
14:17 the death of King Jehoash son of Jehoahaz of I.
14:23 King Jeroboam son of Joash of I began to reign
14:24 of Jeroboam son of Nebat, which he caused I
14:25 the border of I from Lebo-hamath as far as the Sea
14:25 God of I, which he spoke by his servant Jonah A
14:26 LORD saw that the distress of I was very bitter;
14:26 bond or free, and no one to help I.
14:27 not said that he would blot out the name of I from
14:28 how he recovered for I Damascus and Hamath,
14:28 in the Book of the Annals of the Kings of I? H
14:29 Jeroboam slept with his ancestors, the kings of I; H
15: 1 of I King Azariah son of Amaziah of Judah began
15: 8 of Jeroboam reigned over I in Samaria six months.
15: 9 which he caused I to sin.
15:11 in the Book of the Annals of the Kings of I. H
15:12 on the throne of I to the fourth generation."
15:15 in the Book of the Annals of the Kings of I. H
15:17 Menahem son of Gadi began to reign over I;
15:18 of Jeroboam son of Nebat, which he caused I
15:20 Menahem exacted the money from I, that is,
15:21 in the Book of the Annals of the Kings of I? H
15:23 Pekahiah son of Menahem began to reign over I
15:24 of Jeroboam son of Nebat, which he caused I
15:26 in the Book of the Annals of the Kings of I. H
15:27 of Remaliah began to reign over I in Samaria;
15:28 of Jeroboam son of Nebat, which he caused I
15:29 In the days of King Pekah of I,
15:31 in the Book of the Annals of the Kings of I. H
15:32 of King Pekah son of Remaliah of I,
16: 3 but he walked in the way of the kings of I. H
16: 3 the LORD drove out before the people of I. B
16: 5 and King Pekah son of Remaliah of I came up
16: 7 of Aram and from the hand of the king of I, F
17: 1 of Elah began to reign in Samaria over I;
17: 2 yet not like the kings of I who were before him. H
17: 7 occurred because the people of I had sinned B
17: 8 the LORD drove out before the people of I, B
17: 8 the customs that the kings of I had introduced. H
17: 9 people of I secretly did things that were not B
17:13 the LORD warned I and Judah by every prophet M
17:18 Therefore the LORD was very angry with I
17:19 but walked in the customs that I had introduced.
17:20 The LORD rejected all the descendants of I;
17:21 When he had torn I from the house of David,
17:21 Jeroboam drove I from following the LORD
17:22 The people of I continued in all the sins B
17:23 until the LORD removed I out of his sight,
17:23 So I was exiled from their own land to Assyria
17:24 the cities of Samaria in place of the people of I; B
17:34 the children of Jacob, whom he named I.
18: 1 In the third year of King Hoshea son of Elah of I,
18: 4 the people of I had made offerings to it; B
18: 5 He trusted in the LORD the God of I; A
18: 9 the seventh year of King Hoshea son of Elah of I,
18:10 which was the ninth year of King Hoshea of I,
19:15 "O LORD the God of I, who are enthroned A
19:20 saying, "Thus says the LORD, the God of I: A
19:22 Against the Holy One of I!
21: 2 that the LORD drove out before the people of I. B
21: 3 made a sacred pole, as King Ahab of I had done,
21: 7 which I have chosen out of all the tribes of I, G
21: 8 of I to wander any more out of the land that I gave
21: 9 that the LORD destroyed before the people of I. B
21:12 therefore thus says the LORD, the God of I, A
22:15 "Thus says the LORD, the God of I: A
22:18 Thus says the LORD, the God of I: A
23:13 which King Solomon of I had built for Astarte
23:15 by Jeroboam son of Nebat, who caused I to sin—
23:19 which kings of I had made, H
23:22 the judges who judged I, or during all the days
23:22 during all the days of the kings of I or H
23:27 also out of my sight, as I have removed I;
24:13 which King Solomon of I had made,
1Ch 1:34 The sons of Isaac: Esau and I.
2: 1 These are the sons of I: P
2: 7 The sons of Carmi: Achar, the troubler of I,
4:10 Jabez called on the God of I, saying, A
5: 1 The sons of Reuben the firstborn of I.
5: 1 of I, so that he is not enrolled in the genealogy
5: 3 The sons of Reuben, the firstborn of I:
5:17 and in the days of King Jeroboam of I.
5:26 So the God of I stirred up the spirit of King Pul A
6:38 son of Izhar, son of Kohath, son of Levi, son of I;
6:49 of the most holy place, to make atonement for I,
6:64 So the people of I gave the Levites the towns B
7:29 In these lived the sons of Joseph son of I.
9: 1 So all I was enrolled by genealogies; C
9: 1 these are written in the Book of the Kings of I. H
10: 1 Now the Philistines fought against I;
10: 1 and the men of I fled before the Philistines, L
10: 7 When all the men of I who were in the valley L
11: 1 Then all I gathered together to David at Hebron C

1Ch 11: 2 it was you who commanded the army of I.
11: 2 It is you who shall be shepherd of my people I, E
11: 2 you who shall be ruler over my people I." E
11: 3 So all the elders of I came to the king at Hebron, J
11: 3 And they anointed David king over I, K
11: 4 David and all I marched to Jerusalem, C
11:10 together with all I, to make him king, C
11:10 according to the word of the LORD concerning I.
12:32 to know what I ought to do, two hundred chiefs,
12:38 with full intent to make David king over all I; CK
12:38 of I were of a single mind to make David king.
12:40 wine, oil, oxen, and sheep, for there was joy in I.
13: 2 David said to the whole assembly of I, O
13: 2 to our kindred who remain in all the land of I, I
13: 5 So David assembled all I from the Shihor C
13: 6 And David and all I went up to Baalah, that is, C
13: 8 David and all I were dancing before God C
14: 2 the LORD had established him as king over I, K
14: 2 for the sake of his people I. E
14: 8 that David had been anointed king over all I, CK
15: 3 David assembled all I in Jerusalem to bring up C
15:12 up the ark of the LORD, the God of I, A
15:14 to bring up the ark of the LORD, the God of I. A
15:25 So David and the elders of I, J
15:28 So all I brought up the ark of the covenant of C
16: 3 and he distributed to every person in I—
16: 4 to thank, and to praise the LORD, the God of I. A
16:13 O offspring of his servant I,
16:17 to I as an everlasting covenant,
16:36 Blessed be the LORD, the God of I, A
16:40 in the law of the LORD that he commanded I.
17: 5 not lived in a house since the day I brought out I
17: 6 Wherever I have moved about among all I, C
17: 6 a word with any of the judges of I,
17: 7 to be ruler over my people I; E
17: 9 I will appoint a place for my people I, E
17:10 time that I appointed judges over my people I; E
17:21 Who is like your people I, E
17:22 made your people I to be your people forever; E
17:24 'The LORD of hosts, the God of I, A
18:14 So David reigned over all I; C
19:10 of the picked men of I and arrayed them against L
19:16 Arameans saw that they had been defeated by I,
19:17 David was informed, he gathered all I together, C
19:18 The Arameans fled before I;
19:19 that they had been defeated by I,
20: 7 When he taunted I, Jonathan son of Shimea,
21: 1 up against I, and incited David to count the people
21: 1 and incited David to count the people of I. B
21: 2 "Go, number I, from Beer-sheba to Dan,
21: 3 Why should he bring guilt on I?"
21: 4 So Joab departed and went throughout all I, C
21: 5 In all I there were one million one hundred C
21: 7 with this thing, and he struck I.
21:12 throughout all the territory of I.'
21:14 So the LORD sent a pestilence on I;
21:14 and seventy thousand persons fell in I.
22: 1 and here the altar of burnt offering for I."
22: 2 the aliens who were residing in the land of I, I
22: 6 to build a house for the LORD, the God of I. A
22: 9 and I will give peace and quiet to I in his days.
22:10 and I will establish his royal throne in I forever.'
22:12 when he gives you charge over I you may keep
22:13 that the LORD commanded Moses for I.
22:17 David also commanded all the leaders of I
23: 1 he made his son Solomon king over I. K
23: 2 the leaders of I and the priests and the Levites.
23:25 For David said, "The LORD, the God of I, A
24:19 as the LORD God of I had commanded him. A
26:29 to outside duties for I, as officers and judges.
26:30 had the oversight of I west of the Jordan for all
27: 1 This is the list of the people of I, B
27:16 Over the tribes of I, for the Reubenites, G
27:22 These were the leaders of the tribes of I. G
27:23 the LORD had promised to make I as numerous
27:24 yet wrath came upon I for this,
28: 1 at Jerusalem all the officials of I,
28: 4 God of I chose me from all my ancestral house A
28: 4 to be king over I forever; K
28: 4 in making me king over all I. CK
28: 5 the throne of the kingdom of the LORD over I.
28: 8 Now therefore in the sight of all I, C
29:10 the God of our ancestor I, forever and ever.
29:18 O LORD, the God of Abraham, Isaac, and I,
29:21 and sacrifices in abundance for all I; C
29:23 he prospered, and all I obeyed him. C
29:25 in the sight of all I, C
29:25 as had not been on any king before him in I.
29:26 Thus David son of Jesse reigned over all I. C
29:27 The period that he reigned over I was forty years;
29:30 and of the events that befell him and I and all
2Ch 1: 2 Solomon summoned all I, C
1: 2 and all the leaders of all I, the heads of families. C
1:13 And he reigned over I.
2: 4 of the LORD our God, as ordained forever for I.
2:12 "Blessed be the LORD God of I, A
2:17 all the aliens who were residing in the land of I, I
5: 2 Then Solomon assembled the elders of I and all J
5: 2 leaders of the ancestral houses of the people of I, B
5: 4 And all the elders of I came, J
5: 6 King Solomon and all the congregation of I, Q
5:10 the people of I after they came out of Egypt. B
6: 3 around and blessed all the assembly of I, O
6: 3 while all the assembly of I stood. O
6: 4 he said, "Blessed be the LORD, the God of I, A
6: 5 not chosen a city from any of the tribes of I G
6: 5 and I chose no one as ruler over my people I; E

2Ch 6: 6 I have chosen David to be over my people I.' E
6: 7 a house for the name of the LORD, the God of I. A
6:10 and sit on the throne of I,
6:10 for the name of the LORD, the God of I. A
6:11 of the LORD that he made with the people of I." B
6:12 in the presence of the whole assembly of I, O
6:13 in the presence of the whole assembly of I, O
6:14 He said, "O LORD, God of I, A
6:16 Therefore, O LORD, God of I, A
6:16 a successor before me to sit on the throne of I,
6:17 Therefore, O LORD, God of I, A
6:21 the plea of your servant and of your people I, E
6:24 "When your people I, having sinned against you, E
6:25 and forgive the sin of your people I, E
6:27 forgive the sin of your servants, your people I, E
6:29 from any individual or from all your people I, E
6:32 who are not of your people I, E
6:33 as do your people I, and that they may know E
7: 3 all the people of I saw the fire come down B
7: 6 the priests sounded trumpets; and all I stood. C
7: 8 and all I with him, a very great congregation, C
7:10 to David and to Solomon and to his people I. E
7:18 'You shall never lack a successor to rule over I.'
8: 2 and settled the people of I in them. B
8: 7 the Hivites, and the Jebusites, who were not of I,
8: 8 whom the people of I had not destroyed— B
8: 9 But of the people of I Solomon made no slaves B
8:11 not live in the house of King David of I,
9: 8 Because your God loved I
9:30 in Jerusalem over all I forty years. C
10: 1 all I had come to Shechem to make him king. C
10: 3 Jeroboam and all I came and said to Rehoboam, C
10:16 all I saw that the king would not listen to them, C
10:16 Each of you to your tents, O I!
10:16 So all I departed to their tents. C
10:17 the people of I who were living in the cities B
10:18 the people of I stoned him to death. B
10:19 So I has been in rebellion against the house
11: 1 of Judah and Benjamin to fight against I,
11: 3 and to all I in Judah and Benjamin, C
11:13 Levites who were in all I presented themselves C
11:16 God of I came after them from all the tribes of A
11:16 from all the tribes of I to Jerusalem to sacrifice G
12: 1 he and all I with him. C
12: 6 the officers of I and the king humbled themselves
12:13 the LORD had chosen out of all the tribes of I G
13: 4 and said, "Listen to me, Jeroboam and all I! C
13: 5 God of I gave the kingship over Israel forever A
13: 5 over I forever to David and his sons by a covenant
13:15 God defeated Jeroboam and all I before Abijah C
13:17 five hundred thousand picked men of I fell slain. L
15: 3 For a long time I was without the true God,
15: 4 the God of I, and sought him, A
15: 9 for great numbers had deserted to him from I
15:13 the God of I, should be put to death, A
15:17 But the high places were not taken out of I.
16: 1 King Baasha of I went up against Judah,
16: 3 go, break your alliance with King Baasha of I,
16: 4 of his armies against the cities of I.
16:11 in the Book of the Kings of Judah and I. R
17: 1 and strengthened himself against I.
17: 4 and not according to the ways of I.
18: 3 King Ahab of I said to King Jehoshaphat
18: 4 But Jehoshaphat also said to the king of I, F
18: 5 the king of I gathered the prophets together, F
18: 7 The king of I said to Jehoshaphat, F
18: 8 the king of I summoned an officer and said, F
18: 9 the king of I and King Jehoshaphat of Judah F
18:16 "I saw all I scattered on the mountains, C
18:17 The king of I said to Jehoshaphat, F
18:19 LORD said, 'Who will entice King Ahab of I,
18:25 The king of I then ordered, "Take Micaiah, F
18:28 the king of I and King Jehoshaphat of Judah F
18:29 The king of I said to Jehoshaphat, F
18:29 So the king of I disguised himself, F
18:30 but only with the king of I." F
18:31 they said, "It is the king of I." F
18:32 of the chariots saw that it was not the king of I, F
18:33 the king of I between the scale armor and F
18:34 king of I propped himself up in his chariot F
19: 8 and priests and heads of families of I,
20: 7 the inhabitants of this land before your people I, E
20:10 whom you would not let I invade when they came
20:19 stood up to praise the LORD, the God of I, A
20:29 the LORD had fought against the enemies of I.
20:34 are recorded in the Book of the Kings of I. H
20:35 of Judah joined with King Ahaziah of I,
21: 4 and also some of the officials of I.
21: 6 He walked in the way of the kings of I, H
21:13 but have walked in the way of the kings of I, H
21:13 as the house of Ahab led I into unfaithfulness,
22: 5 with Jehoram son of King Ahab of I to make war
23: 2 and the heads of families of I,
24: 5 the cities of Judah and gather money from all I C
24: 6 on the congregation of I for the tent of Q
24: 9 the tax that Moses the servant of God laid on I in
24:16 because he had done good in I,
25: 6 from I for one hundred talents of silver.
25: 7 "O king, do not let the army of I go with you,
25: 7 for the LORD is not with I—all these Ephraimites.
25: 9 that I have given to the army of I?"
25:17 to King Joash son of Jehoahaz son of Jehu of I,
25:18 King Joash of I sent word to King Amaziah
25:21 So King Joash of I went up;
25:22 Judah was defeated by I; everyone fled home.
25:23 King Joash of I captured King Amaziah of Judah,
25:25 after the death of King Joash son of Jehoahaz of I.

2Ch 25:26 in the Book of the Kings of Judah and **I**? R
27: 7 in the Book of the Kings of **I** and Judah. HM
28: 2 but he walked in the ways of the kings of **I**. H
28: 3 the LORD drove out before the people of **I**. B
28: 5 He was also given into the hand of the king of **I**, F
28: 8 people of **I** took captive two hundred thousand B
28:13 and there is fierce wrath against **I**."
28:19 because of King Ahaz of **I**,
28:23 But they were the ruin of him, and of all **I**. C
28:26 in the Book of the Kings of Judah and **I**. R
28:27 not bring him into the tombs of the kings of **I**. H
29: 7 in the holy place to the God of **I**. A
29:10 a covenant with the LORD, the God of **I**, A
29:24 to make atonement for all **I**. C
29:24 and the sin offering should be made for all **I**. C
29:27 by the instruments of King David of **I**.
30: 1 Hezekiah sent word to all **I** and Judah, CM
30: 1 to keep the passover to the LORD the God of **I**. A
30: 5 proclamation throughout all **I**, from Beer-sheba C
30: 5 and keep the passover to the LORD the God of **I**, A
30: 6 So couriers went throughout all **I** and Judah CM
30: 6 saying, "O people of **I**, return to the LORD, B
30: 6 the God of Abraham, Isaac, and **I**,
30:21 people of **I** who were present at Jerusalem kept B
30:25 and the whole assembly that came out of **I**,
30:25 the resident aliens who came out of the land of **I**, I
30:26 of **I** there had been nothing like this in Jerusalem.
31: 1 all **I** who were present went out to the cities C
31: 1 Then all the people of **I** returned to their cities, B
31: 5 the people of **I** gave in abundance the first fruits B
31: 6 people of **I** and Judah who lived in the cities BM
31: 8 they blessed the LORD and his people **I**. E
32:17 to throw contempt on the LORD the God of **I** A
32:32 Amoz in the Book of the Kings of Judah and **I**. R
33: 2 the LORD drove out before the people of **I**. B
33: 7 which I have chosen out of all the tribes of **I**, G
33: 8 I will never again remove the feet of **I** from
33: 9 the LORD had destroyed before the people of **I**. B
33:16 to serve the LORD the God of **I**. A
33:18 to him in the name of the LORD God of **I**, A
33:18 these are in the Annals of the Kings of **I**. H
34: 7 the incense altars throughout all the land of **I**. I
34: 9 the remnant of **I** and from all Judah and Benjamin
34:21 and for those who are left in **I** and in Judah, M
34:23 "Thus says the LORD, the God of **I**: A
34:26 Thus says the LORD, the God of **I**: A
34:33 the territory that belonged to the people of **I**, B
34:33 and made all who were in **I** worship
35: 3 the Levites who taught all **I** and who were holy C
35: 3 the house that Solomon son of David, king of **I**, F
35: 3 Now serve the LORD your God and his people **I**. E
35: 4 of **I** and the written directions of his son Solomon.
35:17 people of **I** who were present kept the passover B
35:18 No passover like it had been kept in **I** since
35:18 none of the kings of **I** had kept such a passover H
35:18 by all Judah and **I** who were present, R
35:25 They made these a custom in **I**;
35:27 in the Book of the Kings of **I** and Judah. HM
36: 8 in the Book of the Kings of **I** and Judah; HM
36:13 against turning to the LORD, the God of **I**. A
Ezr 1: 3 rebuild the house of the LORD, the God of **I**— A
2:59 whether they belonged to **I**:
2:70 temple servants lived in their towns, and all **I** C
3: 2 to build the altar of the God of **I**, A
3:10 according to the directions of King David of **I**;
3:11 for his steadfast love endures forever toward **I**."
4: 1 a temple to the LORD, the God of **I**, A
4: 3 the rest of the heads of families in **I** said to them,
4: 3 we alone will build to the LORD, the God of **I**, A
5: 1 in the name of the God of **I** who was over them. A
5:11 which a great king of **I** built and finished. F
6:14 of the God of **I** and by decree of Cyrus, Darius, A
6:16 The people of **I**, the priests and the Levites, B
6:17 hundred lambs, and as a sin offering for all **I**, C
6:17 according to the number of the tribes of **I**. G
6:21 It was eaten by the people of **I** who had returned B
6:21 of the land to worship the LORD, the God of **I**. A
6:22 in the work on the house of God, the God of **I**. A
7: 6 of Moses that the LORD the God of **I** had given; A
7: 7 Some of the people of **I**, B
7:10 and to teach the statutes and ordinances in **I**.
7:11 of the LORD and his statutes for **I**:
7:13 decree that any of the people of **I** or their priests B
7:15 to the God of **I**, whose dwelling is A
7:28 and I gathered leaders from **I** to go up with me.
8:18 of the descendants of Mahli son of Levi son of **I**,
8:25 his lords, and all **I** there present had offered; C
8:29 and the Levites and the heads of families in **I**
8:35 offered burnt offerings to the God of **I**, A
8:35 twelve bulls for all **I**, ninety-six rams, C
9: 1 "The people of **I**, the priests, B
9: 4 all who trembled at the words of the God of **I**, A
9:15 O LORD, God of **I**, you are just, A
10: 1 women, and children gathered to him out of **I**;
10: 2 but even now there is hope for **I** in spite of this.
10: 5 all **I** swear that they would do as had been said. C
10:10 and so increased the guilt of **I**.
10:25 And of **I**: of the descendants of Parosh:
Ne 1: 6 the people of **I**, confessing the sins of the people B
1: 6 confessing the sins of the people of **I**, B
2:10 to seek the welfare of the people of **I**. B
7:61 whether they belonged to **I**:
7:73 and all **I** settled in their towns. C
7:73 the people of **I** being settled in their towns— B
8: 1 which the LORD had given to **I**.
8:14 that the people of **I** should live in booths during B
8:17 to that day the people of **I** had not done so. B
Ne 9: 1 the people of **I** were assembled with fasting B
10:33 and the sin offerings to make atonement for **I**,
10:39 the people of **I** and the sons of Levi shall bring B
11: 3 **I**, the priests, the Levites, the temple servants,
11:20 of **I**, and of the priests and the Levites, were in all
12:47 days of Nehemiah all **I** gave the daily portions C
13: 3 they separated from **I** all those of foreign descent.
13:18 Yet you bring more wrath on **I** by profaning
13:26 Did not King Solomon of **I** sin on account
13:26 and God made him king over all **I**; CK
Ps 14: 7 O that deliverance for **I** would come from Zion!
14: 7 Jacob will rejoice; **I** will be glad.
22: 3 Yet you are holy, enthroned on the praises of **I**.
22:23 stand in awe of him, all you offspring of **I**!
25:22 Redeem **I**, O God, out of all its troubles.
41:13 Blessed be the LORD, the God of **I**, A
50: 7 and I will speak, O **I**, I will testify against you.
53: 6 O that deliverance for **I** would come from Zion!
53: 6 Jacob will rejoice; **I** will be glad.
59: 5 You, LORD God of hosts, are God of **I**. A
68: 8 at the presence of God, the God of **I**. A
68:34 Ascribe power to God, whose majesty is over **I**;
68:35 Awesome is God in his sanctuary, the God of **I**; A
69: 6 be dishonored because of me, O God of **I**. A
71:22 to you with the lyre, O Holy One of **I**.
72:18 Blessed be the LORD, the God of **I**, A
76: 1 In Judah God is known, his name is great in **I**.
78: 5 and appointed a law in **I**, which he commanded
78:21 his anger mounted against **I**,
78:31 and laid low the flower of **I**.
78:41 and provoked the Holy One of **I**.
78:55 for a possession and settled the tribes of **I** G
78:59 he was full of wrath, and he utterly rejected **I**.
78:71 to be the shepherd of his people Jacob, of **I**,
80: 1 O Shepherd of **I**, you who lead Joseph like
81: 4 For it is a statute for **I**,
81: 8 O **I**, if you would but listen to me!
81:11 **I** would not submit to me.
81:13 that **I** would walk in my ways!
83: 4 let the name of **I** be remembered no more."
89:18 our king to the Holy One of **I**.
98: 3 and faithfulness to the house of **I**. D
103: 7 his acts to the people of **I**. B
105:10 to **I** as an everlasting covenant,
105:23 Then **I** came to Egypt; Jacob lived
105:37 Then he brought **I** out with silver and gold,
106:48 Blessed be the LORD, the God of **I**, A
114: 1 When **I** went out from Egypt,
114: 2 Judah became God's sanctuary, **I** his dominion.
115: 9 O **I**, trust in the LORD!
115:12 he will bless the house of **I**; D
118: 2 Let **I** say, "His steadfast love endures forever."
121: 4 He who keeps **I** will neither slumber nor sleep.
122: 4 as was decreed for **I**, to give thanks to the name
124: 1 not been the LORD who was on our side—let **I**
125: 5 away with evildoers. Peace be upon **I**!
128: 6 see your children's children. Peace be upon **I**!
129: 1 attacked me from my youth"—let **I** now say—
130: 7 O **I**, hope in the LORD!
130: 8 It is he who will redeem **I** from all its iniquities.
131: 3 O **I**, hope in the LORD from this time on
135: 4 For the LORD has chosen Jacob for himself, **I**
135:12 a heritage to his people **I**. E
135:19 O house of **I**, bless the LORD! D
136:11 and brought **I** out from among them,
136:14 and made **I** pass through the midst of it,
136:22 a heritage to his servant **I**,
147: 2 he gathers the outcasts of **I**.
147:19 his statutes and ordinances to **I**.
148:14 for the people of **I** who are close to him. B
149: 2 Let **I** be glad in its Maker;
Pr 1: 1 proverbs of Solomon son of David, king of **I**: F
Ecc 1:12 I, the Teacher, when king over **I** in Jerusalem, K
SS 3: 7 sixty mighty men of the mighty men of **I**, L
Isa 1: 3 but **I** does not know, my people do not understand.
1: 4 who have despised the Holy One of **I**,
1:24 the LORD of hosts, the Mighty One of **I**:
4: 2 be the pride and glory of the survivors of **I**.
5: 7 vineyard of the LORD of hosts is the house of **I**, D
5:19 the plan of the Holy One of **I** hasten to fulfillment,
5:24 and have despised the word of the Holy One of **I**.
7: 1 and King Pekah son of Remaliah of **I** went up
8:14 of **I** he will become a rock one stumbles over—
8:18 and portents in **I** from the LORD of hosts,
9: 8 Lord sent a word against Jacob, and it fell on **I**;
9:12 and they devoured **I** with open mouth.
9:14 So the LORD cut off from **I** head and tail,
10:17 The light of **I** will become a fire,
10:20 On that day the remnant of **I** and the survivors of
10:20 but will lean on the LORD, the Holy One of **I**,
10:22 your people **I** were like the sand of the sea, E
11:12 and will assemble the outcasts of **I**,
11:16 for **I** when they came up from the land of Egypt.
12: 6 for great in your midst is the Holy One of **I**.
14: 1 and will again choose **I**, and will set them
14: 2 and the house of **I** will possess the nations D
17: 3 of Aram will be like the glory of the children of **I**,
17: 6 says the LORD God of **I**. A
17: 7 and their eyes will look to the Holy One of **I**;
17: 9 which they deserted because of the children of **I**,
19:24 On that day **I** will be the third with Egypt
19:25 the work of my hands, and **I** my heritage."
21:10 the God of **I**, I announce to you. A
21:17 for the LORD, the God of **I**, has spoken. A
24:15 the name of the LORD, the God of **I**. A
27: 6 **I** shall blossom and put forth shoots,
27:12 be gathered one by one, O people of **I**. B
Isa 29:19 neediest people shall exult in the Holy One of **I**.
29:23 and will stand in awe of the God of **I**. A
30:11 let us hear no more about the Holy One of **I**."
30:12 Therefore thus says the Holy One of **I**:
30:15 For thus said the Lord GOD, the Holy One of **I**:
30:29 to the mountain of the LORD, to the Rock of **I**.
31: 1 but do not look to the Holy One of **I** or consult
31: 6 whom you have deeply betrayed, O people of **I**. B
37:16 God of **I**, who are enthroned above the cherubim, A
37:21 "Thus says the LORD, the God of **I**: A
37:23 Against the Holy One of **I**!
40:27 Why do you say, O Jacob, and speak, O **I**,
41: 8 But you, **I**, my servant, Jacob,
41:14 Do not fear, you worm Jacob, you insect **I**!
41:14 your Redeemer is the Holy One of **I**.
41:16 in the Holy One of **I** you shall glory.
41:17 I the God of **I** will not forsake them. A
41:20 the Holy One of **I** has created it.
42:24 up Jacob to the spoiler, and **I** to the robbers?
43: 1 O Jacob, he who formed you, O **I**:
43: 3 For I am the LORD your God, the Holy One of **I**,
43:14 your Redeemer, the Holy One of **I**:
43:15 I am the LORD, your Holy One, the Creator of **I**,
43:22 but you have been weary of me, O **I**!
43:28 to utter destruction, and **I** to reviling.
44: 1 hear, O Jacob my servant, **I** whom I have chosen!
44: 5 "The LORD's," and adopt the name of **I**.
44: 6 Thus says the LORD, the King of **I**, F
44:21 Remember these things, O Jacob, and **I**,
44:21 O **I**, you will not be forgotten by me.
44:23 and will be glorified in **I**.
45: 3 the God of **I**, who call you by your name. A
45: 4 the sake of my servant Jacob, and **I** my chosen,
45:11 Thus says the LORD, the Holy One of **I**,
45:15 you are a God who hides himself, O God of **I**, A
45:17 But **I** is saved by the LORD
45:25 In the LORD all the offspring of **I** shall triumph
46: 3 all the remnant of the house of **I**, D
46:13 I will put salvation in Zion, for **I** my glory.
47: 4 is the Holy One of **I**.
48: 1 who are called by the name of **I**,
48: 1 and invoke the God of **I**, but not in truth or right. A
48: 2 and lean on the God of **I**; A
48:12 Listen to me, O Jacob, and **I**, whom I called:
48:17 your Redeemer, the Holy One of **I**:
49: 3 And he said to me, "You are my servant, **I**,
49: 5 and that **I** might be gathered to him,
49: 6 of Jacob and to restore the survivors of **I**;
49: 7 the Redeemer of **I** and his Holy One,
49: 7 the Holy One of **I**, who has chosen you."
52:12 and the God of **I** will be your rear guard. A
54: 5 the Holy One of **I** is your Redeemer,
55: 5 the Holy One of **I**, for he has glorified you.
56: 8 who gathers the outcasts of **I**,
60: 9 and for the Holy One of **I**,
60:14 the Zion of the Holy One of **I**.
63: 7 the house of **I** that he has shown them according D
63:16 though Abraham does not know us and **I** does
Jer 2: 3 **I** was holy to the LORD,
2: 4 and all the families of the house of **I**. D
2:14 Is **I** a slave? Is he a homeborn servant?
2:26 so the house of **I** shall be shamed— D
2:31 Have I been a wilderness to **I**,
3: 6 Have you seen what she did, that faithless one, **I**,
3: 8 **I**, I had sent her away with a decree of divorce;
3:11 Faithless **I** has shown herself less guilty than false Judah.
3:12 Return, faithless **I**, says the LORD.
3:18 the house of Judah shall join the house of **I**, D
3:20 so you have been faithless to me, O house of **I**, D
3:23 Truly in the LORD our God is the salvation of **I**.
4: 1 If you return, O **I**, says the LORD,
5:11 For the house of **I** and the house of Judah D
5:15 O house of **I**, says the LORD. D
6: 9 Glean thoroughly as a vine the remnant of **I**;
7: 3 Thus says the LORD of hosts, the God of **I**: A
7:12 to it for the wickedness of my people **I**. E
7:21 Thus says the LORD of hosts, the God of **I**: A
9:15 thus says the LORD of hosts, the God of **I**: A
9:26 and all the house of **I** is uncircumcised in heart. D
10: 1 that the LORD speaks to you, O house of **I**. D
10:16 and **I** is the tribe of his inheritance;
11: 3 Thus says the LORD, the God of **I**: A
11:10 house of **I** and the house of Judah have broken D
11:17 the house of **I** and the house of Judah have done, D
12:14 the heritage that I have given my people **I** E
13:11 house of **I** and the whole house of Judah cling D
13:12 Thus says the LORD, the God of **I**: A
14: 8 O hope of **I**, its savior in time of trouble,
16: 9 For thus says the LORD of hosts, the God of **I**: A
16:14 "As the LORD lives who brought the people of **I** B
16:15 "As the LORD lives who brought the people of **I** B
17:13 O hope of **I**! O LORD! All who forsake you shall
18: 6 O house of **I**, just as this potter has done? D
18: 6 so are you in my hand, O house of **I**. D
18:13 The virgin **I** has done a most horrible thing.
19: 3 Thus says the LORD of hosts, the God of **I**: A
19:15 the LORD of hosts, the God of **I**: A
21: 4 Thus says the LORD, the God of **I**: A
23: 2 Therefore thus says the LORD, the God of **I**, A
23: 6 In his days Judah will be saved and **I** will live
23: 7 "As the LORD lives who brought the people of **I** B
23: 8 the house of **I** out of the land of the north and D
23:13 by Baal and led my people **I** astray. E
24: 5 the LORD, the God of **I**: A
25:15 For thus the LORD, the God of **I**, said to me: A
25:27 Thus says the LORD of hosts, the God of **I**: A

Jer 27: 4 Thus says the LORD of hosts, the God of I: A
27:21 the God of I, concerning the vessels left A
28: 2 the LORD of hosts, the God of I: A
28:14 For thus says the LORD of hosts, the God of I: A
29: 4 the God of I, to all the exiles whom I have sent A
29: 8 For thus says the LORD of hosts, the God of I: A
29:21 the God of I, concerning Ahab son of Kolaiah A
29:23 because they have perpetrated outrage in I
29:25 the LORD of hosts, the God of I: A
30: 2 the LORD, the God of I: A
30: 3 my people, I and Judah, says the LORD, M
30: 4 that the LORD spoke concerning I and Judah: M
30:10 says the LORD, and do not be dismayed, O I;
31: 1 I will be the God of all the families of I,
31: 2 in the wilderness; when I sought for rest,
31: 4 and you shall be built, O virgin I!
31: 7 "Save, O LORD, your people, the remnant of I."
31: 9 for I have become a father to I,
31:10 say, "He who scattered I will gather him,
31:21 Return, O virgin I, return to these your cities.
31:23 Thus says the LORD of hosts, the God of I: A
31:27 when I will sow the house of I and the house D
31:31 a new covenant with the house of I and D
31:33 covenant that I will make with the house of I D
31:36 of I would cease to be a nation before me forever.
31:37 then I will reject all the offspring of I
32:14 the LORD of hosts, the God of I: A
32:15 For thus says the LORD of hosts, the God of I: A
32:20 and to this day in I and among all humankind,
32:21 You brought your people I out of the land E
32:30 people of I and the people of Judah have done B
32:30 people of I have done nothing but provoke me B
32:32 evil of the people of I and the people of Judah B
32:36 Now therefore thus says the LORD, the God of I, A
33: 4 For thus says the LORD, the God of I, A
33: 7 the fortunes of Judah and the fortunes of I,
33:14 the promise I made to the house of I and D
33:17 a man to sit on the throne of the house of I, D
34: 2 the LORD, the God of I: A
34:13 the LORD, the God of I: A
35:13 the LORD of hosts, the God of I: A
35:17 the God of hosts, the God of I: A
35:18 Thus says the LORD of hosts, the God of I: A
35:19 the LORD of hosts, the God of I: A
36: 2 to you against I and Judah and all the nations, M
37: 7 Thus says the LORD, God of I: A
38:17 the God of hosts, the God of I, A
39:16 Thus says the LORD of hosts, the God of I: A
41: 9 for defense against King Baasha of I;
42: 9 "Thus says the LORD, the God of I, A
42:15 Thus says the LORD of hosts, the God of I: A
42:18 "For thus says the LORD of hosts, the God of I: A
43:10 Thus says the LORD of hosts, the God of I: A
44: 2 the LORD of hosts, the God of I: A
44: 7 thus says the LORD God of hosts, the God of I: A
44:11 thus says the LORD of hosts, the God of I: A
44:25 the LORD of hosts, the God of I: A
45: 2 the God of I, to you, O Baruch: A
46:25 The LORD of hosts, the God of I, said: A
46:27 my servant Jacob, and do not be dismayed, O I;
48: 1 Thus says the LORD of hosts, the God of I: A
48:13 as the house of I was ashamed of Bethel, D
48:27 I was a laughingstock for you,
49: 1 Has I no sons? Has he no heir?
49: 2 I shall dispossess those who dispossessed him,
50: 4 says the LORD, the people of I shall come, B
50:17 I is a hunted sheep driven away by lions.
50:18 thus says the LORD of hosts, the God of I: A
50:19 I will restore I to its pasture,
50:20 says the LORD, the iniquity of I shall be sought,
50:29 the LORD, the Holy One of I.
50:33 The people of I are oppressed, B
51: 5 I and Judah have not been forsaken by their M
51: 5 their land is full of guilt before the Holy One of I.
51:19 and I is the tribe of his inheritance;
51:33 For thus says the LORD of hosts, the God of I: A
51:49 Babylon must fall for the slain of I,
La 2: 1 down from heaven to earth the splendor of I;
2: 3 He has cut down in fierce anger all the might of I;
2: 5 like an enemy; he has destroyed I;
Eze 2: 3 Mortal, I am sending you to the people of I, B
3: 1 eat this scroll, and go, speak to the house of I. D
3: 4 the house of I and speak my very words to them. D
3: 5 but to the house of I— D
3: 7 But the house of I will not listen to you, D
3: 7 because all the house of I have a hard forehead D
3:17 I have made you a sentinel for the house of I; D
4: 3 This is a sign for the house of I. D
4: 4 place the punishment of the house of I upon it; D
4: 5 you shall bear the punishment of the house of I. D
4:13 "Thus shall the people of I eat their bread, B
5: 4 a fire will come out against all the house of I. D
6: 2 set your face toward the mountains of I, N
6: 3 and say, You mountains of I, hear the word of N
6: 5 I will lay the corpses of the people of I in front B
6:11 for all the vile abominations of the house of I! D
7: 2 thus says the Lord GOD to the land of I: An end! I
8: 4 And the glory of the God of I was there, A
8: 6 that the house of I are committing here, D
8:10 and all the idols of the house of I. D
8:11 stood seventy of the elders of the house of I, D
8:12 elders of the house of I are doing in the dark, D
9: 3 the glory of the God of I had gone up from A
9: 8 of I as you pour out your wrath upon Jerusalem?"
9: 9 the house of I and Judah is exceedingly great; DM
10:19 and the glory of the God of I was above them. A
10:20 that I saw underneath the God of I by A

Eze 11: 5 This is what you think, O house of I; D
11:10 I will judge you at the border of I.
11:11 I will judge you at the border of I.
11:13 will you make a full end of the remnant of I?"
11:15 your fellow exiles, the whole house of I, D
11:17 and I will give you the land of I. I
11:22 and the glory of the God of I was above them. A
12: 6 for I have made you a sign for the house of I. D
12: 9 has not the house of I, the rebellious house, D
12:10 the prince in Jerusalem and all the house of I D
12:19 the inhabitants of Jerusalem in the land of I: I
12:22 what is this proverb of yours about the land of I, I
12:23 and they shall use it no more as a proverb in I."
12:24 or flattering divination within the house of I. D
12:27 house of I is saying, "The vision that he sees D
13: 2 against the prophets of I who are prophesying;
13: 4 like jackals among ruins, O I.
13: 5 or repaired a wall for the house of I, D
13: 9 nor be enrolled in the register of the house of I, D
13: 9 nor shall they enter the land of I; I
13:16 of I who prophesied concerning Jerusalem
14: 1 Certain elders of I came to me and sat down J
14: 4 house of I who take their idols into their hearts D
14: 5 of the hearts of the house of I, D
14: 6 say to the house of I, Thus says the Lord GOD: D
14: 7 For any of those of the house of I, D
14: 7 or of the aliens who reside in I,
14: 9 will destroy him from the midst of my people I. E
14:11 the house of I may no longer go astray from me, D
17: 2 and speak an allegory to the house of I. D
17:23 On the mountain height of I I will plant it,
18: 2 repeating this proverb concerning the land of I, I
18: 3 this proverb shall no more be used by you in I.
18: 6 or lift up his eyes to the idols of the house of I, D
18:15 or lift up his eyes to the idols of the house of I, D
18:25 Hear now, O house of I: Is my way unfair? D
18:29 house of I says, "The way of the Lord is unfair." D
18:29 O house of I, are my ways unfair? D
18:30 Therefore I will judge you, O house of I, D
18:31 Why will you die, O house of I? D
19: 1 raise up a lamentation for the princes of I,
19: 9 be heard no more on the mountains of I. N
20: 1 certain elders of I came to consult the LORD, J
20: 3 speak to the elders of I, and say to them: J
20: 5 On the day when I chose I,
20:13 house of I rebelled against me in the wilderness; D
20:27 mortal, speak to the house of I and say to them, D
20:30 say to the house of I, Thus says the Lord GOD: D
20:31 And shall I be consulted by you, O house of I? D
20:38 but they shall not enter the land of I. I
20:39 for you, O house of I, thus says the Lord GOD: D
20:40 on my holy mountain, the mountain height of I,
20:40 says the Lord GOD, there all the house of I, D
20:42 when I bring you into the land of I, I
20:44 O house of I, says the Lord GOD. D
21: 2 prophesy against the land of I I
21: 3 and say to the land of I, Thus says the LORD: I
21:25 As for you, vile, wicked prince of I,
22: 6 The princes of I in you,
22:18 the house of I has become dross to me; D
24:21 Say to the house of I, Thus says the Lord GOD: D
25: 3 over the land of I when it was made desolate, I
25: 6 the malice within you against the land of I, I
25:14 upon Edom by the hand of my people I; E
27:17 Judah and the land of I traded with you; I
28:24 house of I shall no longer find a pricking brier D
28:25 When I gather the house of I from the peoples D
29: 6 you were a staff of reed to the house of I; D
29:16 be the reliance of the house of I; D
29:21 a horn to sprout up for the house of I, D
33: 7 I have made a sentinel for the house of I; D
33:10 Now you, mortal, say to the house of I, D
33:11 for why will you die, O house of I? D
33:20 O house of I, I will judge all of you according D
33:24 these waste places in the land of I keep saying, I
33:28 and the mountains of I shall be so desolate N
34: 2 prophesy against the shepherds of I:
34: 2 of I who have been feeding yourselves!
34:13 and I will feed them on the mountains of I, N
34:14 the mountain heights of I shall be their pasture;
34:14 on rich pasture on the mountains of I. N
34:30 and that they, the house of I, are my people, D
35: 5 over the people of I to the power of the sword B
35:12 that you uttered against the mountains of I, N
35:15 the house of I, because it was desolate, so I will D
36: 1 you, mortal, prophesy to the mountains of I, N
36: 1 O mountains of I, hear the word of the LORD. N
36: 4 mountains of I, hear the word of the Lord GOD: N
36: 6 Therefore prophesy concerning the land of I, I
36: 8 But you, O mountains of I, N
36: 8 and yield your fruit to my people I; E
36:10 the whole house of I, all of it; D
36:12 I will lead people upon you—my people I— E
36:17 when the house of I lived on their own soil, D
36:21 the house of I had profaned among the nations D
36:22 say to the house of I, Thus says the Lord GOD: D
36:22 It is not for your sake, O house of I, D
36:32 and dismayed for your ways, O house of I. D
36:37 also let the house of I ask me to do this for them: D
37:11 "Mortal, these bones are the whole house of I. D
37:12 and I will bring you back to the land of I. I
37:16 of Ephraim) and all the house of I associated D
37:19 of Ephraim) and the tribes of I associated G
37:21 I will take the people of I from the nations B
37:22 in the land, on the mountains of I; N
37:28 nations shall know that I the LORD sanctify I,
38: 8 the mountains of I, which had long lain waste; N

Eze 38:14 that day when my people I are living securely, E
38:16 you will come up against my people I, E
38:17 in former days by my servants the prophets of I,
38:18 when Gog comes against the land of I, I
38:19 be a great shaking in the land of I; I
39: 2 and lead you against the mountains of I. N
39: 4 You shall fall upon the mountains of I, N
39: 7 My holy name I will make known among my people I; E
39: 7 that I am the LORD, the Holy One in I.
39: 9 Then those who live in the towns of I will go out
39:11 that day I will give to Gog a place for burial in I,
39:12 the house of I shall spend burying them, D
39:17 a great sacrificial feast on the mountains of I, N
39:22 house of I shall know that I am the LORD their D
39:23 the nations shall know that the house of I went D
39:25 and have mercy on the whole house of I; D
39:29 when I pour out my spirit upon the house of I, D
40: 2 brought me, in visions of God, to the land of I, I
40: 4 declare all that you see to the house of I." D
43: 2 glory of the God of I was coming from the east; A
43: 7 I will reside among the people of I forever. B
43: 7 house of I shall no more defile my holy name, D
43:10 mortal, describe the temple to the house of I, D
44: 2 for the LORD, the God of I, has entered by it; A
44: 6 Say to the rebellious house, to the house of I, D
44: 6 O house of I, let there be an end D
44: 9 the foreigners who are among the people of I, B
44:10 from me after their idols when I went astray,
44:12 their idols and made the house of I stumble D
44:15 my sanctuary when the people of I went astray B
44:22 but only a virgin of the stock of the house of I, D
44:28 and you shall give them no holding in I;
44:29 and every devoted thing in I shall be theirs.
45: 6 it shall belong to the whole house of I. D
45: 8 It is to be his property in I.
45: 8 but they shall let the house of I have the land D
45: 9 Thus says the Lord GOD: Enough, O princes of I!
45:15 of two hundred, from the pastures of I.
45:16 with the prince in I in making this offering.
45:17 all the appointed festivals of the house of I: D
45:17 to make atonement for the house of I. D
47:13 for inheritance among the twelve tribes of I. G
47:18 the Jordan between Gilead and the land of I; I
47:21 among you according to the tribes of I. G
47:22 They shall be to you as citizens of I;
47:22 be allotted an inheritance among the tribes of I. G
48:11 not go astray when the people of I went astray, B
48:19 The workers of the city, from all the tribes of I, G
48:29 as an inheritance among the tribes of I, G
48:31 gates of the city being named after the tribes of I. G
Da 9: 7 the inhabitants of Jerusalem, and all I, C
9:11 "All I has transgressed your law and turned C
9:20 confessing my sin and the sin of my people I, E
Hos 1: 1 in the days of King Jeroboam son of Joash of I.
1: 4 put an end to the kingdom of the house of I. D
1: 5 On that day I will break the bow of I in the valley
1: 6 for I will no longer have pity on the house of I D
1:10 the people of I shall be like the sand of the sea, B
1:11 and the people of I shall be gathered together, B
3: 1 just as the LORD loves the people of I, B
4: 1 Hear the word of the LORD, O people of I; B
4:15 Though you play the whore, O I,
4:16 Like a stubborn heifer, I is stubborn;
5: 1 Give heed, O house of I! D
5: 3 I know Ephraim, and I is not hidden from me;
5: 3 you have played the whore; I is defiled.
5: 9 among the tribes of I I declare what is sure. G
6:10 In the house of I I have seen a horrible thing; D
6:10 Ephraim's whoredom is there, I is defiled.
7: 1 when I would heal I, the corruption
8: 2 I cries to me, "My God, we—I—know you!"
8: 3 I has spurned the good; the enemy shall pursue
8: 6 For it is from I, an artisan made it; it is not God.
8: 8 I is swallowed up; now they are among the
8:14 I has forgotten his Maker, and built palaces;
9: 1 Do not rejoice, O I!
9: 7 I cries, "The prophet is a fool,
9:10 Like grapes in the wilderness, I found I.
10: 1 I is a luxuriant vine that yields its fruit.
10: 6 and I shall be ashamed of his idol.
10: 8 The high places of Aven, the sin of I,
10: 9 Since the days of Gibeah you have sinned, O I;
10:15 At dawn the king of I shall be utterly cut off. F
11: 1 When I was a child, I loved him,
11: 8 How can I hand you over, O I?
11:12 and the house of I with deceit; D
12:12 there I served for a wife,
12:13 By a prophet the LORD brought I up from Egypt,
13: 1 there was trembling; he was exalted in I;
13: 9 I will destroy you, O I; who can help you?
14: 1 Return, O I, to the LORD your God,
14: 5 I will be like the dew to I;
Joel 2:27 You shall know that I am in the midst of I,
3: 2 on account of my people and my heritage I,
3:16 a stronghold for the people of I. B
Am 1: 1 concerning I in the days of King Uzziah of Judah
1: 1 in the days of King Jeroboam son of Joash of I,
2: 6 For three transgressions of I, and for four,
2:11 Is it not indeed so, O people of I? B
3: 1 O people of I, against the whole family that I B
3:12 a piece of an ear, so shall the people of I who B
3:14 On the day I punish I for its transgressions,
4: 5 for so you love to do, O people of I! B
4:12 Therefore thus I will do to you, O I;
4:12 prepare to meet your God, O I!
5: 1 up over you in lamentation, O house of I: D

Am 5: 2 no more to rise, is maiden **I**;
5: 4 For thus says the LORD to the house of **I**: D
5:25 the forty years in the wilderness, O house of **I**? D
6: 1 to whom the house of **I** resorts! D
6:14 raising up against you a nation, O house of **I**, D
7: 8 a plumb line in the midst of my people **I**; E
7: 9 and the sanctuaries of **I** shall be laid waste,
7:10 the priest of Bethel, sent to King Jeroboam of **I**,
7:10 against you in the very center of the house of **I**; D
7:11 and **I** must go into exile away from his land.' "
7:15 'Go, prophesy to my people **I**.' E
7:16 You say, 'Do not prophesy against **I**,
7:17 **I** shall surely go into exile away from its land.' "
8: 2 "The end has come upon my people **I**; E
9: 7 not like the Ethiopians to me, O people of **I**? B
9: 7 Did I not bring **I** up from the land of Egypt,
9: 9 and shake the house of **I** among all the nations D
9:14 I will restore the fortunes of my people **I**, E
Mic 1: 5 of Jacob and for the sins of the house of **I**. D
1:13 for in you were found the transgressions of **I**.
1:14 of Achzib shall be a deception to the kings of **I**. H
1:15 the glory of **I** shall come to Adullam.
2:12 O Jacob, I will gather the survivors of **I**;
3: 1 you heads of Jacob and rulers of the house of **I**! D
3: 8 to Jacob his transgression and to **I** his sin.
3: 9 the house of Jacob and chiefs of the house of **I**, D
5: 1 a rod they strike the ruler of **I** upon the cheek.
5: 2 for me one who is to rule in **I**,
5: 3 rest of his kindred shall return to the people of **I**. B
6: 2 and he will contend with **I**.
Na 2: 2 as well as the majesty of **I**,
Zep 2: 9 as I live, says the LORD of hosts, the God of **I**, A
3:13 the remnant of **I**; they shall do no wrong
3:14 Sing aloud, O daughter Zion; shout, O **I**!
3:15 The king of **I**, the LORD, is in your midst; F
Zec 1:19 "These are the horns that have scattered Judah, **I**,
8:13 O house of Judah and house of **I**, D
9: 1 as do all the tribes of **I**; G
11:14 annulling the family ties between Judah and **I**. R
12: 1 The word of the LORD concerning **I**:
Mal 1: 1 The word of the LORD to **I** by Malachi.
1: 5 "Great is the LORD beyond the borders of **I**!"
2:11 and abomination has been committed in **I** and
2:16 For I hate divorce, says the LORD, the God of **I**, A
4: 4 that I commanded him at Horeb for all **I**. C
Mt 2: 6 a ruler who is to shepherd my people **I**.' " E
2:20 and go to the land of **I**, I
2:21 and went to the land of **I**. I
8:10 in no one in **I** have I found such faith.
9:33 "Never has anything like this been seen in **I**."
10: 6 but go rather to the lost sheep of the house of **I**. D
10:23 you will not have gone through all the towns of **I**
15:24 to the lost sheep of the house of **I**." D
15:31 And they praised the God of **I**. A
19:28 judging the twelve tribes of **I**. G
27: 9 on whom some of the people of **I** had set a price, B
27:42 He is the King of **I**; F
Mk 12:29 Jesus answered, "The first is, 'Hear, O **I**:
15:32 Let the Messiah, the King of **I**, F
Lk 1:16 of the people of **I** to the Lord their God. B
1:54 He has helped his servant **I**,
1:68 "Blessed be the Lord God of **I**, A
1:80 until the day he appeared publicly to **I**.
2:25 looking forward to the consolation of **I**,
2:32 to the Gentiles and for glory to your people **I**." E
2:34 for the falling and the rising of many in **I**,
4:25 there were many widows in **I** in the time of Elijah,
4:27 There were also many lepers in **I** in the time of
7: 9 "I tell you, not even in **I** have I found such faith."
22:30 on thrones judging the twelve tribes of **I**. G
24:21 But we had hoped that he was the one to redeem **I**.
Jn 1:31 that he might be revealed to **I**."
1:49 You are the King of **I**!" F
3:10 Jesus answered him, "Are you a teacher of **I**,
12:13 of the Lord—the King of **I**!" F
Ac 1: 6 the time when you will restore the kingdom to **I**?"
2:36 house of **I** know with certainty that God has D
4:10 and to all the people of **I**, B
4:27 with the Gentiles and the peoples of **I**,
5:21 the council and the whole body of the elders of **I**, J
5:31 that he might give repentance to **I** and forgiveness
7:42 in the wilderness, O house of **I**? D
9:15 and kings and before the people of **I**; B
10:36 know the message he sent to the people of **I**, B
13:17 of this people **I** chose our ancestors and made E
13:23 Of this man's posterity God has brought to **I**
13:24 a baptism of repentance to all the people of **I**. B
28:20 of the hope of **I** that I am bound with this chain."
Ro 9: 6 For not all Israelites truly belong to **I**,
9:27 And Isaiah cries out concerning **I**,
9:27 "Though the number of the children of **I** were like
9:31 but **I**, who did strive for the righteousness
10:19 Again I ask, did **I** not understand?
10:21 But of **I** he says, "All day long I have held out my
11: 2 how he pleads with God against **I**?
11: 7 **I** failed to obtain what it was seeking.
11:11 so as to make **I** jealous.
11:23 of **I**, if they do not persist in unbelief, will
11:25 a hardening has come upon part of **I**,
11:26 And so all **I** will be saved; C
1Co 10:18 Consider the people of **I**; B
2Co 3: 7 the people of **I** could not gaze at Moses' face B
3:13 people of **I** from gazing at the end of the glory B
Gal 6:16 and mercy, and upon the **I** of God.
Eph 2:12 being aliens from the commonwealth of **I**,
Php 3: 5 a member of the people of **I**, B
Heb 8: 8 with the house of **I** and with the house of Judah; D
8:10 the house of **I** after those days, says the Lord: D
11:28 of the firstborn would not touch the firstborn of **I**.
Rev 2:14 to put a stumbling block before the people of **I**, B
7: 4 sealed out of every tribe of the people of **I**: B
Tob 1: 4 When I was in my own country, in the land of **I**, I
1: 4 from among all the tribes of **I**, G
1: 4 where all the tribes of **I** should offer sacrifice G
1: 5 of **I** had erected in Dan and on all the mountains
1: 6 it is prescribed for all **I** by an everlasting decree. C
1: 8 to the converts who had attached themselves to **I**.
13: 3 before the nations, O children of **I**;
13:17 Blessed be the God of **I**!' A
14: 4 everything that was spoken by the prophets of **I**,
14: 4 All of our kindred, inhabitants of the land of **I**, I
14: 4 and the whole land of **I** will be desolate, I
14: 5 and God will bring them back into the land of **I**; I
14: 5 just as the prophets of **I** have said concerning it.
Jdt 4: 8 and the senate of the whole people of **I**, B
4: 9 every man of **I** cried out to God with great fervor,
4:12 God of **I** not to allow their infants to be carried A
4:15 to look with favor on the whole house of **I**. D
5: 1 people of **I** had prepared for war and had closed B
6: 2 tell us not to make war against the people of **I** B
6:17 had boasted he would do against the house of **I**. D
6:21 that night they called on the God of **I** for help. A
8: 1 of Salamiel son of Sarasadai son of **I**.
8: 6 festivals and days of rejoicing of the house of **I**. D
8:33 the Lord will deliver **I** by my hand.
9:12 God of my father, God of the heritage of **I**,
9:14 there is no other who protects the people of **I** B
10: 1 Judith had stopped crying out to the God of **I**, A
10: 8 the people of **I** may glory and Jerusalem may B
12: 8 she prayed the Lord God of **I** to direct her way A
13: 7 "Give me strength today, O Lord God of **I**!" A
13:11 still showing his power in **I** and his strength
13:14 not withdrawn his mercy from the house of **I**, D
14: 4 the borders of **I** will pursue them and cut them
14: 5 the man who despised the house of **I** and sent D
14:10 When Achior saw all that the God of **I** had done, A
14:10 he was circumcised, and joined the house of **I**, D
15: 4 and to all the frontiers of **I**,
15: 8 the good things that the Lord had done for **I**,
15: 9 you are the great boast of **I**,
15:10 you have done great good to **I**,
15:12 All the women of **I** gathered to see her,
15:13 while all the men of **I** followed, L
15:14 Judith began this thanksgiving before all **I**, C
16: 7 to exalt the oppressed in **I**.
16:24 and the house of **I** mourned her for seven days. D
AdE 10: 9 this is **I**, who cried out to God and were saved.
10:13 to generation forever among his people **I**." E
13: 9 when it is your will to save **I**,
13:13 to kiss the soles of his feet to save **I**!
13:18 And all **I** cried out mightily, C
14: 3 She prayed to the Lord God of **I**, and said: A
14: 5 O Lord, took **I** out of all the nations,
Sir Pr: 1 and for these we should praise **I** for instruction
17:17 but **I** is the Lord's own portion.
24: 8 and in **I** receive your inheritance.'
36:17 O Lord, on the people called by your name, on **I**,
37:25 but the days of **I** are without number.
45: 5 the covenant, and **I** his decrees.
45:11 in engraved letters each of the tribes of **I**; G
45:17 and to enlighten **I** with his law.
45:23 and he made atonement for **I**.
46: 1 so that he might give **I** its inheritance.
47:11 a covenant of kingship and a glorious throne in **I**.
47:18 who is called the God of **I**, A
47:23 of Nebat led **I** into sin and started Ephraim
50:13 their hands before the whole congregation of **I**. Q
50:23 and may there be peace in our days in **I**,
51:12 *Give thanks to the guardian of **I**,*
51:12 *Give thanks to the redeemer of **I**,*
51:12 *Give thanks to him who gathers the dispersed of **I**,*
51:12 *For the children of **I**, the people close to him.*
Bar 2: 1 against our judges who ruled **I**,
2: 1 and our rulers and the people of **I** and Judah. BM
2:11 And now, O Lord God of **I**, A
2:15 for **I** and his descendants are called by your name.
2:26 the wickedness of the house of **I** and the house D
2:28 in the presence of the people of **I**, B
2:35 and I will never again remove my people **I** from E
3: 1 O Lord Almighty, God of **I**, A
3: 4 O Lord Almighty, God of **I**, A
3: 4 hear now the prayer of the people of **I**, B
3: 9 Hear the commandments of life, O **I**;
3:10 O **I**, why is it that you are in the land
3:24 O **I**, how great is the house of God,
3:36 and gave her to his servant Jacob and to **I**,
4: 4 O **I**, for we know what is pleasing to God.
5: 7 so that **I** may walk safely in the glory of God.
5: 8 The woods and every fragrant tree have shaded **I**
5: 9 For God will lead **I** with joy,
Aza 1:12 the sake of your servant Isaac and **I** your holy one,
1:61 Bless the Lord, O **I**; sing praise to him
Sus 1:48 to condemn a daughter of **I** without examination
1:57 how you have been treating the daughters of **I**,
1Mc 1:11 In those days certain renegades came out from **I**
1:20 He went up against **I** and came to Jerusalem with
1:25 **I** mourned deeply in every community,
1:30 and destroyed many people of **I**. B
1:36 an evil adversary of **I** at all times.
1:43 Many even from **I** gladly adopted his religion;
1:53 they drove **I** into hiding in every place
1:58 They kept using violence against **I**,
1:62 in **I** stood firm and were resolved in their hearts
1:64 Very great wrath came upon **I**.
1Mc 2:16 Many from **I** came to them;
2:42 a company of Hasideans, mighty warriors of **I**,
2:46 that they found within the borders of **I**.
2:55 the command, became a judge in **I**.
2:70 all **I** mourned for him with great lamentation. C
3: 2 helped him; they gladly fought for **I**.
3: 8 thus he turned away wrath from **I**.
3:10 and a large force from Samaria to fight against **I**.
3:35 the strength of **I** and the remnant of Jerusalem;
3:46 **I** formerly had a place of prayer in Mizpah.
4:11 that there is one who redeems and saves **I**."
4:25 Thus **I** had a great deliverance that day.
4:27 things had not happened to **I** as he had intended,
4:30 saying, "Blessed are you, O Savior of **I**,
4:31 Hem in this army by the hand of your people **I**, E
4:59 the assembly of **I** determined that every year at O
5: 3 because they kept lying in wait for **I**.
5:60 as two thousand of the people of **I** fell that day. B
5:62 through whom deliverance was given to **I**.
5:63 and his brothers were greatly honored in all **I** C
6:18 the garrison in the citadel kept hemming **I** in
7: 5 to him all the renegade and godless men of **I**; L
7:22 of the land of Judah and did great damage in **I**.
7:26 who hated and detested **I**.
8:18 of the Greeks was enslaving **I** completely.
9:20 All **I** made great lamentation for him; C
9:21 "How is the mighty fallen, the savior of **I**!"
9:23 the renegades emerged in all parts of **I**;
9:27 So there was great distress in **I**,
9:51 And he placed garrisons in them to harass **I**.
9:73 Thus the sword ceased from **I**.
9:73 and he destroyed the godless out of **I**.
10:46 the great wrongs that Demetrius had done in **I** and
10:61 A group of malcontents from **I**, renegades,
11:23 He chose some of the elders of **I** and some of J
11:41 for they kept fighting against **I**.
12:52 and all **I** mourned deeply. C
13: 4 all my brothers have perished for the sake of **I**,
13:26 All **I** bewailed him with great lamentation, C
13:41 the yoke of the Gentiles was removed from **I**,
13:51 enemy had been crushed and removed from **I**.
14:11 and **I** rejoiced with great joy.
16: 2 and my father's house have fought the wars of **I**
16: 2 so that we have delivered **I** many times.
2Mc 1:25 You rescue **I** from every evil;
1:26 this sacrifice on behalf of all your people **I** E
9: 5 But the all-seeing Lord, the God of **I**, A
10:38 the Lord who shows great kindness to **I**
11: 6 prayed the Lord to send a good angel to save **I**.
15:14 the family of **I** and prays much for the people and
1Es 1: 3 He told the Levites, the temple servants of **I**,
1: 4 the Lord your God and serve his people **I**; E
1: 5 of **I** and the magnificence of his son Solomon.
1: 5 minister before your kindred the people of **I**, B
1:19 the people of **I** who were present at that time B
1:20 No passover like it had been kept in **I** since
1:21 none of the kings of **I** had kept such a passover H
1:21 the people of Judah and all of **I** who were living
1:24 so that the words of the Lord fell upon **I**.
1:32 be done throughout the whole nation of **I**.
1:33 in the book of the kings of **I** and Judah. HM
1:48 the laws of the Lord, the God of **I**. A
2: 3 The Lord of **I**, the Lord Most High,
2: 5 and build the house of the Lord of **I**—
5:37 or lineage that they belonged to **I**:
5:41 All those of **I**, twelve or more years of age,
5:46 the gatekeepers, and all **I** in their towns. C
5:48 and prepared the altar of the God of **I**, A
5:60 according to the directions of King David of **I**; C
5:61 goodness and his glory are forever upon all **I**." C
5:67 the temple for the Lord God of **I**. A
5:70 the heads of the ancestral houses in **I** said to them,
5:71 for we alone will build it for the Lord of **I**,
6: 1 to them in the name of the Lord God of **I**. A
6:14 by a king of **I** who was great and strong, F
6:15 against the Lord of **I** who is in heaven,
7: 4 by the command of the Lord God of **I**. A
7: 6 And the people of **I**, the priests, the Levites, B
7: 8 for the sin of all **I**, according to the number of C
7: 8 of the twelve leaders of the tribes of **I**; G
7: 9 the Lord God of **I** in accordance with the book A
7:10 The people of **I** who came from exile kept B
7:13 people of **I** who had returned from exile ate it, B
7:15 for the service of the Lord God of **I**. A
8: 3 which was given by the God of **I**; A
8: 5 the people of **I** and some of the priests and B
8: 7 taught all **I** all the ordinances and judgments. C
8:13 the Lord of **I** that I and my Friends have vowed,
8:27 and I gathered men from **I** to go up with me."
8:47 son of **I**, namely Sherebiah with his descendants
8:55 and the nobles and all **I** had given. C
8:59 and to the heads of the ancestral houses of **I**,
8:65 the God of **I**, twelve bulls for all Israel, A
8:65 the God of Israel, twelve bulls for all **I**, C
8:69 "The people of **I** and the rulers and the priests B
8:72 at the word of the Lord of **I** gathered around me,
8:89 O Lord of **I**, you are faithful;
8:92 Shecaniah son of Jehiel, one of the men of **I**, L
8:92 but even now there is hope for **I**.
8:96 leaders of the priests and Levites of all **I** swear C
9: 7 and so have increased the sin of **I**.
9:26 Of **I**: of the descendants of Parosh:
9:37 when the people of **I** were in their settlements, B
9:39 that had been given by the Lord God of **I**. A
Pm 151: 7 and took away disgrace from the people of **I**. B
3Mc 2: 6 Pharaoh who had enslaved your holy people **I**. E
2:10 And because you love the house of **I**, D

3Mc 2:16 bestowed your glory on your people I, E
6: 4 the light of your mercy on the nation of I.
6: 9 reveal yourself quickly to those of the nation of I—
7:16 of their ancestors, the eternal Savior of I, in words
7:23 Blessed be the Deliverer of I through all times!
2Es 2:10 which I was going to give to I.
2:11 which I had prepared for I.
2:33 from the Lord on Mount Horeb to go to I.
3:19 and your commandment to the posterity of I.
3:32 Or has another nation known you besides I?
4:23 why I has been given over to the Gentiles
5:17 Or do you not know that I has been entrusted
5:33 "Are you greatly disturbed in mind over I?
5:35 of Jacob and the exhaustion of the people of I?" B
7:*107* [37] Joshua after him for I in the days of Achan,
8:16 and about I, for whom I am sad,
9:30 'Hear me, O I, and give heed to my words,
12:46 "Take courage, O I; and do
14:28 "Hear these words, O I.
4Mc 17:22 divine Providence preserved I

ISRAEL'S‡ (18) [ISRAEL]

Ge 47:29 When the time of I death drew near,
48:13 Ephraim in his right hand toward I left,
48:13 and Manasseh in his left hand toward I right,
Ex 18: 8 to Pharaoh and to the Egyptians for I sake,
Nu 1:20 The descendants of Reuben, I firstborn,
Dt 1:38 he is the one who will secure I possession of it.
Jdg 20: 6 sent her throughout the whole extent of I territory;
1Sa 9:20 And on whom is all I desire fixed,
1Ch 17:24 'The LORD of hosts, the God of Israel, is I God';
Ps 68:26 the LORD, O you who are of I fountain!"
Isa 56:10 I sentinels are blind, they are all
Jer 3:21 the plaintive weeping of I children,
Eze 21:12 against all I princes; they are thrown to the sword,
Hos 5: 5 I pride testifies against him;
7:10 I pride testifies against him;
Bar 4: 5 Take courage, my people, who perpetuate I name!
1Mc 14:26 they have fought and repulsed I enemies
2Es 7:10 He said to me, "So also is I portion.

ISRAELITE‡ (31) [ISRAEL]

Ex 1: 9 "Look, the I people are more numerous
5:15 Then the I supervisors came to Pharaoh and cried,
5:19 The I supervisors saw that they were in trouble
14:19 before the I army moved and went behind them;
35:29 All the I men and women whose hearts made them
Lev 24:10 an I and whose father was an Egyptian came out
24:10 the I woman's son and a certain I began fighting
24:11 I woman's son blasphemed the Name in a curse.
Nu 15:13 Every native I shall do these things in this way,
16: 2 two hundred fifty I men, leaders of
25: 8 he went after the I man into the tent,
25: 8 and pierced the two of them, the I and the woman,
25:14 The name of the slain I man,
32:28 to the heads of the ancestral houses of the I tribes.
36: 3 But if they are married into another I tribe,
Dt 3:18 over armed as the vanguard of your I kin.
23:19 not charge interest on loans to another I,
23:20 on loans to another I you may not charge interest,
24: 7 If someone is caught kidnaping another I,
enslaving or selling the I,
Jdg 11:39 So there arose an I custom that
2Sa 15: 6 to every I who came to the king for judgment;
Ezr 2: 2 The number of the I people:
Ne 7: 7 The number of the I people:
9: 2 Then those of I descent separated themselves
Jn 1:47 "Here is truly an I in whom there is no deceit!"
Ro 11: 1 I myself am an I, a descendant of Abraham,
Tob 5: 9 a man who is one of our own I kindred!"
Jdt 4:11 And all the I men, women,
4Mc 18: 1 O I children, offspring of the seed of Abraham,

ISRAELITES‡ (538) [ISRAEL]

A. ALL THE ISRAELITES (37)
B. CONGREGATION OF [THE] ISRAELITES (25)
C. TRIBES OF THE ISRAELITES (8)

Ge 32:32 to this day the I do not eat the thigh muscle that is
36:31 before any king reigned over the I.
46: 8 Now these are the names of the I,
50:25 So Joseph made the I swear, saying,
Ex 1: 7 But the I were fruitful and prolific;
1:12 so that the Egyptians came to dread the I.
1:13 in imposing tasks on the I,
2:23 The I groaned under their slavery, and cried out.
2:25 God looked upon the I, and God took notice
3: 9 The cry of the I has now come to me;
3:10 to Pharaoh to bring my people, the I, out
3:11 and bring the I out of Egypt?"
3:13 "If I come to the I and say to them,
3:14 He said further, "Thus you shall say to the I,
3:15 "Thus you shall say to the I, 'The LORD,
4:29 and assembled all the elders of the I.
4:31 that the LORD had given heed to the I and
5:14 And the supervisors of the I,
6: 5 of the I whom the Egyptians are holding as slaves,
6: 6 Say therefore to the I, 'I am the LORD,
6: 9 Moses told this to the I;
6:11 and tell Pharaoh king of Egypt to let the I go out
6:12 "The I have not listened to me;
6:13 and gave them orders regarding the I
6:13 charging them to free the I from the land of Egypt.
6:26 "Bring the I out of the land of Egypt,
6:27 to Pharaoh king of Egypt to bring the I out

Ex 7: 2 to let the I go out of his land.
7: 4 upon Egypt and bring my people the I,
7: 5 and bring the I out from among them."
9: 4 that nothing shall die of all that belongs to the I.' "
9: 6 but of the livestock of the I not one died.
9: 7 that not one of the livestock of the I was dead.
9:26 Only in the land of Goshen, where the I were,
9:35 and he would not let the I go,
10:20 and he would not let the I go.
10:23 but all the I had light where they lived. A
11: 7 But not a dog shall growl at any of the I—
12:27 for he passed over the houses of the I in Egypt,
12:28 The I went and did just as
12:31 go away from my people, both you and the I!
12:35 The I had done as Moses told them;
12:37 The I journeyed from Rameses to Succoth,
12:40 The time that the I had lived
12:42 a vigil to be kept for the LORD by all the I A
12:50 All the I did just as the LORD had commanded A
12:51 the LORD brought the I out of the land of Egypt,
13: 2 the first to open the womb among the I,
13:18 The I went up out of the land of Egypt prepared
13:19 a solemn oath of the I, saying,
14: 2 the I to turn back and camp in front of Pi-hahiroth,
14: 3 Pharaoh will say of the I,
14: 8 of Pharaoh king of Egypt and he pursued the I,
14:10 As Pharaoh drew near, the I looked back,
14:10 In great fear the I cried out to the LORD.
14:15 Tell the I to go forward.
14:16 that the I may go into the sea on dry ground.
14:22 The I went into the sea on dry ground,
14:25 The Egyptians said, "Let us flee from the I,
14:29 But the I walked on dry ground through the sea,
15: 1 Moses and the I sang this song to the LORD:
15:19 but the I walked through the sea on dry ground.
16: 1 whole congregation of the I set out from Elim; B
16: 2 congregation of the I complained against Moses B
16: 3 The I said to them, "If only we had died by
16: 6 So Moses and Aaron said to all the I, A
16: 9 "Say to the whole congregation of the I, B
16:10 Aaron spoke to the whole congregation of the I, B
16:12 "I have heard the complaining of the I;
16:15 the I saw it, they said to one another, "What is it?"
16:17 The I did so, some gathering more, some less.
16:35 The I ate manna forty years,
17: 1 the whole congregation of the I journeyed B
17: 7 because the I quarreled and tested the LORD,
19: 1 On the third new moon after the I had gone out of
19: 3 to the house of Jacob, and tell the I:
19: 6 These are the words that you shall speak to the I."
20:22 Thus you shall say to the I:
25: 2 Tell the I to take for me an offering;
25:22 I will deliver to you all my commands for the I.
27:20 the I to bring you pure oil of beaten olives for
27:21 be observed throughout their generations by the I.
28: 1 from among the I, to serve me as priests—
28:30 the I on his heart before the LORD continually.
28:38 that the I consecrate as their sacred donations;
29:28 and his sons from the I, for this is an offering;
29:28 be an offering by the I from their sacrifice
29:43 I will meet with the I there,
29:45 I will dwell among the I, and I will be their God.
30:12 When you take a census of the I to register them,
30:16 from the I and shall designate it for the service of
30:16 before the LORD it will be a reminder to the I of
30:31 You shall say to the I,
31:13 You yourself are to speak to the I:
31:16 Therefore the I shall keep the sabbath,
32:20 scattered it on the water, and made the I drink it.
33: 5 For the LORD had said to Moses, "Say to the I,
33: 6 the I stripped themselves of their ornaments,
34:30 When Aaron and all the I saw Moses, A
34:32 Afterward all the I came near, A
34:34 and told the I what he had been commanded,
34:35 the I would see the face of Moses, that the skin
35: 1 Moses assembled all the congregation of the I B
35: 4 Moses said to all the congregation of the I: B
35:20 Then all the congregation of the I withdrew B
35:30 Then Moses said to the I:
36: 3 that the I had brought for doing the work on
39:32 the I had done everything just as
39:42 The I had done all of the work just as
40:36 the I would set out on each stage of their journey;
Lev 25:46 but as for your fellow I,
Nu 1: 2 the whole congregation of I, in their clans, B
1:45 So the whole number of the I,
1:49 not take a census of them with the other I.
1:52 The other I shall camp in their
1:53 be no wrath on the congregation of the I; B
1:54 The I did so; they did just
2: 2 The I shall camp each in their
2:32 the enrollment of the I by their ancestral houses;
2:33 the Levites were not enrolled among the other I.
2:34 I did just as the LORD had commanded Moses:
3: 8 and attend to the duties for the I as they do service
3: 9 to him from among the I.
3:12 the Levites from among the I as substitutes for all
3:12 the firstborn that open the womb among the I.
3:38 whatever had to be done for the I;
3:40 Enroll all the firstborn males of the I,
3:41 as substitutes for all the firstborn among the I,
3:41 for all the firstborn among the livestock of the I.
3:42 So Moses enrolled all the firstborn among the I,
3:45 as substitutes for all the firstborn among the I, and
3:46 of the firstborn of the I,
3:50 from the firstborn of the I he took the money,
5: 2 Command the I to put out of

Nu 5: 4 The I did so, putting them outside the camp;
5: 4 as the LORD had spoken to Moses, so the I did.
5: 6 Speak to the I: When a man
5: 9 Among all the sacred donations of the I,
5:12 Speak to the I and say to them:
6: 2 Speak to the I and say to them:
6:23 saying, Thus you shall bless the I:
6:27 So they shall put my name on the I,
8: 6 the Levites from among the I and cleanse them.
8: 9 and assemble the whole congregation of the I. B
8:10 the I shall lay their hands on the Levites,
8:11 the LORD as an elevation offering from the I,
8:14 the Levites from among the other I,
8:16 to me from among the I;
8:16 that open the womb, the firstborn of all the I. A
8:17 For all the firstborn among the I are mine,
8:18 in place of all the firstborn among the I.
8:19 as a gift to Aaron and his sons from among the I,
8:19 to do the service for the I at the tent of meeting,
8:19 and to make atonement for the I,
8:19 among the I for coming too close to the sanctuary.
8:20 Aaron and the whole congregation of the I did B
8:20 the I did with the Levites just as
9: 2 Let the I keep the passover at its appointed time.
9: 4 So Moses told the I that they should keep
9: 5 the LORD had commanded Moses, so the I did.
9: 7 at its appointed time among the I?"
9:10 Speak to the I, saying: Anyone of you
9:17 then the I would set out;
9:17 the cloud settled down, there the I would camp.
9:18 the command of the LORD the I would set out,
9:19 the I would keep the charge of the LORD,
9:22 the I would remain in camp and would not set out;
10:12 I set out by stages from the wilderness of Sinai,
10:28 This was the order of march of the I,
11: 4 and the I also wept again, and said,
13: 2 which I am giving to the I;
13: 3 all of them leading men among the I.
13:24 of the cluster that the I cut down from there.
13:26 and Aaron and to all the congregation of the I B
13:32 So they brought to the I an unfavorable report of
14: 2 all the I complained against Moses and Aaron; A
14: 5 the assembly of the congregation of the I. B
14: 7 and said to all the congregation of the I, B
14:10 at the tent of meeting to all the I. A
14:27 I have heard the complaints of the I,
14:39 When Moses told these words to all the I, A
15: 2 Speak to the I and say to them:
15:18 Speak to the I and say to them:
15:25 for all the congregation of the I, and they shall B
15:26 All the congregation of the I shall be forgiven, B
15:29 among the I and the alien residing among them—
15:32 When the I were in the wilderness,
15:38 the I, and tell them to make fringes on the corners
16:38 Thus they shall be a sign to the I.
16:40 a reminder to the I that no outsider, who is not of
16:41 of the I rebelled against Moses and against Aaron B
17: 2 to the I, and get twelve staffs from them, one
17: 5 the complaints of the I that they continually make
17: 6 Moses spoke to the I;
17: 9 the staffs from before the LORD to all the I; A
17:12 The I said to Moses, "We are perishing;
18: 5 so that wrath may never again come upon the I.
18: 6 now take your brother Levites from among the I;
18: 8 all the holy gifts of the I;
18:11 the gifts of all the elevation offerings of the I;
18:19 the I present to the LORD I have given to you,
18:20 I am your share and your possession among the I.
18:22 the I shall no longer approach the tent of meeting,
18:23 But among the I they shall have no allotment,
18:24 to the Levites as their portion the tithe of the I,
18:24 that they shall have no allotment among the I.
18:26 the I the tithe that I have given you from them
18:28 from all the tithes that you receive from the I;
18:32 But you shall not profane the holy gifts of the I,
19: 2 Tell the I to bring you a red heifer without defect,
19: 9 they shall be kept for the congregation of the I B
19:10 This shall be a perpetual statute for the I and for
20: 1 The I, the whole congregation,
20:12 to show my holiness before the eyes of the I,
20:19 The I said to him, "We will stay on the highway;
20:22 They set out from Kadesh, and the I,
20:24 not enter the land that I have given to the I,
21: 6 and they bit the people, so that many I died.
21:10 The I set out, and camped in Oboth.
22: 1 The I set out, and camped in the plains of Moab
25: 6 of the I came and brought a Midianite woman
25: 6 in the sight of the whole congregation of the I, B
25:11 from the I by manifesting such zeal among them
25:11 that in my jealousy I did not consume the I.
25:13 and made atonement for the I.' "
26: 2 a census of the whole congregation of the I, B
26: 4 The I, who came out of the land of Egypt, were:
26:51 This was the number of the I enrolled:
26:62 among the I because there was no allotment given
26:62 no allotment given to them among the I.
26:63 who enrolled the I in the plains of Moab by
26:64 who had enrolled the I in the wilderness of Sinai.
27: 8 You shall also say to the I, "If a man dies,
27:11 It shall be for the I a statute and ordinance,
27:12 and see the land that I have given to the I.
27:20 so that all the congregation of the I may obey. B
27:21 both he and all the I with him, A
28: 2 Command the I, and say to them:
29:40 So Moses told the I everything just as
30: 1 Moses said to the heads of the tribes of the I: C
31: 2 "Avenge the I on the Midianites;

Nu 31: 9 The I took the women of Midian
31:12 and to the congregation of the I, B
31:16 made the I act treacherously against the LORD in
31:54 the tent of meeting as a memorial for the I before
32: 7 the hearts of the I from going over into the land
32: 9 they discouraged the hearts of the I from going
32:17 we will take up arms as a vanguard before the I,
32:18 until all the I have obtained their inheritance. A
33: 1 These are the stages by which the I went out of
33: 3 on the day after the passover the I went out boldly
33: 5 I set out from Rameses, and camped at Succoth.
33:38 in the fortieth year after the I had come out of
33:40 heard of the coming of the I.
33:51 Speak to the I, and say to them:
34: 2 Command the I, and say to them:
34:13 Moses commanded the I, saying:
34:29 to apportion the inheritance for the I in the land
35: 2 Command the I to give, from the inheritance
35: 8 the I, from the larger tribes you shall take many,
35:10 Speak to the I, and say to them:
35:15 These six cities shall serve as refuge for the I,
35:34 for I the LORD dwell among the I.
36: 1 the heads of the ancestral houses of the I;
36: 2 to give the land for inheritance by lot to the I;
36: 4 And when the jubilee of the I comes,
36: 5 Then Moses commanded the I according to
36: 7 the I shall be transferred from one tribe to another;
36: 7 for all I shall retain the inheritance
36: 8 an inheritance in any tribe of the I shall marry one
36: 8 so that all I may continue to possess
36: 9 tribes of the I shall retain its own inheritance.'" C
36:13 the LORD commanded through Moses to the I in
Dt 1: 3 to the I just as the LORD had commanded him
4:44 This is the law that Moses set before the I.
4:45 that Moses spoke to the I when they had come out
4:46 and the I defeated when they came out of Egypt.
10: 6 (The I journeyed from Beeroth-bene-jaakan
24:14 whether other I or aliens who reside in your land
27:14 Levites shall declare in a loud voice to all the I: A
29: 1 the LORD commanded Moses to make with the I
31:19 therefore write this song, and teach it to the I;
31:19 be a witness for me against the I.
31:22 and taught it to the I.
31:23 the I into the land that I promised them;
32:49 which I am giving to the I for a possession;
32:51 among the I at the waters of Meribath-kadesh in
32:51 by failing to maintain my holiness among the I.
32:52 the land that I am giving to the I."
33: 1 the man of God, blessed the I before his death.
34: 8 The I wept for Moses in the plains
34: 9 and the I obeyed him, doing as
Jos 1: 2 into the land that I am giving to them, to the I.
2: 2 "Some I have come here tonight to search out
3: 1 and set out from Shittim with all the I, A
3: 9 Joshua then said to the I,
4: 4 Joshua summoned the twelve men from the I,
4: 5 one for each of the tribes of the I, C
4: 7 these stones shall be to the I a memorial forever."
4: 8 The I did as Joshua commanded.
4: 8 according to the number of the tribes of the I, C
4:12 of Manasseh crossed over armed before the I,
4:21 to the I, "When your children ask their parents
5: 1 of the Jordan for the I until they had crossed over,
5: 1 in them, because of the I.
5: 2 "Make flint knives and circumcise the I
5: 3 and circumcised the I at Gibeath-haaraloth.
5: 6 For the I traveled forty years in the wilderness,
5:10 While the I were camped in Gilgal they kept
5:12 and the I no longer had manna;
6: 1 up inside and out because of the I;
7: 1 the I broke faith in regard to the devoted things:
7: 1 and the anger of the LORD burned against the I.
7:12 the I are unable to stand before their enemies;
7:23 and brought them to Joshua and all the I; A
8:22 so they were surrounded by I, some on one side,
8:31 the LORD had commanded the I, as it is written
8:32 And there, in the presence of the I,
9: 6 and said to him and to the I,
9: 7 I said to the Hivites, "Perhaps you live among us;
9:17 I set out and reached their cities on the third day
9:18 But the I did not attack them,
9:26 he saved them from the I;
10: 4 for it has made peace with Joshua and with the I."
10:11 of the hailstones than the I killed with the sword.
10:12 when the LORD gave the Amorites over to the I,
10:20 the I had finished inflicting a very great slaughter
10:21 no one dared to speak against any of the I.
10:24 Joshua summoned all the I, A
11:14 and the livestock, the I took for their booty;
11:19 There was not a town that made peace with the I,
11:22 None of the Anakim was left in the land of the I;
12: 1 the I defeated, whose land they occupied beyond
12: 6 of the LORD, and the I defeated them;
12: 7 and the I defeated on the west side of the Jordan,
13: 6 I will myself drive them out from before the I;
13:13 Yet the I did not drive out the Geshurites or
13:22 the I also put to the sword Balaam son of Beor,
14: 1 These are the inheritances that the I received in
14: 1 of the families of the tribes of the I distributed C
14: 5 The I did as the LORD commanded Moses;
17:13 But when the I grew strong,
18: 1 whole congregation of the I assembled at Shiloh, B
18: 2 among the I seven tribes whose inheritance had
18: 3 So Joshua said to the I,
18:10 and there Joshua apportioned the land to the I,
19:49 the I gave an inheritance among them
19:51 families of the tribes of the I distributed by lot C
Jos 20: 2 "Say to the I, 'Appoint the cities of refuge,
20: 9 These were the cities designated for all the I, A
21: 1 to the heads of the families of the tribes of the I; C
21: 3 the I gave to the Levites the following towns
21: 8 These towns and their pasture lands the I gave
21:41 the holdings of the I were in all forty-eight towns
22: 7 a possession beside their fellow I in the land west
22: 9 parting from the I at Shiloh,
22:11 The I heard that the Reubenites and the Gadites
22:11 on the side that belongs to the I.
22:12 the whole assembly of the I gathered at Shiloh,
22:13 Then the I sent the priest Phinehas son of Eleazar
22:31 now you have saved the I from the hand of
22:32 to the I, and brought back word to them.
22:33 The report pleased the I;
22:33 and the I blessed God and spoke no more
24:32 which the I had brought up from Egypt,
Jdg 1: 1 the death of Joshua, the I inquired of the LORD,
2: 4 of the LORD spoke these words to all the I, A
2: 6 the I all went to their own inheritances
2:11 the I did what was evil in the sight of the LORD
3: 2 that successive generations of I might know war,
3: 5 So the I lived among the Canaanites, the Hittites,
3: 7 The I did what was evil in the sight of the LORD,
3: 8 and the I served Cushan-rishathaim eight years.
3: 9 But when the I cried out to the LORD,
3: 9 the LORD raised up a deliverer for the I,
3:12 The I again did what was evil in the sight of
3:14 the I served King Eglon of Moab eighteen years.
3:15 But when the I cried out to the LORD,
3:15 The I sent tribute by him to King Eglon of Moab.
3:27 the I went down with him from the hill country,
4: 1 The I again did what was evil in the sight of
4: 3 Then the I cried out to the LORD for help;
4: 3 and had oppressed the I cruelly twenty years.
4: 5 and the I came up to her for judgment.
4:23 God subdued King Jabin of Canaan before the I.
4:24 Then the hand of the I bore harder and harder
6: 1 The I did what was evil in the sight of the LORD,
6: 2 the I provided for themselves hiding places in
6: 3 For whenever the I put in seed,
6: 6 and the I cried out to the LORD for help.
6: 7 When the I cried to the LORD on account of
6: 8 the LORD sent a prophet to the I;
8:22 Then the I said to Gideon, "Rule over us,
8:28 So Midian was subdued before the I,
8:33 the I relapsed and prostituted themselves with
8:34 The I did not remember the LORD their God,
9:55 When the I saw that Abimelech was dead,
10: 6 The I again did what was evil in the sight of
10: 8 and they crushed and oppressed the I that year.
10: 8 oppressed all the I that were beyond the Jordan A
10:10 So the I cried out to the LORD, saying,
10:11 And the LORD said to the I,
10:15 And the I said to the LORD, "We have sinned;
10:17 I came together, and they encamped at Mizpah.
11:27 decide today for the I or for the Ammonites."
13: 1 The I again did what was evil in the sight of
19:30 saying, "Thus shall you say to all the I, A
19:30 the day that the I came up from the land of Egypt
20: 1 all the I came out, from Dan to Beer-sheba, A
20: 3 And the I said, "Tell us, how did this criminal act
20: 7 So now, you I, all of you, give your advice
20:13 not listen to their kinsfolk, the I.
20:14 to go out to battle against the I.
20:17 And the I, apart from Benjamin,
20:18 The I proceeded to go up to Bethel,
20:19 Then the I got up in the morning,
20:20 The I went out to battle against Benjamin;
20:20 I drew up the battle line against them at Gibeah.
20:21 down on that day twenty-two thousand of the I.
20:22 The I took courage, and again formed
20:23 The I went up and wept before the LORD until
20:24 So the I advanced against the Benjaminites
20:25 and struck down eighteen thousand of the I,
20:26 Then all the I, the whole army, A
20:27 And the I inquired of the LORD (for the ark of
20:30 Then the I went up against the Benjaminites on
20:32 But the I said, "Let us retreat and draw them away
20:33 The main body of the I drew back its battle line
20:33 while those I who were in ambush rushed out
20:35 I destroyed twenty-five thousand one hundred men
20:36 The I gave ground to Benjamin,
20:39 Benjamin had begun to inflict casualties on the I,
20:42 from the I in the direction of the wilderness;
20:48 the I turned back against the Benjaminites,
21: 1 Now the I had sworn at Mizpah,
21: 5 the I said, "Which of all the tribes of Israel did
21: 6 But the I had compassion for Benjamin their kin,
21:18 the I had sworn, "Cursed be anyone who gives
21:24 So the I departed from there at that time by tribes
1Sa 2:14 at Shiloh to all the I who came there. A
10:27 of the I across the Jordan whose right eye Nahash,
11:15 and there Saul and all the I rejoiced greatly. A
13: 6 When the I saw that they were in distress (for
13:20 so all the I went down to the Philistines A
14:18 For at that time the ark of God went with the I.
14:21 and joined the I who were with Saul and Jonathan.
14:22 when all the I who had gone into hiding A
15: 2 in opposing the I when they came up out of Egypt.
17: 2 the I gathered and encamped in the valley of Elah,
17:24 All the I, when they saw the man, A
17:25 The I said, "Have you seen this man who has come
17:53 The I came back from chasing the Philistines,
29: 1 I were encamped by the fountain that is in Jezreel.
2Sa 15:13 "The hearts of the I have gone after Absalom."
16:15 Now Absalom and all the I came to Jerusalem; A
2Sa 16:18 and this people and all the I have chosen, A
17:26 I and Absalom encamped in the land of Gilead.
18:17 Meanwhile all the I fled to their homes. A
19: 8 Meanwhile, all the I had fled to their homes. A
23: 9 for battle. The I withdrew,
1Ki 6: 1 after the I came out of the land of Egypt,
8: 1 the leaders of the ancestral houses of the I,
8: 9 where the LORD made a covenant with the I,
9:21 whom the I were unable to destroy completely—
9:22 But of the I Solomon made no slaves;
11: 2 the LORD had said to the I, "You shall not enter
12:17 But Rehoboam reigned over the I who were living
18:20 So Ahab sent to all the I, A
19:10 for the I have forsaken your covenant,
19:14 for the I have forsaken your covenant,
20:27 After the I had been mustered and provisioned,
20:29 I killed one hundred thousand Aramean
21:26 whom the LORD drove out before the I.)
2Ki 3:24 the I rose up and attacked the Moabites,
17: 6 he carried the I away to Assyria.
18:11 The king of Assyria carried the I away to Assyria,
1Ch 1:43 of Edom before any king reigned over the I:
9: 2 in their possessions in their towns were I,
2Ch 5: 3 And all the I assembled before the king at A
13:12 O I, do not fight against the LORD,
13:16 The I fled before Judah, and God gave them
13:18 Thus the I were subdued at that time,
Ezr 3: 1 seventh month came, and the I were in the towns,
Ne 13: 2 the I with bread and water, but hired Balaam
Isa 66:20 just as the I bring a grain offering in a clean vessel
Eze 37:16 "For Judah, and the I associated with it";
Da 1: 3 to bring some of the I of the royal family and of
Hos 3: 4 I shall remain many days without king or prince,
3: 5 the I shall return and seek the LORD their God,
Ob 1:20 of the I who are in Halah shall possess Phoenicia
Ac 2:22 "You that are I, listen to what I have to say:
2:29 "Fellow I, I may say to you confidently
3:12 Peter saw it, he addressed the people, "You I,
5:35 Then he said to them, "Fellow I,
7:23 it came into his heart to visit his relatives, the I.
7:37 This is the Moses who said to the I,
13:16 "You I, and others who fear God, listen.
21:28 "Fellow I, help! This is the man who is teaching
everyone everywhere against our
Ro 9: 4 They are I, and to them belong the adoption,
9: 6 For not all I truly belong to Israel,
2Co 11:22 Are they Hebrews? So am I. Are they I?
Heb 11:22 of the I and gave instructions about his burial.
Rev 21:12 the names of the twelve tribes of the I; C
Tob 1:18 For in his anger he put to death many I;
5: 5 "From your kindred, the I," he replied,
14: 7 All the I who are saved in those days A
Jdt 4: 1 When the I living in Judea heard of everything
4: 8 So the I did as they had been ordered by
5:23 They said, "We are not afraid of the I;
6:10 to Bethulia and hand him over to the I.
6:14 the I came down from their town and found him;
7: 1 up into the hill country and make war on the I.
7: 4 When the I saw their vast numbers,
7: 6 in full view of the I in Bethulia.
7:10 the I, do not rely on their spears but on the height
7:17 the water supply and the springs of the I.
7:19 The I then cried out to the Lord their God,
10:19 They marveled at her beauty and admired the I,
15: 3 Then the I, everyone that was a soldier,
15: 5 When the I heard it, with one accord they fell
15: 7 And the I, when they returned from the slaughter,
15: 8 of the I who lived in Jerusalem came to witness
16:25 No one ever again spread terror among the I
Sir 46:10 that all the I might see how good it is to follow A
47: 2 so David was set apart from the I.
50:20 over the whole congregation of I, to pronounce B
Sus 1:48 "Are you such fools, O I,
1Mc 3:15 to take vengeance on the I.
3:41 and went to the camp to get the I for slaves.
5: 9 against the I who lived in their territory,
5:45 Then Judas gathered together all the I in Gilead, A
6:21 the siege and some of the ungodly I joined them.
7: 9 he commanded him to take vengeance on the I.
7:13 among the I to seek peace from them,
7:23 and those with him had done among the I;
1Es 5:47 and the I were all in their own homes,
9:37 and the Levites and the I settled in Jerusalem and
4Mc 18: 5 in no way whatever was he able to compel the I

ISRAELITES' (3) [ISRAEL]

Nu 31:30 the I half you shall take one out of every fifty,
31:42 for the I half, which Moses separated from that of
31:47 From the I half Moses took one of every fifty,

ISSACHAR (42) [ISSACHARITES]

Ge 30:18 my maid to my husband"; so she named him I.
35:23 Simeon, Levi, Judah, I, and Zebulun.
46:13 children of I: Tola, Puvah, Jashub, and Shimron.
49:14 I is a strong donkey, lying down between
Ex 1: 3 I, Zebulun, and Benjamin,
Nu 1: 8 From I, Nethanel son of Zuar.
1:28 The descendants of I, their lineage, in their clans,
1:29 of I were fifty-four thousand four hundred.
2: 5 Those to camp next to him shall be the tribe of I.
7:18 the leader of I, presented an offering;
10:15 the company of the tribe of I was Nethanel son
13: 7 from the tribe of I, Igal son of Joseph;
26:23 The descendants of I by their clans:
26:25 These are the clans of I:
Dt 27:12 Simeon, Levi, Judah, I, Joseph, and Benjamin.

Dt 33:18 Zebulun, in your going out; and **I**,
Jos 17:10 on the north Asher is reached, and on the east **I**.
17:11 Within **I** and Asher, Manasseh had Beth-shean
19:17 The fourth lot came out for **I**, for the tribe of **I**,
19:23 This is the inheritance of the tribe of **I**,
21: 6 from the families of the tribe of **I**,
21:28 Out of the tribe of **I**:
Jdg 5:15 chiefs of **I** came with Deborah, and **I** faithful to
10: 1 Tola son of Puah son of Dodo, a man of **I**,
1Ki 4:17 Jehoshaphat son of Paruah, in **I**;
15:27 Baasha son of Ahijah, of the house of **I**,
1Ch 2: 1 Reuben, Simeon, Levi, Judah, **I**, Zebulun,
6:62 of the tribes of **I**, Asher, Naphtali, and Manasseh
6:72 and out of the tribe of **I**:
7: 1 sons of **I**: Tola, Puah, Jashub, and Shimron, four.
7: 5 to all the families of **I** were
12:32 Of **I**, those who had understanding of the times,
12:40 from as far away as **I** and Zebulun and Naphtali,
26: 5 **I** the seventh, Peullethai the eighth;
27:18 for **I**, Omri son of Michael;
2Ch 30:18 **I**, and Zebulun, had not cleansed themselves,
Eze 48:25 from the east side to the west, **I**, one portion.
48:26 Adjoining the territory of **I**,
48:33 three gates, the gate of Simeon, the gate of **I**,
Rev 7: 7 from the tribe of **I** twelve thousand,

ISSACHARITES (2) [ISSACHAR]
Nu 2: 5 The leader of the **I** shall be Nethanel son of Zuar,
34:26 Of the tribe of the **I** a leader, Paltiel son of Azzan.

ISSHIAH (6)
1Ch 7: 3 Michael, Obadiah, Joel, and **I**, five,
12: 6 **I**, Azarel, Joezer, and Jashobeam, the Korahites;
23:20 sons of Uzziel: Micah the chief and **I** the second.
24:21 Of Rehabiah: of the sons of Rehabiah, **I** the chief.
24:25 brother of Micah, **I**; of the sons of **I**, Zechariah.

ISSHIJAH (1)
Ezr 10:31 Eliezer, **I**, Malchijah, Shemaiah, Shimeon,

ISSUE (17) [ISSUED]
Ge 15: 4 no one but your very own **i** shall be your heir."
Nu 18:15 The first **i** of the womb of all creatures,
Dt 7:13 the increase of your cattle and the **i** of your flock,
21:17 since he is the first **i** of his virility,
28: 4 the increase of your cattle and the **i** of your flock.
28:18 the increase of your cattle and the **i** of your flock.
28:51 the increase of your cattle and the **i** of your flock,
Ezr 4:21 **i** an order that these people be made to cease,
Ps 78:51 the first **i** of their strength in the tents of Ham.
105:36 the first **i** of all their strength.
Isa 22:24 the offspring and **i**, every small vessel,
Eze 21:19 both of them shall **i** from the same land.
AdE 1:19 it pleases the king, let him **i** a royal decree,
Sir 27:28 Mockery and abuse **i** from the proud,
2Mc 4:28 by the king on account of this **i**.
14:18 shrank from deciding the **i** by bloodshed.
15:20 all were now looking forward to the coming **i**,

ISSUED (20) [ISSUE]
Jos 8:27 to the word of the LORD that he had **i** to Joshua.
Ezr 5:17 to see whether a decree was **i** by King Cyrus for
6: 3 the first year of his reign, King Cyrus **i** a decree:
Est 3: 9 let a decree be **i** for their destruction,
3:14 A copy of the document was to be **i** as a decree
3:15 and the decree was **i** in the citadel of Susa.
4: 8 the written decree **i** in Susa for their destruction,
8:13 to be **i** as a decree in every province and published
8:14 The decree was **i** in the citadel of Susa.
9:14 a decree was **i** in Susa,
Eze 1:13 the fire was bright, and lightning **i** from the fire.
Da 2:13 The decree was **i**, and the wise men were about to
7:10 stream of fire **i** and flowed out from his presence.
1Mc 5:58 So they **i** orders to the men of the forces that were
2Mc 6: 8 a decree was **i** to the neighboring Greek cities
15:10 he had aroused their courage, he **i** his orders,
1Es 2:28 now **i** orders to prevent these people from building
3Mc 1: 2 of the Ptolemaic arms that had been previously **i**
2Es 13: 4 and whenever his voice **i** from his mouth,
4Mc 4:23 and after he had plundered them he **i** a decree that

ISUAH (KJV) See ISHVAH

ISUI (KJV) See ISHVI

ISTALCURUS (1)
1Es 8:40 Of the descendants of Bigvai, Uthai son of **I**,

IT (6836) [ITS, ITSELF] See Index of Articles Etc.

ITALIAN (1) [ITALY]
Ac 10: 1 a centurion of the **I** Cohort, as it was called.

ITALY (4) [ITALIAN]
Ac 18: 2 who had recently come from **I**
27: 1 When it was decided that we were to sail for **I**,
27: 6 an Alexandrian ship bound for **I** and put us
Heb 13:24 Those from **I** send you greetings.

ITCH (15) [ITCHING]
Lev 13:30 it is an **i**, a leprous disease of the head or
13:32 priest shall examine the **i**; if the **i** has not spread,
13:32 and the **i** appears to be no deeper than the skin,
13:33 but the **i** he shall not shave.
13:33 The priest shall confine the person with the **i**
13:34 priest shall examine the **i**; if the **i** has not spread
13:35 But if the **i** spreads in the skin
13:36 If the **i** has spread in the skin,
13:37 But if in his eyes the **i** is checked,
13:37 and black hair has grown in it, the **i** is healed,
14:54 This is the ritual for any leprous disease: for an **i**,
22:22 or having a discharge or an **i** or scabs—
Dt 28:27 scurvy, and **i**, of which you cannot be healed.

ITCHING (4) [ITCH]
Lev 13:31 If the priest examines the **i** disease,
13:31 the person with the **i** disease for seven days.
21:20 or a man with a blemish in his eyes or an **i** disease
2Ti 4: 3 not put up with sound doctrine, but having **i** ears,

ITEM (1)
Nu 31:28 one **i** out of every five hundred, whether persons,

ITHAI (1)
1Ch 11:31 **I** son of Ribai of Gibeah of the Benjaminites,

ITHAMAR (22)
Ex 6:23 and she bore him Nadab, Abihu, Eleazar, and **I**.
28: 1 Nadab and Abihu, Eleazar and **I**.
38:21 of the Levites being under the direction of **I** son of
Lev 10: 6 to Aaron and to his sons Eleazar and **I**,
10:12 to Aaron and to his remaining sons, Eleazar and **I**:
10:16 He was angry with Eleazar and **I**,
Nu 3: 2 Nadab the firstborn, and Abihu, Eleazar, and **I**;
3: 4 Eleazar and **I** served as priests in the lifetime
4:28 be under the oversight of **I** son of Aaron the priest.
4:33 under the hand of **I** son of Aaron the priest.
7: 8 under the direction of **I** son of Aaron the priest.
26:60 To Aaron were born Nadab, Abihu, Eleazar, and **I**.
1Ch 6: 3 The sons of Aaron: Nadab, Abihu, Eleazar, and **I**.
24: 1 The sons of Aaron: Nadab, Abihu, Eleazar, and **I**.
24: 2 so Eleazar and **I** became the priests.
24: 3 and Ahimelech of the sons of **I**,
24: 4 the sons of Eleazar than among the sons of **I**,
24: 4 and eight of the sons of **I**.
24: 5 among both the sons of Eleazar and the sons of **I**.
24: 6 for Eleazar and one chosen for **I**.
Ezr 8: 2 of Phinehas, Gershom. Of **I**, Daniel.
1Es 8:29 Of the descendants of **I**, Gamael.

ITHIEL (1)
Ne 11: 7 of Kolaiah son of Maaseiah son of **I** son

ITHLAH (1)
Jos 19:42 Shaalabbin, Aijalon, **I**,

ITHMAH (1)
1Ch 11:46 and Joshaviah sons of Elnaam, and **I** the Moabite,

ITHNAN (1)
Jos 15:23 Kedesh, Hazor, **I**,

ITHRA (1)
2Sa 17:25 the son of a man named **I** the Ishmaelite,

ITHRAN (3)
Ge 36:26 Hemdan, Eshban, **I**, and Cheran.
1Ch 1:41 sons of Dishon: Hamran, Eshban, **I**, and Cheran.
7:37 Bezer, Hod, Shamma, Shilshah, **I**, and Beera.

ITHREAM (2)
2Sa 3: 5 and the sixth, **I**, of David's
1Ch 3: 3 the sixth **I**, by his wife Eglah;

ITHRITE (4) [ITHRITES]
2Sa 23:38 Ira the **I**; Gareb the **I**;
1Ch 11:40 Ira the **I**, Gareb the **I**,

ITHRITES (1) [ITHRITE]
1Ch 2:53 And the families of Kiriath-jearim: the **I**,

ITINERANT (1)
Ac 19:13 Then some **i** Jewish exorcists tried to use the name

ITS (1757) [IT] See Index of Articles Etc.

ITSELF (96) [IT] See Index of Articles Etc.

ITTAH-KAZIN (KJV) See ETH-KAZIN

ITTAI (8)
2Sa 15:19 Then the king said to **I** the Gittite,
15:21 But **I** answered the king, "As the LORD lives,
15:22 David said to **I**, "Go then, march on."
15:22 So **I** the Gittite marched on,
18: 2 and one third under the command of **I** the Gittite.
18: 5 The king ordered Joab and Abishai and **I**, saying,
2Sa 18:12 the king commanded you and Abishai and **I**,
23:29 **I** son of Ribai of Gibeah of the Benjaminites;

ITURAEA (1)
Lk 3: 1 and his brother Philip ruler of the region of **I**

IVAH (KJV) See IVVAH

IVORY (13)
1Ki 10:18 The king also made a great **i** throne,
10:22 silver, **i**, apes, and peacocks.
22:39 and all that he did, and the **i** house that he built,
2Ch 9:17 The king also made a great **i** throne,
9:21 silver, **i**, apes, and peacocks.
Ps 45: 8 From **i** palaces stringed instruments make you glad
SS 5:14 His body is **i** work, encrusted with sapphires.
7: 4 Your neck is like an **i** tower.
Eze 27: 6 of pines from the coasts of Cyprus, inlaid with **i**.
27:15 they brought you in payment **i** tusks and ebony.
Am 3:15 and the houses of **i** shall perish,
6: 4 Alas for those who lie on beds of **i**,
Rev 18:12 all articles of **i**, all articles of costly wood, bronze,

IVVAH (3)
2Ki 18:34 Where are the gods of Sepharvaim, Hena, and **I**?
19:13 the king of Hena, or the king of **I**?"
Isa 37:13 the king of Hena, or the king of **I**?"

IVY (1) [IVY-LEAF, IVY-WREATHED]
2Mc 6: 7 they were compelled to wear wreathes of **i** and

IVY-LEAF (1) [IVY, LEAF]
3Mc 2:29 branded on their bodies by fire with the **i** symbol

IVY-WREATHED (2) [IVY, WREATH]
Jdt 15:12 She took **i** wands in her hands
2Mc 10: 7 carrying **i** wands and beautiful branches and

IYE-ABARIM (2) [ABARIM]
Nu 21:11 They set out from Oboth, and camped at **I**,
33:44 They set out from Oboth and camped at **I**,

IYIM (1)
Nu 33:45 They set out from **I** and camped at Dibon-gad.

IZHAR (10) [IZHARITES]
Ex 6:18 The sons of Kohath: Amram, **I**, Hebron,
6:21 The sons of **I**: Korah, Nepheg, and Zichri.
Nu 3:19 Amram, **I**, Hebron, and Uzziel.
16: 1 Now Korah son of **I** son of Kohath son of Levi,
1Ch 4: 7 The sons of Helah: Zereth, **I**, and Ethnan.
6: 2 sons of Kohath: Amram, **I**, Hebron, and Uzziel.
6:18 sons of Kohath: Amram, **I**, Hebron, and Uzziel.
6:38 son of **I**, son of Kohath, son of Levi, son of Israel;
23:12 Amram, **I**, Hebron, and Uzziel, four.
23:18 The sons of **I**: Shelomith the chief.

IZHARITES (4) [IZHAR]
Nu 3:27 the clan of the **I**, the clan of the Hebronites,
1Ch 24:22 Of the **I**, Shelomoth;
26:23 Of the Amramites, the **I**, the Hebronites,
26:29 Of the **I**, Chenaniah and his sons were appointed

IZLIAH (1)
1Ch 8:18 Ishmerai, **I**, and Jobab were the sons of Elpaal.

IZRAHIAH (2)
1Ch 7: 3 The son of Uzzi: **I**. And the sons of **I**: Michael,

IZRAHITE (1)
1Ch 27: 8 the **I**; in his division were twenty-four thousand.

IZRI (1)
1Ch 25:11 the fourth to **I**, his sons and his brothers, twelve;

IZZIAH (2)
Ezr 10:25 Ramiah, **I**, Malchijah, Mijamin, Eleazar,
1Es 9:26 Ramiah, **I**, Malchijah, Mijamin, and Eleazar,

J

JAAKAN (1)
1Ch 1:42 The sons of Ezer: Bilhan, Zaavan, and **J**.

JAAKOBAH (1)
1Ch 4:36 **J**, Jeshohaiah, Asaiah, Adiel, Jesimiel, Benaiah,

JAALA (1) [=JAALAH]
Ne 7:58 of J, of Darkon, of Giddel,

JAALAH (2) [=JAALA]
Ezr 2:56 J, Darkon, Giddel,
1Es 5:33 the descendants of Peruda, the descendants of J,

JAALAM (KJV) See JALAM

JAANAI (KJV) See JANAI

JAAR (1)
Ps 132: 6 we found it in the fields of J.

JAARE-OREGIM (1)
2Sa 21:19 and Elhanan son of J, the Bethlehemite,

JAARESHIAH (1)
1Ch 8:27 J, Elijah, and Zichri were the sons of Jeroham.

JAASIEL (2)
1Ch 11:47 Eliel, and Obed, and J the Mezobaite.
27:21 for Benjamin, J son of Abner;

JAASU (1)
Ezr 10:37 Mattaniah, Mattenai, and J.

JAAZANIAH (4)
2Ki 25:23 and J son of the Maacathite.
Jer 35: 3 So I took J son of Jeremiah son of Habazziniah,
Eze 8:11 with J son of Shaphan standing among them.
11: 1 among them I saw J son of Azzur,

JAAZER (KJV) See JAZER

JAAZIAH (2)
1Ch 24:26 The sons of J: Beno.
24:27 of J, Beno, Shoham, Zaccur, and Ibri.

JAAZIEL (1)
1Ch 15:18 Zechariah, J, Shemiramoth, Jehiel, Unni, Eliab,

JABAL (1)
Ge 4:20 Adah bore J; he was the ancestor of those

JABBOK (7)
Ge 32:22 and crossed the ford of the J.
Nu 21:24 the Arnon to the J, as far as to the Ammonites;
Dt 2:37 the whole upper region of the Wadi J as well as
3:16 and up to the J, the wadi being boundary of
Jos 12: 2 from the middle of the valley as far as the river J,
Jdg 11:13 took away my land from the Arnon to the J and to
11:22 of the Amorites from the Arnon to the J and from

JABESH (12) [JABESH-GILEAD]
1Sa 11: 1 and all the men of J said to Nahash,
11: 3 The elders of J said to him,
11: 5 the message from the inhabitants of J.
11: 9 messengers came and told the inhabitants of J,
11:10 So the inhabitants of J said,
31:12 They came to J and burned them there.
31:13 and buried them under the tamarisk tree in J,
2Ki 15:10 Shallum son of J conspired against him,
15:13 of J began to reign in the thirty-ninth year
15:14 he struck down Shallum son of J in Samaria
1Ch 10:12 and the bodies of his sons, and brought them to J.
10:12 Then they buried their bones under the oak in J,

JABESH-GILEAD‡ (13) [GILEAD, JABESH]
Jdg 21: 8 It turned out that no one from J had come to
21: 9 not one of the inhabitants of J was there.
21:10 "Go, put the inhabitants of J to the sword,
21:12 of J four hundred young virgins who had never
21:14 whom they had saved alive of the women of J;
1Sa 10:27 from the Ammonites and had entered J.
11: 1 Nahash the Ammonite went up and besieged J;
11: 9 "Thus shall you say to the inhabitants of J:
31:11 of J heard what the Philistines had done to Saul,
2Sa 2: 4 "It was the people of J who buried Saul,"
2: 5 David sent messengers to the people of J,
21:12 of his son Jonathan from the people of J,
1Ch 10:11 But when all J heard everything that

JABEZ (4)
1Ch 2:55 The families also of the scribes that lived at J:
4: 9 J was honored more than his brothers;
4: 9 and his mother named him J, saying,
4:10 J called on the God of Israel, saying,

JABIN‡ (8) [JABIN'S]
Jos 11: 1 When King J of Hazor heard of this,
Jdg 4: 2 So the LORD sold them into the hand of King J
4:17 for there was peace between King J of Hazor and
4:23 that day God subdued King J of Canaan before
4:24 of the Israelites bore harder and harder on King J
4:24 until they destroyed King J of Canaan.
1Sa 12: 9 commander of the army of King J of Hazor,
Ps 83: 9 as to Sisera and J at the Wadi Kishon,

JABIN'S (1) [JABIN]
Jdg 4: 7 I will draw out Sisera, the general of J army,

JABNEEL (2)
Jos 15:11 along to Mount Baalah, and goes out to J;
19:33 and Adami-nekeb, and J, as far as Lakkum;

JABNEH (1) [JAMNIA]
2Ch 26: 6 of Gath and the wall of J and the wall of Ashdod;

JACAN (1)
1Ch 5:13 Michael, Meshullam, Sheba, Jorai, J, Zia,

JACHIN (8) [JACHINITES]
Ge 46:10 The children of Simeon: Jemuel, Jamin, Ohad, J,
Ex 6:15 The sons of Simeon: Jemuel, Jamin, Ohad, J,
Nu 26:12 of J, the clan of the Jachinites;
1Ki 7:21 he set up the pillar on the south and called it J;
1Ch 9:10 Of the priests: Jedaiah, Jehoiarib, J,
24:17 the twenty-first to J, the twenty-second to Gamul,
2Ch 3:17 the one on the right he called J,
Ne 11:10 Of the priests: Jedaiah son of Joiarib, J,

JACHINITES (1) [JACHIN]
Nu 26:12 of Jachin, the clan of the J;

JACINTH (3)
Ex 28:19 and the third row a j, an agate, and an amethyst;
39:12 and the third row, a j, an agate, and an amethyst;
Rev 21:20 the tenth chrysoprase, the eleventh j,

JACKALS (17)
Job 30:29 I am a brother of j, and a companion of ostriches.
Ps 44:19 yet you have broken us in the haunt of j,
63:10 they shall be prey for j.
Isa 13:22 and j in the pleasant palaces;
34:13 It shall be the haunt of j, an abode for ostriches.
35: 7 the haunt of j shall become a swamp,
43:20 The wild animals will honor me, the j and
Jer 9:11 I will make Jerusalem a heap of ruins, a lair of j;
10:22 the cities of Judah a desolation, a lair of j.
14: 6 they pant for air like j;
49:33 Hazor shall become a lair of j,
51:37 a den of j, an object of horror and of hissing,
La 4: 3 Even the j offer the breast and nurse their young,
5:18 which lies desolate; j prowl over it.
Eze 13: 4 Your prophets have been like j among ruins,
Mic 1: 8 I will make lamentation like the j,
Mal 1: 3 a desolation and his heritage a desert for j.

JACOB‡ (415) [=ISRAEL, JACOB'S, =JESHURUN]
A. HOUSE OF JACOB (25)
B. *GOD OF JACOB (22)
C. SERVANT JACOB (11)

Ge 25:26 his hand gripping Esau's heel; so he was named J.
25:27 a man of the field, while J was a quiet man,
25:28 of game; but Rebekah loved J.
25:29 Once when J was cooking a stew,
25:30 Esau said to J, "Let me eat some of that red stuff,
25:31 J said, "First sell me your birthright."
25:33 J said, "Swear to me first."
25:33 So he swore to him, and sold his birthright to J.
25:34 Then J gave Esau bread and lentil stew,
27: 6 Rebekah said to her son J,
27:11 But J said to his mother Rebekah, "Look,
27:15 and put them on her younger son J;
27:17 and the bread that she had prepared, to her son J.
27:19 J said to his father, "I am Esau your firstborn.
27:21 Then Isaac said to J, "Come near,
27:22 So J went up to his father Isaac,
27:30 As soon as Isaac had finished blessing J,
27:30 when J had scarcely gone out from the presence
27:36 Esau said, "Is he not rightly named J?
27:41 Now Esau hated J because of the blessing
27:41 then I will kill my brother J."
27:42 so she sent and called her younger son J and said
27:46 J marries one of the Hittite women such as these,
28: 1 Then Isaac called J and blessed him,
28: 5 Thus Isaac sent J away;
28: 6 that Isaac had blessed J and sent him away
28: 7 and that J had obeyed his father and his mother
28:10 J left Beer-sheba and went toward Haran.
28:16 Then J woke from his sleep and said,
28:18 So J rose early in the morning,
28:20 Then J made a vow, saying,
29: 1 Then J went on his journey,
29: 4 J said to them, "My brothers,
29:10 Now when J saw Rachel,
29:10 J went up and rolled the stone from
29:11 Then J kissed Rachel, and wept aloud.
29:12 J told Rachel that he was her father's kinsman,
29:13 Laban heard the news about his sister's son J,
29:13 J told Laban all these things,
29:15 to J, "Because you are my kinsman, should you
29:18 J loved Rachel; so he said,
29:20 So J served seven years for Rachel,
29:21 Then J said to Laban, "Give me my wife
29:23 he took his daughter Leah and brought her to J;
29:25 And J said to Laban, "What is this you have done
29:28 J did so, and completed her week;
Ge 29:30 So J went in to Rachel also,
30: 1 When Rachel saw that she bore J no children,
30: 1 she said to J, "Give me children, or I shall die!"
30: 2 J became very angry with Rachel and said,
30: 4 and J went in to her.
30: 5 And Bilhah conceived and bore J a son.
30: 7 Rachel's maid Bilhah conceived again and bore J
30: 9 she took her maid Zilpah and gave her to J as
30:10 Then Leah's maid Zilpah bore J a son.
30:12 Leah's maid Zilpah bore J a second son.
30:16 When J came from the field in the evening,
30:17 and she conceived and bore J a fifth son.
30:19 Leah conceived again, and she bore J a sixth son.
30:25 When Rachel had borne Joseph, J said to Laban,
30:29 J said to him, "You yourself know
30:31 J said, "You shall not give me anything;
30:36 of three days' journey between himself and J,
30:36 while J was pasturing the rest of Laban's flock.
30:37 J took fresh rods of poplar and almond and plane,
30:40 J separated the lambs, and set the faces of
30:41 J laid the rods in the troughs before the eyes of
31: 1 Now J heard that the sons of Laban were saying,
31: 1 "J has taken all that was our father's;
31: 2 And J saw that Laban did not regard him
31: 3 Then the LORD said to J,
31: 4 So J sent and called Rachel and Leah into
31:11 the angel of God said to me in the dream, 'J,'
31:17 So J arose, and set his children and his wives
31:20 And J deceived Laban the Aramean,
31:22 On the third day Laban was told that J had fled.
31:24 "Take heed that you say not a word to J,
31:25 Laban overtook J. Now J had pitched his tent in
31:26 Laban said to J, "What have you done?
31:29 'Take heed that you speak to J neither good
31:31 J answered Laban, "Because I was afraid,
31:32 J did not know that Rachel had stolen the gods.
31:36 Then J became angry, and upbraided Laban.
31:36 J said to Laban, "What is my offense?
31:43 Then Laban answered and said to J,
31:45 So J took a stone, and set it up as a pillar.
31:46 And J said to his kinsfolk, "Gather stones,"
31:47 called it Jegar-sahadutha: but J called it Galeed.
31:51 Then Laban said to J, "See this heap and see
31:53 So J swore by the Fear of his father Isaac,
31:54 and J offered a sacrifice on the height
32: 1 J went on his way and the angels
32: 2 and when J saw them he said,
32: 3 J sent messengers before him to his brother Esau
32: 4 Thus says your servant J, C
32: 6 The messengers returned to J, saying,
32: 7 Then J was greatly afraid and distressed;
32: 9 And J said, "O God of my father Abraham
32:18 you shall say, 'They belong to your servant J; C
32:20 'Moreover your servant J is behind us.' " C
32:24 J was left alone; and a man wrestled with him
32:25 the man saw that he did not prevail against J,
32:26 But J said, "I will not let you go,
32:27 "What is your name?" And he said, "J."
32:28 "You shall no longer be called J, but Israel,
32:29 Then J asked him, "Please tell me your name."
32:30 So J called the place Peniel, saying,
32:32 he struck J on the hip socket at the thigh muscle.
33: 1 Now J looked up and saw Esau coming,
33: 5 "Who are these with you?" J said,
33: 8 J answered, "To find favor with my lord."
33:10 J said, "No, please; if I find favor with you,
33:13 But J said to him, "My lord knows that
33:17 But J journeyed to Succoth,
33:18 J came safely to the city of Shechem,
33: 1 whom she had borne to J,
34: 3 And his soul was drawn to Dinah daughter of J;
34: 5 J heard that Shechem had defiled his daughter
34: 5 so J held his peace until they came.
34: 6 And Hamor the father of Shechem went out to J
34: 7 just as the sons of J came in from the field.
34:13 The sons of J answered Shechem
34:25 when they were still in pain, two of the sons of J,
34:27 And the other sons of J came upon the slain,
34:30 Then J said to Simeon and Levi,
35: 1 God said to J, "Arise, go up to Bethel,
35: 2 So J said to his household and to all who were
35: 4 they gave to J all the foreign gods that they had,
35: 4 J hid them under the oak that was near Shechem.
35: 6 J came to Luz (that is, Bethel),
35: 9 to J again when he came from Paddan-aram,
35:10 God said to him, "Your name is J;
35:10 no longer shall you be called J,
35:14 J set up a pillar in the place where he had spoken
35:15 So J called the place where God had spoken
35:20 and J set up a pillar at her grave;
35:22 Now the sons of J were twelve.
35:26 These were the sons of J who were born to him
35:27 J came to his father Isaac at Mamre,
35:29 and his sons Esau and J buried him.
36: 6 to a land some distance from his brother J.
37: 1 J settled in the land where his father had lived as
37: 2 This is the story of the family of J.
37:34 Then J tore his garments,
42: 1 When J learned that there was grain in Egypt,
42: 4 But J did not send Joseph's brother Benjamin
42:29 they came to their father J in the land of Canaan,
42:36 And their father J said to them,
45:25 and came to their father J in the land of Canaan.
45:27 the spirit of their father J revived.
46: 2 to Israel in visions of the night, and said, "J, J."
46: 5 Then J set out from Beer-sheba;
46: 5 and the sons of Israel carried their father J,

Ge 46: 6 J and all his offspring with him,
46: 8 J and his offspring, who came to Egypt.
46:15 whom she bore to J in Paddan-aram,
46:18 and these she bore to J—sixteen persons).
46:22 who were born to J—fourteen persons in all).
46:25 and these she bore to J—seven persons in all).
46:26 the persons belonging to J who came into Egypt,
46:27 all the persons of the house of J who came A
47: 7 Then Joseph brought in his father J, and presented him before Pharaoh, and J blessed Pharaoh.
47: 8 Pharaoh said to J, "How many are the years
47: 9 J said to Pharaoh, "The years
47:10 Then J blessed Pharaoh, and went out from
47:28 J lived in the land of Egypt seventeen years;
47:28 so the days of J, the years of his life,
48: 2 When J was told, "Your son Joseph has come
48: 3 And J said to Joseph, "God Almighty appeared
49: 1 Then J called his sons, and said:
49: 2 Assemble and hear, O sons of J;
49: 7 I will divide them in J, and scatter them in Israel.
49:24 by the hands of the Mighty One of J,
49:33 When J ended his charge to his sons,
50:24 that he swore to Abraham, to Isaac, and to J."
Ex 1: 1 the sons of Israel who came to Egypt with J, each
1: 5 total number of people born to J was seventy.
2:24 with Abraham, Isaac, and J.
3: 6 the God of Isaac, and the God of J." B
3:15 and the God of J, has sent me to you': B
3:16 of Isaac, and of J, has appeared to me, saying:
4: 5 and the God of J, has appeared to you." B
6: 3 Isaac, and J as God Almighty,
6: 8 and J; I will give it to you for a possession.
19: 3 saying, "Thus you shall say to the house of J, A
33: 1 of which I swore to Abraham, Isaac, and J,
Lev 26:42 then will I remember my covenant with J;
Nu 23: 7 'Come, curse J for me; Come, denounce Israel!'
23:10 Who can count the dust of J,
23:21 He has not beheld misfortune in J;
23:23 Surely there is no enchantment against J,
23:23 now it shall be said of J and Israel,
24: 5 O J, your encampments, O Israel!
24:17 a star shall come out of J,
24:19 One out of J shall rule,
32:11 and to J, because they have
Dt 1: 8 to Abraham, to Isaac, and to J,
6:10 to Abraham, to Isaac, and to J, to give you—
9: 5 to Abraham, to Isaac, and to J.
9:27 Remember your servants, Abraham, Isaac, and J;
29:13 to Abraham, to Isaac, and to J.
30:20 to Abraham, to Isaac, and to J.
32: 9 LORD's own portion was his people, J his allotted
32:15 J ate his fill; Jeshurun grew fat, and kicked.
33: 4 as a possession for the assembly of J.
33:10 They teach J your ordinances,
34: 4 to Isaac, and to J, saying,
Jos 24: 4 and to Isaac I gave J and Esau.
24: 4 but J and his children went down to Egypt.
24:32 in the portion of ground that J had bought from
1Sa 12: 8 When J went into Egypt and
2Sa 23: 1 the anointed of the God of J, B
1Ki 18:31 the number of the tribes of the sons of J, to whom
2Ki 13:23 Isaac, and J, and would not destroy them;
17:34 that the LORD commanded the children of J,
1Ch 16:13 children of J, his chosen ones.
16:17 which he confirmed to J as a statute,
Ps 14: 7 J will rejoice; Israel will be glad.
20: 1 The name of the God of J protect you! B
22:23 All you offspring of J, glorify him;
24: 6 who seek the face of the God of J. B
44: 4 you command victories for J.
46: 7 the God of J is our refuge. B
46:11 the God of J is our refuge. B
47: 4 the pride of J whom he loves.
53: 6 J will rejoice; Israel will be glad.
59:13 to the ends of the earth that God rules over J.
75: 9 I will sing praises to the God of J. B
76: 6 At your rebuke, O God of J, B
77:15 the descendants of J and Joseph.
78: 5 He established a decree in J,
78:21 a fire was kindled against J,
78:71 to be the shepherd of his people J,
79: 7 For they have devoured J
81: 1 shout for joy to the God of J. B
81: 4 an ordinance of the God of J. B
84: 8 give ear, O God of J! B
85: 1 you restored the fortunes of J.
87: 2 the gates of Zion more than all the dwellings of J.
94: 7 the God of J does not perceive." B
99: 4 you have executed justice and righteousness in J.
105: 6 children of J, his chosen ones.
105:10 which he confirmed to J as a statute,
105:23 J lived as an alien in the land of Ham.
114: 1 house of J from a people of strange language, A
114: 7 at the presence of the God of J, B
132: 2 to the LORD and vowed to the Mighty One of J,
132: 5 a dwelling place for the Mighty One of J."
135: 4 For the LORD has chosen J for himself,
146: 5 Happy are those whose help is the God of J, B
147:19 He declares his word to J,
Isa 2: 3 to the house of the God of J; B
2: 5 O house of J, come, let us walk in the light of A
2: 6 the ways of your people, O house of J. A
8:17 who is hiding his face from the house of J, A
9: 8 Lord sent a word against J, and it fell on Israel;
10:20 survivors of the house of J will no more lean A
10:21 A remnant will return, the remnant of J,
14: 1 But the LORD will have compassion on J
14: 1 and attach themselves to the house of J. A
17: 4 On that day the glory of J will be brought low,
27: 6 In days to come J shall take root,
27: 9 Therefore by this the guilt of J will be expiated,
29:22 concerning the house of J: A
29:22 No longer shall J be ashamed,
29:23 they will sanctify the Holy One of J,
40:27 Why do you say, O J, and speak, O Israel,
41: 8 But you, Israel, my servant, J,
41:14 Do not fear, you worm J, you insect Israel!
41:21 bring your proofs, says the King of J.
42:24 Who gave up J to the spoiler,
43: 1 thus says the LORD, he who created you, O J,
43:22 Yet you did not call upon me, O J;
43:28 I delivered J to utter destruction,
44: 1 hear, O J my servant, Israel whom I have chosen!
44: 2 Do not fear, O J my servant,
44: 5 another will be called by the name of J,
44:21 Remember these things, O J, and Israel,
44:23 For the LORD has redeemed J,
45: 4 For the sake of my servant J, C
45:19 I did not say to the offspring of J,
46: 3 Listen to me, O house of J, A
48: 1 house of J, who are called by the name of Israel, A
48:12 Listen to me, O J, and Israel, whom I called:
48:20 say, "The LORD has redeemed his servant J!" C
49: 5 to bring J back to him, and that Israel might be
49: 6 up the tribes of J and to restore the survivors
49:26 and your Redeemer, the Mighty One of J.
58: 1 to the house of J their sins. A
58:14 with the heritage of your ancestor J,
59:20 to those in J who turn from transgression,
60:16 and your Redeemer, the Mighty One of J.
65: 9 I will bring forth descendants from J,
Jer 2: 4 Hear the word of the LORD, O house of J, A
5:20 Declare this in the house of J, A
10:16 Not like these is the LORD, the portion of J,
10:25 for they have devoured J;
30: 7 it is a time of distress for J;
30:10 But as for you, have no fear, my servant J, C
30:10 J shall return and have quiet and ease,
30:18 of J, and have compassion on his dwellings;
31: 7 Sing aloud with gladness for J,
31:11 For the LORD has ransomed J,
33:26 of J and of my servant David and not choose any
33:26 over the offspring of Abraham, Isaac, and J.
46:27 But as for you, have no fear, my servant J, C
46:27 J shall return and have quiet and ease,
46:28 As for you, have no fear, my servant J, C
51:19 Not like these is the LORD, the portion of J,
La 1:17 the LORD has commanded against J
2: 2 without mercy all the dwellings of J;
2: 3 he has burned like a flaming fire in J,
Eze 20: 5 I swore to the offspring of the house of J— A
28:25 on their own soil that I gave to my servant J. C
37:25 to my servant J, in which your ancestors lived; C
39:25 Now I will restore the fortunes of J,
Hos 10:11 J must harrow for himself.
12: 2 and will punish J according to his ways,
12:12 J fled to the land of Aram,
Am 3:13 Hear, and testify against the house of J, A
6: 8 I abhor the pride of J and hate his strongholds;
7: 2 I beg you! How can J stand?
7: 5 I beg you! How can J stand?
8: 7 The LORD has sworn by the pride of J:
9: 8 that I will not utterly destroy the house of J, A
Ob 1:10 the slaughter and violence done to your brother J,
1:17 and the house of J shall take possession A
1:18 The house of J shall be a fire, A
Mic 1: 5 for the transgression of J and for the sins of
1: 5 What is the transgression of J?
2: 7 Should this be said, O house of J? A
2:12 I will surely gather all of you, O J,
3: 1 you heads of J and rulers of the house of Israel!
3: 8 to J his transgression and to Israel his sin.
3: 9 the house of J and chiefs of the house of Israel, A
4: 2 to the house of the God of J; B
5: 7 of J, surrounded by many peoples, shall be
5: 8 And among the nations the remnant of J,
7:20 to J and unswerving loyalty to Abraham,
Na 2: 2 (For the LORD is restoring the majesty of J,
Mal 1: 2 says the LORD. Yet I have loved J
2:12 from the tents of J anyone who does this—
3: 6 therefore you, O children of J, have not perished.
Mt 1: 2 and Isaac the father of J, and J the father of Judah and his brothers,
1:15 and Matthan the father of J,
1:16 and J the father of Joseph the husband of Mary,
8:11 with Abraham and Isaac and J in the kingdom
22:32 the God of Isaac, and the God of J'? B
Mk 12:26 the God of Isaac, and the God of J'? B
Lk 1:33 He will reign over the house of J forever, A
3:34 son of J, son of Isaac, son of Abraham, son
13:28 and J and all the prophets in the kingdom of God,
20:37 the God of Isaac, and the God of J. B
Jn 4: 5 of ground that J had given to his son Joseph.
4:12 Are you greater than our ancestor J,
Ac 3:13 the God of Isaac, and the God of J, B
7: 8 Isaac became the father of J, and J of the twelve
7:12 But when J heard that there was grain in Egypt,
7:14 and invited his father J and all his relatives
7:15 so J went down to Egypt.
7:32 the God of Abraham, Isaac, and J.'
7:46 a dwelling place for the house of J. A
Ro 9:13 "I have loved J, but I have hated Esau."
11:26 he will banish ungodliness from J."
Heb 11: 9 living in tents, as did Isaac and J,
Heb 11:20 for the future on J and Esau.
11:21 By faith J, when dying, blessed each of the sons
Tob 4:12 Abraham, Isaac, and J, our ancestors of old,
Jdt 8:26 and what happened to J in Syrian Mesopotamia,
Sir 23:12 may it never be found in the inheritance of J!
24: 8 He said, 'Make your dwelling in J,
24:23 as an inheritance for the congregations of J.
36:13 Gather all the tribes of J,
44:23 he made to rest on the head of J;
45: 5 so that he might teach J the covenant,
45:17 to teach J the testimonies,
46:14 and the Lord watched over J.
47:22 So he gave a remnant to J,
48:10 and to restore the tribes of J.
49:10 of J and delivered them with confident hope.
51:12 *Give thanks to the mighty one of J,*
Bar 2:34 Isaac, and J, and they will rule over it;
3:36 and gave her to his servant J and to Israel, C
4: 2 O J, and take her; walk toward the
1Mc 1:28 and all the house of J was clothed with shame. A
3: 7 but he made J glad by his deeds,
3:45 Joy was taken from J; the flute and the harp
5: 2 the descendants of J who lived among them.
2Mc 1: 2 with Abraham and Isaac and J,
Man 1: 1 and Isaac and J and of their righteous offspring;
1: 8 for Abraham and Isaac and J,
3Mc 6: 3 O Father, upon the children of the sainted J,
6:13 who have power to save the nation of J.
2Es 1:24 "What shall I do to you, O J?
1:39 and J, and Hosea and Amos and Micah and Joel
3:15 and to Isaac you gave J and Esau.
3:16 You set apart J for yourself,
3:16 and J became a great multitude.
3:19 to give the law to the descendants of J,
3:32 so believed the covenants as these tribes of J?
5:35 of J and the exhaustion of the people of Israel?"
6: 8 because from him were born J and Esau,
6: 9 and J is the beginning of the age that follows.
8:16 and about the seed of J, for whom I am troubled.
9:30 and give heed to my words, O descendants of J.
12:46 and do not be sorrowful, O house of J; A
4Mc 2:19 Why else did J, our most wise father,
7:19 like our patriarchs Abraham and Isaac and J,
13:17 Abraham and Isaac and J will welcome us,
16:25 as do Abraham and Isaac and J and all

JACOB'S (14) [JACOB]

Ge 27:22 who felt him and said, "The voice is J voice,
28: 5 the brother of Rebekah, J and Esau's mother.
30:42 so the feebler were Laban's, and the stronger J.
31:33 So Laban went into J tent, and into Leah's tent,
32:25 J hip was put out of joint as he wrestled with him.
34: 7 an outrage in Israel by lying with J daughter,
34:19 because he was delighted with J daughter.
35:23 The sons of Leah: Reuben (J firstborn), Simeon,
46: 8 to Egypt. Reuben, J firstborn,
46:19 children of J wife Rachel: Joseph and Benjamin.
Dt 33:28 untroubled is J abode in a land of grain and wine,
Mal 1: 2 Is not Esau J brother?
Jn 4: 6 J well was there, and Jesus, tired out by his
2Es 6: 8 for J hand held Esau's heel from the beginning.

JADA (2)

1Ch 2:28 The sons of Onam: Shammai and J.
2:32 The sons of J, Shammai's brother:

JADDAI (1)

Ezr 10:43 Jeiel, Mattithiah, Zabad, Zebina, J, Joel,

JADDUA (3)

Ne 10:21 Meshezabel, Zadok, J,
12:11 and Jonathan the father of J.
12:22 in the days of Eliashib, Joiada, Johanan, and J,

JADDUS (1)

1Es 5:38 and the descendants of J who had married Agia,

JADINUS (1)

1Es 9:48 Jeshua and Anniuth and Sherebiah, J, Akkub,

JADON (1)

Ne 3: 7 the Gibeonite and J the Meronothite—

JAEL (6)

Jdg 4:17 on foot to the tent of J wife of Heber the Kenite;
4:18 J came out to meet Sisera, and said to him,
4:21 But J wife of Heber took a tent peg,
4:22 J went out to meet him, and said to him, "Come,
5: 6 the days of J, caravans ceased and travelers kept
5:24 "Most blessed of women be J,

JAGUR (1)

Jos 15:21 the boundary of Edom, were Kabzeel, Eder, J,

JAH (KJV) See †LORD

JAHATH (8)

1Ch 4: 2 Reaiah son of Shobal became the father of J,
4: 2 and J became the father of Ahumai and Lahad.
6:20 Libni his son, J his son, Zimmah his son,
6:43 son of J, son of Gershom, son of Levi.
23:10 the sons of Shimei: J, Zina, Jeush, and Beriah.

1Ch 23:11 **J** was the chief, and Zizah the second;
24:22 of the sons of Shelomoth, **J**.
2Ch 34:12 Over them were appointed the Levites **J**

JAHAZ (6)

Nu 21:23 he came to **J**, and fought against Israel.
Dt 2:32 he and all his people for battle at **J**,
Jos 13:18 and **J**, and Kedemoth, and Mephaath,
Jdg 11:20 and encamped at **J**, and fought with Israel.
Isa 15: 4 their voices are heard as far as **J**;
Jer 48:34 as far as **J** they utter their voice,

JAHAZA (KJV) See JAHAZ

JAHAZAH (KJV) See JAHZAH

JAHAZIAH (KJV) See JAHZEIAH

JAHAZIEL (7)

1Ch 12: 4 Jeremiah, **J**, Johanan, Jozabad of Gederah,
16: 6 and **J** were to blow trumpets regularly,
23:19 Jeriah the chief, Amariah the second, **J** the third,
24:23 Jeriah the chief, Amariah the second, **J** the third,
2Ch 20:14 Then the spirit of the LORD came upon **J** son
Ezr 8: 5 Of the descendants of Zattu, Shecaniah son of **J**,
1Es 8:32 Of the descendants of Zattu, Shecaniah son of **J**,

JAHDAI (1)

1Ch 2:47 The sons of **J**: Regem, Jotham,

JAHDIEL (1)

1Ch 5:24 Hodaviah, and **J**, mighty warriors, famous men,

JAHDO (1)

1Ch 5:14 son of Michael, son of Jeshishai, son of **J**,

JAHLEEL (2) [JAHLEELITES]

Ge 46:14 The children of Zebulun: Sered, Elon, and **J**
Nu 26:26 of **J**, the clan of the Jahleelites.

JAHLEELITES (1) [JAHLEEL]

Nu 26:26 of Jahleel, the clan of the **J**.

JAHMAI (1)

1Ch 7: 2 Uzzi, Rephaiah, Jeriel, **J**, Ibsam, and Shemuel,

JAHZAH (3)

Jos 21:36 with its pasture lands, **J** with its pasture lands,
1Ch 6:78 with its pasture lands, **J** with its pasture lands,
Jer 48:21 upon Holon, and **J**, and Mephaath,

JAHZEEL (2) [JAHZEELITES]

Ge 46:24 The children of Naphtali: **J**, Guni, Jezer,
Nu 26:48 of **J**, the clan of the Jahzeelites;

JAHZEELITES (1) [JAHZEEL]

Nu 26:48 of Jahzeel, the clan of the **J**;

JAHZEIAH (2)

Ezr 10:15 of Asahel and **J** son of Tikvah opposed this,
1Es 9:14 and **J** son of Tikvah undertook the matter

JAHZERAH (1)

1Ch 9:12 son of **J**, son of Meshullam, son of Meshillemith,

JAHZIEL (1)

1Ch 7:13 The descendants of Naphtali: **J**, Guni, Jezer,

JAILER (7)

Ge 39:21 he gave him favor in the sight of the chief **j**.
39:22 The chief **j** committed to Joseph's care all
39:23 The chief **j** paid no heed to anything that was
Ac 16:23 they threw them into prison and ordered the **j**
16:27 **j** woke up and saw the prison doors wide open,
16:29 The **j** called for lights, and rushing in,
16:36 And the **j** reported the message to Paul, saying,

JAIR‡ (11) [HAVVOTH-JAIR, JAIRITE]

Nu 32:41 **J** son of Manasseh went and captured
Dt 3:14 **J** the Manassite acquired the whole region
Jos 13:30 and all the settlements of **J**, which are in Bashan,
Jdg 10: 3 After him came **J** the Gileadite,
10: 5 **J** died, and was buried in Kamon.
1Ki 4:13 in Ramoth-gilead (he had the villages of **J** son
1Ch 2:22 and Segub became the father of **J**,
20: 5 and Elhanan son of **J** killed Lahmi the brother
Est 2: 5 of Susa whose name was Mordecai son of **J** son
AdE 2: 5 of **J** son of Shimei son of Kish, of the tribe
11: 2 Mordecai son of **J** son of Shimei son of Kish,

JAIRITE (1) [JAIR]

2Sa 20:26 and Ira the **J** was also David's priest.

JAIRUS (3)

Mk 5:22 the leaders of the synagogue named **J** came and,
Lk 8:41 Just then there came a man named **J**,
1Es 5:31 the descendants of **J**, the descendants of Daisan,

JAKAN (KJV) See JAAKAN

JAKEH (1)

Pr 30: 1 The words of Agur son of **J**.

JAKIM (2)

1Ch 8:19 **J**, Zichri, Zabdi,
24:12 the eleventh to Eliashib, the twelfth to **J**,

JALAM (4)

Ge 36: 5 and Oholibamah bore Jeush, **J**,
36:14 she bore to Esau Jeush, **J**, and Korah.
36:18 the clans Jeush, **J**, and Korah;
1Ch 1:35 Eliphaz, Reuel, Jeush, **J**, and Korah.

JALON (1)

1Ch 4:17 The sons of Ezrah: Jether, Mered, Epher, and **J**.

JAMBRES (1)

2Ti 3: 8 As Jannes and **J** opposed Moses, so these people,

JAMBRI (2)

1Mc 9:36 of **J** from Medeba came out and seized John
9:37 "The family of **J** are celebrating a great wedding,

JAMES (42)

Mt 4:21 **J** son of Zebedee and his brother John,
10: 2 **J** son of Zebedee, and his brother John;
10: 3 **J** son of Alphaeus, and Thaddaeus;
13:55 And are not his brothers **J** and Joseph and Simon
17: 1 and **J** and his brother John and led them up
27:56 and Mary the mother of **J** and Joseph,
Mk 1:19 he saw **J** son of Zebedee and his brother John,
1:29 the house of Simon and Andrew, with **J** and John.
3:17 **J** son of Zebedee and John the brother of **J**
3:18 and **J** son of Alphaeus, and Thaddaeus,
5:37 He allowed no one to follow him except Peter, **J**, and John, the brother of **J**.
6: 3 and brother of **J** and Joses and Judas and Simon,
9: 2 Jesus took with him Peter and **J** and John,
10:35 **J** and John, the sons of Zebedee,
10:41 they began to be angry with **J** and John.
13: 3 Peter, **J**, John, and Andrew asked him privately,
14:33 He took with him Peter and **J** and John,
15:40 Mary the mother of **J** the younger and of Joses,
16: 1 Mary Magdalene, and Mary the mother of **J**,
Lk 5:10 and so also were **J** and John,
6:14 and **J**, and John, and Philip, and Bartholomew,
6:15 and Thomas, and **J** son of Alphaeus, and Simon,
6:16 of **J**, and Judas Iscariot, who became
8:51 John, and **J**, and the child's father and mother.
9:28 with him Peter and John and **J**,
9:54 When his disciples **J** and John saw it, they said,
24:10 Joanna, Mary the mother of **J**,
Ac 1:13 and John, and **J**, and Andrew, Philip and Thomas, Bartholomew and Matthew, **J** son of Alphaeus, and Simon the Zealot, and Judas son of **J**.
12: 2 had **J**, the brother of John, killed with the sword.
12:17 he added, "Tell this to **J** and to the believers."
15:13 After they finished speaking, **J** replied,
21:18 The next day Paul went with us to visit **J**;
1Co 15: 7 Then he appeared to **J**, then to all the apostles.
Gal 1:19 but I did not see any other apostle except **J**
2: 9 and when **J** and Cephas and John,
2:12 for until certain people came from **J**,
Jas 1: 1 **J**, a servant of God and of the Lord Jesus Christ,
Jude 1: 1 Jude, a servant of Jesus Christ and brother of **J**,

JAMIN (6) [JAMINITES]

Ge 46:10 The children of Simeon: Jemuel, **J**, Ohad, Jachin,
Ex 6:15 The sons of Simeon: Jemuel, **J**, Ohad, Jachin,
Nu 26:12 of **J**, the clan of the Jaminites;
1Ch 2:27 the firstborn of Jerahmeel: Maaz, **J**,
4:24 Nemuel, **J**, Jarib, Zerah, Shaul;
Ne 8: 7 Also Jeshua, Bani, Sherebiah, **J**, Akkub,

JAMINITES (1) [JAMIN]

Nu 26:12 of Jamin, the clan of the **J**;

JAMLECH (1)

1Ch 4:34 Meshobab, **J**, Joshah son of Amaziah,

JAMNIA (7) [JABNEH, JAMNITES]

Jdt 2:28 in Sur and Ocina and all who lived in **J**.
1Mc 4:15 and to the plains of Idumea, and to Azotus and **J**;
5:58 that were with them and marched against **J**.
10:69 a large force and encamped against **J**.
15:40 So Cendebeus came to **J** and began to provoke
2Mc 12: 8 the people in **J** meant in the same way to wipe out
12:40 of the idols of **J**, which the law forbids the Jews

JAMNITES (1) [JAMNIA]

2Mc 12: 9 the **J** by night and set fire to the harbor and

JANAI (1)

1Ch 5:12 Shapham the second, **J**, and Shaphat in Bashan.

JANGLING (KJV) See TALK

JANIM (1)

Jos 15:53 **J**, Beth-tappuah, Aphekah,

JANNAI (1)

Lk 3:24 son of Melchi, son of **J**, son of Joseph,

JANNES (1)

2Ti 3: 8 As **J** and Jambres opposed Moses,

JANOAH (3)

Jos 16: 6 and passes along beyond it on the east to **J**,
16: 7 it goes down from **J** to Ataroth and to Naarah,
2Ki 15:29 Abel-beth-maacah, **J**, Kedesh, Hazor, Gilead,

JANUM (KJV) See JANIM

JAPHETH‡ (13)

Ge 5:32 Noah became the father of Shem, Ham, and **J**.
6:10 And Noah had three sons, Shem, Ham, and **J**.
7:13 Shem and Ham and **J**, and Noah's wife and
9:18 of the ark were Shem, Ham, and **J**.
9:23 Then Shem and **J** took a garment,
9:27 May God make space for **J**,
10: 1 and **J**; children were born to them after the flood.
10: 2 The descendants of **J**: Gomer,
10: 5 These are the descendants of **J** in their lands,
10:21 the elder brother of **J**, children were born.
1Ch 1: 4 Noah, Shem, Ham, and **J**.
1: 5 The descendants of **J**: Gomer,
Jdt 2:25 Then he came to the southern borders of **J**,

JAPHIA (5)

Jos 10: 3 to King **J** of Lachish, and to King Debir of Eglon,
19:12 from there it goes to Daberath, then up to **J**;
2Sa 5:15 Ibhar, Elishua, Nepheg, **J**,
1Ch 3: 7 Nogah, Nepheg, **J**,
14: 6 Nogah, Nepheg, and **J**;

JAPHLET (3) [JAPHLETITES]

1Ch 7:32 Heber became the father of **J**, Shomer, Hotham,
7:33 The sons of **J**: Pasach, Bimhal, and Ashvath.
7:33 These are the sons of **J**.

JAPHLETITES (1) [JAPHLET]

Jos 16: 3 it goes down westward to the territory of the **J**,

JAPHO (KJV) See JOPPA

JAR (30) [JARS, WINE-JAR]

Ge 24:14 'Please offer your **j** that I may drink,'
24:15 coming out with her water **j** on her shoulder.
24:16 She went down to the spring, filled her **j**,
24:17 "Please let me sip a little water from your **j**."
24:18 and quickly lowered her **j** upon her hand
24:20 So she quickly emptied her **j** into the trough
24:43 "Please give me a little water from your **j**
24:45 there was Rebekah coming out with her water **j**
24:46 She quickly let down her **j** from her shoulder,
Ex 16:33 And Moses said to Aaron, "Take a **j**,
1Sa 26:11 take the spear that is at his head, and the water **j**,
26:12 the spear that was at Saul's head and the water **j**,
26:16 or the water **j** that was at his head?"
1Ki 14: 3 some cakes, and a **j** of honey, and go to him;
17:12 only a handful of meal in a **j**,
17:14 The **j** of meal will not be emptied and the jug
17:16 The **j** of meal was not emptied,
19: 6 a cake baked on hot stones, and a **j** of water.
2Ki 4: 2 in the house, except a **j** of oil."
Jer 32:14 and put them in an earthenware **j**,
Mt 26: 7 to him with an alabaster **j** of very costly ointment,
Mk 14: 3 an alabaster **j** of very costly ointment of nard,
14: 3 and she broke open the **j** and poured the ointment
14:13 and a man carrying a **j** of water will meet you;
Lk 7:37 brought an alabaster **j** of ointment,
8:16 "No one after lighting a lamp hides it under a **j**,
22:10 a man carrying a **j** of water will meet you;
Jn 4:28 woman left her water **j** and went back to the city.
19:29 A **j** full of sour wine was standing there.
Sir 21:14 The mind of a fool is like a broken **j**;

JARAH (2)

1Ch 9:42 the father of **J**, and **J** of Alemeth, Azmaveth,

JAREB (KJV) See GREAT

JARED (7)

Ge 5:15 he became the father of **J**.
5:16 after the birth of **J** eight hundred thirty years,
5:18 **J** had lived one hundred sixty-two years he became
5:19 **J** lived after the birth of Enoch
5:20 the days of **J** were nine hundred sixty-two years;
1Ch 1: 2 Kenan, Mahalalel, **J**;
Lk 3:37 son of **J**, son of Mahalaleel, son of Cainan,

JARESIAH (KJV) See JAARESHIAH

JARHA (2)

1Ch 2:34 an Egyptian slave, whose name was **J**.
2:35 in marriage to his slave **J**;

JARIB (5)
1Ch 4:24 Nemuel, Jamin, **J**, Zerah, Shaul;
Ezr 8:16 I sent for Eliezer, Ariel, Shemaiah, Elnathan, **J**,
10:18 Maaseiah, Eliezer, **J**, and Gedaliah.
1Es 8:44 **J**, Nathan, Elnathan, Zechariah, and Meshullam,
9:19 Maaseiah, Eliezar, **J**, and Jodan.

JARMUTH (7)
Jos 10:3 to King Piram of **J**, to King Japhia of Lachish,
10:5 the king of **J**, the king of Lachish,
10:23 the king of **J**, the king of Lachish,
12:11 the king of **J** one the king of Lachish one
15:35 **J**, Adullam, Socoh, Azekah,
21:29 **J** with its pasture lands, En-gannim
Ne 11:29 in En-rimmon, in Zorah, in **J**,

JAROAH (1)
1Ch 5:14 son of **J**, son of Gilead, son of Michael,

JARS (10) [JAR]
Jdg 7:8 So he took the **j** of the troops from their hands,
7:16 and empty **j**, with torches inside the **j**,
7:19 and they blew the trumpets and smashed the **j**
7:20 the **j**, holding in their left hands the torches,
1Ki 18:33 "Fill four **j** with water and pour it on
Jer 48:12 and empty his vessels, and break his **j** in pieces.
Jn 2:6 Now standing there were six stone water **j** for
2:7 Jesus said to them, "Fill the **j** with water."
2Co 4:7 But we have this treasure in clay **j**,

JASHAR (2)
Jos 10:13 Is this not written in the Book of **J**?
2Sa 1:18 it is written in the Book of **J**.)

JASHEN (1)
2Sa 23:32 Eliahba of Shaalbon; the sons of **J**: Jonathan

JASHER (KJV) See JASHAR

JASHOBEAM (3)
1Ch 11:11 **J**, son of Hachmoni, was chief of the Three;
12:6 Isshiah, Azarel, Joezer, and **J**, the Korahites;
27:2 **J** son of Zabdiel was in charge of

JASHUB (5) [JASHUBITES]
Ge 46:13 Tola, Puvah, **J**, and Shimron.
Nu 26:24 of **J**, the clan of the Jashubites;
1Ch 7:1 Tola, Puah, **J**, and Shimron, four.
Ezr 10:29 Meshullam, Malluch, Adaiah, **J**, Sheal,
1Es 9:30 Olamus, Mamuchus, Adaiah, **J**,

JASHUBI-LAHEM See Index to Footnotes

JASHUBITES (1) [JASHUB]
Nu 26:24 of Jashub, the clan of the **J**;

JASIEL (KJV) See JAASIEL

JASON (22) [JASON'S]
Ac 17:6 they dragged **J** and some believers before
17:7 and **J** has entertained them as guests.
17:9 after they had taken bail from **J** and the others,
Ro 16:21 so do Lucius and **J** and Sosipater, my relatives.
1Mc 8:17 of Accos, and **J** son of Eleazar, and sent them
12:16 of Antiochus and Antipater son of **J**,
14:22 of Antiochus and Antipater son of **J**,
2Mc 1:7 in those years after **J** and his company revolted
2:23 which has been set forth by **J** of Cyrene
4:7 **J** the brother of Onias obtained
4:10 When the king assented and **J** came to office,
4:13 because of the surpassing wickedness of **J**,
4:19 the vile **J** sent envoys, chosen
4:22 He was welcomed magnificently by **J** and
4:23 After a period of three years **J** sent Menelaus,
4:24 outbidding **J** by three hundred talents of silver.
4:26 So **J**, who after supplanting his own brother was
5:5 **J** took no fewer than a thousand men
5:6 **J** kept relentlessly slaughtering his compatriots,
4Mc 4:16 the priesthood and appointed Onias's brother **J**
4:17 **J** agreed that if the office were conferred
4:19 **J** changed the nation's way of life

JASON'S (1) [JASON]
Ac 17:5 to the assembly, they attacked **J** house.

JASPER (7)
Ex 28:20 an onyx, and a **j**; they shall be set in gold filigree.
39:13 a beryl, an onyx, and a **j**;
Eze 28:13 chrysolite, and moonstone, beryl, onyx, and **j**,
Rev 4:3 the one seated there looks like **j** and carnelian,
21:11 and a radiance like a very rare jewel, like **j**, clear
21:18 The wall is built of **j**, while the city is pure gold,
21:19 the first was **j**, the second sapphire,

JATHAN See Index to Footnotes

JATHNIEL (1)
1Ch 26:2 Zebadiah the third, **J** the fourth,

JATTIR (4)
Jos 15:48 And in the hill country, Shamir, **J**, Socoh,
21:14 **J** with its pasture lands, Eshtemoa
1Sa 30:27 in Ramoth of the Negeb, in **J**,
1Ch 6:57 Hebron, Libnah with its pasture lands, **J**,

JAVAN (7)
Ge 10:2 Gomer, Magog, Madai, **J**, Tubal, Meshech,
10:4 The descendants of **J**: Elishah,
1Ch 1:5 Gomer, Magog, Madai, **J**, Tubal, Meshech,
1:7 The descendants of **J**: Elishah,
Isa 66:19 and **J**, to the coastlands far away that have
Eze 27:13 **J**, Tubal, and Meshech traded with you;
27:19 Vedan and **J** from Uzal entered into trade

JAVELIN (6) [JAVELINS]
1Sa 17:6 and a **j** of bronze slung between his shoulders.
17:45 "You come to me with sword and spear and **j**;
Job 39:23 the flashing spear, and the **j**.
41:26 nor does the spear, the dart, or the **j**.
Ps 35:3 Draw the spear and **j** against my pursuers;
Jer 6:23 They grasp the bow and the **j**,

JAVELINS (1) [JAVELIN]
Job 41:29 it laughs at the rattle of **j**.

JAW (2) [JAWBONE, JAWS]
1Sa 17:35 if it turned against me, I would catch it by the **j**,
Job 41:2 or pierce its **j** with a hook?

JAWBONE[‡] (4) [JAW, BONE]
Jdg 15:15 Then he found a fresh **j** of a donkey,
15:16 "With the **j** of a donkey, heaps upon heaps, with
the **j** of a donkey I have slain a thousand men."
15:17 he had finished speaking, he threw away the **j**;

JAWS[‡] (4) [JAW]
Ps 22:15 and my tongue sticks to my **j**;
Isa 30:28 the **j** of the peoples a bridle that leads them astray.
Eze 29:4 I will put hooks in your **j**,
38:4 I will turn you around and put hooks into your **j**,

JAZER (14)
Nu 21:32 Moses sent to spy out **J**;
32:1 When they saw that the land of **J** and the land
32:3 Dibon, **J**, Nimrah, Heshbon, Elealeh, Sebam,
32:35 Atroth-shophan, **J**, Jogbehah,
Jos 13:25 Their territory was **J**, and all the towns of Gilead,
21:39 **J** with its pasture lands—four towns in all.
2Sa 24:5 toward Gad and on to **J**.
1Ch 6:81 and **J** with its pasture lands.
26:31 of great ability among them were found at **J**
Isa 16:8 reached to **J** and strayed to the desert;
16:9 with the weeping of **J** for the vines of Sibmah;
Jer 48:32 More than for **J** I weep for you,
48:32 over the sea, reached as far as **J**;
1Mc 5:8 He also took **J** and its villages;

JAZIZ (1)
1Ch 27:30 Over the flocks was **J** the Hagrite.

JEALOUS[‡] (36) [JEALOUSLY, JEALOUSY]
Ge 37:11 So his brothers were **j** of him,
Ex 20:5 for I the LORD your God am a **j** God,
34:14 because the LORD, whose name is **J**, is a **j** God).
Nu 5:14 and he is **j** of his wife who has defiled herself;
5:14 and he is **j** of his wife,
5:30 a spirit of jealousy comes on a man and he is **j**
11:29 But Moses said to him, "Are you **j** for my sake?
Dt 4:24 the LORD your God is a devouring fire, a **j** God.
5:9 for I the LORD your God am a **j** God,
6:15 who is present with you, is a **j** God.
32:16 They made him **j** with strange gods,
32:19 and was **j** he spurned his sons and daughters.
32:21 They made me **j** with what is no god,
32:21 So I will make them **j** with what is no people,
Jos 24:19 for he is a holy God. He is a **j** God;
Job 36:33 he is **j** with anger against iniquity.
Ps 79:5 Will your **j** wrath burn like fire?
106:16 They were **j** of Moses in the camp, and of Aaron,
Isa 11:13 Ephraim shall not be **j** of Judah,
Eze 36:6 I am speaking in my **j** wrath,
39:25 and I will be **j** for my holy name.
Joel 2:18 Then the LORD became **j** for his land,
Na 1:2 A **j** and avenging God is the LORD,
Zec 1:14 I am very **j** for Jerusalem and for Zion.
8:2 I am **j** for Zion with great jealousy,
8:2 and I am **j** for her with great wrath.
Ac 7:9 "The patriarchs, **j** of Joseph, sold him into Egypt;
17:5 But the Jews became **j**, and with the help
Ro 10:19 "I will make you **j** of those who are not a nation;
11:11 so as to make Israel **j**.
11:14 in order to make my own people **j**,
Wis 1:10 because a **j** ear hears all things,
Sir 9:1 Do not be **j** of the wife of your bosom,
26:6 But it is heartache and sorrow when a wife is **j** of
37:10 hide your intentions from those who are **j** of you.

JEALOUSLY (1) [JEALOUS]
Jas 4:5 "God yearns **j** for the spirit that he has made

JEALOUSY (35) [JEALOUS]
Nu 5:14 if a spirit of **j** comes on him, and he is jealous
5:14 or if a spirit of **j** comes on him,
5:15 for it is a grain offering of **j**,
5:18 which is the grain offering of **j**.
5:25 The priest shall take the grain offering of **j** out of
5:29 This is the law in cases of **j**, when a wife,
5:30 of **j** comes on a man and he is jealous of his wife;
25:11 that in my **j** I did not consume the Israelites.
1Ki 14:22 to **j** with their sins that they committed,
Job 5:2 vexation kills the fool, and **j** slays the simple.
Ps 78:58 they moved him to **j** with their idols.
Pr 6:34 For **j** arouses a husband's fury,
27:4 but who is able to stand before **j**?
Isa 11:13 The **j** of Ephraim shall depart,
Eze 5:13 the LORD, have spoken in my **j**,
8:3 to the seat of the image of **j**, which provokes to **j**.
8:5 in the entrance, was this image of **j**.
16:38 and bring blood upon you in wrath and **j**.
16:42 and my **j** shall turn away from you;
36:5 I am speaking in my hot **j** against the rest of
38:19 For in my **j** and in my blazing wrath I declare:
Zec 8:2 I am jealous for Zion with great **j**,
Mt 27:18 that it was out of **j** that they had handed him over.
Mk 15:10 of **j** that the chief priests had handed him over.
Ac 5:17 the sect of the Sadducees), being filled with **j**,
13:45 the Jews saw the crowds, they were filled with **j**;
Ro 13:13 and licentiousness, not in quarreling and **j**.
1Co 3:3 as long as there is **j** and quarreling among you,
10:22 Or are we provoking the Lord to **j**?
2Co 11:2 I feel a divine **j** for you,
12:20 I fear that there may perhaps be quarreling, **j**,
Gal 5:20 enmities, strife, **j**, anger, quarrels, dissensions,
Sir 30:24 **J** and anger shorten life, and anxiety brings
1Mc 8:16 and there is no envy or **j** among them.

JEARIM (1) [=CHESALON, KIRIATH-JEARIM]
Jos 15:10 the northern slope of Mount **J** (that is, Chesalon),

JEATHERAI (1)
1Ch 6:21 Iddo his son, Zerah his son, **J** his son.

JEBERECHIAH (1)
Isa 8:2 the priest Uriah and Zechariah son of **J**.

JEBUS (5) [JEBUSITE, JEBUSITES, =JERUSALEM]
Jos 18:28 Haeleph, **J** (that is, Jerusalem),
Jdg 19:10 and arrived opposite **J** (that is, Jerusalem).
19:11 When they were near **J**, the day was far spent,
1Ch 11:4 that is **J**, where the Jebusites were,
11:5 The inhabitants of **J** said to David,

JEBUSI (KJV) See JEBUSITES

JEBUSITE[‡] (7) [JEBUS]
2Sa 24:16 then by the threshing floor of Araunah the **J**.
24:18 on the threshing floor of Araunah the **J**."
1Ch 21:15 by the threshing floor of Ornan the **J**.
21:18 the LORD on the threshing floor of Ornan the **J**.
21:28 at the threshing floor of Ornan the **J**,
2Ch 3:1 on the threshing floor of Ornan the **J**.
Ne 9:8 the Hittite, the Amorite, the Perizzite, the **J**,

JEBUSITES (35) [JEBUS]
Ge 10:16 and the **J**, the Amorites, the Girgashites,
15:21 the Canaanites, the Girgashites, and the **J**."
Ex 3:8 the Perizzites, the Hivites, and the **J**.
3:17 and the **J**, a land flowing with milk and honey.'
13:5 the Hittites, the Amorites, the Hivites, and the **J**,
23:23 the Hivites, and the **J**, and I blot them out,
33:2 the Hittites, the Perizzites, the Hivites, and the **J**.
34:11 the Hittites, the Perizzites, the Hivites, and the **J**.
Nu 13:29 the **J**, and the Amorites live in the hill country;
Dt 7:1 the Perizzites, the Hivites, and the **J**,
20:17 and the Perizzites, the Hivites and the **J**—
Jos 3:10 Hivites, Perizzites, Girgashites, Amorites, and **J**:
9:1 the Perizzites, the Hivites, and the **J**—
11:3 the Perizzites, and the **J** in the hill country,
12:8 Amorites, Canaanites, Perizzites, Hivites, and **J**):
15:8 at the southern slope of the **J** (that is, Jerusalem);
15:63 But the people of Judah could not drive out the **J**,
15:63 the **J** live with the people of Judah in Jerusalem
18:16 south of the slope of the **J**,
24:11 and the **J**; and I handed them over to you.
Jdg 1:21 the Benjaminites did not drive out the **J** who lived
1:21 so the **J** have lived in Jerusalem among
3:5 the Perizzites, the Hivites, and the **J**;
19:11 "Come now, let us turn aside to this city of the **J**,
2Sa 5:6 and his men marched to Jerusalem against the **J**,
5:8 "Whoever would strike down the **J**,
1Ki 9:20 and the **J**, who were not of the people of Israel—
1Ch 1:14 and the **J**, the Amorites, the Girgashites,
11:4 where the **J** were, the inhabitants of the land.
11:6 "Whoever attacks the **J** first shall be chief
2Ch 8:7 the Hivites, and the **J**, who were not of Israel,
Ezr 9:1 the Hittites, the Perizzites, the **J**, the Ammonites,
Zec 9:7 and Ekron shall be like the **J**.
Jdt 5:16 the **J**, the Shechemites, and all the Gergesites,
1Es 8:69 the Perizzites, the **J**, the Moabites, the Egyptians,

JECAMIAH (KJV) See JEKAMIAH

JECHOLIAH (KJV) See JECOLIAH

JECHONIAH (2) [=JEHOIACHIN]

Mt 1:11 and Josiah the father of **J** and his brothers,
1:12 **J** was the father of Salathiel,

JECHONIAS (KJV) See JECHONIAH

JECOLIAH (2)

2Ki 15: 2 His mother's name was **J** of Jerusalem.
2Ch 26: 3 His mother's name was **J** of Jerusalem.

JECONIAH (13) [=JEHOIACHIN]

1Sa 6:19 The descendants of **J** did not rejoice with
1Ch 3:16 **J** his son, Zedekiah his son;
3:17 and the sons of **J**, the captive: Shealtiel his son,
Est 2: 6 the captives carried away with King **J** of Judah,
Jer 24: 1 from Jerusalem King **J** son of Jehoiakim
27:20 into exile from Jerusalem to Babylon King **J** son
28: 4 to this place King **J** son of Jehoiakim of Judah,
29: 2 This was after King **J**, and the queen mother,
AdE 11: 4 from Jerusalem with King **J** of Judea.
Bar 1: 3 the words of this book to **J** son of Jehoiakim,
1: 9 of Babylon had carried away from Jerusalem **J**
1Es 1: 9 And **J** and Shemaiah and his brother Nethanel,
1:34 The men of the nation took **J** son of Josiah,

JEDAIAH (14)

1Ch 4:37 of Shiphi son of Allon son of **J** son of Shimri son
9:10 Of the priests: **J**, Jehoiarib, Jachin,
24: 7 The first lot fell to Jehoiarib, the second to **J**,
Ezr 2:36 the descendants of **J**, of the house of Jeshua,
Ne 3:10 Next to them **J** son of Harumaph
7:39 the descendants of **J**, namely the house of Jeshua,
11:10 Of the priests: **J** son of Joiarib, Jachin,
12: 6 Shemaiah, Joiarib, **J**,
12: 7 Amok, Hilkiah, **J**. These were the leaders of the
12:19 of Joiarib, Mattenai; of **J**, Uzzi;
12:21 of Hilkiah, Hashabiah; of **J**, Nethanel.
Zec 6:10 from Heldai, Tobijah, and **J**—
6:14 crown shall be in the care of Heldai, Tobijah, **J**,
1Es 5:24 The priests: the descendants of **J** son of Jeshua,

JEDIAEL (6)

1Ch 7: 6 The sons of Benjamin: Bela, Becher, and **J**, three.
7:10 The sons of **J**: Bilhan.
7:11 All these were the sons of **J** according to
11:45 **J** son of Shimri, and his brother Joha the Tizite,
12:20 Adnah, Jozabad, **J**, Michael, Jozabad, Elihu,
26: 2 Zechariah the firstborn, **J** the second,

JEDIDAH (1)

2Ki 22: 1 His mother's name was **J** daughter of Adaiah

JEDIDIAH (1) [=SOLOMON]

2Sa 12:25 so he named him **J**, because of the LORD.

JEDUTHUN (17)

1Ch 9:16 son of Galal, son of **J**, and Berechiah son of Asa,
16:38 while Obed-edom son of **J** and Hosah were to
16:41 With them were Heman and **J**,
16:42 and **J** had with them trumpets and cymbals for
16:42 The sons of **J** were appointed to the gate.
25: 1 and of **J**, who should prophesy with lyres, harps,
25: 3 Of **J**, the sons of **J**: Gedaliah, Zeri, Jeshaiah,
25: 3 six, under the direction of their father **J**,
25: 6 **J**, and Heman were under the order of the king.
2Ch 5:12 Asaph, Heman, and **J**, their sons and kindred,
29:14 and of the sons of **J**, Shemaiah and Uzziel.
35:15 and Asaph, and Heman, and the king's seer **J**.
Ne 11:17 and Abda son of Shammua son of Galal son of **J**.
Ps 39: T *To the leader: to* **J**. *A Psalm of David.*
62: T *To the leader: to* **J**. *A Psalm of David.*
77: T *To the leader: to* **J**. *Of Asaph. A Psalm.*

JEERED (1)

2Ki 2:23 some small boys came out of the city and **j** at him,

JEEZER (KJV) See IEZER

JEEZERITES (KJV) See IEZERITES

JEGAR-SAHADUTHA (1) [=GALEED]

Ge 31:47 Laban called it **J**: but Jacob called it Galeed.

JEHALLELEL (2)

1Ch 4:16 The sons of **J**: Ziph, Ziphah, Tiria, and Asarel.
2Ch 29:12 Kish son of Abdi, and Azariah son of **J**;

JEHDEIAH (2)

1Ch 24:20 of the sons of Shubael, **J**.
27:30 Over the donkeys was **J** the Meronothite.

JEHEZKEL (1)

1Ch 24:16 the nineteenth to Pethahiah, the twentieth to **J**,

JEHIAH (1)

1Ch 15:24 Obed-edom and **J** also were to be gatekeepers for

JEHIEL (17)

1Ch 15:18 Shemiramoth, **J**, Unni, Eliab, Benaiah, Maaseiah,
15:20 Aziel, Shemiramoth, **J**, Unni, Eliab, Maaseiah,
16: 5 Shemiramoth, **J**, Mattithiah, Eliab, Benaiah,
23: 8 **J** the chief, Zetham, and Joel, three.
27:32 **J** son of Hachmoni attended the king's sons.
29: 8 into the care of **J** the Gershonite.
2Ch 21: 2 Azariah, **J**, Zechariah, Azariah, Michael,
31:13 while **J**, Azaziah, Nahath,
35: 8 Hilkiah, Zechariah, and **J**,
Ezr 8: 9 Of the descendants of Joab, Obadiah son of **J**,
10: 2 Shecaniah son of **J**, of the descendants of Elam,
10:21 Maaseiah, Elijah, Shemaiah, **J**, and Uzziah.
10:26 Mattaniah, Zechariah, **J**, Abdi, Jeremoth,
1Es 1: 8 Hilkiah, Zechariah, and **J**,
8:35 Of the descendants of Joab, Obadiah son of **J**,
8:92 Then Shecaniah son of **J**,
9:21 and Zebadiah and Maaseiah and Shemaiah and **J**

JEHIELI (2)

1Ch 26:21 to Ladan the Gershonite: **J**.
26:22 The sons of **J**, Zetham and his brother Joel,

JEHIZKIAH (1)

2Ch 28:12 **J** son of Shallum, and Amasa son of Hadlai,

JEHOADDAH (2)

1Ch 8:36 Ahaz became the father of **J**;
8:36 and **J** became the father of Alemeth, Azmaveth,

JEHOADDAN (1) [=JEHOADDIN]

2Ch 25: 1 His mother's name was **J** of Jerusalem.

JEHOADDIN (1) [=JEHOADDAN]

2Ki 14: 2 His mother's name was **J** of Jerusalem.

JEHOAHAZ‡ (21) [=JOAHAZ]

2Ki 10:35 His son **J** succeeded him.
13: 1 **J** son of Jehu began to reign over Israel
13: 4 But **J** entreated the LORD,
13: 7 So **J** was left with an army of
13: 8 Now the rest of the acts of **J** and all that he did,
13: 9 So **J** slept with his ancestors,
13:10 Jehoash son of **J** began to reign over Israel
13:22 of Aram oppressed Israel all the days of **J**.
13:25 of **J** took again from Ben-hadad son of Hazael
13:25 the towns that he had taken from his father **J**
14: 8 to King Jehoash son of **J**,
14:17 after the death of King Jehoash son of **J** of Israel.
23:30 The people of the land took **J** son of Josiah,
23:31 **J** was twenty-three years old when he began
23:34 he took **J** away; he came to Egypt, and died there.
2Ch 21:17 so that no son was left to him except **J**,
25:17 to King Joash son of **J** son of Jehu of Israel,
25:25 after the death of King Joash son of **J** of Israel.
36: 1 the land took **J** son of Josiah and made him king
36: 2 **J** was twenty-three years old when he began
36: 4 Neco took his brother **J** and carried him to Egypt.

JEHOASH (17) [=JOASH]

2Ki 11:21 **J** was seven years old when he began to reign.
12: 1 In the seventh year of Jehu, **J** began to reign;
12: 2 **J** did what was right in the sight of
12: 4 **J** said to the priests, "All the money offered
12: 6 of King **J** the priests had made no repairs on
12: 7 Therefore King **J** summoned the priest Jehoiada
12:18 King **J** of Judah took all the votive gifts
13:10 **J** son of Jehoahaz began to reign over Israel
13:25 Then **J** son of Jehoahaz took again
14: 8 Then Amaziah sent messengers to King **J** son
14: 9 King **J** of Israel sent word to King Amaziah
14:11 So King **J** of Israel went up;
14:13 King **J** of Israel captured King Amaziah
14:13 of **J**, son of Ahaziah, at Beth-shemesh;
14:15 Now the rest of the acts that **J** did, his might,
14:16 **J** slept with his ancestors,
14:17 the death of King **J** son of Jehoahaz of Israel.

JEHOHANAN (10) [=JOHANAN]

1Ch 26: 3 Elam the fifth, **J** the sixth, Eliehoenai the seventh.
2Ch 17:15 and next to him **J** the commander,
23: 1 Azariah son of Jeroham, Ishmael son of **J**,
Ezr 10: 6 and went to the chamber of **J** son of Eliashib,
10:28 **J**, Hananiah, Zabbai, and Athlai.
Ne 6:18 and his son **J** had married the daughter
12:13 of Ezra, Meshullam; of Amariah, **J**;
12:42 Shemaiah, Eleazar, Uzzi, **J**, Malchijah, Elam,
1Es 9: 1 of the temple to the chamber of **J** son of Eliashib,
9:29 **J** and Hananiah and Zabbai and Emathis.

JEHOIACHIN (14) [=CONIAH, =JECHONIAH, =JECONIAH, JEHOIACHIN'S]

2Ki 24: 6 then his son **J** succeeded him.
24: 8 **J** was eighteen years old when he began to reign;
24:12 King **J** of Judah gave himself up to the king
24:15 He carried away **J** to Babylon;
25:27 the exile of King **J** of Judah, in the twelfth month,
25:27 released King **J** of Judah from prison;
25:29 So **J** put aside his prison clothes.
2Ch 36: 8 and his son **J** succeeded him.
36: 9 **J** was eight years old when he began to reign;
Jer 52:31 the exile of King **J** of Judah, in the twelfth month,
52:31 to King **J** of Judah and brought him out of prison;
52:33 So **J** put aside his prison clothes,
Eze 1: 2 the fifth year of the exile of King **J**),
1Es 1:43 His son **J** became king in his place;

JEHOIACHIN'S (1) [JEHOIACHIN]

2Ki 24:17 The king of Babylon made Mattaniah, **J** uncle,

JEHOIADA (53)

2Sa 8:18 of **J** was over the Cherethites and the Pelethites;
20:23 of **J** was in command of the Cherethites and
23:20 of **J** was a valiant warrior from Kabzeel, a doer
23:22 Such were the things Benaiah son of **J** did,
1Ki 1: 8 But the priest Zadok, and Benaiah son of **J**,
1:26 and Benaiah son of **J**, and your servant Solomon.
1:32 the prophet Nathan, and Benaiah son of **J**."
1:36 Benaiah son of **J** answered the king, "Amen!
1:38 the prophet Nathan, and Benaiah son of **J**,
1:44 the prophet Nathan, and Benaiah son of **J**,
2:25 So King Solomon sent Benaiah son of **J**;
2:29 Solomon sent Benaiah son of **J**, saying, "Go,
2:34 of **J** went up and struck him down and killed him;
2:35 The king put Benaiah son of **J** over the army
2:46 Then the king commanded Benaiah son of **J**;
4: 4 Benaiah son of **J** was in command of the army;
2Ki 11: 4 But in the seventh year **J** summoned the captains
11: 9 according to all that the priest **J** commanded;
11: 9 on duty on the sabbath, and came to the priest **J**.
11:15 Then the priest **J** commanded
11:17 **J** made a covenant between the LORD and
12: 2 because the priest **J** instructed him.
12: 7 Therefore King Jehoash summoned the priest **J**
12: 9 Then the priest **J** took a chest,
1Ch 11:22 Benaiah son of **J** was a valiant man of Kabzeel,
11:24 Such were the things Benaiah son of **J** did,
12:27 **J**, leader of the house of Aaron,
18:17 of **J** was over the Cherethites and the Pelethites;
27: 5 was Benaiah son of the priest **J**, as chief;
27:34 Ahithophel came **J** son of Benaiah, and Abiathar.
2Ch 22:11 daughter of King Jehoram and wife of the priest **J**
23: 1 But in the seventh year **J** took courage,
23: 3 **J** said to them, "Here is the king's son!
23: 8 according to all that the priest **J** commanded;
23: 8 for the priest **J** did not dismiss the divisions.
23: 9 The priest **J** delivered to the captains the spears
23:11 and **J** and his sons anointed him;
23:14 the priest **J** brought out the captains who were set
23:16 **J** made a covenant between himself and all
23:18 **J** assigned the care of the house of the LORD to
24: 2 of the LORD all the days of the priest **J**.
24: 3 **J** got two wives for him,
24: 6 So the king summoned **J** the chief,
24:12 The king and **J** gave it to those who had charge of
24:14 the rest of the money to the king and **J**,
24:14 of the LORD regularly all the days of **J**.
24:15 But **J** grew old and full of days, and died;
24:17 of **J** the officials of Judah came and did obeisance
24:20 of Zechariah son of the priest **J**;
24:22 King Joash did not remember the kindness that **J**,
24:25 because of the blood of the son of the priest **J**,
Ne 13:28 And one of the sons of **J**,
Jer 29:26 of the priest **J**, so that there may be officers in

JEHOIAKIM‡ (42) [=ELIAKIM]

2Ki 23:34 of his father Josiah, and changed his name to **J**.
23:35 **J** gave the silver and the gold to Pharaoh,
23:36 **J** was twenty-five years old when he began
24: 1 **J** became his servant for three years;
24: 5 Now the rest of the deeds of **J**, and all that he did,
24: 6 So **J** slept with his ancestors;
24:19 in the sight of the LORD, just as **J** had done.
1Ch 3:15 Johanan the firstborn, the second **J**,
3:16 The descendants of **J**: Jeconiah his son,
2Ch 36: 4 and changed his name to **J**;
36: 5 **J** was twenty-five years old when he began
36: 8 Now the rest of the acts of **J**,
Jer 1: 3 also in the days of King **J** son of Josiah of Judah,
22:18 the LORD concerning King **J** son of Josiah
22:24 even if King Coniah son of **J** of Judah were
24: 1 into exile from Jerusalem King Jeconiah son of **J**
25: 1 the fourth year of King **J** son of Josiah of Judah
26: 1 the beginning of the reign of King **J** son of Josiah
26:21 And when King **J**, with all his warriors and all
26:22 Then King **J** sent Elnathan son of Achbor
26:23 from Egypt and brought him to King **J**,
27:20 to Babylon King Jeconiah son of **J** of Judah,
28: 4 to this place King Jeconiah son of **J** of Judah,
35: 1 the LORD in the days of King **J** son of Josiah
36: 1 of King **J** son of Josiah of Judah, this word came
36: 9 In the fifth year of King **J** son of Josiah of Judah,
36:28 which King **J** of Judah has burned.
36:29 And concerning King **J** of Judah you shall say:
36:30 thus says the LORD concerning King **J** of Judah:
36:32 of the scroll that King **J** of Judah had burned in
37: 1 succeeded Coniah son of **J**.
45: 1 the fourth year of King **J** son of Josiah of Judah:
46: 2 the fourth year of King **J** son of Josiah of Judah:
52: 2 in the sight of the LORD, just as **J** had done.
Da 1: 1 In the third year of the reign of King **J** of Judah,
1: 2 The Lord let King **J** of Judah fall into his power,

Bar 1: 3 the words of this book to Jeconiah son of J,
1: 7 to the high priest J son of Hilkiah son of Shallum,
1Es 1:37 The king of Egypt made his brother J king
1:38 J put the nobles in prison,
1:39 J was twenty-five years old when he began
1:42 But the things that are reported about J,

JEHOIARIB (2) [=JOIARIB]

1Ch 9:10 Of the priests: Jedaiah, J, Jachin,
24: 7 The first lot fell to J, the second to Jedaiah,

JEHONADAB (3) [=JONADAB]

2Ki 10:15 he met J son of Rechab coming to meet him;
10:15 as mine is to yours?" J answered,
10:23 Then Jehu entered the temple of Baal with J son

JEHONATHAN (2)

2Ch 17: 8 Nethaniah, Zebadiah, Asahel, Shemiramoth, J,
Ne 12:18 of Bilgah, Shammua; of Shemaiah, J;

JEHORAM (22) [=JORAM]

1Ki 22:50 his son J succeeded him.
2Ki 1:17 J succeeded him as king in the second year
1:17 in the second year of King J son of Jehoshaphat
3: 1 J son of Ahab became king over Israel
3: 6 So King J marched out of Samaria at that time
3: 8 J answered, "By the way of the wilderness
8:16 J son of King Jehoshaphat of Judah began
8:25 Ahaziah son of King J of Judah began to reign.
8:29 King Ahaziah son of J of Judah went down
12:18 J, and Ahaziah, his ancestors, the kings of Judah,
2Ch 17: 8 with these Levites, the priests Elishama and J.
21: 1 his son J succeeded him.
21: 3 but he gave the kingdom to J,
21: 4 When J had ascended the throne of his father
21: 5 J was thirty-two years old when he began
21: 9 Then J crossed over with his commanders
21:16 against J the anger of the Philistines and of
22: 1 So Ahaziah son of J reigned as king of Judah.
22: 5 with J son of King Ahab of Israel to make war
22: 6 And Ahaziah son of King J of Judah went down
22: 7 For when he came there he went out with J
22:11 of King J and wife of the priest Jehoiada—

JEHOSHABEATH (2)

2Ch 22:11 But J, the king's daughter, took Joash
22:11 Thus J, daughter of King Jehoram and wife of

JEHOSHAPHAT[‡] (85)

2Sa 8:16 J son of Ahilud was recorder;
20:24 J son of Ahilud was the recorder;
1Ki 4: 3 J son of Ahilud was recorder;
4:17 J son of Paruah, in Issachar;
15:24 his son J succeeded him.
22: 2 But in the third year King J of Judah came down
22: 4 He said to J, "Will you go with me to battle
22: 4 J replied to the king of Israel, "I am as you are;
22: 5 But J also said to the king of Israel,
22: 7 But J said, "Is there no other prophet of
22: 8 The king of Israel said to J,
22: 8 J said, "Let the king not say such a thing."
22:10 and King J of Judah were sitting on their thrones,
22:18 The king of Israel said to J,
22:29 So the king of Israel and King J of Judah went up
22:30 The king of Israel said to J,
22:32 When the captains of the chariots saw J,
22:32 they turned to fight against him; and J cried out.
22:41 J son of Asa began to reign over Judah in
22:42 J was thirty-five years old when he began
22:44 J also made peace with the king of Israel.
22:45 Now the rest of the acts of J,
22:48 J made ships of the Tarshish type to go to Ophir
22:49 Then Ahaziah son of Ahab said to J,
22:49 but J was not willing.
22:50 J slept with his ancestors and was buried
22:51 in Samaria in the seventeenth year of King J
2Ki 1:17 in the second year of King Jehoram son of J
3: 1 In the eighteenth year of King J of Judah,
3: 7 As he went he sent word to King J of Judah,
3:11 But J said, "Is there no prophet of
3:12 J said, "The word of the LORD is with him."
3:12 of Israel and J and the king of Edom went down
3:14 were it not that I have regard for King J of Judah,
8:16 Jehoram son of King J of Judah began to reign.
9: 2 When you arrive, look there for Jehu son of J,
9:14 of J son of Nimshi conspired against Joram.
12:18 of Judah took all the votive gifts that J,
1Ch 3:10 Rehoboam, Abijah his son, Asa his son, J his son,
18:15 J son of Ahilud was recorder;
2Ch 17: 1 His son J succeeded him,
17: 3 The LORD was with J, because he walked in
17: 5 All Judah brought tribute to J,
17:10 and they did not make war against J.
17:11 Some of the Philistines brought J presents,
17:12 J grew steadily greater. He built fortresses
18: 1 Now J had great riches and honor;
18: 3 King Ahab of Israel said to King J of Judah,
18: 4 But J also said to the king of Israel,
18: 6 But J said, "Is there no other prophet of
18: 7 The king of Israel said to J,
18: 7 J said, "Let the king not say such a thing."
18: 9 and King J of Judah were sitting on their thrones,
18:17 The king of Israel said to J,
18:28 So the king of Israel and King J of Judah went up
2Ch 18:29 The king of Israel said to J,
18:31 When the captains of the chariots saw J,
18:31 and J cried out, and the LORD helped him.
19: 1 King J of Judah returned in safety to his house
19: 2 the seer went out to meet him and said to King J,
19: 4 J resided at Jerusalem;
19: 8 in Jerusalem J appointed certain Levites
20: 1 came against J for battle.
20: 2 Messengers came and told J,
20: 3 J was afraid; he set himself to seek
20: 5 J stood in the assembly of Judah and Jerusalem,
20:15 and inhabitants of Jerusalem, and King J:
20:18 Then J bowed down with his face to the ground,
20:20 and as they went out, J stood and said,
20:25 When J and his people came to take the booty
20:27 of Judah and Jerusalem, with J at their head,
20:30 And the realm of J was quiet,
20:31 So J reigned over Judah.
20:34 Now the rest of the acts of J, from first to last,
20:35 After this King J of Judah joined
20:37 of Dodavahu of Mareshah prophesied against J,
21: 1 J slept with his ancestors and was buried
21: 2 He had brothers, the sons of J:
21: 2 all these were the sons of King J of Judah.
21:12 not walked in the ways of your father J or in
22: 9 for they said, "He is the grandson of J,
Joel 3: 2 and bring them down to the valley of J,
3:12 and come up to the valley of J;
Mt 1: 8 Asaph the father of J, and J the father of Joram,

JEHOSHEBA (1)

2Ki 11: 2 But J, King Joram's daughter, Ahaziah's sister,

JEHOSHUA (KJV) See HOSHEA

JEHOSHUAH (KJV) See JOSHUA

JEHOVAH (KJV) See †LORD; See also Index to Footnotes

JEHOVAH-JIREH (KJV) See †LORD WILL PROVIDE

JEHOVAH-NISSI (KJV) See †LORD IS MY BANNER

JEHOVAH-SHALOM (KJV) See †LORD IS PEACE

JEHOZABAD (4)

2Ki 12:21 It was Jozacar son of Shimeath and J son
1Ch 26: 4 Shemaiah the firstborn, J the second,
2Ch 17:18 to him J with one hundred eighty thousand armed
24:26 and J son of Shimrith the Moabite.

JEHOZADAK (8) [=JOZADAK]

1Ch 6:14 Azariah of Seraiah, Seraiah of J;
6:15 and J went into exile when the LORD sent Judah
Hag 1: 1 governor of Judah, and to Joshua son of J,
1:12 Zerubbabel son of Shealtiel, and Joshua son of J,
1:14 and the spirit of Joshua son of J, the high priest,
2: 2 governor of Judah, and to Joshua son of J,
2: 4 take courage, O Joshua, son of J, the high priest;
Zec 6:11 on the head of the high priest Joshua son of J;

JEHU[‡] (62)

1Ki 16: 1 The word of the LORD came to J son of Hanani
16: 7 the LORD came by the prophet J son of Hanani
16:12 which he spoke against Baasha by the prophet J—
19:16 Also you shall anoint J son of Nimshi as king
19:17 from the sword of Hazael, J shall kill;
19:17 and whoever escapes from the sword of J,
2Ki 9: 2 you arrive, look there for J son of Jehoshaphat,
9: 5 "For which one of us?" asked J.
9: 6 So J got up and went inside;
9:11 When J came back to his master's officers,
9:13 and proclaimed, "J is king."
9:14 Thus J son of Jehoshaphat son
9:15 So J said, "If this is your wish,
9:16 Then J mounted his chariot and went to Jezreel,
9:17 on the tower spied the company of J arriving,
9:18 J responded, "What have you to do with peace?
9:19 J answered, "What have you to do with peace?
9:20 It looks like the driving of J son of Nimshi;
9:21 each in his chariot, and went to meet J;
9:22 When Joram saw J, he said, "Is it peace, J?"
9:24 J drew his bow with all his strength,
9:25 J said to his aide Bidkar, "Lift him out,
9:27 J pursued him, saying, "Shoot him also!"
9:30 When J came to Jezreel, Jezebel heard of it;
9:31 As J entered the gate, she said, "Is it peace,
10: 1 So J wrote letters and sent them to Samaria,
10: 5 with the elders and the guardians, sent word to J:
10:11 So J killed all who were left of the house of Ahab
10:13 J met relatives of King Ahaziah of Judah
10:15 J said, "If it is, give me your hand."
10:15 J took him up with him into the chariot.
10:18 Then J assembled all the people and said to them,
10:18 but J will offer much more.
10:19 But J was acting with cunning in order to destroy
2Ki 10:20 J decreed, "Sanctify a solemn assembly
10:21 J sent word throughout all Israel;
10:23 Then J entered the temple of Baal
10:24 Now J had stationed eighty men outside, saying,
10:25 J said to the guards and to the officers,
10:28 Thus J wiped out Baal from Israel.
10:29 But J did not turn aside from the sins
10:30 to J, "Because you have done well
10:31 But J was not careful to follow the law of
10:34 Now the rest of the acts of J, all that he did,
10:35 So J slept with his ancestors,
10:36 The time that J reigned over Israel
12: 1 In the seventh year of J, Jehoash began to reign;
13: 1 Jehoahaz son of J began to reign over Israel
14: 8 son of J, of Israel, saying, "Come,
15:12 the promise of the LORD that he gave to J,
1Ch 2:38 Obed became the father of J, and J of Azariah.
4:35 J son of Joshibiah son of Seraiah son of Asiel,
12: 3 of Azmaveth; Beracah, J of Anathoth,
2Ch 19: 2 J son of Hanani the seer went out to meet him
20:34 are written in the Annals of J son of Hanani,
22: 7 with Jehoram to meet J son of Nimshi,
22: 8 J was executing judgment on the house of Ahab,
22: 9 while hiding in Samaria and was brought to J,
25:17 to King Joash son of Jehoahaz son of J of Israel,
Hos 1: 4 for in a little while I will punish the house of J for

JEHUBBAH (KJV) See HUBBAH

JEHUCAL (1)

Jer 37: 3 King Zedekiah sent J son of Shelemiah and

JEHUD (1)

Jos 19:45 J, Bene-berak, Gath-rimmon,

JEHUDI (4)

Jer 36:14 Then all the officials sent J son of Nethaniah son
36:21 Then the king sent J to get the scroll,
36:21 and J read it to the king and all
36:23 As J read three or four columns,

JEHUDIJAH (KJV) See JUDEAN

JEHUEL (1)

2Ch 29:14 and of the sons of Heman, J and Shimei;

JEHUSH (KJV) See JEUSH

JEIEL[‡] (12)

1Ch 5: 7 the chief, J, and Zechariah,
8:29 J the father of Gibeon lived in Gibeon,
9:35 In Gibeon lived the father of Gibeon, J,
11:44 Shama and J sons of Hotham the Aroerite,
15:18 and the gatekeepers Obed-edom and J.
15:21 Eliphelehu, Mikneiah, Obed-edom, J,
16: 5 and second to him Zechariah, J, Shemiramoth,
16: 5 Mattithiah, Eliab, Benaiah, Obed-edom, and J,
2Ch 20:14 son of Benaiah, son of J, son of Mattaniah,
26:11 by the secretary J and the officer Maaseiah,
35: 9 and Hashabiah and J and Jozabad,
Ezr 10:43 Of the descendants of Nebo: J, Mattithiah,

JEKABZEEL (1)

Ne 11:25 and in J and its villages,

JEKAMEAM (2)

1Ch 23:19 Jahaziel the third, and J the fourth.
24:23 Jahaziel the third, J the fourth.

JEKAMIAH (3)

1Ch 2:41 Shallum became the father of J, and J of Elishama.
3:18 Pedaiah, Shenazzar, J, Hoshama, and Nedabiah;

JEKUTHIEL (1)

1Ch 4:18 Heber father of Soco, and J father of Zanoah.

JEMIMAH (1)

Job 42:14 He named the first J, the second Keziah,

JEMUEL (2)

Ge 46:10 The children of Simeon: J, Jamin, Ohad, Jachin,
Ex 6:15 The sons of Simeon: J, Jamin, Ohad, Jachin,

JEOPARDED (KJV) See SCORNED

JEPHTHAE (KJV) See JEPHTHAH

JEPHTHAH (30)

Jdg 11: 1 Now J the Gileadite, the son of a prostitute,
11: 1 Gilead was the father of J.
11: 2 when his wife's sons grew up, they drove J away,
11: 3 Then J fled from his brothers and lived in
11: 3 Outlaws collected around J and went raiding
11: 5 the elders of Gilead went to bring J from the land
11: 6 They said to J, "Come and be our commander,
11: 7 But J said to the elders of Gilead,
11: 8 The elders of Gilead said to J, "Nevertheless,
11: 9 J said to the elders of Gilead,
11:10 And the elders of Gilead said to J,

Jdg 11:11 So **J** went with the elders of Gilead,
11:11 and **J** spoke all his words before the LORD
11:12 Then **J** sent messengers to the king of
11:13 of the Ammonites answered the messengers of **J**,
11:14 Once again **J** sent messengers to the king of
11:15 and said to him: "Thus says **J**:
11:28 not heed the message that **J** sent him.
11:29 Then the spirit of the LORD came upon **J**,
11:30 And **J** made a vow to the LORD, and said,
11:32 So **J** crossed over to the Ammonites to fight
11:34 Then **J** came to his home at Mizpah;
11:40 of Israel would go out to lament the daughter of **J**
12: 1 and they crossed to Zaphon and said to **J**,
12: 2 **J** said to them, "My people and I were engaged
12: 4 Then **J** gathered all the men of Gilead and fought
12: 7 **J** judged Israel six years.
12: 7 Then **J** the Gileadite died,
1Sa 12:11 And the LORD sent Jerubbaal and Barak, and **J**,
Heb 11:32 **J**, of David and Samuel and the prophets—

JEPHUNNEH (17)

Nu 13: 6 from the tribe of Judah, Caleb son of **J**;
14: 6 And Joshua son of Nun and Caleb son of **J**,
14:30 except Caleb son of **J** and Joshua son of Nun.
14:38 of Nun and Caleb son of **J** alone remained alive,
26:65 except Caleb son of **J** and Joshua son of Nun.
32:12 of **J** the Kenizzite and Joshua son of Nun,
34:19 Of the tribe of Judah, Caleb son of **J**.
Dt 1:36 except Caleb son of **J**. He shall see it,
Jos 14: 6 and Caleb son of **J** the Kenizzite said to him,
14:13 gave Hebron to Caleb son of **J** for an inheritance.
14:14 the inheritance of Caleb son of **J** the Kenizzite
15:13 to Caleb son of **J** a portion among the people
21:12 and its villages had been given to Caleb son of **J**
1Ch 4:15 The sons of Caleb son of **J**:
6:56 and its villages they gave to Caleb son of **J**.
7:38 The sons of Jether: **J**, Pispa, and Ara.
Sir 46: 7 he and Caleb son of **J**:

JERAH (2)

Ge 10:26 Sheleph, Hazarmaveth, **J**,
1Ch 1:20 Sheleph, Hazarmaveth, **J**,

JERAHMEEL (8) [JERAHMEELITES]

1Ch 2: 9 The sons of Hezron, who were born to him: **J**,
2:25 The sons of **J**, the firstborn of Hezron:
2:26 **J** also had another wife, whose name was Atarah;
2:27 The sons of Ram, the firstborn of **J**:
2:33 These were the descendants of **J**.
2:42 The sons of Caleb brother of **J**:
24:29 Of Kish, the sons of Kish: **J**.
Jer 36:26 And the king commanded **J** the king's son

JERAHMEELITES (2) [JERAHMEEL]

1Sa 27:10 or "Against the Negeb of the **J**," or,
30:29 in the towns of the **J**, in the towns of the Kenites,

JERECHUS (1)

1Es 5:22 The descendants of **J**, three hundred forty-five.

JERED (1)

1Ch 4:18 And his Judean wife bore **J** father of Gedor,

JEREMAI (2)

Ezr 10:33 Mattenai, Mattattah, Zabad, Eliphelet, **J**,
1Es 9:34 Of the descendants of Bani: **J**, Momdius, Maerus,

JEREMIAH (159) [JEREMIAH'S]

2Ki 23:31 His mother's name was Hamutal daughter of **J**
24:18 His mother's name was Hamutal daughter of **J**
1Ch 5:24 Epher, Ishi, Eliel, Azriel, **J**, Hodaviah,
12: 4 **J**, Jahaziel, Johanan, Jozabad of Gederah,
12:10 Mishmannah fourth, **J** fifth,
12:13 **J** tenth, Machbannai eleventh.
2Ch 35:25 **J** also uttered a lament for Josiah,
36:12 before the prophet **J** who spoke from the mouth
36:21 the word of the LORD by the mouth of **J**,
36:22 of the LORD spoken by **J**, the LORD stirred up
Ezr 1: 1 the word of the LORD by the mouth of **J** might
Ne 10: 2 Seraiah, Azariah, **J**,
12: 1 of Shealtiel, and Jeshua: Seraiah, **J**,
12:12 Meraiah; of **J**, Hananiah;
12:34 Judah, Benjamin, Shemaiah, and **J**,
Jer 1: 1 The words of **J** son of Hilkiah,
1:11 The word of the LORD came to me, saying, "**J**,
7: 1 The word that came to **J** from the LORD:
11: 1 The word that came to **J** from the LORD:
14: 1 of the LORD that came to **J** concerning
18: 1 The word that came to **J** from the LORD:
18:18 they said, "Come, let us make plots against **J**—
19:14 When **J** came from Topheth,
20: 1 heard **J** prophesying these things.
20: 2 Then Pashhur struck the prophet **J**,
20: 3 The next morning when Pashhur released **J** from
20: 3 **J** said to him, The LORD has named you
21: 1 This is the word that came to **J** from the LORD,
21: 3 Then **J** said to them:
24: 3 the LORD said to me, "What do you see, **J**?"
25: 1 The word that came to **J** concerning all the people
25: 2 the prophet **J** spoke to all the people of Judah
25:13 which **J** prophesied against all the nations.
26: 7 and all the people heard **J** speaking these words
26: 8 And when **J** had finished speaking all that
Jer 26: 9 And all the people gathered around **J** in the house
26:12 **J** spoke to all the officials and all the people,
26:20 against this land in words exactly like those of **J**.
26:24 of Shaphan was with **J** so that he was not given
27: 1 this word came to **J** from the LORD.
28: 5 Then the prophet **J** spoke to the prophet Hananiah
28: 6 and the prophet **J** said, "Amen!
28:10 the yoke from the neck of the prophet **J**,
28:11 At this, the prophet **J** went his way.
28:12 the yoke from the neck of the prophet **J**, the word of the LORD came to **J**:
28:15 And the prophet **J** said to the prophet Hananiah,
29: 1 the letter that the prophet **J** sent from Jerusalem
29:27 not rebuked **J** of Anathoth who plays the prophet
29:29 in the hearing of the prophet **J**.
29:30 Then the word of the LORD came to **J**:
30: 1 The word that came to **J** from the LORD:
32: 1 that came to **J** from the LORD in the tenth year
32: 2 and the prophet **J** was confined in the court of
32: 6 **J** said, The word of the LORD came to me:
32:26 The word of the LORD came to **J**:
33: 1 The word of the LORD came to **J** a second time,
33:19 The word of the LORD came to **J**:
33:23 The word of the LORD came to **J**:
34: 1 The word that came to **J** from the LORD,
34: 6 Then the prophet **J** spoke all these words
34: 8 The word that came to **J** from the LORD,
34:12 word of the LORD came to **J** from the LORD:
35: 1 The word that came to **J** from the LORD in
35: 3 So I took Jaazaniah son of **J** son of Habazziniah,
35:12 Then the word of the LORD came to **J**:
35:18 But to the house of the Rechabites **J** said:
36: 1 this word came to **J** from the LORD:
36: 4 Then **J** called Baruch son of Neriah,
36: 5 And **J** ordered Baruch, saying,
36: 8 that the prophet **J** ordered him about reading from
36:10 Baruch read the words of **J** from the scroll,
36:19 officials said to Baruch, "Go and hide, you and **J**,
36:26 to arrest the secretary Baruch and the prophet **J**.
36:27 the word of the LORD came to **J**:
36:32 Then **J** took another scroll and gave it to
37: 2 the LORD that he spoke through the prophet **J**.
37: 3 of Maaseiah to the prophet **J** saying,
37: 4 **J** was still going in and out among the people,
37: 6 the word of the LORD came to the prophet **J**:
37:12 **J** set out from Jerusalem to go to the land
37:13 of Hananiah arrested the prophet **J** saying,
37:14 And **J** said, "That is a lie;
37:14 and arrested **J** and brought him to the officials.
37:15 The officials were enraged at **J**,
37:16 Thus **J** was put in the cistern house, in the cells,
37:17 from the LORD?" **J** said,
37:18 **J** also said to King Zedekiah,
37:21 and they committed **J** to the court of the guard;
37:21 So **J** remained in the court of the guard.
38: 1 of Malchiah heard the words that **J** was saying
38: 6 So they took **J** and threw him into the cistern
38: 6 in the court of the guard, letting **J** down by ropes.
38: 6 but only mud, and **J** sank in the mud.
38: 7 heard that they had put **J** into the cistern.
38: 9 to the prophet **J** by throwing him into the cistern
38:10 the prophet **J** up from the cistern before he dies."
38:11 which he let down to **J** in the cistern by ropes.
38:12 Then Ebed-melech the Ethiopian said to **J**,
38:12 between your armpits and the ropes." **J** did so.
38:13 Then they drew **J** up by the ropes
38:13 And **J** remained in the court of the guard.
38:14 for the prophet **J** and received him at
38:14 The king said to **J**, "I have something to ask you;
38:15 **J** said to Zedekiah, "If I tell you,
38:16 So King Zedekiah swore an oath in secret to **J**,
38:17 Then **J** said to Zedekiah, "Thus says the LORD,
38:19 King Zedekiah said to **J**,
38:20 **J** said, "That will not happen.
38:24 Then Zedekiah said to **J**,
38:27 the officials did come to **J** and questioned him;
38:28 And **J** remained in the court of the guard until
39:11 of Babylon gave command concerning **J**
39:14 and took **J** from the court of the guard.
39:15 of the LORD came to **J** while he was confined in
40: 1 The word that came to **J** from the LORD
40: 2 The captain of the guard took **J** and said to him,
40: 6 **J** went to Gedaliah son of Ahikam at Mizpah,
42: 2 the prophet **J** and said, "Be good enough to listen
42: 4 The prophet **J** said to them, "Very well:
42: 5 They in their turn said to **J**,
42: 7 of ten days the word of the LORD came to **J**.
43: 1 When **J** finished speaking to all
43: 2 of Kareah and all the other insolent men said to **J**,
43: 6 also the prophet **J** and Baruch son of Neriah.
43: 8 the word of the LORD came to **J** in Tahpanhes:
44: 1 The word that came to **J** for all the Judeans living
44:15 in Pathros in the land of Egypt, answered **J**:
44:20 Then **J** said to all the people, men and women,
44:24 **J** said to all the people and all the women,
45: 1 that the prophet **J** spoke to Baruch son of Neriah,
45: 1 in a scroll at the dictation of **J**, in the fourth year
46: 1 that came to the prophet **J** concerning the nations.
46:13 The word that the LORD spoke to the prophet **J**
47: 1 the LORD that came to the prophet **J** concerning
49:34 that came to the prophet **J** concerning Elam,
50: 1 the land of the Chaldeans, by the prophet **J**:
51:59 that the prophet **J** commanded Seraiah son
51:60 **J** wrote in a scroll all the disasters
51:61 And **J** said to Seraiah:
51:64 Thus far are the words of **J**.
52: 1 His mother's name was Hamutal daughter of **J**
Da 9: 2 to the word of the LORD to the prophet **J**,
Mt 2:17 what had been spoken through the prophet **J**:
16:14 and still others **J** or one of the prophets."
27: 9 the prophet **J**, "And they took the thirty pieces
Sir 49: 6 and made its streets desolate, as **J** had foretold.
LtJ 6: 1 A copy of a letter that **J** sent to those who were to
2Mc 2: 1 prophet **J** ordered those who were being deported
2: 5 **J** came and found a cave-dwelling,
2: 7 **J** learned of it, he rebuked them and declared:
15:14 people and the holy city—**J**, the prophet of God."
15:15 **J** stretched out his right hand and gave to Judas
1Es 1:28 and did not heed the words of the prophet **J** from
1:32 The prophet **J** lamented for Josiah,
1:47 that were spoken by the prophet **J** from the mouth
1:57 of the word of the Lord by the mouth of **J**,
2: 1 that the word of the Lord by the mouth of **J** might
2Es 2:18 I will send you help, my servants Isaiah and **J**.

JEREMIAH'S (3) [JEREMIAH]

Jer 36: 4 a scroll at **J** dictation all the words of the LORD
36:27 with the words that Baruch wrote at **J** dictation,
36:32 who wrote on it at **J** dictation all the words of

JEREMIAS, JEREMY (KJV) See JEREMIAH

JEREMIEL (1)

2Es 4:36 And the archangel **J** answered and said,

JEREMOTH (10)

1Ch 7: 8 Zemirah, Joash, Eliezer, Elioenai, Omri, **J**,
8:14 and Ahio, Shashak, and **J**.
23:23 The sons of Mushi: Mahli, Eder, and **J**, three.
25:22 to **J**, his sons and his brothers, twelve;
Ezr 10:26 Mattaniah, Zechariah, Jehiel, Abdi, **J**, and Elijah.
10:27 Elioenai, Eliashib, Mattaniah, **J**, Zabad,
10:29 Malluch, Adaiah, Jashub, Sheal, and **J**.
1Es 9:27 Jezrielus and Abdi, and **J** and Elijah.
9:28 Eliadas, Eliashib, Othoniah, **J**,
9:30 Mamuchus, Adaiah, Jashub, and Sheal and **J**.

JERIAH (2) [=JERIJAH]

1Ch 23:19 **J** the chief, Amariah the second,
24:23 **J** the chief, Amariah the second,

JERIBAI (1)

1Ch 11:46 and **J** and Joshaviah sons of Elnaam,

JERICHO (70)

Nu 22: 1 in the plains of Moab across the Jordan from **J**.
26: 3 in the plains of Moab by the Jordan opposite **J**,
26:63 in the plains of Moab by the Jordan opposite **J**.
31:12 on the plains of Moab by the Jordan at **J**.
33:48 in the plains of Moab by the Jordan at **J**;
33:50 In the plains of Moab by the Jordan at **J**,
34:15 beyond the Jordan at **J** eastward,
35: 1 In the plains of Moab by the Jordan at **J**,
36:13 in the plains of Moab by the Jordan at **J**.
Dt 32:49 which is in the land of Moab, across from **J**,
34: 1 to the top of Pisgah, which is opposite **J**,
34: 3 that is, the valley of **J**, the city of palm trees—
Jos 2: 1 saying, "Go, view the land, especially **J**."
2: 2 The king of **J** was told,
2: 3 Then the king of **J** sent orders to Rahab,
3:16 Then the people crossed over opposite **J**.
4:13 before the LORD to the plains of **J** for battle.
4:19 and they camped in Gilgal on the east border of **J**.
5:10 the fourteenth day of the month in the plains of **J**.
5:13 Once when Joshua was by **J**,
6: 1 Now **J** was shut up inside and out because of
6: 2 "See, I have handed **J** over to you,
6:25 the messengers whom Joshua sent to spy out **J**.
6:26 to build this city—this **J**!
7: 2 Joshua sent men from **J** to Ai,
8: 2 You shall do to Ai and its king as you did to **J**
9: 3 of Gibeon heard what Joshua had done to **J** and
10: 1 to Ai and its king as he had done to **J** and its king,
10:28 of Makkedah as he had done to the king of **J**.
10:30 he did to its king as he had done to the king of **J**.
12: 9 the king of **J** one the king of Ai,
13:32 beyond the Jordan east of **J**.
16: 1 the Jordan by **J**, east of the waters of **J**,
16: 1 going up from **J** into the hill country to Bethel;
16: 7 and touches **J**, ending at the Jordan.
18:12 boundary goes up to the slope of **J** on the north,
18:21 of Benjamin according to their families were **J**,
20: 8 And beyond the Jordan east of **J**,
24:11 When you went over the Jordan and came to **J**,
24:11 the citizens of **J** fought against you,
2Sa 10: 5 "Remain at **J** until your beards have grown,
1Ki 16:34 In his days Hiel of Bethel built **J**;
2Ki 2: 4 for the LORD has sent me to **J**."
2: 4 So they came to **J**.
2: 5 of prophets who were at **J** drew near to Elisha,
2:15 of prophets who were at **J** saw him at a distance,
2:18 they came back to him (he had remained at **J**),
25: 5 and overtook him in the plains of **J**;
1Ch 6:78 and across the Jordan from **J**, on the east side of
19: 5 "Remain at **J** until your beards have grown,
2Ch 28:15 they brought them to their kindred at **J**,
Ezr 2:34 Of **J**, three hundred forty-five.
Ne 3: 2 And the men of **J** built next to him.
7:36 Of **J**, three hundred forty-five.

Jer 39: 5 and overtook Zedekiah in the plains of **J;**
52: 8 and overtook Zedekiah in the plains of **J;**
Mt 20:29 they were leaving **J,** a large crowd followed him.
Mk 10:46 They came to **J.**
10:46 and a large crowd were leaving **J,**
Lk 10:30 "A man was going down from Jerusalem to **J,**
18:35 As he approached **J,** a blind man was sitting by
19: 1 He entered **J** and was passing through it.
Heb 11:30 the walls of **J** fell after they had been encircled
Jdt 4: 4 Belmain, and **J,** and to Choba and Aesora,
Sir 24:14 and like rosebushes in **J;**
1Mc 9:50 the fortress in **J,** and Emmaus, and Beth-horon,
16:11 had been appointed governor over the plain of **J;**
16:14 and he went down to **J** with his sons Mattathias
2Mc 12:15 or engines of war overthrew **J** in the days

JERIEL (1)

1Ch 7: 2 Uzzi, Rephaiah, **J,** Jahmai, Ibsam, and Shemuel,

JERIJAH (1) [=JERIAH]

1Ch 26:31 Of the Hebronites, **J** was chief of the Hebronites.

JERIMOTH (7)

1Ch 7: 7 The sons of Bela: Ezbon, Uzzi, Uzziel, **J,** and Iri,
12: 5 **J,** Bealiah, Shemariah, Shephatiah the Haruphite;
24:30 The sons of Mushi: Mahli, Eder, and **J.**
25: 4 Bukkiah, Mattaniah, Uzziel, Shebuel, and **J,**
27:19 for Naphtali, **J** son of Azriel;
2Ch 11:18 as his wife Mahalath daughter of **J** son of David,
31:13 Asahel, **J,** Jozabad, Eliel, Ismachiah, Mahath,

JERIOTH (1)

1Ch 2:18 by his wife Azubah, and by **J;**

JEROBOAM (104) [JEROBOAM'S]

1Ki 11:26 **J** son of Nebat, an Ephraimite of Zeredah,
11:28 The man **J** was very able,
11:29 About that time, when **J** was leaving Jerusalem,
11:31 He then said to **J:** Take
11:40 Solomon sought therefore to kill **J;** but **J** promptly fled to Egypt,
12: 2 When **J** son of Nebat heard of it (for he was still
12: 2 then **J** returned from Egypt.
12: 3 and **J** and all the assembly of Israel came and said
12:12 So **J** and all the people came to Rehoboam
12:15 by Ahijah the Shilonite to **J** son of Nebat.
12:20 When all Israel heard that **J** had returned,
12:25 **J** built Shechem in the hill country of Ephraim,
12:26 Then **J** said to himself,
12:32 **J** appointed a festival on the fifteenth day of
13: 1 **J** was standing by the altar to offer incense,
13: 4 **J** stretched out his hand from the altar, saying,
13:33 after this event **J** did not turn from his evil way,
13:34 This matter became sin to the house of **J,**
14: 1 At that time Abijah son of **J** fell sick.
14: 2 **J** said to his wife, "Go, disguise yourself,
14: 2 it will not be known that you are the wife of **J,**
14: 5 "The wife of **J** is coming to inquire of you
14: 6 wife of **J;** why do you pretend to be another?
14: 7 Go, tell **J,** 'Thus says the LORD,
14:10 I will bring evil upon the house of **J.**
14:10 I will cut off from **J** every male,
14:10 and will consume the house of **J,**
14:11 Anyone belonging to **J** who dies in the city,
14:13 the God of Israel, in the house of **J.**
14:14 who shall cut off the house of **J** today,
14:16 He will give Israel up because of the sins of **J,**
14:19 Now the rest of the acts of **J,**
14:20 The time that **J** reigned was twenty-two years;
14:30 between Rehoboam and **J** continually.
15: 1 in the eighteenth year of King **J** son of Nebat,
15: 6 between Rehoboam and **J** continued all the days
15: 7 There was war between Abijam and **J.**
15: 9 In the twentieth year of King **J** of Israel,
15:25 of **J** began to reign over Israel in the second year
15:29 soon as he was king, he killed all the house of **J;**
15:29 he left to the house of **J** not one that breathed,
15:30 of **J** that he committed and that he caused Israel
15:34 in the way of **J** and in the sin that he caused Israel
16: 2 and you have walked in the way of **J,**
16: 3 like the house of **J** son of Nebat.
16: 7 in being like the house of **J,**
16:19 walking in the way of **J,**
16:26 For he walked in all the way of **J** son of Nebat,
16:31 a light thing for him to walk in the sins of **J** son
21:22 like the house of **J** son of Nebat,
22:52 and in the way of **J** son of Nebat,
2Ki 3: 3 he clung to the sin of **J** son of Nebat,
9: 9 the house of Ahab like the house of **J** son
10:29 the sins of **J** son of Nebat, which he caused Israel
10:31 he did not turn from the sins of **J,**
13: 2 and followed the sins of **J** son of Nebat,
13: 6 the sins of the house of **J,** which he caused Israel
13:11 not depart from all the sins of **J** son of Nebat,
13:13 and **J** sat upon his throne;
14:16 then his son **J** succeeded him.
14:23 King **J** son of Joash of Israel began to reign
14:24 not depart from all the sins of **J** son of Nebat,
14:27 so he saved them by the hand of **J** son of Joash.
14:28 Now the rest of the acts of **J,** and all that he did,
14:29 **J** slept with his ancestors, the kings of Israel;
15: 1 of King **J** of Israel King Azariah son of Amaziah
15: 8 of **J** reigned over Israel in Samaria six months.
15: 9 He did not depart from the sins of **J** son of Nebat,
2Ki 15:18 from any of the sins of **J** son of Nebat,
15:24 not turn away from the sins of **J** son of Nebat,
15:28 he did not depart from the sins of **J** son of Nebat,
17:21 they made **J** son of Nebat king.
17:21 **J** drove Israel from following the LORD
17:22 in all the sins that **J** committed;
23:15 the high place erected by **J** son of Nebat,
23:16 when **J** stood by the altar at the festival;
1Ch 5:17 and in the days of King **J** of Israel.
2Ch 9:29 in the visions of the seer Iddo concerning **J** son
10: 2 **J** son of Nebat heard of it (for he was in Egypt,
10: 2 then **J** returned from Egypt.
10: 3 and **J** and all Israel came and said to Rehoboam,
10:12 So **J** and all the people came to Rehoboam
10:15 by Ahijah the Shilonite to **J** son of Nebat.
11: 4 and turned back from the expedition against **J.**
11:14 because **J** and his sons had prevented them
12:15 between Rehoboam and **J.**
13: 1 In the eighteenth year of King **J,**
13: 2 Now there was war between Abijah and **J.**
13: 3 and **J** drew up his line of battle against him
13: 4 and said, "Listen to me, **J** and all Israel!
13: 6 Yet **J** son of Nebat, a servant of Solomon son
13: 8 and have with you the golden calves that **J** made
13:13 **J** had sent an ambush around to come on them
13:15 God defeated **J** and all Israel before Abijah
13:19 Abijah pursued **J,** and took cities from him:
13:20 **J** did not recover his power in the days of Abijah;
Hos 1: 1 and in the days of King **J** son of Joash of Israel.
Am 1: 1 and in the days of King **J** son of Joash of Israel,
7: 9 I will rise against the house of **J** with the sword."
7:10 the priest of Bethel, sent to King **J** of Israel,
7:11 thus Amos has said, '**J** shall die by the sword,
Tob 1: 5 to the calf that King **J** of Israel had erected in Dan
Sir 47:23 Then **J** son of Nebat led Israel into sin

JEROBOAM'S (3) [JEROBOAM]

1Ki 14: 4 **J** wife did so; she set out
14:13 for he alone of **J** family shall come to the grave,
14:17 Then **J** wife got up and went away,

JEROHAM (10)

1Sa 1: 1 of **J** son of Elihu son of Tohu son of Zuph,
1Ch 6:27 Eliab his son, **J** his son, Elkanah his son.
6:34 son of **J,** son of Eliel, son of Toah,
8:27 Jaareshiah, Elijah, and Zichri were the sons of **J.**
9: 8 Ibneiah son of **J,** Elah son of Uzzi, son of Michri,
9:12 and Adaiah son of **J,** son of Pashhur, son
12: 7 and Joelah and Zebadiah, sons of **J** of Gedor.
27:22 for Dan, Azarel son of **J.**
2Ch 23: 1 Azariah son of **J,** Ishmael son of Jehohanan,
Ne 11:12 and Adaiah son of **J** son of Pelaliah son

JERUBBAAL (15) [=GIDEON]

Jdg 6:32 Therefore on that day Gideon was called **J,**
7: 1 Then **J** (that is, Gideon) and all the troops
8:29 **J** son of Joash went to live in his own house.
8:35 and they did not exhibit loyalty to the house of **J**
9: 1 of **J** went to Shechem to his mother's kinsfolk
9: 2 that all seventy of the sons of **J** rule over you,
9: 5 and killed his brothers the sons of **J,**
9: 5 but Jotham, the youngest son of **J,** survived,
9:16 and if you have dealt well with **J** and his house,
9:19 with **J** and with his house this day, then rejoice
9:24 the violence done to the seventy sons of **J** might
9:28 the son of **J** and Zebul his officer serve the men
9:57 and on them came the curse of Jotham son of **J.**
1Sa 12:11 And the LORD sent **J** and Barak, and Jephthah,
2Sa 11:21 Who killed Abimelech son of **J?**

JERUBBESHETH See Index to Footnotes

JERUEL (1)

2Ch 20:16 before the wilderness of **J.**

JERUSALEM‡ (1028) [=JEBUS, JERUSALEM'S, =SALEM]

A. INHABITANTS OF JERUSALEM (49)
B. JUDAH AND JERUSALEM (35)
C. STREETS OF JERUSALEM (13)
D. DAUGHTERS OF JERUSALEM (8)
E. DAUGHTER JERUSALEM (7)
F. JERUSALEM AND JUDAH (7)

Jos 10: 1 of **J** heard how Joshua had taken Ai,
10: 3 of **J** sent a message to King Hoham of Hebron,
10: 5 the king of **J,** the king of Hebron,
10:23 the king of **J,** the king of Hebron,
12:10 the king of **J** one the king of Hebron one
15: 8 at the southern slope of the Jebusites (that is, **J**);
15:63 not drive out the Jebusites, the inhabitants of **J;** A
15:63 so the Jebusites live with the people of Judah in **J**
18:28 Jebus (that is, **J**), Gibeah and Kiriath-jearim—
Jdg 1: 7 They brought him to **J,** and he died there.
1: 8 the people of Judah fought against **J** and took it.
1:21 not drive out the Jebusites who lived in **J;**
1:21 in **J** among the Benjaminites to this day.
19:10 and arrived opposite Jebus (that is, **J**).
1Sa 17:54 the head of the Philistine and brought it to **J;**
2Sa 5: 5 and at **J** he reigned over all Israel
5: 6 and his men marched to **J** against the Jebusites,
5:13 In **J,** after he came from Hebron,
5:14 the names of those who were born to him in **J:**
2Sa 8: 7 the servants of Hadadezer, and brought them to **J.**
9:13 Mephibosheth lived in **J,**
10:14 against the Ammonites, and came to **J.**
11: 1 But David remained at **J.**
11:12 So Uriah remained in **J** that day.
12:31 Then David and all the people returned to **J.**
14:23 went to Geshur, and brought Absalom to **J.**
14:28 So Absalom lived two full years in **J,**
15: 8 If the LORD will indeed bring me back to **J,**
15:11 Two hundred men from **J** went with Absalom;
15:14 to all his officials who were with him at **J,**
15:29 and Abiathar carried the ark of God back to **J,**
15:37 just as Absalom was entering **J.**
16: 3 Ziba said to the king, "He remains in **J;**
16:15 Now Absalom and all the Israelites came to **J;**
17:20 and could not find them, they returned to **J.**
19:19 on the day my lord the king left **J;**
19:25 When he came from **J** to meet the king,
19:33 and I will provide for you in **J** at my side."
19:34 that I should go up with the king to **J?**
20: 2 their king steadfastly from the Jordan to **J.**
20: 3 David came to his house at **J;**
20: 7 they went out from **J** to pursue Sheba son
20:22 while Joab returned to **J** to the king.
24: 8 to **J** at the end of nine months and twenty days.
24:16 when the angel stretched out his hand toward **J**
1Ki 2:11 and thirty-three years in **J.**
2:36 and said to him, "Build yourself a house in **J,**
2:38 So Shimei lived in **J** many days.
2:41 that Shimei had gone from **J** to Gath
3: 1 the house of the LORD and the wall around **J.**
3:15 to **J** where he stood before the ark of the covenant
8: 1 before King Solomon in **J,**
9:15 the Millo and the wall of **J,** Hazor, Megiddo,
9:19 and whatever Solomon desired to build, in **J,**
10: 2 She came to **J** with a very great retinue,
10:26 in the chariot cities and with the king in **J.**
10:27 The king made silver as common in **J** as stones,
11: 7 on the mountain east of **J.**
11:13 sake of my servant David and for the sake of **J,**
11:29 About that time, when Jeroboam was leaving **J,**
11:32 sake of my servant David and for the sake of **J,**
11:36 a lamp before me in **J,**
11:42 The time that Solomon reigned in **J**
12:18 then hurriedly mounted his chariot to flee to **J.**
12:21 When Rehoboam came to **J,**
12:27 to offer sacrifices in the house of the LORD at **J,**
12:28 "You have gone up to **J** long enough.
14:21 and he reigned seventeen years in **J,**
14:25 King Shishak of Egypt came up against **J;**
15: 2 He reigned for three years in **J.**
15: 4 the LORD his God gave him a lamp in **J,** setting up his son after him, and establishing **J;**
15:10 he reigned forty-one years in **J.**
22:42 and he reigned twenty-five years in **J.**
2Ki 8:17 and he reigned eight years in **J.**
8:26 he reigned one year in **J.**
9:28 His officers carried him in a chariot to **J,**
12: 1 he reigned forty years in **J.**
12:17 But when Hazael set his face to go up against **J,**
12:18 Then Hazael withdrew from **J.**
14: 2 and he reigned twenty-nine years in **J.**
14: 2 His mother's name was Jehoaddin of **J.**
14:13 he came to **J,** and broke down the wall of **J**
14:19 They made a conspiracy against him in **J,**
14:20 he was buried in **J** with his ancestors in the city
15: 2 and he reigned fifty-two years in **J.**
15: 2 His mother's name was Jecoliah of **J.**
15:33 to reign and reigned sixteen years in **J.**
16: 2 he reigned sixteen years in **J.**
16: 5 of Remaliah of Israel came up to wage war on **J;**
18: 2 he reigned twenty-nine years in **J.**
18:17 a great army from Lachish to King Hezekiah at **J.**
18:17 They went up and came to **J.**
18:22 saying to Judah and to **J,**
18:22 'You shall worship before this altar in **J**'?
18:35 the LORD should deliver **J** out of my hand?' "
19:10 that **J** will not be given into the hand of the king
19:21 behind your back, daughter **J.** E
19:31 for from **J** a remnant shall go out,
21: 1 he reigned fifty-five years in **J.**
21: 4 "In **J** I will put my name."
21: 7 and in **J,** which I have chosen out of all the tribes
21:12 I am bringing upon **J** and Judah such evil that F
21:13 over **J** the measuring line for Samaria,
21:13 I will wipe **J** as one wipes a dish,
21:16 until he had filled **J** from one end to another,
21:19 he reigned two years in **J.**
22: 1 he reigned thirty-one years in **J.**
22:14 she resided in **J** in the Second Quarter,
23: 1 the elders of Judah and **J** should be gathered B
23: 2 all the inhabitants of **J,** the priests, the prophets, A
23: 4 he burned them outside **J** in the fields of
23: 5 at the cities of Judah and around **J;**
23: 6 outside **J,** to the Wadi Kidron,
23: 9 did not come up to the altar of the LORD in **J,**
23:13 king defiled the high places that were east of **J,**
23:20 Then he returned to **J.**
23:23 Josiah this passover was kept to the LORD in **J.**
23:24 that were seen in the land of Judah and in **J,**
23:27 and I will reject this city that I have chosen, **J,**
23:30 from Megiddo, brought him to **J,** and buried him
23:31 he reigned three months in **J.**
23:33 so that he might not reign in **J,**
23:36 he reigned eleven years in **J.**
24: 4 for he filled **J** with innocent blood,
24: 8 he reigned three months in **J.**

2Ki 24: 8 name was Nehushta daughter of Elnathan of **J.**
24:10 of Babylon came up to **J,**
24:14 He carried away all **J,** all the officials,
24:15 he took into captivity from **J** to Babylon.
24:18 he reigned eleven years in **J.**
24:20 **J** and Judah so angered the LORD F
25: 1 with all his army against **J,** and laid siege to it;
25: 8 a servant of the king of Babylon, came to **J.**
25: 9 the king's house, and all the houses of **J;**
25:10 of the guard broke down the walls around **J.**
1Ch 3: 4 And he reigned thirty-three years in **J.**
3: 5 These were born to him in **J:**
6:10 as priest in the house that Solomon built in **J).**
6:15 sent Judah and **J** into exile by the hand of B
6:32 the house of the LORD in **J;**
8:28 to their generations, chiefs. These lived in **J.**
8:32 Now these also lived opposite their kindred in **J,**
9: 3 Benjamin, Ephraim, and Manasseh lived in **J:**
9:34 to their generations; these leaders lived in **J.**
9:38 and these also lived opposite their kindred in **J,**
11: 4 David and all Israel marched to **J,** that is Jebus,
14: 3 David took more wives in **J,**
14: 4 the names of the children whom he had in **J:**
15: 3 David assembled all Israel in **J** to bring up the ark
18: 7 the servants of Hadadezer, and brought them to **J.**
19:15 Then Joab came to **J.**
20: 1 But David remained at **J.**
20: 3 Then David and all the people returned to **J.**
21: 4 throughout all Israel, and came back to **J.**
21:15 And God sent an angel to **J** to destroy it;
21:16 in his hand a drawn sword stretched out over **J.**
23:25 and he resides in **J** forever.
28: 1 David assembled at **J** all the officials of Israel,
29:27 and thirty-three years in **J.**
2Ch 1: 4 for he had pitched a tent for it in **J.)**
1:13 from the tent of meeting, to **J.**
1:14 in the chariot cities and with the king in **J.**
1:15 The king made silver and gold as common in **J**
2: 7 with me in Judah and **J,** B
2:16 you will take it up to **J."**
3: 1 the house of the LORD in **J** on Mount Moriah,
5: 2 of the people of Israel, in **J,** to bring up the ark of
6: 6 but I have chosen **J** in order that my name may
8: 6 and whatever Solomon desired to build, in **J,**
9: 1 she came to **J** to test him with hard questions,
9:25 in the chariot cities and with the king in **J.**
9:27 The king made silver as common in **J** as stone,
9:30 Solomon reigned in **J** over all Israel forty years.
10:18 hurriedly mounted his chariot to flee to **J.**
11: 1 When Rehoboam came to **J,**
11: 5 Rehoboam resided in **J,** and he built cities
11:14 and their holdings and had come to Judah and **J,** B
11:16 the tribes of Israel to **J** to sacrifice to the LORD,
12: 2 King Shishak of Egypt came up against **J**
12: 4 the fortified cities of Judah and came as far as **J.**
12: 5 who had gathered at **J** because of Shishak,
12: 7 not be poured out on **J** by the hand of Shishak.
12: 9 So King Shishak of Egypt came up against **J;**
12:13 So King Rehoboam established himself in **J**
12:13 he reigned seventeen years in **J,**
13: 2 He reigned for three years in **J.**
14:15 Then they returned to **J.**
15:10 They were gathered at **J** in the third month of
17:13 He had soldiers, mighty warriors, in **J.**
19: 1 of Judah returned in safety to his house in **J.**
19: 4 Jehoshaphat resided at **J;**
19: 8 in **J** Jehoshaphat appointed certain Levites
19: 8 They had their seat at **J.**
20: 5 in the assembly of Judah and **J,** B
20:15 He said, "Listen, all Judah and inhabitants of **J,** A
20:17 of the LORD on your behalf, O Judah and **J.'** B
20:18 the inhabitants of **J** fell down before the LORD, A
20:20 "Listen to me, O Judah and inhabitants of **J!** A
20:27 Then all the people of Judah and **J,** B
20:27 to **J** with joy, for the LORD had enabled them
20:28 to **J,** with harps and lyres and trumpets,
20:31 he reigned twenty-five years in **J.**
21: 5 he reigned eight years in **J.**
21:11 and led the inhabitants of **J** into unfaithfulness, A
21:13 and the inhabitants of **J** into unfaithfulness, A
21:20 he reigned eight years in **J.**
22: 1 inhabitants of **J** made his youngest son Ahaziah A
22: 2 he reigned one year in **J.**
23: 2 of families of Israel, and they came to **J.**
24: 1 he reigned forty years in **J;**
24: 6 in from Judah and **J** the tax levied by Moses, B
24: 9 throughout Judah and **J** to bring in for the LORD B
24:18 And wrath came upon Judah and **J** for this guilt B
24:23 They came to Judah and **J,** B
25: 1 and he reigned twenty-nine years in **J.**
25: 1 His mother's name was Jehoaddan of **J.**
25:23 to **J,** and broke down the wall of Jerusalem from
25:23 to Jerusalem, and broke down the wall of **J** from
25:27 a conspiracy against him in **J,**
26: 3 and he reigned fifty-two years in **J.**
26: 3 His mother's name was Jecoliah of **J.**
26: 9 Uzziah built towers in **J** at the Corner Gate,
26:15 In **J** he set up machines,
27: 1 he reigned sixteen years in **J.**
27: 8 he reigned sixteen years in **J.**
28: 1 he reigned sixteen years in **J.**
28:10 to subjugate the people of Judah and **J,** B
28:24 and made himself altars in every corner of **J.**
28:27 and they buried him in the city, in **J;**
29: 1 he reigned twenty-nine years in **J.**
29: 8 the wrath of the LORD came upon Judah and **J,** B
30: 1 they should come to the house of the LORD at **J,**
2Ch 30: 2 in **J** had taken counsel to keep the passover in
30: 3 nor had the people assembled in **J).**
30: 5 to the LORD the God of Israel, at **J;**
30:11 and Zebulun humbled themselves and came to **J.**
30:13 in **J** to keep the festival of unleavened bread in
30:14 to work and removed the altars that were in **J,**
30:21 The people of Israel who were present at **J** kept
30:26 There was great joy in **J,**
30:26 of Israel there had been nothing like this in **J.**
31: 4 He commanded the people who lived in **J** to give
32: 2 and intended to fight against **J,**
32: 9 he sent his servants to **J** to King Hezekiah
32: 9 and to all the people of Judah that were in **J,**
32:10 that you undergo the siege of **J?**
32:12 and his altars and commanded Judah and **J,** B
32:18 of Judah to the people of **J** who were on the wall,
32:19 of **J** as if he were like the gods of the peoples of
32:22 and the inhabitants of **J** from the hand of A
32:23 in **J** and precious things to King Hezekiah
32:25 wrath came upon him and upon Judah and **J.** B
32:26 both he and the inhabitants of **J,** A
32:33 the inhabitants of **J** did him honor at his death. A
33: 1 he reigned fifty-five years in **J.**
33: 4 "In **J** shall my name be forever."
33: 7 and in **J,** which I have chosen out of all the tribes
33: 9 Manasseh misled Judah and the inhabitants of **J,** A
33:13 and restored him again to **J** and to his kingdom.
33:15 the mountain of the house of the LORD and in **J,**
33:21 he reigned two years in **J.**
34: 1 he reigned thirty-one years in **J.**
34: 3 the twelfth year he began to purge Judah and **J** B
34: 5 on their altars, and purged Judah and **J.** B
34: 7 Then he returned to **J.**
34: 9 and Benjamin and from the inhabitants of **J.** A
34:22 in **J** in the Second Quarter) and spoke to her to
34:29 the elders of Judah and **J.** B
34:30 with all the people of Judah, the inhabitants of **J,** A
34:32 in **J** and in Benjamin pledge themselves to it.
34:32 inhabitants of **J** acted according to the covenant A
35: 1 Josiah kept a passover to the LORD in **J;**
35:18 and by the inhabitants of **J.** A
35:24 in his second chariot and brought him to **J.**
35:24 All Judah and **J** mourned for Josiah. B
36: 1 and made him king to succeed his father in **J.**
36: 2 he reigned three months in **J.**
36: 3 Then the king of Egypt deposed him in **J** and laid
36: 4 his borther Eliakim king over Judah and **J,** B
36: 5 he reigned eleven years in **J.**
36: 9 he reigned three months and ten days in **J.**
36:10 his brother Zedekiah king over Judah and **J.** B
36:11 he reigned eleven years in **J.**
36:14 of the LORD that he had consecrated in **J.**
36:19 broke down the wall of **J,**
36:23 and he has charged me to build him a house at **J,**
Ezr 1: 2 and he has charged me to build him a house at **J**
1: 3 are now permitted to go up to **J** in Judah,
1: 3 he is the God who is in **J;**
1: 4 for the house of God in **J."**
1: 5 to go up and rebuild the house of the LORD in **J.**
1: 7 that Nebuchadnezzar had carried away from **J**
1:11 the exiles were brought up from Babylonia to **J.**
2: 1 they returned to **J** and Judah, F
2:68 as they came to the house of the LORD in **J,**
2:70 and some of the people lived in **J** and its vicinity;
3: 1 the people gathered together in **J.**
3: 8 after their arrival at the house of God at **J,**
3: 8 and the Levites and all who had come to **J** from
4: 6 against the inhabitants of Judah and **J.** B
4: 8 and Shimshai the scribe wrote a letter against **J**
4:12 up from you to us have gone to **J.**
4:20 **J** has had mighty kings who ruled over
4:23 in **J** and by force and power made them cease.
4:24 of God in **J** stopped and was discontinued until
5: 1 prophesied to the Jews who were in Judah and **J,** B
5: 2 to rebuild the house of God in **J;**
5:14 of the temple in **J** and had brought into the temple
5:15 go and put them in the temple in **J,**
5:16 the foundations of the house of God in **J;**
5:17 for the rebuilding of this house of God in **J.**
6: 3 Concerning the house of God at **J,**
6: 5 of the temple in **J** and brought to Babylon,
6: 5 be restored and brought back to the temple in **J,**
6: 9 salt, wine, or oil, as the priests in **J** require—
6:12 or to destroy this house of God in **J.**
6:18 in their courses for the service of God at **J,**
7: 7 and the temple servants also went up to **J,**
7: 8 They came to **J** in the fifth month,
7: 9 on the first day of the fifth month he came to **J,**
7:13 to go to **J** may go with you.
7:14 to make inquiries about Judah and **J** according B
7:15 to the God of Israel, whose dwelling is in **J,**
7:16 given willingly for the house of their God in **J.**
7:17 on the altar of the house of your God in **J.**
7:19 you shall deliver before the God of **J.**
7:27 the king to glorify the house of the LORD in **J,**
8:29 and the heads of families in Israel at **J,**
8:30 to bring them to **J,** to the house of our God.
8:31 on the twelfth day of the first month, to go to **J;**
8:32 We came to **J** and remained there three days.
9: 9 and to give us a wall in Judea and **J.**
10: 7 throughout Judah and **J** to all the returned exiles B
10: 7 the returned exiles that they should assemble at **J,**
10: 9 the people of Judah and Benjamin assembled at **J**
Ne 1: 2 those who had escaped the captivity, and about **J.**
1: 3 the wall of **J** is broken down,
2:11 So I came to **J** and was there for three days.
2:12 into my heart to do for **J.**
Ne 2:13 of **J** that had been broken down and its gates
2:17 how **J** lies in ruins with its gates burned.
2:17 Come, let us rebuild the wall of **J,**
2:20 you have no share or claim or historic right in **J."**
3: 8 and they restored **J** as far as the Broad Wall.
3: 9 ruler of half the district of **J,** made repairs.
3:12 ruler of half the district of **J,** made repairs,
4: 7 the repairing of the walls of **J** was going forward
4: 8 and fight against **J** and to cause confusion in it.
4:22 and his servant pass the night inside **J,**
6: 7 You have also set up prophets to proclaim in **J**
7: 2 over **J,** along with Hananiah the commander of
7: 3 of **J** are not to be opened until the sun is hot;
7: 3 Appoint guards from among the inhabitants of **J,** A
7: 6 they returned to **J** and Judah, each to his town. F
8:15 and proclaim in all their towns and in **J**
11: 1 Now the leaders of the people lived in **J;**
11: 1 to bring one out of ten to live in the holy city **J,**
11: 2 blessed all those who willingly offered to live in **J.**
11: 3 the leaders of the province who lived in **J;**
11: 4 And in **J** lived some of the Judahites and of
11: 6 in **J** were four hundred sixty-eight valiant warriors.
11:22 in **J** was Uzzi son of Bani son of Hashabiah son
12:27 of **J** they sought out the Levites in all their places,
12:27 to **J** to celebrate the dedication with rejoicing,
12:28 from the circuit around **J** and from the villages of
12:29 for themselves villages around **J.**
12:43 The joy of **J** was heard far away.
13: 6 While this was taking place I was not in **J,**
13: 7 and returned to **J.** I then discovered the wrong
13:15 which they brought into **J** on the sabbath day;
13:16 on the sabbath to the people of Judah, and in **J.**
13:19 When it began to be dark at the gates of **J** before
13:20 of merchandise spent the night outside **J** once
Est 2: 6 Kish had been carried away from **J** among
Ps 51:18 in your good pleasure; rebuild the walls of **J,**
68:29 of your temple at **J** kings bear gifts to you.
79: 1 they have laid **J** in ruins.
79: 3 like water all around **J,** and there was no one
102:21 be declared in Zion, and his praise in **J,**
116:19 of the house of the LORD, in your midst, O **J.**
122: 2 Our feet are standing within your gates, O **J.**
122: 3 **J**—built as a city that is bound firmly together.
122: 6 Pray for the peace of **J:**
125: 2 As the mountains surround **J,**
128: 5 May you see the prosperity of **J** all the days
135:21 be the LORD from Zion, he who resides in **J.**
137: 5 If I forget you, O **J,** let my right hand wither!
137: 6 if I do not set **J** above my highest joy.
147: 2 The LORD builds up **J;**
147:12 Praise the LORD, O **J!** Praise your God, O Zion!
Ecc 1: 1 words of the Teacher, the son of David, king in **J.**
1:12 I, the Teacher, when king over Israel in **J,**
1:16 surpassing all who were over **J** before me;
2: 7 more than any who had been before me in **J.**
2: 9 and surpassed all who were before me in **J;**
SS 1: 5 I am black and beautiful, O daughters of **J,** D
2: 7 I adjure you, O daughters of **J,** D
3: 5 I adjure you, O daughters of **J,** D
3:10 inlaid with love. Daughters of **J,** D
5: 8 I adjure you, O daughters of **J,** D
5:16 and this is my friend, O daughters of **J.** D
6: 4 comely as **J,** terrible as an army with banners.
8: 4 I adjure you, O daughters of **J,** D
Isa 1: 1 which he saw concerning Judah and **J** B
2: 1 Isaiah son of Amoz saw concerning Judah and **J.** B
2: 3 and the word of the LORD from **J.**
3: 1 is taking away from **J** and from Judah support
3: 8 For **J** has stumbled and Judah has fallen,
4: 3 Whoever is left in Zion and remains in **J** will
4: 3 everyone who has been recorded for life in **J,**
4: 4 of **J** from its midst by a spirit of judgment and by
5: 3 And now, inhabitants of **J** and people of Judah, A
5:14 the nobility of **J** and her multitude go down,
7: 1 of Remaliah of Israel went up to attack **J,**
7: 6 up against Judah and cut off **J** and conquer it
8:14 a trap and a snare for the inhabitants of **J.** A
10:10 images were greater than those of **J** and Samaria,
10:11 shall I not do to **J** and her idols what I have done
10:12 on Mount Zion and on **J,**
10:32 at the mount of daughter Zion, the hill of **J.**
22:10 You counted the houses of **J,**
22:21 a father to the inhabitants of **J** and to the house A
24:23 of hosts will reign on Mount Zion and in **J,**
27:13 the LORD on the holy mountain at **J.**
28:14 you scoffers who rule this people in **J.**
29: 2 and **J** shall be to me like an Ariel.
30:19 Truly, O people in Zion, inhabitants of **J,** A
31: 5 so the LORD of hosts will protect **J;**
31: 9 whose fire is in Zion, and whose furnace is in **J.**
33:20 Your eyes will see **J,** a quiet habitation,
36: 2 from Lachish to King Hezekiah at **J,**
36: 7 saying to Judah and to **J,**
36:20 that the LORD should save **J** out of my hand?' "
37:10 that **J** will not be given into the hand of the king
37:22 behind your back, daughter **J.** E
37:32 for from **J** a remnant shall go out,
40: 2 to **J,** and cry to her that she has served her term,
40: 9 lift up your voice with strength, O **J,**
41:27 and I give to **J** a herald of good tidings.
44:26 who says of **J,** "It shall be inhabited,"
44:28 and who says of **J,** "It shall be rebuilt,"
51:17 up, O **J,** you who have drunk at the hand of
52: 1 Put on your beautiful garments, O **J,**
52: 2 from the dust, rise up, O captive **J;**
52: 9 Break forth together into singing, you ruins of **J;**
52: 9 has comforted his people, he has redeemed **J.**

Isa 62: 6 Upon your walls, O J, I have posted sentinels;
62: 7 until he establishes J and makes it renowned
64: 10 Zion has become a wilderness, J a desolation.
65: 18 for I am about to create J as a joy,
65: 19 I will rejoice in J, and delight in my people;
66: 10 Rejoice with J, and be glad for her,
66: 13 you shall be comforted in J.
66: 20 and on dromedaries, to my holy mountain J,
Jer 1: 3 until the captivity of J in the fifth month.
1: 15 at the entrance of the gates of J,
2: 2 Go and proclaim in the hearing of J,
3: 17 At that time J shall be called the throne of
3: 17 to the presence of the LORD in J,
4: 3 the people of Judah and to the inhabitants of J: A
4: 4 O people of Judah and inhabitants of J, A
4: 5 Declare in Judah, and proclaim in J, and say:
4: 10 how utterly you have deceived this people and J,
4: 11 At that time it will be said to this people and to J:
4: 14 O J, wash your heart clean of wickedness
4: 16 against J, "Besiegers come from a distant land;
5: 1 Run to and fro through the streets of J, C
5: 1 so that I may pardon J.
6: 1 O children of Benjamin, from the midst of J!
6: 6 cast up a siege ramp against J.
6: 8 O J, or I shall turn from you in disgust,
7: 17 in the towns of Judah and in the streets of J? C
7: 34 in the cities of Judah and in the streets of J; C
8: 1 of the inhabitants of J shall be brought out A
9: 11 I will make J a heap of ruins, a lair of jackals;
11: 2 to the people of Judah and the inhabitants of J. A
11: 6 in the cities of Judah, and in the streets of J: C
11: 9 the people of Judah and the inhabitants of J. A
11: 12 cities of Judah and the inhabitants of J will go A
11: 13 as the streets of J are the altars you have set up C
13: 9 the pride of Judah and the great pride of J.
13: 13 and all the inhabitants of J—with drunkenness. A
13: 27 Woe to you, O J! How long will it be
14: 2 and the cry of J goes up.
14: 16 be thrown out into the streets of J, C
15: 4 of Hezekiah of Judah did in J.
15: 5 Who will have pity on you, O J,
17: 19 and in all the gates of J,
17: 20 and all Judah, and all the inhabitants of J, A
17: 21 on the sabbath day or bring it in by the gates of J.
17: 25 the people of Judah and the inhabitants of J; A
17: 26 from the towns of Judah and the places around J,
17: 27 and to carry in no burden through the gates of J
17: 27 it shall devour the palaces of J and shall not
18: 11 to the people of Judah and the inhabitants of J: A
19: 3 O kings of Judah and inhabitants of J. A
19: 7 the plans of Judah and J, B
19: 13 And the houses of J and the houses of the kings
22: 19 dragged off and thrown out beyond the gates of J.
23: 14 of J I have seen a more shocking thing:
23: 15 of J ungodliness has spread throughout the land."
24: 1 into exile from J King Jeconiah son of Jehoiakim
24: 8 the remnant of J who remain in this land,
25: 2 the people of Judah and all the inhabitants of J: A
25: 18 J and the towns of Judah, its kings and officials,
26: 18 J shall become a heap of ruins,
27: 3 the envoys who have come to J to King Zedekiah
27: 18 and in J may not go to Babylon.
27: 20 into exile from J to Babylon King Jeconiah son
27: 20 and all the nobles of Judah and J— B
27: 21 in the house of the king of Judah, and in J:
29: 1 of the letter that the prophet Jeremiah sent from J
29: 1 into exile from J to Babylon.
29: 2 the court officials, the leaders of Judah and J, B
29: 2 the artisans, and the smiths had departed from J.
29: 4 the exiles whom I have sent into exile from J
29: 20 from J to Babylon, hear the word of the LORD:
29: 25 a letter to all the people who are in J,
32: 2 the army of the king of Babylon was besieging J,
32: 32 the citizens of Judah and the inhabitants of J. A
32: 44 in the places around J, and in the cities of Judah,
33: 10 of Judah and the streets of J that are desolate, C
33: 13 the places around J, and in the towns of Judah,
33: 16 In those days Judah will be saved and J will live
34: 1 under his dominion were fighting against J
34: 6 to Zedekiah king of Judah, in J,
34: 7 of the king of Babylon was fighting against J and
34: 8 the people in J to make a proclamation of liberty
34: 19 the officials of J, the eunuchs, the priests,
35: 11 to J for fear of the army of the Chaldeans and
35: 11 That is why we are living in J."
35: 13 to the people of Judah and the inhabitants of J, A
35: 17 and on all the inhabitants of J every disaster A
36: 9 the people in J and all the people who came from
36: 9 the towns of Judah to J proclaimed a fast before
36: 31 I will bring on them, and on the inhabitants of J, A
37: 5 the Chaldeans who were besieging J heard news
37: 5 of them, they withdrew from J.
37: 11 when the Chaldean army had withdrawn from J
37: 12 Jeremiah set out from J to go to the land
38: 28 of the guard until the day that J was taken.
39: 1 and all his army came against J and besieged it;
39: 3 When J was taken, all the officials of the king
39: 8 and broke down the walls of J.
40: 1 along with all the captives of J and Judah F
42: 18 wrath were poured out on the inhabitants of J, A
44: 2 the disaster that I have brought on J and on all
44: 6 in the towns of Judah and in the streets of J; C
44: 9 in the land of Judah and in the streets of J? C
44: 13 as I have punished J, with the sword,
44: 17 do in the towns of Judah and in the streets of J. C
44: 21 in the towns of Judah and in the streets of J, C
51: 35 on the inhabitants of Chaldea," J shall say.

Jer 51: 50 and let J come into your mind:
52: 1 he reigned eleven years in J.
52: 3 J and Judah so angered the LORD F
52: 4 with all his army against J, and they laid siege
52: 12 the king of Babylon, entered J.
52: 13 the king's house, and all the houses of J;
52: 14 broke down all the walls around J.
52: 29 from J eight hundred thirty-two persons;
La 1: 7 J remembers, in the days of her affliction
1: 8 J sinned grievously, so she has become
1: 17 J has become a filthy thing among them.
2: 10 the young girls of J have bowed their heads
2: 13 to what compare you, O daughter J? E
2: 15 they hiss and wag their heads at daughter J; E
4: 12 that foe or enemy could enter the gates of J.
Eze 4: 1 On it portray a city, J;
4: 7 You shall set your face toward the siege of J,
4: 16 I am going to break the staff of bread in J;
5: 5 Thus says the Lord GOD: This is J;
8: 3 and brought me in visions of God to J,
9: 4 "Go through the city, through J,
9: 8 of Israel as you pour out your wrath upon J?"
11: 15 those of whom the inhabitants of J have said, A
12: 10 the prince in J and all the house of Israel in it."
12: 19 the Lord GOD concerning the inhabitants of J A
13: 16 concerning J and saw visions of peace for it,
14: 21 upon J my four deadly acts of judgment,
14: 22 for the evil that I have brought upon J,
15: 6 so I will give up the inhabitants of J. A
16: 2 Mortal, make known to J her abominations,
16: 3 Thus says the Lord GOD to J:
17: 12 Tell them: The king of Babylon came to J,
21: 2 toward J and preach against the sanctuaries;
21: 20 to Rabbah of the Ammonites or to Judah and to J
21: 22 Into his right hand comes the lot for J,
22: 19 I will gather you into the midst of J.
23: 4 Oholah is Samaria, and Oholibah is J.
24: 2 king of Babylon has laid siege to J this very day.
26: 2 because Tyre said concerning J, "Aha,
33: 21 someone who had escaped from J came to me
36: 38 like the flock at J during her appointed festivals,
Da 1: 1 King Nebuchadnezzar of Babylon came to J
5: 2 in J, so that the king and his lords, his wives,
5: 3 the house of God in J, and the king and his lords,
6: 10 in its upper room open toward J,
9: 2 must be fulfilled for the devastation of J, namely,
9: 7 the people of Judah, the inhabitants of J, A
9: 12 that what has been done against J has never
9: 16 turn away from your city J, your holy mountain;
9: 16 of our ancestors, J and your people have become
9: 25 and rebuild J until the time of an anointed prince,
Joel 2: 32 and in J there shall be those who escape,
3: 1 when I restore the fortunes of Judah and J, B
3: 6 You have sold the people of Judah and J to B
3: 16 and utters his voice from J,
3: 17 And J shall be holy, and strangers shall never
3: 20 be inhabited forever, and J to all generations.
Am 1: 2 and utters his voice from J;
2: 5 and it shall devour the strongholds of J.
Ob 1: 11 foreigners entered his gates and cast lots for J,
1: 20 of J who are in Sepharad shall possess the towns
Mic 1: 1 which he saw concerning Samaria and J.
1: 5 And what is the high place of Judah? Is it not J?
1: 9 it has reached to the gate of my people, to J.
1: 12 down from the LORD to the gate of J.
3: 10 who build Zion with blood and J with wrong!
3: 12 J shall become a heap of ruins,
4: 2 and the word of the LORD from J.
4: 8 the sovereignty of daughter J. E
Zep 1: 4 and against all the inhabitants of J; A
1: 12 At that time I will search J with lamps,
3: 14 and exult with all your heart, O daughter J! E
3: 16 On that day it shall be said to J:
Zec 1: 12 how long will you withhold mercy from J and
1: 14 I am very jealous for J and for Zion.
1: 16 I have returned to J with compassion;
1: 16 the measuring line shall be stretched out over J.
1: 17 LORD will again comfort Zion and again choose J.
1: 19 the horns that have scattered Judah, Israel, and J."
2: 2 He answered me, "To measure J,
2: 4 J shall be inhabited like villages without walls,
2: 12 in the holy land, and will again choose J.
3: 2 The LORD who has chosen J rebuke you!
7: 7 when J was inhabited and in prosperity,
8: 3 and will dwell in the midst of J;
8: 3 J shall be called the faithful city,
8: 4 and old women shall again sit in the streets of J, C
8: 8 and I will bring them to live in J.
8: 15 in these days to do good to J and to the house
8: 22 to seek the LORD of hosts in J,
9: 9 Shout aloud, O daughter J! E
9: 10 from Ephraim and the war horse from J;
12: 2 I am about to make J a cup of reeling for all
12: 2 it will be against Judah also in the siege against J.
12: 3 On that day I will make J a heavy stone for all
12: 5 inhabitants of J have strength through the LORD A
12: 6 while J shall again be inhabited in its place,
12: 6 be inhabited in its place, in J.
12: 7 David and the glory of the inhabitants of J may A
12: 8 the LORD will shield the inhabitants of J so that A
12: 9 to destroy all the nations that come against J.
12: 10 on the house of David and the inhabitants of J, A
12: 11 On that day the mourning in J will be as great as
13: 1 for the house of David and the inhabitants of J, A
14: 2 For I will gather all the nations against J to battle,
14: 4 which lies before J on the east;
14: 8 On that day living waters shall flow out from J,

Zec 14: 10 into a plain from Geba to Rimmon south of J.
14: 10 But J shall remain aloft on its site from the Gate
14: 11 to destruction; J shall abide in security.
14: 12 the peoples that wage war against J:
14: 14 even Judah will fight at J.
14: 16 of the nations that have come against J shall go
14: 17 of the earth do not go up to J to worship the King,
14: 21 in J and Judah shall be sacred to the LORD F
Mal 2: 11 abomination has been committed in Israel and in J;
3: 4 the offering of Judah and J will be pleasing B
Mt 2: 1 wise men from the East came to J,
2: 3 he was frightened, and all J with him;
3: 5 people of J and all Judea were going out to him,
4: 25 J, Judea, and from beyond the Jordan.
5: 35 or by J, for it is the city of the great King.
15: 1 Then Pharisees and scribes came to Jesus from J
16: 21 that he must go to J and undergo great suffering
20: 17 While Jesus was going up to J,
20: 18 up to J, and the Son of Man will be handed over
21: 1 they had come near J and had reached Bethphage,
21: 10 When he entered J, the whole city was in turmoil,
23: 37 "J, J, the city that kills the prophets
Mk 1: 5 and all the people of J were going out to him,
3: 8 they came to him in great numbers from Judea, J,
3: 22 And the scribes who came down from J said,
7: 1 of the scribes who had come from J gathered
10: 32 They were on the road, going up to J,
10: 33 "See, we are going up to J,
11: 1 When they were approaching J,
11: 11 Then he entered J and went into the temple;
11: 15 Then they came to J.
11: 27 Again they came to J.
15: 41 other women who had come up with him to J.
Lk 2: 22 they brought him up to J to present him to
2: 25 there was a man in J whose name was Simeon;
2: 38 to all who were looking for the redemption of J.
2: 41 Now every year his parents went to J for
2: 43 the boy Jesus stayed behind in J,
2: 45 they returned to J to search for him.
4: 9 Then the devil took him to J,
5: 17 of Galilee and Judea and from J);
6: 17 J, and the coast of Tyre and Sidon.
9: 31 which he was about to accomplish at J.
9: 51 he set his face to go to J.
9: 53 because his face was set toward J.
10: 30 "A man was going down from J to Jericho,
13: 4 worse offenders than all the others living in J?
13: 22 teaching as he made his way to J.
13: 33 for a prophet to be killed outside of J.'
13: 34 J, J, the city that kills the prophets
17: 11 the way to J Jesus was going through the region
18: 31 "See, we are going up to J,
19: 11 on to tell a parable, because he was near J, and
19: 28 he had said this, he went on ahead, going up to J.
21: 20 "When you see J surrounded by armies,
21: 24 and J will be trampled on by the Gentiles,
23: 7 who was himself in J at that time.
23: 28 Jesus turned to them and said, "Daughters of J, D
24: 13 about seven miles from J,
24: 18 the only stranger in J who does not know
24: 33 That same hour they got up and returned to J;
24: 47 in his name to all nations, beginning from J.
24: 52 and returned to J with great joy;
Jn 1: 19 when the Jews sent priests and Levites from J
2: 13 and Jesus went up to J.
2: 23 When he was in J during the Passover festival,
4: 20 that the place where people must worship is in J."
4: 21 the Father neither on this mountain nor in J.
4: 45 since they had seen all that he had done in J at
5: 1 and Jesus went up to J.
5: 2 Now in J by the Sheep Gate there is a pool,
7: 25 Now some of the people of J were saying,
10: 22 the festival of the Dedication took place in J.
11: 18 Now Bethany was near J, some two miles away,
11: 55 and many went up from the country to J before
12: 12 to the festival heard that Jesus was coming to J.
Ac 1: 4 he ordered them not to leave J,
1: 8 and you will be my witnesses in J,
1: 12 they returned to J from the mount called Olivet,
1: 12 which is near J, a sabbath day's journey away.
1: 19 This became known to all the residents of J,
2: 5 from every nation under heaven living in J.
2: 14 "Men of Judea and all who live in J,
4: 5 elders, and scribes assembled in J,
4: 16 For it is obvious to all who live in J that
5: 16 also gather from the towns around J,
5: 28 yet here you have filled J with your teaching
6: 7 the number of the disciples increased greatly in J,
8: 1 in J, and all except the apostles were scattered
8: 14 the apostles at J heard that Samaria had accepted
8: 25 to J, proclaiming the good news to many villages
8: 26 to the road that goes down from J to Gaza."
8: 27 He had come to J to worship
9: 2 men or women, he might bring them bound to J.
9: 13 how much evil he has done to your saints in J;
9: 21 in J among those who invoked this name?
9: 26 When he had come to J, he attempted to join
9: 28 So he went in and out among them in J,
10: 39 to all that he did both in Judea and in J.
11: 2 So when Peter went up to J,
11: 22 News of this came to the ears of the church in J,
11: 27 that time prophets came down from J to Antioch.
12: 25 and Saul returned to J and brought
13: 13 John, however, left them and returned to J;
13: 27 Because the residents of J and their leaders did
13: 31 to those who came up with him from Galilee to J,
15: 2 to J to discuss this question with the apostles and

Ac 15: 4 When they came to **J**, they were welcomed by
16: 4 by the apostles and elders who were in **J**.
18:22 he went up to **J** and greeted the church,
19:21 and then to go on to **J**.
20:16 he was eager to be in **J**, if possible,
20:22 as a captive to the Spirit, I am on my way to **J**,
21: 4 the Spirit they told Paul not to go on to **J**.
21:11 in **J** will bind the man who owns this belt
21:12 and the people there urged him not to go up to **J**.
21:13 even to die in **J** for the name of the Lord Jesus."
21:15 these days we got ready and started to go up to **J**.
21:17 When we arrived in **J**, the brothers welcomed us
21:31 to the tribune of the cohort that all **J** was in
22: 5 and to bring them back to **J** for punishment.
22:17 "After I had returned to **J** and while I was praying
22:18 'Hurry and get out of **J** quickly,
23:11 For just as you have testified for me in **J**,
24:11 since I went up to worship in **J**.
25: 1 he went up from Caesarea to **J**
25: 3 to have him transferred to **J**.
25: 7 Jews who had gone down from **J** surrounded him,
25: 9 "Do you wish to go up to **J** and be tried there
25:15 When I was in **J**, the chief priests and the elders
25:20 to go to **J** and be tried there on these charges.
25:24 both in **J** and here, shouting that he ought not
26: 4 the beginning among my own people and in **J**.
26:10 And that is what I did in **J**;
26:20 then in **J** and throughout the countryside of Judea,
28:17 yet I was arrested in **J** and handed over to
Ro 15:19 so that from **J** and as far around
15:25 I am going to **J** in a ministry to the saints;
15:26 with the poor among the saints at **J**.
15:31 my ministry to **J** may be acceptable to the saints,
1Co 16: 3 with letters to take your gift to **J**.
Gal 1:17 up to **J** to those who were already apostles
1:18 after three years I did go up to **J** to visit Cephas
2: 1 Then after fourteen years I went up again to **J**
4:25 in Arabia and corresponds to the present **J**,
4:26 But the other woman corresponds to the **J** above;
Heb 12:22 to the city of the living God, the heavenly **J**, and
Rev 3:12 the new **J** that comes down from my God out
21: 2 And I saw the holy city, the new **J**,
21:10 and showed me the holy city **J** coming down out
Tob 1: 4 the house of David and **J**.
1: 6 But I alone went often to **J** for the festivals,
1: 6 I would hurry off to **J** with the first fruits of
1: 7 the fruits to the sons of Levi who ministered at **J**.
1: 7 in money and go and distribute it in **J**.
5:14 to go with me to **J** and worshiped with me there,
13: 8 and acknowledge him in **J**.
13: 9 O **J**, the holy city, he afflicted you for the deeds
13:16 For **J** will be built as his house for all ages.
13:16 gates of **J** will be built with sapphire and emerald,
13:16 The towers of **J** will be built with gold,
13:16 streets of **J** will be paved with ruby and with C
13:17 The gates of **J** will sing hymns of joy,
14: 4 even Samaria and **J** will be desolate.
14: 5 from their exile and will rebuild **J** in splendor;
14: 7 they will go to **J** and live in safety forever in
Jdt 1: 9 as far as **J** and Bethany and Chelous and Kadesh
4: 2 they were alarmed both for **J** and for the temple
4: 6 The high priest, Joakim, who was in **J** at the time,
4: 8 of the whole people of Israel, in session at **J**,
4:11 and children living at **J** prostrated themselves
4:13 throughout Judea and in **J** before the sanctuary of
5:19 and have occupied **J**, where their sanctuary is,
9: 1 in the house of God in **J**,
10: 8 people of Israel may glory and **J** may be exalted."
11:13 in the presence of our God in **J**—
11:14 Since even the people in **J** have been doing this,
11:19 until you come to **J**; there I will set your throne.
13: 4 on the work of my hands for the exaltation of **J**.
15: 5 Those in **J** and all the hill country also came,
15: 8 of the Israelites who lived in **J** came to witness
15: 9 "You are the glory of **J**,
16:18 When they arrived at **J**, they worshiped God.
16:20 the people continued feasting in **J** before
AdE 2: 6 from **J** among those whom King Nebuchadnezzar
11: 1 one of the residents of **J**.
11: 4 from **J** with King Jeconiah of Judea.
Sir 24:11 and in **J** was my domain.
36:18 **J**, the place of your dwelling.
50:27 Jesus son of Eleazar son of Sirach of **J**,
Bar 1: 2 the time when the Chaldeans took **J** and burned it
1: 7 and sent it to **J** to the high priest Jehoiakim son
1: 7 to all the people who were present with him in **J**.
1: 9 of Babylon had carried away from **J** Jeconiah and
1:15 on the people of Judah, on the inhabitants of **J**, A
2: 2 not been done the like of what he has done in **J**,
2:23 the towns of Judah and from the region around **J**
4: 8 who brought you up, and you grieved **J**,
4:30 Take courage, O **J**, for the one who named you
4:36 Look toward the east, O **J**,
5: 1 and affliction, O **J**, and put on forever the beauty
5: 5 Arise, O **J**, stand upon the height;
Aza 1: 5 in all you have brought upon us and upon **J**,
1Mc 1:14 So they built a gymnasium in **J**,
1:20 against Israel and came to **J** with a strong force.
1:29 and he came to **J** with a large force.
1:35 collecting the spoils of **J** they stored them there,
1:38 Because of them the residents of **J** fled;
1:44 And the king sent letters by messengers to **J** and
2: 1 moved from **J** and settled in Modein.
2: 6 blasphemies being committed in Judah and **J**, B
2:18 of Judah and those that are left in **J** have done.
2:31 and to the troops in **J** the city of David,
3:34 As for the residents of Judea and **J**,
1Mc 3:35 the strength of Israel and the remnant of **J**;
3:45 **J** was uninhabited like a wilderness;
3:46 opposite **J**, because Israel formerly had a place
6: 7 that he had erected on the altar in **J**;
6:12 But now I remember the wrong I did in **J**.
6:26 today they have encamped against the citadel in **J**
6:48 of the king's army went up to **J** against them,
7:17 and their blood they poured out all around **J**,
7:19 Then Bacchides withdrew from **J** and encamped
7:27 So Nicanor came to **J** with a large force,
7:39 Now Nicanor went out from **J** and encamped
7:47 brought them and displayed them just outside **J**.
8:22 to **J** to remain with them there as a memorial
9: 3 they encamped against **J**;
9:50 to **J** and built strong cities in Judea:
9:53 and put them under guard in the citadel at **J**.
10: 7 Then Jonathan came to **J** and read the letter in
10:10 up residence in **J** and began to rebuild and restore
10:31 **J** and its environs, its tithes and its revenues,
10:32 also my control of the citadel in **J** and give it to
10:39 as a gift to the sanctuary in **J**,
10:43 And all who take refuge at the temple in **J**,
10:45 of rebuilding the walls of **J** and fortifying it all
10:66 And Jonathan returned to **J** in peace and gladness.
10:74 He chose ten thousand men and set out from **J**,
10:87 then returned to **J** with a large amount of booty.
11: 7 the river called Eleutherus; then he returned to **J**.
11:20 the Judeans to attack the citadel in **J**,
11:34 in **J** we have granted release from the royal taxes
11:41 the troops of the citadel from **J**, and the troops in
11:51 they returned to **J** with a large amount of spoil.
11:62 of their rulers as hostages and sent them to **J**.
11:74 And Jonathan returned to **J**.
12:25 from **J** and met them in the region of Hamath,
12:36 to build the walls of **J** still higher,
13: 2 So he went up to **J**,
13:10 and hurried to complete the walls of **J**,
13:39 in **J** shall be collected no longer.
13:49 at **J** were prevented from going in and out to buy
14:19 And these were read before the assembly in **J**.
14:36 as were also those in the city of David in **J**,
14:37 and built the walls of **J** higher.
15: 7 and I grant freedom to **J** and the sanctuary.
15:28 of Joppa and Gazara and the citadel in **J**;
15:32 So Athenobius, the king's Friend, came to **J**,
16:20 and he sent other troops to take possession of **J**
2Mc 1: 1 The Jews in **J** and those in the land of Judea,
1:10 The people of **J** and of Judea and the senate
3: 6 and reported to him that the treasury in **J** was full
3: 9 at **J** and had been kindly welcomed by
3:37 be suitable to send on another mission to **J**,
4: 9 to enroll the people of **J** as citizens of Antioch.
4:19 chosen as being Antiochian citizens from **J**,
4:21 upon arriving at Joppa he proceeded to **J**.
5:22 He left governors to oppress the people: at **J**,
5:25 When this man arrived in **J**,
6: 2 to pollute the temple in **J** and to call it the temple
8:31 the rest of the spoils they carried to **J**.
8:36 by the capture of the people of **J** proclaimed that
9: 4 I get there I will make **J** a cemetery of Jews."
10:15 they received those who were banished from **J**,
11: 5 a fortified place about five stadia from **J**,
11: 8 And there, while they were still near **J**,
12: 9 so that the glow of the light was seen in **J**,
12:29 which is seventy-five miles from **J**.
12:31 Then they went up to **J**,
12:43 and sent it to **J** to provide for a sin offering.
14:23 Nicanor stayed on in **J** and did nothing out of
14:37 A certain Razis, one of the elders of **J**,
15:30 and arm and carry them to **J**.
1Es 1: 1 Josiah kept the passover to his Lord in **J**;
1:21 of Judah and all of Israel who were living in **J**.
1:31 and after he was brought back to **J** he died,
1:35 He reigned three months in Judah and **J**. B
1:35 king of Egypt deposed him from reigning in **J**,
1:37 made his brother Jehoiakim king of Judea and **J**.
1:39 when he began to reign in Judea and **J**;
1:44 and he reigned three months and ten days in **J**.
1:46 and made Zedekiah king of Judea and **J**.
1:49 and polluted the temple of the Lord in **J**—
1:55 broke down the walls of **J**,
2: 4 he has commanded me to build him a house at **J**,
2: 5 go up to **J**, which is in Judea,
2: 5 he is the Lord who dwells in **J**,
2: 7 for the temple of the Lord that is in **J**."
2: 8 to go up to build the house in **J** for the Lord;
2:10 that Nebuchadnezzar had carried away from **J**
2:15 with the returning exiles from Babylon to **J**.
2:16 against those who were living in Judea and **J**:
2:18 up from you to us have gone to **J** and are building
2:27 and cruel kings ruled in **J** and exacted tribute
2:30 and their associates went quickly to **J**,
2:30 of the temple in **J** stopped until the second year of
4:43 on the day when you became king, to build **J**,
4:44 the vessels that were taken from **J**,
4:47 and to all who were going up with him to build **J**.
4:48 to bring cedar timber from Lebanon to **J**,
4:55 when the temple would be finished and **J** built.
4:57 also commanded to be done and to be sent to **J**.
4:58 he lifted up his face to heaven toward **J**,
4:63 to go up and build **J** and the temple that is called
5: 2 to **J** in safety, with the music of drums and flutes;
5: 8 and who returned to **J** and the rest of Judea,
5:44 when they came to the temple of God that is in **J**,
5:46 some of the people settled in **J** and its vicinity;
5:56 of God in **J**, in the second month, Zerubbabel son
5:56 and all who had come back to **J** from exile;
1Es 5:57 in the second year after they came to Judea and **J**.
6: 1 to the Jews who were in Judea and **J**;
6: 2 to build the house of the Lord that is in **J**,
6: 8 to the country of Judea and entered the city of **J**,
6: 9 in the city of **J** a great new house for the Lord,
6:18 of the house in **J** and stored in his own temple,
6:19 and put them in the temple at **J**,
6:20 of the house of the Lord that is in **J**.
6:22 in **J** was done with the consent of King Cyrus,
6:24 of the house of the Lord in **J**, where they sacrifice
6:26 which Nebuchadnezzar took out of the house in **J**
6:26 should be restored to the house in **J**,
6:30 for daily use as the priests in **J** may indicate,
6:33 to hinder or damage that house of the Lord in **J**.
8: 5 There came up with him to **J** some of the people
8: 6 the first month and arrived in **J** on the new moon
8:10 may go with you to **J**.
8:12 in order to look into matters in Judea and **J**,
8:13 to carry to **J** the gifts for the Lord of Israel that I
8:13 to collect for the Lord in **J** all the gold and silver
8:14 the nation for the temple of their Lord that is in **J**,
8:15 on the altar of their Lord that is in **J**.
8:17 for the use of the temple of your God that is in **J**.
8:25 to glorify his house that is in **J**,
8:59 in **J**, in the chambers of the house of our Lord."
8:60 and the vessels that had been in **J** carried them to
8:61 we arrived in **J** by the mighty hand of our Lord,
8:61 on the way, and so we came to **J**.
8:81 to give us a stronghold in Judea and **J**.
8:91 of men and women and youths from **J**;
9: 3 a proclamation was made throughout Judea and **J**
9: 3 from exile that they should assemble at **J**,
9: 5 of the tribe of Judah and Benjamin assembled at **J**
9:37 and the Levites and the Israelites settled in **J** and
3Mc 1: 9 After he had arrived in **J**,
3:16 we came on to **J** also,
2Es 2:10 that I will give them the kingdom of **J**,
10:20 and be consoled because of the sorrow of **J**.
10:47 that was the period of residence in **J**.
10:48 this was the destruction that befell **J**.
4Mc 4: 3 that in the **J** treasuries there are deposited tens
4:22 and that the people of **J** had rejoiced greatly.
18: 5 he left **J** and marched against the Persians.

JERUSALEM'S (2) [JERUSALEM]

Ps 137: 7 O LORD, against the Edomites the day of **J** fall,
Isa 62: 1 and for **J** sake I will not rest,

JERUSHA (1) [=JERUSHAH]

2Ki 15:33 His mother's name was **J** daughter of Zadok.

JERUSHAH (1) [=JERUSHA]

2Ch 27: 1 His mother's name was **J** daughter of Zadok.

JESAIAH (KJV) See JESHAIAH

JESARELAH (1)

1Ch 25:14 seventh to **J**, his sons and his brothers, twelve;

JESHAIAH (9)

1Ch 3:21 Pelatiah and **J**, his son Rephaiah, his son Arnan,
25: 3 Gedaliah, Zeri, **J**, Shimei, Hashabiah,
25:15 the eighth to **J**, his sons and his brothers, twelve;
26:25 from Eliezer were his son Rehabiah, his son **J**,
Ezr 8: 7 Of the descendants of Elam, **J** son of Athaliah,
8:19 also Hashabiah and with him **J** of the descendants
Ne 11: 7 of Kolaiah son of Maaseiah son of Ithiel son of **J**.
1Es 8:33 Of the descendants of Elam, **J** son of Gotholiah,
8:48 also Hashabiah and Annunus and his brother **J**, of

JESHANAH (2)

1Sa 7:12 between Mizpah and **J**, and named it Ebenezer;
2Ch 13:19 Bethel with its villages and **J** with its villages

JESHARELAH (KJV) See JESARELAH

JESHEBEAB (1)

1Ch 24:13 the thirteenth to Huppah, the fourteenth to **J**,

JESHER (1)

1Ch 2:18 these were her sons: **J**, Shobab,

JESHIMON‡ (4)

1Sa 23:19 on the hill of Hachilah, which is south of **J**.
23:24 in the Arabah to the south of **J**.
26: 1 on the hill of Hachilah, which is opposite **J**."
26: 3 which is opposite **J** beside the road.

JESHISHAI (1)

1Ch 5:14 son of Gilead, son of Michael, son of **J**,

JESHOHAIAH (1)

1Ch 4:36 Jaakobah, **J**, Asaiah, Adiel, Jesimiel, Benaiah,

JESHUA (46) [=JOSHUA]

1Ch 24:11 the ninth to **J**, the tenth to Shecaniah,
2Ch 31:15 Eden, Miniamin, **J**, Shemaiah, Amariah,
Ezr 2: 2 They came with Zerubbabel, **J**, Nehemiah,
2: 6 namely the descendants of **J** and Joab,
2:36 the descendants of Jedaiah, of the house of **J**,

Ezr 2:40 The Levites: the descendants of J and Kadmiel,
3: 2 Then J son of Jozadak, with his fellow priests,
3: 8 and J son of Jozadak made a beginning,
3: 9 And J with his sons and his kin,
4: 3 J, and the rest of the heads of families
5: 2 and J son of Jozadak set out to rebuild the house
8:33 Jozabad son of J and Noadiah son of Binnui.
10:18 of the descendants of J son of Jozadak
Ne 3:19 next to him Ezer son of J,
7: 7 They came with Zerubbabel, J, Nehemiah,
7:11 namely the descendants of J and Joab,
7:39 descendants of Jedaiah, namely the house of J,
7:43 The Levites: the descendants of J,
8: 7 Also J, Bani, Sherebiah, Jamin, Akkub,
8:17 the days of J son of Nun to that day the people
9: 4 Then J, Bani, Kadmiel, Shebaniah, Bunni,
9: 5 Then the Levites, J, Kadmiel, Bani, Hashabneiah,
10: 9 J son of Azaniah, Binnui of the sons of Henadad,
11:26 and in J and in Moladah and Beth-pelet,
12: 1 up with Zerubbabel son of Shealtiel, and J:
12: 7 the priests and of their associates in the days of J.
12: 8 And the Levites: J, Binnui, Kadmiel, Sherebiah,
12:10 J was the father of Joiakim,
12:24 Hashabiah, Sherebiah, and J son of Kadmiel,
12:26 These were in the days of Joiakim son of J son
Sir 49:12 and so was J son of Jozadak;
1Es 5: 5 J son of Jozadak son of Seraiah and Joakim son
5: 8 They came with Zerubbabel and J, Nehemiah,
5:11 of the descendants of J and Joab,
5:24 The priests: the descendants of Jedaiah son of J,
5:26 the descendants of J and Kadmiel and Bannas
5:48 Then J son of Jozadak, with his fellow priests,
5:56 and J son of Jozadak made a beginning, together
5:58 And J arose, and his sons and kindred
5:58 the sons of J Emadabun and the sons of Joda son
5:68 and J and the heads of the ancestral houses
5:70 and J and the heads of the ancestral houses
6: 2 and J son of Jozadak began to build the house of
8:63 with them were Jozabad son of J and Moeth son
9:19 of the descendants of J son of Jozadak
9:48 J and Anniuth and Sherebiah, Jadinus, Akkub,

JESHURUN (4) [=JACOB]

Dt 32:15 Jacob ate his fill; J grew fat, and kicked.
33: 5 in J, when the leaders of the people assembled—
33:26 There is none like God, O J,
Isa 44: 2 O Jacob my servant, J whom I have chosen.

JESIAH (KJV) See ISSHIAH

JESIMIEL (1)

1Ch 4:36 Jaakobah, Jeshohaiah, Asaiah, Adiel, J, Benaiah,

JESSE (48)

A. SON OF JESSE (21)

Ru 4:17 he became the father of J, the father of David.
4:22 Obed of J, and J of David.
1Sa 16: 1 I will send you to J the Bethlehemite,
16: 3 Invite J to the sacrifice,
16: 5 And he sanctified J and his sons and invited them
16: 8 Then J called Abinadab, and made him pass
16: 9 Then J made Shammah pass by.
16:10 J made seven of his sons pass before Samuel,
16:10 and Samuel said to J, "The LORD has
16:11 Samuel said to J, "Are all your sons here?"
16:11 And Samuel said to J, "Send and bring him;
16:18 a son of J the Bethlehemite who is skillful in A
16:19 So Saul sent messengers to J, and said,
16:20 J took a donkey loaded with bread,
16:22 to J, saying, "Let David remain in my service,
17:12 named J, who had eight sons.
17:13 The three eldest sons of J had followed Saul to
17:17 J said to his son David, "Take for your brothers
17:20 and went as J had commanded him.
17:58 the son of your servant J the Bethlehemite."
20:27 "Why has the son of J not come to the feast, A
20:30 Do I not know that you have chosen the son of J A
20:31 For as long as the son of J lives upon the earth, A
22: 7 the son of J give every one of you fields and A
22: 8 when my son makes a league with the son of J, A
22: 9 answered, "I saw the son of J coming to Nob, A
22:13 you and the son of J, A
25:10 Who is the son of J? A
2Sa 20: 1 no share in the son of J! A
23: 1 The oracle of David, son of J, A
1Ki 12:16 We have no inheritance in the son of J. A
1Ch 2:12 Boaz of Obed, Obed of J.
2:13 J became the father of Eliab his firstborn,
10:14 and turned the kingdom over to David son of J. A
12:18 and with you, O son of J! A
29:26 Thus David son of J reigned over all Israel. A
2Ch 10:16 We have no inheritance in the son of J. A
11:18 and of Abihail daughter of Eliab son of J. A
Ps 72:20 The prayers of David son of J are ended. A
Isa 11: 1 A shoot shall come out from the stump of J,
11:10 the root of J shall stand as a signal to the peoples;
Mt 1: 5 and Obed the father of J,
1: 6 and J the father of King David.
Lk 3:32 son of J, son of Obed, son of Boaz, son of Sala, A
Ac 13:22 son of J, to be a man after my heart, A
Ro 15:12 "The root of J shall come,
Sir 45:25 a covenant was established with David son of J A

JESTING (1)

Ge 19:14 But he seemed to his sons-in-law to be j.

JESTING (KJV) See also VULGAR TALK

JESUI (KJV) See ISHVI

JESUITES (KJV) See ISHVITES

JESURUN (KJV) See JESHURUN

JESUS‡ (994) [JESUS']

A. JESUS CHRIST (138)
B. *LORD JESUS (103)
C. CHRIST JESUS (86)
D. JESUS OF NAZARETH (15)
E. NAME OF JESUS (11)

Mt 1: 1 An account of the genealogy of J the Messiah,
1:16 of whom J was born, who is called the Messiah.
1:18 the birth of J the Messiah took place in this way.
1:21 She will bear a son, and you are to name him J,
1:25 until she had borne a son; and he named him J.
2: 1 after J was born in Bethlehem of Judea,
3:13 Then J came from Galilee to John at the Jordan,
3:15 But J answered him, "Let it be so now;
3:16 And when J had been baptized,
4: 1 Then J was led up by the Spirit into
4: 7 J said to him, "Again it is written,
4:10 J said to him, "Away with you, Satan!
4:12 Now when J heard that John had been arrested,
4:17 From that time J began to proclaim, "Repent,
4:23 J went throughout Galilee,
5: 1 J saw the crowds, he went up the mountain;
7:28 Now when J had finished saying these things,
8: 1 When J had come down from the mountain,
8: 4 Then J said to him, "See that you say nothing
8:10 When J heard him, he was amazed and said
8:13 And to the centurion J said, "Go;
8:14 When J entered Peter's house,
8:18 Now when J saw great crowds around him,
8:20 And J said to him, "Foxes have holes,
8:22 But J said to him, "Follow me,
8:34 Then the whole town came out to meet J;
9: 2 When J saw their faith, he said to the paralytic,
9: 4 But J, perceiving their thoughts, said,
9: 9 As J was walking along, he saw
9:15 J said to them, "The wedding guests cannot mourn
9:19 J got up and followed him, with his disciples.
9:22 J turned, and seeing her he said, "Take heart,
9:23 When J came to the leader's house and saw
9:27 As J went on from there,
9:28 and J said to them, "Do you believe
9:30 Then J sternly ordered them,
9:35 Then J went about all the cities and villages,
10: 1 Then J summoned his twelve disciples
10: 5 These twelve J sent out with
11: 1 J had finished instructing his twelve disciples,
11: 4 J answered them, "Go
11: 7 J began to speak to the crowds about John:
11:25 At that time J said, "I thank you, Father,
12: 1 At that time J went through the grainfields on
12:15 When J became aware of this, he departed.
12:48 But to the one who had told him this, J replied,
13: 1 That same day J went out of the house and sat
13:34 J told the crowds all these things in parables;
13:53 J had finished these parables, he left that place.
13:57 But J said to them, "Prophets are not
14: 1 that time Herod the ruler heard reports about J;
14:12 then they went and told J.
14:13 Now when J heard this, he withdrew from there
14:16 J said to them, "They need not go away;
14:27 But immediately J spoke to them and said,
14:29 started walking on the water, and came toward J.
14:31 J immediately reached out his hand
15: 1 and scribes came to J from Jerusalem and said,
15:21 J left that place and went away to the district
15:28 J answered her, "Woman, great is your faith!
15:29 After J had left that place,
15:32 Then J called his disciples to him and said,
15:34 J asked them, "How many loaves have you?"
16: 1 and to test J they asked him to show them a sign
16: 6 J said to them, "Watch out,
16: 8 And becoming aware of it, J said,
16:13 J came into the district of Caesarea Philippi,
16:17 And J answered him, "Blessed are you,
16:21 J began to show his disciples that he must go
16:24 Then J told his disciples,
17: 1 J took with him Peter and James
17: 4 Peter said to J, "Lord, it is good for us to be here;
17: 7 But J came and touched them, saying,
17: 8 they saw no one except J himself alone.
17: 9 the mountain, J ordered them, "Tell no one about
17:17 J answered, "You faithless
17:18 And J rebuked the demon,
17:19 Then the disciples came to J privately and said,
17:22 As they were gathering in Galilee, J said to them,
17:25 And when he came home, J spoke of it first,
17:26 When Peter said, "From others," J said to him,
18: 1 At that time the disciples came to J and asked,
18:22 J said to him, "Not seven times, but, I tell you,
19: 1 When J had finished saying these things,
19:14 but J said, "Let the little children come to me,
19:18 And J said, "You shall not murder;
Mt 19:21 J said to him, "If you wish to be perfect, go,
19:23 Then J said to his disciples, "Truly I tell you,
19:26 But J looked at them and said,
19:28 J said to them, "Truly I tell you,
20:17 While J was going up to Jerusalem,
20:22 But J answered, "You do
20:25 But J called them to him and said,
20:30 When they heard that J was passing by,
20:32 J stood still and called them, saying,
20:34 Moved with compassion, J touched their eyes.
21: 1 at the Mount of Olives, J sent two disciples,
21: 6 disciples went and did as J had directed them;
21:11 "This is the prophet J from Nazareth in Galilee."
21:12 Then J entered the temple and drove out all who
21:16 J said to them, "Yes; have you never read,
21:21 J answered them, "Truly I tell you,
21:24 J said to them, "I will also ask you one question;
21:27 So they answered J, "We do not know."
21:31 J said to them, "Truly I tell you,
21:42 J said to them, "Have you never read in
22: 1 Once more J spoke to them in parables, saying:
22:18 But J, aware of their malice, said,
22:29 J answered them, "You are wrong,
22:41 J asked them this question:
23: 1 Then J said to the crowds and to his disciples,
24: 1 As J came out of the temple and was going away,
24: 4 J answered them, "Beware
26: 1 When J had finished saying all these things,
26: 4 they conspired to arrest J by stealth and kill him.
26: 6 J was at Bethany in the house of Simon the leper,
26:10 But J, aware of this, said to them,
26:17 of Unleavened Bread the disciples came to J,
26:19 So the disciples did as J had directed them,
26:26 While they were eating, J took a loaf of bread,
26:31 J said to them, "You will all become deserters
26:34 J said to him, "Truly I tell you, this very night,
26:36 J went with them to a place called Gethsemane;
26:49 At once he came up to J and said, "Greetings,
26:50 J said to him, "Friend, do what you are here
26:50 they came and laid hands on J and arrested him.
26:51 one of those with J put his hand on his sword,
26:52 J said to him, "Put your sword back into its place;
26:55 At that hour J said to the crowds,
26:57 Those who had arrested J took him to Caiaphas
26:59 against J so that they might put him to death,
26:63 But J was silent. Then the high priest said to him,
26:64 J said to him, "You have said so.
26:69 "You also were with J the Galilean."
26:71 "This man was with J of Nazareth." D
26:75 Then Peter remembered what J had said:
27: 1 of the people conferred together against J in order
27: 3 Judas, his betrayer, saw that J was condemned,
27:11 Now J stood before the governor;
27:11 J said, "You say so."
27:16 a notorious prisoner, called J Barabbas.
27:17 J Barabbas or J who is called the Messiah?"
27:20 to ask for Barabbas and to have J killed.
27:22 "Then what should I do with J who is called
27:26 flogging J, he handed him over to be crucified.
27:27 Then the soldiers of the governor took J into
27:37 which read, "This is J, the King of the Jews."
27:46 about three o'clock J cried with a loud voice,
27:50 Then J cried again with a loud voice
27:54 who were keeping watch over J,
27:55 they had followed J from Galilee
27:57 named Joseph, who was also a disciple of J.
27:58 He went to Pilate and asked for the body of J;
28: 5 that you are looking for J who was crucified.
28: 9 Suddenly J met them and said, "Greetings!"
28:10 Then J said to them, "Do not be afraid;
28:16 to the mountain to which J had directed them.
28:18 And J came and said to them,
Mk 1: 1 The beginning of the good news of J Christ, A
1: 9 In those days J came from Nazareth of Galilee
1:14 Now after John was arrested, J came to Galilee,
1:16 As J passed along the Sea of Galilee,
1:17 And J said to them, "Follow me
1:24 "What have you to do with us, J of Nazareth? D
1:25 But J rebuked him, saying, "Be silent,
1:41 J stretched out his hand and touched him,
1:45 so that J could no longer go into a town openly,
2: 4 to J because of the crowd, they removed the roof
2: 5 When J saw their faith, he said to the paralytic,
2: 8 At once J perceived in his spirit
2:13 J went out again beside the sea;
2:15 also sitting with J and his disciples—
2:17 When J heard this, he said to them,
2:19 J said to them, "The wedding guests cannot fast
3: 7 J departed with his disciples to the sea,
5: 6 When he saw J from a distance,
5: 7 "What have you to do with me, J,
5: 9 Then J asked him, "What is your name?"
5:15 to J and saw the demoniac sitting there, clothed
5:17 they began to beg J to leave their neighborhood.
5:19 But J refused, and said to him,
5:20 in the Decapolis how much J had done for him;
5:21 J had crossed again in the boat to the other side,
5:27 She had heard about J, and came up behind him
5:30 J turned about in the crowd and said,
5:36 J said to the leader of the synagogue,
6: 4 Then J said to them, "Prophets are not
6:30 The apostles gathered around J,
7:36 Then J ordered them to tell no one;
8:17 And becoming aware of it, J said to them,
8:25 Then J laid his hands on his eyes again;
8:27 J went on with his disciples to the villages
9: 2 J took with him Peter and James and John,

Mk 9: 4 who were talking with J.
9: 5 Then Peter said to J, "Rabbi,
9: 8 they saw no one with them any more, but only J.
9:21 J asked the father,
9:23 J said to him, "If you are able!—
9:25 When J saw that a crowd came running together,
9:27 But J took him by the hand and lifted him up,
9:39 But J said, "Do not stop him;
10: 5 But J said to them, "Because of your hardness
10:14 But when J saw this, he was indignant and said
10:18 J said to him, "Why do you call me good?
10:21 J, looking at him, loved him and said,
10:23 Then J looked around and said to his disciples,
10:24 But J said to them again, "Children,
10:27 J looked at them and said,
10:29 J said, "Truly I tell you, there is no one who has
10:32 and J was walking ahead of them;
10:38 But J said to them, "You do
10:39 Then J said to them, "The cup
10:42 So J called them and said to them,
10:47 When he heard that it was J of Nazareth, D
10:47 he began to shout out and say, "J, Son of David,
10:49 J stood still and said, "Call him here."
10:50 he sprang up and came to J.
10:51 Then J said to him, "What do you want me to do
10:52 J said to him, "Go; your faith has made you well."
11: 6 They told them what J had said;
11: 7 the colt to J and threw their cloaks on it;
11:19 J and his disciples went out of the city.
11:22 J answered them, "Have faith in God.
11:29 J said to them, "I will ask you one question;
11:33 So they answered J, "We do not know."
11:33 And J said to them, "Neither will I tell you
12:17 J said to them, "Give to the emperor the things
12:24 J said to them, "Is not this
12:29 J answered, "The first is, 'Hear, O Israel:
12:34 When J saw that he answered wisely,
12:35 While J was teaching in the temple, he said,
13: 2 J asked him, "Do you see these great buildings?
13: 5 Then J began to say to them,
14: 1 and the scribes were looking for a way to arrest J
14: 6 J said, "Let her alone; why do you trouble her?
14:18 and were eating, J said, "Truly I tell you, one
14:27 J said to them, "You will all become deserters;
14:30 J said to him, "Truly I tell you, this day,
14:48 Then J said to them, "Have you come out
14:53 They took J to the high priest;
14:55 for testimony against J to put him to death;
14:60 the high priest stood up before them and asked J,
14:62 J said, "I am; and 'you will see the Son of Man
14:67 "You also were with J, the man from Nazareth."
14:72 Then Peter remembered that J had said to him,
15: 1 They bound J, led him away,
15: 5 But J made no further reply,
15:15 flogging J, he handed him over to be crucified.
15:22 Then they brought J to the place called Golgotha
15:34 At three o'clock J cried out with a loud voice,
15:37 Then J gave a loud cry and breathed his last.
15:43 went boldly to Pilate and asked for the body of J.
16: 6 you are looking for J of Nazareth, D
16:19 ⟦then the Lord J, after he had spoken to them,⟧ B
16: S ⟦And afterward J himself sent out through them,⟧
Lk 1:31 and you will name him J.
2:21 and he was called J, the name given by the angel
2:27 and when the parents brought in the child J,
2:43 the boy J stayed behind in Jerusalem,
2:52 And J increased in wisdom and in years,
3:21 when J also had been baptized and was praying,
3:23 J was about thirty years old
4: 1 J, full of the Holy Spirit,
4: 4 J answered him, "It is written,
4: 8 J answered him, "It is written,
4:12 J answered him, "It is said,
4:14 Then J, filled with the power of the Spirit,
4:34 What have you to do with us, J of Nazareth? D
4:35 But J rebuked him, saying, "Be silent,
5: 1 Once while J was standing beside the lake
5:10 Then J said to Simon, "Do not be afraid;
5:12 When he saw J, he bowed with his face to
5:13 Then J stretched out his hand, touched him,
5:15 more than ever the word about J spread abroad;
5:18 to bring him in and lay him before J;
5:19 the tiles into the middle of the crowd in front of J.
5:22 When J perceived their questionings,
5:31 J answered, "Those who are well have no need of
5:34 J said to them, "You cannot make wedding guests
6: 1 while J was going through the grainfields,
6: 3 J answered, "Have you not read what David did
6: 9 Then J said to them, "I ask you,
6:11 with one another what they might do to J.
7: 1 After J had finished all his sayings in the hearing
7: 3 about J, he sent some Jewish elders
7: 4 When they came to J, they appealed
7: 6 And J went with them, but when he was not far
7: 9 When J heard this he was amazed at him,
7:15 and J gave him to his mother.
7:21 J had just then cured many people of diseases,
7:24 J began to speak to the crowds about John:
7:36 One of the Pharisees asked J to eat with him,
7:40 J spoke up and said to him, "Simon,
7:43 And J said to him, "You have judged rightly."
8:28 When he saw J, he fell down before him
8:28 "What have you to do with me, J,
8:29 for J had commanded the unclean spirit
8:30 J then asked him, "What is your name?"
8:32 and the demons begged J to let them enter these.
8:35 and when they came to J,

Lk 8:35 the demons had gone sitting at the feet of J,
8:37 the surrounding country of the Gerasenes asked J
8:38 but J sent him away, saying,
8:39 throughout the city how much J had done
8:40 Now when J returned, the crowd welcomed him,
8:45 Then J asked, "Who touched me?"
8:46 But J said, "Someone touched me;
8:50 When J heard this, he replied, "Do not fear.
9: 1 Then J called the twelve together
9:10 the apostles told J all they had done.
9:18 Once when J was praying alone,
9:28 Now about eight days after these sayings J took
9:33 Just as they were leaving him, Peter said to J,
9:36 When the voice had spoken, J was found alone.
9:41 J answered, "You faithless
9:42 But J rebuked the unclean spirit, healed the boy,
9:47 But J, aware of their inner thoughts,
9:50 But J said to him, "Do not stop him;
9:58 And J said to him, "Foxes have holes,
9:60 J said to him, "Let the dead bury their own dead;
9:62 J said to him, "No one who puts a hand to
10:21 At that same hour J rejoiced in the Holy Spirit
10:23 turning to the disciples, J said to them privately,
10:25 Just then a lawyer stood up to test J.
10:29 But wanting to justify himself, he asked J,
10:30 J replied, "A man was going down
10:37 J said to him, "Go and do likewise."
13:12 When J saw her, he called her over and said,
13:14 indignant because J had cured on the sabbath,
13:22 J went through one town and village
14: 1 On one occasion when J was going to the house
14: 3 And J asked the lawyers and Pharisees,
14: 4 J took him and healed him, and sent him away.
14:16 Then J said to him, "Someone gave a great dinner
15:11 J said, "There was a man who had two sons.
16: 1 Then J said to the disciples,
17: 1 J said to his disciples, "Occasions
17:11 On the way to Jerusalem J was going through
17:13 saying, "J, Master, have mercy on us!"
17:17 Then J asked, "Were not ten made clean?
17:20 Once J was asked by the Pharisees when
18: 1 Then J told them a parable about their need
18:16 But J called for them and said,
18:19 J said to him, "Why do you call me good?
18:22 When J heard this, he said to him,
18:24 J looked at him and said,
18:37 They told him, "J of Nazareth is passing by." D
18:38 Then he shouted, "J, Son of David,
18:40 J stood still and ordered the man to be brought
18:42 J said to him, "Receive your sight;
19: 3 He was trying to see who J was,
19: 5 When J came to the place,
19: 9 Then J said to him, "Today salvation has come
19:35 Then they brought it to J;
19:35 throwing their cloaks on the colt, they set J on it.
20: 8 Then J said to them, "Neither will I tell you
20:34 J said to them, "Those who belong
22: 2 and the scribes were looking for a way to put J
22: 8 So J sent Peter and John, saying,
22:34 J said, "I tell you, Peter, the cock will
22:47 He approached J to kiss him;
22:48 but J said to him, "Judas, is it with a kiss
22:51 But J said, "No more of this!"
22:52 Then J said to the chief priests,
22:63 the men who were holding J began to mock him
23: 1 Then the assembly rose as a body and brought J
23: 8 When Herod saw J, he was very glad,
23: 9 but J gave him no answer.
23:20 Pilate, wanting to release J,
23:25 and he handed J over as they wished.
23:26 and made him carry it behind J.
23:28 But J turned to them and said,
23:33 they crucified J there with the criminals,
23:34 ⟦Then J said, "Father, forgive them;⟧
23:42 Then he said, "J, remember me when you come
23:46 Then J, crying with a loud voice, said, "Father,
23:52 to Pilate and asked for the body of J.
24:15 J himself came near and went with them,
24:19 They replied, "The things about J of Nazareth, D
24:36 J himself stood among them and said to them,
Jn 1:17 grace and truth came through J Christ. A
1:29 The next day he saw J coming toward him
1:36 and as he watched J walk by,
1:37 disciples heard him say this, and they followed J.
1:38 When J turned and saw them following,
1:42 He brought Simon to J, who looked at him
1:43 The next day J decided to go to Galilee.
1:45 J son of Joseph from Nazareth."
1:47 When J saw Nathanael coming toward him,
1:48 J answered, "I saw you under the fig tree
1:50 J answered, "Do you believe because I told you
2: 1 and the mother of J was there.
2: 2 J and his disciples had also been invited to
2: 3 the wine gave out, the mother of J said to him,
2: 4 And J said to her, "Woman,
2: 7 J said to them, "Fill the jars with water."
2:11 J did this, the first of his signs,
2:13 and J went up to Jerusalem.
2:19 J answered them, "Destroy this temple,
2:22 the scripture and the word that J had spoken.
2:24 J on his part would not entrust himself to them,
3: 2 He came to J by night and said to him, "Rabbi,
3: 3 J answered him, "Very truly, I tell you,
3: 5 J answered, "Very truly, I tell you,
3:10 J answered him, "Are you a teacher of Israel,
3:22 After this J and his disciples went into
4: 1 Now when J learned that the Pharisees had heard,

Jn 4: 1 that the Pharisees had heard, "J is making
4: 2 not J himself but his disciples who baptized—
4: 6 Jacob's well was there, and J,
4: 7 and J said to her, "Give me a drink."
4:10 J answered her, "If you knew the gift of God,
4:13 J said to her, "Everyone who drinks
4:16 J said to her, "Go, call your husband,
4:17 J said to her, "You are right in saying,
4:21 J said to her, "Woman, believe me,
4:26 J said to her, "I am he,
4:34 J said to them, "My food is to do the will
4:44 (for J himself had testified that
4:47 he heard that J had come from Judea to Galilee,
4:48 Then J said to him, "Unless you see signs
4:50 J said to him, "Go; your son will live."
4:50 The man believed the word that J spoke to him
4:53 that this was the hour when J had said to him,
4:54 that J did after coming from Judea to Galilee.
5: 1 and J went up to Jerusalem.
5: 6 When J saw him lying there and knew
5: 8 J said to him, "Stand up, take your mat
5:13 for J had disappeared in the crowd that was there.
5:14 Later J found him in the temple and said to him,
5:15 the Jews that it was J who had made him well.
5:16 Therefore the Jews started persecuting J,
5:17 But J answered them, "My Father is still working,
5:19 J said to them, "Very truly, I tell you,
6: 1 this J went to the other side of the Sea of Galilee,
6: 3 J went up the mountain and sat down there
6: 5 and saw a large crowd coming toward him, J said
6:10 J said, "Make the people sit down."
6:11 Then J took the loaves,
6:15 When J realized that they were about to come
6:17 It was now dark, and J had not yet come to them.
6:19 they saw J walking on the sea and coming near
6:22 that J had not got into the boat with his disciples,
6:24 that neither J nor his disciples were there,
6:24 the boats and went to Capernaum looking for J.
6:26 J answered them, "Very truly, I tell you,
6:29 J answered them, "This is the work of God,
6:32 Then J said to them, "Very truly, I tell you,
6:35 J said to them, "I am the bread of life.
6:42 They were saying, "Is not this J,
6:43 J answered them, "Do not complain
6:53 So J said to them, "Very truly, I tell you,
6:61 But J, being aware that his disciples were
6:64 For J knew from the first who were the ones
6:67 So J asked the twelve, "Do you also wish
6:70 J answered them, "Did I not choose you,
7: 1 After this J went about in Galilee.
7: 6 J said to them, "My time has not yet come,
7:14 the festival J went up into the temple and began
7:16 Then J answered them, "My teaching is not mine
7:21 J answered them, "I performed one work,
7:28 Then J cried out as he was teaching in the temple,
7:33 J then said, "I will be with you a little
7:37 the great day, while J was standing there,
7:39 because J was not yet glorified.
7:50 Nicodemus, who had gone to J before,
8: 1 ⟦while J went to the Mount of Olives.⟧
8: 6 ⟦J bent down and wrote with his finger on⟧
8: 9 ⟦and J was left alone with the woman standing⟧
8:10 ⟦J straightened up and said to her, "Woman,⟧
8:11 ⟦And J said, "Neither do I condemn you.⟧
8:12 Again J spoke to them, saying,
8:14 J answered, "Even if I testify on my own behalf,
8:19 J answered, "You know neither me
8:25 J said to them, "Why do I speak to you at all?
8:28 So J said, "When you have lifted up the Son
8:31 Then J said to the Jews who had believed in him,
8:34 J answered them, "Very truly, I tell you,
8:39 J said to them, "If you were Abraham's children,
8:42 J said to them, "If God were your Father,
8:49 J answered, "I do not have a demon;
8:54 J answered, "If I glorify myself,
8:58 J said to them, "Very truly, I tell you,
8:59 but J hid himself and went out of the temple.
9: 3 J answered, "Neither this man
9:11 He answered, "The man called J made mud
9:14 Now it was a sabbath day when J made the mud
9:22 that anyone who confessed J to be
9:35 J heard that they had driven him out,
9:37 J said to him, "You have seen him,
9:39 J said, "I came into this world for judgment so
9:41 J said to them, "If you were blind,
10: 6 J used this figure of speech with them,
10: 7 So again J said to them, "Very truly, I tell you,
10:23 and J was walking in the temple,
10:25 J answered, "I have told you,
10:32 J replied, "I have shown you many good works
10:34 J answered, "Is it not written in your law, 'I said,
11: 3 So the sisters sent a message to J, "Lord,
11: 4 But when J heard it, he said,
11: 5 though J loved Martha and her sister and Lazarus,
11: 9 J answered, "Are there not twelve hours
11:13 J, however, had been speaking about his death,
11:14 Then J told them plainly, "Lazarus is dead.
11:17 When J arrived, he found
11:20 When Martha heard that J was coming,
11:21 Martha said to J, "Lord, if you had been here,
11:23 J said to her, "Your brother will rise again."
11:25 J said to her, "I am the resurrection and the life.
11:30 Now J had not yet come to the village,
11:32 When Mary came where J was and saw him,
11:33 When J saw her weeping,
11:35 J began to weep.
11:38 J, again greatly disturbed, came to the tomb.

Jn 11:39 J said, "Take away the stone."
11:40 J said to her, "Did I not tell you that
11:41 And J looked upward and said, "Father,
11:44 J said to them, "Unbind him, and let him go."
11:45 with Mary and had seen what J did,
11:51 that year he prophesied that J was about to die for
11:54 J therefore no longer walked about openly among
11:56 for J and were asking one another as they stood
11:57 where J was should let them know,
12: 1 Six days before the Passover J came to Bethany,
12: 7 J said, "Leave her alone.
12: 9 not only because of J but also to see Lazarus,
12:11 the Jews were deserting and were believing in J.
12:12 the festival heard that J was coming to Jerusalem.
12:14 J found a young donkey and sat on it;
12:16 but when J was glorified,
12:21 and said to him, "Sir, we wish to see J."
12:22 then Andrew and Philip went and told J.
12:23 J answered them, "The hour has come for the Son
12:30 J answered, "This voice has come for your sake,
12:35 J said to them, "The light is with you for
12:36 J had said this, he departed and hid from them.
12:44 Then J cried aloud: "Whoever believes in me
13: 1 J knew that his hour had come to depart
13: 3 J, knowing that the Father had given all things
13: 7 J answered, "You do not know
13: 8 J answered, "Unless I wash you,
13:10 J said to him, "One who has bathed does not need
13:21 After saying this J was troubled in spirit,
13:23 One of his disciples—the one whom J loved—
13:24 Simon Peter therefore motioned to him to ask J
13:25 So while reclining next to J, he asked him, "Lord,
13:26 J answered, "It is the one
13:27 J said to him, "Do quickly what you are going
13:29 J was telling him, "Buy what we need for
13:31 When he had gone out, J said,
13:36 J answered, "Where I am going,
13:38 J answered, "Will you lay down your life for me?
14: 6 J said to him, "I am the way, and the truth,
14: 9 J said to him, "Have I been with you all this time,
14:23 J answered him, "Those who love me will keep my word,
16:19 J knew that they wanted to ask him,
16:31 J answered them, "Do you now believe?
17: 1 After J had spoken these words,
17: 3 true God, and J Christ whom you have sent. A
18: 1 After J had spoken these words,
18: 2 because J often met there with his disciples.
18: 4 Then J, knowing all that was to happen to him,
18: 5 They answered, "J of Nazareth." D
18: 5 J replied, "I am he."
18: 6 When J said to them, "I am he,"
18: 7 And they said, "J of Nazareth." D
18: 8 J answered, "I told you that I am he.
18:11 J said to Peter, "Put your sword back
18:12 and the Jewish police arrested J and bound him.
18:15 Simon Peter and another disciple followed J.
18:15 with J into the courtyard of the high priest,
18:19 the high priest questioned J about his disciples
18:20 J answered, "I have spoken openly to the world;
18:22 of the police standing nearby struck J on the face,
18:23 J answered, "If I have spoken wrongly,
18:28 Then they took J from Caiaphas
18:32 to fulfill what J had said when he indicated
18:33 summoned J, and asked him,
18:34 J answered, "Do you ask this on your own,
18:36 J answered, "My kingdom is not from this world.
18:37 J answered, "You say that I am a king.
19: 1 Then Pilate took J and had him flogged.
19: 5 So J came out, wearing the crown of thorns and
19: 9 He entered his headquarters again and asked J,
19: 9 But J gave him no answer.
19:11 J answered him, "You would have no power
19:13 he brought J outside and sat on the judge's bench
19:16 be crucified. So they took J;
19:18 one on either side, with J between them.
19:19 It read, "J of Nazareth, the King of the Jews." D
19:20 the place where J was crucified was near the city;
19:23 When the soldiers had crucified J,
19:25 standing near the cross of J were his mother,
19:26 When J saw his mother and the disciple
19:28 this, when J knew that all was now finished,
19:30 J had received the wine, he said, "It is finished."
19:33 they came to J and saw that he was already dead,
19:38 Joseph of Arimathea, who was a disciple of J,
19:38 asked Pilate to let him take away the body of J.
19:39 Nicodemus, who had at first come to J by night,
19:40 They took the body of J and wrapped it with
19:42 and the tomb was nearby, they laid J there.
20: 2 the one whom J loved, and said to them,
20:12 sitting where the body of J had been lying,
20:14 she turned around and saw J standing there,
20:14 but she did not know that it was J.
20:15 J said to her, "Woman, why are you weeping?
20:16 J said to her, "Mary!"
20:17 J said to her, "Do not hold on to me,
20:19 J came and stood among them and said,
20:21 J said to them again, "Peace be with you.
20:24 was not with them when J came.
20:26 J came and stood among them and said,
20:29 J said to him, "Have you believed
20:30 Now J did many other signs in the presence
20:31 so that you may come to believe that J is
21: 1 After these things J showed himself again to
21: 4 Just after daybreak, J stood on the beach;
21: 4 but the disciples did not know that it was J.
21: 5 J said to them, "Children, you have no fish,

Jn 21: 7 That disciple whom J loved said to Peter,
21:10 J said to them, "Bring some of the fish
21:12 J said to them, "Come and have breakfast."
21:13 J came and took the bread and gave it to them,
21:14 that J appeared to the disciples after he was raised
21:15 J said to Simon Peter, "Simon son of John,
21:15 J said to him, "Feed my lambs."
21:16 J said to him, "Tend my sheep."
21:17 J said to him, "Feed my sheep.
21:20 the disciple whom J loved following them;
21:20 the one who had reclined next to J at the supper
21:21 When Peter saw him, he said to J, "Lord,
21:22 J said to him, "If it is my will that he remain
21:23 Yet J did not say to him that he would not die,
21:25 But there are also many other things that J did;
Ac 1: 1 about all that J did and taught from the beginning
1:11 This J, who has been taken up from you
1:14 including Mary the mother of J,
1:16 who became a guide for those who arrested J—
1:21 all the time that the Lord J went in and out B
2:22 J of Nazareth, a man attested to you by God D
2:32 This J God raised up, and of that all
2:36 this J whom you crucified."
2:38 in the name of J Christ so that your sins AE
3: 6 in the name of J Christ of Nazareth, AE
3:13 God of our ancestors has glorified his servant J,
3:16 that is through J has given him this perfect health
3:20 the Messiah appointed for you, that is, J,
4: 2 and proclaiming that in J there is the resurrection
4:10 in good health by the name of J Christ AE
4:11 This J is 'the stone that was rejected by you,
4:13 and recognized them as companions of J.
4:18 not to speak or teach at all in the name of J. E
4:27 gathered together against your holy servant J,
4:30 through the name of your holy servant J."
4:33 to the resurrection of the Lord J, B
5:30 The God of our ancestors raised up J,
5:40 they ordered them not to speak in the name of J, E
5:42 not cease to teach and proclaim J as the Messiah.
6:14 that this J of Nazareth will destroy this place D
7:55 the glory of God and J standing at the right hand
7:59 they were stoning Stephen, he prayed, "Lord J, B
8:12 the kingdom of God and the name of J Christ, AE
8:16 in the name of the Lord J). B
8:35 he proclaimed to him the good news about J.
9: 5 reply came, "I am J, whom you are persecuting.
9:17 "Brother Saul, the Lord J, who appeared to you B
9:20 and immediately he began to proclaim J in
9:22 in Damascus by proving that J was the Messiah.
9:27 he had spoken boldly in the name of J. E
9:34 Peter said to him, "Aeneas, J Christ heals you; A
10:36 preaching peace by J Christ—he is Lord of all. A
10:38 how God anointed J of Nazareth with D
10:48 to be baptized in the name of J Christ. AE
11:17 when we believed in the Lord J Christ, AB
11:20 to the Hellenists also, proclaiming the Lord J. B
13:23 to Israel a Savior, J, as he promised;
13:33 their children, by raising J;
13:39 by this J everyone who believes is set free
15:11 be saved through the grace of the Lord J, B
15:26 for the sake of our Lord J Christ. AB
16: 7 but the Spirit of J did not allow them;
16:18 order you in the name of J Christ to come out AE
16:31 They answered, "Believe on the Lord J, B
17: 3 J whom I am proclaiming to you."
17: 7 saying that there is another king named J."
17:18 because he was telling the good news about J and
18: 5 testifying to the Jews that the Messiah was J.
18:25 and taught accurately the things concerning J,
18:28 showing by the scriptures that the Messiah is J.
19: 4 the one who was to come after him, that is, in J."
19: 5 they were baptized in the name of the Lord J. B
19:13 of the Lord J over those who had evil spirits, B
19:13 "I adjure you by the J whom Paul proclaims."
19:15 the evil spirit said to them in reply, "J I know,
19:17 and the name of the Lord J was praised. B
20:21 toward God and faith toward our Lord J. B
20:24 and the ministry that I received from the Lord J, B
20:35 remembering the words of the Lord J, B
21:13 to die in Jerusalem for the name of the Lord J." B
22: 8 'I am J of Nazareth whom you are persecuting.' D
22:18 and saw J saying to me,
24:24 heard him speak concerning faith in Christ J. C
25:19 about their own religion and about a certain J,
26: 9 many things against the name of J of Nazareth. DE
26:15 'I am J whom you are persecuting.
28:23 of God and trying to convince them about J both
28:31 about the Lord J Christ with all boldness and AB
Ro 1: 1 a servant of J Christ, called to be an apostle, A
1: 4 resurrection from the dead, J Christ our Lord, A
1: 6 yourselves who are called to belong to J Christ, A
1: 7 from God our Father and the Lord J Christ. AB
1: 8 I thank my God through J Christ for all of you, A
2:16 according to my gospel, God, through J Christ, A
3:22 righteousness of God through faith in J Christ A
3:24 through the redemption that is in Christ J, C
3:26 and that he justifies the one who has faith in J.
4:24 to us who believe in him who raised J our Lord
5: 1 with God through our Lord J Christ, AB
5:11 even boast in God through our Lord J Christ, AB
5:15 J Christ, abounded for the many. A
5:17 in life through the one man, J Christ. A
5:21 to eternal life through J Christ our Lord. A
6: 3 into Christ J were baptized into his death? C
6:11 to sin and alive to God in Christ J. C
6:23 of God is eternal life in Christ J our Lord. C
7:25 Thanks be to God through J Christ our Lord! A

Ac 8: 1 for those who are in Christ J. C
8: 2 the Spirit of life in Christ J has set you free C
8:11 of him who raised J from the dead dwells in you,
8:34 It is Christ J, who died, yes, who was raised, C
8:39 from the love of God in Christ J our Lord. C
10: 9 if you confess with your lips that J is Lord
13:14 Instead, put on the Lord J Christ, AB
14:14 in the Lord J that nothing is unclean in itself; B
15: 5 in accordance with Christ J, C
15: 6 the God and Father of our Lord J Christ. AB
15:16 Christ J to the Gentiles in the priestly service C
15:17 In Christ J, then, I have reason to boast C
15:30 our Lord J Christ and by the love of the Spirit, AB
16: 3 who work with me in Christ J, C
16:20 The grace of our Lord J Christ be with you. AB
16:25 to my gospel and the proclamation of J Christ, A
16:27 through J Christ, to whom be the glory forever! A
1Co 1: 1 to be an apostle of Christ J by the will of God, C
1: 2 to those who are sanctified in Christ J, C
1: 2 the name of our Lord J Christ, both their Lord AB
1: 3 from God our Father and the Lord J Christ. AB
1: 4 of God that has been given you in Christ J, C
1: 7 wait for the revealing of our Lord J Christ. AB
1: 8 be blameless on the day of our Lord J Christ. AB
1: 9 the fellowship of his Son, J Christ our Lord. A
1:10 by the name of our Lord J Christ, AB
1:30 He is the source of your life in Christ J, C
2: 2 to know nothing among you except J Christ, A
3:11 that foundation is J Christ. A
4:15 in Christ J I became your father through C
4:17 to remind you of my ways in Christ J, C
5: 4 Lord J on the man who has done such a thing. B
5: 4 spirit is present with the power of our Lord J, B
6:11 the name of the Lord J Christ and in the Spirit AB
8: 6 for whom we exist, and one Lord, J Christ, AB
9: 1 Have I not seen J our Lord?
11:23 that the Lord J on the night B
12: 3 by the Spirit of God ever says "Let J be cursed!"
12: 3 and no one can say "J is Lord" except by
15:31 a boast that I make in Christ J our Lord. C
15:57 the victory through our Lord J Christ. AB
16:23 The grace of the Lord J be with you. B
16:24 My love be with all of you in Christ J. C
2Co 1: 1 Paul, an apostle of Christ J by the will of God, C
1: 2 from God our Father and the Lord J Christ. AB
1: 3 be the God and Father of our Lord J Christ, AB
1:14 on the day of the Lord J we are your boast even B
1:19 For the Son of God, J Christ, A
4: 5 we proclaim J Christ as Lord and ourselves A
4: 6 of the glory of God in the face of J Christ. A
4:10 always carrying in the body the death of J,
4:10 life of J may also be made visible in our bodies.
4:11 life of J may be made visible in our mortal flesh.
4:14 the one who raised the Lord J will raise us also B
4:14 raised the Lord Jesus will raise us also with J,
8: 9 know the generous act of our Lord J Christ, AB
11: 4 if someone comes and proclaims another J than
11:31 and Father of the Lord J (blessed be he forever!) B
13: 5 Do you not realize that J Christ is in you?— A
13:13 grace of the Lord J Christ, the love of God, AB
Gal 1: 1 but through J Christ and God the Father, A
1: 3 from God our Father and the Lord J Christ, AB
1:12 but I received it through a revelation of J Christ. A
2: 4 in to spy on the freedom we have in Christ J, C
2:16 works of the law but through faith in J Christ. A
2:16 And we have come to believe in Christ J, C
3: 1 that J Christ was publicly exhibited as crucified! A
3:14 in Christ J the blessing of Abraham might come C
3:22 in J Christ might be given to those who believe. A
3:26 for in Christ J you are all children of God C
3:28 for all of you are one in Christ J. C
4:14 welcomed me as an angel of God, as Christ J. C
5: 6 For in Christ J neither circumcision C
5:24 those who belong to Christ J have crucified C
6:14 anything except the cross of our Lord J Christ, AB
6:17 for I carry the marks of J branded on my body.
6:18 grace of our Lord J Christ be with your spirit, AB
Eph 1: 1 Paul, an apostle of Christ J by the will of God, C
1: 1 in Ephesus and are faithful in Christ J: C
1: 2 from God our Father and the Lord J Christ. AB
1: 3 be the God and Father of our Lord J Christ, AB
1: 5 for adoption as his children through J Christ, A
1:15 the Lord J and your love toward all the saints, B
1:17 I pray that the God of our Lord J Christ, AB
2: 6 with him in the heavenly places in Christ J, C
2: 7 of his grace in kindness toward us in Christ J. C
2:10 created in Christ J for good works, C
2:13 in Christ J you who once were far off have C
2:20 with Christ J himself as the cornerstone. C
3: 1 I Paul am a prisoner for Christ J for the sake C
3: 6 and sharers in the promise in Christ J through C
3:11 that he has carried out in Christ J our Lord, C
3:21 in the church and in Christ J to all generations, C
4:21 about him and were taught in him, as truth is in J.
5:20 everything in the name of our Lord J Christ. AB
6:23 from God the Father and the Lord J Christ. AB
6:24 an undying love for our Lord J Christ. AB
Php 1: 1 Paul and Timothy, servants of Christ J, C
1: 1 To all the saints in Christ J who are in Philippi, C
1: 2 from God our Father and the Lord J Christ. AB
1: 6 to completion by the day of J Christ. A
1: 8 for all of you with the compassion of Christ J. C
1:11 through J Christ for the glory and praise of God. A
1:19 help of the Spirit of J Christ this will turn out A
1:26 in your boasting in Christ J when I come C
2: 5 Let the same mind be in you that was in Christ J, C
2:10 that at the name of J every knee should bend, E

Php 2:11 tongue should confess that J Christ is Lord, A
2:19 hope in the Lord J to send Timothy to you soon, B
2:21 seeking their own interests, not those of J Christ. A
3: 3 in Christ J and have no confidence in the flesh— C
3: 8 of knowing Christ J my Lord. C
3:12 because Christ J has made me his own. C
3:14 the prize of the heavenly call of God in Christ J. C
3:20 we are expecting a Savior, the Lord J Christ. AB
4: 7 guard your hearts and your minds in Christ J. C
4:19 according to his riches in glory in Christ J. C
4:21 Greet every saint in Christ J. C
4:23 grace of the Lord J Christ be with your spirit. AB
Col 1: 1 Paul, an apostle of Christ J by the will of God, C
1: 3 the Father of our Lord J Christ, AB
1: 4 for we have heard of your faith in Christ J and C
2: 6 you therefore have received Christ J the Lord, C
3:17 do everything in the name of the Lord J, B
4:11 And J who is called Justus greets you.
4:12 who is one of you, a servant of Christ J, C
1Th 1: 1 in God the Father and the Lord J Christ: AB
1: 3 steadfastness of hope in our Lord J Christ. AB
1:10 J, who rescues us from the wrath that is coming.
2:14 churches of God in Christ J that are in Judea, C
2:15 the Lord J and the prophets, and drove us out; B
2:19 or joy or crown of boasting before our Lord J B
3:11 Father himself and our Lord J direct our way B
3:13 at the coming of our Lord J with all his saints. B
4: 1 we ask and urge you in the Lord J that, B
4: 2 instructions we gave you through the Lord J. B
4:14 For since we believe that J died and rose again,
4:14 that Jesus died and rose again, even so, through J,
5: 9 obtaining salvation through our Lord J Christ, AB
5:18 for this is the will of God in Christ J for you. C
5:23 blameless at the coming of our Lord J Christ. AB
5:28 The grace of our Lord J Christ be with you. AB
2Th 1: 1 in God our Father and the Lord J Christ: AB
1: 2 from God our Father and the Lord J Christ. AB
1: 7 when the Lord J is revealed from heaven B
1: 8 not obey the gospel of our Lord J. B
1:12 the name of our Lord J may be glorified in you, B
1:12 to the grace of our God and the Lord J Christ. AB
2: 1 As to the coming of our Lord J Christ AB
2: 8 whom the Lord J will destroy with the breath B
2:14 you may obtain the glory of our Lord J Christ. AB
2:16 Now may our Lord J Christ himself AB
3: 6 beloved, in the name of our Lord J Christ, AB
3:12 in the Lord J Christ to do their work quietly AB
3:18 The grace of our Lord J Christ be with all AB
1Ti 1: 1 of Christ J by the command of God our Savior C
1: 1 of God our Savior and of Christ J our hope, C
1: 2 from God the Father and Christ J our Lord. C
1:12 I am grateful to Christ J our Lord, C
1:14 with the faith and love that are in Christ J. C
1:15 Christ J came into the world to save sinners— C
1:16 J Christ might display the utmost patience, A
2: 5 Christ J, himself human, C
3:13 great boldness in the faith that is in Christ J. C
4: 6 you will be a good servant of Christ J, C
5:21 of God and of Christ J and of the elect angels, C
6: 3 with the sound words of our Lord J Christ AB
6:13 who gives life to all things, and of Christ J, C
6:14 until the manifestation of our Lord J Christ, AB
2Ti 1: 1 Paul, an apostle of Christ J by the will of God, C
1: 1 the sake of the promise of life that is in Christ J, C
1: 2 from God the Father and Christ J our Lord. C
1: 9 This grace was given to us in Christ J before C
1:10 through the appearing of our Savior Christ J, C
1:13 in the faith and love that are in Christ J. C
2: 1 be strong in the grace that is in Christ J; C
2: 3 in suffering like a good soldier of Christ J. C
2: 8 Remember J Christ, raised from the dead, A
2:10 also obtain the salvation that is in Christ J, C
3:12 live a godly life in Christ J will be persecuted. C
3:15 for salvation through faith in Christ J. C
4: 1 In the presence of God and of Christ J, C
Tit 1: 1 a servant of God and an apostle of J Christ, A
1: 4 from God the Father and Christ J our Savior. C
2:13 the glory of our great God and Savior, J Christ. A
3: 6 on us richly through J Christ our Savior, A
Phm 1: 1 Paul, a prisoner of Christ J, C
1: 3 from God our Father and the Lord J Christ. AB
1: 5 all the saints and your faith toward the Lord J. B
1: 9 and now also as a prisoner of Christ J. C
1:23 Epaphras, my fellow prisoner in Christ J, C
1:25 grace of the Lord J Christ be with your spirit. AB
Heb 2: 9 but we do see J, who for a little
2:11 For this reason J is not ashamed
3: 1 in a heavenly calling, consider that J, the apostle
3: 3 Yet J is worthy of more glory than Moses,
4:14 the heavens, J, the Son of God, let us hold fast
5: 7 J offered up prayers and supplications,
6:20 where J, a forerunner on our
7:22 accordingly J has also become the guarantee of
8: 6 J has now obtained a more excellent ministry,
10:10 through the offering of the body of J Christ A
10:19 to enter the sanctuary by the blood of J,
12: 2 looking to J the pioneer and perfecter of our faith,
12:24 and to J, the mediator of a new covenant,
13: 8 J Christ is the same yesterday and today A
13:12 Therefore J also suffered outside the city gate
13:20 who brought back from the dead our Lord J, B
13:21 through J Christ, to whom be the glory forever A
Jas 1: 1 a servant of God and of the Lord J Christ, AB
2: 1 in our glorious Lord J Christ? AB
1Pe 1: 1 Peter, an apostle of J Christ, A
1: 2 to J Christ and to be sprinkled with his blood: A
1: 3 be the God and Father of our Lord J Christ! AB
1Pe 1: 3 living hope through the resurrection of J Christ A
1: 7 and glory and honor when J Christ is revealed. A
1:13 that J Christ will bring you when he is revealed. A
2: 5 sacrifices acceptable to God through J Christ. A
3:21 through the resurrection of J Christ, A
4:11 be glorified in all things through J Christ. A
2Pe 1: 1 Simeon Peter, a servant and apostle of J Christ, A
1: 1 righteousness of our God and Savior J Christ: A
1: 2 in the knowledge of God and of J our Lord.
1: 8 in the knowledge of our Lord J Christ. AB
1:11 and Savior J Christ will be richly provided A
1:14 our Lord J Christ has made clear to me. AB
1:16 the power and coming of our Lord J Christ, AB
2:20 the knowledge of our Lord and Savior J Christ, A
3:18 and knowledge of our Lord and Savior J Christ. A
1Jn 1: 3 with the Father and with his Son J Christ. A
1: 7 the blood of J his Son cleanses us from all sin.
2: 1 with the Father, J Christ the righteous; A
2:22 Who is the liar but the one who denies that J is
3:23 of his Son J Christ and love one another, A
4: 2 every spirit that confesses that J Christ has A
4: 3 and every spirit that does not confess J is not
4:15 God abides in those who confess that J is the Son
5: 1 that J is the Christ has been born of God,
5: 5 the one who believes that J is the Son of God?
5: 6 the one who came by water and blood, J Christ, A
5:20 we are in him who is true, in his Son J Christ. A
2Jn 1: 3 with us from God the Father and from J Christ, A
1: 7 who do not confess that J Christ has come in A
Jude 1: 1 Jude, a servant of J Christ and brother of James, A
1: 1 in God the Father and kept safe for J Christ: A
1: 4 and deny our only Master and Lord, J Christ. AB
1:17 of the apostles of our Lord J Christ; AB
1:21 look forward to the mercy of our Lord J Christ AB
1:25 through J Christ our Lord, be glory, majesty, A
Rev 1: 1 The revelation of J Christ, A
1: 2 word of God and to the testimony of J Christ, A
1: 5 from J Christ, the faithful witness, the firstborn A
1: 9 with you in J the persecution and the kingdom
1: 9 of the word of God and the testimony of J.
12:17 of God and hold the testimony of J.
14:12 of God and hold fast to the faith of J.
17: 6 of the saints and the blood of the witnesses to J.
19:10 and your comrades who hold the testimony of J.
19:10 For the testimony of J is the spirit of prophecy."
20: 4 for their testimony to J and for the word of God.
22:16 J, who sent my angel to you with this testimony
22:20 I am coming soon." Amen. Come, Lord J! B
22:21 The grace of the Lord J be with all the saints. B
Sir Pr: 1 to help the outsiders. So my grandfather J,
50:27 J son of Eleazar son of Sirach of Jerusalem,
51: 1 PRAYER OF J SON OF SIRACH I give you thanks,

JESUS' (8) [JESUS]

Mk 6:14 for J name had become known.
Lk 5: 8 Simon Peter saw it, he fell down at J knees,
8:41 at J feet and begged him to come to his house,
17:16 He prostrated himself at J feet and thanked him.
Jn 12: 3 anointed J feet, and wiped them with her hair.
20: 7 and the cloth that had been on J head,
2Co 4: 5 as Lord and ourselves as your slaves for J sake.
4:11 we are always being given up to death for J sake,

JETHER (8)

Jdg 8:20 So he said to J his firstborn, "Go kill them!"
1Ki 2: 5 and Amasa son of J, whom he murdered,
2:32 of Israel, and Amasa son of J, commander of
1Ch 2:17 and the father of Amasa was J the Ishmaelite.
2:32 J and Jonathan; and J died childless.
4:17 The sons of Ezrah: J, Mered, Epher, and Jalon.
7:38 The sons of J: Jephunneh, Pispa, and Ara.

JETHETH (2)

Ge 36:40 the clans Timna, Alvah, J,
1Ch 1:51 The clans of Edom were: clans Timna, Aliah, J,

JETHLAH (KJV) See ITHLAH

JETHRO (10)

Ex 3: 1 of his father-in-law J, the priest of Midian;
4:18 Moses went back to his father-in-law J and said
4:18 And J said to Moses, "Go in peace."
18: 1 J, the priest of Midian, Moses' father-in-law,
18: 2 his father-in-law J took her back,
18: 5 J, Moses' father-in-law, came into the wilderness
18: 6 He sent word to Moses, "I, your father-in-law J,
18: 9 J rejoiced for all the good that
18:10 J said, "Blessed be the LORD,
18:12 And J, Moses' father-in-law,

JETUR (3)

Ge 25:15 Hadad, Tema, J, Naphish, and Kedemah.
1Ch 1:31 J, Naphish, and Kedemah.
5:19 They made war on the Hagrites, J, Naphish,

JEUEL (4)

1Ch 9: 6 J and their kin, six hundred ninety.
2Ch 29:13 and of the sons of Elizaphan, Shimri and J;
Ezr 8:13 their names being Eliphelet, J, and Shemaiah,
1Es 8:39 J, and Shemaiah, and with them seventy men.

JEUSH (9)

Ge 36: 5 and Oholibamah bore J, Jalam,
Ge 36:14 she bore to Esau J, Jalam, and Korah.
36:18 the clans J, Jalam, and Korah;
1Ch 1:35 Eliphaz, Reuel, J, Jalam, and Korah.
7:10 J, Benjamin, Ehud, Chenaanah, Zethan, Tarshish,
8:39 Ulam his firstborn, J the second,
23:10 the sons of Shimei: Jahath, Zina, J, and Beriah.
23:11 but J and Beriah did not have many sons,
2Ch 11:19 She bore him sons: J, Shemariah, and Zaham.

JEUZ (1)

1Ch 8:10 J, Sachia, and Mirmah. These were his sons,

JEW (43) [JEWISH, JEWS, JEWS', JUDAISM]

Est 2: 5 Now there was a J in the citadel
3: 4 for he had told them that he was a J.
5:13 as I see the J Mordecai sitting at the king's gate."
6:10 so to the J Mordecai who sits at the king's gate.
8: 7 to Queen Esther and to the J Mordecai,
9:29 along with the J Mordecai,
9:31 as the J Mordecai and Queen Esther enjoined on
10: 3 the J was next in rank to King Ahasuerus,
Zec 8:23 of every language shall take hold of a J,
Jn 3:25 between John's disciples and a J.
4: 9 a J, ask a drink of me, a woman of Samaria?"
18:35 Pilate replied, "I am not a J, am I?
Ac 10:28 "You yourselves know that it is unlawful for a J
18: 2 There he found a J named Aquila,
18:24 Now there came to Ephesus a J named Apollos,
19:34 But when they recognized that he was a J,
21:39 Paul replied, "I am a J, from Tarsus in Cilicia,
22: 3 "I am a J, born in Tarsus in Cilicia, but brought
Ro 1:16 to the J first and also to the Greek.
2: 9 the J first and also the Greek,
2:10 the J first and also the Greek.
2:17 a J and rely on the law and boast of your relation
2:28 For a person is not a J who is one outwardly,
2:29 Rather, a person is a J who is one inwardly,
3: 1 Then what advantage has the J?
10:12 For there is no distinction between J and Greek;
1Co 9:20 To the Jews I became as a J,
Gal 2:14 though a J, live like a Gentile and not like a J,
3:28 There is no longer J or Greek,
Col 3:11 In that renewal there is no longer Greek and J,
AdE 2: 5 Now there was a J in Susa
3: 4 Mordecai had told them that he was a J.
5: 9 But when he saw Mordecai the J in the courtyard,
5:13 as long as I see Mordecai the J in the courtyard."
6:10 Do just as you have said for Mordecai the J,
9:29 of Aminadab along with Mordecai the J wrote
11: 3 He was a J living in the city of Susa, a great man,
Bel 1:28 saying, "The king has become a J;
1Mc 2:23 a J came forward in the sight of all
2Mc 9:17 in addition to all this he also would become a J
3Mc 1: 3 a J by birth who later changed his religion
3:29 a J is to be made unapproachable and burned

JEWEL (4) [JEWELER, JEWELRY, JEWELS]

Pr 20:15 the lips informed by knowledge are a precious j.
SS 4: 9 with one j of your necklace.
Rev 21:11 the glory of God and a radiance like a very rare j,
21:19 of the wall of the city are adorned with every j;

JEWELER (1) [JEWEL]

Sir 45:11 in a setting of gold, the work of a j,

JEWELRY (5) [JEWEL]

Ge 24:53 the servant brought out j of silver and of gold,
Ex 3:22 in the neighbor's house for j of silver and of gold,
12:35 they had asked the Egyptians for j of silver
Hos 2:13 to them and decked herself with her ring and j,
Jdt 10: 4 bracelets, rings, earrings, and all her other j.

JEWELS (15) [JEWEL]

Job 28:17 nor can it be exchanged for j of fine gold.
Pr 3:15 She is more precious than j,
8:11 for wisdom is better than j,
31:10 She is far more precious than j.
SS 1:10 your neck with strings of j.
5:14 His arms are rounded gold, set with j.
7: 1 Your rounded thighs are like j,
Isa 54:12 of rubies, your gates of j, and all your wall
61:10 and as a bride adorns herself with her j.
Eze 16:17 You also took your beautiful j of my gold
23:26 of your clothes and take away your fine j.
Zec 9:16 like the j of a crown they shall shine on his land.
Rev 17: 4 and adorned with gold and j and pearls,
18:12 j and pearls, fine linen, purple, silk and scarlet,
18:16 in purple and scarlet, adorned with gold, with j,

JEWISH (37) [JEW]

Ne 5: 1 the people and of their wives against their J kin.
5: 8 have bought back our J kindred who had been sold
Est 6:13 of the J people, you will not prevail against him,
Lk 7: 3 he sent some J elders to him,
23:51 He came from the J town of Arimathea,
Jn 2: 6 for the J rites of purification,
7: 2 Now the J festival of Booths was near.
18:12 and the J police arrested Jesus and bound him.
19:42 And so, because it was the J day of Preparation,
Ac 10:22 who is well spoken of by the whole J nation,
12:11 and from all that the J people were expecting."
13: 6 they met a certain magician, a J false prophet,

Ac 14: 1 into the **J** synagogue and spoke in such a way that
16: 1 the son of a **J** woman who was a believer;
17:10 when they arrived, they went to the **J** synagogue.
19:13 Then some itinerant **J** exorcists tried to use
19:14 of a **J** high priest named Sceva were doing this.
24:24 who was **J**, he sent for Paul and heard him speak
25:24 the whole **J** community petitioned me,
Tit 1:14 not paying attention to **J** myths or
AdE 3:13 the **J** people on a given day of the twelfth month,
6:13 "If Mordecai is of the **J** people,
1Mc 8:29 the Romans make a treaty with the **J** people.
12: 3 and the **J** nation have sent us to renew
12: 6 rest of the **J** people to their brothers the Spartans,
14:20 and the priests and the rest of the **J** people,
15:17 by the high priest Simon and by the **J** people
2Mc 1: 1 To their **J** kindred in Egypt,
5:23 In his malice toward the **J** citizens,
8: 1 in the **J** faith, and so they gathered
8:11 inviting them to buy **J** slaves and promising
9:19 "To his worthy **J** citizens,
1Es 8:10 I have given orders that those of the **J** nation and
3Mc 2:27 to inflict public disgrace on the **J** community,
2:33 considering them to be enemies of the **J** nation,
3: 2 against the **J** nation by some who conspired
7:10 of the **J** nation who had willfully transgressed

JEWRY (KJV) See JUDAH, JUDEA

JEWS‡ (407) [JEW]

A. ALL [THE] JEWS (22)
B. KING OF THE JEWS (18)
C. ELDERS OF THE JEWS (9)
D. NATION OF THE JEWS (9)

Ezr 4:12 that the **J** who came up from you to us have gone
4:23 they hurried to the **J** in Jerusalem and by force
5: 1 to the **J** who were in Judah and Jerusalem,
5: 5 eye of their God was upon the elders of the **J**, C
6: 7 the **J** and the elders of the Jews rebuild this house
6: 7 Jews and the elders of the **J** rebuild this house C
6: 8 elders of the **J** for the rebuilding of this house C
6:14 So the elders of the **J** built and prospered, C
Ne 1: 2 and I asked them about the **J** that survived,
2:16 I had not yet told the **J**, the priests, the nobles,
4: 1 and greatly enraged, and he mocked the **J**.
4: 2 "What are these feeble **J** doing?
4:12 When the **J** who lived near them came,
5:17 **J** and officials, besides those who came to us
6: 6 that you and the **J** intend to rebel;
13:23 also I saw **J** who had married women of Ashdod,
Est 3: 6 Haman plotted to destroy all the **J**, A
3:10 of Hammedatha the Agagite, the enemy of the **J**.
3:13 to kill, and to annihilate all **J**, young and old, A
4: 3 there was great mourning among the **J**,
4: 7 the king's treasuries for the destruction of the **J**.
4:13 you will escape any more than all the other **J**.
4:14 relief and deliverance will rise for the **J**
4:16 gather all the **J** to be found in Susa, A
8: 1 the house of Haman, the enemy of the **J**;
8: 3 and the plot that he had devised against the **J**.
8: 5 to destroy the **J** who are in all the provinces of
8: 7 because he plotted to lay hands on the **J**.
8: 8 You may write as you please with regard to the **J**,
8: 9 to the **J** and to the satraps and the governors and
8: 9 and also to the **J** in their script and their language.
8:11 By these letters the king allowed the **J** who were
8:13 the **J** were to be ready on that day to take revenge
8:16 the **J** there was light and gladness, joy and honor.
8:17 there was gladness and joy among the **J**,
8:17 of the peoples of the country professed to be **J**,
8:17 because the fear of the **J** had fallen upon them.
9: 1 on the very day when the enemies of the **J** hoped
9: 1 when the **J** would gain power over their foes,
9: 2 the **J** gathered in their cities throughout all
9: 3 and the royal officials were supporting the **J**,
9: 5 **J** struck down all their enemies with the sword,
9: 6 the **J** killed and destroyed five hundred people.
9:10 of Hammedatha, the enemy of the **J**;
9:12 of Susa the **J** have killed five hundred people and
9:13 the **J** who are in Susa be allowed tomorrow also
9:15 The **J** who were in Susa gathered also on
9:16 Now the other **J** who were in the king's provinces
9:18 But the **J** who were in Susa gathered on
9:19 Therefore the **J** of the villages,
9:20 and sent letters to all the **J** who were in all A
9:22 on which the **J** gained relief from their enemies,
9:23 **J** adopted as a custom what they had begun to do,
9:24 the enemy of all the **J**, had plotted against A
9:24 had plotted against the **J** to destroy them,
9:25 against the **J** should come upon his own head,
9:27 the **J** established and accepted as a custom
9:28 among the **J**, nor should the commemoration
9:30 and security to all the **J**, A
9:31 and Queen Esther enjoined on the **J**,
10: 3 among the **J** and popular with his many kindred,
Da 3: 8 Chaldeans came forward and denounced the **J**.
3:12 There are certain **J** whom you have appointed
Mt 2: 2 is the child who has been born king of the **J**? B
27:11 asked him, "Are you the King of the **J**?" B
27:29 saying, "Hail, King of the **J**!" B
27:37 which read, "This is Jesus, the King of the **J**." B
28:15 And this story is still told among the **J** to this day.
Mk 7: 3 (For the Pharisees, and all the **J**, A
15: 2 Pilate asked him, "Are you the King of the **J**?" B
15: 9 to release for you the King of the **J**?" B
15:12 to do with the man you call the King of the **J**?" B
Mk 15:18 they began saluting him, "Hail, King of the **J**!" B
15:26 charge against him read, "The King of the **J**." B
Lk 23: 3 Pilate asked him, "Are you the king of the **J**?" B
23:37 "If you are the King of the **J**, save yourself!" B
23:38 "This is the King of the **J**." B
Jn 1:19 the **J** sent priests and Levites from Jerusalem
2:13 The Passover of the **J** was near,
2:18 The **J** then said to him,
2:20 The **J** then said, "This temple has been
3: 1 a Pharisee named Nicodemus, a leader of the **J**.
4: 9 (**J** do not share things in common
4:22 for salvation is from the **J**.
5: 1 After this there was a festival of the **J**,
5:10 So the **J** said to the man who had been cured,
5:15 the **J** that it was Jesus who had made him well.
5:16 Therefore the **J** started persecuting Jesus,
5:18 For this reason the **J** were seeking all the more
6: 4 Now the Passover, the festival of the **J**, was near.
6:41 **J** began to complain about him because he said,
6:52 The **J** then disputed among themselves, saying,
7: 1 the **J** were looking for an opportunity to kill him.
7:11 **J** were looking for him at the festival and saying,
7:13 about him for fear of the **J**.
7:15 The **J** were astonished at it, saying,
7:35 The **J** said to one another,
8:22 Then the **J** said, "Is he going to kill himself?
8:31 Then Jesus said to the **J** who had believed in him,
8:48 The **J** answered him, "Are we not right in saying
8:52 The **J** said to him, "Now we know that you have
8:57 Then the **J** said to him,
9:18 The **J** did not believe that he had been blind
9:22 because they were afraid of the **J**;
9:22 for the **J** had already agreed
10:19 Again the **J** were divided because of these words.
10:24 So the **J** gathered around him and said to him,
10:31 The **J** took up stones again to stone him.
10:33 The **J** answered, "It is not for a good work
11: 8 "Rabbi, the **J** were just now trying to stone you,
11:19 and many of the **J** had come to Martha and Mary
11:31 The **J** who were with her in the house,
11:33 and the **J** who came with her also weeping,
11:36 So the **J** said, "See how he loved him!"
11:45 of the **J** therefore, who had come with Mary
11:54 about openly among the **J**, but went from there to
11:55 Now the Passover of the **J** was near,
12: 9 the great crowd of the **J** learned that he was there,
12:11 the **J** were deserting and were believing in Jesus.
13:33 and as I said to the **J** so now I say to you,
18:14 the **J** that it was better to have one person die for
18:20 where all the **J** come together. A
18:31 The **J** replied, "We are not permitted
18:33 and asked him, "Are you the King of the **J**?" B
18:36 to keep me from being handed over to the **J**.
18:38 he went out to the **J** again and told them,
18:39 to release for you the King of the **J**?" B
19: 3 saying, "Hail, King of the **J**!" B
19: 7 The **J** answered him, "We have a law,
19:12 but the **J** cried out, "If you release this man,
19:14 He said to the **J**, "Here is your King!"
19:19 It read, "Jesus of Nazareth, the King of the **J**." B
19:20 Many of the **J** read this inscription,
19:21 Then the chief priests of the **J** said to Pilate,
19:21 "Do not write, 'The King of the **J**,' but, B
19:21 but, 'This man said, I am King of the **J**.' " B
19:31 the **J** did not want the bodies left on the cross
19:38 though a secret one because of his fear of the **J**,
19:40 according to the burial custom of the **J**.
20:19 of the **J**, Jesus came and stood among them
Ac 2: 5 Now there were devout **J** from every nation
2:10 and visitors from Rome, both **J** and proselytes,
9:22 and confounded the **J** who lived in Damascus
9:23 some time had passed, the **J** plotted to kill him,
11:19 and they spoke the word to no one except **J**.
12: 3 After he saw that it pleased the **J**,
13: 5 the word of God in the synagogues of the **J**.
13:43 many **J** and devout converts
13:45 **J** saw the crowds, they were filled with jealousy;
13:50 the **J** incited the devout women of high standing
14: 1 in such a way that a great number of both **J**
14: 2 But the unbelieving **J** stirred up the Gentiles
14: 4 some sided with the **J**, and some with
14: 5 an attempt was made by both Gentiles and **J**,
14:19 But **J** came there from Antioch and Iconium
16: 3 because of the **J** who were in those places,
16:20 disturbing our city; they are **J**
17: 1 where there was a synagogue of the **J**.
17: 5 But the **J** became jealous,
17:11 These **J** were more receptive than those
17:13 when the **J** of Thessalonica learned that the word
17:17 the synagogue with the **J** and the devout persons,
18: 2 Claudius had ordered all **J** to leave Rome. A
18: 4 in the synagogue and would try to convince **J**
18: 5 testifying to the **J** that the Messiah was Jesus.
18:12 the **J** made a united attack on Paul
18:14 Gallio said to the **J**, "If it were a matter of crime
18:14 be justified in accepting the complaint of you **J**;
18:19 the synagogue and had a discussion with the **J**.
18:28 for he powerfully refuted the **J** in public,
19:10 both **J** and Greeks, heard the word of the Lord.
19:17 both **J** and Greeks, everyone was awestruck;
19:33 whom the **J** had pushed forward.
20: 3 when a plot was made against him by the **J**,
20:19 that came to me through the plots of the **J**.
20:21 both **J** and Greeks about repentance toward God
21:11 'This is the way the **J** in Jerusalem will bind
21:20 of believers there are among the **J**,
21:21 all the **J** living among the Gentiles to forsake A
Ac 21:27 the **J** from Asia, who had seen him in the temple,
22:12 and well spoken of by all the **J** living there, A
22:30 the **J**, the next day he released him and ordered
23:12 In the morning the **J** joined in a conspiracy
23:20 "The **J** have agreed to ask you to bring Paul down
23:27 This man was seized by the **J** and was about to
24: 5 agitator among all the **J** throughout the world, A
24: 9 The **J** also joined in the charge by asserting
24:19 But there were some **J** from Asia—
24:27 and since he wanted to grant the **J** a favor,
25: 2 the chief priests and the leaders of the **J** gave him
25: 7 the **J** who had gone down
25: 8 an offense against the law of the **J**,
25: 9 But Festus, wishing to do the **J** a favor,
25:10 I have done no wrong to the **J**,
25:15 and the elders of the **J** informed me about him C
26: 2 against all the accusations of the **J**,
26: 3 with all the customs and controversies of the **J**;
26: 4 "All the **J** know my way of life from my youth, A
26: 7 your Excellency, that I am accused by **J**!
26:21 the **J** seized me in the temple and tried to kill me.
28:17 the local leaders of the **J**.
28:19 But when the **J** objected,
Ro 3: 2 For in the first place the **J** were entrusted with
3: 9 both **J** and Greeks, are under the power of sin,
3:29 Or is God the God of **J** only?
9:24 not from the **J** only but also from the Gentiles?
1Co 1:22 For **J** demand signs and Greeks desire wisdom,
1:23 stumbling block to **J** and foolishness to Gentiles,
1:24 both **J** and Greeks, Christ the power of God and
9:20 To the **J** I became as a Jew, in order to win **J**.
10:32 Give no offense to **J** or to Greeks or to the church
12:13 **J** or Greeks, slaves or free—
2Co 11:24 from the **J** the forty lashes minus one.
Gal 2:13 And the other **J** joined him in this hypocrisy,
2:14 how can you compel the Gentiles to live like **J**?"
2:15 We ourselves are **J** by birth and
1Th 2:14 as they did from the **J**,
Rev 2: 9 the part of those who say that they are **J** and are
3: 9 of the synagogue of Satan who say that they are **J**
Tob 11:17 among all the **J** who were in Nineveh. A
AdE 3: 6 to destroy all the **J** under Artaxerxes' rule. A
3:10 the decree that was to be written against the **J**.
4: 3 of mourning and lamentation among the **J**,
4: 7 to bring about the destruction of the **J**.
4:13 that you alone among all the **J** will escape alive. A
4:14 help and protection will come to the **J**
4:16 "Go and gather all the **J** who are in Susa and A
8: 3 the evil that Haman had planned against the **J**.
8: 5 that Haman wrote and sent to destroy the **J**
8: 7 on a tree because he acted against the **J**,
8: 9 to the **J** was given in writing to the administrators
8:11 the **J** in every city to observe their own laws,
8:13 and let all the **J** be ready on that day to fight A
8:16 And the **J** had light and gladness
8:17 the **J** had joy and gladness,
8:17 and became **J** out of fear of the **J**.
9: 2 On that same day the enemies of the **J** perished;
9: 3 the royal secretaries were paying honor to the **J**,
9: 6 the city of Susa the **J** killed five hundred people,
9:10 the Bougean, the enemy of the **J**—
9:12 the **J** have destroyed five hundred people.
9:13 "Let the **J** be allowed to do the same tomorrow.
9:14 to the **J** of the city the bodies of Haman's sons
9:15 The **J** who were in Susa gathered on
9:16 Now the other **J** in the kingdom gathered
9:18 The **J** who were in Susa, the capital,
9:19 On this account then the **J** who are scattered
9:20 and sent it to the **J** in the kingdom of Artaxerxes
9:22 on these days the **J** got relief from their enemies.
9:23 the **J** accepted what Mordecai had written to them
9:25 against the **J** came back upon himself,
9:27 and the **J** took upon themselves,
10: 3 as well as honored by the **J**.
10: 8 that gathered to destroy the name of the **J**.
16:15 "But we find that the **J**,
16:19 and permit the **J** to live under their own laws.
Sus 1: 4 the **J** used to come to him because he was
1Mc 4: 2 upon the camp of the **J** and attack them suddenly.
4:20 and that the **J** were burning the camp,
5:23 Then he took the **J** of Galilee and Arbatta,
5:30 and attacking the **J** within.
6: 6 but had turned and fled before the **J**;
6: 6 that the **J** had grown strong from the arms,
6:31 but the **J** sallied out and burned these with fire,
6:47 the **J** saw the royal might and the fierce attack of
6:52 The **J** also made engines of war to match theirs,
6:60 and he sent to the **J** an offer of peace,
6:61 On these conditions the **J** evacuated
7:45 The **J** pursued them a day's journey,
7:47 Then the **J** seized the spoils and the plunder;
8:20 of the **J** have sent us to you to establish alliance
8:23 the Romans and with the nation of the **J** at sea D
8:25 the nation of the **J** shall act as their allies D
8:27 if war comes first to the nation of the **J**, D
8:31 on our friends and allies the **J**?
9:40 and the **J** took all their goods.
10:23 ahead of us in forming a friendship with the **J**
10:25 "King Demetrius to the nation of the **J**, D
10:29 free you and exempt all the **J** from payment A
10:33 of the **J** taken as a captive from the land of Judah
10:34 and release for all the **J** who are in my kingdom. A
10:36 "Let **J** be enrolled in the king's forces to
11:30 his brother Jonathan and to the nation of the **J**, D
11:33 to do good to the nation of the **J**, D
11:47 So the king called the **J** to his aid,
11:49 of the city saw that the **J** had gained control of

1Mc 11:50 make the **J** stop fighting against us and our city."
11:51 So the **J** gained glory in the sight of the king and
12:21 the **J** that they are brothers and are of the family
12:26 up in formation to attack the **J** by night.
13:36 and to the elders and nation of the **J**, greetings. D
13:42 and commander and leader of the **J**."
13:51 the **J** entered it with praise and palm branches,
14:22 the **J**, have come to us to renew their friendship
14:33 and he placed there a garrison of **J**.
14:34 He settled **J** there, and provided
14:37 He settled **J** in it and fortified it for the safety of
14:40 the **J** were addressed by the Romans as friends
14:41 "The **J** and their priests have resolved
14:47 be commander and ethnarch of the **J** and priests,
15: 1 the priest and ethnarch of the **J**,
15: 2 and ethnarch and to the nation of the **J**, D
15:17 of the **J** have come to us as our friends and allies
2Mc 1: 1 The **J** in Jerusalem and those in the land of Judea,
1: 7 in the one hundred sixty-ninth year, we **J** wrote
1:10 and to the **J** in Egypt, Greetings and good health.
3:32 that some foul play had been perpetrated by the **J**
4:11 the existing royal concessions to the **J**, secured
4:35 For this reason not only **J**,
4:36 the **J** in the city appealed to him with regard to
4:41 But when the **J** became aware
5:25 then, finding the **J** not at work,
6: 1 the king sent an Athenian senator to compel the **J**
6: 6 nor so much as confess themselves to be **J**.
6: 7 the **J** were taken, under bitter constraint,
6: 8 the **J** and make them partake of the sacrifices,
8:10 by selling the captured **J** into slavery.
8:20 when eight thousand **J** fought along
8:32 and one who had greatly troubled the **J**.
8:34 the thousand merchants to buy the **J**,
8:36 the people of Jerusalem proclaimed that the **J** had
8:36 and that therefore the **J** were invulnerable,
9: 4 the **J** the injury done by those who had put him
9: 4 I get there I will make Jerusalem a cemetery of **J**."
9: 7 breathing fire in his rage against the **J**,
9:15 the **J**, whom he had not considered worth burying
9:18 for himself and wrote to the **J** the following letter,
10: 8 whole nation of the **J** should observe these days D
10:12 to the **J** because of the wrong that had been done
10:14 and at every turn kept attacking the **J**.
10:15 of important strongholds, were harassing the **J**;
10:24 Timothy, who had been defeated by the **J** before,
10:29 and they were leading the **J**.
11: 2 and all his cavalry and came against the **J**.
11:15 of the **J** which Maccabeus delivered to Lysias
11:16 letter written to the **J** by Lysias was to this effect:
11:16 "Lysias to the people of the **J**, greetings.
11:24 that the **J** do not consent to our father's change
11:27 "King Antiochus to the senate of the **J** and to
11:27 to the senate of the Jews and to the other **J**,
11:31 for the **J** to enjoy their own food and laws,
11:34 envoys of the Romans, to the people of the **J**,
12: 1 and the **J** went about their farming.
12: 3 they invited the **J** who lived among them
12: 3 as though there were no ill will to the **J**;
12: 8 the same way to wipe out the **J** who were living
12:17 to the **J** who are called Toubiani.
12:28 But the **J** called upon the Sovereign who
12:30 the **J** who lived there bore witness to the goodwill
12:34 it happened that a few of the **J** fell.
12:40 which the law forbids the **J** to wear.
13: 9 to show the **J** things far worse than those
13:18 king, having had a taste of the daring of the **J**,
13:19 a strong fortress of the **J**, was turned back,
13:21 But Rhodocus, a man from the ranks of the **J**,
13:23 he was dismayed, called in the **J**,
14: 5 about the attitude and intentions of the **J**.
14: 6 "Those of the **J** who are called Hasideans,
14:14 of the **J** would mean prosperity for themselves.
14:15 When the **J** heard of Nicanor's coming and
14:37 of and for his goodwill was called father of the **J**.
14:39 for the **J**, sent more than five hundred soldiers
15: 2 the **J** who were compelled to follow him said,
15:12 for the whole body of the **J**.
1Es 2:18 that the **J** who came up from you to us have gone
2:23 the **J** were rebels and kept setting up blockades
4:49 He wrote in behalf of all the **J** who were going A
4:50 the Idumeans should give up the villages of the **J**
6: 1 of Iddo prophesied to the **J** who were in Judea
6: 5 Yet the elders of the **J** were dealt with kindly, C
6: 8 we found the elders of the **J**, C
6:27 elders of the **J** to build this house of the Lord C
7: 2 assisting the elders of the **J** and the chief officers C
3Mc 1: 8 the **J** had sent some of their council and elders
2:28 and all **J** shall be subjected to a registration A
3: 1 against those **J** who lived in Alexandria,
3: 3 The **J**, however, continued to maintain goodwill
3:27 But those who shelter any of the **J**,
4: 2 But among the **J** there was incessant mourning,
4:17 of the **J** because of their immense number,
4:21 of him who was aiding the **J** from heaven.
5: 2 so that the **J** might meet their doom.
5: 3 the army who were especially hostile toward the **J**.
5: 5 of the **J** went out in the evening and bound
5: 6 For to the Gentiles it appeared that the **J** were left
5:13 Then the **J**, since they had escaped
5:18 the **J** had been allowed to remain alive through
5:20 said that the **J** were benefited by today's sleep,
5:20 the same way for the destruction of the lawless **J**!"
5:25 But the **J**, at their last gasp—
5:31 for the savage animals instead of the **J**,
5:35 Then the **J**, on hearing what the king had said,
5:38 for the destruction of the **J** tomorrow!"
3Mc 5:42 about within him for the protection of the **J**,
5:48 When the **J** saw the dust raised by
6:17 when the **J** observed this they raised great cries
6:18 visible to all but the **J**.
6:29 These then were the things he said; and the **J**,
6:30 the revenues and ordered him to provide to the **J**
6:34 that the **J** would be destroyed and become food
6:35 The **J**, as we have said before,
7: 3 to gather together the **J** of the kingdom in a body
7: 6 that the God of heaven surely defends the **J**,
7:10 On receiving this letter the **J** did
4Mc 5: 7 when you observe the religion of the **J**.

JEWS' (1) [JEW]
3Mc 4:12 hearing that the **J** compatriots from the city

JEZANIAH‡ (1)
Jer 40: 8 **J** son of the Maacathite, they and their troops.

JEZEBEL (22) [JEZEBEL'S]
1Ki 16:31 he took as his wife **J** daughter of King Ethbaal of
18: 4 **J** was killing off the prophets of the LORD,
18:13 not been told my lord what I did when **J** killed
19: 1 Ahab told **J** all that Elijah had done,
19: 2 Then **J** sent a messenger to Elijah, saying,
21: 5 His wife **J** came to him and said,
21: 7 His wife **J** said to him,
21:11 did as **J** had sent word to them.
21:14 they sent to **J**, saying, "Naboth has been stoned;
21:15 As soon as **J** heard that Naboth had been stoned
21:15 **J** said to Ahab, "Go, take possession of
21:23 Also concerning **J** the LORD said,
21:23 dogs shall eat **J** within the bounds of Jezreel.'
21:25 urged on by his wife **J**.
2Ki 9: 7 that I may avenge on **J** the blood of my servants
9:10 The dogs shall eat **J** in the territory of Jezreel,
9:22 and sorceries of your mother **J** continue?"
9:30 When Jehu came to Jezreel, **J** heard of it;
9:36 of Jezreel the dogs shall eat the flesh of **J**;
9:37 of **J** shall be like dung on the field in the territory
9:37 so that no one can say, This is **J**.' "
Rev 2:20 you tolerate that woman **J**,

JEZEBEL'S (1) [JEZEBEL]
1Ki 18:19 of Asherah, who eat at **J** table."

JEZER (3) [JEZERITES]
Ge 46:24 The children of Naphtali: Jahzeel, Guni, **J**,
Nu 26:49 of **J**, the clan of the Jezerites;
1Ch 7:13 The descendants of Naphtali: Jahziel, Guni, **J**,

JEZERITES (1) [JEZER]
Nu 26:49 of Jezer, the clan of the **J**;

JEZIAH (KJV) See IZZIAH

JEZIEL (1)
1Ch 12: 3 also **J** and Pelet sons of Azmaveth;

JEZLIAH (KJV) See IZLIAH

JEZOAR (KJV) See IZHAR

JEZRAHIAH (1)
Ne 12:42 And the singers sang with **J** as their leader.

JEZREEL (40) [JEZREELITE]
Jos 15:56 **J**, Jokdeam, Zanoah,
17:16 and its villages and those in the Valley of **J**."
19:18 Its territory included **J**, Chesulloth, Shunem,
Jdg 6:33 the Jordan they encamped in the Valley of **J**.
1Sa 25:43 David also married Ahinoam of **J**;
27: 3 and David with his two wives, Ahinoam of **J**,
29: 1 by the fountain that is in **J**.
29:11 But the Philistines went up to **J**.
30: 5 Ahinoam of **J**, and Abigail the widow of Nabal
2Sa 2: 2 along with his two wives, Ahinoam of **J**,
2: 9 He made him king over Gilead, the Ashurites, **J**,
3: 2 his firstborn was Amnon, of Ahinoam of **J**;
4: 4 the news about Saul and Jonathan came from **J**.
1Ki 4:12 which is beside Zarethan below **J**,
18:45 Ahab rode off and went to **J**.
18:46 and ran in front of Ahab to the entrance of **J**.
21: 1 Naboth the Jezreelite had a vineyard in **J**,
21:23 dogs shall eat Jezebel within the bounds of **J**.'
2Ki 8:29 King Joram returned to be healed in **J** of
8:29 down to see Joram son of Ahab in **J**,
9:10 The dogs shall eat Jezebel in the territory of **J**,
9:15 but King Joram had returned to be healed in **J** of
9:15 of the city to go and tell the news in **J**."
9:16 Then Jehu mounted his chariot and went to **J**,
9:17 In **J**, the sentinel standing on the tower spied
9:30 When Jehu came to **J**, Jezebel heard of it;
9:36 'In the territory of **J** the dogs shall eat the flesh
9:37 be like dung on the field in the territory of **J**,
10: 1 to the rulers of **J**, to the elders,
10: 6 and come to me at **J** tomorrow at this time."
10: 7 in baskets and sent them to him at **J**.
10:11 of the house of Ahab in **J**,
1Ch 4: 3 These were the sons of Etam: **J**, Ishma,
2Ch 22: 6 in **J** of the wounds that he had received at Ramah,
2Ch 22: 6 down to see Joram son of Ahab in **J**,
Hos 1: 4 And the LORD said to him, "Name him **J**;
1: 4 the house of Jehu for the blood of **J**,
1: 5 the bow of Israel in the valley of **J**."
1:11 for great shall be the day of **J**.
2:22 the wine, and the oil, and they shall answer **J**;

JEZREELITE (9) [JEZREEL]
1Ki 21: 1 Naboth the **J** had a vineyard in Jezreel,
21: 4 and sullen because of what Naboth the **J** had said
21: 6 "Because I spoke to Naboth the **J** and said to him,
21: 7 I will give you the vineyard of Naboth the **J**."
21:15 take possession of the vineyard of Naboth the **J**,
21:16 to go down to the vineyard of Naboth the **J**,
2Ki 9:21 they met him at the property of Naboth the **J**.
9:25 on the plot of ground belonging to Naboth the **J**;
1Ch 3: 1 the firstborn Amnon, by Ahinoam the **J**;

JEZREELITESS (KJV) See [AHINOAM OF] JEZREEL, JEZREELITE

JEZRIELUS (1)
1Es 9:27 Mattaniah and Zechariah, **J** and Abdi,

JIBSAM (KJV) See IBSAM

JIDLAPH (1)
Ge 22:22 Chesed, Hazo, Pildash, **J**, and Bethuel."

JIMNA, JIMNAH (KJV) See IMNAH

JIMNITES (KJV) See IMNITE

JIPHTAH (KJV) See IPHTAH

JIPHTHAH-EL (KJV) See IPHTAH-EL

JIREH See Index to Footnotes

JOAB (142) [JOAB'S]
2Sa 2:13 **J** son of Zeruiah, and the servants of David,
2:14 to **J**, "Let the young men come forward and have
2:14 **J** said, "Let them come forward."
2:18 The three sons of Zeruiah were there, **J**, Abishai,
2:22 then could I show my face to your brother **J**?"
2:24 But **J** and Abishai pursued Abner.
2:26 Then Abner called to **J**, "Is the sword
2:27 **J** said, "As God lives, if you had not spoken,
2:28 **J** sounded the trumpet and all the people stopped;
2:30 **J** returned from the pursuit of Abner;
2:32 **J** and his men marched all night,
3:22 the servants of David arrived with **J** from a raid,
3:23 When **J** and all the army that was with him came,
3:23 it was told **J**, "Abner son of Ner came to the king,
3:24 Then **J** went to the king and said,
3:26 When **J** came out from David's presence,
3:27 **J** took him aside in the gateway to speak
3:29 May the guilt fall on the head of **J**,
3:29 of **J** never be without one who has a discharge,
3:30 So **J** and his brother Abishai murdered Abner
3:31 to **J** and to all the people who were with him,
8:16 **J** son of Zeruiah was over the army;
10: 7 he sent **J** and all the army with the warriors.
10: 9 When **J** saw that the battle was set against him
10:13 So **J** and the people who were
10:14 **J** returned from fighting against the Ammonites,
11: 1 David sent **J** with his officers and all Israel
11: 6 So David sent word to **J**,
11: 6 And **J** sent Uriah to David.
11: 7 David asked how **J** and the people fared,
11:11 and my lord **J** and the servants
11:14 In the morning David wrote a letter to **J**,
11:16 As **J** was besieging the city,
11:17 The men of the city came out and fought with **J**;
11:18 Then **J** sent and told David all the news about
11:22 and came and told David all that **J** had sent him
11:25 "Thus you shall say to **J**,
12:26 Now **J** fought against Rabbah of the Ammonites,
12:27 **J** sent messengers to David, and said,
14: 1 Now **J** son of Zeruiah perceived that
14: 2 **J** sent to Tekoa and brought from there
14: 3 And **J** put the words into her mouth.
14:19 king said, "Is the hand of **J** with you in all this?"
14:19 For it was your servant **J** who commanded me;
14:20 the course of affairs your servant **J** did this.
14:21 Then the king said to **J**, "Very well, I grant this;
14:22 **J** prostrated himself with his face to the ground
14:22 and **J** said, "Today your servant knows
14:23 So **J** set off, went to Geshur,
14:29 Then Absalom sent for **J** to send him to the king;
14:29 but **J** would not come to him.
14:29 He sent a second time, but **J** would not come.
14:31 Then **J** rose and went to Absalom at his house,
14:32 Absalom answered **J**, "Look, I sent word to you:
14:33 Then **J** went to the king and told him;
17:25 over the army in the place of **J**.
18: 2 one third under the command of **J**,
18: 5 The king ordered **J** and Abishai and Ittai, saying,
18:10 A man saw it, and told **J**,
18:11 **J** said to the man who told him, "What,
18:12 But the man said to **J**, "Even if I felt in my hand

2Sa 18:14 J said, "I will not waste time like this with you."
18:16 Then J sounded the trumpet,
18:16 for J restrained the troops.
18:20 J said to him, "You are not to carry tidings today;
18:21 Then J said to a Cushite, "Go,
18:21 The Cushite bowed before J, and ran.
18:22 Then Ahimaaz son of Zadok said again to J,
18:22 And J said, "Why will you run, my son,
18:29 Ahimaaz answered, "When J sent your servant,
19: 1 It was told J, "The king is weeping and mourning
19: 5 Then J came into the house to the king, and said,
19:13 of my army from now on, in place of J.' "
20: 8 Now J was wearing a soldier's garment and
20: 9 J said to Amasa, "Is it well with you,
20: 9 And J took Amasa by the beard
20:10 J struck him in the belly so that his entrails
20:10 Then J and his brother Abishai pursued Sheba
20:11 "Whoever favors J, and whoever is for David,
20:11 and whoever is for David, let him follow J."
20:13 all the people went on after J to pursue Sheba son
20:16 Tell J, 'Come here, I want to speak to you.' "
20:17 and the woman said, "Are you J?"
20:20 J answered, "Far be it from me, far be it,
20:21 The woman said to J, "His head shall be thrown
20:22 and threw it out to J.
20:22 while J returned to Jerusalem to the king.
20:23 Now J was in command of all the army of Israel;
23:18 Now Abishai son of Zeruiah, the brother of J,
23:24 Among the Thirty were Asahel brother of J;
23:37 the armor-bearer of J son of Zeruiah;
24: 2 king said to J and the commanders of the army,
24: 3 But J said to the king,
24: 4 But the king's word prevailed against J and
24: 4 So J and the commanders of the army went out
24: 9 J reported to the king the number
1Ki 1: 7 He conferred with J son of Zeruiah and with
1:19 and J the commander of the army;
1:25 J the commander of the army,
1:41 When J heard the sound of the trumpet, he said,
2: 5 you know also what J son of Zeruiah did to me,
2:22 for the priest Abiathar and for J son of Zeruiah!"
2:28 When the news came to J—
2:28 for J had supported Adonijah though he had
2:28 J fled to the tent of the LORD and grasped
2:29 "J has fled to the tent of the LORD and now is
2:30 saying, "Thus said J, and thus he answered me."
2:31 the guilt for the blood that J shed without cause.
2:33 of J and on the head of his descendants forever;
11:15 and J the commander of the army went up to bury
11:16 (for J and all Israel remained there six months,
11:21 and that J the commander of the army was dead,
1Ch 2:16 sons of Zeruiah: Abishai, J, and Asahel, three.
4:14 and Seraiah became the father of J father
11: 6 And J son of Zeruiah went up first,
11: 8 and J repaired the rest of the city.
11:20 Abishai, the brother of J, was chief of the Thirty.
11:26 warriors of the armies were Asahel brother of J,
11:39 the armor-bearer of J son of Zeruiah,
18:15 J son of Zeruiah was over the army;
19: 8 he sent J and all the army of the warriors.
19:10 When J saw that the line of battle was set
19:14 So J and the troops who were with him advanced
19:15 Then J came to Jerusalem.
20: 1 to battle, J led out the army, ravaged the country
20: 1 J attacked Rabbah, and overthrew it.
21: 2 David said to J and the commanders of the army,
21: 3 But J said, "May the LORD increase the number
21: 4 But the king's word prevailed against J.
21: 4 So J departed and went throughout all Israel,
21: 5 J gave the total count of the people to David.
21: 6 for the king's command was abhorrent to J.
26:28 and J son of Zeruiah had dedicated—
27: 7 Asahel brother of J was fourth,
27:24 J son of Zeruiah began to count them,
27:34 J was commander of the king's army.
Ezr 2: 6 namely the descendants of Jeshua and J,
8: 9 Of the descendants of J, Obadiah son of Jehiel,
Ne 7:11 namely the descendants of Jeshua and J,
Ps 60: T *and when J on his return killed twelve thousand*
1Es 5:11 of the descendants of Jeshua and J,
8:35 Of the descendants of J, Obadiah son of Jehiel,

JOAB'S (12) [JOAB]

1Sa 26: 6 and to J brother Abishai son of Zeruiah,
2Sa 3:27 for shedding the blood of Asahel, J brother.
14:30 J field is next to mine, and he has barley there;
17:25 sister of Zeruiah, J mother.
18: 2 of Abishai son of Zeruiah, J brother,
18:15 And ten young men, J armor-bearers,
20: 7 J men went out after him,
20:10 But Amasa did not notice the sword in J hand;
20:11 And one of J men took his stand by Amasa,
20:15 J forces came and besieged him in Abel
20:15 J forces were battering the wall to break it down.
1Ch 19:15 they likewise fled before Abishai, J brother,

JOAH (11)

2Ki 18:18 and Shebnah the secretary, and J son of Asaph,
18:26 and Shebnah, and J said to the Rabshakeh,
18:37 and Shebna the secretary, and J son of Asaph,
1Ch 6:21 J his son, Iddo his son, Zerah his son,
26: 4 J the third, Sachar the fourth, Nethanel the fifth,
2Ch 29:12 Gershonites, J son of Zimmah, and Eden son of J;
34: 8 and J son of Joahaz, the recorder,
Isa 36: 3 and Shebna the secretary, and J son of Asaph,
36:11 Eliakim, Shebna, and J said to the Rabshakeh,
36:22 and Shebna the secretary, and J son of Asaph,

JOAHAZ (2) [=JEHOAHAZ]

2Ki 14: 1 the second year of King Joash son of J of Israel,
2Ch 34: 8 and Joah son of J, the recorder,

JOAKIM (10) [JOAKIM'S]

Jdt 4: 6 J, who was in Jerusalem at the time,
4: 8 as they had been ordered by the high priest J and
4:14 The high priest J and all the priests who stood
15: 8 Then the high priest J and the elders of
Sus 1: 1 a man living in Babylon whose name was J.
1: 4 J was very rich, and had a fine garden
1:28 people gathered at the house of her husband J,
1:29 for Susanna daughter of Hilkiah, the wife of J."
1:63 and so did her husband J and all her relatives,
1Es 5: 5 Jeshua son of Jozadak son of Seraiah and J son

JOAKIM'S (1) [JOAKIM]

Sus 1: 6 These men were frequently at J house,

JOANAN (1)

Lk 3:27 son of J, son of Rhesa, son of Zerubbabel, son

JOANNA (2)

Lk 8: 3 and J, the wife of Herod's steward Chuza,
24:10 Now it was Mary Magdalene, J,

JOARIB (2)

1Mc 2: 1 a priest of the family of J,
14:29 Simon son of Mattathias, a priest of the sons of J,

JOASH‡ (50) [=JEHOASH]

Jdg 6:11 which belonged to J the Abiezrite,
6:29 they were told, "Gideon son of J did it."
6:30 Then the townspeople said to J,
6:31 But J said to all who were arrayed against him,
7:14 the sword of Gideon son of J, a man of Israel;
8:13 When Gideon son of J returned from the battle by
8:29 Jerubbaal son of J went to live in his own house.
8:32 Then Gideon son of J died at a good old age,
8:32 of his father J at Ophrah of the Abiezrites.
1Ki 22:26 the governor of the city and to J the king's son,
2Ki 11: 2 Ahaziah's sister, took J son of Ahaziah,
12:19 Now the rest of the acts of J, and all that he did,
12:20 and killed J in the house of Millo,
13: 1 In the twenty-third year of King J son of Ahaziah
13: 9 then his son J succeeded him.
13:10 In the thirty-seventh year of King J of Judah,
13:12 Now the rest of the acts of J, and all that he did,
13:13 So J slept with his ancestors,
13:13 J was buried in Samaria with the kings of Israel.
13:14 King J of Israel went down to him,
13:25 Three times J defeated him and recovered
14: 1 the second year of King J son of Joahaz of Israel,
14: 1 King Amaziah son of J of Judah, began to reign.
14: 3 in all things he did as his father J had done.
14:17 of J of Judah lived fifteen years after the death
14:23 In the fifteenth year of King Amaziah son of J
14:23 King Jeroboam son of J of Israel began to reign
14:27 he saved them by the hand of Jeroboam son of J.
1Ch 3:11 Joram his son, Ahaziah his son, J his son,
4:22 and the men of Cozeba, and J, and Saraph,
7: 8 Zemirah, J, Eliezer, Elioenai, Omri, Jeremoth,
12: 3 The chief was Ahiezer, then J,
27:28 Over the stores of oil was J.
2Ch 18:25 the governor of the city and to J the king's son;
22:11 the king's daughter, took J son of Ahaziah,
24: 1 J was seven years old when he began to reign;
24: 2 J did what was right in the sight of the LORD all
24: 4 Some time afterward J decided to restore
24:22 King J did not remember the kindness
24:23 of the year the army of Aram came up against J.
24:24 Thus they executed judgment on J.
25:17 to King J son of Jehoahaz son of Jehu of Israel,
25:18 King J of Israel sent word to King Amaziah
25:21 So King J of Israel went up;
25:23 King J of Israel captured King Amaziah of Judah,
25:23 son of J, son of Ahaziah, at Beth-shemesh;
25:25 King Amaziah son of J of Judah,
25:25 lived fifteen years after the death of King J son
Hos 1: 1 in the days of King Jeroboam son of J of Israel.
Am 1: 1 in the days of King Jeroboam son of J of Israel,

JOATHAM (KJV) See JOTHAM

JOB (59) [JOB'S]

Job 1: 1 a man in the land of Uz whose name was J.
1: 5 J would send and sanctify them,
1: 5 for J said, "It may be that my children have sinned,
1: 5 This is what J always did.
1: 8 "Have you considered my servant J?
1: 9 "Does J fear God for nothing?
1:14 a messenger came to J and said,
1:20 Then J arose, tore his robe, shaved his head,
1:22 In all this J did not sin or charge God
2: 3 "Have you considered my servant J?
2: 7 and inflicted loathsome sores on J from the sole
2: 8 J took a potsherd with which to scrape himself,
2:10 In all this J did not sin with his lips.
3: 1 After this J opened his mouth and cursed the day
3: 2 J said:
6: 1 Then J answered:
9: 1 Then J answered:
12: 1 Then J answered:
16: 1 Then J answered:
19: 1 Then J answered:
21: 1 Then J answered:
23: 1 Then J answered:
26: 1 Then J answered:
27: 1 J again took up his discourse and said:
29: 1 J again took up his discourse and said:
31:40 The words of J are ended.
32: 1 So these three men ceased to answer J,
32: 2 at J because he justified himself rather than God;
32: 3 though they had declared J to be in the wrong.
32: 4 Now Elihu had waited to speak to J,
32:12 but there was in fact no one that confuted J,
33: 1 hear my speech, O J, and listen to all my words.
33:31 Pay heed, J, listen to me;
34: 5 For J has said, 'I am innocent,
34: 7 Who is there like J, who drinks up scoffing
34:35 'J speaks without knowledge,
34:36 Would that J were tried to the limit,
35:16 J opens his mouth in empty talk,
37:14 "Hear this, O J; stop
38: 1 the LORD answered J out of the whirlwind:
40: 1 And the LORD said to J:
40: 3 Then J answered the LORD:
40: 6 the LORD answered J out of the whirlwind:
42: 1 Then J answered the LORD:
42: 7 After the LORD had spoken these words to J,
42: 7 spoken of me what is right, as my servant J has.
42: 8 go to my servant J, and offer up for yourselves
42: 8 and my servant J shall pray for you,
42: 8 of me what is right, as my servant J has done."
42:10 And the LORD restored the fortunes of J
42:10 LORD gave J twice as much as he had before.
42:12 the latter days of J more than his beginning;
42:16 After this J lived one hundred and forty years,
42:17 And J died, old and full of days.
Eze 14:14 Daniel, and J, these three, were in it,
14:20 and J were in it, as I live, says the Lord GOD,
Jas 5:11 You have heard of the endurance of J,
Sir 11:21 but trust in the Lord and keep at your j;
49: 9 also mentioned J who held fast to all the ways

JOB'S (4) [JOB]

Job 2:11 when J three friends heard of all these troubles
32: 3 he was angry also at J three friends
42: 9 and the LORD accepted J prayer.
42:15 no women so beautiful as J daughters;

JOBAB (9)

Ge 10:29 and J; all these were the descendants of Joktan.
36:33 J son of Zerah of Bozrah succeeded him as king.
36:34 J died, and Husham of the land of
Jos 11: 1 he sent to King J of Madon,
1Ch 1:23 and J; all these were the descendants of Joktan.
1:44 J son of Zerah of Bozrah succeeded him.
1:45 When J died, Husham of the land of
8: 9 He had sons by his wife Hodesh: J, Zibia, Mesha,
8:18 Ishmerai, Izliah, and J were the sons of Elpaal.

JOCHEBED (2)

Ex 6:20 Amram married J his father's sister
Nu 26:59 name of Amram's wife was J daughter of Levi,

JODA (2)

Lk 3:26 son of Semein, son of Josech, son of J,
1Es 5:58 of Jeshua Emadabun and the sons of J son

JODAN (1)

1Es 9:19 Maaseiah, Eliezar, Jarib, and J.

JOED (1)

Ne 11: 7 of Meshullam son of J son of Pedaiah son

JOEL‡ (24)

1Sa 8: 2 The name of his firstborn son was J,
1Ch 4:35 J, Jehu son of Joshibiah son of Seraiah son
5: 4 The sons of J: Shemaiah his son,
5: 8 son of Shema, son of J, who lived in Aroer,
5:12 J the chief, Shapham the second, Janai,
6:28 J his firstborn, the second Abijah.
6:33 Heman, the singer, son of J, son of Samuel,
6:36 son of J, son of Azariah, son of Zephaniah,
7: 3 And the sons of Izrahiah: Michael, Obadiah, J,
11:38 J the brother of Nathan, Mibhar son of Hagri,
15: 7 J the chief, with one hundred thirty
15:11 and the Levites Uriel, Asaiah, J, Shemaiah, Eliel,
15:17 So the Levites appointed Heman son of J;
23: 8 Jehiel the chief, Zetham, and J, three.
26:22 The sons of Jehieli, Zetham and his brother J,
27:20 for the half-tribe of Manasseh, J son of Pedaiah;
2Ch 29:12 Mahath son of Amasai, and J son of Azariah,
Ezr 10:43 Jeiel, Mattithiah, Zabad, Zebina, Jaddai, J,
Ne 11: 9 J son of Zichri was their overseer;
Joel 1: 1 word of the LORD that came to J son of Pethuel:
Ac 2:16 this is what was spoken through the prophet J:
1Es 9:34 Jeremai, Momdius, Maerus, J,
9:35 Mazitias, Zabad, Iddo, J, Benaiah.
2Es 1:39 and Amos and Micah and J and Obadiah

JOELAH (1)
1Ch 12: 7 and **J** and Zebadiah, sons of Jeroham of Gedor.

JOEZER (1)
1Ch 12: 6 Isshiah, Azarel, **J**, and Jashobeam, the Korahites;

JOGBEHAH (2)
Nu 32:35 Atroth-shophan, Jazer, **J**,
Jdg 8:11 up by the caravan route east of Nobah and **J**,

JOGLI (1)
Nu 34:22 the tribe of the Danites a leader, Bukki son of **J**.

JOHA (2)
1Ch 8:16 Michael, Ishpah, and **J** were sons of Beriah.
11:45 Jediael son of Shimri, and his brother **J** the Tizite,

JOHANAN (27) [=JEHOHANAN]
2Ki 25:23 Ishmael son of Nethaniah, **J** son of Kareah,
1Ch 3:15 **J** the firstborn, the second Jehoiakim,
3:24 Hodaviah, Eliashib, Pelaiah, Akkub, **J**, Delaiah,
6: 9 Ahimaaz of Azariah, Azariah of **J**,
6:10 and **J** of Azariah (it was he who served as priest
12: 4 Jeremiah, Jahaziel, **J**, Jozabad of Gederah,
12:12 **J** eighth, Elzabad ninth,
2Ch 28:12 Azariah son of **J**, Berechiah son of Meshillemoth,
Ezr 8:12 Of the descendants of Azgad, **J** son of Hakkatan,
Ne 12:22 for the Levites, in the days of Eliashib, Joiada, **J**,
12:23 in the Book of the Annals until the days of **J** son
Jer 40: 8 Ishmael son of Nethaniah, **J** son of Kareah,
40:13 Now **J** son of Kareah and all the leaders of
40:15 Then **J** son of Kareah spoke secretly to Gedaliah
40:16 Gedaliah son of Ahikam said to **J** son of Kareah,
41:11 But when **J** son of Kareah and all the leaders of
41:13 the people who were with Ishmael saw **J** son
41:14 and went to **J** son of Kareah.
41:15 But Ishmael son of Nethaniah escaped from **J**
41:16 Then **J** son of Kareah and all the leaders of
41:16 and eunuchs, whom **J** brought back from Gibeon.
42: 1 **J** son of Kareah and Azariah son of Hoshaiah,
42: 8 Then he summoned **J** son of Kareah and all
43: 2 Azariah son of Hoshaiah and **J** son of Kareah
43: 4 So **J** son of Kareah and all the commanders of
43: 5 But **J** son of Kareah and all the commanders of
1Es 8:38 Of the descendants of Azgad, **J** son of Hakkatan,

JOHN (148) [=GADDI, JOHN'S]
Mt 3: 1 In those days **J** the Baptist appeared in
3: 4 Now **J** wore clothing of camel's hair with
3:13 Then Jesus came from Galilee to **J** at the Jordan,
3:14 **J** would have prevented him, saying,
4:12 Now when Jesus heard that **J** had been arrested,
4:21 James son of Zebedee and his brother **J**,
9:14 Then the disciples of **J** came to him, saying,
10: 2 James son of Zebedee, and his brother **J**;
11: 2 **J** heard in prison what the Messiah was doing,
11: 4 "Go and tell **J** what you hear and see:
11: 7 Jesus began to speak to the crowds about **J**:
11:11 of women no one has arisen greater than **J**
11:12 the days of **J** the Baptist until now the kingdom
11:13 the prophets and the law prophesied until **J** came;
11:18 For **J** came neither eating nor drinking,
14: 2 and he said to his servants, "This is **J** the Baptist;
14: 3 For Herod had arrested **J**, bound him,
14: 4 because **J** had been telling him,
14: 8 the head of **J** the Baptist here on a platter."
14:10 he sent and had **J** beheaded in the prison.
16:14 And they said, "Some say **J** the Baptist,
17: 1 and James and his brother **J** and led them up
17:13 that he was speaking to them about **J** the Baptist.
21:25 Did the baptism of **J** come from heaven,
21:26 for all regard **J** as a prophet."
21:32 For **J** came to you in the way of righteousness
Mk 1: 4 **J** the baptizer appeared in the wilderness,
1: 6 Now **J** was clothed with camel's hair,
1: 9 from Nazareth of Galilee and was baptized by **J**
1:14 Now after **J** was arrested, Jesus came to Galilee,
1:19 he saw James son of Zebedee and his brother **J**,
1:29 of Simon and Andrew, with James and **J**.
3:17 James son of Zebedee and **J** the brother of James
5:37 James, and **J**, the brother of James.
6:14 "**J** the baptizer has been raised from the dead;
6:16 But when Herod heard of it, he said, "**J**,
6:17 For Herod himself had sent men who arrested **J**,
6:18 For **J** had been telling Herod,
6:20 for Herod feared **J**, knowing that he was
6:24 She replied, "The head of **J** the baptizer."
6:25 to give me at once the head of **J** the Baptist on
8:28 And they answered him, "**J** the Baptist;
9: 2 Jesus took with him Peter and James and **J**,
9:38 **J** said to him, "Teacher, we saw someone casting
10:35 James and **J**, the sons of Zebedee,
10:41 they began to be angry with James and **J**.
11:30 Did the baptism of **J** come from heaven,
11:32 for all regarded **J** as truly a prophet.
13: 3 Peter, James, **J**, and Andrew asked him privately,
14:33 He took with him Peter and James and **J**,
Lk 1:13 and you will name him **J**.
1:60 But his mother said, "No; he is to be called **J**."
1:63 for a writing tablet and wrote, "His name is **J**."
3: 2 the word of God came to **J** son of Zechariah in
3: 7 **J** said to the crowds that came out to be baptized
3:15 all were questioning in their hearts concerning **J**,
Lk 3:16 **J** answered all of them by saying, "I baptize you
3:20 added to them all by shutting up **J** in prison.
5:10 and so also were James and **J**,
6:14 and James, and **J**, and Philip, and Bartholomew,
7:18 The disciples of **J** reported all these things to him.
7:18 So **J** summoned two of his disciples
7:20 they said, "**J** the Baptist has sent us to you to ask,
7:22 "Go and tell **J** what you have seen and heard:
7:24 Jesus began to speak to the crowds about **J**:
7:28 of women no one is greater than **J**;
7:33 For **J** the Baptist has come eating no bread
8:51 **J**, and James, and the child's father and mother.
9: 7 by some that **J** had been raised from the dead,
9: 9 Herod said, "**J** I beheaded;
9:19 They answered, "**J** the Baptist;
9:28 with him Peter and **J** and James,
9:49 **J** answered, "Master, we saw someone casting out
9:54 When his disciples James and **J** saw it, they said,
11: 1 "Lord, teach us to pray, as **J** taught his disciples."
16:16 law and the prophets were in effect until **J** came;
20: 4 Did the baptism of **J** come from heaven,
20: 6 for they are convinced that **J** was a prophet."
22: 8 So Jesus sent Peter and **J**, saying,
Jn 1: 6 a man sent from God, whose name was **J**.
1:15 (**J** testified to him and cried out,
1:19 by **J** when the Jews sent priests and Levites
1:26 **J** answered them, "I baptize with water.
1:28 across the Jordan where **J** was baptizing.
1:32 And **J** testified, "I saw the Spirit descending
1:35 The next day **J** again was standing with two
1:40 One of the two who heard **J** speak
1:42 "You are Simon son of **J**.
3:23 **J** also was baptizing at Aenon near Salim
3:24 **J**, of course, had not yet been thrown into prison.
3:26 They came to **J** and said to him, "Rabbi,
3:27 **J** answered, "No one can receive anything except
4: 1 making and baptizing more disciples than **J**"
5:33 You sent messengers to **J**,
10:40 to the place where **J** had been baptizing earlier,
10:41 and they were saying, "**J** performed no sign,
10:41 everything that **J** said about this man was true."
21:15 Jesus said to Simon Peter, "Simon son of **J**,
21:16 A second time he said to him, "Simon son of **J**,
21:17 He said to him the third time, "Simon son of **J**,
Ac 1: 5 for **J** baptized with water,
1:13 Peter, and **J**, and James, and Andrew,
1:22 the baptism of **J** until the day when he was taken
3: 1 One day Peter and **J** were going up to the temple
3: 3 he saw Peter and **J** about to go into the temple,
3: 4 Peter looked intently at him, as did **J**, and said,
3:11 While he clung to Peter and **J**,
4: 1 While Peter and **J** were speaking to the people,
4: 6 Caiaphas, **J**, and Alexander,
4:13 Now when they saw the boldness of Peter and **J**
4:19 But Peter and **J** answered them,
8:14 they sent Peter and **J** to them.
8:17 Then Peter and **J** laid their hands on them,
8:25 Now after Peter and **J** had testified and spoken
10:37 in Galilee after the baptism that **J** announced:
11:16 how he had said, '**J** baptized with water,
12: 2 He had James, the brother of **J**,
12:12 the mother of **J** whose other name was Mark,
12:25 to Jerusalem and brought with them **J**,
13: 5 And they had **J** also to assist them.
13:13 **J**, however, left them and returned to Jerusalem;
13:24 before his coming **J** had already proclaimed
13:25 And as **J** was finishing his work, he said,
15:37 to take with them **J** called Mark.
18:25 though he knew only the baptism of **J**.
19: 4 "**J** baptized with the baptism of repentance,
Gal 2: 9 and when James and Cephas and **J**,
Rev 1: 1 by sending his angel to his servant **J**,
1: 4 **J** to the seven churches that are in Asia:
1: 9 **J**, your brother who share with you in Jesus
22: 8 I, **J**, am the one who heard and saw these things.
1Mc 2: 1 In those days Mattathias son of **J** son of Simeon,
2: 2 He had five sons, **J** surnamed Gaddi,
8:17 So Judas chose Eupolemus son of **J** son of Accos,
9:36 of Jambri from Medeba came out and seized **J**
9:38 how their brother **J** had been killed,
13:53 Simon saw that his son **J** had reached manhood,
16: 1 **J** went up from Gazara and reported
16: 2 Simon called in his two eldest sons Judas and **J**,
16: 4 So **J** chose out of the country twenty thousand
16: 9 At that time Judas the brother of **J** was wounded,
16: 9 **J** pursued them until Cendebeus reached Kedron,
16:10 and **J** burned it with fire,
16:19 to Gazara to do away with **J**;
16:21 ahead and reported to **J** at Gazara that his father
16:23 of **J** and his wars and the brave deeds that he did,
2Mc 4:11 secured through **J** the father of Eupolemus,
11:17 **J** and Absalom, who were sent by you,

JOHN'S (9) [JOHN]
Mk 2:18 Now **J** disciples and the Pharisees were fasting;
2:18 to him, "Why do **J** disciples and the disciples of
6:27 a soldier of the guard with orders to bring **J** head.
Lk 5:33 Then they said to him, "**J** disciples,
7:24 When **J** messengers had gone,
7:29 because they had been baptized with **J** baptism.
Jn 3:25 about purification arose between **J** disciples and
5:36 But I have a testimony greater than **J**.
Ac 19: 3 They answered, "Into **J** baptism."

JOIADA (4)
Ne 3: 6 **J** son of Paseah and Meshullam son
Ne 12:10 the father of Eliashib, Eliashib the father of **J**,
12:11 **J** the father of Jonathan, and Jonathan the father
12:22 As for the Levites, in the days of Eliashib, **J**,

JOIAKIM (4)
Ne 12:10 Jeshua was the father of **J**, **J** the father of Eliashib,
12:12 In the days of **J** the priests,
12:26 These were in the days of **J** son of Jeshua son

JOIARIB (5) [=JEHOIARIB]
Ezr 8:16 who were leaders, and for **J** and Elnathan,
Ne 11: 5 of Adaiah son of **J** son of Zechariah son of
11:10 Of the priests: Jedaiah son of **J**, Jachin,
12: 6 Shemaiah, **J**, Jedaiah,
12:19 of **J**, Mattenai; of Jedaiah, Uzzi;

JOIN (41) [ADJOINING, JOINED, JOINING]
Ex 1:10 **j** our enemies and fight against us and escape
12: 4 it shall **j** its closest neighbor in obtaining one;
23: 1 You shall not **j** hands with the wicked to act as
26: 6 and **j** the curtains to one another with the clasps,
26: 9 You shall **j** five curtains by themselves,
26:11 of bronze, and put the clasps into the loops, and **j**
36:18 of bronze to **j** the tent together so that it might
Jos 23:12 and **j** the survivors of these nations left here
1Sa 13: 4 the people were called out to **j** Saul at Gilgal.
13:15 rest of the people followed Saul to **j** the army;
2Sa 23:13 the thirty chiefs went down to **j** David at the cave
1Ki 5: 6 My servants will **j** your servants,
2Ch 2: 7 to **j** the skilled workers who are with me in Judah
Ne 10:29 **j** with their kin, their nobles, and enter into
Job 16: 4 I could **j** words together against you,
Isa 5: 8 Ah, you who **j** house to house,
14: 1 and aliens will **j** them and attach themselves to
56: 6 the foreigners who **j** themselves to the LORD,
Jer 3:18 In those days the house of Judah shall **j** the house
50: 5 and they shall come and **j** themselves to
Eze 37:17 and **j** them together into one stick,
45:16 All the people of the land shall **j** with the prince
Da 11:34 and many shall **j** them insincerely.
Zec 2:11 Many nations shall **j** themselves to the LORD on
Ac 5:13 None of the rest dared to **j** them,
8:29 "Go over to this chariot and **j** it."
9:26 he attempted to **j** the disciples;
17:15 to have Silas and Timothy **j** him as soon
21:24 **J** these men, go through the rite of purification
Ro 15:30 to **j** me in earnest prayer to God on my behalf,
2Co 1:11 as you also **j** in helping us by your prayers,
Php 3:17 Brothers and sisters, **j** in imitating me,
2Ti 1: 8 but **j** with me in suffering for the gospel,
1Pe 4: 4 They are surprised that you no longer **j** them in
Jdt 1:11 and refused to **j** him in the war;
12:11 in your care to **j** us and to eat and drink with us.
AdE 9:27 and upon all who would **j** them,
Wis 5:20 and creation will **j** with him to fight
1Mc 13:14 and that he was about to **j** battle with him,
2Mc 14:14 who had fled before Judas, flocked to **j** Nicanor,
3Mc 2:30 of them prefer to **j** those who have been initiated

JOINED‡ (74) [JOIN]
Ge 14: 3 All these **j** forces in the Valley of Siddim (that is,
14: 8 and they **j** battle in the Valley of Siddim
29:34 "Now this time my husband will be **j** to me,
49: 6 may I not be **j** to their company—
Ex 26: 3 Five curtains shall be **j** to one another;
26: 3 the other five curtains shall be **j** to one another.
26:24 but **j** at the top, at the first ring;
28: 7 so that it may be **j** together.
36:10 He **j** five curtains to one another,
36:10 and the other five curtains he **j** to one another.
36:13 and **j** the curtains one to the other with clasps;
36:16 He **j** five curtains by themselves,
36:29 They were separate beneath, but **j** at the top,
39: 4 **j** to it at its two edges.
Nu 18: 2 in order that they may be **j** to you,
Jos 11: 5 All these kings **j** their forces,
1Sa 4: 2 and when the battle was **j**,
14:21 into the camp turned and **j** the Israelites who were
1Ki 6:10 and it was **j** to the house with timbers of cedar.
2Ki 23: 3 All the people **j** in the covenant.
2Ch 3:12 was **j** to the wing of the first cherub.
20:35 of Judah **j** with King Ahaziah of Israel,
20:36 He **j** him in building ships to go to Tarshish;
20:37 saying, "Because you have **j** with Ahaziah,
35:22 but **j** battle in the plain of Megiddo.
Ezr 6:21 by all who had **j** them and separated themselves
Ne 4: 6 and all the wall was **j** together to half its height;
11:36 of the Levites in Judah were **j** to Benjamin.
Est 9:27 and their descendants and all who **j** them,
Job 41:17 They are **j** one to another;
Ps 83: 8 Assyria also has **j** them; they are the strong arm
Ecc 9: 4 But whoever is **j** with all the living has hope,
Isa 14:20 You will not be **j** with them in burial,
56: 3 Do not let the foreigner **j** to the LORD say,
Hos 4:17 Ephraim is **j** to idols—let him alone.
Ob 1:13 not have **j** in the gloating over Judah's disaster on
Mt 19: 5 a man shall leave his father and mother and be **j**
19: 6 what God has **j** together, let no one separate."
Mk 10: 7 a man shall leave his father and mother and be **j**
10: 9 what God has **j** together, let no one separate."
Ac 5:36 and a number of men, about four hundred, **j** him;
16:22 The crowd **j** in attacking them,
17: 4 of them were persuaded and **j** Paul and Silas,
17:34 But some of them **j** him and became believers,
20: 6 and in five days we **j** them in Troas,

Ac 23:12 the Jews j in a conspiracy and bound themselves
23:13 There were more than forty who j
24: 9 The Jews also j in the charge by asserting
Gal 2:13 And the other Jews j him in this hypocrisy,
Eph 2:21 In him the whole structure is j together and grows
4:16 j and knit together by every ligament
5:31 a man will leave his father and mother and be j
Jdt 1: 6 Thus, many nations j the forces of the Chaldeans.
7: 1 and all the allies who had j him,
14:10 So he was circumcised, and j the house of Israel,
1Mc 1:15 They j with the Gentiles and sold themselves
1:52 everyone who forsook the law, j them,
2:43 to escape their troubles j them
3: 2 and all who had j his father helped him;
3:41 from Syria and the land of the Philistines j
6:21 and some of the ungodly Israelites j them.
7:22 and all who were troubling their people j him.
7:39 and the Syrian army j him.
11:69 in ambush emerged from their places and j battle.
11:73 to him and j him in the pursuit as far as Kadesh,
15:14 and the ships j battle from the sea;
2Mc 8:23 the first division himself, he j battle with Nicanor.
10:28 the two armies j battle, the one having as pledge
12:34 When they j battle, it happened that a few of
13: 3 Menelaus also j them and
13:12 When they had all j in the same petition
1Es 1:29 He j battle with him in the plain of Megiddo,
5:50 some j them from the other peoples of the land.
7: 6 rest of those who returned from exile who j them,

JOINING (3) [JOIN]

Ex 28:27 at its j above the decorated band of the ephod.
39:20 at its j above the decorated band of the ephod.
4Mc 9:21 the ligaments j his bones were already severed,

JOINT (4) [JOINT-DISLOCATORS, JOINTED, JOINTS]

Ge 32:25 and Jacob's hip was put out of j as he wrestled
Ps 22:14 and all my bones are out of j;
Ro 8:17 then heirs, heirs of God and j heirs with Christ—
Heb 12:13 so that what is lame may not be put out of j,

JOINT-DISLOCATORS (1) [DISLOCATED, JOINT]

4Mc 8:13 the guards had placed before them wheels and j,

JOINTED (1) [JOINT]

Lev 11:21 you may eat those that have j legs above their feet,

JOINTS (2) [JOINT]

Heb 4:12 until it divides soul from spirit, j from marrow;
4Mc 9:17 Cut my limbs, burn my flesh, and twist my j;

JOKDEAM (1)

Jos 15:56 Jezreel, J, Zanoah,

JOKIM (1)

1Ch 4:22 and J, and the men of Cozeba, and Joash,

JOKING (1)

Pr 26:19 who deceives a neighbor and says, "I am only j!"

JOKMEAM (2)

1Ki 4:12 as far as the other side of J;
1Ch 6:68 J with its pasture lands, Beth-horon

JOKNEAM (3)

Jos 12:22 king of Kedesh one the king of J in Carmel one
19:11 then the wadi that is east of J;
21:34 J with its pasture lands, Kartah

JOKSHAN (4)

Ge 25: 2 She bore him Zimran, J, Medan, Midian, Ishbak,
25: 3 J was the father of Sheba and Dedan.
1Ch 1:32 she bore Zimran, J, Medan, Midian, Ishbak,
1:32 The sons of J: Sheba and Dedan.

JOKTAN (6)

Ge 10:25 and his brother's name was J.
10:26 J became the father of Almodad, Sheleph,
10:29 all these were the descendants of J.
1Ch 1:19 and the name of his brother J.
1:20 J became the father of Almodad, Sheleph,
1:23 all these were the descendants of J.

JOKTHE-EL (2)

Jos 15:38 Dilan, Mizpeh, J,
2Ki 14: 7 he called it J, which is its name to this day.

JONA (KJV) See JOHN

JONADAB (12) [=JEHONADAB]

2Sa 13: 3 But Amnon had a friend whose name was J,
13: 3 and J was a very crafty man.
13: 5 J said to him, "Lie down on your bed,
13:32 But J, the son of David's brother Shimeah, said,
13:35 J said to the king, "See,
Jer 35: 6 for our ancestor J son of Rechab commanded us,
35: 8 We have obeyed the charge of our ancestor J son
Jer 35:10 and done all that our ancestor J commanded us.
35:14 The command has been carried out that J son
35:16 of J son of Rechab have carried out the command
35:18 the command of your ancestor J,
35:19 J son of Rechab shall not lack a descendant

JONAH (32)

2Ki 14:25 which he spoke by his servant J son of Amittai,
Jnh 1: 1 the word of the LORD came to J son of Amittai,
1: 3 But J set out to flee to Tarshish from the presence
1: 5 J, meanwhile, had gone down into the hold of
1: 7 So they cast lots, and the lot fell on J.
1:15 So they picked J up and threw him into the sea;
1:17 LORD provided a large fish to swallow up J;
1:17 and J was in the belly of the fish three days
2: 1 Then J prayed to the LORD his God from
2:10 and it spewed J out upon the dry land.
3: 1 The word of the LORD came to J a second time,
3: 3 So J set out and went to Nineveh,
3: 4 J began to go into the city, going a day's walk.
4: 1 But this was very displeasing to J,
4: 5 Then J went out of the city and sat down east of
4: 6 and made it come up over J,
4: 6 so J was very happy about the bush.
4: 8 on the head of J so that he was faint and asked
4: 9 But God said to J, "Is it right for you to be angry
Mt 12:39 be given to it except the sign of the prophet J.
12:40 as J was three days and three nights in the belly
12:41 because they repented at the proclamation of J,
12:41 and see, something greater than J is here!
16: 4 no sign will be given to it except the sign of J."
16:17 "Blessed are you, Simon son of J!
Lk 11:29 no sign will be given to it except the sign of J.
11:30 just as J became a sign to the people of Nineveh,
11:32 because they repented at the proclamation of J,
11:32 and see, something greater than J is here!
1Es 9:23 who was Kelita, and Pethahiah and Judah and J.
3Mc 6: 8 And J, wasting away in the belly of a huge,
2Es 1:39 and Amos and Micah and Joel and Obadiah and J

JONAM (1)

Lk 3:30 son of Joseph, son of J, son of Eliakim,

JONAN (KJV) See JONAM

JONAS (KJV) See JONAH

JONATHAN[‡] (218) [=APPHUS, JONATHAN'S]

Jdg 18:30 J son of Gershom, son of Moses,
1Sa 13: 2 a thousand were with J in Gibeah of Benjamin;
13: 3 J defeated the garrison of the Philistines that was
13:16 his son J, and the people who were present
13:22 of any of the people with Saul and J;
13:22 but Saul and his son J had them.
14: 1 One day J son of Saul said to
14: 3 Now the people did not know that J had gone.
14: 4 by which J tried to go over to
14: 6 J said to the young man who carried his armor,
14: 8 Then J said, "Now we will cross over
14:12 men of the garrison hailed J and his armor-bearer,
14:12 J said to his armor-bearer, "Come up after me;
14:13 Then J climbed up on his hands and feet,
14:13 The Philistines fell before J,
14:14 that first slaughter J and his armor-bearer killed
14:17 J and his armor-bearer were not there.
14:21 the Israelites who were with Saul and J.
14:27 But J had not heard his father charge the troops
14:29 Then J said, "My father has troubled the land;
14:39 even if it is in my son J, he shall surely die!"
14:40 and I and my son J will be on the other side."
14:41 If this guilt is in me or in my son J,
14:41 And J and Saul were indicated by the lot,
14:42 Saul said, "Cast the lot between me and my son
J." And J was taken.
14:43 Saul said to J, "Tell me what you have done."
14:43 J told him, "I tasted a little honey with the tip of
14:44 and more also; you shall surely die, J!"
14:45 Then the people said to Saul, "Shall J die,
14:45 So the people ransomed J, and he did not die.
14:49 the sons of Saul were J, Ishvi, and Malchishua;
18: 1 the soul of J was bound to the soul of David, and
J loved him as his own soul.
18: 3 Then J made a covenant with David,
18: 4 J stripped himself of the robe
19: 1 with his son J and with all his servants
19: 1 But Saul's son J took great delight in David.
19: 2 J told David, "My father Saul is trying
19: 4 J spoke well of David to his father Saul,
19: 6 Saul heeded the voice of J;
19: 7 J called David and related all these things to him.
19: 7 J then brought David to Saul,
20: 1 He came before J and said, "What have I done?
20: 3 and he thinks, 'Do not let J know this,
20: 4 Then J said to David, "Whatever you say,
20: 5 David said to J, "Tomorrow is the new moon,
20: 9 J said, "Far be it from you!
20:10 Then David said to J, "Who will tell me
20:11 J replied to David, "Come,
20:12 J said to David, "By the LORD,
20:13 the LORD do so to J, and more also,
20:16 Thus J made a covenant with the house of David,
20:17 J made David swear again by his love for him;
20:18 J said to him, "Tomorrow is the new moon;
1Sa 20:25 J stood, while Abner sat by Saul's side;
20:27 And Saul said to his son J,
20:28 J answered Saul, "David earnestly asked leave
20:30 Then Saul's anger was kindled against J.
20:32 Then J answered his father Saul,
20:33 so J knew that it was the decision of his father
20:34 J rose from the table in fierce anger
20:35 In the morning J went out into the field to
20:37 J called after the boy and said,
20:38 J called after the boy, "Hurry, be quick,
20:39 only J and David knew the arrangement.
20:40 J gave his weapons to the boy and said to him,
20:42 Then J said to David, "Go in peace,
20:42 He got up and left; and J went into the city.
23:16 Saul's son J set out and came to David at Horesh;
23:18 David remained at Horesh, and J went home.
31: 2 and the Philistines killed J and Abinadab
2Sa 1: 4 and Saul and his son J also died."
1: 5 "How do you know that Saul and his son J died?"
1:12 fasted until evening for Saul and for his son J,
1:17 over Saul and his son J.
1:22 the bow of J did not turn back,
1:23 Saul and J, beloved and lovely!
1:25 J lies slain upon your high places.
1:26 I am distressed for you, my brother J;
4: 4 Saul's son J had a son who was crippled
4: 4 the news about Saul and J came from Jezreel.
9: 3 Ziba said to the king, "There remains a son of J;
9: 6 Mephibosheth son of J son of Saul came
9: 7 for the sake of your father J;
15:27 Ahimaaz your son, and J son of Abiathar.
15:36 Zadok's son Ahimaaz and Abiathar's son J;
17:17 J and Ahimaaz were waiting at En-rogel;
17:20 they said, "Where are Ahimaaz and J?"
21: 7 the son of Saul's son J,
21: 7 between David and J son of Saul.
21:12 of Saul and the bones of his son J from the people
21:13 the bones of Saul and the bones of his son J;
21:14 They buried the bones of Saul and of his son J in
21:21 J son of David's brother Shimei, killed him.
23:32 Eliahba of Shaalbon; the sons of Jashen: J
1Ki 1:42 J son of the priest Abiathar arrived.
1:43 J answered Adonijah, "No,
1Ch 2:32 Jether and J; and Jether died childless.
2:33 The sons of J: Peleth and Zaza.
8:33 Saul of J, Malchishua, Abinadab, and Esh-baal;
8:34 and the son of J was Merib-baal;
9:39 Saul of J, Malchishua, Abinadab, and Esh-baal;
9:40 and the son of J was Merib-baal;
10: 2 and the Philistines killed J and Abinadab
11:34 J son of Shagee the Hararite,
20: 7 When he taunted Israel, J son of Shimea,
27:25 in the villages and in the towers, was J son
27:32 J, David's uncle, was a counselor,
Ezr 8: 6 Of the descendants of Adin, Ebed son of J,
10:15 Only J son of Asahel and Jahzeiah son
Ne 12:11 Joiada the father of J, and J the father of Jaddua.
12:14 of Malluchi, J; of Shebaniah, Joseph;
12:35 of J son of Shemaiah son of Mattaniah son
Jer 37:15 in the house of the secretary J,
37:20 not send me back to the house of the secretary J
38:26 to the king not to send me back to the house of J
1Mc 2: 5 Eleazar called Avaran, and J called Apphus.
4:30 the camp of the Philistines into the hands of J son
5:17 J my brother and I will go to Gilead."
5:24 Judas Maccabeus and his brother J crossed
5:55 and J were in Gilead and their brother Simon was
9:19 Then J and Simon took their brother Judas
9:28 all the friends of Judas assembled and said to J,
9:31 So J accepted the leadership at that time in place
9:33 But J and his brother Simon and all who were
9:35 So J sent his brother as leader of the multitude
9:37 After these things it was reported to J
9:44 And J said to those with him,
9:47 and J stretched out his hand to strike Bacchides,
9:48 Then J and the men with him leaped into
9:58 J and his men are living in quiet and confidence.
9:60 telling them to seize J and his men;
9:62 Then J with his men, and Simon,
9:65 But J left his brother Simon in the town,
9:70 When J learned of this, he sent ambassadors
9:71 to J that he would not try to harm him as long
9:73 J settled in Michmash and began to judge
10: 3 Demetrius sent J a letter in peaceable words
10: 7 Then J came to Jerusalem and read the letter in
10: 9 But those in the citadel released the hostages to J,
10:10 And J took up residence in Jerusalem and began
10:15 of all the promises that Demetrius had sent to J,
10:15 of the battles that J and his brothers had fought,
10:18 "King Alexander to his brother J, greetings.
10:21 So J put on the sacred vestments in
10:46 When J and the people heard these words,
10:59 Then King Alexander wrote to J to come
10:66 J returned to Jerusalem in peace and gladness.
10:69 he sent the following message to the high priest J:
10:74 When J heard the words of Apollonius,
10:76 and J gained possession of Joppa.
10:78 J pursued him to Azotus,
10:80 J learned that there was an ambush behind him,
10:81 But his men stood fast, as J had commanded,
10:84 But J burned Azotus and the surrounding towns
10:86 Then J left there and encamped against Askalon,
10:88 of these things, he honored J still more;
11: 4 the charred bodies of those whom J had burned in
11: 5 They also told the king what J had done,
11: 6 J met the king at Joppa with pomp,
11: 7 And J went with the king as far as

1Mc 11:20 In those days **J** assembled the Judeans to attack
11:21 the king and reported to him that **J** was besieging
11:22 and he wrote **J** not to continue the siege,
11:23 **J** heard this, he gave orders to continue the siege.
11:28 Then **J** asked the king to free Judea and
11:29 and wrote a letter to **J** about all these things;
11:30 to his brother **J** and to the nation of the Jews,
11:37 be given to **J** and put up in a conspicuous place
11:41 Now **J** sent to King Demetrius the request
11:42 And Demetrius sent this message back to **J:**
11:44 So **J** sent three thousand stalwart men to him
11:53 from **J** and did not repay the favors that **J** had done
11:57 Then the young Antiochus wrote to **J,** saying,
11:60 Then **J** set out and traveled beyond the river and
11:62 Then the people of Gaza pleaded with **J,**
11:63 Then **J** heard that the officers
11:67 **J** and his army encamped by the waters
11:70 All the men with **J** fled;
11:71 **J** tore his clothes, put dust on his head,
11:74 And **J** returned to Jerusalem.
12: 1 when **J** saw that the time was favorable for him,
12: 3 the senate chamber and said, "The high priest **J**
12: 5 a copy of the letter that **J** wrote to the Spartans:
12: 6 "The high priest **J,** the senate of the nation,
12:24 Now **J** heard that the commanders
12:27 **J** commanded his troops to be alert and
12:28 that **J** and his troops were prepared for battle,
12:29 **J** and his troops did not know it until morning,
12:30 Then **J** pursued them, but he did
12:31 So **J** turned aside against the Arabs
12:35 When **J** returned he convened the elders of
12:40 He feared that **J** might not permit him to do so,
12:41 **J** went out to meet him
12:44 said to **J,** "Why have you put all these people to
12:46 **J** trusted him and did as he said;
12:48 But when **J** entered Ptolemais,
12:50 that **J** had been seized and had perished along
12:52 for **J** and his companions and were in great fear;
13: 8 in place of Judas and your brother **J.**
13:11 He sent **J** son of Absalom to Joppa,
13:12 and **J** was with him under guard.
13:14 that Simon had risen up in place of his brother **J,**
13:15 "It is for the money that your brother **J** owed
13:18 the money and the sons, that **J** perished."
13:19 but Trypho broke his word and did not release **J.**
13:23 When he approached Baskama, he killed **J,**
13:25 Simon sent and took the bones of his brother **J,**
14:16 that **J** had died, and they were deeply grieved.
14:18 with his brothers Judas and **J.**
14:30 **J** rallied the nation, became their high priest,
2Mc 1:23 **J** led, and the rest responded, as did Nehemiah.
8:22 Simon and Joseph and **J,**
1Es 8:32 Of the descendants of Adin, Obed son of **J,**
9:14 **J** son of Asahel and Jahzeiah son

JONATHAN'S (7) [JONATHAN]

1Sa 20:37 boy came to the place where **J** arrow had fallen,
20:38 So **J** boy gathered up the arrows and came
2Sa 9: 1 to whom I may show kindness for **J** sake?"
1Mc 9:61 And **J** men seized about fifty of the men of
10:62 to take off **J** garments and to clothe him in purple,
11:59 He appointed **J** brother Simon governor from
12:49 and the Great Plain to destroy all **J** soldiers.

JOPPA (29)

Jos 19:46 Me-jarkon, and Rakkon at the border opposite **J.**
2Ch 2:16 and bring it to you as rafts by sea to **J;**
Ezr 3: 7 to bring cedar trees from Lebanon to the sea, to **J,**
Jnh 1: 3 down to **J** and found a ship going to Tarshish;
Ac 9:36 in **J** there was a disciple whose name was Tabitha,
9:38 Since Lydda was near **J,** the disciples,
9:42 This became known throughout **J,**
9:43 Meanwhile he stayed in **J** for some time with
10: 5 to **J** for a certain Simon who is called Peter;
10: 8 after telling them everything, he sent them to **J.**
10:23 some of the believers from **J** accompanied him.
10:32 Send therefore to **J** and ask for Simon,
11: 5 "I was in the city of **J** praying,
11:13 'Send to **J** and bring Simon, who is called Peter;
1Mc 10:75 He encamped before **J,** but the people of
10:75 for Apollonius had a garrison in **J.**
10:76 and Jonathan gained possession of **J.**
11: 6 Jonathan met the king at **J** with pomp,
12:33 He turned aside to **J** and took it by surprise,
13:11 He sent Jonathan son of Absalom to **J,**
14: 5 To crown all his honors he took **J** for a harbor,
14:34 He also fortified **J,** which is by the sea,
15:28 "You hold control of **J** and Gazara and the citadel
15:35 As for **J** and Gazara, which you demand,
2Mc 4:21 upon arriving at **J** he proceeded to Jerusalem.
12: 3 And the people of **J** did so ungodly a deed as this:
12: 4 of **J** took them out to sea and drowned them,
12: 7 and root out the whole community of **J.**
1Es 5:55 and convey them in rafts to the harbor of **J,**

JORAH (1)

Ezr 2:18 Of **J,** one hundred twelve.

JORAI (1)

1Ch 5:13 Michael, Meshullam, Sheba, **J,** Jacan, Zia,

JORAM (31) [=HADORAM, =JEHORAM, JORAM'S]

2Sa 8:10 Toi sent his son **J** to King David,
2Sa 8:10 **J** brought with him articles of silver, gold,
2Ki 8:16 In the fifth year of King **J** son of Ahab of Israel,
8:21 Then **J** crossed over to Zair with all his chariots.
8:23 Now the rest of the acts of **J,** and all that he did,
8:24 So **J** slept with his ancestors,
8:25 the twelfth year of King **J** son of Ahab of Israel,
8:28 He went with **J** son of Ahab to wage war
8:28 where the Arameans wounded **J.**
8:29 King **J** returned to be healed in Jezreel of
8:29 son of Jehoram of Judah went down to see **J** son of
9:14 son of Nimshi conspired against **J.**
9:14 **J** with all Israel had been on guard
9:15 but King **J** had returned to be healed in Jezreel of
9:16 and went to Jezreel, where **J** was lying ill.
9:16 King Ahaziah of Judah had come down to visit **J.**
9:17 **J** said, "Take a horseman;
9:21 **J** said, "Get ready." And they got his chariot ready.
9:21 Then King **J** of Israel and King Ahaziah
9:22 When **J** saw Jehu, he said, "Is it peace, Jehu?"
9:23 Then **J** reined about and fled, saying to Ahaziah,
9:24 and shot **J** between the shoulders,
9:29 In the eleventh year of **J** son of Ahab,
1Ch 3:11 **J** his son, Ahaziah his son, Joash his son,
26:25 his son **J,** his son Zichri, and his son Shelomoth.
2Ch 22: 5 The Arameans wounded **J,**
22: 6 of King Jehoram of Judah went down to see **J** son
22: 7 about through his going to visit **J.**
Mt 1: 8 and Jehoshaphat the father of **J,** and **J** the father of Uzziah,
1Es 1: 9 and Hashabiah and Ochiel and **J,**

JORAM'S (1) [JORAM]

2Ki 11: 2 But Jehosheba, King **J** daughter, Ahaziah's sister,

JORDAN‡ (211)

Ge 13:10 the plain of the **J** was well watered everywhere
13:11 So Lot chose for himself all the plain of the **J,**
32:10 for with only my staff I crossed this **J;**
50:10 beyond the **J,** they held there a very great
50:11 place was named Abel-mizraim; it is beyond the **J.**
Nu 13:29 the Canaanites live by the sea, and along the **J.**"
22: 1 in the plains of Moab across the **J** from Jericho.
26: 3 in the plains of Moab by the **J** opposite Jericho,
26:63 in the plains of Moab by the **J** opposite Jericho.
31:12 at the camp on the plains of Moab by the **J**
32: 5 do not make us cross the **J.**"
32:19 with them on the other side of the **J** and beyond,
32:19 to us on this side of the **J** to the east."
32:21 and all those of you who bear arms cross the **J**
32:29 over the **J** with you and the land shall be subdued
32:32 with us on this side of the **J.**"
33:48 and camped in the plains of Moab by the **J**
33:49 they camped by the **J** from Beth-jeshimoth as far
33:50 In the plains of Moab by the **J** at Jericho,
33:51 you cross over the **J** into the land of Canaan,
34:12 and the boundary shall go down to the **J,**
34:15 beyond the **J** at Jericho eastward,
35: 1 In the plains of Moab by the **J** at Jericho,
35:10 When you cross the **J** into the land of Canaan,
35:14 you shall designate three cities beyond the **J,**
36:13 to the Israelites in the plains of Moab by the **J**
Dt 1: 1 that Moses spoke to all Israel beyond the **J**—
1: 5 Beyond the **J** in the land of Moab,
2:29 until I cross the **J** into the land that
3: 8 of the Amorites the land beyond the **J,**
3:17 with the **J** and its banks,
3:20 the **J,** then each of you may return to the property
3:25 over to see the good land beyond the **J,**
3:27 Look well, for you shall not cross over this **J.**
4:21 and he vowed that I should not cross the **J** and
4:22 to die in this land without crossing over the **J,**
4:26 the land that you are crossing the **J** to occupy;
4:41 on the east side of the **J** three cities
4:46 beyond the **J** in the valley opposite Beth-peor,
4:47 of the Amorites on the eastern side of the **J:**
4:49 with all the Arabah on the east side of the **J** as far
9: 1 You are about to cross the **J** today,
11:30 As you know, they are beyond the **J,**
11:31 When you cross the **J** to go in to occupy the land
12:10 When you cross over the **J** and live in the land
27: 2 the day that you cross over the **J** into the land that
27: 4 So when you have crossed over the **J,**
27:12 over the **J,** these shall stand on Mount Gerizim
30:18 that you are crossing the **J** to enter and possess.
31: 2 'You shall not cross over this **J.**'
31:13 that you are crossing over the **J** to possess."
32:47 that you are crossing over the **J** to possess."
Jos 1: 2 Now proceed to cross the **J,**
1:11 for in three days you are to cross over the **J,**
1:14 in the land that Moses gave you beyond the **J.**
1:15 of the LORD gave you beyond the **J** to the east."
2: 7 the men pursued them on the way to the **J** as far
2:10 of the Amorites that were beyond the **J,**
3: 1 and they came to the **J.**
3: 8 you come to the edge of the waters of the **J,**
3: 8 you shall stand still in the **J.**' "
3:11 the earth is going to pass before you into the **J.**
3:13 rest in the waters of the **J,**
3:13 of the **J** flowing from above shall be cut off;
3:14 people set out from their tents to cross over the **J,**
3:15 the **J** overflows all its banks throughout the time
3:15 when those who bore the ark had come to the **J,**
3:17 on dry ground in the middle of the **J,**
3:17 the entire nation finished crossing over the **J.**
4: 1 the entire nation had finished crossing over the **J,**
4: 3 from here out of the middle of the **J,**
Jos 4: 5 of the LORD your God into the middle of the **J,**
4: 7 the waters of the **J** were cut off in front of the ark
4: 7 When it crossed over the **J,**
4: 7 the waters of the **J** were cut off.
4: 8 up twelve stones out of the middle of the **J,**
4: 9 the middle of the **J,** in the place where the feet of
4:10 the ark remained standing in the middle of the **J,**
4:16 to come up out of the **J.**"
4:17 "Come up out of the **J.**"
4:18 of the LORD came up from the middle of the **J,**
4:18 the waters of the **J** returned to their place
4:19 up out of the **J** on the tenth day of the first month,
4:20 which they had taken out of the **J,**
4:22 'Israel crossed over the **J** here on dry ground.'
4:23 the waters of the **J** for you until you crossed over,
5: 1 When all the kings of the Amorites beyond the **J**
5: 1 the **J** for the Israelites until they had crossed over,
7: 7 Why have you brought this people across the **J**
7: 7 that we had been content to settle beyond the **J!**
9: 1 Now when all the kings who were beyond the **J**
9:10 of the Amorites who were beyond the **J,**
12: 1 whose land they occupied beyond the **J** toward
12: 7 the Israelites defeated on the west side of the **J,**
13: 8 which Moses gave them, beyond the **J** eastward,
13:23 border of the Reubenites was the **J** and its banks.
13:27 of the kingdom of King Sihon of Heshbon, the **J**
13:27 of the Sea of Chinnereth, eastward beyond the **J.**
13:32 beyond the **J** east of Jericho.
14: 3 to the two and one-half tribes beyond the **J;**
15: 5 to the mouth of the **J.**
15: 5 from the bay of the sea at the mouth of the **J;**
16: 1 the Josephites went from the **J** by Jericho, east of
16: 7 and touches Jericho, ending at the **J.**
17: 5 which is on the other side of the **J,**
18: 7 beyond the **J** eastward, which Moses the servant
18:12 On the north side their boundary began at the **J;**
18:19 at the south end of the **J:**
18:20 The **J** forms its boundary on the eastern side.
19:22 Beth-shemesh, and its boundary ends at the **J**—
19:33 and it ended at the **J;**
19:34 and Judah on the east at the **J.**
20: 8 And beyond the **J** east of Jericho,
22: 4 of the LORD gave you on the other side of the **J.**
22: 7 in the land west of the **J.**
22:10 When they came to the region near the **J** that lies
22:10 of Manasseh built there an altar by the **J,**
22:11 in the region near the **J,**
22:25 For the LORD has made the **J** a boundary
23: 4 from the **J** to the Great Sea in the west.
24: 8 who lived on the other side of the **J;**
24:11 When you went over the **J** and came to Jericho,
Jdg 3:28 and seized the fords of the **J** against the Moabites,
5:17 Gilead stayed beyond the **J;**
6:33 and crossing the **J** they encamped in the Valley
7:24 as far as Beth-barah, and also the **J.**"
7:24 the waters as far as Beth-barah, and also the **J.**
7:25 of Oreb and Zeeb to Gideon beyond the **J.**
8: 4 Then Gideon came to the **J** and crossed over,
10: 8 the Israelites that were beyond the **J** in the land of
10: 9 the **J** to fight against Judah and against Benjamin
11:13 from the Arnon to the Jabbok and to the **J;**
11:22 to the Jabbok and from the wilderness to the **J.**
12: 5 Then the Gileadites took the fords of the **J** against
12: 6 and killed him at the fords of the **J.**
1Sa 10:27 across the **J** whose right eye Nahash,
13: 7 Some Hebrews crossed the **J** to the land of Gad
31: 7 beyond the **J** saw that the men of Israel had fled
2Sa 2:29 they crossed the **J,** and, marching
10:17 he gathered all Israel together, and crossed the **J,**
16:14 with him arrived weary at the **J;**
17:22 with him set out and crossed the **J;**
17:22 not one was left who had not crossed the **J.**
17:24 Absalom crossed the **J** with all the men of Israel.
19:15 So the king came back to the **J;**
19:15 to meet the king and to bring him over the **J.**
19:17 rushed down to the **J** ahead of the king,
19:18 as he was about to cross the **J,**
19:31 with the king to the **J,** to escort him over the **J.**
19:36 Your servant will go a little way over the **J** with
19:39 Then all the people crossed over the **J,**
19:41 brought the king and his household over the **J,**
20: 2 their king steadfastly from the **J** to Jerusalem.
24: 5 They crossed the **J,** and began from Aroer and
1Ki 2: 8 but when he came down to meet me at the **J,**
7:46 In the plain of the **J** the king cast them,
17: 3 which is east of the **J.**
17: 5 by the Wadi Cherith, which is east of the **J.**
2Ki 2: 6 for the LORD has sent me to the **J.**"
2: 7 as they both were standing by the **J.**
2:13 and went back and stood on the bank of the **J.**
5:10 saying, "Go, wash in the **J** seven times,
5:14 down and immersed himself seven times in the **J,**
6: 2 Let us go to the **J,** and let us collect logs there,
6: 4 When they came to the **J,** they cut down trees.
7:15 So they went after them as far as the **J;**
10:33 the **J** eastward, all the land of Gilead, the Gadites,
1Ch 6:78 across the **J** from Jericho, on the east side of the **J,**
12:15 the men who crossed the **J** in the first month,
12:37 the half-tribe of Manasseh from beyond the **J,**
19:17 he gathered all Israel together, crossed the **J,**
26:30 of the **J** for all the work of the LORD and for
2Ch 4:17 In the plain of the **J** the king cast them,
Job 40:23 it is confident though **J** rushes against its mouth.
Ps 42: 6 therefore I remember you from the land of **J** and
114: 3 The sea looked and fled; **J** turned back.
114: 5 O **J,** that you turn back?
Isa 9: 1 the land beyond the **J,** Galilee of the nations.

Jer 12: 5 how will you fare in the thickets of the J?
49:19 Like a lion coming up from the thickets of the J
50:44 Like a lion coming up from the thickets of the J
Eze 47:18 along the J between Gilead and the land of Israel;
Zec 11: 3 for the thickets of the J are destroyed!
Mt 3: 5 and all the region along the J,
3: 6 and they were baptized by him in the river J,
3:13 Then Jesus came from Galilee to John at the J,
4:15 across the J, Galilee of the Gentiles—
4:25 Jerusalem, Judea, and from beyond the J.
19: 1 and went to the region of Judea beyond the J.
Mk 1: 5 and were baptized by him in the river J,
1: 9 of Galilee and was baptized by John in the J.
3: 8 Jerusalem, Idumea, beyond the J,
10: 1 and went to the region of Judea and beyond the J.
Lk 3: 3 He went into all the region around the J,
4: 1 the J and was led by the Spirit in the wilderness,
Jn 1:28 This took place in Bethany across the J
3:26 "Rabbi, the one who was with you across the J,
10:40 He went away again across the J to the place
Jdt 1: 9 and beyond the J as far as Jerusalem and Bethany
5:15 the J they took possession of all the hill country.
Sir 24:26 with understanding, and like the J at harvest time.
1Mc 5:24 the J and made three days' journey into
5:52 Then they crossed the J into the large plain
9:34 and he with all his army crossed the J.
9:42 they returned to the marshes of the J.
9:43 on the sabbath day to the banks of the J.
9:45 the water of the J is on this side and on that,
9:48 and the men with him leaped into the J and swam
9:48 and the enemy did not cross the J to attack them.

JORIM (1)

Lk 3:29 son of Eliezer, son of J, son of Matthat,

JORKEAM (1)

1Ch 2:44 Shema became father of Raham, father of J;

JORKOAM (KJV) See JORKEAM

JOSABAD (KJV) See JOZABAD

JOSAPHAT (KJV) See JEHOSHAPHAT

JOSE (KJV) See JOSHUA

JOSECH (1)

Lk 3:26 son of Mattathias, son of Semein, son of J,

JOSEDECH (KJV) See JEHOZADAK

JOSEPH (236) =BARNABAS, =BARSABBAS, JOSEPH'S, JOSEPHITE, JOSEPHITES, =JOSES, =ZAPHENATH-PANEAH]

Ge 30:24 and she named him J, saying, "May
30:25 When Rachel had borne J, Jacob said to Laban,
33: 2 and Rachel and J last of all.
33: 7 and finally J and Rachel drew near,
35:24 The sons of Rachel: J and Benjamin.
37: 2 J, being seventeen years old,
37: 2 and J brought a bad report of them to their father.
37: 3 Israel loved J more than any other of his children,
37: 5 Once J had a dream, and when he told it
37:13 to J, "Are not your brothers pasturing the flock
37:17 So J went after his brothers,
37:23 So when J came to his brothers,
37:28 they drew J up, lifting him out of the pit,
37:28 And they took J to Egypt.
37:29 to the pit and saw that J was not in the pit,
37:33 J is without doubt torn to pieces."
39: 1 Now J was taken down to Egypt, and Potiphar,
39: 2 with J, and he became a successful man;
39: 4 So J found favor in his sight and attended him;
39: 6 Now J was handsome and good-looking.
39: 7 time his master's wife cast her eyes on J and said,
39:10 And although she spoke to J day after day,
39:21 with J and showed him steadfast love;
40: 3 in the prison where J was confined.
40: 4 The captain of the guard charged J with them,
40: 6 When J came to them in the morning,
40: 8 to interpret them." And J said to them, "Do
40: 9 So the chief cupbearer told his dream to J,
40:12 Then J said to him, "This is its interpretation:
40:16 he said to J, "I also had a dream:
40:18 And J answered, "This is its interpretation:
40:22 just as J had interpreted to them.
40:23 Yet the chief cupbearer did not remember J,
41:14 Then Pharaoh sent for J,
41:15 And Pharaoh said to J, "I have had a dream,
41:16 J answered Pharaoh, "It is not I;
41:17 to J, "In my dream I was standing on the banks of
41:25 Then J said to Pharaoh, "Pharaoh's dreams are one
41:39 So Pharaoh said to J,
41:41 And Pharaoh said to J, "See,
41:44 Moreover Pharaoh said to J, "I am Pharaoh,
41:45 Pharaoh gave J the name Zaphenath-paneah;
41:45 Thus J gained authority over the land of Egypt.
41:46 J was thirty years old when he entered the service
41:46 And J went out from the presence of Pharaoh,
41:49 So J stored up grain in such abundance—
Ge 41:50 Before the years of famine came, J had two sons,
41:51 J named the firstborn Manasseh, "For," he said,
41:54 of famine began to come, just as J had said.
41:55 Pharaoh said to all the Egyptians, "Go to J;
41:56 J opened all the storehouses,
41:57 all the world came to J in Egypt to buy grain,
42: 6 Now J was governor over the land;
42: 7 When J saw his brothers, he recognized them,
42: 8 Although J had recognized his brothers,
42: 9 J also remembered the dreams
42:14 J said to them, "It is just as I have said to you;
42:18 On the third day J said to them,
42:23 They did not know that J understood them,
42:25 J then gave orders to fill their bags with grain,
42:36 J is no more, and Simeon is no more,
43:15 on their way down to Egypt, and stood before J.
43:16 When J saw Benjamin with them,
43:17 The man did as J said,
43:26 When J came home, they brought him the present
43:30 that, J hurried out, because he was overcome
44: 2 And he did as J told him.
44: 4 J said to his steward, "Go, follow after the men;
44:15 J said to them, "What deed is this
45: 1 Then J could no longer control himself
45: 1 when J made himself known to his brothers.
45: 3 J said to his brothers, "I am J.
45: 4 Then J said to his brothers, "Come closer to me."
45: 4 He said, "I am your brother, J,
45: 9 'Thus says your son J, God has made me lord
45:17 Pharaoh said to J, "Say to your brothers,
45:21 J gave them wagons according to the instruction
45:26 And they told him, "J is still alive!
45:27 But when they told him all the words of J
45:27 he saw the wagons that J had sent to carry him,
45:28 My son J is still alive.
46:19 children of Jacob's wife Rachel: J and Benjamin.
46:20 To J in the land of Egypt were born Manasseh
46:27 of J, who were born to him in Egypt, were two;
46:28 to J to lead the way before him into Goshen.
46:29 J made ready his chariot and went up
46:30 Israel said to J, "I can die now,
46:31 J said to his brothers and
47: 1 So J went and told Pharaoh,
47: 5 to J, "Your father and your brothers have come
47: 7 Then J brought in his father Jacob,
47:11 J settled his father and his brothers,
47:12 And J provided his father, his brothers,
47:14 J collected all the money to be found in the land
47:14 and J brought the money into Pharaoh's house.
47:15 all the Egyptians came to J, and said,
47:16 And J answered, "Give me your livestock,
47:17 So they brought their livestock to J;
47:17 and J gave them food in exchange for the horses,
47:20 So J bought all the land of Egypt for Pharaoh.
47:23 Then J said to the people,
47:26 J made it a statute concerning the land of Egypt,
47:29 he called his son J and said to him,
48: 1 After this J was told, "Your father is ill."
48: 2 Jacob was told, "Your son J has come to you,"
48: 3 And Jacob said to J, "God Almighty appeared
48: 9 J said to his father, "They are my sons,
48:10 So J brought them near him;
48:11 Israel said to J, "I did not expect to see your face;
48:12 Then J removed them from his father's knees,
48:13 J took them both, Ephraim in his right hand
48:15 He blessed J, and said, "The God
48:17 When J saw that his father laid his right hand on
48:18 J said to his father, "Not so, my father!
48:21 Then Israel said to J, "I am about to die,
49:22 J is a fruitful bough, a fruitful bough by a spring;
49:26 may they be on the head of J,
50: 1 Then J threw himself on his father's face
50: 2 J commanded the physicians in his service
50: 4 J addressed the household of Pharaoh,
50: 7 So J went up to bury his father.
50: 8 as well as all the household of J,
50:14 J returned to Egypt with his brothers
50:15 "What if J still bears a grudge against us
50:16 So they approached J, saying,
50:17 'Say to J: I beg you, forgive the crime of your
50:17 J wept when they spoke to him.
50:19 But J said to them, "Do not be afraid!
50:22 So J remained in Egypt,
50:22 and J lived one hundred ten years.
50:23 J saw Ephraim's children of the third generation;
50:24 Then J said to his brothers, "I am about to die;
50:25 So J made the Israelites swear, saying,
50:26 And J died, being one hundred ten years old;
Ex 1: 5 J was already in Egypt.
1: 6 Then J died, and all his brothers,
1: 8 new king arose over Egypt, who did not know J.
13:19 the bones of J who had required a solemn oath of
Nu 1:10 From the sons of J: from Ephraim,
1:32 The descendants of J, namely,
13: 7 from the tribe of Issachar, Igal son of J;
13:11 from the tribe of J (that is, from the tribe
26:28 sons of J by their clans: Manasseh and Ephraim.
26:37 These are the descendants of J by their clans.
27: 1 of Machir son of Manasseh son of J,
32:33 and to the half-tribe of Manasseh son of J—
36: 5 of the tribe of J are right in what they are saying.
36:12 of the descendants of Manasseh son of J,
Dt 27:12 Simeon, Levi, Judah, Issachar, J, and Benjamin.
33:13 And of J he said: Blessed by the
33:16 Let these come on the head of J,
Jos 14: 4 For the people of J were two tribes,
17: 1 for he was the firstborn of J.
Jos 17: 2 the male descendants of Manasseh son of J,
17:14 The tribe of J spoke to Joshua, saying,
17:16 of J said, "The hill country is not enough for us;
17:17 Then Joshua said to the house of J,
18: 5 and the house of J in their territory on the north.
18:11 between the tribe of Judah and the tribe of J.
24:32 The bones of J, which the Israelites had brought
24:32 it became an inheritance of the descendants of J.
Jdg 1:22 The house of J also went up against Bethel;
1:23 The house of J sent out spies to Bethel (the name
1:35 the hand of the house of J rested heavily on them,
2Sa 19:20 of J to come down to meet my lord the king."
1Ki 11:28 over all the forced labor of the house of J.
1Ch 2: 2 Dan, J, Benjamin, Naphtali, Gad, and Asher.
5: 1 of J son of Israel, so that he is not enrolled in
5: 2 yet the birthright belonged to J.)
7:29 In these lived the sons of J son of Israel.
25: 2 Zaccur, J, Nethaniah, and Asarelah,
25: 9 The first lot fell for Asaph to J;
Ezr 10:42 Shallum, Amariah, and J.
Ne 12:14 of Malluchi, Jonathan; of Shebaniah, J;
Ps 77:15 the descendants of Jacob and J.
78:67 He rejected the tent of J,
80: 1 O Shepherd of Israel, you who lead J like a flock!
81: 5 He made it a decree in J,
105:17 J, who was sold as a slave.
Eze 37:16 "For J (the stick of Ephraim) and all the house
37:19 about to take the stick of J (which is in the hand
47:13 J shall have two portions.
48:32 three gates, the gate of J, the gate of Benjamin,
Am 5: 6 he will break out against the house of J like fire,
5:15 will be gracious to the remnant of J.
6: 6 but are not grieved over the ruin of J!
Ob 1:18 house of J a flame, and the house of Esau stubble;
Zec 10: 6 and I will save the house of J.
Mt 1:16 and Jacob the father of J the husband of Mary,
1:18 When his mother Mary had been engaged to J,
1:19 Her husband J, being a righteous man
1:20 the Lord appeared to him in a dream and said, "J,
1:24 When J awoke from sleep,
2:13 the Lord appeared to J in a dream and said, "Get
2:14 Then J got up, took the child and his mother
2:19 of the Lord suddenly appeared in a dream to J
2:21 Then J got up, took the child and his mother,
13:55 And are not his brothers James and J and Simon
27:56 and Mary the mother of James and J,
27:57 there came a rich man from Arimathea, named J,
27:59 So J took the body and wrapped it in
Mk 15:43 J of Arimathea, a respected member of
15:45 he granted the body to J.
15:46 Then J bought a linen cloth,
Lk 1:27 to a virgin engaged to a man whose name was J,
2: 4 J also went from the town of Nazareth in Galilee
2:16 So they went with haste and found Mary and J,
3:23 He was the son (as was thought) of J son of Heli,
3:24 son of Melchi, son of Jannai, son of J,
3:30 son of J, son of Jonam, son of Eliakim,
23:50 there was a good and righteous man named J,
Jn 1:45 Jesus son of J from Nazareth."
4: 5 of ground that Jacob had given to his son J.
6:42 They were saying, "Is not this Jesus, the son of J,
19:38 After these things, J of Arimathea,
Ac 1:23 So they proposed two, J called Barsabbas,
4:36 There was a Levite, a native of Cyprus, J,
7: 9 patriarchs, jealous of J, sold him into Egypt;
7:13 On the second visit J made himself known
7:14 Then J sent and invited his father Jacob
7:18 until another king who had not known J ruled
Heb 11:21 when dying, blessed each of the sons of J,
11:22 By faith J, at the end of his life,
Rev 7: 8 from the tribe of J twelve thousand,
Jdt 8: 1 the daughter of Merari son of Ox son of J son
Sir 49:15 Nor was anyone ever born like J;
1Mc 2:53 J in the time of his distress kept
5:18 But he left J, son of Zechariah, and Azariah,
5:56 J son of Zechariah, and Azariah, the commanders
5:60 Then J and Azariah were routed,
2Mc 8:22 Simon and J and Jonathan,
10:19 Maccabeus left Simon and J, and also Zacchaeus
1Es 9:34 Shashai, Azarel, Azael, Samatus, Zambris, J.
4Mc 2: 2 certainly, that the temperate J is praised,
18:11 as a burnt offering, and about J in prison.

JOSEPH'S (24) [JOSEPH]

Ge 37:31 Then they took J robe, slaughtered a goat,
39: 5 LORD blessed the Egyptian's house for J sake;
39: 6 So he left all that he had in J charge;
39:20 J master took him and put him into the prison,
39:22 to J care all the prisoners who were in the prison,
39:23 in J care, because the LORD was with him;
41:42 Pharaoh put it on J hand;
42: 3 of J brothers went down to buy grain in Egypt.
42: 4 not send J brother Benjamin with his brothers,
42: 6 And J brothers came and bowed themselves
43:17 and brought the men to J house.
43:18 because they were brought to J house,
43:19 up to the steward of J house and spoke with him
43:24 the steward had brought the men into J house,
43:25 they made the present ready for J coming
43:34 Portions were taken to them from J table,
44:14 Judah and his brothers came to J house
45:16 in Pharaoh's house, "J brothers have come,"
46: 4 and J own hand shall close your eyes."
48: 8 Israel saw J sons, he said, "Who are these?"
50:15 that their father was dead, J brothers said, "What
50:23 of Manasseh were also born on J knees.

Lk 4:22 They said, "Is not this **J** son?"
Ac 7:13 and **J** family became known to Pharaoh.

JOSEPHITE (1) [JOSEPH]

Nu 36: 1 of the **J** clans, came forward and spoke in

JOSEPHITES (3) [JOSEPH]

Nu 34:23 Of the **J:** of the tribe of the
Jos 16: 1 of the **J** went from the Jordan by Jericho, east of
16: 4 The **J**—Manasseh and Ephraim—

JOSES (3) [=JOSEPH]

Mk 6: 3 and brother of James and **J** and Judas and Simon,
15:40 Mary the mother of James the younger and of **J,**
15:47 Mary Magdalene and Mary the mother of **J** saw

JOSHAH (1)

1Ch 4:34 Meshobab, Jamlech, **J** son of Amaziah,

JOSHAPHAT (2)

1Ch 11:43 Hanan son of Maacah, and **J** the Mithnite,
15:24 Shebaniah, **J,** Nethanel, Amasai, Zechariah,

JOSHAVIAH (1)

1Ch 11:46 and Jeribai and **J** sons of Elnaam,

JOSHBEKASHAH (2)

1Ch 25: 4 Hanani, Eliathah, Giddalti, and Romamti-ezer, **J,**
25:24 to **J,** his sons and his brothers, twelve;

JOSHEB-BASSHEBETH (1)

2Sa 23: 8 the warriors whom David had: **J** a Tahchemonite;

JOSHIBIAH (1)

1Ch 4:35 Joel, Jehu son of **J** son of Seraiah son of Asiel,

JOSHUA‡ (227) [=HOSHEA, =JESHUA]

Ex 17: 9 to **J,** "Choose some men for us and go out, fight
17:10 So **J** did as Moses told him,
17:13 **J** defeated Amalek and his people with the sword.
17:14 in a book and recite it in the hearing of **J:**
24:13 So Moses set out with his assistant **J,**
32:17 **J** heard the noise of the people as they shouted,
33:11 but his young assistant, **J** son of Nun,
Nu 11:28 And **J** son of Nun, the assistant of Moses,
13:16 the name of Hoshea son of Nun to **J.**
14: 6 And **J** son of Nun and Caleb son of Jephunneh,
14:30 except Caleb son of Jephunneh and **J** son of Nun.
14:38 But **J** son of Nun and Caleb son
26:65 except Caleb son of Jephunneh and **J** son of Nun.
27:18 the LORD said to Moses, "Take **J** son of Nun,
27:22 He took **J** and had him stand before Eleazar
32:12 of Jephunneh the Kenizzite and **J** son of Nun,
32:28 concerning them to Eleazar the priest, to **J** son
34:17 the priest Eleazar and **J** son of Nun.
Dt 1:38 **J** son of Nun, your assistant, shall enter there;
3:21 And I charged **J** as well at that time, saying:
3:28 But charge **J,** and encourage and strengthen him,
31: 3 **J** also will cross over before you,
31: 7 Then Moses summoned **J** and said to him in
31:14 call **J** and present yourselves in the tent
31:14 So Moses and **J** went and presented themselves in
31:23 the LORD commissioned **J** son of Nun and said,
32:44 he and **J** son of Nun.
34: 9 **J** son of Nun was full of the spirit of wisdom,
Jos 1: 1 the LORD spoke to **J** son of Nun,
1:10 Then **J** commanded the officers of the people,
1:12 and the half-tribe of Manasseh **J** said,
1:16 They answered **J:** "All
2: 1 Then **J** son of Nun sent two men secretly
2:23 They crossed over, came to **J** son of Nun,
2:24 They said to **J,** "Truly the LORD has given all
3: 1 in the morning **J** rose and set out from Shittim
3: 5 Then **J** said to the people, "Sanctify yourselves;
3: 6 To the priests **J** said, "Take up the ark of
3: 7 The LORD said to **J,** "This day I will begin
3: 9 **J** then said to the Israelites,
3:10 **J** said, "By this you shall know that among you is
4: 1 over the Jordan, the LORD said to **J:**
4: 4 **J** summoned the twelve men from the Israelites,
4: 5 **J** said to them, "Pass on before the ark of
4: 8 The Israelites did as **J** commanded.
4: 8 the LORD told **J,** carried them over with them to
4: 9 (**J** set up twelve stones in the middle of
4:10 that the LORD commanded **J** to tell the people,
4:10 according to all that Moses had commanded **J.**
4:14 the LORD exalted **J** in the sight of all Israel;
4:15 The LORD said to **J,**
4:17 **J** therefore commanded the priests,
4:20 of the Jordan, **J** set up in Gilgal,
5: 2 At that time the LORD said to **J,**
5: 3 So **J** made flint knives, and circumcised
5: 4 This is the reason why **J** circumcised them:
5: 7 up in their place, that **J** circumcised;
5: 9 The LORD said to **J,** "Today I have rolled away
5:13 Once when **J** was by Jericho,
5:13 **J** went to him and said to him,
5:14 And **J** fell on his face to the earth and worshiped,
5:15 commander of the army of the LORD said to **J,**
5:15 where you stand is holy." And **J** did so.
6: 2 The LORD said to **J,** "See,
6: 6 So **J** son of Nun summoned the priests and said
Jos 6: 8 As **J** had commanded the people,
6:10 To the people **J** gave this command:
6:12 Then **J** rose early in the morning,
6:16 **J** said to the people, "Shout!
6:22 **J** said to the two men who had spied out the land,
6:25 and all who belonged to her, **J** spared.
6:25 the messengers whom **J** sent to spy out Jericho.
6:26 **J** then pronounced this oath, saying,
6:27 So the LORD was with **J;**
7: 2 **J** sent men from Jericho to Ai,
7: 3 Then they returned to **J** and said to him,
7: 6 Then **J** tore his clothes, and fell to the ground
7: 7 **J** said, "Ah, Lord GOD!
7:10 The LORD said to **J,** "Stand up!
7:16 So **J** rose early in the morning,
7:19 Then **J** said to Achan, "My son,
7:20 And Achan answered **J,** "It is true;
7:22 So **J** sent messengers, and they ran to the tent;
7:23 and brought them to **J** and all the Israelites;
7:24 Then **J** and all Israel with him took Achan son
7:25 **J** said, "Why did you bring trouble on us?
8: 1 LORD said to **J,** "Do not fear or be dismayed;
8: 3 So **J** and all the fighting men set out to go up
8: 3 **J** chose thirty thousand warriors
8: 9 So **J** sent them out; and they went to the
8: 9 but **J** spent that night in the camp.
8:10 the morning **J** rose early and mustered the people,
8:13 But **J** spent that night in the valley.
8:15 And **J** and all Israel made a pretense
8:16 as they pursued **J** they were drawn away from
8:18 Then the LORD said to **J,**
8:18 And **J** stretched out the sword that was
8:21 When **J** and all Israel saw that
8:23 the king of Ai was taken alive and brought to **J.**
8:26 For **J** did not draw back his hand,
8:27 to the word of the LORD that he had issued to **J.**
8:28 So **J** burned Ai, and made it forever a heap
8:29 and at sunset **J** commanded,
8:30 **J** built on Mount Ebal an altar to the LORD,
8:32 **J** wrote on the stones a copy of the law of Moses,
8:35 of all that Moses commanded that **J** did not read
9: 2 they gathered together with one accord to fight **J**
9: 3 the inhabitants of Gibeon heard what **J** had done
9: 6 They went to **J** in the camp at Gilgal,
9: 8 They said to **J,** "We are your servants."
9: 8 And **J** said to them, "Who are you?
9:15 And **J** made peace with them,
9:22 **J** summoned them, and said to them,
9:24 They answered **J,** "Because it was told
9:27 But on that day **J** made them hewers of wood
10: 1 of Jerusalem heard how **J** had taken Ai,
10: 4 it has made peace with **J** and with the Israelites."
10: 6 the Gibeonites sent to **J** at the camp in Gilgal,
10: 7 So **J** went up from Gilgal,
10: 8 The LORD said to **J,** "Do not fear them,
10: 9 So **J** came upon them suddenly,
10:12 the Amorites over to the Israelites, **J** spoke to
10:15 Then **J** returned, and all Israel with him,
10:17 it was told **J,** "The five kings have been found,
10:18 **J** said, "Roll large stones against the mouth of
10:20 When **J** and the Israelites had finished inflicting
10:21 all the people returned safe to **J** in the camp
10:22 Then **J** said, "Open the mouth of the cave,
10:24 When they brought the kings out to **J,**
10:24 **J** summoned all the Israelites,
10:25 **J** said to them, "Do not be afraid or dismayed;
10:26 Afterward **J** struck them down and put them
10:27 At sunset **J** commanded, and they took them
10:28 **J** took Makkedah on that day,
10:29 Then **J** passed on from Makkedah,
10:31 Next **J** passed on from Libnah,
10:33 and **J** struck him and his people,
10:34 From Lachish **J** passed on with all Israel
10:36 **J** went up with all Israel from Eglon to Hebron;
10:38 Then **J,** with all Israel, turned back to Debir
10:40 So **J** defeated the whole land,
10:41 **J** defeated them from Kadesh-barnea to Gaza,
10:42 **J** took all these kings and their land at one time,
10:43 Then **J** returned, and all Israel with him,
11: 6 And the LORD said to **J,**
11: 7 So **J** came suddenly upon them
11: 9 **J** did to them as the LORD commanded him;
11:10 **J** turned back at that time, and took Hazor,
11:12 and all their kings, **J** took,
11:13 on mounds except Hazor, which **J** did burn.
11:15 so Moses commanded **J,** and so **J** did;
11:16 So **J** took all that land:
11:18 **J** made war a long time with all those kings.
11:21 that time **J** came and wiped out the Anakim from
11:21 **J** utterly destroyed them with their towns.
11:23 So **J** took the whole land,
11:23 and **J** gave it for an inheritance to Israel
12: 7 of the land whom **J** and the Israelites defeated on
12: 7 toward Seir (and **J** gave their land to the tribes
13: 1 Now **J** was old and advanced in years;
14: 1 which the priest Eleazar, and **J** son of Nun,
14: 6 Then the people of Judah came to **J** at Gilgal;
14:13 Then **J** blessed him, and gave Hebron
15:13 to the commandment of the LORD to **J,**
17: 4 before the priest Eleazar and **J** son of Nun and
17:14 The tribe of Joseph spoke to **J,** saying,
17:15 And **J** said to them, "If you are
17:17 Then **J** said to the house of Joseph,
18: 3 So **J** said to the Israelites,
18: 8 and **J** charged those who went to write
18: 9 then they came back to **J** in the camp at Shiloh,
18:10 **J** cast lots for them in Shiloh before the LORD;
Jos 18:10 and there **J** apportioned the land to the Israelites,
19:49 an inheritance among them to **J** son of Nun.
19:51 the priest Eleazar and **J** son of Nun and the heads
20: 1 Then the LORD spoke to **J,** saying,
21: 1 to **J** son of Nun and to the heads of the families of
22: 1 Then **J** summoned the Reubenites, the Gadites,
22: 6 So **J** blessed them and sent them away,
22: 7 but to the other half **J** had given a possession
22: 7 **J** sent them away to their tents and blessed them,
23: 1 and **J** was old and well advanced in years,
23: 2 **J** summoned all Israel, their elders
24: 1 **J** gathered all the tribes of Israel to Shechem,
24: 2 And **J** said to all the people,
24:19 But **J** said to the people,
24:21 people said to **J,** "No, we will serve the LORD!"
24:22 Then **J** said to the people,
24:24 to **J,** "The LORD our God we will serve,
24:25 So **J** made a covenant with the people that day,
24:26 **J** wrote these words in the book of the law
24:27 **J** said to all the people, "See,
24:28 So **J** sent the people away to their inheritances.
24:29 After these things **J** son of Nun,
24:31 Israel served the LORD all the days of **J,**
24:31 of the elders who outlived **J** and had known all
Jdg 1: 1 After the death of **J,** the Israelites inquired of
2: 6 When **J** dismissed the people,
2: 7 people worshiped the LORD all the days of **J,**
2: 7 and all the days of the elders who outlived **J,**
2: 8 **J** son of Nun, the servant of the LORD,
2:21 before them any of the nations that **J** left
2:23 and had not handed them over to **J.**
1Sa 6:14 cart came into the field of **J** of Beth-shemesh,
6:18 to this day in the field of **J** of Beth-shemesh.
1Ki 16:34 which he spoke by **J** son of Nun.
2Ki 23: 8 the gates that were at the entrance of the gate of **J**
1Ch 7:27 Nun his son, **J** his son.
Hag 1: 1 governor of Judah, and to **J** son of Jehozadak,
1:12 and **J** son of Jehozadak, the high priest,
1:14 and the spirit of **J** son of Jehozadak,
2: 2 governor of Judah, and to **J** son of Jehozadak,
2: 4 take courage, O **J,** son of Jehozadak,
Zec 3: 1 Then he showed me the high priest **J** standing
3: 3 Now **J** was dressed with filthy clothes as he stood
3: 6 Then the angel of the LORD assured **J,** saying
3: 8 Now listen, **J,** high priest,
3: 9 For on the stone that I have set before **J,**
6:11 on the head of the high priest **J** son of Jehozadak;
Lk 3:29 son of **J,** son of Eliezer, son of Jorim, son
Ac 7:45 in with **J** when they dispossessed the nations
Heb 4: 8 For if **J** had given them rest,
Sir 46: 1 **J** son of Nun was mighty in war,
1Mc 2:55 **J,** because he fulfilled the command,
2Mc 12:15 of war overthrew Jericho in the days of **J,**
2Es 7:*107* [37] **J** after him for Israel in the days of Achan,

JOSIAH (74)

1Ki 13: 2 'A son shall be born to the house of David, **J**
2Ki 21:24 of the land made his son **J** king in place of him.
21:26 then his son **J** succeeded him.
22: 1 **J** was eight years old when he began to reign;
22: 3 In the eighteenth year of King **J,**
23:16 **J** turned, he saw the tombs there on the mount;
23:19 **J** removed all the shrines of the high places
23:23 of King **J** this passover was kept to the LORD
23:24 Moreover **J** put away the mediums, wizards,
23:28 Now the rest of the acts of **J,** and all that he did,
23:29 King **J** went to meet him;
23:30 The people of the land took Jehoahaz son of **J,**
23:34 made Eliakim son of **J** king in place of his father **J,**
1Ch 3:14 Amon his son, **J** his son.
3:15 The sons of **J:** Johanan the firstborn,
2Ch 33:25 of the land made his son **J** king to succeed him.
34: 1 **J** was eight years old when he began to reign;
34:33 **J** took away all the abominations from all
35: 1 **J** kept a passover to the LORD in Jerusalem;
35: 7 Then **J** contributed to the people,
35:16 according to the command of King **J.**
35:18 a passover as was kept by **J,**
35:19 of the reign of **J** this passover was kept.
35:20 After all this, when **J** had set the temple in order,
35:20 and **J** went out against him.
35:22 But **J** would not turn away from him,
35:23 The archers shot King **J;**
35:24 All Judah and Jerusalem mourned for **J.**
35:25 Jeremiah also uttered a lament for **J,**
35:25 and singing women have spoken of **J**
35:26 the acts of **J** and his faithful deeds in accordance
36: 1 The people of the land took Jehoahaz son of **J**
Jer 1: 2 of the LORD came in the days of King **J** son
1: 3 in the days of King Jehoiakim son of **J** of Judah,
1: 3 of the eleventh year of King Zedekiah son of **J**
3: 6 The LORD said to me in the days of King **J:**
22:11 the LORD concerning Shallum son of King **J**
22:11 who succeeded his father **J,**
22:18 the LORD concerning King Jehoiakim son of **J**
25: 1 of King Jehoiakim son of **J** of Judah (that was
25: 3 from the thirteenth year of King **J** son of Amon
26: 1 of the reign of King Jehoiakim son of **J** of Judah,
27: 1 of the reign of King Zedekiah son of **J** of Judah,
35: 1 in the days of King Jehoiakim son of **J** of Judah:
36: 1 of **J** of Judah, this word came to Jeremiah from
36: 2 from the days of **J** until today.
36: 9 In the fifth year of King Jehoiakim son of **J**
37: 1 Zedekiah son of **J,** whom King Nebuchadrezzar
45: 1 in the fourth year of King Jehoiakim son of **J**
46: 2 in the fourth year of King Jehoiakim son of **J**

Zep 1: 1 in the days of King **J** son of Amon of Judah.
Zec 6:10 the same day to the house of **J** son of Zephaniah.
6:14 Tobijah, Jedaiah, and **J** son of Zephaniah,
Mt 1:10 and Amos the father of **J**,
1:11 and **J** the father of Jechoniah and his brothers,
Sir 49: 1 of **J** is like blended incense prepared by the skill
49: 4 Except for David and Hezekiah and **J**,
Bar 1: 8 the silver vessels that Zedekiah son of **J**,
1Es 1: 1 **J** kept the passover to his Lord in Jerusalem;
1: 7 who were present **J** gave thirty thousand lambs
1:18 according to the command of King **J**.
1:21 as was kept by **J** and the priests and Levites and
1:22 of the reign of **J** this passover was kept.
1:23 deeds of **J** were upright in the sight of the Lord,
1:25 After all these acts of **J**, it happened that Pharaoh,
1:25 and **J** went out against him.
1:28 **J**, however, did not turn back to his chariot,
1:29 and the commanders came down against King **J**.
1:32 In all Judea they mourned for **J**.
1:32 The prophet Jeremiah lamented for **J**,
1:33 and every one of the acts of **J**, and his splendor,
1:34 The men of the nation took Jeconiah son of **J**,
1:34 and made him king in succession to his father **J**.

JOSIAS (KJV) See JOSIAH

JOSIBIAH (KJV) See JOSHIBIAH

JOSIPHIAH (2)

Ezr 8:10 Of the descendants of Bani, Shelomith son of **J**,
1Es 8:36 Of the descendants of Bani, Shelomith son of **J**,

JOSTLE (1)

Joel 2: 8 They do not **j** one another,

JOT (KJV) See ONE LETTER

JOTBAH (1)

2Ki 21:19 name was Meshullemeth daughter of Haruz of **J**.

JOTBATH (KJV) See JOTBATHAH

JOTBATHAH (3)

Nu 33:33 from Hor-haggidgad and camped at **J**.
33:34 They set out from **J** and camped at Abronah.
Dt 10: 7 and from Gudgodah to **J**,

JOTHAM (26)

Jdg 9: 5 but **J**, the youngest son of Jerubbaal, survived,
9: 7 When it was told to **J**,
9:21 Then **J** ran away and fled, going to Beer,
9:57 and on them came the curse of **J** son of Jerubbaal.
2Ki 15: 5 **J** the king's son was in charge of the palace,
15: 7 his son **J** succeeded him.
15:30 in the twentieth year of **J** son of Uzziah.
15:32 King **J** son of Uzziah of Judah began to reign.
15:36 Now the rest of the acts of **J**, and all that he did,
15:38 **J** slept with his ancestors,
16: 1 King Ahaz son of **J** of Judah began to reign.
1Ch 2:47 Regem, **J**, Geshan, Pelet, Ephah, and Shaaph.
3:12 Amaziah his son, Azariah his son, **J** his son,
5:17 by genealogies in the days of King **J** of Judah,
2Ch 26:21 His son **J** was in charge of the palace of the king,
26:23 His son **J** succeeded him.
27: 1 **J** was twenty-five years old when he began
27: 6 So **J** became strong because he ordered his ways
27: 7 Now the rest of the acts of **J**,
27: 9 **J** slept with his ancestors,
Isa 1: 1 **J**, Ahaz, and Hezekiah, kings of Judah.
7: 1 In the days of Ahaz son of **J** son of Uzziah,
Hos 1: 1 in the days of Kings Uzziah, **J**, Ahaz,
Mic 1: 1 to Micah of Moresheth in the days of Kings **J**,
Mt 1: 9 Uzziah the father of **J**, and **J** the father of Ahaz,

JOURNEY‡ (82) [JOURNEYED, JOURNEYING, JOURNEYS]

Ge 24:21 or not the LORD had made his **j** successful.
24:56 since the LORD has made my **j** successful;
29: 1 Then Jacob went on his **j**,
30:36 of three days' **j** between himself and Jacob,
33:12 Then Esau said, "Let us **j** on our way,
42:25 and to give them provisions for their **j**.
42:38 If harm should come to him on the **j** that you are
45:21 and he gave them provisions for the **j**.
45:23 bread, and provision for his father on the **j**.
46: 1 When Israel set out on his **j** with all that he had
Ex 3:18 let us now go a three days' **j** into the wilderness,
5: 3 a three days' **j** into the wilderness to sacrifice to
8:27 a three days' **j** into the wilderness and sacrifice to
40:36 Israelites would set out on each stage of their **j**;
40:38 of all the house of Israel at each stage of their **j**.
Nu 9:10 through touching a corpse, or is away on a **j**,
9:13 But anyone who is clean and is not on a **j**,
10:33 from the mount of the LORD three days' **j** with
10:33 of the LORD going before them three days' **j**,
11:31 about a day's **j** on this side and a day's **j** on
33: 8 went a three days' **j** in the wilderness of Etham,
Dt 1: 7 Resume your **j**, and go into the hill country of
1:40 But as for you, **j** back into the wilderness,
2:24 "Proceed on your **j** and cross the Wadi Arnon.
10:11 "Get up, go on your **j** at the head of the people,
23: 4 not meet you with food and water on your **j** out
24: 9 the LORD your God did to Miriam on your **j** out
25:17 Remember what Amalek did to you on your **j** out
Jos 5: 4 of Egypt, all the warriors, had died during the **j**
5: 5 the people born on the **j** through the wilderness
9:11 'Take provisions in your hand for the **j**;
9:12 the **j**, on the day we set out to come to you,
9:13 of ours are worn out from the very long **j**."
Jdg 18:21 So they resumed their **j**, putting the little ones,
19: 9 up early in the morning for your **j**,
1Sa 9: 6 about the **j** on which we have set out."
21: 5 even when it is a common **j**;
2Sa 11:10 "You have just come from a **j**.
1Ki 18:27 or he has wandered away, or he is on a **j**,
19: 4 But he himself went a day's **j** into the wilderness,
19: 7 otherwise the **j** will be too much for you."
Ezr 7: 9 the first month the **j** up from Babylon was begun,
8:21 to seek from him a safe **j** for ourselves,
Pr 7:19 he has gone on a long **j**.
Mt 10:10 for your **j**, or two tunics, or sandals, or a staff;
25:14 "For it is as if a man, going on a **j**,
Mk 6: 8 He ordered them to take nothing for their **j** except
10:17 As he was setting out on a **j**,
13:34 It is like a man going on a **j**,
Lk 2:44 in the group of travelers, they went a day's **j**.
9: 3 He said to them, "Take nothing for your **j**,
Jn 4: 6 tired out by his **j**, was sitting by the well.
Ac 1:12 which is near Jerusalem, a sabbath day's **j** away.
10: 9 as they were on their **j** and approaching the city,
21: 5 we left and proceeded on our **j**;
Ro 15:24 For I do hope to see you on my **j** and to be sent on
3Jn 1: 7 for they began their **j** for the sake of Christ,
Tob 5: 6 It is a **j** of two days from Ecbatana to Rages;
5:17 for the **j** and set out with your brother.
5:17 Before he went out to start his **j**,
5:17 Tobit then said to him, "Have a safe **j**."
5:22 his **j** will be successful, and he will come back
7:12 the God of heaven prosper your **j** with his peace."
10: 5 the light of my eyes, that I let you make the **j**."
10:11 "Farewell, my child; have a safe **j**.
10:13 because he had made his **j** a success.
11:15 to his father that his **j** had been successful,
Wis 13:18 for a prosperous **j**, a thing that cannot take a step;
18: 3 of fire as a guide for your people's unknown **j**,
19: 5 that your people might experience an incredible **j**,
Sir 8:16 and do not **j** with them through lonely country,
21:16 A fool's chatter is like a burden on a **j**,
1Mc 5:24 and made three days' **j** into the wilderness.
7:45 The Jews pursued them a day's **j**,
8:19 They went to Rome, a very long **j**;
2Mc 3: 8 Heliodorus at once set out on his **j**,
9: 4 to drive without stopping until he completed the **j**.
1Es 8: 6 by the prosperous **j** that the Lord gave them.
8:50 to seek from him a prosperous **j** for ourselves and
3Mc 7:18 to them for their **j** until all of them arrived
2Es 13:45 a **j** of a year and a half;

JOURNEYED (21) [JOURNEY]

Ge 12: 9 And Abram **j** on by stages toward the Negeb.
13: 3 He **j** on by stages from the Negeb as far as Bethel,
13:11 the plain of the Jordan, and Lot **j** eastward;
20: 1 From there Abraham **j** toward the region of
33:17 But Jacob **j** to Succoth, and built himself a house,
35: 5 As they **j**, a terror from God fell upon
35:16 Then they **j** from Bethel;
35:21 Israel **j** on, and pitched his tent beyond the tower
Ex 12:37 The Israelites **j** from Rameses to Succoth,
17: 1 the whole congregation of the Israelites **j** by stages,
19: 2 They had **j** from Rephidim,
Nu 11:35 From Kibroth-hattaavah the people **j** to Hazeroth.
Dt 2: 1 we **j** back into the wilderness,
10: 6 Israelites **j** from Beeroth-bene-jaakan to Moserah.
10: 7 From there they **j** to Gudgodah,
Jdg 11:18 Then they **j** through the wilderness,
1Ch 4:39 They **j** to the entrance of Gedor,
Isa 57: 9 You **j** to Molech with oil,
Tob 6: 2 So they both **j** along,
Wis 5: 7 and we **j** through trackless deserts,
11: 2 They **j** through an uninhabited wilderness,

JOURNEYING (1) [JOURNEY]

Jos 14:10 while Israel was **j** through the wilderness;

JOURNEYS (1) [JOURNEY]

2Co 11:26 on frequent **j**, in danger from rivers, danger

JOWLS (1)

Dt 18: 3 the two **j**, and the stomach.

JOY‡ (219) [JOYFUL, JOYFULLY, JOYFULNESS, JOYOUS, JOYOUSLY, JOYS, OVERJOYED]

Jdg 19: 3 the girl's father saw him and came with **j**
1Sa 18: 6 with songs of **j**, and with musical instruments.
1Ki 1:40 playing on pipes and rejoicing with great **j**,
1Ch 12:40 oil, oxen, and sheep, for there was **j** in Israel.
15:16 to raise loud sounds of **j**.
16:27 strength and **j** are in his place.
16:33 Then shall the trees of the forest sing for **j** before
29:22 before the LORD on that day with great **j**.
2Ch 20:27 returned to Jerusalem with **j**,
30:26 There was great **j** in Jerusalem,
Ezr 3:12 though many shouted aloud for **j**,
6:16 the dedication of this house of God with **j**.
6:22 With **j** they celebrated the festival
Ne 8:10 for the **j** of the LORD is your strength."
12:43 for God had made them rejoice with great **j**;
12:43 The **j** of Jerusalem was heard far away.
Est 8:16 Jews there was light and gladness, **j** and honor.
8:17 there was gladness and **j** among the Jews,
Job 8:21 and your lips with shouts of **j**.
20: 5 and the **j** of the godless is but for a moment?
29:13 and I caused the widow's heart to sing for **j**.
33:26 he comes into his presence with **j**,
38: 7 and all the heavenly beings shouted for **j**?
Ps 5:11 let them ever sing for **j**.
16:11 In your presence there is fullness of **j**;
19: 5 and like a strong man runs its course with **j**.
20: 5 May we shout for **j** over your victory,
21: 6 you make him glad with the **j** of your presence.
27: 6 I will offer in his tent sacrifices with shouts of **j**;
30: 5 but **j** comes with the morning.
30:11 have taken off my sackcloth and clothed me with **j**,
32:11 and shout for **j**, all you upright in heart.
35:27 Let those who desire my vindication shout for **j**
43: 4 to the altar of God, to God my exceeding **j**;
45:15 With **j** and gladness they are led along
47: 1 shout to God with loud songs of **j**.
48: 2 is the **j** of all the earth, Mount Zion,
51: 8 Let me hear **j** and gladness;
51:12 Restore to me the **j** of your salvation,
63: 7 and in the shadow of your wings I sing for **j**.
65: 8 of the morning and the evening shout for **j**.
65:12 the hills gird themselves with **j**,
65:13 they shout and sing together for **j**.
67: 4 Let the nations be glad and sing for **j**,
68: 3 let them be jubilant with **j**.
71:23 My lips will shout for **j** when I sing praises
81: 1 shout for **j** to the God of Jacob.
84: 2 and my flesh sing for **j** to the living God.
92: 4 at the works of your hands I sing for **j**.
96:12 Then shall all the trees of the forest sing for **j**
97:11 and **j** for the upright in heart.
98: 8 let the hills sing together for **j**
105:43 So he brought his people out with **j**,
107:22 and tell of his deeds with songs of **j**.
119:111 they are the **j** of my heart.
126: 2 and our tongue with shouts of **j**;
126: 5 May those who sow in tears reap with shouts of **j**.
126: 6 shall come home with shouts of **j**,
132: 9 and let your faithful shout for **j**.
132:16 and its faithful will shout for **j**.
137: 6 if I do not set Jerusalem above my highest **j**.
149: 5 let them sing for **j** on their couches.
Pr 12:20 but those who counsel peace have **j**.
14:10 and no stranger shares its **j**.
14:13 and the end of **j** is grief.
15:21 Folly is a **j** to one who has no sense,
15:23 To make an apt answer is a **j** to anyone,
17:21 the parent of a fool has no **j**.
21:15 When justice is done, it is a **j** to the righteous,
Ecc 2:26 God gives wisdom and knowledge and **j**;
5:20 because God keeps them occupied with the **j**
Isa 9: 3 you have increased its **j**;
9: 3 they rejoice before you as with **j** at the harvest,
12: 3 With **j** you will draw water from the wells
12: 6 Shout aloud and sing for **j**, O royal Zion,
16:10 **J** and gladness are taken away from
22:13 but instead there was **j** and festivity,
24:11 all **j** has reached its eventide;
24:14 They lift up their voices, they sing for **j**;
26:19 O dwellers in the dust, awake and sing for **j**!
29:19 The meek shall obtain fresh **j** in the LORD,
32:14 the **j** of wild asses, a pasture for flocks;
35: 2 and rejoice with **j** and singing.
35: 6 and the tongue of the speechless sing for **j**.
35:10 everlasting **j** shall be upon their heads;
35:10 they shall obtain **j** and gladness,
42:11 let the inhabitants of Sela sing for **j**,
48:20 flee from Chaldea, declare this with a shout of **j**,
49:13 Sing for **j**, O heavens, and exult, O earth;
51: 3 **j** and gladness will be found in her,
51:11 everlasting **j** shall be upon their heads;
51:11 they shall obtain **j** and gladness,
52: 8 up their voices, together they sing for **j**;
55:12 you shall go out in **j**, and be led back in peace;
60:15 a **j** from age to age.
61: 7 everlasting **j** shall be theirs.
65:18 for I am about to create Jerusalem as a **j**,
66: 5 so that we may see your **j**";
66:10 rejoice with her in **j**, all you who mourn over her—
Jer 8:18 My **j** is gone, grief is upon me, my heart is sick.
15:16 and your words became to me a **j** and the delight
31:13 I will turn their mourning into **j**,
33: 9 And this city shall be to me a name of **j**,
48:33 and **j** have been taken away from the fruitful land
48:33 no one treads them with shouts of **j**;
48:33 the shouting is not the shout of **j**.
51:48 shall shout for **j** over Babylon;
La 2:15 the perfection of beauty, the **j** of all the earth?"
5:15 The **j** of our hearts has ceased;
Eze 24:25 when I take from them their stronghold, their **j**
36: 5 who, with wholehearted **j** and utter contempt,
Joel 1:12 surely, **j** withers away among the people.
1:16 **j** and gladness from the house of our God?
Zec 8:19 shall be seasons of **j** and gladness,
Mt 2:10 they were overwhelmed with **j**.
13:20 the word and immediately receives it with **j**;
13:44 in his **j** he goes and sells all that he has and buys
25:21 enter into the **j** of your master.'
25:23 enter into the **j** of your master.'
28: 8 they left the tomb quickly with fear and great **j**,

Mk 4:16 they immediately receive it with j.
Lk 1:14 You will have j and gladness,
1:44 the child in my womb leaped for j.
2:10 I am bringing you good news of great j for all
6:23 Rejoice in that day and leap for j,
8:13 when they hear the word, receive it with j.
10:17 The seventy returned with j, saying, "Lord,
15: 7 there will be more j in heaven
15:10 there is j in the presence of the angels of God
24:41 While in their j they were disbelieving
24:52 and returned to Jerusalem with great j;
Jn 3:29 For this reason my j has been fulfilled.
15:11 I have said these things to you so that my j may
15:11 and that your j may be complete.
16:20 you will have pain, but your pain will turn into j.
16:21 because of the j of having brought a human being
16:22 and no one will take your j from you.
16:24 so that your j may be complete.
17:13 so that they may have my j made complete
Ac 8: 8 So there was great j in that city.
13:52 And the disciples were filled with j and with
14:17 and filling you with food and your hearts with j."
15: 3 and brought great j to all the believers.
Ro 14:17 and drink but righteousness and peace and j in
15:13 May the God of hope fill you with all j and peace
15:32 that by God's will I may come to you with j and
2Co 1:24 rather, we are workers with you for your j,
2: 3 that my j would be the j of all of you.
7:13 we rejoiced still more at the j of Titus,
8: 2 a severe ordeal of affliction, their abundant j
Gal 5:22 By contrast, the fruit of the Spirit is love, j, peace,
Php 1: 4 with j in every one of my prayers for all of you,
1:25 with all of you for your progress and j in faith,
2: 2 make my j complete:
2:29 Welcome him then in the Lord with all j,
4: 1 whom I love and long for, my j and crown,
1Th 1: 6 the word with j inspired by the Holy Spirit,
2:19 or j or crown of boasting before our Lord Jesus
2:20 Yes, you are our glory and j!
3: 9 the j that we feel before our God because of you?
2Ti 1: 4 I long to see you so that I may be filled with j.
Phm 1: 7 I have indeed received much j and encouragement
Heb 12: 2 of the j that was set before him endured the cross,
13:17 Let them do this with j and not with sighing—
Jas 1: 2 of any kind, consider it nothing but j,
4: 9 be turned into mourning and your j into dejection.
1Pe 1: 8 and rejoice with an indescribable and glorious j,
4:13 be glad and shout for j when his glory is revealed.
1Jn 1: 4 We are writing these things so that our j may
2Jn 1:12 so that our j may be complete.
3Jn 1: 4 I have no greater j than this,
Tob 5:10 Tobit retorted, "What j is left for me any more?
7:16 of heaven grant you j in place of your sorrow.
10:13 Tobias parted from Raguel with happiness and j,
11:17 and welcome, with blessing and j.
11:18 also present to share Tobit's j.
13:10 so that his tent may be rebuilt in you in j.
13:17 The gates of Jerusalem will sing hymns of j,
Jdt 12: 2 and desecrated to the malicious j of the Gentiles.
12:14 and it will be a j to me until the day of my death."
AdE 8:17 the Jews had j and gladness,
9:17 celebrating it with j and gladness.
9:18 They celebrated the fifteenth with j and gladness.
10:13 with an assembly and j and gladness before God,
14:18 Your servant has had no j since the day
16:21 to be a j for his chosen people instead of a day
Wis 8:16 and life with her has no pain, but gladness and j.
Sir 1:12 and gives gladness and j and long life.
2: 9 hope for good things, for lasting j and mercy.
3: 5 Those who honor their father will have j
4:12 from early morning are filled with j.
6:28 and she will be changed into j for you.
26: 2 A loyal wife brings j to her husband,
30: 5 in his life he looked upon with j and at death,
30:16 and no gladness above j of heart.
41: 9 When you stumble, there is lasting j;
Bar 4:11 With j I nurtured them, but I sent them away
4:22 and j has come to me from the Holy One,
4:23 but God will give you back to me with j
4:29 upon you will bring you everlasting j
4:36 and see the j that is coming to you from God.
5: 9 For God will lead Israel with j,
1Mc 3:45 J was taken from Jacob; the flute and the harp
4:58 There was very great j among the people,
4:59 the altar should be observed with j and gladness
5:54 they went up to Mount Zion with j and gladness,
14:11 and Israel rejoiced with great j.
2Mc 3:30 was filled with j and gladness,
15:28 action was over and they were returning with j,
3Mc 4: 6 to share married life exchanged j for wailing,
4:16 king was greatly and continually filled with j,
5:44 the Friends and officers departed with great j,
6:31 of j they apportioned to celebrants the place
6:32 they formed choruses as a sign of peaceful j.
2Es 2:19 by these I will fill your children with j.
2:36 receive the j of your glory;
7:*91* with great j the glory of him who receives them,
7:*131* [61] as j over those to whom salvation is assured."

JOYFUL (28) [JOY]

1Ki 8:66 to their tents, j and in good spirits because of all
2Ch 7:10 j and in good spirits because of the goodness that
Ezr 3:13 not distinguish the sound of the j shout from
6:22 for the LORD had made them j,
Job 3: 7 let no j cry be heard in it.
Ps 63: 5 and my mouth praises you with j lips
66: 1 Make a j noise to God, all the earth;
68: 3 But let the righteous be j;
95: 1 let us make a j noise to the rock of our salvation!
95: 2 let us make a j noise to him with songs of praise!
98: 4 Make a j noise to the LORD, all the earth;
98: 6 and the sound of the horn make a j noise before
100: 1 Make a j noise to the LORD, all the earth.
Ecc 7:14 In the day of prosperity be j,
Isa 56: 7 and make them j in my house of prayer;
Jer 49:25 How the famous city is forsaken, the j town!
Tob 13:11 Generation after generation will give j praise
Jdt 14: 9 the people raised a great shout and made a j noise
AdE 5: 9 Haman went out from the king j and glad of heart.
9:19 the fourteenth of Adar as a j holiday,
9:19 the fifteenth day of Adar as their j holiday,
Sir 30:22 A j heart is life itself,
1Es 5:64 while many came with trumpets and a j noise,
3Mc 5:17 and to make the present portion of the banquet j
7:15 and they kept the day as a j festival,
2Es 2:37 the Lord has entrusted to you and be j,
12:34 and he will make them j until the end comes,
13:13 some of whom were j and some sorrowful;

JOYFULLY (8) [JOY]

Dt 28:47 Because you did not serve the LORD your God j
Lk 19:37 to praise God j with a loud voice for all the deeds
Col 1:11 to endure everything with patience, while j
1Mc 4:56 and j offered burnt offerings;
3Mc 5:21 and j with one accord gave their approval,
6:34 and had j registered them,
7:13 multitude shouted the Hallelujah and j departed.
7:16 j and loudly giving thanks to the one God

JOYFULNESS (1) [JOY]

3Mc 6:30 that they should celebrate their rescue with all j in

JOYOUS (7) [JOY]

Ps 98: 4 break forth into j song and sing praises.
113: 9 making her the j mother of children.
Isa 32:13 yes, for all the j houses in the jubilant city.
Tob 5:10 He replied, "J greetings to you!"
7: 1 and he replied, "J greetings, brothers;
3Mc 6:35 the accompaniment of j thanksgiving and psalms.
7:19 as a j festival during the time of their stay.

JOYOUSLY (2) [JOY]

1Ch 29:17 who are present here, offering freely and j to you.
Ps 89:12 Tabor and Hermon j praise your name.

JOYS (1) [JOY]

4Mc 9:31 I lighten my pain by the j that come from virtue,

JOZABAD (13)

1Ch 12: 4 Jeremiah, Jahaziel, Johanan, J of Gederah,
12:20 Adnah, J, Jediael, Michael, J, Elihu,
2Ch 31:13 Asahel, Jerimoth, J, Eliel, Ismachiah, Mahath,
35: 9 and Hashabiah and Jeiel and J,
Ezr 8:33 J son of Jeshua and Noadiah son of Binnui.
10:22 Elioenai, Maaseiah, Ishmael, Nethanel, J,
10:23 J, Shimei, Kelaiah (that is, Kelita), Pethahiah,
Ne 8: 7 Kelita, Azariah, J, Hanan, Pelaiah, the Levites,
11:16 and J, of the leaders of the Levites, who were
1Es 8:63 with them were J son of Jeshua and Moeth son
9:23 And of the Levites: J and Shimei and Kelaiah,
9:48 Hodiah, Maiannas and Kelita, Azariah and J,

JOZACAR (1) [=ZABAD]

2Ki 12:21 It was J son of Shimeath and Jehozabad son

JOZADAK (11) [=JEHOZADAK]

Ezr 3: 2 Then Jeshua son of J, with his fellow priests,
3: 8 and Jeshua son of J made a beginning,
5: 2 of Shealtiel and Jeshua son of J set out to rebuild
10:18 of the descendants of Jeshua son of J
Ne 12:26 in the days of Joiakim son of Jeshua son of J,
Sir 49:12 and so was Jeshua son of J;
1Es 5: 5 Jeshua son of J son of Seraiah and Joakim son
5:48 Then Jeshua son of J, with his fellow priests,
5:56 and Jeshua son of J made a beginning, together
6: 2 of J began to build the house of the Lord that is
9:19 of the descendants of Jeshua son of J

JUBAL (1)

Ge 4:21 His brother's name was J;

JUBILANT (3) [JUBILATION]

Ps 68: 3 let them be j with joy.
Isa 24: 8 the noise of the j has ceased,
32:13 yes, for all the joyous houses in the j city.

JUBILATION (1) [JUBILANT]

Pr 11:10 and when the wicked perish, there is j.

JUBILEE (21)

Lev 25:10 It shall be a j for you:
25:11 That fiftieth year shall be a j for you:
25:12 For it is a j; it shall be holy
25:13 In this year of j you shall return,
25:15 for the number of years since the j;
25:28 with the purchaser until the year of j;
25:28 in the j it shall be released,
25:30 it shall not be released in the j.
25:31 and they shall be released in the j.
25:33 shall be released in the j;
25:40 They shall serve with you until the year of the j.
25:50 to the alien until the j year;
25:52 until the j year, they shall compute thus:
25:54 with them shall go free in the j year.
27:17 person consecrates the field as of the year of j,
27:18 but if the field is consecrated after the j,
27:18 to the years that remain until the year of j,
27:21 But when the field is released in the j,
27:23 the proportionate assessment up to the year of j,
27:24 In the year of j the field shall return to the one
Nu 36: 4 And when the j of the Israelites comes,

JUCAL (1)

Jer 38: 1 Gedaliah son of Pashhur, J son of Shelemiah,

JUDAH‡ (879) [JUDAH'S, JUDAHITES, JUDEA]

A. PEOPLE OF JUDAH (72)
B. LAND OF JUDAH (46)
C. HOUSE OF JUDAH (41)
D. KINGS OF JUDAH (39)
E. JUDAH AND JERUSALEM (35)
F. CITIES OF JUDAH (32)
G. ALL JUDAH (26)
H. TOWNS OF JUDAH (26)
I. TRIBE OF JUDAH (25)
J. ISRAEL AND JUDAH (21)
K. KING OF JUDAH (20)
L. JUDAH AND BENJAMIN (17)
M. JUDAH AND ISRAEL (8)
N. JERUSALEM AND JUDAH (7)

Ge 29:35 therefore she named him J;
35:23 Reuben (Jacob's firstborn), Simeon, Levi, J,
37:26 Then J said to his brothers,
38: 1 at that time that J went down from his brothers
38: 2 There J saw the daughter of
38: 6 J took a wife for Er his firstborn;
38: 8 Then J said to Onan, "Go in
38:11 Then J said to his daughter-in-law Tamar,
38:12 In course of time the wife of J, Shua's daughter,
38:15 When J saw her, he thought her to be a prostitute,
38:20 When J sent the kid by his friend the Adullamite,
38:22 he returned to J, and said, "I have not found her;
38:23 J replied, "Let her keep the things as her own,
38:24 About three months later J was told,
38:24 J said, "Bring her out, and let her be burned."
38:26 Then J acknowledged them and said,
43: 3 But J said to him, "The man solemnly warned us,
43: 8 Then J said to his father Israel,
44:14 J and his brothers came to Joseph's house
44:16 And J said, "What can we say to my lord?
44:18 Then J stepped up to him and said, "O my lord,
46:12 The children of J: Er, Onan,
46:28 Israel sent J ahead to Joseph to lead the way
49: 8 J, your brothers shall praise you;
49: 9 J is a lion's whelp;
49:10 The scepter shall not depart from J,
Ex 1: 2 Reuben, Simeon, Levi, and J,
31: 2 of Uri son of Hur, of the tribe of J: I
35:30 of Uri son of Hur, of the tribe of J; I
38:22 Bezalel son of Uri son of Hur, of the tribe of J, I
Nu 1: 7 From J, Nahshon son of Amminadab.
1:26 The descendants of J, their lineage, in their clans,
1:27 of the tribe of J were seventy-four thousand six I
2: 3 of the regimental encampment of J by companies.
2: 3 of the people of J shall be Nahshon son of A
2: 9 The total enrollment of the camp of J,
7:12 of Amminadab, of the tribe of J; I
10:14 The standard of the camp of J set out first,
13: 6 from the tribe of J, Caleb son of Jephunneh; I
26:19 The sons of J: Er and Onan;
26:20 The descendants of J by their clans were:
26:22 These are the clans of J:
34:19 Of the tribe of J, Caleb son of Jephunneh. I
Dt 27:12 Simeon, Levi, J, Issachar, Joseph, and Benjamin.
33: 7 And this he said of J: O LORD, give heed to J,
34: 2 all the land of J as far as the Western Sea, B
Jos 7: 1 of the tribe of J, took some of the devoted things; I
7:16 and the tribe of J was taken. I
7:17 He brought near the clans of J,
7:18 of the tribe of J, was taken. I
11:21 from Anab, and from all the hill country of J,
14: 6 Then the people of J came to Joshua at Gilgal; A
15: 1 The lot for the tribe of the people of J according A
15:12 This is the boundary surrounding the people of J A
15:13 of Jephunneh a portion among the people of J, A
15:20 of the people of J according to their families. A
15:21 the tribe of the people of J in the extreme South, A
15:63 the people of J could not drive out the Jebusites, A
15:63 with the people of J in Jerusalem to this day. A
18: 5 J continuing in its territory on the south,
18:11 between the tribe of J and the tribe of Joseph. I
18:14 a town belonging to the tribe of J. I
19: 1 within the inheritance of the tribe of J. I
19: 9 of Simeon formed part of the territory of J;
19: 9 portion of the tribe of J was too large for them, I
19:34 and J on the east at the Jordan.
20: 7 Hebron) in the hill country of J.
21: 4 by lot thirteen towns from the tribes of J,
21: 9 the tribe of J and the tribe of Simeon they gave I
21:11 that is Hebron, in the hill country of J,

Jdg 1: 2 The LORD said, "J shall go up.
1: 3 J said to his brother Simeon,
1: 4 Then J went up and the LORD gave
1: 8 people of J fought against Jerusalem and took it. A
1: 9 Afterward the people of J went down to fight A
1:10 J went against the Canaanites who lived
1:16 with the people of J from the city of palms into A
1:16 from the city of palms into the wilderness of J,
1:17 J went with his brother Simeon,
1:18 J took Gaza with its territory,
1:19 with J, and he took possession of the hill country,
10: 9 the Jordan to fight against J and against Benjamin
15: 9 Then the Philistines came up and encamped in J,
15:10 The men of J said, "Why have you come up
15:11 of J went down to the cleft of the rock of Etam,
17: 7 a young man of Bethlehem in J, of the clan of J.
17: 8 This man left the town of Bethlehem in J,
17: 9 He replied, "I am a Levite of Bethlehem in J,
18:12 and went up and encamped at Kiriath-jearim in J.
19: 1 took to himself a concubine from Bethlehem in J.
19: 2 from him to her father's house at Bethlehem in J,
19:18 from Bethlehem in J to the remote parts of
19:18 I went to Bethlehem in J;
20:18 And the LORD answered, "J shall go up first."
Ru 1: 1 and a certain man of Bethlehem in J went to live
1: 2 they were Ephrathites from Bethlehem in J.
1: 7 on their way to go back to the land of J. B
4:12 like the house of Perez, whom Tamar bore to J."
1Sa 11: 8 and those from J seventy thousand.
15: 4 and ten thousand soldiers of J.
17: 1 they were gathered at Socoh, which belongs to J,
17:12 the son of an Ephrathite of Bethlehem in J,
17:52 of Israel and J rose up with a shout and pursued J
18:16 But all Israel and J loved David; J
22: 5 leave, and go into the land of J." B
23: 3 "Look, we are afraid here in J;
23:23 among all the thousands of J."
27: 6 Ziklag has belonged to the kings of J to this day. D
27:10 David would say, "Against the Negeb of J,"
30:14 of the Cherethites and on that which belongs to J
30:16 the land of the Philistines and from the land of J. B
30:26 the elders of J, saying, "Here is a present for you
2Sa 1:18 of the Bow be taught to the people of J; A
2: 1 "Shall I go up into any of the cities of J?" F
2: 4 Then the people of J came, A
2: 4 they anointed David king over the house of J. C
2: 7 the house of J has anointed me king over them." C
2:10 But the house of J followed David. C
2:11 the house of J was seven years and six months. C
3: 8 he said, "Am I a dog's head for J?
3:10 set up the throne of David over Israel and over J,
5: 5 At Hebron he reigned over J seven years
5: 5 over all Israel and J thirty-three years. J
11:11 "The ark and Israel and J remain in booths; J
12: 8 and gave you the house of Israel and of J;
19:11 "Say to the elders of J,
19:14 Amasa swayed the hearts of all the people of J A
19:15 and J came to Gilgal to meet the king and
19:16 down with the people of J to meet King David; A
19:40 people of J, and also half the people of Israel, A
19:41 the people of J stolen you away, A
19:42 the people of J answered the people of Israel, A
19:43 the people of Israel answered the people of J, A
19:43 the words of the people of J were fiercer than A
20: 2 the people of J followed their king steadfastly A
20: 4 the men of J together to me within three days,
20: 5 So Amasa went to summon J;
21: 2 in his zeal for the people of Israel and J.) J
24: 1 saying, "Go, count the people of Israel and J." J
24: 7 they went out to the Negeb of J at Beer-sheba.
24: 9 and those of J were five hundred thousand.
1Ki 1: 9 the king's sons, and all the royal officials of J,
1:35 to be ruler over Israel and over J."
2:32 commander of the army of J.
4:19 And there was one official in the land of J. B
4:20 J and Israel were as numerous as the sand by M
4:25 During Solomon's lifetime J and Israel lived M
12:17 the Israelites who were living in the towns of J. H
12:20 except the tribe of J alone. I
12:21 he assembled all the house of J and the tribe C
12:23 Say to King Rehoboam of J,
12:23 and to all the house of J and Benjamin, CL
12:27 to their master, King Rehoboam of J;
12:27 and return to King Rehoboam of J."
12:32 of the eighth month like the festival that was in J,
13: 1 of God came out of J by the word of the LORD
13:12 that the man of God who came from J had gone.
13:14 "Are you the man of God who came from J?"
13:21 to the man of God who came from J, "Thus says
14:21 Now Rehoboam son of Solomon reigned in J.
14:22 J did what was evil in the sight of the LORD;
14:29 in the Book of the Annals of the Kings of J? D
15: 1 Abijam began to reign over J.
15: 7 in the Book of the Annals of the Kings of J? D
15: 9 Asa began to reign over J;
15:17 King Baasha of Israel went up against J,
15:17 from going out or coming in to King Asa of J.
15:22 Then King Asa made a proclamation to all J, G
15:23 in the Book of the Annals of the Kings of J? D
15:25 over Israel in the second year of King Asa of J;
15:28 in the third year of King Asa of J,
15:33 In the third year of King Asa of J,
16: 8 In the twenty-sixth year of King Asa of J,
16:10 in the twenty-seventh year of King Asa of J,
16:15 In the twenty-seventh year of King Asa of J,
16:23 In the thirty-first year of King Asa of J,
16:29 In the thirty-eighth year of King Asa of J,
1Ki 19: 3 and came to Beer-sheba, which belongs to J;
22: 2 But in the third year King Jehoshaphat of J came
22:10 of Israel and King Jehoshaphat of J were sitting
22:29 the king of Israel and King Jehoshaphat of J went
22:41 over J in the fourth year of King Ahab of Israel.
22:45 in the Book of the Annals of the Kings of J? D
22:51 in the seventeenth year of King Jehoshaphat of J;
2Ki 1:17 of King Jehoram son of Jehoshaphat of J,
3: 1 In the eighteenth year of King Jehoshaphat of J,
3: 7 he went he sent word to King Jehoshaphat of J,
3: 9 So the king of Israel, the king of J, K
3:14 not that I have regard for King Jehoshaphat of J,
8:16 Jehoram son of King Jehoshaphat of J began
8:19 Yet the LORD would not destroy J,
8:20 In his days Edom revolted against the rule of J,
8:22 So Edom has been in revolt against the rule of J
8:23 in the Book of the Annals of the Kings of J? D
8:25 Ahaziah son of King Jehoram of J began to reign.
8:29 King Ahaziah son of Jehoram of J went down
9:16 King Ahaziah of J had come down to visit Joram.
9:21 and King Ahaziah of J set out, each in his chariot,
9:27 When King Ahaziah of J saw this,
9:29 Ahaziah began to reign over J.
10:13 Jehu met relatives of King Ahaziah of J and said,
12:18 of J took all the votive gifts that Jehoshaphat,
12:18 his ancestors, the kings of J, had dedicated, D
12:19 in the Book of the Annals of the Kings of J? D
13: 1 of King Joash son of Ahaziah of J, Jehoahaz son
13:10 In the thirty-seventh year of King Joash of J,
13:12 with which he fought against King Amaziah of J,
14: 1 King Amaziah son of Joash of J, began to reign.
14: 9 of J, "A thornbush on Lebanon sent to a cedar
14:10 so that you fall, you and J with you?"
14:11 of J faced one another in battle at Beth-shemesh,
14:11 in battle at Beth-shemesh, which belongs to J.
14:12 J was defeated by Israel; everyone fled home.
14:13 of Israel captured King Amaziah of J son
14:15 and how he fought with King Amaziah of J,
14:17 of Joash of J lived fifteen years after the death
14:18 in the Book of the Annals of the Kings of J? D
14:21 All the people of J took Azariah, A
14:22 He rebuilt Elath and restored it to J,
14:23 of J, King Jeroboam son of Joash of Israel began
14:28 which had belonged to J,
15: 1 of Israel King Azariah son of Amaziah of J began
15: 6 in the Book of the Annals of the Kings of J? D
15: 8 In the thirty-eighth year of King Azariah of J,
15:13 in the thirty-ninth year of King Uzziah of J;
15:17 In the thirty-ninth year of King Azariah of J,
15:23 In the fiftieth year of King Azariah of J,
15:27 In the fifty-second year of King Azariah of J,
15:32 King Jotham son of Uzziah of J began to reign.
15:36 in the Book of the Annals of the Kings of J? D
15:37 of Aram and Pekah son of Remaliah against J.
16: 1 King Ahaz son of Jotham of J began to reign.
16:19 in the Book of the Annals of the Kings of J? D
17: 1 In the twelfth year of King Ahaz of J,
17:13 the LORD warned Israel and J by every prophet J
17:18 none was left but the tribe of J alone. I
17:19 J also did not keep the commandments of
18: 1 Hezekiah son of King Ahaz of J began to reign.
18: 5 like him among all the kings of J after him, D
18:13 the fortified cities of J and captured them. F
18:14 King Hezekiah of J sent to the king of Assyria
18:14 of King Hezekiah of J three hundred talents
18:16 that King Hezekiah of J had overlaid and gave it
18:22 saying to J and to Jerusalem,
18:26 of J within the hearing of the people who are on
18:28 in a loud voice in the language of J,
19:10 "Thus shall you speak to King Hezekiah of J:
19:30 the house of J shall again take root downward, C
20:20 in the Book of the Annals of the Kings of J? D
21:11 of J has committed these abominations,
21:11 and has caused J also to sin with his idols;
21:12 I am bringing upon Jerusalem and J such evil N
21:16 besides the sin that he caused J to sin so
21:17 in the Book of the Annals of the Kings of J? D
21:25 in the Book of the Annals of the Kings of J? D
22:13 for the people, and for all J, G
22:16 words of the book that the king of J has read. K
22:18 But as to the king of J, K
23: 1 elders of J and Jerusalem should be gathered E
23: 2 and with him went all the people of J, A
23: 5 the kings of J had ordained to make offerings D
23: 5 at the cities of J and around Jerusalem; F
23: 8 He brought all the priests out of the towns of J, H
23:11 that the kings of J had dedicated to the sun, D
23:12 which the kings of J had made, D
23:17 the tomb of the man of God who came from J
23:22 of the kings of Israel or of the kings of J; D
23:24 that were seen in the land of J and in Jerusalem, B
23:26 by which his anger was kindled against J,
23:27 "I will remove J also out of my sight,
23:28 in the Book of the Annals of the Kings of J? D
24: 2 he sent them against J to destroy it,
24: 3 this came upon J at the command of the LORD,
24: 5 in the Book of the Annals of the Kings of J? D
24:12 King Jehoiachin of J gave himself up to the king
24:20 Jerusalem and J so angered the LORD N
25:21 So J went into exile out of its land.
25:22 over the people who remained in the land of J, B
25:27 of King Jehoiachin of J, in the twelfth month,
25:27 released King Jehoiachin of J from prison;
1Ch 2: 1 Reuben, Simeon, Levi, J, Issachar, Zebulun,
2: 3 The sons of J: Er, Onan,
2: 4 J had five sons in all.
2:10 prince of the sons of J.
1Ch 4: 1 sons of J: Perez, Hezron, Carmi, Hur, and Shobal.
4:21 The sons of Shelah son of J:
4:41 came in the days of King Hezekiah of J,
5: 2 though J became prominent among his brothers
5:17 by genealogies in the days of King Jotham of J,
6:15 when the LORD sent J and Jerusalem into exile E
6:55 the land of J and its surrounding pasture lands, B
6:65 They also gave them by lot out of the tribes of J,
9: 1 And J was taken into exile in Babylon because
9: 3 some of the people of J, Benjamin, Ephraim, A
9: 4 son of Bani, from the sons of Perez son of J.
12:24 The people of J bearing shield and spear A
13: 6 that is, to Kiriath-jearim, which belongs to J,
21: 5 and in J four hundred seventy thousand who drew
27:18 for J, Elihu, one of David's brothers;
28: 4 for he chose J as leader,
28: 4 and in the house of J my father's house, C
2Ch 2: 7 workers who are with me in J and Jerusalem, E
9:11 the like of them before in the land of J. B
10:17 of Israel who were living in the cities of J. F
11: 1 house of J and Benjamin to fight against Israel, CL
11: 3 Say to King Rehoboam of J,
11: 3 and to all Israel in J and Benjamin, L
11: 5 and he built cities for defense in J.
11:10 fortified cities that are in J and in Benjamin.
11:12 So he held J and Benjamin. L
11:14 holdings and had come to J and Jerusalem, E
11:17 They strengthened the kingdom of J,
11:23 through all the districts of J and Benjamin, L
12: 4 He took the fortified cities of J and came as far F
12: 5 the officers of J, who had gathered at Jerusalem
12:12 moreover, conditions were good in J.
13: 1 Abijah began to reign over J.
13:13 thus his troops were in front of J,
13:14 When J turned, the battle was in front of them
13:15 Then the people of J raised the battle shout. A
13:15 And when the people of J shouted, A
13:15 and all Israel before Abijah and J.
13:16 The Israelites fled before J,
13:18 and the people of J prevailed, A
14: 4 and commanded J to seek the LORD,
14: 5 cities of J the high places and the incense altars. F
14: 6 He built fortified cities in J while
14: 7 He said to J, "Let us build these cities,
14: 8 an army of three hundred thousand from J, armed
14:12 the Ethiopians before Asa and before J,
14:13 The people of J carried away a great quantity A
15: 2 "Hear me, Asa, and all J and Benjamin: GL
15: 8 land of J and Benjamin and from the towns BL
15: 9 He gathered all J and Benjamin, GL
15:15 All J rejoiced over the oath; G
16: 1 King Baasha of Israel went up against J,
16: 1 or coming into the territory of King Asa of J.
16: 6 Then King Asa brought all J, G
16: 7 that time the seer Hanani came to King Asa of J,
16:11 in the Book of the Kings of J and Israel. DM
17: 2 He placed forces in all the fortified cities of J, F
17: 2 and set garrisons in the land of J, B
17: 5 All J brought tribute to Jehoshaphat, G
17: 6 the high places and the sacred poles from J.
17: 7 Nethanel, and Micaiah, to teach in the cities of J. F
17: 9 They taught in J, having the book of the law of
17: 9 around through all the cities of J and taught F
17:10 on all the kingdoms of the lands around J,
17:12 He built fortresses and storage cities in J.
17:13 He carried out great works in the cities of J. F
17:14 Of J, the commanders of the thousands:
17:19 in the fortified cities throughout all J. G
18: 3 of Israel said to King Jehoshaphat of J,
18: 9 of Israel and King Jehoshaphat of J were sitting
18:28 the king of Israel and King Jehoshaphat of J went
19: 1 of J returned in safety to his house in Jerusalem.
19: 5 in the land in all the fortified cities of J, F
19:11 the governor of the house of J, C
20: 3 and proclaimed a fast throughout all J. G
20: 4 J assembled to seek help from the LORD;
20: 4 the towns of J they came to seek the LORD. H
20: 5 stood in the assembly of J and Jerusalem, E
20:13 Meanwhile all J stood before the LORD, G
20:15 "Listen, all J and inhabitants of Jerusalem, G
20:17 the LORD on your behalf, O J and Jerusalem.' E
20:18 and all J and the inhabitants of Jerusalem fell G
20:20 "Listen to me, O J and inhabitants of Jerusalem!
20:22 Moab, and Mount Seir, who had come against J,
20:24 J came to the watchtower of the wilderness,
20:27 Then all the people of J and Jerusalem, AE
20:31 So Jehoshaphat reigned over J.
20:35 of J joined with King Ahaziah of Israel,
21: 2 all these were the sons of King Jehoshaphat of J.
21: 3 together with fortified cities in J;
21: 8 In his days Edom revolted against the rule of J
21:10 So Edom has been in revolt against the rule of J
21:11 he made high places in the hill country of J,
21:11 into unfaithfulness, and made J go astray.
21:12 or in the ways of King Asa of J,
21:13 and have led J and the inhabitants of Jerusalem
21:17 They came up against J, invaded it,
22: 1 So Ahaziah son of Jehoram reigned as king of J. K
22: 6 And Ahaziah son of King Jehoram of J went
22: 8 of J and the sons of Ahaziah's brothers,
22:10 to destroy all the royal family of the house of J. C
23: 2 through J and gathered the Levites from all
23: 2 and gathered the Levites from all the towns of J, H
23: 8 The Levites and all J did according to all that G
24: 5 the cities of J and gather money from all Israel F
24: 6 from J and Jerusalem the tax levied by Moses, E
24: 9 throughout J and Jerusalem to bring in for E

2Ch 24:17 after the death of Jehoiada the officials of **J** came
24:18 upon **J** and Jerusalem for this guilt of theirs. E
24:23 They came to **J** and Jerusalem, E
25: 5 Amaziah assembled the people of **J**, A
25: 5 and of the hundreds for all **J** and Benjamin. GL
25:10 But they became very angry with **J**,
25:12 people of **J** captured another ten thousand alive, A
25:13 on the cities of **J** from Samaria to Beth-horon; F
25:17 Then King Amaziah of **J** took counsel and sent
25:18 of **J**, "A thornbush on Lebanon sent to a cedar
25:19 so that you fall, you and **J** with you?"
25:21 of **J** faced one another in battle at Beth-shemesh,
25:21 in battle at Beth-shemesh, which belongs to **J**.
25:22 **J** was defeated by Israel; everyone fled home.
25:23 King Joash of Israel captured King Amaziah of **J**,
25:25 King Amaziah son of Joash of **J**,
25:26 in the Book of the Kings of **J** and Israel? DM
26: 1 Then all the people of **J** took Uzziah, A
26: 2 He rebuilt Eloth and restored it to **J**,
27: 4 Moreover he built cities in the hill country of **J**,
27: 7 in the Book of the Kings of Israel and **J**. J
28: 6 in **J** in one day, all of them valiant warriors,
28: 9 was angry with **J**, he gave them into your hand,
28:10 to subjugate the people of **J** and Jerusalem, AE
28:17 the Edomites had again invaded and defeated **J**,
28:18 on the cities in the Shephelah and the Negeb of **J**,
28:19 the LORD brought **J** low because of King Ahaz
28:19 without restraint in **J** and had been faithless to
28:25 of **J** he made high places to make offerings
28:26 in the Book of the Kings of **J** and Israel. DM
29: 8 wrath of the LORD came upon **J** and Jerusalem, E
29:21 for the kingdom and for the sanctuary and for **J**.
30: 1 Hezekiah sent word to all Israel and **J**, J
30: 6 all Israel and **J** with letters from the king and J
30:12 on **J** to give them one heart to do what the king
30:24 For King Hezekiah of **J** gave the assembly
30:25 The whole assembly of **J**,
30:25 and the resident aliens who lived in **J**, rejoiced.
31: 1 to the cities of **J** and broke down the pillars, F
31: 1 the altars throughout all **J** and Benjamin, GL
31: 6 The people of Israel and **J** who lived in the cities J
31: 6 the cities of **J** also brought in the tithe of cattle F
31:20 Hezekiah did this throughout all **J**; G
32: 1 King Sennacherib of Assyria came and invaded **J**
32: 8 by the words of King Hezekiah of **J**.
32: 9 to Jerusalem to King Hezekiah of **J** and to all
32: 9 and to all the people of **J** that were in Jerusalem, A
32:12 and his altars and commanded **J** and Jerusalem, E
32:18 a loud voice in the language of **J** to the people
32:23 and precious things to King Hezekiah of **J**,
32:25 wrath came upon him and upon **J** and Jerusalem. E
32:32 in the Book of the Kings of **J** and Israel. DM
32:33 and all **J** and the inhabitants G
33: 9 Manasseh misled **J** and the inhabitants
33:14 of the army in all the fortified cities in **J**.
33:16 and he commanded **J** to serve the LORD
34: 3 to purge **J** and Jerusalem of the high places, E
34: 5 and purged **J** and Jerusalem. E
34: 9 remnant of Israel and from all **J** and Benjamin GL
34:11 buildings that the kings of **J** had let go to ruin. D
34:21 and for those who are left in Israel and in **J**, J
34:24 in the book that was read before the king of **J**. K
34:26 But as to the king of **J**, K
34:29 together all the elders of **J** and Jerusalem. E
34:30 the people of **J**, the inhabitants of Jerusalem, A
35:18 by all **J** and Israel who were present, GM
35:21 saying, "What have I to do with you, king of **J**? K
35:24 All **J** and Jerusalem mourned for Josiah. EG
35:27 in the Book of the Kings of Israel and **J**. J
36: 4 his brother Eliakim king over **J** and Jerusalem, E
36: 8 in the Book of the Kings of Israel and **J**; J
36:10 his brother Zedekiah king over **J** and Jerusalem. E
36:23 to build him a house at Jerusalem, which is in **J**.
Ezr 1: 2 to build him a house at Jerusalem in **J**.
1: 3 are now permitted to go up to Jerusalem in **J**,
1: 5 The heads of the families of **J** and Benjamin, L
1: 8 to Sheshbazzar the prince of **J**.
2: 1 they returned to Jerusalem and **J**, N
4: 1 When the adversaries of **J** and Benjamin heard L
4: 4 people of the land discouraged the people of **J**, A
4: 6 against the inhabitants of **J** and Jerusalem. E
5: 1 to the Jews who were in **J** and Jerusalem, E
5: 8 to the king that we went to the province of **J**,
7:14 about **J** and Jerusalem according to the law E
10: 7 a proclamation throughout **J** and Jerusalem E
10: 9 the people of **J** and Benjamin assembled at AL
10:23 Shimei, Kelaiah (that is, Kelita), Pethahiah, **J**,
Ne 1: 2 Hanani, came with certain men from **J**;
2: 5 I ask that you send me to **J**,
2: 7 they may grant me passage until I arrive in **J**;
4:10 But **J** said, "The strength of
4:16 behind the whole house of **J**, C
5:14 to be their governor in the land of **J**, B
6: 7 'There is a king in **J**!'
6:17 in those days the nobles of **J** sent many letters
6:18 For many in **J** were bound by oath to him,
7: 6 they returned to Jerusalem and **J**, N
11: 3 but in the towns of **J** all lived on their property H
11: 9 and **J** son of Hassenuah was second in charge of
11:20 were in all the towns of **J**, H
11:24 of the descendants of Zerah son of **J**,
11:25 some of the people of **J** lived in Kiriath-arba A
11:36 of the Levites in **J** were joined to Benjamin.
12: 8 Jeshua, Binnui, Kadmiel, Sherebiah, **J**,
12:31 Then I brought the leaders of **J** up onto the wall,
12:32 them went Hoshaiah and half the officials of **J**,
12:34 **J**, Benjamin, Shemaiah, and Jeremiah,
Ne 12:36 Milalai, Gilalai, Maai, Nethanel, **J**, and Hanani,
12:44 for **J** rejoiced over the priests and
13:12 Then all **J** brought the tithe of the grain, wine, G
13:15 in **J** people treading wine presses on the sabbath,
13:16 and sold them on the sabbath to the people of **J**, A
13:17 Then I remonstrated with the nobles of **J** and said
13:24 and they could not speak the language of **J**,
Est 2: 6 with King Jeconiah of **J**,
Ps 48:11 towns of **J** rejoice because of your judgments. H
60: 7 Ephraim is my helmet; **J** is my scepter.
63: T *of David, when he was in the Wilderness of* **J**.
68:27 the princes of **J** in a body, the princes of Zebulun,
69:35 God will save Zion and rebuild the cities of **J**; F
76: 1 In **J** God is known, his name is great in Israel.
78:68 but he chose the tribe of **J**, I
97: 8 hears and is glad, and the towns of **J** rejoice, H
108: 8 Ephraim is my helmet; **J** is my scepter.
114: 2 **J** became God's sanctuary, Israel his dominion.
Pr 25: 1 that the officials of King Hezekiah of **J** copied.
Isa 1: 1 which he saw concerning **J** and Jerusalem in E
1: 1 Jotham, Ahaz, and Hezekiah, kings of **J**. D
2: 1 of Amoz saw concerning **J** and Jerusalem. E
3: 1 from Jerusalem and from **J** support and staff—
3: 8 For Jerusalem has stumbled and **J** has fallen,
5: 3 now, inhabitants of Jerusalem and people of **J**, A
5: 7 and the people of **J** are his pleasant planting; A
7: 1 of Ahaz son of Jotham son of Uzziah, king of **J**, K
7: 6 up against **J** and cut off Jerusalem and conquer it
7:17 since the day that Ephraim departed from **J**—
8: 8 into **J** as a flood, and, pouring over, it will reach
9:21 and together they were against **J**.
11:12 the dispersed of **J** from the four corners of
11:13 the hostility of **J** shall be cut off;
11:13 Ephraim shall not be jealous of **J**,
11:13 and **J** shall not be hostile towards Ephraim.
19:17 land of **J** will become a terror to the Egyptians; B
22: 8 He has taken away the covering of **J**.
22:21 inhabitants of Jerusalem and to the house of **J**. C
26: 1 that day this song will be sung in the land of **J**: B
36: 1 the fortified cities of **J** and captured them. F
36: 7 saying to **J** and to Jerusalem,
36:11 of **J** within the hearing of the people who are on
36:13 in a loud voice in the language of **J**,
37:10 "Thus shall you speak to King Hezekiah of **J**:
37:31 the house of **J** shall again take root downward, C
38: 9 A writing of King Hezekiah of **J**,
40: 9 say to the cities of **J**, "Here is your God!" F
44:26 "It shall be inhabited," and of the cities of **J**, F
48: 1 and who came forth from the loins of **J**;
65: 9 and from **J** inheritors of my mountains;
Jer 1: 2 in the days of King Josiah son of Amon of **J**,
1: 3 in the days of King Jehoiakim son of Josiah of **J**,
1: 3 of King Zedekiah son of Josiah of **J**,
1:15 and against all the cities of **J**. F
1:18 against the kings of **J**, its princes, its priests, D
2:28 you have as many gods as you have towns, O **J**.
3: 7 she did not return, and her false sister **J** saw it.
3: 8 yet her false sister **J** did not fear,
3:10 for all this her false sister **J** did not return to me
3:11 Faithless Israel has shown herself less guilty than false **J**.
3:18 In those days the house of **J** shall join the house C
4: 3 For thus says the LORD to the people of **J** and to A
4: 4 O people of **J** and inhabitants of Jerusalem, A
4: 5 Declare in **J**, and proclaim in Jerusalem, and say:
4:16 they shout against the cities of **J**. F
5:11 the house of **J** have been utterly faithless to me, C
5:20 in the house of Jacob, proclaim it in **J**:
7: 2 Hear the word of the LORD, all you people of **J**, A
7:17 not see what they are doing in the towns of **J** H
7:30 For the people of **J** have done evil in my sight, A
7:34 bridegroom in the cities of **J** and in the streets F
8: 1 says the LORD, the bones of the kings of **J**, D
9:11 and I will make the towns of **J** a desolation, H
9:26 **J**, Edom, the Ammonites, Moab,
10:22 from the land of the north to make the cities of **J** F
11: 2 the people of **J** and the inhabitants of Jerusalem. A
11: 6 Proclaim all these words in the cities of **J**, F
11: 9 the people of **J** and the inhabitants of Jerusalem. A
11:10 and the house of **J** have broken the covenant C
11:12 the cities of **J** and the inhabitants of Jerusalem F
11:13 as many as your towns, O **J**;
11:17 the house of Israel and the house of **J** have done, C
12:14 I will pluck up the house of **J** from among them. C
13: 9 the pride of **J** and the great pride of Jerusalem.
13:11 of Israel and the whole house of **J** cling to me, C
13:19 all **J** is taken into exile, wholly taken into exile. G
14: 2 **J** mourns and her gates languish;
14:19 Have you completely rejected **J**?
15: 4 of what King Manasseh son of Hezekiah of **J** did
17: 1 The sin of **J** is written with an iron pen;
17:19 the People's Gate, by which the kings of **J** enter D
17:20 Hear the word of the LORD, you kings of **J**, D
17:20 and all **J**, and all the inhabitants of Jerusalem, G
17:25 the people of **J** and the inhabitants of Jerusalem; A
17:26 the towns of **J** and the places around Jerusalem, H
18:11 the people of **J** and the inhabitants of Jerusalem: A
19: 3 O kings of **J** and inhabitants of Jerusalem. D
19: 4 their ancestors nor the kings of **J** have known; D
19: 7 I will make void the plans of **J** and Jerusalem, E
19:13 houses of the kings of **J** shall be defiled like D
20: 4 And I will give all **J** into the hand of the king G
20: 5 of the kings of **J** into the hand of their enemies, D
21: 7 says the LORD, I will give King Zedekiah of **J**,
21:11 To the house of the king of **J** say: K
22: 1 Go down to the house of the king of **J**, K
22: 2 O King of **J** sitting on the throne of David— K
Jer 22: 6 the LORD concerning the house of the king of **J**: K
22:11 concerning Shallum son of King Josiah of **J**,
22:18 concerning King Jehoiakim son of Josiah of **J**:
22:24 even if King Coniah son of Jehoiakim of **J** were
22:30 on the throne of David, and ruling again in **J**.
23: 6 In his days **J** will be saved and Israel will live
24: 1 of Jehoiakim of **J**, together with the officials of **J**,
24: 5 so I will regard as good the exiles from **J**,
24: 8 so will I treat King Zedekiah of **J**, his officials,
25: 1 to Jeremiah concerning all the people of **J**, A
25: 1 of King Jehoiakim son of Josiah of **J** (that was
25: 2 prophet Jeremiah spoke to all the people of **J** A
25: 3 of King Josiah son of Amon of **J**,
25:18 and the towns of **J**, its kings and officials, H
26: 1 of the reign of King Jehoiakim son of Josiah of **J**,
26: 2 the cities of **J** that come to worship in the house F
26:10 When the officials of **J** heard these things,
26:18 during the days of King Hezekiah of **J**, said to all
26:18 said to all the people of **J**: A
26:19 Did King Hezekiah of **J** and all Judah
26:19 of Judah and all **J** actually put him to death? G
27: 1 of the reign of King Zedekiah son of Josiah of **J**,
27: 3 to Jerusalem to King Zedekiah of **J**.
27:12 I spoke to King Zedekiah of **J** in the same way:
27:18 in the house of the king of **J**, K
27:20 of **J**, and all the nobles of Judah and Jerusalem—
27:20 and all the nobles of **J** and Jerusalem— E
27:21 in the house of the king of **J**, and in Jerusalem: K
28: 1 the beginning of the reign of King Zedekiah of **J**,
28: 4 to this place King Jeconiah son of Jehoiakim of **J**,
28: 4 and all the exiles from **J** who went to Babylon,
29: 2 court officials, the leaders of **J** and Jerusalem, E
29: 3 of **J** sent to Babylon to King Nebuchadnezzar
29:22 be used by all the exiles from **J** in Babylon:
30: 3 Israel and **J**, says the LORD, J
30: 4 that the LORD spoke concerning Israel and **J**: J
31:23 in the land of **J** and in its towns when I restore B
31:24 And **J** and all its towns shall live there together,
31:27 and the house of **J** with the seed of humans and C
31:31 with the house of Israel and the house of **J**. C
32: 1 in the tenth year of King Zedekiah of **J**,
32: 2 the guard that was in the palace of the king of **J**, K
32: 3 where King Zedekiah of **J** had confined him.
32: 4 King Zedekiah of **J** shall not escape out of
32:30 of Israel and the people of **J** have done nothing A
32:32 evil of the people of Israel and the people of **J** A
32:32 the citizens of **J** and the inhabitants of Jerusalem.
32:35 that they should do this abomination, causing **J**
32:44 and in the cities of **J**, of the hill country, F
33: 4 the houses of the kings of **J** that were torn down D
33: 7 I will restore the fortunes of **J** and the fortunes
33:10 in the towns of **J** and the streets of Jerusalem H
33:13 and in the towns of **J**, H
33:14 to the house of Israel and the house of **J**. C
33:16 In those days **J** will be saved
34: 2 and speak to King Zedekiah of **J** and say to him:
34: 4 the word of the LORD, O King Zedekiah of **J**!
34: 6 spoke all these words to Zedekiah king of **J**, K
34: 7 cities of **J** that were left, Lachish and Azekah; F
34: 7 the only fortified cities of **J** that remained. F
34:19 of **J**, the officials of Jerusalem, the eunuchs,
34:21 And as for King Zedekiah of **J** and his officials,
34:22 The towns of **J** I will make a desolation H
35: 1 in the days of King Jehoiakim son of Josiah of **J**:
35:13 and say to the people of **J** and the inhabitants A
35:17 I am going to bring on **J** and on all the inhabitants
36: 1 of Josiah of **J**, this word came to Jeremiah from
36: 2 to you against Israel and **J** and all the nations, J
36: 3 when the house of **J** hears of all the disasters C
36: 6 in the hearing of all the people of **J** who come A
36: 9 of King Jehoiakim son of Josiah of **J**,
36: 9 all the people who came from the towns of **J** H
36:28 which King Jehoiakim of **J** has burned.
36:29 concerning King Jehoiakim of **J** you shall say:
36:30 the LORD concerning King Jehoiakim of **J**:
36:31 of Jerusalem, and on the people of **J**, A
36:32 of the scroll that King Jehoiakim of **J** had burned
37: 1 of Babylon made king in the land of **J**, B
37: 7 the two of you shall say to the king of **J**, K
38:22 of the king of **J** being led out to the officials of K
39: 1 In the ninth year of King Zedekiah of **J**,
39: 4 King Zedekiah of **J** and all the soldiers saw them,
39: 6 king of Babylon slaughtered all the nobles of **J**.
39:10 left in the land of **J** some of the poor people B
40: 1 of Jerusalem and **J** who were being exiled N
40: 5 Babylon appointed governor of the towns of **J**, H
40:11 that the king of Babylon had left a remnant in **J**
40:12 came to the land of **J**, to Gedaliah at Mizpah; B
40:15 and the remnant of **J** would perish?"
42:15 the word of the LORD, O remnant of **J**.
42:19 The LORD has said to you, O remnant of **J**,
43: 4 to stay in the land of **J**. B
43: 5 the remnant of **J** who had returned to settle in
43: 5 to settle in the land of **J** from all the nations B
44: 2 on Jerusalem and on all the towns of **J**. H
44: 6 in the towns of **J** and in the streets of Jerusalem; H
44: 7 child and infant, from the midst of **J**,
44: 9 of the kings of **J**, of their wives, D
44: 9 in the land of **J** and in the streets of Jerusalem? B
44:11 to bring all **J** to an end. G
44:12 the remnant of **J** who are determined to come to
44:14 so that none of the remnant of **J** who have come
44:14 or survive or return to the land of **J**. B
44:17 in the towns of **J** and in the streets of Jerusalem. H
44:21 the offerings that you made in the towns of **J** H
44:26 on the lips of any of the people of **J** in all A
44:27 all the people of **J** who are in the land of Egypt A

Jer 44:28 land of Egypt to the land of **J**, few in number; B
44:28 and all the remnant of **J**,
44:30 just as I gave King Zedekiah of **J** into the hand
45: 1 of King Jehoiakim son of Josiah of **J**:
46: 2 of King Jehoiakim son of Josiah of **J**:
49:34 the beginning of the reign of King Zedekiah of **J**.
50: 4 they and the people of **J** together; A
50:20 and the sins of **J**, and none shall be found;
50:33 and so too are the people of **J**; A
51: 5 Israel and **J** have not been forsaken by their God, J
51:59 he went with King Zedekiah of **J** to Babylon,
52: 3 Jerusalem and **J** so angered the LORD N
52:10 and also killed all the officers of **J** at Riblah.
52:27 So **J** went into exile out of its land.
52:31 of **J**, in the twelfth month, on the twenty-fifth day
52:31 to King Jehoiachin of **J** and brought him out
La 1: 3 **J** has gone into exile with suffering
1:15 as in a wine press the virgin daughter **J**.
2: 2 down the strongholds of daughter **J**;
2: 5 in daughter **J** mourning and lamentation.
5:11 virgins in the towns of **J**. H
Eze 4: 6 and bear the punishment of the house of **J**; C
8: 1 with the elders of **J** sitting before me,
8:17 Is it not bad enough that the house of **J** commits C
9: 9 of the house of Israel and **J** is exceedingly great; J
21:20 to come to Rabbah of the Ammonites or to **J** and
25: 3 and over the house of **J** when it went into exile; C
25: 8 The house of **J** is like all the other nations, C
25:12 the house of **J** and has grievously offended C
27:17 **J** and the land of Israel traded with you;
37:16 "For **J**, and the Israelites associated with it";
37:19 and I will put the stick of **J** upon it,
48: 7 from the east side to the west, **J**, one portion.
48: 8 Adjoining the territory of **J**,
48:22 the prince shall lie between the territory of **J** and
48:31 the gate of **J**, and the gate of Levi,
Da 1: 1 the third year of the reign of King Jehoiakim of **J**,
1: 2 Lord let King Jehoiakim of **J** fall into his power,
1: 6 Mishael, and Azariah, from the tribe of **J**. I
2:25 the exiles from **J** a man who can tell the king
5:13 "So you are Daniel, one of the exiles of **J**,
5:13 whom my father the king brought from **J**?
6:13 one of the exiles from **J**, pays no attention to you,
9: 7 the people of **J**, the inhabitants of Jerusalem, A
Hos 1: 1 Jotham, Ahaz, and Hezekiah of **J**,
1: 7 But I will have pity on the house of **J**, C
1:11 The people of **J** and the people of Israel shall A
4:15 O Israel, do not let **J** become guilty.
5: 5 **J** also stumbles with them.
5:10 of **J** have become like those who remove
5:12 and like rottenness to the house of **J**. C
5:13 Ephraim saw his sickness, and **J** his wound,
5:14 and like a young lion to the house of **J**. C
6: 4 What shall I do with you, O **J**?
6:11 For you also, O **J**, a harvest is appointed.
8:14 and **J** has multiplied fortified cities;
10:11 **J** must plow; Jacob must harrow for himself.
11:12 but **J** still walks with God,
12: 2 The LORD has an indictment against **J**,
Joel 3: 1 when I restore the fortunes of **J** and Jerusalem, E
3: 6 You have sold the people of **J** and Jerusalem AE
3: 8 daughters into the hand of the people of **J**, A
3:18 and all the stream beds of **J** shall flow with water;
3:19 because of the violence done to the people of **J**, A
3:20 But **J** shall be inhabited forever,
Am 1: 1 concerning Israel in the days of King Uzziah of **J**
2: 4 For three transgressions of **J**, and for four,
2: 5 So I will send a fire on **J**,
7:12 flee away to the land of **J**, earn your bread there, B
Ob 1:12 should not have rejoiced over the people of **J** A
Mic 1: 1 Ahaz, and Hezekiah of **J**,
1: 5 And what is the high place of **J**?
1: 9 For her wound is incurable. It has come to **J**;
5: 2 who are one of the little clans of **J**,
Na 1:15 Celebrate your festivals, O **J**, fulfill your vows,
Zep 1: 1 in the days of King Josiah son of Amon of **J**.
1: 4 I will stretch out my hand against **J**,
2: 7 the possession of the remnant of the house of **J**, C
Hag 1: 1 governor of **J**, and to Joshua son of Jehozadak,
1:14 of **J**, and the spirit of Joshua son of Jehozadak,
2: 2 governor of **J**, and to Joshua son of Jehozadak,
2:21 of **J**, saying, I am about to shake the heavens and
Zec 1:12 from Jerusalem and the cities of **J**, F
1:19 "These are the horns that have scattered **J**, Israel,
1:21 "These are the horns that scattered **J**,
1:21 that lifted up their horns against the land of **J** B
2:12 The LORD will inherit **J** as his portion in
8:13 O house of **J** and house of Israel, C
8:15 to do good to Jerusalem and to the house of **J**; C
8:19 and cheerful festivals for the house of **J**: C
9: 7 it shall be like a clan in **J**,
9:13 For I have bent **J** as my bow;
10: 3 of hosts cares for his flock, the house of **J**, C
10: 6 I will strengthen the house of **J**, C
11:14 annulling the family ties between **J** and Israel. M
12: 2 be against **J** also in the siege against Jerusalem.
12: 4 But on the house of **J** I will keep a watchful eye, C
12: 5 Then the clans of **J** shall say to themselves,
12: 6 the clans of **J** like a blazing pot on a pile of wood,
12: 7 the LORD will give victory to the tents of **J** first,
12: 7 of Jerusalem may not be exalted over that of **J**.
14: 5 the earthquake in the days of King Uzziah of **J**.
14:14 even **J** will fight at Jerusalem.
14:21 in Jerusalem and **J** shall be sacred to the LORD N
Mal 2:11 **J** has been faithless, and abomination has been
2:11 for **J** has profaned the sanctuary of the LORD,
3: 4 the offering of **J** and Jerusalem will be pleasing E

Mt 1: 2 and Jacob the father of **J** and his brothers,
1: 3 and **J** the father of Perez and Zerah by Tamar,
2: 6 Bethlehem, in the land of **J**, B
2: 6 are by no means least among the rulers of **J**;
Lk 3:30 son of **J**, son of Joseph, son of Jonam,
3:33 son of Hezron, son of Perez, son of **J**,
Heb 7:14 it is evident that our Lord was descended from **J**,
8: 8 with the house of Israel and with the house of **J**; C
Rev 5: 5 See, the Lion of the tribe of **J**, the Root of David, I
7: 5 From the tribe of **J** twelve thousand sealed, I
Jdt 14: 7 and said, "Blessed are you in every tent of **J**!
Sir 45:25 with David son of Jesse of the tribe of **J**, I
49: 4 the kings of **J** came to an end. D
Bar 1: 3 to Jeconiah son of Jehoiakim, king of **J**, K
1: 8 to return them to the land of **J**— B
1: 8 that Zedekiah son of Josiah, king of **J**, K
1:15 on us today, on the people of **J**, A
2: 1 and our rulers and the people of Israel and **J**. J
2:23 I will make to cease from the towns of **J** H
2:26 of the house of Israel and the house of **J**. C
Sus 1:56 "You offspring of Canaan and not of **J**,
1:57 daughter of **J** would not tolerate your wickedness.
1Mc 1:29 the king sent to the cities of **J** a chief collector F
1:44 by messengers to Jerusalem and the towns of **J**; H
1:51 commanded the towns of **J** to offer sacrifice, H
1:54 also built altars in the surrounding towns of **J**, H
2: 6 being committed in **J** and Jerusalem, E
2:18 as all the Gentiles and the people of **J** and A
3: 8 He went through the cities of **J**; F
3:39 to go into the land of **J** and destroy it, B
5:45 a very large company, to go to the land of **J**. B
5:53 the way until he came to the land of **J**. B
5:68 the towns and returned to the land of **J**. B
6: 5 that had gone into the land of **J** had been routed; B
6:12 the inhabitants of **J** without good reason.
7:10 and came with a large force into the land of **J**; B
7:22 of the land of **J** and did great damage in Israel. B
7:50 So the land of **J** had rest for a few days. B
9: 1 sent Bacchides and Alcimus into the land of **J** B
9:57 and the land of **J** had rest for two years. B
9:72 he had taken previously from the land of **J**; B
10:30 land of **J** or from the three districts added to it B
10:33 the Jews taken as a captive from the land of **J** B
10:37 just as the king has commanded in the land of **J**. B
12: 4 for the envoys safe conduct to the land of **J**. B
12:46 and they returned to the land of **J**. B
12:52 So they all reached the land of **J** safely, B
13: 1 to invade the land of **J** and destroy it, B
13:12 with a large army to invade the land of **J**, B
1Es 1:21 the priests and Levites and the people of **J** A
1:33 in the book of the kings of Israel and **J**. J
1:35 He reigned three months in **J** and Jerusalem. E
2: 8 of families of the tribes of **J** and Benjamin, L
5: 5 of the lineage of Phares, of the tribe of **J**, I
5:66 enemies of the tribe of **J** and Benjamin heard it, IL
9: 5 men of the tribe of **J** and Benjamin assembled IL
9:23 who was Kelita, and Pethahiah and **J** and Jonah.
2Es 1:24 You, **J**, would not obey me.

JUDAH'S (4) [JUDAH]

Ge 38: 7 But Er, **J** firstborn, was wicked in the sight of
38:12 when **J** time of mourning was over,
1Ch 2: 3 Now Er, **J** firstborn, was wicked in the sight of
Ob 1:13 not have joined in the gloating over **J** disaster on

JUDAHITES (3) [JUDAH]

1Ch 12:16 Some Benjaminites and **J** came to the stronghold
Ne 11: 4 some of the **J** and of the Benjaminites. Of the **J**:

JUDAISM (7) [JEW]

Ac 13:43 and devout converts to **J** followed Paul
Gal 1:13 You have heard, no doubt, of my earlier life in **J**.
1:14 I advanced in **J** beyond many among my people
2Mc 2:21 from heaven to those who fought bravely for **J**,
14:38 he had been accused of **J**,
14:38 he had most zealously risked body and life for **J**.
4Mc 4:26 the nation to eat defiling foods and to renounce **J**.

JUDAS‡ (167) [=BARSABBAS, ISCARIOT, JUDAS'S, =JUDE, MACCABEUS, =THADDAEUS]

Mt 10: 4 and **J** Iscariot, the one who betrayed him.
13:55 and Joseph and Simon and **J**?
26:14 one of the twelve, who was called **J** Iscariot,
26:25 **J**, who betrayed him, said, "Surely not I, Rabbi?"
26:47 While he was still speaking, **J**, one of the twelve,
27: 3 When **J**, his betrayer, saw
Mk 3:19 and **J** Iscariot, who betrayed him.
6: 3 and brother of James and Joses and **J** and Simon,
14:10 Then **J** Iscariot, who was one of the twelve,
14:43 Immediately, while he was still speaking, **J**,
Lk 6:16 and **J** son of James, and Judas Iscariot,
6:16 and **J** Iscariot, who became a traitor.
22: 3 Then Satan entered into **J** called Iscariot,
22:47 suddenly a crowd came, and the one called **J**,
22:48 "**J**, is it with a kiss that you are betraying the Son
Jn 6:71 He was speaking of **J** son of Simon Iscariot,
12: 4 But **J** Iscariot, one of his disciples
13: 2 The devil had already put it into the heart of **J** son
13:26 he gave it to **J** son of Simon Iscariot.
13:29 because **J** had the common purse,
14:22 **J** (not Iscariot) said to him, "Lord,
18: 2 Now **J**, who betrayed him, also knew the place,
18: 3 So **J** brought a detachment of soldiers together

Jn 18: 5 **J**, who betrayed him, was standing with them.
Ac 1:13 and Simon the Zealot, and **J** son of James.
1:16 through David foretold concerning **J**,
1:25 and apostleship from which **J** turned aside to go
5:37 After him **J** the Galilean rose up at the time of
9:11 of **J** look for a man of Tarsus named Saul.
15:22 They sent **J** called Barsabbas, and Silas,
15:27 We have therefore sent **J** and Silas,
15:32 **J** and Silas, who were themselves prophets,
1Mc 2: 4 **J** called Maccabeus,
2:66 **J** Maccabeus has been a mighty warrior
3: 1 Then his son **J**, who was called Maccabeus,
3:11 When **J** learned of it, he went out to meet him,
3:12 and **J** took the sword of Apollonius,
3:13 heard that **J** had gathered a large company,
3:14 I will make war on **J** and his companions,
3:16 **J** went out to meet him with a small company.
3:17 they said to **J**, "How can we, few as we are,
3:18 **J** replied, "It is easy for many to be hemmed in
3:25 Then **J** and his brothers began to be feared,
3:26 and the Gentiles talked of the battles of **J**.
3:42 Now **J** and his brothers saw
3:55 After this **J** appointed leaders of the people,
3:58 And **J** said, "Arm yourselves and be courageous.
4: 3 But **J** heard of it, and he
4: 5 When Gorgias entered the camp of **J** by night,
4: 6 At daybreak **J** appeared in the plain
4: 8 But **J** said to those who were with him,
4:13 Then the men with **J** blew their trumpets
4:16 **J** and his force turned back from pursuing them,
4:19 Just as **J** was finishing this speech,
4:21 and when they also saw the army of **J** drawn up
4:23 Then **J** returned to plunder the camp,
4:29 and **J** met them with ten thousand men.
4:35 the boldness that inspired those of **J**,
4:36 Then **J** and his brothers said, "See,
4:41 Then **J** detailed men to fight against those in
4:59 Then **J** and his brothers and all the assembly
4:61 **J** stationed a garrison there to guard it;
5: 3 But **J** made war on the descendants of Esau
5:10 and sent to **J** and his brothers a letter that said,
5:16 When **J** and the people heard these messages,
5:17 Then **J** said to his brother Simon,
5:20 and eight thousand to **J** for Gilead.
5:24 **J** Maccabeus and his brother Jonathan crossed
5:28 Then **J** and his army quickly turned back by
5:31 So **J** saw that the battle had begun and that
5:38 **J** sent men to spy out the camp,
5:39 And **J** went to meet them.
5:40 **J** and his army drew near to the stream of water,
5:42 When **J** approached the stream of water,
5:44 they could stand before **J** no longer.
5:45 **J** gathered together all the Israelites in Gilead,
5:48 **J** sent them this friendly message,
5:49 Then **J** ordered proclamation to be made to
5:53 **J** kept rallying the laggards and encouraging
5:55 Now while **J** and Jonathan were in Gilead
5:61 they did not listen to **J** and his brothers.
5:63 The man **J** and his brothers were greatly honored
5:65 Then **J** and his brothers went out and fought
5:68 But **J** turned aside to Azotus in the land of
6:19 **J** therefore resolved to destroy them,
6:32 Then **J** marched away from the citadel
6:42 But **J** and his army advanced to the battle,
7: 6 "**J** and his brothers have destroyed all your
7: 7 the ruin that **J** has brought on us and on the land
7:10 and he sent messengers to **J** and his brothers
7:23 And **J** saw all the wrongs that Alcimus and those
7:24 **J** went out into all the surrounding parts of Judea,
7:25 that **J** and those with him had grown strong,
7:27 to **J** and his brothers this peaceable message,
7:29 to **J**, and they greeted one another peaceably;
7:29 but the enemy were preparing to kidnap **J**.
7:30 It became known to **J** that Nicanor had come
7:31 to meet **J** in battle near Caphar-salama.
7:35 "Unless **J** and his army are delivered
7:40 **J** encamped in Adasa with three thousand men.
7:40 with three thousand men. Then **J** prayed and said,
8: 1 Now **J** heard of the fame of the Romans,
8:17 So **J** chose Eupolemus son of John son of Accos,
8:20 "**J**, who is also called Maccabeus,
9: 5 Now **J** was encamped in Elasa,
9: 7 When **J** saw that his army had slipped away and
9:10 But **J** said, "Far be it from us to do such a thing
9:12 and the men with **J** also blew their trumpets.
9:14 **J** saw that Bacchides and the strength
9:16 and followed close behind **J** and his men.
9:18 **J** also fell, and the rest fled.
9:19 and Simon took their brother **J** and buried him in
9:22 Now the rest of the acts of **J**,
9:23 the death of **J**, the renegades emerged in all parts
9:26 and searched for the friends of **J**,
9:28 the friends of **J** assembled and said to Jonathan,
9:29 the death of your brother **J** there has been no one
9:31 at that time in place of his brother **J**.
11:70 of Absalom and **J** son of Chalphi,
13: 8 in place of **J** and your brother Jonathan.
14:18 that they had established with his brothers **J**
16: 2 Simon called in his two eldest sons **J** and John,
16: 9 At that time **J** the brother of John was wounded,
16:14 down to Jericho with his sons Mattathias and **J**,
2Mc 1:10 of Jerusalem and of Judea and the senate and **J**,
2:14 In the same way **J** also collected all the books
2:19 The story of **J** Maccabeus and his brothers,
5:27 But **J** Maccabeus, with about nine others,
8: 1 Meanwhile **J**, who was also called Maccabeus,
8:12 Word came to **J** concerning Nicanor's invasion;

2Mc 12: 5 **J** heard of the cruelty visited on his compatriots,
12:11 After a hard fight, **J** and his companions,
12:11 The defeated nomads begged **J**
12:12 **J,** realizing that they might indeed be useful
12:14 behaved most insolently toward **J** and his men,
12:15 But **J** and his men, calling against
12:21 When Timothy learned of the approach of **J,**
12:23 **J** pressed the pursuit with the utmost vigor,
12:26 Then **J** marched against Carnaim and the temple
12:36 **J** called upon the Lord to show himself their ally
12:38 Then **J** assembled his army and went to the city
12:39 **J** and his men went to take up the bodies of
12:42 The noble **J** exhorted the people
13: 1 the one hundred forty-ninth year word came to **J**
13:10 But when **J** heard of this,
13:12 **J** exhorted them and ordered them to stand ready.
13:20 **J** sent in to the garrison whatever was necessary.
13:22 received theirs, withdrew, attacked **J** and his men,
14: 1 word came to **J** and his men that Demetrius son
14: 6 whose leader is **J** Maccabeus,
14:10 For as long as **J** lives,
14:11 of the king's Friends, who were hostile to **J,**
14:13 with orders to kill **J** and scatter his troops,
14:14 who had fled before **J,** flocked to join Nicanor,
14:17 the brother of **J,** had encountered Nicanor,
14:18 of the valor of **J** and his troops and their courage
14:22 **J** posted armed men in readiness at key places
14:24 And he kept **J** always in his presence;
14:25 so **J** married, settled down,
14:26 that conspirator against the kingdom, **J,** to
14:33 "If you do not hand **J** over to me as a prisoner,
15: 1 When Nicanor heard that **J** and his troops were in
15: 6 to erect a public monument of victory over **J**
15:15 and gave to **J** a golden sword,
15:17 Encouraged by the words of **J,**
15:26 but **J** and his troops met the enemy in battle
15:35 **J** hung Nicanor's head from the citadel,

JUDAS'S (1) [JUDAS]

2Mc 12:22 But when **J** first division appeared,

JUDE (1) [=JUDAS]

Jude 1: 1 **J,** a servant of Jesus Christ and brother of James,

JUDEA (119) [JUDAH, JUDEAN, JUDEANS]

Ezr 9: 9 and to give us a wall in **J** and Jerusalem.
Mt 2: 1 after Jesus was born in Bethlehem of **J,**
2: 5 They told him, "In Bethlehem of **J;**
2:22 when he heard that Archelaus was ruling over **J**
3: 1 the Baptist appeared in the wilderness of **J,**
3: 5 the people of Jerusalem and all **J** were going out
4:25 Jerusalem, **J,** and from beyond the Jordan.
19: 1 he left Galilee and went to the region of **J** beyond
24:16 then those in **J** must flee to the mountains;
Mk 3: 8 they came to him in great numbers from **J,**
10: 1 that place and went to the region of **J** and beyond
13:14 then those in **J** must flee to the mountains;
Lk 1: 5 In the days of King Herod of **J,**
1:65 about throughout the entire hill country of **J.**
2: 4 from the town of Nazareth in Galilee to **J,**
3: 1 when Pontius Pilate was governor of **J,**
4:44 the message in the synagogues of **J.**
5:17 from every village of Galilee and **J** and
6:17 and a great multitude of people from all **J,**
7:17 This word about him spread throughout **J** and all
21:21 Then those in **J** must flee to the mountains,
23: 5 up the people by teaching throughout all **J,**
Jn 4: 3 he left **J** and started back to Galilee.
4:47 he heard that Jesus had come from **J** to Galilee,
4:54 the second sign that Jesus did after coming from **J**
7: 1 to go about in **J** because the Jews were looking
7: 3 and go to **J** so that your disciples also may see
11: 7 "Let us go to **J** again."
Ac 1: 8 in all **J** and Samaria, and to the ends of the earth."
2: 9 and residents of Mesopotamia, **J** and Cappadocia,
2:14 "Men of **J** and all who live in Jerusalem,
8: 1 throughout the countryside of **J** and Samaria
9:31 Meanwhile the church throughout **J,** Galilee,
10:37 That message spread throughout **J,**
10:39 We are witnesses to all that he did both in **J** and
11: 1 in **J** heard that the Gentiles had also accepted
11:29 to the believers living in **J;**
12:19 down from **J** to Caesarea and stayed there.
15: 1 down from **J** and were teaching the brothers,
21:10 a prophet named Agabus came down from **J.**
26:20 in Jerusalem and throughout the countryside of **J,**
28:21 "We have received no letters from **J** about you,
Ro 15:31 that I may be rescued from the unbelievers in **J,**
2Co 1:16 from Macedonia and have you send me on to **J.**
Gal 1:22 by sight to the churches of **J** that are in Christ;
1Th 2:14 the churches of God in Christ Jesus that are in **J,**
Tob 1:18 from **J** in those days of judgment that the king
Jdt 1:12 and the people of Ammon, and all **J,**
3: 9 near Dothan, facing the great ridge of **J;**
4: 1 the Israelites living in **J** heard of everything
4: 3 all the people of **J** had just now gathered together,
4: 7 since by them **J** could be invaded;
4:13 for the people fasted many days throughout **J** and
8:21 all **J** will be captured and our sanctuary will
11:19 Then I will lead you through **J,**
AdE 11: 4 from Jerusalem with King Jeconiah of **J.**
Bel 1:33 Now the prophet Habakkuk was in **J;**
1Mc 3:34 As for the residents of **J** and Jerusalem,
4:35 to invade **J** again with an even larger army.
5: 8 and its villages; then he returned to **J.**
1Mc 5:18 with the rest of the forces, in **J** to guard it;
5:23 and led them to **J** with great rejoicing.
5:60 and were pursued to the borders of **J;**
6:48 and the king encamped in **J** and at Mount Zion.
6:53 in **J** from the Gentiles had consumed the last of
7:24 Judas went out into all the surrounding parts of **J,**
7:46 the surrounding villages of **J,** and they outflanked
9:50 to Jerusalem and built strong cities in **J:**
9:60 and secretly sent letters to all his allies in **J,**
9:63 and sent orders to the men of **J.**
10:38 the three districts that have been added to **J** from
10:38 be annexed to **J** so that they may be considered to
10:45 and the cost of rebuilding the walls in **J,**
11:28 Then Jonathan asked the king to free **J** and
11:34 as their possession both the territory of **J** and
11:34 were added to **J** from Samaria.
12:35 and planned with them to build strongholds in **J,**
13:33 the strongholds of **J** and walled them all around,
14:33 He fortified the towns of **J,**
14:33 and Beth-zur on the borders of **J,**
15:30 that you have conquered outside the borders of **J;**
15:39 He commanded him to encamp against **J,**
15:40 and began to provoke the people and invade **J**
15:41 and make raids along the highways of **J,**
16:10 He then returned to **J** safely.
2Mc 1: 1 The Jews in Jerusalem and those in the land of **J,**
1:10 The people of Jerusalem and of **J** and the senate
5:11 he took it to mean that **J** was in revolt.
8: 9 to wipe out the whole race of **J.**
10:24 He came on, intending to take **J** by storm.
11: 5 Invading **J,** he approached Beth-zur,
13: 1 with a great army against **J,**
13:13 the king's army could enter **J** and get possession
14:12 appointed him governor of **J,**
14:14 And the Gentiles throughout **J,**
15:22 in the time of King Hezekiah of **J,**
1Es 1:26 to do with each other, O king of **J?**
1:32 In all **J** they mourned for Josiah.
1:33 in the book of the histories of the kings of **J;**
1:37 of Egypt made his brother Jehoiakim king of **J**
1:39 when he began to reign in **J** and Jerusalem;
1:46 and made Zedekiah king of **J** and Jerusalem.
2: 4 to build him a house at Jerusalem, which is in **J.**
2: 5 go up to Jerusalem, which is in **J,**
2:12 to Sheshbazzar, the governor of **J.**
2:16 against those who were living in **J** and Jerusalem:
4:45 the Edomites burned when **J** was laid waste by
4:49 up from his kingdom to **J,** in the interest
5: 8 and who returned to Jerusalem and the rest of **J,**
5:57 in the second year after they came to **J**
5:72 peoples of the land pressed hard upon those in **J,**
6: 1 of Iddo prophesied to the Jews who were in **J**
6: 8 the country of **J** and entered the city of Jerusalem,
6:27 the servant of the Lord and governor of **J,**
6:28 of **J,** until the house of the Lord is finished;
8:12 in order to look into matters in **J** and Jerusalem,
8:81 to give us a stronghold in **J** and Jerusalem.
9: 3 And a proclamation was made throughout **J**
3Mc 5:43 also march against **J** and rapidly level it to

JUDEAN (5) [JUDEA]

1Ch 4:18 And his **J** wife bore Jered father of Gedor,
Jer 34: 9 so that no one should hold another **J** in slavery.
Mk 1: 5 And people from the whole **J** countryside and all
Lk 1:39 with haste to a **J** town in the hill country,
Jn 3:22 and his disciples went into the **J** countryside,

JUDEANS (17) [JUDEA]

2Ki 16: 6 and drove the **J** from Elath;
25:25 down Gedaliah so that he died, along with the **J**
1Ch 4:27 nor did all their family multiply like the **J.**
Jer 32:12 and in the presence of all the **J** who were sitting
38:19 of the **J** who have deserted to the Chaldeans,
40:11 when all the **J** who were in Moab and among
40:12 then all the **J** returned from all the places
40:15 that all the **J** who are gathered around you would
41: 3 also killed all the **J** who were with Gedaliah
40: 9 Let the **J** see you do it,
44: 1 that came to Jeremiah for all the **J** living in
44:24 all you **J** who are in the land of Egypt,
44:26 all you **J** who live in the land of Egypt:
52:28 three thousand twenty-three **J;**
52:30 of the **J** seven hundred forty-five persons;
1Mc 11:20 In those days Jonathan assembled the **J** to attack
1Es 5: 7 These are the **J** who came up out of their sojourn

JUDGE‡ (176) [JUDGE'S, JUDGED, JUDGES, JUDGING, JUDGMENT, JUDGMENTS, JUDICIAL, JUDICIOUS]

Ge 16: 5 May the LORD **j** between you and me!"
18:25 Shall not the **J** of all the earth do what is just?"
19: 9 and he would play the **j!**
31:53 —the God of their father—"**j** between us."
49:16 Dan shall **j** his people as one of the tribes
Ex 2:14 "Who made you a ruler and **j** over us?
5:21 "The LORD look upon you and **j!**
18:13 The next day Moses sat as **j** for the people,
Lev 19:15 with justice you shall **j** your neighbor.
Nu 35:24 then the congregation shall **j** between the slayer
Dt 1:16 and **j** rightly between one person and another,
17: 9 with the levitical priests and the **j** who is in office
17:12 or the **j,** that person shall die.
25: 2 the **j** shall make that person lie down and
Jdg 2:18 the LORD was with the **j,**
Jdg 2:18 the hand of their enemies all the days of the **j;**
2:19 But whenever the **j** died, they would relapse
11:27 Let the LORD, who is **j,**
1Sa 2:10 The LORD will **j** the ends of the earth;
24:12 May the LORD **j** between me and you!
24:15 May the LORD therefore be **j,**
2Sa 15: 4 "If only I were **j** in the land!
1Ki 8:32 and act, and **j** your servants,
1Ch 16:33 for he comes to **j** the earth.
2Ch 6:23 and act, and **j** your servants,
19: 6 for you **j** not on behalf of human beings but on
Ezr 7:25 appoint magistrates and judges who may **j** all
Job 22:13 Can he **j** through the deep darkness?
23: 7 and I should be acquitted forever by my **j.**
Ps 7: 8 The LORD judges the peoples; **j** me, O LORD,
7:11 God is a righteous **j,** and a God who has
50: 4 that he may **j** his people:
50: 6 declare his righteousness, for God himself is **j.**
58: 1 Do you **j** people fairly?
67: 4 for you **j** the peoples with equity and guide
72: 2 May he **j** your people with righteousness,
75: 2 At the set time that I appoint I will **j** with equity.
82: 2 "How long will you **j** unjustly and show partiality
82: 8 Rise up, O God, **j** the earth;
94: 2 Rise up, O **j** of the earth;
96:10 He will **j** the peoples with equity."
96:13 for he is coming, for he is coming to **j** the earth.
96:13 He will **j** the world with righteousness,
98: 9 for he is coming to **j** the earth.
98: 9 He will **j** the world with righteousness,
119:84 When will you **j** those who persecute me?
Pr 31: 9 **j** righteously, defend the rights of the poor
Ecc 3:17 God will **j** the righteous and the wicked,
Isa 2: 4 He shall **j** between the nations,
3: 2 **j** and prophet, diviner and elder,
3:13 he stands to **j** the peoples.
5: 3 **j** between me and my vineyard.
11: 3 He shall not **j** by what his eyes see,
11: 4 with righteousness he shall **j** the poor, and decide
33:22 For the LORD is our **j,** the LORD is our ruler,
Jer 5:28 they do not **j** with justice the cause of the orphan,
11:20 But you, O LORD of hosts, who **j** righteously,
La 3:59 to me, O LORD; **j** my cause.
Eze 7: 3 I will **j** you according to your ways,
7: 8 I will **j** you according to your ways,
7:27 according to their own judgments I will **j** them.
11:10 I will **j** you at the border of Israel.
11:11 I will **j** you at the border of Israel.
16:38 I will **j** you as women who commit adultery
18:30 Therefore I will **j** you, O house of Israel,
20: 4 Will you **j** them, mortal, will you **j** them?
21:30 in the land of your origin, I will **j** you.
22: 2 mortal, will you **j,** will you **j** the bloody city?
23:24 and they shall **j** you according to their ordinances.
23:36 Mortal, will you **j** Oholah and Oholibah?
24:14 to your ways and your doings I will **j** you,
33:20 I will **j** all of you according to your ways!
34:17 I shall **j** between sheep and sheep,
34:20 I myself will **j** between the fat sheep and
34:22 and I will **j** between sheep and sheep.
35:11 among you, when I **j** you.
Joel 3:12 for there I will sit to **j** all the neighboring nations.
Mic 4: 3 He shall **j** between many peoples,
7: 3 the official and the **j** ask for a bribe,
Mt 5:25 or your accuser may hand you over to the **j,** and
the **j** to the guard,
7: 1 "Do not **j,** so that you may not be judged.
Lk 6:37 "Do not **j,** and you will not be judged;
12:14 who set me to be a **j** or arbitrator over you?"
12:57 why do you not **j** for yourselves what is right?
12:58 or you may be dragged before the **j,** and the **j** hand
you over to the officer,
18: 2 a **j** who neither feared God nor had respect
18: 6 the Lord said, "Listen to what the unjust **j** says.
19:22 He said to him, 'I will **j** you by your own words,
Jn 5:30 on my own. As I hear, I **j;**
7:24 Do not **j** by appearances, but **j** with right judgment.
7:51 not **j** people without first giving them a hearing
8:15 You **j** by human standards; I **j** no one.
8:16 Yet even if I do **j,** my judgment is valid; for it is
not I alone who **j,**
8:50 there is one who seeks it and he is the **j.**
12:47 I do not **j** anyone who hears my words and does
12:47 for I came not to **j** the world,
12:48 and does not receive my word has a **j;**
12:48 the word that I have spoken will serve as **j,**
18:31 "Take him yourselves and **j** him according
Ac 4:19 to listen to you rather than to God, you must **j;**
7: 7 'But I will **j** the nation that they serve,' said God,
7:27 saying, 'Who made you a ruler and a **j** over us?
7:35 'Who made you a ruler and a **j?'**
10:42 to testify that he is the one ordained by God as **j**
13:46 and **j** yourselves to be unworthy of eternal life,
18:15 I do not wish to be a **j** of these matters."
23: 3 Are you sitting there to **j** me according to the law,
24:10 for many years you have been a **j** over this nation.
Ro 2: 1 whoever you are, when you **j** others;
2: 1 the **j,** are doing the very same things.
2: 3 that when you **j** those who do such things and
2:16 will **j** the secret thoughts of all.
3: 6 For then how could God **j** the world?
14: 5 Some **j** one day to be better than another,
14: 5 while others **j** all days to be alike.
1Co 4: 3 I do not even **j** myself.
5:12 Is it not those who are inside that you are to **j?**
5:13 God will **j** those outside.
6: 2 Do you not know that the saints will **j** the world?

1Co 6: 3 Do you not know that we are to **j** angels—
10:15 **j** for yourselves what I say.
11:13 **J** for yourselves: is it proper
2Ti 4: 1 who is to **j** the living and the dead,
4: 8 the righteous **j**, will give me on that day,
Heb 4:12 to **j** the thoughts and intentions of the heart.
10:30 And again, "The Lord will **j** his people."
12:23 and to God the **j** of all,
13: 4 for God will **j** fornicators and adulterers.
Jas 4:11 but if you **j** the law, you are not a doer of the law but a **j**.
4:12 There is one lawgiver and **j** who is able to save
4:12 So who, then, are you to **j** your neighbor?
5: 9 See, the **J** is standing at the doors!
1Pe 2:12 and glorify God when he comes to **j**.
4: 5 an accounting to him who stands ready to **j**
Rev 6:10 be before you **j** and avenge our blood on
20: 4 those seated on them were given authority to **j**.
Tob 3: 2 and truth; you **j** the world.
Jdt 7:24 "Let God **j** between you and us!
Wis 9: 7 be king of your people and to be **j** over your sons
9:12 and I shall **j** your people justly,
12:18 Although you are sovereign in strength, you **j**
12:22 when we **j**, we may meditate upon your goodness,
Sir 4:15 Those who obey her will **j** the nations,
7: 6 Do not seek to become a **j**,
8:14 Do not go to law against a **j**,
10: 2 As the people's **j** is, so are his officials;
10:24 The prince and the **j** and the ruler are honored,
11: 9 and do not sit with sinners when they **j** a case.
31:15 **J** your neighbor's feelings by your own,
35:15 Lord is the **j**, and with him there is no partiality.
41:18 of a crime, before a **j** or magistrate;
45:26 of mind to **j** his people with justice,
LtJ 6:14 One of them holds a scepter, like a district **j**,
6:54 They cannot **j** their own cause
1Mc 2:55 because he fulfilled the command, became a **j**
7:42 and **j** him according to this wickedness."
9:73 Jonathan settled in Michmash and began to **j**
2Mc 12: 6 calling upon God, the righteous **j**,
12:41 the righteous **j**, who reveals the things
1Es 3: 9 of Persia **j** to be wisest the victory shall be given
8:23 to **j** all those who know the law of your God,
3Mc 2: 3 and you **j** those who have done anything
2Es 4:18 If now you were a **j** between them,
7:19 "You are not a better **j** than the Lord,
7:57 **J** therefore which things are precious
7:*139* [69] and the **j**, because if he did not pardon
14:32 And since he is a righteous **j**,
16:67 Indeed, God is the **j**; fear him!

JUDGE'S‡ (2) [JUDGE]

Jn 19:13 the **j** bench at a place called The Stone Pavement,
Sir 38:33 They do not sit in the **j** seat,

JUDGED‡ (58) [JUDGE]

Ge 30: 6 Then Rachel said, "God has **j** me,
Ex 18:26 And they **j** the people at all times;
Jdg 3:10 spirit of the LORD came upon him, and he **j** Israel;
10: 2 He **j** Israel twenty-three years.
10: 3 Jair the Gileadite, who **j** Israel twenty-two years.
12: 7 Jephthah **j** Israel six years.
12: 8 After him Ibzan of Bethlehem **j** Israel.
12: 9 He **j** Israel seven years.
12:11 After him Elon the Zebulunite **j** Israel;
12:11 and he **j** Israel ten years.
12:13 Abdon son of Hillel the Pirathonite **j** Israel.
12:14 on seventy donkeys; he **j** Israel eight years.
15:20 And he **j** Israel in the days of the Philistines
16:31 He had **j** Israel twenty years.
1Sa 4:18 He had **j** Israel forty years.
7: 6 And Samuel **j** the people of Israel at Mizpah.
7:15 Samuel **j** Israel all the days of his life.
7:16 and he **j** Israel in all these places.
25:39 the LORD who has **j** the case of Nabal's insult
2Ki 23:22 the judges who **j** Israel, or during all the days of
Ps 9:19 let the nations be **j** before you.
Jer 22:16 He **j** the cause of the poor and needy;
Eze 16:38 and shed blood are **j**, and bring blood upon you
36:19 with their conduct and their deeds I **j** them.
Mt 7: 1 "Do not judge, so that you may not be **j**.
7: 2 For with the judgment you make you will be **j**,
Lk 6:37 "Do not judge, and you will not be **j**;
7:43 And Jesus said to him, "You have **j** rightly."
Ac 16:15 "If you have **j** me to be faithful to the Lord,
17:31 a day on which he will have the world **j**
Ro 2:12 and all who have sinned under the law will be **j**
1Co 4: 3 with me it is a very small thing that I should be **j**
6: 2 And if the world is to be **j** by you,
11:31 But if we **j** ourselves, we would not be **j**.
11:32 But when we are **j** by the Lord,
1Ti 1:12 he **j** me faithful and appointed me to his service,
Jas 2:12 So speak and so act as those who are to be **j** by
3: 1 that we who teach will be **j** with greater strictness.
5: 9 so that you may not be **j**.
1Pe 4: 6 they had been **j** in the flesh as everyone is **j**,
Rev 16: 5 who are and were, for you have **j** these things;
19: 2 he has **j** the great whore who corrupted the earth
20:12 And the dead were **j** according to their works,
20:13 and all were **j** according to what they had done.
Wis 11: 9 how the ungodly were tormented when **j** in wrath.
12:13 that you have not **j** unjustly;
12:21 with what strictness you have **j** your children,
12:22 and when we are **j**, we may expect mercy.
15:18 which are worse than all others when **j**
Sir 46:14 By the law of the Lord he **j** the congregation,
2Es 4:20 He answered me and said, "You have **j** rightly,
4:20 but why have you not **j** so in your own case?
7:11 what had been made was **j**.
7:*87* and in whose presence they are to be **j** in
11:41 You have **j** the earth, but not with truth,
12: 9 For you have **j** me worthy to be shown the end of

JUDGES‡ (68) [JUDGE]

Ex 18:22 Let them sit as **j** for the people at all times;
21:22 paying as much as the **j** determine.
Nu 25: 5 And Moses said to the **j** of Israel,
Dt 1:16 I charged your **j** at that time:
16:18 You shall appoint **j** and officials
19:17 priests and the **j** who are in office in those days,
19:18 and the **j** shall make a thorough inquiry.
21: 2 then your elders and your **j** shall come out
25: 1 and the **j** decide between them,
Jos 8:33 with their elders and officers and their **j**,
23: 2 their elders and heads, their **j** and officers,
24: 1 and summoned the elders, the heads, the **j**,
Jdg 2:16 Then the LORD raised up **j**,
2:17 Yet they did not listen even to their **j**;
2:18 Whenever the LORD raised up **j** for them,
Ru 1: 1 In the days when the **j** ruled,
1Sa 8: 1 he made his sons **j** over Israel.
8: 2 they were **j** in Beer-sheba.
2Sa 7:11 the time that I appointed **j** over my people Israel;
2Ki 23:22 the **j** who judged Israel, or during all the days of
1Ch 17: 6 did I ever speak a word with any of the **j** of Israel,
17:10 the time that I appointed **j** over my people Israel;
23: 4 six thousand shall be officers and **j**,
26:29 to outside duties for Israel, as officers and **j**.
2Ch 1: 2 the **j**, and all the leaders of all Israel,
19: 5 He appointed **j** in the land in all the fortified cities
19: 6 and said to the **j**, "Consider what you are doing,
Ezr 4: 9 and the rest of their associates, the **j**, the envoys,
7:25 appoint magistrates and **j** who may judge all
10:14 and with them the elders and **j** of every town,
Job 9:24 he covers the eyes of its **j**—
12:17 counselors away stripped, and makes fools of **j**.
21:22 seeing that he **j** those that are on high?
31:28 also would be an iniquity to be punished by the **j**,
Ps 7: 8 The LORD **j** the peoples;
9: 8 He **j** the world with righteousness;
9: 8 he **j** the peoples with equity.
58:11 surely there is a God who **j** on earth."
Pr 29:14 If a king **j** the poor with equity,
Isa 1:26 And I will restore your **j** as at the first,
Eze 23:45 But righteous **j** shall declare them guilty
44:24 In a controversy they shall act as **j**,
Zep 3: 3 its **j** are evening wolves that leave nothing until
Mt 12:27 Therefore they will be your **j**.
Lk 11:19 Therefore they will be your **j**.
Jn 5:22 The Father **j** no one but has given all judgment to
Ac 13:20 After that he gave them **j** until the time of
1Co 4: 4 It is the Lord who **j** me.
6: 4 do you appoint as **j** those who have no standing in
Jas 2: 4 and become **j** with evil thoughts?
4:11 Whoever speaks evil against another or **j** another, speaks evil against the law and **j** the law;
1Pe 1:17 the one who **j** all people impartially according
2:23 but he entrusted himself to the one who **j** justly.
Rev 18: 8 for mighty is the Lord God who **j** her."
19:11 and in righteousness he **j** and makes war.
Wis 6: 1 learn, O **j** of the ends of the earth.
Sir 16:12 he **j** a person according to one's deeds.
35:25 until he **j** the case of his people
46:11 The **j** also, with their respective names,
Bar 2: 1 against our **j** who ruled Israel,
Sus 1: 5 from the people were appointed as **j**.
1: 5 from Babylon, from elders who were **j**,
1:41 Because they were elders of the people and **j**,
1Es 2:17 and the **j** in Coelesyria and Phoenicia:
8:23 appoint **j** and justices to judge all those who know
9:13 with the elders and **j** of each place,
9:14 and Levi and Shabbethai served with them as **j**.

JUDGING (11) [JUDGE]

Dt 1:17 You must not be partial in **j**:
Jdg 4: 4 a prophetess, wife of Lappidoth, was **j** Israel.
Pr 24:23 Partiality in **j** is not good.
Mt 19:28 **j** the twelve tribes of Israel.
Lk 22:30 and you will sit on thrones **j** the twelve tribes
Ro 3: 4 be justified in your words, and prevail in your **j**."
1Co 5:12 For what have I to do with **j** those outside?
Rev 11:18 and the time for **j** the dead,
Jdt 10:19 at her beauty and admired the Israelites, **j** them
AdE 16: 9 and always **j** what comes before our eyes
Wis 12:10 But **j** them little by little you gave them

JUDGMENT‡ (222) [JUDGE]

A. DAY OF JUDGMENT (14)

Ge 15:14 but I will bring **j** on the nation that they serve,
Ex 6: 6 an outstretched arm and with mighty acts of **j**.
7: 4 out of the land of Egypt by great acts of **j**.
28:15 You shall make a breastpiece of **j**,
28:29 the breastpiece of **j** on his heart when he goes into
28:30 In the breastpiece of **j** you shall put the Urim and
28:30 thus Aaron shall bear the **j** of the Israelites
Lev 19:15 You shall not render an unjust **j**;
Dt 1:17 not be intimidated by anyone, for the **j** is God's.
32:41 and my hand takes hold on **j**;
Jdg 4: 5 and the Israelites came up to her for **j**.
1Sa 12: 7 I may enter into **j** with you before the LORD,
2Sa 15: 2 when anyone brought a suit before the king for **j**,
15: 6 to every Israelite who came to the king for **j**;
1Ki 3:28 of the **j** that the king had rendered;
7: 7 of the Throne where he was to pronounce **j**,
20:40 The king of Israel said to him, "So shall your **j** be;
1Ch 12:17 then may the God of our ancestors see and give **j**."
2Ch 19: 6 he is with you in giving **j**.
19: 8 to give **j** for the LORD and to decide
20: 9 the sword, **j**, or pestilence, or famine,
20:12 O our God, will you not execute **j** upon them?
22: 8 When Jehu was executing **j** on the house of Ahab,
24:24 Thus they executed **j** on Joash.
Ezr 7:26 let **j** be strictly executed on them,
Job 11:10 and assembles for **j**, who can hinder him?
14: 3 Do you bring me into **j** with you?
19:29 so that you may know there is a **j**."
22: 4 and enters into **j** with you?
34:23 a time for anyone to go before God in **j**.
36:17 of the wicked; **j** and justice seize you.
Ps 1: 5 Therefore the wicked will not stand in the **j**,
7: 6 O my God; you have appointed a **j**.
9: 4 you have sat on the throne giving righteous **j**.
9: 7 he has established his throne for **j**.
9:16 has made himself known, he has executed **j**;
51: 4 in your sentence and blameless when you pass **j**.
75: 7 but it is God who executes **j**,
76: 8 From the heavens you uttered **j**;
76: 9 when God rose up to establish **j**,
82: 1 in the midst of the gods he holds **j**:
110: 6 He will execute **j** among the nations,
119:66 Teach me good **j** and knowledge,
122: 5 For there the thrones for **j** were set up,
143: 2 Do not enter into **j** with your servant,
149: 9 to execute on them the **j** decreed.
Pr 16:10 his mouth does not sin in **j**.
18: 1 showing contempt for all who have sound **j**.
18: 5 or to subvert the innocent in **j**.
20: 8 on the throne of **j** winnows all evil with his eyes.
Ecc 11: 9 that for all these things God will bring you into **j**.
12:14 For God will bring every deed into **j**,
Isa 3:14 into **j** with the elders and princes of his people:
4: 4 of Jerusalem from its midst by a spirit of **j** and by
28: 6 and a spirit of justice to the one who sits in **j**,
28: 7 they err in vision, they stumble in giving **j**.
32: 4 The minds of the rash will have good **j**,
34: 5 upon the people I have doomed to **j**.
41: 1 let us together draw near for **j**.
54:17 that rises against you in **j**.
66:16 For by fire will the LORD execute **j**,
Jer 2:35 Now I am bringing you to **j** for saying,
4:12 Now it is I who speak in **j** against them.
25:31 he is entering into **j** with all flesh,
48:21 **J** has come upon the tableland, upon Holon,
48:47 Thus far is the **j** on Moab.
51: 9 for her **j** has reached up to heaven
Eze 14:21 upon Jerusalem my four deadly acts of **j**,
16:52 about for your sisters a more favorable **j**;
17:20 to Babylon and enter into **j** with him there for
20:35 and there I will enter into **j** with you face to face.
20:36 into **j** with your ancestors in the wilderness of
20:36 so I will enter into **j** with you,
23:10 **J** was executed upon her,
23:24 and helmet, and I will commit the **j** to them,
30:14 and will execute acts of **j** on Thebes.
30:19 Thus I will execute acts of **j** on Egypt.
38:22 With pestilence and bloodshed I will enter into **j**
39:21 all the nations shall see my **j** that I have executed,
Da 7:10 The court sat in **j**, and the books were opened.
7:22 **j** was given for the holy ones of the Most High,
7:26 Then the court shall sit in **j**,
Hos 5: 1 For the **j** pertains to you;
5:11 Ephraim is oppressed, crushed in **j**,
6: 5 and my **j** goes forth as the light.
Joel 3: 2 and I will enter into **j** with them there,
Mic 3:11 Its rulers give **j** for a bribe,
7: 9 until he takes my side and executes **j** for me.
Hab 1: 4 therefore **j** comes forth perverted.
1:12 O LORD, you have marked them for **j**;
Zep 3: 5 Every morning he renders his **j**,
Mal 3: 5 Then I will draw near to you for **j**;
Mt 5:21 and 'whoever murders shall be liable to **j**.'
5:22 you will be liable to **j**;
7: 2 For with the **j** you make you will be judged,
10:15 Gomorrah on the day of **j** than for that town. A
11:22 the day of **j** it will be more tolerable for Tyre A
11:24 the day of **j** it will be more tolerable for the land A
12:36 on the day of **j** you will have to give an account A
12:41 up at the **j** with this generation and condemn it,
12:42 the South will rise up at the **j** with this generation
27:19 While he was sitting on the **j** seat,
Lk 10:14 But at the **j** it will be more tolerable for Tyre
11:31 The queen of the South will rise at the **j** with
11:32 up at the **j** with this generation and condemn it,
Jn 3:19 And this is the **j**, that the light has come into
5:22 The Father judges no one but has given all **j** to
5:24 and does not come under **j**,
5:27 and he has given him authority to execute **j**,
5:30 As I hear, I judge; and my **j** is just,
7:24 not judge by appearances, but judge with right **j**."
8:16 Yet even if I do judge, my **j** is valid;
9:39 "I came into this world for **j** so that those who do
12:31 Now is the **j** of this world;
16: 8 about sin and righteousness and **j**:
16:11 about **j**, because the ruler of this world has been
Ac 21:25 a letter with our **j** that they should abstain
24:25 self-control, and the coming **j**,
Ro 2: 1 for in passing **j** on another you condemn yourself,

Ro 2: 2 that God's j on those who do such things is
2: 3 you will escape the j of God?
2: 5 when God's righteous j will be revealed.
5:16 j following one trespass brought condemnation,
12: 3 but to think with sober j,
13: 2 and those who resist will incur j.
14: 3 and those who abstain must not pass j
14: 4 Who are you to pass j on servants of another?
14:10 Why do you pass j on your brother or sister?
14:10 For we will all stand before the j seat of God.
14:13 Let us therefore no longer pass j on one another,
1Co 4: 5 Therefore do not pronounce j before the time,
5: 3 and as if present I have already pronounced j
7:40 But in my j she is more blessed if she remains
10:29 be subject to the j of someone else's conscience?
11:29 eat and drink j against themselves.
2Co 5:10 all of us must appear before the j seat of Christ,
2Th 1: 5 This is evidence of the righteous j of God,
1Ti 5:24 and precede them to j, while the sins
Heb 6: 2 resurrection of the dead, and eternal j.
9:27 for mortals to die once, and after that the j,
10:27 but a fearful prospect of j,
Jas 2:13 For j will be without mercy to anyone who has
shown no mercy; mercy triumphs over j.
1Pe 4:17 for j to begin with the household of God;
2Pe 2: 4 of deepest darkness to be kept until the j;
2: 9 under punishment until the day of j A
2:11 do not bring against them a slanderous j from
3: 7 until the day of j and destruction of the godless. A
1Jn 4:17 that we may have boldness on the day of j, A
Jude 1: 6 in eternal chains in deepest darkness for the j of
1:15 to execute j on all, and to convict everyone of all
Rev 14: 7 for the hour of his j has come;
17: 1 the j of the great whore who is seated
18:10 For in one hour your j has come."
18:20 For God has given j for you against her."
Tob 1:18 in those days of j that the king of heaven executed
Jdt 9: 6 and your j is with foreknowledge.
16:17 take vengeance on them in the day of j; A
AdE 1:13 Give therefore your ruling and j on this matter."
13: 3 who excels among us in sound j,
Wis 3:18 and no consolation on the day of j. A
6: 5 because severe j falls on those in high places.
7:15 May God grant me to speak with j,
8:11 I shall be found keen in j,
9: 3 and pronounce j in uprightness of soul,
9: 5 with little understanding of j and laws;
12:12 Or will resist your j?
12:25 you sent your j to mock them.
12:26 of mild rebukes will experience the deserved j
16:18 that they were being pursued by the j of God;
Sir 3:24 and wrong opinion has impaired their j.
6:23 Listen, my child, and accept my j;
18:20 Before j comes, examine yourself;
21: 5 and his j comes speedily.
25: 4 How attractive is sound j in the gray-haired,
35:22 and does justice for the righteous, and executes j.
38:33 they cannot expound discipline or j,
42: 2 and of rendering j to acquit the ungodly;
43:13 and speeds the lightnings of his j.
45:10 with the oracle of j, Urim and Thummim;
Aza 1: 5 a true j you have brought all this upon us because
1: 8 you have done by a true j.
2Mc 1:17 in every way be our God, who has brought j
2:29 such in my j is the case with us.
7:35 You have not yet escaped the j of the almighty,
7:36 but you, by the j of God,
8:11 not expecting the j from the Almighty that was
9: 4 But the j of heaven rode with him!
9:18 for the j of God had justly come upon him,
11:37 and send messengers so that we may have your j.
1Es 4:40 and there is nothing unrighteous in its j.
3Mc 2:22 since he was smitten by a righteous j.
2Es 5:34 and to search out some part of his j."
5:40 so you cannot discover my j,
5:42 He said to me, "I shall liken my j to a circle;
5:43 so that you might show your j the sooner?"
6:20 and all shall see my j together.
7:*33* The Most High shall be revealed on the seat of j,
7:*34* Only j shall remain, truth shall stand,
7:*38* Thus he will speak to them on the day of j— A
7:*44* This is my j and its prescribed order;
7:*60* So also will be the j that I have promised;
7:*66* for they do not look for a j,
7:*69* And if after death we were not to come into j,
7:*70* prepared the j and the things that pertain to the j.
7:*73* What, then, will they have to say in the j,
7:*102* day of j the righteous will be able to intercede A
7:*104* day of j is decisive and displays to all the seal A
7:*113* [43] But the day of j will be the end of this age A
7:*115* [45] someone who has been condemned in the j,
8:18 and now also I have heard of the swiftness of the j
8:38 or about their death, their j, or their destruction;
8:61 Therefore my j is now drawing near;
11:46 for the j and mercy of him who made it.' "
12:33 For first he will bring them alive before his j seat,
12:34 the end comes, the day of j, of which I spoke A
14:35 death the j will come, when we shall live again;
4Mc 1: 2 I mean, of course, rational j.
1:18 Now the kinds of wisdom are rational j, justice,
1:19 Rational j is supreme over all of these,
1:30 that rational j is sovereign over the emotions

JUDGMENTS (44) [JUDGE]

Ex 12:12 on all the gods of Egypt I will execute j:
Nu 33: 4 The LORD executed j even against their gods.
1Ch 16:12 his miracles, and the j he uttered,
16:14 his j are in all the earth.
Ps 10: 5 your j are on high, out of their sight;
36: 6 your j are like the great deep;
48:11 let the towns of Judah rejoice because of your j.
97: 8 and the towns of Judah rejoice, because of your j,
105: 5 his miracles, and the j he uttered,
105: 7 his j are in all the earth.
119:75 I know, O LORD, that your j are right,
119:120 and I am afraid of your j.
119:137 O LORD, and your j are right.
Isa 26: 8 In the path of your j, O LORD, we wait for you;
26: 9 For when your j are in the earth,
58: 2 they ask of me righteous j,
Jer 1:16 And I will utter my j against them,
Eze 5: 8 I will execute j among you in the sight of
5:10 I will execute j on you,
5:15 when I execute j on you in anger and fury,
7:27 according to their own j I will judge them.
11: 9 the hands of foreigners, and execute j upon you.
16:41 and execute j on you in the sight of many women;
25:11 and I will execute j upon Moab.
28:22 when I execute j in it, and manifest my holiness
28:26 in safety, when I execute j
44:24 and they shall decide it according to my j.
Zep 3:15 The LORD has taken away the j against you,
Zec 7: 9 Render true j, show kindness and mercy
8:16 to one another, render in your gates j that are true
Ro 11:33 How unsearchable are his j and
Rev 15: 4 for your j have been revealed."
16: 7 the Almighty, your j are true and just!"
19: 2 for his j are true and just;
Tob 3: 5 And now your many j are true in exacting penalty
Wis 17: 1 Great are your j and hard to describe;
Sir 32:16 Those who fear the Lord will form true j,
45:17 and statutes and j, to teach Jacob the testimonies,
48: 7 You heard rebuke at Sinai and j of vengeance
Aza 1: 4 and your ways right, and all your j are true.
1: 5 You have executed true j in all you have brought
Sus 1:53 pronouncing unjust j, condemning the innocent
1Es 8: 7 but taught all Israel all the ordinances and j.
4Mc 9:32 the j of the divine wrath."

JUDICIAL (1) [JUDGE]

Dt 17: 8 If a j decision is too difficult for you to make

JUDICIOUS (1) [JUDGE]

Pr 16:23 The mind of the wise makes their speech j,

JUDITH (33) [JUDITH'S]

Ge 26:34 he married J daughter of Beeri the Hittite,
Jdt 8: 1 Now in those days J heard about these things:
8: 4 J remained as a widow for three years
8: 9 When J heard the harsh words spoken by
8:32 Then J said to them, "Listen to me.
9: 1 Then J prostrated herself, put ashes on her head,
9: 1 J cried out to the Lord with a loud voice,
10: 1 J had stopped crying out to the God of Israel,
10:10 When they had done this, J went out,
10:23 When J came into the presence of Holofernes
11: 5 J answered him, "Accept the words of your slave,
12: 2 But J said, "I cannot partake of them,
12: 4 J replied, "As surely as you live, my lord,
12:14 J replied, "Who am I to refuse my lord?
12:16 Then J came in and lay down.
12:18 J said, "I will gladly drink, my lord,
13: 2 But J was left alone in the tent,
13: 3 Now J had told her maid to stand outside
13: 4 Then J, standing beside his bed, said in her heart,
13:11 a distance J called out to the sentries at the gates,
14: 1 Then J said to them, "Listen to me, my friends.
14: 8 So J told him in the presence of the people all
14:14 for he supposed that he was sleeping with J.
14:17 Then he went to the tent where J had stayed,
15: 8 and to see J and to wish her well.
15:11 They gave J the tent of Holofernes
15:14 J began this thanksgiving before all Israel,
16: 1 And J said, Begin a song to my God
16: 6 but J daughter of Merari with the beauty of her
countenance undid him.
16:19 J also dedicated to God all the possessions
16:20 and J remained with them.
16:21 J went to Bethulia, and remained on her estate.
16:25 among the Israelites during the lifetime of J,

JUDITH'S (1) [JUDITH]

Jdt 14: 7 they raised him up he threw himself at J feet,

JUG (5) [JUGS]

1Ki 17:12 handful of meal in a jar, and a little oil in a j;
17:14 not be emptied and the j of oil will not fail until
17:16 neither did the j of oil fail,
Jer 19: 1 Go and buy a potter's earthenware j.
19:10 the j in the sight of those who go with you,

JUGS (1) [JUG]

Lk 16: 6 He answered, 'A hundred j of olive oil.'

JUICE (5)

Nu 6: 3 and shall not drink any grape j or eat grapes,
Job 6: 6 or is there any flavor in the j of mallows?
SS 8: 2 the j of my pomegranates.
Isa 63: 3 their j spattered on my garments,
1Mc 6:34 the elephants the j of grapes and mulberries,

JULIA[‡] (1)

Ro 16:15 Greet Philologus, J, Nereus and his sister,

JULIUS (2)

Ac 27: 1 to a centurion of the Augustan Cohort, named J.
27: 3 and J treated Paul kindly,

JUMP (1) [JUMPED, JUMPING]

Ac 27:43 to j overboard first and make for the land,

JUMPED (3) [JUMP]

2Ki 5:21 he j down from the chariot to meet him and said,
Jn 21: 7 for he was naked, and j into the sea.
Tob 7: 6 At that Raguel j up and kissed him and wept.

JUMPING (1) [JUMP]

Ac 3: 8 J up, he stood and began to walk,

JUNGLE (1)

4Mc 1:29 and so tames the j of habits and emotions.

JUNIA (1)

Ro 16: 7 and J, my relatives who were in prison with me;

JUNIAS See Index to Footnotes

JUPITER (KJV) See HEAVEN, ZEUS

JURISDICTION (3)

Ne 3: 7 the j of the governor of the province Beyond
Lk 20:20 so as to hand him over to the j and authority of
23: 7 when he learned that he was under Herod's j,

JUSHAB-HESED (1)

1Ch 3:20 Ohel, Berechiah, Hasadiah, and J, five.

JUST[‡] (433) [JUSTICE, JUSTICES, JUSTIFICATION, JUSTIFIED, JUSTIFIES, JUSTIFY, JUSTLY]

Ge 9: 3 and j as I gave you the green plants,
18:25 Shall not the Judge of all the earth do what is j?"
18:32 not let the Lord be angry if I speak j once more.
26:29 j as we have not touched you and have done
34: 7 j as the sons of Jacob came in from the field.
38:29 But j then he drew back his hand,
40:13 j as you used to do when you were his cupbearer.
40:22 j as Joseph had interpreted to them.
41:54 and the seven years of famine began to come, j
42:14 Joseph said to them, "It is j as I have said to you;
47:19 j give us seed, so that we may live and not die,
48: 5 j as Reuben and Simeon are.
Ex 7: 6 they did j as the LORD commanded them.
7:20 and Aaron did j as the LORD commanded.
8:15 j as the LORD had said.
8:19 j as the LORD had said.
9:12 j as the LORD had spoken to Moses.
9:35 j as the LORD had spoken through Moses.
10:17 Do forgive my sin j this once,
10:29 Moses said, "J as you say!
12:28 and did j as the LORD had commanded Moses
12:50 All the Israelites did j as the LORD
27: 8 be made j as you were shown on the mountain.
29:35 j as I have commanded you;
31:11 They shall do j as I have commanded you.
39:32 the Israelites had done everything j as the LORD
39:42 the work j as the LORD had commanded Moses.
39:43 the work j as the LORD had commanded,
40:16 Moses did everything j as the LORD
Lev 4:10 j as these are removed from the ox of the sacrifice
4:20 He shall do with the bull j as is done with the bull
16: 2 not to come j at any time into the sanctuary inside
Nu 1:54 they did j as the LORD commanded Moses.
2:17 they shall set out j as they camp, each in position,
2:33 J as the LORD had commanded Moses,
2:34 The Israelites did j as the LORD had commanded
8:20 the Israelites did with the Levites j as
9: 5 J as the LORD had commanded Moses,
14:19 j as you have pardoned this people,
14:20 LORD said, "I do forgive, j as you have asked;
15:20 you shall present it j as you present a donation
15:36 j as the LORD had commanded Moses.
16:40 j as the LORD had said to him through Moses.
17:11 j as the LORD commanded him, so he did.
18:18 j as the breast that is elevated and as
20:19 j let us pass through on foot."
22: 8 j as the LORD speaks to me";
22:33 j now I would have killed you and let it live."
22:38 but do I have power to say j anything?
25: 6 J then one of the Israelites came and brought
29:40 So Moses told the Israelites everything j as
32:27 to do battle for the LORD, j as my lord orders."
Dt 1: 3 Moses spoke to the Israelites j as the LORD
1:19 Then, j as the LORD our God had ordered us,
1:30 j as he did for you in Egypt
1:31 j as one carries a child,
1:41 j as the LORD our God commanded us."
2:16 J as soon as all the warriors had died off from
2:29 j as the descendants of Esau who live

Dt 2:37 **j** as the LORD our God had charged.
4: 5 See, **j** as the LORD my God has charged me,
4: 8 as **j** as this entire law that I am setting
7:18 **J** remember what the LORD your God did
12:22 Indeed, **j** as gazelle or deer is eaten,
16:18 and they shall render **j** decisions for the people.
19:19 the false witness **j** as the false witness had meant
20:17 **j** as the LORD your God has commanded,
23:23 **j** as you have freely vowed to the LORD
24: 8 **j** as I have commanded them.
26:14 doing **j** as you commanded me.
28:63 And **j** as the LORD took delight
30: 2 **j** as I am commanding you today,
30: 9 **j** as he delighted in prospering your ancestors,
32: 4 Rock, his work is perfect, and all his ways are **j.**
32: 4 A faithful God, without deceit, **j** and upright is he;
Jos 1:17 **J** as we obeyed Moses in all things,
8:31 **j** as Moses the servant of the LORD
10:37 **j** as he had done to Eglon,
10:39 **j** as he had done to Hebron, and,
11:20 **j** as the LORD had commanded Moses.
21:44 on every side **j** as he had sworn to their ancestors;
23:15 But **j** as all the good things that
Jdg 6:39 please, make trial with the fleece **j** once more;
7:19 when they had **j** set the watch;
Ru 2: 4 **J** then Boaz came from Bethlehem.
3: 6 and did **j** as her mother-in-law had instructed her.
1Sa 4:16 man said to Eli, "I have **j** come from the battle;
8: 8 **J** as they have done to me,
9:12 They answered, "Yes, there he is **j** ahead of you.
9:12 Hurry; he has come **j** now to the town,
17:28 for you have come down **j** to see the battle."
17:33 for you are **j** a boy,
28:17 The LORD has done to you **j** as he spoke by me;
2Sa 3: 9 For **j** what the LORD has sworn to David,
3:22 **J** then the servants of David arrived with Joab
3:36 **j** as everything the king did pleased all the people.
5:25 David did **j** as the LORD had commanded him;
10: 2 **j** as his father dealt loyally with me."
10: 3 that David is honoring your father **j** because he
11:10 "You have **j** come from a journey.
15:37 **j** as Absalom was entering Jerusalem.
16:19 **J** as I have served your father,
1Ki 8:53 **j** as you promised through Moses, your servant,
14:10 **j** as one burns up dung until it is all gone.
21:11 **J** as it was written in the letters that she had sent
22:53 to anger, **j** as his father had done.
2Ki 4: 3 empty vessels and not **j** a few.
5: 4 in and told his lord **j** what the girl from the land
5: 7 **J** look and see how he is trying to pick a quarrel
5:22 of a company of prophets have **j** come to me from
7: 7 and their donkeys leaving the camp **j** as it was,
7:17 **j** as the man of God had said when the king came
9:12 So he said, "This is **j** what he said to me:
15: 3 **j** as his father Amaziah had done.
15:34 **j** as his father Uzziah had done.
16:11 **j** so did the priest Uriah build it,
18: 3 He did what was right in the sight of the LORD **j** as
23:19 he did to them **j** as he had done at Bethel.
23:32 **j** as his ancestors had done.
23:37 **j** as all his ancestors had done.
24: 9 **j** as his father had done.
24:19 the sight of the LORD, **j** as Jehoiakim had done.
1Ch 26:12 had duties, **j** as their kindred did,
2Ch 26: 4 **j** as his father Amaziah had done.
27: 2 He did what was right in the sight of the LORD **j** as
29: 2 **j** as his ancestor David had done.
32:17 "**J** as the gods of the nations in other lands did
Ezr 9:15 O LORD, God of Israel, you are **j,**
Ne 9:33 You have been **j** in all that has come upon us,
Est 2:20 for Esther obeyed Mordecai **j** as
4:14 Perhaps you have come to royal dignity for **j** such
6: 4 Now Haman had **j** entered the outer court of
9:31 **j** as they had laid down for themselves and
Job 5: 7 but human beings are born to trouble **j**
9: 2 but how can a mortal be **j** before God?
12: 4 a **j** and blameless man, I am a laughingstock.
27:17 but the **j** will wear it,
31: 6 in a **j** balance, and let God know my integrity!—
35: 2 "Do you think this to be **j**?
40:15 which I made **j** as I made you;
Ps 9: 4 For you have maintained my **j** cause;
17: 1 Hear a **j** cause, O LORD;
50:21 you thought that I was one **j** like yourself.
111: 7 The works of his hands are faithful and **j;**
119:121 I have done what is **j** and right;
145:17 The LORD is **j** in all his ways,
Pr 2:20 and keep to the paths of the **j.**
8:15 By me kings reign, and rulers decree what is **j;**
12: 5 The thoughts of the righteous are **j;**
21: 7 because they refuse to do what is **j.**
27:19 **J** as water reflects the face,
Ecc 2:16 How can the wise die **j** like fools?
5:16 **j** as they came, so shall they go;
11: 5 **J** as you do not know how the breath comes to
Isa 4: 1 **j** let us be called by your name;
20: 3 "**J** as my servant Isaiah has walked naked
26: 7 The way of the righteous is level; O **J** One,
29: 8 **J** as when a hungry person dreams of eating
52:14 **J** as there were many who were astonished at him
54: 9 **J** as I swore that the waters
56: 3 and do not let the eunuch say, "I am **j** a dry tree."
66:20 **j** as the Israelites bring a grain offering in
Jer 3: 4 Have you not **j** now called to me, "My Father,
7:14 **j** what I did to Shiloh.
7:15 **j** as I cast out all your kinsfolk,
10:24 Correct me, O LORD, but in **j** measure;
Jer 13: 9 **J** so I will ruin the pride of Judah and
18: 6 O house of Israel, **j** as this potter has done?
18: 6 **J** like the clay in the potter's hand,
23:27 **j** as their ancestors forgot my name for Baal.
30:11 I will chastise you in **j** measure,
31:28 And **j** as I have watched over them to pluck up
32:42 **J** as I have brought all this great disaster
33:22 **J** as the host of heaven cannot be numbered and
38:12 "**J** put the rags and clothes between your armpits
38:20 **J** obey the voice of the LORD in what I say
38:25 '**J** tell us what you said to the king;
40: 4 I have **j** released you today from the fetters
42:18 **J** as my anger and my wrath were poured out on
44:17 **j** as we and our ancestors,
44:30 **j** as I gave King Zedekiah of Judah into the hand
46:28 I will chastise you in **j** measure,
50:29 **j** as she has done, do to her—
52: 2 the sight of the LORD, **j** as Jehoiakim had done.
Eze 12: 7 I did **j** as I was commanded.
24:24 you shall do **j** as he has done.
33:17 your people say, "The way of the Lord is not **j,**"
33:17 when it is their own way that is not **j.**
33:20 Yet you say, "The way of the Lord is not **j.**"
45: 9 and do what is **j** and right.
Da 2:40 **j** as iron crushes and smashes everything,
2:43 **j** as iron does not mix with clay.
2:45 **j** as you saw that a stone was cut from
6:10 **j** as he had done previously.
9:13 **J** as it is written in the law of Moses,
Hos 3: 1 **j** as the LORD loves the people of Israel,
Am 2:13 **j** as a cart presses down when it is full of sheaves.
5:14 will be with you, **j** as you have said.
Zec 1: 6 **j** as he planned to do."
7:13 **J** as, when I called, they would not hear, so,
8:13 **J** as you have been a cursing among the nations,
8:14 **J** as I purposed to bring disaster upon you,
Mt 1:20 But **j** when he had resolved to do this,
3:16 **j** as he came up from the water,
9: 2 And **j** then some people were carrying
9:18 saying, "My daughter has **j** died;
12:40 For **j** as Jonah was three days and three nights in
13:40 **J** as the weeds are collected and burned up
15:22 **J** then a Canaanite woman from
20:28 **j** as the Son of Man came not to be served but
21: 3 If anyone says anything to you, **j** say this,
25:40 **j** as you did it to one of the least
25:45 **j** as you did not do it to one of the least of these,
Mk 1:10 And **j** as he was coming up out of the water,
1:23 **J** then there was in their synagogue a man with
4:36 they took him with them in the boat, **j** as he was.
11: 3 **j** say this, 'The Lord needs it
16: 7 there you will see him, **j** as he told you."
Lk 1: 2 **j** as they were handed on to us by those who from
5:18 **J** then some men came, carrying a paralyzed man
6:36 Be merciful, **j** as your Father is merciful.
7:21 Jesus had **j** then cured many people of diseases,
8:41 **J** then there came a man named Jairus,
9:33 **J** as they were leaving him, Peter said to Jesus,
9:38 **J** then a man from the crowd shouted, "Teacher,
10:25 **J** then a lawyer stood up to test Jesus.
11:30 For **j** as Jonah became a sign to the people
13: 5 you repent, you will all perish **j** as they did."
13:11 And **j** then there appeared a woman with a spirit
14: 2 **J** then, in front of him, there was
14:20 Another said, 'I have **j** been married,
15: 7 **J** so, I tell you, there will be more joy in heaven
15:10 **J** so, I tell you, there is joy in the presence of
17: 7 to your slave who has **j** come in from plowing
17:26 **J** as it was in the days of Noah,
17:28 Likewise, **j** as it was in the days of Lot:
19:31 **j** say this, 'The Lord needs it.' "
22:29 **j** as my Father has conferred on me, a kingdom,
24:24 to the tomb and found it **j** as the women had said;
Jn 3:14 **j** as Moses lifted up the serpent in the wilderness,
4:27 **J** then his disciples came.
5:21 **j** as the Father raises the dead and gives them life,
5:23 all may honor the Son **j** as they honor the Father.
5:26 For **j** as the Father has life in himself,
5:30 As I hear, I judge; and my judgment is **j,**
6:57 **J** as the living Father sent me,
10:15 **j** as the Father knows me and I know the Father.
11: 8 "Rabbi, the Jews were **j** now trying to stone you,
12:24 it remains **j** a single grain;
12:50 therefore, I speak **j** as the Father has told me."
13:34 **J** as I have loved you,
15: 4 **J** as the branch cannot bear fruit by itself
15:10 **j** as I have kept my Father's commandments
17:14 **j** as I do not belong to the world.
17:16 **j** as I do not belong to the world.
21: 4 **J** after daybreak, Jesus stood on the beach;
21:10 "Bring some of the fish that you have **j** caught."
Ac 7:51 **j** as your ancestors used to do.
10:47 the Holy Spirit **j** as we have?"
11:15 the Holy Spirit fell upon them **j** as it had upon us
14:13 whose temple was **j** outside the city,
14:15 We are mortals **j** like you,
15: 8 **j** as he did to us;
15:11 be saved through the grace of the Lord Jesus, **j**
18:14 **J** as Paul was about to speak,
21:37 **J** as Paul was about to be brought into
22: 3 being zealous for God, **j** as all of you are today.
23:11 For **j** as you have testified for me in Jerusalem,
27:33 **J** before daybreak, Paul urged all of them
Ro 5:12 **j** as sin came into the world through one man,
5:18 Therefore **j** as one man's trespass led
5:19 For **j** as by the one man's disobedience
5:21 **j** as sin exercised dominion in death,
Ro 6: 4 **j** as Christ was raised from the dead by the glory
6:19 For **j** as you once presented your members
7:12 and the commandment is holy and **j** and good.
8: 4 **j** requirement of the law might be fulfilled in us,
11:30 **J** as you were once disobedient to God but have
15: 7 therefore, **j** as Christ has welcomed you,
1Co 1: 6 **j** as the testimony of Christ has been strengthened
7:22 **j** as whoever was free when called is a slave
9:18 What then is my reward? **J** this:
10:33 **j** as I try to please everyone in everything I do,
11: 2 and maintain the traditions **j** as I handed them on
11:12 For **j** as woman came from man,
12:11 to each one individually **j** as the Spirit chooses.
12:12 For **j** as the body is one and has many members,
15:49 **J** as we have borne the image of the man of dust,
16: 7 I do not want to see you now **j** in passing,
16:10 for he is doing the work of the Lord **j** as I am;
2Co 1: 5 **j** as the sufferings of Christ are abundant for us,
4:13 But **j** as we have the same spirit of faith that is
7:14 but **j** as everything we said to you was true,
10: 7 that **j** as you belong to Christ, so also do we.
Gal 2: 7 **j** as Peter had been entrusted with the gospel for
3: 6 **J** as Abraham "believed God,
4:29 But **j** as at that time the child who was born
Eph 1: 4 **J** as he chose us in Christ before the foundation of
4: 4 **j** as you were called to the one hope
5:23 the husband is the head of the wife **j** as Christ is
5:24 **J** as the church is subject to Christ,
5:25 **j** as Christ loved the church and gave himself up
5:29 **j** as Christ does for the church,
Php 1:18 **J** this, that Christ is proclaimed in every way,
2:12 my beloved, **j** as you have always obeyed me,
4: 8 whatever is honorable, whatever is **j,**
Col 1: 6 **J** as it is bearing fruit and growing in
2: 7 **j** as you were taught, abounding in thanksgiving.
3:13 **j** as the Lord has forgiven you,
1Th 1: 5 **j** as you know what kind of persons we proved to
2: 4 but **j** as we have been approved by God to
3: 6 But Timothy has **j** now come to us from you,
3: 6 **j** as we long to see you.
3:12 **j** as we abound in love for you.
4: 6 **j** as we have already told you beforehand
2Th 1: 6 For it is indeed **j** of God to repay
3: 1 **j** as it is among you,
Heb 2: 2 or disobedience received a **j** penalty,
3: 2 **j** as Moses also "was faithful in all God's house."
3: 3 **j** as the builder of a house has more honor than
4: 2 For indeed the good news came to us **j** as to them;
4: 3 **j** as God has said, "As in my anger I swore,
5: 4 but takes it only when called by God, **j**
9:27 And **j** as it is appointed for mortals to die once,
Jas 2:26 For **j** as the body without the spirit is dead,
2Pe 2: 1 **j** as there will be false teachers among you,
2:18 of the flesh they entice people who have **j** escaped
1Jn 1: 9 he who is faithful and **j** will forgive us our sins
2: 6 "I abide in him," ought to walk **j** as he walked.
2:27 and **j** as it has taught you, abide in him.
3: 3 in him purify themselves, **j** as he is pure.
3: 7 does what is right is righteous, **j** as he is righteous.
3:23 **j** as he has commanded us.
2Jn 1: 4 **j** as we have been commanded by the Father.
1: 6 this is the commandment **j** as you have heard it
3Jn 1: 2 **j** as it is well with your soul.
Rev 3:21 **j** as I myself conquered and sat down
15: 3 **J** and true are your ways, King of the nations!
16: 5 I heard the angel of the waters say, "You are **j,**
16: 7 the Almighty, your judgments are true and **j!**"
19: 2 for his judgments are true and **j;**
Tob 3: 2 O Lord, and all your deeds are **j;**
5: 9 "I have **j** found a man who is one
14: 5 **j** as the prophets of Israel have said concerning it.
Jdt 2: 1 on the whole region, **j** as he had said.
4: 3 the people of Judea had **j** now gathered together,
10: 9 and accomplish the things you have **j** said to me."
10:16 but tell him what you have **j** said,
AdE 1:17 "And **j** as she defied King Artaxerxes,
2:20 **j** as she had done when she was with him.
6:10 Do **j** as you have said for Mordecai the Jew,
Wis 14:30 But **j** penalties will overtake them on two counts:
14:31 but the **j** penalty for those who sin,
19:17 **j** as were those at the door of the righteous man—
Sir 18: 2 the Lord alone is **j.**
18: 7 human beings have finished, they are **j** beginning,
20:18 downfall of the wicked will occur **j** as speedily.
45:25 **J** as a covenant was established with David son
Bar 2: 9 for the Lord is **j** in all the works
4:28 For **j** as you were disposed to go astray from God,
4:33 For **j** as she rejoiced at your fall and was glad
LtJ 6:17 **j** as someone's dish is useless when it is broken,
6:18 And **j** as the gates are shut on every side
6:20 They are **j** like a beam of the temple,
6:27 Gifts are placed before them **j** as before the dead.
Aza 1: 4 For you are **j** in all you have done;
Sus 1:45 **J** as she was being led off to execution,
1Mc 2:26 **j** as Phinehas did against Zimri son of Salu.
4:19 **J** as Judas was finishing this speech,
7:12 before Alcimus and Bacchides to ask for **j** terms.
7:47 and displayed them **j** outside Jerusalem.
8:26 arms, money, or ships, **j** as Rome has decided;
8:28 arms, money, or ships, **j** as Rome has decided;
10:37 **j** as the king has commanded in the land of Judah.
2Mc 1:24 you are awe-inspiring and strong and **j**
1:25 you alone are **j** and almighty and eternal.
2:10 **J** as Moses prayed to the Lord,
2:27 **j** as it is not easy for one who prepares a banquet
3:28 this man who had **j** entered the aforesaid treasury
5:18 **j** as Heliodorus had been,

2Mc 7:36 will receive **j** punishment for your arrogance.
10:28 **J** as dawn was breaking, the two armies joined
11:14 persuaded them to settle everything on **j** terms,
11:31 **j** as formerly, and none of them shall be molested
13: 8 And this was eminently **j**;
13:11 to let the people who had **j** begun to revive fall
13:17 This happened, **j** as day was dawning,
15:39 For **j** as it is harmful to drink wine alone, or,
1Es 5:69 For we obey your Lord **j** as you do
8:11 so disposed, therefore, leave with you, **j** as I and
3Mc 2: 3 of all things and the governor of all, are a **j** Ruler,
2:25 who were strangers to everything **j**.
4: 6 And young women who had **j** entered
6:15 but **j** as you have said,
6:16 **J** as Eleazar was ending his prayer,
2Es 3:10 **j** as death came upon Adam,
3:26 in everything doing **j** as Adam
4:42 For **j** as a woman who is in labor makes haste
4:50 for **j** as the rain is more than the drops,
5:40 "**J** as you cannot do one of the things
5:42 **j** as for those who are last there is no slowness,
6: 6 **j** as the end shall come through me alone and not
7:*52* "If you have **j** a few precious stones,
7:*104* **J** as now a father does not send his son,
8: 2 **J** as, when you ask the earth,
8:41 "For **j** as the farmer sows many seeds in
8:59 For **j** as the things that I have predicted await you,
9: 5 For **j** as with everything that has occurred in
10:14 '**J** as you brought forth in sorrow,
10:16 For if you acknowledge the decree of God to be **j**,
11:33 **j** as the wings had done.
13:52 "**J** as no one can explore or know what is in
15:21 **J** as they have done to my elect until this day,
16:16 **J** as an arrow shot by a mighty archer does
16:29 **J** as in an olive orchard three or four olives may
16:30 or **j** as when a vineyard is gathered,
16:38 **J** as a pregnant woman, in the ninth month when
16:49 **J** as a respectable and virtuous woman abhors
4Mc 1:14 We shall decide **j** what reason is
1:28 **J** as pleasure and pain are two plants growing
2: 6 **J** so it is with the emotions that hinder one
2:16 all these malicious emotions, **j** as it repels anger—
2:23 to this will rule a kingdom that is temperate, **j**,
3:21 **j** at that time certain persons attempted
7:11 For **j** as our father Aaron, armed with the censer,
8: 5 as that of the old man who has **j** been tortured,
8: 6 **J** as I am able to punish
9:24 Thereby the **j** Providence
10:16 from them that I am a brother to those who have **j**
13: 6 For **j** as towers jutting out over harbors hold back
14: 6 **J** as the hands and feet are moved in harmony
14: 7 For **j** as the seven days of creation move
15:31 **J** as Noah's ark, carrying the world in

JUSTICE (165) [JUST]

Ge 18:19 of the LORD by doing righteousness and **j**;
Ex 23: 2 not side with the majority so as to pervert **j**;
23: 6 You shall not pervert the **j** due to your poor
Lev 19:15 with **j** you shall judge your neighbor.
Dt 10:18 who executes **j** for the orphan and the widow,
16:19 You must not distort **j**; you must
16:20 **J**, and only **j**, you shall pursue,
24:17 not deprive a resident alien or an orphan of **j**;
27:19 the orphan, and the widow of **j**."
33:21 he executed the **j** of the LORD,
1Sa 7:17 he administered **j** there to Israel,
8: 3 they took bribes and perverted **j**.
2Sa 8:15 David administered **j** and equity to all his people.
15: 4 and I would give them **j**."
1Ki 3:28 that the wisdom of God was in him, to execute **j**.
7: 7 to pronounce judgment, the Hall of **J**,
10: 9 he has made you king to execute **j**
1Ch 18:14 and he administered **j** and equity to all his people.
2Ch 9: 8 that you may execute **j** and righteousness."
19: 7 for there is no perversion of **j** with
Job 8: 3 Does God pervert **j**? Or does the Almighty pervert
9:19 If it is a matter of **j**, who can summon him?
19: 7 I am not answered; I call aloud, but there is no **j**.
29:14 my **j** was like a robe and a turban.
34:12 and the Almighty will not pervert **j**.
34:17 Shall one who hates **j** govern?
36:17 judgment and **j** seize you.
37:23 he is great in power and **j**,
Ps 10:18 to do **j** for the orphan and the oppressed,
33: 5 He loves righteousness and **j**;
37: 6 and the **j** of your cause like the noonday.
37:28 the LORD loves **j**; he will not forsake his faithful
37:30 and their tongues speak **j**.
72: 1 the king your **j**, O God, and your righteousness to
72: 2 with righteousness, and your poor with **j**.
82: 3 Give **j** to the weak and the orphan;
89:14 and **j** are the foundation of your throne;
94:15 for **j** will return to the righteous,
97: 2 righteousness and **j** are the foundation
99: 4 lover of **j**, you have established equity;
99: 4 you have executed **j** and righteousness in Jacob.
101: 1 I will sing of loyalty and of **j**;
103: 6 The LORD works vindication and **j**
106: 3 Happy are those who observe **j**,
112: 5 who conduct their affairs with **j**.
119:149 O LORD, in your **j** preserve my life.
119:156 give me life according to your **j**.
140:12 and executes **j** for the poor.
146: 7 who executes **j** for the oppressed;
Pr 1: 3 righteousness, **j**, and equity;
2: 8 of **j** and preserving the way of his faithful ones.
Pr 2: 9 Then you will understand righteousness and **j**
8:20 in the way of righteousness, along the paths of **j**,
17:23 a concealed bribe to pervert the ways of **j**.
19:28 A worthless witness mocks at **j**,
21: 3 To do righteousness and **j** is more acceptable to
21:15 When **j** is done, it is a joy to the righteous,
28: 5 The evil do not understand **j**,
29: 4 By **j** a king gives stability to the land,
29:26 but it is from the LORD that one gets **j**.
Ecc 3:16 I saw under the sun that in the place of **j**,
5: 8 oppression of the poor and the violation of **j** and
Isa 1:17 seek **j**, rescue the oppressed,
1:21 that was full of **j**, righteousness lodged in her—
1:27 Zion shall be redeemed by **j**,
5: 7 he expected **j**, but saw bloodshed;
5:16 But the LORD of hosts is exalted by **j**,
9: 7 and uphold it with **j** and with righteousness
10: 2 the needy from **j** and to rob the poor of my people
16: 3 "Give counsel, grant **j**; make your shade like night
16: 5 a ruler who seeks **j** and is swift to do what is right.
28: 6 and a spirit of **j** to the one who sits in judgment,
28:17 And I will make **j** the line,
29:21 and without grounds deny **j** to the one in the right.
30:18 For the LORD is a God of **j**;
32: 1 and princes will rule with **j**.
32:16 Then **j** will dwell in the wilderness,
33: 5 he filled Zion with **j** and righteousness;
40:14 and who taught him the path of **j**?
42: 1 he will bring forth **j** to the nations.
42: 3 he will faithfully bring forth **j**.
42: 4 be crushed until he has established **j** in the earth;
51: 4 and my **j** for a light to the peoples.
53: 8 By a perversion of **j** he was taken away.
56: 1 Thus says the LORD: Maintain **j**, and do what is right,
59: 8 and there is no **j** in their paths.
59: 9 Therefore **j** is far from us,
59:11 We wait for **j**, but there is none;
59:14 **J** is turned back, and righteousness stands at
59:15 and it displeased him that there was no **j**.
61: 8 For I the LORD love **j**, I hate robbery
Jer 4: 2 in truth, in **j**, and in uprightness,
5:28 they do not judge with **j** the cause of the orphan,
9:24 I act with steadfast love, **j**,
21:12 Thus says the LORD: Execute **j** in the morning,
22: 3 Act with **j** and righteousness,
22:15 Did not your father eat and drink and do **j**
23: 5 and shall execute **j** and righteousness in the land.
33:15 he shall execute **j** and righteousness in the land.
Eze 18: 8 executes true **j** between contending parties,
34:16 I will feed them with **j**.
Da 4:37 for all his works are truth, and his ways are **j**;
Hos 2:19 for my wife in righteousness and in **j**,
12: 6 you, return to your God, hold fast to love and **j**,
Am 5: 7 Ah, you that turn **j** to wormwood,
5:15 and establish **j** in the gate;
5:24 But let **j** roll down like waters,
6:12 But you have turned **j** into poison and the fruit
Mic 3: 1 Should you not know **j**?—
3: 8 of the LORD, and with **j** and might, to declare
3: 9 who abhor **j** and pervert all equity,
6: 8 what does the LORD require of you but to do **j**,
7: 3 dictate what they desire; thus they pervert **j**.
Hab 1: 4 So the law becomes slack and **j** never prevails.
1: 7 their **j** and dignity proceed from themselves.
Mal 2:17 Or by asking, "Where is the God of **j**?"
Mt 12:18 and he will proclaim **j** to the Gentiles.
12:20 a smoldering wick until he brings **j** to victory.
23:23 of the law: **j** and mercy and faith.
Lk 7:29 acknowledged the **j** of God,
11:42 and neglect **j** and the love of God;
18: 3 'Grant me **j** against my opponent.'
18: 5 I will grant her **j**, so that she may not wear me out
18: 7 not God grant **j** to his chosen ones who cry
18: 8 I tell you, he will quickly grant **j** to them.
Ac 8:33 In his humiliation **j** was denied him.
24:25 And as he discussed **j**, self-control,
28: 4 **j** has not allowed him to live."
Ro 3: 5 But if our injustice serves to confirm the **j** of God,
Heb 11:33 administered **j**, obtained promises,
AdE 16: 4 that they will escape the evil-hating **j** of God,
Wis 1: 8 and **j**, when it punishes, will not pass them by.
5:18 and wear impartial **j** as a helmet;
8: 7 for she teaches self-control and prudence, **j**
11:20 at a single breath when pursued by **j** and scattered
Sir 16:22 Who is to announce his acts of **j**?
27: 8 If you pursue **j**, you will attain it and wear it like
35:22 and does **j** for the righteous,
45:26 of mind to judge his people with **j**,
49: 9 to all the ways of **j**.
Bar 2:17 will not ascribe glory or **j** to the Lord;
Sus 1: 9 or remembering their duty to administer **j**.
1Mc 2:29 and **j** went down to the wilderness to live there,
6:22 "How long will you fail to do **j** and
7:18 for they said, "There is no truth or **j** in them,
14:35 of the **j** and loyalty that he had maintained
2Mc 4:34 then, with no regard for **j**,
8:13 and distrustful of God's **j** ran off and got away.
10:12 took the lead in showing **j** to the Jews because of
2Es 2:20 secure **j** for the ward, give to the needy,
4Mc 1: 4 the emotions that hinder one from **j**,
1: 6 but those that are opposed to **j**, courage,
1:18 the kinds of wisdom are rational judgment, **j**,
2: 6 so it is with the emotions that hinder one from **j**.
4:13 by human treachery and not by divine **j**.
4:21 The divine **j** was angered by these acts
5:24 in **j**, so that in all our dealings we act impartially,
4Mc 8:14 whatever **j** you revere will be merciful to you
8:22 divine **j** will excuse us for fearing the king
9: 9 from the divine **j** eternal torment by fire."
9:15 enemy of heavenly **j**, savage of mind,
11: 3 from the heavenly **j** for even more crimes.
12:12 **j** has laid up for you intense and eternal fire
18:22 For these crimes divine **j** pursued and will pursue

JUSTICES (3) [JUST]

Da 3: 2 the treasurers, the **j**, the magistrates,
3: 3 the treasurers, the **j**, the magistrates,
1Es 8:23 appoint judges and **j** to judge all those who know

JUSTIFICATION (6) [JUST]

Ro 4:25 for our trespasses and was raised for our **j**.
5:16 the free gift following many trespasses brings **j**.
5:18 so one man's act of righteousness leads to **j**
5:21 also exercise dominion through **j** leading
2Co 3: 9 much more does the ministry of **j** abound
Gal 2:21 for if **j** comes through the law,

JUSTIFIED‡ (32) [JUST]

Job 32: 2 at Job because he **j** himself rather than God;
40: 8 Will you condemn me that you may be **j**?
Ps 51: 4 so that you are **j** in your sentence and blameless
Mt 12:37 for by your words you will be **j**,
Lk 18:14 this man went down to his home **j** rather than
Ac 18:14 be **j** in accepting the complaint of you Jews;
Ro 2:13 but the doers of the law who will be **j**.
3: 4 "So that you may be **j** in your words,
3:20 be **j** in his sight" by deeds prescribed by the law,
3:24 they are now **j** by his grace as a gift,
3:28 a person is **j** by faith apart from works prescribed
4: 2 For if Abraham was **j** by works,
5: 1 Therefore, since we are **j** by faith,
5: 9 now that we have been **j** by his blood,
8:30 and those whom he called he also **j**; and those whom he **j** he also glorified.
10:10 For one believes with the heart and so is **j**,
1Co 6:11 you were **j** in the name of the Lord Jesus Christ
Gal 2:16 yet we know that a person is **j** not by the works of
2:16 so that we might be **j** by faith in Christ,
2:16 because no one will be **j** by the works of the law.
2:17 But if, in our effort to be **j** in Christ,
3:11 Now it is evident that no one is **j** before God by
3:24 so that we might be **j** by faith.
5: 4 to be **j** by the law have cut yourselves off
Tit 3: 7 having been **j** by his grace,
Jas 2:21 Was not our ancestor Abraham **j** by works
2:24 that a person is **j** by works and not by faith alone.
2:25 the prostitute also **j** by works when she welcomed
Sir 1:22 Unjust anger cannot be **j**,
23:11 if he swears a false oath, he will not be **j**,
31: 5 One who loves gold will not be **j**;

JUSTIFIES (4) [JUST]

Pr 17:15 One who **j** the wicked and one who condemns
Ro 3:26 and that he **j** the one who has faith in Jesus.
4: 5 But to one who without works trusts him who **j**
8:33 It is God who **j**.

JUSTIFY (9) [JUST]

Job 33:32 speak, for I desire to **j** you.
Isa 43: 9 Let them bring their witnesses to **j** them,
Lk 10:29 But wanting to **j** himself, he asked Jesus,
16:15 "You are those who **j** yourselves in the sight
Ac 19:40 that we can give to **j** this commotion."
Ro 3:30 and he will **j** the circumcised on the ground
Gal 3: 8 foreseeing that God would **j** the Gentiles by faith,
Sir 13:22 he speaks unseemly words, but they **j** him.
2Es 4:18 which would you undertake to **j**,

JUSTLE (KJV) See RUSH

JUSTLY (13) [JUST]

2Sa 23: 3 One who rules over people **j**,
Isa 59: 4 No one brings suit **j**, no one goes to law honestly;
Jer 5: 1 who acts **j** and seeks truth—
7: 5 if you truly act **j** one with another,
Lk 23:41 And we indeed have been condemned **j**,
Col 4: 1 Masters, treat your slaves **j** and fairly,
1Pe 2:23 but he entrusted himself to the one who judges **j**.
Wis 9:12 and I shall judge your people **j**,
19:13 for they **j** suffered because of their wicked acts;
2Mc 7:38 an end the wrath of the Almighty that has **j** fallen
9: 6 and that very **j**, for he had tortured the bowels
9:18 for the judgment of God had **j** come upon him,
3Mc 7: 7 we **j** have acquitted them of every charge

JUSTUS (3) [=BARSABBAS]

Ac 1:23 who was also known as **J**, and Matthias.
18: 7 the house of a man named Titius **J**, a worshiper
Col 4:11 And Jesus who is called **J** greets you.

JUTTAH (2)

Jos 15:55 Maon, Carmel, Ziph, **J**,
21:16 **J** with its pasture lands, and Beth-shemesh

JUTTING (2)

4Mc 7: 5 For in setting his mind firm like a **j** cliff,
13: 6 For just as towers **j** out over harbors hold back

K

KAB (1)
2Ki 6:25 of a **k** of dove's dung for five shekels of silver.

KABZEEL (3)
Jos 15:21 toward the boundary of Edom, were **K**, Eder,
2Sa 23:20 of Jehoiada was a valiant warrior from **K**, a doer
1Ch 11:22 Benaiah son of Jehoiada was a valiant man of **K**,

KADESH (18) [=EN-MISHPAT, KADESH-BARNEA]
Ge 14: 7 to En-mishpat (that is, **K**), and subdued all
16:14 it lies between **K** and Bered.
20: 1 and settled between **K** and Shur.
Nu 13:26 of the Israelites in the wilderness of Paran, at **K**;
20: 1 and the people stayed in **K**.
20:14 Moses sent messengers from **K** to the king
20:16 and here we are in **K**,
20:22 They set out from **K**, and the Israelites,
33:36 and camped in the wilderness of Zin (that is, **K**).
33:37 They set out from **K** and camped at Mount Hor,
Dt 1:46 you had stayed at **K** as many days as you did,
Jdg 11:16 the wilderness to the Red Sea and came to **K**.
11:17 So Israel remained at **K**.
2Sa 24: 6 and to **K** in the land of the Hittites;
Ps 29: 8 the LORD shakes the wilderness of **K**.
Jdt 1: 9 as Jerusalem and Bethany and Chelous and **K** and
1Mc 11:63 the officers of Demetrius had come to **K** in Galilee
11:73 to him and joined him in the pursuit as far as **K**,

KADESH-BARNEA (11) [KADESH]
Nu 32: 8 when I sent them from **K** to see the land.
34: 4 and its outer limit shall be south of **K**;
Dt 1: 2 of Mount Seir it takes eleven days to reach **K**
1:19 of the Amorites, until we reached **K**.
2:14 of time we had traveled from **K** until we crossed
9:23 And when the LORD sent you from **K**, saying,
Jos 10:41 And Joshua defeated them from **K** to Gaza,
14: 6 the LORD said to Moses the man of God in **K**
14: 7 of the LORD sent me from **K** to spy out the land;
15: 3 passes along to Zin, and goes up south of **K**,
Jdt 5:14 and he led them by the way of Sinai and **K**.

KADMIEL (10)
Ezr 2:40 The Levites: the descendants of Jeshua and **K**,
3: 9 and **K** and his sons, Binnui and Hodaviah along
Ne 7:43 namely of **K** of the descendants of Hodevah,
9: 4 Then Jeshua, Bani, **K**, Shebaniah, Bunni,
9: 5 Then the Levites, Jeshua, **K**, Bani, Hashabneiah,
10: 9 Binnui of the sons of Henadad, **K**;
12: 8 And the Levites: Jeshua, Binnui, **K**, Sherebiah,
12:24 Hashabiah, Sherebiah, and Jeshua son of **K**,
1Es 5:26 the descendants of Jeshua and **K** and Bannas
5:58 and his sons and kindred and his brother **K** and

KADMONITES (1)
Ge 15:19 the land of the Kenites, the Kenizzites, the **K**,

KAIN‡ (2)
Nu 24:22 yet **K** is destined for burning.
Jos 15:57 **K**, Gibeah, and Timnah: ten towns with their

KAIWAN (1)
Am 5:26 and **K** your star-god, your images,

KALLAI (1)
Ne 12:20 of Sallai, **K**; of Amok, Eber;

KAMON (1)
Jdg 10: 5 Jair died, and was buried in **K**.

KANAH (3)
Jos 16: 8 the boundary goes westward to the Wadi **K**,
17: 9 Then the boundary went down to the Wadi **K**.
19:28 Ebron, Rehob, Hammon, **K**, as far as Great Sidon;

KAREAH (14)
2Ki 25:23 Ishmael son of Nethaniah, Johanan son of **K**,
Jer 40: 8 Ishmael son of Nethaniah, Johanan son of **K**,
40:13 Now Johanan son of **K** and all the leaders of
40:15 Then Johanan son of **K** spoke secretly to Gedaliah
40:16 Gedaliah son of Ahikam said to Johanan son of **K**,
41:11 But when Johanan son of **K** and all the leaders of
41:13 of **K** and all the leaders of the forces with him,
41:14 and went to Johanan son of **K**.
41:16 Then Johanan son of **K** and all the leaders of
42: 1 Johanan son of **K** and Azariah son of Hoshaiah,
42: 8 Then he summoned Johanan son of **K** and all
43: 2 Azariah son of Hoshaiah and Johanan son of **K**
43: 4 of **K** and all the commanders of the forces and all
43: 5 son of **K** and all the commanders of the forces

KARKA (1)
Jos 15: 3 along by Hezron, up to Addar, makes a turn to **K**,

KARKOR (1)
Jdg 8:10 Zebah and Zalmunna were in **K** with their army,

KARNAIM (1)
Am 6:13 not by our own strength taken **K** for ourselves?"

KARTAH (1)
Jos 21:34 with its pasture lands, **K** with its pasture lands,

KARTAN (1)
Jos 21:32 and **K** with its pasture lands—three towns.

KARYOT See Index to Footnotes

KASDIM See Index to Footnotes

KASERIN (1)
Tob 11: 1 When they came near to **K**,

KATTATH (1)
Jos 19:15 **K**, Nahalal, Shimron, Idalah, and Bethlehem—

KEDAR (11) [KEDAR'S]
Ge 25:13 the firstborn of Ishmael; and **K**,
1Ch 1:29 of Ishmael, Nebaioth; and **K**,
Ps 120: 5 that I must live among the tents of **K**.
SS 1: 5 like the tents of **K**, like the curtains of Solomon.
Isa 21:16 all the glory of **K** will come to an end;
42:11 the villages that **K** inhabits;
60: 7 All the flocks of **K** shall be gathered to you,
Jer 2:10 send to **K** and examine with care;
49:28 Concerning **K** and the kingdoms of Hazor
49:28 Rise up, advance against **K**!
Eze 27:21 and all the princes of **K** were your favored dealers

KEDAR'S (1) [KEDAR]
Isa 21:17 and the remaining bows of **K** warriors will be few;

KEDEMAH (2)
Ge 25:15 Hadad, Tema, Jetur, Naphish, and **K**.
1Ch 1:31 Naphish, and **K**. These are the sons of Ishmael.

KEDEMOTH (4)
Dt 2:26 So I sent messengers from the wilderness of **K**
Jos 13:18 and Jahaz, and **K**, and Mephaath,
21:37 **K** with its pasture lands, and Mephaath
1Ch 6:79 **K** with its pasture lands, and Mephaath

KEDESH (13) [KEDESH NAPHTALI]
Jos 12:22 king of **K** one the king of Jokneam in Carmel one
15:23 **K**, Hazor, Ithnan,
19:37 **K**, Edrei, En-hazor,
20: 7 So they set apart **K** in Galilee in the hill country
21:32 **K** in Galilee with its pasture lands,
Jdg 4: 6 and summoned Barak son of Abinoam from **K**
4: 9 Then Deborah got up and went with Barak to **K**.
4:10 Barak summoned Zebulun and Naphtali to **K**;
4:11 as Elon-bezaanannim, which is near **K**.
2Ki 15:29 Abel-beth-maacah, Janoah, **K**, Hazor, Gilead,
1Ch 6:72 **K** with its pasture lands, Daberath
6:76 **K** in Galilee with its pasture lands,
Tob 1: 2 to the south of **K** Naphtali in Upper Galilee,

KEDESH NAPHTALI See KEDESH, NAPHTALI

KEDRON (3)
1Mc 15:39 to build up **K** and fortify its gates,
15:41 up **K** and stationed horsemen and troops there,
16: 9 John pursued them until Cendebeus reached **K**,

KEEL (1)
Wis 5:10 no track of its **k** in the waves;

KEEN (2)
Wis 7:22 invulnerable, loving the good, **k**, irresistible,
8:11 I shall be found **k** in judgment,

KEEP‡ (461) [DOORKEEPER, DOORKEEPERS, GATEKEEPER, GATEKEEPERS, INNKEEPER, KEEPER, KEEPERS, KEEPING, KEEPS, KEPT, SAFEKEEPING]
Ge 2:15 and put him in the garden of Eden to till it and **k** it.
6:19 to **k** them alive with you;
6:20 of every kind shall come in to you, to **k** them alive.
7: 3 to **k** their kind alive on the face of all the earth.
17: 9 "As for you, you shall **k** my covenant,
17:10 This is my covenant, which you shall **k**,
18:19 to **k** the way of the LORD by doing righteousness
28:15 with you and will **k** you wherever you go,
28:20 and will **k** me in this way that I go,
30:31 I will again feed your flock and **k** it:
33: 9 **k** what you have for yourself."
38:23 Judah replied, "Let her **k** the things as her own,
41:35 of Pharaoh for food in the cities, and let them **k** it.
42: 1 "Why do you **k** looking at one another?
45: 7 and to **k** alive for you many survivors.
Ex 12: 6 You shall **k** it until the fourteenth day
12:25 as he has promised, you shall **k** this observance.
13: 5 you shall **k** this observance in this month.
13:10 You shall **k** this ordinance at its proper time
14:14 and you have only to **k** still."
15:26 and **k** all his statutes, I will not bring upon you any
16:28 to **k** my commandments and instructions?
19: 5 if you obey my voice and **k** my covenant,
19:23 'Set limits around the mountain and **k** it holy.' "
20: 6 of those who love me and **k** my commandments.
20: 8 Remember the sabbath day, and **k** it holy.
21:36 the owner shall restore ox for ox, but **k**
23: 7 **K** far from a false charge,
31:13 "You shall **k** my sabbaths,
31:14 You shall **k** the sabbath, because it is holy for you;
31:16 Therefore the Israelites shall **k** the sabbath,
34:18 You shall **k** the festival of unleavened bread.
Lev 7: 8 priest who offers anyone's burnt offering shall **k**
15:31 Thus you shall **k** the people of Israel separate
18: 4 and my statutes you shall **k**, following them:
18: 5 You shall **k** my statutes and my ordinances;
18:26 But you shall **k** my statutes and my ordinances
18:30 So **k** my charge not to commit any
19: 3 and you shall **k** my sabbaths:
19:13 and you shall not **k** for yourself the wages of
19:19 You shall **k** my statutes.
19:30 You shall **k** my sabbaths
19:37 You shall **k** all my statutes and all my ordinances,
20: 8 **K** my statutes, and observe them;
20:22 You shall **k** all my statutes and all my ordinances,
22: 9 They shall **k** my charge, so that they may
22:31 Thus you shall **k** my commandments
23:32 from evening to evening you shall **k** your sabbath.
23:39 you shall **k** the festival of the LORD,
23:41 You shall **k** it as a festival to
23:41 you shall **k** it in the seventh month as
25:18 and faithfully **k** my ordinances,
25:46 You may **k** them as a possession for your children
26: 2 You shall **k** my sabbaths
26: 3 you follow my statutes and **k** my commandments
Nu 6:24 The LORD bless you and **k** you;
9: 2 the Israelites **k** the passover at its appointed time.
9: 3 at twilight, you shall **k** it at its appointed time;
9: 3 and all its regulations you shall **k** it.
9: 4 So Moses told the Israelites that they should **k**
9: 6 so that they could not **k** the passover on that day.
9:10 shall still **k** the passover to the LORD.
9:11 on the fourteenth day, at twilight, they shall **k** it;
9:12 to all the statute for the passover they shall **k** it.
9:14 Any alien residing among you who wishes to **k**
9:19 the Israelites would **k** the charge of the LORD,
31:18 a man by sleeping with him, **k** alive for yourselves.
Dt 4: 2 but **k** the commandments of the LORD your God
4:40 **K** his statutes and his commandments,
5:10 of those who love me and **k** my commandments.
5:12 Observe the sabbath day and **k** it holy,
5:15 the LORD your God commanded you to **k**
5:29 to fear me and to **k** all my commandments always,
6: 2 and **k** all his decrees and his commandments
6: 6 **K** these words that I am commanding you today
6:17 You must diligently **k** the commandments of
6:24 for our lasting good, so as to **k** us alive,
7: 9 and **k** his commandments,
8: 2 whether or not you would **k** his commandments.
8: 6 **k** the commandments of the LORD your God,
8:11 by failing to **k** his commandments, his ordinances,
10:13 to **k** the commandments of the LORD your God
11: 1 and **k** his charge, his decrees, his ordinances,
11: 8 **K**, then, this entire commandment
13: 4 his commandments you shall **k**,
16:10 Then you shall **k** the festival of weeks for
16:13 You shall **k** the festival of booths for seven days,
16:15 Seven days you shall **k** the festival for
26:17 and for you to walk in his ways, to **k** his statutes,
26:18 as he promised you, and to **k** his commandments;
27: 1 **K** the entire commandment
27: 9 **K** silence and hear, O Israel!
28: 9 if you **k** the commandments of
Jos 6:18 **k** away from the things devoted to destruction,
22: 3 to **k** the charge of the LORD your God.
22: 5 to **k** his commandments, and to hold fast to him,
Jdg 18:19 They said to him, "**K** quiet!
Ru 2: 8 but **k** close to my young women.
2: 9 **K** your eyes on the field that is being reaped,
1Sa 17:34 "Your servant used to **k** sheep for his father;
19:11 Saul sent messengers to David's house to **k** watch
2Sa 2:26 "Is the sword to **k** devouring forever?
3: 8 Today I **k** showing loyalty to the house
14:11 may the king **k** the LORD your God in mind,
14:14 to **k** an outcast banished forever from his presence.
18:18 "I have no son to **k** my name in remembrance";
1Ki 2: 3 and **k** the charge of the LORD your God,
6:12 and **k** all my commandments by walking in them,
8:25 **k** for your servant my father David
8:58 and to **k** his commandments, his statutes,
9: 6 and do not **k** my commandments and my statutes
11:34 and who did **k** my commandments
18: 5 perhaps we may find grass to **k** the horses
2Ki 2: 3 And he said, "Yes, I know; **k** silent."
17:13 from your evil ways and **k** my commandments
17:19 not **k** the commandments of the LORD their God
23:21 "**K** the passover to the LORD your God

1Ch 4:10 and that you would **k** me from hurt and harm!"
10:13 to the LORD in that he did not **k** the command of
12:29 the majority had continued to **k** their allegiance to
22:12 when he gives you charge over Israel you may **k**
23:32 Thus they shall **k** charge of the tent of meeting and
29:18 **k** forever such purposes and thoughts in the hearts
29:19 with single mind he may **k** your commandments,
2Ch 6:16 O LORD, God of Israel, **k** for your servant,
6:16 if only your children **k** to their way,
13:11 for we **k** the charge of the LORD our God,
14:4 and to **k** the law and the commandment.
30:1 to **k** the passover to the LORD the God of Israel.
30:2 in Jerusalem had taken counsel to **k** the passover in
30:3 (for they could not **k** it at its proper time because
30:5 and **k** the passover to the LORD the God of Israel,
30:13 in Jerusalem to **k** the festival of unleavened bread
30:23 Then the whole assembly agreed together to **k**
34:21 our ancestors did not **k** the word of the LORD,
35:16 to **k** the passover and to offer burnt offerings on
Ezr 6:6 in the province Beyond the River, **k** away;
8:29 Guard them and **k** them until you weigh them
Ne 1:5 and **k** his commandments;
1:7 failing to **k** the commandments, the statutes,
1:9 but if you return to me and **k** my commandments
13:22 to **k** the sabbath day holy.
Est 3:8 and they do not **k** the king's laws,
4:14 For if you **k** silence at such a time as this,
9:21 that they should **k** the fourteenth day of
Job 4:2 But who can **k** from speaking?
13:5 If you would only **k** silent,
14:16 you would not **k** watch over my sin;
16:3 Or what provokes you that you **k** on talking?
22:15 Will you **k** to the old way that
30:10 They abhor me, they **k** aloof from me;
33:17 from their deeds, and **k** them from pride,
36:6 He does not **k** the wicked alive,
36:19 Will your cry avail to **k** you from distress,
41:12 "I will not **k** silence concerning its limbs,
Ps 16:8 I **k** the LORD always before me;
19:13 **K** back your servant also from the insolent;
25:10 for those who **k** his covenant and his decrees.
33:19 and to **k** them alive in famine.
34:13 **K** your tongue from evil, and your lips
37:21 but the righteous are generous and **k** giving;
37:34 Wait for the LORD, and **k** to his way,
39:1 I will **k** a muzzle on my mouth as long as
40:11 and your faithfulness **k** me safe forever.
50:3 Our God comes and does not **k** silence,
50:18 and you **k** company with adulterers.
66:7 whose eyes **k** watch on the nations—
74:11 why do you **k** your hand in your bosom?
75:3 it is I who **k** its pillars steady.
77:4 You **k** my eyelids from closing;
78:7 the works of God, but **k** his commandments;
78:10 They did not **k** God's covenant,
78:42 They did not **k** in mind his power,
83:1 O God, do not **k** silence; do
89:28 Forever I will **k** my steadfast love for him,
89:31 and do not **k** my commandments,
103:9 nor will he **k** his anger forever.
103:18 to those who **k** his covenant and remember
105:45 that they might **k** his statutes and observe his laws.
119:2 Happy are those who **k** his decrees,
119:9 How can young people **k** their way pure?
119:34 that I may **k** your law and observe it
119:44 I will **k** your law continually, forever and ever.
119:55 O LORD, and **k** your law.
119:57 LORD is my portion; I promise to **k** your words.
119:60 I hurry and do not delay to **k** your commandments.
119:63 of those who **k** your precepts.
119:67 but now I **k** your word.
119:69 but with my whole heart I **k** your precepts.
119:88 so that I may **k** the decrees of your mouth.
119:100 the aged, for I **k** your precepts.
119:101 in order to **k** your word.
119:115 that I may **k** the commandments of my God.
119:133 **K** my steps steady according to your promise,
119:134 that I may **k** your precepts.
119:145 I will **k** your statutes
119:158 because they do not **k** your commands.
119:168 I **k** your precepts and decrees,
121:7 LORD will **k** you from all evil; he will **k** your life.
121:8 The LORD will **k** your going out
132:12 If your sons **k** my covenant and my decrees
141:3 **k** watch over the door of my lips.
141:9 **K** me from the trap that they have laid for me,
Pr 1:15 **k** your foot from their paths;
2:20 and **k** to the paths of the just.
3:1 but let your heart **k** my commandments;
3:21 **k** sound wisdom and prudence,
3:26 be your confidence and will **k** your foot
4:4 **k** my commandments, and live.
4:6 Do not forsake her, and she will **k** you;
4:13 **K** hold of instruction; do
4:21 from your sight; **k** them within your heart.
4:23 **K** your heart with all vigilance,
4:26 **K** straight the path of your feet,
5:6 She does not **k** straight to the path of life;
5:8 **K** your way far from her, and do not go near
6:20 My child, **k** your father's commandment,
7:1 **k** my words and store up my commandments
7:2 **k** my commandments and live, **k** my teachings as
7:5 that they may **k** you from the loose woman,
8:32 happy are those who **k** my ways.
17:28 Even fools who **k** silent are considered wise;
19:8 to **k** understanding is to prosper.
19:16 Those who **k** the commandment will live;
Pr 21:23 over mouth and tongue is to **k** out of trouble.
22:5 the cautious will **k** far from them.
22:12 The eyes of the LORD **k** watch over knowledge,
22:18 for it will be pleasant if you **k** them within you,
23:30 those who **k** trying mixed wines.
28:4 but those who **k** the law struggle against them.
28:7 Those who **k** the law are wise children,
29:3 but to **k** company with prostitutes is
29:18 but happy are those who **k** the law.
Ecc 2:10 Whatever my eyes desired I did not **k** from them;
3:6 a time to **k**, and a time to throw away;
3:7 a time to **k** silence, and a time to speak;
4:11 Again, if two lie together, they **k** warm;
4:11 but how can one **k** warm alone?
5:1 for they do not know how to **k** from doing evil.
8:2 **K** the king's command because
12:13 Fear God, and **k** his commandments;
Isa 6:9 '**K** listening, but do not comprehend;
6:9 **k** looking, but do not understand.'
7:21 On that day one will **k** alive a young cow
26:3 Those of steadfast mind you **k** in peace—
33:23 the mast firm in its place, or **k** the sail spread out.
45:20 and **k** on praying to a god that cannot save.
56:4 To the eunuchs who **k** my sabbaths,
56:6 and to be his servants, all who **k** the sabbath,
57:20 wicked are like the tossing sea that cannot **k** still;
62:1 For Zion's sake I will not **k** silent,
64:12 Will you **k** silent, and punish us so severely?
65:5 "**K** to yourself, do not come near me,
65:6 I will not **k** silent, but I will repay;
Jer 2:25 **K** your feet from going unshod and your throat
4:19 My heart is beating wildly; I cannot **k** silent;
17:22 but **k** the sabbath day holy,
17:24 but **k** the sabbath day holy and do no work on it,
17:27 you do not listen to me, to **k** the sabbath day holy,
23:17 They **k** saying to those who despise the word of
31:10 and will **k** him as a shepherd a flock."
31:16 **K** your voice from weeping,
34:18 not **k** the terms of the covenant that they made
42:4 I will **k** nothing back from you."
44:25 **k** your vows and make your libations!
49:11 Leave your orphans, I will **k** them alive;
La 4:22 is accomplished, he will **k** you in exile no longer;
Eze 7:26 they shall **k** seeking a vision from the prophet;
11:20 and **k** my ordinances and obey them.
18:21 that they have committed and **k** all my statutes
33:24 of these waste places in the land of Israel **k** saying,
38:7 Be ready and **k** ready, you and all the companies
44:14 Yet I will appoint them to **k** charge of the temple,
44:16 to minister to me, and they shall **k** my charge.
44:24 shall **k** my laws and my statutes regarding all my
44:24 and they shall **k** my sabbaths holy.
46:17 only his sons may **k** a gift from his inheritance.
Da 5:19 kept alive those he wanted to **k** alive,
9:4 and **k** your commandments,
12:4 **k** the words secret and the book sealed until
Hos 13:2 And now they **k** on sinning and make a cast image
Am 5:13 Therefore the prudent will **k** silent in such a time;
Hab 1:17 Is he then to **k** on emptying his net,
2:1 I will **k** watch to see what he will say to me,
2:20 let all the earth **k** silence before him!
Zec 3:7 you will walk in my ways and **k** my requirements,
11:12 give me my wages; but if not, **k** them."
12:4 But on the house of Judah I will **k** a watchful eye,
14:16 and to **k** the festival of booths.
14:18 on the nations that do not go up to **k** the festival
14:19 of all the nations that do not go up to **k** the festival
Mt 19:17 you wish to enter into life, **k** the commandments."
24:42 **K** awake therefore, for you do not know
25:13 **K** awake therefore, for you know neither the day
26:18 I will **k** the Passover at your house
28:14 we will satisfy him and **k** you out of trouble."
Mk 7:9 of God in order to **k** your tradition!
13:33 **k** alert; for you do not know
13:35 **k** awake—for you do not know
13:37 And what I say to you I say to all: **K** awake."
14:34 remain here, and **k** awake."
14:37 Could you not **k** awake one hour?
14:38 **K** awake and pray that you may not come into
Lk 12:29 And do not **k** striving for what you are to eat
12:29 and what you are to drink, and do not **k** worrying.
17:33 but those who lose their life will **k** it.
Jn 4:15 be thirsty or have to **k** coming here to draw water."
8:55 But I do know him and I **k** his word.
10:24 "How long will you **k** us in suspense?
12:7 She bought it so that she might **k** it for the day
12:25 and those who hate their life in this world will **k** it
12:47 not **k** them, for I came not to judge the world,
14:15 "If you love me, you will **k** my commandments.
14:21 and **k** them are those who love me;
14:23 "Those who love me will **k** my word,
14:24 Whoever does not love me does not **k** my words;
15:10 If you **k** my commandments,
15:20 if they kept my word, they will **k** yours also.
16:1 "I have said these things to you to **k** you
18:36 be fighting to **k** me from being handed over to
Ac 4:17 to **k** it from spreading further among the people,
4:20 for we cannot **k** from speaking
5:3 the Holy Spirit and to **k** back part of the proceeds
5:38 **k** away from these men and let them alone;
15:5 for them to be circumcised and ordered to **k**
15:29 If you **k** yourselves from these, you will do well.
16:23 and ordered the jailer to **k** them securely.
20:28 **K** watch over yourselves and over all the flock,
23:11 That night the Lord stood near him and said, "**K**
24:23 Then he ordered the centurion to **k** him in custody,
27:22 I urge you now to **k** up your courage,
Ac 27:25 So **k** up your courage, men,
Ro 2:26 if those who are uncircumcised **k** the requirements
2:27 but **k** the law will condemn you that have
11:10 and **k** their backs forever bent."
16:17 to **k** an eye on those who cause dissensions
1Co 7:37 and has determined in his own mind to **k** her
16:13 **K** alert, stand firm in your faith, be courageous,
2Co 3:13 over his face to **k** the people of Israel from gazing
4:4 to **k** them from seeing the light of the gospel of
10:13 will **k** within the field that God has assigned to us,
12:7 Therefore, to **k** me from being too elated,
12:7 to **k** me from being too elated.
Eph 6:18 To that end **k** alert and always persevere
Php 4:9 **K** on doing the things that you have learned
1Th 5:6 but let us **k** awake and be sober;
2Th 3:6 to **k** away from believers who are living in idleness
1Ti 2:12 over a man; she is to **k** silent.
5:21 to **k** these instructions without prejudice,
5:22 in the sins of others; **k** yourself pure.
6:14 to **k** the commandment without spot or blame until
Phm 1:13 I wanted to **k** him with me,
Heb 13:5 **K** your lives free from the love of money,
Jas 1:27 and to **k** oneself unstained by the world.
2:16 **k** warm and eat your fill,"
3:2 able to **k** the whole body in check with a bridle.
1Pe 3:10 let them **k** their tongues from evil and their lips
3:16 **K** your conscience clear, so that,
5:8 Discipline yourselves, **k** alert.
2Pe 1:8 they **k** you from being ineffective and unfruitful in
1:12 I intend to **k** on reminding you of these things,
2:9 and to **k** the unrighteous under punishment until
1Jn 5:21 Little children, **k** yourselves from idols.
Jude 1:6 And the angels who did not **k** their own position,
1:21 **k** yourselves in the love of God;
1:24 Now to him who is able to **k** you from falling,
Rev 1:3 and who **k** what is written in it;
3:10 I will **k** you from the hour of trial that is coming on
3:18 to clothe you and to **k** the shame of your nakedness
12:17 those who **k** the commandments of God and hold
14:12 those who **k** the commandments of God
22:9 and with those who **k** the words of this book.
Tob 3:15 or other kindred for whom I should **k** myself
4:14 "Do not **k** over until the next day the wages
6:5 **K** them with you, but throw away the intestines.
6:13 For I know that Raguel can by no means **k** her
8:17 Be merciful to them, O Master, and **k** them safe;
Jdt 7:12 and **k** all the men in your forces with you;
7:13 of the nearby mountains and camp there to **k** watch
11:10 but **k** it in your mind, for it is true.
AdE 2:20 but she was to fear God and **k** his laws,
3:8 and they do not **k** the laws of the king.
3:11 The king told Haman, "**K** the money,
4:14 For if you **k** quiet at such a time as this,
9:19 the country outside Susa **k** the fourteenth of Adar
9:19 in the large cities **k** the fifteenth day of Adar
9:21 that they should **k** the fourteenth and fifteenth days
Wis 1:11 and **k** your tongue from slander;
6:4 not rule rightly, or **k** the law, or walk according to
13:7 while they live among his works, they **k** searching,
14:24 they no longer **k** either their lives
Sir 1:26 If you desire wisdom, **k** the commandments,
1:29 and **k** watch over your lips.
2:15 and those who love him **k** his ways.
4:1 and do not **k** needy eyes waiting.
6:13 **K** away from your enemies,
6:26 and **k** her ways with all your might.
7:22 if they are profitable to you, **k** them.
8:17 for they cannot **k** a secret.
9:13 **K** far from those who have power to kill,
11:21 but trust in the Lord and **k** at your job;
13:12 Cruel are those who do not **k** your secrets;
15:15 If you choose, you can **k** the commandments,
17:22 and he will **k** a person's kindness like the apple
20:1 there is the person who is wise enough to **k** silent.
20:5 Some people **k** silent and are thought to be wise,
20:6 Some people **k** silent because they have nothing
20:6 others **k** silent because they know when to speak.
26:10 **K** strict watch over a headstrong daughter, or else,
26:19 *My child, **k** sound the bloom of your youth,*
26:29 A merchant can hardly **k** from wrongdoing,
27:17 Love your friend and **k** faith with him;
27:22 and those who know him will **k** their distance.
29:1 a helping hand they **k** the commandments.
29:3 **K** your promise and be honest with him,
29:8 and do not **k** him waiting for your alms.
33:16 Now I was the last to **k** vigil;
35:5 To **k** from wickedness is pleasing to the Lord,
42:11 **K** strict watch over a headstrong daughter,
LtJ 6:35 if one makes a vow to them and does not **k** it,
1Mc 4:60 to **k** the Gentiles from coming and trampling them
8:26 and they shall **k** their obligations
8:28 and they shall **k** these obligations and do so
10:20 and you are to take our side and **k** friendship
10:27 Now continue still to **k** faith with us,
12:27 to **k** their arms at hand so as to be ready all night
2Mc 1:9 And now see that you **k** the festival of booths in
2:16 Will you therefore please **k** the days?
3:15 that he should **k** them safe
3:22 that he would **k** what had been entrusted safe
6:6 People could neither **k** the sabbath,
7:17 **K** on, and see how his mighty power will torture
9:25 and the neighbors of my kingdom **k** watching
10:15 and endeavored to **k** up the war.
12:42 the people to **k** themselves free from sin,
14:36 **k** undefiled forever this house that has been
15:8 to **k** in mind the former times when help had come
1Es 1:6 and **k** the passover according to the commandment

1Es 1:58 it shall **k** sabbath all the time of its desolation until
4:11 but they **k** watch around him,
6:27 to **k** away from the place,
8:51 and an escort to **k** us safe from our adversaries;
2Es 1:24 so that they may **k** my statutes.
2: 5 because they would not **k** my covenant,
4:40 her womb can **k** the fetus within her any longer."
7:*45* and **k** your commandments!
7:*72* the commandments, they did not **k** them;
7:*89* so that they might **k** the law of
9:32 they did not **k** it and did not observe the statutes;
9:33 they did not **k** what had been sown in them.
10:15 Now, therefore, **k** your sorrow to yourself,
12:38 to comprehend and **k** these secrets.
13:42 at least they might **k** their statutes that they had
14: 6 and these you shall **k** secret.'
14:30 and received the law of life, which they did not **k**,
14:31 and did not **k** the ways that
14:46 but **k** the seventy that were written last,
16:76 You who **k** my commandments and precepts,
4Mc 14:17 If they are not able to **k** the intruder away,

KEEPER (20) [KEEP]

Ge 4: 2 Now Abel was a **k** of sheep,
4: 9 He said, "I do not know; am I my brother's **k?"**
1Sa 17:20 left the sheep with a **k**, took the provisions,
17:22 the things in charge of the **k** of the baggage,
2Ki 10:22 He said to the **k** of the wardrobe,
22:14 son of Harhas, **k** of the wardrobe;
2Ch 31:14 Kore son of Imnah the Levite, **k** of the east gate,
34:22 **k** of the wardrobe (who lived in Jerusalem in
Ne 2: 8 the **k** of the king's forest,
3:29 the **k** of the East Gate, made repairs.
Ps 121: 5 The LORD is your **k**; the LORD is your shade
SS 1: 6 they made me **k** of the vineyards,
Isa 27: 3 I, the LORD, am its **k**; every moment I water it.
Jer 35: 4 above the chamber of Maaseiah son of Shallum, **k**
Ac 19:35 the temple **k** of the great Artemis and of the statue
Tob 1:22 Now Ahikar was chief cupbearer, **k** of the signet,
Sir 37:12 with a godly person whom you know to be a **k** of
3Mc 5: 1 so he summoned Hermon, **k** of the elephants,
5: 4 And Hermon, **k** of the elephants,
5:45 with frightful devices, the elephant **k**

KEEPERS (6) [KEEP]

Ge 46:32 for they have been **k** of livestock;
46:34 'Your servants have been **k** of livestock
2Ki 22: 4 which the **k** of the threshold have collected from
2Ch 34: 9 which the Levites, the **k** of the threshold,
SS 8:11 he entrusted the vineyard to **k**;
8:12 and the **k** of the fruit two hundred!

KEEPING‡ (52) [KEEP]

Ex 3: 1 Moses was **k** the flock of his father-in-law Jethro,
21:34 giving money to its owner, but **k** the dead animal.
34: 7 **k** steadfast love for the thousandth generation,
Lev 8:35 **k** the LORD's charge so that you do not die;
Nu 9:13 and yet refrains from **k** the passover,
Dt 13:18 the LORD your God by **k** all his commandments
16: 1 Observe the month of Abib by **k** the passover for
1Sa 16:11 but he is **k** the sheep."
25:16 all the while we were with them **k** the sheep.
1Ki 2: 3 walking in his ways and **k** his statutes,
3:14 **k** my statutes and my commandments,
8:23 **k** covenant and steadfast love
8:61 walking in his statutes and **k** his commandments,
9: 4 and **k** my statutes and my ordinances,
11:33 in my sight and **k** my statutes and my ordinances,
11:38 and do what is right in my sight by **k** my statutes
2Ki 23: 3 **k** his commandments, his decrees, and his statutes,
1Ch 28: 7 if he continues resolute in **k** my commandments
2Ch 6:14 **k** covenant in steadfast love
7:17 that I have commanded you and **k** my statutes
31:18 for they were faithful in **k** themselves holy.
34:31 **k** his commandments, his decrees, and his statutes,
Ne 9:32 **k** covenant and steadfast love—
Ps 19:11 in **k** them there is great reward.
42: 4 and songs of thanksgiving, a multitude **k** festival.
119: 5 that my ways may be steadfast in **k** your statutes!
Pr 15: 3 **k** watch on the evil and the good.
Eze 13:19 not die and **k** alive persons who should not live,
17:14 and that by **k** his covenant it might stand.
44: 8 to act for you in **k** my charge in my sanctuary.
Da 9: 4 **k** covenant and steadfast love
Mal 3:14 by **k** his command or by going about as mourners
Mt 27:54 who were **k** watch over Jesus,
Lk 2: 8 **k** watch over their flock by night.
17:12 ten lepers approached him. **K** their distance,
Ac 12: 6 in front of the door were **k** watch over the prison.
22:20 and **k** the coats of those who killed him.'
Col 4: 2 **k** alert in it with thanksgiving.
1Ti 3: 4 **k** his children submissive and respectful
Heb 13:17 for they are **k** watch over your souls and will give
Wis 6:18 and love of her is the **k** of her laws,
Sir 32:23 for this is the **k** of the commandments.
42: 3 of **k** accounts with a partner or
1Mc 10:54 to you and to her in **k** with your position."
2Mc 8:17 **k** before their eyes the lawless outrage that
14: 6 are **k** up war and stirring up sedition,
15: 3 a sovereign in heaven who had commanded the **k**
3Mc 5:44 at the places in the city most favorable for **k** guard.
2Es 8: 9 and that which is kept shall both be kept by your **k**.
13:26 this is he whom the Most High has been **k**
4Mc 5:29 the sacred oaths of my ancestors concerning the **k**
15:10 they obeyed her even to death in **k** the ordinances.

KEEPS‡ (37) [KEEP]

Ne 1: 5 the great and awesome God who **k** covenant
Ps 34:20 He **k** all their bones; not one of them
41: 2 The LORD protects them and **k** them alive;
119:129 decrees are wonderful; therefore my soul **k** them.
119:167 My soul **k** your decrees; I love them exceedingly.
121: 3 he who **k** you will not slumber.
121: 4 He who **k** Israel will neither slumber nor sleep.
127: 1 LORD guards the city, the guard **k** watch in vain.
146: 6 and all that is in them; who **k** faith forever;
Pr 11: 5 of the blameless **k** their ways straight,
11:13 but one who is trustworthy in spirit **k** a confidence.
24:12 Does not he who **k** watch over your soul know it?
Ecc 5:20 God **k** them occupied with the joy of their hearts.
Isa 26: 2 that the righteous nation that **k** faith may enter in.
56: 2 the one who holds it fast, who **k** the sabbath,
Jer 5:24 and **k** for us the weeks appointed for the harvest."
6: 7 As a well **k** its water fresh, so she **k** fresh her wickedness;
48:10 the one who **k** back the sword from bloodshed.
Joel 2: 7 Each **k** to its own course, they do not swerve from
2: 8 each **k** to its own track;
Mt 15:23 "Send her away, for she **k** shouting after us."
Mk 9:25 that **k** this boy from speaking and hearing,
Lk 18: 5 yet because this widow **k** bothering me,
Jn 7:19 Yet none of you **k** the law.
8:51 whoever **k** my word will never see death."
8:52 'Whoever **k** my word will never taste death.'
Jas 2:10 For whoever **k** the whole law but fails
Rev 22: 7 the one who **k** the words of the prophecy
Tob 4:10 For almsgiving delivers from death and **k** you
Sir 19:28 Even if lack of strength **k** him from sinning,
21:11 Whoever **k** the law controls his thoughts,
28: 1 for he **k** a strict account of their sins.
32:24 The one who **k** the law preserves himself,
35: 1 The one who **k** the law makes many offerings;
37:14 our own mind sometimes **k** us better informed
2Es 8: 9 But that which **k** and that which is kept shall both

KEHELATHAH (2)

Nu 33:22 They set out from Rissah and camped at **K.**
33:23 from **K** and camped at Mount Shepher.

KEILAH (17)

Jos 15:44 **K,** Achzib, and Mareshah:
1Sa 23: 1 "The Philistines are fighting against **K,**
23: 2 "Go and attack the Philistines and save **K."**
23: 3 how much more then if we go to **K** against
23: 4 The LORD answered him, "Yes, go down to **K;**
23: 5 So David and his men went to **K,**
23: 5 Thus David rescued the inhabitants of **K.**
23: 6 Abiathar son of Ahimelech fled to David at **K,**
23: 7 Now it was told Saul that David had come to **K.**
23: 8 to go down to **K,** to besiege David and his men.
23:10 that Saul seeks to come to **K,**
23:12 "Will the men of **K** surrender me and my men into
23:13 who were about six hundred, set out and left **K;**
23:13 Saul was told that David had escaped from **K,**
1Ch 4:19 were the fathers of **K** the Garmite and Eshtemoa
Ne 3:17 ruler of half the district of **K,**
3:18 son of Henadad, ruler of half the district of **K;**

KELAIAH (2) [KELITA]

Ezr 10:23 Jozabad, Shimei, **K** (that is, Kelita), Pethahiah,
1Es 9:23 And of the Levites: Jozabad and Shimei and **K,**

KELITA (5) [KELAIAH]

Ezr 10:23 Jozabad, Shimei, Kelaiah (that is, **K**), Pethahiah,
Ne 8: 7 **K,** Azariah, Jozabad, Hanan, Pelaiah, the Levites,
10:10 Shebaniah, Hodiah, **K,** Pelaiah, Hanan,
1Es 9:23 Jozabad and Shimei and Kelaiah, who was **K,**
9:48 Hodiah, Maiannas and **K,** Azariah and Jozabad,

KEMUEL (3)

Ge 22:21 Buz his brother, **K** the father of Aram,
Nu 34:24 and of the tribe of the Ephraimites a leader, **K** son
1Ch 27:17 for Levi, Hashabiah son of **K;** for Aaron, Zadok;

KENAN (6) [=CAINAN]

Ge 5: 9 he became the father of **K.**
5:10 after the birth of **K** eight hundred fifteen years,
5:12 When **K** had lived seventy years,
5:13 **K** lived after the birth of Mahalalel eight hundred
5:14 the days of **K** were nine hundred and ten years;
1Ch 1: 2 **K,** Mahalalel, Jared;

KENATH (2)

Nu 32:42 And Nobah went and captured **K** and its villages,
1Ch 2:23 **K** and its villages, sixty towns.

KENAZ (11)

Ge 36:11 Omar, Zepho, Gatam, and **K.**
36:15 the clans Teman, Omar, Zepho, **K,**
36:42 **K,** Teman, Mibzar,
Jos 15:17 Othniel son of **K,** the brother of Caleb, took it;
Jdg 1:13 Othniel son of **K,** Caleb's younger brother, took it;
3: 9 Othniel son of **K,** Caleb's younger brother.
3:11 Then Othniel son of **K** died.
1Ch 1:36 Teman, Omar, Zephi, Gatam, **K,** Timna,
1:53 **K,** Teman, Mibzar,
4:13 The sons of **K:** Othniel
4:15 and Naam; and the son of Elah: **K.**

KENEZITE (KJV) See KENIZZITE

KENITE (6) [KENITES]

Nu 24:21 he looked on the **K,** and uttered his oracle, saying:
Jdg 1:16 The descendants of Hobab the **K,**
4:11 Heber the **K** had separated from the other Kenites,
4:17 on foot to the tent of Jael wife of Heber the **K;**
4:17 of Hazor and the clan of Heber the **K.**
5:24 the wife of Heber the **K,**

KENITES (7) [KENITE]

Ge 15:19 the land of the **K,** the Kenizzites, the Kadmonites,
Jdg 4:11 Heber the Kenite had separated from the other **K,**
1Sa 15: 6 Saul said to the **K,** "Go!
15: 6 So the **K** withdrew from the Amalekites.
27:10 or, "Against the Negeb of the **K."**
30:29 in the towns of the **K,**
1Ch 2:55 These are the **K** who came from Hammath,

KENIZZITE (3) [KENIZZITES]

Nu 32:12 of Jephunneh the **K** and Joshua son of Nun,
Jos 14: 6 and Caleb son of Jephunneh the **K** said to him,
14:14 the inheritance of Caleb son of Jephunneh the **K**

KENIZZITES (1) [KENIZZITE]

Ge 15:19 the land of the Kenites, the **K,** the Kadmonites,

KEPHA See Index to Footnotes

KEPT‡ (289) [KEEP]

Ge 20: 6 furthermore it was I who **k** you from sinning
26: 5 Abraham obeyed my voice and **k** my charge,
29: 9 with her father's sheep; for she **k** them.
37:11 but his father **k** the matter in mind.
39: 9 has he **k** back anything from me except yourself,
39:16 Then she **k** his garment by her
Ex 12:42 a vigil to be **k** for the LORD by all the Israelites
16:23 that is left over put aside to be **k** until morning.' "
16:32 an omer of it be **k** throughout your generations,
16:33 to be **k** throughout your generations."
36: 3 They still **k** bringing him freewill offerings every
Lev 6: 9 while the fire on the altar shall be **k** burning.
6:12 The fire on the altar shall be **k** burning;
6:13 A perpetual fire shall be **k** burning on the altar;
24: 2 that a light may be **k** burning regularly.
Nu 9: 5 They **k** the passover in the first month,
9: 7 be **k** from presenting the LORD's offering
9:23 They **k** the charge of the LORD,
17:10 to be **k** as a warning to rebels,
19: 9 be **k** for the congregation of the Israelites for
Dt 2:35 Only the livestock we **k** as spoil for ourselves,
3: 7 the livestock and the plunder of the towns we **k**
7: 8 the LORD loved you and **k** the oath that he swore
33: 9 For they observed your word, and **k** your covenant.
Jos 5:10 While the Israelites were camped in Gilgal they **k**
14:10 And now, as you see, the LORD has **k** me alive,
Jdg 5: 6 caravans ceased and travelers **k** to the byways.
16: 2 They **k** quiet all night, thinking,
19: 7 his father-in-law **k** urging him until he spent
1Sa 9:24 Samuel said, "See, what was **k** is set before you.
13:13 not **k** the commandment of the LORD your God,
13:14 you have not **k** what the LORD commanded you."
21: 4 the young men have **k** themselves from women."
21: 5 "Indeed women have been **k** from us as always
25:33 who have **k** me today from bloodguilt and
25:39 and has **k** back his servant from evil;
26:15 then have you not **k** watch over your lord the king?
26:16 because you have not **k** watch over your lord,
2Sa 13:34 When the young man who **k** watch looked up,
15:12 and the people with Absalom **k** increasing.
18:25 He **k** coming, and drew near.
22:22 For I have **k** the ways of the LORD,
22:24 and I **k** myself from guilt.
22:44 you **k** me as the head of the nations;
1Ki 2:43 Why then have you not **k** your oath to the LORD
3: 6 you have **k** for him this great and steadfast love,
8:24 that you **k** for your servant my father David
11:11 and you have not **k** my covenant and my statutes
13:21 the LORD, and have not **k** the commandment that
14: 8 like my servant David, who **k** my commandments
14:27 who **k** the door of the king's house.
2Ki 2:12 Elisha **k** watching and crying out, "Father, father!
4: 5 they **k** bringing vessels to her, and she **k** pouring.
18: 6 from following him but **k** the commandments that
23:22 No such passover had been **k** since the days of
23:23 of King Josiah this passover was **k** to the LORD
1Ch 4:33 And they **k** a genealogical record.
12:22 Indeed from day to day people **k** coming to David
2Ch 6:15 you who have **k** for your servant,
12:10 who **k** the door of the king's house.
30: 5 they had not **k** it in great numbers as prescribed.
30:21 of Israel who were present at Jerusalem **k**
30:23 so they **k** it for another seven days with gladness.
35: 1 Josiah **k** a passover to the LORD in Jerusalem;
35:17 of Israel who were present **k** the passover at
35:18 No passover like it had been **k** in Israel since
35:18 none of the kings of Israel had **k** such a passover as was **k** by Josiah,
35:19 of the reign of Josiah this passover was **k.**
36:16 but they **k** mocking the messengers of God,
36:21 All the days that it lay desolate it **k** sabbath,
Ezr 3: 4 And they **k** the festival of booths, as prescribed,
6:19 the first month the returned exiles **k** the passover.

Ne 4:23 each **k** his weapon in his right hand.
8:18 They **k** the festival seven days;
9:34 not **k** your law or heeded the commandments and
11:19 who **k** watch at the gates,
Est 9:28 be remembered and **k** throughout every generation,
Job 21:32 a watch is **k** over their tomb.
23:11 I have **k** his way and have not turned aside.
24: 1 "Why are times not **k** by the Almighty,
29:21 and waited, and **k** silence for my counsel.
31:34 so that I **k** silence, and did not go out of doors—
Ps 18:21 For I have **k** the ways of the LORD,
18:23 and I **k** myself from guilt.
22: 9 you **k** me safe on my mother's breast.
32: 3 While I **k** silence, my body wasted away
37:28 The righteous shall be **k** safe forever,
55:14 with whom I **k** pleasant company;
56: 8 You have **k** count of my tossings;
66: 9 who has **k** us among the living,
73:13 All in vain I have **k** my heart clean
99: 7 they **k** his decrees, and the statutes
105:19 the word of the LORD **k** testing him.
116:10 I **k** my faith, even when I said,
119: 4 have commanded your precepts to be **k** diligently.
119:22 for I have **k** your decrees.
119:56 for I have **k** your precepts.
119:136 of tears because your law is not **k.**
Ecc 2:10 I **k** my heart from no pleasure,
5:13 riches were **k** by their owners to their hurt,
SS 1: 6 but my own vineyard I have not **k!**
Isa 30:29 a song as in the night when a holy festival is **k;**
42: 6 I have taken you by the hand and **k** you;
42:14 I have **k** still and restrained myself;
49: 8 I have **k** you and given you as a covenant to
57:11 Have I not **k** silent and closed my eyes,
57:17 but they **k** turning back to their own ways.
Jer 16:11 and have forsaken me and have not **k** my law;
35:18 of your ancestor Jonadab, and **k** all his precepts,
Eze 5: 7 have not followed my statutes or **k** my ordinances,
11:12 and whose ordinances you have not **k,**
44: 8 And you have not **k** charge of my sacred offerings;
44:15 who **k** the charge of my sanctuary when the people
48:11 the descendants of Zadok, who **k** my charge,
Da 5:19 **k** alive those he wanted to keep alive,
7:28 but I **k** the matter in my mind.
8:12 and **k** prospering in what it did.
9:14 So the LORD **k** watch over this calamity
Hos 11: 2 they **k** sacrificing to the Baals,
13:12 his sin is **k** in store.
Am 1:11 his anger perpetually, and **k** his wrath forever.
2: 4 and have not **k** his statutes,
Mic 6:16 For you have **k** the statutes of Omri and all
Mal 2: 9 not **k** my ways but have shown partiality
3: 7 from my statutes and have not **k** them.
Mt 19:20 The young man said to him, "I have **k** all these;
27:36 then they sat down there and **k** watch over him.
Mk 1:27 and they **k** on asking one another, "What is this?
9:10 So they **k** the matter to themselves,
10:20 "Teacher, I have **k** all these since my youth."
11:18 they **k** looking for a way to kill him;
Lk 1:22 He **k** motioning to them and remained unable
4:36 They were all amazed and **k** saying to one another,
8:29 he was **k** under guard and bound with chains
9:36 And they **k** silent and in those days told no one any
11:16 **k** demanding from him a sign from heaven.
13:14 **k** saying to the crowd, "There are six days
18: 3 that city there was a widow who **k** coming to him
18:21 He replied, "I have **k** all these since my youth."
19:36 people **k** spreading their cloaks on the road.
19:47 and the leaders of the people **k** looking for a way
22:59 Then about an hour later still another **k** insisting,
22:64 they also blindfolded him and **k** asking him,
22:65 They **k** heaping many other insults on him.
23:21 but they **k** shouting, "Crucify, crucify him!"
23:23 But they **k** urgently demanding with loud shouts
23:39 criminals who were hanged there **k** deriding him
24:16 but their eyes were **k** from recognizing him.
Jn 2:10 But you have **k** the good wine until now."
3:23 and people **k** coming and were being baptized
6: 2 A large crowd **k** following him,
8: 7 ‖When they **k** on questioning him,‖
9: 9 He **k** saying, "I am the man."
9:10 But they **k** asking him,
11:37 of the blind man have **k** this man from dying?"
12: 6 he **k** the common purse and used
15:10 as I have **k** my Father's commandments and abide
15:20 if they **k** my word, they will keep yours also.
17: 6 and they have **k** your word.
19: 3 They **k** coming up to him, saying, "Hail,
Ac 5: 2 he **k** back some of the proceeds,
7:53 and yet you have not **k** it."
12: 5 While Peter was **k** in prison,
12:22 The people **k** shouting, "The voice of a god,
15:12 The whole assembly **k** silence,
16:18 She **k** doing this for many days.
21:36 crowd that followed **k** shouting, "Away with him!"
23:35 that he be **k** under guard in Herod's headquarters.
25: 4 Festus replied that Paul was being **k** at Caesarea,
25:21 But when Paul had appealed to be **k** in custody for
27:43 **k** them from carrying out their plan.
Ro 11: 4 "I have **k** for myself seven thousand who have
16:25 to the revelation of the mystery that was **k** secret
Gal 2:12 he drew back and **k** himself separate for fear of
1Th 5:23 and may your spirit and soul and body be **k** sound
2Ti 4: 7 I have finished the race, I have **k** the faith.
Heb 11:28 By faith he **k** the Passover and the sprinkling
13: 4 and let the marriage bed be **k** undefiled;
Jas 5: 4 which you **k** back by fraud, cry out,
1Pe 1: 4 undefiled, and unfading, **k** in heaven for you,
2Pe 2: 4 of deepest darkness to be **k** until the judgment;
3: 7 being **k** until the day of judgment and destruction
Jude 1: 1 who are beloved in God the Father and **k** safe
1: 6 he has **k** in eternal chains in deepest darkness for
Rev 3: 8 and yet you have **k** my word and have
3:10 Because you have **k** my word of patient endurance,
8:12 a third of the day was **k** from shining,
Tob 1:11 but I **k** myself from eating the food of the Gentiles.
3: 5 For we have not **k** your commandments and have
6: 6 and ate some of the fish, and **k** some to be salted.
8: 5 to pray and implore that they might be **k** safe.
10: 1 Now, day by day, Tobit **k** counting
10: 6 But Tobit **k** saying to her, "Be quiet
12:22 They **k** blessing God and singing his praises,
Jdt 6:12 and all the slingers **k** them from coming up
12: 1 to bring her in where his silver dinnerware was **k,**
AdE 9:27 These days of Purim should be a memorial and **k**
12: 1 the two eunuchs of the king who **k** watch in
Wis 4:17 and for what he **k** them safe.
10: 5 and **k** him strong in the face of his compassion
10:12 and **k** him safe from those who lay in wait for him;
14:16 grown strong with time, was **k** as a law,
17:16 thus was **k** shut up in a prison not made of iron;
18: 4 those who had **k** your children imprisoned,
19: 6 so that your children might be **k** unharmed.
Sir 3: 1 act accordingly, that you may be **k** in safety.
8:18 of strangers do nothing that is to be **k** secret,
20: 3 the one who admits his fault will be **k** from failure.
44:17 in the time of wrath he **k** the race alive;
44:20 He **k** the law of the Most High,
48:22 and he **k** firmly to the ways of his ancestor David,
49: 3 He **k** his heart fixed on the Lord;
Bar 2: 9 And the Lord has **k** the calamities ready,
Aza 1: 7 not **k** them or done what you have commanded us
1:23 the king's servants who threw them in **k** stoking
1Mc 1:58 They **k** using violence against Israel,
2:53 in the time of his distress **k** the commandment,
5: 3 because they **k** lying in wait for Israel.
5:53 Judas **k** rallying the laggards and encouraging
6:18 the garrison in the citadel **k** hemming Israel in
7:45 as they followed they **k** sounding the battle call on
8:12 and those who rely on them they have **k** friendship.
10:26 Since you have **k** your agreement with us
11: 5 on him; but the king **k** silent.
11: 8 he **k** devising wicked designs against Alexander.
11:25 of his nation **k** making complaints against him,
11:41 for they **k** fighting against Israel.
12:40 so he **k** seeking to seize and kill him,
12:47 He **k** with himself three thousand men,
12:50 and they encouraged one another and **k** marching
13:20 and his army **k** marching along opposite him
13:21 the citadel **k** sending envoys to Trypho urging him
15:25 he shut Trypho up and **k** him from going out or in.
2Mc 2:12 Likewise Solomon also **k** the eight days.
3:19 the young women who were **k** indoors ran together
4:28 the captain of the citadel **k** requesting payment—
5: 6 Jason **k** relentlessly slaughtering his compatriots,
5:27 and **k** himself and his companions alive in
6:11 their piety **k** them from defending themselves,
8:27 the enemy and stripped them of their spoils, they **k**
10:14 and at every turn **k** attacking the Jews.
10:30 they **k** him from being wounded.
10:34 **k** blaspheming terribly and uttering wicked words.
12:38 according to the custom, and **k** the sabbath there.
14: 4 During that day he **k** quiet.
14:24 And he **k** Judas always in his presence;
15:34 "Blessed is he who has **k** his own place undefiled!"
1Es 1: 1 Josiah **k** the passover to his Lord in Jerusalem;
1:17 that day: the passover was **k**
1:19 the people of Israel who were present at that time **k**
1:20 No passover like it had been **k** in Israel since
1:21 none of the kings of Israel had **k** such a passover
1:21 as was **k** by Josiah and the priests and Levites and
1:22 of the reign of Josiah this passover was **k.**
2:23 the Jews were rebels and **k** setting up blockades
3: 4 who **k** guard over the person of the king,
5:51 They **k** the festival of booths,
5:73 They were **k** from building for two years,
7:10 from exile **k** the passover on the fourteenth day of
7:14 also **k** the festival of unleavened bread seven days,
3Mc 3: 4 they **k** their separateness with respect to foods.
6:25 those who faithfully **k** our country's fortresses,
7:15 and they **k** the day as a joyful festival,
2Es 3:35 what nation has **k** your commandments so well?
3:36 find individuals who have **k** your commandments,
6:42 up and **k** so that some of them might be planted
6:49 "Then you **k** in existence two living creatures;
6:52 you have **k** them to be eaten by whom you wish,
7:*75* as everyone of us yields up the soul, we shall be **k**
7:*79* of those who have shown scorn and have not **k**
7:*88* of those who have **k** the ways of the Most High,
7:*94* that throughout their life they **k** the law
8: 9 But that which keeps and that which is **k** shall
both be **k** by your keeping.
8:27 those who have **k** your covenants amid afflictions.
11:20 I **k** looking, and in due time the wings
11:24 As I **k** looking I saw that two little wings separated
11:26 As I **k** looking, one was set up,
12:21 be **k** for the time when its end approaches,
12:21 but two shall be **k** until the end.
12:30 It is these whom the Most High has **k** for
12:32 this is the Messiah whom the Most High has **k**
13: 3 As I **k** looking the wind made something like
13:42 that they had not **k** in their own land.
14: 4 where I **k** him with me many days.
14:34 and discipline your hearts, you shall be **k** alive,
4Mc 6: 7 he **k** his reason upright and unswerving.

KERCHIEFS (KJV) See VEILS

KEREN-HAPPUCH (1)

Job 42:14 the second Keziah, and the third **K.**

KERIOTH‡ (2)

Jer 48:24 and **K,** and Bozrah, and all the towns of the land
Am 2: 2 and it shall devour the strongholds of **K,**

KERIOTH-HEZRON (1) [HAZOR]

Jos 15:25 Hazor-hadattah, **K** (that is, Hazor),

KEROS (3)

Ezr 2:44 **K,** Siaha, Padon,
Ne 7:47 of **K,** of Sia, of Padon,
1Es 5:29 the descendants of **K,** the descendants of Sua,

KETAB (1)

1Es 5:30 the descendants of **K,** the descendants of Hagab,

KETTLE (3) [KETTLES]

1Sa 2:14 or **k,** or caldron, or pot;
Mic 3: 3 and chop them up like meat in a **k,**
Sir 13: 2 How can the clay pot associate with the iron **k?**

KETTLES (1) [KETTLE]

Mk 7: 4 the washing of cups, pots, and bronze **k.)**

KETURAH (4)

Ge 25: 1 Abraham took another wife, whose name was **K.**
25: 4 All these were the children of **K.**
1Ch 1:32 The sons of **K,** Abraham's concubine:
1:33 All these were the descendants of **K.**

KEY (7) [KEYS]

Jdg 3:25 they took the **k** and opened them.
Isa 22:22 I will place on his shoulder the **k** of the house
Lk 11:52 For you have taken away the **k** of knowledge;
Rev 3: 7 the true one, who has the **k** of David,
9: 1 the **k** to the shaft of the bottomless pit;
20: 1 holding in his hand the **k** to the bottomless pit and
2Mc 14:22 at **k** places to prevent sudden treachery on the part

KEYS (2) [KEY]

Mt 16:19 I will give you the **k** of the kingdom of heaven,
Rev 1:18 and I have the **k** of Death and of Hades.

KEYSTONE See Index to Footnotes

KEZIAH (1)

Job 42:14 He named the first Jemimah, the second **K,**

KIBROTH-HATTAAVAH (5)

Nu 11:34 So that place was called **K,**
11:35 From **K** the people journeyed to Hazeroth.
33:16 from the wilderness of Sinai and camped at **K.**
33:17 They set out from **K** and camped at Hazeroth.
Dt 9:22 At Taberah also, and at Massah, and at **K,**

KIBZAIM (1)

Jos 21:22 **K** with its pasture lands, and Beth-horon

KICK‡ (2) [KICKED]

Ac 26:14 It hurts you to **k** against the goads.'
4Mc 6: 8 the cruel guards rushed at him and began to **k** him

KICKED (1) [KICK]

Dt 32:15 Jacob ate his fill; Jeshurun grew fat, and **k.**

KID (13) [KIDS]

Ge 38:17 He answered, "I will send you a **k** from the flock."
38:20 Judah sent the **k** by his friend the Adullamite,
38:23 you see, I sent this **k,** and you could not find her."
Ex 23:19 You shall not boil a **k** in its mother's milk.
34:26 You shall not boil a **k** in its mother's milk.
Dt 14:21 You shall not boil a **k** in its mother's milk.
Jdg 6:19 So Gideon went into his house and prepared a **k,**
13:15 "Allow us to detain you, and prepare a **k** for you."
13:19 So Manoah took the **k** with the grain offering,
14: 6 as one might tear apart a **k.**
15: 1 Samson went to visit his wife, bringing along a **k.**
1Sa 16:20 and a **k,** and sent them by his son David to Saul.
Isa 11: 6 the leopard shall lie down with the **k,**

KIDNAP (1) [KIDNAPER, KIDNAPING, KIDNAPS]

1Mc 7:29 but the enemy were preparing to **k** Judas.

KIDNAPER (1) [KIDNAP]

Dt 24: 7 or selling the Israelite, then that **k** shall die.

KIDNAPING (1) [KIDNAP]

Dt 24: 7 If someone is caught **k** another Israelite,

KIDNAPS (1) [KIDNAP]

Ex 21:16 Whoever **k** a person, whether that person has been

KIDNEYS (18)

Ex 29:13 and the two **k** with the fat that is on them,
29:22 the two **k** with the fat that is on them,
Lev 3: 4 the two **k** with the fat that is on them at the loins,
3: 4 which he shall remove with the **k.**
3:10 the two **k** with the fat that is on them at the loins,
3:10 which you shall remove with the **k.**
3:15 the two **k** with the fat that is on them at the loins,
3:15 which you shall remove with the **k.**
4: 9 the two **k** with the fat that is on them at the loins;
4: 9 which he shall remove with the **k,**
7: 4 the two **k** with the fat that is on them at the loins,
7: 4 which shall be removed with the **k.**
8:16 and the two **k** with their fat,
8:25 and the two **k** with their fat—and the right thigh.
9:10 the **k,** and the appendage of the liver from
9:19 the two **k** and the fat on them,
Job 16:13 He slashes open my **k,** and shows no mercy;
Isa 34: 6 with the fat of the **k** of rams.

KIDRON (12)

2Sa 15:23 the king crossed the Wadi **K,**
1Ki 2:37 For on the day you go out, and cross the Wadi **K,**
15:13 down her image and burned it at the Wadi **K.**
2Ki 23: 4 in the fields of the **K,**
23: 6 to the Wadi **K,** burned it at the Wadi **K,**
23:12 and threw the rubble into the Wadi **K.**
2Ch 15:16 crushed it, and burned it at the Wadi **K.**
29:16 and carried them out to the Wadi **K.**
30:14 and threw into the Wadi **K.**
Jer 31:40 and all the fields as far as the Wadi **K,**
Jn 18: 1 he went out with his disciples across the **K** valley

KIDS (10) [KID]

Ge 27: 9 Go to the flock, and get me two choice **k,**
27:16 and she put the skins of the **k** on his hands and on
Nu 15:11 or for each of the male lambs or the **k.**
1Sa 10: 3 at Bethel will meet you there, one carrying three **k,**
2Ch 35: 7 lambs and **k** from the flock to the number
35: 8 and **k** and three hundred bulls.
35: 9 the passover offerings five thousand lambs and **k**
SS 1: 8 and pasture your **k** beside the shepherds' tents.
Isa 5:17 fatlings and **k** shall feed among the ruins.
1Es 1: 7 and **k,** and three thousand calves;

KILAN (1)

1Es 5:15 The descendants of **K** and Azetas, sixty-seven.

KILL‡ (211) [KILLED, KILLER, KILLER'S, KILLERS, KILLING, KILLS]

Ge 4:14 and anyone who meets me may **k** me."
4:15 so that no one who came upon him would **k** him.
12:12 then they will **k** me, but they will let you live.
20:11 and they will **k** me because of my wife.
22:10 and took the knife to **k** his son.
26: 7 of the place might **k** me for the sake of Rebekah,
27:41 then I will **k** my brother Jacob."
27:42 Esau is consoling himself by planning to **k** you.
32:11 he may come and **k** us all,
37:18 near to them, they conspired to **k** him.
37:20 let us **k** him and throw him into one of the pits;
37:26 if we **k** our brother and conceal his blood?
42:37 "You may **k** my two sons if I do
Ex 1:16 and see them on the birthstool, if it is a boy, **k** him;
2:14 Do you mean to **k** me as you killed the Egyptian?"
2:15 When Pharaoh heard of it, he sought to **k** Moses.
4:23 now I will **k** your firstborn son.' "
4:24 the LORD met him and tried to **k** him.
5:21 and have put a sword in their hand to **k** us."
16: 3 into this wilderness to **k** this whole assembly
17: 3 to **k** us and our children and livestock with thirst?"
22:24 and I will **k** you with the sword,
23: 7 and do not **k** the innocent and those in the right,
32:12 with evil intent that he brought them out to **k** them
32:27 and each of you **k** your brother, your friend,
Lev 20:15 and you shall **k** the animal.
20:16 you shall **k** the woman and the animal;
Nu 14:15 Now if you **k** this people all at one time,
16:13 of a land flowing with milk and honey to **k** us in
22:29 I would **k** you right now!"
25: 5 "Each of you shall **k** any
31:17 Now therefore, **k** every male among the little ones,
31:17 and **k** every woman who has known a man
Dt 13: 9 But you shall surely **k** them;
32:39 I **k** and I make alive; I wound and I heal;
Jos 9:26 and they did not **k** them.
Jdg 8:19 if you had saved them alive, I would not **k** you."
8:20 So he said to Jether his firstborn, "Go **k** them!"
8:21 Zebah and Zalmunna said, "You come and **k** us;
8:21 So Gideon proceeded to **k** Zebah and Zalmunna;
9:24 who strengthened his hands to **k** his brothers.
9:54 "Draw your sword and **k** me,
13:23 "If the LORD had meant to **k** us,
15:13 into their hands; we will not **k** you."
16: 2 of the morning; then we will **k** him."
20: 5 intended to **k** me, and they raped my concubine
1Sa 2:25 for it was the will of the LORD to **k** them.
5:10 around to us the ark of the God of Israel to **k** us
5:11 that it may not **k** us and our people."
15: 3 do not spare them, but **k** both man and woman,
1Sa 16: 2 If Saul hears of it, he will **k** me."
17: 9 If he is able to fight with me and **k** me,
17: 9 but if I prevail against him and **k** him,
17:35 I would catch it by the jaw, strike it down, and **k** it.
19: 2 "My father Saul is trying to **k** you;
19:11 planning to **k** him in the morning.
19:15 "Bring him up to me in the bed, that I may **k** him."
19:17 'Let me go; why should I **k** you?' "
20: 8 But if there is guilt in me, **k** me yourself;
22:17 "Turn and **k** the priests of the LORD,
24:10 and some urged me to **k** you, but I spared you.
24:11 the corner of your cloak, and did not **k** you,
24:18 not **k** me when the LORD put me into your hands.
30:15 "Swear to me by God that you will not **k** me,
2Sa 1: 9 He said to me, 'Come, stand over me and **k** me;
13:28 'Strike Amnon,' then **k** him.
14: 7 so that we may **k** him for the life
14:11 so that the avenger of blood may **k** no more,
14:32 if there is guilt in me, let him **k** me!"
21:16 with new weapons, said he would **k** David.
1Ki 1:51 that he will not **k** his servant with the sword.' "
3:26 give her the living boy; certainly do not **k** him!"
3:27 "Give the first woman the living boy; do not **k** him.
11:40 Solomon sought therefore to **k** Jeroboam;
12:27 they will **k** me and return to King Rehoboam
18: 9 would hand your servant over to Ahab, to **k** me?
18:12 and tell Ahab and he cannot find you, he will **k** me,
18:14 that Elijah is here'; he will surely **k** me."
19:17 from the sword of Hazael, Jehu shall **k;**
19:17 from the sword of Jehu, Elisha shall **k.**
20:36 as soon as you have left me, a lion will **k** you."
2Ki 6:21 to Elisha, "Father, shall I **k** them? Shall I **k** them?"
6:22 and your bow those whom you want to **k?**
7: 4 and if they **k** us, we shall but die."
8:12 you will **k** their young men with the sword,
10:25 "Come in and **k** them; let no one escape."
11:15 and **k** with the sword anyone who follows her."
2Ch 22:11 hid him from Athaliah, so that she did not **k** him;
Ne 4:11 before we come upon them and **k** them and stop
6:10 for they are coming to **k** you; indeed, tonight they
are coming to **k** you."
Est 3:13 to **k,** and to annihilate all Jews, young and old,
8:11 to assemble and defend their lives, to destroy, to **k,**
Job 13:15 he will **k** me; I have no hope;
20:16 the tongue of a viper will **k** them.
24:14 murderer rises at dusk to **k** the poor and needy,
Ps 37:14 to **k** those who walk uprightly;
37:32 for the righteous, and seek to **k** them.
59: T *ordered his house to be watched in order to **k** him.*
59:11 Do not **k** them, or my people may forget;
94: 6 They **k** the widow and the stranger,
139:19 O that you would **k** the wicked, O God,
Pr 1:18 in wait—to **k** themselves!
Ecc 3: 3 a time to **k,** and a time to heal;
Isa 11: 4 with the breath of his lips he shall **k** the wicked.
14:30 and your remnant I will **k.**
27: 1 and he will **k** the dragon that is in the sea.
Jer 5: 6 Therefore a lion from the forest shall **k** them,
15: 3 the sword to **k,** the dogs to drag away,
18:23 you, O LORD, know all their plotting to **k** me.
20: 4 and shall **k** them with the sword.
20:17 because he did not **k** me in the womb;
29:21 and he shall **k** them before your eyes.
40:15 "Please let me go and **k** Ishmael son of Nethaniah,
41: 8 "Do not **k** us, for we have stores of wheat, barley,
41: 8 and did not **k** them along with their companions.
43: 3 in order that they may **k** us or take us into exile
50:27 **K** all her bulls, let them go down to the slaughter.
Eze 9: 5 "Pass through the city after him, and **k;**
23:47 they shall **k** their sons and their daughters,
28: 9 "I am a god," in the presence of those who **k** you,
Da 5:19 He killed those he wanted to **k,**
Hos 2: 3 and turn her into a parched land, and **k** her
9:16 I will **k** the cherished offspring of their womb.
Am 2: 3 and will **k** all its officials with him,
9: 1 and those who are left I will **k** with the sword;
9: 4 the sword, and it shall **k** them;
Zec 11: 5 Those who buy them **k** them and go unpunished;
Mt 10:28 Do not fear those who **k** the body but cannot **k** the
soul;
17:23 and they will **k** him, and on the third day he will
21:38 come, let us **k** him and get his inheritance.'
23:34 and scribes, some of whom you will **k** and crucify,
26: 4 they conspired to arrest Jesus by stealth and **k** him.
Mk 3: 4 to save life or to **k?"**
6:19 a grudge against him, and wanted to **k** him.
9:31 be betrayed into human hands, and they will **k** him,
10:34 and **k** him; and after three days he will rise again."
11:18 they kept looking for a way to **k** him;
12: 7 let us **k** him, and the inheritance will be ours.'
14: 1 for a way to arrest Jesus by stealth and **k** him;
Lk 11:49 some of whom they will **k** and persecute,'
12: 4 my friends, do not fear those who **k** the body,
13:31 "Get away from here, for Herod wants to **k** you."
15:23 And get the fatted calf and **k** it,
18:33 After they have flogged him, they will **k** him,
19:47 of the people kept looking for a way to **k** him;
20:14 let us **k** him so that the inheritance may be ours.'
Jn 5:18 the Jews were seeking all the more to **k** him,
7: 1 the Jews were looking for an opportunity to **k** him.
7:19 Why are you looking for an opportunity to **k** me?"
7:20 Who is trying to **k** you?"
7:25 "Is not this the man whom they are trying to **k?**
8:22 Then the Jews said, "Is he going to **k** himself?
8:37 yet you look for an opportunity to **k** me,
8:40 but now you are trying to **k** me,
10:10 The thief comes only to steal and **k** and destroy.
Jn 16: 2 when those who **k** you will think that by doing
Ac 5:33 they were enraged and wanted to **k** them.
7:28 to **k** me as you killed the Egyptian yesterday?'
9:23 some time had passed, the Jews plotted to **k** him,
9:24 the gates day and night so that they might **k** him;
9:29 but they were attempting to **k** him.
10:13 he heard a voice saying, "Get up, Peter; **k** and eat."
11: 7 to me, 'Get up, Peter; **k** and eat.'
16:27 he drew his sword and was about to **k** himself,
21:31 While they were trying to **k** him,
23:21 by an oath neither to eat nor drink until they **k** him.
25: 3 planning an ambush to **k** him along the way.
26:21 the Jews seized me in the temple and tried to **k** me.
27:42 The soldiers' plan was to **k** the prisoners,
1Ti 1: 9 for those who **k** their father or mother,
Rev 6: 8 to **k** with sword, famine, and pestilence,
9: 5 not to **k** them, and their torture was like the torture
9:15 the month, and the year, to **k** a third of humankind.
11: 7 on them and conquer them and **k** them,
13:10 if you **k** with the sword, with the sword you must
be killed.
Tob 14:10 because he tried to **k** Ahikar.
Jdt 1:12 that he would **k** with his sword also all
11:12 to **k** their livestock and have determined to use all
16: 4 and **k** my young men with the sword,
AdE 2:21 and they plotted to **k** King Artaxerxes.
Wis 11: 7 in rebuke for the decree to **k** the infants,
11:19 but the mere sight of them could **k** by fright.
14:23 For whether they **k** children in their initiations,
14:24 but they either treacherously **k** one another,
18: 5 When they had resolved to **k** the infants
Sir 9:13 Keep far from those who have power to **k,**
47: 4 In his youth did he not **k** a giant,
Bel 1:26 and I will **k** the dragon without sword or club."
1:29 or else we will **k** you and your household."
1Mc 5: 2 So they began to **k** and destroy among the people.
9:32 When Bacchides learned of this, he tried to **k** him.
11:10 for he has tried to **k** me."
11:45 and they wanted to **k** the king.
12:40 so he kept seeking to seize and **k** him,
15:40 and take the people captive and **k** them.
16:21 and that "he has sent men to **k** you also."
2Mc 4:34 taking Andronicus aside, urged him to **k** Onias.
5:12 and to **k** those who went into their houses.
5:24 and commanded him to **k** all the grown men and
6: 9 and should **k** those who did not choose to change
14:13 with orders to **k** Judas and scatter his troops,
1Es 1: 6 and **k** the passover lamb and prepare the sacrifices
4: 5 They **k** and are killed, and do not disobey
4: 7 If he tells them to **k,** they **k;**
3Mc 1: 2 intending single-handed to **k** him and thereby end
2Es 1:18 'Why have you led us into this wilderness to **k** us?
4Mc 18:19 'I **k** and I make alive:

KILLED‡ (330) [KILL]

Ge 4: 8 Cain rose up against his brother Abel, and **k** him.
4:23 I have **k** a man for wounding me,
4:25 child instead of Abel, because Cain **k** him."
34:25 against the city unawares, and **k** all the males.
34:26 They **k** Hamor and his son Shechem with
49: 6 for in their anger they **k** men,
Ex 2:12 and seeing no one he **k** the Egyptian and hid him in
2:14 Do you mean to kill me as you **k** the Egyptian?"
13:15 the LORD **k** all the firstborn in the land of Egypt,
Nu 3:13 when I **k** all the firstborn in the land of Egypt,
16:41 saying, "You have **k** the people of the LORD."
19:16 in the open field touches one who has been **k** by
21:35 So they **k** him, his sons, and all his people,
22:33 surely just now I would have **k** you and let it live."
25:14 who was **k** with the Midianite woman,
25:15 Midianite woman who was **k** was Cozbi daughter
25:18 she was **k** on the day of the plague that resulted
31: 7 LORD had commanded Moses, and **k** every male.
31: 8 They **k** the kings of Midian:
31: 8 they also **k** Balaam son of Beor with the sword.
31:19 of you has **k** any person or touched a corpse,
35:27 and is **k** by the avenger,
Dt 19: 4 someone who has **k** another person unintentionally
Jos 7: 5 The men of Ai **k** about thirty-six of them,
10:11 because of the hailstones than the Israelites **k** with
20: 5 because the neighbor was **k** by mistake,
20: 9 that anyone who **k** a person
Jdg 3:29 At that time they **k** about ten thousand of
3:31 who **k** six hundred of the Philistines with
7:25 they **k** Oreb at the rock of Oreb, and Zeeb they **k**
at the wine press of Zeeb,
8:17 and **k** the men of the city.
8:18 "What about the men whom you **k** at Tabor?"
9: 5 and **k** his brothers the sons of Jerubbaal,
9:18 and have **k** his sons, seventy men on one stone,
9:24 who **k** them, and on the lords of Shechem,
9:43 he rose against them and **k** them.
9:44 on all who were in the fields and **k** them.
9:45 he took the city, and **k** the people that were in it;
9:54 not say about me, 'A woman **k** him.' "
12: 6 Then they seized him and **k** him at the fords of
14:19 He **k** thirty men of the town, took their spoil,
15:15 and with it he **k** a thousand men.
16:24 the ravager of our country, who has **k** many of us."
16:30 So those he **k** at his death were more than those he
had **k** during his life.
1Sa 4: 2 who **k** about four thousand men on the field
6:19 and he **k** seventy men of them.
14:13 and his armor-bearer, coming after him, **k** them.
14:14 that first slaughter Jonathan and his armor-bearer **k**
17:36 Your servant has **k** both lions and bears;

1Sa 17:51 and **k** him; then he cut off his head with it.
18: 7 "Saul has **k** his thousands, and David his ten
18:27 and **k** one hundred of the Philistines;
19:11 not save your life tonight, tomorrow you will be **k.**
21: 9 whom you **k** in the valley of Elah,
21:11 'Saul has **k** his thousands, and David his ten
22:18 on that day he **k** eighty-five who wore
22:21 Abiathar told David that Saul had **k** the priests of
29: 5 'Saul has **k** his thousands, and David his ten
30: 2 they **k** none of them, but carried them off,
31: 2 and the Philistines **k** Jonathan and Abinadab
2Sa 1:10 So I stood over him, and **k** him,
1:16 saying, 'I have **k** the LORD's anointed.' "
2:31 of David had **k** of Benjamin three hundred sixty
3:30 because he had **k** their brother Asahel in the battle
4: 7 they attacked him, **k** him, and beheaded him.
4:10 I seized him and **k** him at Ziklag—
4:11 when wicked men have **k** a righteous man
4:12 the young men, and they **k** them;
8: 5 David **k** twenty-two thousand men of
8:13 he **k** eighteen thousand Edomites in the Valley
10:18 before Israel; and David **k** of
11:17 Uriah the Hittite was **k** as well.
11:21 Who **k** Abimelech son of Jerubbaal?
12: 9 and have **k** him with the sword of the Ammonites.
13:30 to David that Absalom had **k** all the king's sons,
13:32 that they have **k** all the young men the king's sons;
14: 6 and one struck the other and **k** him.
18:15 surrounded Absalom and struck him, and **k** him.
21:12 on the day the Philistines **k** Saul on Gilboa.
21:17 and attacked the Philistine and **k** him.
21:18 then Sibbecai the Hushathite **k** Saph,
21:19 the Bethlehemite, **k** Goliath the Gittite,
21:21 Jonathan son of David's brother Shimei, **k** him.
23: 8 against eight hundred whom he **k** at one time.
23:12 defended it, and **k** the Philistines;
23:18 against three hundred men and **k** them,
23:20 He also went down and **k** a lion in a pit on a day
23:21 And he **k** an Egyptian, a handsome man.
23:21 and **k** him with his own spear.
1Ki 2:32 and **k** with the sword two men more righteous
2:34 up and struck him down and **k** him;
9:16 had **k** the Canaanites who lived in the city,
11:15 he **k** every male in Edom
13:24 a lion met him on the road and **k** him.
13:26 the lion, which has torn him and **k** him according
15:28 So Baasha **k** Nadab in the third year of King Asa
15:29 he **k** all the house of Jeroboam;
16:10 Zimri came in and struck him down and **k** him,
16:11 he **k** all the house of Baasha;
16:16 "Zimri has conspired, and he has **k** the king";
18:13 not been told my lord what I did when Jezebel **k**
18:40 down to the Wadi Kishon, and **k** them there.
19: 1 and how he had **k** all the prophets with the sword.
19:10 and **k** your prophets with the sword.
19:14 and **k** your prophets with the sword.
20:20 Each **k** his man; the Arameans fled
20:29 **k** one hundred thousand Aramean foot soldiers
20:36 when he had left him, a lion met him and **k** him.
21:19 Have you **k,** and also taken possession?"
2Ki 3:23 must have fought together, and **k** one another.
10: 7 they took the king's sons and **k** them,
10: 9 against my master and **k** him;
10:11 So Jehu **k** all who were left of the house of Ahab
10:17 he **k** all who were left to Ahab in Samaria,
11: 2 the king's children who were about to be **k;**
11: 2 so that he was not **k;**
11: 8 and whoever approaches the ranks is to be **k.**
11:15 "Let her not be **k** in the house of the LORD."
11:18 and they **k** Mattan, the priest of Baal,
11:20 the city was quiet after Athaliah had been **k** with
12:20 and **k** Joash in the house of Millo,
14: 5 he **k** his servants who had murdered his father
14: 7 He **k** ten thousand Edomites in the Valley of Salt
14:19 they sent after him to Lachish, and **k** him there.
15:10 and struck him down in public and **k** him,
15:14 down Shallum son of Jabesh in Samaria and **k** him;
15:25 he **k** him, and reigned in place of him.
15:30 of Remaliah, attacked him, and **k** him;
16: 9 carrying its people captive to Kir, then he **k** Rezin.
17:25 the LORD sent lions among them, which **k** some
19:37 his sons Adrammelech and Sharezer **k** him with
21:23 and **k** the king in his house.
21:24 of the land **k** all those who had conspired
23:29 Pharaoh Neco met him at Megiddo, he **k** him.
1Ch 7:21 people of Gath, who were born in the land, **k** them,
10: 2 and the Philistines **k** Jonathan and Abinadab
11:11 against three hundred whom he **k** at one time.
11:14 defended it, and **k** the Philistines;
11:20 against three hundred and **k** them,
11:22 He also went down and **k** a lion in a pit on a day
11:23 And he **k** an Egyptian, a man of great stature,
11:23 and **k** him with his own spear.
18: 5 David **k** twenty-two thousand Arameans.
18:12 of Zeruiah **k** eighteen thousand Edomites in
19:18 and David **k** seven thousand Aramean charioteers
19:18 and also **k** Shophach the commander of their army.
20: 4 then Sibbecai the Hushathite **k** Sippai,
20: 5 of Jair **k** Lahmi the brother of Goliath the Gittite,
20: 7 Jonathan son of Shimea, David's brother, **k** him.
2Ch 21:13 and because you also have **k** your brothers,
22: 1 the Arabs to the camp had **k** all the older sons.
22: 8 who attended Ahaziah, and he **k** them.
22:11 the king's children who were about to be **k;**
23: 7 and whoever enters the house shall be **k.**
23:17 and they **k** Mattan, the priest of Baal,
23:21 the city was quiet after Athaliah had been **k** with
2Ch 24:22 Zechariah's father, had shown him, but **k** his son.
24:25 and they **k** him on his bed.
25: 3 he **k** his servants who had murdered his father
25:13 they **k** three thousand people in them,
25:27 they sent after him to Lachish, and **k** him there.
28: 6 of Remaliah **k** one hundred twenty thousand
28: 7 **k** the king's son Maaseiah,
28: 9 but you have **k** them in a rage that has reached up
33:24 His servants conspired against him and **k** him
33:25 of the land **k** all those who had conspired
36:17 who **k** their youths with the sword in the house
Ezr 6:20 they **k** the passover lamb for all the returned exiles,
Ne 9:26 behind their backs and **k** your prophets,
Est 7: 4 to be destroyed, to be **k,** and to be annihilated.
9: 6 the Jews **k** and destroyed five hundred people.
9: 7 They **k** Parshandatha, Dalphon, Aspatha,
9:11 That very day the number of those **k** in the citadel
9:12 of Susa the Jews have **k** five hundred people and
9:15 of Adar and they **k** three hundred persons in Susa;
9:16 **k** seventy-five thousand of those who hated them;
Job 1:15 and **k** the servants with the edge of the sword;
1:17 and **k** the servants with the edge of the sword;
Ps 44:22 Because of you we are being **k** all day long,
60: T *Joab on his return* ***k*** *twelve thousand Edomites*
78:31 of God rose against them and he **k** the strongest
78:34 When he **k** them, they sought for him;
135:10 struck down many nations and **k** mighty kings—
136:18 and **k** famous kings, for his steadfast love endures
Pr 22:13 I shall be **k** in the streets!"
Isa 14:20 have destroyed your land, you have **k** your people.
27: 7 Or have they been **k** as their killers were **k?**
37:38 his sons Adrammelech and Sharezer **k** him with
Jer 14:18 look—those **k** by the sword!
41: 2 Ahikam son of Shaphan with the sword and **k** him,
41: 3 also **k** all the Judeans who were with Gedaliah
41: 9 that cistern with those whom he had **k.**
41:18 of Nethaniah had **k** Gedaliah son of Ahikam,
52:10 of Babylon **k** the sons of Zedekiah before his eyes,
52:10 and also **k** all the officers of Judah at Riblah.
La 2: 4 he has **k** all in whom we took pride in the tent
2:20 Should priest and prophet be **k** in the sanctuary of
2:21 in the day of your anger you have **k** them,
Eze 9: 7 So they went out and **k** in the city.
11: 6 You have **k** many in this city,
23:10 and they **k** her with the sword.
26: 6 and its daughter-towns in the country shall be **k** by
31:17 to those **k** by the sword, along with its allies,
31:18 with those who are **k** by the sword.
32:20 They shall fall among those who are **k** by
32:21 they lie still, the uncircumcised, **k** by the sword."
32:22 their graves all around it, all of them **k,**
32:23 Its company is all around its grave, all of them **k,**
32:24 all of them **k,** fallen by the sword,
32:25 all of them uncircumcised, **k** by the sword;
32:26 all of them uncircumcised, **k** by the sword;
32:28 with those who are **k** by the sword.
32:29 for all their might are laid with those who are **k** by
32:30 they lie uncircumcised with those who are **k** by
32:31 Pharaoh and all his army, **k** by the sword,
35: 8 and in all your watercourses those **k** with
Da 3:22 the raging flames **k** the men who lifted Shadrach,
5:19 He **k** those he wanted to kill,
5:30 very night Belshazzar, the Chaldean king, was **k.**
Hos 6: 5 I have **k** them by the words of my mouth,
Am 4:10 I **k** your young men with the sword;
Zep 2:12 You also, O Ethiopians, shall be **k** by my sword.
Mt 2:16 and he sent and **k** all the children in and
16:21 and be **k,** and on the third day be raised.
21:35 tenants seized his slaves and beat one, **k** another,
21:39 threw him out of the vineyard, and **k** him.
22: 6 mistreated them, and **k** them.
27:20 to ask for Barabbas and to have Jesus **k.**
Mk 8:31 the chief priests, and the scribes, and be **k,**
9:31 and they will kill him, and three days after being **k,**
12: 5 Then he sent another, and that one they **k.**
12: 5 some they beat, and others they **k.**
12: 8 So they seized him, **k** him,
Lk 9:22 and be **k,** and on the third day be raised."
11:47 the tombs of the prophets whom your ancestors **k.**
11:48 for they **k** them, and you build their tombs
12: 5 fear him who, after he has **k,**
13: 4 Or those eighteen who were **k** when the tower
13:33 for a prophet to be **k** outside of Jerusalem.'
15:27 and your father has **k** the fatted calf,
15:30 you **k** the fatted calf for him!'
20:15 So they threw him out of the vineyard and **k** him.
Ac 2:23 you crucified and **k** by the hands of those outside
3:15 and you **k** the Author of life,
5:30 whom you had **k** by hanging him on a tree.
5:36 about four hundred, joined him; but he was **k,**
7:28 to kill me as you **k** the Egyptian yesterday?'
7:52 They **k** those who foretold the coming of
12: 2 the brother of John, **k** with the sword.
13:28 they asked Pilate to have him **k.**
22:20 and keeping the coats of those who **k** him.'
23:12 to eat nor drink until they had **k** Paul.
23:14 by an oath to taste no food until we have **k** Paul.
23:27 by the Jews and was about to be **k** by them,
Ro 7:11 deceived me and through it **k** me.
8:36 "For your sake we are being **k** all day long;
11: 3 "Lord, they have **k** your prophets,
2Co 6: 9 as punished, and yet not **k;**
1Th 2:15 who **k** both the Lord Jesus and the prophets,
Heb 11:37 they were sawn in two, they were **k** by the sword;
2Pe 2:12 mere creatures of instinct, born to be caught and **k.**
Rev 2:13 who was **k** among you, where Satan lives.
6:11 to be **k** as they themselves had been **k.**
Rev 9:18 a third of humankind was **k,**
9:20 who were not **k** by these plagues,
11: 5 anyone who wants to harm them must be **k**
11:13 seven thousand people were **k** in the earthquake,
13:10 with the sword you must be **k.**
13:15 not worship the image of the beast to be **k.**
19:21 rest were **k** by the sword of the rider on the horse,
Tob 1:21 before two of Sennacherib's sons **k** him,
3: 8 the wicked demon Asmodeus had **k** each of them
6:14 that it was a demon that **k** them.
Jdt 2:25 and **k** everyone who resisted him.
9: 3 So you gave up their rulers to be **k,** and their bed,
AdE 9: 6 in the city of Susa the Jews **k** five hundred people,
9:11 the number of those **k** in Susa was reported to
9:15 on the fourteenth and **k** three hundred people,
Wis 10: 3 he perished because in rage he **k** his brother.
16: 9 For they were **k** by the bites of locusts and flies,
Bel 1:28 he has destroyed Bel, and **k** the dragon,
1Mc 2: 9 Her infants have been **k** in her streets,
2:24 he ran and **k** him on the altar.
2:25 At the same time he **k** the king's officer
3:11 and he defeated and **k** him.
5:13 in the land of Tob have been **k;**
5:28 and **k** every male by the edge of the sword;
5:35 and he **k** every male in it, plundered it,
6:45 he **k** men right and left,
6:46 stabbed it from beneath, and **k** it;
7: 4 So the army **k** them, and Demetrius took his seat
7:16 but he seized sixty of them and **k** them in one day,
7:19 and **k** them and threw them into a great pit.
9: 2 and they took it and **k** many people.
9:38 Remembering how their brother John had been **k,**
9:61 in this treachery, and **k** them.
9:69 and he **k** many of them.
11:18 in the strongholds were **k** by the inhabitants of
11:47 they **k** on that day about one hundred thousand.
12:48 and they **k** with the sword all who had entered
13:23 When he approached Baskama, he **k** Jonathan,
13:31 the young King Antiochus; he **k** him
16:16 in the banquet hall and **k** him and his two sons,
16:22 the men who came to destroy him and **k** them,
2Mc 4:42 a result, they wounded many of them, and **k** some,
4:42 temple robber himself they **k** close by the treasury.
5:14 and as many were sold into slavery as were **k.**
5:26 with his armed warriors and **k** great numbers
8:24 they **k** more than nine thousand of the enemy,
8:30 and Bacchides they **k** more than twenty thousand
8:32 They **k** the commander of Timothy's forces,
10:22 Then he **k** these men who had turned traitor,
10:37 They **k** Timothy, who was hiding in a cistern,
12:28 and **k** as many as twenty-five thousand
13:15 and **k** as many as two thousand men in the camp.
15:22 and he **k** fully one hundred eighty-five thousand in
1Es 1: 1 he **k** the passover lamb on the fourteenth day of
1:53 These **k** their young men with the sword
4: 5 and are **k,** and do not disobey the king's command;
2Es 1:11 and Sidon; I **k** all their enemies.
1:32 and **k** them and torn their bodies in pieces;
15:53 if you had not **k** my chosen people continually,
16:34 Their bridegrooms shall be **k** in war,
4Mc 3: 7 with the soldiers of his nation had **k** many of them.
5: 3 they were to be broken on the wheel and **k.**
12:14 for having **k** without cause the contestants

KILLER (5) [KILL]

Ex 21:13 for you a place to which the **k** may flee.
21:14 you shall take the **k** from my altar for execution.
Dt 19: 5 the **k** may flee to one of these cities and live.
19: 6 and overtake and put the **k** to death,
Pr 28:17 let that **k** be a fugitive until death;

KILLER'S (1) [KILL]

Dt 19:12 of the **k** city shall send to have the culprit taken

KILLERS (2) [KILL]

Isa 27: 7 Or have they been killed as their **k** were killed?
Jer 4:31 I am fainting before **k!"**

KILLING‡ (22) [KILL]

Jos 7: 5 as far as Shebarim and **k** them on the slope.
Jdg 9:56 against his father in **k** his seventy brothers;
20:31 **k** about thirty men of Israel.
20:39 to inflict casualties on the Israelites, **k** about thirty
1Sa 17:50 striking down the Philistine and **k** him;
17:57 On David's return from **k** the Philistine,
18: 6 when David returned from **k** the Philistine,
19: 1 and with all his servants about **k** David.
19: 5 an innocent person by **k** David without cause?"
2Sa 3:37 the king had no part in the **k** of Abner son of Ner.
1Ki 17:20 the widow with whom I am staying, by **k** her son?"
18: 4 Jezebel was **k** off the prophets of the LORD,
2Ki 17:26 they are **k** them, because they do not know the law
Isa 22:13 **k** oxen and slaughtering sheep,
La 3:43 with anger and pursued us, **k** without pity;
Eze 9: 8 While they were **k,** and I was left alone,
21:14 Let the sword fall twice, thrice; it is a sword for **k.**
Ac 8: 1 And Saul approved of their **k** him.
1Mc 2:37 and earth testify for us that you are **k** us unjustly."
9:40 on them from the ambush and began **k** them.
2Mc 10:17 **k** no fewer than twenty thousand.
4Mc 13:14 Let us not fear him who thinks he is **k** us,

KILLS (26) [KILL]

Ge 4:15 Whoever **k** Cain will suffer a sevenfold vengeance.

Ex 21:14 But if someone willfully attacks and **k** another
21:29 and it **k** a man or a woman, the ox shall be stoned,
Lev 24:17 Anyone who **k** a human being shall be put
24:18 Anyone who **k** an animal shall make restitution
24:21 One who **k** an animal shall make restitution for it;
24:21 but one who **k** a human being shall be put to death.
Nu 35:11 so that a slayer who **k** a person
35:15 so that anyone who **k** a person
35:30 If anyone **k** another, the murderer shall be put
Dt 4:42 someone who unintentionally **k** another person,
Jos 20: 3 so that anyone who **k** a person without intent or
1Sa 2: 6 The LORD **k** and brings to life;
17:25 The king will greatly enrich the man who **k** him,
17:26 be done for the man who **k** this Philistine,
17:27 "So shall it be done for the man who **k** him."
Job 5: 2 vexation **k** the fool, and jealousy slays the simple.
Pr 1:32 For waywardness **k** the simple,
Isa 66: 3 Whoever slaughters an ox is like one who **k**
Mt 23:37 that **k** the prophets and stones those who are sent
Lk 13:34 that **k** the prophets and stones those who are sent
2Co 3: 6 for the letter **k**, but the Spirit gives life.
Tob 3: 8 "You are the one who **k** your husbands!
6:15 but it **k** anyone who desires to approach her.
Wis 16:14 A person in wickedness **k** another,
Sir 34:24 Like one who **k** a son before his father's eyes is

KILN (5)

Ex 9: 8 "Take handfuls of soot from the **k**,
9:10 So they took soot from the **k**,
19:18 the smoke went up like the smoke of a **k**,
Sir 27: 5 The **k** tests the potter's vessels;
38:30 and he takes care in firing the **k**.

KIN (56) [KINDRED, KINSFOLK, KINSHIP, KINSMAN, KINSMAN'S, KINSMEN, KINSWOMAN, NEXT-OF-KIN]

Ge 16:12 and he shall live at odds with all his **k**."
24:27 on the way to the house of my master's **k**."
Lev 7:20 a state of uncleanness shall be cut off from their **k**.
7:21 you shall be cut off from your **k**.
7:25 you who eat it shall be cut off from your **k**.
7:27 be cut off from your **k**.
18: 6 None of you shall approach anyone near of **k**
19:17 You shall not hate in your heart anyone of your **k**;
21: 2 except for his nearest **k**: his mother,
21:14 He shall marry a virgin of his own **k**,
21:15 that he may not profane his offspring among his **k**;
25:25 If anyone of your **k** falls into difficulty and sells
25:25 then the next of **k** shall come and redeem what
25:35 of your **k** fall into difficulty and become dependent
25:47 and if any of your **k** fall into difficulty with one
Nu 5: 8 of **k** to whom restitution may be made for
Dt 2: 8 So we passed by our **k**,
3:18 over armed as the vanguard of your Israelite **k**.
23: 7 not abhor any of the Edomites, for they are your **k**.
32:50 be gathered to your **k**, as your brother Aaron died
32:50 on Mount Hor and was gathered to his **k**;
33: 9 he ignored his **k**, and did not acknowledge his
Jos 17: 4 to give us an inheritance along with our male **k**."
Jdg 5:14 following you, Benjamin, with your **k**;
14: 3 "Is there not a woman among your **k**,
21: 6 the Israelites had compassion for Benjamin their **k**,
Ru 2:20 a relative of ours, one of our nearest **k**."
2Sa 19:12 You are my **k**, you are my bone and my flesh;
19:42 "Because the king is near of **k** to us.
2Ki 10:13 They answered, "We are **k** of Ahaziah;
1Ch 9: 6 Jeuel and their **k**, six hundred ninety.
2Ch 28: 8 of their **k**, women, sons, and daughters;
Ezr 3: 2 and Zerubbabel son of Shealtiel with his **k** set out
3: 9 And Jeshua with his sons and his **k**,
3: 9 the Levites, their sons and **k**,
8:18 namely Sherebiah, with his sons and **k**, eighteen;
8:19 with his **k** and their sons, twenty;
8:24 Hashabiah, and ten of their **k** with them.
Ne 3:18 After him their **k** made repairs:
4:14 who is great and awesome, and fight for your **k**,
5: 1 and of their wives against their Jewish **k**.
5: 8 but now you are selling your own **k**,
10:29 with their **k**, their nobles, and enter into a curse
Ps 50:20 You sit and speak against your **k**;
Pr 18: 9 One who is slack in work is close **k** to a vandal.
18:24 but a true friend sticks closer than one's nearest **k**.
19: 7 If the poor are hated even by their **k**,
Isa 58: 7 and not to hide yourself from your own **k**?
Jer 9: 4 and put no trust in any of your **k**;
9: 4 for all your **k** are supplanters,
Eze 11:15 your kinsfolk, your own **k**, your fellow exiles,
Mk 6: 4 except in their hometown, and among their own **k**,
Tob 6:12 and you, as next of **k** to her,
10: 6 with him is trustworthy and is one of our own **k**.
Jdt 16:24 to all those who were next of **k**
Sir 23:16 of **k** will never cease until the fire burns him up.

KINAH (1)

Jos 15:22 **K**, Dimonah, Adadah,

KIND‡ (112) [KINDLINESS, KINDLY, KINDNESS, KINDS]

A. EVERY KIND (39)

Ge 1:11 and fruit trees of every **k** on earth that bear fruit A
1:12 plants yielding seed of every **k**, A
1:12 trees of every **k** bearing fruit with the seed in it. A
1:21 of every **k**, with which the waters swarm, A
1:21 and every winged bird of every **k**. A
1:24 the earth bring forth living creatures of every **k**: A
1:24 and wild animals of the earth of every **k**." A
1:25 made the wild animals of the earth of every **k**, A
1:25 and the cattle of every **k**, A
1:25 that creeps upon the ground of every **k**. A
6:19 you shall bring two of every **k** into the ark, A
6:20 of the ground according to its **k**,
6:20 two of every **k** shall come in to you, A
6:21 Also take with you every **k** of food that is eaten, A
7: 3 to keep their **k** alive on the face of all the earth.
7:14 they and every wild animal of every **k**, A
7:14 and all domestic animals of every **k**, A
7:14 and every bird of every **k**— A
33:15 But he said, "Why should my lord be so **k** to me?"
37:10 "What **k** of dream is this that you have had?
Ex 1:14 in mortar and brick and in every **k** of field labor. A
31: 3 intelligence, and knowledge in every **k** of craft, A
31: 5 and in carving wood, in every **k** of craft. A
35:31 intelligence, and knowledge in every **k** of craft, A
35:33 and in carving wood, in every **k** of craft. A
35:35 skill to do every **k** of work done by an artisan A
Lev 11:14 the buzzard, the kite of any **k**;
11:15 every raven of any **k**;
11:16 the nighthawk, the sea gull, the hawk of any **k**;
11:19 the heron of any **k**, the hoopoe, and the bat.
11:22 Of them you may eat: the locust according to its **k**,
11:22 the bald locust according to its **k**,
11:22 the cricket according to its **k**,
11:22 and the grasshopper according to its **k**.
11:29 the mouse, the great lizard according to its **k**,
19:19 not let your animals breed with a different **k**;
Dt 14:13 the buzzard, the kite, of any **k**;
14:14 every raven of any **k**;
14:15 the nighthawk, the sea gull, the hawk, of any **k**;
14:18 the heron, of any **k**; the hoopoe and the bat.
17: 8 to make between one **k** of bloodshed and another,
one **k** of legal right and another, or one **k** of
assault and another—
22: 9 You shall not sow your vineyard with a second **k**
24:10 When you make your neighbor a loan of any **k**,
1Ki 9:13 "What **k** of cities are these that you have given me,
1Ch 28:21 be every volunteer who has skill for any **k**
2Ch 10: 7 "If you will be **k** to this people and please them,
34:13 and directed all who did work in every **k** A
Ps 107:18 they loathed any **k** of food,
144:13 our barns be filled, with produce of every **k**; A
145:17 and **k** in all his doings.
Pr 11:17 Those who are **k** reward themselves,
14:21 but happy are those who are **k** to the poor.
14:31 but those who are **k** to the needy honor him.
19:17 Whoever is **k** to the poor lends to the LORD,
28: 8 for another who is **k** to the poor.
Eze 17:23 Under it every **k** of bird will live; A
17:23 branches will nest winged creatures of every **k**. A
27:18 because of your great wealth of every **k**— A
39: 4 every **k** and to the wild animals to be devoured. A
39:17 the birds of every **k** and to all the wild animals: A
Da 6:23 and no **k** of harm was found on him,
Hag 2:12 or oil, or any **k** of food, does it become holy?
Mt 13:47 into the sea and caught fish of every **k**; A
Mk 9:29 "This **k** can come out only through prayer."
Lk 4:36 "What **k** of utterance is this?
6:35 for he is **k** to the ungrateful and the wicked.
7:39 he would have known who and what **k**
Jn 12:33 He said this to indicate the **k** of death he was
18:32 when he indicated the **k** of death he was to die.)
21:19 the **k** of death by which he would glorify God.)
Ac 7:49 What **k** of house will you build for me,
10:33 and you have been **k** enough to come.
Ro 1:29 They were filled with every **k** of wickedness, A
1Co 1: 5 in speech and knowledge of every **k**— A
5: 1 and of a **k** that is not found even among pagans;
7: 7 one having one **k** and another a different **k**.
13: 4 Love is patient; love is **k**;
15:35 With what **k** of body do they come?"
15:38 and to each **k** of seed its own body.
Eph 4:19 greedy to practice every **k** of impurity. A
4:32 and be **k** to one another,
5: 3 But fornication and impurity of any **k**, or greed,
5:27 without a spot or wrinkle or anything of the **k**—
Php 4:14 In any case, it was **k** of you to share my distress.
1Th 1: 5 just as you know what **k** of persons we proved to
1: 9 the people of those regions report about us what **k**
2Th 2:10 and every **k** of wicked deception A
Tit 2: 5 chaste, good managers of the household, **k**,
Jas 1: 2 whenever you face trials of any **k**,
1:18 so that we would become a **k** of first fruits
3:16 also be disorder and wickedness of every **k**. A
1Pe 2:18 not only those who are **k** and gentle but
Rev 11: 6 and to strike the earth with every **k** of plague, A
Tob 4:12 "Beware, my son, of every **k** of fornication. A
Wis 12:19 that the righteous must be **k**,
15: 1 But you, our God, are **k** and true, patient,
19:11 Afterward they saw also a new **k** of birds,
19:21 quick-melting **k** of heavenly food.
Sir 13:16 All living beings associate with their own **k**,
27: 9 Birds roost with their own **k**,
41:16 nor is every **k** of abashment to be approved. A
47:25 For they sought out every **k** of wickedness, A
1Mc 6:11 For I was **k** and beloved in my power.'
2Mc 1:24 you alone are king and are **k**,
12:30 and their **k** treatment of them in times
3Mc 7: 7 of every charge of whatever **k**.
4Mc 3: 2 No one of us can eradicate that **k** of desire,
8:17 and exhorted us to accept **k** treatment
9:29 "How sweet is any **k** of death for the religion

KINDLE (14) [KINDLED, KINDLERS, KINDLES, KINDLING, REKINDLE, REKINDLED, SELF-KINDLED]

Ex 35: 3 You shall **k** no fire in all your dwellings on
Jer 7:18 The children gather wood, the fathers **k** fire,
17:27 then I will **k** a fire in its gates;
21:14 I will **k** a fire in its forest,
43:12 He shall **k** a fire in the temples of the gods
49:27 And I will **k** a fire at the wall of Damascus,
50:32 and I will **k** a fire in his cities,
Eze 20:47 Thus says the Lord GOD, I will **k** a fire in you,
24:10 Heap up the logs, **k** the fire;
Am 1:14 So I will **k** a fire against the wall of Rabbah,
Mal 1:10 so that you would not **k** fire on my altar in vain!
Sir 8:10 Do not **k** the coals of sinners,
28: 8 for the hot-tempered **k** strife,
32:16 and they will **k** righteous deeds like a light.

KINDLED (62) [KINDLE]

Ex 4:14 Then the anger of the LORD was **k** against Moses
Nu 11: 1 the LORD heard it and his anger was **k**.
11:33 the anger of the LORD was **k** against the people,
12: 9 And the anger of the LORD was **k** against them,
22:22 God's anger was **k** because he was going,
22:27 and Balaam's anger was **k**,
24:10 Then Balak's anger was **k** against Balaam,
25: 3 and the LORD's anger was **k** against Israel.
32:10 LORD's anger was **k** on that day and he swore,
32:13 And the LORD's anger was **k** against Israel,
Dt 6:15 be **k** against you and he would destroy you from
7: 4 the anger of the LORD would be **k** against you,
11:17 then the anger of the LORD will be **k** against you
29:27 so the anger of the LORD was **k** against that land,
31:17 My anger will be **k** against them in that day.
32:22 For a fire is **k** by my anger,
Jos 23:16 then the anger of the LORD will be **k** against you,
Jdg 2:14 So the anger of the LORD was **k** against Israel,
2:20 So the anger of the LORD was **k** against Israel;
3: 8 the anger of the LORD was **k** against Israel,
9:30 the words of Gaal son of Ebed, his anger was **k**.
10: 7 So the anger of the LORD was **k** against Israel,
1Sa 11: 6 and his anger was greatly **k**.
17:28 and Eliab's anger was **k** against David.
20:30 Then Saul's anger was **k** against Jonathan.
2Sa 6: 7 The anger of the LORD was **k** against Uzzah;
12: 5 Then David's anger was greatly **k** against the man.
24: 1 the anger of the LORD was **k** against Israel,
2Ki 13: 3 The anger of the LORD was **k** against Israel,
22:13 for great is the wrath of the LORD that is **k**
22:17 therefore my wrath will be **k** against this place,
23:26 by which his anger was **k** against Judah,
1Ch 13:10 The anger of the LORD was **k** against Uzzah;
Job 19:11 He has **k** his wrath against me,
42: 7 "My wrath is **k** against you and
Ps 2:12 for his wrath is quickly **k**.
78:21 a fire was **k** against Jacob,
106:40 the anger of the LORD was **k** against his people,
124: 3 when their anger was **k** against us;
Isa 5:25 the anger of the LORD was **k** against his people,
9:18 it **k** the thickets of the forest,
10:16 and under his glory a burning will be **k**,
50:11 and among the brands that you have **k**!
Jer 15:14 for in my anger a fire is **k** that shall burn forever.
17: 4 for in my anger a fire is **k** that shall burn forever.
44: 6 So my wrath and my anger were poured out and **k**
La 4:11 and **k** a fire in Zion that consumed its foundations.
Eze 20:48 All flesh shall see that I the LORD have **k** it;
Hos 7: 6 For they are **k** like an oven,
Lk 12:49 and how I wish it were already **k**!
22:55 When they had **k** a fire in the middle of
Ac 28: 2 they **k** a fire and welcomed all of us around it.
Jdt 7: 5 and when they had **k** fires on their towers,
Wis 2: 2 reason is a spark **k** by the beating of our hearts;
Sir 9: 8 and by it passion is **k** like a fire.
11:32 From a spark many coals are **k**,
16: 6 In an assembly of sinners a fire is **k**,
51: 4 and from the midst of fire that I had not **k**,
1Mc 12:28 so they **k** fires in their camp and withdrew.
2Mc 10:36 they **k** fires and burned the blasphemers alive.
2Es 16:15 The fire is **k**, and shall not be put out
16:68 burning wrath of a great multitude is **k** over you;

KINDLERS (1) [KINDLE]

Isa 50:11 But all of you are **k** of fire, lighters of firebrands.

KINDLES (6) [KINDLE]

Job 41:21 Its breath **k** coals, and a flame comes out
Isa 30:33 breath of the LORD, like a stream of sulfur, **k** it.
44:15 he **k** a fire and bakes bread.
64: 2 as when fire **k** brushwood and the fire causes water
Sir 28:11 A hasty quarrel **k** a fire,
40:30 but it **k** a fire inside him.

KINDLINESS (1) [KIND]

AdE 16:10 and quite devoid of our **k**),

KINDLING (1) [KINDLE]

Pr 26:21 so is a quarrelsome person for **k** strife.

KINDLY (23) [KIND]

Ge 50:21 In this way he reassured them, speaking **k** to them.
Ex 8: 9 "**K** tell me when I am to pray for you and
Jos 2:12 Now then, since I have dealt **k** with you,

Jos 2:12 to me by the LORD that you in turn will deal **k**
2:14 then we will deal **k** and faithfully with you when
Jdg 1:24 and we will deal **k** with you."
Ru 1: 8 May the LORD deal **k** with you,
2:13 for you have comforted me and spoken **k**
1Sa 20: 8 Therefore deal **k** with your servant,
2Sa 19: 7 So go out at once and speak **k** to your servants;
2Ki 25:28 he spoke **k** to him, and gave him a seat above
Jer 52:32 he spoke **k** to him, and gave him a seat above
Ac 27: 3 and Julius treated Paul **k**, and allowed him to go
1Co 4:13 when slandered, we speak **k**.
1Th 3: 6 He has told us also that you always remember us **k**
2Ti 2:24 the Lord's servant must not be quarrelsome but **k**
Jdt 6:19 and look **k** today on the faces
Wis 1: 6 a **k** spirit, but will not free blasphemers from
Sir 11:12 but the eyes of the Lord look **k** upon them;
13: 6 he will speak to you **k** and say,
2Mc 3: 9 and had been **k** welcomed by the high priest of
6:22 and be treated **k** on account of his old friendship
1Es 6: 5 Yet the elders of the Jews were dealt with **k**,

KINDNESS‡ (52) [KIND]

Ge 19:19 and you have shown me great **k** in saving my life;
20:13 I said to her, 'This is the **k** you must do me:
40:14 please do me the **k** to make mention of me
Ru 2:20 whose **k** has not forsaken the living or the dead!"
1Sa 15: 6 for you showed **k** to all the people of Israel
2Sa 9: 1 to whom I may show **k** for Jonathan's sake?"
9: 3 of the house of Saul to whom I may show the **k**
9: 7 for I will show you **k** for the sake
2Ch 24:22 King Joash did not remember the **k** that Jehoiada,
Job 6:14 "Those who withhold **k** from a friend forsake
Ps 109:12 May there be no one to do him a **k**,
109:16 For he did not remember to show **k**,
Pr 21:21 Whoever pursues righteousness and **k** will find life
31:26 and the teaching of **k** is on her tongue.
Hos 11: 4 I led them with cords of human **k**,
Mic 6: 8 and to love **k**, and to walk humbly with your God?
Zec 7: 9 show **k** and mercy to one another;
Mk 14: 7 and you can show **k** to them whenever you wish;
Ac 28: 2 The natives showed us unusual **k**.
Ro 2: 4 the riches of his **k** and forbearance and patience?
2: 4 that God's **k** is meant to lead you to repentance?
3:12 there is no one who shows **k**,
11:22 the **k** and the severity of God: severity toward
those who have fallen, but God's **k** toward you,
provided you continue in his **k**;
2Co 6: 6 patience, **k**, holiness of spirit, genuine love,
Gal 5:22 joy, peace, patience, **k**, generosity, faithfulness,
Eph 2: 7 of his grace in **k** toward us in Christ Jesus.
Col 3:12 clothe yourselves with compassion, **k**, humility,
Tit 3: 4 and loving **k** of God our Savior appeared,
AdE 13: 2 but always acting reasonably and with **k**),
16: 2 with the most generous **k** of their benefactors,
Wis 16: 2 of this punishment you showed **k** to your people,
16:11 and become unresponsive to your **k**.
16:24 in **k** relaxes on behalf of those who trust in you.
Sir 3:14 For **k** to a father will not be forgotten,
7:33 do not withhold **k** even from the dead.
17:22 he will keep a person's **k** like the apple of his eye.
29:15 Do not forget the **k** of your guarantor,
30: 6 and one to repay the **k** of his friends.
35: 3 The one who returns a **k** offers choice flour,
36:28 If **k** and humility mark her speech,
37:11 about generosity or with the merciless about **k**,
40:17 but **k** is like a garden of blessings,
51: 8 O Lord, and your **k** from of old,
Bar 2:27 in all your **k** and in all your great compassion,
2Mc 2:22 the Lord with great **k** became gracious to them—
6:13 it is a sign of great **k** not to let the impious alone
9:27 and will treat you with moderation and **k**."
10:38 the Lord who shows great **k** to Israel
14: 9 and our hard-pressed nation with the gracious **k**
Man 1:11 the knee of my heart, imploring you for your **k**.

KINDRED‡ (153) [KIN]

Ge 12: 1 and your **k** and your father's house to the land
13: 8 and my herders; for we are **k**.
24: 4 but will go to my country and to my **k** and get
24:38 to my **k**, and get a wife for my son.'
24:40 You shall get a wife for my son from my **k**,
24:41 when you come to my **k**;
31: 3 to the land of your ancestors and to your **k**,
32: 9 'Return to your country and to your **k**,
43: 7 about ourselves and our **k**,
Ex 4:18 "Please let me go back to my **k** in Egypt
Lev 10: 6 but your **k**, the whole house of Israel,
Nu 10:30 but I will go back to my own land and to my **k**."
20: 3 "Would that we had died when our **k** died before
Dt 1:28 Our **k** have made our hearts melt by reporting,
2: 4 about to pass through the territory of your **k**,
3:20 When the LORD gives rest to your **k**, as to you,
10: 9 Levi has no allotment or inheritance with his **k**;
Jos 1:14 among you shall cross over armed before your **k**
1:15 the LORD gives rest to your **k** as well as to you,
6:23 they brought all her **k** out—
22: 3 you have not forsaken your **k** these many days,
22: 4 now the LORD your God has given rest to your **k**,
22: 8 divide the spoil of your enemies with your **k**."
Ru 4:10 of the dead may not be cut off from his **k** and from
2Sa 19:41 "Why have our **k** the people
1Ki 12:24 up or fight against your **k** the people of Israel.
16:11 not leave him a single male of his **k** or his friends.
2Ki 23: 9 but ate unleavened bread among their **k**.
1Ch 5: 7 And his **k** by their families,
5:13 And their **k** according to their clans:
6:44 On the left were their **k** the sons of Merari:
6:48 and their **k** the Levites were appointed for all
7: 5 Their **k** belonging to all the families
8:32 Now these also lived opposite their **k** in Jerusalem,
8:32 in Jerusalem, with their **k**.
9: 9 and their **k** according to their generations,
9:13 besides their **k**, heads of their
9:17 and their **k** Shallum was the chief,
9:19 and his **k** of his ancestral house, the Korahites,
9:25 and their **k** who were in their villages were obliged
9:32 of their **k** of the Kohathites had charge of the rows
9:38 and these also lived opposite their **k** in Jerusalem,
9:38 in Jerusalem, with their **k**.
12: 2 they were Benjaminites, Saul's **k**.
12:29 Of the Benjaminites, the **k** of Saul, three thousand,
12:32 and all their **k** under their command.
12:39 for their **k** had provided for them.
13: 2 let us send abroad to our **k** who remain in all
15: 5 Uriel the chief, with one hundred twenty of his **k**;
15: 6 with two hundred twenty of his **k**;
15: 7 Joel the chief, with one hundred thirty of his **k**;
15: 8 Shemaiah the chief, with two hundred of his **k**;
15: 9 Eliel the chief, with eighty of his **k**;
15:10 with one hundred twelve of his **k**.
15:12 sanctify yourselves, you and your **k**,
15:16 the Levites to appoint their **k** as the singers to play
15:17 and of his **k** Asaph son of Berechiah;
15:17 and of the sons of Merari, their **k**,
15:18 and with them their **k** of the second order,
16: 7 of praises to the LORD by Asaph and his **k**.
16:39 And he left the priest Zadok and his **k** the priests
23:22 their **k**, the sons of Kish, married them.
23:32 and shall attend the descendants of Aaron, their **k**,
24:31 These also cast lots corresponding to their **k**,
25: 7 They and their **k**, who were trained in singing to
26:12 had duties, just as their **k** did,
2Ch 5:12 Asaph, Heman, and Jeduthun, their sons and **k**,
11: 4 You shall not go up or fight against your **k**.
19:10 to you from your **k** who live in their cities,
19:10 and wrath may not come on you and your **k**.
28:11 the captives whom you have taken from your **k**,
28:15 they brought them to their **k** at Jericho,
29:34 their **k**, the Levites, helped them until
30: 7 Do not be like your ancestors and your **k**,
30: 9 your **k** and your children will find compassion
31:15 to distribute the portions to their **k**,
35: 5 to the groupings of the ancestral houses of your **k**
35: 6 and on behalf of your **k** make preparations,
35:15 for their **k** the Levites made preparations for them.
Ne 5: 5 Now our flesh is the same as that of our **k**;
5: 8 have bought back our Jewish **k** who had been sold
12:36 and his **k**, Shemaiah, Azarel,
Est 2:10 Esther did not reveal her people or **k**,
2:20 Now Esther had not revealed her **k** or her people,
8: 6 Or how can I bear to see the destruction of my **k**?"
10: 3 among the Jews and popular with his many **k**,
Ps 69: 8 I have become a stranger to my **k**,
133: 1 and pleasant it is when **k** live together in unity!
Pr 27:10 to the house of your **k** in the day of your calamity.
27:10 a neighbor who is nearby than **k** who are far away.
Isa 9:20 they devoured the flesh of their own **k**;
66:20 They shall bring all your **k** from all the nations as
Mic 5: 3 the rest of his **k** shall return to the people of Israel.
Ro 9: 3 my **k** according to the flesh.
Heb 7: 5 from the people, that is, from their **k**, though these
Tob 1: 3 of charity for my **k** and my people who had gone
1: 5 All my **k** and our ancestral house
1:10 everyone of my **k** and my people ate the food of
1:16 I performed many acts of charity to my **k**,
2:10 All my **k** were sorry for me,
3:15 or other **k** for whom I should keep myself as wife.
4:12 all took wives from among their **k**.
4:13 So now, my son, love your **k**,
4:13 and in your heart do not disdain your **k**,
5: 5 "From your **k**, the Israelites," he replied,
5: 9 a man who is one of our own Israelite **k**!"
5:14 Your **k** are good people; you come of good stock.
14: 4 All of our **k**, inhabitants of the land of Israel,
Jdt 8:22 The slaughter of our **k** and the captivity of the land
8:24 my brothers, let us set an example for our **k**,
16:24 and to her own nearest **k**.
Wis 7: 3 and fell upon the **k** earth;
Sir 40:24 **K** and helpers are for a time of trouble,
1Mc 2:40 "If we all do as our **k** have done and refuse to fight
2:41 not all die as our **k** died in their hiding places."
5:13 and all our **k** who were in the land
5:16 for their **k** who were in distress
5:17 "Choose your men and go and rescue your **k**
5:25 and told them all that had happened to their **k**
5:32 to the men of his forces, "Fight today for your **k**!"
6:22 to do justice and to avenge our **k**?
9: 9 and let us come back with our **k** and fight them;
9:10 If our time has come, let us die bravely for our **k**,
9:66 He struck down Odomera and his **k** and the people
2Mc 1: 1 To their Jewish **k** in Egypt,
5: 6 not realizing that success at the cost of one's **k** is
8: 1 the villages and summoned their **k**
10:21 and accused these men of having sold their **k**
11: 7 the others to risk their lives with him to aid their **k**.
12: 6 attacked the murderers of his **k**.
12:25 they let him go, for the sake of saving their **k**.
12:39 the fallen and to bring them back to lie with their **k**
1Es 1: 4 prepare yourselves by your families and **k**,
1: 5 who minister before your **k** the people of Israel,
1: 6 and prepare the sacrifices for your **k**,
1:10 stood in proper order according to **k**
1:13 the passover for themselves and for their **k**
1Es 1:14 for themselves and for their **k** the priests,
1:16 their **k** the Levites prepared the passover for them.
3:22 to be friendly with friends and **k**,
4:61 and went to Babylon and told this to all his **k**.
5: 3 all their **k** were making merry.
5:56 together with their **k** and the levitical priests
5:58 and his sons and **k** and his brother Kadmiel and
5:58 with their sons and **k**, all the Levites,
7: 9 according to **k**, for the services of the Lord God
7:12 the returned captives and for their **k** the priests and
8:16 Whatever you and your **k** are minded to do with
8:46 and ordered them to tell Iddo and his **k** and
8:77 we with our **k** and our kings
9:19 of Jeshua son of Jozadak and his **k**,
3Mc 4:12 to lament bitterly the ignoble misfortune of their **k**,
2Es 7:*103* brothers for brothers, relatives for their **k**,

KINDRED[S] (KJV) See also BIRTH, FAMILY, FELLOW EXILES, KINSMAN, RACE, RELATIVES, TRIBE

KINDS‡ (54) [KIND]

Ge 4:22 who made all **k** of bronze and iron tools.
6:20 to their **k**, and of the animals according to their **k**,
24:10 taking all **k** of choice gifts from his master;
Lev 19:19 you shall not sow your field with two **k** of seed;
19:23 into the land and plant all **k** of trees for food,
Dt 25:13 You shall not have in your bag two **k** of weights,
25:14 not have in your house two **k** of measures,
2Ki 8: 9 all **k** of goods of Damascus, forty camel loads.
1Ch 22:15 carpenters, and all **k** of artisans without number,
2Ch 16:14 on a bier that had been filled with various **k**
32:27 for shields, and for all **k** of costly objects;
32:28 and stalls for all **k** of cattle, and sheepfolds.
Ne 13:15 and also wine, grapes, figs, and all **k** of burdens,
13:16 in fish and all **k** of merchandise and sold them on
13:20 and sellers of all **k** of merchandise spent
Est 1: 7 of different **k**, and the royal wine was lavished
Ps 45:13 with all **k** of wealth. The princess is decked in her
Pr 1:13 We shall find all **k** of costly things;
Ecc 2: 5 and planted in them all **k** of fruit trees.
Jer 15: 3 And I will appoint over them four **k** of destroyers,
Eze 8:10 were all **k** of creeping things,
27:22 they exchanged for your wares the best of all **k**
39:20 with warriors and all **k** of soldiers,
44:30 The first of all the first fruits of all **k**,
44:30 and every offering of all **k** from all your offerings,
47:10 its fish will be of a great many **k**,
47:12 there will grow all **k** of trees for food.
Mt 5:11 and utter all **k** of evil against you falsely
23:27 of the bones of the dead and of all **k** of filth.
Lk 4:40 with various **k** of diseases brought them to him;
11:42 For you tithe mint and rue and herbs of all **k**,
12:15 Be on your guard against all **k** of greed;
Ac 10:12 In it were all **k** of four-footed creatures and reptiles
Ro 7: 8 produced in me all **k** of covetousness.
1Co 12:10 to another various **k** of tongues,
12:28 forms of leadership, various **k** of tongues.
14:10 There are doubtless many different **k** of sounds in
1Ti 6:10 For the love of money is a root of all **k** of evil,
2Ti 3: 6 overwhelmed by their sins and swayed by all **k**
Heb 13: 9 not be carried away by all **k** of strange teachings;
1Pe 5: 9 the world are undergoing the same **k** of suffering.
Rev 18:12 purple, silk and scarlet, all **k** of scented wood,
22: 2 the river is the tree of life with its twelve **k** of fruit,
Sir 16:30 With all **k** of living beings he covered its surface,
23:16 Two **k** of individuals multiply sins,
25: 2 I hate three **k** of people, and I loathe their manner
36:24 As the palate tastes the **k** of game,
43:25 all **k** of living things, and huge sea-monsters.
50: 9 like a vessel of hammered gold studded with all **k**
2Mc 5: 3 the flash of golden trappings, and armor of all **k**.
3Mc 7:16 in words of praise and all **k** of melodious songs.
4Mc 1:14 how many **k** of emotions there are,
1:18 Now the **k** of wisdom are rational judgment,

KINE (KJV) See CATTLE, COWS, HERD

KING‡ (2922) [KING'S, KINGDOM, KINGDOMS, KINGLY, KINGS, KINGS', KINGSHIP]

A. KING OF BABYLON (85)
B. KING OF ISRAEL (82)
C. KING OF ASSYRIA (63)
D. *LORD THE KING (63)
E. KING SOLOMON (54)
F. KING NEBUCHADNEZZAR (50)
G. KING DAVID (49)
H. KING OF EGYPT (48)
I. KING HEZEKIAH (31)
J. KING ZEDEKIAH (31)
K. KING NEBUCHADREZZAR (29)
L. KING OVER [ALL] ISRAEL (29)
M. KING OF JUDAH (20)
N. GREAT KING (18)
O. KING OF THE JEWS (18)
P. KING OF KINGS (8)

Ge 14: 1 In the days of **K** Amraphel of Shinar, **K** Arioch of
Ellasar, **K** Chedorlaomer of Elam, and **K** Tidal of
14: 2 these kings made war with **K** Bera of Sodom, **K**
Birsha of Gomorrah, **K** Shinab of Admah, **K**
Shemeber of Zeboiim, and the **k** of Bela

Ge 14: 8 Then the **k** of Sodom, the **k** of Gomorrah, the **k** of Admah, the **k** of Zeboiim, and the **k** of Bela
14: 9 with **K** Chedorlaomer of Elam, **K** Tidal of Goiim, **K** Amraphel of Shinar, and **K** Arioch of Ellasar,
14:17 the **k** of Sodom went out to meet him at the Valley
14:18 And **K** Melchizedek of Salem brought out bread
14:21 Then the **k** of Sodom said to Abram,
14:22 But Abram said to the **k** of Sodom,
20: 2 And **K** Abimelech of Gerar sent and took Sarah.
26: 1 to **K** Abimelech of the Philistines.
26: 8 **K** Abimelech of the Philistines looked out of
36:31 before any **k** reigned over the Israelites.
36:33 Jobab son of Zerah of Bozrah succeeded him as **k.**
36:34 of the land of the Temanites succeeded him as **k.**
36:35 in the country of Moab, succeeded him as **k,**
36:36 and Samlah of Masrekah succeeded him as **k.**
36:37 of Rehoboth on the Euphrates succeeded him as **k.**
36:38 and Baal-hanan son of Achbor succeeded him as **k.**
36:39 and Hadar succeeded him as **k,**
40: 1 of the **k** of Egypt and his baker offended their H
40: 1 his baker offended their lord the **k** of Egypt. DH
40: 5 the cupbearer and the baker of the **k** of Egypt, H
41:46 he entered the service of Pharaoh **k** of Egypt. H
Ex 1: 8 new **k** arose over Egypt, who did not know Joseph.
1:15 The **k** of Egypt said to the Hebrew midwives, H
1:17 not do as the **k** of Egypt commanded them, H
1:18 the **k** of Egypt summoned the midwives and said H
2:23 After a long time the **k** of Egypt died. H
3:18 Israel shall go to the **k** of Egypt and say to him, H
3:19 the **k** of Egypt will not let you go unless H
5: 4 But the **k** of Egypt said to them, H
6:11 "Go and tell Pharaoh **k** of Egypt to let H
6:13 the Israelites and Pharaoh **k** of Egypt, H
6:27 to Pharaoh **k** of Egypt to bring the Israelites out H
6:29 tell Pharaoh **k** of Egypt all that I am speaking H
14: 5 the **k** of Egypt was told that the people had fled, H
14: 8 the heart of Pharaoh **k** of Egypt and he pursued H
Nu 20:14 to the **k** of Edom, "Thus says your brother Israel:
21: 1 When the Canaanite, the **k** of Arad,
21:21 Israel sent messengers to **K** Sihon of the Amorites,
21:26 Heshbon was the city of **K** Sihon of the Amorites,
21:26 the former **k** of Moab and captured all his land
21:29 and his daughters captives, to an Amorite **k,** Sihon.
21:33 and **K** Og of Bashan came out against them,
21:34 to him as you did to **K** Sihon of the Amorites,
22: 4 Balak son of Zippor was **k** of Moab at that time.
22:10 "**K** Balak son of Zippor of Moab,
23: 7 the **k** of Moab from the eastern mountains:
23:21 acclaimed as a **k** among them.
24: 7 his **k** shall be higher than Agag,
32:33 the kingdom of **K** Sihon of the Amorites and the kingdom of **K** Og of Bashan,
33:40 The Canaanite, the **k** of Arad,
Dt 1: 4 after he had defeated **K** Sihon of the Amorites,
1: 4 who reigned in Heshbon, and **K** Og of Bashan,
2:24 I have handed over to you **K** Sihon the Amorite
2:26 to **K** Sihon of Heshbon with the following terms
2:30 But **K** Sihon of Heshbon was not willing
3: 1 **K** Og of Bashan came out against us,
3: 2 Do to him as you did to **K** Sihon of the Amorites,
3: 3 the LORD our God also handed over to us **K** Og
3: 6 as we had done to **K** Sihon of Heshbon,
3:11 (Now only **K** Og of Bashan was left of
4:46 in the land of **K** Sihon of the Amorites,
4:47 of **K** Og of Bashan, the two kings of the Amorites
7: 8 from the hand of Pharaoh **k** of Egypt. H
11: 3 the **k** of Egypt, and to all his land; H
17:14 and you say, "I will set a **k** over me,
17:15 a **k** whom the LORD your God will choose.
17:15 One of your own community you may set as **k**
28:36 and the **k** whom you set over you,
29: 7 **K** Sihon of Heshbon and King Og
29: 7 and **K** Og of Bashan came out against us for battle,
33: 5 There arose a **k** in Jeshurun,
Jos 2: 2 The **k** of Jericho was told,
2: 3 Then the **k** of Jericho sent orders to Rahab,
6: 2 along with its **k** and soldiers.
8: 1 over to you the **k** of Ai with his people,
8: 2 You shall do to Ai and its **k** as you did to Jericho
8: 2 to Ai and its king as you did to Jericho and its **k;**
8:14 When the **k** of Ai saw this, he and all his people,
8:23 the **k** of Ai was taken alive and brought to Joshua.
8:29 And he hanged the **k** of Ai on a tree until evening;
9:10 the Jordan, **K** Sihon of Heshbon, and King Og
9:10 and **K** Og of Bashan who lived in Ashtaroth.
10: 1 When **K** Adoni-zedek of Jerusalem heard
10: 1 and its **k** as he had done to Jericho and its **k,**
10: 3 So **K** Adoni-zedek of Jerusalem sent a message
10: 3 a message to **K** Hoham of Hebron, to **K** Piram of Jarmuth, to **K** Japhia of Lachish, and to **K** Debir
10: 5 the **k** of Jerusalem, the **k** of Hebron, the **k** of Jarmuth, the **k** of Lachish, and the **k** of Eglon—
10:23 the **k** of Jerusalem, the **k** of Hebron, the **k** of Jarmuth, the **k** of Lachish, and the **k** of Eglon.
10:28 and struck it and its **k** with the edge of the sword;
10:28 did to the **k** of Makkedah as he had done to the **k**
10:30 The LORD gave it also and its **k** into the hand
10:30 to its **k** as he had done to the **k** of Jericho.
10:33 Then **K** Horam of Gezer came up to help Lachish;
10:37 and its **k** and its towns, and every person in it;
10:39 and he took it with its **k** and all its towns;
10:39 to Libnah and its **k,** so he did to Debir and its **k.**
11: 1 When **K** Jabin of Hazor heard of this, he sent to **K** Jobab of Madon, to the **k** of Shimron, to the **k** of Achshaph,
11:10 and struck its **k** down with the sword.
12: 2 **K** Sihon of the Amorites who lived at Heshbon,
Jos 12: 4 and **K** Og of Bashan, one of the last of
12: 5 of Gilead to the boundary of **K** Sihon of Heshbon.
12: 9 the **k** of Jericho one the **k** of Ai, which is next to
12:10 the **k** of Jerusalem one the **k** of Hebron one
12:11 the **k** of Jarmuth one the **k** of Lachish one
12:12 the **k** of Eglon one the **k** of Gezer one
12:13 the **k** of Debir one the **k** of Geder one
12:14 the **k** of Hormah one the **k** of Arad one
12:15 the **k** of Libnah one the **k** of Adullam one
12:16 the **k** of Makkedah one the **k** of Bethel one
12:17 the **k** of Tappuah one the **k** of Hepher one
12:18 the **k** of Aphek one the **k** of Lasharon one
12:19 the **k** of Madon one the **k** of Hazor one
12:20 **k** of Shimron-meron one the **k** of Achshaph one
12:21 the **k** of Taanach one the **k** of Megiddo one
12:22 the **k** of Kedesh one the **k** of Jokneam in Carmel
12:23 the **k** of Dor in Naphath-dor one the **k** of Goiim
12:24 the **k** of Tirzah one thirty-one kings in all.
13:10 the cities of **K** Sihon of the Amorites, who reigned
13:21 and all the kingdom of **K** Sihon of the Amorites,
13:27 the rest of the kingdom of **K** Sihon of Heshbon,
13:30 the whole kingdom of **K** Og of Bashan,
24: 9 Then **K** Balak son of Zippor of Moab,
Jdg 3: 8 of **K** Cushan-rishathaim of Aram-naharaim;
3:10 to war, and the LORD gave **K** Cushan-rishathaim
3:12 and the LORD strengthened **K** Eglon of Moab
3:14 Israelites served **K** Eglon of Moab eighteen years.
3:15 Israelites sent tribute by him to **K** Eglon of Moab.
3:17 Then he presented the tribute to **K** Eglon of Moab.
3:19 and said, "I have a secret message for you, O **k.**"
3:19 So the **k** said, "Silence!"
4: 2 So the LORD sold them into the hand of **K** Jabin
4:17 for there was peace between **K** Jabin of Hazor and
4:23 that day God subdued **K** Jabin of Canaan before
4:24 of the Israelites bore harder and harder on **K** Jabin
4:24 until they destroyed **K** Jabin of Canaan.
8:18 they resembled the sons of a **k.**"
9: 6 and they went and made Abimelech **k,**
9: 8 trees once went out to anoint a **k** over themselves.
9:15 'If in good faith you are anointing me **k** over you,
9:16 and honor when you made Abimelech **k,** and
9:18 **k** over the lords of Shechem,
11:12 Then Jephthah sent messengers to the **k** of
11:13 The **k** of the Ammonites answered the messengers
11:14 Once again Jephthah sent messengers to the **k** of
11:17 Israel then sent messengers to the **k** of Edom,
11:17 but the **k** of Edom would not listen.
11:17 They also sent to the **k** of Moab,
11:19 then sent messengers to **K** Sihon of the Amorites, **k** of Heshbon;
11:25 Now are you any better than **K** Balak son
11:28 the **k** of the Ammonites did not heed the message
17: 6 In those days there was no **k** in Israel;
18: 1 In those days there was no **k** in Israel.
19: 1 In those days, when there was no **k** in Israel,
21:25 In those days there was no **k** in Israel;
1Sa 2:10 he will give strength to his **k,**
8: 5 appoint for us, then, a **k** to govern us,
8: 6 "Give us a **k** to govern us."
8: 7 but they have rejected me from being **k** over them.
8: 9 and show them the ways of the **k** who shall reign
8:10 to the people who were asking him for a **k.**
8:11 "These will be the ways of the **k** who will reign
8:18 And in that day you will cry out because of your **k,**
8:19 but we are determined to have a **k** over us,
8:20 and that our **k** may govern us and go out before us
8:22 "Listen to their voice and set a **k** over them."
10:19 but set a **k** over us.'
10:24 And all the people shouted, "Long live the **k!**"
10:27 Now Nahash, **k** of the Ammonites,
10:27 **k** of the Ammonites, had not gouged out.
11:15 and there they made Saul **k** before the LORD
12: 1 and have set a **k** over you.
12: 2 See, it is the **k** who leads you now;
12: 9 commander of the army of **K** Jabin of Hazor,
12: 9 and into the hand of the **k** of Moab;
12:12 that **K** Nahash of the Ammonites came
12:12 you said to me, 'No, but a **k** shall reign over us,'
12:12 though the LORD your God was your **k.**
12:13 See, here is the **k** whom you have chosen,
12:13 see, the LORD has set a **k** over you.
12:14 and the **k** who reigns over you will follow
12:15 hand of the LORD will be against you and your **k.**
12:17 the sight of the LORD is great in demanding a **k**
12:19 the evil of demanding a **k** for ourselves."
12:25 you shall be swept away, both you and your **k.**"
15: 1 to anoint you **k** over his people Israel;
15: 8 He took **K** Agag of the Amalekites alive,
15:11 "I regret that I made Saul **k,**
15:17 The LORD anointed you **k** over Israel. L
15:20 I have brought Agag the **k** of Amalek,
15:23 he has also rejected you from being **k.**"
15:26 LORD has rejected you from being **k** over Israel." L
15:32 "Bring Agag **k** of the Amalekites here to me."
15:35 was sorry that he had made Saul **k** over Israel. L
16: 1 I have rejected him from being **k** over Israel. L
16: 1 I have provided for myself a **k** among his sons."
17:25 The **k** will greatly enrich the man who kills him,
17:55 Abner said, "As your soul lives, O **k,**
17:56 The **k** said, "Inquire whose son the stripling is."
18: 6 singing and dancing, to meet **K** Saul,
18:18 that I should be son-in-law to the **k?**"
18:22 'See, the **k** is delighted with you,
18:25 'The **k** desires no marriage present except
18:27 which were given in full number to the **k,**
19: 4 "The **k** should not sin against his servant David,
20: 5 and I should not fail to sit with the **k** at the meal;
1Sa 20:24 the new moon came, the **k** sat at the feast to eat.
20:25 The **k** sat upon his seat, as at other times,
21: 2 "The **k** has charged me with a matter,
21:10 he went to **K** Achish of Gath.
21:11 "Is this not David the **k** of the land?
21:12 and was very much afraid of **K** Achish of Gath.
22: 3 He said to the **k** of Moab,
22: 4 He left them with the **k** of Moab,
22:11 The **k** sent for the priest Ahimelech son of Ahitub
22:11 and all of them came to the **k.**
22:14 Then Ahimelech answered the **k,**
22:15 Do not let the **k** impute anything to his servant or
22:16 The **k** said, "You shall surely die, Ahimelech,
22:17 The **k** said to the guard who stood around him,
22:17 But the servants of the **k** would not raise their hand
22:18 Then the **k** said to Doeg, "You, Doeg,
23:17 you shall be **k** over Israel, and I shall be second L
23:20 O **k,** whenever you wish to come down, do so;
24: 8 the cave and called after Saul, "My lord the **k!**" D
24:14 Against whom has the **k** of Israel come out? B
24:20 Now I know that you shall surely be **k,**
25:36 a feast in his house, like the feast of a **k.**
26:14 Abner replied, "Who are you that calls to the **k?**"
26:15 not kept watch over your lord the **k?** D
26:15 of the people came in to destroy your lord the **k.** D
26:17 David said, "It is my voice, my lord, O **k.**"
26:19 let my lord the **k** hear the words of his servant. D
26:20 the **k** of Israel has come out to seek a single flea, B
26:22 David replied, "Here is the spear, O **k!**
27: 2 to **K** Achish son of Maoch of Gath.
28:13 **k** said to her, "Have no fear; what do you see?"
29: 3 "Is this not David, the servant of **K** Saul of Israel,
29: 8 fight against the enemies of my lord the **k?**" D
2Sa 2: 4 and there they anointed David **k** over the house
2: 7 the house of Judah has anointed me **k** over them."
2: 9 He made him **k** over Gilead, the Ashurites, Jezreel,
2:11 that David was **k** in Hebron over the house
3: 3 daughter of **K** Talmai of Geshur;
3:17 past you have been seeking David as **k** over you.
3:21 "Let me go and rally all Israel to my lord the **k,** D
3:23 it was told Joab, "Abner son of Ner came to the **k,**
3:24 Joab went to the **k** and said, "What have you done?
3:31 And **K** David followed the bier. G
3:32 The **k** lifted up his voice and wept at the grave
3:33 The **k** lamented for Abner, saying,
3:36 just as everything the **k** did pleased all the people.
3:37 that the **k** had no part in the killing of Abner son
3:38 And the **k** said to his servants,
3:39 Today I am powerless, even though anointed **k;**
4: 8 and said to the **k,** "Here is the head of Ishbaal, son
4: 8 the LORD has avenged my lord the **k** this day D
5: 2 For some time, while Saul was **k** over us,
5: 3 So all the elders of Israel came to the **k** at Hebron;
5: 3 and **K** David made a covenant with them G
5: 3 and they anointed David **k** over Israel. L
5: 6 The **k** and his men marched to Jerusalem against
5:11 **K** Hiram of Tyre sent messengers to David,
5:12 that the LORD had established him **k** over Israel, L
5:17 that David had been anointed **k** over Israel, all L
6:12 It was told **K** David, "The LORD has blessed G
6:16 and saw **K** David leaping and dancing before G
6:20 "How the **k** of Israel honored himself today, B
7: 1 Now when the **k** was settled in his house,
7: 2 the **k** said to the prophet Nathan,
7: 3 Nathan said to the **k,** "Go,
7:18 Then **K** David went in and sat before the LORD, G
8: 3 also struck down **K** Hadadezer son of Rehob
8: 5 of Damascus came to help **K** Hadadezer of Zobah,
8: 8 **K** David took a great amount of bronze. G
8: 9 When **K** Toi of Hamath heard
8:10 Toi sent his son Joram to **K** David, G
8:11 these also **K** David dedicated to the LORD, G
8:12 the spoil of **K** Hadadezer son of Rehob of Zobah.
9: 2 The **k** said to him, "Are you Ziba?"
9: 3 The **k** said, "Is there anyone remaining of
9: 3 to the **k,** "There remains a son of Jonathan;
9: 4 The **k** said to him, "Where is he?"
9: 4 to the **k,** "He is in the house of Machir son
9: 5 Then **K** David sent and brought him from G
9: 9 Then the **k** summoned Saul's servant Ziba,
9:11 Then Ziba said to the **k,**
9:11 to all that my lord the **k** commands his servant, D
10: 1 the **k** of the Ammonites died,
10: 5 The **k** said, "Remain at Jericho
10: 6 as well as the **k** of Maacah, one thousand men,
11: 8 and there followed him a present from the **k.**
11:19 "When you have finished telling the **k** all the news
12: 7 I anointed you **k** over Israel, L
13: 4 He said to him, "O son of the **k,**
13: 6 and when the **k** came to see him,
13: 6 the king came to see him, Amnon said to the **k,**
13:13 Now therefore, I beg you, speak to the **k;**
13:18 how the virgin daughters of the **k** were clothed
13:21 When **K** David heard of all these things, G
13:24 Absalom came to the **k,** and said,
13:24 will the **k** and his servants please go
13:25 But the **k** said to Absalom, "No, my son,
13:26 The **k** said to him, "Why should he go with you?"
13:31 **k** rose, tore his garments, and lay on the ground;
13:33 do not let my lord the **k** take it to heart, D
13:35 Jonadab said to the **k,** "See,
13:36 the **k** and all his servants also wept very bitterly.
13:37 and went to Talmai son of Ammihud, **k** of Geshur.
13:39 the heart of the **k** went out, yearning for Absalom;
14: 3 Go to the **k** and speak to him as follows."
14: 4 When the woman of Tekoa came to the **k,**
14: 4 and did obeisance, and said, "Help, O **k!**"

2Sa 14: 5 The **k** asked her, "What is your trouble?"
14: 8 Then the **k** said to the woman, "Go to your house,
14: 9 The woman of Tekoa said to the **k**,
14: 9 my lord the **k**, and on my father's house; D
14: 9 let the **k** and his throne be guiltless."
14:10 The **k** said, "If anyone says anything to you,
14:11 may the **k** keep the LORD your God in mind,
14:12 a word to my lord the **k**." D
14:13 For in giving this decision the **k** convicts himself,
14:13 the **k** does not bring his banished one home again.
14:15 I have come to say this to my lord the **k** because D
14:15 your servant thought, 'I will speak to the **k**;
14:15 that the **k** will perform the request of his servant.
14:16 For the **k** will hear, and deliver his servant from
14:17 'The word of my lord the **k** will set me at rest'; D
14:17 for my lord the **k** is like the angel of God, D
14:18 Then the **k** answered the woman,
14:18 The woman said, "Let my lord the **k** speak." D
14:19 **k** said, "Is the hand of Joab with you in all this?"
14:19 "As surely as you live, my lord the **k**, D
14:19 or left from anything that my lord the **k** has said. D
14:21 Then the **k** said to Joab, "Very well, I grant this;
14:22 the ground and did obeisance, and blessed the **k**;
14:22 in your sight, my lord the **k**, D
14:22 in that the **k** has granted the request of his servant."
14:24 The **k** said, "Let him go to his own house;
14:29 Then Absalom sent for Joab to send him to the **k**;
14:32 that I may send you to the **k** with the question,
14:33 Then Joab went to the **k** and told him;
14:33 to the **k** and prostrated himself with his face to the ground before the **k**;
14:33 and the **k** kissed Absalom.
15: 2 anyone brought a suit before the **k** for judgment,
15: 3 but there is no one deputed by the **k** to hear you."
15: 6 to every Israelite who came to the **k** for judgment;
15: 7 At the end of four years Absalom said to the **k**,
15: 9 The **k** said to him, "Go in peace."
15:10 Absalom has become **k** at Hebron!"
15:15 The king's officials said to the **k**,
15:15 to do whatever our lord the **k** decides." D
15:16 So the **k** left, followed by all his household,
15:17 The **k** left, followed by all the people;
15:18 from Gath, passed on before the **k**.
15:19 Then the **k** said to Ittai the Gittite,
15:19 Go back, and stay with the **k**;
15:21 But Ittai answered the **k**, "As the LORD lives,
15:21 "As the LORD lives, and as my lord the **k** lives, D
15:21 wherever my lord the **k** may be, D
15:23 the **k** crossed the Wadi Kidron,
15:25 Then the **k** said to Zadok,
15:27 The **k** also said to the priest Zadok, "Look,
15:34 'I will be your servant, O **k**;
16: 2 **k** said to Ziba, "Why have you brought these?"
16: 3 The **k** said, "And where is your master's son?"
16: 3 Ziba said to the **k**, "He remains in Jerusalem;
16: 4 Then the **k** said to Ziba,
16: 4 let me find favor in your sight, my lord the **k**." D
16: 5 When **K** David came to Bahurim, G
16: 6 at David and at all the servants of **K** David; G
16: 9 Then Abishai son of Zeruiah said to the **k**,
16: 9 "Why should this dead dog curse my lord the **k**? D
16:10 But the **k** said, "What have I to do with you,
16:14 The **k** and all the people who were
16:16 "Long live the **k**! Long live the **k**!"
17: 2 I will strike down only the **k**,
17:16 the **k** and all the people who are with him will
17:17 and they would go and tell **K** David; G
17:21 and went and told **K** David. G
18: 2 The **k** said to the men,
18: 4 The **k** said to them, "Whatever seems best
18: 4 So the **k** stood at the side of the gate,
18: 5 The **k** ordered Joab and Abishai and Ittai, saying,
18: 5 And all the people heard when the **k** gave orders
18:12 in our hearing the **k** commanded you and Abishai
18:13 (and there is nothing hidden from the **k**),
18:19 to the **k** that the LORD has delivered him from
18:21 "Go, tell the **k** what you have seen."
18:25 The sentinel shouted and told the **k**.
18:25 The **k** said, "If he is alone
18:26 The **k** said, "He also is bringing tidings."
18:27 The **k** said, "He is a good man,
18:28 Then Ahimaaz cried out to the **k**, "All is well!"
18:28 He prostrated himself before the **k** with his face to
18:28 who raised their hand against my lord the **k**." D
18:29 **k** said, "Is it well with the young man Absalom?"
18:30 The **k** said, "Turn aside, and stand here."
18:31 Cushite said, "Good tidings for my lord the **k**! D
18:32 The **k** said to the Cushite,
18:32 "May the enemies of my lord the **k**, D
18:33 The **k** was deeply moved, and went up to
19: 1 "The **k** is weeping and mourning for Absalom."
19: 2 "The **k** is grieving for his son."
19: 4 The **k** covered his face, and the **k** cried
19: 5 Then Joab came into the house to the **k**, and said,
19: 8 Then the **k** got up and took his seat in the gate.
19: 8 "See, the **k** is sitting in the gate";
19: 8 and all the troops came before the **k**.
19: 9 "The **k** delivered us from the hand of our enemies,
19:10 about bringing the **k** back?"
19:11 **K** David sent this message to the priests Zadok G
19:11 'Why should you be the last to bring the **k** back
19:11 The talk of all Israel has come to the **k**.
19:12 then should you be the last to bring back the **k**?'
19:14 and they sent word to the **k**, "Return,
19:15 So the **k** came back to the Jordan;
19:15 to meet the **k** and to bring him over the Jordan.
19:16 down with the people of Judah to meet **K** David; G

2Sa 19:17 rushed down to the Jordan ahead of the **k**,
19:18 Shimei son of Gera fell down before the **k**,
19:19 and said to the **k**, "May my lord not hold me guilty
19:19 on the day my lord the **k** left Jerusalem; D
19:19 may the **k** not bear it in mind.
19:20 of Joseph to come down to meet my lord the **k**." D
19:22 do I not know that I am this day **k** over Israel?" L
19:23 The **k** said to Shimei, "You shall not die."
19:23 And the **k** gave him his oath.
19:24 of Saul came down to meet the **k**;
19:24 or washed his clothes, from the day the **k** left until
19:25 When he came from Jerusalem to meet the **k**,
19:25 the **k** said to him, "Why did you not go with me,
19:26 He answered, "My lord, O **k**,
19:26 so that I may ride on it and go with the **k**.'
19:27 He has slandered your servant to my lord the **k**. D
19:27 But my lord the **k** is like the angel of God; D
19:28 to death before my lord the **k**; D
19:28 further right have I, then, to appeal to the **k**?"
19:29 The **k** said to him, "Why speak any more
19:30 Mephibosheth said to the **k**, "Let him take it all,
19:30 since my lord the **k** has arrived home safely." D
19:31 he went on with the **k** to the Jordan,
19:32 He had provided the **k** with food while he stayed
19:33 The **k** said to Barzillai, "Come over with me,
19:34 But Barzillai said to the **k**,
19:34 that I should go up with the **k** to Jerusalem?
19:35 be an added burden to my lord the **k**? D
19:36 a little way over the Jordan with the **k**.
19:36 Why should the **k** recompense me with such
19:37 let him go over with my lord the **k**; D
19:38 The **k** answered, "Chimham shall go over with me,
19:39 over the Jordan, and the **k** crossed over;
19:39 the **k** kissed Barzillai and blessed him,
19:40 The **k** went on to Gilgal, and Chimham went on
19:40 and also half the people of Israel, brought the **k**
19:41 Then all the people of Israel came to the **k**,
19:41 brought the **k** and his household over the Jordan,
19:42 "Because the **k** is near of kin to us.
19:43 "We have ten shares in the **k**,
19:43 not the first to speak of bringing back our **k**?"
20: 2 but the people of Judah followed their **k** steadfastly
20: 3 the **k** took the ten concubines whom he had left
20: 4 Then the **k** said to Amasa,
20:21 has lifted up his hand against **K** David; G
20:22 while Joab returned to Jerusalem to the **k**.
21: 2 So the **k** called the Gibeonites and spoke to them.
21: 5 to the **k**, "The man who consumed us and planned
21: 6 The **k** said, "I will hand them over."
21: 7 But the **k** spared Mephibosheth,
21: 8 **k** took the two sons of Rizpah daughter of Aiah,
21:14 they did all that the **k** commanded.
22:51 He is a tower of salvation for his **k**,
24: 2 **k** said to Joab and the commanders of the army,
24: 3 But Joab said to the **k**,
24: 3 while the eyes of my lord the **k** can still see it! D
24: 3 But why does my lord the **k** want to do this?" D
24: 4 the presence of the **k** to take a census of the people
24: 9 the **k** the number of those who had been recorded:
24:20 he saw the **k** and his servants coming toward him;
24:20 and prostrated himself before the **k** with his face
24:21 "Why has my lord the **k** come to his servant?" D
24:22 lord the **k** take and offer up what seems good D
24:23 All this, O **k**, Araunah gives to the king."
24:23 All this, O king, Araunah gives to the **k**."
24:23 And Araunah said to the **k**,
24:24 But the **k** said to Araunah, "No,
1Ki 1: 1 **K** David was old and advanced in years; G
1: 2 "Let a young virgin be sought for my lord the **k**, D
1: 2 and let her wait on the **k**, and be his attendant;
1: 2 so that my lord the **k** may be warm." D
1: 3 and brought her to the **k**.
1: 4 but the **k** did not know her sexually.
1: 5 of Haggith exalted himself, saying, "I will be **k**";
1:11 of Haggith has become **k** and our lord David does
1:13 Go in at once to **K** David, and say to him, G
1:13 you not, my lord the **k**, swear to your servant, D
1:13 Your son Solomon shall succeed me as **k**,
1:13 Why then is Adonijah **k**?'
1:14 Then while you are still there speaking with the **k**,
1:15 So Bathsheba went to the **k** in his room.
1:15 in his room. The **k** was very old;
1:15 Abishag the Shunammite was attending the **k**.
1:16 Bathsheba bowed and did obeisance to the **k**,
1:16 and the **k** said, "What do you wish?"
1:17 Your son Solomon shall succeed me as **k**,
1:18 But now suddenly Adonijah has become **k**,
1:18 though you, my lord the **k**, do not know it. D
1:19 and has invited all the children of the **k**,
1:20 But you, my lord the **k**—the eyes of all D
1:20 on the throne of my lord the **k** after him. D
1:21 when my lord the **k** sleeps with his ancestors, D
1:22 While she was still speaking with the **k**,
1:23 The **k** was told, "Here is the prophet Nathan."
1:23 When he came in before the **k**,
1:23 he did obeisance to the **k**,
1:24 Nathan said, "My lord the **k**, have you said, D
1:24 have you said, 'Adonijah shall succeed me as **k**,
1:25 and saying, 'Long live **K** Adonijah!'
1:27 this thing been brought about by my lord the **k** D
1:27 on the throne of my lord the **k** after him?" D
1:28 **K** David answered, "Summon Bathsheba to me. G
1:28 into the king's presence, and stood before the **k**.
1:29 The **k** swore, saying, "As the LORD lives,
1:30 'Your son Solomon shall succeed me as **k**,
1:31 and did obeisance to the **k**, and said,
1:31 and said, "May my lord **K** David live forever!" G

1Ki 1:32 **K** David said, "Summon to me the priest Zadok, G
1:32 When they came before the **k**,
1:33 the **k** said to them, "Take with you the servants
1:34 and the prophet Nathan anoint him **k** over Israel; L
1:34 and say, 'Long live **K** Solomon!' E
1:35 he shall be **k** in my place;
1:36 Benaiah son of Jehoiada answered the **k**, "Amen!
1:36 May the LORD, the God of my lord the **k**, D
1:37 As the LORD has been with my lord the **k**, D
1:37 the throne of my lord **K** David." G
1:38 down and had Solomon ride on **K** David's mule,
1:39 and all the people said, "Long live **K** Solomon!" E
1:43 for our lord **K** David has made Solomon king; G
1:43 for our lord King David has made Solomon **k**;
1:44 the **k** has sent with him the priest Zadok,
1:45 the prophet Nathan have anointed him **k** at Gihon;
1:47 to congratulate our lord **K** David, G
1:47 The **k** bowed in worship on the bed
1:51 "Adonijah is afraid of **K** Solomon; E
1:51 altar, saying, 'Let **K** Solomon swear to me first E
1:53 **K** Solomon sent to have him brought down E
1:53 He came to do obeisance to **K** Solomon; E
2:17 He said, "Please ask **K** Solomon— E
2:18 I will speak to the **k** on your behalf."
2:19 So Bathsheba went to **K** Solomon, E
2:19 The **k** rose to meet her, and bowed down to her;
2:20 the **k** said to her, "Make your request, my mother;
2:22 **K** Solomon answered his mother, E
2:23 Then **K** Solomon swore by the LORD, E
2:25 So **K** Solomon sent Benaiah son of Jehoiada; E
2:26 The **k** said to the priest Abiathar, "Go to Anathoth,
2:29 When it was told **K** Solomon, E
2:30 "The **k** commands, 'Come out.' "
2:30 Then Benaiah brought the **k** word again, saying,
2:31 The **k** replied to him, "Do as he has said,
2:35 The **k** put Benaiah son of Jehoiada over the army
2:35 the **k** put the priest Zadok in the place of Abiathar.
2:36 Then the **k** sent and summoned Shimei,
2:38 And Shimei said to the **k**, "The sentence is fair;
2:38 my lord the **k** has said, so will your servant do." D
2:39 of Shimei's slaves ran away to **K** Achish son
2:42 the **k** sent and summoned Shimei,
2:44 The **k** also said to Shimei,
2:45 But **K** Solomon shall be blessed, E
2:46 Then the **k** commanded Benaiah son of Jehoiada;
3: 1 a marriage alliance with Pharaoh **k** of Egypt; H
3: 4 The **k** went to Gibeon to sacrifice there,
3: 7 you have made your servant **k** in place
3:13 no other **k** shall compare with you.
3:16 two women who were prostitutes came to the **k**
3:22 So they argued before the **k**.
3:23 Then the **k** said, "The one says,
3:24 So the **k** said, "Bring me a sword," and they brought a sword before the **k**.
3:25 The **k** said, "Divide the living boy in two;
3:26 the woman whose son was alive said to the **k**—
3:27 the **k** responded: "Give the first woman the living
3:28 heard of the judgment that the **k** had rendered; and they stood in awe of the **k**,
4: 1 **K** Solomon was king over all Israel, E
4: 1 King Solomon was **k** over all Israel, L
4: 7 who provided food for the **k** and his household;
4:19 of **K** Sihon of the Amorites and of **K** Og
4:27 officials supplied provisions for **K** Solomon E
4:27 for all who came to **K** Solomon's table, each one
5: 1 **K** Hiram of Tyre sent his servants to Solomon,
5: 1 that they had anointed him **k** in place of his father;
5:13 **K** Solomon conscripted forced labor out E
6: 2 The house that **K** Solomon built for E
7:13 **K** Solomon invited and received Hiram from E
7:14 He came to **K** Solomon, and did all his work. E
7:40 the work that he did for **K** Solomon on the house E
7:45 all these vessels that Hiram made for **K** Solomon E
7:46 In the plain of the Jordan the **k** cast them,
7:51 the work that **K** Solomon did on the house of E
8: 1 before **K** Solomon in Jerusalem, E
8: 2 Israel assembled to **K** Solomon at the festival in E
8: 5 **K** Solomon and all the congregation of Israel, E
8:14 the **k** turned around and blessed all the assembly
8:62 Then the **k**, and all Israel with him,
8:63 So the **k** and all the people of Israel dedicated
8:64 the **k** consecrated the middle of the court that was
8:66 and they blessed the **k**, and went to their tents,
9:11 **K** Hiram of Tyre having supplied Solomon
9:11 **K** Solomon gave to Hiram twenty cities in the E
9:14 to the **k** one hundred twenty talents of gold.
9:15 **K** Solomon conscripted to build the house of E
9:16 (Pharaoh **k** of Egypt had gone up H
9:26 **K** Solomon built a fleet of ships at Ezion-geber, E
9:28 which they delivered to **K** Solomon. E
10: 3 there was nothing hidden from the **k** that he could
10: 6 So she said to the **k**,
10: 9 he has made you **k** to execute justice
10:10 she gave the **k** one hundred twenty talents of gold,
10:10 which the queen of Sheba gave to **K** Solomon. E
10:12 the almug wood the **k** made supports for the house
10:13 Meanwhile **K** Solomon gave to the queen E
10:16 **K** Solomon made two hundred large shields E
10:17 **k** put them in the House of the Forest of Lebanon.
10:18 The **k** also made a great ivory throne,
10:21 All **K** Solomon's drinking vessels were of gold,
10:22 the **k** had a fleet of ships of Tarshish at sea with
10:23 **K** Solomon excelled all the kings of the earth E
10:26 in the chariot cities and with the **k** in Jerusalem.
10:27 **k** made silver as common in Jerusalem as stones,
11: 1 **K** Solomon loved many foreign women along E
11:18 to Pharaoh **k** of Egypt, who gave him a house, H

1Ki 11:23 from his master, **K** Hadadezer of Zobah.
11:24 settled there, and made him **k** in Damascus.
11:26 a widow, rebelled against the **k.**
11:27 following was the reason he rebelled against the **k.**
11:37 you shall be **k** over Israel. L
11:40 to Egypt, to **K** Shishak of Egypt,
12: 1 all Israel had come to Shechem to make him **k.**
12: 2 where he had fled from **K** Solomon), E
12: 6 Then **K** Rehoboam took counsel with
12:12 the third day, as the **k** had said, "Come to me again
12:13 The **k** answered the people harshly.
12:15 So the **k** did not listen to the people,
12:16 all Israel saw that the **k** would not listen to them,
12:16 the people answered the **k,**
12:18 When **K** Rehoboam sent Adoram,
12:18 **K** Rehoboam then hurriedly mounted his chariot
12:20 the assembly and made him **k** over all Israel. L
12:23 Say to **K** Rehoboam of Judah,
12:27 to their master, **K** Rehoboam of Judah;
12:27 they will kill me and return to **K** Rehoboam
12:28 the **k** took counsel, and made two calves of gold.
13: 4 the **k** heard what the man of God cried out against
13: 6 The **k** said to the man of God,
13: 7 Then the **k** said to the man of God,
13: 8 But the man of God said to the **k,**
13:11 the words also that he had spoken to the **k,**
14: 2 who said of me that I should be **k** over this people.
14:14 LORD will raise up for himself a **k** over Israel, L
14:25 In the fifth year of **K** Rehoboam,
14:25 **K** Shishak of Egypt came up against Jerusalem;
14:27 so **K** Rehoboam made shields of bronze instead,
14:28 often as the **k** went into the house of the LORD,
15: 1 the eighteenth year of **K** Jeroboam son of Nebat,
15: 9 In the twentieth year of **K** Jeroboam of Israel,
15:16 between Asa and **K** Baasha of Israel all their days.
15:17 **K** Baasha of Israel went up against Judah,
15:17 from going out or coming in to **K** Asa of Judah.
15:18 **K** Asa sent them to **K** Ben-hadad
15:19 go, break your alliance with **K** Baasha of Israel,
15:20 Ben-hadad listened to **K** Asa,
15:22 Then **K** Asa made a proclamation to all Judah,
15:22 with them **K** Asa built Geba of Benjamin
15:25 over Israel in the second year of **K** Asa of Judah;
15:28 So Baasha killed Nadab in the third year of **K** Asa
15:29 as he was **k,** he killed all the house of Jeroboam;
15:32 between Asa and **K** Baasha of Israel all their days.
15:33 In the third year of **K** Asa of Judah,
16: 8 In the twenty-sixth year of **K** Asa of Judah,
16:10 in the twenty-seventh year of **K** Asa of Judah,
16:15 In the twenty-seventh year of **K** Asa of Judah,
16:16 "Zimri has conspired, and he has killed the **k";**
16:16 **k** over Israel that day in the camp. L
16:21 to make him **k,** and half followed Omri.
16:22 so Tibni died, and Omri became **k.**
16:23 In the thirty-first year of **K** Asa of Judah,
16:29 In the thirty-eighth year of **K** Asa of Judah,
16:31 he took as his wife Jezebel daughter of **K** Ethbaal
19:15 you shall anoint Hazael as **k** over Aram.
19:16 anoint Jehu son of Nimshi as **k** over Israel; L
20: 1 **K** Ben-hadad of Aram gathered all his army
20: 2 into the city to **K** Ahab of Israel, and said to him:
20: 4 The **k** of Israel answered, "As you say, my lord, B
20: 4 my lord, O **k,** I am yours, and all that I have."
20: 7 the **k** of Israel called all the elders of the land, B
20: 9 messengers of Ben-hadad, "Tell my lord the **k:** D
20:11 The **k** of Israel answered, "Tell him: B
20:13 a certain prophet came up to **K** Ahab of Israel
20:20 but **K** Ben-hadad of Aram escaped on a horse
20:21 The **k** of Israel went out, B
20:22 approached the **k** of Israel and said to him, B
20:22 for in the spring the **k** of Aram will come up
20:23 The servants of the **k** of Aram said to him,
20:28 of God approached and said to the **k** of Israel, B
20:31 and go out to the **k** of Israel; B
20:32 put ropes on their heads, went to the **k** of Israel, B
20:34 The **k** of Israel responded, B
20:38 and waited for the **k** along the road,
20:39 As the **k** passed by, he cried to the **k** and said,
20:40 **k** of Israel said to him, "So shall your judgment B
20:41 The **k** of Israel recognized him as one of the B
20:43 The **k** of Israel set out toward home, B
21: 1 beside the palace of **K** Ahab of Samaria.
21:10 saying, 'You have cursed God and the **k.'**
21:13 saying, "Naboth cursed God and the **k."**
21:18 to meet **K** Ahab of Israel, who rules in Samaria;
22: 2 But in the third year **K** Jehoshaphat of Judah
22: 2 of Judah came down to the **k** of Israel. B
22: 3 The **k** of Israel said to his servants, B
22: 3 to take it out of the hand of the **k** of Aram?"
22: 4 Jehoshaphat replied to the **k** of Israel, B
22: 5 But Jehoshaphat also said to the **k** of Israel, B
22: 6 the **k** of Israel gathered the prophets together, B
22: 6 for the LORD will give it into the hand of the **k."**
22: 8 The **k** of Israel said to Jehoshaphat, B
22: 8 Jehoshaphat said, "Let the **k** not say such a thing."
22: 9 Then the **k** of Israel summoned an officer and B
22:10 Now the **k** of Israel and King Jehoshaphat B
22:10 of Israel and **K** Jehoshaphat of Judah were sitting
22:12 the LORD will give it into the hand of the **k."**
22:13 with one accord are favorable to the **k;**
22:15 When he had come to the **k,** the **k** said to him,
22:15 the LORD will give it into the hand of the **k."**
22:16 But the **k** said to him,
22:18 The **k** of Israel said to Jehoshaphat, B
22:26 The **k** of Israel then ordered, "Take Micaiah, B
22:27 and say, 'Thus says the **k:** Put this fellow in prison,
22:29 the **k** of Israel and King Jehoshaphat of Judah B

1Ki 22:29 and **K** Jehoshaphat of Judah went up
22:30 The **k** of Israel said to Jehoshaphat, B
22:30 **k** of Israel disguised himself and went into B
22:31 Now the **k** of Aram had commanded
22:31 but only with the **k** of Israel." B
22:32 they said, "It is surely the **k** of Israel." B
22:33 of the chariots saw that it was not the **k** of Israel, B
22:34 and unknowingly struck the **k** of Israel between B
22:35 and the **k** was propped up in his chariot facing
22:37 So the **k** died, and was brought to Samaria;
22:37 they buried the **k** in Samaria.
22:41 over Judah in the fourth year of **K** Ahab of Israel.
22:44 Jehoshaphat also made peace with the **k** of Israel. B
22:47 There was no **k** in Edom; a deputy was **k.**
22:51 in the seventeenth year of **K** Jehoshaphat of Judah;
2Ki 1: 3 go to meet the messengers of the **k** of Samaria,
1: 5 The messengers returned to the **k,**
1: 6 'Go back to the **k** who sent you, and say to him:
1: 9 **k** sent to him a captain of fifty with his fifty men.
1: 9 "O man of God, the **k** says, 'Come down.' "
1:11 Again the **k** sent to him another captain of fifty
1:13 the **k** sent the captain of a third fifty with his fifty.
1:15 So he set out and went down with him to the **k,**
1:17 Jehoram succeeded him as **k** in the second year
1:17 the second year of **K** Jehoram son of Jehoshaphat
3: 1 In the eighteenth year of **K** Jehoshaphat of Judah,
3: 1 Jehoram son of Ahab became **k** over Israel L
3: 4 Now **K** Mesha of Moab was a sheep breeder,
3: 4 to the **k** of Israel one hundred thousand lambs, B
3: 5 the **k** of Moab rebelled against the king of Israel.
3: 5 the king of Moab rebelled against the **k** of Israel. B
3: 6 So **K** Jehoram marched out of Samaria at that time
3: 7 he went he sent word to **K** Jehoshaphat of Judah,
3: 7 "The **k** of Moab has rebelled against me;
3: 9 So the **k** of Israel, the king of Judah, B
3: 9 So the king of Israel, the **k** of Judah, M
3: 9 the king of Judah, and the **k** of Edom set out;
3:10 Then the **k** of Israel said, "Alas! B
3:11 one of the servants of the **k** of Israel answered, B
3:12 So the **k** of Israel and Jehoshaphat and B
3:12 and Jehoshaphat and the **k** of Edom went
3:13 Elisha said to the **k** of Israel, B
3:13 But the **k** of Israel said to him, "No; B
3:14 not that I have regard for **K** Jehoshaphat of Judah,
3:26 When the **k** of Moab saw that the battle was going
3:26 opposite the **k** of Edom; but they could not.
4:13 on your behalf to the **k** or to the commander of
5: 1 commander of the army of the **k** of Aram,
5: 5 And the **k** of Aram said, "Go then,
5: 5 and I will send along a letter to the **k** of Israel." B
5: 6 He brought the letter to the **k** of Israel, B
5: 7 When the **k** of Israel read the letter, B
5: 8 Elisha the man of God heard that the **k** of Israel B
5: 8 he sent a message to the **k,**
6: 8 Once when the **k** of Aram was at war with Israel,
6: 9 But the man of God sent word to the **k** of Israel, B
6:10 The **k** of Israel sent word to the place of which B
6:11 The mind of the **k** of Aram was greatly perturbed
6:11 who among us sides with the **k** of Israel?" B
6:12 Then one of his officers said, "No one, my lord **k.**
6:12 tells the **k** of Israel the words that you speak B
6:21 When the **k** of Israel saw them he said to Elisha, B
6:24 Some time later **K** Ben-hadad of Aram
6:26 as the **k** of Israel was walking on the city wall, B
6:26 a woman cried out to him, "Help, my lord **k!"**
6:28 then the **k** asked her, "What is your complaint?"
6:30 When the **k** heard the words of
6:33 the **k** came down to him and said,
7: 2 Then the captain on whose hand the **k** leaned said
7: 6 "The **k** of Israel has hired the kings of the Hittites B
7:12 The **k** got up in the night, and said to his servants,
7:14 and the **k** sent them after the Aramean army,
7:15 So the messengers returned, and told the **k.**
7:17 Now the **k** had appointed the captain
7:17 as the man of God had said when the **k** came down
7:18 For when the man of God had said to the **k,**
8: 3 to appeal to the **k** for her house and her land.
8: 4 Now the **k** was talking with Gehazi the servant of
8: 5 the **k** how Elisha had restored a dead person to life,
8: 5 to life appealed to the **k** for her house and her land.
8: 5 Gehazi said, "My lord **k,** here is the woman,
8: 6 When the **k** questioned the woman, she told him.
8: 6 So the **k** appointed an official for her, saying,
8: 7 to Damascus while **K** Ben-hadad of Aram was ill.
8: 8 the **k** said to Hazael, "Take a present with you
8: 9 "Your son **K** Ben-hadad of Aram has sent me
8:13 "The LORD has shown me that you are to be **k**
8:16 In the fifth year of **K** Joram son of Ahab of Israel,
8:16 Jehoram son of **K** Jehoshaphat of Judah began
8:17 He was thirty-two years old when he became **k,**
8:20 and set up a **k** of their own.
8:25 the twelfth year of **K** Joram son of Ahab of Israel,
8:25 Ahaziah son of **K** Jehoram of Judah began
8:26 a granddaughter of **K** Omri of Israel.
8:28 of Ahab to wage war against **K** Hazael of Aram
8:29 **K** Joram returned to be healed in Jezreel of
8:29 when he fought against **K** Hazael of Aram.
8:29 **K** Ahaziah son of Jehoram of Judah went down
9: 3 I anoint you **k** over Israel.' L
9: 6 I anoint you **k** over the people of the LORD,
9:12 I anoint you **k** over Israel.' " L
9:13 blew the trumpet, and proclaimed, "Jehu is **k."**
9:14 at Ramoth-gilead against **K** Hazael of Aram;
9:15 but **K** Joram had returned to be healed in Jezreel
9:15 when he fought against **K** Hazael of Aram.
9:16 **K** Ahaziah of Judah had come down
9:18 he said, "Thus says the **k,** 'Is it peace?' "

2Ki 9:19 who came to them and said, "Thus says the **k,**
9:21 **K** Joram of Israel and **K** Ahaziah of Judah set out,
9:27 When **K** Ahaziah of Judah saw this,
10: 5 We will not make anyone **k;**
10:13 Jehu met relatives of **K** Ahaziah of Judah and said,
11: 2 But Jehosheba, **K** Joram's daughter,
11: 8 shall surround the **k,** each with weapons in hand;
11: 8 Be with the **k** in his comings and goings."
11:10 that had been **K** David's, which were in the house
11:11 to guard the **k** on every side.
11:12 they proclaimed him **k,** and anointed him;
11:12 and shouted, "Long live the **k!"**
11:14 there was the **k** standing by the pillar,
11:14 with the captains and the trumpeters beside the **k,**
11:17 the LORD and the **k** and people, that they should
11:17 also between the **k** and the people.
11:19 then they brought the **k** down from the house of
12: 6 of **K** Jehoash the priests had made no repairs on
12: 7 Therefore **K** Jehoash summoned
12:17 At that time **K** Hazael of Aram went up,
12:18 **K** Jehoash of Judah took all the votive gifts
12:18 and sent these to **K** Hazael of Aram.
13: 1 In the twenty-third year of **K** Joash son of Ahaziah
13: 3 into the hand of **K** Hazael of Aram,
13: 4 how the **k** of Aram oppressed them.
13: 7 the **k** of Aram had destroyed them and made them
13:10 In the thirty-seventh year of **K** Joash of Judah,
13:12 with which he fought against **K** Amaziah of Judah,
13:14 **K** Joash of Israel went down to him,
13:16 Then he said to the **k** of Israel, "Draw the bow"; B
13:18 He said to the **k** of Israel, B
13:22 Now **K** Hazael of Aram oppressed Israel all
13:24 When **K** Hazael of Aram died,
14: 1 the second year of **K** Joash son of Joahaz of Israel,
14: 1 **K** Amaziah son of Joash of Judah, began to reign.
14: 5 servants who had murdered his father the **k.**
14: 8 Then Amaziah sent messengers to **K** Jehoash son
14: 9 **K** Jehoash of Israel sent word to **K** Amaziah
14:11 So **K** Jehoash of Israel went up;
14:11 he and **K** Amaziah of Judah faced one another
14:13 **K** Jehoash of Israel captured **K** Amaziah
14:15 and how he fought with **K** Amaziah of Judah,
14:17 **K** Amaziah son of Joash of Judah
14:17 the death of **K** Jehoash son of Jehoahaz of Israel.
14:21 and made him **k** to succeed his father Amaziah.
14:22 after **K** Amaziah slept with his ancestors.
14:23 In the fifteenth year of **K** Amaziah son of Joash
14:23 **K** Jeroboam son of Joash of Israel began to reign
15: 1 In the twenty-seventh year of **K** Jeroboam of Israel **K** Azariah son of
15: 5 The LORD struck the **k,** so that he was leprous to
15: 8 In the thirty-eighth year of **K** Azariah of Judah,
15:13 in the thirty-ninth year of **K** Uzziah of Judah;
15:17 In the thirty-ninth year of **K** Azariah of Judah,
15:19 **K** Pul of Assyria came against the land;
15:20 to give to the **k** of Assyria. C
15:20 So the **k** of Assyria turned back, C
15:23 In the fiftieth year of **K** Azariah of Judah,
15:27 In the fifty-second year of **K** Azariah of Judah,
15:29 In the days of **K** Pekah of Israel,
15:29 **K** Tiglath-pileser of Assyria came
15:32 In the second year of **K** Pekah son of Remaliah
15:32 **K** Jotham son of Uzziah of Judah began to reign.
15:37 In those days the LORD began to send **K** Rezin
16: 1 **K** Ahaz son of Jotham of Judah began to reign.
16: 5 **K** Rezin of Aram and **K** Pekah son of Remaliah
16: 6 that time the **k** of Edom recovered Elath for Edom,
16: 7 Ahaz sent messengers to **K** Tiglath-pileser
16: 7 and rescue me from the hand of the **k** of Aram
16: 7 of Aram and from the hand of the **k** of Israel, B
16: 8 and sent a present to the **k** of Assyria. C
16: 9 The **k** of Assyria listened to him; C
16: 9 the **k** of Assyria marched up against Damascus, C
16:10 When **K** Ahaz went to Damascus
16:10 to Damascus to meet **K** Tiglath-pileser of Assyria,
16:10 **K** Ahaz sent to the priest Uriah a model of
16:11 with all that **K** Ahaz had sent from Damascus,
16:11 before **K** Ahaz arrived from Damascus.
16:12 **k** came from Damascus, the **k** viewed the altar.
16:12 Then the **k** drew near to the altar, went up on it,
16:15 **K** Ahaz commanded the priest Uriah, saying,
16:16 The priest Uriah did everything that **K** Ahaz
16:17 Then **K** Ahaz cut off the frames of the stands,
16:18 and the outer entrance for the **k** he removed from
16:18 He did this because of the **k** of Assyria. C
17: 1 In the twelfth year of **K** Ahaz of Judah,
17: 3 **K** Shalmaneser of Assyria came up against him;
17: 4 But the **k** of Assyria found treachery in Hoshea; C
17: 4 for he had sent messengers to **K** So of Egypt,
17: 4 and offered no tribute to the **k** of Assyria, C
17: 4 the **k** of Assyria confined him and imprisoned C
17: 5 the **k** of Assyria invaded all the land and came C
17: 6 of Hoshea the **k** of Assyria captured Samaria; C
17: 7 from under the hand of Pharaoh **k** of Egypt. H
17:21 they made Jeroboam son of Nebat **k.**
17:24 The **k** of Assyria brought people from Babylon, C
17:26 So the **k** of Assyria was told, C
17:27 Then the **k** of Assyria commanded, C
18: 1 In the third year of **K** Hoshea son of Elah of Israel,
18: 1 Hezekiah son of **K** Ahaz of Judah began to reign.
18: 7 the **k** of Assyria and would not serve him. C
18: 9 In the fourth year of **K** Hezekiah, I
18: 9 seventh year of **K** Hoshea son of Elah of Israel,
18: 9 **K** Shalmaneser of Assyria came up
18:10 which was the ninth year of **K** Hoshea of Israel,
18:11 **k** of Assyria carried the Israelites away to C
18:13 In the fourteenth year of **K** Hezekiah, I

2Ki 18:13 **K** Sennacherib of Assyria came up against all
18:14 **K** Hezekiah of Judah sent to the king of Assyria I
18:14 King Hezekiah of Judah sent to the **k** of Assyria C
18:14 The **k** of Assyria demanded of King Hezekiah C
18:14 The king of Assyria demanded of **K** Hezekiah I
18:16 that **K** Hezekiah of Judah had overlaid and I
18:16 had overlaid and gave it to the **k** of Assyria. C
18:17 The **k** of Assyria sent the Tartan, the Rabsaris, C
18:17 with a great army from Lachish to **K** Hezekiah I
18:18 When they called for the **k**,
18:19 Thus says the great **k**, the king of Assyria: N
18:19 Thus says the great king, the **k** of Assyria: C
18:21 Pharaoh **k** of Egypt to all who rely on him. H
18:23 make a wager with my master the **k** of Assyria: C
18:28 "Hear the word of the great **k**, N
18:28 the word of the great king, the **k** of Assyria! C
18:29 says the **k**: 'Do not let Hezekiah deceive you,
18:30 not be given into the hand of the **k** of Assyria.' C
18:31 for thus says the **k** of Assyria: C
18:33 of the hand of the **k** of Assyria? C
19: 1 When **K** Hezekiah heard it, he tore his clothes, I
19: 4 his master the **k** of Assyria has sent to mock C
19: 5 When the servants of **K** Hezekiah came to Isaiah, I
19: 6 the servants of the **k** of Assyria have reviled me. C
19: 8 found the **k** of Assyria fighting against Libnah; C
19: 8 for he had heard that the **k** had left Lachish.
19: 9 the **k** heard concerning **K** Tirhakah of Ethiopia,
19:10 "Thus shall you speak to **K** Hezekiah of Judah: I
19:10 not be given into the hand of the **k** of Assyria. C
19:13 the **k** of Hamath, the **k** of Arpad, the **k** of the city
of Sepharvaim, the **k** of Hena, or the **k** of Ivvah?"
19:20 to me about **K** Sennacherib of Assyria.
19:32 thus says the LORD concerning the **k** of Assyria: C
19:36 Then **K** Sennacherib of Assyria left, went home,
20: 6 and this city out of the hand of the **k** of Assyria; C
20:12 At that time **K** Merodach-baladan son of Baladan
20:14 Then the prophet Isaiah came to **K** Hezekiah, I
20:18 be eunuchs in the palace of the **k** of Babylon." A
21: 3 made a sacred pole, as **K** Ahab of Israel had done,
21:11 "Because **K** Manasseh of Judah
21:23 and killed the **k** in his house.
21:24 all those who had conspired against **K** Amon,
21:24 of the land made his son Josiah **k** in place of him.
22: 3 In the eighteenth year of **K** Josiah,
22: 3 the **k** sent Shaphan son of Azaliah,
22: 9 Then Shaphan the secretary came to the **k**,
22: 9 the **k**, "Your servants have emptied out the money
22:10 Shaphan the secretary informed the **k**,
22:10 Shaphan then read it aloud to the **k**.
22:11 the **k** heard the words of the book of the law,
22:12 Then the **k** commanded the priest Hilkiah,
22:16 words of the book that the **k** of Judah has read. M
22:18 But as to the **k** of Judah, M
22:20 They took the message back to the **k**.
23: 1 Then the **k** directed that all the elders of Judah
23: 2 The **k** went up to the house of the LORD,
23: 3 The **k** stood by the pillar and made a covenant
23: 4 The **k** commanded the high priest Hilkiah,
23:13 The **k** defiled the high places that were east
23:13 which **K** Solomon of Israel had built for Astarte E
23:21 The **k** commanded all the people,
23:23 of **K** Josiah this passover was kept to the LORD
23:25 Before him there was no **k** like him,
23:29 In his days Pharaoh Neco **k** of Egypt went up H
23:29 up to the **k** of Assyria to the river Euphrates. C
23:29 **K** Josiah went to meet him;
23:30 and made him **k** in place of his father.
23:34 Pharaoh Neco made Eliakim son of Josiah **k**
24: 1 In his days **K** Nebuchadnezzar F
24: 7 The **k** of Egypt did not come again out of his H
24: 7 the **k** of Babylon had taken over all that A
24: 7 belonged to the **k** of Egypt from the Wadi H
24:10 At that time the servants of **K** Nebuchadnezzar F
24:11 **K** Nebuchadnezzar of Babylon came to the city, F
24:12 **K** Jehoiachin of Judah gave himself up to
24:12 gave himself up to the **k** of Babylon, A
24:12 The **k** of Babylon took him prisoner in A
24:13 which **K** Solomon of Israel had made, E
24:16 The **k** of Babylon brought captive to Babylon A
24:17 The **k** of Babylon made Mattaniah A
24:17 **k** in his place, and changed his name to Zedekiah.
24:20 Zedekiah rebelled against the **k** of Babylon. A
25: 1 **K** Nebuchadnezzar of Babylon came F
25: 2 until the eleventh year of **K** Zedekiah. J
25: 4 the **k** with all the soldiers fled by night by the way
25: 5 But the army of the Chaldeans pursued the **k**,
25: 6 Then they captured the **k** and brought him up to
25: 6 brought him up to the **k** of Babylon at Riblah, A
25: 8 the nineteenth year of **K** Nebuchadnezzar, F
25: 8 year of King Nebuchadnezzar, **k** of Babylon— A
25: 8 servant of the **k** of Babylon, came to Jerusalem. A
25:11 deserters who had defected to the **k** of Babylon A
25:20 and brought them to the **k** of Babylon at Riblah. A
25:21 The **k** of Babylon struck them down and A
25:22 whom **K** Nebuchadnezzar of Babylon had left. F
25:23 that the **k** of Babylon had appointed Gedaliah A
25:24 live in the land, serve the **k** of Babylon, A
25:27 thirty-seventh year of the exile of **K** Jehoiachin
25:27 **K** Evil-merodach of Babylon,
25:27 released **K** Jehoiachin of Judah from prison;
25:30 a regular allowance was given him by the **k**,
1Ch 1:43 of Edom before any **k** reigned over the Israelites:
3: 2 son of Maacah, daughter of **K** Talmai of Geshur;
4:23 they lived there with the **k** in his service.
4:31 These were their towns until David became **k**.
4:41 came in the days of **K** Hezekiah of Judah, I
5: 6 whom **K** Tilgath-pilneser of Assyria carried away
1Ch 5:17 by genealogies in the days of **K** Jotham of Judah,
5:17 and in the days of **K** Jeroboam of Israel.
5:26 So the God of Israel stirred up the spirit of **K** Pul
5:26 the spirit of **K** Tilgath-pilneser of Assyria,
11: 2 For some time now, even while Saul was **k**,
11: 3 So all the elders of Israel came to the **k** at Hebron,
11: 3 And they anointed David **k** over Israel, L
11:10 together with all Israel, to make him **k**,
12:31 to come and make David **k**.
12:38 with full intent to make David **k** over all Israel; L
12:38 of Israel were of a single mind to make David **k**.
14: 1 **K** Hiram of Tyre sent messengers to David,
14: 2 the LORD had established him as **k** over Israel, L
14: 8 that David had been anointed **k** over all Israel, L
15:29 and saw **K** David leaping and dancing; G
16:31 say among the nations, "The LORD is **k**!"
17:16 Then **K** David went in and sat before the LORD, G
18: 3 David also struck down **K** Hadadezer of Zobah,
18: 5 of Damascus came to help **K** Hadadezer of Zobah,
18: 9 When **K** Tou of Hamath heard that David had
18: 9 the whole army of **K** Hadadezer of Zobah,
18:10 he sent his son Hadoram to **K** David, G
18:11 these also **K** David dedicated to the LORD, G
18:17 the chief officials in the service of the **k**.
19: 1 **K** Nahash of the Ammonites died,
19: 5 The **k** said, "Remain at Jericho
19: 7 They hired thirty-two thousand chariots and the **k**
21: 3 Are they not, my lord the **k**, D
21:23 let my lord the **k** do what seems good to him; D
21:24 But **K** David said to Ornan, "No; G
23: 1 he made his son Solomon **k** over Israel. L
24: 6 a Levite, recorded them in the presence of the **k**,
24:31 in the presence of **K** David, Zadok, Ahimelech, G
25: 2 who prophesied under the direction of the **k**.
25: 6 and Heman were under the order of the **k**.
26:26 treasuries of the dedicated gifts that **K** David, G
26:30 of the LORD and for the service of the **k**.
26:32 **K** David appointed him and his brothers, G
26:32 to God and for the affairs of the **k**.
27: 1 and their officers who served the **k** in all matters
27:24 into the account of the Annals of **K** David. G
27:31 All these were stewards of **K** David's property.
28: 1 the officers of the divisions that served the **k**,
28: 1 of all the property and cattle of the **k** and his sons,
28: 2 Then **K** David rose to his feet and said: G
28: 4 from all my ancestral house to be **k** over Israel L
28: 4 he took delight in making me **k** over all Israel. L
29: 1 **K** David said to the whole assembly, G
29: 9 **K** David also rejoiced greatly. G
29:20 before the LORD and the **k**.
29:22 They made David's son Solomon **k** a second time;
29:23 succeeding his father David as **k**;
29:24 and also all the sons of **K** David, G
29:24 pledged their allegiance to **K** Solomon. E
29:25 as had not been on any **k** before him in Israel.
29:29 Now the acts of **K** David, from first to last, G
2Ch 1: 8 and have made me succeed him as **k**.
1: 9 for you have made me **k** over a people
1:11 over whom I have made you **k**,
1:14 in the chariot cities and with the **k** in Jerusalem.
1:15 The **k** made silver and gold as common
2: 3 Solomon sent word to **K** Huram of Tyre:
2:11 Then **K** Huram of Tyre answered in a letter
2:11 the LORD loves his people he has made you **k**
2:12 who has given **K** David a wise son, G
4:11 work that he did for **K** Solomon on the house E
4:16 burnished bronze for **K** Solomon for the house E
4:17 In the plain of the Jordan the **k** cast them,
5: 3 the Israelites assembled before the **k** at the festival
5: 6 **K** Solomon and all the congregation of Israel, E
6: 3 the **k** turned around and blessed all the assembly
7: 4 the **k** and all the people offered sacrifice before
7: 5 **K** Solomon offered as a sacrifice E
7: 5 **k** and all the people dedicated the house of God.
7: 6 for music to the LORD that **K** David had made G
8:10 These were the chief officers of **K** Solomon, E
8:11 "My wife shall not live in the house of **K** David G
8:15 not turn away from what the **k** had commanded
8:18 of gold and brought it to **K** Solomon. E
9: 5 So she said to the **k**,
9: 8 on his throne as **k** for the LORD your God.
9: 8 he has made you **k** over them,
9: 9 she gave the **k** one hundred twenty talents of gold,
9: 9 that the queen of Sheba gave to **K** Solomon. E
9:11 the **k** made steps for the house of the LORD and
9:12 Meanwhile **K** Solomon granted the queen E
9:12 well beyond what she had brought to the **k**.
9:15 **K** Solomon made two hundred large shields E
9:16 **k** put them in the House of the Forest of Lebanon.
9:17 The **k** also made a great ivory throne,
9:20 All **K** Solomon's drinking vessels were of gold,
9:22 **K** Solomon excelled all the kings of the earth E
9:25 in the chariot cities and with the **k** in Jerusalem.
9:27 **k** made silver as common in Jerusalem as stone,
10: 1 all Israel had come to Shechem to make him **k**.
10: 2 where he had fled from **K** Solomon), E
10: 6 Then **K** Rehoboam took counsel with
10:12 the third day, as the **k** had said, "Come to me again
10:13 The **k** answered them harshly.
10:13 **K** Rehoboam rejected the advice of the older men;
10:15 So the **k** did not listen to the people,
10:16 all Israel saw that the **k** would not listen to them,
10:16 the people answered the **k**,
10:18 When **K** Rehoboam sent Hadoram,
10:18 **K** Rehoboam hurriedly mounted his chariot to flee
11: 3 Say to **K** Rehoboam of Judah,
11:22 for he intended to make him **k**.
2Ch 12: 2 In the fifth year of **K** Rehoboam,
12: 2 **K** Shishak of Egypt came up against Jerusalem
12: 6 the officers of Israel and the **k** humbled themselves
12: 9 So **K** Shishak of Egypt came up against Jerusalem;
12:10 but **K** Rehoboam made in place of them shields
12:11 Whenever the **k** went into the house of the LORD,
12:13 So **K** Rehoboam established himself in Jerusalem
13: 1 In the eighteenth year of **K** Jeroboam,
15:16 **K** Asa even removed his mother Maacah
16: 1 **K** Baasha of Israel went up against Judah,
16: 1 or coming into the territory of **K** Asa of Judah.
16: 2 and sent them to **K** Ben-hadad of Aram,
16: 3 go, break your alliance with **K** Baasha of Israel,
16: 4 Ben-hadad listened to **K** Asa,
16: 6 Then **K** Asa brought all Judah,
16: 7 that time the seer Hanani came to **K** Asa of Judah,
16: 7 "Because you relied on the **k** of Aram,
16: 7 the army of the **k** of Aram has escaped you.
17:19 These were in the service of the **k**,
17:19 besides those whom the **k** had placed in
18: 3 **K** Ahab of Israel said to **K** Jehoshaphat
18: 4 But Jehoshaphat also said to the **k** of Israel, B
18: 5 the **k** of Israel gathered the prophets together, B
18: 5 for God will give it into the hand of the **k**."
18: 7 The **k** of Israel said to Jehoshaphat, B
18: 7 Jehoshaphat said, "Let the **k** not say such a thing."
18: 8 the **k** of Israel summoned an officer and said, B
18: 9 Now the **k** of Israel and King Jehoshaphat B
18: 9 of Israel and **K** Jehoshaphat of Judah were sitting
18:11 the LORD will give it into the hand of the **k**."
18:12 with one accord are favorable to the **k**;
18:14 When he had come to the **k**, the **k** said to him,
18:15 But the **k** said to him,
18:17 The **k** of Israel said to Jehoshaphat, B
18:19 LORD said, 'Who will entice **K** Ahab of Israel,
18:25 The **k** of Israel then ordered, "Take Micaiah, B
18:26 and say, 'Thus says the **k**: Put this fellow in prison,
18:28 the **k** of Israel and King Jehoshaphat of Judah B
18:28 of Israel and **K** Jehoshaphat of Judah went up
18:29 The **k** of Israel said to Jehoshaphat, B
18:29 So the **k** of Israel disguised himself, B
18:30 Now the **k** of Aram had commanded the captains
18:30 but only with the **k** of Israel." B
18:31 they said, "It is the **k** of Israel." B
18:32 of the chariots saw that it was not the **k** of Israel, B
18:33 and unknowingly struck the **k** of Israel between B
18:34 and the **k** of Israel propped himself up B
19: 1 **K** Jehoshaphat of Judah returned in safety
19: 2 to meet him and said to **K** Jehoshaphat,
20:15 and inhabitants of Jerusalem, and **K** Jehoshaphat:
20:35 After this **K** Jehoshaphat of Judah joined
20:35 of Judah joined with **K** Ahaziah of Israel,
21: 2 all these were the sons of **K** Jehoshaphat of Judah.
21: 8 the rule of Judah and set up a **k** of their own.
21:12 of your father Jehoshaphat or in the ways of **K** Asa
22: 1 of Jerusalem made his youngest son Ahaziah **k**
22: 1 Ahaziah son of Jehoram reigned as **k** of Judah. M
22: 5 Jehoram son of **K** Ahab of Israel to make war
against **K** Hazael of Aram
22: 6 when he fought **K** Hazael of Aram.
22: 6 And Ahaziah son of **K** Jehoram of Judah went
22:11 of **K** Jehoram and wife of the priest Jehoiada—
23: 3 the whole assembly made a covenant with the **k** in
23: 7 The Levites shall surround the **k**,
23: 7 Stay with the **k** in his comings and goings."
23: 9 that had been **K** David's, which were in the house
23:10 and he set all the people as a guard for the **k**,
23:11 they proclaimed him **k**, and Jehoiada
23:11 and they shouted, "Long live the **k**!"
23:12 the noise of the people running and praising the **k**,
23:13 the **k** standing by his pillar at the entrance,
23:13 and the captains and the trumpeters beside the **k**,
23:16 and the **k** that they should be the LORD's people.
23:20 and they brought the **k** down from the house of
23:20 They set the **k** on the royal throne.
24: 6 So the **k** summoned Jehoiada the chief,
24: 8 So the **k** gave command, and they made a chest,
24:12 The **k** and Jehoiada gave it
24:14 the rest of the money to the **k** and Jehoiada,
24:17 of Judah came and did obeisance to the **k**;
24:17 then the **k** listened to them.
24:21 and by command of the **k** they stoned him to death
24:22 **K** Joash did not remember the kindness
24:23 sent all the booty they took to the **k** of Damascus.
25: 3 his servants who had murdered his father the **k**.
25: 7 But a man of God came to him and said, "O **k**,
25:16 But as he was speaking the **k** said to him,
25:17 Then **K** Amaziah of Judah took counsel and sent
25:17 to **K** Joash son of Jehoahaz son of Jehu of Israel,
25:18 **K** Joash of Israel sent word to **K** Amaziah
25:21 So **K** Joash of Israel went up;
25:21 he and **K** Amaziah of Judah faced one another
25:23 **K** Joash of Israel captured **K** Amaziah of Judah,
25:25 **K** Amaziah son of Joash of Judah,
25:25 lived fifteen years after the death of **K** Joash son
26: 1 and made him **k** to succeed his father Amaziah.
26: 2 after the **k** slept with his ancestors.
26:13 to help the **k** against the enemy.
26:18 they withstood **K** Uzziah, and said to him,
26:21 **K** Uzziah was leprous to the day of his death,
26:21 in charge of the palace of the **k**,
27: 5 with the **k** of the Ammonites and prevailed
28: 5 into the hand of the **k** of Aram,
28: 5 was also given into the hand of the **k** of Israel, B
28: 7 and Elkanah the next in authority to the **k**.
28:16 At that time **K** Ahaz sent to the king of Assyria
28:16 At that time King Ahaz sent to the **k** of Assyria C

2Ch 28:19 the LORD brought Judah low because of **K** Ahaz
28:20 **K** Tilgath-pilneser of Assyria came against him,
28:21 the house of the LORD and the houses of the **k**
28:21 and gave tribute to the **k** of Assyria; C
28:22 more faithless to the LORD—this same **K** Ahaz.
29:15 and went in as the **k** had commanded,
29:18 Then they went inside to **K** Hezekiah and said, I
29:19 that **K** Ahaz repudiated during his reign
29:20 Then **K** Hezekiah rose early, I
29:23 for the sin offering were brought to the **k** and
29:24 For the **k** commanded that the burnt offering and
29:27 accompanied by the instruments of **K** David G
29:29 the **k** and all who were present with him bowed
29:30 **K** Hezekiah and the officials commanded I
30: 2 For the **k** and his officials and all the assembly
30: 4 plan seemed right to the **k** and all the assembly.
30: 6 and Judah with letters from the **k** and his officials,
30: 6 as the **k** had commanded, saying,
30:12 the **k** and the officials commanded by the word of
30:24 For **K** Hezekiah of Judah gave the assembly I
30:26 for since the time of Solomon son of **K** David G
31: 3 of the **k** from his own possessions was for
31:13 by the appointment of **K** Hezekiah and of I
32: 1 **K** Sennacherib of Assyria came and invaded Judah
32: 7 **k** of Assyria and all the horde that is with him; C
32: 8 by the words of **K** Hezekiah of Judah. I
32: 9 while **K** Sennacherib of Assyria was at Lachish
32: 9 he sent his servants to Jerusalem to **K** Hezekiah I
32:10 "Thus says **K** Sennacherib of Assyria:
32:11 from the hand of the **k** of Assyria'? C
32:20 Then **K** Hezekiah and the prophet Isaiah son I
32:21 and officers in the camp of the **k** of Assyria. C
32:22 of **K** Sennacherib of Assyria and from the hand
32:23 in Jerusalem and precious things to **K** Hezekiah I
33:11 commanders of the army of the **k** of Assyria, C
33:25 all those who had conspired against **K** Amon;
33:25 of the land made his son Josiah **k** to succeed him.
34:16 Shaphan brought the book to the **k**,
34:16 and further reported to the **k**,
34:18 The secretary Shaphan informed the **k**,
34:18 Shaphan then read it aloud to the **k**.
34:19 **k** heard the words of the law he tore his clothes.
34:20 Then the **k** commanded Hilkiah,
34:22 So Hilkiah and those whom the **k** had sent
34:24 in the book that was read before the **k** of Judah. M
34:26 But as to the **k** of Judah, M
34:28 They took the message back to the **k**.
34:29 the **k** sent word and gathered together all the elders
34:30 The **k** went up to the house of the LORD,
34:31 The **k** stood in his place and made a covenant
35: 3 house that Solomon son of David, **k** of Israel, B
35: 4 of **K** David of Israel and the written directions G
35:16 according to the command of **K** Josiah.
35:20 **K** Neco of Egypt went up to fight at Carchemish
35:21 "What have I to do with you, **k** of Judah? M
35:23 The archers shot **K** Josiah;
35:23 and the **k** said to his servants, "Take me away,
36: 1 made him **k** to succeed his father in Jerusalem.
36: 3 the **k** of Egypt deposed him in Jerusalem and H
36: 4 The **k** of Egypt made his brother Eliakim king H
36: 4 of Egypt made his brother Eliakim **k** over Judah
36: 6 Against him **K** Nebuchadnezzar of Babylon F
36:10 year **K** Nebuchadnezzar sent and brought him F
36:10 and made his brother Zedekiah **k** over Judah
36:13 He also rebelled against **K** Nebuchadnezzar, F
36:17 he brought up against them the **k** of the Chaldeans,
36:18 and the treasures of the **k** and of his officials,
36:22 In the first year of **K** Cyrus of Persia,
36:22 the LORD stirred up the spirit of **K** Cyrus of Persia
36:23 "Thus says **K** Cyrus of Persia:
Ezr 1: 1 In the first year of **K** Cyrus of Persia,
1: 1 the LORD stirred up the spirit of **K** Cyrus of Persia
1: 2 "Thus says **K** Cyrus of Persia:
1: 7 **K** Cyrus himself brought out the vessels of
1: 8 **K** Cyrus of Persia had them released into
2: 1 those captive exiles whom **K** Nebuchadnezzar F
3: 7 according to the grant that they had from **K** Cyrus
3:10 according to the directions of **K** David of Israel; G
4: 2 to him ever since the days of **K** Esar-haddon
4: 3 as **K** Cyrus of Persia has commanded us."
4: 5 throughout the reign of **K** Cyrus of Persia and
4: 5 of Persia and until the reign of **K** Darius of Persia.
4: 7 of their associates wrote to **K** Artaxerxes of Persia;
4: 8 against Jerusalem to **K** Artaxerxes as follows
4:11 "To **K** Artaxerxes: Your servants, the people of
4:12 may it be known to the **k** that the Jews who came
4:13 Now may it be known to the **k** that,
4:14 therefore we send and inform the **k**,
4:16 We make known to the **k** that,
4:17 The **k** sent an answer: "To Rehum
4:22 why should damage grow to the hurt of the **k**?"
4:23 when the copy of **K** Artaxerxes' letter was read
4:24 the second year of the reign of **K** Darius of Persia.
5: 6 in the province Beyond the River sent to **K** Darius;
5: 7 "To Darius the **k**, all peace!
5: 8 be known to the **k** that we went to the province
5:11 which a great **k** of Israel built and finished. BN
5:12 gave them into the hand of **K** Nebuchadnezzar F
5:13 However, **K** Cyrus of Babylon,
5:14 these **K** Cyrus took out of the temple of Babylon,
5:17 And now, if it seems good to the **k**,
5:17 by **K** Cyrus for the rebuilding of this house of God
5:17 Let the **k** send us his pleasure in this matter."
6: 1 Then **K** Darius made a decree,
6: 3 the first year of his reign, **K** Cyrus issued a decree:
6:10 and pray for the life of the **k** and his children.
6:12 has established his name there overthrow any **k**

Ezr 6:13 Then, according to the word sent by **K** Darius,
6:13 with all diligence what **K** Darius had ordered.
6:14 Darius, and **K** Artaxerxes of Persia;
6:15 in the sixth year of the reign of **K** Darius.
6:22 had turned the heart of the **k** of Assyria to them, C
7: 1 After this, in the reign of **K** Artaxerxes of Persia,
7: 6 and the **k** granted him all that he asked,
7: 7 in the seventh year of **K** Artaxerxes.
7: 8 which was in the seventh year of the **k**.
7:11 letter that **K** Artaxerxes gave to the priest Ezra,
7:12 "Artaxerxes, **k** of kings, to the priest Ezra, P
7:14 For you are sent by the **k** and his seven counselors
7:15 that the **k** and his counselors have freely offered to
7:21 **K** Artaxerxes, decree to all the treasurers in
7:23 or wrath will come upon the realm of the **k**
7:26 not obey the law of your God and the law of the **k**,
7:27 as this into the heart of the **k** to glorify the house
7:28 and who extended to me steadfast love before the **k**
8: 1 in the reign of **K** Artaxerxes:
8:22 to ask the **k** for a band of soldiers and cavalry
8:22 the **k** that the hand of our God is gracious
8:25 the offering for the house of our God that the **k**,
Ne 1:11 At the time, I was cupbearer to the **k**.
2: 1 in the twentieth year of **K** Artaxerxes,
2: 1 I carried the wine and gave it to the **k**.
2: 2 So the **k** said to me, "Why is your face sad,
2: 3 I said to the **k**, "May the **k** live forever!
2: 4 Then the **k** said to me, "What do you request?"
2: 5 Then I said to the **k**, "If it pleases the **k**,
2: 6 The **k** said to me (the queen also was sitting
2: 6 So it pleased the **k** to send me, and I set him a date.
2: 7 Then I said to the **k**, "If it pleases the **k**,
2: 8 And the **k** granted me what I asked,
2: 9 the **k** had sent officers of the army and cavalry
2:18 and also the words that the **k** had spoken to me.
2:19 Are you rebelling against the **k**?"
3:25 the tower projecting from the upper house of the **k**
5:14 to the thirty-second year of **K** Artaxerxes,
6: 6 to this report you wish to become their **k**.
6: 7 'There is a **k** in Judah!'
6: 7 And now it will be reported to the **k** according
7: 6 of those exiles whom **K** Nebuchadnezzar F
9:22 of **K** Sihon of Heshbon and the land of **K** Og
11:23 there was a command from the **k** concerning them,
13: 6 of **K** Artaxerxes of Babylon I went to the **k**.
13: 6 After some time I asked leave of the **k**
13:26 Did not **K** Solomon of Israel sin on account E
13:26 Among the many nations there was no **k** like him,
13:26 and God made him **k** over all Israel; L
Est 1: 2 when **K** Ahasuerus sat on his royal throne in
1: 5 the **k** gave for all the people present in the citadel
1: 7 according to the bounty of the **k**.
1: 8 for the **k** had given orders to all the officials
1: 9 for the women in the palace of **K** Ahasuerus.
1:10 when the **k** was merry with wine,
1:11 the **k**, wearing the royal crown, in order to show
1:12 At this the **k** was enraged,
1:13 Then the **k** consulted the sages who knew the laws
1:14 who had access to the **k**, and sat first in
1:15 of **K** Ahasuerus conveyed by the eunuchs?"
1:16 Then Memucan said in the presence of the **k** and
1:16 "Not only has Queen Vashti done wrong to the **k**,
1:16 in all the provinces of **K** Ahasuerus.
1:17 '**K** Ahasuerus commanded Queen Vashti to
1:19 the **k**, let a royal order go out from him, and let it
1:19 Vashti is never again to come before **K** Ahasuerus;
1:19 and let the **k** give her royal position
1:20 by the **k** is proclaimed throughout all his kingdom,
1:21 This advice pleased the **k** and the officials,
1:21 and the **k** did as Memucan proposed;
2: 1 when the anger of **K** Ahasuerus had abated,
2: 2 be sought out for the **k**.
2: 3 the **k** appoint commissioners in all the provinces
2: 4 And let the girl who pleases the **k** be queen instead
2: 4 This pleased the **k**, and he did so.
2: 6 among the captives carried away with **K** Jeconiah
2: 6 whom **K** Nebuchadnezzar of Babylon F
2:12 turn came for each girl to go in to **K** Ahasuerus,
2:13 the **k** she was given whatever she asked for to take
2:14 she did not go in to the **k** again,
2:14 not go in to the king again, unless the **k** delighted
2:15 to go in to the **k**,
2:16 When Esther was taken to **K** Ahasuerus
2:17 the **k** loved Esther more than all the other women;
2:18 Then the **k** gave a great banquet to all his officials
2:21 and conspired to assassinate **K** Ahasuerus.
2:22 and Esther told the **k** in the name of Mordecai.
2:23 in the book of the annals in the presence of the **k**.
3: 1 these things **K** Ahasuerus promoted Haman son
3: 2 for the **k** had so commanded concerning him.
3: 7 in the twelfth year of **K** Ahasuerus,
3: 8 Then Haman said to **K** Ahasuerus,
3: 8 that it is not appropriate for the **k** to tolerate them.
3: 9 the **k**, let a decree be issued for their destruction,
3:10 the **k** took his signet ring from his hand and gave it
3:11 The **k** said to Haman, "The money is given to you,
3:12 of **K** Ahasuerus and sealed with the king's ring.
3:15 The couriers went quickly by order of the **k**,
3:15 The **k** and Haman sat down to drink;
4: 8 and charge her to go to the **k** to make supplication
4:11 to the **k** inside the inner court without being called,
4:11 if the **k** holds out the golden scepter to someone,
4:11 not been called to come in to the **k** for thirty days."
4:16 that I will go to the **k**, though it is against the law;
5: 1 The **k** was sitting on his royal throne inside
5: 2 as the **k** saw Queen Esther standing in the court,
5: 3 The **k** said to her, "What is it, Queen Esther?

Est 5: 4 Then Esther said, "If it pleases the **k**, let the **k** and
Haman come today to a banquet that I have
prepared for the **k**."
5: 5 Then the **k** said, "Bring Haman quickly,
5: 5 So the **k** and Haman came to the banquet
5: 6 they were drinking wine, the **k** said to Esther,
5: 8 the **k** to grant my petition and fulfill my request,
5: 8 the **k** and Haman come tomorrow to the banquet
5: 8 and then I will do as the **k** has said."
5:11 the promotions with which the **k** had honored him,
5:11 above the officials and the ministers of the **k**.
5:12 with the **k** to the banquet that she prepared.
5:12 also I am invited by her, together with the **k**.
5:14 in the morning tell the **k** to have Mordecai hanged
5:14 then go with the **k** to the banquet in good spirits."
6: 1 On that night the **k** could not sleep,
6: 1 the annals, and they were read to the **k**.
6: 2 who had conspired to assassinate **K** Ahasuerus.
6: 3 Then the **k** said, "What honor or distinction
6: 4 The **k** said, "Who is in the court?"
6: 4 to speak to the **k** about having Mordecai hanged on
6: 5 The **k** said, "Let him come in."
6: 6 So Haman came in, and the **k** said to him,
6: 6 be done for the man whom the **k** wishes to honor?"
6: 6 "Whom would the **k** wish to honor more than me?"
6: 7 So Haman said to the **k**,
6: 7 "For the man whom the **k** wishes to honor,
6: 8 be brought, which the **k** has worn, and a horse that
the **k** has ridden,
6: 9 let him robe the man whom the **k** wishes to honor,
6: 9 for the man whom the **k** wishes to honor.' "
6:10 Then the **k** said to Haman, "Quickly,
6:11 be done for the man whom the **k** wishes to honor."
7: 1 **k** and Haman went in to feast with Queen Esther.
7: 2 the **k** again said to Esther, "What is your petition,
7: 3 "If I have won your favor, O **k**,
7: 3 and if it pleases the **k**, let my life be given me—
7: 4 no enemy can compensate for this damage to the **k**.
7: 5 Then **K** Ahasuerus said to Queen Esther,
7: 6 Haman was terrified before the **k** and the queen.
7: 7 The **k** rose from the feast in wrath and went into
7: 7 he saw that the **k** had determined to destroy him.
7: 8 When the **k** returned from the palace garden to
7: 8 and the **k** said, "Will he even assault the queen
7: 8 As the words left the mouth of the **k**,
7: 9 one of the eunuchs in attendance on the **k**, said,
7: 9 whose word saved the **k**, stands at Haman's house,
7: 9 And the **k** said, "Hang him on that."
7:10 Then the anger of the **k** abated.
8: 1 On that day **K** Ahasuerus gave to Queen Esther
8: 1 and Mordecai came before the **k**,
8: 2 Then the **k** took off his signet ring,
8: 3 Then Esther spoke again to the **k**;
8: 4 The **k** held out the golden scepter to Esther,
8: 5 and Esther rose and stood before the **k**.
8: 5 She said, "If it pleases the **k**,
8: 5 and if the thing seems right before the **k**,
8: 5 the Jews who are in all the provinces of the **k**.
8: 7 Then **K** Ahasuerus said to Queen Esther and to
8: 8 the name of the **k**, and seal it with the king's ring;
8: 8 for an edict written in the name of the **k** and sealed
8:10 He wrote letters in the name of **K** Ahasuerus,
8:11 By these letters the **k** allowed the Jews who were
8:12 throughout all the provinces of **K** Ahasuerus,
8:15 Mordecai went out from the presence of the **k**,
9: 2 throughout all the provinces of **K** Ahasuerus
9:11 in the citadel of Susa was reported to the **k**.
9:12 The **k** said to Queen Esther,
9:13 Esther said, "If it pleases the **k**,
9:14 So the **k** commanded this to be done;
9:20 in all the provinces of **K** Ahasuerus,
9:25 but when Esther came before the **k**,
10: 1 **K** Ahasuerus laid tribute on the land and on
10: 2 to which the **k** advanced him,
10: 3 the Jew was next in rank to **K** Ahasuerus,
Job 15:24 like a **k** prepared for battle.
18:14 and are brought to the **k** of terrors.
29:25 and I lived like a **k** among his troops,
34:18 who says to a **k**, 'You scoundrel!'
41:34 it is **k** over all that are proud."
Ps 2: 6 "I have set my **k** on Zion, my holy hill."
5: 2 Listen to the sound of my cry, my **K** and my God,
10:16 The LORD is **k** forever and ever;
18:50 Great triumphs he gives to his **k**,
20: 9 Give victory to the **k**, O LORD;
21: 1 In your strength the **k** rejoices,
21: 7 For the **k** trusts in the LORD,
24: 7 that the **K** of glory may come in.
24: 8 Who is the **K** of glory?
24: 9 that the **K** of glory may come in.
24:10 Who is this **K** of glory?
24:10 The LORD of hosts, he is the **K** of glory.
29:10 the LORD sits enthroned as **k** forever.
33:16 A **k** is not saved by his great army;
44: 4 You are my **K** and my God;
45: 1 I address my verses to the **k**;
45:11 and the **k** will desire your beauty.
45:14 in many-colored robes she is led to the **k**;
45:15 along as they enter the palace of the **k**.
45:16 In the place of ancestors you, O **k**, shall have sons;
47: 2 is awesome, a great **k** over all the earth. N
47: 6 sing praises to our **K**, sing praises.
47: 7 For God is the **k** of all the earth;
47: 8 God is **k** over the nations;
48: 2 in the far north, the city of the great **K**. N
61: 6 Prolong the life of the **k**;
63:11 But the **k** shall rejoice in God;

Ps 68:24 O God, the processions of my God, my **K**,
72: 1 the **k** your justice, O God, and your righteousness
74:12 Yet God my **K** is from of old,
84: 3 O LORD of hosts, my **K** and my God.
89:18 our **k** to the Holy One of Israel.
93: 1 The LORD is **k**, he is robed in majesty;
95: 3 and a great **K** above all gods. N
96:10 Say among the nations, "The LORD is **k**!
97: 1 The LORD is **k**! Let the earth rejoice;
98: 6 of the horn make a joyful noise before the **K**,
99: 1 The LORD is **k**; let the peoples tremble!
99: 4 Mighty **K**, lover of justice,
105:20 The **k** sent and released him;
135:11 **k** of the Amorites, and Og, king of Bashan,
135:11 **k** of Bashan, and all the kingdoms of Canaan—
136:19 **k** of the Amorites, for his steadfast love endures
136:20 **k** of Bashan, for his steadfast love endures forever;
145: 1 my God and **K**, and bless your name forever
149: 2 let the children of Zion rejoice in their **K**.
Pr 1: 1 proverbs of Solomon son of David, **k** of Israel: B
14:28 The glory of a **k** is a multitude of people;
16:10 Inspired decisions are on the lips of a **k**;
16:13 Righteous lips are the delight of a **k**,
20: 2 dread anger of a **k** is like the growling of a lion;
20: 8 A **k** who sits on the throne
20:26 A wise **k** winnows the wicked,
20:28 Loyalty and faithfulness preserve the **k**,
22:11 and are gracious in speech will have the **k** as
24:21 My child, fear the LORD and the **k**,
25: 1 that the officials of **K** Hezekiah of Judah copied. I
25: 5 take away the wicked from the presence of the **k**,
29: 4 By justice a **k** gives stability to the land,
29:14 If a **k** judges the poor with equity,
30:22 when he becomes **k**, and a fool when glutted
30:27 locusts have no **k**, yet all of them march in rank;
30:31 the he-goat, and a **k** striding before his people.
31: 1 The words of **K** Lemuel.
Ecc 1: 1 the son of David, **k** in Jerusalem.
1:12 I, the Teacher, when **k** over Israel in Jerusalem, L
2:12 for what can the one do who comes after the **k**?
4:13 a poor but wise youth than an old but foolish **k**,
4:15 follow that youth who replaced the **k**;
5: 9 a **k** for a plowed field.
8: 4 For the word of the **k** is powerful,
9:14 A great **k** came against it and besieged it, N
10:16 Alas for you, O land, when your **k** is a servant,
10:17 O land, when your **k** is a nobleman,
10:20 Do not curse the **k**, even in your thoughts,
SS 1: 4 The **k** has brought me into his chambers.
1:12 While the **k** was on his couch,
3: 9 **K** Solomon made himself a palanquin from E
3:11 Look, O daughters of Zion, at **K** Solomon, E
7: 5 a **k** is held captive in the tresses.
Isa 6: 1 In the year that **K** Uzziah died,
6: 5 my eyes have seen the **K**, the LORD of hosts!"
7: 1 Ahaz son of Jotham son of Uzziah, **k** of Judah, M
7: 1 **K** Rezin of Aram and **K** Pekah son of Remaliah
7: 6 for ourselves and make the son of Tabeel **k** in it;
7:17 departed from Judah—the **k** of Assyria." C
7:20 beyond the River—with the **k** of Assyria— C
8: 4 will be carried away by the **k** of Assyria. C
8: 7 the **k** of Assyria and all his glory; C
8:21 be enraged and will curse their **k** and their gods.
10:12 punish the arrogant boasting of the **k** of Assyria C
14: 4 will take up this taunt against the **k** of Babylon: A
14:28 In the year that **K** Ahaz died this oracle came:
19: 4 a fierce **k** will rule over them, says the Sovereign,
20: 1 who was sent by **K** Sargon of Assyria,
20: 4 shall the **k** of Assyria lead away the Egyptians C
20: 6 for help and deliverance from the **k** of Assyria! C
23:15 for seventy years, the lifetime of one **k**.
30:33 truly it is made ready for the **k**,
32: 1 See, a **k** will reign in righteousness,
33:17 Your eyes will see the **k** in his beauty;
33:22 the LORD is our ruler, the LORD is our **k**;
36: 1 In the fourteenth year of **K** Hezekiah, I
36: 1 **K** Sennacherib of Assyria came up against all
36: 2 The **k** of Assyria sent the Rabshakeh from C
36: 2 the Rabshakeh from Lachish to **K** Hezekiah I
36: 4 Thus says the great **k**, the king of Assyria. N
36: 4 Thus says the great king, the **k** of Assyria: C
36: 6 Pharaoh **k** of Egypt to all who rely on him. H
36: 8 make a wager with my master the **k** of Assyria: C
36:13 "Hear the words of the great **k**, N
36:13 the words of the great king, the **k** of Assyria! C
36:14 Thus says the **k**: 'Do not let Hezekiah deceive you,
36:15 not be given into the hand of the **k** of Assyria.' C
36:16 for thus says the **k** of Assyria: C
36:18 their land out of the hand of the **k** of Assyria? C
37: 1 When **K** Hezekiah heard it, he tore his clothes, I
37: 4 his master the **k** of Assyria has sent to mock C
37: 5 When the servants of **K** Hezekiah came to Isaiah, I
37: 6 the servants of the **k** of Assyria have reviled me. C
37: 8 found the **k** of Assyria fighting against Libnah; C
37: 8 for he had heard that the **k** had left Lachish.
37: 9 the **k** heard concerning **K** Tirhakah of Ethiopia,
37:10 "Thus shall you speak to **K** Hezekiah of Judah: I
37:10 not be given into the hand of the **k** of Assyria. C
37:13 the **k** of Hamath, the **k** of Arpad, the **k** of the city
of Sepharvaim, the **k** of Hena, or the **k** of Ivvah?"
37:21 to me concerning **K** Sennacherib of Assyria,
37:33 thus says the LORD concerning the **k** of Assyria: C
37:37 Then **K** Sennacherib of Assyria left, went home,
38: 6 and this city out of the hand of the **k** of Assyria, C
38: 9 A writing of **K** Hezekiah of Judah, I
39: 1 At that time **K** Merodach-baladan son of Baladan
39: 3 the prophet Isaiah came to **K** Hezekiah and said I

Isa 39: 7 be eunuchs in the palace of the **k** of Babylon." A
41:21 bring your proofs, says the **K** of Jacob.
43:15 your Holy One, the Creator of Israel, your **K**.
44: 6 Thus says the LORD, the **K** of Israel, B
Jer 1: 2 word of the LORD came in the days of **K** Josiah
1: 3 in the days of **K** Jehoiakim son of Josiah of Judah,
1: 3 of the eleventh year of **K** Zedekiah son of Josiah J
3: 6 The LORD said to me in the days of **K** Josiah:
4: 9 courage shall fail the **k** and the officials;
8:19 Is her **K** not in her?"
10: 7 Who would not fear you, O **K** of the nations?
10:10 he is the living God and the everlasting **K**.
13:18 Say to the **k** and the queen mother;
15: 4 what **K** Manasseh son of Hezekiah of Judah did
20: 4 give all Judah into the hand of the **k** of Babylon; A
21: 1 when **K** Zedekiah sent to him Pashhur son J
21: 2 **K** Nebuchadrezzar of Babylon is making war K
21: 4 you are fighting against the **k** of Babylon A
21: 7 says the LORD, I will give **K** Zedekiah of Judah, J
21: 7 into the hands of **K** Nebuchadrezzar of Babylon, K
21:10 be given into the hands of the **k** of Babylon, A
21:11 To the house of the **k** of Judah say: M
22: 1 Go down to the house of the **k** of Judah, M
22: 2 O **K** of Judah sitting on the throne of David— M
22: 6 LORD concerning the house of the **k** of Judah: M
22:11 the LORD concerning Shallum son of **K** Josiah
22:15 Are you a **k** because you compete in cedar?
22:18 the LORD concerning **K** Jehoiakim son of Josiah
22:24 even if **K** Coniah son of Jehoiakim of Judah were
22:25 into the hands of **K** Nebuchadrezzar of Babylon K
23: 5 and he shall reign as **k** and deal wisely,
24: 1 after **K** Nebuchadrezzar of Babylon had taken K
24: 1 from Jerusalem **K** Jeconiah son of Jehoiakim
24: 8 so will I treat **K** Zedekiah of Judah, his officials, J
25: 1 of **K** Jehoiakim son of Josiah of Judah (that was
25: 1 the first year of **K** Nebuchadrezzar of Babylon), K
25: 3 from the thirteenth year of **K** Josiah son of Amon
25: 9 even for **K** Nebuchadrezzar of Babylon, K
25:11 and these nations shall serve the **k** of Babylon A
25:12 I will punish the **k** of Babylon and that nation, A
25:19 Pharaoh **k** of Egypt, his servants, his officials, H
25:26 And after them the **k** of Sheshach shall drink.
26: 1 of the reign of **K** Jehoiakim son of Josiah of Judah,
26:18 during the days of **K** Hezekiah of Judah, I
26:19 Did **K** Hezekiah of Judah and all Judah I
26:21 when **K** Jehoiakim, with all his warriors and all
26:21 heard his words, the **k** sought to put him to death;
26:22 Then **K** Jehoiakim sent Elnathan son of Achbor
26:23 from Egypt and brought him to **K** Jehoiakim,
27: 1 the reign of **K** Zedekiah son of Josiah of Judah, J
27: 3 word to the **k** of Edom, the **k** of Moab, the **k** of the
Ammonites, the **k** of Tyre, and the **k** of Sidon
27: 3 to Jerusalem to **K** Zedekiah of Judah. J
27: 6 into the hand of **K** Nebuchadnezzar of Babylon, F
27: 8 But if any nation or kingdom will not serve this **k**,
27: 8 put its neck under the yoke of the **k** of Babylon, A
27: 9 'You shall not serve the **k** of Babylon.' A
27:11 under the yoke of the **k** of Babylon and serve A
27:12 I spoke to **K** Zedekiah of Judah in the same way: J
27:12 your necks under the yoke of the **k** of Babylon, A
27:13 any nation that will not serve the **k** of Babylon? A
27:14 are telling you not to serve the **k** of Babylon, A
27:17 serve the **k** of Babylon and live. A
27:18 in the house of the **k** of Judah, M
27:20 which **K** Nebuchadnezzar of Babylon did F
27:20 to Babylon **K** Jeconiah son of Jehoiakim of Judah,
27:21 the house of the **k** of Judah, and in Jerusalem: M
28: 1 beginning of the reign of **K** Zedekiah of Judah, J
28: 2 I have broken the yoke of the **k** of Babylon. A
28: 3 which **K** Nebuchadnezzar of Babylon took F
28: 4 I will also bring back to this place **K** Jeconiah son
28: 4 for I will break the yoke of the **k** of Babylon." A
28:11 the yoke of **K** Nebuchadnezzar of Babylon from F
28:14 so that they may serve **K** Nebuchadnezzar F
29: 2 This was after **K** Jeconiah, and the queen mother,
29: 3 whom **K** Zedekiah of Judah sent to Babylon J
29: 3 of Judah sent to Babylon to **K** Nebuchadnezzar F
29:16 Thus says the LORD concerning the **k** who sits on
29:21 deliver them into the hand of **K** Nebuchadrezzar K
29:22 whom the **k** of Babylon roasted in the fire," A
30: 9 the LORD their God and David their **k**,
32: 1 from the LORD in the tenth year of **K** Zedekiah J
32: 2 of the **k** of Babylon was besieging Jerusalem, A
32: 2 guard that was in the palace of the **k** of Judah, M
32: 3 where **K** Zedekiah of Judah had confined him. J
32: 3 give this city into the hand of the **k** of Babylon, A
32: 4 **K** Zedekiah of Judah shall not escape out of J
32: 4 the hands of the **k** of Babylon, and shall speak A
32:28 into the hand of **K** Nebuchadrezzar of Babylon, K
32:36 being given into the hand of the **k** of Babylon A
34: 1 when **K** Nebuchadrezzar of Babylon K
34: 2 speak to **K** Zedekiah of Judah and say to him: J
34: 2 give this city into the hand of the **k** of Babylon, A
34: 3 you shall see the **k** of Babylon eye to eye A
34: 4 the word of the LORD, O **K** Zedekiah of Judah! J
34: 6 spoke all these words to Zedekiah **k** of Judah, M
34: 7 the **k** of Babylon was fighting against Jerusalem A
34: 8 after **K** Zedekiah had made a covenant with all J
34:21 as for **K** Zedekiah of Judah and his officials, J
34:21 to the army of the **k** of Babylon, A
35: 1 in the days of **K** Jehoiakim son of Josiah of Judah:
35:11 when **K** Nebuchadrezzar of Babylon came up K
36: 1 In the fourth year of **K** Jehoiakim son of Josiah
36: 9 In the fifth year of **K** Jehoiakim son of Josiah
36:16 We certainly must report all these words to the **k**."
36:20 they went to the court of the **k**;
36:20 and they reported all the words to the **k**.

Jer 36:21 Then the **k** sent Jehudi to get the scroll,
36:21 the **k** and all the officials who stood beside the **k**.
36:22 the **k** was sitting in his winter apartment (it was
36:23 the **k** would cut them off with a penknife
36:24 Yet neither the **k**, nor any of his
36:25 and Delaiah and Gemariah urged the **k** not to burn
36:26 And the **k** commanded Jerahmeel the king's son
36:27 after the **k** had burned the scroll with the words
36:28 which **K** Jehoiakim of Judah has burned.
36:29 concerning **K** Jehoiakim of Judah you shall say:
36:29 in it that the **k** of Babylon will certainly come A
36:30 the LORD concerning **K** Jehoiakim of Judah:
36:32 of the scroll that **K** Jehoiakim of Judah had burned
37: 1 whom **K** Nebuchadrezzar of Babylon made king K
37: 1 Nebuchadrezzar of Babylon made **k** in the land
37: 3 **K** Zedekiah sent Jehucal son of Shelemiah and J
37: 7 the two of you shall say to the **k** of Judah, M
37:17 Then **K** Zedekiah sent for him, and received him. J
37:17 The **k** questioned him secretly in his house,
37:17 "You shall be handed over to the **k** of Babylon." A
37:18 Jeremiah also said to **K** Zedekiah, J
37:19 'The **k** of Babylon will not come against you A
37:20 Now please hear me, my lord **k**:
37:21 So **K** Zedekiah gave orders, J
38: 3 to the army of the **k** of Babylon and be taken. A
38: 4 Then the officials said to the **k**,
38: 5 **K** Zedekiah said, "Here he is; J
38: 5 for the **k** is powerless against you."
38: 7 The **k** happened to be sitting at the Benjamin Gate,
38: 8 the king's house and spoke to the **k**,
38: 9 "My lord **k**, these men have acted wickedly
38:10 the **k** commanded Ebed-melech the Ethiopian,
38:11 the men with him and went to the house of the **k**,
38:14 **K** Zedekiah sent for the prophet Jeremiah J
38:14 **k** said to Jeremiah, "I have something to ask you;
38:16 **K** Zedekiah swore an oath in secret to Jeremiah, J
38:17 surrender to the officials of the **k** of Babylon, A
38:18 not surrender to the officials of the **k** of Babylon, A
38:19 **K** Zedekiah said to Jeremiah, J
38:22 remaining in the house of the **k** of Judah M
38:22 to the officials of the **k** of Babylon and saying, A
38:23 but shall be seized by the **k** of Babylon; A
38:25 'Just tell us what you said to the **k**;
38:25 What did the **k** say to you?'
38:26 the **k** not to send me back to the house of Jonathan
38:27 in the very words the **k** had commanded.
39: 1 In the ninth year of **K** Zedekiah of Judah, J
39: 1 **K** Nebuchadrezzar of Babylon K
39: 3 all the officials of the **k** of Babylon came and A
39: 3 the rest of the officials of the **k** of Babylon. A
39: 4 When **K** Zedekiah of Judah and all J
39: 5 up to **K** Nebuchadrezzar of Babylon, at Riblah, K
39: 6 **k** of Babylon slaughtered the sons of Zedekiah A
39: 6 **k** of Babylon slaughtered all the nobles of Judah. A
39:11 **K** Nebuchadrezzar of Babylon gave command K
39:13 all the chief officers of the **k** of Babylon sent A
40: 5 **k** of Babylon appointed governor of the towns A
40: 7 that the **k** of Babylon had appointed Gedaliah A
40: 9 Stay in the land and serve the **k** of Babylon, A
40:11 other lands heard that the **k** of Babylon had left A
40:14 "Are you at all aware that Baalis **k** of
41: 1 one of the chief officers of the **k**,
41: 2 the **k** of Babylon had appointed him governor A
41: 9 the large cistern that **K** Asa had made for defense
41: 9 for defense against **K** Baasha of Israel;
41:18 **k** of Babylon had made governor over the land. A
42:11 Do not be afraid of the **k** of Babylon, A
43:10 to send and take my servant **K** Nebuchadrezzar K
44:30 I am going to give Pharaoh Hophra, **k** of Egypt, H
44:30 just as I gave **K** Zedekiah of Judah into the hand J
44:30 into the hand of **K** Nebuchadrezzar of Babylon, K
45: 1 in the fourth year of **K** Jehoiakim son of Josiah
46: 2 about the army of Pharaoh Neco, **k** of Egypt, H
46: 2 which **K** Nebuchadrezzar of Babylon defeated K
46: 2 in the fourth year of **K** Jehoiakim son of Josiah
46:13 **K** Nebuchadrezzar of Babylon to attack the land K
46:17 Give Pharaoh, **k** of Egypt, H
46:18 says the **K**, whose name is the LORD of hosts,
46:26 **K** Nebuchadrezzar of Babylon and his officers. K
48:15 says the **K**, whose name is the LORD of hosts,
49:28 the kingdoms of Hazor that **K** Nebuchadrezzar K
49:30 For **K** Nebuchadrezzar of Babylon has made K
49:34 beginning of the reign of **K** Zedekiah of Judah. J
49:38 and destroy their **k** and officials, says the LORD.
50:17 First the **k** of Assyria devoured it, C
50:17 and now at the end **K** Nebuchadrezzar K
50:18 to punish the **k** of Babylon and his land, A
50:18 as I punished the **k** of Assyria. C
50:43 The **k** of Babylon heard news of them, A
51:31 to tell the **k** of Babylon that his city is taken A
51:34 "**K** Nebuchadrezzar of Babylon has devoured K
51:57 says the **K**, whose name is the LORD of hosts.
51:59 he went with **K** Zedekiah of Judah to Babylon, J
52: 3 Zedekiah rebelled against the **k** of Babylon. A
52: 4 **K** Nebuchadrezzar of Babylon came K
52: 5 until the eleventh year of **K** Zedekiah. J
52: 8 But the army of the Chaldeans pursued the **k**,
52: 9 Then they captured the **k**, and brought him
52: 9 **k** of Babylon at Riblah in the land of Hamath, A
52:10 The **k** of Babylon killed the sons of Zedekiah A
52:11 and the **k** of Babylon took him to Babylon, A
52:12 the nineteenth year of **K** Nebuchadrezzar, K
52:12 year of King Nebuchadrezzar, **k** of Babylon— A
52:12 of the bodyguard who served the **k** of Babylon, A
52:15 deserters who had defected to the **k** of Babylon, A
52:20 which **K** Solomon had made for the house of E
52:26 and brought them to the **k** of Babylon at Riblah. A

Jer 52:27 And the **k** of Babylon struck them down, A
52:31 thirty-seventh year of the exile of **K** Jehoiachin
52:31 **K** Evil-merodach of Babylon,
52:31 to **K** Jehoiachin of Judah and brought him out
52:34 allowance was given him by the **k** of Babylon, A
La 2:6 in his fierce indignation has spurned **k** and priest.
2:9 her **k** and princes are among the nations;
Eze 1:2 the fifth year of the exile of **K** Jehoiachin),
7:27 The **k** shall mourn, the prince shall be wrapped
17:12 Tell them: The **k** of Babylon came to Jerusalem, A
17:12 took its **k** and its officials,
17:16 the place where the **k** resides who made him **k**,
19:9 and brought him to the **k** of Babylon; A
20:33 and with wrath poured out, I will be **k** over you.
21:19 for the sword of the **k** of Babylon to come; A
21:21 **k** of Babylon stands at the parting of the way, A
24:2 The **k** of Babylon has laid siege to Jerusalem A
26:7 against Tyre from the north **K** Nebuchadrezzar K
26:7 **k** of kings, together with horses, chariots, P
28:12 raise a lamentation over the **k** of Tyre,
29:2 set your face against Pharaoh **k** of Egypt, H
29:3 I am against you, Pharaoh **k** of Egypt, H
29:18 **K** Nebuchadrezzar of Babylon K
29:19 give the land of Egypt to **K** Nebuchadrezzar K
30:10 by the hand of **K** Nebuchadrezzar of Babylon. K
30:21 I have broken the arm of Pharaoh **k** of Egypt; H
30:22 I am against Pharaoh **k** of Egypt, H
30:24 I will strengthen the arms of the **k** of Babylon, A
30:25 I will strengthen the arms of the **k** of Babylon, A
30:25 put my sword into the hand of the **k** of Babylon. A
31:2 say to Pharaoh **k** of Egypt and to his hordes: H
32:2 raise a lamentation over Pharaoh **k** of Egypt, H
32:11 sword of the **k** of Babylon shall come against A
37:22 and one **k** shall be **k** over them all.
37:24 My servant David shall be **k** over them;
Da 1:1 In the third year of the reign of **K** Jehoiakim
1:1 **K** Nebuchadnezzar of Babylon came to F
1:2 Lord let **K** Jehoiakim of Judah fall into his power,
1:3 the **k** commanded his palace master Ashpenaz
1:5 The **k** assigned them a daily portion of
1:10 "I am afraid of my lord the **k**; D
1:10 you would endanger my head with the **k**."
1:18 At the end of the time that the **k** had set for them to
1:19 and the **k** spoke with them.
1:20 concerning which the **k** inquired of them,
1:21 until the first year of **K** Cyrus.
2:2 So the **k** commanded that the magicians,
2:2 Chaldeans be summoned to tell the **k** his dreams.
2:2 When they came in and stood before the **k**,
2:4 The Chaldeans said to the **k** (in Aramaic), "O **k**,
2:5 The **k** answered the Chaldeans,
2:7 "Let the **k** first tell his servants the dream,
2:8 The **k** answered, "I know with certainty
2:10 The Chaldeans answered the **k**,
2:10 on earth who can reveal what the **k** demands!
2:10 In fact no **k**, however great and powerful,
2:11 The thing that the **k** is asking is too difficult,
2:11 and no one can reveal it to the **k** except the gods,
2:12 the **k** flew into a violent rage and commanded
2:15 "Why is the decree of the **k** so urgent?"
2:16 that the **k** give him time and he would tell the **k**
2:23 for you have revealed to us what the **k** ordered."
2:24 whom the **k** had appointed to destroy the wise men
2:24 bring me in before the **k**,
2:24 and I will give the **k** the interpretation."
2:25 Then Arioch quickly brought Daniel before the **k**
2:25 the exiles from Judah a man who can tell the **k**
2:26 **k** said to Daniel, whose name was Belteshazzar,
2:27 Daniel answered the **k**, "No wise men, enchanters,
magicians, or diviners can show to the **k** the
mystery that the **k** is asking,
2:28 **K** Nebuchadnezzar what will happen at the end F
2:29 O **k**, as you lay in bed,
2:30 to the **k** and that you may understand the thoughts
2:31 "You were looking, O **k**, and lo!
2:36 now we will tell the **k** its interpretation.
2:37 You, O **k**, the king of kings—
2:37 You, O king, the **k** of kings— P
2:45 The great God has informed the **k** what shall
2:46 Then **K** Nebuchadnezzar fell on his face, F
2:47 The **k** said to Daniel, "Truly,
2:48 Then the **k** promoted Daniel,
2:49 Daniel made a request of the **k**,
3:1 **K** Nebuchadnezzar made a golden statue F
3:2 Then **K** Nebuchadnezzar sent for the satraps, F
3:2 of the statue that **K** Nebuchadnezzar had set up. F
3:3 of the statue that **K** Nebuchadnezzar had set up. F
3:5 that **K** Nebuchadnezzar has set up. F
3:7 that **K** Nebuchadnezzar had set up. F
3:9 They said to **K** Nebuchadnezzar, "O king, F
3:9 They said to King Nebuchadnezzar, "O **k**,
3:10 You, O **k**, have made a decree,
3:12 These pay no heed to you, O **K**.
3:13 so they brought those men before the **k**.
3:16 Meshach, and Abednego answered the **k**,
3:17 of blazing fire and out of your hand, O **k**,
3:18 But if not, be it known to you, O **k**,
3:24 Then **K** Nebuchadnezzar was astonished and F
3:24 They answered the **k**, "True, O **k**."
3:30 Then the **k** promoted Shadrach, Meshach,
4:1 **K** Nebuchadnezzar to all peoples, nations, F
4:18 the dream that I, **K** Nebuchadnezzar, saw. F
4:19 The **k** said, "Belteshazzar,
4:22 it is you, O **k**! You have grown great
4:23 And whereas the **k** saw a holy watcher coming
4:24 O **k**, and it is a decree of the Most High
4:24 Most High that has come upon my lord the **k**: D
Da 4:27 O **k**, may my counsel be acceptable to you:
4:28 All this came upon **K** Nebuchadnezzar. F
4:30 and the **k** said, "Is this not magnificent Babylon,
4:31 "O **K** Nebuchadnezzar, to you it is declared: F
4:37 praise and extol and honor the **K** of heaven,
5:1 **K** Belshazzar made a great festival for a thousand
5:2 so that the **k** and his lords, his wives,
5:3 and the **k** and his lords, his wives,
5:5 The **k** was watching the hand as it wrote.
5:7 The **k** cried aloud to bring in the enchanters,
5:7 and the **k** said to the wise men of Babylon,
5:8 not read the writing or tell the **k** the interpretation.
5:9 Then **K** Belshazzar became greatly terrified
5:10 she heard the discussion of the **k** and his lords,
5:10 The queen said, "O **k**, live forever!
5:11 Your father, **K** Nebuchadnezzar, F
5:12 Daniel, whom the **k** named Belteshazzar.
5:13 Then Daniel was brought in before the **k**.
5:13 The **k** said to Daniel, "So you are Daniel,
5:13 whom my father the **k** brought from Judah?
5:17 Then Daniel answered in the presence of the **k**,
5:17 to the **k** and let him know the interpretation.
5:18 O **k**, the Most High God gave your father
5:30 very night Belshazzar, the Chaldean **k**, was killed.
6:2 so that the **k** might suffer no loss.
6:3 **k** planned to appoint him over the whole kingdom.
6:6 to the **k** and said to him, "O **K** Darius, live forever!
6:7 the governors are agreed that the **k** should establish
6:7 O **k**, shall be thrown into a den of lions.
6:8 O **k**, establish the interdict and sign the document,
6:9 **K** Darius signed the document and interdict.
6:12 the **k** and said concerning the interdict, "O **k**!
6:12 O **k**, shall be thrown into a den of lions?"
6:12 The **k** answered, "The thing stands fast,
6:13 Then they responded to the **k**, "Daniel,
6:13 O **k**, or to the interdict you have signed,
6:14 **k** heard the charge, he was very much distressed.
6:15 came to the **k** and said to him, "Know, O **k**,
6:15 that the **k** establishes can be changed."
6:16 Then the **k** gave the command,
6:16 The **k** said to Daniel, "May your God,
6:17 and the **k** sealed it with his own signet and with
6:18 the **k** went to his palace and spent the night fasting;
6:19 the **k** got up and hurried to the den of lions.
6:21 Daniel then said to the **k**, "O **k**, live forever!
6:22 and also before you, O **k**, I have done no wrong."
6:23 Then the **k** was exceedingly glad and commanded
6:24 The **k** gave a command,
6:25 Then **K** Darius wrote to all peoples and nations
7:1 In the first year of **K** Belshazzar of Babylon,
8:1 the reign of **K** Belshazzar a vision appeared to me,
8:21 The male goat is the **k** of Greece, and the great
horn between its eyes is the first **k**.
8:23 a **k** of bold countenance shall arise,
9:1 who became **k** over the realm of the Chaldeans—
10:1 of **K** Cyrus of Persia a word was revealed
11:3 Then a warrior **k** shall arise,
11:5 "Then the **k** of the south shall grow strong,
11:6 and the daughter of the **k** of the south shall come
to the **k** of the north to ratify the agreement.
11:7 against the army and enter the fortress of the **k** of
11:8 from attacking the **k** of the north;
11:9 latter shall invade the realm of the **k** of the south,
11:11 the **k** of the south shall go out and do battle
against the **k** of the north,
11:13 For the **k** of the north shall again raise a multitude,
11:14 "In those times many shall rise against the **k** of
11:15 **k** of the north shall come and throw up siegeworks,
11:25 and determination against the **k** of the south with
11:25 and the **k** of the south shall wage war with
11:36 "The **k** shall act as he pleases.
11:40 time of the end the **k** of the south shall attack him.
11:40 But the **k** of the north shall rush upon him like
Hos 1:1 in the days of **K** Jeroboam son of Joash of Israel.
3:4 For the Israelites shall remain many days without **k**
3:5 and seek the LORD their God, and David their **k**;
5:1 Listen, O house of the **k**! For the judgment pertains
5:13 and sent to the great **k**. N
7:3 By their wickedness they make the **k** glad,
7:5 On the day of our **k** the officials became sick with
10:3 "We have no **k**, for we do not fear the LORD,
10:3 for we do not fear the LORD, and a **k**—
10:6 be carried to Assyria as tribute to the great **k**. N
10:7 Samaria's **k** shall perish like a chip on the face of
10:15 At dawn the **k** of Israel shall be utterly cut off. B
11:5 and Assyria shall be their **k**,
13:10 Where now is your **k**, that he may save you?
13:10 of whom you said, "Give me a **k** and rulers"?
13:11 I gave you a **k** in my anger,
Am 1:1 concerning Israel in the days of **K** Uzziah of Judah
1:1 in the days of **K** Jeroboam son of Joash of Israel,
1:15 then their **k** shall go into exile,
2:1 he burned to lime the bones of the **k** of Edom.
5:26 You shall take up Sakkuth your **k**,
7:10 the priest of Bethel, sent to **K** Jeroboam of Israel,
Jnh 3:6 When the news reached the **k** of Nineveh,
3:7 "By the decree of the **k** and his nobles:
Mic 2:13 Their **k** will pass on before them,
4:9 Is there no **k** in you?
6:5 remember now what **K** Balak of Moab devised,
Na 3:18 Your shepherds are asleep, O **k** of Assyria; C
Zep 1:1 in the days of **K** Josiah son of Amon of Judah.
3:15 The **K** of Israel, the LORD, is in your midst; B
Hag 1:1 In the second year of **K** Darius, in the sixth month,
1:15 In the second year of **K** Darius,
Zec 7:1 In the fourth year of **K** Darius,
9:5 The **k** shall perish from Gaza;
Zec 9:9 your **k** comes to you; triumphant and victorious
11:6 and each into the hand of the **k**;
14:5 the earthquake in the days of **K** Uzziah of Judah.
14:9 And the LORD will become **k** over all the earth;
14:16 up year after year to worship the **K**,
14:17 not go up to Jerusalem to worship the **K**,
Mal 1:14 for I am a great **K**, says the LORD of hosts, N
Mt 1:6 and Jesse the father of **K** David. G
2:1 In the time of **K** Herod,
2:2 is the child who has been born **k** of the Jews? O
2:3 When **K** Herod heard this, he was frightened,
2:9 When they had heard the **k**, they set out;
5:35 or by Jerusalem, for it is the city of the great **K**. N
14:9 The **k** was grieved, yet out of regard for his oaths
18:23 be compared to a **k** who wished to settle accounts
21:5 Look, your **k** is coming to you, humble,
22:2 be compared to a **k** who gave a wedding banquet
22:7 The **k** was enraged. He sent his troops,
22:11 "But when the **k** came in to see the guests,
22:13 Then the **k** said to the attendants,
25:34 Then the **k** will say to those at his right hand,
25:40 And the **k** will answer them, 'Truly I tell you,
27:11 asked him, "Are you the **K** of the Jews?" O
27:29 saying, "Hail, **K** of the Jews!" O
27:37 which read, "This is Jesus, the **K** of the Jews." O
27:42 He is the **K** of Israel; B
Mk 6:14 **K** Herod heard of it, for Jesus' name had become
6:22 and the **k** said to the girl,
6:25 Immediately she rushed back to the **k**
6:26 The **k** was deeply grieved;
6:27 Immediately the **k** sent a soldier of the guard
15:2 Pilate asked him, "Are you the **K** of the Jews?" O
15:9 want me to release for you the **K** of the Jews?" O
15:12 to do with the man you call the **K** of the Jews?" O
15:18 they began saluting him, "Hail, **K** of the Jews!" O
15:26 charge against him read, "The **K** of the Jews." O
15:32 Let the Messiah, the **K** of Israel, B
Lk 1:5 In the days of **K** Herod of Judea,
14:31 Or what **k**, going out to wage war
14:31 going out to wage war against another **k**,
19:27 of mine who did not want me to be **k** over them—
19:38 the **k** who comes in the name of the Lord!
23:2 and saying that he himself is the Messiah, a **k**."
23:3 Pilate asked him, "Are you the **k** of the Jews?" O
23:37 "If you are the **K** of the Jews, save yourself!" O
23:38 "This is the **K** of the Jews." O
Jn 1:49 You are the **K** of Israel!" B
6:15 to come and take him by force to make him **k**,
12:13 comes in the name of the Lord—the **K** of Israel! B
12:15 your **k** is coming, sitting on a donkey's colt!"
18:33 and asked him, "Are you the **K** of the Jews?" O
18:37 Pilate asked him, "So you are a **k**?"
18:37 Jesus answered, "You say that I am a **k**.
18:39 want me to release for you the **K** of the Jews?" O
19:3 saying, "Hail, **K** of the Jews!" O
19:12 Everyone who claims to be a **k** sets himself against
19:14 He said to the Jews, "Here is your **K**!"
19:15 Pilate asked them, "Shall I crucify your **K**?"
19:15 "We have no **k** but the emperor."
19:19 It read, "Jesus of Nazareth, the **K** of the Jews." O
19:21 'The **K** of the Jews,' but, 'This man said, O
19:21 but, 'This man said, I am **K** of the Jews.' " O
Ac 7:10 when he stood before Pharaoh, **k** of Egypt, H
7:18 until another **k** who had not known Joseph ruled
12:1 About that time **K** Herod laid violent hands
13:21 Then they asked for a **k**;
13:22 When he had removed him, he made David their **k**.
17:7 saying that there is another **k** named Jesus."
25:13 **K** Agrippa and Bernice arrived at Caesarea
25:14 Festus laid Paul's case before the **k**, saying,
25:24 "**K** Agrippa and all here present with us,
25:26 **K** Agrippa, so that, after we have examined him,
26:2 **K** Agrippa, I am to make my defense today
26:19 "After that, **K** Agrippa, I was not disobedient to
26:26 Indeed the **k** knows about these things,
26:27 **K** Agrippa, do you believe the prophets?
26:30 Then the **k** got up, and with him the governor
2Co 11:32 under **K** Aretas guarded the city of Damascus
1Ti 1:17 To the **K** of the ages, immortal, invisible,
6:15 the **K** of kings and Lord of lords. P
Heb 7:1 This "**K** Melchizedek of Salem,
7:2 in the first place, means "**k** of righteousness";
7:2 next he is also **k** of Salem, that is, "**k** of peace."
Rev 9:11 as **k** over them the angel of the bottomless pit;
15:3 Just and true are your ways, **K** of the nations!
17:14 for he is Lord of lords and **K** of kings, P
19:16 "**K** of kings and Lord of lords." P
Tob 1:2 **K** Shalmaneser of the Assyrians was taken
1:5 of Naphtali sacrificed to the calf that **K** Jeroboam
1:18 also buried any whom **K** Sennacherib put to death
1:18 that the **k** of heaven executed upon him because
1:19 Then one of the Ninevites went and informed the **k**
1:19 the **k** knew about me and that I was being searched
1:22 of the accounts under **K** Sennacherib of Assyria;
10:13 praising the Lord of heaven and earth, **K** over all,
12:7 It is good to conceal the secret of a **k**,
12:11 'It is good to conceal the secret of a **k**,
13:6 and exalt the **K** of the ages.
13:7 and my soul rejoices in the **K** of heaven.
13:10 for he is good, and bless the **K** of the ages,
13:11 bearing gifts in their hands for the **K** of heaven.
13:15 My soul blesses the Lord, the great **K**! N
13:16 to see your glory and acknowledge the **K**
14:15 into Media, those whom **K** Cyaxares
Jdt 1:5 Then **K** Nebuchadnezzar made war F
1:5 against **K** Arphaxad in the great plain that is on
1:6 and, on the plain, Arioch, **k** of the Elymeans.

Jdt 1: 7 Then Nebuchadnezzar, **k** of the Assyrians,
1:11 **k** of the Assyrians, and refused to join him in
1:13 against **K** Arphaxad and defeated him in battle,
2: 1 the palace of Nebuchadnezzar, **k** of the Assyrians,
2: 4 **k** of the Assyrians, called Holofernes,
2: 5 the Great **K,** the lord of the whole earth: N
2:19 **K** Nebuchadnezzar and to cover the whole face F
3: 2 the servants of Nebuchadnezzar, the Great **K,** N
4: 1 the **k** of the Assyrians, had done to the nations,
5: 3 Who rules over them as **k** and leads their army?
5:11 So the **k** of Egypt became hostile to them; H
6: 4 says **K** Nebuchadnezzar, lord of the whole earth. F
9:12 Creator of the waters, **K** of all your creation,
11: 1 to serve Nebuchadnezzar, **k** of all the earth.
11: 4 the servants of my lord **K** Nebuchadnezzar." F
11: 7 the life of Nebuchadnezzar, **k** of the whole earth,
11:23 palace of **K** Nebuchadnezzar and be renowned F
14:18 on the house of **K** Nebuchadnezzar. F
AdE 1: 2 **K** Artaxerxes was enthroned in the city of Susa,
1: 5 the end of the festivity the **k** gave a drinking party
1: 7 such as the **k** himself drank.
1: 8 but the **k** wished to have it so,
1: 9 the women in the palace where **K** Artaxerxes was.
1:10 when the **k** was in good humor, he told Haman,
1:10 the seven eunuchs who served **K** Artaxerxes,
1:12 This offended the **k** and he became furious.
1:14 Persians and Medes who were closest to the **k—**
1:15 for not obeying the order that the **k** had sent her by
1:16 Then Muchaeus said to the **k** and the governors,
1:16 not only the **k** but also all the king's governors
1:17 the queen had said and how she had defied the **k**).
1:17 "And just as she defied **K** Artaxerxes,
1:18 on hearing what she has said to the **k,**
1:19 If therefore it pleases the **k,**
1:19 but let the **k** give her royal rank to
1:20 Let whatever law the **k** enacts be proclaimed
1:21 This speech pleased the **k** and the governors,
1:21 and the **k** did as Muchaeus had recommended.
1:22 The **k** sent the decree into all his kingdom,
2: 2 and virtuous girls be sought out for the **k.**
2: 3 The **k** shall appoint officers in all the provinces
2: 4 And the woman who pleases the **k** shall
2: 4 This pleased the **k,** and he did so.
2: 6 among those whom **K** Nebuchadnezzar F
2: 8 So, when the decree of the **k** was proclaimed,
2:12 a girl was to go to the **k** was twelve months.
2:13 Then she goes in to the **k;**
2:14 in to the **k** again unless she is summoned by name.
2:15 the brother of Mordecai's father, to go in to the **k,**
2:16 in to **K** Artaxerxes in the twelfth month,
2:17 the **k** loved Esther and she found favor beyond all
2:18 Then the **k** gave a banquet lasting seven days
2:21 and they plotted to kill **K** Artaxerxes.
2:22 who in turn revealed the plot to the **k.**
2:23 Then the **k** ordered a memorandum to be deposited
3: 1 these events **K** Artaxerxes promoted Haman son
3: 2 for so the **k** had commanded to be done.
3: 7 In the twelfth year of **K** Artaxerxes Haman came
3: 8 Then Haman said to **K** Artaxerxes,
3: 8 and they do not keep the laws of the **k.**
3: 8 It is not expedient for the **k** to tolerate them.
3: 9 If it pleases the **k,** let it be decreed that they are to
3:10 the **k** took off his signet ring and gave it to Haman
3:11 The **k** told Haman, "Keep the money,
3:12 in the name of **K** Artaxerxes to the magistrates and
3:15 And while the **k** and Haman caroused together,
4: 8 to go in to the **k** and plead for his favor in behalf of
4: 8 for Haman, who stands next to the **k,**
4: 8 then speak to the **k** in our behalf,
4:11 to the **k** inside the inner court without being called,
4:11 the **k** stretches out the golden scepter is safe—
4:11 now thirty days since I was called to go to the **k.'** "
4:16 After that I will go to the **k,** contrary to the law,
5: 3 The **k** said to her, "What do you wish, Esther?
5: 4 If it pleases the **k,** let him and Haman come to
5: 5 Then the **k** said, "Bring Haman quickly,
5: 6 they were drinking wine, the **k** said to Esther,
5: 8 if I have found favor in the sight of the **k,**
5: 8 let the **k** and Haman come to the dinner
5: 9 So Haman went out from the **k** joyful and glad
5:11 and the honor that the **k** had bestowed on him,
5:12 to the dinner with the **k** except me;
5:14 in the morning tell the **k** to have Mordecai hanged
5:14 Then, go merrily with the **k** to the dinner."
6: 1 That night the Lord took sleep from the **k,**
6: 2 told the **k** about the two royal eunuchs who were on guard and sought to lay hands on **K** Artaxerxes.
6: 3 The **k** said, "What honor or dignity did we bestow
6: 4 the **k** was inquiring about the goodwill shown
6: 4 The **k** asked, "Who is in the courtyard?"
6: 4 to the **k** about hanging Mordecai on the gallows
6: 5 The servants of the **k** answered,
6: 5 And the **k** said, "Summon him."
6: 6 Then the **k** said to Haman,
6: 6 "Whom would the **k** wish to honor more than me?"
6: 7 So he said to the **k,**
6: 7 "For a person whom the **k** wishes to honor,
6: 8 the fine linen robe that the **k** has worn,
6: 8 and the horse on which the **k** rides,
6: 9 the person whom the **k** loves and mount him on
6: 9 be done to everyone whom the **k** honors.' "
6:10 Then the **k** said to Haman,
6:11 be done to everyone whom the **k** wishes to honor."
7: 1 the **k** and Haman went in to drink with the queen.
7: 2 second day, as they were drinking wine, the **k** said,
7: 3 "If I have found favor with the **k,**
7: 5 the **k** said, "Who is the person that would dare
AdE 7: 6 Haman was terrified in the presence of the **k**
7: 7 **k** rose from the banquet and went into the garden,
7: 8 When the **k** returned from the garden,
7: 8 The **k** said, "Will he dare even assault my wife
7: 9 Then Bugathan, one of the eunuchs, said to the **k,**
7: 9 who gave information of concern to the **k;**
7: 9 So the **k** said, "Let Haman be hanged on that."
7:10 With that the anger of the **k** abated.
8: 1 that very day **K** Artaxerxes granted to Esther all
8: 1 Mordecai was summoned by the **k,**
8: 1 for Esther had told the **k** that he was related to her.
8: 2 **k** took the ring that had been taken from Haman,
8: 3 Then she spoke once again to the **k** and,
8: 4 The **k** extended his golden scepter to Esther,
8: 4 and she rose and stood before the **k.**
8: 7 The **k** said to Esther, "Now that I have granted all
8:14 to perform what the **k** had commanded;
9: 1 which is Adar, the decree written by the **k** arrived.
9:11 of those killed in Susa was reported to the **k.**
9:12 The **k** said to Esther, "In Susa, the capital,
9:13 And Esther said to the **k,**
9:25 he went in to the **k,** telling him to hang Mordecai;
10: 1 The **k** levied a tax upon his kingdom both by land
10: 3 of **K** Artaxerxes and was great in the kingdom,
10: 6 whom the **k** married and made queen.
11: 3 a great man, serving in the court of the **k.**
11: 4 of the captives whom **K** Nebuchadnezzar F
11: 4 from Jerusalem with **K** Jeconiah of Judea.
12: 1 the two eunuchs of the **k** who kept watch in
12: 2 to lay hands on **K** Artaxerxes;
12: 2 and he informed the **k** concerning them.
12: 3 Then the **k** examined the two eunuchs,
12: 4 The **k** made a permanent record of these things,
12: 5 And the **k** ordered Mordecai to serve in the court,
12: 6 a Bougean, who was in great honor with the **k,**
12: 6 because of the two eunuchs of the **k.**
13: 1 This is a copy of the letter: "The Great **K,** N
13: 9 "O Lord, Lord, you rule as **K** over all things,
13:15 And now, O Lord God and **K,** God of Abraham,
14: 3 "O my Lord, you only are our **k;**
14:10 and to magnify forever a mortal **k.**
14:12 O **K** of the gods and Master of all dominion!
15: 6 through all the doors, she stood before the **k.**
15: 8 Then God changed the spirit of the **k** to gentleness,
15:16 Then the **k** was agitated, and all his servants tried
16: 1 "The Great **K,** Artaxerxes, N
Wis 6:24 and a sensible **k** is the stability of any people.
7: 5 no **k** has had a different beginning of existence;
9: 7 be **k** of your people and to be judge over your sons
11:10 but you examined the ungodly as a stern **k** does
12:14 nor can any **k** or monarch confront you
14:17 made a visible image of the **k** whom they honored,
14:18 not know the **k** to intensify their worship.
18:11 and the commoner suffered the same loss as the **k;**
Sir 7: 4 or the seat of honor from the **k.**
7: 5 or display your wisdom before the **k.**
10: 3 An undisciplined **k** ruins his people,
10:10 the **k** of today will die tomorrow.
38: 2 and they are rewarded by the **k.**
46:20 he prophesied and made known to the **k** his death,
48:23 and he prolonged the life of the **k.**
50:15 a pleasing odor to the Most High, the **k** of all.
51: 1 O Lord and **K,** and praise you, O God my Savior.
51: 6 the slander of an unrighteous tongue to the **k.**
51:12 *Give thanks to the **K** of the kings of the kings,*
Bar 1: 3 to Jeconiah son of Jehoiakim, **k** of Judah, M
1: 8 vessels that Zedekiah son of Josiah, **k** of Judah, M
1: 9 after **K** Nebuchadnezzar of Babylon F
1:11 for the life of **K** Nebuchadnezzar of Babylon, F
1:12 the protection of **K** Nebuchadnezzar of Babylon, F
2:21 Bend your shoulders and serve the **k** of Babylon, A
2:22 of the Lord and will not serve the **k** of Babylon, A
2:24 to serve the **k** of Babylon; A
LtJ 6: 1 to Babylon as exiles by the **k** of the Babylonians,
6: 2 exiles by Nebuchadnezzar, **k** of the Babylonians.
6:18 against anyone who has offended a **k,**
6:34 They cannot set up a **k** or depose one.
6:53 up a **k** over a country or give rain to people.
6:56 they can offer no resistance to **k** or enemy.
6:59 So it is better to be a **k** who shows his courage,
Aza 1: 9 lawless and hateful rebels, and to an unjust **k,**
Bel 1: 1 **K** Astyages was laid to rest with his ancestors,
1: 2 Daniel was a companion of the **k,**
1: 4 The **k** revered it and went every day to worship it.
1: 4 the **k** said to him, "Why do you not worship Bel?"
1: 6 The **k** said to him, "Do you not think that Bel is
1: 7 and said, "Do not be deceived, O **k,**
1: 8 Then the **k** was angry and called the priests of Bel
1: 9 Daniel said to the **k,** "Let it be done
1:10 So the **k** went with Daniel into the temple of Bel.
1:11 O **k,** set out the food and prepare the wine,
1:14 they had gone out, the **k** set out the food for Bel.
1:14 the whole temple in the presence of the **k** alone.
1:16 Early in the morning the **k** rose and came,
1:17 The **k** said, "Are the seals unbroken, Daniel?"
1:17 He answered, "They are unbroken, O **k.**"
1:18 the **k** looked at the table,
1:19 Daniel laughed and restrained the **k** from going in.
1:20 The **k** said, "I see the footprints of men and women
1:21 Then the **k** was enraged, and he arrested the priests
1:22 Therefore the **k** put them to death,
1:24 The **k** said to Daniel, "You cannot deny that this is
1:26 But give me permission, O **k,**
1:26 The **k** said, "I give you permission."
1:28 against the **k,** saying, "The king has become a Jew;
1:28 saying, "The **k** has become a Jew;
1:29 Going to the **k,** they said, "Hand Daniel over to us,
Bel 1:30 The **k** saw that they were pressing him hard,
1:40 the seventh day the **k** came to mourn for Daniel.
1:41 The **k** shouted with a loud voice, "You are great,
1Mc 1: 1 had defeated **K** Darius of the Persians and the Medes, he succeeded him as **k.**
1: 1 (He had previously become **k** of Greece.)
1:10 Antiochus Epiphanes, son of **K** Antiochus;
1:13 and some of the people eagerly went to the **k,**
1:16 he determined to become **k** of the land of Egypt,
1:18 He engaged **K** Ptolemy of Egypt in battle,
1:29 the **k** sent to the cities of Judah a chief collector
1:41 the **k** wrote to his whole kingdom that all should
1:43 All the Gentiles accepted the command of the **k.**
1:44 And the **k** sent letters by messengers to Jerusalem
1:50 not obey the command of the **k** shall die."
1:57 was condemned to death by decree of the **k.**
2:18 be the first to come and do what the **k** commands,
2:18 be numbered among the Friends of the **k,**
2:19 that live under the rule of the **k** obey him,
2:33 Come out and do what the **k** commands,
2:34 the **k** commands and so profane the sabbath day."
3:26 His fame reached the **k,** and the Gentiles talked of
3:27 When **K** Antiochus heard these reports,
3:37 Then the **k** took the remaining half of his forces
3:38 able men among the Friends of the **k,**
3:39 of Judah and destroy it, as the **k** had commanded.
3:42 also learned what the **k** had commanded to do to
4:27 nor had they turned out as the **k** had ordered.
6: 1 **K** Antiochus was going through
6: 2 Macedonian **k** who first reigned over the Greeks.
6: 8 When the **k** heard this news,
6:15 and bring him up to be **k.**
6:16 Thus **K** Antiochus died there in
6:17 When Lysias learned that the **k** was dead,
6:22 They went to the **k** and said,
6:28 The **k** was enraged when he heard this.
6:32 opposite the camp of the **k.**
6:33 the **k** set out and took his army by a forced march
6:43 and he supposed that the **k** was on it.
6:48 and the **k** encamped in Judea and at Mount Zion.
6:50 So the **k** took Beth-zur and stationed a guard there
6:55 Then Lysias heard that Philip, whom **K** Antiochus
6:55 to bring up his son Antiochus to be **k,**
6:56 with the forces that had gone with the **k,**
6:57 and said to the **k,** to the commanders of the forces,
6:60 The speech pleased the **k** and the commanders,
6:61 So the **k** and the commanders gave them their oath.
6:62 But when the **k** entered Mount Zion and saw what
7: 6 They brought to the **k** this accusation against
7: 7 on us and on the land of the **k,**
7: 8 So the **k** chose Bacchides,
7: 8 in the kingdom and was faithful to the **k.**
7:20 then Bacchides went back to the **k.**
7:25 he returned to the **k** and brought malicious charges
7:26 Then the **k** sent Nicanor, one
7:33 the burnt offering that was being offered for the **k.**
7:41 the messengers from the **k** spoke blasphemy,
8: 5 and **K** Perseus of the Macedonians,
8: 6 also had defeated Antiochus the Great, **k** of Asia,
8: 8 These they took from him and gave to **K** Eumenes.
8:31 "Concerning the wrongs that **K** Demetrius is doing
9:57 he returned to the **k,** and the land of Judah had rest
10: 2 When **K** Demetrius heard of it,
10: 8 that the **k** had given him authority to recruit troops.
10:15 Now **K** Alexander heard of all the promises
10:18 "**K** Alexander to his brother Jonathan, greetings.
10:25 "**K** Demetrius to the nation of the Jews, greetings.
10:36 be given them that is due to all the forces of the **k.**
10:37 be stationed in the great strongholds of the **k,**
10:37 just as the **k** has commanded in the land of Judah.
10:43 because they owe money to the **k** or are in debt,
10:44 the sanctuary be paid from the revenues of the **k.**
10:45 also be paid from the revenues of the **k.**"
10:48 Now **K** Alexander assembled large forces
10:51 Ptolemy **k** of Egypt with the following message: H
10:55 Ptolemy the **k** replied and said,
10:58 **K** Alexander met him,
10:59 Then **K** Alexander wrote to Jonathan to come
10:61 but the **k** paid no attention to them.
10:62 The **k** gave orders to take off Jonathan's garments
10:63 The **k** also seated him at his side;
10:65 Thus the **k** honored him and enrolled him
10:68 When **K** Alexander heard of it,
10:88 When **K** Alexander heard of these things,
11: 1 Then the **k** of Egypt gathered great forces, H
11: 2 **K** Alexander had commanded them to meet him,
11: 5 They also told the **k** what Jonathan had done, to throw blame on him; but the **k** kept silent.
11: 6 Jonathan met the **k** at Joppa with pomp,
11: 7 with the **k** as far as the river called Eleutherus;
11: 8 So **K** Ptolemy gained control of the coastal cities
11: 9 He sent envoys to **K** Demetrius, saying, "Come,
11:14 Now **K** Alexander was in Cilicia at that time,
11:16 and **K** Ptolemy was triumphant.
11:18 But **K** Ptolemy died three days later,
11:19 So Demetrius became **k** in
11:21 to the **k** and reported to him
11:24 for he went to the **k** at Ptolemais,
11:26 **k** treated him as his predecessors had treated him;
11:28 Then Jonathan asked the **k** to free Judea and
11:29 The **k** consented, and wrote a letter to Jonathan
11:30 "**K** Demetrius to his brother Jonathan and to
11:32 '**K** Demetrius to his father Lasthenes, greetings.
11:34 that the **k** formerly received from them each year,
11:38 When **K** Demetrius saw that the land was quiet
11:40 to become **k** in place of his father.
11:41 Now Jonathan sent to **K** Demetrius the request

1Mc 11:44 they came to the **k**, the **k** rejoiced at their arrival.
11:45 and they wanted to kill the **k**.
11:46 But the **k** fled into the palace.
11:47 So the **k** called the Jews to his aid,
11:48 of spoil on that day, and saved the **k**.
11:49 their courage failed and they cried out to the **k**
11:51 So the Jews gained glory in the sight of the **k** and
11:52 So **K** Demetrius sat on the throne of his kingdom,
12: 7 to the high priest Onias from Arius, who was **k**
12:20 "**K** Arius of the Spartans,
12:39 Then Trypho attempted to become **k** in Asia
12:39 and to raise his hand against **K** Antiochus.
13:31 with the young **K** Antiochus;
13:32 and became **k** in his place, putting on the crown
13:34 to **K** Demetrius with a request to grant relief to
13:35 **K** Demetrius sent him a favorable reply
13:36 "**K** Demetrius to Simon, the high priest and friend
14: 1 **K** Demetrius assembled his forces
14: 2 When **K** Arsaces of Persia and Media heard
14:38 of these things **K** Demetrius confirmed him in
15: 1 Antiochus, son of **K** Demetrius,
15: 2 "**K** Antiochus to Simon the high priest
15:16 consul of the Romans, to **K** Ptolemy, greetings.
15:22 The consul wrote the same thing to **K** Demetrius
15:25 **K** Antiochus besieged Dor for the second time,
15:36 in wrath to the **k** and reported to him these words,
15:36 And the **k** was very angry.
15:38 Then the **k** made Cendebeus commander-in-chief
15:39 on the people; but the **k** pursued Trypho.
15:41 as the **k** had ordered him.
16:18 a report about these things and sent it to the **k**,
2Mc 1:10 teacher of **K** Ptolemy, and to the Jews in Egypt,
1:11 for taking our side against the **k**,
1:20 having been commissioned by the **k** of Persia,
1:24 you alone are **k** and are kind,
1:33 and it was reported to the **k** of the Persians that,
1:34 the **k** investigated the matter,
1:35 the **k** favored he exchanged many excellent gifts.
3: 3 to the extent that **K** Seleucus of Asia defrayed
3: 6 for them to fall under the control of the **k**.
3: 7 When Apollonius met the **k**,
3: 7 The **k** chose Heliodorus, who was in charge
3:13 because of the orders he had from the **k**,
3:32 fearing that the **k** might get the notion
3:35 he marched off with his forces to the **k**.
3:37 the **k** asked Heliodorus what sort of person would
4: 5 So he appealed to the **k**,
4: 8 the **k** at an interview three hundred sixty talents
4:10 When the **k** assented and Jason came to office,
4:18 at Tyre and the **k** was present,
4:21 to Egypt for the coronation of Philometor as **k**,
4:23 the money to the **k** and to complete the records
4:24 But he, when presented to the **k**,
4:27 of the money promised to the **k**.
4:28 of them were summoned by the **k** on account
4:31 So the **k** went hurriedly to settle the trouble,
4:36 When the **k** returned from the region of Cilicia,
4:44 When the **k** came to Tyre,
4:45 to Ptolemy son of Dorymenes to win over the **k**.
4:46 the **k** aside into a colonnade as if for refreshment,
4:46 induced the **k** to change his mind.
5:11 When news of what had happened reached the **k**,
5:18 whom **K** Seleucus sent to inspect the treasury.
6: 1 the **k** sent an Athenian senator to compel the Jews
6:21 that had been commanded by the **k**,
7: 1 and were being compelled by the **k**,
7: 3 The **k** fell into a rage,
7: 5 the **k** ordered them to take him to the fire,
7: 9 but the **K** of the universe will raise us up to
7:12 the **k** himself and those with him were astonished
7:16 But he looked at the **k**, and said,
7:25 the **k** called the mother to him and urged her
7:39 The **k** fell into a rage,
8:10 to make up for the **k** the tribute due to the Romans,
9:19 "To his worthy Jewish citizens, Antiochus their **k**
9:25 So I have appointed my son Antiochus to be **k**,
11:14 promising that he would persuade the **k**,
11:15 For the **k** granted every request in behalf of
11:18 I have informed the **k** of everything that needed to
11:22 "**K** Antiochus to his brother Lysias, greetings.
11:27 "**K** Antiochus to the senate of the Jews and to
11:35 the kinsman of the **k** has granted you,
11:36 that he decided are to be referred to the **k**,
12: 1 Lysias returned to the **k**, and the Jews went
13: 4 the **K** of kings aroused the anger of Antiochus P
13: 9 The **k** with barbarous arrogance was coming
13:18 The **k**, having had a taste of the daring of the Jews,
13:22 The **k** negotiated a second time with the people
14: 4 and went to **K** Demetrius in about
14: 8 for the interests of the **k**,
14: 9 Since you are acquainted, O **k**,
14:27 The **k** became excited and,
14:29 Since it was not possible to oppose the **k**,
15:22 you sent your angel in the time of **K** Hezekiah I
1Es 1: 3 house that **K** Solomon, son of David, had built; E
1: 5 in accordance with the directions of **K** David G
1:15 Zechariah, and Eddinus, who represented the **k**.
1:18 according to the command of **K** Josiah.
1:25 it happened that Pharaoh, **k** of Egypt, H
1:26 And the **k** of Egypt sent word to him saying, H
1:26 to do with each other, O **k** of Judea?
1:29 and the commanders came down against **K** Josiah.
1:30 The **k** said to his servants,
1:34 and made him **k** in succession to his father Josiah.
1:35 Then the **k** of Egypt deposed him from reigning H
1:37 The **k** of Egypt made his brother Jehoiakim king H
1:37 The king of Egypt made his brother Jehoiakim **k**

1Es 1:40 **K** Nebuchadnezzar of Babylon came up F
1:43 His son Jehoiachin became **k** in his place;
1:43 when he was made **k** he was eighteen years old,
1:46 and made Zedekiah **k** of Judea and Jerusalem.
1:48 **K** Nebuchadnezzar had made him swear F
2: 1 In the first year of Cyrus as **k** of the Persians,
2: 2 the spirit of **K** Cyrus of the Persians, and he made
2: 3 "Thus says Cyrus **k** of the Persians:
2: 3 the Lord Most High, has made me **k** of the world,
2:10 **K** Cyrus also brought out the holy vessels of
2:11 When **K** Cyrus of the Persians brought these out,
2:16 In the time of **K** Artaxerxes of the Persians,
2:17 "To **K** Artaxerxes our lord, your servants
2:18 be known to our lord the **k** that the Jews who D
2:21 but to speak to our lord the **k**, D
2:24 we now make known to you, O lord and **k**,
2:25 Then the **k**, in reply to the recorder Rehum,
2:30 Then, when the letter from **K** Artaxerxes was read,
2:30 until the second year of the reign of **K** Darius of
3: 1 Now **K** Darius gave a great banquet for all
3: 3 and **K** Darius went to his bedroom;
3: 4 who kept guard over the person of the **k**,
3: 5 **K** Darius will give rich gifts and great honors
3: 8 and put them under the pillow of **K** Darius,
3: 9 "When the **k** wakes, they will give him the writing;
3: 9 the one whose statement the **k** and the three nobles
3:11 The second wrote, "The **k** is strongest."
3:13 the **k** awoke, they took the writing and gave it
3:19 It makes equal the mind of the **k** and the orphan,
4: 1 second, who had spoken of the strength of the **k**,
4: 3 But the **k** is stronger; he is their lord
4: 5 win the victory, they bring everything to the **k**—
4: 6 and reap, and bring some to the **k**;
4: 6 and they compel one another to pay taxes to the **k**.
4:12 Gentlemen, why is not the **k** the strongest,
4:14 is not the **k** great, and are not men many,
4:15 Women gave birth to the **k** and to every people
4:28 "Is not the **k** great in his power?
4:30 and slap the **k** with her left hand.
4:31 At this the **k** would gaze at her with mouth agape.
4:33 Then the **k** and the nobles looked at one another;
4:37 Wine is unrighteous, the **k** is unrighteous,
4:42 Then the **k** said to him, "Ask what you wish,
4:43 Then he said to the **k**,
4:43 that you made on the day when you became **k**,
4:46 O lord the **k**, this is what I ask and request D
4:46 the vow whose fulfillment you vowed to the **K**
4:47 Then **K** Darius got up and kissed him,
4:58 and praised the **K** of heaven, saying,
5: 6 who spoke wise words before **K** Darius of
5: 7 whom **K** Nebuchadnezzar of Babylon F
5:55 the decree that they had in writing from **K** Cyrus
5:60 according to the directions of **K** David of Israel; G
5:69 since the days of **K** Esar-haddon of the Assyrians,
5:71 the **k** of the Persians, has commanded us."
5:73 of the building as long as **K** Cyrus lived.
6: 8 "To **K** Darius, greetings. Let it be fully
6: 8 Let it be fully known to our lord the **k** that, D
6:14 house was built many years ago by a **k** of Israel B
6:15 the hands of **K** Nebuchadnezzar of Babylon, F
6:15 Nebuchadnezzar of Babylon, **k** of the Chaldeans;
6:17 **K** Cyrus wrote that this house should be rebuilt.
6:18 these **K** Cyrus took out again from the temple
6:21 Now therefore, O **k**, if it seems wise to do so,
6:21 be made in the royal archives of our lord the **k** D
6:22 with the consent of **K** Cyrus,
6:22 and if it is approved by our lord the **k**, D
6:24 of the reign of **K** Cyrus, he ordered the building of
6:25 the cost to be paid from the treasury of **K** Cyrus;
6:31 to the Most High God for the **k** and his children,
6:32 and all property forfeited to the **k**.
6:33 destroy every **k** and nation
6:34 **K** Darius, have decreed that it be done
7: 1 following the orders of **K** Darius,
7: 5 in the sixth year of **K** Darius.
7:15 the will of the **k** of the Assyrians concerning them,
8: 1 the **k** of the Persians, was reigning, Ezra came,
8: 4 and the **k** showed him honor,
8: 4 for he found favor before the **k** in all his requests.
8: 8 of the written commission from **K** Artaxerxes
8: 9 "**K** Artaxerxes to Ezra the priest and reader of
8:19 **K** Artaxerxes, have commanded the treasurers
8:21 not come upon the kingdom of the **k** and his sons.
8:25 who put this into the heart of the **k**,
8:26 of the **k** and his counselors and all his Friends
8:28 in the reign of **K** Artaxerxes:
8:51 the **k** for foot soldiers and cavalry and an escort
8:52 for we had said to the **k**,
8:55 the **k** himself and his counselors and the nobles
3Mc 1: 3 had led the **k** away and arranged that
1: 3 the vengeance meant for the **k**.
1:11 the **k** was by no means persuaded.
1:15 "But since this has happened," the **k** said,
1:21 because of what the **k** was profanely plotting.
1:25 while the elders near the **k** tried in various ways
2: 2 **k** of the heavens, and sovereign of all creation,
2: 9 O **K**, when you had created the boundless
2:13 now, O holy **K**, that because of our many
2:31 by their future association with the **k**.
3: 1 When the impious **k** comprehended this situation,
3: 7 that these people were loyal neither to the **k** nor
3:11 Then the **k**, boastful of his present good fortune,
3:12 "**K** Ptolemy Philopator to his generals and soldiers
4:11 the voyage was concluded as the **k** had decreed,
4:12 And when this had happened, the **k**,
4:16 The **k** was greatly and continually filled with joy,
4:17 to the **k** that they were no longer able to take

3Mc 5: 1 Then the **k**, completely inflexible,
5:10 to report to the **k** about these preparations.
5:11 But the Lord sent upon the **k** a portion of sleep,
5:14 approached the **k** and nudged him.
5:16 The **k**, after considering this,
5:18 the **k** summoned Hermon and
5:20 the **k**, possessed by a savagery worse than that
5:21 When the **k** had spoken, all those present readily
5:26 and while the **k** was receiving his Friends,
5:26 that what the **k** desired was ready for action.
5:29 "O **k**, according to your eager purpose."
5:35 Then the Jews, on hearing what the **k** had said,
5:35 praised the manifest Lord God, **K** of kings, P
5:36 The **k**, however, reconvened the party in
5:40 "O **k**, how long will you put us to the test,
5:42 At this the **k**, a Phalaris in everything and filled
5:46 and urged the **k** on to the matter at hand.
6: 2 "**K** of great power, Almighty God Most High,
6: 5 oppressive **k** of the Assyrians,
6:16 the **k** arrived at the hippodrome with the animals
6:20 Even the **k** began to shudder bodily,
6:30 Then the **k**, when he had returned to the city,
6:33 also the **k**, after convening a great banquet
6:37 Then they petitioned the **k**,
6:40 being provided with everything by the **k**,
6:41 The **k** granted their request at once and wrote
7: 1 "**K** Ptolemy Philopator to the generals in Egypt
7:10 of the **k** that at their own hands those of
7:12 The **k** then, admitting and approving the truth
7:18 the **k** had generously provided all things to them
2Es 1: 3 of the Medes in the reign of Artaxerxes, **k** of
13:40 the days of **K** Hoshea, whom Shalmaneser, **k** of
the Assyrians,
15:16 they shall in their might have no respect for their **k**
4Mc 3: 6 by the story of **K** David's thirst.
3:10 but the **k** was extremely thirsty,
3:14 and from it boldly brought the **k** a drink.
3:20 so that even Seleucus Nicanor, **k** of Asia,
4: 3 of the temple but belong to **K** Seleucus."
4: 4 he praised Simon for his service to the **k** and went
4:13 for him so that **K** Seleucus would not suppose
4:14 went away to report to the **k** what had happened
4:15 **K** Seleucus died, his son Antiochus Epiphanes
4:17 **k** three thousand six hundred sixty talents annually.
4:18 **k** appointed him high priest and ruler of the nation.
5: 4 leader of the flock, was brought before the **k**.
5:36 O **k**, shall not defile the honorable mouth
7:10 O supreme **k** over the passions, Eleazar!
8:17 Since the **k** has summoned and exhorted us
8:22 for fearing the **k** when we are under compulsion.
8:26 when we can live in peace if we obey the **k?**"
10:13 but obey the **k** and save yourself."
12: 8 let me speak to the **k** and to all his friends that are

KING'S‡ (335) [KING]

A. KING'S HOUSE (39)
B. KING'S COMMAND (23)
C. KING'S SONS (15)
D. KING'S SON (14)
E. KING'S GATE (13)
F. KING'S SERVANTS (13)

Ge 14:17 at the Valley of Shaveh (that is, the **K** Valley).
39:20 the place where the **k** prisoners were confined;
Nu 20:17 we will go along the **K** Highway,
21:22 we will go by the **K** Highway until we have passed
1Sa 18:22 now then, become the **k** son-in-law.' "
18:23 to you a little thing to become the **k** son-in-law,
18:25 that he may be avenged on the **k** enemies.' "
18:26 David was well pleased to be the **k** son-in-law.
18:27 that he might become the **k** son-in-law.
20:29 For this reason he has not come to the **k** table."
21: 8 because the **k** business required haste."
22:14 the **k** son-in-law, and is quick to do your bidding,
23:20 our part will be to surrender him into the **k** hand."
26:16 See now, where is the **k** spear,
2Sa 9:11 like one of the **k** sons. C
9:13 for he always ate at the **k** table.
11: 2 was walking about on the roof of the **k** house, A
11: 8 Uriah went out of the **k** house, A
11: 9 the entrance of the **k** house with all the servants A
11:20 if the **k** anger rises, and if he says to you,
11:24 some of the **k** servants are dead; F
13:23 and Absalom invited all the **k** sons. C
13:27 he let Amnon and all the **k** sons go with him. C
13:27 Absalom made a feast like a **k** feast.
13:29 Then all the **k** sons rose, C
13:30 to David that Absalom had killed all the **k** sons, C
13:32 they have killed all the young men the **k** sons; C
13:33 as if all the **k** sons were dead; C
13:35 "See, the **k** sons have come; C
13:36 **k** sons arrived, and raised their voices and wept; C
14: 1 of Zeruiah perceived that the **k** mind was
14:24 and did not come into the **k** presence.
14:26 two hundred shekels by the **k** weight.
14:28 without coming into the **k** presence.
14:32 Now let me go into the **k** presence;
15:15 The **k** officials said to the king,
15:35 So whatever you hear from the **k** house, A
16: 2 "The donkeys are for the **k** household to ride,
18:12 I would not raise my hand against the **k** son; D
18:18 that is in the **K** Valley, for he said, "I have no son
18:20 because the **k** son is dead." D
19:18 to bring over the **k** household,
19:42 Have we eaten at all at the **k** expense?
24: 4 But the **k** word prevailed against Joab and

1Ki 1: 4 She became the **k** attendant and served him,
1: 9 the **k** sons, and all the royal officials of Judah, C
1:25 and has invited all the **k** children,
1:28 So she came into the **k** presence,
1:44 and they had him ride on the **k** mule;
1:47 Moreover the **k** servants came F
2:19 and had a throne brought for the **k** mother,
4: 5 Zabud son of Nathan was priest and **k** friend;
5:17 At the **k** command, they quarried out great, B
9: 1 **k** house and all that Solomon desired to build, A
9:10 the house of the LORD and the **k** house, A
10:12 the **k** house, lyres also and harps for the singers; A
10:28 the **k** traders received them from Kue at a price.
10:29 the **k** traders they were exported to all the kings
13: 6 and the **k** hand was restored to him,
14:26 of the LORD and the treasures of the **k** house; A
14:27 who kept the door of the **k** house. A
15:18 of the LORD and the treasures of the **k** house, A
16:18 he went into the citadel of the **k** house; A
16:18 burned down the **k** house over himself with fire, A
22:26 the governor of the city and to Joash the **k** son, D
2Ki 1:11 this is the **k** order: Come down quickly!"
7: 9 therefore let us go and tell the **k** household."
7:11 and proclaimed it to the **k** household.
8:15 dipped it in water and spread it over the **k** face,
9:34 for she is a **k** daughter."
10: 6 Now the **k** sons, seventy persons, C
10: 7 they took the **k** sons and killed them, C
10: 8 "They have brought the heads of the **k** sons," C
11: 2 among the **k** children who were about to be killed;
11: 4 then he showed them the **k** son. D
11: 5 on the sabbath and guard the **k** house A
11:12 Then he brought out the **k** son, D
11:16 through the horses' entrance to the **k** house, A
11:19 through the gate of the guards to the **k** house. A
11:20 with the sword at the **k** house. A
12:10 the **k** secretary and the high priest went up,
12:18 of the house of the LORD and of the **k** house, A
13:16 Elisha laid his hands on the **k** hands.
14:14 of the LORD and in the treasuries of the **k** house, A
15: 5 Jotham the **k** son was in charge of the palace, D
16: 8 of the LORD and in the treasures of the **k** house, A
16:15 and the **k** burnt offering, and his grain offering,
18:15 of the LORD and in the treasuries of the **k** house. A
18:36 for the **k** command was, "Do not answer him." B
22:12 Shaphan the secretary, and the **k** servant Asaiah,
24:13 and the treasures of the **k** house; A
24:15 the **k** mother, the **k** wives, his officials,
25: 4 of the gate between the two walls, by the **k** garden,
25: 9 He burned the house of the LORD, the **k** house, A
25:19 and five men of the **k** council who were found in
25:29 of his life he dined regularly in the **k** presence.
1Ch 9:18 previously in the **k** gate on the east side. E
21: 4 But the **k** word prevailed against Joab.
21: 6 for the **k** command was abhorrent to Joab. B
25: 5 All these were the sons of Heman the **k** seer,
27:25 Over the **k** treasuries was Azmaveth son of Adiel.
27:32 Jehiel son of Hachmoni attended the **k** sons. C
27:33 Ahithophel was the **k** counselor,
27:33 and Hushai the Archite was the **k** friend.
27:34 Joab was commander of the **k** army.
29: 6 and the officers over the **k** work.
2Ch 1:16 the **k** traders received them from Kue at
7:11 the house of the LORD and the **k** house; A
9:11 the house of the LORD and for the **k** house, A
9:21 For the **k** ships went to Tarshish with the servants
12: 9 of the LORD and the treasures of the **k** house; A
12:10 who kept the door of the **k** house. A
16: 2 of the house of the LORD and the **k** house, A
18:25 the governor of the city and to Joash the **k** son; D
19:11 of the house of Judah, in all the **k** matters;
21:17 that belonged to the **k** house, A
22:11 But Jehoshabeath, the **k** daughter,
22:11 among the **k** children who were about to be killed;
23: 3 Jehoiada said to them, "Here is the **k** son! D
23: 5 one third shall be at the **k** house, and one third A
23:11 Then he brought out the **k** son, D
23:15 the entrance of the Horse Gate of the **k** house, A
23:20 marching through the upper gate to the **k** house. A
24:11 Whenever the chest was brought to the **k** officers
24:11 the **k** secretary and the officer of the chief priest
25:24 he seized also the treasuries of the **k** house, A
26:11 of Hananiah, one of the **k** commanders.
28: 7 killed the **k** son Maaseiah, D
29:25 the commandment of David and of Gad the **k** seer
34:20 the secretary Shaphan, and the **k** servant Asaiah:
35: 7 these were from the **k** possessions.
35:10 in their divisions according to the **k** command. B
35:15 and Asaph, and Heman, and the **k** seer Jeduthun.
Ezr 4:14 and it is not fitting for us to witness the **k** dishonor,
7:20 you may provide out of the **k** treasury.
7:28 and before all the **k** mighty officers.
8:36 the **k** commissions to the king's satraps and to
8:36 the **k** satraps and to the governors of the province
Ne 2: 8 the keeper of the **k** forest,
2: 9 and gave them the **k** letters.
2:14 I went on to the Fountain Gate and to the **K** Pool;
3:15 the wall of the Pool of Shelah of the **k** garden,
5: 4 on our fields and vineyards to pay the **k** tax.
11:24 at the **k** hand in all matters concerning the people.
Est 1: 5 in the court of the garden of the **k** palace.
1:12 at the **k** command conveyed by the eunuchs. B
1:13 the **k** procedure toward all who were versed in law
1:18 against the **k** officials, and there will be no end
2: 2 Then the **k** servants who attended him said, F
2: 3 the **k** eunuch, who is in charge of the women;
2: 8 when the **k** order and his edict were proclaimed,
Est 2: 8 also was taken into the **k** palace and put in custody
2: 9 and with seven chosen maids from the **k** palace,
2:13 for to take with her from the harem to the **k** palace.
2:14 of Shaashgaz, the **k** eunuch, who was in charge of
2:15 for nothing except what Hegai the **k** eunuch,
2:19 Mordecai was sitting at the **k** gate. E
2:21 while Mordecai was sitting at the **k** gate, E
2:21 two of the **k** eunuchs, who guarded the threshold,
3: 2 the **k** servants who were at the king's gate F
3: 2 the king's servants who were at the **k** gate E
3: 3 the **k** servants who were at the king's gate said F
3: 3 the king's servants who were at the **k** gate said E
3: 3 "Why do you disobey the **k** command?" B
3: 8 and they do not keep the **k** laws,
3: 9 of those who have charge of the **k** business,
3: 9 so that they may put it into the **k** treasuries."
3:12 Then the **k** secretaries were summoned on
3:12 was written to the **k** satraps and to the governors
3:12 of King Ahasuerus and sealed with the **k** ring.
3:13 Letters were sent by couriers to all the **k** provinces,
4: 2 he went up to the entrance of the **k** gate, E
4: 2 for no one might enter the **k** gate clothed E
4: 3 wherever the **k** command and his decree came, B
4: 5 Esther called for Hathach, one of the **k** eunuchs,
4: 6 the open square of the city in front of the **k** gate, E
4: 7 into the **k** treasuries for the destruction of the Jews.
4:11 "All the **k** servants and the people of the king's F
4:11 the people of the **k** provinces know that if any man
4:13 in the **k** palace you will escape any more than all
5: 1 and stood in the inner court of the **k** palace,
5: 1 of the king's palace, opposite the **k** hall.
5: 8 If I have won the **k** favor,
5: 9 But when Haman saw Mordecai in the **k** gate, E
5:13 as I see the Jew Mordecai sitting at the **k** gate." E
6: 2 two of the **k** eunuchs, who guarded the threshold,
6: 3 The **k** servants who attended him said, F
6: 4 the outer court of the **k** palace to speak to the king
6: 5 So the **k** servants told him, "Haman is there, F
6: 9 over to one of the **k** most noble officials;
6:10 do so to the Jew Mordecai who sits at the **k** gate. E
6:12 Then Mordecai returned to the **k** gate, E
6:14 the **k** eunuchs arrived and hurried Haman off to
8: 8 in the name of the king, and seal it with the **k** ring;
8: 8 and sealed with the **k** ring cannot be revoked."
8: 9 The **k** secretaries were summoned at that time,
8:10 sealed them with the **k** ring,
8:14 hurried out, urged by the **k** command. B
8:17 wherever the **k** command and his edict came, B
9: 1 **k** command and edict were about to be executed, B
9: 4 For Mordecai was powerful in the **k** house, A
9:12 in the rest of the **k** provinces?
9:16 the **k** provinces also gathered to defend their lives,
Ps 45: 5 in the heart of the **k** enemies;
72: 1 O God, and your righteousness to a **k** son. D
Pr 14:35 A servant who deals wisely has the **k** favor,
16:14 A **k** wrath is a messenger of death,
16:15 In the light of a **k** face there is life,
19:12 A **k** anger is like the growling of a lion,
21: 1 The **k** heart is a stream of water in the hand of
25: 6 not put yourself forward in the **k** presence or stand
Ecc 8: 2 Keep the **k** command because of your sacred B
Isa 36:21 for the **k** command was, "Do not answer him." B
Jer 26:10 up from the **k** house to the house of the LORD A
36:12 he went down to the **k** house, A
36:26 And the king commanded Jerahmeel the **k** son D
38: 6 the **k** son, which was in the court of the guard, D
38: 7 a eunuch in the **k** house, A
38: 8 So Ebed-melech left the **k** house and spoke to A
39: 4 of the city at night by way of the **k** garden through
39: 8 The Chaldeans burned the **k** house and the A
41:10 the **k** daughters and all the people who were left
52: 7 of the gate between the two walls, by the **k** garden,
52:13 He burned the house of the LORD, the **k** house, A
52:25 and seven men of the **k** council who were found in
52:33 of his life he dined regularly at the **k** table.
Da 1: 4 and competent to serve in the **k** palace;
1: 5 of that time they could be stationed in the **k** court.
1:19 therefore they were stationed in the **k** court.
2:14 the **k** chief executioner, who had gone out
2:49 But Daniel remained at the **k** court.
3:22 the **k** command was urgent and the furnace was B
3:27 the **k** counselors gathered together and saw that
3:28 They disobeyed the **k** command and yielded B
4:31 While the words were still in the **k** mouth,
5: 6 **k** face turned pale, and his thoughts terrified him.
5: 8 Then all the **k** wise men came in,
8:27 then I arose and went about the **k** business.
Am 7: 1 the latter growth after the **k** mowings).
7:13 for it is the **k** sanctuary,
Zep 1: 8 and the **k** sons and all who dress themselves C
Zec 14:10 from the Tower of Hananel to the **k** wine presses.
Ac 12:20 and after winning over Blastus, the **k** chamberlain,
12:20 their country depended on the **k** country for food.
Heb 11:23 and they were not afraid of the **k** edict.
11:27 By faith he left Egypt, unafraid of the **k** anger;
Jdt 6: 3 we the **k** servants will destroy them as one man. F
AdE 1:16 the king but also all the **k** governors and officials"
2: 1 After these things, the **k** anger abated,
2: 2 Then the **k** servants said, "Let beautiful F
2: 3 be entrusted to the **k** eunuch who is in charge of
2:13 and goes with him from the harem to the **k** palace.
2:14 where Gai the **k** eunuch is in charge of the women;
2:21 Now the **k** eunuchs, who were chief bodyguards,
3: 1 and granting him precedence over all the **k** Friends.
3: 3 Then the **k** courtiers said to Mordecai,
3: 3 Mordecai, why do you disobey the **k** command? B
3: 4 that Mordecai was resisting the **k** command. B
AdE 3: 9 of silver into the **k** treasury."
3:12 the first month the **k** secretaries were summoned,
4: 2 He got as far as the **k** gate, and there he stopped, E
4: 3 the **k** proclamation had been posted there was
6: 3 on Mordecai?"The **k** servants said, F
6: 8 let the **k** servants bring out the fine linen robe F
6: 9 let both be given to one of the **k** honored Friends,
7: 4 Our antagonist brings shame on the **k** court."
8: 8 the **k** command and sealed with my ring cannot B
8:10 with the **k** authority and sealed with his ring,
9: 4 The **k** decree required that Mordecai's name
14:17 and I have not honored the **k** feast or drunk
Sir 45:25 that the **k** heritage passes only from son to son,
Aza 1:23 the **k** servants who threw them in kept stoking F
Bel 1:14 shut the door and sealed it with the **k** signet,
1Mc 2:15 The **k** officers who were enforcing
2:17 Then the **k** officers spoke to Mattathias as follows:
2:22 the **k** words by turning aside from our religion to
2:23 according to the **k** command. B
2:25 the **k** officer who was forcing them to sacrifice,
2:31 And it was reported to the **k** officers,
2:31 the **k** command had gone down to B
3:14 who scorn the **k** command." B
3:32 in charge of the **k** affairs from the river Euphrates
4: 3 and his warriors moved out to attack the **k** force
6:17 he set up Antiochus the **k** son to reign. D
6:40 part of the **k** army was spread out on the high hills,
6:42 and six hundred of the **k** army fell.
6:48 of the **k** army went up to Jerusalem against them,
7: 8 So the **k** chose Bacchides, one of the **k** Friends,
10:20 be called the **k** Friend and you are to take our side
10:36 "Let Jews be enrolled in the **k** forces to the number
10:40 of the **k** revenues from appropriate places.
10:89 such as it is the custom to give to the **K** Kinsmen.
11:57 and make you one of the **k** Friends."
15:32 So Athenobius, the **k** Friend, came to Jerusalem,
15:32 When he reported to him the **k** message,
2Mc 3: 8 but in fact to carry out the **k** purpose.
3:13 in any case be confiscated for the **k** treasury.
4: 6 the **k** attention public affairs could not again reach
4:25 After receiving the **k** orders he returned,
4:30 as a present to Antiochis, the **k** concubine.
6: 7 On the monthly celebration of the **k** birthday,
7:30 I will not obey the **k** command, B
8: 8 to come to the aid of the **k** government.
8: 9 one of the **k** chief Friends, and sent him,
10:13 before Eupator by the **k** Friends.
11: 1 Lysias, the **k** guardian and kinsman,
11:22 The **k** letter ran thus: "King Antiochus to his
11:27 To the nation the **k** letter was as follows:
13:13 the **k** army could enter Judea and get possession of
13:15 he attacked the **k** pavilion at night and killed
13:26 how the **k** attack and withdrawal turned out.
14:11 When he had said this, the rest of the **k** Friends,
15: 5 to take up arms and finish the **k** business."
1Es 1: 7 these were given from the **k** possessions,
4: 5 and do not disobey the **k** command; B
4:29 Yet I have seen him with Apame, the **k** concubine,
4:29 she would sit at the **k** right hand
4:30 the crown from the **k** head and put it on her own,
8: 6 in the fifth month (this was the **k** seventh year);
8:67 They delivered the **k** orders to the royal stewards
3Mc 2:26 intently observing the **k** purpose,
4:11 with the **k** forces nor in any way claim to be inside
5:28 for he had implanted in the **k** mind a forgetfulness
5:29 Then Hermon and all the **k** Friends pointed out that
5:34 The **k** Friends one by one sullenly slipped away
6:22 the **k** anger was turned to pity and tears because of
7:11 be favorably disposed toward the **k** government.
7:20 since at the **k** command they had all of them B
4Mc 3:12 complained bitterly because of the **k** craving,
3:12 respecting the **k** desire, armed themselves fully,
4: 3 because I am loyal to the **k** government,
4: 6 with the **k** authority to seize the private funds in
6: 4 who faced him cried out, "Obey the **k** commands!"
6:13 some of the **k** retinue came to him and said,

KINGDOM‡ (413) [KING]

A. KINGDOM OF *GOD (00)
B. KINGDOM OF HEAVEN (32)
C. WHOLE KINGDOM (10)

Ge 10:10 The beginning of his **k** was Babel, Erech,
20: 9 have brought such great guilt on me and my **k?**
Ex 19: 6 you shall be for me a priestly **k** and a holy nation.
Nu 24: 7 and his **k** shall be exalted.
32:33 the **k** of King Sihon of the Amorites and
32:33 of the Amorites and the **k** of King Og of Bashan,
Dt 3: 4 the whole region of Argob, the **k** of Og in Bashan.
3:10 towns of Og's **k** in Bashan.
3:13 the rest of Gilead and all of Bashan, Og's **k.**
17:18 When he has taken the throne of his **k,**
17:20 and his descendants may reign long over his **k**
Jos 13:12 the **k** of Og in Bashan, who reigned in Ashtaroth
13:21 and all the **k** of King Sihon of the Amorites,
13:27 the rest of the **k** of King Sihon of Heshbon,
13:30 the whole **k** of King Og of Bashan, C
13:31 and Edrei, the towns of the **k** of Og in Bashan;
1Sa 13:13 The LORD would have established your **k**
13:14 but now your **k** will not continue;
15:28 the **k** of Israel from you this very day,
18: 8 what more can he have but the **k?"**
20:31 neither you nor your **k** shall be established.
24:20 the **k** of Israel shall be established in your hand.
28:17 for the LORD has torn the **k** out of your hand,
2Sa 3:10 to transfer the **k** from the house of Saul,

2Sa 3:28 and my **k** are forever guiltless before the LORD
5:12 and that he had exalted his **k** for the sake
7:12 and I will establish his **k**.
7:13 and I will establish the throne of his **k** forever.
7:16 Your house and your **k** shall be made sure forever
16: 3 of Israel will give me back my grandfather's **k**.' "
16: 8 and the LORD has given the **k** into the hand
1Ki 2:12 and his **k** was firmly established.
2:15 He said, "You know that the **k** was mine,
2:15 the **k** has turned about and become my brother's,
2:22 Ask for him the **k** as well!
2:46 So the **k** was established in the hand of Solomon.
10:20 Nothing like it was ever made in any **k**.
11:11 I will surely tear the **k** from you and give it
11:13 I will not, however, tear away the entire **k**;
11:31 I am about to tear the **k** from the hand of Solomon,
11:34 Nevertheless I will not take the whole **k** away C
11:35 but I will take the **k** away from his son and give it
12:21 to restore the **k** to Rehoboam son of Solomon.
12:26 "Now the **k** may well revert to the house of David.
13: 8 "If you give me half your **k**,
14: 8 the **k** away from the house of David to give it
18:10 or **k** to which my lord has not sent to seek you;
18:10 he would require an oath of the **k** or nation,
1Ch 10:14 the LORD put him to death and turned the **k** over
11:10 who gave him strong support in his **k**,
12:23 to David in Hebron to turn the **k** of Saul over
14: 2 and that his **k** was highly exalted for the sake
16:20 from one **k** to another people,
17:11 one of your own sons, and I will establish his **k**.
17:14 in my house and in my **k** forever,
28: 5 upon the throne of the **k** of the LORD over Israel.
28: 7 I will establish his **k** forever
29:11 yours is the **k**, O LORD, and you are exalted
2Ch 1: 1 of David established himself in his **k**;
9:19 The like of it was never made in any **k**.
11: 1 to restore the **k** to Rehoboam.
11:17 They strengthened the **k** of Judah,
13: 8 "And now you think that you can withstand the **k**
14: 5 And the **k** had rest under him.
17: 5 the LORD established the **k** in his hand.
21: 3 but he gave the **k** to Jehoram,
22: 9 the house of Ahaziah had no one able to rule the **k**.
29:21 a sin offering for the **k** and for the sanctuary and
32:15 or **k** has been able to save his people from my hand
33:13 and restored him again to Jerusalem and to his **k**.
36:20 and to his sons until the establishment of the **k**
36:22 a herald throughout all his **k** and also declared in
Ezr 1: 1 that he sent a herald throughout all his **k**, and also
7:13 or their priests or Levites in my **k** who freely offers
Ne 9:35 Even in their own **k**, and in
Est 1: 4 of his **k** and the splendor and pomp of his majesty
1:14 who had access to the king, and sat first in the **k**):
1:20 by the king is proclaimed throughout all his **k**,
2: 3 of his **k** to gather all the beautiful young virgins to
3: 6 throughout the whole **k** of Ahasuerus. C
3: 8 among the peoples in all the provinces of your **k**;
5: 3 It shall be given you, even to the half of my **k**."
5: 6 Even to the half of my **k**, it shall be fulfilled."
7: 2 Even to the half of my **k**, it shall be fulfilled."
9:30 to the one hundred twenty-seven provinces of the **k**
Ps 103:19 and his **k** rules over all.
105:13 from one **k** to another people,
145:11 They shall speak of the glory of your **k**,
145:12 and the glorious splendor of your **k**.
145:13 Your **k** is an everlasting **k**,
Ecc 4:14 even though born poor in the **k**.
Isa 9: 7 be endless peace for the throne of David and his **k**.
17: 3 and the **k** from Damascus;
19: 2 city against city, **k** against **k**;
34:12 They shall name it No K There,
60:12 nation and **k** that will not serve you shall perish;
Jer 18: 7 concerning a nation or a **k**,
18: 9 a nation or a **k** that I will build and plant it,
27: 8 But if any nation or **k** will not serve this king,
La 2: 2 down to the ground in dishonor the **k** and its rulers.
Eze 17:14 so that the **k** might be humble and not lift itself up,
29:14 and there they shall be a lowly **k**.
Da 1:20 the magicians and enchanters in his whole **k**. C
2:37 to whom the God of heaven has given the **k**,
2:39 After you shall arise another **k** inferior to yours,
2:39 and yet a third **k** of bronze,
2:40 And there shall be a fourth **k**, strong as iron;
2:41 it shall be a divided **k**;
2:42 so the **k** shall be partly strong and partly brittle.
2:44 the God of heaven will set up a **k** that shall never
2:44 nor shall this **k** be left to another people.
4: 3 His **k** is an everlasting **k**,
4:17 the Most High is sovereign over the **k** of mortals;
4:18 of my **k** are unable to tell me the interpretation.
4:25 that the Most High has sovereignty over the **k**
4:26 your **k** shall be re-established for you from
4:31 The **k** has departed from you!
4:32 the **k** of mortals and gives it to whom he will."
4:34 and his **k** endures from generation to generation.
4:36 to me for the glory of my **k**,
4:36 I was re-established over my **k**,
5: 7 of gold around his neck, and rank third in the **k**."
5:11 a man in your **k** who is endowed with a spirit of
5:16 and rank third in the **k**."
5:21 that the Most High God has sovereignty over the **k**
5:26 the days of your **k** and brought it to an end;
5:28 your **k** is divided and given to the Medes
5:29 concerning him that he should rank third in the **k**.
5:31 And Darius the Mede received the **k**,
6: 1 to set over the **k** one hundred twenty satraps,
6: 1 stationed throughout the whole **k**, C

Da 6: 3 king planned to appoint him over the whole **k**. C
6: 4 against Daniel in connection with the **k**.
6: 7 All the presidents of the **k**,
6:26 His **k** shall never be destroyed,
7:18 the holy ones of the Most High shall receive the **k**
and possess the **k** forever—
7:22 when the holy ones gained possession of the **k**.
7:23 the fourth beast, there shall be a fourth **k** on earth
7:24 for the ten horns, out of this **k** ten kings shall arise,
7:27 their **k** shall be an everlasting **k**,
10:13 of the **k** of Persia opposed me twenty-one days.
10:13 I left him there with the prince of the **k** of Persia,
11: 2 he shall stir up all against the **k** of Greece.
11: 4 his **k** shall be broken and divided toward
11: 4 for his **k** shall be uprooted and go to others
11:17 to come with the strength of his whole **k**, C
11:17 the **k**, he shall give him a woman in marriage;
11:20 an official for the glory of the **k**;
11:21 without warning and obtain the **k** through intrigue.
Hos 1: 4 and I will put an end to the **k** of the house of Israel.
Am 7:13 and it is a temple of the **k**."
9: 8 The eyes of the Lord GOD are upon the sinful **k**,
Ob 1:21 and the **k** shall be the LORD's.
Mt 3: 2 "Repent, for the **k** of heaven has come near." B
4:17 "Repent, for the **k** of heaven has come near." B
4:23 the **k** and curing every disease and every sickness
5: 3 for theirs is the **k** of heaven. B
5:10 for theirs is the **k** of heaven. B
5:19 will be called least in the **k** of heaven; B
5:19 will be called great in the **k** of heaven. B
5:20 you will never enter the **k** of heaven. B
6:10 Your **k** come. Your will be done,
6:33 first for the **k** of God and his righteousness, A
7:21 'Lord, Lord,' will enter the **k** of heaven, B
8:11 Abraham and Isaac and Jacob in the **k** of heaven, B
8:12 of the **k** will be thrown into the outer darkness,
9:35 and proclaiming the good news of the **k**,
10: 7 'The **k** of heaven has come near.' B
11:11 yet the least in the **k** of heaven is greater than he. B
11:12 of John the Baptist until now the **k** of heaven B
12:25 "Every **k** divided against itself is laid waste,
12:26 how then will his **k** stand?
12:28 then the **k** of God has come to you. A
13:11 to know the secrets of the **k** of heaven, B
13:19 When anyone hears the word of the **k** and does
13:24 "The **k** of heaven may be compared B
13:31 "The **k** of heaven is like a mustard seed B
13:33 "The **k** of heaven is like yeast that a woman B
13:38 and the good seed are the children of the **k**;
13:41 and they will collect out of his **k** all causes of sin
13:43 Then the righteous will shine like the sun in the **k**
13:44 "The **k** of heaven is like treasure hidden in a B
13:45 the **k** of heaven is like a merchant in search B
13:47 the **k** of heaven is like a net that was thrown B
13:52 for the **k** of heaven is like the master of B
16:19 I will give you the keys of the **k** of heaven, B
16:28 before they see the Son of Man coming in his **k**."
18: 1 "Who is the greatest in the **k** of heaven?" B
18: 3 you will never enter the **k** of heaven. B
18: 4 like this child is the greatest in the **k** of heaven. B
18:23 this reason the **k** of heaven may be compared B
19:12 for the sake of the **k** of heaven. B
19:14 to such as these that the **k** of heaven belongs." B
19:23 hard for a rich person to enter the **k** of heaven. B
19:24 for someone who is rich to enter the **k** of God." A
20: 1 "For the **k** of heaven is like a landowner B
20:21 at your right hand and one at your left, in your **k**."
21:31 the prostitutes are going into the **k** of God ahead A
21:43 the **k** of God will be taken away from you A
21:43 to a people that produces the fruits of the **k**.
22: 2 "The **k** of heaven may be compared to B
23:13 For you lock people out of the **k** of heaven. B
24: 7 and **k** against **k**, and there will be famines
24:14 the **k** will be proclaimed throughout the world,
25: 1 "Then the **k** of heaven will be like this. B
25:34 inherit the **k** prepared for you from the foundation
26:29 when I drink it new with you in my Father's **k**."
Mk 1:15 and the **k** of God has come near; A
3:24 If a **k** is divided against itself, that **k** cannot stand.
4:11 has been given the secret of the **k** of God, A
4:26 "The **k** of God is as if someone would scatter A
4:30 "With what can we compare the **k** of God, A
6:23 I will give you, even half of my **k**."
9: 1 until they see that the **k** of God has come A
9:47 the **k** of God with one eye than to have two eyes A
10:14 it is to such as these that the **k** of God belongs. A
10:15 the **k** of God as a little child will never enter it." A
10:23 those who have wealth to enter the **k** of God!" A
10:24 "Children, how hard it is to enter the **k** of God! A
10:25 for someone who is rich to enter the **k** of God." A
11:10 Blessed is the coming **k** of our ancestor David!
12:34 "You are not far from the **k** of God." A
13: 8 nation will rise against nation, and **k** against **k**;
14:25 that day when I drink it new in the **k** of God." A
15:43 himself waiting expectantly for the **k** of God, A
Lk 1:33 and of his **k** there will be no end."
4:43 "I must proclaim the good news of the **k** of God A
6:20 for yours is the **k** of God. A
7:28 yet the least in the **k** of God is greater than he." A
8: 1 and bringing the good news of the **k** of God. A
8:10 to know the secrets of the **k** of God; A
9: 2 and he sent them out to proclaim the **k** of God A
9:11 and spoke to them about the **k** of God, A
9:27 not taste death before they see the **k** of God." A
9:60 but as for you, go and proclaim the **k** of God." A
9:62 the plow and looks back is fit for the **k** of God." A
10: 9 'The **k** of God has come near to you.' A

Lk 10:11 Yet know this: the **k** of God has come near.' A
11: 2 be your name. Your **k** come.
11:17 "Every **k** divided against itself becomes a desert,
11:18 against himself, how will his **k** stand?
11:20 then the **k** of God has come to you. A
12:31 for his **k**, and these things will be given to you
12:32 it is your Father's good pleasure to give you the **k**.
13:18 He said therefore, "What is the **k** of God like? A
13:20 "To what should I compare the **k** of God? A
13:28 Jacob and all the prophets in the **k** of God, A
13:29 north and south, and will eat in the **k** of God. A
14:15 anyone who will eat bread in the **k** of God!" A
16:16 the good news of the **k** of God is proclaimed, A
17:20 asked by the Pharisees when the **k** of God A
17:20 "The **k** of God is not coming with things that A
17:21 For, in fact, the **k** of God is among you." A
18:16 it is to such as these that the **k** of God belongs. A
18:17 the **k** of God as a little child will never enter it." A
18:24 those who have wealth to enter the **k** of God! A
18:25 for someone who is rich to enter the **k** of God." A
18:29 for the sake of the **k** of God, A
19:11 and because they supposed that the **k** of God A
21:10 "Nation will rise against nation, and **k** against **k**;
21:31 you know that the **k** of God is near. A
22:16 not eat it until it is fulfilled in the **k** of God." A
22:18 the fruit of the vine until the **k** of God comes." A
22:29 just as my Father has conferred on me, a **k**,
22:30 so that you may eat and drink at my table in my **k**,
23:42 "Jesus, remember me when you come into your **k**."
23:51 he was waiting expectantly for the **k** of God. A
Jn 3: 3 no one can see the **k** of God without being born A
3: 5 can enter the **k** of God without being born A
18:36 Jesus answered, "My **k** is not from this world.
18:36 If my **k** were from this world,
18:36 But as it is, my **k** is not from here."
Ac 1: 3 forty days and speaking about the **k** of God. A
1: 6 the time when you will restore the **k** to Israel?"
8:12 about the **k** of God and the name of Jesus Christ, A
14:22 that we must enter the **k** of God." A
19: 8 and argued persuasively about the **k** of God. A
20:25 whom I have gone about proclaiming the **k**,
28:23 to the **k** of God and trying to convince them A
28:31 proclaiming the **k** of God and teaching about A
Ro 14:17 For the **k** of God is not food and drink A
1Co 4:20 the **k** of God depends not on talk but on power. A
6: 9 that wrongdoers will not inherit the **k** of God? A
6:10 none of these will inherit the **k** of God. A
15:24 when he hands over the **k** to God the Father,
15:50 flesh and blood cannot inherit the **k** of God, A
Gal 5:21 do such things will not inherit the **k** of God. A
Eph 5: 5 has any inheritance in the **k** of Christ and of God.
Col 1:13 and transferred us into the **k** of his beloved Son,
4:11 among my co-workers for the **k** of God, A
1Th 2:12 who calls you into his own **k** and glory.
2Th 1: 5 intended to make you worthy of the **k** of God, A
2Ti 4: 1 and in view of his appearing and his **k**,
4:18 and save me for his heavenly **k**.
Heb 1: 8 and the righteous scepter is the scepter of your **k**.
12:28 since we are receiving a **k** that cannot be shaken,
Jas 2: 5 the world to be rich in faith and to be heirs of the **k**
2Pe 1:11 entry into the eternal **k** of our Lord
Rev 1: 6 and made us to be a **k**,
1: 9 with you in Jesus the persecution and the **k** and
5:10 to be a **k** and priests serving our God,
11:15 "The **k** of the world has become the **k** of our Lord
12:10 the **k** of our God and the authority of his Messiah,
16:10 and its **k** was plunged into darkness;
17:12 yet received a **k**, but they are to receive authority
17:17 to carry out his purpose by agreeing to give their **k**
Tob 1:21 over all the accounts of his **k**,
13: 1 because his **k** lasts throughout all ages.
Jdt 1:12 by his throne and **k** that he would take revenge on
2:12 For as I live, and by the power of my **k**,
11: 8 that you alone are the best in the whole **k**, C
AdE 1: 4 when he had displayed to them the riches of his **k**
1:20 the king enacts be proclaimed in his **k**,
1:22 The king sent the decree into all his **k**,
2: 3 in all the provinces of his **k**,
3: 8 among the other nations in all your **k**;
5: 3 It shall be given you, even to half of my **k**."
5:11 how he had advanced him to be the first in the **k**.
7: 2 It shall be granted to you, even to half of my **k**."
8: 5 and sent to destroy the Jews in your **k**.
8:12 which is Adar, throughout all the **k** of Artaxerxes.
8:13 of the decree be posted conspicuously in all the **k**,
9: 4 be held in honor throughout the **k**.
9:16 other Jews in the **k** gathered to defend themselves,
9:20 and sent it to the Jews in the **k** of Artaxerxes both
10: 1 king levied a tax upon his **k** both by land and sea.
10: 2 and the wealth and glory of his **k**,
10: 3 of King Artaxerxes and was great in the **k**,
13: 2 in order to make my **k** peaceable and open to travel
13: 3 and has attained the second place in the **k**—
13: 4 of the **k** that we honorably intend cannot
13: 5 doing all the harm they can so that our **k** may
16: 8 In the future we will take care to render our **k** quiet
16:12 he undertook to deprive us of our **k** and our life,
16:13 and of Esther, the blameless partner of our **k**,
16:14 and would transfer the **k** of the Persians to
16:16 the **k** both for us and for our ancestors in
Wis 6: 4 as servants of his **k** you did not rule rightly,
6:20 so the desire for wisdom leads to a **k**.
10:10 she showed him the **k** of God, A
10:14 the scepter of a **k** and authority over his masters.
Sir 46:13 the Lord, he established the **k** and anointed rulers
47:21 the sovereignty was divided and a rebel **k** arose out
Aza 1:33 Blessed are you on the throne of your **k**,

Bel 1: 1 Cyrus the Persian succeeded to his **k.**
1Mc 1: 6 divided his **k** among them while he was still alive.
1:10 in the one hundred thirty-seventh year of the **k** of
1:16 When Antiochus saw that his **k** was established,
1:41 the king wrote to his whole **k** that all should C
1:51 In such words he wrote to his whole **k.** C
2:57 inherited the throne of the **k** forever.
3:14 a name for myself and win honor in the **k.**
3:27 and he sent and gathered all the forces of his **k,**
6:14 and made him ruler over all his **k.**
6:57 and the affairs of the **k** press urgently on us.
7: 4 and Demetrius took his seat on the throne of his **k.**
7: 8 a great man in the **k** and was faithful to the king.
8:18 for they saw that the **k** of the Greeks
10:33 into any part of my **k,** I set free without payment;
10:34 and release for all the Jews who are in my **k.**
10:37 of them be put in positions of trust in the **k.**
10:43 and receive back all their property in my **k.**
10:52 to my **k** and have taken my seat on the throne
10:53 and we have taken our seat on the throne of his **k**—
10:55 and took your seat on the throne of their **k.**
11: 1 and he tried to get possession of Alexander's **k**
11: 1 by trickery and add it to his own **k.**
11: 9 and you shall reign over your father's **k.**
11:11 on Alexander because he coveted his **k.**
11:51 the sight of the king and of all the people in his **k,**
11:52 So King Demetrius sat on the throne of his **k,**
15: 3 of the **k** of our ancestors,
15: 3 to the **k** so that I may restore it as it formerly was,
15: 4 those who have devastated many cities in my **k,**
15: 9 When we gain control of our **k,**
15:28 they are cities of my **k.**
15:29 you have taken possession of many places in my **k.**
2Mc 1: 7 from the holy land and the **k**
4: 7 who was called Epiphanes, succeeded to the **k,**
9:25 and the neighbors of my **k** keep watching
10:11 This man, when he succeeded to the **k,**
11:23 the **k** be undisturbed in caring for their own affairs.
14: 6 and will not let the **k** attain tranquility.
14:26 he had appointed that conspirator against the **k,**
1Es 1:24 toward the Lord beyond any other people or **k,**
2: 2 a proclamation throughout all his **k** and also put it
4:49 the Jews who were going up from his **k** to Judea,
8:21 so that wrath may not come upon the **k** of the king
8:24 or the law of the **k** shall be strictly punished,
3Mc 6:24 by secretly devising acts of no advantage to the **k.**
7: 3 persuaded us to gather together the Jews of the **k**
7:12 in his **k** who had transgressed the law of God.
2Es 2:10 "Tell my people that I will give them the **k**
2:13 The **k** is already prepared for you; be on the watch!
2:35 Be ready for the rewards of the **k,**
12:11 up from the sea is the fourth **k** that appeared in
12:13 The days are coming when a **k** shall rise on earth,
12:18 of that **k** great struggles shall arise, and it shall be
13:31 people against people, and **k** against **k.**
4Mc 2:23 and one who lives subject to this will rule a **k**
12: 5 and a leader in the government of the **k."**
12:11 and also your **k** from God,

KINGDOMS‡ (63) [KING]

A. ALL THE ... KINGDOMS (27)
B. KINGDOMS OF THE EARTH (14)

Dt 3:21 the LORD will do to all the **k** into which you are A
28:25 an object of horror to all the **k** of the earth. AB
Jos 11:10 Before that time Hazor was the head of all those **k.**
1Sa 10:18 the hand of all the **k** that were oppressing you.' A
1Ki 4:21 over all the **k** from the Euphrates to the land of A
2Ki 19:15 God, you alone, of all the **k** of the earth; AB
19:19 that all the **k** of the earth may know that you, AB
1Ch 29:30 befell him and Israel and all the **k** of the earth. AB
2Ch 12: 8 between serving me and serving the **k**
17:10 fear of the LORD fell on all the **k** of the lands A
20: 6 Do you not rule over all the **k** of the nations? A
20:29 fear of God came on all the **k** of the countries A
36:23 has given me all the **k** of the earth, AB
Ezr 1: 2 has given me all the **k** of the earth, AB
Ne 9:22 And you gave them **k** and peoples,
Ps 46: 6 The nations are in an uproar, the **k** totter;
68:32 Sing to God, O **k** of the earth; B
79: 6 and on the **k** that do not call on your name.
102:22 and **k,** to worship the LORD.
135:11 Og, king of Bashan, and all the **k** of Canaan— A
Isa 10:10 As my hand has reached to the **k** of the idols
13: 4 an uproar of **k,** of nations gathering together!
13:19 And Babylon, the glory of **k,**
14:16 the earth tremble, who shook **k,**
23:11 over the sea, he has shaken the **k;**
23:17 all the **k** of the world on the face of the earth. A
37:16 God, you alone, of all the **k** of the earth; AB
37:20 that all the **k** of the earth may know that you AB
47: 5 For you shall no more be called the mistress of **k.**
Jer 1:10 See, today I appoint you over nations and over **k,**
1:15 now I am calling all the tribes of the **k** of the north,
10: 7 of the nations and in all their **k** there is no one
15: 4 make them a horror to all the **k** of the earth AB
24: 9 an evil thing, to all the **k** of the earth— AB
25:26 all the **k** of the world that are on the face of A
28: 8 pestilence against many countries and great **k.**
29:18 make them a horror to all the **k** of the earth, AB
34: 1 and all his army and all the **k** of the earth AB
34:17 make you a horror to all the **k** of the earth. AB
49:28 and the **k** of Hazor that King Nebuchadrezzar
51:20 with you I smash nations; with you I destroy **k;**
51:27 summon against her the **k,** Ararat, Minni,
Eze 29:15 It shall be the most lowly of the **k,**
Eze 37:22 and never again shall they be divided into two **k.**
Da 2:44 It shall crush all these **k** and bring them to an end,
7:23 that shall be different from all the other **k;** A
7:27 the greatness of the **k** under the whole heaven shall
8:22 four **k** shall arise from his nation,
Am 6: 2 Are you better than these **k?**
Na 3: 5 and I will let nations look on your nakedness and **k**
Zep 3: 8 my decision is to gather nations, to assemble **k,**
Hag 2:22 and to overthrow the throne of **k;**
2:22 the strength of the **k** of the nations, and overthrow
Mt 4: 8 and showed him all the **k** of the world A
Lk 4: 5 showed him in an instant all the **k** of the world. A
Heb 11:33 who through faith conquered **k,**
Sir 44: 3 There were those who ruled in their **k,**
Bar 2: 4 He made them subject to all the **k** around us, A
1Mc 1:16 in order that he might reign over both **k.**
6:29 also came to him from other **k** and from islands of
8:11 The remaining **k** and islands,
2Es 2:37 to him who has called you to the celestial **k.**
12:13 be more terrifying than all the **k** that have been A

KINGLY (1) [KING]

Da 5:20 he was deposed from his **k** throne,

KINGS‡ (390) [KING]

A. KINGS OF ISRAEL (42)
B. KINGS OF JUDAH (39)
C. ALL THE KINGS (32)
D. KINGS OF THE EARTH (26)
E. BOOK OF THE KINGS (11)
F. KING OF KINGS (8)

Ge 14: 2 these **k** made war with King Bera of Sodom,
14: 5 and the **k** who were with him came and subdued
14: 9 and King Arioch of Ellasar, four **k** against five.
14:10 and as the **k** of Sodom and Gomorrah fled,
14:17 the defeat of Chedorlaomer and the **k** who were
17: 6 and **k** shall come from you.
17:16 **k** of peoples shall come from her."
35:11 and **k** shall spring from you.
36:31 These are the **k** who reigned in the land of Edom,
Nu 31: 8 They killed the **k** of Midian:
31: 8 Rekem, Zur, Hur, and Reba, the five **k** of Midian,
Dt 3: 8 that time we took from the two **k** of the Amorites
3:21 the LORD your God has done to these two **k;**
4:47 the two **k** of the Amorites on the eastern side of
7:24 He will hand their **k** over to you
31: 4 the **k** of the Amorites, and to their land,
Jos 2:10 and what you did to the two **k** of the Amorites
5: 1 all the **k** of the Amorites beyond the Jordan C
5: 1 and all the **k** of the Canaanites by the sea, C
9: 1 when all the **k** who were beyond the Jordan C
9:10 that he did to the two **k** of the Amorites who were
10: 5 Then the five **k** of the Amorites—
10: 6 for all the **k** of the Amorites who live in C
10:16 these five **k** fled and hid themselves in the cave
10:17 it was told Joshua, "The five **k** have been found,
10:22 and bring those five **k** out to me from the cave."
10:23 and brought the five **k** out to him from the cave,
10:24 When they brought the **k** out to Joshua,
10:24 "Come near, put your feet on the necks of these **k."**
10:40 and the lowland and the slopes, and all their **k;**
10:42 Joshua took all these **k** and their land at one time,
11: 2 and to the **k** who were in the northern hill country,
11: 5 All these **k** joined their forces,
11:12 And all the towns of those **k,** and all their kings,
11:12 And all the towns of those kings, and all their **k,**
11:17 He took all their **k,** struck them down,
11:18 Joshua made war a long time with all those **k.**
12: 1 Now these are the **k** of the land,
12: 7 The following are the **k** of the land whom Joshua
12:24 the king of Tirzah one thirty-one **k** in all.
24:12 drove out before you the two **k** of the Amorites;
Jdg 1: 7 "Seventy **k** with their thumbs and big toes cut off
5: 3 O **k;** give ear, O princes;
5:19 "The **k** came, they fought;
5:19 then fought the **k** of Canaan, at Taanach,
8: 5 and I am pursuing Zebah and Zalmunna, the **k**
8:12 and he pursued them and took the two **k** of Midian,
8:26 and the purple garments worn by the **k** of Midian,
1Sa 14:47 the **k** of Zobah, and against the Philistines;
27: 6 Ziklag has belonged to the **k** of Judah to this B
2Sa 10:19 all the **k** who were servants of Hadadezer C
11: 1 the time when **k** go out to battle,
1Ki 4:24 over all the **k** west of the Euphrates; C
4:34 from all the **k** of the earth who had heard of CD
10:15 from all the **k** of Arabia and the governors of C
10:23 King Solomon excelled all the **k** of the earth CD
10:29 they were exported to all the **k** of the Hittites C
10:29 to all the kings of the Hittites and the **k** of Aram.
14:19 in the Book of the Annals of the **K** of Israel. A
14:29 in the Book of the Annals of the **K** of Judah? B
15: 7 in the Book of the Annals of the **K** of Judah? B
15:23 in the Book of the Annals of the **K** of Judah? B
15:31 in the Book of the Annals of the **K** of Israel? A
16: 5 in the Book of the Annals of the **K** of Israel? A
16:14 in the Book of the Annals of the **K** of Israel? A
16:20 in the Book of the Annals of the **K** of Israel? A
16:27 in the Book of the Annals of the **K** of Israel? A
16:33 had all the **k** of Israel who were before him. AC
20: 1 thirty-two **k** were with him,
20:12 he had been drinking with the **k** in the booths—
20:16 he and the thirty-two **k** allied with him.
20:24 Also do this: remove the **k,** each from his post,
20:31 that the **k** of the house of Israel are merciful **k;**
22:39 in the Book of the Annals of the **K** of Israel? A
1Ki 22:45 in the Book of the Annals of the **K** of Judah? B
2Ki 1:18 in the Book of the Annals of the **K** of Israel? A
3:10 The LORD has summoned us, three **k,**
3:13 it is the LORD who has summoned us, three **k,**
3:21 the Moabites heard that the **k** had come up to fight
3:23 the **k** must have fought together,
7: 6 the **k** of the Hittites and the **k** of Egypt to fight
8:18 He walked in the way of the **k** of Israel, A
8:23 in the Book of the Annals of the **K** of Judah? B
10: 4 "Look, two **k** could not withstand him;
10:34 in the Book of the Annals of the **K** of Israel? A
11:19 He took his seat on the throne of the **k.**
12:18 his ancestors, the **k** of Judah, had dedicated, B
12:19 in the Book of the Annals of the **K** of Judah? B
13: 8 in the Book of the Annals of the **K** of Israel? A
13:12 in the Book of the Annals of the **K** of Israel? A
13:13 Joash was buried in Samaria with the **k** of Israel. A
14:15 in the Book of the Annals of the **K** of Israel? A
14:16 and was buried in Samaria with the **k** of Israel; A
14:18 in the Book of the Annals of the **K** of Judah? B
14:28 in the Book of the Annals of the **K** of Israel? A
14:29 slept with his ancestors, the **k** of Israel; A
15: 6 in the Book of the Annals of the **K** of Judah? B
15:11 in the Book of the Annals of the **K** of Israel. A
15:15 in the Book of the Annals of the **K** of Israel. A
15:21 in the Book of the Annals of the **K** of Israel? A
15:26 in the Book of the Annals of the **K** of Israel. A
15:31 in the Book of the Annals of the **K** of Israel. A
15:36 in the Book of the Annals of the **K** of Judah? B
16: 3 but he walked in the way of the **k** of Israel. A
16:19 in the Book of the Annals of the **K** of Judah? B
17: 2 yet not like the **k** of Israel who were before him. A
17: 8 the customs that the **k** of Israel had introduced. A
18: 5 no one like him among all the **k** of Judah BC
19:11 you have heard what the **k** of Assyria have done
19:17 the **k** of Assyria have laid waste the nations
20:20 in the Book of the Annals of the **K** of Judah? B
21:17 in the Book of the Annals of the **K** of Judah? B
21:25 in the Book of the Annals of the **K** of Judah? B
23: 5 the **k** of Judah had ordained to make offerings in B
23:11 that the **k** of Judah had dedicated to the sun, B
23:12 which the **k** of Judah had made, B
23:19 which **k** of Israel had made, A
23:22 during all the days of the **k** of Israel or of the A
23:22 days of the kings of Israel or of the **k** of Judah; B
23:28 in the Book of the Annals of the **K** of Judah? B
24: 5 in the Book of the Annals of the **K** of Judah? B
25:28 above the other seats of the **k** who were with him
1Ch 1:43 These are the **k** who reigned in the land of Edom
9: 1 these are written in the Book of the **K** of Israel. AE
16:21 he rebuked **k** on their account,
19: 9 and the **k** who had come were by themselves in
20: 1 the time when **k** go out to battle,
2Ch 1:12 such as none of the **k** had who were before you,
1:17 were exported to all the **k** of the Hittites C
1:17 to all the kings of the Hittites and the **k** of Aram.
9:14 and all the **k** of Arabia and the governors of C
9:22 King Solomon excelled all the **k** of the earth CD
9:23 All the **k** of the earth sought the presence of CD
9:26 over all the **k** from the Euphrates to the land of C
16:11 are written in the Book of the **K** of Judah BE
20:34 are recorded in the Book of the **K** of Israel. AE
21: 6 He walked in the way of the **k** of Israel, A
21:13 but have walked in the way of the **k** of Israel, A
21:20 but not in the tombs of the **k.**
24:16 they buried him in the city of David among the **k,**
24:25 but they did not bury him in the tombs of the **k.**
24:27 in the Commentary on the Book of the **K.** E
25:26 they not written in the Book of the **K** of Judah BE
26:23 in the burial field that belonged to the **k,**
27: 7 are written in the Book of the **K** of Israel AE
28: 2 but he walked in the ways of the **k** of Israel. A
28:23 "Because the gods of the **k** of Aram helped them,
28:26 are written in the Book of the **K** of Judah BE
28:27 not bring him into the tombs of the **k** of Israel. A
30: 6 of you who have escaped from the hand of the **k**
32: 4 "Why should the Assyrian **k** come and find water
32:32 in the Book of the **K** of Judah and Israel. BE
33:18 these are in the Annals of the **K** of Israel. A
34:11 buildings that the **k** of Judah had let go to ruin B
35:18 none of the **k** of Israel had kept such a passover A
35:27 in the Book of the **K** of Israel and Judah. AE
36: 8 in the Book of the **K** of Israel and Judah; AE
Ezr 4:15 hurtful to **k** and provinces,
4:19 and discovered that this city has risen against **k**
4:20 Jerusalem has had mighty **k** who ruled over
7:12 "Artaxerxes, king of **k,** to the priest Ezra, F
9: 7 and for our iniquities we, our **k,**
9: 7 and our priests have been handed over to the **k** of
9: 9 to us his steadfast love before the **k** of Persia,
Ne 9:24 with their **k** and the peoples of the land,
9:32 upon our **k,** our officials, our priests, our prophets,
9:32 since the time of the **k** of Assyria until today.
9:34 our **k,** our officials, our priests,
9:37 Its rich yield goes to the **k** whom you have set
Est 10: 2 are they not written in the annals of the **k** of Media
Job 3:14 **k** and counselors of the earth who rebuild ruins
12:18 He looses the sash of **k,**
36: 7 but with **k** on the throne he sets them forever,
Ps 2: 2 The **k** of the earth set themselves, D
2:10 O **k,** be wise; be warned, O rulers of the earth.
45: 9 daughters of **k** are among your ladies of honor;
48: 4 Then the **k** assembled, they came on together.
68:12 "The **k** of the armies, they flee,
68:14 Almighty scattered **k** there, snow fell on Zalmon.
68:29 of your temple at Jerusalem **k** bear gifts to you.
72:10 May the **k** of Tarshish and of the isles

Ps 72:10 may the **k** of Sheba and Seba bring gifts.
72:11 May all **k** fall down before him,
76:12 who inspires fear in the **k** of the earth. D
89:27 the highest of the **k** of the earth. D
102:15 and all the **k** of the earth your glory. CD
105:14 he rebuked **k** on their account,
105:30 even in the chambers of their **k.**
110: 5 he will shatter **k** on the day of his wrath.
119:46 I will also speak of your decrees before **k,**
135:10 struck down many nations and killed mighty **k—**
136:17 who struck down great **k,**
136:18 and killed famous **k,** for his steadfast love endures
138: 4 All the **k** of the earth shall praise you, O LORD, CD
144:10 the one who gives victory to **k,**
148:11 **K** of the earth and all peoples, D
149: 8 to bind their **k** with fetters and their nobles
Pr 8:15 By me **k** reign, and rulers decree what is just;
16:12 It is an abomination to **k** to do evil,
22:29 in their work? they will serve **k;**
25: 2 but the glory of **k** is to search things out.
25: 3 so the mind of **k** is unsearchable.
31: 3 your ways to those who destroy **k.**
31: 4 It is not for **k,** O Lemuel, it is not for **k** to drink wine,
Ecc 2: 8 for myself silver and gold and the treasure of **k**
Isa 1: 1 Jotham, Ahaz, and Hezekiah, **k** of Judah. B
7:16 the land before whose two **k** you are in dread will
10: 8 For he says: "Are not my commanders all **k?**
14: 9 from their thrones all who were **k** of the nations.
14:18 All the **k** of the nations lie in glory, C
19:11 "I am one of the sages, a descendant of ancient **k"?**
24:21 and on earth the **k** of the earth. D
37:11 you have heard what the **k** of Assyria have done
37:18 the **k** of Assyria have laid waste all the nations
41: 2 and tramples **k** under foot;
45: 1 before him and strip **k** of their robes, to open doors
49: 7 the slave of rulers, **"K** shall see and stand up,
49:23 **K** shall be your foster fathers,
52:15 **k** shall shut their mouths because of him;
60: 3 and **k** to the brightness of your dawn.
60:10 and their **k** shall minister to you;
60:11 with their **k** led in procession.
60:16 you shall suck the breasts of **k;**
62: 2 and all the **k** your glory; C
Jer 1:18 against the **k** of Judah, its princes, its priests, B
2:26 they, their **k,** their officials, their priests,
8: 1 says the LORD, the bones of the **k** of Judah, B
13:13 the **k** who sit on David's throne, the priests,
17:19 in the People's Gate, by which the **k** of Judah B
17:20 Hear the word of the LORD, you **k** of Judah, B
17:25 of this city **k** who sit on the throne of David,
19: 3 O **k** of Judah and inhabitants of Jerusalem. B
19: 4 their ancestors nor the **k** of Judah have known; B
19:13 Jerusalem and the houses of the **k** of Judah shall B
20: 5 all the treasures of the **k** of Judah into the hand B
22: 4 of this house shall enter **k** who sit on the throne
25:14 For many nations and great **k** shall make slaves
25:18 its **k** and officials, to make them a desolation and
25:20 all the **k** of the land of Uz; C
25:20 all the **k** of the land of the Philistines— C
25:22 all the **k** of Tyre, all the kings of Sidon, C
25:22 all the **k** of Sidon, and the kings of the coastland C
25:22 and the **k** of the coastland across the sea;
25:24 all the **k** of Arabia and all the kings of C
25:24 all the **k** of the mixed peoples that live in the C
25:25 all the **k** of Zimri, all the kings of Elam, C
25:25 all the **k** of Elam, and all the kings of Media; C
25:25 all the kings of Elam, and all the **k** of Media; C
25:26 all the **k** of the north, far and near, C
27: 7 and great **k** shall make him their slave.
32:32 they, their **k** and their officials,
33: 4 the houses of the **k** of Judah that were torn down B
34: 5 the earlier **k** who preceded you,
44: 9 of the **k** of Judah, of their wives, B
44:17 as we and our ancestors, our **k** and our officials,
44:21 you and your ancestors, your **k** and your officials,
46:25 and Pharaoh, and Egypt and her gods and her **k,**
50:41 and many **k** are stirring from the farthest parts of
51:11 The LORD has stirred up the spirit of the **k** of
51:28 the nations for war against her, the **k** of the Medes,
52:32 above the seats of the other **k** who were with him
La 4:12 The **k** of the earth did not believe, D
Eze 26: 7 king of **k,** together with horses, chariots, F
27:33 merchandise you enriched the **k** of the earth. D
27:35 and their **k** are horribly afraid,
28:17 I exposed you before **k,** to feast their eyes on you.
32:10 their **k** shall shudder because of you.
32:29 Edom is there, its **k** and all its princes,
43: 7 neither they nor their **k,** by their whoring,
43: 7 and by the corpses of their **k** at their death.
43: 9 and the corpses of their **k** far from me,
Da 2:21 times and seasons, deposes **k** and sets up **k;**
2:37 You, O king, the king of **k—** F
2:44 those **k** the God of heaven will set up a kingdom
2:47 of gods and Lord of **k** and a revealer of mysteries,
7:17 four **k** shall arise out of the earth.
7:24 the ten horns, out of this kingdom ten **k** shall arise,
7:24 and shall put down three **k.**
8:20 these are the **k** of Media and Persia.
9: 6 who spoke in your name to our **k,** our princes,
9: 8 Open shame, O LORD, falls on us, our **k,**
11: 2 Three more **k** shall arise in Persia.
11:27 The two **k,** their minds bent on evil,
Hos 1: 1 in the days of **K** Uzziah, Jotham, Ahaz,
7: 7 their **k** have fallen; none of them calls upon me.
8: 4 They made **k,** but not through me;
8:10 They shall soon writhe under the burden of **k**

Mic 1: 1 to Micah of Moresheth in the days of **K** Jotham,
1:14 Achzib shall be a deception to the **k** of Israel. A
Hab 1:10 At **k** they scoff, and of rulers they make sport.
Mt 10:18 be dragged before governors and **k** because of me,
17:25 whom do **k** of the earth take toll or tribute? D
Mk 13: 9 and you will stand before governors and **k** because
Lk 10:24 For I tell you that many prophets and **k** desired
21:12 and you will be brought before **k** and governors
22:25 "The **k** of the Gentiles lord it over them;
Ac 4:26 The **k** of the earth took their stand, D
9:15 to bring my name before Gentiles and **k** and
1Co 4: 8 Quite apart from us you have become **k!** Indeed, I wish that you had become **k,** so that we might be **k** with you!
1Ti 2: 2 for **k** and all who are in high positions,
6:15 the King of **k** and Lord of lords. F
Heb 7: 1 as he was returning from defeating the **k**
Rev 1: 5 and the ruler of the **k** of the earth. D
6:15 Then the **k** of the earth and the magnates and D
10:11 and nations and languages and **k."**
16:12 in order to prepare the way for the **k** from the east.
16:14 who go abroad to the **k** of the whole world,
17: 2 the **k** of the earth have committed fornication, D
17: 9 which the woman is seated; also, they are seven **k,**
17:12 And the ten horns that you saw are ten **k** who
17:12 but they are to receive authority as **k** for one hour,
17:14 for he is Lord of lords and King of **k,** F
17:18 the great city that rules over the **k** of the earth." D
18: 3 the **k** of the earth have committed fornication D
18: 9 the **k** of the earth, who committed fornication D
19:16 "King of **k** and Lord of lords." F
19:18 to eat the flesh of **k,** the flesh of captains,
19:19 and the **k** of the earth with their armies gathered D
21:24 the **k** of the earth will bring their glory into it. D
AdE 10: 2 the annals of the **k** of the Persians and the Medes.
13: 4 and continually disregard the ordinances of **k,**
Wis 6: 1 Listen therefore, O **k,** and understand;
10:16 and withstood dread **k** with wonders and signs.
Sir 8: 2 and has perverted the minds of **k.**
11: 5 Many **k** have had to sit on the ground,
45: 3 the Lord glorified him in the presence of **k.**
48: 6 You sent **k** down to destruction, and famous men,
48: 8 You anointed **k** to inflict retribution,
49: 4 the **k** of Judah came to an end. B
51:12 *Give thanks to the King of the* **k** *of* **k,**
Bar 1:16 and on our **k,** our rulers, our priests, our prophets,
2: 1 and against our **k** and our rulers and the people
2:19 of any righteous deeds of our ancestors or our **k**
2:24 the prophets, that the bones of our **k** and the bones
LtJ 6:51 to all the nations and **k** that they are not gods but
6:66 They can neither curse nor bless **k;**
1Mc 1: 2 and put to death the **k** of the earth. D
2:48 the law out of the hands of the Gentiles and **k,**
3: 7 He embittered many **k,** but he made Jacob glad
3:30 to give more lavishly than preceding **k.**
8: 4 They also subdued the **k** who came against them
8:12 They have subdued **k** far and near,
8:13 they wish to help and to make **k,** they make **k,**
10:49 The two **k** met in battle,
10:58 at Ptolemais with great pomp, as **k** do.
10:60 with pomp to Ptolemais and met the two **k;**
12:13 the **k** around us have waged war against us.
13:36 the high priest and friend of **k,**
14:13 and the **k** were crushed in those days.
15: 5 that the **k** before me have granted you,
15:15 with letters to the **k** and countries,
15:19 to write to the **k** and countries that they should
2Mc 2:13 and collected the books about the **k** and prophets,
2:13 and letters of **k** about votive offerings.
3: 2 the **k** themselves honored the place and glorified
5:16 that other **k** had made to enhance the glory
13: 4 the King of **k** aroused the anger of Antiochus F
1Es 1:21 none of the **k** of Israel had kept such a passover A
1:33 in the book of the histories of the **k** of Judea;
1:33 are recorded in the book of the **k** of Israel AE
1:42 are written in the annals of the **k.**
1:52 to bring against them the **k** of the Chaldeans.
2:19 not only refuse to pay tribute but will even resist **k.**
2:22 troubling both **k** and other cities,
2:26 that this city from of old has fought against **k,**
2:27 and cruel **k** ruled in Jerusalem and exacted tribute
2:29 go no further to the annoyance of **k."**
3:21 It makes all hearts feel rich, forgets **k** and satraps,
7: 4 and Darius and Artaxerxes, **k** of the Persians,
8:77 and our **k** and our priests were given over to
8:77 our priests were given over to the **k** of the earth, D
8:80 he brought us into favor with the **k** of the Persians,
3Mc 3:19 in defiance of **k** and their own benefactors,
5:35 praised the manifest Lord God, King of **k,** F
2Es 1:10 For their sake I have overthrown many **k;**
12:14 And twelve **k** shall reign in it, one after another.
12:20 Eight **k** shall arise in it, whose times shall be short
12:23 In its last days the Most High will raise up three **k,**
12:26 one of the **k** shall die in his bed, but in agonies.
15:20 I am calling together all the **k** of the earth CD
15:33 and indecision upon their **k.**
4Mc 14: 2 more royal than **k** and freer than the free!

KINGS' (1) [KING]

Pr 30:28 yet it is found in **k** palaces.

KINGSHIP (12) [KING]

1Sa 10:16 But about the matter of the **k,**
10:25 the people the rights and duties of the **k;**
11:14 "Come, let us go to Gilgal and there renew the **k."**
14:47 When Saul had taken the **k** over Israel,

2Ch 13: 5 not know that the LORD God of Israel gave the **k**
Da 5:18 God gave your father Nebuchadnezzar **k,**
7:14 To him was given dominion and glory and **k,**
7:14 and his **k** is one that shall never be destroyed.
7:27 The **k** and dominion and the greatness of
Sir 47:11 he gave him a covenant of **k** and a glorious throne
2Mc 2:17 and the **k** and the priesthood and the consecration,
1Es 4:40 the **k** and the power and the majesty of all the ages.

KINSFOLK‡ (28) [KIN]

Ge 31:23 So he took his **k** with him and pursued him
31:25 and Laban with his **k** camped in the hill country
31:32 In the presence of our **k,**
31:37 Set it here before my **k** and your **k,**
31:46 And Jacob said to his **k,** "Gather stones,"
31:54 on the height and called his **k** to eat bread;
Ex 2:11 an Egyptian beating a Hebrew, one of his **k.**
Jdg 9: 1 to Shechem to his mother's **k** and said to them and
9: 3 So his mother's **k** spoke all these words
9:26 Gaal son of Ebed moved into Shechem with his **k,**
9:31 Gaal son of Ebed and his **k** have come to Shechem,
9:41 and Zebul drove out Gaal and his **k,**
18: 8 When they came to their **k** at Zorah and Eshtaol,
20:13 But the Benjaminites would not listen to their **k,**
20:23 "Shall we again draw near to battle against our **k**
20:28 "Shall we go out once more to battle against our **k**
1Sa 18:18 David said to Saul, "Who am I and who are my **k,**
2Sa 15:20 Go back, and take your **k** with you;
1Ch 16:37 David left Asaph and his **k** there before the ark of
16:38 and also Obed-edom and his sixty-eight **k;**
Pr 17:17 and **k** are born to share adversity.
Jer 7:15 just as I cast out all your **k,**
12: 6 For even your **k** and your own family,
29:16 your **k** who did not go out with you into exile:
49:10 his **k** and his neighbors; and he is no more.
Eze 11:15 your **k,** your own kin, your fellow exiles,
Ac 7:25 He supposed that his **k** would understand that God

KINSHIP (4) [KIN]

Am 1: 9 and did not remember the covenant of **k.**
Wis 8:17 that in **k** with wisdom there is immortality,
2Mc 5: 9 in hope of finding protection because of their **k.**
4Mc 10: 3 I do not renounce the noble **k** that binds me

KINSMAN (20) [KIN, MAN]

Ge 24:48 to obtain the daughter of my master's **k** for his son.
29:12 And Jacob told Rachel that he was her father's **k,**
29:15 Then Laban said to Jacob, "Because you are my **k,**
Nu 27:11 then you shall give his inheritance to the nearest **k**
Jdg 9:18 over the lords of Shechem, because he is your **k—**
Ru 2: 1 Now Naomi had a **k** on her husband's side,
3: 2 Now here is our **k** Boaz,
3:12 But now, though it is true that I am a near **k,**
3:12 there is another **k** more closely related than I.
4: 3 of land that belonged to our **k** Elimelech.
Tob 5: 6 with our **k** Gabael who lives in Rages of Media.
5:14 It turns out that you are a **k,**
7: 2 much the young man resembles my **k** Tobit!"
7: 4 She said to them, "Do you know our **k** Tobit?"
7: 7 He then embraced his **k** Tobias and wept.
1Mc 11:31 concerning you to our **k** Lasthenes we have written
2Mc 11: 1 Lysias, the king's guardian and **k,**
11:35 to what Lysias the **k** of the king has granted you,
1Es 3: 7 to Darius and shall be called **K** of Darius."
4:42 You shall sit next to me, and be called my **K."**

KINSMAN'S (1) [KIN, MAN]

Lev 18:20 not have sexual relations with your **k** wife,

KINSMEN (9) [KIN, MAN]

Lev 10: 4 and carry your **k** away from the front of
Jos 17: 4 an inheritance among the **k** of their father.
2Sa 2:26 to turn from the pursuit of their **k?"**
2:27 the people would have continued to pursue their **k,**
Tob 7:11 I have given her to seven men of our **k,**
1Mc 10:89 such as it is the custom to give to the King's **K.**
1Es 5:48 and Zerubbabel son of Shealtiel, with his **k,**
8:47 namely Sherebiah with his descendants and **k,**
8:54 and ten of their **k** with them;

KINSWOMAN (4) [KIN, WOMAN]

Tob 6:18 of Raphael and learned that she was his **k,**
7: 9 ask Raguel to give me my **k** Sarah."
7:11 be given to you. Take your **k;**
8: 7 I now am taking this **k** of mine, not because of lust,

KIR (5) [KIR-HARESETH, KIR-HERES]

2Ki 16: 9 and took it, carrying its people captive to **K;**
Isa 15: 1 **K** is laid waste in a night, Moab is undone.
22: 6 and **K** uncovered the shield.
Am 1: 5 and the people of Aram shall go into exile to **K,**
9: 7 from Caphtor and the Arameans from **K?**

KIR-HARASETH (KJV) See KIR-HARESETH

KIR-HARESH (KJV) See KIR-HERES

KIR-HARESETH (2) [KIR]

2Ki 3:25 Only at **K** did the stone walls remain,
Isa 16: 7 Mourn, utterly stricken, for the raisin cakes of **K.**

KIR-HERES (3) [KIR]
Isa 16:11 and my very soul for **K**.
Jer 48:31 for the people of **K** I mourn.
48:36 my heart moans like a flute for the people of **K**;

KIRAMA (1)
1Es 5:20 Those from **K** and Geba, six hundred twenty-one.

KIRIATH See Index to Footnotes

KIRIATH-ARBA (9) [=HEBRON]
Ge 23: 2 And Sarah died at **K** (that is, Hebron) in the land
35:27 at Mamre, or **K** (that is, Hebron), where Abraham
Jos 14:15 Now the name of Hebron formerly was **K**;
15:13 **K**, that is, Hebron (Arba was the father of Anak).
15:54 **K** (that is, Hebron), and Zior:
20: 7 hill country of Ephraim, and **K** (that is, Hebron)
21:11 They gave them **K** (Arba being the father
Jdg 1:10 in Hebron (the name of Hebron was formerly **K**);
Ne 11:25 of the people of Judah lived in **K** and its villages,

KIRIATH-BAAL (2) [BAAL, =KIRIATH-JEARIM]
Jos 15:60 **K** (that is, Kiriath-jearim), and Rabbah:
18:14 and it ends at **K** (that is, Kiriath-jearim),

KIRIATH-HUZOTH (1)
Nu 22:39 Balaam went with Balak, and they came to **K**.

KIRIATH-JEARIM (19) [=BAALAH, JEARIM, =KIRIATH-BAAL]
Jos 9:17 Chephirah, Beeroth, and **K**.
15: 9 the boundary bends around to Baalah (that is, **K**);
15:60 Kiriath-baal (that is, **K**), and Rabbah:
18:14 **K**), a town belonging to the tribe of Judah.
18:15 The southern side begins at the outskirts of **K**;
18:28 Jebus (that is, Jerusalem), Gibeah and **K**—
Jdg 18:12 and went up and encamped at **K** in Judah.
18:12 to this day; it is west of **K**.
1Sa 6:21 So they sent messengers to the inhabitants of **K**,
7: 1 And the people of **K** came and took up the ark of
7: 2 From the day that the ark was lodged at **K**,
1Ch 2:50 of Ephrathah: Shobal father of **K**,
2:52 Shobal father of **K** had other sons:
2:53 And the families of **K**: the Ithrites,
13: 5 to bring the ark of God from **K**.
13: 6 that is, to **K**, which belongs to Judah,
2Ch 1: 4 from **K** to the place that David had prepared for it;
Ne 7:29 Of **K**, Chephirah, and Beeroth,
Jer 26:20 Uriah son of Shemaiah from **K**.

KIRIATH-SANNAH (1) [=DEBIR]
Jos 15:49 Dannah, **K** (that is, Debir),

KIRIATH-SEPHER (4) [=DEBIR]
Jos 15:15 now the name of Debir formerly was **K**.
15:16 And Caleb said, "Whoever attacks **K** and takes it,
Jdg 1:11 of Debir (the name of Debir was formerly **K**).
1:12 Then Caleb said, "Whoever attacks **K** and takes it,

KIRIATHAIM (6)
Nu 32:37 And the Reubenites rebuilt Heshbon, Elealeh, **K**,
Jos 13:19 and **K**, and Sibmah, and Zereth-shahar on the hill
1Ch 6:76 and **K** with its pasture lands.
Jer 48: 1 **K** is put to shame, it is taken;
48:23 and **K**, and Beth-gamul, and Beth-meon,
Eze 25: 9 Beth-jeshimoth, Baal-meon, and **K**.

KIRIATHARIM (2)
Ezr 2:25 Of **K**, Chephirah, and Beeroth,
1Es 5:19 Those from **K**, twenty-five.

KIRIOTH (KJV) See KERIOTH

KIRJATH (KJV) See KIRIATH

KIRJATH-ARBA (KJV) See KIRIATH-ARBA

KIRJATH-ARIM (KJV) See KIRIATHARIM

KIRJATH-BAAL (KJV) See KIRIATH-BAAL

KIRJATH-HUZOTH (KJV) See KIRIATH-HUZOTH

KIRJATH-JEARIM (KJV) See KIRIATH-JEARIM

KIRJATH-SANNAH (KJV) See KIRIATH-SANNAH

KIRJATH-SEPHER (KJV) See KIRIATH-SEPHER

KIRJATHAIM (KJV) See KIRIATHAIM

KISH (25)
1Sa 9: 1 of Benjamin whose name was **K** son of Abiel son
9: 3 Now the donkeys of **K**, Saul's father, had strayed.
9: 3 So **K** said to his son Saul,
10:11 "What has come over the son of **K**?
10:21 and Saul the son of **K** was taken by lot.
14:51 **K** was the father of Saul,
2Sa 21:14 in the tomb of his father **K**;
1Ch 8:30 His firstborn son: Abdon, then Zur, **K**, Baal,
8:33 Ner became the father of **K**, **K** of Saul,
9:36 His firstborn son was Abdon, then Zur, **K**, Baal,
9:39 Ner became the father of **K**, **K** of Saul,
12: 1 not move about freely because of Saul son of **K**;
23:21 The sons of Mahli: Eleazar and **K**.
23:22 their kindred, the sons of **K**, married them.
24:29 Of **K**, the sons of **K**: Jerahmeel.
26:28 Also all that Samuel the seer, and Saul son of **K**,
2Ch 29:12 and of the sons of Merari, **K** son of Abdi,
Est 2: 5 of Jair son of Shimei son of **K**,
2: 6 **K** had been carried away from Jerusalem among
Ac 13:21 and God gave them Saul son of **K**,
AdE 2: 5 of Shimei son of **K**, of the tribe of Benjamin;
11: 2 Mordecai son of Jair son of Shimei son of **K**,

KISHI (1)
1Ch 6:44 Ethan son of **K**, son of Abdi, son of Malluch,

KISHION (2)
Jos 19:20 Rabbith, **K**, Ebez,
21:28 **K** with its pasture lands, Daberath

KISHON (6)
Jdg 4: 7 by the Wadi **K** with his chariots and his troops;
4:13 from Harosheth-ha-goiim to the Wadi **K**.
5:21 The torrent **K** swept them away,
5:21 the onrushing torrent, the torrent **K**.
1Ki 18:40 and Elijah brought them down to the Wadi **K**,
Ps 83: 9 as to Sisera and Jabin at the Wadi **K**,

KISON (KJV) See KISHON

KISS (21) [KISSED, KISSES, KISSING]
Ge 27:26 his father Isaac said to him, "Come near and **k** me,
31:28 And why did you not permit me to **k** my sons
2Sa 15: 5 and take hold of them, and **k** them.
20: 9 by the beard with his right hand to **k** him.
1Ki 19:20 and said, "Let me **k** my father and my mother,
Ps 2:12 **k** his feet, or he will be angry, and you will perish
85:10 righteousness and peace will **k** each other.
Pr 24:26 One who gives an honest answer gives a **k** on
SS 1: 2 Let him **k** me with the kisses of his mouth!
8: 1 If I met you outside, I would **k** you,
Mt 26:48 saying, "The one I will **k** is the man; arrest him."
Mk 14:44 saying, "The one I will **k** is the man;
Lk 7:45 You gave me no **k**, but from the time I came
22:47 He approached Jesus to **k** him;
22:48 with a **k** that you are betraying the Son of Man?"
Ro 16:16 Greet one another with a holy **k**.
1Co 16:20 Greet one another with a holy **k**.
2Co 13:12 Greet one another with a holy **k**.
1Th 5:26 Greet all the brothers and sisters with a holy **k**.
1Pe 5:14 Greet one another with a **k** of love.
AdE 13:13 for I would have been willing to **k** the soles

KISSED (28) [KISS]
Ge 27:27 So he came near and **k** him;
29:11 Then Jacob **k** Rachel, and wept aloud.
29:13 he embraced him and **k** him,
31:55 and **k** his grandchildren and his daughters
33: 4 and embraced him, and fell on his neck and **k** him,
45:15 And he **k** all his brothers and wept upon them;
48:10 and he **k** them and embraced them.
50: 1 on his father's face and wept over him and **k** him.
Ex 4:27 and he met him at the mountain of God and **k** him.
18: 7 he bowed down and **k** him;
Ru 1: 9 Then she **k** them, and they wept aloud.
1:14 Orpah **k** her mother-in-law, but Ruth clung to her.
1Sa 10: 1 a vial of oil and poured it on his head, and **k** him;
20:41 He bowed three times, and they **k** each other,
2Sa 14:33 before the king; and the king **k** Absalom.
19:39 the king **k** Barzillai and blessed him,
1Ki 19:18 and every mouth that has not **k** him."
Job 31:27 and my mouth has **k** my hand;
Mt 26:49 "Greetings, Rabbi!" and **k** him.
Mk 14:45 and said, "Rabbi!" and **k** him.
Lk 15:20 he ran and put his arms around him and **k** him.
Ac 20:37 they embraced Paul and **k** him,
Tob 5:17 he **k** his father and mother.
7: 6 At that Raguel jumped up and **k** him and wept.
10:12 Then he **k** his daughter Sarah and said to her,
10:12 Then she **k** them both and saw them safely off.
1Es 4:47 Then King Darius got up and **k** him,
3Mc 5:49 and groans they **k** each other, embracing relatives

KISSES (5) [KISS]
Pr 7:13 She seizes him and **k** him,
27: 6 but profuse are the **k** of an enemy.
SS 1: 2 Let him kiss me with the **k** of his mouth!
7: 9 your **k** like the best wine that goes down smoothly,
Sir 29: 5 One **k** another's hands until he gets a loan,

KISSING (3) [KISS]
Hos 13: 2 they say. People are **k** calves!
Lk 7:38 Then she continued **k** his feet and anointing them
7:45 the time I came in she has not stopped **k** my feet.

KITCHENS (1)
Eze 46:24 "These are the **k** where those who serve at

KITE (2)
Lev 11:14 the buzzard, the **k** of any kind;
Dt 14:13 the buzzard, the **k**, of any kind;

KITHLISH (KJV) See CHITLISH

KITRON (1)
Jdg 1:30 Zebulun did not drive out the inhabitants of **K**,

KITTIM‡ (5)
Ge 10: 4 Elishah, Tarshish, **K**, and Rodanim.
Nu 24:24 from **K** and shall afflict Asshur and Eber;
1Ch 1: 7 Elishah, Tarshish, **K**, and Rodanim.
Da 11:30 For ships of **K** shall come against him,
1Mc 1: 1 the Macedonian, who came from the land of **K**,

KNEAD (2) [KNEADED, KNEADING, KNEADS]
Ge 18: 6 three measures of choice flour, **k** it,
Jer 7:18 the fathers kindle fire, and the women **k** dough,

KNEADED (2) [KNEAD]
1Sa 28:24 She quickly slaughtered it, and she took flour, **k** it,
2Sa 13: 8 She took dough, **k** it, made cakes in his sight,

KNEADING (5) [KNEAD]
Ex 8: 3 and into your ovens and your **k** bowls.
12:34 with their **k** bowls wrapped up in their cloaks
Dt 28: 5 Blessed shall be your basket and your **k** bowl.
28:17 Cursed shall be your basket and your **k** bowl.
Hos 7: 4 from the **k** of the dough until it is leavened.

KNEADS (1) [KNEAD]
Wis 15: 7 A potter **k** the soft earth

KNEE (6) [KNEE-DEEP, KNEES]
Ge 41:43 and they cried out in front of him, "Bow the **k**!"
Isa 45:23 "To me every **k** shall bow,
Ro 11: 4 not bowed the **k** to Baal."
14:11 "As I live, says the Lord, every **k** shall bow to me,
Php 2:10 so that at the name of Jesus every **k** should bend,
Man 1:11 And now I bend the **k** of my heart,

KNEE-DEEP (1) [DEEP, KNEE]
Eze 47: 4 through the water; and it was **k**.

KNEEL‡ (4) [KNEELING, KNELT]
Ge 24:11 He made the camels **k** down outside the city by
Jdg 7: 5 all those who **k** down to drink,
Job 31:10 and let other men **k** over her.
Ps 95: 6 let us **k** before the LORD, our Maker!

KNEELING‡ (3) [KNEEL]
Mt 20:20 and **k** before him, she asked a favor of him.
Mk 1:40 and **k** he said to him, "If you choose,
1Es 8:73 **k** down and stretching out my hands to the Lord

KNEES (28) [KNEE]
Ge 30: 3 go in to her, that she may bear upon my **k** and
48:12 Then Joseph removed them from his father's **k**,
50:23 of Manasseh were also born on Joseph's **k**.
Dt 28:35 on the **k** and on the legs with grievous boils
1Ki 18:42 upon the earth and put his face between his **k**.
19:18 all the **k** that have not bowed to Baal,
2Ki 1:13 and came and fell on his **k** before Elijah,
2Ch 6:13 on his **k** in the presence of the whole assembly
Ezr 9: 5 and fell on my **k**, spread out my hands to
Job 3:12 Why were there **k** to receive me,
4: 4 and you have made firm the feeble **k**.
Ps 109:24 My **k** are weak through fasting;
Isa 35: 3 and make firm the feeble **k**.
66:12 and be carried on her arm, and dandled on her **k**.
Eze 7:17 All hands shall grow feeble, all **k** turn to water.
21: 7 every spirit will faint and all **k** will turn to water.
Da 5: 6 His limbs gave way, and his **k** knocked together.
6:10 down on his **k** three times a day to pray to his God
10:10 and roused me to my hands and **k**.
Na 2:10 Hearts faint and **k** tremble, all loins quake,
Mt 18:26 So the slave fell on his **k** before him, saying,
Lk 5: 8 when Simon Peter saw it, he fell down at Jesus' **k**,
Eph 3:14 For this reason I bow my **k** before the Father,
Heb 12:12 and strengthen your weak **k**,
Sir 25:23 and weak **k** come from the wife who does
3Mc 2: 1 bending his **k** and extending his hands
5:42 mangled by the **k** and feet of the animals,
4Mc 11:10 they tied him to it on his **k**,

KNELT (17) [KNEEL]
Jdg 7: 6 but all the rest of the troops **k** down to drink water.
1Ki 8:54 he had **k** with hands outstretched toward heaven;
2Ch 6:13 Then he **k** on his knees in the presence of

Mt 2:11 and they **k** down and paid him homage.
8: 2 and there was a leper who came to him and **k**
9:18 suddenly a leader of the synagogue came in and **k**
15:25 But she came and **k** before him, saying, "Lord,
17:14 a man came to him, **k** before him,
27:29 They put a reed in his right hand and **k** before him
Mk 10:17 a man ran up and **k** before him, and asked him,
15:19 spat upon him, and **k** down in homage to him.
Lk 22:41 from them about a stone's throw, **k** down,
Jn 11:32 she **k** at his feet and said to him, "Lord,
Ac 7:60 Then he **k** down and cried out in a loud voice,
9:40 and then he **k** down and prayed.
20:36 he **k** down with them all and prayed.
21: 5 There we **k** down on the beach and prayed

KNEW‡ (83) [KNOW]

Ge 3: 7 and they **k** that they were naked;
4: 1 Now the man **k** his wife Eve,
4:17 Cain **k** his wife, and she conceived
4:25 Adam **k** his wife again, and she bore a son
8:11 so Noah **k** that the waters had subsided from
9:24 and **k** what his youngest son had done to him,
38: 9 since Onan **k** that the offspring would not be his,
Dt 34:10 whom the LORD **k** face to face.
1Sa 1:19 Elkanah **k** his wife Hannah,
3:13 for the iniquity that he **k**,
3:20 from Dan to Beer-sheba **k** that Samuel was
10:11 When all who **k** him before saw
20: 9 If I **k** that it was decided by my father
20:33 so Jonathan **k** that it was the decision of his father
20:39 But the boy **k** nothing; only Jonathan and David **k** the arrangement.
22:17 they **k** that he fled, and did not disclose it to me."
22:22 David said to Abiathar, "I **k** on that day,
26:12 No one saw it, or **k** it, nor did anyone awake;
28:14 So Saul **k** that it was Samuel,
2Sa 1:10 for I **k** that he could not live after he had fallen.
11:16 to the place where he **k** there were valiant warriors.
2Ch 33:13 Manasseh **k** that the LORD indeed was God.
Ne 9:10 for you **k** that they acted insolently
Est 1:13 Then the king consulted the sages who **k** the laws
Job 20:20 "They **k** no quiet in their bellies;
23: 3 Oh, that I **k** where I might find him,
Isa 9: 9 and all the people **k** it—
48: 7 so that you could not say, "I already **k** them."
48: 8 For I **k** that you would deal very treacherously,
Jer 1: 5 "Before I formed you in the womb I **k** you,
11:18 and I **k**; then you showed me their evil deeds.
32: 8 Then I **k** that this was the word of the LORD.
41: 4 after the murder of Gedaliah, before anyone **k** of it,
Eze 10:20 and I **k** that they were cherubim.
Da 5:22 even though you **k** all this!
6:10 Daniel **k** that the document had been signed,
Jnh 1:10 the men **k** that he was fleeing from the presence of
4: 2 for I **k** that you are a gracious God and merciful,
Zec 11:11 **k** that it was the word of the LORD.
Mt 7:23 Then I will declare to them, 'I never **k** you;
12:25 He **k** what they were thinking and said to them,
24:39 and they **k** nothing until the flood came
25:24 saying, 'Master, I **k** that you were a harsh man,
25:26 You **k**, did you, that I reap where I did not sow,
Mk 1:34 the demons to speak, because they **k** him.
Lk 4:41 because they **k** that he was the Messiah.
6: 8 Even though he **k** what they were thinking,
11:17 But he **k** what they were thinking and said to them,
12:47 That slave who **k** what his master wanted,
19:22 You **k**, did you, that I was a harsh man,
Jn 2: 9 (though the servants who had drawn the water **k**),
2:24 to them, because he **k** all people
2:25 for he himself **k** what was in everyone.
4:10 Jesus answered her, "If you **k** the gift of God,
5: 6 and **k** that he had been there a long time,
6: 6 for he himself **k** what he was going to do.
6:64 For Jesus **k** from the first who were the ones
8:19 If you **k** me, you would know my Father also."
11:42 I **k** that you always hear me,
11:57 the Pharisees had given orders that anyone who **k**
13: 1 Jesus **k** that his hour had come to depart
13:11 For he **k** who was to betray him;
13:28 Now no one at the table **k** why he said this to him.
16:19 Jesus **k** that they wanted to ask him,
18: 2 Now Judas, who betrayed him, also **k** the place,
19:28 After this, when Jesus **k** that all was now finished,
21:12 because they **k** it was the Lord.
Ac 2:30 he **k** that God had sworn with an oath to him
16: 3 for they all **k** that his father was a Greek.
18:25 though he **k** only the baptism of John.
Ro 1:21 though they **k** God, they did not honor him as God
2Co 5:16 we once **k** Christ from a human point of view,
5:21 For our sake he made him to be sin who **k** no sin,
Tob 1:19 the king **k** about me and that I was being searched
5:14 For I **k** Hananiah and Nathan,
Wis 19: 1 for God **k** in advance even their future actions:
1Mc 13:17 Simon **k** that they were speaking deceitfully
15:12 for he **k** that troubles had converged on him,
2Mc 15:21 for he **k** that it is not by arms,
2Es 8:58 though they **k** well that they must die.
10:52 I **k** that the Most High would reveal these things
4Mc 16:25 They **k** also that those who die for the sake

KNIFE (5) [KNIVES, PENKNIFE]

Ge 22: 6 and he himself carried the fire and the **k**.
22:10 Then Abraham reached out his hand and took the **k**
Jdg 19:29 When he had entered his house, he took a **k**,
Pr 23: 2 put a **k** to your throat if you have a big appetite.
4Mc 16:20 and when Isaac saw his father's hand wielding a **k**

KNIT (5)

1Ch 12:17 to help me, then my heart will be **k** to you;
Job 10:11 and **k** me together with bones and sinews.
40:17 the sinews of its thighs are **k** together.
Ps 139:13 you **k** me together in my mother's womb.
Eph 4:16 joined and **k** together by every ligament

KNIVES (4) [KNIFE]

Jos 5: 2 "Make flint **k** and circumcise the Israelites
5: 3 So Joshua made flint **k**, and circumcised
Ezr 1: 9 one thousand; **k**, twenty-nine;
Pr 30:14 whose teeth are **k**, to devour the poor from off

KNOCK (3) [KNOCKED, KNOCKING, KNOCKS]

Mt 7: 7 **k**, and the door will be opened for you.
Lk 11: 9 **k**, and the door will be opened for you.
13:25 and you begin to stand outside and to **k** at the door,

KNOCKED (3) [KNOCK]

Da 5: 6 His limbs gave way, and his knees **k** together.
Ac 12:13 When he **k** at the outer gate,
Jdt 14:14 So Bagoas went in and **k** at the entry of the tent,

KNOCKING (3) [KNOCK]

SS 5: 2 but my heart was awake. Listen! my beloved is **k**.
Ac 12:16 Meanwhile Peter continued **k**;
Rev 3:20 I am standing at the door, **k**; if you hear my voice

KNOCKS (4) [KNOCK]

Ex 21:27 the owner **k** out a tooth of a male or female slave,
Mt 7: 8 and for everyone who **k**, the door will be opened.
Lk 11:10 and for everyone who **k**, the door will be opened.
12:36 the door for him as soon as he comes and **k**.

KNOP, KNOPS (KJV) See CALYX, CALYXES, GOURDS, PANELS

KNOTS (1)

Wis 13:13 useful for nothing, a stick crooked and full of **k**,

KNOW‡ (1054) [FOREKNEW, FOREKNOWLEDGE, KNEW, KNOWING, KNOWLEDGE, KNOWLEDGEABLE, KNOWN, KNOWS, WELL-KNOWN]

Ge 4: 9 He said, "I do not **k**; am I my brother's keeper?"
12:11 "I **k** well that you are a woman beautiful
15: 8 how am I to **k** that I shall possess it?"
15:13 the LORD said to Abram, "**K** this for certain,
18:21 and if not, I will **k**."
19: 5 Bring them out to us, so that we may **k** them."
19:33 he did not **k** when she lay down or when she rose.
19:35 he did not **k** when she lay down or when she rose.
20: 6 I **k** that you did this in the integrity of your heart;
20: 7 you do not restore her, **k** that you shall surely die,
21:26 "I do not **k** who has done this;
22:12 for now I **k** that you fear God,
24:14 By this I shall **k** that you have shown steadfast love
27: 2 I do not **k** the day of my death.
27:21 to **k** whether you are really my son Esau or not."
28:15 **K** that I am with you
28:16 and I did not **k** it!"
29: 5 He said to them, "Do you **k** Laban son of Nahor?"
30:26 for you **k** very well the service I have given you."
30:29 "You yourself **k** how I have served you,
31: 6 You **k** that I have served your father
31:32 Jacob did not **k** that Rachel had stolen the gods.
38:16 for he did not **k** that she was his daughter-in-law.
42:23 They did not **k** that Joseph understood them,
42:33 'By this I shall **k** that you are honest men:
42:34 and I shall **k** that you are not spies but honest men.
43: 7 Could we in any way **k** that he would say,
43:22 We do not **k** who put our money in our sacks."
44:15 not **k** that one such as I can practice divination?"
44:27 'You **k** that my wife bore me two sons;
47: 6 if you **k** that there are capable men among them,
48:19 his father refused, and said, "I **k**, my son, I **k**;
Ex 1: 8 new king arose over Egypt, who did not **k** Joseph.
3: 7 Indeed, I **k** their sufferings,
3:19 I **k**, however, that the king of Egypt will
4:14 I **k** that he can speak fluently;
5: 2 I do not **k** the LORD, and I will not let Israel go."
6: 7 You shall **k** that I am the LORD your God,
7: 5 The Egyptians shall **k** that I am the LORD,
7:17 "By this you shall **k** that I am the LORD."
8:10 So that you may **k** that there is no one like
8:22 that you may **k** that I the LORD am in this land.
9:14 so that you may **k** that there is no one like me in all
9:29 so that you may **k** that the earth is the LORD's.
9:30 I **k** that you do not yet fear the LORD God."
10: 2 so that you may **k** that I am the LORD."
10:26 the LORD our God, and we will not **k** what to use
11: 7 that you may **k** that the LORD makes a distinction
14: 4 and the Egyptians shall **k** that I am the LORD.
14:18 And the Egyptians shall **k** that I am the LORD,
16: 6 "In the evening you shall **k** that it was
16:12 then you shall **k** that I am the LORD your God.' "
16:15 For they did not **k** what it was.
18:11 Now I **k** that the LORD is greater than all gods,
23: 9 you **k** the heart of an alien,
29:46 And they shall **k** that I am the LORD their God,
31:13 given in order that you may **k** that I, the LORD,
32: 1 we do not **k** what has become of him."
32:22 you **k** the people, that they are bent on evil.
32:23 we do not **k** what has become of him.'
33:12 but you have not let me **k** whom you will send
33:12 Yet you have said, 'I **k** you by name,
33:13 so that I may **k** you and find favor in your sight.
33:17 for you have found favor in my sight, and I **k** you
34:29 Moses did not **k** that the skin of his face shone
36: 1 the LORD has given skill and understanding to **k**
Lev 5: 3 and are unaware of it, when you come to **k** it,
5: 4 and are unaware of it, when you come to **k** it,
23:43 that your generations may **k** that I made the people
Nu 10:31 for you **k** where we should camp in the wilderness,
11:16 whom you **k** to be the elders of the people
14:31 and they shall **k** the land that you have despised.
14:34 forty years, and you shall **k** my displeasure."
16:28 how you shall **k** that the LORD has sent me
16:30 then you shall **k** that these men have despised
20:14 You **k** all the adversity that has befallen us:
22: 6 for I **k** that whomever you bless is blessed,
22:34 for I did not **k** that you were standing in the road
Dt 1:39 who today do not yet **k** right from wrong,
3:19 I **k** that you have much livestock—
7: 9 **K** therefore that the LORD your God is God,
8: 2 testing you to **k** what was in your heart,
8: 5 **K** then in your heart that as a parent disciplines
8:16 with manna that your ancestors did not **k**,
9: 2 the offspring of the Anakim, whom you **k**.
9: 3 **K** then today that the LORD your God is the one
9: 6 **K**, then, that the LORD your God is not giving you
11:30 As you **k**, they are beyond the Jordan,
13: 3 to **k** whether you indeed love the LORD your God
20:20 You may destroy only the trees that you **k** do
22: 2 or you do not **k** who the owner is, you shall bring it
28:33 A people whom you do not **k** shall eat up the fruit
29: 6 so that you may **k** that I am the LORD your God.
29:16 You **k** how we lived in the land of Egypt,
31:21 For I **k** what they are inclined to do even now,
31:27 For I **k** well how rebellious and stubborn you are.
31:29 For I **k** that after my death you will
Jos 2: 4 but I did not **k** where they came from.
2: 5 Where the men went I do not **k**.
2: 9 "I **k** that the LORD has given you the land,
3: 4 so that you may **k** the way you should go,
3: 7 so that they may **k** that I will be with you as I was
3:10 "By this you shall **k** that among you is
4:22 then you shall let your children **k**,
4:24 that all the peoples of the earth may **k** that the hand
8:14 not **k** that there was an ambush against him behind
14: 6 "You **k** what the LORD said to Moses the man
22:22 He knows; and let Israel itself **k**!
22:31 "Today we **k** that the LORD is among us,
23:13 **k** assuredly that the LORD your God will
23:14 and you **k** in your hearts and souls, all of you,
Jdg 2:10 not **k** the LORD or the work that he had done
3: 2 successive generations of Israelites might **k** war,
3: 4 to **k** whether Israel would obey the commandments
6:37 I shall **k** that you will deliver Israel by my hand,
13:16 (For Manoah did not **k** that he was the angel of
14: 4 His father and mother did not **k** that this was from
15:11 "Do you not **k** that the Philistines are rulers
16:20 But he did not **k** that the LORD had left him.
17:13 "Now I **k** that the LORD will prosper me,
18: 5 "Inquire of God that we may **k** whether
18:14 "Do you **k** that in these buildings there are
Ru 2:11 and came to a people that you did not **k** before.
3:11 for all the assembly of my people **k** that you are
4: 4 but if you will not, tell me, so that I may **k**;
1Sa 3: 7 Now Samuel did not yet **k** the LORD,
6: 9 then we shall **k** that it is not his hand that struck us;
12:17 and you shall **k** and see that the wickedness
14: 3 Now the people did not **k** that Jonathan had gone.
17:28 I **k** your presumption and the evil of your heart;
17:46 that all the earth may **k** that there is a God in Israel,
17:47 that all this assembly may **k** that the LORD does
17:55 "As your soul lives, O king, I do not **k**."
20: 3 and he thinks, 'Do not let Jonathan **k** this,
20: 7 then **k** that evil has been determined by him.
20:30 Do I not **k** that you have chosen the son of Jesse
21: 2 'No one must **k** anything of the matter
22: 3 until I **k** what God will do for me."
24:11 of your cloak, and did not kill you, you may **k**
24:20 Now I **k** that you shall surely be king,
25:11 give it to men who come from I do not **k** where?"
25:17 therefore **k** this and consider what you should do;
28: 1 Achish said to David, "You **k**, of course,
28: 2 then you shall **k** what your servant can do."
28: 9 "Surely you **k** what Saul has done,
29: 9 "I **k** that you are as blameless in my sight as
2Sa 1: 5 do you **k** that Saul and his son Jonathan died?"
2:26 Do you not **k** that the end will be bitter?
3:25 You **k** that Abner son of Ner came to deceive you,
3:26 but David did not **k** about it.
3:38 "Do you not **k** that a prince and
7:20 For you **k** your servant, O Lord GOD!
7:21 so that your servant may **k** it.
11:20 Did you not **k** that they would shoot from the wall?
14:20 like the wisdom of the angel of God to **k** all things
17: 8 "You **k** that your father and his men are warriors,
18:29 I saw a great tumult, but I do not **k** what it was."
19:22 For do I not **k** that I am this day king over Israel?"
24: 2 so that I may **k** how many there are."
1Ki 1: 4 but the king did not **k** her sexually.
1:11 and our lord David does not **k** it?
1:18 though you, my lord the king, do not **k** it.

1Ki 1:27 not let your servants **k** who should sit on the throne
2: 5 you **k** also what Joab son of Zeruiah did to me,
2: 9 you will **k** what you ought to do to him,
2:15 He said, "You **k** that the kingdom was mine,
2:37 **k** for certain that you shall die;
2:42 '**K** for certain that on the day you go out and go
2:44 "You **k** in your own heart all the evil that you did
3: 7 I do not **k** how to go out or come in.
5: 3 "You **k** that my father David could not build
5: 6 for you **k** that there is no one among us who knows
8:39 forgive, act, and render to all whose hearts you **k—**
8:39 for only you **k** what is in every human heart—
8:43 that all the peoples of the earth may **k** your name
8:43 that they may **k** that your name has been invoked
8:60 so that all the peoples of the earth may **k** that
17:24 "Now I **k** that you are a man of God,
18:12 spirit of the LORD will carry you I **k** not where;
18:37 answer me, so that this people may **k** that you,
20:13 and you shall **k** that I am the LORD."
20:28 and you shall **k** that I am the LORD."
22: 3 "Do you **k** that Ramoth-gilead belongs to us,
2Ki 2: 3 to Elisha, and said to him, "Do you **k** that today
2: 3 And he said, "Yes, I **k**; keep silent."
2: 5 to Elisha, and said to him, "Do you **k** that today
2: 5 And he answered, "Yes, I **k**; be silent."
4: 1 and you **k** that your servant feared the LORD,
5: 6 **k** that I have sent to you my servant Naaman,
5:15 before him and said, "Now I **k** that there is no God
7:12 They **k** that we are starving;
8:12 I **k** the evil that you will do to the people of Israel;
9:11 "You **k** the sort and how they babble."
10:10 **K** then that there shall fall to the earth nothing of
17:26 and placed in the cities of Samaria do not **k** the law
17:26 they do not **k** the law of the god of the land."
19:19 that all the kingdoms of the earth may **k** that you,
19:27 "But I **k** your rising and your sitting,
1Ch 12:32 to **k** what Israel ought to do, two hundred chiefs,
17:18 for honoring your servant? You **k** your servant.
21: 2 so that I may **k** their number."
28: 9 you, my son Solomon, **k** the God of your father,
29:17 I **k**, my God, that you search the heart,
2Ch 2: 8 for I **k** that your servants are skilled
6:30 forgive, and render to all whose heart you **k**,
6:30 for only you **k** the human heart.
6:33 that all the peoples of the earth may **k** your name
6:33 that they may **k** that your name has been invoked
12: 8 that they may **k** the difference between serving me
13: 5 Do you not **k** that the LORD God of Israel gave
20:12 We do not **k** what to do, but our eyes are on you."
25:16 "I **k** that God has determined to destroy you,
32:13 Do you not **k** what I and my ancestors have done
32:31 to test him and to **k** all that was in his heart.
Ezr 7:25 the people in the province Beyond the River who **k**
7:25 and you shall teach those who do not **k** them.
Ne 2:16 not **k** where I had gone or what I was doing;
4:11 "They will not **k** or see anything before we come
Est 4:11 and the people of the king's provinces **k** that
Job 5:24 You shall **k** that your tent is safe,
5:25 You shall **k** that your descendants will be many,
5:27 Hear, and **k** it for yourself."
7:10 nor do their places **k** them any more.
8: 9 but of yesterday, and we **k** nothing, for our days
9: 2 "Indeed I **k** that this is so;
9: 5 not **k** it, when he overturns them in his anger;
9:21 I am blameless; I do not **k** myself; I loathe my life.
9:28 for I **k** you will not hold me innocent.
9:35 for I **k** I am not what I am thought to be.
10: 2 let me **k** why you contend against me.
10: 7 although you **k** that I am not guilty,
10:13 I **k** that this was your purpose.
11: 6 **K** then that God exacts of you less than your guilt
11: 8 Deeper than Sheol—what can you **k?**
12: 3 Who does not **k** such things as these?
12: 9 Who among all these does not **k** that the hand of
13: 2 What you **k**, I also **k**; I am not inferior to you.
13:18 I **k** that I shall be vindicated.
13:23 Make me **k** my transgression and my sin.
14:21 Their children come to honor, and they do not **k** it;
15: 9 What do you **k** that we do not **k?**
15:23 They **k** that a day of darkness is ready at hand;
18:21 such is the place of those who do not **k** God."
19: 6 **k** then that God has put me in the wrong,
19:25 For I **k** that my Redeemer lives,
19:29 so that you may **k** there is a judgment."
20: 4 Do you not **k** this from of old,
21:14 We do not desire to **k** your ways.
21:19 Let it be paid back to them, so that they may **k** it.
21:27 I **k** your thoughts, and your schemes to wrong me.
22:13 Therefore you say, 'What does God **k?**
24: 1 and why do those who **k** him never see his days?
24:16 they do not **k** the light.
28:13 Mortals do not **k** the way to it,
30:23 I **k** that you will bring me to death,
31: 6 and let God **k** my integrity!—
32:22 For I do not **k** how to flatter—
33: 3 and what my lips **k** they speak sincerely.
34: 2 you wise men, and give ear to me, you who **k**;
34:33 therefore declare what you **k**.
36:26 Surely God is great, and we do not **k** him;
37: 7 so that all whom he has made may **k** it.
37:15 Do you **k** how God lays his command upon them,
37:16 Do you **k** the balancings of the clouds,
38: 5 Who determined its measurements—surely you **k!**
38:12 and caused the dawn to **k** its place,
38:18 Declare, if you **k** all this.
38:21 Surely you **k**, for you were born then,
38:33 Do you **k** the ordinances of the heavens?
Job 39: 1 "Do you **k** when the mountain goats give birth?
39: 2 and do you **k** the time when they give birth,
42: 2 "I **k** that you can do all things,
42: 3 things too wonderful for me, which I did not **k**.
Ps 4: 3 But **k** that the LORD has set apart the faithful
9:10 And those who **k** your name put their trust in you,
9:20 let the nations **k** that they are only human.
20: 6 Now I **k** that the LORD will help his anointed;
25: 4 Make me to **k** your ways, O LORD;
35:11 they ask me about things I do not **k**.
35:15 ruffians whom I did not **k** tore at me without
36:10 O continue your steadfast love to those who **k** you,
39: 4 let me **k** my end, and what is the measure
39: 4 let me **k** how fleeting my life is.
39: 6 they heap up, and do not **k** who will gather.
40: 9 see, I have not restrained my lips, as you **k**,
41:11 By this I **k** that you are pleased with me;
46:10 "Be still, and **k** that I am God!
50:11 I **k** all the birds of the air,
51: 3 For I **k** my transgressions,
56: 9 This I **k**, that God is for me.
69: 5 O God, you **k** my folly; the wrongs I have done are
69:19 You **k** the insults I receive,
73:11 And they say, "How can God **k?**
78: 6 that the next generation might **k** them,
79: 6 on the nations that do not **k** you,
83:18 Let them **k** that you alone,
87: 4 Among those who **k** me I mention Rahab
89:15 Happy are the people who **k** the festal shout,
91:14 I will protect those who **k** my name.
92: 6 dullard cannot **k**, the stupid cannot understand this:
100: 3 **K** that the LORD is God.
101: 4 I will **k** nothing of evil.
109:27 Let them **k** that this is your hand;
119:75 I **k**, O LORD, that your judgments are right,
119:79 so that they may **k** your decrees.
119:125 so that I may **k** your decrees.
135: 5 For I **k** that the LORD is great;
139: 2 You **k** when I sit down and when I rise up;
139: 4 O LORD, you **k** it completely.
139:14 Wonderful are your works; that I **k** very well.
139:23 Search me, O God, and **k** my heart;
139:23 test me and **k** my thoughts.
140:12 I **k** that the LORD maintains the cause of
142: 3 When my spirit is faint, you **k** my way.
147:20 they do not **k** his ordinances.
Pr 4:19 they do not **k** what they stumble over.
5: 6 her ways wander, and she does not **k** it.
9:18 But they do not **k** that the dead are there,
10:32 The lips of the righteous **k** what is acceptable,
12:10 The righteous **k** the needs of their animals,
24:12 "Look, we did not **k** this"—
24:12 Does not he who keeps watch over your soul **k** it?
24:14 **K** that wisdom is such to your soul;
27: 1 for you do not **k** what a day may bring.
27:23 **K** well the condition of your flocks,
28:22 to get rich and does not **k** that loss is sure to come.
29: 7 The righteous **k** the rights of the poor;
30: 4 of the person's child? Surely you **k!**
Ecc 1:17 to **k** wisdom and to **k** madness and folly.
3:12 I **k** that there is nothing better for them than to
3:14 I **k** that whatever God does endures forever;
5: 1 for they do not **k** how to keep from doing evil.
6: 8 the poor have who **k** how to conduct themselves
7:25 to **k** and to search out and to seek wisdom and
7:25 and to **k** that wickedness is folly and
8: 5 and the wise mind will **k** the time and way.
8: 7 Indeed, they do not **k** what is to be,
8:12 yet I **k** that it will be well with those who fear God,
8:16 When I applied my mind to **k** wisdom,
8:17 even though those who are wise claim to **k**,
9: 1 whether it is love or hate one does not **k**.
9: 5 living **k** that they will die, but the dead **k** nothing;
10:15 for they do not even **k** the way to town.
11: 2 you do not **k** what disaster may happen on earth.
11: 5 as you do not **k** how the breath comes to the bones
11: 5 so you do not **k** the work of God,
11: 6 for you do not **k** which will prosper, this or that,
11: 9 but **k** that for all these things God will bring you
SS 1: 8 If you do not **k**, O fairest among women,
Isa 1: 3 but Israel does not **k**, my people do not understand.
5:19 of Israel hasten to fulfillment, that we may **k** it!"
19:21 and the Egyptians will **k** the LORD on that day,
37:20 the kingdoms of the earth may **k** that you alone are
37:28 I **k** your rising up and your sitting down,
41:20 so that all may see and **k**,
41:22 and that we may **k** their outcome;
41:23 that we may **k** that you are gods;
41:26 so that we might **k**, and beforehand,
42:16 I will lead the blind by a road they do not **k**,
43:10 so that you may **k** and believe me and understand
44: 8 There is no other rock; I **k** not one.
44: 9 their witnesses neither see nor **k**.
44:18 They do not **k**, nor do they comprehend;
45: 3 so that you may **k** that it is I, the LORD,
45: 4 I surname you, though you do not **k** me.
45: 5 I arm you, though you do not **k** me,
45: 6 so that they may **k**, from the rising of the sun and
47: 8 not sit as a widow or **k** the loss of children"—
47:11 on you suddenly, of which you **k** nothing.
48: 4 Because I **k** that you are obstinate,
49:23 Then you will **k** that I am the LORD;
49:26 all flesh shall **k** that I am the LORD your Savior,
50: 4 that I may **k** how to sustain the weary with a word.
50: 7 and I **k** that I shall not be put to shame;
51: 7 Listen to me, you who **k** righteousness,
52: 6 Therefore my people shall **k** my name;
Isa 52: 6 in that day they shall **k** that it is I who speak;
55: 5 See, you shall call nations that you do not **k**,
55: 5 and nations that do not **k** you shall run to you,
58: 2 and delight to **k** my ways, as if they were a nation
59: 8 The way of peace they do not **k**,
59:12 with us, and we **k** our iniquities:
60:16 and you shall **k** that I, the LORD,
63:16 though Abraham does not **k** us and Israel does
66:18 For I **k** their works and their thoughts,
Jer 1: 6 Truly I do not **k** how to speak,
2: 8 Those who handle the law did not **k** me;
2:19 **K** and see that it is evil and bitter for you
2:23 in the valley; **k** what you have done—
4:22 "For my people are foolish, they do not **k** me;
4:22 but do not **k** how to do good."
5: 4 for they do not **k** the way of the LORD,
5: 5 surely they **k** the way of the LORD,
5:15 a nation whose language you do not **k**,
5:28 They **k** no limits in deeds of wickedness;
6:15 they did not **k** how to blush.
6:18 Therefore hear, O nations, and **k**, O congregation,
6:27 and a refiner among my people so that you may **k**
7:11 You **k**, I too am watching, says the LORD.
8: 7 but my people do not **k** the ordinance of the LORD.
8:12 they did not **k** how to blush.
9: 3 and they do not **k** me, says the LORD.
9: 6 They refuse to **k** me, says the LORD.
9:24 that they understand and **k** me,
10:23 I **k**, O LORD, that the way of human beings is not
10:25 the nations that do not **k** you, and on the peoples
11:19 not **k** it was against me that they devised schemes,
12: 3 But you, O LORD, **k** me;
13:12 not **k** that every wine-jar should be filled
15:14 in a land that you do not **k**,
15:15 O LORD, you **k**; remember me
15:15 **k** that on your account I suffer insult.
16:21 and they shall **k** that my name is the LORD."
17: 4 in a land that you do not **k**,
17:16 You **k** what came from my lips;
18:23 Yet you, O LORD, **k** all their plotting to kill me.
22:16 Is not this to **k** me? says the LORD.
22:28 and cast away in a land that they do not **k?**
24: 7 I will give them a heart to **k** that I am the LORD;
26:15 Only **k** for certain that if you put me to death,
29:11 For surely I **k** the plans I have for you,
31:34 "**K** the LORD," for they shall all **k** me,
36:19 and let no one **k** where you are."
38:24 "Do not let anyone else **k** of this conversation,
40:15 and no one else will **k**.
44:28 shall **k** whose words will stand, mine or theirs!
44:29 that you may **k** that my words against you will
48:17 all you his neighbors, and all who **k** his name;
48:30 I myself **k** his insolence, says the LORD;
50:24 O Babylon, but you did not **k** it;
Eze 2: 5 they shall **k** that there has been a prophet
5:13 and they shall **k** that I, the LORD, have spoken
6: 7 then you shall **k** that I am the LORD.
6:10 And they shall **k** that I am the LORD;
6:13 And you shall **k** that I am the LORD,
6:14 Then they shall **k** that I am the LORD.
7: 4 Then you shall **k** that I am the LORD.
7: 9 Then you shall **k** that it is I the LORD who strike.
7:27 And they shall **k** that I am the LORD.
11: 5 I **k** the things that come into your mind.
11:10 And you shall **k** that I am the LORD.
11:12 Then you shall **k** that I am the LORD,
12:15 And they shall **k** that I am the LORD,
12:16 then they shall **k** that I am the LORD.
12:20 and you shall **k** that I am the LORD.
13: 9 and you shall **k** that I am the Lord GOD.
13:14 and you shall **k** that I am the LORD.
13:21 and you shall **k** that I am the LORD.
13:23 Then you will **k** that I am the LORD.
14: 8 and you shall **k** that I am the LORD.
14:23 and you shall **k** that it was not without cause
15: 7 and you shall **k** that I am the LORD,
16:62 and you shall **k** that I am the LORD,
17:12 Do you not **k** what these things mean?
17:21 and you shall **k** that I, the LORD, have spoken.
17:24 the trees of the field shall **k** that I am the LORD
18: 4 **K** that all lives are mine;
20: 4 let them **k** the abominations of their ancestors,
20:12 that they might **k** that I the LORD sanctify them.
20:20 so that you may **k** that I the LORD am your God.
20:26 so that they might **k** that I am the LORD.
20:38 Then you shall **k** that I am the LORD.
20:42 You shall **k** that I am the LORD,
20:44 And you shall **k** that I am the LORD,
21: 5 and all flesh shall **k** that I the LORD have drawn my
22:16 and you shall **k** that I am the LORD.
22:22 and you shall **k** that I the LORD have poured out
23:49 and you shall **k** that I am the Lord GOD.
24:24 then you shall **k** that I am the Lord GOD.
24:27 and they shall **k** that I am the LORD.
25: 5 Then you shall **k** that I am the LORD.
25: 7 Then you shall **k** that I am the LORD.
25:11 Then they shall **k** that I am the LORD.
25:14 they shall **k** my vengeance, says the Lord GOD.
25:17 Then they shall **k** that I am the LORD,
26: 6 Then they shall **k** that I am the LORD.
28:19 All who **k** you among the peoples are appalled
28:22 They shall **k** that I am the LORD
28:23 And they shall **k** that I am the LORD.
28:24 And they shall **k** that I am the Lord GOD.
28:26 And they shall **k** that I am the LORD their God.
29: 6 Then all the inhabitants of Egypt shall **k** that I am
29: 9 Then they shall **k** that I am the LORD.

Eze 29:16 Then they shall **k** that I am the Lord GOD.
29:21 Then they shall **k** that I am the LORD.
30: 8 Then they shall **k** that I am the LORD,
30:19 Then they shall **k** that I am the LORD.
30:25 And they shall **k** that I am the LORD,
30:26 Then they shall **k** that I am the LORD.
32:15 then they shall **k** that I am the LORD.
33:29 Then they shall **k** that I am the LORD,
33:33 they shall **k** that a prophet has been among them.
34:27 and they shall **k** that I am the LORD,
34:30 They shall **k** that I, the LORD their God,
35: 4 and you shall **k** that I am the LORD.
35: 9 Then you shall **k** that I am the LORD.
35:12 You shall **k** that I, the LORD,
35:15 Then they shall **k** that I am the LORD.
36:11 Then you shall **k** that I am the LORD.
36:23 and the nations shall **k** that I am the LORD,
36:36 nations that are left all around you shall **k** that I,
36:38 Then they shall **k** that I am the LORD.
37: 3 I answered, "O Lord GOD, you **k.**"
37: 6 and you shall **k** that I am the LORD."
37:13 And you shall **k** that I am the LORD,
37:14 then you shall **k** that I, the LORD,
37:28 the nations shall **k** that I the LORD sanctify Israel,
38:16 so that the nations may **k** me, when through you,
38:23 Then they shall **k** that I am the LORD.
39: 6 and they shall **k** that I am the LORD.
39: 7 and the nations shall **k** that I am the LORD,
39:22 of Israel shall **k** that I am the LORD their God,
39:23 the nations shall **k** that the house of Israel went
39:28 Then they shall **k** that I am the LORD their God
Da 2: 8 "I **k** with certainty that you are trying to gain time,
2: 9 I shall **k** that you can give me its interpretation."
4: 9 I **k** that you are endowed with a spirit of
4:17 in order that all who live may **k** that
5:17 to the king and let him **k** the interpretation.
5:23 wood, and stone, which do not see or hear or **k;**
6:15 conspirators came to the king and said to him, "**K,**
7:19 I desired to **k** the truth concerning the fourth beast,
9:25 **K** therefore and understand:
10:20 Then he said, "Do you **k** why I have come to you?
11:38 a god whom his ancestors did not **k** he shall honor
Hos 2: 8 She did not **k** that it was I who gave her the grain,
2:20 and you shall **k** the LORD.
5: 3 I **k** Ephraim, and Israel is not hidden from me;
5: 4 and they do not **k** the LORD.
6: 3 Let us **k,** let us press on to **k** the LORD;
7: 9 but he does not **k** it;
7: 9 upon him, but he does not **k** it.
8: 2 "My God, we—Israel—**k** you!"
11: 3 but they did not **k** that I healed them.
13: 4 you **k** no God but me, and besides me there is no
14: 9 those who are discerning **k** them.
Joel 2:27 You shall **k** that I am in the midst of Israel,
3:17 So you shall **k** that I, the LORD your God,
Am 3:10 They do not **k** how to do right, says the LORD,
5:12 For I **k** how many are your transgressions,
Jnh 1: 7 let us cast lots, so that we may **k**
1:12 for I **k** it is because of me
4:11 not **k** their right hand from their left,
Mic 3: 1 Should you not **k** justice?—
4:12 But they do not **k** the thoughts of the LORD;
6: 5 that you may **k** the saving acts of the LORD."
Zec 2: 9 you will **k** that the LORD of hosts has sent me.
2:11 And you shall **k** that the LORD
4: 5 "Do you not **k** what these are?"
4: 9 Then you will **k** that the LORD
4:13 He said to me, "Do you not **k** what these are?"
6:15 and you shall **k** that the LORD of hosts has sent me
Mal 2: 4 **K,** then, that I have sent this command to you,
Mt 6: 3 let your left hand **k** what your right hand is doing,
7:11 **k** how to give good gifts to your children,
7:16 You will **k** them by their fruits.
7:20 Thus you will **k** them by their fruits.
9: 6 that you may **k** that the Son of Man has authority
13:11 "To you it has been given to **k** the secrets of
15:12 "Do you **k** that the Pharisees took offense
16: 3 You **k** how to interpret the appearance of the sky,
20:22 "You do not **k** what you are asking.
20:25 "You **k** that the rulers of the Gentiles lord it
21:27 So they answered Jesus, "We do not **k.**"
22:16 saying, "Teacher, we **k** that you are sincere,
22:29 you **k** neither the scriptures nor the power of God.
24:32 you **k** that summer is near.
24:33 when you see all these things, you **k** that he is near,
24:42 for you do not **k** on what day your Lord is coming.
24:50 not expect him and at an hour that he does not **k.**
25:12 But he replied, 'Truly I tell you, I do not **k** you.'
25:13 for you **k** neither the day nor the hour.
26: 2 "You **k** that after two days the Passover is coming,
26:70 saying, "I do not **k** what you are talking about."
26:72 "I do not **k** the man."
26:74 and he swore an oath, "I do not **k** the man!"
28: 5 I **k** that you are looking
Mk 1:24 I **k** who you are, the Holy One of God."
2:10 that you may **k** that the Son of Man has authority
4:27 and grow, he does not **k** how.
5:43 He strictly ordered them that no one should **k** this,
7:24 a house and did not want anyone to **k** he was there.
9: 6 He did not **k** what to say, for they were terrified.
9:30 He did not want anyone to **k** it;
10:19 You **k** the commandments:
10:38 "You do not **k** what you are asking.
10:42 So Jesus called them and said to them, "You **k** that
11:33 So they answered Jesus, "We do not **k.**"
12:14 "Teacher, we **k** that you are sincere,
12:24 you **k** neither the scriptures nor the power of God?
Mk 13:28 you **k** that summer is near.
13:29 you **k** that he is near, at the very gates.
13:33 for you do not **k** when the time will come.
13:35 not **k** when the master of the house will come,
14:40 and they did not **k** what to say to him.
14:68 not **k** or understand what you are talking about."
14:71 "I do not **k** this man you are talking about."
Lk 1: 4 so that you may **k** the truth concerning the things
1:18 "How will I **k** that this is so?
2:43 but his parents did not **k** it.
2:49 not **k** that I must be in my Father's house?"
4:34 I **k** who you are, the Holy One of God."
5:24 that you may **k** that the Son of Man has authority
8:10 "To you it has been given to **k** the secrets of
10:11 Yet **k** this: the kingdom of God has come near.'
11:13 **k** how to give good gifts to your children,
12:39 "But **k** this: if the owner of the
12:46 not expect him and at an hour that he does not **k,**
12:48 not **k** and did what deserved a beating will receive
12:56 You **k** how to interpret the appearance of earth
12:56 not **k** how to interpret the present time?
13:25 'I do not **k** where you come from.'
13:27 But he will say, 'I do not **k** where you come from;
18:20 You **k** the commandments:
20: 7 that they did not **k** where it came from.
20:21 we **k** that you are right in what you say and teach,
21:20 then **k** that its desolation has come near.
21:30 for yourselves and **k** that summer is already near.
21:31 you **k** that the kingdom of God is near.
22:34 until you have denied three times that you **k** me."
22:57 But he denied it, saying, "Woman, I do not **k** him."
22:60 "Man, I do not **k** what you are talking about!"
23:34 ⟦for they do not **k** what they are doing."⟧
24:18 the only stranger in Jerusalem who does not **k**
Jn 1:10 yet the world did not **k** him.
1:26 Among you stands one whom you do not **k,**
1:31 I myself did not **k** him;
1:33 I myself did not **k** him,
1:48 "Where did you get to **k** me?"
2: 9 and did not **k** where it came from
3: 2 we **k** that you are a teacher who has come
3: 8 you do not **k** where it comes from or where it goes.
3:11 of what we **k** and testify to what we have seen;
4:22 You worship what you do not **k;**
4:22 we worship what we **k,** for salvation is from
4:25 The woman said to him, "I **k**
4:32 "I have food to eat that you do not **k** about."
4:42 and we **k** that this is truly the Savior of the world."
5:13 the man who had been healed did not **k** who it was,
5:32 and I **k** that his testimony to me is true.
5:42 I **k** that you do not have the love of God in you.
6:42 the son of Joseph, whose father and mother we **k?**
6:69 We have come to believe and **k** that you are
7:17 to do the will of God will **k** whether the teaching is
7:26 Can it be that the authorities really **k** that this is
7:27 Yet we **k** where this man is from;
7:27 Messiah comes, no one will **k** where he is from."
7:28 "You **k** me, and you **k** where I am from.
7:28 the one who sent me is true, and you do not **k** him.
7:29 I **k** him, because I am from him, and he sent me."
7:49 But this crowd, which does not **k** the law—
8:14 because I **k** where I have come from and
8:14 not **k** where I come from or where I am going.
8:19 Jesus answered, "You **k** neither me nor my Father.
8:19 If you knew me, you would **k** my Father also."
8:32 and you will **k** the truth,
8:37 I **k** that you are descendants of Abraham;
8:52 "Now we **k** that you have a demon.
8:55 though you do not **k** him. But I **k** him; if I would
say that I do not **k** him,
8:55 But I do **k** him and I keep his word.
9:12 He said, "I do not **k.**"
9:20 His parents answered, "We **k** that this is our son,
9:21 but we do not **k** how it is that now he sees,
9:21 nor do we **k** who opened his eyes.
9:24 We **k** that this man is a sinner."
9:25 He answered, "I do not **k** whether he is a sinner.
9:25 One thing I do **k,** that though I was blind,
9:29 We **k** that God has spoken to Moses,
9:29 we do not **k** where he comes from."
9:30 You do not **k** where he comes from,
9:31 We **k** that God does not listen to sinners,
10: 4 and the sheep follow him because they **k** his voice.
10: 5 but they will run from him because they do not **k**
10:14 I **k** my own and my own **k** me,
10:15 just as the Father knows me and I **k** the Father.
10:27 I **k** them, and they follow me.
10:38 so that you may **k** and understand that the Father is
11:22 now I **k** that God will give you whatever you ask
11:24 "I **k** that he will rise again in the resurrection on
11:49 said to them, "You **k** nothing at all!
11:57 where Jesus was should let them **k,**
12:35 you do not **k** where you are going.
12:50 And I **k** that his commandment is eternal life.
13: 7 "You do not **k** now what I am doing,
13:12 "Do you **k** what I have done to you?
13:17 you **k** these things, you are blessed if you do them.
13:18 I **k** whom I have chosen.
13:35 By this everyone will **k** that you are my disciples,
14: 4 And you **k** the way to the place where I am going."
14: 5 "Lord, we do not **k** where you are going.
14: 5 How can we **k** the way?"
14: 7 If you **k** me, you will **k** my Father also. From now
on you do **k** him and have seen him."
14: 9 Philip, and you still do not **k** me?
14:17 You **k** him, because he abides with you,
14:20 On that day you will **k** that I am in my Father,
Jn 14:31 so that the world may **k** that I love the Father.
15:15 the servant does not **k** what the master is doing;
15:21 because they do not **k** him who sent me.
16:18 We do not **k** what he is talking about."
16:30 Now we **k** that you **k** all things,
17: 3 And this is eternal life, that they may **k** you,
17: 7 Now they **k** that everything you have given me is
17: 8 and they have received them and **k** in truth
17:23 so that the world may **k** that you have sent me
17:25 "Righteous Father, the world does not **k** you, but I
k you; and these **k** that you have sent me.
18:21 heard what I said to them; they **k** what I said."
19: 4 to you to let you **k** that I find no case against him."
19:10 Do you not **k** that I have power to release you,
20: 2 and we do not **k** where they have laid him."
20:13 and I do not **k** where they have laid him."
20:14 but she did not **k** that it was Jesus.
21: 4 but the disciples did not **k** that it was Jesus.
21:15 He said to him, "Yes, Lord; you **k** that I love you."
21:16 He said to him, "Yes, Lord; you **k** that I love you."
21:17 And he said to him, "Lord, you **k** everything; you
k that I love you."
21:24 and we **k** that his testimony is true.
Ac 1: 7 to **k** the times or periods that the Father has set
1:24 "Lord, you **k** everyone's heart.
2:22 through him among you, as you yourselves **k—**
2:36 of Israel **k** with certainty that God has made him
3:16 has made this man strong, whom you see and **k;**
3:17 "And now, friends, I **k** that you acted in ignorance,
7:40 we do not **k** what has happened to him.'
10:28 "You yourselves **k** that it is unlawful for a Jew
10:36 You **k** the message he sent to the people of Israel,
15: 7 you **k** that in the early days God made a choice
17:19 "May we **k** what this new teaching is
17:20 so we would like to **k** what it means."
19:15 reply, "Jesus I **k,** and Paul I **k;** but who are you?"
19:25 you **k** that we get our wealth from this business.
19:32 of them did not **k** why they had come together.
19:35 that does not **k** that the city of the Ephesians is
19:39 If there is anything further you want to **k,**
20:18 "You yourselves **k** how I lived among you
20:25 "And now I **k** that none of you,
20:29 I **k** that after I have gone,
20:34 You **k** for yourselves that I worked
21:24 Thus all will **k** that there is nothing
21:37 The tribune replied, "Do you **k** Greek?
22:14 God of our ancestors has chosen you to **k** his will,
22:19 And I said, 'Lord, they themselves **k** that
23:28 to **k** the charge for which they accused him,
25:10 to the Jews, as you very well **k.**
26: 4 "All the Jews **k** my way of life from my youth,
26:27 I **k** that you believe."
28:22 for with regard to this sect we **k**
Ro 1:13 I want you to **k,** brothers and sisters,
1:32 They **k** God's decree, that those who practice such
2: 2 "We **k** that God's judgment on those who do such
2:18 and **k** his will and determine what is best
3:19 Now we **k** that whatever the law says,
6: 3 Do you not **k** that all of us who have been baptized
6: 6 We **k** that our old self was crucified with him so
6: 9 We **k** that Christ, being raised from the dead,
6:16 not **k** that if you present yourselves to anyone
7: 1 Do you not **k,** brothers and sisters—
7: 1 for I am speaking to those who **k** the law—
7:14 For we **k** that the law is spiritual;
7:18 For I **k** that nothing good dwells within me, that is,
8:22 We **k** that the whole creation has been groaning
8:26 for we do not **k** how to pray as we ought,
8:28 We **k** that all things work together for good
11: 2 Do you not **k** what the scripture says of Elijah,
13:11 Besides this, you **k** what time it is,
14:14 I **k** and am persuaded in the Lord Jesus
15:29 and I **k** that when I come to you,
1Co 1:16 I do not **k** whether I baptized anyone else.)
1:21 the world did not **k** God through wisdom,
2: 2 to **k** nothing among you except Jesus Christ,
3:16 Do you not **k** that you are God's temple and
5: 6 not **k** that a little yeast leavens the whole batch
6: 2 Do you not **k** that the saints will judge the world?
6: 3 Do you not **k** that we are to judge angels—
6: 9 not **k** that wrongdoers will not inherit the kingdom
6:15 not **k** that your bodies are members of Christ?
6:16 Do you not **k** that whoever is united to
6:19 not **k** that your body is a temple of the Holy Spirit
7:16 Wife, for all you **k,** you might save your husband.
7:16 Husband, for all you **k,** you might save your wife.
8: 1 we **k** that "all of us possess knowledge."
8: 2 Anyone who claims to **k** something does not
8: 4 we **k** that "no idol in the world really exists,"
9:13 Do you not **k** that those who are employed in
9:24 Do you not **k** that in a race the runners all compete,
12: 2 You **k** that when you were pagans,
13: 9 we **k** only in part, and we prophesy only in part;
13:12 Now I **k** only in part;
13:12 I will **k** fully, even as I have been fully known.
14: 7 how will anyone **k** what is being played?
14: 9 how will anyone **k** what is being said?
14:11 If then I do not **k** the meaning of a sound,
14:16 since the outsider does not **k** what you are saying?
14:35 If there is anything they desire to **k,**
15:58 you **k** that in the Lord your labor is not in vain.
16:15 you **k** that members of the household
2Co 1: 7 for we **k** that as you share in our sufferings,
2: 4 to let you **k** the abundant love that I have for you.
2: 9 and to **k** whether you are obedient in everything.
4:14 because we **k** that the one who raised
5: 1 we **k** that if the earthly tent we live in is destroyed,

2Co 5: 6 even though we **k** that while we are at home in
5:16 we **k** him no longer in that way.
8: 1 We want you to **k,** brothers and sisters,
8: 9 you **k** the generous act of our Lord Jesus Christ,
9: 2 for I **k** your eagerness, which is the subject
12: 2 I **k** a person in Christ who fourteen years ago was
12: 2 whether in the body or out of the body I do not **k;**
12: 3 And I **k** that such a person—
12: 3 whether in the body or out of the body I do not **k;**
Gal 1:11 For I want you to **k,** brothers and sisters,
2:16 yet we **k** that a person is justified not by the works
4: 8 Formerly, when you did not **k** God,
4: 9 Now, however, that you have come to **k** God,
4:13 You **k** that it was because of a physical infirmity
Eph 1:17 of wisdom and revelation as you come to **k** him,
1:18 you may **k** what is the hope
3:19 to **k** the love of Christ that surpasses knowledge,
6: 9 for you **k** that both of you have the same Master
6:21 you also may **k** how I am and what I am doing,
6:22 to let you **k** how we are,
Php 1:12 I want you to **k,** beloved, that what has happened
1:19 for I **k** that through your prayers and the help of
1:22 and I do not **k** which I prefer.
1:25 I **k** that I will remain and continue with all of you
1:27 I will **k** that you are standing firm in one spirit,
2:22 But Timothy's worth you **k,**
3:10 I want to **k** Christ and the power of his resurrection
4:12 I **k** what it is to have little, and I **k** what it is to have plenty.
4:15 You Philippians indeed **k** that in the early days of
Col 2: 1 I want you to **k** how much I am struggling for you,
3:24 since you **k** that from the Lord you will receive
4: 1 for you **k** that you also have a Master in heaven.
4: 6 that you may **k** how you ought to answer everyone.
4: 8 so that you may **k** how we are and
1Th 1: 4 For we **k,** brothers and sisters beloved by God,
1: 5 just as you **k** what kind of persons we proved to be
2: 1 You yourselves **k,** brothers and sisters,
2: 2 at Philippi, as you **k,** we had courage in our God
2: 5 As you **k** and as God is our witness,
2:11 As you **k,** we dealt with each one of you like
3: 3 you yourselves **k** that this is what we are destined
3: 4 so it turned out, as you **k.**
4: 2 For you **k** what instructions we gave you through
4: 4 of you **k** how to control your own body in holiness
4: 5 like the Gentiles who do not **k** God;
5: 2 For you yourselves **k** very well that the day of
2Th 1: 8 on those who do not **k** God and on those who do
2: 6 And you **k** what is now restraining him,
3: 7 For you yourselves **k** how you ought to imitate us;
1Ti 1: 8 Now we **k** that the law is good,
3: 5 not **k** how to manage his own household,
3:15 you may **k** how one ought to behave in
4: 3 with thanksgiving by those who believe and **k**
2Ti 1:12 for I **k** the one in whom I have put my trust,
1:18 that day! And you **k** very well
2:23 you **k** that they breed quarrels.
2:25 that they will repent and come to **k** the truth,
Tit 1:16 They profess to **k** God, but they deny him
3:11 you **k** that such a person is perverted and sinful,
Heb 8:11 '**K** the Lord,' for they shall all **k** me, from the least
10:30 For we **k** the one who said, "Vengeance is mine,
12:17 You **k** that later, when he wanted to inherit
13:23 to **k** that our brother Timothy has been set free;
Jas 1: 3 because you **k** that the testing
3: 1 for you **k** that we who teach will be judged
4: 4 not **k** that friendship with the world is enmity
4:14 Yet you do not even **k** what tomorrow will bring.
5:20 you should **k** that whoever brings back a sinner
1Pe 1:18 You **k** that you were ransomed from
5: 9 for you **k** that your brothers and sisters in all
2Pe 1:12 though you **k** them already and are established in
1:14 since I **k** that my death will come soon,
1Jn 2: 3 Now by this we may be sure that we **k** him,
2: 4 Whoever says, "I have come to **k** him,"
2:11 and does not **k** the way to go,
2:13 because you **k** him who is from the beginning.
2:14 I write to you, children, because you **k** the Father.
2:14 because you **k** him who is from the beginning.
2:18 From this we **k** that it is the last hour.
2:21 I write to you, not because you do not **k** the truth, but because you **k** it, and you **k** that no lie comes from the truth.
2:29 If you **k** that he is righteous,
3: 1 the world does not **k** us is that it did not **k** him.
3: 2 What we do **k** is this:
3: 5 You **k** that he was revealed to take away sins,
3:14 We **k** that we have passed from death to life
3:15 and you **k** that murderers do
3:16 We **k** love by this, that he laid down his life
3:19 And by this we will **k** that we are from the truth
3:24 And by this we **k** that he abides in us,
4: 2 By this you **k** the Spirit of God:
4: 6 From this we **k** the spirit of truth and the spirit
4: 8 Whoever does not love does not **k** God,
4:13 By this we **k** that we abide in him and he in us,
5: 2 By this we **k** that we love the children of God,
5:13 so that you may **k** that you have eternal life.
5:15 And if we **k** that he hears us in whatever we ask,
5:15 we **k** that we have obtained the requests made
5:18 We **k** that those who are born of God do not sin,
5:19 We **k** that we are God's children,
5:20 And we **k** that the Son of God has come
5:20 so that we may **k** him who is true;
2Jn 1: 1 and not only I but also all who **k** the truth,
3Jn 1:12 and you **k** that our testimony is true.
Jude 1:10 like irrational animals, they **k** by instinct.

Rev 2: 2 "I **k** your works, your toil
2: 2 I **k** that you cannot tolerate evildoers;
2: 3 I also **k** that you are enduring patiently and bearing
2: 9 "I **k** your affliction and your poverty,
2: 9 I **k** the slander on the part of those who say
2:13 "I **k** where you are living,
2:19 "I **k** your works—your love,
2:19 I **k** that your last works are greater than the first.
2:23 And all the churches will **k** that I am
3: 1 and the seven stars: "I **k** your works;
3: 3 and you will not **k** at what hour I will come to you.
3: 8 "I **k** your works. Look, I have set
3: 8 I **k** that you have but little power,
3:15 "I **k** your works; you are neither cold
Tob 2:10 I did not **k** that there were sparrows on the wall;
3:14 You **k,** O Master, that I am innocent
5: 2 since he does not **k** me and I do not **k** him?
5: 2 I do not **k** the roads to Media, or how to get there."
5: 5 "Do you **k** the way to go to Media?"
5: 6 I am acquainted with it and **k** all the roads.
5:10 "I can go with him and I **k** all the roads,
5:12 He replied, "Why do you need to **k** my tribe?"
6:13 For I **k** that Raguel can by no means keep her
6:16 I **k** that this very night she will be given to you
7: 4 She said to them, "Do you **k** our kinsman Tobit?"
7: 4 And they replied, "Yes, we **k** him."
9: 4 you **k** that my father must be counting the days,
10: 7 for I **k** that my father and mother do not believe
11: 7 "I **k** that his eyes will be opened.
14: 4 For I **k** and believe that whatever God has said will
Jdt 5: 8 the God they had come to **k,**
8:20 But we **k** no other god but him,
9: 7 not **k** that you are the Lord who crushes wars;
9:14 and every tribe **k** and understand that you are God,
AdE 4:11 of the empire **k** that if any man or woman goes to
13:12 You **k** all things; you **k,** O Lord,
14:15 and you **k** that I hate the splendor of the wicked
14:16 You **k** my necessity—
16: 4 carried away by the boasts of those who **k** nothing
Wis 2:22 not **k** the secret purposes of God, nor hoped for
7:12 but I did not **k** that she was their mother.
7:17 to **k** the structure of the world and the activity of
8:21 it was a mark of insight to **k** whose gift she was—
12:17 you rebuke any insolence among those who **k** it.
12:27 the one whom they had before refused to **k.**
13: 1 to **k** the one who exists, nor did they recognize
13: 3 people assumed them to be gods, let them **k**
13: 9 to **k** so much that they could investigate the world,
14:18 of the artisan impelled even those who did not **k**
15: 2 because we **k** that you acknowledge us as yours.
15: 3 For to **k** you is complete righteousness,
15: 3 and to **k** your power is the root of immortality.
15:11 because they failed to **k** the one who formed them
15:13 **k** that they sin when they make
16:16 for the ungodly, refusing to **k** you, were flogged by
16:18 but that seeing this they might **k**
16:22 so that they might **k** that the crops
Sir 5:10 Stand firm for what you **k,**
5:12 If you **k** what to say, answer your neighbor;
8:18 for you do not **k** what they will divulge.
9:11 for you do not **k** what their end will be like.
9:13 **K** that you are stepping among snares,
9:14 As much as you can, aim to **k** your neighbors,
11:19 not **k** how long it will be until he leaves them
12: 1 If you do good, **k** to whom you do it,
20: 6 others keep silent because they **k** when to speak.
24:28 The first man did not **k** wisdom fully,
27:22 and those who **k** him will keep their distance.
27:27 and he will not **k** where it came from.
36: 5 Then they will **k,** as we have known
36:22 and all who are on the earth will **k** that you are
37:12 with a godly person whom you **k** to be a keeper of
46: 6 so that the nations might **k** his armament,
Bar 2:15 all the earth may **k** that you are the Lord our God,
2:30 For I **k** that they will not obey me,
2:31 and **k** that I am the Lord their God.
4: 4 O Israel, for we **k** what is pleasing to God.
LtJ 6:23 From this you will **k** that they are not gods;
6:29 Since you **k** by these things that they are not gods,
6:52 Who then can fail to **k** that they are not gods?
6:65 you **k** then that they are not gods, do not fear them.
6:72 the purple and linen that rot upon them you will **k**
Aza 1:22 Let them **k** that you alone are the Lord God,
Sus 1:42 you **k** what is secret and are aware of all things
1:43 you **k** that these men have given false evidence
Bel 1:35 and I **k** nothing about the den."
1Mc 2:65 "Here is your brother Simeon who, I **k,**
3:52 you **k** what they plot against us.
4:11 the Gentiles will **k** that there is one who redeems
4:33 let all who **k** your name praise you with hymns."
6:13 I **k** that it is because of this
11:31 so that you may **k** what it says.
12:29 Jonathan and his troops did not **k** it until morning,
13: 3 "You yourselves **k** what great things my brothers
13: 3 you **k** also the wars and the difficulties
2Mc 1:27 and let the Gentiles **k** that you are our God.
7:22 "I do not **k** how you came into being in my womb.
9:24 they would **k** to whom the government was left.
11:26 so that they may **k** our policy and be of good cheer
14:32 When they declared on oath that they did not **k**
1Es 8:23 to judge all those who **k** the law of your God,
8:23 and you shall teach it to those who do not **k** it.
3Mc 3:14 as you yourselves **k,** it was brought to conclusion,
5:18 and with sharp threats demanded to **k** why
7: 9 For you should **k** that if we devise any evil
2Es 4:46 For I **k** what has gone by, but I do not **k** what is to
4:52 to tell you concerning your life, for I do not **k.**

2Es 5: 7 the many do not **k** shall make his voice heard
5:17 Or do you not **k** that Israel has been entrusted
5:38 to **k** these things except he whose dwelling is not
6:16 for they **k** that their end must be changed."
7:*64* because we perish and we **k** it.
7:*66* not **k** of any torment or salvation promised to them
7:*132* [62] I answered and said, "I **k,** O Lord,
8:15 About all humankind you **k** best;
9: 2 then you will **k** that it is the very time when
9: 4 then you will **k** that it was of these that
10:35 For I have seen what I did not **k,**
12:38 whose hearts you **k** are able to comprehend
13:52 as no one can explore or **k** what is in the depths of
14:42 using characters that they did not **k.**
4Mc 5:25 that the law was established by God, we **k** that in
6:27 "You **k,** O God, that though I might have saved
10: 2 "Do you not **k** that the same father begot me

KNOWING (36) [KNOW]

Ge 3: 5 and you will be like God, **k** good and evil."
3:22 the man has become like one of us, **k** good
Lev 5:17 If any of you sin without **k** it,
2Sa 15:11 and they went in their innocence, **k** nothing of
1Ki 8:38 all **k** the afflictions of their own hearts so
2Ki 4:39 up into the pot of stew, not **k** what they were.
2Ch 6:29 all **k** their own suffering and their own sorrows so
Job 34:25 **k** their works, he overturns them in the night,
Pr 7:23 not **k** that it will cost him his life.
Mk 5:33 But the woman, **k** what had happened to her,
6:20 **k** that he was a righteous and holy man,
12:15 But **k** their hypocrisy, he said to them,
Lk 8:53 And they laughed at him, **k** that she was dead.
9:33 and one for Elijah"—not **k** what he said.
Jn 13: 3 **k** that the Father had given all things
18: 4 Then Jesus, **k** all that was to happen to him,
Ac 5: 7 in, not **k** what had happened.
20:22 not **k** what will happen to me there,
24:10 **k** that for many years you have been a judge
Ro 5: 3 **k** that suffering produces endurance,
2Co 2:14 the fragrance that comes from **k** him.
5:11 **k** the fear of the Lord, we try to persuade others;
Eph 6: 8 **k** that whatever good we do,
Php 1:16 **k** that I have been put here for the defense of
3: 8 of the surpassing value of **k** Christ Jesus my Lord.
2Ti 3:14 **k** from whom you learned it,
Phm 1:21 **k** that you will do even more than I say.
Heb 10:34 **k** that you yourselves possessed something better
11: 8 and he set out, not **k** where he was going.
13: 2 that some have entertained angels without **k** it.
2Pe 2:21 of righteousness than, after **k** it, to turn back from
Tob 8:12 if he is dead, let us bury him without anyone **k** it."
Wis 8: 9 **k** that she would give me good counsel
15: 2 For even if we sin we are yours, **k** your power;
18:19 they might not perish without **k** why they suffered.
4Mc 18: 2 **k** that devout reason is master of all emotions,

KNOWLEDGE‡ (186) [KNOW]

Ge 2: 9 and the tree of the **k** of good and evil.
2:17 the tree of the **k** of good and evil you shall not eat,
Ex 31: 3 intelligence, and **k** in every kind of craft,
35:31 intelligence, and **k** in every kind of craft,
Nu 15:24 then if it was done unintentionally without the **k** of
24:16 and knows the **k** of the Most High,
1Sa 2: 3 for the LORD is a God of **k,**
1Ki 2:32 because, without the **k** of my father David,
7:14 intelligence, and **k** in working bronze.
2Ch 1:10 Give me now wisdom and **k** to go out and come in
1:11 and **k** for yourself that you may rule my people
1:12 wisdom and **k** are granted to you.
Ne 10:28 their daughters, all who have **k** and understanding,
Est 2:22 But the matter came to the **k** of Mordecai,
Job 15: 2 "Should the wise answer with windy **k,**
21:22 Will any teach God **k,** seeing that he judges those
34:35 'Job speaks without **k,** his words are without
35:16 he multiplies words without **k."**
36: 3 I will bring my **k** from far away,
36: 4 one who is perfect in **k** is with you.
36:12 they shall perish by the sword, and die without **k.**
37:16 the wondrous works of the one whose **k** is perfect,
38: 2 that darkens counsel by words without **k?**
42: 3 'Who is this that hides counsel without **k?'**
Ps 14: 4 Have they no **k,** all the evildoers who eat
19: 2 and night to night declares **k.**
53: 4 Have they no **k,** those evildoers,
71:15 though their number is past my **k.**
73:11 Is there **k** in the Most High?"
82: 5 They have neither **k** nor understanding,
94:10 he who teaches **k** to humankind,
119:66 Teach me good judgment and **k,**
139: 6 Such **k** is too wonderful for me;
Pr 1: 4 **k** and prudence to the young—
1: 7 The fear of the LORD is the beginning of **k;**
1:22 in their scoffing and fools hate **k?**
1:29 Because they hated **k** and did not choose the fear
2: 5 the fear of the LORD and find the **k** of God.
2: 6 from his mouth come **k** and understanding;
2:10 and **k** will be pleasant to your soul;
3:20 by his **k** the deeps broke open,
5: 2 and your lips may guard **k.**
8: 9 and right to those who find **k.**
8:10 and **k** rather than choice gold;
8:12 live with prudence, and I attain **k** and discretion.
9:10 and the **k** of the Holy One is insight.
10:14 The wise lay up **k,** but the babbling of
11: 9 but by **k** the righteous are delivered.
12: 1 Whoever loves discipline loves **k,**

Pr 12:23 One who is clever conceals **k**,
14: 6 but **k** is easy for one who understands.
14: 7 for there you do not find words of **k**.
14:18 but the clever are crowned with **k**.
15: 2 The tongue of the wise dispenses **k**,
15: 7 The lips of the wise spread **k**;
15:14 The mind of one who has understanding seeks **k**,
18:15 An intelligent mind acquires **k**,
18:15 and the ear of the wise seeks **k**.
19: 2 Desire without **k** is not good,
19:25 reprove the intelligent, and they will gain **k**.
19:27 Cease straying, my child, from the words of **k**,
20:15 but the lips informed by **k** are a precious jewel.
21:11 when the wise are instructed, they increase in **k**.
22:12 The eyes of the LORD keep watch over **k**,
22:20 for you thirty sayings of admonition and **k**,
23:12 to instruction and your ear to words of **k**.
24: 4 by **k** the rooms are filled with all precious
24: 5 those who have **k** than those who have strength;
30: 3 nor have I **k** of the holy ones.
Ecc 1:16 mind has had great experience of wisdom and **k**."
1:18 and those who increase **k** increase sorrow.
2:21 with wisdom and **k** and skill must leave all to
2:26 the one who pleases him God gives wisdom and **k**
7:12 and the advantage of **k** is that wisdom gives life to
9:10 for there is no work or thought or **k** or wisdom
12: 9 the Teacher also taught the people **k**,
Isa 5:13 Therefore my people go into exile without **k**;
11: 2 the spirit of **k** and the fear of the LORD.
11: 9 of the **k** of the LORD as the waters cover the sea.
28: 9 "Whom will he teach **k**, and
33: 6 and **k**; the fear of the LORD is Zion's treasure.
40:14 Who taught him **k**, and showed him the way of
44:19 nor is there **k** or discernment to say,
44:25 and makes their **k** foolish;
45:20 They have no **k**—those who carry about their
47:10 Your wisdom and your **k** led you astray,
53:11 he shall find satisfaction through his **k**.
56:10 Israel's sentinels are blind, they are all without **k**;
Jer 3:15 who will feed you with **k** and understanding.
10:14 Everyone is stupid and without **k**;
14:18 throughout the land, and have no **k**.
51:17 Everyone is stupid and without **k**;
Da 1: 4 endowed with **k** and insight,
1:17 To these four young men God gave **k** and skill
2:21 to the wise and **k** to those who have understanding.
5:12 **k**, and understanding to interpret dreams,
Hos 4: 1 and no **k** of God in the land.
4: 6 My people are destroyed for lack of **k**;
4: 6 because you have rejected **k**,
6: 6 the **k** of God rather than burnt offerings.
8: 4 they set up princes, but without my **k**.
Hab 2:14 But the earth will be filled with the **k** of the glory
Mal 2: 7 For the lips of a priest should guard **k**,
Lk 1:77 to give **k** of salvation to his people
11:52 For you have taken away the key of **k**;
Ac 5: 2 with his wife's **k**, he kept back some of
Ro 2:20 having in the law the embodiment of **k** and truth,
3:20 for through the law comes the **k** of sin.
11:33 the depth of the riches and wisdom and **k** of God!
15:14 filled with all **k**, and able to instruct one another.
1Co 1: 5 in speech and **k** of every kind—
8: 1 we know that "all of us possess **k**."
8: 1 **K** puffs up, but love builds up.
8: 2 not yet have the necessary **k**;
8: 7 It is not everyone, however, who has this **k**.
8:10 For if others see you, who possess **k**,
8:11 So by your **k** those weak believers
12: 8 the utterance of **k** according to the same Spirit,
13: 2 and understand all mysteries and all **k**,
13: 8 as for **k**, it will come to an end.
14: 6 in some revelation or **k** or prophecy or teaching?
15:34 for some people have no **k** of God.
2Co 4: 6 in our hearts to give the light of the **k** of the glory
6: 6 **k**, patience, kindness, holiness of spirit,
8: 7 in faith, in speech, in **k**, in utmost eagerness,
10: 5 and every proud obstacle raised up against the **k**
11: 6 I may be untrained in speech, but not in **k**;
Eph 3:19 and to know the love of Christ that surpasses **k**,
4:13 come to the unity of the faith and of the **k** of the
Php 1: 9 that your love may overflow more and more with **k**
Col 1: 9 with the **k** of God's will in all spiritual wisdom
1:10 in every good work and as you grow in the **k**
2: 2 the riches of assured understanding and have the **k**
2: 3 the treasures of wisdom and **k**.
3:10 which is being renewed in **k** according to
1Ti 2: 4 to be saved and to come to the **k** of the truth.
6:20 and contradictions of what is falsely called **k**;
2Ti 3: 7 and can never arrive at a **k** of the truth.
Tit 1: 1 the faith of God's elect and the **k** of the truth that
Heb 10:26 in sin after having received the **k** of the truth,
2Pe 1: 2 and peace be yours in abundance in the **k** of God
1: 3 the **k** of him who called us by his own glory
1: 5 with goodness, and goodness with **k**,
1: 6 and **k** with self-control, and self-control
1: 8 and unfruitful in the **k** of our Lord Jesus Christ.
2:20 through the **k** of our Lord and Savior Jesus Christ,
3:18 and **k** of our Lord and Savior Jesus Christ.
1Jn 2:20 and all of you have **k**.
AdE 7: 4 This has come to my **k**.
14:15 You have **k** of all things,
Wis 2:13 He professes to have **k** of God,
6:22 and make **k** of her clear, and I will not pass by
7:17 For it is he who gave me unerring **k** of what exists,
8: 4 For she is an initiate in the **k** of God,
10:10 and gave him **k** of holy things;
14:22 Then it was not enough for them to err about the **k**
Wis 18: 6 so that they might rejoice in sure **k** of the oaths
Sir 1:19 She rained down **k** and discerning comprehension,
3:25 without **k** there is no wisdom.
6:33 If you love to listen you will gain **k**,
10:30 The poor are honored for their **k**,
16:24 Listen to me, my child, and acquire **k**,
16:25 discipline precisely and declare **k** accurately.
17: 7 He filled them with **k** and understanding,
17:11 He bestowed **k** upon them,
19:22 The **k** of wickedness is not wisdom,
21:13 The **k** of the wise will increase like a flood,
21:14 mind of a fool is like a broken jar; it can hold no **k**.
21:18 and to the ignorant, **k** is talk that has no meaning.
32: 3 but with accurate **k**, and do not interrupt the music.
33:11 In the fullness of his **k** the Lord distinguished them
39: 7 The Lord will direct his counsel and **k**,
44: 4 the people by their counsels and by their **k** of
45: 5 the law of life and **k**,
50:27 in understanding and **k** I have written in this book,
Bar 3:20 but they have not learned the way to **k**,
3:27 or give them the way to **k**;
3:36 He found the whole way to **k**,
2Mc 6:30 "It is clear to the Lord in his holy **k** that,
1Es 8: 7 For Ezra possessed great **k**,
2Es 14:47 the fountain of wisdom, and the river of **k**."
4Mc 1: 2 subject is essential to everyone who is seeking **k**,
1:16 the **k** of divine and human matters and the causes
5:35 honored priesthood and **k** of the law.
11:21 For religious **k**, O tyrant, is invincible.
16:23 It is unreasonable for people who have religious **k**

KNOWLEDGEABLE (1) [KNOW]

Pr 17:27 One who spares words is **k**;

KNOWN‡ (238) [KNOW]

Ge 19: 8 Look, I have two daughters who have not **k** a man;
24:16 a virgin, whom no man had **k**.
41:21 when they had eaten them no one would have **k**
41:31 The plenty will no longer be **k** in the land because
45: 1 when Joseph made himself **k** to his brothers.
Ex 2:14 and thought, "Surely the thing is **k**."
6: 3 by my name 'The LORD' I did not make myself **k**
18:16 and I make **k** to them the statutes and instructions
18:20 the statutes and instructions and make **k** to them
21:36 But if it was **k** that the ox was accustomed to gore
33:16 shall it be **k** that I have found favor in your sight,
Lev 4:14 when the sin that they have committed becomes **k**,
4:23 the sin that he has committed is made **k** to him,
4:28 the sin that you have committed is made **k** to you,
Nu 12: 6 I the LORD make myself **k** to them in visions;
16: 5 the morning the LORD will make **k** who is his,
31:17 and kill every woman who has **k** a man by sleeping
31:18 the young girls who have not **k** a man by sleeping
31:35 women who had not **k** a man by sleeping with him.
Dt 4: 9 make them **k** to your children
9:24 against the LORD as long as he has **k** you.
11: 2 that it was not your children (who have not **k**
11:28 to follow other gods that you have not **k**.
13: 2 "Let us follow other gods" (whom you have not **k**)
13: 6 whom neither you nor your ancestors have **k**,
13:13 and worship other gods," whom you have not **k**,
21: 1 and it is not **k** who struck the person down,
25:10 Throughout Israel his family shall be **k** as
28:36 that neither you nor your ancestors have **k**,
28:64 which neither you nor your ancestors have **k**.
29:26 gods whom they had not **k** and whom he had
31:13 so that their children, who have not **k** it, may hear
32:17 not God, to deities they had never **k**,
Jos 24:31 of the elders who outlived Joshua and had **k** all
Jdg 16: 9 So the secret of his strength was not **k**.
Ru 3: 3 but do not make yourself **k** to the man
3:14 for he said, "It must not be **k** that the woman came
1Sa 9:27 that I may make **k** to you the word of God."
22:15 for your servant has **k** nothing of all this,
2Sa 17:19 and nothing was **k** of it.
22:44 people whom I had not **k** served me.
1Ki 14: 2 it will not be **k** that you are the wife of Jeroboam,
18:36 let it be **k** this day that you are God in Israel,
1Ch 16: 8 make **k** his deeds among the peoples.
17:19 making **k** all these great things.
Ezr 4:12 may it be **k** to the king that the Jews who came up
4:13 Now may it be **k** to the king that,
4:16 We make **k** to the king that,
5: 8 be **k** to the king that we went to the province
Ne 4:15 our enemies heard that their plot was **k** to us,
9:14 and you made **k** your holy sabbath to them
Est 1:17 of the queen will be made **k** to all women,
Job 14: 5 and the number of their months is **k** to you,
42:11 and all who had **k** him before, and they ate bread
Ps 9:16 The LORD has made himself **k**,
18:43 people whom I had not **k** served me.
25:14 and he makes his covenant **k** to them.
38: 9 O Lord, all my longing is **k** to you;
59:13 be **k** to the ends of the earth that God rules
67: 2 that your way may be **k** upon earth,
69:19 my foes are all **k** to you.
76: 1 In Judah God is **k**, his name is great in Israel.
78: 3 things that we have heard and **k**,
79:10 the outpoured blood of your servants be **k** among
81: 5 I hear a voice I had not **k**:
88:12 Are your wonders **k** in the darkness,
98: 2 The LORD has made **k** his victory;
103: 7 He made **k** his ways to Moses,
105: 1 make **k** his deeds among the peoples.
106: 8 so that he might make **k** his mighty power.
139: 1 O LORD, you have searched me and **k** me.
Ps 145:12 to make **k** to all people your mighty deeds,
Pr 1:23 I will make my words **k** to you.
14:33 but it is not **k** in the heart of fools.
20:11 Even children make themselves **k** by their acts,
22:19 I have made them **k** to you today—yes, to you.
31:23 Her husband is **k** in the city gates,
Ecc 6: 5 moreover it has not seen the sun or **k** anything;
6:10 and it is **k** what human beings are,
Isa 12: 4 make **k** his deeds among the nations;
12: 5 let this be **k** in all the earth.
19:12 and make **k** what the LORD of hosts has planned
19:21 The LORD will make himself **k** to the Egyptians;
38:19 fathers make **k** to children your faithfulness.
40:21 Have you not **k**? Have you not heard?
40:28 Have you not **k**? Have you not heard?
42:16 by paths they have not **k** I will guide them.
48: 3 they went out from my mouth and I made them **k**;
48: 6 hidden things that you have not **k**.
48: 8 You have never heard, you have never **k**,
61: 9 Their descendants shall be **k** among the nations,
64: 2 to make your name **k** to your adversaries,
66:14 and it shall be **k** that the hand of the LORD is
Jer 7: 9 and go after other gods that you have not **k**,
9:16 that neither they nor their ancestors have **k**;
11:18 It was the LORD who made it **k** to me,
16:13 a land that neither you nor your ancestors have **k**,
19: 4 nor their ancestors nor the kings of Judah have **k**;
28: 9 be **k** that the LORD has truly sent the prophet."
33: 3 and hidden things that you have not **k**.
44: 3 and serve other gods that they had not **k**,
Eze 16: 2 Mortal, make **k** to Jerusalem her abominations,
20: 5 making myself **k** to them in the land of Egypt—
20: 9 in whose sight I made myself **k** to them
32: 9 into countries you have not **k**.
35:11 and I will make myself **k** among you,
36:32 let that be **k** to you.
38:23 and make myself **k** in the eyes of many nations.
39: 7 My holy name I will make **k**
43:11 make **k** to them the plan of the temple,
Da 2:30 in order that the interpretation may be **k** to the king
3:18 But if not, be it **k** to you, O king,
Am 3: 2 You only have I **k** of all the families of the earth;
Hab 3: 2 in our own time make it **k**;
Zec 7:14 among all the nations that they had not **k**.
14: 7 there shall be continuous day (it is **k** to the LORD),
Mt 10: 2 first, Simon, also **k** as Peter,
10:26 and nothing secret that will not become **k**.
12: 7 But if you had **k** what this means,
12:16 and he ordered them not to make him **k**.
12:33 for the tree is **k** by its fruit.
24:43 if the owner of the house had **k** in what part of
Mk 3:12 But he sternly ordered them not to make him **k**.
6:14 for Jesus' name had become **k**.
Lk 2:15 which the Lord has made **k** to us."
2:17 they made **k** what had been told them
6:44 for each tree is **k** by its own fruit.
7:39 he would have **k** who and what kind
8:17 nor is anything secret that will not become **k**
12: 2 and nothing secret that will not become **k**.
12:39 the house had **k** at what hour the thief was coming,
24:35 how he had been made **k** to them in the breaking of
Jn 1:18 to the Father's heart, who has made him **k**.
7: 4 for no one who wants to be widely **k** acts in secret.
15:15 because I have made **k** to you everything
16: 3 And they will do this because they have not **k**
17: 6 "I have made your name **k**
17:26 I made your name **k** to them, and I will make it **k**,
18:15 Since that disciple was **k** to the high priest,
18:16 So the other disciple, who was **k** to the high priest,
Ac 1:19 This became **k** to all the residents of Jerusalem,
1:23 Joseph called Barsabbas, who was also **k** as Justus,
2:14 let this be **k** to you, and listen to what I say.
2:28 You have made **k** to me the ways of life;
4:10 let it be **k** to all of you,
7:13 On the second visit Joseph made himself **k**
7:13 and Joseph's family became **k** to Pharaoh.
7:18 until another king who had not **k** Joseph ruled
9:24 but their plot became **k** to Saul.
9:42 This became **k** throughout Joppa,
13: 9 But Saul, also **k** as Paul, filled with the Holy Spirit,
13:38 Let it be **k** to you therefore, my brothers,
15:18 **k** from long ago.'
19:17 When this became **k** to all residents of Ephesus,
26: 5 They have **k** for a long time,
28:28 Let it be **k** to you then that this salvation
Ro 1:19 For what can be **k** about God is plain to them,
3:17 and the way of peace they have not **k**."
7: 7 it had not been for the law, I would not have **k** sin.
7: 7 not have **k** what it is to covet if the law had not
9:22 to show his wrath and to make **k** his power,
9:23 to make **k** the riches of his glory for the objects
11:34 "For who has **k** the mind of the Lord?
16:19 For while your obedience is **k** to all,
16:26 the prophetic writings is made **k** to all the Gentiles,
1Co 2:16 "For who has **k** the mind of the Lord so as
8: 3 but anyone who loves God is **k** by him.
13:12 then I will know fully, even as I have been fully **k**.
2Co 3: 2 written on our hearts, to be **k** and read by all;
5:11 but we ourselves are well **k** to God,
5:11 I hope that we are also well **k** to your consciences.
6: 9 as unknown, and yet are well **k**;
7:12 but in order that your zeal for us might be made **k**
Gal 4: 9 or rather to be **k** by God,
Eph 1: 9 he has made **k** to us the mystery of his will,
3: 3 how the mystery was made **k** to me by revelation,
3: 5 In former generations this mystery was not made **k**
3:10 of God in its rich variety might now be made **k** to

Eph 6:19 to make **k** with boldness the mystery of the gospel,
Php 1:13 so that it has become **k** throughout
4:5 Let your gentleness be **k** to everyone.
4:6 with thanksgiving let your requests be made **k**
Col 1:8 and he has made **k** to us your love in the Spirit.
1:25 to make the word of God fully **k,**
1:27 To them God chose to make **k** how great among
1Th 1:8 but in every place your faith in God has become **k,**
1Ti 1:4 the divine training that is **k** by faith.
2Ti 3:15 from childhood you have **k** the sacred writings
Heb 3:10 and they have not **k** my ways.'
2Pe 1:16 when we made **k** to you the power and coming
2:21 to have **k** the way of righteousness than,
1Jn 3:6 no one who sins has either seen him or **k** him.
4:16 we have **k** and believe the love that God has for us.
Rev 1:1 he made it **k** by sending his angel
Tob 2:14 These things are **k** about you!"
AdE 2:10 for Mordecai had commanded her not to make it **k.**
2:22 The matter became **k** to Mordecai,
14:12 make yourself **k** in this time of our affliction,
Wis 2:1 and no one has been **k** to return from Hades.
4:1 because it is **k** both by God and by mortals.
5:7 but the way of the Lord we have not **k.**
6:13 to make herself **k** to those who desire her.
16:28 to make it **k** that one must rise before the sun
18:6 night was made **k** beforehand to our ancestors,
18:18 made **k** why they were dying;
Sir 4:24 For wisdom becomes **k** through speech,
6:27 Search out and seek, and she will become **k** to you;
11:28 by how he ends, a person becomes **k.**
12:8 A friend is not **k** in prosperity,
17:15 Their ways are always **k** to him;
19:29 A person is **k** by his appearance,
19:29 and a sensible person is **k** when first met,
21:7 The mighty in speech are widely **k;**
23:20 Before the universe was created, it was **k** to him,
26:6 and a tongue-lashing makes it **k** to all.
26:26 *in her pride she will be k to all as ungodly.*
36:5 as we have **k** that there is no God but you, O Lord.
38:5 with a tree in order that its power might be **k?**
42:18 For the Most High knows all that may be **k;**
46:15 by his words he became **k** as a trustworthy seer.
46:20 he prophesied and made **k** to the king his death,
LtJ 6:50 it will afterward be **k** that they are false.
1Mc 6:3 but he could not because his plan had become **k** to
7:3 But when this act became **k** to him, he said,
7:30 It became **k** to Judas that Nicanor had come to him
8:10 but this became **k** to them,
9:60 because their plan became **k.**
2Mc 1:33 When this matter became **k,**
1Es 2:18 be **k** to our lord the king that the Jews who came
2:24 Therefore we now make **k** to you, O lord and king,
6:8 Let it be fully **k** to our lord the king that,
3Mc 1:3 But Dositheus, **k** as the son of Drimylus,
2:6 You made **k** your mighty power by inflicting many
3:21 we made **k** to all our amnesty
2Es 3:32 Or has another nation **k** you besides Israel?
4Mc 4:25 though they had **k** beforehand
5:4 and **k** to many in the tyrant's court because

KNOWS‡ (106) [KNOW]

Ge 3:5 for God **k** that when you eat of it your eyes will
33:13 "My lord **k** that the children are frail and that
Nu 24:16 and **k** the knowledge of the Most High,
Dt 2:7 he **k** your going through this great wilderness.
34:6 but no one **k** his burial place to this day.
Jos 22:22 He **k;** and let Israel itself know!
1Sa 20:3 "Your father **k** well that you like me;
23:17 my father Saul also **k** that this is so."
2Sa 12:22 and wept; for I said, 'Who **k?**
14:22 "Today your servant **k** that I have found favor
17:10 for all Israel **k** that your father is a warrior,
19:20 For your servant **k** that I have sinned;
1Ki 5:6 for you know that there is no one among us who **k**
Est 4:14 Who **k?** Perhaps you have come to royal dignity
Job 11:11 For he **k** those who are worthless;
23:10 But he **k** the way that I take;
28:7 "That path no bird of prey **k,**
28:23 "God understands the way to it, and he **k** its place.
Ps 37:18 The LORD **k** the days of the blameless,
44:21 For he **k** the secrets of the heart.
74:9 and there is no one among us who **k** how long.
94:11 The LORD **k** our thoughts,
103:14 For he **k** how we were made;
103:16 and it is gone, and its place **k** it no more.
104:19 the sun **k** its time for setting.
Pr 9:13 she is ignorant and **k** nothing.
14:10 The heart **k** its own bitterness,
24:22 and who **k** the ruin that both can bring?
Ecc 2:19 and who **k** whether they will be wise or foolish?
3:21 Who **k** whether the human spirit goes upward and
6:12 For who **k** what is good for mortals while they live
7:22 heart **k** that many times you have yourself cursed
8:1 And who **k** the interpretation of a thing?
10:14 No one **k** what is to happen,
Isa 1:3 ox **k** its owner, and the donkey its master's crib;
7:15 He shall eat curds and honey by the time he **k** how
7:16 child **k** how to refuse the evil and choose the good,
8:4 child **k** how to call "My father" or "My mother,"
29:15 "Who sees us? Who **k** us?"
59:8 no one who walks in them **k** peace.
Jer 8:7 Even the stork in the heavens **k** its times;
29:23 I am the one who **k** and bears witness,
Da 2:22 he **k** what is in the darkness,
Joel 2:14 Who **k** whether he will not turn and relent,
Jnh 3:9 Who **k?** God may relent
Na 3:17 no one **k** where they have gone.
Zep 3:5 but the unjust **k** no shame.
Mt 6:8 your Father **k** what you need before you ask him.
6:32 and indeed your heavenly Father **k**
9:30 "See that no one **k** of this."
11:27 no one **k** the Son except the Father, and no one **k**
24:36 "But about that day and hour no one **k,**
Mk 13:32 "But about that day or hour no one **k,**
Lk 10:22 and no one **k** who the Son is except the Father,
12:30 and your Father **k** that you need them.
16:15 of others; but God **k** your hearts;
Jn 10:15 just as the Father **k** me and I know the Father.
14:17 because it neither sees him nor **k** him.
19:35 and he **k** that he tells the truth.)
Ac 15:8 And God, who **k** the human heart,
26:26 Indeed the king **k** about these things,
Ro 8:27 **k** what is the mind of the Spirit,
1Co 2:11 what human being **k** what is truly human except
3:20 "The Lord **k** the thoughts of the wise,
2Co 11:11 And why? Because I do not love you? God **k** I do!
11:31 **k** that I do not lie.
12:2 of the body I do not know; God **k.**
12:3 of the body I do not know; God **k**—
2Ti 2:19 "The Lord **k** those who are his," and,
Jas 4:17 then, who **k** the right thing to do and fails to do it,
2Pe 2:9 then the Lord **k** how to rescue the godly from trial,
1Jn 3:20 God is greater than our hearts, and he **k** everything.
4:6 Whoever **k** God listens to us,
4:7 everyone who loves is born of God and **k** God.
Rev 2:17 that no one **k** except the one who receives it.
7:14 I said to him, "Sir, you are the one that **k.**"
12:12 because he **k** that his time is short!"
19:12 he has a name inscribed that no one **k** but himself.
Tob 6:13 Indeed he **k** that you, rather than any other man,
AdE 4:14 who **k** whether it was not for such a time as this
Wis 1:7 that which holds all things together **k** what is said,
5:12 so that no one **k** its pathway.
8:8 she **k** the things of old, and infers the things
9:9 she who **k** your works and was present
9:11 For she **k** and understands all things,
13:16 because he **k** that it cannot help itself,
Sir 1:6 Her subtleties—who **k** them?
15:19 and he **k** every human action.
18:28 Every intelligent person **k** wisdom,
21:7 when they slip, the sensible person **k** it.
32:8 be as one who **k** and can still hold his tongue.
34:9 An educated person **k** many things,
34:9 with much experience **k** what he is talking about.
34:10 An inexperienced person **k** few things,
42:18 For the Most High **k** all that may be known;
Bar 3:31 No one **k** the way to her,
3:32 But the one who **k** all things **k** her,
2Es 14:21 and so no one **k** the things which have been done
15:26 For God **k** all who sin against him;
16:54 The Lord certainly **k** everything that people do;
16:54 he **k** their imaginations and their thoughts
16:56 and he **k** the number of the stars.
16:63 He **k** your imaginations and what you think
4Mc 7:22 and **k** that it is blessed to endure any suffering for

KOA (1)

Eze 23:23 the Chaldeans, Pekod and Shoa and **K,** and all

KOHATH (19) [KOHATH'S, KOHATHITE, KOHATHITES]

Ge 46:11 The children of Levi: Gershon, **K,** and Merari.
Ex 6:16 Gershon, **K,** and Merari, and the length
6:18 The sons of **K:** Amram, Izhar,
Nu 3:17 by their names: Gershon, **K,**
3:19 The sons of **K** by their clans:
3:27 To **K** belonged the clan of the Amramites,
16:1 Now Korah son of Izhar son of **K** son of Levi,
26:57 of **K,** the clan of the Kohathites;
26:58 Now **K** was the father of Amram.
1Ch 6:1 The sons of Levi: Gershom, **K,** and Merari.
6:2 The sons of **K:** Amram, Izhar, Hebron, and Uzziel.
6:16 The sons of Levi: Gershom, **K,** and Merari.
6:18 The sons of **K:** Amram, Izhar, Hebron, and Uzziel.
6:22 The sons of **K:** Amminadab his son,
6:38 son of Izhar, son of **K,** son of Levi, son of Israel;
6:66 of the sons of **K** had towns of their territory out of
15:5 of **K,** Uriel the chief, with one hundred twenty
23:6 to the sons of Levi: Gershon, **K,**
23:12 The sons of **K:** Amram, Izhar,

KOHATH'S (1) [KOHATH]

Ex 6:18 of **K** life was one hundred thirty-three years.

KOHATHITE (1) [KOHATH]

Jos 21:20 of the Kohathites belonging to the **K** families of

KOHATHITES (27) [KOHATH]

Nu 3:27 these are the clans of the **K.**
3:29 The clans of the **K** were to camp on the south side
3:30 of the ancestral house of the clans of the **K.**
4:2 a census of the **K** separate from the other Levites,
4:4 of the **K** relating to the tent of meeting concerns
4:15 after that the **K** shall come to carry these,
4:15 the things of the tent of meeting that the **K** are
4:18 not let the tribe of the clans of the **K** be destroyed
4:20 But the **K** must not go in to look on the holy things
4:34 and the leaders of the congregation enrolled the **K,**
4:37 This was the enrollment of the clans of the **K,**
7:9 But to the **K** he gave none,
Nu 10:21 Then the **K,** who carried the holy things, set out;
26:57 of Kohath, the clan of the **K;**
Jos 21:4 The lot came out for the families of the **K.**
21:5 the **K** received by lot ten towns from the families
21:10 the families of the **K** who belonged to the Levites,
21:20 of the **K** belonging to the Kohathite families of
21:26 of the families of the rest of the **K** were ten in all,
1Ch 6:33 and their sons were: Of the **K:**
6:54 to the sons of Aaron of the families of **K**—
6:61 of the **K** were given by lot out of the family of
6:70 for the rest of the families of the **K.**
9:32 Also some of their kindred of the **K** had charge of
2Ch 20:19 And the Levites, of the **K** and the Korahites,
29:12 and Joel son of Azariah, of the sons of the **K;**
34:12 of the sons of the **K,** to have oversight.

KOLA (1)

Jdt 15:4 to Betomasthaim and Choba and **K,**

KOLAIAH (2)

Ne 11:7 of **K** son of Maaseiah son of Ithiel son of Jeshaiah.
Jer 29:21 concerning Ahab son of **K** and Zedekiah son

KONA (1)

Jdt 4:4 and to **K,** Beth-horon, Belmain, and Jericho,

KORAH (27) [KORAH'S, KORAHITE, KORAHITES]

Ge 36:5 and Oholibamah bore Jeush, Jalam, and **K.**
36:14 she bore to Esau Jeush, Jalam, and **K.**
36:16 **K,** Gatam, and Amalek; these are the clans of Eliphaz
36:18 the clans Jeush, Jalam, and **K;**
Ex 6:21 The sons of Izhar: **K,** Nepheg, and Zichri.
6:24 The sons of **K:** Assir, Elkanah,
Nu 16:1 Now **K** son of Izhar son of Kohath son of Levi,
16:5 Then he said to **K** and all his company,
16:6 Do this: take censers, **K** and all your company,
16:8 Then Moses said to **K,** "Hear now, you Levites!
16:16 to **K,** "As for you and all your company,
16:19 Then **K** assembled the whole congregation
16:24 Get away from the dwellings of **K,** Dathan,
16:27 So they got away from the dwellings of **K,**
16:32 everyone who belonged to **K** and all their goods.
16:40 so as not to become like **K** and his company—
16:49 besides those who died in the affair of **K.**
26:9 against Moses and Aaron in the company of **K,**
26:10 up along with **K,** when that company died,
26:11 Notwithstanding, the sons of **K** did not die.
27:3 against the LORD in the company of **K,** but died
1Ch 1:35 sons of Esau: Eliphaz, Reuel, Jeush, Jalam, and **K.**
2:43 sons of Hebron: **K,** Tappuah, Rekem, and Shema.
6:22 Amminadab his son, **K** his son, Assir his son,
6:37 son of Assir, son of Ebiasaph, son of **K,**
9:19 Shallum son of Kore, son of Ebiasaph, son of **K,**
Sir 45:18 and their followers and the company of **K,**

KORAH'S (1) [KORAH]

Jude 1:11 for the sake of gain, and perish in **K** rebellion.

KORAHITE (1) [KORAH]

1Ch 9:31 one of the Levites, the firstborn of Shallum the **K,**

KORAHITES (18) [KORAH]

Ex 6:24 these are the families of the **K.**
Nu 26:58 the clan of the Mushites, the clan of the **K.**
1Ch 9:19 the **K,** were in charge of the work of the service,
12:6 Isshiah, Azarel, Joezer, and Jashobeam, the **K;**
26:1 As for the divisions of the gatekeepers: of the **K,**
26:19 the divisions of the gatekeepers among the **K** and
2Ch 20:19 And the Levites, of the Kohathites and the **K,**
Ps 42:T *To the leader. A Maskil of the K.*
44:T *To the leader. Of the K. A Maskil.*
45:T *according to Lilies. Of the K. A Maskil.*
46:T *Of the K. According to Alamoth. A Song.*
47:T *To the leader. Of the K. A Psalm.*
48:T *A Song. A Psalm of the K.*
49:T *To the leader. Of the K. A Psalm.*
84:T *according to The Gittith. Of the K. A Psalm.*
85:T *To the leader. Of the K. A Psalm.*
87:T *Of the K. A Psalm. A Song.*
88:T *A Song. A Psalm of the K. To the leader:*

KORATHITES, KORHITES (KJV) See KORAHITES

KORE (3)

1Ch 9:19 Shallum son of **K,** son of Ebiasaph, son of Korah,
26:1 of the Korahites, Meshelemiah son of **K,**
2Ch 31:14 **K** son of Imnah the Levite, keeper of the east gate,

KOZ (1)

1Ch 4:8 **K** became the father of Anub, Zobebah,

KUE (4)

1Ki 10:28 import of horses was from Egypt and **K,**
10:28 the king's traders received them from **K** at a price.
2Ch 1:16 horses were imported from Egypt and **K;**
1:16 the king's traders received them from **K** at

KUSHAIAH (1)
1Ch 15:17 their kindred, Ethan son of **K**;

L

LAADAH (1)
1Ch 4:21 Er father of Lecah, **L** father of Mareshah,

LAADEN (KJV) See LADAN

LABAN (56) [LABAN'S]
Ge 24:29 Rebekah had a brother whose name was **L**; and **L** ran out to the man, to the spring.
24:32 and **L** unloaded the camels,
24:50 Then **L** and Bethuel answered,
25:20 of Paddan-aram, sister of **L** the Aramean.
27:43 flee at once to my brother **L** in Haran,
28: 2 take as wife from there one of the daughters of **L**,
28: 5 to **L** son of Bethuel the Aramean,
29: 5 He said to them, "Do you know **L** son of Nahor?"
29:10 the daughter of his mother's brother **L**,
29:10 and the sheep of his mother's brother **L**,
29:10 and watered the flock of his mother's brother **L**.
29:13 **L** heard the news about his sister's son Jacob,
29:13 Jacob told **L** all these things,
29:14 and **L** said to him, "Surely you are my bone
29:15 Then **L** said to Jacob,
29:16 Now **L** had two daughters;
29:19 **L** said, "It is better that I give her to you than
29:21 to **L**, "Give me my wife that I may go in to her,
29:22 So **L** gathered together all the people of the place,
29:24 (**L** gave his maid Zilpah to his daughter Leah to
29:25 And Jacob said to **L**, "What is this you have done
29:26 **L** said, "This is not done in our country—
29:28 then **L** gave him his daughter Rachel as a wife.
29:29 (**L** gave his maid Bilhah to his daughter Rachel to
29:30 He served **L** for another seven years.
30:25 When Rachel had borne Joseph, Jacob said to **L**,
30:27 But **L** said to him, "If you will allow me to say
30:34 **L** said, "Good! Let it be as you have said."
30:35 But that day **L** removed the male goats
30:40 the completely black animals in the flock of **L**;
31: 1 Now Jacob heard that the sons of **L** were saying,
31: 2 And Jacob saw that **L** did not regard him
31:12 for I have seen all that **L** is doing to you.
31:19 Now **L** had gone to shear his sheep,
31:20 And Jacob deceived **L** the Aramean,
31:22 On the third day **L** was told that Jacob had fled.
31:24 God came to **L** the Aramean in a dream by night,
31:25 **L** overtook Jacob. Now Jacob had pitched his tent
31:25 and **L** with his kinsfolk camped in the hill country
31:26 **L** said to Jacob, "What have you done?
31:31 Jacob answered **L**, "Because I was afraid,
31:33 So **L** went into Jacob's tent, and into Leah's tent,
31:34 **L** felt all about in the tent, but did not find them.
31:36 Then Jacob became angry, and upbraided **L**.
31:36 Jacob said to **L**, "What is my offense?
31:43 Then **L** answered and said to Jacob,
31:47 **L** called it Jegar-sahadutha:
31:48 **L** said, "This heap is a witness between you
31:51 Then **L** said to Jacob, "See this heap and see
31:55 Early in the morning **L** rose up,
32: 4 'I have lived with **L** as an alien,
46:18 whom **L** gave to his daughter Leah;
46:25 whom **L** gave to his daughter Rachel,
Dt 1: 1 between Paran and Tophel, **L**, Hazeroth,
Jdt 8:26 while he was tending the sheep of **L**,

LABAN'S (3) [LABAN]
Ge 30:36 while Jacob was pasturing the rest of **L** flock.
30:40 and did not put them with **L** flock.
30:42 so the feebler were **L**, and the stronger Jacob's.

LABOR (109) [LABORED, LABORER, LABORERS, LABORIOUSLY, LABORS]
A. WOMAN IN LABOR (17)
Ge 31:42 God saw my affliction and the **l** of my hands,
35:16 Rachel was in childbirth, and she had hard **l**.
35:17 When she was in her hard **l**,
38:28 While she was in **l**, one put out a hand;
49:15 and became a slave at forced **l**.
Ex 1:11 over them to oppress them with forced **l**.
1:14 in mortar and brick and in every kind of field **l**.
2:11 he went out to his people and saw their forced **l**.
5: 9 then they will **l** at it and pay no attention
20: 9 Six days you shall **l** and do all your work.
23:16 of the first fruits of your **l**,
23:16 you gather in from the field the fruit of your **l**.
Dt 5:13 Six days you shall **l** and do all your work.
20:11 all the people in it shall serve you at forced **l**.
26: 6 by imposing hard **l** on us,
Jos 16:10 to this day but have been made to do forced **l**.
Jos 17:13 they put the Canaanites to forced **l**,
Jdg 1:28 they put the Canaanites to forced **l**,
1:30 and became subject to forced **l**.
1:33 and of Beth-anath became subject to forced **l**
1:35 and they became subject to forced **l**.
1Sa 4:19 for her **l** pains overwhelmed her.
2Sa 20:24 Adoram was in charge of the forced **l**;
1Ki 4: 6 of Abda was in charge of the forced **l**.
5:13 King Solomon conscripted forced **l** out
5:14 Adoniram was in charge of the forced **l**.
9:15 of the forced **l** that King Solomon conscripted
9:21 these Solomon conscripted for slave **l**,
11:28 over all the forced **l** of the house of Joseph.
12:18 who was taskmaster over the forced **l**,
2Ch 8: 8 these Solomon conscripted for forced **l**,
10:18 who was taskmaster over the forced **l**,
Ne 4:22 be a guard for us by night and may **l** by day."
5:18 because of the heavy burden of **l** on the people.
Job 9:29 I shall be condemned; why then do I **l** in vain?
39:11 and will you hand over your **l** to it?
39:16 though its **l** should be in vain, yet it has no fear;
Ps 48: 6 pains as of a woman in **l**, A
78:46 and the fruit of their **l** to the locust.
104:23 People go out to their work and to their **l** until
107:12 Their hearts were bowed down with hard **l**;
127: 1 those who build it **l** in vain.
128: 2 You shall eat the fruit of the **l** of your hands;
Pr 12:14 and manual **l** has its reward.
12:24 while the lazy will be put to forced **l**.
21:25 for lazy hands refuse to **l**.
SS 8: 5 There your mother was in **l** with you;
8: 5 there she who bore you was in **l**.
Isa 13: 8 they will be in anguish like a woman in **l**. A
21: 3 like the pangs of a woman in **l**; A
31: 8 and his young men shall be put to forced **l**.
42:14 now I will cry out like a woman in **l**, A
45:10 or to a woman, "With what are you in **l**?"
54: 1 you who have not been in **l**!
55: 2 and your **l** for that which does not satisfy?
65:23 not **l** in vain, or bear children for calamity;
66: 7 Before she was in **l** she gave birth;
66: 8 soon as Zion was in **l** she delivered her children.
Jer 4:31 For I heard a cry as of a woman in **l**, A
6:24 pain as of a woman in **l**. A
13:21 like those of a woman in **l**? A
22:23 pain as of a woman in **l**! A
30: 6 with his hands on his loins like a woman in **l**? A
31: 8 those with child and those in **l**, together;
48:41 shall be like the heart of a woman in **l**. A
49:22 that day shall be like the heart of a woman in **l**. A
49:24 of her, as of a woman in **l**. A
50:43 pain like that of a woman in **l**. A
Eze 23:29 and take away all the fruit of your **l**,
29:18 of Babylon made his army **l** hard against Tyre;
29:18 from Tyre to pay for the **l** that he had expended
Jnh 4:10 which you did not **l** and which you did not grow;
Mic 4: 9 that pangs have seized you like a woman in **l**? A
4:10 O daughter Zion, like a woman in **l**; A
5: 3 the time when she who is in **l** has brought forth;
Hab 2:13 not from the LORD of hosts that peoples **l** only
Jn 4:38 I sent you to reap that for which you did not **l**.
4:38 and you have entered into their **l**."
16:21 When a woman is in **l**, she has pain,
Ro 8:22 the whole creation has been groaning in **l** pains
1Co 3: 8 and each will receive wages according to the **l**
15:58 you know that in the Lord your **l** is not in vain.
Eph 4:28 rather let them **l** and work honestly
Php 1:22 that means fruitful **l** for me;
2:16 on the day of Christ that I did not run in vain or **l**
1Th 1: 3 of faith and **l** of love and steadfastness of hope
2: 9 You remember our **l** and toil,
3: 5 and that our **l** had been in vain.
5: 3 as **l** pains come upon a pregnant woman,
5:12 to respect those who **l** among you,
2Th 3: 8 but with toil and **l** we worked night and day,
1Ti 5:17 especially those who **l** in preaching and teaching;
Wis 9:10 that she may **l** at my side,
9:16 and what is at hand we find with **l**;
Sir Pr: 2 despite our diligent **l** in translating,
Pr: 3 that I should myself devote some diligence and **l**
7:15 Do not hate hard **l** or farm work,
19:11 the fool suffers birth pangs like a woman in **l** A
34: 5 and like a woman in **l**, the mind has fantasies. A
48:19 and they were in anguish, like women in **l**.
1Es 4:22 "Do you not **l** and toil,
3Mc 4:14 the hard **l** that has been briefly mentioned before,
2Es 3:33 not appeared and their **l** has borne no fruit.
4:42 as a woman who is in **l** makes haste to escape
5:12 they shall **l**, but their ways shall not prosper.
8:14 with so great **l** was fashioned by your command,
9:22 because with much **l** I have perfected them.
16:45 Because of this those who **l**, **l** in vain;

LABORED (15) [LABOR]
Jos 24:13 I gave you a land on which you had not **l**,
2Ch 24:13 So those who were engaged in the work **l**,
Ne 4:17 a way that each **l** on the work with one hand and
4:21 So we **l** at the work,
Isa 23: 4 "I have neither **l** nor given birth,
47:12 with which you have **l** from your youth;
47:15 Such to you are those with whom you have **l**,
49: 4 But I said, "I have **l** in vain,
62: 8 not drink the wine for which you have **l**;
Jer 3:24 for which our ancestors had **l**,
Eze 29:20 the land of Egypt as his payment for which he **l**,
Jn 4:38 Others have **l**, and you have entered
Sir 24:34 Observe that I have not **l** for myself alone,
33:18 Consider that I have not **l** for myself alone,
51:27 See with your own eyes that I have **l** but little

LABORER (8) [LABOR]
Lev 19:13 for yourself the wages of a **l** until morning.
25:50 the owner shall be rated as the time of a hired **l**.
25:53 As a **l** hired by the year they shall be under
Job 7: 1 and are not their days like the days of a **l**?
Lk 10: 7 for the **l** deserves to be paid.
1Ti 5:18 and, "The **l** deserves to be paid."
Jdt 4:10 and every resident alien and hired **l**
Sir 37:11 with an idler about any work or with a seasonal **l**

LABORERS (20) [LABOR]
Lev 25: 6 your hired and your bound **l** who live with you;
25:40 They shall remain with you as hired or bound **l**.
Dt 15:18 given you services worth the wages of hired **l**;
24:14 not withhold the wages of poor and needy **l**,
1Ki 5:15 Solomon also had seventy thousand **l**
2Ch 2: 2 Solomon conscripted seventy thousand **l**
2:18 Seventy thousand of them he assigned as **l**,
Job 7: 2 and like **l** who look for their wages,
14: 6 and desist, that they may enjoy, like **l**, their days.
Ecc 5:12 the sleep of **l**, whether they eat little or much;
Mt 9:37 "The harvest is plentiful, but the **l** are few;
9:38 therefore ask the Lord of the harvest to send out **l**
10:10 or a staff; for **l** deserve their food.
20: 1 in the morning to hire **l** for his vineyard.
20: 2 agreeing with the **l** for the usual daily wage,
20: 8 'Call the **l** and give them their pay,
Lk 10: 2 "The harvest is plentiful, but the **l** are few;
10: 2 therefore ask the Lord of the harvest to send out **l**
Jas 5: 4 The wages of the **l** who mowed your fields,
Sir 7:20 or hired **l** who devote themselves to their task.

LABORIOUSLY (2) [LABOR]
Wis 15: 7 and **l** molds each vessel for our service,
2Es 7:89 they **l** served the Most High,

LABORS (20) [LABOR]
Ex 5: 4 away from their work? Get to your **l**!"
Dt 28:33 up the fruit of your ground and of all your **l**;
Pr 5:10 and your **l** will go to the house of an alien;
Ecc 2:20 to despair concerning all the toil of my **l** under
Isa 3:10 for they shall eat the fruit of their **l**.
Hag 1:11 on human beings and animals, and on all their **l**.
2Co 6: 5 imprisonments, riots, **l**, sleepless nights, hunger;
10:15 that is, in the **l** of others;
11:23 with far greater **l**, far more imprisonments,
Heb 4:10 also cease from their **l** as God did from his.
Rev 14:13 says the Spirit, "they will rest from their **l**,
Wis 3:11 Their hope is vain, their **l** are unprofitable,
3:15 For the fruit of good **l** is renowned,
5: 1 and those who make light of their **l**.
8: 7 if anyone loves righteousness, her **l** are virtues;
8:18 and in the **l** of her hands, unfailing wealth,
10:10 she prospered him in his **l**,
10:17 She gave to holy people the reward of their **l**;
Sir 14:15 Will you not leave the fruit of your **l** to another,
38:27 So too is every artisan and master artisan who **l**

LACCUNUS (1)
1Es 9:31 Naathus and Moossias, **L** and Naidus,

LACE (KJV) See CORD

LACEDAEMONIANS (1)
2Mc 5: 9 to the **L** in hope of finding protection because

LACERATE (1)
Dt 14: 1 not **l** yourselves or shave your forelocks for

LACHISH‡ (24)
Jos 10: 3 to King Japhia of **L**, and to King Debir of Eglon,
10: 5 the king of **L**, and the king of Eglon—
10:23 the king of **L**, and the king of Eglon.
10:31 and all Israel with him, to **L**, and laid siege to it,
10:32 The LORD gave **L** into the hand of Israel,
10:33 Then King Horam of Gezer came up to help **L**;
10:34 From **L** Joshua passed on with all Israel to Eglon;
10:35 that day, as he had done to **L**.
12:11 the king of Jarmuth one the king of **L** one
15:39 **L**, Bozkath, Eglon,
2Ki 14:19 against him in Jerusalem, and he fled to **L**.
14:19 But they sent after him to **L**, and killed him there.
18:14 of Assyria at **L**, saying, "I have done wrong;
18:17 and the Rabshakeh with a great army from **L**
19: 8 for he had heard that the king had left **L**.
2Ch 11: 9 Adoraim, **L**, Azekah,
25:27 against him in Jerusalem, and he fled to **L**.
25:27 But they sent after him to **L**, and killed him there.
32: 9 while King Sennacherib of Assyria was at **L**
Ne 11:30 **L** and its fields, and Azekah and its villages.
Isa 36: 2 The king of Assyria sent the Rabshakeh from **L**
37: 8 for he had heard that the king had left **L**.
Jer 34: 7 and against all the cities of Judah that were left, **L**
Mic 1:13 the steeds to the chariots, inhabitants of **L**;

LACK (47) [LACKED, LACKING, LACKS]
Ge 18:28 Will you destroy the whole city for **l** of five?"
Dt 8: 9 where you will **l** nothing,

Dt 28:48 in nakedness and l of everything.
28:57 she is eating them in secret for l of anything else,
Jdg 18:10 a place where there is no l of anything on earth."
1Sa 21:15 Do I l madmen, that you have brought this fellow
1Ki 11:22 "What do you l with me that you now seek to go
2Ch 7:18 'You shall never l a successor to rule
Job 4:11 The strong lion perishes for l of prey,
31:19 if I have seen anyone perish for l of clothing,
38:41 and wander about for l of food?
39:13 though its pinions l plumage.
Ps 34:10 but those who seek the LORD l no good thing.
Pr 5:23 They die for l of discipline,
8: 5 acquire intelligence, you who l it.
10:21 but fools die for l of sense.
12: 9 than to be self-important and l food.
26:20 For l of wood the fire goes out,
28:27 Whoever gives to the poor will l nothing,
31:11 and he will have no l of gain.
Ecc 6: 2 so that they l nothing of all that they desire,
10: 3 Even when fools walk on the road, they l sense,
Isa 24:11 There is an outcry in the streets for l of wine;
50: 2 their fish stink for l of water, and die of thirst.
51:14 and go down to the Pit, nor shall they l bread.
Jer 33:17 David shall never l a man to sit on the throne of
33:18 and the levitical priests shall never l a man
35:19 not l a descendant to stand before me for all time.
Hos 4: 6 My people are destroyed for l of knowledge;
Am 4: 6 and l of bread in all your places,
Zec 10: 2 they suffer for l of a shepherd.
Mt 19:20 "I have kept all these; what do I still l?"
Mk 10:21 loved him and said, "You l one thing;
16:14 ⟦and he upbraided them for their l of faith⟧
Lk 8: 6 and as it grew up, it withered for l of moisture.
22:35 bag, or sandals, did you l anything?"
1Co 7: 5 that Satan may not tempt you because of your l
Tit 3:13 and see that they l nothing.
Jdt 8: 9 because they were faint for l of water,
Wis 11:17 not l the means to send upon them a multitude
15:18 when judged by their l of intelligence;
Sir 11:12 who l strength and abound in poverty;
19:24 the God-fearing who l understanding than
19:28 Even if l of strength keeps him from sinning,
22:13 and you will never be wearied by his l of sense.
23:10 under scrutiny will not l bruises,
1Mc 2:61 of those who put their trust in him will l strength.

LACKED (4) [LACK]

Dt 2: 7 God has been with you; you have l nothing."
Ne 9:21 in the wilderness so that they l nothing;
Jer 44:18 we have l everything and have perished by
Wis 19: 4 up the punishment that their torments still l,

LACKEYS (1)

4Mc 9:17 "You abominable l, your wheel is not so powerful

LACKING (19) [LACK]

Ge 18:28 Suppose five of the fifty righteous are l?
Jdg 18: 7 quiet and unsuspecting, l nothing on earth,
21: 3 that today there should be one tribe l in Israel?"
1Ki 4:27 in his month; they let nothing be l.
Pr 10:19 When words are many, transgression is not l,
Ecc 1:15 and what is l cannot be counted.
9: 8 do not let oil be l on your head.
Isa 59:15 Truth is l, and whoever turns
Eze 4:17 L bread and water, they will look at one another
Lk 18:22 he said to him, "There is still one thing l.
1Co 1: 7 that you are not l in any spiritual gift as you wait
Col 1:24 and in my flesh I am completing what is l
1Th 3:10 to face and restore whatever is l in your faith.
Jas 1: 4 so that you may be mature and complete, l
1: 5 If any of you is l in wisdom, ask God,
Sir 14:10 A miser begrudges bread, and it is l at his table.
37:21 since he is l in all wisdom.
47:23 broad in folly and l in sense, Rehoboam,
51:24 Why do you say you are l in these things,

LACKS (11) [LACK]

2Sa 3:29 or who falls by the sword, or who l food!"
Pr 10:13 but a rod is for the back of one who l sense.
11:12 Whoever belittles another l sense,
25:28 without walls, is one who l self-control.
28:16 A ruler who l understanding is a cruel oppressor;
SS 7: 2 a rounded bowl that never l mixed wine.
Jas 2:15 If a brother or sister is naked and l daily food,
2Pe 1: 9 For anyone who l these things is nearsighted
Wis 14: 4 so that even a person who l skill may put to sea.
Sir 10:27 in plenty than the boaster who l bread.
19:23 and there is a fool who merely l wisdom.

LAD (2)

Tob 7:10 But Raguel overheard it and said to the l,
Sus 1:45 up the holy spirit of a young l named Daniel,

LAD (KJV) See also ATTENDANT, BOY, HELPER

LADAN (7)

1Ch 7:26 L his son, Ammihud his son, Elishama his son,
23: 7 The sons of Gershon were L and Shimei.
23: 8 The sons of L: Jehiel the chief,
23: 9 These were the heads of families of L.
26:21 of L, the sons of the Gershonites belonging to L,
26:21 heads of families belonging to L the Gershonite:

LADDER (2) [LADDERS]

Ge 28:12 he dreamed that there was a l set up on the earth,
1Mc 11:59 from the L of Tyre to the borders of Egypt.

LADDERS (1) [LADDER]

1Mc 5:30 carrying l and engines of war to capture

LADE, LADED, LADING (KJV) See CARGO, LAID, LOAD, LOADED, LOADS, PUT ON BOARD

LADEN (3)

Isa 1: 4 Ah, sinful nation, people l with iniquity,
Eze 27:25 So you were filled and heavily l in the heart of
Sir 50:10 like an olive tree l with fruit,

LADIES (4) [LADY]

Jdg 5:29 Her wisest l make answer, indeed,
Est 1:18 the noble l of Persia and Media who have heard
Ps 45: 9 daughters of kings are among your l of honor;
AdE 1:18 so now the other l who are wives of the Persian

LADLES (4)

2Ch 4:22 basins, l, and firepans, of pure gold.
24:14 and l, and vessels of gold and silver.
Jer 52:18 the shovels, the snuffers, the basins, the l,
52:19 the lampstands, the l, and the bowls for libation,

LADY (2) [LADIES]

2Jn 1: 1 The elder to the elect l and her children,
1: 5 But now, dear l, I ask you,

LAEL (1)

Nu 3:24 Eliasaph son of L as head of the ancestral house

LAG (1)

Ro 12:11 Do not l in zeal, be ardent in spirit,

LAGGARDS (1)

1Mc 5:53 the l and encouraging the people all the way

LAGGED (1)

Dt 25:18 and struck down all who l behind you;

LAHAD (1)

1Ch 4: 2 and Jahath became the father of Ahumai and L.

LAHAI-ROI (KJV) See BEER LAHAI ROI

LAHMAM (1)

Jos 15:40 Cabbon, L, Chitlish,

LAHMI (1)

1Ch 20: 5 of Jair killed L the brother of Goliath the Gittite,

LAID‡ (249) [LAY]

Ge 9:23 l it on both their shoulders,
22: 6 of the burnt offering and l it on his son Isaac,
22: 9 Abraham built an altar there and l the wood
22: 9 He bound his son Isaac, and l him on the altar,
30:41 Jacob l the rods in the troughs before the eyes of
48:14 But Israel stretched out his right hand and l it on
48:17 When Joseph saw that his father l his right hand
Ex 5: 9 Let heavier work be l on them;
22: 8 the owner had l hands on the neighbor's goods.
22:11 the two of them that the one has not l hands on
40:18 Moses set up the tabernacle; he l its bases,
Lev 8:14 and his sons l their hands upon the head of the bull
8:18 and his sons l their hands on the head of the ram,
8:22 and his sons l their hands on the head of the ram,
9:20 They first l the fat on the breasts,
10: 1 put fire in it, and l incense on it;
20:18 he has l bare her flow and she has l bare her flow
Nu 16:18 they put fire in the censers and l incense on them,
19: 2 and on which no yoke has been l.
21:30 and we l waste until fire spread to Medeba."
27:23 he l his hands on him and commissioned him—
Dt 32:34 Is not this l up in store with me,
34: 9 because Moses had l his hands on him;
Jos 2: 6 the stalks of flax that she had l out on the roof.
2:19 but if a hand is l upon any who are with you in
4: 8 where they camped, and l them down there.
10:31 to Lachish, and l siege to it, and assaulted it.
10:34 and they l siege to it, and assaulted it;
Jdg 9:24 and their blood be l on their brother Abimelech,
9:48 and took it up and l it on his shoulder.
Ru 4:16 Naomi took the child and l him in her bosom,
1Sa 10:25 and he wrote them in a book and l it up before
14:24 He had l an oath on the troops, saying,
19:13 Michal took an idol and l it on the bed;
2Sa 22:16 the foundations of the world were l bare at
1Ki 1:51 see, he has l hold of the horns of the altar,
3:20 She l him at her breast, and l her dead son at my
6:37 the foundation of the house of the LORD was l,
11:30 Ahijah l hold of the new garment he was wearing
12:11 Now, whereas my father l on you a heavy yoke,
13:29 l it on the donkey, and brought it back to the city,
13:30 He l the body in his own grave;
1Ki 16:34 he l its foundation at the cost
17:19 and l him on his own bed.
18:33 cut the bull in pieces, and l it on the wood.
20: 1 He marched against Samaria, l siege to it,
2Ki 4:21 She went up and l him on the bed of the man
4:31 Gehazi went on ahead and l the staff on the face
6:24 he marched against Samaria and l siege to it.
11:16 So they l hands on her;
13:16 Elisha l his hands on the king's hands.
19:17 the kings of Assyria have l waste the nations
25: 1 with all his army against Jerusalem, and l siege
2Ch 8:16 the house of the LORD was l until the house of
10:11 Now, whereas my father l on you a heavy yoke,
16:14 They l him on a bier that had been filled
23:15 So they l hands on her;
24: 9 the tax that Moses the servant of God l on Israel
29:23 they l their hands on them,
31: 6 to the LORD their God, and l them in heaps.
36: 3 the king of Egypt deposed him in Jerusalem and l
Ezr 3: 6 of the temple of the LORD was not yet l.
3:10 When the builders l the foundation of the temple
3:11 the foundation of the house of the LORD was l.
4:15 On that account this city was l waste.
5: 8 and timber is l in the walls;
5:16 and l the foundations of the house of God
Ne 3: 3 they l its beams and set up its doors, its bolts,
3: 6 they l its beams and set up its doors, its bolts,
5:15 before me l heavy burdens on the people,
Est 9:16 but they l no hands on the plunder.
9:31 just as they had l down for themselves and
10: 1 King Ahasuerus l tribute on the land and on
Job 6: 2 and all my calamity l in the balances!
14:10 But mortals die, and are l low;
15:20 through all the years that are l up for the ruthless.
16:15 and have l my strength in the dust.
20:26 Utter darkness is l up for their treasures;
29: 9 and l their hands on their mouths;
34:13 Who gave him charge over the earth and who l
38: 4 were you when I l the foundation of the earth?
38: 6 were its bases sunk, or who l its cornerstone
Ps 18:15 and the foundations of the world were l bare
31:19 O how abundant is your goodness that you have l
55:20 My companion l hands on a friend and violated
66:11 you l burdens on our backs;
78:31 and l low the flower of Israel.
79: 1 they have l Jerusalem in ruins.
79: 7 and l waste his habitation.
89:40 you have l his strongholds in ruins.
102:25 Long ago you l the foundation of the earth,
116: 3 the pangs of Sheol l hold on me;
119:110 The wicked have l a snare for me,
141: 9 Keep me from the trap that they have l for me,
Pr 7:26 for many are those she has l low,
13:22 but the sinner's wealth is l up for the righteous.
Ecc 9: 1 All this I l to heart, examining it all,
SS 7:13 new as well as old, which I have l up for you,
Isa 14: 8 Since you were l low, no one comes to cut us down
14:12 you who l the nations low!
15: 1 Ar is l waste in a night, Moab is undone;
15: 1 Kir is l waste in a night, Moab is undone.
15: 7 and what they have l up they carry away over
24: 3 be utterly l waste and utterly despoiled;
25:11 their pride will be l low despite the struggle
25:12 l low, cast to the ground, even to the dust.
32:19 and the city will be utterly l low.
37:18 the kings of Assyria have l waste all the nations
44:28 and of the temple, "Your foundation shall be l."
48:13 My hand l the foundation of the earth,
49:17 and those who l you waste go away from you.
51:13 the heavens and l the foundations of the earth.
53: 6 the LORD has l on him the iniquity of us all.
60:12 those nations shall be utterly l waste.
Jer 4:20 the whole land is l waste.
4:26 all its cities were l in ruins before the LORD,
9:10 they are l waste so that no one passes through,
9:12 the land ruined and l waste like a wilderness,
10:25 and have l waste his habitation.
18:22 and l snares for my feet.
26: 8 and the prophets and all the people l hold of him,
48: 1 Alas for Nebo, it is l waste!
48:20 Tell it by the Arnon, that Moab is l waste.
49: 3 Wail, O Heshbon, for Ai is l waste!
52: 4 and they l siege to it;
La 2: 5 l in ruins its strongholds,
4: 6 though no hand was l on it.
Eze 12:20 The inhabited cities shall be l waste,
13:14 so that its foundation will be l bare;
19: 7 ravaged their strongholds, and l waste their towns;
24: 2 The king of Babylon has l siege
26:19 When I make you a city l waste,
29:12 among cities that are l waste.
30: 7 and their cities shall lie among cities l waste.
32:19 Be l to rest with the uncircumcised!"
32:27 whose swords were l under their heads,
32:29 for all their might are l with those who are killed
32:32 he shall be l to rest among the uncircumcised,
35:12 saying, "They are l desolate,
39:21 and my hand that I have l on them.
40:42 on which the instruments were to be l with which
40:43 on the tables the flesh of the offering was to be l.
Da 2: 5 and your houses shall be l in ruins.
3:29 and their houses l in ruins;
6:17 stone was brought and l on the mouth of the den,
Joel 1: 7 It has l waste my vines,
Am 4: 9 I l waste your gardens and your vineyards;
7: 9 and the sanctuaries of Israel shall be l waste,
Mic 5: 1 with a wall; siege is l against us;

Zep 1:13 and their houses l waste.
2:14 for its cedar work will be l bare.
3:6 I have l waste their streets so that no one walks
Hag 2:18 the foundation of the LORD's temple was l,
Zec 4:9 "The hands of Zerubbabel have l the foundation
8:9 when the foundation was l for the rebuilding of
10:11 The pride of Assyria shall be l low,
Mt 12:25 "Every kingdom divided against itself is l waste,
19:15 And he l his hands on them and went on his way.
26:50 they came and l hands on Jesus and arrested him.
27:60 and l it in his own new tomb,
Mk 6:5 except that he l his hands on a few sick people
6:29 they came and took his body, and l it in a tomb.
6:56 they l the sick in the marketplaces,
8:23 on his eyes and l his hands on him,
8:25 Then Jesus l his hands on his eyes again;
10:16 he took them up in his arms, l his hands on them,
14:46 Then they l hands on him and arrested him.
15:46 l it in a tomb that had been hewn out of the rock.
15:47 the mother of Joses saw where the body was l.
16:6 Look, there is the place they l him.
Lk 2:7 and l him in a manger,
4:40 he l his hands on each of them and cured them.
6:48 who dug deeply and l the foundation on rock;
12:19 you have ample goods l up for many years;
13:13 When he l his hands on her,
14:29 he has l a foundation and is not able to finish,
23:26 and they l the cross on him,
23:53 and l it in a rock-hewn tomb where no one had ever been l.
23:55 and they saw the tomb and how his body was l.
Jn 7:30 but no one l hands on him,
7:44 but no one l hands on him.
11:34 He said, "Where have you l him?"
19:41 a new tomb in which no one had ever been l.
19:42 and the tomb was nearby, they l Jesus there.
20:2 and we do not know where they have l him."
20:13 and I do not know where they have l him."
20:15 tell me where you have l him,
Ac 4:35 They l it at the apostles' feet,
4:37 and l it at the apostles' feet.
5:2 brought only a part and l it at the apostles' feet.
5:15 and l them on cots and mats,
6:6 who prayed and l their hands on them.
7:16 and l in the tomb that Abraham had bought for
7:58 and the witnesses l their coats at the feet of
8:17 Then Peter and John l their hands on them,
9:17 He l his hands on Saul and said, "Brother Saul,
9:37 they l her in a room upstairs.
12:1 About that time King Herod l violent hands
13:3 Then after fasting and praying they l their hands
13:29 they took him down from the tree and l him in
13:36 died, was l beside his ancestors,
19:6 When Paul had l his hands on them,
24:14 believing everything l down according to the law
25:14 Festus l Paul's case before the king, saying,
1Co 3:10 like a skilled master builder I l a foundation,
3:11 the one that has been l;
9:16 for an obligation is l on me,
Gal 2:2 Then I l before them (though only in
Col 1:5 because of the hope l up for you in heaven.
1Ti 1:9 that the law is l down not for the innocent but for
Heb 4:13 but all are naked and l bare to the eyes of the one
Jas 5:3 You have l up treasure for the last days.
1Jn 3:16 that he l down his life for us—
Rev 18:17 For in one hour all this wealth has been l waste!"
18:19 For in one hour she has been l waste.
Tob 2:4 and removed the body from the square and l it
14:11 Then they l him on his bed, and he died;
Sir 21:4 thus the house of the proud will be l waste.
40:1 and a heavy yoke is l on the children of Adam,
50:2 He l the foundations for the high double walls,
51:2 and from the trap l by a slanderous tongue,
Bar 3:20 nor understood her paths, nor l hold of her.
Sus 1:34 before the people and l their hands on her head.
Bel 1:1 King Astyages was l to rest with his ancestors,
1Mc 2:12 our beauty, and our glory have been l waste;
2Mc 1:21 the liquid on the wood and on the things l
11:11 and l low eleven thousand of them
12:45 that is l up for those who fall asleep in godliness,
14:7 Therefore I have l aside my ancestral glory—
15:27 they l low at least thirty-five thousand,
1Es 2:23 That is why this city was l waste.
4:45 the Edomites burned when Judea was l waste by
5:57 and they l the foundation of the temple of God
6:9 of hewn stone, with costly timber l in the walls.
6:20 l the foundations of the house of the Lord that is
8:22 that no tribute or any other tax is to be l on any
2Es 3:7 And you l upon him one commandment of yours;
6:2 and before the foundations of paradise were l,
7:*83* the reward l up for those who have trusted
7:*84* the torment l up for themselves in the last days.
8:33 righteous, who have many works l up with you,
10:21 For you see how our sanctuary has been l waste,
10:22 our harp has been l low,
11:42 of those who brought forth fruit, and have l low
13:56 for there is a reward l up with the Most High.
4Mc 12:12 justice has l up for you intense and eternal fire

LAIN (8) [LIE]

Ge 26:10 of the people might easily have l with your wife,
Nu 5:19 saying, "If no man has l with you,
Jdg 21:11 every male and every woman that has l with
Job 31:9 and I have l in wait at my neighbor's door;
Jer 3:2 Where have you not been l with?
Eze 23:8 for in her youth men had l with her
Eze 38:8 the mountains of Israel, which had long l waste;
Jnh 1:5 had gone down into the hold of the ship and had l

LAIR (4) [LAIRS]

Jer 9:11 a heap of ruins, a l of jackals;
10:22 the cities of Judah a desolation, a l of jackals.
49:33 Hazor shall become a l of jackals,
Zep 2:15 a desolation it has become, a l for wild animals!

LAIRS (1) [LAIR]

Job 37:8 animals go into their l and remain in their dens.

LAISH (6) [=DAN]

Jdg 18:7 The five men went on, and when they came to L,
18:14 L) said to their comrades,
18:27 and the priest who belonged to him, came to L,
18:29 but the name of the city was formerly L.
1Sa 25:44 to Palti son of L, who was from Gallim.
2Sa 3:15 from her husband Paltiel the son of L.

LAISHAH (1)

Isa 10:30 O daughter Gallim! Listen, O L!

LAKE (13)

Job 14:11 As waters fail from a l,
Lk 5:1 Once while Jesus was standing beside the l
5:2 he saw two boats there at the shore of the l;
8:22 "Let us go across to the other side of the l."
8:23 A windstorm swept down on the l,
8:33 down the steep bank into the l and was drowned.
Rev 19:20 These two were thrown alive into the l of fire
20:10 into the l of fire and sulfur,
20:14 Death and Hades were thrown into the l of fire.
20:14 This is the second death, the l of fire;
20:15 in the book of life was thrown into the l of fire.
21:8 their place will be in the l that burns with fire
2Mc 12:16 so that the adjoining l, a quarter of a mile wide,

LAKKUM (1)

Jos 19:33 and Adami-nekeb, and Jabneel, as far as L;

LAMB (111) [LAMB'S, LAMBS, LAMBSKINS]

Ge 22:7 but where is the l for a burnt offering?"
22:8 "God himself will provide the l for
30:32 and every black l, and the spotted and speckled
30:35 and every l that was black,
Ex 12:3 on the tenth of this month they are to take a l for each family, a l for each household.
12:4 If a household is too small for a whole l,
12:4 the l shall be divided in proportion to the number
12:5 Your l shall be without blemish, a year-old male;
12:8 They shall eat the l that same night;
12:21 and slaughter the passover l.
29:39 One l you shall offer in the morning, and the other l you shall offer in the evening;
29:40 and with the first l one-tenth of a measure
29:41 And the other l you shall offer in the evening,
34:20 firstborn of a donkey you shall redeem with a l,
Lev 9:3 a calf and a l, yearlings without blemish,
12:6 of meeting a l in its first year for a burnt offering,
14:10 and one ewe l in its first year without blemish,
14:13 the l in the place where the sin offering and
14:21 he shall take one male l for a guilt offering to
14:24 and the priest shall take the l of the guilt offering
14:25 the l of the guilt offering and shall take some of
17:3 of the house of Israel slaughters an ox or a l or
22:23 An ox or a l that has a limb too long
23:12 you shall offer a l a year old, without blemish,
Nu 6:12 and bring a male l a year old as a guilt offering.
6:14 one male l a year old without blemish as
6:14 one ewe l a year old without blemish as
7:15 one male l a year old, for a burnt offering;
7:21 one male l a year old, as a burnt offering;
7:27 one male l a year old, for a burnt offering;
7:33 one male l a year old, for a burnt offering;
7:39 one male l a year old, for a burnt offering;
7:45 one male l a year old, for a burnt offering;
7:51 one male l a year old, for a burnt offering;
7:57 one male l a year old, for a burnt offering;
7:63 one male l a year old, for a burnt offering;
7:69 one male l a year old, for a burnt offering;
7:75 one male l a year old, for a burnt offering;
7:81 one male l a year old, for a burnt offering;
15:5 the burnt offering or the sacrifice, for each l.
28:4 One l you shall offer in the morning,
28:4 and the other l you shall offer at twilight
28:7 be one-fourth of a hin for each l;
28:8 The other l you shall offer at twilight with
28:13 with oil as a grain offering for every l—
28:14 and one-fourth of a hin for a l.
1Sa 7:9 So Samuel took a sucking l and offered it as
17:34 and took a l from the flock,
17:35 rescuing the l from its mouth;
2Sa 12:3 the poor man had nothing but one little ewe l,
12:4 but he took the poor man's l,
12:6 he shall restore the l fourfold,
2Ch 30:15 the passover l on the fourteenth day of
30:17 to slaughter the passover l for everyone who was
35:1 the passover l on the fourteenth day of
35:6 Slaughter the passover l, sanctify yourselves,
35:11 They slaughtered the passover l,
35:13 They roasted the passover l with fire according
Ezr 6:20 the passover l for all the returned exiles,
Isa 11:6 The wolf shall live with the l,
53:7 like a l that is led to the slaughter,
65:25 The wolf and the l shall feed together,
66:3 whoever sacrifices a l, like one who breaks
Jer 11:19 But I was like a gentle l led to the slaughter.
Eze 46:13 He shall provide a l, a yearling, without blemish,
46:15 Thus the l and the grain offering and the oil shall
Hos 4:16 now feed them like a l in a broad pasture?
Mk 14:12 when the Passover l is sacrificed,
Lk 22:7 on which the Passover l had to be sacrificed.
Jn 1:29 "Here is the L of God who takes away the sin of
1:36 he exclaimed, "Look, here is the L of God!"
Ac 8:32 and like a l silent before its shearer,
1Co 5:7 For our paschal l, Christ, has been sacrificed.
1Pe 1:19 like that of a l without defect or blemish.
Rev 5:6 a L standing as if it had been slaughtered,
5:8 and the twenty-four elders fell before the L,
5:12 the L that was slaughtered to receive power
5:13 on the throne and to the L be blessing and honor
6:1 Then I saw the L open one of the seven seals,
6:16 on the throne and from the wrath of the L;
7:9 standing before the throne and before the L,
7:10 on the throne, and to the L!"
7:14 and made them white in the blood of the L.
7:17 for the L at the center of the throne will
8:1 When the L opened the seventh seal,
12:11 of the L and by the word of their testimony,
13:8 in the book of life of the L that was slaughtered.
13:11 it had two horns like a l and it spoke like
14:1 Then I looked, and there was the L,
14:4 these follow the L wherever he goes.
14:4 from humankind as first fruits for God and the L,
14:10 of the holy angels and in the presence of the L.
15:3 the servant of God, and the song of the L:
17:14 they will make war on the L, and the L will conquer them,
19:7 for the marriage of the L has come,
19:9 to the marriage supper of the L."
21:9 I will show you the bride, the wife of the L."
21:14 the twelve names of the twelve apostles of the L.
21:22 the Lord God the Almighty and the L.
21:23 and its lamp is the L.
22:1 flowing from the throne of God and of the L
22:3 But the throne of God and of the L will be in it,
Sir 13:17 What does a wolf have in common with a l?
46:16 and he offered in sacrifice a suckling l.
1Es 1:1 he killed the passover l on the fourteenth day of
1:6 and kill the passover l and prepare the sacrifices
1:12 They roasted the passover l with fire, as required;
7:12 the passover l for all the returned captives and

LAMB'S (1) [LAMB]

Rev 21:27 only those who are written in the L book of life.

LAMBS (94) [LAMB]

Ge 21:28 Abraham set apart seven ewe l of the flock.
21:29 of these seven ewe l that you have set apart?"
21:30 "These seven ewe l you shall accept
30:33 among the goats and black among the l,
30:40 the l, and set the faces of the flocks toward
Ex 12:21 "Go, select l for your families,
29:38 two l a year old regularly each day.
Lev 14:10 On the eighth day he shall take two male l
14:12 The priest shall take one of the l,
23:18 the bread seven l a year old without blemish,
23:19 two male l a year old as a sacrifice of well-being.
23:20 before the LORD, together with the two l;
Nu 7:17 five male goats, and five male l a year old.
7:23 five male goats, and five male l a year old.
7:29 five male goats, and five male l a year old.
7:35 five male goats, and five male l a year old.
7:41 five male goats, and five male l a year old.
7:47 five male goats, and five male l a year old.
7:53 five male goats, and five male l a year old.
7:59 five male goats, and five male l a year old.
7:65 five male goats, and five male l a year old.
7:71 five male goats, and five male l a year old.
7:77 five male goats, and five male l a year old.
7:83 five male goats, and five male l a year old.
7:87 twelve rams, twelve male l a year old,
7:88 the male goats sixty, the male l a year old sixty.
15:11 or for each of the male l or the kids.
28:3 two male l a year old without blemish, daily,
28:9 two male l a year old without blemish,
28:11 seven male l a year old without blemish;
28:19 one ram, and seven male l a year old;
28:21 one-tenth shall you offer for each of the seven l;
28:27 one ram, seven male l a year old.
28:29 one-tenth for each of the seven l;
29:2 seven male l a year old without blemish.
29:4 and one-tenth for each of the seven l;
29:8 one young bull, one ram, seven male l a year old.
29:10 one-tenth for each of the seven l;
29:13 two rams, fourteen male l a year old.
29:15 and one-tenth for each of the fourteen l;
29:17 fourteen male l a year old without blemish,
29:18 for the rams, and for the l,
29:20 fourteen male l a year old without blemish,
29:21 for the rams, and for the l,
29:23 fourteen male l a year old without blemish,
29:24 for the rams, and for the l,
29:26 fourteen male l a year old without blemish,
29:27 for the rams, and for the l,
29:29 fourteen male l a year old without blemish,
29:30 for the rams, and for the l,
29:32 fourteen male l a year old without blemish,

Nu 29:33 for the rams, and for the **l**,
29:36 seven male **l** a year old without blemish,
29:37 for the ram, and for the **l**,
Dt 32:14 and milk from the flock, with fat of **l** and rams;
1Sa 15: 9 and the **l**, and all that was valuable,
2Ki 3: 4 to the king of Israel one hundred thousand **l**,
1Ch 29:21 and a thousand **l**, with their libations,
2Ch 29:21 They brought seven bulls, seven rams, seven **l**,
29:22 the **l** and their blood was dashed against the altar.
29:32 one hundred rams, and two hundred **l**;
35: 7 **l** and kids from the flock to the number
35: 8 passover offerings two thousand six hundred **l**
35: 9 the passover offerings five thousand **l** and kids
Ezr 6:17 four hundred **l**, and as a sin offering for all Israel,
7:17 with all diligence buy bulls, rams, and **l**,
8:35 ninety-six rams, seventy-seven **l**,
Ps 114: 4 The mountains skipped like rams, the hills like **l**.
114: 6 like rams? O hills, like **l**?
Pr 27:26 the **l** will provide your clothing, and the goats
Isa 1:11 I do not delight in the blood of bulls, or of **l**,
5:17 Then the **l** shall graze as in their pasture,
16: 1 Send **l** to the ruler of the land, from Sela,
34: 6 with the blood of **l** and goats,
40:11 he will gather the **l** in his arms,
Jer 51:40 I will bring them down like **l** to the slaughter,
Eze 27:21 of Kedar were your favored dealers in **l**, rams,
39:18 of rams, of **l**, and of goats, of bulls,
46: 4 on the sabbath day shall be six **l** without blemish
46: 5 and the grain offering with the **l** shall be as much
46: 6 six **l** and a ram, which shall be without blemish;
46: 7 and with the **l** as much as he wishes,
46:11 and with the **l** as much as one wishes to give,
Am 6: 4 and eat **l** from the flock, and calves from the stall;
Lk 10: 3 I am sending you out like **l** into the midst
Jn 21:15 Jesus said to him, "Feed my **l**."
Wis 19: 9 For they ranged like horses, and leaped like **l**,
Sir 47: 3 and with bears as though they were **l** of the flock.
Aza 1:17 or with tens of thousands of fat **l**;
1Es 1: 7 who were present Josiah gave thirty thousand **l**
6:29 for bulls and rams and **l**,
7: 7 two hundred rams, four hundred **l**,
8:14 and silver for bulls and rams and **l** and what goes
8:66 seventy-two **l**, and as a thank offering twelve

LAMBSKINS (1) [LAMB, SKIN]

Jdt 12:15 before Holofernes the **l** she had received

LAME (31) [LAMENESS]

Lev 21:18 one who is blind or **l**,
2Sa 4: 4 it happened that he fell and became **l**.
5: 6 even the blind and the **l** will turn you back"—
5: 8 let him get up the water shaft to attack the **l** and
5: 8 blind and the **l** shall not come into the house."
9:13 Now he was **l** in both his feet.
19:26 For your servant is **l**.
Job 29:15 I was eyes to the blind, and feet to the **l**.
Pr 25:19 a bad tooth or a **l** foot is trust in a faithless person
Isa 33:23 even the **l** will fall to plundering.
35: 6 then the **l** shall leap like a deer,
Jer 31: 8 among them the blind and the **l**,
Mic 4: 6 that day, says the LORD, I will assemble the **l**
4: 7 The **l** I will make the remnant,
Zep 3:19 And I will save the **l** and gather the outcast,
Mal 1: 8 And when you offer those that are **l** or sick,
1:13 by violence or is **l** or sick,
Mt 11: 5 the **l** walk, the lepers are cleansed, the deaf hear,
15:30 bringing with them the **l**, the maimed, the blind,
15:31 the **l** walking, and the blind seeing.
18: 8 to enter life maimed or **l** than to have two hands
21:14 The blind and the **l** came to him in the temple,
Mk 9:45 for you to enter life **l** than to have two feet and to
Lk 7:22 the blind receive their sight, the **l** walk,
14:13 invite the poor, the crippled, the **l**, and the blind.
14:21 the crippled, the blind, and the **l**.'
Jn 5: 3 In these lay many invalids—blind, **l**,
Ac 3: 2 And a man **l** from birth was being carried in.
8: 7 many others who were paralyzed or **l** were cured.
Heb 12:13 so that what is **l** may not be put out of joint,
2Es 2:21 do not ridicule the **l**, protect the maimed,

LAMECH (12)

Ge 4:18 and Methushael the father of **L**.
4:19 **L** took two wives; the name of the
4:23 **L** said to his wives: "Adah and Zillah,
4:23 you wives of **L**, listen to what I say:
4:24 truly **L** seventy-sevenfold."
5:25 he became the father of **L**.
5:26 the birth of **L** seven hundred eighty-two years,
5:28 When **L** had lived one hundred eighty-two years,
5:30 **L** lived after the birth of Noah
5:31 of **L** were seven hundred seventy-seven years;
1Ch 1: 3 Enoch, Methuselah, **L**;
Lk 3:36 son of Shem, son of Noah, son of **L**,

LAMENESS (1) [LAME]

Dt 15:21 any serious defect, such as **l** or blindness—

LAMENT (28) [LAMENTABLE, LAMENTATION, LAMENTATIONS, LAMENTED, LAMENTING, LAMENTS]

Jdg 11:40 to **l** the daughter of Jephthah the Gileadite.
2Ch 35:25 Jeremiah also uttered a **l** for Josiah,
Isa 3:26 And her gates shall **l** and mourn;
19: 8 all who cast hooks in the Nile will **l**,
Jer 4: 8 Because of this put on sackcloth, **l** and wail:
9:20 and each to her neighbor a **l**.
16: 5 Do not enter the house of mourning, or go to **l**,
16: 6 and no one shall **l** for them;
22:18 They shall not **l** for him, saying, "Alas,
22:18 They shall not **l** for him, saying, "Alas, lord!"
34: 5 so they shall burn spices for you and **l** for you,
49: 3 **l**, and slash yourselves with whips!
La 2: 8 he caused rampart and wall to **l**;
Eze 27:32 a lamentation for you, and **l** over you:
Joel 1: 8 **L** like a virgin dressed in sackcloth for
1:13 Put on sackcloth and **l**, you priests;
Mic 1: 8 For this I will **l** and wail;
Jas 4: 9 **L** and mourn and weep.
Wis 18:10 of their enemies echoed back, and their piteous **l**
Sir 38:16 and as one in great pain begin the **l**.
1Mc 1:27 Every bridegroom took up the **l**;
3Mc 4: 6 all together raising a **l** instead of a wedding song,
4:12 the city frequently went out in secret to **l** bitterly
2Es 7:*65* Let the human race **l**, but let the wild animals of
7:*65* let all who have been born **l**,
8:16 for whom I **l**, and about Israel,
16: 2 and **l** for them; for your destruction is at hand.
4Mc 16:12 not wail with such a **l** for any of them,

LAMENTABLE (1) [LAMENT]

3Mc 6:31 of deliverance instead of a bitter and **l** death,

LAMENTATION (42) [LAMENT]

Ge 50:10 they held there a very great and sorrowful **l**;
2Sa 1:17 David intoned this **l** over Saul
11:26 that her husband was dead, she made **l** for him.
Job 27:15 and their widows make no **l**.
Ps 78:64 and their widows made no **l**.
Isa 29: 2 and there shall be moaning and **l**,
43:14 the shouting of the Chaldeans will be turned to **l**.
Jer 6:26 as for an only child, most bitter **l**:
7:29 raise a **l** on the bare heights,
9:10 and a **l** for the pastures of the wilderness,
31:15 A voice is heard in Ramah, **l** and bitter weeping.
48:38 and in the squares there is nothing but **l**;
La 2: 5 and multiplied in daughter Judah mourning and **l**.
Eze 2:10 and written on it were words of **l** and mourning
19: 1 As for you, raise up a **l** for the princes of Israel,
19:14 This is a **l**, and it is used as a **l**.
26:17 And they shall raise a **l** over you, and say to you:
27: 2 Now you, mortal, raise a **l** over Tyre,
27:32 In their wailing they raise a **l** for you,
28:12 raise a **l** over the king of Tyre, and say to him,
32: 2 raise a **l** over Pharaoh king of Egypt,
32:16 This is a **l**; it shall be chanted.
Am 5: 1 Hear this word that I take up over you in **l**,
5:16 and those skilled in **l**, to wailing;
8:10 and all your songs into **l**;
Mic 1: 8 I will make **l** like the jackals,
2: 4 and wail with bitter **l**, and say,
Mt 2:18 and loud **l**, Rachel weeping for her children;
Ac 8: 2 Devout men buried Stephen and made loud **l**
Tob 2: 6 and all your songs into **l**."
Jdt 7:29 and general **l** arose throughout the assembly,
AdE 4: 3 a loud cry of mourning and **l** among the Jews,
1Mc 2:70 And all Israel mourned for him with great **l**.
4:39 they tore their clothes and mourned with great **l**;
9:20 All Israel made great **l** for him;
13:26 All Israel bewailed him with great **l**,
1Es 1:32 with the women, have made **l** for him to this day;
3Mc 4: 2 among the Jews there was incessant mourning, **l**,
5:49 to **l** and groans they kissed each other,
2Es 10:12 But if you say to me, 'My **l** is not like the earth's,
16:18 when there shall be much **l**;

LAMENTATIONS (4) [LAMENT]

Est 9:31 concerning their fasts and their **l**.
2Mc 11: 6 they and all the people, with **l** and tears,
3Mc 1:18 and filled the streets with groans and **l**.
4: 8 in **l** instead of good cheer and youthful revelry,

LAMENTED (7) [LAMENT]

1Sa 7: 2 and all the house of Israel **l** after the LORD.
2Sa 3:33 The king **l** for Abner, saying,
Jer 16: 4 They shall not be **l**, nor shall they be buried;
25:33 They shall not be **l**, or gathered, or buried;
Zec 7: 5 When you fasted and **l** in the fifth month and in
Sir 51:19 and **l** my ignorance of her.
1Es 1:32 The prophet Jeremiah **l** for Josiah,

LAMENTING (2) [LAMENT]

Est 4: 3 with fasting and weeping and **l**,
Wis 19: 3 and were **l** at the graves of their dead,

LAMENTS (3) [LAMENT]

2Ch 35:25 of Josiah in their **l** to this day.
35:25 they are recorded in the **L**.
Ps 35:14 I went about as one who **l** for a mother,

LAMP (41) [LAMPS, LAMPSTAND, LAMPSTANDS]

Ex 27:20 so that a **l** may be set up to burn regularly.
Lev 24: 2 to bring you pure oil of beaten olives for the **l**,
1Sa 3: 3 the **l** of God had not yet gone out,
2Sa 21:17 so that you do not quench the **l** of Israel."
22:29 Indeed, you are my **l**, O LORD,
1Ki 11:36 so that my servant David may always have a **l**
1Ki 15: 4 the LORD his God gave him a **l** in Jerusalem,
2Ki 4:10 a table, a chair, and a **l**,
8:19 to give a **l** to him and to his descendants forever.
2Ch 21: 7 to give a **l** to him and to his descendants forever.
Job 18: 6 and the **l** above them is put out.
21:17 "How often is the **l** of the wicked put out?
29: 3 when his **l** shone over my head,
Ps 18:28 It is you who light my **l**;
119:105 Your word is a **l** to my feet and a light
132:17 I have prepared a **l** for my anointed one.
Pr 6:23 the commandment is a **l** and the teaching a light,
13: 9 but the **l** of the wicked goes out.
20:20 your **l** will go out in utter darkness.
20:27 The human spirit is the **l** of the LORD,
21: 4 the **l** of the wicked—are sin.
24:20 the **l** of the wicked will go out.
31:18 Her **l** does not go out at night.
Jer 25:10 the sound of the millstones and the light of the **l**.
Mt 5:15 after lighting a **l** puts it under the bushel basket,
6:22 "The eye is the **l** of the body.
Mk 4:21 a **l** brought in to be put under the bushel basket,
Lk 8:16 "No one after lighting a **l** hides it under a jar,
11:33 "No one after lighting a **l** puts it in a cellar,
11:34 Your eye is the **l** of your body.
11:36 of light as when a **l** gives you light with its rays."
15: 8 if she loses one of them, does not light a **l**,
Jn 5:35 He was a burning and shining **l**,
2Pe 1:19 to be attentive to this as to a **l** shining in
Rev 18:23 and the light of a **l** will shine in you no more;
21:23 glory of God is its light, and its **l** is the Lamb.
22: 5 they need no light of **l** or sun, for the Lord God
Tob 8:13 they sent the maid, lit a **l**, and opened the door;
Sir 26:17 Like the shining **l** on the holy lampstand,
2Es 12:42 and like a **l** in a dark place,
14:25 I will light in your heart the **l** of understanding,

LAMPS (39) [LAMP]

Ex 25: 6 oil for the **l**, spices for the anointing oil and for
25:37 You shall make the seven **l** for it;
25:37 and the **l** shall be set up so as to give light on
30: 7 when he dresses the **l** he shall offer it,
30: 8 and when Aaron sets up the **l** in the evening,
35:14 with its utensils and its **l**, and the oil for the light;
37:23 He made its seven **l** and its snuffers and its trays
39:37 with its **l** set on it and all its utensils, and the oil
40: 4 you shall bring in the lampstand, and set up its **l**.
40:25 and set up the **l** before the LORD;
Lev 24: 4 up the **l** on the lampstand of pure gold before
Nu 4: 9 and cover the lampstand for the light, with its **l**,
8: 2 When you set up the **l**,
8: 2 seven **l** shall give light in front of the lampstand.
8: 3 up its **l** to give light in front of the lampstand,
1Ki 7:49 the flowers, the **l**, and the tongs, of gold;
1Ch 28:15 the weight of the golden lampstands and their **l**,
28:15 the weight of gold for each lampstand and its **l**,
28:15 the weight of silver for a lampstand and its **l**,
2Ch 4:20 the lampstands and their **l** of pure gold to burn
4:21 the flowers, the **l**, and the tongs, of purest gold;
13:11 so that its **l** may burn every evening;
29: 7 the doors of the vestibule and put out the **l**,
Zep 1:12 At that time I will search Jerusalem with **l**,
Zec 4: 2 there are seven **l** on it, with seven lips on each of
the **l** that are on the top
Mt 25: 1 Ten bridesmaids took their **l** and went to meet
25: 3 foolish took their **l**, they took no oil with them;
25: 4 but the wise took flasks of oil with their **l**.
25: 7 all those bridesmaids got up and trimmed their **l**.
25: 8 for our **l** are going out.'
Lk 12:35 "Be dressed for action and have your **l** lit;
Ac 20: 8 There were many **l** in the room upstairs
Jdt 10:22 with silver **l** carried before him.
LtJ 6:19 They light more **l** for them than they light
1Mc 4:50 on the altar and lit the **l** on the lampstand,
2Mc 1: 8 and we lit the **l** and set out the loaves.
10: 3 and they offered incense and lighted **l** and set out
2Es 10: 2 So all of us put out our **l**,

LAMPSTAND (44) [LAMP]

Ex 25:31 You shall make a **l** of pure gold. The base and the
shaft of the **l** shall be made
25:32 three branches of the **l** out of one side of it and
three branches of the **l** out of the other
25:33 so for the six branches going out of the **l**.
25:34 On the **l** itself there shall be four cups shaped
25:35 so for the six branches that go out of the **l**.
26:35 the **l** on the south side of the tabernacle opposite
30:27 and the **l** and its utensils, and the altar of incense,
31: 8 and the pure **l** with all its utensils,
35:14 the **l** also for the light, with its utensils
37:17 He also made the **l** of pure gold.
37:17 the shaft of the **l** were made of hammered work;
37:18 three branches of the **l** out of one side of it and
three branches of the **l** out of the other
37:19 so for the six branches going out of the **l**.
37:20 On the **l** itself there were four cups shaped
39:37 the pure **l** with its lamps set on it
40: 4 and you shall bring in the **l**, and set up its lamps.
40:24 He put the **l** in the tent of meeting,
Lev 24: 4 the **l** of pure gold before the LORD regularly.
Nu 3:31 the table, the **l**, the altars,
4: 9 and cover the **l** for the light, with its lamps,
8: 2 the seven lamps shall give light in front of the **l**.
8: 3 he set up its lamps to give light in front of the **l**,
8: 4 Now this was how the **l** was made,
8: 4 the LORD had shown Moses, so he made the **l**.
1Ch 28:15 the weight of gold for each **l** and its lamps,

1Ch 28:15 the weight of silver for a l and its lamps,
2Ch 13:11 and care for the golden l so
Da 5: 5 of the wall of the royal palace, next to the l.
Zec 4: 2 And I said, "I see a l all of gold,
4:11 on the right and the left of the l?"
Mt 5:15 but on the l, and it gives light to all in the house.
Mk 4:21 or under the bed, and not on the l?
Lk 8:16 or puts it under a bed, but puts it on a l,
11:33 on the l so that those who enter may see the light.
Heb 9: 2 the first one, in which were the l, the table,
Rev 2: 5 to you and remove your l from its place,
Sir 26:17 Like the shining lamp on the holy l,
1Mc 1:21 the l for the light, and all its utensils.
4:49 They made new holy vessels, and brought the l,
4:50 on the altar and lit the lamps on the l,
2Es 10:22 the light of our l has been put out,

LAMPSTANDS (11) [LAMP]

1Ki 7:49 the l of pure gold, five on the south side and five
1Ch 28:15 the weight of the golden l and their lamps,
2Ch 4: 7 He made ten golden l as prescribed,
4:20 the l and their lamps of pure gold to burn before
Jer 52:19 the firepans, the basins, the pots, the l, the ladles,
Rev 1:12 and on turning I saw seven golden l,
1:13 the midst of the l I saw one like the Son of Man,
1:20 in my right hand, and the seven golden l:
1:20 and the seven l are the seven churches.
2: 1 who walks among the seven golden l:
11: 4 the two olive trees and the two l that stand before

LANCES (3)

1Ki 18:28 with swords and l until the blood gushed out
Jer 46: 4 whet your l, put on your coats of mail!
2Mc 5: 2 in companies fully armed with l

LANCETS (KJV) See LANCES

LAND‡ (1961) [BORDERLANDS, COASTLAND, COASTLANDS, HIGHLANDS, HOMELAND, LAND'S, LANDED, LANDHOLDING, LANDING, LANDINGS, LANDMARK, LANDMARKS, LANDOWNER, LANDS, LOWLAND, MAINLAND, TABLELAND, WASTELAND]

A. LAND OF EGYPT (233)
B. LAND OF CANAAN (67)
C. ALL THE LAND (53)
D. PEOPLE OF THE LAND (52)
E. LAND OF JUDAH (46)
F. WHOLE LAND (38)
G. LAND OF ISRAEL (35)
H. LAND FLOWING WITH MILK AND HONEY (20)
I. LIVE IN THE LAND (19)
J. GOOD LAND (17)
K. LAND OF GILEAD (17)
L. LAND OF THE LIVING (15)
M. PEOPLES OF THE LAND (15)
N. POSSESS[ED] THE LAND (12)

Ge 1: 9 and let the dry l appear."
1:10 God called the dry l Earth,
2:11 the one that flows around the whole l of Havilah, F
2:12 and the gold of that l is good;
2:13 the one that flows around the whole l of Cush. F
4:16 and settled in the l of Nod, east of Eden.
7:22 everything on dry l in whose nostrils was
10:10 Erech, and Accad, all of them in the l of Shinar.
10:11 From that l he went into Assyria,
11: 2 upon a plain in the l of Shinar and settled there.
11:28 before his father Terah in the l of his birth,
11:31 of the Chaldeans to go into the l of Canaan; B
12: 1 and your kindred and your father's house to the l
12: 5 and they set forth to go to the l of Canaan. B
12: 5 When they had come to the l of Canaan, B
12: 6 Abram passed through the l to the place
12: 6 At that time the Canaanites were in the l.
12: 7 and said, "To your offspring I will give this l."
12:10 Now there was a famine in the l.
12:10 for the famine was severe in the l.
13: 6 l could not support both of them living together;
13: 7 the Canaanites and the Perizzites lived in the l.
13: 9 Is not the whole l before you? F
13:10 like the l of Egypt, in the direction of Zoar; A
13:12 Abram settled in the l of Canaan, B
13:15 for all the l that you see I will give to you and C
13:17 walk through the length and the breadth of the l,
15: 7 to give you this l to possess."
15:13 in a l that is not theirs, and shall be slaves there,
15:18 saying, "To your descendants I give this l,
15:19 the l of the Kenites, the Kenizzites,
16: 3 Abram had lived ten years in the l of Canaan, B
17: 8 the l where you are now an alien,
17: 8 all the l of Canaan, for a perpetual holding; BC
19:28 toward all the l of the Plain and saw the smoke C
19:28 of the Plain and saw the smoke of the l going up
20:15 Abimelech said, "My l is before you;
21:21 got a wife for him from the l of Egypt. A
21:23 with me and with the l where you have resided
21:32 left and returned to the l of the Philistines.
21:34 as an alien many days in the l of the Philistines.
22: 2 whom you love, and go to the l of Moriah,
23: 2 Hebron) in the l of Canaan; B

Ge 23: 7 and bowed to the Hittites, the people of the l. D
23:12 Abraham bowed down before the people of the l. D
23:13 to Ephron in the hearing of the people of the l, D
23:15 piece of l worth four hundred shekels of silver—
23:19 Mamre (that is, Hebron) in the l of Canaan. B
24: 5 not be willing to follow me to this l;
24: 5 must I then take your son back to the l
24: 7 from my father's house and from the l
24: 7 'To your offspring I will give this l,'
24:37 the daughters of the Canaanites, in whose l I live;
26: 1 Now there was a famine in the l,
26: 2 settle in the l that I shall show you.
26: 3 Reside in this l as an alien,
26:12 Isaac sowed seed in that l,
26:22 and we shall be fruitful in the l."
27:46 one of the women of the l,
28: 4 that you may take possession of the l where you
28: 4 l that God gave to Abraham."
28:13 the l on which you lie I will give to you and
28:15 and will bring you back to this l;
29: 1 and came to the l of the people of the east.
31: 3 to the l of your ancestors and to your kindred,
31:13 Now leave this l at once and return to the l of your
31:18 to go to his father Isaac in the l of Canaan. B
32: 3 before him to his brother Esau in the l of Seir,
33:18 which is in the l of Canaan, B
33:19 the plot of l on which he had pitched his tent.
34:10 and the l shall be open to you;
34:21 let them live in the l and trade in it, I
34:21 for the l is large enough for them;
34:30 by making me odious to the inhabitants of the l,
35: 6 Bethel), which is in the l of Canaan, B
35:12 The l that I gave to Abraham
35:12 and I will give the l to your offspring after you."
35:22 While Israel lived in that l,
36: 5 of Esau who were born to him in the l of Canaan. B
36: 6 the property he had acquired in the l of Canaan; B
36: 6 to a l some distance from his brother Jacob.
36: 7 the l where they were staying could
36:16 these are the clans of Eliphaz in the l of Edom;
36:17 these are the clans of Reuel in the l of Edom;
36:20 of Seir the Horite, the inhabitants of the l:
36:21 the sons of Seir in the l of Edom.
36:30 clan by clan in the l of Seir.
36:31 These are the kings who reigned in the l
36:34 of the l of the Temanites succeeded him as king.
36:43 of Edom), according to their settlements in the l
37: 1 Jacob settled in the l where his father had lived
37: 1 father had lived as an alien, the l of Canaan. B
40:15 in fact I was stolen out of the l of the Hebrews;
41:19 had I seen such ugly ones in all the l of Egypt. AC
41:29 of great plenty throughout all the l of Egypt. AC
41:30 all the plenty will be forgotten in the l of Egypt; A
41:30 the famine will consume the l.
41:31 in the l because of the famine that will follow,
41:33 and set him over the l of Egypt. A
41:34 to appoint overseers over the l,
41:34 the l of Egypt during the seven plenteous years. A
41:36 the l against the seven years of famine that are
41:36 years of famine that are to befall the l of Egypt, A
41:36 so that the l may not perish through the famine."
41:41 "See, I have set you over all the l of Egypt." AC
41:43 Thus he set him over all the l of Egypt. AC
41:44 up hand or foot in all the l of Egypt." AC
41:45 Joseph gained authority over the l of Egypt. A
41:46 and went through all the l of Egypt. AC
41:48 in the l of Egypt, and stored up food in the cities; A
41:52 "For God has made me fruitful in the l
41:53 plenty that prevailed in the l of Egypt came to A
41:54 but throughout the l of Egypt there was bread. A
41:55 When all the l of Egypt was famished, AC
41:56 And since the famine had spread over all the l, C
41:56 for the famine was severe in the l of Egypt. A
42: 5 for the famine had reached the l of Canaan. B
42: 6 Now Joseph was governor over the l;
42: 6 it was he who sold to all the people of the l. D
42: 7 They said, "From the l of Canaan, to buy food." B
42: 9 you have come to see the nakedness of the l!"
42:12 you have come to see the nakedness of the l!"
42:13 the sons of a certain man in the l of Canaan; B
42:29 came to their father Jacob in the l of Canaan, B
42:30 the lord of the l, spoke harshly to us,
42:30 and charged us with spying on the l.
42:32 is now with our father in the l of Canaan.' B
42:33 Then the man, the lord of the l, said to us,
42:34 and you may trade in the l.' "
43: 1 Now the famine was severe in the l.
43:11 of the l in your bags, and carry them down as
44: 8 we brought back to you from the l of Canaan; B
45: 6 For the famine has been in the l these two years;
45: 8 all his house and ruler over all the l of Egypt. AC
45:10 You shall settle in the l of Goshen,
45:17 your animals and go back to the l of Canaan. B
45:18 so that I may give you the best of the l of Egypt, A
45:18 and you may enjoy the fat of the l.'
45:19 from the l of Egypt for your little ones and A
45:20 for the best of all the l of Egypt is yours.' " AC
45:25 came to their father Jacob in the l of Canaan. B
45:26 He is even ruler over all the l of Egypt." AC
46: 6 goods that they had acquired in the l of Canaan, B
46:12 (but Er and Onan died in the l of Canaan); B
46:20 in the l of Egypt were born Manasseh and A
46:28 When they came to the l of Goshen,
46:31 who were in the l of Canaan, have come to me. B
46:34 in order that you may settle in the l of Goshen,
47: 1 have come from the l of Canaan; B
47: 1 they are now in the l of Goshen."

Ge 47: 4 "We have come to reside as aliens in the l;
47: 4 because the famine is severe in the l of Canaan. B
47: 4 let your servants settle in the l of Goshen."
47: 6 The l of Egypt is before you; A
47: 6 and your brothers in the best part of the l;
47: 6 let them live in the l of Goshen; I
47:11 and granted them a holding in the l of Egypt, A
47:11 in the best part of the l, in the l of Rameses,
47:13 Now there was no food in all the l, C
47:13 The l of Egypt and the land of Canaan A
47:13 l of Canaan languished because of the famine. B
47:14 the money to be found in the l of Egypt and in A
47:14 in the l of Canaan, in exchange for the grain B
47:15 the money from the l of Egypt and from the A
47:15 from the land of Egypt and from the l of Canaan B
47:19 before your eyes, both we and our l?
47:19 Buy us and our l in exchange for food.
47:19 We with our l will become slaves to Pharaoh;
47:19 and that the l may not become desolate."
47:20 Joseph bought all the l of Egypt for Pharaoh. AC
47:20 and the l became Pharaoh's.
47:22 Only the l of the priests he did not buy;
47:22 therefore they did not sell their l.
47:23 "Now that I have this day bought you and your l
47:23 here is seed for you; sow the l.
47:26 made it a statute concerning the l of Egypt, A
47:26 l of the priests alone did not become Pharaoh's.
47:27 Thus Israel settled in the l of Egypt, A
47:28 Jacob lived in the l of Egypt seventeen years; A
48: 3 appeared to me at Luz in the l of Canaan, B
48: 4 and will give this l to your offspring after you for
48: 5 the l of Egypt before I came to you in Egypt, A
48: 7 Rachel, alas, died in the l of Canaan on the way, B
48:21 be with you and will bring you again to the l
49:15 and that the l was pleasant;
49:30 near Mamre, in the l of Canaan, B
50: 5 that I hewed out for myself in the l of Canaan, B
50: 7 and all the elders of the l of Egypt, A
50: 8 and their herds were left in the l of Goshen.
50:11 of the l saw the mourning on the threshing floor
50:13 to the l of Canaan and buried him in the cave B
50:24 and bring you up out of this l to the l that he swore
Ex 1: 7 so that the l was filled with them.
1:10 and fight against us and escape from the l."
2:15 He settled in the l of Midian,
2:22 "I have been an alien residing in a foreign l."
3: 8 bring them up out of that l to a good and broad l,
3: 8 a l flowing with milk and honey, H
3:17 to the l of the Canaanites, the Hittites,
3:17 a l flowing with milk and honey.' H
4:20 on a donkey and went back to the l of Egypt; A
5: 5 people of the l and yet you want them to stop D
5:12 the people scattered throughout the l of Egypt, A
6: 1 by a mighty hand he will drive them out of his l."
6: 4 to give them the l of Canaan, B
6: 4 the l in which they resided as aliens.
6: 8 into the l that I swore to give to Abraham, Isaac,
6:11 of Egypt to let the Israelites go out of his l."
6:13 to free the Israelites from the l of Egypt. A
6:26 "Bring the Israelites out of the l of Egypt, A
6:28 when the LORD spoke to Moses in the l of Egypt, A
7: 2 to let the Israelites go out of his l.
7: 3 multiply my signs and wonders in the l of Egypt. A
7: 4 out of the l of Egypt by great acts of judgment. A
7:19 be blood throughout the whole l of Egypt, AF
7:21 was blood throughout the whole l of Egypt. AF
8: 5 and make frogs come up on the l of Egypt.' " A
8: 6 the frogs came up and covered the l of Egypt. A
8: 7 and brought frogs up on the l of Egypt. A
8:14 in heaps, and the l stank.
8:16 become gnats throughout the whole l of Egypt. AF
8:17 into gnats throughout the whole l of Egypt. AF
8:21 so also the l where they live.
8:22 But on that day I will set apart the l of Goshen,
8:22 you may know that I the LORD am in this l.
8:24 of Egypt the l was ruined because of the flies.
8:25 and said, "Go, sacrifice to your God within the l."
9: 5 the LORD will do this thing in the l."
9: 9 It shall become fine dust all over the l of Egypt, A
9: 9 and animals throughout the whole l of Egypt." AF
9:22 so that hail may fall on the whole l of Egypt, AF
9:22 and all the plants of the field in the l of Egypt." A
9:23 And the LORD rained hail on the l of Egypt; A
9:24 hail as had never fallen in all the l of Egypt AC
9:25 in the open field throughout all the l of Egypt, AC
9:26 Only in the l of Goshen,
10: 5 They shall cover the surface of the l,
10: 5 so that no one will be able to see the l.
10:12 "Stretch out your hand over the l of Egypt, A
10:12 upon it and eat every plant in the l,
10:13 Moses stretched out his staff over the l of Egypt, A
10:13 the LORD brought an east wind upon the l all
10:14 The locusts came upon all the l of Egypt and AC
10:15 They covered the surface of the whole l, F
10:15 so that the l was black;
10:15 the plants in the l and all the fruit of the trees that
10:15 no plant in the field, in all the l of Egypt. AC
10:21 that there may be darkness over the l of Egypt, A
10:22 there was dense darkness in all the l of Egypt AC
11: 3 a man of great importance in the l of Egypt, A
11: 5 Every firstborn in the l of Egypt shall die, A
11: 6 be a loud cry throughout the whole l of Egypt, AF
11: 9 wonders may be multiplied in the l of Egypt." A
11:10 he did not let the people of Israel go out of his l.
12: 1 LORD said to Moses and Aaron in the l of Egypt: A
12:12 For I will pass through the l of Egypt that night, A
12:12 the l of Egypt, both human beings and animals; A

Ex 12:13 when I strike the **l** of Egypt. A
12:17 I brought your companies out of the **l** of Egypt: A
12:19 whether an alien or a native of the **l.**
12:25 you come to the **l** that the LORD will give you,
12:29 struck down all the firstborn in the **l** of Egypt, A
12:33 the people to hasten their departure from the **l,**
12:41 of the LORD went out from the **l** of Egypt. A
12:42 to bring them out of the **l** of Egypt. A
12:48 he shall be regarded as a native of the **l.**
12:51 LORD brought the Israelites out of the **l** of Egypt, A
13: 5 LORD brings you into the **l** of the Canaanites,
13: 5 a **l** flowing with milk and honey, H
13:11 "When the LORD has brought you into the **l** of
13:15 LORD killed all the firstborn in the **l** of Egypt, A
13:17 the **l** of the Philistines, although that was nearer;
13:18 up out of the **l** of Egypt prepared for battle. A
14: 3 'They are wandering aimlessly in the **l;**
14:21 and turned the sea into dry **l;**
16: 1 after they had departed from the **l** of Egypt. A
16: 3 of the LORD in the **l** of Egypt, when we sat by A
16: 6 the LORD who brought you out of the **l** of Egypt, A
16:32 when I brought you out of the **l** of Egypt.' " A
16:35 until they came to a habitable **l;**
16:35 until they came to the border of the **l** of Canaan. B
18: 3 "I have been an alien in a foreign **l**"),
19: 1 the Israelites had gone out of the **l** of Egypt, A
20: 2 who brought you out of the **l** of Egypt, A
20:12 in the **l** that the LORD your God is giving you.
22:21 for you were aliens in the **l** of Egypt. A
23: 9 for you were aliens in the **l** of Egypt. A
23:10 For six years you shall sow your **l** and gather
23:26 No one shall miscarry or be barren in your **l;**
23:29 or the **l** would become desolate and
23:30 until you have increased and possess the **l.** N
23:31 I will hand over to you the inhabitants of the **l,**
23:33 They shall not live in your **l,**
29:46 of the **l** of Egypt that I might dwell among them; A
32: 1 the man who brought us up out of the **l** of Egypt, A
32: 4 who brought you up out of the **l** of Egypt!" A
32: 7 whom you brought up out of the **l** of Egypt, A
32: 8 who brought you up out of the **l** of Egypt!' " A
32:11 out of the **l** of Egypt with great power and A
32:13 and all this **l** that I have promised I will give
32:23 the man who brought us up out of the **l** of Egypt, A
33: 1 up out of the **l** of Egypt, A
33: 1 and go to the **l** of which I swore to Abraham,
33: 3 Go up to a **l** flowing with milk and honey; H
34:12 to make a covenant with the inhabitants of the **l**
34:15 not make a covenant with the inhabitants of the **l,**
34:24 no one shall covet your **l** when you go up
Lev 11: 2 From among all the **l** animals,
11:30 the **l** crocodile, the lizard, the sand lizard,
11:45 LORD who brought you up from the **l** of Egypt, A
11:46 This is the law pertaining to **l** animal and bird
14:34 When you come into the **l** of Canaan, B
14:34 and I put a leprous disease in a house in the **l**
18: 3 You shall not do as they do in the **l** of Egypt, A
18: 3 you shall not do as they do in the **l** of Canaan, B
18:25 Thus the **l** became defiled;
18:25 and the **l** vomited out its inhabitants.
18:27 of the **l,** who were before you, committed all
18:27 and the **l** became defiled);
18:28 otherwise the **l** will vomit you out for defiling it,
19: 9 When you reap the harvest of your **l,**
19:23 into the **l** and plant all kinds of trees for food,
19:29 **l** not become prostituted and full of depravity.
19:33 When an alien resides with you in your **l,**
19:34 for you were aliens in the **l** of Egypt: A
19:36 who brought you out of the **l** of Egypt. A
20: 2 the people of the **l** shall stone them to death. D
20: 4 if the people of the **l** should ever close their eyes D
20:22 so that the **l** to which I bring you to settle in may
20:24 But I have said to you: You shall inherit their **l,**
20:24 a **l** flowing with milk and honey. H
22:24 such you shall not do within your **l,**
22:33 I who brought you out of the **l** of Egypt to A
23:10 When you enter the **l** that I am giving you
23:22 When you reap the harvest of your **l,**
23:39 when you have gathered in the produce of the **l,**
23:43 when I brought them out of the **l** of Egypt: A
25: 2 When you enter the **l** that I am giving you,
25: 2 the **l** shall observe a sabbath for the LORD.
25: 4 a sabbath of complete rest for the **l,** a sabbath for
25: 5 it shall be a year of complete rest for the **l.**
25: 6 the **l** yields during its sabbath—
25: 7 for the wild animals in your **l** all its yield shall be
25: 9 the trumpet sounded throughout all your **l.**
25:10 and you shall proclaim liberty throughout the **l**
25:18 so that you may live on the **l** securely.
25:19 The **l** will yield its fruit,
25:23 The **l** shall not be sold in perpetuity, for the **l** is mine;
25:24 Throughout the **l** that you hold, you shall provide for the redemption of the **l.**
25:34 the open **l** around their cities may not be sold;
25:38 who brought you out of the **l** of Egypt, A
25:38 to give you the **l** of Canaan, to be your God. B
25:42 whom I brought out of the **l** of Egypt; A
25:45 who have been born in your **l;**
25:55 whom I brought out from the **l** of Egypt: A
26: 1 and you shall not place figured stones in your **l,**
26: 4 and the **l** shall yield its produce,
26: 5 and live securely in your **l.**
26: 6 And I will grant peace in the **l,**
26: 6 I will remove dangerous animals from the **l,**
26: 6 and no sword shall go through your **l.**
26:13 of the **l** of Egypt, to be their slaves no more; A

Lev 26:20 your **l** shall not yield its produce,
26:20 and the trees of the **l** shall not yield their fruit.
26:32 the **l,** so that your enemies who come to settle
26:33 your **l** shall be a desolation,
26:34 Then the **l** shall enjoy its sabbath years as long
26:34 while you are in the **l** of your enemies;
26:34 then the **l** shall rest, and enjoy its sabbath years.
26:38 and the **l** of your enemies shall devour you.
26:39 the **l** of your enemies because of their iniquities;
26:41 and brought them into the **l** of their enemies;
26:42 and I will remember the **l.**
26:43 For the **l** shall be deserted by them,
26:44 all that, when they are in the **l** of their enemies,
26:45 ancestors whom I brought out of the **l** of Egypt A
27:24 from whom it was bought, whose holding the **l** is.
27:30 from the **l,** whether the seed from the ground or
Nu 1: 1 after they had come out of the **l** of Egypt, A
3:13 when I killed all the firstborn in the **l** of Egypt, A
8:17 firstborn in the **l** of Egypt I consecrated them A
9: 1 after they had come out of the **l** of Egypt, A
10: 9 When you go to war in your **l** against
10:30 I will go back to my own **l** and to my kindred."
11:12 to the **l** that you promised on oath
13: 2 to spy out the **l** of Canaan, which I am giving B
13:16 of the men whom Moses sent to spy out the **l.**
13:17 Moses sent them to spy out the **l** of Canaan, B
13:18 and see what the **l** is like,
13:19 and whether the **l** they live in is good or bad,
13:20 and whether the **l** is rich or poor,
13:20 Be bold, and bring some of the fruit of the **l.**"
13:21 up and spied out the **l** from the wilderness of Zin
13:25 of forty days they returned from spying out the **l.**
13:26 and showed them the fruit of the **l.**
13:27 "We came to the **l** to which you sent us;
13:28 Yet the people who live in the **l** are strong, I
13:29 The Amalekites live in the **l** of the Negeb; I
13:32 of the **l** that they had spied out, saying, "The land
13:32 "The **l** that we have gone through as spies is
13:32 as spies is a **l** that devours its inhabitants;
14: 2 "Would that we had died in the **l** of Egypt! A
14: 3 Why is the LORD bringing us into this **l** to fall
14: 6 who were among those who had spied out the **l,**
14: 7 "The **l** that we went through as spies is
14: 7 through as spies is an exceedingly good **l.** J
14: 8 he will bring us into this **l** and give it to us,
14: 8 a **l** that flows with milk and honey.
14: 9 and do not fear the people of the **l,** D
14:14 and they will tell the inhabitants of this **l.**
14:16 not able to bring this people into the **l** he swore
14:23 the **l** that I swore to give to their ancestors;
14:24 I will bring into the **l** into which he went,
14:30 of you shall come into the **l** in which I swore
14:31 and they shall know the **l** that you have despised.
14:34 of the days in which you spied out the **l,**
14:36 And the men whom Moses sent to spy out the **l,**
14:36 against him by bringing a bad report about the **l**—
14:37 about the **l** died by a plague before the LORD.
14:38 of those men who went to spy out the **l.**
15: 2 When you come into the **l** you are to inhabit,
15:18 you come into the **l** to which I am bringing you,
15:19 whenever you eat of the bread of the **l,**
15:41 who brought you out of the **l** of Egypt, A
16:13 of a **l** flowing with milk and honey to kill us H
16:14 into a **l** flowing with milk and honey, H
18:13 The first fruits of all that is in their **l,**
18:20 You shall have no allotment in their **l,**
20:12 into the **l** that I have given them."
20:17 Now let us pass through your **l.**
20:23 on the border of the **l** of Edom,
20:24 not enter the **l** that I have given to the Israelites,
21: 4 to go around the **l** of Edom;
21:22 "Let me pass through your **l;**
21:24 of his **l** from the Arnon to the Jabbok, as far as to
21:26 the former king of Moab and captured all his **l**
21:31 Thus Israel settled in the **l** of the Amorites.
21:34 with all his people, and all his **l.**
21:35 and they took possession of his **l.**
22: 5 which is on the Euphrates, in the **l** of Amaw,
22: 6 to defeat them and drive them from the **l;**
22:13 to the officials of Balak, "Go to your own **l,** for
26: 4 Israelites, who came out of the **l** of Egypt, were: A
26:19 Er and Onan died in the **l** of Canaan. B
26:53 the **l** shall be apportioned for inheritance
26:55 But the **l** shall be apportioned by lot;
27:12 and see the **l** that I have given to the Israelites.
32: 1 When they saw that the **l** of Jazer and the land
32: 1 and the **l** of Gilead was a good place for cattle, K
32: 4 the **l** that the LORD subdued before
32: 4 is a **l** for cattle; and your servants have cattle."
32: 5 let this **l** be given to your servants for
32: 7 over into the **l** that the LORD has given them?
32: 8 I sent them from Kadesh-barnea to see the **l.**
32: 9 they went up to the Wadi Eshcol and saw the **l,**
32: 9 the hearts of the Israelites from going into the **l**
32:11 shall see the **l** that I swore to give to Abraham,
32:17 because of the inhabitants of the **l.**
32:22 and the **l** is subdued before the LORD—
32:22 this **l** shall be your possession before the LORD.
32:29 with you and the **l** shall be subdued before you,
32:29 then you shall give them the **l** of Gilead for K
32:30 have possessions among you in the **l** of Canaan. B
32:32 armed before the LORD into the **l** of Canaan, B
32:33 and the kingdom of King Og of Bashan, the **l**
33: 1 which the Israelites went out of the **l** of Egypt A
33:37 on the edge of the **l** of Edom.
33:38 the Israelites had come out of the **l** of Egypt, A
33:40 who lived in the Negeb in the **l** of Canaan, B

Nu 33:51 you cross over the Jordan into the **l** of Canaan, B
33:52 you shall drive out all the inhabitants of the **l**
33:53 You shall take possession of the **l** and settle in it,
33:53 for I have given you the **l** to possess.
33:54 You shall apportion the **l** by lot according
33:55 if you do not drive out the inhabitants of the **l**
33:55 in the **l** where you are settling.
34: 2 When you enter the **l** of Canaan (this is the land B
34: 2 (this is the **l** that shall fall to you for an inheritance,
34: 2 the **l** of Canaan, defined by its boundaries), B
34:12 be your **l** with its boundaries all around.
34:13 This is the **l** that you shall inherit by lot,
34:17 the names of the men who shall apportion the **l**
34:18 of every tribe to apportion the **l** for inheritance.
34:29 inheritance for the Israelites in the **l** of Canaan. B
35: 5 this shall belong to them as pasture **l**
35:10 When you cross the Jordan into the **l** of Canaan, B
35:14 and three cities in the **l** of Canaan, B
35:32 to live in the **l** before the death of the high priest. I
35:33 You shall not pollute the **l** in which you live;
35:33 the **l,** and no expiation can be made for the **l,**
35:34 You shall not defile the **l** in which you live,
36: 2 "The LORD commanded my lord to give the **l**
Dt 1: 5 Beyond the Jordan in the **l** of Moab,
1: 7 the **l** of the Canaanites and the Lebanon,
1: 8 See, I have set the **l** before you;
1: 8 go in and take possession of the **l** that I swore
1:21 See, the LORD your God has given the **l** to you;
1:22 ahead of us to explore the **l** for us and bring back
1:25 a good **l** that the LORD our God is giving us." J
1:27 that he has brought us out of the **l** of Egypt, A
1:35 the good **l** that I swore to give to your ancestors, J
1:36 to him and to his descendants I will give the **l**
2: 5 even so much as a foot's length of their **l,**
2: 9 I will not give you any of its **l** as a possession,
2:12 the **l** that the LORD gave them as a possession.)
2:19 for I will not give the **l** of the Ammonites to you
2:20 (It also is usually reckoned as a **l** of Rephaim.
2:24 the Amorite of Heshbon, and his **l.**
2:27 through your **l,** I will travel only along the road;
2:29 into the **l** that the LORD our God is giving us."
2:31 I have begun to give Sihon and his **l** over to you.
2:31 Begin now to take possession of his **l.**"
2:37 however, on the **l** of the Ammonites,
3: 2 along with his people and his **l.**
3: 8 from the two kings of the Amorites the **l** beyond
3:12 for the **l** that we took possession of at that time,
3:13 all that portion of Bashan used to be called a **l**
3:18 LORD your God has given you this **l** to occupy,
3:20 the **l** that the LORD your God is giving them
3:25 Let me cross over to see the good **l** beyond J
3:28 and who shall secure their possession of the **l**
4: 1 that you may live to enter and occupy the **l** that
4: 5 in the **l** that you are about to enter and occupy.
4:14 to observe in the **l** that you are about to cross into
4:21 the Jordan and that I should not enter the good **l** J
4:22 to die in this **l** without crossing over the Jordan,
4:22 to cross over to take possession of that good **l.** J
4:25 and become complacent in the **l,**
4:26 the **l** that you are crossing the Jordan to occupy;
4:38 giving you their **l** for a possession,
4:40 in the **l** that the LORD your God is giving you
4:46 in the **l** of King Sihon of the Amorites,
4:47 They occupied his **l** and the **l** of King Og
5: 6 who brought you out of the **l** of Egypt, A
5:15 that you were a slave in the **l** of Egypt, A
5:16 be long and that it may go well with you in the **l**
5:31 in the **l** that I am giving them to possess."
5:33 you may live long in the **l** that you are to possess.
6: 1 to observe in the **l** that you are about to cross into
6: 3 greatly in a **l** flowing with milk and honey, H
6:10 the LORD your God has brought you into the **l**
6:10 a **l** with fine, large cities that you did not build,
6:12 who brought you out of the **l** of Egypt, A
6:18 so that you may go in and occupy the good **l** that J
6:23 the **l** that he promised on oath to our ancestors.
7: 1 When the LORD your God brings you into the **l**
7:13 and the issue of your flock, in the **l** that he swore
8: 1 in and occupy the **l** that the LORD promised
8: 7 LORD your God is bringing you into a good **l,** J
8: 7 a **l** with flowing streams,
8: 8 a **l** of wheat and barley,
8: 8 a **l** of olive trees and honey,
8: 9 a **l** where you may eat bread without scarcity,
8: 9 a **l** whose stones are iron and from whose hills
8:10 and bless the LORD your God for the good **l** J
8:14 who brought you out of the **l** of Egypt, A
9: 4 the LORD has brought me in to occupy this **l**";
9: 5 that you are going in to occupy their **l;**
9: 6 not giving you this good **l** to occupy because J
9: 7 from the day you came out of the **l** of Egypt A
9:23 "Go up and occupy the **l** that I have given you,"
9:28 the **l** from which you have brought us might say,
9:28 the LORD was not able to bring them into the **l**
10: 7 a **l** with flowing streams.
10:11 the **l** that I swore to their ancestors to give them."
10:19 for you were strangers in the **l** of Egypt. A
11: 3 the king of Egypt, and to all his **l;**
11: 8 to go in and occupy the **l** that you are crossing
11: 9 in the **l** that the LORD swore to your ancestors
11: 9 a **l** flowing with milk and honey. H
11:10 For the **l** that you are about to enter to occupy is
11:10 to enter to occupy is not like the **l** of Egypt, A
11:11 But the **l** that you are crossing over to occupy is a **l** of hills and valleys,
11:12 a **l** that the LORD your God looks after.
11:14 the rain for your **l** in its season, the early rain and

Dt 11:17 there will be no rain and the **l** will yield no fruit;
11:17 then you will perish quickly off the good **l** that J
11:21 in the **l** that the LORD swore to your ancestors
11:25 of you on all the **l** on which you set foot, C
11:29 the LORD your God has brought you into the **l**
11:30 in the **l** of the Canaanites who live in the Arabah,
11:31 the **l** that the LORD your God is giving you,
12: 1 that you must diligently observe in the **l** that
12:10 When you cross over the Jordan and live in the **l** I
12:19 the Levite as long as you live in your **l.**
12:29 you have dispossessed them and live in their **l,**
13: 5 the **l** of Egypt and redeemed you from the house A
13:10 who brought you out of the **l** of Egypt, A
15: 4 the **l** that the LORD your God is giving you as
15: 7 the **l** that the LORD your God is giving you,
15:11 to the poor and needy neighbor in your **l.**"
15:15 that you were a slave in the **l** of Egypt, A
16: 3 you came out of the **l** of Egypt in great haste, A
16: 3 the day of your departure from the **l** of Egypt. A
16:20 the **l** that the LORD your God is giving you.
17:14 the **l** that the LORD your God is giving you,
18: 9 the **l** that the LORD your God is giving you,
19: 1 the LORD your God has cut off the nations whose **l**
19: 2 in the **l** that the LORD your God is giving you
19: 3 the distances and divide into three regions the **l**
19: 8 all the **l** that he promised your ancestors C
19:10 an innocent person may not be shed in the **l** that
19:14 in the **l** that the LORD your God is giving you
20: 1 who brought you up from the **l** of Egypt. A
21: 1 in the **l** that the LORD your God is giving you
21:23 the **l** that the LORD your God is giving you
23: 7 because you were an alien residing in their **l.**
23:20 in the **l** that you are about to enter and possess.
24: 4 the LORD, and you shall not bring guilt on the **l**
24:14 or aliens who reside in your **l** in one
24:22 that you were a slave in the **l** of Egypt; A
25:15 in the **l** that the LORD your God is giving you.
25:19 the **l** that the LORD your God is giving you as
26: 1 into the **l** that the LORD your God is giving you
26: 2 the **l** that the LORD your God is giving you,
26: 3 that I have come into the **l** that the LORD swore
26: 9 he brought us into this place and gave us this **l,**
26: 9 a **l** flowing with milk and honey. H
26:15 a **l** flowing with milk and honey." H
27: 2 the day that you cross over the Jordan into the **l**
27: 3 the **l** that the LORD your God is giving you,
27: 3 a **l** flowing with milk and honey, as the LORD, H
28: 8 in the **l** that the LORD your God is giving you.
28:11 in the **l** that the LORD swore to your ancestors
28:12 to give the rain of your **l** in its season and
28:21 to you until it has consumed you off the **l**
28:24 The LORD will change the rain of your **l**
28:52 come down throughout your **l;**
28:52 the **l** that the LORD your God has given you.
28:63 be plucked off the **l** that you are entering
29: 1 to make with the Israelites in the **l** of Moab,
29: 2 LORD did before your eyes in the **l** of Egypt, A
29: 2 to Pharaoh and to all his servants and to all his **l,**
29: 8 We took their **l** and gave it as an inheritance to
29:16 You know how we lived in the **l** of Egypt, A
29:22 the devastation of that **l** and the afflictions
29:24 "Why has the LORD done thus to this **l?**
29:25 when he brought them out of the **l** of Egypt. A
29:27 anger of the LORD was kindled against that **l,**
29:28 The LORD uprooted them from their **l** in anger,
29:28 and cast them into another **l,** as is now the case."
30: 5 The LORD your God will bring you into the **l**
30:16 and the LORD your God will bless you in the **l**
30:18 in the **l** that you are crossing the Jordan to enter
30:20 that you may live in the **l** that the LORD swore I
31: 4 the kings of the Amorites, and to their **l,**
31: 7 the **l** that the LORD has sworn to their ancestors
31:13 as long as you live in the **l** that you are crossing I
31:16 the gods of the **l** into which they are going;
31:20 into the **l** flowing with milk and honey, H
31:21 into the **l** that I promised them on oath."
31:23 the Israelites into the **l** that I promised them;
32:10 He sustained him in a desert **l,**
32:13 He set him atop the heights of the **l,**
32:43 and cleanse the **l** for his people.
32:47 in the **l** that you are crossing over the Jordan
32:49 which is in the **l** of Moab, across from Jericho,
32:49 across from Jericho, and view the **l** of Canaan, B
32:52 Although you may view the **l** from a distance,
32:52 the **l** that I am giving to the Israelites."
33:13 Blessed by the LORD be his **l,**
33:28 in a **l** of grain and wine, where the heavens
34: 1 and the LORD showed him the whole **l:** F
34: 2 the **l** of Ephraim and Manasseh,
34: 2 all the **l** of Judah as far as the Western Sea, CE
34: 4 "This is the **l** of which I swore to Abraham,
34: 5 died there in the **l** of Moab,
34: 6 He was buried in a valley in the **l** of Moab,
34:11 the LORD sent him to perform in the **l** of Egypt, A
34:11 and all his servants and his entire **l,**
Jos 1: 2 into the **l** that I am giving to them,
1: 4 the river Euphrates, all the **l** of the Hittites, C
1: 6 the **l** that I swore to their ancestors to give them.
1:11 the Jordan, to go in to take possession of the **l**
1:13 and will give you this **l.**'
1:14 in the **l** that Moses gave you beyond the Jordan.
1:15 of the **l** that the LORD your God is giving them.
1:15 to your own **l** and take possession of it,
1:15 the **l** that Moses the servant of the LORD
2: 1 saying, "Go, view the **l,** especially Jericho."
2: 2 have come here tonight to search out the **l.**"
2: 3 they have come only to search out the whole **l.**" F

Jos 2: 9 "I know that the LORD has given you the **l,**
2: 9 the inhabitants of the **l** melt in fear before you.
2:14 with you when the LORD gives us the **l.**"
2:18 the **l** and you do not tie this crimson cord in
2:24 the LORD has given all the **l** into our hands; C
2:24 all the inhabitants of the **l** melt in fear before us."
5: 6 the **l** that he had sworn to their ancestors
5: 6 a **l** flowing with milk and honey. H
5:11 on that very day, they ate the produce of the **l,**
5:12 of the **l,** and the Israelites no longer had manna;
5:12 they ate the crops of the **l** of Canaan that year. B
6:22 to the two men who had spied out the **l,**
6:27 and his fame was in all the **l.** C
7: 2 and said to them, "Go up and spy out the **l.**"
7: 9 and all the inhabitants of the **l** will hear of it,
8: 1 the king of Ai with his people, his city, and his **l.**
9:24 his servant Moses to give you all the **l,** C
9:24 to destroy all the inhabitants of the **l** before you;
10:40 So Joshua defeated the whole **l,** F
10:42 Joshua took all these kings and their **l**
11: 3 and the Hivites under Hermon in the **l** of Mizpah.
11:16 So Joshua took all that **l:**
11:16 all the **l** of Goshen and the lowland and C
11:22 of the Anakim was left in the **l** of the Israelites;
11:23 So Joshua took the whole **l,** F
11:23 And the **l** had rest from war.
12: 1 Now these are the kings of the **l,**
12: 1 whose **l** they occupied beyond the Jordan toward
12: 6 and Moses the servant of the LORD gave their **l**
12: 7 the **l** whom Joshua and the Israelites defeated on
12: 7 toward Seir (and Joshua gave their **l** to the tribes
12: 8 and in the Negeb, the **l** of the Hittites, Amorites,
13: 1 very much of the **l** still remains to be possessed.
13: 2 This is the **l** that still remains:
13: 4 all the **l** of the Canaanites, C
13: 5 and the **l** of the Gebalites,
13: 6 only allot the **l** to Israel for an inheritance,
13: 7 Now therefore divide this **l** for an inheritance to
13:21 as princes of Sihon, who lived in the **l.**
13:25 and half the **l** of the Ammonites, to Aroer,
14: 1 that the Israelites received in the **l** of Canaan, B
14: 4 and no portion was given to the Levites in the **l,**
14: 5 as the LORD commanded Moses; they allotted the **l.**
14: 7 from Kadesh-barnea to spy out the **l;**
14: 9 the **l** on which your foot has trodden shall be
14:15 And the **l** had rest from war.
15:19 since you have set me in the **l** of the Negeb,
17: 5 besides the **l** of Gilead and Bashan, K
17: 6 The **l** of Gilead was allotted to the rest of K
17: 8 The **l** of Tappuah belonged to Manasseh,
17:10 The **l** to the south is Ephraim's and that to
17:12 but the Canaanites continued to live in that **l.**
17:15 and clear ground there for yourselves in the **l** of
18: 1 The **l** lay subdued before them.
18: 3 in and taking possession of the **l** that the LORD,
18: 4 that they may begin to go throughout the **l,**
18: 6 You shall describe the **l** in seven divisions
18: 8 the **l,** saying, "Go throughout the land and write
18: 8 the **l** and write a description of it, and come back
18: 9 the men went and traversed the **l** and set down in
18:10 there Joshua apportioned the **l** to the Israelites,
19:49 the several territories of the **l** as inheritances,
19:51 So they finished dividing the **l.**
21: 2 they said to them at Shiloh in the **l** of Canaan, B
21:43 to Israel all the **l** that he swore to their ancestors C
22: 4 to your tents in the **l** where your possession lies,
22: 7 beside their fellow Israelites in the **l** west of
22: 9 which is in the **l** of Canaan, B
22: 9 to go to the **l** of Gilead, K
22: 9 their own **l** of which they had taken possession
22:10 near the Jordan that lies in the **l** of Canaan, B
22:11 an altar at the frontier of the **l** of Canaan, B
22:13 the half-tribe of Manasseh, in the **l** of Gilead, K
22:15 the half-tribe of Manasseh, in the **l** of Gilead, K
22:19 But now, if your **l** is unclean,
22:19 the LORD's **l** where the LORD's tabernacle
22:32 Reubenites and the Gadites in the **l** of Gilead K
22:32 in the land of Gilead to the **l** of Canaan, B
22:33 of making war against them, to destroy the **l**
23: 5 and you shall possess their **l,**
23:13 in your eyes, until you perish from this good **l** J
23:15 until he has destroyed you from this good **l** that J
23:16 and you shall perish quickly from the good **l** J
24: 3 and led him through all the **l** of Canaan BC
24: 8 Then I brought you to the **l** of the Amorites,
24: 8 and you took possession of their **l,**
24:13 I gave you a **l** on which you had not labored,
24:15 of the Amorites in whose **l** you are living;
24:17 and our ancestors up from the **l** of Egypt, A
24:18 the Amorites who lived in the **l.**
Jdg 1: 2 I hereby give the **l** into his hand."
1:15 since you have set me in the **l** of the Negeb,
1:26 man went to the **l** of the Hittites and built a city,
1:27 but the Canaanites continued to live in that **l.**
1:32 among the Canaanites, the inhabitants of the **l;**
1:33 among the Canaanites, the inhabitants of the **l;**
2: 1 into the **l** that I had promised to your ancestors.
2: 2 a covenant with the inhabitants of this **l;**
2: 6 to take possession of the **l.**
2:12 who had brought them out of the **l** of Egypt; A
3:11 So the **l** had rest forty years.
3:30 And the **l** had rest eighty years.
5:31 And the **l** had rest forty years.
6: 4 against them and destroy the produce of the **l,**
6: 5 so they wasted the **l** as they came in.
6: 9 before you, and gave you their **l;**
6:10 to the gods of the Amorites, in whose **l** you live.'

Jdg 8:28 the **l** had rest forty years in the days of Gideon.
10: 4 which are in the **l** of Gilead, K
10: 8 the Israelites that were beyond the Jordan in the **l**
11: 3 from his brothers and lived in the **l** of Tob.
11: 5 of Gilead went to bring Jephthah from the **l**
11:12 that you have come to me to fight against my **l?**"
11:13 took away my **l** from the Arnon to the Jabbok
11:15 Israel did not take away the **l** of Moab or the **l** of
11:17 saying, 'Let us pass through your **l'**;
11:18 went around the **l** of Edom and the **l** of Moab,
11:18 arrived on the east side of the **l** of Moab,
11:19 'Let us pass through your **l** to our country.'
11:21 so Israel occupied all the **l** of the Amorites, C
12:12 and was buried at Aijalon in the **l** of Zebulun.
12:15 and was buried at Pirathon in the **l** of Ephraim,
18: 2 to spy out the **l** and to explore it;
18: 2 and they said to them, "Go, explore the **l.**"
18: 9 for we have seen the **l,** and it is very good.
18: 9 but enter in and possess the **l.** N
18:10 to an unsuspecting people. The **l** is broad—
18:14 five men who had gone to spy out the **l** (that is,
18:17 to spy out the **l** proceeded to enter and take
18:30 the tribe of the Danites until the time the **l** went
19:30 that the Israelites came up from the **l** of Egypt A
20: 1 including the **l** of Gilead, K
21:12 which is in the **l** of Canaan. B
21:21 and go to the **l** of Benjamin.
Ru 1: 1 there was a famine in the **l,**
1: 7 went on their way to go back to the **l** of Judah. E
2:11 and mother and your native **l** and came to
4: 3 of **l** that belonged to our kinsman Elimelech.
1Sa 6: 5 of your mice that ravage the **l,** and give glory to
6: 5 on you and your gods and your **l.**
6: 9 And watch; if it goes up on the way to its own **l,**
9: 4 and passed through the **l** of Shalishah,
9: 4 And they passed through the **l** of Shaalim,
9: 4 Then he passed through the **l** of Benjamin,
9: 5 When they came to the **l** of Zuph,
9:16 to you a man from the **l** of Benjamin,
12: 6 brought your ancestors up out of the **l** of Egypt. A
13: 3 And Saul blew the trumpet throughout all the **l,** C
13: 7 Some Hebrews crossed the Jordan to the **l** of Gad
13:17 one company turned toward Ophrah, to the **l**
13:19 to be found throughout all the **l** of Israel; CG
14:14 an area about half a furrow long in an acre of **l.**
14:29 Jonathan said, "My father has troubled the **l;**
21:11 "Is this not David the king of the **l?**
22: 5 leave, and go into the **l** of Judah." E
23:23 Then I will go with you; and if he is in the **l,**
23:27 for the Philistines have made a raid on the **l.**"
27: 1 for me than to escape to the **l** of the Philistines;
27: 8 on the way to Shur and on to the **l** of Egypt. A
27: 9 the **l,** leaving neither man nor woman alive,
28: 3 the mediums and the wizards from the **l.**
28: 9 the mediums and the wizards from the **l.**
29:11 to return to the **l** of the Philistines.
30:16 from the **l** of the Philistines and from the land
30:16 of the Philistines and from the **l** of Judah. E
31: 9 the **l** of the Philistines to carry the good news to
2Sa 3:12 saying, "To whom does the **l** belong?
5: 6 the inhabitants of the **l,** who said to David,
9: 7 to you all the **l** of your grandfather Saul, C
9:10 till the **l** for him, and shall bring in the produce,
10: 2 When David's envoys came into the **l** of
15: 4 "If only I were judge in the **l!**
17:26 and Absalom encamped in the **l** of Gilead. K
19: 9 now he has fled out of the **l** because of Absalom.
19:29 I have decided: you and Ziba shall divide the **l.**"
21:14 the bones of Saul and of his son Jonathan in the **l**
21:14 After that, God heeded supplications for the **l.**
23: 4 gleaming from the rain on the grassy **l.**
24: 6 and to Kadesh in the **l** of the Hittites;
24: 8 So when they had gone through all the **l,** C
24:13 of famine come to you on your **l?**
24:13 shall there be three days' pestilence in your **l?**
24:25 the LORD answered his supplication for the **l,**
1Ki 4:10 (to him belonged Socoh and all the **l** of Hepher); C
4:19 in the **l** of Gilead, the country of King Sihon of K
4:19 And there was one official in the **l** of Judah. E
4:21 over all the kingdoms from the Euphrates to the **l**
6: 1 after the Israelites came out of the **l** of Egypt, A
8: 9 when they came out of the **l** of Egypt. A
8:21 when he brought them out of the **l** of Egypt." A
8:34 and bring them again to the **l** that you gave
8:36 and grant rain on your **l,**
8:37 "If there is famine in the **l,** if there is plague,
8:40 the days that they live in the **l** that you gave I
8:41 comes from a distant **l** because of your name
8:46 so that they are carried away captive to the **l** of
8:47 in the **l** to which they have been taken captive,
8:47 and plead with you in the **l** of their captors,
8:48 if they repent with all their heart and soul in the **l**
8:48 and pray to you toward their **l,**
9: 7 then I will cut Israel off from the **l**
9: 8 'Why has the LORD done such a thing to this **l**
9: 9 brought their ancestors out of the **l** of Egypt, A
9:11 to Hiram twenty cities in the **l** of Galilee.
9:13 So they are called the **l** of Cabul to this day.
9:18 Baalath, Tamar in the wilderness, within the **l,**
9:19 in Lebanon, and in all the **l** of his dominion. C
9:21 their descendants who were still left in the **l,**
9:26 near Eloth on the shore of the Red Sea, in the **l**
10: 6 "The report was true that I heard in my own **l**
10:13 she returned to her own **l,** with her servants.
10:15 the kings of Arabia and the governors of the **l.**
11:18 an allowance of food, and gave him **l.**
12:28 who brought you up out of the **l** of Egypt." A

1Ki 14:15 of this good **l** that he gave to their ancestors, J
14:24 there were also male temple prostitutes in the **l**.
15:12 the male temple prostitutes out of the **l**,
15:20 and all Chinneroth, with all the **l** of Naphtali. C
17: 7 wadi dried up, because there was no rain in the **l**.
18: 5 through the **l** to all the springs of water and to all
18: 6 So they divided the **l** between them to pass
20: 7 the king of Israel called all the elders of the **l**,
22:46 the male temple prostitutes who were still in the **l**
2Ki 2:19 but the water is bad, and the **l** is unfruitful."
3:19 every good piece of **l** you shall ruin with stones."
3:25 on every good piece of **l** everyone threw a stone,
3:27 from him and returned to their own **l**.
4:38 there was a famine in the **l**.
5: 2 a young girl captive from the **l** of Israel, G
5: 4 what the girl from the **l** of Israel had said. G
6:23 no longer came raiding into the **l** of Israel. G
8: 1 and it will come on the **l** for seven years."
8: 2 and settled in the **l** of the Philistines seven years.
8: 3 the woman returned from the **l** of the Philistines,
8: 3 to appeal to the king for her house and her **l**.
8: 5 to the king for her house and her **l**.
8: 6 of the fields from the day that she left the **l**
10:33 all the **l** of Gilead, the Gadites, the Reubenites, CK
11: 3 while Athaliah reigned over the **l**.
11:14 and all the people of the **l** rejoicing and D
11:18 all the people of the **l** went to the house of Baal, D
11:19 the guards, and all the people of the **l**; D
11:20 So all the people of the **l** rejoiced; D
13:20 Moabites used to invade the **l** in the spring of
15: 5 governing the people of the **l**. D
15:19 King Pul of Assyria came against the **l**;
15:20 and did not stay there in the **l**.
15:29 Hazor, Gilead, and Galilee, all the **l** of Naphtali; C
16:15 with the burnt offering of all the people of the **l**, D
17: 5 Assyria invaded all the **l** and came to Samaria; C
17: 7 who had brought them up out of the **l** of Egypt A
17:23 So Israel was exiled from their own **l** to Assyria
17:26 not know the law of the god of the **l**;
17:26 they do not know the law of the god of the **l**."
17:27 and teach them the law of the god of the **l**."
17:36 out of the **l** of Egypt with great power and A
18:25 The LORD said to me, Go up against this **l**,
18:32 and take you away to a **l** like your own **l**, a **l** of
grain and wine, a **l** of bread and vineyards, a **l** of
olive oil and honey,
18:33 the nations ever delivered its **l** out of the hand of
19: 7 he shall hear a rumor and return to his own **l**;
19: 7 to fall by the sword in his own **l**.' "
19:37 and they escaped into the **l** of Ararat.
21: 8 the feet of Israel to wander any more out of the **l**
21:24 the people of the **l** killed all those who had D
21:24 people of the **l** made his son Josiah king in D
23:24 were seen in the **l** of Judah and in Jerusalem, E
23:30 The people of the **l** took Jehoahaz son of Josiah, D
23:33 Pharaoh Neco confined him at Riblah in the **l**
23:33 the **l** of one hundred talents of silver and a talent
23:35 the **l** in order to meet Pharaoh's demand
23:35 the silver and the gold from the people of the **l**, D
24: 7 king of Egypt did not come again out of his **l**,
24:14 except the poorest people of the **l**. D
24:15 his officials, and the elite of the **l**,
25: 3 that there was no food for the people of the **l**. D
25:12 guard left some of the poorest people of the **l** D
25:19 of the army who mustered the people of the **l**; D
25:19 the people of the **l** who were found in the city. D
25:21 down and put them to death at Riblah in the **l**
25:21 So Judah went into exile out of its **l**.
25:22 over the people who remained in the **l** of Judah, E
25:24 live in the **l**, serve the king of Babylon, I
1Ch 1:43 These are the kings who reigned in the **l** of Edom
1:45 Husham of the **l** of the Temanites succeeded him.
2:22 who had twenty-three towns in the **l** of Gilead. K
4:40 good pasture, and the **l** was very broad, quiet,
5: 9 their cattle had multiplied in the **l** of Gilead. K
5:11 of Gad lived beside them in the **l** of Bashan as far
5:23 of the half-tribe of Manasseh lived in the **l**;
5:25 to the gods of the peoples of the **l**, M
6:55 the **l** of Judah and its surrounding pasture lands, E
7:21 Now the people of Gath, who were born in the **l**,
10: 9 the **l** of the Philistines to carry the good news
11: 4 where the Jebusites were, the inhabitants of the **l**.
13: 2 to our kindred who remain in all the **l** of Israel, CG
16:18 "To you I will give the **l** of Canaan B
16:19 of little account, and strangers in the **l**,
19: 2 When David's servants came to Hanun in the **l** of
19: 3 to search and to overthrow and to spy out the **l**?"
21:12 of the sword of the LORD, pestilence on the **l**,
22: 2 the aliens who were residing in the **l** of Israel, G
22:18 For he has delivered the inhabitants of the **l**
22:18 **l** is subdued before the LORD and his people.
28: 8 that you may possess this good **l**, J
2Ch 2:17 the aliens who were residing in the **l** of Israel, G
6: 5 I brought my people out of the **l** of Egypt, A
6:25 the **l** that you gave to them and to their ancestors.
6:27 and send down rain upon your **l**,
6:28 "If there is famine in the **l**, if there is plague,
6:31 in your ways all the days that they live in the **l** I
6:32 from a distant **l** because of your great name,
6:36 they are carried away captive to a **l** far or near;
6:37 in the **l** to which they have been taken captive,
6:37 and plead with you in the **l** of their captivity,
6:38 if they repent with all their heart and soul in the **l**
6:38 toward their **l**, which you gave to their ancestors,
7:13 or command the locust to devour the **l**,
7:14 and will forgive their sin and heal their **l**.
7:20 up from the **l** that I have given you;

2Ch 7:21 'Why has the LORD done such a thing to this **l**
7:22 who brought them out of the **l** of Egypt, A
8: 6 in Lebanon, and in all the **l** of his dominion. C
8: 8 in the **l**, whom the people of Israel had
8:17 and Eloth on the shore of the sea, in the **l**
9: 5 "The report was true that I heard in my own **l**
9:11 the like of them before in the **l** of Judah. E
9:12 she returned to her own **l**, with her servants.
9:14 and the governors of the **l** brought gold and silver
9:26 over all the kings from the Euphrates to the **l** of
14: 1 In his days the **l** had rest for ten years.
14: 6 in Judah while the **l** had rest.
14: 7 the **l** is still ours because we have sought
15: 8 the abominable idols from all the **l** of Judah CE
17: 2 and set garrisons in the **l** of Judah, E
19: 3 for you destroyed the sacred poles out of the **l**,
19: 5 in the **l** in all the fortified cities of Judah,
20: 7 the inhabitants of this **l** before your people Israel,
20:10 invade when they came from the **l** of Egypt, A
22:12 while Athaliah reigned over the **l**.
23:13 and all of the people of the **l** rejoicing D
23:20 and all the people of the **l**, D
23:21 So all the people of the **l** rejoiced, D
26:21 governing the people of the **l**. D
30: 9 with their captors, and return to this **l**.
30:25 resident aliens who came out of the **l** of Israel, G
31:19 the fields of common **l** belonging to their towns,
32: 4 and the wadi that flowed through the **l**,
32:21 So he returned in disgrace to his own **l**.
32:31 about the sign that had been done in the **l**,
33: 8 from the **l** that I appointed for your ancestors,
33:25 the people of the **l** killed all those who had D
33:25 the people of the **l** made his son Josiah king D
34: 7 the incense altars throughout all the **l** of Israel. CG
34: 8 when he had purged the **l** and the house,
36: 1 The people of the **l** took Jehoahaz son of Josiah D
36: 3 on the **l** a tribute of one hundred talents of silver
36:21 until the **l** had made up for its sabbaths.
Ezr 4: 4 people of the **l** discouraged the people of Judah, D
6:21 the pollutions of the nations of the **l** to worship
9:11 'The **l** that you are entering to possess is
9:11 a **l** unclean with the pollutions of the peoples of
9:12 that you may be strong and eat the good of the **l**
10: 2 foreign women from the peoples of the **l**, M
10:11 separate yourselves from the peoples of the **l** M
Ne 4: 4 and give them over as plunder in a **l** of captivity.
5:14 appointed to be their governor in the **l** of Judah, E
5:16 to the work on this wall, and acquired no **l**;
9: 8 to give to his descendants the **l** of the Canaanite,
9:10 and all his servants and all the people of his **l**,
9:11 so that they passed through the sea on dry **l**,
9:15 in to possess the **l** that you swore to give them. N
9:22 of the **l** of King Sihon of Heshbon and the land
9:22 of King Sihon of Heshbon and the **l** of King Og
9:23 the **l** that you had told their ancestors to enter
9:24 So the descendants went in and possessed the **l**, N
9:24 you subdued before them the inhabitants of the **l**,
9:24 with their kings and the peoples of the **l**, M
9:25 And they captured fortress cities and a rich **l**,
9:35 in the large and rich **l** that you set before them,
9:36 slaves in the **l** that you gave to our ancestors
10:30 not give our daughters to the peoples of the **l** M
10:31 and if the peoples of the **l** bring in merchandise M
Est 10: 1 King Ahasuerus laid tribute on the **l** and on
Job 1: 1 a man in the **l** of Uz whose name was Job.
1:10 and his possessions have increased in the **l**.
10:21 to the **l** of gloom and deep darkness,
10:22 the **l** of gloom and chaos,
12:15 if he sends them out, they overwhelm the **l**.
15:19 to whom alone the **l** was given,
22: 8 powerful possess the **l**, and the favored live in it. N
24:18 their portion in the **l** is cursed;
28:13 and it is not found in the **l** of the living. L
30: 8 they have been whipped out of the **l**.
31:38 "If my **l** has cried out against me,
37:13 Whether for correction, or for his **l**, or for love,
38:26 to bring rain on a **l** where no one lives,
38:27 to satisfy the waste and desolate **l**,
39: 6 the salt **l** for its dwelling place?
42:15 In all the **l** there were no women so beautiful C
Ps 10:16 the nations shall perish from his **l**.
16: 3 As for the holy ones in the **l**, they are the noble,
25:13 and their children shall possess the **l**. N
27:13 the goodness of the LORD in the **l** of the living. L
35:20 against those who are quiet in the **l**.
37: 3 so you will live in the **l**, and enjoy security. I
37: 9 those who wait for the LORD shall inherit the **l**.
37:11 But the meek shall inherit the **l**,
37:22 those blessed by the LORD shall inherit the **l**,
37:29 righteous shall inherit the **l**, and live in it forever.
37:34 and he will exalt you to inherit the **l**;
41: 2 they are called happy in the **l**.
42: 6 therefore I remember you from the **l** of Jordan
44: 3 the **l**, nor did their own arm give them victory;
52: 5 he will uproot you from the **l** of the living. L
60: 2 You have caused the **l** to quake;
63: 1 as in a dry and weary **l** where there is no water.
66: 6 He turned the sea into dry **l**;
68: 6 but the rebellious live in a parched **l**.
72:16 May there be abundance of grain in the **l**;
74: 8 the meeting places of God in the **l**.
74:20 for the dark places of the **l** are full of the haunts
78:12 he worked marvels in the **l** of Egypt, A
80: 9 it took deep root and filled the **l**.
81: 5 when he went out over the **l** of Egypt. A
81:10 who brought you up out of the **l** of Egypt. A
85: 1 you were favorable to your **l**;

Ps 85: 9 that his glory may dwell in our **l**.
85:12 and our **l** will yield its increase.
88:12 or your saving help in the **l** of forgetfulness?
94:17 my soul would soon have lived in the **l**
95: 5 The sea is his, for he made it, and the dry **l**,
101: 6 I will look with favor on the faithful in the **l**,
101: 8 by morning I will destroy all the wicked in the **l**,
105:11 "To you I will give the **l** of Canaan B
105:16 When he summoned famine against the **l**,
105:23 Jacob lived as an alien in the **l** of Ham.
105:27 and miracles in the **l** of Ham.
105:28 He sent darkness, and made the **l** dark;
105:30 Their **l** swarmed with frogs,
105:32 and lightning that flashed through their **l**.
105:35 they devoured all the vegetation in their **l**,
105:36 He struck down all the firstborn in their **l**,
106:22 wondrous works in the **l** of Ham,
106:24 Then they despised the pleasant **l**,
106:38 and the **l** was polluted with blood.
107:34 a fruitful **l** into a salty waste,
107:35 a parched **l** into springs of water.
112: 2 Their descendants will be mighty in the **l**;
116: 9 I walk before the LORD in the **l** of the living. L
119:19 I live as an alien in the **l**;
125: 3 of wickedness shall not rest on the **l** allotted to
135:12 and gave their **l** as a heritage,
136:21 and gave their **l** as a heritage,
137: 4 could we sing the LORD's song in a foreign **l**?
140:11 Do not let the slanderer be established in the **l**;
141: 7 a rock that one breaks apart and shatters on the **l**,
142: 5 my portion in the **l** of the living." L
143: 6 my soul thirsts for you like a parched **l**.
Pr 2:21 For the upright will abide in the **l**,
2:22 but the wicked will be cut off from the **l**,
10:30 but the wicked will not remain in the **l**.
12:11 Those who till their **l** will have plenty of food,
21:19 to live in a desert **l** than with a contentious
28: 2 When a **l** rebels it has many rulers;
28:19 Anyone who tills the **l** will have plenty of bread,
29: 4 By justice a king gives stability to the **l**,
31:23 taking his seat among the elders of the **l**.
Ecc 5: 9 all things considered, this is an advantage for a **l**:
10:16 Alas for you, O **l**, when your king is a servant,
10:17 O **l**, when your king is a nobleman,
SS 2:12 and the voice of the turtledove is heard in our **l**.
Isa 1: 7 in your very presence aliens devour your **l**;
1:19 you shall eat the good of the **l**;
2: 7 Their **l** is filled with silver and gold,
2: 7 their **l** is filled with horses,
2: 8 Their **l** is filled with idols;
4: 2 the **l** shall be the pride and glory of the survivors
5: 8 you are left to live alone in the midst of the **l**!
5:30 if one look to the **l**—only darkness and distress;
6:11 and the **l** is utterly desolate;
6:12 and vast is the emptiness in the midst of the **l**.
7:16 the **l** before whose two kings you are
7:18 and for the bee that is in the **l** of Assyria.
7:22 for everyone that is left in the **l** shall eat curds
7:24 for all the **l** will be briers and thorns; C
8: 8 its outspread wings will fill the breadth of your **l**,
8:21 They will pass through the **l**,
9: 1 In the former time he brought into contempt the **l**
of Zebulun and the **l** of Naphtali,
9: 1 the **l** beyond the Jordan, Galilee of the nations.
9: 2 those who lived in a **l** of deep darkness—
9:19 wrath of the LORD of hosts the **l** was burned,
10:18 and his fruitful **l** the LORD will destroy,
11:16 Israel when they came up from the **l** of Egypt. A
13: 5 They come from a distant **l**,
14: 1 and will set them in their own **l**;
14: 2 as male and female slaves in the LORD's **l**;
14:20 because you have destroyed your **l**,
14:25 in my **l**, and on my mountains trample him
15: 8 For a cry has gone around the **l** of Moab;
15: 9 of Moab who escape, for the remnant of the **l**.
16: 1 Send lambs to the ruler of the **l**, from Sela,
16: 4 and marauders have vanished from the **l**,
18: 1 **l** of whirring wings beyond the rivers
18: 2 whose **l** the rivers divide,
18: 7 whose **l** the rivers divide, to Mount Zion,
19:17 **l** of Judah will become a terror to the Egyptians; E
19:18 **l** of Egypt that speak the language of Canaan A
19:19 altar to the LORD in the center of the **l** of Egypt, A
19:20 witness to the LORD of hosts in the **l** of Egypt; A
21: 1 it comes from the desert, from a terrible **l**.
21:14 O inhabitants of the **l** of Tema.
22:18 and throw you like a ball into a wide **l**;
23:10 Cross over to your own **l**, O ships of Tarshish;
23:13 Look at the **l** of the Chaldeans!
26: 1 that day this song will be sung in the **l** of Judah: E
26:10 the **l** of uprightness they deal perversely and do
26:15 you have enlarged all the borders of the **l**.
27:13 the **l** of Assyria and those who were driven out to
27:13 those who were driven out to the **l** of Egypt A
28:22 from the Lord GOD of hosts upon the whole **l**. F
30: 6 Through a **l** of trouble and distress,
32: 2 like the shade of a great rock in a weary **l**.
33: 9 The **l** mourns and languishes;
33:17 they will behold a **l** that stretches far away.
34: 6 a great slaughter in the **l** of Edom.
34: 7 Their **l** shall be soaked with blood,
34: 9 her **l** shall become burning pitch.
35: 1 The wilderness and the dry **l** shall be glad,
36:10 that I have come up against this **l** to destroy it?
36:10 The LORD said to me, Go up against this **l**,
36:17 and take you away to a **l** like your own **l**, a **l** of
grain and wine, a **l** of bread and vineyards.

Isa 36:18 gods of the nations saved their l out of the hand of
37: 7 and return to his own l;
37: 7 to fall by the sword in his own l.' "
37:38 and they escaped into the l of Ararat.
38:11 I shall not see the LORD in the l of the living; L
41:18 and the dry l springs of water.
44: 3 For I will pour water on the thirsty l,
45:19 I did not speak in secret, in a l of darkness;
49: 8 establish the l, to apportion the desolate heritages;
49:12 and these from the l of Syene.
49:19 and your desolate places and your devastated l—
53: 8 For he was cut off from the l of the living, L
57:13 possess the l and inherit my holy mountain. N
60:18 Violence shall no more be heard in your l,
60:21 they shall possess the l forever. N
61: 5 foreigners shall till your l and dress your vines;
62: 4 and your l shall no more be termed Desolate;
62: 4 My Delight is in Her, and your l Married;
62: 4 and your l shall be married.
65:16 in the l shall bless by the God of faithfulness,
65:16 and whoever takes an oath in the l shall swear by
66: 8 Shall a l be born in one day?
Jer 1: 1 of the priests who were in Anathoth in the l
1:14 on all the inhabitants of the l.
1:18 and a bronze wall, against the whole l— F
1:18 its princes, its priests, and the people of the l. D
2: 2 how you followed me in the wilderness, in a l
2: 6 the LORD who brought us up from the l of Egypt, A
2: 6 in a l of deserts and pits, in a l of drought and deep darkness, in a l that no one passes through,
2: 7 a plentiful l to eat its fruits and its good things.
2: 7 But when you entered you defiled my l,
2:15 They have made his l a waste;
2:31 or a l of thick darkness?
3: 1 Would not such a l be greatly polluted?
3: 2 You have polluted the l with your whoring and
3: 9 she polluted the l, committing adultery
3:16 when you have multiplied and increased in the l,
3:18 and together they shall come from the l of the north to the l that I gave your ancestors
3:19 and give you a pleasant l,
4: 5 Blow the trumpet through the l;
4: 7 to make your l a waste; your cities will be ruins
4:16 "Besiegers come from a distant l;
4:20 the whole l is laid waste. F
4:26 I looked, and lo, the fruitful l was a desert,
4:27 The whole l shall be a desolation; F
5:19 and served foreign gods in your l,
5:19 you shall serve strangers in a l that is not yours."
5:30 and horrible thing has happened in the l:
6: 8 and make you a desolation, an uninhabited l.
6:12 against the inhabitants of the l,
6:20 or sweet cane from a distant l?
6:22 See, a people is coming from the l of the north,
7: 7 the l that I gave of old to your ancestors forever
7:22 I brought your ancestors out of the l of Egypt, A
7:25 that your ancestors came out of the l of Egypt A
7:34 for the l shall become a waste.
8:16 neighing of their stallions the whole l quakes. F
8:16 They come and devour the l and all that fills it,
8:19 cry of my poor people from far and wide in the l:
9: 3 they have grown strong in the l for falsehood,
9:12 the l ruined and laid waste like a wilderness,
9:19 because we have left the l,
10:18 to sling out the inhabitants of the l at this time,
10:22 from the l of the north to make the cities of Judah
11: 4 when I brought them out of the l of Egypt, A
11: 5 to give them a l flowing with milk and honey, H
11: 7 when I brought them up out of the l of Egypt, A
11:19 let us cut him off from the l of the living, L
12: 4 How long will the l mourn,
12: 5 And if in a safe l you fall down,
12:11 The whole l is made desolate, F
12:12 of the LORD devours from one end of the l to
12:14 I am about to pluck them up from their l,
12:15 to their heritage and to their l,
13:13 I am about to fill all the inhabitants of this l—
14: 4 Because there has been no rain on the l
14: 8 why should you be like a stranger in the l,
14:15 "Sword and famine shall not come on this l":
14:18 and priest ply their trade throughout the l,
15: 7 with a winnowing fork in the gates of the l;
15:10 a man of strife and contention to the whole l! F
15:14 I will make you serve your enemies in a l
16: 3 and the fathers who beget them in this l:
16: 6 Both great and small shall die in this l;
16:13 Therefore I will hurl you out of this l into a land
16:13 Therefore I will hurl you out of this land into a l
16:14 the people of Israel up out of the l of Egypt," A
16:15 of Israel up out of the l of the north and out of all
16:15 to their own l that I gave to their ancestors.
16:18 because they have polluted my l with
17: 4 and I will make you serve your enemies in a l
17: 6 of the wilderness, in an uninhabited salt l.
17:26 from the l of Benjamin, from the Shephelah,
18:16 making their l a horror, a thing to be hissed
22:10 for he shall return no more to see his native l.
22:12 and he shall never see this l again.
22:27 not return to the l to which they long to return.
22:28 and his offspring hurled out and cast away in a l
22:29 O l, l, l, hear the word of the LORD!
23: 5 shall execute justice and righteousness in the l.
23: 7 the people of Israel up out of the l of Egypt," A
23: 8 the offspring of the house of Israel out of the l of
23: 8 Then they shall live in their own l.
23:10 For the l is full of adulterers;
23:10 because of the curse the l mourns,
Jer 23:15 ungodliness has spread throughout the l."
24: 5 whom I have sent away from this place to the l of
24: 6 and I will bring them back to this l.
24: 8 the remnant of Jerusalem who remain in this l,
24: 8 and those who live in the l of Egypt. AI
24:10 from the l that I gave to them and their ancestors.
25: 5 upon the l that the LORD has given to you
25: 9 against this l and its inhabitants,
25:11 This whole l shall become a ruin and a waste, F
25:12 the l of the Chaldeans, for their iniquity,
25:12 making the l an everlasting waste.
25:13 that l all the words that I have uttered against it,
25:20 all the kings of the l of Uz; all the kings of the l of the Philistines—
25:38 for their l has become a waste because of
26:17 the l arose and said to all the assembled people,
26:20 He prophesied against this city and against this l
27: 7 until the time of his own l comes;
27:10 that you will be removed far from your l;
27:11 I will leave on its own l, says the LORD,
30: 3 and I will bring them back to the l that I gave
30:10 and your offspring from the l of their captivity.
31: 8 I am going to bring them from the l of the north,
31:16 they shall come back from the l of the enemy;
31:23 they shall use these words in the l of Judah E
31:32 by the hand to bring them out of the l of Egypt A
32: 8 in the l of Benjamin, for the right of possession
32:15 and vineyards shall again be bought in this l.
32:20 showed signs and wonders in the l of Egypt, A
32:21 of the l of Egypt with signs and wonders, A
32:22 and you gave them this l, which you swore
32:22 a l flowing with milk and honey; H
32:41 and I will plant them in this l in faithfulness,
32:43 be bought in this l of which you are saying, It is
32:44 in the l of Benjamin, in the places
33:11 For I will restore the fortunes of the l as at first,
33:13 and of the Negeb, in the l of Benjamin,
33:15 and righteousness in the l.
34:13 when I brought them out of the l of Egypt, A
34:19 people of the l who passed between the parts D
35: 7 that you may live many days in the l
35:11 of Babylon came up against the l,
35:15 then you shall live in the l that I gave to you I
36:29 and destroy this l, and will cut off
37: 1 of Babylon made king in the l of Judah, E
37: 2 nor his servants nor the people of the l listened D
37: 7 is going to return to its own l, to Egypt.
37:12 the l of Benjamin to receive his share of property
37:19 not come against you and against this l'?
39: 5 at Riblah, in the l of Hamath;
39:10 the guard left in the l of Judah some of the E
40: 4 See, the whole l is before you; F
40: 6 among the people who were left in the l.
40: 7 of Ahikam governor in the l,
40: 7 of the poorest of the l who had not been taken
40: 9 Stay in the l and serve the king of Babylon,
40:12 to the l of Judah, to Gedaliah at Mizpah; E
41: 2 of Babylon had appointed him governor in the l.
41:18 of Babylon had made governor over the l.
42:10 in this l, then I will build you up and
42:13 you continue to say, 'We will not stay in this l,'
42:14 'No, we will go to the l of Egypt, A
42:16 shall overtake you there, in the l of Egypt; A
43: 4 to stay in the l of Judah. E
43: 5 to settle in the l of Judah from all the nations E
43: 7 And they came into the l of Egypt, A
43:11 He shall come and ravage the l of Egypt, A
43:12 and he shall pick clean the l of Egypt, A
43:13 which is in the l of Egypt; A
44: 1 for all the Judeans living in the l of Egypt, A
44: 1 at Memphis, and in the l of Pathros,
44: 8 in the l of Egypt where you have come to settle? A
44: 9 in the l of Judah and in the streets of Jerusalem? E
44:12 who are determined to come to the l of Egypt A
44:12 in the l of Egypt they shall fall; A
44:13 I will punish those who live in the l of Egypt, AI
44:14 the l of Egypt shall escape or survive or return A
44:14 escape or survive or return to the l of Judah. E
44:15 people who lived in Pathros in the l of Egypt, A
44:21 and the people of the l, D
44:22 therefore your l became a desolation and a waste
44:24 all you Judeans who are in the l of Egypt, A
44:26 all you Judeans who live in the l of Egypt: AI
44:26 the people of Judah in all the l of Egypt, AC
44:27 Judah who are in the l of Egypt shall perish by A
44:28 from the l of Egypt to the land of Judah, few A
44:28 from the land of Egypt to the l of Judah, few E
44:28 who have come to the l of Egypt to settle, A
45: 4 up what I have planted—that is, the whole l. F
46:10 the Lord GOD of hosts holds a sacrifice in the l
46:13 of Babylon to attack the l of Egypt: A
46:16 let us go back to our own people and to the l
46:27 and your offspring from the l of their captivity.
47: 2 they shall overflow the l and all that fills it,
47: 2 and all the inhabitants of the l shall wail.
48:24 and all the towns of the l of Moab, far and near.
48:33 and joy have been taken away from the fruitful l
50: 1 concerning the l of the Chaldeans,
50: 3 it shall make her l a desolation,
50: 8 and go out of the l of the Chaldeans,
50: 9 a company of great nations from the l of
50:12 a wilderness, dry l, and a desert.
50:16 and all of them shall flee to their own l.
50:18 to punish the king of Babylon and his l,
50:21 Go up to the l of Merathaim;
50:22 noise of battle is in the l, and great destruction!
50:25 of hosts has a task to do in the l of the Chaldeans.
Jer 50:28 and refugees from the l of Babylon are coming
50:38 For it is a l of images, and they go mad over idols.
50:45 that he has formed against the l of the Chaldeans:
51: 2 They shall empty her l when they come against her
51: 4 down slain in the l of the Chaldeans,
51: 5 though their l is full of guilt before the Holy One
51:27 Raise a standard in the l,
51:28 and every l under their dominion.
51:29 The l trembles and writhes,
51:29 to make the l of Babylon a desolation,
51:43 a l of drought and a desert, a l in which no one
51:46 or fearful at the rumors heard in the l—
51:46 the next year another, rumors of violence in the l
51:47 her whole l shall be put to shame, F
51:50 Remember the LORD in a distant l,
51:52 and through all her l the wounded shall groan.
51:54 A great crashing from the l of the Chaldeans!
52: 6 that there was no food for the people of the l. D
52: 9 the king of Babylon at Riblah in the l of Hamath,
52:16 guard left some of the poorest people of the l D
52:25 of the army who mustered the people of the l; D
52:25 of the people of the l who were found inside D
52:27 put them to death at Riblah in the l of Hamath.
52:27 So Judah went into exile out of its l.
La 3:34 all the prisoners of the l are crushed under foot,
4:21 O daughter Edom, you that live in the l of Uz; I
Eze 1: 3 in the l of the Chaldeans by the river Chebar;
6:14 and make the l desolate and waste,
7: 2 thus says the Lord GOD to the l of Israel: G
7: 2 The end has come upon the four corners of the l.
7: 7 to you, O inhabitant of the l.
7:23 For the l is full of bloody crimes;
7:27 the hands of the people of the l shall tremble. D
8:12 the LORD has forsaken the l.' "
8:17 Must they fill the l with violence,
9: 9 the l is full of bloodshed and the city full
9: 9 for they say, 'The LORD has forsaken the l,
11:15 to us this l is given for a possession."
11:17 and I will give you the l of Israel. G
12: 6 so that you may not see the l;
12:12 so that he may not see the l with his eyes.
12:13 the l of the Chaldeans, yet he shall not see it;
12:19 to the people of the l, Thus says the Lord GOD D
12:19 the inhabitants of Jerusalem in the l of Israel: G
12:19 because their l shall be stripped of all it contains,
12:20 and the l shall become a desolation;
12:22 is this proverb of yours about the l of Israel, G
13: 9 nor shall they enter the l of Israel; G
14:13 when a l sins against me by acting faithlessly,
14:15 If I send wild animals through the l to ravage it,
14:16 but the l would be desolate.
14:17 Or if I bring a sword upon that l and say,
14:17 'Let a sword pass through the l,'
14:19 Or if I send a pestilence into that l,
15: 8 And I will make the l desolate,
16: 3 and your birth were in the l of the Canaanites;
16:29 with Chaldea, the l of merchants;
17: 4 He carried it to a l of trade,
17: 5 he took a seed from the l, placed it in fertile soil;
17:13 the chief men of the l),
18: 2 repeating this proverb concerning the l of Israel, G
19: 4 they brought him with hooks to the l of Egypt. A
19: 7 the l was appalled, and all in it,
19:13 into a dry and thirsty l.
20: 5 making myself known to them in the l of Egypt A
20: 6 that I would bring them out of the l of Egypt A
20: 6 into a l that I had searched out for them,
20: 6 a l flowing with milk and honey, H
20: 8 against them in the midst of the l of Egypt. A
20: 9 to them in bringing them out of the l of Egypt. A
20:10 out of the l of Egypt and brought them into A
20:15 not bring them into the l that I had given them,
20:15 a l flowing with milk and honey, H
20:28 when I had brought them into the l that I swore
20:36 ancestors in the wilderness of the l of Egypt, A
20:38 I will bring them out of the l where they reside
20:38 but they shall not enter the l of Israel. G
20:40 all of them, shall serve me in the l;
20:42 when I bring you into the l of Israel, G
20:46 and prophesy against the forest l in the Negeb;
21: 2 prophesy against the l of Israel G
21: 3 and say to the l of Israel, Thus says the LORD: G
21:19 both of them shall issue from the same l.
21:30 in the l of your origin, I will judge you.
22:24 You are a l that is not cleansed,
22:29 The people of the l have practiced extortion D
22:30 on behalf of the l, so that I would not destroy it;
23:15 of Babylonians whose native l was Chaldea.
23:19 when she played the whore in the l of Egypt A
23:27 and your whoring brought from the l of Egypt; A
23:48 Thus will I put an end to lewdness in the l,
25: 3 over the l of Israel when it was made desolate, G
25: 6 the malice within you against the l of Israel, G
26:20 be inhabited or have a place in the l of the living. L
27:17 Judah and the l of Israel traded with you; G
29: 9 the l of Egypt shall be a desolation and a waste. A
29:10 and I will make the l of Egypt an utter waste A
29:12 I will make the l of Egypt a desolation A
29:14 back to the l of Pathros, the l of their origin;
29:19 the l of Egypt to King Nebuchadrezzar A
29:20 I have given him the l of Egypt as his payment A
30: 5 and the people of the allied l shall fall with them
30:11 shall be brought in to destroy the l,
30:11 and fill the l with the slain.
30:12 and will sell the l into the hand of evildoers;
30:12 I will bring desolation upon the l and everything
30:13 shall no longer be a prince in the l of Egypt; A

Eze 30:13 so I will put fear in the l of Egypt. A
30:25 He shall stretch it out against the l of Egypt, A
31:12 in all the watercourses of the l;
32: 6 I will drench the l with your flowing blood up to
32: 8 and put darkness on your l, says the Lord GOD.
32:15 When I make the l of Egypt desolate and when A
32:15 and when the l is stripped of all that fills it,
32:23 who spread terror in the l of the living. L
32:24 who spread terror in the l of the living. L
32:25 terror of them was spread in the l of the living, L
32:26 for they spread terror in the l of the living. L
32:27 terror of the warriors was in the l of the living. L
32:32 For he spread terror in the l of the living; L
33: 2 If I bring the sword upon a l,
33: 2 and the people of the l take one of their number D
33: 3 if the sentinel sees the sword coming upon the l
33:24 of these waste places in the l of Israel G
33:24 yet he got possession of the l;
33:24 the l is surely given us to possess."
33:25 shall you then possess the l? N
33:26 shall you then possess the l? N
33:28 I will make the l a desolation and a waste,
33:29 when I have made the l a desolation and a waste
34:13 and will bring them into their own l;
34:13 and in all the inhabited parts of the l.
34:14 there they shall lie down in good grazing l,
34:25 of peace and banish wild animals from the l,
34:28 nor shall the animals of the l devour them;
34:29 be consumed with hunger in the l,
36: 5 took my l as their possession,
36: 6 Therefore prophesy concerning the l of Israel, G
36:18 for the blood that they had shed upon the l,
36:20 and yet they had to go out of his l."
36:24 and bring you into your own l.
36:28 Then you shall live in the l that I gave to your I
36:34 The l that was desolate shall be tilled,
36:35 "This l that was desolate has become like
37:12 and I will bring you back to the l of Israel. G
37:21 and bring them to their own l.
37:22 I will make them one nation in the l,
37:25 live in the l that I gave to my servant Jacob, I
38: 2 set your face toward Gog, of the l of Magog,
38: 8 the latter years you shall go against a l restored
38: 8 from war, a l where people were gathered
38: 9 you shall be like a cloud covering the l,
38:11 "I will go up against the l of unwalled villages;
38:16 In the latter days I will bring you against my l,
38:18 when Gog comes against the l of Israel, G
38:19 there shall be a great shaking in the l of Israel; G
39:12 in order to cleanse the l.
39:13 All the people of the l shall bury them; D
39:14 the l regularly and bury any invaders who remain
39:14 on the face of the l, so as to cleanse it;
39:15 As the searchers pass through the l,
39:16 Thus they shall cleanse the l.
39:26 when they live securely in their l with no one
39:28 and then gathered them into their own l.
40: 2 in visions of God, to the l of Israel, G
45: 1 When you allot the l as an inheritance,
45: 1 the LORD a portion of the l as a holy district,
45: 4 It shall be a holy portion of the l;
45: 7 And to the prince shall belong the l on both sides
45: 8 of the l. It is to be his property in Israel.
45: 8 but they shall let the house of Israel have the l
45:16 All the people of the l shall join with the prince D
45:22 people of the l a young bull for a sin offering. D
46: 3 people of the l shall bow down at the entrance D
46: 9 the people of the l come before the LORD at D
47:13 the boundaries by which you shall divide the l
47:14 and this l shall fall to you as your inheritance.
47:15 This shall be the boundary of the l:
47:18 the Jordan between Gilead and the l of Israel; G
47:21 So you shall divide this l among you according
48:12 a special portion from the holy portion of the l,
48:14 they shall not transfer this choice portion of the l,
48:17 The city shall have open l:
48:29 the l that you shall allot as an inheritance among
Dn 1: 2 These he brought to the l of Shinar,
8: 9 toward the east, and toward the beautiful l.
9: 6 and our ancestors, and to all the people of the l. D
9:15 who brought your people out of the l of Egypt A
11: 9 but will return to his own l.
11:16 He shall take a position in the beautiful l,
11:19 toward the fortresses of his own l,
11:28 He shall return to his l with great wealth,
11:28 He shall work his will, and return to his own l.
11:39 and shall distribute the l for a price.
11:41 He shall come into the beautiful l,
11:42 and the l of Egypt shall not escape. A
Hos 1: 2 for the l commits great whoredom by forsaking
1:11 and they shall take possession of the l,
2: 3 and turn her into a parched l,
2:15 at the time when she came out of the l of Egypt. A
2:18 the sword, and war from the l;
2:23 and I will sow him for myself in the l.
4: 1 an indictment against the inhabitants of the l.
4: 1 and no knowledge of God in the l.
4: 3 the l mourns, and all who live in it languish;
7:16 So much for their babbling in the l of Egypt. A
9: 3 They shall not remain in the l of the LORD;
11: 5 They shall return to the l of Egypt, A
11:11 and like doves from the l of Assyria;
12: 9 I am the LORD your God from the l of Egypt; A
12:12 Jacob fled to the l of Aram,
13: 4 the LORD your God ever since the l of Egypt; A
13: 5 in the wilderness, in the l of drought.
Joel 1: 2 O elders, give ear, all inhabitants of the l!
Joel 1: 6 For a nation has invaded my l,
1:14 Gather the elders and all the inhabitants of the l
2: 1 Let all the inhabitants of the l tremble,
2: 3 Before them the l is like the garden of Eden,
2:18 Then the LORD became jealous for his l,
2:20 and drive it into a parched and desolate l,
3: 2 They have divided my l,
3:19 in whose l they have shed innocent blood.
Am 2:10 Also I brought you up out of the l of Egypt, A
2:10 to possess the l of the Amorite. N
3: 1 family that I brought up out of the l of Egypt: A
3: 9 to the strongholds in the l of Egypt, and say, A
3:11 An adversary shall surround the l,
5: 2 forsaken on her l, with no one to raise her up.
7: 2 When they had finished eating the grass of the l,
7: 4 the great deep and was eating up the l.
7:10 the l is not able to bear all his words.
7:11 and Israel must go into exile away from his l.' "
7:12 "O seer, go, flee away to the l of Judah, E
7:17 and your l shall be parceled out by line;
7:17 you yourself shall die in an unclean l,
7:17 Israel shall surely go into exile away from its l.' "
8: 4 and bring to ruin the poor of the l,
8: 8 Shall not the l tremble on this account,
8:11 when I will send a famine on the l;
9: 7 Did I not bring Israel up from the l of Egypt, A
9:15 I will plant them upon their l,
9:15 be plucked up out of the l that I have given them,
Ob 1:19 those of the Shephelah the l of the Philistines;
1:19 they shall possess the l of Ephraim and the N
1:19 of Ephraim and the l of Samaria,
Jnh 1: 9 who made the sea and the dry l."
1:13 the men rowed hard to bring the ship back to l,
2: 6 I went down to the l whose bars closed upon me
2:10 and it spewed Jonah out upon the dry l.
Mic 5: 5 If the Assyrians come into our l and tread
5: 6 They shall rule the l of Assyria with the sword,
5: 6 and the l of Nimrod with the drawn sword;
5: 6 if they come into our l or tread within our border.
5:11 of your l and throw down all your strongholds;
6: 4 For I brought you up from the l of Egypt, A
7: 2 The faithful have disappeared from the l,
7:14 in a forest in the midst of a garden l;
7:15 the days when you came out of the l of Egypt, A
Na 3:13 The gates of your l are wide open to your foes;
Hab 3: 7 the tent-curtains of the l of Midian trembled.
Zep 2: 3 Seek the LORD, all you humble of the l,
2: 5 O Canaan, l of the Philistines;
2: 9 a l possessed by nettles and salt pits,
Hag 1:11 I have called for a drought on the l and the hills,
2: 4 take courage, all you people of the l, D
2: 6 and the earth and the sea and the dry l;
Zec 1:21 that lifted up their horns against the l of Judah E
2: 6 Flee from the l of the north, says the LORD;
2:12 as his portion in the holy l,
3: 9 I will remove the guilt of this l in a single day.
5: 3 that goes out over the face of the whole l; F
5: 6 And he said, "This is their iniquity in all the l." C
5:11 He said to me, "To the l of Shinar,
7: 5 Say to all the people of the l and the priests: D
7:14 Thus the l they left was desolate,
7:14 and a pleasant l was made desolate.
9: 1 the l of Hadrach and will rest upon Damascus.
9:16 the jewels of a crown they shall shine on his l.
10:10 I will bring them home from the l of Egypt, A
10:10 I will bring them to the l of Gilead and K
11:16 now raising up in the l a shepherd who does
12:12 The l shall mourn, each family by itself;
13: 2 I will cut off the names of the idols from the l,
13: 2 and also I will remove from the l the prophets
13: 5 the l has been my possession since my youth."
13: 8 In the whole l, says the LORD, F
14:10 The whole l shall be turned into a plain F
Mal 3:12 for you will be a l of delight,
4: 6 that I will not come and strike the l with a curse.
Mt 2: 6 Bethlehem, in the l of Judah, E
2:20 and go to the l of Israel, G
2:21 and went to the l of Israel. G
4:15 L of Zebulun, l of Naphtali, on the road by the sea,
10:15 for the l of Sodom and Gomorrah on the day
11:24 of judgment it will be more tolerable for the l
14:24 battered by the waves, was far from the l,
14:34 they came to l at Gennesaret.
23:15 For you cross sea and l to make a single convert,
27:45 darkness came over the whole l until three in F
Mk 4: 1 the whole crowd was beside the sea on the l.
6:47 and he was alone on the l.
6:53 they came to l at Gennesaret and moored
15:33 darkness came over the whole l until three in F
Lk 4:25 and there was a severe famine over all the l; C
8:27 As he stepped out on l,
12:16 "The l of a rich man produced abundantly.
14:18 The first said to him, 'I have bought a piece of l,
23:44 darkness came over the whole l until three in F
Jn 6:21 and immediately the boat reached the l
21: 8 for they were not far from the l,
Ac 5: 3 and to keep back part of the proceeds of the l?
5: 8 and your husband sold the l for such and such
7: 3 and go to the l that I will show you.'
7:29 Moses fled and became a resident alien in the l
7:40 this Moses who led us out from the l of Egypt, A
13:17 during their stay in the l of Egypt, A
13:19 had destroyed seven nations in the l of Canaan, B
13:19 he gave them their l as an inheritance
20:13 intending to go by l himself.
27:27 the sailors suspected that they were nearing l.
27:39 In the morning they did not recognize the l,
Ac 27:43 to jump overboard first and make for the l,
27:44 And so it was that all were brought safely to l.
Heb 8: 9 by the hand to lead them out of the l of Egypt; A
11: 9 for a time in the l he had been promised,
11: 9 as in a foreign l, living in tents,
11:15 If they had been thinking of the l
11:29 through the Red Sea as if it were dry l,
Jude 1: 5 once for all saved a people out of the l of Egypt, A
Rev 10: 2 on the sea and his left foot on the l,
10: 5 the sea and the l raised his right hand to heaven
10: 8 the angel who is standing on the sea and on the l."
Tob 1: 3 in exile to Nineveh in the l of the Assyrians.
1: 4 I was in my own country, in the l of Israel, G
3:15 or the name of my father in the l of my exile.
4:12 and their posterity will inherit the l.
6: 4 the fish and drew it up on the l.
13: 6 In the l of my exile I acknowledge him,
14: 4 All of our kindred, inhabitants of the l of Israel, G
14: 4 and taken as captives from the good l; J
14: 4 and the whole l of Israel will be desolate, FG
14: 5 God will bring them back into the l of Israel; G
14: 7 and live in safety forever in the l of Abraham,
Jdt 1: 9 and Tahpanhes and Raamses and the whole l F
1:12 with his sword also all the inhabitants of the l
2: 6 March out against all the l to the west, C
3: 3 and all our l and all our wheat fields
3: 8 to destroy all the gods of the l,
5: 9 they were living and go to the l of Canaan. B
5:10 a famine spread over the l of Canaan they went B
5:12 the whole l of Egypt with incurable plagues. AF
5:15 and took up residence in the l of the Amorites,
5:18 and were led away captive to a foreign l.
7: 4 "They will now strip clean the whole l; F
7:18 and covered the whole face of the l.
8:22 of the l and the desolation of our inheritance—
AdE 10: 1 The king levied a tax upon his kingdom both by l
13:16 redeemed for yourself out of the l of Egypt. A
Wis 12: 3 Those who lived long ago in your holy l
12: 7 the l most precious of all to you might receive
14: 5 the billows on a raft they come safely to l.
16:19 to destroy the crops of the unrighteous l.
18:15 into the midst of the l that was doomed,
19: 7 dry l emerging where water had stood before,
19:19 l animals were transformed into water creatures,
19:19 and creatures that swim moved over to the l.
Sir 37: 3 why were you formed to cover the l with deceit?
39:22 "His blessing covers the dry l like a river,
39:23 as when he turned a watered l into salt.
43: 3 At noon it parches the l,
45:22 But in the l of the people he has no inheritance,
46: 8 the l flowing with milk and honey. H
47:24 until they were exiled from their l.
48:15 as plunder from their l, and were scattered
Bar 1: 8 to return them to the l of Judah— E
1: 9 and the nobles and the people of the l, D
1:19 brought our ancestors out of the l of Egypt A
1:20 of the l of Egypt to give to us a land flowing A
1:20 to give to us a l flowing with milk and honey. H
2:11 out of the l of Egypt with a mighty hand and A
2:21 the king of Babylon, and you will remain in the l
2:23 whole l will be a desolation without inhabitants. F
2:30 the l of their exile they will come to themselves
2:32 they will praise me in the l of their exile,
2:34 into the l that I swore to give to their ancestors,
2:35 from the l that I have given them."
3:10 why is it that you are in the l of your enemies,
LtJ 6:61 and the wind likewise blows in every l.
6:72 and be a reproach in the l.
1Mc 1: 1 the Macedonian, who came from the l of Kittim,
1:16 he determined to become king of the l of Egypt, A
1:19 captured the fortified cities in the l of Egypt, A
1:19 and he plundered the l of Egypt. A
1:24 Taking them all, he went into his own l.
1:28 Even the l trembled for its inhabitants,
1:44 to follow customs strange to the l,
1:52 joined them, and they did evil in the l;
2:56 received an inheritance in the l.
3: 8 he destroyed the ungodly out of the l;
3:24 and the rest fled into the l of the Philistines.
3:29 the l by abolishing the laws that had existed from
3:36 and distribute their l by lot.
3:39 seven thousand cavalry to go into the l of Judah E
3:41 from Syria and the l of the Philistines joined
4:22 they all fled into the l of the Philistines.
5:13 and all our kindred who were in the l
5:45 a very large company, to go to the l of Judah. E
5:48 "Let us pass through your l to get to our l.
5:53 all the way until he came to the l of Judah. E
5:65 and fought the descendants of Esau in the l to
5:66 he marched off to go into the l of the Philistines,
5:68 But Judas turned aside to Azotus in the l of
5:68 the towns and returned to the l of Judah. E
6: 5 had gone into the l of Judah had been routed; E
6:13 perishing of bitter disappointment in a strange l."
6:49 since it was a sabbatical year for the l.
7: 6 and have driven us out of our l.
7: 7 the ruin that Judas has brought on us and on the l
7:10 and came with a large force into the l of Judah; E
7:22 of the l of Judah and did great damage in Israel. E
7:50 So the l of Judah had rest for a few days. E
8: 3 in the l of Spain to get control of the silver
8:10 they plundered them, conquered the l,
8:16 to rule over them and to control all their l;
8:23 the nation of the Jews at sea and on l forever,
8:32 and fight you on sea and on l.' "
9: 1 and Alcimus into the l of Judah a second time, E
9:53 the leading men of the l as hostages and put them

1Mc 9:57 and the l of Judah had rest for two years. E
9:69 Then he decided to go back to his own l.
9:72 he had taken previously from the l of Judah; E
9:72 then he turned and went back to his own l,
10:30 the l of Judah or from the three districts added E
10:33 the Jews taken as a captive from the l of Judah E
10:37 as the king has commanded in the l of Judah. E
10:39 Ptolemais and the l adjoining it I have given as
10:55 on which you returned to the l of your ancestors
10:67 of Demetrius came from Crete to the l
10:72 to flight in their own l.
11:34 from the crops of the l and the fruit of the trees.
11:38 When King Demetrius saw that the l was quiet
11:52 and the l was quiet before him.
12: 4 for the envoys safe conduct to the l of Judah. E
12:46 and they returned to the l of Judah. E
12:52 So they all reached the l of Judah safely, E
13: 1 to invade the l of Judah and destroy it, E
13:12 with a large army to invade the l of Judah, E
13:22 He marched off and went into the l of Gilead. K
13:24 Then Trypho turned and went back to his own l.
13:32 and he brought great calamity on the l.
14: 4 The l had rest all the days of Simon.
14: 8 They tilled their l in peace;
14:11 He established peace in the l,
14:13 No one was left in the l to fight them,
15:10 and invaded the l of his ancestors.
15:14 he pressed the town hard from l and sea,
15:29 you have done great damage in the l,
15:33 "We have neither taken foreign l nor seized
15:35 among the people and to our l;
2Mc 1: 1 Jews in Jerusalem and those in the l of Judea,
1: 7 and his company revolted from the holy l and
2:21 in number they seized the whole l and pursued F
4:26 was driven as a fugitive into the l of Ammon.
5:21 that he could sail on the l and walk on the sea,
9:28 among the mountains in a strange l.
1Es 1:58 "Until the l has enjoyed its sabbaths,
4: 2 who rule over l and sea and all that is in them?
4:15 and to every people that rules over sea and l.
4:56 He wrote that l and wages should be provided
5:50 joined them from the other peoples of the l. M
5:50 for all the peoples of the l were hostile to them M
5:72 But the peoples of the l pressed hard upon M
7:13 from the abominations of the peoples of the l M
8:69 the alien peoples of the l and their pollutions, M
8:70 with the alien peoples of the l; M
8:83 'The l that you are entering to take possession of is
a l polluted with the pollution of the aliens of the l,
8:85 and eat the good things of the l and leave it for
8:87 with the uncleanness of the peoples of the l. M
8:92 from the peoples of the l; M
9: 9 separate yourselves from the peoples of the l M
3Mc 6: 3 as foreigners in a foreign l.
6:15 in the l of their enemies did I neglect them,'
7:20 by l and sea and river to their own homes.
2Es 1: 7 not I who brought them out of the l of Egypt, A
2: 9 whose l lies in lumps of pitch and heaps of ashes.
4:19 for the l has been assigned to the forest,
4:21 the l has been assigned to the forest and the sea
5: 1 and the l shall be barren of faith.
5: 3 And the l that you now see ruling shall be
5:17 that Israel has been entrusted to you in the l
7:26 and the l that now is hidden shall be disclosed.
9: 8 and will see my salvation in my l and
13:40 that were taken away from their own l into exile
13:40 and they were taken into another l.
13:42 that they had not kept in their own l.
14:31 Then l was given to you for a possession in
14:31 to you for a possession in the l of Zion;
15: 6 because iniquity has spread throughout every l,
15:10 allow them to live any longer in the l of Egypt, A
15:11 as before, and will destroy all its l.
15:30 of the l of the Assyrians with their teeth.
15:33 And from the l of the Assyrians an enemy
15:60 of your l and abolish a portion of your glory,
15:62 your l and your mountains;
4Mc 1:11 and thus their native l was purified through them.
4:20 at the very citadel of our native l,

LAND'S (1) [LAND]

Dt 1:25 and gathered some of the l produce,

LANDED (5) [LAND]

1Sa 27: 8 the l settlements from Telam on the way to Shur
Ac 18:22 When he had l at Caesarea,
21: 3 we sailed to Syria and l at Tyre,
1Mc 10: 1 son of Antiochus, l and occupied Ptolemais.
3Mc 7:19 And when they had all l in peace

LANDHOLDING (3) [LAND]

Lev 27:16 person consecrates to the LORD any inherited l,
27:22 which is not a part of the inherited l,
27:28 or inherited l, may be sold or redeemed;

LANDING (1) [LAND]

1Mc 15: 4 to make a l in the country so that I may proceed

LANDINGS (1) [LAND]

Jdg 5:17 at the coast of the sea, settling down by his l.

LANDMARK (3) [LAND]

Pr 22:28 the ancient l that your ancestors set up.
23:10 not remove an ancient l or encroach on the fields
Hos 5:10 like those who remove the l;

LANDMARK (KJV) See also BOUNDARY MARKER

LANDMARKS (1) [LAND]

Job 24: 2 The wicked remove l; they seize flocks

LANDOWNER (3) [LAND, OWN]

Mt 20: 1 like a l who went out early in the morning
20:11 they received it, they grumbled against the l,
21:33 There was a l who planted a vineyard,

LANDS‡ (165) [LAND]

Ge 10: 5 These are the descendants of Japheth in their l,
10:20 their languages, their l, and their nations.
10:31 their languages, their l, and their nations.
26: 3 and to your descendants I will give all these l,
26: 4 and will give to your offspring all these l;
47:18 in the sight of my lord but our bodies and our l.
Lev 26:36 I will send faintness into their hearts in the l
Nu 35: 2 to the Levites pasture l surrounding the towns.
35: 3 and their pasture l shall be for their cattle,
35: 4 The pasture l of the towns,
35: 7 Levites shall total forty-eight, with their pasture l.
Jos 14: 4 with their pasture l for their flocks and herds.
21: 2 along with their pasture l for our livestock."
21: 3 the Levites the following towns and pasture l out
21: 8 and their pasture l the Israelites gave by lot to
21:11 along with the pasture l around it.
21:13 with its pasture l, Libnah with its pasture l,
21:14 Jattir with its pasture l, Eshtemoa with its pasture l,
21:15 Holon with its pasture l, Debir with its pasture l,
21:16 Ain with its pasture l, Juttah with its pasture l, and
Beth-shemesh with its pasture l—
21:17 Gibeon with its pasture l, Geba with its pasture l,
21:18 Anathoth with its pasture l, and Almon with its
pasture l—four towns.
21:19 were thirteen in all, with their pasture l.
21:21 with its pasture l in the hill country of Ephraim,
Gezer with its pasture l,
21:22 Kibzaim with its pasture l, and Beth-horon with its
pasture l—four towns.
21:23 Out of the tribe of Dan: Elteke with its pasture l,
Gibbethon with its pasture l,
21:24 Aijalon with its pasture l, Gath-rimmon with its
pasture l—four towns.
21:25 Taanach with its pasture l, and Gath-rimmon with
its pasture l—two towns.
21:26 ten in all, with their pasture l.
21:27 Golan in Bashan with its pasture l,
21:27 and Beeshterah with its pasture l—two towns.
21:28 Kishion with its pasture l, Daberath with its
pasture l,
21:29 Jarmuth with its pasture l, En-gannim with its
pasture l—
21:30 Mishal with its pasture l, Abdon with its pasture l,
21:31 Helkath with its pasture l, and Rehob with its
pasture l—four towns.
21:32 Kedesh in Galilee with its pasture l,
21:32 Hammoth-dor with its pasture l, and Kartan with
its pasture l—three towns.
21:33 in all thirteen, with their pasture l.
21:34 Jokneam with its pasture l, Kartah with its pasture l
21:35 Dimnah with its pasture l, Nahalal with its pasture l
21:36 Bezer with its pasture l, Jahzah with its pasture l,
21:37 Kedemoth with its pasture l, and Mephaath with
its pasture l—four towns.
21:38 Ramoth in Gilead with its pasture l,
21:38 Mahanaim with its pasture l,
21:39 Heshbon with its pasture l, Jazer with its pasture l
21:41 in all forty-eight towns with their pasture l.
21:42 Each of these towns had its pasture l around it;
2Ki 19:11 the kings of Assyria have done to all l,
19:17 of Assyria have laid waste the nations and their l,
1Ch 5:16 and in all the pasture l of Sharon to their limits.
6:55 the land of Judah and its surrounding pasture l,
6:57 Hebron, Libnah with its pasture l, Jattir, Eshtemoa
with its pasture l,
6:58 Hilen with its pasture l, Debir with its pasture l,
6:59 Ashan with its pasture l, and Beth-shemesh with
its pasture l.
6:60 Geba with its pasture l, Alemeth with its pasture l,
and Anathoth with its pasture l.
6:64 the Levites the towns with their pasture l.
6:67 Shechem with its pasture l in the hill country of
Ephraim, Gezer with its pasture l,
6:68 Jokmeam with its pasture l, Beth-horon with its
pasture l,
6:69 Aijalon with its pasture l, Gath-rimmon with its
pasture l;
6:70 with its pasture l, and Bileam with its pasture l,
6:71 Golan in Bashan with its pasture l and Ashtaroth
with its pasture l;
6:72 Kedesh with its pasture l, Daberath with its
pasture l,
6:73 Ramoth with its pasture l, and Anem with its
pasture l;
6:74 Mashal with its pasture l, Abdon with its pasture l,
6:75 Hukok with its pasture l, and Rehob with its
pasture l;
6:76 Kedesh in Galilee with its pasture l, Hammon with
its pasture l, and Kiriathaim with its pasture l.
6:77 with its pasture l, Tabor with its pasture l,
1Ch 6:78 Bezer in the steppe with its pasture l, Jahzah with
its pasture l,
6:79 Kedemoth with its pasture l, and Mephaath with
its pasture l;
6:80 Ramoth in Gilead with its pasture l, Mahanaim
with its pasture l,
6:81 Heshbon with its pasture l, and Jazer with its
pasture l.
13: 2 and Levites in the cities that have pasture l,
14:17 The fame of David went out into all l,
22: 5 famous and glorified throughout all l;
2Ch 6:28 in any of the settlements of the l;
9:28 for Solomon from Egypt and from all l.
11:14 The Levites had left their common l
12: 8 and serving the kingdoms of other l."
13: 9 for yourselves like the peoples of other l?
15: 5 disturbances afflicted all the inhabitants of the l.
17:10 of the LORD fell on all the kingdoms of the l
26:10 and vinedressers in the hills and in the fertile l,
32:13 to all the peoples of other l?
32:13 Were the gods of the nations of those l at all able
to save their l out of
32:17 the nations in other l did not rescue their people
Ezr 9: 1 from the peoples of the l with their abominations,
9: 2 with the peoples of the l,
9: 7 over to the kings of the l,
9:11 with the pollutions of the peoples of the l,
Ne 9:30 you handed them over to the peoples of the l.
10:28 the peoples of the l to adhere to the law of God,
Ps 49:11 though they named l their own.
105:44 He gave them the l of the nations,
106:27 scattering them over the l.
107: 3 and gathered in from the l,
Isa 13:14 and all will flee to their own l.
37:11 the kings of Assyria have done to all l,
37:18 Assyria have laid waste all the nations and their l,
Jer 16:15 up out of the land of the north and out of all the l
23: 3 the remnant of my flock out of all the l
23: 8 and out of all the l where he had driven them."
27: 6 Now I have given all these l into the hand
32:37 from all the l to which I drove them in my anger
40:11 the Ammonites and in Edom and in other l heard
Eze 20: 6 the most glorious of all l.
20:15 the most glorious of all l,
30:23 and disperse them throughout the l.
39:27 and gathered them from their enemies' l,
Da 9: 7 in all the l to which you have driven them,
Ac 4:34 as owned l or houses sold them and brought
28: 7 that place were l belonging to the leading man of
2Co 10:16 we may proclaim the good news in l beyond you,
Jdt 2:27 and ravaged their l and put all their young men to
Sir 10:16 The Lord lays waste the l of the nations,
39: 4 he travels in foreign l and learns what is good and
1Mc 6:25 they have also attacked all the l on their borders.
10:13 and went back to their own l.
1Es 4:28 Do not all l fear to touch him?
2Es 1:21 I divided fertile l among you;
5:24 and from all the l of the world you have chosen
13:33 all the nations shall leave their own l and

LANE (1) [LANES]

Ac 12:10 and they went outside and walked along a l,

LANES (2) [LANE]

Lk 14:21 'Go out at once into the streets and l of the town
14:23 'Go out into the roads and l,

LANGUAGE‡ (55) [LANGUAGES]

Ge 10: 5 with their own l, by their families,
11: 1 the whole earth had one l and the same words.
11: 6 they are one people, and they have all one l;
11: 7 Come, let us go down, and confuse their l there,
11: 9 there the LORD confused the l of all the earth;
Dt 28:49 a nation whose l you do not understand,
2Ki 18:26 "Please speak to your servants in the Aramaic l,
18:26 to us in the l of Judah within the hearing of
18:28 and called out in a loud voice in the l of Judah,
2Ch 32:18 with a loud voice in the l of Judah to the people
Ne 13:24 and half of their children spoke the l of Ashdod,
13:24 and they could not speak the l of Judah,
13:24 but spoke the l of various peoples.
Est 1:22 in its own script and to every people in its own l,
3:12 in its own script and every people in its own l;
8: 9 in its own script and to every people in its own l,
8: 9 and also to the Jews in their script and their l.
Ps 114: 1 the house of Jacob from a people of strange l,
Isa 19:18 be five cities in the land of Egypt that speak the l
33:19 stammering in a l that you cannot understand.
36:11 to us in the l of Judah within the hearing of
36:13 and called out in a loud voice in the l of Judah,
Jer 5:15 a nation whose l you do not know,
Eze 3: 5 of obscure speech and difficult l,
3: 6 of obscure speech and difficult l,
Da 1: 4 to be taught the literature and l of the Chaldeans.
3:29 Any people, nation, or l that utters blasphemy
6:25 to all peoples and nations of every l throughout
Zec 8:23 from nations of every l shall take hold of a Jew,
Ac 1:19 so that the field was called in their l Hakeldama,
2: 6 in the native l of each.
2: 8 each of us, in our own native l?
14:11 they shouted in the Lycaonian l,
21:40 he addressed them in the Hebrew l, saying:
26:14 I heard a voice saying to me in the Hebrew l,
Col 3: 8 malice, slander, and abusive l from your mouth.
Rev 5: 9 for God saints from every tribe and l and people

Rev 13: 7 over every tribe and people and **l** and nation,
14: 6 to every nation and tribe and **l** and people.
AdE 1:22 to every province in its own **l**,
3:12 the governors were addressed each in his own **l**.
8: 9 to each province in its own **l**.
9:26 (for in their **l** this is the word that means "lots").
Sir Pr: 2 the same sense when translated into another **l**.
23:13 Do not accustom your mouth to coarse, foul **l**,
23:15 to using abusive **l** will never become disciplined
Bar 4:15 a nation ruthless and of a strange **l**,
2Mc 7: 8 He replied in the **l** of his ancestors and said
7:21 She encouraged each of them in the **l**
7:27 she spoke in their native **l** as follows,
12:37 In the **l** of their ancestors he raised the battle cry,
15:29 the Sovereign Lord in the **l** of their ancestors.
15:36 which is called Adar in the Aramaic **l**—
4Mc 12: 7 his mother had exhorted him in the Hebrew **l**,
16:15 and said to your sons in the Hebrew **l**,

LANGUAGES (13) [LANGUAGE]

Ge 10:20 their **l**, their lands, and their nations.
10:31 their **l**, their lands, and their nations.
Da 3: 4 "You are commanded, O peoples, nations, and **l**,
3: 7 and **l** fell down and worshiped the golden statue
4: 1 nations, and **l** that live throughout the earth:
5:19 nations, and **l** trembled and feared before him.
7:14 that all peoples, nations, and **l** should serve him.
Ac 2: 4 the Holy Spirit and began to speak in other **l**,
2:11 in our own **l** we hear them speaking
Rev 7: 9 from all tribes and peoples and **l**,
10:11 about many peoples and nations and **l**
11: 9 the peoples and tribes and **l** and nations will gaze
17:15 are peoples and multitudes and nations and **l**.

LANGUISH (9) [LANGUISHED, LANGUISHES, LANGUISHING]

Lev 26:39 And those of you who survive shall **l** in the land
26:39 also they shall **l** because of the iniquities
Isa 16: 8 For the fields of Heshbon **l**,
19: 8 and those who spread nets on the water will **l**.
24: 4 the heavens **l** together with the earth.
Jer 14: 2 Judah mourns and her gates **l**;
31:12 and they shall never **l** again.
La 2: 8 to lament; they **l** together.
Hos 4: 3 the land mourns, and all who live in it **l**;

LANGUISHED (3) [LANGUISH]

Ge 47:13 and the land of Canaan **l** because of the famine.
Ps 68: 9 you restored your heritage when it **l**;
Jer 15: 9 She who bore seven has **l**;

LANGUISHES (4) [LANGUISH]

Ps 119:81 My soul **l** for your salvation;
Isa 24: 4 The earth dries up and withers, the world **l**
24: 7 The wine dries up, the vine **l**,
33: 9 The land mourns and **l**; Lebanon is confounded

LANGUISHING (2) [LANGUISH]

Dt 28:65 failing eyes, and a **l** spirit.
Ps 6: 2 Be gracious to me, O LORD, for I am **l**;

LANTERNS (1)

Jn 18: 3 they came there with **l** and torches and weapons.

LAODICEA (6) [LAODICEANS]

Col 2: 1 for you, and for those in **L**, and for all who have
4:13 for you and for those in **L** and in Hierapolis.
4:15 to the brothers and sisters in **L**,
4:16 and see that you read also the letter from **L**.
Rev 1:11 to Thyatira, to Sardis, to Philadelphia, and to **L**."
3:14 "And to the angel of the church in **L** write:

LAODICEANS (1) [LAODICEA]

Col 4:16 have it read also in the church of the **L**;

LAP (6) [LAPFUL, LAPPED, LAPS]

Jdg 7: 5 "All those who **l** the water with their tongues,
16:19 She let him fall asleep on her **l**;
2Ki 4:20 the child sat on her **l** until noon, and he died.
Pr 16:33 The lot is cast into the **l**,
Lk 6:38 running over, will be put into your **l**;
2Es 15:55 The reward of a prostitute is in your **l**;

LAPFUL (1) [LAP]

2Ki 4:39 he found a wild vine and gathered from it a **l**

LAPIDOTH (KJV) See LAPPIDOTH

LAPIS See Index to Footnotes

LAPPED (2) [LAP]

Jdg 7: 6 The number of those that **l** was three hundred;
7: 7 "With the three hundred that **l** I will deliver you,

LAPPIDOTH (1)

Jdg 4: 4 At that time Deborah, a prophetess, wife of **L**,

LAPS (4) [LAP]

Jdg 7: 5 as a dog **l**, you shall put to one side;
Isa 65: 6 I will indeed repay into their **l**
65: 7 the hills, I will measure into their **l** full payment
Jer 32:18 of parents into the **l** of their children after them,

LAPSE (1)

2Mc 10: 3 they offered sacrifices, after a **l** of two years,

LAPWING (KJV) See HOOPOE

LARGE‡ (128) [ENLARGE, ENLARGED, ENLARGEMENT, ENLARGES, LARGER]

Ge 29: 2 The stone on the well's mouth was **l**,
30:43 and had **l** flocks, and male and female slaves,
34:21 for the land is **l** enough for them;
Nu 13:28 and the towns are fortified and very **l**;
20:20 And Edom came out against them with a **l** force,
26:54 To a **l** tribe you shall give a **l** inheritance,
33:54 to a **l** one you shall give a **l** inheritance,
Dt 1:28 the cities are **l** and fortified up to heaven!
2:10 a **l** and numerous people, as tall as the Anakim—
6:10 a land with fine, **l** cities that you did not build,
25:13 in your bag two kinds of weights, **l** and small.
25:14 in your house two kinds of measures, **l** and small.
27: 2 you shall set up **l** stones and cover them
Jos 10: 2 because Gibeon was a **l** city,
10:18 "Roll **l** stones against the mouth of the cave,
10:27 they set **l** stones against the mouth of the cave,
19: 9 portion of the tribe of Judah was too **l** for them,
24:26 and he took a **l** stone,
1Sa 6:14 and stopped there. A **l** stone was there;
6:15 and set them upon the **l** stone.
14:33 roll a **l** stone before me here."
2Sa 20: 8 When they were at the **l** stone that is in Gibeon,
1Ki 10:16 King Solomon made two hundred **l** shields
10:16 of gold went into each **l** shield.
18:32 **l** enough to contain two measures of seed.
2Ki 4:38 he said to his servant, "Put the **l** pot on,
2Ch 9:15 King Solomon made two hundred **l** shields
9:15 of beaten gold went into each **l** shield.
11:12 He also put **l** shields and spears in all the cities,
14: 8 armed with **l** shields and spears,
23: 9 the captains the spears and the **l** and small shields
24:11 when they saw that there was a **l** amount
26:10 and hewed out many cisterns, for he had **l** herds,
26:15 and the corners for shooting arrows and **l** stones.
30:13 in the second month, a very **l** assembly.
36:18 All the vessels of the house of God, **l** and small,
Ne 7: 4 The city was wide and **l**,
9:35 in the **l** and rich land that you set before them,
13: 5 a **l** room where they had previously put
Pr 16: 8 Better is a little with righteousness than **l** income
Isa 5: 9 **l** and beautiful houses, without inhabitant.
8: 1 a **l** tablet and write on it in common characters,
Jer 22:14 a spacious house with **l** upper rooms,"
41: 9 the **l** cistern that King Asa had made for defense
43: 9 Take some **l** stones in your hands,
Eze 17:15 that they might give him horses and a **l** army.
31: 5 its boughs grew **l** and its branches long,
Jnh 1:17 LORD provided a **l** fish to swallow up Jonah;
3: 3 Now Nineveh was an exceedingly **l** city,
Mt 8:30 a **l** herd of swine was feeding at some distance
19: 2 **L** crowds followed him, and he cured them there.
20:29 As they were leaving Jericho, a **l** crowd followed
21: 8 A very **l** crowd spread their cloaks on the road,
26: 9 this ointment could have been sold for a **l** sum,
26:47 with him was a **l** crowd with swords and clubs,
28:12 they devised a plan to give a **l** sum of money to
Mk 4: 1 a very **l** crowd gathered around him that he got
4:32 and puts forth **l** branches,
5:24 a **l** crowd followed him and pressed in on him.
10:46 and a **l** crowd were leaving Jericho,
12:37 the **l** crowd was listening to him with delight.
12:41 Many rich people put in **l** sums.
13: 1 what **l** stones and what **l** buildings!"
14:15 He will show you a **l** room upstairs,
16: 4 which was very **l**, had already been rolled back.
Lk 5:29 a **l** crowd of tax collectors and others sitting at
7:11 and his disciples and a **l** crowd went with him.
7:12 and with her was a **l** crowd from the town.
8:32 on the hillside a **l** herd of swine was feeding;
14:25 Now **l** crowds were traveling with him;
22:12 He will show you a **l** room upstairs,
Jn 6: 2 A **l** crowd kept following him,
6: 5 When he looked up and saw a **l** crowd coming
21:11 full of **l** fish, a hundred fifty-three of them;
Ac 10:11 and something like a **l** sheet coming down,
11: 5 There was something like a **l** sheet coming down
22:28 a **l** sum of money to get my citizenship."
Ro 8:29 that he might be the firstborn within a **l** family.
Gal 6:11 See what **l** letters I make when I am writing
2Ti 2:20 In a **l** house there are utensils not only of gold
Jas 3: 4 though they are so **l** that it takes strong winds
Tob 6: 3 Suddenly a **l** fish leaped up from the water
Jdt 5: 3 How **l** is their army,
AdE 9:19 in the **l** cities keep the fifteenth day of Adar
1Mc 1:17 and elephants and cavalry and with a **l** fleet.
1:29 and he came to Jerusalem with a **l** force.
3:10 and a **l** force from Samaria to fight against Israel.
3:13 heard that Judas had gathered a **l** company,
3:31 from those regions and raise a **l** fund.
5:26 all these towns were strong and **l**—
5:30 At dawn they looked out and saw a **l** company,
5:38 it is a very **l** force.
5:45 a very **l** company, to go to the land of Judah.
5:46 This was a **l** and very strong town on the road,
5:52 Then they crossed the Jordan into the **l** plain
6:41 trembled, for the army was very **l** and strong.
7:10 So they marched away and came with a **l** force
7:11 for they saw that they had come with a **l** force.
7:27 So Nicanor came to Jerusalem with a **l** force,
8: 6 and with cavalry and chariots and a very **l** army.
9:37 from Nadabath with a **l** escort."
9:43 with a **l** force on the sabbath day to the banks of
9:60 He started to come with a **l** force,
10: 2 he assembled a very **l** army and marched out
10:48 Now King Alexander assembled **l** forces
10:69 and he assembled a **l** force and encamped
10:77 he mustered three thousand cavalry and a **l** army,
10:77 for he had a **l** troop of cavalry and put confidence
10:87 then returned to Jerusalem with a **l** amount
11:48 They set fire to the city and seized a **l** amount
11:51 and they returned to Jerusalem with a **l** amount
11:63 to Kadesh in Galilee with a **l** army,
12:42 Trypho saw that he had come with a **l** army,
13: 1 Simon heard that Trypho had assembled a **l** army
13:12 with a **l** army to invade the land of Judah,
14:24 a **l** gold shield weighing one thousand minas,
15:26 and gold and a **l** amount of military equipment.
16: 5 a **l** force of infantry and cavalry was coming
16:11 he had a **l** store of silver and gold,
2Mc 1:31 that was left should be poured on **l** stones.
8:30 and they divided a very **l** amount of plunder,
1Es 2:30 with cavalry and a **l** number of armed troops,
3Mc 5: 2 with **l** handfuls of frankincense and plenty
2Es 8: 2 it will tell you that it provides a **l** amount of clay
12:26 As for your seeing that the **l** head disappeared,

LARGER (12) [LARGE]

Nu 26:56 be apportioned according to lot between the **l** and
35: 8 from the **l** tribes you shall take many,
Dt 9: 1 and dispossess nations **l** and mightier than you,
11:23 and you will dispossess nations **l** and mightier
20: 1 an army **l** than your own,
Jos 10: 2 and was **l** than Ai, and all its men were warriors.
Eze 43:14 and from the smaller ledge to the **l** ledge,
Da 11:13 of the north shall again raise a multitude, **l** than
Lk 12:18 I will pull down my barns and build **l** ones,
1Mc 4:35 to invade Judea again with an even **l** army.
12:24 with a **l** force than before,
2Es 11: 4 the middle head was **l** than the other heads,

LASCIVIOUSNESS (KJV) See LICENTIOUSNESS

LASEA (1)

Ac 27: 8 to a place called Fair Havens, near the city of **L**.

LASHA (1)

Ge 10:19 Gomorrah, Admah, and Zeboiim, as far as **L**.

LASHARON (1)

Jos 12:18 the king of Aphek one the king of **L** one

LASHED (1) [LASHES]

Wis 5:11 the light air, **l** by the beat of its pinions

LASHES‡ (4) [LASHED]

Dt 25: 2 with the number of **l** proportionate to the offense.
25: 3 Forty **l** may be given but not more; if more **l** than these are given,
2Co 11:24 from the Jews the forty **l** minus one.

LAST‡ (156) [EVERLASTING, LASTED, LASTING, LASTS]

A. LAST DAYS (14)
B. FROM FIRST TO LAST (8)
C. LAST DAY (8)
D. LAST TIMES (7)

Ge 2:23 at **l** is bone of my bones and flesh of my flesh;
19: 4 all the people to the **l** man, surrounded the house;
19:34 "Look, I lay **l** night with my father;
25: 8 Abraham breathed his **l** and died in
25:17 he breathed his **l** and died,
31:29 but the God of your father spoke to me **l** night,
31:42 and rebuked you **l** night."
33: 2 and Rachel and Joseph **l** of all.
35:29 And Isaac breathed his **l**;
49:33 he drew up his feet into the bed, breathed his **l**,
Ex 10: 5 They shall devour the **l** remnant left you after
25:35 and a calyx of one piece with it under the **l** pair
37:21 of one piece with it under the **l** pair of branches.
Nu 2:31 They shall set out **l**, by companies.
14:33 the **l** of your dead bodies lies in the wilderness.
Dt 28:54 and to the **l** of his remaining children,
Jos 8:24 to the very **l** had fallen by the edge of the sword,
12: 4 one of the **l** of the Rephaim,
Ru 3:10 this **l** instance of your loyalty is better than
1Sa 15:16 the LORD said to me **l** night."
2Sa 15:17 and they stopped at the **l** house.
19:11 'Why should you be the **l** to bring the king back
19:12 then should you be the **l** to bring back the king?'
23: 1 Now these are the **l** words of David:
1Ch 23:27 to the **l** words of David these were the number of
29:29 Now the acts of King David, from first to **l**, B
2Ch 9:29 the rest of the acts of Solomon, from first to **l**, B
12:15 Now the acts of Rehoboam, from first to **l**, B

2Ch 16:11 The acts of Asa, from first to l, B
20:34 rest of the acts of Jehoshaphat, from first to l, B
25:26 the rest of the deeds of Amaziah, from first to l, B
26:22 the rest of the acts of Uzziah, from first to l, B
28:26 rest of his acts and all his ways, from first to l, B
35:27 first and l, are written in the Book of the Kings
Ne 8:18 And day by day, from the first day to the l day, C
Job 11:20 and their hope is to breathe their l."
14: 2 flees like a shadow and does not l.
19:25 and that at the l he will stand upon the earth;
Ps 68:25 the singers in front, the musicians l,
76:10 you bind the l bit of your wrath around you.
81:15 and their doom would l forever.
Pr 23:32 At the l it bites like a serpent,
27:24 for riches do not l forever,
Isa 41: 4 I, the LORD, am first, and will be with the l.
44: 6 I am the first and I am the l;
48:12 I am the first, and I am the l.
Jer 32:14 in order that they may l for a long time.
50:12 Lo, she shall be the l of the nations, a wilderness,
50:21 the inhabitants of Pekod and utterly destroy the l
La 2:16 at l we have seen it!"
Da 4: 8 At l Daniel came in before me—
Am 4: 2 even the l of you with fishhooks.
Mt 5:26 until you have paid the l penny.
12:45 the l state of that person is worse than the first.
19:30 many who are first will be l, and the l will be first.
20: 8 beginning with the l and then going to the first.'
20:12 'These l worked only one hour,
20:14 I choose to give to this l the same as I give
20:16 So the l will be first, and the first will be l."
22:27 L of all, the woman herself died.
26:60 false witnesses came forward. At l two came
27:50 with a loud voice and breathed his l.
27:64 the l deception would be worse than the first."
Mk 9:35 to be first must be l of all and servant of all."
10:31 many who are first will be l, and the l will be first."
12:22 L of all the woman herself died.
15:37 Then Jesus gave a loud cry and breathed his l.
15:39 saw that in this way he breathed his l, he said,
Lk 11:26 the l state of that person is worse than the first."
12:59 until you have paid the very l penny."
13:30 Indeed, some are l who will be first, and some are first who will be l."
23:46 Having said this, he breathed his l.
Jn 6:39 but raise it up on the l day. C
6:40 and I will raise them up on the l day." C
6:44 and I will raise that person up on the l day. C
6:54 and I will raise them up on the l day; C
7:37 On the l day of the festival, the great day, C
11:24 in the resurrection on the l day." C
12:48 the l day the word that I have spoken will serve C
15:16 to go and bear fruit, fruit that will l, so that
Ac 2:17 'In the l days it will be, A
27:20 all hope of our being saved was at l abandoned.
27:23 For l night there stood by me an angel of the God
Ro 1:10 that by God's will I may somehow at l succeed
1Co 4: 9 For I think that God has exhibited us apostles as l
15: 8 L of all, as to one untimely born,
15:26 The l enemy to be destroyed is death.
15:45 the l Adam became a life-giving spirit.
15:52 in the twinkling of an eye, at the l trumpet.
2Co 8:10 it is appropriate for you who began l year
9: 2 saying that Achaia has been ready since l year;
Php 4:10 now at l you have revived your concern for me;
1Th 2:16 but God's wrath has overtaken them at l.
2Ti 3: 1 that in the l days distressing times will come. A
Heb 1: 2 but in these l days he has spoken to us by a Son, A
Jas 5: 3 You have laid up treasure for the l days. A
1Pe 1: 5 for a salvation ready to be revealed in the l time.
2Pe 2:20 l state has become worse for them than the first.
3: 3 that in the l days scoffers will come, A
1Jn 2:18 Children, it is the l hour!
2:18 From this we know that it is the l hour.
Jude 1:18 "In the l time there will be scoffers,
Rev 1:17 I am the first and the l,
2: 8 These are the words of the first and the l,
2:19 that your l works are greater than the first.
15: 1 seven angels with seven plagues, which are the l,
21: 9 the seven bowls full of the seven l plagues came
22:13 the first and the l, the beginning and the end."
Jdt 7:27 our wives and children drawing their l breath.
Wis 2:16 he calls the l end of the righteous happy,
14:13 from the beginning, nor will they l forever.
Sir 2: 3 so that your l days may be prosperous. A
6:28 For at l you will find the rest she gives,
12:12 and at l you will realize the truth of my words,
24:28 nor will the l one fathom her.
32:11 Leave in good time and do not be the l;
33:16 Now I was the l to keep vigil;
40:12 but good faith will l forever.
1Mc 6:53 in Judea from the Gentiles had consumed the l of
2Mc 3:31 to one who was lying quite at his l breath.
5: 5 on the wall had been forced back and at l
7: 9 And when he was at his l breath, he said,
7:41 L of all, the mother died, after her sons.
1Es 8:39 Of the descendants of Adonikam, the l ones,
3Mc 5:25 But the Jews, at their l gasp—
5:49 they thought that this was their l moment of life,
5:49 at their breasts who were drawing their l milk.
2Es 5:42 just as for those who are l there is no slowness,
6:12 the l of your signs of which you showed me
6:34 then you will not act hastily in the l times.' " D
7:*43* It will l as though for a week of years.
7:*73* or how will they answer in the l times? D
7:*77* but it will not be shown to you until the l times. D
7:*84* the torment laid up for themselves in the l days. A
7:*87* to be judged in the l times. D
7:*95* and the glory waiting for them in the l days. A
7:*116* [46] "This is my first and l comment:
8:50 the world in the l times, D
8:63 of the signs that you will do in the l times, D
10:59 to those who inhabit the earth in the l days." A
11: 9 but let the heads be reserved for the l."
12: 9 be shown the end of the times and the l events of
12:23 In its l days the Most High will raise A
12:25 up his wickedness and perform his l actions.
12:28 but he also shall fall by the sword in the l days. A
13:18 the things that are reserved for the l days, A
13:20 and not to see what will happen in the l days." A
13:46 "Then they lived there until the l times; D
14:22 those who want to live in the l days may do so." A
14:46 but keep the seventy that were written l,
4Mc 2: 9 nor gathers the l grapes from the vineyard.
15:18 When the firstborn breathed his l,

LASTED (2) [LAST]

Jdg 14:17 before him the seven days that their feast l;
Jdt 13: 1 for they all were weary because the banquet had l

LASTHENES (2)

1Mc 11:31 concerning you to our kinsman L we have written
11:32 'King Demetrius to his father L, greetings.

LASTING (17) [LAST]

Lev 23:34 of this seventh month, and l seven days,
23:39 the festival of the LORD, l seven days;
Dt 6:24 to fear the LORD our God, for our l good,
28:59 and your offspring with severe and l afflictions
28:59 and grievous and l maladies.
Est 1: 5 both great and small, a banquet l for seven days,
Pr 28: 2 but with an intelligent ruler there is l order.
Heb 10:34 yourselves possessed something better and more l.
13:14 For here we have no l city,
1Pe 3: 4 be the inner self with the l beauty of a gentle
AdE 2:18 a banquet l seven days for all his Friends and
13: 2 to settle the lives of my subjects in l tranquility
Sir 2: 9 hope for good things, for l joy and mercy.
11:17 and his favor brings l success.
41: 9 When you stumble, there is l joy;
49:13 The memory of Nehemiah also is l;
1Mc 4:45 a l shame to them that the Gentiles had defiled it.

LASTS (6) [LAST]

Pr 12:19 but a lying tongue l only a moment.
Tob 13: 1 because his kingdom l throughout all ages.
Sir 22:12 Mourning for the dead l seven days,
22:12 but for the foolish or the ungodly it l all the days
41: 4 Whether life l for ten years or a hundred or
41:13 but a good name l forever.

LATCHET (KJV) See SANDAL-THONG, THONG

LATE (11) [LATER, LATTER]

Ex 9:32 for they are l in coming up.)
2Sa 11: 2 It happened, l one afternoon,
Ps 127: 2 It is in vain that you rise up early and go l to rest,
Pr 23:30 Those who linger l over wine,
Mt 14:15 "This is a deserted place, and the hour is now l;
Mk 6:35 When it grew l, his disciples came to him
6:35 and the hour is now very l;
11:11 around at everything, as it was already l,
Jas 5: 7 with it until it receives the early and the l rains.
1Mc 10:80 at his men from early morning until l afternoon.
2Mc 8:25 to return because the hour was l.

LATER‡ (47) [LATE]

Ge 30:33 So my honesty will answer for me l,
38:24 About three months l Judah was told,
Dt 11:14 the early rain and the l rain,
1Sa 11: 1 About a month l, Nahash the Ammonite went up
25:38 About ten days l the LORD struck Nabal,
1Ki 3:16 L, two women who were prostitutes came to
21: 1 L the following events took place:
2Ki 6:24 Some time l King Ben-hadad
Ezr 8:13 those who came l, their names being Eliphelet,
Ecc 4:16 Yet those who come l will not rejoice in him.
Da 8:19 and I will tell you what will take place l in
Joel 2:23 the early and the l rain, as before.
Mt 17: 1 Six days l, Jesus took with him Peter and James
21:29 but l he changed his mind and went.
25:11 L the other bridesmaids came also, saying, 'Lord,
Mk 9: 2 Six days l, Jesus took with him Peter and James
16:14 ⟦L he appeared to the eleven themselves⟧
Lk 15:13 A few days l the younger son gathered all he had
17: 8 l you may eat and drink'?
18: 4 For a while he refused; but l he said to himself,
22:58 A little l someone else, on seeing him, said,
22:59 Then about an hour l still another kept insisting,
Jn 5:14 L Jesus found him in the temple and said to him,
13: 7 but l you will understand."
20:26 A week l his disciples were again in the house,
Ac 24: 1 Five days l the high priest Ananias came down
24:24 Some days l when Felix came
28:11 Three months l we set sail on a ship
28:17 Three days l he called together the local leaders
Gal 3:17 the law, which came four hundred thirty years l,
1Ti 4: 1 that in l times some will renounce the faith
Heb 3: 5 to testify to the things that would be spoken l.
4: 7 "today"—saying through David much l,
4: 8 God would not speak l about another day.
7:28 which came l than the law,
12:11 but l it yields the peaceful fruit of righteousness
12:17 You know that l, when he wanted to inherit
Sir 27:23 but l he will twist his speech and
Bar 3:20 L generations have seen the light of day,
1Mc 1:29 Two years l the king sent to the cities of Judah
11:18 But King Ptolemy died three days l,
2Mc 4:17 a fact that l events will make clear.
14: 1 Three years l, word came to Judas and his men
1Es 1:45 A year l Nebuchadnezzar sent and removed him
3Mc 1: 3 a Jew by birth who l changed his religion
3:24 if a sudden disorder l arises against us,
4Mc 12: 7 as we shall tell a little l,

LATIN‡ (1)

Jn 19:20 and it was written in Hebrew, in L, and in Greek.

LATRINE (1)

2Ki 10:27 and made it a l to this day.

LATTER (17) [LATE]

Job 8: 7 your l days will be very great.
42:12 the l days of Job more than his beginning;
Isa 9: 1 but in the l time he will make glorious the way of
Jer 23:20 In the l days you will understand it clearly.
30:24 In the l days you will understand this.
48:47 I will restore the fortunes of Moab in the l days,
49:39 in the l days I will restore the fortunes of Elam,
Eze 38: 8 in the l years you shall go against a land restored
38:16 In the l days I will bring you against my land,
Da 11: 9 l shall invade the realm of the king of the south,
Hos 3: 5 to the LORD and to his goodness in the l days.
Am 7: 1 at the time the l growth began to sprout (it was the l growth after the king's mowings).
Hag 2: 9 The l splendor of this house shall be greater than
Wis 16:16 the l, having first received them
1Mc 11:34 the l, with all the region bordering them,
2Mc 14:31 When the l became aware

LATTICE (5) [LATTICEWORK, LATTICEWORKS]

Jdg 5:28 the mother of Sisera gazed through the l:
2Ki 1: 2 through the l in his upper chamber in Samaria,
Pr 7: 6 of my house I looked out through my l,
SS 2: 9 gazing in at the windows, looking through the l.
Sir 42:11 See that there is no l in her room,

LATTICEWORK (8) [LATTICE]

1Ki 7:18 with two rows around each l to cover the capitals
7:20 the rounded projection that was beside the l;
7:42 two rows of pomegranates for each l,
2Ki 25:17 l and pomegranates, all of bronze,
25:17 The second pillar had the same, with the l.
2Ch 4:13 two rows of pomegranates for each l,
Jer 52:22 l and pomegranates, all of bronze,
52:23 the l numbered one hundred.

LATTICEWORKS (4) [LATTICE]

1Ki 7:41 the two l to cover the two bowls of the capitals
7:42 the four hundred pomegranates for the two l,
2Ch 4:12 the two l to cover the two bowls of the capitals
4:13 the four hundred pomegranates for the two l,

LAUD (1)

Ps 145: 4 One generation shall l your works to another,

LAUD (KJV) See also PRAISE

LAUGH (19) [LAUGHED, LAUGHING, LAUGHINGSTOCK, LAUGHS, LAUGHTER]

Ge 18:13 The LORD said to Abraham, "Why did Sarah l,
18:15 But Sarah denied, saying, "I did not l";
18:15 He said, "Oh yes, you did l."
21: 6 everyone who hears will l with me."
Job 5:22 At destruction and famine you shall l,
22:19 the innocent l them to scorn,
Ps 52: 6 and fear, and will l at the evildoer, saying,
59: 8 But you l at them, O LORD;
80: 6 our enemies l among themselves.
Pr 1:26 I also will l at your calamity;
Ecc 3: 4 a time to weep, and a time to l;
Hab 1:10 They l at every fortress, and heap up earth to take
Lk 6:21 "Blessed are you who weep now, for you will l.
Jdt 12:12 If we do not seduce her, she will l at us."
AdE 14:11 and do not let them l at our downfall;
Wis 4:18 but the Lord will l them to scorn.
Sir 13: 7 and finally he will l at you.
30:10 not l with him, or you will have sorrow with him,
4Mc 5:28 But you shall have no such occasion to l at me,

LAUGHED (10) [LAUGH]

Ge 17:17 Then Abraham fell on his face and l,
18:12 So Sarah l to herself, saying,
38:23 otherwise we will be l at;
2Ch 30:10 but they l them to scorn, and mocked them.
Mt 9:24 And they l at him.
Mk 5:40 And they l at him.
Lk 8:53 And they l at him, knowing that she was dead.
Tob 2: 8 my neighbors l and said, "Is he still not afraid?

Bel 1: 7 And Daniel l, and said, "Do not be deceived,
1:19 Daniel l and restrained the king from going in.

LAUGHING (1) [LAUGH]

Lk 6:25 "Woe to you who are l now,

LAUGHINGSTOCK (12) [LAUGH]

Job 12: 4 I am a l to my friends;
12: 4 a just and blameless man, I am a l.
Ps 44:14 among the nations, a l among the peoples.
Jer 20: 7 I have become a l all day long;
48:26 he too shall become a l.
48:27 Israel was a l for you, though he was not caught
La 3:14 I have become the l of all my people,
Jdt 5:21 and we shall become the l of the whole world."
Sir 6: 4 and makes them the l of their enemies.
18:31 it will make you the l of your enemies.
42:11 or she may make you a l to your enemies,
4Mc 6:20 for a little while and during that time be a l to all

LAUGHS‡ (9) [LAUGH]

Job 39:18 it l at the horse and its rider.
39:22 It l at fear, and is not dismayed;
41:29 it l at the rattle of javelins.
Ps 2: 4 He who sits in the heavens l;
37:13 but the LORD l at the wicked,
Pr 31:25 and she l at the time to come.
Sir 21:15 he l at it and throws it behind his back.
21:20 A fool raises his voice when he l,
1Es 4:31 If she smiles at him, he l;

LAUGHTER (11) [LAUGH]

Ge 21: 6 Now Sarah said, "God has brought l for me;
Job 8:21 He will yet fill your mouth with l,
Ps 126: 2 Then our mouth was filled with l,
Pr 14:13 in l the heart is sad, and the end of joy is grief.
Ecc 2: 2 I said of l, "It is mad," and of pleasure,
7: 3 Sorrow is better than l, for by sadness
7: 6 so is the l of fools; this also is vanity.
10:19 Feasts are made for l; wine gladdens life,
Jas 4: 9 Let your l be turned into mourning and your joy
Sir 19:30 A person's attire and hearty l,
27:13 and their l is wantonly sinful.

LAUNCHED (3)

1Sa 19: 8 He l a heavy attack on them,
2Mc 4:40 about three thousand men and l an unjust attack,
2Es 9:34 or what was l or what was put in is destroyed,

LAVER (1)

2Ki 16:17 and removed the l from them;

LAVER (KJV) See also BASIN

LAVISH (4) [LAVISHED, LAVISHING, LAVISHLY]

Isa 46: 6 Those who l gold from the purse,
Hab 1:16 for by them his portion is l, and his food is rich.
Sir 1:26 and the Lord will l her upon you.
3Mc 5: 2 maddened by the l abundance of drink,

LAVISHED (5) [LAVISH]

Est 1: 7 and the royal wine was l according to the bounty
Eze 16:15 and l your whorings on any passer-by.
Hos 2: 8 and who l upon her silver and gold that they used
Eph 1: 8 that he l on us. With all wisdom and insight
Sir 1:10 he l her upon those who love him.

LAVISHING (1) [LAVISH]

Da 11:24 l plunder, spoil, and wealth on them.

LAVISHLY (2) [LAVISH]

1Mc 3:30 that he used to give more l than preceding kings.
3Mc 6:33 gave thanks to heaven unceasingly and l for

LAW‡ (588) [LAW'S, LAW-ABIDING, LAWBREAKER, LAWBREAKERS, LAWFUL, LAWFULLY, LAWGIVER, LAWLESS, LAWLESSLY, LAWLESSNESS, LAWS, LAWSUIT, LAWSUITS, LAWYER, LAWYERS]

A. LAW OF MOSES (28)
B. LAW OF ... *GOD (26)
C. BOOK OF THE/THIS LAW (22)
D. WRITTEN IN ... LAW (18)
E. LAW OF THE †LORD (16)
F. UNDER [THE] LAW (14)
G. WORDS OF THE/THIS LAW (14)
H. THIS IS THE LAW (10)
I. WORKS OF THE LAW (7)

Ex 12:49 there shall be one l for the native and for
24:12 with the l and the commandment,
Lev 11:46 This is the l pertaining to land animal and bird H
12: 7 This is the l for her who bears a child, H
24:22 You shall have one l for the alien and for
Nu 5:29 This is the l in cases of jealousy, when a wife, H
5:30 and the priest shall apply this entire l to her.
6:13 This is the l for the nazirites when the time H
Nu 6:21 This is the l for the nazirites who take a vow. H
6:21 following the l for their consecration.
15:16 the same l and the same ordinance.
15:29 you shall have the same l for anyone who acts
19: 2 of the l that the LORD has commanded:
19:14 This is the l when someone dies in a tent: H
31:21 of the l that the LORD has commanded Moses:
Dt 1: 5 Moses undertook to expound this l as follows:
4: 8 as this entire l that I am setting before you today?
4:44 This is the l that Moses set before the Israelites. H
17:11 You must carry out fully the l that they interpret
17:18 a copy of this l written for him in the presence of
17:19 diligently observing all the words of this l G
27: 3 the words of this l when you have crossed over, G
27: 8 on the stones all the words of this l very clearly. G
27:26 the words of this l by observing them." G
28:58 the words of this l that are written in this book, G
28:61 even though not recorded in the book of this l, C
29:21 of the covenant written in this book of the l. C
29:29 to observe all the words of this l. G
30:10 and decrees that are written in this book of the l, C
31: 9 Then Moses wrote down this l,
31:11 you shall read this l before all Israel
31:12 and to observe diligently all the words of this l, G
31:24 in a book the words of this l to the very end, G
31:26 "Take this book of the l and put it beside the ark C
32:46 may diligently observe all the words of this l. G
33: 4 Moses charged us with the l,
33:10 teach Jacob your ordinances, and Israel your l;
Jos 1: 7 being careful to act in accordance with all the l
1: 8 book of the l shall not depart out of your mouth; C
8:31 as it is written in the book of the l of Moses, AC
8:32 wrote on the stones a copy of the l of Moses, A
8:34 And afterward he read all the words of the l, G
8:34 to all that is written in the book of the l. C
23: 6 that is written in the book of the l of Moses, AC
24:26 wrote these words in the book of the l of God; BC
1Ki 2: 3 as it is written in the l of Moses, AD
2Ki 10:31 not careful to follow the l of the LORD the God E
14: 6 what is written in the book of the l of Moses, AC
17:13 with all the l that I commanded your ancestors
17:26 cities of Samaria do not know the l of the god B
17:26 they do not know the l of the god of the land." B
17:27 and teach them the l of the god of the land." B
17:34 the ordinances or the l or the commandment that
17:37 the ordinances and the l and the commandment
21: 8 the l that my servant Moses commanded them."
22: 8 "I have found the book of the l in the house of C
22:11 the king heard the words of the book of the l, C
23:24 the words of the l that were written in the book G
23:25 according to all the l of Moses; A
1Ch 16:40 all that is written in the l of the LORD DE
22:12 over Israel you may keep the l of the LORD E
2Ch 6:16 to walk in my l as you have walked before me.'
12: 1 he abandoned the l of the LORD, E
14: 4 and to keep the l and the commandment.
15: 3 and without a teaching priest, and without l;
17: 9 the book of the l of the LORD with them; CE
19:10 concerning bloodshed, l or commandment,
23:18 as it is written in the l of Moses, AD
25: 4 according to what is written in the l, D
30:16 according to the l of Moses the man of God; A
31: 3 as it is written in the l of the LORD. DE
31: 4 might devote themselves to the l of the LORD. E
31:21 in accordance with the l and the commandments,
33: 8 to do all that I have commanded them, all the l,
34:14 book of the l of the LORD given through Moses. CE
34:15 "I have found the book of the l in the house of C
34:19 king heard the words of the l he tore his clothes. G
35:26 with what is written in the l of the LORD, DE
Ezr 3: 2 as prescribed in the l of Moses the man of God. A
7: 6 a scribe skilled in the l of Moses that the LORD A
7:10 Ezra had set his heart to study the l of the LORD, E
7:12 the scribe of the l of the God of heaven: Peace. B
7:14 and Jerusalem according to the l of your God, B
7:21 the scribe of the l of the God of heaven, B
7:26 All who will not obey the l of your God and B
7:26 the law of your God and the l of the king,
10: 3 and let it be done according to the l.
Ne 8: 1 Ezra to bring the book of the l of Moses, AC
8: 2 the priest Ezra brought the l before the assembly,
8: 3 the people were attentive to the book of the l. C
8: 7 helped the people to understand the l,
8: 8 So they read from the book, from the l of God, B
8: 9 when they heard the words of the l. G
8:13 in order to study the words of the l. G
8:14 And they found it written in the l, D
8:18 he read from the book of the l of God. BC
9: 3 from the book of the l of the LORD their God CE
9:14 and statutes and a l through your servant Moses.
9:26 against you and cast your l behind their backs
9:29 in order to turn them back to your l.
9:34 not kept your l or heeded the commandments and
10:28 peoples of the lands to adhere to the l of God, B
10:29 enter into a curse and an oath to walk in God's l,
10:34 as it is written in the l. D
10:36 as it is written in the l, D
12:44 to gather into them the portions required by the l
13: 3 When the people heard the l,
Est 1:13 toward all who were versed in l and custom,
1:15 to the l, what is to be done to Queen Vashti
4:11 there is but one l—all alike are to be put to death.
4:16 I will go to the king, though it is against the l;
Ps 1: 2 but their delight is in the l of the LORD, E
1: 2 and on his l they meditate day and night.
19: 7 The l of the LORD is perfect, reviving the soul; E
37:31 The l of their God is in their hearts; B
Ps 40: 8 your l is within my heart."
78: 5 and appointed a l in Israel,
78:10 but refused to walk according to his l.
89:30 If his children forsake my l and do not walk
94:12 O LORD, and whom you teach out of your l,
119: 1 who walk in the l of the LORD. E
119:18 that I may behold wondrous things out of your l.
119:29 and graciously teach me your l.
119:34 that I may keep your l and observe it
119:44 I will keep your l continually, forever and ever.
119:51 but I do not turn away from your l.
119:53 those who forsake your l.
119:55 O LORD, and keep your l.
119:61 I do not forget your l.
119:70 but I delight in your l.
119:72 The l of your mouth is better
119:77 for your l is my delight.
119:85 for me; they flout your l.
119:92 If your l had not been my delight,
119:97 Oh, how I love your l!
119:109 but I do not forget your l.
119:113 I hate the double-minded, but I love your l.
119:126 for your l has been broken.
119:136 My eyes shed streams of tears because your l is
119:142 and your l is the truth.
119:150 they are far from your l.
119:153 for I do not forget your l.
119:163 I hate and abhor falsehood, but I love your l.
119:165 Great peace have those who love your l;
119:174 O LORD, and your l is my delight.
Pr 28: 4 Those who forsake the l praise the wicked,
28: 4 but those who keep the l struggle against them.
28: 7 Those who keep the l are wise children,
28: 9 When one will not listen to the l,
29: 9 If the wise go to l with fools,
29:18 but happy are those who keep the l.
Isa 42:24 and whose l they would not obey?
59: 4 no one goes to l honestly;
Jer 2: 8 Those who handle the l did not know me;
5: 4 the way of the LORD, the l of their God. B
5: 5 know the way of the LORD, the l of their God." B
8: 8 and the l of the LORD is with us," when, in fact, E
9:13 they have forsaken my l that I set before them,
16:11 and have forsaken me and have not kept my l;
26: 4 to walk in my l that I have set before you,
31:33 I will put my l within them,
32:23 they did not obey your voice or follow your l;
44:10 in my l and my statutes that I set before you and
44:23 not obey the voice of the LORD or walk in his l
Eze 43:12 This is the l of the temple: H
43:12 This is the l of the temple. H
Da 6: 5 we find it in connection with the l of his God." B
6: 8 according to the l of the Medes and the Persians,
6:12 according to the l of the Medes and Persians,
6:15 a l of the Medes and Persians that no interdict
7:25 to change the sacred seasons and the l;
9:11 "All Israel has transgressed your l
9:11 curse and the oath written in the l of Moses, AD
9:13 Just as it is written in the l of Moses, AD
Hos 4: 6 And since you have forgotten the l of your God, B
8: 1 broken my covenant, and transgressed my l.
Am 2: 4 because they have rejected the l of the LORD, E
Hab 1: 4 So the l becomes slack and justice never prevails.
Zep 3: 4 they have done violence to the l.
Zec 7:12 not to hear the l and the words that the LORD
Mt 5:17 "Do not think that I have come to abolish the l or
5:18 will pass from the l until all is accomplished.
7:12 for this is the l and the prophets. H
11:13 For all the prophets and the l prophesied
12: 5 not read in the l that on the sabbath the priests in
22:36 which commandment in the l is the greatest?"
22:40 On these two commandments hang all the l and
23:23 and have neglected the weightier matters of the l:
Lk 2:22 their purification according to the l of Moses, A
2:23 (as it is written in the l of the Lord, D
2:24 according to what is stated in the l of the Lord,
2:27 to do for him what was customary under the l, F
2:39 everything required by the l of the Lord,
5:17 Pharisees and teachers of the l were sitting near
10:26 He said to him, "What is written in the l? D
16:16 l and the prophets were in effect until John came;
16:17 for one stroke of a letter in the l to be dropped.
24:44 everything written about me in the l of Moses, A
Jn 1:17 The l indeed was given through Moses;
1:45 "We have found him about whom Moses in the l
7:19 "Did not Moses give you the l?
7:19 Yet none of you keeps the l.
7:23 the sabbath in order that the l of Moses may not A
7:49 But this crowd, which does not know the l—
7:51 "Our l does not judge people
8: 5 ⟦the l Moses commanded us to stone such women⟧
8:17 In your l it is written that the testimony
10:34 Jesus answered, "Is it not written in your l, D
12:34 from the l that the Messiah remains forever.
15:25 It was to fulfill the word that is written in their l, D
18:31 and judge him according to your l."
19: 7 The Jews answered him, "We have a l,
19: 7 that l he ought to die because he has claimed to
Ac 2:23 and killed by the hands of those outside the l.
5:34 a teacher of the l, respected by all the people,
6:13 against this holy place and the l;
7:53 You are the ones that received the l as ordained
13:15 After the reading of the l and the prophets,
13:39 which you could not be freed by the l of Moses. A
15: 5 circumcised and ordered to keep the l of Moses." A
18:13 to worship God in ways that are contrary to the l."
18:15 and names and your own l, see to it yourselves;

Ac 21:20 and they are all zealous for the **l**.
21:24 but that you yourself observe and guard the **l**.
21:28 against our people, our **l**, and this place;
22: 3 educated strictly according to our ancestral **l**,
22:12 a devout man according to the **l** and well spoken
23: 3 to judge me according to the **l**,
23: 3 in violation of the **l** you order me to be struck?"
23:29 concerning questions of their **l**,
24:14 believing everything laid down according to the **l**
25: 8 in no way committed an offense against the **l** of
28:23 both from the **l** of Moses and from the prophets. A
Ro 2:12 apart from the **l** will also perish apart from the **l**,
2:12 and all who have sinned under the **l** F
2:12 sinned under the law will be judged by the **l**.
2:13 For it is not the hearers of the **l** who are righteous
2:13 but the doers of the **l** who will be justified.
2:14 When Gentiles, who do not possess the **l**, do instinctively what the **l** requires, these, though not having the **l**, are a **l** to themselves.
2:15 that what the **l** requires is written on their hearts,
2:17 a Jew and rely on the **l** and boast of your relation
2:18 because you are instructed in the **l**,
2:20 in the **l** the embodiment of knowledge and truth,
2:23 You that boast in the **l**, do you dishonor God by breaking the **l**?
2:25 of value if you obey the **l**; but if you break the **l**,
2:26 the requirements of the **l**,
2:27 the **l** will condemn you that have the written code
2:27 and circumcision but break the **l**.
3:19 Now we know that whatever the **l** says,
3:19 it speaks to those who are under the **l**, F
3:20 in his sight" by deeds prescribed by the **l**,
3:20 for through the **l** comes the knowledge of sin.
3:21 But now, apart from **l**, the righteousness
3:21 and is attested by the **l** and the prophets,
3:27 It is excluded. By what **l**?
3:27 No, but by the **l** of faith.
3:28 by faith apart from works prescribed by the **l**.
3:31 Do we then overthrow the **l** by this faith?
3:31 On the contrary, we uphold the **l**.
4:13 to Abraham or to his descendants through the **l**
4:14 it is the adherents of the **l** who are to be the heirs,
4:15 For the **l** brings wrath; but where there is no **l**,
4:16 the adherents of the **l** but also to those who share
5:13 sin was indeed in the world before the **l**, but sin is not reckoned when there is no **l**.
5:20 But **l** came in, with the result that
6:14 since you are not under **l** but under grace. F
6:15 Should we sin because we are not under **l** but F
7: 1 for I am speaking to those who know the **l**—that the **l** is binding on a person only during
7: 2 by the **l** to her husband as long as he lives; but if her husband dies, she is discharged from the **l**
7: 3 But if her husband dies, she is free from that **l**,
7: 4 you have died to the **l** through the body of Christ,
7: 5 our sinful passions, aroused by the **l**,
7: 6 But now we are discharged from the **l**,
7: 7 That the **l** is sin?
7: 7 Yet, if it had not been for the **l**,
7: 7 not have known what it is to covet if the **l** had
7: 8 Apart from the **l** sin lies dead.
7: 9 I was once alive apart from the **l**,
7:12 So the **l** is holy, and the commandment is holy
7:14 For we know that the **l** is spiritual;
7:16 I do what I do not want, I agree that the **l** is good.
7:21 to be a **l** that when I want to do what is good,
7:22 For I delight in the **l** of God in my inmost self, B
7:23 in my members another **l** at war with the **l** of my mind, making me captive to the **l** of sin that dwells
7:25 then, with my mind I am a slave to the **l** of God, B
7:25 but with my flesh I am a slave to the **l** of sin.
8: 2 For the **l** of the Spirit of life in Christ Jesus has set you free from the **l** of sin and death.
8: 3 For God has done what the **l**,
8: 4 just requirement of the **l** might be fulfilled in us,
8: 7 it does not submit to God's **l**—
9: 4 the covenants, the giving of the **l**, the worship,
9:31 for the righteousness that is based on the **l**, did not succeed in fulfilling that **l**.
10: 4 For Christ is the end of the **l** so that there may
10: 5 the righteousness that comes from the **l**,
13: 8 for the one who loves another has fulfilled the **l**.
13:10 therefore, love is the fulfilling of the **l**.
1Co 9: 8 Does not the **l** also say the same?
9: 9 For it is written in the **l** of Moses, AD
9:20 To those under the **l** I became as one under F
9:20 I became as one under the **l** (though I myself F
9:20 (though I myself am not under the **l**) F
9:20 so that I might win those under the **l**. F
9:21 To those outside the **l** I became as one outside the **l** (though I am not free from God's **l** but am under Christ's **l**) so that I might win those outside the **l**.
14:21 the **l** it is written, "By people of strange tongues
14:34 but should be subordinate, as the **l** also says.
15:56 sting of death is sin, and the power of sin is the **l**.
Gal 2:16 that a person is justified not by the works of the **l** I
2:16 and not by doing the works of the **l**, I
2:16 no one will be justified by the works of the **l**. I
2:19 the **l** I died to the **l**, so that I might live to God.
2:21 for if justification comes through the **l**,
3: 2 works of the **l** or by believing what you heard? I
3: 5 among you by your doing the works of the **l**, I
3:10 who rely on the works of the **l** are under a curse; I
3:10 the things written in the book of the **l**." C
3:11 that no one is justified before God by the **l**;
3:12 But the **l** does not rest on faith;
3:12 "Whoever does the works of the **l** will live I
Gal 3:13 the curse of the **l** by becoming a curse for us—
3:17 the **l**, which came four hundred thirty years later,
3:18 For if the inheritance comes from the **l**,
3:19 Why then the **l**? It was added
3:21 Is the **l** then opposed to the promises of God?
3:21 For if a **l** had been given that could make alive,
3:21 righteousness would indeed come through the **l**.
3:23 we were imprisoned and guarded under the **l** F
3:24 the **l** was our disciplinarian until Christ came,
4: 4 born of a woman, born under the **l**, F
4: 5 in order to redeem those who were under the **l**, F
4:21 Tell me, you who desire to be subject to the **l**,
4:21 will you not listen to the **l**?
5: 3 that he is obliged to obey the entire **l**.
5: 4 to be justified by the **l** have cut yourselves off
5:14 whole **l** is summed up in a single commandment,
5:18 you are not subject to the **l**.
5:23 There is no **l** against such things.
6: 2 and in this way you will fulfill the **l** of Christ.
6:13 the circumcised do not themselves obey the **l**,
Eph 2:15 He has abolished the **l** with its commandments
Php 3: 5 Hebrew born of Hebrews; as to the **l**, a Pharisee;
3: 6 as to righteousness under the **l**, blameless. F
3: 9 a righteousness of my own that comes from the **l**,
1Ti 1: 7 desiring to be teachers of the **l**,
1: 8 Now we know that the **l** is good,
1: 9 that the **l** is laid down not for the innocent but for
Tit 3: 9 dissensions, and quarrels about the **l**,
Heb 7: 5 the priestly office have a commandment in the **l**
7:11 the people received the **l** under this priesthood—
7:12 there is necessarily a change in the **l** as well.
7:19 (for the **l** made nothing perfect);
7:28 For the **l** appoints as high priests those who are
7:28 the oath, which came later than the **l**,
8: 4 there are priests who offer gifts according to the **l**.
9:19 the people by Moses in accordance with the **l**,
9:22 under the **l** almost everything is purified with F
10: 1 Since the **l** has only a shadow of the good things
10: 8 (these are offered according to the **l**),
10:28 Anyone who has violated the **l** of Moses dies A
Jas 1:25 But those who look into the perfect **l**,
1:25 the **l** of liberty, and persevere,
2: 8 if you really fulfill the royal **l** according to
2: 9 and are convicted by the **l** as transgressors.
2:10 For whoever keeps the whole **l** but fails
2:11 you have become a transgressor of the **l**.
2:12 and so act as those who are to be judged by the **l**
4:11 speaks evil against the **l** and judges the **l**; but if you judge the **l**, you are not a doer of the **l** but
Tob 1: 8 concerning it in the **l** of Moses and according to A
7:12 the **l** and decree written in the book of Moses.
7:13 wife according to the decree of the **l** of Moses. A
AdE 1:20 Let whatever **l** the king enacts be proclaimed
4:16 After that I will go to the king, contrary to the **l**,
15:10 for our **l** applies only to our subjects.
Wis 2:11 But let our might be our **l** of right,
2:12 he reproaches us for sins against the **l**,
6: 4 not rule rightly, or keep the **l**, or walk according
14:16 grown strong with time, was kept as a **l**,
18: 4 through whom the imperishable light of the **l** was
18: 9 and with one accord agreed to the divine **l**,
Sir Pr: 1 through the **L** and the Prophets and the others
Pr: 1 of the **L** and the Prophets and the other books
Pr: 1 even greater progress in living according to the **l**.
Pr: 2 Not only this book, but even the **L** itself,
Pr: 3 and are disposed to live according to the **l**.
2:16 and those who love him are filled with his **l**.
8:14 Do not go to **l** against a judge,
9:15 and let all your discussion be about the **l** of
15: 1 and whoever holds to the **l** will obtain wisdom.
17:11 and allotted to them the **l** of life.
19:17 and let the **l** of the Most High take its course.
19:20 and in all wisdom there is the fulfillment of the **l**.
19:24 the highly intelligent who transgress the **l**.
21:11 Whoever keeps the **l** controls his thoughts,
23:23 she has disobeyed the **l** of the Most High;
24:23 the **l** that Moses commanded us as an inheritance
32:15 The one who seeks the **l** will be filled with it,
32:24 The one who keeps the **l** preserves himself,
33: 2 The wise will not hate the **l**,
33: 3 The sensible person will trust in the **l**;
33: 3 a one the **l** is as dependable as a divine oracle.
34: 8 Without such deceptions the **l** will be fulfilled,
35: 1 The one who keeps the **l** makes many offerings;
38:34 the one who devotes himself to the study of the **l**
39: 8 and will glory in the **l** of the Lord's covenant.
41: 8 who have forsaken the **l** of the Most High God!
41:18 and of a breach of the **l**,
42: 2 of the **l** of the Most High and his covenant,
44:20 He kept the **l** of the Most High,
45: 5 the **l** of life and knowledge,
45:17 and to enlighten Israel with his **l**.
46:14 By the **l** of the Lord he judged the congregation,
49: 4 for they abandoned the **l** of the Most High;
Bar 2: 2 the threats that were written in the **l** of Moses. AD
2:28 when you commanded him to write your **l** in
4: 1 the **l** that endures forever.
4:12 because they turned away from the **l** of God. B
Aza 1: 6 and broken your **l** in turning away from you;
Sus 1: 3 their daughter according to the **l** of Moses. A
1:62 Acting in accordance with the **l** of Moses, A
1Mc 1:49 so that they would forget the **l** and change all
1:52 Many of the people, everyone who forsook the **l**,
1:56 The books of the **l** that they found they tore
1:57 or anyone who adhered to the **l**,
2:21 be it from us to desert the **l** and the ordinances.
2:26 Thus he burned with zeal for the **l**,
1Mc 2:27 for the **l** and supports the covenant come out
2:42 all who offered themselves willingly for the **l**.
2:48 the **l** out of the hands of the Gentiles and kings,
2:50 Now, my children, show zeal for the **l**,
2:58 Elijah, because of great zeal for the **l**,
2:64 be courageous and grow strong in the **l**,
2:67 You shall rally around you all who observe the **l**,
2:68 and obey the commands of the **l**."
3: 5 and pursued those who broke the **l**;
3:48 the book of the **l** to inquire into those matters C
3:56 he told to go home again, according to the **l**.
4:42 He chose blameless priests devoted to the **l**,
4:47 Then they took unhewn stones, as the **l** directs,
4:53 as the **l** directs, on the new altar of burnt offering
10:14 the **l** and the commandments,
13:48 and settled in it those who observed the **l**.
14:14 the **l**, and did away with all the renegades
14:29 that their sanctuary and the **l** might be preserved;
15:21 so that he may punish them according to their **l**."
2Mc 1: 4 to his **l** and his commandments,
2: 2 the **l**, instructed those who were being deported
2: 3 that the **l** should not depart from their hearts.
2:18 as he promised through the **l**.
3:15 upon him who had given the **l** about deposits,
4:11 and introduced new customs contrary to the **l**.
6:23 and moreover according to the holy God-given **l**,
7:30 but I obey the command of the **l** that was given
10:26 to their adversaries, as the **l** declares.
12:40 which the **l** forbids the Jews to wear.
13:10 of being deprived of the **l** and their country and
15: 9 Encouraging them from the **l** and the prophets,
1Es 1:33 and his understanding of the **l** of the Lord,
5:51 as it is commanded in the **l**,
8: 3 in the **l** of Moses, which was given by the God A
8: 7 so that he omitted nothing from the **l** of the Lord
8: 8 to Ezra the priest and reader of the **l** of the Lord:
8: 9 to Ezra the priest and reader of the **l** of the Lord,
8:12 in accordance with what is in the **l** of the Lord,
8:19 that whatever Ezra the priest and reader of the **l**
8:21 in the **l** of God be scrupulously fulfilled for B
8:23 to judge all those who know the **l** of your God, B
8:24 the **l** of your God or the law of the kingdom B
8:24 or the **l** of the kingdom shall be strictly punished,
8:87 but we turned back again to transgress your **l**
8:94 as seems good to you and to all who obey the **l** of
9: 7 the **l** and married foreign women,
9:39 chief priest and reader to bring the **l** of Moses A
9:40 So Ezra the chief priest brought the **l**,
9:40 men and women, and all the priests to hear the **l**,
9:41 and all the multitude gave attention to the **l**.
9:42 and reader of the **l** stood on the wooden platform
9:45 up the book of the **l** in the sight of the multitude, C
9:46 When he opened the **l**, they all stood erect.
9:48 Pelaiah, the Levites, taught the **l** of the Lord,
9:50 now they were all weeping as they heard the **l**—
3Mc 1:12 Even after the **l** had been read to him,
1:23 and die courageously for the ancestral **l**,
3: 4 and conducted themselves by his **l**,
7:10 the holy God and the **l** of God should receive B
7:12 his kingdom who had transgressed the **l** of God. B
2Es 1: 8 for they have not obeyed my **l**—
2:40 who have fulfilled the **l** of the Lord.
3:19 to give the **l** to the descendants of Jacob,
3:20 so that your **l** might produce fruit in them.
3:22 the **l** was in the hearts of the people along with
4:23 and the **l** of our ancestors has been brought
5:27 you have given the **l** that is approved by all.
7:17 you have ordained in your **l** that
7:20 that the **l** of God that is set before them B
7:24 They scorned his **l**, and denied his covenants;
7:*72* and though they obtained the **l**,
7:*79* of the Most High, who have despised his **l**
7:*81* they have scorned the **l** of the Most High.
7:*89* the **l** of the Lawgiver perfectly.
7:*94* that throughout their life they kept the **l**
7:*133* [63] to those who turn in repentance to his **l**;
8:12 and instructed it in your **l**,
8:29 regard those who have gloriously taught your **l**.
8:56 and were contemptuous of his **l**,
9:11 as scorned my **l** while they still had freedom,
9:31 For I sow my **l** in you,
9:32 But though our ancestors received the **l**,
9:32 yet the fruit of the **l** did not perish—
9:36 the **l** and sinned will perish, as well as our hearts
9:37 the **l**, however, does not perish but survives
13:38 by means of the **l** (which was symbolized by
13:54 and have searched out my **l**;
14:21 For your **l** has been burned,
14:22 the things that were written in your **l**, D
14:30 and received the **l** of life,
4Mc 1:17 This, in turn, is education in the **l**,
1:34 of foods that are forbidden to us by the **l**,
2: 5 Thus the **l** says, "You shall
2: 6 In fact, since the **l** has told us not to covet,
2: 8 a way of life in accordance with the **l**,
2: 9 by the **l** through reason so that one neither gleans
2:10 For the **l** prevails even over affection for parents,
2:11 so that one rebukes her when she breaks the **l**.
2:14 through the **l**, can prevail even over enmity.
2:23 To the mind he gave the **l**;
3:20 of their observance of the **l** and were prospering,
4:19 of government in complete violation of the **l**,
4:23 the ancestral **l** they should die.
4:24 to put an end to the people's observance of the **l**,
5: 4 He was a man of priestly family, learned in the **l**,
5:16 to govern our lives by the divine **l**,
5:16 more powerful than our obedience to the **l**.

4Mc 5:18 our **l** were not truly divine
5:20 to transgress the **l** in matters either small
5:21 for in either case the **l** is equally despised.
5:25 we believe that the **l** was established by God,
5:25 in giving us the **l** has shown sympathy toward us.
5:27 for you to compel us not only to transgress the **l**,
5:29 of my ancestors concerning the keeping of the **l**,
5:33 not so pity my old age as to break the ancestral **l**
5:34 I will not play false to you, O **l** that trained me,
5:35 honored priesthood and knowledge of the **l**.
6:18 in accordance with **l** the reputation of such a life,
6:21 by not contending even to death for our divine **l**.
6:27 in burning torments for the sake of the **l**.
6:30 by virtue of reason, for the sake of the **l**.
7: 7 O man in harmony with the **l** and philosopher
7: 8 be those who are administrators of the **l**,
7: 9 to the **l** through your glorious endurance,
8:25 even the **l** itself would arbitrarily put us to death
9: 2 to the **l** and to Moses our counselor.
9: 4 through transgression of the **l**,
9:15 but because I protect the divine **l**."
11: 5 and live according to his virtuous **l**?
11:12 an opportunity to show our endurance for the **l**."
11:27 of the tyrant but those of the divine **l** that are set
13: 9 let us die like brothers for the sake of the **l**;
13:13 and let us use our bodies as a bulwark for the **l**.
13:22 education and our discipline in the **l** of God.
13:24 by the same **l** and trained in the same virtues
15: 9 of her sons and their ready obedience to the **l**,
15:29 vindicator of the **l** and champion of religion,
15:32 the **l**, overwhelmed from every side by the flood
16:16 Fight zealously for our ancestral **l**.
18: 1 obey this **l** and exercise piety in every way,
18: 4 of the **l** in the homeland they ravaged the enemy.
18:10 he taught you the **l** and the prophets.

LAW'S (1) [LAW]

Wis 16: 6 to remind them of your **l** command.

LAW-ABIDING (1) [LAW]

4Mc 7:15 and of venerable gray hair and of **l** life,

LAWAH See Index to Footnotes

LAWBREAKER (1) [BREAK, LAW]

2Mc 13: 7 a fate it came about that Menelaus the **l** died,

LAWBREAKERS (2) [BREAK, LAW]

Sir 40:14 to rejoice, so **l** will utterly fail.
1Mc 3: 6 **L** shrank back for fear of him;

LAWFUL (36) [LAW]

Ezr 7:24 We also notify you that it shall not be **l**
Eze 18: 5 a man is righteous and does what is **l** and right—
18:19 When the son has done what is **l** and right,
18:21 and do what is **l** and right, they shall surely live;
18:27 and do what is **l** and right,
33:14 yet if they turn from their sin and do what is **l**
33:16 they have done what is **l** and right,
33:19 and do what is **l** and right, they shall live by it.
Mt 12: 2 your disciples are doing what is not **l** to do on
12: 4 which it was not **l** for him or his companions
12:10 "Is it **l** to cure on the sabbath?"
12:12 So it is **l** to do good on the sabbath."
14: 4 "It is not **l** for you to have her."
19: 3 "Is it **l** for a man to divorce his wife
22:17 Is it **l** to pay taxes to the emperor, or not?"
27: 6 said, "It is not **l** to put them into the treasury,
Mk 2:24 why are they doing what is not **l** on the sabbath?"
2:26 which it is not **l** for any but the priests to eat,
3: 4 "Is it **l** to do good or to do harm on the sabbath,
6:18 "It is not **l** for you to have your brother's wife."
10: 2 "Is it **l** for a man to divorce his wife?"
12:14 Is it **l** to pay taxes to the emperor, or not?
Lk 6: 2 "Why are you doing what is not **l** on
6: 4 which it is not **l** for any but the priests to eat,
6: 9 is it **l** to do good or to do harm on the sabbath,
14: 3 "Is it **l** to cure people on the sabbath, or not?"
20:22 Is it **l** for us to pay taxes to the emperor, or not?"
Jn 5:10 it is not **l** for you to carry your mat."
Ac 16:21 and are advocating customs that are not **l** for us
1Co 6:12 "All things are **l** for me," but not all things are
6:12 "All things are **l** for me," but I will not be
10:23 "All things are **l**," but not all things are beneficial.
10:23 "All things are **l**," but not all things build up.
Jdt 11:13 things it is not **l** for any of the people even
2Mc 4:11 the **l** ways of living and introduced new customs
3Mc 2:21 having heard the **l** supplication,

LAWFULLY (1) [LAW]

4Mc 5:36 nor my long life lived **l**.

LAWGIVER (3) [GIVE, LAW]

Jas 4:12 There is one **l** and judge who is able to save and
Sir 10: 5 and it is he who confers honor upon the **l**.
2Es 7:*89* so that they might keep the law of the **L** perfectly.

LAWLESS‡ (28) [LAW]

Da 11:14 **l** among your own people shall lift themselves up
Lk 22:37 'And he was counted among the **l**';
2Th 2: 3 and the **l** one is revealed,
2: 8 And then the **l** one will be revealed,
2Th 2: 9 of the **l** one is apparent in the working of Satan,
1Ti 1: 9 not for the innocent but for the **l** and disobedient,
Heb 10:17 and their **l** deeds no more."
1Pe 4: 3 drunkenness, revels, carousing, and **l** idolatry.
2Pe 2: 7 by the licentiousness of the **l**
2: 8 in his righteous soul by their **l** deeds that he saw
3:17 the error of the **l** and lose your own stability.
Wis 1: 9 to convict them of their **l** deeds;
3:14 the eunuch whose hands have done no **l** deed,
4:20 and their **l** deeds will convict them to their face.
15:17 and what they make with **l** hands is dead;
17: 2 For when **l** people supposed that they held
Sir 26:23 *A godless wife is given as a portion to a **l** man,*
34:22 the gifts of the **l** are not acceptable.
49: 3 in **l** times he made godliness prevail.
Aza 1: 9 **l** and hateful rebels, and to an unjust king,
1Mc 9:58 Then all the **l** plotted and said, "See!
2Mc 8: 4 also the **l** destruction of the innocent babies and
8:17 the **l** outrage that the Gentiles had committed
3Mc 5:12 in his **l** purpose and was completely frustrated
5:20 the same way for the destruction of the **l** Jews!"
6: 4 exalted with **l** insolence and boastful tongue,
6: 9 by the abominable and **l** Gentiles.
6:12 of the **l** are being deprived of life in the manner

LAWLESSLY (1) [LAW]

3Mc 6:26 Who is it that has so **l** encompassed

LAWLESSNESS‡ (12) [LAW]

Mt 23:28 but inside you are full of hypocrisy and **l**.
24:12 And because of the increase of **l**,
2Co 6:14 between righteousness and **l**?
2Th 2: 7 For the mystery of **l** is already at work,
1Jn 3: 4 Everyone who commits sin is guilty of **l**; sin is **l**.
Wis 5: 7 We took our fill of the paths of **l** and destruction,
5:23 **L** will lay waste the whole earth,
Sir 21: 3 All **l** is like a two-edged sword;
1Mc 3:20 against us in great insolence and **l** to destroy us
1Es 1:49 of sacrilege and **l** beyond all the unclean deeds
4Mc 9: 3 Tyrant and counselor of **l**,

LAWS (55) [LAW]

Ge 26: 5 my commandments, my statutes, and my **l**."
Lev 26:46 and ordinances and **l** that the LORD established
Ezr 7:25 in the province Beyond the River who know the **l**
Ne 9:13 and gave them right ordinances and true **l**,
Est 1:13 the king consulted the sages who knew the **l**
1:19 the **l** of the Persians and the Medes so that it may
3: 8 their **l** are different from those
3: 8 and they do not keep the king's **l**,
Ps 105:45 they might keep his statutes and observe his **l**.
Isa 24: 5 for they have transgressed **l**, violated the statutes,
Eze 43:11 all its ordinances and its entire plan and all its **l**;
44: 5 of the temple of the LORD and all its **l**;
44:24 keep my **l** and my statutes regarding all my
Da 9:10 of the LORD our God by following his **l**,
Heb 8:10 I will put my **l** in their minds,
10:16 I will put my **l** in their hearts,
Jdt 11:12 to use all that God by his **l** has forbidden them
AdE 1:19 the **l** of the Medes and Persians so that it may not
2:20 but she was to fear God and keep his **l**,
3: 8 their **l** are different from those
3: 8 and they do not keep the **l** of the king.
8:11 the Jews in every city to observe their own **l**,
13: 4 who have **l** contrary to those of every nation
13: 5 a strange manner of life and **l**,
16:15 but are governed by most righteous **l**
16:19 and permit the Jews to live under their own **l**.
Wis 6:18 and love of her is the keeping of her **l**,
6:18 giving heed to her **l** is assurance of immortality,
9: 5 with little understanding of judgment and **l**;
1Mc 3:21 but we fight for our lives and our **l**.
3:29 the land by abolishing the **l** that had existed from
6:59 to let them live by their **l** as they did before;
6:59 for it was on account of their **l** that we abolished
10:37 and let them live by their own **l**,
13: 3 the house of my father have done for the **l** and
2Mc 2:22 the **l** that were about to be abolished,
3: 1 the **l** were strictly observed because of the piety
4: 2 and a zealot for the **l**.
4:17 to show irreverence to the divine **l**—
5: 8 hated as a rebel against the **l**,
5:15 who had become a traitor both to the **l** and
6: 1 to forsake the **l** of their ancestors and no longer to live by the **l** of God;
6: 5 that were forbidden by the **l**.
6:28 and nobly for the revered and holy **l**."
7: 2 to die rather than transgress the **l**
7: 9 because we have died for his **l**."
7:11 and because of his **l** I disdain them,
7:23 you now forget yourselves for the sake of his **l**."
7:37 give up body and life for the **l** of our ancestors,
8:21 and made them ready to die for their **l**
8:36 because they followed the **l** ordained by him.
11:31 for the Jews to enjoy their own food and **l**,
13:14 to fight bravely to the death for the **l**,
1Es 1:48 and hardened his heart and transgressed the **l** of

LAWSUIT (3) [LAW, SUE]

Ex 23: 2 when you bear witness in a **l**,
23: 3 nor shall you be partial to the poor in a **l**.
Isa 29:21 those who cause a person to lose a **l**,

LAWSUITS (3) [LAW, SUE]

Ex 23: 6 not pervert the justice due to your poor in their **l**.
1Co 6: 7 to have **l** at all with one another is already
Sir 29:19 his pursuit of gain involves him in **l**.

LAWYER (3) [LAW]

Mt 22:35 a **l**, asked him a question to test him.
Lk 10:25 Just then a **l** stood up to test Jesus.
Tit 3:13 to send Zenas the **l** and Apollos on their way,

LAWYERS (5) [LAW]

Lk 7:30 and the **l** rejected God's purpose for themselves.)
11:45 One of the **l** answered him, "Teacher,
11:46 "Woe also to you **l**! For you load people with
11:52 Woe to you **l**! For you have taken away the key of
14: 3 And Jesus asked the **l** and Pharisees,

LAY‡ (234) [LAID, LAYING, LAYS, LIE]

Ge 9:21 and he **l** uncovered in his tent.
19: 4 But before they **l** down, the men of the city,
19:33 and the firstborn went in, and **l** with her father;
19:33 not know when she **l** down or when she rose.
19:34 "Look, I **l** last night with my father;
19:35 and the younger rose, and **l** with him;
19:35 not know when she **l** down or when she rose.
22:12 not **l** your hand on the boy or do anything to him;
28:11 he put it under his head and **l** down in that place.
30:16 So he **l** with her that night.
30:42 the feebler of the flock he did not **l** them there;
34: 2 saw her, he seized her and **l** with her by force.
35:22 and **l** with Bilhah his father's concubine;
37:22 but **l** no hand on him"—
37:27 and not **l** our hands on him, for he is our brother,
41:35 and **l** up grain under the authority of Pharaoh
Ex 7: 4 I will **l** my hand upon Egypt and bring my people
24:11 not **l** his hand on the chief men of the people
29:10 and his sons shall **l** their hands on the head of
29:15 and his sons shall **l** their hands on the head of
29:19 and his sons shall **l** their hands on the head of
Lev 1: 4 You shall **l** your hand on the head of
2:15 You shall add oil to it and **l** frankincense on it;
3: 2 You shall **l** your hand on the head of the offering
3: 8 and **l** your hand on the head of the offering.
3:13 and **l** your hand on its head;
4: 4 before the LORD and **l** his hand on the head of
4:15 The elders of the congregation shall **l** their hands
4:24 He shall **l** his hand on the head of the goat;
4:29 You shall **l** your hand on the head of
4:33 You shall **l** your hand on the head of
5:11 you shall not put oil on it or **l** frankincense on it,
6:12 **l** out the burnt offering on it,
16:21 Then Aaron shall **l** both his hands on the head of
20:19 for that is to **l** bare one's own flesh;
22:10 No **l** person shall eat of the sacred donations.
22:13 No **l** person shall eat of it.
24:14 and let all who were within hearing **l** their hands
26:31 I will **l** your cities waste,
Nu 8:10 the Israelites shall **l** their hands on the Levites,
8:12 The Levites shall **l** their hands on the heads of
11:11 that you **l** the burden of all this people on me?
16: 7 and **l** incense on them before the LORD;
16:46 put fire on it from the altar and **l** incense on it,
22:27 it **l** down under Balaam;
24: 9 He crouched, he **l** down like a lion,
27:18 and **l** your hand upon him;
Dt 7:15 but he will **l** them on all who hate you.
9:18 Then I **l** prostrate before the LORD as before,
9:25 the forty days and forty nights that I **l** prostrate
15:15 for this reason I **l** this command upon you today.
22:14 but when I **l** with her,
22:22 the man who **l** with the woman as well as
22:25 then only the man who **l** with her shall die.
22:29 the man who **l** with her shall give fifty shekels
Jos 4: 3 and **l** them down in the place
6:26 the cost of his firstborn he shall **l** its foundation,
8: 9 and **l** between Bethel and Ai, to the west of Ai;
18: 1 The land **l** subdued before them.
19: 1 its inheritance **l** within the inheritance of the tribe
Jdg 5:27 He sank, he fell, he **l** still at her feet;
6:37 to **l** a fleece of wool on the threshing floor;
7:12 of the east **l** along the valley as thick as locusts;
9:34 and **l** in wait against Shechem in four companies.
9:43 and **l** in wait in the fields.
16: 2 and **l** in wait for him all night at the city gate.
16: 3 But Samson **l** only until midnight.
Ru 3: 7 and uncovered his feet, and **l** down.
3:14 So she **l** at his feet until morning,
1Sa 2:22 and how they **l** with the women who served at
3: 5 So he went and **l** down.
3: 9 So Samuel went and **l** down in his place.
3:15 Samuel **l** there until morning;
9:25 and he **l** down to sleep.
15: 5 Saul came to the city of the Amalekites and **l**
19:24 He **l** naked all that day and all that night.
26: 5 and David saw the place where Saul **l**,
26: 7 there Saul **l** sleeping within the encampment,
26: 7 and Abner and the army **l** around him.
2Sa 2:23 He fell there, and died where he **l**.
11: 4 and she came to him, and he **l** with her.
12:16 and went in and **l** all night on the ground.
12:24 and went to her, and **l** with her;
13: 6 So Amnon **l** down, and pretended to be ill;
13:14 he forced her and **l** with her.
13:31 king rose, tore his garments, and **l** on the ground;
20:12 Amasa **l** wallowing in his blood on the highway,

1Ki 3:19 in the night, because she l on him.
5:17 costly stones in order to l the foundation of
13:31 l my bones beside his bones.
18:23 and l it on the wood, but put no fire to it;
18:23 I will prepare the other bull and l it on the wood,
19: 5 he l down under the broom tree and fell asleep.
19: 6 He ate and drank, and l down again.
20: 6 and l hands on whatever pleases them,
21: 4 He l down on his bed, turned away his face,
21:27 he fasted, l in the sackcloth,
2Ki 1: 2 in his upper chamber in Samaria, and l injured;
4:11 he went up to the chamber and l down there.
4:29 and l my staff on the face of the child."
4:34 Then he got up on the bed and l upon the child,
4:34 and while he l bent over him,
10: 8 "L them in two heaps at the entrance of the gate
1Ch 9:27 for on them l the duty of watching,
2Ch 36:21 All the days that it l desolate it kept sabbath,
Ne 10:32 We also l on ourselves the obligation
13:21 If you do so again, I will l hands on you."
Est 3: 6 But he thought it beneath him to l hands
4: 3 and most of them l in sackcloth and ashes.
8: 7 because he plotted to l hands on the Jews.
9: 2 to l hands on those who had sought their ruin;
Job 9:33 who might l his hand on us both.
17: 3 "L down a pledge for me with yourself;
21: 5 and l your hand upon your mouth.
22:22 and l up his words in your heart.
23: 4 I would l my case before him,
40: 4 I l my hand on my mouth.
41: 8 L hands on it; think of the
Ps 7: 5 and l my soul in the dust.
22:15 you l me in the dust of death.
38:12 Those who seek my life l their snares;
50:21 now I rebuke you, and l the charge before you.
76: 6 O God of Jacob, both rider and horse l stunned.
83: 3 They l crafty plans against your people;
84: 3 where she may l her young, at your altars,
139: 5 behind and before, and l your hand upon me.
Pr 3:18 She is a tree of life to those who l hold of her;
9: 6 L aside immaturity, and live,
10:14 The wise l up knowledge,
Ecc 2: 3 and how to l hold on folly,
7: 2 and the living will l it to heart.
SS 7: 8 I say I will climb the palm tree and l hold
Isa 3:17 and the LORD will l bare their secret parts.
13:11 and l low the insolence of tyrants.
21: 2 Go up, O Elam, l siege, O Media;
24: 1 about to l waste the earth and make it desolate,
34:15 and l and hatch and brood in its shadow;
42:15 I will l waste mountains and hills,
47: 7 not l these things to heart or remember their end.
54:11 and l your foundations with sapphires.
Jer 9: 8 but inwardly are planning to l an ambush.
12: 1 O LORD, when I l charges against you;
17:11 Like the partridge hatching what it did not l,
La 2: 8 The LORD determined to l in ruins the wall
4:19 they l in wait for us in the wilderness.
Eze 3:20 and I l a stumbling block before them,
6: 5 I will l the corpses of the people of Israel in front
16: 6 As you l in your blood, I said to you, "Live!
19: 2 She l down among young lions, rearing her cubs.
25: 9 therefore I will l open the flank of Moab from
25:14 I will l my vengeance upon Edom by the hand
25:17 when I l my vengeance on them.
35: 4 I l your towns in ruins;
36:29 and make it abundant and l no famine upon you.
37: 6 I will l sinews on you, and will cause flesh
44:19 and l them in the holy chambers;
Da 2:28 Your dream and the visions of your head as you l
2:29 O king, as you l in bed,
4:13 in the visions of my head as I l in bed,
7: 1 a dream and visions of his head as he l in bed.
8:27 Daniel, was overcome and l sick for some days;
Hos 2:12 I will l waste her vines and her fig trees,
Am 2: 8 they l themselves down beside every altar
Mic 1: 7 and all her idols I will l waste;
7:16 they shall l their hands on their mouths;
Hab 3: 4 where his power l hidden.
Mal 2: 2 not l it to heart to give glory to my name, says
2: 2 because you do not l it to heart.
Mt 8:20 but the Son of Man has nowhere to l his head."
9:18 come and l your hand on her, and she will live."
12:11 will you not l hold of it and lift it out?
19:13 to him in order that he might l his hands on them
23: 4 and l them on the shoulders of others;
28: 6 Come, see the place where he l.
Mk 2: 4 they let down the mat on which the paralytic l.
5:23 Come and l your hands on her,
7:32 and they begged him to l his hand on him.
16:18 ⟦they will l their hands on the sick,⟧
Lk 5:18 They were trying to bring him in and l him
9:58 but the Son of Man has nowhere to l his head."
16:20 And at his gate l a poor man named Lazarus,
20:19 they wanted to l hands on him at that very hour,
22:53 you did not l hands on me.
Jn 4:46 Now there was a royal official whose son l ill
5: 3 In these l many invalids—
10:15 And I l down my life for the sheep.
10:17 I l down my life in order to take it up again.
10:18 but I l it down of my own accord.
10:18 I have power to l it down,
13:37 I will l down my life for you."
13:38 "Will you l down your life for me?
15:13 to l down one's life for one's friends.
Ac 3: 2 People would l him daily at the gate of
8:19 that anyone on whom I l my hands may receive
Ac 9:12 a man named Ananias come in and l his hands
18:10 and no one will l a hand on you to harm you,
28: 8 of Publius l sick in bed with fever and dysentery.
Ro 13:12 Let us then l aside the works of darkness and put
1Co 3:11 For no one can l any foundation other than
2Co 12:14 for children ought not to l up for their parents,
Heb 12: 1 also l aside every weight and the sin that clings
1Jn 3:16 and we ought to l down our lives for one another.
Rev 2:24 to you I say, I do not l on you any other burden;
Tob 12: 8 It is better to give alms than to l up gold.
Jdt 10: 2 she rose from where she l prostrate.
12:16 Then Judith came in and l down.
13:15 and here is the canopy beneath which he l
AdE 6: 2 and sought to l hands on King Artaxerxes.
12: 2 and learned that they were preparing to l hands
Wis 5:23 Lawlessness will l waste the whole earth,
10:12 kept him safe from those who l in wait for him;
17: 2 they themselves l as captives of darkness
17: 7 The delusions of their magic art l humbled,
Sir 3: 4 like those who l up treasure.
5:14 not be called double-tongued and do not l traps
29:11 L up your treasure according to the
38:16 L out the body with due ceremony,
50:28 and those who l them to heart will become wise.
Sus 1:37 who was hiding there, came to her and l with her.
1Mc 6: 9 He l there for many days,
14:31 to invade their country and l hands
15: 3 to l claim to the kingdom so that I may restore it
16: 5 and a stream l between them.
2Mc 3:29 While he l prostrate, speechless because of
15:18 l upon them less heavily;
1Es 4: 8 if he tells them to l waste, they l waste;
3Mc 2:22 so that he l helpless on the ground and,
2Es 3: 1 I was troubled as I l on my bed,
7:105 neither shall anyone l a burden on another;
9:27 After seven days, while I l on the grass,
10:24 and l aside your many sorrows,
14: 8 L up in your heart the signs that I have shown
14:15 l to one side the thoughts that are most grievous

LAYER (3)

Ex 16:13 and in the morning there was a l of dew around
16:14 When the l of dew lifted,
1Ki 7:12 to one l of cedar beams all around;

LAYING (20) [LAY]

Ge 15:10 l each half over against the other;
1Sa 28: 9 Why then are you l a snare for my life to bring
1Ki 15:27 Nadab and all Israel were l siege to Gibbethon.
Ps 64: 5 they talk of l snares secretly, thinking,
Isa 28:16 I am l in Zion a foundation stone, a tested stone,
51:16 stretching out the heavens and l the foundations
Jer 6:21 See, I am l before this people stumbling blocks
51:55 For the LORD is l Babylon waste,
Eze 42:14 into the outer court without l there the vestments
Hab 3:13 l it bare from foundation to roof.
Ac 8:18 that the Spirit was given through the l on of
Ro 9:33 I am l in Zion a stone
1Ti 4:14 to you through prophecy with the l on of hands
2Ti 1: 6 the gift of God that is within you through the l on
Heb 6: 1 and not l again the foundation:
6: 2 l on of hands, resurrection of the dead,
1Pe 2: 6 "See, I am l in Zion a stone,
Tob 4: 9 So you will be l up a good treasure for yourself
1Es 2:18 and walls and l the foundations for a temple.
6:11 and l the foundations of this structure?'

LAYMAN (1)

Lev 22:12 If a priest's daughter marries a l,

LAYS (11) [LAY]

Job 8:15 if one l hold of it, it will not endure.
18: 9 a snare l hold of them.
37:15 Do you know how God l his command
Pr 29:25 The fear of others l a snare,
Isa 26: 5 the lofty city he l low.
26: 5 He l it low to the ground, casts it to the dust.
30:32 that the LORD l upon him will be to the sound
Jer 12:11 but no one l it to heart.
Lk 15: 5 he l it on his shoulders and rejoices.
Jn 10:11 The good shepherd l down his life for the sheep.
Sir 10:16 The Lord l waste the lands of the nations,

LAZARUS (17)

Lk 16:20 And at his gate lay a poor man named L,
16:23 up and saw Abraham far away with L by his side.
16:24 and send L to dip the tip of his finger in water
16:25 and L in like manner evil things;
Jn 11: 1 Now a certain man was ill, L of Bethany,
11: 2 with her hair; her brother L was ill.
11: 5 though Jesus loved Martha and her sister and L,
11: 6 after having heard that L was ill,
11:11 he told them, "Our friend L has fallen asleep,
11:14 Then Jesus told them plainly, "L is dead.
11:17 that L had already been in the tomb four days.
11:43 he cried with a loud voice, "L, come out!"
12: 1 to Bethany, the home of L, whom he had raised
12: 2 and L was one of those at the table with him.
12: 9 not only because of Jesus but also to see L,
12:10 the chief priests planned to put L to death as well,
12:17 when he called L out of the tomb and raised him

LAZINESS (1) [LAZY]

Pr 19:15 L brings on deep sleep; an idle person will suffer

LAZULI See Index to Footnotes

LAZY (21) [LAZINESS, LAZYBONES]

Ex 5: 8 do not diminish it, for they are l;
5:17 He said, "You are l, l;
Pr 10:26 so are the l to their employers.
12:24 while the l will be put to forced labor.
12:27 The l do not roast their game,
13: 4 The appetite of the l craves, and gets nothing,
15:19 The way of the l is overgrown with thorns,
19:24 The l person buries a hand in the dish,
20: 4 The l person does not plow in season;
21:25 The craving of the l person is fatal,
21:25 for l hands refuse to labor.
22:13 The l person says, "There is a lion outside!
24:30 I passed by the field of one who was l,
26:13 The l person says, "There is a lion in the road!
26:14 so does a l person in bed.
26:15 The l person buries a hand in the dish,
26:16 The l person is wiser in self-esteem
Mt 25:26 But his master replied, 'You wicked and l slave!
Tit 1:12 always liars, vicious brutes, l gluttons."
Sir 37:11 with a l servant about a big task—

LAZYBONES (2) [LAZY]

Pr 6: 6 you l; consider its ways, and be wise.
6: 9 How long will you lie there, O l?

LEAD‡ (89) [LEADEN, LEADER, LEADER'S, LEADERS, LEADERSHIP, LEADING, LEADS, LED, RINGLEADER]

Ge 33:14 and I will l on slowly,
46:28 to Joseph to l the way before him into Goshen.
Ex 13:17 not l them by way of the land of the Philistines,
13:21 to l them along the way,
15:10 they sank like l in the mighty waters.
32:34 l the people to the place
Nu 27:17 who shall l them out and bring them in,
31:22 gold, silver, bronze, iron, tin, and l—
Dt 4:27 among the nations where the LORD will l you.
28:37 the peoples where the LORD will l you.
Jdg 4: 9 on which you are going will not l to your glory,
5:12 Arise, Barak, l away your captives,
1Ch 15:21 and Azaziah were to l with lyres according to
Job 19:24 and with l they were engraved on a rock forever!
38:32 Can you l forth the Mazzaroth in their season,
Ps 5: 8 L me, O LORD, in your righteousness because
25: 5 L me in your truth, and teach me,
27:11 and l me on a level path because of my enemies.
31: 3 for your name's sake l me and guide me,
43: 3 and your truth; let them l me;
60: 9 Who will l me to Edom?
61: 2 L me to the rock that is higher than I;
68:27 There is Benjamin, the least of them, in the l,
80: 1 you who l Joseph like a flock!
108:10 Who will l me to Edom?
110: 3 the day you l your forces on the holy mountains.
119:35 L me in the path of your commandments,
125: 5 the LORD will l away with evildoers.
139:10 even there your hand shall l me,
139:24 and l me in the way everlasting.
143:10 Let your good spirit l me on a level path.
Pr 6:22 When you walk, they will l you;
16:29 and l them in a way that is not good.
21: 5 The plans of the diligent l surely to abundance,
22:16 and giving to the rich, will l only to loss.
Ecc 5: 6 Do not let your mouth l you into sin,
SS 8: 2 I would l you and bring you into the house
Isa 11: 6 and a little child shall l them.
20: 4 so shall the king of Assyria l away the Egyptians
40:11 and gently l the mother sheep.
42:16 I will l the blind by a road they do not know,
49:10 for he who has pity on them will l them,
57:18 I will l them and repay them with comfort,
Jer 6:29 the l is consumed by the fire;
23:32 and who l my people astray by their lies
31: 9 and with consolations I will l them back,
Eze 22:18 all of them, silver, bronze, tin, iron, and l.
22:20 As one gathers silver, bronze, iron, l,
27:12 iron, tin, and l they exchanged for your wares.
36:12 I will l people upon you—
38: 4 and I will l you out with all your army,
39: 2 and l you against the mountains of Israel.
Da 12: 3 and those who l many to righteousness,
Hos 9:13 Ephraim must l out his children for slaughter.
Mic 3: 5 concerning the prophets who l my people astray,
Mt 24: 5 and they will l many astray.
24:11 many false prophets will arise and l many astray.
24:24 to l astray, if possible, even the elect.
Mk 13: 6 and they will l many astray.
13:22 to l astray, if possible, the elect.
14:44 arrest him and l him away under guard."
Lk 13:15 and l it away to give it water?
Jn 11: 4 he said, "This illness does not l to death;
Ac 7:40 'Make gods for us who will l the way for us;
13:11 about groping for someone to l him by the hand.
Ro 2: 4 not realize that God's kindness is meant to l you
1Co 7:17 of you l the life that the Lord has assigned,
Eph 4: 1 beg you to l a life worthy of the calling
Col 1:10 so that you may l lives worthy of the Lord,
1Th 2:12 and pleading that you l a life worthy of God,
1Ti 2: 2 so that we may l a quiet and peaceable life
2Ti 2:16 for it will l people into more and more impiety,
Heb 8: 9 by the hand to l them out of the land of Egypt;

Jdt 2: 9 I will **l** them away captive to the ends of
11:19 Then I will **l** you through Judea,
Wis 16:13 you **l** mortals down to the gates of Hades
Sir 19: 2 Wine and women **l** intelligent men astray,
22:14 What is heavier than **l**?
40:28 My child, do not **l** the life of a beggar;
46: 8 to **l** the people into their inheritance,
47:18 like tin and amassed silver like **l**.
Bar 5: 9 For God will **l** Israel with joy,
2Mc 10:12 took the **l** in showing justice to the Jews because
2Es 7:*52* will you add to them **l** and clay?"
7:*55* and also iron and **l** and clay;
7:*56* iron than bronze, and **l** than iron, and clay than **l**.'
7:*92* it might not **l** them astray from life into death.
16:67 so God will **l** you forth and deliver you

LEADEN (2) [LEAD]

Zec 5: 7 Then a **l** cover was lifted,
5: 8 and pressed the **l** weight down on its mouth.

LEADER‡ (148) [LEAD]

Ex 22:28 or curse a **l** of your people.
Nu 2: 3 The **l** of the people of Judah shall
2: 5 The **l** of the Issacharites shall be Nethanel son
2: 7 **l** of the Zebulunites shall be Eliab son of Helon,
2:10 The **l** of the Reubenites shall be Elizur son
2:12 The **l** of the Simeonites shall be Shelumiel son
2:14 **l** of the Gadites shall be Eliasaph son of Reuel,
2:18 The **l** of the people of Ephraim shall
2:20 The **l** of the people of Manasseh shall
2:22 The **l** of the Benjaminites shall be Abidan son
2:25 The **l** of the Danites shall be Ahiezer son
2:27 **l** of the Asherites shall be Pagiel son of Ochran,
2:29 **l** of the Naphtalites shall be Ahira son of Enan,
7:11 They shall present their offerings, one **l** each day,
7:18 the **l** of Issachar, presented an offering;
7:24 On the third day Eliab son of Helon, the **l** of
7:30 On the fourth day Elizur son of Shedeur, the **l** of
7:36 the fifth day Shelumiel son of Zurishaddai, the **l**
7:42 On the sixth day Eliasaph son of Deuel, the **l** of
7:48 the **l** of the Ephraimites:
7:54 the eighth day Gamaliel son of Pedahzur, the **l** of
7:60 the **l** of the Benjaminites:
7:66 the tenth day Ahiezer son of Ammishaddai, the **l**
7:72 On the eleventh day Pagiel son of Ochran, the **l**
7:78 On the twelfth day Ahira son of Enan, the **l** of
13: 2 every one a **l** among them."
17: 6 all their leaders gave him staffs, one for each **l**,
25:18 the daughter of a **l** of Midian, their sister;
34:18 You shall take one **l** of every tribe to apportion
34:22 Of the tribe of the Danites a **l**,
34:23 of the tribe of the Manassites a **l**,
34:24 and of the tribe of the Ephraimites a **l**,
34:25 Of the tribe of the Zebulunites a **l**,
34:26 Of the tribe of the Issacharites a **l**,
34:27 And of the tribe of the Asherites a **l**,
34:28 Of the tribe of the Naphtalites a **l**,
1Ki 11:24 He gathered followers around him and became **l**
14: 7 made you **l** over my people Israel,
16: 2 of the dust and made you **l** over my people Israel,
1Ch 11:42 a **l** of the Reubenites, and thirty with him,
12: 4 warrior among the Thirty and a **l** over the Thirty;
12:27 Jehoiada, **l** of the house of Aaron,
13: 1 the thousands and of the hundreds, with every **l**.
15:22 Chenaniah, **l** of the Levites in music,
15:27 and Chenaniah the **l** of the music of the singers;
28: 4 for he chose Judah as **l**,
Ezr 8:17 the **l** at the place called Casiphia,
Ne 11:17 the **l** to begin the thanksgiving in prayer,
12:42 And the singers sang with Jezrahiah as their **l**.
12:46 and Asaph long ago there was a **l** of the singers,
Ps 4: T *To the **l**: with stringed instruments. A Psalm*
5: T *To the **l**: for the flutes. A Psalm of David.*
6: T *To the **l**: with stringed instruments: according to*
8: T *To the **l**: according to The Gittith. A Psalm*
9: T *To the **l**: according Muth-labben. A Psalm*
11: T *To the **l**. Of David.*
12: T *To the **l**: according to the Sheminith. A Psalm*
13: T *To the **l**. A Psalm of David.*
14: T *To the **l**. Of David.*
18: T *To the **l**. A Psalm of David the servant of the LORD.*
19: T *To the **l**. A Psalm of David.*
20: T *To the **l**. A Psalm of David.*
21: T *To the **l**. A Psalm of David.*
22: T *To the **l**: according to The Deer of the Dawn.*
31: T *To the **l**. A Psalm of David.*
36: T *To the **l**. Of David, the servant of the LORD.*
39: T *To the **l**: to Jeduthun. A Psalm of David.*
40: T *To the **l**. Of David. A Psalm.*
41: T *To the **l**. A Psalm of David.*
42: T *To the **l**. A Maskil of the Korahites.*
44: T *To the **l**. Of the Korahites. A Maskil.*
45: T *To the **l**: according to Lilies. Of the Korahites.*
46: T *To the **l**. Of the Korahites. According to Alamoth.*
47: T *To the **l**. Of the Korahites. A Psalm.*
49: T *To the **l**. Of the Korahites. A Psalm.*
51: T *To the **l**. A Psalm of David, when the prophet*
52: T *To the **l**. A Maskil of David, when Doeg*
53: T *To the **l**: according to Mahalath. A Maskil*
54: T *To the **l**: with stringed instruments. A Maskil*
55: T *To the **l**: with stringed instruments. A Maskil*
56: T *To the **l**: according to The Dove on Far-off*
57: T *To the **l**: Do Not Destroy. Of David. A Miktam,*
58: T *To the **l**: Do Not Destroy. Of David. A Miktam,*
59: T *To the **l**: Do Not Destroy. Of David. A Miktam,*
60: T *To the **l**: according to the Lily of the Covenant.*
Ps 61: T *To the **l**: with stringed instruments. Of David.*
62: T *To the **l**: according to Jeduthun. A Psalm of David.*
64: T *To the **l**. A Psalm of David.*
65: T *To the **l**. A Psalm of David. A Song.*
66: T *To the **l**. A Song. A Psalm.*
67: T *To the **l**: with stringed instruments. A Psalm.*
68: T *To the **l**. Of David. A Psalm. A Song.*
69: T *To the **l**: according to Lilies. Of David.*
70: T *To the **l**. Of David, for the memorial offering.*
75: T *To the **l**: Do Not Destroy. A Psalm of Asaph.*
76: T *To the **l**: with stringed instruments. A Psalm*
77: T *To the **l**: according to Jeduthun. Of Asaph.*
80: T *To the **l**: on Lilies, a Covenant. Of Asaph.*
81: T *To the **l**: according to The Gittith. Of Asaph.*
84: T *To the **l**: according to The Gittith.*
85: T *To the **l**. Of the Korahites. A Psalm.*
88: T *To the **l**: according to Mahalath Leannoth.*
109: T *To the **l**. Of David. A Psalm.*
139: T *To the **l**. Of David. A Psalm.*
140: T *To the **l**. A Psalm of David.*
Isa 3: 6 you shall be our **l**, and this heap of ruins shall be
3: 7 you shall not make me **l** of the people."
55: 4 a **l** and commander for the peoples.
Hab 3:19 To the **l**: with stringed instruments.
Mt 9:18 suddenly a **l** of the synagogue came in and knelt
Mk 5:36 Jesus said to the **l** of the synagogue,
5:38 they came to the house of the **l** of the synagogue,
Lk 8:41 then there came a man named Jairus, a **l** of
13:14 But the **l** of the synagogue,
14: 1 the house of a **l** of the Pharisees to eat a meal on
22:26 and the **l** like one who serves.
Jn 3: 1 Now there was a Pharisee named Nicodemus, a **l**
Ac 5:31 God exalted him at his right hand as **L** and Savior
23: 5 'You shall not speak evil of a **l** of your people.' "
Ro 12: 8 in generosity; the **l**, in diligence;
Jdt 5: 5 Then Achior, the **l** of all the Ammonites,
13:18 who has guided you to cut off the head of the **l**
Sir 9:17 so a people's **l** is proved wise by his words.
10: 4 over it he will raise up the right **l** for the time.
10:20 Among family members their **l** is worthy
45:24 he should be **l** of the sanctuary and of his people,
50: 1 The **l** of his brothers and the pride
Aza 1:15 In our day we have no ruler, or prophet, or **l**,
1Mc 2:17 "You are a **l**, honored and great in this town,
5: 6 and many people, with Timothy as their **l**.
5:18 son of Zechariah, and Azariah, a **l** of the people,
9:30 to take his place as our ruler and **l**,
9:35 So Jonathan sent his brother as **l** of the multitude
12:53 for they said, "They have no **l** or helper.
13: 8 "You are our **l** in place of Judas
13:42 the great high priest and commander and **l** of
14:35 and they made him their **l** and high priest,
14:41 be their **l** and high priest forever,
2Mc 1:13 When the **l** reached Persia with a force
1:16 they threw stones and struck down the **l**
10:28 while the other made rage their **l** in the fight.
12:36 upon the Lord to show himself their ally and **l** in
14: 6 whose **l** is Judas Maccabeus,
14:16 At the command of the **l**,
14:20 and the **l** had informed the people,
2Es 1:13 I gave you Moses as **l** and Aaron as priest;
4Mc 5: 4 **l** of the flock, was brought before the king.
12: 5 to persuasion you will be my friend and a **l** in

LEADER'S (3) [LEAD]

Mt 9:23 to the **l** house and saw the flute players and
Mk 5:35 some people came from the **l** house to say,
Lk 8:49 someone came from the **l** house to say,

LEADERS‡ (121) [LEAD]

Ex 15:15 trembling seized the **l** of Moab;
16:22 the **l** of the congregation came and told Moses,
34:31 and all the **l** of the congregation returned to him,
35:27 And the **l** brought onyx stones and gems to be set
Nu 1:16 the **l** of their ancestral tribes,
1:44 and Aaron enrolled with the help of the **l**
3:32 of Aaron the priest was to be chief over the **l** of
4:34 the **l** of the congregation enrolled the Kohathites,
4:46 and Aaron and the **l** of Israel enrolled,
7: 2 the **l** of Israel, heads of their ancestral houses, the **l** of the tribes,
7: 3 a wagon for every two of the **l**,
7:10 The **l** also presented offerings for the dedication
7:10 the **l** presented their offering before the altar.
7:84 at the time when it was anointed, from the **l**
10: 4 But if only one is blown, then the **l**,
16: 2 **l** of the congregation, chosen from the assembly,
17: 2 from all the **l** of their ancestral houses.
17: 6 and all their **l** gave him staffs,
21:18 the well that the **l** sank,
27: 2 Eleazar the priest, the **l**, and all the congregation,
31:13 and all the **l** of the congregation went
32: 2 and to the **l** of the congregation, saying,
36: 1 in the presence of Moses and the **l**, the heads of
Dt 1:13 discerning, and reputable to be your **l**."
1:15 So I took the **l** of your tribes,
1:15 and installed them as **l** over you,
29:10 the **l** of your tribes, your elders,
33: 5 when the **l** of the people assembled—
Jos 9:14 So the **l** partook of their provisions,
9:15 the **l** of the congregation swore an oath to them.
9:18 the **l** of the congregation had sworn to them by
9:18 all the congregation murmured against the **l**.
9:19 But all the **l** said to all the congregation,
9:21 The **l** said to them, "Let them live."
9:21 as the **l** had decided concerning them.
Jos 13:21 whom Moses defeated with the **l** of Midian,
17: 4 and Joshua son of Nun and the **l**,
1Sa 14:38 Saul said, "Come here, all you **l** of the people;
2Sa 7: 7 did I ever speak a word with any of the tribal **l**
1Ki 8: 1 the **l** of the ancestral houses of the Israelites,
2Ki 10: 6 seventy persons, were with the **l** of the city,
10:11 all his **l**, close friends, and priests,
1Ch 4:38 these mentioned by name were **l** in their families,
4:42 went to Mount Seir, having as their **l** Pelatiah,
9:34 these **l** lived in Jerusalem.
22:17 David also commanded all the **l** of Israel
23: 2 David assembled all the **l** of Israel and the priests
26:12 corresponding to their **l**, had duties,
27:22 These were the **l** of the tribes of Israel.
29: 6 Then the **l** of ancestral houses made their freewill offerings, as did also the **l** of the tribes,
29:24 All the **l** and the mighty warriors,
2Ch 1: 2 and all the **l** of all Israel, the heads of families.
5: 2 **l** of the ancestral houses of the people of Israel,
24:10 All the **l** and all the people rejoiced
Ezr 7:28 and I gathered **l** from Israel to go up with me.
8:16 Nathan, Zechariah, and Meshullam, who were **l**,
9: 2 in this faithlessness the officials and **l** have led
Ne 4:16 the **l** posted themselves behind the whole house
10:14 The **l** of the people: Parosh,
11: 1 Now the **l** of the people lived in Jerusalem;
11: 3 the **l** of the province who lived in Jerusalem;
11:16 of the **l** of the Levites, who were over
12: 7 the **l** of the priests and of their associates in
12:24 And the **l** of the Levites:
12:31 Then I brought the **l** of Judah up onto the wall,
Job 12:24 He strips understanding from the **l** of the earth,
Isa 3:12 O my people, your **l** mislead you,
14: 9 all who were **l** of the earth;
Jer 29: 2 the court officials, the **l** of Judah and Jerusalem,
40: 7 When all the **l** of the forces in the open country
40:13 Now Johanan son of Kareah and all the **l** of
41:11 But when Johanan son of Kareah and all the **l** of
41:13 of Kareah and all the **l** of the forces with him,
41:16 the **l** of the forces with him took all the rest of
Zec 10: 3 and I will punish the **l**;
Mk 5:22 of the **l** of the synagogue named Jairus came and,
6:21 for his courtiers and officers and for the **l**
Lk 19:47 **l** of the people kept looking for a way to kill him;
23:13 Pilate then called together the chief priests, the **l**,
23:35 the **l** scoffed at him, saying, "He saved others;
24:20 and **l** handed him over to be condemned to death
Ac 13:27 Because the residents of Jerusalem and their **l** did
15:22 and Silas, **l** among the brothers,
25: 2 the **l** of the Jews gave him a report against Paul.
28:17 Three days later he called together the local **l** of
1Co 3:21 So let no one boast about human **l**.
Gal 2: 2 in a private meeting with the acknowledged **l**)
2: 6 those who were supposed to be acknowledged **l**
2: 6 those **l** contributed nothing to me.
Heb 13: 7 Remember your **l**, those who spoke the word
13:17 Obey your **l** and submit to them,
13:24 Greet all your **l** and all the saints.
Jdt 6:17 that he had said in the presence of the Assyrian **l**,
7: 8 and all the **l** of the Moabites and the commanders
14:19 When the **l** of the Assyrian army heard this,
Sir 33:19 and you **l** of the congregation, pay heed!
46:18 he subdued the **l** of the enemy and all the rulers
1Mc 3:55 After this Judas appointed **l** of the people,
9:61 about fifty of the men of the country who were **l**
10:37 Let their officers and **l** be of their own number,
2Mc 10:21 he gathered the **l** of the people,
14:21 The **l** set a day on which to meet by themselves.
1Es 1:49 Even the **l** of the people and of
5: 8 Reeliah, Rehum, and Baanah, their **l**.
5: 9 The number of those of the nation and their **l**:
6:12 in writing who the **l** are,
7: 8 the number of the twelve **l** of the tribes of Israel;
8:28 the **l**, according to their ancestral houses
8:44 who were **l** and men of understanding;
8:49 and the **l** had given for the service of the Levites,
8:54 Then I set apart twelve of the **l** of the priests,
8:59 until you deliver them to the **l** of the priests and
8:68 the **l** came to me and said,
8:70 and from the beginning of this matter the **l** and
8:96 the **l** of the priests and Levites of all Israel swear
9:12 So let the **l** of the multitude stay,
2Es 1:39 to them I will give as **l** Abraham,
9: 3 wavering of **l**, confusion of princes,
15:16 for their king or the chief of their **l**.

LEADERSHIP (7) [LEAD]

Nu 33: 1 in military formation under the **l** of Moses
1Co 12:28 forms of **l**, various kinds of tongues.
Heb 3:16 Was it not all those who left Egypt under the **l**
Sir 32: 2 and receive a wreath for your excellent **l**.
1Mc 9:31 So Jonathan accepted the **l** at that time in place
2Mc 4:40 under the **l** of a certain Auranus,
1Es 5:36 under the **l** of Cherub, Addan, and Immer,

LEADING‡ (30) [LEAD]

Nu 13: 3 all of them **l** men among the Israelites.
1Sa 18:13 and David marched out and came in, **l** the army.
18:16 it was he who marched out and came in **l** them.
2Ch 23:13 and the singers with their musical instruments **l**
36:14 All the **l** priests and the people
Ezr 8:24 Then I set apart twelve of the **l** priests:
10: 5 Then Ezra stood up and made the **l** priests,
Ps 68:18 **l** captives in your train and receiving gifts
Jer 50: 8 and be like male goats **l** the flock.
Eze 21:19 make it for a fork in the road **l** to a city;

Eze 40:26 There were seven steps l up to it;
Lk 22:47 one of the twelve, was l them.
Ac 12:10 they came before the iron gate l into the city.
13:50 the devout women of high standing and the l men
16:12 which is a l city of the district of Macedonia and
17: 4 the devout Greeks and not a few of the l women.
28: 7 that place were lands belonging to the l man of
Ro 5:21 also exercise dominion through justification l
2Th 2:11 l them to believe what is false,
2Pe 3:11 of persons ought you to be in l lives of holiness
Tob 11:16 along in full vigor and with no one l him,
Jdt 15:13 in the dance, l all the women, while all the men
1Mc 5:11 and Timothy is l their forces.
9:53 of the l men of the land as hostages and put them
2Mc 8:23 then, l the first division himself,
10: 1 the Lord l them on, recovered the temple and
10:29 and they were l the Jews.
13:15 He stabbed the l elephant and its rider.
1Es 8:45 who was the l man at the place of the treasury,
9:16 for himself the l men of their ancestral houses,

LEADS (40) [LEAD]

1Sa 12: 2 See, it is the king who l you now;
Job 12:17 He l counselors away stripped,
12:19 He l priests away stripped,
12:23 he enlarges nations, then l them away.
Ps 23: 2 he l me beside still waters;
23: 3 He l me in right paths for his name's sake.
25: 9 He l the humble in what is right,
37: 8 Do not fret—it l only to evil.
68: 6 he l out the prisoners to prosperity,
Pr 2:18 for her way l down to death, and her paths to
10:16 The wage of the righteous l to life,
12:26 but the way of the wicked l astray.
14:23 but mere talk l only to poverty.
15:24 For the wise the path of life l upward,
19: 3 One's own folly l to ruin,
Isa 30:28 of the peoples a bridle that l them astray.
48:17 who l you in the way you should go.
Mt 7:13 for the gate is wide and the road is easy that l
7:14 gate is narrow and the road is hard that l to life,
24: 4 "Beware that no one l you astray.
Mk 13: 5 "Beware that no one l you astray.
Jn 10: 3 He calls his own sheep by name and l them out.
Ac 11:18 even to the Gentiles the repentance that l to life."
Ro 5:18 of righteousness l to justification and life for all.
6:16 either of sin, which l to death, or of obedience,
6:16 or of obedience, which l to righteousness?
2Co 2:14 in Christ always l us in triumphal procession,
7:10 For godly grief produces a repentance that l
Jude 1:21 of our Lord Jesus Christ that l to eternal life.
Tob 13: 2 he l down to Hades in the lowest regions of
Jdt 5: 3 Who rules over them as king and l their army?
Wis 6:20 so the desire for wisdom l to a kingdom.
7:12 I rejoiced in them all, because wisdom l them;
Sir 4:21 For there is a shame that l to sin,
20:26 A liar's way l to disgrace,
27:15 The strife of the proud l to bloodshed,
31:29 Wine drunk to excess l to bitterness of spirit,
37:30 and gluttony l to nausea.
1Mc 9: 2 that l to Gilgal and encamped against Mesaloth
1Es 3:18 It l astray the minds of all who drink it.

LEAF (8) [IVY-LEAF, LEAFY, LEAVES]

Ge 8:11 there in its beak was a freshly plucked olive l;
Ex 39: 3 Gold l was hammered out and cut into threads
Lev 26:36 the sound of a driven l shall put them to flight,
Job 13:25 a windblown l and pursue dry chaff?
Isa 1:30 For you shall be like an oak whose l withers,
34: 4 All their host shall wither like a l withering on
64: 6 We all fade like a l, and our iniquities,
Mk 11:13 Seeing in the distance a fig tree in l,

LEAFY (6) [LEAF]

Lev 23:40 boughs of l trees, and willows of the brook;
Dt 12: 2 on the hills, and under every l tree.
Ne 8:15 and other l trees to make booths, as it is written."
Eze 6:13 under every green tree, and under every l oak,
20:28 wherever they saw any high hill or any l tree,
Mk 11: 8 and others spread l branches that they had cut in

LEAGUE (2)

1Sa 22: 8 No one discloses to me when my son makes a l
Job 5:23 For you shall be in l with the stones of the field,

LEAGUE (KJV) See also ALLIANCE, ALLIED, COVENANT, TREATY

LEAH (28) [LEAH'S]

Ge 29:16 the name of the elder was L,
29:23 But in the evening he took his daughter L
29:24 (Laban gave his maid Zilpah to his daughter L to
29:25 When morning came, it was L!
29:30 and he loved Rachel more than L.
29:31 When the LORD saw that L was unloved,
29:32 L conceived and bore a son,
30: 9 When L saw that she had ceased bearing children,
30:11 And L said, "Good fortune!"
30:13 And L said, "Happy am I!
30:14 and brought them to his mother L.
30:14 Then Rachel said to L, "Please give me some
30:16 L went out to meet him, and said,
30:17 And God heeded L, and she conceived
Ge 30:18 L said, "God has given me my hire
30:19 And L conceived again, and she bore Jacob
30:20 Then L said, "God has endowed me with
31: 4 So Jacob sent and called Rachel and L into
31:14 Then Rachel and L answered him,
33: 1 So he divided the children among L and Rachel
33: 2 then L with her children,
33: 7 L likewise and her children drew near
34: 1 Now Dinah the daughter of L,
35:23 The sons of L: Reuben (Jacob's firstborn),
46:15 (these are the sons of L, whom she bore to Jacob
46:18 whom Laban gave to his daughter L;
49:31 Rebekah were buried; and there I buried L—
Ru 4:11 into your house like Rachel and L,

LEAH'S (6) [LEAH]

Ge 29:17 L eyes were lovely, and Rachel was graceful
30:10 Then L maid Zilpah bore Jacob a son.
30:12 L maid Zilpah bore Jacob a second son.
31:33 So Laban went into Jacob's tent, and into L tent,
31:33 And he went out of L tent, and entered Rachel's.
35:26 The sons of Zilpah, L maid: Gad and Asher.

LEAKS (1)

Ecc 10:18 and through indolence the house l.

LEAN (9) [LEANED, LEANING, LEANNESS, LEANS]

Ge 41:27 The seven l and ugly cows that came up
Jdg 16:26 so that I may l against them."
Isa 10:20 of the house of Jacob will no more l on the one
10:20 but will l on the LORD, the Holy One of Israel,
17: 4 and the fat of his flesh will grow l.
48: 2 and l on the God of Israel;
Eze 34:20 between the fat sheep and the l sheep.
Mic 3:11 yet they l upon the LORD and say,
Sir 15: 4 He will l on her and not fall,

LEANED (6) [LEAN]

Jdg 16:29 and he l his weight against them,
2Ki 7: 2 on whose hand the king l said to the man of God,
7:17 the captain on whose hand he l to have charge of
Ps 71: 6 Upon you I have l from my birth;
Eze 29: 7 and when they l on you, you broke,
AdE 15: 3 on one she l gently for support,

LEANFLESHED (KJV) See THIN

LEANING (6) [LEAN]

2Sa 1: 6 and there was Saul l on his spear,
2Ki 5:18 into the house of Rimmon to worship there, l
Ps 62: 3 as you would a l wall, a tottering fence?
SS 8: 5 up from the wilderness, l upon her beloved?
Sir 41:19 and of l on your elbow at meals;
2Mc 7:27 l close to him, she spoke in their native language

LEANNESS (1) [LEAN]

Job 16: 8 my l has risen up against me,

LEANNOTH (1)

Ps 88: T *To the leader: according to Mahalath L.*

LEANS (3) [LEAN]

2Ki 18:21 which will pierce the hand of anyone who l on it.
Job 8:15 If one l against its house, it will not stand;
Isa 36: 6 which will pierce the hand of anyone who l on it.

LEAP (14) [LEAPED, LEAPING, LEAPS]

Ge 31:12 the goats that l on the flock are striped, speckled,
Lev 11:21 with which to l on the ground.
2Sa 22:30 and by my God I can l over a wall.
Job 39:20 Do you make it l like the locust?
41:19 its mouth go flaming torches; sparks of fire l out.
Ps 18:29 and by my God I can l over a wall.
Isa 33: 4 as locusts l, they leaped upon it.
35: 6 then the lame shall l like a deer,
Joel 2: 5 they l on the tops of the mountains,
2: 9 They l upon the city, they run upon the walls;
Zep 1: 9 On that day I will punish all who l over
Lk 6:23 Rejoice in that day and l for joy,
Wis 5:21 and will l from the clouds to the target,
2Es 6:21 and these shall live and l about.

LEAPED (11) [LEAP]

Ge 31:10 the male goats that l upon the flock were striped,
Isa 33: 4 as locusts leap, they l upon it.
Lk 1:41 the child l in her womb.
1:44 the child in my womb l for joy.
Ac 19:16 Then the man with the evil spirit l on them,
Tob 6: 3 Suddenly a large fish l up from the water
Wis 18:15 your all-powerful word l from heaven,
19: 9 For they ranged like horses, and l like lambs,
1Mc 9:48 and the men with him l into the Jordan and swam
13:44 The men in the siege engine l out into the city,
4Mc 11: 1 after being cruelly tortured, the fifth l up, saying,

LEAPING (6) [LEAP]

2Sa 6:16 and saw King David l and dancing before
1Ch 15:29 and saw King David l and dancing;
SS 2: 8 l upon the mountains, bounding over the hills.
Mal 4: 2 You shall go out l like calves from the stall.
Ac 3: 8 walking and l and praising God.
Wis 17:19 or the unseen running of l animals,

LEAPS (2) [LEAP]

Dt 33:22 Dan is a lion's whelp that l forth from Bashan.
Job 37: 1 my heart trembles, and l out of its place.

LEARN (74) [LEARNED, LEARNING, LEARNS]

Ge 24:21 The man gazed at her in silence to l whether or
Nu 22:19 I may l what more the LORD may say to me."
Dt 4:10 that they may l to fear me as long as they live on
5: 1 you shall l them and observe them diligently.
14:23 you may l to fear the LORD your God always.
17:19 so that he may l to fear the LORD his God,
18: 9 you must not l to imitate the abhorrent practices
31:12 and l to fear the LORD your God and
31:13 may hear and l to fear the LORD your God,
Ru 3:18 until you l how the matter turns out,
1Sa 19: 3 if I l anything I will tell you."
23:23 around and l all the hiding places where he lurks,
2Sa 3:25 to l your comings and goings and to l all that you
2Ki 5: 8 that he may l that there is a prophet in Israel."
Est 2:11 to l how Esther was and how she fared.
4: 5 to Mordecai to l what was happening and why.
Job 23: 5 I would l what he would answer me,
Ps 119: 7 when I l your righteous ordinances.
119:71 so that I might l your statutes.
119:73 that I may l your commandments.
141: 6 then they shall l that my words were pleasant.
Pr 8: 5 O simple ones, l prudence;
17:16 when they have no mind to l?
19:25 Strike a scoffer, and the simple will l prudence;
22:25 or you may l their ways and entangle yourself in
Isa 1:17 l to do good; seek justice,
2: 4 neither shall they l war any more.
26: 9 the inhabitants of the world l righteousness.
26:10 they do not l righteousness;
Jer 10: 2 Do not l the way of the nations,
12:16 if they will diligently l the ways of my people,
35:13 Can you not l a lesson and obey my words?
Da 4:26 be re-established for you from the time that you l
Mic 4: 3 neither shall they l war any more;
Mt 9:13 Go and l what this means, 'I desire mercy,
11:29 Take my yoke upon you, and l from me;
24:32 "From the fig tree l its lesson:
Mk 13:28 "From the fig tree l its lesson:
Ac 21:34 as he could not l the facts because of the uproar,
24: 8 By examining him yourself you will be able to l
1Co 4: 6 you may l through us the meaning of the saying,
14:31 so that all may l and all be encouraged.
Gal 3: 2 The only thing I want to l from you is this:
1Ti 1:20 so that they may l not to blaspheme.
2:11 Let a woman l in silence with full submission.
5: 4 they should first l their religious duty
5:13 Besides that, they l to be idle,
Tit 3:14 And let people l to devote themselves
Rev 3: 9 and they will l that I have loved you.
14: 3 No one could l that song except
Tob 5: 9 so that I may l about his family and
Jdt 8:13 but you will never l anything!
Wis 6: 1 l, O judges of the ends of the earth.
6: 9 so that you may l wisdom and not transgress.
9:10 and that I may l what is pleasing to you.
9:13 For who can l the counsel of God?
10:12 the victory, so that he might l
11:16 so that they might l that one is punished by
16:26 might l that it is not the production of crops
Sir 8: 8 because from them you will l discipline and how
8: 9 from them you l how to understand and to give
18:19 Before you speak, l;
37: 8 and l first what is his interest,
Bar 3: 9 O Israel; give ear, and l wisdom!
3:14 L where there is wisdom, where there is strength,
1Mc 7:42 let the rest l that Nicanor has spoken wickedly
10:72 Ask and l who I am and who the others are
2Mc 7: 2 said, "What do you intend to ask and l from us?
1Es 2:22 And will l that this city was rebellious,
2Es 12:36 And you alone were worthy to l this secret of
4Mc 1:17 by which we l divine matters reverently
2: 7 a glutton, or even a drunkard can l a better way,
10:16 so that you may l from them that I am a brother

LEARNED (76) [LEARN]

Ge 30:27 I have l by divination that the LORD has blessed me
42: 1 When Jacob l that there was grain in Egypt,
Lev 5: 1 though able to testify as one who has seen or l of
1Sa 4: 6 When they l that the ark of the LORD had come
23: 9 David l that Saul was plotting evil against him,
23:15 when he l that Saul had come out to seek his life.
26: 3 he l that Saul came after him into the wilderness,
26: 4 and l that Saul had indeed arrived.
Est 4: 1 When Mordecai l all that had been done,
Ps 106:35 but they mingled with the nations and l to do
119:152 Long ago I l from your decrees
Pr 30: 3 I have not l wisdom, nor have I knowledge of
Isa 23: 1 When they came in from Cyprus they l of it.
29:13 of me is a human commandment l by rote;
Eze 19: 3 and he l to catch prey; he devoured humans.
19: 6 and he l to catch prey; he devoured people.
Da 4:25 until you have l that the Most High God has
4:32 until you have l that the Most High God has
5:21 until he l that the Most High God has sovereignty
Mt 2: 7 for the wise men and l from them the exact time
2:16 to the time that he had l from the wise men.

Mk 15:45 When he l from the centurion that he was dead,
Lk 7:37 having l that he was eating in
23: 7 when he l that he was under Herod's jurisdiction,
Jn 4: 1 Now when Jesus l that the Pharisees had heard,
6:45 Everyone who has heard and l from
12: 9 the great crowd of the Jews l that he was there,
Ac 9:30 When the believers l of it,
14: 6 the apostles l of it and fled to Lystra and Derbe,
17:13 when the Jews of Thessalonica l that the word
23:27 but when I had l that he was a Roman citizen,
23:34 and when he l that he was from Cilicia,
28: 1 we then l that the island was called Malta.
Ro 16:17 in opposition to the teaching that you have l;
Eph 4:20 That is not the way you l Christ!
Php 4: 9 the things that you have l and received and heard
4:11 for I have l to be content with whatever I have.
4:12 In any and all circumstances I have l the secret
Col 1: 7 This you l from Epaphras,
1Th 4: 1 as you l from us how you ought to live and
2Ti 3:14 continue in what you have l and firmly believed,
3:14 knowing from whom you l it,
Heb 5: 8 he l obedience through what he suffered;
Rev 2:24 not l what some call 'the deep things of Satan,'
Tob 6:18 When Tobias heard the words of Raphael and l
Jdt 11:16 when I, your slave, l all this, I fled from them.
AdE 3: 5 So when Haman l that Mordecai was
4: 1 When Mordecai l of all that had been done,
12: 2 and l that they were preparing to lay hands
Wis 7:13 I l without guile and I impart without grudging;
7:21 I l both what is secret and what is manifest,
9:17 Who has l your counsel,
11: 9 they l how the ungodly were tormented
Sir 8: 9 for they themselves l from their parents;
39: 8 He will show the wisdom of what he has l,
Bar 3:20 but they have not l the way to knowledge,
3:23 have not l the way to wisdom,
1Mc 2:39 When Mattathias and his friends l of it,
3:11 When Judas l of it, he went out to meet him,
3:42 They also l what the king had commanded to do
6:17 When Lysias l that the king was dead,
7:31 When Nicanor l that his plan had been disclosed,
9:32 When Bacchides l of this, he tried to kill him.
9:63 When Bacchides l of this,
9:70 When Jonathan l of this,
10:80 Jonathan l that there was an ambush behind him,
12:22 And now that we have l this,
13:14 Trypho l that Simon had risen up in place
2Mc 2: 7 Jeremiah l of it, he rebuked them and declared:
4:21 Antiochus l that Philometor had become hostile
12:21 When Timothy l of the approach of Judas,
1Es 5:67 They l that those who had returned
3Mc 1: 1 When Philopator l from those who returned that
4Mc 4: 4 When Apollonius l the details of these things,
5: 4 He was a man of priestly family, l in the law,
9: 5 a short time ago you l nothing from Eleazar.

LEARNING (11) [LEARN]

Pr 1: 2 For l about wisdom and instruction,
1: 5 Let the wise also hear and gain in l,
9: 9 teach the righteous and they will gain in l.
Jn 7:15 saying, "How does this man have such l,
Ac 26:24 Too much l is driving you insane!"
Sir Pr: 1 of l be able through the spoken and written word
Pr: 1 also with his book those who love l might make
Pr: 3 to gain l and are disposed to live according to
15: 3 She will feed him with the bread of l,
Sus 1:48 without examination and without l the facts?
2Mc 12: 8 But l that the people in Jamnia meant in

LEARNS (1) [LEARN]

Sir 39: 4 in foreign lands and l what is good and evil in

LEASE (1) [LEASED]

Mt 21:41 to a miserable death, and l the vineyard

LEASED (3) [LEASE]

Mt 21:33 he l it to tenants and went to another country.
Mk 12: 1 he l it to tenants and went to another country.
Lk 20: 9 "A man planted a vineyard, and l it to tenants,

LEASH (1)

Job 41: 5 or will you put it on l for your girls?

LEASING (KJV) See LIES

LEAST (45) [LESS]

Ge 24:55 at l ten days; after that she may go."
32:10 I am not worthy of the l of all the steadfast love
Ex 5:11 but your work will not be lessened in the l.' "
10:17 at the l he remove this deadly thing from me."
Nu 11:32 the l anyone gathered was ten homers;
Jdg 6:15 and I am the l in my family."
1Sa 9:21 from the l of the tribes of Israel,
2Ki 18:24 then can you repulse a single captain among the l
1Ch 12:14 the l equal to a hundred and the greatest to
Ps 68:27 There is Benjamin, the l of them, in the lead,
Isa 36: 9 then can you repulse a single captain among the l
60:22 The l of them shall become a clan,
Jer 6:13 For from the l to the greatest of them,
8:10 from the l to the greatest everyone is greedy
31:34 from the l of them to the greatest,
42: 1 and all the people from the l to the greatest,
42: 8 and all the people from the l to the greatest,
44:12 from the l to the greatest,
49:15 For I will make you l among the nations,
Ob 1: 2 I will surely make you l among the nations;
Mt 2: 6 are by no means l among the rulers of Judah;
5:19 the l of these commandments, and teaches others
5:19 will be called l in the kingdom of heaven;
11:11 the l in the kingdom of heaven is greater than he.
25:40 of the l of these who are members of my family,
25:45 just as you did not do it to one of the l of these,
Lk 7:28 the l in the kingdom of God is greater than he."
9:48 for the l among all of you is the greatest."
11: 8 at l because of his persistence he will get up
Ac 8:10 All of them, from the l to the greatest,
1Co 9: 2 If I am not an apostle to others, at l I am to you;
15: 9 For I am the l of the apostles,
2Co 11: 5 not in the l inferior to these super-apostles.
Eph 3: 8 Although I am the very l of all the saints,
Heb 8:11 from the l of them to the greatest.
Wis 16: 3 might lose the l remnant of appetite because of
Sir 23:21 and where he l suspects it, he will be seized.
2Mc 8:35 as of the l account, took off his splendid uniform
10:18 When at l nine thousand took refuge
12: 4 to sea and drowned them, at l two hundred.
12:10 against Timothy, at l five thousand Arabs
15:27 they laid low at l thirty-five thousand,
3Mc 1:15 the king said, "why should not I at l enter,
2Es 12:40 from the l to the greatest,
13:42 at l they might keep their statutes that they had

LEATHER (17)

Ex 25: 5 tanned rams' skins, fine l, acacia wood,
26:14 and an outer covering of fine l.
35: 7 tanned rams' skins, and fine l; acacia wood,
35:23 or goats' hair or tanned rams' skins or fine l,
36:19 and an outer covering of fine l.
39:34 of tanned rams' skins and the covering of fine l,
Nu 4: 6 then they shall put on it a covering of fine l,
4: 8 and cover it with a covering of fine l,
4:10 with all its utensils in a covering of fine l,
4:11 and cover it with a covering of fine l,
4:12 and cover them with a covering of fine l,
4:14 and they shall spread on it a covering of fine l,
4:25 the outer covering of fine l that is on top of it,
2Ki 1: 8 "A hairy man, with a l belt around his waist."
Eze 16:10 and with sandals of fine l;
Mt 3: 4 of camel's hair with a l belt around his waist,
Mk 1: 6 with a l belt around his waist,

LEATHERN (KJV) See LEATHER

LEAVE (165) [LEAVES, LEAVING, LEFT]

Ge 28:15 for I will not l you
31:13 Now l this land at once and return to the land
33:15 "Let me l with you some of the people who are
42:15 as Pharaoh lives, you shall not l this place
42:33 l one of your brothers with me,
44:22 We said to my lord, 'The boy cannot l his father,
for if he should l his father, his father would die.'
Ex 2:20 Why did you l the man?
8:11 the frogs shall l you and your houses
8:29 Then Moses said, "As soon as I l you,
11: 8 'L us, you and all the people who follow you.'
11: 8 After that I will l."
14: 5 letting Israel l our service?"
16:19 "Let no one l any of it over until morning."
16:29 do not l your place on the seventh day."
23:11 and what they l the wild animals may eat.
33: 1 The LORD said to Moses, "Go, l this place,
33:11 Joshua son of Nun, would not l the tent.
Lev 7:15 you shall not l any of it until morning.
16:23 into the holy place, and shall l them there.
19:10 you shall l them for the poor and the alien:
22:30 you shall not l any of it until morning:
23:22 you shall l them for the poor and for the alien:
Nu 9:12 They shall l none of it until morning,
10:31 not l us, for you know where we should camp in
11:20 saying, 'Why did we ever l Egypt?' "
Jos 11:14 and they did not l any who breathed.
Jdg 6: 4 and l no sustenance in Israel,
16:17 then my strength would l me;
19: 8 the fifth day he got up early in the morning to l;
19: 9 with his concubine and his servant got up to l,
Ru 1:16 to l you or to turn back from following you!
2: 8 do not go to glean in another field or l this one,
2:16 and l them for her to glean,
1Sa 10: 9 As he turned away to l Samuel,
14:36 let us not l one of them."
15: 6 Saul said to the Kenites, "Go! L!
20: 6 'David earnestly asked l of me to run
20:28 "David earnestly asked l of me to go
22: 5 l, and go into the land of Judah."
25:22 if by morning I l so much as one male
29:10 and l as soon as you have light."
30:22 each man may take his wife and children, and l."
2Sa 14: 7 and l to my husband neither name nor remnant
1Ki 8:57 may he not l us or abandon us,
16:11 he did not l him a single male of his kindred
19:18 Yet I will l seven thousand in Israel,
2Ki 1: 4 'You shall not l the bed to which you have gone,
1: 6 you shall not l the bed to which you have gone,
1:16 you shall not l the bed to which you have gone,
2: 2 and as you yourself live, I will not l you."
2: 4 and as you yourself live, I will not l you."
2: 6 and as you yourself live, I will not l you."
4:30 I will not l without you."
9: 2 go in and get him to l his companions,
1Ch 28: 8 that you may possess this good land, and l it for
Ezr 9:12 be strong and eat the good of the land and l it for
Ne 6: 3 the work stop while I l it to come down to you?"
9:19 of cloud that led them in the way did not l them
13: 6 After some time I asked l of the king
Est 6:10 L out nothing that you have mentioned."
Job 21:14 They say to God, 'L us alone!
22:17 They said to God, 'L us alone,'
Ps 17:14 may they l something over to their little ones.
49:10 fool and dolt perish together and l their wealth
119:121 do not l me to my oppressors.
141: 8 in you I seek refuge; do not l me defenseless.
Pr 13:22 good l an inheritance to their children's children,
14: 7 L the presence of a fool,
Ecc 2:18 seeing that I must l it to those who come after me
2:21 and knowledge and skill must l all to be enjoyed
10: 4 of the ruler rises against you, do not l your post,
Isa 10: 3 and where will you l your wealth,
30:11 l the way, turn aside from
32: 6 to l the craving of the hungry unsatisfied,
65:15 You shall l your name to my chosen to use as
Jer 9: 2 that I might l my people and go away from them!
17:11 in mid-life it will l them,
18:14 Does the snow of Lebanon l the crags of Sirion?
27:11 I will l on its own land, says the LORD,
30:11 and I will by no means l you unpunished.
46:28 and I will by no means l you unpunished.
48:28 L the towns, and live on the rock,
49: 9 would they not l gleanings?
49:11 L your orphans, I will keep them alive;
Eze 16:39 and take your beautiful objects and l you naked
23:29 and l you naked and bare,
39:28 I will l none of them behind;
Da 4:15 But l its stump and roots in the ground,
4:23 but l its stump and roots in the ground,
4:26 As it was commanded to l the stump and roots of
Joel 2:14 and l a blessing behind him,
2:16 Let the bridegroom l his room,
3: 7 to l the places to which you have sold them,
Am 4: 3 Through breaches in the wall you shall l,
Ob 1: 5 would they not l gleanings?
Zep 3: 3 its judges are evening wolves that l nothing until
3:12 For I will l in the midst of you a people humble
Mal 4: 1 so that it will l them neither root nor branch.
Mt 5:24 l your gift there before the altar and go;
8:34 they begged him to l their neighborhood.
10:11 and stay there until you l.
10:14 from your feet as you l that house or town.
18:12 does he not l the ninety-nine on the mountains
19: 5 a man shall l his father and mother and be joined
Mk 5:17 they began to beg Jesus to l their neighborhood.
6:10 stay there until you l the place.
6:11 as you l, shake off the dust that is on your feet as
10: 7 a man shall l his father and mother and be joined
Lk 8:37 of the Gerasenes asked Jesus to l them;
9: 4 stay there, and l from there.
9:39 it mauls him and will scarcely l him.
15: 4 not l the ninety-nine in the wilderness and go
19:44 not l within you one stone upon another;
21:21 and those inside the city must l it,
Jn 7: 3 "L here and go to Judea so that your disciples
12: 7 Jesus said, "L her alone.
14:18 "I will not l you orphaned; I am coming to you.
14:27 Peace I l with you; my peace I give to you.
16:32 each one to his home, and you will l me alone.
Ac 1: 4 he ordered them not to l Jerusalem,
4:15 to l the council while they discussed the matter
7: 3 'L your country and your relatives and go to
16:39 they took them out and asked them to l the city.
18: 2 Claudius had ordered all Jews to l Rome.
18:21 but on taking l of them,
20: 7 since he intended to l the next day,
23:23 to l by nine o'clock tonight for Caesarea
Ro 12:19 but l room for the wrath of God;
2Co 12: 8 to the Lord about this, that it would l me,
Eph 5:31 a man will l his father and mother and be joined
Heb 13: 5 he has said, "I will never l you or forsake you."
Rev 11: 2 l that out, for it is given over to the nations,
Tob 5:16 We shall l in good health and return to you
5:21 our child will l in good health and return to us
8:20 "You shall not l here for fourteen days,
12:13 up and l your dinner to go and bury the dead,
14:8,9 So now, my son, l Nineveh; do not remain here.
Jdt 2: 5 L my presence and take with you men confident
5: 9 Then their God commanded them to l the place
10:19 It is not wise to l one of their men alive,
AdE 13: 7 and l our government completely secure
Wis 1: 5 and will l foolish thoughts behind,
2: 9 everywhere let us l signs of enjoyment,
8:13 and l an everlasting remembrance
10:14 and when he was in prison she did not l him,
19: 3 those whom they had begged and compelled to l.
Sir 14:15 Will you not l the fruit of your labors to another,
23:11 and the scourge will not l his house.
23:26 She will l behind an accursed memory
24:33 and l it to all future generations.
32:11 L in good time and do not be the last;
33:26 l his hands idle, and he will seek liberty.
38:12 do not let him l you, for you need him.
39:11 he will l a name greater than a thousand,
1Mc 1:48 and to l their sons uncircumcised.
9:10 and l no cause to question our honor."
15:14 and permitted no one to l or enter it.
2Mc 6:28 and l to the young a noble example of how to die
1Es 8:11 as many as are so disposed, therefore, l with you,
8:78 to l to us a root and a name in your holy place,

1Es 8:85 and eat the good things of the land and l it for
2Es 13:33 all the nations shall l their own lands and
13:41 that they would l the multitude of the nations
4Mc 9:23 "Do not l your post in my struggle

LEAVED [GATES] (KJV) DOORS

LEAVEN (9) [LEAVENED, LEAVENS]

Ex 12:15 on the first day you shall remove l
12:19 seven days no l shall be found in your houses;
13: 7 no l shall be seen among you in all your territory.
34:25 not offer the blood of my sacrifice with l,
Lev 2:11 to the LORD shall be made with l,
2:11 not turn any l or honey into smoke as an offering
6:17 It shall not be baked with l.
23:17 they shall be of choice flour, baked with l,
Dt 16: 4 No l shall be seen with you in all your territory

LEAVEN (KJV) See also YEAST

LEAVENED (14) [LEAVEN]

Ex 12:15 from your houses, for whoever eats l bread from
12:19 for whoever eats what is l shall be cut off from
12:20 You shall eat nothing l;
12:34 So the people took their dough before it was l,
12:39 not l, because they were driven out of Egypt
13: 3 no l bread shall be eaten.
13: 7 no l bread shall be seen in your possession,
23:18 the blood of my sacrifice with anything l,
Lev 7:13 you shall bring your offering with cakes of l bread.
Dt 16: 3 You must not eat with it anything l.
Hos 7: 4 from the kneading of the dough until it is l.
Am 4: 5 bring a thank offering of l bread,
Mt 13:33 with three measures of flour until all of it was l."
Lk 13:21 with three measures of flour until all of it was l."

LEAVENS (2) [LEAVEN]

1Co 5: 6 that a little yeast l the whole batch of dough?
Gal 5: 9 A little yeast l the whole batch of dough.

LEAVES (40) [LEAF, LEAVE]

Ge 2:24 a man l his father and his mother and clings
3: 7 and they sewed fig l together
Ex 21:33 If someone l a pit open,
Dt 18: 6 If a Levite l any of your towns,
24: 1 of his house; she then l his house
1Ki 6:34 the two l of the one door were folding,
6:34 and the two l of the other door were folding.
Job 16: 6 and if I forbear, how much of it l me?
30: 4 they pick mallow and the l of bushes,
39:14 For it l its eggs to the earth,
41:32 It l a shining wake behind it;
Ps 1: 3 and their l do not wither.
Pr 11:28 but the righteous will flourish like green l.
28: 3 the poor is a beating rain that l no food.
Isa 33: 9 and Bashan and Carmel shake off their l.
Jer 3:20 Instead, as a faithless wife l her husband,
8:13 even the l are withered, and what I gave them
17: 8 and its l shall stay green;
Eze 17: 9 its fresh sprouting l to fade?
41:24 The doors had two l apiece,
41:24 two swinging l for each door.
47:12 Their l will not wither nor their fruit fail,
47:12 be for food, and their l for healing."
Mt 21:19 he went to it and found nothing at all on it but l.
24:32 as its branch becomes tender and puts forth its l,
Mk 11:13 When he came to it, he found nothing but l,
13:28 as its branch becomes tender and puts forth its l,
13:34 when he l home and puts his slaves in charge,
Lk 21:30 as they sprout l you can see for yourselves
Jn 10:12 the wolf coming and l the sheep and runs away—
Rev 22: 2 the l of the tree are for the healing of the nations.
Sir 6: 3 Your l will be devoured and your fruit destroyed,
11:19 not know how long it will be until he l them
14:18 Like abundant l on a spreading tree
23:22 a woman who l her husband and presents him
33:32 If you ill-treat him, and he l you and runs away,
1Es 4:20 A man l his own father, who brought him up,
2Es 1:20 of the heat I clothed you with the l of trees.
5:18 like a shepherd who l the flock in the power
7:78 that a person shall die, as the spirit l the body

LEAVING (35) [LEAVE]

Ge 45:24 and as they were l he said to them,
Dt 2: 8 l behind the route of the Arabah,
2: 8 and l behind Elath and Ezion-geber.
28:51 l you neither grain, wine, and oil,
Jos 10:33 and his people, l him no survivors.
1Sa 27: 9 l neither man nor woman alive,
1Ki 11:29 when Jeroboam was l Jerusalem,
2Ki 7: 7 and their donkeys l the camp just as it was,
2Ch 24:25 they had withdrawn, l him severely wounded,
Jer 36:20 L the scroll in the chamber of Elishama
44: 7 l yourselves without a remnant?
Mt 20:29 they were l Jericho, a large crowd followed him.
22:25 and died childless, l the widow to his brother.
26:44 So l them again, he went away and prayed for
Mk 4:36 And l the crowd behind,
10:46 and a large crowd were l Jericho,
12:19 l a wife but no child,
12:21 the second married her and died, l no children;
Lk 4:38 After l the synagogue he entered Simon's house.
4:42 they wanted to prevent him from l them.
Lk 9: 5 as you are l that town shake the dust off your feet
9:33 Just as they were l him, Peter said to Jesus,
10:30 beat him, and went away, l him half dead.
20:28 l a wife but no children,
Jn 16:28 I am l the world and am going to the Father."
Ac 16:40 After l the prison they went to Lydia's home;
21: 3 We came in sight of Cyprus; and l it on our left,
26:31 and as they were l, they said
28:25 as they were l, Paul made one further statement:
Heb 6: 1 l behind the basic teaching about Christ,
1Pe 2:21 l you an example, so that you should follow
2Mc 2:28 l the responsibility for exact details to
4:31 l Andronicus, a man of high rank,
6:31 l in his death an example of nobility and
1Es 8:88 not angry enough with us to destroy us without l

LEB-QAMAI (1)

Jer 51: 1 against Babylon and against the inhabitants of L;

LEBANA (1)

Ne 7:48 of L, of Hagaba, of Shalmai,

LEBANAH (2)

Ezr 2:45 L, Hagabah, Akkub,
1Es 5:29 the descendants of Padon, the descendants of L,

LEBANON (80)

Dt 1: 7 the land of the Canaanites and the L,
3:25 that good hill country and the L."
11:24 from the wilderness to the L and from the River,
Jos 1: 4 the wilderness and the L as far as the great river,
9: 1 along the coast of the Great Sea toward L—
11:17 in the valley of L below Mount Hermon.
12: 7 from Baal-gad in the valley of L to Mount Halak,
13: 5 and all L, toward the east,
13: 6 of the hill country from L to Misrephoth-maim,
Jdg 3: 3 and the Hivites who lived on Mount L,
9:15 of the bramble and devour the cedars of L.'
1Ki 4:33 the cedar that is in the L to the hyssop that grows
5: 6 command that cedars from the L be cut for me.
5: 9 down to the sea from the L;
5:14 He sent them to the L, ten thousand a month
5:14 they would be a month in the L and two months
7: 2 of the Forest of the L one hundred cubits long,
9:19 in L, and in all the land of his dominion.
10:17 the king put them in the House of the Forest of L.
10:21 of the House of the Forest of L were of pure gold;
2Ki 14: 9 "A thornbush on L sent to a cedar on L,
14: 9 of L passed by and trampled down the thornbush.
19:23 to the far recesses of L;
2Ch 2: 8 cypress, and algum timber from L,
2: 8 that your servants are skilled in cutting L timber.
2:16 We will cut whatever timber you need from L,
8: 6 in L, and in all the land of his dominion.
9:16 the king put them in the House of the Forest of L.
9:20 of the House of the Forest of L were of pure gold;
25:18 "A thornbush on L sent to a cedar on L,
25:18 of L passed by and trampled down the thornbush.
Ezr 3: 7 the Tyrians to bring cedar trees from L to the sea,
Ps 29: 5 the LORD breaks the cedars of L.
29: 6 He makes L skip like a calf,
37:35 and towering like a cedar of L.
72:16 may its fruit be like L;
92:12 and grow like a cedar in L.
104:16 the cedars of L that he planted.
SS 3: 9 a palanquin from the wood of L.
4: 8 Come with me from L, my bride; come with me from L.
4:11 the scent of your garments is like the scent of L.
4:15 and flowing streams from L.
5:15 His appearance is like L, choice as the cedars.
7: 4 Your nose is like a tower of L,
Isa 2:13 against all the cedars of L, lofty and lifted up;
10:34 and L with its majestic trees will fall.
14: 8 The cypresses exult over you, the cedars of L,
29:17 not L in a very little while become a fruitful field,
33: 9 L is confounded and withers away;
35: 2 The glory of L shall be given to it,
37:24 to the far recesses of L;
40:16 L would not provide fuel enough,
60:13 The glory of L shall come to you, the cypress,
Jer 18:14 Does the snow of L leave the crags of Sirion?
22: 6 You are like Gilead to me, like the summit of L;
22:20 Go up to L, and cry out,
22:23 O inhabitant of L, nested among the cedars,
Eze 17: 3 rich in plumage of many colors, came to the L.
27: 5 they took a cedar from L to make a mast for you.
31: 3 Consider Assyria, a cedar of L,
31:15 I clothed L in gloom for it,
31:16 all the trees of Eden, the choice and best of L,
Hos 14: 5 he shall strike root like the forests of L.
14: 6 and his fragrance like that of L.
14: 7 their fragrance shall be like the wine of L.
Na 1: 4 and the bloom of L fades.
Hab 2:17 For the violence done to L will overwhelm you;
Zec 10:10 I will bring them to the land of Gilead and to L,
11: 1 O L, so that fire may devour your cedars!
Jdt 1: 7 in Cilicia and Damascus, L and Antilebanon,
Sir 24:13 "I grew tall like a cedar in L,
50: 8 like a green shoot on L on a summer day;
50:12 like a young cedar on L surrounded by the trunks
1Es 4:48 in Coelesyria and Phoenicia and to those in L,
4:48 to bring cedar timber from L to Jerusalem,
5:55 from L and convey them in rafts to the harbor
2Es 15:20 from the east and from L;

LEBAOTH (1) [BETH-LEBAOTH]

Jos 15:32 L, Shilhim, Ain, and Rimmon:

LEBBAEUS (KJV) See THADDAEUS; See also Index to Footnotes

LEBO-HAMATH (12) [HAMATH]

Nu 13:21 from the wilderness of Zin to Rehob, near L.
34: 8 to L, and the outer limit of the boundary shall be
Jos 13: 5 from Baal-gad below Mount Hermon to L,
Jdg 3: 3 from Mount Baal-hermon as far as L.
1Ki 8:65 people from L to the Wadi of Egypt—
2Ki 14:25 He restored the border of Israel from L as far as
1Ch 13: 5 from the Shihor of Egypt to L,
2Ch 7: 8 from L to the Wadi of Egypt.
Eze 47:15 from the Great Sea by way of Hethlon to L,
47:20 be the boundary to a point opposite L.
48: 1 on the Hethlon road, from L,
Am 6:14 and they shall oppress you from L to

LEBO-ZEDAD See Index to Footnotes

LEBONAH (1)

Jdg 21:19 up from Bethel to Shechem, and south of L."

LECAH (1)

1Ch 4:21 The sons of Shelah son of Judah: Er father of L,

LECTURE (1)

Ac 19: 9 and argued daily in the l hall of Tyrannus.

LED (162) [LEAD]

Ge 14:14 he l forth his trained men, born in his house,
24:27 the LORD has l me on the way to the house
24:48 who had l me by the right way to obtain
Ex 3: 1 he l his flock beyond the wilderness,
13:18 So God l the people by the roundabout way of
15:13 "In your steadfast love you l the people
Lev 8:14 He l forward the bull of sin offering;
Dt 4:19 do not be l astray and bow down to them
8: 2 the LORD your God has l you these forty years
8:15 who l you through the great
13:13 among you have gone out and l the inhabitants of
29: 5 I have l you forty years in the wilderness.
30:17 but are l astray to bow down to other gods
Jos 24: 3 beyond the River and l him through all the land
Jdg 6: 8 I l you up from Egypt, and brought you out of
1Sa 12: 2 I have l you from my youth until this day.
2Sa 5: 2 it was you who l out Israel and brought it in.
1Ki 1:38 on King David's mule, and l him to Gihon.
2Ki 6:19 And he l them to Samaria.
1Ch 20: 1 when kings go out to battle, Joab l out the army,
2Ch 21:11 l the inhabitants of Jerusalem into unfaithfulness,
21:13 and have l Judah and the inhabitants
21:13 as the house of Ahab l Israel into unfaithfulness,
25:11 Amaziah took courage, and l out his people;
Ezr 9: 2 the officials and leaders have l the way."
Ne 9:12 you l them by day with a pillar of cloud,
9:19 that l them in the way did not leave them by day,
Est 6:11 the horse and robed Mordecai and l him riding
Ps 42: 4 and l them in procession to the house of God,
45:14 in many-colored robes she is l to the king;
45:15 and gladness they are l along as they enter
77:20 You l your people like a flock by the hand
78:14 In the daytime he l them with a cloud,
78:26 and by his power he l out the south wind;
78:52 Then he l out his people like sheep,
78:53 He l them in safety, so that they were not afraid;
106: 9 he l them through the deep as through a desert.
107: 7 he l them by a straight way,
136:16 who l his people through the wilderness,
Pr 4:11 I have l you in the paths of uprightness.
20: 1 and whoever is l astray by it is not wise.
Ecc 4:16 there was no end to all those people whom he l.
Isa 9:16 for those who l this people l them astray,
9:16 those who were l by them were left in confusion.
19:13 the cornerstones of its tribes have l Egypt astray.
44:20 a deluded mind has l him astray,
47:10 Your wisdom and your knowledge l you astray,
48:21 not thirst when he l them through the deserts;
53: 7 like a lamb that is l to the slaughter,
55:12 you shall go out in joy, and be l back in peace;
60:11 with their kings l in procession.
63:13 who l them through the depths?
63:14 Thus you l your people, to make for yourself a
Jer 2: 6 who l us in the wilderness,
2:17 while he l you in the way?
11:19 But I was like a gentle lamb l to the slaughter.
23: 8 but "As the LORD lives who brought out and l
23:13 by Baal and l my people Israel astray.
29:31 and has l you to trust in a lie,
38:22 of the king of Judah being l out to the officials of
38:23 All your wives and your children shall be l out to
50: 6 their shepherds have l them astray,
La 3:11 he l me off my way and tore me to pieces;
Eze 20:10 So I l them out of the land of Egypt
37: 2 He l me all around them;
40:22 Seven steps l up to it;
40:24 Then he l me toward the south,
40:49 ten steps l up to it;
42: 1 Then he l me out into the outer court,
42:15 he l me out by the gate that faces east,

Eze 46:21 and l me past the four corners of the court;
47: 2 and l me around on the outside to the outer gate
47: 3 and then l me through the water;
47: 4 and l me through the water;
47: 4 and l me through the water;
47: 6 Then he l me back along the bank of the river.
Hos 4:12 For a spirit of whoredom has l them astray,
11: 4 I l them with cords of human kindness,
Am 2: 4 not kept his statutes, but they have been l astray
2:10 and l you forty years in the wilderness,
Na 2: 7 that the city be exiled, its slave women l away,
Mt 4: 1 Then Jesus was l up by the Spirit into
17: 1 and James and his brother John and l them up
27: 2 They bound him, l him away,
27:31 Then they l him away to crucify him.
Mk 8:23 He took the blind man by the hand and l him out
9: 2 and l them up a high mountain apart,
15: 1 They bound Jesus, l him away,
15:16 the soldiers l him into the courtyard of the palace
15:20 Then they l him out to crucify him.
Lk 4: 1 returned from the Jordan and was l by the Spirit
4: 5 Then the devil l him up and showed him in
4:29 and l him to the brow of the hill
21: 8 And he said, "Beware that you are not l astray;
22:54 Then they seized him and l him away,
23:26 As they l him away, they seized a man,
23:32 were l away to be put to death with him.
24:50 Then he l them out as far as Bethany, and,
Ac 7:36 He l them out, having performed wonders
7:40 this Moses who l us out from the land of Egypt,
8:32 "Like a sheep he was l to the slaughter,
9: 8 so they l him by the hand and brought him
13:17 and with uplifted arm he l them out of it.
21:38 a revolt and l the four thousand assassins out into
22:11 those who were with me took my hand and l me
Ro 5:18 as one man's trespass l to condemnation for all,
8:14 For all who are l by the Spirit
1Co 12: 2 you were enticed and l astray to idols that could
2Co 7: 9 but because your grief l to repentance;
11: 3 your thoughts will be l astray from a sincere
Gal 2:13 even Barnabas was l astray by their hypocrisy.
5:18 But if you are l by the Spirit,
Tit 3: 3 l astray, slaves to various passions and pleasures,
Tob 5:14 with me there, and were not l astray.
12: 3 For he has l me back to you safely,
14: 6 which deceitfully have l them into their error;
14:15 and he saw its prisoners being l into Media,
Jdt 1:13 In the seventeenth year he l his forces
5:14 and he l them by the way of Sinai
5:18 in many battles and were l away captive to
6:11 So the slaves took him and l him out of the camp
7: 6 the second day Holofernes l out all his cavalry
10:20 and all his servants came out and l her into
AdE 12: 3 they were l away to execution.
Wis 2:21 Thus they reasoned, but they were l astray,
10:18 and l them through deep waters;
11:15 which l them astray to worship irrational serpents
19:11 when desire l them to ask for luxurious food;
Sir Pr: 1 also l to write something pertaining to instruction
3:24 For their conceit has l many astray,
13: 8 Take care not to be l astray and humiliated
15:12 Do not say, "It was he who l me astray";
31: 5 one who pursues money will be l astray by it.
44: 4 those who l the people by their counsels and
45: 5 and l him into the dark cloud,
47:23 of Nebat l Israel into sin and started Ephraim
Bar 4:16 They l away the widow's beloved sons,
5: 6 l away by their enemies;
LtJ 6:43 of them is l off by one of the passers-by
Sus 1:45 Just as she was being l off to execution,
1Mc 5:23 and l them to Judea with great rejoicing.
7: 5 they were l by Alcimus, who wanted to
2Mc 1:19 our ancestors were being l captive to Persia,
1:23 Jonathan l, and the rest responded,
2: 2 to be l astray in their thoughts on seeing the gold
4:38 and l him around the whole city to
6:25 they would be l astray because of me,
1Es 1:56 survivors he l away to Babylon with the sword,
3Mc 1: 3 had l the king away and arranged that
4: 5 sluggish and bent with age, was being l away,
5: 5 also l them out with harsh treatment as slaves,
2Es 1:18 'Why have you l us into this wilderness
3: 6 And you l him into the garden
3:17 And when you l his descendants out of Egypt,
7:*122* [52] of the Most High will defend those who have l
14: 4 and I sent him and l my people out of Egypt;
14: 4 and I l him up on Mount Sinai,
15:10 my people are being l like a flock to
4Mc 10: 1 a glorious death, the third was l in,
11:13 he too had died, the sixth, a mere boy, was l in.
11:17 When he had said this, they l him to the wheel.

LEDGE (8)

Ex 27: 5 You shall set it under the l of the altar so that
38: 4 under its l, extending halfway down.
Eze 43:14 the lower l, two cubits, with a width of one cubit;
43:14 and from the smaller l to the larger l,
43:17 The l also shall be square,
43:20 and on the four corners of the l,
45:19 the four corners of the l of the altar,

LEE (3)

Ac 27: 4 we sailed under the l of Cyprus,
27: 7 we sailed under the l of Crete off Salmone.
27:16 running under the l of a small island called Cauda

LEECH (1)

Pr 30:15 The l has two daughters; "Give, give," they cry.

LEEKS (1)

Nu 11: 5 the cucumbers, the melons, the l, the onions,

LEES (KJV) See DREGS, WELL-AGED

LEFT‡ (547) [LEAVE, LEFT-HANDED]

A. LEFT HAND (18)

Ge 7:23 Only Noah was l, and those that were with him
11: 8 and they l off building the city.
13: 9 If you take the l hand, then I will go to the right; A
13: 9 if you take the right hand, then I will go to the l."
19:16 they brought him out and l him outside the city.
21:32 l and returned to the land of the Philistines.
24:49 that I may turn either to the right hand or to the l."
28:10 Jacob l Beer-sheba and went toward Haran.
31:14 or inheritance l to us in our father's house?
32: 8 then the company that is l will escape."
32:24 Jacob was l alone; and a man wrestled with him
39: 6 So he l all that he had in Joseph's charge;
39:12 But he l his garment in her hand,
39:13 When she saw that he had l his garment
39:15 he l his garment beside me, and fled outside."
39:18 he l his garment beside me, and fled outside."
42:38 for his brother is dead, and he alone is l.
44:20 he alone is l of his mother's children,
44:28 one l me, and I said, Surely he has been torn
47:18 There is nothing l in the sight of my lord
48:13 Ephraim in his right hand toward Israel's l,
48:13 and Manasseh in his l hand toward Israel's right, A
48:14 and his l hand on the head of Manasseh, A
50: 8 and their herds were l in the land of Goshen.
Ex 5:20 As they l Pharaoh, they came upon Moses
8: 9 and your houses and be l only in the Nile."
8:11 they shall be l only in the Nile."
9:21 not regard the word of the LORD l their slaves
9:33 So Moses l Pharaoh, went out of the city,
10: 5 They shall devour the last remnant l you after
10:12 all that the hail has l."
10:15 and all the fruit of the trees that the hail had l;
10:15 nothing green was l, no tree, no plant in the field,
10:19 a single locust was l in all the country of Egypt.
10:26 not a hoof shall be l behind,
11: 8 And in hot anger he l Pharaoh.
13:22 of fire by night l its place in front of the people.
14:22 a wall for them on their right and on their l.
14:29 a wall for them on their right and on their l.
16:20 some l part of it until morning,
16:23 to boil, and all that is l over put aside to be kept
34:25 of the festival of the passover shall not be l until
Lev 2: 3 And what is l of the grain offering shall be
2:10 And what is l of the grain offering shall be
6:16 Aaron and his sons shall eat what is l of it;
7:16 and what is l of it shall be eaten the next day;
7:17 but what is l of the flesh of the sacrifice shall
10:12 that is l from the LORD's offerings by fire,
14:15 and pour it into the palm of his own l hand, A
14:16 the oil that is in his l hand and sprinkle some oil A
14:26 of the oil into the palm of his own l hand, A
14:27 of the oil that is in his l hand seven times before A
19: 6 and anything l over until the third day shall
Nu 14:44 and Moses, had not l the camp.
20:17 to the right hand or to the l until we have passed
21:35 and all his people, until there was no survivor l;
22:26 to turn either to the right or to the l.
25: 7 saw it, he got up and l the congregation.
26:65 Not one of them was l,
Dt 2:27 I will turn aside neither to the right nor to the l.
2:34 We l not a single survivor.
3: 3 down until not a single survivor was l.
3:11 of Bashan was l of the remnant of the Rephaim.
4:27 a few of you will be l among the nations where
5:32 you shall not turn to the right or to the l.
17:11 either to the right or to the l.
17:20 either to the right or to the l,
24:19 it shall be l for the alien, the orphan,
24:20 you beat your olive trees, do not strip what is l;
24:21 do not glean what is l;
28:14 either to the right or to the l,
28:62 you shall be l few in number,
Jos 1: 7 do not turn from it to the right hand or to the l,
2:11 and there was no courage l in any of us because
8:17 There was not a man l in Ai or Bethel who did
8:17 they l the city open, and pursued Israel.
8:22 until no one was l who survived or escaped.
10:28 in it; he l no one remaining.
10:30 he l no one remaining in it;
10:37 he l no one remaining, just as he had done
10:39 in it; he l no one remaining;
10:40 he l no one remaining, but utterly destroyed all
11: 8 until they had l no one remaining.
11:11 there was no one l who breathed,
11:15 he l nothing undone of all that
11:22 of the Anakim was l in the land of the Israelites;
13:12 and in Edrei (he alone was l of the survivors of
23: 6 from it neither to the right nor to the l,
23: 7 be mixed with these nations l here among you,
23:12 the survivors of these nations l here among you,
Jdg 2:21 before them any of the nations that Joshua l
2:23 the LORD had l those nations,
3: 1 the nations that the LORD l to test all those
3:21 Then Ehud reached with his l hand, A
4:16 by the sword; no one was l.
7:20 holding in their l hands the torches,
8:10 all who were l of all the army of the people of
16:19 He began to weaken, and his strength l him.
16:20 But he did not know that the LORD had l him.
16:29 his right hand on the one and his l hand on A
17: 8 This man l the town of Bethlehem in Judah,
18:24 and the priest, and go away, and what have I l?
21: 7 What shall we do for wives for those who are l,
21:16 "What shall we do for wives for those who are l,
21:16 since there are no women l in Benjamin?"
Ru 1: 3 died, and she was l with her two sons.
1: 5 so that the woman was l without her two sons
2:11 and how you l your father and mother
2:14 and she had some l over.
2:18 Then she took out and gave her what was l over
4:14 who has not l you this day without next-of-kin;
1Sa 1:28 She l him there for the LORD.
2:36 Everyone who is l in your family shall come
5: 4 only the trunk of Dagon was l to him.
6:12 they turned neither to the right nor to the l,
10:27 No one was l of the Israelites across
11:11 so that no two of them were l together.
13:15 And Samuel l and went on his way from Gilgal.
17:20 l the sheep with a keeper, took the provisions,
17:22 David l the things in charge of the keeper of
17:28 With whom have you l those few sheep in
20:42 He got up and l; and Jonathan went into the city.
22: 1 David l there and escaped to the cave
22: 4 He l them with the king of Moab,
22: 5 So David l, and went into the forest of Hereth.
23:13 about six hundred, set out and l Keilah;
24: 7 Saul got up and l the cave, and went on his way.
25:34 by morning there would not have been l to Nabal
27:11 David l neither man nor woman alive to
30: 9 where those stayed who were l behind.
30:13 master l me behind because I fell sick three days
30:21 and who had been l at the Wadi Besor.
2Sa 2:19 to the right nor to the l as he followed him.
2:21 "Turn to your right or to your l,
8: 4 but l enough for a hundred chariots.
9: 1 "Is there still anyone l of the house of Saul
13:30 and not one of them was l.
14:19 or l from anything that my lord the king has said.
15:16 So the king l, followed by all his household,
15:16 except ten concubines whom he l behind to look
15:17 The king l, followed by all the people;
16: 6 the warriors were on his right and on his l.
16:21 the ones he has l to look after the house;
17:22 by daybreak not one was l who had not crossed
18: 9 and he was l hanging between heaven and earth,
19:19 on the day my lord the king l Jerusalem;
19:24 the king l until the day he came back in safety.
20: 3 the king took the ten concubines whom he had l
1Ki 7:47 Solomon l all the vessels unweighed,
9:20 All the people who were l of the Amorites,
9:21 their descendants who were still l in the land,
15:18 the silver and the gold that were l in the treasures
15:29 he l to the house of Jeroboam not one
17:17 so severe that there was no breath l in him.
18:22 "I, even I only, am l a prophet of the LORD;
19: 3 to Judah; he l his servant there.
19:10 I alone am l, and they are seeking my life,
19:14 I alone am l, and they are seeking my life,
19:20 He l the oxen, ran after Elijah, and said,
20: 9 The messengers l and brought him word again.
20:30 on twenty-seven thousand men that were l.
20:36 as soon as you have l me, a lion will kill you."
20:36 he had l him, a lion met him and killed him.
22:19 beside him to the right and to the l of him.
2Ki 4: 5 So she l him and shut the door behind her
4:21 closed the door on him, and l.
4:37 then she took her son and l.
4:43 'They shall eat and have some l.' "
4:44 He set it before them, they ate, and had some l,
5:24 he dismissed the men, and they l.
5:26 in spirit when someone l his chariot to meet you?
5:27 So he l his presence leprous, as white as snow.
7:12 so they have l the camp to hide themselves in
7:13 since those l here will suffer the fate of
8: 6 the revenue of the fields from the day that she l
8:14 Then he l Elisha, and went
10:11 So Jehu killed all who were l of the house
10:11 and priests, until he l him no survivor.
10:15 When he l there, he met Jehonadab son
10:17 he killed all who were l to Ahab in Samaria,
10:21 so that there was no one l who did not come.
13: 7 So Jehoahaz was l with an army of
14:26 there was no one l, bond or free,
17:18 none was l but the tribe of Judah alone.
19: 4 lift up your prayer for the remnant that is l."
19: 8 for he had heard that the king had l Lachish.
19:36 Then King Sennacherib of Assyria l, went home,
20:17 nothing shall be l, says the LORD.
22: 2 he did not turn aside to the right or to the l.
23: 8 which were on the l at the gate of the city.
25:11 the rest of the people who were l in the city and
25:12 of the guard l some of the poorest people of
25:22 whom King Nebuchadnezzar of Babylon had l.
1Ch 6:44 On the l were their kindred the sons of Merari:
12: 2 with either the right hand or the l;
16:37 David l Asaph and his kinsfolk there before
16:39 And he l the priest Zadok and his kindred
18: 4 but l one hundred of them.
2Ch 3:17 one on the right, the other on the l;
3:17 and the one on the l, Boaz.
4: 6 and set five on the right side, and five on the l.

2Ch 4: 8 five on the right side and five on the l.
8: 7 All the people who were l of the Hittites,
8: 8 from their descendants who were still l in
9: 4 there was no more spirit l in her.
11:14 The Levites had l their common lands
18:18 of heaven standing to the right and to the l
21:17 so that no son was l to him except Jehoahaz,
28:14 the warriors l the captives and the booty before
31:10 so that we have this great supply l over."
32:31 God l him to himself, in order to test him and
34: 2 he did not turn aside to the right or to the l.
34:21 and for those who are l in Israel and in Judah,
Ezr 8:31 Then we l the river Ahava on the twelfth day of
9: 8 who has l us a remnant,
Ne 6: 1 the wall and that there was no gap l in it (though
8: 4 Zechariah, and Meshullam on his l hand. A
12:38 of those who gave thanks went to the l,
Est 7: 8 As the words l the mouth of the king,
Job 20:21 There was nothing l after they had eaten;
20:26 what is l in their tent will be consumed.
21:34 There is nothing l of your answers
22:20 and what they l, the fire has consumed.'
23: 9 on the l he hides, and I cannot behold him;
Ps 106:11 not one of them was l.
Pr 3:16 in her l hand are riches and honor. A
4:27 Do not swerve to the right or to the l;
19: 4 but the poor are l friendless.
Ecc 10: 2 but the heart of a fool to the l.
SS 2: 6 O that his l hand were under my head, A
8: 3 O that his l hand were under my head, A
Isa 1: 8 And daughter Zion is l like a booth in a vineyard,
1: 9 the LORD of hosts had not l us a few survivors,
4: 3 Whoever is l in Zion and remains
5: 8 you are l to live alone in the midst of the land!
7:22 for everyone that is l in the land shall eat curds
9:16 those who were led by them were l in confusion.
9:20 but still were hungry, and they devoured on the l,
11:11 yet a second time to recover the remnant that is l
11:16 a highway from Assyria for the remnant that is l
17: 6 Gleanings will be l in it,
18: 6 be l to the birds of prey of the mountains and to
24: 6 of the earth dwindled, and few people are l.
24:12 Desolation is l in the city,
30:17 you are l like a flagstaff on the top of a mountain,
30:21 you turn to the right or when you turn to the l,
37: 4 lift up your prayer for the remnant that is l."
37: 8 for he had heard that the king had l Lachish.
37:37 Then King Sennacherib of Assyria l, went home,
39: 6 nothing shall be l, says the LORD.
49:21 I was l all alone—where then have these come
54: 3 For you will spread out to the right and to the l,
Jer 9:19 because we have l the land,
11:23 and not even a remnant shall be l of them.
25:38 Like a lion he has l his covert;
27:18 that the vessels l in the house of the LORD,
27:19 and the rest of the vessels that are l in this city,
27:21 the vessels l in the house of the LORD,
34: 7 against all the cities of Judah that were l, Lachish
38: 4 because he is discouraging the soldiers who are l
38: 8 So Ebed-melech l the king's house and spoke to
38: 9 for there is no bread l in the city."
39: 9 to Babylon the rest of the people who were l in
39:10 of the guard l in the land of Judah some of
40: 6 with him among the people who were l in
40:11 that the king of Babylon had l a remnant in Judah
41:10 and all the people who were l at Mizpah,
42: 2 For there are only a few of us l out of many,
43: 6 the guard had l with Gedaliah son of Ahikam son
44:27 by the sword and by famine, until not one is l.
50:26 let nothing be l of her.
52:15 the people and the rest of the people who were l
52:16 But Nebuzaradan the captain of the guard l some
La 1:13 he has l me stunned, faint all day long.
5:14 The old men have l the city gate,
Eze 1:10 the face of an ox on the l side,
4: 4 Then lie on your l side, and place the punishment
6:12 any who are l and are spared shall die of famine.
9: 8 While they were killing, and I was l alone,
11:24 Then the vision that I had seen l me.
14:22 Yet, survivors shall be l in it,
21:16 to the right! Engage to the l!
24:21 and your daughters whom you l behind shall fall
31:12 of the nations have cut it down and l it.
31:12 of the earth went away from its shade and l it.
36:36 the nations that are l all around you shall know
39: 3 I will strike your bow from your l hand, A
41:11 The side chambers opened onto the area l free,
41:11 the part that was l free was five cubits all around.
47:11 they are to be l for salt.
Da 2: 1 that his spirit was troubled and his sleep l him.
2:44 nor shall this kingdom be l to another people.
7: 7 and stamping what was l with its feet.
7:19 and stamped what was l with its feet;
10: 8 So I was l alone to see this great vision.
10: 8 to see this great vision. My strength l me,
10:13 and I l him there with the prince of the kingdom
10:17 and no breath is l in me."
12: 7 raised his right hand and his l hand A
Hos 9:12 I will bereave them until no one is l.
Joel 1: 4 What the cutting locust l,
1: 4 What the swarming locust l,
1: 4 and what the hopping locust l,
Am 5: 3 a thousand shall have a hundred l,
5: 3 which marched out a hundred shall have ten l.
9: 1 and those who are l I will kill with the sword;
Jnh 4:11 not know their right hand from their l,
Mic 7: 2 and there is no one l who is upright;
Zep 2: 5 and I will destroy you until no inhabitant is l.
Hag 2: 3 Who is l among you that saw this house
2:19 Is there any seed l in the barn?
Zec 4: 3 on the right of the bowl and the other on its l."
4:11 on the right and the l of the lampstand?"
7:14 Thus the land they l was desolate,
11: 9 that are l devour the flesh of one another!"
12: 6 the right and to the l all the surrounding peoples,
12:14 and all the families that are l,
13: 8 and one-third shall be l alive.
Mt 2:12 they l for their own country by another road.
2:13 after they had l, an angel of the Lord appeared
4:11 Then the devil l him, and suddenly angels came
4:13 He l Nazareth and made his home in Capernaum
4:20 Immediately they l their nets and followed him.
4:22 Immediately they l the boat and their father,
6: 3 your l hand know what your right hand is doing, A
8:15 and the fever l her, and she got up and began
12: 9 He l that place and entered their synagogue;
13:36 Then he l the crowds and went into the house.
13:53 Jesus had finished these parables, he l that place.
14:20 up what was l over of the broken pieces,
15:21 Jesus l that place and went away to the district
15:29 After Jesus had l that place,
15:37 and they took up the broken pieces l over,
16: 4 Then he l them and went away.
19: 1 he l Galilee and went to the region of Judea
19:27 "Look, we have l everything and followed you.
19:29 And everyone who has l houses or brothers
20:21 one at your right hand and one at your l,
20:23 but to sit at my right hand and at my l,
21:17 He l them, went out of the city to Bethany,
22:22 and they l him and went away.
23:38 See, your house is l to you, desolate.
24: 2 not one stone will be l here upon another;
24:40 one will be taken and one will be l.
24:41 one will be taken and one will be l.
25:33 the sheep at his right hand and the goats at the l.
25:41 Then he will say to those at his l hand, A
27:38 one on his right and one on his l.
28: 8 they l the tomb quickly with fear and great joy,
Mk 1:18 immediately they l their nets and followed him.
1:20 and they l their father Zebedee in the boat with
1:29 As soon as they l the synagogue,
1:31 the fever l her, and she began to serve them.
1:42 Immediately the leprosy l him,
6: 1 He l that place and came to his hometown,
7:17 When he had l the crowd and entered the house,
7:29 the demon has l your daughter."
8: 8 and they took up the broken pieces l over,
8:13 And he l them, and getting into the boat again,
10: 1 He l that place and went to the region of Judea
10:28 "Look, we have l everything and followed you."
10:29 there is no one who has l house or brothers
10:37 one at your right hand and one at your l,
10:40 but to sit at my right hand or at my l is not mine
12:12 So they l him and went away.
12:20 the first married and, when he died, l no children;
12:22 none of the seven l children.
13: 2 Not one stone will be l here upon another;
14:52 but he l the linen cloth and ran off naked.
15:27 one on his right and one on his l.
Lk 2:15 the angels had l them and gone into heaven,
2:37 She never l the temple but worshiped there
4:39 over her and rebuked the fever, and it l her.
5:11 they l everything and followed him.
5:13 Immediately the leprosy l him.
5:28 And he got up, l everything, and followed him.
9:17 What was l over was gathered up,
10:40 not care that my sister has l me to do all the work
13:35 See, your house is l to you.
17:29 but on the day that Lot l Sodom,
17:34 one will be taken and the other l.
17:35 one will be taken and the other l."
18:28 "Look, we have l our homes and followed you."
18:29 there is no one who has l house or wife
21: 6 the days will come when not one stone will be l
23:33 one on his right and one on his l.
Jn 4: 3 he l Judea and started back to Galilee.
4:28 woman l her water jar and went back to the city.
4:30 They l the city and were on their way to him.
4:52 at one in the afternoon the fever l him."
6:12 "Gather up the fragments l over,
6:13 l by those who had eaten,
8: 9 ⟦and Jesus was l alone with the woman standing⟧
8:29 he has not l me alone,
19:31 the Jews did not want the bodies l on the cross
Ac 5:41 As they l the council, they rejoiced
7: 4 Then he l the country of the Chaldeans
10: 7 When the angel who spoke to him had l,
12:10 when suddenly the angel l him.
12:17 Then he l and went to another place.
13:13 John, however, l them and returned to Jerusalem;
14:17 not l himself without a witness in doing good—
17:15 as soon as possible, they l him.
17:33 At that point Paul l them.
18: 1 After this Paul l Athens and went to Corinth.
18: 7 Then he l the synagogue and went to the house
18:19 When they reached Ephesus, he l them there,
19: 9 he l them, taking the disciples with him,
19:12 to the sick, their diseases l them,
20: 1 after encouraging them and saying farewell, he l
20:11 with them until dawn; then he l.
21: 3 and leaving it on our l,
21: 5 we l and proceeded on our journey;
21: 8 The next day we l and came to Caesarea;
24:27 to grant the Jews a favor, Felix l Paul in prison.
Ac 25:14 "There is a man here who was l in prison
27:40 they cast off the anchors and l them in the sea.
Ro 9:29 "If the Lord of hosts had not l survivors to us,
11: 3 I alone am l, and they are seeking my life."
2Co 6: 7 of righteousness for the right hand and for the l;
Php 4:15 the early days of the gospel, when I l Macedonia,
1Th 3: 1 we decided to be l alone in Athens;
4:15 who are l until the coming of the Lord,
4:17 Then we who are alive, who are l,
1Ti 5: 5 The real widow, l alone,
2Ti 4:13 bring the cloak that I l with Carpus at Troas,
4:20 Trophimus I l ill in Miletus.
Tit 1: 5 I l you behind in Crete for this reason,
Heb 2: 8 God l nothing outside their control.
3:16 not all those who l Egypt under the leadership
11:15 of the land that they had l behind,
11:27 By faith he l Egypt, unafraid of the king's anger;
2Pe 2:15 They have l the straight road
Jude 1: 6 but l their proper dwelling,
Rev 10: 2 Setting his right foot on the sea and his l foot on
Tob 1: 8 for my father had died and l me an orphan.
1:14 of Media I l bags of silver worth ten talents
1:20 nothing was l to me that was not taken into
2: 4 I sprang up, l the dinner before even tasting it,
4: 1 the money that he had l in trust with Gabael
4:20 let me explain to you that I l ten talents of silver
5: 3 since I l this money in trust.
5:10 Tobit retorted, "What joy is l for me any more?
10: 7 I have already explained to you how I l him."
11: 2 "You are aware of how we l your father.
Jdt 2:14 So Holofernes l the presence of his lord,
6:13 they bound Achior and l him lying at the foot of
8: 7 Her husband Manasseh had l her gold and silver,
12:13 So Bagoas l the presence of Holofernes,
13: 2 But Judith was l alone in the tent,
13: 4 either small or great, was l in the bedchamber.
14: 8 from the day she l until
Wis 4:19 they will be l utterly dry and barren,
10: 8 also l for humankind a reminder of their folly,
12:11 that you l them unpunished for their sins.
14: 6 and guided by your hand l to the world the seed
Sir 6: 3 and you will be l like a withered tree.
15:14 he l them in the power of their own free choice.
22:11 Weep for the dead, for he has l the light behind;
22:11 for he has l intelligence behind.
30: 4 for he has l behind him one like himself,
30: 6 He has l behind him an avenger
39:32 and have thought it out and l it in writing:
44: 8 Some of them have l behind a name,
44:17 remnant was l on the earth when the flood came.
47:23 and l behind him one of his sons,
48:15 The people were l very few in number,
Bar 2:13 Let your anger turn away from us, for we are l,
4:12 I was l desolate because of the sins
4:19 Go, my children, go; for I have been l desolate.
LtJ 6:47 They have l only lies and reproach
Sus 1: 7 When the people l at noon,
1:13 So they both l and parted from each other.
1Mc 2:18 and those that are l in Jerusalem have done.
2:22 from our religion to the right hand or to the l."
2:28 Then he and his sons fled to the hills and l all
3:32 He l Lysias, a distinguished man
3:37 and l Antioch his capital in the one hundred
5:18 But he l Joseph, son of Zechariah, and Azariah,
5:29 He l the place at night,
5:46 not go around it to the right or to the l;
6: 2 and weapons l there by Alexander son of Philip,
6: 4 So he fled and in great disappointment l there
6:36 they went with it, and they never l it.
6:45 he killed men right and l,
6:54 Only a few men were l in the sanctuary;
7:20 of the country and l with him a force to help him;
7:46 not even one of them was l.
9: 6 until no more than eight hundred of them were l.
9: 8 He became faint, but he said to those who were l,
9:16 the l wing saw that the right wing was crushed,
9:36 and seized John and all that he had, and l with it.
9:65 But Jonathan l his brother Simon in the town,
10:13 all of them l their places and went back
10:79 Now Apollonius had secretly l
10:86 Jonathan l there and encamped against Askalon,
11:64 but l his brother Simon in the country.
11:70 of them was l except Mattathias son of Absalom
12:47 two thousand of whom he l in Galilee,
13: 4 for the sake of Israel, and I alone am l.
13:12 Then Trypho l Ptolemais with a large army
14:13 No one was l in the land to fight them,
2Mc 1:31 that was l should be poured on large stones.
4:29 Menelaus l his own brother Lysimachus
4:29 while Sostratus l Crates,
5:11 he l Egypt and took the city by storm.
5:22 He l governors to oppress the people:
9:24 to whom the government was l.
10:19 Maccabeus l Simon and Joseph,
12:18 by then l there without accomplishing anything,
12:18 in one place he had l a very strong garrison.
12:19 and destroyed those whom Timothy had l in
13:23 who had been l in charge of the government,
13:24 l Hegemonides as governor from Ptolemais
1Es 4:30 and slap the king with her l hand. A
8: 6 for they l Babylon on the new moon of
8:61 We l the river Theras on the twelfth day of
8:89 for we are l as a root to this day.
9:44 and on his l Pedaiah, Mishael,
3Mc 3: 9 be l to its fate when it had committed no offense.
5: 6 to the Gentiles it appeared that the Jews were l
2Es 3:11 But you l one of them, Noah with his household,

2Es 5:19 He heard what I said and **l** me.
7: 7 on the right hand and deep water on the **l**.
7:30 so that no one shall be **l**.
7:*140* [70] there would probably be **l** only very few of
11:35 the head on the right side devour the one on the **l**.
12: 5 and not even a little strength is **l** in me,
12:39 to show you." Then he **l** me.
12:42 For of all the prophets you alone are **l** to us,
13:16 alas for those who will be **l** in those days!
13:16 And still more, alas for those who are not **l**!
13:17 For those who are not **l** will be sad
13:19 But alas for those also who are **l**,
13:24 those who are **l** are more blessed than those who
13:26 and he will direct those who are **l**.
13:48 But those who are **l** of your people,
16:23 for the earth shall be **l** desolate,
16:24 No one shall be **l** to cultivate the earth or
16:28 For ten shall be **l** out of a city;
16:29 in an olive orchard three or four olives may be **l**
16:30 be **l** by those who search carefully through
16:31 be **l** by those who search their houses with
16:32 The earth shall be **l** desolate,
4Mc 13:18 Those who were **l** behind said to each of
13:27 those who were **l** endured for the sake
18: 5 he **l** Jerusalem and marched against the Persians.

LEFT-HANDED (2) [HAND, LEFT]
Jdg 3:15 Ehud son of Gera, the Benjaminite, a **l** man.
20:16 there were seven hundred picked men who were **l**;

LEGAL (4)
Dt 17: 8 one kind of **l** right and another,
Ac 22:25 "Is it **l** for you to flog
Col 2:14 that stood against us with its **l** demands.
Heb 7:16 a **l** requirement concerning physical descent,

LEGION (3) [LEGIONS]
Mk 5: 9 He replied, "My name is **L**; for we are many."
5:15 the very man who had had the **l**;
Lk 8:30 He said, "**L**"; for many demons had entered him.

LEGIONS (1) [LEGION]
Mt 26:53 and he will at once send me more than twelve **l**

LEGISLATION (1)
4Mc 17:16 Who did not admire the athletes of the divine **l**?

LEGITIMATELY (1)
1Ti 1: 8 we know that the law is good, if one uses it **l**.

LEGS‡ (26)
Ex 12: 9 but roasted over the fire, with its head, **l**,
25:26 fasten the rings to the four corners at its four **l**.
29:17 and wash its entrails and its **l**,
37:13 fastened the rings to the four corners at its four **l**.
Lev 1: 9 its entrails and its **l** shall be washed with water.
1:13 the entrails and the **l** shall be washed with water.
4:11 as well as its head, its **l**, its entrails,
8:21 the entrails and the **l** were washed with water,
9:14 He washed the entrails and the **l** and,
11:21 on all fours you may eat those that have jointed **l**
Dt 28:35 on the **l** with grievous boils of which you cannot
1Sa 17: 6 of bronze on his **l** and a javelin of bronze slung
Pr 26: 7 The **l** of a disabled person hang limp;
SS 5:15 His **l** are alabaster columns,
Isa 47: 2 uncover your **l**, pass through the rivers.
Eze 1: 7 Their **l** were straight, and the soles
29: 7 you broke, and made all their **l** unsteady.
Da 2:33 its **l** of iron, its feet partly of iron and partly
10: 6 and **l** like the gleam of burnished bronze,
Am 3:12 from the mouth of the lion two **l**,
Jn 19:31 to have the **l** of the crucified men broken and
19:32 the soldiers came and broke the **l** of the first and
19:33 they did not break his **l**.
Rev 10: 1 and his **l** like pillars of fire.
Sir 26:18 so are shapely **l** and steadfast feet
4Mc 10: 6 breaking his fingers and arms and **l** and elbows.

LEHABIM (2)
Ge 10:13 Egypt became the father of Ludim, Anamim, **L**,
1Ch 1:11 Egypt became the father of Ludim, Anamim, **L**,

LEHEM (1)
1Ch 4:22 but returned to **L** (now the records are ancient).

LEHI (5) [RAMATH-LEHI]
Jdg 15: 9 and made a raid on **L**.
15:14 to **L**, the Philistines came shouting to meet him;
15:19 So God split open the hollow place that is at **L**,
15:19 which is at **L** to this day.
2Sa 23:11 The Philistines gathered together at **L**,

LEISURE (4)
Mk 6:31 and they had no **l** even to eat.
AdE 14:16 and I do not wear it on the days when I am at **l**.
Wis 13:13 he takes and carves with care in his **l**,
Sir 38:24 of the scribe depends on the opportunity of **l**;

LEMA (2)
Mt 27:46 "Eli, Eli, **l** sabachthani?"
Mk 15:34 "Eloi, Eloi, **l** sabachthani?"

LEMUEL (2)
Pr 31: 1 The words of King **L**.
31: 4 It is not for kings, O **L**,

LEND (18) [LENDER, LENDING, LENDS, LENT, MONEYLENDER]
Ex 22:25 If you **l** money to my people,
Lev 25:37 You shall not **l** them your money at interest taken
Dt 15: 6 as he promised you, you will **l** to many nations,
28:12 You will **l** to many nations,
28:44 They shall **l** to you but you shall not **l**
Ps 15: 5 who do not **l** money at interest,
112: 5 It is well with those who deal generously and **l**,
Lk 6:34 If you **l** to those from whom you hope to receive,
6:34 sinners **l** to sinners, to receive as much again.
6:35 But love your enemies, do good, and **l**,
11: 5 'Friend, **l** me three loaves of bread;
Sir 8:12 Do not **l** to one who is stronger than you;
8:12 but if you do **l** anything, count it as a loss.
29: 1 The merciful **l** to their neighbors;
29: 2 **L** to your neighbor in his time of need;
29: 7 Many refuse to **l**, not because of meanness,
4Mc 2: 8 contrary to natural ways and to **l** without interest

LENDER (2) [LEND]
Pr 22: 7 and the borrower is the slave of the **l**.
Isa 24: 2 as with the **l**, so with the borrower;

LENDING (3) [LEND]
Dt 15: 8 willingly **l** enough to meet the need,
Ne 5:10 and my servants are **l** them money and grain.
Ps 37:26 They are ever giving liberally and **l**,

LENDS (2) [LEND]
Pr 19:17 Whoever is kind to the poor **l** to the LORD,
Sir 20:15 Today he **l** and tomorrow he asks it back;

LENGTH‡ (64) [LONG]
Ge 6:15 the **l** of the ark three hundred cubits,
13:17 walk through the **l** and the breadth of the land,
23: 1 this was the **l** of Sarah's life.
25: 7 This is the **l** of Abraham's life,
25:17 (This is the **l** of the life of Ishmael,
Ex 6:16 Gershon, Kohath, and Merari, and the **l**
6:18 Amram, Izhar, Hebron, and Uzziel, and the **l**
6:20 and she bore him Aaron and Moses, and the **l**
25:17 two cubits and a half shall be its **l**,
26: 2 The **l** of each curtain shall be twenty-eight cubits,
26: 8 The **l** of each curtain shall be thirty cubits,
26:13 of what remains in the **l** of the curtains of
26:16 Ten cubits shall be the **l** of a frame,
27:11 Likewise for its **l** on the north side there shall
27:18 The **l** of the court shall be one hundred cubits,
28:16 a span in **l** and a span in width.
36: 9 The **l** of each curtain was twenty-eight cubits,
36:15 The **l** of each curtain was thirty cubits,
36:21 Ten cubits was the **l** of a frame,
37: 6 two cubits and a half was its **l**,
39: 9 a span in **l** and a span in width when doubled.
Lev 19:35 You shall not cheat in measuring **l**, weight,
Dt 2: 5 for I will not give you even so much as a foot's **l**
2:14 And the **l** of time we had traveled
30:20 for that means life to you and **l** of days,
Jdg 3:16 for himself a sword with two edges, a cubit in **l**;
1Sa 27: 7 The **l** of time that David lived in the country of
28:20 Immediately Saul fell full **l** on the ground,
2Sa 8: 2 and one **l** for those who were to be spared.
1Ki 6:24 Five cubits was the **l** of one wing of the cherub,
6:24 five cubits the **l** of the other wing of the cherub;
2Ch 3: 3 the **l**, in cubits of the old standard,
3: 8 its **l**, corresponding to the width of the house,
Job 12:12 and understanding in **l** of days?
Ps 21: 4 **l** of days forever and ever.
Pr 3: 2 for **l** of days and years of life
Eze 31: 7 in the **l** of its branches;
40: 5 The **l** of the measuring reed in
40: 5 each being a cubit and a handbreadth in **l**;
40:18 corresponding to the **l** of the gates;
41: 2 He measured the **l** of the nave, forty cubits,
42: 2 The **l** of the building that was on
42:11 to the chambers on the north, of the same **l**
45: 7 corresponding in **l** to one of the tribal portions,
48: 8 and in **l** equal to one of the tribal portions,
48: 9 be twenty-five thousand cubits in **l**,
48:10 twenty-five thousand in **l** on the southern side,
48:13 an allotment twenty-five thousand cubits in **l**
48:13 The whole **l** shall be twenty-five thousand cubits
48:15 in width and twenty-five thousand in **l**,
48:18 of the **l** alongside the holy portion shall
Zec 2: 2 to see what is its width and what is its **l**."
5: 2 its **l** is twenty cubits, and its width ten cubits."
Lk 23: 9 He questioned him at some **l**,
Ac 7: 5 not even a foot's **l**, but promised to give it to him
Eph 3:18 what is the breadth and **l** and height and depth,
Rev 21:16 city lies foursquare, its **l** the same as its width;
21:16 its **l** and width and height are equal.
Jdt 7: 3 in breadth over Dothan as far as Balbaim and in **l**
Wis 4: 8 For old age is not honored for **l** of time,
8:12 if I speak at greater **l**,
Bar 3:14 at the same time discern where there is **l** of days,
4Mc 13:20 There each of the brothers spent the same **l**
18:19 this is your life and the **l** of your days.' "

LENGTHEN (5) [LONG]
1Ki 3:14 then I will **l** your life."
2Ki 20:10 "It is normal for the shadow to **l** ten intervals;
Isa 54: 2 **l** your cords and strengthen your stakes.
Jer 6: 4 for the day declines, the shadows of evening **l**!"
2Mc 2:32 be foolish to **l** the preface while cutting short

LENGTHENS (1) [LONG]
Sir 30:22 and rejoicing **l** one's life span.

LENGTHS (1) [LONG]
2Sa 8: 2 he measured two **l** of cord for those who were to

LENGTHY (1) [LONG]
Sir 13:11 or trust his **l** conversations;

LENIENT (1)
2Co 13: 2 that if I come again, I will not be **l**—

LENT (3) [LEND]
Dt 23:19 interest on anything that is **l**.
1Sa 1:28 Therefore I have **l** him to the LORD;
Jer 15:10 I have not **l**, nor have I borrowed,

LENTIL (1) [LENTILS]
Ge 25:34 Then Jacob gave Esau bread and **l** stew,

LENTILES (KJV) See LENTILS, LENTIL STEW

LENTILS (3) [LENTIL]
2Sa 17:28 wheat, barley, meal, parched grain, beans and **l**,
23:11 where there was a plot of ground full of **l**;
Eze 4: 9 And you, take wheat and barley, beans and **l**,

LEOPARD (6) [LEOPARD-LIKE, LEOPARDS]
Isa 11: 6 the **l** shall lie down with the kid,
Jer 5: 6 A **l** is watching against their cities;
Da 7: 6 this, as I watched, another appeared, like a **l**.
Hos 13: 7 like a **l** I will lurk beside the way.
Rev 13: 2 And the beast that I saw was like a **l**,
Sir 28:23 like a **l** it will mangle them.

LEOPARD-LIKE (1) [LEOPARD]
4Mc 9:28 These **l** beasts tore out his sinews with

LEOPARDS (3) [LEOPARD]
SS 4: 8 from the dens of lions, from the mountains of **l**.
Jer 13:23 Can Ethiopians change their skin or **l** their spots?
Hab 1: 8 Their horses are swifter than **l**,

LEPER (4) [LEPROSY]
Mt 8: 2 and there was a **l** who came to him and knelt
26: 6 at Bethany in the house of Simon the **l**,
Mk 1:40 A **l** came to him begging him,
14: 3 he was at Bethany in the house of Simon the **l**,

LEPERS (5) [LEPROSY]
Mt 10: 8 Cure the sick, raise the dead, cleanse the **l**,
11: 5 the lame walk, the **l** are cleansed, the deaf hear,
Lk 4:27 There were also many **l** in Israel in the time of
7:22 the lame walk, the **l** are cleansed, the deaf hear,
17:12 As he entered a village, ten **l** approached him.

LEPROSY (10) [LEPER, LEPERS, LEPROUS]
2Ki 5: 1 man, though a mighty warrior, suffered from **l**.
5: 3 He would cure him of his **l**."
5: 6 that you may cure him of his **l**."
5: 7 to me to cure a man of his **l**?
5:11 over the spot, and cure the **l**!
5:27 Therefore the **l** of Naaman shall cling to you,
Mt 8: 3 Immediately his **l** was cleansed.
Mk 1:42 Immediately the **l** left him,
Lk 5:12 there was a man covered with **l**.
5:13 Immediately the **l** left him.

LEPROUS (46) [LEPROSY]
Ex 4: 6 he took it out, his hand was **l**, as white as snow.
Lev 13: 2 it turns into a **l** disease on the skin of his body,
13: 3 the skin of his body, it is a **l** disease;
13: 8 priest shall pronounce him unclean; it is a **l** disease.
13: 9 When a person contracts a **l** disease,
13:11 it is a chronic **l** disease in the skin of his body.
13:15 Raw flesh is unclean, for it is a **l** disease.
13:20 this is a **l** disease, broken out in the boil.
13:25 it is a **l** disease; it has broken out in the burn,
13:25 This is a **l** disease.
13:27 This is a **l** disease.
13:30 it is an itch, a **l** disease of the head or the beard.
13:42 it is a **l** disease breaking out on his bald head
13:43 on his bald forehead, which resembles a **l** disease
13:44 he is **l**, he is unclean.
13:45 the **l** disease shall wear torn clothes and let
13:47 when a **l** disease appears in it,
13:49 it is a **l** disease and shall be shown to the priest.
13:51 this is a spreading **l** disease; it is unclean.

Lev 13:52 or anything of skin, for it is a spreading **l** disease;
13:55 you shall burn it in fire, whether the **l** spot is on
13:59 This is the ritual for a **l** disease in a cloth of wool
14: 2 This shall be the ritual for the **l** person at the time
14: 3 If the disease is healed in the **l** person,
14: 7 the one who is to be cleansed of the **l** disease;
14:32 This is the ritual for the one who has a **l** disease,
14:34 and I put a **l** disease in a house in the land
14:44 it is a spreading **l** disease in the house;
14:54 This is the ritual for any **l** disease: for an itch,
14:55 for **l** diseases in clothing and houses,
14:57 This is the ritual for **l** diseases.
22: 4 No one of Aaron's offspring who has a **l** disease
Nu 5: 2 to put out of the camp everyone who is **l**, or has
12:10 Miriam had become **l**, as white as snow.
12:10 and saw that she was **l**.
Dt 24: 8 Guard against an outbreak of a **l** skin disease
2Sa 3:29 or who is **l**, or who holds a spindle,
2Ki 5:27 So he left his presence **l**, as white as snow.
7: 3 Now there were four **l** men outside the city gate,
7: 8 these **l** men had come to the edge of the camp,
15: 5 so that he was **l** to the day of his death,
2Ch 26:19 the priests a **l** disease broke out on his forehead,
26:20 looked at him, he was **l** in his forehead.
26:21 King Uzziah was **l** to the day of his death,
26:21 and being **l** lived in a separate house,
26:23 that belonged to the kings, for they said, "He is **l**."

LESHEM (2) [=DAN]

Jos 19:47 the Danites went up and fought against **L**,
19:47 calling **L**, Dan, after their ancestor Dan.

LESS (31) [LEAST, LESSEN, LESSENED, LESSER, LESSON]

Ex 16:17 Israelites did so, some gathering more, some **l**.
30:15 and the poor shall not give **l**, than the half shekel,
Nu 22:18 the command of the LORD my God, to do **l**
1Sa 15:23 For rebellion is no **l** a sin than divination,
1Ki 8:27 much **l** this house that I have built!
2Ch 6:18 how much **l** this house that I have built!
32:15 much **l** will your God save you out of my hand!"
Ezr 9:13 have punished us **l** than our iniquities deserved
Job 11: 6 that God exacts of you **l** than your guilt deserves.
15:16 how much **l** one who is abominable and corrupt,
25: 6 how much **l** a mortal, who is a maggot,
35:14 much **l** when you say that you do not see him,
Pr 17: 7 still **l** is false speech to a ruler.
19:10 much **l** for a slave to rule over princes.
Isa 40:17 they are accounted by him as **l** than nothing
Jer 3:11 Faithless Israel has shown herself **l** guilty than false Judah.
Eze 15: 5 for nothing; how much **l**—
1Co 12:15 that would not make it any **l** a part of the body.
12:16 that would not make it any **l** a part of the body.
12:23 of the body that we think **l** honorable we clothe
12:23 and our **l** respectable members are treated
2Co 12:15 If I love you more, am I to be loved **l**?
Php 2:28 and that I may be **l** anxious.
1Ti 5: 9 on the list if she is not **l** than sixty years old
Heb 12:25 on earth, how much **l** will we escape if we reject
Wis 15:10 and their lives are of **l** worth than clay,
Sir 19: 6 but one who hates gossip has **l** evil.
22:11 Weep **l** bitterly for the dead, for he is at rest;
2Mc 4:40 a man advanced in years and no **l** advanced
15:18 lay upon them **l** heavily;
2Es 7:*58* what is plentiful is of **l** worth,

LESSEN (2) [LESS]

Ex 5:19 "You shall not **l** your daily number of bricks."
Sir 17:25 pray in his presence and **l** your offense.

LESSENED (1) [LESS]

Ex 5:11 but your work will not be **l** in the least.' "

LESSER (1) [LESS]

Ge 1:16 to rule the day and the **l** light to rule the night—

LESSON (5) [LESS]

Jer 35:13 Can you not learn a **l** and obey my words?
Mt 24:32 "From the fig tree learn its **l**:
Mk 13:28 "From the fig tree learn its **l**:
1Co 14:26 you come together, each one has a hymn, a **l**,
Sir 9: 1 or you will teach her an evil **l** to your own hurt.

LET‡ (1679) [LETS, LETTING]

Ge 1: 3 God said, "**L** there be light"; and there was light.
1: 6 "**L** there be a dome in the midst of the waters,
1: 6 and **l** it separate the waters from the waters."
1: 9 "**L** the waters under the sky be gathered together
1: 9 and **l** the dry land appear."
1:11 Then God said, "**L** the earth put forth vegetation:
1:14 "**L** there be lights in the dome of the sky
1:14 and **l** them be for signs and for seasons and
1:15 and **l** them be lights in the dome of the sky
1:20 "**L** the waters bring forth swarms
1:20 and **l** birds fly above the earth across the dome of
1:22 and **l** birds multiply on the earth."
1:24 "**L** the earth bring forth living creatures
1:26 God said, "**L** us make humankind in our image,
1:26 **l** them have dominion over the fish of the sea,
4: 8 "**L** us go out to the field."
9:26 and **l** Canaan be his slave.
9:27 and **l** him live in the tents of Shem;
Ge 9:27 and **l** Canaan be his slave."
11: 3 **l** us make bricks, and burn them thoroughly."
11: 4 they said, "Come, **l** us build ourselves a city,
11: 4 and **l** us make a name for ourselves;
11: 7 **l** us go down, and confuse their language there,
12:12 then they will kill me, but they will **l** you live.
13: 8 "**L** there be no strife between you and me,
14:24 **L** them take their share."
18: 4 **L** a little water be brought, and wash your feet,
18: 5 **L** me bring a little bread,
18:27 "**L** me take it upon myself to speak to the Lord,
18:30 "Oh do not **l** the Lord be angry if I speak.
18:31 "**L** me take it upon myself to speak to the Lord.
18:32 not **l** the Lord be angry if I speak just once more.
19: 8 **l** me bring them out to you,
19:20 **L** me escape there—is it not a little one?
19:32 Come, **l** us make our father drink wine,
19:34 **l** us make him drink wine tonight also;
20: 6 Therefore I did not **l** you touch her.
21:16 "Do not **l** me look on the death of the child."
23: 9 the full price **l** him give it to me in your presence
24:14 **L** the girl to whom I shall say,
24:14 **l** her be the one whom you have appointed
24:17 "Please **l** me sip a little water from your jar."
24:43 **l** the young woman who comes out to draw,
24:44 **l** her be the woman whom
24:45 I said to her, 'Please **l** me drink.'
24:46 She quickly **l** down her jar from her shoulder,
24:51 and **l** her be the wife of your master's son,
24:55 "**L** the girl remain with us a while,
24:56 **l** me go that I may go to my master."
25:30 "**L** me eat some of that red stuff,
26:28 **l** there be an oath between you us, and **l** us make a
27:13 His mother said to him, "**L** your curse be on me,
27:29 **L** peoples serve you, and nations bow down
27:31 "**L** my father sit up and eat of his son's game,
30:26 for whom I have served you, and **l** me go;
30:32 **l** me pass through all your flock today, removing
30:34 Laban said, "Good! **L** it be as you have said."
31:35 "**L** not my lord be angry that I cannot rise
31:44 Come now, **l** us make a covenant, you and I;
31:44 and **l** it be a witness between you and me."
32:26 Then he said, "**L** me go, for the day is breaking."
32:26 But Jacob said, "I will not **l** you go,
33:12 Then Esau said, "**L** us journey on our way,
33:14 **L** my lord pass on ahead of his servant,
33:15 "**L** me leave with you some of the people who are
34:11 "**L** me find favor with you,
34:21 **l** them live in the land and trade in it,
34:21 **l** us take their daughters in marriage,
34:21 and **l** us give them our daughters.
34:23 Only **l** us agree with them,
35: 3 **l** us go up to Bethel,
37:17 for I heard them say, '**L** us go to Dothan.' "
37:20 **l** us kill him and throw him into one of the pits;
37:21 saying, "**L** us not take his life."
37:27 Come, **l** us sell him to the Ishmaelites,
38:16 and said, "Come, **l** me come in to you,"
38:23 Judah replied, "**L** her keep the things as her own,
38:24 Judah said, "Bring her out, and **l** her be burned."
41:33 Now therefore **l** Pharaoh select
41:34 **L** Pharaoh proceed to appoint overseers over
41:35 **L** them gather all the food of these good years
41:35 for food in the cities, and **l** them keep it.
42:16 **L** one of you go and bring your brother,
42:19 **l** one of your brothers stay here
43: 8 "Send the boy with me, and **l** us be on our way,
43: 9 then **l** me bear the blame forever.
44: 9 with any one of your servants, **l** him die;
44:10 in accordance with your words, **l** it be:
44:18 **l** your servant please speak a word
44:33 please **l** your servant remain as a slave to my lord
44:33 and **l** the boy go back with his brothers.
47: 4 **l** your servants settle in the land of Goshen."
47: 6 **l** them live in the land of Goshen;
48:11 and here God has **l** me see your children also."
48:16 and in them **l** my name be perpetuated,
48:16 and **l** them grow into a multitude on the earth."
49:21 Naphtali is a doe **l** loose that bears lovely fawns.
50: 5 **l** me go up, so that I may bury my father;
Ex 1:10 Come, **l** us deal shrewdly with them,
1:17 as the king of Egypt commanded them, but they **l**
1:22 but you shall **l** every girl live."
3:18 **l** us now go a three days' journey into
3:19 not **l** you go unless compelled by a mighty hand.
3:20 after that he will **l** you go.
4:18 "Please **l** me go back to my kindred in Egypt
4:21 so that he will not **l** the people go.
4:23 "**L** my son go that he may worship me."
4:23 But you refused to **l** him go;
4:26 So he **l** him alone.
5: 1 the God of Israel, '**L** my people go,
5: 2 that I should heed him and **l** Israel go?
5: 2 and I will not **l** Israel go."
5: 3 **l** us go a three days' journey into the wilderness
5: 7 **l** them go and gather straw for themselves.
5: 8 '**L** us go and offer sacrifice to our God.'
5: 9 **L** heavier work be laid on them;
5:17 '**L** us go and sacrifice to the LORD.'
6: 1 Indeed, by a mighty hand he will **l** them go;
6:11 of Egypt to **l** the Israelites go out of his land."
7: 2 and your brother Aaron shall tell Pharaoh to **l**
7:14 he refuses to **l** the people go.
7:16 sent me to you to say, "**L** my people go,
8: 1 **L** my people go, so that they may worship me.
8: 2 If you refuse to **l** them go,
8: 8 I will **l** the people go to sacrifice to the LORD."
Ex 8:20 **L** my people go, so that they may worship me.
8:21 For if you will not **l** my people go,
8:28 "I will **l** you go to sacrifice to
8:29 not **l** Pharaoh again deal falsely by not letting
8:32 and would not **l** the people go.
9: 1 **L** my people go, so that they may worship me.
9: 2 For if you refuse to **l** them go and still hold them,
9: 7 and he would not **l** the people go.
9: 8 and **l** Moses throw it in the air in the sight
9:13 **L** my people go, so that they may worship me.
9:16 But this is why I have **l** you live:
9:17 and will not **l** them go.
9:28 I will **l** you go; you need stay no longer."
9:35 and he would not **l** the Israelites go,
10: 3 **L** my people go, so that they may worship me.
10: 4 For if you refuse to **l** my people go,
10: 7 **L** the people go, so that they may worship
10:10 if ever I **l** your little ones go with you!
10:20 and he would not **l** the Israelites go.
10:25 also **l** us have sacrifices and burnt offerings
10:27 and he was unwilling to **l** them go.
11: 1 afterwards he will **l** you go from here;
11:10 not **l** the people of Israel go out of his land.
12:10 You shall **l** none of it remain until the morning;
12:36 so that they **l** them have what they asked.
13:15 When Pharaoh stubbornly refused to **l** us go,
13:17 When Pharaoh **l** the people go,
14:12 '**L** us alone and let us serve the Egyptians'?
14:12 'Let us alone and **l** us serve the Egyptians'?
14:25 The Egyptians said, "**L** us flee from the Israelites,
16:19 "**L** no one leave any of it over until morning."
16:32 '**L** an omer of it be kept
18:22 **L** them sit as judges for the people at all times;
18:22 **l** them bring every important case to you,
18:27 Then Moses **l** his father-in-law depart,
19:24 but do not **l** either the priests or the people break
20:19 but do not **l** God speak to us, or we will die."
21: 8 then he shall **l** her be redeemed;
21:26 the owner shall **l** the slave go, a free person,
21:27 the slave shall be **l** go, a free person,
22:13 **l** it be brought as evidence;
23:11 the seventh year you shall **l** it rest and lie fallow,
23:13 do not **l** them be heard on your lips.
23:18 **l** the fat of my festival remain until the morning.
32:10 Now **l** me alone, so that my wrath may burn hot
32:22 "Do not **l** the anger of my lord burn hot;
32:25 (for Aaron had **l** them run wild,
33:12 but you have not **l** me know whom you will send
34: 3 and do not **l** anyone be seen throughout all
34: 3 and do not **l** flocks or herds graze in front of
34: 9 O Lord, I pray, **l** the Lord go with us.
35: 5 **l** whoever is of a generous heart bring
Lev 13:45 the leprous disease shall wear torn clothes and **l**
14: 7 he shall **l** the living bird go into the open field.
14:53 and he shall **l** the living bird go out of the city
19:19 not **l** your animals breed with a different kind;
24:14 and **l** all who were within hearing lay their hands
24:14 and **l** the whole congregation stone him.
25:36 but fear your God; **l** them live with you.
26:22 I will **l** loose wild animals against you,
27:33 **L** no one inquire whether it is good or bad,
Nu 4:18 not **l** the tribe of the clans of the Kohathites
5:21 —**l** the priest make the woman take the oath of
6: 5 they shall **l** the locks of the head grow long.
8: 8 Then **l** them take a young bull
9: 2 **L** the Israelites keep the passover
10:35 "Arise, O LORD, **l** your enemies be scattered,
11:15 and do not **l** me see my misery."
11:31 and it brought quails from the sea and **l** them fall
12:12 Do not **l** her be like one stillborn,
12:14 **L** her be shut out of the camp for seven days,
13:30 and said, "**L** us go up at once and occupy it,
14: 4 they said to one another, "**L** us choose a captain,
14:17 **l** the power of the LORD be great in the way
14:42 do not **l** yourselves be struck down
16:17 and **l** each one of you take his censer,
20:17 Now **l** us pass through your land.
20:19 just **l** us pass through on foot."
20:24 "**L** Aaron be gathered to his people.
21:22 "**L** me pass through your land;
21:27 **l** it be built; **l** the city of Sihon be established.
22:13 for the LORD has refused to **l** me go with you."
22:16 not **l** anything hinder you from coming to me;
22:33 just now I would have killed you and **l** it live."
23:10 **L** me die the death of the upright, and **l** my end be like his!"
24:14 **l** me advise you what this people will do
27: 7 you shall indeed **l** them possess an inheritance
27:16 "**L** the LORD, the God of the spirits
32: 5 **l** this land be given to your servants for
33:55 then those whom you **l** remain shall be as barbs
36: 6 '**L** them marry whom they think best;
Dt 1:22 "**L** us send men ahead of us to explore the land
2:27 "If you **l** me pass through your land,
2:30 of Heshbon was not willing to **l** us pass through,
3:25 **L** me cross over to see the good land beyond
4: 9 nor to **l** them slip from your mind all the days
4:10 and I will **l** them hear my words,
9:14 **L** me alone that I may destroy them
9:28 he has brought them out to **l** them die in
13: 2 "**L** us follow other gods" (whom you have not known) "and **l** us serve them,"
13: 6 saying, "**L** us go worship other gods,"
13:13 saying, "**L** us go and worship other gods,"
13:17 Do not **l** anything devoted to destruction stick
20:16 not **l** anything that breathes remain alive.
21: 8 do not **l** the guilt of innocent blood remain in

Dt 21:14 you shall l her go free and not sell her for money.
22: 7 L the mother go, taking only the young
31:26 l it remain there as a witness against you.
32: 1 l the earth hear the words of my mouth.
32:38 L them rise up and help you, l them be your protection!
33:16 L these come on the head of Joseph,
34: 4 I have l you see it with your eyes,
Jos 2:15 she l them down by a rope through the window,
2:18 in the window through which you l us down,
4:22 then you shall l your children know,
5: 6 the LORD swore that he would not l them see
6:10 "You shall not shout or l your voice be heard,
9:20 We will l them live, so that wrath may not come
9:21 The leaders said to them, "L them live."
10: 4 up and help me, and l us attack Gibeon;
10:19 Do not l them enter their towns,
22:22 He knows; and l Israel itself know!
22:26 Therefore we said, 'L us now build an altar,
Jdg 1:25 but they l the man and all his family go.
6:31 If he is a god, l him contend for himself,
6:32 that is to say, "L Baal contend against him,"
6:39 "Do not l your anger burn against me, l me speak one more time; l me, please, make trial with the fleece just once more; l it be dry only on the fleece, and on all the ground l there be dew."
7: 3 and trembling, l him return home.' "
7: 7 L all the others go to their homes."
8:24 "L me make a request of you;
9:15 if not, l fire come out of the bramble and devour
9:19 and l him also rejoice in you;
9:20 l fire come out from Abimelech,
9:20 and l fire come out from the lords of Shechem,
10:14 l them deliver you in the time of your distress."
11:17 saying, 'L us pass through your land';
11:19 'L us pass through your land to our country.'
11:27 L the LORD, who is judge,
11:37 "L this thing be done for me:
12: 5 of the fugitives of Ephraim said, "L me go over,"
13: 8 l the man of God whom you sent come
13:13 "L the woman give heed to all that I said to her.
14:12 "L me now put a riddle to you.
14:13 they said to him, "Ask your riddle; l us hear it."
15: 5 he l the foxes go into the standing grain of
16: 2 "L us wait until the light of the morning;
16:19 She l him fall asleep on her lap;
16:25 they said, "Call Samson, and l him entertain us."
16:26 "L me feel the pillars on which the house rests,
16:30 Samson said, "L me die with the Philistines."
18: 9 They said, "Come, l us go up against them;
18:25 "You had better not l your voice be heard
19:11 l us turn aside to this city of the Jebusites,
19:13 "Come, l us try to reach one of these places,
19:24 l me bring them out now.
19:25 And as the dawn began to break, they l her go.
20:32 "L us retreat and draw them away from the city
Ru 2: 2 "L me go to the field and glean among the ears
2: 7 l me glean and gather among the sheaves behind
2:15 "L her glean even among the standing sheaves,
3:13 for you, good; l him do it.
1Sa 1:18 "L your servant find favor in your sight."
2: 3 l not arrogance come from your mouth;
2:16 if the man said to him, "L them burn the fat first,
3:18 l him do what seems good to him."
3:19 and l none of his words fall to the ground.
4: 3 L us bring the ark of the covenant of
5: 8 "L the ark of God be moved on to us."
5:11 and l it return to its own place,
6: 6 did they not l the people go, and they departed?
6: 8 Then send it off, and l it go its way.
9: 5 "L us turn back, or my father will stop worrying
9: 6 he says always comes true. L us go there now;
9: 9 "Come, l us go to the seer";
9:10 Saul said to the boy, "Good; come, l us go."
9:19 the morning I will l you go and will tell you all
11:14 l us go to Gilgal and there renew the kingship."
13: 3 saying, "L the Hebrews hear!"
14: 1 l us go over to the Philistine garrison on
14: 6 l us go over to the garrison
14:34 'L all bring their oxen or their sheep,
14:36 "L us go down after the Philistines by night
14:36 l us not leave one of them."
14:36 But the priest said, "L us draw near to God here."
14:38 and l us find out how this sin has arisen today.
16:16 L our lord now command
16:22 saying, "L David remain in my service,
17: 8 and l him come down to me.
17:32 "L no one's heart fail because of him;
18: 2 and would not l him return to his father's house.
18:17 l the Philistines deal with him."
18:21 "L me give her to him that she may be a snare
19:12 So Michal l David down through the window;
19:17 and l my enemy go, so that he has escaped?"
19:17 Michal answered Saul, "He said to me, 'L me go;
20: 3 and he thinks, 'Do not l Jonathan know this,
20: 5 but l me go, so that I may hide in the field until
20:11 "Come, l us go out into the field."
20:29 'L me go; for our family is holding a sacrifice in
20:29 I have found favor in your sight, l me get away,
21:13 and l his spittle run down his beard.
22: 3 "Please l my father and mother come to you,
22:15 Do not l the king impute anything to his servant
25: 8 l my young men find favor in your sight;
25:24 please l your servant speak in your ears,
25:26 now l your enemies and those who seek
25:27 now l this present that your servant has brought
26: 8 now therefore l me pin him to the ground
1Sa 26:11 and the water jar, and l us go."
26:19 l my lord the king hear the words of his servant.
26:20 therefore, do not l my blood fall to the ground,
26:22 L one of the young men come over and get it.
27: 5 l a place be given me in one of
28:22 l me set a morsel of bread before you.
2Sa 1:21 l there be no dew or rain upon you,
2: 7 Therefore l your hands be strong, and be valiant;
2:14 "L the young men come forward and have
2:14 Joab said, "L them come forward."
3:21 "L me go and rally all Israel to my lord the king,
5: 8 l him get up the water shaft to attack the lame
10:12 l us be courageous for the sake of our people,
11:25 'Do not l this matter trouble you,
13: 5 'L my sister Tamar come and give me something
13: 6 "Please l my sister Tamar come and make
13:25 "No, my son, l us not all go,
13:26 "If not, please l my brother Amnon go with us."
13:27 But Absalom pressed him until he l Amnon
13:32 "L not my lord suppose that they have killed all
13:33 do not l my lord the king take it to heart,
14: 9 l the king and his throne be guiltless."
14:12 "Please l your servant speak a word to my lord
14:18 The woman said, "L my lord the king speak."
14:24 The king said, "L him go to his own house;
14:32 Now l me go into the king's presence; if there is guilt in me, l him kill me!"
15: 7 "Please l me go to Hebron and pay the vow
15:14 L us flee, or there will be no escape for us
15:25 and l me see both it and the place where it stays.
15:26 l him do to me what seems good to him."
16: 4 l me find favor in your sight, my lord the king."
16: 9 L me go over and take off his head."
16:11 L him alone, and l him curse;
17: 1 "L me choose twelve thousand men,
17: 5 and l us hear too what he has to say."
18:19 Then Ahimaaz son of Zadok said, "L me run,
18:22 l me also run after the Cushite."
19:30 Mephibosheth said to the king, "L him take it all,
19:37 Please l your servant return,
19:37 l him go over with my lord the king,
20:11 and whoever is for David, l him follow Joab."
20:18 'L them inquire at Abel';
21: 6 l seven of his sons be handed over to us,
24:14 l us fall into the hand of the LORD,
24:14 but l me not fall into human hands."
24:17 L your hand, I pray, be against me and
24:22 "L my lord the king take and offer
1Ki 1: 2 "L a young virgin be sought for my lord the king, and l her wait on the king, and be his attendant; l her lie in your bosom,
1:12 Now therefore come, l me give you advice,
1:27 not l your servants know who should sit on
1:34 There l the priest Zadok and
1:35 L him enter and sit on my throne;
1:51 'L King Solomon swear to me first that he will
2: 6 do not l his gray head go down to Sheol in peace.
2: 7 and l them be among those who eat at your table;
2:21 "L Abishag the Shunammite be given
4:27 they l nothing be lacking.
8:26 O God of Israel, l your word be confirmed,
8:52 L your eyes be open to the plea of your servant,
8:59 L these words of mine, with which I pleaded
11:21 "L me depart, that I may go to my own country."
11:22 And he said, "No, do l me go."
12:24 L everyone go home, for this thing is from me."
15:19 "L there be an alliance between me and you,
17:21 l this child's life come into him again."
18:23 L two bulls be given to us; l them choose one bull
18:36 l it be known this day that you are God in Israel,
18:40 do not l one of them escape."
19:20 and said, "L me kiss my father and my mother,
20:23 but l us fight against them in the plain,
20:31 l us put sackcloth around our waists and ropes
20:32 "Your servant Ben-hadad says, 'Please l me live.' "
20:34 "I will l you go on those terms."
20:34 So he made a treaty with him and l him go.
20:42 the LORD, 'Because you have l
22: 8 "L the king not say such a thing."
22:13 l your word be like the word of one of them,
22:17 l each one go home in peace.' "
22:49 "L my servants go with your servants in
2Ki 1:10 l fire come down from heaven and consume you
1:12 l fire come down from heaven and consume you
1:13 "O man of God, please l my life,
1:14 but now l my life be precious in your sight."
2: 9 "Please l me inherit a double share
2:16 please l them go and seek your master;
4:10 L us make a small roof chamber with walls,
4:27 But the man of God said, "L her alone,
4:41 and said, "Serve the people and l them eat."
4:42 "Give it to the people and l them eat."
4:43 "Give it to the people and l them eat,
5: 8 L him come to me, that he may learn that there is
5:17 please l two mule-loads of earth be given
5:20 the man of God, thought, "My master has l
6: 2 L us go to the Jordan,
6: 2 and l us collect logs there, one for each of us,
6:22 and l them go to their master."
6:27 L the LORD help you.
7: 4 If we say, 'L us enter the city,'
7: 4 Therefore, l us desert to the Aramean camp;
7: 9 therefore l us go and tell the king's household."
7:13 "L some men take five of the remaining horses,
7:13 l us send and find out."
9:15 then l no one slip out of the city to go and tell
9:17 send him to meet them, and l him say,
2Ki 10:19 l none be missing, for I have a great sacrifice
10:25 and kill them; l no one escape."
11:15 "L her not be killed in the house of the LORD."
12: 5 l the priests receive from each of the donors;
12: 5 and l them repair the house wherever any need
14: 8 "Come, l us look one another in the face."
17:27 l him go and live there,
18:29 'Do not l Hezekiah deceive you,
18:30 Do not l Hezekiah make you rely on the LORD
19:10 not l your God on whom you rely deceive you
20: 7 L them take it and apply it to the boil,
20:10 rather l the shadow retreat ten intervals."
22: 5 l it be given into the hand of the workers
22: 5 l them give it to the workers who are at the house
22: 6 and l them use it to buy timber
23:18 He said, "L him rest; l no one move his bones."
23:18 So they l his bones alone,
1Ch 13: 2 l us send abroad to our kindred who remain in all
13: 3 Then l us bring again the ark of our God to us;
16:10 l the hearts of those who seek
16:31 L the heavens be glad, and l the earth rejoice,
16:31 and l them say among the nations,
16:32 L the sea roar, and all that fills it;
16:32 l the field exult, and everything in it.
17:23 l it be established forever,
19:13 and l us be courageous for our people and for
21:13 l me fall into the hand of the LORD,
21:13 but l me not fall into human hands."
21:17 L your hand, I pray, O LORD my God,
21:17 but do not l your people be plagued!"
21:23 l my lord the king do what seems good to him;
2Ch 1: 9 l your promise to my father David now
2:15 l him send them to his servants.
6:17 God of Israel, l your word be confirmed,
6:40 l your eyes be open and your ears attentive
6:41 L your priests, O LORD God,
6:41 and l your faithful rejoice in your goodness.
11: 4 L everyone return home,
14: 7 He said to Judah, "L us build these cities,
14:11 l no mortal prevail against you."
15: 7 Do not l your hands be weak,
16: 3 "L there be an alliance between me and you,
16: 5 he stopped building Ramah, and l his work cease.
18: 7 "L the king not say such a thing."
18:12 l your word be like the word of one of them,
18:16 l each one go home in peace.' "
19: 7 Now, l the fear of the LORD be upon you;
20:10 not l Israel invade when they came from the land
23: 3 L him reign, as the LORD promised concerning
23: 6 Do not l anyone enter the house of
25: 7 "O king, do not l the army of Israel go with you,
25:17 "Come, l us look one another in the face."
32:15 Now therefore do not l Hezekiah deceive you
34:11 for the buildings that the kings of Judah had l go
35: 5 and l there be Levites for each division of
36:23 may the LORD his God be with him! L him go up."
Ezr 1: 4 and l all survivors, in whatever place they reside,
4: 2 "L us build with you, for we worship your God
5:15 and l the house of God be rebuilt on its site."
5:17 L the king send us his pleasure in this matter."
6: 3 at Jerusalem, l the house be rebuilt, the place
6: 4 l the cost be paid from the royal treasury.
6: 5 l the gold and silver vessels of the house of God,
6: 7 l the work on this house of God alone;
6: 7 l the governor of the Jews and the elders of
6: 9 l that be given to them day by day without fail,
6:12 l it be done with all diligence."
7:21 requires of you, l it be done with all diligence,
7:23 l it be done with zeal for the house of the God
7:26 l judgment be strictly executed on them,
10: 3 So now l us make a covenant with our God
10: 3 and l it be done according to the law.
10:14 L our officials represent the whole assembly, and l all in our towns
Ne 1: 6 l your ear be attentive and your eyes open to hear
1:11 l your ear be attentive to the prayer
2: 7 l letters be given me to the governors of
2:17 Come, l us rebuild the wall of Jerusalem,
2:18 Then they said, "L us start building!"
4: 5 do not l their sin be blotted out from your sight;
4:22 "L every man and his servant pass the night
5:10 L us stop this taking of interest.
6: 2 and l us meet together in one of the villages in
6: 7 So come, therefore, and l us confer together."
6:10 he said, "L us meet together in the house of God,
6:10 and l us close the doors of the temple,
7: 3 l them shut and bar the doors.
Est 1:19 l a royal order go out from him,
1:19 and l it be written among the laws of the Persians
1:19 and l the king give her royal position
2: 2 "L beautiful young virgins be sought out for
2: 3 And l the king appoint commissioners in all
2: 3 l their cosmetic treatments be given them.
2: 4 And l the girl who pleases the king
3: 9 l a decree be issued for their destruction,
5: 4 l the king and Haman come today to a banquet
5: 8 l the king and Haman come tomorrow to
5:12 "Even Queen Esther l no one but myself come
5:14 "L a gallows fifty cubits high be made,
6: 5 The king said, "L him come in."
6: 8 l royal robes be brought,
6: 9 L the robes and the horse be handed over to one
6: 9 l him robe the man whom the king wishes
6: 9 and l him conduct the man on horseback through
7: 3 and if it pleases the king, l my life be given me—
8: 5 l an order be written to revoke the letters devised
9:13 l the Jews who are in Susa be allowed tomorrow

Est 9:13 and l the ten sons of Haman be hanged on
Job 3: 3 "L the day perish in which I was born,
3: 4 L that day be darkness!
3: 5 L gloom and deep darkness claim it. L clouds settle upon it; l the blackness of the day terrify it.
3: 6 That night—l thick darkness seize it! l it not rejoice among the days of the year; l it not come into the number of the months.
3: 7 Yes, l that night be barren; l no joyful cry be heard
3: 8 L those curse it who curse the Sea,
3: 9 L the stars of its dawn be dark; l it hope for light,
6: 9 that he would l loose his hand and cut me off!
6:29 Turn, I pray, l no wrong be done.
7:16 L me alone, for my days are a breath.
7:19 l me alone until I swallow my spittle?
9:18 he will not l me get my breath,
9:34 and not l dread of him terrify me,
10: 2 l me know why you contend against me.
10:20 L me alone, that I may find
11:14 and do not l wickedness reside in your tents.
13:13 "L me have silence, and l come on me what may.
13:17 and l my declaration be in your ears.
13:21 and do not l dread of you terrify me.
13:22 or l me speak, and you reply to me.
15:13 and l such words go out of your mouth?
15:31 L them not trust in emptiness,
16:18 l my outcry find no resting place.
17: 4 therefore you will not l them triumph.
20:13 though they are loath to l it go,
20:20 in their greed they l nothing escape.
21: 2 and l this be your consolation.
21:19 L it be paid back to them,
21:20 L their own eyes see their destruction,
21:20 and l them drink of the wrath of the Almighty.
27: 6 I hold fast my righteousness, and will not l it go;
31: 6 l me be weighed in a just balance, and l God know my integrity!—
31: 8 then l me sow, and another eat; and l what grows for me be rooted out.
31:10 then l my wife grind for another, and l other men kneel over her.
31:22 then l my shoulder blade fall from my shoulder, and l my arm be broken from its socket.
31:30 not l my mouth sin by asking for their lives with
31:35 l the Almighty answer me!)
31:40 l thorns grow instead of wheat,
32: 7 'L days speak, and many years teach wisdom.'
32:10 l me also declare my opinion.'
33:25 l his flesh become fresh with youth; l him return to the days of his youthful vigor.'
34: 4 L us choose what is right; l us determine among ourselves what is good.
36:18 not l the greatness of the ransom turn you aside.
39: 5 "Who has l the wild ass go free?
Ps 2: 3 "L us burst their bonds asunder,
4: 6 L the light of your face shine on us, O LORD!"
5:10 l them fall by their own counsels;
5:11 But l all who take refuge in you rejoice; l them ever sing for joy.
7: 5 then l the enemy pursue and overtake me,
7: 7 L the assembly of the peoples be gathered
7: 9 O l the evil of the wicked come to an end,
9:19 Do not l mortals prevail; l the nations be judged before you.
9:20 l the nations know that they are only human.
10: 2 l them be caught in the schemes they have devised.
16:10 or l your faithful one see the Pit.
17: 2 From you l my vindication come; l your eyes see the right.
19:13 do not l them have dominion over me.
19:14 L the words of my mouth and the meditation
22: 8 "Commit your cause to the LORD; l him deliver—l him rescue the one in whom he delights!"
25: 2 do not l me be put to shame; do not l my enemies exult over me.
25: 3 Do not l those who wait for you be put to shame; l them be ashamed who are wantonly treacherous.
25:20 do not l me be put to shame,
27:14 be strong, and l your heart take courage;
30: 1 and did not l my foes rejoice over me.
31: 1 do not l me ever be put to shame;
31:16 L your face shine upon your servant;
31:17 Do not l me be put to shame, O LORD,
31:17 l the wicked be put to shame; l them go dumbfounded to Sheol.
31:18 L the lying lips be stilled that speak insolently
31:24 Be strong, and l your heart take courage,
32: 6 l all who are faithful offer prayer to you;
33: 8 L all the earth fear the LORD; l all the inhabitants of the world stand in awe
33:22 L your steadfast love, O LORD, be upon us,
34: 2 l the humble hear and be glad.
34: 3 and l us exalt his name together.
35: 4 L them be put to shame and dishonor who seek
35: 4 L them be turned back and confounded
35: 5 L them be like chaff before the wind,
35: 6 L their way be dark and slippery,
35: 8 L ruin come on them unawares.
35: 8 And l the net that they hid ensnare them; l them fall in it—to their ruin.
35:19 not l my treacherous enemies rejoice over me,
35:24 and do not l them rejoice over me.
35:25 Do not l them say to themselves, "Aha,
35:25 Do not l them say, "We have swallowed you up."
35:26 L all those who rejoice at my calamity be put
35:26 l those who exalt themselves against me
35:27 L those who desire my vindication shout for joy

Ps 36:11 Do not l the foot of the arrogant tread on me,
37:33 or l them be condemned when they are brought
38:16 For I pray, "Only do not l them rejoice over me,
39: 4 l me know my end, and what is the measure
39: 4 l me know how fleeting my life is.
40:11 l your steadfast love and your faithfulness keep me
40:14 L all those be put to shame
40:14 l those be turned back and brought
40:15 L those be appalled because
43: 3 l them lead me; l them bring me to your holy hill
45: 4 l your right hand teach you dread deeds.
48:11 L Mount Zion be glad, l the towns of Judah rejoice
51: 8 L me hear joy and gladness; l the bones that you have crushed rejoice.
55:15 L death come upon them; l them go down alive to
57: 5 L your glory be over all the earth.
57:11 L your glory be over all the earth.
58: 7 L them vanish like water that runs away; like grass l them be trodden down and wither.
58: 8 L them be like the snail that dissolves into slime;
59:10 my God will l me look in triumph
59:12 l them be trapped in their pride.
61: 4 L me abide in your tent forever,
64:10 L the righteous rejoice in the LORD
64:10 L all the upright in heart glory.
66: 7 l the rebellious not exalt themselves.
66: 8 O peoples, l the sound of his praise be heard,
66: 9 and has not l our feet slip.
66:12 you l people ride over our heads;
67: 3 L the peoples praise you, O God; l all the peoples praise you.
67: 4 L the nations be glad and sing for joy,
67: 5 L the peoples praise you, O God; l all the peoples praise you.
67: 7 l all the ends of the earth revere him.
68: 1 L God rise up, l his enemies be scattered; l those who hate him flee before him.
68: 2 l the wicked perish before God.
68: 3 But l the righteous be joyful; l them exult before God; l them be jubilant with joy.
68:31 L bronze be brought from Egypt; l Ethiopia hasten
69: 6 Do not l those who hope in you be put to shame
69: 6 not l those who seek you be dishonored because
69:14 l me be delivered from my enemies and from
69:15 Do not l the flood sweep over me,
69:22 L their table be a trap for them,
69:23 L their eyes be darkened so that they cannot see,
69:24 and l your burning anger overtake them.
69:25 l no one live in their tents.
69:28 L them be blotted out of the book of the living; l them not be enrolled among the righteous.
69:29 l your salvation, O God, protect me.
69:32 L the oppressed see it and be glad; you who seek God, l your hearts revive.
69:34 L heaven and earth praise him,
70: 2 L those be put to shame
70: 2 L those be turned back and brought
70: 3 L those who say, "Aha, Aha!"
70: 4 L all who seek you rejoice and be glad in you.
70: 4 L those who love your salvation say evermore,
71: 1 l me never be put to shame.
71:13 L my accusers be put to shame and consumed; l those who seek to hurt me be covered with scorn
74:21 Do not l the downtrodden be put to shame; l the poor and needy praise your name.
76:11 l all who are around him bring gifts to
78:13 He divided the sea and l them pass through it,
78:28 he l them fall within their camp,
78:49 He l loose on them his fierce anger, wrath,
79: 8 l your compassion come speedily to meet us,
79:10 L the avenging of the outpoured blood
79:11 L the groans of the prisoners come before you;
80: 3 l your face shine, that we may be saved.
80: 7 l your face shine, that we may be saved.
80:17 l your hand be upon the one at your right hand,
80:19 l your face shine, that we may be saved.
83: 4 They say, "Come, l us wipe them out as a nation; l the name of Israel be remembered no more."
83:12 "L us take the pastures of God
83:17 L them be put to shame and dismayed forever; l them perish in disgrace.
83:18 L them know that you alone,
85: 8 L me hear what God the LORD will speak,
88: 2 l my prayer come before you;
89: 5 L the heavens praise your wonders,
90:16 L your work be manifest to your servants,
90:17 L the favor of the Lord our God be upon us,
95: 1 l us sing to the LORD; l us make a joyful noise to
95: 2 L us come into his presence with thanksgiving; l us make a joyful noise to him with songs
95: 6 O come, l us worship and bow down, l us kneel before the LORD, our Maker!
96:11 L the heavens be glad, and l the earth rejoice; l the sea roar, and all that fills it;
96:12 l the field exult, and everything
97: 1 The LORD is king! L the earth rejoice; l the many coastlands be glad!
98: 7 L the sea roar, and all that fills it;
98: 8 L the floods clap their hands; l the hills sing together for joy
99: 1 The LORD is king; l the peoples tremble!
99: 1 enthroned upon the cherubim; l the earth quake!
99: 3 L them praise your great and awesome name.
102: 1 l my cry come to you.
102:18 L this be recorded for a generation to come,
104:35 L sinners be consumed from the earth, and l the wicked be no more.

Ps 105: 3 l the hearts of those who seek
106:48 And l all the people say, "Amen."
107: 2 L the redeemed of the LORD say so,
107: 8 L them thank the LORD for his steadfast love,
107:15 L them thank the LORD for his steadfast love,
107:21 L them thank the LORD for his steadfast love,
107:22 And l them offer thanksgiving sacrifices,
107:31 L them thank the LORD for his steadfast love,
107:32 L them extol him in the congregation of
107:38 and he does not l their cattle decrease.
107:43 L those who are wise give heed to these things,
108: 5 and l your glory be over all the earth.
109: 6 l an accuser stand on his right.
109: 7 When he is tried, l him be found guilty; l his prayer be counted as sin.
109:14 and do not l the sin of his mother be blotted out.
109:15 L them be before the LORD continually,
109:17 He loved to curse; l curses come on him.
109:27 L them know that this is your hand;
109:28 L them curse, but you will bless.
109:28 L my assailants be put to shame;
118: 2 L Israel say, "His steadfast love endures forever."
118: 3 L the house of Aaron say,
118: 4 L those who fear the LORD say,
118:24 l us rejoice and be glad in it.
119:10 do not l me stray from your commandments.
119:31 l me not be put to shame.
119:41 L your steadfast love come to me, O LORD,
119:76 L your steadfast love become my comfort
119:77 L your mercy come to me, that I may live;
119:78 L the arrogant be put to shame,
119:79 L those who fear you turn to me,
119:116 and l me not be put to shame in my hope.
119:122 do not l the godless oppress me.
119:133 and never l iniquity have dominion over me.
119:169 L my cry come before you, O LORD;
119:170 L my supplication come before you;
119:173 L your hand be ready to help me,
119:175 L me live that I may praise you,
119:175 and l your ordinances help me.
121: 3 He will not l your foot be moved;
122: 1 "L us go to the house of the LORD!"
124: 1 not been the LORD who was on our side —l Israel
129: 1 from my youth" —l Israel now say—
129: 6 L them be like the grass on the housetops
130: 2 L your ears be attentive to the voice of my
132: 7 "L us go to his dwelling place; l us worship at his footstool."
132: 9 L your priests be clothed with righteousness, and l your faithful shout for joy.
137: 5 O Jerusalem, l my right hand wither!
137: 6 L my tongue cling to the roof of my mouth,
140: 9 l the mischief of their lips overwhelm them!
140:10 L burning coals fall on them!
140:10 L them be flung into pits, no more to rise!
140:11 Do not l the slanderer be established in the land; l evil speedily hunt down the violent!
141: 2 L my prayer be counted as incense before you,
141: 4 do not l me eat of their delicacies.
141: 5 L the righteous strike me; l the faithful correct me.
141: 5 Never l the oil of the wicked anoint my head,
141:10 L the wicked fall into their own nets,
143: 8 L me hear of your steadfast love in the morning,
143:10 L your good spirit lead me on a level path.
148: 5 L them praise the name of the LORD,
148:13 L them praise the name of the LORD,
149: 2 L Israel be glad in its Maker;
149: 2 l the children of Zion rejoice in their King.
149: 3 L them praise his name with dancing,
149: 5 L the faithful exult in glory; l them sing for joy on
149: 6 L the high praises of God be in their throats
150: 6 L everything that breathes praise the LORD!
Pr 1: 5 L the wise also hear and gain in learning,
1:11 "Come with us, l us lie in wait for blood; l us wantonly ambush the innocent;
1:12 like Sheol l us swallow them alive and whole,
3: 1 but l your heart keep my commandments;
3: 3 Do not l loyalty and faithfulness forsake you;
3:21 My child, do not l these escape from your sight:
4: 4 and said to me, "L your heart hold fast my words;
4:13 do not l go; guard her, for she is your life.
4:21 Do not l them escape from your sight;
4:25 L your eyes look directly forward,
5:17 L them be for yourself alone,
5:18 L your fountain be blessed,
6:25 and do not l her capture you with her eyelashes;
7:18 Come, l us take our fill of love until morning; l us delight ourselves with love.
7:25 Do not l your hearts turn aside to her ways;
10: 3 The LORD does not l the righteous go hungry,
23:17 Do not l your heart envy sinners,
23:25 L your father and mother be glad; l her who bore you rejoice.
23:26 and l your eyes observe my ways.
24:17 do not l your heart be glad when they stumble,
25:17 L your foot be seldom in your neighbor's house,
27: 2 L another praise you, and not your own mouth—
28:17 l that killer be a fugitive until death; l no one offer assistance.
31: 7 l them drink and forget their poverty,
31:31 and l her works praise her in the city gates.
Ecc 5: 2 l your heart be quick to utter a word before God,
5: 2 therefore l your words be few.
5: 6 Do not l your mouth lead you into sin,
5:12 but the surfeit of the rich will not l them sleep.
9: 8 L your garments always be white; do not l oil be lacking on your head.

Ecc 11: 6 and at evening do not l your hands be idle;
11: 8 yet l them remember that the days
11: 9 l your heart cheer you in the days of your youth.
SS 1: 2 L him kiss me with the kisses of his mouth!
1: 4 Draw me after you, l us make haste.
2:14 l me see your face, l me hear your voice;
3: 4 and would not l him go until I brought him
4:16 L my beloved come to his garden,
7:11 Come, my beloved, l us go forth into the fields,
7:12 l us go out early to the vineyards,
8:13 listening for your voice; l me hear it.
Isa 1:18 Come now, l us argue it out, says the LORD:
2: 3 l us go up to the mountain of the LORD,
2: 5 come, l us walk in the light of the LORD!
4: 1 just l us be called by your name;
5: 1 L me sing for my beloved my love-song
5:19 "L him make haste, l him speed his work
5:19 l the plan of the Holy One of Israel hasten
7: 4 and do not l your heart be faint because
7: 6 L us go up against Judah and cut off Jerusalem
7:11 l it be deep as Sheol or high as heaven.
7:25 where cattle are l loose and where sheep tread.
8:13 l him be your fear, and l him be your dread.
12: 5 l this be known in all the earth.
14:17 who would not l his prisoners go home?"
14:21 L them never rise to possess the earth or cover
16: 4 l the outcasts of Moab settle among you;
16: 7 l Moab wail, l everyone wail for Moab.
19:12 L them tell you and make known what
21: 6 post a lookout, l him announce what he sees.
21: 7 l him listen diligently, very diligently."
22: 4 Look away from me, l me weep bitter tears;
22:13 "L us eat and drink, for tomorrow we die."
25: 9 l us be glad and rejoice in his salvation.
26:11 L them see your zeal for your people,
26:11 L the fire for your adversaries consume them.
27: 5 Or else l it cling to me for protection, l it make peace with me, l it make peace with me.
29: 1 Add year to year; l the festivals run their round.
30:11 l us hear no more about the Holy One of Israel."
32:20 who l the ox and the donkey range freely.
34: 1 L the earth hear, and all that fills it;
36:14 'Do not l Hezekiah deceive you,
36:15 Do not l Hezekiah make you rely on the LORD
36:18 Do not l Hezekiah mislead you by saying,
37:10 not l your God on whom you rely deceive you
38:21 Now Isaiah had said, "L them take a lump of figs,
41: 1 l the peoples renew their strength; l them approach, then l them speak; l us together draw near for judgment.
41:22 L them bring them, and tell us what is to happen.
42:10 L the sea roar and all that fills it,
42:11 L the desert and its towns lift up their voice,
42:11 l the inhabitants of Sela sing for joy, l them shout from the tops of the mountains.
42:12 L them give glory to the LORD,
43: 9 L all the nations gather together, and l the peoples assemble.
43: 9 L them bring their witnesses to justify them, and l them hear and say, "It is true."
43:26 Accuse me, l us go to trial;
44: 7 L them proclaim it, l them declare and set it forth
44: 7 L them tell us what is yet to be.
44:11 L them all assemble, l them stand up;
45: 8 and l the skies rain down righteousness; l the earth
45: 8 and l it cause righteousness to sprout up also;
45:21 l them take counsel together!
47:13 l those who study the heavens stand up
50: 8 L us stand up together.
50: 8 Who are my adversaries? L them confront me.
54: 2 and l the curtains of your habitations
55: 7 l the wicked forsake their way,
55: 7 l them return to the LORD,
56: 3 Do not l the foreigner joined to the LORD say,
56: 3 do not l the eunuch say, "I am just a dry tree."
56:12 "Come," they say, "l us get wine; l us fill ourselves with strong drink.
57:13 l your collection of idols deliver you!
58: 6 to l the oppressed go free,
66: 5 "L the LORD be glorified,
Jer 2:28 L them come, if they can save you,
3:25 L us lie down in our shame, and l our dishonor cover us;
4: 5 and l us go into the fortified cities!"
5: 5 L me go to the rich and speak to them;
5:24 "L us fear the LORD our God,
6: 4 up, and l us attack at noon!"
6: 5 "Up, and l us attack by night,
7: 3 and l me dwell with you in this place.
8:14 l us go into the fortified cities and perish there;
9:18 l them quickly raise a dirge over us,
9:20 and l your ears receive the word of his mouth;
9:23 Do not l the wise boast in their wisdom, do not l the mighty boast in their might, do not l the wealthy boast in their wealth;
9:24 but l those who boast boast in this,
11:19 saying, "L us destroy the tree with its fruit, l us cut him off from the land of the living,
11:20 l me see your retribution upon them,
12: 1 but l me put my case to you.
14:17 L my eyes run down with tears night and day, and l them not cease, for the virgin daughter—
15: 1 Send them out of my sight, and l them go!
17:15 of the LORD? L it come!"
17:18 L my persecutors be shamed, but do not l me be shamed;
17:18 l them be dismayed, but do not l me be dismayed;
Jer 18: 2 and there I will l you hear my words."
18:18 "Come, l us make plots against Jeremiah—
18:18 Come, l us bring charges against him, and l us not heed any of his words."
18:21 l their wives become childless and widowed.
18:23 L them be tripped up before you;
20:10 Denounce him! L us denounce him!"
20:12 l me see your retribution upon them,
20:14 day when my mother bore me, l it not be blessed!
20:16 L that man be like the cities that
20:16 l him hear a cry in the morning and an alarm
23:28 L the prophet who has a dream tell the dream, but l the one who has my word
27:18 then l them intercede with the LORD of hosts,
29: 8 Do not l the prophets and the diviners who are
29:14 I will l you find me,
29:17 I am going to l loose on them sword, famine,
31: 6 "Come, l us go up to Zion,
31: 9 I will l them walk by brooks of water,
31:18 Bring me back, l me come back,
35:11 and l us go to Jerusalem for fear of the army of
36:19 and l no one know where you are."
38:11 which he l down to Jeremiah in the cistern
38:24 "Do not l anyone else know of this conversation,
40: 1 of the guard had l him go from Ramah,
40: 5 an allowance of food and a present, and l him go.
40:15 "Please l me go and kill Ishmael son
42: 3 L the LORD your God show us
43: 9 L the Judeans see you do it,
46: 8 It said, L me rise, l me cover the earth, l me destroy cities and their inhabitants.
46: 9 L the warriors go forth: Ethiopia and Put who
46:16 l us go back to our own people and to the land
48: 2 "Come, l us cut her off from being a nation!"
48:26 l Moab wallow in his vomit;
49:11 and l your widows trust in me.
50:26 l nothing be left of her.
50:27 l them go down to the slaughter.
50:29 Encamp all around her; l no one escape.
50:33 and refuse to l them go.
51: 3 L not the archer bend his bow, and l him not array himself in his coat of mail.
51: 9 and l each of us go to our own country;
51:10 come, l us declare in Zion the work of
51:50 and l Jerusalem come into your mind:
La 1:21 and l them be as I am.
1:22 L all their evil doing come before you;
2:18 L tears stream down like a torrent day and night!
3:40 L us test and examine our ways,
3:41 L us lift up our hearts as well as our hands to God
Eze 1:24 when they stopped, they l down their wings.
1:25 when they stopped, they l down their wings.
3:27 l those who will hear, hear; and l those who refuse
4: 3 and l it be in a state of siege,
4:15 I will l you have cow's dung instead
5:16 which I will l loose to destroy you,
7: 3 I will l loose my anger upon you;
7:12 l not the buyer rejoice, nor the seller mourn,
12:16 But I will l a few of them escape from the sword,
13:20 from your arms, and l the lives go free,
14: 3 shall I l myself be consulted by them?
14:17 'L a sword pass through the land,'
20: 4 l them know the abominations of their ancestors,
20:32 the thought, "L us be like the nations,
21:14 L the sword fall twice, thrice;
24:10 mix in the spices, l the bones be burned.
32: 4 and I will l the wild animals of
36:15 and no longer will I l you hear the insults of
36:32 l that be known to you.
36:37 I will also l the house of Israel ask me to do this
39: 7 I will not l my holy name be profaned any more;
43: 9 Now l them put away their idolatry and
43:10 and l them measure the pattern; and l them be ashamed of their iniquities.
44: 6 l there be an end to all your abominations
44:20 not shave their heads or l their locks grow long;
45: 8 but they shall l the house of Israel have the land
Da 1: 2 The Lord l King Jehoiakim of Judah fall
1:12 L us be given vegetables to eat and water
2: 7 "L the king first tell his servants the dream,
3:17 O king, l him deliver us.
4:14 L the animals flee from beneath it and the birds
4:15 L him be bathed with the dew of heaven.
4:15 and l his lot be with the animals of the field in
4:16 L his mind be changed from that of a human, and l the mind of an animal be given to him.
4:16 And l seven times pass over him.
4:19 not l the dream or the interpretation terrify you."
4:23 and l him be bathed with the dew of heaven, and l his lot be with the animals of the field,
5:10 Do not l your thoughts terrify you
5:12 Now l Daniel be called, and he will give
5:17 "L your gifts be for yourself,
5:17 to the king and l him know the interpretation.
9:16 l your anger and wrath, we pray,
9:17 l your face shine upon your desolated sanctuary.
10:19 I was strengthened and said, "L my lord speak,
Hos 4: 4 Yet l no one contend, and l none accuse,
4:15 O Israel, do not l Judah become guilty.
4:17 Ephraim is joined to idols—l him alone.
6: 1 l us return to the LORD;
6: 3 L us know, l us press on to know the LORD;
Joel 1: 3 and l your children tell their children,
2: 1 L all the inhabitants of the land tremble,
2:16 L the bridegroom leave his room,
2:17 Between the vestibule and the altar l the priests,
2:17 L them say, "Spare your people, O LORD,
Joel 3: 9 L all the soldiers draw near, l them come up.
3:10 l the weakling say, "I am a warrior."
3:12 L the nations rouse themselves,
Am 5:24 But l justice roll down like waters,
Ob 1: 1 L us rise against it for battle!"
Jnh 1: 7 sailors said to one another, "Come, l us cast lots,
1:14 do not l us perish on account of this man's life.
Mic 1: 2 and l the Lord GOD be a witness against you,
4: 2 l us go up to the mountain of the LORD,
4:11 saying, "L her be profaned,
4:11 and l our eyes gaze upon Zion."
6: 1 and l the hills hear your voice.
7:14 l them feed in Bashan and Gilead as in the days
Na 3: 5 and I will l nations look on your nakedness
Hab 2:20 l all the earth keep silence before him!
Zep 3:16 do not l your hands grow weak.
Zec 3: 5 I said, "L them put a clean turban on his head."
8: 9 L your hands be strong—
8:13 Do not be afraid, but l your hands be strong.
8:21 l us go to entreat the favor of the LORD,
8:23 a Jew, grasping his garment and saying, "L us go
11: 9 What is to die, l it die;
11: 9 what is to be destroyed, l it be destroyed;
11: 9 and l those that are left devour the flesh
11:17 L his arm be completely withered,
Mal 2:15 not l anyone be faithless to the wife of his youth.
Mt 3:15 But Jesus answered him, "L it be so now;
5:16 In the same way, l your light shine before others,
5:31 l him give her a certificate of divorce.'
5:37 L your word be 'Yes, Yes' or 'No, No';
6: 3 do not l your left hand know what your right hand
7: 4 'L me take the speck out of your eye,'
8:13 l it be done for you according to your faith."
8:21 "Lord, first l me go and bury my father."
8:22 "Follow me, and l the dead bury their own dead."
9:29 "According to your faith l it be done to you."
10:13 the house is worthy, l your peace come upon it;
10:13 but if it is not worthy, l your peace return to you.
11:15 L anyone with ears listen!
13: 9 L anyone with ears listen!"
13:30 L both of them grow together until the harvest;
13:43 L anyone with ears listen!
15:14 L them alone; they are blind guides of the blind.
15:28 L it be done for you as you wish."
16:24 l them deny themselves and take up their cross
18:17 to the church, l such a one be to you as a Gentile
19: 6 what God has joined together, l no one separate."
19:12 L anyone accept this who can."
19:14 "L the little children come to me,
20:33 They said to him, "Lord, l our eyes be opened."
21:38 come, l us kill him and get his inheritance.'
24:15 by the prophet Daniel (l the reader understand),
24:43 and would not have l his house be broken into.
26:39 if it is possible, l this cup pass from me;
26:46 Get up, l us be going.
27:22 All of them said, "L him be crucified!"
27:23 they shouted all the more, "L him be crucified!"
27:42 l him come down from the cross now,
27:43 l God deliver him now, if he wants to;
27:49 l us see whether Elijah will come to save him."
Mk 1:38 "L us go on to the neighboring towns,
2: 4 they l down the mat on which the paralytic lay.
4: 9 And he said, "L anyone with ears to hear listen!"
4:23 L anyone with ears to hear listen!"
4:35 "L us go across to the other side."
5:12 into the swine; l us enter them."
7:27 He said to her, "L the children be fed first,
8:34 l them deny themselves and take up their cross
9: 5 l us make three dwellings, one for you,
10: 9 what God has joined together, l no one separate."
10:14 "L the little children come to me;
10:51 "My teacher, l me see again."
12: 7 l us kill him, and the inheritance will be ours.'
12:15 Bring me a denarius and l me see it."
13:14 not to be (l the reader understand), then those
14: 6 Jesus said, "L her alone; why do you trouble her?
14:42 Get up, l us be going.
14:49 But l the scriptures be fulfilled."
15:32 L the Messiah, the King of Israel,
15:36 l us see whether Elijah will come
Lk 1:38 l it be with me according to your word."
2:15 "L us go now to Bethlehem and see this thing
4:18 to l the oppressed go free,
4:34 "L us alone! What have you to do
5: 4 the deep water and l down your nets for a catch."
5: 5 Yet if you say so, I will l down the nets."
5:19 on the roof and l him down with his bed through
6:42 'Friend, l me take out the speck in your eye,'
7: 7 only speak the word, and l my servant be healed.
8: 8 he called out, "L anyone with ears to hear listen!"
8:22 "L us go across to the other side of the lake."
8:32 the demons begged Jesus to l them enter these.
9:23 l them deny themselves and take
9:33 l us make three dwellings, one for you,
9:44 "L these words sink into your ears:
9:59 he said, "Lord, first l me go and bury my father."
9:60 "L the dead bury their own dead;
9:61 but l me first say farewell to those at my home."
12:39 he would not have l his house be broken into.
13: 8 He replied, 'Sir, l it alone for one more year,
14:35 L anyone with ears to hear listen!"
15:23 and l us eat and celebrate;
18:16 "L the little children come to me,
18:41 He said, "Lord, l me see again."
20:14 l us kill him so that the inheritance may be ours.'
23:35 l him save himself if he is the Messiah of God,
Jn 1:22 L us have an answer for those who sent us.

Jn 7:37 "L anyone who is thirsty come to me,
7:38 and l the one who believes in me drink.
8: 7 [["L anyone among you who is without sin be]]
11: 7 "L us go to Judea again."
11:15 But l us go to him."
11:16 "L us also go, that we may die with him."
11:44 Jesus said to them, "Unbind him, and l him go."
11:48 If we l him go on like this,
11:57 where Jesus was should l them know,
14: 1 "Do not l your hearts be troubled.
14:27 Do not l your hearts be troubled, and do not l them be afraid.
14:31 Rise, l us be on our way.
18: 8 So if you are looking for me, l these men go."
19: 4 to l you know that I find no case against him."
19:24 So they said to one another, "L us not tear it,
19:38 asked Pilate to l him take away the body
Ac 1:20 'L his homestead become desolate, and l there be no one to live in it';
1:20 and 'L another take his position of overseer.'
2:14 l this be known to you, and listen to what I say.
2:27 or l your Holy One experience corruption.
2:36 Therefore l the entire house of Israel know
4:10 l it be known to all of you,
4:17 l us warn them to speak no more to anyone
4:21 After threatening them again, they l them go,
5:38 keep away from these men and l them alone;
5:40 not to speak in the name of Jesus, and l them go.
9:25 and l him down through an opening in the wall,
13:35 not l your Holy One experience corruption.'
13:38 L it be known to you therefore, my brothers,
15:36 l us return and visit the believers in every city
16:35 saying, "L those men go."
16:36 saying, "The magistrates sent word to l you go;
16:37 L them come and take us out themselves."
17: 9 from Jason and the others, they l them go.
19:30 but the disciples would not l him;
19:38 l them bring charges there against one another.
21:39 I beg you, l me speak to the people."
23:32 next day they l the horsemen go on with him,
24:20 l these men here tell what crime they had found
24:23 to l him have some liberty and not to prevent any
25: 5 "l those of you who have the authority come
25: 5 about the man, l them accuse him."
27:29 they l down four anchors from the stern
28:28 L it be known to you then that this salvation
Ro 3: 4 everyone is a liar, l God be proved true,
3: 8 "L us do evil so that good may come"?
6:12 do not l sin exercise dominion
11: 9 "L their table become a snare and a trap,
11:10 l their eyes be darkened so that they cannot see,
12: 9 L love be genuine; hate what is evil,
13: 1 L every person be subject to
13:12 L us then lay aside the works of darkness and put
13:13 l us live honorably as in the day,
14: 5 L all be fully convinced in their own minds.
14:13 L us therefore no longer pass judgment
14:15 Do not l what you eat cause the ruin of one
14:16 So do not l your good be spoken of as evil.
14:19 L us then pursue what makes for peace and
15:11 and l all the peoples praise him";
1Co 1:31 "L the one who boasts, boast in the Lord."
3:21 So l no one boast about human leaders.
5: 8 Therefore, l us celebrate the festival,
7:11 l her remain unmarried or else be reconciled
7:15 if the unbelieving partner separates, l it be so;
7:17 l each of you lead the life that
7:18 L him not seek to remove the marks
7:18 L him not seek circumcision.
7:20 L each of you remain in the condition
7:29 from now on, l even those who have wives be as
7:36 and so it has to be, l him marry as he wishes;
7:36 it is no sin. L them marry.
10:13 he will not l you be tested beyond your strength,
12: 3 the Spirit of God ever says "L Jesus be cursed!"
14:26 L all things be done for building up.
14:27 l there be only two or at most three, and in turn; and l one interpret.
14:28 l them be silent in church and speak
14:29 L two or three prophets speak, and l the others weigh what is said.
14:30 l the first person be silent.
14:35 l them ask their husbands at home.
15:32 "L us eat and drink, for tomorrow we die."
16:11 therefore l no one despise him.
16:14 L all that you do be done in love.
16:22 L anyone be accursed who has no love for
2Co 2: 4 but to l you know the abundant love that I have
4: 6 "L light shine out of darkness,"
7: 1 l us cleanse ourselves from every defilement
10:11 L such people understand that what we say
10:17 "L the one who boasts, boast in the Lord."
11:16 I repeat, l no one think that I am a fool;
11:33 but I was l down in a basket through a window in
12:16 L it be assumed that I did not burden you.
Gal 1: 8 contrary to what we proclaimed to you, l that one
1: 9 a gospel contrary to what you received, l that one
5: 2 that if you l yourselves be circumcised,
5:25 l us also be guided by the Spirit.
5:26 L us not become conceited,
6: 9 So l us not grow weary in doing what is right,
6:10 l us work for the good of all,
6:17 From now on, l no one make trouble for me;
Eph 4:25 l all of us speak the truth to our neighbors,
4:26 do not l the sun go down on your anger,
4:28 rather l them labor and work honestly
4:29 L no evil talk come out of your mouths,
Eph 5: 4 but instead, l there be thanksgiving.
5: 6 L no one deceive you with empty words,
6:22 to l you know how we are,
Php 2: 4 L each of you look not to your own interests,
2: 5 L the same mind be in you that was
3:15 L those of us then who are mature be of
3:16 Only l us hold fast to what we have attained.
4: 5 L your gentleness be known to everyone.
4: 6 with thanksgiving l your requests
Col 2:16 not l anyone condemn you in matters of food
2:18 Do not l anyone disqualify you,
3:15 And l the peace of Christ rule in your hearts,
3:16 L the word of Christ dwell in you richly;
4: 6 L your speech always be gracious,
1Th 5: 6 So then l us not fall asleep as others do, but l us keep awake and be sober;
5: 8 But since we belong to the day, l us be sober,
2Th 2: 3 L no one deceive you in any way;
1Ti 2:11 L a woman learn in silence with full submission.
3:10 And l them first be tested;
3:10 l them serve as deacons.
3:12 L deacons be married only once, and l them manage their children
4:12 L no one despise your youth,
5: 9 L a widow be put on the list if she is
5:16 relatives who are really widows, l her assist them;
5:16 l the church not be burdened,
5:17 L the elders who rule well be considered worthy
6: 1 L all who are under the yoke of slavery
2Ti 2:19 and, "L everyone who calls on the name of
Tit 2:15 L no one look down on you.
3:14 And l people learn to devote themselves
Phm 1:20 l me have this benefit from you in the Lord!
Heb 1: 6 he says, "L all God's angels worship him."
4: 1 l us take care that none of you should seem
4:11 L us therefore make every effort to enter that rest,
4:14 the Son of God, l us hold fast to our confession.
4:16 L us therefore approach the throne of grace
6: 1 Therefore l us go on toward perfection,
10:22 l us approach with a true heart in full assurance
10:23 L us hold fast to the confession of our hope
10:24 And l us consider how to provoke one another
12: 1 l us also lay aside every weight and the sin
12: 1 and l us run with perseverance the race that is set
12:28 l us give thanks, by which we offer to God
13: 1 L mutual love continue.
13: 4 L marriage be held in honor by all, and l the marriage bed be kept undefiled;
13:13 L us then go to him outside the camp and bear
13:15 l us continually offer a sacrifice of praise to God,
13:17 L them do this with joy and not with sighing—
Jas 1: 4 and l endurance have its full effect,
1: 9 L the believer who is lowly boast in being raised
1:19 l everyone be quick to listen, slow to speak,
4: 9 L your laughter be turned into mourning
5:12 but l your "Yes" be yes and your "No" be no,
1Pe 2: 5 l yourselves be built into a spiritual house,
3: 4 l your adornment be the inner self with
3: 6 and never l fears alarm you.
3:10 l them keep their tongues from evil and their lips
3:11 l them turn away from evil and do good; l them seek peace and pursue it.
4:15 But l none of you suffer as a murderer, a thief,
4:19 l those suffering in accordance
1Jn 2:24 L what you heard from the beginning abide
3: 7 Little children, l no one deceive you.
3:18 Little children, l us love, not in word or speech,
4: 7 Beloved, l us love one another,
2Jn 1: 5 from the beginning, l us love one another.
Rev 2: 7 L anyone who has an ear listen to what the Spirit
2:11 L anyone who has an ear listen to what the Spirit
2:17 L anyone who has an ear listen to what the Spirit
2:29 L anyone who has an ear listen to what the Spirit
3: 6 L anyone who has an ear listen to what the Spirit
3:13 L anyone who has an ear listen to what the Spirit
3:22 L anyone who has an ear listen to what the Spirit
11: 9 and refuse to l them be placed in a tomb;
13: 9 L anyone who has an ear listen:
13:18 l anyone with understanding calculate
19: 7 L us rejoice and exult and give him the glory,
20: 3 After that he must be l out for a little while.
22:11 L the evildoer still do evil,
22:17 And l everyone who hears say, "Come."
22:17 And l everyone who is thirsty come.
22:17 L anyone who wishes take the water of life as
Tob 3:11 l all your works praise you forever.
4: 7 and do not l your eye begrudge the gift
4:15 Do not drink wine to excess or l drunkenness go
4:16 do not l your eye begrudge your giving of alms.
4:19 and do not l them be erased from your heart.
4:20 l me explain to you that I left ten talents of silver
5:19 but l it be a ransom for our child.
7:10 l me explain to you the true situation more fully,
8: 4 and l us pray and implore our Lord
8: 5 L the heavens and the whole creation bless you
8: 6 l us make a helper for him like himself.'
8:12 l us bury him without anyone knowing it."
8:15 l all your chosen ones bless you.
8:15 L them bless you forever.
10: 5 that I l you make the journey."
10: 7 to l me go so that I may return to my own father.
10:12 Then he bade them farewell and l them go.
11: 3 L us run ahead of your wife and prepare
13: 8 L all people speak of his majesty,
Jdt 5:21 then l my lord pass them by;
5:24 Therefore l us go ahead, Lord Holofernes,
7:12 l your servants take possession of the spring
Jdt 7:24 "L God judge between you and us!
7:30 L us hold out for five days more;
8:17 l us call upon him to help us,
8:24 my brothers, l us set an example for our kindred,
8:25 In spite of everything l us give thanks to
9:14 L your whole nation and every tribe know
10:19 for if we l them go they will be able to beguile
11: 5 and l your servant speak in your presence.
12: 6 "L my lord now give orders to allow your servant
12:12 For it would be a disgrace if we l such
12:13 "L this pretty girl not hesitate to come to my lord
14: 2 and l every able-bodied man go out of the town;
16:14 L all your creatures serve you, for you spoke,
AdE 1:19 it pleases the king, l him issue a royal decree,
1:19 but l the king give her royal rank to
1:20 L whatever law the king enacts be proclaimed
2: 2 "L beautiful and virtuous girls be sought out for
2: 3 L them be entrusted to the king's eunuch who is
2: 3 and l ointments and whatever else they need
3: 9 l it be decreed that they are to be destroyed,
5: 4 l him and Haman come to the dinner
5: 8 l the king and Haman come to the dinner
5:14 "L a gallows be made, fifty cubits high,
6: 8 l the king's servants bring out the fine linen robe
6: 9 and l both be given to one of the king's honored
6: 9 and l him robe the person whom the king loves
6: 9 and l it be proclaimed through the open square of
6:10 And l nothing be omitted
7: 3 l my life be granted me at my petition,
7: 9 So the king said, "L Haman be hanged on that."
8: 5 l an order be sent rescinding the letters
8:13 "L copies of the decree be posted conspicuously
8:13 and l all the Jews be ready on that day to fight
9:13 "L the Jews be allowed to do the same tomorrow.
14:11 and do not l them laugh at our downfall;
Wis 2: 6 therefore, l us enjoy the good things that exist,
2: 7 L us take our fill of costly wine and perfumes, and l no flower of spring pass us by.
2: 8 L us crown ourselves with rosebuds
2: 9 L none of us fail to share in our revelry; everywhere l us leave signs of enjoyment,
2:10 L us oppress the righteous poor man; l us not spare the widow or regard the gray hairs
2:11 But l our might be our law of right,
2:12 "L us lie in wait for the righteous man,
2:17 L us see if his words are true, and l us test what
2:19 L us test him with insult and torture,
2:20 L us condemn him to a shameful death, for,
13: 3 people assumed them to be gods, l them know
13: 4 l them perceive from them
Sir 2:17 L us fall into the hands of the Lord,
4:31 Do not l your hand be stretched out to receive
5:10 and l your speech be consistent.
6: 6 L those who are friendly with you be many, but l your advisers be one in a thousand.
6:27 and when you get hold of her, do not l her go.
6:35 and l no wise proverbs escape you.
6:36 l your foot wear out his doorstep.
7:21 L your soul love intelligent slaves;
8:11 Do not l the insolent bring you to your feet,
9: 2 a woman and l her trample down your strength.
9:15 L your conversation be with intelligent people,
9:15 and l all your discussion be about the law of
9:16 L the righteous be your dinner companions, and l your glory be in the fear of the Lord.
12:12 Do not l him sit at your right hand,
14:14 do not l your share of desired good pass by you.
18:22 L nothing hinder you from paying
19:10 L it die with you.
19:17 and l the law of the Most High take its course.
23: 1 and do not l me fall because of them!
23: 6 L neither gluttony nor lust overcome me,
27:19 so you have l your neighbor go,
29:10 and do not l it rust under a stone and be lost.
29:26 l me eat what you have there."
31:10 L it be for him a ground for boasting.
33:21 do not l anyone take your place.
36: 3 and l them see your might.
36:10 and l people recount your mighty deeds.
36:11 L survivors be consumed in the fiery wrath,
36:21 for you and l your prophets be found trustworthy.
38:12 do not l him leave you, for you need him.
38:16 My child, l your tears fall for the dead,
38:17 L your weeping be bitter
38:23 the dead is at rest, l his remembrance rest too,
42:12 Do not l her parade her beauty before any man,
43:27 l the final word be: "He is the all."
44: 1 L us now sing the praises of famous men,
51:26 and l your souls receive instruction;
Bar 2:13 L your anger turn away from us, for we are left,
4:12 L no one rejoice over me,
4:14 L the neighbors of Zion come;
Aza 1:21 L all who do harm to your servants be put
1:21 l them be disgraced and deprived of all power,
1:21 and l their strength be broken.
1:22 L them know that you alone are the Lord God,
1:52 "L the earth bless the Lord; l it sing praise to him
Sus 1:13 One day they said to each other, "L us go home,
Bel 1: 9 "L it be done as you have said."
1Mc 1:11 "L us go and make a covenant with the Gentiles
2:27 "L every one who is zealous for the law
2:37 "L us all die in our innocence;
2:41 "L us fight against anyone who comes
2:41 l us not all die as our kindred died
2:48 and they never l the sinner gain the upper hand.
3:43 "L us restore the ruins of our people,
4:10 And now, l us cry to Heaven,

1Mc 4:31 and **l** them be ashamed of their troops
4:32 **l** them tremble in their destruction.
4:33 and **l** all who know your name praise you
4:36 **l** us go up to cleanse the sanctuary
5:48 "**L** us pass through your land to get to our land.
5:57 they said, "**L** us also make a name for ourselves;
5:57 **l** us go and make war on the Gentiles around us."
6:58 Now then **l** us come to terms with these people,
6:59 **L** us agree to **l** them live by their laws as they did
7: 3 he said, "Do not **l** me see their faces!"
7: 7 **l** him go and see all the ruin
7: 7 and **l** him punish them and all who help them."
7:28 "**L** there be no fighting between you and me;
7:38 and **l** them fall by the sword;
7:38 and **l** them live no longer."
7:42 **l** the rest learn that Nicanor has spoken wickedly
9: 8 "**L** us get up and go against our enemies.
9: 9 **L** us rather save our own lives now,
9: 9 **l** us come back with our kindred and fight them;
9:10 **l** us die bravely for our kindred,
9:44 "**L** us get up now and fight for our lives,
9:58 So now **l** us bring Bacchides back,
10: 4 "**L** us act first to make peace with him
10:33 and **l** all officials cancel also the taxes
10:34 **l** them all be days of immunity and release for all
10:36 "**L** Jews be enrolled in the king's forces to
10:36 and **l** the maintenance be given them that is due
10:37 **L** some of them be stationed in
10:37 and **l** some of them be put in positions of trust in
10:37 **L** their officers and leaders be
10:37 and **l** them live by their own laws,
10:38 **l** them be annexed to Judea so that they may
10:43 to the king or are in debt, **l** them be released
10:44 "**L** the cost of rebuilding and restoring
10:45 And **l** the cost of rebuilding the walls
10:54 **l** us establish friendship with one another;
10:63 and **l** no one annoy him for any reason."
10:71 and **l** us match strength with each other there,
11: 9 "Come, **l** us make a covenant with each other,
11:37 and **l** it be given to Jonathan and put up in
12:53 therefore **l** us make war on them and blot out
13:38 and **l** the strongholds that you have built
13:40 **l** them be enrolled, and **l** there be peace between
2Mc 1:27 and **l** the Gentiles know that you are our God.
2:32 At this point therefore **l** us begin our narrative,
6:13 of great kindness not to **l** the impious alone
6:17 **L** what we have said serve as a reminder;
7:42 **L** this be enough, then, about the eating
10:20 on receiving seventy thousand drachmas **l** some
10:36 Others broke open the gates and **l** in the rest of
12: 2 would not **l** them live quietly and in peace.
12:24 With great guile he begged them to **l** him go
12:25 to restore them unharmed, they **l** him go,
13:11 to **l** the people who had just begun to revive fall
14: 6 and will not **l** the kingdom attain tranquility.
15:36 by public vote never to **l** this day go unobserved,
1Es 2: 6 and **l** each of you, wherever you may live,
2:18 **L** it now be known to our lord the king that
3: 5 "**L** each of us state what one thing is strongest;
4:19 they **l** all those things go,
6: 8 **L** it be fully known to our lord the king that,
6:21 **l** search be made in the royal archives of our lord
6:22 by our lord the king, **l** him send us directions
8:11 **L** as many as are so disposed, therefore,
8:21 **L** all things prescribed in the law of God
8:93 **L** us take an oath to the Lord about this,
9:12 So **l** the leaders of the multitude stay, and **l** all
3Mc 2:20 Speedily **l** your mercies overtake us,
6:11 **L** not the vain-minded praise their vanities at
6:13 And **l** the Gentiles cower today in fear
6:15 **L** it be shown to all the Gentiles that you are
2Es 2: 7 **L** them be scattered among the nations; **l** their names be blotted out from the earth,
2:21 and **l** the blind have a vision of my splendor.
4:14 'Come, **l** us go and make war against the sea,
4:15 **l** us go up and subdue the forest of the plain so
5:50 now given me the opportunity, **l** me speak
6:38 '**L** heaven and earth be made,'
7: 20 **l** many perish who are now living,
7:65 **L** the human race lament, but **l** the wild animals of the field be glad; **l** all who have been born lament, but **l** the cattle and the flocks rejoice.
8:42 "If I have found favor in your sight, **l** me speak.
9:22 **l** the multitude perish that has been born in vain, but **l** my grape and my plant be saved,
9:23 "Now, if you will **l** seven days more pass—
9:41 She said to me, "**L** me alone, my lord,
10:20 but **l** yourself be persuaded—
10:55 and do not **l** your heart be terrified;
11: 8 **l** each sleep in its own place,
11: 9 but **l** the heads be reserved for the last."
14:19 "**L** me speak in your presence, Lord.
14:36 But **l** no one come to me now, and **l** no one seek
14:45 and **l** the worthy and the unworthy read them;
15:12 **L** Egypt mourn, and its foundations,
15:13 **L** the farmers that till the ground mourn,
16:41 **L** the one who sells be like one who will flee; **l** the one who buys be like one who will lose;
16:42 **l** the one who does business be like one who will
16:42 and **l** the one who builds a house be
16:43 **l** the one who sows be like one who will
16:55 He said, "**L** the earth be made," and it was made, and "**L** the heaven be made," and it was made.
16:76 must not **l** your sins weigh you down,
4Mc 6:28 and **l** our punishment suffice for them.
8:16 **L** us consider, on the other hand,
8:20 **L** us take pity on our youth and have compassion

4Mc 8:21 and **l** us seriously consider that
8:24 **L** us not struggle against compulsion
10:20 we **l** our bodily members be mutilated.
12: 8 "**L** me loose, **l** me speak to the king and to all
12:12 and these throughout all time will never **l** you go.
13: 9 **l** us die like brothers for the sake of the law; **l** us imitate the three youths
13:10 **L** us not be cowardly in the demonstration
13:13 "**L** us with all our hearts consecrate ourselves
13:13 and **l** us use our bodies as a bulwark for the law.
13:14 **L** us not fear him who thinks he is killing us,
13:16 **l** us put on the full armor of self-control,

LETHECH See Index to Footnotes

LETS (7) [LET]

Ex 11: 1 indeed, when he **l** you go,
22: 5 **l** livestock loose to graze in someone else's field,
Job 37: 3 Under the whole heaven he **l** it loose,
39:14 and **l** them be warmed on the ground,
Ps 107:36 And there he **l** the hungry live,
Isa 44:14 and **l** it grow strong among the trees of the forest.
Gal 5: 3 Once again I testify to every man who **l** himself

LETTER (93) [LETTERS]

2Sa 11:14 In the morning David wrote a **l** to Joab,
11:15 In the **l** he wrote, "Set Uriah in the forefront of
2Ki 5: 5 and I will send along a **l** to the king of Israel."
5: 6 He brought the **l** to the king of Israel, which read, "When this **l** reaches you,
5: 7 When the king of Israel read the **l**,
10: 6 Then he wrote them a second **l**, saying,
10: 7 When the **l** reached them,
19:14 the **l** from the hand of the messengers and read it;
2Ch 2:11 of Tyre answered in a **l** that he sent to Solomon,
21:12 A **l** came to him from the prophet Elijah, saying:
Ezr 4: 7 the **l** was written in Aramaic and translated.
4: 8 a **l** against Jerusalem to King Artaxerxes
4:11 this is a copy of the **l** that they sent):
4:18 the **l** that you sent to us has been read
4:23 when the copy of King Artaxerxes' **l** was read
5: 5 and then answer was returned by **l** in reply to it.
5: 6 of the **l** that Tattenai the governor of the province
7:11 This is a copy of the **l** that King Artaxerxes gave
Ne 2: 8 and a **l** to Asaph, the keeper of
6: 5 to me with an open **l** in his hand.
Est 9:26 Thus because of all that was written in this **l**,
9:29 confirming this second **l** about Purim.
Isa 37:14 the **l** from the hand of the messengers and read it;
Jer 29: 1 the words of the **l** that the prophet Jeremiah sent
29: 3 The **l** was sent by the hand of Elasah son
29:25 a **l** to all the people who are in Jerusalem,
29:29 The priest Zephaniah read this **l** in the hearing of
Mt 5:18 until heaven and earth pass away, not one **l**, not one stroke of a **l**, will pass from the law
Lk 16:17 for one stroke of a **l** in the law to be dropped.
Ac 15:23 with the following **l**: "The brothers,
15:30 the congregation together, they delivered the **l**.
21:25 a **l** with our judgment that they should abstain
23:25 He wrote a **l** to this effect:
23:33 When they came to Caesarea and delivered the **l**
23:34 the **l**, he asked what province he belonged to,
Ro 16:22 I Tertius, the writer of this **l**,
1Co 5: 9 I wrote to you in my **l** not to associate
2Co 3: 2 You yourselves are our **l**, written on our hearts,
3: 3 and you show that you are a **l** of Christ,
3: 6 not of **l** but of spirit; for the **l** kills, but the Spirit gives life.
7: 8 For even if I made you sorry with my **l**,
7: 8 for I see that I grieved you with that **l**,
10:11 Let such people understand that what we say by **l**
Col 4:16 And when this **l** has been read among you,
4:16 and see that you read also the **l** from Laodicea.
1Th 5:27 I solemnly command you by the Lord that this **l**
2Th 2: 2 either by spirit or by word or by **l**,
2:15 either by word of mouth or by our **l**.
3:14 of those who do not obey what we say in this **l**;
3:17 This is the mark in every **l** of mine;
1Pe 5:12 I have written this short **l** to encourage you and
2Pe 3: 1 beloved, the second **l** I am writing to you;
AdE 9:26 And so, because of what was written in this **l**,
9:29 and gave full authority to the **l** about Purim.
11: 1 to Egypt the preceding **L** about Purim,
13: 1 This is a copy of the **l**:
16: 1 The following is a copy of this **l**:
16:19 post a copy of this **l** publicly in every place,
LtJ 6: 1 of a **l** that Jeremiah sent to those who were to
1Mc 5:10 and sent to Judas and his brothers a **l** that said,
5:14 While the **l** was still being read,
8:22 the **l** that they wrote in reply, on bronze tablets,
10: 3 Demetrius sent Jonathan a **l** in peaceable words
10: 7 and read the **l** in the hearing of all the people and
10:17 And he wrote a **l** and sent it to him,
11:29 and wrote a **l** to Jonathan about all these things;
11:31 This copy of the **l** that we wrote concerning you
12: 5 This is a copy of the **l** that Jonathan wrote to
12: 7 in time past a **l** was sent to the high priest Onias
12: 8 with honor, and received the **l**, which contained
12:10 since you sent your **l** to us.
12:17 also to you and greet you and deliver to you this **l**
12:19 This is a copy of the **l** that they sent to Onias:
13:35 and wrote him a **l** as follows,
14:20 This is a copy of the **l** that the Spartans sent:
15: 1 sent a **l** from the islands of the sea to Simon,
2Mc 9:18 for himself and wrote to the Jews the following **l**,

2Mc 11:16 **l** written to the Jews by Lysias was to this effect:
11:22 The king's **l** ran thus: "King Antiochus to his
11:27 To the nation the king's **l** was as follows:
11:34 The Romans also sent them a **l**, which read thus:
1Es 2:16 wrote him the following **l**,
2:26 "I have read the **l** that you sent me.
2:30 when the **l** from King Artaxerxes was read,
6: 7 of the **l** that Sisinnes the governor of Syria
3Mc 3:11 wrote this **l** against them:
3:25 as soon as this **l** arrives,
3:30 The **l** was written in the above form.
6:41 at once and wrote the following **l** for them to
7:10 On receiving this **l** the Jews did

LETTERS‡ (46) [LETTER]

1Ki 21: 8 So she wrote **l** in Ahab's name and sealed them
21: 8 the **l** to the elders and the nobles who lived
21: 9 She wrote in the **l**, "Proclaim a fast,
21:11 Just as it was written in the **l** that she had sent
2Ki 10: 1 So Jehu wrote **l** and sent them to Samaria,
20:12 of Baladan of Babylon sent envoys with **l** and
2Ch 30: 1 and wrote **l** also to Ephraim and Manasseh,
30: 6 and Judah with **l** from the king and his officials,
32:17 He also wrote **l** to throw contempt on the LORD
Ne 2: 7 let **l** be given me to the governors of the province
2: 9 and gave them the king's **l**.
6:17 in those days the nobles of Judah sent many **l**
6:17 and Tobiah's **l** came to them.
6:19 And Tobiah sent **l** to intimidate me.
Est 1:22 he sent **l** to all the royal provinces,
3:13 **L** were sent by couriers to all
8: 5 be written to revoke the **l** devised by Haman son
8:10 He wrote **l** in the name of King Ahasuerus,
8:11 By these **l** the king allowed the Jews who were
9:20 and sent **l** to all the Jews who were in all
9:30 **L** were sent wishing peace and security to all
Isa 39: 1 of Baladan of Babylon sent envoys with **l** and
Ac 9: 2 asked him for **l** to the synagogues at Damascus,
22: 5 also received **l** to the brothers in Damascus,
28:21 "We have received no **l** from Judea about you,
1Co 16: 3 I will send any whom you approve with **l**
2Co 3: 1 **l** of recommendation to you or from you, do we?
3: 7 ministry of death, chiseled in **l** on stone tablets,
10: 9 as though I am trying to frighten you with my **l**.
10:10 For they say, "His **l** are weighty and strong,
Gal 6:11 See what large **l** I make when I am writing
2Pe 3:16 speaking of this as he does in all his **l**.
AdE 8: 5 the **l** that Haman wrote and sent to destroy
13: 6 in the **l** written by Haman, who is in charge
16:17 not to put in execution the **l** sent by Haman son
Sir 45:11 a jeweler, to commemorate in engraved **l** each of
1Mc 1:44 And the king sent **l** by messengers to Jerusalem
9:60 and secretly sent **l** to all his allies in Judea,
12: 2 also sent **l** to the same effect to the Spartans and
12: 4 Romans gave them **l** to the people in every place,
15:15 with **l** to the kings and countries,
16:19 he sent **l** to the captains asking them to come
2Mc 2:13 and **l** of kings about votive offerings.
1Es 4:47 and wrote **l** for him to all the treasurers
4:48 And he wrote **l** to all the governors in Coelesyria
4:61 So he took the **l**, and went to Babylon

LETTING (10) [LET]

Ex 8:29 not **l** the people go to sacrifice to the LORD."
14: 5 "What have we done, **l** Israel leave our service?"
Dt 8: 3 He humbled you by **l** you hunger,
2Ch 25:10 to him from Ephraim, **l** them go home again.
25:13 not **l** them go with him to battle,
Pr 17:14 The beginning of strife is like **l** out water;
Ecc 7:18 without **l** go of the other;
Jer 8:17 See, I am **l** snakes loose among you,
38: 6 **l** Jeremiah down by ropes.
LtJ 6: 5 of becoming at all like the foreigners or of **l** fear

LETUSHIM (1)

Ge 25: 3 sons of Dedan were Asshurim, **L**, and Leummim.

LEUMMIM (1)

Ge 25: 3 sons of Dedan were Asshurim, Letushim, and **L**.

LEVEL (13) [LEVELED]

Ps 26:12 My foot stands on **l** ground;
27:11 and lead me on a **l** path because of my enemies.
143:10 Let your good spirit lead me on a **l** path.
Pr 15:19 but the path of the upright is a **l** highway.
Isa 26: 7 The way of the righteous is **l**;
40: 4 the uneven ground shall become **l**,
42:16 the rough places into **l** ground.
45: 2 I will go before you and **l** the mountains,
Lk 6:17 He came down with them and stood on a **l** place,
Bar 5: 7 to make **l** ground, so that Israel may walk safely
2Mc 9:14 which he was hurrying to **l** to the ground and
14:33 to me as a prisoner, I will **l** this shrine of God to
3Mc 5:43 and rapidly **l** it to the ground with fire and spear,

LEVELED (3) [LEVEL]

Isa 28:25 When they have **l** its surface,
Jer 51:58 broad wall of Babylon shall be **l** to the ground,
2Mc 8: 3 that was being destroyed and about to be **l** to

LEVI‡ (68) [FELLOW-LEVITES, LEVI'S, LEVITE, LEVITES, LEVITICAL, =MATTHEW]

A. SONS OF LEVI (13)
B. TRIBE OF LEVI (11)

Ge 29:34 therefore he was named L.
34:25 two of the sons of Jacob, Simeon and L,
34:30 Then Jacob said to Simeon and L,
35:23 Reuben (Jacob's firstborn), Simeon, L, Judah,
46:11 The children of L: Gershon, Kohath, and Merari.
49: 5 Simeon and L are brothers;
Ex 1: 2 Reuben, Simeon, L, and Judah,
2: 1 the house of L went and married a Levite woman.
6:16 of the sons of L according to their genealogies: A
32:26 And all the sons of L gathered around him. A
32:28 The sons of L did as Moses commanded, A
Nu 1:49 Only the tribe of L you shall not enroll, B
3: 6 Bring the tribe of L near, B
3:17 following were the sons of L, by their names: A
16: 1 Now Korah son of Izhar son of Kohath son of L,
17: 3 and write Aaron's name on the staff of L.
17: 8 staff of Aaron for the house of L had sprouted.
18: 2 with you also your brothers of the tribe of L, B
26:58 These are the clans of L:
26:59 of Amram's wife was Jochebed daughter of L,
26:59 who was born to L in Egypt;
Dt 10: 8 the LORD set apart the tribe of L to carry the ark B
10: 9 Therefore L has no allotment or inheritance
18: 1 The levitical priests, the whole tribe of L, B
18: 5 For the LORD your God has chosen L out
21: 5 Then the priests, the sons of L, A
27:12 Simeon, L, Judah, Issachar, Joseph,
31: 9 and gave it to the priests, the sons of L, A
33: 8 And of L he said: Give to L your Thummim,
Jos 13:14 the tribe of L alone Moses gave no inheritance; B
13:33 But to the tribe of L Moses gave no inheritance; B
1Ch 2: 1 These are the sons of Israel: Reuben, Simeon, L,
6: 1 The sons of L: Gershom, Kohath, and Merari. A
6:16 The sons of L: Gershom, Kohath, and Merari. A
6:38 son of Kohath, son of L, son of Israel;
6:43 son of Jahath, son of Gershom, son of L.
6:47 son of Mushi, son of Merari, son of L;
21: 6 not include L and Benjamin in the numbering,
23: 6 in divisions corresponding to the sons of L: A
23:14 to be reckoned among the tribe of L. B
23:24 the sons of L by their ancestral houses, A
24:20 And of the rest of the sons of L: A
27:17 for L, Hashabiah son of Kemuel;
Ezr 8:15 I found there none of the descendants of L.
8:18 the descendants of Mahli son of L son of Israel,
Ne 10:39 sons of L shall bring the contribution of grain, A
Ps 135:20 O house of L, bless the LORD!
Eze 40:46 who alone among the descendants of L may come
48:31 the gate of Judah, and the gate of L,
Zec 12:13 of L by itself, and their wives by themselves;
Mal 2: 4 that my covenant with L may hold,
2: 8 you have corrupted the covenant of L,
3: 3 the descendants of L and refine them like gold
Mk 2:14 he saw L son of Alphaeus sitting at the tax booth,
Lk 3:24 son of L, son of Melchi, son of Jannai,
3:29 son of Jorim, son of Matthat, son of L,
5:27 this he went out and saw a tax collector named L,
5:29 Then L gave a great banquet for him in his house;
Heb 7: 5 of L who receive the priestly office have
7: 9 One might even say that L himself,
Rev 7: 7 from the tribe of L twelve thousand, B
Tob 1: 7 to the sons of L who ministered at Jerusalem. A
Sir 45: 6 Moses who was his brother, of the tribe of L. B
1Es 8:47 of the descendants of Mahli son of L, son
9:14 and L and Shabbethai served with them as judges.
2Es 1: 3 of Aaron, of the tribe of L, who was a captive in B
4Mc 2:19 of Simeon and L for their irrational slaughter of

LEVI'S (2) [LEVI]

Ex 6:16 of L life was one hundred thirty-seven years.
Mk 2:15 And as he sat at dinner in L house,

LEVIATHAN (8)

Job 3: 8 those who are skilled to rouse up L.
41: 1 "Can you draw out L with a fishhook,
Ps 74:14 You crushed the heads of L;
104:26 and L that you formed to sport in it.
Isa 27: 1 and great and strong sword will punish L
27: 1 L the twisting serpent, and he will kill the dragon
2Es 6:49 and the name of the other L.
6:52 to L you gave the seventh part, the watery part;

LEVIED (2) [LEVY]

2Ch 24: 6 in from Judah and Jerusalem the tax l by Moses,
AdE 10: 1 The king l a tax upon his kingdom both by land

LEVIES (2) [LEVY]

Am 5:11 from them l of grain, you have built houses
1Mc 10:29 from payment of tribute and salt tax and crown l,

LEVITAS See Index to Footnotes

LEVITE‡ (20) [LEVI]

Ex 2: 1 the house of Levi went and married a L woman.
4:14 "What of your brother Aaron, the L?
Dt 12:19 not neglect the L as long as you live in your land.
18: 6 If a L leaves any of your towns,
Jdg 17: 7 He was a L residing there.
17: 9 He replied, "I am a L of Bethlehem in Judah,
17:11 The L agreed to stay with the man;
17:12 So Micah installed the L,
17:13 because the L has become my priest."
18: 3 they recognized the voice of the young L;
18:15 and came to the house of the young L,
19: 1 when there was no king in Israel, a certain L,
20: 4 The L, the husband of the woman who was
1Ch 24: 6 The scribe Shemaiah son of Nethanel, a L,
2Ch 20:14 son of Mattaniah, a L of the sons of Asaph,
31:12 the L, with his brother Shimei as second;
31:14 Kore son of Imnah the L, keeper of the east gate,
Lk 10:32 So likewise a L, when he came to the place
Ac 4:36 There was a L, a native of Cyprus, Joseph,
AdE 11: 1 Dositheus, who said that he was a priest and a L,

LEVITES (306) [LEVI]

A. PRIESTS AND [THE] LEVITES (56)

Ex 6:19 These are the families of the L according
6:25 of the ancestral houses of the L by their families.
38:21 the L being under the direction of Ithamar son of
Lev 25:32 As for the cities of the L,
25:32 the L shall forever have the right of redemption
25:33 Such property as may be redeemed from the L—
25:33 in the cities of the L are their possession among
Nu 1:47 The L, however, were not numbered
1:50 Rather you shall appoint the L over the tabernacle
1:51 tabernacle is to set out, the L shall take it down;
1:51 tabernacle is to be pitched, the L shall set it up.
1:53 but the L shall camp around the tabernacle of
1:53 and the L shall perform the guard duty of
2:17 The tent of meeting, with the camp of the L,
2:33 L were not enrolled among the other Israelites.
3: 9 the L to Aaron and his descendants;
3:12 I hereby accept the L from among the Israelites
3:12 The L shall be mine,
3:15 Enroll the L by ancestral houses and by clans.
3:20 These are the clans of the L,
3:32 to be chief over the leaders of the L,
3:39 of the L whom Moses and Aaron enrolled at
3:41 But you shall accept the L for me—
3:41 of the L as substitutes for all the firstborn among
3:45 Accept the L as substitutes for all the firstborn
3:45 of the L as substitutes for their livestock;
3:45 and the L shall be mine.
3:46 over and above the number of the L,
3:49 over and above those redeemed by the L;
4: 2 of the Kohathites separate from the other L,
4:18 of the Kohathites be destroyed from among the L.
4:46 All those who were enrolled of the L,
7: 5 and give them to the L,
7: 6 and gave them to the L.
8: 6 the L from among the Israelites and cleanse them.
8: 9 You shall bring the L before the tent of meeting,
8:10 When you bring the L before the LORD,
8:10 the Israelites shall lay their hands on the L,
8:11 and Aaron shall present the L before the LORD
8:12 L shall lay their hands on the heads of the bulls,
8:12 to make atonement for the L.
8:13 Then you shall have the L stand before Aaron
8:14 Thus you shall separate the L from among
8:14 and the L shall be mine.
8:15 Thereafter the L may go in to do service at
8:18 but I have taken the L in place of all the firstborn
8:19 I have given the L as a gift to Aaron and his sons
8:20 of the Israelites did with the L accordingly;
8:20 the L just as the LORD had commanded Moses
8:21 The L purified themselves from sin
8:22 Thereafter the L went in to do their service in
8:22 concerning the L, so they did
8:24 This applies to the L: from twenty-five
8:26 with the L in assigning their duties.
16: 7 You L have gone too far!"
16: 8 Then Moses said to Korah, "Hear now, you L!
16:10 and all your brother L with you;
18: 6 It is I who now take your brother L from among
18:21 To the L I have given every tithe in Israel for
18:23 L shall perform the service of the tent of meeting,
18:24 to the L as their portion the tithe of the Israelites,
18:26 You shall speak to the L, saying:
18:30 the rest shall be reckoned to the L as produce of
26:57 This is the enrollment of the L by their clans:
31:30 to the L who have charge of the tabernacle of
31:47 to the L who had charge of the tabernacle of
35: 2 towns for the L to live in;
35: 2 to the L pasture lands surrounding the towns.
35: 4 which you shall give to the L,
35: 6 that you give to the L shall include the six cities
35: 7 that you give to the L shall total forty-eight,
35: 8 shall give of its towns to the L.
Dt 12:12 and the L who reside in your towns
12:18 and the L resident in your towns,
14:27 As for the L resident in your towns,
14:29 the L, because they have no allotment
16:11 the L resident in your towns,
16:14 your male and female slaves, as well as the L,
26:11 with the L and the aliens who reside among you,
26:12 giving it to the L, the aliens, the orphans,
26:13 and I have given it to the L, the resident aliens,
27:14 L shall declare in a loud voice to all the Israelites:
31:25 Moses commanded the L who carried the ark of
Jos 14: 3 but to the L he gave no inheritance among them.
14: 4 and no portion was given to the L in the land,
18: 7 The L have no portion among you,
Jos 21: 1 the L came to the priest Eleazar and to Joshua son
21: 3 the L the following towns and pasture lands out
21: 4 So those L who were descendants of Aaron
21: 8 the Israelites gave by lot to the L,
21:10 of the Kohathites who belonged to the L,
21:20 to the Kohathite families of the L,
21:27 To the Gershonites, one of the families of the L,
21:34 To the rest of the L—
21:40 that is, the remainder of the families of the L,
21:41 of the L within the holdings of the Israelites were
1Sa 6:15 The L took down the ark of the LORD and
2Sa 15:24 Abiathar came up, and Zadok also, with all the L,
1Ki 8: 4 the priests and the L brought them up. A
12:31 from among all the people, who were not L.
1Ch 6:19 the clans of the L according to their ancestry.
6:48 and their kindred the L were appointed for all
6:64 So the people of Israel gave the L the towns
9: 2 priests, L, and temple servants.
9:14 Of the L: Shemaiah son of Hasshub,
9:18 These were the gatekeepers of the camp of the L.
9:26 who were L, were in charge of the chambers and
9:31 the L, the firstborn of Shallum the Korahite, was
9:33 the heads of ancestral houses of the L,
9:34 These were heads of ancestral houses of the L,
12:26 Of the L four thousand six hundred.
13: 2 the priests and L in the cities that have pasture A
15: 2 that no one but the L were to carry the ark
15: 4 the descendants of Aaron and the L:
15:11 and the L Uriel, Asaiah, Joel, Shemaiah, Eliel,
15:12 "You are the heads of families of the L;
15:14 priests and the L sanctified themselves to bring A
15:15 the L carried the ark of God on their shoulders
15:16 of the L to appoint their kindred as the singers
15:17 So the L appointed Heman son of Joel;
15:22 Chenaniah, leader of the L in music,
15:26 the L who were carrying the ark of the covenant
15:27 as also were all the L who were carrying the ark,
16: 4 He appointed certain of the L as ministers before
23: 2 the leaders of Israel and the priests and the L. A
23: 3 The L, thirty years old and upward,
23:26 so the L no longer need to carry the tabernacle
23:27 of the L from twenty years old and upward—
24: 6 of ancestral houses of the priests and of the L; A
24:30 of the L according to their ancestral houses.
24:31 of ancestral houses of the priests and of the L, A
26:17 On the east there were six L each day,
26:20 And of the L, Ahijah had charge of the treasuries
28:13 of the priests and the L, and all the work A
28:21 of the priests and the L for all the service A
2Ch 5: 4 and the L carried the ark.
5: 5 the priests and the L brought them up. A
7: 6 The priests stood at their posts; the L also,
8:14 and the L for their offices of praise
8:15 the priests and L regarding anything at all, A
11:13 The priests and the L who were in all Israel A
11:14 The L had left their common lands
13: 9 the descendants of Aaron, and the L,
13:10 the LORD who are descendants of Aaron, and L
17: 8 With them were the L, Shemaiah, Nethaniah,
17: 8 with these L, the priests Elishama and Jehoram.
19: 8 in Jerusalem Jehoshaphat appointed certain L
19:11 and the L will serve you as officers.
20:19 And the L, of the Kohathites and the Korahites,
23: 2 around through Judah and gathered the L from all
23: 4 one third of you, priests and L, A
23: 6 the LORD except the priests and ministering L;
23: 7 The L shall surround the king,
23: 8 The L and all Judah did according to all that
24: 5 the priests and the L and said to them, "Go out A
24: 5 But the L did not act quickly.
24: 6 "Why have you not required the L to bring in
24:11 to the king's officers by the L,
29: 4 the priests and the L and assembled them A
29: 5 He said to them, "Listen to me, L!
29:12 Then the L arose, Mahath son of Amasai,
29:16 and the L took them and carried them out to
29:25 the L in the house of the LORD with cymbals,
29:26 The L stood with the instruments of David,
29:30 and the officials commanded the L to sing praises
29:34 the L, helped them until the work was finished—
29:34 for the L were more conscientious than the priests
30:15 The priests and the L were ashamed, A
30:16 that they received from the hands of the L.
30:17 the L had to slaughter the passover lamb
30:21 L and the priests praised the LORD day by day,
30:22 to all the L who showed good skill in the service
30:25 whole assembly of Judah, the priests and the L, A
30:27 priests and the L stood up and blessed the A
31: 2 the divisions of the priests and of the L, A
31: 2 according to his service, the priests and the L, A
31: 4 to give the portion due to the priests and the L, A
31: 9 Hezekiah questioned the priests and the L about A
31:17 of the L from twenty years old and upwards was
31:19 and to everyone among the L who was enrolled.
34: 9 which the L, the keepers of the threshold,
34:12 Over them were appointed the L Jahath
34:12 Other L, all skillful with instruments of music,
34:13 and some of the L were scribes, and officials,
34:30 the priests and the L, all the people both great A
35: 3 the L who taught all Israel and who were holy to
35: 5 be L for each division of an ancestral house.
35: 8 to the priests, and to the L. A
35: 9 and Jeiel and Jozabad, the chiefs of the L, gave to
35: 9 the chiefs of the Levites, gave to the L for
35:10 and the L in their divisions according to
35:11 while the L did the skinning.
35:14 the L made preparations for themselves and for

2Ch 35:15 their kindred the **L** made preparations for them.
35:18 as was kept by Josiah, by the priests and the **L**, A
Ezr 1: 5 and the priests and the **L**— A
2:40 The **L**: the descendants of Jeshua
2:70 the **L**, and some of the people lived in Jerusalem
3: 8 the priests and the **L** and all who had come A
3: 8 the **L**, from twenty years old and upward, to have
3: 9 the **L**, their sons and kin,
3:10 and the **L**, the sons of Asaph, with cymbals,
3:12 many of the priests and **L** and heads of families, A
6:16 The people of Israel, the priests and the **L**, A
6:18 and the **L** in their courses for the service of God
6:20 the priests and the **L** had purified themselves; A
7: 7 and some of the priests and **L**, A
7:13 or **L** in my kingdom who freely offers to go
7:24 or toll on any of the priests, the **L**, the singers,
8:20 and his officials had set apart to attend the **L**.
8:29 before the chief priests and the **L** and the heads A
8:30 So the priests and the **L** took over the silver, A
8:33 and with them were the **L**,
9: 1 priests, and the **L** have not separated themselves A
10: 5 the leading priests, the **L**, and all Israel swear
10:15 Meshullam and Shabbethai the **L** supported them.
10:23 Of the **L**: Jozabad, Shimei,
Ne 3:17 After him the **L** made repairs:
7: 1 the singers, and the **L** had been appointed,
7:43 The **L**: the descendants of Jeshua,
7:73 So the priests, the **L**, the gatekeepers, the singers,
8: 7 Kelita, Azariah, Jozabad, Hanan, Pelaiah, the **L**,
8: 9 the **L** who taught the people said to all the people,
8:11 So the **L** stilled all the people, saying, "Be quiet,
8:13 with the priests and the **L**, came together A
9: 4 the stairs of the **L** and cried out with a loud voice
9: 5 Then the **L**, Jeshua, Kadmiel, Bani, Hashabneiah,
9:38 the names of our officials, our **L**,
10: 9 And the **L**: Jeshua son of Azaniah,
10:28 The rest of the people, the priests, the **L**,
10:34 We have also cast lots among the priests, the **L**,
10:37 and to bring to the **L** the tithes from our soil,
10:37 the **L** who collect the tithes in all our rural towns.
10:38 be with the **L** when the **L** receive the tithes;
10:38 and the **L** shall bring up a tithe of the tithes to
11: 3 Israel, the priests, the **L**, the temple servants,
11:15 And of the **L**: Shemaiah son of Hasshub
11:16 of the **L**, who were over the outside work of
11:18 **L** in the holy city were two hundred eighty-four.
11:20 the rest of Israel, and of the priests and the **L**, A
11:22 The overseer of the **L** in Jerusalem was Uzzi son
11:36 of the **L** in Judah were joined to Benjamin.
12: 1 priests and the **L** who came up with Zerubbabel A
12: 8 And the **L**: Jeshua, Binnui,
12:22 As for the **L**, in the days of Eliashib, Joiada,
12:23 The **L**, heads of ancestral houses,
12:24 And the leaders of the **L**:
12:27 of the wall of Jerusalem they sought out the **L**
12:30 And the priests and the **L** purified themselves; A
12:44 the priests and for the **L** from the fields A
12:44 over the priests and the **L** who ministered. A
12:47 They set apart that which was for the **L**;
12:47 the **L** set apart that which was for the descendants
13: 5 which were given by commandment to the **L**,
13:10 the portions of the **L** had not been given to them;
13:10 so that the **L** and the singers,
13:13 the scribe Zadok, and Pedaiah of the **L**,
13:22 the **L** that they should purify themselves
13:29 the covenant of the priests and the **L**. A
13:30 and I established the duties of the priests and **L**, A
Isa 66:21 I will also take some of them as priests and as **L**, A
Jer 33:21 and my covenant with my ministers the **L**.
33:22 and the **L** who minister to me.
Eze 44:10 But the **L** who went far from me,
45: 5 shall be for the **L** who minister at the temple,
48:11 the people of Israel went astray, as the **L** did.
48:12 a most holy place, adjoining the territory of the **L**.
48:13 the territory of the priests, the **L** shall have
48:22 and the property of the **L** and of the city,
Jn 1:19 the Jews sent priests and **L** from Jerusalem A
1Es 1: 3 He told the **L**, the temple servants of Israel,
1: 5 to the groupings of the ancestral houses of you **L**,
1: 7 to the people and the priests and **L**. A
1: 9 gave the **L** for the passover five thousand sheep
1:10 priests and the **L**, having the unleavened bread, A
1:14 so the **L** prepared it for themselves and
1:16 for their kindred the **L** prepared the passover
1:21 the priests and **L** and the people of Judah and all A
2: 8 and the priests and the **L**, A
4:55 that the support for the **L** should be provided until
5:26 The **L**: the descendants of Jeshua
5:46 the **L**, and some of the people settled
5:58 the **L** who were twenty or more years of age
5:58 with their sons and kindred, all the **L**,
5:59 and the **L**, the sons of Asaph, with cymbals,
7: 6 And the people of Israel, the priests, the **L**,
7: 9 the priests and the **L** stood arrayed in their A
7:10 the priests and the **L** were purified together. A
7:11 but the **L** were all purified together,
8: 5 people of Israel and some of the priests and **L** A
8:10 and of the priests and **L** and others in our realm, A
8:22 the priests or **L** or temple singers or gatekeepers
8:42 of the descendants of the priests or of the **L**,
8:49 and the leaders had given for the service of the **L**,
8:59 to the leaders of the priests and the **L**, A
8:60 So the priests and the **L** who took the silver A
8:63 of Jeshua and Moeth son of Binnui, the **L**.
8:69 the priests and the **L** have not put away from A
8:96 leaders of the priests and **L** of all Israel swear A
9:23 And of the **L**: Jozabad
9:37 priests and the **L** and the Israelites settled in A
9:48 Hanan, Pelaiah, the **L**, taught the law of the Lord,
9:49 and to the **L** who were teaching the multitude,
9:53 The **L** commanded all the people, saying,
2Es 10:22 our **L** have gone into exile,

LEVITICAL (15) [LEVI]

Dt 17: 9 with the **l** priests and the judge who is in office
17:18 for him in the presence of the **l** priests.
18: 1 The **l** priests, the whole tribe of Levi,
24: 8 the **l** priests instruct you,
27: 9 Then Moses and the **l** priests spoke to all Israel,
Jos 3: 3 by the **l** priests, then you shall set out
8:33 the **l** priests who carried the ark of the covenant
2Ch 5:12 and all the **l** singers, Asaph, Heman,
23:18 to the **l** priests whom David had organized to be
Jer 33:18 and the **l** priests shall never lack a man
Eze 43:19 you shall give to the **l** priests of the family
44:15 But the **l** priests, the descendants of Zadok,
Heb 7:11 had been attainable through the **l** priesthood—
1Es 5:56 and the **l** priests and all who had come back
5:63 of the **l** priests and heads of ancestral houses,

LEVY (2) [LEVIED, LEVIES]

1Ki 5:13 the **l** numbered thirty thousand men.
2Mc 11: 3 and to **l** tribute on the temple as he did on

LEWD (1) [LEWDLY, LEWDNESS]

Eze 16:27 who were ashamed of your **l** behavior.

LEWDLY (1) [LEWD]

Eze 22:11 another **l** defiles his daughter-in-law;

LEWDNESS (12) [LEWD]

Eze 16:43 not committed **l** beyond all your abominations?
16:58 the penalty of your **l** and your abominations,
22: 9 who commit **l** in your midst.
23:21 Thus you longed for the **l** of your youth,
23:27 to your **l** and your whoring brought from the land
23:29 Your **l** and your whorings
23:35 bear the consequences of your **l** and whorings.
23:48 Thus will I put an end to **l** in the land,
23:48 and not commit **l** as you have done.
23:49 They shall repay you for your **l**,
24:13 Yet, when I cleansed you in your filthy **l**,
Hos 4:18 they love **l** more than their glory.

LIABILITY (1) [LIABLE]

Ex 21:19 then the assailant shall be free of **l**,

LIABLE (6) [LIABILITY]

Ex 21:28 but the owner of the ox shall not be **l**.
Mt 5:21 and 'whoever murders shall be **l** to judgment.'
5:22 with a brother or sister, you will be **l** to judgment;
5:22 a brother or sister, you will be **l** to the council;
5:22 'You fool,' you will be **l** to the hell of fire.
1Mc 14:45 or rejects any of them shall be **l** to punishment."

LIAR (17) [LIE]

2Ki 9:12 They said, "**L**! Come on, tell us!"
Job 24:25 If it is not so, who will prove me a **l**,
34: 6 in spite of being right I am counted a **l**;
Ps 116:11 I said in my consternation, "Everyone is a **l**."
Pr 17: 4 and a **l** gives heed to a mischievous tongue.
19: 5 and a **l** will not escape.
19: 9 not go unpunished, and the **l** will perish.
19:22 and it is better to be poor than a **l**.
30: 6 and you will be found a **l**.
Jn 8:44 for he is a **l** and the father of lies.
8:55 I would be a **l** like you.
Ro 3: 4 Although everyone is a **l**, let God be proved true,
1Jn 1:10 we make him a **l**, and his word is not in us.
2: 4 but does not obey his commandments, is a **l**,
2:22 Who is the **l** but the one who denies that Jesus is
5:10 in God have made him a **l** by not believing in
Sir 20:25 A thief is preferable to a habitual **l**,

LIAR'S (1) [LIE]

Sir 20:26 A **l** way leads to disgrace,

LIARS (9) [LIE]

Ps 63:11 for the mouths of **l** will be stopped.
Isa 44:25 who frustrates the omens of **l**, and makes fools
1Ti 1:10 sodomites, slave traders, **l**, perjurers,
4: 2 the hypocrisy of **l** whose consciences are seared
Tit 1:12 who said, "Cretans are always **l**, vicious brutes,
1Jn 4:20 and hate their brothers or sisters, are **l**;
Rev 21: 8 the sorcerers, the idolaters, and all **l**,
Sir 15: 8 and **l** will never think of her.
2Es 11:42 the truth, and have loved **l**;

LIBATION (3) [LIBATIONS]

Jer 52:19 the lampstands, the ladles, and the bowls for **l**,
Php 2:17 if I am being poured out as a **l** over the sacrifice
2Ti 4: 6 As for me, I am already being poured out as a **l**,

LIBATIONS (12) [LIBATION]

Dt 32:38 and drank the wine of their **l**?
1Ch 29:21 and a thousand lambs, with their **l**,
Jer 19:13 and **l** have been poured out to other gods.
32:29 to Baal and **l** have been poured out to other gods,
44:17 to the queen of heaven and pour out **l** to her,
44:18 to the queen of heaven and pouring out **l** to her,
44:19 to the queen of heaven and pouring out **l** to her;
44:19 for her, marked with her image, and poured out **l**
44:25 to the queen of heaven and to pour out **l** to her.'
44:25 By all means, keep your vows and make your **l**!
AdE 14:17 the king's feast or drunk the wine of **l**.
1Es 6:31 that **l** may be made to the Most High God

LIBERAL (1) [LIBERALITY, LIBERALLY]

Sir 31:23 People bless the one who is **l** with food,

LIBERALITY (1) [LIBERAL]

Est 2:18 and gave gifts with royal **l**.

LIBERALLY (4) [LIBERAL]

Dt 15:10 Give **l** and be ungrudging when you do so,
15:14 Provide **l** out of your flock, your threshing floor,
Ps 37:26 They are ever giving **l** and lending,
3Mc 3:21 with us and the myriad affairs **l** entrusted to them

LIBERATED (2) [LIBERTY]

2Mc 2:22 and **l** the city, and re-established the laws
2Es 14:29 and they were **l** from there

LIBERATOR (1) [LIBERTY]

Ac 7:35 both ruler and **l** through the angel who appeared

LIBERTINES (KJV) See FREEDMEN

LIBERTY‡ (15) [LIBERATED, LIBERATOR]

Lev 25:10 and you shall proclaim **l** throughout the land
Ps 119:45 I shall walk at **l**, for I have sought your precepts.
Isa 61: 1 to proclaim **l** to the captives,
Jer 34: 8 in Jerusalem to make a proclamation of **l**
34:15 by proclaiming **l** to one another, and you made
Eze 46:17 it shall be his to the year of **l**;
Ac 24:23 but to let him have some **l** and not to prevent any
1Co 8: 9 that this **l** of yours does not somehow become
10:29 For why should my **l** be subject to the judgment
Jas 1:25 those who look into the perfect law, the law of **l**,
2:12 as those who are to be judged by the law of **l**.
Tob 7:10 at **l** to give her to any other man than yourself,
Sir 26:10 or else, when she finds **l**, she will make use of it.
33:26 leave his hands idle, and he will seek **l**.
2Es 7:96 the spacious **l** that they are to receive and enjoy

LIBNAH (18)

Nu 33:20 from Rimmon-perez and camped at **L**.
33:21 They set out from **L** and camped at Rissah.
Jos 10:29 to **L**, and fought against **L**.
10:31 Next Joshua passed on from **L**,
10:32 and every person in it, as he had done to **L**.
10:39 and, as he had done to **L** and its king,
12:15 the king of **L** one the king of Adullam one
15:42 **L**, Ether, Ashan,
21:13 with its pasture lands, **L** with its pasture lands,
2Ki 8:22 **L** also revolted at the same time.
19: 8 and found the king of Assyria fighting against **L**;
23:31 name was Hamutal daughter of Jeremiah of **L**.
24:18 name was Hamutal daughter of Jeremiah of **L**.
1Ch 6:57 Hebron, **L** with its pasture lands, Jattir,
2Ch 21:10 At that time **L** also revolted against his rule,
Isa 37: 8 and found the king of Assyria fighting against **L**;
Jer 52: 1 name was Hamutal daughter of Jeremiah of **L**.

LIBNI (5) [LIBNITES]

Ex 6:17 sons of Gershon: **L** and Shimei, by their families.
Nu 3:18 by their clans: **L** and Shimei.
1Ch 6:17 of Gershom: **L** and Shimei.
6:20 **L** his son, Jahath his son, Zimmah his son,
6:29 Mahli, **L** his son, Shimei his son, Uzzah his son,

LIBNITES (2) [LIBNI]

Nu 3:21 the clan of the **L** and the clan of the Shimeites;
26:58 These are the clans of Levi: the clan of the **L**,

LIBRARY (2)

AdE 2:23 in the royal **l** in praise of the goodwill shown
2Mc 2:13 that he founded a **l** and collected the books about

LIBYA (2) [LIBYANS]

Eze 30: 5 Ethiopia, and Put, and Lud, and all Arabia, and **L**,
Ac 2:10 Egypt and the parts of **L** belonging to Cyrene,

LIBYANS (4) [LIBYA]

2Ch 12: 3 **L**, Sukkiim, and Ethiopians.
16: 8 Were not the Ethiopians and the **L** a huge army
Da 11:43 the **L** and the Ethiopians shall follow in his train.
Na 3: 9 Put and the **L** were her helpers.

LICE (KJV) See GNAT[S]

LICENSE‡ (1)

3Mc 7:12 granted them a general **l** so that freely,

LICENTIOUS (3) [LICENTIOUSNESS]

2Pe 2: 2 Even so, many will follow their **l** ways,
2:18 and with **l** desires of the flesh they entice people

3Mc 2:26 He was not content with his uncounted l deeds,

LICENTIOUSNESS (8) [LICENTIOUS]

Mk 7:22 wickedness, deceit, l, envy, slander, pride, folly.
Ro 13:13 not in debauchery and l,
2Co 12:21 sexual immorality, and l that they have practiced.
Gal 5:19 of the flesh are obvious: fornication, impurity, l,
Eph 4:19 and have abandoned themselves to l,
1Pe 4:3 living in l, passions, drunkenness, revels,
2Pe 2:7 a righteous man greatly distressed by the l of
Jude 1:4 of our God into l and deny our only Master

LICK (6) [LICKED, LICKS]

Nu 22:4 "This horde will now l up all that is around us,
1Ki 21:19 dogs will also l up your blood."
Ps 72:9 and his enemies l the dust.
Isa 49:23 and l the dust of your feet.
Mic 7:17 they shall l dust like a snake,
Lk 16:21 even the dogs would come and l his sores.

LICKED (3) [LICK]

1Ki 18:38 and even l up the water that was in the trench.
21:19 In the place where dogs l up the blood of Naboth,
22:38 the dogs l up his blood,

LICKS (1) [LICK]

Nu 22:4 as an ox l up the grass of the field."

LID (1)

2Ki 12:9 priest Jehoiada took a chest, made a hole in its l,

LIDEBIR See Index to Footnotes

LIE‡ (165) [LAIN, LAY, LIAR, LIAR'S, LIARS, LIED, LIES, LYING]

Ge 19:32 and we will l with him,
19:34 then you go in and l with him,
28:13 the land on which you l I will give to you and
30:15 "Then he may l with you tonight
38:26 And he did not l with her again.
39:7 on Joseph and said, "L with me."
39:10 he would not consent to l beside her or to be
39:12 of his garment, saying, "L with me!"
39:14 He came in to me to l with me,
47:30 When I l down with my ancestors,
Ex 23:11 the seventh year you shall let it rest and l fallow,
28:28 that it may l on the decorated band of the ephod,
39:21 it should l on the decorated band of the ephod,
Lev 18:22 You shall not l with a male as with a woman;
19:11 and you shall not l to one another.
26:6 And I will grant peace in the land, and you shall l
Nu 21:15 and l along the border of Moab."
23:19 God is not a human being, that he should l,
23:24 not l down until it has eaten the prey and drunk
Dt 6:7 when you l down and when you rise.
11:19 when you l down and when you rise.
25:2 that person l down and be beaten in his presence
28:30 but another man shall l with her.
31:16 "Soon you will l down with your ancestors.
Jos 7:21 They now l hidden in the ground inside my tent,
8:4 "You shall l in ambush against the city,
Jdg 9:32 and l in wait in the fields.
21:20 saying, "Go and l in wait in the vineyards,
Ru 3:4 then, go and uncover his feet and l down;
3:7 he went to l down at the end of the heap of grain.
3:13 L down until the morning."
1Sa 3:5 But he said, "I did not call; l down again."
3:6 he said, "I did not call, my son; l down again."
3:9 Therefore Eli said to Samuel, "Go, l down;
22:8 to l in wait, as he is doing today."
22:13 so that he has risen against me, to l in wait,
2Sa 7:12 When your days are fulfilled and you l down
8:2 making them l down on the ground,
11:11 to eat and to drink, and to l with my wife?
11:13 in the evening he went out to l on his couch with
12:3 and drink from his cup, and l in his bosom,
12:11 to your neighbor, and he shall l with your wives
13:5 Jonadab said to him, "L down on your bed,
13:11 and said to her, "Come, l with me, my sister."
1Ki 1:2 let her l in your bosom,
Job 6:28 for I will not l to your face.
7:4 When I l down I say, 'When shall I rise?'
7:21 For now I shall l in the earth;
11:19 You will l down, and no one will make you afraid;
14:12 so mortals l down and do not rise again;
20:11 will l down in the dust with them.
21:26 They l down alike in the dust,
24:7 They l all night naked, without clothing,
38:40 or l in wait in their covert?
Ps 3:5 I l down and sleep; I wake again,
4:8 I will both l down and sleep in peace;
4:8 you alone, O LORD, make me l down in safety.
23:2 He makes me l down in green pastures;
36:12 There the evildoers l prostrate;
41:8 that I will not rise again from where I l.
57:4 I l down among lions
59:3 Even now they l in wait for my life;
88:5 like the slain that l in the grave,
89:35 I will not l to David.
102:7 I l awake; I am like a
104:22 they withdraw and l down in their dens.
119:95 The wicked l in wait to destroy me,
Pr 1:11 "Come with us, let us l in wait for blood;
Pr 1:18 yet they l in wait—to kill themselves!
3:24 when you l down, your sleep will be sweet.
6:9 How long will you l there, O lazybones?
6:22 when you l down, they will watch over you;
14:5 A faithful witness does not l,
15:11 Sheol and Abaddon l open before the LORD,
24:15 Do not l in wait like an outlaw against the home
Ecc 4:11 Again, if two l together, they keep warm;
8:6 the troubles of mortals l heavy upon them.
11:3 in the place where the tree falls, there it will l.
SS 1:7 where you make it l down at noon;
Isa 6:11 "Until cities l waste without inhabitant,
11:6 the leopard shall l down with the kid,
11:7 their young shall l down together;
13:20 shepherds will not make their flocks l down there.
13:21 But wild animals will l down there,
14:18 All the kings of the nations l in glory,
14:30 and the needy l down in safety;
17:2 they will be places for flocks, which will l down,
21:9 and all the images of her gods l shattered on
22:18 and there your splendid chariots shall l,
27:10 the calves graze there, there they l down,
34:10 From generation to generation it shall l waste;
43:17 they l down, they cannot rise,
50:11 you shall l down in torment.
51:20 they l at the head of every street like an antelope
58:5 and to l in sackcloth and ashes?
65:10 the Valley of Achor a place for herds to l down,
Jer 3:25 Let us l down in our shame,
8:8 the false pen of the scribes has made it into a l?
14:2 they l in gloom on the ground,
27:10 For they are prophesying a l to you,
27:14 for they are prophesying a l to you.
27:16 for they are prophesying a l to you.
28:15 and you made this people trust in a l.
29:9 a l that they are prophesying to you in my name;
29:21 who are prophesying a l to you in my name:
29:31 and has led you to trust in a l,
37:14 And Jeremiah said, "That is a l;
40:16 for you are telling a l about Ishmael."
43:2 to Jeremiah, "You are telling a l.
La 4:1 The sacred stones l scattered at the head
Eze 4:4 Then l on your left side, and place
4:4 for the number of the days that you l there.
4:6 you shall l down a second time,
4:9 the number of days that you l on your side,
6:13 their slain l among their idols around their altars,
30:7 and their cities shall l among cities laid waste.
31:12 and its boughs l broken in all the watercourses of
31:18 you shall l among the uncircumcised,
32:21 "They have come down, they l still,
32:27 And they do not l with the fallen warriors
32:28 be broken and l among the uncircumcised,
32:29 they l with the uncircumcised,
32:30 they l uncircumcised with those who are killed
34:14 there they shall l down in good grazing land,
34:15 and I will make them l down,
48:22 the prince shall l between the territory of Judah
Hos 2:18 and I will make you l down in safety.
6:9 As robbers l in wait for someone,
Am 6:4 Alas for those who l on beds of ivory,
Mic 7:2 they all l in wait for blood,
Hab 2:3 it speaks of the end, and does not l.
Zep 2:7 and in the houses of Ashkelon they shall l down
2:14 Herds shall l down in it, every wild animal;
3:13 Then they will pasture and l down,
Ac 5:3 to l to the Holy Spirit and to keep back part of
5:4 You did not l to us but to God!"
Ro 1:25 about God for a l and worshiped and served
2Co 11:31 knows that I do not l.
Gal 1:20 writing to you, before God, I do not l!
Col 3:9 Do not l to one another,
1Jn 1:6 we l and do not do what is true;
2:21 and you know that no l comes from the truth.
2:27 and is true and is not a l,
Rev 11:8 and their dead bodies will l in the street of
14:5 and in their mouth no l was found;
Tob 5:10 the light of heaven, but I l in darkness like
Jdt 3:2 the Great King, l prostrate before you.
3:3 and herds and all our encampments l before you;
Wis 2:12 "Let us l in wait for the righteous man,
Sir 7:12 Do not devise a l against your brother,
7:13 Refuse to utter any l, for it is a habit that results
8:11 or they may l in ambush against your words.
11:31 for they l in wait, turning good into evil,
20:24 A l is an ugly blot on a person;
41:17 and of a l, before a prince or a ruler;
43:32 Many things greater than these l hidden,
46:12 from where they l, and may the names
47:19 But you brought in women to l at your side,
49:10 from where they l, for they comforted the people
Sus 1:20 so give your consent, and l with us.
1:55 This l has cost you your head,
1:59 This l has cost you also your head,
2Mc 5:10 to l unburied had no one to mourn for him;
12:39 and to bring them back to l with their kindred in
4Mc 17:9 "Here l buried an aged priest and an aged woman

LIED (3) [LIE]

Lev 6:3 or have found something lost and l about it—
Ps 78:36 they l to him with their tongues.
Isa 57:11 Whom did you dread and fear so that you l,

LIEN (KJV) See LAIN, STAY

LIES (125) [LIE]

Ge 16:14 it l between Kadesh and Bered.
49:25 blessings of the deep that l beneath,
Ex 22:16 a virgin who is not engaged to be married, and l
22:19 Whoever l with an animal shall be put to death.
Lev 15:4 the one with the discharge l shall be unclean;
15:18 If a man l with a woman and has an emission
15:20 upon which she l during her impurity shall
15:24 If any man l with her, and her impurity falls
15:24 and every bed on which he l shall be unclean.
15:26 Every bed on which she l during all the days
15:33 for the man who l with a woman who is unclean.
20:11 The man who l with his father's wife has
20:12 If a man l with his daughter-in-law,
20:13 If a man l with a male as with a woman,
20:18 If a man l with a woman having her sickness
20:20 If a man l with his uncle's wife,
26:34 as long as it l desolate, while you are in the land
26:35 As long as it l desolate,
Nu 14:33 the last of your dead bodies l in the wilderness.
Dt 19:11 But if someone at enmity with another l in wait
22:23 and a man meets her in the town and l with her,
22:25 and the man seizes her and l with her,
22:28 and seizes her and l with her,
27:20 "Cursed be anyone who l with his father's wife,
27:21 "Cursed be anyone who l with any animal."
27:22 "Cursed be anyone who l with his sister,
27:23 be anyone who l with his mother-in-law."
33:13 and of the deep that l beneath;
Jos 15:8 up to the top of the mountain that l over against
18:13 the mountain that l south of Lower Beth-horon.
18:14 from the mountain that l to the south,
22:4 to your tents in the land where your possession l,
22:10 to the region near the Jordan that l in the land
Jdg 1:16 which l in the Negeb near Arad.
16:10 "You have mocked me and told me l;
16:13 "Until now you have mocked me and told me l;
Ru 3:4 When he l down, observe the place where he l;
2Sa 1:19 O Israel, l slain upon your high places!
1:25 Jonathan l slain upon your high places.
2:24 which l before Giah on the way to the wilderness
Ne 2:3 the place of my ancestors' graves, l waste,
2:17 how Jerusalem l in ruins with its gates burned.
Job 13:4 As for you, you whitewash with l;
40:21 Under the lotus plants it l,
Ps 4:2 long will you love vain words, and seek after l?
5:6 You destroy those who speak l;
7:14 and are pregnant with mischief, and bring forth l.
12:2 They utter l to each other;
58:3 they err from their birth, speaking l.
59:12 For the cursing and l that they utter,
88:7 Your wrath l heavy upon me,
101:7 no one who utters l shall continue in my presence.
119:69 The arrogant smear me with l,
144:8 mouths speak l, and whose right hands are false.
144:11 mouths speak l, and whose right hands are false.
Pr 7:12 and at every corner she l in wait.
14:5 but a false witness breathes out l.
14:25 but one who utters l is a betrayer.
23:28 She l in wait like a robber and increases
23:34 You will be like one who l down in the midst of
23:34 like one who l on the top of a mast.
Ecc 6:1 and it l heavy upon humankind:
SS 1:13 to me a bag of myrrh that l between my breasts.
Isa 1:7 Your country l desolate,
9:15 and prophets who teach l are the tail;
24:5 The earth l polluted under its inhabitants;
24:20 its transgression l heavy upon it, and it falls,
28:15 for we have made l our refuge,
28:17 hail will sweep away the refuge of l,
59:3 your lips have spoken l, your tongue mutters
59:4 they rely on empty pleas, they speak l,
Jer 6:16 for the ancient paths, where the good way l;
9:5 they have taught their tongues to speak l;
13:25 because you have forgotten me and trusted in l.
14:14 The prophets are prophesying l in my name;
16:19 Our ancestors have inherited nothing but l,
23:14 they commit adultery and walk in l;
23:25 the prophets have said who prophesy l
23:26 those who prophesy l, and who prophesy
23:32 by their l and their recklessness, when I did
La 5:18 which l desolate; jackals prowl over it.
Eze 13:8 you have uttered falsehood and envisioned l,
13:19 by your l to my people, who listen to l.
21:29 Offering false visions for you, divining l for you,
22:28 seeing false visions and divining l for them,
47:16 Sibraim (which l between the border
Da 11:27 shall sit at one table and exchange l.
Hos 7:13 but they speak l against me.
10:13 you have eaten the fruit of l.
11:12 Ephraim has surrounded me with l,
Am 2:4 by the same l after which their ancestors walked.
Mic 6:12 your inhabitants speak l,
7:5 of your mouth from her who l in your embrace;
Hab 2:18 a cast image, a teacher of l?
Zep 3:13 they shall do no wrong and utter no l,
Hag 1:4 while this house l in ruins?
1:9 Because my house l in ruins,
Zec 10:2 teraphim utter nonsense, and the diviners see l;
13:3 for you speak l in the name of the LORD";
14:4 which l before Jerusalem on the east;
Jn 8:44 When he l, he speaks according to his own nature,
8:44 for he is a liar and the father of l.
Ro 7:8 Apart from the law sin l dead.
7:21 that when I want to do what is good, evil l close
2Co 3:15 a veil l over their minds;

Php 3:13 forgetting what l behind and straining forward to what l ahead,
Tit 1: 2 God, who never l, promised before the ages began
1Jn 5:19 whole world l under the power of the evil one.
Rev 21:16 city l foursquare, its length the same as its width;
Tob 2: 3 and now he l there strangled."
5: 6 for it l in a mountainous area,
Wis 14:28 or prophesy l, or live unrighteously,
Sir 11:32 and a sinner l in wait to shed blood.
25: 2 a pauper who boasts, a rich person who l,
27:10 lion l in wait for prey; so does sin for evildoers.
27:28 but vengeance l in wait for them like a lion.
38:13 when recovery l in the hands of physicians,
51: 2 from lips that fabricate l.
LtJ 6:47 They have left only l and reproach
Bel 1:12 otherwise Daniel will, who is telling l about us."
2Es 2: 9 whose land l in lumps of pitch and heaps
14:20 For the world l in darkness,

LIEUTENANTS (KJV) See SATRAPS

LIFE‡ (749) [LIVE]

A. ETERNAL LIFE (44)
B. THE DAYS OF ... LIFE (34)
C. WAY OF LIFE (15)
D. TREE OF LIFE (14)
E. LIFE ... DEATH (10)
F. BREATH OF ... LIFE (8)
G. BOOK OF LIFE (7)

Ge 1:30 everything that has the breath of l, F
2: 7 and breathed into his nostrils the breath of l; F
2: 9 the tree of l also in the midst of the garden, D
3:14 and dust you shall eat all the days of your l. B
3:17 in toil you shall eat of it all the days of your l; B
3:22 from the tree of l, and eat, and live forever"— D
3:24 and turning to guard the way to the tree of l. D
6:17 in which is the breath of l; F
7:11 In the six hundredth year of Noah's l,
7:15 of all flesh in which there was the breath of l. F
7:22 in whose nostrils was the breath of l died. F
9: 4 Only, you shall not eat flesh with its l, that is,
9: 5 I will require a reckoning for human l.
12:13 and that my l may be spared on your account."
19:17 they said, "Flee for your l;
19:19 you have shown me great kindness in saving my l;
19:20 and my l will be saved!"
23: 1 this was the length of Sarah's l.
25: 7 This is the length of Abraham's l,
25:17 (This is the length of the l of Ishmael,
26:35 and they made l bitter for Isaac and Rebekah.
27:46 of my l because of the Hittite women.
27:46 what good will my l be to me?"
32:30 and yet my l is preserved."
37:21 saying, "Let us not take his l."
44:30 then, as his l is bound up in the boy's l,
44:32 the blame in the sight of my father all my l.'
45: 5 for God sent me before you to preserve l.
47: 8 "How many are the years of your l?"
47: 9 few and hard have been the years of my l.
47: 9 the l of my ancestors during their long sojourn."
47:28 so the days of Jacob, the years of his l,
48:15 the God who has been my shepherd all my l
Ex 4:19 for all those who were seeking your l are dead."
6:16 of Levi's l was one hundred thirty-seven years.
6:18 of Kohath's l was one hundred thirty-three years.
6:20 of Amram's l was one hundred thirty-seven years.
21: 6 and he shall serve him for l.
21:23 If any harm follows, then you shall give l for l,
21:30 for the redemption of the victim's l.
Lev 17:11 For the l of the flesh is in the blood;
17:11 for, as l, it is the blood that makes atonement.
17:14 For the l of every creature—its blood is its l;
17:14 for the l of every creature is its blood;
24:18 an animal shall make restitution for it, l for l.
26:16 that waste the eyes and cause l to pine away.
Nu 22:30 which you have ridden all your l to this day?
35:31 Moreover you shall accept no ransom for the l of
Dt 4: 9 from your mind all the days of your l; B
6: 2 the LORD your God all the days of your l, B
12:23 for the blood is the l, and you shall not eat the l with the meat.
16: 3 so that all the days of your l you may remember B
17:19 and he shall read in it all the days of his l, B
19:11 in wait and attacks and takes the l of that person,
19:21 l for l, eye for eye, tooth for tooth,
24: 6 for that would be taking a l in pledge.
28:66 Your l shall hang in doubt before you;
28:66 with no assurance of your l.
30:15 See, I have set before you today l and prosperity,
30:19 today that I have set before you l and death, E
30:19 l so that you and your descendants may
30:20 for that means l to you and length of days,
32:47 for you, but rather your very l;
Jos 1: 5 to stand against you all the days of your l. B
2:14 The men said to her, "Our l for yours!
4:14 in awe of Moses, all the days of his l. B
Jdg 9:17 and risked his l, and rescued you from the hand
12: 3 I took my l in my hand,
13:12 what is to be the boy's rule of l;
16:30 were more than those he had killed during his l.
18:25 and you will lose your l and the lives
Ru 4:15 He shall be to you a restorer of l and a nourisher
1Sa 2: 6 The LORD kills and brings to l;
7:15 Samuel judged Israel all the days of his l. B
19: 5 for he took his l in his hand when he attacked
1Sa 19:11 "If you do not save your l tonight,
20: 1 that he is trying to take my l?"
20:17 for he loved him as he loved his own l.
22:23 for the one who seeks my l seeks your l;
23:15 that Saul had come out to seek his l.
24:11 though you are hunting me to take my l.
25:29 to seek your l, the l of my lord shall be bound
26:21 because my l was precious in your sight today;
26:24 As your l was precious today in my sight,
26:24 may my l be precious in the sight of the LORD,
28: 2 "Very well, I will make you my bodyguard for l."
28: 9 Why then are you laying a snare for my l to bring
28:21 I have taken my l in my hand,
2Sa 1: 9 and yet my l still lingers.'
1:23 In l and in death they were not divided; E
4: 8 son of Saul, your enemy, who sought your l;
4: 9 who has redeemed my l out of every adversity,
14: 7 for the l of his brother whom he murdered,
14:14 But God will not take away a l;
15:21 whether for death or for l,
16:11 "My own son seeks my l;
17: 3 You seek the l of only one man,
18:13 if I had dealt treacherously against his l
19: 5 of all your officers who have saved your l today,
1Ki 1:12 so that you may save your own l and the l of your
1:29 who has saved my l from every adversity,
2:23 at the risk of his l!
3:11 and have not asked for yourself long l or riches, or for the l of your enemies,
3:13 both riches and honor all your l;
3:14 then I will lengthen your l."
4:21 and served Solomon all the days of his l. B
11:34 but will make him ruler all the days of his l, B
15: 5 that he commanded him all the days of his l, B
15: 6 and Jeroboam continued all the days of his l. B
17:21 let this child's l come into him again."
17:22 the l of the child came into him again,
19: 2 if I do not make your l like the l of one of them
19: 3 Then he was afraid; he got up and fled for his l,
19: 4 now, O LORD, take away my l,
19:10 I alone am left, and they are seeking my l,
19:14 I alone am left, and they are seeking my l,
20:31 perhaps he will spare your l."
20:39 if he is missing, your l shall be given for his l,
20:42 therefore your l shall be for his l,
2Ki 1:13 "O man of God, please let my l, and the l of these fifty servants of yours,
1:14 but now let my l be precious in your sight."
4:31 but there was no sound or sign of l.
5: 7 "Am I God, to give death or l,
8: 1 the woman whose son he had restored to l,
8: 5 how Elisha had restored a dead person to l,
8: 5 to l appealed to the king for her house
8: 5 and here is her son whom Elisha restored to l."
10:24 into your hands shall forfeit his l."
13:21 he came to l and stood on his feet.
20: 6 I will add fifteen years to your l.
25:29 of his l he dined regularly in the king's presence.
2Ch 1:11 wealth, honor, or the l of those who hate you, and have not even asked for long l,
Ezr 6:10 and pray for the l of the king and his children.
9: 9 to give us new l to set up the house of our God,
Ne 6:11 a man like me go into the temple to save his l?
9: 6 To all of them you give l,
Est 7: 3 and if it pleases the king, let my l be given me—
7: 7 Haman stayed to beg his l from Queen Esther,
Job 2: 6 in your power; only spare his l."
3:20 and l to the bitter in soul,
7: 7 "Remember that my l is a breath;
7:16 I loathe my l; I would not live forever.
9:21 not know myself; I loathe my l.
10: 1 "I loathe my l; I will give free utterance to my
10:12 You have granted me l and steadfast love,
10:20 Are not the days of my l few? B
11:17 And your l will be brighter than the noonday;
12:10 In his hand is the l of every living thing and
13:14 and put my l in my hand.
24:22 God prolongs the l of the mighty by his power;
24:22 they rise up when they despair of l.
33: 4 and the breath of the Almighty gives me l.
33:28 and my l shall see the light.'
33:30 so that they may see the light of l.
36:14 and their l ends in shame.
38:26 on the desert, which is empty of human l,
Ps 6: 4 Turn, O LORD, save my l;
7: 5 trample my l to the ground,
16:11 You show me the path of l.
17:13 By your sword deliver my l from the wicked,
17:14 from mortals whose portion in l is in this world.
21: 4 He asked you for l; you gave it to him—
22:20 my l from the power of the dog!
23: 6 and mercy shall follow me all the days of my l, B
23: 6 in the house of the LORD my whole l long.
25:20 O guard my l, and deliver me;
26: 9 nor my l with the bloodthirsty,
27: 1 The LORD is the stronghold of my l;
27: 4 in the house of the LORD all the days of my l, B
30: 3 restored me to l from among those gone down to
31:10 For my l is spent with sorrow,
31:13 as they plot to take my l.
34:12 Which of you desires l, and covets many days
34:22 The LORD redeems the l of his servants;
35: 4 to shame and dishonor who seek after my l.
35: 7 without cause they dug a pit for my l.
35:17 from their ravages, my l from the lions!
36: 9 For with you is the fountain of l;
38:12 Those who seek my l lay their snares;
Ps 39: 4 let me know how fleeting my l is.
40:14 and confusion who seek to snatch away my l;
42: 8 a prayer to the God of my l.
49: 7 Truly, no ransom avails for one's l,
49: 8 For the ransom of l is costly,
54: 3 against me, the ruthless seek my l;
54: 4 the Lord is the upholder of my l.
56: 6 As they hoped to have my l,
56:13 so that I may walk before God in the light of l.
59: 3 Even now they lie in wait for my l;
61: 6 Prolong the l of the king;
63: 3 Because your steadfast love is better than l,
63: 9 to destroy my l shall go down into the depths of
64: 1 preserve my l from the dread enemy.
70: 2 be put to shame and confusion who seek my l.
71:10 and those who watch for my l consult together.
72:14 and violence he redeems their l;
74:19 do not forget the l of your poor forever.
80:18 give us l, and we will call on your name.
86: 2 Preserve my l, for I am devoted to you;
86:14 a band of ruffians seeks my l,
88: 3 and my l draws near to Sheol.
90:10 The days of our l are seventy years, B
91:16 With long l I will satisfy them,
94:21 They band together against the l of the righteous,
102:24 "do not take me away at the mid-point of my l,
103: 4 who redeems your l from the Pit,
109:20 of those who speak evil against my l.
116: 4 "O LORD, I pray, save my l!"
119:37 give me l in your ways.
119:40 in your righteousness give me l.
119:50 that your promise gives me l.
119:88 In your steadfast love spare my l,
119:93 for by them you have given me l.
119:107 give me l, O LORD, according to your word.
119:109 I hold my l in my hand continually,
119:149 O LORD, in your justice preserve my l.
119:154 give me l according to your promise.
119:156 give me l according to your justice.
119:159 preserve my l according to your steadfast love.
121: 7 from all evil; he will keep your l.
128: 5 the prosperity of Jerusalem all the days of your l. B
133: 3 the LORD ordained his blessing, l forevermore.
143: 3 crushing my l to the ground,
143:11 For your name's sake, O LORD, preserve my l.
146: 2 I will sing praises to my God all my l long.
Pr 1:19 it takes away the l of its possessors.
2:19 nor do they regain the paths of l.
3: 2 of l and abundant welfare they will give you.
3:16 Long l is in her right hand;
3:18 She is a tree of l to those who lay hold of her; D
3:22 be l for your soul and adornment for your neck.
4:10 that the years of your l may be many.
4:13 guard her, for she is your l.
4:22 For they are l to those who find them,
4:23 for from it flow the springs of l.
5: 6 She does not keep straight to the path of l;
5:11 and at the end of your l you will groan,
6:23 and the reproofs of discipline are the way of l, C
6:26 but the wife of another stalks a man's very l.
7:23 not knowing that it will cost him his l.
8:35 For whoever finds me finds l and obtains favor
9:11 and years will be added to your l.
10:11 The mouth of the righteous is a fountain of l,
10:16 The wage of the righteous leads to l,
10:17 Whoever heeds instruction is on the path to l,
10:27 The fear of the LORD prolongs l,
11:30 The fruit of the righteous is a tree of l, D
12:28 In the path of righteousness there is l,
13: 8 Wealth is a ransom for a person's l,
13:12 but a desire fulfilled is a tree of l. D
13:14 The teaching of the wise is a fountain of l,
14:27 The fear of the LORD is a fountain of l,
14:30 A tranquil mind gives l to the flesh,
15: 4 A gentle tongue is a tree of l, D
15:24 For the wise the path of l leads upward,
16:15 In the light of a king's face there is l,
16:22 Wisdom is a fountain of l to one who has it,
16:31 it is gained in a righteous l.
18:21 Death and l are in the power of the tongue
19:23 The fear of the LORD is l indeed;
20: 2 anyone who provokes him to anger forfeits l itself.
21:21 and kindness will find l and honor.
22: 4 and fear of the LORD is riches and honor and l.
22:23 and despoils of l those who despoil them.
28:16 but one who hates unjust gain will enjoy a long l.
29:10 and they seek the l of the upright.
29:24 To be a partner of a thief is to hate one's own l;
31:12 and not harm, all the days of her l. B
Ecc 2: 3 do under heaven during the few days of their l. B
2:17 So I hated l, because what is done under
5:18 under the sun the few days of the l God gives us; B
6:12 while they live the few days of their vain l, B
7:12 that wisdom gives l to the one who possesses it.
7:15 In my vain l I have seen everything;
7:15 and there are wicked people who prolong their l
8:15 the days of l that God gives them under the sun. B
9: 9 Enjoy l with the wife whom you love,
9: 9 the days of your vain l that are given you under B
9: 9 because that is your portion in l and in your toil
10:19 wine gladdens l, and money meets every need.
11:10 for youth and the dawn of l are vanity.
Isa 4: 3 everyone who has been recorded for l
38: 5 I will add fifteen years to your l.
38:12 like a weaver I have rolled up my l;
38:16 and in all these is the l of my spirit.
38:17 but you have held back my l from the pit

Isa 43: 4 nations in exchange for your l.
53:10 When you make his l an offering for sin,
Jer 4:30 Your lovers despise you; they seek your l.
8: 3 be preferred to l by all the remnant that remains
11:21 the people of Anathoth, who seek your l,
15:11 Surely I have intervened in your l for good,
18:20 Yet they have dug a pit for my l.
19: 7 and by the hand of those who seek their l.
19: 9 and those who seek their l afflict them.
20:13 the l of the needy from the hands of evildoers.
21: 8 before you the way of l and the way of death. C
22:25 give you into the hands of those who seek your l,
31:12 their l shall become like a watered garden,
38:16 or hand you over to these men who seek your l."
38:17 then your l shall be spared,
38:20 and your l shall be spared.
39:18 but you shall have your l as a prize of war,
40:14 of Nethaniah to take your l?"
40:15 Why should he take your l,
44:30 the hands of his enemies, those who seek his l,
44:30 his enemy who sought his l."
45: 5 but I will give you your l as a prize of war
46:26 I will hand them over to those who seek their l,
49:37 and before those who seek their l;
51:13 your end has come, the thread of your l is cut.
52:33 of his l he dined regularly at the king's table.
La 2:12 as their l is poured out on their mothers' bosom.
3:58 O Lord, you have redeemed my l.
4: 9 whose l drains away, deprived of the produce of
4:20 The LORD's anointed, the breath of our l, F
Eze 3:18 to save their l, those wicked persons shall die
3:19 but you will have saved your l.
3:21 and you will have saved your l.
18: 4 the l of the parent as well as the l of the child
18:27 lawful and right, they shall save their l.
33: 9 but you will have saved your l.
33:15 and walk in the statutes of l,
Da 12: 2 of the earth shall awake, some to everlasting l,
Jnh 1:14 do not let us perish on account of this man's l.
2: 6 yet you brought up my l from the Pit,
2: 7 As my l was ebbing away,
4: 3 And now, O LORD, please take my l from me,
Hab 2:10 you have forfeited your l.
Mal 2: 5 with him was a covenant of l and well-being,
Mt 2:20 those who were seeking the child's l are dead."
6:25 "Therefore I tell you, do not worry about your l,
6:25 Is not l more than food,
6:27 by worrying add a single hour to your span of l?
7:14 gate is narrow and the road is hard that leads to l,
10:39 Those who find their l will lose it,
10:39 those who lose their l for my sake will find it.
16:25 For those who want to save their l will lose it,
those who lose their l for my sake will find it.
16:26 if they gain the whole world but forfeit their l?
16:26 Or what will they give in return for their l?
18: 8 to enter l maimed or lame than to have two hands
18: 9 to enter l with one eye than to have two eyes and
19:16 what good deed must I do to have eternal l?" A
19:17 If you wish to enter into l,
19:29 and will inherit eternal l. A
20:28 and to give his l a ransom for many."
25:46 but the righteous into eternal l." A
Mk 3: 4 to save l or to kill?"
8:35 For those who want to save their l will lose it,
8:35 and those who lose their l for my sake,
8:36 to gain the whole world and forfeit their l?
8:37 Indeed, what can they give in return for their l?
9:43 for you to enter l maimed than to have two hands
9:45 for you to enter l lame than to have two feet and
10:17 what must I do to inherit eternal l?" A
10:30 and in the age to come eternal l. A
10:45 and to give his l a ransom for many."
Lk 6: 9 on the sabbath, to save l or to destroy it?"
8:14 by the cares and riches and pleasures of l,
9:24 For those who want to save their l will lose it,
9:24 those who lose their l for my sake will save it.
10:25 he said, "what must I do to inherit eternal l?" A
12:15 for one's l does not consist in the abundance
12:20 This very night your l is being demanded of you.
12:22 "Therefore I tell you, do not worry about your l,
12:23 For l is more than food,
12:25 by worrying add a single hour to your span of l?
14:26 yes, and even l itself, cannot be my disciple.
15:32 of yours was dead and has come to l;
17:33 Those who try to make their l secure will lose it,
17:33 but those who lose their l will keep it.
18:18 what must I do to inherit eternal l?" A
18:30 and in the age to come eternal l." A
21:34 and drunkenness and the worries of this l,
Jn 1: 4 in him was l, and the l was the light of all people.
3:15 that whoever believes in him may have eternal l. A
3:16 in him may not perish but may have eternal l. A
3:36 Whoever believes in the Son has eternal l; A
3:36 whoever disobeys the Son will not see l,
4:14 a spring of water gushing up to eternal l." A
4:36 and is gathering fruit for eternal l, A
5:21 as the Father raises the dead and gives them l,
5:21 so also the Son gives l to whomever he wishes.
5:24 and believes him who sent me has eternal l, A
5:24 but has passed from death to l.
5:26 For just as the Father has l in himself,
5:26 he has granted the Son also to have l in himself;
5:29 who have done good, to the resurrection of l,
5:39 that in them you have eternal l; A
5:40 Yet you refuse to come to me to have l.
6:27 but for the food that endures for eternal l, A
6:33 that which comes down from heaven and gives l
Jn 6:35 Jesus said to them, "I am the bread of l.
6:40 the Son and believe in him may have eternal l; A
6:47 I tell you, whoever believes has eternal l. A
6:48 I am the bread of l.
6:51 that I will give for the l of the world is my flesh."
6:53 you have no l in you.
6:54 and drink my blood have eternal l, A
6:63 It is the spirit that gives l; the flesh is useless.
6:63 words that I have spoken to you are spirit and l.
6:68 You have the words of eternal l. A
8:12 in darkness but will have the light of l."
10:10 I came that they may have l,
10:11 The good shepherd lays down his l for the sheep.
10:15 And I lay down my l for the sheep.
10:17 I lay down my l in order to take it up again.
10:28 I give them eternal l, and they will never perish. A
11:25 Jesus said to her, "I am the resurrection and the l.
12:25 Those who love their l lose it, and those who hate
their l in this world
12:25 in this world will keep it for eternal l. A
12:50 And I know that his commandment is eternal l. A
13:37 I will lay down my l for you."
13:38 "Will you lay down your l for me?
14: 6 "I am the way, and the truth, and the l.
15:13 to lay down one's l for one's friends.
17: 2 give eternal l to all whom you have given him. A
17: 3 And this is eternal l, that they may know you, A
20:31 through believing you may have l in his name.
Ac 2:28 You have made known to me the ways of l;
3:15 and you killed the Author of l,
5:20 the people the whole message about this l."
8:33 For his l is taken away from the earth."
11:18 to the Gentiles the repentance that leads to l."
13:46 judge yourselves to be unworthy of eternal l, A
13:48 for eternal l became believers. A
17:25 since he himself gives to all mortals l and breath
20:10 and said, "Do not be alarmed, for his l is in him."
20:24 But I do not count my l of any value to myself,
23: 1 up to this day I have lived my l with
26: 4 "All the Jews know my way of l from my youth, C
26: 4 a l spent from the beginning among my own
27:22 for there will be no loss of l among you,
Ro 2: 7 and immortality, he will give eternal l; A
4:17 who gives l to the dead and calls into existence
5:10 will we be saved by his l.
5:17 of righteousness exercise dominion in l through
5:18 of righteousness leads to justification and l
5:21 to eternal l through Jesus Christ our Lord. A
6: 4 so we too might walk in newness of l.
6:10 but the l he lives, he lives to God.
6:13 as those who have been brought from death to l,
6:22 The end is eternal l. A
6:23 gift of God is eternal l in Christ Jesus our Lord. A
7: 6 the old written code but in the new l of the Spirit.
7:10 the very commandment that promised l proved to
8: 2 of l in Christ Jesus has set you free from the law
8: 6 but to set the mind on the Spirit is l and peace.
8:10 the Spirit is l because of righteousness.
8:11 from the dead will give l to your mortal bodies
8:38 For I am convinced that neither death, nor l,
11: 3 I alone am left, and they are seeking my l."
11:15 what will their acceptance be but l from
16: 4 and who risked their necks for my l,
1Co 1:30 He is the source of your l in Christ Jesus,
3:22 or Apollos or Cephas or the world or l or death E
7:17 of you lead the l that the Lord has assigned,
7:28 those who marry will experience distress in this l,
15:19 If for this l only we have hoped in Christ,
15:36 What you sow does not come to l unless it dies.
2Co 1: 8 unbearably crushed that we despaired of l itself.
2:16 to the other a fragrance from l to l.
3: 6 for the letter kills, but the Spirit gives l.
4:10 l of Jesus may also be made visible in our bodies.
4:11 so that the l of Jesus may be made visible
4:12 So death is at work in us, but l in you.
5: 4 so that what is mortal may be swallowed up by l.
Gal 1:13 no doubt, of my earlier l in Judaism.
2:20 And the l I now live in the flesh I live by faith in
3:15 I give an example from daily l:
6: 8 you will reap eternal l from the Spirit. A
Eph 2:10 God prepared beforehand to be our way of l. C
4: 1 beg you to lead a l worthy of the calling
4:18 from the l of God because of their ignorance
4:22 to put away your former way of l, C
Php 1:20 whether by l or by death. E
1:27 live your l in a manner worthy of the gospel
2:16 of l that I can boast on the day of Christ that I did
2:30 risking his l to make up for those services
4: 3 whose names are in the book of l. G
Col 3: 3 and your l is hidden with Christ in God.
3: 4 When Christ who is your l is revealed,
3: 7 when you were living that l.
1Th 2:12 and pleading that you lead a l worthy of God,
1Ti 1:16 to believe in him for eternal l. A
2: 2 and peaceable l in all godliness and dignity.
4: 8 promise for both the present l and the l to come.
6:12 take hold of the eternal l, A
6:13 In the presence of God, who gives l to all things,
6:19 that they may take hold of the l that really is l.
2Ti 1: 1 sake of the promise of l that is in Christ Jesus,
1:10 and brought l and immortality to light through
3:10 my conduct, my aim in l, my faith, my patience,
3:12 all who want to live a godly l in Christ Jesus will
Tit 1: 2 of eternal l that God, who never lies, promised A
3: 7 according to the hope of eternal l. A
Heb 7: 3 having neither beginning of days nor end of l,
7:16 but through the power of an indestructible l.
Heb 11:22 By faith Joseph, at the end of his l,
13: 7 consider the outcome of their way of l, C
Jas 1:11 in the midst of a busy l, they will wither away.
1:12 the test and will receive the crown of l that
3:13 Show by your good l that your works are done
4:14 What is your l? For you are a mist
1Pe 3: 7 in your l together, paying honor to the woman as
3: 7 they too are also heirs of the gracious gift of l—
3:10 "Those who desire l and desire to see good days,
4: 2 of your earthly l no longer by human desires but
2Pe 1: 3 for l and godliness, through the knowledge
1Jn 1: 1 touched with our hands, concerning the word of l
1: 2 this l was revealed, and we have seen it
1: 2 and declare to you the eternal l that was with A
2:25 And this is what he has promised us, eternal l. A
3:14 We know that we have passed from death to l
3:15 that murderers do not have eternal l abiding A
3:16 that he laid down his l for us—
5:11 God gave us eternal l, and this life is in his Son. A
5:11 God gave us eternal life, and this l is in his Son.
5:12 Whoever has the Son has l; whoever does not
have the Son of God does not have l.
5:13 so that you may know that you have eternal l. A
5:16 you will ask, and God will give l to such a one—
5:20 He is the true God and eternal l. A
Jude 1:21 of our Lord Jesus Christ that leads to eternal l. A
Rev 2: 7 from the tree of l that is in the paradise of God. D
2: 8 who was dead and came to l:
2:10 and I will give you the crown of l.
3: 5 I will not blot your name out of the book of l; G
7:17 he will guide them to springs of the water of l,
11:11 the breath of l from God entered them, F
12:11 they did not cling to l even in the face of death.
13: 8 the foundation of the world in the book of l G
17: 8 the book of l from the foundation of the world, G
20: 4 came to l and reigned with Christ a thousand years.
20: 5 (The rest of the dead did not come to l until
20:12 Also another book was opened, the book of l. G
20:15 name was not found written in the book of l G
21: 6 as a gift from the spring of the water of l.
21:27 who are written in the Lamb's book of l. G
22: 1 the angel showed me the river of the water of l,
22: 2 of the river is the tree of l with its twelve kinds D
22:14 the right to the tree of l and may enter the city D
22:17 Let anyone who wishes take the water of l as
22:19 that person's share in the tree of l and in D
Tob 1: 3 of truth and righteousness all the days of my l. B
3: 6 for me to die than to see so much distress in my l
3:15 if it is not pleasing to you, O Lord, to take my l,
4: 3 and do not abandon her all the days of her l. B
4: 5 Live uprightly all the days of your l, B
5:20 For the l that is given to us by the Lord is enough
6:15 and mother's l down to their grave, grieving
10:12 do nothing to grieve her all the days of your l. B
10:13 by the Lord to honor you all the days of my l." B
12: 9 Those who give alms will enjoy a full l,
Jdt 8:29 but from the beginning of your l all
10:15 "You have saved your l by hurrying down
11: 7 By the l of Nebuchadnezzar,
12:18 because today is the greatest day in my whole l."
13:20 because you risked your own l
16:21 For the rest of her l she was honored throughout
16:22 days of her l after her husband Manasseh died B
AdE 2:20 So Esther did not change her mode of l.
7: 3 let my l be granted me at my petition,
7: 7 Haman began to beg for his l from the queen,
10: 3 His way of l was such as to make him beloved C
13: 5 perversely following a strange manner of l
16:12 to deprive us of our kingdom and our l,
Wis 1:12 Do not invite death by the error of your l,
2: 1 "Short and sorrowful is our l,
2: 1 and there is no remedy when a l comes to its end,
2: 4 our l will pass away like the traces of a cloud,
2:15 because his manner of l is unlike that of others,
2:17 let us test what will happen at the end of his l;
4: 9 and a blameless l is ripe old age.
7: 6 there is for all one entrance into l,
8: 5 If riches are a desirable possession in l,
8: 7 in l is more profitable for mortals than these.
8:16 and l with her has no pain, but gladness and joy.
12:23 those who lived unrighteously, in a l of folly,
13:18 for l he prays to a thing that is dead;
14:12 the invention of them was the corruption of l;
15: 9 to die or that their l is brief, but they compete
15:12 and l a festival held for profit,
15:17 since they have l, but the idols never had.
16:13 For you have power over l and death; E
Sir 1:12 and gives gladness and joy and long l.
1:20 and her branches are long l.
3: 6 Those who respect their father will have long l,
4:12 Whoever loves her loves l,
7:36 In all you do, remember the end of your l,
9:13 make no misstep, or they may rob you of your l.
10: 9 Even in l the human body decays.
11:14 Good things and bad, l and death, E
11:27 at the close of one's l one's deeds are revealed.
15:17 Before each person are l and death, E
17:11 and allotted to them the law of l.
18: 9 in their l is great if they reach one hundred years.
20:22 One may lose his l through shame,
22:11 but the l of the fool is worse than death.
23: 1 O Lord, Father and Master of my l,
23: 4 O Lord, Father and God of my l,
25: 2 and I loathe their manner of l:
28: 6 Remember the end of your l,
29:15 for he has given his l for you.
29:21 The necessities of l are water, bread,

Sir 29:22 Better is the l of the poor
29:24 It is a miserable l to go from house to house;
30: 5 in his l he looked upon with joy and at death,
30:17 Death is better than a l of misery,
30:22 A joyful heart is l itself,
30:22 and rejoicing lengthens one's l span.
30:24 Jealousy and anger shorten l,
31:27 Wine is very l to human beings if taken in
31:27 What is l to one who is without wine?
33:14 and l the opposite of death; E
33:24 At the time when you end the days of your l, B
33:31 for you will need him as you need your l.
34:20 he gives health and l and blessing.
34:25 The bread of the needy is the l of the poor;
37:18 good and evil, l and death; E
37:25 The days of a person's l are numbered, B
37:31 but the one who guards against it prolongs his l.
38:14 for the sake of preserving l.
38:19 but the l of the poor weighs down the heart.
39:26 of human l are water and fire and iron and salt
40:18 Wealth and wages make l sweet,
40:28 My child, do not lead the l of a beggar;
40:29 one's way of l cannot be considered a life. C
40:29 one's way of life cannot be considered a l.
41: 4 Whether l lasts for ten years or a hundred or
41:13 The days of a good l are numbered, B
45: 5 the law of l and knowledge,
46:12 May their bones send forth new l from
48:14 In his l he did wonders,
48:23 and he prolonged the l of the king.
49:10 of the Twelve Prophets send forth new l from
50: 1 who in his l repaired the house,
51: 3 from the hand of those seeking my l,
51: 6 and my l was on the brink of Hades below.
Bar 1:11 for the l of King Nebuchadnezzar of Babylon,
1:11 and for the l of his son Belshazzar,
3: 9 Hear the commandments of l, O Israel;
3:14 and l, where there is light for the eyes,
1Mc 3:12 and used it in battle the rest of his l.
6:44 So he gave his l to save his people and to win
13: 5 from me to spare my l in any time of distress,
2Mc 3:31 to grant l to one who was lying quite
3:33 for his sake the Lord has granted you your l.
3:35 and made very great vows to the Savior of his l,
4:10 over to the Greek way of l. C
6:19 welcoming death with honor rather than l
6:20 even for the natural love of l.
6:23 and his excellent l even from childhood,
6:24 "Such pretense is not worthy of our time of l,"
6:27 Therefore, by bravely giving up my l now,
7: 9 you dismiss us from this present l,
7: 9 up to an everlasting renewal of l,
7:14 But for you there will be no resurrection to l!"
7:22 It was not I who gave you l and breath,
7:23 in his mercy give l and breath back to you again,
7:27 and brought you up to this point in your l,
7:36 a brief suffering have drunk of ever-flowing l,
7:37 give up body and l for the laws of our ancestors,
8:17 the overthrow of their ancestral way of l. C
9:28 came to the end of his l by a most pitiable fate,
10:13 he took poison and ended his l.
14:25 settled down, and shared the common l.
14:38 and he had most zealously risked body and l
14:46 upon the Lord of l and spirit to give them back
Man 1:15 I will praise you continually all the days of my l. B
3Mc 2:23 and fearing that he would lose his l,
2:32 in exchange for l they confidently attempted
3: 5 of l with the good deeds of upright people,
3:23 in accordance with their infamous way of l, C
4: 4 reflected on the uncertainty of l and shed tears at
4: 6 to share married l exchanged joy for wailing,
5:32 In fact you would have been deprived of l instead
5:49 they thought that this was their last moment of l,
6: 1 and throughout his l had been adorned
6:12 the lawless are being deprived of l in the manner
6:24 and l by secretly devising acts of no advantage to
2Es 2:12 The tree of l shall give them fragrant perfume, D
3: 5 and you breathed into him the breath of l, F
4:24 and our l is like a mist,
4:52 but I was not sent to tell you concerning your l,
5:45 to your servant that you will certainly give l
7:*48* the paths of perdition and removed us far from l—
7:*92* it might not lead them astray from l into death. E
7:*94* that throughout their l they kept the law
7:*98* to see the face of him whom they served in l and
7:*122* [52] a pure l, but we have walked in
7:*129* [59] 'Choose l for yourself, so that you may live!'
7:*137* [67] with those who inhabit it would not have l—
7:*138* [68] ten-thousandth of humankind could have l;
8: 8 And because you give l to the body that is
8:52 paradise is opened, the tree of l is planted, D
8:60 and have been ungrateful to him who prepared l
13:55 for you have devoted your l to wisdom,
14:13 And now renounce the l that is corruptible,
14:30 and received the law of l,
16:61 gave each person breath and l and understanding
4Mc 1:15 that with sound logic prefers the l of wisdom.
2: 8 as soon as one adopts a way of l in accordance C
4: 1 Onias, who then held the high priesthood for l.
4:19 the nation's way of l and altered its form C
5:36 nor my long l lived lawfully.
6:18 in accordance with law the reputation of such a l,
6:29 and take my l in exchange for theirs."
7: 4 his sacred l was consumed by tortures and racks,
7: 7 with the law and philosopher of divine l!
7:15 and of venerable gray hair and of law-abiding l,
8: 7 the ancestral tradition of your national l.
4Mc 8: 8 by adopting the Greek way of l and by changing C
8:23 from this most pleasant l and deprive ourselves
9:25 the saintly youth broke the thread of l.
10:15 and by the everlasting l of the pious,
12:18 both in this present l and when you are dead."
12:19 into the braziers and so ended his l.
13:20 from the same blood and through the same l,
15: 3 the religion that preserves them for eternal l A
16:18 a share in the world and have enjoyed l,
17: 9 wished to destroy the way of l of the Hebrews. C
17:12 The prize was immortality in endless l.
17:18 now stand before the divine throne and live the l
18: 9 who lived out his l with good children,
18:16 'There is a tree of l for those who do his will.' D
18:19 this is your l and the length of your days.' "

LIFE'S (2) [LIVE]

Ecc 6: 3 if he does not enjoy l good things,
Wis 13:11 a useful vessel that serves l needs,

LIFE-GIVING‡ (2) [GIVE, LIVE]

1Co 15:45 the last Adam became a l spirit.
Sir 21:13 and their counsel like a l spring.

LIFE-SAVING (1) [LIVE, SAVE]

Sir 6:16 Faithful friends are l medicine;

LIFEBLOOD (3) [BLOOD, LIVE]

Ge 9: 5 For your own l I will surely require a reckoning:
Isa 63: 6 and I poured out their l on the earth."
Jer 2:34 on your skirts is found the l of the innocent poor,

LIFELESS (6) [LIVE]

1Co 14: 7 with l instruments that produce sound,
Wis 13:17 he is not ashamed to address a l thing.
14:29 in l idols they swear wicked oaths and expect
15: 5 so that they desire the l form of a dead image.
2Es 3: 5 and it gave you Adam, a l body?
6:48 The dumb and l water produced living creatures,

LIFELIKE (1) [LIVE]

Sir 38:27 they set their heart on painting a l image,

LIFETIME (14) [LIVE]

Nu 3: 4 Eleazar and Ithamar served as priests in the l
2Sa 18:18 in his l had taken and set up for himself a pillar
1Ki 4:25 During Solomon's l Judah and Israel lived
11:12 of your father David I will not do it in your l;
Ps 30: 5 his anger is but for a moment; his favor is for a l.
39: 5 and my l is as nothing in your sight.
49:18 Though in their l they count themselves happy
Isa 23:15 be forgotten for seventy years, the l of one king.
65:20 or an old person who does not live out a l;
Lk 16:25 that during your l you received your good things,
Ro 7: 1 on a person only during that person's l?
Jdt 16:25 among the Israelites during the l of Judith,
Sir 48:12 Never in his l did he tremble before any ruler,
2Es 9:10 as many as did not acknowledge me in their l,

LIFT‡ (87) [LIFTED, LIFTING, LIFTS, UPLIFTED]

Ge 21:18 l up the boy and hold him fast with your hand,
40:13 within three days Pharaoh will l up your head
40:19 within three days Pharaoh will l up your head—
41:44 and without your consent no one shall l up hand
Ex 14:16 But you l up your staff,
Nu 6:26 the LORD l up his countenance upon you,
Dt 22: 4 you shall help to l it up.
32:40 For I l up my hand to heaven, and swear:
2Sa 1:14 "Were you not afraid to l your hand to destroy
2Ki 9:25 Jehu said to his aide Bidkar, "L him out,
9:26 l him out and throw him on the plot of ground,
19: 4 l up your prayer for the remnant that is left."
Ezr 9: 6 I am too ashamed and embarrassed to l my face
Job 10:15 If I am righteous, I cannot l up my head,
11:15 then you will l up your face without blemish;
22:26 and l up your face to God.
30:22 You l me up on the wind,
38:34 "Can you l up your voice to the clouds,
Ps 7: 6 l yourself up against the fury of my enemies;
10:12 Rise up, O LORD; O God, l up your hand;
24: 4 who do not l up their souls to what is false,
24: 7 L up your heads, O gates!
24: 9 L up your heads, O gates!
25: 1 To you, O LORD, I l up my soul.
28: 2 I l up my hands toward your most holy sanctuary.
63: 4 I will l up my hands and call on your name.
68: 4 l up a song to him who rides upon the clouds—
75: 4 and to the wicked, "Do not l up your horn;
75: 5 do not l up your horn on high,
76: 5 none of the troops was able to l a hand.
86: 4 for to you, O Lord, I l up my soul.
93: 3 the floods l up their roaring.
110: 7 therefore he will l up his head.
116:13 I will l up the cup of salvation and call on
121: 1 I l up my eyes to the hills—
123: 1 To you I l up my eyes,
134: 2 L up your hands to the holy place,
139:20 and l themselves up against you for evil!
140: 9 Those who surround me l up their heads;
143: 8 for to you I l up my soul.
Pr 30:13 how lofty are their eyes, how high their eyelids l!
Ecc 4:10 For if they fall, one will l up the other;
Isa 2: 4 nation shall not l up sword against nation,
10:15 or as if a staff should l the one who is not wood!
10:24 when they beat you with a rod and l up their staff
10:26 and he will l it as he did in Egypt.
24:14 They l up their voices, they sing for joy;
33:10 "now I will l myself up; now I will be exalted.
37: 4 l up your prayer for the remnant that is left."
40: 9 l up your voice with strength, O Jerusalem, herald of good tidings, l it up,
40:26 L up your eyes on high and see:
42: 2 He will not cry or l up his voice,
42:11 Let the desert and its towns l up their voice,
46: 7 They l it to their shoulders, they carry it,
49:18 L up your eyes all around and see;
49:22 I will soon l up my hand to the nations,
51: 6 L up your eyes to the heavens,
52: 8 Your sentinels l up their voices,
58: 1 L up your voice like a trumpet!
60: 4 L up your eyes and look around;
62:10 clear it of stones, l up an ensign over the peoples.
Jer 11:14 or l up a cry or prayer on their behalf,
13:20 L up your eyes and see those who come from
13:26 I myself will l up your skirts over your face,
22:20 and cry out, and l up your voice in Bashan;
23:39 I will surely l you up and cast you away
La 2:19 L your hands to him for the lives of your children,
3:41 Let us l up our hearts as well as our hands to God
Eze 8: 5 l up your eyes now in the direction of the north."
12: 6 In their sight you shall l the baggage
12:12 the prince who is among them shall l his baggage
17:14 the kingdom might be humble and not l itself up,
18: 6 or l up his eyes to the idols of the house of Israel,
18:15 or l up his eyes to the idols of the house of Israel,
33:25 and l up your eyes to your idols, and shed blood;
Da 11:14 among your own people shall l themselves up
Hos 11: 4 to them like those who l infants to their cheeks.
Mic 4: 3 nation shall not l up sword against nation,
Na 3: 5 and will l up your skirts over your face;
Zec 12: 3 all who l it shall grievously hurt themselves.
Mt 12:11 will you not lay hold of it and l it out?
23: 4 but they themselves are unwilling to l a finger
Lk 11:46 you yourselves do not l a finger to ease them.
Heb 12:12 Therefore l your drooping hands
Sir 13: 2 Do not l a weight too heavy for you,
36: 3 L up your hand against foreign nations

LIFTED (84) [LIFT]

Ge 21:16 she l up her voice and wept.
27:38 And Esau l up his voice and wept.
40:20 and l up the head of the chief cupbearer and
Ex 7:20 In the sight of Pharaoh and of his officials he l up
10:19 which l the locusts and drove them into
16:14 When the layer of dew l,
Lev 9:22 Aaron l his hands toward the people
Nu 9:17 Whenever the cloud l from over the tent,
9:21 and when the cloud l in the morning,
9:21 when the cloud l they would set out.
9:22 but when it l they would set out.
10:11 cloud l from over the tabernacle of the covenant.
20:11 Then Moses l up his hand and struck
Jdg 2: 4 the people l up their voices and wept.
8:28 and they l up their heads no more.
21: 2 and they l up their voices and wept bitterly.
1Sa 24:16 Saul l up his voice and wept.
2Sa 3:32 The king l up his voice and wept at the grave
20:21 has l up his hand against King David;
2Ki 14:10 and your heart has l you up.
19:22 and haughtily l your eyes?
2Ch 25:19 and your heart has l you up in boastfulness.
Job 5:11 and those who mourn are l to safety.
Ps 24: 7 and be l up, O ancient doors!
24: 9 and be l up, O ancient doors!
27: 6 my head is l up above my enemies all around me,
41: 9 who ate of my bread, has l the heel against me.
93: 3 The floods have l up, O LORD, the floods have l up
102:10 for you have l me up and thrown me aside.
107:25 which l up the waves of the sea.
131: 1 not l up, my eyes are not raised too high;
Isa 2:12 against all that is l up and high;
2:13 against all the cedars of Lebanon, lofty and l up;
26:11 O LORD, your hand is l up,
37:23 and haughtily l your eyes?
40: 4 Every valley shall be l up,
52:13 he shall be exalted and l up,
63: 9 he l them up and carried them all the days of old.
Jer 12: 8 she has l up her voice against me—
13:22 of your iniquity that your skirts are l up,
51: 9 up to heaven and has been l up even to the skies.
Eze 3:12 Then the spirit l me up, and as the glory of
3:14 The spirit l me up and bore me away;
8: 3 and the spirit l me up between earth and heaven,
8: 5 So I l up my eyes toward the north, and there,
10:16 and when the cherubim l up their wings to rise
10:19 The cherubim l up their wings and rose up from
11: 1 The spirit l me up and brought me to
11:22 Then the cherubim l up their wings,
11:24 The spirit l me up and brought me in a vision by
43: 5 the spirit l me up, and brought me into
Da 3:22 the raging flames killed the men who l Shadrach,
4:34 I, Nebuchadnezzar, l my eyes to heaven,
5:20 But when his heart was l up
7: 4 and it was l up from the ground and made
Mic 5: 9 Your hand shall be l up over your adversaries,
Zec 1:21 the nations that l up their horns against the land
5: 7 Then a leaden cover was l,
5: 9 and they l up the basket between earth and sky.

Mt 21:21 'Be l up and thrown into the sea,' it will be done.
Mk 1:31 He came and took her by the hand and l her up.
9:27 But Jesus took him by the hand and l him up,
Lk 1:52 down the powerful from their thrones, and l up
Jn 3:14 just as Moses l up the serpent in the wilderness,
3:14 so must the Son of Man be l up,
8:28 Jesus said, "When you have l up the Son of Man,
12:32 And I, when I am l up from the earth,
12:34 can you say that the Son of Man must be l up?
13:18 one who ate my bread has l his heel against me.'
Ac 1: 9 as they were watching, he was l up,
Jdt 11: 2 I would never have l my spear against them.
16:11 they l up their voices,
Sir 46: 2 when he l his hands and brandished his sword
46:20 and l up his voice from the ground in prophecy,
1Mc 1: 3 he was exalted, and his heart was l up.
16:13 His heart was l up; he determined to get
1Es 4:58 he l up his face to heaven toward Jerusalem,
8:86 l the burden of our sins
9:47 They l up their hands, and fell to the ground
3Mc 6: 5 by the spear and was l up against your holy city,
2Es 6: 4 and before the heights of the air were l up,
13: 9 he neither l his hand nor held a spear
4Mc 6:26 he l up his eyes to God and said,

LIFTING (8) [LIFT]

Ge 37:28 they drew Joseph up, l him out of the pit,
Ne 8: 6 "Amen, Amen," l up their hands.
Ps 75: 6 the west and not from the wilderness comes l up;
75: 7 putting down one and l up another.
141: 2 and the l up of my hands as an evening sacrifice.
Lk 24:50 and, l up his hands, he blessed them.
1Ti 2: 8 l up holy hands without anger or argument;
AdE 15: 7 L his face, flushed with splendor,

LIFTS (12) [LIFT]

1Sa 2: 8 he l the needy from the ash heap,
Job 27:21 The east wind l them up and they are gone;
Ps 3: 3 my glory, and the one who l up my head.
9:13 the one who l me up from the gates of death,
113: 7 and l the needy from the ash heap,
146: 8 The LORD l up those who are bowed down;
147: 6 The LORD l up the downtrodden;
Isa 10:15 As if a rod should raise the one who l it up,
Eze 18:12 l up his eyes to the idols, commits abomination,
Sir 11: 1 The wisdom of the humble l their heads high,
11:12 he l them out of their lowly condition
34:20 He l up the soul and makes the eyes sparkle;

LIGAMENT (1) [LIGAMENTS]

Eph 4:16 knit together by every l with which it is equipped,

LIGAMENTS (2) [LIGAMENT]

Col 2:19 nourished and held together by its l and sinews,
4Mc 9:21 the l joining his bones were already severed,

LIGHT‡ (295) [DAYLIGHT, ENLIGHTEN, ENLIGHTENED, ENLIGHTENING, ENLIGHTENMENT, ENLIGHTENS, FIRELIGHT, LIGHTED, LIGHTEN, LIGHTENED, LIGHTENS, LIGHTER, LIGHTERS, LIGHTING, LIGHTLY, LIGHTS, LIT]

Ge 1: 3 God said, "Let there be l"; and there was l.
1: 4 And God saw that the l was good;
1: 4 and God separated the l from the darkness.
1: 5 God called the l Day,
1:15 in the dome of the sky to give l upon the earth."
1:16 the greater l to rule the day and the lesser l to rule the night—
1:17 in the dome of the sky to give l upon the earth,
1:18 and to separate the l from the darkness.
44: 3 As soon as the morning was l,
Ex 10:23 but all the Israelites had l where they lived.
13:21 and in a pillar of fire by night, to give them l,
25:37 and the lamps shall be set up so as to give l on
27:20 to bring you pure oil of beaten olives for the l,
35: 8 oil for the l, spices for the anointing oil and for
35:14 also for the l, with its utensils and its lamps,
35:14 and the oil for the l;
35:28 and spices and oil for the l,
39:37 and the oil for the l;
Lev 24: 2 that a l may be kept burning regularly.
Nu 4: 9 and cover the lampstand for the l, with its lamps,
4:16 the priest shall have charge of the oil for the l,
8: 2 the lamps, the seven lamps shall give l in front of
8: 3 up its lamps to give l in front of the lampstand,
Jdg 9:38 Are not these the troops you made l of?
16: 2 thinking, "Let us wait until the l of the morning;
19:26 where her master was, until it was l.
1Sa 14:36 by night and despoil them until the morning l;
25:36 so she told him nothing at all until the morning l.
29:10 and leave as soon as you have l."
2Sa 17:12 we shall l on him as the dew falls on the ground;
23: 4 is like the l of morning,
1Ki 16:31 if it had been a l thing for him to walk in the sins
2Ki 7: 9 if we are silent and wait until the morning l,
Ne 9:12 to give them l on the way
9:19 nor the pillar of fire by night that gave them l on
Est 8:16 the Jews there was l and gladness, joy and honor.
Job 3: 4 May God above not seek it, or l shine on it.
3: 9 let it hope for l, but have none;
Job 3:16 like an infant that never sees the l?
3:20 "Why is l given to one in misery,
3:23 Why is l given to one who cannot see the way,
10:22 where l is like darkness."
12:22 and brings deep darkness to l.
12:25 They grope in the dark without l;
17:12 'The l,' they say, 'is near to the darkness.'
18: 5 "Surely the l of the wicked is put out,
18: 6 The l is dark in their tent,
18:18 They are thrust from l into darkness,
22:28 and l will shine on your ways.
24:13 "There are those who rebel against the l,
24:16 they do not know the l.
25: 3 Upon whom does his l not arise?
26:10 at the boundary between l and darkness.
28:11 hidden things they bring to l.
29: 3 and by his l I walked through darkness;
29:24 the l of my countenance they did not extinguish.
30:26 and when I waited for l, darkness came.
33:28 and my life shall see the l.'
33:30 so that they may see the l of life.
37:21 no one can look on the l when it is bright in
38:15 L is withheld from the wicked,
38:19 "Where is the way to the dwelling of l,
38:24 the way to the place where the l is distributed,
41:18 Its sneezes flash forth l, and its eyes are like
Ps 4: 6 Let the l of your face shine on us, O LORD!"
13: 3 Give l to my eyes, or I will sleep the sleep
18:28 It is you who l my lamp;
27: 1 The LORD is my l and my salvation;
36: 9 in your l we see l.
37: 6 He will make your vindication shine like the l,
38:10 as for the l of my eyes—
43: 3 O send out your l and your truth;
44: 3 and your arm, and the l of your countenance,
49:19 who will never again see the l.
56:13 so that I may walk before God in the l of life.
78:14 and all night long with a fiery l.
89:15 O LORD, in the l of your countenance;
90: 8 our secret sins in the l of your countenance.
97: 4 His lightnings l up the world;
97:11 L dawns for the righteous,
104: 2 wrapped in l as with a garment.
105:39 and fire to give l by night.
112: 4 They rise in the darkness as a l for the upright;
118:27 The LORD is God, and he has given us l.
119:105 Your word is a lamp to my feet and a l
119:130 The unfolding of your words gives l;
139:11 and the l around me become night,"
139:12 for darkness is as l to you.
Pr 4:18 the path of the righteous is like the l of dawn,
6:23 the commandment is a lamp and the teaching a l,
13: 9 The l of the righteous rejoices,
15:30 The l of the eyes rejoices the heart,
16:15 In the l of a king's face there is life,
23: 5 When your eyes l upon it, it is gone;
29:13 the LORD gives l to the eyes of both.
Ecc 2:13 that wisdom excels folly as l excels darkness.
11: 7 L is sweet, and it is pleasant for the eyes to see
12: 2 the l and the moon and the stars are darkened and
Isa 2: 5 come, let us walk in the l of the LORD!
5:20 who put darkness for l and l for darkness,
5:30 and the l grows dark with clouds.
9: 2 in darkness have seen a great l;
9: 2 land of deep darkness—on them l has shined.
10:17 The l of Israel will become a fire,
13:10 and their constellations will not give their l;
13:10 and the moon will not shed its l.
30:26 the l of the moon will be like the l of the sun,
30:26 and the l of the sun will be sevenfold,
30:26 like the l of seven days,
42: 6 I have given you as a covenant to the people, a l
42:16 I will turn the darkness before them into l,
45: 7 I form l and create darkness,
49: 6 "It is too l a thing that you should be my servant
49: 6 I will give you as a l to the nations,
50:10 who walks in darkness and has no l,
51: 4 and my justice for a l to the peoples.
53:11 Out of his anguish he shall see l;
58: 8 Then your l shall break forth like the dawn,
58:10 then your l shall rise in the darkness
59: 9 not reach us; we wait for l,
60: 1 Arise, shine; for your l has come,
60: 3 Nations shall come to your l,
60:19 The sun shall no longer be your l by day, nor for brightness shall the moon give l to you by night; but the LORD will be your everlasting l,
60:20 for the LORD will be your everlasting l,
Jer 4:23 and to the heavens, and they had no l.
13:16 while you look for l, he turns it into gloom
25:10 the sound of the millstones and the l of the lamp.
31:35 the sun for l by day and the fixed order of the moon and the stars for l by night,
La 3: 2 and brought me into darkness without any l;
Eze 32: 7 and the moon shall not give its l.
Da 2:22 he knows what is in the darkness, and l dwells
Hos 6: 5 and my judgment goes forth as the l.
Am 5:18 of the LORD? It is darkness, not l;
5:20 Is not the day of the LORD darkness, not l,
Mic 7: 8 I sit in darkness, the LORD will be a l to me.
7: 9 He will bring me out to the l;
Hab 3:11 at the l of your arrows speeding by,
Zec 14: 7 for at evening time there shall be l.
Mt 4:16 people who sat in darkness have seen a great l,
4:16 in the region and shadow of death l has dawned."
5:14 "You are the l of the world.
5:15 and it gives l to all in the house.
Mt 5:16 In the same way, let your l shine before others,
6:22 your whole body will be full of l;
6:23 l in you is darkness, how great is the darkness!
10:27 What I say to you in the dark, tell in the l;
11:30 For my yoke is easy, and my burden is l."
22: 5 But they made l of it and went away,
24:29 and the moon will not give its l;
Mk 4:22 nor is anything secret, except to come to l.
13:24 and the moon will not give its l,
Lk 1:79 to give l to those who sit in darkness and in
2:32 a l for revelation to the Gentiles and for glory
8:16 so that those who enter may see the l.
8:17 that will not become known and come to l.
11:33 so that those who enter may see the l.
11:34 your eye is healthy, your whole body is full of l;
11:35 consider whether the l in you is not darkness.
11:36 If then your whole body is full of l,
11:36 be as full of l as when a lamp gives you l
12: 3 you have said in the dark will be heard in the l,
12:48 deserved a beating will receive a l beating.
15: 8 if she loses one of them, does not l a lamp,
16: 8 with their own generation than are the children of l.
23:45 while the sun's l failed;
Jn 1: 4 and the life was the l of all people.
1: 5 The l shines in the darkness,
1: 7 He came as a witness to testify to the l,
1: 8 was not the l, but he came to testify to the l.
1: 9 The true l, which enlightens everyone,
3:19 that the l has come into the world, and people loved darkness rather than l
3:20 all who do evil hate the l and do not come to the l,
3:21 But those who do what is true come to the l,
5:35 you were willing to rejoice for a while in his l.
8:12 saying, "I am the l of the world.
8:12 never walk in darkness but will have the l of life."
9: 5 I am the l of the world."
11: 9 because they see the l of this world.
11:10 because the l is not in them."
12:35 "The l is with you for a little longer.
12:35 Walk while you have the l,
12:36 While you have the l, believe in the l, so that you may become children of l."
12:46 I have come as l into the world,
Ac 9: 3 suddenly a l from heaven flashed around him.
12: 7 an angel of the Lord appeared and a l shone in
13:47 saying, 'I have set you to be a l for the Gentiles,
22: 6 about noon a great l from heaven suddenly shone
22: 9 Now those who were with me saw the l but did
22:11 not see because of the brightness of that l,
26:13 I saw a l from heaven, brighter than the sun,
26:18 from darkness to l and from the power of Satan
26:23 he would proclaim l both to our people and to
Ro 2:19 a l to those who are in darkness,
13:12 the works of darkness and put on the armor of l;
1Co 4: 5 who will bring to l the things now hidden
2Co 4: 4 to keep them from seeing the l of the gospel of
4: 6 "Let l shine out of darkness,"
4: 6 in our hearts to give the l of the knowledge of
6:14 what fellowship is there between l and darkness?
11:14 Even Satan disguises himself as an angel of l.
Eph 5: 8 but now in the Lord you are l.
5: 8 Live as children of l—
5: 9 for the fruit of the l is found in all that is good
5:13 but everything exposed by the l becomes visible,
5:14 for everything that becomes visible is l.
Col 1:12 to share in the inheritance of the saints in the l.
1Th 5: 5 you are all children of l and children of the day;
1Ti 6:16 in unapproachable l, whom no one has ever seen
2Ti 1:10 and brought life and immortality to l through
1Pe 2: 9 of darkness into his marvelous l.
1Jn 1: 5 God is l and in him there is no darkness at all.
1: 7 if we walk in the l as he himself is in the l,
2: 8 and the true l is already shining.
2: 9 Whoever says, "I am in the l,"
2:10 Whoever loves a brother or sister lives in the l,
Rev 8:12 so that a third of their l was darkened;
18:23 and the l of a lamp will shine in you no more;
21:23 for the glory of God is its l,
21:24 The nations will walk by its l,
22: 5 they need no l of lamp or sun, for the Lord God will be their l,
Tob 3:17 so that he might see God's l with his eyes;
5:10 I cannot see the l of heaven,
5:10 in darkness like the dead who no longer see the l.
10: 5 my child, the l of my eyes,
11: 8 and your father will regain his sight and see the l."
11:14 "I see you, my son, the l of my eyes!"
13:11 A bright l will shine to all the ends of the earth;
14:10 Ahikar came out into the l,
Jdt 13:13 Then they lit a fire to give l,
AdE 8:16 And the Jews had l and gladness
10: 6 and there was l and sun and abundant water—
11:11 l came, and the sun rose,
Wis 5: 1 and those who make l of their labors.
5: 6 and the l of righteousness did not shine on us,
5:11 the l air, lashed by the beat of its pinions
5:14 and like a l frost driven away by a storm;
7:10 and I chose to have her rather than l,
7:26 For she is a reflection of eternal l,
7:29 Compared with the l she is found to be superior,
16:28 and must pray to you at the dawning of the l;
17: 5 And no power of fire was able to give l,
17:20 the whole world was illumined with brilliant l,
18: 1 But for your holy ones there was very great l.
18: 4 to be deprived of l and imprisoned in darkness,
18: 4 through whom the imperishable l of the law was
Sir 3:25 Without eyes there is no l;

Sir 22:11 Weep for the dead, for he has left the l behind;
32:16 and they will kindle righteous deeds like a l.
42:16 The sun looks down on everything with its l,
43: 7 a l that wanes when it completes its course.
Bar 1:12 The Lord will give us strength, and l to our eyes;
3:14 and life, where there is l for the eyes, and peace.
3:20 Later generations have seen the l of day,
3:33 the one who sends forth the l, and it goes;
4: 2 walk toward the shining of her l.
5: 9 in the l of his glory,
LtJ 6:19 They l more lamps for them than they l for
6:67 or shine like the sun or give l like the moon.
Aza 1:48 Bless the Lord, l and darkness;
1Mc 1:21 the lampstand for the l, and all its utensils.
4:50 and these gave l in the temple.
2Mc 1:32 when the l from the altar shone back, it went out.
2:26 it is no l matter but calls for sweat and loss
4:17 It is no l thing to show irreverence to
12: 9 so that the glow of the l was seen in Jerusalem,
1Es 8:79 a l for us in the house of the Lord our God,
3Mc 6: 4 manifesting the l of your mercy on the nation
6: 7 you brought up to the l unharmed.
2Es 1:14 I provided l for you from a pillar of fire,
2:35 perpetual l will shine on you forevermore.
6:40 of l to be brought out from your store-chambers,
6:45 the l of the moon, and the arrangement of
7:*42* or dawn or shining or brightness or l,
7:*97* how they are to be made like the l of the stars,
10:22 the l of our lampstand has been put out,
14:20 and its inhabitants are without l.
14:25 I will l in your heart the lamp of understanding,
4Mc 13:20 they were brought to the l of day.

LIGHTED‡ (1) [LIGHT]

2Mc 10: 3 and l lamps and set out the bread of the Presence.

LIGHTEN (9) [LIGHT]

1Sa 6: 5 perhaps he will l his hand on you and your gods
1Ki 12: 4 Now therefore l the hard service of your father
12: 9 'L the yoke that your father put on us'?"
12:10 but you must l it for us';
2Ch 10: 4 Now therefore l the hard service of your father
10: 9 'L the yoke that your father put on us'?"
10:10 but you must l it for us';
Jnh 1: 5 the cargo that was in the ship into the sea, to l it
4Mc 9:31 I l my pain by the joys that come from virtue,

LIGHTENED (1) [LIGHT]

Ac 27:38 they l the ship by throwing the wheat into the sea.

LIGHTENS (1) [LIGHT]

2Sa 22:29 my lamp, O LORD, the LORD l my darkness.

LIGHTER (1) [LIGHT]

Ps 62: 9 they are together l than a breath.

LIGHTERS (1) [LIGHT]

Isa 50:11 But all of you are kindlers of fire, l of firebrands.

LIGHTING (4) [LIGHT]

Mt 5:15 after l a lamp puts it under the bushel basket,
Lk 8:16 "No one after l a lamp hides it under a jar,
11:33 "No one after l a lamp puts it in a cellar,
4Mc 17: 5 l the way of your star-like seven sons to piety,

LIGHTLY (5) [LIGHT]

2Ki 5:20 that Aramean Naaman off too l by not accepting
Ne 9:32 not treat l all the hardship that has come upon us,
Jer 2:36 How l you gad about, changing your ways!
3: 9 Because she took her whoredom so l,
Heb 12: 5 do not regard l the discipline of the Lord,

LIGHTNING (33) [LIGHTNINGS]

Ex 19:16 of the third day there was thunder and l,
20:18 When all the people witnessed the thunder and l,
2Sa 22:15 He sent out arrows, and scattered them —l,
Job 36:30 He scatters his l around him and covers the roots
36:32 He covers his hands with the l,
37: 3 and his l to the corners of the earth.
37:11 with moisture; the clouds scatter his l.
37:15 and causes the l of his cloud to shine?
Ps 105:32 and l that flashed through their land.
144: 6 Make the l flash and scatter them;
Eze 1:13 the fire was bright, and l issued from the fire.
1:14 to and fro, like a flash of l.
21:10 for slaughter, honed to flash like l!
21:28 for slaughter Polished to consume, to flash like l.
Da 10: 6 His body was like beryl, his face like l,
Na 2: 4 their appearance is like torches, they dart like l.
Zec 9:14 and his arrow go forth like l;
Mt 24:27 as the l comes from the east and flashes as far as
28: 3 His appearance was like l,
Lk 10:18 from heaven like a flash of l.
17:24 the l flashes and lights up the sky from one side
Rev 4: 5 Coming from the throne are flashes of l,
8: 5 rumblings, flashes of l, and an earthquake.
11:19 and there were flashes of l, rumblings,
16:18 And there came flashes of l, rumblings,
Wis 5:21 Shafts of l will fly with true aim,
Sir 32:10 L travels ahead of the thunder,
LtJ 6:61 So also the l, when it flashes, is widely seen;
2Es 6: 2 and before the flashes of l shone,
7:*40* or cloud or thunder or l,
10:25 her countenance flashed like l,
16:10 He will flash l, and who will not be afraid?
4Mc 4:10 with l flashing from their weapons appeared

LIGHTNINGS (10) [LIGHTNING]

Job 37: 4 not restrain the l when his voice is heard.
38:35 Can you send forth l, so that they may go
Ps 18:14 he flashed forth l, and routed them.
77:18 your l lit up the world;
97: 4 His l light up the world;
135: 7 he makes l for the rain and brings out the wind
Jer 10:13 He makes l for the rain, and he brings out the wind
51:16 He makes l for the rain, and he brings out the wind
Sir 43:13 the driving snow and speeds the l of his judgments.
Aza 1:51 Bless the Lord, l and clouds;

LIGHTS (11) [LIGHT]

Ge 1:14 "Let there be l in the dome of the sky to separate
1:15 be l in the dome of the sky to give light upon
1:16 God made the two great l—
Ps 18:28 the LORD, my God, l up my darkness.
136: 7 the great l, for his steadfast love endures forever;
Jer 46:20 a gadfly from the north l upon her.
Eze 32: 8 All the shining l of the heavens I will darken
Lk 17:24 For as the lightning flashes and l up the sky
Ac 16:29 The jailer called for l, and rushing in,
Jas 1:17 coming down from the Father of l,
Sir 36:27 A woman's beauty l up a man's face,

LIGN (KJV) See ALOES

LIGURE (KJV) See JACINTH

LIKE‡ (1772) [ALIKE, LIKE-MINDED, LIKED, LIKELY, LIKEN, LIKENED, LIKENESS, LIKENESSES, LIKES, LIKEWISE, LIKING]

Ge 3: 5 and you will be l God, knowing good and evil."
3:22 "See, the man has become l one of us,
10: 9 "L Nimrod a mighty hunter before the LORD."
13:10 Jordan was well watered everywhere l the garden
13:10 l the land of Egypt, in the direction of Zoar;
13:16 I will make your offspring l the dust of the earth;
19:28 the smoke of the land going up l the smoke of
25:25 first came out red, all his body l a hairy mantle;
27: 4 Then prepare for me savory food, such as I l,
27:23 his hands were hairy l his brother Esau's hands;
27:27 and said, "Ah, the smell of my son is l the smell
28:14 and your offspring shall be l the dust of the earth,
31:26 and carried away my daughters l captives of
31:40 It was l this with me:
33:10 to see your face is l seeing the face of God—
34:12 as you l, and I will give whatever you ask me;
34:31 "Should our sister be treated l a whore?"
38:11 for he feared that he too would die, l his brothers.
41:38 "Can we find anyone else l this—
41:49 l the sand of the sea—
42: 7 but he treated them l strangers and spoke harshly
44:18 for you are l Pharaoh himself.
48:20 'God make you l Ephraim and l Manasseh.' "
49: 9 he stretches out l a lion, l a lioness—
Ex 1:19 Hebrew women are not l the Egyptian women;
4: 7 it was restored l the rest of his body—
5:15 "Why do you treat your servants l this?
7: 1 "See, I have made you l God to Pharaoh,
8:10 that you may know that there is no one l the LORD
9:14 so that you may know that there is no one l me
15: 5 they went down into the depths l a stone.
15: 7 it consumed them l stubble.
15:10 they sank l lead in the mighty waters.
15:11 "Who is l you, O LORD, among the gods?
15:11 Who is l you, majestic in holiness,
16:31 it was l coriander seed, white, and the taste of it was l wafers made with honey.
19:18 the smoke went up l the smoke of a kiln,
24:10 Under his feet there was something l a pavement
24:10 l the very heaven for clearness.
24:17 the glory of the LORD was l a devouring fire on
25:33 three cups shaped l almond blossoms,
25:33 and three cups shaped l almond blossoms,
25:34 be four cups shaped l almond blossoms,
28:14 and two chains of pure gold, twisted l cords;
28:21 be l signets, each engraved with its name,
28:22 for the breastpiece chains of pure gold, twisted l
28:32 l the opening in a coat of mail,
28:36 and engrave on it, l the engraving of a signet,
30:32 and you shall make no other l it in composition;
30:33 Whoever compounds any l it
30:38 Whoever makes any l it to use as perfume shall
32:13 'I will multiply your descendants l the stars
34: 1 "Cut two tablets of stone l the former ones,
34: 4 Moses cut two tablets of stone l the former ones;
37:19 three cups shaped l almond blossoms,
37:19 and three cups shaped l almond blossoms,
37:20 lampstand itself there were four cups shaped l
39: 6 of gold filigree and engraved l the engravings of
39: 8 in skilled work, l the work of the ephod, of gold,
39:14 they were l signets, each engraved with its name,
39:15 on the breastpiece chains of pure gold, twisted l
39:23 of the robe in the middle of it was l the opening
39:30 l the engraving of a signet,
Lev 4:26 l the fat of the sacrifice of well-being.
5:13 L the grain offering, the rest shall be for
6:17 l the sin offering and the guilt offering.
7: 7 The guilt offering is l the sin offering,
9:15 and presented it as a sin offering l the first one.
14:13 for the guilt offering, l the sin offering,
26:19 and I will make your sky l iron and your earth
26:19 like iron and your earth l copper.
Nu 11: 7 Now the manna was l coriander seed,
11: 7 and its color was l the color of gum resin.
11: 8 taste of it was l the taste of cakes baked with oil.
12:12 Do not let her be l one stillborn,
13:18 and see what the land is l,
13:33 and to ourselves we seemed l grasshoppers,
16:40 so as not to become l Korah and his company—
23:10 and let my end be l his!"
23:22 is l the horns of a wild ox for them.
23:24 Look, a people rising up l a lioness, and rousing itself l a lion!
24: 6 L palm groves that stretch far away, l gardens beside a river, l aloes that the LORD has planted, l cedar trees beside the waters.
24: 8 is l the horns of a wild ox for him;
24: 9 He crouched, he lay down l a lion, and l a lioness;
27:17 that the congregation of the LORD may not be l
28: 8 a grain offering and a drink offering l the one in
Dt 2:11 L the Anakim, they are usually reckoned
3:24 or on earth can perform deeds and mighty acts l
4:32 so great as this ever happened or has its l
7:26 or you will be set apart for destruction l it.
8:20 L the nations that the LORD is destroying
10: 1 "Carve out two tablets of stone l the former ones,
10: 3 cut two tablets of stone l the former ones,
11:10 that you are about to enter to occupy is not l
11:10 where you sow your seed and irrigate by foot l
12:16 you shall pour it out on the ground l water.
12:24 you shall pour it out on the ground l water.
15:23 you shall pour it out on the ground l water.
17:14 l all the nations that are around me,"
18: 7 l all his fellow-Levites who stand
18:15 a prophet l me from among your own people;
18:18 a prophet l you from among their own people;
20: 8 the heart of his comrades to melt l his own."
22:26 by death, because this case is l that
28:49 to swoop down on you l an eagle,
29:23 l the destruction of Sodom and Gomorrah,
32: 2 May my teaching drop l the rain, my speech condense l the dew; l gentle rain on grass, l showers on new growth.
32:31 Indeed their rock is not l our Rock;
33:20 Gad lives l a lion; he tears at arm and scalp.
33:26 There is none l God, O Jeshurun,
33:29 Who is l you, a people saved by the LORD,
34:10 since has there arisen a prophet in Israel l Moses,
Jos 10: 2 l one of the royal cities, and was larger than Ai,
10:14 There has been no day l it before or since,
11: 4 in number l the sand on the seashore,
Jdg 5:31 But may your friends be l the sun as it rises
9:36 shadows on the mountains look l people to you."
13: 6 and his appearance was l that of an angel of God,
15:14 and the ropes that were on his arms became l flax
16: 7 then I shall become weak, and be l anyone else."
16:11 then I shall become weak, and be l anyone else."
16:12 But he snapped the ropes off his arms l a thread.
16:13 then I shall become weak, and be l anyone else."
16:17 I would become weak, and be l anyone else."
17:11 the young man became to him l one of his sons.
Ru 4:11 the woman who is coming into your house l
4:12 may your house be l the house of Perez,
1Sa 2: 2 "There is no Holy One l the LORD,
2: 2 there is no Rock l our God.
4: 7 For nothing l this has happened before.
8: 5 then, a king to govern us, l other nations."
8:20 so that we also may be l other nations,
10:24 There is no one l him among all the people."
13: 5 troops l the sand on the seashore in multitude;
15:23 and stubbornness is l iniquity and idolatry.
17: 7 The shaft of his spear was l a weaver's beam,
17:36 and this uncircumcised Philistine shall be l one
19:17 "Why have you deceived me l this,
20: 3 "Your father knows well that you l me;
21: 9 David said, "There is none l it; give it to me."
25:26 and those who seek to do evil to my lord be l
25:36 he was holding a feast in his house, l the feast of
25:37 within him; he became l a stone.
26:15 Who is l you in Israel?
26:20 l one who hunts a partridge in the mountains."
2Sa 5:20 against my enemies before me, l
7: 9 l the name of the great ones of the earth.
7:22 for there is no one l you,
7:23 Who is l your people, l Israel?
9:11 l one of the king's sons.
12: 3 and it was l a daughter to him.
13:27 Absalom made a feast l a king's feast.
14: 2 not anoint yourself with oil, but behave l
14:14 we are l water spilled on the ground,
14:17 for my lord the king is l the angel of God,
14:20 But my lord has wisdom l the wisdom of
17: 8 l a bear robbed of her cubs in the field.
17:10 whose heart is l the heart of a lion,
17:11 l the sand by the sea for multitude,
18:14 Joab said, "I will not waste time l this with you."
18:27 of the first one is l the running of Ahimaaz son
18:32 the king, and all who rise up to do you harm, be l
19:27 But my lord the king is l the angel of God;
21:19 the shaft of whose spear was l a weaver's beam.
22:34 He made my feet l the feet of deer,
22:43 I beat them fine l the dust of the earth,
22:43 and stamped them down l the mire of the streets.
23: 4 is l the light of morning,

2Sa 23: 4 l the sun rising on a cloudless morning,
23: 5 Is not my house l this with God?
23: 6 the godless are all l thorns that are thrown away;
1Ki 3:12 no one l you has been before you and no one
3:12 no one like you has been before you and no one l
5: 6 among us who knows how to cut timber l
7: 8 a house l this hall for Pharaoh's daughter,
7:26 its brim was made l the brim of a cup,
7:26 l the flower of a lily; it held two thousand baths.
7:33 The wheels were made l a chariot wheel;
8:23 there is no God l you in heaven above or
10:20 Nothing l it was ever made in any kingdom.
12:32 the eighth month l the festival that was in Judah,
14: 8 yet you have not been l my servant David,
15: 3 l the heart of his father David.
15:19 l that between my father and your father:
16: 3 and I will make your house l the house
16: 7 in being l the house of Jeroboam,
19: 2 if I do not make your life l the life of one of them
20:11 on armor should not brag l one who takes it off."
20:25 and muster an army l the army that you have lost,
20:27 the people of Israel encamped opposite them l
21:22 I will make your house l the house of Jeroboam
21:22 and l the house of Baasha son of Ahijah,
21:25 (Indeed, there was no one l Ahab,
22:13 let your word be l the word of one of them,
22:17 l sheep that have no shepherd;
2Ki 3: 2 though not l his father and mother,
5:14 his flesh was restored l the flesh of a young boy,
9: 9 the house of Ahab l the house of Jeroboam son
9: 9 and l the house of Baasha son of Ahijah.
9:20 It looks l the driving of Jehu son of Nimshi;
9:20 for he drives l a maniac."
9:37 the corpse of Jezebel shall be l dung on the field
13: 7 of Aram had destroyed them and made them l
14: 3 yet not l his ancestor David;
17: 2 yet not l the kings of Israel who were before him.
18: 5 that there was no one l him among all the kings
18:32 and take you away to a land l your own land,
19:26 become l plants of the field and l tender grass, l
grass on the housetops,
23:25 Before him there was no king l him,
23:25 nor did any l him arise after him.
1Ch 4:27 nor did all their family multiply l the Judeans.
11:23 The Egyptian had in his hand a spear l
12: 8 whose faces were l the faces of lions,
12:22 until there was a great army, l an army of God.
14:11 against my enemies by my hand, l
17: 8 l the name of the great ones of the earth.
17:20 There is no one l you, O LORD,
17:21 Who is l your people Israel,
20: 5 the shaft of whose spear was l a weaver's beam.
29:15 our days on the earth are l a shadow,
2Ch 1:12 and none after you shall have the l."
4: 5 its rim was made l the rim of a cup,
4: 5 l the flower of a lily; it held three thousand baths.
6:14 "O LORD, God of Israel, there is no God l you,
9:11 there never was seen the l of them before in
9:19 The l of it was never made in any kingdom.
13: 9 and made priests for yourselves l the peoples
16: 3 l that between my father and your father;
18:12 let your word be l the word of one of them,
18:16 l sheep without a shepherd;
21:19 l the fires made for his ancestors.
30: 7 Do not be l your ancestors and your kindred,
30:26 of King David of Israel there had been nothing l
32:19 the God of Jerusalem as if he were l the gods of
35:18 No passover l it had been kept in Israel since
Ne 6:11 But I said, "Should a man l me run away?
6:11 a man l me go into the temple to save his life?
9:11 l a stone into mighty waters.
9:23 You multiplied their descendants l the stars
13:26 Among the many nations there was no king l
Job 1: 8 There is no one l him on the earth,
2: 3 There is no one l him on the earth,
3:16 Or why was I not buried l a stillborn child,
3:16 l an infant that never sees the light?
3:24 For my sighing comes l my bread,
3:24 and my groanings are poured out l water.
4:19 who are crushed l a moth.
5:25 and your offspring l the grass of the earth.
6: 7 they are l food that is loathsome to me.
6:15 My companions are treacherous l a torrent-bed,
6:15 l freshets that pass away,
7: 1 and are not their days l the days of a laborer?
7: 2 L a slave who longs for the shadow,
7: 2 and l laborers who look for their wages,
9:26 They go by l skiffs of reed,
9:26 l an eagle swooping on the prey.
10: 5 Are your days l the days of mortals,
10: 5 or your years l human years,
10: 9 Remember that you fashioned me l clay;
10:10 not pour me out l milk and curdle me l cheese?
10:22 where light is l darkness."
11:17 its darkness will be l the morning.
12:25 he makes them stagger l a drunkard.
13:28 One wastes away l a rotten thing,
13:28 l a garment that is moth-eaten.
14: 2 comes up l a flower and withers,
14: 2 flees l a shadow and does not last.
14: 6 and desist, that they may enjoy, l laborers,
14: 9 of water it will bud and put forth branches l
15:16 one who drinks iniquity l water!
15:24 l a king prepared for battle.
15:33 They will shake off their unripe grape, l the vine,
15:33 and cast off their blossoms, l the olive tree.
16:14 he rushes at me l a warrior.
Job 17: 7 and all my members are l a shadow.
19:10 and I am gone, he has uprooted my hope l a tree.
19:22 Why do you, l God, pursue me,
20: 7 they will perish forever l their own dung;
20: 8 They will fly away l a dream, and not be found;
20: 8 they will be chased away l a vision of the night.
21:11 They send out their little ones l a flock,
21:18 How often are they l straw before the wind,
21:18 and l chaff that the storm carries away?
22:24 if you treat gold l dust,
22:24 and gold of Ophir l the stones of the torrent-bed,
23:10 when he has tested me, I shall come out l gold.
24: 5 L wild asses in the desert they go out to their toil,
24:14 and in the night is l a thief.
24:20 so wickedness is broken l a tree.
24:24 they wither and fade l the mallow;
24:24 they are cut off l the heads of grain.
27: 7 "May my enemy be l the wicked,
27: 7 and may my opponent be l the unrighteous.
27:16 Though they heap up silver l dust,
27:16 and pile up clothing l clay—
27:18 They build their houses l nests,
27:18 l booths made by sentinels of the vineyard.
27:20 Terrors overtake them l a flood;
29:14 my justice was l a robe and a turban.
29:18 and I shall multiply my days l the phoenix;
29:22 and my word dropped upon them l dew.
29:25 and I lived l a king among his troops,
29:25 l one who comforts mourners.
30:15 and my prosperity has passed away l a cloud.
30:19 and I have become l dust and ashes.
31:18 from my youth I reared the orphan l a father,
31:36 I would bind it on me l a crown;
31:37 l a prince I would approach him.
32:19 My heart is indeed l wine that has no vent;
32:19 l new wineskins, it is ready to burst.
34: 7 Who is there l Job, who drinks up scoffing l water,
35: 8 Your wickedness affects others l you,
36:22 who is a teacher l him?
37:18 Can you, l him, spread out the skies,
38: 3 Gird up your loins l a man, I will question you,
38:14 It is changed l clay under the seal,
38:14 and it is dyed l a garment.
38:30 The waters become hard l stone,
39:20 Do you make it leap l the locust?
40: 7 "Gird up your loins l a man;
40: 9 Have you an arm l God,
40: 9 and can you thunder with a voice l his?
40:15 it eats grass l an ox.
40:17 It makes its tail stiff l a cedar;
40:18 its limbs l bars of iron.
41:18 and its eyes are l the eyelids of the dawn.
41:30 Its underparts are l sharp potsherds;
41:30 it spreads itself l a threshing sledge on the mire.
41:31 It makes the deep boil l a pot;
41:31 it makes the sea l a pot of ointment.
Ps 1: 3 They are l trees planted by streams of water,
1: 4 but are l chaff that the wind drives away.
2: 9 and dash them in pieces l a potter's vessel."
7: 2 or l a lion they will tear me apart;
10: 9 they lurk in secret l a lion in its covert;
11: 1 "Flee l a bird to the mountains;
17:12 They are l a lion eager to tear,
17:12 l a young lion lurking in ambush.
18:33 He made my feet l the feet of a deer,
18:42 I beat them fine, l dust before the wind;
18:42 I cast them out l the mire of the streets.
19: 5 which comes out l a bridegroom
19: 5 and l a strong man runs its course with joy.
21: 9 You will make them l a fiery furnace
22:13 l a ravening and roaring lion.
22:14 I am poured out l water, and all my bones are out
22:14 my heart is l wax; it is melted within my breast;
22:15 up l a potsherd, and my tongue sticks to my jaws;
28: 1 I shall be l those who go down to the Pit.
29: 6 He makes Lebanon skip l a calf,
29: 6 and Sirion l a young wild ox.
31:12 I have passed out of mind l one who is dead;
31:12 I have become l a broken vessel.
32: 9 Do not be l a horse or a mule,
35: 5 Let them be l chaff before the wind,
35:10 "O LORD, who is l you?
36: 6 Your righteousness is l the mighty mountains,
36: 6 your judgments are l the great deep;
37: 2 for they will soon fade l the grass,
37: 2 and wither l the green herb.
37: 6 He will make your vindication shine l the light,
37: 6 and the justice of your cause l the noonday.
37:20 and the enemies of the LORD are l the glory of
37:20 l smoke they vanish away.
37:35 and towering l a cedar of Lebanon.
38: 4 they weigh l a burden too heavy for me.
38:13 But I am l the deaf, I do not hear;
38:13 l the mute, who cannot speak.
38:14 Truly, I am l one who does not hear,
39: 6 Surely everyone goes about l a shadow.
39:11 consuming l a moth what is dear to them;
39:12 an alien, l all my forebears.
44:11 You have made us l sheep for slaughter,
45: 1 my tongue is l the pen of a ready scribe.
48:10 Your name, O God, l your praise,
49:12 they are l the animals that perish.
49:14 L sheep they are appointed for Sheol;
49:20 they are l the animals that perish.
50:21 you thought that I was one just l yourself.
52: 2 Your tongue is l a sharp razor,
52: 8 But I am l a green olive tree in the house of God.
Ps 55: 6 And I say, "O that I had wings l a dove!
58: 4 They have venom l the venom of a serpent,
58: 4 l the deaf adder that stops its ear,
58: 7 Let them vanish l water that runs away;
58: 7 l grass let them be trodden down and wither.
58: 8 Let them be l the snail that dissolves into slime;
58: 8 l the untimely birth that never sees the sun.
59: 6 howling l dogs and prowling about the city.
59:14 howling l dogs and prowling about the city.
64: 3 who whet their tongues l swords,
64: 3 who aim bitter words l arrows,
71: 7 I have been l a portent to many,
71:19 who have done great things, O God, who is l you?
72: 6 May he be l rain that falls on the mown grass,
72: 6 l showers that water the earth.
72:16 may its fruit be l Lebanon;
72:16 and may people blossom in the cities l the grass
73: 5 they are not plagued l other people.
73: 6 violence covers them l a garment.
73:20 They are l a dream when one awakes;
73:22 I was l a brute beast toward you.
77:20 You led your people l a flock by the hand
78: 8 and that they should not be l their ancestors,
78:13 and made the waters stand l a heap.
78:16 and caused waters to flow down l rivers.
78:27 rained flesh upon them l dust, winged birds l the
sand of the seas;
78:33 So he made their days vanish l a breath,
78:52 Then he led out his people l sheep,
78:52 and guided them in the wilderness l a flock.
78:57 turned away and were faithless l their ancestors;
78:57 they twisted l a treacherous bow.
78:65 l a warrior shouting because of wine.
78:69 He built his sanctuary l the high heavens,
78:69 l the earth, which he has founded forever.
79: 3 They have poured out their blood l water all
79: 5 Will your jealous wrath burn l fire?
80: 1 you who lead Joseph l a flock!
82: 7 you shall die l mortals, and fall l any prince."
83:11 Make their nobles l Oreb and Zeeb,
83:11 all their princes l Zebah and Zalmunna,
83:13 make them l whirling dust, l chaff before the wind.
86: 8 There is none l you among the gods, O Lord,
86: 8 O Lord, nor are there any works l yours.
88: 4 I am l those who have no help,
88: 5 l those forsaken among the dead,
88: 5 l the slain that lie in the grave,
88: 5 l those whom you remember no more,
88:17 They surround me l a flood all day long;
89: 6 Who among the heavenly beings is l the LORD,
89:10 You crushed Rahab l a carcass;
89:36 and his throne endure before me l the sun.
89:37 It shall be established forever l the moon,
89:46 How long will your wrath burn l fire?
90: 4 For a thousand years in your sight are l yesterday
90: 4 or l a watch in the night.
90: 5 You sweep them away; they are l a dream,
90: 5 l grass that is renewed in the morning;
90: 9 our years come to an end l a sigh.
92: 7 wicked sprout l grass and all evildoers flourish,
92:10 you have exalted my horn l that of the wild ox;
92:12 The righteous flourish l the palm tree,
92:12 and grow l a cedar in Lebanon.
97: 5 The mountains melt l wax before the LORD,
102: 3 For my days pass away l smoke,
102: 3 and my bones burn l a furnace.
102: 4 My heart is stricken and withered l grass;
102: 6 I am l an owl of the wilderness,
102: 6 l a little owl of the waste places.
102: 7 I lie awake; I am l a lonely bird on the housetop.
102: 9 For I eat ashes l bread,
102:11 My days are l an evening shadow;
102:11 like an evening shadow; I wither away l grass.
102:26 they will all wear out l a garment.
102:26 You change them l clothing, and they pass away;
103: 5 so that your youth is renewed l the eagle's.
103:15 As for mortals, their days are l grass;
103:15 they flourish l a flower of the field;
104: 2 You stretch out the heavens l a tent,
105:41 it flowed through the desert l a river.
107:27 they reeled and staggered l drunkards,
107:41 and makes their families l flocks.
109:17 He did not l blessing; may it be far from him.
109:18 soak into his body l water, l oil into his bones.
109:19 be l a garment that he wraps around himself,
109:19 l a belt that he wears every day."
109:23 I am gone l a shadow at evening;
109:23 I am shaken off l a locust.
110: 3 From the womb of the morning, l dew,
113: 5 Who is l the LORD our God,
114: 4 mountains skipped l rams, the hills l lambs.
114: 6 mountains, that you skip l rams? O hills, l lambs?
115: 8 Those who make them are l them;
118:12 They surrounded me l bees;
118:12 they blazed l a fire of thorns;
119:83 For I have become l a wineskin in the smoke,
119:162 I rejoice at your word l one who finds great spoil.
119:176 I have gone astray l a lost sheep;
124: 7 We have escaped l a bird from the snare of
125: 1 Those who trust in the LORD are l Mount Zion,
126: 1 we were l those who dream.
126: 4 O LORD, l the watercourses in the Negeb.
127: 4 L arrows in the hand of a warrior are the sons
128: 3 be l a fruitful vine within your house;
128: 3 be l olive shoots around your table.
129: 6 be l the grass on the housetops that withers
131: 2 l a weaned child with its mother;

Ps 131: 2 my soul is l the weaned child that is with me.
133: 2 It is l the precious oil on the head,
133: 3 It is l the dew of Hermon,
135:18 and all who trust them shall become l them.
141: 7 L a rock that one breaks apart and shatters on
143: 3 making me sit in darkness l those long dead.
143: 6 my soul thirsts for you l a parched land.
143: 7 or I shall be l those who go down to the Pit.
144: 4 are l a breath; their days are l a passing shadow.
144:12 in their youth be l plants full grown,
144:12 our daughters l corner pillars,
147:16 He gives snow l wool; he scatters frost l ashes.
147:17 He hurls down hail l crumbs—
Pr 1:12 l Sheol let us swallow them alive and whole,
1:12 l those who go down to the Pit.
1:27 when panic strikes you l a storm,
1:27 and your calamity comes l a whirlwind,
2: 4 if you seek it l silver, and search for it as
4:18 the path of the righteous is l the light of dawn,
4:19 The way of the wicked is l deep darkness;
6: 5 save yourself l a gazelle from the hunter,
6: 5 l a bird from the hand of the fowler.
6:11 and poverty will come upon you l a robber,
6:11 and want, l an armed warrior.
7:10 decked out l a prostitute, wily of heart.
7:22 and goes l an ox to the slaughter,
7:22 or bounds l a stag toward the trap
7:23 He is l a bird rushing into a snare,
8:30 then I was beside him, l a master worker;
10:23 Doing wrong is l sport to a fool,
10:26 L vinegar to the teeth, and smoke to the eyes,
11:22 L a gold ring in a pig's snout is
11:28 but the righteous will flourish l green leaves.
12: 4 but she who brings shame is l rottenness
12:18 Rash words are l sword thrusts,
15:12 Scoffers do not l to be rebuked;
16:15 his favor is l the clouds that bring the spring rain.
16:24 Pleasant words are l a honeycomb,
16:27 and their speech is l a scorching fire.
17: 8 A bribe is l a magic stone in the eyes
17:14 The beginning of strife is l letting out water;
18: 8 The words of a whisperer are l delicious morsels;
18:11 in their imagination it is l a high wall.
18:19 such quarreling is l the bars of a castle.
19:12 A king's anger is l the growling of a lion,
19:12 but his favor is l dew on the grass.
20: 2 dread anger of a king is l the growling of a lion;
20: 5 purposes in the human mind are l deep water,
23: 5 flying l an eagle toward heaven.
23: 7 for l a hair in the throat,
23:28 in wait l a robber and increases the number of
23:32 At the last it bites l a serpent, and stings l the adder
23:34 You will be l one who lies down in the midst of
23:34 l one who lies on the top of a mast.
24:15 Do not lie in wait l an outlaw against the home of
24:34 and poverty will come upon you l a robber,
24:34 and want, l an armed warrior.
25: 3 L the heavens for height, l the earth for depth,
25:11 A word fitly spoken is l apples of gold in
25:12 L a gold ring or an ornament of gold is
25:13 L the cold of snow in the time of harvest
25:14 L clouds and wind without rain is one who boasts
25:18 L a war club, a sword,
25:19 L a bad tooth or a lame foot is trust in
25:20 L vinegar on a wound is one who sings songs to
25:20 L a moth in clothing or a worm in wood,
25:25 L cold water to a thirsty soul,
25:26 L a muddied spring or a polluted fountain are
25:28 L a city breached, without walls,
26: 1 L snow in summer or rain in harvest,
26: 2 L a sparrow in its flitting, l a swallow in its flying,
26: 6 It is l cutting off one's foot and drinking down
26: 8 It is l binding a stone in a sling to give honor to
26: 9 L a thornbush brandished by the hand of
26:10 L an archer who wounds everybody is one who
26:11 L a dog that returns to its vomit is a fool
26:17 L somebody who takes a passing dog by
26:18 L a maniac who shoots deadly firebrands
26:22 The words of a whisperer are l delicious morsels;
26:23 L the glaze covering an earthen vessel are smooth
27: 8 L a bird that strays from its nest is one who strays
28:15 L a roaring lion or a charging bear is
29:20 more hope for a fool than for anyone l that.
31:14 She is l the ships of the merchant,
Ecc 2:16 How can the wise die just l fools?
6:12 which they pass l a shadow?
7: 6 For l the crackling of thorns under a pot,
7:12 For the protection of wisdom is l the protection
8: 1 Who is l the wise man?
8:13 neither will they prolong their days l a shadow,
9: 2 those who swear are l those who shun an oath.
9:12 L fish taken in a cruel net, and l birds caught in a
10: 7 and princes walking on foot l slaves.
12:11 The sayings of the wise are l goads,
12:11 and l nails firmly fixed are the collected sayings
SS 1: 5 l the tents of Kedar, l the curtains of Solomon.
1: 7 for why should I be l one who is veiled beside
2: 9 My beloved is l a gazelle or a young stag.
2:17 be l a gazelle or a young stag on
3: 6 that coming up from the wilderness, l a column
4: 1 Your hair is l a flock of goats,
4: 2 Your teeth are l a flock of shorn ewes
4: 3 Your lips are l a crimson thread,
4: 3 Your cheeks are l halves of a pomegranate
4: 4 Your neck is l the tower of David,
4: 5 Your two breasts are l two fawns,
4:11 scent of your garments is l the scent of Lebanon.
SS 5:12 His eyes are l doves beside springs of water,
5:13 His cheeks are l beds of spices,
5:15 His appearance is l Lebanon,
6: 5 Your hair is l a flock of goats,
6: 6 Your teeth are l a flock of ewes,
6: 7 Your cheeks are l halves of a pomegranate
6:10 "Who is this that looks forth l the dawn,
7: 1 Your rounded thighs are l jewels,
7: 3 Your two breasts are l two fawns,
7: 4 Your neck is l an ivory tower.
7: 4 Your nose is l a tower of Lebanon,
7: 5 Your head crowns you l Carmel,
7: 5 and your flowing locks are l purple;
7: 7 and your breasts are l its clusters.
7: 8 Oh, may your breasts be l clusters of the vine,
7: 8 and the scent of your breath l apples,
7: 9 and your kisses l the best wine that goes
8: 1 O that you were l a brother to me,
8:10 I was a wall, and my breasts were l towers;
8:14 be l a gazelle or a young stag upon the mountains
Isa 1: 8 daughter Zion is left l a booth in a vineyard, l a
shelter in a cucumber field, l a besieged city.
1: 9 have been l Sodom, and become l Gomorrah.
1:18 your sins are l scarlet, they shall be l snow;
1:18 they are red l crimson, they shall become l wool.
1:30 For you shall be l an oak whose leaf withers,
1:30 and l a garden without water.
1:31 The strong shall become l tinder,
1:31 and their work l a spark;
2: 6 from the east and of soothsayers l the Philistines,
3: 9 they proclaim their sin l Sodom,
5:24 and their blossom go up l dust;
5:25 and their corpses were l refuse in the streets.
5:28 their horses' hoofs seem l flint,
5:28 and their wheels l the whirlwind.
5:29 Their roaring is l a lion, l young lions they roar;
5:30 l the roaring of the sea.
6:13 l a terebinth or an oak whose stump remains
8:20 those who speak l this will have no dawn!
9:18 For wickedness burned l a fire,
9:19 and the people became l fuel for the fire;
10: 6 and to tread them down l the mire of the streets.
10: 9 Is not Calno l Carchemish? Is not Hamath l
Arpad? Is not Samaria l Damascus?
10:13 l a bull I have brought down those who sat
10:14 My hand has found, l a nest,
10:16 and under his glory a burning will be kindled, l
10:22 your people Israel were l the sand of the sea,
11: 7 and the lion shall eat straw l the ox.
13: 6 it will come l destruction from the Almighty!
13: 8 they will be in anguish l a woman in labor.
13:14 L a hunted gazelle, or l sheep with no one to gather
13:19 will be l Sodom and Gomorrah
14:10 You have become l us!"
14:14 I will make myself l the Most High."
14:17 the world l a desert and overthrew its cities,
14:19 away from your grave, l loathsome carrion,
14:19 l a corpse trampled underfoot.
16: 2 L fluttering birds, l scattered nestlings,
16: 3 make your shade l night at the height of noon;
16:11 Therefore my heart throbs l a harp for Moab,
16:14 In three years, l the years of a hired worker,
17: 3 and the remnant of Aram will be l the glory of
17: 9 be l the deserted places of the Hivites and
17:12 they thunder l the thundering of the sea!
17:12 they roar l the roaring of mighty waters!
17:13 The nations roar l the roaring of many waters,
17:13 chased l chaff on the mountains before the wind
18: 4 I will quietly look from my dwelling l clear heat
18: 4 l a cloud of dew in the heat of harvest.
19:16 On that day the Egyptians will be l women,
21: 3 l the pangs of a woman in labor;
22:18 and throw you l a ball into a wide land;
22:23 I will fasten him l a peg in a secure place,
24:20 earth staggers l a drunkard, it sways l a hut;
24:22 They will be gathered together l prisoners in
25: 4 the blast of the ruthless was l a winter rainstorm,
25: 5 of aliens l heat in a dry place, you subdued
26: 1 he sets up victory l walls and bulwarks.
26:17 L a woman with child, who writhes and cries out
27: 9 the stones of the altars l chalkstones crushed
27:10 a habitation deserted and forsaken, l
28: 2 l a storm of hail, a destroying tempest, l a storm of
28: 4 will be l a first-ripe fig before the summer;
29: 2 and Jerusalem shall be to me l an Ariel.
29: 3 And l David I will encamp against you;
29: 4 your voice shall come from the ground l
29: 5 the multitude of your foes shall be l small dust,
29: 5 and the multitude of tyrants l flying chaff.
29: 7 and who distress her, shall be l a dream,
29:11 of all this has become for you l the words of
30:13 for you l a break in a high wall, bulging out,
30:14 its breaking is l that of a potter's vessel
30:17 until you are left l a flagstaff on the top of
30:17 l a signal on a hill.
30:22 You will scatter them l filthy rags;
30:26 light of the moon will be l the light of the sun,
30:26 l the light of seven days,
30:27 and his tongue is l a devouring fire;
30:28 his breath is l an overflowing stream that reaches
30:33 the breath of the LORD, l a stream of sulfur,
31: 5 L birds hovering overhead,
32: 2 Each will be l a hiding place from the wind,
32: 2 l streams of water in a dry place,
32: 2 l the shade of a great rock in a weary land.
33: 9 Sharon is l a desert; and Bashan and Carmel shake
33:12 l thorns cut down, that are burned in the fire."
Isa 34: 4 and the skies roll up l a scroll.
34: 4 All their host shall wither l a leaf withering on
35: 1 desert shall rejoice and blossom; l the crocus
35: 6 then the lame shall leap l a deer,
36:17 and take you away to a land l your own land,
37:27 become l plants of the field and l tender grass,
37:27 l grass on the housetops,
38:12 up and removed from me l a shepherd's tent;
38:12 l a weaver I have rolled up my life;
38:13 l a lion he breaks all my bones;
38:14 L a swallow or a crane I clamor, I moan l a dove.
40: 6 their constancy is l the flower of the field.
40:11 He will feed his flock l a shepherd;
40:15 Even the nations are l a drop from a bucket,
40:15 see, he takes up the isles l fine dust.
40:22 and its inhabitants are l grasshoppers;
40:22 who stretches out the heavens l a curtain,
40:22 and spreads them l a tent to live in;
40:24 and the tempest carries them off l stubble.
40:31 they shall mount up with wings l eagles,
41: 2 he makes them l dust with his sword,
41: 2 l driven stubble with his bow.
41:15 and you shall make the hills l chaff.
42:13 The LORD goes forth l a soldier,
42:13 l a warrior he stirs up his fury;
42:14 now I will cry out l a woman in labor,
42:19 or deaf l my messenger whom I send?
42:19 Who is blind l my dedicated one,
42:19 or blind l the servant of the LORD?
43:17 they are extinguished, quenched l a wick:
44: 4 They shall spring up l a green tamarisk,
44: 4 l willows by flowing streams.
44: 7 Who is l me? Let them proclaim it,
44:22 I have swept away your transgressions l a cloud,
and your sins l mist;
46: 9 I am God, and there is no one l me,
47:14 See, they are l stubble, the fire consumes them;
48:10 See, I have refined you, but not l silver;
48:18 Then your prosperity would have been l a river,
48:18 and your success l the waves of the sea;
48:19 your offspring would have been l the sand,
48:19 and your descendants l its grains;
49: 2 He made my mouth l a sharp sword,
49:18 you shall put all of them on l an ornament,
49:18 and l a bride you shall bind them on.
50: 7 therefore I have set my face l flint,
50: 9 All of them will wear out l a garment;
51: 3 and will make her wilderness l Eden,
51: 3 her desert l the garden of the LORD;
51: 6 for the heavens will vanish l smoke,
51: 6 the earth will wear out l a garment,
51: 6 and those who live on it will die l gnats;
51: 8 For the moth will eat them up l a garment,
51: 8 and the worm will eat them l wool;
51:12 a human being who fades l grass?
51:20 at the head of every street l an antelope in a net;
51:23 you have made your back l the ground and l the
street for them to walk on.
53: 2 For he grew up before him l a young plant,
53: 2 and l a root out of dry ground;
53: 6 All we l sheep have gone astray;
53: 7 l a lamb that is led to the slaughter,
53: 7 and l a sheep that before its shearers is silent,
54: 6 For the LORD has called you l a wife forsaken
54: 6 l the wife of a man's youth when she is cast off,
54: 9 This is l the days of Noah to me:
56:12 And tomorrow will be l today,
57:20 wicked are l the tossing sea that cannot keep still;
58: 1 Lift up your voice l a trumpet!
58: 5 Is it to bow down the head l a bulrush,
58: 8 Then your light shall break forth l the dawn,
58:10 in the darkness and your gloom be l the noonday.
58:11 you shall be l a watered garden, l a spring of water,
59:10 We grope l the blind along a wall,
59:10 groping l those who have no eyes;
59:11 We all growl l bears; like doves
59:11 l doves we moan mournfully.
59:17 He put on righteousness l a breastplate,
59:19 for he will come l a pent-up stream that the wind
60: 8 Who are these that fly l a cloud,
60: 8 and l doves to their windows?
62: 1 until her vindication shines out l the dawn,
62: 1 and her salvation l a burning torch.
63: 2 and your garments l theirs who tread
63:13 L a horse in the desert, they did not stumble.
63:14 L cattle that go down into the valley,
63:19 We have long been l those whom you do
63:19 l those not called by your name.
64: 6 We have all become l one who is unclean,
64: 6 and all our righteous deeds are l a filthy cloth.
64: 6 We all fade l a leaf, and our iniquities, l the wind,
65:22 for l the days of a tree shall the days
65:25 the lion shall eat straw l the ox;
66: 3 slaughters an ox is l one who kills a human being,
66: 3 l one who breaks a dog's neck;
66: 3 l one who offers swine's blood;
66: 3 l one who blesses an idol.
66:12 I will extend prosperity to her l a river,
66:12 wealth of the nations l an overflowing stream;
66:14 your bodies shall flourish l the grass;
66:15 and his chariots l the whirlwind,
Jer 2:30 Your own sword devoured your prophets l
3: 2 l a nomad in the wilderness.
4: 4 or else my wrath will go forth l fire,
4:13 He comes up l clouds, his chariots l the whirlwind;
4:17 They have closed in around her l watchers of
5:16 Their quiver is l an open tomb;

Jer 5:26 L fowlers they set a trap;
5:27 L a cage full of birds, their houses are full
6: 9 l a grape-gatherer, pass your hand again
6:23 their sound is l the roaring sea;
6:23 equipped l a warrior for battle, against you,
8: 2 they shall be l dung on the surface of the ground.
8: 6 l a horse plunging headlong into battle.
9: 3 They bend their tongues l bows;
9: 4 and every neighbor goes around l a slanderer.
9:12 the land ruined and laid waste l a wilderness,
9:22 "Human corpses shall fall l dung upon
9:22 l sheaves behind the reaper,
10: 5 Their idols are l scarecrows in a cucumber field,
10: 6 There is none l you, O LORD;
10: 7 and in all their kingdoms there is no one l you.
10:16 Not l these is the LORD, the portion of Jacob,
11:19 But I was l a gentle lamb led to the slaughter.
12: 3 Pull them out l sheep for the slaughter,
12: 8 My heritage has become to me l a lion in
13:10 and worship them, shall be l this loincloth,
13:21 l those of a woman in labor?
13:24 I will scatter you l chaff driven by the wind from
14: 6 they pant for air l jackals;
14: 8 why should you be l a stranger in the land,
14: 8 l a traveler turning aside for the night?
14: 9 Why should you be l someone confused,
14: 9 l a mighty warrior who cannot give help?
15:18 Truly, you are to me l a deceitful brook,
15:18 to me like a deceitful brook, l waters that fail.
16: 4 they shall become l dung on the surface of
17: 6 They shall be l a shrub in the desert,
17: 8 They shall be l a tree planted by water,
17:11 L the partridge hatching what it did not lay,
18: 6 Just l the clay in the potter's hand,
18:13 Who has heard the l of this?
18:17 L the wind from the east,
19:12 and to its inhabitants, making this city l Topheth.
19:13 of Judah shall be defiled l the place of Topheth—
20: 9 within me there is something l a burning fire shut
20:11 But the LORD is with me l a dread warrior;
20:16 be l the cities that the LORD overthrew
21:12 or else my wrath will go forth l fire, and burn,
22: 6 You are l Gilead to me, l the summit of Lebanon;
23: 9 become l a drunkard, l one overcome by wine,
23:12 be to them l slippery paths in the darkness,
23:14 all of them have become l Sodom to me,
23:14 and its inhabitants l Gomorrah.
23:29 Is not my word l fire, says the LORD,
23:29 and l a hammer that breaks a rock in pieces?
24: 2 One basket had very good figs, l first-ripe figs,
24: 5 L these good figs, so I will regard as good
24: 8 L the bad figs that are so bad they cannot
25:30 and shout, l those who tread grapes,
25:34 and you shall fall l a choice vessel.
25:38 L a lion he has left his covert;
26: 6 then I will make this house l Shiloh,
26: 9 saying, 'This house shall be l Shiloh,
26:20 and against this land in words exactly l those
29:17 and I will make them l rotten figs that are
29:22 "The LORD make you l Zedekiah and Ahab,
30: 6 with his hands on his loins l a woman in labor?
30: 7 that day is so great there is none l it;
31:12 their life shall become l a watered garden,
31:18 I was l a calf untrained.
31:32 be l the covenant that I made with their ancestors
34:18 I will make l the calf when they cut it in two
46: 7 rising l the Nile, l rivers whose waters surge?
46: 8 Egypt rises l the Nile, l rivers whose waters surge.
46:18 one is coming l Tabor among the mountains,
46:18 and l Carmel by the sea.
46:21 her mercenaries in her midst are l fatted calves;
46:22 She makes a sound l a snake gliding away;
46:22 against her with axes, l those who fell trees.
48: 6 Be l a wild ass in the desert!
48:11 settled l wine on its dregs;
48:28 Be l the dove that nests on the sides of the mouth
48:36 Therefore my heart moans for Moab l a flute,
48:36 and my heart moans l a flute for the people
48:38 I have broken Moab l a vessel that no one wants,
48:40 Look, he shall swoop down l an eagle,
48:41 shall be l the heart of a woman in labor.
49:19 L a lion coming up from the thickets of
49:19 For who is l me?
49:22 he shall mount up and swoop down l an eagle,
49:22 that day shall be l the heart of a woman in labor.
49:23 they are troubled l the sea that cannot be quiet.
50: 8 and be l male goats leading the flock.
50: 9 Their arrows are l the arrows of
50:11 about l a heifer on the grass, and neigh l stallions,
50:26 pile her up l heaps of grain,
50:42 The sound of them is l the roaring sea;
50:43 pain l that of a woman in labor.
50:44 L a lion coming up from the thickets of
50:44 For who is l me?
51:14 I will fill you with troops l a swarm of locusts,
51:19 Not l these is the LORD, the portion of Jacob,
51:27 bring up horses l bristling locusts.
51:33 Daughter Babylon is l a threshing floor at
51:34 he has swallowed me l a monster;
51:38 L lions they shall roar together;
51:38 they shall growl l lions' whelps.
51:40 down l lambs to the slaughter, l rams and goats.
51:55 Their waves roar l mighty waters,
La 1: 1 How l a widow she has become,
1: 6 Her princes have become l stags
1:12 Look and see if there is any sorrow l my sorrow,
1:20 in the house it is l death.
La 2: 3 he has burned l a flaming fire in Jacob,
2: 4 He has bent his bow l an enemy,
2: 4 with his right hand set l a foe;
2: 4 he has poured out his fury l fire.
2: 5 The Lord has become l an enemy;
2: 6 He has broken down his booth l a garden,
2:12 they faint l the wounded in the streets of the city,
2:18 Let tears stream down l a torrent day and night!
2:19 Pour out your heart l water before the presence
3: 6 he has made me sit in darkness l the dead
3:52 without cause have hunted me l a bird;
4: 3 l the ostriches in the wilderness.
4: 7 were more ruddy than coral, their hair l sapphire.
5: 3 our mothers are l widows.
Eze 1: 4 something l gleaming amber.
1: 5 of it was something l four living creatures.
1: 7 soles of their feet were l the sole of a calf's foot;
1: 7 and they sparkled l burnished bronze.
1:13 that looked l burning coals of fire,
1:13 l torches moving to and fro among
1:14 The living creatures darted to and fro, l a flash
1:16 their appearance was l the gleaming of beryl;
1:16 their construction being something l a wheel
1:22 living creatures there was something l a dome,
1:22 shining l crystal, spread out above their heads.
1:24 of their wings l the sound of mighty waters,
1:24 l the thunder of the Almighty,
1:24 a sound of tumult l the sound of an army;
1:26 over their heads there was something l a throne,
1:26 in appearance l sapphire;
1:26 throne was something that seemed l a human form.
1:27 from what appeared l the loins I saw something
1:27 like the loins I saw something l gleaming amber,
1:27 something that looked l fire enclosed all around;
1:27 from what looked l the loins I saw something that
looked l fire,
1:28 L the bow in a cloud on a rainy day,
2: 8 do not be rebellious l that rebellious house;
3: 9 L the hardest stone, harder than flint,
3:13 that sounded l a loud rumbling.
3:23 l the glory that I had seen by the river Chebar;
5: 9 and the l of which I will never do again.
7:16 be found on the mountains l doves of the valleys,
8: 2 there was a figure that looked l a human being;
8: 2 l the appearance of brightness, l gleaming amber.
8: 4 l the vision that I had seen in the valley.
10: 1 above them something l a sapphire,
10: 5 l the voice of God Almighty when he speaks.
10: 9 appearance of the wheels was l gleaming beryl.
10:10 something l a wheel within a wheel.
10:21 underneath their wings something l human hands.
10:22 As for what their faces were l,
12: 3 you shall go l an exile from your place
13: 4 Your prophets have been l jackals among ruins,
13:20 the lives that you hunt down l birds.
15: 6 L the wood of the vine among the trees of
16: 7 and grow up l a plant of the field."
16:16 nothing l this has ever been or ever shall be.
16:31 Yet you were not l a whore,
16:44 "L mother, l daughter."
17: 5 he set it l a willow twig.
19:10 Your mother was l a vine in
20:32 the thought, "Let us be l the nations,
20:32 l the tribes of the countries,
21:10 honed to flash l lightning!
21:23 But to them it will seem l a false divination;
21:28 for slaughter Polished to consume, to flash l
22:25 Its princes within it are l a roaring lion tearing
22:27 Its officials within it are l wolves tearing
23:15 all of them looking l officers—
23:20 whose members were l those of donkeys,
23:20 and whose emission was l that of stallions.
25: 8 The house of Judah is l all the other nations,
26:10 when he enters your gates l those entering
26:19 l cities that are not inhabited,
27:32 "Who was ever destroyed l Tyre in the midst of
31: 2 Whom are you l in your greatness?
31: 8 no tree in the garden of God was l it in beauty.
31:18 among the trees of Eden was l you in glory and
32: 2 but you are l a dragon in the seas;
32:14 and cause their streams to run l oil,
33:32 To them you are l a singer of love songs,
36:17 their conduct in my sight was l the uncleanness
36:35 "This land that was desolate has become l
36:37 to increase their population l a flock.
36:38 L the flock for sacrifices, l the flock at Jerusalem
38: 9 You shall advance, coming on l a storm;
38: 9 you shall be l a cloud covering the land,
38:16 l a cloud covering the earth.
40: 2 on which was a structure l a city to the south.
40: 3 whose appearance shone l bronze,
40:25 l the windows of the others;
42: 6 they had no pillars l the pillars of the outer court;
43: 2 the sound was l the sound of mighty waters;
43: 3 The vision I saw was l the vision that I had seen
43: 3 l the vision that I had seen by the river Chebar;
45:14 l the homer, contains ten baths);
47:10 l the fish of the Great Sea.
Da 2:35 were all broken in pieces and became l the chaff
4:25 You shall be made to eat grass l oxen,
4:32 You shall be made to eat grass l oxen,
4:33 ate grass l oxen, and his body was bathed with
4:33 and his nails became l birds' claws.
5:11 and wisdom l the wisdom of the gods.
5:21 and his mind was made l that of an animal.
5:21 he was fed grass l oxen,
7: 4 The first was l a lion and had eagles' wings.
Da 7: 4 from the ground and made to stand on two feet l
7: 5 a second one, that looked l a bear.
7: 6 this, as I watched, another appeared, l a leopard.
7: 8 There were eyes l human eyes in this horn,
7: 9 and the hair of his head l pure wool;
7:13 I saw one l a human being coming with the clouds
10: 6 His body was l beryl, his face l lightning, his eyes
l flaming torches, his arms and legs l the gleam of
burnished bronze, and the sound of his words l the
roar of a multitude.
11:10 which shall advance l a flood and pass through,
11:40 king of the north shall rush upon him l a whirlwind
11:40 against countries and pass through l a flood.
12: 3 Those who are wise shall shine l the brightness
12: 3 l the stars forever and ever.
Hos 1:10 the people of Israel shall be l the sand of the sea,
2: 3 and make her l a wilderness,
4: 9 And it shall be l people, l priest;
4:16 L a stubborn heifer, Israel is stubborn;
4:16 now feed them l a lamb in a broad pasture?
5:10 of Judah have become l those who remove
5:10 on them I will pour out my wrath l water.
5:12 Therefore I am l maggots to Ephraim,
5:12 and l rottenness to the house of Judah.
5:14 For I will be l a lion to Ephraim,
5:14 and l a young lion to the house of Judah.
6: 3 he will come to us l the showers,
6: 3 l the spring rains that water the earth."
6: 4 Your love is l a morning cloud,
6: 4 l the dew that goes away early.
7: 4 They are all adulterers; they are l a heated oven,
7: 6 For they are kindled l an oven,
7: 6 in the morning it blazes l a flaming fire.
7:11 Ephraim has become l a dove,
7:12 I will bring them down l birds of the air;
7:16 they have become l a defective bow;
8: 1 One l a vulture is over the house of the LORD,
9: 4 Such sacrifices shall be l mourners' bread;
9:10 L grapes in the wilderness, I found Israel.
9:10 L the first fruit on the fig tree, in its first season,
9:10 and became detestable l the thing they loved.
9:11 Ephraim's glory shall fly away l a bird—
10: 4 up l poisonous weeds in the furrows of the field.
10: 7 Samaria's king shall perish l a chip on the face of
11: 4 was to them l those who lift infants to their cheeks.
11: 8 How can I make you l Admah?
11: 8 How can I treat you l Zeboiim?
11:10 after the LORD, who roars l a lion;
11:11 They shall come trembling l birds from Egypt,
11:11 and l doves from the land of Assyria;
12:11 be l stone heaps on the furrows of the field.
13: 3 Therefore they shall be l the morning mist or l the
dew that goes away early, l chaff that swirls from
the threshing floor or l smoke from a window.
13: 7 So I will become l a lion to them,
13: 7 l a leopard I will lurk beside the way.
13: 8 I will fall upon them l a bear robbed of her cubs,
13: 8 there I will devour them l a lion,
14: 5 I will be l the dew to Israel; he shall blossom l the
lily, he shall strike root l the forests of Lebanon.
14: 6 his beauty shall be l the olive tree,
14: 6 and his fragrance l that of Lebanon.
14: 7 they shall blossom l the vine,
14: 7 their fragrance shall be l the wine of Lebanon.
14: 8 I am l an evergreen cypress;
Joel 1: 8 Lament l a virgin dressed in sackcloth for
2: 2 L blackness spread upon the mountains a great
2: 2 their l has never been from of old,
2: 3 Before them the land is l the garden of Eden,
2: 4 and l war-horses they charge.
2: 5 l the crackling of a flame of fire devouring
2: 5 l a powerful army drawn up for battle.
2: 7 L warriors they charge, l soldiers they scale the
2: 9 they enter through the windows l a thief.
Am 2: 9 whose height was l the height of cedars,
4:11 and you were l a brand snatched from the fire;
5: 6 or he will break out against the house of Joseph l
5:24 But let justice roll down l waters,
5:24 and righteousness l an ever-flowing stream.
6: 5 and l David improvise on instruments of music;
8: 8 and all of it rise l the Nile,
8: 8 and be tossed about and sink again, l the Nile
8:10 I will make it l the mourning for an only son,
8:10 and the end of it l a bitter day.
9: 5 all of it rises l the Nile, and sinks again, l the Nile
9: 7 Are you not l the Ethiopians to me,
Ob 1: 4 Though you soar aloft l the eagle,
1:11 you too were l one of them.
Mic 1: 4 l wax near the fire,l waters poured down a steep
1: 8 I will make lamentation l the jackals,
1: 8 and mourning l the ostriches.
2:12 I will set them together l sheep in a fold,
2:12 l a flock in its pasture; it will resound with people.
3: 3 chop them up l meat in a kettle, l flesh in a
4: 9 that pangs have seized you l a woman in labor?
4:10 O daughter Zion, l a woman in labor;
5: 7 be l dew from the LORD, l showers on the grass,
5: 8 shall be l a lion among the animals of the forest,
5: 8 l a young lion among the flocks of sheep, which,
7: 1 For I have become l one who,
7: 4 The best of them is l a brier,
7:10 she will be trodden down l the mire of the streets.
7:17 they shall lick dust l a snake,
7:17 l the crawling things of the earth;
7:18 Who is a God l you,
Na 1: 6 His wrath is poured out l fire,
1:10 L thorns they are entangled,

Na 1:10 l drunkards they are drunk;
1:10 they are consumed l dry straw.
2: 4 their appearance is l torches, they dart l lightning.
2: 7 moaning l doves and beating their breasts.
2: 8 Nineveh is l a pool whose waters run away.
3:12 All your fortresses are l fig trees
3:15 It will devour you l the locust.
3:15 Multiply yourselves l the locust, multiply l the grasshopper!
3:17 Your guards are l grasshoppers, your scribes l swarms of locusts
Hab 1: 8 they fly l an eagle swift to devour.
1: 9 they gather captives l sand.
1:11 Then they sweep by l the wind;
1:14 You have made people l the fish of the sea,
1:14 l crawling things that have no ruler.
2: 5 l Death they never have enough.
3: 4 The brightness was l the sun;
3:14 who came l a whirlwind to scatter us,
3:19 he makes my feet l the feet of a deer,
Zep 1:17 upon people that they shall walk l the blind;
1:17 their blood shall be poured out l dust, and their flesh l dung.
2: 2 before you are driven away l the drifting chaff,
2: 9 Moab shall become l Sodom and the Ammonites l Gomorrah,
2:13 a desolation, a dry waste l the desert.
Hag 2:23 says the LORD, and make you l a signet ring;
Zec 1: 4 Do not be l your ancestors,
2: 4 Jerusalem shall be inhabited l villages
2: 6 for I have spread you abroad l the four winds
5: 9 they had wings l the wings of a stork,
9: 3 and heaped up silver l dust, and gold l the dirt
9: 7 it shall be l a clan in Judah,
9: 7 and Ekron shall be l the Jebusites.
9:13 O Greece, and wield you l a warrior's sword.
9:14 and his arrow go forth l lightning;
9:15 shall drink their blood l wine, and be full l a bowl,
9:15 drenched l the corners of the altar.
9:16 for l the jewels of a crown they shall shine
10: 2 Therefore the people wander l sheep;
10: 3 and will make them l his proud war horse.
10: 5 Together they shall be l warriors in battle,
10: 7 the people of Ephraim shall become l warriors,
12: 6 of Judah l a blazing pot on a pile of wood,
12: 6 l a flaming torch among sheaves;
12: 8 feeblest among them on that day shall be l David,
12: 8 and the house of David shall be l God,
12: 8 l the angel of the LORD, at their head.
14:15 a plague l this plague shall fall on the horses,
Mal 3: 2 For he is l a refiner's fire and l fullers' soap;
3: 3 the descendants of Levi and refine them l gold
4: 1 See, the day is coming, burning l an oven,
4: 2 You shall go out leaping l calves from the stall.
Mt 3:16 of God descending l a dove and alighting on him.
6: 5 whenever you pray, do not be l the hypocrites;
6: 8 be l them, for your Father knows what you need
6:16 do not look dismal, l the hypocrites,
6:29 even Solomon in all his glory was not clothed l
7:24 on them will be l a wise man who built his house
7:26 be l a foolish man who built his house on sand.
9:33 "Never has anything l this been seen in Israel."
9:36 l sheep without a shepherd.
10:16 I am sending you out l sheep into the midst
10:25 it is enough for the disciple to be l the teacher,
10:25 and the slave l the master.
11:16 It is l children sitting in the marketplaces
13:31 kingdom of heaven is l a mustard seed
13:33 kingdom of heaven is l yeast that a woman took
13:43 the righteous will shine l the sun in the kingdom
13:44 kingdom of heaven is l treasure hidden in a field,
13:45 of heaven is l a merchant in search of fine pearls;
13:47 the kingdom of heaven is l a net that was thrown
13:52 for the kingdom of heaven is l the master of
17: 2 and his face shone l the sun,
18: 3 unless you change and become l children,
18: 4 Whoever becomes humble l this child is
20: 1 kingdom of heaven is l a landowner who went out
22:30 but are l angels in heaven.
22:39 And a second is l it:
23:27 For you are l whitewashed tombs,
25: 1 "Then the kingdom of heaven will be l this.
28: 3 His appearance was l lightning,
28: 4 of him the guards shook and became l dead men.
Mk 1:10 and the Spirit descending l a dove on him.
2:12 saying, "We have never seen anything l this!"
4:31 It is l a mustard seed, which,
6:15 "It is a prophet, l one of the prophets of old."
6:34 because they were l sheep without a shepherd;
7:13 And you do many things l this."
8:24 "I can see people, but they look l trees, walking."
9:26 it came out, and the boy was l a corpse,
12:25 but are l angels in heaven.
12:38 who l to walk around in long robes,
13:34 It is l a man going on a journey,
Lk 2:48 "Child, why have you treated us l this?
3:22 upon him in bodily form l a dove.
5:33 "John's disciples, l the disciples of the Pharisees,
6:40 but everyone who is fully qualified will be l
6:47 I will show you what someone is l who comes
6:48 That one is l a man building a house,
6:49 and does not act is l a man who built a house on
7:31 of this generation, and what are they l?
7:32 They are l children sitting in the marketplace
10: 3 I am sending you out l lambs into the midst
10:18 "I watched Satan fall from heaven l a flash
11:44 For you are l unmarked graves,
Lk 12:27 even Solomon in all his glory was not clothed l
12:36 be l those who are waiting for their master
13:18 "What is the kingdom of God l?
13:19 It is l a mustard seed that someone took
13:21 It is l yeast that a woman took and mixed in
15:19 treat me l one of your hired hands." '
15:29 For all these years I have been working l a slave
16:25 and Lazarus in l manner evil things;
17:30 —it will be l that on the day that the Son of Man
18:11 'God, I thank you that I am not l other people:
18:11 rogues, adulterers, or even l this tax collector.
20:36 they are l angels and are children of God,
20:46 who l to walk around in long robes,
21:35 l a trap. For it will come upon all
22:26 rather the greatest among you must become l
22:26 and the leader l one who serves.
22:31 Satan has demanded to sift all of you l wheat,
22:44 ⟦and his sweat became l great drops of blood⟧
Jn 1:32 the Spirit descending from heaven l a dove,
6:58 not l that which your ancestors ate,
7:46 "Never has anyone spoken l this!"
8:55 I would be a liar l you.
9: 9 "No, but it is someone l him."
11:48 If we let him go on l this,
15: 6 Whoever does not abide in me is thrown away l
Ac 2: 2 And suddenly from heaven there came a sound l
3:22 up for you from your own people a prophet l me.
6:15 they saw that his face was l the face of an angel.
8:32 "L a sheep he was led to the slaughter,
8:32 and l a lamb silent before its shearer,
9:18 And immediately something l scales fell
10:11 and something l a large sheet coming down,
11: 5 There was something l a large sheet coming
14:15 We are mortals just l you,
17:20 so we would l to know what it means."
17:29 we ought not to think that the deity is l gold,
25:22 "I would l to hear the man myself."
28:22 But we would l to hear from you what you think,
Ro 5:14 even over those whose sins were not l
5:15 But the free gift is not l the trespass.
5:16 free gift is not l the effect of the one man's sin.
6: 5 if we have been united with him in a death l his,
6: 5 be united with him in a resurrection l his.
9:20 "Why have you made me l this?"
9:27 the children of Israel were l the sand of the sea,
9:29 have fared l Sodom and been made l Gomorrah."
1Co 3:10 l a skilled master builder I laid a foundation,
4:13 We have become l the rubbish of the world,
13:11 When I was a child, I spoke l a child, I thought l a child, I reasoned l a child;
14: 5 Now I would l all of you to speak in tongues,
2Co 2:17 we are not peddlers of God's word l so many;
3:13 not l Moses, who put a veil over his face to keep
11:23 I am talking l a madman—
Gal 2:14 though a Jew, live l a Gentile and not l a Jew,
2:14 how can you compel the Gentiles to live l Jews?"
4:28 my friends, are children of the promise, l Isaac.
5:21 drunkenness, carousing, and things l these.
Eph 2: 3 by nature children of wrath, l everyone else.
Php 2:15 in which you shine l stars in the world.
2:20 I have no one l him who will
2:22 how l a son with a father he has served with me
3:10 of his sufferings by becoming l him in his death,
1Th 2: 7 l a nurse tenderly caring for her own children.
2:11 with each one of you l a father with his children,
4: 5 l the Gentiles who do not know God;
5: 2 that the day of the Lord will come l a thief in
5: 4 for that day to surprise you l a thief;
2Ti 2: 3 in suffering l a good soldier of Christ Jesus.
2: 9 even to the point of being chained l a criminal.
2:17 and their talk will spread l gangrene.
Heb 1:11 they will all wear out l clothing;
1:12 l a cloak you will roll them up,
1:12 and l clothing they will be changed.
2:17 Therefore he had to become l his brothers
8: 9 not l the covenant that I made with their ancestors,
12:16 See to it that no one becomes l Esau,
Jas 1: 6 for the one who doubts is l a wave of the sea,
1:10 the rich will disappear l a flower in the field.
1:23 they are l those who look at themselves in
1:24 immediately forget what they were l.
5: 3 and it will eat your flesh l fire.
5:17 Elijah was a human being l us,
1Pe 1:14 L obedient children, do not be conformed to
1:18 not with perishable things l silver or gold,
1:19 l that of a lamb without defect or blemish.
1:24 "All flesh is l grass and all its glory l the flower
2: 2 L newborn infants, long for the pure,
2: 5 l living stones, let yourselves be built into
2:25 For you were going astray l sheep,
4: 3 in doing what the Gentiles l to do,
4:10 L good stewards of the manifold grace of God,
5: 8 L a roaring lion your adversary the devil prowls
2Pe 2:12 These people, however, are l irrational animals,
3: 8 that with the Lord one day is l a thousand years, and a thousand years are l one day.
3:10 But the day of the Lord will come l a thief,
1Jn 3: 2 when he is revealed, we will be l him,
3:12 not be l Cain who was from the evil one
Jude 1:10 l irrational animals, they know by instinct.
Rev 1:10 and I heard behind me a loud voice l a trumpet
1:13 the midst of the lampstands I saw one l the Son
1:14 his eyes were l a flame of fire,
1:15 his feet were l burnished bronze,
1:15 and his voice was l the sound of many waters.
1:16 and his face was l the sun shining with full force.
2:18 who has eyes l a flame of fire,
Rev 2:18 and whose feet are l burnished bronze:
3: 3 If you do not wake up, I will come l a thief,
3: 5 you will be clothed l them in white robes,
4: 1 which I had heard speaking to me l a trumpet,
4: 3 the one seated there looks l jasper and carnelian,
4: 3 the throne is a rainbow that looks l an emerald.
4: 6 throne there is something l a sea of glass, l crystal.
4: 7 the first living creature l a lion, the second living creature l an ox, the third living creature with a face l a human face, and the fourth living creature l a flying eagle.
6:12 the full moon became l blood,
6:14 The sky vanished l a scroll rolling itself up,
8: 8 and something l a great mountain,
8:10 a great star fell from heaven, blazing l a torch,
9: 2 and from the shaft rose smoke l the smoke of
9: 3 and they were given authority l the authority
9: 5 and their torture was l the torture of a scorpion
9: 7 In appearance the locusts were l horses equipped
9: 7 On their heads were what looked l crowns
9: 7 their faces were l human faces,
9: 8 their hair l women's hair, and their teeth l lions'
9: 9 they had scales l iron breastplates,
9: 9 of their wings was l the noise of many chariots
9:10 They have tails l scorpions, with stingers,
9:17 the heads of the horses were l lions' heads,
9:19 their tails are l serpents, having heads;
10: 1 his face was l the sun, and his legs l pillars of fire.
10: 3 a great shout, l a lion roaring.
11: 1 Then I was given a measuring rod l a staff,
12:15 from his mouth the serpent poured water l a river
13: 2 And the beast that I saw was l a leopard, its feet were l a bear's, and its mouth was l a lion's mouth.
13: 4 saying, "Who is l the beast,
13:11 it had two horns l a lamb and it spoke l a dragon.
14: 2 heaven l the sound of many waters and l the sound
14: 2 the voice I heard was l the sound of harpists
14:14 seated on the cloud was one l the Son of Man,
16: 3 and it became l the blood of a corpse,
16:13 And I saw three foul spirits l frogs coming from
16:15 ("See, I am coming l a thief!
18: 7 so give her a l measure of torment and grief.
18:18 "What city was l the great city?"
18:21 a mighty angel took up a stone l a great millstone
19: 6 l the sound of many waters and l the sound of
19:12 His eyes are l a flame of fire,
21:11 of God and a radiance l a very rare jewel, l jasper,
Tob 5:10 but I lie in darkness l the dead who no longer see
8: 6 let us make a helper for him l himself.'
14: 5 and they will rebuild the temple of God, but not l
Jdt 2:20 crowd l a swarm of locusts, l the dust of the earth
8:16 for God is not l a human being, to be threatened,
8:16 or l a mere mortal, to be won over by pleading.
10:19 who have women l this among them?
11:19 You will drive them l sheep
12:13 and to become today l one of the Assyrian women
16:12 and wounded them l the children of fugitives;
16:15 before your glance the rocks shall melt l wax.
AdE 14:16 I abhor it l a filthy rag,
15:13 "I saw you, my lord, l an angel of God,
Wis 2: 3 and the spirit will dissolve l empty air.
2: 4 our life will pass away l the traces of a cloud,
2: 4 and be scattered l mist that is chased by
3: 6 l gold in the furnace he tried them,
3: 6 l a sacrificial burnt offering he accepted them.
3: 7 and will run l sparks through the stubble.
5: 9 "All those things have vanished l a shadow,
5: 9 and l a rumor that passes by;
5:10 l a ship that sails through the billowy water,
5:14 the ungodly is l thistledown carried by the wind,
5:14 and l a light frost driven away by a storm;
5:14 it is dispersed l smoke before the wind,
5:14 and it passes l the remembrance of a guest
5:23 and l a tempest it will winnow them away.
7: 1 I also am mortal, l everyone else,
11:22 Because the whole world before you is l a speck
11:22 l a drop of morning dew that falls on the ground.
12:24 they were deceived l foolish infants.
13:14 or makes it l some worthless animal, giving it
15:16 for none can form gods that are l themselves.
16:29 of an ungrateful person will melt l wintry frost,
16:29 and flow away l waste water.
19: 9 For they ranged l horses, and leaped l lambs,
Sir 3: 4 and those who respect their mother are l
3:15 l frost in fair weather, your sins will melt away.
3:16 Whoever forsakes a father is l a blasphemer,
4:10 and be l a husband to their mother;
4:10 you will then be l a son of the Most High,
4:30 Do not be l a lion in your home,
6: 3 and you will be left l a withered tree.
6:19 Come to her l one who plows and sows,
6:21 She will be l a heavy stone to test them,
6:22 For wisdom is l her name;
6:31 You will wear her l a glorious robe,
6:31 and put her on l a splendid crown.
9: 8 and by it passion is kindled l a fire.
9:10 A new friend is l new wine;
9:11 for you do not know what their end will be l.
11:30 L a decoy partridge in a cage,
11:30 and l spies they observe your weakness;
12:10 for l corrosion in copper, so is his wickedness.
12:11 Be to him l one who polishes a mirror,
13: 1 with a proud person becomes l him.
13:15 Every creature loves its l,
13:16 and people stick close to those l themselves.
14:17 All living beings become old l a garment,
14:18 L abundant leaves on a spreading tree

Sir 14:22 pursuing her l a hunter, and lying in wait
15: 2 She will come to meet him l a mother,
15: 2 and l a young bride she will welcome him.
16:21 L a tempest that no one can see,
17: 3 He endowed them with strength l his own,
17:22 One's almsgiving is l a signet ring with the Lord,
17:22 and he will keep a person's kindness l the apple
18:10 L a drop of water from the sea and a grain
18:23 do not be l one who puts the Lord to the test.
19:11 the fool suffers birth pangs l a woman in labor
19:12 L an arrow stuck in a person's thigh,
20: 4 L a eunuch lusting to violate a girl is
20:15 he opens his mouth l a town crier.
20:19 A coarse person is l an inappropriate story,
20:29 l a muzzle on the mouth they stop reproofs.
21: 3 All lawlessness is l a two-edged sword;
21: 8 with other people's money is l one who gathers
21: 9 An assembly of the wicked is l a bundle of tow,
21:13 knowledge of the wise will increase l a flood,
21:13 and their counsel l a life-giving spring.
21:14 The mind of a fool is l a broken jar;
21:16 A fool's chatter is l a burden on a journey,
21:18 L a house in ruins is wisdom to a fool,
21:19 and l manacles on his right hand.
21:21 To the sensible person education is l
21:21 and l a bracelet on the right arm.
22: 1 The idler is l a filthy stone,
22: 2 The idler is l the filth of dunghills;
22: 6 L music in time of mourning
22: 9 a fool is l one who glues potsherds together,
22:17 on an intelligent thought is l stucco decoration
23:14 and behave l a fool through bad habit;
23:16 that blazes l a fire will not be quenched
24: 3 and covered the earth l a mist.
24:13 "I grew tall l a cedar in Lebanon,
24:13 and l a cypress on the heights of Hermon.
24:14 I grew tall l a palm tree in En-gedi,
24:14 and l rosebushes in Jericho;
24:14 l a fair olive tree in the field,
24:14 and l a plane tree beside water I grew tall.
24:15 L cassia and camel's thorn I gave forth perfume,
24:15 and l choice myrrh I spread my fragrance,
24:15 l galbanum, onycha, and stacte,
24:15 and l the odor of incense in the tent.
24:16 L a terebinth I spread out my branches,
24:17 L the vine I bud forth delights,
24:25 It overflows, l the Pishon, with wisdom,
24:25 and l the Tigris at the time of the first fruits.
24:26 It runs over, l the Euphrates, with understanding,
24:26 and l the Jordan at harvest time.
24:27 It pours forth instruction l the Nile,
24:27 l the Gihon at the time of vintage.
24:30 As for me, I was l a canal from a river,
24:30 l a water channel into a garden.
24:32 I will again make instruction shine forth l the dawn
24:33 I will again pour out teaching l prophecy,
25:17 and darkens her face l that of a bear.
26: 7 taking hold of her is l grasping a scorpion.
26:16 L the sun rising in the heights of the Lord,
26:17 L the shining lamp on the holy lampstand,
26:18 L golden pillars on silver bases,
26:27 *A loud-voiced and garrulous wife is l a trumpet*
26:27 *and every person l this lives in the anarchy*
27: 8 you will attain it and wear it l a glorious robe.
27:11 but the fool changes l the moon.
27:20 and has escaped l a gazelle from a snare.
27:28 but vengeance lies in wait for them l a lion.
28: 4 If one has no mercy toward another l himself,
28:23 It will be sent out against them l a lion;
28:23 l a leopard it will mangle them.
29:18 and has tossed them about l waves of the sea;
29:25 and besides this you will hear rude words l these:
30: 4 for he has left behind him one l himself,
30:18 that is closed are l offerings of food placed upon
31:16 before you l a well brought-up person,
32:16 and they will kindle righteous deeds l a light.
33: 2 but the one who is hypocritical about it is l a boat
33: 5 The heart of a fool is l a cart wheel,
33: 5 and his thoughts l a turning axle.
33: 6 A mocking friend is l a stallion
33:13 L clay in the hand of the potter,
33:16 I was l a gleaner following the grape-pickers;
33:17 and l a grape-picker I filled my wine press.
33:31 If you have but one slave, treat him l yourself,
33:31 If you have but one slave, treat him l a brother,
34: 5 and l a woman in labor, the mind has fantasies.
34:24 L one who kills a son before his father's eyes is
35:22 and l a warrior will not be patient
37: 2 Is it not a sorrow l that for death itself when
38:22 Remember his fate, for yours is l it;
39:12 I am full l the full moon.
39:13 blossom l a rose growing by a stream of water.
39:14 Send out fragrance l incense,
39:14 and put forth blossoms l a lily.
39:22 "His blessing covers the dry land l a river,
39:22 and drenches it l a flood.
40: 6 by the visions of his mind l one who has escaped
40:13 The wealth of the unjust will dry up l a river,
40:13 and crash l a loud clap of thunder in a storm.
40:17 but kindness is l a garden of blessings,
40:27 The fear of the Lord is l a garden of blessing,
43:14 and the clouds fly out l birds.
43:17 He scatters the snow l birds flying down,
43:17 and its descent is l locusts alighting.
43:19 He pours frost over the earth l salt,
43:19 and icicles form l pointed thorns.
43:20 and the water puts it on l a breastplate.
Sir 43:21 and withers the tender grass l fire.
44:19 and no one has been found l him in glory.
44:21 and exalt his offspring l the stars,
45: 6 a holy man l Moses who was his brother,
45:11 with precious stones engraved l seals,
45:12 inscribed l a seal with "Holiness,"
47:14 You overflowed l the Nile with understanding.
47:18 you gathered gold l tin and amassed silver l lead.
48: 1 Then Elijah arose, a prophet l fire, and his word burned l a torch.
48:19 and they were in anguish, l women in labor.
49: 1 The name of Josiah is l blended incense prepared
49: 1 and l music at a banquet of wine.
49:11 He was l a signet ring on the right hand,
49:14 Few have ever been created on earth l Enoch,
49:15 Nor was anyone ever born l Joseph;
50: 3 a reservoir l the sea in circumference.
50: 6 L the morning star among the clouds,
50: 6 l the full moon at the festal season;
50: 7 l the sun shining on the temple of the Most High,
50: 7 l the rainbow gleaming in splendid clouds;
50: 8 l roses in the days of first fruits,
50: 8 l lilies by a spring of water,
50: 8 l a green shoot on Lebanon on a summer day;
50: 9 l fire and incense in the censer,
50: 9 l a vessel of hammered gold studded
50:10 l an olive tree laden with fruit,
50:10 and l a cypress towering in the clouds.
50:12 he was l a young cedar on Lebanon surrounded
Bar 1:11 their days on earth may be l the days of heaven.
2: 2 the whole heaven there has not been done the l
4:26 they were taken away l a flock carried off by
LtJ 6: 5 So beware of becoming at all l the foreigners or
6:11 They deck their gods out with garments l
6:14 One of them holds a scepter, l a district judge,
6:20 They are just l a beam of the temple,
6:39 of wood and overlaid with gold and silver are l
6:55 they are l crows between heaven and earth.
6:55 but the gods will be burned up l timbers.
6:67 or shine l the sun or give light l the moon.
6:70 L a scarecrow in a cucumber bed,
6:71 are l a thornbush in a garden
6:71 or l a corpse thrown out in the darkness.
Aza 1:13 to multiply their descendants l the stars of heaven and l the sand on the shore of the sea.
Sus 1:27 nothing l this had ever been said about Susanna.
1Mc 1:39 Her sanctuary became desolate l a desert;
2: 8 Her temple has become l a person without honor;
3: 3 L a giant he put on his breastplate;
3: 4 He was l a lion in his deeds,
3: 4 l a lion's cub roaring for prey.
3:45 Jerusalem was uninhabited l a wilderness;
4:47 and built a new altar l the former one.
6:39 the hills were ablaze with them and gleamed l
9:29 of your brother Judas there has been no one l him
11: 1 l the sand by the seashore, and many ships;
2Mc 7:37 l my brothers, give up body and life for the laws
8:35 and made his way alone l a runaway slave across
10: 6 in the mountains and caves l wild animals.
11:11 They hurled themselves l lions against
1Es 1:20 No passover l it had been kept in Israel since
8:57 of fine bronze that glittered l gold.
3Mc 4: 9 They were brought on board l wild animals,
7:19 in l manner they decided to observe these days as
2Es 4:15 In l manner the waves of the sea also made
4:24 We pass from the world l locusts,
4:24 and our life is l a mist,
4:36 the number of those l yourselves is completed;
4:41 the chambers of the souls are l the womb.
5:18 l a shepherd who leaves the flock in the power
5:52 not l those whom you bore before,
6:17 and its sound was l the sound of mighty waters.
6:24 friends shall make war on friends l enemies,
6:56 and that they are l spittle,
7: 4 so that it is l a river.
7:*61* for it is they who are now l a mist,
7:*62* of the dust l the other created things?
7:*97* shown them how their face is to shine l the sun,
7:*97* how they are to be made l the light of the stars,
8:44 because they are made l you,
8:44 have you also made them l the farmer's seed?
8:51 concerning the glory of those who are l yourself,
8:62 but only to you and a few l you."
10:12 'My lamentation is not l the earth's,
10:25 her countenance flashed l lightning,
10:30 lying there l a corpse, deprived
10:33 He said to me, "Stand up l a man,
11:14 so that it disappeared l the first.
11:34 which also in l manner ruled over the earth
12:42 l a cluster of grapes from the vintage,
12:42 and l a lamp in a dark place,
12:42 and l a haven for a ship saved from a storm.
13: 3 looking the wind made something l the figure of
13:10 he sent forth from his mouth something l a stream
13:20 than to pass from the world l a cloud,
14: 9 with my Son and with those who are l you,
14:39 full of something l water, but its color was l fire.
15:10 my people are being led l a flock to
15:23 of the earth and the sinners, l burnt straw.
15:30 shall go forth l wild boars from the forest,
15:47 For you have made yourself l her;
15:50 the glory of your strength shall wither l a flower
15:51 be weakened l a wretched woman who is beaten
15:61 You shall be broken down by them l stubble,
15:61 and they shall be l fire to you.
16:23 And the dead shall be thrown out l dung,
16:40 and in the midst of the calamities be l strangers
2Es 16:41 Let the one who sells be l one who will flee;
16:41 let the one who buys be l one who will lose;
16:42 let the one who does business be l one who will
16:42 the one who builds a house be l one who will
16:43 let the one who sows be l one who will not reap;
16:43 l one who will not gather the grapes;
16:44 l those who will have no children;
16:44 l those who are widowed.
16:51 Therefore do not be l her or her works.
16:59 the heaven l a dome and made it secure upon
16:71 They shall be l maniacs, sparing no one,
16:73 l gold that is tested by fire.
16:77 They are l a field choked with underbrush
4Mc 6: 5 the courageous and noble man, l a true Eleazar,
6:10 L a noble athlete the old man, while being beaten,
7: 1 For l a most skillful pilot,
7: 5 For in setting his mind firm l a jutting cliff,
7:14 and by reason l that of Isaac he rendered
7:19 l our patriarchs Abraham and Isaac and Jacob,
11:10 that he was completely curled back l a scorpion,
12:13 to cut out the tongues of men who have feelings l
13: 9 let us die l brothers for the sake of the law;
15:15 the flesh of the head to the chin exposed l masks.
16:13 a mind l adamant and giving rebirth
17: 3 Nobly set l a roof on the pillars of your sons,

LIKE-MINDED (1) [LIKE, MIND]

Sir 37:12 who is l with yourself, and who will grieve with

LIKED (1) [LIKE]

Mk 6:20 and yet he l to listen to him.

LIKELY (1) [LIKE]

Wis 9:14 and our designs are l to fail;

LIKEN (5) [LIKE]

Isa 40:18 To whom then will you l God,
46: 5 To whom will you l me and make me equal,
La 2:13 To what can I l you, that I may comfort you,
Wis 7: 9 Neither did I l to her any priceless gem,
2Es 5:42 He said to me, "I shall l my judgment to a circle;

LIKENED‡ (1) [LIKE]

Jer 6: 2 I have l daughter Zion to the loveliest pasture.

LIKENESS (22) [LIKE]

Ge 1:26 make humankind in our image, according to our l;
5: 1 he made them in the l of God.
5: 3 he became the father of a son in his l,
Dt 4:16 the l of male or female,
4:17 the l of any animal that is on the earth,
4:17 the l of any winged bird that flies in the air,
4:18 the l of anything that creeps on the ground,
4:18 l of any fish that is in the water under the earth.
Ps 17:15 I awake I shall be satisfied, beholding your l.
Isa 40:18 or what l compare with him?
Eze 1:26 and seated above the l of a throne was something
1:28 This was the appearance of the l of the glory of
Ro 8: 3 by sending his own Son in the l of sinful flesh,
Eph 4:24 the l of God in true righteousness and holiness.
Php 2: 7 the form of a slave, being born in human l.
Jas 3: 9 and with it we curse those who are made in the l
Wis 13:13 he forms it in the l of a human being,
14:19 the l to take more beautiful form,
Sir 34: 3 the l of a face looking at itself.
2Es 8: 6 the l of a human being may be able to live.
10:49 So you saw her l, how she mourned for her son,
4Mc 15: 4 upon the character of a small child a wondrous l

LIKENESSES (2) [LIKE]

Wis 13:10 and l of animals, or a useless stone,
1Mc 3:48 the Gentiles consulted the l of their gods.

LIKES (2) [LIKE]

Ge 27: 9 savory food for your father, such as he l;
3Jn 1: 9 but Diotrephes, who l to put himself first,

LIKEWISE (58) [LIKE]

Ge 32:19 He l instructed the second and the third
32:23 and l everything that he had.
33: 7 Leah l and her children drew near
Ex 26: 4 and l you shall make loops on the edge of
27:11 L for its length on the north side there shall
36:11 l he made them on the edge of
Lev 21: 3 l, for a virgin sister, close to him
Nu 35:20 L, if someone pushes another from hatred,
Dt 2:29 done for me and l the Moabites who live in Ar—
1Sa 14:22 L, when all the Israelites who had gone
2Sa 10:14 they l fled before Abishai, and entered the city.
1Ki 8:41 "L when a foreigner, who is not
1Ch 12:38 l all the rest of Israel were of a single mind
19:15 they l fled before Abishai, Joab's brother,
23:30 and praising the LORD, and l at evening,
2Ch 6:32 "L when foreigners, who are not
32:29 He l provided cities for himself,
Ecc 5:19 L all to whom God gives wealth and possessions
Jer 40:11 L, when all the Judeans who were in Moab and
Eze 18:14 considers, and does not do l,
Mk 12:21 leaving no children; and the third l;
Lk 3:11 and whoever has food must do l."
10:32 So l a Levite, when he came to the place
10:37 Jesus said to him, "Go and do l."

Lk 17:28 L, just as it was in the days of Lot:
17:31 and l anyone in the field must not turn back.
22:36 the one who has a purse must take it, and l a bag.
Jn 5:19 for whatever the Father does, the Son does l.
Ro 4:12 and l the ancestor of the circumcised who are
8:26 L the Spirit helps us in our weakness;
1Co 7: 3 and l the wife to her husband.
7: 4 l the husband does not have authority
1Ti 3: 8 Deacons l must be serious, not double-tongued,
3:11 Women l must be serious, not slanderers,
Tit 2: 3 L, tell the older women to be reverent
2: 6 L, urge the younger men to be self-controlled.
Heb 2:14 he himself l shared the same things,
Jas 2:25 L, was not Rahab the prostitute also justified
Jude 1: 7 L, Sodom and Gomorrah and
Rev 8:12 of the day was kept from shining, and l the night.
Tob 1: 7 l the tenth of the grain, wine, olive oil,
7: 8 and their daughter Sarah l wept.
7:10 L I am not at liberty to give her
12:12 and l whenever you would bury the dead.
AdE 1:18 will l dare to insult their husbands.
Sir 13:19 l the poor are feeding grounds for the rich.
13:20 l the poor are an abomination to the rich.
49: 7 and l to build and to plant.
LtJ 6:28 L their wives preserve some of the meat with salt,
6:35 L they are not able to give either wealth
6:61 and the wind l blows in every land.
2Mc 2:12 L Solomon also kept the eight days.
1Es 4: 6 L those who do not serve in the army
6:30 and l wheat and salt and wine and oil,
8:20 and l up to a hundred cors of wheat,
3Mc 6:33 L also the king, after convening a great banquet
2Es 4:17 l also the plan of the waves of the sea was
4Mc 11:15 we ought l to die for the same principles.

LIKHI (1)
1Ch 7:19 The sons of Shemida were Ahian, Shechem, L,

LIKING (2) [LIKE]
Wis 16:21 was changed to suit everyone's l.
Sir 32:17 and will find a decision according to his l.

LILIES (13) [LILY]
Ps 45: T *To the leader: according to L. Of the Korahites.*
69: T *To the leader: according to L. Of David.*
80: T *To the leader: on L, a Covenant. Of Asaph.*
SS 2:16 he pastures his flock among the l.
4: 5 twins of a gazelle, that feed among the l.
5:13 His lips are l, distilling liquid myrrh.
6: 2 in the gardens, and to gather l.
6: 3 he pastures his flock among the l.
7: 2 Your belly is a heap of wheat, encircled with l.
Mt 6:28 Consider the l of the field, how they grow;
Lk 12:27 Consider the l, how they grow:
Sir 50: 8 like l by a spring of water,
2Es 2:19 on which roses and l grow;

LILITH (1)
Isa 34:14 there too L shall repose, and find a place to rest.

LILY (8) [LILIES, LILY-WORK]
1Ki 7:26 like the flower of a l; it held two thousand baths.
2Ch 4: 5 like the rim of a cup, like the flower of a l;
Ps 60: T *To the leader: according to the L of the Covenant.*
SS 2: 1 I am a rose of Sharon, a l of the valleys.
2: 2 l among brambles, so is my love among maidens.
Hos 14: 5 he shall blossom like the l,
Sir 39:14 and put forth blossoms like a l.
2Es 5:24 of the world you have chosen for yourself one l,

LILY-WORK (2) [LILY]
1Ki 7:19 the tops of the pillars in the vestibule were of l,
7:22 On the tops of the pillars was l.

LIMB (11) [LIMBS]
Lev 21:18 or one who has a mutilated face or a l too long,
22:23 that has a l too long or too short you may present
Jdg 19:29 l by l, and sent her throughout all the territory
Da 2: 5 you shall be torn l from l,
3:29 and Abednego shall be torn l from l,
2Mc 7: 7 eat rather than have your body punished l by l?"
9: 7 fall was so hard as to torture every l of his body.

LIMBS‡ (8) [LIMB]
Job 18:13 the firstborn of Death consumes their l.
40:18 bones are tubes of bronze, its l like bars of iron.
41:12 "I will not keep silence concerning its l,
Da 5: 6 His l gave way, and his knees knocked together.
3Mc 2:22 besides being paralyzed in his l,
4Mc 9:13 stretched around this, his l were dislocated,
9:17 Cut my l, burn my flesh, and twist my joints;
10: 5 dismembering him by prying his l from their

LIME (2)
Isa 33:12 And the peoples will be as if burned to l,
Am 2: 1 he burned to l the bones of the king of Edom.

LIMIT (12) [LIMITATIONS, LIMITED, LIMITS]
Nu 34: 4 and its outer l shall be south of Kadesh-barnea;
34: 8 and the outer l of the boundary shall be at Zedad;
Job 11: 7 Can you find out the l of the Almighty?
15: 8 And do you l wisdom to yourself?
16: 3 Have windy words no l?
34:36 Would that Job were tried to the l,
Ps 119:96 I have seen a l to all perfection,
Pr 8:29 when he assigned to the sea its l,
Na 3: 9 Egypt too, and that without l;
Sir 27:12 Among stupid people l your time,
39:18 and none can l his saving power.
2Es 15: 6 and their harmful doings have reached their l.

LIMITATIONS (1) [LIMIT]
Ro 6:19 in human terms because of your natural l.

LIMITED (2) [LIMIT]
Nu 11:23 "Is the LORD's power l?
3Mc 2:29 also be reduced to their former l status."

LIMITS (8) [LIMIT]
Ex 19:12 You shall set l for the people all around, saying,
19:23 'Set l around the mountain and keep it holy.' "
1Ch 5:16 and in all the pasture lands of Sharon to their l.
Ps 139: 9 the morning and settle at the farthest l of the sea,
Jer 5:28 They know no l in deeds of wickedness;
2Co 10:13 We, however, will not boast beyond l,
10:14 not overstepping our l when we reached you;
10:15 We do not boast beyond l, that is,

LIMP (1) [LIMPED, LIMPING]
Pr 26: 7 The legs of a disabled person hang l;

LIMPED (1) [LIMP]
1Ki 18:26 They l about the altar that they had made.

LIMPING (2) [LIMP]
Ge 32:31 The sun rose upon him as he passed Penuel, l
1Ki 18:21 long will you go l with two different opinions?

LINE‡ (42) [LINEAGE, LINED, LINES]
Nu 34: 7 from the Great Sea you shall mark out your l
Jdg 20:20 the Israelites drew up the battle l against them
20:22 and again formed the battle l in the same place
20:33 the Israelites drew back its battle l to Baal-tamar,
1Sa 4: 2 The Philistines drew up in l against Israel,
4:12 A man of Benjamin ran from the battle l,
17:20 as the army was going forth to the battle l,
17:48 David ran quickly toward the battle l to meet
1Ki 7:23 A l of thirty cubits would encircle it completely.
2Ki 21:13 the measuring l for Samaria, and the plummet for
1Ch 19:10 the l of battle was set against him both in front
2Ch 4: 2 A l of thirty cubits would encircle it completely.
13: 3 and Jeroboam drew up his l of battle against him
Job 38: 5 Or who stretched the l upon it?
Ps 89:29 I will establish his l forever,
89:36 His l shall continue forever,
Isa 28:10 precept upon precept, l upon l, l upon l,
28:13 precept upon precept, l upon l, l upon l,
28:17 And I will make justice the l,
34:11 He shall stretch the l of confusion over it,
34:17 his hand has portioned it out to them with the l;
44:13 The carpenter stretches a l,
Jer 31:39 And the measuring l shall go out farther,
La 2: 8 he stretched the l; he did not withhold his hand
Am 7: 7 beside a wall built with a plumb l, with a plumb l
in his hand.
7: 8 And I said, "A plumb l."
7: 8 a plumb l in the midst of my people Israel;
7:17 and your land shall be parceled out by l;
Mic 2: 5 to cast the l by lot in the assembly of the LORD.
Zec 1:16 the LORD of hosts, and the measuring l shall
2: 1 up and saw a man with a measuring l in his hand.
Sir 47:20 and defiled your family l,
47:22 or destroy the family l of him who loved him.
1Mc 7:14 priest of the l of Aaron has come with the army,
1Es 1:30 his servants took him out of the l of battle.

LINEAGE (18) [LINE]
Nu 1:20 descendants of Reuben, Israel's firstborn, their l,
1:22 The descendants of Simeon, their l,
1:24 The descendants of Gad, their l, in their clans,
1:26 The descendants of Judah, their l, in their clans,
1:28 The descendants of Issachar, their l,
1:30 The descendants of Zebulun, their l,
1:32 the descendants of Ephraim, their l,
1:34 The descendants of Manasseh, their l,
1:36 The descendants of Benjamin, their l,
1:38 The descendants of Dan, their l, in their clans,
1:40 The descendants of Asher, their l, in their clans,
1:42 The descendants of Naphtali, their l,
3: 1 This is the l of Aaron and Moses at the time
Tob 5:14 and of good and noble l.
6:18 related through his father's l,
1Mc 3:32 He left Lysias, a distinguished man of royal l,
1Es 5: 5 of the house of David, of the l of Phares,
5:37 by their ancestral houses or l that they belonged

LINEAGE (KJV) See also FAMILY

LINED (4) [LINE]
1Ki 6:15 He l the walls of the house on the inside
2Ch 3: 5 The nave he l with cypress,
3: 7 So he l the house with gold—
1Mc 16: 6 Then he and his army l up against them.

LINEN (111)
A. FINE LINEN (32)
B. FINE TWISTED LINEN (22)

Ge 41:42 he arrayed him in garments of fine l, A
Ex 25: 4 purple, and crimson yarns and fine l, goats' hair, A
26: 1 the tabernacle with ten curtains of fine twisted l, B
26:31 purple, and crimson yarns, and of fine twisted l; B
26:36 purple, and crimson yarns, and of fine twisted l, B
27: 9 of fine twisted l one hundred cubits long for B
27:16 purple, and crimson yarns, and of fine twisted l, B
27:18 with hangings of fine twisted l and bases B
28: 5 blue, purple, and crimson yarns, and fine l. A
28: 6 purple, and crimson yarns, and of fine twisted l, B
28: 8 purple, and crimson yarns, and of fine twisted l. B
28:15 and of fine twisted l you shall make it. B
28:39 You shall make the checkered tunic of fine l, A
28:39 and you shall make a turban of fine l, A
28:42 You shall make for them l undergarments
35: 6 purple, and crimson yarns, and fine l; A
35:23 or purple or crimson yarn or fine l or goats' hair A
35:25 in blue and purple and crimson yarns and fine l; A
35:35 purple, and crimson yarns, and in fine l, A
36: 8 they were made of fine twisted l, and blue, B
36:35 purple, and crimson yarns, and fine twisted l, B
36:37 and fine twisted l, embroidered with needlework; B
38: 9 the hangings of the court were of fine twisted l, B
38:16 around the court were of fine twisted l. B
38:18 purple, and crimson yarns and fine twisted l. B
38:23 purple, and crimson yarns, and in fine l. A
39: 2 purple, and crimson yarns, and of fine twisted l. B
39: 3 and crimson yarns and into the fine twisted l, B
39: 5 purple, and crimson yarns, and of fine twisted l; B
39: 8 purple, and crimson yarns, and of fine twisted l. B
39:24 purple, and crimson yarns, and of fine twisted l. B
39:27 They also made the tunics, woven of fine l, A
39:28 and the turban of fine l, A
39:28 and the headdresses of fine l, A
39:28 and the l undergarments of fine twisted linen,
39:28 and the linen undergarments of fine twisted l, B
39:29 the sash of fine twisted l, and of blue, purple, B
Lev 6:10 The priest shall put on his l vestments
6:10 after putting on his l undergarments next
13:47 leprous disease appears in it, in woolen or l cloth,
13:48 in warp or woof of l or wool,
13:52 whether diseased in warp or woof, woolen or l,
13:59 for a leprous disease in a cloth of wool or l,
16: 4 He shall put on the holy l tunic,
16: 4 shall have the l undergarments next to his body,
16: 4 fasten the l sash, and wear the linen turban;
16: 4 fasten the linen sash, and wear the l turban;
16:23 the l vestments that he put on when he went into
16:32 wearing the l vestments, the holy vestments.
Dt 22:11 of wool and l woven together.
Jdg 14:12 then I will give you thirty l garments
14:13 then you shall give me thirty l garments
1Sa 2:18 before the LORD, a boy wearing a l ephod.
22:18 he killed eighty-five who wore the l ephod.
2Sa 6:14 David was girded with a l ephod.
1Ch 4:21 families of the guild of l workers at Beth-ashbea;
15:27 David was clothed with a robe of fine l, A
15:27 and David wore a l ephod.
2Ch 2:14 blue, and crimson fabrics and fine l, A
3:14 blue and purple and crimson fabrics and fine l, A
5:12 arrayed in fine l, with cymbals, harps, and lyres, A
Est 1: 6 with cords of fine l and purple to silver rings A
8:15 a great golden crown and a mantle of fine l A
Pr 7:16 colored spreads of Egyptian l;
31:22 her clothing is fine l and purple. A
31:24 She makes l garments and sells them;
Isa 3:23 the l garments, the turbans, and the veils.
Jer 13: 1 "Go and buy yourself a l loincloth,
Eze 9: 2 among them was a man clothed in l,
9: 3 The LORD called to the man clothed in l,
9:11 Then the man clothed in l,
10: 2 He said to the man clothed in l,
10: 6 When he commanded the man clothed in l,
10: 7 and put it into the hands of the man clothed in l,
16:10 in fine l and covered you with rich fabric, A
16:13 while your clothing was of fine l, rich fabric, A
27: 7 Of fine embroidered l from Egypt was your sail,
27:16 embroidered work, fine l, coral, and rubies. A
40: 3 with a l cord and a measuring reed in his hand;
44:17 they shall wear l vestments;
44:18 They shall have l turbans on their heads,
44:18 and l undergarments on their loins;
Da 10: 5 I looked up and saw a man clothed in l,
12: 6 One of them said to the man clothed in l,
12: 7 The man clothed in l, who was upstream,
Mt 27:59 the body and wrapped it in a clean l cloth
Mk 14:51 wearing nothing but a l cloth.
14:52 but he left the l cloth and ran off naked.
15:46 Then Joseph bought a l cloth,
15:46 wrapped it in the l cloth,
Lk 16:19 a rich man who was dressed in purple and fine l A
23:53 Then he took it down, wrapped it in a l cloth,
24:12 he saw the l cloths by themselves;
Jn 19:40 and wrapped it with the spices in l cloths,
20: 5 to look in and saw the l wrappings lying there,
20: 6 He saw the l wrappings lying there,
20: 7 the l wrappings but rolled up in a place by itself.
Rev 15: 6 with the seven plagues, robed in pure bright l,
18:12 jewels and pearls, fine l, purple, silk and scarlet, A
18:16 clothed in fine l, in purple and scarlet, A
19: 8 to be clothed with fine l, bright and pure"— A
19: 8 for the fine l is the righteous deeds of the saints. A

Rev 19:14 And the armies of heaven, wearing fine l, A
Jdt 16: 8 with a tiara and put on a l gown to beguile him.
AdE 1: 6 which was adorned with curtains of fine l A
1: 6 of purple l attached to gold and silver blocks
6: 8 the king's servants bring out the fine l robe that A
8:15 a gold crown and a turban of purple l.
Sir 45: 8 the l undergarments, the long robe,
LtJ 6:72 and l that rot upon them you will know
1Es 3: 6 turban of fine l, and a necklace around his neck; A

LINES (2) [LINE]

2Ch 14:10 and they drew up their l of battle in the valley
Ps 16: 6 boundary l have fallen for me in pleasant places;

LINGER‡ (8) [LINGERED, LINGERS]

1Sa 20:38 "Hurry, be quick, do not l."
2Ki 9: 3 Then open the door and flee; do not l."
Ps 30: 5 Weeping may l for the night,
Pr 23:30 Those who l late over wine,
Isa 5:11 who l in the evening to be inflamed by wine,
Jer 51:50 You survivors of the sword, go, do not l!
Sir 27:12 but among thoughtful people l on.
32:11 go home quickly and do not l.

LINGERED (2) [LINGER]

Ge 19:16 But he l; so the men seized him
Jdg 19: 8 So they l until the day declined,

LINGERS (1) [LINGER]

2Sa 1: 9 and yet my life still l.'

LINTEL (4)

Ex 12: 7 on the two doorposts and the l of the houses
12:22 the l and the two doorposts with the blood in
12:23 the blood on the l and on the two doorposts,
1Ki 6:31 the l and the doorposts were five-sided.

LINTEL (KJV) See also CAPITALS

LINUS (1)

2Ti 4:21 and L and Claudia and all the brothers and sisters.

LION‡ (102) [LION'S, LIONESS, LIONESSES, LIONS, LIONS']

Ge 49: 9 He crouches down, he stretches out like a l,
Nu 23:24 and rousing itself like a l!
24: 9 He crouched, he lay down like a l,
Dt 33:20 Gad lives like a l; he tears at arm and scalp.
Jdg 14: 5 suddenly a young l roared at him.
14: 6 the l apart barehanded as one might tear apart
14: 8 and he turned aside to see the carcass of the l,
14: 8 there was a swarm of bees in the body of the l,
14: 9 the honey from the carcass of the l.
14:18 What is stronger than a l?"
1Sa 17:34 and whenever a l or a bear came,
17:37 who saved me from the paw of the l and from
2Sa 17:10 whose heart is like the heart of a l,
23:20 He also went down and killed a l in a pit on a day
1Ki 13:24 a l met him on the road and killed him.
13:24 the l also stood beside the body.
13:25 with the l standing by the body.
13:26 therefore the LORD has given him to the l,
13:28 the donkey and the l standing beside the body.
13:28 l had not eaten the body or attacked the donkey.
20:36 as soon as you have left me, a l will kill you."
20:36 when he had left him, a l met him and killed him.
1Ch 11:22 He also went down and killed a l in a pit on a day
Job 4:10 The roar of the l, the voice of the fierce l,
4:11 The strong l perishes for lack of prey,
10:16 Bold as a l you hunt me;
28: 8 the l has not passed over it.
38:39 "Can you hunt the prey for the l,
Ps 7: 2 or like a l they will tear me apart;
10: 9 they lurk in secret like a l in its covert;
17:12 They are like a l eager to tear,
17:12 like a young l lurking in ambush.
22:13 like a ravening and roaring l.
22:21 Save me from the mouth of the l!
91:13 You will tread on the l and the adder,
91:13 the young l and the serpent you will trample
Pr 19:12 A king's anger is like the growling of a l,
20: 2 dread anger of a king is like the growling of a l;
22:13 The lazy person says, "There is a l outside!
26:13 The lazy person says, "There is a l in the road!
26:13 There is a l in the streets!"
28: 1 but the righteous are as bold as a l.
28:15 a roaring l or a charging bear is a wicked ruler
30:30 the l, which is mightiest among wild animals
Ecc 9: 4 for a living dog is better than a dead l.
Isa 5:29 like a l, like young lions they roar;
11: 6 the calf and the l and the fatling together,
11: 7 and the l shall eat straw like the ox.
15: 9 a l for those of Moab who escape,
30: 6 of trouble and distress, of lioness and roaring l,
31: 4 As a l or a young l growls over its prey,
35: 9 No l shall be there, nor shall any ravenous beast
38:13 like a l he breaks all my bones;
65:25 the l shall eat straw like the ox;
Jer 2:30 sword devoured your prophets like a ravening l.
4: 7 A l has gone up from its thicket,
5: 6 Therefore a l from the forest shall kill them,
12: 8 My heritage has become to me like a l in
25:38 Like a l he has left his covert;
Jer 49:19 a l coming up from the thickets of the Jordan
50:44 a l coming up from the thickets of the Jordan
La 3:10 He is a bear lying in wait for me, a l in hiding;
Eze 1:10 the face of a l on the right side,
10:14 that of a human being, the third that of a l,
19: 3 a young l, and he learned to catch prey;
19: 5 of her cubs and made him a young l.
19: 6 a young l, and he learned to catch prey;
22:25 Its princes within it are like a roaring l tearing
32: 2 You consider yourself a l among the nations,
41:19 the face of a young l turned toward the palm tree
Da 7: 4 The first was like a l and had eagles' wings.
Hos 5:14 For I will be like a l to Ephraim,
5:14 and like a young l to the house of Judah.
11:10 after the LORD, who roars like a l;
13: 7 So I will become like a l to them,
13: 8 there I will devour them like a l,
Am 3: 4 Does a l roar in the forest, when it has no prey?
3: 4 Does a young l cry out from its den,
3: 8 The l has roared; who will not fear?
3:12 from the mouth of the l two legs,
5:19 if someone fled from a l, and was met by a bear;
Mic 5: 8 shall be like a l among the animals of the forest,
5: 8 like a young l among the flocks of sheep, which,
Na 2:11 where the l goes, and the lion's cubs, with no one
2:12 The l has torn enough for his whelps
1Pe 5: 8 Like a roaring l your adversary the devil prowls
Rev 4: 7 the first living creature like a l,
5: 5 See, the L of the tribe of Judah,
10: 3 a great shout, like a l roaring.
AdE 14:13 Put eloquent speech in my mouth before the l,
Sir 4:30 Do not be like a l in your home,
25:16 I would rather live with a l and a dragon than live
27:10 l lies in wait for prey; so does sin for evildoers.
27:28 but vengeance lies in wait for them like a l.
28:23 It will be sent out against them like a l;
1Mc 3: 4 He was like a l in his deeds,
2Es 11:37 I saw what seemed to be a l roused from
12: 1 While the l was saying these words to the eagle,
12:31 the l whom you saw rousing up out of the forest
16: 6 Can one drive off a hungry l in the forest,

LION'S (7) [LION]

Ge 49: 9 Judah is a l whelp;
Dt 33:22 Dan is a l whelp that leaps forth from Bashan.
Na 2:11 and the l cubs, with no one to disturb them?
2Ti 4:17 So I was rescued from the l mouth.
Rev 13: 2 and its mouth was like a l mouth.
Sir 21: 2 Its teeth are l teeth, and can destroy human lives.
1Mc 3: 4 like a l cub roaring for prey.

LIONESS (7) [LION]

Ge 49: 9 he stretches out like a lion, like a l—
Nu 23:24 Look, a people rising up like a l,
24: 9 and like a l; who will rouse him up?
Job 4:11 and the whelps of the l are scattered.
Isa 30: 6 land of trouble and distress, of l and roaring lion,
Eze 19: 2 What a l was your mother among lions!
Joel 1: 6 and it has the fangs of a l.

LIONESSES (1) [LION]

Na 2:12 for his whelps and strangled prey for his l;

LIONLIKE (KJV) See SONS OF ARIEL

LIONS‡ (51) [LION]

1Sa 17:36 Your servant has killed both l and bears;
2Sa 1:23 they were stronger than l.
1Ki 7:29 on the borders that were set in the frames were l,
7:29 both above and below the l and oxen,
7:36 l, and palm trees, where each had space,
10:19 the seat were arm rests and two l standing beside
10:20 while twelve l were standing,
2Ki 17:25 therefore the LORD sent l among them,
17:26 therefore he has sent l among them;
1Ch 12: 8 whose faces were like the faces of l,
2Ch 9:18 the seat were arm rests and two l standing beside
9:19 while twelve l were standing,
Job 4:10 and the teeth of the young l are broken.
38:39 or satisfy the appetite of the young l,
Ps 34:10 The young l suffer want and hunger,
35:17 from their ravages, my life from the l!
57: 4 down among l that greedily devour human prey;
58: 6 tear out the fangs of the young l, O LORD!
104:21 The young l roar for their prey,
SS 4: 8 from the dens of l, from the mountains of leopards.
Isa 5:29 like a lion, like young l they roar;
Jer 2:15 The l have roared against him,
50:17 Israel is a hunted sheep driven away by l.
51:38 Like l they shall roar together;
Eze 19: 2 What a lioness was your mother among l!
19: 2 She lay down among young l, rearing her cubs.
19: 6 He prowled among the l;
Da 6: 7 O king, shall be thrown into a den of l.
6:12 O king, shall be thrown into a den of l?"
6:16 Daniel was brought and thrown into the den of l.
6:19 the king got up and hurried to the den of l.
6:20 to deliver you from the l?"
6:24 and thrown into the den of l—
6:24 the l overpowered them and broke all their bones
6:27 for he has saved Daniel from the power of the l."
Na 2:11 the cave of the young l, where the lion goes,
2:13 and the sword shall devour your young l;
Zep 3: 3 The officials within it are roaring l;
Zec 11: 3 Listen, the roar of the l, for the thickets of the
Heb 11:33 obtained promises, shut the mouths of l,
Wis 11:17 to send upon them a multitude of bears, or bold l,
Sir 13:19 Wild asses in the wilderness are the prey of l;
47: 3 with l as though they were young goats,
Bel 1:32 There were seven l in the den,
1Mc 2:60 was delivered from the mouth of the l.
2Mc 11:11 They hurled themselves like l against the enemy,
1Es 4:24 he faces l, and he walks in darkness,
3Mc 6: 7 into the ground to l as food for wild animals,
4Mc 16: 3 The l surrounding Daniel were not so savage,
16:21 Daniel the righteous was thrown to the l,
18:13 He praised Daniel in the den of the l

LIONS' (8) [LION]

Jer 51:38 they shall growl like l whelps.
Da 6:22 My God sent his angel and shut the l mouths so
Joel 1: 6 its teeth are l teeth, and it has the fangs of a lioness.
Na 2:11 What became of the l den,
Rev 9: 8 and their teeth like l teeth;
9:17 the heads of the horses were like l heads,
Bel 1:31 They threw Daniel into the l den,
1:34 to Babylon, to Daniel, in the l den."

LIP (4) [LIPS]

Lev 13:45 and he shall cover his upper l and cry out,
Isa 28:11 with stammering l and with alien
Eze 24:17 do not cover your upper l or eat the bread
24:22 you shall not cover your upper l or eat the bread

LIPS‡ (130) [LIP]

Ex 13: 9 the teaching of the LORD may be on your l;
23:13 do not let them be heard on your l.
Nu 30: 6 by her vows or any thoughtless utterance of her l
30: 8 or the thoughtless utterance of her l,
30:12 then whatever proceeds out of her l
Dt 23:23 Whatever your l utter you must diligently perform,
1Sa 1:13 only her l moved, but her voice was not heard;
Job 2:10 In all this Job did not sin with his l.
8:21 and your l with shouts of joy.
11: 5 oh, that God would speak, and open his l to you,
13: 6 and listen to the pleadings of my l.
15: 6 your own l testify against you.
16: 5 and the solace of my l would assuage your pain.
23:12 not departed from the commandment of his l;
27: 4 my l will not speak falsehood,
32:20 I must open my l and answer.
33: 3 and what my l know they speak sincerely.
Ps 12: 2 with flattering l and a double heart they speak.
12: 3 May the LORD cut off all flattering l,
12: 4 our l are our own—who is our master?"
16: 4 not pour out or take their names upon my l.
17: 1 give ear to my prayer from l free of deceit.
17: 4 by the word of your l I have avoided the ways of
21: 2 and have not withheld the request of his l.
31:18 the lying l be stilled that speak insolently against
34:13 and your l from speaking deceit.
40: 9 see, I have not restrained my l, as you know,
45: 2 grace is poured upon your l;
50:16 or take my covenant on your l?
51:15 O Lord, open my l, and my mouth will declare
59: 7 with sharp words on their l—
59:12 For the sin of their mouths, the words of their l,
63: 3 love is better than life, my l will praise you.
63: 5 and my mouth praises you with joyful l
66:14 those that my l uttered and my mouth promised
71:23 My l will shout for joy when I sing praises
89:34 or alter the word that went forth from my l.
119:13 With my l I declare all the ordinances
119:171 My l will pour forth praise,
120: 2 from lying l, from a deceitful tongue."
140: 3 and under their l is the venom of vipers.
140: 9 let the mischief of their l overwhelm them!
141: 3 keep watch over the door of my l.
Pr 5: 2 and your l may guard knowledge.
5: 3 For the l of a loose woman drip honey,
6: 2 you are snared by the utterance of your l,
8: 6 and from my l will come what is right;
8: 7 wickedness is an abomination to my l.
10:13 On the l of one who has understanding wisdom is
10:18 Lying l conceal hatred,
10:21 The l of the righteous feed many,
10:32 The l of the righteous know what is acceptable,
12:13 evil are ensnared by the transgression of their l,
12:19 Truthful l endure forever,
12:22 Lying l are an abomination to the LORD,
13: 3 those who open wide their l come to ruin.
14: 3 but the l of the wise preserve them.
15: 7 The l of the wise spread knowledge;
16:10 Inspired decisions are on the l of a king;
16:13 Righteous l are the delight of a king,
16:23 and adds persuasiveness to their l.
16:30 one who compresses the l brings evil to pass.
17: 4 An evildoer listens to wicked l;
17:28 they close their l, they are deemed intelligent.
18: 6 A fool's l bring strife, and a fool's mouth invites
18: 7 and their l a snare to themselves.
18:20 the yield of the l brings satisfaction.
20:15 l informed by knowledge are a precious jewel.
22:18 if all of them are ready on your l.
23:16 when your l speak what is right.
24: 2 and their l talk of mischief.
24:26 an honest answer gives a kiss on the l.
24:28 and do not deceive with your l.
26:23 the glaze covering an earthen vessel are smooth l

Pr 27: 2 a stranger, and not your own **l**.
Ecc 10:12 but the **l** of fools consume them.
SS 4: 3 Your **l** are like a crimson thread,
4:11 Your **l** distill nectar, my bride;
5:13 His **l** are lilies, distilling liquid myrrh.
7: 9 down smoothly, gliding over **l** and teeth.
Isa 6: 5 I am lost, for I am a man of unclean **l**, and I live among a people of unclean **l**;
6: 7 "Now that this has touched your **l**,
11: 4 with the breath of his **l** he shall kill the wicked.
29:13 near with their mouths and honor me with their **l**,
30:27 his **l** are full of indignation,
57:18 creating for their mourners the fruit of the **l**.
59: 3 your **l** have spoken lies, your tongue mutters
Jer 7:28 it is cut off from their **l**.
17:16 You know what came from my **l**;
44:26 the **l** of any of the people of Judah in all the land
Eze 29:21 and I will open your **l** among them.
33:31 For flattery is on their **l**,
Da 10:16 Then one in human form touched my **l**,
Hos 8: 1 Set the trumpet to your **l**!
14: 2 and we will offer the fruit of our **l**.
Mic 3: 7 they shall all cover their **l**,
Hab 3:16 my **l** quiver at the sound.
Zec 4: 2 there are seven lamps on it, with seven **l** on each
Mal 2: 6 and no wrong was found on his **l**.
2: 7 For the **l** of a priest should guard knowledge,
Mt 15: 8 with their **l**, but their hearts are far from me;
Mk 7: 6 'This people honors me with their **l**,
Lk 22:71 We have heard it ourselves from his own **l**!"
Ro 3:13 "The venom of vipers is under their **l**."
10: 8 "The word is near you, on your **l** and in your heart"
10: 9 if you confess with your **l** that Jesus is Lord
1Co 14:21 by the **l** of foreigners I will speak to this people;
Heb 13:15 that is, the fruit of **l** that confess his name.
1Pe 3:10 let them keep their tongues from evil and their **l**
Jdt 2: 2 with his own **l**, all the wickedness of the region.
9:10 of my **l** strike down the slave with the prince and
AdE 13:17 do not destroy the **l** of those who praise you."
Sir 1:24 then the **l** of many tell of their good sense.
1:29 and keep watch over your **l**.
12:16 An enemy speaks sweetly with his **l**,
14: 1 Happy are those who do not blunder with their **l**,
15: 9 Praise is unseemly on the **l** of a sinner,
20:19 continually on the **l** of the ignorant.
20:20 A proverb from a fool's **l** will be rejected,
20:24 it is continually on the **l** of the ignorant.
21: 5 of the poor goes from their **l** to the ears of God,
21:25 **l** of babblers speak of what is not their concern.
22:27 and an effective seal upon my **l**,
23: 8 Sinners are overtaken through their **l**;
39:15 with songs on your **l**, and with harps;
50:20 to pronounce the blessing of the Lord with his **l**,
51: 2 from **l** that fabricate lies.
1Es 4:46 to the King of heaven with your own **l**."
2Es 13:10 and from his **l** a flaming breath,

LIQUID (8) [LIQUIDS]

Ex 30:23 of **l** myrrh five hundred shekels,
Lev 11:34 and any **l** that could be drunk shall be unclean
SS 5: 5 my fingers with **l** myrrh,
5:13 His lips are lilies, distilling **l** myrrh.
2Mc 1:20 that they had not found fire but only a thick **l**,
1:21 Nehemiah ordered the priests to sprinkle the **l** on
1:31 Nehemiah ordered that the **l** that was left should
1:33 the **l** had appeared with which Nehemiah

LIQUIDS (1) [LIQUID]

4Mc 6:25 and poured stinking **l** into his nostrils.

LIQUOR (KJV) See JUICE, MIXED WINE

LIST (8) [LISTED]

Ge 5: 1 This is the **l** of the descendants of Adam.
1Ch 25: 1 The **l** of those who did the work and
27: 1 This is the **l** of the people of Israel,
1Ti 5: 9 on the **l** if she is not less than sixty years old
5:11 But refuse to put younger widows on the **l**;
1Es 6:12 a **l** of the names of those who are at their head.
8:49 the **l** of all their names was reported.
2Es 2:40 and close the **l** of your people who are clothed

LISTED (1) [LIST]

Jdg 8:14 he **l** for him the officials and elders of Succoth,

LISTEN‡ (332) [LISTENED, LISTENER, LISTENERS, LISTENING, LISTENS]

Ge 4:10 **L**; your brother's blood is crying out to me
4:23 you wives of Lamech, **l** to what I say:
23:13 "If you only will **l** to me!
23:15 "My lord, **l** to me; a piece of land
34:17 But if you will not **l** to us and be circumcised,
37: 6 He said to them, "**L** to this dream that I dreamed.
42:21 when he pleaded with us, but we would not **l**.
42:22 But you would not **l**.
49: 2 of Jacob; **l** to Israel your father.
Ex 3:18 They will **l** to your voice;
4: 1 "But suppose they do not believe me or **l** to me,
6: 9 but they would not **l** to Moses,
6:12 shall Pharaoh **l** to me, poor speaker that I am?"
6:30 why would Pharaoh **l** to me?"
7: 4 When Pharaoh does not **l** to you,
7:13 and he would not **l** to them,
Ex 7:22 and he would not **l** to them;
8:15 he hardened his heart, and would not **l** to them,
8:19 and he would not **l** to them,
9:12 and he would not **l** to them,
11: 9 "Pharaoh will not **l** to you,
15:26 "If you will **l** carefully to the voice of the LORD
16:20 But they did not **l** to Moses;
18:19 Now **l** to me. I will give you counsel,
20:19 "You speak to us, and we will **l**;
22:27 And if your neighbor cries out to me, I will **l**,
23:21 Be attentive to him and **l** to his voice;
23:22 you **l** attentively to his voice and do all that I say,
Nu 20:10 and he said to them, "**L**, you rebels,
23:18 **l** to me, O son of Zippor:
Dt 1:43 Although I told you, you would not **l**.
5:27 and we will **l** and do it."
Jos 24:10 but I would not **l** to Balaam;
Jdg 2:17 Yet they did not **l** even to their judges;
9: 7 and cried aloud and said to them, "**L** to me, you lords of Shechem, so that God may **l** to you.
11:17 but the king of Edom would not **l**.
19:25 But the men would not **l** to him.
20:13 the Benjaminites would not **l** to their kinsfolk,
Ru 2: 8 Then Boaz said to Ruth, "Now **l**, my daughter,
1Sa 2:25 But they would not **l** to the voice of their father;
8: 7 "**L** to the voice of the people in all that they say
8: 9 Now then, **l** to their voice;
8:19 the people refused to **l** to the voice of Samuel;
8:22 "**L** to their voice and set a king over them."
15: 1 now therefore **l** to the words of the LORD.
22:12 Saul said, "**L** now, son of Ahitub."
24: 9 "Why do you **l** to the words of those who say,
28:22 Now therefore, you also **l** to your servant;
30:24 Who would **l** to you in this matter?
2Sa 12:18 we spoke to him, and he did not **l** to us;
13:14 But he would not **l** to her;
13:16 But he would not **l** to her.
19:35 Can I still **l** to the voice of singing men
20:16 Then a wise woman called from the city, "**L**! **L**!
20:17 she said to him, "**L** to the words of your servant."
1Ki 11:38 If you will **l** to all that I command you,
12:15 So the king did not **l** to the people,
12:16 all Israel saw that the king would not **l** to them,
20: 8 the people said to him, "Do not **l** or consent."
2Ki 14:11 But Amaziah would not **l**.
17:14 They would not **l** but were stubborn,
17:40 They would not **l**, however,
18:31 Do not **l** to Hezekiah;
18:32 Do not **l** to Hezekiah when he misleads you
21: 9 But they did not **l**; Manasseh misled them to do
2Ch 10:15 So the king did not **l** to the people,
10:16 all Israel saw that the king would not **l** to them,
13: 4 and said, "**L** to me, Jeroboam and all Israel!
20:15 "**L**, all Judah and inhabitants of Jerusalem,
20:20 "**L** to me, O Judah and inhabitants of Jerusalem!
24:19 they testified against them, but they would not **l**.
25:20 But Amaziah would not **l**—
29: 5 He said to them, "**L** to me, Levites!
35:22 not **l** to the words of Neco from the mouth
Ne 9:30 through your prophets; yet they would not **l**.
13:27 Shall we then **l** to you and do all this great evil
Est 3: 4 to him day after day and he would not **l** to them,
Job 9:16 I do not believe that he would **l** to my voice.
13: 6 and **l** to the pleadings of my lips.
13:17 **L** carefully to my words,
15:17 "I will show you; **l** to me;
21: 2 "**L** carefully to my words,
32:10 I say, '**L** to me; let me also declare my opinion.'
33: 1 hear my speech, O Job, and **l** to all my words.
33:31 Pay heed, Job, **l** to me; be silent, and I will speak.
33:33 **l** to me; be silent, and I will teach you wisdom."
34:16 hear this; **l** to what I say.
36:11 If they **l**, and serve him, they complete their days
36:12 But if they do not **l**,
37: 2 **L**, **l** to the thunder of his voice
Ps 5: 2 **L** to the sound of my cry, my King and my God,
34:11 Come, O children, **l** to me;
61: 1 Hear my cry, O God; **l** to my prayer.
68:33 **l**, he sends out his voice, his mighty voice.
81: 8 O Israel, if you would but **l** to me!
81:11 "But my people did not **l** to my voice;
81:13 O that my people would **l** to me,
86: 6 **l** to my cry of supplication.
95: 7 O that today you would **l** to his voice!
Pr 1:33 but those who **l** to me will be secure and will live
4: 1 **L**, children, to a father's instruction,
5: 7 And now, my child, **l** to me,
5:13 I did not **l** to the voice of my teachers
7:24 And now, my children, **l** to me,
8:32 And now, my children, **l** to me:
12:15 but the wise **l** to advice.
13: 1 but a scoffer does not **l** to rebuke.
19:20 **L** to advice and accept instruction,
23:22 **L** to your father who begot you,
28: 9 When one will not **l** to the law,
Ecc 5: 1 to **l** is better than the sacrifice offered by fools;
SS 5: 2 **L**! my beloved is knocking.
Isa 1: 2 Hear, O heavens, and **l**, O earth;
1:10 **L** to the teaching of our God,
1:15 though you make many prayers, I will not **l**;
6:10 so that they may not look with their eyes, and **l**
8: 9 Band together, you peoples, and be dismayed; **l**,
10:30 Cry aloud, O daughter Gallim! **L**,
13: 4 **L**, a tumult on the mountains as of
13: 4 **L**, an uproar of kingdoms,
18: 3 When a trumpet is blown, **l**!
19:22 and he will **l** to their supplications and heal them.
Isa 21: 7 let him **l** diligently, very diligently."
28:23 **L**, and hear my voice; Pay attention,
32: 3 and the ears of those who have hearing will **l**.
32: 9 you complacent daughters, **l** to my speech.
33: 7 **L**! the valiant cry in the streets;
36:16 Do not **l** to Hezekiah;
41: 1 **L** to me in silence, O coastlands;
42:18 **L**, you that are deaf; and you
42:23 who will attend and **l** for the time to come?
46: 3 **L** to me, O house of Jacob,
46:12 **L** to me, you stubborn of heart,
48:12 **L** to me, O Jacob, and Israel, whom I called:
49: 1 **L** to me, O coastlands, pay attention,
50: 4 wakens my ear to **l** as those who are taught.
51: 1 **L** to me, you that pursue righteousness,
51: 4 **L** to me, my people, and give heed to me,
51: 7 **L** to me, you who know righteousness,
52: 8 **L**! Your sentinels lift up their
55: 2 **L** carefully to me, and eat what is good,
55: 3 Incline your ear, and come to me; **l**,
65:12 you did not answer, when I spoke, you did not **l**,
66: 4 no one answered, when I spoke, they did not **l**;
66: 6 **L**, an uproar from the city!
Jer 6:10 See, their ears are closed, they cannot **l**.
7:13 you did not **l**, and when I called you,
7:26 yet they did not **l** to me,
7:27 but they will not **l** to you.
10:22 Hear, a noise! **L**, it is coming—
11: 4 **L** to my voice, and do all that I command you.
11:11 though they cry out to me, I will not **l** to them.
11:14 for I will not **l** when they call to me in the time
12:17 But if any nation will not **l**,
13:11 But they would not **l**.
13:17 But if you will not **l**, my soul will weep in secret
16:12 your stubborn evil will, refusing to **l** to me.
17:23 Yet they did not **l** or incline their ear;
17:24 But if you **l** to me, says the LORD,
17:27 But if you do not **l** to me,
18:19 O LORD, and **l** to what my adversaries say!
22:21 but you said, "I will not **l**."
23:16 not **l** to the words of the prophets who prophesy
25: 7 Yet you did not **l** to me, says the LORD,
26: 3 It may be that they will **l**, all of them,
26: 4 If you will not **l** to me,
27: 9 You, therefore, must not **l** to your prophets,
27:14 Do not **l** to the words of the prophets who are
27:16 Do not **l** to the words of your prophets who are
27:17 Do not **l** to them; serve the king of Babylon
28: 7 But **l** now to this word that I speak
28:15 "**L**, Hananiah, the LORD has not sent you,
29: 8 and do not **l** to the dreams that they dream,
29:19 but they would not **l**, says the LORD.
32:33 they would not **l** and accept correction.
34:14 not **l** to me or incline their ears to me.
36:25 he would not **l** to them.
36:31 I have threatened them—but they would not **l**.
37:14 But Irijah would not **l** to him,
37:20 be good enough to **l** to my plea,
38:15 And if I give you advice, you will not **l** to me."
42: 2 "Be good enough to **l** to our plea,
44: 5 But they did not **l** or incline their ear,
44:16 we are not going to **l** to you.
50:28 **L**! Fugitives and refugees from the land
51:54 **L**!—a cry from Babylon!
Eze 3: 6 Surely, if I sent you to them, they would **l** to you.
3: 7 But the house of Israel will not **l** to you,
3: 7 for they are not willing to **l** to me;
8:18 in my hearing with a loud voice, I will not **l**
13:19 by your lies to my people, who **l** to lies.
20: 8 they rebelled against me and would not **l** to me;
20:39 if you will not **l** to me;
40: 4 "Mortal, look closely and **l** attentively,
44: 5 Mortal, mark well, look closely, and **l** attentively
Da 8:19 "**L**, and I will tell you what will take place later
9:17 **l** to the prayer of your servant and
9:19 O Lord, **l** and act and do not delay!
Hos 5: 1 **L**, O house of the king! For the judgment pertains
Am 5:23 I will not **l** to the melody of your harps.
Mic 1: 2 **l**, O earth, and all that is in it;
3: 1 **L**, you heads of Jacob and rulers of the house of
Hab 1: 2 for help, and you will not **l**?
Zec 3: 8 Now **l**, Joshua, high priest,
7:11 to **l**, and turned a stubborn shoulder,
11: 3 **L**, the wail of the shepherds,
11: 3 **L**, the roar of the lions, for the thickets of the
Mal 2: 2 not **l**, if you will not lay it to heart to give glory
Mt 10:14 anyone will not welcome you or **l** to your words,
11:15 Let anyone with ears **l**!
12:42 because she came from the ends of the earth to **l**
13: 3 he told them many things in parables, saying: "**L**!
13: 9 Let anyone with ears **l**!"
13:13 and hearing they do not **l**,
13:14 'You will indeed **l**, but never understand,
13:15 and **l** with their ears, and understand with their
13:43 Let anyone with ears **l**!
15:10 to him and said to them, "**L** and understand:
17: 5 with him I am well pleased; **l** to him!"
18:17 member refuses to **l** to them, tell it to the church;
18:17 if the offender refuses to **l** even to the church,
21:33 "**L** to another parable. There was a landowner
Mk 4: 3 "**L**! A sower went out to sow.
4: 9 And he said, "Let anyone with ears to hear **l**!"
4:12 and may indeed **l**, but not understand;
4:23 Let anyone with ears to hear **l**!"
6:20 and yet he liked to **l** to him.
7:14 "**L** to me, all of you, and understand:
9: 7 "This is my Son, the Beloved; **l** to him!"

Mk 15:35 they said, "L, he is calling for Elijah."
Lk 6:27 "But I say to you that l, Love your enemies,
8: 8 he called out, "Let anyone with ears to hear l!"
8:18 Then pay attention to how you l;
9:35 "This is my Son, my Chosen; l to him!"
11:31 because she came from the ends of the earth to l
13:32 He said to them, "Go and tell that fox for me, 'L,
14:35 Let anyone with ears to hear l!"
15: 1 and sinners were coming near to l to him.
15:29 But he answered his father, 'L!
16:29 and the prophets; they should l to them.'
16:31 'If they do not l to Moses and the prophets,
18: 6 the Lord said, "L to what the unjust judge says.
21:38 the people would get up early in the morning to l
22:10 "L," he said to them, "when you have entered
22:31 Simon, l! Satan has demanded to sift all of you
Jn 9:27 "I have told you already, and you would not l.
9:31 We know that God does not l to sinners,
9:31 but he does l to one who worships him
10: 8 but the sheep did not l to them.
10:16 and they will l to my voice.
10:20 and is out of his mind. Why l to him?"
Ac 2:14 let this be known to you, and l to what I say.
2:22 "You that are Israelites, l to what I have to say:
3:22 You must l to whatever he tells you.
3:23 that everyone who does not l to that prophet will
4:19 to l to you rather than to God, you must judge;
7: 2 Stephen replied: "Brothers and fathers, l to me.
10:33 now all of us are here in the presence of God to l
13:11 now l—the hand of the Lord is against you,
13:16 "You Israelites, and others who fear God, l.
15:13 James replied, "My brothers, l to me.
16:14 The Lord opened her heart to l eagerly
22: 1 l to the defense that I now make before you."
26: 3 therefore I beg of you to l to me patiently.
28:26 You will indeed l, but never understand,
28:27 so that they might not look with their eyes, and l
28:28 to the Gentiles; they will l."
1Co 14:21 even then they will not l to me," says the Lord.
15:51 L, I will tell you a mystery!
2Co 13:11 Put things in order, l to my appeal,
Gal 4:21 will you not l to the law?
5: 2 L! I, Paul, am telling you that if you let yourselves
Jas 1:19 let everyone be quick to l, slow to speak,
2: 5 L, my beloved brothers and sisters.
5: 4 L! The wages of the laborers who mowed your
1Jn 4: 6 and whoever is not from God does not l to us.
Rev 2: 7 who has an ear l to what the Spirit is saying to
2:11 who has an ear l to what the Spirit is saying to
2:17 who has an ear l to what the Spirit is saying to
2:29 who has an ear l to what the Spirit is saying to
3: 6 who has an ear l to what the Spirit is saying to
3:13 who has an ear l to what the Spirit is saying to
3:20 L! I am standing at the door,
3:22 who has an ear l to what the Spirit is saying to
13: 9 Let anyone who has an ear l:
Tob 3: 6 because I have had to l to undeserved insults,
3: 6 so much distress in my life and to l to insults."
3:10 but to pray the Lord that I may die and not l
3:13 the earth and not l to such reproaches any more.
6:13 So l to me, brother;
6:13 So now l to me, brother,
6:16 Now l to me, brother, and say no more
Jdt 5: 5 "May my lord please l to a report from the mouth
7: 9 "L to what we have to say,
8:11 They came to her, and she said to them, "L to me,
8:32 Then Judith said to them, "L to me.
14: 1 Then Judith said to them, "L to me, my friends.
AdE 3: 4 but he would not l to them.
Wis 6: 1 L therefore, O kings, and understand;
Sir 3: 1 L to me your father, O children;
4:15 and all who l to her will live secure.
6:23 L, my child, and accept my judgment;
6:33 If you love to l you will gain knowledge,
6:35 Be ready to l to every godly discourse,
11: 8 Do not answer before you l,
16:24 L to me, my child, and acquire knowledge,
21:24 It is ill-mannered for a person to l at a door;
23: 7 L, my children, to instruction concerning the
31:22 L to me, my child, and do not disregard me,
34:29 to whose voice will the Lord l?
34:31 who will l to his prayer?
35:16 but he will l to the prayer of one who is wronged.
39:13 L to me, my faithful children,
Bar 1:21 We did not l to the voice of the Lord our God
4: 9 L, you neighbors of Zion,
1Mc 2:65 always l to him; he shall be your father.
5:61 they did not l to Judas and his brothers.
2Mc 7:25 Since the young man would not l to him at all,
3Mc 2:10 you would l to our petition when we come
2Es 1:26 When you call to me, I will not l to you;
2: 1 but they would not l to them,
5:32 He said to me, "L to me, and I will instruct you;
7: 2 l to the words that I have come to speak to you."
7:49 He answered me and said, "L to me, Ezra,
10:38 He answered me and said, "L to me,
11:16 "L to me, you who have ruled
11:38 "L and I will speak to you.
16:35 L now to these things, and understand them,
16:74 L, my elect ones, says the Lord;

LISTENED (50) [LISTEN]

Ge 3:17 "Because you have l to the voice of your wife,
16: 2 And Abram l to the voice of Sarai.
Ex 6:12 "The Israelites have not l to me;
7:16 But until now you have not l.'
Ex 18:24 So Moses l to his father-in-law and did all
Nu 21: 3 The LORD l to the voice of Israel,
Dt 9:19 But the LORD l to me that time also.
10:10 And once again the LORD l to me.
Jos 5: 6 perished, not having l to the voice of the LORD.
Jdg 13: 9 God l to Manoah, and the angel
1Sa 12: 1 "I have l to you in all that you have said to me,
28:21 she said to him, "Your servant has l to you;
28:21 and have l to what you have said to me.
28:23 and he l to their words.
1Ki 15:20 Ben-hadad l to King Asa,
17:22 The LORD l to the voice of Elijah;
2Ki 16: 9 The king of Assyria l to him;
18:12 they neither l nor obeyed.
2Ch 16: 4 Ben-hadad l to King Asa,
24:17 then the king l to them.
25:16 you have done this and have not l to my advice."
Ezr 8:23 and he l to our entreaty.
Job 15: 8 Have you l in the council of God?
29:21 "They l to me, and waited,
32:11 I l for your wise sayings,
Ps 66:18 the Lord would not have l.
66:19 But truly God has l; he has given heed to the
Jer 8: 6 and l, but they do not speak honestly;
25: 3 to you, but you have not l.
25: 4 you have neither l nor inclined your ears to hear
35:17 I have spoken to them and they have not l,
37: 2 nor his servants nor the people of the land l to
Da 9: 6 We have not l to your servants the prophets,
Hos 9:17 they have not l to him, my God will reject them;
Zep 3: 2 It has l to no voice; it has accepted no correction.
Mal 3:16 The LORD took note and l,
Mt 18:16 But if you are not l to,
Lk 10:39 at the Lord's feet and l to what he was saying.
Ac 8: 6 with one accord l eagerly to what was said
8:10 from the least to the greatest, l to him eagerly,
8:11 And they l eagerly to him because for
14: 9 He l to Paul as he was speaking.
15:12 and l to Barnabas and Paul as they told of all
22:22 Up to this point they l to him,
27:21 you should have l to me and not have set sail
2Co 6: 2 he says, "At an acceptable time I have l to you,
Heb 4: 2 they were not united by faith with those who l.
Sir 33: 4 Prepare what to say, and then you will be l to;
2Es 2: 9 is what I will do to those who have not l to me,
6:17 When I heard this, I got to my feet and l;

LISTENER (1) [LISTEN]

Pr 21:28 but a good l will testify successfully.

LISTENERS (1) [LISTEN]

Sir 25: 9 and the one who speaks to attentive l.

LISTENING‡ (19) [LISTEN]

Ge 18:10 And Sarah was l at the tent entrance behind him.
27: 5 Rebekah was l when Isaac spoke to his son Esau.
1Sa 3: 9 'Speak, LORD, for your servant is l.' "
3:10 And Samuel said, "Speak, for your servant is l."
2Sa 20:17 He answered, "I am l."
1Ki 8:52 l to them whenever they call to you.
Pr 25:12 or an ornament of gold is a wise rebuke to a l ear.
SS 8:13 my companions are l for your voice;
Isa 6: 9 'Keep l, but do not comprehend;
Jer 18:10 but if it does evil in my sight, not l to my voice,
Mk 12:37 And the large crowd was l to him with delight.
Lk 2:46 l to them and asking them questions.
8:10 and l they may not understand.'
19:11 As they were l to this,
Ac 16:14 Lydia, a worshiper of God, was l to us;
16:25 and the prisoners were l to them.
26:29 to God that not only you but also all who are l
2Ti 2:14 but only ruins those who are l.
4: 4 from l to the truth and wander away to myths.

LISTENS (10) [LISTEN]

Pr 8:34 Happy is the one who l to me,
17: 4 An evildoer l to wicked lips;
29:12 If a ruler l to falsehood,
Mt 18:15 the member l to you, you have regained that one.
Lk 10:16 "Whoever l to you l to me,
Jn 18:37 Everyone who belongs to the truth l
1Jn 4: 5 from the world, and the world l to them.
4: 6 Whoever knows God l to us,
Sir 14:23 through her windows and l at her doors;

LISTETH (KJV) See CHOOSES, DIRECTS

LISTLESS (1)

Jdt 7:22 Their children were l, and the women

LIT (7) [LIGHT]

Ex 14:20 and it l up the night;
Ps 77:18 your lightnings l up the world;
Lk 12:35 "Be dressed for action and have your lamps l;
Tob 8:13 So they sent the maid, l a lamp,
Jdt 13:13 Then they l a fire to give light,
1Mc 4:50 on the altar and l the lamps on the lampstand,
2Mc 1: 8 and we l the lamps and set out the loaves.

LITERAL (1)

Ro 2:29 a matter of the heart—it is spiritual and not l.

LITERATURE (2)

Da 1: 4 to be taught the l and language of the Chaldeans.
1:17 and skill in every aspect of l and wisdom;

LITIGATION (2)

Dt 25: 1 a dispute and enter into l,
Hos 10: 4 so l springs up like poisonous weeds in

LITTER (2) [LITTERED, LITTERS]

SS 3: 7 Look, it is the l of Solomon!
2Mc 9: 8 was brought down to earth and carried in a l,

LITTERED (1) [LITTER]

2Ki 7:15 the whole way was l with garments

LITTERS (1) [LITTER]

Isa 66:20 and in l, and on mules, and on dromedaries,

LITTLE‡ (273)

A. LITTLE CHILDREN (16)
B. LITTLE CHILD (6)
C. LITTLE FAITH (6)

Ge 18: 4 Let a l water be brought, and wash your feet,
18: 5 a l bread, that you may refresh yourselves,
19:20 near enough to flee to, and it is a l one.
19:20 is it not a l one?—and my life will be saved!"
24:17 "Please let me sip a l water from your jar."
24:43 "Please give me a l water from your jar to drink,"
30:30 For you had l before I came,
34:29 All their wealth, all their l ones and their wives,
43: 2 "Go again, buy us a l more food."
43: 8 you and we and also our l ones.
43:11 a l balm and a l honey, gum, resin,
44:25 when our father said, 'Go again, buy us a l food,'
45:19 of Egypt for your l ones and for your wives,
46: 5 their l ones, and their wives,
47:24 and as food for your l ones."
50:21 I myself will provide for you and your l ones."
Ex 10:10 if ever I let your l ones go with you!
16:18 and those who gathered l had no shortage;
23:30 L by l I will drive them out from before you,
Lev 11:17 the l owl, the cormorant, the great owl,
Nu 14: 3 Our wives and our l ones will become booty;
14:31 your l ones, who you said would become booty,
16: 9 Is it too l for you that the God
16:13 Is it too l that you have brought us up out of
16:27 their children, and their l ones.
31: 9 the women of Midian and their l ones captive;
31:17 Now therefore, kill every male among the l ones,
32:16 and towns for our l ones,
32:17 Meanwhile our l ones will stay in
32:24 Build towns for your l ones,
32:26 Our l ones, our wives, our flocks,
Dt 1:39 And as for your l ones,
7:22 will clear away these nations before you l by l;
14:16 the l owl and the great owl, the water hen
28:38 into the field but shall gather l in,
Jos 1:14 Your wives, your l ones,
8:35 and the women, and the l ones,
Jdg 4:19 he said to her, "Please give me a l water to drink;
18:21 So they resumed their journey, putting the l ones,
21:10 including the women and the l ones.
1Sa 2:19 for him a l robe and take it to him each year,
14:29 how my eyes have brightened because I tasted a l
14:43 "I tasted a l honey with the tip of the staff
15:17 "Though you are l in your own eyes,
18:23 to you a l thing to become the king's son-in-law,
20:35 and with him was a l boy.
22:15 of all this, much or l."
2Sa 12: 3 the poor man had nothing but one l ewe lamb,
12: 8 and if that had been too l,
15:22 with all his men and all the l ones who were
16: 1 When David had passed a l beyond the summit,
19:36 Your servant will go a l way over the Jordan
1Ki 3: 7 although I am only a l child; B
12:10 'My l finger is thicker than my father's loins.
17:10 "Bring me a l water in a vessel,
17:12 and a l oil in a jug;
17:13 first make me a l cake of it and bring it to me,
18:44 a l cloud no bigger than a person's hand
18:45 In a l while the heavens grew black with clouds
20:27 like two l flocks of goats,
2Ki 8:12 dash in pieces their l ones,
1Ch 16:19 When they were few in number, of l account,
2Ch 10:10 'My l finger is thicker than my father's loins.
20:13 with their l ones, their wives, and their children.
31:18 priests were enrolled with all their l children, A
Ezr 9: 8 and grant us a l sustenance in our slavery.
Job 10:20 that I may find a l comfort
21:11 They send out their l ones like a flock,
24:24 They are exalted a l while, and then are gone;
36: 2 a l, and I will show you, for I have yet something
Ps 8: 5 Yet you have made them a l lower than God,
17:14 may they leave something over to their l ones.
37:10 Yet a l while, and the wicked will be no more;
37:16 Better is a l that the righteous person has than
102: 6 like a l owl of the waste places.
105:12 When they were few in number, of l account,
137: 9 be who take your l ones and dash them against
Pr 6:10 A l sleep, a l slumber, a l folding of the hands
10:20 the mind of the wicked is of l worth.
13:11 but those who gather l by l will increase it.
15:16 a l with the fear of the LORD than great treasure

Pr 16: 8 Better is a l with righteousness than large income
23: 8 You will vomit up the l you have eaten,
24:33 A l sleep, a l slumber, a l folding of the hands
Ecc 5:12 whether they eat l or much;
9:14 There was a l city with few people in it.
10: 1 so a l folly outweighs wisdom and honor.
SS 2:15 Catch us the foxes, the l foxes,
8: 8 We have a l sister, and she has no breasts.
Isa 7:13 Is it too l for you to weary mortals,
10:25 For in a very l while my indignation will come to
11: 6 and a l child shall lead them. B
26:20 for a l while until the wrath is past.
28:10 line upon line, line upon line, here a l, there a l."
28:13 line upon line, line upon line, here a l, there a l;"
29:17 Shall not Lebanon in a very l while become
32:10 In l more than a year you will shudder,
63:18 Your holy people took possession for a l while;
Jer 48: 4 "Moab is destroyed!" her l ones cry out.
49:20 the l ones of the flock shall be dragged away;
50:45 the l ones of the flock shall be dragged away;
51:33 yet a l while and the time of her harvest will come.
Eze 9: 6 l children and women, but touch no one who A
11:16 a sanctuary to them for a l while in the countries
16:47 a very l time you were more corrupt than they
Da 7: 8 a l one coming up among them;
8: 9 Out of one of them came another horn, a l one,
11:34 When they fall victim, they shall receive a l help,
Hos 1: 4 for in a l while I will punish the house of Jehu
13:16 their l ones shall be dashed in pieces,
Am 6:11 and the l house to pieces.
Mic 5: 2 who are one of the l clans of Judah,
Hag 1: 6 You have sown much, and harvested l;
1: 9 You have looked for much, and, lo, it came to l;
2: 6 Once again, in a l while,
Zec 1:15 for while I was only a l angry,
13: 7 I will turn my hand against the l ones.
Mt 6:30 not much more clothe you—you of l faith? C
8:26 "Why are you afraid, you of l faith?" C
10:42 even a cup of cold water to one of these l ones in
14:31 "You of l faith, why did you doubt?" C
16: 8 becoming aware of it, Jesus said, "You of l faith, C
17:20 He said to them, "Because of your l faith. C
18: 6 before one of these l ones who believe in me,
18:10 that you do not despise one of these l ones;
18:14 in heaven that one of these l ones should be lost.
19:13 Then l children were being brought to him A
19:14 "Let the l children come to me, A
26:39 a l farther, he threw himself on the ground
26:73 l while the bystanders came up and said to Peter,
Mk 1:19 As he went a l farther,
5:23 "My l daughter is at the point of death.
5:41 "Talitha cum," which means, "L girl, get up!"
7:25 but a woman whose l daughter had an unclean
9:36 Then he took a l child and put it among them; B
9:42 before one of these l ones who believe in me,
10:13 People were bringing l children to him in order A
10:14 "Let the l children come to me; A
10:15 kingdom of God as a l child will never enter it." B
14:35 a l farther, he threw himself on the ground
14:70 after a l while the bystanders again said to Peter,
Lk 5: 3 and asked him to put out a l way from the shore.
7:47 But the one to whom l is forgiven, loves l."
9:47 took a l child and put it by his side, B
12:28 much more will he clothe you—you of l faith! C
12:32 "Do not be afraid, l flock,
16:10 "Whoever is faithful in a very l is faithful also
16:10 and whoever is dishonest in a very l is dishonest
17: 2 the sea than for you to cause one of these l ones
18:16 "Let the l children come to me, A
18:17 kingdom of God as a l child will never enter it." B
22:58 A l later someone else, on seeing him, said,
Jn 4:49 "Sir, come down before my l boy dies."
6: 7 not buy enough bread for each of them to get a l."
7:33 "I will be with you a l while longer,
12:35 "The light is with you for a l longer.
13:33 L children, I am with you only a little longer. A
13:33 Little children, I am with you only a l longer.
14:19 In a l while the world will no longer see me,
16:16 "A l while, and you will no longer see me,
16:16 and again a l while, and you will see me."
16:17 "What does he mean by saying to us, 'A l while,
16:17 and again a l while, and you will see me';
16:18 "What does he mean by this 'a l while'?
16:19 'A l while, and you will no longer see me,
16:19 and again a l while, and you will see me'?
Ac 19:23 that time no l disturbance broke out concerning
19:24 brought no l business to the artisans.
20:12 the boy away alive and were not a l comforted.
27:28 a l farther on they took soundings again
Ro 15:24 once I have enjoyed your company for a l while.
1Co 5: 6 that a l yeast leavens the whole batch of dough?
2Co 8:15 and the one who had l did not have too l."
10: 8 even if I boast a l too much of our authority,
11: 1 I wish you would bear with me in a l foolishness.
11:16 so that I too may boast a l.
Gal 4:19 My l children, for whom I am again in the pain A
5: 9 A l yeast leavens the whole batch of dough.
Php 4:12 I know what it is to have l,
1Ti 5:23 but take a l wine for the sake of your stomach
Heb 2: 7 You have made them for a l while lower than
2: 9 for a l while was made lower than the angels,
10:37 For yet "in a very l while,
Jas 4:14 For you are a mist that appears for a l while and
1Pe 1: 6 for a l while you have had to suffer various trials,
5:10 And after you have suffered for a l while,
1Jn 2: 1 My l children, I am writing these things to you A
2:12 I am writing to you, l children, A
1Jn 2:28 And now, l children, abide in him, A
3: 7 L children, let no one deceive you. A
3:18 L children, let us love, not in word or speech, A
4: 4 L children, you are from God, A
5:21 L children, keep yourselves from idols. A
Rev 3: 8 I know that you have but l power,
6:11 a white robe and told to rest a l longer,
10: 2 He held a l scroll open in his hand.
10: 9 to the angel and told him to give me the l scroll;
10:10 the l scroll from the hand of the angel and ate it;
17:10 when he comes, he must remain only a l while.
20: 3 After that he must be let out for a l while.
Tob 4: 8 not be afraid to give according to the l you have.
12: 8 A l with righteousness is better than wealth
Jdt 7:27 not witness our l ones dying before our eyes,
16:16 to you is a very l thing;
AdE 10: 6 There was the l spring that became a river,
Wis 3: 5 Having been disciplined a l,
7: 9 because all gold is but a l sand in her sight,
9: 5 with l understanding of judgment and laws;
12: 2 you correct l by l those who trespass,
12: 8 as forerunners of your army to destroy them l
12: 8 of your army to destroy them little by l,
12:10 But judging them l by l you gave them an opportunity to repent,
13: 6 Yet these people are l to be blamed,
15: 8 of earth a short time before and after a l while go
16: 6 they were troubled for a l while as a warning,
Sir Pr: 2 the books differ not a l when read in the original.
Pr: 3 I found opportunity for no l instruction.
6:19 For when you cultivate her you will toil but l,
19: 1 one who despises small things will fail l by l.
20:12 Some buy much for l, but pay
20:15 He gives l and upbraids much;
29:23 Be content with l or much,
31:19 How ample a l is for a well-disciplined person!
38:24 the one who has l business can become wise.
40: 6 He gets l or no rest;
42: 4 and of acquiring much or l;
51:16 I inclined my ear a l and received her,
51:27 See with your own eyes that I have labored but l
51:28 Hear but a l of my instruction,
1Mc 16:15 the l stronghold called Dok, which he had built;
2Mc 3:14 There was no l distress throughout
3:30 a l while before was full of fear and disturbance,
5:17 that the Lord was angered for a l while because
6:29 a l before had acted toward him with goodwill
7:33 And if our living Lord is angry for a l while,
8: 8 that the man was gaining ground l by l,
8:33 who had fled into one l house;
9: 8 Thus he who only a l while before had thought
9:10 a l while before had thought that he could touch
15:19 to remain in the city were in no l distress,
2Es 6:29 l by little the place where I was standing began
6:29 by l the place where I was standing began to rock
8: 2 but only a l dust from which gold comes,
10:22 our l ones have been cast out,
10:41 The woman who appeared to you a l while ago,
11: 3 but they became l, puny wings.
11:22 and the two l wings had disappeared,
11:23 the three heads that were at rest and six l wings.
11:24 that two l wings separated from the six
11:25 that these l wings planned to set themselves up
11:31 and devoured the two l wings that were planning
11:45 your most evil l wings, your malicious heads,
12: 5 and not even a l strength is left in me,
12:19 your seeing eight l wings clinging to its wings,
12:29 As for your seeing two l wings passing over to
4Mc 6:20 a l while and during that time be a laughingstock
12: 7 as we shall tell a l later,

LIVE‡ (641) [ALIVE, LIFE, LIFE'S, LIFE-GIVING, LIFE-SAVING, LIFEBLOOD, LIFELESS, LIFELIKE, LIFETIME, LIVED, LIVES, LIVING, MID-LIFE, OUTLIVE, OUTLIVED, SHORT-LIVED]

A. AS I LIVE (31)
B. LIVE IN THE LAND (10)
C. LIVE FOREVER (17)

Ge 3:22 from the tree of life, and eat, and l forever"— C
4:20 he was the ancestor of those who l in tents
9:27 and let him l in the tents of Shem;
12:12 then they will kill me, but they will let you l.
13: 6 so great that they could not l together,
16:12 and he shall l at odds with all his kin."
17:18 "O that Ishmael might l in your sight!"
20: 7 and he will pray for you and you shall l.
24: 3 of the Canaanites, among whom I l,
24:37 of the Canaanites, in whose land I l;
25:22 and she said, "If it is to be this way, why do I l?"
27:40 By your sword you shall l,
28: 4 of the land where you now l as an alien—
31:32 with whom you find your gods shall not l.
34:10 You shall l with us; and the land shall be open
34:10 l and trade in it, and get property in it."
34:16 we will l among you and become one people.
34:21 let them l in the land and trade in it, B
34:22 on this condition will they agree to l among us,
34:23 and they will l among us."
36: 7 possessions were too great for them to l together;
38:11 So Tamar went to l in her father's house.
42: 2 that we may l and not die."
42:18 "Do this and you will l, for I fear God:
43: 8 so that we may l and not die—
Ge 47: 6 let them l in the land of Goshen; B
47:19 just give us seed, so that we may l and not die,
Ex 1:16 but if it is a girl, she shall l."
1:17 but they let the boys l.
1:18 and allowed the boys to l?"
1:22 but you shall let every girl l."
8:21 so also the land where they l.
8:22 the land of Goshen, where my people l, so
9:16 But this is why I have let you l:
12:13 be a sign for you on the houses where you l:
19:13 whether animal or human being, they shall not l.'
21:35 they shall sell the l ox and divide the price of it;
22:18 You shall not permit a female sorcerer to l.
23:33 They shall not l in your land,
33:20 for no one shall see me and l."
34:10 the people among whom you l shall see the work
Lev 13:46 he is unclean. He shall l alone;
14: 8 but shall l outside his tent seven days.
16:20 he shall present the l goat.
16:21 both his hands on the head of the l goat,
18: 5 by doing so one shall l: I am the LORD.
23:42 You shall l in booths for seven days;
23:42 all that are citizens in Israel shall l in booths,
23:43 of Israel l in booths when I brought them out of
25: 6 your hired and your bound laborers who l
25:18 so that you may l on the land securely.
25:19 and you will eat your fill and l on it securely.
25:35 they shall l with you as though resident aliens.
25:36 but fear your God; let them l with you.
26: 5 and l securely in your land.
Nu 4:19 that they may l and not die when they come near
13:18 and whether the people who l in it are strong
13:19 and whether the land they l in is good or bad,
13:19 and whether the towns that they l in are unwalled
13:28 Yet the people who l in the land are strong, B
13:29 The Amalekites l in the land of the Negeb; B
13:29 and the Amorites l in the hill country;
13:29 Canaanites l by the sea, and along the Jordan."
14:21 as I l, and as all the earth shall be filled with A
14:25 Amalekites and the Canaanites l in the valleys,
14:28 Say to them, "As I l," says the LORD, A
21: 8 and everyone who is bitten shall look at it and l."
21: 9 person would look at the serpent of bronze and l.
22:33 just now I would have killed you and let it l."
24:23 "Alas, who shall l when God does this?
31:15 "Have you allowed all the women to l?
35: 2 towns for the Levites to l in;
35: 3 The towns shall be theirs to l in,
35:25 The slayer shall l in it until the death of
35:29 throughout your generations wherever you l.
35:32 l in the land before the death of the high priest. B
35:33 You shall not pollute the land in which you l;
35:34 You shall not defile the land in which you l,
Dt 2: 4 the descendants of Esau, who l in Seir.
2: 8 the descendants of Esau who l in Seir,
2:22 of Esau, who l in Seir, by destroying the Horim
2:29 the descendants of Esau who l in Seir have done for me and likewise the Moabites who l in Ar—
4: 1 that you may l to enter and occupy the land that
4:10 that they may learn to fear me as long as they l
4:26 you will not l long on it,
4:42 homicide could flee to one of these cities and l:
5:24 to someone and the person may still l.
5:33 that you may l, and that it may go well with you,
5:33 and that you may l long in the land that you are
8: 1 so that you may l and increase,
8: 3 to make you understand that one does not l
8:12 and have built fine houses and l in them,
11: 9 and so that you may l long in the land that
11:30 the land of the Canaanites who l in the Arabah,
11:31 and when you occupy it and l in it,
12: 1 has given you to occupy all the days that you l on
12:10 you cross over the Jordan and l in the land B
12:10 from your enemies all around so that you l
12:19 the Levite as long as you l in your land.
12:29 you have dispossessed them and l in their land,
13:12 that the LORD your God is giving you to l in,
14: 9 Of all that l in water you may eat these:
16:20 so that you may l and occupy the land that
19: 4 of a homicide who might flee there and l,
19: 5 the killer may flee to one of these cities and l.
22: 7 that it may go well with you and you may l long.
23: 6 or their prosperity as long as you l.
28:30 You shall build a house, but not l in it.
30: 6 in order that you may l.
30:16 then you shall l and become numerous,
30:18 not l long in the land that you are crossing
30:19 so that you and your descendants may l,
30:20 that you may l in the land that the LORD swore B
31:13 long as you l in the land that you are crossing B
32:40 my hand to heaven, and swear: As I l forever, AC
32:47 through it you may l long in the land
33: 6 May Reuben l, and not die out,
Jos 6:17 with her in her house shall l because she hid
9: 7 "Perhaps you l among us;
9:20 We will let them l, so that wrath may not come
9:21 The leaders said to them, "Let them l."
10: 6 for all the kings of the Amorites who l in
13:13 Geshur and Maacath l within Israel to this day.
14: 4 to the Levites in the land, but only towns to l in,
15:63 so the Jebusites l with the people of Judah
17:12 but the Canaanites continued to l in that land.
17:16 the Canaanites who l in the plain have chariots
21: 2 through Moses that we be given towns to l in,
24:13 and towns that you had not built, and you l
Jdg 1:27 but the Canaanites continued to l in that land.
1:35 The Amorites continued to l in Har-heres,

Jdg 6:10 the gods of the Amorites, in whose land you l.'
8:29 of Joash went to l in his own house.
9:41 so that they could not l on at Shechem.
17: 8 to l wherever he could find a place.
17: 9 and I am going to l wherever I can find a place."
18: 1 for itself a territory to l in;
Ru 1: 1 a certain man of Bethlehem in Judah went to l in
1Sa 1:26 As you l, my lord, I am
2:31 so that no one in your family will l to old age.
2:32 and no one in your family shall ever l to old age.
10:24 And all the people shouted, "Long l the king!"
20: 3 truly, as the LORD lives and as you yourself l,
25:26 as the LORD lives, and as you yourself l,
25:28 evil shall not be found in you so long as you l.
27: 5 so that I may l there;
27: 5 for why should your servant l in the royal city
2Sa 1:10 for I knew that he could not l after he had fallen.
7: 5 Are you the one to build me a house to l in?
7:10 so that they may l in their own place,
11:11 As you l, and as your soul lives,
12:22 be gracious to me, and the child may l.'
14:19 woman answered and said, "As surely as you l,
16:16 to Absalom, "Long l the king! Long l the king!"
19:34 "How many years have I still to l,
1Ki 1:25 and saying, 'Long l King Adonijah!'
1:31 and said, "May my lord King David l forever!" C
1:34 and say, 'Long l King Solomon!'
1:39 and all the people said, "Long l King Solomon!"
2:36 "Build yourself a house in Jerusalem, and l there,
3:17 my lord, this woman and I l in the same house;
8:40 may fear you all the days that they l in the land B
17: 9 which belongs to Sidon, and l there;
20:32 "Your servant Ben-hadad says, 'Please let me l.' "
2Ki 2: 2 "As the LORD lives, and as you yourself l,
2: 4 "As the LORD lives, and as you yourself l,
2: 6 "As the LORD lives, and as you yourself l,
4: 7 and you and your children can l on the rest."
4:13 She answered, "I l among my own people."
4:30 "As the LORD lives, and as you yourself l,
6: 1 where we l under your charge is too small for us.
6: 2 and build a place there for us to l."
7: 4 if they spare our lives, we shall l;
10:19 whoever is missing shall not l."
11:12 they clapped their hands and shouted, "Long l
16: 6 Edomites came to Elath, where they l to this day.
17:27 let him go and l there,
18:32 that you may l and not die.
25:24 l in the land, serve the king of Babylon, B
1Ch 9: 2 Now the first to l again in their possessions
17: 4 You shall not build me a house to l in.
17: 9 so that they may l in their own place,
2Ch 2: 3 to build himself a house to l in.
6:31 in your ways all the days that they l in the land B
8:11 "My wife shall not l in the house of King David
19:10 to you from your kindred who l in their cities,
23:11 and they shouted, "Long l the king!"
Ezr 4:17 the rest of their associates who l in Samaria and
Ne 2: 3 I said to the king, "May the king l forever! C
4:12 "From all the places where they l they will come
8:14 that the people of Israel should l in booths during
9:29 by the observance of which a person shall l.
11: 1 of the people cast lots to bring one out of ten to l
11: 2 all those who willingly offered to l in Jerusalem.
Est 4:11 the golden scepter to someone, may that person l.
9:19 the Jews of the villages, who l in the open towns,
Job 4:19 how much more those who l in houses of clay,
7:16 I loathe my life; I would not l forever. C
8:17 around the stoneheap; they l among the rocks.
14:14 If mortals die, will they l again?
15:28 they will l in desolate cities, in houses
18:19 and no survivor where they used to l.
21: 7 Why do the wicked l on, reach old age,
22: 8 powerful possess the land, and the favored l in it.
30: 6 In the gullies of wadis they must l,
Ps 22:26 May your hearts l forever! C
22:29 down to the dust, and I shall l for him.
24: 1 the world, and those who l in it;
27: 4 to l in the house of the LORD all the days
37: 3 so you will l in the land, and enjoy security. B
37:29 The righteous shall inherit the land, and l
49: 9 one should l on forever and never see the grave.
55:23 and treacherous shall not l out half their days.
63: 4 So I will bless you as long as I l; A
65: 4 and bring near to l in your courts.
65: 8 Those who l at earth's farthest bounds are awed
68: 6 God gives the desolate a home to l in;
68: 6 but the rebellious l in a parched land.
68:30 Rebuke the wild animals that l among the reeds,
69:25 let no one l in their tents.
69:35 and his servants shall l there and possess it;
69:36 and those who love his name shall l in it.
72: 5 May he l while the sun endures,
72:15 Long may he l! May gold of Sheba be given to him
84: 4 Happy are those who l in your house,
84:10 than l in the tents of wickedness.
89:48 Who can l and never see death?
91: 1 You who l in the shelter of the Most High,
98: 7 the world and those who l in it.
101: 6 so that they may l with me;
102:28 The children of your servants shall l secure;
103: 5 who satisfies you with good as long as you l so
104:33 I will sing to the LORD as long as I l; A
107:36 And there he lets the hungry l,
107:36 and they establish a town to l in;
116: 2 therefore I will call on him as long as I l. A
118:17 I shall not die, but I shall l,
119:17 so that I may l and observe your word.
Ps 119:19 I l as an alien in the land;
119:77 Let your mercy come to me, that I may l;
119:116 to your promise, that I may l, and let me not
119:144 give me understanding that I may l.
119:175 Let me l that I may praise you,
120: 5 that I must l among the tents of Kedar.
133: 1 and pleasant it is when kindred l together
140:13 the upright shall l in your presence.
146: 2 I will praise the LORD as long as I l; A
Pr 1:33 to me will be secure and will l at ease,
4: 4 keep my commandments, and l.
7: 2 and l, keep my teachings as the apple
8: 4 O people, I call, and my cry is to all that l.
8:12 I, wisdom, l with prudence,
9: 6 Lay aside immaturity, and l,
11:19 Whoever is steadfast in righteousness will l,
15:27 but those who hate bribes will l.
19:10 It is not fitting for a fool to l in luxury,
19:16 Those who keep the commandment will l;
21: 9 It is better to l in a corner of the housetop than in
21:19 to l in a desert land than with a contentious
24:15 to the place where the righteous l;
25:24 It is better to l in a corner of the housetop than in
Ecc 3:12 be happy and enjoy themselves as long as they l;
6: 3 a hundred children, and l many years;
6: 6 though he should l a thousand years twice over,
6:12 while they l the few days of their vain life,
9: 3 madness is in their hearts while they l,
11: 8 Even those who l many years should rejoice
Isa 5: 8 you are left to l alone in the midst of the land!
6: 5 and I l among a people of unclean lips;
6: 6 a l coal that had been taken from the altar with
10:24 O my people, who l in Zion,
11: 6 The wolf shall l with the lamb,
13:21 ostriches will l, and there goat-demons will dance.
18: 3 you who l on the earth,
23:18 and fine clothing for those who l in the presence
26:14 The dead do not l; shades do not rise—
26:19 Your dead shall l, their corpses shall rise.
33:14 "Who among us can l with the devouring fire?
33:14 Who among us can l with everlasting flames?"
33:16 they will l on the heights;
33:24 people who l there will be forgiven their iniquity.
34:11 the owl and the raven shall l in it.
34:17 from generation to generation they shall l in it.
38:16 O Lord, by these things people l,
38:16 Oh, restore me to health and make me l!
40:22 and spreads them like a tent to l in;
49:18 As I l, says the LORD, you shall put all of them A
51: 6 and those who l on it will die like gnats;
55: 3 listen, so that you may l.
58:12 the restorer of streets to l in.
65:20 or an old person who does not l out a lifetime;
Jer 8:16 the city and those who l in it.
9:26 all those with shaven temples who l in the desert.
10:17 O you who l under siege!
12: 4 the wickedness of those who l in it the animals
17: 6 They shall l in the parched places of
20: 6 And you, Pashhur, and all who l in your house,
21: 9 to the Chaldeans who are besieging you shall l
22:24 As I l, says the LORD, even if King Coniah A
23: 6 In his days Judah will be saved and Israel will l
23: 8 Then they shall l in their own land.
24: 8 and those who l in the land of Egypt. B
25:24 and all the kings of the mixed peoples that l in
27:11 says the LORD, to till it and l there.
27:12 and serve him and his people, and l.
27:17 serve the king of Babylon and l.
29: 5 Build houses and l in them;
29:16 and concerning all the people who l in this city,
29:28 build houses and l in them,
31:24 And Judah and all its towns shall l there together,
33:16 be saved and Jerusalem will l in safety.
35: 7 shall l in tents all your days, that you may l many
35: 9 and not to build houses to l in.
35:15 then you shall l in the land that I gave to you B
38: 2 but those who go out to the Chaldeans shall l;
38: 2 as a prize of war, and l.
38:17 and you and your house shall l.
40:10 and l in the towns that you have taken over."
44:13 I will punish those who l in the land of Egypt, B
44:14 Although they long to go back to l there,
44:26 all you Judeans who l in the land of Egypt: B
46:18 As I l, says the King, whose name is the LORD A
47: 2 the city and those who l in it.
48:28 Leave the towns, and l on the rock,
49:16 you who l in the clefts of the rock,
49:18 no one shall l there, nor shall anyone settle in it.
49:33 no one shall l there, nor shall anyone settle in it.
50: 3 and no one shall l in it;
50:39 wild animals shall l with hyenas in Babylon,
50:40 says the LORD, so no one shall l there,
51:13 You who l by mighty waters, rich in treasures,
51:62 so that neither human beings nor animals shall l
La 4:20 of whom we said, "Under his shadow we shall l
4:21 O daughter Edom, you that l in the land of Uz; B
Eze 2: 6 though briers and thorns surround you and you l
3:21 they shall surely l, because they took warning;
5:11 Therefore, as I l, says the Lord GOD, surely, A
6: 6 Wherever you l, your towns shall be waste
12:19 on account of the violence of all those who l
13:19 and keeping alive persons who should not l,
14:16 three men were in it, as I l, says the Lord GOD, A
14:18 three men were in it, as I l, says the Lord GOD, A
14:20 and Job were in it, as I l, says the Lord GOD, A
16: 6 As you lay in your blood, I said to you, "L!
16:48 As I l, says the Lord GOD, A
Eze 17:16 As I l, says the Lord GOD, A
17:19 Therefore thus says the Lord GOD: As I l, A
17:23 Under it every kind of bird will l;
18: 3 As I l, says the Lord GOD, A
18: 9 he shall surely l, says the Lord GOD.
18:13 or accrued interest; shall he then l?
18:17 for his father's iniquity; he shall surely l.
18:19 to observe all my statutes, he shall surely l.
18:21 they shall surely l; they shall not die.
18:22 righteousness that they have done they shall l.
18:23 that they should turn from their ways and l?
18:24 that the wicked do, shall they l?
18:28 they shall surely l; they shall not die.
18:32 says the Lord GOD. Turn, then, and l.
20: 3 As I l, says the Lord GOD, A
20:11 by whose observance everyone shall l.
20:13 by whose observance everyone shall l;
20:21 by whose observance everyone shall l;
20:25 and ordinances by which they could not l.
20:31 As I l, says the Lord GOD, A
20:33 As I l, says the Lord GOD, A
26:20 and I will make you l in the world below,
28:26 They shall l in safety in it,
28:26 They shall l in safety, when I execute judgments
32:15 when I strike down all who l in it,
33:10 of them; how then can we l?"
33:11 Say to them, As I l, says the Lord GOD, A
33:11 but that the wicked turn from their ways and l;
33:12 be able to l by their righteousness when they sin.
33:13 I say to the righteous that they shall surely l,
33:15 they shall surely l, they shall not die.
33:16 and right, they shall surely l.
33:19 and do what is lawful and right, they shall l by it.
33:27 As I l, surely those who are in the waste places A
34: 8 As I l, says the Lord GOD, A
34:25 so that they may l in the wild and sleep in
34:28 of the land devour them; they shall l in safety,
35: 6 as I l, says the Lord GOD, A
35:11 as I l, says the Lord GOD, A
36:28 Then you shall l in the land that I gave B
37: 3 He said to me, "Mortal, can these bones l?"
37: 5 I will cause breath to enter you, and you shall l.
37: 6 and put breath in you, and you shall l;
37: 9 and breathe upon these slain, that they may l."
37:14 I will put my spirit within you, and you shall l,
37:25 They shall l in the land that I gave B
37:25 and their children's children shall l there forever;
38:11 I will fall upon the quiet people who l in safety,
38:12 who l at the center of the earth.
39: 6 and on those who l securely in the coastlands;
39: 9 Then those who l in the towns
39:26 when they l securely in their land with no one
45: 5 as their holding for cities to l in.
47: 9 every living creature that swarms will l,
47: 9 and everything will l where the river goes.
Da 2: 4 to the king (in Aramaic), "O king, l forever! C
2:38 wherever they l, the wild animals of the field,
3: 9 to King Nebuchadnezzar, "O king, l forever! C
4: 1 and languages that l throughout the earth:
4:17 in order that all who l may know that
5:10 The queen said, "O king, l forever! C
6: 6 "O King Darius, l forever! C
6:21 Daniel then said to the king, "O king, l forever! C
Hos 4: 3 the land mourns, and all who l in it languish;
6: 2 that we may l before him.
12: 9 I will make you l in tents again,
14: 7 They shall again l beneath my shadow,
Am 3:12 the people of Israel who l in Samaria be rescued,
5: 4 of Israel: Seek me and l;
5: 6 the LORD and l, or he will break out against
5:11 but you shall not l in them;
5:14 Seek good and not evil, that you may l;
9: 5 and all who l in it mourn,
Ob 1: 3 you that l in the clefts of the rock,
Jnh 4: 3 for it is better for me to die than to l."
4: 8 He said, "It is better for me to die than to l."
Mic 5: 4 And they shall l secure, for now he shall be great
Na 1: 5 the world and all who l in it.
Hab 2: 4 but the righteous l by their faith.
2: 8 to cities and all who l in them.
2:17 to cities and all who l in them.
Zep 2: 9 Therefore, as I l, says the LORD of hosts, A
Hag 1: 4 for you yourselves to l in your paneled houses,
Zec 1: 5 And the prophets, do they l forever? C
2: 7 you that l with daughter Babylon.
8: 8 and I will bring them to l in Jerusalem.
13: 3 "You shall not l, for you speak lies in the name
Mt 4: 4 "It is written, 'One does not l by bread alone,
9:18 come and lay your hand on her, and she will l."
12:45 and they enter and l there;
Mk 5:23 so that she may be made well, and l."
7: 5 not l according to the tradition of the elders,
12:44 in everything she had, all she had to l on."
Lk 4: 4 "It is written, 'One does not l by bread alone.' "
7:25 those who put on fine clothing and l in luxury are
8:27 and he did not l in a house but in the tombs.
10:28 do this, and you will l."
11:26 and they enter and l there;
21: 4 of her poverty has put in all she had to l on."
21:35 For it will come upon all who l on the face of
Jn 4:50 Jesus said to him, "Go; your son will l."
4:53 when Jesus had said to him, "Your son will l."
5:25 and those who hear will l.
6:51 Whoever eats of this bread will l forever; C
6:57 and I l because of the Father,
6:57 so whoever eats me will l because of me.
6:58 But the one who eats this bread will l forever." C

Jn 11:25 even though they die, will l,
14:19 because I l, you also will l.
Ac 1:20 and let there be no one to l in it';
2:14 "Men of Judea and all who l in Jerusalem,
2:26 moreover my flesh will l in hope.
4:16 For it is obvious to all who l in Jerusalem that
17:24 does not l in shrines made by human hands,
17:26 the boundaries of the places where they would l,
17:28 For 'In him we l and move and have our being';
22:22 For he should not be allowed to l."
25:24 shouting that he ought not to l any longer.
28: 4 justice has not allowed him to l."
28:16 Paul was allowed to l by himself,
Ro 1:17 "The one who is righteous will l by faith."
6: 8 we believe that we will also l with him.
8: 5 For those who l according to the flesh
8: 5 but those who l according to the Spirit
8:12 not to the flesh, to l according to the flesh—
8:13 for if you l according to the flesh, you will die;
8:13 to death the deeds of the body, you will l.
10: 5 person who does these things will l by them."
12:16 L in harmony with one another;
12:18 so far as it depends on you, l peaceably with all.
13:13 let us l honorably as in the day,
14: 7 We do not l to ourselves,
14: 8 If we l, we l to the Lord, and if we die,
14: 8 so then, whether we l or whether we die,
14:11 For it is written, "As I l, says the Lord, A
15: 5 and encouragement grant you to l in harmony
1Co 7:12 is an unbeliever, and she consents to l with him,
7:13 is an unbeliever, and he consents to l with her,
2Co 4:11 For while we l, we are always being given up
5: 1 that if the earthly tent we l in is destroyed,
5:15 those who l might l no longer for themselves,
6:16 "I will l in them and walk among them,
7: 3 to die together and to l together.
10: 3 Indeed, we l as human beings,
13: 4 but in dealing with you we will l with him by
13:11 agree with one another, l in peace;
Gal 2:14 though a Jew, l like a Gentile and not like a Jew,
2:14 how can you compel the Gentiles to l like Jews?"
2:19 the law I died to the law, so that I might l to God.
2:20 and it is no longer I who l,
2:20 And the life I now l in the flesh I l by faith in
3:11 for "The one who is righteous will l by faith."
3:12 "Whoever does the works of the law will l
5:16 L by the Spirit, I say, and do not gratify
5:25 If we l by the Spirit,
Eph 1:12 might l for the praise of his glory.
4:17 you must no longer l as the Gentiles l,
5: 2 and l in love, as Christ loved us and gave himself
5: 8 in the Lord you are light. L as children of light—
5:15 Be careful then how you l,
6: 3 that it may be well with you and you may l long
Php 1:22 If I am to l in the flesh,
1:27 l your life in a manner worthy of the gospel
3:17 and observe those who l according to
3:18 For many l as enemies of the cross of Christ;
Col 2: 6 continue to l your lives in him,
2:20 why do you l as if you still belonged to
1Th 3: 8 For we now l, if you continue to stand firm in
4: 1 as you learned from us how you ought to l and
4:11 to aspire to l quietly, to mind your own affairs,
5:10 so that whether we are awake or asleep we may l
2Ti 2:11 we have died with him, we will also l with him;
3:12 all who want to l a godly life in Christ Jesus will
Tit 2:12 the present age to l lives that are self-controlled,
Heb 10:38 but my righteous one will l by faith.
12: 9 to be subject to the Father of spirits and l?
Jas 4:15 we will l and do this or that."
1Pe 1:17 l in reverent fear during the time of your exile.
2:16 As servants of God, l as free people,
2:24 free from sins, we might l for righteousness;
4: 2 as to l for the rest of your earthly life no longer
4: 6 they might l in the spirit as God does.
2Pe 2:18 from those who l in error.
1Jn 2:17 but those who do the will of God l forever. C
4: 9 into the world so that we might l through him.
Rev 14: 6 with an eternal gospel to proclaim to those who l
Tob 3: 6 For it is better for me to die than to l,
3:15 Why should I still l?
4: 5 L uprightly all the days of your life,
10:12 hear a good report about you as long as I l." A
10:12 and may I l long enough to see children of you
14: 7 they will go to Jerusalem and l in safety forever
Jdt 2:12 For as I l, and by the power of my kingdom, A
5: 4 why have they alone, of all who l in the west,
7:10 but on the height of the mountains where they l,
7:14 be strewn about in the streets where they l.
11: 2 if your people who l in the hill country had
11: 3 You will l tonight and ever after.
11: 7 and the cattle and the birds of the air will l,
11:23 and you shall l in the palace
12: 4 Judith replied, "As surely as you l, my lord,
14: 4 Then you and all who l within the borders
AdE 9:19 while those who l in the large cities keep
13:17 turn our mourning into feasting that we may l
16:19 and permit the Jews to l under their own laws.
Wis 3:17 if they l long they will be held of no account,
5:15 But the righteous l forever, C
8: 9 Therefore I determined to take her to l with me,
13: 7 For while they l among his works,
14:28 or l unrighteously, or readily commit perjury;
Sir Pr: 3 to gain learning and are disposed to l according
4:15 and all who listen to her will l secure.
10: 3 to l in through the understanding of its rulers.
13: 5 If you own something, he will l with you;
Sir 14: 4 and others will l in luxury on his goods.
23:15 will never become disciplined as long as they l.
25: 1 and a wife and a husband who l in harmony.
25:16 I would rather l with a lion and a dragon than l
with an evil woman.
33:20 not give power over yourself, as long as you l;
34:14 The spirit of those who fear the Lord will l,
37:26 and his name will l forever. C
37:27 My child, test yourself while you l;
38:32 and wherever they l, they will not go hungry.
39: 9 and his name will l through all generations.
41:19 in the place where you l.
42:23 All these things l and remain forever;
46:12 of those who have been honored l again
48:11 For we also shall surely l.
50:26 Those who l in Seir, and the Philistines, and the
foolish people that l in Shechem.
51:18 For I resolved to l according to wisdom,
Bar 1:12 we shall l under the protection
4: 1 All who hold her fast will l,
LtJ 6:46 not l very long themselves;
1Mc 2: 7 to l there when it was given over to the enemy,
2:13 Why should we l any longer?"
2:19 "Even if all the nations that l under the rule of
2:20 I and my sons and my brothers will continue to l
2:29 down to the wilderness to l there,
2:33 and do what the king commands, and you will l."
4:35 how ready they were either to l or to die nobly,
6:23 to l by what he said,
6:59 to let them l by their laws as they did before;
7:38 and let them l no longer."
10:37 and let them l by their own laws,
2Mc 5:27 they continued to l on what grew wild,
6: 1 of their ancestors and no longer to l by the laws
6:26 yet whether I l or die I shall not escape the hands
11:25 and that they shall l according to the customs
12: 2 would not let them l quietly and in peace.
12: 4 to l peaceably and suspected nothing,
1Es 2: 6 wherever you may l, be helped by the people
3Mc 3:25 you are to send to us those who l among you,
2Es 4:12 be here than to come here and l in ungodliness,
4:26 "If you are alive, you will see, and if you l long,
4:51 "Do you think that I shall l until those days?
5: 4 But if the Most High grants that you l,
5:45 If therefore all creatures will l at one time and
6:21 and these shall l and leap about.
6:51 to l in it, where there are a thousand mountains;
7:21 when they came, what they should do to l,
7:72 those who l on earth shall be tormented,
7:82 now make a good repentance so that they may l.
7:109 [39] and for the one who was dead, that he might l,
7:117 [47] they l in sorrow now and expect punishment
7:129 [59] 'Choose life for yourself, so that you may l!'
8: 5 for you have been given only a short time to l.
8: 6 the likeness of a human being may be able to l.
8:13 and make it l as your work.
8:25 For as long as I l I will speak, A
8:46 "Things that are present are for those who l now,
8:46 that are future are for those who will l hereafter.
9: 9 with contempt shall l in torments.
9:18 before the world was made for them to l in,
14: 9 and henceforth you shall l with my Son and
14:22 those who want to l in the last days may do so."
14:35 the judgment will come, when we shall l again;
15:10 I will not allow them to l any longer in the land
15:14 Alas for the world and for those who l in it!
16:22 For many of those who l on the earth shall perish
16:42 a house be like one who will not l in it;
4Mc 7:19 do not die to God, but l to God.
8:26 when we can l in peace if we obey the king?"
11: 5 of all things and l according to his virtuous law?
16:25 that those who die for the sake of God l to God,
17:18 now stand before the divine throne and l the life
18:17 'Shall these dry bones l?'

LIVED[‡] (260) [LIVE]

Ge 5: 3 When Adam had l one hundred thirty years,
5: 5 that Adam l were nine hundred thirty years;
5: 6 When Seth had l one hundred five years,
5: 7 Seth l after the birth of Enosh
5: 9 When Enosh had l ninety years,
5:10 Enosh l after the birth of Kenan
5:12 When Kenan had l seventy years,
5:13 Kenan l after the birth of Mahalalel
5:15 When Mahalalel had l sixty-five years,
5:16 Mahalalel l after the birth of Jared
5:18 Jared had l one hundred sixty-two years he became
5:19 Jared l after the birth of Enoch
5:21 When Enoch had l sixty-five years,
5:25 Methuselah had l one hundred eighty-seven years,
5:26 Methuselah l after the birth of Lamech
5:28 Lamech had l one hundred eighty-two years,
5:30 Lamech l after the birth of Noah
9:28 After the flood Noah l three hundred fifty years.
10:30 in which they l extended from Mesha in
11:11 and Shem l after the birth of Arpachshad
11:12 When Arpachshad had l thirty-five years,
11:13 and Arpachshad l after the birth of Shelah
11:14 When Shelah had l thirty years,
11:15 and Shelah l after the birth of Eber
11:16 When Eber had l thirty-four years,
11:17 and Eber l after the birth of Peleg
11:18 When Peleg had l thirty years,
11:19 and Peleg l after the birth of Reu
11:20 When Reu had l thirty-two years,
11:21 and Reu l after the birth of Serug
Ge 11:22 When Serug had l thirty years,
11:23 and Serug l after the birth of Nahor
11:24 When Nahor had l twenty-nine years,
11:25 and Nahor l after the birth of Terah
11:26 When Terah had l seventy years,
13: 7 At that time the Canaanites and the Perizzites l in
14: 7 and also the Amorites who l in Hazazon-tamar.
14:12 who l in Sodom, and his goods, and departed.
16: 3 Abram had l ten years in the land of Canaan,
19:30 so he l in a cave with his two daughters.
21:20 he l in the wilderness, and became an expert with
21:21 He l in the wilderness of Paran;
22:19 and Abraham l at Beer-sheba.
23: 1 Sarah l one hundred twenty-seven years;
32: 4 'I have l with Laban as an alien,
35:22 While Israel l in that land,
37: 1 Jacob settled in the land where his father had l as
47:22 and l on the allowance that Pharaoh gave them;
47:28 Jacob l in the land of Egypt seventeen years;
50:22 and Joseph l one hundred ten years.
Ex 10:23 but all the Israelites had light where they l.
12:40 The time that the Israelites had l
Lev 18: 3 in the land of Egypt, where you l, and you shall
Nu 14:45 Then the Amalekites and the Canaanites who l in
20:15 and we l in Egypt a long time;
21: 1 Canaanite, the king of Arad, who l in the Negeb,
33:40 who l in the Negeb in the land of Canaan,
Dt 1:44 The Amorites who l in that hill country
2:23 who had l in settlements in the vicinity of Gaza,
4:33 as you have heard, and l?
26: 5 he went down into Egypt and l there as an alien,
29:16 You know how we l in the land of Egypt,
Jos 6:25 Her family has l in Israel ever since.
9:10 and King Og of Bashan who l in Ashtaroth.
12: 2 King Sihon of the Amorites who l at Heshbon,
12: 4 who l at Ashtaroth and at Edrei
13:21 as princes of Sihon, who l in the land.
16:10 drive out the Canaanites who l in Gezer:
16:10 the Canaanites have l within Ephraim to this day
24: 2 l beyond the Euphrates and served other gods.
24: 7 Afterwards you l in the wilderness a long time.
24: 8 who l on the other side of the Jordan;
24:18 the Amorites who l in the land.
Jdg 1: 9 against the Canaanites who l in the hill country,
1:10 the Canaanites who l in Hebron (the name
1:21 not drive out the Jebusites who l in Jerusalem;
1:21 so the Jebusites have l in Jerusalem among
1:29 not drive out the Canaanites who l in Gezer;
1:29 but the Canaanites l among them in Gezer.
1:30 but the Canaanites l among them,
1:32 but the Asherites l among the Canaanites,
1:33 but l among the Canaanites,
3: 3 and the Hivites who l on Mount Lebanon,
3: 5 So the Israelites l among the Canaanites,
4: 2 who l in Harosheth-ha-goiim.
10: 1 who l at Shamir in the hill country of Ephraim,
11: 3 Then Jephthah fled from his brothers and l in
11:26 While Israel l in Heshbon and its villages,
18:28 They rebuilt the city, and l in it.
21:23 and rebuilt the towns, and l in them.
Ru 1: 4 When they had l there about ten years,
2:23 and she l with her mother-in-law.
1Sa 12:11 on every side; and you l in safety.
23:29 and l in the strongholds of En-gedi.
27: 7 The length of time that David l in the country of
27:11 the time he l in the country of the Philistines.
2Sa 7: 6 I have not l in a house since the day I brought up
9:12 And all who l in Ziba's house became
9:13 Mephibosheth l in Jerusalem,
14:28 So Absalom l two full years in Jerusalem,
15: 8 For your servant made a vow while I l at Geshur
1Ki 2:38 So Shimei l in Jerusalem many days.
4:25 During Solomon's lifetime Judah and Israel l
9:16 had killed the Canaanites who l in the city,
13:11 Now there l an old prophet in Bethel.
13:25 and told it in the town where the old prophet l.
15:21 he stopped building Ramah and l in Tirzah.
17: 5 he went and l by the Wadi Cherith,
21: 8 to the elders and the nobles who l with Naboth
21:11 the elders and the nobles who l in his city
2Ki 4: 8 where a wealthy woman l,
13: 5 the people of Israel l in their homes as formerly.
14:17 son of Joash of Judah l fifteen years after the death
15: 5 to the day of his death, and l in a separate house.
17:28 from Samaria came and l in Bethel;
17:29 every nation in the cities in which they l;
19:36 went home, and l at Nineveh.
25:30 a portion every day, as long as he l.
1Ch 2:55 The families also of the scribes that l at Jabez:
4:23 they l there with the king in his service.
4:28 They l in Beer-sheba, Moladah, Hazar-shual,
4:43 and they have l there to this day.
5: 8 who l in Aroer, as far as Nebo and Baal-meon.
5: 9 He also l to the east as far as the beginning of
5:10 and they l in their tents throughout all
5:11 of Gad l beside them in the land of Bashan as far
5:16 and they l in Gilead, in Bashan and in its towns,
5:22 And they l in their territory until the exile.
5:23 The members of the half-tribe of Manasseh l in
7:29 In these l the sons of Joseph son of Israel.
8:28 These l in Jerusalem.
8:29 Jeiel the father of Gibeon l in Gibeon,
8:32 these also l opposite their kindred in Jerusalem,
9: 3 Ephraim, and Manasseh l in Jerusalem:
9:16 who l in the villages of the Netophathites.
9:34 these leaders l in Jerusalem.
9:35 In Gibeon l the father of Gibeon, Jeiel,

1Ch 9:38 these also **l** opposite their kindred in Jerusalem,
17: 5 not **l** in a house since the day I brought out Israel
17: 5 but I have **l** in a tent and a tabernacle.
2Ch 20: 8 They have **l** in it, and in it have built you
25:25 **l** fifteen years after the death of King Joash son
26: 7 against the Arabs who **l** in Gur-baal,
26:21 and being leprous **l** in a separate house,
30:25 and the resident aliens who **l** in Judah, rejoiced.
31: 4 He commanded the people who **l** in Jerusalem
31: 6 The people of Israel and Judah who **l** in the cities
34:22 keeper of the wardrobe (who **l** in Jerusalem in
Ezr 2:70 of the people **l** in Jerusalem and its vicinity;
2:70 and the temple servants **l** in their towns,
Ne 4:12 When the Jews who **l** near them came,
8:17 from the captivity made booths and **l** in them;
11: 1 Now the leaders of the people **l** in Jerusalem;
11: 3 the leaders of the province who **l** in Jerusalem;
11: 3 but in the towns of Judah all **l** on their property
11: 4 And in Jerusalem **l** some of the Judahites and of
11: 6 All the descendants of Perez who **l**
11:21 But the temple servants **l** on Ophel;
11:25 some of the people of Judah **l** in Kiriath-arba
11:31 people of Benjamin also **l** from Geba onward,
13:16 Tyrians also, who **l** in the city,
Job 21:28 Where is the tent in which the wicked **l**?'
29:25 and I **l** like a king among his troops,
42:16 After this Job **l** one hundred and forty years,
Ps 94:17 my soul would soon have **l** in the land of silence.
105:23 Jacob **l** as an alien in the land of Ham.
Isa 9: 2 those who **l** in a land of deep darkness—
13:20 be inhabited or **l** in for all generations;
37:37 went home, and **l** at Nineveh.
Jer 35:10 but we have **l** in tents,
44:15 the people who **l** in Pathros in the land of Egypt,
52:34 as long as he **l**, up to the day of his death.
Eze 3:15 who **l** by the river Chebar.
16:46 who **l** with her daughters to the north of you;
16:46 your younger sister, who **l** to the south of you,
20: 9 in the sight of the nations among whom they **l**,
31: 6 and in its shade all great nations **l**.
31:17 those who **l** in its shade among the nations.
36:17 when the house of Israel **l** on their own soil,
37:10 and the breath came into them, and they **l**,
37:25 in which your ancestors **l**;
Da 4:21 under which animals of the field **l**,
Zep 2:15 Is this the exultant city that **l** secure,
Mt 1:18 but before they **l** together,
23:30 'If we had **l** in the days of our ancestors,
Mk 5: 3 He **l** among the tombs;
Lk 2:36 having **l** with her husband seven years
Jn 1:14 And the Word became flesh and **l** among us,
7:42 the village where David **l**?"
Ac 7: 2 when he was in Mesopotamia, before he **l**
9:22 and confounded the Jews who **l** in Damascus
20:18 "You yourselves know how I **l** among you
23: 1 up to this day I have **l** my life with
26: 5 to the strictest sect of our religion and I **l** as
28:30 He **l** there two whole years at his own expense
Ro 14: 9 For to this end Christ died and **l** again,
Eph 2: 2 in which you once **l**, following the course
2: 3 All of us once **l** among them in the passions
2Ti 1: 5 a faith that **l** first in your grandmother Lois
Jas 5: 5 You have **l** on the earth in luxury and
Rev 13:14 that had been wounded by the sword and yet **l**;
18: 7 As she glorified herself and **l** luxuriously,
18: 9 and **l** in luxury with her, will weep and wail
Tob 14: 2 and after regaining it he **l** in prosperity,
Jdt 1: 6 the people of the hill country and all those who **l**
1: 7 to all who **l** in Persia and to all who **l** in the west,
those who **l** in Cilicia and Damascus,
1: 7 and all who **l** along the seacoast,
1:10 and all who **l** in Egypt as far as the borders
1:11 But all who **l** in the whole region disregarded
2:28 dread of him fell upon all the people who **l** along
2:28 who **l** in Sur and Ocina and all who **l** in Jamnia.
2:28 who **l** in Azotus and Ascalon feared him greatly.
5: 7 At one time they **l** in Mesopotamia,
5: 8 and **l** there for a long time.
5:10 of Canaan they went down to Egypt and **l** there
5:16 and all the Gergesites, and **l** there a long time.
10: 2 down into the house where she **l** on sabbaths and
15: 8 the Israelites who **l** in Jerusalem came to witness
AdE 1: 5 the people of various nations who **l** in the city.
Wis 12: 3 Those who **l** long ago in your holy land
12:23 Therefore those who **l** unrighteously,
14:17 since they **l** at a distance,
Sir 47:12 a wise son rose up who because of him **l**
Bar 1: 4 all who **l** in Babylon by the river Sud.
3:20 and have **l** upon the earth;
3:37 Afterward she appeared on earth and **l**
1Mc 5: 2 the descendants of Jacob who **l** among them.
5: 9 against the Israelites who **l** in their territory,
9:71 that he would not try to harm him as long as he **l**.
13:52 and he and his men **l** there.
13:53 of all the forces; and he **l** at Gazara.
14:34 where the enemy formerly **l**.
2Mc 5:17 a little while because of the sins of those who **l** in
6: 2 as did the people who **l** in that place.
12: 3 they invited the Jews who **l** among them
12:27 a fortified town where Lysias **l** with multitudes
12:30 the Jews who **l** there bore witness to the goodwill
1Es 5:73 of the building as long as King Cyrus **l**.
3Mc 3: 1 against those Jews who **l** in Alexandria,
3: 8 for they **l** under tyranny.
2Es 3: 2 and the wealth of those who **l** in Babylon.
3:12 "When those who **l** on earth began to multiply,
5:41 but what will those do who **l** before me, or we,

2Es 7:*89* During the time that they **l** in it,
7:*121* [51] but we have **l** wickedly?
7:*124* [54] because we have **l** in perverse ways?
7:*126* [56] For while we **l** and committed iniquity we did
8:28 of those who have **l** wickedly in your sight,
9:43 though I **l** with my husband for thirty years.
11:40 for so long you have **l** on the earth with deceit.
13:41 where no human beings had ever **l**,
13:46 "Then they **l** there until the last times;
14:29 At first our ancestors **l** as aliens in Egypt,
4Mc 5:36 nor my long life **l** lawfully.
6:18 if having **l** in accordance with truth up to old age
9: 6 of the Hebrews because of their religion **l** piously
18: 9 who **l** out his life with good children,

LIVELIHOOD (1)

Dt 24:15 they are poor and their **l** depends on them;

LIVELY (KJV) See LIVING, VIGOROUS

LIVER (19)

Ex 29:13 and the appendage of the **l**,
29:22 that covers the entrails, the appendage of the **l**,
Lev 3: 4 and the appendage of the **l**,
3:10 and the appendage of the **l**,
3:15 and the appendage of the **l**,
4: 9 and the appendage of the **l**,
7: 4 and the appendage of the **l**,
8:16 and the appendage of the **l**,
8:25 around the entrails, the appendage of the **l**, and
9:10 the **l** from the sin offering he turned into smoke
9:19 and the appendage of the **l**.
Eze 21:21 he consults the teraphim, he inspects the **l**.
Tob 6: 5 the fish and take out its gall, heart, and **l**.
6: 5 For its gall, heart, and **l** are useful as medicine."
6: 6 young man gathered together the gall, heart, and **l**;
6: 7 in the fish's heart and **l**,
6: 8 He replied, "As for the fish's heart and **l**,
6:17 take some of the fish's **l** and heart,
8: 2 and he took the fish's **l** and heart out of the bag

LIVES‡ (226) [LIVE]

A. AS THE †LORD LIVES (35)
B. WHO LIVES FOREVER (8)

Ge 9: 3 Every moving thing that **l** shall be food for you;
42:15 Here is how you shall be tested: as Pharaoh **l**,
42:16 or else, as Pharaoh **l**, surely you are spies."
47:25 They said, "You have saved our **l**;
Ex 1:14 and made their **l** bitter with hard service
30:12 of them shall give a ransom for their **l** to
30:15 to the LORD to make atonement for your **l**.
30:16 to the Israelites of the ransom given for your **l**.
Lev 17:11 for making atonement for your **l** on the altar;
Nu 15:14 An alien who **l** with you,
16:38 at the cost of their **l**.
Dt 22:19 not be permitted to divorce her as long as he **l**.
22:29 not be permitted to divorce her as long as he **l**.
33:20 Gad **l** like a lion; he tears at arm and scalp.
33:28 So Israel **l** in safety, untroubled is Jacob's abode
Jos 2:13 and deliver our **l** from death."
9:15 guaranteeing their **l** by a treaty;
9:24 so we were in great fear for our **l** because of you,
Jdg 8:19 as the LORD **l**, if you had saved them alive, A
18:25 and you will lose your life and the **l**
Ru 3:13 as the LORD **l**, I will act as next-of-kin for you. A
1Sa 1:28 as long as he **l**, he is given to the LORD."
14:39 For as the LORD **l** who saves Israel, A
14:45 As the LORD **l**, not one hair of his head shall fall A
17:55 Abner said, "As your soul **l**, O king,
19: 6 Saul swore, "As the LORD **l**, A
20: 3 truly, as the LORD **l** and as you yourself live, A
20:21 then you are to come, for, as the LORD **l**, A
20:31 For as long as the son of Jesse **l** upon the earth,
22:22 for the **l** of all your father's house.
25:26 Now then, my lord, as the LORD **l**, A
25:29 the **l** of your enemies he shall sling out as from
25:34 For as surely as the LORD the God of Israel **l**,
26:10 David said, "As the LORD **l**, A
26:16 As the LORD **l**, you deserve to die, A
28:10 "As the LORD **l**, no punishment shall come A
29: 6 "As the LORD **l**, you have been honest, A
2Sa 2:27 Joab said, "As God **l**, if you had not spoken,
4: 9 "As the LORD **l**, who has redeemed my life out A
11:11 As you live, and as your soul **l**,
12: 5 He said to Nathan, "As the LORD **l**, A
14:11 He said, "As the LORD **l**, A
15:21 But Ittai answered the king, "As the LORD **l**, A
15:21 "As the LORD lives, and as my lord the king **l**,
19: 5 and the **l** of your sons and your daughters,
19: 5 and the **l** of your wives and your concubines,
22:47 The LORD **l**! Blessed be my rock,
23:17 of the men who went at the risk of their **l**?"
1Ki 1:29 The king swore, saying, "As the LORD **l**, A
2:24 Now therefore as the LORD **l**, A
17: 1 said to Ahab, "As the LORD the God of Israel **l**,
17:12 But she said, "As the LORD your God **l**,
18:10 As the LORD your God **l**,
18:15 Elijah said, "As the LORD of hosts **l**,
22:14 But Micaiah said, "As the LORD **l**, A
2Ki 2: 2 But Elisha said, "As the LORD **l**, A
2: 4 But he said, "As the LORD **l**, A
2: 6 But he said, "As the LORD **l**, A
3:14 Elisha said, "As the LORD of hosts **l**,
4:30 the mother of the child said, "As the LORD **l**, A

2Ki 5:16 But he said, "As the LORD **l**, whom I serve, A
5:20 As the LORD **l**, I will run after him A
7: 4 if they spare our **l**, we shall live;
7: 7 the camp just as it was, and fled for their **l**.
1Ch 11:19 For at the risk of their **l** they brought it."
2Ch 18:13 But Micaiah said, "As the LORD **l**, A
Est 7: 3 and the **l** of my people—that is my request.
8:11 in every city to assemble and defend their **l**,
9:16 also gathered to defend their **l**, and gained relief
Job 2: 4 All that people have they will give to save their **l**.
19:25 For I know that my Redeemer **l**,
27: 2 "As God **l**, who has taken away my right,
27: 8 when God takes away their **l**?
31:30 I have not let my mouth sin by asking for their **l**
33:18 their **l** from traversing the River.
33:20 so that their **l** loathe bread,
33:22 and their **l** to those who bring death.
38:26 to bring rain on a land where no one **l**,
39:28 It **l** on the rock and makes its home in
Ps 18:46 The LORD **l**! Blessed be my rock,
72:13 and saves the **l** of the needy.
78:50 but gave their **l** over to the plague.
97:10 he guards the **l** of his faithful;
Pr 1:18 and set an ambush—for their own **l**!
3:29 against your neighbor who **l** trustingly
11:30 but violence takes **l** away.
13: 3 Those who guard their mouths preserve their **l**;
14:25 A truthful witness saves **l**,
16:17 those who guard their way preserve their **l**.
18: 1 The one who **l** alone is self-indulgent,
23:14 you will save their **l** from Sheol.
Ecc 5:20 they will scarcely brood over the days of their **l**,
8:12 a hundred times and prolong their **l**,
Isa 38:20 all the days of our **l**, at the house of the LORD.
65:20 that **l** but a few days, or an old person who does
Jer 2: 6 that no one passes through, where no one **l**?"
4: 2 and if you swear, "As the LORD **l**!" A
4:29 all the towns are forsaken, and no one **l** in them.
5: 2 Although they say, "As the LORD **l**," A
12:16 to swear by my name, "As the LORD **l**," A
16:14 "As the LORD **l** who brought the people of Israel A
16:15 "As the LORD **l** who brought the people of Israel A
17:21 Thus says the LORD: For the sake of your **l**,
21: 7 into the hands of those who seek their **l**.
21: 9 and shall have their **l** as a prize of war.
23: 7 "As the LORD **l** who brought the people of Israel A
23: 8 "As the LORD **l** who brought out and led A
34:20 to their enemies and to those who seek their **l**.
34:21 to their enemies and to those who seek their **l**,
38: 2 they shall have their **l** as a prize of war, and live.
38:16 "As the LORD **l**, who gave us our lives, A
38:16 "As the LORD lives, who gave us our **l**,
44:26 saying, 'As the Lord GOD **l**.'
49:31 advance against a nation at ease, that **l** secure,
49:31 that has no gates or bars, that **l** alone.
51: 6 Flee from the midst of Babylon, save your **l**,
51:43 a land in which no one **l**,
51:45 Save your **l**, each of you,
La 1: 3 she **l** now among the nations,
2:19 Lift your hands to him for the **l** of your children,
5: 9 We get our bread at the peril of our **l**,
Eze 7:13 of their iniquity, they cannot maintain their **l**.
13:18 of every height, in the hunt for human **l**!
13:18 Will you hunt down **l** among my people,
13:18 and maintain your own **l**?
13:20 I am against your bands with which you hunt **l**;
13:20 from your arms, and let the **l** go free,
13:20 the **l** that you hunt down like birds.
13:22 to turn from their wicked way and save their **l**;
14:14 they would save only their own **l**
14:20 they would save only their own **l**
17:17 up and siege walls built to cut off many **l**.
18: 4 Know that all **l** are mine;
22:25 they have devoured human **l**;
22:27 destroying **l** to get dishonest gain.
32:10 they shall tremble every moment for their **l**,
33: 5 they would have saved their **l**.
Da 4:34 and praised and honored the one who **l** forever. B
7:12 their **l** were prolonged for a season and a time.
12: 7 the one who **l** forever that it would be for a time, B
Hos 4:15 and do not swear, "As the LORD **l**." A
Am 2:14 nor shall the mighty save their **l**;
2:15 nor shall those who ride horses save their **l**;
8: 8 and everyone mourn who **l** in it,
8:14 and say, "As your god **l**, O Dan," and,
8:14 O Dan," and, "As the way of Beer-sheba **l**"—
Mic 7:14 which **l** alone in a forest in the midst of a garden
Jn 11:26 and everyone who **l** and believes
Ac 15:26 who have risked their **l** for the sake
27:10 of the cargo and the ship, but also of our **l**."
Ro 6:10 but the life he **l**, he **l** to God.
7: 2 by the law to her husband as long as he **l**;
7: 3 be called an adulteress if she **l** with another man
1Co 7:39 A wife is bound as long as her husband **l**.
2Co 13: 4 but **l** by the power of God.
Gal 2:20 but it is Christ who **l** in me.
Col 1:10 so that you may lead **l** worthy of the Lord,
2: 6 continue to live your **l** in him,
1Ti 5: 6 widow who **l** for pleasure is dead even while she **l**.
2Ti 1: 5 and your mother Eunice and now, I am sure, **l**
Tit 2:12 the present age to live **l** that are self-controlled,
Heb 2:15 and free those who all their **l** were held in slavery
5:13 for everyone who **l** on milk,
7: 8 by one of whom it is testified that he **l**.
7:25 since he always **l** to make intercession for them.
13: 5 Keep your **l** free from the love of money,
1Pe 3: 2 when they see the purity and reverence of your **l**.

2Pe 3:11 what sort of persons ought you to be in leading **l**
1Jn 2:10 Whoever loves a brother or sister **l** in the light,
3:16 and we ought to lay down our **l** for one another.
4:12 if we love one another, God **l** in us,
Rev 2:13 who was killed among you, where Satan **l**.
4:9 on the throne, who **l** forever and ever, B
4:10 on the throne and worship the one who **l** forever B
10:6 and swore by him who **l** forever and ever, B
15:7 of the wrath of God, who **l** forever and ever; B
18:13 and chariots, slaves—and human **l**.
Tob 5:6 and would stay with our kinsman Gabael who **l**
8:17 bring their **l** to fulfillment in happiness
10:12 May we all prosper together all the days of our **l**."
13:1 Then Tobit said: "Blessed be God who **l** forever, B
Jdt 5:3 what people is this that **l** in the hill country?
5:5 about this people that **l** in the mountain district
7:27 but our **l** will be spared,
8:24 for their **l** depend upon us, and the sanctuary—
13:16 As the Lord **l**, who has protected me in
AdE 13:2 to settle the **l** of my subjects in lasting tranquility
Wis 5:4 that their **l** were madness and that their end was
7:28 so much as the person who **l** with wisdom.
12:6 these parents who murder helpless **l**,
14:5 therefore people trust their **l** even to
14:24 either their **l** or their marriages pure,
15:10 and their **l** are of less worth than clay,
Sir 3:12 and do not grieve him as long as he **l**;
9:12 that they will not be held guiltless all their **l**.
18:1 He who **l** forever created the whole universe; B
21:2 and can destroy human **l**.
22:12 or the ungodly it lasts all the days of their **l**.
25:7 a man who **l** to see the downfall of his foes.
25:8 Happy the man who **l** with a sensible wife,
26:27 *every person like this l in the anarchy of war.*
39:11 If he **l** long, he will leave a name greater than
44:14 but their name **l** on generation after generation.
LtJ 6:7 and he is watching over your **l**.
1Mc 2:40 and refuse to fight with the Gentiles for our **l** and
2:50 and give your **l** for the covenant of our ancestors.
3:21 but we fight for our **l** and our laws.
9:9 Let us rather save our own **l** now,
9:44 "Let us get up now and fight for our **l**,
12:51 that they would fight for their **l**,
2Mc 11:7 and he urged the others to risk their **l** with him
14:10 For as long as Judas **l**,
1Es 4:38 and **l** and prevails forever and ever.
6:31 and prayers be offered for their **l**."
3Mc 6:6 in Babylon who had voluntarily surrendered their **l**
6:10 if our **l** have become entangled in impieties
7:6 toward all people we barely spared their **l**.
2Es 8:31 and our ancestors have passed our **l** in ways
4Mc 2:23 and one who **l** subject to this will rule a kingdom
5:16 who have been persuaded to govern our **l** by
5:26 to eat what will be most suitable for our **l**,
7:21 What person who **l** as a philosopher by
9:7 and if you take our **l** because of our religion,
13:13 who gave us our **l**, and let us use our bodies as

LIVESTOCK (92)

Ge 4:20 the ancestor of those who live in tents and have **l**.
13:2 Abram was very rich in **l**, in silver, and in gold.
13:7 the herders of Abram's **l** and the herders of Lot's **l**.
31:9 Thus God has taken away the **l** of your father,
31:18 and he drove away all his **l**,
31:18 the **l** in his possession that he had acquired
34:23 Will not their **l**, their property,
36:6 all his **l**, and all the property he had acquired in
36:7 not support them because of their **l**.
46:6 They also took their **l** and the goods
46:32 for they have been keepers of **l**;
46:34 of **l** from our youth even until now, both we
47:6 put them in charge of my **l**."
47:16 And Joseph answered, "Give me your **l**, and I will give you food in exchange for your **l**,
47:17 So they brought their **l** to Joseph;
47:17 with food in exchange for all their **l**.
Ex 9:3 with a deadly pestilence your **l** in the field:
9:4 the LORD will make a distinction between the **l** of Israel and the **l** of Egypt,
9:6 all the **l** of the Egyptians died, but of the **l** of the Israelites not one died.
9:7 Pharaoh inquired and found that not one of the **l**
9:19 and have your **l** and everything that you have in
9:20 of the LORD hurried their slaves and **l** off to
9:21 the word of the LORD left their slaves and **l** in
10:26 Our **l** also must go with us;
11:5 and all the firstborn of the **l**.
12:29 and all the firstborn of the **l**.
12:38 and **l** in great numbers, both flocks and herds.
13:12 All the firstborn of your **l** that are males shall be
17:3 to kill us and our children and **l** with thirst?"
20:10 your **l**, or the alien resident in your towns.
22:5 or lets **l** loose to graze in someone else's field,
34:19 all your male **l**, the firstborn of cow and sheep.
Lev 1:2 any of you bring an offering of **l** to the LORD,
5:2 of an unclean beast or the carcass of unclean **l** or
25:7 for your **l** also, and for the wild animals
26:22 of your children and destroy your **l**;
Nu 3:41 the firstborn among the Israelites, and the **l** of
3:41 for all the firstborn among the **l** of the Israelites.
3:45 the **l** of the Levites as substitutes for their **l**;
7:87 all the **l** for the burnt offering twelve bulls,
7:88 and all the **l** for the sacrifice
20:4 into this wilderness for us and our **l** to die here?
20:8 for the congregation and their **l**.
20:11 and the congregation and their **l** drank.
Nu 20:19 and if we drink of your water, we and our **l**,
32:26 and all our **l** shall remain there in the towns
35:3 for their **l**, and for all their animals.
Dt 2:35 Only the **l** we kept as spoil for ourselves,
3:7 But all the **l** and the plunder of the towns we kept
3:19 Only your wives, your children, and your **l**—
3:19 I know that you have much **l**—
5:14 or your ox or your donkey, or any of your **l**,
7:14 nor barrenness among you or your **l**.
11:15 and he will give grass in your fields for your **l**,
13:15 even putting its **l** to the sword.
20:14 the children, **l**, and everything else in the town,
28:4 the fruit of your ground, and the fruit of your **l**,
28:11 in the fruit of your womb, in the fruit of your **l**,
28:51 It shall consume the fruit of your **l** and the fruit
30:9 in the fruit of your **l**, and in the fruit of your soil.
Jos 1:14 and your **l** shall remain in the land
8:2 and its **l** you may take as booty for yourselves.
8:27 Only the **l** and the spoil of that city Israel took
11:14 All the spoil of these towns, and the **l**,
21:2 along with their pasture lands for our **l**."
22:8 and with very much **l**, with silver, gold, bronze,
Jdg 6:5 For they and their **l** would come up,
18:21 the **l**, and the goods in front of them.
1Sa 23:5 fought with the Philistines, brought away their **l**,
1Ch 5:21 They captured their **l**: fifty thousand of their
2Ch 14:15 They also attacked the tents of those who had **l**,
20:25 they found **l** in great numbers, goods, clothing,
Ne 9:37 over our bodies and over our **l** at their pleasure,
10:36 the firstborn of our sons and of our **l**,
Eze 32:13 I will destroy all its **l** from
Jdt 5:9 in gold and silver and very much **l**.
8:7 **l**, and fields; and she maintained this estate.
11:12 to kill their **l** and have determined to use all
1Mc 1:32 the women and children, and seized the **l**.
2:30 their sons, their wives, and their **l**,
2:38 with their wives and children and **l**,
10:33 let all officials cancel also the taxes on their **l**.
12:23 to you that your **l** and your property belong to us,
2Mc 12:11 promising to give him **l** and to help his people
1Es 5:1 and their male and female servants, and their **l**.
8:50 and for our children and the **l** that were with us.
9:4 their **l** would be seized for sacrifice and

LIVING‡ (298) [LIVE]

A. LIVING CREATURES (36)
B. LIVING *GOD (36)
C. LIVING CREATURE (18)
D. LAND OF THE LIVING (15)
E. LIVING THING (9)
F. LIVING BEING (7)
G. LIVING WATER (6)

Ge 1:20 Let the waters bring forth swarms of **l** creatures, A
1:21 the great sea monsters and every **l** creature C
1:24 the earth bring forth **l** creatures of every kind: A
1:28 and over every **l** thing that moves upon E
2:7 and the man became a **l** being. F
2:19 and whatever the man called every **l** creature, C
3:20 because she was the mother of all **l**.
6:19 And of every **l** thing, of all flesh, E
7:4 and every **l** thing that I have made I will blot out E
7:23 He blotted out every **l** thing that was on the face E
8:17 Bring out with you every **l** thing that is with you E
8:21 nor will I ever again destroy every **l** creature C
9:10 and with every **l** creature that is with you, C
9:12 between me and you and every **l** creature that is C
9:15 that is between me and you and every **l** creature C
9:16 between God and every **l** creature of all flesh C
13:6 land could not support both of them **l** together;
14:13 who was **l** by the oaks of Mamre the Amorite,
25:6 while he was still **l**, and he sent them away
25:27 while Jacob was a quiet man, **l** in tents.
Ex 3:22 and any woman **l** in the neighbor's house
4:18 in Egypt and see whether they are still **l**."
Lev 11:10 in the waters and among all the other **l** creatures A
11:46 and bird and every **l** creature that moves through C
11:47 and between the **l** creature that may be eaten and C
11:47 be eaten and the **l** creature that may not be eaten. C
14:4 the priest shall command that two **l** clean birds
14:6 He shall take the **l** bird with the cedarwood and
14:6 and dip them and the **l** bird in the blood of
14:7 and he shall let the **l** bird go into the open field.
14:51 along with the **l** bird, and dip them in the blood
14:52 and with the fresh water, and with the **l** bird,
14:53 and he shall let the **l** bird go out of the city into
26:35 not have on your sabbaths when you were **l** on it.
Nu 16:48 He stood between the dead and the **l**;
23:9 Here is a people **l** alone,
Dt 5:26 the voice of the **l** God speaking out of fire, B
11:6 their tents, and every **l** being in their company; F
Jos 3:10 the **l** God who without fail will drive out from B
9:16 that they were their neighbors and were **l**
9:22 while in fact you are **l** among us?
24:15 of the Amorites in whose land you are **l**;
Jdg 17:10 a set of clothes, and your **l**."
18:7 the people who were there **l** securely,
Ru 1:7 she set out from the place where she had been **l**,
2:20 whose kindness has not forsaken the **l** or
1Sa 17:26 that he should defy the armies of the **l** God?" B
17:36 since he has defied the armies of the **l** God." B
25:29 be bound in the bundle of the **l** under the care of
2Sa 7:2 "See now, I am **l** in a house of cedar,
20:3 until the day of their death, **l** as if in widowhood.
1Ki 3:22 But the other woman said, "No, the **l** son is mine,
3:22 the dead son is yours, and the **l** son is mine."
1Ki 3:23 Your son is dead, and my son is the **l** one.' "
3:25 The king said, "Divide the **l** boy in two;
3:26 "Please, my lord, give her the **l** boy;
3:27 "Give the first woman the **l** boy; do not kill him.
12:17 the Israelites who were **l** in the towns of Judah.
2Ki 19:4 the king of Assyria has sent to mock the **l** God, B
19:16 which he has sent to mock the **l** God. B
1Ch 9:33 **l** in the chambers of the temple free
17:1 "I am **l** in a house of cedar,
2Ch 10:17 over the people of Israel who were **l** in the cities
Ne 3:26 and the temple servants **l** on Ophel made repairs
3:30 of Berechiah made repairs opposite his **l** quarters.
Job 12:10 In his hand is the life of every **l** thing and E
28:13 and it is not found in the land of the **l**. D
28:21 It is hidden from the eyes of all **l**,
30:23 and to the house appointed for all **l**.
Ps 27:13 the goodness of the LORD in the land of the **l**. D
42:2 My soul thirsts for God, for the **l** God. B
52:5 he will uproot you from the land of the **l**. D
66:9 who has kept us among the **l**,
69:28 Let them be blotted out of the book of the **l**;
84:2 my heart and my flesh sing for joy to the **l** God. B
104:25 **l** things both small and great.
116:9 I walk before the LORD in the land of the **l**. D
142:5 my portion in the land of the **l**." D
143:2 for no one **l** is righteous before you.
145:16 satisfying the desire of every **l** thing. E
Ecc 4:2 who have already died, more fortunate than the **l**,
4:15 I saw all the **l** who, moving about under the sun,
6:8 how to conduct themselves before the **l**?
7:2 and the **l** will lay it to heart.
9:4 But whoever is joined with all the **l** has hope,
9:4 for a **l** dog is better than a dead lion.
9:5 The **l** know that they will die,
SS 4:15 a well of **l** water, and flowing streams G
Isa 8:19 the dead on behalf of the **l**,
37:4 the king of Assyria has sent to mock the **l** God, B
37:17 which he has sent to mock the **l** God. B
38:11 I shall not see the LORD in the land of the **l**; D
38:19 The **l**, the **l**, they thank you, as I do this day;
53:8 For he was cut off from the land of the **l**, D
Jer 2:13 the fountain of **l** water, and dug out cisterns G
10:10 he is the **l** God and the everlasting King. B
11:19 let us cut him off from the land of the **l**, D
17:13 for they have forsaken the fountain of **l** water, G
23:36 and so you pervert the words of the **l** God, B
29:32 he shall not have anyone **l** among this people
35:11 That is why we are **l** in Jerusalem."
44:1 that came to Jeremiah for all the Judeans **l** in
Eze 1:5 of it was something like four **l** creatures. A
1:13 middle of the **l** creatures there was something A
1:13 to and fro among the **l** creatures; A
1:14 The **l** creatures darted to and fro, A
1:15 As I looked at the **l** creatures, A
1:15 I saw a wheel on the earth beside the **l** creatures, A
1:19 When the **l** creatures moved, A
1:19 **l** creatures rose from the earth, the wheels rose. A
1:20 for the spirit of the **l** creatures was in the wheels. A
1:21 for the spirit of the **l** creatures was in the wheels. A
1:22 the **l** creatures there was something like a dome, A
3:13 the sound of the wings of the **l** creatures A
10:15 the **l** creatures that I saw by the river Chebar. A
10:17 for the spirit of the **l** creatures was in them. A
10:20 These were the **l** creatures that I saw underneath A
12:2 you are **l** in the midst of a rebellious house,
26:20 be inhabited or have a place in the land of the **l**. D
32:23 who spread terror in the land of the **l**. D
32:24 who spread terror in the land of the **l**. D
32:25 terror of them was spread in the land of the **l**, D
32:26 for they spread terror in the land of the **l**. D
32:27 terror of the warriors was in the land of the **l**. D
32:32 For he spread terror in the land of the **l**; D
38:8 from the nations and now are **l** in safety,
38:11 all of them **l** without walls,
38:14 that day when my people Israel are **l** securely,
47:9 every **l** creature that swarms will live, C
Da 2:30 that I have more than any other **l** being, F
4:4 was **l** at ease in my home and prospering
4:12 and from it all **l** beings were fed.
6:20 O Daniel, servant of the **l** God, B
6:26 For he is the **l** God, enduring forever. B
Hos 1:10 it shall be said to them, "Children of the **l** God." B
Zec 14:8 that day **l** waters shall flow out from Jerusalem,
Mt 16:16 "You are the Messiah, the Son of the **l** God." B
22:32 He is God not of the dead, but of the **l**."
26:63 "I put you under oath before the **l** God, B
Mk 12:27 He is God not of the dead, but of the **l**;
Lk 1:6 **l** blamelessly according to all the commandments
2:8 that region there were shepherds **l** in the fields,
13:4 the others **l** in Jerusalem?
15:13 there he squandered his property in dissolute **l**.
20:38 Now he is God not of the dead, but of the **l**;
24:5 "Why do you look for the **l** among the dead?
Jn 4:10 and he would have given you **l** water." G
4:11 Where do you get that **l** water? G
6:51 I am the **l** bread that came down from heaven.
6:57 Just as the **l** Father sent me,
7:38 the believer's heart shall flow rivers of **l** water.' G
Ac 2:5 from every nation under heaven **l** in Jerusalem.
7:4 to this country in which you are now **l**.
7:38 and he received **l** oracles to give to us.
9:31 **L** in the fear of the Lord and in the comfort of
9:32 he came down also to the saints **l** in Lydda.
10:42 the one ordained by God as judge of the **l** and
11:29 each would send relief to the believers **l** in Judea;
14:15 from these worthless things to the **l** God, B
17:21 and the foreigners **l** there would spend their time

Ac 21:21 the Jews l among the Gentiles to forsake Moses,
22:12 and well spoken of by all the Jews l there,
Ro 6: 2 How can we who died to sin go on l in it?
7: 5 While we were l in the flesh, our sinful passions,
9:26 they shall be called children of the l God." B
12: 1 to present your bodies as a l sacrifice,
14: 9 that he might be Lord of both the dead and the l.
1Co 5: 1 for a man is l with his father's wife.
9: 6 to refrain from working for a l?
9:14 the gospel should get their l by the gospel.
15:45 "The first man, Adam, became a l being"; F
2Co 3: 3 not with ink but with the Spirit of the l God, B
6:16 For we are the temple of the l God; B
13: 5 Examine yourselves to see whether you are l in
Php 1:21 For to me, l is Christ and dying is gain.
Col 3: 7 when you were l that life.
1Th 1: 9 to serve a l and true God,
2Th 3: 6 to keep away from believers who are l in idleness
3:11 For we hear that some of you are l in idleness,
3:12 to do their work quietly and to earn their own l.
1Ti 3:15 which is the church of the l God, B
4:10 because we have our hope set on the l God, B
2Ti 1:14 with the help of the Holy Spirit l in us.
4: 1 who is to judge the l and the dead,
Heb 3:12 heart that turns away from the l God. B
4:12 Indeed, the word of God is l and active,
9:14 from dead works to worship the l God! B
10:20 the new and l way that he opened for us through
10:31 fearful thing to fall into the hands of the l God. B
11: 9 l in tents, as did Isaac and Jacob,
12:22 to Mount Zion and to the city of the l God, B
1Pe 1: 3 a new birth into a l hope through the resurrection
1:23 through the l and enduring word of God.
2: 4 a l stone, though rejected by mortals yet chosen
2: 5 like l stones, let yourselves be built into
4: 3 l in licentiousness, passions, drunkenness, revels,
4: 5 to him who stands ready to judge the l and
2Pe 2: 8 l among them day after day,
Rev 1:18 and the l one. I was dead, and see, I am alive
2:13 "I know where you are l,
4: 6 are four l creatures, full of eyes in front A
4: 7 the first l creature like a lion, C
4: 7 the second l creature like an ox, C
4: 7 third l creature with a face like a human face, C
4: 7 and the fourth l creature like a flying eagle. C
4: 8 And the four l creatures, A
4: 9 the l creatures give glory and honor and thanks A
5: 6 between the throne and the four l creatures and A
5: 8 he had taken the scroll, the four l creatures A
5:11 the throne and the l creatures and the elders; A
5:14 And the four l creatures said, "Amen!" A
6: 1 and I heard one of the four l creatures call out, A
6: 3 I heard the second l creature call out, "Come!" C
6: 5 I heard the third l creature call out, "Come!" C
6: 6 voice in the midst of the four l creatures saying, A
6: 7 heard the voice of the fourth l creature call out, C
7: 2 having the seal of the l God, B
7:11 and around the elders and the four l creatures, A
8: 9 a third of the l creatures in the sea died, A
14: 3 before the four l creatures and before the elders. A
15: 7 Then one of the four l creatures gave A
16: 3 and every l thing in the sea died. E
17:10 one is l, and the other has not yet come;
19: 4 and the four l creatures fell down A
Tob 10: 4 and is no longer among the l."
12: 6 and acknowledge him in the presence of all the l
13: 4 Exalt him in the presence of every l being, F
Jdt 4: 1 the Israelites l in Judea heard of everything
4:11 and children l at Jerusalem prostrated themselves
5: 9 where they were l and go to the land of Canaan.
10: 3 to wear while her husband Manasseh was l.
11: 7 of him who has sent you to direct every l being! F
AdE 6:13 because the l God is with him. B
11: 3 He was a Jew l in the city of Susa, a great man,
16:16 and are children of the l God, B
Wis 1:13 and he does not delight in the death of the l.
4:10 and while l among sinners were taken up.
4:16 the ungodly who are l, and youth
8: 3 She glorifies her noble birth by l with God,
11:26 for they are yours, O Lord, you who love the l.
14:22 but though l in great strife due to ignorance,
15:11 with active souls and breathed a l spirit
18:12 For the l were not sufficient even to bury them,
18:23 and cut off its way to the l.
Sir Pr: 1 even greater progress in l according to the law.
Pr: 3 for those l abroad who wished to gain learning
1:10 upon all the l according to his gift;
4: 1 My child, do not cheat the poor of their l,
7:33 Give graciously to all the l;
13:16 All l beings associate with their own kind,
14:17 All l beings become old like a garment,
16:30 With all kinds of l beings he covered its surface,
17: 4 He put the fear of them in all l beings,
17:27 in Hades in place of the l who give thanks?
18:13 the compassion of the Lord is for every l thing. E
31: 4 The poor person toils to make a meager l,
34:26 To take away a neighbor's l is to commit murder;
40: 1 until the day they return to the mother of all the l.
43:25 all kinds of l things, and huge sea-monsters.
44: 6 l peacefully in their homes—
45:16 He chose him out of all the l to offer sacrifice to
49:16 but above every other created l being was Adam. F
Bar 3:13 you would be l in peace forever.
Sus 1: 1 a man l in Babylon whose name was Joakim.
Bel 1: 5 not revere idols made with hands, but the l God, B
1: 5 earth and has dominion over all l creatures." A
1: 6 "Do you not think that Bel is a l god? B
Bel 1:24 "You cannot deny that this is a l god; B
1:25 "I worship the Lord my God, for he is the l God. B
1Mc 6:55 whom King Antiochus while still l had appointed
9:58 and his men are l in quiet and confidence.
2Mc 4:11 the lawful ways of l and introduced new customs
4:16 and those whose ways of l they admired
6:25 for the sake of l a brief moment longer,
7:33 And if our l Lord is angry for a little while,
9: 9 and while he was still l in anguish and pain,
11:24 but prefer their own way of l and ask
12: 8 in the same way to wipe out the Jews who were l
15: 4 When they declared, "It is the l Lord himself,
1Es 1:21 the people of Judah and all of Israel who were l
2:16 l in Samaria and other places,
2:16 against those who were l in Judea and Jerusalem:
2:25 the others associated with them and l in Samaria
3Mc 6:28 children of the almighty and l God of heaven, B
2Es 2:14 for I am the L One, says the Lord.
6:47 to bring forth l creatures, birds, and fishes; A
6:48 dumb and lifeless water produced l creatures, A
6:49 "Then you kept in existence two l creatures; A
7:14 Therefore unless the l pass through the difficult
7:20 Let many perish who are now l,
7:46 For who among the l is there that has not sinned,
7:*136* [66] who are now l and to those who are gone
14:20 and I will reprove the people who are now l;
4Mc 5:22 You scoff at our philosophy as though l
5:24 proper reverence we worship the only l God. B
8: 8 of life and by changing your manner of l.
13:24 in the same virtues and brought up in right l,

LIZARD (4)

Lev 11:29 the mouse, the great l according to its kind,
11:30 the l, the sand l, and the chameleon.
Pr 30:28 the l can be grasped in the hand,

LO (31)

Isa 17:14 At evening time, l, terror!
25: 9 It will be said on that day, L, this is our God;
34: 5 my sword has drunk its fill in the heavens, l,
49:12 L, these shall come from far away, and l,
59: 9 we wait for light, and l!
Jer 4:23 I looked on the earth, and l,
4:24 I looked on the mountains, and l,
4:25 I looked, and l, there was no one at all,
4:26 I looked, and l, the fruitful land was a desert,
44:26 L, I swear by my great name, says the LORD,
50:12 L, she shall be the last of the nations,
Eze 44: 4 of the temple; and I looked, and l!
Da 2:31 "You were looking, O king, and l!
Am 4:13 For l, the one who forms the mountains,
9: 9 For l, I will command, and shake the house
Mic 1: 3 For l, the LORD is coming out of his place,
Hag 1: 9 You have looked for much, and, l,
Zec 1:11 and l, the whole earth remains at peace."
2:10 For l, I will come and dwell in your midst,
6: 8 Then he cried out to me, "L,
9: 9 L, your king comes to you;
Mal 4: 5 L, I will send you the prophet Elijah before
Sir 16:18 L, heaven and the highest heaven,
24:31 l, my canal became a river, and my river a sea.
2Es 4:48 So I stood and looked, and l,
4:48 and when the flame had gone by I looked, and l,
5: 1 "Now concerning the signs: l,
10:10 and, l, almost all go to perdition,
10:32 and l, what I have seen I saw, and can still see,
13: 2 And l, a wind arose from the sea and stirred

LO-AMMI (2) [AMMI]

Hos 1: 9 "Name him L, for you are not my people
2:23 and I will say to L, "You are my people";

LO-DEBAR (4)

2Sa 9: 4 in the house of Machir son of Ammiel, at L."
9: 5 from the house of Machir son of Ammiel, at L.
17:27 and Machir son of Ammiel from L,
Am 6:13 you who rejoice in L, who say, "Have we not

LO-RUHAMAH (3) [RUHAMAH]

Hos 1: 6 "Name her L, for I will no longer have pity on
1: 8 she had weaned L, she conceived and bore a son.
2:23 And I will have pity on L,

LOAD (4) [LOADED, LOADING, LOADS, MULE-LOADS]

Ge 45:17 l your animals and go back to the land
Isa 22:25 and the l that was on it will perish,
Hab 2: 6 How long will you l yourselves with goods taken
Lk 11:46 For you l people with burdens hard to bear,

LOADED (10) [LOAD]

Ge 42:26 They l their donkeys with their grain,
44:13 Then each one l his donkey,
45:23 ten donkeys l with the good things of Egypt,
45:23 and ten female donkeys l with grain, bread,
1Sa 16:20 Jesse took a donkey l with bread, a skin of wine,
25:18 two hundred cakes of figs. She l them on donkeys
Isa 46: 1 these things you carry are l as burdens
Tob 9: 5 then they l them on the camels.
Jdt 15:11 She took them and l her mules and hitched
2Es 2:18 for you twelve trees l with various fruits,

LOADING (1) [LOAD]

Ne 13:15 and bringing in heaps of grain and l them

LOADS (5) [LOAD]

2Ki 8: 9 all kinds of goods of Damascus, forty camel l.
Ne 4:17 The burden bearers carried their l in such a way
Job 37:11 He l the thick cloud with moisture;
La 5:13 and boys stagger under l of wood.
Gal 6: 5 For all must carry their own l.

LOAF (13) [LOAVES]

Ex 29:23 and one l of bread, one cake of bread made
Lev 24: 5 two-tenths of an ephah shall be in each l.
Nu 15:20 of dough you shall present a l as a donation;
1Sa 2:36 to implore him for a piece of silver or a l
1Ch 16: 3 to each a l of bread, a portion of meat,
Pr 6:26 for a prostitute's fee is only a l of bread,
Jer 37:21 and a l of bread was given him daily from
Mt 26:26 While they were eating, Jesus took a l of bread,
Mk 8:14 and they had only one l with them in the boat.
14:22 While they were eating, he took a l of bread,
Lk 4: 3 command this stone to become a l of bread."
22:19 Then he took a l of bread,
1Co 11:23 the night when he was betrayed took a l of bread,

LOAN (5) [LOANS]

Dt 24:10 When you make your neighbor a l of any kind,
24:11 the person to whom you are making the l brings
Sir 29: 2 repay your neighbor when a l falls due.
29: 4 Many regard a l as a windfall,
29: 5 One kisses another's hands until he gets a l,

LOANS (4) [LOAN]

Dt 23:19 not charge interest on l to another Israelite,
23:20 On l to a foreigner you may charge interest,
23:20 but on l to another Israelite you may
Pr 11:15 To guarantee l for a stranger brings trouble,

LOATH (2) [LOATHE]

2Sa 12: 4 and he was l to take one of his own flock or herd
Job 20:13 though they are l to let it go,

LOATHE (10) [LOATH, LOATHED, LOATHING, LOATHSOME]

Job 7:16 I l my life; I would not live forever.
9:21 not know myself; I l my life.
10: 1 "I l my life; I will give free utterance to my
33:20 so that their lives l bread,
Ps 139:21 And do I not l those who rise up against you?
Jer 14:19 Does your heart l Zion?
Eze 20:43 and you shall l yourselves for all the evils
36:31 and you shall l yourselves for your iniquities
Sir 11: 2 or l anyone because of appearance alone.
25: 2 and I l their manner of life:

LOATHED‡ (5) [LOATHE]

Ps 95:10 For forty years I l that generation and said,
107:18 they l any kind of food,
Eze 16:45 who l her husband and her children;
16:45 who l their husbands and their children.
Sir 16: 8 whom he l on account of their arrogance.

LOATHING (2) [LOATHE]

2Sa 13:15 Amnon was seized with a very great l for her;
13:15 his l was even greater than the lust he had felt

LOATHSOME (7) [LOATHE]

Nu 11:20 until it comes out of your nostrils and becomes l
Job 2: 7 and inflicted l sores on Job from the sole
6: 7 they are like food that is l to me.
19:17 I am l to my own family.
Isa 14:19 away from your grave, like l carrion,
Eze 6: 9 Then they will be l in their own sight for
8:10 were all kinds of creeping things, and l animals,

LOAVES‡ (36) [LOAF]

Lev 23:17 You shall bring from your settlements two l
24: 5 and bake twelve l of it;
Jdg 8: 5 "Please give some l of bread to my followers,
1Sa 10: 3 another carrying three l of bread,
10: 4 They will greet you and give you two l of bread,
17:17 an ephah of this parched grain and these ten l,
21: 3 Give me five l of bread, or whatever is here."
25:18 Then Abigail hurried and took two hundred l,
2Sa 16: 1 carrying two hundred l of bread,
1Ki 14: 3 Take with you ten l, some cakes,
2Ki 4:42 twenty l of barley and fresh ears of grain
Mt 4: 3 command these stones to become l of bread."
14:17 "We have nothing here but five l and two fish."
14:19 Taking the five l and the two fish,
14:19 and blessed and broke the l,
15:34 Jesus asked them, "How many l have you?"
15:36 he took the seven l and the fish;
16: 9 not remember the five l for the five thousand,
16:10 Or the seven l for the four thousand,
Mk 6:38 And he said to them, "How many l have you?
6:41 Taking the five l and the two fish,
6:41 and blessed and broke the l,
6:44 the l numbered five thousand men.
6:52 for they did not understand about the l,
8: 5 He asked them, "How many l do you have?"

Mk 8: 6 and he took the seven l, and
8:19 When I broke the five l for the five thousand,
Lk 9:13 "We have no more than five l and two fish—
9:16 And taking the five l and the two fish,
11: 5 'Friend, lend me three l of bread;
Jn 6: 9 a boy here who has five barley l and two fish.
6:11 Then Jesus took the l, and
6:13 and from the fragments of the five barley l,
6:26 but because you ate your fill of the l.
Tob 8:19 this he asked his wife to bake many l of bread;
2Mc 1: 8 and we lit the lamps and set out the l.

LOBE (6) [LOBES]
Ex 29:20 on the l of Aaron's right ear and on the lobes of
Lev 8:23 Moses took some of its blood and put it on the l
14:14 on the l of the right ear of the one to be cleansed,
14:17 on the l of the right ear of the one to be cleansed,
14:25 on the l of the right ear of the one to be cleansed,
14:28 on the l of the right ear of the one to be cleansed,

LOBES (2) [LOBE]
Ex 29:20 of Aaron's right ear and on the l of the right ears
Lev 8:24 put some of the blood on the l of their right ears

LOCAL (3)
Ac 28:17 Three days later he called together the l leaders
1Es 6: 7 the l rulers in Syria and Phoenicia, wrote
6:27 and those who were appointed as l rulers in Syria

LOCALE (1) [LOCALITIES]
2Es 4:19 and the l of the sea a place to carry its waves."

LOCALITIES (2) [LOCALE]
Ge 36:40 to their families and their l by their names:
3Mc 2:26 that he framed evil reports in the various l;

LOCATED (2) [LOCATION]
1Sa 22: 6 and those who were with him had been l.
1Mc 13:47 the houses in which the idols were l,

LOCATION (1) [LOCATED]
2Ki 2:19 "The l of this city is good, as my lord sees;

LOCK (4) [LOCKED, LOCKS]
Eze 8: 3 and took me by a l of my head;
Mt 23:13 For you l people out of the kingdom of heaven.
Sir 28:24 As you l up your silver and gold,
42: 6 and where there are many hands, l things up.

LOCKED (9) [LOCK]
Jdg 3:23 of the roof chamber on him, and l them.
3:24 that the doors of the roof chamber were l,
SS 4:12 A garden l is my sister, my bride, a garden l,
Lk 11: 7 the door has already been l,
Jn 20:19 the disciples had met were l for fear of the Jews,
Ac 5:23 the prison securely l and the guards standing at
26:10 I not only l up many of the saints in prison,
Rev 20: 3 and l and sealed it over him,

LOCKS (11) [LOCK]
Nu 6: 5 they shall let the l of the head grow long.
Jdg 5: 2 "When l are long in Israel,
16:13 "If you weave the seven l of my head with
16:14 the seven l of his head and wove them into
16:19 and had him shave off the seven l of his head.
SS 5: 2 my l with the drops of the night."
5:11 his l are wavy, black as a raven.
7: 5 and your flowing l are like purple;
Eze 44:20 not shave their heads or let their l grow long;
LtJ 6:18 with doors and l and bars,
3Mc 1: 4 and tears, her l all disheveled, and exhorted them

LOCKS (KJV) See also BOLTS, VEIL

LOCUST (22) [LOCUSTS]
Ex 10:19 not a single l was left in all the country of Egypt.
Lev 11:22 you may eat: the l according to its kind, the bald l
Dt 28:38 for the l shall consume it.
1Ki 8:37 if there is plague, blight, mildew, l, or caterpillar;
2Ch 6:28 if there is plague, blight, mildew, l, or caterpillar;
7:13 or command the l to devour the land,
Job 39:20 Do you make it leap like the l?
Ps 78:46 and the fruit of their labor to the l.
109:23 I am shaken off like a l.
Joel 1: 4 What the cutting l left, the swarming l has eaten.
1: 4 What the swarming l left, the hopping l has eaten,
1: 4 what the hopping l left, the destroying l has eaten.
2:25 for the years that the swarming l has eaten,
Am 4: 9 the l devoured your fig trees and your olive trees;
Na 3:15 It will devour you like the l.
3:15 Multiply yourselves like the l,
3:16 The l sheds its skin and flies away.
Mal 3:11 I will rebuke the l for you,

LOCUSTS (25) [LOCUST]
Ex 10: 4 tomorrow I will bring l into your country.
10:12 that the l may come upon it and eat every plant in
10:13 morning came, the east wind had brought the l.
10:14 The l came upon all the land of Egypt and settled
10:14 a dense swarm of l as had never been before,
10:19 the l and drove them into the Red Sea;
Jdg 6: 5 even bring their tents, as thick as l;
7:12 of the east lay along the valley as thick as l;
Ps 105:34 and the l came, and young l without number;
Pr 30:27 the l have no king, yet all of them march in rank;
Isa 33: 4 as l leap, they leaped upon it.
Jer 46:23 because they are more numerous than l;
51:14 I will fill you with troops like a swarm of l,
51:27 bring up horses like bristling l.
Am 7: 1 he was forming l at the time
Na 3:17 of l settling on the fences on a cold day—
Mt 3: 4 and his food was l and wild honey.
Mk 1: 6 and he ate l and wild honey.
Rev 9: 3 Then from the smoke came l on the earth,
9: 7 In appearance the l were like horses equipped
Jdt 2:20 with them went a mixed crowd like a swarm of l,
Wis 16: 9 For they were killed by the bites of l and flies,
Sir 43:17 and its descent is like l alighting.
2Es 4:24 We pass from the world like l,

LOD (4)
1Ch 8:12 and Shemed, who built Ono and L with its towns,
Ezr 2:33 Of L, Hadid, and Ono, seven hundred twenty-five.
Ne 7:37 Of L, Hadid, and Ono, seven hundred twenty-one.
11:35 L, and Ono, the valley of artisans.

LODGE (13) [LODGED, LODGES, LODGING, LODGINGS]
Ru 1:16 Where you l, I will l;
2Sa 17:16 'Do not l tonight at the fords of the wilderness,
Ps 55: 7 I would l in the wilderness;
Pr 15:31 The ear that heeds wholesome admonition will l
SS 7:11 into the fields, and l in the villages;
Isa 10:29 at Geba they l for the night;
21:13 In the scrub of the desert plain you will l,
Jer 4:14 How long shall your evil schemes l within you?
Eze 31:13 and among its boughs l all the wild animals.
Zep 2:14 and the screech owl shall l on its capitals;
Lk 9:12 the surrounding villages and countryside, to l
Sir 51:23 and l in the house of instruction.

LODGED (4) [LODGE]
1Sa 7: 2 From the day that the ark was l at Kiriath-jearim,
Job 31:32 the stranger has not l in the street;
Isa 1:21 righteousness l in her—but now murderers!
2Mc 3:17 to those who looked at him the pain l in his heart.

LODGES (3) [LODGE]
Ecc 7: 9 for anger l in the bosom of fools.
Sir 14:26 under her shelter, and l under her boughs;
36:31 but l wherever night overtakes him?

LODGING (9) [LODGE]
Ge 42:27 to give his donkey fodder at the l place,
43:21 we came to the l place we opened our sacks,
1Ki 17:19 up into the upper chamber where he was l,
Jer 9: 2 O that I had in the desert a traveler's l place,
Ac 10: 6 he is l with Simon, a tanner, whose house is by
10:23 So Peter invited them in and gave them l.
Sir 14:25 and so occupies an excellent l place;
29:28 for a sensible person to bear scolding about l and
1Mc 3:45 it was a l place for the Gentiles.

LODGINGS (1) [LODGE]
Ac 28:23 they came to him at his l in great numbers.

LOFT (KJV) UPPER CHAMBER

LOFTILY (1) [LOFTY]
Ps 73: 8 l they threaten oppression.

LOFTINESS (1) [LOFTY]
Jer 48:29 of his l, his pride, and his arrogance,

LOFTY‡ (20) [LOFTILY, LOFTINESS]
Job 22:12 See the highest stars, how l they are!
41:34 It surveys everything that is l;
Ps 104:13 From your l abode you water the mountains;
Pr 30:13 how l are their eyes, how high their eyelids lift!
Isa 2:12 of hosts has a day against all that is proud and l,
2:13 against all the cedars of Lebanon, l and lifted up;
2:14 and against all the l hills;
6: 1 I saw the Lord sitting on a throne, high and l;
10:33 and the l will be brought low.
26: 5 the l city he lays low.
30:25 On every l mountain
57: 7 a high and l mountain you have set your bed,
57:15 the high and l one who inhabits eternity,
Eze 16:24 and made yourself a l place in every square;
16:25 at the head of every street you built your l place
16:31 and making your l place in every square!
16:39 and break down your l places;
17:22 I myself will take a sprig from the l top of
17:22 I myself will plant it on a high and l mountain.
31:14 the waters may grow to l height or set their tops
Zep 1:16 the fortified cities and against the l battlements.
1Co 2: 1 the mystery of God to you in l words or wisdom.
2Es 15:40 and shall pour out upon every high and l place

LOG (12) [LOGS]
Lev 14:10 of choice flour mixed with oil, and one l of oil.
14:12 along with the l of oil,
14:15 The priest shall take some of the l of oil
14:21 with oil for a grain offering and a l of oil;
14:24 the lamb of the guilt offering and the l of oil,
2Ki 6: 5 But as one was felling a l,
Mt 7: 3 but do not notice the l in your own eye?
7: 4 while the l is in your own eye?
7: 5 first take the l out of your own eye,
Lk 6:41 but do not notice the l in your own eye?
6:42 you yourself do not see the l in your own eye?
6:42 first take the l out of your own eye,

LOGIC (1)
4Mc 1:15 Now reason is the mind that with sound l prefers

LOGS (7) [LOG]
2Ki 6: 2 Let us go to the Jordan, and let us collect l there,
1Ch 14: 1 with cedar l, and masons and carpenters to build
22: 4 and cedar l without number—
Ecc 10: 9 and whoever splits l will be endangered by them.
Eze 24: 5 the choicest one of the flock, pile the l under it;
24:10 Heap up the l, kindle the fire;
1Es 5:55 to bring cedar l from Lebanon and convey them

LOINCLOTH (9) [CLOTH, LOINS]
Isa 5:27 not a l is loose, not a sandal-thong broken;
Jer 13: 1 "Go and buy yourself a linen l,
13: 2 I bought a l according to the word of the LORD,
13: 4 "Take the l that you bought and are wearing,
13: 6 and take from there the l that I commanded you
13: 7 I took the l from the place where I had hidden it.
13: 7 now the l was ruined; it was good for nothing.
13:10 shall be like this l, which is good for nothing.
13:11 For as the l clings to one's loins,

LOINCLOTHS (1) [CLOTH, LOINS]
Ge 3: 7 and they sewed fig leaves together and made l

LOINS‡ (46) [LOINCLOTH, LOINCLOTHS]
Ge 37:34 and put sackcloth on his l,
Ex 12:11 This is how you shall eat it: your l girded,
Lev 3: 4 two kidneys with the fat that is on them at the l,
3:10 two kidneys with the fat that is on them at the l,
3:15 two kidneys with the fat that is on them at the l,
4: 9 two kidneys with the fat that is on them at the l;
7: 4 two kidneys with the fat that is on them at the l,
Dt 33:11 crush the l of his adversaries,
1Ki 12:10 'My little finger is thicker than my father's l.
18:46 up his l and ran in front of Ahab to the entrance
2Ki 4:29 He said to Gehazi, "Gird up your l,
9: 1 of prophets and said to him, "Gird up your l;
2Ch 10:10 'My little finger is thicker than my father's l.
Job 12:18 and binds a waistcloth on their l.
15:27 and gathered fat upon their l,
21:24 his l full of milk and the marrow
31:20 whose l have not blessed me, and who was
38: 3 Gird up your l like a man, I will question you,
40: 7 "Gird up your l like a man;
40:16 Its strength is in its l,
Ps 38: 7 For my l are filled with burning,
69:23 and make their l tremble continually.
Isa 11: 5 and faithfulness the belt around his l.
15: 4 therefore the l of Moab quiver; his soul trembles.
20: 2 from your l and take your sandals off your feet,"
21: 3 Therefore my l are filled with anguish;
32:11 and put sackcloth on your l.
48: 1 and who came forth from the l of Judah;
Jer 1:17 But you, gird up your l;
13: 1 and put it on your l, but do not dip it in water."
13: 2 and put it on my l.
13:11 For as the loincloth clings to one's l,
30: 6 then do I see every man with his hands on his l
48:37 the hands there are gashes, and on the l sackcloth.
Eze 1:27 like the l I saw something like gleaming amber,
1:27 like the l I saw something that looked like fire,
8: 2 below what appeared to be its l it was fire, and
above the l it was like the appearance of
44:18 and linen undergarments on their l,
Am 8:10 I will bring sackcloth on all l,
Na 2: 1 gird your l; collect all your strength.
2:10 all l quake, all faces grow pale!
Heb 7:10 the l of his ancestor when Melchizedek met him.
Jdt 4:14 with sackcloth around their l,
Sir 35:22 a warrior will not be patient until he crushes the l
2Mc 10:25 on their heads and girded their l with sackcloth,

LOIS (1)
2Ti 1: 5 in your grandmother L and your mother Eunice

LONELY (5) [ALONE]
Ps 25:16 for I am l and afflicted.
102: 7 I lie awake; I am like a l bird on the housetop.
La 1: 1 How l sits the city that once was full of people!
Sir 8:16 and do not journey with them through l country,
Bar 4:16 and bereaved the l woman of her daughters.

LONG‡ (417) [LENGTH, LENGTHEN, LENGTHENS, LENGTHS, LENGTHY, LONG-HAIRED, LONG-SUFFERING, LONGED, LONGER, LONGING, LONGINGLY, LONGS]
Ge 8:22 As l as the earth endures, seedtime and harvest,

Ge 26: 8 When Isaac had been there a l time,
37: 3 and he had made him a l robe with sleeves.
37:23 the l robe with sleeves that he wore;
37:32 the l robe with sleeves taken to their father,
47: 9 the life of my ancestors during their l sojourn."
Ex 2:23 After a l time the king of Egypt died.
10: 3 l will you refuse to humble yourself before me?
10: 7 "How l shall this fellow be a snare to us?
16:28 to Moses, "How l will you refuse
19:13 When the trumpet sounds a l blast,
20:12 so that your days may be l in the land that
25:10 it shall be two and a half cubits l,
25:23 two cubits l, one cubit wide,
27: 1 five cubits l and five cubits wide;
27: 9 of fine twisted linen one hundred cubits l for
27:11 be hangings one hundred cubits l,
27:16 the court there shall be a screen twenty cubits l,
30: 2 It shall be one cubit l, and one cubit wide;
37: 1 it was two and a half cubits l,
37:10 two cubits l, one cubit wide,
37:25 one cubit l, and one cubit wide;
38: 1 it was five cubits l, and five cubits wide;
38: 9 of fine twisted linen, one hundred cubits l;
38:11 side there were hangings one hundred cubits l;
38:12 the west side there were hangings fifty cubits l,
38:18 It was twenty cubits l and, along the width of it,
Lev 13:46 He shall remain unclean as l as he has
21:18 or one who has a mutilated face or a limb too l,
22:23 that has a limb too l or too short you may present
26:10 You shall eat old grain l stored,
26:34 as l as it lies desolate, while you are in the land
26:35 As l as it lies desolate,
Nu 6: 5 they shall let the locks of the head grow l.
9:18 As l as the cloud rested over the tabernacle,
14:11 "How l will this people despise me?
14:11 And how l will they refuse to believe in me,
14:27 How l shall this wicked congregation complain
20:15 and we lived in Egypt a l time;
24:22 How l shall Asshur take you away captive?"
Dt 1: 6 "You have stayed l enough at this mountain.
2: 3 "You have been skirting this hill country l enough.
3:11 By the common cubit it is nine cubits l
4:10 that they may learn to fear me as l as they live on
4:26 you will not live l on it,
4:32 ask now about former ages, l before your own,
4:40 so that you may l remain in the land that
5:16 be l and that it may go well with you in the land
5:33 you may live l in the land that you are to possess.
6: 2 so that your days may be l.
8: 2 Remember the l way that the LORD your God
9:24 You have been rebellious against the LORD as l
11: 9 and so that you may live l in the land that
11:21 as l as the heavens are above the earth.
12:19 that you do not neglect the Levite as l as you live
17:20 so that he and his descendants may reign l
20:19 If you besiege a town for a l time,
22: 7 that it may go well with you and you may live l.
22:19 not be permitted to divorce her as l as he lives.
22:29 not be permitted to divorce her as l as he lives.
23: 6 or their prosperity as l as you live.
25:15 and honest measure, so that your days may be l
30:18 not live l in the land that you are crossing
31:13 as l as you live in the land that you are crossing
32: 7 consider the years l past;
32:47 through it you may live l in the land
33:12 the High God surrounds him all day l—
Jos 6: 5 When they make a l blast with the ram's horn,
9:13 of ours are worn out from the very l journey."
11:18 Joshua made war a l time with all those kings.
18: 3 "How l will you be slack about going in
23: 1 A l time afterward,
24: 2 L ago your ancestors—Terah and his sons
24: 7 Afterwards you lived in the wilderness a l time.
Jdg 5: 2 "When locks are l in Israel,
5:28 'Why is his chariot so l in coming?
18:31 as l as the house of God was at Shiloh.
1Sa 1:14 l will you make a drunken spectacle of yourself?
1:28 as l as he lives, he is given to the LORD."
7: 2 a l time passed, some twenty years,
10:24 And all the people shouted, "L live the king!"
14:14 an area about half a furrow l in an acre of land.
16: 1 "How l will you grieve over Saul?
20:19 you shall go a l way down;
20:31 For as l as the son of Jesse lives upon the earth,
25:15 as l as we were with them;
25:28 evil shall not be found in you so l as you live.
31:12 traveled all night l, and took the body of Saul
2Sa 2:26 How l will it be before you order your people
3: 1 There was a l war between the house of Saul and
4: 7 and traveled by way of the Arabah all night l.
13:18 (Now she was wearing a l robe with sleeves;
13:19 and tore the l robe that she was wearing;
16:16 to Absalom, "L live the king! L live the king!"
1Ki 1:25 and saying, 'L live King Adonijah!'
1:34 and say, 'L live King Solomon!'
1:39 and all the people said, "L live King Solomon!"
3:11 and have not asked for yourself l life or riches,
6: 2 for the LORD was sixty cubits l,
6:17 in front of the inner sanctuary, was forty cubits l.
6:20 of the inner sanctuary was twenty cubits l,
7: 2 the Forest of the Lebanon one hundred cubits l,
7: 6 of Pillars fifty cubits l and thirty cubits wide.
7:27 each stand was four cubits l, four cubits wide,
8: 8 so l that the ends of the poles were seen from
12:28 "You have gone up to Jerusalem l enough.
18:21 "How l will you go limping
2Ki 9:22 so l as the many whoredoms and sorceries
2Ki 11:12 they clapped their hands and shouted, "L live
19:25 Have you not heard that I determined it l ago?
25:30 a portion every day, as l as he lived.
2Ch 1:11 and have not even asked for l life,
3: 4 the nave of the house was twenty cubits l, across
3:11 one wing of the one, five cubits l,
3:11 and its other wing, five cubits l,
3:12 five cubits l, touched the wall of the house,
3:12 and the other wing, also five cubits l,
4: 1 He made an altar of bronze, twenty cubits l,
5: 9 so l that the ends of the poles were seen from
6:13 a bronze platform five cubits l, five cubits wide,
15: 3 For a l time Israel was without the true God,
23:11 and they shouted, "L live the king!"
26: 5 and as l as he sought the LORD,
Ezr 4:15 and that sedition was stirred up in it from l ago.
4:19 that this city has risen against kings from l ago,
Ne 2: 6 "How l will you be gone,
12:46 and Asaph l ago there was a leader of the singers,
Est 5:13 Yet all this does me no good so l as I see
Job 3:21 who l for death, but it does not come, and dig
7: 4 the night is l, and I am full of tossing until dawn.
8: 2 "How l will you say these things,
14:15 you would l for the work of your hands.
18: 2 "How l will you hunt for words?
19: 2 "How l will you torment me,
27: 3 as l as my breath is in me and the spirit of God is
36:20 Do not l for the night,
Ps 4: 2 How l, you people, shall my honor suffer shame?
4: 2 l will you love vain words, and seek after lies?
6: 3 while you, O LORD—how l?
12: 5 "I will place them in the safety for which they l."
13: 1 How l, O LORD? Will you forget me forever?
13: 1 How l will you hide your face from me?
13: 2 How l must I bear pain in my soul,
13: 2 and have sorrow in my heart all day l?
13: 2 How l shall my enemy be exalted over me?
23: 6 in the house of the LORD my whole life l.
25: 5 for you I wait all day l.
32: 3 through my groaning all day l.
35:17 How l, O LORD, will you look on?
35:28 and of your praise all day l.
38: 6 all day l I go around mourning.
38:12 and meditate treachery all day l.
39: 1 a muzzle on my mouth as l as the wicked are
44:15 All day l my disgrace is before me,
44:22 Because of you we are being killed all day l,
52: 1 mischief done against the godly? All day l
56: 1 all day l foes oppress me;
56: 2 my enemies trample on me all day l,
56: 5 All day l they seek to injure my cause;
62: 3 How l will you assail a person,
63: 4 So I will bless you as l as I live;
71: 8 and with your glory all day l.
71:15 of your deeds of salvation all day l,
71:24 All day l my tongue will talk
72: 5 and as l as the moon, throughout all generations.
72:15 L may he live! May gold of Sheba
72:15 and blessings invoked for him all day l.
72:17 his fame continue as l as the sun.
73:14 For all day l I have been plagued,
74: 2 which you acquired l ago,
74: 9 and there is no one among us who knows how l.
74:10 How l, O God, is the foe to scoff?
74:22 remember how the impious scoff at you all day l.
77: 5 and remember the years of l ago.
78:14 and all night l with a fiery light.
79: 5 How l, O LORD? Will you be angry
80: 4 l will you be angry with your people's prayers?
82: 2 "How l will you judge unjustly
86: 3 O Lord, for to you do I cry all day l.
88:17 They surround me like a flood all day l;
89:16 they exult in your name all day l,
89:29 and his throne as l as the heavens endure.
89:46 How l, O LORD? Will you hide yourself forever?
89:46 How l will your wrath burn like fire?
90:13 O LORD! How l? Have compassion on your
91:16 With l life I will satisfy them,
94: 3 O LORD, how l shall the wicked,
94: 3 how l shall the wicked exult?
102: 8 All day l my enemies taunt me;
102:25 L ago you laid the foundation of the earth,
103: 5 as l as you live so that your youth is renewed like
104:33 I will sing to the LORD as l as I live;
116: 2 therefore I will call on him as l as I live.
119:84 How l must your servant endure?
119:97 It is my meditation all day l.
119:131 because I l for your commandments.
119:152 L ago I learned from your decrees
119:174 I l for your salvation, O LORD,
120: 6 Too l have I had my dwelling
129: 3 they made their furrows l."
143: 3 making me sit in darkness like those l dead.
146: 2 I will praise the LORD as l as I live;
146: 2 I will sing praises to my God all my life l.
Pr 1:22 How l, O simple ones, will you love being simple?
1:22 How l will scoffers delight in their scoffing
3:16 L life is in her right hand;
6: 9 How l will you lie there, O lazybones?
7:19 he has gone on a l journey.
8:22 the first of his acts of l ago.
21:26 All day l the wicked covet,
28:16 but one who hates unjust gain will enjoy a l life.
Ecc 1:11 The people of l ago are not remembered,
2:16 in the days to come all will have been l forgotten.
3:12 be happy and enjoy themselves as l as they live;
9: 7 for God has l ago approved what you do.
Isa 6:11 Then I said, "How l, O Lord?"
22:11 or have regard for him who planned it l ago.
26:19 and the earth will give birth to those l dead.
30:33 For his burning place has l been prepared;
37:26 Have you not heard that I determined it l ago?
42:14 For a l time I have held my peace,
45:21 Who told this l ago? Who declared it of old?
48: 3 The former things I declared l ago,
48: 5 I declared them to you from l ago,
48: 7 They are created now, not l ago;
51: 9 as in days of old, the generations of l ago!
51:13 You fear continually all day l because of the fury
52: 4 For thus says the Lord GOD: L ago,
52: 5 and continually, all day l, my name is despised.
63:19 We have l been like those whom you do not rule,
65: 2 I held out my hands all day l to
65: 5 a fire that burns all day l.
65:22 my chosen shall l enjoy the work of their hands.
Jer 2:20 l ago you broke your yoke and burst your bonds,
4:14 How l shall your evil schemes lodge within you?
4:21 How l must I see the standard,
12: 4 How l will the land mourn,
13:27 How l will it be before you are made clean?
20: 7 I have become a laughingstock all day l;
20: 8 for me a reproach and derision all day l.
22:27 not return to the land to which they l to return.
23:26 How l? Will the hearts of the prophets ever turn
29:28 saying, "It will be a l time;
31:22 How l will you waver, O faithless daughter?
32:14 in order that they may last for a l time.
44:14 Although they l to go back to live there,
47: 5 How l will you gash yourselves?
47: 6 How l until you are quiet?
52:34 as l as he lived, up to the day of his death.
La 1:13 he has left me stunned, faint all day l.
2:17 he ordained l ago, he has demolished without pity;
3: 3 again and again, all day l.
3: 6 in darkness like the dead of l ago.
3:14 the object of their taunt-songs all day l.
3:62 of my assailants are against me all day l.
Eze 7:13 to what has been sold as l as they remain alive.
17: 3 A great eagle, with great wings and l pinions,
23:27 you shall not l for them,
26:20 to the people of l ago,
31: 5 its boughs grew large and its branches l,
32:27 not lie with the fallen warriors of l ago who went
38: 8 the mountains of Israel, which had l lain waste;
40: 5 in the man's hand was six l cubits, each being
40:42 a cubit and a half l,
40:43 There were pegs, one handbreadth l,
41: 8 a full reed of six l cubits.
41:22 two cubits l, and two cubits wide;
42: 7 opposite the chambers, fifty cubits l.
42: 8 chambers on the outer court were fifty cubits l,
42: 8 the temple were one hundred cubits l.
42:20 a wall around it, five hundred cubits l
43:16 twelve cubits l by twelve wide.
43:17 fourteen cubits l by fourteen wide,
44:20 not shave their heads or let their locks grow l;
45: 1 twenty-five thousand cubits l
45: 3 a section twenty-five thousand cubits l
45: 5 twenty-five thousand cubits l
45: 6 and twenty-five thousand cubits l;
46:22 forty cubits l and thirty wide;
Da 4:33 as l as eagles' feathers and his nails became
8: 3 Both horns were l, but one was longer than
8:13 "For how l is this vision concerning
12: 6 l shall it be until the end of these wonders?"
Hos 8: 5 How l will they be incapable of innocence?
12: 1 and pursues the east wind all day l;
Hab 1: 2 O LORD, how l shall I cry for help,
2: 6 How l will you load yourselves with goods taken
Zec 1:12 how l will you withhold mercy from Jerusalem
Mt 9:15 "The wedding guests cannot mourn as l as
11:21 they would have repented l ago in sackcloth
23: 5 make their phylacteries broad and their fringes l.
25:19 After a l time the master of those slaves came
Mk 2:19 As l as they have the bridegroom with them,
9:21 "How l has this been happening to him?"
12:38 who like to walk around in l robes,
12:40 and for the sake of appearance say l prayers.
Lk 5: 5 we have worked all night l
8:27 For a l time he had worn no clothes,
10:13 they would have repented l ago,
13:16 for eighteen l years, be set free
17:22 "The days are coming when you will l to see one
18: 7 Will he delay l in helping them?
20: 9 and went to another country for a l time.
20:46 who like to walk around in l robes,
20:47 and for the sake of appearance say l prayers.
23: 8 for he had been wanting to see him for a l time,
Jn 5: 6 and knew that he had been there a l time,
9: 5 As l as I am in the world,
10:24 "How l will you keep us in suspense?
Ac 3:21 of universal restoration that God announced l ago
8:11 for a l time he had amazed them with his magic.
14: 3 So they remained for a l time,
15:18 known from l ago.'
24: 2 because of you we have l enjoyed peace,
26: 5 They have known for a l time,
27:21 Since they had been without food for a l time,
28: 6 but after they had waited a l time and saw
Ro 7: 2 by the law to her husband as l as he lives;
8:36 "For your sake we are being killed all day l;
10:21 "All day l I have held out my hands to
16:25 of the mystery that was kept secret for l ages
1Co 3: 3 l as there is jealousy and quarreling among you,

1Co 7:39 A wife is bound as l as her husband lives.
11:14 that if a man wears l hair, it is degrading to him,
11:15 but if a woman has l hair, it is her glory?
2Co 9:14 while they l for you and pray for you because of
Gal 4: 1 My point is this: heirs, as l as they are minors,
Eph 6: 3 that it may be well with you and you may live l
Php 1: 8 how I l for all of you with the compassion
4: 1 my brothers and sisters, whom I love and l for,
1Th 3: 6 and l to see us—just as we l to see you.
2Ti 1: 4 I l to see you so that I may be filled with joy.
Heb 1: 1 L ago God spoke to our ancestors in many
3:13 as l as it is called "today,"
9: 8 into the sanctuary has not yet been disclosed as l
9:17 not in force as l as the one who made it is alive.
1Pe 1:12 things into which angels l to look!
2: 2 Like newborn infants, l for the pure,
3: 5 in this way l ago the holy women who hoped
3: 6 You have become her daughters as l
2Pe 1:13 I think it right, as l as I am in this body,
2: 3 pronounced against them l ago, has not been idle,
3: 5 that by the word of God heavens existed l ago
Jude 1: 4 people who l ago were designated
Rev 1:13 a l robe and with a golden sash across his chest.
6:10 how l will it be before you judge
9: 6 they will l to die, but death will flee from them.
Tob 5: 8 but do not take too l."
10: 7 in and mourn and weep all night l,
10:12 may I hear a good report about you as l as I live."
10:12 and may I live l enough to see children of you
Jdt 1: 2 hewn stones three cubits thick and six cubits l;
5: 8 and lived there for a l time.
5:10 to Egypt and lived there as l as they had food.
5:16 and all the Gergesites, and lived there a l time.
5:17 "As l as they did not sin
13: 1 because the banquet had lasted so l.
16:25 or for a l time after her death.
AdE 5:13 as l as I see Mordecai the Jew in the courtyard."
13: 7 so that those who have l been hostile and remain
Wis 3:17 if they live l they will be held of no account,
4: 2 and they l for it when it has gone;
4:13 in a short time, they fulfilled l years;
6:11 l for them, and you will be instructed.
11:14 though they had mockingly rejected him who l
12: 3 Those who lived l ago in your holy land
17: 2 as captives of darkness and prisoners of l night,
18:20 but the wrath did not l continue.
18:24 For on his l robe the whole world was depicted,
Sir 1:12 and gives gladness and joy and l life.
1:20 and her branches are l life.
3: 6 Those who respect their father will have l life,
3:12 and do not grieve him as l as he lives;
10:10 A l illness baffles the physician;
11:19 not know how l it will be until he leaves them
23:15 will never become disciplined as l as they live.
33:20 do not give power over yourself, as l as you live;
39:11 If he lives l, he will leave a name greater than
45: 8 the linen undergarments, the l robe,
45:15 for his descendants as l as the heavens endure,
46: 4 that the sun stood still and one day become as l
Bar 4:35 and for a l time she will be inhabited by demons.
LtJ 6: 3 for a l time, up to seven generations;
6:46 not live very l themselves;
1Mc 6:22 "How l will you fail to do justice and
8:19 They went to Rome, a very l journey;
9:71 that he would not try to harm him as l
2Mc 6: 1 Not l after this, the king sent an Athenian senator
6:13 not to let the impious alone for l,
6:21 the man aside because of their l acquaintance
10: 6 remembering how not l before,
12:36 and his men had been fighting for a l time
14:10 For as l as Judas lives,
1Es 3:22 and before l they draw their swords.
5:73 of the building as l as King Cyrus lived.
3Mc 4: 1 for the inveterate enmity that had l ago been
5:40 how l will you put us to the test,
2Es 1: 9 How l shall I endure them,
4:26 "If you are alive, you will see, and if you live l,
4:33 Then I answered and said, "How l?
4:33 saying, 'How l are we to remain here?
6:28 and the truth, which has been so l without fruit,
6:59 How l will this be so?"
7:74 How l the Most High has been patient
8:25 For as l as I live I will speak,
8:25 and as l as I have understanding I will answer.
11:13 and it continued to reign a l time.
11:17 you no one shall rule as l as you have ruled,
11:17 as long as you have ruled, not even half as l."
11:40 for so l you have lived on the earth with deceit.
13:45 Through that region there was a l way to go,
16:27 a person will l to see another human being,
4Mc 3: 7 the Philistines all day l, and together with
5: 7 Although you have had them for so l a time,
5:36 nor my l life lived lawfully.

LONG-HAIRED (1) [HAIR, LONG]

Dt 32:42 of the slain and the captives, from the l enemy.

LONG-SUFFERING (1) [LONG]

Man 1: 7 of great compassion, l, and very merciful,

LONGED (10) [LONG]

Ge 31:30 Even though you had to go because you l greatly
Ps 119:40 See, I have l for your precepts;
Isa 21: 4 the twilight I l for has been turned for me
La 2:16 Ah, this is the day we l for;
Eze 23:21 Thus you l for the lewdness of your youth,
Mt 13:17 and righteous people l to see what you see,
Lk 16:21 who l to satisfy his hunger with what fell from
1Th 2:17 we l with great eagerness to see you face to face.
2Ti 4: 8 and not only to me but also to all who have l
Rev 18:14 fruit for which your soul l has gone from you,

LONGER‡ (201) [LONG]

Ge 4:12 it will no l yield to you its strength;
17: 5 No l shall your name be Abram,
32:28 the man said, "You shall no l be called Jacob,
35:10 no l shall you be called Jacob,
41:31 The plenty will no l be known in the land
45: 1 Then Joseph could no l control himself
49: 4 you shall no l excel because you went
Ex 2: 3 When she could hide him no l she got
5: 7 "You shall no l give the people straw
9:28 I will let you go; you need stay no l."
9:33 and the rain no l poured down on the earth.
Lev 17: 7 so that they may no l offer their sacrifices
27:20 it shall no l be redeemable.
Nu 9:22 Whether it was two days, or a month, or a l time,
18:22 now on the Israelites shall no l approach the tent
Dt 5:25 we hear the voice of the LORD our God any l,
10:16 and do not be stubborn any l.
31: 2 I am no l able to get about,
Jos 5: 1 and there was no l any spirit in them,
5:12 and the Israelites no l had manna;
Jdg 2:14 so that they could no l withstand their enemies.
2:21 I will no l drive out before them any of
10:16 and he could no l bear to see Israel suffer.
Ru 1:20 "Call me no l Naomi, call me Mara,
1Sa 1:18 and her countenance was sad no l.
27: 1 then Saul will despair of seeking me any l within
27: 4 he no l sought for him.
2Sa 2:28 they no l pursued Israel or engaged
21:17 "You shall not go out with us to battle any l,
2Ki 2:12 But when he could no l see him,
5:17 for your servant will no l offer burnt offering
6:23 the Arameans no l came raiding into the land
6:33 Why should I hope in the LORD any l?"
1Ch 23:26 so the Levites no l need to carry the tabernacle
2Ch 35: 3 you need no l carry it on your shoulders."
Ne 2:17 so that we may no l suffer disgrace."
Job 11: 9 Its measure is l than the earth,
20: 9 nor will their place behold them any l.
24:20 they are no l remembered;
Ps 12: 1 O LORD, for there is no l anyone who is godly;
74: 9 there is no l any prophet,
Ecc 4:13 who will no l take advice.
Isa 7: 8 be shattered, no l a people.)
23:12 You will exult no l, O oppressed virgin daughter
24: 9 No l do they drink wine with singing;
26:21 and will no l cover its slain.
29:22 No l shall Jacob be ashamed,
29:22 no l shall his face grow pale.
32: 5 A fool will no l be called noble,
33:19 No l will you see the insolent people,
60:19 The sun shall no l be your light by day,
Jer 3:16 says the LORD, they shall no l say,
3:17 shall no l stubbornly follow their own evil will.
11:19 so that his name will no l be remembered!"
16:14 says the LORD, when it shall no l be said,
23: 4 and they shall not fear any l, or be dismayed,
23: 7 says the LORD, when it shall no l be said,
31:29 In those days they shall no l say:
31:34 No l shall they teach one another,
33:24 in such contempt that they no l regard them as
44:22 The LORD could no l bear the sight
44:26 that my name shall no l be pronounced on
49: 7 Is there no l wisdom in Teman?
51:44 The nations shall no l stream to him;
La 4:15 "They shall stay here no l."
4:22 is accomplished, he will keep you in exile no l;
Eze 12:24 For there shall no l be any false vision
12:25 It will no l be delayed;
12:28 None of my words will be delayed any l,
13:21 they shall no l be prey in your hands;
13:23 therefore you shall no l see false visions
14:11 the house of Israel may no l go astray from me,
16:42 I will be calm, and will be angry no l.
24:27 and you shall speak and no l be silent.
28:24 of Israel shall no l find a pricking brier or
30:13 there shall no l be a prince in the land of Egypt;
33:22 and I was no l unable to speak.
34:10 no l shall the shepherds feed themselves.
34:22 and they shall no l be ravaged;
34:29 and no l suffer the insults of the nations.
36:12 No l shall you bereave them of children.
36:14 therefore you shall no l devour people
36:14 and no l bereave your nation of children,
36:15 and no l will I let you hear the insults of
36:15 no l shall you bear the disgrace of the peoples;
36:15 and no l shall you cause your nation to stumble,
45: 8 And my princes shall no l oppress my people;
Da 8: 3 horns were long, but one was l than the other,
8: 3 and the l one came up second.
Hos 1: 6 for I will no l have pity on the house of Israel
2:16 "My husband," and no l will you call me,
Na 1:14 "Your name shall be perpetuated no l;
Zep 3:11 you shall no l be haughty in my holy mountain.
Zec 11: 6 For I will no l have pity on the inhabitants of
14:21 And there shall no l be traders in the house of
Mal 2:13 and groaning because he no l regards the offering
Mt 5:13 It is no l good for anything,
17:17 how much l must I be with you?
Mt 17:17 How much l must I put up with you?
19: 6 So they are no l two, but one flesh.
Mk 1:45 so that Jesus could no l go into a town openly,
2: 2 around that there was no l room for them,
7:12 then you no l permit doing anything for a father
9:19 how much l must I be among you?
9:19 How much l must I put up with you?
10: 8 So they are no l two, but one flesh.
Lk 8:49 do not trouble the teacher any l."
9:41 much l must I be with you and bear with you?
15:19 I am no l worthy to be called your son;
15:21 I am no l worthy to be called your son.'
16: 2 because you cannot be my manager any l.'
20:40 For they no l dared to ask him another question.
Jn 4:42 "It is no l because of what you said
6:66 of his disciples turned back and no l went about
7:33 "I will be with you a little while l,
11: 6 he stayed two days l in the place where he was.
11:54 Jesus therefore no l walked about openly among
12:35 "The light is with you for a little l.
13:33 Little children, I am with you only a little l.
14:19 In a little while the world will no l see me,
14:30 I will no l talk much with you,
15:15 I do not call you servants any l,
16:10 to the Father and you will see me no l;
16:16 "A little while, and you will no l see me,
16:17 and you will no l see me, and again a little while,
16:19 and you will no l see me, and again a little while,
16:21 she no l remembers the anguish because of
16:25 The hour is coming when I will no l speak to you
17:11 And now I am no l in the world,
Ac 18:20 When they asked him to stay l, he declined;
19:22 while he himself stayed for some time l in Asia.
20: 9 into a deep sleep while Paul talked still l.
25:24 shouting that he ought not to live any l.
Ro 6: 6 and we might no l be enslaved to sin.
6: 9 death no l has dominion over him.
6:13 No l present your members to sin as instruments
7:17 But in fact it is no l I that do it,
7:20 if I do what I do not want, it is no l I that do it,
11: 6 if it is by grace, it is no l on the basis of works,
11: 6 otherwise grace would no l be grace.
14:13 therefore no l pass judgment on one another,
14:15 you are no l walking in love.
2Co 5:15 those who live might live no l for themselves,
5:16 we know him no l in that way.
Gal 2:20 and it is no l I who live,
3:18 it no l comes from the promise;
3:25 we are no l subject to a disciplinarian,
3:28 There is no l Jew or Greek,
3:28 there is no l slave or free,
3:28 there is no l male and female;
4: 7 So you are no l a slave but a child,
Eph 2:19 So then you are no l strangers and aliens,
4:14 We must no l be children,
4:17 you must no l live as the Gentiles live,
Col 3:11 In that renewal there is no l Greek and Jew,
1Th 3: 1 Therefore when we could bear it no l,
3: 5 For this reason, when I could bear it no l,
1Ti 5:23 No l drink only water, but take a little wine for
Phm 1:16 no l as a slave but more than a slave,
Heb 10: 2 would no l have any consciousness of sin?
10:18 there is no l any offering for sin.
10:26 there no l remains a sacrifice for sins,
1Pe 4: 2 the rest of your earthly life no l by human desires
4: 4 They are surprised that you no l join them in
Rev 6:11 a white robe and told to rest a little l,
12: 8 and there was no l any place for them in heaven.
Tob 1:15 and I could no l go there.
5:10 in darkness like the dead who no l see the light.
6: 8 and never remain with that person any l.
10: 4 "My child has perished and is no l among
13: 6 to you and will no l hide his face from you.
Jdt 7:22 they no l had any strength.
8:31 Then we will no l feel faint from thirst."
AdE 1:19 that the queen may no l come into his presence;
2: 1 and he no l was concerned about Vashti
Wis 14:24 they no l keep either their lives
Sir 41:12 since it will outlive you l than a thousand hoards
1Mc 2:11 no l free, she has become a slave
2:13 Why should we live any l?"
5:44 they could stand before Judas no l.
7:38 and let them live no l."
9:55 that he could no l say a word or give commands
13:39 in Jerusalem shall be collected no l.
2Mc 4:14 that the priests were no l intent upon their service
6: 1 to forsake the laws of their ancestors and no l
6:25 for the sake of living a brief moment l,
9:13 who would no l have mercy on him,
1Es 1: 4 "You need no l carry it on your shoulders.
2:24 you will no l have access to Coelesyria
8:90 for we can no l stand in your presence because
3Mc 4:17 that they were no l able to take the census of
2Es 4:23 and the written covenants no l exist.
4:40 her womb can keep the fetus within her any l."
5:49 not bring forth any l, so I have made
10:27 I looked up, the woman was no l visible to me,
11:13 so that even its place was no l visible.
12:15 for a l time than any other one of the twelve.
14:41 and my mouth was opened and was no l closed.
15: 8 I will be silent no l concerning their ungodly acts
15:10 not allow them to live any l in the land of Egypt,
4Mc 7:13 his body no l tense and firm, his muscles flabby,

LONGING (8) [LONG]

Ps 38: 9 O Lord, all my l is known to you;

Ps 119:20 My soul is consumed with l for your ordinances
Ro 1:11 For I am l to see you so that I may share
8:19 the creation waits with eager l for the revealing
2Co 5: 2 l to be clothed with our heavenly dwelling—
7: 7 as he told us of your l, your mourning,
7:11 what alarm, what l, what zeal, what punishment!
Php 2:26 for he has been l for all of you,

LONGINGLY (2) [LONG]

2Sa 23:15 David said l, "O that someone would give me
1Ch 11:17 David said l, "O that someone would give me

LONGS (6) [LONG]

Ge 34: 8 heart of my son Shechem l for your daughter;
Job 7: 2 Like a slave who l for the shadow,
Ps 42: 1 As a deer l for flowing streams,
42: 1 so my soul l for you, O God.
84: 2 My soul l, indeed it faints for the courts of
Wis 8: 8 And if anyone l for wide experience,

LONGSUFFERING (KJV) See FORBEARANCE, LONG-SUFFERING, PATIENCE, SLOW TO ANGER

LOOK‡ (371) [LOOKED, LOOKING, LOOKOUT, LOOKOUTS, LOOKS]

Ge 11: 6 And the LORD said, "L, they are one people,
13:14 and l from the place where you are,
15: 5 "L toward heaven and count the stars,
19: 8 L, I have two daughters who have not known
19:17 do not l back or stop anywhere in the Plain;
19:20 L, that city is near enough to flee to,
19:34 the firstborn said to the younger, "L,
20:16 "L, I have given your brother a thousand pieces
21:16 "Do not let me l on the death of the child."
24:16 The girl was very fair to l upon, a virgin,
24:51 L, Rebekah is before you, take her and go,
27:11 But Jacob said to his mother Rebekah, "L,
27:36 and l, now he has taken away my blessing."
29: 7 He said, "L, it is still broad daylight;
30:33 when you come to l into my wages with you.
31:12 'L up and see that all the goats that leap on
37: 9 saying, "L, I have had another dream:
39: 8 But he refused and said to his master's wife, "L,
44: 8 L, the money that we found at the top
Ex 1: 9 He said to his people, "L,
3: 3 "I must turn aside and l at this great sight,
3: 6 Moses hid his face, for he was afraid to l at God.
5:16 L how your servants are beaten!
5:21 "The LORD l upon you and judge!
18:21 You should also l for able men among all
19:21 not to break through to the LORD to l;
Lev 26: 9 I will l with favor upon you
Nu 4:20 in to l on the holy things even for a moment;
11: 6 and there is nothing at all but this manna to l at."
21: 8 and everyone who is bitten shall l at it and live."
21: 9 person would l at the serpent of bronze and live.
23:24 L, a people rising up like a lioness,
24: 1 so he did not go, as at other times, to l for omens,
Dt 3:27 to the top of Pisgah and l around you to the west,
3:27 L well, for you shall not cross over this Jordan.
4:19 when you l up to the heavens and see the sun,
5:24 "L, the LORD our God has shown us his glory
26:15 L down from your holy habitation, from heaven,
28:32 be given to another people, while you l on;
Jos 22:28 'L at this copy of the altar of the LORD,
Jdg 7:17 "L at me, and do the same;
9:31 "L, Gaal son of Ebed and his kinsfolk have come
9:36 And when Gaal saw them, he said to Zebul, "L,
9:36 shadows on the mountains l like people to you."
9:37 Gaal spoke again and said, "L,
14:16 "L, I have not told my father or my mother.
19: 9 the girl's father, said to him, "L,
21:19 So they said, "L, the yearly festival of
1Sa 1:11 if only you will l on the misery of your servant,
2:29 Why then l with greedy eye at my sacrifices
2:32 Then in distress you will l with greedy eye on all
9: 3 go and l for the donkeys."
14:11 and the Philistines said, "L,
14:33 Then it was reported to Saul, "L,
16: 7 "Do not l on his appearance or on the height
16: 7 they l on the outward appearance,
16:16 now command the servants who attend you to l
20:21 If I say to the boy, 'L,
20:22 But if I say to the young man, 'L,
21:14 Achish said to his servants, "L,
23: 3 But David's men said to him, "L,
23:23 L around and learn all the hiding places
24: 2 to l for David and his men in the direction of
2Sa 5: 1 and said, "L, we are your bone and flesh.
9: 8 that you should l upon a dead dog such as I?"
14:30 Then he said to his servants, "L,
14:32 Absalom answered Joab, "L, I sent word to you:
15:16 except ten concubines whom he left behind to l
15:27 The king also said to the priest Zadok, "L,
16:12 It may be that the LORD will l on my distress,
16:21 the ones he has left to l after the house;
20: 3 the ten concubines whom he had left to l after
1Ki 8:25 if only your children l to their way,
12:16 L now to your own house, O David."
18:43 "Go up now, l toward the sea."
18:44 At the seventh time he said, "L,
20: 7 the elders of the land, and said, "L now!
20:13 L, I will give it into your hand today;
1Ki 20:31 His servants said to him, "L,
22:13 "L, the words of the prophets
2Ki 1:14 L, fire came down from heaven and consumed
3:14 I would give you neither a l nor a glance.
4: 9 She said to her husband, "L,
4:25 "L, there is the Shunammite woman;
5: 7 Just l and see how he is trying to pick a quarrel
9: 2 you arrive, l there for Jehu son of Jehoshaphat,
10: 4 But they were utterly terrified and said, "L,
14: 8 saying, "Come, let us l one another in the face."
2Ch 10:16 L now to your own house, O David."
18:12 "L, the words of the prophets
25:17 saying, "Come, let us l one another in the face."
Est 1:17 to l with contempt on their husbands,
7: 9 the eunuchs in attendance on the king, said, "L,
Job 6:19 caravans of Tema l, the travelers of Sheba hope.
6:28 "But now, be pleased to l at me;
7: 2 and like laborers who l for their wages,
7:19 Will you not l away from me for a while,
9:11 L, he passes by me, and I do not see him;
10:15 with disgrace and l upon my affliction.
13: 1 "L, my eye has seen all this,
14: 6 l away from them, and desist,
17:13 If I l for Sheol as my house,
20:17 They will not l on the rivers,
21: 5 L at me, and be appalled,
30:20 I stand, and you merely l at me.
31: 1 how then could I l upon a virgin?
33:10 L, he finds occasions against me,
34:26 for their wickedness while others l on,
35: 5 L at the heavens and see;
37:21 no one can l on the light when it is bright in
40:11 and l on all who are proud, and abase them.
40:12 L on all who are proud, and bring them low;
40:15 "L at Behemoth, which I made just
Ps 8: 3 When I l at your heavens,
11: 2 for l, the wicked bend the bow,
34: 5 L to him, and be radiant;
35:17 How long, O LORD, will you l on?
37:10 though you l diligently for their place,
37:34 you will l on the destruction of the wicked.
49:10 When we l at the wise, they die;
59:10 my God will let me l in triumph on my enemies.
68:16 Why do you l with envy,
80:14 l down from heaven, and see;
84: 9 l on the face of your anointed.
85:11 and righteousness will l down from the sky.
91: 8 You will only l with your eyes and see
101: 5 A haughty l and an arrogant heart I will
101: 6 I will l with favor on the faithful in the land,
104:27 These all l to you to give them their food
112: 8 in the end they will l in triumph on their foes.
118: 7 I shall l in triumph on those who hate me.
119:153 L on my misery and rescue me,
119:158 I l at the faithless with disgust,
123: 2 the eyes of servants l to the hand of their master,
123: 2 so our eyes l to the LORD our God,
142: 4 L on my right hand and see—
145:15 The eyes of all l to you,
Pr 4:25 Let your eyes l directly forward,
23:31 Do not l at wine when it is red,
24:12 "L, we did not know this"—
29:16 but the righteous will l upon their downfall.
Ecc 4: 1 L, the tears of the oppressed—
12: 3 and those who l through the windows see dimly;
SS 2: 8 L, he comes, leaping upon the mountains,
2: 9 L, there he stands behind our wall,
3: 7 L, it is the litter of Solomon!
3:11 L, O daughters of Zion, at King Solomon,
6:11 to l at the blossoms of the valley,
6:13 Return, return, that we may l upon you.
6:13 Why should you l upon the Shulammite,
Isa 3: 9 The l on their faces bears witness against them;
5:30 And if one l to the land—
6:10 so that they may not l with their eyes,
7:14 L, the young woman is with child and shall bear
8:22 or they will l to the earth,
10:33 L, the Sovereign, the LORD of hosts,
13: 8 They will l aghast at one another;
17: 7 and their eyes will l to the Holy One of Israel;
17: 8 not l to what their own fingers have made,
18: 3 when a signal is raised on the mountains, l!
18: 4 I will quietly l from my dwelling like clear heat
21: 9 L, there they come, riders, horsemen in pairs!"
22: 4 L away from me, let me weep bitter tears;
22:11 But you did not l to him who did it,
23:13 L at the land of the Chaldeans!
31: 1 but do not l to the Holy One of Israel or consult
33:20 L on Zion, the city of our appointed festivals!
38:11 I shall l upon mortals no more among
41:28 But when I l there is no one;
42:18 and you that are blind, l up and see!
44:11 L, all its devotees shall be put to shame;
51: 1 L to the rock from which you were hewn,
51: 2 L to Abraham your father and
51: 6 and l at the earth beneath;
53: 2 he had no form or majesty that we should l
58: 3 L, you serve your own interest on your fast day,
58: 4 L, you fast only to quarrel and to fight and
60: 4 Lift up your eyes and l around;
63:15 L down from heaven and see,
66: 2 But this is the one to whom I will l,
66:24 And they shall go out and l at the dead bodies of
Jer 2:10 Cross to the coasts of Cyprus and l,
2:23 L at your way in the valley;
3: 2 L up to the bare heights, and see!
3:12 I will not l on you in anger, for I am merciful,
Jer 4:13 L! He comes up like clouds,
5: 1 and fro through the streets of Jerusalem, l around
5: 3 O LORD, do your eyes not l for truth?
6:16 Stand at the crossroads, and l,
8:15 We l for peace, but find no good,
13:16 while you l for light, he turns it into gloom
14:18 If I go out into the field, l—those killed by
14:18 And if I enter the city, l—those sick with famine!
14:19 We l for peace, but find no good;
18:11 L, I am a potter shaping evil against you
20: 4 by the sword of their enemies while you l on.
23:19 L, the storm of the LORD!
30:23 L, the storm of the LORD!
39:12 l after him well and do him no harm,
40: 4 Now l, I have just released you today from
44: 2 on all the towns of Judah. L at them;
46: 5 They do not l back—terror is all around!
48:40 L, he shall swoop down like an eagle,
49:22 L, he shall mount up and swoop down like
50:41 L, a people is coming from the north;
La 1: 9 "O LORD, l at my affliction,
1:11 L, O LORD, and see how worthless I have become.
1:12 L and see if there is any sorrow like my sorrow,
2:20 L, O LORD, and consider!
5: 1 Remember, O LORD, what has befallen us; l,
Eze 4:17 they will l at one another in dismay,
40: 4 "Mortal, l closely and listen attentively,
44: 5 Mortal, mark well, l closely,
Da 9:18 Open your eyes and l at our desolation and
Hos 5: 8 l behind you, Benjamin!
14: 8 It is I who answer and l after you.
Am 5:22 of your fatted animals I will not l upon.
Jnh 2: 4 how shall I l again upon your holy temple?'
Mic 7: 7 But as for me, I will l to the LORD,
Na 1:15 L! On the mountains the feet of one
3: 5 and I will let nations l on your nakedness
3:13 L at your troops: they are women in your midst.
Hab 1: 3 Why do you make me see wrongdoing and l
1: 5 L at the nations, and see!
1:13 and you cannot l on wrongdoing;
1:13 why do you l on the treacherous,
2: 4 L at the proud! Their spirit is
Hag 2: 3 How does it l to you now?
Zec 5: 5 "L up and see what this is that is coming out."
12:10 when they l on the one whom they have pierced,
Mal 2:15 So l to yourselves, and do not let anyone
Mt 1:23 "L, the virgin shall conceive and bear a son,
6:16 "And whenever you fast, do not l dismal,
6:26 L at the birds of the air;
11: 7 "What did you go out into the wilderness to l at?
11: 8 L, those who wear soft robes are in royal palaces.
11:19 and they say, 'L, a glutton and a drunkard,
12: 2 When the Pharisees saw it, they said to him, "L,
12:47 Someone told him, "L, your mother
13:14 but never understand, and you will indeed l,
13:15 so that they might not l with their eyes,
19:27 Then Peter said in reply, "L,
21: 5 L, your king is coming to you, humble,
22: 4 L, I have prepared my dinner,
23:27 which on the outside l beautiful,
23:28 So you also on the outside l righteous to others,
24:23 Then if anyone says to you, 'L!
24:26 So, if they say to you, 'L!
24:26 not go out. If they say, 'L!
25: 6 But at midnight there was a shout, 'L!
26:16 that moment he began to l for an opportunity
Mk 2:24 The Pharisees said to him, "L,
4:12 that 'they may indeed l, but not perceive,
8:24 "I can see people, but they l like trees, walking."
10:28 Peter began to say to him, "L,
11:21 Peter remembered and said to him, "Rabbi, l!
13: 1 one of his disciples said to him, "L, Teacher,
13:21 'L! Here is the Messiah!' or 'L! There he is!'
14:11 So he began to l for an opportunity to betray him.
16: 6 L, there is the place they laid him.
Lk 2:44 to l for him among their relatives and friends.
2:48 L, your father and I have been searching for you
7:24 "What did you go out into the wilderness to l at?
7:25 L, those who put on fine clothing and live
7:34 and you say, 'L, a glutton and a drunkard,
9:38 I beg you to l at my son; he is my only child.
17:21 nor will they say, 'L, here it is!'
17:23 They will say to you, 'L there!' or 'L here!'
18:13 standing far off, would not even l up to heaven,
18:28 "L, we have left our homes and followed you."
19: 8 Zacchaeus stood there and said to the Lord, "L,
21:29 "L at the fig tree and all the trees;
22: 6 and began to l for an opportunity to betray him
22:38 They said, "Lord, l, here are two swords."
24: 5 "Why do you l for the living among the dead?
24:39 L at my hands and my feet; see that it is I myself.
Jn 1:36 he exclaimed, "L, here is the Lamb of God!"
4:35 But I tell you, l around you,
8:37 yet you l for an opportunity to kill me,
12:15 L, your king is coming, sitting on a donkey's colt!"
12:19 L, the world has gone after him!"
12:40 so that they might not l with their eyes,
13:33 with you only a little longer. You will l for me;
19: 4 Pilate went out again and said to them, "L,
19:37 of scripture says, "They will l on
20: 5 to l in and saw the linen wrappings lying there,
20:11 As she wept, she bent over to l into the tomb;
Ac 3: 4 as did John, and said, "L at us."
4:29 And now, Lord, l at their threats,
5: 9 L, the feet of those who have buried your husband
5:25 Then someone arrived and announced, "L,
7:31 and as he approached to l,

Ac 7:32 Moses began to tremble and did not dare to l.
7:56 "L," he said, "I see the heavens opened and
8:36 and the eunuch said, "L, here is water!
9:11 of Judas l for a man of Tarsus named Saul.
10:19 "L, three men are searching for you.
11:25 Then Barnabas went to Tarsus to l for Saul,
13:41 'L, you scoffers! Be amazed
28:26 but never understand, and you will indeed l,
28:27 so that they might not l with their eyes,
2Co 4:18 because we l not at what can be seen but
10: 7 L at what is before your eyes.
Php 2: 4 Let each of you l not to your own interests,
Tit 2:15 Let no one l down on you.
Heb 8: 7 there would have been no need to l for
Jas 1:23 like those who l at themselves in a mirror;
1:24 for they l at themselves and,
1:25 But those who l into the perfect law,
3: 4 Or l at ships: though they are
1Pe 1:12 things into which angels long to l!
Jude 1:21 l forward to the mercy of our Lord Jesus Christ
Rev 1: 7 L! He is coming with the
3: 8 L, I have set before you an open door,
5: 3 under the earth was able to open the scroll or to l
5: 4 to open the scroll or to l into it.
Tob 2: 3 So Tobias went to l for some poor person
2: 3 Then he went on to say, "L, father,
3: 3 O Lord, remember me and l favorably upon me.
5: 4 So Tobias went out to l for a man to go with him
11: 6 she said to his father, "L, your son is coming,
13: 6 perhaps he may l with favor upon you
Jdt 4:15 they cried out to the Lord with all their might to l
6: 9 not be taken, then do not l downcast!
6:19 and l kindly today on the faces
9: 9 L at their pride, and send your wrath
13: 4 l in this hour on the work of my hands for
14:18 L, Holofernes is lying on the ground,
AdE 7: 9 one of the eunuchs, said to the king, "L,
8: 6 How can I l on the ruin of my people?
Wis 17:10 refusing to l even at the air,
Sir 7:22 Do you have cattle? L after them;
9: 5 Do not l intently at a virgin,
9: 7 Do not l around in the streets of a city,
11:12 but the eyes of the Lord l kindly upon them;
14:16 because in Hades one cannot l for luxury.
23:19 they l upon every aspect of human behavior
33:15 L at all the works of the Most High;
33:22 that you should l to the hand of your children.
34:18 To whom does he l? And who is his support?
43:11 L at the rainbow, and praise him who made it;
Bar 2:16 O Lord, l down from your holy dwelling,
4:36 L toward the east, O Jerusalem,
4:37 L, your children are coming,
5: 5 l toward the east, and see your children gathered
Aza 1:32 Blessed are you who l into the depths
Sus 1:20 They said, "L, the garden doors are shut,
Bel 1:19 from going in. "L at the floor," he said,
1Mc 9:45 For l! the battle is in front
2Mc 1:27 l on those who are rejected and despised,
7:28 to l at the heaven and the earth
8: 2 to l upon the people who were oppressed by all;
11:29 to return home and l after your own affairs.
15: 8 and so to l for the victory that
1Es 8:12 in order to l into matters in Judea and Jerusalem,
Man 1: 9 not worthy to l up and see the height of heaven
3Mc 1:20 and without a backward l they crowded together
5:30 and with a threatening l he said,
6: 3 l upon the descendants of Abraham,
2Es 1:38 l with pride and see the people coming from
7: 5 to l at it or to navigate it,
7:37 'L now, and understand whom you have denied,
7:38 L on this side and on that;
7:66 for they do not l for a judgment,
8:23 whose l dries up the depths
8:26 O do not l on the sins of your people,
11:28 to l the two that remained were planning
11:36 "L in front of you and consider what you see."
13: 3 and wherever he turned his face to l,

LOOKED‡ (201) [LOOK]

Ge 8:13 and Noah removed the covering of the ark, and l,
13:10 Lot l about him, and saw that the plain of
16: 4 she l with contempt on her mistress.
16: 5 she l on me with contempt.
18: 2 He l up and saw three men standing near him.
18:16 and they l toward Sodom;
19:26 But Lot's wife, behind him, l back,
19:28 and he l down toward Sodom and Gomorrah and
22: 4 On the third day Abraham l up and saw
22:13 And Abraham l up and saw a ram,
24:64 And Rebekah l up, and when she saw Isaac,
26: 8 King Abimelech of the Philistines l out of
29: 2 As he l, he saw a well in the field
29:32 "Because the LORD has l on my affliction;
31:10 of the flock I once had a dream in which I l up
33: 1 Now Jacob l up and saw Esau coming,
33: 5 Esau l up and saw the women and children,
43:29 Then he l up and saw his brother Benjamin,
43:33 the men l at one another in amazement.
Ex 2:12 He l this way and that,
2:25 God l upon the Israelites,
3: 2 he l, and the bush was blazing,
14:10 As Pharaoh drew near, the Israelites l back,
14:24 of fire and cloud l down upon the Egyptian army,
16:10 they l toward the wilderness,
Nu 17: 9 and they l, and each man took his staff.
24: 2 Balaam l up and saw Israel camping tribe
Nu 24:20 he l on Amalek, and uttered his oracle, saying:
24:21 he l on the Kenite, and uttered his oracle, saying:
Jos 5:13 he l up and saw a man standing before him with
8:20 So when the men of Ai l back,
Jdg 9:43 he l and saw the people coming out of the city,
13:20 of the altar while Manoah and his wife l on;
16:27 who l on while Samson performed.
19:17 When the old man l up and saw the wayfarer in
20:40 the Benjaminites l behind them—
1Sa 6:13 When they l up and saw the ark,
16: 6 When they came, he l on Eliab and thought,
17:42 When the Philistine l and saw David,
24: 8 When Saul l behind him,
2Sa 1: 7 he l behind him, he saw me, and called to me.
2:20 Then Abner l back and said, "Is it you, Asahel?"
6:16 Michal daughter of Saul l out of the window,
13:34 When the young man who kept watch l up,
18:24 and when he l up, he saw a man running alone.
22:42 They l, but there was no one to save them;
24:20 When Araunah l down, he saw the king
1Ki 3:21 but when I l at him closely in the morning,
18:43 He went up and l, and said, "There is nothing."
19: 6 He l, and there at his head was a cake baked
2Ki 9:30 and adorned her head, and l out of the window.
9:32 He l up to the window and said,
9:32 Two or three eunuchs l out at him.
11:14 when she l, there was the king standing by
23:16 he turned and l up at the tomb of the man
1Ch 15:29 Michal daughter of Saul l out of the window,
21:16 David l up and saw the angel of
21:21 David came to Ornan, Ornan l and saw David;
2Ch 20:24 they l toward the multitude;
23:13 and when she l, there was the king standing
26:20 chief priest Azariah, and all the priests, l at him,
Ezr 2:62 These l for their entries in
Ne 4:14 After I l these things over,
Job 30:26 But when I l for good, evil came;
31:26 if I have l at the sun when it shone,
36:25 All people have l on it;
Ps 54: 7 and my eye has l in triumph on my enemies.
63: 2 So I have l upon you in the sanctuary,
69:20 I l for pity, but there was none;
102:19 that he l down from his holy height,
102:19 from heaven the LORD l at the earth,
114: 3 The sea l and fled; Jordan turned back.
Pr 7: 6 of my house I l out through my lattice,
24:32 I l and received instruction.
Isa 22: 8 On that day you l to the weapons of the House of
63: 5 I l, but there was no helper;
Jer 4:23 I l on the earth, and lo, it was waste and void;
4:24 I l on the mountains, and lo, they were quaking,
4:25 I l, and lo, there was no one at all,
4:26 I l, and lo, the fruitful land was a desert,
7:24 and l backward rather than forward.
31:26 Thereupon I awoke and l,
La 1: 7 the foe l on mocking over her downfall.
Eze 1: 4 As I l, a stormy wind came out of the north:
1:13 of the living creatures there was something that l
1:15 As I l at the living creatures,
1:27 something that l like fire enclosed all around;
1:27 from what l like the loins I saw something that l like fire,
2: 9 I l, and a hand was stretched out to me,
8: 2 I l, and there was a figure that l like a human being;
8: 7 I l, and there was a hole in the wall.
8:10 So I went in and l;
10: 1 Then I l, and above the dome that was over
10: 2 He went in as I l on.
10: 9 I l, and there were four wheels beside
10:10 And as for their appearance, the four l alike,
16: 8 I passed by you again and l on you;
37: 8 I l, and there were sinews on them,
44: 4 to the front of the temple; and I l,
Da 2:13 and they l for Daniel and his companions,
2:34 As you l on, a stone was cut out,
7: 5 a second one, that l like a bear.
7:21 As I l, this horn made war with the holy ones
8: 3 I l up and saw a ram standing beside the river.
10: 5 I l up and saw a man clothed in linen,
12: 5 Then I, Daniel, l, and two others appeared,
Hab 3: 6 he l and made the nations tremble.
Hag 1: 9 You have l for much, and, lo, it came to little;
Zec 1:18 And I l up and saw four horns.
2: 1 I l up and saw a man with a measuring line
5: 1 Again I l up and saw a flying scroll.
5: 9 Then I l up and saw two women coming forward.
6: 1 And again I l up and saw four chariots coming out
Mt 14:19 and the two fish, he l up to heaven, and blessed
17: 8 when they l up, they saw no one except Jesus
19:26 But Jesus l at them and said,
Mk 3: 5 He l around at them with anger;
5:32 He l all around to see who had done it.
6:41 he l up to heaven, and blessed and broke
8:24 And the man l up and said, "I can see people,
8:25 and he l intently and his sight was restored,
9: 8 Suddenly when they l around,
10:23 Then Jesus l around and said to his disciples,
10:27 Jesus l at them and said,
11:11 and when he had l around at everything,
16: 4 When they l up, they saw that the stone,
Lk 1:25 for me when he l favorably on me and took away
1:48 for he has l with favor on the lowliness
1:68 for he has l favorably on his people
6:20 Then he l up at his disciples and said:
7:16 and "God has l favorably on his people!"
9:16 he l up to heaven, and blessed and broke them,
16:23 he l up and saw Abraham far away with Lazarus
Lk 18:24 Jesus l at him and said,
19: 5 Jesus came to the place, he l up and said to him,
20:17 But he l at them and said,
21: 1 He l up and saw rich people putting their gifts
22:61 The Lord turned and l at Peter.
Jn 1:42 who l at him and said,
6: 5 When he l up and saw a large crowd coming
11:41 And Jesus l upward and said, "Father,
13:22 The disciples l at one another,
17: 1 he l up to heaven and said, "Father,
Ac 3: 4 Peter l intently at him, as did John, and said,
6:15 And all who sat in the council l intently at him,
11: 6 As I l at it closely I saw four-footed animals,
13: 9 as Paul, filled with the Holy Spirit, l intently
15:14 Simeon has related how God first l favorably on
17:23 For as I went through the city and l carefully at
21: 4 We l up the disciples and stayed there
Heb 11:10 For he l forward to the city that has foundations,
1Jn 1: 1 what we have l at and touched with our hands,
Rev 4: 1 this I l, and there in heaven a door stood open!
5:11 Then I l, and I heard the voice
6: 2 I l, and there was a white horse!
6: 5 I l, and there was a black horse!
6: 8 I l and there was a pale green horse!
6:12 When he opened the sixth seal, I l,
7: 9 After this I l, and there was a great multitude
8:13 Then I l, and I heard an eagle crying with
9: 7 On their heads were what l like crowns of gold;
14: 1 Then I l, and there was the Lamb,
14:14 Then I l, and there was a white cloud,
15: 5 After this I l, and the temple of the tent
Tob 1:18 Sennacherib l for them he could not find them.
AdE 15: 5 and she l happy, as if beloved,
15: 7 flushed with splendor, he l at her in fierce anger.
Sir 16:29 Then the Lord l upon the earth,
30: 5 whom in his life he l upon with joy and at death,
51: 7 I l for human assistance, and there was none.
Sus 1:35 Through her tears she l up toward Heaven,
Bel 1:18 the king l at the table,
1:40 he came to the den he l in, and there sat Daniel!
1Mc 4: 5 so he l for them in the hills, because he said,
4:12 When the foreigners l up and saw them coming
5:30 At dawn they l out and saw a large company,
9:39 They l out and saw a tumultuous procession with
2Mc 3:17 to those who l at him the pain lodged in his heart.
7: 4 while the rest of the brothers and the mother l on.
7:16 But he l at the king, and said,
1Es 4:33 Then the king and the nobles l at one another;
2Es 4:48 So I stood and l, and lo,
4:48 and when the flame had gone by I l, and lo,
9:38 When I said these things in my heart, I l around,
9:45 and l upon my low estate,
10:27 When I l up, the woman was no longer visible
11:10 I l again and saw that the voice did not come
11:22 And after this I l and saw that the twelve wings
11:33 After this I l again and saw the head in
11:35 while I l, I saw the head on the right side devour
11:37 When I l, I saw what seemed to be a lion roused
11:44 The Most High has l at his times;
12: 1 the lion was saying these words to the eagle, I l
12: 3 When I l again, they were already vanishing.
13: 5 After this I l and saw that
13: 6 And I l and saw that he carved out for himself
13: 8 After this I l and saw
4Mc 15:18 when the second in torments l at you piteously
15:19 nor did you weep when you l at the eyes

LOOKING‡ (71) [LOOK]

Ge 24:63 and l up, he saw camels coming.
37:25 and l up they saw a caravan
42: 1 "Why do you keep l at one another?
Dt 28:32 you will strain your eyes l for them all day but
Ps 119:37 Turn my eyes from l at vanities;
Pr 1:17 For in vain is the net baited while the bird is l on;
SS 2: 9 gazing in at the windows, l through the lattice.
Isa 6: 9 keep l, but do not understand.'
33:15 of bloodshed and shut their eyes from l on evil,
38:14 My eyes are weary with l upward.
Eze 23:15 all of them l like officers
Da 2:31 "You were l, O king, and lo!
4:13 I continued l, in the visions of my head as I lay
8: 2 In the vision I was l and saw myself in Susa
Mt 12:43 through waterless regions l for a resting place,
26:59 and the whole council were l for false testimony
27:55 also there, l on from a distance;
28: 5 that you are l for Jesus who was crucified.
Mk 3:34 And l at those who sat around him, he said,
7:34 Then l up to heaven, he sighed and said to him,
8:33 But turning and l at his disciples,
10:21 Jesus, l at him, loved him and said,
11:18 they kept l for a way to kill him;
14: 1 The chief priests and the scribes were l for a way
14:55 the chief priests and the whole council were l
15:40 There were also women l on from a distance;
16: 6 you are l for Jesus of Nazareth,
Lk 2:25 l forward to the consolation of Israel,
2:38 and to speak about the child to all who were l for
4:42 And the crowds were l for him;
6:10 After l around at all of them, he said to him,
8:10 so that 'l they may not perceive,
11:24 through waterless regions l for a resting place,
13: 6 and he came l for fruit on it and found none.
13: 7 three years I have come l for fruit on this fig tree,
19:47 leaders of the people kept l for a way to kill him;
22: 2 the scribes were l for a way to put Jesus to death,
24:12 and l in, he saw the linen cloths by themselves;

Lk 24:17 They stood still, l sad.
Jn 1:38 he said to them, "What are you l for?"
6:24 into the boats and went to Capernaum l for Jesus.
6:26 you are l for me, not because you saw signs,
7: 1 to go about in Judea because the Jews were l for
7:11 Jews were l for him at the festival and saying,
7:19 Why are you l for an opportunity to kill me?"
11:56 They were l for Jesus
18: 4 and asked them, "Whom are you l for?"
18: 7 Again he asked them, "Whom are you l for?"
18: 8 So if you are l for me, let these men go."
20:15 Whom are you l for?"
Ac 1:11 why do you stand l up toward heaven?
10:21 "I am the one you are l for;
14: 9 l at him intently and seeing that he had faith to
23: 1 While Paul was l intently at the council he said,
Heb 11:26 for he was l ahead to the reward.
12: 2 l to Jesus the pioneer and perfecter of our faith,
13:14 but we are l for the city that is to come.
1Pe 5: 8 l for someone to devour.
Tob 11: 5 Meanwhile Anna sat l intently down the road
Sir 34: 3 the likeness of a face l at itself.
41:20 before those who greet you; of l at a prostitute,
Sus 1: 9 and turned away their eyes from l to Heaven
2Mc 12:45 But if he was l to the splendid reward that is laid
15:20 all were now l forward to the coming issue,
15:34 And they all, l to heaven,
2Es 11:20 I kept l, and in due time the wings that followed
11:24 As I kept l I saw that two little wings separated
11:26 As I kept l, one was set up,
13: 3 As I kept l the wind made something like
4Mc 13:13 of them and all of them together l at one another,
17:10 l to God and enduring torture even to death."

LOOKINGGLASSES (KJV) See MIRRORS

LOOKOUT (1) [LOOK]
Isa 21: 6 "Go, post a l, let him announce what he sees.

LOOKOUTS (1) [LOOK]
1Sa 14:16 Saul's l in Gibeah of Benjamin were watching as

LOOKS (27) [LOOK]
Dt 11:12 a land that the LORD your God l after.
1Sa 13:18 toward the mountain that l down upon the valley
16: 7 but the LORD l on the heart."
2Ki 9:20 It l like the driving of Jehu son of Nimshi;
Job 28:24 For he l to the ends of the earth,
Ps 14: 2 The LORD l down from heaven on humankind
33:13 The LORD l down from heaven;
53: 2 God l down from heaven on humankind to see
104:32 who l on the earth and it trembles,
113: 6 who l far down on the heavens and the earth?
Pr 17:24 The discerning person l to wisdom,
25:23 and a backbiting tongue, angry l.
31:27 She l well to the ways of her household,
SS 6:10 "Who is this that l forth like the dawn,
La 3:50 until the LORD from heaven l down and sees.
Eze 2: 6 and do not be dismayed at their l,
3: 9 do not fear them or be dismayed at their l,
Mt 5:28 But I say to you that everyone who l at a woman
Lk 9:62 to the plow and l back is fit for the kingdom
Rev 4: 3 the one seated there l like jasper and carnelian,
4: 3 the throne is a rainbow that l like an emerald.
Jdt 11:21 of the earth to the other l so beautiful or speaks
Sir 11: 2 Do not praise individuals for their good l,
16:19 the earth quiver and quake when he l upon them.
20:14 for he l for recompense sevenfold.
40:29 When one l to the table of another,
42:16 The sun l down on everything with its light,

LOOM (3) [LOOMS]
Jdg 16:14 and pulled away the pin, the l, and the web.
Isa 19: 9 and the carders and those at the l will grow pale.
38:12 he cuts me off from the l;

LOOMS (1) [LOOM]
Jer 6: 1 for evil l out of the north, and great destruction.

LOOPS (14)
Ex 26: 4 You shall make l of blue on the edge of
26: 4 and likewise you shall make l on the edge of
26: 5 You shall make fifty l on the one curtain,
26: 5 and you shall make fifty l on the edge of
26: 5 the l shall be opposite one another.
26:10 You shall make fifty l on the edge of the curtain
26:10 and fifty l on the edge of the curtain
26:11 and put the clasps into the l,
36:11 He made l of blue on the edge of
36:12 fifty l on the one curtain, and he made fifty l on
36:12 the l were opposite one another.
36:17 He made fifty l on the edge of
36:17 and fifty l on the edge of

LOOSE (30) [LOOSED, LOOSENED, LOOSES]
Ge 27:40 but when you break l, you shall break his yoke
49:21 Naphtali is a doe let l that bears lovely fawns.
Ex 22: 5 lets livestock l to graze in someone else's field,
28:28 the breastpiece shall not come l from the ephod.
39:21 breastpiece should not come l from the ephod;
Lev 26:22 I will let l wild animals against you,
Job 6: 9 that he would let l his hand and cut me off!
37: 3 Under the whole heaven he lets it l,
38:31 or l the cords of Orion?
Ps 78:49 He let l on them his fierce anger, wrath,
Pr 2:16 You will be saved from the l woman,
5: 3 For the lips of a l woman drip honey,
7: 5 that they may keep you from the l woman,
22:14 The mouth of a l woman is a deep pit;
Isa 5:27 not a loincloth is l, not a sandal-thong broken;
7:25 where cattle are let l and where sheep tread.
20: 2 and l the sackcloth from your loins
33:23 Your rigging hangs l; it cannot hold the mast firm
52: 2 l the bonds from your neck,
58: 6 to l the bonds of injustice,
Jer 8:17 See, I am letting snakes l among you,
29:17 I am going to let l on them sword, famine,
Eze 5:16 I l against you my deadly arrows of famine,
5:16 which I will let l to destroy you,
7: 3 end is upon you, I will let l my anger upon you;
Mt 16:19 and whatever you l on earth will be loosed
18:18 whatever you l on earth will be loosed in heaven.
Sir 9: 3 Do not go near a l woman,
3Mc 6:27 L and untie their unjust bonds!
4Mc 12: 8 "Let me l, let me speak to the king and

LOOSED‡ (5) [LOOSE]
Job 30:11 God has l my bowstring and humbled me,
39: 5 Who has l the bonds of the swift ass,
Ps 116:16 You have l my bonds.
Mt 16:19 whatever you loose on earth will be l in heaven."
18:18 whatever you loose on earth will be l in heaven.

LOOSENED (2) [LOOSE]
Ac 27:40 At the same time they l the ropes that tied
Sir 22:16 into a building is not l by an earthquake;

LOOSES (2) [LOOSE]
Job 12:18 He l the sash of kings,
12:21 and l the belt of the strong.

LOOT (1) [LOOTED]
Eze 26:12 will plunder your riches and l your merchandise;

LOOTED (2) [LOOT]
Ob 1:13 not have l his goods on the day of his calamity.
Zec 14: 2 be taken and the houses l and the women raped;

LOP (1)
Isa 10:33 will l the boughs with terrifying power;

*LORD‡ (2039) [*LORD'S, LORDED, LORDLY, LORDS]
A. THUS SAYS THE *LORD †GOD (134)
B. *LORD JESUS (103)
C. SAYS THE *LORD †GOD (93)
D. *LORD THE KING (63)
E. *LORD MY/HIS/OUR/THEIR/YOUR *GOD (47)
F. *LORD *GOD (44)
G. BLESS THE *LORD (37)
H. SAYS THE *LORD (32)
I. NAME OF THE *LORD (26)
J. WORD OF THE *LORD (25)
K. FEAR OF THE *LORD (24)
L. FEAR THE *LORD (23)
M. BEFORE THE *LORD (21)
N. *LORD †GOD OF HOSTS (16)
O. ANGEL OF THE *LORD (14)
P. HOUSE OF THE *LORD (14)
Q. *LORD ALMIGHTY (14)
R. SOVEREIGN *LORD (13)
S. *LORD OF HEAVEN (11)
T. THUS SAYS THE *LORD (11)
U. TEMPLE OF THE *LORD (10)
V. WAY OF THE *LORD (10)
W. DAY OF THE/OUR *LORD (7)
X. HAND OF THE *LORD (7)
Y. GLORY OF THE *LORD (6)
Z. SPIRIT OF THE *LORD (6)
VOICE OF THE *LORD (6) See VOICE
BLESSED BE THE *LORD (4) See BLESSED
LOVE THE *LORD (3) See LOVE

Ge 15: 2 But Abram said, "O L GOD,
15: 8 But he said, "O L GOD,
18: 3 He said, "My l, if I find favor with you,
18:27 "Let me take it upon myself to speak to the L,
18:30 he said, "Oh do not let the L be angry if I speak.
18:31 "Let me take it upon myself to speak to the L.
18:32 not let the L be angry if I speak just once more.
20: 4 he said, "L, will you destroy an innocent people?
23: 6 my l; you are a mighty prince among us.
23:11 my l, hear me; I give you the field,
23:15 "My l, listen to me; a piece of land
24:18 my l," she said, and quickly lowered her jar
27:29 Be l over your brothers, and may your mother's
27:37 "I have already made him your l,
31:35 not my l be angry that I cannot rise before you,
32: 4 "Thus you shall say to my l Esau:
32: 5 and I have sent to tell my l,
32:18 they are a present sent to my l Esau;
33: 8 Jacob answered, "To find favor with my l."
33:13 "My l knows that the children are frail and that
33:14 Let my l pass on ahead of his servant,
33:14 until I come to my l in Seir."
33:15 he said, "Why should my l be so kind to me?"
40: 1 and his baker offended their l the king of Egypt. D
42:10 They said to him, "No, my l;
42:30 the l of the land, spoke harshly to us,
42:33 Then the man, the l of the land, said to us,
43:20 my l, we came down the first time to buy food;
44: 5 Is it not from this that my l drinks?
44: 7 "Why does my l speak such words as these?
44:16 And Judah said, "What can we say to my l?
44:18 Then Judah stepped up to him and said, "O my l,
44:19 My l asked his servants, saying,
44:20 And we said to my l, 'We have a father,
44:22 to my l, 'The boy cannot leave his father,
44:24 servant my father we told him the words of my l.
44:33 please let your servant remain as a slave to my l
45: 8 and l of all his house and ruler over all the land
45: 9 God has made me l of all Egypt;
47:18 not hide from my l that our money is all spent;
47:18 in the sight of my l but our bodies and our lands.
47:25 may it please my l, we will be slaves
Ex 4:10 But Moses said to the LORD, "O my L,
4:13 But he said, "O my L, please send someone else."
23:17 all your males shall appear before the L GOD. M
32:22 "Do not let the anger of my l burn hot;
34: 9 in your sight, O L, I pray, let the L go with us.
Nu 11:28 one of his chosen men, said, "My l Moses,
12:11 Then Aaron said to Moses, "Oh, my l,
16:13 that you must also l it over us?
32:25 "Your servants will do as my l commands.
32:27 to do battle for the LORD, just as my l orders."
36: 2 "The LORD commanded my l to give the land
36: 2 and my l was commanded by the LORD to give
Dt 3:24 "O L GOD, you have only begun
9:26 to the LORD and said, "L GOD, do not destroy
10:17 LORD your God is God of gods and L of lords,
Jos 3:11 the L of all the earth is going to pass before you
3:13 the L of all the earth, rest in the waters of
5:14 "What do you command your servant, my l?"
7: 7 Joshua said, "Ah, L GOD!
7: 8 O L, what can I say,
Jdg 3:25 There was their l lying dead on the floor.
4:18 my l, turn aside to me; have no fear."
6:22 and Gideon said, "Help me, L GOD!
16:28 Samson called to the LORD and said, "L GOD,
Ru 2:13 "May I continue to find favor in your sight, my l,
1Sa 1:15 But Hannah answered, "No, my l,
1:26 And she said, "Oh, my l!
1:26 my l, I am the woman who was standing here
16:16 Let our l now command the servants who attend
22:12 He answered, "Here I am, my l."
24: 6 LORD forbid that I should do this thing to my l,
24: 8 the cave and called after Saul, "My l the king!" D
24:10 I said, 'I will not raise my hand against my l;
25:24 "Upon me alone, my l, be the guilt;
25:25 My l, do not take seriously this ill-natured fellow,
25:25 your servant, did not see the young men of my l,
25:26 Now then, my l, as the LORD lives,
25:26 and those who seek to do evil to my l be
25:27 that your servant has brought to my l be given to
25:27 be given to the young men who follow my l.
25:28 LORD will certainly make my l a sure house,
25:28 my l is fighting the battles of the LORD;
25:29 of my l shall be bound in the bundle of the living
25:30 When the LORD has done to my l according
25:31 my l shall have no cause of grief,
25:31 And when the LORD has dealt well with my l,
25:41 a slave to wash the feet of the servants of my l."
26:15 have you not kept watch over your l the king? D
26:15 of the people came in to destroy your l the king. D
26:16 because you have not kept watch over your l,
26:17 David said, "It is my voice, my l, O king."
26:18 he added, "Why does my l pursue his servant?
26:19 let my l the king hear the words of his servant. D
29: 4 how could this fellow reconcile himself to his l?
29: 8 and fight against the enemies of my l the king?" D
29:10 and the servants of your l who came with you,
2Sa 1:10 and I have brought them here to my l."
2: 5 because you showed this loyalty to Saul your l,
2: 7 for Saul your l is dead,
3:21 "Let me go and rally all Israel to my l the king, D
4: 8 the LORD has avenged my l the king this day D
7:18 "Who am I, O L GOD, and what is my house,
7:19 this was a small thing in your eyes, O L GOD;
7:19 be instruction for the people, O L GOD!
7:20 For you know your servant, O L GOD!
7:28 And now, O L GOD, you are God,
7:29 for you, O L GOD, have spoken,
9:11 to all that my l the king commands his servant, D
10: 3 princes of the Ammonites said to their l Hanun,
11: 9 of the king's house with all the servants of his l,
11:11 and my l Joab and the servants
11:11 and the servants of my l are camping in
11:13 to lie on his couch with the servants of his l,
13:32 "Let not my l suppose that they have killed all
13:33 do not let my l the king take it to heart, D
14: 9 my l the king, and on my father's house; D
14:12 let your servant speak a word to my l the king." D
14:15 Now I have come to say this to my l the king D
14:17 'The word of my l the king will set me at rest'; D
14:17 for my l the king is like the angel of God, D
14:18 The woman said, "Let my l the king speak." D
14:19 "As surely as you live, my l the king, D
14:19 or left from anything that my l the king has said. D
14:20 But my l has wisdom like the wisdom of
14:22 have found favor in your sight, my l the king, D
15:15 servants are ready to do whatever our l the king D
15:21 "As the LORD lives, and as my l the king lives, D

*LORD distinguishes the words translated "Lord" and "lord" from the proper name of God, *Yahweh,* indicated in the NRSV by "LORD" and indexed under the heading †LORD on pages 804-25.

2Sa 15:21 wherever my l the king may be, D
16: 4 let me find favor in your sight, my l the king." D
16: 9 "Why should this dead dog curse my l the king? D
18:28 who raised their hand against my l the king." D
18:31 Cushite said, "Good tidings for my l the king! D
18:32 "May the enemies of my l the king, D
19:19 "May my l not hold me guilty or remember
19:19 servant did wrong on the day my l the king left D
19:20 of Joseph to come down to meet my l the king." D
19:26 He answered, "My l, O king,
19:27 He has slandered your servant to my l the king. D
19:27 But my l the king is like the angel of God; D
19:28 to death before my l the king; D
19:30 since my l the king has arrived home safely." D
19:35 be an added burden to my l the king? D
19:37 let him go over with my l the king; D
24: 3 while the eyes of my l the king can still see it! D
24: 3 But why does my l the king want to do this?" D
24:21 "Why has my l the king come to his servant?" D
24:22 "Let my l the king take and offer D
1Ki 1: 2 "Let a young virgin be sought for my l the king, D
1: 2 so that my l the king may be warm." D
1:11 and our l David does not know it?
1:13 my l the king, swear to your servant, saying: D
1:17 "My l, you swore to your servant by
1:18 though you, my l the king, do not know it. D
1:20 But you, my l the king— D
1:20 who shall sit on the throne of my l the king D
1:21 when my l the king sleeps with his ancestors, D
1:24 Nathan said, "My l the king, have you said, D
1:27 this thing been brought about by my l the king D
1:27 on the throne of my l the king after him?" D
1:31 and said, "May my l King David live forever!"
1:33 "Take with you the servants of your l,
1:36 May the LORD, the God of my l the king, D
1:37 As the LORD has been with my l the king, D
1:37 the throne of my l King David."
1:43 for our l King David has made Solomon king;
1:47 to congratulate our l King David,
2:26 the ark of the L GOD before my father David,
2:38 my l the king has said, so will your servant do." D
3:10 It pleased the L that Solomon had asked this.
3:17 The one woman said, "Please, my l,
3:26 "Please, my l, give her the living boy;
8:53 you brought our ancestors out of Egypt, O L GOD."
18: 7 fell on his face, and said, "Is it you, my l Elijah?"
18: 8 Go, tell your l that Elijah is here."
18:10 there is no nation or kingdom to which my l has
18:11 now you say, 'Go, tell your l that Elijah is here.'
18:13 not been told my l what I did when Jezebel killed
18:14 now you say, 'Go, tell your l that Elijah is here';
20: 4 The king of Israel answered, "As you say, my l,
20: 9 messengers of Ben-hadad, "Tell my l the king: D
2Ki 2:19 "The location of this city is good, as my l sees;
4:16 She replied, "No, my l, O man of God;
4:28 Then she said, "Did I ask my l for a son?
5: 3 "If only my l were with the prophet who is
5: 4 in and told his l just what the girl from the land
6:12 one of his officers said, "No one, my l king.
6:26 a woman cried out to him, "Help, my l king!"
7: 6 For the L had caused the Aramean army to hear
8: 5 Gehazi said, "My l king, here is the woman,
8:12 Hazael asked, "Why does my l weep?"
19:23 By your messengers you have mocked the L,
1Ch 21: 3 Are they not, my l the king, D
21: 3 Why then should my l require this?
21:23 let my l the king do what seems good to him; D
2Ch 2:14 with your artisans, the artisans of my l,
2:15 barley, oil, and wine, of which my l has spoken,
13: 6 rose up and rebelled against his l;
32:16 His servants said still more against the L GOD
Ezr 10: 3 to the counsel of my l and of those who tremble
Ne 1:11 O L, let your ear be attentive to the prayer
3: 5 not put their shoulders to the work of their L.
10:29 the commandments of the LORD our L
Job 28:28 he said to humankind, 'Truly, the fear of the L, K
Ps 16: 2 I say to the LORD, "You are my L;
22:30 future generations will be told about the L,
35:22 O L, do not be far from me!
35:23 for my cause, my God and my L!
38: 9 O L, all my longing is known to you;
38:22 make haste to help me, O L, my salvation.
39: 7 "And now, O L, what do I wait for?
40:17 but the L takes thought for me.
44:23 Why do you sleep, O L?
45:11 Since he is your l, bow to him;
51:15 O L, open my lips, and my mouth will declare
54: 4 the L is the upholder of my life.
55: 9 Confuse, O L, confound their speech;
57: 9 I will give thanks to you, O L,
59:11 and bring them down, O L, our shield.
62:12 and steadfast love belongs to you, O L.
66:18 the L would not have listened.
68:11 The L gives the command;
68:17 the L came from Sinai into the holy place.
68:19 Blessed be the L, who daily bears us up;
68:20 and to GOD, the L, belongs escape from death.
68:22 The L said, "I will bring them back from Bashan,
68:32 of the earth; sing praises to the L,
69: 6 to shame because of me, O L GOD of hosts; N
71: 5 For you, O L, are my hope, my trust, O LORD,
71:16 the mighty deeds of the L GOD,
73:28 I have made the L GOD my refuge,
77: 2 In the day of my trouble I seek the L;
77: 7 "Will the L spurn forever,
78:65 Then the L awoke as from sleep,
79:12 the taunts with which they taunted you, O L!

Ps 86: 3 O L, for to you do I cry all day long.
86: 4 Gladden the soul of your servant, for to you, O L,
86: 5 For you, O L, are good and forgiving,
86: 8 There is none like you among the gods, O L,
86: 9 O L, and shall glorify your name.
86:12 I give thanks to you, O L my God, E
86:15 But you, O L, are a God merciful and gracious,
89:49 L, where is your steadfast love of old, which
89:50 Remember, O L, how your servant is taunted;
90: 1 L, you have been our dwelling place
90:17 Let the favor of the L our God be upon us, E
97: 5 before the L of all the earth. M
105:21 He made him l of his house,
109:21 But you, O LORD my L,
110: 1 The LORD says to my l,
110: 5 The L is at your right hand;
130: 2 L, hear my voice! Let your ears be attentive
130: 3 If you, O LORD, should mark iniquities, L,
130: 6 for the L more than those who watch for
135: 5 our L is above all gods.
136: 3 O give thanks to the L of lords,
140: 7 O LORD, my L, my strong deliverer,
141: 8 my eyes are turned toward you, O GOD, my L;
147: 5 Great is our L, and abundant in power;
Isa 3:15 says the L GOD of hosts. CN
3:17 the L will afflict with scabs the heads of
3:18 the L will take away the finery of the anklets,
4: 4 the L has washed away the filth of the daughters
6: 1 I saw the L sitting on a throne, high and lofty;
6: 8 Then I heard the voice of the L saying,
6:11 Then I said, "How long, O L?"
7: 7 therefore thus says the L GOD: A
7:14 Therefore the L himself will give you a sign.
7:20 On that day the L will shave with a razor hired
8: 7 the L is bringing up against it
9: 8 L sent a word against Jacob, and it fell on Israel;
9:17 the L did not have pity on their young people,
10:12 the L has finished all his work on Mount Zion
10:23 For the L GOD of hosts will make a full end, N
10:24 Therefore thus says the L GOD of hosts: AN
11:11 the L will extend his hand yet a second time
21: 6 For thus the L said to me:
21: 8 "Upon a watchtower I stand, O L,
21:16 For thus the L said to me:
22: 5 For the L GOD of hosts has a day of tumult N
22:12 that day the L GOD of hosts called to weeping N
22:14 says the L GOD of hosts. CN
22:15 Thus says the L GOD of hosts: AN
25: 8 L GOD will wipe away the tears from all faces,
28: 2 See, the L has one who is mighty and strong;
28:16 therefore thus says the L GOD, See, I am laying A
28:22 a decree of destruction from the L GOD of hosts N
29:13 The L said: Because these people draw near with
30:15 thus said the L GOD, the Holy One of Israel:
30:20 the L may give you the bread of adversity and
37:24 By your servants you have mocked the L,
38:14 O L, I am oppressed; be my security!
38:16 O L, by these things people live,
40:10 See, the L GOD comes with might,
48:16 And now the L GOD has sent me and his spirit.
49:14 LORD has forsaken me, my L has forgotten me."
49:22 Thus says the L GOD: I will soon lift up my A
50: 4 L GOD has given me the tongue of a teacher,
50: 5 The L GOD has opened my ear,
50: 7 The L GOD helps me;
50: 9 It is the L GOD who helps me;
52: 4 For thus says the L GOD: A
56: 8 Thus says the L GOD, who gathers the outcasts A
61: 1 The spirit of the L GOD is upon me, Z
61:11 the L GOD will cause righteousness and praise
65:13 Therefore thus says the L GOD: A
65:15 and the L GOD will put you to death;
Jer 1: 6 Then I said, "Ah, L GOD!
2:19 says the L GOD of hosts. CN
2:22 of your guilt is still before me, says the L GOD. C
4:10 Then I said, "Ah, L GOD,
7:20 Therefore thus says the L GOD: A
14:13 Then I said: "Ah, L GOD!
22:18 They shall not lament for him, saying, "Alas, l!"
32:17 Ah L GOD! It is you who made the heavens
32:25 Yet you, O L GOD, have said to me,
34: 5 for you and lament for you, saying, "Alas, l!"
37:20 Now please hear me, my l king:
38: 9 "My l king, these men have acted wickedly
44:26 saying, 'As the L GOD lives.'
46:10 That day is the day of the L GOD of hosts, NW
46:10 the L GOD of hosts holds a sacrifice in the land N
49: 5 says the L GOD of hosts, CN
50:25 the L GOD of hosts has a task to do in the land N
50:31 O arrogant one, says the L GOD of hosts; CN
La 1:14 the L handed me over to those whom I cannot
1:15 the L has trodden as in a wine press
2: 1 the L in his anger has humiliated daughter Zion!
2: 2 The L has destroyed without mercy all
2: 5 The L has become like an enemy;
2: 7 L has scorned his altar, disowned his sanctuary;
2:18 Cry aloud to the L!
2:19 like water before the presence of the L!
2:20 and prophet be killed in the sanctuary of the L?
3:28 to sit alone in silence when the L has imposed it,
3:31 For the L will not reject forever.
3:36 one's case is subverted—does the L not see it?
3:37 if the L has not ordained it?
3:58 You have taken up my cause, O L,
Eze 2: 4 "Thus says the L GOD." A
3:11 Say to them, "Thus says the L GOD"; A
3:27 "Thus says the L GOD"; A

Eze 4:14 Then I said, "Ah L GOD!
5: 5 Thus says the L GOD: This is Jerusalem; A
5: 7 Therefore thus says the L GOD: A
5: 8 therefore thus says the L GOD: A
5:11 Therefore, as I live, says the L GOD, surely, C
6: 3 hear the word of the L GOD! J
6: 3 Thus says the L GOD to the mountains A
6:11 Thus says the L GOD: Clap your hands A
7: 2 thus says the L GOD to the land of Israel: A
7: 5 Thus says the L GOD: Disaster after disaster! A
8: 1 the hand of the L GOD fell upon me there. X
9: 8 on my face and cried out, "Ah L GOD!
11: 7 Therefore thus says the L GOD: A
11: 8 the sword upon you, says the L GOD. C
11:13 cried with a loud voice, and said, "Ah L GOD!
11:16 Therefore say: Thus says the L GOD: A
11:17 Therefore say: Thus says the L GOD: A
11:21 upon their own heads, says the L GOD. C
12:10 Say to them, "Thus says the L GOD: A
12:19 Thus says the L GOD concerning the inhabitants A
12:23 Tell them therefore, "Thus says the L GOD: A
12:25 the word and fulfill it, says the L GOD. C
12:28 Therefore say to them, Thus says the L GOD: A
12:28 that I speak will be fulfilled, says the L GOD. C
13: 3 Thus says the L GOD, Alas for A
13: 8 Therefore thus says the L GOD: A
13: 8 I am against you, says the L GOD. C
13: 9 and you shall know that I am the L GOD.
13:13 Therefore thus says the L GOD: A
13:16 when there was no peace, says the L GOD. C
13:18 and say, Thus says the L GOD: A
13:20 Therefore thus says the L GOD: A
14: 4 and say to them, Thus says the L GOD: A
14: 6 say to the house of Israel, Thus says the L GOD: A
14:11 and I will be their God, says the L GOD. C
14:14 by their righteousness, says the L GOD. C
14:16 as I live, says the L GOD, C
14:18 as I live, says the L GOD, C
14:20 and Job were in it, as I live, says the L GOD, C
14:21 For thus says the L GOD: A
14:23 that I have done in it, says the L GOD. C
15: 6 Therefore thus says the L GOD: A
15: 8 they have acted faithlessly, says the L GOD. C
16: 3 Thus says the L GOD to Jerusalem: A
16: 8 says the L GOD, and you became mine. C
16:14 that I had bestowed on you, says the L GOD. C
16:19 and so it was, says the L GOD. C
16:23 to you! says the L GOD), C
16:30 How sick is your heart, says the L GOD, C
16:36 Thus says the L GOD, Because your lust was A
16:43 upon your head, says the L GOD. C
16:48 As I live, says the L GOD, C
16:59 Yes, thus says the L GOD: A
16:63 that you have done, says the L GOD. C
17: 3 Say: Thus says the L GOD: A
17: 9 Say: Thus says the L GOD: Will it prosper? A
17:16 As I live, says the L GOD, C
17:19 Therefore thus says the L GOD: A
17:22 Thus says the L GOD: I myself will take a sprig A
18: 3 As I live, says the L GOD, C
18: 9 he shall surely live, says the L GOD. C
18:23 in the death of the wicked, says the L GOD, C
18:25 Yet you say, "The way of the L is unfair." V
18:29 of Israel says, "The way of the L is unfair." V
18:30 you according to your ways, says the L GOD. C
18:32 in the death of anyone, says the L GOD. C
20: 3 Thus says the L GOD: Why are you coming? A
20: 3 As I live, says the L GOD, C
20: 5 to them: Thus says the L GOD: A
20:27 of Israel and say to them, Thus says the L GOD: A
20:30 say to the house of Israel, Thus says the L GOD: A
20:31 As I live, says the L GOD, C
20:33 As I live, says the L GOD, C
20:36 into judgment with you, says the L GOD. C
20:39 for you, O house of Israel, thus says the L GOD: A
20:40 the mountain height of Israel, says the L GOD, C
20:44 O house of Israel, says the L GOD. C
20:47 Thus says the L GOD, I will kindle a fire in you, A
20:49 Then I said, "Ah L GOD!
21: 7 and it will be fulfilled," says the L GOD. C
21: 9 and say: Thus says the L; T
21:13 not happen? says the L GOD. C
21:24 Therefore thus says the L GOD: A
21:26 thus says the L GOD: Remove the turban, A
21:28 Thus says the L GOD concerning the A
22: 3 You shall say, Thus says the L GOD: A city! A
22:12 and you have forgotten me, says the L GOD. C
22:19 Therefore thus says the L GOD: A
22:28 saying, "Thus says the L GOD," A
22:31 upon their heads, says the L GOD. C
23:22 Therefore, O Oholibah, thus says the L GOD: A
23:28 For thus says the L GOD: A
23:32 Thus says the L GOD: You shall drink your A
23:34 for I have spoken, says the L GOD. C
23:35 Therefore thus says the L GOD: A
23:46 For thus says the L GOD: A
23:49 and you shall know that I am the L GOD.
24: 3 and say to them, Thus says the L GOD: A
24: 6 Therefore thus says the L GOD: A
24: 9 thus says the L GOD: Woe to the bloody city! A
24:14 your doings I will judge you, says the L GOD. C
24:21 to the house of Israel, Thus says the L GOD: A
24:24 then you shall know that I am the L GOD.
25: 3 Hear the word of the L GOD: J
25: 3 Thus says the L GOD, Because you said, A
25: 6 For thus says the L GOD: A
25: 8 Thus says the L GOD: A

***LORD** distinguishes the words translated "Lord" and "lord" from the proper name of God, *Yahweh,* indicated in the NRSV by "LORD" and indexed under the heading †**LORD** on pages 804-25.

Eze 25:12 Thus says the L GOD: A
25:13 thus says the L GOD, I will stretch out my hand A
25:14 they shall know my vengeance, says the L GOD. C
25:15 Thus says the L GOD: A
25:16 therefore thus says the L GOD, A
26: 3 Therefore, thus says the L GOD: A
26: 5 I have spoken, says the L GOD. C
26: 7 For thus says the L GOD: A
26:14 for I the LORD have spoken, says the L GOD. C
26:15 Thus says the L GOD to Tyre: A
26:19 For thus says the L GOD: A
26:21 you will never be found again, says the L GOD. C
27: 3 on many coastlands, Thus says the L GOD: A
28: 2 say to the prince of Tyre, Thus says the L GOD: A
28: 6 Therefore thus says the L GOD: A
28:10 for I have spoken, says the L GOD. C
28:12 and say to him, Thus says the L GOD: A
28:22 and say, Thus says the L GOD: A
28:24 And they shall know that I am the L GOD.
28:25 Thus says the L GOD: A
29: 3 and say, Thus says the L GOD: A
29: 8 Therefore, thus says the L GOD: A
29:13 Further, thus says the L GOD: A
29:16 Then they shall know that I am the L GOD.
29:19 Therefore thus says the L GOD: A
29:20 because they worked for me, says the L GOD. C
30: 2 Thus says the L GOD: Wail, "Alas for the day!" A
30: 6 within it by the sword, says the L GOD. C
30:10 Thus says the L GOD: I will put an end to the A
30:13 Thus says the L GOD: I will destroy the idols A
30:22 Therefore thus says the L GOD: A
31:10 Therefore thus says the L GOD: A
31:15 Thus says the L GOD: A
31:18 and all his horde, says the L GOD. C
32: 3 Thus says the L GOD: A
32: 8 and put darkness on your land, says the L GOD. C
32:11 For thus says the L GOD: A
32:14 to run like oil, says the L GOD. C
32:16 they shall chant it, says the L GOD. C
32:31 killed by the sword, says the L GOD. C
32:32 Pharaoh and all his multitude, says the L GOD. C
33:11 Say to them, As I live, says the L GOD, C
33:17 your people say, "The way of the L is not just," V
33:20 Yet you say, "The way of the L is not just." V
33:25 Therefore say to them, Thus says the L GOD: A
33:27 Say this to them, Thus says the L GOD: A
34: 2 to the shepherds: Thus says the L GOD: A
34: 8 says the L GOD, because my sheep C
34:10 Thus says the L GOD, I am against the A
34:11 For thus says the L GOD: A
34:15 and I will make them lie down, says the L GOD. C
34:17 As for you, my flock, thus says the L GOD: A
34:20 Therefore, thus says the L GOD to them: A
34:30 are my people, says the L GOD. C
34:31 and I am your God, says the L GOD. C
35: 3 and say to it, Thus says the L GOD: A
35: 6 says the L GOD, I will prepare you for blood, C
35:11 as I live, says the L GOD, C
35:14 Thus says the L GOD: A
36: 2 Thus says the L GOD: A
36: 3 and say: Thus says the L GOD: A
36: 4 hear the word of the L GOD: J
36: 4 Thus says the L GOD to the mountains and A
36: 5 therefore thus says the L GOD: A
36: 6 Thus says the L GOD: A
36: 7 therefore thus says the L GOD: A
36:13 Thus says the L GOD: A
36:14 of children, says the L GOD; C
36:15 to stumble, says the L GOD. C
36:22 say to the house of Israel, Thus says the L GOD: A
36:23 that I am the LORD, says the L GOD, C
36:32 says the L GOD; let that be known to you. C
36:33 Thus says the L GOD: A
36:37 Thus says the L GOD: I will A
37: 3 I answered, "O L GOD, you know."
37: 5 Thus says the L GOD to these bones: A
37: 9 to the breath: Thus says the L GOD: A
37:12 and say to them, Thus says the L GOD: A
37:19 say to them, Thus says the L GOD: A
37:21 then say to them, Thus says the L GOD: A
38: 3 and say: Thus says the L GOD: A
38:10 Thus says the L GOD: A
38:14 to Gog: Thus says the L GOD: A
38:17 Thus says the L GOD: Are you he of whom A
38:18 says the L GOD, my wrath shall be aroused. C
38:21 in all my mountains, says the L GOD; C
39: 1 and say: Thus says the L GOD: A
39: 5 for I have spoken, says the L GOD. C
39: 8 It has happened, says the L GOD. C
39:10 those who plundered them, says the L GOD. C
39:13 the day that I show my glory, says the L GOD. C
39:17 As for you, mortal, thus says the L GOD: A
39:20 and all kinds of soldiers, says the L GOD. C
39:25 Therefore thus says the L GOD: A
39:29 upon the house of Israel, says the L GOD. C
43:18 Mortal, thus says the L GOD: A
43:19 says the L GOD, a bull for a sin offering. C
43:27 and I will accept you, says the L GOD. C
44: 6 to the house of Israel, Thus says the L GOD: A
44: 9 Thus says the L GOD: No foreigner, A
44:12 concerning them, says the L GOD, C
44:15 the fat and the blood, says the L GOD. C
44:27 he shall offer his sin offering, says the L GOD. C
45: 9 Thus says the L GOD: Enough, A
45: 9 of my people, says the L GOD. C
45:15 to make atonement for them, says the L GOD. C
45:18 Thus says the L GOD: In the first month, A

Eze 46: 1 Thus says the L GOD: The gate of the A
46:16 Thus says the L GOD: If the prince A
47:13 Thus says the L GOD: These are the boundaries A
47:23 assign them their inheritance, says the L GOD. C
48:29 and these are their portions, says the L GOD. C
Da 1: 2 L let King Jehoiakim of Judah fall into his power,
1:10 "I am afraid of my l the king; D
2:47 your God is God of gods and L of kings and
4:19 Belteshazzar answered, "My l,
4:24 Most High that has come upon my l the king: D
5:23 have exalted yourself against the L of heaven! S
9: 3 Then I turned to the L God, F
9: 4 saying, "Ah, L, great and awesome God,
9: 7 "Righteousness is on your side, O L,
9: 9 To the L our God belong mercy and forgiveness, E
9:15 "And now, O L our God, E
9:16 O L, in view of all your righteous acts,
9:17 and for your own sake, L,
9:19 O L, hear; O L, forgive; O L, listen and act
10:16 and said to the one who stood before me, "My l,
10:17 How can my lord's servant talk with my l?
10:19 "Let my l speak, for you have strengthened me."
12: 8 so I said, "My l, what shall be the outcome
Hos 12:14 so his L will bring his crimes down on him
Am 1: 8 of the Philistines shall perish, says the L GOD. C
3: 7 Surely the L GOD does nothing,
3: 8 The L GOD has spoken; who can but prophesy?
3:11 Therefore thus says the L GOD: A
3:13 says the L GOD, the God of hosts: C
4: 2 The L GOD has sworn by his holiness:
4: 5 O people of Israel! says the L GOD. C
5: 3 For thus says the L GOD: A
5:16 thus says the LORD, the God of hosts, the L:
6: 8 The L GOD has sworn by himself (says the LORD,
7: 1 This is what the L GOD showed me:
7: 2 I said, "O L GOD, forgive, I beg you!
7: 4 This is what the L GOD showed me:
7: 4 the L GOD was calling for a shower of fire,
7: 5 Then I said, "O L GOD, cease, I beg you!
7: 6 "This also shall not be," said the L GOD.
7: 7 the L was standing beside a wall built with
7: 8 Then the L said, "See, I am setting a plumb line
8: 1 This is what the L GOD showed me—
8: 3 in that day," says the L GOD; C
8: 9 On that day, says the L GOD, C
8:11 The time is surely coming, says the L GOD, C
9: 5 The L, GOD of hosts, he who touches the earth N
9: 8 eyes of the L GOD are upon the sinful kingdom,
Ob 1: 1 Thus says the L GOD concerning Edom: A
Mic 1: 2 and let the L GOD be a witness against you,
1: 2 the L from his holy temple.
4:13 their wealth to the L of the whole earth.
Hab 3:19 GOD, the L, is my strength;
Zep 1: 7 Be silent before the L GOD! M
Zec 1: 9 Then I said, "What are these, my l?"
4: 4 with me, "What are these, my l?"
4: 5 I said, "No, my l."
4:13 I said, "No, my l."
4:14 the two anointed ones who stand by the L of
6: 4 with me, "What are these, my l?"
9: 4 the L will strip it of its possessions
9:14 the L GOD will sound the trumpet
Mal 1:14 and yet sacrifices to the L what is blemished;
3: 1 and the L whom you seek will suddenly come
Mt 1:20 an angel of the L appeared to him in a dream O
1:22 to fulfill what had been spoken by the L through
1:24 he did as the angel of the L commanded him; O
2:13 an angel of the L appeared to Joseph in a dream O
2:15 This was to fulfill what had been spoken by the L
2:19 an angel of the L suddenly appeared in a dream O
3: 3 'Prepare the way of the L, V
4: 7 'Do not put the L your God to the test.' " E
4:10 for it is written, 'Worship the L your God, E
5:33 but carry out the vows you have made to the L.'
7:21 "Not everyone who says to me, 'L, L,'
7:22 On that day many will say to me, 'L, L,
8: 2 "L, if you choose, you can make me clean."
8: 6 "L, my servant is lying at home paralyzed,
8: 8 The centurion answered, "L,
8:21 Another of his disciples said to him, "L,
8:25 they went and woke him up, saying, "L, save us!
9:28 They said to him, "Yes, L."
9:38 the L of the harvest to send out laborers
11:25 "I thank you, Father, L of heaven and earth, S
12: 8 For the Son of Man is l of the sabbath."
14:28 Peter answered him, "L, if it is you,
14:30 and beginning to sink, he cried out, "L, save me!"
15:22 "Have mercy on me, L, Son of David;
15:25 But she came and knelt before him, saying, "L,
15:27 L, yet even the dogs eat the crumbs that fall
16:22 saying, "God forbid it, L!
17: 4 Then Peter said to Jesus, "L,
17:15 "L, have mercy on my son,
18:21 Then Peter came and said to him, "L,
18:25 as he could not pay, his l ordered him to be sold,
18:27 the l of that slave released him and forgave him
18:31 and reported to their l all that had taken place.
18:32 Then his l summoned him and said to him,
18:34 And in anger his l handed him over to be tortured
20:25 "You know that the rulers of the Gentiles l it
20:30 "L, have mercy on us, Son of David!"
20:31 "Have mercy on us, L, Son of David!"
20:33 They said to him, "L, let our eyes be opened."
21: 3 just say this, 'The L needs them.'
21: 9 the one who comes in the name of the L! I
22:37 love the L your God with all your heart, E
22:43 is it then that David by the Spirit calls him L,

Mt 22:44 'The L said to my L, "Sit at my right hand,
22:45 David thus calls him L, how can he be his son?"
23:39 the one who comes in the name of the L.' " I
24:42 you do not know on what day your L is coming.
25:11 saying, 'L, l, open to us.'
25:37 Then the righteous will answer him, 'L,
25:44 Then they also will answer, 'L,
26:22 to say to him one after another, "Surely not I, L?"
27:10 as the L commanded me."
28: 2 for an angel of the L, descending from heaven, O
Mk 1: 3 'Prepare the way of the L, V
2:28 so the Son of Man is l even of the sabbath."
5:19 and tell them how much the L has done for you,
10:42 as their rulers l it over them,
11: 3 just say this, 'The L needs it
11: 9 the one who comes in the name of the L! I
12:29 the L our God, the Lord is one; E
12:29 the Lord our God, the L is one;
12:30 shall love the L your God with all your heart, E
12:36 'The L said to my L, "Sit at my right hand,
12:37 David himself calls him L;
13:20 And if the L had not cut short those days,
16:19 ⟦then the L Jesus, after he had spoken to them,⟧ B
16:20 ⟦while the L worked with them and confirmed⟧
Lk 1: 6 the commandments and regulations of the L.
1: 9 to enter the sanctuary of the L and offer incense.
1:11 Then there appeared to him an angel of the L, O
1:15 for he will be great in the sight of the L.
1:16 of the people of Israel to the L their God. E
1:17 to make ready a people prepared for the L."
1:25 the L has done for me when he looked favorably
1:28 The L is with you."
1:32 and the L God will give to him the throne F
1:38 Mary said, "Here am I, the servant of the L;
1:43 that the mother of my L comes to me?
1:45 a fulfillment of what was spoken to her by the L."
1:46 And Mary said, "My soul magnifies the L,
1:58 that the L had shown his great mercy to her,
1:66 For, indeed, the hand of the L was with him. X
1:68 "Blessed be the L God of Israel, F
1:76 you will go before the L to prepare his ways, M
2: 9 Then an angel of the L stood before them, O
2: 9 and the glory of the L shone around them, Y
2:11 a Savior, who is the Messiah, the L.
2:15 which the L has made known to us."
2:22 up to Jerusalem to present him to the L
2:23 (as it is written in the law of the L,
2:23 be designated as holy to the L"),
2:24 according to what is stated in the law of the L,
2:39 by the law of the L,
3: 4 'Prepare the way of the L, V
4: 8 'Worship the L your God, and serve only him.' " E
4:12 'Do not put the L your God to the test.' " E
4:18 "The Spirit of the L is upon me, Z
5: 8 "Go away from me, L, for I am a sinful man!"
5:12 "L, if you choose, you can make me clean."
5:17 and the power of the L was with him to heal.
6: 5 "The Son of Man is l of the sabbath."
6:46 "Why do you call me 'L, L,'
7: 6 the centurion sent friends to say to him, "L,
7:13 the L saw her, he had compassion for her and said
7:19 and sent them to the L to ask,
9:54 his disciples James and John saw it, they said, "L,
9:59 he said, "L, first let me go and bury my father."
9:61 Another said, "I will follow you, L;
10: 1 the L appointed seventy others and sent them on
10: 2 the L of the harvest to send out laborers
10:17 The seventy returned with joy, saying, "L,
10:21 "I thank you, Father, L of heaven and earth, S
10:27 love the L your God with all your heart, E
10:40 so she came to him and asked, "L,
10:41 But the L answered her, "Martha, Martha,
11: 1 "L, teach us to pray, as John taught his disciples."
11:39 Then the L said to him,
12:41 "L, are you telling this parable for us or
12:42 And the L said, "Who then is the faithful
13:15 the L answered him and said, "You hypocrites!
13:23 Someone asked him, "L,
13:25 'L, open to us,' then in reply he will say to you,
13:35 the one who comes in the name of the L.' " I
17: 5 The apostles said to the L, "Increase our faith!"
17: 6 The L replied, "If you had faith the size of
17:37 Then they asked him, "Where, L?"
18: 6 And the L said, "Listen to what the unjust judge says.
18:41 He said, "L, let me see again."
19: 8 Zacchaeus stood there and said to the L, "Look,
19: 8 half of my possessions, L, I will give to the poor;
19:16 The first came forward and said, 'L,
19:18 Then the second came, saying, 'L,
19:20 the other came, saying, 'L, here is your pound.
19:25 (And they said to him, 'L, he has ten pounds!')
19:31 just say this, 'The L needs it.' "
19:34 They said, "The L needs it."
19:38 the king who comes in the name of the L! I
20:37 where he speaks of the L as the God of Abraham,
20:42 'The L said to my L, "Sit at my right hand,
20:44 David thus calls him L;
22:25 "The kings of the Gentiles l it over them;
22:33 to him, "L, I am ready to go with you to prison
22:38 They said, "L, look, here are two swords."
22:49 they asked, "L, should we strike with the sword?"
22:61 The L turned and looked at Peter.
22:61 Then Peter remembered the word of the L, J
24:34 They were saying, "The L has risen indeed,
Jn 1:23 'Make straight the way of the L,' " V
6:23 the bread after the L had given thanks.
6:68 Simon Peter answered him, "L,

*LORD distinguishes the words translated "Lord" and "lord" from the proper name of God, *Yahweh*, indicated in the NRSV by "LORD" and indexed under the heading †LORD on pages 804-25.

Jn 9:38 He said, "**L**, I believe." And he worshiped him.
11: 2 the one who anointed the **L** with perfume
11: 3 So the sisters sent a message to Jesus, "**L**,
11:12 The disciples said to him, "**L**,
11:21 Martha said to Jesus, "**L**, if you had been here,
11:27 She said to him, "Yes, **L**,
11:32 she knelt at his feet and said to him, "**L**,
11:34 They said to him, "**L**, come and see."
11:39 the sister of the dead man, said to him, "**L**,
12:13 the one who comes in the name of the **L**— I
12:38 "**L**, who has believed our message,
12:38 to whom has the arm of the **L** been revealed?"
13: 6 He came to Simon Peter, who said to him, "**L**,
13: 9 Simon Peter said to him, "**L**,
13:13 You call me Teacher and **L**—
13:14 So if I, your **L** and Teacher,
13:25 while reclining next to Jesus, he asked him, "**L**,
13:36 Simon Peter said to him, "**L**,
13:37 "**L**, why can I not follow you now?
14: 5 "**L**, we do not know where you are going.
14: 8 Philip said to him, "**L**, show us the Father,
14:22 Judas (not Iscariot) said to him, "**L**,
20: 2 "They have taken the **L** out of the tomb,
20:13 She said to them, "They have taken away my **L**,
20:18 to the disciples, "I have seen the **L**";
20:20 Then the disciples rejoiced when they saw the **L**.
20:25 the other disciples told him, "We have seen the **L**."
20:28 Thomas answered him, "My **L** and my God!"
21: 7 whom Jesus loved said to Peter, "It is the **L**!"
21: 7 When Simon Peter heard that it was the **L**,
21:12 because they knew it was the **L**.
21:15 He said to him, "Yes, **L**;
21:16 He said to him, "Yes, **L**;
21:17 And he said to him, "**L**, you know everything;
21:20 "**L**, who is it that is going to betray you?"
21:21 When Peter saw him, he said to Jesus, "**L**,
Ac 1: 6 they had come together, they asked him, "**L**,
1:21 during all the time that the **L** Jesus went in B
1:24 Then they prayed and said, "**L**,
2:21 on the name of the **L** shall be saved.' I
2:25 'I saw the **L** always before me,
2:34 'The **L** said to my **L**, "Sit at my right hand,
2:36 with certainty that God has made him both **L**
2:39 everyone whom the **L** our God calls to him." E
2:47 And day by day the **L** added
3:20 from the presence of the **L**,
3:22 'The **L** your God will raise up for you E
4:24 and said, "Sovereign **L**, who made the heaven R
4:26 the rulers have gathered together against the **L**
4:29 And now, **L**, look at their threats,
4:33 to the resurrection of the **L** Jesus, B
5: 9 to put the Spirit of the **L** to the test? Z
5:14 more than ever believers were added to the **L**,
5:19 But during the night an angel of the **L** opened O
7:31 there came the voice of the **L**:
7:33 Then the **L** said to him,
7:49 says the **L**, or what is the place of my rest? H
7:59 they were stoning Stephen, he prayed, "**L** Jesus, B
7:60 he knelt down and cried out in a loud voice, "**L**,
8:16 baptized in the name of the **L** Jesus). BI
8:22 and pray to the **L** that, if possible,
8:24 Simon answered, "Pray for me to the **L**,
8:25 and spoken the word of the **L**, J
8:26 Then an angel of the **L** said to Philip, O
8:39 the Spirit of the **L** snatched Philip away; Z
9: 1 and murder against the disciples of the **L**,
9: 5 He asked, "Who are you, **L**?"
9:10 The **L** said to him in a vision, "Ananias."
9:10 He answered, "Here I am, **L**."
9:11 The **L** said to him, "Get up and go to
9:13 But Ananias answered, "**L**,
9:15 But the **L** said to him, "Go,
9:17 "Brother Saul, the **L** Jesus, B
9:27 for them how on the road he had seen the **L**,
9:28 speaking boldly in the name of the **L**. I
9:31 Living in the fear of the **L** and in the comfort K
9:35 of Lydda and Sharon saw him and turned to the **L**.
9:42 and many believed in the **L**.
10: 4 at him in terror and said, "What is it, **L**?"
10:14 But Peter said, "By no means, **L**;
10:33 to listen to all that the **L** has commanded you
10:36 by Jesus Christ—he is **L** of all.
11: 8 But I replied, 'By no means, **L**;
11:16 And I remembered the word of the **L**, J
11:17 when we believed in the **L** Jesus Christ, B
11:20 to the Hellenists also, proclaiming the **L** Jesus. B
11:21 The hand of the **L** was with them, X
11:21 great number became believers and turned to the **L**.
11:23 to the **L** with steadfast devotion;
11:24 And a great many people were brought to the **L**.
12: 7 an angel of the **L** appeared and a light shone in O
12:11 that the **L** has sent his angel and rescued me from
12:17 how the **L** had brought him out of the prison.
12:23 an angel of the **L** struck him down, O
13: 2 While they were worshiping the **L** and fasting,
13:10 the straight paths of the **L**?
13:11 the hand of the **L** is against you, X
13:12 for he was astonished at the teaching about the **L**.
13:44 whole city gathered to hear the word of the **L**. J
13:47 For so the **L** has commanded us, saying,
13:48 they were glad and praised the word of the **L**; J
13:49 the word of the **L** spread throughout the region. J
14: 3 speaking boldly for the **L**,
14:23 to the **L** in whom they had come to believe.
15:11 be saved through the grace of the **L** Jesus, B
15:17 so that all other peoples may seek the **L**—
15:17 Thus says the **L**, who has been making these T
Ac 15:26 for the sake of our **L** Jesus Christ. B
15:35 they taught and proclaimed the word of the **L**. J
15:36 where we proclaimed the word of the **L** and J
15:40 believers commending him to the grace of the **L**.
16:14 The **L** opened her heart to listen eagerly
16:15 "If you have judged me to be faithful to the **L**,
16:31 They answered, "Believe on the **L** Jesus, B
16:32 They spoke the word of the **L** to him J
17:24 he who is **L** of heaven and earth, S
18: 8 became a believer in the **L**,
18: 9 One night the **L** said to Paul in a vision,
18:25 He had been instructed in the Way of the **L**; V
19: 5 they were baptized in the name of the **L** Jesus. BI
19:10 both Jews and Greeks, heard the word of the **L**. J
19:13 name of the **L** Jesus over those who had evil BI
19:17 and the name of the **L** Jesus was praised. BI
19:20 the word of the **L** grew mightily and prevailed. J
20:19 serving the **L** with all humility and with tears,
20:21 toward God and faith toward our **L** Jesus. B
20:24 the ministry that I received from the **L** Jesus, B
20:35 remembering the words of the **L** Jesus, B
21:13 die in Jerusalem for the name of the **L** Jesus." BI
22: 8 I answered, 'Who are you, **L**?'
22:10 I asked, 'What am I to do, **L**?'
22:10 The **L** said to me, 'Get up and go to Damascus;
22:19 And I said, '**L**, they themselves know that
23:11 That night the **L** stood near him and said,
26:15 I asked, 'Who are you, **L**?'
26:15 'Who are you, Lord?' The **L** answered,
28:31 about the **L** Jesus Christ with all boldness B
Ro 1: 4 by resurrection from the dead, Jesus Christ our **L**,
1: 7 from God our Father and the **L** Jesus Christ. B
4: 8 the one against whom the **L** will not reckon sin."
4:24 to us who believe in him who raised Jesus our **L**
5: 1 with God through our **L** Jesus Christ, B
5:11 even boast in God through our **L** Jesus Christ, B
5:21 to eternal life through Jesus Christ our **L**.
6:23 of God is eternal life in Christ Jesus our **L**.
7:25 Thanks be to God through Jesus Christ our **L**!
8:39 from the love of God in Christ Jesus our **L**.
9:28 for the **L** will execute his sentence on
9:29 "If the **L** of hosts had not left survivors to us,
10: 9 if you confess with your lips that Jesus is **L**
10:12 the same **L** is **L** of all and is generous
10:13 "Everyone who calls on the name of the **L** shall I
10:16 Isaiah says, "**L**, who has believed our message?"
11: 3 "**L**, they have killed your prophets,
11:34 "For who has known the mind of the **L**?
12:11 Do not lag in zeal, be ardent in spirit, serve the **L**.
12:19 "Vengeance is mine, I will repay, says the **L**." H
13:14 Instead, put on the **L** Jesus Christ, B
14: 4 It is before their own **l** that they stand or fall.
14: 4 for the **L** is able to make them stand.
14: 6 observe it in honor of the **L**.
14: 6 Also those who eat, eat in honor of the **L**,
14: 6 abstain in honor of the **L** and give thanks to God.
14: 8 If we live, we live to the **L**, and if we die, we die
to the **L**;
14: 9 he might be **L** of both the dead and the living.
14:11 For it is written, "As I live, says the **L**, H
14:14 in the **L** Jesus that nothing is unclean in itself; B
15: 6 the God and Father of our **L** Jesus Christ. B
15:11 "Praise the **L**, all you Gentiles,
15:30 by our **L** Jesus Christ and by the love of B
16: 2 so that you may welcome her in the **L** as is fitting
16: 8 Greet Ampliatus, my beloved in the **L**.
16:11 in the **L** who belong to the family of Narcissus.
16:12 Greet those workers in the **L**,
16:12 who has worked hard in the **L**.
16:13 Greet Rufus, chosen in the **L**;
16:18 For such people do not serve our **L** Christ,
16:20 The grace of our **L** Jesus Christ be with you. B
16:22 the writer of this letter, greet you in the **L**.
1Co 1: 2 on the name of our **L** Jesus Christ, B
1: 2 our Lord Jesus Christ, both their **L** and ours:
1: 3 from God our Father and the **L** Jesus Christ. B
1: 7 for the revealing of our **L** Jesus Christ. B
1: 8 blameless on the day of our **L** Jesus Christ. BW
1: 9 into the fellowship of his Son, Jesus Christ our **L**.
1:10 by the name of our **L** Jesus Christ, B
1:31 "Let the one who boasts, boast in the **L**."
2: 8 they would not have crucified the **L** of glory.
2:16 "For who has known the mind of the **L** so as
3: 5 as the **L** assigned to each.
3:20 "The **L** knows the thoughts of the wise,
4: 4 It is the **L** who judges me.
4: 5 before the **L** comes, who will bring to light the M
4:17 who is my beloved and faithful child in the **L**,
4:19 But I will come to you soon, if the **L** wills,
5: 4 in the name of the **L** Jesus on the man who has BI
5: 4 spirit is present with the power of our **L** Jesus, B
5: 5 that his spirit may be saved in the day of the **L**. W
6:11 justified in the name of the **L** Jesus Christ and BI
6:13 body is meant not for fornication but for the **L**,
and the **L** for the body.
6:14 And God raised the **L** and will also raise us
6:17 But anyone united to the **L** becomes one spirit
7:10 the married I give this command—not I but the **L**
7:12 To the rest I say—I and not the **L**—
7:17 of you lead the life that the **L** has assigned,
7:22 called in the **L** as a slave is a freed person
belonging to the **L**,
7:25 concerning virgins, I have no command of the **L**,
7:32 about the affairs of the **L**, how to please the **L**;
7:34 the **L**, so that they may be holy in body and spirit;
7:35 and unhindered devotion to the **L**.
7:39 to marry anyone she wishes, only in the **L**.
1Co 8: 6 and for whom we exist, and one **L**, Jesus Christ, B
9: 1 Have I not seen Jesus our **L**?
9: 1 Are you not my work in the **L**?
9: 2 for you are the seal of my apostleship in the **L**.
9: 5 as do the other apostles and the brothers of the **L**
9:14 the **L** commanded that those who proclaim
10:21 drink the cup of the **L** and the cup of demons.
10:21 of the table of the **L** and the table of demons.
10:22 Or are we provoking the **L** to jealousy?
11:11 in the **L** woman is not independent of man
11:23 For I received from the **L** what I also handed on
11:23 that the **L** Jesus on the night B
11:27 the **L** in an unworthy manner will be answerable
for the body and blood of the **L**.
11:32 But when we are judged by the **L**,
12: 3 no one can say "Jesus is **L**" except by the Holy
12: 5 of services, but the same **L**;
14:21 even then they will not listen to me," says the **L**. H
14:37 to you is a command of the **L**.
15:31 a boast that I make in Christ Jesus our **L**.
15:57 the victory through our **L** Jesus Christ. B
15:58 always excelling in the work of the **L**,
15:58 you know that in the **L** your labor is not in vain.
16: 7 to spend some time with you, if the **L** permits.
16:10 for he is doing the work of the **L** just as I am;
16:19 greet you warmly in the **L**.
16:22 Let anyone be accursed who has no love for the **L**.
16:22 Our **L**, come!
16:23 The grace of the **L** Jesus be with you. B
2Co 1: 2 from God our Father and the **L** Jesus Christ. B
1: 3 be the God and Father of our **L** Jesus Christ, B
1:14 on the day of the **L** Jesus we are your boast BW
1:24 not mean to imply that we **l** it over your faith;
2:12 a door was opened for me in the **L**;
3:16 but when one turns to the **L**, the veil is removed.
3:17 Now the **L** is the Spirit,
3:17 and where the Spirit of the **L** is, Z
3:18 the glory of the **L** as though reflected in a mirror, Y
3:18 for this comes from the **L**, the Spirit.
4: 5 as **L** and ourselves as your slaves for Jesus' sake.
4:14 the one who raised the **L** Jesus will raise us also B
5: 6 at home in the body we are away from the **L**—
5: 8 be away from the body and at home with the **L**.
5:11 Therefore, knowing the fear of the **L**, K
6:17 says the **L**, and touch nothing unclean; H
6:18 my sons and daughters, says the **L** Almighty." HQ
8: 5 they gave themselves first to the **L** and,
8: 9 you know the generous act of our **L** Jesus Christ, B
8:19 for the glory of the **L** himself and to show Y
10: 8 which the **L** gave for building you up and not
10:17 "Let the one who boasts, boast in the **L**."
10:18 but those whom the **L** commends.
11:31 Father of the **L** Jesus (blessed be he forever!) B
12: 1 I will go on to visions and revelations of the **L**.
12: 8 Three times I appealed to the **L** about this,
13:10 the authority that the **L** has given me for building
13:13 The grace of the **L** Jesus Christ, the love of God, B
Gal 1: 3 from God our Father and the **L** Jesus Christ, B
5:10 I am confident about you in the **L** that you will
6:14 the cross of our **L** Jesus Christ, B
6:18 of our **L** Jesus Christ be with your spirit, B
Eph 1: 2 from God our Father and the **L** Jesus Christ. B
1: 3 be the God and Father of our **L** Jesus Christ, B
1:15 your faith in the **L** Jesus and your love toward B
1:17 I pray that the God of our **L** Jesus Christ, B
2:21 and grows into a holy temple in the **L**;
3:11 that he has carried out in Christ Jesus our **L**,
4: 1 I therefore, the prisoner in the **L**,
4: 5 one **L**, one faith, one baptism,
4:17 Now this I affirm and insist on in the **L**:
5: 8 but now in the **L** you are light.
5:10 Try to find out what is pleasing to the **L**.
5:17 but understand what the will of the **L** is.
5:19 and making melody to the **L** in your hearts,
5:20 everything in the name of our **L** Jesus Christ. B
5:22 be subject to your husbands as you are to the **L**.
6: 1 Children, obey your parents in the **L**,
6: 4 up in the discipline and instruction of the **L**.
6: 7 as to the **L** and not to men and women,
6: 8 we will receive the same again from the **L**,
6:10 in the **L** and in the strength of his power.
6:21 a dear brother and a faithful minister in the **L**.
6:23 from God the Father and the **L** Jesus Christ. B
6:24 an undying love for our **L** Jesus Christ. B
Php 1: 2 from God our Father and the **L** Jesus Christ. B
1:14 having been made confident in the **L**
2:11 that Jesus Christ is **L**, to the glory of God
2:19 in the **L** Jesus to send Timothy to you soon, B
2:24 and I trust in the **L** that I will also come soon.
2:29 Welcome him then in the **L** with all joy,
3: 1 Finally, my brothers and sisters, rejoice in the **L**.
3: 8 of knowing Christ Jesus my **L**.
3:20 we are expecting a Savior, the **L** Jesus Christ. B
4: 1 stand firm in the **L** in this way, my beloved.
4: 2 to be of the same mind in the **L**.
4: 4 Rejoice in the **L** always; again I will say, Rejoice.
4: 5 gentleness be known to everyone. The **L** is near.
4:10 I rejoice in the **L** greatly that now
4:23 grace of the **L** Jesus Christ be with your spirit. B
Col 1: 3 the Father of our **L** Jesus Christ, B
1:10 so that you may lead lives worthy of the **L**,
2: 6 you therefore have received Christ Jesus the **L**,
3:13 just as the **L** has forgiven you,
3:17 do everything in the name of the **L** Jesus, BI
3:18 be subject to your husbands, as is fitting in the **L**.
3:20 for this is your acceptable duty in the **L**.
3:22 but wholeheartedly, fearing the **L**.

***LORD** distinguishes the words translated "Lord" and "lord" from the proper name of God, *Yahweh*, indicated in the NRSV by "LORD" and indexed under the heading †**LORD** on pages 804-25.

Col 3:23 as done for the L and not for your masters,
3:24 since you know that from the L you will receive
3:24 as your reward; you serve the L Christ.
4: 7 a faithful minister, and a fellow servant in the L.
4:17 the task that you have received in the L."
1Th 1: 1 in God the Father and the L Jesus Christ: B
1: 3 and steadfastness of hope in our L Jesus Christ. B
1: 6 And you became imitators of us and of the L,
1: 8 the word of the L has sounded forth from you J
2:15 the L Jesus and the prophets, and drove us out; B
2:19 or joy or crown of boasting before our L Jesus B
3: 8 if you continue to stand firm in the L.
3:11 Father himself and our L Jesus direct our way B
3:12 And may the L make you increase and abound
3:13 at the coming of our L Jesus with all his saints. B
4: 1 we ask and urge you in the L Jesus that, B
4: 2 instructions we gave you through the L Jesus. B
4: 6 because the L is an avenger in all these things,
4:15 For this we declare to you by the word of the L, J
4:15 who are left until the coming of the L,
4:16 For the L himself, with a cry of command,
4:17 up in the clouds together with them to meet the L
4:17 and so we will be with the L forever.
5: 2 that the day of the L will come like a thief in W
5: 9 through our L Jesus Christ, B
5:12 have charge of you in the L and admonish you;
5:23 at the coming of our L Jesus Christ. B
5:27 I solemnly command you by the L that this letter
5:28 The grace of our L Jesus Christ be with you. B
2Th 1: 1 in God our Father and the L Jesus Christ: B
1: 2 from God our Father and the L Jesus Christ. B
1: 7 when the L Jesus is revealed from heaven B
1: 8 not obey the gospel of our L Jesus. B
1: 9 separated from the presence of the L and from
1:12 the name of our L Jesus may be glorified in you, B
1:12 to the grace of our God and the L Jesus Christ. B
2: 1 As to the coming of our L Jesus Christ B
2: 2 the effect that the day of the L is already here. W
2: 8 whom the L Jesus will destroy with the breath B
2:13 brothers and sisters beloved by the L,
2:14 you may obtain the glory of our L Jesus Christ. B
2:16 Now may our L Jesus Christ himself B
3: 1 so that the word of the L may spread rapidly J
3: 3 But the L is faithful; he will strengthen you
3: 4 And we have confidence in the L concerning you,
3: 5 the L direct your hearts to the love of God and to
3: 6 beloved, in the name of our L Jesus Christ, B
3:12 in the L Jesus Christ to do their work quietly B
3:16 the L of peace himself give you peace at all times
3:16 The L be with all of you.
3:18 grace of our L Jesus Christ be with all of you. B
1Ti 1: 2 from God the Father and Christ Jesus our L.
1:12 I am grateful to Christ Jesus our L,
1:14 and the grace of our L overflowed for me with
6: 3 with the sound words of our L Jesus Christ B
6:14 until the manifestation of our L Jesus Christ, B
6:15 the King of kings and L of lords.
2Ti 1: 2 from God the Father and Christ Jesus our L.
1: 8 the testimony about our L or of me his prisoner,
1:16 May the L grant mercy to the household
1:18 the L grant that he will find mercy from the L
2: 7 the L will give you understanding in all things.
2:19 "The L knows those who are his," and,
2:19 the name of the L turn away from wickedness." I
2:22 with those who call on the L from a pure heart.
3:11 Yet the L rescued me from all of them.
4: 8 which the L, the righteous judge,
4:14 the L will pay him back for his deeds.
4:17 But the L stood by me and gave me strength,
4:18 The L will rescue me from every evil attack
4:22 The L be with your spirit. Grace be with you.
Phm 1: 3 from God our Father and the L Jesus Christ. B
1: 5 the saints and your faith toward the L Jesus. B
1:16 both in the flesh and in the L.
1:20 let me have this benefit from you in the L!
1:25 grace of the L Jesus Christ be with your spirit. B
Heb 1:10 And, "In the beginning, L, you founded the earth,
2: 3 It was declared at first through the L,
7:14 For it is evident that our L was descended
7:21 "The L has sworn and will not change his mind,
8: 2 in the sanctuary and the true tent that the L,
8: 8 "The days are surely coming, says the L, H
8: 9 and so I had no concern for them, says the L. H
8:10 the house of Israel after those days, says the L: H
8:11 'Know the L,' for they shall all know me,
10:16 with them after those days, says the L: H
10:30 And again, "The L will judge his people."
12: 5 do not regard lightly the discipline of the L,
12: 6 for the L disciplines those whom he loves,
12:14 the holiness without which no one will see the L.
13: 6 "The L is my helper; I will not be afraid.
13:20 who brought back from the dead our L Jesus, B
Jas 1: 1 James, a servant of God and of the L Jesus B
1:7,8 must not expect to receive anything from the L.
1:12 that the L has promised to those who love him.
2: 1 believe in our glorious L Jesus Christ? B
3: 9 With it we bless the L and Father, G
4:10 Humble yourselves before the L, M
4:15 Instead you ought to say, "If the L wishes,
5: 4 of the harvesters have reached the ears of the L
5: 7 therefore, beloved, until the coming of the L.
5: 8 for the coming of the L is near.
5:10 the prophets who spoke in the name of the L. I
5:11 and you have seen the purpose of the L,
5:11 how the L is compassionate and merciful.
5:14 anointing them with oil in the name of the L. I
5:15 and the L will raise them up;
1Pe 1: 3 be the God and Father of our L Jesus Christ! B
1:25 but the word of the L endures forever." J
2: 3 if indeed you have tasted that the L is good.
3: 6 Thus Sarah obeyed Abraham and called him l.
3:12 For the eyes of the L are on the righteous,
3:12 the face of the L is against those who do evil."
3:15 but in your hearts sanctify Christ as L.
5: 3 Do not l it over those in your charge,
2Pe 1: 2 in the knowledge of God and of Jesus our L.
1: 8 in the knowledge of our L Jesus Christ. B
1:11 entry into the eternal kingdom of our L
1:14 indeed our L Jesus Christ has made clear to me. B
1:16 the power and coming of our L Jesus Christ, B
2: 9 the L knows how to rescue the godly from trial,
2:11 against them a slanderous judgment from the L.
2:20 the knowledge of our L and Savior Jesus Christ,
3: 2 of the L and Savior spoken through your apostles.
3: 8 that with the L one day is like a thousand years,
3: 9 The L is not slow about his promise,
3:10 But the day of the L will come like a thief, W
3:15 and regard the patience of our L as salvation.
3:18 and knowledge of our L and Savior Jesus Christ.
Jude 1: 4 and deny our only Master and L, Jesus Christ. B
1: 5 though you are fully informed, that the L,
1: 9 but said, "The L rebuke you!"
1:14 L is coming with ten thousands of his holy ones,
1:17 of the apostles of our L Jesus Christ; B
1:21 look forward to the mercy of our L Jesus Christ B
1:25 through Jesus Christ our L, be glory, majesty,
Rev 1: 8 the Alpha and the Omega," says the L God, HF
4: 8 the L God the Almighty, who was and is and F
4:11 our L and God, to receive glory and honor
6:10 "Sovereign L, holy and true, R
11: 4 lampstands that stand before the L of the earth. M
11: 8 where also their L was crucified.
11:15 the world has become the kingdom of our L and
11:17 L God Almighty, who are and who were, F
14:13 the dead who from now on die in the L."
15: 3 "Great and amazing are your deeds, L God F
15: 4 L, who will not fear and glorify your name?
16: 7 And I heard the altar respond, "Yes, O L God, F
17:14 for he is L of lords and King of kings,
18: 8 for mighty is the L God who judges her." F
19: 6 For the L our God the Almighty reigns. E
19:16 "King of kings and L of lords."
21:22 for its temple is the L God the Almighty and F
22: 5 for the L God will be their light, F
22: 6 "These words are trustworthy and true, for the L,
22:20 I am coming soon." Amen. Come, L Jesus! B
22:21 The grace of the L Jesus be with all the saints. B
Tob 3: 2 O L, and all your deeds are just;
3: 3 O L, remember me and look favorably upon me.
3: 6 O L, that I be released from this distress;
3: 6 and do not, O L, turn your face away from me.
3:10 but to pray the L that I may die and not listen
3:12 And now, L, I turn my face to you,
3:15 But if it is not pleasing to you, O L,
4: 5 "Revere the L all your days, my son,
4:19 At all times bless the L God, GF
4:19 but the L himself will give them good counsel;
4:21 in the sight of the L your God." E
5:20 life that is given to us by the L is enough for us."
6:18 the L of heaven that mercy and safety may S
7:11 and the L will act on behalf of you both."
7:11 May the L of heaven, my child, S
7:16 the L of heaven grant you joy in place S
8: 4 and implore our L that he grant us mercy
9: 6 May the L grant the blessing of heaven to you
10:11 L of heaven prosper you and your wife Sarah, S
10:12 the L of heaven bring you back safely, S
10:12 In the sight of the L I entrust my daughter to you;
10:13 praising the L of heaven and earth, King over all, S
10:13 by the L to honor you all the days of my life."
12:12 of your prayer before the glory of the L, Y
12:15 and enter before the glory of the L." Y
13: 4 because he is our L and he is our God;
13: 6 Bless the L of righteousness, G
13:10 Acknowledge the L, for he is good,
13:13 be gathered together and will praise the L of
13:15 My soul blesses the L, the great King!
14:15 and he blessed the L God forever and ever. F
Jdt 2: 5 the l of the whole earth:
2:14 So Holofernes left the presence of his l,
2:15 by divisions as his l had ordered him to do,
4: 2 and for the temple of the L their God. EU
4:11 and spread out their sackcloth before the L. M
4:13 The L heard their prayers and had regard
4:13 before the sanctuary of the L Almighty. Q
4:14 priests who stood before the L and ministered M
4:14 before the Lord and ministered to the L,
4:15 they cried out to the L with all their might to look
5: 5 "May my l please listen to a report from
5:20 "So now, my master and l,
5:21 then let my l pass them by;
5:21 for their L and God will defend them,
5:24 Therefore let us go ahead, L Holofernes,
6: 4 says King Nebuchadnezzar, l of the whole earth.
6:19 "O L God of heaven, see their arrogance, F
7: 9 my l, and your army will suffer no losses.
7:11 Therefore, my l, do not fight against them
7:19 The Israelites then cried out to the L their God, E
7:28 the L of our ancestors, who punishes us
7:29 they cried out to the L God with a loud voice. F
7:30 by that time the L our God will turn his mercy E
8:11 to our enemies unless the L turns and helps us
8:13 You are putting the L Almighty to the test, Q
8:14 No, my brothers, do not anger the L our God. E
Jdt 8:16 Do not try to bind the purposes of the L our God; E
8:23 but the L our God will turn it to dishonor. E
8:25 everything let us give thanks to the L our God, E
8:27 but the L scourges those who are close to him
8:31 so that the L may send us rain to fill our cisterns.
8:33 the L will deliver Israel by my hand.
8:35 "Go in peace, and may the L God go before you, F
9: 1 Judith cried out to the L with a loud voice,
9: 2 "O L God of my ancestor Simeon, F
9: 7 the L who crushes wars; the L is your name.
9:12 L of heaven and earth, Creator of the waters, S
10:15 by hurrying down to see our l.
11: 4 the servants of my l King Nebuchadnezzar."
11: 5 I will say nothing false to my l this night.
11: 6 and my l will not fail to achieve his purposes.
11:10 l and master, do not disregard what he said,
11:11 in order that my l may not be defeated
11:17 So, my l, I will remain with you;
11:22 on those who have despised my l.
12: 4 Judith replied, "As surely as you live, my l,
12: 4 with me before the L carries out M
12: 6 "Let my l now give orders to allow your servant
12: 8 she prayed the L God of Israel to direct her way F
12:13 "Let this pretty girl not hesitate to come to my l
12:14 Judith replied, "Who am I to refuse my l?
12:18 Judith said, "I will gladly drink, my l,
13: 4 said in her heart, "O L God of all might, F
13: 7 "Give me strength today, O L God of Israel!" F
13:15 L has struck him down by the hand of a woman.
13:16 As the L lives, who has protected me in
13:18 and blessed be the L God, F
14:13 "Wake up our l, for the slaves have been so bold
15: 8 to witness the good things that the L had done
15:10 May the Almighty L bless you forever!"
16: 1 sing to my L with cymbals.
16: 2 For the L is a God who crushes wars;
16: 5 But the L Almighty has foiled them by the hand Q
16:12 they perished before the army of my L.
16:13 I will sing to my God a new song: O L,
16:16 but whoever fears the L is great forever.
16:17 The L Almighty will take vengeance on them Q
AdE 4: 8 and demands our death. Call upon the L;
6: 1 That night the L took sleep from the king,
10: 9 The L has saved his people;
10: 9 the L has rescued us from all these evils;
13: 8 Then Mordecai prayed to the L,
13: 8 calling to remembrance all the works of the L.
13: 9 "O L, L, you rule as King over all things,
13:11 are L of all, and there is no one who can resist you,
13:11 and there is no one who can resist you, the L.
13:12 You know all things; you know, O L,
13:14 not bow down to anyone but you, who are my L;
13:15 And now, O L God and King, God of Abraham, F
13:17 and sing praise to your name, O L;
14: 1 seized with deadly anxiety, fled to the L.
14: 3 She prayed to the L God of Israel, and said: F
14: 3 "O my L, you only are our king;
14: 5 O L, took Israel out of all the nations,
14: 7 You are righteous, O L!
14:11 "O L, do not surrender your scepter
14:12 O L; make yourself known in this
14:14 who am alone and have no helper but you, O L.
14:18 except in you, O L God of Abraham. F
15:13 She said to him, "I saw you, my l,
15:14 For you are wonderful, my l,
Wis 1: 1 of the L in goodness and seek him with sincerity
1: 7 Because the spirit of the L has filled the world, Z
1: 9 and a report of their words will come to the L,
2:13 and calls himself a child of the L.
3: 8 and the L will reign over them forever.
3:10 the righteous and rebelled against the L;
3:14 who has not devised wicked things against the L;
3:14 a place of great delight in the temple of the L. U
4:14 for their souls were pleasing to the L,
4:17 not understand what the L purposed for them,
4:18 but the L will laugh them to scorn.
5: 7 but the way of the L we have not known. V
5:15 and their reward is with the L;
5:16 and a beautiful diadem from the hand of the L, X
5:17 The L will take his zeal as his whole armor,
6: 3 For your dominion was given you from the L,
6: 7 For the L of all will not stand in awe of anyone,
8: 3 and the L of all loves her.
8:21 so I appealed to the L and implored him,
9: 1 "O God of my ancestors and L of mercy,
9:13 Or who can discern what the L wills?
10:16 She entered the soul of a servant of the L,
10:20 they sang hymns, O L, to your holy name,
11:26 You spare all things, for they are yours, O L,
12: 2 from wickedness and put their trust in you, O L.
13: 3 how much better than these is their L,
13: 9 did they fail to find sooner the L of these things?
16:12 but it was your word, O L, that heals all people.
16:26 so that your children, whom you loved, O L,
19: 9 and leaped like lambs, praising you, O L,
19:22 O L, you have exalted and glorified your people,
Sir 1: 1 All wisdom is from the L,
1: 8 seated upon his throne—the L.
1:11 The fear of the L is glory and exultation, K
1:12 The fear of the L delights the heart, K
1:13 Those who fear the L will have a happy end; L
1:14 To fear the L is the beginning of wisdom; L
1:16 To fear the L is fullness of wisdom; L
1:18 The fear of the L is the crown of wisdom, K
1:20 To fear the L is the root of wisdom, L
1:26 and the L will lavish her upon you.
1:27 For the fear of the L is wisdom and discipline, K

*LORD distinguishes the words translated "Lord" and "lord" from the proper name of God, *Yahweh*, indicated in the NRSV by "LORD" and indexed under the heading †LORD on pages 804-25.

Sir 1:28 Do not disobey the fear of the L; K
1:30 The L will reveal your secrets and overthrow you
1:30 because you did not come in the fear of the L, K
2: 1 My child, when you come to serve the L,
2: 7 You who fear the L, wait for his mercy; L
2: 8 You who fear the L, trust in him, L
2: 9 You who fear the L, hope for good things, L
2:10 in the L and been disappointed?
2:10 Or has anyone persevered in the fear of the L K
2:11 For the L is compassionate and merciful;
2:15 Those who fear the L do not disobey his words, L
2:16 Those who fear the L seek to please him, L
2:17 Those who fear the L prepare their hearts, L
2:17 Let us fall into the hands of the L,
3: 2 For the L honors a father above his children,
3: 6 and those who honor their mother obey the L;
3:16 and whoever angers a mother is cursed by the L.
3:18 so you will find favor in the sight of the L.
3:20 For great is the might of the L;
4:13 and the L blesses the place she enters.
4:14 the L loves those who love her.
4:28 and the L God will fight for you. F
5: 3 for the L will surely punish you.
5: 4 for the L is slow to anger.
5: 7 Do not delay to turn back to the L,
5: 7 suddenly the wrath of the L will come upon you,
6:11 and l it over your servants;
6:16 and those who fear the L will find them. L
6:17 who fear the L direct their friendship aright, L
6:37 Reflect on the statutes of the L,
7: 4 Do not seek from the L high office,
7: 5 Do not assert your righteousness before the L, M
7:29 With all your soul fear the L, L
7:31 Fear the L and honor the priest, L
9:16 and let your glory be in the fear of the L. K
10: 4 government of the earth is in the hand of the L, X
10: 5 Human success is in the hand of the L, X
10: 7 Arrogance is hateful to the L and to mortals,
10:12 beginning of human pride is to forsake the L;
10:13 the L brings upon them unheard-of calamities,
10:14 The L overthrows the thrones of rulers,
10:15 The L plucks up the roots of the nations,
10:16 The L lays waste the lands of the nations,
10:19 Those who fear the L. L
10:20 but those who fear the L are worthy of honor L
10:22 their glory is the fear of the L. K
10:24 of them is greater than the one who fears the L.
11: 4 for the works of the L are wonderful,
11:12 but the eyes of the L look kindly upon them;
11:14 poverty and wealth, come from the L.
11:21 but trust in the L and keep at your job;
11:21 the sight of the L to make the poor rich suddenly,
11:22 The blessing of the L is the reward of the pious,
11:26 the L on the day of death to reward individuals
14:11 and present worthy offerings to the L.
15: 1 Whoever fears the L will do this,
15: 9 for it has not been sent from the L.
15:10 and the L will make it prosper.
15:13 The L hates all abominations;
15:18 For great is the wisdom of the L;
16: 2 unless the fear of the L is in them. K
16:11 For mercy and wrath are with the L;
16:17 Do not say, "I am hidden from the L,
16:26 the L created his works from the beginning,
16:29 Then the L looked upon the earth,
17: 1 The L created human beings out of earth,
17:20 and all their sins are before the L. M
17:22 One's almsgiving is like a signet ring with the L,
17:25 Turn back to the L and forsake your sins;
17:29 How great is the mercy of the L,
18: 2 the L alone is just.
18: 6 nor is it possible to fathom the wonders of the L.
18:11 That is why the L is patient with them
18:13 the compassion of the L is for every living thing.
18:23 do not be like one who puts the L to the test.
18:26 all things move swiftly before the L. M
19:20 The whole of wisdom is fear of the L, K
21: 6 but those who fear the L repent in their heart. L
21:11 the fulfillment of the fear of the L is wisdom. K
23: 1 O L, Father and Master of my life,
23: 4 O L, Father and God of my life,
23:19 of the L are ten thousand times brighter than
23:27 that nothing is better than the fear of the L, K
23:27 to heed the commandments of the L.
24:12 in the portion of the L, his heritage.
25: 6 and their boast is the fear of the L. K
25:10 But none is superior to the one who fears the L.
25:11 Fear of the L surpasses everything; K
26: 3 among the blessings of the man who fears the L.
26:14 A silent wife is a gift from the L,
26:16 Like the sun rising in the heights of the L,
26:23 *a pious wife is given to the man who fears the L.*
26:25 *one who has a sense of shame will fear the L.* L
26:28 the L will prepare him for the sword!
27: 3 If a person is not steadfast in the fear of the L, K
27:24 above all; even the L hates him.
28: 3 and expect healing from the L?
28:23 Those who forsake the L will fall into its power;
30:19 So is the one punished by the L;
32:16 Those who fear the L will form true judgments, L
32:24 and the one who trusts the L will not suffer loss.
33: 1 No evil will befall the one who fears the L,
33:11 of his knowledge the L distinguished them
33:17 by the blessing of the L I arrived first,
34:14 The spirit of those who fear the L will live, L
34:16 Those who fear the L will not be timid, L
34:17 Happy is the soul that fears the L!

Sir 34:19 The eyes of the L are on those who love him,
34:29 to whose voice will the L listen?
35: 5 To keep from wickedness is pleasing to the L,
35: 6 Do not appear before the L empty-handed, M
35:10 Be generous when you worship the L,
35:13 For the L is the one who repays,
35:15 L is the judge, and with him there is no partiality.
35:20 The one whose service is pleasing to the L will
35:22 Indeed, the L will not delay,
36: 5 that there is no God but you, O L.
36:17 O L, on the people called by your name,
36:22 Hear, O L, the prayer of your servants,
36:22 on the earth will know that you are the L,
37:21 for the L has withheld the gift of charm,
38: 1 for their services, for the L created them;
38: 4 The L created medicines out of the earth,
38: 9 when you are ill, do not delay, but pray to the L,
38:12 the physician his place, for the L created him;
38:14 the L that he grant them success in diagnosis and
39: 5 to rise early to seek the L who made him,
39: 6 If the great L is willing, he will be filled with
39: 6 of wisdom of his own and give thanks to the L
39: 7 The L will direct his counsel and knowledge,
39:14 bless the L for all his works. G
39:16 "All the works of the L are very good,
39:33 All the works of the L are good,
39:35 and bless the name of the L. I
40:26 but the fear of the L is better than either. K
40:26 There is no want in the fear of the L, K
40:27 The fear of the L is like a garden of blessing, K
42:15 I will now call to mind the works of the L,
42:15 By the word of the L his works are made; J
42:16 and the work of the L is full of his glory.
42:17 The L has not empowered even his holy ones
42:17 which the L the Almighty has established so that
43: 5 Great is the L who made it;
43: 9 a glittering array in the heights of the L.
43:29 Awesome is the L and very great,
43:30 Glorify the L and exalt him as much as you can,
43:33 For the L has made all things,
44: 2 The L apportioned to them great glory,
44:16 Enoch pleased the L and was taken up,
44:21 Therefore the L assured him with an oath that
44:23 From his descendants the L brought forth
45: 3 the L glorified him in the presence of kings.
45:15 as long as the heavens endure, to minister to the L
45:16 of all the living to offer sacrifice to the L,
45:19 The L saw it and was not pleased,
45:21 for they eat the sacrifices of the L,
45:22 for the L himself is his portion and inheritance.
45:23 in glory for being zealous in the fear of the L, K
45:26 bless the L who has crowned you with glory. G
45:26 May the L grant you wisdom of mind
46: 3 For he waged the wars of the L.
46: 5 and the great L answered him with hailstones
46: 6 that he was fighting in the sight of the L;
46: 9 The L gave Caleb strength,
46:10 how good it is to follow the L.
46:11 and who did not turn away from the L—
46:13 Samuel was beloved by his L;
46:13 a prophet of the L, he established the kingdom
46:14 By the law of the L he judged the congregation,
46:14 and the L watched over Jacob.
46:16 He called upon the L, the Mighty One,
46:17 Then the L thundered from heaven,
46:19 Samuel bore witness before the L M
47: 5 For he called on the L, the Most High,
47: 6 praised him for the blessings bestowed by the L,
47:11 The L took away his sins,
47:18 In the name of the L God, FI
47:22 But the L will never give up his mercy,
48: 3 By the word of the L he shut up the heavens, J
48:20 But they called upon the L who is merciful,
48:21 The L struck down the camp of the Assyrians,
48:22 For Hezekiah did what was pleasing to the L,
49: 3 He kept his heart fixed on the L;
49:12 the house and raised a temple holy to the L,
50:17 to worship their L, the Almighty, God Most High.
50:19 of the L Most High offered their prayers before
50:19 until the order of worship of the L was ended,
50:20 to pronounce the blessing of the L with his lips,
50:29 for the fear of the L is their path. K
51: 1 O L and King, and praise you, O God my Savior.
51: 8 Then I remembered your mercy, O L,
51:10 I cried out, "L, you are my Father;
51:12 and I bless the name of the L. I
51:22 The L gave me my tongue as a reward,
Bar 1: 5 they wept, and fasted, and prayed before the L; M
1: 8 Baruch took the vessels of the house of the L, P
1:10 and offer them on the altar of the L our God; E
1:12 The L will give us strength, and light to our eyes;
1:13 Pray also for us to the L our God, E
1:13 for we have sinned against the L our God, E
1:13 to this day the anger of the L and his wrath have
1:14 the house of the L on the days of the festivals P
1:15 And you shall say: The L our God is in the right, E
1:17 because we have sinned before the L. M
1:18 and have not heeded the voice of the L our God, E
1:18 in the statutes of the L that he set before us.
1:19 the time when the L brought our ancestors out of
1:19 we have been disobedient to the L our God, E
1:20 that the L declared through his servant Moses at
1:21 to the voice of the L our God in all the words E
1:22 in the sight of the L our God. E
2: 1 the L carried out the threat he spoke against us:
2: 4 where the L has scattered them.
2: 5 because our nation sinned against the L our God, E

Bar 2: 6 The L our God is in the right, E
2: 7 with which the L threatened us have come
2: 8 not entreated the favor of the L by turning away,
2: 9 And the L has kept the calamities ready,
2: 9 and the L has brought them upon us,
2: 9 for the L is just in all the works
2:10 in the statutes of the L that he set before us.
2:11 And now, O L God of Israel, F
2:12 O L our God, against all your ordinances. E
2:14 Hear, O L, our prayer and our supplication,
2:15 the earth may know that you are the L our God, E
2:16 O L, look down from your holy dwelling,
2:16 Incline your ear, O L, and hear;
2:17 O L, and see, for the dead who are in Hades,
2:17 will not ascribe glory or justice to the L;
2:18 will declare your glory and righteousness, O L.
2:19 before you our prayer for mercy, O L our God. E
2:21 Thus says the L: Bend your shoulders T
2:22 of the L and will not serve the king of Babylon,
2:27 Yet you have dealt with us, O L our God, E
2:31 and know that I am the L their God. E
2:33 who sinned before the L. M
3: 1 O L Almighty, God of Israel, Q
3: 2 Hear, O L, and have mercy,
3: 4 O L Almighty, God of Israel, Q
3: 4 who did not heed the voice of the L their God, E
3: 6 For you are the L our God, and it is you, E
3: 6 and it is you, O L, whom we will praise.
3: 8 who forsook the L our God. E
LtJ 6: 6 But say in your heart, "It is you, O L,
Aza 1: 1 singing hymns to God and blessing the L.
1: 3 O L, God of our ancestors, and worthy of praise;
1:14 O L, have become fewer than any other nation,
1:20 and bring glory to your name, O L.
1:22 Let them know that you alone are the L God, F
1:26 the angel of the L came down into the furnace O
1:29 O L, God of our ancestors,
1:35 "Bless the L, all you works of the Lord; G
1:35 "Bless the Lord, all you works of the L;
1:36 Bless the L, you heavens; G
1:37 Bless the L, you angels of the Lord; G
1:37 Bless the Lord, you angels of the L;
1:38 Bless the L, all you waters above the heavens; G
1:39 Bless the L, all you powers of the Lord; G
1:39 Bless the Lord, all you powers of the L;
1:40 Bless the L, sun and moon; G
1:41 Bless the L, stars of heaven; G
1:42 "Bless the L, all rain and dew; G
1:43 Bless the L, all you winds; G
1:44 Bless the L, fire and heat; G
1:45 Bless the L, winter cold and summer heat; G
1:46 Bless the L, dews and falling snow; G
1:47 Bless the L, nights and days; G
1:48 Bless the L, light and darkness; G
1:49 Bless the L, ice and cold; G
1:50 Bless the L, frosts and snows; G
1:51 Bless the L, lightnings and clouds; G
1:52 "Let the earth bless the L; G
1:53 Bless the L, mountains and hills; G
1:54 Bless the L, all that grows in the ground; G
1:55 Bless the L, seas and rivers; G
1:56 Bless the L, you springs; G
1:57 Bless the L, you whales and all that swim G
1:58 Bless the L, all birds of the air; G
1:59 Bless the L, all wild animals and cattle; G
1:60 "Bless the L, all people on earth; G
1:61 Bless the L, O Israel; sing praise to him G
1:62 Bless the L, you priests of the Lord; G
1:62 Bless the Lord, you priests of the L;
1:63 Bless the L, you servants of the Lord; G
1:63 Bless the Lord, you servants of the L;
1:64 Bless the L, spirits and souls of the righteous; G
1:65 Bless the L, you who are holy and humble G
1:66 "Bless the L, Hananiah, Azariah, and Mishael; G
1:67 Give thanks to the L, for he is good,
1:68 All who worship the L, bless the God of gods,
Sus 1: 2 very beautiful woman and one who feared the L.
1: 5 Concerning them the L had said:
1:23 rather than sin in the sight of the L."
1:35 for her heart trusted in the L.
1:44 The L heard her cry.
1:53 though the L said, 'You shall not put an innocent
Bel 1:25 Daniel said, "I worship the L my God, E
1:34 But the angel of the L said to Habakkuk, O
1:36 Then the angel of the L took him by the crown O
1:41 "You are great, O L, the God of Daniel,
1Mc 2:53 the commandment, and became l of Egypt.
2Mc 1: 8 We prayed to the L and were heard,
1:24 The prayer was to this effect: "O L, Lord God,
1:24 The prayer was to this effect: "O Lord, L God, F
2: 2 not to forget the commandments of the L,
2: 8 Then the L will disclose these things,
2: 8 and the glory of the L and the cloud will appear, Y
2:10 Just as Moses prayed to the L,
2:22 L with great kindness became gracious to them—
3:22 While they were calling upon the Almighty L
3:30 they praised the L who had acted marvelously
3:30 now that the Almighty L had appeared.
3:33 since for his sake the L has granted you your life.
3:35 to the L and made very great vows to the Savior
4:38 The L thus repaid him with
5:17 that the L was angered for a little while because
5:19 But the L did not choose the nation for the sake
5:20 when the great L became reconciled.
6:14 the case of the other nations the L waits patiently
6:30 "It is clear to the L in his holy knowledge that,
7: 6 "The L God is watching over us and F

***LORD** distinguishes the words translated "Lord" and "lord" from the proper name of God, *Yahweh*, indicated in the NRSV by "LORD" and indexed under the heading **†LORD** on pages 804-25.

2Mc 7:20 with good courage because of her hope in the L.
7:33 And if our living L is angry for a little while,
7:40 putting his whole trust in the L.
8: 2 They implored the L to look upon
8: 5 for the wrath of the L had turned to mercy.
8:14 the L to rescue those who had been sold by
8:27 giving great praise and thanks to the L,
8:29 the merciful L to be wholly reconciled
8:35 the help of the L by opponents whom he regarded
9: 5 But the all-seeing L, the God of Israel,
9:13 Then the abominable fellow made a vow to the L,
10: 1 the L leading them on, recovered the temple and
10: 4 they fell prostrate and implored the L
10:28 but also their reliance on the L,
10:38 the L who shows great kindness to Israel
11: 6 prayed the L to send a good angel to save Israel.
11:10 for the L had mercy on them.
12:36 Judas called upon the L to show himself their ally
12:41 So they all blessed the ways of the L,
13:10 he ordered the people to call upon the L day
13:12 and had implored the merciful L with weeping
14:35 "O L of all, though you have need
14:36 O holy One, L of all holiness,
14:46 upon the L of life and spirit to give them back
15: 4 When they declared, "It is the living L himself,
15: 7 that he would get help from the L.
15:21 and called upon the L who works wonders;
15:21 that it is not by arms, but as the L decides,
15:22 He called upon him in these words: "O L,
15:29 they blessed the Sovereign L in the language R
15:34 blessed the L who had manifested himself,
15:35 to everyone of the help of the L.
1Es 1: 1 Josiah kept the passover to his L in Jerusalem;
1: 2 in their vestments, in the temple of the L. U
1: 3 that they should sanctify themselves to the L
1: 3 of the L in the house that King Solomon, son
1: 4 the L your God and serve his people Israel; E
1: 6 to the commandment of the L that was given
1:11 the offering to the L as it is written in the book
1:17 with the sacrifices to the L were accomplished
1:18 the sacrifices were offered on the altar of the L,
1:23 deeds of Josiah were upright in the sight of the L,
1:24 the L beyond any other people or kingdom,
1:24 and how they grieved the L deeply,
1:24 so that the words of the L fell upon Israel.
1:27 I was not sent against you by the L God, F
1:27 And now the L is with me!
1:27 The L is with me, urging me on!
1:27 Stand aside, and do not oppose the L."
1:28 of the prophet Jeremiah from the mouth of the L.
1:33 and his understanding of the law of the L,
1:39 he did what was evil in the sight of the L.
1:41 also took some holy vessels of the L,
1:44 He did what was evil in the sight of the L.
1:45 with the holy vessels of the L,
1:47 He also did what was evil in the sight of the L,
1:47 by the prophet Jeremiah from the mouth of the L.
1:48 made him swear by the name of the L, I
1:48 and transgressed the laws of the L,
1:49 and polluted the temple of the L in Jerusalem— U
1:51 and whenever the L spoke,
1:54 They took all the holy vessels of the L,
1:54 the treasure chests of the L, and the royal stores,
1:55 They burned the house of the L, P
1:57 in fulfillment of the word of the L by the mouth J
2: 1 the word of the L by the mouth of Jeremiah J
2: 2 the L stirred up the spirit of King Cyrus of
2: 3 The L of Israel, the L Most High,
2: 5 are of his people, may your L be with you;
2: 5 and build the house of the L of Israel— P
2: 5 he is the L who dwells in Jerusalem,
2: 7 as votive offerings for the temple of the L U
2: 8 and all whose spirit the L had stirred to go up
2: 8 up to build the house in Jerusalem for the L;
2:10 of the L that Nebuchadnezzar had carried away
2:17 "To King Artaxerxes our l, your servants
2:18 to our l the king that the Jews who came up D
2:21 but to speak to our l the king, D
2:24 we now make known to you, O l and king,
4: 3 But the king is stronger; he is their l and master,
4:46 now, O l the king, this is what I ask and request D
4:60 I give you thanks, O L of our ancestors."
5:50 and burnt offerings to the L morning and evening.
5:58 of age to have charge of the work of the L.
5:58 So the builders built the temple of the L. U
5:60 praising the L and blessing him,
5:61 the L, "For his goodness and his glory are forever
5:62 the L for the erection of the house of the Lord.
5:62 the Lord for the erection of the house of the L. P
5:67 the temple for the L God of Israel. F
5:69 For we obey your L just as you do
5:70 with us in building the house for the L our God, E
5:71 for we alone will build it for the L of Israel,
6: 1 prophesied to them in the name of the L God FI
6: 2 to build the house of the L that is in Jerusalem, P
6: 2 with the help of the prophets of the L who were
6: 5 for the providence of the L was over the captives;
6: 8 Let it be fully known to our l the king that, D
6: 9 the city of Jerusalem a great new house for the L,
6:13 the servants of the L who created the heaven and
6:15 But when our ancestors sinned against the L
6:19 this temple of the L should be rebuilt on its site. U
6:20 laid the foundations of the house of the L that is P
6:21 be made in the royal archives of our l the king D
6:22 of the house of the L in Jerusalem was done P
6:22 and if it is approved by our l the king, D
6:24 the building of the house of the L in Jerusalem, P
1Es 6:26 and that the holy vessels of the house of the L, P
6:27 the servant of the L and governor of Judea,
6:27 the Jews to build this house of the L on its site. P
6:28 until the house of the L is finished; P
6:29 the governor, for sacrifices to the L, for bulls
6:33 the L, whose name is there called
6:33 or damage that house of the L in Jerusalem. P
7: 4 by the command of the L God of Israel. F
7: 7 of the temple of the L one hundred bulls, U
7: 9 the services of the L God of Israel in accordance F
7:13 of the peoples of the land and sought the L.
7:14 seven days, rejoicing before the L, M
7:15 for the service of the L God of Israel. F
8: 6 by the prosperous journey that the L gave them.
8: 7 so that he omitted nothing from the law of the L
8: 8 to Ezra the priest and reader of the law of the L:
8: 9 to Ezra the priest and reader of the law of the L,
8:12 in accordance with what is in the law of the L,
8:13 the L of Israel that I and my Friends have vowed,
8:13 the L in Jerusalem all the gold and silver that may
8:14 for the temple of their L that is in Jerusalem,
8:15 as to offer sacrifices on the altar of their L that is
8:17 the L that are given you for the use of the temple
8:25 Ezra the scribe said, "Blessed be the L alone,
8:27 I was encouraged by the help of the L my God, E
8:46 to serve as priests in the house of our L.
8:47 of our L they brought us competent men of
8:50 a fast for the young men before our L,
8:52 power of our L will be with those who seek him,
8:53 And again we prayed to our L about these things,
8:55 and the holy vessels of the house of our L,
8:58 And I said to them, "You are holy to the L,
8:58 gold are vowed to the L, the L of our ancestors.
8:59 in the chambers of the house of our L."
8:60 in Jerusalem carried them to the temple of the L. U
8:61 by the mighty hand of our L, which was upon us;
8:62 in the house of our L to the priest Meremoth son
8:65 from exile offered sacrifices to the L,
8:66 all as a sacrifice to the L.
8:67 the people and the temple of the L. U
8:72 the word of the L of Israel gathered around me, J
8:73 down and stretching out my hands to the L
8:74 "O L, I am ashamed and confused
8:78 from you, O L, to leave to us a root and a name
8:79 a light for us in the house of the L our God, EP
8:80 in our bondage we were not forsaken by our L,
8:81 and glorified the temple of our L,
8:82 "And now, O L, what shall we say,
8:86 For you, O L, lifted the burden
8:89 O L of Israel, you are faithful;
8:92 and said to Ezra, "We have sinned against the L,
8:93 Let us take an oath to the L about this,
8:94 to you and to all who obey the law of the L.
9: 8 and give glory to the L the God of our ancestors,
9:13 until we are freed from the wrath of the L
9:39 of Moses that had been given by the L God F
9:46 And Ezra blessed the L God Most High, F
9:47 and fell to the ground and worshiped the L.
9:48 Pelaiah, the Levites, taught the law of the L,
9:50 "This day is holy to the L"—
9:52 for the day is holy to the L;
9:52 and do not be sorrowful, for the L will exalt you."
Man 1: 1 O L Almighty, God of our ancestors, Q
1: 7 for you are the L Most High,
1: 7 L, according to your great goodness you have
1: 8 Therefore you, O L, God of the righteous,
1: 9 my transgressions are multiplied, O L,
1:12 I have sinned, O L, I have sinned,
1:13 I earnestly implore you, forgive me, O L,
1:13 For you, O L, are the God of those who repent,
Pm 151: 3 And who will tell my L?
151: 3 The L himself; it is he who hears.
151: 5 but the L was not pleased with them.
3Mc 2: 2 "L, L, king of the heavens, and sovereign
5: 7 to silence they all called upon the Almighty L
5:11 But the L sent upon the king a portion of sleep,
5:12 the L he was overcome by so pleasant and deep
5:35 praised the manifest L God, King of kings, F
6: 5 you, O L, broke in pieces,
6:10 and destroy us, L, by whatever fate you choose.
6:15 O L, and have not turned your face from us;
6:15 did I neglect them,' so accomplish it, O L."
6:39 the L of all most gloriously revealed his mercy
2Es 1: 4 The word of the L came to me, saying, J
1:12 "But speak to them and say, Thus says the L: T
1:14 Yet you have forgotten me, says the L. H
1:15 "Thus says the L Almighty: QT
1:21 What more can I do for you? says the L. H
1:22 Thus says the L Almighty: QT
1:27 you have forsaken yourselves, says the L. H
1:28 "Thus says the L Almighty: QT
1:32 I will require their blood of you, says the L. H
1:33 "Thus says the L Almighty: QT
1:40 who is also called the messenger of the L.
2: 1 "Thus says the L: I brought this people out T
2: 3 sinned before the L God and have done FM
2: 4 Go, my children, and ask for mercy from the L.'
2: 9 not listened to me, says the L Almighty." HQ
2:10 Thus says the L to Ezra: T
2:14 for I am the Living One, says the L. H
2:15 because I have chosen you, says the L. H
2:17 for I have chosen you, says the L. H
2:28 be able to do anything against you, says the L. H
2:30 because I will deliver you, says the L. H
2:31 for I am merciful, says the L Almighty. HQ
2:33 received a command from the L on Mount Horeb
2:37 Receive what the L has entrusted to you and
2Es 2:38 at the feast of the L.
2:39 have received glorious garments from the L.
2:40 who have fulfilled the law of the L.
2:42 and they all were praising the L with songs.
2:44 Then I asked an angel, "Who are these, my l?"
2:47 for the name of the L. I
2:48 the wonders of the L God that you have seen." F
3: 4 "O sovereign L, did you not speak at R
4: 3 Then I said, "Yes, my l."
4: 5 I said, "Speak, my l."
4:22 Then I answered and said, "I implore you, my l,
4:38 Then I answered and said, "But, O sovereign L, R
4:41 And I said, "No, l, it cannot."
5:23 "O sovereign L, from every forest of the earth R
5:28 now, O L, why have you handed the one over to
5:33 Then I said, "Speak, my l."
5:34 my l, but because of my grief I have spoken;
5:35 And I said, "Why not, my l?
5:38 "O sovereign L, who is able R
5:41 O L, you have charge of those who are alive at
5:56 I said, "I implore you, O L,
6:11 I answered and said, "O sovereign L, R
6:38 "O L, you spoke at the beginning of creation,
6:55 "All this I have spoken before you, O L,
6:57 And now, O L, these nations,
7: 3 I said, "Speak, my l."
7:10 I said, "That is right, l."
7:17 Then I answered and said, "O sovereign L, R
7:19 "You are not a better judge than the L,
7:21 the L strictly commanded those who came into
7:*45* I answered and said, "O sovereign L, R
7:*53* I said, "L, how could that be?"
7:*58* O sovereign L, what is plentiful is of less worth, R
7:*75* "If I have found favor in your sight, O L,
7:*132* [62] I answered and said, "I know, O L,
8: 6 O L above us, grant to your servant
8:20 "O L, you who inhabit eternity,
8:24 O L, the prayer of your servant,
8:36 O L, your righteousness and goodness will
8:45 Surely not, O L above!
8:63 "O L, you have already shown me a great number
9:29 "O L, you showed yourself among us,
9:41 She said to me, "Let me alone, my l,
10:34 I said, "Speak, my l; only do
12: 7 Then I said, "O sovereign L, R
13:51 I said, "O sovereign L, explain this to me: R
14: 2 I answered, "Here I am, L," and I rose to my feet.
14:19 "Let me speak in your presence, L.
15: 1 that I will put in your mouth, says the L, H
15: 5 says the L, I am bringing evils upon the world, H
15: 7 Therefore, says the L, H
15: 9 I will surely avenge them, says the L, H
15:12 and castigation that the L will bring upon it.
15:21 into their bosom. Thus says the L God: FT
15:24 not observe my commandments, says the L; H
15:52 with you so violently, says the L, H
15:56 As you will do to my chosen people, says the L, H
16: 8 The L God sends calamities, F
16:11 The L will threaten, and who will not
16:12 be troubled at the presence of the L and the glory
16:35 you who are servants of the L.
16:36 This is word of the L; J
16:36 receive it and do not disbelieve what the L says.
16:48 be with them for their sins, says the L. H
16:54 The L certainly knows everything that people do;
16:64 The L will strictly examine all their works,
16:66 Or how will you hide your sins before the L M
16:70 be a great uprising against those who fear the L. L
16:71 and destroying those who continue to fear the L. L
16:74 Listen, my elect ones, says the L; H
16:76 says the L God, must not let your sins weigh FH
4Mc 2: 7 unless reason is clearly l of the emotions?

†LORD‡ (6490) [†GOD, †LORD'S]

A. †LORD MY/HIS/OUR/THEIR/YOUR *GOD (642)
B. SAYS THE †LORD (330)
C. THUS SAYS THE †LORD (283)
D. BEFORE THE †LORD (255)
E. †LORD OF HOSTS (245)
F. HOUSE OF THE †LORD (240)
G. WORD OF THE †LORD (237)
H. I AM THE †LORD (155)
I. NAME OF THE †LORD (83)
J. †LORD *GOD (61)
K. ANGEL OF THE †LORD (56)
L. EVIL IN THE SIGHT OF THE †LORD (53)
M. PRAISE THE †LORD (42)
N. ARK OF THE †LORD (38)
O. COVENANT OF THE †LORD (38)
P. VOICE OF THE †LORD (38)
Q. AS THE †LORD LIVES (35)
R. GLORY OF THE †LORD (35)
S. HAND OF THE †LORD (32)
T. BLESSED BE THE †LORD (26)
U. FEAR OF THE †LORD (24)
V. TEMPLE OF THE †LORD (24)
W. BLESS THE †LORD (23)
X. FEAR THE †LORD (28)
Y. SERVANT OF THE †LORD (23)
Z. †LORD ... APPEARED (21)
SPIRIT OF THE †LORD (22) See SPIRIT
DAY OF THE †LORD (18) See DAY
LAW OF THE †LORD (16) See LAW
ASSEMBLY OF THE †LORD (10) See ASSEMBLY
PEOPLE OF THE †LORD (10) See PEOPLE

***LORD** distinguishes the words translated "Lord" and "lord" from the proper name of God, *Yahweh*, indicated in the NRSV by "LORD" and indexed under the heading **†LORD** on pages 804-25.
†LORD distinguishes the proper name of God, *Yahweh*, indicated in the NRSV by "LORD," from the words translated "Lord" and "lord," indexed under the heading ***LORD** on pages 798-804.

LOVE THE †LORD (8) See LOVE
DEEDS OF THE †LORD (7) See DEEDS
†LORD BLESSED (7) See BLESSED
WAY OF THE †LORD (7) See WAY

Ge 2: 4 that the L God made the earth and the heavens, J
2: 5 L God had not caused it to rain upon the earth, J
2: 7 then the L God formed man from the dust of J
2: 8 the L God planted a garden in Eden, in the east; J
2: 9 the ground the L God made to grow every tree J
2:15 The L God took the man and put him in J
2:16 And the L God commanded the man, J
2:18 Then the L God said, "It is not good that J
2:19 of the ground the L God formed every animal of J
2:21 L God caused a deep sleep to fall upon the man, J
2:22 the L God had taken from the man he made into J
3: 1 that the L God had made. J
3: 8 the sound of the L God walking in the garden at J
3: 8 from the presence of the L God among the trees J
3: 9 But the L God called to the man, J
3:13 Then the L God said to the woman, J
3:14 The L God said to the serpent, J
3:21 the L God made garments of skins for the man J
3:22 Then the L God said, "See, J
3:23 L God sent him forth from the garden of Eden, J
4: 1 "I have produced a man with the help of the L."
4: 3 to the L an offering of the fruit of the ground,
4: 4 And the L had regard for Abel and his offering,
4: 6 The L said to Cain, "Why are you angry,
4: 9 L said to Cain, "Where is your brother Abel?"
4:10 And the L said, "What have you done?
4:13 Cain said to the L, "My punishment is greater than
4:15 Then the L said to him, "Not so!
4:15 And the L put a mark on Cain,
4:16 Cain went away from the presence of the L,
4:26 people began to invoke the name of the L. I
5:29 the L has cursed this one shall bring us relief
6: 3 Then the L said, "My spirit shall not abide
6: 5 The L saw that the wickedness
6: 6 the L was sorry that he had made humankind on
6: 7 So the L said, "I will blot out from the earth
6: 8 But Noah found favor in the sight of the L.
7: 1 Then the L said to Noah, "Go into the ark,
7: 5 Noah did all that the L had commanded him.
7:16 and the L shut him in.
8:20 Then Noah built an altar to the L,
8:21 And when the L smelled the pleasing odor,
8:21 the L said in his heart, "I will never again curse
9:26 "Blessed by the L my God be Shem; A
10: 9 He was a mighty hunter before the L; D
10: 9 "Like Nimrod a mighty hunter before the L." D
11: 5 The L came down to see the city and the tower,
11: 6 And the L said, "Look, they are one people,
11: 8 So the L scattered them abroad from there over
11: 9 because there the L confused the language of all
11: 9 and from there the L scattered them abroad over
12: 1 Now the L said to Abram,
12: 4 So Abram went, as the L had told him;
12: 7 Then the L appeared to Abram, and said, Z
12: 7 built there an altar to the L, who had appeared Z
12: 8 and there he built an altar to the L and invoked
12: 8 to the LORD and invoked the name of the L. I
12:17 But the L afflicted Pharaoh and his house
13: 4 and there Abram called on the name of the L. I
13:10 like the garden of the L, like the land of Egypt,
13:10 before the L had destroyed Sodom and D
13:13 great sinners against the L.
13:14 The L said to Abram, after Lot had separated
13:18 and there he built an altar to the L.
14:22 "I have sworn to the L, God Most High,
15: 1 the word of the L came to Abram in a vision, G
15: 4 But the word of the L came to him, G
15: 6 And he believed the L; and the L reckoned it to
him as righteousness.
15: 7 "I am the L who brought you from Ur of H
15:13 Then the L said to Abram,
15:18 On that day the L made a covenant with Abram,
16: 2 the L has prevented me from bearing children;
16: 5 May the L judge between you and me!"
16: 7 The angel of the L found her by a spring K
16: 9 The angel of the L said to her, K
16:10 The angel of the L also said to her, K
16:11 And the angel of the L said to her, K
16:11 for the L has given heed to your affliction.
16:13 So she named the L who spoke to her,
17: 1 the L appeared to Abram, and said to him, Z
18: 1 L appeared to Abraham by the oaks of Mamre, Z
18:13 The L said to Abraham, "Why did Sarah laugh,
18:14 Is anything too wonderful for the L?
18:17 The L said, "Shall I hide
18:19 to keep the way of the L by doing righteousness
18:19 so that the L may bring about
18:20 Then the L said, "How great is the outcry
18:22 while Abraham remained standing before the L. D
18:26 the L said, "If I find at Sodom fifty righteous in
18:33 And the L went his way,
19:13 against its people has become great before the L, D
19:13 and the L has sent us to destroy it."
19:14 for the L is about to destroy the city."
19:16 the L being merciful to him,
19:24 the L rained on Sodom and Gomorrah sulfur and
fire from the L
19:27 to the place where he had stood before the L; D
20:18 the L had closed fast all the wombs of the house
21: 1 The L dealt with Sarah as he had said,
21: 1 and the L did for Sarah as he had promised.
21:33 and called there on the name of the L, I

Ge 22:11 the angel of the L called to him from heaven, K
22:14 Abraham called that place "The L will provide";
22:14 "On the mount of the L it shall be provided."
22:15 angel of the L called to Abraham a second time K
22:16 "By myself I have sworn, says the L: B
24: 1 and the L had blessed Abraham in all things.
24: 3 and I will make you swear by the L,
24: 7 The L, the God of heaven,
24:12 And he said, "O L, God of my master Abraham,
24:21 or not the L had made his journey successful.
24:26 The man bowed his head and worshiped the L
24:27 "Blessed be the L, the God of my master T
24:27 the L has led me on the way to the house
24:31 He said, "Come in, O blessed of the L.
24:35 The L has greatly blessed my master,
24:40 But he said to me, 'The L, before whom I walk,
24:42 "I came today to the spring, and said, 'O L,
24:44 let her be the woman whom the L has appointed
24:48 Then I bowed my head and worshiped the L,
24:48 and worshiped the LORD, and blessed the L,
24:50 "The thing comes from the L;
24:51 of your master's son, as the L has spoken."
24:52 he bowed himself to the ground before the L. D
24:56 since the L has made my journey successful;
25:21 Isaac prayed to the L for his wife,
25:21 and the L granted his prayer,
25:22 So she went to inquire of the L.
25:23 And the L said to her, "Two nations are
26: 2 The L appeared to Isaac and said, Z
26:12 The L blessed him,
26:22 saying, "Now the L has made room for us,
26:24 that very night the L appeared to him and said, Z
26:25 called on the name of the L, I
26:28 "We see plainly that the L has been with you;
26:29 You are now the blessed of the L."
27: 7 that I may bless you before the L before I die.' D
27:20 "Because the L your God granted me success." A
27:27 like the smell of a field that the L has blessed.
28:13 And the L stood beside him and said,
28:13 LORD stood beside him and said, "I am the L, H
28:16 "Surely the L is in this place—
28:21 then the L shall be my God,
29:31 When the L saw that Leah was unloved,
29:32 "Because the L has looked on my affliction;
29:33 "Because the L has heard that I am hated,
29:35 and said, "This time I will praise the L"; M
30:24 saying, "May the L add to me another son!"
30:27 by divination that the L has blessed me because
30:30 and the L has blessed you wherever I turned.
31: 3 Then the L said to Jacob,
31:49 for he said, "The L watch between you and me,
32: 9 O L who said to me,
38: 7 Er, Judah's firstborn, was wicked in the sight of
the L, and the L put him to death.
38:10 in the sight of the L,
39: 2 The L was with Joseph,
39: 3 His master saw that the L was with him,
39: 3 L caused all that he did to prosper in his hands.
39: 5 the L blessed the Egyptian's house
39: 5 the blessing of the L was on all that he had,
39:21 But the L was with Joseph
39:23 because the L was with him;
39:23 and whatever he did, the L made it prosper.
49:18 I wait for your salvation, O L.
Ex 3: 2 the angel of the L appeared to him in a flame KZ
3: 4 When the L saw that he had turned aside to see,
3: 7 Then the L said, "I have observed the misery
3:15 "Thus you shall say to the Israelites, 'The L,
3:16 'The L, the God of your ancestors,
3:18 'The L, the God of the Hebrews,
3:18 so that we may sacrifice to the L our God.' A
4: 1 but say, 'The L did not appear to you.' "
4: 2 The L said to him, "What is that in your hand?"
4: 4 Then the L said to Moses,
4: 5 "so that they may believe that the L,
4: 6 Again, the L said to him,
4:10 But Moses said to the L, "O my Lord,
4:11 L said to him, "Who gives speech to mortals?
4:11 Is it not I, the L?
4:14 of the L was kindled against Moses and he said,
4:19 L said to Moses in Midian, "Go back to Egypt;
4:21 And the L said to Moses,
4:22 you shall say to Pharaoh, 'Thus says the L: C
4:24 the L met him and tried to kill him.
4:27 The L said to Aaron, "Go into the wilderness
4:28 the words of the L with which he had sent him,
4:30 Aaron spoke all the words that the L had spoken
4:31 and when they heard that the L had given heed
5: 1 "Thus says the L, the God of Israel, C
5: 2 But Pharaoh said, "Who is the L,
5: 2 I do not know the L,
5: 3 into the wilderness to sacrifice to the L our God, A
5:17 'Let us go and sacrifice to the L.'
5:21 "The L look upon you and judge!
5:22 Then Moses turned again to the L and said,
5:22 "O L, why have you mistreated this people?
6: 1 Then the L said to Moses,
6: 2 and said to him: "I am the L. H
6: 3 'The L' I did not make myself known to them.
6: 6 Say therefore to the Israelites, 'I am the L, H
6: 7 You shall know that I am the L your God, AH
6: 8 for a possession. I am the L.' " H
6:10 Then the L spoke to Moses,
6:12 But Moses spoke to the L,
6:13 Thus the L spoke to Moses and Aaron,
6:26 and Moses to whom the L said,
6:28 when the L spoke to Moses in the land of Egypt,

Ex 6:29 he said to him, "I am the L; H
7: 1 The L said to Moses, "See,
7: 5 The Egyptians shall know that I am the L, H
7: 6 they did just as the L commanded them.
7: 8 The L said to Moses and Aaron,
7:10 to Pharaoh and did as the L had commanded;
7:13 not listen to them, as the L had said.
7:14 L said to Moses, "Pharaoh's heart is hardened;
7:16 Say to him, 'The L, the God of the Hebrews,
7:17 Thus says the L, "By this you shall know C
7:17 "By this you shall know that I am the L." H
7:19 The L said to Moses, "Say to Aaron,
7:20 Moses and Aaron did just as the L commanded.
7:22 would not listen to them; as the L had said.
7:25 Seven days passed after the L had struck
8: 1 Then the L said to Moses,
8: 1 to Pharaoh and say to him, 'Thus says the L: C
8: 5 And the L said to Moses, "Say to Aaron,
8: 8 "Pray to the L to take away the frogs from me
8: 8 and I will let the people go to sacrifice to the L."
8:10 that there is no one like the L our God, A
8:12 the L concerning the frogs that he had brought
8:13 And the L did as Moses requested:
8:15 just as the L had said.
8:16 Then the L said to Moses, "Say to Aaron,
8:19 just as the L had said.
8:20 Then the L said to Moses,
8:20 and say to him, 'Thus says the L: C
8:22 that you may know that I the L am in this land.
8:24 The L did so, and great swarms of flies came
8:26 to the L our God are offensive to the Egyptians. A
8:27 the wilderness and sacrifice to the L our God A
8:28 to sacrifice to the L your God in the wilderness, A
8:29 I will pray to the L that the swarms
8:29 by not letting the people go to sacrifice to the L."
8:30 from Pharaoh and prayed to the L.
8:31 And the L did as Moses asked:
9: 1 Then the L said to Moses, "Go to Pharaoh,
9: 1 'Thus says the L, the God of the Hebrews: C
9: 3 the hand of the L will strike with S
9: 4 But the L will make a distinction between
9: 5 The L set a time, saying,
9: 5 "Tomorrow the L will do this thing in the land."
9: 6 And on the next day the L did so;
9: 8 Then the L said to Moses and Aaron,
9:12 But the L hardened the heart of Pharaoh,
9:12 just as the L had spoken to Moses.
9:13 Then the L said to Moses,
9:13 'Thus says the L, the God of the Hebrews: C
9:20 who feared word of the L hurried their slaves G
9:21 the word of the L left their slaves and livestock G
9:22 The L said to Moses, "Stretch out your hand
9:23 and the L sent thunder and hail,
9:23 And the L rained hail on the land of Egypt;
9:27 the L is in the right,
9:28 Pray to the L! Enough of God's thunder
9:29 I will stretch out my hands to the L;
9:30 I know that you do not yet fear the L God." JX
9:33 and stretched out his hands to the L;
9:35 just as the L had spoken through Moses.
10: 1 Then the L said to Moses, "Go to Pharaoh;
10: 2 so that you may know that I am the L." H
10: 3 "Thus says the L, the God of the Hebrews, C
10: 7 so that they may worship the L their God; A
10: 8 "Go, worship the L your God! A
10:10 "The L indeed will be with you,
10:11 Your men may go and worship the L,
10:12 Then the L said to Moses,
10:13 and the L brought an east wind upon the land all
10:16 "I have sinned against the L your God, A
10:17 and pray to the L your God that at A
10:18 he went out from Pharaoh and prayed to the L.
10:19 The L changed the wind into
10:20 But the L hardened Pharaoh's heart,
10:21 Then the L said to Moses,
10:24 and said, "Go, worship the L.
10:25 to sacrifice to the L our God. A
10:26 of them for the worship of the L our God, A
10:26 to use to worship the L until we arrive there."
10:27 But the L hardened Pharaoh's heart
11: 1 The L said to Moses, "I will bring one more
11: 3 The L gave the people favor in the sight of
11: 4 Moses said, "Thus says the L: C
11: 7 that the L makes a distinction between Egypt
11: 9 The L said to Moses, "Pharaoh will not listen
11:10 but the L hardened Pharaoh's heart,
12: 1 L said to Moses and Aaron in the land of Egypt:
12:11 It is the passover of the L.
12:12 of Egypt I will execute judgments: I am the L. H
12:14 You shall celebrate it as a festival to the L;
12:23 For the L will pass through to strike down
12:23 the two doorposts, the L will pass over that door
12:25 you come to the land that the L will give you,
12:27 'It is the passover sacrifice to the L,
12:28 and did just as the L had commanded Moses
12:29 At midnight the L struck down all the firstborn
12:31 Go, worship the L, as you said.
12:36 and the L had given the people favor in the sight
12:41 the companies of the L went out from the land
12:42 That was for the L a night of vigil,
12:42 a vigil to be kept for the L by all the Israelites
12:43 The L said to Moses and Aaron:
12:48 to the L, all his males shall be circumcised;
12:50 as the L had commanded Moses and Aaron.
12:51 That very day the L brought the Israelites out of
13: 1 The L said to Moses:
13: 3 the L brought you out from there by strength

†**LORD** distinguishes the proper name of God, *Yahweh,* indicated in the NRSV by "LORD," from the words translated "Lord" and "lord," indexed under the heading ***LORD** on pages 798-804.

Ex 13: 5 the **L** brings you into the land of the Canaanites,
13: 6 the seventh day there shall be a festival to the **L.**
13: 8 the **L** did for me when I came out of Egypt.'
13: 9 that the teaching of the **L** may be on your lips;
13: 9 a strong hand the **L** brought you out of Egypt.
13:11 "When the **L** has brought you into the land of
13:12 you shall set apart to the **L** all that first opens
13:14 'By strength of hand the **L** brought us out
13:15 the **L** killed all the firstborn in the land of Egypt,
13:15 to the **L** every male that first opens the womb,
13:16 that by strength of hand the **L** brought us out
13:21 The **L** went in front of them in a pillar of cloud
14: 1 Then the **L** said to Moses:
14: 4 and the Egyptians shall know that I am the **L.** H
14: 8 The **L** hardened the heart of Pharaoh king
14:10 In great fear the Israelites cried out to the **L.**
14:13 the deliverance that the **L** will accomplish
14:14 The **L** will fight for you,
14:15 **L** said to Moses, "Why do you cry out to me?
14:18 And the Egyptians shall know that I am the **L,** H
14:21 The **L** drove the sea back by
14:24 the **L** in the pillar of fire and cloud looked down
14:25 for the **L** is fighting for them against Egypt."
14:26 Then the **L** said to Moses,
14:27 the **L** tossed the Egyptians into the sea.
14:30 the **L** saved Israel that day from the Egyptians;
14:31 Israel saw the great work that the **L** did against
14:31 So the people feared the **L** and believed in
14:31 and believed in the **L** and in his servant Moses.
15: 1 Moses and the Israelites sang this song to the **L:**
15: 1 sing to the **L,** for he has triumphed gloriously;
15: 2 The **L** is my strength and my might,
15: 3 The **L** is a warrior; the **L** is his name.
15: 6 Your right hand, O **L,** glorious in power—
15: 6 your right hand, O **L,** shattered the enemy.
15:11 "Who is like you, O **L,** among the gods?
15:16 as a stone until your people, O **L,**
15:17 O **L,** that you made your abode, the sanctuary,
15:17 that you made your abode, the sanctuary, O **L,**
15:18 The **L** will reign forever and ever."
15:19 **L** brought back the waters of the sea upon them;
15:21 "Sing to the **L,** for he has triumphed gloriously;
15:25 He cried out to the **L;**
15:25 and the **L** showed him a piece of wood;
15:25 the **L** made for them a statute and an ordinance
15:26 voice of the **L** your God, and do what is right AP
15:26 for I am the **L** who heals you." H
16: 3 died by the hand of the **L** in the land of Egypt, S
16: 4 Then the **L** said to Moses,
16: 6 the **L** who brought you out of the land of Egypt,
16: 7 in the morning you shall see the glory of the **L,** R
16: 7 he has heard your complaining against the **L.**
16: 8 the **L** gives you meat to eat in the evening
16: 8 the **L** has heard the complaining that you utter
16: 8 not against us but against the **L.**"
16: 9 of the Israelites, 'Draw near to the **L,**
16:10 and the glory of the **L** appeared in the cloud. RZ
16:11 The **L** spoke to Moses and said,
16:12 you shall know that I am the **L** your God.' " AH
16:15 "It is the bread that the **L** has given you to eat.
16:16 This is what the **L** has commanded:
16:23 "This is what the **L** has commanded:
16:23 a holy sabbath to the **L;**
16:25 "Eat it today, for today is a sabbath to the **L;**
16:28 The **L** said to Moses, "How long will you refuse
16:29 The **L** has given you the sabbath,
16:32 "This is what the **L** has commanded:
16:33 and place it before the **L,** D
16:34 As the **L** commanded Moses,
17: 1 journeyed by stages, as the **L** commanded.
17: 2 Why do you test the **L?**"
17: 4 So Moses cried out to the **L,**
17: 5 The **L** said to Moses, "Go on ahead of
17: 7 because the Israelites quarreled and tested the **L,**
17: 7 saying, "Is the **L** among us or not?"
17:14 Then the **L** said to Moses,
17:15 an altar and called it, The **L** is my banner.
17:16 He said, "A hand upon the banner of the **L!**
17:16 The **L** will have war with Amalek
18: 1 how the **L** had brought Israel out of Egypt.
18: 8 the **L** had done to Pharaoh and to the Egyptians
18: 8 and how the **L** had delivered them.
18: 9 for all the good that the **L** had done to Israel,
18:10 Jethro said, "Blessed be the **L,** T
18:11 Now I know that the **L** is greater than all gods,
19: 3 the **L** called to him from the mountain, saying,
19: 7 that the **L** had commanded him.
19: 8 "Everything that the **L** has spoken we will do."
19: 8 Moses reported the words of the people to the **L.**
19: 9 Then the **L** said to Moses,
19: 9 Moses had told the words of the people to the **L,**
19:10 the **L** said to Moses: "Go to the
19:11 because on the third day the **L** will come down
19:18 because the **L** had descended upon it in fire;
19:20 When the **L** descended upon Mount Sinai,
19:20 **L** summoned Moses to the top of the mountain,
19:21 Then the **L** said to Moses,
19:21 the people not to break through to the **L** to look;
19:22 the **L** must consecrate themselves or
19:22 or the **L** will break out against them."
19:23 the **L,** "The people are not permitted to come up
19:24 The **L** said to him, "Go down,
19:24 the people break through to come up to the **L;**
20: 2 I am the **L** your God, who brought you out of AH
20: 5 for I the **L** your God am a jealous God, A
20: 7 of the name of the **L** your God, AI
20: 7 **L** will not acquit anyone who misuses his name.

Ex 20:10 the seventh day is a sabbath to the **L** your God; A
20:11 For in six days the **L** made heaven and earth,
20:11 the **L** blessed the sabbath day and consecrated it.
20:12 in the land that the **L** your God is giving you. A
20:22 The **L** said to Moses: Thus you shall say to the
22:11 an oath before the **L** shall decide between D
22:20 to any god, other than the **L** alone, shall
23:19 into the house of the **L** your God. AF
23:25 You shall worship the **L** your God, A
24: 1 Then he said to Moses, "Come up to the **L,**
24: 2 Moses alone shall come near the **L;**
24: 3 and told the people all the words of the **L** and all
24: 3 the words that the **L** has spoken we will do."
24: 4 And Moses wrote down all the words of the **L.**
24: 5 as offerings of well-being to the **L.**
24: 7 they said, "All that the **L** has spoken we will do,
24: 8 the blood of the covenant that the **L** has made
24:12 The **L** said to Moses, "Come up to me on
24:16 The glory of the **L** settled on Mount Sinai, R
24:17 the glory of the **L** was like a devouring fire on R
25: 1 The **L** said to Moses:
27:21 from evening to morning before the **L.** D
28:12 and Aaron shall bear their names before the **L** D
28:29 for a continual remembrance before the **L.** D
28:30 on Aaron's heart when he goes in before the **L;** D
28:30 on his heart before the **L** continually. D
28:35 when he goes into the holy place before the **L,** D
28:36 like the engraving of a signet, "Holy to the **L.**"
28:38 in order that they may find favor before the **L.** D
29:11 and you shall slaughter the bull before the **L,** D
29:18 it is a burnt offering to the **L;**
29:18 it is a pleasing odor, an offering by fire to the **L.**
29:23 of unleavened bread that is before the **L;** D
29:24 raise them as an elevation offering before the **L.** D
29:25 of pleasing odor before the **L;** D
29:25 it is an offering by fire to the **L.**
29:26 as an elevation offering before the **L;** D
29:28 of well-being, their offering to the **L.**
29:41 for a pleasing odor, an offering by fire to the **L.**
29:42 the entrance of the tent of meeting before the **L,** D
29:46 they shall know that I am the **L** their God, AH
29:46 I am the **L** their God. AH
30: 8 before the **L** throughout your generations. D
30:10 It is most holy to the **L.**
30:11 The **L** spoke to Moses:
30:12 a ransom for their lives to the **L,**
30:13 half a shekel as an offering to the **L.**
30:15 to the **L** to make atonement for your lives.
30:16 before the **L** it will be a reminder to the Israelites D
30:17 The **L** spoke to Moses:
30:20 to make an offering by fire to the **L,**
30:22 The **L** spoke to Moses:
30:34 The **L** said to Moses: Take sweet spices,
30:37 it shall be regarded by you as holy to the **L.**
31: 1 The **L** spoke to Moses:
31:12 The **L** said to Moses:
31:13 given in order that you may know that I, the **L,**
31:15 a sabbath of solemn rest, holy to the **L;**
31:17 that in six days the **L** made heaven and earth,
32: 5 "Tomorrow shall be a festival to the **L.**"
32: 7 The **L** said to Moses, "Go down at once!
32: 9 The **L** said to Moses, "I have seen this people,
32:11 But Moses implored the **L** his God, and said, A
32:11 and said, "O **L,** why does your wrath burn hot
32:14 And the **L** changed his mind about the disaster
32:27 He said to them, "Thus says the **L,** C
32:29 for the service of the **L,**
32:30 But now I will go up to the **L;**
32:31 So Moses returned to the **L** and said, "Alas,
32:33 But the **L** said to Moses,
32:35 Then the **L** sent a plague on the people,
33: 1 The **L** said to Moses, "Go, leave this place,
33: 5 For the **L** had said to Moses,
33: 7 And everyone who sought the **L** would go out to
33: 9 and the **L** would speak with Moses.
33:11 Thus the **L** used to speak to Moses face to face,
33:12 Moses said to the **L,** "See, you have said to me,
33:17 The **L** said to Moses, "I will do the very thing
33:19 proclaim before you the name, 'The **L**';
33:21 And the **L** continued, "See,
34: 1 The **L** said to Moses, "Cut two tablets of stone
34: 4 as the **L** had commanded him,
34: 5 The **L** descended in the cloud and stood
34: 5 and proclaimed the name, "The **L.**"
34: 6 The **L** passed before him, and proclaimed, "The **L,**
the **L,**
34:10 among whom you live shall see the work of the **L;**
34:14 because the **L,** whose name is Jealous,
34:23 before the **L** God, the God of Israel. DJ
34:24 to appear before the **L** your God three times AD
34:26 to the house of the **L** your God. AF
34:27 The **L** said to Moses: Write these words;
34:28 with the **L** forty days and forty nights;
34:32 that the **L** had spoken with him on Mount Sinai.
34:34 Moses went in before the **L** to speak with him, D
35: 1 the things that the **L** has commanded you to do:
35: 2 a holy sabbath of solemn rest to the **L;**
35: 4 This is the thing that the **L** has commanded:
35: 5 Take from among you an offering to the **L;**
35:10 and make all that the **L** has commanded:
35:22 everyone bringing an offering of gold to the **L.**
35:29 that the **L** had commanded by Moses to be done,
35:29 brought it as a freewill offering to the **L.**
35:30 the **L** has called by name Bezalel son of Uri son
36: 1 the **L** has given skill and understanding to know
36: 1 with all that the **L** has commanded.
36: 2 to whom the **L** had given skill,

Ex 36: 5 for doing the work that the **L** has commanded us
38:22 made all that the **L** commanded Moses;
39: 1 as the **L** had commanded Moses.
39: 5 as the **L** had commanded Moses.
39: 7 as the **L** had commanded Moses.
39:21 as the **L** had commanded Moses.
39:26 as the **L** had commanded Moses.
39:29 as the **L** had commanded Moses.
39:30 like the engraving of a signet, "Holy to the **L.**"
39:31 as the **L** had commanded Moses.
39:32 as the **L** had commanded Moses.
39:42 the work just as the **L** had commanded Moses.
39:43 the work just as the **L** had commanded,
40: 1 The **L** spoke to Moses:
40:16 as the **L** had commanded him.
40:19 as the **L** had commanded Moses.
40:21 as the **L** had commanded Moses.
40:23 and set the bread in order on it before the **L;** D
40:23 as the **L** had commanded Moses.
40:25 and set up the lamps before the **L;** D
40:25 as the **L** had commanded Moses.
40:27 as the **L** had commanded Moses.
40:29 as the **L** had commanded Moses.
40:32 as the **L** had commanded Moses.
40:34 and the glory of the **L** filled the tabernacle. R
40:35 and the glory of the **L** filled the tabernacle. R
40:38 the cloud of the **L** was on the tabernacle by day,
Lev 1: 1 The **L** summoned Moses and spoke to him from
1: 2 of you bring an offering of livestock to the **L,**
1: 3 for acceptance in your behalf before the **L.** D
1: 5 The bull shall be slaughtered before the **L;** D
1: 9 an offering by fire of pleasing odor to the **L.**
1:11 on the north side of the altar before the **L,** D
1:13 an offering by fire of pleasing odor to the **L.**
1:14 If your offering to the **L** is a burnt offering
1:17 an offering by fire of pleasing odor to the **L.**
2: 1 When anyone presents a grain offering to the **L,**
2: 2 an offering by fire of pleasing odor to the **L.**
2: 3 a most holy part of the offerings by fire to the **L.**
2: 8 the **L** the grain offering that is prepared in any
2: 9 an offering by fire of pleasing odor to the **L.**
2:10 a most holy part of the offerings by fire to the **L.**
2:11 No grain offering that you bring to the **L** shall
2:11 into smoke as an offering by fire to the **L.**
2:12 You may bring them to the **L** as an offering
2:14 you bring a grain offering of first fruits to the **L,**
2:16 it is an offering by fire to the **L.**
3: 1 without blemish before the **L.** D
3: 3 as an offering by fire to the **L,**
3: 5 as an offering by fire of pleasing odor to the **L.**
3: 6 for a sacrifice of well-being to the **L** is from
3: 7 you shall bring it before the **L** D
3: 9 as an offering by fire to the **L:**
3:11 on the altar as a food offering by fire to the **L.**
3:12 you shall bring it before the **L** D
3:14 as an offering by fire to the **L,**
4: 1 The **L** spoke to Moses, saying,
4: 3 without blemish as a sin offering to the **L.**
4: 4 tent of meeting before the **L** and lay his hand D
4: 4 the bull shall be slaughtered before the **L.** D
4: 6 the blood seven times before the **L** in front of D
4: 7 that is in the tent of meeting before the **L;** D
4:15 on the head of the bull before the **L,** D
4:15 and the bull shall be slaughtered before the **L.** D
4:17 and sprinkle it seven times before the **L,** D
4:18 on the horns of the altar that is before the **L** in D
4:22 that by commandments of the **L** his God ought A
4:24 the burnt offering is slaughtered before the **L;** D
4:31 on the altar for a pleasing odor to the **L.**
4:35 with the offerings by fire to the **L.**
5: 6 And you shall bring to the **L,**
5: 7 you shall bring to the **L,**
5:12 with the offerings by fire to the **L;**
5:14 The **L** spoke to Moses, saying:
5:15 of the **L,** you shall bring, as your guilt offering
5:15 you shall bring, as your guilt offering to the **L,**
5:19 you have incurred guilt before the **L.** D
6: 1 The **L** spoke to Moses, saying:
6: 2 a trespass against the **L** by deceiving a neighbor
6: 6 as your guilt offering to the **L,**
6: 7 on your behalf before the **L,** D
6: 8 The **L** spoke to Moses, saying:
6:14 The sons of Aaron shall offer it before the **L,** D
6:15 on the altar as a pleasing odor to the **L.**
6:19 The **L** spoke to Moses, saying:
6:20 that Aaron and his sons shall offer to the **L** on
6:21 you shall present it as a pleasing odor to the **L.**
6:24 The **L** spoke to Moses, saying:
6:25 be slaughtered before the **L** at the spot where D
7: 5 on the altar as an offering by fire to the **L;**
7:11 of well-being that one may offer to the **L.**
7:14 one cake from each offering, as a gift to the **L;**
7:22 The **L** spoke to Moses, saying:
7:25 an offering by fire may be made to the **L,**
7:28 The **L** spoke to Moses, saying:
7:29 of you who would offer to the **L** your sacrifice
7:29 to the **L** your offering from your sacrifice
7:30 be raised as an elevation offering before the **L.** D
7:35 to the **L,** once they have been brought forward to
serve the **L** as priests;
7:36 these the **L** commanded to be given them,
7:38 the **L** commanded Moses on Mount Sinai,
7:38 of Israel to bring their offerings to the **L,**
8: 1 The **L** spoke to Moses, saying:
8: 4 And Moses did as the **L** commanded him.
8: 5 "This is what the **L** has commanded to
8: 9 the holy crown, as the **L** commanded Moses.

†LORD distinguishes the proper name of God, *Yahweh*, indicated in the NRSV by "LORD," from the words translated "Lord" and "lord," indexed under the heading ***LORD** on pages 798-804.

Lev 8:13 as the L commanded Moses.
8:17 as the L commanded Moses.
8:21 an offering by fire to the L,
8:21 as the L commanded Moses.
8:26 of unleavened bread that was before the L, D
8:27 as an elevation offering before the L. D
8:28 an offering by fire to the L.
8:29 as an elevation offering before the L; D
8:29 as the L commanded Moses.
8:34 the L has commanded to be done
8:36 that the L commanded through Moses.
9: 2 without blemish, and offer them before the L. D
9: 4 of well-being to sacrifice before the L; D
9: 4 For today the L will appear to you.' "
9: 5 near and stood before the L. D
9: 6 "This is the thing that the L commanded you
9: 6 so that the glory of the L may appear to you." R
9: 7 as the L has commanded."
9:10 as the L commanded Moses;
9:21 as an elevation offering before the L, D
9:23 the glory of the L appeared to all the people. RZ
9:24 from the L and consumed the burnt offering
10: 1 and they offered unholy fire before the L, D
10: 2 from the presence of the L and consumed them,
10: 2 and they died before the L. D
10: 3 "This is what the L meant when he said,
10: 6 may mourn the burning that the L has sent.
10: 7 for the anointing oil of the L is on you."
10: 8 And the L spoke to Aaron:
10:11 that the L has spoken to them through Moses.
10:13 from the offerings by fire to the L;
10:15 to raise for an elevation offering before the L; D
10:15 as the L has commanded.
10:17 to make atonement on their behalf before the L. D
10:19 and their burnt offering before the L; D
10:19 would it have been agreeable to the L?"
11: 1 L spoke to Moses and Aaron, saying to them:
11:44 For I am the L your God; AH
11:45 For I am the L who brought you up from H
12: 1 The L spoke to Moses, saying:
12: 7 He shall offer it before the L, D
13: 1 The L spoke to Moses and Aaron, saying:
14: 1 The L spoke to Moses, saying:
14:11 along with these things, before the L, D
14:12 raise them as an elevation offering before the L. D
14:16 with his finger seven times before the L. D
14:18 on his behalf before the L: D
14:23 of the tent of meeting, before the L; D
14:24 as an elevation offering before the L. D
14:27 that is in his left hand seven times before the L. D
14:29 to make atonement on his behalf before the L. D
14:31 the priest shall make atonement before the L D
14:33 The L spoke to Moses and Aaron, saying:
15: 1 The L spoke to Moses and Aaron, saying:
15:14 and come before the L to the entrance of the tent D
15:15 on his behalf before the L for his discharge. D
15:30 before the L for her unclean discharge. D
16: 1 The L spoke to Moses after the death of
16: 1 when they drew near before the L and died. D
16: 2 The L said to Moses: Tell your brother Aaron
16: 7 and set them before the L at the entrance of D
16: 8 one lot for the L and the other lot for Azazel.
16: 9 on which the lot fell for the L, and offer it as
16:10 for Azazel shall be presented alive before the L D
16:12 of coals of fire from the altar before the L, D
16:13 and put the incense on the fire before the L, D
16:18 before the L and make atonement on its behalf, D
16:30 all your sins you shall be clean before the L. D
16:34 And Moses did as the L had commanded him.
17: 1 The L spoke to Moses:
17: 2 This is what the L has commanded.
17: 4 an offering to the L before the tabernacle of the L,
17: 5 that they may bring them to the L,
17: 5 offer them as sacrifices of well-being to the L.
17: 6 of the L at the entrance of the tent of meeting,
17: 6 the fat into smoke as a pleasing odor to the L,
17: 9 to sacrifice it to the L,
18: 1 The L spoke to Moses, saying:
18: 2 I am the L your God. AH
18: 4 I am the L your God. AH
18: 5 by doing so one shall live: I am the L. H
18: 6 to uncover nakedness: I am the L. H
18:21 so profane the name of your God: I am the L. H
18:30 I am the L your God. AH
19: 1 The L spoke to Moses, saying:
19: 2 You shall be holy, for I the L your God am holy. A
19: 3 I am the L your God. AH
19: 4 I am the L your God. AH
19: 5 you offer a sacrifice of well-being to the L,
19: 8 they have profaned what is holy to the L;
19:10 I am the L your God. AH
19:12 of your God: I am the L. H
19:14 you shall fear your God: I am the L. H
19:16 of your neighbor: I am the L. H
19:18 love your neighbor as yourself: I am the L. H
19:21 a guilt offering for himself to the L,
19:22 the ram of guilt offering before the L for his sin D
19:24 be set apart for rejoicing in the L.
19:25 I am the L your God. AH
19:28 or tattoo any marks upon you: I am the L. H
19:30 and reverence my sanctuary: I am the L. H
19:31 I am the L your God. AH
19:32 and you shall fear your God: I am the L. H
19:34 I am the L your God. AH
19:36 I am the L your God, AH
19:37 and observe them: I am the L. H
20: 1 The L spoke to Moses, saying:

Lev 20: 7 for I am the L your God. AH
20: 8 I am the L; I sanctify you. H
20:24 I am the L your God; AH
20:26 You shall be holy to me; for I the L am holy,
21: 1 The L said to Moses: Speak to the
21: 8 they shall be holy to you, for I the L,
21:12 of his God is upon him: I am the L. H
21:15 for I am the L; I sanctify him. H
21:16 The L spoke to Moses, saying:
21:23 for I am the L; I sanctify them. H
22: 1 The L spoke to Moses, saying:
22: 2 not profane my holy name; I am the L. H
22: 3 which the people of Israel dedicate to the L,
22: 3 from my presence: I am the L. H
22: 8 becoming unclean by it: I am the L. H
22: 9 I am the L; I sanctify them. H
22:15 which they offer to the L,
22:16 for I am the L; I sanctify them. H
22:17 The L spoke to Moses, saying:
22:18 as a freewill offering that is offered to the L as
22:21 anyone offers a sacrifice of well-being to the L,
22:22 the L or put any of them on the altar as offerings
22:22 of them on the altar as offerings by fire to the L.
22:24 you shall not offer to the L;
22:26 The L spoke to Moses, saying:
22:29 you sacrifice a thanksgiving offering to the L,
22:30 until morning: I am the L. H
22:31 and observe them: I am the L. H
22:32 among the people of Israel: I am the L; H
22:33 be your God: I am the L. H
23: 1 The L spoke to Moses, saying:
23: 2 These are the appointed festivals of the L
23: 3 a sabbath to the L throughout your settlements.
23: 4 These are the appointed festivals of the L,
23: 5 there shall be a passover offering to the L,
23: 6 the festival of unleavened bread to the L;
23: 9 The L spoke to Moses:
23:11 He shall raise the sheaf before the L, D
23:12 without blemish, as a burnt offering to the L.
23:13 an offering by fire of pleasing odor to the L;
23:16 an offering of new grain to the L.
23:17 baked with leaven, as first fruits to the L.
23:18 they shall be a burnt offering to the L,
23:18 an offering by fire of pleasing odor to the L.
23:20 an elevation offering before the L, together with D
23:20 they shall be holy to the L for the priest.
23:22 I am the L your God. AH
23:23 The L spoke to Moses, saying:
23:26 The L spoke to Moses, saying:
23:28 on your behalf before the L your God. AD
23:33 The L spoke to Moses, saying:
23:34 there shall be the festival of booths to the L.
23:37 These are the appointed festivals of the L,
23:37 for presenting to the L offerings by fire—
23:38 apart from the sabbaths of the L,
23:38 which you give to the L.
23:39 you shall keep the festival of the L,
23:40 and you shall rejoice before the L your God AD
23:41 as a festival to the L seven days in the year;
23:43 I am the L your God. AH
23:44 of Israel the appointed festivals of the L.
24: 1 The L spoke to Moses, saying:
24: 3 from evening to morning before the L regularly; D
24: 4 of pure gold before the L regularly. D
24: 7 as an offering by fire to the L.
24: 8 in order before the L regularly as a commitment D
24: 9 for him from the offerings by fire to the L,
24:12 until the decision of the L should be made clear
24:13 The L said to Moses, saying:
24:16 One who blasphemes the name of the L shall I
24:22 for I am the L your God. AH
24:23 of Israel did as the L had commanded Moses.
25: 1 The L spoke to Moses on Mount Sinai, saying:
25: 2 the land shall observe a sabbath for the L.
25: 4 for the land, a sabbath for the L:
25:17 for I am the L your God. AH
25:38 I am the L your God, AH
25:55 I am the L your God. AH
26: 1 for I am the L your God. AH
26: 2 and reverence my sanctuary: I am the L. H
26:13 I am the L your God who brought you out of AH
26:44 for I am the L their God; AH
26:45 to be their God: I am the L. H
26:46 and laws that the L established between himself
27: 1 The L spoke to Moses, saying:
27: 2 When a person makes an explicit vow to the L
27: 9 that may be brought as an offering to the L,
27: 9 any such that may be given to the L shall
27:11 that may not be brought as an offering to the L,
27:14 If a person consecrates a house to the L,
27:16 to the L any inherited landholding,
27:21 it shall be holy to the L as a devoted field;
27:22 to the L a field that has been purchased,
27:23 a sacred donation to the L.
27:26 however, which as a firstling belongs to the L,
27:28 to destruction for the L, be it human or animal,
27:28 every devoted thing is most holy to the L.
27:30 they are holy to the L.
27:32 shall be holy to the L.
27:34 the commandments that the L gave to Moses for
Nu 1: 1 L spoke to Moses in the wilderness of Sinai,
1:19 as the L commanded Moses.
1:48 The L had said to Moses:
1:54 they did just as the L commanded Moses.
2: 1 The L spoke to Moses and Aaron, saying:
2:33 Just as the L had commanded Moses,
2:34 as the L had commanded Moses:

Nu 3: 1 when the L spoke with Moses on Mount Sinai.
3: 4 before the L when they offered illicit fire before D
3: 4 when they offered illicit fire before the L in D
3: 5 Then the L spoke to Moses, saying:
3:11 Then the L spoke to Moses, saying:
3:13 they shall be mine. I am the L. H
3:14 the L spoke to Moses in the wilderness of Sinai,
3:16 according to the word of the L, G
3:39 at the commandment of the L,
3:40 Then the L said to Moses:
3:41 shall accept the Levites for me—I am the L— H
3:42 as the L commanded him.
3:44 Then the L spoke to Moses, saying:
3:45 and the Levites shall be mine. I am the L. H
3:51 according to the word of the L, G
3:51 as the L had commanded Moses.
4: 1 The L spoke to Moses and Aaron, saying:
4:17 Then the L spoke to Moses and Aaron, saying:
4:21 Then the L spoke to Moses, saying:
4:37 to the commandment of the L by Moses.
4:41 according to the commandment of the L.
4:45 to the commandment of the L by Moses.
4:49 of the L through Moses they were appointed
4:49 as the L commanded Moses.
5: 1 The L spoke to Moses, saying:
5: 4 the L had spoken to Moses, so the Israelites did.
5: 5 The L spoke to Moses, saying:
5: 6 breaking faith with the L,
5: 8 the restitution for wrong shall go to the L for
5:11 The L spoke to Moses, saying:
5:16 and set her before the L; D
5:18 The priest shall set the woman before the L, D
5:21 "the L make you an execration and an oath
5:21 when the L makes your uterus drop,
5:25 and shall elevate the grain offering before the L D
5:30 then he shall set the woman before the L, D
6: 1 The L spoke to Moses, saying:
6: 2 to separate themselves to the L,
6: 5 for which they separate themselves to the L,
6: 6 that they separate themselves to the L they shall
6: 8 All their days as nazirites they are holy to the L.
6:12 and separate themselves to the L for their days
6:14 and they shall offer their gift to the L,
6:16 The priest shall present them before the L D
6:17 to the L, with the basket of unleavened bread;
6:20 as an elevation offering before the L; D
6:21 Their offering to the L must be in accordance
6:22 The L spoke to Moses, saying:
6:24 The L bless you and keep you;
6:25 the L make his face to shine upon you,
6:26 the L lift up his countenance upon you,
7: 3 They brought their offerings before the L, D
7: 4 Then the L said to Moses:
7:11 The L said to Moses: They shall present their
7:89 the L, he would hear the voice speaking to him
8: 1 The L spoke to Moses, saying:
8: 3 as the L had commanded Moses.
8: 4 to the pattern that the L had shown Moses,
8: 5 The L spoke to Moses, saying:
8:10 When you bring the Levites before the L, D
8:11 and Aaron shall present the Levites before the L D
8:11 that they may do the service of the L.
8:12 and the other for a burnt offering to the L,
8:13 as an elevation offering to the L.
8:20 the Levites just as the L had commanded Moses
8:21 as an elevation offering before the L, D
8:22 As the L had commanded Moses concerning
8:23 The L spoke to Moses, saying:
9: 1 L spoke to Moses in the wilderness of Sinai,
9: 5 Just as the L had commanded Moses,
9: 8 so that I may hear what the L will command
9: 9 The L spoke to Moses, saying:
9:10 shall still keep the passover to the L.
9:14 to the L shall do so according to the statute of
9:18 of the L the Israelites would set out,
9:18 and at the command of the L they would camp.
9:19 the Israelites would keep the charge of the L,
9:20 to the command of the L they would remain
9:20 to the command of the L they would set out.
9:23 At the command of the L they would camp,
9:23 and at the command of the L they would set out.
9:23 They kept the charge of the L,
9:23 at the command of the L by Moses.
10: 1 The L spoke to Moses, saying:
10: 9 be remembered before the L your God and AD
10:10 on your behalf before the L your God: AD
10:10 I am the L your God. AH
10:13 for the first time at the command of the L
10:29 for the place of which the L said, 'I will give it
10:29 for the L has promised good to Israel."
10:32 whatever good the L does for us,
10:33 from the mount of the L three days' journey
10:33 ark of the covenant of the L going before O
10:34 the L being over them by day when they set out
10:35 "Arise, O L, let your enemies be scattered,
10:36 O L of the ten thousand thousands of Israel."
11: 1 in the hearing of the L about their misfortunes,
11: 1 the L heard it and his anger was kindled.
11: 1 Then the fire of the L burned against them,
11: 2 and Moses prayed to the L, and the fire abated.
11: 3 because the fire of the L burned against them.
11:10 Then the L became very angry,
11:11 So Moses said to the L,
11:16 So the L said to Moses,
11:18 for you have wailed in the hearing of the L,
11:18 the L will give you meat, and you shall eat.
11:20 you have rejected the L who is among you,

†LORD distinguishes the proper name of God, *Yahweh*, indicated in the NRSV by "LORD," from the words translated "Lord" and "lord," indexed under the heading ***LORD** on pages 798-804.

Nu 11:23 The **L** said to Moses, "Is
11:24 and told the people the words of the **L**;
11:25 the **L** came down in the cloud and spoke to him,
11:29 and that the **L** would put his spirit on them!"
11:31 Then a wind went out from the **L**,
11:33 anger of the **L** was kindled against the people,
11:33 the **L** struck the people with a very great plague.
12: 2 "Has the **L** spoken only through Moses?
12: 2 And the **L** heard it.
12: 4 Suddenly the **L** said to Moses, Aaron,
12: 5 Then the **L** came down in a pillar of cloud,
12: 6 I the **L** make myself known to them in visions;
12: 8 and he beholds the form of the **L**.
12: 9 the anger of the **L** was kindled against them,
12:13 Moses cried to the **L**, "O God, please heal her."
12:14 But the **L** said to Moses,
13: 1 The **L** said to Moses,
13: 3 according to the command of the **L**,
14: 3 Why is the **L** bringing us into this land to fall by
14: 8 If the **L** is pleased with us,
14: 9 Only, do not rebel against the **L**;
14: 9 and the **L** is with us; do not fear them."
14:10 glory of the **L** appeared at the tent of meeting RZ
14:11 And the **L** said to Moses,
14:13 But Moses said to the **L**,
14:14 They have heard that you, O **L**,
14:14 for you, O **L**, are seen face to face,
14:16 because the **L** was not able to bring this people
14:17 of the **L** be great in the way that you promised
14:18 'The **L** is slow to anger,
14:20 the **L** said, "I do forgive, just as you have asked;
14:21 the earth shall be filled with the glory of the **L**— R
14:26 And the **L** spoke to Moses and to Aaron, saying:
14:28 Say to them, "As I live," says the **L**, B
14:35 I the **L** have spoken;
14:37 about the land died by a plague before the **L**. D
14:40 up to the place that the **L** has promised,
14:41 to transgress the command of the **L**?
14:42 Do not go up, for the **L** is not with you;
14:43 you have turned back from following the **L**,
14:43 the **L** will not be with you."
14:44 even though the ark of the covenant of the **L**, O
15: 1 The **L** spoke to Moses, saying:
15: 3 and you make an offering by fire to the **L** from
15: 3 to make a pleasing odor for the **L**,
15: 4 to the **L** shall present also a grain offering,
15: 7 a pleasing odor to the **L**.
15: 8 a vow or as an offering of well-being to the **L**,
15:10 as an offering by fire, a pleasing odor to the **L**.
15:13 a pleasing odor to the **L**.
15:14 a pleasing odor to the **L**, shall do as you do.
15:15 you and the alien shall be alike before the **L**. D
15:17 The **L** spoke to Moses, saying:
15:19 you shall present a donation to the **L**.
15:21 to the **L** a donation from the first of your batch
15:22 that the **L** has spoken to Moses—
15:23 that the **L** has commanded you by Moses,
15:23 the **L** gave commandment and thereafter,
15:24 a pleasing odor to the **L**,
15:25 an offering by fire to the **L**,
15:25 and their sin offering before the **L**, D
15:28 the priest shall make atonement before the **L** D
15:30 whether a native or an alien, affronts the **L**,
15:31 Because of having despised the word of the **L** G
15:35 **L** said to Moses, "The man shall be put to death;
15:36 just as the **L** had commanded Moses.
15:37 The **L** said to Moses:
15:39 the commandments of the **L** and do them,
15:41 I am the **L** your God, who brought you out AH
15:41 I am the **L** your God. AH
16: 3 everyone of them, and the **L** is among them.
16: 3 above the assembly of the **L**?"
16: 5 the morning the **L** will make known who is his,
16: 7 and lay incense on them before the **L**; D
16: 7 man whom the **L** chooses shall be the holy one.
16:11 company have gathered together against the **L**.
16:15 Moses was very angry and said to the **L**,
16:16 be present tomorrow before the **L**, D
16:17 each one of you present his censer before the **L**, D
16:19 the glory of the **L** appeared to the whole RZ
16:20 the **L** spoke to Moses and to Aaron, saying:
16:23 And the **L** spoke to Moses, saying:
16:28 that the **L** has sent me to do all these works;
16:29 then the **L** has not sent me.
16:30 But if the **L** creates something new,
16:30 that these men have despised the **L**."
16:35 And fire came out from the **L** and consumed
16:36 Then the **L** spoke to Moses, saying:
16:38 for they presented them before the **L** D
16:40 shall approach to offer incense before the **L**, D
16:40 just as the **L** had said to him through Moses.
16:41 saying, "You have killed the people of the **L**."
16:42 and the glory of the **L** appeared. RZ
16:44 and the **L** spoke to Moses, saying,
16:46 For wrath has gone out from the **L**;
17: 1 The **L** spoke to Moses, saying:
17: 7 So Moses placed the staffs before the **L** in D
17: 9 the staffs from before the **L** to all the Israelites; D
17:10 And the **L** said to Moses,
17:11 just as the **L** commanded him, so he did.
17:13 the tabernacle of the **L** will die.
18: 1 The **L** said to Aaron: You
18: 6 they are now yours as a gift, dedicated to the **L**,
18: 8 The **L** spoke to Aaron: I have given you charge of
18:12 the choice produce that they give to the **L**,
18:13 which they bring to the **L**, shall be yours;
18:15 human and animal, which is offered to the **L**,

Nu 18:17 an offering by fire for a pleasing odor to the **L**;
18:19 that the Israelites present to the **L** I have given
18:19 a covenant of salt forever before the **L** for you D
18:20 Then the **L** said to Aaron:
18:24 which they set apart as an offering to the **L**.
18:25 Then the **L** spoke to Moses, saying:
18:26 you shall set apart an offering from it to the **L**,
18:28 Thus you also shall set apart an offering to the **L**
18:29 you shall set apart every offering due to the **L**;
19: 1 The **L** spoke to Moses and Aaron, saying:
19: 2 a statute of the law that the **L** has commanded:
19:13 defile the tabernacle of the **L**;
19:20 for they have defiled the sanctuary of the **L**.
20: 3 when our kindred died before the **L**! D
20: 4 the assembly of the **L** into this wilderness for us
20: 6 and the glory of the **L** appeared to them. RZ
20: 7 The **L** spoke to Moses, saying:
20: 9 So Moses took the staff from before the **L**, D
20:12 But the **L** said to Moses and Aaron,
20:13 where the people of Israel quarreled with the **L**,
20:16 and when we cried to the **L**, he heard our voice,
20:23 the **L** said to Moses and Aaron at Mount Hor,
20:27 Moses did as the **L** had commanded;
21: 2 Then Israel made a vow to the **L** and said,
21: 3 The **L** listened to the voice of Israel,
21: 6 the **L** sent poisonous serpents among the people,
21: 7 "We have sinned by speaking against the **L** and
21: 7 pray to the **L** to take away the serpents from us."
21: 8 And the **L** said to Moses,
21:14 in the Book of the Wars of the **L**,
21:16 that is the well of which the **L** said to Moses,
21:34 the **L** said to Moses, "Do not be afraid of him;
22: 8 just as the **L** speaks to me";
22:13 for the **L** has refused to let me go with you."
22:18 not go beyond the command of the **L** my God, A
22:19 I may learn what more the **L** may say to me."
22:22 the angel of the **L** took his stand in the road K
22:23 saw the angel of the **L** standing in the road, K
22:24 Then the angel of the **L** stood in a narrow path K
22:25 When the donkey saw the angel of the **L**, K
22:26 Then the angel of the **L** went ahead, K
22:27 When the donkey saw the angel of the **L**, K
22:28 Then the **L** opened the mouth of the donkey,
22:31 Then the **L** opened the eyes of Balaam,
22:31 he saw the angel of the **L** standing in the road, K
22:32 The angel of the **L** said to him, K
22:34 Then Balaam said to the angel of the **L**, K
22:35 The angel of the **L** said to Balaam, K
23: 3 Perhaps the **L** will come to meet me.
23: 5 The **L** put a word in Balaam's mouth, and said,
23: 8 How can I denounce those whom the **L** has
23:12 "Must I not take care to say what the **L** puts
23:15 while I meet the **L** over there.
23:16 The **L** met Balaam, put a word into his mouth,
23:17 Balak said to him, "What has the **L** said?"
23:21 The **L** their God is with them, A
23:26 'Whatever the **L** says, that is what I must do'?"
24: 1 Balaam saw that it pleased the **L** to bless Israel,
24: 6 like aloes that the **L** has planted,
24:11 but the **L** has denied you any reward."
24:13 beyond the word of the **L**, to do either good or G
24:13 what the **L** says, that is what I will say'?
25: 4 The **L** said to Moses, "Take all the chiefs of
25: 4 and impale them in the sun before the **L**, D
25: 4 that the fierce anger of the **L** may turn away
25:10 The **L** spoke to Moses, saying:
25:16 The **L** said to Moses,
26: 1 the **L** said to Moses and to Eleazar son of Aaron
26: 4 as the **L** commanded Moses.
26: 9 when they rebelled against the **L**,
26:52 The **L** spoke to Moses, saying:
26:61 when they offered illicit fire before the **L**. D
26:65 For the **L** had said of them,
27: 3 against the **L** in the company of Korah, but died
27: 5 Moses brought their case before the **L**. D
27: 6 And the **L** spoke to Moses, saying:
27:11 as the **L** commanded Moses."
27:12 The **L** said to Moses, "Go up this mountain of
27:15 Moses spoke to the **L**, saying,
27:16 "Let the **L**, the God of the spirits
27:17 the congregation of the **L** may not be like sheep
27:18 So the **L** said to Moses,
27:21 by the decision of the Urim before the **L**; D
27:22 So Moses did as the **L** commanded him.
27:23 as the **L** had directed through Moses.
28: 1 The **L** spoke to Moses, saying:
28: 3 the offering by fire that you shall offer to the **L**:
28: 6 an offering by fire to the **L**.
28: 7 a drink offering of strong drink to the **L**.
28: 8 a pleasing odor to the **L**.
28:11 a burnt offering to the **L**:
28:13 an offering by fire to the **L**.
28:15 be one male goat for a sin offering to the **L**;
28:16 be a passover offering to the **L**.
28:19 a burnt offering to the **L**:
28:24 a pleasing odor to the **L**;
28:26 to the **L** at your festival of weeks, you shall have
28:27 a pleasing odor to the **L**:
29: 2 a pleasing odor to the **L**:
29: 6 a pleasing odor, an offering by fire to the **L**.
29: 8 You shall offer a burnt offering to the **L**,
29:12 a festival to the **L** seven days.
29:13 an offering by fire, a pleasing odor to the **L**:
29:36 an offering by fire, a pleasing odor to the **L**:
29:39 to the **L** at your appointed festivals,
29:40 as the **L** had commanded Moses.
30: 1 This is what the **L** has commanded.

Nu 30: 2 When a man makes a vow to the **L**,
30: 3 When a woman makes a vow to the **L**,
30: 5 and the **L** will forgive her,
30: 8 and the **L** will forgive her.
30:12 and the **L** will forgive her.
30:16 the **L** commanded Moses concerning a husband
31: 1 The **L** spoke to Moses, saying,
31: 7 as the **L** had commanded Moses,
31:16 the Israelites act treacherously against the **L** in
31:16 plague came among the congregation of the **L**.
31:21 of the law that the **L** has commanded Moses:
31:25 The **L** spoke to Moses, saying,
31:28 set aside as tribute for the **L**,
31:29 to Eleazar the priest as an offering to the **L**.
31:30 of the tabernacle of the **L**."
31:31 the priest did as the **L** had commanded Moses:
31:41 Moses gave the tribute, the offering for the **L**,
31:41 as the **L** had commanded Moses.
31:47 of the tabernacle of the **L**;
31:47 as the **L** had commanded Moses.
31:50 to make atonement for ourselves before the **L**." D
31:52 of the offering that they offered to the **L**,
31:54 as a memorial for the Israelites before the **L**. D
32: 4 that the **L** subdued before the congregation
32: 7 over into the land that the **L** has given them?
32: 9 into the land that the **L** had given them.
32:12 for they have unreservedly followed the **L**.'
32:13 done evil in the sight of the **L** had disappeared. L
32:20 you take up arms to go before the **L** for the war, D
32:21 cross the Jordan before the **L**, D
32:22 and the land is subdued before the **L**— D
32:22 and be free of obligation to the **L** and to Israel,
32:22 this land shall be your possession before the **L**. D
32:23 you have sinned against the **L**;
32:27 everyone armed for war, to do battle for the **L**,
32:29 everyone armed for battle before the **L**, D
32:31 "As the **L** has spoken to your servants,
32:32 We will cross over armed before the **L** into D
33: 2 stage by stage, by command of the **L**;
33: 4 whom the **L** had struck down among them.
33: 4 **L** executed judgments even against their gods.
33:38 of the **L** and died there in the fortieth year after
33:50 the **L** spoke to Moses, saying:
34: 1 The **L** spoke to Moses, saying:
34:13 the **L** has commanded to give to the nine tribes
34:16 The **L** spoke to Moses, saying:
34:29 the ones whom the **L** commanded to apportion
35: 1 the **L** spoke to Moses, saying:
35: 9 The **L** spoke to Moses, saying:
35:34 for I the **L** dwell among the Israelites.
36: 2 "The **L** commanded my lord to give the land
36: 2 and my lord was commanded by the **L** to give
36: 5 the Israelites according to the word of the **L**, G
36: 6 the **L** commands concerning the daughters
36:10 as the **L** had commanded Moses.
36:13 and the ordinances that the **L** commanded

Dt 1: 3 as the **L** had commanded him to speak to them.
1: 6 The **L** our God spoke to us at Horeb, A
1:10 The **L** your God has multiplied you, A
1:11 May the **L**, the God of your ancestors,
1:19 Then, just as the **L** our God had ordered us, A
1:20 which the **L** our God is giving us. A
1:21 See, the **L** your God has given the land to you; A
1:21 go up, take possession, as the **L**,
1:25 a good land that the **L** our God is giving us." A
1:26 against the command of the **L** your God; A
1:27 the **L** hates us that he has brought us out of
1:30 The **L** your God, who goes before you, A
1:31 where you saw how the **L** your God carried you, A
1:32 you have no trust in the **L** your God, A
1:34 **L** heard your words, he was wrathful and swore:
1:36 because of his complete fidelity to the **L**."
1:37 Even with me the **L** was angry on your account,
1:41 "We have sinned against the **L**!
1:41 just as the **L** our God commanded us." A
1:42 The **L** said to me, "Say to them,
1:43 the command of the **L** and presumptuously went
1:45 When you returned and wept before the **L**, D
1:45 the **L** would neither heed your voice
2: 1 as the **L** had told me and skirted Mount Seir
2: 2 Then the **L** said to me:
2: 7 Surely the **L** your God has blessed you A
2: 7 These forty years the **L** your God has been A
2: 9 the **L** said to me: "Do not harass Moab
2:12 the land that the **L** gave them as a possession.)
2:14 as the **L** had sworn concerning them.
2:17 the **L** spoke to me, saying,
2:21 But the **L** destroyed them from before
2:29 into the land that the **L** our God is giving us." A
2:30 for the **L** your God had hardened his spirit A
2:31 The **L** said to me, "See,
2:33 the **L** our God gave him over to us; A
2:36 The **L** our God gave everything to us. A
2:37 just as the **L** our God had charged. A
3: 2 The **L** said to me, "Do not fear him,
3: 3 the **L** our God also handed over to us King Og A
3:18 **L** your God has given you this land to occupy, A
3:20 When the **L** gives rest to your kindred,
3:20 the land that the **L** your God is giving them A
3:21 the **L** your God has done to these two kings; A
3:21 so the **L** will do to all the kingdoms
3:22 for it is the **L** your God who fights for you." A
3:23 At that time, too, I entreated the **L**, saying:
3:26 But the **L** was angry with me on your account
3:26 The **L** said to me, "Enough from you!
4: 1 to enter and occupy the land that the **L**,
4: 2 but keep the commandments of the **L** your God A

Dt 4: 3 You have seen for yourselves what the L did
4: 3 how the L your God destroyed from A
4: 4 to the L your God are all alive today. A
4: 5 See, just as the L my God has charged me, A
4: 7 near to it as the L our God is whenever we call A
4:10 stood before the L your God at Horeb, AD
4:10 the L said to me, "Assemble the people for me,
4:12 Then the L spoke to you out of the fire.
4:14 And the L charged me at that time
4:15 Since you saw no form when the L spoke to you
4:19 things that the L your God has allotted to all A
4:20 But the L has taken you and brought you out of
4:21 The L was angry with me because of you,
4:21 the L your God is giving for your possession. A
4:23 to forget the covenant that the L your God made A
4:23 that the L your God has forbidden you. A
4:24 L your God is a devouring fire, a jealous God. A
4:25 evil in the sight of the L your God, AL
4:27 The L will scatter you among the peoples;
4:27 among the nations where the L will lead you.
4:29 From there you will seek the L your God, A
4:30 you will return to the L your God and heed him. A
4:31 Because the L your God is a merciful God, A
4:34 as the L your God did for you in Egypt A
4:35 that you would acknowledge that the L is God;
4:39 to heart that the L is God in heaven above and
4:40 that the L your God is giving you for all time. A
5: 2 L our God made a covenant with us at Horeb. A
5: 3 with our ancestors did the L make this covenant,
5: 4 L spoke with you face to face at the mountain,
5: 5 that time I was standing between the L and you
5: 5 and you to declare to you the words of the L;
5: 6 I am the L your God, who brought you out of AH
5: 9 for I the L your God am a jealous God, A
5:11 of the name of the L your God, AI
5:11 L will not acquit anyone who misuses his name.
5:12 as the L your God commanded you. A
5:14 the seventh day is a sabbath to the L your God; A
5:15 the L your God brought you out from there with A
5:15 therefore the L your God commanded you A
5:16 as the L your God commanded you, A
5:16 in the land that the L your God is giving you. A
5:22 These words the L spoke with a loud voice
5:24 L our God has shown us his glory and greatness, A
5:25 we hear the voice of the L our God any longer, AP
5:27 and hear all that the L our God will say. A
5:27 tell us everything that the L our God tells you, A
5:28 The L heard your words when you spoke to me,
5:28 and the L said to me:
5:32 to do as the L your God has commanded you; A
5:33 that the L your God has commanded you, A
6: 1 that the L your God charged me to teach you A
6: 2 fear the L your God all the days of your life, AX
6: 3 as the L, the God of your ancestors,
6: 4 The L is our God, the L alone.
6: 5 love the L your God with all your heart, A
6:10 the L your God has brought you into the land A
6:12 take care that you do not forget the L,
6:13 The L your God you shall fear; A
6:15 because the L your God, A
6:15 of the L your God would be kindled against you A
6:16 Do not put the L your God to the test, A
6:17 the commandments of the L your God, A
6:18 Do what is right and good in the sight of the L,
6:18 the good land that the L swore to your ancestors
6:19 from before you, as the L has promised.
6:20 that the L our God has commanded you?" A
6:21 L brought us out of Egypt with a mighty hand.
6:22 The L displayed before our eyes great
6:24 L commanded us to observe all these statutes,
6:24 to fear the L our God, for our lasting good, AX
6:25 entire commandment before the L our God, AD
7: 1 When the L your God brings you into the land A
7: 2 when the L your God gives them over to you A
7: 4 the anger of the L would be kindled against you,
7: 6 For you are a people holy to the L your God; A
7: 6 the L your God has chosen you out of all A
7: 7 that the L set his heart on you and chose you—
7: 8 the L loved you and kept the oath that he swore
7: 8 the L has brought you out with a mighty hand,
7: 9 Know therefore that the L your God is God, A
7:12 the L your God will maintain with you A
7:15 The L will turn away from you every illness;
7:16 the peoples that the L your God is giving over A
7:18 the L your God did to Pharaoh and to all Egypt, A
7:19 by which the L your God brought you out. A
7:19 The L your God will do the same to all A
7:20 the L your God will send the pestilence A
7:21 Have no dread of them, for the L your God, A
7:22 The L your God will clear away these nations A
7:23 But the L your God will give them over to you, A
7:25 for it is abhorrent to the L your God. A
8: 1 and occupy the land that the L promised on oath
8: 2 the L your God has led you these forty years in A
8: 3 that comes from the mouth of the L.
8: 5 a child so the L your God disciplines you. A
8: 6 keep the commandments of the L your God, A
8: 7 the L your God is bringing you into a good land, A
8:10 shall eat your fill and bless the L your God AW
8:11 care that you do not forget the L your God, A
8:14 forgetting the L your God, A
8:18 But remember the L your God, A
8:19 the L your God and follow other gods to serve A
8:20 the nations that the L is destroying before you,
8:20 not obey the voice of the L your God. AP
9: 3 that the L your God is the one who crosses over A
9: 3 as the L has promised you.

Dt 9: 4 the L your God thrusts them out before you, A
9: 4 of my righteousness that the L has brought me
9: 4 of these nations that the L is dispossessing them
9: 5 the L your God is dispossessing them A
9: 5 in order to fulfill the promise that the L made
9: 6 the L your God is not giving you this good land A
9: 7 how you provoked the L your God to wrath in A
9: 7 the L from the day you came out of the land
9: 8 Even at Horeb you provoked the L to wrath,
9: 8 the L was so angry with you that he was ready
9: 9 the tablets of the covenant that the L made
9:10 the L gave me the two stone tablets written with
9:10 that the L had spoken to you at the mountain out
9:11 of forty days and forty nights the L gave me
9:12 Then the L said to me, "Get up,
9:13 Furthermore the L said to me,
9:16 the L your God, by casting for yourselves A
9:16 from the way that the L had commanded you.
9:18 Then I lay prostrate before the L as before, D
9:18 the sin you had committed, provoking the L
9:19 that the anger that the L bore against you was
9:19 But the L listened to me that time also.
9:20 The L was so angry with Aaron
9:22 you provoked the L to wrath.
9:23 And when the L sent you from Kadesh-barnea,
9:23 against the command of the L your God, A
9:24 You have been rebellious against the L as long
9:25 that I lay prostrate before the L D
9:25 when the L intended to destroy you,
9:26 I prayed to the L and said,
9:28 'Because the L was not able to bring them into
10: 1 At that time the L said to me,
10: 4 the L had spoken to you on the mountain out of
10: 4 and the L gave them to me.
10: 5 and there they are, as the L commanded me.
10: 8 the L set apart the tribe of Levi to carry the ark
10: 8 Levi to carry the ark of the covenant of the L, O
10: 8 to stand before the L to minister to him, D
10: 9 the L is his inheritance,
10: 9 as the L your God promised him.) A
10:10 And once again the L listened to me.
10:10 The L was unwilling to destroy you.
10:11 The L said to me, "Get up,
10:12 what does the L your God require of you? A
10:12 Only to fear the L your God, AX
10:12 to serve the L your God with all your heart and A
10:13 to keep the commandments of the L your God A
10:14 of heavens belong to the L your God, A
10:15 yet the L set his heart in love
10:17 L your God is God of gods and Lord of lords, A
10:20 You shall fear the L your God; AX
10:22 now the L your God has made you as numerous A
11: 1 You shall love the L your God, therefore, A
11: 2 or seen the discipline of the L your God), A
11: 4 so that the L has destroyed them to this day;
11: 7 that have seen every great deed that the L did.
11: 9 that the L swore to your ancestors to give them
11:12 a land that the L your God looks after. A
11:12 The eyes of the L your God are always on it, A
11:13 loving the L your God, and serving him A
11:17 the anger of the L will be kindled against you
11:17 the good land that the L is giving you.
11:21 that the L swore to your ancestors to give them,
11:22 loving the L your God, walking in all his ways, A
11:23 the L will drive out all these nations before you,
11:25 the L your God will put the fear and dread A
11:27 the commandments of the L your God A
11:28 not obey the commandments of the L your God, A
11:29 the L your God has brought you into the land A
11:31 the land that the L your God is giving you, A
12: 1 in the land that the L,
12: 4 not worship the L your God in such ways. A
12: 5 the L your God will choose out of all your tribes A
12: 7 in the presence of the L your God, A
12: 7 in which the L your God has blessed you. A
12: 9 that the L your God is giving you. A
12:10 the land that the L your God is allotting to you, A
12:11 to the place that the L your God will choose as A
12:11 that you vow to the L.
12:12 And you shall rejoice before the L your God, AD
12:14 that the L will choose in one of your tribes—
12:15 the blessing that the L your God has given you; A
12:18 the presence of the L your God at the place that A
12:18 at the place that the L your God will choose, A
12:18 rejoicing in the presence of the L your God A
12:20 When the L your God enlarges your territory, A
12:21 If the place where the L your God will choose A
12:21 of your herd or flock that the L has given you,
12:25 you do what is right in the sight of the L.
12:26 to the place that the L will choose.
12:27 on the altar of the L your God; A
12:27 beside the altar of the L your God, A
12:28 and right in the sight of the L your God. A
12:29 When the L your God has cut off before you A
12:31 You must not do the same for the L your God, A
12:31 that the L hates they have done for their gods.
13: 3 for the L your God is testing you, A
13: 3 the L your God with all your heart and soul. A
13: 4 The L your God you shall follow, A
13: 5 against the L your God— A
13: 5 in which the L your God commanded you A
13:10 to turn you away from the L your God, A
13:12 of the towns that the L your God is giving you A
13:16 as a whole burnt offering to the L your God. A
13:17 so that the L may turn from his fierce anger
13:18 if you obey the voice of the L your God AP
13:18 in the sight of the L your God. A

Dt 14: 1 You are children of the L your God. A
14: 2 For you are a people holy to the L your God; A
14: 2 the L has chosen out of all the peoples on earth
14:21 For you are a people holy to the L your God. A
14:23 In the presence of the L your God, A
14:23 you may learn to fear the L your God always. AX
14:24 But if, when the L your God has blessed you, A
14:24 the place where the L your God will choose A
14:25 go to the place that the L your God will choose; A
14:26 in the presence of the L your God, A
14:29 the L your God may bless you in all the work A
15: 4 because the L is sure to bless you in the land
15: 4 in the land that the L your God is giving you as A
15: 5 if only you will obey the L your God A
15: 6 When the L your God has blessed you, A
15: 7 the land that the L your God is giving you, A
15: 9 your neighbor might cry to the L against you,
15:10 the L your God will bless you in all your work A
15:14 with which the L your God has blessed you. A
15:15 and the L your God redeemed you; A
15:18 the L your God will bless you in all that you do. A
15:19 flock you shall consecrate to the L your God; A
15:20 of the L your God year by year at the place that A
15:20 by year at the place that the L will choose.
15:21 you shall not sacrifice it to the L your God; A
16: 1 by keeping the passover for the L your God, A
16: 1 the L your God brought you out of Egypt A
16: 2 the passover sacrifice for the L your God, A
16: 2 at the place that the L will choose as a dwelling
16: 5 of your towns that the L your God is giving you. A
16: 6 But at the place that the L your God will choose A
16: 7 at the place that the L your God will choose; A
16: 8 be a solemn assembly for the L your God, A
16:10 the festival of weeks for the L your God, A
16:10 that you have received from the L your God. A
16:11 Rejoice before the L your God— AD
16:11 at the place that the L your God will choose as A
16:15 the festival for the L your God at the place that A
16:15 at the place that the L will choose;
16:15 for the L your God will bless you A
16:16 appear before the L your God at the place AD
16:16 not appear before the L empty-handed; D
16:17 according to the blessing of the L your God A
16:18 that the L your God is giving you, A
16:20 the land that the L your God is giving you. A
16:21 the altar that you make for the L your God; A
16:22 things that the L your God hates. A
17: 1 not sacrifice to the L your God an ox or a sheep A
17: 1 for that is abhorrent to the L your God. A
17: 2 of your towns that the L your God is giving you, A
17: 2 what is evil in the sight of the L your God, AL
17: 8 up to the place that the L your God will choose, A
17:10 to you from the place that the L will choose,
17:12 to minister there to the L your God, A
17:14 into the land that the L your God is giving you, A
17:15 a king whom the L your God will choose. A
17:16 since the L has said to you,
17:19 so that he may learn to fear the L his God, AX
18: 2 the L is their inheritance, as he promised them.
18: 5 For the L your God has chosen Levi out A
18: 5 to stand and minister in the name of the L, I
18: 6 and comes to the place that the L will choose
18: 7 he may minister in the name of the L his God, AI
18: 7 to minister there before the L. D
18: 9 into the land that the L your God is giving you, A
18:12 whoever does these things is abhorrent to the L;
18:12 the L your God is driving them out before you. A
18:13 remain completely loyal to the L your God. A
18:14 the L your God does not permit you to do so. A
18:15 The L your God will raise up for you a prophet A
18:16 This is what you requested of the L your God A
18:16 "If I hear the voice of the L my God any more, AP
18:17 Then the L replied to me:
18:21 "How can we recognize a word that the L has
18:22 If a prophet speaks in the name of the L but I
18:22 it is a word that the L has not spoken.
19: 1 When the L your God has cut off A
19: 1 the L your God is giving you, A
19: 2 that the L your God is giving you to possess. A
19: 3 that the L your God gives you as a possession, A
19: 8 If the L your God enlarges your territory, A
19: 9 by loving the L your God and walking always A
19:10 in the land that the L your God is giving you as A
19:14 that the L your God is giving you to possess. A
19:17 parties to the dispute shall appear before the L, D
20: 1 for the L your God is with you, A
20: 4 for it is the L your God who goes with you, A
20:13 when the L your God gives it into your hand, A
20:14 which the L your God has given you. A
20:16 the L your God is giving you as an inheritance, A
20:17 just as the L your God has commanded, A
20:18 and you thus sin against the L your God. A
21: 1 that the L your God is giving you to possess, A
21: 5 for the L your God has chosen them to minister A
21: 5 to pronounce blessings in the name of the L, I
21: 8 Absolve, O L, your people Israel,
21: 9 you must do what is right in the sight of the L.
21:10 and the L your God hands them over to you A
21:23 the L your God is giving you for possession. A
22: 5 does such things is abhorrent to the L your God. A
23: 1 be admitted to the assembly of the L.
23: 2 not be admitted to the assembly of the L.
23: 2 be admitted to the assembly of the L.
23: 3 be admitted to the assembly of the L.
23: 3 be admitted to the assembly of the L,
23: 5 (Yet the L your God refused to heed Balaam; A
23: 5 the L your God turned the curse into a blessing A

†LORD distinguishes the proper name of God, *Yahweh*, indicated in the NRSV by "LORD," from the words translated "Lord" and "lord," indexed under the heading *LORD on pages 798-804.

Dt 23: 5 because the L your God loved you.) A
23: 8 be admitted to the assembly of the L.
23:14 the L your God travels along with your camp, A
23:18 into the house of the L your God in payment AF
23:18 both of these are abhorrent to the L your God. A
23:20 so that the L your God may bless you A
23:21 If you make a vow to the L your God, A
23:21 for the L your God will surely require it of you, A
23:23 as you have freely vowed to the L your God A
24: 4 for that would be abhorrent to the L,
24: 4 on the land that the L your God is giving you as A
24: 9 Remember what the L your God did to Miriam A
24:13 it will be to your credit before the L your God. AD
24:15 otherwise they might cry to the L against you,
24:18 and the L your God redeemed you from there; A
24:19 so that the L your God may bless you A
25:15 in the land that the L your God is giving you. A
25:16 are abhorrent to the L your God. A
25:19 when the L your God has given you rest A
25:19 in the land that the L your God is giving you as A
26: 1 into the land that the L your God is giving you A
26: 2 from the land that the L your God is giving you, A
26: 2 to the place that the L your God will choose as A
26: 3 to the L your God that I have come into the land A
26: 3 that I have come into the land that the L swore
26: 4 down before the altar of the L your God, A
26: 5 make this response before the L your God: AD
26: 7 we cried to the L, the God of our ancestors;
26: 7 the L heard our voice and saw our affliction,
26: 8 The L brought us out of Egypt with
26:10 the first of the fruit of the ground that you, O L,
26:10 before the L your God and bow down before AD
26:10 and bow down before the L your God. AD
26:11 the bounty that the L your God has given to you A
26:13 then you shall say before the L your God: AD
26:14 I have obeyed the L my God, A
26:16 the L your God is commanding you A
26:18 Today the L has obtained your agreement:
26:19 for you to be a people holy to the L your God, A
27: 2 into the land that the L your God is giving you, A
27: 3 the land that the L your God is giving you, A
27: 3 a land flowing with milk and honey, as the L,
27: 5 you shall build an altar there to the L your God, A
27: 6 the altar of the L your God of unhewn stones. A
27: 6 offer up burnt offerings on it to the L your God, A
27: 7 rejoicing before the L your God. AD
27: 9 the people of the L your God. A
27:10 Therefore obey the L your God, A
27:15 anything abhorrent to the L,
28: 1 If you will only obey the L your God, A
28: 1 the L your God will set you high above all A
28: 2 if you obey the L your God: A
28: 7 The L will cause your enemies who rise
28: 8 The L will command the blessing upon you
28: 8 in the land that the L your God is giving you. A
28: 9 The L will establish you as his holy people,
28: 9 the commandments of the L your God and walk A
28:10 that you are called by the name of the L, I
28:11 The L will make you abound in prosperity,
28:11 that the L swore to your ancestors to give you.
28:12 The L will open for you his rich storehouse,
28:13 The L will make you the head, and not the tail;
28:13 obey the commandments of the L your God, A
28:15 But if you will not obey the L your God A
28:20 The L will send upon you disaster, panic,
28:21 The L will make the pestilence cling to you
28:22 The L will afflict you with consumption, fever,
28:24 L will change the rain of your land into powder,
28:25 The L will cause you to be defeated
28:27 The L will afflict you with the boils of Egypt,
28:28 The L will afflict you with madness, blindness,
28:35 The L will strike you on the knees and on
28:36 The L will bring you,
28:37 the peoples where the L will lead you.
28:45 because you did not obey the L your God, A
28:47 the L your God joyfully and with gladness A
28:48 the L will send against you,
28:49 The L will bring a nation from far away,
28:52 the land that the L your God has given you. A
28:53 the L your God has given you. A
28:58 and awesome name, the L your God, A
28:59 then the L will overwhelm both you
28:61 the L will inflict on you until you are destroyed.
28:62 because you did not obey the L your God. A
28:63 as the L took delight in making you prosperous
28:63 so the L will take delight in bringing you to ruin
28:64 The L will scatter you among all peoples,
28:65 There the L will give you a trembling heart,
28:68 The L will bring you back in ships to Egypt,
29: 1 of the covenant that the L commanded Moses
29: 2 the L did before your eyes in the land of Egypt,
29: 4 But to this day the L has not given you a mind
29: 6 that you may know that I am the L your God. AH
29:10 all of you, before the L your God— AD
29:12 into the covenant of the L your God, sworn by AO
29:12 the L your God is making with you today; A
29:14 with us today before the L our God, AD
29:18 L our God to serve the gods of those nations. A
29:20 the L will be unwilling to pardon them,
29:20 L will blot out their names from under heaven.
29:21 The L will single them out from all the tribes
29:22 with which the L has afflicted it—
29:23 which the L destroyed in his fierce anger—
29:24 "Why has the L done thus to this land?
29:25 because they abandoned the covenant of the L, O
29:27 the anger of the L was kindled against that land,
29:28 The L uprooted them from their land in anger,

Dt 29:29 The secret things belong to the L our God, A
30: 1 where the L your God has driven you, A
30: 2 and return to the L your God, A
30: 3 then the L your God will restore your fortunes A
30: 3 among whom the L your God has scattered you. A
30: 4 from there the L your God will gather you, A
30: 5 The L your God will bring you into the land A
30: 6 the L your God will circumcise your heart and A
30: 6 the L your God with all your heart and A
30: 7 The L your God will put all these curses A
30: 8 Then you shall again obey the L,
30: 9 L your God will make you abundantly A
30: 9 the L will again take delight in prospering you,
30:10 when you obey the L your God A
30:10 to the L your God with all your heart and A
30:16 the commandments of the L your God A
30:16 by loving the L your God, walking in his ways, A
30:16 and the L your God will bless you in the land A
30:20 the L your God, obeying him, and holding fast A
30:20 so that you may live in the land that the L swore
31: 2 and the L has told me,
31: 3 L your God himself will cross over before you. A
31: 3 over before you, as the L promised.
31: 4 L will do to them as he did to Sihon and Og,
31: 5 The L will give them over to you
31: 6 because it is the L your God who goes with you; A
31: 7 the L has sworn to their ancestors to give them;
31: 8 It is the L who goes before you.
31: 9 who carried the ark of the covenant of the L, O
31:11 appear before the L your God at the place AD
31:12 fear the L your God and to observe diligently AX
31:13 may hear and learn to fear the L your God, AX
31:14 The L said to Moses, "Your time to die is near;
31:15 the L appeared at the tent in a pillar of cloud; Z
31:16 The L said to Moses, "Soon you will lie down
31:23 L commissioned Joshua son of Nun and said,
31:25 the ark of the covenant of the L, O
31:26 the ark of the covenant of the L your God; AO
31:27 so rebellious toward the L while I am still alive
31:29 you will do what is evil in the sight of the L, L
32: 3 For I will proclaim the name of the L; I
32: 6 Do you thus repay the L,
32:12 the L alone guided him;
32:19 The L saw it, and was jealous he spurned his sons
32:27 it was not the L who did all this."
32:30 the L had given them up?
32:36 Indeed the L will vindicate his people,
32:48 that very day the L addressed Moses as follows:
33: 2 He said: The L came from Sinai,
33: 7 And this he said of Judah: O L,
33:11 Bless, O L, his substance,
33:12 The beloved of the L rests in safety—
33:13 Blessed by the L be his land,
33:21 he executed the justice of the L,
33:23 sated with favor, full of the blessing of the L,
33:29 Who is like you, a people saved by the L,
34: 1 and the L showed him the whole land:
34: 4 The L said to him, "This is the land
34: 5 Then Moses, the servant of the L, died there Y
34: 9 doing as the L had commanded Moses.
34:10 whom the L knew face to face.
34:11 for all the signs and wonders that the L sent him
Jos 1: 1 After the death of Moses the servant of the L, Y
1: 1 the L spoke to Joshua son of Nun,
1: 9 the L your God is with you wherever you go." A
1:11 that the L your God gives you to possess.' " A
1:13 the servant of the L commanded you, Y
1:13 L your God is providing you a place of rest, A
1:15 until the L gives rest to your kindred as well as
1:15 of the land that the L your God is giving them. A
1:15 that Moses the servant of the L gave you Y
1:17 Only may the L your God be with you, A
2: 9 "I know that the L has given you the land,
2:10 For we have heard how the L dried up the water
2:11 The L your God is indeed God in heaven above A
2:12 to me by the L that you in turn will deal kindly
2:14 and faithfully with you when the L gives us
2:24 the L has given all the land into our hands;
3: 3 the covenant of the L your God being carried AO
3: 5 tomorrow the L will do wonders among you."
3: 7 The L said to Joshua, "This day I will begin
3: 9 near and hear the words of the L your God." A
3:13 bear the ark of the L, the Lord of all the earth, N
3:17 of the covenant of the L stood on dry ground in O
4: 1 over the Jordan, the L said to Joshua:
4: 5 the ark of the L your God into the middle AN
4: 7 in front of the ark of the covenant of the L. O
4: 8 the Israelites, as the L told Joshua, carried them
4:10 that the L commanded Joshua to tell the people,
4:11 the ark of the L, and the priests, N
4:13 for war crossed over before the L to the plains D
4:14 the L exalted Joshua in the sight of all Israel;
4:15 The L said to Joshua,
4:18 covenant of the L came up from the middle O
4:23 For the L your God dried up the waters of A
4:23 as the L your God did to the Red Sea, A
4:24 that the hand of the L is mighty, S
4:24 so that you may fear the L your God forever." AX
5: 1 that the L had dried up the waters of the Jordan
5: 2 At that time the L said to Joshua,
5: 6 not having listened to the voice of the L. P
5: 6 the L swore that he would not let them see
5: 9 The L said to Joshua, "Today I have rolled away
5:14 but as commander of the army of the L I have
5:15 commander of the army of the L said to Joshua,
6: 2 The L said to Joshua, "See,
6: 6 of rams' horns in front of the ark of the L." N

Jos 6: 7 the armed men pass on before the ark of the L." N
6: 8 of rams' horns before the L went forward, D
6: 8 the ark of the covenant of the L following them. O
6:11 So the ark of the L went around the city, N
6:12 and the priests took up the ark of the L. N
6:13 rams' horns before the ark of the L passed on, N
6:13 and the rear guard came after the ark of the L, N
6:16 For the L has given you the city.
6:17 in it shall be devoted to the L for destruction.
6:19 of bronze and iron, are sacred to the L;
6:19 they shall go into the treasury of the L."
6:24 they put into the treasury of the house of the L. F
6:26 "Cursed before the L be anyone who tries to D
6:27 So the L was with Joshua;
7: 1 the anger of the L burned against the Israelites.
7: 6 to the ground on his face before the ark of the L N
7:10 The L said to Joshua, "Stand up!
7:13 for thus says the L, the God of Israel, C
7:14 tribe that the L takes shall come near by clans,
7:14 that the L takes shall come near by households,
7:14 and the household that the L takes shall come
7:15 for having transgressed the covenant of the L, O
7:19 the L God of Israel and make confession to him. J
7:20 the one who sinned against the L God of Israel. J
7:23 and they spread them out before the L. D
7:25 The L is bringing trouble on you today."
7:26 Then the L turned from his burning anger.
8: 1 L said to Joshua, "Do not fear or be dismayed;
8: 7 for the L your God will give it into your hand. A
8: 8 doing as the L has ordered;
8:18 Then the L said to Joshua,
8:27 the word of the L that he had issued to Joshua. G
8:30 Joshua built on Mount Ebal an altar to the L,
8:31 as Moses the servant of the L had commanded Y
8:31 and they offered on it burnt offerings to the L,
8:33 the ark of the covenant of the L, O
8:33 the servant of the L had commanded at the first, Y
9: 9 because of the name of the L your God; AI
9:14 and did not ask direction from the L.
9:18 of the congregation had sworn to them by the L,
9:19 "We have sworn to them by the L,
9:24 L your God had commanded his servant Moses A
9:27 for the congregation and for the altar of the L,
10: 8 The L said to Joshua, "Do not fear them,
10:10 And the L threw them into a panic before Israel,
10:11 the L threw down huge stones from heaven
10:12 On the day when the L gave the Amorites over
10:12 over to the Israelites, Joshua spoke to the L;
10:14 when the L heeded a human voice;
10:14 for the L fought for Israel.
10:19 the L your God has given them into your hand." A
10:25 for thus the L will do to all the enemies
10:30 The L gave it also and its king into the hand
10:32 The L gave Lachish into the hand of Israel,
10:40 as the L God of Israel commanded. J
10:42 because the L God of Israel fought for Israel. J
11: 6 And the L said to Joshua,
11: 8 And the L handed them over to Israel,
11: 9 Joshua did to them as the L commanded him;
11:12 as Moses the servant of the L had commanded. Y
11:15 As the L had commanded his servant Moses,
11:15 of all that the L had commanded Moses.
11:20 just as the L had commanded Moses.
11:23 according to all that the L had spoken to Moses;
12: 6 Moses, the servant of the L, Y
12: 6 and Moses the servant of the L gave their land Y
13: 1 and the L said to him,
13: 8 as Moses the servant of the L gave them: Y
13:14 to the L God of Israel are their inheritance, J
13:33 the L God of Israel is their inheritance, J
14: 2 as the L had commanded Moses for the nine
14: 5 The Israelites did as the L commanded Moses;
14: 6 "You know what the L said to Moses the man
14: 7 servant of the L sent me from Kadesh-barnea Y
14: 8 yet I wholeheartedly followed the L my God. A
14: 9 have wholeheartedly followed the L my God.' A
14:10 And now, as you see, the L has kept me alive,
14:10 the time that the L spoke this word to Moses,
14:12 of which the L spoke on that day;
14:12 it may be that the L will be with me,
14:12 and I shall drive them out, as the L said."
14:14 because he wholeheartedly followed the L,
15:13 According to the commandment of the L
17: 4 "The L commanded Moses to give us
17: 4 of the L he gave them an inheritance among
17:14 whom all along the L has blessed?"
18: 3 in and taking possession of the land that the L,
18: 6 for you here before the L our God. AD
18: 7 for the priesthood of the L is their heritage;
18: 7 which Moses the servant of the L gave them." Y
18: 8 and I will cast lots for you here before the L D
18:10 for them in Shiloh before the L; D
19:50 the L they gave him the town that he asked for,
19:51 by lot at Shiloh before the L, D
20: 1 Then the L spoke to Joshua, saying,
21: 2 "The L commanded through Moses that we
21: 3 So by command of the L the Israelites gave to
21: 8 as the L had commanded through Moses.
21:43 the L gave to Israel all the land that he swore
21:44 And the L gave them rest on every side just
21:44 L had given all their enemies into their hands.
21:45 the L had made to the house of Israel had failed;
22: 2 Moses the servant of the L commanded you, Y
22: 3 to keep the charge of the L your God. A
22: 4 the L your God has given rest to your kindred, A
22: 4 the servant of the L gave you on the other side Y
22: 5 the servant of the L commanded you, Y

†**LORD** distinguishes the proper name of God, *Yahweh*, indicated in the NRSV by "LORD," from the words translated "Lord" and "lord," indexed under the heading ***LORD** on pages 798-804.

Jos 22: 5 to love the L your God, to walk in all his ways, A
22: 9 by command of the L through Moses.
22:16 "Thus says the whole congregation of the L,
22:16 in turning away today from following the L,
22:16 an altar today in rebellion against the L?
22:17 a plague came upon the congregation of the L,
22:18 you must turn away today from following the L!
22:18 If you rebel against the L today,
22:19 only do not rebel against the L,
22:19 an altar other than the altar of the L our God. A
22:22 "The L, God of gods! The L, God of gods!
22:22 in rebellion or in breach of faith toward the L,
22:23 an altar to turn away from following the L;
22:23 may the L himself take vengeance.
22:24 'What have you to do with the L,
22:25 For the L has made the Jordan a boundary
22:25 you have no portion in the L.'
22:25 might make our children cease to worship the L.
22:27 of the L in his presence with our burnt offerings
22:27 "You have no portion in the L." '
22:28 'Look at this copy of the altar of the L,
22:29 be it from us that we should rebel against the L,
22:29 and turn away this day from following the L
22:29 other than the altar of the L our God that stands A
22:31 "Today we know that the L is among us,
22:31 not committed this treachery against the L;
22:31 the Israelites from the hand of the L." S
22:34 "it is a witness between us that the L is God."
23: 1 when the L had given rest to Israel
23: 3 the L your God has done to all these nations A
23: 3 for it is the L your God who has fought for you. A
23: 5 L your God will push them back before you, A
23: 5 as the L your God promised you. A
23: 8 but hold fast to the L your God, A
23: 9 For the L has driven out before you great
23:10 since it is the L your God who fights for you, A
23:11 therefore, to love the L your God. A
23:13 know assuredly that the L your God will A
23:13 that the L your God has given you. A
23:14 that the L your God promised concerning you; A
23:15 the good things that the L your God promised A
23:15 so the L will bring upon you all the bad things,
23:15 that the L your God has given you. A
23:16 transgress the covenant of the L your God, AO
23:16 the anger of the L will be kindled against you,
24: 2 Joshua said to all the people, "Thus says the L, C
24: 7 When they cried out to the L,
24:14 "Now therefore revere the L,
24:14 beyond the River and in Egypt, and serve the L.
24:15 Now if you are unwilling to serve the L,
24:15 for me and my household, we will serve the L."
24:16 that we should forsake the L to serve other gods;
24:17 L our God who brought us and our ancestors A
24:18 and the L drove out before us all the peoples,
24:18 we also will serve the L, for he is our God."
24:19 "You cannot serve the L, for he is a holy God.
24:20 If you forsake the L and serve foreign gods,
24:21 people said to Joshua, "No, we will serve the L!"
24:22 against yourselves that you have chosen the L,
24:23 and incline your hearts to the L,
24:24 "The L our God we will serve, A
24:26 up there under the oak in the sanctuary of the L.
24:27 the words of the L that he spoke to us;
24:29 Joshua son of Nun, the servant of the L, died, Y
24:31 Israel served the L all the days of Joshua,
24:31 and had known all the work that the L did
Jdg 1: 1 death of Joshua, the Israelites inquired of the L,
1: 2 The L said, "Judah shall go up.
1: 4 and the L gave the Canaanites and the Perizzites
1:19 The L was with Judah, and he took possession
1:22 and the L was with them.
2: 1 angel of the L went up from Gilgal to Bochim, K
2: 4 the angel of the L spoke these words to all K
2: 5 and there they sacrificed to the L.
2: 7 people worshiped the L all the days of Joshua,
2: 7 the great work that the L had done for Israel.
2: 8 Joshua son of Nun, the servant of the L, Y
2:10 the L or the work that he had done for Israel.
2:11 evil in the sight of the L and worshiped the L
2:12 and they abandoned the L, the God
2:12 and they provoked the L to anger.
2:13 They abandoned the L, and worshiped Baal and
2:14 So the anger of the L was kindled against Israel,
2:15 the hand of the L was against them to bring S
2:15 as the L had warned them and sworn to them;
2:16 Then the L raised up judges,
2:17 who had obeyed the commandments of the L;
2:18 Whenever the L raised up judges for them,
2:18 the L was with the judge,
2:18 the L would be moved to pity by their groaning
2:20 So the anger of the L was kindled against Israel;
2:22 in the way of the L as their ancestors did,
2:23 the L had left those nations,
3: 1 the nations that the L left to test all those
3: 4 the commandments of the L,
3: 7 Israelites did what was evil in the sight of the L, L
3: 7 forgetting the L their God, A
3: 8 the anger of the L was kindled against Israel,
3: 9 But when the Israelites cried out to the L,
3: 9 the L raised up a deliverer for the Israelites,
3:10 The spirit of the L came upon him,
3:10 to war, and the L gave King Cushan-rishathaim
3:12 evil in the sight of the L; L
3:12 and the L strengthened King Eglon of Moab
3:12 evil in the sight of the L. L
3:15 But when the Israelites cried out to the L,
3:15 the L raised up for them a deliverer,

Jdg 3:28 for the L has given your enemies the Moabites
4: 1 evil in the sight of the L, L
4: 2 So the L sold them into the hand of King Jabin
4: 3 Then the Israelites cried out to the L for help;
4: 6 "The L, the God of Israel, commands you, 'Go,
4: 9 the L will sell Sisera into the hand of a woman."
4:14 on which the L has given Sisera into your hand.
4:14 The L is indeed going out before you."
4:15 And the L threw Sisera and all his chariots
5: 2 people offer themselves willingly—bless the L! W
5: 3 to the L I will sing,
5: 3 I will make melody to the L, the God of Israel.
5: 4 "L, when you went out from Seir,
5: 5 The mountains quaked before the L, D
5: 5 before the L, the God of Israel. D
5: 9 among the people. Bless the L. W
5:11 there they repeat the triumphs of the L,
5:11 down to the gates marched the people of the L.
5:13 the L marched down for him against the mighty.
5:23 "Curse Meroz, says the angel of the L, K
5:23 because they did not come to the help of the L,
5:23 to the help of the L against the mighty.
5:31 "So perish all your enemies, O L!
6: 1 Israelites did what was evil in the sight of the L, L
6: 1 and the L gave them into the hand
6: 6 and the Israelites cried out to the L for help.
6: 7 When the Israelites cried to the L on account of
6: 8 the L sent a prophet to the Israelites;
6: 8 and he said to them, "Thus says the L, C
6:10 'I am the L your God; AH
6:11 angel of the L came and sat under the oak K
6:12 angel of the L appeared to him and said to him, KZ
6:12 "The L is with you, you mighty warrior."
6:13 "But sir, if the L is with us,
6:13 saying, 'Did not the L bring us up from Egypt?'
6:13 But now the L has cast us off,
6:14 Then the L turned to him and said,
6:16 The L said to him, "But I will be with you,
6:21 the angel of the L reached out the tip of the staff K
6:21 and the angel of the L vanished from his sight. K
6:22 Gideon perceived that it was the angel of the L; K
6:22 For I have seen the angel of the L face to face." K
6:23 But the L said to him, "Peace be to you;
6:24 Then Gideon built an altar there to the L,
6:24 and called it, The L is peace.
6:25 That night the L said to him,
6:26 and build an altar to the L your God on the top A
6:27 and did as the L had told him;
6:34 the spirit of the L took possession of Gideon;
7: 2 The L said to Gideon, "The troops
7: 4 L said to Gideon, "The troops are still too many;
7: 5 and the L said to Gideon,
7: 7 Then the L said to Gideon,
7: 9 That same night the L said to him, "Get up,
7:15 L has given the army of Midian into your hand."
7:18 and shout, 'For the L and for Gideon!' "
7:20 they cried, "A sword for the L and for Gideon!"
7:22 the L set every man's sword against his fellow
8: 7 L has given Zebah and Zalmunna into my hand,
8:19 as the L lives, if you had saved them alive, Q
8:23 the L will rule over you."
8:34 Israelites did not remember the L their God, A
10: 6 did what was evil in the sight of the L, L
10: 6 Thus they abandoned the L,
10: 7 So the anger of the L was kindled against Israel,
10:10 So the Israelites cried to the L, saying,
10:11 And the L said to the Israelites,
10:15 the Israelites said to the L, "We have sinned;
10:16 from among them and worshiped the L;
11: 9 and the L gives them over to me,
11:10 "The L will be witness between us;
11:11 and Jephthah spoke all his words before the L D
11:21 Then the L, the God of Israel,
11:23 So now the L, the God of Israel,
11:24 the L our God has conquered for our benefit? A
11:27 Let the L, who is judge,
11:29 Then the spirit of the L came upon Jephthah,
11:30 And Jephthah made a vow to the L, and said,
11:32 and the L gave them into his hand.
11:35 For I have opened my mouth to the L,
11:36 if you have opened your mouth to the L,
11:36 now that the L has given you vengeance
12: 3 and the L gave them into my hand.
13: 1 did what was evil in the sight of the L, L
13: 1 and the L gave them into the hand of
13: 3 the angel of the L appeared to the woman KZ
13: 8 Then Manoah entreated the L, and said, "O,
13: 8 Manoah entreated the LORD, and said, "O, L,
13:13 The angel of the L said to Manoah, K
13:15 Manoah said to the angel of the L, K
13:16 The angel of the L said to Manoah, K
13:16 to prepare a burnt offering, then offer it to the L."
13:16 not know that he was the angel of the L.) K
13:17 Then Manoah said to the angel of the L, K
13:18 But the angel of the L said to him, K
13:19 and offered it on the rock to the L,
13:20 the angel of the L ascended in the flame of K
13:21 angel of the L did not appear again to Manoah K
13:21 Manoah realized that it was the angel of the L. K
13:23 "If the L had meant to kill us,
13:24 The boy grew, and the L blessed him.
13:25 of the L began to stir him in Mahaneh-dan,
14: 4 not know that this was from the L;
14: 6 The spirit of the L rushed on him,
14:19 Then the spirit of the L rushed on him,
15:14 and the spirit of the L rushed on him,
15:18 and he called on the L, saying,

Jdg 16:20 But he did not know that the L had left him.
16:28 Then Samson called to the L and said,
17: 2 "May my son be blessed by the L!"
17: 3 "I consecrate the silver to the L from my hand
17:13 "Now I know that the L will prosper me,
18: 6 mission you are on is under the eye of the L."
20: 1 in one body before the L at Mizpah. D
20:18 And the L answered, "Judah shall go up first."
20:23 The Israelites went up and wept before the L D
20:23 and they inquired of the L,
20:23 And the L said, "Go up against them."
20:26 sitting there before the L; D
20:26 and sacrifices of well-being before the L. D
20:27 And the Israelites inquired of the L (for the ark
20:28 The L answered, "Go up,
20:35 The L defeated Benjamin before Israel;
21: 3 They said, "O L, the God of Israel,
21: 5 not come up in the assembly to the L?"
21: 5 concerning whoever did not come up to the L
21: 7 since we have sworn by the L that we will
21: 8 the tribes of Israel who did not come up to the L
21:15 on Benjamin because the L had made a breach
21:19 yearly festival of the L is taking place at Shiloh,
Ru 1: 6 of Moab that the L had considered his people
1: 8 May the L deal kindly with you,
1: 9 The L grant that you may find security,
1:13 the hand of the L has turned against me." S
1:17 May the L do thus and so to me,
1:21 but the L has brought me back empty;
1:21 when the L has dealt harshly with me,
2: 4 He said to the reapers, "The L be with you."
2: 4 They answered, "The L bless you."
2:12 May the L reward you for your deeds,
2:12 and may you have a full reward from the L,
2:20 "Blessed be he by the L,
3:10 He said, "May you be blessed by the L,
3:13 as the L lives, I will act as next-of-kin for you. Q
4:11 May the L make the woman who is coming
4:12 that the L will give you by this young woman,
4:13 they came together, the L made her conceive,
4:14 the women said to Naomi, "Blessed be the L, T
1Sa 1: 3 to worship and to sacrifice to the L of hosts E
1: 3 Hophni and Phinehas, were priests of the L.
1: 5 though the L had closed her womb.
1: 6 because the L had closed her womb.
1: 7 as often as she went up to the house of the L, F
1: 9 Hannah rose and presented herself before the L. D
1: 9 beside the doorpost of the temple of the L. V
1:10 She was deeply distressed and prayed to the L,
1:11 She made this vow: "O L of hosts, E
1:12 As she continued praying before the L, D
1:15 I have been pouring out my soul before the L. D
1:19 in the morning and worshiped before the L; D
1:19 and the L remembered her.
1:20 for she said, "I have asked him of the L."
1:21 and all his household went up to offer to the L
1:22 that he may appear in the presence of the L,
1:23 may the L establish his word."
1:24 She brought him to the house of the L at Shiloh; F
1:26 in your presence, praying to the L.
1:27 the L has granted me the petition that I made
1:28 Therefore I have lent him to the L;
1:28 as long as he lives, he is given to the L."
1:28 She left him there for the L.
2: 1 "My heart exults in the L;
2: 2 "There is no Holy One like the L,
2: 3 for the L is a God of knowledge,
2: 6 The L kills and brings to life;
2: 7 The L makes poor and makes rich;
2:10 The L! His adversaries shall be shattered;
2:10 The L will judge the ends of the earth;
2:11 while the boy remained to minister to the L,
2:12 they had no regard for the L
2:17 in the sight of the L;
2:17 for they treated the offerings of the L
2:18 Samuel was ministering before the L, D
2:20 the L repay you with children by this woman for
2:20 for the gift that she made to the L";
2:21 And the L took note of Hannah;
2:21 boy Samuel grew up in the presence of the L.
2:24 that I hear the people of the L spreading abroad.
2:25 for the sinner with the L;
2:25 but if someone sins against the L,
2:25 for it was the will of the L to kill them.
2:26 both in stature and in favor with the L and with
2:27 to him, "Thus the L has said, 'I revealed myself
2:30 Therefore the L the God of Israel declares:
2:30 but now the L declares:
3: 1 boy Samuel was ministering to the L under Eli.
3: 1 The word of the L was rare in those days; G
3: 3 Samuel was lying down in the temple of the L, V
3: 4 Then the L called, "Samuel!
3: 6 The L called again, "Samuel!"
3: 7 Now Samuel did not yet know the L,
3: 7 word of the L had not yet been revealed to him. G
3: 8 The L called Samuel again, a third time.
3: 8 Eli perceived that the L was calling the boy.
3: 9 and if he calls you, you shall say, 'Speak, L,
3:10 Now the L came and stood there,
3:11 Then the L said to Samuel, "See,
3:15 then he opened the doors of the house of the L. F
3:18 Then he said, "It is the L;
3:19 the L was with him and let none
3:20 that Samuel was a trustworthy prophet of the L.
3:21 The L continued to appear at Shiloh,
3:21 for the L revealed himself to Samuel at Shiloh
3:21 to Samuel at Shiloh by the word of the L. G

1Sa 4: 3 the L put us to rout today before the Philistines?
4: 3 of the covenant of the L here from Shiloh, O
4: 4 the ark of the covenant of the L of hosts, OE
4: 5 ark of the covenant of the L came into the camp, O
4: 6 that the ark of the L had come to the camp, N
5: 3 on his face to the ground before the ark of the L. N
5: 4 on his face to the ground before the ark of the L, N
5: 6 The hand of the L was heavy upon the people S
5: 9 the hand of the L was against the city, S
6: 1 The ark of the L was in the country of N
6: 2 "What shall we do with the ark of the L? N
6: 8 Take the ark of the L and place it on the cart, N
6: 11 They put the ark of the L on the cart, N
6: 14 the cows as a burnt offering to the L.
6: 15 the ark of the L and the box that was beside it, N
6: 15 and presented sacrifices on that day to the L.
6: 17 as a guilt offering to the L:
6: 18 beside which they set down the ark of the L, N
6: 19 when they greeted the ark of the L; N
6: 19 because the L had made a great slaughter among
6: 20 "Who is able to stand before the L, D
6: 21 "The Philistines have returned the ark of the L. N
7: 1 and took up the ark of the L, N
7: 1 Eleazar, to have charge of the ark of the L. N
7: 2 and all the house of Israel lamented after the L.
7: 3 "If you are returning to the L with all your heart,
7: 3 Direct your heart to the L, and serve him only,
7: 4 and they served the L only.
7: 5 and I will pray to the L for you."
7: 6 and drew water and poured it out before the L. D
7: 6 and said, "We have sinned against the L."
7: 8 "Do not cease to cry out to the L our God for us, A
7: 9 as a whole burnt offering to the L;
7: 9 Samuel cried out to the L for Israel,
7: 9 and the L answered him.
7: 10 the L thundered with a mighty voice that day
7: 12 for he said, "Thus far the L has helped us."
7: 13 the hand of the L was against the Philistines all S
7: 17 and built there an altar to the L.
8: 6 Samuel prayed to the L,
8: 7 and the L said to Samuel, "Listen to the voice of
8: 10 of the L to the people who were asking him for
8: 18 but the L will not answer you in that day."
8: 21 he repeated them in the ears of the L.
8: 22 The L said to Samuel, "Listen to their voice
9: 15 the L had revealed to Samuel:
9: 17 When Samuel saw Saul, the L told him,
10: 1 L has anointed you ruler over his people Israel.
10: 1 the people of the L and you will save them from
10: 1 the sign to you that the L has anointed you ruler
10: 6 Then the spirit of the L will possess you,
10: 17 Samuel summoned the people to the L
10: 18 "Thus says the L, the God of Israel, C
10: 19 before the L by your tribes and by your clans." D
10: 22 So they inquired again of the L,
10: 22 the L said, "See, he has hidden himself among
10: 24 "Do you see the one whom the L has chosen?
10: 25 in a book and laid it up before the L. D
11: 7 Then the dread of the L fell upon the people,
11: 13 today the L has brought deliverance to Israel."
11: 15 and there they made Saul king before the L D
11: 15 offerings of well-being before the L, D
12: 3 against me before the L and before his anointed. D
12: 5 He said to them, "The L is witness against you,
12: 6 Samuel said to the people, "The L is witness,
12: 7 into judgment with you before the L, D
12: 7 the saving deeds of the L that he performed
12: 8 to the L and the L sent Moses and Aaron,
12: 9 But they forgot the L their God; A
12: 10 Then they cried to the L, and said,
12: 10 because we have forsaken the L,
12: 11 And the L sent Jerubbaal and Barak,
12: 12 though the L your God was your king. A
12: 13 see, the L has set a king over you.
12: 14 fear the L and serve him and heed his voice X
12: 14 the commandment of the L, and if both you and
12: 14 over you will follow the L your God, it will A
12: 15 but if you will not heed the voice of the L, P
12: 15 but rebel against the commandment of the L,
12: 15 hand of the L will be against you and your king. S
12: 16 and see this great thing that the L will do
12: 17 I will call upon the L, that he may send thunder
12: 17 in the sight of the L is great in demanding a king
12: 18 So Samuel called upon the L,
12: 18 and the L sent thunder and rain that day;
12: 18 all the people greatly feared the L and Samuel.
12: 19 "Pray to the L your God for your servants, A
12: 20 yet do not turn aside from following the L,
12: 20 but serve the L with all your heart;
12: 22 For the L will not cast away his people,
12: 22 because it has pleased the L to make you
12: 23 that I should sin against the L by ceasing to pray
12: 24 Only fear the L, and serve him faithfully X
13: 12 and I have not entreated the favor of the L';
13: 13 not kept the commandment of the L your God, A
13: 13 The L would have established your kingdom
13: 14 the L has sought out a man after his own heart;
13: 14 L has appointed him to be ruler over his people,
13: 14 you have not kept what the L commanded you."
14: 3 the priest of the L in Shiloh, carrying an ephod.
14: 6 it may be that the L will act for us;
14: 6 for nothing can hinder the L from saving
14: 10 for the L has given them into our hand.
14: 12 the L has given them into the hand of Israel."
14: 23 So the L gave Israel the victory that day.
14: 33 the troops are sinning against the L by eating
14: 34 not sin against the L by eating with the blood.'"

1Sa 14: 35 And Saul built an altar to the L;
14: 35 it was the first altar that he built to the L.
14: 39 For as the L lives who saves Israel, Q
14: 41 Then Saul said, "O L God of Israel, J
14: 41 O L God of Israel, give Urim; J
14: 45 As the L lives, not one hair of his head shall fall Q
15: 1 "The L sent me to anoint you king
15: 1 now therefore listen to the words of the L.
15: 2 Thus says the L of hosts, CE
15: 10 The word of the L came to Samuel: G
15: 11 and he cried out to the L all night.
15: 13 "May you be blessed by the L;
15: 13 I have carried out the command of the L."
15: 15 to sacrifice to the L your God; A
15: 16 I will tell you what the L said to me last night."
15: 17 The L anointed you king over Israel.
15: 18 And the L sent you on a mission, and said, 'Go,
15: 19 Why then did you not obey the voice of the L? P
15: 19 and do what was evil in the sight of the L?" L
15: 20 "I have obeyed the voice of the L, P
15: 20 on the mission on which the L sent me,
15: 21 to sacrifice to the L your God in Gilgal." A
15: 22 "Has the L as great delight in burnt offerings
15: 22 as in obeying the voice of the L? P
15: 23 Because you have rejected the word of the L, G
15: 24 the commandment of the L and your words,
15: 25 and return with me, so that I may worship the L."
15: 26 for you have rejected the word of the L, G
15: 26 L has rejected you from being king over Israel."
15: 28 "The L has torn the kingdom of Israel
15: 30 so that I may worship the L your God." A
15: 31 and Saul worshiped the L.
15: 33 And Samuel hewed Agag in pieces before the L D
15: 35 And the L was sorry that he had made Saul king
16: 1 The L said to Samuel,
16: 2 And the L said, "Take a heifer with you,
16: 2 and say, 'I have come to sacrifice to the L.'
16: 4 Samuel did what the L commanded,
16: 5 I have come to sacrifice to the L;
16: 6 the LORD's anointed is now before the L." D
16: 7 But the L said to Samuel,
16: 7 for the L does not see as mortals see;
16: 7 but the L looks on the heart."
16: 8 He said, "Neither has the L chosen this one."
16: 9 he said, "Neither has the L chosen this one."
16: 10 "The L has not chosen any of these."
16: 12 The L said, "Rise and anoint him;
16: 13 the spirit of the L came mightily upon David
16: 14 Now the spirit of the L departed from Saul,
16: 14 and an evil spirit from the L tormented him.
16: 18 and the L is with him."
17: 37 "The L, who saved me from the paw of the lion
17: 37 "Go, and may the L be with you!"
17: 45 but I come to you in the name of the L of hosts, EI
17: 46 the L will deliver you into my hand,
17: 47 that all this assembly may know that the L does
18: 12 the L was with him but had departed from Saul.
18: 14 for the L was with him.
18: 28 when Saul realized that the L was with David,
19: 5 the L brought about a great victory for all Israel.
19: 6 Saul swore, "As the L lives, Q
19: 9 Then an evil spirit from the L came upon Saul,
20: 3 But truly, as the L lives and as you yourself live, Q
20: 12 Jonathan said to David, "By the L,
20: 13 the L do so to Jonathan, and more also,
20: 13 May the L be with you,
20: 14 show me the faithful love of the L;
20: 15 if the L were to cut off every one of the enemies
20: 16 "May the L seek out the enemies of David."
20: 21 then you are to come, for, as the L lives, Q
20: 22 for the L has sent you away.
20: 23 the L is witness between you and me forever."
20: 42 both of us have sworn in the name of the L, I
20: 42 saying, 'The L shall be between me and you,
21: 6 which is removed from before the L, D
21: 7 that day, detained before the L; D
22: 10 he inquired of the L for him,
22: 17 "Turn and kill the priests of the L,
22: 17 not raise their hand to attack the priests of the L.
22: 21 that Saul had killed the priests of the L.
23: 2 David inquired of the L,
23: 2 The L said to David, "Go and attack
23: 4 Then David inquired of the L again.
23: 4 The L answered him, "Yes, go down to Keilah;
23: 10 David said, "O L, the God of Israel,
23: 11 O L, the God of Israel, I beseech you,
23: 11 The L said, "He will come down."
23: 12 The L said, "They will surrender you."
23: 14 but the L did not give him into his hand.
23: 16 there he strengthened his hand through the L.
23: 18 the two of them made a covenant before the L; D
23: 21 by the L for showing me compassion!
24: 4 "Here is the day of which the L said to you,
24: 6 L forbid that I should do this thing to my lord,
24: 10 how the L gave you into my hand in the cave;
24: 12 May the L judge between me and you!
24: 12 May the L avenge me on you;
24: 15 May the L therefore be judge,
24: 18 not kill me when the L put me into your hands.
24: 19 So may the L reward you with good
24: 21 the L that you will not cut off my descendants
25: 26 Now then, my lord, as the L lives, Q
25: 26 since the L has restrained you from bloodguilt
25: 28 the L will certainly make my lord a sure house,
25: 28 because my lord is fighting the battles of the L;
25: 29 of the living under the care of the L your God; A
25: 30 When the L has done to my lord according to all

1Sa 25: 31 And when the L has dealt well with my lord,
25: 32 David said to Abigail, "Blessed be the L, T
25: 34 For as surely as the L the God of Israel lives,
25: 38 About ten days later the L struck Nabal,
25: 39 "Blessed be the L who has judged the case of T
25: 39 the L has returned the evildoing of Nabal
26: 10 David said, "As the L lives, Q
26: 10 the L will strike him down;
26: 11 The L forbid that I should raise my hand against
26: 12 a deep sleep from the L had fallen upon them.
26: 16 As the L lives, you deserve to die, Q
26: 19 If it is the L who has stirred you up against me,
26: 19 if it is mortals, may they be cursed before the L, D
26: 19 from my share in the heritage of the L,
26: 20 away from the presence of the L;
26: 23 The L rewards everyone for his righteousness
26: 23 for the L gave you into my hand today,
26: 24 so may my life be precious in the sight of the L,
28: 6 When Saul inquired of the L,
28: 6 the L did not answer him, not by dreams,
28: 10 But Saul swore to her by the L,
28: 10 "As the L lives, no punishment shall come Q
28: 16 L has turned from you and become your enemy?
28: 17 The L has done to you just as he spoke by me;
28: 17 for the L has torn the kingdom out of your hand,
28: 18 Because you did not obey the voice of the L, P
28: 18 therefore the L has done this thing to you today.
28: 19 Moreover the L will give Israel along with you
28: 19 the L will also give the army of Israel into
29: 6 "As the L lives, you have been honest, Q
30: 6 David strengthened himself in the L his God. A
30: 8 David inquired of the L,
30: 23 my brothers, with what the L has given us;
30: 26 for you from the spoil of the enemies of the L";
2Sa 1: 12 for the army of the L and for the house of Israel,
2: 1 After this David inquired of the L,
2: 1 The L said to him, "Go up."
2: 5 and said to them, "May you be blessed by the L,
2: 6 the L show steadfast love and faithfulness
3: 9 For just what the L has sworn to David,
3: 18 for the L has promised David:
3: 28 before the L for the blood of Abner son of Ner. D
3: 39 The L pay back the one who does wickedly
4: 8 the L has avenged my lord the king this day
4: 9 "As the L lives, who has redeemed my life out Q
5: 2 and brought it in. The L said to you:
5: 3 a covenant with them at Hebron before the L, D
5: 10 David became greater and greater, for the L,
5: 12 that the L had established him king over Israel,
5: 19 David inquired of the L,
5: 19 The L said to David, "Go up;
5: 20 L has burst forth against my enemies before me,
5: 23 When David inquired of the L, he said,
5: 24 for then the L has gone out before you to strike
5: 25 David did just as the L had commanded him;
6: 2 the name of the L of hosts who is enthroned on EI
6: 5 the house of Israel were dancing before the L D
6: 7 The anger of the L was kindled against Uzzah;
6: 8 David was angry because the L had burst forth
6: 9 David was afraid of the L that day;
6: 9 "How can the ark of the L come into my care?" N
6: 10 So David was unwilling to take the ark of the L N
6: 11 The ark of the L remained in the house of N
6: 11 the L blessed Obed-edom and all his household.
6: 12 "The L has blessed the household
6: 13 the ark of the L had gone six paces, N
6: 14 David danced before the L with all his might; D
6: 15 the house of Israel brought up the ark of the L N
6: 16 As the ark of the L came into the city of David, N
6: 16 and dancing before the L; D
6: 17 They brought in the ark of the L, N
6: 17 and offerings of well-being before the L. D
6: 18 blessed the people in the name of the L of hosts, EI
6: 21 David said to Michal, "It was before the L, D
6: 21 the people of the L, that I have danced before
6: 21 that I have danced before the L. D
7: 1 the L had given him rest from all his enemies
7: 3 for the L is with you."
7: 4 same night the word of the L came to Nathan: G
7: 5 and tell my servant David: Thus says the L: C
7: 8 Thus says the L of hosts: CE
7: 11 Moreover the L declares to you that
7: 11 to you that the L will make you a house.
7: 18 Then King David went in and sat before the L, D
7: 22 Therefore you are great, O L God; J
7: 24 and you, O L, became their God.
7: 25 O L God, as for the word that you have spoken J
7: 26 'The L of hosts is God over Israel'; E
7: 27 For you, O L of hosts, the God of Israel, E
8: 6 The L gave victory to David wherever he went.
8: 11 these also King David dedicated to the L,
8: 14 the L gave victory to David wherever he went.
10: 12 and may the L do what seems good to him."
11: 27 the thing that David had done displeased the L,
12: 1 and the L sent Nathan to David.
12: 5 He said to Nathan, "As the L lives, Q
12: 7 Thus says the L, the God of Israel: C
12: 9 Why have you despised the word of the L, G
12: 11 Thus says the L: I will raise up trouble C
12: 13 "I have sinned against the L."
12: 13 "Now the L has put away your sin;
12: 14 by this deed you have utterly scorned the L,
12: 15 The L struck the child that Uriah's wife bore
12: 20 He went into the house of the L, and worshiped; F
12: 22 The L may be gracious to me,
12: 24 and he named him Solomon. The L loved him,
12: 25 so he named him Jedidiah, because of the L.

†**LORD** distinguishes the proper name of God, *Yahweh*, indicated in the NRSV by "LORD," from the words translated "Lord" and "lord," indexed under the heading ***LORD** on pages 798-804.

2Sa 14:11 may the king keep the L your God in mind, A
14:11 He said, "As the L lives, Q
14:17 The L your God be with you!" A
15: 7 and pay the vow that I have made to the L.
15: 8 If the L will indeed bring me back to Jerusalem,
15: 8 then I will worship the L in Hebron."
15:20 the L show steadfast love and faithfulness
15:21 But Ittai answered the king, "As the L lives, Q
15:25 If I find favor in the eyes of the L,
15:31 And David said, "O L, I pray you,
16: 8 The L has avenged on all of you the blood of
16: 8 and the L has given the kingdom into the hand
16:10 If he is cursing because the L has said to him,
16:11 for the L has bidden him.
16:12 It may be that the L will look on my distress,
16:12 the L will repay me with good for this cursing
16:18 but the one whom the L and this people and all
17:14 the L had ordained to defeat the good counsel
17:14 so that the L might bring ruin on Absalom.
18:19 to the king that the L has delivered him from
18:28 and said, "Blessed be the L your God, AT
18:31 For the L has vindicated you this day,
19: 7 for I swear by the L, if you do not go,
20:19 why will you swallow up the heritage of the L?"
21: 1 and David inquired of the L.
21: 1 The L said, "There is bloodguilt on Saul and
21: 3 that you may bless the heritage of the L?"
21: 6 and we will impale them before the L at Gibeon D
21: 6 the LORD at Gibeon on the mountain of the L."
21: 7 of the oath of the L that was between them,
21: 9 on the mountain before the L. D
22: 1 to the L the words of this song on the day when
22: 1 the day when the L delivered him from the hand
22: 2 The L is my rock, my fortress, and my deliverer,
22: 4 I call upon the L, who is worthy to be praised,
22: 7 In my distress I called upon the L;
22:14 The L thundered from heaven;
22:16 at the rebuke of the L, at the blast of the breath
22:19 but the L was my stay.
22:21 L rewarded me according to my righteousness;
22:22 For I have kept the ways of the L,
22:25 Therefore the L has recompensed me according
22:29 Indeed, you are my lamp, O L,
22:29 the L lightens my darkness.
22:31 the promise of the L proves true;
22:32 For who is God, but the L?
22:42 they cried to the L, but he did not answer them.
22:47 The L lives! Blessed be my rock,
22:50 For this I will extol you, O L,
23: 2 The spirit of the L speaks through me,
23:10 The L brought about a great victory that day.
23:12 and the L brought about a great victory.
23:16 he poured it out to the L,
23:17 "The L forbid that I should do this.
24: 1 the anger of the L was kindled against Israel,
24: 3 "May the L your God increase the number of A
24:10 David said to the L, "I have sinned greatly
24:10 But now, O L, I pray you,
24:11 the word of the L came to the prophet Gad, G
24:12 to David: Thus says the L: C
24:14 let us fall into the hand of the L, S
24:15 So the L sent a pestilence on Israel from
24:16 the L relented concerning the evil,
24:16 angel of the L was then by the threshing floor K
24:17 he said to the L, "I alone have sinned,
24:18 and erect an altar to the L on the threshing floor
24:19 David went up, as the L had commanded.
24:21 from you in order to build an altar to the L,
24:23 the L your God respond favorably to you." A
24:24 I will not offer burnt offerings to the L my God A
24:25 David built there an altar to the L,
24:25 So the L answered his supplication for the land,
1Ki 1:17 you swore to your servant by the L your God, A
1:29 The king swore, saying, "As the L lives, Q
1:30 as I swore to you by the L,
1:36 May the L, the God of my lord the king,
1:37 As the L has been with my lord the king,
1:48 'Blessed be the L, the God of Israel, T
2: 3 and keep the charge of the L your God, A
2: 4 Then the L will establish his word that he spoke
2: 8 I swore to him by the L,
2:15 for it was his from the L.
2:23 Then King Solomon swore by the L,
2:24 Now therefore as the L lives, Q
2:27 from being priest to the L,
2:27 the word of the L that he had spoken concerning G
2:28 to the tent of the L and grasped the horns of
2:29 to the tent of the L and now is beside the altar,"
2:30 So Benaiah came to the tent of the L and said
2:32 The L will bring back his bloody deeds
2:33 there shall be peace from the L forevermore."
2:42 "Did I not make you swear by the L,
2:43 Why then have you not kept your oath to the L
2:44 L will bring back your evil on your own head.
2:45 be established before the L forever." D
3: 1 house of the L and the wall around Jerusalem. F
3: 2 yet been built for the name of the L. I
3: 3 Solomon loved the L, walking in the statutes
3: 5 the L appeared to Solomon in a dream by night; Z
3: 7 And now, O L my God, A
3:15 before the ark of the covenant of the L. O
5: 3 build a house for the name of the L his God AI
5: 3 until the L put them under the soles of his feet.
5: 4 the L my God has given me rest on every side; A
5: 5 to build a house for the name of the L my God, AI
5: 5 as the L said to my father David, 'Your son,
5: 7 and said, "Blessed be the L today, T
1Ki 5:12 L gave Solomon wisdom, as he promised him.
6: 1 he began to build the house of the L. F
6: 2 for the L was sixty cubits long,
6:11 Now the word of the L came to Solomon, G
6:19 to set there the ark of the covenant of the L. O
6:37 the foundation of the house of the L was laid, F
7:12 so had the inner court of the house of the L, F
7:40 for King Solomon on the house of the L: F
7:45 for the house of the L were of burnished bronze. F
7:48 the vessels that were in the house of the L: F
7:51 on the house of the L was finished. F
7:51 in the treasuries of the house of the L. F
8: 1 of the covenant of the L out of the city of David, O
8: 4 So they brought up the ark of the L, N
8: 6 the ark of the covenant of the L to its place, O
8: 9 where the L made a covenant with the Israelites,
8:10 a cloud filled the house of the L, F
8:11 glory of the L filled the house of the LORD. R
8:11 glory of the LORD filled the house of the L. F
8:12 "The L has said that he would dwell
8:15 He said, "Blessed be the L, the God of Israel, T
8:17 in mind to build a house for the name of the L, I
8:18 But the L said to my father David,
8:20 Now the L has upheld the promise that he made;
8:20 I sit on the throne of Israel, as the L promised,
8:20 and have built the house for the name of the L, I
8:21 in which is the covenant of the L that he made O
8:22 Then Solomon stood before the altar of the L in
8:23 He said, "O L, God of Israel,
8:25 Therefore, O L, God of Israel,
8:28 O L my God, heeding the cry and the prayer A
8:44 the L toward the city that you have chosen and
8:54 and this plea to the L, he arose from facing
8:54 he arose from facing the altar of the L,
8:56 "Blessed be the L, who has given rest T
8:57 The L our God be with us, A
8:59 with which I pleaded before the L, D
8:59 be near to the L our God day and night, A
8:60 of the earth may know that the L is God;
8:61 devote yourselves completely to the L our God, A
8:62 offered sacrifice before the L. D
8:63 to the L twenty-two thousand oxen
8:63 people of Israel dedicated the house of the L. F
8:64 the court that was in front of the house of the L; F
8:64 that was before the L was too small to receive D
8:65 before the L our God, seven days. AD
8:66 that the L had shown to his servant David and
9: 1 the house of the L and the king's house and all F
9: 2 the L appeared to Solomon a second time, Z
9: 3 The L said to him, "I have heard your prayer
9: 8 'Why has the L done such a thing to this land
9: 9 'Because they have forsaken the L their God, A
9: 9 the L has brought this disaster upon them.' "
9:10 the house of the L and the king's house, F
9:15 to build the house of the L and his own house, F
9:25 of well-being on the altar that he built for the L,
9:25 offering incense before the L. D
10: 1 (fame due to the name of the L), I
10: 5 that he offered at the house of the L, F
10: 9 Blessed be the L your God, AT
10: 9 Because the L loved Israel forever,
10:12 the king made supports for the house of the L, F
11: 2 the nations concerning which the L had said to
11: 4 and his heart was not true to the L his God, A
11: 6 Solomon did what was evil in the sight of the L, L
11: 6 and did not completely follow the L,
11: 9 Then the L was angry with Solomon,
11: 9 because his heart had turned away from the L,
11:10 but he did not observe what the L commanded.
11:11 Therefore the L said to Solomon,
11:14 the L raised up an adversary against Solomon,
11:31 for thus says the L, the God of Israel, "See, C
12:15 about by the L that he might fulfill his word,
12:15 which the L had spoken by Ahijah the Shilonite
12:24 "Thus says the L, You shall not go up or fight C
12:24 the word of the L and went home again, G
12:24 according to the word of the L. G
12:27 to go up to offer sacrifices in the house of the L F
13: 1 of God came out of Judah by the word of the L G
13: 2 the word of the L, and said, "O altar, altar, G
13: 2 and said, "O altar, altar, thus says the L: C
13: 3 saying, "This is the sign that the L has spoken:
13: 5 the man of God had given by the word of the L. G
13: 6 "Entreat now the favor of the L your God, A
13: 6 So the man of God entreated the L;
13: 9 thus I was commanded by the word of the L: G
13:17 for it was said to me by the word of the L: G
13:18 and an angel spoke to me by the word of the L: G
13:20 the word of the L came to the prophet G
13:21 who came from Judah, "Thus says the L: C
13:21 Because you have disobeyed the word of the L, G
13:21 that the L your God commanded you, A
13:26 of God who disobeyed the word of the L; G
13:26 therefore the L has given him to the lion,
13:26 according to the word that the L spoke to him."
13:32 that he proclaimed by the word of the L against G
14: 5 But the L said to Ahijah,
14: 7 Go, tell Jeroboam, 'Thus says the L, C
14:11 of the air shall eat; for the L has spoken.'
14:13 to the L, the God of Israel, in the house
14:14 the L will raise up for himself a king over Israel,
14:15 "The L will strike Israel,
14:15 provoking the L to anger.
14:18 according to the word of the L, G
14:21 the L had chosen out of all the tribes of Israel,
14:22 Judah did what was evil in the sight of the L; L
14:24 that the L drove out before the people of Israel.
1Ki 14:26 he took away the treasures of the house of the L F
14:28 often as the king went into the house of the L, F
15: 3 his heart was not true to the L his God, A
15: 4 for David's sake the L his God gave him a lamp A
15: 5 David did what was right in the sight of the L,
15:11 Asa did what was right in the sight of the L,
15:14 the heart of Asa was true to the L all his days.
15:15 the house of the L the votive gifts of his father F
15:18 house of the L and the treasures of the king's F
15:26 He did what was evil in the sight of the L, L
15:29 according to the word of the L that he spoke G
15:30 of the anger to which he provoked the L,
15:34 He did what was evil in the sight of the L, L
16: 1 The word of the L came to Jehu son of Hanani G
16: 7 the word of the L came by the prophet Jehu son G
16: 7 of all the evil that he did in the sight of the L,
16:12 according to the word of the L, G
16:13 the L God of Israel to anger with their idols. J
16:19 doing evil in the sight of the L, L
16:25 Omri did what was evil in the sight of the L; L
16:26 provoking the L, the God of Israel, to anger
16:30 did evil in the sight of the L more than all L
16:33 Ahab did more to provoke the anger of the L,
16:34 according to the word of the L, G
17: 1 said to Ahab, "As the L the God of Israel lives,
17: 2 The word of the L came to him, saying, G
17: 5 he went and did according to the word of the L; G
17: 8 Then the word of the L came to him, saying, G
17:12 But she said, "As the L your God lives, A
17:14 For thus says the L the God of Israel: C
17:14 until the day that the L sends rain on the earth."
17:16 according to the word of the L that he spoke G
17:20 He cried out to the L, "O LORD my God,
17:20 He cried out to the LORD, "O L my God, A
17:21 and cried out to the L, "O LORD my God,
17:21 and cried out to the LORD, "O L my God, A
17:22 The L listened to the voice of Elijah;
17:24 that the word of the L in your mouth is truth." G
18: 1 many days the word of the L came to Elijah, G
18: 3 (Now Obadiah revered the L greatly;
18: 4 Jezebel was killing off the prophets of the L,
18:10 As the L your God lives, A
18:12 spirit of the L will carry you I know not where;
18:12 although I your servant have revered the L
18:13 when Jezebel killed the prophets of the L,
18:15 Elijah said, "As the L of hosts lives, E
18:18 the commandments of the L and followed
18:21 If the L is God, follow him;
18:22 "I, even I only, am left a prophet of the L;
18:24 and I will call on the name of the L; I
18:30 the altar of the L that had been thrown down;
18:31 to whom the word of the L came, saying, G
18:32 the stones he built an altar in the name of the L. I
18:36 the prophet Elijah came near and said, "O L,
18:37 Answer me, O L, answer me,
18:37 so that this people may know that you, O L,
18:38 of the L fell and consumed the burnt offering,
18:39 "The L indeed is God; the L indeed is God."
18:46 But the hand of the L was on Elijah; S
19: 4 now, O L, take away my life,
19: 7 The angel of the L came a second time, K
19: 9 Then the word of the L came to him, saying, G
19:10 "I have been very zealous for the L,
19:11 "Go out and stand on the mountain before the L, D
19:11 for the L is about to pass by."
19:11 breaking rocks in pieces before the L, D
19:11 but the L was not in the wind;
19:11 but the L was not in the earthquake;
19:12 but the L was not in the fire;
19:14 "I have been very zealous for the L,
19:15 Then the L said to him, "Go,
20:13 of Israel and said, "Thus says the L, C
20:13 and you shall know that I am the L." H
20:14 He said, "Thus says the L, C
20:28 and said to the king of Israel, "Thus says the L: C
20:28 'The L is a god of the hills but he is not a god of
20:28 and you shall know that I am the L." H
20:35 At the command of the L a certain member of
20:36 you have not obeyed the voice of the L, P
20:42 Then he said to him, "Thus says the L, C
21: 3 But Naboth said to Ahab, "The L forbid
21:17 the word of the L came to Elijah the Tishbite, G
21:19 You shall say to him, "Thus says the L: C
21:19 You shall say to him, "Thus says the L: C
21:20 to do what is evil in the sight of the L, L
21:23 Also concerning Jezebel the L said,
21:25 to do what was evil in the sight of the L, L
21:26 whom the L drove out before the Israelites.)
21:28 the word of the L came to Elijah the Tishbite: G
22: 5 "Inquire first for the word of the L." G
22: 6 for the L will give it into the hand of the king."
22: 7 of the L here of whom we may inquire?"
22: 8 by whom we may inquire of the L, Micaiah son
22:11 and he said, "Thus says the L: C
22:12 the L will give it into the hand of the king."
22:14 But Micaiah said, "As the L lives, Q
22:14 whatever the L says to me, that I will speak."
22:15 the L will give it into the hand of the king."
22:16 nothing but the truth in the name of the L?" I
22:17 and the L said, 'These have no master;
22:19 Micaiah said, "Therefore hear the word of the L: G
22:19 I saw the L sitting on his throne,
22:20 And the L said, 'Who will entice Ahab,
22:21 a spirit came forward and stood before the L, D
22:22 the L asked him. He replied,
22:22 Then the L said, 'You are to entice him,
22:23 the L has put a lying spirit in the mouth

†**LORD** distinguishes the proper name of God, *Yahweh,* indicated in the NRSV by "LORD," from the words translated "Lord" and "lord," indexed under the heading ***LORD** on pages 798-804.

1Ki 22:23 the L has decreed disaster for you."
22:24 "Which way did the spirit of the L pass from me
22:28 the L has not spoken by me."
22:38 to the word of the L that he had spoken. G
22:43 doing what was right in the sight of the L;
22:52 He did what was evil in the sight of the L, L
22:53 he provoked the L, the God of Israel, to anger,
2Ki 1: 3 the angel of the L said to Elijah the Tishbite, K
1: 4 Now therefore thus says the L, C
1: 6 and say to him: Thus says the L: C
1:15 Then the angel of the L said to Elijah, K
1:16 and said to him, "Thus says the L: C
1:17 to the word of the L that Elijah had spoken. G
2: 1 the L was about to take Elijah up to heaven by
2: 2 for the L has sent me as far as Bethel."
2: 2 But Elisha said, "As the L lives, Q
2: 3 the L will take your master away from you?"
2: 4 for the L has sent me to Jericho."
2: 4 But he said, "As the L lives, Q
2: 5 the L will take your master away from you?"
2: 6 for the L has sent me to the Jordan."
2: 6 But he said, "As the L lives, Q
2:14 and struck the water, saying, "Where is the L,
2:16 it may be that the spirit of the L has caught him
2:21 and said, "Thus says the L, C
2:24 he cursed them in the name of the L. I
3: 2 He did what was evil in the sight of the L, L
3:10 The L has summoned us, three kings,
3:11 "Is there no prophet of the L here,
3:11 through whom we may inquire of the L?"
3:12 "The word of the L is with him." G
3:13 it is the L who has summoned us, three kings,
3:14 Elisha said, "As the L of hosts lives, E
3:15 the power of the L came on him.
3:16 And he said, "Thus says the L, C
3:17 For thus says the L, 'You shall see neither wind C
3:18 This is only a trifle in the sight of the L,
4: 1 and you know that your servant feared the L,
4:27 L has hidden it from me and has not told me."
4:30 the mother of the child said, "As the L lives, Q
4:33 on the two of them, and prayed to the L.
4:43 the people and let them eat, for thus says the L, C
4:44 according to the word of the L. G
5: 1 by him the L had given victory to Aram.
5:11 stand and call on the name of the L his God, AI
5:16 But he said, "As the L lives, whom I serve, Q
5:17 or sacrifice to any god except the L.
5:18 may the L pardon your servant on one count:
5:18 the L pardon your servant on this one count."
5:20 As the L lives, I will run after him Q
6:17 "O L, please open his eyes that he may see."
6:17 L opened the eyes of the servant, and he saw;
6:18 Elisha prayed to the L, and said,
6:20 soon as they entered Samaria, Elisha said, "O L,
6:20 The L opened their eyes,
6:27 Let the L help you.
6:33 "This trouble is from the L!
6:33 Why should I hope in the L any longer?"
7: 1 But Elisha said, "Hear the word of the L: G
7: 1 thus says the L, Tomorrow about this time C
7: 2 if the L were to make windows in the sky,
7:16 according to the word of the L. G
7:19 if the L were to make windows in the sky,
8: 1 for the L has called for a famine,
8: 8 Inquire of the L through him,
8:10 the L has shown me that he shall certainly die."
8:13 "The L has shown me that you are to be king
8:18 He did what was evil in the sight of the L. L
8:19 Yet the L would not destroy Judah,
8:27 doing what was evil in the sight of the L, L
9: 3 'Thus says the L: I anoint you king over Israel.' C
9: 6 "Thus says the L the God of Israel: C
9: 6 I anoint you king over the people of the L,
9: 7 and the blood of all the servants of the L.
9:12 'Thus says the L, I anoint you king C
9:25 how the L uttered this oracle against him:
9:26 says the L, I swear I will repay you B
9:26 in accordance with the word of the L." G
9:36 he said, "This is the word of the L, G
10:10 to the earth nothing of the word of the L, G
10:10 the L spoke concerning the house of Ahab;
10:10 for the L has done what he said
10:16 "Come with me, and see my zeal for the L."
10:17 according to the word of the L that he spoke G
10:23 and see that there is no worshiper of the L here
10:30 The L said to Jehu,
10:31 not careful to follow the law of the L the God
10:32 In those days the L began to trim off parts
11: 3 hidden in the house of the L, F
11: 4 and had them come to him in the house of the L. F
11: 4 and put them under oath in the house of the L; F
11: 7 on the sabbath and guard the house of the L F
11:10 which were in the house of the L; F
11:13 she went into the house of the L to the people; F
11:15 "Let her not be killed in the house of the L." F
11:17 the L and the king and people, that they should
11:18 priest posted guards over the house of the L. F
11:19 the king down from the house of the L, F
12: 2 in the sight of the L all his days,
12: 4 that is brought into the house of the L, F
12: 4 into the house of the L, F
12: 9 the right side as one entered the house of the L; F
12: 9 that was brought into the house of the L. F
12:10 the money that was found in the house of the L, F
12:11 the oversight of the house of the L; F
12:11 the builders who worked on the house of the L, F
12:12 for making repairs on the house of the L, F
2Ki 12:13 But for the house of the L no basins of silver, F
12:13 that was brought into the house of the L, F
12:14 repairing the house of the L with it. F
12:16 not brought into the house of the L; F
12:18 of the house of the L and of the king's house, F
13: 2 He did what was evil in the sight of the L, L
13: 3 The anger of the L was kindled against Israel,
13: 4 But Jehoahaz entreated the L,
13: 4 the LORD, and the L heeded him;
13: 5 Therefore the L gave Israel a savior,
13:11 He also did what was evil in the sight of the L; L
13:23 the L was gracious to them and had compassion
14: 3 He did what was right in the sight of the L,
14: 6 where the L commanded,
14:14 the vessels that were found in the house of the L F
14:24 He did what was evil in the sight of the L; L
14:25 according to the word of the L, G
14:26 L saw that the distress of Israel was very bitter;
14:27 But the L had not said that he would blot out
15: 3 He did what was right in the sight of the L,
15: 5 The L struck the king, so that he was leprous to
15: 9 He did what was evil in the sight of the L, L
15:12 This was the promise of the L that he gave
15:18 He did what was evil in the sight of the L; L
15:24 He did what was evil in the sight of the L; L
15:28 He did what was evil in the sight of the L; L
15:34 He did what was right in the sight of the L,
15:35 He built the upper gate of the house of the L. F
15:37 In those days the L began to send King Rezin
16: 2 right in the sight of the L his God, A
16: 3 of the nations whom the L drove out before
16: 8 house of the L and in the treasures of the king's F
16:14 that was before the L he removed from the front D
16:14 between his altar and the house of the L, F
16:18 the king he removed from the house of the L. F
17: 2 He did what was evil in the sight of the L, L
17: 7 of Israel had sinned against the L their God, A
17: 8 of the nations whom the L drove out before
17: 9 that were not right against the L their God. A
17:11 as the nations did whom the L carried away
17:11 provoking the L to anger;
17:12 of which the L had said to them,
17:13 the L warned Israel and Judah by every prophet
17:14 who did not believe in the L their God. A
17:15 concerning whom the L had commanded them
17:16 all the commandments of the L their God A
17:17 to do evil in the sight of the L, L
17:18 Therefore the L was very angry with Israel
17:19 not keep the commandments of the L their God A
17:20 The L rejected all the descendants of Israel;
17:21 Jeroboam drove Israel from following the L
17:23 until the L removed Israel out of his sight,
17:25 they did not worship the L;
17:25 therefore the L sent lions among them,
17:28 he taught them how they should worship the L.
17:32 They also worshiped the L and appointed from
17:33 worshiped the L but also served their own gods,
17:34 the L and they do not follow the statutes or
17:34 that the L commanded the children of Jacob,
17:35 The L had made a covenant with them
17:36 the L, who brought you out of the land of Egypt
17:39 but you shall worship the L your God; A
17:41 So these nations worshiped the L,
18: 3 He did what was right in the sight of the L just
18: 5 He trusted in the L the God of Israel;
18: 6 For he held fast to the L;
18: 6 that the L commanded Moses.
18: 7 The L was with him; wherever he went,
18:12 did not obey the voice of the L their God but AP
18:12 the servant of the L had commanded; Y
18:15 in the house of the L and in the treasuries of F
18:16 the gold from the doors of the temple of the L, V
18:22 if you say to me, 'We rely on the L our God,' A
18:25 the L that I have come up against this place
18:25 The L said to me, Go up against this land,
18:30 Do not let Hezekiah make you rely on the L
18:30 The L will surely deliver us,
18:32 by saying, The L will deliver us.
18:35 L should deliver Jerusalem out of my hand?' "
19: 1 and went into the house of the L. F
19: 4 be that the L your God heard all the words of A
19: 4 the words that the L your God has heard; A
19: 6 "Say to your master, 'Thus says the L: C
19:14 then Hezekiah went up to the house of the L F
19:14 of the LORD and spread it before the L. D
19:15 And Hezekiah prayed before the L, and said: D
19:15 "O L the God of Israel, who are enthroned
19:16 Incline your ear, O L, and hear;
19:16 open your eyes, O L, and see;
19:17 O L, the kings of Assyria have laid waste
19:19 So now, O L our God, save us, I pray you, A
19:19 of the earth may know that you, O L,
19:20 saying, "Thus says the L, the God of Israel: C
19:21 the word that the L has spoken concerning him:
19:31 The zeal of the L of hosts will do this. E
19:32 thus says the L concerning the king of Assyria: C
19:33 he shall not come into this city, says the L. B
19:35 That very night the angel of the L set out K
20: 1 and said to him, "Thus says the L: C
20: 2 to the wall and prayed to the L:
20: 3 now, O L, I implore you, how I have walked
20: 4 the word of the L came to him: G
20: 5 Thus says the L, the God of your ancestor C
20: 5 go up to the house of the L. F
20: 8 "What shall be the sign that the L will heal me,
20: 8 and that I shall go up to the house of the L on F
20: 9 Isaiah said, "This is the sign to you from the L,
2Ki 20: 9 that the L will do the thing that he has promised:
20:11 The prophet Isaiah cried to the L;
20:16 "Hear the word of the L: G
20:17 nothing shall be left, says the L. B
20:19 word of the L that you have spoken is good." G
21: 2 He did what was evil in the sight of the L, L
21: 2 that the L drove out before the people of Israel.
21: 4 He built altars in the house of the L, F
21: 4 of which the L had said,
21: 5 in the two courts of the house of the L. F
21: 6 He did much evil in the sight of the L, L
21: 7 in the house of which the L said to David and
21: 9 the nations had done that the L destroyed before
21:10 The L said by his servants the prophets,
21:12 therefore thus says the L, C
21:16 that they did what was evil in the sight of the L. L
21:20 He did what was evil in the sight of the L, L
21:22 he abandoned the L, the God of his ancestors,
21:22 and did not walk in the way of the L.
22: 2 He did what was right in the sight of the L,
22: 3 the secretary, to the house of the L, saying, F
22: 4 that has been brought into the house of the L, F
22: 5 the oversight of the house of the L; F
22: 5 to the workers who are at the house of the L, F
22: 8 the book of the law in the house of the L." F
22: 9 of the house of the L." F
22:13 inquire of the L for me, for the people,
22:13 for great is the wrath of the L that is kindled
22:15 She declared to them, "Thus says the L, C
22:16 Thus says the L, I will indeed bring disaster C
22:18 who sent you to inquire of the L,
22:18 thus shall you say to him, Thus says the L, C
22:19 and you humbled yourself before the L, D
22:19 I also have heard you, says the L. B
23: 2 The king went up to the house of the L, F
23: 2 that had been found in the house of the L. F
23: 3 by the pillar and made a covenant before the L, D
23: 3 to follow the L, keeping his commandments,
23: 4 temple of the L all the vessels made for Baal, V
23: 6 the image of Asherah from the house of the L, F
23: 7 that were in the house of the L, F
23: 9 not come up to the altar of the L in Jerusalem,
23:11 at the entrance to the house of the L, F
23:12 in the two courts of the house of the L, F
23:16 and defiled it, according to the word of the L G
23:19 provoking the L to anger;
23:21 to the L your God as prescribed in this book of A
23:23 of King Josiah this passover was kept to the L
23:24 in the house of the L. F
23:25 who turned to the L with all his heart,
23:26 Still the L did not turn from the fierceness
23:27 The L said, "I will remove Judah also out
23:32 He did what was evil in the sight of the L, L
23:37 He did what was evil in the sight of the L, L
24: 2 The L sent against him bands of the Chaldeans,
24: 2 the word of the L that he spoke by his servants G
24: 3 this came upon Judah at the command of the L,
24: 4 and the L was not willing to pardon.
24: 9 He did what was evil in the sight of the L, L
24:13 house of the L, and the treasures of the king's F
24:13 the vessels of gold in the temple of the L, V
24:13 all this as the L had foretold.
24:19 He did what was evil in the sight of the L, L
24:20 the L that he expelled them from his presence.
25: 9 He burned the house of the L, the king's house, F
25:13 bronze pillars that were in the house of the L, F
25:13 the bronze sea that were in the house of the L, F
25:16 for the house of the L, F
1Ch 2: 3 was wicked in the sight of the L,
6:15 when the L sent Judah and Jerusalem into exile
6:31 of the service of song in the house of the L, F
6:32 until Solomon had built the house of the L F
9:19 in charge of the camp of the L,
9:20 in former times; the L was with him.
9:23 in charge of the gates of the house of the L, F
10:13 he was unfaithful to the L in that he did not keep the command of the L;
10:14 and did not seek guidance from the L.
10:14 the L put him to death and turned the kingdom
11: 2 The L your God said to you: A
11: 3 a covenant with them at Hebron before the L. D
11: 3 according to the word of the L by Samuel. G
11: 9 for the L of hosts was with him. E
11:10 to the word of the L concerning Israel. G
11:14 and the L saved them by a great victory.
11:18 he poured it out to the L,
12:23 according to the word of the L. G
13: 2 and if it is the will of the L our God, A
13: 6 to bring up from there the ark of God, the L, N
13:10 The anger of the L was kindled against Uzzah;
13:11 David was angry because the L had burst out
13:14 and the L blessed the household of Obed-edom
14: 2 the L had established him as king over Israel,
14:10 The L said to him, "Go up,
14:17 and the L brought the fear of him on all nations.
15: 2 for the L had chosen them to carry the ark of
15: 2 the ark of the L and to minister to him forever. N
15: 3 in Jerusalem to bring up the ark of the L N
15:12 so that you may bring up the ark of the L, N
15:13 the L our God burst out against us, A
15:14 to bring up the ark of the L, N
15:15 according to the word of the L. G
15:25 went to bring up the ark of the covenant of the L O
15:26 the ark of the covenant of the L, O
15:28 the ark of the covenant of the L with shouting, O
15:29 the ark of the covenant of the L came to the city O
16: 2 he blessed the people in the name of the L; I

†**LORD** distinguishes the proper name of God, *Yahweh*, indicated in the NRSV by "LORD," from the words translated "Lord" and "lord," indexed under the heading ***LORD** on pages 798-804.

1Ch 16: 4 the Levites as ministers before the ark of the **L**, N
16: 4 to thank, and to praise the **L**, the God of Israel. M
16: 7 of praises to the **L** by Asaph and his kindred.
16: 8 O give thanks to the **L**, call on his name,
16:10 let the hearts of those who seek the **L** rejoice.
16:11 Seek the **L** and his strength,
16:14 He is the **L** our God; A
16:23 Sing to the **L**, all the earth.
16:25 For great is the **L**, and greatly to be praised;
16:26 but the **L** made the heavens.
16:28 Ascribe to the **L**, O families of the peoples,
16:28 ascribe to the **L** glory and strength.
16:29 Ascribe to the **L** the glory due his name;
16:29 Worship the **L** in holy splendor;
16:31 among the nations, "The **L** is king!"
16:33 the trees of the forest sing for joy before the **L**, D
16:34 O give thanks to the **L**, for he is good;
16:36 Blessed be the **L**, the God of Israel, T
16:36 all the people said "Amen!" and praised the **L**.
16:37 of the covenant of the **L** to minister regularly O
16:39 the tabernacle of the **L** in the high place that was
16:40 to the **L** on the altar of burnt offering regularly,
16:40 in the law of the **L** that he commanded Israel.
16:41 and expressly named to render thanks to the **L**,
17: 1 the ark of the covenant of the **L** is under a tent." O
17: 3 same night the word of the **L** came to Nathan, G
17: 4 and tell my servant David: Thus says the **L**: C
17: 7 Thus says the **L** of hosts: CE
17:10 to you that the **L** will build you a house.
17:16 Then King David went in and sat before the **L**, D
17:16 "Who am I, O **L** God, and what is my house, J
17:17 as someone of high rank, O **L** God! J
17:19 For your servant's sake, O **L**,
17:20 There is no one like you, O **L**,
17:22 and you, O **L**, became their God.
17:23 now, O **L**, as for the word that you have spoken
17:24 'The **L** of hosts, the God of Israel, E
17:26 And now, O **L**, you are God,
17:27 you, O **L**, have blessed and are blessed forever."
18: 6 The **L** gave victory to David wherever he went.
18:11 these also King David dedicated to the **L**,
18:13 the **L** gave victory to David wherever he went.
19:13 and may the **L** do what seems good to him."
21: 3 "May the **L** increase the number of his people
21: 9 The **L** spoke to Gad, David's seer, saying,
21:10 and say to David, 'Thus says the **L**: C
21:11 "Thus says the **L**, 'Take your choice: C
21:12 or three days of the sword of the **L**,
21:12 and the angel of the **L** destroying throughout all K
21:13 let me fall into the hand of the **L**, S
21:14 So the **L** sent a pestilence on Israel;
21:15 when he was about to destroy it, the **L** took note
21:15 The angel of the **L** was then standing by K
21:16 the angel of the **L** standing between earth and K
21:17 Let your hand, I pray, O **L** my God, A
21:18 angel of the **L** commanded Gad to tell David K
21:18 and erect an altar to the **L** on the threshing floor
21:19 which he had spoken in the name of the **L**. I
21:22 that I may build on it an altar to the **L**—
21:24 I will not take for the **L** what is yours,
21:26 an altar to the **L** and presented burnt offerings
21:26 He called upon the **L**, and he answered him
21:27 Then the **L** commanded the angel,
21:28 when David saw that the **L** had answered him at
21:29 For the tabernacle of the **L**,
21:30 he was afraid of the sword of the angel of the **L**. K
22: 1 the house of the **L** God and here the altar FJ
22: 5 the **L** must be exceedingly magnificent, famous
22: 6 and charged him to build a house for the **L**,
22: 7 to build a house to the name of the **L** my God. AI
22: 8 But the word of the **L** came to me, saying, G
22:11 Now, my son, the **L** be with you,
22:11 in building the house of the **L** your God, AF
22:12 the **L** grant you discretion and understanding,
22:12 the law of the **L** your God. A
22:13 the ordinances that the **L** commanded Moses
22:14 the house of the **L** one hundred thousand talents F
22:16 Now begin the work, and the **L** be with you."
22:18 "Is not the **L** your God with you? A
22:18 the land is subdued before the **L** and his people. D
22:19 set your mind and heart to seek the **L** your God. A
22:19 Go and build the sanctuary of the **L** God so that J
22:19 of the covenant of the **L** and the holy vessels O
22:19 into a house built for the name of the **L**." I
23: 4 of the work in the house of the **L**, F
23: 5 to the **L** with the instruments that I have made
23:13 before the **L**, and minister to him D
23:24 the work for the service of the house of the **L**. F
23:25 For David said, "The **L**, the God of Israel,
23:28 the house of the **L**, having the care of the courts F
23:30 thanking and praising the **L**,
23:31 to the **L** on sabbaths, new moons,
23:31 of them, regularly before the **L**. D
23:32 for the service of the house of the **L**." F
24:19 the house of the **L** according to the procedure F
24:19 as the **L** God of Israel had commanded him. J
25: 3 with the lyre in thanksgiving and praise to the **L**.
25: 6 the music in the house of the **L** with cymbals, F
25: 7 who were trained in singing to the **L**,
26:12 ministering in the house of the **L**; F
26:22 in charge of the treasuries of the house of the **L**. F
26:27 for the maintenance of the house of the **L**. F
26:30 the work of the **L** and for the service of the king.
27:23 the **L** had promised to make Israel as numerous
28: 2 of rest for the ark of the covenant of the **L**, O
28: 4 Yet the **L** God of Israel chose me J
28: 5 of all my sons, for the **L** has given me many,

1Ch 28: 5 the throne of the kingdom of the **L** over Israel.
28: 8 in the sight of all Israel, the assembly of the **L**,
28: 8 the commandments of the **L** your God; A
28: 9 for the **L** searches every mind,
28:10 for the **L** has chosen you to build a house as
28:12 for the courts of the house of the **L**, F
28:13 all the work of the service in the house of the **L**; F
28:13 the vessels for the service in the house of the **L**, F
28:18 and covered the ark of the covenant of the **L**. O
28:20 for the **L** God, my God, is with you. J
28:20 for the service of the house of the **L** is finished. F
29: 1 temple will not be for mortals but for the **L** God. J
29: 5 consecrating themselves today to the **L**?"
29: 8 to the treasury of the house of the **L**, F
29: 9 with single mind they had offered freely to the **L**;
29:10 Then David blessed the **L** in the presence of all
29:10 O **L**, the God of our ancestor Israel,
29:11 Yours, O **L**, are the greatness, the power,
29:11 yours is the kingdom, O **L**,
29:16 O **L** our God, all this abundance A
29:18 O **L**, the God of Abraham, Isaac, and Israel,
29:20 "Bless the **L** your God." AW
29:20 And all the assembly blessed the **L**,
29:20 and prostrated themselves before the **L** and D
29:21 to the **L**, a thousand bulls, a thousand rams,
29:22 and they ate and drank before the **L** on that day D
29:23 Then Solomon sat on the throne of the **L**,
29:25 The **L** highly exalted Solomon in the sight
2Ch 1: 1 the **L** his God was with him A
1: 3 the servant of the **L** had made in the wilderness, Y
1: 5 was there in front of the tabernacle of the **L**.
1: 6 up there to the bronze altar before the **L**, D
1: 9 O **L** God, let your promise to my father David J
2: 1 to build a temple for the name of the **L**, I
2: 4 name of the **L** my God and dedicate it to him AI
2: 4 and the appointed festivals of the **L** our God, A
2:11 the **L** loves his people he has made you king
2:12 "Blessed be the **L** God of Israel, JT
2:12 who will build a temple for the **L**,
3: 1 Solomon began to build the house of the **L** F
3: 1 where the **L** had appeared to his father David, Z
4:16 for King Solomon for the house of the **L**. F
5: 1 for the house of the **L** was finished. F
5: 2 of the covenant of the **L** out of the city of David, O
5: 7 the ark of the covenant of the **L** to its place, O
5:10 the **L** made a covenant with the people of Israel
5:13 in unison in praise and thanksgiving to the **L**,
5:13 in praise to the **L**, "For he is good,
5:13 the house of the **L**, was filled with a cloud, F
5:14 for the glory of the **L** filled the house of God. R
6: 1 "The **L** has said that he would reside
6: 4 And he said, "Blessed be the **L**, T
6: 7 in mind to build a house for the name of the **L**, I
6: 8 But the **L** said to my father David,
6:10 the **L** has fulfilled his promise that he made;
6:10 on the throne of Israel, as the **L** promised,
6:10 and have built the house for the name of the **L**, I
6:11 covenant of the **L** that he made with the people O
6:12 Then Solomon stood before the altar of the **L** in
6:14 He said, "O **L**, God of Israel,
6:16 Therefore, O **L**, God of Israel,
6:17 Therefore, O **L**, God of Israel,
6:19 and his plea, O **L** my God, heeding the cry and A
6:41 "Now rise up, O **L** God, J
6:41 Let your priests, O **L** God, J
6:42 O **L** God, do not reject your anointed one. J
7: 1 and the glory of the **L** filled the temple. R
7: 2 The priests could not enter the house of the **L**, F
7: 2 the glory of the **L** filled the LORD's house. R
7: 3 the fire come down and the glory of the **L** on R
7: 3 and worshiped and gave thanks to the **L**, saying,
7: 4 and all the people offered sacrifice before the **L**. D
7: 6 for music to the **L** that King David had made
7: 6 for giving thanks to the **L**—
7: 7 the court that was in front of the house of the **L**; F
7:10 the goodness that the **L** had shown to David and
7:11 Thus Solomon finished the house of the **L** and F
7:11 to do in the house of the **L** and F
7:12 the **L** appeared to Solomon in the night and said Z
7:21 'Why has the **L** done such a thing to this land
7:22 'Because they abandoned the **L** the God
8: 1 the house of the **L** and his own house, F
8:11 to which the ark of the **L** has come are holy." N
8:12 to the **L** on the altar of the **L** that he had built
8:16 of the house of the **L** was laid until the house F
8:16 the house of the **L** was finished completely. F
9: 4 that he offered at the house of the **L**, F
9: 8 Blessed be the **L** your God, AT
9: 8 on his throne as king for the **L** your God. A
9:11 for the house of the **L** and for the king's house, F
10:15 by God so that the **L** might fulfill his word,
11: 2 the word of the **L** came to Shemaiah the man G
11: 4 "Thus says the **L**: You shall not go up C
11: 4 heeded the word of the **L** and turned back from G
11:14 from serving as priests of the **L**,
11:16 the **L** God of Israel came after them from all J
11:16 of Israel to Jerusalem to sacrifice to the **L**,
12: 1 he abandoned the law of the **L**,
12: 2 because they had been unfaithful to the **L**,
12: 5 and said to them, "Thus says the **L**: C
12: 6 "The **L** is in the right."
12: 7 When the **L** saw that they humbled themselves,
12: 7 the word of the **L** came to Shemaiah, saying: G
12: 9 he took away the treasures of the house of the **L** F
12:11 Whenever the king went into the house of the **L**, F
12:12 the wrath of the **L** turned from him,
12:13 in Jerusalem, the city that the **L** had chosen out

2Ch 12:14 for he did not set his heart to seek the **L**.
13: 5 Do you not know that the **L** God of Israel gave J
13: 8 that you can withstand the kingdom of the **L** in
13: 9 Have you not driven out the priests of the **L**,
13:10 But as for us, the **L** is our God,
13:10 to the **L** who are descendants of Aaron,
13:11 They offer to the **L** every morning
13:11 for we keep the charge of the **L** our God, A
13:12 O Israelites, do not fight against the **L**,
13:14 They cried out to the **L**,
13:18 because they relied on the **L**,
13:20 the **L** struck him down, and he died.
14: 2 and right in the sight of the **L** his God. A
14: 4 and commanded Judah to seek the **L**,
14: 6 for the **L** gave him peace.
14: 7 because we have sought the **L** our God; A
14:11 Asa cried to the **L** his God, "O LORD, A
14:11 Asa cried to the LORD his God, "O **L**, A
14:11 Help us, O **L** our God, for we rely on you, A
14:11 O **L**, you are our God;
14:12 So the **L** defeated the Ethiopians before Asa and
14:13 for they were broken before the **L** and his army. D
14:14 for the fear of the **L** was on them. U
15: 2 The **L** is with you, while you are with him.
15: 4 but when in their distress they turned to the **L**,
15: 8 He repaired the altar of the **L** that was in front of
15: 8 in front of the vestibule of the house of the **L**. F
15: 9 when they saw that the **L** his God was with him. A
15:11 They sacrificed to the **L** on that day,
15:12 They entered into a covenant to seek the **L**,
15:13 Whoever would not seek the **L**,
15:14 They took an oath to the **L** with a loud voice,
15:15 and the **L** gave them rest all around.
16: 2 from the treasures of the house of the **L** and F
16: 7 and did not rely on the **L** your God, A
16: 8 Yet because you relied on the **L**,
16: 9 eyes of the **L** range throughout the entire earth,
16:12 yet even in his disease he did not seek the **L**,
17: 3 The **L** was with Jehoshaphat,
17: 5 the **L** established the kingdom in his hand.
17: 6 His heart was courageous in the ways of the **L**;
17: 9 having the book of the law of the **L** with them;
17:10 The fear of the **L** fell on all the kingdoms U
17:16 a volunteer for the service of the **L**,
18: 4 "Inquire first for the word of the **L**." G
18: 6 prophet of the **L** here of whom we may inquire?"
18: 7 by whom we may inquire of the **L**, Micaiah son
18:10 and he said, "Thus says the **L**: C
18:11 the **L** will give it into the hand of the king."
18:13 But Micaiah said, "As the **L** lives, Q
18:15 but the truth in the name of the **L**?" I
18:16 and the **L** said, 'These have no master;
18:18 Micaiah said, "Therefore hear the word of the **L**: G
18:18 I saw the **L** sitting on his throne,
18:19 And the **L** said, 'Who will entice King Ahab
18:20 a spirit came forward and stood before the **L**, D
18:20 The **L** asked him, 'How?'
18:21 Then the **L** said, 'You are to entice him,
18:22 the **L** has put a lying spirit in the mouth
18:22 the **L** has decreed disaster for you."
18:23 "Which way did the spirit of the **L** pass from me
18:27 the **L** has not spoken by me."
18:31 Jehoshaphat cried out, and the **L** helped him.
19: 2 the wicked and love those who hate the **L**?
19: 2 wrath has gone out against you from the **L**.
19: 4 and brought them back to the **L**,
19: 7 Now, let the fear of the **L** be upon you; U
19: 7 of justice with the **L** our God, A
19: 8 for the **L** and to decide disputed cases.
19: 9 in the fear of the **L**, in faithfulness, U
19:10 before the **L** and wrath may not come on you D
19:11 over you in all matters of the **L**;
19:11 and may the **L** be with the good!"
20: 3 he set himself to seek the **L**,
20: 4 Judah assembled to seek help from the **L**;
20: 4 the towns of Judah they came to seek the **L**.
20: 5 in the house of the **L**, before the new court, F
20: 6 "O **L**, God of our ancestors,
20:13 Meanwhile all Judah stood before the **L**, D
20:14 Then the spirit of the **L** came upon Jahaziel son
20:15 Thus says the **L** to you: C
20:17 and see the victory of the **L** on your behalf,
20:17 and the **L** will be with you."
20:18 of Jerusalem fell down before the **L**, D
20:18 down before the LORD, worshiping the **L**.
20:19 stood up to praise the **L**, the God of Israel, M
20:20 in the **L** your God and you will be established; A
20:21 to sing to the **L** and praise him in holy splendor,
20:21 "Give thanks to the **L**, for his steadfast love
20:22 the **L** set an ambush against the Ammonites,
20:26 for there they blessed the **L**;
20:27 for the **L** had enabled them to rejoice
20:28 to the house of the **L**. F
20:29 the **L** had fought against the enemies of Israel.
20:32 doing what was right in the sight of the **L**.
20:37 the **L** will destroy what you have made."
21: 6 He did what was evil in the sight of the **L**. L
21: 7 Yet the **L** would not destroy the house of David
21:10 because he had forsaken the **L**,
21:12 "Thus says the **L**, the God of your father David: C
21:14 the **L** will bring a great plague on your people,
21:16 The **L** aroused against Jehoram the anger of
21:18 After all this the **L** struck him in his bowels with
22: 4 He did what was evil in the sight of the **L**, L
22: 7 whom the **L** had anointed to destroy the house
22: 9 who sought the **L** with all his heart."
23: 3 as the **L** promised concerning the sons of David.

†LORD distinguishes the proper name of God, *Yahweh*, indicated in the NRSV by "LORD," from the words translated "Lord" and "lord," indexed under the heading ***LORD** on pages 798-804.

2Ch 23: 5 be in the courts of the house of the L. F
23: 6 enter the house of the L except the priests and F
23: 6 the instructions of the L.
23:12 she went into the house of the L to the people; F
23:14 "Do not put her to death in the house of the L." F
23:18 Jehoiada assigned the care of the house of the L F
23:18 to be in charge of the house of the L, F
23:18 to offer burnt offerings to the L,
23:19 the house of the L so that no one should enter F
23:20 the king down from the house of the L, F
24: 2 Joash did what was right in the sight of the L all
24: 4 to restore the house of the L. F
24: 6 the tax levied by Moses, the servant of the L, Y
24: 7 the dedicated things of the house of the L for F
24: 8 and set it outside the gate of the house of the L. F
24: 9 the L the tax that Moses the servant of God laid
24:12 of the work of the house of the L, F
24:12 and carpenters to restore the house of the L, F
24:12 in iron and bronze to repair the house of the L. F
24:14 for the house of the L, F
24:14 in the house of the L regularly all the days F
24:18 They abandoned the house of the L, F
24:19 among them to bring them back to the L;
24:20 the commandments of the L,
24:20 Because you have forsaken the L,
24:21 to death in the court of the house of the L. F
24:22 he said, "May the L see and avenge!"
24:24 L delivered into their hand a very great army,
24:24 because they had abandoned the L,
25: 2 He did what was right in the sight of the L,
25: 4 in the book of Moses, where the L commanded,
25: 7 for the L is not with Israel—
25: 9 L is able to give you much more than this."
25:15 The L was angry with Amaziah and sent to him
25:27 that Amaziah turned away from the L they made
26: 4 He did what was right in the sight of the L,
26: 5 long as he sought the L, God made him prosper.
26:16 For he was false to the L his God, A
26:16 entered the temple of the L to make offering V
26:17 with eighty priests of the L who were men
26:18 Uzziah, to make offering to the L,
26:18 and it will bring you no honor from the L God." J
26:19 the presence of the priests in the house of the L, F
26:20 because the L had struck him.
26:21 for he was excluded from the house of the L. F
27: 2 He did what was right in the sight of the L just
27: 2 only he did not invade the temple of the L. V
27: 3 He built the upper gate of the house of the L, F
27: 6 he ordered his ways before the L his God. AD
28: 1 not do what was right in the sight of the L,
28: 3 of the nations whom the L drove out before
28: 5 L his God gave him into the hand of the king A
28: 6 because they had abandoned the L,
28: 9 But a prophet of the L was there,
28: 9 "Because the L, the God of your ancestors,
28:10 against the L your God? A
28:11 for the fierce wrath of the L is upon you."
28:13 the L in addition to our present sins and guilt.
28:19 the L brought Judah low because of King Ahaz
28:19 in Judah and had been faithless to the L.
28:21 the house of the L and the houses of the king F
28:22 yet more faithless to the L—
28:24 house of the L and made himself altars in every F
28:25 provoking to anger the L,
29: 2 He did what was right in the sight of the L,
29: 3 he opened the doors of the house of the L F
29: 5 and sanctify the house of the L, F
29: 6 what was evil in the sight of the L our God; AL
29: 6 from the dwelling of the L,
29: 8 wrath of the L came upon Judah and Jerusalem,
29:10 it is in my heart to make a covenant with the L,
29:11 for the L has chosen you to stand in his presence
29:15 by the words of the L,
29:15 to cleanse the house of the L. F
29:16 the inner part of the house of the L to cleanse it, F
29:16 the temple of the L into the court of the house V
29:16 the LORD into the court of the house of the L; F
29:17 the month they came to the vestibule of the L;
29:17 for eight days they sanctified the house of the L, F
29:18 "We have cleansed all the house of the L, F
29:19 see, they are in front of the altar of the L."
29:20 and went up to the house of the L. F
29:21 of Aaron to offer them on the altar of the L.
29:25 the Levites in the house of the L with cymbals, F
29:25 for the commandment was from the L
29:27 the song to the L began also, and the trumpets,
29:30 to sing praises to the L with the words of David
29:31 now consecrated yourselves to the L;
29:31 and thank offerings to the house of the L." F
29:32 all these were for a burnt offering to the L.
29:35 the service of the house of the L was restored. F
30: 1 that they should come to the house of the L F
30: 1 to keep the passover to the L the God of Israel.
30: 5 and keep the passover to the L the God of Israel,
30: 6 return to the L, the God of Abraham, Isaac,
30: 7 who were faithless to the L God J
30: 8 but yield yourselves to the L and come
30: 8 and serve the L your God, A
30: 9 For as you return to the L,
30: 9 For the L your God is gracious and merciful, A
30:12 the officials commanded by the word of the L. G
30:15 into the house of the L. F
30:17 to make it holy to the L.
30:18 saying, "The good L pardon all
30:19 the L the God of their ancestors,
30:20 The L heard Hezekiah, and healed the people.
30:21 Levites and the priests praised the L day by day,

2Ch 30:21 accompanied by loud instruments for the L.
30:22 showed good skill in the service of the L.
30:22 offerings of well-being and giving thanks to the L
31: 2 the gates of the camp of the L and to give thanks
31: 3 as it is written in the law of the L.
31: 4 devote themselves to the law of the L.
31: 6 that had been consecrated to the L their God, A
31: 8 they blessed the L and his people Israel.
31:10 the house of the L, we have had enough to eat F
31:10 for the L has blessed his people,
31:11 to prepare store-chambers in the house of the L; F
31:14 to apportion the contribution reserved for the L
31:16 all who entered the house of the L as the duty F
31:20 and right and faithful before the L his God. AD
32: 8 but with us is the L our God, A
32:11 'The L our God will save us from the hand of A
32:17 the L the God of Israel and to speak against him,
32:21 And the L sent an angel who cut off all
32:22 So the L saved Hezekiah and the inhabitants
32:23 to the L in Jerusalem and precious things
32:24 to the L, and he answered him and gave him
32:26 that the wrath of the L did not come upon them
33: 2 He did what was evil in the sight of the L, L
33: 2 of the nations whom the L drove out before
33: 4 He built altars in the house of the L, F
33: 4 of which the L had said,
33: 5 in the two courts of the house of the L. F
33: 6 He did much evil in the sight of the L, L
33: 9 the L had destroyed before the people of Israel.
33:10 The L spoke to Manasseh and to his people,
33:11 the L brought against them the commanders of
33:12 of the L his God and humbled himself greatly A
33:13 Manasseh knew that the L indeed was God.
33:15 and the idol from the house of the L, F
33:15 on the mountain of the house of the L and F
33:16 the L and offered on it sacrifices of well-being
33:16 and he commanded Judah to serve the L
33:17 but only to the L their God. A
33:18 to him in the name of the L God of Israel, IJ
33:22 He did what was evil in the sight of the L, L
33:23 He did not humble himself before the L, D
34: 2 He did what was right in the sight of the L,
34: 8 to repair the house of the L his God. AF
34:10 the oversight of the house of the L, F
34:10 house of the L gave it for repairing and F
34:14 that had been brought into the house of the L, F
34:14 of the law of the L given through Moses.
34:15 the book of the law in the house of the L"; F
34:17 the money that was found in the house of the L F
34:21 the L for me and for those who are left in Israel
34:21 wrath of the L that is poured out on us is great,
34:21 our ancestors did not keep the word of the L, G
34:23 She declared to them, "Thus says the L, C
34:24 Thus says the L: I will indeed bring disaster C
34:26 who sent you to inquire of the L,
34:26 Thus says the L, the God of Israel: C
34:27 I also have heard you, says the L. B
34:30 The king went up to the house of the L, F
34:30 that had been found in the house of the L. F
34:31 in his place and made a covenant before the L, D
34:31 to follow the L, keeping his commandments,
34:33 in Israel worship the L their God. A
34:33 from following the L the God of their ancestors.
35: 1 Josiah kept a passover to the L in Jerusalem;
35: 2 in the service of the house of the L. F
35: 3 and who were holy to the L, "Put the holy ark in
35: 3 Now serve the L your God and his people Israel. A
35: 6 according to the word of the L by Moses." G
35:12 of the people, to offer to the L, as it is written in
35:16 all the service of the L was prepared that day,
35:16 and to offer burnt offerings on the altar of the L,
35:26 with what is written in the law of the L,
36: 5 evil in the sight of the L his God. AL
36: 7 of the vessels of the house of the L to Babylon F
36: 9 He did what was evil in the sight of the L. L
36:10 with the precious vessels of the house of the L, F
36:12 what was evil in the sight of the L his God. AL
36:12 from the mouth of the L.
36:13 and hardened his heart against turning to the L,
36:14 the house of the L that he had consecrated F
36:15 The L, the God of their ancestors,
36:16 the wrath of the L against his people became
36:18 and the treasures of the house of the L, F
36:21 the word of the L by the mouth of Jeremiah, G
36:22 the word of the L spoken by Jeremiah, G
36:22 the L stirred up the spirit of King Cyrus
36:23 The L, the God of heaven,
36:23 may the L his God be with him! A
Ezr 1: 1 in order that the word of the L by the mouth G
1: 1 the L stirred up the spirit of King Cyrus
1: 2 The L, the God of heaven,
1: 3 and rebuild the house of the L, F
1: 5 up and rebuild the house of the L in Jerusalem. F
1: 7 house of the L that Nebuchadnezzar had carried F
2:68 as they came to the house of the L in Jerusalem, F
3: 3 they offered burnt offerings upon it to the L,
3: 5 and at all the sacred festivals of the L,
3: 5 a freewill offering to the L.
3: 6 to offer burnt offerings to the L.
3: 6 But the foundation of the temple of the L was V
3: 8 the oversight of the work on the house of the L. F
3:10 the foundation of the temple of the L, the priests V
3:10 in their vestments were stationed to praise the L M
3:11 praising and giving thanks to the L,
3:11 with a great shout when they praised the L,
3:11 the foundation of the house of the L was laid. F
4: 1 a temple to the L, the God

Ezr 4: 3 but we alone will build to the L,
6:21 of the nations of the land to worship the L,
6:22 for the L had made them joyful,
7: 6 of Moses that the L the God of Israel had given;
7: 6 for the hand of the L his God was upon him. AS
7:10 Ezra had set his heart to study the law of the L,
7:11 of the commandments of the L and his statutes
7:27 Blessed be the L, the God of our ancestors, T
7:27 to glorify the house of the L in Jerusalem, F
7:28 for the hand of the L my God was upon me, AS
8:28 And I said to them, "You are holy to the L,
8:28 and the gold are a freewill offering to the L,
8:29 within the chambers of the house of the L." F
8:35 all this was a burnt offering to the L.
9: 5 spread out my hands to the L my God, A
9: 8 by the L our God, who has left us a remnant, A
9:15 O L, God of Israel, you are just,
10:11 the L the God of your ancestors, and do his will;
Ne 1: 5 I said, "O L God of heaven, J
4:14 Remember the L, who is great and awesome,
5:13 "Amen," and praised the L.
8: 1 which the L had given to Israel.
8: 6 Then Ezra blessed the L, the great God,
8: 6 and worshiped the L with their faces to
8: 9 "This day is holy to the L your God; A
8:10 for this day is holy to our L;
8:10 for the joy of the L is your strength."
8:14 which the L had commanded by Moses,
9: 3 the law of the L their God for a fourth part of A
9: 3 and worshiped the L their God. A
9: 4 with a loud voice to the L their God. A
9: 5 bless the L your God from everlasting to AW
9: 6 And Ezra said: "You are the L, you alone;
9: 7 You are the L, the God who chose Abram
10:29 and do all the commandments of the L our Lord
10:34 to burn on the altar of the L our God, A
10:35 year by year, to the house of the L; F
Job 1: 6 to present themselves before the L, D
1: 7 L said to Satan, "Where have you come from?"
1: 7 the L, "From going to and fro on the earth,
1: 8 The L said to Satan, "Have you considered my
1: 9 Then Satan answered the L,
1:12 The L said to Satan, "Very well,
1:12 So Satan went out from the presence of the L.
1:21 the L gave, and the LORD has taken away;
1:21 the LORD gave, and the L has taken away;
1:21 blessed be the name of the L." I
2: 1 to present themselves before the L, D
2: 1 among them to present himself before the L. D
2: 2 L said to Satan, "Where have you come from?"
2: 2 the L, "From going to and fro on the earth,
2: 3 The L said to Satan, "Have you considered my
2: 4 Then Satan answered the L, "Skin for skin!
2: 6 L said to Satan, "Very well, he is in your power;
2: 7 So Satan went out from the presence of the L,
12: 9 not know that the hand of the L has done this? S
38: 1 Then the L answered Job out of the whirlwind:
40: 1 And the L said to Job:
40: 3 Then Job answered the L:
40: 6 Then the L answered Job out of the whirlwind:
42: 1 Then Job answered the L:
42: 7 After the L had spoken these words to Job,
42: 7 the L said to Eliphaz the Temanite:
42: 9 and did what the L had told them;
42: 9 and the L accepted Job's prayer.
42:10 And the L restored the fortunes of Job
42:10 the L gave Job twice as much as he had before.
42:11 for all the evil that the L had brought upon him;
42:12 The L blessed the latter days
Ps 1: 2 but their delight is in the law of the L,
1: 6 for the L watches over the way of the righteous,
2: 2 against the L and his anointed, saying,
2: 4 the L has them in derision.
2: 7 I will tell of the decree of the L:
2:11 Serve the L with fear, with trembling
3: 1 O L, how many are my foes!
3: 3 O L, are a shield around me, my glory,
3: 4 I cry aloud to the L,
3: 5 I wake again, for the L sustains me.
3: 7 Rise up, O L! Deliver me,
3: 8 Deliverance belongs to the L;
4: 3 that the L has set apart the faithful for himself;
4: 3 the L hears when I call to him.
4: 5 and put your trust in the L.
4: 6 Let the light of your face shine on us, O L!"
4: 8 for you alone, O L, make me lie down in safety.
5: 1 O L; give heed to my sighing.
5: 3 O L, in the morning you hear my voice;
5: 6 the L abhors the bloodthirsty and deceitful.
5: 8 O L, in your righteousness because
5:12 For you bless the righteous, O L;
6: 1 O L, do not rebuke me in your anger,
6: 2 Be gracious to me, O L, for I am languishing;
6: 2 O L, heal me, for my bones are shaking
6: 3 while you, O L—how long?
6: 4 Turn, O L, save my life;
6: 8 for the L has heard the sound of my weeping.
6: 9 The L has heard my supplication;
6: 9 the L accepts my prayer.
7: T *of David, which he sang to the L concerning Cush,*
7: 1 O L my God, in you I take refuge; A
7: 3 O L my God, if I have done this, A
7: 6 Rise up, O L, in your anger;
7: 8 The L judges the peoples;
7: 8 The LORD judges the peoples; judge me, O L,
7:17 to the L the thanks due to his righteousness,
7:17 and sing praise to the name of the L, I

†**LORD** distinguishes the proper name of God, *Yahweh*, indicated in the NRSV by "LORD," from the words translated "Lord" and "lord," indexed under the heading ***LORD** on pages 798-804.

Ps 8: 1 O L, our Sovereign, how majestic is your name
8: 9 O L, our Sovereign, how majestic is your name
9: 1 I will give thanks to the L with my whole heart;
9: 7 But the L sits enthroned forever,
9: 9 The L is a stronghold for the oppressed,
9:10 O L, have not forsaken those who seek you.
9:11 Sing praises to the L, who dwells in Zion.
9:13 Be gracious to me, O L.
9:16 The L has made himself known,
9:19 Rise up, O L! Do not let mortals prevail;
9:20 Put them in fear, O L; let the nations know
10: 1 O L, do you stand far off?
10: 3 those greedy for gain curse and renounce the L.
10:12 Rise up, O L; O God, lift up your
10:16 The L is king forever and ever;
10:17 O L, you will hear the desire of the meek;
11: 1 In the L I take refuge;
11: 4 The L is in his holy temple;
11: 5 The L tests the righteous and the wicked,
11: 7 For the L is righteous; he loves righteous deeds;
12: 1 O L, for there is no longer anyone who is godly;
12: 3 May the L cut off all flattering lips,
12: 5 I will now rise up," says the L; B
12: 6 promises of the L are promises that are pure,
12: 7 You, O L, will protect us;
13: 1 How long, O L? Will you forget me forever?
13: 3 Consider and answer me, O L my God! A
13: 6 I will sing to the L,
14: 2 The L looks down from heaven on humankind
14: 4 and do not call upon the L?
14: 6 but the L is their refuge.
14: 7 When the L restores the fortunes of his people,
15: 1 O L, who may abide in your
15: 4 but who honor those who fear the L; X
16: 2 I say to the L, "You are my Lord;
16: 5 The L is my chosen portion and my cup;
16: 7 I bless the L who gives me counsel; W
16: 8 I keep the L always before me;
17: 1 Hear a just cause, O L;
17:13 Rise up, O L, confront them, overthrow them!
17:14 from mortals—by your hand, O L—
18: T *A Psalm of David the servant of the L,* Y
18: T *who addressed the words of this song to the L*
18: T *the L delivered him from the hand of all his*
18: 1 I love you, O L, my strength.
18: 2 The L is my rock, my fortress, and my deliverer,
18: 3 I call upon the L, who is worthy to be praised,
18: 6 In my distress I called upon the L;
18:13 The L also thundered in the heavens,
18:15 at your rebuke, O L, at the blast of the breath of
18:18 but the L was my support.
18:20 L rewarded me according to my righteousness;
18:21 For I have kept the ways of the L,
18:24 Therefore the L has recompensed me according
18:28 the L, my God, lights up my darkness. A
18:30 the promise of the L proves true;
18:31 For who is God except the L?
18:41 they cried to the L, but he did not answer them.
18:46 The L lives! Blessed be my
18:49 For this I will extol you, O L,
19: 7 The law of the L is perfect, reviving the soul;
19: 7 the decrees of the L are sure,
19: 8 precepts of the L are right, rejoicing the heart;
19: 8 the commandment of the L is clear,
19: 9 the fear of the L is pure, enduring forever; U
19: 9 of the L are true and righteous altogether.
19:14 O L, my rock and my redeemer.
20: 1 The L answer you in the day of trouble!
20: 5 May the L fulfill all your petitions.
20: 6 Now I know that the L will help his anointed;
20: 7 but our pride is in the name of the L our God. AI
20: 9 Give victory to the king, O L;
21: 1 O L, and in your help how greatly he exults!
21: 7 For the king trusts in the L,
21: 9 The L will swallow them up in his wrath,
21:13 Be exalted, O L, in your strength!
22: 8 "Commit your cause to the L;
22:19 But you, O L, do not be far away!
22:23 You who fear the L, praise him! X
22:26 those who seek him shall praise the L. M
22:27 of the earth shall remember and turn to the L;
22:28 For dominion belongs to the L,
23: 1 The L is my shepherd, I shall not want.
23: 6 in the house of the L my whole life long. F
24: 3 Who shall ascend the hill of the L?
24: 5 They will receive blessing from the L,
24: 8 The L, strong and mighty, the L,
24:10 The L of hosts, he is the King of glory. E
25: 1 To you, O L, I lift up my soul.
25: 4 Make me to know your ways, O L;
25: 6 Be mindful of your mercy, O L,
25: 7 for your goodness' sake, O L!
25: 8 Good and upright is the L;
25:10 of the L are steadfast love and faithfulness,
25:11 For your name's sake, O L, pardon my guilt,
25:12 Who are they that fear the L? X
25:14 friendship of the L is for those who fear him,
25:15 My eyes are ever toward the L,
26: 1 O L, for I have walked in my integrity,
26: 1 and I have trusted in the L without wavering.
26: 2 Prove me, O L, and try me;
26: 6 and go around your altar, O L,
26: 8 O L, I love the house in which you dwell,
26:12 in the great congregation I will bless the L. W
27: 1 The L is my light and my salvation;
27: 1 The L is the stronghold of my life;
27: 4 One thing I asked of the L, that will I seek after:

Ps 27: 4 in the house of the L all the days of my life, F
27: 4 to behold the beauty of the L,
27: 6 I will sing and make melody to the L.
27: 7 Hear, O L, when I cry aloud,
27: 8 Your face, L, do I seek.
27:10 the L will take me up.
27:11 Teach me your way, O L,
27:13 I believe that I shall see the goodness of the L in
27:14 Wait for the L; be strong,
27:14 and let your heart take courage; wait for the L!
28: 1 To you, O L, I call; my rock,
28: 5 Because they do not regard the works of the L,
28: 6 Blessed be the L, for he has heard the sound T
28: 7 The L is my strength and my shield;
28: 8 The L is the strength of his people;
29: 1 Ascribe to the L, O heavenly beings, ascribe to
29: 1 ascribe to the L glory and strength.
29: 2 Ascribe to the L the glory of his name;
29: 2 worship the L in holy splendor.
29: 3 The voice of the L is over the waters; P
29: 3 the God of glory thunders, the L,
29: 4 The voice of the L is powerful; P
29: 4 the voice of the L is full of majesty. P
29: 5 The voice of the L breaks the cedars; P
29: 5 the L breaks the cedars of Lebanon.
29: 7 The voice of the L flashes forth flames of fire. P
29: 8 The voice of the L shakes the wilderness; P
29: 8 the L shakes the wilderness of Kadesh.
29: 9 The voice of the L causes the oaks to whirl, P
29:10 The L sits enthroned over the flood;
29:10 the L sits enthroned as king forever.
29:11 May the L give strength to his people!
29:11 May the L bless his people with peace!
30: 1 O L, for you have drawn me up,
30: 2 O L my God, I cried to you for help, A
30: 3 O L, you brought up my soul from Sheol,
30: 4 Sing praises to the L, O you his faithful ones,
30: 7 O L, you had established me as
30: 8 O L, I cried,
30: 8 I cried, and to the L I made supplication:
30:10 Hear, O L, and be gracious to me!
30:10 O L, be my helper!"
30:12 O L my God, I will give thanks to you forever. A
31: 1 In you, O L, I seek refuge;
31: 5 you have redeemed me, O L, faithful God.
31: 6 but I trust in the L.
31: 9 Be gracious to me, O L, for I am in distress;
31:14 I trust in you, O L; I say, "You are my God."
31:17 Do not let me be put to shame, O L,
31:21 Blessed be the L, for he has wondrously shown T
31:23 Love the L, all you his saints.
31:23 The L preserves the faithful,
31:24 all you who wait for the L.
32: 2 to whom the L imputes no iniquity,
32: 5 "I will confess my transgressions to the L,"
32:10 steadfast love surrounds those who trust in the L.
32:11 Be glad in the L and rejoice, O righteous,
33: 1 Rejoice in the L, O you righteous.
33: 2 Praise the L with the lyre; M
33: 4 For the word of the L is upright, G
33: 5 the earth is full of the steadfast love of the L.
33: 6 By the word of the L the heavens were made, G
33: 8 Let all the earth fear the L; X
33:10 L brings the counsel of the nations to nothing;
33:11 The counsel of the L stands forever,
33:12 Happy is the nation whose God is the L,
33:13 The L looks down from heaven;
33:18 Truly the eye of the L is on those who fear him,
33:20 Our soul waits for the L;
33:22 Let your steadfast love, O L, be upon us,
34: 1 I will bless the L at all times; W
34: 2 My soul makes its boast in the L;
34: 3 O magnify the L with me,
34: 4 I sought the L, and he answered me,
34: 6 This poor soul cried, and was heard by the L,
34: 7 angel of the L encamps around those who fear K
34: 8 O taste and see that the L is good;
34: 9 O fear the L, you his holy ones, X
34:10 but those who seek the L lack no good thing.
34:11 I will teach you the fear of the L. U
34:15 The eyes of the L are on the righteous,
34:16 The face of the L is against evildoers,
34:17 When the righteous cry for help, the L hears,
34:18 The L is near to the brokenhearted,
34:19 but the L rescues them from them all.
34:22 The L redeems the life of his servants;
35: 1 O L, with those who contend with me;
35: 5 with the angel of the L driving them on. K
35: 6 with the angel of the L pursuing them. K
35: 9 Then my soul shall rejoice in the L,
35:10 All my bones shall say, "O L, who is like you?
35:17 How long, O L, will you look on?
35:22 You have seen, O L; do not be silent!
35:24 Vindicate me, O L, my God, A
35:27 "Great is the L, who delights in the welfare of
36: T *Of David, the servant of the L.* Y
36: 5 Your steadfast love, O L,
36: 6 you save humans and animals alike, O L.
37: 3 Trust in the L, and do good;
37: 4 Take delight in the L, and he will give you
37: 5 Commit your way to the L;
37: 7 Be still before the L, and wait patiently for him; D
37: 9 those who wait for the L shall inherit the land.
37:13 but the L laughs at the wicked,
37:17 but the L upholds the righteous.
37:18 The L knows the days of the blameless,
37:20 and the enemies of the L are like the glory of

Ps 37:22 for those blessed by the L shall inherit the land,
37:23 Our steps are made firm by the L,
37:24 for the L holds us by the hand.
37:28 For the L loves justice; he will
37:33 The L will not abandon them to their power,
37:34 Wait for the L, and keep to his way,
37:39 The salvation of the righteous is from the L;
37:40 The L helps them and rescues them;
38: 1 O L, do not rebuke me in your anger,
38:15 But it is for you, O L, that I wait;
38:15 it is you, O L my God, who will answer. A
38:21 Do not forsake me, O L;
39: 4 "L, let me know my end, and what is
39:12 O L, and give ear to my cry;
40: 1 I waited patiently for the L;
40: 3 and put their trust in the L.
40: 4 Happy are those who make the L their trust,
40: 5 You have multiplied, O L my God, A
40: 9 I have not restrained my lips, as you know, O L.
40:11 Do not, O L, withhold your mercy from me;
40:13 Be pleased, O L, to deliver me;
40:13 O L, make haste to help me.
40:16 say continually, "Great is the L!"
41: 1 the L delivers them in the day of trouble.
41: 2 The L protects them and keeps them alive;
41: 3 The L sustains them on their sickbed;
41: 4 As for me, I said, "O L, be gracious to me;
41:10 But you, O L, be gracious to me,
41:13 Blessed be the L, the God of Israel, T
42: 8 By day the L commands his steadfast love,
46: 7 The L of hosts is with us; E
46: 8 behold the works of the L;
46:11 The L of hosts is with us; E
47: 2 For the L, the Most High, is awesome,
47: 5 the L with the sound of a trumpet.
48: 1 Great is the L and greatly to be praised in
48: 8 so have we seen in the city of the L of hosts, E
50: 1 God the L, speaks and summons the earth from
54: 6 I will give thanks to your name, O L,
55:16 But I call upon God, and the L will save me.
55:22 Cast your burden on the L,
56:10 In God, whose word I praise, in the L,
58: 6 tear out the fangs of the young lions, O L!
59: 3 For no transgression or sin of mine, O L,
59: 5 You, L God of hosts, are God of Israel. J
59: 8 But you laugh at them, O L;
64:10 the righteous rejoice in the L and take refuge
68: 4 his name is the L—be exultant before him.
68:16 where the L will reside forever?
68:18 against the L God's abiding there.
68:26 the L, O you who are of Israel's fountain!"
69:13 But as for me, my prayer is to you, O L.
69:16 O L, for your steadfast love is good;
69:31 This will please the L more than an ox or a bull
69:33 For the L hears the needy,
70: 1 O L, make haste to help me!
70: 5 You are my help and my deliverer; O L,
71: 1 In you, O L, I take refuge;
71: 5 For you, O Lord, are my hope, my trust, O L,
72:18 Blessed be the L, the God of Israel, T
74:18 Remember this, O L, how the enemy scoffs,
75: 8 hand of the L there is a cup with foaming wine, S
76:11 Make vows to the L your God, A
77:11 I will call to mind the deeds of the L;
78: 4 the glorious deeds of the L,
78:21 when the L heard, he was full of rage;
79: 5 How long, O L? Will you be angry
80: 4 O L God of hosts, how long will you be angry J
80:19 Restore us, O L God of hosts; J
81:10 I am the L your God, AH
81:15 Those who hate the L would cringe before him,
83:16 so that they may seek your name, O L.
83:18 whose name is the L, are the Most High over all
84: 1 lovely is your dwelling place, O L of hosts! E
84: 2 indeed it faints for the courts of the L;
84: 3 O L of hosts, my King and my God. E
84: 8 O L God of hosts, hear my prayer; J
84:11 For the L God is a sun and shield; J
84:11 the L withhold from those who walk uprightly.
84:12 O L of hosts, happy is everyone who trusts E
85: 1 L, you were favorable to your land;
85: 7 Show us your steadfast love, O L,
85: 8 Let me hear what God the L will speak,
85:12 The L will give what is good,
86: 1 O L, and answer me, for I am poor and needy.
86: 6 Give ear, O L, to my prayer;
86:11 Teach me your way, O L,
86:17 L, have helped me and comforted me.
87: 2 the L loves the gates of Zion more than all
87: 6 The L records, as he registers the peoples,
88: 1 O L, God of my salvation, when,
88: 9 Every day I call on you, O L;
88:13 But I, O L, cry out to you;
88:14 O L, why do you cast me off?
89: 1 of your steadfast love, O L, forever;
89: 5 O L, your faithfulness in the assembly of
89: 6 For who in the skies can be compared to the L?
89: 6 Who among the heavenly beings is like the L,
89: 8 O L God of hosts, who is as mighty as you, J
89: 8 who is as mighty as you, O L?
89:15 O L, in the light of your countenance;
89:18 For our shield belongs to the L,
89:46 How long, O L? Will you hide yourself forever?
89:51 O L, with which they taunted the footsteps
89:52 Blessed be the L forever. Amen and Amen. T
90:13 O L! How long? Have compassion on your
91: 2 will say to the L, "My refuge and my fortress;

†**LORD** distinguishes the proper name of God, *Yahweh,* indicated in the NRSV by "LORD," from the words translated "Lord" and "lord," indexed under the heading ***LORD** on pages 798-804.

Ps 91: 9 Because you have made the **L** your refuge,
92: 1 It is good to give thanks to the **L**, to sing praises
92: 4 For you, O **L**, have made me glad by your work;
92: 5 How great are your works, O **L**!
92: 8 but you, O **L**, are on high forever.
92: 9 For your enemies, O **L**,
92:13 They are planted in the house of the **L**; F
92:15 showing that the **L** is upright;
93: 1 The **L** is king, he is robed in majesty;
93: 1 the **L** is robed, he is girded with strength.
93: 3 The floods have lifted up, O **L**,
93: 4 majestic on high is the **L**!
93: 5 holiness befits your house, O **L**, forevermore.
94: 1 O **L**, you God of vengeance,
94: 3 O **L**, how long shall the wicked,
94: 5 They crush your people, O **L**,
94: 7 and they say, "The **L** does not see;
94:11 The **L** knows our thoughts,
94:12 Happy are those whom you discipline, O **L**,
94:14 For the **L** will not forsake his people;
94:17 If the **L** had not been my help,
94:18 "My foot is slipping," your steadfast love, O **L**,
94:22 But the **L** has become my stronghold,
94:23 the **L** our God will wipe them out. A
95: 1 O come, let us sing to the **L**;
95: 3 For the **L** is a great God,
95: 6 let us kneel before the **L**, our Maker! D
96: 1 O sing to the **L** a new song;
96: 1 sing to the **L**, all the earth.
96: 2 Sing to the **L**, bless his name;
96: 4 For great is the **L**, and greatly to be praised;
96: 5 but the **L** made the heavens.
96: 7 Ascribe to the **L**, O families of the peoples,
96: 7 ascribe to the **L** glory and strength.
96: 8 Ascribe to the **L** the glory due his name;
96: 9 Worship the **L** in holy splendor;
96:10 Say among the nations, "The **L** is king!
96:13 before the **L**; for he is coming, D
97: 1 The **L** is king! Let the earth rejoice;
97: 5 The mountains melt like wax before the **L**, D
97: 9 For you, O **L**, are most high over all the earth;
97:10 The **L** loves those who hate evil;
97:12 Rejoice in the **L**, O you righteous,
98: 1 O sing to the **L** a new song,
98: 2 The **L** has made known his victory;
98: 4 Make a joyful noise to the **L**, all the earth;
98: 5 Sing praises to the **L** with the lyre,
98: 6 a joyful noise before the King, the **L**.
98: 9 at the presence of the **L**,
99: 1 The **L** is king; let the peoples tremble!
99: 2 The **L** is great in Zion;
99: 5 Extol the **L** our God; worship at his footstool. A
99: 6 They cried to the **L**, and he answered them.
99: 8 O **L** our God, you answered them; A
99: 9 Extol the **L** our God, and worship A
99: 9 for the **L** our God is holy. A
100: 1 Make a joyful noise to the **L**, all the earth.
100: 2 Worship the **L** with gladness;
100: 3 Know that the **L** is God.
100: 5 the **L** is good; his steadfast love endures forever,
101: 1 to you, O **L**, I will sing.
101: 8 cutting off all evildoers from the city of the **L**.
102: T *when faint and pleading before the* ***L***. D
102: 1 Hear my prayer, O **L**; let my cry come to you.
102:12 But you, O **L**, are enthroned forever;
102:15 The nations will fear the name of the **L**, I
102:16 **L** will build up Zion; he will appear in his glory.
102:18 so that a people yet unborn may praise the **L**: M
102:19 from heaven the **L** looked at the earth,
102:21 that the name of the **L** may be declared in Zion, I
102:22 and kingdoms, to worship the **L**.
103: 1 Bless the **L**, O my soul, and all that is within W
103: 2 Bless the **L**, O my soul, W
103: 6 The **L** works vindication and justice
103: 8 The **L** is merciful and gracious,
103:13 so the **L** has compassion for those who fear him.
103:17 the steadfast love of the **L** is from everlasting
103:19 The **L** has established his throne in the heavens,
103:20 Bless the **L**, O you his angels, W
103:21 Bless the **L**, all his hosts, W
103:22 Bless the **L**, all his works, W
103:22 Bless the **L**, O my soul. W
104: 1 Bless the **L**, O my soul. W
104: 1 O **L** my God, you are very great. A
104:16 The trees of the **L** are watered abundantly,
104:24 O **L**, how manifold are your works!
104:31 May the glory of the **L** endure forever; R
104:31 may the **L** rejoice in his works—
104:33 I will sing to the **L** as long as I live;
104:34 for I rejoice in the **L**.
104:35 Bless the **L**, O my soul. W
104:35 O my soul. Praise the **L**! M
105: 1 O give thanks to the **L**, call on his name,
105: 3 let the hearts of those who seek the **L** rejoice.
105: 4 Seek the **L** and his strength;
105: 7 He is the **L** our God; A
105:19 the word of the **L** kept testing him. G
105:24 And the **L** made his people very fruitful,
105:45 and observe his laws. Praise the **L**! M
106: 1 Praise the **L**! O give thanks to the LORD, M
106: 1 O give thanks to the **L**, for he is good;
106: 2 Who can utter the mighty doings of the **L**,
106: 4 O **L**, when you show favor to your people;
106:16 and of Aaron, the holy one of the **L**.
106:25 and did not obey the voice of the **L**. P
106:29 they provoked the **L** to anger with their deeds,
106:32 They angered the **L** at the waters of Meribah,
Ps 106:34 as the **L** commanded them,
106:40 anger of the **L** was kindled against his people,
106:47 O **L** our God, and gather us from among A
106:48 Blessed be the **L**, the God of Israel, T
106:48 let all the people say, "Amen." Praise the **L**! M
107: 1 O give thanks to the **L**, for he is good;
107: 2 Let the redeemed of the **L** say so,
107: 6 Then they cried to the **L** in their trouble,
107: 8 Let them thank the **L** for his steadfast love,
107:13 Then they cried to the **L** in their trouble,
107:15 Let them thank the **L** for his steadfast love,
107:19 Then they cried to the **L** in their trouble,
107:21 Let them thank the **L** for his steadfast love,
107:24 they saw the deeds of the **L**,
107:28 Then they cried to the **L** in their trouble,
107:31 Let them thank the **L** for his steadfast love,
107:43 and consider the steadfast love of the **L**.
108: 3 I will give thanks to you, O **L**,
109:14 of his father be remembered before the **L**, D
109:15 Let them be before the **L** continually, D
109:20 that be the reward of my accusers from the **L**,
109:21 O **L** my Lord, act on my behalf
109:26 Help me, O **L** my God! A
109:27 Let them know that this is your hand; you, O **L**,
109:30 With my mouth I will give great thanks to the **L**;
110: 1 The **L** says to my lord,
110: 2 The **L** sends out from Zion your mighty scepter.
110: 4 The **L** has sworn and will not change his mind,
111: 1 Praise the **L**! I will give thanks to the LORD M
111: 1 I will give thanks to the **L** with my whole heart,
111: 2 Great are the works of the **L**,
111: 4 the **L** is gracious and merciful.
111:10 The fear of the **L** is the beginning of wisdom; U
112: 1 Praise the **L**! Happy are those who fear M
112: 1 Happy are those who fear the **L**, X
112: 7 their hearts are firm, secure in the **L**.
113: 1 Praise the **L**! Praise, O servants of the LORD; M
113: 1 Praise, O servants of the **L**;
113: 1 praise the name of the **L**. I
113: 2 Blessed be the name of the **L** from this time on I
113: 3 to its setting the name of the **L** is to be praised. I
113: 4 The **L** is high above all nations,
113: 5 Who is like the **L** our God, A
113: 9 of children. Praise the **L**! M
114: 7 Tremble, O earth, at the presence of the **L**,
115: 1 Not to us, O **L**, not to us,
115: 9 O Israel, trust in the **L**!
115:10 O house of Aaron, trust in the **L**!
115:11 You who fear the **L**, trust in the LORD! X
115:11 You who fear the LORD, trust in the **L**!
115:12 The **L** has been mindful of us;
115:13 he will bless those who fear the **L**, X
115:14 May the **L** give you increase,
115:15 May you be blessed by the **L**,
115:17 The dead do not praise the **L**, M
115:18 But we will bless the **L** from this time on W
115:18 and forevermore. Praise the **L**! M
116: 1 I love the **L**, because he has heard my voice
116: 4 Then I called on the name of the **L**: I
116: 4 "O **L**, I pray, save my life!"
116: 5 Gracious is the **L**, and righteous;
116: 6 The **L** protects the simple;
116: 7 for the **L** has dealt bountifully with you.
116: 9 I walk before the **L** in the land of the living. D
116:12 What shall I return to the **L** for all his bounty
116:13 of salvation and call on the name of the **L**, I
116:14 I will pay my vows to the **L** in the presence
116:15 Precious in the sight of the **L** is the death
116:16 O **L**, I am your servant;
116:17 and call on the name of the **L**. I
116:18 I will pay my vows to the **L** in the presence
116:19 in the courts of the house of the **L**, F
116:19 O Jerusalem. Praise the **L**! M
117: 1 Praise the **L**, all you nations! M
117: 2 and the faithfulness of the **L** endures forever.
117: 2 of the LORD endures forever. Praise the **L**! M
118: 1 O give thanks to the **L**, for he is good;
118: 4 Let those who fear the **L** say, X
118: 5 Out of my distress I called on the **L**;
118: 5 the **L** answered me and set me in a broad place.
118: 6 With the **L** on my side I do not fear.
118: 7 The **L** is on my side to help me;
118: 8 to take refuge in the **L** than to put confidence
118: 9 to take refuge in the **L** than to put confidence
118:10 in the name of the **L** I cut them off! I
118:11 in the name of the **L** I cut them off! I
118:12 in the name of the **L** I cut them off! I
118:13 so that I was falling, but the **L** helped me.
118:14 The **L** is my strength and my might;
118:15 "The right hand of the **L** does valiantly; S
118:16 the right hand of the **L** is exalted; S
118:16 the right hand of the **L** does valiantly." S
118:17 but I shall live, and recount the deeds of the **L**.
118:18 The **L** has punished me severely,
118:19 through them and give thanks to the **L**.
118:20 This is the gate of the **L**;
118:24 This is the day that the **L** has made;
118:25 Save us, we beseech you, O **L**!
118:25 O **L**, we beseech you, give us success!
118:26 the one who comes in the name of the **L**. I
118:26 We bless you from the house of the **L**. F
118:27 The **L** is God, and he has given us light.
118:29 O give thanks to the **L**, for he is good,
119: 1 who walk in the law of the **L**.
119:12 Blessed are you, O **L**; teach me your statutes.
119:31 I cling to your decrees, O **L**;
119:33 Teach me, O **L**, the way of your statutes,
Ps 119:41 Let your steadfast love come to me, O **L**,
119:52 from of old, I take comfort, O **L**.
119:55 I remember your name in the night, O **L**,
119:57 **L** is my portion; I promise to keep your words.
119:64 The earth, O **L**, is full of your steadfast love;
119:65 You have dealt well with your servant, O **L**,
119:75 I know, O **L**, that your judgments are right,
119:89 The **L** exists forever; your word is firmly fixed in
119:107 give me life, O **L**, according to your word.
119:108 Accept my offerings of praise, O **L**,
119:126 It is time for the **L** to act,
119:137 You are righteous, O **L**,
119:145 With my whole heart I cry; answer me, O **L**.
119:149 O **L**, in your justice preserve my life.
119:151 O **L**, and all your commandments are true.
119:156 Great is your mercy, O **L**;
119:166 I hope for your salvation, O **L**,
119:169 Let my cry come before you, O **L**;
119:174 I long for your salvation, O **L**,
120: 1 to the **L**, that he may answer me:
120: 2 O **L**, from lying lips, from a deceitful tongue."
121: 2 My help comes from the **L**,
121: 5 The **L** is your keeper;
121: 5 the **L** is your shade at your right hand.
121: 7 The **L** will keep you from all evil;
121: 8 The **L** will keep your going out
122: 1 "Let us go to the house of the **L**!" F
122: 4 To it the tribes go up, the tribes of the **L**,
122: 4 to give thanks to the name of the **L**. I
122: 9 For the sake of the house of the **L** our God, AF
123: 2 so our eyes look to the **L** our God, A
123: 3 Have mercy upon us, O **L**, have mercy upon us,
124: 1 If it not been the **L** who was on our side—
124: 2 if it had not been the **L** who was on our side,
124: 6 Blessed be the **L**, who has not given us as prey T
124: 8 Our help is in the name of the **L**, I
125: 1 Those who trust in the **L** are like Mount Zion,
125: 2 so the **L** surrounds his people,
125: 4 Do good, O **L**, to those who are good,
125: 5 to their own crooked ways the **L** will lead away
126: 1 When the **L** restored the fortunes of Zion,
126: 2 "The **L** has done great things for them."
126: 3 **L** has done great things for us, and we rejoiced.
126: 4 Restore our fortunes, O **L**,
127: 1 Unless the **L** builds the house,
127: 1 **L** guards the city, the guard keeps watch in vain.
127: 3 Sons are indeed a heritage from the **L**,
128: 1 Happy is everyone who fears the **L**,
128: 4 Thus shall the man be blessed who fears the **L**.
128: 5 The **L** bless you from Zion.
129: 4 The **L** is righteous; he has cut the cords of the
129: 8 "The blessing of the **L** be upon you!
129: 8 We bless you in the name of the **L**!" I
130: 1 Out of the depths I cry to you, O **L**.
130: 3 If you, O **L**, should mark iniquities, Lord,
130: 5 I wait for the **L**, my soul waits,
130: 7 O Israel, hope in the **L**!
130: 7 For with the **L** there is steadfast love,
131: 1 O **L**, my heart is not lifted up, my eyes are
131: 3 in the **L** from this time on and forevermore.
132: 1 O **L**, remember in David's favor all
132: 2 to the **L** and vowed to the Mighty One of Jacob,
132: 5 until I find a place for the **L**,
132: 8 Rise up, O **L**, and go to your resting place,
132:11 The **L** swore to David a sure oath
132:13 For the **L** has chosen Zion;
133: 3 For there the **L** ordained his blessing,
134: 1 bless the **L**, all you servants of the LORD, W
134: 1 bless the LORD, all you servants of the **L**,
134: 1 who stand by night in the house of the **L**! F
134: 2 your hands to the holy place, and bless the **L**. W
134: 3 May the **L**, maker of heaven and earth,
135: 1 Praise the **L**! Praise the name of the LORD; M
135: 1 Praise the name of the **L**; I
135: 1 give praise, O servants of the **L**,
135: 2 you that stand in the house of the **L**, F
135: 3 Praise the **L**, for the LORD is good; M
135: 3 Praise the LORD, for the **L** is good;
135: 4 For the **L** has chosen Jacob for himself,
135: 5 For I know that the **L** is great;
135: 6 Whatever the **L** pleases he does,
135:13 Your name, O **L**, endures forever, your renown,
135:13 O LORD, endures forever, your renown, O **L**,
135:14 For the **L** will vindicate his people,
135:19 O house of Israel, bless the **L**! W
135:19 O house of Aaron, bless the **L**! W
135:20 O house of Levi, bless the **L**! W
135:20 You that fear the **L**, bless the LORD! X
135:20 You that fear the LORD, bless the **L**! W
135:21 Blessed be the **L** from Zion, T
135:21 in Jerusalem. Praise the **L**! M
136: 1 O give thanks to the **L**, for he is good,
137: 7 O **L**, against the Edomites the day
138: 1 O **L**, with my whole heart;
138: 4 All the kings of the earth shall praise you, O **L**,
138: 5 They shall sing of the ways of the **L**,
138: 5 for great is the glory of the **L**. R
138: 6 For though the **L** is high, he regards the lowly;
138: 8 The **L** will fulfill his purpose for me;
138: 8 your steadfast love, O **L**, endures forever.
139: 1 O **L**, you have searched me and known me.
139: 4 Even before a word is on my tongue, O **L**,
139:21 Do I not hate those who hate you, O **L**?
140: 1 Deliver me, O **L**, from evildoers;
140: 4 O **L**, from the hands of the wicked;
140: 6 I say to the **L**, "You are my God;
140: 6 give ear, O **L**, to the voice of my supplications."

†LORD distinguishes the proper name of God, *Yahweh*, indicated in the NRSV by "LORD," from the words translated "Lord" and "lord," indexed under the heading ***LORD** on pages 798-804.

Ps 140: 7 O L, my Lord, my strong deliverer,
140: 8 Do not grant, O L, the desires of the wicked;
140:12 that the L maintains the cause of the needy,
141: 1 I call upon you, O L; come quickly to me;
141: 3 Set a guard over my mouth, O L;
142: 1 With my voice I cry to the L;
142: 1 with my voice I make supplication to the L.
142: 5 I cry to you, O L; I say,
143: 1 Hear my prayer, O L; give ear to my
143: 7 Answer me quickly, O L;
143: 9 Save me, O L, from my enemies;
143:11 For your name's sake, O L, preserve my life.
144: 1 Blessed be the L, my rock, T
144: 3 O L, what are human beings
144: 5 Bow your heavens, O L, and come down;
144:15 happy are the people whose God is the L.
145: 3 Great is the L, and greatly to be praised;
145: 8 The L is gracious and merciful,
145: 9 The L is good to all,
145:10 All your works shall give thanks to you, O L,
145:13 The L is faithful in all his words,
145:14 The L upholds all who are falling,
145:17 The L is just in all his ways,
145:18 The L is near to all who call on him,
145:20 The L watches over all who love him,
145:21 My mouth will speak the praise of the L,
146: 1 Praise the L! Praise the LORD, O my soul! M
146: 1 Praise the LORD! Praise the L, O my soul! M
146: 2 I will praise the L as long as I live; M
146: 5 whose hope is in the L their God, A
146: 7 The L sets the prisoners free;
146: 8 the L opens the eyes of the blind.
146: 8 The L lifts up those who are bowed down;
146: 8 the L loves the righteous.
146: 9 The L watches over the strangers;
146:10 The L will reign forever, your God, O Zion,
146:10 for all generations. Praise the L! M
147: 1 Praise the L! How good it is to sing M
147: 2 The L builds up Jerusalem;
147: 6 The L lifts up the downtrodden;
147: 7 Sing to the L with thanksgiving;
147:11 but the L takes pleasure in those who fear him,
147:12 Praise the L, O Jerusalem! M
147:20 not know his ordinances. Praise the L! M
148: 1 Praise the L! Praise the LORD from the M
148: 1 Praise the L from the heavens; M
148: 5 Let them praise the name of the L, I
148: 7 Praise the L from the earth, M
148:13 Let them praise the name of the L, I
148:14 of Israel who are close to him. Praise the L! M
149: 1 Praise the L! Sing to the LORD M
149: 1 Sing to the L a new song,
149: 4 For the L takes pleasure in his people;
149: 9 for all his faithful ones. Praise the L! M
150: 1 Praise the L! Praise God in his sanctuary; M
150: 6 Let everything that breathes praise the L! M
150: 6 that breathes praise the LORD! Praise the L! M
Pr 1: 7 The fear of the L is the beginning of knowledge; U
1:29 and did not choose the fear of the L, U
2: 5 the fear of the L and find the knowledge of God. U
2: 6 For the L gives wisdom;
3: 5 Trust in the L with all your heart,
3: 7 fear the L, and turn away from evil. X
3: 9 Honor the L with your substance and with
3:12 for the L reproves the one he loves,
3:19 The L by wisdom founded the earth;
3:26 for the L will be your confidence
3:32 for the perverse are an abomination to the L,
5:21 For human ways are under the eyes of the L,
6:16 There are six things that the L hates,
8:13 The fear of the L is hatred of evil. U
8:22 The L created me at the beginning of his work,
8:35 and obtains favor from the L;
9:10 The fear of the L is the beginning of wisdom, U
10: 3 The L does not let the righteous go hungry,
10:22 The blessing of the L makes rich,
10:27 The fear of the L prolongs life, U
10:29 The way of the L is a stronghold for the upright,
11: 1 A false balance is an abomination to the L,
11:20 Crooked minds are an abomination to the L,
12: 2 The good obtain favor from the L,
12:22 Lying lips are an abomination to the L,
14: 2 Those who walk uprightly fear the L, X
14:26 In the fear of the L one has strong confidence, U
14:27 The fear of the L is a fountain of life, U
15: 3 The eyes of the L are in every place,
15: 8 of the wicked is an abomination to the L,
15: 9 way of the wicked is an abomination to the L,
15:11 Sheol and Abaddon lie open before the L, D
15:16 a little with the fear of the L than great treasure U
15:25 The L tears down the house of the proud,
15:26 Evil plans are an abomination to the L,
15:29 The L is far from the wicked,
15:33 The fear of the L is instruction in wisdom, U
16: 1 but the answer of the tongue is from the L.
16: 2 but the L weighs the spirit.
16: 3 Commit your work to the L,
16: 4 The L has made everything for its purpose,
16: 5 an abomination to the L;
16: 6 and by the fear of the L one avoids evil. U
16: 7 When the ways of people please the L,
16: 9 but the L directs the steps.
16:20 and happy are those who trust in the L.
17: 3 but the L tests the heart.
17:15 both alike an abomination to the L.
18:10 The name of the L is a strong tower; I
18:22 and obtains favor from the L.
Pr 19: 3 yet the heart rages against the L.
19:14 but a prudent wife is from the L.
19:17 Whoever is kind to the poor lends to the L,
19:21 it is the purpose of the L that will be established.
19:23 The fear of the L is life indeed; U
20:10 both alike an abomination to the L.
20:12 the L has made them both.
20:22 wait for the L, and he will help you.
20:23 Differing weights are an abomination to the L,
20:24 All our steps are ordered by the L;
20:27 The human spirit is the lamp of the L,
21: 1 a stream of water in the hand of the L; S
21: 2 but the L weighs the heart.
21: 3 justice is more acceptable to the L than sacrifice.
21:30 no counsel, can avail against the L.
21:31 but the victory belongs to the L.
22: 2 the L is the maker of them all.
22: 4 and fear of the L is riches and honor and life. U
22:12 The eyes of the L keep watch over knowledge,
22:14 he with whom the L is angry falls into it.
22:19 So that your trust may be in the L,
22:23 for the L pleads their cause and despoils
23:17 but always continue in the fear of the L. U
24:18 or else the L will see it and be displeased,
24:21 My child, fear the L and the king, X
25:22 and the L will reward you.
28: 5 those who seek the L understand it completely.
28:25 but whoever trusts in the L will be enriched.
29:13 the L gives light to the eyes of both.
29:25 but one who trusts in the L is secure.
29:26 but it is from the L that one gets justice.
30: 9 and deny you, and say, "Who is the L?"
31:30 but a woman who fears the L is to be praised.
Isa 1: 2 O earth; for the L has spoken:
1: 4 who have forsaken the L,
1: 9 If the L of hosts had not left us a few survivors, E
1:10 Hear the word of the L, you rulers of Sodom! G
1:11 the multitude of your sacrifices? says the L; B
1:18 Come now, let us argue it out, says the L: B
1:20 for the mouth of the L has spoken.
1:24 Therefore says the Sovereign, the L of hosts, E
1:28 and those who forsake the L shall be consumed.
2: 3 "Come, let us go up to the mountain of the L,
2: 3 and the word of the L from Jerusalem. G
2: 5 come, let us walk in the light of the L!
2:10 and hide in the dust from the terror of the L,
2:11 and the L alone will be exalted in that day.
2:12 the L of hosts has a day against all that is proud E
2:17 and the L alone will be exalted on that day.
2:19 from the terror of the L,
2:21 from the terror of the L,
3: 1 For now the Sovereign, the L of hosts, E
3: 8 their speech and their deeds are against the L,
3:13 The L rises to argue his case;
3:14 The L enters into judgment with the elders
3:16 The L said: Because the daughters of Zion
3:17 and the L will lay bare their secret parts.
4: 2 that day the branch of the L shall be beautiful
4: 5 Then the L will create over the whole site
5: 7 vineyard of the L of hosts is the house of Israel, E
5: 9 The L of hosts has sworn in my hearing: E
5:12 but who do not regard the deeds of the L,
5:16 But the L of hosts is exalted by justice, E
5:24 rejected the instruction of the L of hosts, E
5:25 anger of the L was kindled against his people,
6: 3 "Holy, holy, holy is the L of hosts; E
6: 5 yet my eyes have seen the King, the L of hosts!" E
6:12 until the L sends everyone far away,
7: 3 Then the L said to Isaiah, Go out to meet Ahaz,
7:10 Again the L spoke to Ahaz, saying,
7:11 Ask a sign of the L your God; A
7:12 I will not ask, and I will not put the L to the test.
7:17 The L will bring on you and on your people and
7:18 On that day the L will whistle for the fly that is
8: 1 Then the L said to me,
8: 3 L said to me, Name him Maher-shalal-hash-baz;
8: 5 The L spoke to me again:
8:11 For the L spoke thus to me
8:13 But the L of hosts, him you shall regard as holy; E
8:17 I will wait for the L,
8:18 the children whom the L has given me are signs
8:18 and portents in Israel from the L of hosts, E
9: 7 The zeal of the L of hosts will do this. E
9:11 So the L raised adversaries against them,
9:13 or seek the L of hosts. E
9:14 So the L cut off from Israel head and tail,
9:19 the wrath of the L of hosts the land was burned, E
10:16 Therefore the Sovereign, the L of hosts, E
10:18 and his fruitful land the L will destroy,
10:20 but will lean on the L, the Holy One of Israel,
10:26 The L of hosts will wield a whip against them, E
10:33 Look, the Sovereign, the L of hosts, E
11: 2 The spirit of the L shall rest on him,
11: 2 the spirit of knowledge and the fear of the L. U
11: 3 His delight shall be in the fear of the L. U
11: 9 the earth will be full of the knowledge of the L
11:15 the L will utterly destroy the tongue of the sea
12: 1 I will give thanks to you, O L,
12: 2 for the L GOD is my strength and my might;
12: 4 Give thanks to the L, call on his name;
12: 5 to the L, for he has done gloriously;
13: 4 The L of hosts is mustering an army for battle. E
13: 5 the L and the weapons of his indignation,
13: 6 Wail, for the day of the L is near;
13: 9 See, the day of the L comes, cruel,
13:13 of the L of hosts in the day of his fierce anger. E
14: 1 But the L will have compassion on Jacob
Isa 14: 3 When the L has given you rest from your pain
14: 5 The L has broken the staff of the wicked,
14:22 I will rise up against them, says the L of hosts, BE
14:22 offspring and posterity, says the L. B
14:23 the broom of destruction, says the L of hosts. BE
14:24 The L of hosts has sworn: E
14:27 L of hosts has planned, and who will annul it? E
14:32 "The L has founded Zion,
16:13 the word that the L spoke concerning Moab in
16:14 But now the L says, In three years,
17: 3 the children of Israel, says the L of hosts. BE
17: 6 says the L God of Israel. BJ
18: 4 For thus the L said to me:
18: 7 to the L of hosts from a people tall and smooth, E
18: 7 the place of the name of the L of hosts. EI
19: 1 L is riding on a swift cloud and comes to Egypt;
19: 4 says the Sovereign, the L of hosts. E
19:12 and make known what the L of hosts has E
19:14 L has poured into them a spirit of confusion;
19:16 with fear before the hand that the L of hosts E
19:17 that the L of hosts is planning against them. E
19:18 and swear allegiance to the L of hosts. E
19:19 On that day there will be an altar to the L in
19:19 and a pillar to the L at its border.
19:20 a sign and a witness to the L of hosts in the land E
19:20 when they cry to the L because of oppressors,
19:21 L will make himself known to the Egyptians;
19:21 and the Egyptians will know the L on that day,
19:21 they will make vows to the L and perform them.
19:22 The L will strike Egypt, striking and healing;
19:22 they will return to the L,
19:25 whom the L of hosts has blessed, E
20: 2 at that time the L had spoken to Isaiah son
20: 3 Then the L said, "Just as my servant Isaiah
21:10 what I have heard from the L of hosts, E
21:17 for the L, the God of Israel, has spoken.
22:14 The L of hosts has revealed himself in my ears: E
22:17 The L is about to hurl you away violently,
22:25 On that day, says the L of hosts, BE
22:25 that was on it will perish, for the L has spoken.
23: 9 The L of hosts has planned it— E
23:11 the L has given command concerning Canaan
23:17 the end of seventy years, the L will visit Tyre,
23:18 and her wages will be dedicated to the L;
23:18 for those who live in the presence of the L.
24: 1 Now the L is about to lay waste the earth
24: 3 for the L has spoken this word.
24:14 from the west over the majesty of the L.
24:15 Therefore in the east give glory to the L;
24:15 of the sea glorify the name of the L, I
24:21 On that day the L will punish the host of heaven
24:23 for the L of hosts will reign on Mount Zion and E
25: 1 O L, you are my God;
25: 6 the L of hosts will make for all peoples a feast E
25: 8 from all the earth, for the L has spoken.
25: 9 This is the L for whom we have waited;
25:10 For the hand of the L will rest on this mountain. S
26: 4 Trust in the L forever,
26: 4 for in the L GOD you have an everlasting rock.
26: 8 In the path of your judgments, O L,
26:10 and do not see the majesty of the L.
26:11 O L, your hand is lifted up,
26:12 O L, you will ordain peace for us, for indeed,
26:13 O L our God, other lords besides you have ruled A
26:15 But you have increased the nation, O L,
26:16 O L, in distress they sought you,
26:17 so were we because of you, O L;
26:21 For the L comes out from his place to punish
27: 1 On that day the L with his cruel and great
27: 3 I, the L, am its keeper; every moment I water it.
27:12 On that day the L will thresh from the channel
27:13 the land of Egypt will come and worship the L
28: 5 the L of hosts will be a garland of glory, E
28:13 Therefore the word of the L will be to them, G
28:14 Therefore hear the word of the L, G
28:21 For the L will rise up as on Mount Perazim,
28:29 This also comes from the L of hosts; E
29: 6 by the L of hosts with thunder and earthquake E
29:10 For the L has poured out upon you a spirit
29:15 You who hide a plan too deep for the L,
29:19 The meek shall obtain fresh joy in the L,
29:22 Therefore thus says the L, C
30: 1 Oh, rebellious children, says the L, B
30: 9 not hear the instruction of the L;
30:18 Therefore the L waits to be gracious to you;
30:18 For the L is a God of justice;
30:26 when the L binds up the injuries of his people,
30:27 See, the name of the L comes from far away, I
30:29 of the flute to go to the mountain of the L,
30:30 the L will cause his majestic voice to be heard
30:31 be terror-stricken at the voice of the L, P
30:32 of punishment that the L lays upon him will be
30:33 the breath of the L, like a stream of sulfur,
31: 1 to the Holy One of Israel or consult the L!
31: 3 When the L stretches out his hand,
31: 4 For thus the L said to me,
31: 4 at their noise, so the L of hosts will come down E
31: 5 so the L of hosts will protect Jerusalem; E
31: 9 says the L, whose fire is in Zion, B
32: 6 to utter error concerning the L,
33: 2 O L, be gracious to us; we wait for you.
33: 5 The L is exalted, he dwells on high;
33: 6 the fear of the L is Zion's treasure. U
33:10 "Now I will arise," says the L, B
33:21 But there the L in majesty will be for us a place
33:22 For the L is our judge, the L is our ruler, the L is our king;

†LORD distinguishes the proper name of God, *Yahweh,* indicated in the NRSV by "LORD," from the words translated "Lord" and "lord," indexed under the heading *LORD on pages 798-804.

Isa 34: 2 For the L is enraged against all the nations,
34: 6 The L has a sword; it is sated with blood,
34: 6 For the L has a sacrifice in Bozrah,
34: 8 For the L has a day of vengeance,
34:16 Seek and read from the book of the L:
34:16 For the mouth of the L has commanded,
35: 2 They shall see the glory of the L, R
35:10 And the ransomed of the L shall return,
36: 7 if you say to me, 'We rely on the L our God,' A
36:10 the L that I have come up against this land
36:10 The L said to me, Go up against this land,
36:15 Do not let Hezekiah make you rely on the L
36:15 The L will surely deliver us;
36:18 by saying, The L will save us.
36:20 the L should save Jerusalem out of my hand?' "
37: 1 and went into the house of the L. F
37: 4 It may be that the L your God heard the words A
37: 4 the words that the L your God has heard; A
37: 6 "Say to your master, 'Thus says the L: C
37:14 then Hezekiah went up to the house of the L F
37:14 of the LORD and spread it before the L. D
37:15 And Hezekiah prayed to the L, saying:
37:16 "O L of hosts, God of Israel, who are enthroned E
37:17 Incline your ear, O L, and hear;
37:17 open your eyes, O L, and see;
37:18 O L, the kings of Assyria have laid waste all
37:20 So now, O L our God, save us from his hand, A
37:20 of the earth may know that you alone are the L."
37:21 "Thus says the L, the God of Israel: C
37:22 the word that the L has spoken concerning him:
37:32 The zeal of the L of hosts will do this. E
37:33 thus says the L concerning the king of Assyria: C
37:34 he shall not come into this city, says the L. B
37:36 Then the angel of the L set out and struck K
38: 1 and said to him, "Thus says the L: C
38: 2 to the wall, and prayed to the L:
38: 3 now, O L, I implore you, how I have walked
38: 4 Then the word of the L came to Isaiah: G
38: 5 Thus says the L, the God of your ancestor C
38: 7 "This is the sign to you from the L,
38: 7 the L will do this thing that he has promised:
38:11 I shall not see the L in the land of the living;
38:20 The L will save me, and we will sing
38:20 at the house of the L. F
38:22 that I shall go up to the house of the L?" F
39: 5 "Hear the word of the L of hosts: EG
39: 6 nothing shall be left, says the L. B
39: 8 word of the L that you have spoken is good." G
40: 3 "In the wilderness prepare the way of the L,
40: 5 Then the glory of the L shall be revealed, R
40: 5 for the mouth of the L has spoken."
40: 7 when the breath of the L blows upon it;
40:13 Who has directed the spirit of the L,
40:27 O Israel, "My way is hidden from the L,
40:28 The L is the everlasting God,
40:31 for the L shall renew their strength,
41: 4 I, the L, am first, and will be with the last.
41:13 For I, the L your God, hold your right hand; A
41:14 I will help you, says the L; B
41:16 Then you shall rejoice in the L;
41:17 I the L will answer them,
41:20 that the hand of the L has done this, S
41:21 Set forth your case, says the L; B
42: 5 the L, who created the heavens
42: 6 I am the L, I have called you H
42: 8 I am the L, that is my name; H
42:10 Sing to the L a new song,
42:12 Let them give glory to the L,
42:13 The L goes forth like a soldier,
42:19 or blind like the servant of the L? Y
42:21 The L was pleased, for the sake
42:24 Was it not the L, against whom we have sinned,
43: 1 But now thus says the L, he who created you, C
43: 3 For I am the L your God, AH
43:10 You are my witnesses, says the L, B
43:11 I, I am the L, and besides me there is no savior. H
43:12 and you are my witnesses, says the L. B
43:14 Thus says the L, your Redeemer, C
43:15 I am the L, your Holy One, H
43:16 Thus says the L, who makes a way in the sea, C
44: 2 Thus says the L who made you, C
44: 6 Thus says the L, the King of Israel, C
44: 6 and his Redeemer, the L of hosts: E
44:23 Sing, O heavens, for the L has done it;
44:23 For the L has redeemed Jacob,
44:24 Thus says the L, your Redeemer, C
44:24 I am the L, who made all things, H
45: 1 Thus says the L to his anointed, to Cyrus, C
45: 3 so that you may know that it is I, the L,
45: 5 I am the L, and there is no other; H
45: 6 I am the L, and there is no other. H
45: 7 I the L do all these things.
45: 8 I the L have created it.
45:11 Thus says the L, the Holy One of Israel, C
45:13 not for price or reward, says the L of hosts. BE
45:14 Thus says the L: The wealth of Egypt C
45:17 by the L with everlasting salvation;
45:18 For thus says the L, who created C
45:18 I am the L, and there is no other. H
45:19 I the L speak the truth, I declare what is right.
45:21 Was it not I, the L? There is no other god besides
45:24 Only in the L, it shall be said of me,
45:25 In the L all the offspring of Israel shall triumph
47: 4 Our Redeemer—the L of hosts is his name— E
48: 1 who swear by the name of the L, I
48: 2 the L of hosts is his name. E
48:14 The L loves him; he shall perform his purpose

Isa 48:17 Thus says the L, your Redeemer, C
48:17 I am the L your God, who teaches you AH
48:20 say, "The L has redeemed his servant Jacob!"
48:22 "There is no peace," says the L, for the wicked." B
49: 1 The L called me before I was born,
49: 4 yet surely my cause is with the L,
49: 5 now the L says, who formed me in the womb to
49: 5 for I am honored in the sight of the L,
49: 7 Thus says the L, the Redeemer of Israel C
49: 7 because of the L, who is faithful,
49: 8 Thus says the L: In a time of favor C
49:13 For the L has comforted his people,
49:14 But Zion said, "The L has forsaken me,
49:18 As I live, says the L, you shall put all of them B
49:23 Then you will know that I am the L; H
49:25 But thus says the L: C
49:26 all flesh shall know that I am the L your Savior, H
50: 1 Thus says the L: C
50:10 Who among you fears the L and obeys the voice
50:10 in the name of the L and relies upon his God? I
51: 1 that pursue righteousness, you that seek the L.
51: 3 For the L will comfort Zion;
51: 3 her desert like the garden of the L;
51: 9 Awake, awake, put on strength, O arm of the L!
51:11 So the ransomed of the L shall return,
51:13 You have forgotten the L, your Maker,
51:15 For I am the L your God, AH
51:15 the L of hosts is his name. E
51:17 you who have drunk at the hand of the L the cup S
51:20 they are full of the wrath of the L,
51:22 L, your God who pleads the cause of his people:
52: 3 For thus says the L: You were sold C
52: 5 Now therefore what am I doing here, says the L, B
52: 5 Their rulers howl, says the L, and continually, B
52: 8 for in plain sight they see the return of the L
52: 9 for the L has comforted his people,
52:10 The L has bared his holy arm before the eyes
52:11 you who carry the vessels of the L.
52:12 for the L will go before you,
53: 1 to whom has the arm of the L been revealed?
53: 6 and the L has laid on him the iniquity of us all.
53:10 it was the will of the L to crush him with pain.
53:10 through him the will of the L shall prosper.
54: 1 the children of her that is married, says the L. B
54: 5 the L of hosts is his name; E
54: 6 For the L has called you like a wife forsaken
54: 8 says the L, your Redeemer. B
54:10 says the L, who has compassion on you. B
54:13 All your children shall be taught by the L,
54:17 of the servants of the L and their vindication
54:17 and their vindication from me, says the L. B
55: 5 because of the L your God, A
55: 6 Seek the L while he may be found,
55: 7 let them return to the L,
55: 8 nor are your ways my ways, says the L. B
55:13 and it shall be to the L for a memorial,
56: 1 Thus says the L: Maintain justice, C
56: 3 Do not let the foreigner joined to the L say,
56: 3 L will surely separate me from his people";
56: 4 For thus says the L: To the eunuchs C
56: 6 the foreigners who join themselves to the L,
56: 6 to minister to him, to love the name of the L, I
57:19 Peace, peace, to the far and the near, says the L; B
58: 5 a day acceptable to the L?
58: 8 the glory of the L shall be your rear guard. R
58: 9 Then you shall call, and the L will answer;
58:11 The L will guide you continually,
58:13 a delight and the holy day of the L honorable;
58:14 the L, and I will make you ride upon the heights
58:14 for the mouth of the L has spoken.
59:13 and denying the L, and turning away
59:15 The L saw it, and it displeased him
59:19 those in the west shall fear the name of the L, I
59:19 that the wind of the L drives on.
59:20 who turn from transgression, says the L. B
59:21 me, this is my covenant with them, says the L: B
59:21 says the L, from now on and forever. B
60: 1 and the glory of the L has risen upon you. R
60: 2 but the L will arise upon you,
60: 6 and shall proclaim the praise of the L.
60: 9 for the name of the L your God, AI
60:14 they shall call you the City of the L,
60:16 and you shall know that I, the L,
60:19 but the L will be your everlasting light,
60:20 for the L will be your everlasting light,
60:22 I am the L; in its time I will accomplish it H
61: 1 because the L has anointed me;
61: 3 the planting of the L, to display his glory.
61: 6 the L, you shall be named ministers of our God;
61: 8 For I the L love justice,
61: 9 that they are a people whom the L has blessed.
61:10 I will greatly rejoice in the L,
62: 2 a new name that the mouth of the L will give.
62: 3 be a crown of beauty in the hand of the L, S
62: 4 for the L delights in you,
62: 6 You who remind the L, take no rest,
62: 8 The L has sworn by his right hand and
62: 9 those who garner it shall eat it and praise the L, M
62:11 The L has proclaimed to the end of the earth:
62:12 "The Holy People, The Redeemed of the L";
63: 7 I will recount the gracious deeds of the L,
63: 7 the praiseworthy acts of the L,
63: 7 because of all that the L has done for us,
63:14 the spirit of the L gave them rest.
63:16 you, O L, are our father;
63:17 O L, do you make us stray from your ways
64: 8 Yet, O L, you are our Father;

Isa 64: 9 Do not be exceedingly angry, O L,
64:12 After all this, will you restrain yourself, O L?
65: 7 their ancestors' iniquities together, says the L; B
65: 8 Thus says the L: As the wine is found in the C
65:11 But you who forsake the L,
65:23 for they shall be offspring blessed by the L—
65:25 or destroy on all my holy mountain, says the L. B
66: 1 Thus says the L: Heaven is my throne C
66: 2 and so all these things are mine, says the L. B
66: 5 Hear the word of the L, G
66: 5 the L be glorified, so that we may see your joy";
66: 6 The voice of the L, dealing retribution to his P
66: 9 open the womb and not deliver? says the L; B
66:12 For thus says the L: I will extend prosperity C
66:14 and it shall be known that the hand of the L is S
66:15 For the L will come in fire,
66:16 For by fire will the L execute judgment,
66:16 and those slain by the L shall be many.
66:17 shall come to an end together, says the L. B
66:20 from all the nations as an offering to the L,
66:20 to my holy mountain Jerusalem, says the L, B
66:20 in a clean vessel to the house of the L. F
66:21 of them as priests and as Levites, says the L. B
66:22 shall remain before me, says the L; B
66:23 to worship before me, says the L. B
Jer 1: 2 word of the L came in the days of King Josiah G
1: 4 Now the word of the L came to me saying, G
1: 7 the L said to me, "Do not say, 'I am only a boy';
1: 8 for I am with you to deliver you, says the L." B
1: 9 the L put out his hand and touched my mouth;
1: 9 and the L said to me,
1:11 The word of the L came to me, saying, G
1:12 Then the L said to me, "You have seen well,
1:13 The word of the L came to me a second time, G
1:14 Then the L said to me:
1:15 of the kingdoms of the north, says the L; B
1:19 for I am with you, says the L, to deliver you. B
2: 1 The word of the L came to me, saying: G
2: 2 in the hearing of Jerusalem, Thus says the L: C
2: 3 Israel was holy to the L,
2: 3 disaster came upon them, says the L. B
2: 4 Hear the word of the L, O house of Jacob, G
2: 5 Thus says the L: What wrong did your C
2: 6 the L who brought us up from the land of Egypt,
2: 8 The priests did not say, "Where is the L?"
2: 9 says the L, and I accuse your children's B
2:12 be shocked, be utterly desolate, says the L, B
2:17 upon yourself by forsaking the L your God, A
2:19 and bitter for you to forsake the L your God; A
2:29 You have all rebelled against me, says the L. B
2:31 you, O generation, behold the word of the L! G
2:37 for the L has rejected those in whom you trust,
3: 1 and would you return to me? says the L. B
3: 6 The L said to me in the days of King Josiah:
3:10 but only in pretense, says the L. B
3:11 Then the L said to me:
3:12 Return, faithless Israel, says the L. B
3:12 says the L; I will not be angry forever. B
3:13 that you have rebelled against the L your God, A
3:13 and have not obeyed my voice, says the L. B
3:14 says the L, for I am your master; B
3:16 says the L, they shall no longer say, B
3:16 "The ark of the covenant of the L." O
3:17 be called the throne of the L,
3:17 to the presence of the L in Jerusalem,
3:20 O house of Israel, says the L. B
3:21 they have forgotten the L their God: A
3:22 for you are the L our God. A
3:23 Truly in the L our God is the salvation of Israel. A
3:25 for we have sinned against the L our God, A
3:25 not obeyed the voice of the L our God." AP
4: 1 If you return, O Israel, says the L, B
4: 2 and if you swear, "As the L lives!" Q
4: 3 For thus says the L to the people of Judah and C
4: 4 Circumcise yourselves to the L,
4: 8 "The fierce anger of the L has not turned away
4: 9 On that day, says the L, B
4:17 because she has rebelled against me, says the L. B
4:26 and all its cities were laid in ruins before the L, D
4:27 For thus says the L: The whole land shall be a C
5: 2 Although they say, "As the L lives," Q
5: 3 O L, do your eyes not look for truth?
5: 4 for they do not know the way of the L,
5: 5 surely they know the way of the L,
5: 9 says the L; and shall I not bring retribution B
5:11 have been utterly faithless to me, says the L. B
5:12 They have spoken falsely of the L,
5:14 Therefore thus says the L, the God of hosts: C
5:15 O house of Israel, says the L. B
5:18 But even in those days, says the L, B
5:19 "Why has the L our God done all these things A
5:22 says the L; Do you not tremble before me? B
5:24 "Let us fear the L our God, AX
5:29 says the L, and shall I not bring retribution B
6: 6 For thus says the L of hosts: CE
6: 9 Thus says the L of hosts: CE
6:10 The word of the L is to them an object of scorn; G
6:11 But I am full of the wrath of the L;
6:12 against the inhabitants of the land, says the L. B
6:15 they shall be overthrown, says the L. B
6:16 Thus says the L: Stand at the C
6:21 Therefore thus says the L: C
6:22 Thus says the L: See, a people is coming from C
6:30 for the L has rejected them.
7: 1 The word that came to Jeremiah from the L:
7: 2 Hear the word of the L, all you people of Judah, G
7: 2 you that enter these gates to worship the L.

†**LORD** distinguishes the proper name of God, *Yahweh,* indicated in the NRSV by "LORD," from the words translated "Lord" and "lord," indexed under the heading ***LORD** on pages 798-804.

Jer 7: 3 Thus says the **L** of hosts, the God of Israel: CE
7: 4 "This is the temple of the **L**, V
7: 4 the temple of the **L**, the temple of the LORD." V
7: 4 the temple of the LORD, the temple of the **L**." V
7: 11 You know, I too am watching, says the **L**. B
7: 13 you have done all these things, says the **L**, B
7: 19 Is it I whom they provoke? says the **L**. B
7: 21 Thus says the **L** of hosts, the God of Israel: CE
7: 28 voice of the **L** their God, and did not accept AP
7: 29 the **L** has rejected and forsaken the generation
7: 30 of Judah have done evil in my sight, says the **L**; B
7: 32 the days are surely coming, says the **L**, B
8: 1 At that time, says the **L**, B
8: 3 I have driven them, says the **L** of hosts. BE
8: 4 You shall say to them, Thus says the **L**: C
8: 7 my people do not know the ordinance of the **L**.
8: 8 "We are wise, and the law of the **L** is with us,"
8: 9 since they have rejected the word of the **L**, G
8: 12 they shall be overthrown, says the **L**. B
8: 13 When I wanted to gather them, says the **L**, B
8: 14 for the **L** our God has doomed us to perish, A
8: 14 because we have sinned against the **L**.
8: 17 and they shall bite you, says the **L**. B
8: 19 "Is the **L** not in Zion? Is her King not in her?"
9: 3 and they do not know me, says the **L**. B
9: 6 They refuse to know me, says the **L**. B
9: 7 Therefore thus says the **L** of hosts: CE
9: 9 for these things? says the **L**; B
9: 12 To whom has the mouth of the **L** spoken,
9: 13 And the **L** says:
9: 15 thus says the **L** of hosts, the God of Israel: CE
9: 17 Thus says the **L** of hosts: CE
9: 20 Hear, O women, the word of the **L**, G
9: 22 Thus says the **L**: "Human corpses shall fall C
9: 23 Thus says the **L**: Do C
9: 24 and know me, that I am the **L**; H
9: 24 for in these things I delight, says the **L**. B
9: 25 The days are surely coming, says the **L**, B
10: 1 Hear the word that the **L** speaks to you,
10: 2 Thus says the **L**: Do not let the wise boast C
10: 6 There is none like you, O **L**;
10: 10 But the **L** is the true God;
10: 16 Not like these is the **L**, the portion of Jacob,
10: 16 the **L** of hosts is his name. E
10: 18 For thus says the **L**: I am going to sling C
10: 21 and do not inquire of the **L**;
10: 23 O **L**, that the way of human beings is not
10: 24 Correct me, O **L**, but in just measure;
11: 1 The word that came to Jeremiah from the **L**:
11: 3 You shall say to them, Thus says the **L**, C
11: 5 Then I answered, "So be it, **L**."
11: 6 And the **L** said to me:
11: 9 And the **L** said to me:
11: 11 Therefore, thus says the **L**, C
11: 16 The **L** once called you, "A green olive tree,
11: 17 The **L** of hosts, who planted you, E
11: 18 It was the **L** who made it known to me,
11: 20 But you, O **L** of hosts, who judge righteously, E
11: 21 Therefore thus says the **L** concerning the people C
11: 21 "You shall not prophesy in the name of the **L**, I
11: 22 therefore thus says the **L** of hosts: CE
12: 1 You will be in the right, O **L**,
12: 3 But you, O **L**, know me;
12: 12 for the sword of the **L** devours from one end of
12: 13 because of the fierce anger of the **L**.
12: 14 Thus says the **L** concerning all C
12: 16 to swear by my name, "As the **L** lives," Q
12: 17 and destroy it, says the **L**. B
13: 1 Thus said the **L** to me,
13: 2 a loincloth according to the word of the **L**, G
13: 3 the word of the **L** came to me a second time, G
13: 5 as the **L** commanded me.
13: 6 And after many days the **L** said to me,
13: 8 Then the word of the **L** came to me: G
13: 9 Thus says the **L**: Just so I will ruin the pride C
13: 11 says the **L**, in order that they might be for me B
13: 12 Thus says the **L**, the God of Israel: C
13: 13 Then you shall say to them: Thus says the **L**: C
13: 14 parents and children together, says the **L**. B
13: 15 do not be haughty, for the **L** has spoken.
13: 16 the **L** your God before he brings darkness, A
13: 25 says the **L**, because you have forgotten me B
14: 1 word of the **L** that came to Jeremiah concerning G
14: 7 our iniquities testify against us, act, O **L**,
14: 9 Yet you, O **L**, are in the midst of us,
14: 10 Thus says the **L** concerning this people: C
14: 10 therefore the **L** does not accept them,
14: 11 The **L** said to me: Do
14: 14 And the **L** said to me:
14: 15 thus says the **L** concerning the prophets who C
14: 20 We acknowledge our wickedness, O **L**,
14: 22 Is it not you, O **L** our God? A
15: 1 Then the **L** said to me:
15: 2 you shall say to them: Thus says the **L**: C
15: 3 over them four kinds of destroyers, says the **L**: B
15: 6 You have rejected me, says the **L**, B
15: 9 to the sword before their enemies, says the **L**. B
15: 11 The **L** said: Surely I have intervened in your
15: 15 O **L**, you know; remember me
15: 16 I am called by your name, O **L**, God of hosts.
15: 19 Therefore thus says the **L**: C
15: 20 to save you and deliver you, says the **L**. B
16: 1 The word of the **L** came to me: G
16: 3 For thus says the **L** concerning the sons C
16: 5 For thus says the **L**: Do C
16: 5 says the **L**, my steadfast love and mercy. B
16: 9 For thus says the **L** of hosts, the God of Israel: CE

Jer 16: 10 the **L** pronounced all this great evil against us?
16: 10 that we have committed against the **L** our God?" A
16: 11 says the **L**, and have gone after other gods B
16: 14 the days are surely coming, says the **L**, B
16: 14 "As the **L** lives who brought the people of Israel Q
16: 15 "As the **L** lives who brought the people of Israel Q
16: 16 says the **L**, and they shall catch them; B
16: 19 O **L**, my strength and my stronghold,
16: 21 and they shall know that my name is the **L**."
17: 5 Thus says the **L**: Cursed are those who trust in C
17: 5 whose hearts turn away from the **L**.
17: 7 Blessed are those who trust in the **L**,
17: 7 in the LORD, whose trust is the **L**.
17: 10 I the **L** test the mind and search the heart,
17: 13 O hope of Israel! O **L**! All who forsake you shall
17: 13 the fountain of living water, the **L**.
17: 14 Heal me, O **L**, and I shall be healed;
17: 15 "Where is the word of the **L**? G
17: 19 Thus said the **L** to me:
17: 20 Hear the word of the **L**, you kings of Judah, G
17: 21 Thus says the **L**: For the sake of your C
17: 24 But if you listen to me, says the **L**, B
17: 26 bringing thank offerings to the house of the **L**. F
18: 1 The word that came to Jeremiah from the **L**:
18: 5 Then the word of the **L** came to me: G
18: 6 as this potter has done? says the **L**. B
18: 11 of Jerusalem: Thus says the **L**: C
18: 13 Therefore thus says the **L**: C
18: 19 O **L**, and listen to what my adversaries say!
18: 23 Yet you, O **L**, know all their plotting to kill me.
19: 1 Thus said the **L**: Go and buy a potter's
19: 3 You shall say: Hear the word of the **L**, G
19: 3 Thus says the **L** of hosts, the God of Israel: CE
19: 6 the days are surely coming, says the **L**, B
19: 11 Thus says the **L** of hosts: CE
19: 12 Thus will I do to this place, says the **L**, B
19: 14 where the **L** had sent him to prophesy,
19: 15 Thus says the **L** of hosts, the God of Israel: CE
20: 1 who was chief officer in the house of the **L**, F
20: 2 the upper Benjamin Gate of the house of the **L**. F
20: 3 The **L** has named you not Pashhur
20: 4 For thus says the **L**: I am making you a terror C
20: 7 O **L**, you have enticed me, and I was enticed;
20: 8 the word of the **L** has become for me a reproach G
20: 11 But the **L** is with me like a dread warrior;
20: 12 O **L** of hosts, you test the righteous, E
20: 13 Sing to the **L**; praise the LORD!
20: 13 Sing to the LORD; praise the **L**! M
20: 16 like the cities that the **L** overthrew without pity;
21: 1 the word that came to Jeremiah from the **L**,
21: 2 of the **L** on our behalf, for King Nebuchadrezzar
21: 2 perhaps the **L** will perform a wonderful deed
21: 4 Thus says the **L**, the God of Israel: C
21: 7 says the **L**, I will give King Zedekiah of Judah, B
21: 8 to this people you shall say: Thus says the **L**: C
21: 10 for evil and not for good, says the **L**: B
21: 11 Hear the word of the **L**, G
21: 12 O house of David! Thus says the **L**: C
21: 13 O rock of the plain, says the **L**; B
21: 14 says the **L**; I will kindle a fire in its forest, B
22: 1 Thus says the **L**: Go down to C
22: 2 Hear the word of the **L**, G
22: 3 Thus says the **L**: Act with justice C
22: 5 I swear by myself, says the **L**, B
22: 6 thus says the **L** concerning the house of the king C
22: 8 the **L** dealt in this way with that great city?"
22: 9 abandoned the covenant of the **L** their God, AO
22: 11 thus says the **L** concerning Shallum son of King C
22: 16 Is not this to know me? says the **L**. B
22: 18 thus says the **L** concerning King Jehoiakim C
22: 24 As I live, says the **L**, even if King Coniah son B
22: 29 O land, land, land, hear the word of the **L**! G
22: 30 Thus says the **L**: Record this man C
23: 1 the sheep of my pasture! says the **L**. B
23: 2 Therefore thus says the **L**, the God of Israel, C
23: 2 to you for your evil doings, says the **L**. B
23: 4 nor shall any be missing, says the **L**. B
23: 5 The days are surely coming, says the **L**, B
23: 6 "The **L** is our righteousness."
23: 7 the days are surely coming, says the **L**, B
23: 7 "As the **L** lives who brought the people of Israel Q
23: 8 but "As the **L** lives who brought out and led Q
23: 9 because of the **L** and because of his holy words.
23: 11 I have found their wickedness, says the **L**. B
23: 12 in the year of their punishment, says the **L**. B
23: 15 Therefore thus says the **L** of hosts concerning CE
23: 16 Thus says the **L** of hosts: CE
23: 16 not from the mouth of the **L**.
23: 17 to those who despise the word of the **L**, G
23: 18 For who has stood in the council of the **L** so as
23: 19 Look, the storm of the **L**!
23: 20 of the **L** will not turn back until he has executed
23: 23 Am I a God near by, says the **L**, B
23: 24 that I cannot see them? says the **L**. B
23: 24 not fill heaven and earth? says the **L**. B
23: 28 in common with wheat? says the **L**. B
23: 29 Is not my word like fire, says the **L**, B
23: 30 therefore, I am against the prophets, says the **L**, B
23: 31 See, I am against the prophets, says the **L**, B
23: 31 use their own tongues and say, "Says the **L**." B
23: 32 says the **L**, and who tell them, B
23: 32 they do not profit this people at all, says the **L**. B
23: 33 "What is the burden of the **L**?"
23: 33 and I will cast you off, says the **L**." B
23: 34 or the people who say, "The burden of the **L**,"
23: 35 among yourselves, "What has the **L** answered?"
23: 35 or "What has the **L** spoken?"

Jer 23: 36 "the burden of the **L**" you shall mention no more,
23: 36 the **L** of hosts, our God. E
23: 37 "What has the **L** answered you?"
23: 37 or "What has the **L** spoken?"
23: 38 But if you say, "the burden of the **L**,"
23: 38 "the burden of the LORD," thus says the **L**: C
23: 38 you have said these words, "the burden of the **L**,"
23: 38 saying, You shall not say, "the burden of the **L**,"
24: 1 The **L** showed me two baskets of figs placed
24: 1 of figs placed before the temple of the **L**. V
24: 3 the **L** said to me, "What do you see, Jeremiah?"
24: 4 Then the word of the **L** came to me: G
24: 5 Thus says the **L**, the God of Israel: C
24: 7 a heart to know that I am the **L**; H
24: 8 But thus says the **L**: Like the bad figs C
25: 3 to this day, the word of the **L** has come to me, G
25: 4 the **L** persistently sent you all his servants
25: 5 the **L** has given to you and your ancestors from
25: 7 Yet you did not listen to me, says the **L**, B
25: 8 Therefore thus says the **L** of hosts: CE
25: 9 says the **L**, even for King Nebuchadrezzar B
25: 12 for their iniquity, says the **L**, B
25: 15 For thus the **L**, the God of Israel, said to me:
25: 17 the nations to whom the **L** sent me drink it:
25: 27 shall say to them, Thus says the **L** of hosts, CE
25: 28 Thus says the **L** of hosts: You must drink! CE
25: 29 inhabitants of the earth, says the **L** of hosts. BE
25: 30 The **L** will roar from on high,
25: 31 for the **L** has an indictment against the nations;
25: 31 the guilty he will put to the sword, says the **L**. B
25: 32 Thus says the **L** of hosts: CE
25: 33 by the **L** on that day shall extend from one end
25: 36 For the **L** is despoiling their pasture,
25: 37 because of the fierce anger of the **L**.
26: 1 this word came from the **L**:
26: 2 Thus says the **L**: Stand in the C
26: 2 that come to worship in the house of the **L**; F
26: 4 You shall say to them: Thus says the **L**: C
26: 7 in the house of the **L**. F
26: 8 that the **L** had commanded him to speak to all
26: 9 Why have you prophesied in the name of the **L**, I
26: 9 around Jeremiah in the house of the **L**. F
26: 10 up from the king's house to the house of the **L** F
26: 10 the entry of the New Gate of the house of the **L**. F
26: 12 "It is the **L** who sent me to prophesy
26: 13 and obey the voice of the **L** your God, AP
26: 13 the **L** will change his mind about the disaster
26: 15 the **L** sent me to you to speak all these words
26: 16 to us in the name of the **L** our God." AI
26: 18 'Thus says the **L** of hosts, CE
26: 19 Did he not fear the **L** and entreat the favor of X
26: 19 the LORD and entreat the favor of the **L**,
26: 19 not the **L** change his mind about the disaster
26: 20 in the name of the **L**, I
27: 1 this word came to Jeremiah from the **L**.
27: 2 Thus the **L** said to me:
27: 4 Thus says the **L** of hosts, the God of Israel: CE
27: 8 with famine, and with pestilence, says the **L**, B
27: 11 I will leave on its own land, says the **L**, B
27: 13 the **L** has spoken concerning any nation that will
27: 15 I have not sent them, says the **L**, B
27: 16 saying, Thus says the **L**: C
27: 18 and if the word of the **L** is with them, G
27: 18 then let them intercede with the **L** of hosts, E
27: 18 that the vessels left in the house of the **L**, F
27: 19 thus says the **L** of hosts concerning the pillars, CE
27: 21 thus says the **L** of hosts, the God of Israel, CE
27: 21 concerning the vessels left in the house of the **L**, F
27: 22 when I give attention to them, says the **L**. B
28: 1 from Gibeon, spoke to me in the house of the **L**, F
28: 2 "Thus says the **L** of hosts, the God of Israel: CE
28: 4 to Babylon, says the **L**, for I will break the yoke B
28: 5 in the house of the **L**; F
28: 6 "Amen! May the **L** do so;
28: 6 the **L** fulfill the words that you have prophesied,
28: 6 from Babylon the vessels of the house of the **L**, F
28: 9 be known that the **L** has truly sent the prophet."
28: 11 saying, "Thus says the **L**: C
28: 12 the word of the **L** came to Jeremiah: G
28: 13 tell Hananiah, Thus says the **L**: C
28: 14 For thus says the **L** of hosts, the God of Israel: CE
28: 15 "Listen, Hananiah, the **L** has not sent you,
28: 16 Therefore thus says the **L**: C
28: 16 you have spoken rebellion against the **L**."
29: 4 Thus says the **L** of hosts, the God of Israel, CE
29: 7 and pray to the **L** on its behalf,
29: 8 For thus says the **L** of hosts, the God of Israel: CE
29: 9 I did not send them, says the **L**. B
29: 10 For thus says the **L**: Only when Babylon's C
29: 11 I know the plans I have for you, says the **L**, B
29: 14 says the **L**, and I will restore your fortunes B
29: 14 the places where I have driven you, says the **L**, B
29: 15 **L** has raised up prophets for us in Babylon,"—
29: 16 Thus says the **L** concerning the king C
29: 17 Thus says the **L** of hosts, CE
29: 19 because they did not heed my words, says the **L**, B
29: 19 but they would not listen, says the **L**. B
29: 20 hear the word of the **L**: G
29: 21 Thus says the **L** of hosts, the God of Israel, CE
29: 22 "The **L** make you like Zedekiah and Ahab,
29: 23 and bears witness, says the **L**. B
29: 25 Thus says the **L** of hosts, the God of Israel: CE
29: 26 The **L** himself has made you priest instead of
29: 26 that there may be officers in the house of the **L** F
29: 30 Then the word of the **L** came to Jeremiah: G
29: 31 Thus says the **L** concerning Shemaiah C
29: 32 therefore thus says the **L**: C

†LORD distinguishes the proper name of God, *Yahweh,* indicated in the NRSV by "LORD," from the words translated "Lord" and "lord," indexed under the heading ***LORD** on pages 798-804.

Jer 29:32 that I am going to do to my people, says the **L**, B
29:32 for he has spoken rebellion against the **L**.
30: 1 The word that came to Jeremiah from the **L**:
30: 2 Thus says the **L**, the God of Israel: C
30: 3 For the days are surely coming, says the **L**, B
30: 3 Israel and Judah, says the **L**, B
30: 4 that the **L** spoke concerning Israel and Judah:
30: 5 Thus says the **L**: We have heard a cry of panic, C
30: 8 On that day, says the **L** of hosts, BE
30: 9 the **L** their God and David their king, A
30:10 you, have no fear, my servant Jacob, says the **L**, B
30:11 For I am with you, says the **L**, to save you; B
30:12 For thus says the **L**: Your hurt is incurable, C
30:17 and your wounds I will heal, says the **L**, B
30:18 Thus says the **L**: I am going to restore C
30:21 to approach me? says the **L**. B
30:23 Look, the storm of the **L**!
30:24 of the **L** will not turn back until he has executed
31: 1 At that time, says the **L**, B
31: 2 Thus says the **L**: The people who survived C
31: 3 the **L** appeared to him from far away. Z
31: 6 "Come, let us go up to Zion, to the **L** our God." A
31: 7 For thus says the **L**: Sing aloud with gladness C
31: 7 proclaim, give praise, and say, "Save, O **L**,
31:10 Hear the word of the **L**, O nations, G
31:11 For the **L** has ransomed Jacob,
31:12 they shall be radiant over the goodness of the **L**,
31:14 be satisfied with my bounty, says the **L**. B
31:15 Thus says the **L**: A voice is heard in Ramah, C
31:16 Thus says the **L**: Keep your voice from weeping, C
31:16 says the **L**: they shall come back from the land B
31:17 says the **L**: your children shall come back B
31:18 let me come back, for you are the **L** my God. A
31:20 I will surely have mercy on him, says the **L**. B
31:22 For the **L** has created a new thing on the earth:
31:23 Thus says the **L** of hosts, the God of Israel: CE
31:23 "The **L** bless you, O abode of righteousness,
31:27 The days are surely coming, says the **L**, B
31:28 over them to build and to plant, says the **L**. B
31:31 The days are surely coming, says the **L**, B
31:32 though I was their husband, says the **L**. B
31:33 the house of Israel after those days, says the **L**: B
31:34 "Know the **L**," for they shall all know me,
31:34 the least of them to the greatest, says the **L**; B
31:35 Thus says the **L**, who gives the sun for light C
31:35 the **L** of hosts is his name: E
31:36 to cease from my presence, says the **L**, B
31:37 Thus says the **L**: If the heavens above can C
31:37 because of all they have done, says the **L**. B
31:38 The days are surely coming, says the **L**, B
31:38 be rebuilt for the **L** from the tower of Hananel to
31:40 shall be sacred to the **L**.
32: 1 The word that came to Jeremiah from the **L** in
32: 3 and say: Thus says the **L**: C
32: 5 until I attend to him, says the **L**; B
32: 6 Jeremiah said, The word of the **L** came to me: G
32: 8 in accordance with the word of the **L**, G
32: 8 Then I knew that this was the word of the **L**. G
32:14 Thus says the **L** of hosts, the God of Israel: CE
32:15 For thus says the **L** of hosts, the God of Israel: CE
32:16 I prayed to the **L**, saying:
32:18 and mighty God whose name is the **L** of hosts, E
32:26 The word of the **L** came to Jeremiah: G
32:27 I am the **L**, the God of all flesh; H
32:28 Therefore, thus says the **L**: C
32:30 to anger by the work of their hands, says the **L**. B
32:36 Now therefore thus says the **L**, C
32:42 For thus says the **L**: Just as I have brought C
32:44 for I will restore their fortunes, says the **L**. B
33: 1 word of the **L** came to Jeremiah a second time, G
33: 2 Thus says the **L** who made the earth, C
33: 2 the **L** who formed it to establish it—the **L** is his name:
33: 4 For thus says the **L**, the God of Israel, C
33:10 Thus says the **L**: In this C
33:11 they bring thank offerings to the house of the **L**: F
33:11 "Give thanks to the **L** of hosts, E
33:11 to the LORD of hosts, for the **L** is good,
33:11 the fortunes of the land as at first, says the **L**. B
33:12 Thus says the **L** of hosts: CE
33:13 of the one who counts them, says the **L**. B
33:14 The days are surely coming, says the **L**, B
33:16 "The **L** is our righteousness."
33:17 For thus says the **L**: David shall never lack C
33:19 The word of the **L** came to Jeremiah: G
33:20 Thus says the **L**: If any of you C
33:23 The word of the **L** came to Jeremiah: G
33:24 that the **L** chose have been rejected by him,"
33:25 Thus says the **L**: Only if I had not C
34: 1 The word that came to Jeremiah from the **L**,
34: 2 "Thus says the **L**, the God of Israel: C
34: 2 and say to him: Thus says the **L**: C
34: 4 Yet hear the word of the **L**, G
34: 4 Thus says the **L** concerning you: C
34: 5 For I have spoken the word, says the **L**. B
34: 8 The word that came to Jeremiah from the **L**,
34:12 The word of the **L** came to Jeremiah G
34:12 word of the LORD came to Jeremiah from the **L**:
34:13 Thus says the **L**, the God of Israel: C
34:17 Therefore, thus says the **L**: C
34:17 I am going to grant a release to you, says the **L** B
34:22 I am going to command, says the **L**, B
35: 1 The word that came to Jeremiah from the **L** in
35: 2 and bring them to the house of the **L**, F
35: 4 the house the **L** into the chamber of the sons of F
35:12 Then the word of the **L** came to Jeremiah: G
35:13 Thus says the **L** of hosts, the God of Israel: CE

Jer 35:13 and obey my words? says the **L**. B
35:17 Therefore, thus says the **L**, the God of hosts, C
35:18 Thus says the **L** of hosts, the God of Israel: CE
35:19 thus says the **L** of hosts, the God of Israel: CE
36: 1 this word came to Jeremiah from the **L**:
36: 4 the words of the **L** that he had spoken to him.
36: 5 from entering the house of the **L**; F
36: 6 of the **L** from the scroll that you have written
36: 7 It may be that their plea will come before the **L**, D
36: 7 that the **L** has pronounced against this people."
36: 8 about reading from the scroll the words of the **L**
36: 9 to Jerusalem proclaimed a fast before the **L**. D
36:10 in the house of the **L**, F
36:11 of Shaphan heard all the words of the **L** from
36:26 But the **L** hid them.
36:27 the word of the **L** came to Jeremiah: G
36:29 Thus says the **L**, You have dared C
36:30 thus says the **L** concerning King Jehoiakim C
37: 2 to the words of the **L** that he spoke through
37: 3 "Please pray for us to the **L** our God." A
37: 6 the word of the **L** came to the prophet Jeremiah: G
37: 7 Thus says the **L**, God of Israel: C
37: 9 Thus says the **L**: Do not deceive yourselves, C
37:17 and said, "Is there any word from the **L**?"
38: 2 Thus says the **L**, Those who stay in this city C
38: 3 Thus says the **L**, This city shall surely be C
38:14 at the third entrance of the temple of the **L**. V
38:16 "As the **L** lives, who gave us our lives, Q
38:17 Jeremiah said to Zedekiah, "Thus says the **L**, C
38:20 Just obey the voice of the **L** in what I say to you, P
38:21 this is what the **L** has shown me—
39:15 The word the **L** came to Jeremiah G
39:16 Thus says the **L** of hosts, the God of Israel: CE
39:17 But I will save you on that day, says the **L**, B
39:18 because you have trusted in me, says the **L**. B
40: 1 from the **L** after Nebuzaradan the captain of
40: 2 "The **L** your God threatened this place A
40: 3 and now the **L** has brought it about,
40: 3 because all of you sinned against the **L** and did
41: 5 and incense to present at the temple of the **L**. V
42: 2 and pray to the **L** your God for us— A
42: 3 the **L** your God show us where we should go A
42: 4 to the **L** your God as you request, and whatever A
42: 4 and whatever the **L** answers you I will tell you;
42: 5 the **L** be a true and faithful witness against us
42: 5 to everything that the **L** your God sends us A
42: 6 obey the voice of the **L** our God to whom AP
42: 6 when we obey the voice of the **L** our God." AP
42: 7 of ten days the word of the **L** came to Jeremiah. G
42: 9 "Thus says the **L**, the God of Israel, C
42:11 do not be afraid of him, says the **L**, B
42:13 thus disobeying the voice of the **L** your God AP
42:15 then hear the word of the **L**, G
42:15 Thus says the **L** of hosts, the God of Israel: CE
42:18 For thus says the **L** of hosts, the God of Israel: CE
42:19 The **L** has said to you, O remnant of Judah,
42:20 For you yourselves sent me to the **L** your God, A
42:20 saying, 'Pray for us to the **L** our God, A
42:20 and whatever the **L** our God says, A
42:21 the voice of the **L** your God in anything AP
43: 1 the people all these words of the **L** their God, A
43: 1 with which the **L** their God had sent him A
43: 2 The **L** our God did not send you to say, A
43: 4 the people did not obey the voice of the **L**, P
43: 7 for they did not obey the voice of the **L**. P
43: 8 word of the **L** came to Jeremiah in Tahpanhes: G
43:10 Thus says the **L** of hosts, the God of Israel: CE
44: 2 Thus says the **L** of hosts, the God of Israel: CE
44: 7 thus says the **L** God of hosts, the God of Israel: CJ
44:11 thus says the **L** of hosts, the God of Israel: CE
44:16 that you have spoken to us in the name of the **L**, I
44:21 did not the **L** remember them?
44:22 The **L** could no longer bear the sight
44:23 because you sinned against the **L** and
44:23 and did not obey the voice of the **L** P
44:24 "Hear the word of the **L**, G
44:25 Thus says the **L** of hosts, the God of Israel: CE
44:26 Therefore hear the word of the **L**, G
44:26 Lo, I swear by my great name, says the **L**, B
44:29 This shall be the sign to you, says the **L**, B
44:30 Thus says the **L**, I am going to give Pharaoh C
45: 2 Thus says the **L**, the God of Israel, to you, C
45: 3 The **L** has added sorrow to my pain;
45: 4 Thus you shall say to him, "Thus says the **L**: C
45: 5 to bring disaster upon all flesh, says the **L**; B
46: 1 word of the **L** that came to the prophet Jeremiah G
46: 5 terror is all around! says the **L**. B
46:13 that the **L** spoke to the prophet Jeremiah about
46:15 —because the **L** thrust him down.
46:18 says the King, whose name is the **L** of hosts, E
46:23 says the **L**, though it is impenetrable, B
46:25 The **L** of hosts, the God of Israel, said: E
46:26 be inhabited as in the days of old, says the **L**. B
46:28 says the **L**, for I am with you. B
47: 1 word of the **L** that came to the prophet Jeremiah G
47: 2 Thus says the **L**: See, waters are rising out of C
47: 4 For the **L** is destroying the Philistines,
47: 6 Ah, sword of the **L**!
47: 7 when the **L** has given it an order?
48: 1 Thus says the **L** of hosts, the God of Israel: CE
48: 8 be destroyed, as the **L** has spoken.
48:10 the one who is slack in doing the work of the **L**;
48:12 Therefore, the time is surely coming, says the **L**, B
48:15 says the King, whose name is the **L** of hosts. E
48:25 and his arm is broken, says the **L**. B
48:26 because he magnified himself against the **L**;
48:30 I myself know his insolence, says the **L**; B

Jer 48:35 And I will bring to an end in Moab, says the **L**, B
48:38 like a vessel that no one wants, says the **L**. B
48:40 For thus says the **L**: Look, C
48:42 because he magnified himself against the **L**.
48:43 O inhabitants of Moab! says the **L**. B
48:44 in the year of their punishment, says the **L**. B
48:47 of Moab in the latter days, says the **L**. B
49: 1 Thus says the **L**: Has Israel no sons? C
49: 2 Therefore, the time is surely coming, says the **L**, B
49: 2 those who dispossessed him, says the **L**. B
49: 6 the fortunes of the Ammonites, says the **L**. B
49: 7 Thus says the **L** of hosts: CE
49:12 For thus says the **L**: If those who do C
49:13 For by myself I have sworn, says the **L**, B
49:14 I have heard tidings from the **L**,
49:16 from there I will bring you down, says the **L**. B
49:18 says the **L**, no one shall live there, B
49:20 the **L** has made against Edom and the purposes
49:26 be destroyed in that day, says the **L** of hosts. BE
49:28 of Babylon defeated. Thus says the **L**: C
49:30 O inhabitants of Hazor! says the **L**. B
49:31 says the **L**, that has no gates or bars, B
49:32 against them from every side, says the **L**. B
49:34 word of the **L** that came to the prophet Jeremiah G
49:35 Thus says the **L** of hosts: CE
49:37 my fierce anger, says the **L**. B
49:38 and destroy their king and officials, says the **L**. B
49:39 the fortunes of Elam, says the **L**. B
50: 1 The word that the **L** spoke concerning Babylon,
50: 4 In those days and in that time, says the **L**, B
50: 4 as they seek the **L** their God. A
50: 5 the **L** by an everlasting covenant that will never
50: 7 because they have sinned against the **L**,
50: 7 the **L**, the hope of their ancestors."
50:10 all who plunder her shall be sated, says the **L**. B
50:13 of the wrath of the **L** she shall not be inhabited,
50:14 for she has sinned against the **L**.
50:15 For this is the vengeance of the **L**:
50:18 thus says the **L** of hosts, the God of Israel: CE
50:20 In those days and at that time, says the **L**, B
50:21 says the **L**; do all that I have commanded you. B
50:24 because you challenged the **L**.
50:25 The **L** has opened his armory,
50:28 in Zion the vengeance of the **L** our God, A
50:29 for she has arrogantly defied the **L**,
50:30 be destroyed on that day, says the **L**. B
50:33 Thus says the **L** of hosts: CE
50:34 the **L** of hosts is his name. E
50:35 A sword against the Chaldeans, says the **L**, B
50:40 says the **L**, so no one shall live there, B
50:45 the plan that the **L** has made against Babylon,
51: 1 Thus says the **L**: I am going to stir C
51: 5 not been forsaken by their God, the **L** of hosts, E
51:10 The **L** has brought forth our vindication;
51:10 let us declare in Zion the work of the **L** our God. A
51:11 The **L** has stirred up the spirit of the kings of
51:11 for that is the vengeance of the **L**,
51:12 the **L** has both planned and done what he spoke
51:14 The **L** of hosts has sworn by himself: E
51:19 Not like these is the **L**, the portion of Jacob,
51:19 the **L** of hosts is his name. E
51:24 that they have done in Zion, says the **L**. B
51:25 says the **L**, that destroys the whole earth; B
51:26 but you shall be a perpetual waste, says the **L**. B
51:33 For thus says the **L** of hosts, the God of Israel: CE
51:36 Therefore thus says the **L**: C
51:39 a perpetual sleep and never wake, says the **L**. B
51:45 each of you, from the fierce anger of the **L**!
51:48 against them out of the north, says the **L**. B
51:50 Remember the **L** in a distant land,
51:52 Therefore the time is surely coming, says the **L**, B
51:53 destroyers would come upon her, says the **L**. B
51:55 For the **L** is laying Babylon waste,
51:56 **L** is a God of recompense, he will repay in full.
51:57 says the King, whose name is the **L** of hosts. E
51:58 Thus says the **L** of hosts: CE
51:62 and say, 'O **L**, you yourself threatened
52: 2 He did what was evil in the sight of the **L**, L
52: 3 the **L** that he expelled them from his presence.
52:13 He burned the house of the **L**, the king's house, F
52:17 pillars of bronze that were in the house of the **L**, F
52:17 the bronze sea that were in the house of the **L**, F
52:20 for the house of the **L**, F
La 1: 5 the **L** has made her suffer for the multitude
1: 9 "O **L**, look at my affliction,
1:11 Look, O **L**, and see how worthless I have become.
1:12 which the **L** inflicted on the day of his fierce anger.
1:15 The **L** has rejected all my warriors in the midst
1:17 the **L** has commanded against Jacob
1:18 The **L** is in the right, for I have rebelled
1:20 See, O **L**, how distressed I am;
2: 6 the **L** has abolished in Zion festival and sabbath,
2: 7 a clamor was raised in the house of the **L** as on F
2: 8 The **L** determined to lay in ruins the wall
2: 9 and her prophets obtain no vision from the **L**.
2:17 The **L** has done what he purposed,
2:20 Look, O **L**, and consider!
2:22 on the day of the anger of the **L** no one escaped
3:18 and all that I had hoped for from the **L**."
3:22 of the **L** never ceases, his mercies never come to
3:24 "The **L** is my portion," says my soul,
3:25 The **L** is good to those who wait for him,
3:26 for the salvation of the **L**.
3:40 and examine our ways, and return to the **L**.
3:50 until the **L** from heaven looks down and sees.
3:55 I called on your name, O **L**,
3:59 You have seen the wrong done to me, O **L**;

†**LORD** distinguishes the proper name of God, *Yahweh,* indicated in the NRSV by "LORD," from the words translated "Lord" and "lord," indexed under the heading ***LORD** on pages 798-804.

La 3:61 You have heard their taunts, O **L**,
3:64 Pay them back for their deeds, O **L**,
4:11 The **L** gave full vent to his wrath;
4:16 The **L** himself has scattered them,
5: 1 Remember, O **L**, what has befallen us;
5:19 But you, O **L**, reign forever;
5:21 Restore us to yourself, O **L**,
Eze 1: 3 the word of the **L** came to the priest Ezekiel son G
1: 3 and the hand of the **L** was on him there. S
1:28 of the likeness of the glory of the **L**. R
3:12 and as the glory of the **L** rose from its place, R
3:14 the hand of the **L** being strong upon me. S
3:16 the word of the **L** came to me: G
3:22 Then the hand of the **L** was upon me there; S
3:23 and the glory of the **L** stood there, R
4:13 The **L** said, "Thus shall the people
5:13 and they shall know that I, the **L**,
5:15 I, the **L**, have spoken—
5:17 I, the **L**, have spoken.
6: 1 The word of the **L** came to me: G
6: 7 then you shall know that I am the **L**. H
6:10 And they shall know that I am the **L**; H
6:13 And you shall know that I am the **L**, H
6:14 Then they shall know that I am the **L**. H
7: 1 The word of the **L** came to me: G
7: 4 Then you shall know that I am the **L**. H
7: 9 you shall know that it is I the **L** who strike.
7:19 on the day of the wrath of the **L**.
7:27 And they shall know that I am the **L**. H
8:12 For they say, 'The **L** does not see us,
8:12 the **L** has forsaken the land.' "
8:14 of the north gate of the house of the **L**; F
8:16 into the inner court of the house of the **L**; F
8:16 there, at the entrance of the temple of the **L**, V
8:16 with their backs to the temple of the **L**, V
9: 3 The **L** called to the man clothed in linen,
9: 9 for they say, 'The **L** has forsaken the land,
9: 9 and the **L** does not see.'
10: 4 the glory of the **L** rose up from the cherub R
10: 4 of the brightness of the glory of the **L**. R
10:18 the glory of the **L** went out from the threshold R
10:19 of the east gate of the house of the **L**; F
11: 1 to the east gate of the house of the **L**, F
11: 5 Then the spirit of the **L** fell upon me,
11: 5 and he said to me, "Say, Thus says the **L**: C
11:10 And you shall know that I am the **L**. H
11:12 Then you shall know that I am the **L**, H
11:14 Then the word of the **L** came to me: G
11:15 "They have gone far from the **L**;
11:23 the glory of the **L** ascended from the middle of R
11:25 the things that the **L** had shown me.
12: 1 The word of the **L** came to me: G
12: 8 In the morning the word of the **L** came to me: G
12:15 And they shall know that I am the **L**, H
12:16 then they shall know that I am the **L**. H
12:17 The word of the **L** came to me: G
12:20 and you shall know that I am the **L**. H
12:21 The word of the **L** came to me: G
12:25 But I the **L** will speak the word that I speak,
12:26 The word of the **L** came to me: G
13: 1 The word of the **L** came to me: G
13: 2 "Hear the word of the **L**!" G
13: 5 that it might stand in battle on the day of the **L**.
13: 6 lying divination; they say, "Says the **L**," B
13: 6 when the **L** has not sent them,
13: 7 "Says the **L**," even though I did not speak? B
13:14 and you shall know that I am the **L**. H
13:21 and you shall know that I am the **L**. H
13:23 Then you will know that I am the **L**. H
14: 2 And the word of the **L** came to me: G
14: 4 I the **L** will answer those who come with
14: 7 I the **L** will answer them myself.
14: 8 and you shall know that I am the **L**. H
14: 9 prophet is deceived and speaks a word, I, the **L**,
14:12 The word of the **L** came to me: G
15: 1 The word of the **L** came to me: G
15: 7 and you shall know that I am the **L**, H
16: 1 The word of the **L** came to me: G
16:35 **Therefore, O whore, hear the word of the L:** G
16:58 and your abominations, says the **L**. B
16:62 and you shall know that I am the **L**, H
17: 1 The word of the **L** came to me: G
17:11 Then the word of the **L** came to me: G
17:21 and you shall know that I, the **L**, have spoken.
17:24 the trees of the field shall know that I am the **L**. H
17:24 I the **L** have spoken; I will accomplish it.
18: 1 The word of the **L** came to me: G
20: 1 certain elders of Israel came to consult the **L**,
20: 2 And the word of the **L** came to me: G
20: 5 I swore to them, saying, I am the **L** your God. AH
20: 7 I am the **L** your God. AH
20:12 that they might know that I the **L** sanctify them.
20:19 I the **L** am your God;
20:20 so that you may know that I the **L** am your God.
20:26 so that they might know that I am the **L**. H
20:38 Then you shall know that I am the **L**. H
20:42 You shall know that I am the **L**, H
20:44 And you shall know that I am the **L**, H
20:45 The word of the **L** came to me: G
20:47 Hear the word of the **L**: G
20:48 All flesh shall see that I the **L** have kindled it;
21: 1 The word of the **L** came to me: G
21: 3 and say to the land of Israel, Thus says the **L**: C
21: 5 the **L** have drawn my sword out of its sheath;
21: 8 And the word of the **L** came to me: G
21:17 I will satisfy my fury; I the **L** have spoken.
21:18 The word of the **L** came to me: G
Eze 21:32 for I the **L** have spoken.
22: 1 The word of the **L** came to me: G
22:14 I the **L** have spoken, and I will do it.
22:16 and you shall know that I am the **L**. H
22:17 The word of the **L** came to me: G
22:22 that I the **L** have poured out my wrath upon you.
22:23 The word of the **L** came to me: G
22:28 when the **L** has not spoken.
23: 1 The word of the **L** came to me: G
23:36 The **L** said to me: Mortal,
24: 1 the word of the **L** came to me: G
24:14 I the **L** have spoken; the time is coming,
24:15 The word of the **L** came to me: G
24:20 The word of the **L** came to me: G
24:27 and they shall know that I am the **L**. H
25: 1 The word of the **L** came to me: G
25: 5 Then you shall know that I am the **L**. H
25: 7 Then you shall know that I am the **L**. H
25:11 Then they shall know that I am the **L**. H
25:17 Then they shall know that I am the **L**, H
26: 1 the word of the **L** came to me: G
26: 6 Then they shall know that I am the **L**. H
26:14 for I the **L** have spoken, says the Lord GOD.
27: 1 The word of the **L** came to me: G
28: 1 The word of the **L** came to me: G
28:11 Moreover the word of the **L** came to me: G
28:20 The word of the **L** came to me: G
28:22 that I am the **L** when I execute judgments in it, H
28:23 And they shall know that I am the **L**. H
28:26 they shall know that I am the **L** their God. AH
29: 1 the word of the **L** came to me: G
29: 6 that I am the **L** because you were a staff of reed H
29: 9 Then they shall know that I am the **L**. H
29:17 the word of the **L** came to me: G
29:21 Then they shall know that I am the **L**. H
30: 1 The word of the **L** came to me: G
30: 3 For a day is near, the day of the **L** is near;
30: 6 Thus says the **L**: Those who support Egypt C
30: 8 Then they shall know that I am the **L**, H
30:12 of foreigners; I the **L** have spoken.
30:19 Then they shall know that I am the **L**. H
30:20 the word of the **L** came to me: G
30:25 And they shall know that I am the **L**, H
30:26 Then they shall know that I am the **L**. H
31: 1 the word of the **L** came to me: G
32: 1 the word of the **L** came to me: G
32:15 then they shall know that I am the **L**. H
32:17 the word of the **L** came to me: G
33: 1 The word of the **L** came to me: G
33:22 the hand of the **L** had been upon me the evening S
33:23 The word of the **L** came to me: G
33:29 Then they shall know that I am the **L**, H
33:30 the word is that comes from the **L**."
34: 1 The word of the **L** came to me: G
34: 7 you shepherds, hear the word of the **L**: G
34: 9 you shepherds, hear the word of the **L**: G
34:24 And I, the **L**, will be their God,
34:24 be prince among them; I, the **L**,
34:27 and they shall know that I am the **L**, H
34:30 They shall know that I, the **L** their God, A
35: 1 The word of the **L** came to me: G
35: 4 and you shall know that I am the **L**. H
35: 9 Then you shall know that I am the **L**. H
35:10 although the **L** was there—
35:12 You shall know that I, the **L**,
35:15 Then they shall know that I am the **L**. H
36: 1 O mountains of Israel, hear the word of the **L**. G
36:11 Then you shall know that I am the **L**. H
36:16 The word of the **L** came to me: G
36:20 "These are the people of the **L**,
36:23 and the nations shall know that I am the **L**, H
36:36 the **L**, have rebuilt the ruined places,
36:36 I, the **L**, have spoken, and I will do it.
36:38 Then they shall know that I am the **L**. H
37: 1 The hand of the **L** came upon me, S
37: 1 the spirit of the **L** and set me down in the middle
37: 4 O dry bones, hear the word of the **L**. G
37: 6 and you shall know that I am the **L**." H
37:13 And you shall know that I am the **L**, H
37:14 then you shall know that I, the **L**,
37:14 have spoken and will act," says the **L**. B
37:15 The word of the **L** came to me: G
37:28 nations shall know that I the **L** sanctify Israel,
38: 1 The word of the **L** came to me: G
38:23 Then they shall know that I am the **L**. H
39: 6 and they shall know that I am the **L**. H
39: 7 and the nations shall know that I am the **L**, H
39:22 of Israel shall know that I am the **L** their God, AH
39:28 they shall know that I am the **L** their God AH
40: 1 the hand of the **L** was upon me, S
40:46 the descendants of Levi may come near to the **L**
41:22 "This is the table that stands before the **L**." D
42:13 where the priests who approach the **L** shall eat
43: 4 the glory of the **L** entered the temple by the gate R
43: 5 and the glory of the **L** filled the temple. R
43:24 You shall present them before the **L**, D
43:24 and offer them up as a burnt offering to the **L**.
44: 2 The **L** said to me: This gate shall remain shut;
44: 2 for the **L**, the God of Israel, has entered by it;
44: 3 may sit in it to eat food before the **L**; D
44: 4 glory of the **L** filled the temple of the LORD; R
44: 4 glory of the LORD filled the temple of the **L**; V
44: 5 The **L** said to me: Mortal,
44: 5 of the temple of the **L** and all its laws; V
45: 1 you shall set aside for the **L** a portion of the land
45: 4 in the sanctuary and approach the **L** to minister
45:23 as a burnt offering to the **L** seven young bulls
Eze 46: 3 down at the entrance of that gate before the **L** D
46: 4 The burnt offering that the prince offers to the **L**
46: 9 come before the **L** at the appointed festivals, D
46:12 to the **L**, the gate facing east shall be opened
46:13 for a burnt offering to the **L** daily;
46:14 as a grain offering to the **L**;
48: 9 for the **L** shall be twenty-five thousand cubits
48:10 with the sanctuary of the **L** in the middle of it.
48:14 for it is holy to the **L**.
48:35 from that time on shall be, The **L** is There.
Da 9: 2 to the word of the **L** to the prophet Jeremiah, G
9: 4 I prayed to the **L** my God and made confession, A
9: 8 Open shame, O **L**, falls on us, our kings,
9:10 have not obeyed the voice of the **L** our God AP
9:13 We did not entreat the favor of the **L** our God, A
9:14 So the **L** kept watch over this calamity
9:14 the **L** our God is right in all that he has done; A
9:20 before the **L** my God on behalf of the holy AD
Hos 1: 1 word of the **L** that came to Hosea son of Beeri, G
1: 2 When the **L** first spoke through Hosea,
1: 2 the **L** said to Hosea, "Go, take for yourself a wife
1: 2 land commits great whoredom by forsaking the **L**."
1: 4 And the **L** said to him, "Name him Jezreel;
1: 6 Then the **L** said to him, "Name her Lo-ruhamah,
1: 7 and I will save them by the **L** their God; A
1: 9 Then the **L** said, "Name him Lo-ammi,
2:13 and forgot me, says the **L**. B
2:16 On that day, says the **L**, you will call me, B
2:20 and you shall know the **L**.
2:21 On that day I will answer, says the **L**, B
3: 1 The **L** said to me again, "Go, love a woman
3: 1 just as the **L** loves the people of Israel,
3: 5 and seek the **L** their God, and David their king; A
3: 5 to the **L** and to his goodness in the latter days.
4: 1 Hear the word of the **L**, O people of Israel; G
4: 1 the **L** has an indictment against the inhabitants
4:10 because they have forsaken the **L**
4:15 and do not swear, "As the **L** lives." Q
4:16 can the **L** now feed them like a lamb in
5: 4 and they do not know the **L**.
5: 6 to seek the **L**, but they will not find him;
5: 7 They have dealt faithlessly with the **L**;
6: 1 let us return to the **L**;
6: 3 Let us know, let us press on to know the **L**;
7:10 yet they do not return to the **L** their God, A
8: 1 One like a vulture is over the house of the **L**, F
8:13 the **L** does not accept them.
9: 3 They shall not remain in the land of the **L**;
9: 4 not pour drink offerings of wine to the **L**,
9: 4 it shall not come to the house of the **L**. F
9: 5 and on the day of the festival of the **L**?
9:14 Give them, O **L**—what will you give?
10: 2 The **L** will break down their altars,
10: 3 "We have no king, for we do not fear the **L**, X
10:12 for it is time to seek the **L**,
11:10 They shall go after the **L**, who roars like a lion;
11:11 I will return them to their homes, says the **L**. B
12: 2 The **L** has an indictment against Judah,
12: 5 The **L** the God of hosts, the **L** is his name!
12: 9 I am the **L** your God from the land of Egypt; AH
12:13 a prophet the **L** brought Israel up from Egypt,
13: 4 the **L** your God ever since the land of Egypt; A
13:15 a blast from the **L**, rising from the wilderness;
14: 1 Return, O Israel, to the **L** your God, A
14: 2 Take words with you and return to the **L**;
14: 9 For the ways of the **L** are right,
Joel 1: 1 word of the **L** that came to Joel son of Pethuel: G
1: 9 from the house of the **L**. F
1: 9 The priests mourn, the ministers of the **L**.
1:14 of the land to the house of the **L** your God, AF
1:14 and cry out to the **L**.
1:15 For the day of the **L** is near,
1:19 To you, O **L**, I cry.
2: 1 for the day of the **L** is coming, it is near—
2:11 The **L** utters his voice at the head of his army;
2:11 Truly the day of the **L** is great;
2:12 Yet even now, says the **L**, B
2:13 Return to the **L**, your God, A
2:14 and a drink offering for the **L**, your God? A
2:17 the ministers of the **L**, weep.
2:17 Let them say, "Spare your people, O **L**,
2:18 Then the **L** became jealous for his land,
2:19 In response to his people the **L** said:
2:21 for the **L** has done great things!
2:23 be glad and rejoice in the **L** your God; A
2:26 and praise the name of the **L** your God, AI
2:27 the **L**, am your God and there is no other.
2:31 before the great and terrible day of the **L** comes.
2:32 who calls on the name of the **L** shall be saved; I
2:32 be those who escape, as the **L** has said,
2:32 the survivors shall be those whom the **L** calls.
3: 8 to a nation far away; for the **L** has spoken.
3:11 Bring down your warriors, O **L**.
3:14 the day of the **L** is near in the valley of decision.
3:16 The **L** roars from Zion, and utters his voice
3:16 But the **L** is a refuge for his people,
3:17 So you shall know that I, the **L** your God, A
3:18 the house of the **L** and water the Wadi Shittim. F
3:21 for the **L** dwells in Zion.
Am 1: 2 The **L** roars from Zion, and utters his voice from
1: 3 Thus says the **L**: For three transgressions of C
1: 5 of Aram shall go into exile to Kir, says the **L**. B
1: 6 Thus says the **L**: For three transgressions of C
1: 9 Thus says the **L**: For three transgressions of C
1:11 Thus says the **L**: For three transgressions of C
1:13 Thus says the **L**: For three transgressions of C
1:15 he and his officials together, says the **L**. B

†LORD distinguishes the proper name of God, *Yahweh*, indicated in the NRSV by "LORD," from the words translated "Lord" and "lord," indexed under the heading ***LORD** on pages 798-804.

Am 2: 1 Thus says the L: For three transgressions of C
2: 3 will kill all its officials with him, says the L. B
2: 4 Thus says the L: For three transgressions of C
2: 4 because they have rejected the law of the L,
2: 6 Thus says the L: For three transgressions of C
2:11 O people of Israel? says the L. B
2:16 shall flee away naked in that day, says the L. B
3: 1 that the L has spoken against you, O people
3: 6 unless the L has done it?
3:10 They do not know how to do right, says the L, B
3:12 Thus says the L: As the shepherd rescues C
3:15 to an end, says the L. B
4: 3 you shall be flung out into Harmon, says the L. B
4: 6 yet you did not return to me, says the L. B
4: 8 yet you did not return to me, says the L. B
4: 9 yet you did not return to me, says the L. B
4:10 yet you did not return to me, says the L. B
4:11 yet you did not return to me, says the L. B
4:13 the L, the God of hosts, is his name!
5: 4 For thus says the L to the house of Israel: C
5: 6 Seek the L and live, or he will break out against
5: 8 on the surface of the earth, the L is his name,
5:14 and so the L, the God of hosts, will be with you,
5:15 it may be that the L, the God of hosts,
5:16 thus says the L, the God of hosts, the Lord: C
5:17 through the midst of you, says the L. B
5:18 Alas for you who desire the day of the L!
5:18 Why do you want the day of the L?
5:20 Is not the day of the L darkness, not light,
5:27 says the L, whose name is the God of hosts. B
6: 8 Lord GOD has sworn by himself (says the L, B
6:10 We must not mention the name of the L." I
6:11 the L commands, and the great house shall
6:14 O house of Israel, says the L, the God of hosts, B
7: 3 The L relented concerning this;
7: 3 "It shall not be," said the L.
7: 6 The L relented concerning this;
7: 8 the L said to me, "Amos, what do you see?"
7:15 and the L took me from following the flock,
7:15 and the L said to me, 'Go,
7:16 "Now therefore hear the word of the L. G
7:17 Therefore thus says the L: C
8: 2 Then the L said to me, "The end has come
8: 7 The L has sworn by the pride of Jacob:
8:11 but of hearing the words of the L.
8:12 seeking the word of the L, G
9: 1 I saw the L standing beside the altar,
9: 6 of the earth—the L is his name.
9: 7 O people of Israel? says the L. B
9: 8 the house of Jacob, says the L. B
9:12 says the L who does this. B
9:13 The time is surely coming, says the L, B
9:15 that I have given them, says the L your God. AB
Ob 1: 1 We have heard a report from the L,
1: 4 from there I will bring you down, says the L. B
1: 8 On that day, says the L, B
1:15 the day of the L is near against all the nations.
1:18 of Esau; for the L has spoken.
Jnh 1: 1 the word of the L came to Jonah son of Amittai, G
1: 3 to flee to Tarshish from the presence of the L.
1: 3 away from the presence of the L.
1: 4 But the L hurled a great wind upon the sea,
1: 9 "I worship the L, the God of heaven,
1:10 that he was fleeing from the presence of the L,
1:14 Then they cried out to the L, "Please,
1:14 they cried out to the LORD, "Please, O L,
1:14 for you, O L, have done as it pleased you."
1:16 Then the men feared the L even more,
1:16 they offered a sacrifice to the L and made vows.
1:17 the L provided a large fish to swallow up Jonah;
2: 1 to the L his God from the belly of the fish, A
2: 2 "I called to the L out of my distress,
2: 6 up my life from the Pit, O L my God. A
2: 7 my life was ebbing away, I remembered the L;
2: 9 Deliverance belongs to the L!"
2:10 Then the L spoke to the fish,
3: 1 The word of the L came to Jonah a second time, G
3: 3 according to the word of the L. G
4: 2 He prayed to the L and said, "O LORD!
4: 2 He prayed to the LORD and said, "O L!
4: 3 And now, O L, please take my life from me,
4: 4 And the L said, "Is it right for you to be angry?"
4: 6 The L God appointed a bush, J
4:10 the L said, "You are concerned about the bush,
Mic 1: 1 word of the L that came to Micah of Moresheth G
1: 3 For lo, the L is coming out of his place,
1:12 down from the L to the gate of Jerusalem.
2: 3 Therefore thus says the L: C
2: 4 the L alters the inheritance of my people;
2: 5 to cast the line by lot in the assembly of the L.
2:13 on before them, the L at their head.
3: 4 Then they will cry to the L,
3: 5 Thus says the L concerning the prophets C
3: 8 I am filled with power, with the spirit of the L,
3:11 yet they lean upon the L and say,
3:11 "Surely the L is with us!
4: 2 "Come, let us go up to the mountain of the L,
4: 2 and the word of the L from Jerusalem. G
4: 4 for the mouth of the L of hosts has spoken. E
4: 5 in the name of the L our God forever and ever. AI
4: 6 In that day, says the L, I will assemble the lame B
4: 7 the L will reign over them in Mount Zion now
4:10 there the L will redeem you from the hands
4:12 But they do not know the thoughts of the L;
4:13 and shall devote their gain to the L,
5: 4 and feed his flock in the strength of the L,
5: 4 in the majesty of the name of the L his God. AI

Mic 5: 7 shall be like dew from the L,
5:10 says the L, I will cut off your horses from B
6: 1 Hear what the L says: Rise,
6: 2 Hear, you mountains, the controversy of the L,
6: 2 for the L has a controversy with his people,
6: 5 that you may know the saving acts of the L."
6: 6 "With what shall I come before the L, D
6: 7 Will the L be pleased with thousands of rams,
6: 8 what does the L require of you but to do justice,
6: 9 The voice of the L cries to the city P
7: 7 But as for me, I will look to the L,
7: 8 I sit in darkness, the L will be a light to me.
7: 9 I must bear the indignation of the L,
7:10 "Where is the L your God?" A
7:17 they shall turn in dread to the L our God, A
Na 1: 2 A jealous and avenging God is the L,
1: 2 the L is avenging and wrathful;
1: 2 the L takes vengeance on his adversaries
1: 3 The L is slow to anger but great in power,
1: 3 and the L will by no means clear the guilty.
1: 7 The L is good, a stronghold in a day of trouble;
1: 9 Why do you plot against the L?
1:11 one has gone out who plots evil against the L,
1:12 Thus says the L, "Though they are at full C
1:14 The L has commanded concerning you:
2: 2 (For the L is restoring the majesty of Jacob,
2:13 See, I am against you, says the L of hosts, BE
3: 5 says the L of hosts, and will lift up your skirts BE
Hab 1: 2 O L, how long shall I cry for help,
1:12 Are you not from of old, O L my God, A
1:12 O L, you have marked them for judgment;
2: 2 Then the L answered me and said:
2:13 not from the L of hosts that peoples labor only E
2:14 with the knowledge of the glory of the L, R
2:20 But the L is in his holy temple;
3: 2 O L, I have heard of your renown,
3: 2 and I stand in awe, O L, of your work.
3: 8 Was your wrath against the rivers, O L?
3:18 yet I will rejoice in the L;
Zep 1: 1 The word of the L that came to Zephaniah G
1: 2 from the face of the earth, says the L. B
1: 3 from the face of the earth, says the L. B
1: 5 those who bow down and swear to the L,
1: 6 from following the L, who have not sought
1: 6 who have not sought the L or inquired of him.
1: 7 For the day of the L is at hand;
1: 7 the L has prepared a sacrifice,
1:10 On that day, says the L, a cry will be heard B
1:12 "The L will not do good, nor will he do harm."
1:14 The great day of the L is near,
1:14 the sound of the day of the L is bitter,
1:17 because they have sinned against the L,
2: 2 there comes upon you the fierce anger of the L,
2: 3 Seek the L, all you humble of the land,
2: 5 The word of the L is against you, O Canaan, G
2: 7 For the L their God will be mindful of them A
2: 9 Therefore, as I live, says the L of hosts, BE
2:10 boasted against the people of the L of hosts. E
2:11 The L will be terrible against them;
3: 2 It has not trusted in the L;
3: 5 The L within it is righteous; he does no wrong.
3: 8 Therefore wait for me, says the L, B
3: 9 that all of them may call on the name of the L I
3:12 They shall seek refuge in the name of the L— I
3:15 L has taken away the judgments against you,
3:15 The king of Israel, the L, is in your midst;
3:17 The L, your God, is in your midst, A
3:20 before your eyes, says the L. B
Hag 1: 1 the word of the L came by the prophet Haggai G
1: 2 Thus says the L of hosts: CE
1: 3 the word of the L came by the prophet Haggai, G
1: 5 Now therefore thus says the L of hosts: CE
1: 7 Thus says the L of hosts: CE
1: 8 in it and be honored, says the L. B
1: 9 says the L of hosts. BE
1:12 obeyed the voice of the L their God, AP
1:12 as the L their God had sent him; A
1:12 and the people feared the L.
1:13 Then Haggai, the messenger of the L,
1:13 saying, I am with you, says the L. B
1:14 And the L stirred up the spirit of Zerubbabel
1:14 and worked on the house of the L of hosts, EF
2: 1 the word of the L came by the prophet Haggai, G
2: 4 now take courage, O Zerubbabel, says the L; B
2: 4 all you people of the land, says the L; B
2: 4 work, for I am with you, says the L of hosts, BE
2: 6 For thus says the L of hosts: CE
2: 7 with splendor, says the L of hosts. BE
2: 8 and the gold is mine, says the L of hosts. BE
2: 9 be greater than the former, says the L of hosts; BE
2: 9 place I will give prosperity, says the L of hosts. BE
2:10 the word of the L came by the prophet Haggai, G
2:11 Thus says the L of hosts: CE
2:14 and with this nation before me, says the L; B
2:17 yet you did not return to me, says the L. B
2:20 word of the L came a second time to Haggai G
2:23 On that day, says the L of hosts, I will take BE
2:23 says the L, and make you like a signet ring; B
2:23 for I have chosen you, says the L of hosts. BE
Zec 1: 1 word of the L came to the prophet Zechariah G
1: 2 The L was very angry with your ancestors.
1: 3 say to them, Thus says the L of hosts: CE
1: 3 Return to me, says the L of hosts, BE
1: 3 and I will return to you, says the L of hosts. BE
1: 4 "Thus says the L of hosts, CE
1: 4 But they did not hear or heed me, says the L. B
1: 6 "The L of hosts has dealt with us according E

Zec 1: 7 word of the L came to the prophet Zechariah G
1:10 "They are those whom the L has sent to patrol
1:11 the angel of the L who was standing among K
1:12 Then the angel of the L said, K
1:12 the angel of the LORD said, "O L of hosts, E
1:13 Then the L replied with gracious
1:14 Thus says the L of hosts; CE
1:16 Therefore, thus says the L, C
1:16 house shall be built in it, says the L of hosts, BE
1:17 Proclaim further: Thus says the L of hosts: CE
1:17 the L will again comfort Zion
1:20 Then the L showed me four blacksmiths.
2: 5 I will be a wall of fire all around it, says the L, B
2: 6 Flee from the land of the north, says the L; B
2: 6 like the four winds of heaven, says the L. B
2: 8 the L of hosts (after his glory sent me) regarding E
2: 9 you will know that the L of hosts has sent me. E
2:10 I will come and dwell in your midst, says the L. B
2:11 Many nations shall join themselves to the L on
2:11 that the L of hosts has sent me to you. E
2:12 The L will inherit Judah as his portion in
2:13 Be silent, all people, before the L; D
3: 1 before the angel of the L, K
3: 2 And the L said to Satan,
3: 2 the LORD said to Satan, "The L rebuke you,
3: 2 The L who has chosen Jerusalem rebuke you!
3: 5 and the angel of the L was standing by. K
3: 6 Then the angel of the L assured Joshua, saying K
3: 7 "Thus says the L of hosts: CE
3: 9 engrave its inscription, says the L of hosts, BE
3:10 On that day, says the L of hosts, BE
4: 6 "This is the word of the L to Zerubbabel: G
4: 6 but by my spirit, says the L of hosts. BE
4: 8 Moreover the word of the L came to me, G
4: 9 that the L of hosts has sent me to you. E
4:10 "These seven are the eyes of the L,
5: 4 I have sent it out, says the L of hosts, BE
6: 5 after presenting themselves before the L of all D
6: 9 The word of the L came to me: G
6:12 Thus says the L of hosts: CE
6:12 and he shall build the temple of the L. V
6:13 It is he that shall build the temple of the L; V
6:14 as a memorial in the temple of the L. V
6:15 and help to build the temple of the L; V
6:15 that the L of hosts has sent me to you. E
6:15 the voice of the L your God. AP
7: 1 word of the L came to Zechariah on the fourth G
7: 2 to entreat the favor of the L,
7: 3 of the house of the L of hosts and the prophets, EF
7: 4 Then the word of the L of hosts came to me: EG
7: 7 Were not these the words that the L proclaimed
7: 8 The word of the L came to Zechariah, saying: G
7: 9 Thus says the L of hosts: CE
7:12 that the L of hosts had sent by his spirit through E
7:12 Therefore great wrath came from the L of hosts. E
7:13 I would not hear, says the L of hosts, BE
8: 1 The word of the L of hosts came to me, saying: EG
8: 2 Thus says the L of hosts: CE
8: 3 Thus says the L: I will return to Zion, C
8: 3 the L of hosts shall be called the holy mountain. E
8: 4 Thus says the L of hosts: CE
8: 6 Thus says the L of hosts: CE
8: 6 seem impossible to me, says the L of hosts? BE
8: 7 Thus says the L of hosts: CE
8: 9 Thus says the L of hosts: CE
8: 9 the house of the L of hosts. EF
8:11 as in the former days, says the L of hosts. BE
8:14 For thus says the L of hosts: CE
8:14 and I did not relent, says the L of hosts, BE
8:17 for all these are things that I hate, says the L. B
8:18 The word of the L of hosts came to me, EG
8:19 Thus says the L of hosts: CE
8:20 Thus says the L of hosts: CE
8:21 "Come, let us go to entreat the favor of the L,
8:21 and to seek the L of hosts; I myself am going." E
8:22 strong nations shall come to seek the L of hosts E
8:22 and to entreat the favor of the L.
8:23 Thus says the L of hosts: CE
9: 1 The word of the L is against the land of Hadrach G
9: 1 For to the L belongs the capital of Aram,
9:14 Then the L will appear over them,
9:15 The L of hosts will protect them, E
9:16 On that day the L their God will save them A
10: 1 from the L in the season of the spring rain,
10: 1 from the L who makes the storm clouds,
10: 3 for the L of hosts cares for his flock, E
10: 5 they shall fight, for the L is with them,
10: 6 I am the L their God and I will answer them. AH
10: 7 their hearts shall exult in the L.
10:12 I will make them strong in the L,
10:12 and they shall walk in his name, says the L. B
11: 4 Thus said the L my God: A
11: 5 and those who sell them say, "Blessed be the L, T
11: 6 on the inhabitants of the earth, says the L. B
11:11 knew that it was the word of the L. G
11:13 the L said to me, "Throw it into the treasury"—
11:13 into the treasury in the house of the L. F
11:15 Then the L said to me:
12: 1 The word of the L concerning Israel: G
12: 1 Thus says the L, who stretched out the heavens C
12: 4 On that day, says the L, B
12: 5 Jerusalem have strength through the L of hosts, E
12: 7 the L will give victory to the tents of Judah first,
12: 8 the L will shield the inhabitants of Jerusalem so
12: 8 like the angel of the L, at their head. K
13: 2 On that day, says the L of hosts, BE
13: 3 for you speak lies in the name of the L"; I

†LORD distinguishes the proper name of God, *Yahweh,* indicated in the NRSV by "LORD," from the words translated "Lord" and "lord," indexed under the heading *LORD on pages 798-804.

Zec 13: 7 man who is my associate," says the **L** of hosts. BE
13: 8 In the whole land, says the **L**, B
13: 9 and they will say, "The **L** is our God."
14: 1 See, a day is coming for the **L**,
14: 3 Then the **L** will go forth and fight
14: 5 Then the **L** my God will come, A
14: 7 be continuous day (it is known to the **L**),
14: 9 And the **L** will become king over all the earth;
14: 9 on that day the **L** will be one and his name one.
14:12 the **L** will strike all the peoples that wage war
14:13 the **L** shall fall on them, so that each will seize
14:16 the King, the **L** of hosts, and to keep the festival E
14:17 the **L** of hosts, there will be no rain upon them. E
14:18 on them shall come the plague that the **L** inflicts
14:20 on the bells of the horses, "Holy to the **L**."
14:20 And the cooking pots in the house of the **L** shall F
14:21 and Judah shall be sacred to the **L** of hosts, E
14:21 be traders in the house of the **L** of hosts on EF
Mal 1: 1 The word of the **L** to Israel by Malachi. G
1: 2 I have loved you, says the **L**. B
1: 2 not Esau Jacob's brother? says the **L**. B
1: 4 the **L** of hosts says: They may build, but I will E
1: 4 the people with whom the **L** is angry forever.
1: 5 "Great is the **L** beyond the borders of Israel!"
1: 6 says the **L** of hosts to you, O priests, BE
1: 8 says the **L** of hosts. BE
1: 9 says the **L** of hosts. BE
1:10 I have no pleasure in you, says the **L** of hosts, BE
1:11 among the nations, says the **L** of hosts. BE
1:13 and you sniff at me, says the **L** of hosts. BE
1:13 from your hand? says the **L**. B
1:14 for I am a great King, says the **L** of hosts, BE
2: 2 says the **L** of hosts, then I will send the curse BE
2: 4 with Levi may hold, says the **L** of hosts. BE
2: 7 for he is the messenger of the **L** of hosts. E
2: 8 the covenant of Levi, says the **L** of hosts, BE
2:11 for Judah has profaned the sanctuary of the **L**,
2:12 May the **L** cut off from the tents
2:12 or to bring an offering to the **L** of hosts. E
2:14 Because the **L** was a witness between you and
2:16 For I hate divorce, says the **L**, the God of Israel, B
2:16 with violence, says the **L** of hosts. BE
2:17 You have wearied the **L** with your words.
2:17 "All who do evil are good in the sight of the **L**,
3: 1 indeed, he is coming, says the **L** of hosts. BE
3: 3 until they present offerings to the **L**
3: 4 of Judah and Jerusalem will be pleasing to the **L**
3: 5 and do not fear me, says the **L** of hosts. BE
3: 6 For I the **L** do not change;
3: 7 and I will return to you, says the **L** of hosts. BE
3:10 and thus put me to the test, says the **L** of hosts; BE
3:11 field shall not be barren, says the **L** of hosts. BE
3:12 a land of delight, says the **L** of hosts. BE
3:13 spoken harsh words against me, says the **L**. B
3:14 as mourners before the **L** of hosts? DE
3:16 those who revered the **L** spoke with one another.
3:16 The **L** took note and listened,
3:16 of those who revered the **L** and thought
3:17 They shall be mine, says the **L** of hosts, BE
4: 1 shall burn them up, says the **L** of hosts, BE
4: 3 on the day when I act, says the **L** of hosts. BE
4: 5 before the great and terrible day of the **L** comes.
Sir 51:12 *Give thanks to the **L**, for he is good,*
51:12 *Israel, the people close to him. Praise the **L**!* M

*LORD'S‡ (42) [*LORD]

Ge 44: 8 or gold from your **l** house?
44: 9 the rest of us will become my **l** slaves."
44:16 here we are then, my **l** slaves,
44:18 let your servant please speak a word in my **l** ears,
47:18 and the herds of cattle are my **l**.
2Sa 20: 6 take your **l** servants and pursue him,
1Ch 21: 3 my lord the king, all of them my **l** servants?
Da 10:17 How can my **l** servant talk with my lord?
Mal 1:12 when you say that the **L** table is polluted,
Mt 21:42 was the **L** doing, and it is amazing in our eyes'?
Mk 12:11 this was the **L** doing, and it is amazing
Lk 2:26 not see death before he had seen the **L** Messiah.
4:19 to proclaim the year of the **L** favor."
10:39 at the **L** feet and listened to what he was saying.
Ac 2:20 the coming of the **L** great and glorious day.
21:14 to say, "The **L** will be done."
Ro 14: 8 whether we live or whether we die, we are the **L**.
1Co 7:25 as one who by the **L** mercy is trustworthy.
10:26 for "the earth and its fullness are the **L**."
11:20 it is not really to eat the **L** supper.
11:26 you proclaim the **L** death until he comes.
2Co 8:21 to do what is right not only in the **L** sight but also
11:17 I am saying not with the **L** authority,
Gal 1:19 any other apostle except James the **L** brother.
2Ti 2:24 the **L** servant must not be quarrelsome but kindly
1Pe 2:13 For the **L** sake accept the authority
Rev 1:10 I was in the spirit on the **L** day,
Jdt 2:13 of your **l** commands, but carry them out exactly
Wis 11:13 they perceived it was the **L** doing.
Sir 2:14 What will you do when the **L** reckoning comes?
11:17 The **L** gift remains with the devout,
15:11 Do not say, "It was the **L** doing that I fell away";
17:17 but Israel is the **L** own portion.
17:28 those who are alive and well sing the **L** praises.
28: 1 The vengeful will face the **L** vengeance,
33: 8 By the **L** wisdom they were distinguished,
39: 8 and will glory in the law of the **L** covenant.
41: 4 This is the **L** decree for all flesh;
50:13 in their splendor held the **L** offering in their hands
2Mc 13:17 because the **L** help protected him.
2Es 2:33 and refused the **L** commandment.
2:41 implore the **L** authority that your people,

†LORD'S (128) [†LORD]

A. †LORD'S HOUSE (13)
B. †LORD'S ANOINTED (12)
C. †LORD'S OFFERING (12)
D. †LORD'S OFFERINGS (7)

Ex 6:30 But Moses said in the **L** presence,
9:29 so that you may know that the earth is the **L**.
10: 9 because we have the **L** festival to celebrate."
13:12 of your livestock that are males shall be the **L**.
30:14 shall give the **L** offering. C
32:26 and said, "Who is on the **L** side?
35: 5 of a generous heart bring the **L** offering: C
35:21 the **L** offering to be used for the tent of meeting, C
35:24 of silver or bronze brought it as the **L** offering; C
Lev 3:16 All fat is the **L**.
4: 2 in any of the **L** commandments about things not
4:13 of the things that by the **L** commandments ought
4:27 of the things that by the **L** commandments ought
5:17 of the things that by the **L** commandments ought
6:18 from the **L** offerings by fire; D
6:22 shall prepare it; it is the **L**—
7:20 the **L** sacrifice of well-being while in a state
7:21 eats flesh from the **L** sacrifice of well-being,
7:30 Your own hands shall bring the **L** offering C
8:35 keeping the **L** charge so that you do not die;
10:12 the **L** offerings by fire, and eat it unleavened D
21: 6 for they offer the **L** offerings by fire, D
21:21 near to offer the **L** offerings by fire; D
22:27 on it shall be acceptable as the **L** offering C
23: 8 For seven days you shall present the **L** offerings D
23:25 and you shall present the **L** offering by fire. C
23:27 and present the **L** offering by fire; C
23:36 Seven days you shall present the **L** offerings D
23:36 a holy convocation and present the **L** offerings D
27:26 whether ox or sheep, it is the **L**.
27:30 are the **L**; they are holy to the LORD.
Nu 9: 7 the **L** offering at its appointed time among C
9:13 the people for not presenting the **L** offering C
11:23 LORD said to Moses, "Is the **L** power limited?
11:29 Would that all the **L** people were prophets,
16: 9 to perform the duties of the **L** tabernacle,
18:28 and from them you shall give the **L** offering to C
25: 3 and the **L** anger was kindled against Israel.
31: 3 to execute the **L** vengeance on Midian.
31:37 and the **L** tribute of sheep
31:38 of which the **L** tribute was seventy-two.
31:39 of which the **L** tribute was sixty-one.
31:40 of which the **L** tribute was thirty-two persons.
31:50 And we have brought the **L** offering, C
32:10 **L** anger was kindled on that day and he swore,
32:13 And the **L** anger was kindled against Israel,
32:14 to increase the **L** fierce anger against Israel!
Dt 2:15 Indeed, the **L** own hand was against them,
15: 2 because the **L** remission has been proclaimed.
18: 1 the sacrifices that are the **L** portion
26:17 Today you have obtained the **L** agreement:
29:20 **L** anger and passion will smoke against them.
32: 9 the **L** own portion was his people,
34: 5 in the land of Moab, at the **L** command.
Jos 11:20 For it was the **L** doing to harden their hearts so
22:19 into the **L** land where the **L** tabernacle now stands
Jdg 11:31 the Ammonites, shall be the **L**, to be offered up
1Sa 2: 8 For the pillars of the earth are the **L**,
16: 6 the **L** anointed is now before the LORD." B
17:47 the **L** and he will give you into our hand."
18:17 only be valiant for me and fight the **L** battles."
24: 6 the **L** anointed, to raise my hand against him; B
24: 6 for he is the **L** anointed." B
24:10 for he is the **L** anointed.' B
26: 9 who can raise his hand against the **L** anointed, B
26:11 I should raise my hand against the **L** anointed; B
26:16 not kept watch over your lord, the **L** anointed. B
26:23 not raise my hand against the **L** anointed. B
2Sa 1:14 to lift your hand to destroy the **L** anointed?" B
1:16 saying, 'I have killed the **L** anointed.'" B
19:21 because he cursed the **L** anointed?" B
1Ki 18:13 I hid a hundred of the **L** prophets fifty to a cave,
2Ki 11:17 that they should be the **L** people;
13:17 Then he said, "The **L** arrow of victory,
1Ch 28:19 "All this, in writing at the **L** direction,
29:22 they anointed him as the **L** prince,
2Ch 7: 2 the glory of the LORD filled the **L** house. A
19: 6 on behalf of human beings but on the **L** behalf;
23:16 and the king that they should be the **L** people.
Ps 11: 4 the **L** throne is in heaven.
24: 1 The earth is the **L** and all that is in it, the world,
115:16 The heavens are the **L** heavens,
118:23 This is the **L** doing; it is marvelous in our eyes.
137: 4 could we sing the **L** song in a foreign land?
Pr 3:11 do not despise the **L** discipline or be weary
3:33 The **L** curse is on the house of the wicked,
16:11 Honest balances and scales are the **L**;
16:33 but the decision is the **L** alone.
Isa 2: 2 the **L** house shall be established as the highest A
14: 2 as male and female slaves in the **L** land;
40: 2 that she has received from the **L** hand double
44: 5 This one will say, "I am the **L**,"
44: 5 yet another will write on the hand, "The **L**,"
59: 1 See, the **L** hand is not too short to save,
61: 2 to proclaim the year of the **L** favor, and the day
Jer 5:10 strip away her branches, for they are not the **L**.
7: 2 Stand in the gate of the **L** house, A
13:17 because the **L** flock has been taken captive.
19:14 he stood in the court of the **L** house and said A
25:17 So I took the cup from the **L** hand,
26: 2 Stand in the court of the **L** house, A
27:16 of the **L** house will soon be brought back A
28: 3 to this place all the vessels of the **L** house, A
36: 6 of the people in the **L** house you shall read A
36: 8 the words of the LORD in the **L** house. A
36:10 at the entry of the New Gate of the **L** house. A
51: 6 for this is the time of the **L** vengeance;
51: 7 Babylon was a golden cup in the **L** hand,
51:29 for the **L** purposes against Babylon stand,
51:51 into the holy places of the **L** house. A
La 3:66 and destroy them from under the **L** heavens.
4:20 The **L** anointed, the breath of our life, B
Ob 1:21 and the kingdom shall be the **L**.
Mic 2: 7 Is the **L** patience exhausted?
4: 1 the **L** house shall be established as the highest of A
Hab 2:16 cup in the **L** right hand will come around to you,
Zep 1: 8 of the **L** sacrifice I will punish the officials and
1:18 be able to save them on the day of the **L** wrath;
2: 2 there comes upon you the day of the **L** wrath.
2: 3 be hidden on the day of the **L** wrath.
Hag 1: 2 not yet come to rebuild the **L** house. A
1:13 spoke to the people with the **L** message, saying,
2:15 a stone was placed upon a stone in the **L** temple,
2:18 day that the foundation of the **L** temple was laid,
Zec 14: 5 you shall flee by the valley of the **L** mountain,
Mal 1: 7 By thinking that the **L** table may be despised.
2:13 You cover the **L** altar with tears,

LORDED (3) [*LORD]

Ne 5:15 Even their servants **l** it over the people.
Bar 3:16 and those who **l** it over the animals on earth;
2Mc 5:23 who **l** it over his compatriots worse than

LORDLY (2) [*LORD]

Jdg 5:25 she brought him curds in a **l** bowl.
Zec 11:13 this **l** price at which I was valued by them.

LORDS‡ (58) [*LORD]

Ge 19: 2 my **l**, turn aside to your servant's house
19:18 And Lot said to them, "Oh, no, my **l**;
Dt 10:17 LORD your God is God of gods and Lord of **l**,
Jdg 3: 3 the five **l** of the Philistines,
9: 2 "Say in the hearing of all the **l** of Shechem,
9: 3 on his behalf in the hearing of all the **l** of Shechem;
9: 6 Then all the **l** of Shechem
9: 7 you **l** of Shechem, so that God may listen to you.
9:18 king over the **l** of Shechem,
9:20 and devour the **l** of Shechem, and Beth-millo;
9:20 and let fire come out from the **l** of Shechem,
9:23 between Abimelech and the **l** of Shechem;
9:23 and the **l** of Shechem dealt treacherously
9:24 who killed them, and on the **l** of Shechem,
9:25 **l** of Shechem set ambushes on the mountain tops.
9:26 the **l** of Shechem put confidence in him.
9:39 Gaal went out at the head of the **l** of Shechem,
9:46 all the **l** of the Tower of Shechem heard of it,
9:47 Abimelech was told that all the **l** of the Tower
9:51 the **l** of the city fled to it and shut themselves in;
16: 5 **l** of the Philistines came to her and said to her,
16: 8 Then the **l** of the Philistines brought her seven
16:18 she sent and called the **l** of the Philistines,
16:18 Then the **l** of the Philistines came up to her,
16:23 Now the **l** of the Philistines gathered to offer
16:27 all the **l** of the Philistines were there,
16:30 on the **l** and all the people who were in it.
20: 5 The **l** of Gibeah rose up against me,
1Sa 5: 8 and gathered together all the **l** of the Philistines,
5:11 and gathered together all the **l** of the Philistines,
6: 4 to the number of the **l** of the Philistines;
6: 4 upon all of you and upon your **l**.
6:12 and the **l** of the Philistines went after them as far
6:16 When the five **l** of the Philistines saw it,
6:18 of the Philistines belonging to the five **l**,
7: 7 the **l** of the Philistines went up against Israel.
29: 2 As the **l** of the Philistines were passing on
29: 6 Nevertheless the **l** do not approve of you.
29: 7 do nothing to displease the **l** of the Philistines."
Ezr 8:25 his **l**, and all Israel there present had offered;
Ps 136: 3 O give thanks to the Lord of **l**,
Isa 16: 8 the **l** of the nations, reached to Jazer and strayed
26:13 other **l** besides you have ruled over us,
Jer 25:34 roll in ashes, you **l** of the flock,
25:35 and there shall be no escape for the **l** of the flock.
25:36 and the wail of the **l** of the flock!
Da 4:36 My counselors and my **l** sought me out,
5: 1 a great festival for a thousand of his **l**,
5: 2 so that the king and his **l**, his wives,
5: 3 and the king and his **l**, his wives,
5: 9 and his **l** were perplexed.
5:10 she heard the discussion of the king and his **l**,
5:23 in before you, and you and your **l**, your wives
6:17 with his own signet and with the signet of his **l**,
1Co 8: 5 as in fact there are many gods and many **l**—
1Ti 6:15 the King of kings and Lord of **l**.
Rev 17:14 for he is Lord of **l** and King of kings,
19:16 "King of kings and Lord of **l**."

LORDSHIP (KJV) See *LORD IT OVER

LORE (1)

Sir 44: 4 and by their knowledge of the people's **l**;

†**LORD** distinguishes the proper name of God, *Yahweh*, indicated in the NRSV by "LORD," from the words translated "Lord" and "lord," indexed under the heading ***LORD** on pages 798-804.
***LORD'S** distinguishes words translated "Lord's" and "lord's" from the proper name of God, *Yahweh's*, indicated in the NRSV by "LORD's," indexed under the heading †**LORD'S** on this page.

LOSE (46) [LOSERS, LOSES, LOSING, LOSS, LOSSES, LOST]

Ge 27:45 Why should I l both of you in one day?"
Dt 20: 3 Do not l heart, or be afraid, or panic,
Jdg 18:25 and you will l your life and the lives
1Ki 18: 5 and not l some of the animals."
Ecc 3: 6 a time to seek, and a time to l;
Isa 29:21 those who cause a person to l a lawsuit,
Jer 17: 4 By your own act you shall l the heritage
Da 11:30 and he shall l heart and withdraw.
Zep 3: 7 it will not l sight of all that I have brought upon it."
Mt 5:29 it is better for you to l one of your members than
5:30 it is better for you to l one of your members than
10:39 Those who find their life will l it, and those who l their life for my sake will find it.
10:42 truly I tell you, none of these will l their reward."
16:25 For those who want to save their life will l it, and those who l their life for my sake will find it.
Mk 8:35 For those who want to save their life will l it, and those who l their life for my sake,
9:41 the name of Christ will by no means l the reward.
Lk 9:24 For those who want to save their life will l it, and those who l their life for my sake will save it.
9:25 but l or forfeit themselves?
17:33 Those who try to make their life secure will l it, but those who l their life will keep it.
18: 1 about their need to pray always and not to l heart.
Jn 6:39 I should l nothing of all that he has given me,
12:25 Those who love their life l it,
18: 9 not l a single one of those whom you gave me."
Ac 27:34 for none of you will l a hair from your heads."
2Co 4: 1 in this ministry, we do not l heart.
4:16 So we do not l heart.
Eph 3:13 that you may not l heart over my sufferings
Col 3:21 not provoke your children, or they may l heart.
Heb 12: 3 so that you may not grow weary or l heart.
12: 5 or l heart when you are punished by him;
2Pe 3:17 the error of the lawless and l your own stability.
2Jn 1: 8 so that you do not l what we have worked for,
Wis 16: 3 might l the least remnant of appetite because of
Sir 9: 6 or you may l your inheritance.
19: 7 and you will l nothing at all.
20:22 One may l his life through shame, or l it because of human respect.
29:10 L your silver for the sake of a brother or a friend,
2Mc 9:11 he began to l much of his arrogance and to come
3Mc 2:23 and fearing that he would l his life,
2Es 16:41 let the one who buys be like one who will l;

LOSERS (1) [LOSE]

Ex 32:18 or the sound made by l;

LOSES‡ (6) [LOSE]

Lev 13:40 If anyone l the hair from his head,
13:41 If he l the hair from his forehead and temples,
Dt 22: 3 the same with anything else that your neighbor l
Lk 15: 8 if she l one of them, does not light a lamp,
Sir 40:29 One l self-respect with another person's food,
1Es 4:31 if she l her temper with him, he flatters her,

LOSING (3) [LOSE]

Lk 15: 4 having a hundred sheep and l one of them,
Jdt 10:13 and capture all the hill country without l one
Sir 17:24 and he encourages those who are l hope.

LOSS (24) [LOSE]

Ge 31:39 I bore the l of it myself;
Ex 21:19 except to pay for the l of time,
22: 9 clothing, or any other l, of which one party says,
Pr 22:16 and giving to the rich, will lead only to l.
28:22 to get rich and does not know that l is sure
Isa 47: 8 not sit as a widow or know the l of children"—
47: 9 the l of children and widowhood shall come
Da 6: 2 so that the king might suffer no l.
Ac 25:20 I was at a l how to investigate these questions,
27:10 be with danger and much heavy l,
27:21 and thereby avoided this damage and l.
27:22 for there will be no l of life among you,
1Co 3:15 the work is burned up, the builder will suffer l;
Php 3: 7 these I have come to regard as l because
3: 8 as l because of the surpassing value
3: 8 For his sake I have suffered the l of all things,
Tob 4:13 And in idleness there is l and dire poverty,
Wis 18:11 the commoner suffered the same l as the king;
19:17 They were stricken also with l of sight—
Sir 8:12 but if you do lend anything, count it as a l.
20: 9 and a windfall may result in a l.
22: 3 and the birth of a daughter is a l.
32:24 and the one who trusts the Lord will not suffer l.
2Mc 2:26 it is no light matter but calls for sweat and l

LOSSES (2) [LOSE]

Jdt 7: 9 my lord, and your army will suffer no l.
Sir 20:11 There are l for the sake of glory,

LOST‡ (60) [LOSE]

Ge 42:28 At this they l heart and turned trembling
Lev 6: 3 or have found something l and lied about it—
6: 4 or the l thing that you found,
Nu 17:12 we are l, all of us are l!
Dt 31:21 not be l from the mouths of their descendants.
Jos 19:47 When the territory of the Danites was l to them,
1Sa 9:20 As for your donkeys that were l three days ago,
2Sa 22:46 Foreigners l heart, and came trembling out
1Ki 20:25 like the army that you have l, horse for horse,
Job 11:20 all way of escape will be l to them,
Ps 18:45 Foreigners l heart, and came trembling out
119:176 I have gone astray like a l sheep;
Pr 5:23 and because of their great folly they are l.
Ecc 5:14 and those riches were l in a bad venture;
9: 5 and even the memory of them is l.
Isa 6: 5 I am l, for I am a man of unclean lips,
27:13 and those who were l in the land of Assyria
Jer 50: 6 My people have been l sheep;
La 3:54 water closed over my head; I said, "I am l."
Eze 19: 5 that her hope was l, she took another of her cubs
34: 4 you have not sought the l,
34:16 I will seek the l, and I will bring back the strayed,
37:11 and our hope is l; we are cut off completely.'
Mt 5:13 but if salt has l its taste,
10: 6 but go rather to the l sheep of the house of Israel.
15:24 "I was sent only to the l sheep of the house
18:14 in heaven that one of these little ones should be l.
Mk 2:22 the wine will burst the skins, and the wine is l,
9:50 if salt has l its saltiness, how can you season it?
Lk 14:34 "Salt is good; but if salt has l its taste,
15: 4 in the wilderness and go after the one that is l
15: 6 for I have found my sheep that was l.'
15: 9 for I have found the coin that I had l.'
15:24 he was l and is found!'
15:32 he was l and has been found.' "
19:10 Son of Man came to seek out and to save the l."
Jn 6:12 so that nothing may be l."
17:12 not one of them was l except the one destined to be l,
Ac 25:17 So when they met here, I l no time,
27: 9 Since much time had been l and sailing was
2Co 3:10 what once had glory has l its glory because of
Eph 4:19 They have l all sensitivity
Heb 10:39 not among those who shrink back and so are l,
Rev 18:14 all your dainties and your splendor are l to you,
Tob 14: 2 when he l his eyesight,
Jdt 10:10 where they l sight of her.
Sir 2: 8 trust in him, and your reward will not be l.
2:14 Woe to you who have l your nerve!
29:10 and do not let it rust under a stone and be l.
29:14 one who has l all sense of shame will fail him.
41: 2 to one who is contrary, and has l all patience!
2Mc 2:14 the books that had been l on account of the war
1Es 4:26 Many men have l their minds because of women,
2Es 2: 3 but with mourning and sorrow I have l you,
9:20 So I considered my world, and saw that it was l.
10:11 she who l so great a multitude,
10:12 for I have l the fruit of my womb,
14:10 The age has l its youth,

LOT‡ (115) [LOT'S, LOTS]

Ge 11:27 and Haran was the father of L.
11:31 Terah took his son Abram and his grandson L son
12: 4 as the LORD had told him; and L went with him.
12: 5 and his brother's son L, and all the possessions
13: 1 and all that he had, and L with him,
13: 5 Now L, who went with Abram,
13: 8 to L, "Let there be no strife between you and me,
13:10 L looked about him, and saw that the plain of
13:11 So L chose for himself all the plain of the Jordan,
13:11 and L journeyed eastward;
13:12 while L settled among the cities of the Plain
13:14 after L had separated from him,
14:12 they also took L, the son
14:16 also brought back his nephew L with his goods,
19: 1 and L was sitting in the gateway of Sodom.
19: 1 When L saw them, he rose to meet them,
19: 5 to L, "Where are the men who came
19: 6 L went out of the door to the men,
19: 9 Then they pressed hard against the man L,
19:10 inside reached out their hands and brought L into
19:12 the men said to L, "Have you anyone else here?
19:14 So L went out and said to his sons-in-law,
19:15 When morning dawned, the angels urged L,
19:18 And L said to them, "Oh, no, my lords;
19:23 sun had risen on the earth when L came to Zoar.
19:29 and sent L out of the midst of the overthrow,
19:29 he overthrew the cities in which L had settled.
19:30 Now L went up out of Zoar and settled in the hills
19:36 Thus both the daughters of L became pregnant
Lev 16: 8 one l for the LORD and the other l for Azazel.
16: 9 on which the l fell for the LORD, and offer it as
16:10 but the goat on which the l fell for Azazel shall
Nu 26:55 But the land shall be apportioned by l;
26:56 according to l between the larger and the smaller.
33:54 You shall apportion the land by l according
33:54 to the person on whom the l falls;
34:13 This is the land that you shall inherit by l,
36: 2 the land for inheritance by l to the Israelites;
Dt 2: 9 as a possession to the descendants of L."
2:19 because I have given it to the descendants of L."
Jos 14: 2 Their inheritance was by l,
15: 1 The l for the tribe of the people of Judah
17:14 but one l and one portion as an inheritance,
17:17 you shall not have one l only,
18:11 The l of the tribe of Benjamin according
19: 1 The second l came out for Simeon,
19:10 The third l came up for the tribe of Zebulun,
19:17 The fourth l came out for Issachar,
19:24 The fifth l came out for the tribe of Asher
19:32 The sixth l came out for the tribe of Naphtali,
19:40 The seventh l came out for the tribe of Dan,
19:51 of the Israelites distributed by l at Shiloh before
Jos 21: 4 The l came out for the families of the Kohathites.
21: 4 of Aaron the priest received by l thirteen towns
21: 5 of the Kohathites received by l ten towns from
21: 6 by l thirteen towns from the families of the tribe
21: 8 and their pasture lands the Israelites gave by l to
21:10 since the l fell to them first.
Jdg 19:22 a perverse l, surrounded the house,
20: 9 we will go up against it by l.
1Sa 10:20 and the tribe of Benjamin was taken by l.
10:21 and the family of the Matrites was taken by l.
10:21 and Saul the son of Kish was taken by l.
14:41 And Jonathan and Saul were indicated by the l,
14:42 "Cast the l between me and my son Jonathan."
1Ch 6:54 for the l fell to them first—
6:61 To the rest of the Kohathites were given by l out
6:65 also gave them by l out of the tribes of Judah,
24: 5 They organized them by l, all alike,
24: 7 The first l fell to Jehoiarib, the second to Jedaiah,
25: 9 The first l fell for Asaph to Joseph;
26:14 The l for the east fell to Shelemiah.
26:14 and his l came out for the north.
Est 3: 7 they cast Pur—which means "the l"—
3: 7 l fell on the thirteenth day of the twelfth month,
9:24 and had cast Pur—that is "the l"—
Ps 16: 5 and my cup; you hold my l.
49:13 the end of those who are pleased with their l.
83: 8 they are the strong arm of the children of L.
Pr 1:14 Throw in your l among us;
16:33 The l is cast into the lap,
18:18 Casting the l puts an end to disputes and decides
Ecc 3:22 that all should enjoy their work, for that is their l;
5:18 of the life God gives us; for this is our l.
5:19 and to accept their l and find enjoyment
Isa 17:14 and the l of those who plunder us.
34:17 He has cast the l for them,
57: 6 of the valley is your portion; they, they, are your l;
61: 7 and dishonor was proclaimed as their l,
Jer 13:25 This is your l, the portion I have measured out
La 1: 4 her young girls grieve, and her l is bitter.
Eze 21:22 Into his right hand comes the l for Jerusalem,
Da 4:15 and let his l be with the animals of the field in
4:23 and let his l be with the animals of the field,
Jnh 1: 7 So they cast lots, and the l fell on Jonah.
Mic 2: 5 the line by l in the assembly of the LORD.
Zep 2:10 This shall be their l in return for their pride,
Lk 1: 9 by l, according to the custom of the priesthood,
17:28 Likewise, just as it was in the days of L:
17:29 but on the day that L left Sodom,
Ac 1:26 they cast lots for them, and the l fell on Matthias;
2Pe 2: 7 if he rescued L, a righteous man greatly distressed
AdE 3: 7 l fell on the fourteenth day of the month of Adar.
Wis 2: 9 because this is our portion, and this our l.
5: 5 And why is their l among the saints?
8:19 and a good soul fell to my l;
Sir 14:15 what you acquired by toil to be divided by l?
16: 8 He did not spare the neighbors of L,
20:25 but the l of both is ruin.
25:19 may a sinner's l befall her!
37: 8 He may cast the l against you
39: 4 and learns what is good and evil in the human l.
41: 9 and when you die, a curse is your l.
1Mc 3:36 and distribute their land by l.

LOT'S (3) [LOT]

Ge 13: 7 and the herders of L livestock.
19:26 But L wife, behind him, looked back,
Lk 17:32 Remember L wife.

LOTAN (5) [LOTAN'S]

Ge 36:20 L, Shobal, Zibeon, Anah,
36:22 The sons of L were Hori and Heman;
36:29 These are the clans of the Horites: the clans L,
1Ch 1:38 The sons of Seir: L, Shobal, Zibeon, Anah,
1:39 The sons of L: Hori and Homam;

LOTAN'S (2) [LOTAN]

Ge 36:22 and Heman; and L sister was Timna.
1Ch 1:39 and Homam; and L sister was Timna.

LOTHASUBUS (1)

1Es 9:44 Mishael, Malchijah, L, Nabariah, and Zechariah.

LOTHE (KJV) LOATHE, LOATHESOME, UNABLE

LOTS‡ (29) [LOT]

Lev 16: 8 and Aaron shall cast l on the two goats,
Jos 18: 6 and I will cast l for you here before
18: 8 and I will cast l for you here before the LORD
18:10 and Joshua cast l for them in Shiloh before
1Ch 24:31 These also cast l corresponding to their kindred,
25: 8 And they cast l for their duties, small and great,
26:13 and they cast l by ancestral houses,
26:14 They cast l also for his son Zechariah,
Ne 10:34 We have also cast l among the priests,
11: 1 of the people cast l to bring one out of ten to live
Job 6:27 You would even cast l over the orphan,
Ps 22:18 and for my clothing they cast l.
Joel 3: 3 and cast l for my people,
Ob 1:11 and foreigners entered his gates and cast l
Jnh 1: 7 sailors said to one another, "Come, let us cast l,
1: 7 So they cast l, and the lot fell on Jonah.
Na 3:10 l were cast for her nobles,

Mt 27:35 among themselves by casting l;
Mk 15:24 casting l to decide what each should take.
Lk 23:34 And they cast l to divide his clothing.
Jn 19:24 but cast l for it to see who will get it."
19:24 and for my clothing they cast l."
Ac 1:26 they cast l for them, and the lot fell on Matthias;
AdE 3: 7 to a decision by casting l,
9:24 how he made a decree and cast l to destroy them,
9:26 "Purim," because of the l (for in their language this is the word that means "l").
10:10 For this purpose he made two l,
10:11 and these two l came to the hour and moment

LOTUS (2)

Job 40:21 Under the l plants it lies,
40:22 The l trees cover it for shade;

LOUD (109) [ALOUD, LOUD-VOICED, LOUDER, LOUDLY]

Ge 39:14 and I cried out with a l voice;
Ex 11: 6 be a l cry throughout the whole land of Egypt,
12:30 and there was a l cry in Egypt,
19:16 of a trumpet so l that all the people who were in
Lev 25: 9 Then you shall have the trumpet sounded l;
Nu 14: 1 Then all the congregation raised a l cry,
Dt 5:22 These words the LORD spoke with a l voice
27:14 Then the Levites shall declare in a l voice to all
Jdg 5:22 "Then l beat the horses' hoofs with the galloping,
1Sa 28:12 woman saw Samuel, she cried out with a l voice;
2Sa 19: 4 and the king cried with a l voice,
1Ki 8:55 the assembly of Israel with a l voice:
2Ki 18:28 the Rabshakeh stood and called out in a l voice
1Ch 15:16 to raise l sounds of joy.
15:28 and made l music on harps and lyres.
2Ch 15:14 They took an oath to the LORD with a l voice,
20:19 the God of Israel, with a very l voice.
30:21 accompanied by l instruments for the LORD.
32:18 a l voice in the language of Judah to the people
Ezr 3:12 wept with a l voice when they saw this house,
10:12 Then all the assembly answered with a l voice,
Ne 9: 4 of the Levites and cried out with a l voice to
Est 4: 1 wailing with a l and bitter cry;
Ps 33: 3 play skillfully on the strings, with l shouts.
47: 1 shout to God with l songs of joy.
102: 5 of my l groaning my bones cling to my skin.
150: 5 praise him with l clashing cymbals!
Pr 7:11 She is l and wayward; her feet do
9:13 The foolish woman is l;
27:14 Whoever blesses a neighbor with a l voice,
Isa 36:13 the Rabshakeh stood and called out in a l voice
Jer 51:55 and stilling her l clamor.
Eze 3:12 I heard behind me the sound of l rumbling;
3:13 that sounded like a l rumbling.
8:18 and though they cry in my hearing with a l voice,
9: 1 Then he cried in my hearing with a l voice,
11:13 Then I fell down on my face, cried with a l voice,
Zep 1:10 a l crash from the hills.
3:17 he will exult over you with l singing
Mt 2:18 wailing and l lamentation,
24:31 he will send out his angels with a l trumpet call,
27:46 about three o'clock Jesus cried with a l voice,
27:50 Then Jesus cried again with a l voice
Mk 1:26 convulsing him and crying with a l voice,
15:34 At three o'clock Jesus cried out with a l voice,
15:37 Then Jesus gave a l cry and breathed his last.
Lk 1:42 and exclaimed with a l cry,
4:33 and he cried out with a l voice,
17:15 turned back, praising God with a l voice.
19:37 to praise God joyfully with a l voice for all
23:23 But they kept urgently demanding with l shouts
23:46 Then Jesus, crying with a l voice, said, "Father,
Jn 11:43 When he had said this, he cried with a l voice,
Ac 7:57 with a l shout all rushed together against him.
7:60 Then he knelt down and cried out in a l voice,
8: 2 and made l lamentation over him.
8: 7 crying with l shrieks, came out
14:10 said in a l voice, "Stand upright
16:28 But Paul shouted in a l voice,
Heb 5: 7 with l cries and tears, to the one who was able
2Pe 3:10 then the heavens will pass away with a l noise,
Rev 1:10 and I heard behind me a l voice like a trumpet
5: 2 I saw a mighty angel proclaiming with a l voice,
6:10 they cried out with a l voice,
7: 2 and he called with a l voice to
7:10 They cried out in a l voice, saying,
8:13 and I heard an eagle crying with a l voice
11:12 they heard a l voice from heaven saying to them,
11:15 and there were l voices in heaven, saying,
12:10 Then I heard a l voice in heaven, proclaiming,
14: 2 of many waters and like the sound of l thunder;
14: 7 in a l voice, "Fear God and give him glory,
14: 9 a third, followed them, crying with a l voice,
14:15 with a l voice to the one who sat on the cloud,
14:18 with a l voice to him who had the sharp sickle,
16: 1 Then I heard a l voice from the temple telling
16:17 and a l voice came out of the temple,
19: 1 After this I heard what seemed to be the l voice
19:17 with a l voice he called to all the birds that fly
21: 3 And I heard a l voice from the throne saying,
Jdt 7:23 of the town and cried out with a l voice,
7:29 and they cried out to the Lord God with a l voice.
9: 1 Judith cried out to the Lord with a l voice,
13:14 Then she said to them with a l voice,
14:16 with a l voice and wept and groaned and shouted,
14:19 and their l cries and shouts rose up throughout
AdE 4: 3 a l cry of mourning and lamentation among
Sir 8: 3 Do not argue with the l of mouth,
9:18 The l of mouth are feared in their city,
40:13 and crash like a l clap of thunder in a storm.
Sus 1:24 Then Susanna cried out with a l voice,
1:42 Then Susanna cried out with a l voice, and said,
1:46 and he shouted with a l voice,
Bel 1:18 and shouted in a l voice, "You are great, O Bel,
1:41 The king shouted with a l voice, "You are great,
1Mc 2:19 But Mattathias answered and said in a l voice:
2:27 Mattathias cried out in the town with a l voice,
3:54 they sounded the trumpets and gave a l shout.
5:31 with trumpets and l shouts,
13: 8 and they answered in a l voice,
13:45 and they cried out with a l voice,
1Es 5:63 of this one with outcries and l weeping,
9:10 all the multitude shouted and said with a l voice,
3Mc 5:48 and heard the l and tumultuous noise,
5:51 and cried out in a very l voice,
2Es 9:38 she was mourning and weeping with a l voice,
10:26 she suddenly uttered a l and fearful cry,
10:27 I was afraid, and cried with a l voice and said,
12:45 And they wept with a l voice.

LOUD-VOICED (1) [LOUD, VOICE]

Sir 26:27 *A l and garrulous wife is like a trumpet*

LOUDER (2) [LOUD]

Ex 19:19 As the blast of the trumpet grew l and l,

LOUDLY (12) [LOUD]

Ge 45: 2 And he wept so l that the Egyptians heard it,
Ezr 3:13 so l that the sound was heard far away.
Jer 2:15 lions have roared against him, they have roared l.
Mt 9:27 crying l, "Have mercy on us, Son of David!"
20:31 but they shouted even more l,
Mk 5:38 people weeping and wailing l.
10:48 but he cried out even more l, "Son of David,
Lk 18:39 but he shouted even more l, "Son of David,
Jdt 15:14 and all the people l sang this song of praise.
AdE 4: 1 through the street of the city, shouting l:
1Es 5:65 For the multitude sounded the trumpets l,
3Mc 7:16 joyfully and l giving thanks to the one God

LOUNGE (1) [LOUNGERS]

Am 6: 4 and l on their couches, and eat lambs from

LOUNGERS (1) [LOUNGE]

Am 6: 7 and the revelry of the l shall pass away.

LOVE‡ (586) [BELOVED, BELOVED'S, BROTHERLY-LOVING, LOVE-FEASTS, LOVE-SONG, LOVED, LOVER, LOVERS, LOVES, LOVING]

A. STEADFAST LOVE (172)
B. STEADFAST LOVE ENDURES FOREVER (43)
C. STEADFAST LOVE AND ... FAITHFULNESS (16)
D. LOVE ONE ANOTHER (15)
E. LOVE OF *GOD (9)
F. LOVE YOUR/ONE'S NEIGHBOR (9)
G. LOVE THE †LORD (8)
H. LOVE THE *LORD (3)

Ge 22: 2 whom you l, and go to the land of Moriah,
24:12 and show steadfast l to my master Abraham. A
24:14 that you have shown steadfast l to my master." A
24:27 not forsaken his steadfast l and his faithfulness AC
29:20 but a few days because of the l he had for her.
29:32 surely now my husband will l me."
32:10 of all the steadfast l and all the faithfulness AC
39:21 with Joseph and showed him steadfast l; A
Ex 15:13 "In your steadfast l you led A
20: 6 but showing steadfast l to the thousandth A
20: 6 of those who l me and keep my commandments.
21: 5 But if the slave declares, "I l my master,
34: 6 and abounding in steadfast l and faithfulness, AC
34: 7 keeping steadfast l for the thousandth generation, A
Lev 19:18 but you shall l your neighbor as yourself: F
19:34 you shall l the alien as yourself,
Nu 14:18 and abounding in steadfast l, A
14:19 according to the greatness of your steadfast l, A
Dt 5:10 but showing steadfast l to A
5:10 of those who l me and keep my commandments.
6: 5 You shall l the LORD your God G
7: 9 maintains covenant loyalty with those who l him
7:13 he will l you, bless you, and multiply you;
10:12 to walk in all his ways, to l him,
10:15 in l on your ancestors alone and chose you,
10:19 You shall also l the stranger,
11: 1 You shall l the LORD your God, therefore, G
13: 3 know whether you indeed l the LORD your God G
30: 6 so that you will l the LORD your God G
Jos 22: 5 to l the LORD your God, G
23:11 therefore, to l the LORD your God. G
Jdg 14:16 you do not really l me.
16: 4 After this he fell in l with a woman in the valley
16:15 she said to him, "How can you say, 'I l you,'
1Sa 18:22 and all his servants l you;
20:14 show me the faithful l of the LORD;
20:15 never cut off your faithful l from my house,
20:17 Jonathan made David swear again by his l
2Sa 1:26 your l to me was wonderful, passing the l of
2: 6 the LORD show steadfast l and faithfulness AC
2Sa 7:15 But I will not take my steadfast l from him, A
13: 1 and David's son Amnon fell in l with her.
13: 4 Amnon said to him, "I l Tamar,
15:20 the LORD show steadfast l and faithfulness AC
19: 6 for l of those who hate you and for hatred of those who l you.
22:51 and shows steadfast l to his anointed, A
1Ki 3: 6 and steadfast l to your servant my father David, A
3: 6 you have kept for him this great and steadfast l, A
8:23 and steadfast l for your servants who walk A
11: 2 Solomon clung to these in l.
1Ch 16:34 for his steadfast l endures forever. AB
16:41 for his steadfast l endures forever. AB
17:13 I will not take my steadfast l from him, A
2Ch 1: 8 "You have shown great and steadfast l A
5:13 for his steadfast l endures forever," the house, AB
6:14 in steadfast l with your servants who walk A
6:42 Remember your steadfast l A
7: 3 for his steadfast l endures forever." AB
7: 6 for his steadfast l endures forever— AB
19: 2 the wicked and l those who hate the LORD?
20:21 for his steadfast l endures forever." AB
Ezr 3:11 his steadfast l endures forever toward Israel." AB
7:28 and who extended to me steadfast l before A
9: 9 to us his steadfast l before the kings of Persia, A
Ne 1: 5 and steadfast l with those who love him A
1: 5 and steadfast love with those who l him
9:17 slow to anger and abounding in steadfast l, A
9:32 keeping covenant and steadfast l— A
13:22 according to the greatness of your steadfast l. A
Job 10:12 You have granted me life and steadfast l, A
37:13 Whether for correction, or for his land, or for l,
Ps 4: 2 long will you l vain words, and seek after lies?
5: 7 But I, through the abundance of your steadfast l, A
5:11 so that those who l your name may exult in you.
6: 4 deliver me for the sake of your steadfast l. A
13: 5 But I trusted in your steadfast l; A
17: 7 Wondrously show your steadfast l, A
18: 1 I l you, O LORD, my strength.
18:50 and shows steadfast l to his anointed, A
21: 7 through the steadfast l of the Most High he shall A
25: 6 O LORD, and of your steadfast l, A
25: 7 according to your steadfast l remember me, A
25:10 of the LORD are steadfast l and faithfulness, AC
26: 3 For your steadfast l is before my eyes, A
26: 8 O LORD, I l the house in which you dwell,
31: 7 I will exult and rejoice in your steadfast l, A
31:16 save me in your steadfast l. A
31:21 for he has wondrously shown his steadfast l A
31:23 L the LORD, all you his saints. G
32:10 but steadfast l surrounds those who trust in A
33: 5 the earth is full of the steadfast l of the LORD. A
33:18 on those who hope in his steadfast l, A
33:22 Let your steadfast l, O LORD, be upon us, A
36: 5 Your steadfast l, O LORD, A
36: 7 How precious is your steadfast l, O God! A
36:10 O continue your steadfast l A
40:10 your steadfast l and your faithfulness AC
40:11 your steadfast l and your faithfulness keep me AC
40:16 may those who l your salvation say continually,
42: 8 By day the LORD commands his steadfast l, A
44:26 Redeem us for the sake of your steadfast l. A
45: T *Of the Korahites. A Maskil. A l song.*
45: 7 you l righteousness and hate wickedness.
48: 9 We ponder your steadfast l, A
51: 1 O God, according to your steadfast l; A
52: 3 You l evil more than good,
52: 4 You l all words that devour, O deceitful tongue.
52: 8 I trust in the steadfast l of God forever and AE
57: 3 send forth his steadfast l and faithfulness AC
57:10 For your steadfast l is as high as the heavens; A
59:10 My God in his steadfast l will meet me; A
59:16 I will sing aloud of your steadfast l in A
59:17 the God who shows me steadfast l. A
60: 5 so that those whom you l may be rescued.
61: 7 appoint steadfast l and faithfulness to watch AC
62:12 and steadfast l belongs to you, A
63: 3 Because your steadfast l is better than life, A
66:20 rejected my prayer or removed his steadfast l A
69:13 in the abundance of your steadfast l, answer me. A
69:16 O LORD, for your steadfast l is good; A
69:36 and those who l his name shall live in it.
70: 4 Let those who l your salvation say evermore,
77: 8 Has his steadfast l ceased forever? A
85: 7 Show us your steadfast l, O LORD, A
85:10 Steadfast l and faithfulness will meet; AC
86: 5 abounding in steadfast l to all who call on you. A
86:13 For great is your steadfast l toward me; A
86:15 and abounding in steadfast l and faithfulness. AC
88:11 Is your steadfast l declared in the grave, A
89: 1 I will sing of your steadfast l, O LORD, forever; A
89: 2 that your steadfast l is established forever; A
89:14 steadfast l and faithfulness go before you. AC
89:24 faithfulness and steadfast l shall be with him; A
89:28 Forever I will keep my steadfast l for him, A
89:33 but I will not remove from him my steadfast l, A
89:49 where is your steadfast l of old, A
90:14 Satisfy us in the morning with your steadfast l, A
91:14 Those who l me, I will deliver;
92: 2 to declare your steadfast l in the morning, A
94:18 your steadfast l, O LORD, held me up. A
98: 3 remembered his steadfast l and faithfulness AC
100: 5 his steadfast l endures forever, AB
103: 4 who crowns you with steadfast l and mercy, A
103: 8 slow to anger and abounding in steadfast l. A
103:11 so great is his steadfast l A
103:17 the steadfast l of the LORD is from everlasting A

Ps 106: 1 for his steadfast l endures forever. AB
106: 7 not remember the abundance of your steadfast l, A
106:45 according to the abundance of his steadfast l. A
107: 1 for his steadfast l endures forever. AB
107: 8 Let them thank the LORD for his steadfast l, A
107:15 Let them thank the LORD for his steadfast l, A
107:21 Let them thank the LORD for his steadfast l, A
107:31 Let them thank the LORD for his steadfast l, A
107:43 and consider the steadfast l of the LORD. A
108: 4 For your steadfast l is higher than the heavens, A
108: 6 so that those whom you l may be rescued.
109: 4 In return for my l they accuse me,
109: 5 for good, and hatred for my l.
109:21 because your steadfast l is good, deliver me. A
109:26 Save me according to your steadfast l. A
115: 1 sake of your steadfast l and your faithfulness. AC
116: 1 I l the LORD, because he has heard my voice G
117: 2 For great is his steadfast l toward us, A
118: 1 his steadfast l endures forever! AB
118: 2 Israel say, "His steadfast l endures forever." AB
118: 3 "His steadfast l endures forever." AB
118: 4 "His steadfast l endures forever." AB
118:29 he is good, for his steadfast l endures forever. AB
119:41 Let your steadfast l come to me, O LORD, A
119:47 in your commandments, because I l them.
119:48 I revere your commandments, which I l,
119:64 The earth, O LORD, is full of your steadfast l; A
119:76 Let your steadfast l become my comfort A
119:88 In your steadfast l spare my life, A
119:97 Oh, how I l your law!
119:113 I hate the double-minded, but I l your law.
119:119 therefore I l your decrees.
119:124 with your servant according to your steadfast l, A
119:127 Truly I l your commandments more than gold,
119:132 as is your custom toward those who l your name.
119:149 In your steadfast l hear my voice; A
119:159 Consider how I l your precepts;
119:159 preserve my life according to your steadfast l. A
119:163 I hate and abhor falsehood, but I l your law.
119:165 Great peace have those who l your law;
119:167 My soul keeps your decrees; I l them exceedingly.
122: 6 "May they prosper who l you.
130: 7 For with the LORD there is steadfast l, A
136: 1 he is good, for his steadfast l endures forever. AB
136: 2 for his steadfast l endures forever. AB
136: 3 for his steadfast l endures forever; AB
136: 4 for his steadfast l endures forever; AB
136: 5 for his steadfast l endures forever; AB
136: 6 for his steadfast l endures forever; AB
136: 7 for his steadfast l endures forever; AB
136: 8 for his steadfast l endures forever; AB
136: 9 for his steadfast l endures forever; AB
136:10 for his steadfast l endures forever; AB
136:11 for his steadfast l endures forever; AB
136:12 for his steadfast l endures forever; AB
136:13 for his steadfast l endures forever; AB
136:14 for his steadfast l endures forever; AB
136:15 for his steadfast l endures forever; AB
136:16 for his steadfast l endures forever; AB
136:17 for his steadfast l endures forever; AB
136:18 for his steadfast l endures forever; AB
136:19 for his steadfast l endures forever; AB
136:20 for his steadfast l endures forever; AB
136:21 for his steadfast l endures forever; AB
136:22 for his steadfast l endures forever. AB
136:23 for his steadfast l endures forever; AB
136:24 for his steadfast l endures forever; AB
136:25 for his steadfast l endures forever. AB
136:26 for his steadfast l endures forever. AB
138: 2 for your steadfast l and faithfulness; AC
138: 8 your steadfast l, O LORD, endures forever. AB
143: 8 Let me hear of your steadfast l in the morning, A
143:12 In your steadfast l cut off my enemies, A
145: 8 slow to anger and abounding in steadfast l. A
145:20 The LORD watches over all who l him,
147:11 in those who hope in his steadfast l. A
Pr 1:22 O simple ones, will you l being simple?
4: 6 l her, and she will guard you.
5:19 may you be intoxicated always by her l.
7:18 Come, let us take our fill of l until morning;
7:18 let us delight ourselves with l.
8:17 I l those who l me,
8:21 endowing with wealth those who l me,
8:36 all who hate me l death."
9: 8 the wise, when rebuked, will l you.
10:12 Hatred stirs up strife, but l covers all offenses.
13:24 those who l them are diligent to discipline them.
15:17 a dinner of vegetables where l is than a fatted ox
18:21 and those who l it will eat its fruits.
19: 8 To get wisdom is to l oneself;
20:13 Do not l sleep, or else you will come to poverty;
22:11 Those who l a pure heart and are gracious
27: 5 Better is open rebuke than hidden l.
Ecc 3: 8 a time to l, and a time to hate;
9: 1 whether it is l or hate one does not know.
9: 6 Their l and their hate
9: 9 Enjoy life with the wife whom you l,
SS 1: 2 For your l is better than wine,
1: 3 therefore the maidens l you.
1: 4 extol your l more than wine; rightly do they l you.
1: 9 my l, to a mare among Pharaoh's chariots.
1:15 Ah, you are beautiful, my l;
2: 2 lily among brambles, so is my l among maidens.
2: 4 and his intention toward me was l.
2: 5 for I am faint with l.
2: 7 do not stir up or awaken l until it is ready!
2:10 "Arise, my l, my fair one, and come away;
SS 2:13 Arise, my l, my fair one, and come away.
3: 5 do not stir up or awaken l until it is ready!
3:10 its interior was inlaid with l.
4: 1 How beautiful you are, my l, how very beautiful!
4: 7 You are altogether beautiful, my l;
4:10 How sweet is your l, my sister, my bride!
4:10 how much better is your l than wine,
5: 1 Eat, friends, drink, and be drunk with l.
5: 2 "Open to me, my sister, my l, my dove,
5: 8 tell him this: I am faint with l.
6: 4 You are beautiful as Tirzah, my l,
7:12 There I will give you my l.
8: 4 do not stir up or awaken l until it is ready!
8: 6 for l is strong as death, passion fierce as the grave.
8: 7 Many waters cannot quench l,
8: 7 If one offered for l all the wealth of his house,
Isa 16: 5 then a throne shall be established in steadfast l A
43: 4 and I l you, I give people in return for you,
54: 8 with everlasting l I will have compassion on you,
54:10 but my steadfast l shall not depart from you, A
55: 3 my steadfast, sure l for David.
56: 6 to minister to him, to l the name of the LORD,
61: 8 For I the LORD l justice,
63: 7 according to the abundance of his steadfast l. A
63: 9 in his l and in his pity he redeemed them;
66:10 and be glad for her, all you who l her;
Jer 2: 2 I remember the devotion of your youth, your l as
5:31 my people l to have it so,
9:24 I act with steadfast l, justice, A
16: 5 says the LORD, my steadfast l and mercy. A
31: 3 I have loved you with an everlasting l;
32:18 show steadfast l to the thousandth generation, A
33:11 for his steadfast l endures forever!" AB
La 3:22 The steadfast l of the LORD never ceases, A
3:32 according to the abundance of his steadfast l; A
Eze 16: 8 you were at the age for l.
23:17 the Babylonians came to her into the bed of l,
33:32 To them you are like a singer of l songs,
Da 9: 4 and steadfast l with those who love you A
9: 4 and steadfast love with those who l you
Hos 2:19 in steadfast l, and in mercy. A
3: 1 l a woman who has a lover and is an adulteress,
3: 1 they turn to other gods and l raisin cakes."
4:18 they l lewdness more than their glory.
6: 4 Your l is like a morning cloud,
6: 6 For I desire steadfast l and not sacrifice, A
9:15 I will l them no more; all their officials are rebels.
10:12 for yourselves righteousness; reap steadfast l; A
11: 4 with cords of human kindness, with bands of l.
12: 6 you, return to your God, hold fast to l and justice,
14: 4 I will heal their disloyalty; I will l them freely,
Joel 2:13 slow to anger, and abounding in steadfast l, A
Am 4: 5 for so you l to do, O people of Israel!
5:15 Hate evil and l good, and establish justice in
Jnh 4: 2 slow to anger, and abounding in steadfast l, A
Mic 3: 2 and l the evil, who tear the skin off my people,
6: 8 of you but to do justice, and to l kindness,
Zep 3:17 he will renew you in his l;
Zec 8:17 against one another, and l no false oath;
8:19 therefore l truth and peace.
Mt 5:43 shall l your neighbor and hate your enemy.' F
5:44 L your enemies and pray
5:46 For if you l those who l you,
6: 5 for they l to stand and pray in the synagogues
6:24 a slave will either hate the one and l the other,
19:19 also, You shall l your neighbor as yourself." F
22:37 " 'You shall l the Lord your God H
22:39 'You shall l your neighbor as yourself.' F
23: 6 They l to have the place of honor at banquets and
24:12 the l of many will grow cold.
Mk 12:30 you shall l the Lord your God with all your heart, H
12:31 'You shall l your neighbor as yourself.' F
12:33 and 'to l him with all the heart, and with all
12:33 and 'to l one's neighbor as oneself,'— F
Lk 6:27 "But I say to you that listen, L your enemies,
6:32 "If you l those who l you,
6:32 For even sinners l those who l them.
6:35 But l your enemies, do good, and lend,
7:42 Now which of them will l him more?"
7:47 hence she has shown great l.
10:27 "You shall l the Lord your God H
11:42 and neglect justice and the l of God; E
11:43 For you l to have the seat of honor in
16:13 a slave will either hate the one and l the other,
20:46 l to be greeted with respect in the marketplaces,
Jn 5:42 I know that you do not have the l of God in you. E
8:42 "If God were your Father, you would l me,
11: 3 "Lord, he whom you l is ill."
12:25 Those who l their life lose it,
13:34 a new commandment, that you l one another. D
13:34 you also should l one another. D
13:35 if you have l for one another."
14:15 "If you l me, you will keep my commandments.
14:21 and keep them are those who l me;
14:21 and those who l me will be loved by my Father,
14:21 and I will l them and reveal myself to them."
14:23 "Those who l me will keep my word,
14:23 and my Father will l them,
14:24 Whoever does not l me does not keep my words;
14:31 so that the world may know that I l the Father.
15: 9 so I have loved you; abide in my l.
15:10 you will abide in my l,
15:10 my Father's commandments and abide in his l.
15:12 that you l one another as I have loved you. D
15:13 No one has greater l than this,
15:17 so that you may l one another. D
15:19 the world would l you as its own.
Jn 17:26 l with which you have loved me may be in them,
21:15 do you l me more than these?"
21:15 "Yes, Lord; you know that I l you."
21:16 "Simon son of John, do you l me?"
21:16 "Yes, Lord; you know that I l you."
21:17 "Simon son of John, do you l me?"
21:17 to him the third time, "Do you l me?"
21:17 you know everything; you know that I l you."
Ro 5: 5 because God's l has been poured into our hearts
5: 8 But God proves his l for us in that
8:28 for good for those who l God,
8:35 Who will separate us from the l of Christ?
8:39 will be able to separate us from the l of God E
12: 9 Let l be genuine; hate what is evil,
12:10 l one another with mutual affection; D
13: 8 Owe no one anything, except to l one another; D
13: 9 "L your neighbor as yourself." F
13:10 L does no wrong to a neighbor;
13:10 therefore, l is the fulfilling of the law.
14:15 you are no longer walking in l.
15:30 by our Lord Jesus Christ and by the l of
1Co 2: 9 what God has prepared for those who l him"—
4:21 or with l in a spirit of gentleness?
8: 1 Knowledge puffs up, but l builds up.
13: 1 of angels, but do not have l, I am a noisy gong or
13: 2 so as to remove mountains, but do not have l,
13: 3 but do not have l, I gain nothing.
13: 4 L is patient; l is kind; l is not envious or boastful
13: 8 L never ends. But as for prophecies,
13:13 l abide, these three; and the greatest of these is l.
14: 1 Pursue l and strive for the spiritual gifts,
16:14 Let all that you do be done in l.
16:22 Let anyone be accursed who has no l for
16:24 My l be with all of you in Christ Jesus.
2Co 2: 4 but to let you know the abundant l that I have
2: 8 So I urge you to reaffirm your l for him.
5:14 For the l of Christ urges us on,
6: 6 patience, kindness, holiness of spirit, genuine l,
8: 7 in utmost eagerness, and in our l for you—
8: 8 but I am testing the genuineness of your l against
8:24 the proof of your l and of our reason for boasting
11:11 Because I do not l you?
12:15 If I l you more, am I to be loved less?
13:11 and the God of l and peace will be with you.
13:13 The grace of the Lord Jesus Christ, the l of God, E
Gal 5: 6 only thing that counts is faith working through l.
5:13 but through l become slaves to one another.
5:14 "You shall l your neighbor as yourself." F
5:22 By contrast, the fruit of the Spirit is l, joy, peace,
Eph 1: 4 to be holy and blameless before him in l.
1:15 in the Lord Jesus and your l toward all the saints,
2: 4 out of the great l with which he loved us
3:17 as you are being rooted and grounded in l.
3:19 to know the l of Christ that surpasses knowledge,
4: 2 with patience, bearing with one another in l,
4:15 But speaking the truth in l,
4:16 the body's growth in building itself up in l.
5: 2 and live in l, as Christ loved us and gave himself
5:25 l your wives, just as Christ loved the church
5:28 husbands should l their wives
5:33 however, should l his wife as himself,
6:23 the whole community, and l with faith, from God
6:24 Grace be with all who have an undying l
Php 1: 9 that your l may overflow more and more
1:16 These proclaim Christ out of l,
2: 1 any consolation from l, any sharing in the Spirit,
2: 2 be of the same mind, having the same l,
4: 1 my brothers and sisters, whom I l and long for,
Col 1: 4 in Christ Jesus and of the l that you have for all
1: 8 and he has made known to us your l in the Spirit.
2: 2 to be encouraged and united in l,
3:14 Above all, clothe yourselves with l,
3:19 l your wives and never treat them harshly.
1Th 1: 3 of faith and labor of l and steadfastness of hope
3: 6 has brought us the good news of your faith and l.
3:12 the Lord make you increase and abound in l
3:12 just as we abound in l for you.
4: 9 Now concerning l of the brothers and sisters,
4: 9 taught by God to l one another; D
4:10 and indeed you do l all the brothers and sisters
5: 8 and put on the breastplate of faith and l,
5:13 esteem them very highly in l because
2Th 1: 3 and the l of everyone of you
2:10 they refused to l the truth and so be saved.
3: 5 to the l of God and to the steadfastness of Christ. E
1Ti 1: 5 the aim of such instruction is l that comes from
1:14 with the faith and l that are in Christ Jesus.
2:15 provided they continue in faith and l
4:12 an example in speech and conduct, in l, in faith,
6:10 For the l of money is a root of all kinds of evil,
6:11 pursue righteousness, godliness, faith, l,
2Ti 1: 7 a spirit of power and of l and of self-discipline.
1:13 in the faith and l that are in Christ Jesus.
2:22 and pursue righteousness, faith, l, and peace,
3:10 my faith, my patience, my l, my steadfastness,
4:10 in l with this present world,
Tit 2: 2 and sound in faith, in l, and in endurance.
2: 4 the young women to l their husbands,
2: 4 to love their husbands, to l their children,
3:15 Greet those who l us in the faith.
Phm 1: 5 of your l for all the saints and your faith toward
1: 7 and encouragement from your l,
1: 9 yet I would rather appeal to you on the basis of l—
Heb 6:10 and the l that you showed for his sake in serving
10:24 how to provoke one another to l and good deeds,
13: 1 Let mutual l continue.
13: 5 Keep your lives free from the l of money,

Jas 1:12 that the Lord has promised to those who l him.
2: 5 that he has promised to those who l him?
2: 8 "You shall l your neighbor as yourself." F
1Pe 1: 8 Although you have not seen him, you l him;
1:22 to the truth so that you have genuine mutual l,
1:22 l one another deeply from the heart. D
2:17 L the family of believers.
3: 8 have unity of spirit, sympathy, l for one another,
4: 8 Above all, maintain constant l for one another,
4: 8 for l covers a multitude of sins.
5:14 Greet one another with a kiss of l.
2Pe 1: 7 and mutual affection with l.
1Jn 2: 5 the l of God has reached perfection. E
2:15 Do not l the world or the things in the world.
2:15 l of the Father is not in those who l the world;
3: 1 See what l the Father has given us,
3:10 are those who do not l their brothers and sisters.
3:11 that we should l one another. D
3:14 from death to life because we l one another. D
3:14 Whoever does not l abides in death.
3:16 We know l by this, that he laid down his life
3:17 How does God's l abide in anyone who has
3:18 Little children, let us l, not in word or speech,
3:23 of his Son Jesus Christ and l one another, D
4: 7 Beloved, let us l one another, D
4: 7 let us love one another, because l is from God;
4: 8 does not l does not know God, for God is l.
4: 9 God's l was revealed among us in this way:
4:10 In this is l, not that we loved God but
4:11 we also ought to l one another. D
4:12 No one has ever seen God; if we l one another, D
4:12 God lives in us, and his l is perfected in us.
4:16 So we have known and believe the l that God has
4:16 God is l, and those who abide in l abide in God,
4:17 L has been perfected among us in this:
4:18 There is no fear in l, but perfect l casts out fear;
4:18 whoever fears has not reached perfection in l.
4:19 We l because he first loved us.
4:20 Those who say, "I l God,"
4:20 do not l a brother or sister whom they have seen,
4:20 cannot l God whom they have not seen.
4:21 those who l God must l their brothers
5: 2 By this we know that we l the children of God,
5: 2 when we l God and obey his commandments.
5: 3 l of God is this, that we obey his commandments. E
2Jn 1: 1 whom I l in the truth,
1: 3 the Father's Son, in truth and l.
1: 5 from the beginning, let us l one another. D
1: 6 And this is l, that we walk according
3Jn 1: 1 elder to the beloved Gaius, whom I l in truth.
1: 6 they have testified to your l before the church.
Jude 1: 2 May mercy, peace, and l be yours in abundance.
1:21 keep yourselves in the l of God; E
Rev 2: 4 that you have abandoned the l you had at first.
2:19 your l, faith, service, and patient endurance.
3:19 I reprove and discipline those whom I l.
Tob 4:13 So now, my son, l your kindred,
13:10 and l all those within you who are distressed,
13:14 Happy are those who l you,
14: 7 Those who sincerely l God will rejoice,
AdE 13:12 that it was not in insolence or pride or for any l
Wis 1: 1 L righteousness, you rulers of the earth,
3: 9 and the faithful will abide with him in l,
6:12 and she is easily discerned by those who l her,
6:17 and concern for instruction is l of her,
6:18 and l of her is the keeping of her laws,
11:24 For you l all things that exist,
11:26 for they are yours, O Lord, you who l the living.
Sir Pr: 1 with his book those who l learning might make
1:10 he lavished her upon those who l him.
2:15 and those who l him keep his ways.
2:16 and those who l him are filled with his law.
4:10 and he will l you more than does your mother.
4:14 the Lord loves those who l her.
6:33 If you l to listen you will gain knowledge,
7:21 Let your soul l intelligent slaves;
7:30 With all your might l your Maker,
27:17 L your friend and keep faith with him;
34:19 The eyes of the Lord are on those who l him,
40:20 but the l of friends is better than either.
48:11 and were adorned with your l!
Bel 1:38 O God, and have not forsaken those who l you."
1Mc 4:33 down with the sword of those who l you,
2Mc 6:20 even for the natural l of life.
3Mc 2:10 And because you l the house of Israel,
2Es 5:33 Or do you l him more than his Maker does?"
5:40 goal of the l that I have promised to my people."
8:30 but l those who have always put their trust
8:47 of being able to l my creation more than I l it.
4Mc 2:11 It is superior to l for one's wife,
2:12 It takes precedence over l for children,
13:26 they could make their brotherly l more fervent
14: 1 but also mastered the emotions of brotherly l.
14:13 how complex is a mother's l for her children,
14:14 a sympathy and parental l for their offspring.
14:17 in circles around them in the anguish of l,
15: 4 the emotions of parents who l their children?
15: 6 in herself tender l toward them,
15:11 to suffer with them out of l for her children,
15:13 O sacred nature and affection of parental l,
15:23 for the time, her parental l.
15:25 nature, family, parental l,
16: 3 as was her innate parental l,

LOVE-FEASTS (1) [FEAST, LOVE]

Jude 1:12 These are blemishes on your l,

LOVE-SONG (1) [LOVE, SING]

Isa 5: 1 for my beloved my l concerning his vineyard:

LOVED‡ (112) [LOVE]

Ge 24:67 and she became his wife; and he l her.
25:28 Isaac l Esau, because he was fond of game; but Rebekah l Jacob.
27:14 mother prepared savory food, such as his father l.
29:18 Jacob l Rachel; so he said,
29:30 and he l Rachel more than Leah.
34: 3 he l the girl, and spoke tenderly to her.
37: 3 Now Israel l Joseph more than any other
37: 4 that their father l him more than all his brothers,
Dt 4:37 And because he l your ancestors,
7: 8 the LORD l you and kept the oath that he swore
21:15 one of them l and the other disliked,
21:15 both the l and the disliked have borne him sons,
21:16 of the l as the firstborn in preference to the son of
23: 5 because the LORD your God l you.)
1Sa 1: 5 a double portion, because he l her,
16:21 and entered his service. Saul l him greatly,
18: 1 and Jonathan l him as his own soul.
18: 3 because he l him as his own soul.
18:16 But all Israel and Judah l David;
18:20 Now Saul's daughter Michal l David.
18:28 and that Saul's daughter Michal l him,
20:17 for he l him as he l his own life.
2Sa 12:24 and he named him Solomon. The LORD l him,
13:21 because he l him, for he was his firstborn.
1Ki 3: 3 Solomon l the LORD, walking in the statutes
10: 9 Because the LORD l Israel forever,
11: 1 King Solomon l many foreign women along with
2Ch 9: 8 Because your God l Israel
11:21 Rehoboam l Maacah daughter
26:10 the hills and in the fertile lands, for he l the soil.
Est 2:17 the king l Esther more than all the other women;
Job 19:19 and those whom I l have turned against me.
Ps 109:17 He l to curse; let curses come on him.
SS 7: 6 How fair and pleasant you are, O l one,
Isa 57: 8 for yourself with them, you have l their bed,
Jer 2:25 you said, "It is hopeless, for I have l strangers,
8: 2 which they have l and served,
14:10 Truly they have l to wander,
31: 3 I have l you with an everlasting love;
Eze 16:37 all those you l and all those you hated;
Hos 9: 1 You have l a prostitute's pay
9:10 and became detestable like the thing they l.
10:11 Ephraim was a trained heifer that l to thresh,
11: 1 When Israel was a child, I l him,
Mic 7: 5 have no confidence in a l one;
Mal 1: 2 I have l you, says the LORD.
1: 2 But you say, "How have you l us?"
1: 2 says the LORD. Yet I have l Jacob
Mk 10:21 Jesus, looking at him, l him and said,
Jn 3:16 God so l the world that he gave his only Son,
3:19 and people l darkness rather than light
11: 5 though Jesus l Martha and her sister and Lazarus,
11:36 So the Jews said, "See how he l him!"
12:43 for they l human glory more than the glory
13: 1 Having l his own who were in the world, he l them to the end.
13:23 One of his disciples—the one whom Jesus l—
13:34 Just as I have l you, you also should love one
14:21 and those who love me will be l by my Father,
14:28 If you l me, you would rejoice that I am going to
15: 9 As the Father has l me, so I have l you;
15:12 that you love one another as I have l you.
16:27 because you have l me and have believed
17:23 and have l them even as you have l me.
17:24 which you have given me because you l me
17:26 love with which you have l me may be in them,
19:26 and the disciple whom he l standing beside her,
20: 2 the one whom Jesus l, and said to them,
21: 7 That disciple whom Jesus l said to Peter,
21:20 the disciple whom Jesus l following them;
Ro 8:37 are more than conquerors through him who l us.
9:13 "I have l Jacob, but I have hated Esau."
2Co 12:15 If I love you more, am I to be l less?
Gal 2:20 who l me and gave himself for me
Eph 2: 4 out of the great love with which he l us
5: 2 as Christ l us and gave himself up for us,
5:25 just as Christ l the church and gave himself up
2Th 2:16 and God our Father, who l us and
Heb 1: 9 You have l righteousness and hated wickedness;
2Pe 2:15 who l the wages of doing wrong,
1Jn 4:10 In this is love, not that we l God but that he l us
4:11 Beloved, since God l us so much,
4:19 We love because he first l us.
Rev 3: 9 and they will learn that I have l you.
Tob 6:18 through his father's lineage, he l her very much,
AdE 2:17 the king l Esther and she found favor beyond all
14: 2 every part that she l to adorn she covered
Wis 4:10 There were some who pleased God and were l
7:10 I l her more than health and beauty,
8: 2 I l her and sought her from my youth;
16:26 whom you l, O Lord, might learn that it is not
Sir 3:17 then you will be l by those whom God accepts.
7:35 because for such deeds you will be l.
15:13 such things are not l by those who fear him.
47: 8 with all his heart, and he l his Maker.
47:16 and you were l for your peaceful reign.
47:22 or destroy the family line of him who l him.
Bar 3:36 to his servant Jacob and to Israel, whom he l.
2Mc 14:37 to Nicanor as a man who l his compatriots
2Es 3:14 you l him, and to him alone you revealed the end
4:23 why the people whom you l has been given over
5:27 and to this people, whom you have l,
11:42 the truth, and have l liars;
4Mc 13:24 they l one another all the more.
15: 3 She l religion more, the religion
15: 6 more than any other mother, l her children.
15:10 and l their brothers and their mother,

LOVELIEST (1) [LOVELY]

Jer 6: 2 I have likened daughter Zion to the l pasture.

LOVELINESS (1) [LOVELY]

2Es 10:50 the brilliance of her glory, and the l of her beauty.

LOVELY (11) [LOVELIEST, LOVELINESS]

Ge 29:17 Leah's eyes were l, and Rachel was graceful
49:21 Naphtali is a doe let loose that bears l fawns.
2Sa 1:23 Saul and Jonathan, beloved and l!
Ps 84: 1 How l is your dwelling place,
Pr 5:19 a l deer, a graceful doe.
SS 1:16 Ah, you are beautiful, my beloved, truly l.
2:14 for your voice is sweet, and your face is l.
4: 3 like a crimson thread, and your mouth is l.
Hos 9:13 as a young palm planted in a l meadow,
Jdt 8: 7 and was very l to behold.
1Es 4:18 then see a woman l in appearance and beauty,

LOVER‡ (9) [LOVE]

Ps 11: 5 and his soul hates the l of violence.
99: 4 Mighty King, l of justice,
Ecc 5:10 The l of money will not be satisfied with money;
5:10 nor the l of wealth, with gain.
Isa 47: 8 Now therefore hear this, you l of pleasures,
Hos 3: 1 love a woman who has a l and is an adulteress,
1Ti 3: 3 not quarrelsome, and not a l of money.
Tit 1: 8 a l of goodness, prudent, upright, devout,
4Mc 2: 8 even though a l of money,

LOVERS (31) [LOVE]

Jer 2:33 How well you direct your course to seek l!
3: 1 You have played the whore with many l;
3: 2 By the waysides you have sat waiting for l,
4:30 Your l despise you; they seek your life.
22:20 cry out from Abarim, for all your l are crushed.
22:22 and your l shall go into captivity;
30:14 All your l have forgotten you;
La 1: 2 among all her l she has no one to comfort her;
1:19 I called to my l but they deceived me;
Eze 16:33 but you gave your gifts to all your l,
16:36 in your whoring with your l,
16:37 I will gather all your l,
23: 5 she lusted after her l the Assyrians,
23: 9 Therefore I delivered her into the hands of her l,
23:22 against you your l from whom you turned
Hos 2: 5 For she said, "I will go after my l;
2: 7 She shall pursue her l, but not overtake them;
2:10 I will uncover her shame in the sight of her l,
2:12 "These are my pay, which my l have given me."
2:13 and went after her l, and forgot me,
8: 9 Ephraim has bargained for l.
Lk 16:14 The Pharisees, who were l of money,
2Ti 3: 2 For people will be l of themselves, l of money,
3: 4 l of pleasure rather than l of God,
Wis 15: 6 L of evil things and fit for such objects
Sir Pr: 1 also as l of learning be able through the spoken
26:22 *a married woman as a tower of death to her l.*
2Es 15:47 for prostitution to please and glory in your l,
15:51 so that you cannot receive your mighty l.

LOVES‡ (71) [LOVE]

Ge 44:20 of his mother's children, and his father l him.'
Dt 10:18 and who l the strangers, providing them food
15:16 because he l you and your household,
Ru 4:15 for your daughter-in-law who l you,
2Ch 2:11 the LORD l his people he has made you king
Ps 11: 7 he l righteous deeds; the upright shall behold his
33: 5 He l righteousness and justice;
37:28 For the LORD l justice;
47: 4 the pride of Jacob whom he l.
78:68 Mount Zion, which he l.
87: 2 the LORD l the gates of Zion more than all
97:10 The LORD l those who hate evil;
119:140 Your promise is well tried, and your servant l it.
146: 8 the LORD l the righteous.
Pr 3:12 for the LORD reproves the one he l,
12: 1 Whoever l discipline l knowledge,
13: 1 A wise child l discipline,
15: 9 but he l the one who pursues righteousness.
16:13 and he l those who speak what is right.
17:17 A friend l at all times,
17:19 One who l transgression l strife;
21:17 Whoever l pleasure will suffer want;
21:17 whoever l wine and oil will not be rich.
29: 3 A child who l wisdom makes a parent glad,
SS 1: 7 Tell me, you whom my soul l,
3: 1 at night I sought him whom my soul l;
3: 2 I will seek him whom my soul l."
3: 3 "Have you seen him whom my soul l?"
3: 4 when I found him whom my soul l.
Isa 1:23 Everyone l a bribe and runs after gifts.
48:14 The LORD l him; he shall perform his purpose
Hos 3: 1 just as the LORD l the people of Israel,
12: 7 A trader, in whose hands are false balances, he l
Mal 2:11 the sanctuary of the LORD, which he l,
Mt 10:37 Whoever l father or mother more than me is

Mt 10:37 and whoever l son or daughter more than me is
Lk 7: 5 for he l our people, and it is he who built our
7:47 But the one to whom little is forgiven, l little."
Jn 3:35 The Father l the Son and has placed all things
5:20 The Father l the Son and shows him all
10:17 For this reason the Father l me,
16:27 for the Father himself l you,
Ro 13: 8 for the one who l another has fulfilled the law.
1Co 8: 3 but anyone who l God is known by him.
2Co 9: 7 for God l a cheerful giver.
Eph 5:28 He who l his wife l himself.
Heb 12: 6 for the Lord disciplines those whom he l,
1Jn 2:10 Whoever l a brother or sister lives in the light,
4: 7 everyone who l is born of God and knows God.
5: 1 and everyone who l the parent l the child.
Rev 1: 5 To him who l us and freed us from our sins
22:15 and everyone who l and practices falsehood.
AdE 6: 9 the person whom the king l and mount him on
Wis 7:28 for God l nothing so much as
8: 3 and the Lord of all l her.
8: 7 if anyone l righteousness, her labors are virtues;
Sir 3:26 and whoever l danger will perish in it.
4:12 Whoever l her l life,
4:14 the Lord l those who love her.
13:15 Every creature l its like, and every person
30: 1 He who l his son will whip him often,
31: 5 One who l gold will not be justified;
LtJ 6: 9 as they might for a girl who l ornaments.
2Mc 15:14 a man who l the family of Israel and prays much
1Es 4:24 he brings it back to the woman he l.
4:25 man l his wife more than his father or his mother.

LOVING (8) [LOVE]

Dt 11:13 l the LORD your God, and serving him
11:22 l the LORD your God, walking in all his ways,
19: 9 by l the LORD your God and walking always
30:16 by l the LORD your God, walking in his ways,
30:20 l the LORD your God, obeying him,
Isa 56:10 dreaming, lying down, l to slumber.
Tit 3: 4 and l kindness of God our Savior appeared,
Wis 7:22 unpolluted, distinct, invulnerable, l the good,

LOVINGKINDNESS (KJV) See EVERLASTING LOVE, STEADFAST LOVE

LOW‡ (63) [LOWER, LOWERED, LOWERING, LOWEST, LOWING, LOWLAND, LOWLIEST, LOWLINESS, LOWLY]

Ex 11: 8 and bow l to me, saying, 'Leave us,
Jdg 11:35 You have brought me very l;
1Sa 2: 7 he brings l, he also exalts.
2Ki 25:26 high and l and the captains of the forces set out
2Ch 28:19 For the LORD brought Judah l because
Est 1:20 to their husbands, high and l alike."
Job 6: 5 or the ox l over its fodder?
14:10 But mortals die, and are laid l;
14:21 they are brought l, and it goes unnoticed.
40:12 Look on all who are proud, and bring them l;
Ps 49: 2 both l and high, rich and poor together.
62: 9 Those of l estate are but a breath, those
78:31 and laid l the flower of Israel.
79: 8 for we are brought very l.
106:43 and were brought l through their iniquity.
107:39 When they are diminished and brought l
116: 6 when I was brought l, he saved me.
136:23 It is he who remembered us in our l estate,
142: 6 Give heed to my cry, for I am brought very l.
Pr 7:26 for many are those she has laid l,
Ecc 10: 6 and the rich sit in a l place.
12: 4 and the sound of the grinding is l,
12: 4 and all the daughters of song are brought l;
Isa 2: 9 people are humbled, and everyone is brought l—
2:11 The haughty eyes of people shall be brought l,
2:17 and the pride of everyone shall be brought l;
5:15 People are bowed down, everyone is brought l,
10:33 and the lofty will be brought l.
13:11 and lay l the insolence of tyrants.
14: 8 you were laid l, no one comes to cut us down."
14:12 you who laid the nations l!
17: 4 On that day the glory of Jacob will be brought l,
25:11 their pride will be laid l despite the struggle
25:12 laid l, cast to the ground, even to the dust.
26: 5 For he has brought l the inhabitants of the height;
26: 5 the lofty city he lays l.
26: 5 He lays it l to the ground, casts it to the dust.
29: 4 from l in the dust your words shall come;
32:19 and the city will be utterly laid l.
40: 4 and every mountain and hill be made l;
60:14 of those who oppressed you shall come bending l
Jer 49: 8 Flee, turn back, get down l,
Eze 17: 6 and became a vine spreading out, but l;
17:24 I bring l the high tree, I make high the l tree;
21:26 Exalt that which is l, abase that which is high.
Da 4:37 and he is able to bring l those who walk in pride.
Hab 3: 6 the everlasting hills sank l.
Zec 10:11 The pride of Assyria shall be laid l,
Lk 3: 5 and every mountain and hill shall be made l,
1Co 1:28 God chose what is l and despised in the world,
Jas 1:10 and the rich in being brought l,
Jdt 13:20 when our nation was brought l,
Sir 4: 7 bow your head l to the great.
6:12 but if you are brought l,
33:12 but some he cursed and brought l,
Bar 5: 7 and the everlasting hills be made l and
Aza 1:14 and are brought l this day in all the world
2Mc 11:11 and laid l eleven thousand of them
15:27 they laid l at least thirty-five thousand,
2Es 9:45 and looked upon my l estate,
10:22 our harp has been laid l,
11:42 of those who brought forth fruit, and have laid l

LOWER (32) [LOW]

Ge 6:16 make it with l, second, and third decks.
Ex 28:27 in front to the l part of the two shoulder-pieces of
28:33 On its l hem you shall make pomegranates
28:33 purple, and crimson yarns, all around the l hem,
28:34 a pomegranate alternating all around the l hem of
39:20 in front to the l part of the two shoulder-pieces of
39:24 the l hem of the robe they made pomegranates
39:25 the bells between the pomegranates on the l hem
39:26 a bell and a pomegranate all around on the l hem
Dt 3:17 with the l slopes of Pisgah on the east.
28:43 while you shall descend l and l.
Jos 13:27 as far as the l end of the Sea of Chinnereth,
15:19 the upper springs and the l springs.
16: 3 as far as the territory of L Beth-horon,
18:13 on the mountain that lies south of L Beth-horon.
Jdg 1:15 So Caleb gave her Upper Gulloth and L Gulloth.
1Ki 9:17 so Solomon rebuilt Gezer), L Beth-horon,
1Ch 7:24 who built both L and Upper Beth-horon,
2Ch 8: 5 also built Upper Beth-horon and L Beth-horon,
Job 41:24 as hard as the l millstone.
Ps 8: 5 Yet you have made them a little l than God,
Pr 25: 7 than to be put l in the presence of a noble.
Isa 22: 9 and you collected the waters of the l pool.
Eze 40:18 of the gates; this was the l pavement.
40:19 of the l gate to the outer front of the inner court,
42: 5 from them than from the l and middle chambers
42: 6 the ground more than the l and the middle ones.
43:14 the l ledge, two cubits, with a width of one cubit;
Eph 4: 9 but that he had also descended into the l parts of
Heb 2: 7 You have made them for a little while l than
2: 9 who for a little while was made l than the angels,

LOWERED (7) [LOW]

Ge 24:18 and quickly l her jar upon her hand and gave him
44:11 Then each one quickly l his sack to the ground,
Ex 17:11 and whenever he l his hand, Amalek prevailed.
Ac 10:11 being l to the ground by its four corners.
11: 5 being l by its four corners;
27:17 they l the sea anchor and so were driven.
27:30 the sailors tried to escape from the ship and had l

LOWERING (1) [LOW]

Ac 9:25 through an opening in the wall, l him in a basket.

LOWEST (7) [LOW]

Ge 9:25 l of slaves shall he be to his brothers."
1Ki 6: 6 The l story was five cubits wide,
Ne 4:13 So in the l parts of the space behind the wall,
Ps 55:23 you, O God, will cast them down into the l pit;
Lk 14: 9 in disgrace you would start to take the l place.
14:10 you are invited, go and sit down at the l place,
Tob 13: 2 down to Hades in the l regions of the earth,

LOWING (3) [LOW]

1Sa 6:12 along one highway, l as they went;
15:14 and the l of cattle that I hear?"
Jer 9:10 and the l of cattle is not heard;

LOWLAND (8) [LAND, LOW]

Jos 9: 1 the hill country and in the l all along the coast of
10:40 the hill country and the Negeb and the l and
11: 2 and in the l, and in Naphoth-dor on the west,
11:16 the l and the Arabah and the hill country of Israel and its l,
12: 8 in the l, in the Arabah, in the slopes,
15:33 And in the L, Eshtaol, Zorah, Ashnah,
Jdg 1: 9 in the Negeb, and in the l.

LOWLIEST (2) [LOW]

Da 4:17 he gives it to whom he will and sets over it the l
Wis 6: 6 For the l may be pardoned in mercy,

LOWLINESS (1) [LOW]

Lk 1:48 he has looked with favor on the l of his servant.

LOWLY‡ (18) [LOW]

Job 5:11 he sets on high those who are l,
Ps 69:29 But I am l and in pain;
82: 3 maintain the right of the l and the destitute.
138: 6 For though the LORD is high, he regards the l;
Pr 16:19 It is better to be of a l spirit among the poor than
29:23 but one who is l in spirit will obtain honor.
Jer 13:18 "Take a l seat, for your beautiful crown has come
Eze 29:14 and there they shall be a l kingdom.
29:15 It shall be the most l of the kingdoms,
Zep 3:12 in the midst of you a people humble and l.
Lk 1:52 from their thrones, and lifted up the l;
Ro 12:16 do not be haughty, but associate with the l;
Jas 1: 9 Let the believer who is l boast in being raised up,
Jdt 9:11 But you are the God of the l,
AdE 11:11 l were exalted and devoured those held in honor.
Sir 10:14 and enthrones the l in their place.
11:12 he lifts them out of their l condition
2Es 14:13 comfort the l among them,

LOWRING (KJV) THREATENING

LOYAL (17) [LOYALLY, LOYALTY]

Dt 18:13 You must remain completely l to the LORD
33: 8 and your Urim to your l one,
2Sa 22:26 With the l you show yourself l;
Ps 18:25 With the l you show yourself l;
Pr 20: 6 Many proclaim themselves l,
Da 11:32 the people who are l to their God shall stand firm
Php 4: 3 Yes, and I ask you also, my l companion,
1Ti 1: 2 my l child in the faith:
Tit 1: 4 my l child in the faith we share:
AdE 16: 1 and to those who are l to our government,
16:23 for you and the l Persians,
Sir 26: 2 A l wife brings joy to her husband,
51:12 *praise for all his l ones.*
3Mc 3: 7 that these people were l neither to the king nor
4Mc 4: 3 because I am l to the king's government,

LOYALLY (8) [LOYAL]

Ge 21:23 but as I have dealt l with you,
24:49 you will deal l and truly with my master, tell me;
47:29 under my thigh and promise to deal l and truly
2Sa 10: 2 "I will deal l with Hanun son of Nahash, just as his father dealt l with me."
1Ki 2: 7 Deal l, however, with the sons of Barzillai
1Ch 19: 2 "I will deal l with Hanun son of Nahash, for his father dealt l with me."

LOYALTY‡ (22) [LOYAL]

Dt 7: 9 the faithful God who maintains covenant l
7:12 the covenant l that he swore to your ancestors;
Jdg 8:35 not exhibit l to the house of Jerubbaal (that is,
Ru 3:10 this last instance of your l is better than the first;
2Sa 2: 5 because you showed this l to Saul your lord,
3: 8 Today I keep showing l to the house
16:17 "Is this your l to your friend?
1Ki 2: 7 for with such l they met me when I fled
Ps 101: 1 I will sing of l and of justice;
Pr 3: 3 Do not let l and faithfulness forsake you;
14:22 Those who plan good find l and faithfulness.
16: 6 By l and faithfulness iniquity is atoned for,
19:22 What is desirable in a person is l,
20:28 L and faithfulness preserve the king,
Hos 4: 1 There is no faithfulness or l,
Jnh 2: 8 Those who worship vain idols forsake their true l.
Mic 7:20 to Jacob and unswerving l to Abraham,
Sir 46: 7 And in the days of Moses he proved his l,
1Mc 14:35 and l that he had maintained toward his nation.
3Mc 3: 3 continued to maintain goodwill and unswerving l
5:31 to an extraordinary degree a full and firm l
4Mc 7: 9 strengthened our l to the law

LOZON (1)

1Es 5:33 the descendants of Jaalah, the descendants of L,

LUBIM[S] (KJV) See LIBYA, LIBYANS

LUCAS (KJV) See LUKE

LUCIFER (KJV) See DAY STAR

LUCIUS (3)

Ac 13: 1 Simeon who was called Niger, L of Cyrene,
Ro 16:21 so do L and Jason and Sosipater, my relatives.
1Mc 15:16 "L, consul of the Romans,

LUCRE (KJV) See GAIN, MONEY, SORDID GAIN

LUD (6) [LUDIM]

Ge 10:22 Elam, Asshur, Arpachshad, L, and Aram.
1Ch 1:17 Elam, Asshur, Arpachshad, L, Aram, Uz, Hul,
Isa 66:19 to the nations, to Tarshish, Put, and L—
Eze 27:10 Paras and L and Put were in your army,
30: 5 Ethiopia, and Put, and L, and all Arabia,
Jdt 2:23 and L, and plundered all the Rassisites and

LUDIM (3) [LUD]

Ge 10:13 Egypt became the father of L, Anamim,
1Ch 1:11 Egypt became the father of L, Anamim,
Jer 46: 9 Ethiopia and Put who carry the shield, the L,

LUHITH (2)

Isa 15: 5 For at the ascent of L they go up weeping;
Jer 48: 5 at the ascent of L they go up weeping bitterly;

LUKE (3)

Col 4:14 L, the beloved physician, and Demas greet you.
2Ti 4:11 Only L is with me.
Phm 1:24 Aristarchus, Demas, and L, my fellow workers.

LUKEWARM (1) [WARM]

Rev 3:16 So, because you are l, and neither cold nor hot,

LUMINARIES (2)

Ps 74:16 you established the l and the sun.

Wis 13: 2 the l of heaven were the gods that rule the world.

LUMP (3) [LUMPS]
2Ki 20: 7 Then Isaiah said, "Bring a l of figs.
Isa 38:21 Now Isaiah had said, "Let them take a l of figs,
Ro 9:21 the same l one object for special use and another

LUMPS (1) [LUMP]
2Es 2: 9 whose land lies in l of pitch and heaps of ashes.

LUNATICK (KJV) EPILEPTIC, EPILEPTICS

LUNCH (1) [LUNCHEON]
Sus 1:13 "Let us go home, for it is time for l."

LUNCHEON (1) [LUNCH]
Lk 14:12 "When you give a l or a dinner,

LURE (2) [LURED]
Mt 13:22 of the world and the l of wealth choke the word,
Mk 4:19 of the world, and the l of wealth, and the desire

LURED (1) [LURE]
Jas 1:14 one's own desire, being l and enticed by it;

LURK (4) [LURKING, LURKS]
Ps 10: 9 they l in secret like a lion in its covert;
10: 9 they l that they may seize the poor;
56: 6 They stir up strife, they l, they watch my steps.
Hos 13: 7 like a leopard I will l beside the way.

LURKING (2) [LURK]
Ge 4: 7 And if you do not do well, sin is l at the door;
Ps 17:12 like a young lion l in ambush.

LURKS (1) [LURK]
1Sa 23:23 around and learn all the hiding places where he l,

LUST (19) [LUSTED, LUSTFUL, LUSTING, LUSTS, LUSTY]
Nu 15:39 the l of your own heart and your own eyes.
2Sa 13:15 even greater than the l he had felt for her.
Ps 68:30 Trample under foot those who l after tribute;
Isa 57: 5 with l among the oaks, under every green tree;
Jer 2:24 Who can restrain her l?
Eze 16:36 Because your l was poured out
23: 8 and poured out their l upon her.
23:17 and they defiled her with their l;
Mt 5:28 a woman with l has already committed adultery
2Pe 1: 4 the corruption that is in the world because of l,
2:10 those who indulge their flesh in depraved l,
Jude 1: 7 in sexual immorality and pursued unnatural l,
Tob 8: 7 not because of l, but with sincerity.
Sir 23: 6 Let neither gluttony nor l overcome me,
Sus 1: 8 and they began to l for her.
1:14 the other for the reason, they confessed their l.
1:56 and l has perverted your heart.
4Mc 1: 3 that hinder self-control, namely, gluttony and l,
2:15 l for power, vainglory, boasting, arrogance,

LUSTED (8) [LUST]
Jdg 2:17 they l after other gods and bowed down to them.
Eze 23: 5 she l after her lovers the Assyrians,
23: 7 with all the idols of everyone for whom she l.
23: 9 into the hands of the Assyrians, for whom she l.
23:12 She l after the Assyrians,
23:16 When she saw them she l after them,
23:20 and l after her paramours there,
2Es 15:47 who have always l after you.

LUSTFUL (3) [LUST]
Eze 16:26 your l neighbors, multiplying your whoring,
1Th 4: 5 not with l passion, like the Gentiles who do
Sus 1:11 for they were ashamed to disclose their l desire

LUSTING (2) [LUST]
Eze 23:11 yet she was more corrupt than she in her l and
Sir 20: 4 Like a eunuch l to violate a girl

LUSTS (5) [LUST]
Ro 1:24 gave them up in the l of their hearts to impurity,
Eph 4:22 your old self, corrupt and deluded by its l,
2Pe 3: 3 scoffing and indulging their own l
Jude 1:16 they indulge their own l;
1:18 indulging their own ungodly l."

LUSTY (1) [LUST]
Jer 5: 8 They were well-fed l stallions,

LUTE (2) [LUTES]
Ps 92: 3 to the music of the l and the harp,
150: 3 praise him with l and harp!

LUTES (1) [LUTE]
1Mc 4:54 it was dedicated with songs and harps and l

LUXURIANT (1) [LUXURY]
Hos 10: 1 Israel is a l vine that yields its fruit.

LUXURIOUS (1) [LUXURY]
Wis 19:11 when desire led them to ask for l food;

LUXURIOUSLY (1) [LUXURY]
Rev 18: 7 As she glorified herself and lived l,

LUXURY (9) [LUXURIANT, LUXURIOUS, LUXURIOUSLY]
2Sa 1:24 in l, who put ornaments of gold on your apparel.
Pr 19:10 It is not fitting for a fool to live in l,
Lk 7:25 on fine clothing and live in l are in royal palaces.
Jas 5: 5 You have lived on the earth in l and in pleasure;
Rev 18: 3 grown rich from the power of her l."
18: 9 and lived in l with her, will weep and wail
Sir 14: 4 and others will live in l on his goods.
14:16 because in Hades one cannot look for l.
18:32 Do not revel in great l,

LUZ (8) [=BETHEL]
Ge 28:19 but the name of the city was L at the first.
35: 6 Jacob came to L (that is, Bethel),
48: 3 "God Almighty appeared to me at L in the land
Jos 16: 2 to L, it passes along to Ataroth, the territory of
18:13 along southward in the direction of L,
18:13 to the slope of L (that is, Bethel),
Jdg 1:23 to Bethel (the name of the city was formerly L).
1:26 and named it L; that is its name to this day.

LYCAONIA (1) [LYCAONIAN]
Ac 14: 6 cities of L, and to the surrounding country;

LYCAONIAN (1) [LYCAONIA]
Ac 14:11 they shouted in the L language,

LYCIA (2)
Ac 27: 5 we came to Myra in L.
1Mc 15:23 and to Pamphylia, and to L, and to Halicarnassus,

LYDDA (4)
Ac 9:32 he came down also to the saints living in L.
9:35 the residents of L and Sharon saw him and turned
9:38 Since L was near Joppa, the disciples,
1Mc 11:34 and the three districts of Aphairema and L

LYDIA (2) [LYDIA'S]
Ac 16:14 A certain woman named L, a worshiper of God,
1Mc 8: 8 the countries of India, Media, and L.

LYDIA'S (1) [LYDIA]
Ac 16:40 After leaving the prison they went to L home;

LYE‡ (3)
Job 9:30 with soap and cleanse my hands with l,
Isa 1:25 I will smelt away your dross as with l
Jer 2:22 you wash yourself with l and use much soap,

LYING‡ (95) [LIE]
Ge 29: 2 in the field and three flocks of sheep l there
34: 7 an outrage in Israel by l with Jacob's daughter,
49:14 l down between the sheepfolds;
Ex 23: 5 When you see the donkey of one who hates you l
Lev 26:43 and enjoy its sabbath years by l desolate
Nu 21:20 to the valley l in the region of Moab by the top
35:20 or hurls something at another, l in wait,
35:22 or hurls any object without l in wait,
Dt 21: 1 a body is found l in open country,
22:22 If a man is caught l with the wife of another man,
Jdg 3:25 There was their lord l dead on the floor.
4:21 he was l fast asleep from weariness—
4:22 and there was Sisera l dead,
16: 9 While men were l in wait in an inner chamber,
16:12 (The men l in wait were in an inner chamber.)
19:27 there was his concubine l at the door of
Ru 3: 8 and turned over, and there, l at his feet,
1Sa 3: 2 was l down in his room;
3: 3 Samuel was l down in the temple of the LORD,
5: 4 both his hands were l cut off upon the threshold;
26: 5 Saul was l within the encampment,
2Sa 4: 7 while he was l on his couch in his bedchamber;
13: 8 her brother Amnon's house, where he was l down.
1Ki 22:22 and be a l spirit in the mouth of all his prophets.'
22:23 a l spirit in the mouth of all these your prophets;
2Ki 4:32 he saw the child l dead on his bed.
9:16 and went to Jezreel, where Joram was l ill.
2Ch 18:21 and be a l spirit in the mouth of all his prophets.'
18:22 a l spirit in the mouth of these your prophets;
20:24 they were corpses l on the ground;
Job 3:13 Now I would be l down and quiet;
Ps 31:18 the l lips be stilled that speak insolently against
52: 3 and l more than speaking the truth.
109: 2 speaking against me with l tongues.
120: 2 O LORD, from l lips, from a deceitful tongue."
139: 3 You search out my path and my l down,
Pr 6:17 a l tongue, and hands that shed innocent blood,
6:19 a l witness who testifies falsely,
10:18 L lips conceal hatred,
12:19 but a l tongue lasts only a moment.
12:22 L lips are an abomination to the LORD,
21: 6 of treasures by a l tongue is a fleeting vapor and
26:28 A l tongue hates its victims,
30: 8 Remove far from me falsehood and l;
Isa 32: 7 to ruin the poor with l words,
56:10 dreaming, l down, loving to slumber.
59:13 conceiving l words and uttering them from
Jer 14:14 They are prophesying to you a l vision,
23:32 See, I am against those who prophesy l dreams,
29:23 and have spoken in my name l words that I did
La 2:21 The young and the old are l on the ground in
3:10 He is a bear l in wait for me, a lion in hiding;
Eze 13: 6 They have envisioned falsehood and l divination;
13: 7 not seen a false vision or uttered a l divination,
13: 9 who see false visions and utter l divinations;
37: 2 there were very many l in the valley,
Da 2: 9 to speak l and misleading words to me
Hos 4: 2 Swearing, l, and murder,
Mt 3:10 Even now the ax is l at the root of the trees;
8: 6 "Lord, my servant is l at home paralyzed,
8:14 he saw his mother-in-law l in bed with a fever;
9: 2 a paralyzed man l on a bed.
Mk 7:30 So she went home, found the child l on the bed,
Lk 2:12 a child wrapped in bands of cloth and l in
2:16 and the child l in the manger.
3: 9 Even now the ax is l at the root of the trees;
5:25 took what he had been l on,
11:54 l in wait for him, to catch him
Jn 5: 6 When Jesus saw him l there and knew
11:38 It was a cave, and a stone was l against it.
20: 5 to look in and saw the linen wrappings l there,
20: 6 He saw the linen wrappings l there,
20: 7 not l with the linen wrappings but rolled up in
20:12 sitting where the body of Jesus had been l,
Ac 23:21 for more than forty of their men are l in ambush
Ro 9: 1 I am speaking the truth in Christ—I am not l;
2Th 2: 9 who uses all power, signs, l wonders,
1Ti 2: 7 and an apostle (I am telling the truth, I am not l),
Rev 3: 9 that they are Jews and are not, but are l—
Jdt 6:13 they bound Achior and left him l at the foot of
14:18 Look, Holofernes is l on the ground,
Wis 1:11 and a l mouth destroys the soul.
Sir 14:22 and l in wait on her paths;
28:26 and fall victim to one l in wait.
51: 5 from an unclean tongue and l words—
1Mc 5: 3 because they kept l in wait for Israel.
11: 4 and the corpses l about, and the charred bodies
2Mc 3:31 to one who was l quite at his last breath.
4:41 and others took handfuls of the ashes that were l
13:12 and l prostrate for three days without ceasing,
15:28 they recognized Nicanor, l dead, in full armor.
1Es 8:91 weeping and l on the ground before the temple,
2Es 7: 8 There is only one path l between them, that is,
10:30 l there like a corpse, deprived
4Mc 13:15 of eternal torment l before those who transgress

LYRE (26) [LYRES]
Ge 4:21 the ancestor of all those who play the l and pipe.
31:27 with mirth and songs, with tambourine and l.
1Sa 10: 5 tambourine, flute, and l playing in front of them;
16:16 for someone who is skillful in playing the l;
16:23 David took the l and played it with his hand,
18:10 while David was playing the l,
1Ch 25: 3 the l in thanksgiving and praise to the LORD.
Job 21:12 They sing to the tambourine and the l,
30:31 My l is turned to mourning,
Ps 33: 2 Praise the LORD with the l;
57: 8 Awake, O harp and l! I will awake the dawn.
71:22 I will sing praises to you with the l,
81: 2 sound the tambourine, the sweet l with the harp.
92: 3 to the melody of the l.
98: 5 Sing praises to the LORD with the l,
98: 5 with the l and the sound of melody.
108: 2 Awake, O harp and l! I will awake the dawn.
147: 7 make melody to our God on the l.
149: 3 making melody to him with tambourine and l.
Isa 5:12 whose feasts consist of l and harp,
24: 8 the mirth of the l is stilled.
Da 3: 5 pipe, l, trigon, harp, drum,
3: 7 pipe, l, trigon, harp, drum,
3:10 pipe, l, trigon, harp, drum,
3:15 pipe, l, trigon, harp, drum,
Pm 151: 2 My hands made a harp; my fingers fashioned a l.

LYRES (16) [LYRE]
2Sa 6: 5 and l and harps and tambourines and castanets
1Ki 10:12 l also and harps for the singers;
1Ch 13: 8 and l and harps and tambourines and cymbals
15:16 on harps and l and cymbals,
15:21 and Azaziah were to lead with l according to
15:28 and made loud music on harps and l.
16: 5 Obed-edom, and Jeiel, with harps and l;
25: 1 who should prophesy with l, harps, and cymbals.
25: 6 harps, and l for the service of the house of God.
2Ch 5:12 arrayed in fine linen, with cymbals, harps, and l,
9:11 l also and harps for the singers;
20:28 with harps and l and trumpets,
29:25 and l, according to the commandment of David
Ne 12:27 with cymbals, harps, and l.
Isa 30:32 upon him will be to the sound of timbrels and l;
Eze 26:13 the sound of your l shall be heard no more.

LYSANIAS (1)
Lk 3: 1 the region of Ituraea and Trachonitis, and L ruler

LYSIAS‡ (31)
Ac 23:26 "Claudius L to his Excellency the governor Felix,
24:22 "When L the tribune comes down,
1Mc 3:32 He left L, a distinguished man of royal lineage,

1Mc 3:33 L was also to take care of his son Antiochus
3:34 And he turned over to L half of his forces and
3:35 L was to send a force against them to wipe out
3:38 L chose Ptolemy son of Dorymenes,
4:26 and reported to L all that had happened.
4:34 and there fell of the army of L five thousand men;
4:35 When L saw the rout of his troops and observed
6: 6 that L had gone first with a strong force,
6:17 When L learned that the king was dead,
6:17 L had brought him up from boyhood;
6:55 Then L heard that Philip,
7: 2 the army seized Antiochus and L to bring them
2Mc 10:11 appointed one L to have charge of
11: 1 L, the king's guardian and kinsman,
11: 6 and his men got word that L was besieging
11:12 and L himself escaped by disgraceful flight.
11:15 agreed to all that L urged.
11:15 of the Jews which Maccabeus delivered to L
11:16 letter written to the Jews by L was to this effect:
11:16 "L to the people of the Jews, greetings.
11:22 "King Antiochus to his brother L, greetings.
11:35 With regard to what L the kinsman of
12: 1 L returned to the king, and the Jews went
12:27 a fortified town where L lived with multitudes
13: 2 and with him L, his guardian, who had charge of
13: 4 when L informed him that this man was to blame
13:26 L took the public platform,
14: 2 with Antiochus and his guardian L.

LYSIMACHUS (7)

AdE 11: 1 and had been translated by L son of Ptolemy,
2Mc 4:29 Menelaus left his own brother L as deputy in
4:39 in the city by L with the connivance of Menelaus,
4:39 the populace gathered against L,
4:40 L armed about three thousand men and launched
4:41 Jews became aware that L was attacking them,
4:41 threw them in wild confusion at L and his men.

LYSTRA (6)

Ac 14: 6 the apostles learned of it and fled to L and Derbe,
14: 8 In L there was a man sitting who could
14:21 and had made many disciples, they returned to L,
16: 1 Paul went on also to Derbe and to L,
16: 2 He was well spoken of by the believers in L
2Ti 3:11 that happened to me in Antioch, Iconium, and L.

M

MAACAH (22) [ABEL-BETH-MAACAH, BETH-MAACAH, ARAM-MAACAH, MAACATH, MAACATHITE, MAACATHITES]

Ge 22:24 bore Tebah, Gaham, Tahash, and M.
2Sa 3: 3 the third, Absalom son of M,
10: 6 as well as the king of M, one thousand men,
10: 8 and the men of Tob and M,
23:34 Eliphelet son of Ahasbai of M;
1Ki 2:39 to King Achish son of M of Gath.
15: 2 His mother's name was M daughter of Abishalom.
15:10 His mother's name was M daughter of Abishalom.
15:13 He also removed his mother M
1Ch 2:48 M, Caleb's concubine, bore Sheber and Tirhanah.
3: 2 son of M, daughter of King Talmai of Geshur;
7:15 The name of his sister was M.
7:16 M the wife of Machir bore a son,
8:29 and the name of his wife was M.
9:35 Jeiel, and the name of his wife was M.
11:43 Hanan son of M, and Joshaphat the Mithnite,
19: 7 and the king of M with his army,
27:16 for the Simeonites, Shephatiah son of M;
2Ch 11:20 After her he took M daughter of Absalom,
11:21 Rehoboam loved M daughter
11:22 of M as chief prince among his brothers,
15:16 King Asa even removed his mother M

MAACATH (1) [MAACAH]

Jos 13:13 but Geshur and M live within Israel to this day.

MAACATHITE (3) [MAACAH]

2Ki 25:23 and Jaazaniah son of the M.
1Ch 4:19 of Keilah the Garmite and Eshtemoa the M.
Jer 40: 8 Jezaniah son of the M, they and their troops.

MAACATHITES (4) [MAACAH]

Dt 3:14 the Geshurites and the M, and he named them—
Jos 12: 5 to the boundary of the Geshurites and the M,
13:11 and the region of the Geshurites and M,
13:13 not drive out the Geshurites or the M;

MAADAI (1)

Ezr 10:34 Of the descendants of Bani: M, Amram, Uel,

MAADIAH (1) [=MOADIAH]

Ne 12: 5 Mijamin, M, Bilgah,

MAAI (1)

Ne 12:36 Milalai, Gilalai, M, Nethanel, Judah, and Hanani,

MAALEH-ACRABBIM (KJV) See AKRABBIM

MAANI (1)

1Es 5:31 the descendants of Asnah, the descendants of M,

MAAPHA (1)

1Mc 5:35 Next he turned aside to M,

MAARATH (1)

Jos 15:59 M, Beth-anoth, and Eltekon:

MAASAI (1)

1Ch 9:12 son of Malchijah, and M son of Adiel,

MAASEIAH (26)

1Ch 15:18 Unni, Eliab, Benaiah, M, Mattithiah, Eliphelehu,
15:20 Aziel, Shemiramoth, Jehiel, Unni, Eliab, M,
2Ch 23: 1 M son of Adaiah, and Elishaphat son of Zichri.
26:11 by the secretary Jeiel and the officer M,
28: 7 killed the king's son M, Azrikam the commander
34: 8 M the governor of the city,
Ezr 10:18 M, Eliezer, Jarib, and Gedaliah.
10:21 M, Elijah, Shemaiah, Jehiel, and Uzziah.
10:22 Of the descendants of Pashhur: Elioenai, M,
10:30 Adna, Chelal, Benaiah, M, Mattaniah, Bezalel,
Ne 3:23 of M son of Ananiah made repairs
8: 4 Anaiah, Uriah, Hilkiah, and M on his right hand;
8: 7 Sherebiah, Jamin, Akkub, Shabbethai, Hodiah, M,
10:25 Rehum, Hashabnah, M,
11: 5 and M son of Baruch son of Col-hozeh son
11: 7 of Kolaiah son of M son of Ithiel son of Jeshaiah.
12:41 M, Miniamin, Micaiah, Elioenai, Zechariah,
12:42 and M, Shemaiah, Eleazar,
Jer 21: 1 of Malchiah and the priest Zephaniah son of M,
29:21 and Zedekiah son of M, who are prophesying a lie
29:25 and to the priest Zephaniah son of M,
35: 4 above the chamber of M son of Shallum,
37: 3 of Shelemiah and the priest Zephaniah son of M to
1Es 9:19 M, Eliezar, Jarib, and Jodan.
9:21 and Zebadiah and M and Shemaiah and Jehiel
9:22 Of the descendants of Pashhur: Elioenai, M,

MAASMAS (1)

1Es 8:43 I sent word to Eliezar, Iduel, M,

MAATH (1)

Lk 3:26 son of M, son of Mattathias, son of Semein, son

MAAZ (1)

1Ch 2:27 The sons of Ram, the firstborn of Jerahmeel: M,

MAAZIAH (2)

1Ch 24:18 to Delaiah, the twenty-fourth to M.
Ne 10: 8 M, Bilgai, Shemaiah; these are the priests.

MACALON (1)

1Es 5:21 Those from M, one hundred twenty-two.

MACCABEUS (31) [JUDAS]

1Mc 2: 4 Judas called M,
2:66 Judas M has been a mighty warrior from his youth;
3: 1 Then his son Judas, who was called M,
5:24 Judas M and his brother Jonathan crossed
5:34 when the army of Timothy realized that it was M,
8:20 also called M, and his brothers and the people of
2Mc 2:19 The story of Judas M and his brothers,
5:27 But Judas M, with about nine others,
8: 1 Meanwhile Judas, who was also called M,
8: 5 As soon as M got his army organized,
8:16 But M gathered his forces together,
10: 1 Now M and his followers,
10:16 But M and his forces,
10:19 M left Simon and Joseph, and also Zacchaeus
10:21 When word of what had happened came to M,
10:25 M and his men sprinkled dust on their heads
10:30 Two of them took M between them,
10:33 Then M and his men were glad,
10:35 twenty young men in the army of M,
11: 6 When M and his men got word
11: 7 M himself was the first to take up arms,
11:15 M, having regard for the common good,
11:15 in behalf of the Jews which M delivered to Lysias
12:19 who were captains under M,
12:20 But M arranged his army in divisions,
13:24 He received M, left Hegemonides as governor
14: 6 whose leader is Judas M, are keeping up war
14:27 with the covenant and commanding him to send M
14:30 But M, noticing that Nicanor was more austere
15: 7 But M did not cease to trust with all confidence
15:21 M, observing the masses that were in front of him

MACEDONIA (24) [MACEDONIAN, MACEDONIANS]

Ac 16: 9 a man of M pleading with him and saying,
16: 9 "Come over to M and help us."
16:10 we immediately tried to cross over to M,
16:12 which is a leading city of the district of M and
18: 5 When Silas and Timothy arrived from M,
19:21 Paul resolved in the Spirit to go through M
19:22 Timothy and Erastus, to M,
20: 1 and saying farewell, he left for M.
20: 3 and so he decided to return through M.
Ro 15:26 for M and Achaia have been pleased
1Co 16: 5 I will visit you after passing through M—
16: 5 for I intend to pass through M—
2Co 1:16 I wanted to visit you on my way to M,
1:16 to you from M and have you send me on to Judea.
2:13 So I said farewell to them and went on to M.
7: 5 For even when we came into M,
8: 1 that has been granted to the churches of M;
9: 2 of my boasting about you to the people of M,
11: 9 by the friends who came from M.
Php 4:15 that in the early days of the gospel, when I left M,
1Th 1: 7 an example to all the believers in M and in Achaia.
1: 8 the Lord has sounded forth from you not only in M
4:10 love all the brothers and sisters throughout M.
1Ti 1: 3 I urge you, as I did when I was on my way to M,

MACEDONIAN (5) [MACEDONIA]

Ac 27: 2 to sea, accompanied by Aristarchus, a M
AdE 9:24 the M, fought against them,
16:10 a M (really an alien to the Persian blood,
1Mc 1: 1 After Alexander son of Philip, the M,
6: 2 the M king who first reigned over the Greeks.

MACEDONIANS (6) [MACEDONIA]

Ac 19:29 M who were Paul's travel companions.
2Co 9: 4 if some M come with me and find that you are
AdE 16:14 the kingdom of the Persians to the M.
1Mc 8: 5 and King Perseus of the M,
2Mc 8:20 along with four thousand M;
8:20 yet when the M were hard pressed,

MACHBANNAI (1)

1Ch 12:13 Jeremiah tenth, M eleventh.

MACHBENAH (1)

1Ch 2:49 Sheva father of M and father of Gibea;

MACHI (1)

Nu 13:15 from the tribe of Gad, Geuel son of M.

MACHINE (2) [MACHINES]

4Mc 9:20 pieces of flesh were falling off the axles of the m.
9:26 they bound him to the torture m and catapult.

MACHINES (5) [MACHINE]

2Ch 26:15 In Jerusalem he set up m,
1Mc 6:51 m to shoot arrows, and catapults.
9:64 he fought against it for many days and made m
9:67 from the town and set fire to the m of war.
4Mc 7: 4 with many ingenious war m has ever held out

MACHIR (21) [MACHIRITES]

Ge 50:23 the children of M son of Manasseh were also born
Nu 26:29 of M, the clan of the Machirites;
26:29 and M was the father of Gilead;
27: 1 of Gilead son of M son of Manasseh son
32:39 descendants of M son of Manasseh went to Gilead,
32:40 so Moses gave Gilead to M son of Manasseh,
36: 1 of the descendants of Gilead son of M son
Dt 3:15 To M I gave Gilead.
Jos 13:31 of M son of Manasseh according to their clans—
17: 1 To M the firstborn of Manasseh,
17: 3 of Gilead son of M son of Manasseh had no sons,
Jdg 5:14 from M marched down the commanders,
2Sa 9: 4 "He is in the house of M son of Ammiel,
9: 5 and brought him from the house of M son
17:27 and M son of Ammiel from Lo-debar,
1Ch 2:21 of M father of Gilead, whom he married
2:23 All these were descendants of M, father of Gilead.
7:14 she bore M the father of Gilead.
7:15 And M took a wife for Huppim and for Shuppim.
7:16 Maacah the wife of M bore a son,
7:17 These were the sons of Gilead son of M,

MACHIRITES (2) [MACHIR]

Nu 26:29 of Machir, the clan of the M;
Jos 13:31 according to their clans—for half the M.

MACHNADEBAI (1)

Ezr 10:40 M, Shashai, Sharai,

MACHPELAH (6)

Ge 23: 9 he may give me the cave of M, which he owns;
23:17 So the field of Ephron in M,
23:19 in the cave of the field of M facing Mamre (that is,
25: 9 and Ishmael buried him in the cave of M,
49:30 in the cave in the field at M,
50:13 and buried him in the cave of the field at M,

MACRON (1) [PTOLEMY]
2Mc 10:12 Ptolemy, who was called **M,**

MAD (8) [MADDENED, MADDENING, MADLY, MADMAN, MADMEN, MADNESS]
Dt 28:34 and driven **m** by the sight that your eyes shall see.
1Sa 21:13 he pretended to be **m** when in their presence.
21:14 "Look, you see the man is **m;**
Ecc 2: 2 I said of laughter, "It is **m,**" and of pleasure,
Jer 50:38 it is a land of images, and they go **m** over idols.
51: 7 and so the nations went **m.**
Hos 9: 7 "The prophet is a fool, the man of the spirit is **m!**"
2Mc 14: 5 that furthered his **m** purpose when he was invited

MADAI (2)
Ge 10: 2 The descendants of Japheth: Gomer, Magog, **M,**
1Ch 1: 5 The descendants of Japheth: Gomer, Magog, **M,**

MADDENED (1) [MAD]
3Mc 5: 2 **m** by the lavish abundance of drink,

MADDENING (1) [MAD]
4Mc 7: 5 father Eleazar broke the **m** waves of the emotions.

MADE‡ (1466) [MAKE]
Ge 1: 7 So God **m** the dome and separated the waters
1:16 God **m** the two great lights—
1:25 God **m** the wild animals of the earth of every kind,
1:31 God saw everything that he had **m,** and indeed,
2: 4 that the LORD God **m** the earth and the heavens,
2: 9 the ground the LORD God **m** to grow every tree
2:22 the LORD God had taken from the man he **m** into
3: 1 any other wild animal that the LORD God had **m.**
3: 7 and **m** loincloths for themselves.
3:21 the LORD God **m** garments of skins for the man
4:22 who **m** all kinds of bronze and iron tools.
5: 1 he **m** them in the likeness of God.
6: 6 the LORD was sorry that he had **m** humankind on
6: 7 for I am sorry that I have **m** them."
7: 4 and every living thing that I have **m** I will blot out
8: 1 And God **m** a wind blow over the earth,
8: 6 the window of the ark that he had **m**
9: 6 for in his own image God **m** humankind.
13: 4 to the place where he had **m** an altar at the first;
14: 2 these kings **m** war with King Bera of Sodom,
14:23 so that you might not say, 'I have **m** Abram rich.'
15:18 On that day the LORD **m** a covenant with Abram,
17: 5 for I have **m** you the ancestor of a multitude
19: 3 and he **m** them a feast,
19:33 So they **m** their father drink wine that night;
19:35 So they **m** their father drink wine that night also;
21: 8 and Abraham **m** a great feast on the day
21:27 and the two men **m** a covenant.
21:32 When they had **m** a covenant at Beer-sheba,
24:11 He **m** the camels kneel down outside the city by
24:21 or not the LORD had **m** his journey successful.
24:37 My master **m** me swear, saying,
24:56 since the LORD has **m** my journey successful;
26:22 saying, "Now the LORD has **m** room for us,
26:30 So he **m** them a feast, and they ate and drank.
26:35 and they **m** life bitter for Isaac and Rebekah.
27:37 "I have already **m** him your lord,
28:20 Then Jacob **m** a vow, saying,
29:22 the people of the place, and **m** a feast.
31:13 where you anointed a pillar and **m** a vow to me.
31:46 and **m** a heap; and they ate there by the heap.
33:17 and **m** booths for his cattle;
34:29 they captured and **m** their prey.
37: 3 and he had **m** him a long robe with sleeves.
38:25 "It was the owner of these who **m** me pregnant."
38:29 she said, "What a breach you have **m** for yourself!"
39: 4 he **m** him overseer of his house and put him
39: 5 From the time that he **m** him overseer in his house
39:23 and whatever he did, the LORD **m** it prosper.
40:20 he **m** a feast for all his servants,
41:51 "God has **m** me forget all my hardship
41:52 "For God has **m** me fruitful in the land
43:25 they **m** the present ready for Joseph's coming
45: 1 when Joseph **m** himself known to his brothers.
45: 8 he has **m** me a father to Pharaoh,
45: 9 God has **m** me lord of all Egypt;
46:29 Joseph **m** ready his chariot and went up
47:21 he **m** slaves of them from one end of Egypt to
47:26 Joseph **m** it a statute concerning the land of Egypt,
49:24 and his arms were **m** agile by the hands of
50: 5 My father **m** me swear an oath;
50: 6 and bury your father, as he **m** you swear to do."
50:25 So Joseph **m** the Israelites swear, saying,
Ex 1:14 and **m** their lives bitter with hard service in mortar
2:14 "Who **m** you a ruler and judge over us?
5: 8 of bricks as they have **m** previously;
7: 1 "See, I have **m** you like God to Pharaoh,
10: 2 and grandchildren how I have **m** fools of
14: 6 So he had his chariot **m** ready,
15:17 that you **m** your abode, the sanctuary, O LORD,
15:25 the LORD **m** for them a statute and an ordinance
16:31 and the taste of it was like wafers **m** with honey.
20:11 For in six days the LORD **m** heaven and earth,
22: 5 be **m** from the best in the owner's field
22:11 and no restitution shall be **m.**
22:12 if it was stolen, restitution shall be **m** to its owner.
22:13 restitution shall not be **m** for the mangled remains.
22:14 not being present, full restitution shall be **m.**
Ex 24: 8 the blood of the covenant that the LORD has **m**
25:31 The base and the shaft of the lampstand shall be **m**
25:39 shall be **m** from a talent of pure gold.
26:31 it shall be **m** with cherubim skillfully worked
27: 8 be **m** just as you were shown on the mountain.
29:23 one cake of bread **m** with oil, and one wafer,
29:33 the food by which atonement is **m,**
31:17 that in six days the LORD **m** heaven and earth,
32: 5 and Aaron **m** proclamation and said,
32:18 But he said, "It is not the sound **m** by victors, or
the sound **m** by losers;
32:20 He took the calf that they had **m,**
32:20 and **m** the Israelites drink it.
32:31 they have **m** for themselves gods of gold.
32:35 a plague on the people, because they **m** the calf—
32:35 because they made the calf—the one that Aaron **m.**
34:27 with these words I have **m** a covenant with you and
35:29 and women whose hearts **m** them willing
36: 8 the workers **m** the tabernacle with ten curtains;
36: 8 they were **m** of fine twisted linen, and blue, purple,
36:11 He **m** loops of blue on the edge of the outermost
36:11 likewise he **m** them on the edge of the outermost
36:12 he **m** fifty loops on the one curtain, and he **m** fifty
loops on the edge of the curtain
36:13 And he **m** fifty clasps of gold,
36:14 He also **m** curtains of goats' hair for a tent over
the tabernacle; he **m** eleven curtains.
36:17 He **m** fifty loops on the edge of the outermost
36:18 He **m** fifty clasps of bronze to join the tent together
36:19 And he **m** for the tent a covering
36:20 Then he **m** the upright frames for the tabernacle
36:23 The frames for the tabernacle he **m** in this way:
36:24 he **m** forty bases of silver under the twenty frames,
36:25 on the north side, he **m** twenty frames
36:27 rear of the tabernacle westward he **m** six frames.
36:28 He **m** two frames for corners of the tabernacle in
36:29 he **m** two of them in this way, for the two corners.
36:31 He **m** bars of acacia wood,
36:33 He **m** the middle bar to pass through from end
36:34 and **m** rings of gold for them to hold the bars,
36:35 He **m** the curtain of blue, purple,
36:36 For it he **m** four pillars of acacia,
36:37 He also **m** a screen for the entrance to the tent,
37: 1 Bezalel **m** the ark of acacia wood;
37: 2 and **m** a molding of gold around it.
37: 4 He **m** poles of acacia wood,
37: 6 He **m** a mercy seat of pure gold;
37: 7 He **m** two cherubim of hammered gold; at the two
ends of the mercy seat he **m** them,
37: 8 the mercy seat he **m** the cherubim at its two ends.
37:10 He also **m** the table of acacia wood,
37:11 and **m** a molding of gold around it.
37:12 He **m** around it a rim a handbreadth wide, and **m** a
molding of gold around the rim.
37:15 He **m** the poles of acacia wood to carry the table,
37:16 And he **m** the vessels of pure gold that were to be
37:17 He also **m** the lampstand of pure gold.
37:17 The base and the shaft of the lampstand were **m**
37:23 He **m** its seven lamps and its snuffers and its trays
37:24 He **m** it and all its utensils of a talent of pure gold.
37:25 He **m** the altar of incense of acacia wood,
37:26 and he **m** for it a molding of gold all around,
37:27 and **m** two golden rings for it under its molding,
37:28 And he **m** the poles of acacia wood,
37:29 He **m** the holy anointing oil also,
38: 1 He **m** the altar of burnt offering also
38: 2 He **m** horns for it on its four corners;
38: 3 He **m** all the utensils of the altar, the pots,
38: 3 all its utensils he **m** of bronze.
38: 4 He **m** for the altar a grating, a network of bronze,
38: 6 He **m** the poles of acacia wood,
38: 7 he **m** it hollow, with boards.
38: 8 He **m** the basin of bronze with its stand of bronze,
38: 9 He **m** the court; for the south side the hangings of
38:22 **m** all that the LORD commanded Moses;
38:28 he **m** hooks for the pillars, and overlaid their
capitals and **m** bands for them.
38:30 with it he **m** the bases for the entrance of the tent
39: 1 crimson yarns they **m** finely worked vestments,
39: 1 they **m** the sacred vestments for Aaron;
39: 2 He **m** the ephod of gold, of blue, purple,
39: 4 They **m** for the ephod shoulder-pieces,
39: 8 He **m** the breastpiece, in skilled work,
39: 9 It was square; the breastpiece was **m** double,
39:15 They **m** on the breastpiece chains of pure gold,
39:16 and they **m** two settings of gold filigree
39:19 Then they **m** two rings of gold,
39:20 They **m** two rings of gold,
39:22 He also **m** the robe of the ephod woven all
39:24 On the lower hem of the robe they **m** pomegranates
39:25 They also **m** bells of pure gold,
39:27 They also **m** the tunics, woven of fine linen,
39:30 They **m** the rosette of the holy diadem
Lev 2: 7 it shall be **m** of choice flour in oil.
2:11 that you bring to the LORD shall be **m** with leaven,
4:23 the sin that he has committed is **m** known to him,
4:28 sin that you have committed is **m** known to you,
6:21 It shall be **m** with oil on a griddle;
7:25 an animal of which an offering by fire may be **m** to
7:35 and to his sons from the offerings **m** by fire to
10:16 Moses **m** inquiry about the goat of the sin offering,
13:48 or in a skin or in anything **m** of skin,
13:49 in warp or woof or in skin or in anything **m** of skin,
15:17 Everything **m** of cloth or of skin on which
16:17 and has **m** atonement for himself and for his house
16:30 For on this day atonement shall be **m** for you,
19:19 on a garment **m** of two different materials.
Lev 22: 4 Whoever touches anything **m** unclean by a corpse
22: 5 be **m** unclean or any human being
22: 5 by whom he may be **m** unclean—
23:17 each **m** of two-tenths of an ephah;
23:43 so that your generations may know that I **m**
24:12 until the decision of the LORD should be **m** clear
26:13 the bars of your yoke and **m** you walk erect.
Nu 5: 8 of kin to whom restitution may be **m** for the wrong,
5: 8 the ram of atonement with which atonement is **m**
5:27 When he has **m** her drink the water, then,
7: 2 over those who were enrolled, **m** offerings.
8: 4 Now this was how the lampstand was **m,**
8: 4 that the LORD had shown Moses, so he **m**
8:21 and Aaron **m** atonement for them to cleanse them.
11: 8 then boiled it in pots and **m** cakes of it;
14:36 who returned and **m** all the congregation complain
16:47 and **m** atonement for the people.
18: 8 I have given you charge of the offerings **m** to me,
21: 2 Then Israel **m** a vow to the LORD and said,
21: 9 So Moses **m** a serpent of bronze,
21:29 He has **m** his sons fugitives,
22:29 "Because you have **m** a fool of me!
25:13 and **m** atonement for the Israelites.' "
30:10 And if she **m** a vow in her husband's house,
31:16 **m** the Israelites act treacherously against
31:20 every article of skin, everything **m** of goats' hair,
32:13 and he **m** them wander in the wilderness
35:33 and no expiation can be **m** for the land,
Dt 1:28 Our kindred have **m** our hearts melt by reporting,
2:30 and **m** his heart defiant in order to hand him over
4:23 to forget the covenant that the LORD your God **m**
4:28 There you will serve other gods **m**
4:36 From heaven he **m** you hear his voice
5: 2 LORD our God **m** a covenant with us at Horeb.
8:15 He **m** water flow for you from flint rock,
9: 5 in order to fulfill the promise that the LORD **m**
9: 9 the tablets of the covenant that the LORD **m**
9:21 Then I took the sinful thing you had **m,** the calf,
10: 3 So I **m** an ark of acacia wood,
10: 5 and put the tablets in the ark that I had **m;**
10:22 now the LORD your God has **m** you as numerous
11: 4 how he **m** the water of the Red Sea flow over them
22:11 You shall not wear clothes **m** of wool
22:17 now he has **m** up charges against her,
26:19 that he has **m,** in praise and in fame and in honor;
28:51 until it has **m** you perish.
29: 1 to the covenant that he had **m** with them at Horeb.
29:25 which he **m** with them when he brought them out
31:16 breaking my covenant that I have **m** with them.
32: 6 who created you, who **m** you and established you?
32:15 He abandoned God who **m** him,
32:16 They **m** him jealous with strange gods,
32:21 They **m** me jealous with what is no god,
Jos 2:17 from this oath that you have **m** us swear to you
2:20 be released from this oath that you **m** us swear
5: 3 So Joshua **m** flint knives, and circumcised
8:15 and all Israel **m** a pretense of being beaten
8:28 Joshua burned Ai, and **m** it forever a heap of ruins,
9:15 And Joshua **m** peace with them,
9:16 But when three days had passed after they had **m**
9:27 But on that day Joshua **m** them hewers of wood
10: 1 the inhabitants of Gibeon had **m** peace with Israel
10: 4 it has **m** peace with Joshua and with the Israelites."
10: 5 and camped against Gibeon, and **m** war against it.
11:18 Joshua **m** war a long time with all those kings.
11:19 that **m** peace with the Israelites, except the Hivites,
14: 8 But my companions who went up with me **m**
16:10 to this day but have been **m** to do forced labor.
17: 1 Then allotment was **m** to the tribe of Manasseh,
17: 2 And allotments were **m** to the rest of the tribe
21:45 the LORD had **m** to the house of Israel had failed;
22:25 For the LORD has **m** the Jordan a boundary
22:28 which our ancestors **m,** not for burnt offerings,
24: 3 the land of Canaan and **m** his offspring many.
24: 7 and **m** the sea come upon them and cover them;
24:25 So Joshua **m** a covenant with the people that day,
24:25 **m** statutes and ordinances for them at Shechem.
Jdg 3:16 Ehud **m** for himself a sword with two edges,
8: 8 and **m** the same request of them;
8:27 Gideon **m** an ephod of it and put it in his town,
9: 6 and they went and **m** Abimelech king,
9:16 and honor when you **m** Abimelech king,
9:18 seventy men on one stone, and have **m** Abimelech,
9:38 Are not these the troops you **m** light of?
9:57 and God also **m** all the wickedness of the people
11: 4 After a time the Ammonites **m** war against Israel.
11: 5 And when the Ammonites **m** war against Israel,
11:11 the people **m** him head and commander over them;
11:30 And Jephthah **m** a vow to the LORD, and said,
11:39 who did with her according to the vow he had **m.**
14:10 and Samson **m** a feast there as
15: 9 and **m** a raid on Lehi.
16:14 and **m** them tight with the pin.
16:25 They **m** him stand between the pillars;
17: 4 who **m** it into an idol of cast metal;
17: 5 and he **m** an ephod and teraphim,
18:24 He replied, "You take my gods that I **m,**
18:27 The Danites, having taken what Micah had **m,**
18:31 as their own Micah's idol that he had **m,**
19: 4 His father-in-law, the girl's father, **m** him stay,
21:15 on Benjamin because the LORD had **m** a breach
Ru 4:13 they came together, the LORD **m** her conceive,
1Sa 1:11 She **m** this vow: "O LORD of hosts,
1:17 of Israel grant the petition you have **m** to him."
1:27 the LORD has granted me the petition that I **m**
2:20 with children by this woman for the gift that she **m**
6: 6 After he had **m** fools of them,

1Sa 6:19 because the LORD had **m** a great slaughter among
8: 1 he **m** his sons judges over Israel.
11:15 and there they **m** Saul king before the LORD
15:11 "I regret that I **m** Saul king,
15:33 "As your sword has **m** women childless,
15:35 And the LORD was sorry that he had **m** Saul king
16: 8 and **m** him pass before Samuel.
16: 9 Then Jesse **m** Shammah pass by.
16:10 Jesse **m** seven of his sons pass before Samuel,
18: 3 Then Jonathan **m** a covenant with David,
18: 7 the women sang to one another as they **m** merry,
18:13 and **m** him a commander of a thousand;
20:16 Thus Jonathan **m** a covenant with the house
20:17 Jonathan **m** David swear again by his love for him;
21: 2 I have **m** an appointment with the young men
23:18 the two of them **m** a covenant before the LORD;
23:27 for the Philistines have **m** a raid on the land."
26:21 I have been a fool, and have **m** a great mistake."
27: 8 up and **m** raids on the Geshurites, the Girzites,
27:10 "Against whom have you **m** a raid today?"
27:12 "He has **m** himself utterly abhorrent
30: 1 the Amalekites had **m** a raid on the Negeb and
30:14 We had **m** a raid on the Negeb of the Cherethites
30:25 that day forward he **m** it a statute and an ordinance
2Sa 2: 9 He **m** him king over Gilead, the Ashurites, Jezreel,
3: 8 The words of Ishbaal **m** Abner very angry;
3:20 David **m** a feast for Abner and the men who were
5: 3 and King David **m** a covenant with them at Hebron
7:16 and your kingdom shall be **m** sure forever
7:27 have **m** this revelation to your servant, saying,
10:19 that they had been defeated by Israel, they **m** peace
11:13 to eat and drink in his presence and **m** him drunk;
11:26 she **m** lamentation for him.
13: 2 that he **m** himself ill because of his sister Tamar,
13: 8 She took dough, kneaded it, **m** cakes in his sight,
13:10 So Tamar took the cakes she had **m**,
13:27 Absalom **m** a feast like a king's feast.
14:15 the king because the people have **m** me afraid;
15: 7 and pay the vow that I have **m** to the LORD.
15: 8 For your servant **m** a vow while I lived at Geshur
16:21 that you have **m** yourself odious to your father,
19: 6 You have **m** it clear today that commanders
22:12 He **m** darkness around him a canopy, thick clouds,
22:34 He **m** my feet like the feet of deer,
22:36 and your help has **m** me great.
22:37 You have **m** me stride freely,
22:40 you **m** my assailants sink under me.
22:41 You **m** my enemies turn their backs to me,
23: 5 For he has **m** with me an everlasting covenant,
1Ki 1:43 "No, for our lord King David has **m** Solomon king;
2:24 and who has **m** me a house as he promised,
3: 1 Solomon **m** a marriage alliance with Pharaoh king
3: 7 you have **m** your servant king in place
5:12 and the two of them **m** a treaty.
6: 4 For the house he **m** windows with recessed frames.
6: 5 and he **m** side chambers all around.
6: 6 for around the outside of the house he **m** offsets on
6:12 which I **m** to your father David.
6:23 In the inner sanctuary he **m** two cherubim
6:31 For the entrance to the inner sanctuary he **m** doors
6:33 So also he **m** for the entrance to the nave doorposts
7: 6 He **m** the Hall of Pillars fifty cubits long
7: 7 He **m** the Hall of the Throne where he was
7: 8 Solomon also **m** a house like this hall
7: 9 All these were **m** of costly stones,
7:16 He also **m** two capitals of molten bronze,
7:18 He **m** the columns with two rows
7:23 Then he **m** the molten sea;
7:26 its brim was **m** like the brim of a cup,
7:27 He also **m** the ten stands of bronze;
7:31 its opening was round, as a pedestal is **m**;
7:33 The wheels were **m** like a chariot wheel;
7:37 In this way he **m** the ten stands;
7:38 He **m** ten basins of bronze;
7:40 Hiram also **m** the pots, the shovels, and the basins.
7:45 all these vessels that Hiram **m** for King Solomon
7:48 So Solomon **m** all the vessels that were in
8: 7 cherubim **m** a covering above the ark and its poles.
8: 9 where the LORD **m** a covenant with the Israelites,
8:20 the LORD has upheld the promise that he **m**;
8:21 in which is the covenant of the LORD that he **m**
9: 3 and your plea, which you **m** before me;
9:22 But of the Israelites Solomon **m** no slaves;
10: 9 he has **m** you king to execute justice
10:12 the almug wood the king **m** supports for the house
10:16 King Solomon **m** two hundred large shields
10:17 He **m** three hundred shields of beaten gold;
10:18 The king also **m** a great ivory throne,
10:20 Nothing like it was ever **m** in any kingdom.
10:27 king **m** silver as common in Jerusalem as stones,
10:27 and he **m** cedars as numerous as the sycamores of
11:24 settled there, and **m** him king in Damascus.
12: 4 "Your father **m** our yoke heavy.
12:10 'Your father **m** our yoke heavy,
12:14 "My father **m** your yoke heavy,
12:20 and called him to the assembly and **m** him king
12:28 the king took counsel, and **m** two calves of gold.
12:31 He also **m** houses on high places,
12:32 sacrificing to the calves that he had **m**.
12:32 the priests of the high places that he had **m**.
12:33 He went up to the altar that he had **m** in Bethel on
13:33 but **m** priests for the high places again from
14: 7 **m** you leader over my people Israel,
14: 9 and have gone and **m** for yourself other gods,
14:15 because they have **m** their sacred poles,
14:26 the shields of gold that Solomon had **m**;
14:27 so King Rehoboam **m** shields of bronze instead,
1Ki 15:12 and removed all the idols that his ancestors had **m**.
15:13 she had **m** an abominable image for Asherah;
15:22 Then King Asa **m** a proclamation to all Judah,
16: 2 of the dust and **m** you leader over my people Israel,
16:16 therefore all Israel **m** Omri,
16:20 and the conspiracy that he **m**,
16:33 Ahab also **m** a sacred pole.
18:26 They limped about the altar that they had **m**.
18:32 Then he **m** a trench around the altar,
20:34 So he **m** a treaty with him and let him go.
22:11 Zedekiah son of Chenaanah **m** for himself horns
22:44 Jehoshaphat also **m** peace with the king of Israel.
22:48 Jehoshaphat **m** ships of the Tarshish type to go
2Ki 2:21 I have **m** this water wholesome;
3: 2 he removed the pillar of Baal that his father had **m**.
3: 9 they had **m** a roundabout march of seven days,
6: 6 and threw it in there, and **m** the iron float.
10:27 and **m** it a latrine to this day.
11: 4 He **m** a covenant with them and put them
11:17 Jehoiada **m** a covenant between the LORD and
12: 6 of King Jehoash the priests had **m** no repairs on
12: 9 the priest Jehoiada took a chest, **m** a hole in its lid,
12:13 were **m** from the money that was brought into
13: 7 the king of Aram had destroyed them and **m** them
13:17 the Arameans in Aphek until you have **m** an end
13:19 down Aram until you had **m** an end of it,
14: 4 the people still sacrificed and **m** offerings on
14:19 They **m** a conspiracy against him in Jerusalem,
14:21 and **m** him king to succeed his father Amaziah.
15: 4 the people still sacrificed and **m** offerings on
15:15 including the conspiracy that he **m**,
15:30 of Elah **m** a conspiracy against Pekah son
15:35 the people still sacrificed and **m** offerings on
16: 3 He even **m** his son pass through fire,
16: 4 He sacrificed and **m** offerings on the high places,
17:11 there they **m** offerings on all the high places,
17:15 and his covenant that he **m** with their ancestors,
17:16 and **m** for themselves cast images of two calves;
17:16 they **m** a sacred pole, worshiped all the host
17:17 They **m** their sons and their daughters pass
17:21 they **m** Jeroboam son of Nebat king.
17:21 the LORD and **m** them commit great sin.
17:29 But every nation still **m** gods of its own
17:29 that the people of Samaria had **m**, every nation in
17:30 the people of Babylon **m** Succoth-benoth,
17:30 the people of Cuth **m** Nergal,
17:30 the people of Hamath **m** Ashima;
17:31 the Avvites **m** Nibhaz and Tartak;
17:35 The LORD had **m** a covenant with them
17:38 not forget the covenant that I have **m** with you.
18: 4 in pieces the bronze serpent that Moses had **m**, for
18: 4 the people of Israel had **m** offerings to it;
19:15 you have **m** heaven and earth.
20:20 how he **m** the pool and the conduit
21: 3 he erected altars for Baal, **m** a sacred pole,
21: 6 He **m** his son pass through fire;
21: 7 The carved image of Asherah that he had **m** he set
21:24 of the land **m** his son Josiah king in place of him.
22:17 and have **m** offerings to other gods,
23: 3 by the pillar and **m** a covenant before the LORD,
23: 4 the LORD all the vessels **m** for Baal, for Asherah,
23: 5 those also who **m** offerings to Baal, to the sun,
23: 8 the high places where the priests had **m** offerings,
23:12 which the kings of Judah had **m**,
23:12 that Manasseh had **m** in the two courts of the house
23:19 which kings of Israel had **m**,
23:30 and **m** him king in place of his father.
23:34 Pharaoh Neco **m** Eliakim son of Josiah king
24:13 which King Solomon of Israel had **m**,
24:17 The king of Babylon **m** Mattaniah,
25: 4 Then a breach was **m** in the city wall;
25:15 What was **m** of gold the captain of
25:15 and what was **m** of silver, for the silver.
25:16 which Solomon had **m** for the house of
1Ch 5:10 in the days of Saul they **m** war on the Hagrites,
5:19 They **m** war on the Hagrites, Jetur, Naphish,
6:49 But Aaron and his sons **m** offerings on the altar
11: 3 and David **m** a covenant with them at Hebron
12:18 and **m** them officers of his troops.
14: 9 the Philistines had come and **m** a raid in the valley
14:13 Once again the Philistines **m** a raid in the valley.
15:28 and cymbals, and **m** loud music on harps and lyres.
16:16 the covenant that he **m** with Abraham,
16:26 but the LORD **m** the heavens.
17:22 And you **m** your people Israel to
18: 8 with it Solomon **m** the bronze sea and the pillars
19: 6 that they had **m** themselves odious to David,
19:19 that they had been defeated by Israel, they **m** peace
21:28 of Ornan the Jebusite, he **m** his sacrifices there.
21:29 which Moses had **m** in the wilderness,
23: 1 he **m** his son Solomon king over Israel.
23: 5 to the LORD with the instruments that I have **m**
26:10 not the firstborn, his father **m** him chief),
26:31 (In the fortieth year of David's reign search was **m**,
28: 2 and I **m** preparations for building.
28:18 altar of incense **m** of refined gold, and its weight;
28:19 he **m** clear to me—the plan of all the works."
29: 6 of ancestral houses **m** their freewill offerings,
29:19 the temple for which I have **m** provision."
29:22 They **m** David's son Solomon king a second time;
2Ch 1: 1 with him and **m** him exceedingly great.
1: 3 the servant of the LORD had **m** in the wilderness,
1: 5 of Hur, had **m**, was there in front of the tabernacle
1: 8 and have **m** me succeed him as king.
1: 9 for you have **m** me king over a people as numerous
1:11 over whom I have **m** you king,
1:15 The king **m** silver and gold as common
2Ch 1:15 and he **m** cedar as plentiful as the sycamore of
2:11 the LORD loves his people he has **m** you king
2:12 be the LORD God of Israel, who **m** heaven
3: 5 and **m** palms and chains on it.
3: 8 He **m** the most holy place;
3:10 In the most holy place he **m** two carved cherubim
3:14 And Solomon **m** the curtain of blue and purple
3:15 the house he **m** two pillars thirty-five cubits high,
3:16 He **m** encircling chains and put them on the tops of
3:16 and he **m** one hundred pomegranates,
4: 1 He **m** an altar of bronze, twenty cubits long,
4: 2 Then he **m** the molten sea;
4: 5 its rim was **m** like the rim of a cup,
4: 6 He also **m** ten basins in which to wash,
4: 7 He **m** ten golden lampstands as prescribed,
4: 8 also **m** ten tables and placed them in the temple,
4: 8 And he **m** one hundred basins of gold.
4: 9 He **m** the court of the priests, and the great court,
4:11 And Huram **m** the pots, the shovels, and the basins.
4:14 He **m** the stands, the basins on the stands,
4:16 and all the equipment for these Huram-abi **m**
4:18 Solomon **m** all these things in great quantities,
4:19 So Solomon **m** all the things that were in the house
5: 8 cherubim **m** a covering above the ark and its poles.
5:10 the LORD **m** a covenant with the people of Israel
6:10 the LORD has fulfilled his promise that he **m**;
6:11 of the LORD that he **m** with the people of Israel."
6:13 Solomon had **m** a bronze platform five cubits long,
7: 6 for music to the LORD that King David had **m**
7: 7 the bronze altar Solomon had **m** could not hold
7:15 and my ears attentive to the prayer that is **m**
7:18 as I **m** covenant with your father David saying,
8: 9 But of the people of Israel Solomon **m** no slaves
9: 8 he has **m** you king over them,
9:11 the king **m** steps for the house of the LORD and
9:15 King Solomon **m** two hundred large shields
9:16 He **m** three hundred shields of beaten gold;
9:17 The king also **m** a great ivory throne,
9:19 The like of it was never **m** in any kingdom.
9:27 king **m** silver as common in Jerusalem as stone,
10: 4 "Your father **m** our yoke heavy.
10:10 'Your father **m** our yoke heavy,
10:14 "My father **m** your yoke heavy, but I will add to it;
11:11 He **m** the fortresses strong,
11:12 and spears in all the cities, and **m** them very strong.
11:15 and for the calves that he had **m**.
11:17 and for three years they **m** Rehoboam son
12: 9 the shields of gold that Solomon had **m**;
12:10 but King Rehoboam **m** in place of them shields
13: 8 the golden calves that Jeroboam **m** as gods for you.
13: 9 and **m** priests for yourselves like the peoples
15:16 from being queen mother because she had **m**
16:14 and they **m** a very great fire in his honor.
18: 1 and he **m** a marriage alliance with Ahab.
18:10 Zedekiah son of Chenaanah **m** for himself horns
20:23 when they had **m** an end of the inhabitants of Seir,
20:37 the LORD will destroy what you have **m**."
21: 7 because of the covenant that he had **m** with David,
21:11 he **m** high places in the hill country of Judah,
21:11 into unfaithfulness, and **m** Judah go astray.
21:19 His people **m** no fire in his honor,
21:19 like the fires **m** for his ancestors.
22: 1 of Jerusalem **m** his youngest son Ahaziah king
23: 3 the whole assembly **m** a covenant with the king in
23:16 Jehoiada **m** a covenant between himself and all
24: 8 So the king gave command, and they **m** a chest,
24: 9 A proclamation was **m** throughout Judah
24:14 and with it were **m** utensils for the house of
25:16 "Have we **m** you a royal counselor?
25:27 that Amaziah turned away from the LORD they **m**
26: 1 and **m** him king to succeed his father Amaziah.
26: 5 long as he sought the LORD, God **m** him prosper.
26: 6 He went out and **m** war against the Philistines,
26:11 the numbers in the muster as **m** by the secretary Jeiel
28: 2 He even **m** cast images for the Baals;
28: 3 he **m** offerings in the valley of the son of Hinnom,
28: 3 and **m** his sons pass through fire,
28: 4 He sacrificed and **m** offerings on the high places,
28:18 And the Philistines had **m** raids on the cities in
28:24 of the LORD and **m** himself altars in every corner
28:25 of Judah he **m** high places to make offerings
29: 7 and have not offered incense or **m** burnt offerings
29: 8 and he has **m** them an object of horror,
29:19 we have **m** ready and sanctified;
29:24 the priests slaughtered them and **m** a sin offering
29:24 the burnt offering and the sin offering should be **m**
30: 7 so that he **m** them a desolation, as you see.
32: 5 and **m** weapons and shields in abundance.
32:27 and he **m** for himself treasuries for silver, for gold,
33: 3 **m** sacred poles, worshiped all the host of heaven,
33: 6 He **m** his son pass through fire in the valley of
33: 7 The carved image of the idol that he had **m** he set
33:22 to all the images that his father Manasseh had **m**,
33:25 of the land **m** his son Josiah king to succeed him.
34: 4 he **m** dust of them and scattered it over the graves
34:25 and have **m** offerings to other gods,
34:31 in his place and **m** a covenant before the LORD,
34:32 Then he **m** all who were present in Jerusalem and
34:33 and **m** all who were in Israel worship
35:14 Afterward they **m** preparations for themselves and
35:14 the Levites **m** preparations for themselves and for
35:15 their kindred the Levites **m** preparations for them.
35:25 They **m** these a custom in Israel;
36: 1 and **m** him king to succeed his father in Jerusalem.
36: 4 of Egypt **m** his brother Eliakim king over Judah
36:10 and **m** his brother Zedekiah king over Judah
36:13 who had **m** him swear by God;

2Ch 36:21 until the land had **m** up for its sabbaths.
Ezr 2:68 some of the heads of families **m** freewill offerings
3: 5 of everyone who **m** a freewill offering to
3: 8 and Jeshua son of Jozadak **m** a beginning,
4: 4 and **m** them afraid to build,
4:15 a search may be **m** in the annals of your ancestors.
4:19 So I **m** a decree, and someone searched
4:19 and that rebellion and sedition have been **m** in it.
4:21 issue an order that these people be **m** to cease,
4:23 and by force and power **m** them cease.
5:13 **m** a decree that this house of God should
5:14 whom he had **m** governor.
5:17 a search **m** in the royal archives there in Babylon,
6: 1 Then King Darius **m** a decree,
6:11 The house shall be **m** a dunghill.
6:22 for the LORD had **m** them joyful,
10: 1 While Ezra prayed and **m** confession,
10: 5 Then Ezra stood up and **m** the leading priests,
10: 7 They **m** a proclamation throughout Judah
Ne 3: 4 of Uriah son of Hakkoz **m** repairs.
3: 4 of Berechiah son of Meshezabel **m** repairs.
3: 4 Next to them Zadok son of Baana **m** repairs.
3: 5 Next to them the Tekoites **m** repairs;
3: 7 to them repairs were **m** by Melatiah the Gibeonite
3: 8 one of the goldsmiths, **m** repairs.
3: 8 one of the perfumers, **m** repairs;
3: 9 ruler of half the district of Jerusalem, **m** repairs.
3:10 of Harumaph **m** repairs opposite his house;
3:10 next to him Hattush son of Hashabneiah **m** repairs.
3:12 ruler of half the district of Jerusalem, **m** repairs,
3:17 After him the Levites **m** repairs:
3:17 the district of Keilah, **m** repairs for his district.
3:18 After him their kin **m** repairs:
3:22 the men of the surrounding area, **m** repairs.
3:23 and Hasshub **m** repairs opposite their house.
3:23 of Ananiah **m** repairs beside his own house.
3:26 the temple servants living on Ophel **m** repairs up to
3:28 Above the Horse Gate the priests **m** repairs,
3:29 of Immer **m** repairs opposite his own house.
3:29 the keeper of the East Gate, **m** repairs.
3:30 of Berechiah **m** repairs opposite his living quarters.
3:31 **m** repairs as far as the house of the temple servants
3:32 the goldsmiths and the merchants **m** repairs.
5:12 **m** them take an oath to do as they had promised.
8: 4 on a wooden platform that had been **m** for
8:16 and **m** booths for themselves,
8:17 from the captivity **m** booths and lived in them;
9: 3 and for another fourth they **m** confession
9: 6 you have **m** heaven, the heaven of heavens,
9: 8 and **m** with him a covenant to give
9:10 You **m** a name for yourself,
9:14 and you **m** known your holy sabbath to them
9:27 the hands of their enemies, who **m** them suffer.
12:43 for God had **m** them rejoice with great joy;
13:25 and I **m** them take an oath in the name of God,
13:26 and God **m** him king over all Israel;
13:26 nevertheless, foreign women **m** even him to sin.
Est 1:17 of the queen will be **m** known to all women,
1:20 So when the decree **m** by the king is proclaimed
2:17 on her head and **m** her queen instead of Vashti.
5:14 "Let a gallows fifty cubits high be **m**,
5:14 and he had the gallows **m**.
9:17 on the fourteenth day they rested and **m** that a day
Job 1:17 **m** a raid on the camels and carried them off,
4: 4 and you have **m** firm the feeble knees.
4:14 and trembling, which **m** all my bones shake.
7:20 Why have you **m** me your target?
9: 9 who **m** the Bear and Orion, the Pleiades and
10: 8 Your hands fashioned and **m** me;
16: 7 he has **m** desolate all my company.
17: 6 "He has **m** me a byword of the peoples,
23:16 God has **m** my heart faint;
26:13 By his wind the heavens were **m** fair;
27: 2 and the Almighty, who has **m** my soul bitter,
27:18 like booths **m** by sentinels of the vineyard.
28:18 No mention shall be **m** of coral or of crystal;
28:26 when he **m** a decree for the rain, and a way for
29:17 and **m** them drop their prey from their teeth.
31: 1 "I have **m** a covenant with my eyes;
31:15 Did not he who **m** me in the womb make them?
31:24 If I have **m** gold my trust,
33: 4 The spirit of God has **m** me,
37: 7 so that all whom he has **m** may know it.
38: 9 when I **m** the clouds its garment,
39:17 because God has **m** it forget wisdom,
40:15 "Look at Behemoth, which I **m** just as I **m** you;
41:15 Its back is **m** of shields in rows,
Ps 7:15 and fall into the hole that they have **m**.
8: 5 Yet you have **m** them a little lower than God,
9:15 The nations have sunk in the pit that they **m**;
9:16 The LORD has **m** himself known,
18:11 He **m** darkness his covering around him,
18:32 with strength, and **m** my way safe.
18:33 He **m** my feet like the feet of a deer,
18:35 your help has **m** me great.
18:39 you **m** my assailants sink under me.
18:40 You **m** my enemies turn their backs to me,
18:43 you **m** me head of the nations;
30: 8 I cried, and to the LORD I **m** supplication:
33: 6 By the word of the LORD the heavens were **m**,
37:23 Our steps are **m** firm by the LORD,
39: 5 You have **m** my days a few handbreadths,
44:10 You **m** us turn back from the foe,
44:11 You have **m** us like sheep for slaughter,
44:13 You have **m** us the taunt of our neighbors,
44:14 You have **m** us a byword among the nations,
50: 5 who **m** a covenant with me by sacrifice!"
Ps 60: 3 You have **m** your people suffer hard things;
60: 3 you have given us wine to drink that **m** us reel.
69:11 When I **m** sackcloth my clothing,
71:20 You who have **m** me see many troubles
72:15 May prayer be **m** for him continually,
73:28 I have **m** the Lord GOD my refuge,
74:17 you **m** summer and winter.
78:13 and **m** the waters stand like a heap.
78:16 He **m** streams come out of the rock,
78:33 So he **m** their days vanish like a breath,
78:50 He **m** a path for his anger;
78:64 and their widows **m** no lamentation.
80:17 the one whom you **m** strong for yourself.
81: 5 He **m** it a decree in Joseph,
86: 9 the nations you have **m** shall come and bow down
88: 8 you have **m** me a thing of horror to them.
89: 3 "I have **m** a covenant with my chosen one,
89:42 you have **m** all his enemies rejoice.
91: 9 Because you have **m** the LORD your refuge,
92: 4 For you, O LORD, have **m** me glad by your work;
95: 5 The sea is his, for he **m** it, and the dry land,
96: 5 but the LORD **m** the heavens.
98: 2 The LORD has **m** known his victory;
100: 3 It is he that **m** us, and we are his;
103: 7 He **m** known his ways to Moses,
103:14 For he knows how we were **m**;
104:19 You have **m** the moon to mark the seasons;
104:24 In wisdom you have **m** them all;
105: 9 the covenant that he **m** with Abraham,
105:21 He **m** him lord of his house,
105:24 And the LORD **m** his people very fruitful,
105:24 and **m** them stronger than their foes,
105:28 He sent darkness, and **m** the land dark;
106:19 They **m** a calf at Horeb and worshiped
106:33 for they **m** his spirit bitter,
107:29 he **m** the storm be still,
115:15 be blessed by the LORD, who **m** heaven
118:24 This is the day that the LORD has **m**;
119:49 in which you have **m** me hope.
119:73 Your hands have **m** and fashioned me;
119:87 They have almost **m** an end of me on earth;
121: 2 from the LORD, who **m** heaven and earth.
124: 8 the name of the LORD, who **m** heaven and earth.
129: 3 they **m** their furrows long."
136: 5 who by understanding **m** the heavens,
136: 7 who **m** the great lights,
136:14 and **m** Israel pass through the midst of it,
139:14 I praise you, for I am fearfully and wonderfully **m**.
139:15 when I was being **m** in secret,
145: 9 and his compassion is over all that he has **m**.
146: 6 who **m** heaven and earth, the sea, and all that is
Pr 4:16 of sleep unless they have **m** someone stumble.
8:26 when he had not yet **m** earth and fields,
8:28 when he **m** firm the skies above,
16: 4 The LORD has **m** everything for its purpose,
20: 9 Who can say, "I have **m** my heart clean;
20:12 the LORD has **m** them both.
21:31 The horse is **m** ready for the day of battle,
22:19 I have **m** them known to you today—yes, to you.
Ecc 1:15 What is crooked cannot be **m** straight,
2: 4 I **m** great works; I built houses
2: 5 I **m** myself gardens and parks,
2: 6 I **m** myself pools from which to water the forest
3:11 He has **m** everything suitable for its time;
7: 3 for by sadness of countenance the heart is **m** glad.
7:13 who can make straight what he has **m** crooked?
7:14 God has **m** the one as well as the other,
7:29 that God **m** human beings straightforward,
10:19 Feasts are **m** for laughter; wine gladdens life,
SS 1: 6 they **m** me keeper of the vineyards,
3: 9 King Solomon **m** himself a palanquin from
3:10 He **m** its posts of silver, its back of gold,
Isa 2: 8 to what their own fingers have **m**.
2:20 which they **m** for themselves to worship,
14: 3 the hard service with which you were **m** to serve,
14:16 "Is this the man who **m** the earth tremble,
14:17 who **m** the world like a desert
16: 8 whose clusters once **m** drunk the lords of
17: 8 not look to what their own fingers have **m**,
19:14 and they have **m** Egypt stagger in all its doings as
22:11 You **m** a reservoir between the two walls for
23:13 they tore down her palaces, they **m** her a ruin.
25: 2 you have **m** the city a heap, the fortified city a ruin;
27:11 he that **m** them will not have compassion on them,
28:15 you have said, "We have **m** a covenant with death,
28:15 for we have **m** lies our refuge,
28:22 do not scoff, or your bonds will be **m** stronger;
29:16 Shall the thing **m** say of its maker,
30:33 truly it is **m** ready for the king, its pyre **m** deep
31: 7 which your hands have sinfully **m** for you.
34: 7 and their soil **m** rich with fat.
37:16 you have **m** heaven and earth.
40: 4 and every mountain and hill be **m** low;
43: 7 for my glory, whom I formed and **m**."
44: 2 Thus says the LORD who **m** you,
44:24 I am the LORD, who **m** all things,
45:12 I **m** the earth, and created humankind upon it;
45:18 who formed the earth and **m** it (he established it;
46: 4 I have **m**, and I will bear; I will carry and will save.
47: 6 on the aged you **m** your yoke exceedingly heavy.
48: 3 from my mouth and I **m** them known;
48:21 he **m** water flow for them from the rock;
49: 2 He **m** my mouth like a sharp sword,
49: 2 he **m** me a polished arrow,
51: 2 but I blessed him and **m** him many.
51:10 who **m** the depths of the sea a way for
51:23 and you have **m** your back like the ground and like
Isa 53: 5 upon him was the punishment that **m** us whole,
53: 9 They **m** his grave with the wicked and his tomb
53:12 and **m** intercession for the transgressors.
55: 4 See, I **m** him a witness to the peoples,
57: 8 you have gone up to it, you have **m** it wide;
57: 8 and you have **m** a bargain for yourself with them,
57:16 even the souls that I have **m**.
59: 8 Their roads they have **m** crooked;
66: 2 All these things my hand has **m**,
Jer 1:16 they have **m** offerings to other gods,
1:18 I for my part have **m** you today a fortified city,
2: 7 and **m** my heritage an abomination.
2:15 They have **m** his land a waste;
2:28 But where are your gods that you **m** for yourself?
3:16 nor shall another one be **m**.
5: 3 They have **m** their faces harder than rock;
6:27 I have **m** you a tester and a refiner
7:12 where I **m** my name dwell at first,
8: 8 the false pen of the scribes has **m** it into a lie?
10:12 It is he who **m** the earth by his power,
11:10 of Judah have broken the covenant that I **m**
11:18 It was the LORD who **m** it known to me,
12:10 they have **m** my pleasant portion
12:11 They have **m** it a desolation;
12:11 The whole land is **m** desolate,
13:11 so I **m** the whole house of Israel and
13:27 How long will it be before you are **m** clean?
15: 8 I have **m** anguish and terror fall upon her suddenly.
19:13 upon whose roofs offerings have been **m** to
25:17 and **m** all the nations to whom
27: 5 and my outstretched arm have **m** the earth,
28:15 and you **m** this people trust in a lie.
29:26 The LORD himself has **m** you priest instead of
31:32 that I **m** with their ancestors when I took them by
32:17 It is you who **m** the heavens and the earth
32:20 and have **m** yourself a name that continues
32:23 you have **m** all these disasters come upon them.
32:29 the houses on whose roofs offerings have been **m**
33: 2 Thus says the LORD who **m** the earth,
33:14 when I will fulfill the promise I **m** to the house
34: 8 after King Zedekiah had **m** a covenant with all
34:13 I myself **m** a covenant with your ancestors
34:15 and you **m** a covenant before me in the house
34:18 of the covenant that they **m** before me, I will make
37: 1 whom King Nebuchadrezzar of Babylon **m** king in
37:15 for it had been **m** a prison.
39: 2 a breach was **m** in the city.
41: 9 the large cistern that King Asa had **m** for defense
41:18 the king of Babylon had **m** governor over the land.
42:20 that you have **m** a fatal mistake.
44:19 do you think that we **m** cakes for her,
44:21 the offerings that you **m** in the towns of Judah and
44:25 to perform the vows that we have **m**,
49:20 the LORD has **m** against Edom and the purposes
49:30 For King Nebuchadrezzar of Babylon has **m** a plan
50:45 the plan that the LORD has **m** against Babylon,
51:15 It is he who **m** the earth by his power,
51:34 he has **m** me an empty vessel,
52: 7 Then a breach was **m** in the city wall;
52:20 which King Solomon had **m** for the house of
La 1: 5 the LORD has **m** her suffer for the multitude
2:17 he has **m** the enemy rejoice over you,
3: 4 He has **m** my flesh and my skin waste away,
3: 6 he has **m** me sit in darkness like the dead
3: 9 he has **m** my paths crooked.
3:11 to pieces; he has **m** me desolate;
3:16 He has **m** my teeth grind on gravel,
3:16 and **m** me cower in ashes;
3:45 You have **m** us filth and rubbish among
5: 6 We have **m** a pact with Egypt and Assyria,
Eze 3: 8 See, I have **m** your face hard against their faces,
3: 9 harder than flint, I have **m** your forehead;
3:17 I have **m** you a sentinel for the house of Israel;
7:14 They have blown the horn and **m** everything ready;
7:20 they **m** their abominable images,
12: 6 for I have **m** you a sign for the house of Israel.
14:15 that it is **m** desolate, and no one may pass through
16:16 and **m** for yourself colorful shrines,
16:17 and **m** for yourself male images,
16:24 and **m** yourself a lofty place in every square,
16:51 and have **m** your sisters appear righteous by all
16:52 for you have **m** your sisters appear righteous.
17:13 of the royal offspring and **m** a covenant with him,
17:16 the place where the king resides who **m** him king,
19: 5 she took another of her cubs and **m** him
20: 9 in whose sight I **m** myself known to them
21:15 Ah! It is **m** for flashing, it is polished for slaughter.
22: 4 and defiled by the idols that you have **m**;
22: 4 I have **m** you a disgrace before the nations,
22:13 at the dishonest gain you have **m**,
22:25 they have **m** many widows within it.
22:26 they have **m** no distinction between the holy and
25: 3 and over the land of Israel when it was **m** desolate,
27: 4 your builders **m** perfect your beauty.
27: 5 They **m** all your planks of fir trees from Senir;
27: 6 From oaks of Bashan they **m** your oars;
27: 6 **m** your deck of pines from the coasts of Cyprus,
27:11 they **m** perfect your beauty.
27:24 bound with cords and **m** secure;
29: 3 "My Nile is my own; I **m** it for myself."
29: 7 you broke, and **m** all their legs unsteady.
29: 9 Because you said, "The Nile is mine, and I **m** it,"
29:18 of Babylon **m** his army labor hard against Tyre;
29:18 head was **m** bald and every shoulder was rubbed
31: 4 The waters nourished it, the deep **m** it grow tall,
31: 6 All the birds of the air **m** their nests in its boughs;
31: 9 I **m** it beautiful with its mass of branches,

Eze 31:16 I **m** the nations quake at the sound of its fall,
32:25 They have **m** Elam a bed among the slain
33: 7 mortal, I have **m** a sentinel for the house of Israel;
33:29 when I have **m** the land a desolation and a waste
36: 3 Because they **m** you desolate indeed,
44:12 before their idols and **m** the house of Israel stumble
46:23 with hearths **m** at the bottom of
Da 2:48 and **m** him ruler over the whole province
2:49 Daniel **m** a request of the king,
3: 1 King Nebuchadnezzar **m** a golden statue whose
3:10 You, O king, have **m** a decree,
3:15 to fall down and worship the statue that I have **m**,
4: 6 So I **m** a decree that all the wise men
4:25 You shall be **m** to eat grass like oxen,
4:32 You shall be **m** to eat grass like oxen,
5: 1 King Belshazzar **m** a great festival for a thousand
5:11 **m** him chief of the magicians, enchanters,
5:21 and his mind was **m** like that of an animal.
5:29 and a proclamation was **m** concerning him
6:14 the sun went down he **m** every effort to rescue him.
7: 4 and it was lifted up from the ground and **m** to stand
7:21 this horn **m** war with the holy ones
9: 4 I prayed to the LORD my God and **m** confession,
9:15 a mighty hand and **m** your name renowned even
11:23 And after an alliance is **m** with him,
Hos 7:12 I will discipline them according to the report **m**
8: 4 They **m** kings, but not through me;
8: 4 and gold they **m** idols for their own destruction.
8: 6 an artisan **m** it; it is not God.
13: 2 idols of silver **m** according to their understanding,
Am 2:12 But you **m** the nazirites drink wine,
3: 3 Do two walk together unless they have **m**
4:10 and I **m** the stench of your camp go up
5: 8 The one who **m** the Pleiades and Orion,
5:26 your images, which you **m** for yourselves;
7: 9 the high places of Isaac shall be **m** desolate,
Jnh 1: 9 who **m** the sea and the dry land."
1:16 they offered a sacrifice to the LORD and **m** vows.
3: 7 Then he had a proclamation **m** in Nineveh:
4: 5 and **m** a booth for himself there.
4: 6 and **m** it come up over Jonah,
Hab 1:14 You have **m** people like the fish of the sea,
2:18 For its maker trusts in what has been **m**,
3: 6 he looked and **m** the nations tremble.
Zep 2: 8 how they have taunted my people and **m** boasts
3: 6 their cities have been **m** desolate, without people,
Hag 2: 5 to the promise that I **m** you when you came out
Zec 1:15 I was only a little angry, they **m** the disaster worse.
7:12 They **m** their hearts adamant in order not to hear
7:14 and a pleasant land was **m** desolate.
9:13 I have **m** Ephraim its arrow.
11:10 the covenant that I had **m** with all the peoples.
Mal 1: 3 I have **m** his hill country a desolation
Mt 2:23 There he **m** his home in a town called Nazareth,
4:13 He left Nazareth and **m** his home in Capernaum by
5:33 but carry out the vows you have **m** to the Lord.'
8: 3 "I do choose. Be **m** clean!"
9:16 and a worse tear is **m**.
9:21 "If I only touch his cloak, I will be **m** well."
9:22 "Take heart, daughter; your faith has **m** you well."
9:22 And instantly the woman was **m** well.
14:22 Immediately he **m** the disciples get into the boat
18:25 and all his possessions, and payment to be **m**.
19: 4 "Have you not read that the one who **m** them at
19: 4 at the beginning '**m** them male and female,'
19:12 and there are eunuchs who have been **m** eunuchs
19:12 there are eunuchs who have **m** themselves eunuchs
20:12 and you have **m** them equal to us who have borne
22: 5 But they **m** light of it and went away,
23:17 gold or the sanctuary that has **m** the gold sacred?
25:16 and traded with them, and **m** five more talents.
25:17 one who had the two talents **m** two more talents.
25:20 see, I have **m** five more talents.'
25:22 see, I have **m** two more talents.'
27:64 Therefore command the tomb to be **m** secure until
27:66 So they went with the guard and **m** the tomb secure
Mk 1:41 "I do choose. Be **m** clean!"
1:42 the leprosy left him, and he was **m** clean.
2:21 the new from the old, and a worse tear is **m**.
2:23 and as they **m** their way his disciples began
2:27 "The sabbath was **m** for humankind,
5:23 so that she may be **m** well, and live."
5:28 "If I but touch his clothes, I will be **m** well."
5:34 "Daughter, your faith has **m** you well;
6:45 Immediately he **m** his disciples get into the boat
10: 6 'God **m** them male and female.'
10:52 Jesus said to him, "Go; your faith has **m** you well."
11:17 But you have **m** it a den of robbers."
14:58 'I will destroy this temple that is **m** with hands,
14:58 three days I will build another, not **m** with hands.'
15: 5 But Jesus **m** no further reply,
Lk 1:55 according to the promise he **m** to our ancestors,
2:15 which the Lord has **m** known to us."
2:17 they **m** known what had been told them
3: 5 and every mountain and hill shall be **m** low,
3: 5 and the crooked shall be **m** straight,
3: 5 and the rough ways **m** smooth;
5:13 "I do choose. Be **m** clean."
8:48 your faith has **m** you well; go in peace."
9:15 They did so and **m** them all sit down.
11:40 the one who **m** the outside make the inside also?
13:19 and the birds of the air **m** nests in its branches."
13:22 teaching as he **m** his way to Jerusalem.
17:14 And as they went, they were **m** clean.
17:17 Then Jesus asked, "Were not ten **m** clean?
17:19 go on your way; your faith has **m** you well."
19:16 'Lord, your pound has **m** ten more pounds.'
Lk 19:18 saying, 'Lord, your pound has **m** five pounds.'
19:46 but you have **m** it a den of robbers."
23:26 and **m** him carry it behind Jesus.
24:35 how he had been **m** known to them in the breaking
Jn 1:18 to the Father's heart, who has **m** him known.
5: 6 he said to him, "Do you want to be **m** well?"
5: 9 At once the man was **m** well,
5:11 "The man who **m** me well said to me,
5:14 "See, you have been **m** well!
5:15 the Jews that it was Jesus who had **m** him well.
8:33 by saying, 'You will be **m** free'?"
9: 6 and **m** mud with the saliva and spread the mud on
9:11 He answered, "The man called Jesus **m** mud,
9:14 Now it was a sabbath day when Jesus **m** the mud
12: 3 a pound of costly perfume **m** of pure nard,
15:15 because I have **m** known to you everything
17: 6 "I have **m** your name known
17:13 so that they may have my joy **m** complete
17:26 I **m** your name known to them,
18:18 the slaves and the police had **m** a charcoal fire
Ac 2:28 You have **m** known to me the ways of life;
2:36 of Israel know with certainty that God has **m** him
3: 7 and immediately his feet and ankles were **m** strong.
3:12 by our own power or piety we had **m** him walk?
3:16 his name itself has **m** this man strong,
4: 7 they had **m** the prisoners stand in their midst,
4:24 "Sovereign Lord, who **m** the heaven and the earth,
7:13 On the second visit Joseph **m** himself known
7:17 for the fulfillment of the promise that God had **m**
7:27 saying, 'Who **m** you a ruler and a judge over us?
7:35 'Who **m** you a ruler and a judge?'
7:41 At that time they **m** a calf,
7:43 the images that you **m** to worship;
7:48 Yet the Most High does not dwell in houses **m**
8: 2 and **m** loud lamentation over him.
9:21 "Is not this the man who **m** havoc in Jerusalem
9:39 that Dorcas had **m** while she was with them.
10:15 a second time, "What God has **m** clean,
10:26 But Peter **m** him get up, saying, "Stand up;
11: 9 from heaven, 'What God has **m** clean, you must
13:17 and **m** the people great during their stay in the land
13:22 When he had removed him, he **m** David their king.
13:34 'I will give you the holy promises **m** to David.'
14: 5 when an attempt was **m** by both Gentiles and Jews,
14:15 who **m** the heaven and the earth and the sea and all
14:21 to that city and had **m** many disciples,
15: 7 that in the early days God **m** a choice among you,
15: 9 by faith he has **m** no distinction between them
17:24 The God who **m** the world and everything in it,
17:24 does not live in shrines **m** by human hands,
17:26 From one ancestor he **m** all nations to inhabit
18:12 the Jews **m** a united attack on Paul
19:24 a silversmith who **m** silver shrines of Artemis,
19:26 of people by saying that gods **m** with hands are
20: 3 to set sail for Syria when a plot was **m** against him
20:13 for he had **m** this arrangement,
20:28 of which the Holy Spirit has **m** you overseers,
21:26 when the sacrifice would be **m** for each of them.
24: 2 and reforms have been **m** for this people because
26: 6 on account of my hope in the promise **m** by God
27:40 then hoisting the foresail to the wind, they **m** for
28:25 as they were leaving, Paul **m** one further statement:
Ro 1:20 and seen through the things he has **m**.
4:17 "I have **m** you the father of many nations")—
4:20 No distrust **m** him waver concerning the promise
5:19 the many were **m** sinners,
5:19 the many will be **m** righteous.
9:20 "Why have you **m** me like this?"
9:22 with much patience the objects of wrath that are **m**
9:29 we would have fared like Sodom and been **m**
16:26 prophetic writings is **m** known to all the Gentiles,
1Co 1:20 Has not God **m** foolish the wisdom of the world?
7:14 unbelieving husband is **m** holy through his wife,
7:14 unbelieving wife is **m** holy through her husband.
9:12 Nevertheless, we have not **m** use of this right,
9:15 But I have **m** no use of any of these rights,
9:19 I have **m** myself a slave to all,
11: 8 Indeed, man was not **m** from woman,
12:13 and we were all **m** to drink of one Spirit.
14:30 If a revelation is **m** to someone else sitting nearby,
15:22 so all will be **m** alive in Christ.
16:17 because they have **m** up for your absence;
2Co 2: 1 So I **m** up my mind not to make you another
2: 3 from those who should have **m** me rejoice;
3: 6 who has **m** us competent to be ministers of
4: 7 be **m** clear that this extraordinary power belongs
4:10 life of Jesus may also be **m** visible in our bodies.
4:11 life of Jesus may be **m** visible in our mortal flesh.
5: 1 a house not **m** with hands, eternal in the heavens.
5:21 For our sake he **m** him to be sin who knew no sin,
7: 8 For even if I **m** you sorry with my letter,
7:12 in order that your zeal for us might be **m** known
8: 6 as he had already **m** a beginning,
9: 7 of you must give as you have **m** up your mind,
11: 6 and in all things we have **m** this evident to you.
11:29 Who is **m** to stumble, and I am not indignant?
12: 9 for power is **m** perfect in weakness."
Gal 3:16 promises were **m** to Abraham and to his offspring;
3:19 to whom the promise had been **m**;
4:18 to be **m** much of for a good purpose at all times,
Eph 1: 9 he has **m** known to us the mystery of his will,
1:22 and has **m** him the head over all things for
2: 5 **m** us alive together with Christ—
2:10 For we are what he has **m** us,
2:11 a physical circumcision **m** in the flesh
2:14 in his flesh he has **m** both groups into one
3: 3 the mystery was **m** known to me by revelation,
Eph 3: 5 not **m** known to humankind, as it has
3:10 of God in its rich variety might now be **m** known
4: 8 he ascended on high he **m** captivity itself a captive;
Php 1:14 having been **m** confident in the Lord
3:12 because Christ Jesus has **m** me his own.
3:13 I do not consider that I have **m** it my own;
4: 6 with thanksgiving let your requests be **m** known
Col 1: 8 and he has **m** known to us your love in the Spirit.
1:11 be **m** strong with all the strength that comes
2:13 God **m** you alive together with him,
2:15 the rulers and authorities and **m** a public example
1Th 2: 7 we might have **m** demands as apostles of Christ.
2:17 we were **m** orphans by being separated from you—
1Ti 1:18 in accordance with the prophecies **m** earlier
2: 1 and thanksgivings be **m** for everyone,
6:12 to which you were called and for which you **m**
6:13 who in his testimony before Pontius Pilate **m**
Heb 1: 3 When he had **m** purification for sins,
2: 7 You have **m** them for a little while lower than
2: 9 who for a little while was **m** lower than the angels,
5: 9 and having been **m** perfect,
6:13 When God **m** a promise to Abraham,
7:19 (for the law **m** nothing perfect);
7:28 appoints a Son who has been **m** perfect forever.
8: 9 not like the covenant that I **m** with their ancestors,
8:13 he has **m** the first one obsolete.
9: 6 Such preparations having been **m**,
9:11 the greater and perfect tent (not **m** with hands,
9:16 the death of the one who **m** it must be established.
9:17 not in force as long as the one who **m** it is alive.
9:24 not enter a sanctuary **m** by human hands,
10:13 "until his enemies would be **m** a footstool
11: 3 what is seen was **m** from things that are not visible.
11:22 **m** mention of the exodus of the Israelites
11:40 they would not, apart from us, be **m** perfect.
12:19 and a voice whose words **m** the hearers beg that
12:23 and to the spirits of the righteous **m** perfect,
Jas 2: 4 have you not **m** distinctions among yourselves,
3: 9 with it we curse those who are **m** in the likeness
4: 5 "God yearns jealously for the spirit that he has **m**
1Pe 1:10 that was to be yours **m** careful search and inquiry,
3:18 but **m** alive in the spirit,
3:19 also he went and **m** a proclamation to the spirits
3:22 authorities, and powers **m** subject to him.
2Pe 1:14 as indeed our Lord Jesus Christ has **m** clear to me.
1:16 when we **m** known to you the power and coming
2: 6 and **m** them an example of what is coming to
1Jn 2:19 But by going out they **m** it plain that none
5:10 Those who do not believe in God have **m** him a liar
5:15 we know that we have obtained the requests **m**
Rev 1: 1 he **m** it known by sending his angel
1: 6 and **m** us to be a kingdom,
5:10 you have **m** them to be a kingdom
7:14 they have washed their robes and **m** them white in
8: 6 the seven trumpets **m** ready to blow them.
8:11 from the water, because it was **m** bitter.
10:10 but when I had eaten it, my stomach was **m** bitter.
14: 7 and worship him who **m** heaven and earth,
14: 8 She has **m** all nations drink of the wine of
18: 1 and the earth was **m** bright with his splendor.
19: 7 and his bride has **m** herself ready;
Tob 2:12 She used to send what she **m** to the owners
4:19 and ask him that your ways may be **m** straight and
6:18 she was set apart for you before the world was **m**.
7:16 and **m** the bed in the room as he had told her,
8: 6 You **m** Adam, and for him you made his wife Eve
8: 6 him you **m** his wife Eve as a helper and support.
8:16 Blessed are you because you have **m** me glad.
10:13 because he had **m** his journey a success.
11:12 and it **m** them smart.
Jdt 1: 2 he **m** the walls seventy cubits high
1: 4 He **m** its gates seventy cubits high
1: 5 Then King Nebuchadnezzar **m** war
6: 1 When the disturbance **m** by the people outside
8:14 to search out God, who **m** all these things,
8:18 or town of ours that worships gods **m** with hands,
8:30 and **m** us take an oath that we cannot break.
10: 4 Thus she **m** herself very beautiful,
14: 9 the people raised a great shout and **m** a joyful noise
16:14 for you spoke, and they were **m**.
AdE 1: 7 and a miniature cup was displayed, **m** of ruby,
4:14 not for such a time as this that you were **m** queen?"
5:14 "Let a gallows be **m**, fifty cubits high,
6:10 "You have **m** an excellent suggestion!
6:11 and **m** him ride through the open square of the city,
7: 4 to be destroyed, plundered, and **m** slaves—
8:17 wherever the proclamation was **m**,
9:17 the fourteenth day they rested and **m** that same day
9:24 how he **m** a decree and cast lots to destroy them,
10: 6 whom the king married and **m** queen.
10:10 For this purpose he **m** two lots,
12: 4 The king **m** a permanent record of these things,
13:10 for you have **m** heaven and earth
16: 5 of authority have been **m** in part responsible for
16:21 has **m** this day to be a joy
16:24 be **m** not only impassable for human beings,
Wis 1: 9 inquiry will be **m** into the counsels of the ungodly,
1:16 they pined away and **m** a covenant with him,
2:23 and **m** us in the image of his own eternity,
5: 4 in derision and **m** a byword of reproach—
6: 7 because he himself **m** both small and great,
6:10 For they will be **m** holy who observe holy things
9: 1 who have **m** all things by your word,
9: 2 to have dominion over the creatures you have **m**,
9: 9 and was present when you **m** the world;
10:11 she stood by him and **m** him rich.
10:21 and **m** the tongues of infants speak clearly.

Wis 11:24 and detest none of the things that you have **m,**
11:24 you would not have **m** anything if you had hated it.
12:12 for the destruction of nations that you **m?**
14: 8 But the idol **m** with hands is accursed,
14: 8 and so is the one who **m** it—
14: 8 he for having **m** it, and the perishable thing
14:15 **m** an image of his child,
14:17 **m** a visible image of the king whom they honored,
15: 8 these mortals who were **m** of earth a short time
15:16 For a human being **m** them,
16:24 For creation, serving you who **m** it,
17:16 and thus was kept shut up in a prison not **m** of iron;
18: 6 night was **m** known beforehand to our ancestors,
18:18 **m** known why they were dying;
19: 4 and **m** them forget what had happened,
19:14 when they came to them, but these **m** slaves
Sir 1:15 She **m** among human beings an eternal foundation,
14:19 and the one who **m** it will pass away with it.
17: 3 and **m** them in his own image.
29: 6 and he has needlessly **m** him an enemy;
33: 9 and some he **m** ordinary days.
33:12 and some he **m** holy and brought near to himself;
38: 5 Was not water **m** sweet with a tree in order
39: 5 to rise early to seek the Lord who **m** him,
42:15 By the word of the Lord his works are **m;**
42:24 and he has **m** nothing incomplete.
43: 5 Great is the Lord who **m** it;
43:11 Look at the rainbow, and praise him who **m** it;
43:33 For the Lord has **m** all things,
44: 3 and **m** a name for themselves by their valor;
44:18 Everlasting covenants were **m** with him
44:23 he **m** to rest on the head of Jacob;
45: 2 He **m** him equal in glory to the holy ones,
45: 2 and **m** him great, to the terror of his enemies.
45: 7 He **m** an everlasting covenant with him,
45:23 and he **m** atonement for Israel.
46:17 and **m** his voice heard with a mighty sound;
46:20 he prophesied and **m** known to the king his death,
47:13 because God **m** all his borders tranquil,
48: 2 and by his zeal he **m** them few in number.
48:18 and **m** great boasts in his arrogance.
49: 3 in lawless times he **m** godliness prevail.
49: 6 and **m** its streets desolate, as Jeremiah had foretold.
50:11 he **m** the court of the sanctuary glorious.
51:17 I **m** progress in her; to him
Bar 1: 8 that Zedekiah son of Josiah, king of Judah, had **m,**
2: 4 He **m** them subject to all the kingdoms around us,
2:11 and **m** yourself a name that continues to this day,
2:26 the house that is called by your name you have **m**
3:17 those who **m** sport of the birds of the air,
3:34 They shone with gladness for him who **m** them.
4: 7 the one who **m** you by sacrificing to demons and
5: 7 the everlasting hills be **m** low and the valleys filled
LtJ 6: 4 in Babylon you will see gods **m** of silver and gold
6:39 These things that are **m** of wood and overlaid
6:45 They are **m** by carpenters and goldsmiths;
6:47 then can the things that are **m** by them be gods?
6:50 Since they are **m** of wood and overlaid with gold
6:57 Gods **m** of wood and overlaid with silver
Aza 1:27 and **m** the inside of the furnace as though
Bel 1: 5 "Because I do not revere idols **m** with hands,
1:13 for beneath the table they had **m** a hidden entrance,
1:27 and hair, and boiled them together and **m** cakes,
1:33 he had **m** a stew and had broken bread into a bowl,
1Mc 2:41 So they **m** this decision that day:
3: 7 but he **m** Jacob glad by his deeds,
4:49 They **m** new holy vessels, and brought
5: 3 But Judas **m** war on the descendants of Esau
5:14 came from Galilee and **m** a similar report;
5:24 and **m** three days' journey into the wilderness.
5:49 Then Judas ordered proclamation to be **m** to
6:14 and **m** him ruler over all his kingdom.
6:33 and his troops **m** ready for battle
6:41 All who heard the noise **m** by their multitude,
6:49 He **m** peace with the people of Beth-zur,
6:52 The Jews also **m** engines of war to match theirs,
7: 9 the ungodly Alcimus, whom he **m** high priest;
8: 1 and were well-disposed toward all who **m**
8:31 'Why have you **m** your yoke heavy on our friends
9:20 All Israel **m** great lamentation for him:
9:26 They **m** inquiry and searched for the friends
9:26 who took vengeance on them and **m** sport of them.
9:64 he fought against it for many days and **m** machines
10:65 and **m** him general and governor of the province.
11:51 And they threw down their arms and **m** peace.
11:62 and he **m** peace with them,
13:27 he **m** it high so that it might be seen,
13:38 All the grants that we have **m** to you remain valid,
13:43 He **m** a siege engine, brought it up to the city,
13:53 and so he **m** him commander of all the forces;
14:15 He **m** the sanctuary glorious,
14:27 So they **m** a record on bronze tablets and put it
14:35 and they **m** him their leader and high priest,
14:39 **m** him one of his Friends,
15:27 and broke all the agreements he formerly had **m**
15:38 Then the king **m** Cendebeus commander-in-chief
16:13 **m** treacherous plans against Simon and his sons,
2Mc 1:34 and enclosed the place and **m** it sacred.
2: 9 It was also **m** clear that being possessed
3: 4 who had been **m** captain of the temple,
3: 9 that had been **m** and stated why he had come,
3:20 up their hands to heaven, they all **m** supplication.
3:35 to the Lord and **m** very great vows to the Savior
5: 1 About this time Antiochus **m** his second invasion
5: 3 attacks and counterattacks **m** on this side and on
5: 5 a thousand men and suddenly **m** an assault on
5:16 that other kings had **m** to enhance the glory
2Mc 8:15 the sake of the covenants **m** with their ancestors,
8:21 and **m** them ready to die for their laws
8:29 they **m** common supplication and implored
8:35 took off his splendid uniform and **m** his way alone
9:13 Then the abominable fellow **m** a vow to the Lord,
9:23 when he **m** expeditions into the upper country,
10: 3 and **m** another altar of sacrifice;
10:28 while the other **m** rage their leader in the fight.
12:27 before the walls and **m** a vigorous defense;
12:45 Therefore he **m** atonement for the dead,
13:26 **m** the best possible defense, convinced them,
14: 2 having **m** away with Antiochus
14:26 he took the covenant that had been **m** and went
15: 1 he **m** plans to attack them with complete safety on
15: 9 he **m** them the more eager.
1Es 1:15 were in their place according to the arrangement **m**
1:32 have **m** lamentation for him to this day;
1:34 and **m** him king in succession to his father Josiah.
1:37 The king of Egypt **m** his brother Jehoiakim king
1:43 when he was **m** king he was eighteen years old,
1:46 and **m** Zedekiah king of Judea and Jerusalem.
1:48 Although King Nebuchadnezzar had **m** him swear
1:49 the temple that God had **m** holy.
2: 2 the spirit of King Cyrus of the Persians, and he **m**
2: 3 the Lord Most High, has **m** me king of the world,
2:21 search may be **m** in the records of your ancestors.
2:26 So I ordered search to be **m,**
4:43 that you **m** on the day when you became king,
5: 3 And he **m** them go up with them.
5:39 a search was **m** in the register and the genealogy
5:53 And all who had **m** any vow to God began
5:56 and Jeshua son of Jozadak **m** a beginning, together
6: 6 be sent to Darius concerning them and a report **m.**
6:21 let search be **m** in the royal archives of our lord
6:23 be **m** in the royal archives that were deposited
6:28 be **m** to help those who have returned from
6:31 that libations may be **m** to the Most High God for
8:96 Then Ezra rose up and **m** the leaders of the priests
9: 3 And a proclamation was **m** throughout Judea
Man 1: 2 you who **m** heaven and earth with all their order;
Pm 151: 2 My hands **m** a harp; my fingers fashioned a lyre.
3Mc 1: 9 and **m** thank offerings and did what was fitting for
2: 5 and you **m** them an example
2: 6 You **m** known your mighty power
2: 9 you **m** it a firm foundation for the glory
3:21 we **m** known to all our amnesty
3:29 to be **m** unapproachable and burned with fire,
4: 1 in their minds was now **m** evident and outspoken.
6:40 also they **m** the petition for their dismissal.
2Es 1:13 **m** safe highways for you where there was no road;
1:23 threw a tree into the water and **m** the stream sweet.
2: 1 not listen to them, and **m** my counsels void.
2:41 from the beginning, may be **m** holy."
3: 5 and he was **m** alive in your presence.
3:15 You **m** an everlasting covenant with him,
4:13 into a forest of trees of the plain, and they **m** a plan
4:15 In like manner the waves of the sea also **m** a plan
4:19 I answered and said, "Each **m** a foolish plan,
5:26 the flocks that have been **m** you have provided
5:49 so I have **m** the same rule for the world
6: 6 and they were **m** through me alone and not
6:38 'Let heaven and earth be **m,'**
6:44 These were **m** on the third day.
6:54 as ruler over all the works that you had **m;**
7:11 For I **m** the world for their sake,
7:11 what had been **m** was judged.
7:12 And so the entrances of this world were **m** narrow
7:*50* For this reason the Most High has **m** not one world
7:*60* it is they who have **m** my glory to prevail now,
7:62 if the mind is **m** out of the dust like
7:*63* so that the mind might not have been **m** from it.
7:*70* "When the Most High **m** the world and Adam
7:*97* and how they are to be **m** like the light of the stars,
8: 1 "The Most High **m** this world for the sake of many,
8: 2 of clay from which earthenware is **m,**
8:14 to what purpose was it **m?**
8:44 and are called your own image because they are **m**
8:44 have you also **m** them like the farmer's seed?
8:54 the end the treasure of immortality is **m** manifest.
8:*60* the name of him who **m** them,
9: 2 about to visit the world that he has **m.**
9:13 age belongs and for whose sake the age was **m."**
9:18 before the world was **m** for them to live in,
10:14 that is, humankind, to him who **m** her.'
10:22 and our strong men **m** powerless.
11:39 that remains of the four beasts that I had **m** to reign
11:46 for the judgment and mercy of him who **m** it.' "
13: 3 As I kept looking the wind **m** something like
13:36 Zion shall come and be **m** manifest to all people,
13:40 king of the Assyrians, **m** captives;
15:47 For you have **m** yourself like her;
16:55 He said, "Let the earth be **m,"** and it was **m,**
16:55 and "Let the heaven be **m,"** and it was **m.**
16:59 like a dome and **m** it secure upon the waters;
16:62 surely **m** all things and searches out hidden things
4Mc 6: 1 in this manner had **m** eloquent response to
7: 9 but by your deeds you **m** your words
12:13 like yours and are **m** of the same elements as you,
17:24 and this **m** them brave and courageous
18: 7 but I guarded the rib from which woman was **m.**

MADIAN (KJV) See MIDIAN

MADLY (2) [MAD]

Jer 46: 9 Advance, O horses, and dash **m,** O chariots!
Na 2: 4 The chariots race **m** through the streets,

MADMAN (4) [MAD, MAN]

1Sa 21:15 that you have brought this fellow to play the **m**
2Ki 9:11 Why did that **m** come to you?"
Jer 29:26 of the LORD to control any **m** who plays
2Co 11:23 I am talking like a **m—**

MADMANNAH (2)

Jos 15:31 Ziklag, **M,** Sansannah,
1Ch 2:49 She also bore Shaaph father of **M,**

MADMEN (2) [MAD, MAN]

1Sa 21:15 Do I lack **m,** that you have brought this fellow
Jer 48: 2 You also, O **M,** shall be brought to silence;

MADMENAH (1)

Isa 10:31 **M** is in flight, the inhabitants of Gebim flee

MADNESS (14) [MAD]

Dt 28:28 The LORD will afflict you with **m,** blindness,
Ps 34: T *Of David, when he feigned* **m** *before Abimelech,*
Ecc 1:17 to know wisdom and to know **m** and folly.
2:12 So I turned to consider wisdom and **m** and folly;
7:25 that wickedness is folly and that foolishness is **m.**
9: 3 **m** is in their hearts while they live,
10:13 and their talk ends in wicked **m;**
Zec 12: 4 with panic, and its rider with **m.**
2Pe 2:16 with a human voice and restrained the prophet's **m.**
Wis 5: 4 that their lives were **m** and that their end was
2Mc 6:29 he had uttered were in their opinion sheer **m.**
3Mc 5:42 a Phalaris in everything and filled with **m,**
5:45 animals had been brought virtually to a state of **m,**
4Mc 8: 5 Not only do I advise you not to display the same **m**

MADON (2)

Jos 11: 1 he sent to King Jobab of **M,**
12:19 the king of **M** one the king of Hazor one

MAERUS (1)

1Es 9:34 Jeremai, Momdius, **M,** Joel,

MAGADAN (1)

Mt 15:39 he got into the boat and went to the region of **M.**

MAGBISH (1)

Ezr 2:30 Of **M,** one hundred fifty-six.

MAGDALA (KJV) See MAGADAN; See also Index to Footnotes

MAGDALAN See Index to Footnotes

MAGDALENE (12)

Mt 27:56 Among them were Mary **M,**
27:61 Mary **M** and the other Mary were there,
28: 1 Mary **M** and the other Mary went to see the tomb.
Mk 15:40 among them were Mary **M,**
15:47 Mary **M** and Mary the mother of Joses saw where
16: 1 When the sabbath was over, Mary **M,**
16: 9 ⟦he appeared first to Mary **M,**⟧
Lk 8: 2 called **M,** from whom seven demons had gone out,
24:10 Now it was Mary **M,** Joanna,
Jn 19:25 Mary the wife of Clopas, and Mary **M.**
20: 1 Mary **M** came to the tomb and saw that
20:18 Mary **M** went and announced to the disciples,

MAGDIEL (2)

Ge 36:43 **M,** and Iram; these are the clans of Edom
1Ch 1:54 **M,** and Iram; these are the clans of Edom.

MAGEDA See Index to Footnotes

MAGGOT (1) [MAGGOTS]

Job 25: 6 who is a **m,** and a human being, who is a worm!"

MAGGOTS (3) [MAGGOT]

Isa 14:11 **m** are the bed beneath you,
Hos 5:12 Therefore I am like **m** to Ephraim,
Sir 10:11 one is dead he inherits **m** and vermin and worms.

MAGI See Index to Footnotes

MAGIC (6) [MAGICIAN, MAGICIANS]

Pr 17: 8 like a **m** stone in the eyes of those who give it;
Ac 8: 9 man named Simon had previously practiced **m**
8:11 for a long time he had amazed them with his **m.**
19:19 of those who practiced **m** collected their books
Wis 17: 7 The delusions of their **m** art lay humbled,
18:13 because of their **m** arts, yet,

MAGICIAN (4) [MAGIC]

Isa 3: 3 counselor and skillful **m** and expert enchanter.
Da 2:10 has ever asked such a thing of any **m** or enchanter
Ac 13: 6 they met a certain **m,** a Jewish false prophet,
13: 8 But the **m** Elymas (for that is the translation

MAGICIANS (15) [MAGIC]

Ge 41: 8 so he sent and called for all the **m** of Egypt

Ge 41:24 But when I told it to the **m**,
Ex 7:11 and they also, the **m** of Egypt,
7:22 the **m** of Egypt did the same by their secret arts;
8: 7 But the **m** did the same by their secret arts,
8:18 The **m** tried to produce gnats by their secret arts,
8:19 the **m** said to Pharaoh, "This is the finger of God!"
9:11 The **m** could not stand before Moses because of
9:11 boils afflicted the **m** as well as all the Egyptians.
Da 1:20 he found them ten times better than all the **m**
2: 2 So the king commanded that the **m**, the enchanters,
2:27 "No wise men, enchanters, **m**,
4: 7 Then the **m**, the enchanters, the Chaldeans,
4: 9 the **m**, I know that you are endowed with a spirit of
5:11 made him chief of the **m**, enchanters, Chaldeans,

MAGISTRATE (3) [MAGISTRATES]

Lk 12:58 Thus, when you go with your accuser before a **m**,
Sir 10: 1 A wise **m** educates his people,
41:18 of a crime, before a judge or **m**;

MAGISTRATES (10) [MAGISTRATE]

Ezr 7:25 appoint **m** and judges who may judge all
Da 3: 2 the counselors, the treasurers, the justices, the **m**,
3: 3 the counselors, the treasurers, the justices, the **m**,
Ac 16:20 When they had brought them before the **m**,
16:22 and the **m** had them stripped of their clothing
16:35 When morning came, the **m** sent the police, saying,
16:36 saying, "The **m** sent word to let you go;
16:38 The police reported these words to the **m**,
Jdt 6:14 and placed him before the **m** of their town,
AdE 3:12 of King Artaxerxes to the **m** and the governors

MAGNANIMOUS (1) [MAGNANIMOUSLY]

4Mc 15:10 and self-controlled and brave and **m**,

MAGNANIMOUSLY (1) [MAGNANIMOUS]

3Mc 6:41 the generals in the cities, **m** expressing his concern:

MAGNATES‡ (2)

Rev 6:15 of the earth and the **m** and the generals and the rich
18:23 for your merchants were the **m** of the earth,

MAGNIFICENCE (2) [MAGNIFICENT]

1Mc 15:32 and his great **m**, he was amazed.
1Es 1: 5 David of Israel and the **m** of his son Solomon.

MAGNIFICENT (4) [MAGNIFICENCE, MAGNIFICENTLY]

1Ch 22: 5 to be built for the LORD must be exceedingly **m**,
Da 4:30 "Is this not **m** Babylon, which I have built as
3Mc 2: 9 when you had glorified it by your **m** manifestation,
3:17 and honor it with **m** and most beautiful offerings,

MAGNIFICENTLY (3) [MAGNIFICENT]

2Mc 3:25 For there appeared to them a **m** caparisoned horse,
4:22 He was welcomed **m** by Jason and the city,
4:49 provided **m** for their funeral.

MAGNIFIED (5) [MAGNIFY]

2Sa 7:26 Thus your name will be **m** forever in the saying,
1Ch 17:24 and **m** forever in the saying, 'The LORD of hosts,
Jer 48:26 because he **m** himself against the LORD;
48:42 because he **m** himself against the LORD.
Eze 35:13 you **m** yourselves against me with your mouth,

MAGNIFIES (1) [MAGNIFY]

Lk 1:46 And Mary said, "My soul **m** the Lord,

MAGNIFY (7) [MAGNIFIED, MAGNIFIES]

Job 19: 5 If indeed you **m** yourselves against me,
Ps 34: 3 O **m** the LORD with me,
69:30 I will **m** him with thanksgiving.
Isa 10:15 or the saw **m** itself against the one who handles it?
42:21 to **m** his teaching and make it glorious.
AdE 14:10 and to **m** forever a mortal king.
Sir 49:11 How shall we **m** Zerubbabel?

MAGOG (5)

Ge 10: 2 The descendants of Japheth: Gomer, **M**, Madai,
1Ch 1: 5 The descendants of Japheth: Gomer, **M**, Madai,
Eze 38: 2 set your face toward Gog, of the land of **M**,
39: 6 on **M** and on those who live securely in
Rev 20: 8 Gog and **M**, in order to gather them for battle;

MAGPIASH (1)

Ne 10:20 **M**, Meshullam, Hezir,

MAHALAB (1)

Jos 19:29 and it ends at the sea; **M**,

MAHALAH (KJV) See MAHLAH

MAHALALEEL (1) [=MAHALALEL]

Lk 3:37 son of Jared, son of **M**, son of Cainan,

MAHALALEL (7) [=MAHALALEEL]

Ge 5:12 he became the father of **M**.
5:13 after the birth of **M** eight hundred and forty years,
5:15 When **M** had lived sixty-five years,
5:16 **M** lived after the birth of Jared
5:17 days of **M** were eight hundred ninety-five years;
1Ch 1: 2 Kenan, **M**, Jared;
Ne 11: 4 of Shephatiah son of **M**, of the descendants

MAHALATH (4)

Ge 28: 9 and took **M** daughter of Abraham's son Ishmael,
2Ch 11:18 as his wife **M** daughter of Jerimoth son of David,
Ps 53: T *To the leader: according to* **M**. *A Maskil of David.*
88: T *To the leader: according to* **M** *Leannoth.*

MAHALI (KJV) See MAHLI

MAHANAIM‡ (13)

Ge 32: 2 So he called that place **M**.
Jos 13:26 and from **M** to the territory of Debir,
13:30 Their territory extended from **M**,
21:38 of refuge for the slayer, **M** with its pasture lands,
2Sa 2: 8 and brought him over to **M**.
2:12 went out from **M** to Gibeon.
2:29 marching the whole forenoon, they came to **M**.
17:24 to **M**, while Absalom crossed the Jordan with all
17:27 When David came to **M**, Shobi son of Nahash
19:32 the king with food while he stayed at **M**,
1Ki 2: 8 with a terrible curse on the day when I went to **M**;
4:14 Ahinadab son of Iddo, in **M**;
1Ch 6:80 with its pasture lands, **M** with its pasture lands,

MAHANEH-DAN (2) [DAN]

Jdg 13:25 The spirit of the LORD began to stir him in **M**,
18:12 On this account that place is called **M** to this day;

MAHARAI (3)

2Sa 23:28 Zalmon the Ahohite; **M** of Netophah;
1Ch 11:30 **M** of Netophah, Heled son of Baanah of Netophah,
27:13 Tenth, for the tenth month, was **M** of Netophah,

MAHATH (3)

1Ch 6:35 son of Elkanah, son of **M**, son of Amasai,
2Ch 29:12 Then the Levites arose, **M** son of Amasai,
31:13 Asahel, Jerimoth, Jozabad, Eliel, Ismachiah, **M**,

MAHAVITE (1)

1Ch 11:46 the **M**, and Jeribai and Joshaviah sons of Elnaam,

MAHAZIOTH (2)

1Ch 25: 4 Joshbekashah, Mallothi, Hothir, **M**.
25:30 to **M**, his sons and his brothers, twelve;

MAHER-SHALAL-HASH-BAZ (2)

Isa 8: 1 on it in common characters, "Belonging to **M**,"
8: 3 Then the LORD said to me, Name him **M**;

MAHLAH (5)

Nu 26:33 the names of the daughters of Zelophehad were **M**,
27: 1 **M**, Noah, Hoglah, Milcah, and Tirzah.
36:11 **M**, Tirzah, Hoglah, Milcah, and Noah,
Jos 17: 3 **M**, Noah, Hoglah, Milcah, and Tirzah.
1Ch 7:18 Hammolecheth bore Ishhod, Abiezer, and **M**.

MAHLI (13) [MAHLITES]

Ex 6:19 The sons of Merari: **M** and Mushi.
Nu 3:20 The sons of Merari by their clans: **M** and Mushi.
1Ch 6:19 The sons of Merari: **M** and Mushi.
6:29 **M**, Libni his son, Shimei his son, Uzzah his son,
6:47 of **M**, son of Mushi, son of Merari, son of Levi;
23:21 The sons of Merari: **M** and Mushi. The sons of **M**:
23:23 The sons of Mushi: **M**, Eder, and Jeremoth, three.
24:26 The sons of Merari: **M** and Mushi.
24:28 Of **M**: Eleazar, who had no sons.
24:30 The sons of Mushi: **M**, Eder, and Jerimoth.
Ezr 8:18 of the descendants of **M** son of Levi son of Israel,
1Es 8:47 of **M** son of Levi, son of Israel, namely Sherebiah

MAHLITES (2) [MAHLI]

Nu 3:33 To Merari belonged the clan of the **M** and the clan
26:58 the clan of the Hebronites, the clan of the **M**,

MAHLON (4)

Ru 1: 2 the names of his two sons were **M** and Chilion;
1: 5 both **M** and Chilion also died,
4: 9 and all that belonged to Chilion and **M**.
4:10 acquired Ruth the Moabite, the wife of **M**,

MAHOL (1)

1Ki 4:31 and Heman, Calcol, and Darda, children of **M**;

MAHSEIAH (3)

Jer 32:12 of purchase to Baruch son of Neriah son of **M**,
51:59 of **M**, when he went with King Zedekiah of Judah
Bar 1: 1 the book that Baruch son of Neriah son of **M** son

MAIANNAS (1)

1Es 9:48 Hodiah, **M** and Kelita, Azariah and Jozabad,

MAID (33) [MAIDS]

Ge 29:24 (Laban gave his **m** Zilpah to his daughter Leah to be her **m**.)
29:29 (Laban gave his **m** Bilhah to his daughter Rachel to be her **m**.)
30: 3 Then she said, "Here is my **m** Bilhah;
30: 4 So she gave him her **m** Bilhah as a wife;
30: 7 Rachel's **m** Bilhah conceived again and bore Jacob
30: 9 she took her **m** Zilpah and gave her to Jacob as
30:10 Then Leah's **m** Zilpah bore Jacob a son.
30:12 Leah's **m** Zilpah bore Jacob a second son.
30:18 "God has given me my hire because I gave my **m**
35:25 The sons of Bilhah, Rachel's **m**: Dan and Naphtali.
35:26 The sons of Zilpah, Leah's **m**: Gad and Asher.
Ex 2: 5 She saw the basket among the reeds and sent her **m**
Ps 123: 2 as the eyes of a **m** to the hand of her mistress,
Pr 30:23 and a **m** when she succeeds her mistress.
Isa 24: 2 as with the **m**, so with her mistress;
Ac 12:13 a **m** named Rhoda came to answer.
Tob 3: 8 So the **m** said to her,
8:13 they sent the **m**, lit a lamp, and opened the door;
8:14 Then the **m** came out and informed them
Jdt 8:10 she sent her **m**, who was in charge
8:33 so that I may go out with my **m**;
10: 2 She called her **m** and went down into the house
10: 5 She gave her **m** a skin of wine and a flask of oil,
10:10 Judith went out, accompanied by her **m**.
10:17 a hundred men to accompany her and her **m**,
12:15 Her **m** went ahead and spread for her on
12:19 Then she took what her **m** had prepared and ate
13: 3 Now Judith had told her **m** to stand outside
13: 9 and gave Holofernes' head to her **m**,
16:23 She set her **m** free.
AdE 15: 7 on the head of the **m** who went in front of her.

MAIDEN (3) [MAIDENS]

SS 7: 1 graceful are your feet in sandals, O queenly **m**!
7: 6 O loved one, delectable **m**!
Am 5: 2 no more to rise, is **m** Israel;

MAIDENS (4) [MAIDEN]

SS 1: 3 perfume poured out; therefore the **m** love you.
2: 2 As a lily among brambles, so is my love among **m**.
6: 8 and eighty concubines, and **m** without number.
6: 9 The **m** saw her and called her happy;

MAIDS (26) [MAID]

Ge 24:61 Then Rebekah and her **m** rose up,
31:33 and into the tent of the two **m**,
32:22 his two **m**, and his eleven children,
33: 1 among Leah and Rachel and the two **m**.
33: 2 He put the **m** with their children in front,
33: 6 Then the **m** drew near, they and their children,
1Sa 25:42 on a donkey; her five **m** attended her.
2Sa 6:20 before the eyes of his servants' **m**,
6:22 but by the **m** of whom you have spoken,
Est 2: 9 and with seven chosen **m** from the king's palace,
2: 9 and advanced her and her **m** to the best place in
4: 4 Esther's **m** and her eunuchs came and told her,
4:16 I and my **m** will also fast as you do.
Tob 3: 7 was reproached by one of her father's **m**.
8:12 of the **m** and have her go in to see if he is alive.
AdE 2: 9 as well as seven **m** chosen from the palace;
2: 9 he treated her and her **m** with special favor in
4: 4 the queen's **m** and eunuchs came and told her,
4:16 and my **m** and I will also go without food.
15: 2 she took two **m** with her;
Sus 1:15 she went in as before with only two **m**,
1:17 to her **m**, "Bring me olive oil and ointments,
1:19 When the **m** had gone out,
1:21 and this was why you sent your **m** away."
1:36 this woman came in with two **m**,
1:36 shut the garden doors, and dismissed the **m**.

MAIL (9)

Ex 28:32 like the opening in a coat of **m**,
39:23 of it was like the opening in a coat of **m**,
1Sa 17: 5 and he was armed with a coat of **m**;
17:38 on his head and clothed him with a coat of **m**.
2Ch 26:14 helmets, coats of **m**, bows, and stones for slinging.
Job 41:13 Who can penetrate its double coat of **m**?
Jer 46: 4 whet your lances, put on your coats of **m**!
51: 3 and let him not array himself in his coat of **m**.
1Mc 6:35 coats of **m**, and with brass helmets on their heads;

MAIMED (7) [MAIMS]

Lev 22:22 Anything blind, or injured, or **m**,
Zec 11:16 or seek the wandering, or heal the **m**,
Mt 15:30 bringing with them the lame, the **m**, the blind,
15:31 the **m** whole, the lame walking,
18: 8 to enter life **m** or lame than to have two hands
Mk 9:43 for you to enter life **m** than to have two hands and
2Es 2:21 do not ridicule the lame, protect the **m**.

MAIMS (1) [MAIMED]

Lev 24:19 Anyone who **m** another shall suffer the same injury

MAIN (13)

Jos 8:13 the **m** encampment that was north of the city
Jdg 20:31 along the **m** roads, one of which goes up to Bethel
20:33 The **m** body of the Israelites drew back its battle
20:38 Now the agreement between the **m** body of Israel
20:39 the **m** body of Israel should turn in battle.
20:41 Then the **m** body of Israel turned,
20:45 of them were cut down on the **m** roads,
Da 11:41 and the **m** part of the Ammonites shall escape

Mt 22: 9 Go therefore into the m streets,
Heb 8: 1 Now the m point in what we are saying is this:
1Mc 11:46 Then the people of the city seized the m streets of
2Mc 12:35 by m strength, wishing to take
4Mc 1:12 I shall begin by stating my m principle,

MAINLAND (1) [LAND]

Eze 26:17 who imposed your terror on all the m!

MAINSAIL (KJV) See FORESAIL

MAINSTAY (1)

Jer 49:35 to break the bow of Elam, the m of their might;

MAINTAIN (25) [MAINTAINED, MAINTAINING, MAINTAINS, MAINTENANCE]

Lev 26: 9 and I will m my covenant with you.
Dt 7:12 the LORD your God will m with you
32:51 by failing to m my holiness among the Israelites.
Ru 4: 5 to m the dead man's name on his inheritance."
4:10 to m the dead man's name on his inheritance,
1Ki 8:45 and their plea, and m their cause.
8:49 and their plea, m their cause
8:59 and may he m the cause of his servant and
2Ch 6:35 and their plea, and m their cause.
6:39 and their pleas, m their cause
Job 16:21 that he would m the right of a mortal with God,
Ps 82: 3 m the right of the lowly and the destitute.
Isa 56: 1 Thus says the LORD: M justice,
Eze 7:13 Because of their iniquity, they cannot m their lives.
13:18 among my people, and m your own lives?
1Co 11: 2 because you remember me in everything and m
Eph 4: 3 making every effort to m the unity of the Spirit in
1Pe 4: 8 Above all, m constant love for one another,
Sir 38:34 But they m the fabric of the world,
1Mc 7:21 Alcimus struggled to m his high priesthood,
2Mc 9:26 to you and to m your present goodwill,
10:12 and attempted to m peaceful relations with them.
11:19 you will m your goodwill toward the government,
3Mc 1:12 he did not cease to m that he ought to enter, saying,
3: 3 continued to m goodwill and unswerving loyalty

MAINTAINED (9) [MAINTAIN]

Jdg 18:31 they m as their own Micah's idol that he had made,
Ps 9: 4 For you have m my just cause;
Am 1:11 he m his anger perpetually,
Jdt 8: 7 slaves, livestock, and fields; and she m this estate.
1Mc 14:35 because of the justice and loyalty that he had m
2Mc 10:14 he m a force of mercenaries,
15:30 the man who m his youthful goodwill
2Es 6:32 and has also observed the purity that you have m
4Mc 6:18 up to old age and having m in accordance with law

MAINTAINING (3) [MAINTAIN]

3Mc 2:31 to be exacted for m the religion of their city,
3:19 By m their manifest ill-will toward us,
4Mc 17: 4 m firm an enduring hope in God.

MAINTAINS (3) [MAINTAIN]

Dt 7: 9 the faithful God who m covenant loyalty
Ps 140:12 I know that the LORD m the cause of the needy,
Pr 15:25 but m the widow's boundaries.

MAINTENANCE (2) [MAINTAIN]

1Ch 26:27 in battles they dedicated gifts for the m of
1Mc 10:36 the m be given them that is due to all the forces of

MAJESTIC (18) [MAJESTY]

Ex 15:11 Who is like you, m in holiness,
Lev 23:40 On the first day you shall take the fruit of m trees,
Dt 33:26 the heavens to your help, m through the skies.
Job 37: 4 he thunders with his m voice and he does
39:20 Its m snorting is terrible.
Ps 8: 1 how m is your name in all the earth!
8: 9 how m is your name in all the earth!
76: 4 more m than the everlasting mountains.
93: 4 More m than the thunders of mighty waters, more m than the waves of the sea, m on high is the LORD
Isa 10:34 and Lebanon with its m trees will fall.
30:30 And the LORD will cause his m voice to be heard
60:15 I will make you m forever, a joy from age to age.
Eze 32:18 with Egypt and the daughters of m nations,
2Pe 1:17 that voice was conveyed to him by the M Glory,
Sir 18: 5 Who can measure his m power?
2Mc 3:34 report to all people the m power of God."

MAJESTICALLY (1) [MAJESTY]

AdE 15: 2 m adorned, after invoking the aid of the all-seeing

MAJESTY (60) [MAJESTIC, MAJESTICALLY]

Ex 15: 7 of your m you overthrew your adversaries;
Dt 33:17 A firstborn bull—m is his!
1Ch 16:27 Honor and m are before him;
29:11 the power, the glory, the victory, and the m;
29:25 and bestowed upon him such royal m as had
Est 1: 4 and the splendor and pomp of his m for many days,
Job 13:11 Will not his m terrify you,
31:23 and I could not have faced his m.
Job 37:22 around God is awesome m.
40:10 "Deck yourself with m and dignity;
Ps 21: 5 splendor and m you bestow on him.
29: 4 the voice of the LORD is full of m.
45: 3 O mighty one, in your glory and m.
45: 4 In your m ride on victoriously for the cause
68:34 Ascribe power to God, whose m is over Israel;
93: 1 The LORD is king, he is robed in m;
96: 6 Honor and m are before him;
104: 1 You are clothed with honor and m,
111: 3 Full of honor and m is his work,
145: 5 On the glorious splendor of your m,
Isa 2:10 and from the glory of his m.
2:19 and from the glory of his m,
2:21 and from the glory of his m,
24:14 they shout from the west over the m of the LORD.
26:10 and do not see the m of the LORD.
33: 3 before your m, nations scattered.
33:21 But there the LORD in m will be for us a place
35: 2 the m of Carmel and Sharon.
35: 2 the glory of the LORD, the m of our God.
53: 2 he had no form or m that we should look at him,
Jer 22:18 "Alas, lord!" or "Alas, his m!"
La 1: 6 From daughter Zion has departed all her m.
Da 4:30 by my mighty power and for my glorious m?"
4:36 and my m and splendor were restored to me for
5:18 Nebuchadnezzar kingship, greatness, glory, and m.
11:21 a contemptible person on whom royal m had
Mic 5: 4 in the m of the name of the LORD his God.
Na 2: 2 (For the LORD is restoring the m of Jacob,
2: 2 as well as the m of Israel,
Ac 19:27 be deprived of her m that brought all Asia and
25:21 in custody for the decision of his Imperial M,
25:25 and when he appealed to his Imperial M,
Heb 1: 3 he sat down at the right hand of the M on high,
8: 1 at the right hand of the throne of the M in
2Pe 1:16 but we had been eyewitnesses of his m.
Jude 1:25 through Jesus Christ our Lord, be glory, m, power,
Tob 13: 6 and show his power and m to a nation of sinners:
13: 8 Let all people speak of his m,
14: 2 and acknowledging God's m.
AdE 15: 6 clothed in the full array of his m,
Wis 18:24 and your m was on the diadem upon his head.
Sir 2:17 for equal to his m is his mercy,
17: 8 the fear of him into their hearts to show them the m
17:13 Their eyes saw his glorious m,
36:19 Fill Zion with your m, and your temple
39:15 Ascribe m to his name and give thanks to him
43:15 In his m he gives the clouds their strength,
44: 2 The Lord apportioned to them great glory, his m
2Mc 15:13 and of marvelous m and authority.
1Es 4:40 and the kingship and the power and the m of all

MAJORITY (6)

Ex 23: 2 You shall not follow a m in wrongdoing;
23: 2 in a lawsuit, you shall not side with the m so as
1Ch 12:29 the m had continued to keep their allegiance to
Ac 27:12 the m was in favor of putting to sea from there,
2Co 2: 6 This punishment by the m is enough for such
3Mc 2:32 the m acted firmly with a courageous spirit and did

MAKAZ (1)

1Ki 4: 9 in M, Shaalbim, Beth-shemesh,

MAKE‡ (1199) [MADE, MAKER, MAKERS, MAKES, MAKING, MERRYMAKERS, MERRYMAKING, MISCHIEF-MAKER, MONEY-MAKING, TENTMAKERS]

Ge 1:26 God said, "Let us m humankind in our image,
2:18 I will m him a helper as his partner."
3: 6 and that the tree was to be desired to m one wise,
6:13 "I have determined to m an end of all flesh,
6:14 M yourself an ark of cypress wood; m rooms in the ark, and cover it inside and out
6:15 This is how you are to m it:
6:16 M a roof for the ark, and finish it to a cubit above;
6:16 m it with lower, second, and third decks.
9:12 of the covenant that I m between me and you
9:27 May God m space for Japheth,
11: 3 they said to one another, "Come, let us m bricks,
11: 4 and let us m a name for ourselves;
12: 2 I will m of you a great nation, and I will bless you, and m your name great,
13:16 I will m your offspring like the dust of the earth;
17: 2 And I will m my covenant between me and you, and will m you exceedingly numerous."
17: 6 I will m you exceedingly fruitful; and I will m nations of you,
17:20 and m him fruitful and exceedingly numerous;
17:20 and I will m him a great nation.
18: 6 "M ready quickly three measures of choice flour,
18: 6 of choice flour, knead it, and m cakes."
19:32 Come, let us m our father drink wine,
19:34 let us m him drink wine tonight also;
21:13 I will m a nation of him also,
21:18 for I will m a great nation of him."
22:17 and I will m your offspring as numerous as
24: 3 and I will m you swear by the LORD,
24:40 with you and m your way successful.
24:42 you will only m successful the way I am going!
26: 4 I will m your offspring as numerous as the stars
26:24 and will bless you and m your offspring numerous
26:28 between you and us, and let us m a covenant
28: 3 May God Almighty bless you and m you fruitful
Ge 31:44 Come now, let us m a covenant, you and I;
32:12 and m your offspring as the sand of the sea,
34: 9 M marriages with us; give your daughters to us,
35: 1 M an altar there to the God who appeared to you
35: 3 that I may m an altar there to
40:14 please do me the kindness to m mention of me
42:38 to him on the journey that you are to m,
43:16 and slaughter an animal and m ready,
43:18 to m slaves of us and take our donkeys."
46: 3 for I will m of you a great nation there.
48: 4 to m you fruitful and increase your numbers; I will m of you a company of peoples,
48:20 'God m you like Ephraim and like Manasseh.' "
Ex 5: 7 the people straw to m bricks, as before;
5:16 yet they say to us, 'M bricks!'
6: 3 'The LORD' I did not m myself known to them.
8: 5 and m frogs come up on the land of Egypt.' "
8:23 Thus I will m a distinction between my people
9: 4 But the LORD will m a distinction between
9:16 and to m my name resound through all the earth.
18:16 and I m known to them the statutes
18:20 the statutes and instructions and m known to them
20: 4 You shall not m for yourself an idol,
20: 7 You shall not m wrongful use of the name of
20:23 You shall not m gods of silver alongside me, nor shall you m for yourselves gods of gold.
20:24 You need m for me only an altar of earth
20:25 But if you m for me an altar of stone,
21:34 the owner of the pit shall m restitution,
22: 1 The thief shall m restitution, but if unable to do so,
22: 6 the one who started the fire shall m full restitution.
22:16 the bride-price for her and m her his wife.
22:29 to m offerings from the fullness of your harvest
23:27 I will m all your enemies turn their backs to you.
23:32 You shall m no covenant with them and their gods.
23:33 or they will m you sin against me;
25: 8 And have them m me a sanctuary,
25: 9 and of all its furniture, so you shall m it.
25:10 They shall m an ark of acacia wood;
25:11 you shall m a molding of gold upon it all around.
25:13 You shall m poles of acacia wood,
25:17 Then you shall m a mercy seat of pure gold;
25:18 You shall m two cherubim of gold;
25:18 you shall m them of hammered work,
25:19 M one cherub at the one end,
25:19 with the mercy seat you shall m the cherubim
25:23 You shall m a table of acacia wood,
25:24 and m a molding of gold around it.
25:25 You shall m around it a rim a handbreadth wide,
25:26 You shall m for it four rings of gold,
25:28 You shall m the poles of acacia wood,
25:29 You shall m its plates and dishes for incense,
25:29 you shall m them of pure gold.
25:31 You shall m a lampstand of pure gold.
25:37 You shall m the seven lamps for it;
25:40 that you m them according to the pattern for them,
26: 1 Moreover you shall m the tabernacle
26: 1 you shall m them with cherubim skillfully worked
26: 4 You shall m loops of blue on the edge of
26: 4 and likewise you shall m loops on the edge of
26: 5 You shall m fifty loops on the one curtain,
26: 5 and you shall m fifty loops on the edge of
26: 6 You shall m fifty clasps of gold,
26: 7 You shall also m curtains of goats' hair for a tent
26: 7 you shall m eleven curtains.
26:10 You shall m fifty loops on the edge of the curtain
26:11 You shall m fifty clasps of bronze,
26:14 You shall m for the tent a covering
26:15 You shall m upright frames of acacia wood for
26:17 you shall m these for all the frames of
26:18 You shall m the frames for the tabernacle:
26:19 and you shall m forty bases of silver under
26:22 of the tabernacle westward you shall m six frames.
26:23 You shall m two frames for corners of
26:26 You shall m bars of acacia wood,
26:29 and shall m their rings of gold to hold the bars;
26:31 You shall m a curtain of blue, purple,
26:36 You shall m a screen for the entrance of the tent,
26:37 You shall m for the screen five pillars of acacia,
27: 1 You shall m the altar of acacia wood,
27: 2 You shall m horns for it on its four corners;
27: 3 You shall m pots for it to receive its ashes,
27: 3 you shall m all its utensils of bronze.
27: 4 You shall also m for it a grating,
27: 4 and on the net you shall m four bronze rings
27: 6 You shall m poles for the altar,
27: 8 You shall m it hollow, with boards.
27: 9 You shall m the court of the tabernacle.
28: 2 You shall m sacred vestments for
28: 3 that they m Aaron's vestments to consecrate him
28: 4 These are the vestments that they shall m:
28: 4 When they m these sacred vestments
28: 6 They shall m the ephod of gold, of blue, purple,
28:13 You shall m settings of gold filigree,
28:15 You shall m a breastpiece of judgment,
28:15 you shall m it in the style of the ephod;
28:15 and of fine twisted linen you shall m it.
28:22 You shall m for the breastpiece chains
28:23 you shall m for the breastpiece two rings of gold,
28:26 You shall m two rings of gold,
28:27 You shall m two rings of gold,
28:31 You shall m the robe of the ephod all of blue.
28:33 On its lower hem you shall m pomegranates
28:36 You shall m a rosette of pure gold,
28:39 You shall m the checkered tunic of fine linen,
28:39 and you shall m a turban of fine linen,
28:39 you shall m a sash embroidered with needlework.

Ex 28:40 For Aaron's sons you shall **m** tunics and sashes
28:40 you shall **m** them for their glorious adornment.
28:42 You shall **m** for them linen undergarments
29: 2 You shall **m** them of choice wheat flour.
29:36 when you **m** atonement for it, and shall anoint it,
29:37 Seven days you shall **m** atonement for the altar,
30: 1 You shall **m** an altar on which to offer incense;
30: 1 you shall **m** it of acacia wood.
30: 3 and you shall **m** for it a molding of gold all around.
30: 4 And you shall **m** two golden rings for it;
30: 4 on two opposite sides of it you shall **m** them,
30: 5 You shall **m** the poles of acacia wood,
30:15 to the LORD to **m** atonement for your lives.
30:18 You shall **m** a bronze basin with a bronze stand
30:20 to **m** an offering by fire to the LORD,
30:25 and you shall **m** of these
30:32 and you shall **m** no other like it in composition;
30:35 and **m** an incense blended as by the perfumer,
30:37 you **m** incense according to this composition,
30:37 you shall not **m** it for yourselves;
31: 6 so that they may **m** all that I have commanded you:
32: 1 "Come, **m** gods for us, who shall go before us;
32:10 and of you I will **m** a great nation."
32:23 They said to me, '**M** us gods,
32:30 perhaps I can **m** atonement for your sin."
33:19 he said, "I will **m** all my goodness pass before you,
34:10 He said: I hereby **m** a covenant.
34:12 not to **m** a covenant with the inhabitants of the land
34:15 You shall not **m** a covenant with the inhabitants of
34:16 to their gods will **m** your sons
34:17 You shall not **m** cast idols.
35:10 and **m** all that the LORD has commanded:
35:24 Everyone who could **m** an offering of silver
36: 6 or woman is to **m** anything else as an offering for
Lev 4:20 The priest shall **m** atonement for them,
4:26 Thus the priest shall **m** atonement on his behalf
4:31 Thus the priest shall **m** atonement on your behalf,
4:35 Thus the priest shall **m** atonement on your behalf
5: 6 and the priest shall **m** atonement on your behalf
5:10 Thus the priest shall **m** atonement on your behalf
5:13 Thus the priest shall **m** atonement on your behalf
5:16 And you shall **m** restitution for the holy thing
5:16 The priest shall **m** atonement on your behalf with
5:18 and the priest shall **m** atonement on your behalf for
6: 7 The priest shall **m** atonement on your behalf before
8:15 Thus he consecrated it, to **m** atonement for it.
8:34 to be done to **m** atonement for you.
9: 7 and **m** atonement for yourself and for the people;
9: 7 and **m** atonement for them;
10:17 to **m** atonement on their behalf before the LORD.
11:43 not **m** yourselves detestable with any creature
11:47 to **m** a distinction between the unclean and
12: 7 and **m** atonement on her behalf;
12: 8 and the priest shall **m** atonement on her behalf,
13: 8 The priest shall **m** an examination,
13:10 The priest shall **m** an examination,
13:13 then the priest shall **m** an examination,
13:20 The priest shall **m** an examination,
13:39 the priest shall **m** an examination, and if the spots
14: 3 and the priest shall **m** an examination.
14:18 the priest shall **m** atonement on his behalf before
14:19 to **m** atonement for the one to be cleansed
14:20 Thus the priest shall **m** atonement on his behalf
14:21 to **m** atonement on his behalf,
14:29 to **m** atonement on his behalf before the LORD.
14:31 and the priest shall **m** atonement before the LORD
14:39 on the seventh day and **m** an inspection;
14:44 the priest shall go and **m** inspection;
14:53 so he shall **m** atonement for the house,
15:15 the priest shall **m** atonement on his behalf before
15:30 the priest shall **m** atonement on her behalf before
16: 6 shall **m** atonement for himself and for his house.
16:10 before the LORD to **m** atonement over it,
16:11 shall **m** atonement for himself and for his house;
16:16 Thus he shall **m** atonement for the sanctuary,
16:17 to **m** atonement in the sanctuary until he comes out
16:18 before the LORD and **m** atonement on its behalf,
16:27 whose blood was brought in to **m** atonement in
16:32 as priest in his father's place shall **m** atonement,
16:33 He shall **m** atonement for the sanctuary,
16:33 and he shall **m** atonement for the tent of meeting
16:33 and he shall **m** atonement for the priests and for all
16:34 to **m** atonement for the people of Israel once in
19: 4 not turn to idols or **m** cast images for yourselves:
19:22 the priest shall **m** atonement for him with the ram
19:28 You shall not **m** any gashes in your flesh for
20:25 therefore **m** a distinction between the clean animal
21: 5 They shall not **m** bald spots upon their heads,
21: 5 or **m** any gashes in their flesh.
23:21 On that same day you shall **m** proclamation;
23:28 a day of atonement, to **m** atonement on your behalf
24:18 Anyone who kills an animal shall **m** restitution
24:21 One who kills an animal shall **m** restitution for it;
25:14 When you **m** a sale to your neighbor or buy
25:36 not take interest in advance or otherwise **m** a profit
25:39 you shall not **m** them serve as slaves.
25:52 to the years involved they shall **m** payment
26: 1 You shall **m** for yourselves no idols
26: 6 and no one shall **m** you afraid;
26: 9 I will look with favor upon you and **m** you fruitful
26:10 and you shall have to clear out the old to **m** way
26:19 and I will **m** your sky like iron and your earth
26:22 they shall **m** you few in number,
26:31 will **m** your sanctuaries desolate,
26:41 and they **m** amends for their iniquity,
26:43 while they shall **m** amends for their iniquity,
27:25 twenty gerahs shall **m** a shekel.
Lev 27:33 or bad, or **m** substitution for it;
Nu 3:10 But you shall **m** a register of Aaron
5: 7 The person shall **m** full restitution for the wrong,
5:19 Then the priest shall **m** her take an oath, saying,
5:21 the priest **m** the woman take the oath of the curse
5:21 "the LORD **m** you an execration and an oath
5:22 and **m** your womb discharge,
5:24 He shall **m** the woman drink the water of bitterness
5:26 and afterward shall **m** the woman drink the water.
6: 2 When either men or women **m** a special vow,
6:11 and **m** atonement for them,
6:17 also shall **m** the accompanying grain offering
6:25 the LORD **m** his face to shine upon you,
8:12 to **m** atonement for the Levites.
8:19 and to **m** atonement for the Israelites,
10: 2 **M** two silver trumpets; you shall make them
10: 2 you shall **m** them of hammered work;
12: 6 I the LORD **m** myself known to them in visions;
14:12 and I will **m** of you a nation greater
15: 3 and you **m** an offering by fire to the LORD from
15: 3 to **m** a pleasing odor for the LORD,
15:25 The priest shall **m** atonement for all
15:28 the priest shall **m** atonement before the LORD for
15:28 to **m** atonement for the person,
15:38 to **m** fringes on the corners of their garments
16: 5 the morning the LORD will **m** known who is his,
16:38 **M** them into hammered plates as a covering for
16:46 to the congregation and **m** atonement for them.
17: 5 the Israelites that they continually **m** against you.
17:10 you may **m** an end of their complaints against me,
21: 8 LORD said to Moses, "**M** a poisonous serpent,
28:22 for a sin offering, to **m** atonement for you.
28:30 with one male goat, to **m** atonement for you.
29: 5 for a sin offering, to **m** atonement for you.
31:26 of the ancestral houses of the congregation **m**
31:50 to **m** atonement for ourselves before the LORD."
32: 5 do not **m** us cross the Jordan."
Dt 4: 9 **m** them known to your children
4:23 to **m** for yourselves an idol in the form of anything
5: 3 with our ancestors did the LORD **m** this covenant,
5: 8 You shall not **m** for yourself an idol,
5:11 You shall not **m** wrongful use of the name of
7: 2 **M** no covenant with them and show them no
7:22 you will not be able to **m** a quick end of them,
8: 3 in order to **m** you understand that one does not live
9:14 and I will **m** of you a nation mightier
10: 1 and **m** an ark of wood.
13:14 you shall inquire and **m** a thorough investigation.
16:21 as a sacred pole beside the altar that you **m** for
17: 4 and you **m** a thorough inquiry,
17: 8 to **m** between one kind of bloodshed and another,
19:18 and the judges shall **m** a thorough inquiry.
22: 8 you shall **m** a parapet for your roof;
22:12 You shall **m** tassels on the four corners of the cloak
23:21 If you **m** a vow to the LORD your God,
24:10 When you **m** your neighbor a loan of any kind,
25: 2 the judge shall **m** that person lie down and
26: 5 you shall **m** this response before
27: 7 **m** sacrifices of well-being,
28:11 The LORD will **m** you abound in prosperity,
28:13 The LORD will **m** you the head, and not the tail;
28:21 The LORD will **m** the pestilence cling to you
29: 1 that the LORD commanded Moses to **m** with
30: 5 he will **m** you more prosperous
30: 9 LORD your God will **m** you abundantly prosperous
32:21 So I will **m** them jealous with what is no people,
32:39 I kill and I **m** alive; I wound and I heal;
32:42 I will **m** my arrows drunk with blood,
Jos 1: 8 For then you shall **m** your way prosperous,
5: 2 "**M** flint knives and circumcise the Israelites
6: 5 When they **m** a long blast with the ram's horn,
6:18 and take any of the devoted things and **m** the camp
7: 3 do not **m** the whole people toil up there."
7:19 the LORD God of Israel and **m** confession to him.
9: 6 so now **m** a treaty with us."
9: 7 then how can we **m** a treaty with you?"
9:11 come now, **m** a treaty with us." '
22:12 of the Israelites gathered at Shiloh, to **m** war
22:25 So your children might **m** our children cease
23: 7 or **m** mention of the names of their gods,
Jdg 2: 2 not **m** a covenant with the inhabitants of this land;
5: 3 I will **m** melody to the LORD, the God of Israel.
5:29 Her wisest ladies **m** answer, indeed,
6:39 please, **m** trial with the fleece just once more;
8:24 Gideon said to them, "Let me **m** a request of you;
16:13 of my head with the web and **m** it tight with
17: 3 to **m** an idol of cast metal."
Ru 3: 3 but do not **m** yourself known to the man
4:11 May the LORD **m** the woman who is coming
1Sa 1:14 long will you **m** a drunken spectacle of yourself?
2: 8 **m** them sit with princes and inherit a seat of honor.
2:19 His mother used to **m** for him a little robe
2:25 against the LORD, who can **m** intercession?"
3:11 in Israel that will **m** both ears of anyone who hears
6: 5 So you must **m** images of your tumors and images
8:12 and to **m** his implements of war and the equipment
9:27 that I may **m** known to you the word of God."
11: 1 "**M** a treaty with us, and we will serve you."
11: 2 "On this condition I will **m** a treaty with you,
12:22 because it has pleased the LORD to **m** you
13:19 "The Hebrews must not **m** swords or spears
17:25 and **m** his family free in Israel."
18:25 Now Saul planned to **m** David fall by the hand of
22: 7 and vineyards, will he **m** you all commanders
23:22 Go and **m** sure once more;
25:28 the LORD will certainly **m** my lord a sure house,
25:39 David sent and wooed Abigail, to **m** her his wife.
1Sa 28: 2 "Very well, I will **m** you my bodyguard for life."
31: 4 not come and thrust me through, and **m** sport
2Sa 3:12 **M** your covenant with me,
3:13 He said, "Good; I will **m** a covenant with you.
3:21 in order that they may **m** a covenant with you,
6:22 I will **m** myself yet more contemptible than this,
7: 9 and I will **m** for you a great name,
7:11 to you that the LORD will **m** you a house.
7:23 and to **m** a name for himself,
13: 6 the king, "Please let my sister Tamar come and **m**
15:20 and shall I today **m** you wander about with us,
21: 3 How shall I **m** expiation, that you may bless
1Ki 1:37 and **m** his throne greater than the throne
1:47 saying, 'May God **m** the name
1:47 and **m** his throne greater than your throne.'
2:16 I have one request to **m** of you; do not refuse me."
2:20 she said, "I have one small request to **m** of you;
2:20 the king said to her, "**M** your request, my mother;
2:42 "Did I not **m** you swear by the LORD,
4: 7 each one had to **m** provision for one month in
5: 9 I will **m** it into rafts to go by sea to
11:34 but will **m** him ruler all the days of his life,
12: 1 for all Israel had come to Shechem to **m** him king.
16: 3 and I will **m** your house like the house
16:21 to **m** him king, and half followed Omri.
17:13 but first **m** me a little cake of it and bring it to me,
17:13 afterwards **m** something for yourself and your son.
19: 2 if I do not **m** your life like the life of one of them
21:22 and I will **m** your house like the house
22:16 "How many times must I **m** you swear
2Ki 3:16 'I will **m** this wadi full of pools.'
4:10 Let us **m** a small roof chamber with walls,
4:38 and **m** some stew for the company of prophets."
7: 2 if the LORD were to **m** windows in the sky,
7:19 if the LORD were to **m** windows in the sky,
9: 9 I will **m** the house of Ahab like the house
10: 5 We will not **m** anyone king;
12: 3 the people continued to sacrifice and **m** offerings
18:23 **m** a wager with my master the king of Assyria:
18:30 Do not let Hezekiah **m** you rely on the LORD
18:31 '**M** your peace with me and come out to me;
19:25 that you should **m** fortified cities crash into heaps
23: 5 the kings of Judah had ordained to **m** offerings in
23:10 so that no one would **m** a son or a daughter pass
1Ch 6:49 of the most holy place, to **m** atonement for Israel,
10: 4 not come and **m** sport of me."
11:10 together with all Israel, to **m** him king,
12:31 to come and **m** David king.
12:38 came to Hebron with full intent to **m** David king
12:38 of Israel were of a single mind to **m** David king.
16: 8 **m** known his deeds among the peoples.
17: 8 and I will **m** for you a name,
22: 5 I will therefore **m** preparation for it."
23:13 so that he and his sons forever should **m** offerings
27:23 the LORD had promised to **m** Israel as numerous
29:12 in your hand to **m** great and to give strength to all.
29:14 that we should be able to **m** this freewill offering?
2Ch 2: 6 except as a place to **m** offerings before him?
2:18 and three thousand six hundred as overseers to **m**
5:13 the trumpeters and singers to **m** themselves heard
7:20 of my sight, and will **m** it a proverb and a byword
10: 1 for all Israel had come to Shechem to **m** him king.
11:22 for he intended to **m** him king.
17:10 and they did not **m** war against Jehoshaphat.
18:15 "How many times must I **m** you swear
22: 5 with Jehoram son of King Ahab of Israel to **m** war
26:13 who could **m** war with mighty power,
26:16 and entered the temple of the LORD to **m** offering
26:18 Uzziah, to **m** offering to the LORD,
26:18 who are consecrated to **m** offering.
26:19 Now he had a censer in his hand to **m** offering,
28:25 of Judah he made high places to **m** offerings
29:10 it is in my heart to **m** a covenant with the LORD,
29:11 and to be his ministers and **m** offerings to him."
29:24 to **m** atonement for all Israel.
30: 5 to **m** a proclamation throughout all Israel,
30:17 to **m** it holy to the LORD.
32:12 and upon it you shall **m** your offerings'?
35: 4 **M** preparations by your ancestral houses
35: 6 and on behalf of your kindred **m** preparations,
Ezr 4:16 We **m** known to the king that,
4:21 and that this city not be rebuilt, until I **m** a decree.
6: 8 Moreover I **m** a decree regarding what you shall do
6:12 **m** a decree; let it be done with all diligence."
7:14 by the king and his seven counselors to **m** inquiries
10: 3 So now let us **m** a covenant with our God
10:11 Now **m** confession to the LORD the God
Ne 2: 8 directing him to give me timber to **m** beams for
6:13 to intimidate me and **m** me sin by acting
6:14 of the prophets who wanted to **m** me afraid.
8:12 and to send portions and to **m** great rejoicing,
8:15 and other leafy trees to **m** booths, as it is written."
9:31 in your great mercies you did not **m** an end of them
9:38 of all this we **m** a firm agreement in writing,
10:33 and the sin offerings to **m** atonement for Israel,
Est 4: 8 and charge her to go to the king to **m** supplication
9:22 they should **m** them days of feasting and gladness,
Job 6:22 Have I said, '**M** me a gift'?
6:24 **m** me understand how I have gone wrong.
7:17 that you **m** so much of them,
8: 5 If you will seek God and **m** supplication to
11:19 You will lie down, and no one will **m** you afraid;
13:23 **M** me know my transgression and my sin.
13:26 and **m** me reap the iniquities of my youth.
17:12 They **m** night into day; 'The light,'
19: 5 and **m** my humiliation an argument against me,
22: 3 or is it gain to him if you **m** your ways blameless?

Job 27:15 and their widows **m** no lamentation.
30: 1 "But now they **m** sport of me,
30:22 You lift me up on the wind, you **m** me ride on it,
31:15 Did not he who made me in the womb **m** them?
34:11 according to their ways he will **m** it befall them.
38:27 and to **m** the ground put forth grass?
39:20 Do you **m** it leap like the locust?
41: 3 Will it **m** many supplications to you?
41: 4 Will it **m** a covenant with you to be taken
41:28 The arrow cannot **m** it flee;
Ps 2: 8 Ask of me, and I will **m** the nations your heritage,
4: 8 for you alone, O LORD, **m** me lie down in safety.
5: 8 **m** your way straight before me.
5:10 **M** them bear their guilt, O God;
7:15 They **m** a pit, digging it out,
21: 6 you **m** him glad with the joy of your presence.
21: 9 You will **m** them like a fiery furnace
22: 7 they **m** mouths at me, they shake their heads;
25: 4 **M** me to know your ways, O LORD;
27: 6 I will sing and **m** melody to the LORD.
33: 2 **m** melody to him with the harp of ten strings.
37: 6 He will **m** your vindication shine like the light,
38:22 **m** haste to help me, O Lord, my salvation.
39: 8 Do not **m** me the scorn of the fool.
40: 4 Happy are those who **m** the LORD their trust,
40:13 O LORD, **m** haste to help me.
45: 8 ivory palaces stringed instruments **m** you glad;
45:16 you will **m** them princes in all the earth.
46: 4 There is a river whose streams **m** glad the city
50:18 You **m** friends with a thief when you see one,
57: 7 I will sing and **m** melody.
59: 4 for no fault of mine, they run and **m** ready.
59:11 **m** them totter by your power,
65: 8 you **m** the gateways of the morning and
66: 1 **M** a joyful noise to God, all the earth;
66:15 I will **m** an offering of bulls and goats.
67: 1 to us and bless us and **m** his face to shine upon us,
69:12 and the drunkards **m** songs about me.
69:17 in distress—**m** haste to answer me.
69:23 and **m** their loins tremble continually.
70: 1 O LORD, **m** haste to help me!
71:12 O my God, **m** haste to help me!
73:18 you **m** them fall to ruin.
76:11 **M** vows to the LORD your God,
80: 6 You **m** us the scorn of our neighbors;
83: 5 against you they **m** a covenant—
83:11 **M** their nobles like Oreb and Zeeb,
83:13 O my God, **m** them like whirling dust,
84: 6 As they go through the valley of Baca they **m** it
85:13 and will **m** a path for his steps.
89:27 I will **m** him the firstborn,
90:15 **M** us glad as many days as you have afflicted us,
95: 1 let us **m** a joyful noise to the rock of our salvation!
95: 2 let us **m** a joyful noise to him with songs of praise!
97: 7 those who **m** their boast in worthless idols;
98: 4 **M** a joyful noise to the LORD, all the earth;
98: 6 and the sound of the horn **m** a joyful noise before
100: 1 **M** a joyful noise to the LORD, all the earth.
104: 3 you **m** the clouds your chariot,
104: 4 you **m** the winds your messengers,
104:10 You **m** springs gush forth in the valleys;
104:15 oil to **m** the face shine, and bread to strengthen the
104:20 You **m** darkness, and it is night,
105: 1 **m** known his deeds among the peoples.
106: 8 so that he might **m** known his mighty power.
106:26 and swore to them that he would **m** them fall in
108: 1 I will sing and **m** melody.
109: 4 even while I **m** prayer for them.
110: 1 until I **m** your enemies your footstool."
113: 8 to **m** them sit with princes,
115: 7 they **m** no sound in their throats.
115: 8 Those who **m** them are like them;
119:27 **M** me understand the way of your precepts,
119:54 have been my songs wherever I **m** my home.
119:135 **M** your face shine upon your servant,
119:165 nothing can **m** them stumble.
135:18 Those who **m** them and all who trust them shall
139: 8 if I **m** my bed in Sheol, you are there.
140: 3 They **m** their tongue sharp as a snake's,
142: 1 with my voice I **m** supplication to the LORD.
144: 6 **M** the lightning flash and scatter them;
145:12 to **m** known to all people your mighty deeds,
147: 7 **m** melody to our God on the lyre.
Pr 1:23 I will **m** my words known to you.
3: 6 and he will **m** straight your paths.
13:10 By insolence the heedless **m** strife,
15:23 To **m** an apt answer is a joy to anyone,
15:27 Those who are greedy for unjust gain **m** trouble
20:11 Even children **m** themselves known by their acts,
20:30 beatings **m** clean the innermost parts.
22:24 **M** no friends with those given to anger,
27: 9 Perfume and incense **m** the heart glad,
27:11 Be wise, my child, and **m** my heart glad,
30:26 yet they **m** their homes in the rocks;
Ecc 2: 1 I will **m** a test of pleasure; enjoy yourself."
5: 4 you **m** a vow to God, do not delay fulfilling it;
7:13 who can **m** straight what he has made crooked?
10: 1 Dead flies **m** the perfumer's ointment give off
SS 1: 4 Draw me after you, let us **m** haste.
1: 7 where you **m** it lie down at noon;
1:11 We will **m** you ornaments of gold,
8:14 **M** haste, my beloved, and be like a gazelle or
Isa 1:15 even though you **m** many prayers, I will not listen;
1:16 Wash yourselves; **m** yourselves clean;
3: 4 And I will **m** boys their princes,
3: 7 you shall not **m** me leader of the people."
5: 6 I will **m** it a waste;

Isa 5:19 "Let him **m** haste, let him speed his work
6:10 **M** the mind of this people dull, and stop their ears,
7: 6 for ourselves and **m** the son of Tabeel king in it;
9: 1 but in the latter time he will **m** glorious the way of
10: 1 Ah, you who **m** iniquitous decrees,
10: 2 and that you may **m** the orphans your prey!
10:23 For the Lord GOD of hosts will **m** a full end,
11:15 and **m** a way to cross on foot;
12: 4 **m** known his deeds among the nations;
13: 9 to **m** the earth a desolation,
13:12 I will **m** mortals more rare than fine gold,
13:13 Therefore I will **m** the heavens tremble,
13:20 shepherds will not **m** their flocks lie down there.
14:14 I will **m** myself like the Most High."
14:23 And I will **m** it a possession of the hedgehog,
14:30 but I will **m** your root die of famine,
16: 3 **m** your shade like night at the height of noon;
17: 2 and no one will **m** them afraid.
17:11 though you **m** them grow on the day
17:11 and **m** them blossom in the morning that you sow;
19:12 Let them tell you and **m** known what the LORD
19:21 LORD will **m** himself known to the Egyptians;
19:21 they will **m** vows to the LORD and perform them.
23:16 **M** sweet melody, sing many songs,
24: 1 about to lay waste the earth and **m** it desolate,
25: 6 of hosts will **m** for all peoples a feast of rich food,
26: 7 you **m** smooth the path of the righteous.
27: 5 let it **m** peace with me, let it **m** peace with me.
27:11 women come and **m** a fire of them.
28:17 And I will **m** justice the line,
29:16 of its maker, "He did not **m** me";
30: 1 who **m** an alliance, but against my will,
32:11 strip, and **m** yourselves bare,
35: 3 and **m** firm the feeble knees.
36: 8 **m** a wager with my master the king of Assyria:
36:15 Do not let Hezekiah **m** you rely on the LORD
36:16 '**M** your peace with me and come out to me;
37:26 that you should **m** fortified cities crash into heaps
38: 8 I will **m** the shadow cast by the declining sun on
38:16 Oh, restore me to health and **m** me live!
38:19 fathers **m** known to children your faithfulness.
40: 3 **m** straight in the desert a highway for our God.
41:15 Now, I will **m** of you a threshing sledge, sharp,
41:15 and you shall **m** the hills like chaff.
41:18 I will **m** the wilderness a pool of water,
42: 2 or **m** it heard in the street;
42:21 to magnify his teaching and **m** it glorious.
43:19 I will **m** a way in the wilderness and rivers in
44: 9 All who **m** idols are nothing,
44:19 Now shall I **m** the rest of it an abomination?
45: 7 I **m** weal and create woe;
45:13 and I will **m** all his paths straight;
45:14 They will **m** supplication to you, saying,
46: 5 To whom will you liken me and **m** me equal,
48: 6 From this time forward I **m** you hear new things,
49:20 **m** room for me to settle."
49:26 I will **m** your oppressors eat their own flesh,
50: 2 I **m** the rivers a desert;
50: 3 and **m** sackcloth their covering.
51: 3 and will **m** her wilderness like Eden,
53:10 When you **m** his life an offering for sin,
53:11 righteous one, my servant, shall **m** many righteous,
54:12 I will **m** your pinnacles of rubies,
55: 3 I will **m** with you an everlasting covenant,
56: 7 and **m** them joyful in my house of prayer;
58: 4 as you do today will not **m** your voice heard
58:11 in parched places, and **m** your bones strong;
58:14 and I will **m** you ride upon the heights of the earth;
59: 6 they cannot cover themselves with what they **m.**
60:15 I will **m** you majestic forever,
61: 8 and I will **m** an everlasting covenant with them.
63:12 before them to **m** for himself an everlasting name,
63:14 to **m** for yourself a glorious name.
63:17 do you **m** us stray from your ways
64: 2 to **m** your name known to your adversaries,
66:22 new heavens and the new earth, which I will **m,**
Jer 4: 7 to **m** your land a waste; your cities will be ruins
4:27 yet I will not **m** a full end.
5:10 but do not **m** a full end;
5:10 says the LORD, I will not **m** a full end of you.
5:28 the cause of the orphan, to **m** it prosper,
6: 8 and **m** you a desolation, an uninhabited land.
6:26 **m** mourning as for an only child,
7: 9 swear falsely, **m** offerings to Baal,
7:18 to **m** cakes for the queen of heaven;
9:11 I will **m** Jerusalem a heap of ruins, a lair of jackals;
9:11 and I will **m** the towns of Judah a desolation,
10:11 not **m** the heavens and the earth shall perish from
10:22 a great commotion from the land of the north to **m**
11:12 and cry out to the gods to whom they **m** offerings,
11:13 altars to **m** offerings to Baal.
15: 4 I will **m** them a horror to all the kingdoms of
15:14 I will **m** you serve your enemies in a land
15:20 And I will **m** you to this people a fortified wall
16:20 Can mortals **m** for themselves gods?
17: 4 and I will **m** you serve your enemies in a land
17: 5 in mere mortals and **m** mere flesh their strength,
18:18 "Come, let us **m** plots against Jeremiah—
19: 7 And in this place I will **m** void the plans of Judah
19: 7 will **m** them fall by the sword before their enemies,
19: 8 I will **m** this city a horror, a thing to be hissed at;
19: 9 And I will **m** them eat the flesh of their sons and
21: 2 and will **m** him withdraw from us."
22: 6 but I swear that I will **m** you a desert,
23:15 "I am going to **m** them eat wormwood,
23:27 to **m** my people forget my name by their dreams
24: 9 I will **m** them a horror, an evil thing,

Jer 25: 9 and **m** them an object of horror and of hissing,
25:14 For many nations and great kings shall **m** slaves
25:15 and **m** all the nations to whom I send you drink it.
25:18 to **m** them a desolation and a waste,
26: 6 then I will **m** this house like Shiloh,
26: 6 and I will **m** this city a curse for all the nations of
27: 2 **M** yourself a yoke of straps and bars,
27: 7 and great kings shall **m** him their slave.
29:17 and I will **m** them like rotten figs that are
29:18 and will **m** them a horror to all the kingdoms of
29:22 "The LORD **m** you like Zedekiah and Ahab,
30: 8 and strangers shall no more **m** a servant of him.
30:10 and no one shall **m** him afraid.
30:11 I will **m** an end of all the nations
30:11 but of you I will not **m** an end.
30:16 and all who prey on you I will **m** a prey.
30:19 I will **m** them many, and they shall not be few;
30:19 I will **m** them honored, and they shall not
31:21 for yourself, **m** yourself guideposts;
31:31 when I will **m** a new covenant with the house
31:33 the covenant that I will **m** with the house of Israel
32:40 I will **m** an everlasting covenant with them,
33: 4 to **m** a defense against the siege ramps and before
33:18 to offer burnt offerings, to **m** grain offerings,
33:18 and to **m** sacrifices for all time.
34: 8 a covenant with all the people in Jerusalem to **m**
34:17 I will **m** you a horror to all the kingdoms of
34:18 I will **m** like the calf when they cut it in two
34:22 of Judah I will **m** a desolation without inhabitant.
44: 3 that they went to **m** offerings and serve other gods
44: 5 to turn from their wickedness and **m** no offerings
44:17 **m** offerings to the queen of heaven
44:25 that we have made, to **m** offerings to the queen
44:25 keep your vows and **m** your libations!
46:27 and no one shall **m** him afraid.
46:28 I will **m** an end of all the nations
46:28 but I will not **m** an end of you!
48:26 **M** him drunk, because he magnified himself
48:35 at a high place and **m** offerings to their gods.
49:15 For I will **m** you least among the nations,
49:16 Although you **m** your nest as high as the eagle's,
50: 3 it shall **m** her land a desolation,
51:12 of Babylon; **m** the watch strong;
51:25 and **m** you a burned-out mountain.
51:29 to **m** the land of Babylon a desolation,
51:36 I will dry up her sea and **m** her fountain dry;
51:39 I will set out their drink and **m** them drunk,
51:44 and **m** him disgorge what he has swallowed.
51:57 I will **m** her officials and her sages drunk,
Eze 3:26 and I will **m** your tongue cling to the roof
4: 9 put them into one vessel, and **m** bread for yourself.
5:14 Moreover I will **m** you a desolation and an object
6:14 and **m** the land desolate and waste,
7:20 therefore I will **m** of it an unclean thing to them.
7:23 **M** a chain! For the land is full of bloody
11:13 will you **m** a full end of the remnant of Israel?"
13:13 In my wrath I will **m** a stormy wind break out,
13:18 **m** veils for the heads of persons of every height,
14: 8 I will **m** them a sign and a byword and cut them off
15: 3 Is wood taken from it to **m** anything?
15: 8 And I will **m** the land desolate,
16: 2 Mortal, **m** known to Jerusalem her abominations,
16:41 and you shall also **m** no more payments.
17:24 I bring low the high tree, I **m** high the low tree;
17:24 I dry up the green tree and **m** the dry tree flourish.
20:13 to **m** an end of them.
20:17 and I did not destroy them or **m** an end of them in
20:31 and **m** your children pass through the fire,
20:37 I will **m** you pass under the staff,
21:10 How can we **m** merry? You have despised the rod,
21:19 And **m** a signpost, make it for a fork in
21:19 **m** it for a fork in the road leading to a city;
21:27 A ruin, a ruin, a ruin—I will **m** it!
22:12 and **m** gain of your neighbors by extortion;
23:46 and **m** them an object of terror and of plunder.
24: 9 I will even **m** the pile great.
24:17 Sigh, but not aloud; **m** no mourning for the dead.
25: 5 I will **m** Rabbah a pasture for camels and Ammon
25: 7 from the peoples and will **m** you perish out of
25:13 and I will **m** it desolate;
26: 4 I will scrape its soil from it and **m** it a bare rock.
26:14 I will **m** you a bare rock;
26:19 When I **m** you a city laid waste,
26:20 and I will **m** you live in the world below,
27: 5 they took a cedar from Lebanon to **m** a mast
27:31 they **m** themselves bald for you,
29: 4 **m** the fish of your channels stick to your scales.
29:10 and I will **m** the land of Egypt an utter waste
29:12 I will **m** the land of Egypt a desolation
29:15 and I will **m** them so small
30:14 I will **m** Pathros a desolation,
30:22 and I will **m** the sword fall from his hand.
32: 7 I will cover the heavens, and **m** their stars dark;
32:10 I will **m** many peoples appalled at you;
32:14 Then I will **m** their waters clear,
32:15 When I **m** the land of Egypt desolate and when
33:12 it shall not **m** them stumble when they turn
33:28 I will **m** the land a desolation and a waste,
34:15 and I will **m** them lie down, says the Lord GOD.
34:25 I will **m** with them a covenant of peace
34:26 I will **m** them and the region around my hill
34:28 and no one shall **m** them afraid.
35: 3 against you to **m** you a desolation and a waste.
35: 7 I will **m** Mount Seir a waste and a desolation;
35: 9 I will **m** you a perpetual desolation,
35:11 and I will **m** myself known among you,
35:14 As the whole earth rejoices, I will **m** you desolate.

Eze 36:27 and **m** you follow my statutes and be careful
36:29 and **m** it abundant and lay no famine upon you.
36:30 I will **m** the fruit of the tree and the produce of
37:19 the stick of Judah upon it, and **m** them one stick,
37:22 I will **m** them one nation in the land,
37:26 I will **m** a covenant of peace with them;
38:23 and **m** myself known in the eyes of many nations.
39: 3 will **m** your arrows drop out of your right hand.
39: 7 My holy name I will **m** known
39: 9 of Israel will go out and **m** fires of the weapons
39: 9 and they will **m** fires of them for seven years.
39:10 for they will **m** their fires of the weapons;
39:14 for seven months they shall **m** their search.
39:26 in their land with no one to **m** them afraid,
42:20 to **m** a separation between the holy and
43:11 **m** known to them the plan of the temple,
43:20 thus you shall purify it and **m** atonement for it.
43:26 Seven days shall they **m** atonement for the altar
45:12 and fifteen shekels shall **m** a mina for you.
45:13 This is the offering that you shall **m:**
45:15 to **m** atonement for them, says the Lord GOD.
45:17 to **m** atonement for the house of Israel.
45:20 so you shall **m** atonement for the temple.
45:25 he shall **m** the same provision for sin offerings,
Da 3:29 Therefore I **m** a decree: Any people,
6:26 I **m** a decree, that in all
7: 8 to **m** room for it, three of
7:20 and to **m** room for which three of them fell out—
8:25 By his cunning he shall **m** deceit prosper
9:27 He shall **m** a strong covenant with many
9:27 he shall **m** sacrifice and offering cease;
11: 6 After some years they shall **m** an alliance,
11:39 who acknowledge him he shall **m** more wealthy,
Hos 2: 3 and **m** her like a wilderness,
2:12 I will **m** them a forest, and the wild animals shall
2:15 and **m** the Valley of Achor a door of hope.
2:18 I will **m** for you a covenant on that day with
2:18 and I will **m** you lie down in safety.
4:13 and **m** offerings upon the hills, under oak, poplar,
7: 3 By their wickedness they **m** the king glad,
10: 4 with empty oaths they **m** covenants;
10:11 but I will **m** Ephraim break the ground;
11: 8 How can I **m** you like Admah?
12: 1 they **m** a treaty with Assyria,
12: 9 I will **m** you live in tents again,
13: 2 And now they keep on sinning and **m** a cast image
Joel 2:17 O LORD, and do not **m** your heritage a mockery,
2:19 will no more **m** you a mockery among the nations.
Am 8: 5 We will **m** the ephah small and the shekel great,
8: 9 I will **m** the sun go down at noon,
8:10 I will **m** it like the mourning for an only son,
9:14 and they shall **m** gardens and eat their fruit.
Ob 1: 2 I will surely **m** you least among the nations;
Jnh 1:14 Do not **m** us guilty of innocent blood;
Mic 1: 6 I will **m** Samaria a heap in the open country,
1: 8 I will **m** lamentation like the jackals,
1:16 **M** yourselves bald and cut off your hair
1:16 **m** yourselves as bald as the eagle,
4: 4 and no one shall **m** them afraid;
4: 7 The lame I will **m** the remnant,
4:13 for I will **m** your horn iron and your hoofs bronze;
6:16 Therefore I will **m** you a desolation,
Na 1: 8 He will **m** a full end of his adversaries,
1: 9 He will **m** an end; no adversary will rise up twice.
1:14 I will **m** your grave, for you are worthless."
3: 6 at you and treat you with contempt, and **m** you
Hab 1: 3 Why do you **m** me see wrongdoing and look
1:10 At kings they scoff, and of rulers they **m** sport.
2: 2 **m** it plain on tablets, so that a runner may read it.
2: 7 and those who **m** you tremble wake up?
2:15 "Alas for you who **m** your neighbors drink,
3: 2 in our own time **m** it known;
Zep 1: 3 I will **m** the wicked stumble.
1:18 a full, a terrible end he will **m** of all the inhabitants
2:13 and he will **m** Nineveh a desolation,
3: 7 the more eager to **m** all their deeds corrupt.
3:13 and no one shall **m** them afraid.
3:20 for I will **m** you renowned and praised among all
Hag 2:23 says the LORD, and **m** you like a signet ring;
Zec 6:11 Take the silver and gold and **m** a crown,
8:16 judgments that are true and **m** for peace,
9: 6 and I will **m** an end of the pride of Philistia.
9:17 Grain shall **m** the young men flourish,
10: 3 and will **m** them like his proud war horse.
10:12 I will **m** them strong in the LORD,
12: 2 I am about to **m** Jerusalem a cup of reeling for all
12: 3 that day I will **m** Jerusalem a heavy stone for all
12: 6 On that day I will **m** the clans of Judah like
Mal 2: 9 I **m** you despised and abased before all the people,
2:15 Did not one God **m** her?
Mt 3: 3 the way of the Lord, **m** his paths straight.' "
4:19 "Follow me, and I will **m** you fish for people."
5:36 for you cannot **m** one hair white or black.
7: 2 For with the judgment you **m** you will be judged,
8: 2 saying, "Lord, if you choose, you can **m** me clean."
12:16 and he ordered them not to **m** him known.
12:33 "Either **m** the tree good, and its fruit good;
12:33 or **m** the tree bad, and its fruit bad;
13:32 birds of the air come and **m** nests in its branches."
15: 6 you **m** void the word of God.
17: 4 if you wish, I will **m** three dwellings here,
23: 5 for they **m** their phylacteries broad
23:15 For you cross sea and land to **m** a single convert,
23:15 and you **m** the new convert twice as much a child
26:17 to **m** the preparations for you to eat the Passover?"
27:13 "Do you not hear how many accusations they **m**
27:65 go, **m** it as secure as you can."
Mt 28:19 Go therefore and **m** disciples of all nations,
Mk 1: 3 the way of the Lord, **m** his paths straight,' "
1:17 "Follow me and I will **m** you fish for people."
1:40 "If you choose, you can **m** me clean."
3:12 But he sternly ordered them not to **m** him known.
4:32 so that the birds of the air can **m** nests in its shade."
5:39 "Why do you **m** a commotion and weep?
9: 5 let us **m** three dwellings, one for you,
14:12 to go and **m** the preparations for you to eat
14:15 **M** preparations for us there."
Lk 1:17 to **m** ready a people prepared for the Lord."
3: 4 'Prepare the way of the Lord, **m** his paths straight.
5:12 "Lord, if you choose, you can **m** me clean."
5:14 **m** an offering for your cleansing,
5:34 "You cannot **m** wedding guests fast while
9:14 **"M** them sit down in groups of about fifty each."
9:33 let us **m** three dwellings, one for you,
9:52 a village of the Samaritans to **m** ready for him;
11:40 the one who made the outside **m** the inside also?
12:33 **M** purses for yourselves that do not wear out,
12:58 on the way **m** an effort to settle the case,
14:18 But they all alike began to **m** excuses.
16: 6 'Take your bill, sit down quickly, and **m** it fifty.'
16: 7 He said to him, 'Take your bill and **m** it eighty.'
16: 9 **m** friends for yourselves by means
17:33 Those who try to **m** their life secure will lose it,
19:42 had only recognized on this day the things that **m**
20:43 until I **m** your enemies your footstool." '
21:14 So **m** up your minds not to prepare your defense
22: 9 "Where do you want us to **m** preparations for it?"
22:12 **M** preparations for us there."
Jn 1:23 **'M** straight the way of the Lord,' "
6:10 Jesus said, **"M** the people sit down."
6:15 to come and take him by force to **m** him king,
8:32 and the truth will **m** you free."
14:23 we will come to them and **m** our home with them.
15: 2 that bears fruit he prunes to **m** it bear more fruit.
17:26 and I will **m** it known,
Ac 2:28 you will **m** me full of gladness
2:35 until I **m** your enemies your footstool." '
7:40 **'M** gods for us who will lead the way for us;
7:44 to **m** it according to the pattern he had seen.
7:50 Did not my hand **m** all these things?'
9:34 get up and **m** your bed!"
10:17 while Peter was greatly puzzled about what to **m** of
11:12 with them and not to **m** a distinction between them
19:33 And Alexander motioned for silence and tried to **m**
22: 1 listen to the defense that I now **m** before you."
23:15 that you want to **m** a more thorough examination
24:10 "I cheerfully **m** my defense,
24:19 to be here before you to **m** an accusation,
25:16 and had been given an opportunity to **m** a defense
26: 2 to **m** my defense today against all the accusations
27:43 to jump overboard first and **m** for the land,
Ro 4:11 to **m** him the ancestor of all who believe
6:12 to **m** you obey their passions.
9:21 to **m** out of the same lump one object
9:22 to show his wrath and to **m** known his power,
9:23 to **m** known the riches of his glory for the objects
9:33 in Zion a stone that will **m** people stumble,
9:33 a rock that will **m** them fall,
10:19 "I will **m** you jealous of those who are not a nation;
10:19 with a foolish nation I will **m** you angry."
11:11 so as to **m** Israel jealous.
11:14 in order to **m** my own people jealous,
13:14 and **m** no provision for the flesh,
14: 4 for the Lord is able to **m** them stand.
14:20 for you to **m** others fall by what you eat;
15:20 Thus I **m** it my ambition to proclaim
1Co 4:14 I am not writing this to **m** you ashamed,
6:15 the members of Christ and **m** them members of
7:21 **m** use of your present condition
9:18 that in my proclamation I may **m** the gospel free
9:18 so as not to **m** full use of my rights in the gospel.
12:15 that would not **m** it any less a part of the body.
12:16 that would not **m** it any less a part of the body.
15:31 a boast that I **m** in Christ Jesus our Lord.
2Co 1:17 Do I **m** my plans according
2: 1 up my mind not to **m** you another painful visit.
2: 2 to **m** me glad but the one whom I have pained?
5: 9 we **m** it our aim to please him.
7: 2 **M** room in your hearts for us;
Gal 2: 2 in order to **m** sure that I was not running,
3:21 For if a law had been given that could **m** alive,
4:17 They **m** much of you, but for no good purpose;
4:17 so that you may **m** much of them.
6:11 See what large letters I **m** when I am writing
6:12 It is those who want to **m** a good showing in
6:17 From now on, let no one **m** trouble for me;
Eph 3: 9 and to **m** everyone see what is the plan of
4:27 and do not **m** room for the devil.
5:26 to **m** her holy by cleansing her with the washing
6:15 for your feet put on whatever will **m** you ready
6:19 to me to **m** known with boldness the mystery of
Php 2: 2 **m** my joy complete:
2:30 risking his life to **m** up for those services
3:12 but I press on to **m** it my own,
3:21 also enables him to **m** all things subject to himself.
Col 1:25 to **m** the word of God fully known,
1:27 To them God chose to **m** known how great among
1Th 3:12 And may the Lord **m** you increase and abound
2Th 1: 5 and is intended to **m** you worthy of the kingdom
1:11 asking that our God will **m** you worthy of his call
1Ti 1: 7 or the things about which they **m** assertions.
5: 4 to their own family and **m** some repayment
2Ti 3: 6 For among them are those who **m** their way
3: 9 But they will not **m** much progress, because,
Tit 3:13 **M** every effort to send Zenas the lawyer
Heb 1:13 at my right hand until I **m** your enemies a footstool
2:10 should **m** the pioneer of their salvation perfect
2:17 to **m** a sacrifice of atonement for the sins of
4:11 Let us therefore **m** every effort to enter that rest,
7:25 since he always lives to **m** intercession for them.
8: 5 the tent, was warned, "See that you **m** everything
8:10 the covenant that I will **m** with the house of Israel
10: 1 **m** perfect those who approach.
10:16 that I will **m** with them after those days, says
11:14 for people who speak in this way **m** it clear
12:13 and **m** straight paths for your feet,
13:21 **m** you complete in everything good so
Jas 3: 2 For all of us **m** many mistakes.
3: 3 into the mouths of horses to **m** them obey us,
3:18 in peace for those who **m** peace.
1Pe 3:15 to **m** your defense to anyone who demands
2Pe 1: 5 you must **m** every effort to support your faith
1:15 And I will **m** every effort so that
1Jn 1:10 If we say that we have not sinned, we **m** him a liar,
Jude 1:24 and to **m** you stand without blemish in the presence
Rev 2:16 I will come to you soon and **m** war against them
3: 9 I will **m** those of the synagogue of Satan who say
3: 9 I will **m** them come and bow down
3:12 I will **m** you a pillar in the temple of my God;
11: 7 that comes up from the bottomless pit will **m** war
12:17 and went off to **m** war on the rest of her children,
13: 7 Also it was allowed to **m** war on the saints and
13:14 to **m** an image for the beast that had been wounded
17:14 they will **m** war on the Lamb,
17:16 they will **m** her desolate and naked;
19:19 of the earth with their armies gathered to **m** war
Tob 4: 7 not let your eye begrudge the gift when you **m** it.
4: 8 **m** your gift from them in proportion;
6: 8 you must burn them to **m** a smoke in the presence
8: 6 let us **m** a helper for him like himself.'
8:19 So they began to **m** preparations.
10: 5 The light of my eyes, that I let you **m** the journey."
11: 8 the medicine will **m** the white films shrink
Jdt 5:11 he exploited them and forced them to **m** bricks.
6: 2 and tell us not to **m** war against the people of Israel
7: 1 up into the hill country and **m** war on the Israelites.
8:21 he will **m** us pay for its desecration with our blood.
9:13 **M** my deceitful words bring wound and bruise
AdE 2:10 Mordecai had commanded her not to **m** it known.
10: 3 His way of life was such as to **m** him beloved
13: 2 to **m** my kingdom peaceable and open to travel
14:11 **m** an example of him who began this against us.
14:12 **m** yourself known in this time of our affliction,
Wis 1:13 because God did not **m** death,
2: 6 and **m** use of the creation to the full as in youth.
2:19 and **m** trial of his forbearance.
5: 1 and those who **m** light of their labors.
6:13 to **m** herself known to those who desire her.
6:22 and **m** knowledge of her clear,
13:11 then with pleasing workmanship **m** a useful vessel
15: 6 for such objects of hope are those who either **m**
15:13 when they **m** from earthy matter fragile vessels
15:17 and what they **m** with lawless hands is dead;
16:28 to **m** it known that one must rise before the sun
Sir Pr: 1 with his book those who love learning might **m**
2: 6 **m** your ways straight, and hope in him.
7: 9 and when I **m** an offering to the Most High God,
7:23 and **m** them obedient from their youth.
8: 4 Do not **m** fun of one who is ill-bred,
9:13 But if you approach them, **m** no misstep,
10:26 Do not **m** a display of your wisdom
11:21 the sight of the Lord to **m** the poor rich suddenly,
11:34 and will **m** you a stranger to your own family.
15:10 and the Lord will **m** it prosper.
18:31 it will **m** you the laughingstock of your enemies.
19:10 Be brave, it will not **m** you burst!
19:16 A person may **m** a slip without intending it.
20:13 wise **m** themselves beloved by only few words,
24: 8 He said, **'M** your dwelling in Jacob,
24:32 I will again **m** instruction shine forth like the dawn,
24:32 and I will **m** it clear from far away.
25:23 from the wife who does not **m** her husband happy.
26:10 or else, when she finds liberty, she will **m** use of it.
27:14 Their cursing and swearing **m** one's hair stand
27:14 and their quarrels **m** others stop their ears.
28: 5 who will **m** an atoning sacrifice for his sins?
28:25 so **m** a door and a bolt for your mouth.
28:25 so **m** balances and scales for your words.
30: 3 who teaches his son will **m** his enemies envious,
30:13 Discipline your son and **m** his yoke heavy,
31: 4 The poor person toils to **m** a meager living,
31:27 It has been created to **m** people happy.
32: 1 If they **m** you master of the feast,
33:30 and if he does not obey, **m** his fetters heavy.
36: 7 **m** your hand and right arm glorious.
38:17 **m** your mourning worthy of the departed,
40:18 Wealth and wages **m** life sweet,
40:19 Cattle and orchards **m** one prosperous;
40:21 The flute and the harp **m** sweet melody,
40:25 Gold and silver **m** one stand firm,
42: 7 When you **m** a deposit, be sure it is counted
42:11 she may **m** you a laughingstock to your enemies,
44:21 that he would **m** him as numerous as the dust of
45: 9 to **m** their ringing heard in the temple as
45:16 to **m** atonement for the people.
47: 9 to **m** sweet melody with their voices.
Bar 1:14 to **m** your confession in the house of the Lord on
2:23 I will **m** to cease from the towns of Judah and from
2:35 I will **m** an everlasting covenant with them to
5: 7 to **m** level ground, so that Israel may walk safely in
LtJ 6: 9 People take gold and **m** crowns for the heads

LtJ 6:18 so the priests **m** their temples secure with doors
6:46 Those who **m** them will certainly
Aza 1:15 to **m** an offering before you and to find mercy.
1Mc 1:11 and **m** a covenant with the Gentiles around us,
1:48 to **m** themselves abominable by everything unclean
2:15 to the town of Modein to **m** them offer sacrifice.
3:14 "I will **m** a name for myself and win honor in
3:14 I will **m** war on Judas and his companions,
5:42 but **m** them all enter the battle."
5:57 So they said, "Let us also **m** a name for ourselves;
5:57 let us go and **m** war on the Gentiles around us."
6:58 and **m** peace with them and with all their nation.
8:13 they wish to help and to **m** kings, they **m** kings,
8:29 Thus on these terms the Romans **m** a treaty with
8:30 and any addition or deletion that they may **m** shall
9:70 to him to **m** peace with him and obtain release of
10: 4 to **m** peace with him before he makes peace
10:16 Come now, we will **m** him our friend and ally."
10:54 and will **m** gifts to you and to her in keeping
11: 9 "Come, let us **m** a covenant with each other,
11:37 Now therefore take care to **m** a copy of this,
11:50 **m** the Jews stop fighting against us and our city."
11:57 and set you over the four districts and **m** you one
12:40 but might **m** war on him,
12:53 Now therefore let us **m** war on them and blot out
13:37 and we are ready to **m** a general peace with you
13:45 asking Simon to **m** peace with them;
13:50 Then they cried to Simon to **m** peace with them,
14: 1 so that he could **m** war against Trypho.
14:12 and there was none to **m** them afraid.
15: 4 to **m** a landing in the country so that I may proceed
15:19 that they should not seek their harm or **m** war
15:19 or **m** alliance with those who war against them.
15:31 Otherwise we will come and **m** war on you."
15:39 and to **m** war on the people;
15:41 so that they might go out and **m** raids along
2Mc 1:26 and preserve your portion and **m** it holy.
2:25 to **m** it easy for those who are inclined
3: 8 to **m** a tour of inspection of the cities of Coelesyria
3:18 also hurried out of their houses in crowds to **m**
4:17 a fact that later events will **m** clear.
6: 8 the Jews and **m** them partake of the sacrifices,
7:24 but promised with oaths that he would **m** him rich
7:28 that God did not **m** them out of things that existed.
7:37 and plagues to **m** you confess that he alone is God,
8:10 to **m** up for the king the tribute due to the Romans,
9: 4 I get there I will **m** Jerusalem a cemetery of Jews."
9:14 to level to the ground and to **m** a cemetery, he was
9:15 he would **m,** all of them, equal to citizens
11: 2 He intended to **m** the city a home for Greeks,
11:36 so that we may **m** proposals appropriate for you.
11:37 Therefore **m** haste and send messengers so
12:12 agreed to **m** peace with them;
1Es 1:11 to **m** the offering to the Lord as it is written in
1:25 went to **m** war at Carchemish on the Euphrates,
2:24 Therefore we now **m** known to you,
4: 4 If he tells them to **m** war on one another, they do it;
4: 6 not serve in the army or **m** war but till the soil;
4:17 Women **m** men's clothes; they bring men glory;
4:52 with the commandment to **m** seventeen offerings;
9: 8 Now then **m** confession and give glory to the Lord
9:54 to those who had none, and to **m** great rejoicing;
3Mc 3:21 and we ventured to **m** a change,
3:21 and to **m** them participants in our regular religious
4:11 to **m** them an obvious spectacle to all coming back
5:17 and to **m** the present portion of the banquet joyful
7:10 not immediately hurry to **m** their departure,
2Es 4:14 'Come, let us go and **m** war against the sea,
4:14 that it may recede before us and so that we may **m**
5: 7 the many do not know shall **m** his voice heard
5:36 and **m** the withered flowers bloom again for me;
6:24 At that time friends shall **m** war on friends
7:*82* because they cannot now **m** a good repentance so
7:*137* [67] for if he did not **m** them abound, the world
8:13 and **m** it live as your work.
12:34 and he will **m** them joyful until the end comes,
13: 5 from the four winds of heaven to **m** war against
13:31 They shall plan to **m** war against one another,
14:26 you have finished, some things you shall **m** public,
14:45 "**M** public the twenty-four books
15:19 but shall **m** an assault upon their houses with
16:42 be like one who will not **m** a profit;
16:64 and will **m** a public spectacle of all of you.
4Mc 4:21 and caused Antiochus himself to **m** war on them.
6: 8 and began to kick him in the side to **m** him get
6:29 **M** my blood their purification,
10:14 "You do not have a fire hot enough to **m** me play
10:19 of this you will not **m** our reason speechless.
13: 6 and **m** it calm for those who sail into
13:26 they could **m** their brotherly love more fervent
18:19 'I kill and I **m** alive:

MAKED (2)

1Mc 5:26 in Alema and Chaspho, **M** and Carnaim"—
5:36 From there he marched on and took Chaspho, **M,**

MAKER (32) [MAKE]

Ge 14:19 by God Most High, **m** of heaven and earth;
14:22 God Most High, **m** of heaven and earth,
Job 4:17 Can human beings be pure before their **M?**
32:22 or my **M** would soon put an end to me!
35:10 But no one says, 'Where is God my **M,**
36: 3 and ascribe righteousness to my **M.**
40:19 only its **M** can approach it with the sword.
Ps 95: 6 let us kneel before the LORD, our **M!**
134: 3 May the LORD, **m** of heaven and earth,
Ps 149: 2 Let Israel be glad in its **M;**
Pr 14:31 Those who oppress the poor insult their **M,**
17: 5 Those who mock the poor insult their **M;**
22: 2 the LORD is the **m** of them all.
Isa 17: 7 On that day people will regard their **M,**
29:16 Shall the thing made say of its **m,**
45: 9 Woe to you who strive with your **M,**
45:11 the Holy One of Israel, and its **M:**
51:13 You have forgotten the LORD, your **M,**
54: 5 For your **M** is your husband,
Eze 20:49 'Is he not a **m** of allegories?' "
Hos 8:14 Israel has forgotten his **M,** and built palaces;
Hab 2:18 What use is an idol once its **m** has shaped it—
2:18 For its **m** trusts in what has been made,
1Pe 4:15 a thief, a criminal, or even as a mischief **m.**
Sir 7:30 With all your might love your **M,**
10:12 the heart has withdrawn from its **M.**
32:13 But above all bless your **M,**
33:13 so all are in the hand of their **M,**
38:15 He who sins against his **M,**
39:28 and calm the anger of their **M.**
47: 8 with all his heart, and he loved his **M.**
2Es 5:33 Or do you love him more than his **M** does?"

MAKERS‡ (1) [MAKE]

Isa 45:16 the **m** of idols go in confusion together.

MAKES‡ (148) [MAKE]

Ex 4:11 Who **m** them mute or deaf, seeing or blind?
11: 7 that you may know that the LORD **m** a distinction
30:38 Whoever **m** any like it to use as perfume shall
Lev 7: 7 the priest who **m** atonement with it shall have it.
13:53 If the priest **m** an examination,
13:56 If the priest **m** an examination,
14:48 If the priest comes and **m** an inspection,
15: 2 his discharge **m** him ceremonially unclean.
17:11 for, as life, it is the blood that **m** atonement.
27: 2 When a person **m** an explicit vow to the LORD
27:33 if one **m** substitution for it,
Nu 5:21 when the LORD **m** your uterus drop,
30: 2 When a man **m** a vow to the LORD,
30: 3 When a woman **m** a vow to the LORD,
Dt 18:10 be found among you who **m** a son or daughter pass
20:12 but **m** war against you, then you shall besiege it;
20:20 in building siegeworks against the town that **m** war
22:14 and **m** up charges against her, slandering her
27:15 be anyone who **m** an idol or casts an image,
Jos 15: 3 along by Hezron, up to Addar, **m** a turn to Karka,
16: 6 the boundary **m** a turn toward Taanath-shiloh,
19:14 the boundary **m** a turn to Hannathon, and it ends at
Jdg 16: 5 and find out what **m** his strength so great,
16: 6 "Please tell me what **m** your strength so great,
16:15 now and have not told me what **m** your strength
1Sa 2: 7 The LORD **m** poor and **m** rich;
22: 8 No one discloses to me when my son **m** a league
Job 12:17 counselors away stripped, and **m** fools of judges.
12:23 He **m** nations great, then destroys them;
12:24 and **m** them wander in a pathless waste.
12:25 he **m** them stagger like a drunkard.
25: 2 he **m** peace in his high heaven.
31:14 When he **m** inquiry, what shall I answer him?
32: 8 in a mortal, the breath of the Almighty, that **m**
35:11 and **m** us wiser than the birds of the air?'
39:27 that the eagle mounts up and **m** its nest on high?
39:28 It lives on the rock and **m** its home in the fastness
40:17 It **m** its tail stiff like a cedar;
41:31 It **m** the deep boil like a pot;
41:31 it **m** the sea like a pot of ointment.
Ps 12: 3 the tongue that **m** great boasts,
23: 2 He **m** me lie down in green pastures;
25:14 and he **m** his covenant known to them.
29: 6 He **m** Lebanon skip like a calf,
34: 2 My soul **m** its boast in the LORD;
46: 9 He **m** wars cease to the end of the earth;
107:40 on princes and **m** them wander in trackless wastes;
107:41 and **m** their families like flocks.
119:98 Your commandment **m** me wiser than my enemies,
135: 7 He it is who **m** the clouds rise at the end of
135: 7 he **m** lightnings for the rain and brings out
147: 8 **m** grass grow on the hills.
147:18 he **m** his wind blow, and the waters flow.
Pr 10: 1 A wise child **m** a glad father,
10: 4 but the hand of the diligent **m** rich.
10:10 but the one who rebukes boldly **m** peace.
10:22 The blessing of the LORD **m** rich,
13:12 Hope deferred **m** the heart sick,
14:30 but passion **m** the bones rot.
15:13 A glad heart **m** a cheerful countenance,
15:20 A wise child **m** a glad father,
16:23 The mind of the wise **m** their speech judicious,
29: 3 A child who loves wisdom **m** a parent glad,
29: 4 but one who **m** heavy exactions ruins it.
31:17 with strength, and **m** her arms strong.
31:22 She **m** herself coverings; her clothing is fine linen
31:24 She **m** linen garments and sells them;
Ecc 7: 7 Surely oppression **m** the wise foolish,
8: 1 Wisdom **m** one's face shine,
11: 5 not know the work of God, who **m** everything.
Isa 27: 9 when he **m** all the stones of the altars
40:23 and **m** the rulers of the earth as nothing.
41: 2 he **m** them like dust with his sword,
43:16 Thus says the LORD, who **m** a way in the sea,
44:13 he **m** it in human form, with human beauty,
44:15 Then he **m** a god and worships it,
44:15 **m** it a carved image and bows down before it.
44:17 The rest of it he **m** into a god, his idol,
Isa 44:25 the omens of liars, and **m** fools of diviners;
44:25 and **m** their knowledge foolish;
46: 6 they hire a goldsmith, who **m** it into a god;
62: 7 until he establishes Jerusalem and **m** it renowned
66: 3 whoever **m** a memorial offering of frankincense,
Jer 10:13 and he **m** the mist rise from the ends of the earth.
10:13 He **m** lightnings for the rain,
13:16 he turns it into gloom and **m** it deep darkness.
22:13 who **m** his neighbors work for nothing,
46:22 She **m** a sound like a snake gliding away;
51:16 and he **m** the mist rise from the ends of the earth.
51:16 He **m** lightnings for the rain,
Eze 46:16 If the prince **m** a gift to any of his sons out
46:17 But if he **m** a gift out of his inheritance to one
Da 8:13 the transgression that **m** desolate,
11:31 and set up the abomination that **m** desolate.
Am 4:13 **m** the morning darkness, and treads on the heights
5: 9 who **m** destruction flash out against the strong,
Na 1: 4 He rebukes the sea and **m** it dry,
Hab 1:16 he sacrifices to his net and **m** offerings to his seine;
3:19 he **m** my feet like the feet of a deer,
3:19 and **m** me tread upon the heights.
Zec 10: 1 from the LORD who **m** the storm clouds,
Mt 5:45 for he **m** his sun rise on the evil and on the good,
23:19 the gift or the altar that **m** the gift sacred?
Mk 7:37 he even **m** the deaf to hear and the mute to speak."
9:17 he has a spirit that **m** him unable to speak;
Jn 8:36 So if the Son **m** you free, you will be free indeed.
Ro 14:19 Let us then pursue what **m** for peace and
14:21 or drink wine or do anything that **m** your brother
2Co 11:20 you put up with it when someone **m** slaves of you,
Gal 2: 6 (what they actually were **m** no difference to me;
Heb 1: 7 "He **m** his angels winds, and his servants flames
Jas 3: 2 Anyone who **m** no mistakes in speaking is perfect,
1Pe 2: 8 and "A stone that **m** them stumble,
2: 8 and a rock that **m** them fall."
Rev 13:12 and it **m** the earth and its inhabitants worship
19:11 and in righteousness he judges and **m** war.
Wis 7:27 into holy souls and **m** them friends of God,
13:14 or **m** it like some worthless animal, giving it a coat
13:15 then he **m** a suitable niche for it,
Sir 6: 4 and **m** them the laughingstock of their enemies.
11:27 An hour's misery **m** one forget past delights,
16:14 He **m** room for every act of mercy;
17: 1 and **m** them return to it again.
18:18 and the gift of a grudging giver **m** the eyes dim.
20:23 Another out of shame **m** promises to a friend,
20:23 and so **m** an enemy for nothing.
22:17 like stucco decoration that **m** a wall smooth.
22:19 and one who pricks the heart **m** clear its feelings.
26: 6 and a tongue-lashing **m** it known to all.
34:20 He lifts up the soul and **m** the eyes sparkle;
35: 1 The one who keeps the law **m** many offerings;
35: 2 one who heeds the commandments **m** an offering
35:25 of his people and **m** them rejoice in his mercy.
38: 3 The skill of physicians **m** them distinguished,
38: 8 the pharmacist **m** a mixture from them.
38:30 the clay with his arm and **m** it pliable with his feet;
51:12 *who* **m** *a horn to sprout for the house of David,*
LtJ 6:35 if one **m** a vow to them and does not keep it,
1Mc 8:26 that **m** war they shall not give or supply grain,
10: 4 before he **m** peace with Alexander against us,
1Es 3:19 It **m** equal the mind of the king and the orphan,
3:21 It **m** all hearts feel rich, forgets kings and satraps,
3:21 and **m** everyone talk in millions.
4:34 for it **m** the circuit of the heavens and returns
2Es 4:42 as a woman who is in labor **m** haste to escape
7:*136* [66] because he **m** his compassions abound more
8:23 up the depths and whose indignation **m**

MAKHELOTH (2)

Nu 33:25 They set out from Haradah and camped at **M.**
33:26 They set out from **M** and camped at Tahath.

MAKING‡ (109) [MAKE]

Ge 34:30 "You have brought trouble on me by **m** me odious
Lev 16:24 **m** atonement for himself and for the people.
17:11 to you for **m** atonement for your lives on the altar;
19:29 not profane your daughter by **m** her a prostitute,
27: 8 according to what each one **m** a vow can afford.
Dt 4:16 not act corruptly by **m** an idol for yourselves,
4:25 if you act corruptly by **m** an idol in the form
20:19 **m** war against it in order to take it,
24:11 to whom you are **m** the loan brings the pledge out
28:63 as the LORD took delight in **m** you prosperous
29:12 which the LORD your God is **m** with you today;
29:14 I am **m** this covenant, sworn by an oath,
Jos 22:33 and spoke no more of **m** war against them,
Jdg 8:33 with the Baals, **m** Baal-berith their god.
11:27 but you are the one who does me wrong by **m** war
2Sa 3: 6 Abner was **m** himself strong in the house of Saul.
8: 2 **m** them lie down on the ground,
1Ki 11:25 the days of Solomon, **m** trouble as Hadad did;
2Ki 12:12 to buy timber and quarried stone for **m** repairs on
1Ch 9:31 was in charge of **m** the flat cakes.
17:19 **m** known all these great things.
17:21 **m** for yourself a name for great and terrible things,
28: 4 in **m** me king over all Israel.
2Ch 25:14 and worshiped them, **m** offerings to them.
Est 9:18 **m** that a day of feasting and gladness.
Ps 7:13 his deadly weapons, **m** his arrows fiery shafts.
19: 7 decrees of the LORD are sure, **m** wise the simple;
40: 2 and set my feet upon a rock, **m** my steps secure.
113: 9 **m** her the joyous mother of children.
143: 3 **m** me sit in darkness like those long dead.
149: 3 **m** melody to him with tambourine and lyre.

Pr 2: 2 **m** your ear attentive to wisdom
20:25 and begin to reflect only after **m** a vow.
28:10 into evil ways will fall into pits of their own **m,**
Ecc 12:12 Of **m** many books there is no end,
SS 5: 7 **M** their rounds in the city the sentinels found me;
Isa 45: 9 to the one who fashions it, "What are you **m**"?
55:10 **m** it bring forth and sprout,
Jer 5:14 I am now **m** my words in your mouth a fire,
11:17 provoking me to anger by **m** offerings to Baal.
18: 4 The vessel he was **m** of clay was spoiled in
18:16 **m** their land a horror, a thing to be hissed
19: 4 and have profaned this place by **m** offerings in it
19:12 and to its inhabitants, **m** this city like Topheth.
20: 4 I am **m** you a terror to yourself and
20:15 "A child is born to you, a son," **m** him very glad.
21: 2 for King Nebuchadrezzar of Babylon is **m** war
25:12 says the LORD, **m** the land an everlasting waste.
44: 8 **m** offerings to other gods in the land of Egypt
44:15 that their wives had been **m** offerings
44:18 from the time we stopped **m** offerings to the queen
44:19 "Indeed we will go on **m** offerings to the queen
51: 7 in the LORD's hand, **m** all the earth drunken;
Eze 16:31 and **m** your lofty place in every square!
20: 5 **m** myself known to them in the land of Egypt—
22: 3 its time has come; **m** its idols,
24: 6 Empty it piece by piece, **m** no choice at all.
31: 4 **m** its rivers flow around the place it was planted,
45:16 with the prince in Israel in **m** this offering.
Mic 6:13 **m** you desolate because of your sins.
Mt 9:23 the flute players and the crowd **m** a commotion,
21:13 but you are **m** it a den of robbers."
Mk 7:13 thus **m** void the word of God
Jn 2:15 **M** a whip of cords, he drove all of them out of
2:16 Stop **m** my Father's house a marketplace!"
4: 1 "Jesus is **m** and baptizing more disciples than
5: 7 and while I am **m** my way,
5:18 thereby **m** himself equal to God.
8: 3 ⟦and **m** her stand before all of them,⟧
10:33 though only a human being, are **m** yourself God."
Ac 13:10 not stop **m** crooked the straight paths of the Lord?
15:17 who has been **m** these things
16:19 that their hope of **m** money was gone,
21:26 **m** public the completion of the days of purification
26:24 While he was **m** this defense, Festus exclaimed,
Ro 7:23 **m** me captive to the law of sin that dwells
2Co 5:20 since God is **m** his appeal through us;
6:10 as poor, yet **m** many rich;
7: 1 **m** holiness perfect in the fear of God.
Gal 2: 8 through Peter **m** him an apostle to the circumcised
Eph 2:15 in place of the two, thus **m** peace,
4: 3 **m** every effort to maintain the unity of the Spirit in
5:16 **m** the most of the time, because the days are evil.
5:19 singing and **m** melody to the Lord in your hearts,
Col 1:20 by **m** peace through the blood of his cross.
4: 5 **m** the most of the time.
1Ti 1:16 **m** me an example to those who would come
Jas 4:13 doing business and **m** money."
Rev 13:13 even **m** fire come down from heaven to earth in
21: 5 "See, I am **m** all things new."
Jdt 5:23 a people with no strength or power for **m** war.
7:24 a great injury in not **m** peace with the Assyrians.
Wis 14:12 idea of **m** idols was the beginning of fornication,
15: 7 and those for contrary uses, **m** all alike;
Sir 1:18 **m** peace and perfect health to flourish.
16:26 and, in **m** them, determined their boundaries,
18:23 Before **m** a vow, prepare yourself;
31:31 and do not distress him by **m** demands of him.
38:27 each is diligent in **m** a great variety;
41:22 and do not be insulting after **m** a gift.
1Mc 11:25 of his nation kept **m** complaints against him,
15:25 against it and **m** engines of war;
2Mc 3:33 While the high priest was **m** an atonement,
6:23 But **m** a high resolve, worthy of his years and
9: 8 **m** the power of God manifest to all.
10:16 after **m** solemn supplication and imploring God
1Es 5: 3 all their kindred were **m** merry.
8:91 While Ezra was praying and **m** his confession,
4Mc 14:19 at the time for **m** honeycombs defend themselves

MAKKEDAH (9)

Jos 10:10 and struck them down as far as Azekah and **M.**
10:16 and hid themselves in the cave at **M.**
10:17 hidden in the cave at **M."**
10:21 to Joshua in the camp at **M;**
10:28 Joshua took **M** on that day,
10:28 And he did to the king of **M** as he had done to
10:29 Then Joshua passed on from **M,**
12:16 the king of **M** one the king of Bethel one
15:41 Naamah, and **M:** sixteen towns with their villages.

MAKTESH (KJV) See MORTAR

MALACHI (2)

Mal 1: 1 An oracle. The word of the LORD to Israel by **M.**
2Es 1:40 Zephaniah, Haggai, Zechariah and **M,**

MALADIES (1) [MALADY]

Dt 28:59 and lasting afflictions and grievous and lasting **m.**

MALADY (1) [MALADIES]

Dt 28:61 Every other **m** and affliction,

MALCAM‡ (1)

1Ch 8: 9 by his wife Hodesh: Jobab, Zibia, Mesha, **M,**

MALCHAM (KJV) See MALCAM, MILCOM

MALCHIAH (3) [=MALCHIJAH]

Jer 21: 1 when King Zedekiah sent to him Pashhur son of **M**
38: 1 of **M** heard the words that Jeremiah was saying
38: 6 and threw him into the cistern of **M,**

MALCHIEL (3) [MALCHIELITES]

Ge 46:17 children of Beriah: Heber and **M**
Nu 26:45 of **M,** the clan of the Malchielites.
1Ch 7:31 Heber and **M,** who was the father of Birzaith.

MALCHIELITES (1) [MALCHIEL]

Nu 26:45 of Malchiel, the clan of the **M.**

MALCHIJAH‡ (14) [=MALCHIAH]

1Ch 6:40 son of Michael, son of Baaseiah, son of **M,**
9:12 son of **M,** and Maasai son of Adiel,
24: 9 the fifth to **M,** the sixth to Mijamin,
Ezr 10:25 Ramiah, Izziah, **M,** Mijamin, Eleazar, Hashabiah,
10:31 Of the descendants of Harim: Eliezer, Isshijah, **M,**
Ne 3:11 **M** son of Harim and Hasshub son
3:14 **M** son of Rechab, ruler of the district
3:31 After him **M,** one of the goldsmiths,
8: 4 and Pedaiah, Mishael, **M,** Hashum,
10: 3 Pashhur, Amariah, **M,**
11:12 of Zechariah son of Pashhur son of **M,**
12:42 Shemaiah, Eleazar, Uzzi, Jehohanan, **M,** Elam,
1Es 9:26 Ramiah, Izziah, **M,** Mijamin, and Eleazar,
9:44 Mishael, **M,** Lothasubus, Nabariah, and Zechariah.

MALCHIRAM (1)

1Ch 3:18 **M,** Pedaiah, Shenazzar, Jekamiah, Hoshama,

MALCHISHUA (5)

1Sa 14:49 the sons of Saul were Jonathan, Ishvi, and **M;**
31: 2 Philistines killed Jonathan and Abinadab and **M,**
1Ch 8:33 Saul of Jonathan, **M,** Abinadab, and Esh-baal;
9:39 Saul of Jonathan, **M,** Abinadab, and Esh-baal;
10: 2 Philistines killed Jonathan and Abinadab and **M,**

MALCHUS (1)

Jn 18:10 The slave's name was **M.**

MALCONTENTS (2)

Jude 1:16 These are grumblers and **m;**
1Mc 10:61 A group of **m** from Israel, renegades,

MALE‡ (234) [MALES]

A. EVERY MALE (28)

Ge 1:27 **m** and female he created them.
5: 2 **M** and female he created them,
6:19 they shall be **m** and female.
7: 2 with you seven pairs of all clean animals, the **m**
7: 2 the animals that are not clean, the **m** and its mate;
7: 3 the air also, **m** and female, to keep their kind alive
7: 9 **m** and female, went into the ark with Noah,
7:16 And those that entered, **m** and female of all flesh,
12:16 had sheep, oxen, **m** donkeys, **m** and female slaves,
17:10 Every **m** among you shall be circumcised. A
17:12 Throughout your generations every **m** A
17:14 Any uncircumcised **m** who is not circumcised in
17:23 every **m** among the men of Abraham's house, A
20:14 and oxen, and **m** and female slaves, and gave them
24:35 **m** and female slaves, camels and donkeys.
30:35 the **m** goats that were striped and spotted, and all
30:43 and **m** and female slaves, and camels and donkeys.
31:10 in which I looked up and saw that the **m** goats
32: 5 donkeys, flocks, **m** and female slaves;
32:14 two hundred female goats and twenty **m** goats,
32:15 twenty female donkeys and ten **m** donkeys.
34:15 and every **m** among you be circumcised. A
34:22 that every **m** among us be circumcised A
34:24 and every **m** was circumcised, A
Ex 12: 5 Your lamb shall be without blemish, a year-old **m;**
13:13 firstborn **m** among your children you shall redeem.
13:15 to the LORD every **m** that first opens the womb, A
20:10 your son or your daughter, your **m** or female slave,
20:17 or **m** or female slave, or ox, or donkey,
21: 2 When you buy a **m** Hebrew slave,
21: 7 she shall not go out as the **m** slaves do.
21:20 a slaveowner strikes a **m** or female slave with a rod
21:26 slaveowner strikes the eye of a **m** or female slave,
21:27 owner knocks out a tooth of a **m** or female slave,
21:32 If the ox gores a **m** or female slave,
34:19 all your **m** livestock, the firstborn of cow
Lev 1: 3 you shall offer a **m** without blemish;
1:10 your offering shall be a **m** without blemish.
3: 1 the herd, whether **m** or female, you shall offer one
3: 6 **m** or female, you shall offer one without blemish.
4:23 as his offering a **m** goat without blemish.
6:18 Every **m** among the descendants of Aaron shall A
6:29 Every **m** among the priests shall eat of it; A
7: 6 Every **m** among the priests shall eat of it; A
9: 3 'Take a **m** goat for a sin offering;
12: 2 If a woman conceives and bears a **m** child,
12: 7 the law for her who bears a child, **m** or female.
14:10 On the eighth day he shall take two **m** lambs
14:21 he shall take one **m** lamb for a guilt offering to
15:33 for anyone, **m** or female, who has a discharge,
16: 5 the people of Israel two **m** goats for a sin offering,
Lev 18:22 You shall not lie with a **m** as with a woman;
20:13 If a man lies with a **m** as with a woman,
22:19 in your behalf it shall be a **m** without blemish,
23:19 You shall also offer one **m** goat for a sin offering,
23:19 and two **m** lambs a year old as a sacrifice
25: 6 you, your **m** and female slaves,
25:44 for the **m** and female slaves whom you may have,
25:44 the nations around you that you may acquire **m**
27: 3 the equivalent for a **m** shall be:
27: 5 the equivalent is twenty shekels for a **m**
27: 6 the equivalent for a **m** is five shekels of silver,
27: 7 then the equivalent for a **m** is fifteen shekels,
Nu 1: 2 to the number of names, every **m** individually; A
1:20 every **m** from twenty years old and upward, A
1:22 every **m** from twenty years old and upward, A
3:15 You shall enroll every **m** from a month old A
5: 3 both **m** and female, putting them outside the camp;
6:12 and bring a **m** lamb a year old as a guilt offering.
6:14 one **m** lamb a year old without blemish as
7:15 one **m** lamb a year old, for a burnt offering;
7:16 one **m** goat for a sin offering;
7:17 five **m** goats, and five **m** lambs a year old.
7:21 one **m** lamb a year old, as a burnt offering;
7:22 one **m** goat as a sin offering;
7:23 five **m** goats, and five **m** lambs a year old.
7:27 one **m** lamb a year old, for a burnt offering;
7:28 one **m** goat for a sin offering;
7:29 five **m** goats, and five **m** lambs a year old.
7:33 one **m** lamb a year old, for a burnt offering;
7:34 one **m** goat for a sin offering;
7:35 five **m** goats, and five **m** lambs a year old.
7:39 one **m** lamb a year old, for a burnt offering;
7:40 one **m** goat for a sin offering;
7:41 five **m** goats, and five **m** lambs a year old.
7:45 one **m** lamb a year old, for a burnt offering;
7:46 one **m** goat for a sin offering;
7:47 five **m** goats, and five **m** lambs a year old.
7:51 one **m** lamb a year old, for a burnt offering;
7:52 one **m** goat for a sin offering;
7:53 five **m** goats, and five **m** lambs a year old.
7:57 one **m** lamb a year old, for a burnt offering;
7:58 one **m** goat for a sin offering;
7:59 five **m** goats, and five **m** lambs a year old.
7:63 one **m** lamb a year old, for a burnt offering;
7:64 one **m** goat for a sin offering;
7:65 five **m** goats, and five **m** lambs a year old.
7:69 one **m** lamb a year old, for a burnt offering;
7:70 one **m** goat for a sin offering;
7:71 five **m** goats, and five **m** lambs a year old.
7:75 one **m** lamb a year old, for a burnt offering;
7:76 one **m** goat for a sin offering;
7:77 five **m** goats, and five **m** lambs a year old.
7:81 one **m** lamb a year old, for a burnt offering;
7:82 one **m** goat for a sin offering;
7:83 five **m** goats, and five **m** lambs a year old.
7:87 twelve rams, twelve **m** lambs a year old,
7:87 and twelve **m** goats for a sin offering;
7:88 the **m** goats sixty, the **m** lambs a year old sixty.
15:11 or for each of the **m** lambs or the kids.
15:24 and one **m** goat for a sin offering.
18:10 every **m** may eat it; it shall be holy to you. A
26:62 every **m** one month old and up; A
28: 3 two **m** lambs a year old without blemish, daily,
28: 9 two **m** lambs a year old without blemish,
28:11 seven **m** lambs a year old without blemish;
28:15 And there shall be one **m** goat for a sin offering to
28:19 one ram, and seven **m** lambs a year old;
28:22 also one **m** goat for a sin offering,
28:27 one ram, seven **m** lambs a year old.
28:30 with one **m** goat, to make atonement for you.
29: 2 seven **m** lambs a year old without blemish.
29: 5 with one **m** goat for a sin offering,
29: 8 one ram, seven **m** lambs a year old.
29:11 with one **m** goat for a sin offering,
29:13 two rams, fourteen **m** lambs a year old.
29:16 also one **m** goat for a sin offering,
29:17 fourteen **m** lambs a year old without blemish,
29:19 also one **m** goat for a sin offering,
29:20 fourteen **m** lambs a year old without blemish,
29:22 also one **m** goat for a sin offering,
29:23 fourteen **m** lambs a year old without blemish,
29:25 also one **m** goat for a sin offering,
29:26 fourteen **m** lambs a year old without blemish,
29:28 also one **m** goat for a sin offering,
29:29 fourteen **m** lambs a year old without blemish,
29:31 also one **m** goat for a sin offering,
29:32 fourteen **m** lambs a year old without blemish,
29:34 also one **m** goat for a sin offering,
29:36 seven **m** lambs a year old without blemish,
29:38 also one **m** goat for a sin offering,
31: 7 had commanded Moses, and killed every **m.** A
31:17 therefore, kill every **m** among the little ones, A
Dt 4:16 the likeness of **m** or female,
5:14 or your **m** or female slave,
5:14 your **m** and female slave may rest as well as you.
5:21 or field, or **m** or female slave, or ox, or donkey,
12:12 your **m** and female slaves,
12:18 your **m** and female slaves,
15:13 you send a **m** slave out from you a free person,
15:19 Every firstling **m** born of your herd
16:11 your **m** and female slaves,
16:14 your **m** and female slaves, as well as the Levites,
23:18 of a prostitute or the wages of a **m** prostitute into
28:68 for sale to your enemies as **m** and female slaves,
Jos 17: 2 these were the **m** descendants of Manasseh son
17: 4 to give us an inheritance along with our **m** kin."
Jdg 21:11 every **m** and every woman that has lain with A

Jdg 21:11 with a **m** you shall devote to destruction."
1Sa 1:11 but will give to your servant a **m** child,
8:16 He will take your **m** and female slaves,
25:22 so much as one **m** of all who belong to him."
25:34 not have been left to Nabal so much as one **m."**
1Ki 11:15 he killed every **m** in Edom A
11:16 until he had eliminated every **m** in Edom); A
14:10 I will cut off from Jeroboam every **m,** A
14:24 there were also **m** temple prostitutes in the land.
15:12 He put away the **m** temple prostitutes out of
16:11 he did not leave him a single **m** of his kindred
21:21 will cut off from Ahab every **m,** bond or free, A
22:46 the **m** temple prostitutes who were still in the land
2Ki 5:26 sheep and oxen, and **m** and female slaves?
9:8 I will cut off from Ahab every **m,** bond or free, A
23:7 the houses of the **m** temple prostitutes that were in
2Ch 17:11 and seven thousand seven hundred **m** goats.
28:10 **m** and female, as your slaves.
29:21 and seven **m** goats for a sin offering for
29:23 Then the **m** goats for the sin offering were brought
31:19 distribute portions to every **m** among the priests A
Ezr 2:65 besides their **m** and female servants,
2:65 and they had two hundred **m** and female singers.
6:17 and as a sin offering for all Israel, twelve **m** goats,
8:35 and as a sin offering twelve **m** goats;
Ne 7:67 besides their **m** and female slaves,
7:67 and they had two hundred forty-five singers, **m**
Job 31:13 I have rejected the cause of my **m** or female slaves,
Ecc 2:7 I bought **m** and female slaves,
Isa 14:2 the house of Israel will possess the nations as **m**
Jer 34:9 that all should set free their Hebrew slaves, **m**
34:10 **m** or female, so that they would not
34:11 the **m** and female slaves they had set free,
34:16 of you took back your **m** and female slaves,
50:8 and be like **m** goats leading the flock.
Eze 16:17 and made for yourself **m** images,
23:14 she saw **m** figures carved on the wall,
43:22 a **m** goat without blemish for a sin offering;
45:23 and a **m** goat daily for a sin offering.
Da 8:5 I was watching, a **m** goat appeared from the west,
8:8 Then the **m** goat grew exceedingly great;
8:21 The **m** goat is the king of Greece,
Joel 2:29 Even on the **m** and female slaves, in those days,
Mal 1:14 be the cheat who has a **m** in the flock and vows
Mt 19:4 at the beginning 'made them **m** and female,'
Mk 10:6 'God made them **m** and female.'
Lk 2:23 "Every firstborn **m** shall be designated as holy to
1Co 6:9 Fornicators, idolaters, adulterers, **m** prostitutes,
Gal 3:28 there is no longer **m** and female;
Rev 12:5 And she gave birth to a son, a **m** child,
12:13 the woman who had given birth to the **m** child.
Tob 6:12 He has no **m** heir and no daughter except Sarah
10:10 **m** and female slaves, oxen and sheep,
AdE 7:4 and our children—**m** and female slaves.
1Mc 5:28 and killed every **m** by the edge of the sword; A
5:35 and he killed every **m** in it, plundered it, A
5:51 He destroyed every **m** by the edge of the sword, A
1Es 5:1 and their **m** and female servants,
5:41 besides **m** and female servants,
5:42 their **m** and female servants were seven thousand
7:8 and twelve **m** goats for the sin of all Israel,
8:66 and as a thank offering twelve **m** goats—

MALEFACTOR[S] (KJV) See CRIMINAL[S]

MALELEEL (KJV) See MAHALALEEL

MALES (28) [MALE]

Ge 34:25 against the city unawares, and killed all the **m.**
Ex 12:48 all his **m** shall be circumcised;
13:12 of your livestock that are **m** shall be the LORD's.
23:17 Three times in the year all your **m** shall appear
34:23 Three times in the year all your **m** shall appear
Nu 3:22 counting all the **m** from a month old and upward,
3:28 Counting all the **m,** from a month old and upward,
3:34 counting all the **m** from a month old and upward,
3:39 all the **m** from a month old and upward,
3:40 Enroll all the firstborn **m** of the Israelites,
3:43 all the firstborn **m** from a month old and upward,
Dt 16:16 Three times a year all your **m** shall appear before
20:13 you shall put all its **m** to the sword.
Jos 5:4 all the **m** of the people who came out of Egypt,
2Ch 31:16 **m** from three years old and upwards,
Ezr 8:3 with whom were registered one hundred fifty **m.**
8:4 and with him two hundred **m.**
8:5 and with him three hundred **m.**
8:6 Ebed son of Jonathan, and with him fifty **m.**
8:7 Jeshaiah son of Athaliah, and with him seventy **m.**
8:8 Zebadiah son of Michael, and with him eighty **m.**
8:9 and with him two hundred eighteen **m.**
8:10 and with him one hundred sixty **m.**
8:11 and with him twenty-eight **m.**
8:12 and with him one hundred ten **m.**
8:13 Jeuel, and Shemaiah, and with them sixty **m.**
8:14 Uthai and Zaccur, and with them seventy **m.**
4Mc 15:30 O more noble than **m** in steadfastness,

MALESEAR (2)

AdE 1:14 Arkesaeus, Sarsathaeus, and **M,**
1:14 Arkesaeus, Sarsathaeus, and **M,**

MALEVOLENT (1)

4Mc 1:25 In pleasure there exists even a **m** tendency,

MALICE‡ (21) [MALICIOUS, MALICIOUSLY]

Ps 41:5 My enemies wonder in **m** when I will die,
73:8 They scoff and speak with **m;**
La 3:60 You have seen all their **m,**
Eze 25:6 with all the **m** within you against the land of Israel,
25:15 and with **m** of heart took revenge in destruction;
Mt 22:18 But Jesus, aware of their **m,** said,
Ro 1:29 of wickedness, evil, covetousness, **m.**
1Co 5:8 not with the old yeast, the yeast of **m** and evil,
Eph 4:31 and wrangling and slander, together with all **m,**
Col 3:8 anger, wrath, **m,** slander, and abusive language
Tit 3:3 passing our days in **m** and envy, despicable,
1Pe 2:1 Rid yourselves, therefore, of all **m,** and all guile,
2Mc 4:4 was intensifying the **m** of Simon.
5:23 In his **m** toward the Jewish citizens,
3Mc 2:25 he arrived in Egypt, he increased in his deeds of **m,**
3:22 in their innate **m** they took this in a contrary spirit,
4Mc 1:4 that hinder one from justice, such as **m,** and those
1:26 covetousness, thirst for honor, rivalry, and **m;**
2:15 vainglory, boasting, arrogance, and **m.**
3:4 No one of us can eradicate **m,**
3:4 at our side so that we are not overcome by **m.**

MALICIOUS (8) [MALICE]

Ex 23:1 with the wicked to act as a **m** witness.
Dt 19:16 If a **m** witness comes forward to accuse someone
Ps 35:11 **M** witnesses rise up; they ask me about things
Jdt 4:12 to be profaned and desecrated to the **m** joy of
1Mc 7:25 to the king and brought **m** charges against them.
3Mc 7:3 frequently urging us with **m** intent,
2Es 11:45 your most evil little wings, your **m** heads,
4Mc 2:16 the temperate mind repels all these **m** emotions,

MALICIOUSLY (2) [MALICE]

Ps 139:20 those who speak of you **m,**
4Mc 6:25 with **m** contrived instruments,

MALIGN‡ (2) [MALIGNED]

Mt 10:25 much more will they **m** those of his household!
1Pe 2:12 so that, though they **m** you as evildoers,

MALIGNED (2) [MALIGN]

1Pe 3:16 so that, when you are **m,** those who abuse you
2Pe 2:2 of these teachers the way of truth will be **m.**

MALIGNITY (KJV) See MALICE

MALLET (1)

Jdg 5:26 and her right hand to the workmen's **m;**

MALLOTHI (2)

1Ch 25:4 Giddalti, and Romamti-ezer, Joshbekashah, **M,**
25:26 to **M,** his sons and his brothers, twelve;

MALLOW (2) [MALLOWS]

Job 24:24 they wither and fade like the **m;**
30:4 they pick **m** and the leaves of bushes,

MALLOWS (1) [MALLOW]

Job 6:6 or is there any flavor in the juice of **m?**

MALLUCH (6)

1Ch 6:44 Ethan son of Kishi, son of Abdi, son of **M,**
Ezr 10:29 Of the descendants of Bani: Meshullam, **M,**
10:32 Benjamin, **M,** and Shemariah.
Ne 10:4 Hattush, Shebaniah, **M,**
10:27 **M,** Harim, and Baanah.
12:2 Amariah, **M,** Hattush,

MALLUCHI (1)

Ne 12:14 of **M,** Jonathan; of Shebaniah, Joseph;

MALLUS (1)

2Mc 4:30 of **M** revolted because their cities had been given

MALTA (1)

Ac 28:1 we then learned that the island was called **M.**

MALTREAT (1) [MALTREATED]

4Mc 12:13 and to **m** and torture them in this way?

MALTREATED (3) [MALTREAT]

2Mc 7:13 they **m** and tortured the fourth in the same way.
7:15 Next they brought forward the fifth and **m** him.
4Mc 13:27 while watching their brothers being **m** and tortured

MAMDAI (1)

1Es 9:34 Maerus, Joel, **M** and Bedeiah and Vaniah,

MAMITANEMUS (1)

1Es 9:34 Carabasion and Eliashib and **M,** Eliasis, Binnui,

MAMMON (KJV) See WEALTH; See also Index to Footnotes

MAMRE (10) [=HEBRON]

Ge 13:18 and came and settled by the oaks of **M,**
14:13 who was living by the oaks of **M** the Amorite,
14:24 with me—Aner, Eshcol, and **M.**
18:1 LORD appeared to Abraham by the oaks of **M,**
23:17 which was to the east of **M,**
23:19 in the cave of the field of Machpelah facing **M**
25:9 of Ephron son of Zohar the Hittite, east of **M,**
35:27 Jacob came to his father Isaac at **M,**
49:30 near **M,** in the land of Canaan,
50:13 near **M,** which Abraham bought as a burial site

MAMUCHUS (1)

1Es 9:30 Of the descendants of Mani: Olamus, **M,** Adaiah,

MAN‡ (1111) [FISHERMEN, FOOTMEN, FREEDMEN, GENTLEMEN, HERDSMAN, HORSEMAN, HORSEMEN, KINSMAN, KINSMAN'S, KINSMEN, MADMAN, MADMEN, MAN'S, MAN-CHILD, MANHOOD, MEN, MEN'S, NOBLEMAN, SPEARMEN, SPOKESMAN, SWORDSMEN, TRADESMAN, WORKMAN, WORKMEN'S]

A. SON OF MAN (85); See also MORTAL
B. MAN OF *GOD (81)
C. YOUNG MAN (71)
D. OLD MAN (18)
E. EVERY MAN (14)
F. RIGHTEOUS MAN (14)

Ge 2:7 then the LORD God formed **m** from the dust of
2:7 and the **m** became a living being.
2:8 and there he put the **m** whom he had formed.
2:15 the **m** and put him in the garden of Eden to till it
2:16 And the LORD God commanded the **m,**
2:18 "It is not good that the **m** should be alone;
2:19 to the **m** to see what he would call them;
2:19 and whatever the **m** called every living creature,
2:20 The **m** gave names to all cattle,
2:20 the **m** there was not found a helper as his partner.
2:21 a deep sleep to fall upon the **m,** and he slept;
2:22 from the **m** he made into a woman and brought her
2:22 into a woman and brought her to the **m.**
2:23 Then the **m** said, "This at last is bone of my bones
2:23 for out of **M** this one was taken."
2:24 a **m** leaves his father and his mother and clings
2:25 And the **m** and his wife were both naked,
3:8 and the **m** and his wife hid themselves from
3:9 But the LORD God called to the **m,**
3:12 The **m** said, "The woman whom you gave to be
3:17 And to the **m** he said, "Because you have listened
3:20 The **m** named his wife Eve,
3:21 the LORD God made garments of skins for the **m**
3:22 "See, the **m** has become like one of us,
3:24 He drove out the **m;** and at the
4:1 Now the **m** knew his wife Eve,
4:1 "I have produced a **m** with the help of the LORD."
4:23 I have killed a **m** for wounding me,
4:23 a young **m** for striking me. C
6:9 a righteous **m,** blameless in his generation; F
9:20 a **m** of the soil, was the first to plant a vineyard.
15:4 "This **m** shall not be your heir;
16:12 He shall be a wild ass of a **m,**
17:17 a child be born to a **m** who is a hundred years old?
19:4 all the people to the last **m,** surrounded the house;
19:8 I have two daughters who have not known a **m;**
19:9 Then they pressed hard against the **m** Lot,
19:31 and there is not a **m** on earth to come in to us after
24:16 a virgin, whom no **m** had known.
24:21 The **m** gazed at her in silence to learn whether or
24:22 the **m** took a gold nose-ring weighing a half shekel,
24:26 The **m** bowed his head and worshiped the LORD
24:29 and Laban ran out to the **m,** to the spring.
24:30 "Thus the **m** spoke to me," he went to the **m;**
24:32 So the **m** came into the house;
24:58 and said to her, "Will you go with this **m?"**
24:61 mounted the camels and followed the **m;**
24:65 "Who is the **m** over there,
25:8 an old **m** and full of years, D
25:27 a **m** of the field, while Jacob was a quiet **m,**
26:11 "Whoever touches this **m** or his wife shall be put
26:13 and the **m** became rich; he prospered more
27:11 Esau is a hairy **m,** and I am a **m** of smooth skin.
29:19 to you than that I should give her to any other **m;**
30:43 Thus the **m** grew exceedingly rich,
32:24 and a **m** wrestled with him until daybreak.
32:25 the **m** saw that he did not prevail against Jacob,
32:28 the **m** said, "You shall no longer be called Jacob,
34:19 And the young **m** did not delay to do the thing, C
37:15 and a **m** found him wandering in the fields;
37:15 the **m** asked him, "What are you seeking?"
37:17 The **m** said, "They have gone away,
39:2 and he became a successful **m;**
41:33 let Pharaoh select a **m** who is discerning and wise,
42:11 We are all sons of one **m;**
42:13 the sons of a certain **m** in the land of Canaan;
42:30 "The **m,** the lord of the land, spoke harshly to us,
42:33 Then the **m,** the lord of the land, said to us,
43:3 Judah said to him, "The **m** solemnly warned us,
43:5 for the **m** said to us, 'You shall not see my face,
43:6 "Why did you treat me so badly as to tell the **m**
43:7 "The **m** questioned us carefully about ourselves
43:11 and carry them down as a present to the **m—**
43:13 and be on your way again to the **m;**

Ge 43:14 may God Almighty grant you mercy before the **m,**
43:17 The **m** did as Joseph said,
43:27 the old **m** of whom you spoke? D
44:20 we said to my lord, 'We have a father, an old **m,** D
Ex 2: 1 Now a **m** from the house of Levi went and married
2:20 Why did you leave the **m?**
2:21 Moses agreed to stay with the **m,**
11: 2 the people that every **m** is to ask his neighbor E
11: 3 Moses himself was a **m** of great importance in
21: 7 When a **m** sells his daughter as a slave,
21:28 When an ox gores a **m** or a woman to death,
21:29 and it kills a **m** or a woman, the ox shall be stoned,
22:16 When a **m** seduces a virgin who is not engaged to
32: 1 the **m** who brought us up out of the land of Egypt,
32:23 the **m** who brought us up out of the land of Egypt,
36: 6 "No **m** or woman is to make anything else as
Lev 13:29 When a **m** or woman has a disease on the head or
13:38 a **m** or a woman has spots on the skin of the body,
15: 2 When any **m** has a discharge from his member,
15:16 If a **m** has an emission of semen,
15:18 If a **m** lies with a woman and has an emission
15:24 If any **m** lies with her, and her impurity falls
15:33 for the **m** who lies with a woman who is unclean.
19:20 If a **m** has sexual relations with a woman who is
19:20 designated for another **m** but not ransomed
20:10 **m** commits adultery with the wife of his neighbor,
20:11 The **m** who lies with his father's wife has
20:12 If a **m** lies with his daughter-in-law,
20:13 If a **m** lies with a male as with a woman,
20:14 **m** takes a wife and her mother also, it is depravity;
20:15 If a **m** has sexual relations with an animal,
20:17 If a **m** takes his sister, a daughter of his father or
20:18 If a **m** lies with a woman having her sickness
20:20 If a **m** lies with his uncle's wife,
20:21 If a **m** takes his brother's wife, it is impurity;
20:27 A **m** or a woman who is a medium or
21:20 a **m** with a blemish in his eyes or an itching disease
22: 4 a corpse or a **m** who has had an emission of semen,
22:14 If a **m** eats of the sacred donation unintentionally,
24:10 A **m** whose mother was an Israelite
Nu 1: 4 A **m** from each tribe shall be with you,
1: 4 each **m** the head of his ancestral house.
5: 6 When a **m** or a woman wrongs another,
5:13 if a **m** has had intercourse with her but it is hidden
5:15 then the **m** shall bring his wife to the priest.
5:19 saying, "If no **m** has lain with you,
5:20 **m** other than your husband has had intercourse
5:30 a spirit of jealousy comes on a **m** and he is jealous
5:31 The **m** shall be free from iniquity,
11:27 And a young **m** ran and told Moses, C
12: 3 Now the **m** Moses was very humble,
13: 2 of their ancestral tribes you shall send a **m,**
15:32 they found a **m** gathering sticks on the sabbath day.
15:35 "The **m** shall be put to death;
16: 7 **m** whom the LORD chooses shall be the holy one.
16:18 So each **m** took his censer,
17: 5 And the staff of the **m** whom I choose shall sprout;
17: 9 and they looked, and each **m** took his staff.
24: 3 the oracle of the **m** whose eye is clear,
24:15 the oracle of the **m** whose eye is clear,
25: 8 he went after the Israelite **m** into the tent,
25:14 The name of the slain Israelite **m,**
27: 8 You shall also say to the Israelites, "If a **m** dies,
27:18 a **m** in whom is the spirit,
30: 2 When a **m** makes a vow to the LORD,
31:17 and kill every woman who has known a **m**
31:18 But all the young girls who have not known a **m**
31:35 women who had not known a **m** by sleeping
Dt 15:12 whether a Hebrew **m** or a Hebrew woman,
17: 2 a **m** or woman who does what is evil in the sight of
17: 5 then you shall bring out to your gates that **m** or
17: 5 and you shall stone the **m** or woman to death.
21:15 If a **m** has two wives,
22: 5 nor shall a **m** put on a woman's garment;
22:13 Suppose a **m** marries a woman,
22:16 "I gave my daughter in marriage to this **m**
22:18 of that town shall take the **m** and punish him;
22:22 a **m** is caught lying with the wife of another **m,**
22:22 **m** who lay with the woman as well as the woman.
22:23 and a **m** meets her in the town and lies with her,
22:24 and the **m** because he violated his neighbor's wife.
22:25 **m** meets the engaged woman in the open country,
22:25 and the **m** seizes her and lies with her,
22:25 then only the **m** who lay with her shall die.
22:28 If a **m** meets a virgin who is not engaged,
22:29 the **m** who lay with her shall give fifty shekels
22:30 A **m** shall not marry his father's wife,
24: 1 Suppose a **m** enters into marriage with a woman,
24: 3 Then suppose the second **m** dislikes her,
24: 3 (or the second **m** who married her dies);
24: 5 When a **m** is newly married,
25: 7 the **m** has no desire to marry his brother's widow,
25: 9 the **m** who does not build up his brother's house."
28:30 but another **m** shall lie with her.
29:18 It may be that there is among you a **m** or woman,
32:25 for young **m** and woman alike, C
33: 1 the blessing with which Moses, the **m** of God, B
Jos 5:13 he looked up and saw a **m** standing before him
8:17 There was not a **m** left in Ai or Bethel who did
14: 6 what the LORD said to Moses the **m** of God B
14:15 this Arba was the greatest **m** among the Anakim.
Jdg 1:24 When the spies saw a **m** coming out of the city,
1:25 but they let the **m** and all his family go.
1:26 **m** went to the land of the Hittites and built a city,
3:15 the Benjaminite, a left-handed **m.**
3:17 Now Eglon was a very fat **m.**
4:22 and I will show you the **m** whom you are seeking."
Jdg 5:30 A girl or two for every **m;** E
7:13 there was a **m** telling a dream to his comrade;
7:14 the sword of Gideon son of Joash, a **m** of Israel;
7:21 Every **m** stood in his place all around the camp, E
8:14 a young **m,** one of the people of Succoth, C
8:21 for as the **m** is, so is his strength."
9:54 to the young **m** who carried his armor and said C
9:54 So the young **m** thrust him through, and he died. C
10: 1 Tola son of Puah son of Dodo, a **m** of Issachar,
11:39 She had never slept with a **m.**
13: 2 There was a certain **m** of Zorah,
13: 6 "A **m** of God came to me, B
13: 8 let the **m** of God whom you sent come to us B
13:10 "The **m** who came to me
13:11 and came to the **m** and said to him,
13:11 "Are you the **m** who spoke to this woman?"
14:20 who had been his best **m.**
16:19 called a **m,** and had him shave off the seven locks
17: 1 There was a **m** in the hill country
17: 5 This **m** Micah had a shrine,
17: 7 there was a young **m** of Bethlehem in Judah, C
17: 8 This **m** left the town of Bethlehem in Judah,
17:11 The Levite agreed to stay with the **m;**
17:11 the young **m** became to him like one of his sons. C
17:12 and the young **m** became his priest, C
19: 6 and the girl's father said to the **m,**
19: 7 When the **m** got up to go,
19: 9 When the **m** with his concubine and his servant got
19:10 But the **m** would not spend the night;
19:16 an old **m** coming from his work in the field. D
19:16 The **m** was from the hill country of Ephraim,
19:17 the old **m** looked up and saw the wayfarer D
19:19 wine for me and the woman and the young **m** C
19:20 The old **m** said, "Peace be to you. D
19:22 They said to the old **m,** the master of the house, D
19:22 "Bring out the **m** who came into your house,
19:23 And the **m,** the master of the house,
19:23 Since this **m** is my guest, do not do this vile thing.
19:24 but against this **m** do not do such a vile thing."
19:25 **m** seized his concubine, and put her out to them.
19:28 and the **m** set out for his home.
21:12 with a **m** and brought them to the camp at Shiloh,
21:22 we did not capture in battle a wife for each **m.**
Ru 1: 1 and a certain **m** of Bethlehem in Judah went to live
1: 2 The name of the **m** was Elimelech and the name
2: 1 a prominent rich **m,** of the family of Elimelech,
2:19 Blessed be the **m** who took notice of you."
2:19 of the **m** with whom I worked today is Boaz."
2:20 "The **m** is a relative of ours,
3: 3 to the **m** until he has finished eating and drinking.
3: 8 At midnight the **m** was startled, and turned over,
3:16 Then she told her all that the **m** had done for her,
3:18 for the **m** will not rest,
4: 5 the widow of the dead **m,**
1Sa 1: 1 There was a certain **m** of Ramathaim,
1: 3 Now this **m** used to go up year by year
1:21 The **m** Elkanah and all his household went up
2:16 And if the **m** said to him,
2:27 A **m** of God came to Eli and said to him, B
4:12 A **m** of Benjamin ran from the battle line,
4:13 When the **m** came into the city and told the news,
4:14 Then the **m** came quickly and told Eli.
4:16 **m** said to Eli, "I have just come from the battle;
4:18 for he was an old **m,** and heavy. D
9: 1 a **m** of Benjamin whose name was Kish son
9: 1 a Benjaminite, a **m** of wealth.
9: 2 whose name was Saul, a handsome young **m.** C
9: 2 There was not a **m** among the people
9: 6 said to him, "There is a **m** of God in this town; B
9: 6 he is a **m** held in honor.
9: 7 "But if we go, what can we bring the **m?**
9: 7 and there is no present to bring to the **m** of God. B
9: 8 I will give it to the **m** of God, to tell us our way. B
9:10 So they went to the town where the **m** of God B
9:16 about this time I will send to you a **m** from the land
9:17 "Here is the **m** of whom I spoke to you.
10:12 A **m** of the place answered,
10:21 the family of the Matrites near **m** by **m,**
10:22 of the LORD, "Did the **m** come here?"
10:27 "How can this **m** save us?"
13:14 the LORD has sought out a **m** after his own heart;
14: 1 said to the young **m** who carried his armor, C
14: 6 to the young **m** who carried his armor, C
15: 3 do not spare them, but kill both **m** and woman,
16:18 a **m** of valor, a warrior, prudent in speech,
16:18 prudent in speech, and a **m** of good presence;
17: 8 Choose a **m** for yourselves,
17:10 Give me a **m,** that we may fight together."
17:12 the **m** was already old and advanced in years.
17:24 All the Israelites, when they saw the **m,**
17:25 "Have you seen this **m** who has come up?
17:25 The king will greatly enrich the **m** who kills him,
17:26 be done for the **m** who kills this Philistine,
17:27 "So shall it be done for the **m** who kills him."
17:55 "Abner, whose son is this young **m?"** C
17:58 said to him, "Whose son are you, young **m?"** C
18:23 seeing that I am a poor **m** and of no repute?"
20:22 But if I say to the young **m,** 'Look, C
21: 7 Now a certain **m** of the servants of Saul was there
21:14 "Look, you see the **m** is mad;
25: 2 There was a **m** in Maon,
25: 2 The **m** was very rich;
25: 3 Now the name of the **m** was Nabal,
25: 3 but the **m** was surly and mean; he was a Calebite.
25:13 "Every **m** strap on his sword!" E
26:15 David said to Abner, "Are you not a **m?**
27: 3 he and his troops, every **m** with his household, E
1Sa 27: 9 leaving neither **m** nor woman alive,
27:11 David left neither **m** nor woman alive to
28:14 She said, "An old **m** is coming up; D
29: 4 of the Philistines said to him, "Send the **m** back,
30:13 He said, "I am a young **m** of Egypt, C
30:22 except that each **m** may take his wife and children,
2Sa 1: 2 On the third day, a **m** came from Saul's camp,
1: 5 David asked the young **m** who was reporting C
1: 6 The young **m** reporting to him said, C
1:13 David said to the young **m** who had reported C
3:38 prince and a great **m** has fallen this day in Israel?
4:11 when wicked men have killed a righteous **m** F
12: 2 The rich **m** had very many flocks and herds;
12: 3 but the poor **m** had nothing but one little ewe lamb,
12: 4 Now there came a traveler to the rich **m,**
12: 5 David's anger was greatly kindled against the **m.**
12: 5 the **m** who has done this deserves to die;
12: 7 Nathan said to David, "You are the **m!**
13: 3 and Jonadab was a very crafty **m.**
13:17 He called the young **m** who served him and said, C
13:34 When the young **m** who kept watch looked up, C
14: 7 They say, 'Give up the **m** who struck his brother,
14:16 the **m** who would cut both me and my son off from
14:21 go, bring back the young **m** Absalom." C
16: 5 a **m** of the family of the house
16: 8 for you are a **m** of blood."
17: 3 You seek the life of only one **m,**
17:18 and came to the house of a **m** at Bahurim,
17:25 the son of a **m** named Ithra the Ishmaelite,
18: 5 for my sake with the young **m** Absalom." C
18:10 A **m** saw it, and told Joab,
18:11 Joab said to the **m** who told him, "What,
18:12 But the **m** said to Joab, "Even if I felt in my hand
18:12 For my sake protect the young **m** Absalom! C
18:24 and when he looked up, he saw a **m** running alone.
18:26 Then the sentinel saw another **m** running;
18:26 "See, another **m** running alone!"
18:27 The king said, "He is a good **m,**
18:29 said, "Is it well with the young **m** Absalom?" C
18:32 "Is it well with the young **m** Absalom?" C
18:32 up to do you harm, be like that young **m."** C
19: 7 not a **m** will stay with you this night;
19:32 Barzillai was a very aged **m,** eighty years old.
19:32 for he was a very wealthy **m.**
20:12 and the **m** saw that all the people were stopping.
20:21 But a **m** of the hill country of Ephraim,
21: 5 **m** who consumed us and planned to destroy us,
21:20 where there was a **m** of great size,
23: 1 the oracle of the **m** whom God exalted,
23:21 And he killed an Egyptian, a handsome **m.**
1Ki 1: 6 He was also a very handsome **m,**
1:42 a worthy **m** and surely you bring good news."
1:52 "If he proves to be a worthy **m,**
2: 9 do not hold him guiltless, for you are a wise **m;**
7:14 a **m** of Tyre, had been an artisan in bronze;
11:28 The **m** Jeroboam was very able,
11:28 young **m** was industrious he gave him charge C
12:22 word of God came to Shemaiah the **m** of God: B
13: 1 a **m** of God came out of Judah by the word of B
13: 4 king heard what the **m** of God cried out against B
13: 5 according to the sign that the **m** of God had B
13: 6 The king said to the **m** of God, B
13: 6 So the **m** of God entreated the LORD; B
13: 7 Then the king said to the **m** of God, B
13: 8 But the **m** of God said to the king, B
13:11 and told him all that the **m** of God had done B
13:12 the **m** of God who came from Judah had gone. B
13:14 He went after the **m** of God, B
13:14 "Are you the **m** of God who came from Judah?" B
13:19 Then the **m** of God went back with him, B
13:21 to the **m** of God who came from Judah, B
13:23 After the **m** of God had eaten food and had B
13:26 "It is the **m** of God who disobeyed the word of B
13:29 The prophet took up the body of the **m** of God, B
13:31 in the grave in which the **m** of God is buried; B
17:18 "What have you against me, O **m** of God? B
17:24 "Now I know that you are a **m** of God, B
20: 7 See how this **m** is seeking trouble;
20:20 Each killed his **m;** the Arameans fled
20:28 A **m** of God approached and said to the king B
20:35 But the **m** refused to strike him.
20:37 Then he found another **m** and said, "Strike me!"
20:37 So the **m** hit him, striking and wounding him.
20:39 brought a **m** to me, and said, 'Guard this **m;**
20:42 the **m** go whom I had devoted to destruction,
22:34 a certain **m** drew his bow and unknowingly struck
22:36 the army, "Every **m** to his city, and every man E
22:36 and every **m** to his country!" E
2Ki 1: 6 They answered him, "There came a **m** to meet us,
1: 7 "What sort of **m** was he who came to meet you
1: 8 They answered him, "A hairy **m,**
1: 9 "O **m** of God, the king says, 'Come down.' " B
1:10 "If I am a **m** of God, B
1:11 He went up and said to him, "O **m** of God, B
1:12 But Elijah answered them, "If I am a **m** of God, B
1:13 entreated him, "O **m** of God, please let my life, B
4: 7 She came and told the **m** of God, and he said, B
4: 9 that this **m** who regularly passes our way is
4: 9 regularly passes our way is a holy **m** of God. B
4:16 She replied, "No, my lord, O **m** of God; B
4:21 and laid him on the bed of the **m** of God, B
4:22 so that I may quickly go to the **m** of God B
4:25 and came to the **m** of God at Mount Carmel. B
4:25 When the **m** of God saw her coming, B
4:27 she came to the **m** of God at the mountain, B
4:27 But the **m** of God said, "Let her alone, B
4:40 "O **m** of God, there is death in the pot!" B

2Ki 4:42 A **m** came from Baal-shalishah,
4:42 food from the first fruits to the **m** of God: B
5: 1 was a great **m** and in high favor with his master,
5: 1 **m,** though a mighty warrior, suffered from leprosy.
5: 7 that this **m** sends word to me to cure a man
5: 7 that this man sends word to me to cure a **m**
5: 8 when Elisha the **m** of God heard that the king B
5:14 according to the word of the **m** of God; B
5:15 Then he returned to the **m** of God, B
5:20 the servant of Elisha the **m** of God, thought, B
6: 6 Then the **m** of God said, "Where did it fall?" B
6: 9 the **m** of God sent word to the king of Israel, B
6:10 sent word to the place of which the **m** of God B
6:15 When an attendant of the **m** of God rose early B
6:19 and I will bring you to the **m** whom you seek."
6:32 So he dispatched a **m** from his presence.
7: 2 said to the **m** of God, "Even if the LORD B
7:17 just as the **m** of God had said when the king B
7:18 For when the **m** of God had said to the king, B
7:19 the captain had answered the **m** of God, B
8: 2 and did according to the word of the **m** of God; B
8: 4 with Gehazi the servant of the **m** of God, B
8: 7 it was told him, "The **m** of God has come here," B
8: 8 a present with you and go to meet the **m** of God. B
8:11 Then the **m** of God wept. B
9: 4 So the young **m,** the young prophet, C
9: 6 the young **m** poured the oil on his head, C
11:11 every **m** with his weapons in his hand, E
13:19 the **m** of God was angry with him, and said, B
13:21 As a **m** was being buried, a marauding band was seen and the **m** was thrown into the grave of
13:21 as soon as the **m** touched the bones of Elisha,
22:15 Tell the **m** who sent you to me,
23:16 the **m** of God proclaimed, when Jeroboam stood B
23:16 of the **m** of God who had predicted these things. B
23:17 the tomb of the **m** of God who came from Judah B
1Ch 11:22 of Jehoiada was a valiant **m** of Kabzeel, a doer
11:23 And he killed an Egyptian, a **m** of great stature,
16: 3 in Israel—**m** and woman alike—
20: 6 where there was a **m** of great size,
22: 9 he shall be a **m** of peace.
23:14 but as for Moses the **m** of God, B
27: 6 the Benaiah who was a mighty **m** of the Thirty
27:32 being a **m** of understanding and a scribe;
2Ch 8:14 for so David the **m** of God had commanded. B
11: 2 of the LORD came to Shemaiah the **m** of God: B
15:13 whether young or old, **m** or woman.
18:33 a certain **m** drew his bow and unknowingly struck
25: 7 But a **m** of God came to him and said, "O king, B
25: 9 Amaziah said to the **m** of God, B
25: 9 The **m** of God answered, "The LORD is able B
30:16 according to the law of Moses the **m** of God; B
34:23 Tell the **m** who sent you to me,
36:17 no compassion on young **m** or young woman, C
Ezr 3: 2 as prescribed in the law of Moses the **m** of God. B
5:14 they were delivered to a **m** named Sheshbazzar,
8:18 they brought us a **m** of discretion,
Ne 1:11 and grant him mercy in the sight of this **m!"**
4:18 The **m** who sounded the trumpet was beside me.
4:22 "Let every **m** and his servant pass the night E
6:11 But I said, "Should a **m** like me run away?
6:11 a **m** like me go into the temple to save his life?
7: 2 a faithful **m** and feared God more than many.
12:24 the commandment of David the **m** of God, B
12:36 the musical instruments of David the **m** of God; B
Est 1:22 that every **m** should be master in his own house. E
4:11 that if any **m** or woman goes to the king inside
6: 6 for the **m** whom the king wishes to honor?"
6: 7 "For the **m** whom the king wishes to honor,
6: 9 let him robe the **m** whom the king wishes to honor,
6: 9 to honor, and let him conduct the **m** on horseback
6: 9 for the **m** whom the king wishes to honor.' "
6:11 be done for the **m** whom the king wishes to honor."
9: 4 as the **m** Mordecai grew more and more powerful.
Job 1: 1 a **m** in the land of Uz whose name was Job.
1: 1 That **m** was blameless and upright,
1: 3 this **m** was the greatest of all the people of the east.
1: 8 and upright **m** who fears God and turns away
2: 3 and upright **m** who fears God and turns away
12: 4 a just and blameless **m,** I am a laughingstock
38: 3 Gird up your loins like a **m,** I will question you,
40: 7 "Gird up your loins like a **m;**
Ps 19: 5 and like a strong **m** runs its course with joy.
90: T A Prayer of Moses, the **m** of God. B
105:17 he had sent a **m** ahead of them,
109: 6 They say, "Appoint a wicked **m** against him;
127: 5 Happy is the **m** who has his quiver full of them.
128: 4 Thus shall the **m** be blessed who fears the LORD.
Pr 7: 7 among the youths, a young **m** without sense, C
30: 1 An oracle. Thus says the **m:**
30:19 and the way of a **m** with a girl.
Ecc 6: 3 A **m** may beget a hundred children,
7:28 One **m** among a thousand I found,
8: 1 Who is like the wise **m?**
9:15 Now there was found in it a poor wise **m,**
9:15 Yet no one remembered that poor **m.**
11: 9 Rejoice, young **m,** while you are young, C
Isa 4: 1 Seven women shall take hold of one **m** in that day,
6: 5 I am lost, for I am a **m** of unclean lips,
14:16 "Is this the **m** who made the earth tremble,
46:11 the **m** for my purpose from a far country.
53: 3 a **m** of suffering and acquainted with infirmity;
62: 5 For as a young **m** marries a young woman, C
Jer 3: 1 If a **m** divorces his wife and she goes from him
15:10 a **m** of strife and contention to the whole land!
20:15 be the **m** who brought the news to my father,
20:16 that **m** be like the cities that the LORD overthrew

Jer 22:28 Is this **m** Coniah a despised broken pot,
22:30 Thus says the LORD: Record this **m** as childless,
22:30 a **m** who shall not succeed in his days;
26:11 "This **m** deserves the sentence of death
26:16 "This **m** does not deserve the sentence of death,
26:20 There was another **m** prophesying in the name of
30: 6 Ask now, and see, can a **m** bear a child?
30: 6 then do I see every **m** with his hands on his loins E
31:22 a woman encompasses a **m.**
33:17 David shall never lack a **m** to sit on the throne of
33:18 and the levitical priests shall never lack a **m**
35: 4 the sons of Hanan son of Igdaliah, the **m** of God, B
38: 4 "This **m** ought to be put to death,
38: 4 For this **m** is not seeking the welfare of this people,
44: 7 to cut off **m** and woman, child and infant,
48:19 Ask the **m** fleeing and the woman escaping;
51:22 with you I smash **m** and woman;
51:22 with you I smash the old **m** and the boy; D
51:22 with you I smash the young **m** and the girl; C
Eze 9: 2 among them was a **m** clothed in linen,
9: 3 The LORD called to the **m** clothed in linen,
9:11 Then the **m** clothed in linen,
10: 2 He said to the **m** clothed in linen,
10: 3 on the south side of the house when the **m** went in;
10: 6 When he commanded the **m** clothed in linen,
10: 7 and put it into the hands of the **m** clothed in linen,
18: 5 **m** is righteous and does what is lawful and right—
18:14 But if this **m** has a son who sees all the sins
33:24 "Abraham was only one **m,**
40: 3 When he brought me there, a **m** was there,
40: 4 The **m** said to me, "Mortal,
43: 6 While the **m** was standing beside me,
47: 3 the **m** measured one thousand cubits,
Da 2:25 the exiles from Judah a **m** who can tell the king
5:11 a **m** in your kingdom who is endowed with a spirit
8:15 having the appearance of a **m,**
8:16 "Gabriel, help this **m** understand the vision."
9:21 the **m** Gabriel, whom I had seen before in a vision,
10: 5 I looked up and saw a **m** clothed in linen,
12: 6 One of them said to the **m** clothed in linen,
12: 7 The **m** clothed in linen, who was upstream,
Hos 3: 3 you shall not have intercourse with a **m,**
9: 7 "The prophet is a fool, the **m** of the spirit is mad!"
Zec 1: 8 In the night I saw a **m** riding on a red horse!
1:10 So the **m** who was standing among
2: 1 up and saw a **m** with a measuring line in his hand.
2: 4 "Run, say to that young **m:** C
3: 2 Is not this **m** a brand plucked from the fire?"
6:12 Here is a **m** whose name is Branch:
13: 7 against the **m** who is my associate,"
Mt 1:19 being a righteous **m** and unwilling to expose her F
7:24 on them will be like a wise **m** who built his house
7:26 be like a foolish **m** who built his house on sand.
8: 9 For I also am a **m** under authority,
8:20 but the Son of **M** has nowhere to lay his head." A
8:27 They were amazed, saying, "What sort of **m** is this,
9: 2 a paralyzed **m** lying on a bed.
9: 3 to themselves, "This **m** is blaspheming."
9: 6 you may know that the Son of **M** has authority A
9: 9 he saw a **m** called Matthew sitting at the tax booth;
10:23 the towns of Israel before the Son of **M** comes. A
10:35 For I have come to set a **m** against his father,
11:19 the Son of **M** came eating and drinking, A
12: 8 For the Son of **M** is lord of the sabbath." A
12:10 a **m** was there with a withered hand,
12:13 Then he said to the **m,** "Stretch out your hand."
12:29 without first tying up the strong **m?**
12:32 Whoever speaks a word against the Son of **M** A
12:40 three nights the Son of **M** will be in the heart A
13:37 one who sows the good seed is the Son of **M;** A
13:41 The Son of **M** will send his angels, A
13:54 "Where did this **m** get this wisdom and these deeds
13:56 Where then did this **m** get all this?"
16:13 "Who do people say that the Son of **M** is?" A
16:27 the Son of **M** is to come with his angels in A
16:28 the Son of **M** coming in his kingdom." A
17: 9 the Son of **M** has been raised from the dead." A
17:12 the Son of **M** is about to suffer at their hands." A
17:14 When they came to the crowd, a **m** came to him,
17:22 Son of **M** is going to be betrayed into human A
19: 3 for a **m** to divorce his wife for any cause?"
19: 5 a **m** shall leave his father and mother and be joined
19:10 "If such is the case of a **m** with his wife,
19:20 The young **m** said to him, "I have kept all these; C
19:22 When the young **m** heard this word, C
19:28 Son of **M** is seated on the throne of his glory, A
20:18 Son of **M** will be handed over to the chief A
20:28 the Son of **M** came not to be served but to serve, A
21:28 "What do you think? A **m** had two sons;
22:11 a **m** there who was not wearing a wedding robe,
22:24 Moses said, 'If a **m** dies childless,
24:27 so will be the coming of the Son of **M.** A
24:30 the sign of the Son of **M** will appear in heaven, A
24:30 Son of **M** coming on the clouds of heaven' A
24:37 so will be the coming of the Son of **M.** A
24:39 so too will be the coming of the Son of **M.** A
24:44 the Son of **M** is coming at an unexpected hour. A
25:14 "For it is as if a **m,** going on a journey,
25:24 saying, 'Master, I knew that you were a harsh **m,**
25:31 "When the Son of **M** comes in his glory, A
26: 2 Son of **M** will be handed over to be crucified." A
26:18 He said, "Go into the city to a certain **m,**
26:24 The Son of **M** goes as it is written of him, A
26:24 to that one by whom the Son of **M** is betrayed! A
26:45 Son of **M** is betrayed into the hands of sinners. A
26:48 saying, "The one I will kiss is the **m;** arrest him."
26:64 the Son of **M** seated at the right hand of Power A

Mt 26:71 "This **m** was with Jesus of Nazareth."
26:72 "I do not know the **m."**
26:74 and he swore an oath, "I do not know the **m!"**
27:19 "Have nothing to do with that innocent **m,**
27:32 they came upon a **m** from Cyrene named Simon;
27:32 they compelled this **m** to carry his cross.
27:47 they said, "This **m** is calling for Elijah."
27:54 "Truly this **m** was God's Son!"
27:57 there came a rich **m** from Arimathea,
Mk 1:23 Just then there was in their synagogue a **m** with
2: 3 some people came, bringing to him a paralyzed **m,**
2:10 you may know that the Son of **M** has authority A
2:28 so the Son of **M** is lord even of the sabbath." A
3: 1 and a **m** was there who had a withered hand.
3: 3 And he said to the **m** who had the withered hand,
3: 5 at their hardness of heart and said to the **m,**
3:27 without first tying up the strong **m;**
5: 2 immediately a **m** out of the tombs with
5: 8 For he had said to him, "Come out of the **m,**
5:15 the very **m** who had had the legion;
5:18 the **m** who had been possessed
6: 2 They said, "Where did this **m** get all this?
6:20 knowing that he was a righteous and holy **m,**
7:32 a deaf **m** who had an impediment in his speech;
8:22 a blind **m** to him and begged him to touch him.
8:23 He took the blind **m** by the hand and led him out of
8:24 And the **m** looked up and said, "I can see people,
8:31 that the Son of **M** must undergo great suffering, A
8:38 Son of **M** will also be ashamed when he comes A
9: 9 until after the Son of **M** had risen from the dead. A
9:12 How then is it written about the Son of **M,** A
9:31 Son of **M** is to be betrayed into human hands, A
10: 2 "Is it lawful for a **m** to divorce his wife?"
10: 4 a **m** to write a certificate of dismissal and
10: 7 a **m** shall leave his father and mother and be joined
10:17 a **m** ran up and knelt before him, and asked him,
10:33 Son of **M** will be handed over to the chief A
10:45 the Son of **M** came not to be served but to serve, A
10:49 And they called the blind **m,** saying to him,
10:51 The blind **m** said to him, "My teacher,
12: 1 "A **m** planted a vineyard, put a fence around it,
12:19 the **m** shall marry the widow and raise up children
13:26 Son of **M** coming in clouds' with great power A
13:34 It is like a **m** going on a journey,
14:13 and a **m** carrying a jar of water will meet you;
14:21 For the Son of **M** goes as it is written of him, A
14:21 to that one by whom the Son of **M** is betrayed! A
14:41 Son of **M** is betrayed into the hands of sinners. A
14:44 saying, "The one I will kiss is the **m;**
14:51 A certain young **m** was following him, C
14:62 Son of **M** seated at the right hand of the Power,' A
14:67 "You also were with Jesus, the **m** from Nazareth."
14:69 "This **m** is one of them."
14:71 "I do not know this **m** you are talking about."
15: 7 Now a **m** called Barabbas was in prison with
15:12 to do with the **m** you call the King of the Jews?"
15:39 he said, "Truly this **m** was God's Son!"
16: 5 As they entered the tomb, they saw a young **m,** C
Lk 1:18 I am an old **m,** and my wife is getting on D
1:27 a virgin engaged to a **m** whose name was Joseph,
2:25 a **m** in Jerusalem whose name was Simeon;
2:25 this **m** was righteous and devout,
4:33 In the synagogue there was a **m** who had the spirit
5: 8 "Go away from me, Lord, for I am a sinful **m!"**
5:12 there was a **m** covered with leprosy.
5:18 carrying a paralyzed **m** on a bed.
5:24 you may know that the Son of **M** has authority A
6: 5 "The Son of **M** is lord of the sabbath." A
6: 6 a **m** there whose right hand was withered.
6: 8 he said to the **m** who had the withered hand,
6:22 and defame you on account of the Son of **M.** A
6:48 That one is like a **m** building a house,
6:49 not act is like a **m** who built a house on the ground
7: 8 For I also am a **m** set under authority,
7:12 a **m** who had died was being carried out.
7:14 And he said, "Young **m,** I say to you, rise!" C
7:15 The dead **m** sat up and began to speak,
7:34 the Son of **M** has come eating and drinking, A
7:39 he said to himself, "If this **m** were a prophet,
8:27 a **m** of the city who had demons met him
8:29 the unclean spirit to come out of the **m.**
8:33 demons came out of the **m** and entered the swine,
8:35 the **m** from whom the demons had gone sitting at
8:38 The **m** from whom the demons had gone begged
8:41 Just then there came a **m** named Jairus,
9:22 "The Son of **M** must undergo great suffering, A
9:26 the Son of **M** will be ashamed when he comes A
9:38 Just then a **m** from the crowd shouted, "Teacher,
9:44 Son of **M** is going to be betrayed into human A
9:58 but the Son of **M** has nowhere to lay his head." A
10:30 "A **m** was going down from Jerusalem to Jericho,
10:36 was a neighbor to the **m** who fell into the hands of
11:21 When a strong **m,** fully armed, guards his castle,
11:30 so the Son of **M** will be to this generation. A
12: 8 the Son of **M** also will acknowledge before the A
12:10 a word against the Son of **M** will be forgiven; A
12:16 "The land of a rich **m** produced abundantly.
12:40 the Son of **M** is coming at an unexpected hour." A
13: 6 "A **m** had a fig tree planted in his vineyard;
14: 2 in front of him, there was a **m** who had dropsy.
15:11 Jesus said, "There was a **m** who had two sons.
16: 1 "There was a rich **m** who had a manager,
16: 1 to him that this **m** was squandering his property.
16:19 a rich **m** who was dressed in purple and fine linen
16:20 And at his gate lay a poor **m** named Lazarus,
16:22 The poor **m** died and was carried away by
16:22 The rich **m** also died and was buried.

Lk 17:22 to see one of the days of the Son of **M**, A
17:24 so will the Son of **M** be in his day. A
17:26 so too it will be in the days of the Son of **M.** A
17:30 that on the day that the Son of **M** is revealed. A
18: 8 Son of **M** comes, will he find faith on earth?" A
18:14 this **m** went down to his home justified rather than
18:31 everything that is written about the Son of **M** A
18:35 a blind **m** was sitting by the roadside begging.
18:40 Jesus stood still and ordered the **m** to be brought
19: 2 A **m** was there named Zacchaeus;
19:10 Son of **M** came to seek out and to save the lost." A
19:14 saying, 'We do not want this **m** to rule over us.'
19:21 because you are a harsh **m;**
19:22 You knew, did you, that I was a harsh **m,**
20: 9 "A **m** planted a vineyard, and leased it to tenants,
20:28 the **m** shall marry the widow and raise up children
21:27 'the Son of **M** coming in a cloud' with power A
21:36 and to stand before the Son of **M."** A
22:10 a **m** carrying a jar of water will meet you;
22:22 the Son of **M** is going as it has been determined, A
22:48 with a kiss that you are betraying the Son of **M?** A
22:56 "This **m** also was with him."
22:58 But Peter said, **"M,** I am not!"
22:59 "Surely this **m** also was with him;
22:60 **"M,** I do not know what you are talking about!"
22:69 the Son of **M** will be seated at the right hand of A
23: 2 saying, "We found this **m** perverting our nation,
23: 4 "I find no basis for an accusation against this **m."**
23: 6 he asked whether the **m** was a Galilean.
23:14 and said to them, "You brought me this **m**
23:14 in your presence and have not found this **m** guilty
23:19 a **m** who had been put in prison for an insurrection
23:25 He released the **m** they asked for,
23:26 As they led him away, they seized a **m,**
23:41 but this **m** has done nothing wrong."
23:47 "Certainly this **m** was innocent."
23:50 there was a good and righteous **m** named Joseph, F
23:52 This **m** went to Pilate and asked for the body
24: 7 the Son of **M** must be handed over to sinners, A
Jn 1: 6 There was a **m** sent from God,
1:13 or of the will of the flesh or of the will of **m,**
1:30 'After me comes a **m** who ranks ahead of me
1:51 and descending upon the Son of **M."** A
3:13 from heaven, the Son of **M.** A
3:14 so must the Son of **M** be lifted up, A
4:29 a **m** who told me everything I have ever done!
4:50 The **m** believed the word that Jesus spoke to him
5: 5 One **m** was there who had been ill
5: 7 The sick **m** answered him, "Sir,
5: 9 At once the **m** was made well,
5:10 So the Jews said to the **m** who had been cured,
5:11 "The **m** who made me well said to me,
5:12 They asked him, "Who is the **m** who said to you,
5:13 **m** who had been healed did not know who it was,
5:15 The **m** went away and told the Jews
5:27 because he is the Son of **M.** A
6:27 which the Son of **M** will give you. A
6:52 saying, "How can this **m** give us his flesh to eat?"
6:53 the flesh of the Son of **M** and drink his blood, A
6:62 Son of **M** ascending to where he was before? A
7:12 While some were saying, "He is a good **m,"**
7:15 saying, "How does this **m** have such learning,
7:22 and you circumcise a **m** on the sabbath.
7:23 a **m** receives circumcision on the sabbath in order
7:25 "Is not this the **m** whom they are trying to kill?
7:27 Yet we know where this **m** is from;
7:31 will he do more signs than this **m** has done?"
7:35 does this **m** intend to go that we will not find him?
8:28 "When you have lifted up the Son of **M,** A
8:40 a **m** who has told you the truth that I heard
9: 1 As he walked along, he saw a **m** blind from birth.
9: 2 this **m** or his parents, that he was born blind?"
9: 3 "Neither this **m** nor his parents sinned;
9: 8 "Is this not the **m** who used to sit and beg?"
9: 9 He kept saying, "I am the **m."**
9:11 He answered, "The **m** called Jesus made mud,
9:13 the Pharisees the **m** who had formerly been blind.
9:16 "This **m** is not from God,
9:16 can a **m** who is a sinner perform such signs?"
9:17 So they said again to the blind **m,**
9:18 the parents of the **m** who had received his sight
9:24 second time they called the **m** who had been blind,
9:24 We know that this **m** is a sinner."
9:29 that God has spoken to Moses, but as for this **m,**
9:30 The **m** answered, "Here is an astonishing thing!
9:33 If this **m** were not from God, he could do nothing."
9:35 he said, "Do you believe in the Son of **M?"** A
10:41 everything that John said about this **m** was true."
11: 1 Now a certain **m** was ill, Lazarus of Bethany,
11:37 of the blind **m** have kept this **m** from dying?"
11:39 Martha, the sister of the dead **m,** said to him,
11:44 The dead **m** came out, his hands and feet bound
11:47 This **m** is performing many signs.
11:50 to have one **m** die for the people than to have
12:23 hour has come for the Son of **M** to be glorified. A
12:34 you say that the Son of **M** must be lifted up? A
12:34 Who is this Son of **M?"** A
13:31 "Now the Son of **M** has been glorified, A
18:26 a relative of the **m** whose ear Peter had cut off,
18:29 "What accusation do you bring against this **m?"**
18:30 They answered, "If this **m** were not a criminal,
18:40 They shouted in reply, "Not this **m,** but Barabbas!"
19: 5 Pilate said to them, "Here is the **m!"**
19:12 but the Jews cried out, "If you release this **m,**
19:21 but, 'This **m** said, I am King of the Jews.' "
Ac 1:18 (Now this **m** acquired a field with the reward
2:22 a **m** attested to you by God with deeds of power,
Ac 2:23 this **m,** handed over to you according to
3: 2 And a **m** lame from birth was being carried in.
3:16 his name itself has made this **m** strong,
4: 9 and are asked how this **m** has been healed,
4:10 that this **m** is standing before you in good health by
4:14 When they saw the **m** who had been cured standing
4:22 For the **m** on whom this sign
5: 1 But a **m** named Ananias, with the consent
6: 5 a **m** full of faith and the Holy Spirit,
6:13 "This **m** never stops saying things
7:24 he defended the oppressed **m** and avenged him
7:27 But the **m** who was wronging his neighbor
7:56 the heavens opened and the Son of **M** standing A
7:58 at the feet of a young **m** named Saul. C
8: 9 **m** named Simon had previously practiced magic
8:10 "This **m** is the power of God that is called Great."
9:11 of Judas look for a **m** of Tarsus named Saul.
9:12 a **m** named Ananias come in and lay his hands
9:13 "Lord, I have heard from many about this **m,**
9:21 "Is not this the **m** who made havoc in Jerusalem
9:33 There he found a **m** named Aeneas,
10: 1 In Caesarea there was a **m** named Cornelius,
10: 2 a devout **m** who feared God with all his household;
10:22 a centurion, an upright and God-fearing **m,**
10:30 I was praying in my house when suddenly a **m**
11:24 for he was a good **m,**
13: 7 Sergius Paulus, an intelligent **m,**
13:21 a **m** of the tribe of Benjamin,
13:22 son of Jesse, to be a **m** after my heart,
13:38 this **m** forgiveness of sins is proclaimed to you;
14: 8 In Lystra there was a **m** sitting who could
14:10 And the **m** sprang up and began to walk.
16: 9 a **m** of Macedonia pleading with him and saying,
17:31 in righteousness by a **m** whom he has appointed,
18: 7 the house of a **m** named Titius Justus, a worshiper
18:13 "This **m** is persuading people to worship God
18:24 He was an eloquent **m,** well-versed in
19:16 Then the **m** with the evil spirit leaped on them,
19:24 A **m** named Demetrius, a silversmith who made
20: 9 A young **m** named Eutychus, C
21:11 the **m** who owns this belt and will hand him over to
21:28 This is the **m** who is teaching everyone everywhere
22:12 a devout **m** according to the law and well spoken
22:26 This **m** is a Roman citizen."
23: 9 "We find nothing wrong with this **m.**
23:17 "Take this young **m** to the tribune, C
23:18 and asked me to bring this young **m** to you; C
23:22 So the tribune dismissed the young **m,** C
23:27 This **m** was seized by the Jews and was about to
23:30 that there would be a plot against the **m,**
24: 5 We have, in fact, found this **m** a pestilent fellow,
25: 5 and if there is anything wrong about the **m,**
25:14 "There is a **m** here who was left in prison by Felix.
25:17 on the tribunal and ordered the **m** to be brought.
25:22 "I would like to hear the **m** myself."
25:24 you see this **m** about whom
26:31 "This **m** is doing nothing to deserve death
26:32 "This **m** could have been set free if he had
28: 4 "This **m** must be a murderer;
28: 7 lands belonging to the leading **m** of that island,
Ro 5:12 just as sin came into the world through one **m,**
5:15 of God and the free gift in the grace of the one **m,**
5:17 in life through the one **m,**
7: 3 be called an adulteress if she lives with another **m**
7: 3 and if she marries another **m,**
7:24 Wretched **m** that I am!
1Co 5: 1 for a **m** is living with his father's wife.
5: 4 of the Lord Jesus on the **m** who has done such
5: 5 to hand this **m** over to Satan for the destruction of
7: 1 "It is well for a **m** not to touch a woman."
7: 2 each **m** should have his own wife
7:32 The unmarried **m** is anxious about the affairs of
7:33 married **m** is anxious about the affairs of the world,
11: 3 to understand that Christ is the head of every **m,** E
11: 4 Any **m** who prays or prophesies with something
11: 7 For a **m** ought not to have his head veiled,
11: 7 but woman is the reflection of **m.**
11: 8 **m** was not made from woman, but woman from **m.**
11: 9 Neither was **m** created for the sake of woman, but
woman for the sake of **m.**
11:11 in the Lord woman is not independent of **m** or **m**
independent of woman.
11:12 For just as woman came from **m,** so **m** comes
through woman;
11:14 that if a **m** wears long hair,
15:45 Thus it is written, "The first **m,** Adam,
15:47 The first **m** was from the earth, a **m** of dust; the
second **m** is from heaven.
15:48 was the **m** of dust, so are those who are of the dust;
15:48 is the **m** of heaven, so are those who are of heaven.
15:49 Just as we have borne the image of the **m** of dust,
we will also bear the image of the **m** of heaven.
Gal 5: 3 Once again I testify to every **m** who lets himself E
Eph 5:31 a **m** will leave his father and mother and be joined
1Ti 1:13 a persecutor, and a **m** of violence.
2:12 to teach or to have authority over a **m;**
5: 1 Do not speak harshly to an older **m,**
6:11 But as for you, **m** of God, shun all this; B
Phm 1: 9 and I, Paul, do this as an old **m,** D
Heb 7: 6 But this **m,** who does not belong to their ancestry,
2Pe 2: 7 a righteous **m** greatly distressed by F
2: 8 (for that righteous **m,** living among them day F
Rev 1:13 of the lampstands I saw one like the Son of **M,** A
14:14 seated on the cloud was one like the Son of **M,** A
Tob 1: 4 in the land of Israel, while I was still a young **m,** C
1: 9 When I became a **m** I married a woman,
3:14 that I am innocent of any defilement with a **m,**
Tob 5: 3 find yourself a trustworthy **m** to go with you,
5: 4 So Tobias went out to look for a **m** to go with him
5: 5 "Where do you come from, young **m?"** C
5: 7 Tobias said to him, "Wait for me, young **m,** C
5: 9 a **m** who is one of our own Israelite kindred!"
5: 9 He replied, "Call the **m** in, my son,
5:10 said, "Young **m,** my father is calling for you." C
5:10 I am a **m** without eyesight;
5:10 But the young **m** said, "Take courage; C
6: 1 young **m** went out and the angel went with him; C
6: 3 Then the young **m** went down to wash his feet C
6: 4 But the angel said to the young **m,** C
6: 4 So the young **m** grasped the fish and drew it up C
6: 6 the fish the young **m** gathered together the gall, C
6: 7 the young **m** questioned the angel and said C
6: 8 presence of a **m** or woman afflicted by a demon
6:11 Raphael said to the young **m,** C
6:12 and very beautiful, and her father is a good **m."**
6:13 to another **m** without incurring the penalty of death
6:13 Indeed he knows that you, rather than any other **m,**
7: 2 the young **m** resembles my kinsman Tobit!" C
7: 7 an upright and beneficent **m** has become blind!"
7:10 at liberty to give her to any other **m** than yourself,
8: 1 the young **m** and brought him into the bedroom. C
8: 6 'It is not good that the **m** should be alone;
10: 6 The **m** who went with him is trustworthy
11: 6 and the **m** who went with him!"
12: 1 to paying the wages of the **m** who went with you,
Jdt 1:11 but regarded him as only one **m.**
4: 9 And every **m** of Israel cried out to God E
6: 3 we the king's servants will destroy them as one **m.**
7:11 and not a **m** of your army will fall.
14: 2 and let every able-bodied **m** go out of the town;
14: 5 that he may see and recognize the **m** who despised
16:22 but she gave herself to no **m** all the days of her life
AdE 4:11 of the empire know that if any **m** or woman goes to
7: 6 Esther said, "Our enemy is this evil **m** Haman!"
11: 3 He was a Jew living in the city of Susa, a great **m,**
14:13 and turn his heart to hate the **m** who is fighting
16:15 to annihilation by this thrice-accursed **m,**
Wis 2:10 Let us oppress the righteous poor **m;**
2:12 "Let us lie in wait for the righteous **m,** F
2:18 for if the righteous **m** is God's child, F
7: 2 from the seed of a **m** and the pleasure of marriage.
9: 5 a **m** who is weak and short-lived,
10: 3 an unrighteous **m** departed from her in his anger,
10: 4 the righteous **m** by a paltry piece of wood. F
10: 5 the righteous **m** and preserved him blameless F
10: 6 a righteous **m** when the ungodly were perishing; F
10:10 a righteous **m** fled from his brother's wrath, F
10:13 When a righteous **m** was sold, F
18:21 a blameless **m** was quick to act as their champion;
19:17 just as were those at the door of the righteous **m** F
Sir 7:25 but give her to a sensible **m.**
19: 2 and the **m** who consorts with prostitutes is reckless.
22:10 a story to a fool tells it to a drowsy **m;**
23:21 This **m** will be punished in the streets of the city,
23:22 and presents him with an heir by another **m.**
23:23 and brought forth children by another **m.**
24:28 The first **m** did not know wisdom fully,
25: 7 a **m** who can rejoice in his children;
25: 7 a **m** who lives to see the downfall of his foes.
25: 8 Happy the **m** who lives with a sensible wife,
26: 3 be granted among the blessings of the **m** who fears
26:23 *godless wife is given as a portion to a lawless **m,***
26:23 *a pious wife is given to the **m** who fears the Lord.*
26:28 a **m** who turns back from righteousness to sin—
36:26 A woman will accept any **m** as a husband,
36:30 a **m** will become a fugitive and a wanderer.
36:31 So who will trust a **m** that has no nest,
42:12 Do not let her parade her beauty before any **m,**
42:14 of a **m** than a woman who does good;
43: 4 A **m** tending a furnace works in burning heat,
44:23 the Lord brought forth a godly **m,**
45: 6 a holy **m** like Moses who was his brother,
Sus 1: 1 a **m** living in Babylon whose name was Joakim.
1:21 we will testify against you that a young **m** was C
1:37 Then a young **m,** who was hiding there, C
1:39 we saw them embracing, we could not hold the **m,**
1:40 this woman and asked who the young **m** was, C
1Mc 3:32 He left Lysias, a distinguished **m** of royal lineage,
4:30 and of the **m** who carried his armor.
5:63 The **m** Judas and his brothers were greatly honored
7: 7 Now then send a **m** whom you trust;
7: 8 he was a great **m** in the kingdom and was faithful
7:38 Take vengeance on this **m** and on his army,
8:16 They trust one **m** each year to rule over them and
8:16 they all heed the one **m,**
10:16 So he said, "Shall we find another such **m?**
2Mc 3: 4 But a **m** named Simon, of the tribe of Benjamin,
3:11 a **m** of very prominent position,
3:17 terror and bodily trembling had come over the **m,**
3:28 this **m** who had just entered the aforesaid treasury
4: 2 as a plotter against the government the **m** who was
4:26 by another **m,** was driven as a fugitive into
4:31 leaving Andronicus, a **m** of high rank,
4:35 and displeased at the unjust murder of the **m.**
4:40 **m** advanced in years and no less advanced in folly.
5:18 this **m** would have been flogged and turned back
5:22 the **m** who appointed him;
5:25 When this **m** arrived in Jerusalem,
6:18 a **m** now advanced in age and of noble presence,
6:21 of that unlawful sacrifice took the **m** aside because
7:25 Since the young **m** would not listen to him at all, C
7:30 While she was still speaking, the young **m** said, C
8: 8 that the **m** was gaining ground little by little,
8: 9 a general and a **m** of experience in military service.

2Mc 8:32 of Timothy's forces, a most wicked **m,**
9:10 the **m** who a little while before had thought
10:10 who was the son of that ungodly **m,**
10:11 This **m,** when he succeeded to the kingdom,
12:35 who was on horseback and was a strong **m,**
12:35 wishing to take the accursed **m** alive,
12:43 He also took up a collection, **m** by **m,**
13:4 and when Lysias informed him that this **m** was
13:21 But Rhodocus, a **m** from the ranks of the Jews,
14:24 he was warmly attached to the **m.**
14:27 by the false accusations of that depraved **m,**
14:28 when the **m** had done no wrong.
14:31 that he had been cleverly outwitted by the **m,**
14:31 and commanded them to hand the **m** over.
14:32 not know where the **m** was whom he wanted,
14:37 to Nicanor as a **m** who loved his compatriots
15:12 who had been high priest, a noble and good **m,**
15:14 a **m** who loves the family of Israel and prays much
15:30 the **m** who was ever in body and soul the defender
15:30 the **m** who maintained his youthful goodwill
1Es 1:53 and did not spare young **m** or young woman, C
1:53 not spare young man or young woman, old **m** D
4:7 And yet he is only one **m!**
4:20 A **m** leaves his own father, who brought him up,
4:23 A **m** takes his sword, and goes out to travel and rob
4:25 A **m** loves his wife more than his father
4:58 When the young **m** went out, C
5:49 directions in the book of Moses the **m** of God. B
8:45 who was the leading **m** at the place of the treasury,
3Mc 1:3 a certain insignificant **m** should sleep in the tent;
1:3 that this **m** incurred the vengeance meant for
2:2 from an impious and profane **m,**
2:14 and profane **m** undertakes to violate the holy place
2Es 2:43 In their midst was a young **m** of great stature, C
2:46 "Who is that young **m** who is placing crowns C
10:33 He said to me, "Stand up like a **m,**
13:3 like the figure of a **m** come up out of the heart of
13:3 I saw that this **m** flew with the clouds of heaven;
13:5 of heaven to make war against the **m** who came
13:12 the same **m** come down from the mountain and call
13:25 your seeing a **m** come up from the heart of the sea,
13:32 whom you saw as a **m** coming up from the sea.
13:51 Why did I see the **m** coming up from the heart of
4Mc 4:1 a political opponent of the noble and good **m,**
4:15 an arrogant and terrible **m,**
5:4 When many persons had been rounded up, one **m,**
5:4 He was a **m** of priestly family, learned in the law,
5:6 old **m,** I would advise you to save yourself D
6:2 First they stripped the old **m,** D
6:5 But the courageous and noble **m,**
6:10 a noble athlete the old **m,** while being beaten, D
6:30 he said this, the holy **m** died nobly in his tortures;
7:4 as did that most holy **m.**
7:7 O **m** in harmony with the law and philosopher
7:10 O aged **m,** more powerful than tortures;
7:13 Most amazing, indeed, though he was an old **m,** D
7:15 O **m** of blessed age and of venerable gray hair and
7:16 of piety an aged **m** despised tortures even to death,
8:2 to compel an aged **m** to eat defiling foods,
8:5 as that of the old **m** who has just been tortured, D
12:13 As a **m,** were you not ashamed,
16:14 you have proved more powerful than a **m.**
16:17 while an aged **m** endures such agonies for the sake
18:9 A happy **m** was he, who lived out his life

MAN'S‡ (52) [MAN]

Ge 20:7 Now then, return the **m** wife;
42:25 to return every **m** money to his sack,
44:1 and put each **m** money in the top of his sack.
44:26 the **m** face unless our youngest brother is with us.'
Nu 5:12 If any **m** wife goes astray and is unfaithful to him,
17:2 Write each **m** name on his staff,
Dt 22:5 A woman shall not wear a **m** apparel,
24:2 and goes off to become another **m** wife,
Jdg 7:22 the LORD set every **m** sword against his fellow
19:26 at the door of the **m** house where her master was,
Ru 4:5 to maintain the dead **m** name on his inheritance."
4:10 to maintain the dead **m** name on his inheritance,
2Sa 12:4 but he took the poor **m** lamb,
17:19 The **m** wife took a covering,
Pr 6:26 But the wife of another stalks a **m** very life.
Ecc 9:16 yet the poor **m** wisdom is despised,
Isa 54:6 like the wife of a **m** youth when she is cast off,
Jer 3:1 from him and becomes another **m** wife,
Eze 40:5 the **m** hand was six long cubits, each being a cubit
Jnh 1:14 do not let us perish on account of this **m** life.
Mt 12:29 a strong **m** house and plunder his property,
27:24 saying, "I am innocent of this **m** blood;
Mk 3:27 a strong **m** house and plunder his property
12:19 Moses wrote for us that 'if a **m** brother dies,
Lk 16:21 with what fell from the rich **m** table;
20:28 Moses wrote for us that if a **m** brother dies,
Jn 7:23 because I healed a **m** whole body on the sabbath?
9:6 with the saliva and spread the mud on the **m** eyes,
18:17 "You are not also one of this **m** disciples,
Ac 5:28 and you are determined to bring this **m** blood
11:12 and we entered the **m** house.
13:23 Of this **m** posterity God has brought to Israel
Ro 5:15 For if the many died through the one **m** trespass,
5:16 the free gift is not like the effect of the one **m** sin.
5:17 If, because of the one **m** trespass,
5:18 just as one **m** trespass led to condemnation for all,
5:18 so one **m** act of righteousness leads to justification
5:19 For just as by the one **m** disobedience the many
5:19 so by the one **m** obedience the many will
Tob 6:3 the water and tried to swallow the young **m** foot,
Sir 9:9 Never dine with another **m** wife,
36:27 A woman's beauty lights up a **m** face,
41:21 and of gazing at another **m** wife;
2Mc 3:32 offered sacrifice for the **m** recovery.
7:12 with him were astonished at the young **m** spirit,
7:21 with a **m** courage, and said
9:9 And so the ungodly **m** body swarmed with worms,
15:32 the vile Nicanor's head and that profane **m** arm,
2Es 15:36 and a **m** thigh and a camel's hock.
4Mc 6:6 yet while the old **m** eyes were raised to heaven,
10:5 Enraged by the **m** boldness,
15:23 a **m** courage in the very midst of her emotions,

MAN-CHILD (1) [CHILD, MAN]

Job 3:3 and the night that said, 'A **m** is conceived.'

MANACLES (2)

2Ch 33:11 who took Manasseh captive in **m,**
Sir 21:19 and like **m** on his right hand.

MANAEN (1)

Ac 13:1 **M** a member of the court of Herod the ruler,

MANAGE (4) [MANAGEMENT, MANAGER, MANAGERS]

1Ti 3:4 He must **m** his own household well,
3:5 not know how to **m** his own household,
3:12 and let them **m** their children
5:14 bear children, and **m** their households,

MANAGEMENT (1) [MANAGE]

Lk 16:2 Give me an accounting of your **m,**

MANAGER (7) [MANAGE]

Mt 20:8 the owner of the vineyard said to his **m,**
Lk 12:42 and prudent **m** whom his master will put in charge
16:1 "There was a rich man who had a **m,**
16:2 because you cannot be my **m** any longer.'
16:3 Then the **m** said to himself, 'What will I do,
16:4 when I am dismissed as **m,**
16:8 the dishonest **m** because he had acted shrewdly;

MANAGERS (1) [MANAGE]

Tit 2:5 chaste, good **m** of the household, kind,

MANAHATH (3) [MANAHATHITES]

Ge 36:23 Alvan, **M,** Ebal, Shepho, and Onam.
1Ch 1:40 Alian, **M,** Ebal, Shephi, and Onam.
8:6 and they were carried into exile to **M):**

MANAHATHITES (1) [MANAHATH]

1Ch 2:54 Atroth-beth-joab, and half of the **M,** the Zorites.

MANAHETHITES (KJV) See MANAHATHITES, MENUHOTH

MANASSEAS (1)

1Es 9:31 and Sesthel, and Belnuus and **M.**

MANASSEH‡ (142) [MANASSEH'S, MANASSITE, MANASSITES]

Ge 41:51 Joseph named the firstborn **M,** "For," he said,
46:20 in the land of Egypt were born **M** and Ephraim,
48:1 So he took with him his two sons, **M** and Ephraim.
48:5 Ephraim and **M** shall be mine,
48:13 and **M** in his left hand toward Israel's right,
48:14 and his left hand on the head of **M,** crossing his hands, for **M** was the firstborn.
48:20 saying, 'God make you like Ephraim and like **M.'**
48:20 So he put Ephraim ahead of **M.**
50:23 the children of Machir son of **M** were also born
Nu 1:10 from **M,** Gamaliel son of Pedahzur.
1:34 The descendants of **M,** their lineage, in their clans,
1:35 of **M** were thirty-two thousand two hundred.
2:20 Next to him shall be the tribe of **M.**
2:20 of the people of **M** shall be Gamaliel son
10:23 the company of the tribe of **M** was Gamaliel son
13:11 from the tribe of **M),** Gaddi son of Susi;
26:28 The sons of Joseph by their clans: **M** and Ephraim.
26:29 The descendants of **M:** of Machir,
26:34 These are the clans of **M;**
27:1 of Gilead son of Machir son of **M** son of Joseph,
32:33 to the Reubenites and to the half-tribe of **M** son
32:39 descendants of Machir son of **M** went to Gilead,
32:40 so Moses gave Gilead to Machir son of **M,**
32:41 Jair son of **M** went and captured their villages,
34:14 and also the half-tribe of **M;**
36:1 the descendants of Gilead son of Machir son of **M,**
36:12 the clans of the descendants of **M** son of Joseph,
Dt 3:13 and I gave to the half-tribe of **M** the rest of Gilead
29:8 the Gadites, and the half-tribe of **M.**
33:17 the myriads of Ephraim, such the thousands of **M.**
34:2 the land of Ephraim and **M,**
Jos 1:12 the Gadites, and the half-tribe of **M** Joshua said,
4:12 and the half-tribe of **M** crossed over armed before
12:6 and the Gadites and the half-tribe of **M.**
13:7 to the nine tribes and the half-tribe of **M."**
13:8 With the other half-tribe of **M** the Reubenites and
13:29 Moses gave an inheritance to the half-tribe of **M;**
13:31 of Machir son of **M** according to their clans—
Jos 14:4 people of Joseph were two tribes, **M** and Ephraim;
16:4 **M** and Ephraim—received their inheritance.
17:1 Then allotment was made to the tribe of **M,**
17:1 To Machir the firstborn of **M,** the father of Gilead,
17:2 allotments were made to the rest of the tribe of **M,**
17:2 these were the male descendants of **M** son
17:3 of Gilead son of Machir son of **M** had no sons,
17:5 Thus there fell to **M** ten portions,
17:6 of **M** received an inheritance along with his sons.
17:7 of **M** reached from Asher to Michmethath,
17:8 The land of Tappuah belonged to **M,**
17:8 on the boundary of **M** belonged to the Ephraimites.
17:9 to the south of the wadi, among the towns of **M,**
17:9 Then the boundary of **M** goes along the north side
17:11 **M** had Beth-shean and its villages,
17:17 and **M,** "You are indeed a numerous people,
18:7 the half-tribe of **M** have received their inheritance
20:8 and Golan in Bashan, from the tribe of **M.**
21:5 from the tribe of Dan, and the half-tribe of **M.**
21:6 and from the half-tribe of **M** in Bashan.
21:25 Out of the half-tribe of **M:**
21:27 were given out of the half-tribe of **M,**
22:1 the Gadites, and the half-tribe of **M,**
22:7 to the one half of the tribe of **M** Moses had given
22:9 the Gadites and the half-tribe of **M** returned home,
22:10 and the Gadites and the half-tribe of **M** built there
22:11 the half-tribe of **M** had built an altar at the frontier
22:13 and the Gadites and the half-tribe of **M,**
22:15 and the half-tribe of **M,** in the land of Gilead,
22:21 and the half-tribe of **M** said in answer to the heads
Jdg 1:27 **M** did not drive out the inhabitants of Beth-shean
6:15 My clan is the weakest in **M,**
6:35 He sent messengers throughout all **M,**
7:23 from Naphtali and from Asher and from all **M,**
11:29 and he passed through Gilead and **M.**
12:4 in the heart of Ephraim and **M."**
1Ki 4:13 the villages of Jair son of **M,** which are in Gilead,
2Ki 20:21 and his son **M** succeeded him.
21:1 **M** was twelve years old when he began to reign;
21:9 **M** misled them to do more evil than
21:11 "Because King **M** of Judah has committed these
21:16 Moreover **M** shed very much innocent blood,
21:17 Now the rest of the acts of **M,** all that he did,
21:18 **M** slept with his ancestors,
21:20 as his father **M** had done.
23:12 and the altars that **M** had made in the two courts of
23:26 the provocations with which **M** had provoked him.
24:3 to remove them out of his sight, for the sins of **M,**
1Ch 3:13 Ahaz his son, Hezekiah his son, **M** his son,
5:18 and the half-tribe of **M** had valiant warriors,
5:23 members of the half-tribe of **M** lived in the land;
5:26 the Gadites, and the half-tribe of **M,**
6:61 out of the half-tribe, the half of **M,** ten towns.
6:62 Asher, Naphtali, and **M** in Bashan.
6:70 and out of the half-tribe of **M,**
6:71 To the Gershomites: out of the half-tribe of **M:**
7:14 The sons of **M:** Asriel, whom his Aramean
7:17 the sons of Gilead son of Machir, son of **M.**
9:3 Benjamin, Ephraim, and **M** lived in Jerusalem:
12:20 Elihu, and Zillethai, chiefs of the thousands in **M.**
12:31 Of the half-tribe of **M,** eighteen thousand,
12:37 the Reubenites and Gadites and the half-tribe of **M**
27:20 for the half-tribe of **M,** Joel son of Pedaiah;
27:21 half-tribe of **M** in Gilead, Iddo son of Zechariah;
2Ch 15:9 and those from Ephraim, **M,**
30:1 and wrote letters also to Ephraim and **M,**
30:10 to city through the country of Ephraim and **M,** and
30:11 Only a few from Asher, **M,**
30:18 many of them from Ephraim, **M,** Issachar,
31:1 and Benjamin, and in Ephraim and **M,**
32:33 His son **M** succeeded him.
33:1 **M** was twelve years old when he began to reign;
33:9 **M** misled Judah and the inhabitants of Jerusalem,
33:10 The LORD spoke to **M** and to his people,
33:11 who took **M** captive in manacles,
33:13 Then **M** knew that the LORD indeed was God.
33:18 Now the rest of the acts of **M,**
33:20 So **M** slept with his ancestors,
33:22 as his father **M** had done.
33:22 to all the images that his father **M** had made,
33:23 as his father **M** had humbled himself,
34:6 In the towns of **M,** Ephraim, and Simeon,
34:9 had collected from **M** and Ephraim and from all
Ezr 10:30 Maaseiah, Mattaniah, Bezalel, Binnui, and **M.**
10:33 Mattenai, Mattattah, Zabad, Eliphelet, Jeremai, **M,**
Ps 60:7 Gilead is mine, and **M** is mine;
80:2 before Ephraim and Benjamin and **M.**
108:8 Gilead is mine; **M** is mine;
Isa 9:21 **M** devoured Ephraim, and Ephraim Manasseh,
9:21 and Ephraim **M,** and together they were
Jer 15:4 the earth because of what King **M** son of Hezekiah
Eze 48:4 from the east side to the west, **M,** one portion.
48:5 Adjoining the territory of **M,**
Mt 1:10 the father of **M,** and **M** the father of Amos,
Rev 7:6 from the tribe of **M** twelve thousand,
Jdt 8:2 Her husband **M,** who belonged to her tribe
8:7 Her husband **M** had left her gold and silver,
10:3 to wear while her husband **M** was living.
16:22 the days of her life after her husband **M** died
16:23 and they buried her in the cave of her husband **M;**
16:24 of kin to her husband **M,**
1Es 9:33 and Mattattah and Zabad and Eliphelet and **M**

MANASSEH'S (2) [MANASSEH]

Ge 48:17 to remove it from Ephraim's head to **M** head.
Jos 17:10 the north is **M,** with the sea forming its boundary;

MANASSES (KJV) See MANASSEH; See also Index to Footnotes

MANASSITE (2) [MANASSEH]

Nu 27: 1 a member of the **M** clans.
Dt 3:14 the **M** acquired the whole region of Argob as far as

MANASSITES (14) [MANASSEH]

Nu 7:54 of Pedahzur, the leader of the **M**:
34:23 Of the Josephites: of the tribe of the **M** a leader,
Dt 4:43 and Golan in Bashan belonging to the **M**.
Jos 13:29 it was allotted to the half-tribe of the **M** according
16: 9 the Ephraimites within the inheritance of the **M**,
17: 6 land of Gilead was allotted to the rest of the **M**.
17:12 the **M** could not take possession of those towns;
22:30 the Reubenites and the Gadites and the **M** spoke,
22:31 and the Gadites and the **M**, "Today we know that
2Ki 10:33 the Gadites, the Reubenites, and the **M**,
1Ch 7:29 also along the borders of the **M**,
12:19 Some of the **M** deserted to David when he came
12:20 As he went to Ziklag these **M** deserted to him:
26:32 of the **M** for everything pertaining to God and for

MANDRAKES (6)

Ge 30:14 of wheat harvest Reuben went and found **m** in
30:14 "Please give me some of your son's **m**."
30:15 Would you take away my son's **m** also?"
30:15 he may lie with you tonight for your son's **m**."
30:16 for I have hired you with my son's **m**."
SS 7:13 The **m** give forth fragrance,

MANE (1)

Job 39:19 Do you clothe its neck with **m**?

MANEH (KJV) See MINA

MANGER (4)

Lk 2: 7 and laid him in a **m**,
2:12 a child wrapped in bands of cloth and lying in a **m**.
2:16 and the child lying in the **m**.
13:15 the sabbath untie his ox or his donkey from the **m**,

MANGLE (2) [MANGLED, MANGLING]

Hos 13: 8 as a wild animal would **m** them.
Sir 28:23 like a leopard it will **m** them.

MANGLED (4) [MANGLE]

Ex 22:13 If it was **m** by beasts, let it be brought as evidence;
22:13 restitution shall not be made for the **m** remains.
22:31 not eat any meat that is **m** by beasts in the field;
3Mc 5:42 **m** by the knees and feet of the animals,

MANGLING (1) [MANGLE]

4Mc 9:15 savage of mind, you are **m** me in this manner,

MANHOOD (2) [MAN]

Hos 12: 3 and in his **m** he strove with God.
1Mc 13:53 Simon saw that his son John had reached **m**,

MANI (1)

1Es 9:30 Of the descendants of **M**: Olamus,

MANIAC (2) [MANIACS]

2Ki 9:20 for he drives like a **m**."
Pr 26:18 Like a **m** who shoots deadly firebrands and arrows,

MANIACS (1) [MANIAC]

2Es 16:71 They shall be like **m**, sparing no one,

MANIFEST‡ (20) [MANIFESTATION, MANIFESTED, MANIFESTING, MANIFESTS]

Ps 90:16 Let your work be **m** to your servants,
Isa 24:23 and before his elders he will **m** his glory.
Eze 20:41 and I will **m** my holiness among you in the sight of
28:22 and **m** my holiness in it;
28:25 **m** my holiness in them in the sight of the nations,
Wis 7:21 I learned both what is secret and what is **m**,
LtJ 6:51 be **m** to all the nations and kings that they are
1Mc 11:12 and their enmity became **m**.
15: 9 so that your glory will become **m** in all the earth."
2Mc 9: 8 making the power of God **m** to all.
Man 1:14 and in me you will **m** your goodness;
3Mc 3:19 By maintaining their **m** ill-will toward us,
5:35 praised the **m** Lord God, King of kings,
5:51 imploring the Ruler over every power to **m** himself
2Es 8:54 in the end the treasure of immortality is made **m**.
9: 5 the beginning is evident, and the end **m**;
9: 6 beginnings are **m** in wonders and mighty works,
13:36 And Zion shall come and be made **m** to all people,
14:35 then the names of the righteous shall become **m**,
16:73 Then the tested quality of my elect shall be **m**,

MANIFESTATION‡ (9) [MANIFEST]

1Co 12: 7 the **m** of the Spirit for the common good.
2Th 2: 8 annihilating him by the **m** of his coming.
1Ti 6:14 or blame until the **m** of our Lord Jesus Christ,
Tit 2:13 and the **m** of the glory of our great God and Savior,
2Mc 3:24 of spirits and of all authority caused so great a **m**
12:22 and fear came over the enemy at the **m** to them
15:27 and were greatly gladdened by God's **m**.
3Mc 2: 9 when you had glorified it by your magnificent **m**,
5: 8 against them and in a glorious **m** rescue them from

MANIFESTED‡ (3) [MANIFEST]

Wis 16:21 For your sustenance **m** your sweetness
2Mc 15:34 blessed the Lord who had **m** himself, saying,
2Es 7:*35* and the reward shall be **m**;

MANIFESTING (3) [MANIFEST]

Nu 25:11 from the Israelites by **m** such zeal among them
2Mc 14:15 and always upholds his own heritage by **m** himself.
3Mc 6: 4 **m** the light of your mercy on the nation of Israel.

MANIFESTS (1) [MANIFEST]

Wis 1: 2 and **m** himself to those who do not distrust him.

MANIFOLD‡ (3)

Ps 104:24 O LORD, how **m** are your works!
1Pe 4:10 Like good stewards of the **m** grace of God,
Wis 7:22 holy, unique, **m**, subtle, mobile, clear, unpolluted,

MANIUS (1)

2Mc 11:34 "Quintus Memmius and Titus **M**,

MANNA‡ (18)

Ex 16:31 The house of Israel called it **m**;
16:33 "Take a jar, and put an omer of **m** in it,
16:35 The Israelites ate **m** forty years,
16:35 they ate **m**, until they came to the border of
Nu 11: 6 and there is nothing at all but this **m** to look at."
11: 7 Now the **m** was like coriander seed,
11: 9 the **m** would fall with it.
Dt 8: 3 then by feeding you with **m**,
8:16 in the wilderness with **m** that your ancestors did
Jos 5:12 The **m** ceased on the day they ate the produce of
5:12 and the Israelites no longer had **m**;
Ne 9:20 and did not withhold your **m** from their mouths,
Ps 78:24 he rained down on them **m** to eat,
Jn 6:31 Our ancestors ate the **m** in the wilderness;
6:49 Your ancestors ate the **m** in the wilderness,
Heb 9: 4 in which there were a golden urn holding the **m**,
Rev 2:17 the hidden **m**, and I will give a white stone,
2Es 1:19 I pitied your groanings and gave you **m** for food;

MANNER‡ (36) [ILL-MANNERED, MANNERS]

Ge 18:11 had ceased to be with Sarah after the **m** of women.
19:31 a man on earth to come in to us after the **m** of all
Dt 15: 2 And this is the **m** of the remission:
Jos 6:15 around the city in the same **m** seven times.
Jdg 18: 7 after the **m** of the Sidonians,
Ru 4: 7 this was the **m** of attesting in Israel.
2Ki 17:33 after the **m** of the nations from
Ne 6: 4 and I answered them in the same **m**.
Eze 20:30 after the **m** of your ancestors and go astray
Am 4:10 I sent among you a pestilence after the **m** of Egypt;
Lk 16:25 and Lazarus in like **m** evil things;
1Co 11:27 in an unworthy **m** will be answerable for the body
Php 1:27 live your life in a **m** worthy of the gospel of Christ,
3Jn 1: 6 You will do well to send them on in a **m** worthy
Jude 1: 7 which, in the same **m** as they,
Rev 1: 5 to harm them must be killed in this **m**.
AdE 13: 5 perversely following a strange **m** of life and laws,
Wis 2:15 because his **m** of life is unlike that of others,
Sir 23:12 There is a **m** of speaking comparable to death;
25: 2 and I loathe their **m** of life:
2Mc 10: 6 in the **m** of the festival of booths,
14:46 This was the **m** of his death.
15:12 of modest bearing and gentle **m**,
3Mc 4: 5 with which they were driven in such a shameful **m**.
5:36 reconvened the party in the same **m** and urged
6:12 of the lawless are being deprived of life in the **m**
7:13 When they had applauded him in fitting **m**,
7:19 in like **m** they decided to observe these days as
2Es 4:15 In like **m** the waves of the sea also made a plan
11:34 in like **m** ruled over the earth and its inhabitants.
4Mc 4: 1 When despite all **m** of slander he was unable
6: 1 in this **m** had made eloquent response to
8: 8 the Greek way of life and by changing your **m**
9:15 savage of mind, you are mangling me in this **m**,
10:12 he too had died in a **m** worthy of his brothers,
15: 4 In what **m** might I express the emotions

MANNERS (1) [MANNER]

Sir 31:17 Be the first to stop, as befits good **m**,

MANOAH‡ (17)

Jdg 13: 2 of the tribe of the Danites, whose name was **M**.
13: 8 Then **M** entreated the LORD, and said, "O,
13: 9 to **M**, and the angel of God came again to
13: 9 but her husband **M** was not with her.
13:11 **M** got up and followed his wife,
13:12 Then **M** said, "Now when your words come true,
13:13 The angel of the LORD said to **M**,
13:15 **M** said to the angel of the LORD,
13:16 The angel of the LORD said to **M**,
13:16 (For **M** did not know that he was the angel of
13:17 Then **M** said to the angel of the LORD,
13:19 So **M** took the kid with the grain offering,
Jdg 13:20 of the altar while **M** and his wife looked on;
13:21 The angel of the LORD did not appear again to **M**
13:21 **M** realized that it was the angel of the LORD.
13:22 And **M** said to his wife, "We shall surely die,
16:31 and Eshtaol in the tomb of his father **M**.

MANSLAYER, MANSLAYERS (KJV) See MURDERERS, SLAYER

MANTELET (1)

Na 2: 5 they hasten to the wall, and the **m** is set up.

MANTLE (18) [MANTLES]

Ge 25:25 The first came out red, all his body like a hairy **m**;
Jos 7:21 I saw among the spoil a beautiful **m** from Shinar,
7:24 with the silver, the **m**, and the bar of gold,
1Ki 19:13 in his **m** and went out and stood at the entrance of
19:19 Elijah passed by him and threw his **m** over him.
2Ki 2: 8 Then Elijah took his **m** and rolled it up,
2:13 He picked up the **m** of Elijah that had fallen
2:14 He took the **m** of Elijah that had fallen from him,
Ezr 9: 3 When I heard this, I tore my garment and my **m**,
9: 5 with my garments and my **m** torn,
Est 8:15 with a great golden crown and a **m** of fine linen
Ps 109:29 may they be wrapped in their own shame as in a **m**.
SS 5: 7 they took away my **m**, those sentinels of the walls.
Isa 59:17 and wrapped himself in fury as in a **m**.
61: 3 the **m** of praise instead of a faint spirit.
Zec 13: 4 they will not put on a hairy **m** in order to deceive,
1Es 8:71 and my holy **m**, and pulled out hair from my head
8:73 with my garments and my holy **m** torn,

MANTLES (1) [MANTLE]

Isa 3:22 the **m**, the cloaks, and the handbags;

MANUAL (1)

Pr 12:14 and **m** labor has its reward.

MANURE (2)

Lk 13: 8 until I dig around it and put **m** on it.
14:35 It is fit neither for the soil nor for the **m** pile;

MANY‡ (737) [MANY-COLORED, MANY-HEADED, MANY-PEAKED, MANY-SIDED]

Ge 9:10 as **m** as came out of the ark.
21:34 as an alien **m** days in the land of the Philistines.
37:34 and mourned for his son **m** days.
45: 7 and to keep alive for you **m** survivors.
47: 8 "How **m** are the years of your life?"
Ex 19:21 otherwise **m** of them will perish.
Lev 11:42 or whatever has **m** feet, all the creatures
15:25 If a woman has a discharge of blood for **m** days,
25:51 If **m** years remain, they shall pay
Nu 9:19 the cloud continued over the tabernacle **m** days,
13:18 whether they are few or **m**,
21: 6 and they bit the people, so that **m** Israelites died.
35: 8 from the larger tribes you shall take **m**,
Dt 1:46 you had stayed at Kadesh as **m** days as you did,
2: 1 and skirted Mount Seir for **m** days.
3: 5 double gates, and bars, besides a great **m** villages.
7: 1 and he clears away **m** nations before you—
15: 6 as he promised you, you will lend to **m** nations,
15: 6 you will rule over **m** nations,
17:16 Even so, he must not acquire **m** horses for himself,
17:17 And he must not acquire **m** wives for himself,
23:24 you may eat your fill of grapes, as **m** as you wish,
28:12 You will lend to **m** nations,
31:17 and **m** terrible troubles will come upon them.
31:21 And when **m** terrible troubles come upon them,
Jos 11: 4 with very **m** horses and chariots.
22: 3 you have not forsaken your kindred these **m** days,
24: 3 the land of Canaan and made his offspring **m**.
Jdg 7: 2 with you are too **m** for me to give the Midianites
7: 4 "The troops are still too **m**;
8:30 his own offspring, for he had **m** wives.
9:40 **M** fell wounded, up to the entrance of the gate.
16:24 the ravager of our country, who has killed **m**
1Sa 2: 5 but she who has **m** children is forlorn.
14: 6 the LORD from saving by **m** or by few."
25:10 There are **m** servants today who are breaking away
26:25 You will do **m** things and will succeed in them."
31: 1 and **m** fell on Mount Gilboa.
2Sa 1: 4 but also **m** of the army fell and died;
12: 2 The rich man had very **m** flocks and herds;
13:34 he saw **m** people coming from the Horonaim road
14: 2 like a woman who has been mourning **m** days for
19:34 "How **m** years have I still to live,
24: 2 so that I may know how **m** there are."
1Ki 2:38 So Shimei lived in Jerusalem **m** days.
7:47 because there were so **m** of them;
8: 5 sacrificing so **m** sheep and oxen that they could not
11: 1 King Solomon loved **m** foreign women along with
17:15 she as well as he and her household ate for **m** days.
18: 1 **m** days the word of the LORD came to Elijah,
18:25 and prepare it first, for you are **m**;
22:16 "How **m** times must I make you swear
2Ki 9:22 so long as the **m** whoredoms and sorceries
19:23 'With my **m** chariots I have gone up the heights of
1Ch 4:27 but his brothers did not have **m** children,
5:22 **M** fell slain, because the war was of God.
7: 4 thirty-six thousand, for they had **m** wives and sons.

1Ch 7:22 And their father Ephraim mourned **m** days,
8:40 archers, having **m** children and grandchildren,
23:11 but Jeush and Beriah did not have **m** sons,
28: 5 of all my sons, for the LORD has given me **m,**
2Ch 5: 6 sacrificing so **m** sheep and oxen that they could not
11:23 and found **m** wives for them.
16: 8 with exceedingly **m** chariots and cavalry?
18:15 "How **m** times must I make you swear
21: 3 Their father gave them **m** gifts, of silver, gold,
24:27 and of the **m** oracles against him,
26:10 in the wilderness and hewed out **m** cisterns,
30:13 **M** people came together in Jerusalem to keep
30:17 For there were **m** in the assembly who had
30:18 multitude of the people, **m** of them from Ephraim,
32: 4 A great **m** people were gathered,
32:23 **M** brought gifts to the LORD in Jerusalem
Ezr 3:12 **m** of the priests and Levites and heads of families,
3:12 though **m** shouted aloud for joy,
5:11 the house that was built **m** years ago,
10:13 the people are **m,** and it is a time of heavy rain;
10:13 for **m** of us have transgressed in this matter.
Ne 5: 2 "With our sons and our daughters, we are **m;**
6:17 in those days the nobles of Judah sent **m** letters
6:18 For **m** in Judah were bound by oath to him,
7: 2 a faithful man and feared God more than **m.**
9:28 from heaven, and **m** times you rescued them
9:30 **M** years you were patient with them,
13:26 Among the **m** nations there was no king like him,
Est 1: 4 the splendor and pomp of his majesty for **m** days,
2: 8 when **m** young women were gathered in the citadel
8:17 **m** of the peoples of the country professed to
10: 3 among the Jews and popular with his **m** kindred,
Job 1: 3 five hundred donkeys, and very **m** servants;
4: 3 See, you have instructed **m;**
5:25 You shall know that your descendants will be **m,**
11:19 will make you afraid; **m** will entreat your favor.
13:23 How **m** are my iniquities and my sins?
16: 2 "I have heard **m** such things;
23:14 and **m** such things are in his mind.
32: 7 'Let days speak, and **m** years teach wisdom.'
41: 3 Will it make **m** supplications to you?
Ps 3: 1 O LORD, how **m** are my foes!
3: 1 **M** are rising against me;
3: 2 **m** are saying to me, "There is no help for you
4: 6 are **m** who say, "O that we might see some good!
5:10 because of their **m** transgressions cast them out,
22:12 **M** bulls encircle me, strong bulls of Bashan
25:19 Consider how **m** are my foes,
31:13 For I hear the whispering of **m—**
32:10 **M** are the torments of the wicked,
34:12 and covets **m** days to enjoy good?
34:19 **M** are the afflictions of the righteous,
37:16 the abundance of **m** wicked.
38:19 and **m** are those who hate me wrongfully.
40: 3 **M** will see and fear, and put their trust in the LORD.
55:18 for **m** are arrayed against me.
56: 2 on me all day long, for **m** fight against me.
69: 4 **m** are those who would destroy me,
71: 7 I have been like a portent to **m,**
71:20 You who have made me see **m** troubles
90:15 Make us glad as **m** days as you have afflicted us,
90:15 and as **m** years as we have seen evil.
94:19 When the cares of my heart are **m,**
97: 1 Let the earth rejoice; let the **m** coastlands be glad!
106:43 **M** times he delivered them,
119:157 **M** are my persecutors and my adversaries,
135:10 down **m** nations and killed mighty kings—
Pr 4:10 that the years of your life may be **m.**
7:26 for **m** are those she has laid low,
10:19 When words are **m,** transgression is not lacking,
10:21 The lips of the righteous feed **m,**
14:20 but the rich have **m** friends.
15:22 plans go wrong, but with **m** advisers they succeed.
19: 4 Wealth brings **m** friends,
19: 6 **M** seek the favor of the generous,
19:21 The human mind may devise **m** plans,
20: 6 **M** proclaim themselves loyal,
28: 2 When a land rebels it has **m** rulers;
28:27 but one who turns a blind eye will get **m** a curse.
29:26 **M** seek the favor of a ruler,
31:29 "**M** women have done excellently,
Ecc 2: 8 and delights of the flesh, and **m** concubines.
5: 3 For dreams come with **m** cares,
5: 3 and a fool's voice with **m** words.
5: 7 With **m** dreams come vanities and a multitude
6: 3 a hundred children, and live **m** years;
6: 3 but however **m** are the days of his years,
7:22 that **m** times you have yourself cursed others.
7:29 but they have devised **m** schemes.
10: 6 folly is set in **m** high places,
11: 1 for after **m** days you will get it back.
11: 8 those who live **m** years should rejoice in them all;
11: 8 that the days of darkness will be **m.**
12: 9 weighing and studying and arranging **m** proverbs.
12:12 Of making **m** books there is no end,
SS 8: 7 **M** waters cannot quench love,
Isa 1:15 even though you make **m** prayers, I will not listen;
2: 3 **M** peoples shall come and say, "Come,
2: 4 and shall arbitrate for **m** peoples;
5: 9 Surely **m** houses shall be desolate,
8:15 And **m** among them shall stumble;
17:12 Ah, the thunder of **m** peoples,
17:13 The nations roar like the roaring of **m** waters,
22: 9 and you saw that there were **m** breaches in the city
23:16 Make sweet melody, sing **m** songs,
24:22 and after **m** days they will be punished.
31: 1 in chariots because they are **m** and in horsemen
Isa 37:24 'With my **m** chariots I have gone up the heights of
42:20 He sees **m** things, but does not observe them;
47: 9 in full measure, in spite of your **m** sorceries and
47:12 and your **m** sorceries, with which you have labored
47:13 You are wearied with your **m** consultations;
51: 2 but I blessed him and made him **m.**
52:14 Just as there were **m** who were astonished at him
52:15 so he shall startle **m** nations;
53:11 righteous one, my servant, shall make **m** righteous,
53:12 yet he bore the sin of **m,** and made intercession for
57:10 You grew weary from your **m** wanderings,
58:12 up the foundations of **m** generations;
59:12 For our transgressions before you are **m,**
61: 4 the devastations of **m** generations.
66:16 and those slain by the LORD shall be **m.**
Jer 2:28 you have as **m** gods as you have towns, O Judah.
3: 1 You have played the whore with **m** lovers;
5: 6 because their transgressions are **m,**
11:13 For your gods have become as **m** as your towns,
11:13 and as **m** as the streets of Jerusalem are
12:10 **M** shepherds have destroyed my vineyard,
13: 6 And after **m** days the LORD said to me,
14: 7 our apostasies indeed are **m,**
16:16 I am now sending for **m** fishermen,
16:16 and afterward I will send for **m** hunters,
20:10 For I hear **m** whispering: "Terror is all around!
22: 8 And **m** nations will pass by this city,
25:14 For **m** nations and great kings shall make slaves
27: 7 of his own land comes; then **m** nations
28: 8 pestilence against **m** countries and great kingdoms.
30:19 I will make them **m,** and they shall not be few;
35: 7 you may live **m** days in the land where you reside.'
36:32 and **m** similar words were added to them.
37:16 in the cells, and remained there **m** days.
42: 2 For there are only a few of us left out of **m,**
46:11 In vain you have used **m** medicines;
50:41 and **m** kings are stirring from the farthest parts of
La 1:22 for my groans are **m** and my heart is faint.
5:20 Why have you forsaken us these **m** days?
Eze 3: 6 not to **m** peoples of obscure speech
11: 6 You have killed **m** in this city,
12:27 "The vision that he sees is for **m** years ahead;
16:41 on you in the sight of **m** women;
17: 3 rich in plumage of **m** colors, came to the Lebanon.
17:17 up and siege walls built to cut off **m** lives.
21:15 therefore hearts melt and **m** stumble.
22:25 they have made **m** widows within it.
23:42 with **m** of the rabble brought in drunken from
26: 3 I will hurl **m** nations against you,
26:10 be so **m** that their dust shall cover you.
27: 3 merchant of the peoples on **m** coastlands,
27:15 **m** coastlands were your own special markets;
27:33 from the seas, you satisfied **m** peoples;
32: 3 In an assembly of **m** peoples I will throw my net
32: 9 I will trouble the hearts of **m** peoples,
32:10 I will make **m** peoples appalled at you;
33:24 of the land; but we are **m;**
37: 2 there were very **m** lying in the valley,
38: 6 with all its troops—**m** peoples are with you.
38: 8 After **m** days you shall be mustered;
38: 8 a land where people were gathered from **m** nations
38: 9 you and all your troops, and **m** peoples with you.
38:15 you and **m** peoples with you,
38:22 and his troops and the **m** peoples that are with him.
38:23 and make myself known in the eyes of **m** nations.
39:27 in the sight of **m** nations.
47: 7 the bank of the river a great **m** trees on the one side
47: 9 and there will be very **m** fish,
47:10 its fish will be of a great **m** kinds,
Da 2:48 the king promoted Daniel, gave him **m** great gifts,
7: 5 "Arise, devour **m** bodies!"
8:25 Without warning he shall destroy **m** and shall
8:26 for it refers to **m** days from now."
9:27 a strong covenant with **m** for one week,
11:14 "In those times **m** shall rise against the king of
11:18 to the coastlands, and shall capture **m.**
11:26 be swept away, and **m** shall fall slain.
11:33 among the people shall give understanding to **m;**
11:34 and **m** shall join them insincerely.
11:39 and shall appoint them as rulers over **m,**
11:40 with chariots and horsemen, and with **m** ships.
11:44 to bring ruin and complete destruction to **m.**
12: 2 **M** of those who sleep in the dust of
12: 3 and those who lead **m** to righteousness,
12: 4 **M** shall be running back and forth,
12:10 **M** shall be purified, cleansed, and refined,
Hos 3: 3 "You must remain as mine for **m** days;
3: 4 For the Israelites shall remain **m** days without king
Am 5:12 For I know how **m** are your transgressions,
8: 3 dead bodies shall be **m,** cast out in every place.
Jnh 4:11 from their left, and also **m** animals?"
Mic 4: 2 and **m** nations shall come and say:
4: 3 He shall judge between **m** peoples,
4:11 Now **m** nations are assembled against you, saying,
4:13 you shall beat in pieces **m** peoples,
5: 7 the remnant of Jacob, surrounded by **m** peoples,
5: 8 of Jacob, surrounded by **m** peoples, shall be like
Na 1:12 "Though they are at full strength and **m,**
Hab 2: 8 Because you have plundered **m** nations,
2:10 for your house by cutting off **m** peoples;
Zec 2:11 **M** nations shall join themselves to the LORD on
7: 3 as I have done for so **m** years?"
8:20 Peoples shall yet come, the inhabitants of **m** cities;
8:22 **M** peoples and strong nations shall come to seek
Mal 2: 6 and he turned **m** from iniquity.
2: 8 you have caused **m** to stumble by your instruction;
Mt 3: 7 when he saw **m** Pharisees and Sadducees coming
Mt 6: 7 that they will be heard because of their **m** words.
7:13 and there are **m** who take it.
7:22 On that day **m** will say to me, 'Lord, Lord,
7:22 and do **m** deeds of power in your name?'
8:11 **m** will come from east and west and will eat
8:16 to him **m** who were possessed with demons;
9:10 **m** tax collectors and sinners came and were sitting
10:31 you are of more value than **m** sparrows.
12:15 **M** crowds followed him, and he cured all of them,
13: 3 he told them **m** things in parables, saying: "Listen!
13:17 **m** prophets and righteous people longed
13:58 And he did not do **m** deeds of power there,
15:30 the maimed, the blind, the mute, and **m** others.
15:34 Jesus asked them, "How **m** loaves have you?"
16: 9 and how **m** baskets you gathered?
16:10 and how **m** baskets you gathered?
18:21 As **m** as seven times?"
19:22 he went away grieving, for he had **m** possessions.
19:30 But **m** who are first will be last,
20:28 and to give his life a ransom for **m."**
22:14 For **m** are called, but few are chosen."
24: 5 For **m** will come in my name, saying,
24: 5 and they will lead **m** astray.
24:10 Then **m** will fall away,
24:11 **m** false prophets will arise and lead **m** astray.
24:12 the love of **m** will grow cold.
25:21 I will put you in charge of **m** things;
25:23 I will put you in charge of **m** things;
26:28 which is poured out for **m** for the forgiveness
26:60 though **m** false witnesses came forward.
27:13 "Do you not hear how **m** accusations they make
27:52 The tombs also were opened, and **m** bodies of
27:53 and entered the holy city and appeared to **m.**
27:55 **M** women were also there,
Mk 1:34 he cured **m** who were sick with various diseases,
and cast out **m** demons;
2: 2 So **m** gathered around
2:15 **m** tax collectors and sinners were also sitting
2:15 for there were **m** who followed him.
3:10 for he had cured **m,** so
4: 2 He began to teach them **m** things in parables,
4:33 With **m** such parables he spoke the word to them,
5: 9 He replied, "My name is Legion; for we are **m."**
5:26 She had endured much under **m** physicians,
6: 2 and **m** who heard him were astounded.
6:13 They cast out **m** demons, and with oil **m** who
6:31 For **m** were coming and going,
6:33 Now **m** saw them going and recognized them,
6:34 and he began to teach them **m** things.
6:38 And he said to them, "How **m** loaves have you?
7: 4 there are also **m** other traditions that they observe,
7:13 And you do **m** things like this."
8: 5 He asked them, "How **m** loaves do you have?"
8:19 **m** baskets full of broken pieces did you collect?"
8:20 **m** baskets full of broken pieces did you collect?"
9:12 that he is to go through **m** sufferings and be treated
10:22 and went away grieving, for he had **m** possessions.
10:31 But **m** who are first will be last,
10:45 and to give his life a ransom for **m."**
10:48 **M** sternly ordered him to be quiet,
11: 8 **M** people spread their cloaks on the road,
12: 5 And so it was with **m** others;
12:41 **M** rich people put in large sums.
13: 6 **M** will come in my name and say, 'I am he!'
13: 6 and they will lead **m** astray.
14:24 which is poured out for **m.**
14:56 For **m** gave false testimony against him,
15: 3 Then the chief priests accused him of **m** things.
15: 4 See how **m** charges they bring against you."
15:41 and there were **m** other women who had come up
Lk 1: 1 Since **m** have undertaken to set down
1:14 and **m** will rejoice at his birth,
1:16 He will turn **m** of the people of Israel to
2:34 for the falling and the rising of **m** in Israel,
2:35 so that the inner thoughts of **m** will be revealed—
3:18 So, with **m** other exhortations,
4:25 there were **m** widows in Israel in the time of Elijah,
4:27 There were also **m** lepers in Israel in the time of
4:41 Demons also came out of **m,** shouting,
5: 6 so **m** fish that their nets were beginning to break
5:15 **m** crowds would gather to hear him and to
7:21 Jesus had just then cured **m** people of diseases,
7:21 and had given sight to **m** who were blind.
7:47 Therefore, I tell you, her sins, which were **m,**
8: 3 and Susanna, and **m** others,
8:29 (For **m** times it had seized him;
8:30 He said, "Legion"; for **m** demons had entered him.
10:24 For I tell you that **m** prophets and kings desired
10:40 But Martha was distracted by her **m** tasks;
10:41 you are worried and distracted by **m** things;
11:53 and to cross-examine him about **m** things,
12: 7 you are of more value than **m** sparrows.
12:19 'Soul, you have ample goods laid up for **m** years;
13:24 **m,** I tell you, will try to enter and will not be able.
14:16 "Someone gave a great dinner and invited **m.**
15:17 But when he came to himself he said, 'How **m**
21: 8 for **m** will come in my name and say, 'I am he!'
22:65 They kept heaping **m** other insults on him.
Jn 2:23 **m** believed in his name because they saw the signs
4:39 **M** Samaritans from that city believed in him
4:41 And **m** more believed because of his word.
5: 3 In these lay **m** invalids—blind,
6: 9 But what are they among so **m** people?"
6:60 When **m** of his disciples heard it, they said,
6:66 Because of this **m** of his disciples turned back
7:31 **m** in the crowd believed in him and were saying,
8:30 As he was saying these things, **m** believed in him.

Jn 10:20 **M** of them were saying, "He has a demon
10:32 "I have shown you **m** good works from the Father.
10:41 **M** came to him, and they were saying,
10:42 And **m** believed in him there.
11:19 and **m** of the Jews had come to Martha and Mary
11:45 **M** of the Jews therefore, who had come with Mary
11:47 This man is performing **m** signs.
11:55 and **m** went up from the country to Jerusalem
12:11 of him that **m** of the Jews were deserting
12:37 he had performed so **m** signs in their presence,
12:42 **m**, even of the authorities, believed in him.
14: 2 In my Father's house there are **m** dwelling places.
16:12 "I still have **m** things to say to you,
19:20 **M** of the Jews read this inscription,
20:30 Now Jesus did **m** other signs in the presence
21: 6 not able to haul it in because there were so **m** fish.
21:11 and though there were so **m**, the net was not torn.
21:25 But there are also **m** other things that Jesus did;
Ac 1: 3 to them by **m** convincing proofs,
1: 5 with the Holy Spirit not **m** days from now."
2:40 with **m** other arguments and exhorted them,
2:43 because **m** wonders and signs were being done by
3:24 And all the prophets, as **m** as have spoken,
4: 4 But **m** of those who heard the word believed;
4:34 for as **m** as owned lands or houses sold them
5:12 Now **m** signs and wonders were done among
6: 7 great **m** of the priests became obedient to the faith.
8: 7 came out of **m** who were possessed;
8: 7 **m** others who were paralyzed or lame were cured.
8:25 the good news to **m** villages of the Samaritans.
9:13 "Lord, I have heard from **m** about this man,
9:42 and **m** believed in the Lord.
10:27 he went in and found that **m** had assembled;
11:24 And a great **m** people were brought to the Lord.
11:26 with the church and taught a great **m** people,
12:12 where **m** had gathered and were praying.
13:31 and for **m** days he appeared to those who came up
13:43 **m** Jews and devout converts
13:48 and as **m** as had been destined
14:21 to that city and had made **m** disciples,
14:22 "It is through **m** persecutions that we must enter
15:35 in Antioch, and there, with **m** others, they taught
16:18 She kept doing this for **m** days.
17: 4 a great **m** of the devout Greeks and not a few of
17:12 **M** of them therefore believed,
18: 8 with all his household; and **m** of
18:10 for there are **m** in this city who are my people."
19:18 Also **m** of those who became believers confessed
20: 8 There were **m** lamps in the room upstairs
21:20 **m** thousands of believers there are among the Jews,
24:10 for **m** years you have been a judge over this nation.
25: 7 bringing **m** serious charges against him,
26: 9 I myself was convinced that I ought to do **m** things
26:10 I not only locked up **m** of the saints in prison,
27:20 When neither sun nor stars appeared for **m** days,
28:10 They bestowed **m** honors on us,
Ro 4:17 "I have made you the father of **m** nations")—
4:18 that he would become "the father of **m** nations,"
5:15 For if the **m** died through the one man's trespass,
5:15 Jesus Christ, abounded for the **m**.
5:16 gift following **m** trespasses brings justification.
5:19 one man's disobedience the **m** were made sinners,
5:19 one man's obedience the **m** will be made righteous
12: 4 For as in one body we have **m** members,
12: 5 who are **m**, are one body in Christ,
15:23 I desire, as I have for **m** years,
16: 2 for she has been a benefactor of **m** and of myself
1Co 1:26 not **m** of you were wise by human standards, not
m were powerful, not **m** were of noble birth.
4:15 you do not have **m** fathers.
8: 5 as in fact there are **m** gods and **m** lords—
10:17 there is one bread, we who are **m** are one body,
10:33 not seeking my own advantage, but that of **m**,
11:30 For this reason **m** of you are weak and ill,
12:12 For just as the body is one and has **m** members,
12:12 though **m**, are one body, so it is with Christ.
12:14 the body does not consist of one member but of **m**.
12:20 As it is, there are **m** members, yet one body.
14:10 There are doubtless **m** different kinds of sounds in
16: 9 and there are **m** adversaries.
2Co 1:11 so that **m** will give thanks on our behalf for
1:11 the blessing granted us through the prayers of **m**.
2: 4 and anguish of heart and with **m** tears,
2:17 For we are not peddlers of God's word like so **m**;
6:10 as poor, yet making **m** rich;
8:22 and found eager in **m** matters,
9:12 the saints but also overflows with **m** thanksgivings
11:18 since **m** boast according to human standards,
11:27 through **m** a sleepless night, hungry and thirsty,
12:21 to mourn over **m** who previously sinned and have
Gal 1:14 I advanced in Judaism beyond **m** among my people
3:16 it does not say, "And to offsprings," as of **m**;
3:27 As **m** of you as were baptized into Christ
Php 3:18 For **m** live as enemies of the cross of Christ;
1Ti 6: 9 and are trapped by **m** senseless and harmful desires
6:10 the faith and pierced themselves with **m** pains.
6:12 in the presence of **m** witnesses.
2Ti 2: 2 from me through **m** witnesses entrust
Tit 1:10 There are also **m** rebellious people,
Heb 1: 1 Long ago God spoke to our ancestors in **m**
2:10 in bringing **m** children to glory,
7:23 Furthermore, the former priests were **m** in number,
9:28 having been offered once to bear the sins of **m**,
11:12 "as **m** as the stars of heaven and as
12:15 and through it **m** become defiled.
Jas 3: 1 Not **m** of you should become teachers,
3: 2 For all of us make **m** mistakes.

2Pe 2: 2 Even so, **m** will follow their licentious ways,
1Jn 2:18 so now **m** antichrists have come.
4: 1 for **m** false prophets have gone out into the world.
2Jn 1: 7 **M** deceivers have gone out into the world,
Rev 1:15 and his voice was like the sound of **m** waters.
5:11 the voice of **m** angels surrounding the throne and
8:11 and **m** died from the water,
9: 9 like the noise of **m** chariots with horses rushing
10:11 "You must prophesy again about **m** peoples
14: 2 from heaven like the sound of **m** waters and like
17: 1 of the great whore who is seated on **m** waters,
19: 6 like the sound of **m** waters and like the sound
19:12 and on his head are **m** diadems;
Tob 1: 3 I performed **m** acts of charity for my kindred
1:16 In the days of Shalmaneser I performed **m** acts
1:18 For in his anger he put to death **m** Israelites;
3: 5 now your **m** judgments are true in exacting penalty
4: 4 because she faced **m** dangers for you
4: 8 If you have **m** possessions,
5: 6 "Yes," he replied, "I have been there **m** times;
8:19 this he asked his wife to bake **m** loaves of bread;
10: 1 how **m** days Tobias would need for going and
11:18 and **m** gifts were given to him.
13:11 **m** nations will come to you from far away,
Jdt 1: 6 Thus, **m** nations joined the forces of the Chaldeans.
4:13 for the people fasted **m** days throughout Judea and
5:18 in **m** battles and were led away captive to
8:11 the Lord turns and helps us within so **m** days.
16:22 **M** desired to marry her, but she gave herself
AdE 2: 8 and **m** girls were gathered in Susa the capital
8:17 And **m** of the Gentiles were circumcised
13: 2 "Having become ruler of **m** nations and master of
16: 2 "**M** people, the more they are honored with
16: 5 And often **m** of those who are set in places
Wis 6: 2 that rule over multitudes, and boast of **m** nations.
18:12 had corpses too **m** to count.
Sir Pr: 1 **M** great teachings have been given to us through
1:24 then the lips of **m** tell of their good sense.
3:24 For their conceit has led **m** astray,
6: 6 Let those who are friendly with you be **m**,
6:22 she is not readily perceived by **m**.
8: 2 for gold has ruined **m**, and has perverted the minds
9: 8 **m** have been seduced by a woman's beauty,
11: 5 **M** kings have had to sit on the ground,
11: 6 **M** rulers have been utterly disgraced,
11:10 My child, do not busy yourself with **m** matters;
11:13 raises up their heads to the amazement of the **m**.
11:29 for **m** are the tricks of the crafty.
11:32 From a spark **m** coals are kindled,
13:22 If the rich person slips, **m** come to the rescue;
16: 5 **M** such things my eye has seen,
16:17 Among so **m** people I am unknown,
20:17 How **m** will ridicule him, and how often!
23:11 The one who swears **m** oaths is full of iniquity,
27: 1 **M** have committed sin for gain,
27:24 I have hated **m** things, but him above all;
27:25 and a treacherous blow opens up **m** wounds.
28:13 for they destroy the peace of **m**.
28:14 Slander has shaken **m**, and scattered them
28:18 **M** have fallen by the edge of the sword,
28:18 but not as **m** as have fallen because of the tongue.
29: 4 **M** regard a loan as a windfall,
29: 7 **M** refuse to lend, not because of meanness,
29:18 Being surety has ruined **m** who were prosperous,
30:23 for sorrow has destroyed **m**,
31: 6 **M** have come to ruin because of gold,
31:18 If you are seated among **m** persons,
31:25 by wine-drinking, for wine has destroyed **m**.
34: 7 For dreams have deceived **m**,
34: 9 An educated person knows **m** things,
34:12 I have seen **m** things in my travels,
35: 1 The one who keeps the law makes **m** offerings;
37:19 Some people may be clever enough to teach **m**,
37:31 **M** have died of gluttony, but the one who guards
39: 9 **M** will praise his understanding;
42: 6 and where there are **m** hands, lock things up.
43:32 **M** things greater than these lie hidden,
45: 9 with **m** golden bells all around,
48:12 He performed twice as **m** signs,
51: 3 from the **m** troubles I endured,
Bar 1:12 and we shall serve them **m** days and find favor
4:12 a widow and bereaved of **m**;
4:35 upon her from the Everlasting for **m** days,
LtJ 6: 3 to Babylon you will remain there for **m** years,
1Mc 1: 2 He fought **m** battles, conquered strongholds,
1: 3 to the ends of the earth, and plundered **m** nations.
1: 9 so did their descendants after them for **m** years;
1: 9 and they caused **m** evils on the earth.
1:11 from Israel and misled **m**, saying, "Let us go
1:11 from them **m** disasters have come upon us."
1:18 and **m** were wounded and fell.
1:30 and destroyed **m** people of Israel.
1:43 **M** even from Israel gladly adopted his religion;
1:52 **M** of the people, everyone who forsook the law,
1:62 But **m** in Israel stood firm and were resolved
2:16 **M** from Israel came to them;
2:18 be honored with silver and gold and **m** gifts."
2:29 At that time **m** who were seeking righteousness
2:32 **M** pursued them, and overtook them;
3: 7 He embittered **m** kings, but he made Jacob glad
3:11 **M** were wounded and fell, and the rest fled.
3:18 "It is easy for **m** to be hemmed in by few,
3:18 between saving by **m** or by few.
5: 6 where he found a strong band and **m** people,
5: 7 He engaged in **m** battles with them,
5:12 for **m** of us have fallen,
5:21 So Simon went to Galilee and fought **m** battles

1Mc 5:22 as **m** as three thousand of the Gentiles fell,
5:26 "**M** of them have been shut up in Bozrah
5:34 As **m** as eight thousand of them fell that day.
5:60 as **m** as two thousand of the people of Israel fell
6: 9 He lay there for **m** days,
6:24 moreover, they have put to death as **m** of us
6:31 for **m** days they fought and built engines of war;
6:51 he encamped before the sanctuary for **m** days.
6:52 of war to match theirs, and fought for **m** days.
7:19 and seized **m** of the men who had deserted to him,
8:10 **M** of them were wounded and fell,
8:11 as **m** as ever opposed them,
8:12 as **m** as have heard of their fame have feared them.
9: 2 and they took it and killed **m** people.
9: 6 and **m** slipped away from the camp,
9:17 and **m** on both sides were wounded and fell.
9:20 they mourned **m** days and said,
9:22 have not been recorded, but they were very **m**.
9:39 with tambourines and musicians and **m** weapons.
9:40 **M** were wounded and fell,
9:64 he fought against it for **m** days and made machines
9:69 and he killed **m** of them.
10:28 We will grant you **m** immunities
10:60 and their Friends silver and gold and **m** gifts,
11: 1 like the sand by the seashore, and **m** ships;
11:20 and he built **m** engines of war to use against it.
11:27 and in as **m** other honors as he had formerly had,
11:40 and he stayed there **m** days.
11:65 and fought against it for **m** days and hemmed it in.
11:74 **m** as three thousand of the foreigners fell that day.
12:13 **m** trials and **m** wars have encircled us;
13:26 and mourned for him **m** days.
13:49 and **m** of them perished from famine.
15: 4 and those who have devastated **m** cities
15:29 and you have taken possession of **m** places
16: 2 so that we have delivered Israel **m** times.
16: 8 **m** of them fell wounded and the rest fled into
2Mc 1:20 But after **m** years had passed, when it pleased God,
1:35 the king favored he exchanged **m** excellent gifts.
2:27 of **m** we will gladly endure the uncomfortable toil,
3:26 inflicting **m** blows on him.
4:35 but **m** also of other nations,
4:39 When **m** acts of sacrilege had been committed in
4:39 **m** of the gold vessels had already been stolen.
4:42 As a result, they wounded **m** of them,
5: 9 There he who had driven **m** from their own country
5:10 He who had cast out **m** to lie unburied had no one
5:14 and as **m** were sold into slavery as were killed.
5:18 not happened that they were involved in **m** sins,
6:24 "for **m** of the young might suppose that Eleazar
9: 6 the bowels of others with **m** and strange inflictions.
9:16 the holy vessels he would give back, **m** times over;
12:12 that they might indeed be useful in **m** ways, agreed
12:23 and destroyed as **m** as thirty thousand.
12:25 **m** words he had confirmed his solemn promise
12:28 as **m** as twenty-five thousand of those who were
13: 8 because he had committed **m** sins against
13:15 and killed as **m** as two thousand men in the camp.
1Es 1:49 of the people and of the priests committed **m** acts
2: 9 from **m** whose hearts were stirred.
4:14 and are not men **m**, and is not wine strong?
4:26 **M** men have lost their minds because of women,
4:27 **M** have perished, or stumbled,
5:64 while **m** came with trumpets and a joyful noise,
6:14 The house was built **m** years ago by a king
8:11 Let as **m** as are so disposed, therefore,
Man 1:10 I am weighted down with **m** an iron fetter,
3Mc 1: 5 and **m** captives also were taken.
2: 6 by inflicting **m** and varied punishments on
2:13 because of our **m** and great sins we are crushed
2:26 and **m** of his friends, intently observing
5:37 "How **m** times, you poor wretch,
6: 5 broke in pieces, showing your power to **m** nations.
2Es 1:10 For their sake I have overthrown **m** kings;
2:48 and how **m** are the wonders of the Lord God
3:12 they produced children and peoples and **m** nations,
3:25 This was done for **m** years;
3:29 and my soul has seen **m** sinners
4: 7 'How **m** dwellings are in the heart of the sea,
4: 7 or how **m** streams are at the source of the deep,
4: 7 or how **m** streams are above the firmament,
4:34 but the Highest is in a hurry on behalf of **m**.
5: 7 the **m** do not know shall make his voice heard
5: 8 There shall be chaos also in **m** places,
5:10 and it shall be sought by **m** but shall not be found,
5:28 why have you handed the one over to the **m**,
5:28 and scattered your only one among the **m**?
7:20 Let **m** perish who are now living,
7:*47* will bring delight to few, but torments to **m**.
7:*51* as you have said that the righteous are not **m**
7:*110* [40] and **m** others prayed for **m**?
8: 1 Most High made this world for the sake of **m**,
8: 3 **M** have been created, but only a few shall
8:33 the righteous, who have **m** works laid up with you,
8:41 "For just as the farmer sows **m** seeds in the ground
8:50 for **m** miseries will affect those who inhabit
9:10 as **m** as did not acknowledge me in their lifetime,
9:11 **m** as scorned my law while they still had freedom,
10: 9 over so **m** who have come into being upon her.
10:20 for how **m** are the adversities of Zion?—
10:24 and lay aside your **m** sorrows,
10:38 for the Most High has revealed **m** secrets to you.
10:57 For you are more blessed than **m**,
12: 7 before you beyond **m** others,
12:23 and they shall renew **m** things in it,
13:13 Then **m** people came to him,
13:26 for **m** ages, who will himself deliver his creation;

2Es 13:50 And then he will show them very **m** wonders."
14: 4 where I kept him with me **m** days.
14: 5 I told him **m** wondrous things,
14:24 But prepare for yourself **m** writing tablets,
15:29 of Arabia shall come out with **m** chariots,
16:18 the beginning of famine, when **m** shall perish;
16:22 For **m** of those who live on the earth shall perish
16:70 in **m** places and in neighboring cities there shall be
4Mc 1: 7 I could prove to you from **m** and various examples
1:14 how **m** kinds of emotions there are,
1:21 of both pleasure and pain have **m** consequences.
1:28 so there are **m** offshoots of these plants,
3: 7 the soldiers of his nation had killed **m** of them.
3:21 and caused **m** and various disasters.
5: 4 When **m** persons had been rounded up, one man,
5: 4 and known to **m** in the tyrant's court because
7: 4 with **m** ingenious war machines has ever held out
7:18 But as **m** as attend to religion with a whole heart,
10: 1 and **m** repeatedly urged him to save himself
11:20 in which so **m** of us brothers have been summoned
12: 6 on her who had been bereaved of so **m** sons and
15: 5 the weaker sex and gave birth to **m**,
15: 7 and because of the **m** pains she suffered with each
15:11 though so **m** factors influenced the mother to suffer
15:20 when you saw the place filled with **m** spectators of
15:22 and how **m** torments the mother then suffered
16: 4 the mother quenched so **m** and such great emotions
16: 6 "O how wretched am I and **m** times unhappy!
16: 8 In vain, my sons, I endured **m** birth pangs for you,
16:10 I who had so **m** and beautiful children am a widow
and alone, with **m** sorrows.
18:15 who said, '**M** are the afflictions of the righteous.'

MANY-COLORED (1) [COLOR, MANY]
Ps 45:14 in **m** robes she is led to the king;

MANY-HEADED (1) [HEAD, MANY]
4Mc 7:14 that of Isaac he rendered the **m** rack ineffective.

MANY-PEAKED (2) [MANY, PEAK]
Ps 68:15 O **m** mountain, mountain of Bashan!
68:16 Why do you look with envy, O **m** mountain,

MANY-SIDED (1) [MANY, SIDE]
Job 11: 6 tell you the secrets of wisdom! For wisdom is **m**.

MAOCH (1)
1Sa 27: 2 to King Achish son of **M** of Gath.

MAON (7) [MAONITES]
Jos 15:55 **M**, Carmel, Ziph, Juttah,
1Sa 23:24 David and his men were in the wilderness of **M**,
23:25 to the rock and stayed in the wilderness of **M**.
23:25 he pursued David into the wilderness of **M**.
25: 2 There was a man in **M**,
1Ch 2:45 of Shammai: **M**; and **M** was the father of Beth-zur.

MAONITES (1) [MAON]
Jdg 10:12 Sidonians also, and the Amalekites, and the **M**,

MAR (3) [MARRED]
Lev 19:27 on your temples or **m** the edges of your beard.
Sir 7: 6 be partial to the powerful, and so **m** your integrity.
2Es 15:63 and **m** the glory of your countenance.

MAR (KJV) See also BREAK UP, DAMAGING, RAVAGE, ROUND OFF, RUIN

MARA (1) [=NAOMI]
Ru 1:20 "Call me no longer Naomi, call me **M**,

MARAH (5)
Ex 15:23 came to **M**, they could not drink the water of **M**
because it was bitter. That is why it was called **M**.
Nu 33: 8 in the wilderness of Etham, and camped at **M**.
33: 9 They set out from **M** and came to Elim;

MARALAH (1)
Jos 19:11 and on to **M**, and touches Dabbesheth,

MARAN, MARANA See Index to Footnotes

MARANATHA (KJV) See OUR LORD COME

MARAUDER (1) [MARAUDERS, MARAUDING]
Jer 18:22 when you bring the **m** suddenly upon them!

MARAUDERS (2) [MARAUDER]
Isa 16: 4 and **m** have vanished from the land,
4Mc 2:14 but one preserves the property of enemies from **m**

MARAUDING (2) [MARAUDER]
1Ki 11:24 and became leader of a **m** band, after the slaughter
2Ki 13:21 a **m** band was seen and the man was thrown into

MARBLE‡ (6)
1Ch 29: 2 all sorts of precious stones, and **m** in abundance.
Est 1: 6 and purple to silver rings and **m** pillars.
1: 6 **m**, mother-of-pearl, and colored stones.
Rev 18:12 all articles of costly wood, bronze, iron, and **m**,
AdE 1: 6 and silver blocks on pillars of **m** and other stones.
1: 6 a mosaic floor of emerald, mother-of-pearl, and **m**.

MARCH (26) [MARCHED, MARCHES, MARCHING]
Nu 2: 9 They shall set out first on the **m**.
2:24 They shall set out third on the **m**.
10:28 This was the order of **m** of the Israelites,
12:15 not set out on the **m** until Miriam had been brought
Jos 6: 3 You shall **m** around the city,
6: 4 On the seventh day you shall **m** around
6: 7 "Go forward and **m** around the city;
Jdg 5:21 **M** on, my soul, with might!
1Sa 29: 6 and to me it seems right that you should **m** out and
2Sa 15:22 David said to Ittai, "Go then, **m** on."
2Ki 3: 8 Then he asked, "By which way shall we **m**?"
3: 9 they had made a roundabout **m** of seven days,
Pr 30:27 the locusts have no king, yet all of them **m** in rank;
Isa 27: 4 I will **m** to battle against it.
63:12 who caused his glorious arm to **m** at the right hand
Jer 46:22 for her enemies **m** in force,
Hab 1: 6 who **m** through the breadth of the earth
Zec 9: 8 so that no one shall **m** to and fro;
9:14 the Lord GOD will sound the trumpet and **m** forth
Jdt 1: 4 and forty cubits wide to allow his armies to **m** out
2: 6 **M** out against all the land to the west,
1Mc 6:33 the king set out and took his army by a forced **m**
2Mc 12:10 on their **m** against Timothy,
13:13 to **m** out and decide the matter by the help of God
3Mc 4: 5 forced to **m** at a swift pace by the violence
5:43 and would also **m** against Judea and rapidly level it

MARCHED (55) [MARCH]
Dt 33: 3 they **m** at your heels, accepted direction from you.
Jos 6:14 On the second day they **m** around the city once and
6:15 **m** around the city in the same manner seven times.
6:15 that day that they **m** around the city seven times.
10: 9 having **m** up all night from Gilgal.
Jdg 2:15 Whenever they **m** out, the hand of the LORD was
5: 4 when you **m** from the region of Edom,
5:11 down to the gates **m** the people of the LORD.
5:13 Then down **m** the remnant of the noble;
5:13 of the LORD **m** down for him against the mighty.
5:14 from Machir **m** down the commanders,
1Sa 18:13 and David **m** out and came in, leading the army.
18:16 for it was he who **m** out and came in leading them.
2Sa 2:32 Joab and his men **m** all night,
5: 6 and his men **m** to Jerusalem against the Jebusites,
15:22 So Ittai the Gittite **m** on,
18: 4 all the army **m** out by hundreds and by thousands.
1Ki 20: 1 He **m** against Samaria, laid siege to it,
2Ki 3: 6 So King Jehoram **m** out of Samaria at that time
6:24 he **m** against Samaria and laid siege to it.
16: 9 the king of Assyria **m** up against Damascus,
1Ch 11: 4 David and all Israel **m** to Jerusalem, that is Jebus,
Ps 68: 7 when you **m** through the wilderness,
Am 5: 3 that **m** out a thousand shall have a hundred left,
5: 3 and that which **m** out a hundred shall have ten left.
Rev 20: 9 They **m** up over the breadth of the earth
Jdt 2:21 They **m** for three days from Nineveh to the plain
7: 2 So all their warriors **m** off that day;
1Mc 3:57 Then the army **m** out and encamped to the south
5:36 From there he **m** on and took Chaspho, Maked,
5:58 to the men of the forces that were with them and **m**
5:66 Then he **m** off to go into the land of the Philistines,
6:32 Then Judas **m** away from the citadel and encamped
7:10 So they **m** away and came with a large force into
9: 4 then they **m** off and went to Berea
9:11 Then the army of Bacchides **m** out from the camp
10: 2 a very large army and **m** out to meet him in battle.
11:15 Ptolemy **m** out and met him with a strong force,
11:67 Early in the morning they **m** to the plain of Hazor,
12:25 So he **m** away from Jerusalem and met them in
12:32 and **m** through all that region.
12:33 and **m** through the country as far as Askalon and
12:40 and he **m** out and came to Beth-shan.
13:22 He **m** off and went into the land of Gilead.
14: 1 and **m** into Media to obtain help,
16: 4 and they **m** against Cendebeus and camped for
16: 5 the morning they started out and **m** into the plain,
2Mc 3:35 he **m** off with his forces to the king.
4:22 Then he **m** his army into Phoenicia.
12:19 **m** out and destroyed those whom Timothy had left
12:26 Then Judas **m** against Carnaim and the temple
12:27 of these, he **m** also against Ephron, a fortified town
3Mc 1: 1 and **m** out to the region near Raphia,
4Mc 4:22 He speedily **m** against them,
18: 5 he left Jerusalem and **m** against the Persians.

MARCHES (1) [MARCH]
Wis 4: 2 throughout all time it **m**, crowned in triumph,

MARCHING (9) [MARCH]
2Sa 2:29 **m** the whole forenoon, they came to Mahanaim.
5:24 the sound of **m** in the tops of the balsam trees,
2Ki 11:19 of the LORD, **m** through the gate of the guards to
1Ch 14:15 of **m** in the tops of the balsam trees, then go out
2Ch 23:20 **m** through the upper gate to the king's house.
Isa 63: 1 so splendidly robed, **m** in his great might?"
1Mc 6:41 by the **m** of the multitude and the clanking
12:50 and they encouraged one another and kept **m**
13:20 and his army kept **m** along opposite him

MARCUS (KJV) See MARK

MARE (1)
SS 1: 9 my love, to a **m** among Pharaoh's chariots.

MARESHAH‡ (8)
Jos 15:44 Achzib, and **M**: nine towns with their villages.
1Ch 2:42 The sons of **M** father of Hebron.
4:21 Er father of Lecah, Laadah father of **M**,
2Ch 11: 8 Gath, **M**, Ziph,
14: 9 and came as far as **M**.
14:10 of battle in the valley of Zephathah at **M**.
20:37 Then Eliezer son of Dodavahu of **M** prophesied
Mic 1:15 a conqueror upon you, inhabitants of **M**;

MARINERS (4)
Eze 27: 9 the ships of the sea with their **m** were within you,
27:27 your merchandise, your **m** and your pilots,
27:29 **m** and all the pilots of the sea stand on the shore
Jnh 1: 5 Then the **m** were afraid, and each cried to his god.

MARISA (2)
1Mc 5:66 the land of the Philistines, and passed through **M**.
2Mc 12:35 so Gorgias escaped and reached **M**.

MARISHES (KJV) See MARSHES

MARITAL (2) [MARRY]
Ex 21:10 clothing, or **m** rights of the first wife.
Mt 1:25 but had no **m** relations with her until she had borne

MARK (41) [=JOHN, MARKED, MARKER, MARKERS, MARKS]
Ge 4:15 And the LORD put a **m** on Cain,
Ex 12: 2 This month shall **m** for you the beginning
Nu 34: 7 from the Great Sea you shall **m** out your line
34: 8 from Mount Hor you shall **m** it out
34:10 You shall **m** out your eastern boundary
1Sa 20:20 as though I shot at a **m**.
Job 36:32 and commands it to strike the **m**.
Ps 37:37 **M** the blameless, and behold the upright,
50:22 "**M** this, then, you who forget God,
104:19 You have made the moon to **m** the seasons;
130: 3 If you, O LORD, should **m** iniquities, Lord,
La 3:12 he bent his bow and set me as a **m** for his arrow.
Eze 9: 4 a **m** on the foreheads of those who sigh and groan
9: 6 but touch no one who has the **m**.
21:19 **m** out two roads for the sword of the king
21:20 **m** out the road for the sword to come to Rabbah of
44: 5 The LORD said to me: Mortal, **m** well,
44: 5 and **m** well those who may be admitted to
Jn 20:25 "Unless I see the **m** of the nails in his hands,
20:25 in the **m** of the nails and my hand in his side,
Ac 12:12 the mother of John whose other name was **M**,
12:25 whose other name was **M**.
15:37 Barnabas wanted to take with them John called **M**.
15:39 Barnabas took **M** with him and sailed away
Col 4:10 as does **M** the cousin of Barnabas,
2Th 3:17 This is the **m** in every letter of mine;
1Ti 6:21 by professing it some have missed the **m** as regards
2Ti 4:11 Get **M** and bring him with you,
Phm 1:24 and so do **M**, Aristarchus, Demas,
1Pe 5:13 and so does my son **M**.
Rev 13:17 no one can buy or sell who does not have the **m**,
14: 9 receive a **m** on their foreheads or on their hands,
14:11 for anyone who receives the **m** of the beast
16: 2 and painful sore came on those who had the **m** of
19:20 those who had received the **m** of the beast
20: 4 the beast or its image and had not received its **m**
Wis 8:21 it was a **m** of insight to know whose gift she was—
Sir 36:28 If kindness and humility **m** her speech,
1Mc 8:14 of them has put on a crown or worn purple as a **m**
2Mc 2: 6 of those who followed him came up intending to **m**
2Es 2:23 commit them to the grave and **m** it,

MARKED (8) [MARK]
Pr 8:29 when he **m** out the foundations of the earth,
Isa 40:12 the hollow of his hand and **m** off the heavens with
Jer 44:19 that we made cakes for her, **m** with her image,
Hab 1:12 O LORD, you have **m** them for judgment;
Eph 1:13 were **m** with the seal of the promised Holy Spirit;
4:30 with which you were **m** with a seal for the day
Rev 7: 3 until we have **m** the servants of our God with a seal
13:16 to be **m** on the right hand or the forehead,

MARKER (2) [MARK]
Dt 19:14 You must not move your neighbor's boundary **m**,
27:17 be anyone who moves a neighbor's boundary **m**."

MARKERS (1) [MARK]
Jer 31:21 Set up road **m** for yourself,

MARKET‡ (5) [MARKETPLACE, MARKETPLACES, MARKETS]
Mk 7: 4 not eat anything from the **m** unless they wash it;
1Co 10:25 in the meat **m** without raising any question on

Tob 2: 3 and thrown into the **m** place,
2Mc 3: 4 about the administration of the city **m.**
1Es 2: 18 repairing its **m** places and walls and laying

MARKETPLACE‡ (6) [MARKET]

Ps 55: 11 oppression and fraud do not depart from its **m.**
Mt 20: 3 he saw others standing idle in the **m;**
Lk 7: 32 They are like children sitting in the **m** and calling
Jn 2: 16 Stop making my Father's house a **m!"**
Ac 16: 19 and dragged them into the **m** before the authorities.
17: 17 also in the **m** every day with those who happened

MARKETPLACES (7) [MARKET]

Mt 11: 16 It is like children sitting in the **m** and calling
23: 7 and to be greeted with respect in the **m,**
Mk 6: 56 they laid the sick in the **m,**
12: 38 and to be greeted with respect in the **m,**
Lk 11: 43 and to be greeted with respect in the **m.**
20: 46 and love to be greeted with respect in the **m,**
Ac 17: 5 the help of some ruffians in the **m** they formed

MARKETS (2) [MARKET]

Eze 27: 15 many coastlands were your own special **m;**
Jdt 1: 14 plundered its **m,** and turned its glory into disgrace.

MARKS (8) [MARK]

Lev 19: 28 in your flesh for the dead or tattoo any **m**
1Sa 21: 13 He scratched **m** on the doors of the gate,
Isa 44: 13 carpenter stretches a line, **m** it out with a stylus,
44: 13 fashions it with planes, and **m** it with a compass;
1Co 7: 18 Let him not seek to remove the **m** of circumcision.
Gal 6: 17 for I carry the **m** of Jesus branded on my body.
Sir 43: 6 It is the moon that **m** the changing seasons,
1Mc 1: 15 and removed the **m** of circumcision,

MARMASIMA (1)

AdE 9: 9 **M,** Aruphaeus, Arsaeus, Zabutheus,

MAROTH (1)

Mic 1: 12 For the inhabitants of **M** wait anxiously for good,

MARRED (1) [MAR]

Isa 52: 14 —so **m** was his appearance, beyond human

MARRIAGE‡ (50) [MARRY]

Ge 34: 8 please give her to him in **m.**
34: 12 Put the **m** present and gift as high as you like,
34: 21 let us take their daughters in **m,**
38: 14 yet she had not been given to him in **m.**
Ex 2: 21 and he gave Moses his daughter Zipporah in **m.**
Dt 22: 16 "I gave my daughter in **m** to this man
24: 1 Suppose a man enters into **m** with a woman,
25: 5 to her, taking her in **m,** and performing the duty of
Jdg 12: 9 He gave his thirty daughters in **m** outside his clan
21: 1 of us shall give his daughter in **m** to Benjamin."
1Sa 18: 25 'The king desires no **m** present except
1Ki 3: 1 Solomon made a **m** alliance with Pharaoh king
7: 8 whom he had taken in **m.**
11: 2 "You shall not enter into **m** with them,
1Ch 2: 35 Sheshan gave his daughter in **m** to his slave Jarha;
2Ch 18: 1 and he made a **m** alliance with Ahab.
Ps 78: 63 and their girls had no **m** song.
Jer 29: 6 and give your daughters in **m,**
Da 2: 43 so will they mix with one another in **m,**
11: 17 he shall give him a woman in **m;**
Mt 22: 30 nor are given in **m,** but are like angels
24: 38 marrying and giving in **m,**
Mk 12: 25 they neither marry nor are given in **m,**
Lk 2: 36 with her husband seven years after her **m,**
17: 27 and marrying and being given in **m,**
20: 34 to this age marry and are given in **m;**
20: 35 from the dead neither marry nor are given in **m.**
1Co 7: 38 and he who refrains from **m** will do better.
2Co 11: 2 for I promised you in **m** to one husband,
1Ti 4: 3 They forbid **m** and demand abstinence from foods,
Heb 13: 4 Let **m** be held in honor by all,
13: 4 and let the **m** bed be kept undefiled;
Rev 19: 7 for the **m** of the Lamb has come,
19: 9 Blessed are those who are invited to the **m** supper
Tob 3: 17 by giving her in **m** to Tobias son of Tobit,
6: 13 "You have every right to take her in **m.**
6: 13 we return from Rages we will celebrate her **m.**
6: 16 that this very night she will be given to you in **m.**
7: 13 and he wrote out a copy of a **m** contract,
AdE 2: 18 and the officers to celebrate his **m** to Esther;
Wis 7: 2 from the seed of a man and the pleasure of **m.**
13: 17 he prays about possessions and his **m** and children,
Sir 7: 25 a daughter in **m,** and you complete a great task;
23: 18 one who sins against his **m** bed says to himself,
1Mc 10: 58 Ptolemy gave him his daughter Cleopatra in **m,**
11: 9 in **m** my daughter who was Alexander's wife,
1Es 8: 84 not give your daughters in **m** to their descendants,
3Mc 1: 19 for **m** abandoned the bridal chambers prepared
4: 8 spent the remaining days of their **m** festival
2Es 9: 47 I set a day for the **m** feast.

MARRIAGES (3) [MARRY]

Ge 34: 9 Make **m** with us; give your daughters to us,
Wis 14: 24 either their lives or their **m** pure,
14: 26 defiling of souls, sexual perversion, disorder in **m,**

MARRIED‡ (84) [MARRY]

Ge 20: 3 for she is a **m** woman."
25: 20 and Isaac was forty years old when he **m** Rebekah,
26: 34 he **m** Judith daughter of Beeri the Hittite,
38: 2 he **m** her and went in to her.
Ex 2: 1 Now a man from the house of Levi went and **m**
6: 20 Amram **m** Jochebed his father's sister
6: 23 Aaron **m** Elisheba, daughter of Amminadab
6: 25 Aaron's son Eleazar **m** one of the daughters
21: 3 he comes in **m,** then his wife shall go out with him.
22: 16 man seduces a virgin who is not engaged to be **m,**
Nu 12: 1 because of the Cushite woman whom he had **m**
12: 1 (for he had indeed **m** a Cushite woman);
36: 3 But if they are **m** into another Israelite tribe,
36: 4 of the tribe into which they have **m;**
36: 6 be into a clan of their father's tribe that they are **m,**
36: 11 **m** sons of their father's brothers.
36: 12 They were **m** into the clans of the descendants
Dt 20: 7 to a woman but not yet **m** her?
22: 14 slandering her by saying, "I **m** this woman;
22: 23 a virgin already engaged to be **m,**
24: 3 of his house (or the second man who **m** her dies);
24: 5 When a man is newly **m,**
24: 5 to be happy with the wife whom he has **m.**
25: 5 of the deceased shall not be **m** outside the family to
1Sa 25: 43 David also **m** Ahinoam of Jezreel;
2Sa 17: 25 who had **m** Abigal daughter of Nahash,
1Ch 2: 19 Azubah died, Caleb **m** Ephrath, who bore him Hur.
2: 21 whom he **m** when he was sixty years old;
4: 17 daughter of Pharaoh, whom Mered **m;**
4: 22 who **m** into Moab but returned to Lehem (now
23: 22 their kindred, the sons of Kish, **m** them.
Ezr 2: 61 of Habaiah, Hakkoz, and Barzillai (who had **m** one
10: 2 and have **m** foreign women from the peoples of
10: 10 "You have trespassed and **m** foreign women,
10: 17 the end of all the men who had **m** foreign women.
10: 18 of the priests who had **m** foreign women,
10: 44 All these had **m** foreign women,
Ne 6: 18 and his son Jehohanan had **m** the daughter
7: 63 of Barzillai (who had **m** one of the daughters
13: 23 In those days also I saw Jews who had **m** women
Isa 54: 1 be more than the children of her that is **m,**
62: 4 be called My Delight Is in Her, and your land **M;**
62: 4 LORD delights in you, and your land shall be **m.**
Mal 2: 11 and has **m** the daughter of a foreign god.
Mt 22: 25 the first **m,** and died childless,
22: 28 For all of them had **m** her."
Mk 6: 17 brother Philip's wife, because Herod had **m** her.
12: 20 the first **m** and, when he died, left no children;
12: 21 the second **m** her and died, leaving no children;
12: 23 For the seven had **m** her."
Lk 14: 20 Another said, 'I have just been **m,**
20: 29 the first **m,** and died childless;
20: 31 and the third **m** her,
20: 33 For the seven had **m** her."
Ro 7: 2 a **m** woman is bound by the law to her husband
1Co 7: 10 To the **m** I give this command—
7: 33 **m** man is anxious about the affairs of the world,
7: 34 **m** woman is anxious about the affairs of the world,
Gal 4: 27 the children of the one who is **m."**
1Ti 3: 2 a bishop must be above reproach, **m** only once,
3: 12 Let deacons be **m** only once,
5: 9 and has been **m** only once;
Tit 1: 6 **m** only once, whose children are believers,
Tob 1: 9 When I became a man I **m** a woman,
3: 8 For she had been **m** to seven husbands,
3: 8 you have already been **m** to seven husbands
6: 14 that she already has been **m** to seven husbands and
9: 5 and informed him that Tobit's son Tobias had **m**
11: 15 that he had **m** Raguel's daughter Sarah,
AdE 10: 6 river is Esther, whom the king **m** and made queen.
Sir 26: 22 *and a **m** woman as a tower of death to her lovers.*
42: 9 she is young, for fear she may not marry, or if **m,**
42: 10 or, though **m,** for fear she may be barren.
42: 12 or spend her time among **m** women;
Sus 1: 2 He **m** the daughter of Hilkiah, named Susanna,
1Mc 3: 56 or were about to be **m,** or were planting a vineyard,
2Mc 14: 25 so Judas **m,** settled down, and shared
1Es 5: 38 and the descendants of Jaddus who had **m** Agia,
8: 70 and their descendants have **m** the daughters
8: 92 and have **m** foreign women from the peoples of
9: 7 "You have broken the law and **m** foreign women,
9: 36 All these had **m** foreign women,
3Mc 4: 6 the bridal chamber to share **m** life exchanged joy
4Mc 16: 9 some unmarried, others **m** and without offspring.

MARRIES‡ (14) [MARRY]

Ge 27: 46 If Jacob **m** one of the Hittite women such as these,
Lev 22: 12 If a priest's daughter **m** a layman,
Nu 30: 6 If she **m,** while obligated by her vows
Dt 22: 13 Suppose a man **m** a woman,
Isa 62: 5 For as a young man **m** a young woman,
Mt 5: 32 whoever **m** a divorced woman commits adultery.
19: 9 and **m** another commits adultery."
Mk 10: 11 and **m** another commits adultery against her;
10: 12 and if she divorces her husband and **m** another,
Lk 16: 18 divorces his wife and **m** another commits adultery,
16: 18 whoever **m** a woman divorced from her husband
Ro 7: 3 she is free from that law, and if she **m** another man,
1Co 7: 28 But if you marry, you do not sin, and if a virgin **m,**
7: 38 So then, he who **m** his fiancée does well;

MARROW (3)

Job 21: 24 his loins full of milk and the **m** of his bones moist.
Isa 25: 6 of rich food filled with **m,**
Heb 4: 12 until it divides soul from spirit, joints from **m;**

MARRY‡ (48) [INTERMARRY, MARITAL, MARRIAGE, MARRIAGES, MARRIED, MARRIES, MARRYING]

Ge 19: 14 who were to **m** his daughters, "Up,
28: 1 "You shall not **m** one of the Canaanite women.
28: 6 "You shall not **m** one of the Canaanite women,"
Lev 21: 7 They shall not **m** a prostitute or
21: 7 neither shall they **m** a woman divorced
21: 13 He shall **m** only a woman who is a virgin.
21: 14 a prostitute, these he shall not **m.**
21: 14 He shall **m** a virgin of his own kin,
Nu 36: 3 to the inheritance of the tribe into which they **m;**
36: 6 'Let them **m** whom they think best;
36: 8 in any tribe of the Israelites shall **m** one from
Dt 20: 7 or he might die in the battle and another **m** her."
21: 11 beautiful woman whom you desire and want to **m,**
22: 30 A man shall not **m** his father's wife,
25: 7 if the man has no desire to **m** his brother's widow,
25: 8 If he persists, saying, "I have no desire to **m** her,"
Jos 23: 12 so that you **m** their women and they yours,
Jdg 14: 8 After a while he returned to **m** her,
Isa 62: 5 so shall your builder **m** you,
Eze 44: 22 They shall not **m** a widow, or a divorced woman,
Mt 19: 10 it is better not to **m."**
22: 24 his brother shall **m** the widow,
22: 30 For in the resurrection they neither **m** nor are given
Mk 12: 19 the man shall **m** the widow and raise up children
12: 25 they neither **m** nor are given in marriage,
Lk 20: 28 the man shall **m** the widow and raise up children
20: 34 "Those who belong to this age **m** and are given
20: 35 from the dead neither **m** nor are given in marriage.
1Co 7: 9 they are not practicing self-control, they should **m.**
7: 9 For it is better to **m** than to be aflame with passion.
7: 28 But if you **m,** you do not sin,
7: 28 those who **m** will experience distress in this life,
7: 36 and so it has to be, let him **m** as he wishes;
7: 36 it is no sin. Let them **m.**
7: 39 husband dies, she is free to **m** anyone she wishes,
1Ti 5: 11 from Christ, they want to **m,**
5: 14 So I would have younger widows **m,** bear children,
Tob 3: 17 before all others who had desired to **m** her.
4: 12 **m** a woman from among the descendants
4: 12 do not **m** a foreign woman,
6: 13 are entitled to **m** his daughter.
7: 10 brother, has the right to **m** my daughter Sarah.
Jdt 16: 22 Many desired to **m** her, but she gave herself
Sir 42: 9 when she is young, for fear she may not **m,**
2Mc 1: 14 On the pretext of intending to **m** her,
14: 25 He urged him to **m** and have children;
2Es 16: 44 those who **m,** like those who will have no children;
16: 44 those who do not **m,** like those who are widowed.

MARRYING (4) [MARRY]

Ru 1: 13 Would you then refrain from **m?**
Ne 13: 27 against our God by **m** foreign women?"
Mt 24: 38 before the flood they were eating and drinking, **m**
Lk 17: 27 They were eating and drinking, and **m**

MARS (KJV) See AREOPAGUS

MARSENA (1)

Est 1: 14 Admatha, Tarshish, Meres, **M,** and Memucan,

MARSH (3) [MARSHES]

Job 8: 11 "Can papyrus grow where there is no **m?**
40: 21 in the covert of the reeds and in the **m.**
1Mc 9: 45 with **m** and thicket; there is no place to turn.

MARSHAL (1) [MARSHAL'S, MARSHALED, MARSHALS]

Jer 51: 27 appoint a **m** against her, bring up horses like bristling locusts.

MARSHAL'S (1) [MARSHAL]

Jdg 5: 14 and from Zebulun those who bear the **m** staff;

MARSHALED (1) [MARSHAL]

Jdt 2: 16 and he organized them as a great army is **m** for

MARSHALS (1) [MARSHAL]

Sir 17: 32 He **m** the host of the height of heaven;

MARSHES (3) [MARSH]

Jer 51: 32 the **m** have been burned with fire,
Eze 47: 11 But its swamps and **m** will not become fresh;
1Mc 9: 42 they returned to the **m** of the Jordan.

MARTHA (13)

Lk 10: 38 a woman named **M** welcomed him into her home.
10: 40 But **M** was distracted by her many tasks;
10: 41 But the Lord answered her, **"M, M,**
Jn 11: 1 the village of Mary and her sister **M.**
11: 5 though Jesus loved **M** and her sister and Lazarus,
11: 19 the Jews had come to **M** and Mary to console them
11: 20 When **M** heard that Jesus was coming,
11: 21 **M** said to Jesus, "Lord, if you had been here,
11: 24 **M** said to him, "I know that he will rise again in
11: 30 but was still at the place where **M** had met him.

Jn 11:39 **M,** the sister of the dead man, said to him, "Lord,
12: 2 **M** served, and Lazarus was one of those at

MARVEL (2) [MARVELED, MARVELING, MARVELOUS, MARVELOUSLY, MARVELS]

Sir 43:24 and we **m** at what we hear.
2Es 4:26 and if you live long, you will often **m,**

MARVELED (9) [MARVEL]

2Th 1:10 be glorified by his saints and to be **m** at on that day
Jdt 10:19 They **m** at her beauty and admired the Israelites,
10:23 they all **m** at the beauty of her face.
11:20 They **m** at her wisdom and said,
Wis 11:14 at the end of the events they **m** at him,
2Mc 1:22 shone out, a great fire blazed up, so that all **m.**
3Mc 1:10 he **m** at the good order of the temple,
4Mc 1:11 **m** at their courage and endurance,
17:17 and all his council **m** at their endurance,

MARVELING (1) [MARVEL]

4Mc 9:26 While all were **m** at his courageous spirit,

MARVELOUS (22) [MARVEL]

1Ch 16:24 his **m** works among all the peoples.
Job 5: 9 and unsearchable, **m** things without number.
9:10 and **m** things without number.
Ps 96: 3 his **m** works among all the peoples.
98: 1 for he has done **m** things.
118:23 This is the LORD's doing; it is **m** in our eyes.
131: 1 not occupy myself with things too great and too **m**
Mic 7:15 of the land of Egypt, show us **m** things.
1Pe 2: 9 called you out of darkness into his **m** light.
Tob 12:22 they acknowledged God for these **m** deeds of his,
Wis 10:17 she guided them along a **m** way,
19: 8 after gazing on **m** wonders.
Sir 38: 6 that he might be glorified in his **m** works.
39:20 and nothing is too **m** for him.
42:17 even his holy ones to recount all his **m** works,
43: 2 proclaims as it rises what a **m** instrument it is,
43: 8 how **m** it is in this change,
43:25 In it are strange and **m** creatures,
43:29 the Lord and very great, and **m** is his power.
48:14 and in death his deeds were **m.**
Aza 1:20 Deliver us in accordance with your **m** works,
2Mc 15:13 and of **m** majesty and authority.

MARVELOUSLY (3) [MARVEL]

2Ch 26:15 for he was **m** helped until he became strong.
Jdt 10:14 she was in their eyes **m** beautiful—
2Mc 3:30 the Lord who had acted **m** for his own place.

MARVELS‡ (3) [MARVEL]

Ex 34:10 Before all your people I will perform **m,**
Ps 78:12 the sight of their ancestors he worked **m** in the land
Sir 48:12 and **m** with every utterance of his mouth.

MARY (53) [MARY'S]

Mt 1:16 and Jacob the father of Joseph the husband of **M,**
1:18 When his mother **M** had been engaged to Joseph,
1:20 do not be afraid to take **M** as your wife,
2:11 they saw the child with **M** his mother;
13:55 Is not his mother called **M?**
27:56 Among them were **M** Magdalene, and **M** the mother of James and Joseph,
27:61 **M** Magdalene and the other **M** were there,
28: 1 **M** Magdalene and the other **M** went to see
Mk 6: 3 of **M** and brother of James and Joses and Judas
15:40 were **M** Magdalene, **M** the mother of James
15:47 **M** Magdalene and **M** the mother of Joses saw
16: 1 **M** Magdalene, and **M** the mother of James,
16: 9 ⟦he appeared first to **M** Magdalene,⟧
Lk 1:27 The virgin's name was **M.**
1:30 The angel said to her, "Do not be afraid, **M,**
1:34 **M** said to the angel, "How can this be,
1:38 Then **M** said, "Here am I, the servant of the Lord;
1:39 In those days **M** set out and went with haste to
1:46 And **M** said, "My soul magnifies the Lord,
1:56 And **M** remained with her about three months and
2: 5 He went to be registered with **M,**
2:16 So they went with haste and found **M** and Joseph,
2:19 But **M** treasured all these words
2:34 Simeon blessed them and said to his mother **M,**
8: 2 and infirmities: **M,** called Magdalene,
10:39 She had a sister named **M,**
10:42 **M** has chosen the better part,
24:10 **M** Magdalene, Joanna, **M** the mother of James,
Jn 11: 1 the village of **M** and her sister Martha.
11: 2 **M** was the one who anointed the Lord
11:19 and many of the Jews had come to Martha and **M**
11:20 she went and met him, while **M** stayed at home.
11:28 she went back and called her sister **M,**
11:31 consoling her, saw **M** get up quickly and go out.
11:32 When **M** came where Jesus was and saw him,
11:45 with **M** and had seen what Jesus did,
12: 3 **M** took a pound of costly perfume made
19:25 **M** the wife of Clopas, and **M** Magdalene.
20: 1 **M** Magdalene came to the tomb and saw that
20:11 But **M** stood weeping outside the tomb.
20:16 Jesus said to her, **"M!"**
20:18 **M** Magdalene went and announced to
Ac 1:14 including **M** the mother of Jesus, as well as his
12:12 he went to the house of **M,** the mother of John
Ro 16: 6 Greet **M,** who has worked very hard among you.

MARY'S (1) [MARY]

Lk 1:41 When Elizabeth heard **M** greeting,

MASH‡ (1)

Ge 10:23 descendants of Aram: Uz, Hul, Gether, and **M.**

MASHAH See Index to Footnotes

MASHAL (1)

1Ch 6:74 **M** with its pasture lands, Abdon

MASIAH (1)

1Es 5:34 the descendants of Sarothie, the descendants of **M,**

MASKIL‡ (13)

Ps 32: T *Of David. A **M**.*
42: T *To the leader. A **M** of the Korahites.*
44: T *To the leader. Of the Korahites. A **M**.*
45: T *Of the Korahites. A **M**. A love song.*
52: T *A **M** of David, when Doeg the Edomite came to*
53: T *according to Mahalath. A **M** of David.*
54: T *A **M** of David, when the Ziphites went and told*
55: T *with stringed instruments. A **M** of David.*
74: T *A **M** of Asaph.*
78: T *A **M** of Asaph.*
88: T *A **M** of Heman the Ezrahite.*
89: T *A **M** of Ethan the Ezrahite.*
142: T *A **M** of David. When he was in the cave.*

MASKS (1)

4Mc 15:15 the flesh of the head to the chin exposed like **m.**

MASONRY (1) [MASONS]

Eze 46:23 around each of the four courts was a row of **m,**

MASONS (8) [MASONRY]

2Sa 5:11 and carpenters and **m** who built David a house.
2Ki 12:12 to the **m** and the stonecutters,
22: 6 to the carpenters, to the builders, to the **m;**
1Ch 14: 1 and **m** and carpenters to build a house for him.
22:15 stonecutters, **m,** carpenters,
2Ch 24:12 and they hired **m** and carpenters to restore
Ezr 3: 7 So they gave money to the **m** and the carpenters,
1Es 5:54 They gave money to the **m** and the carpenters,

MASREKAH (2)

Ge 36:36 and Samlah of **M** succeeded him as king.
1Ch 1:47 When Hadad died, Samlah of **M** succeeded him.

MASS (6) [MASSES, MASSING, MASSIVE]

Job 16:10 they **m** themselves together against me.
38:38 the dust runs into a **m** and the clods cling together?
Eze 19:11 it stood out in its height with its **m** of branches.
31: 9 I made it beautiful with its **m** of branches,
2Mc 2:24 upon the narratives of history because of the **m**
3Mc 2: 7 he pursued them with chariots and a **m** of troops,

MASSA (2)

Ge 25:14 Mishma, Dumah, **M,**
1Ch 1:30 Mishma, Dumah, **M,** Hadad, Tema,

MASSACRE (1) [MASSACRED]

2Mc 5:13 Then there was **m** of young and old,

MASSACRED (1) [MASSACRE]

2Mc 12: 6 and **m** those who had taken refuge there.

MASSAH (5)

Ex 17: 7 He called the place **M** and Meribah,
Dt 6:16 as you tested him at **M.**
9:22 At Taberah also, and at **M,**
33: 8 whom you tested at **M,** with whom you contended
Ps 95: 8 as on the day at **M** in the wilderness,

MASSES (3) [MASS]

2Mc 15:21 observing the **m** that were in front of him and
3Mc 5:41 it is crowded with **m** of people,
5:46 with countless **m** of people crowding their way

MASSING (1) [MASS]

2Mc 5: 3 brandishing of shields, **m** of spears,

MASSIVE (1) [MASS]

Jdg 11:33 He inflicted a **m** defeat on them from Aroer to

MAST (3)

Pr 23:34 like one who lies on the top of a **m.**
Isa 33:23 it cannot hold the **m** firm in its place,
Eze 27: 5 they took a cedar from Lebanon to make a **m**

MASTER‡ (158) [MASTER'S, MASTERED, MASTERS, MASTERS', MASTERY, SHIPMASTERS, TASKMASTER, TASKMASTERS]

Ge 4: 7 its desire is for you, but you must **m** it."
24: 9 the thigh of Abraham his **m** and swore to him
24:10 taking all kinds of choice gifts from his **m;**
24:12 And he said, "O LORD, God of my **m** Abraham,
24:12 and show steadfast love to my **m** Abraham.
24:14 that you have shown steadfast love to my **m."**
24:27 the LORD, the God of my **m** Abraham,
24:27 and his faithfulness toward my **m.**
24:35 The LORD has greatly blessed my **m,**
24:36 And Sarah my master's wife bore a son to my **m**
24:37 My **m** made me swear, saying,
24:39 I said to my **m,** 'Perhaps the woman will
24:42 and said, 'O LORD, the God of my **m** Abraham,
24:48 the LORD, the God of my **m** Abraham,
24:49 you will deal loyally and truly with my **m,** tell me;
24:54 he said, "Send me back to my **m."**
24:56 let me go that I may go to my **m."**
24:65 The servant said, "It is my **m."**
39: 2 he was in the house of his Egyptian **m.**
39: 3 His **m** saw that the LORD was with him,
39: 8 my **m** has no concern about anything in the house,
39:16 by her until his **m** came home,
39:19 his **m** heard the words that his wife spoke to him,
39:20 Joseph's **m** took him and put him into the prison,
Ex 21: 4 If his **m** gives him a wife and she bears him sons
21: 5 But if the slave declares, "I love my **m,** my wife,
21: 6 then his **m** shall bring him before God.
21: 6 and his **m** shall pierce his ear with an awl;
21: 8 If she does not please her **m,**
Jdg 19:11 and the servant said to his **m,** "Come now,
19:12 But his **m** said to him, "We will not turn aside into
19:22 They said to the old man, the **m** of the house,
19:23 And the man, the **m** of the house,
19:26 at the door of the man's house where her **m** was,
19:27 In the morning her **m** got up,
1Sa 20:38 up the arrows and came to his **m.**
25:14 of the wilderness to salute our **m;**
25:17 for evil has been decided against our **m** and
30:13 **m** left me behind because I fell sick three days
30:15 or hand me over to my **m,**
1Ki 11:23 Rezon son of Eliada, who had fled from his **m,**
12:27 the heart of this people will turn again to their **m,**
22:17 and the LORD said, 'These have no **m;**
2Ki 2: 3 the LORD will take your **m** away from you?"
2: 5 the LORD will take your **m** away from you?"
2:16 please let them go and seek your **m;**
5: 1 was a great man and in high favor with his **m,**
5:18 when my **m** goes into the house of Rimmon
5:20 of Elisha the man of God, thought, "My **m** has let
5:22 He replied, "Yes, but my **m** has sent me to say,
5:25 He went in and stood before his **m;**
6: 5 into the water; he cried out, "Alas, **m!**
6:15 His servant said, "Alas, **m!**
6:22 and let them go to their **m."**
6:23 on their way, and they went to their **m.**
8:14 Then he left Elisha, and went to his **m** Ben-hadad,
9: 7 You shall strike down the house of your **m** Ahab,
9:31 she said, "Is it peace, Zimri, murderer of your **m?"**
10: 3 select the son of your **m** who is the best qualified,
10: 9 It was I who conspired against my **m**
18:23 make a wager with my **m** the king of Assyria:
18:27 "Has my **m** sent me to speak these words to your **m** and to you,
19: 4 whom his **m** the king of Assyria has sent to mock
19: 6 "Say to your **m,** 'Thus says the LORD:
1Ch 12:19 "He will desert to his **m** Saul at the cost
2Ch 18:16 and the LORD said, 'These have no **m;**
Est 1:22 that every man should be **m** in his own house.
Ps 12: 4 our lips are our own—who is our **m?"**
123: 2 As the eyes of servants look to the hand of their **m,**
Pr 8:30 then I was beside him, like a **m** worker;
27:18 and anyone who takes care of a **m** will be honored.
30:10 Do not slander a servant to a **m,**
Ecc 2:19 be **m** of all for which I toiled and used my wisdom
SS 7: 1 the work of a **m** hand.
Isa 19: 4 the Egyptians into the hand of a hard **m;**
22:15 who is **m** of the household, and say to him:
24: 2 as with the slave, so with his **m;**
36: 8 make a wager with my **m** the king of Assyria:
36:12 "Has my **m** sent me to speak these words to your **m** and to you,
37: 4 whom his **m** the king of Assyria has sent to mock
37: 6 "Say to your **m,** 'Thus says the LORD:
Jer 3:14 says the LORD, for I am your **m;**
Da 1: 3 Then the king commanded his palace **m** Ashpenaz
1: 7 The palace **m** gave them other names:
1: 8 the palace **m** to allow him not to defile himself.
1: 9 and compassion from the palace **m.**
1:10 The palace **m** said to Daniel,
1:11 the guard whom the palace **m** had appointed
1:18 the palace **m** brought them into the presence
Mal 1: 6 A son honors his father, and servants their **m.**
1: 6 And if I am a **m,** where is the respect due me?
Mt 10:24 nor a slave above the **m;**
10:25 and the slave like the **m.**
10:25 If they have called the **m** of the house Beelzebul,
13:27 **'M,** did you not sow good seed in your field?
13:52 for the kingdom of heaven is like the **m** of
24:45 whom his **m** has put in charge of his household,
24:46 Blessed is that slave whom his **m** will find at work
24:48 wicked slave says to himself, 'My **m** is delayed,'
24:50 the **m** of that slave will come on a day
25:19 the **m** of those slaves came and settled accounts
25:20 saying, **'M,** you handed over to me five talents;
25:21 His **m** said to him, 'Well done,
25:21 enter into the joy of your **m.'**
25:22 saying, **'M,** you handed over to me two talents;
25:23 His **m** said to him, 'Well done,
25:23 enter into the joy of your **m.'**

Mt 25:24 saying, '**M,** I knew that you were a harsh man,
25:26 But his **m** replied, 'You wicked and lazy slave!
Mk 13:35 not know when the **m** of the house will come,
Lk 2:29 "**M,** now you are dismissing your servant in peace,
5: 5 "**M,** we have worked all night long
8:24 shouting, "**M, M,** we are perishing!"
8:45 When all denied it, Peter said, "**M,**
9:33 Peter said to Jesus, "**M,** it is good for us to be here;
9:49 "**M,** we saw someone casting out demons
12:36 be like those who are waiting for their **m** to return
12:37 Blessed are those slaves whom the **m** finds alert
12:42 and prudent manager whom his **m** will put
12:43 Blessed is that slave whom his **m** will find at work
12:45 'My **m** is delayed in coming,'
12:46 the **m** of that slave will come on a day
12:47 That slave who knew what his **m** wanted,
14:21 So the slave returned and reported this to his **m.**
14:23 Then the **m** said to the slave,
16: 3 that my **m** is taking the position away from me?
16: 5 'How much do you owe my **m?'**
16: 8 And his **m** commended the dishonest manager
17:13 saying, "Jesus, **M,** have mercy on us!"
Jn 13:16 I tell you, servants are not greater than their **m,**
15:15 the servant does not know what the **m** is doing;
15:20 'Servants are not greater than their **m.'**
1Co 3:10 like a skilled **m** builder I laid a foundation,
Eph 6: 9 for you know that both of you have the same **M**
Col 4: 1 for you know that you also have a **M** in heaven.
2Pe 2: 1 They will even deny the **M** who bought them—
Jude 1: 4 into licentiousness and deny our only **M** and Lord,
Tob 3:14 O **M,** that I am innocent of any defilement with
8:17 Be merciful to them, O **M,** and keep them safe;
Jdt 5:20 "So now, my **m** and lord, if there is any oversight
6:13 at the foot of the hill, and returned to their **m.**
11:10 lord and **m,** do not disregard what he said,
AdE 13: 2 "Having become ruler of many nations and **m** of
14:12 O King of the gods and **M** of all dominion!
Wis 18:11 the **m,** and the commoner suffered the same loss as
Sir 23: 1 O Lord, Father and **M** of my life,
32: 1 If they make you **m** of the feast,
38:27 So too is every artisan and **m** artisan who labors
2Mc 2:29 as the **m** builder of a new house must be concerned
1Es 4: 3 But the king is stronger; he is their lord and **m,**
2Es 7:*104* or a **m** his servant, or a friend his dearest friend,
4Mc 1:29 each of which the **m** cultivator,
2:24 one might say, that if reason is **m** of the emotions,
5:23 so that we **m** all pleasures and desires,
18: 2 knowing that devout reason is **m** of all emotions,

MASTER'S (29) [MASTER]

Ge 24:10 the servant took ten of his **m** camels and departed,
24:27 on the way to the house of my **m** kin."
24:36 And Sarah my **m** wife bore a son to my master
24:44 the LORD has appointed for my **m** son.'
24:48 the daughter of my **m** kinsman for his son.
24:51 and let her be the wife of your **m** son,
39: 7 a time his **m** wife cast her eyes on Joseph and said,
39: 8 But he refused and said to his **m** wife, "Look,
40: 7 who were with him in custody in his **m** house,
Ex 21: 4 the wife and her children shall be her **m**
2Sa 9: 9 to all his house I have given to your **m** grandson.
9:10 so that your **m** grandson may have food to eat;
9:10 your **m** grandson Mephibosheth shall always eat
12: 8 I gave you your **m** house, and your master's wives
12: 8 and your **m** wives into your bosom,
16: 3 The king said, "And where is your **m** son?"
2Ki 6:32 Is not the sound of his **m** feet behind him?"
9:11 When Jehu came back to his **m** officers,
10: 2 "Since your **m** sons are with you and you have
10: 3 and fight for your **m** house."
10: 6 take the heads of your **m** sons and come to me
18:24 a single captain among the least of my **m** servants,
Isa 1: 3 The ox knows its owner, and the donkey its **m** crib;
22:18 O you disgrace to your **m** house!
36: 9 a single captain among the least of my **m** servants,
Zep 1: 9 who fill their **m** house with violence and fraud.
Mt 25:18 and dug a hole in the ground and hid his **m** money.
Lk 16: 5 So, summoning his **m** debtors one by one,
Jdt 13: 1 and shut out the attendants from his **m** presence.

MASTERBUILDER (KJV) See BUILDER, MASTER

MASTERED (4) [MASTER]

Ac 19:16 with the evil spirit leaped on them, **m** them all,
4Mc 6:35 I have proved not only that reason has **m** agonies,
13: 4 for the brothers **m** both emotions and pains.
14: 1 but also **m** the emotions of brotherly love.

MASTERS (25) [MASTER]

1Sa 25:10 today who are breaking away from their **m.**
Job 3:19 and the slaves are free from their **m.**
Pr 25:13 they refresh the spirit of their **m.**
Jer 27: 4 Give them this charge for their **m:**
27: 4 This is what you shall say to your **m:**
La 1: 5 Her foes have become the **m,** her enemies prosper,
Mt 6:24 "No one can serve two **m;**
Lk 16:13 No slave can serve two **m;**
1Co 7:23 do not become slaves of human **m.**
Eph 6: 5 obey your earthly **m** with fear and trembling,
6: 9 And, **m,** do the same to them.
Col 3:22 Slaves, obey your earthly **m** in everything,
3:23 as done for the Lord and not for your **m,**
4: 1 **M,** treat your slaves justly and fairly,
1Ti 6: 1 under the yoke of slavery regard their **m** as worthy
6: 2 Those who have believing **m** must not
Tit 2: 9 to be submissive to their **m** and to give satisfaction
1Pe 2:18 accept the authority of your **m** with all deference,
2Pe 2:19 for people are slaves to whatever **m** them.
Wis 10:14 the scepter of a kingdom and authority over his **m.**
Sir 3: 7 they will serve their parents as their **m.**
4Mc 1: 4 that it **m** the emotions that hinder one from justice,
6:34 of reason when it **m** even external agonies.
6:35 that it **m** pleasures and in no respect yields to them.
7:23 the wise and courageous are **m** of their emotions.

MASTERS' (1) [MASTER]

Mt 15:27 dogs eat the crumbs that fall from their **m** table."

MASTERLESS See Index to Footnotes

MASTERY (1) [MASTER]

1Es 4:14 then, that rules them, or has the **m** over them?

MASTIC (1)

Sus 1:54 He answered, "Under a **m** tree."

MAT (8) [MATS]

Mk 2: 4 they let down the **m** on which the paralytic lay.
2: 9 or to say, 'Stand up and take your **m** and walk'?
2:11 stand up, take your **m** and go to your home."
2:12 and immediately took the **m** and went out
Jn 5: 8 "Stand up, take your **m** and walk."
5: 9 and he took up his **m** and began to walk.
5:10 it is not lawful for you to carry your **m."**
5:11 'Take up your **m** and walk.' "

MATCH (4) [MATCHED, MATCHING]

Lk 5:36 and the piece from the new will not **m** the old.
2Co 11:15 Their end will **m** their deeds.
1Mc 6:52 The Jews also made engines of war to **m** theirs,
10:71 and let us **m** strength with each other there,

MATCHED (1) [MATCH]

2Co 8:11 so that your eagerness may be **m** by completing it

MATCHING (1) [MATCH]

Eze 42:12 from the east, along the **m** wall.

MATE (4) [MATING]

Ge 7: 2 of all clean animals, the male and its **m;**
7: 2 the animals that are not clean, the male and its **m;**
Isa 34:15 the buzzards shall gather, each one with its **m.**
34:16 none shall be without its **m.**

MATERIAL (7) [MATERIALS]

Nu 19: 6 and crimson **m,** and throw them into the fire
Pr 25: 4 and the smith has **m** for a vessel;
Eze 27:24 and in carpets of colored **m,**
Ro 15:27 also to be of service to them in **m** things.
1Co 9:11 is it too much if we reap your **m** benefits?
Tob 7:13 and told her to bring writing **m;**
2Mc 2:24 the narratives of history because of the mass of **m,**

MATERIALS (7) [MATERIAL]

Ex 28: 8 on it shall be of the same workmanship and **m,**
39: 5 on it was of the same **m** and workmanship, of gold,
Lev 19:19 on a garment made of two different **m.**
1Ch 22: 5 So David provided **m** in great quantity
2Mc 1:21 When the **m** for the sacrifices were presented,
1:31 After the **m** of the sacrifice had been consumed,
1:33 and his associates had burned the **m** of

MATHUSALA (KJV) See METHUSELAH

MATING (1) [MATE]

Ge 31:10 During the **m** of the flock I once had a dream

MATRED (2)

Ge 36:39 the daughter of **M,** daughter of Me-zahab.
1Ch 1:50 and his wife's name Mehetabel daughter of **M,**

MATRITES (2)

1Sa 10:21 and the family of the **M** was taken by lot.
10:21 Finally he brought the family of the **M** near man

MATRI (KJV) See MATRITES

MATRIX (KJV) See WOMB

MATS (2) [MAT]

Mk 6:55 that whole region and began to bring the sick on **m**
Ac 5:15 and laid them on cots and **m,**

MATTAN (3)

2Ki 11:18 and they killed **M,** the priest of Baal,
2Ch 23:17 and they killed **M,** the priest of Baal,
Jer 38: 1 Now Shephatiah son of **M,**

MATTANAH (2)

Nu 21:18 From the wilderness to **M,**
Nu 21:19 from **M** to Nahaliel, from Nahaliel to Bamoth,

MATTANIAH (17) [=ZEDEKIAH]

2Ki 24:17 The king of Babylon made **M,** Jehoiachin's uncle,
1Ch 9:15 Heresh, Galal, and **M** son of Mica, son of Zichri,
25: 4 Of Heman, the sons of Heman: Bukkiah, **M,**
25:16 the ninth to **M,** his sons and his brothers, twelve;
2Ch 20:14 son of **M,** a Levite of the sons of Asaph,
29:13 and of the sons of Asaph, Zechariah and **M;**
Ezr 10:26 **M,** Zechariah, Jehiel, Abdi, Jeremoth, and Elijah.
10:27 Of the descendants of Zattu: Elioenai, Eliashib, **M,**
10:30 Adna, Chelal, Benaiah, Maaseiah, **M,** Bezalel,
10:37 **M,** Mattenai, and Jaasu.
Ne 11:17 and **M** son of Mica son of Zabdi son of Asaph,
11:22 of Bani son of Hashabiah son of **M** son of Mica,
12: 8 Binnui, Kadmiel, Sherebiah, Judah, and **M,**
12:25 **M,** Bakbukiah, Obadiah, Meshullam, Talmon,
12:35 of **M** son of Micaiah son of Zaccur son of Asaph;
13:13 as their assistant Hanan son of Zaccur son of **M,**
1Es 9:27 Of the descendants of Elam: **M** and Zechariah,

MATTATHA (1)

Lk 3:31 son of Menna, son of **M,** son of Nathan,

MATTATHIAH (1) [=MATTITHIAH]

1Es 9:43 and beside him stood **M,** Shema,

MATTATHIAS‡ (16)

Lk 3:25 son of **M,** son of Amos, son of Nahum, son
3:26 son of **M,** son of Semein, son of Josech,
1Mc 2: 1 In those days **M** son of John son of Simeon,
2:14 Then **M** and his sons tore their clothes,
2:16 and **M** and his sons were assembled.
2:17 Then the king's officers spoke to **M** as follows:
2:19 But **M** answered and said in a loud voice:
2:24 When **M** saw it, he burned with zeal
2:27 **M** cried out in the town with a loud voice, saying:
2:39 When **M** and his friends learned of it,
2:45 And **M** and his friends went around and tore down
2:49 Now the days drew near for **M** to die,
11:70 not one of them was left except **M** son of Absalom
14:29 Simon son of **M,** a priest of the sons of Joarib,
16:14 and he went down to Jericho with his sons **M**
2Mc 14:19 and **M** to give and receive pledges of friendship.

MATTATTAH (2)

Ezr 10:33 Of the descendants of Hashum: Mattenai, **M,**
1Es 9:33 and **M** and Zabad and Eliphelet and Manasseh

MATTENAI (4)

Ezr 10:33 Of the descendants of Hashum: **M,** Mattattah,
10:37 Mattaniah, **M,** and Jaasu.
Ne 12:19 of Joiarib, **M;** of Jedaiah, Uzzi;
1Es 9:33 **M** and Mattattah and Zabad and Eliphelet

MATTER (102) [MATTERS]

Ge 21:11 The **m** was very distressing to Abraham on account
24: 9 and swore to him concerning this **m.**
30:15 a small **m** that you have taken away my husband?
37:11 but his father kept the **m** in mind.
Lev 4:13 of Israel errs unintentionally and the **m** escapes
5: 1 testify as one who has seen or learned of the **m—**
6: 2 against the LORD by deceiving a neighbor in a **m**
Nu 20:19 It is only a small **m;**
Dt 3:26 Never speak to me of this **m** again!
32:47 This is no trifling **m** for you,
Jos 22:20 of Zerah break faith in the **m** of the devoted things,
Jdg 18:23 the **m** that you come with such a company?"
18:24 How then can you ask me, 'What is the **m?'** "
Ru 3:18 my daughter, until you learn how the **m** turns out,
3:18 but will settle the **m** today."
1Sa 10:16 But about the **m** of the kingship,
11: 4 they reported the **m** in the hearing of the people;
11: 5 and Saul said, "What is the **m** with the people,
20:23 As for the **m** about which you and I have spoken,
21: 2 "The king has charged me with a **m,**
21: 2 'No one must know anything of the **m**
30:24 Who would listen to you in this **m?**
2Sa 11:25 'Do not let this **m** trouble you,
15:11 knowing nothing of the **m.**
19:42 Why then are you angry over this **m?**
20:18 and so they would settle a **m.**
21: 4 "It is not a **m** of silver or gold between us and Saul
1Ki 5: 8 I will fulfill all your needs in the **m** of cedar
11:10 and had commanded him concerning this **m,**
13:34 This **m** became sin to the house of Jeroboam,
15: 5 except in the **m** of Uriah the Hittite.
1Ch 2: 7 who transgressed in the **m** of the devoted thing;
2Ch 32:31 in the **m** of the envoys of the officials of Babylon,
Ezr 4:22 Moreover, take care not to be slack in this **m;**
5:17 Let the king send us his pleasure in this **m."**
10: 9 because of this **m** and because of the heavy rain.
10:13 for many of us have transgressed in this **m.**
10:16 the tenth month they sat down to examine the **m.**
Est 2:22 But the **m** came to the knowledge of Mordecai,
9:26 and of what they had faced in this **m,**
Job 9:19 If it is a **m** of justice, who can summon him?
19:28 and, 'The root of the **m** is found in him';
22:28 You will decide on a **m,**
Pr 6:35 and refuses a bribe no **m** how great.
16:20 Those who are attentive to a **m** will prosper,
Ecc 3: 1 and a time for every **m** under heaven:
3:17 for he has appointed a time for every **m,**

Ecc 5: 8 do not be amazed at the **m;**
8: 3 do not delay when the **m** is unpleasant,
8: 6 For every **m** has its time and way,
10:20 or some winged creature tell the **m.**
12:13 The end of the **m;** all has been heard.
Da 1:20 In every **m** of wisdom and understanding
2:15 Arioch then explained the **m** to Daniel.
3:16 to present a defense to you in this **m.**
5:15 not able to give the interpretation of the **m.**
5:26 This is the interpretation of the **m:**
7:16 to me the interpretation of the **m:**
7:28 but I kept the **m** in my mind.
Mk 9:10 So they kept the **m** to themselves,
10:10 the disciples asked him again about this **m.**
Ac 4:15 to leave the council while they discussed the **m**
15: 6 and the elders met together to consider this **m.**
18:14 "If it were a **m** of crime or serious villainy,
18:15 since it is a **m** of questions about words and names
28:23 From morning until evening he explained the **m**
Ro 2:29 and real circumcision is a **m** of the heart—
1Co 11:22 In this **m** I do not commend you!
2Co 7:11 you have proved yourselves guiltless in the **m.**
8:10 And in this **m** I am giving my advice:
Php 1:18 What does it **m?** Just this,
4:15 no church shared with me in the **m** of giving
1Th 4: 6 or exploit a brother or sister in this **m,**
2Pe 1:20 of scripture is a **m** of one's own interpretation,
AdE 1:13 your ruling and judgment on this **m."**
2:22 The **m** became known to Mordecai,
3:15 The **m** was expedited also in Susa.
Wis 11:17 which created the world out of formless **m,**
15:13 from earthy **m** fragile vessels and carved images.
Sir 11: 9 Do not argue about a **m** that does not concern you,
15:15 and to act faithfully is a **m** of your own choice.
31:15 and in every **m** be thoughtful.
33: 6 like a stallion that neighs no **m** who the rider is.
1Mc 10:35 from them or annoy any of them about any **m.**
10:63 to bring charges against him about any **m,**
2Mc 1:33 When this **m** became known,
1:34 the king investigated the **m,**
2:26 it is no light **m** but calls for sweat and loss of sleep,
13:13 to march out and decide the **m** by the help of God
14: 9 O king, with the details of this **m,**
15:17 the **m** by fighting hand to hand with all courage,
1Es 2:20 we think it best not to neglect such a **m,**
8:70 and from the beginning of this **m** the leaders and
9:13 from the wrath of the Lord over this **m."**
9:14 and Jahzeiah son of Tikvah undertook the **m**
9:16 they began their sessions to investigate the **m.**
3Mc 4:19 he was clearly convinced about the **m**
5:27 inquired what the **m** was for which this had been
5:40 and again revoking your decree in the **m?**
5:46 and urged the king on to the **m** at hand.
2Es 10:31 "What is the **m** with you?
4Mc 4: 5 On receiving authority to deal with this **m,**

MATTERS‡ (34) [MATTER]

Dt 17: 8 any such **m** of dispute in your towns—
1Ch 27: 1 and their officers who served the king in all **m**
2Ch 19:11 the chief priest is over you in all **m** of the LORD;
19:11 of the house of Judah, in all the king's **m;**
Ne 11:24 at the king's hand in all **m** concerning the people.
Mt 23:23 and have neglected the weightier **m** of the law:
Ac 18:15 I do not wish to be a judge of these **m."**
1Co 6: 3 to say nothing of ordinary **m?**
7: 1 Now concerning the **m** about which you wrote:
2Co 8:22 and found eager in many **m,**
Col 2:16 in **m** of food and drink or of observing festivals,
AdE 10: 5 the dream that I had concerning these **m,**
16: 7 as from investigation of **m** close at hand.
Sir 3:23 Do not meddle in **m** that are beyond you,
5:15 In great and small **m** cause no harm,
11:10 My child, do not busy yourself with many **m;**
Aza 1: 6 in all **m** we have sinned grievously.
1Mc 3:48 into those **m** about which the Gentiles consulted
2Mc 2:30 to discuss **m** from every side,
11:17 and have asked about the **m** indicated in it.
11:20 And concerning such **m** and their details,
11:36 But as to the **m** that he decided are to be referred to
15:37 This, then, is how **m** turned out with Nicanor,
1Es 8:12 in order to look into **m** in Judea and Jerusalem,
3Mc 1: 4 **m** were turning out rather in favor of Antiochus,
3: 2 While these **m** were being arranged,
3: 8 and expected that **m** would change;
5:30 mind had been deranged concerning these **m;**
2Es 4:35 the righteous in their chambers ask about these **m,**
13:56 and explain weighty and wondrous **m** to you."
4Mc 1:16 of divine and human **m** and the causes of these.
1:17 by which we learn divine **m** reverently
2: 9 In all other **m** we can recognize that reason rules
5:20 in **m** either small or great is of equal seriousness,

MATTHAN (2)

Mt 1:15 Eleazar the father of **M,** and **M** the father of Jacob,

MATTHAT (2)

Lk 3:24 son of **M,** son of Levi, son of Melchi, son
3:29 son of Eliezer, son of Jorim, son of **M,**

MATTHEW (5) [=LEVI]

Mt 9: 9 he saw a man called **M** sitting at the tax booth;
10: 3 Thomas and **M** the tax collector;
Mk 3:18 and **M,** and Thomas, and James son of Alphaeus,
Lk 6:15 and **M,** and Thomas, and James son of Alphaeus,
Ac 1:13 Bartholomew and **M,** James son of Alphaeus,

MATTHIAS (2)

Ac 1:23 who was also known as Justus, and **M.**
1:26 And they cast lots for them, and the lot fell on **M;**

MATTIA See Index to Footnotes

MATTITHIAH (8) [=MATTATHIAH]

1Ch 9:31 and **M,** one of the Levites, the firstborn of Shallum
15:18 Benaiah, Maaseiah, **M,** Eliphelehu, and Mikneiah,
15:21 but **M,** Eliphelehu, Mikneiah, Obed-edom, Jeiel,
16: 5 Jehiel, **M,** Eliab, Benaiah, Obed-edom, and Jeiel,
25: 3 Zeri, Jeshaiah, Shimei, Hashabiah, and **M,** six,
25:21 **M,** his sons and his brothers, twelve;
Ezr 10:43 Jeiel, **M,** Zabad, Zebina, Jaddai, Joel, and Benaiah.
Ne 8: 4 and beside him stood **M,** Shema, Anaiah, Uriah,

MATTOCKS (2)

1Sa 13:20 the Philistines to sharpen their plowshare, **m,** axes,
13:21 of a shekel for the plowshares and for the **m,**

MATURE (8) [MATURITY]

Lk 8:14 and pleasures of life, and their fruit does not **m.**
1Co 2: 6 Yet among the **m** we do speak wisdom,
Php 3:15 of us then who are **m** be of the same mind;
Col 1:28 so that we may present everyone **m** in Christ.
4:12 so that you may stand **m** and fully assured
Heb 5:14 But solid food is for the **m,**
Jas 1: 4 so that you may be **m** and complete,
1Mc 16: 3 and you by Heaven's mercy are **m** in years.

MATURITY‡ (4) [MATURE]

Eph 4:13 to **m,** to the measure of the full stature of Christ.
Wis 3:16 But children of adulterers will not come to **m,**
4: 5 branches will be broken off before they come to **m,**
4Mc 18: 9 In the time of my **m** I remained with my husband,

MAUL (1) [MAULED, MAULS]

Mt 7: 6 trample them under foot and turn and **m** you.

MAULED (1) [MAUL]

2Ki 2:24 out of the woods and **m** forty-two of the boys.

MAULS (1) [MAUL]

Lk 9:39 it **m** him and will scarcely leave him.

MAW (KJV) See STOMACH

MAXIMS (2)

Job 13:12 Your **m** are proverbs of ashes,
Sir 8: 8 but busy yourself with their **m;**

MAY (1702) See Index of Articles Etc.

MAZITIAS (1)

1Es 9:35 **M,** Zabad, Iddo, Joel, Benaiah.

MAZZAROTH (1)

Job 38:32 Can you lead forth the **M** in their season,

ME (4470) [I] See Index of Articles Etc.

ME-JARKON (1)

Jos 19:46 **M,** and Rakkon at the border opposite Joppa.

ME-ZAHAB (2)

Ge 36:39 the daughter of Matred, daughter of **M.**
1Ch 1:50 daughter of Matred, daughter of **M.**

MEADOW‡ (1) [MEADOWS]

Hos 9:13 as a young palm planted in a lovely **m,**

MEADOWS (3) [MEADOW]

Ps 65:13 the **m** clothe themselves with flocks,
Zep 2: 6 **m** for shepherds and folds for flocks.
2Es 15:42 trees of the forests, and grass of the **m,**

MEAGER (2)

2Sa 12: 3 it used to eat of his **m** fare, and drink from his cup,
Sir 31: 4 The poor person toils to make a **m** living,

MEAH (KJV) See HUNDRED

MEAL (26) [MEALS, MEALTIME]

Ge 43:31 and controlling himself he said, "Serve the **m."**
1Sa 20: 5 and I should not fail to sit with the king at the **m;**
2Sa 17:28 wheat, barley, **m,** parched grain, beans and lentils,
1Ki 4:22 of choice flour, and sixty cors of **m,**
17:12 only a handful of **m** in a jar, and a little oil in a jug;
17:14 of **m** will not be emptied and the jug of oil will
17:16 The jar of **m** was not emptied,
2Ki 4: 8 who urged him to have a **m.**
4: 8 he would stop there for a **m.**
7: 1 about this time a measure of choice **m** shall be sold
7:16 So a measure of choice **m** was sold for a shekel,
7:18 and a measure of choice **m** for a shekel,
1Ch 12:40 abundant provisions of **m,** cakes of figs,
Isa 47: 2 Take the millstones and grind **m,** remove your veil,
Hos 8: 7 standing grain has no heads, it shall yield no **m;**
Mt 24:41 Two women will be grinding **m** together;
26:19 and they prepared the Passover **m.**
Mk 14:16 and they prepared the Passover **m.**
Lk 14: 1 the house of a leader of the Pharisees to eat a **m** on
17:35 There will be two women grinding **m** together;
22: 8 the Passover **m** for us that we may eat it."
22:13 and they prepared the Passover **m.**
1Co 10:27 If an unbeliever invites you to a **m**
Heb 12:16 who sold his birthright for a single **m.**
Tob 2:12 and also gave her a young goat for a **m.**
2Mc 6:21 of the sacrificial **m** that had been commanded by

MEALS (2) [MEAL]

Sir 41:19 and of leaning on your elbow at **m;**
LtJ 6:30 Women serve **m** for gods of silver and gold

MEALTIME (1) [MEAL]

Ru 2:14 At **m** Boaz said to her, "Come here,

MEAN (37) [MEANING, MEANINGLESS, MEANINGS, MEANNESS, MEANS, MEANT]

Ge 33: 8 "What do you **m** by all this company that I met?"
Ex 2:14 Do you **m** to kill me as you killed the Egyptian?"
12:26 'What do you **m** by this observance?'
13:14 the future your child asks you, 'What does this **m?'**
Dt 15: 9 Be careful that you do not entertain a **m** thought,
Jos 4: 6 'What do those stones **m** to you?'
4:21 'What do these stones **m?'**
1Sa 4: 6 in the camp of the Hebrews **m?"**
25: 3 but the man was surly and **m;** he was a Calebite.
Pr 23: 7 they say to you; but they do not **m** it.
Isa 3:15 What do you **m** by crushing my people,
22: 1 What do you **m** that you have gone up, all of you,
Jer 4:30 what do you **m** that you dress in crimson,
Eze 17:12 Do you not know what these things **m?**
18: 2 What do you **m** by repeating this proverb
24:19 "Will you not tell us what these things **m** for us,
37:18 "Will you not show us what you **m** by these?"
Mk 9:10 what this rising from the dead could **m.**
Lk 20:17 "What then does this text **m:**
Jn 7:36 What does he **m** by saying,
8:33 What do you **m** by saying,
16:17 "What does he **m** by saying to us, 'A little while,
16:18 "What does he **m** by this 'a little while'?
Ac 2:12 saying to one another, "What does this **m?"**
Ro 11:12 how much more will their full inclusion **m!**
1Co 1:12 What I **m** is that each of you says,
7:29 I **m,** brothers and sisters, the appointed time has
10:29 I **m** the other's conscience,
2Co 1:24 I do not **m** to imply that we lord it over your faith;
8:13 I do not **m** that there should be relief for others
Eph 4: 9 what does it **m** but that he had also descended into
Sir 14: 5 one is **m** to himself, to whom will he be generous?
Sus 1:22 For if I do this, it will **m** death for me;
2Mc 5:11 he took it to **m** that Judea was in revolt.
14: 7 my ancestral glory—I **m** the high priesthood—
14:14 of the Jews would **m** prosperity for themselves.
4Mc 1: 2 I **m,** of course, rational judgment.

MEANING (13) [MEAN]

Ge 21:29 "What is the **m** of these seven ewe lambs
40: 5 and each dream with its own **m.**
41:11 he and I, each having a dream with its own **m.**
Dt 6:20 "What is the **m** of the decrees and the statutes and
1Sa 4:21 She named the child Ichabod, **m,**
Lk 9:45 its **m** was concealed from them,
1Co 4: 6 that you may learn through us the **m** of the saying,
5:10 not at all **m** the immoral of this world,
14:11 If then I do not know the **m** of a sound,
Sir 21:18 knowledge is talk that has no **m.**
47:15 and you filled it with proverbs having deep **m.**
2Es 10:40 This therefore is the **m** of the vision.
12: 8 the interpretation and **m** of this terrifying vision so

MEANINGLESS (1) [MEAN]

1Ti 1: 6 from these and turned to **m** talk,

MEANINGS (1) [MEAN]

Sir 39: 3 he seeks out the hidden **m** of proverbs

MEANNESS (3) [MEAN]

Sir 14: 6 this is the punishment for his **m.**
14: 7 and in the end he reveals his **m.**
29: 7 Many refuse to lend, not because of **m,**

MEANS (76) [MEAN]

Ge 41:32 And the doubling of Pharaoh's dream **m** that
Ex 34: 7 yet by no **m** clearing the guilty,
Lev 16:21 into the wilderness by **m** of someone designated
25:26 but then prospers and finds sufficient **m** to do so,
25:28 But if there is not sufficient **m** to recover it,
Nu 14:18 but by no **m** clearing the guilty,
Dt 30:20 for that **m** life to you and length of days,
1Sa 6: 3 but by all **m** return him a guilt offering.
22:15 that I have inquired of God for him? By no **m!**
2Sa 17:16 but by all **m** cross over;
Est 3: 7 they cast Pur—which **m** "the lot"—
Ecc 11: 2 Divide your **m** seven ways, or even eight,
Jer 30:11 and I will by no **m** leave you unpunished.

Jer 44:25 By all **m,** keep your vows and make your libations!
44:28 and I will by no **m** leave you unpunished.
Na 1: 3 and the LORD will by no **m** clear the guilty.
Mt 1:23 and they shall name him Emmanuel," which **m,**
2: 6 are by no **m** least among the rulers of Judah;
9:13 Go and learn what this **m,** 'I desire mercy,
12: 7 But if you had known what this **m,**
27:33 to a place called Golgotha (which **m** Place of
Mk 5:41 "Talitha cum," which **m,** "Little girl, get up!"
9:41 the name of Christ will by no **m** lose the reward.
15:22 to the place called Golgotha (which **m** the place of
15:34 which **m,** "My God, my God,
Lk 16: 9 by **m** of dishonest wealth so that when it is gone,
Jn 1:38 "Rabbi" (which translated **m** Teacher),
8:22 Is that what he **m** by saying, 'Where I am going,
9: 7 "Go, wash in the pool of Siloam" (which **m** Sent).
20:16 "Rabbouni!" (which **m** Teacher).
Ac 4:36 the name Barnabas (which **m** "son
10:14 But Peter said, "By no **m,** Lord;
11: 8 But I replied, 'By no **m,** Lord;
17:20 so we would like to know what it **m."**
Ro 3: 4 By no **m!** Although everyone is a liar,
3: 6 By no **m!** For then how could God judge the
3:31 then overthrow the law by this faith? By no **m!**
6: 2 By no **m!** How can we who died to sin
6:15 under law but under grace? By no **m!**
7: 7 That the law is sin? By no **m!**
7:13 bring death to me? By no **m!**
9: 8 This **m** that it is not the children of the flesh
9:14 Is there injustice on God's part? By no **m!**
11: 1 has God rejected his people? By no **m!**
11:11 stumbled so as to fall? By no **m!**
11:12 Now if their stumbling **m** riches for the world,
11:12 and if their defeat **m** riches for Gentiles,
1Co 9:22 that I might by all **m** save some.
2Co 8: 3 they voluntarily gave according to their **m,** and
even beyond their **m,**
8:11 be matched by completing it according to your **m.**
Php 1:22 that **m** fruitful labor for me;
1Th 4:15 will by no **m** precede those who have died.
1Ti 1: 9 This **m** understanding that the law is laid down not
6: 5 imagining that godliness is a **m** of gain.
Heb 7: 2 in the first place, **m** "king of righteousness";
2Pe 3: 5 and an earth was formed out of water and by **m**
Tob 6:13 For I know that Raguel can by no **m** keep her
AdE 9:26 in their language this is the word that **m** "lots").
Wis 11:17 did not lack the **m** to send upon them a multitude
12:27 being punished by **m** of them,
15:12 however one can, even by base **m.**
18: 8 For by the same **m** by which
Sir 8:13 Do not give surety beyond your **m;**
8:16 because bloodshed **m** nothing to them,
12: 5 for by **m** of it they might subdue you;
14:11 My child, treat yourself well, according to your **m,**
1Mc 14:10 and furnished them with the **m** of defense,
2Mc 1:36 called this "nephthar," which **m** purification,
3Mc 1:11 the king was by no **m** persuaded.
2:24 though he had been punished, he by no **m** repented,
3: 1 and put to death by the most cruel **m.**
4:19 charging that they had been bribed to contrive a **m**
2Es 13:38 and will destroy them without effort by **m** of
4Mc 1:19 since by **m** of it reason rules over the emotions.
4:24 When, by **m** of his decrees, he has not been able

MEANT (13) [MEAN]

Lev 10: 3 "This is what the LORD **m** when he said,
Dt 19:19 to the false witness just as the false witness had **m**
Jdg 13:23 "If the LORD had **m** to kill us,
Pr 27: 6 Well **m** are the wounds a friend inflicts,
Lk 8: 9 Then his disciples asked him what this parable **m.**
Jn 16:19 "Are you discussing among yourselves what I **m**
Ro 2: 4 not realize that God's kindness is **m** to lead you
1Co 6:13 "Food is **m** for the stomach and the stomach
6:13 The body is **m** not for fornication but for the Lord,
2Mc 12: 8 that the people in Jamnia **m** in the same way
1Es 5:66 to find out what the sound of the trumpets **m.**
3Mc 1: 3 that this man incurred the vengeance **m** for
2Es 10:25 While I was wondering what this **m,**

MEANWHILE (29)

Ge 37:36 **M** the Midianites had sold him in Egypt
Nu 32:17 **M** our little ones will stay in the fortified towns
Jos 10:16 **M,** these five kings fled and hid themselves in
Jdg 20:48 **M,** the Israelites turned back against
2Sa 18:17 **M** all the Israelites fled to their homes.
19: 8 **M,** all the Israelites had fled to their homes.
1Ki 10:13 **M** King Solomon gave to the queen
2Ch 9:12 **M** King Solomon granted the queen
20:13 **M** all Judah stood before the LORD,
Jer 37: 5 **M,** the army of Pharaoh had come out of Egypt;
Jnh 1: 5 **m,** had gone down into the hold of the ship
Lk 1:21 **M** the people were waiting for Zechariah,
12: 1 **M,** when the crowd gathered by the thousands,
Jn 4:31 **M** the disciples were urging him, "Rabbi,
19:25 **M,** standing near the cross
Ac 9: 1 **M** Saul, still breathing threats and murder against
9:31 **M** the church throughout Judea, Galilee,
9:43 **M** he stayed in Joppa for some time with
12:16 **M** Peter continued knocking;
19:32 **M,** some were shouting one thing, some another;
20:12 **M** they had taken the boy away alive and were not
Tob 11: 5 **M** Anna sat looking intently down the road
Jdt 7:13 **M,** we and our people will go up to the tops of
AdE 1: 9 **M,** Queen Vashti gave a drinking party for
2:19 **M** Mordecai was serving in the courtyard.
1Mc 6:18 **M** the garrison in the citadel kept hemming Israel
15:37 **M** Trypho embarked on a ship and escaped
2Mc 8: 1 **M** Judas, who was also called Maccabeus,
3Mc 1:24 **M** the crowd, as before, was engaged in prayer,

MEARAH (1)

Jos 13: 4 and **M** that belongs to the Sidonians, to Aphek,

MEASURE‡ (68) [MEASURED, MEASUREMENT, MEASUREMENTS, MEASURES, MEASURING]

Ge 41:49 that he stopped measuring it; it was beyond **m.**
Ex 29:40 a **m** of choice flour mixed with one-fourth of a hin
Nu 35: 5 You shall **m,** outside the town,
Dt 21: 2 and your judges shall come out to **m** the distances
25:15 you shall have only a full and honest **m,**
1Ki 6:25 both cherubim had the same **m** and the same form.
7: 9 cut according to **m,** sawed with saws,
7:11 There were costly stones above, cut to **m,**
2Ki 7: 1 about this time a **m** of choice meal shall be sold for
7:16 So a **m** of choice meal was sold for a shekel,
7:18 and a **m** of choice meal for a shekel,
Job 11: 9 Its **m** is longer than the earth,
28:25 and apportioned out the waters by **m;**
Ps 39: 4 and what is the **m** of my days;
80: 5 and given them tears to drink in full **m.**
147: 5 his understanding is beyond **m.**
Isa 5:14 and opened its mouth beyond **m;**
40:12 enclosed the dust of the earth in a **m,**
47: 9 and widowhood shall come upon you in full **m,**
56:12 tomorrow will be like today, great beyond **m."**
65: 7 will **m** into their laps full payment for their actions.
Jer 10:24 Correct me, O LORD, but in just **m;**
30:11 I will chastise you in just **m,**
46:28 I will chastise you in just **m,**
La 5:22 and are angry with us beyond **m.**
Eze 4:11 you shall drink water by **m,** one-sixth of a hin;
4:16 and they shall drink water by **m** and in dismay.
43:10 and let them **m** the pattern;
45: 3 In the holy district you shall **m** off
45:11 The ephah and the bath shall be of the same **m,**
45:11 the homer shall be the standard **m.**
48:30 to be four thousand five hundred cubits by **m,**
48:33 to be four thousand five hundred cubits by **m,**
Da 8:23 when the transgressions have reached their full **m,**
Hos 3: 2 of silver and a homer of barley and a **m** of wine.
Mic 6:10 and the scant **m** that is accursed?
Zec 2: 2 He answered me, "To **m** Jerusalem,
Mt 7: 2 and the **m** you give will be the **m** you get.
23:32 Fill up, then, the **m** of your ancestors.
Mk 4:24 the **m** you give will be the **m** you get,
7:37 They were astounded beyond **m,** saying,
Lk 6:38 A good **m,** pressed down, shaken together,
6:38 the **m** you give will be the **m** you get back."
Jn 3:34 for he gives the Spirit without **m.**
Ro 7:13 the commandment might become sinful beyond **m.**
12: 3 according to the **m** of faith that God has assigned.
2Co 4:17 for an eternal weight of glory beyond all **m,**
10:12 But when they **m** themselves by one another,
Eph 4: 7 But each of us was given grace according to the **m**
4:13 to maturity, to the **m** of the full stature of Christ.
1Th 2:16 Thus they have constantly been filling up the **m**
Rev 11: 1 "Come and **m** the temple of God and the altar
11: 2 but do not **m** the court outside the temple;
18: 7 so give her a like **m** of torment and grief.
21:15 a measuring rod of gold to **m** the city and its gates
Wis 11:20 But you have arranged all things by **m** and number
Sir 1: 9 he saw her and took her **m;**
18: 5 Who can **m** his majestic power?
2Mc 6:14 to punish them until they have reached the full **m**
1Es 8:78 now in some **m** mercy has come to us from you,
2Es 4: 5 or **m** for me a blast of wind,
4:37 and measured the times by **m,** and numbered
4:37 not move or arouse them until that **m** is fulfilled.' "
8:21 whose throne is beyond **m** and whose glory is
9: 1 **"M** carefully in your mind,

MEASURED (55) [MEASURE]

Ex 16:18 But when they **m** it with an omer,
30:24 of cassia—**m** by the sanctuary shekel—
38:24 shekels, **m** by the sanctuary shekel.
38:25 shekel, **m** by the sanctuary shekel;
38:26 half a shekel, **m** by the sanctuary shekel),
Ru 3:15 So she held it, and he **m** out six measures of barley,
2Sa 8: 2 **m** them off with a cord;
8: 2 he **m** two lengths of cord for those who were to
1Ki 6:25 The other cherub also **m** ten cubits;
7:38 basin held forty baths, each basin **m** four cubits;
Isa 40:12 Who has **m** the waters in the hollow of his hand
Jer 13:25 This is your lot, the portion I have **m** out to you,
31:37 If the heavens above can be **m,**
33:22 be numbered and the sands of the sea cannot be **m,**
Eze 40: 5 so he **m** the thickness of the wall, one reed;
40: 6 going up its steps, and **m** the threshold of the gate,
40: 8 he **m** the inner vestibule of the gateway, one cubit.
40: 9 he **m** the vestibule of the gateway, eight cubits;
40:11 he **m** the width of the opening of the gateway,
40:13 Then he **m** the gate from the back of the one recess
40:14 He **m** also the vestibule, twenty cubits;
40:19 Then he **m** the distance from the inner front of
40:20 he **m** the gate of the outer court that faced north—
40:23 he **m** from gate to gate, one hundred cubits.
40:24 and he **m** its pilasters and its vestibule;
40:27 and he **m** from gate to gate toward the south,
40:28 and he **m** the south gate;
40:32 the inner court on the east side, and he **m** the gate;
40:35 Then he brought me to the north gate, and he **m** it;
40:47 He **m** the court, one hundred cubits deep,
40:48 to the vestibule of the temple and **m** the pilasters of
41: 1 he brought me to the nave, and **m** the pilasters;
41: 2 He **m** the length of the nave, forty cubits,
41: 3 the inner room and **m** the pilasters of the entrance,
41: 4 He **m** the depth of the room, twenty cubits,
41: 5 Then he **m** the wall of the temple, six cubits thick;
41: 8 the foundations of the side chambers **m** a full reed
41:13 Then he **m** the temple, one hundred cubits deep;
41:15 Then he **m** the depth of the building facing
42:15 and **m** the temple area all around.
42:16 He **m** the east side with the measuring reed,
42:17 Then he turned and **m** the north side,
42:18 Then he turned and **m** the south side,
42:19 Then he turned to the west side and **m,**
42:20 He **m** it on the four sides.
47: 3 the man **m** one thousand cubits,
47: 4 Again he **m** one thousand,
47: 4 Again he **m** one thousand,
47: 5 Again he **m** one thousand,
Hos 1:10 which can be neither **m** nor numbered;
Rev 21:16 he **m** the city with his rod, fifteen hundred miles;
21:17 He also **m** its wall, one hundred forty-four cubits
Wis 4: 8 or **m** by number of years;
2Es 4:37 and **m** the times by measure, and numbered
16:57 he has **m** the sea and its contents;

MEASUREMENT (1) [MEASURE]

Rev 21:17 one hundred forty-four cubits by human **m,**

MEASUREMENTS (2) [MEASURE]

2Ch 3: 3 These are Solomon's **m** for building the house
Job 38: 5 Who determined its **m**—surely you know!

MEASURES‡ (20) [MEASURE]

Ge 18: 6 "Make ready quickly three **m** of choice flour,
Dt 25:14 You shall not have in your house two kinds of **m,**
Ru 3:15 she held it, and he measured out six **m** of barley,
3:17 "He gave me these six **m** of barley, for he said,
1Sa 25:18 five sheep ready dressed, five **m** of parched grain,
1Ki 18:32 large enough to contain two **m** of seed.
2Ki 7: 1 and two **m** of barley for a shekel,
7:16 and two **m** of barley for a shekel,
7:18 "Two **m** of barley shall be sold for a shekel,
1Ch 23:29 and all **m** of quantity or size.
Pr 20:10 and diverse **m** are both alike an abomination to
Hag 2:16 When one came to a heap of twenty **m,**
2:16 when one came to the winevat to draw fifty **m,**
Mt 13:33 with three **m** of flour until all of it was leavened."
Lk 13:21 with three **m** of flour until all of it was leavened."
Ac 27:17 hoisting it up they took **m** to undergird the ship;
Bel 1: 3 of choice flour and forty sheep and six **m** of wine.
2Mc 4:21 and he took **m** for his own security.
1Es 8:95 and we are with you to take strong **m."**
2Es 6: 4 and before the **m** of the firmaments were named,

MEASURING (17) [MEASURE]

Ge 41:49 that he stopped **m** it; it was beyond measure.
Lev 19:35 You shall not cheat in **m** length, weight,
2Ki 21:13 the **m** line for Samaria, and the plummet for
Jer 31:39 And the **m** line shall go out farther,
Eze 40: 3 with a linen cord and a **m** reed in his hand;
40: 5 the **m** reed in the man's hand was six long cubits,
42:15 he had finished **m** the interior of the temple area,
42:16 He measured the east side with the **m** reed,
42:16 five hundred cubits by the **m** reed.
42:17 five hundred cubits by the **m** reed.
42:18 five hundred cubits by the **m** reed.
42:19 five hundred cubits by the **m** reed.
48:10 an allotment **m** twenty-five thousand cubits on
Zec 1:16 the **m** line shall be stretched out over Jerusalem.
2: 1 up and saw a man with a **m** line in his hand.
Rev 11: 1 Then I was given a **m** rod like a staff,
21:15 The angel who talked to me had a **m** rod of gold

MEAT (54) [MEATS]

Ex 16: 8 the LORD gives you **m** to eat in the evening
16:12 say to them, 'At twilight you shall eat **m,**
22:31 not eat any **m** that is mangled by beasts in the field;
Nu 11: 4 and said, "If only we had **m** to eat!
11:13 Where am I to get **m** to give to all this people?
11:13 For they come weeping to me and say, 'Give us **m**
11:18 for tomorrow, and you shall eat **m;**
11:18 saying, 'If only we had **m** to eat!
11:18 the LORD will give you **m,** and you shall eat.
11:21 and you say, 'I will give them **m,**
11:33 But while the **m** was still between their teeth,
Dt 12:15 and eat **m** within any of your towns,
12:20 and you say, "I am going to eat some **m,"** because
you wish to eat **m,** you may eat **m** whenever you
12:23 and you shall not eat the life with the **m.**
12:27 both the **m** and the blood, on the altar of
12:27 of the LORD your God, but the **m** you may eat.
14: 8 You shall not eat their **m,**
16: 4 of the **m** of what you slaughter on the evening of
Jdg 6:19 the **m** he put in a basket,
6:20 "Take the **m** and the unleavened cakes,
6:21 and touched the **m** and the unleavened cakes;
6:21 and consumed the **m** and the unleavened cakes;
1Sa 2:13 while the **m** was boiling, with a three-pronged fork
2:15 "Give **m** for the priest to roast; for he will not
accept boiled **m** from you,

1Sa 25:11 and the **m** that I have butchered for my shearers,
2Sa 6:19 to each a cake of bread, a portion of **m**,
1Ki 17: 6 ravens brought him bread and **m** in the morning, and bread and **m** in the evening;
1Ch 16: 3 to each a loaf of bread, a portion of **m**,
Ps 78:20 or provide **m** for his people?"
Pr 23:20 or among gluttonous eaters of **m**;
Isa 22:13 eating **m** and drinking wine.
44:16 over this half he roasts **m**, eats it and is satisfied.
44:19 I roasted **m** and have eaten.
Eze 11: 3 this city is the pot, and we are the **m**.'
11: 7 slain whom you have placed within it are the **m**,
11:11 and you shall not be the **m** inside it;
24:10 Heap up the logs, kindle the fire; boil the **m** well,
Da 10: 3 no **m** or wine had entered my mouth,
Mic 3: 3 and chop them up like **m** in a kettle,
Hag 2:12 If one carries consecrated **m** in the fold
Ro 14:21 it is good not to eat **m** or drink wine or do anything
1Co 8:13 food is a cause of their falling, I will never eat **m**,
10:25 in the **m** market without raising any question on
LtJ 6:28 Likewise their wives preserve some of the **m**
2Mc 6:21 and privately urged him to bring **m**
2Es 9:24 and taste no **m** and drink no wine,
4Mc 5: 8 why should you abhor eating the very excellent **m**
5:14 in this fashion to eat **m** unlawfully,
6:15 We will set before you some cooked **m**;
10: 1 to save himself by tasting the **m**.

MEATS (1) [MEAT]
4Mc 5:26 but he has forbidden us to eat **m** that would be

MEBUNNAI (1)
2Sa 23:27 Abiezer of Anathoth; **M** the Hushathite;

MECHERATHITE (1)
1Ch 11:36 Hepher the **M**, Ahijah the Pelonite,

MECONAH (1)
Ne 11:28 in Ziklag, in **M** and its villages,

MEDAD (2)
Nu 11:26 one named Eldad, and the other named **M**,
11:27 "Eldad and **M** are prophesying in the camp."

MEDAN (2)
Ge 25: 2 She bore him Zimran, Jokshan, **M**, Midian,
1Ch 1:32 she bore Zimran, Jokshan, **M**, Midian, Ishbak,

MEDDLE (1) [MEDDLES, MEDDLING]
Sir 3:23 Do not **m** in matters that are beyond you,

MEDDLES (1) [MEDDLE]
Pr 26:17 by the ears is one who **m** in the quarrel of another.

MEDDLING (1) [MEDDLE]
Sir 41:22 of **m** with his servant-girl—do not approach her

MEDE (3) [MEDIA]
Da 5:31 And Darius the **M** received the kingdom,
9: 1 by birth a **M**, who became king over the realm of
11: 1 As for me, in the first year of Darius the **M**,

MEDEBA (6)
Nu 21:30 and we laid waste until fire spread to **M**."
Jos 13: 9 and all the tableland from **M** as far as Dibon;
13:16 and all the tableland by **M**;
1Ch 19: 7 who came and camped before **M**.
Isa 15: 2 over Nebo and over **M** Moab wails.
1Mc 9:36 of Jambri from **M** came out and seized John

MEDES (18) [MEDIA]
2Ki 17: 6 the river of Gozan, and in the cities of the **M**.
18:11 the river of Gozan, and in the cities of the **M**,
Est 1:10 the laws of the Persians and the **M** so that it may
Isa 13:17 See, I am stirring up the **M** against them,
Jer 51:11 up the spirit of the kings of the **M**,
51:28 the nations for war against her, the kings of the **M**,
Da 5:28 your kingdom is divided and given to the **M**
6: 8 according to the law of the **M** and the Persians,
6:12 according to the law of the **M** and Persians,
6:15 the **M** and Persians that no interdict or ordinance
Ac 2: 9 **M**, Elamites, and residents of Mesopotamia,
Jdt 1: 1 In those days Arphaxad ruled over the **M**
16:10 the **M** were daunted at her daring.
AdE 1:14 the Persians and **M** who were closest to the king—
1:19 of the **M** and Persians so that it may not be altered,
10: 2 the annals of the kings of the Persians and the **M**.
1Mc 1: 1 of the Persians and the **M**,
2Es 1: 3 in the country of the **M** in the reign of Artaxerxes,

MEDIA (38) [MEDE, MEDES, MEDIAN]
Ezr 6: 2 the capital in the province of **M**,
Est 1: 3 of Persia and **M** and the nobles and governors of
1:14 and Memucan, the seven officials of Persia and **M**,
1:18 the noble ladies of Persia and **M** who have heard
10: 2 are they not written in the annals of the kings of **M**
Isa 21: 2 Go up, O Elam, lay siege, O **M**;
Jer 25:25 all the kings of Elam, and all the kings of **M**;
Da 8:20 these are the kings of **M** and Persia.
Tob 1:14 Until his death I used to go into **M**,
1:14 of **M** I left bags of silver worth ten talents in trust
1:15 the highways into **M** became unsafe
3: 7 On the same day, at Ecbatana in **M**,
4: 1 that he had left in trust with Gabael at Rages in **M**,
4:20 in trust with Gabael son of Gabrias, at Rages in **M**.
5: 2 I do not know the roads to **M**, or how to get there."
5: 4 to look for a man to go with him to **M**,
5: 5 "Do you know the way to go to **M**?"
5: 6 I have often traveled to **M**,
5: 6 with our kinsman Gabael who lives in Rages of **M**.
5:10 "My son Tobias wishes to go to **M**.
5:10 to **M** and have crossed all its plains,
6: 6 on their way together until they were near **M**.
6:10 entered **M** and already was approaching Ecbatana,
9: 5 and two camels went to Rages in **M** and stayed
14: 4 and hurry off to **M**, for I believe the word of God
14: 4 it will be safer in **M** than in Assyria and Babylon.
14:12 and his wife and children returned to **M** and settled
14:13 and buried them in Ecbatana of **M**.
14:15 and he saw its prisoners being led into **M**,
14:15 whom King Cyaxares of **M** had taken captive.
AdE 8: 9 and governors of the provinces from **M**
1Mc 6:56 and **M** with the forces that had gone with the king,
8: 8 the countries of India, **M**,
14: 1 and marched into **M** to obtain help,
14: 2 When King Arsaces of Persia and **M** heard
1Es 3: 1 and all the nobles of **M** and Persia,
3:14 and **M** and the satraps and generals and governors
6:23 the fortress that is in the country of **M**,

MEDIAN (2) [MEDIA]
AdE 1: 3 the Persians and **M** nobles,
1:18 of the Persian and **M** governors,

MEDIATE See Index to Footnotes

MEDIATOR (7)
Job 33:23 if there should be for one of them an angel, a **m**,
Gal 3:19 and it was ordained through angels by a **m**.
3:20 a **m** involves more than one party; but God is one.
1Ti 2: 5 there is also one **m** between God and humankind,
Heb 8: 6 and to that degree he is the **m** of a better covenant,
9:15 For this reason he is the **m** of a new covenant,
12:24 the **m** of a new covenant,

MEDICINAL (1) [MEDICINE]
Tob 6: 7 what **m** value is there in the fish's heart and liver,

MEDICINE (6) [MEDICINAL, MEDICINES]
Pr 17:22 A cheerful heart is a good **m**,
Jer 30:13 no **m** for your wound, no healing for you.
Tob 6: 5 For its gall, heart, and liver are useful as **m**."
11: 8 the **m** will make the white films shrink and peel off
11:11 With this he applied the **m** on his eyes,
Sir 6:16 Faithful friends are life-saving **m**;

MEDICINES (2) [MEDICINE]
Jer 46:11 In vain you have used many **m**;
Sir 38: 4 The Lord created **m** out of the earth,

MEDIOCRE (1)
2Mc 15:38 if it is poorly done and **m**,

MEDITATE (17) [MEDITATES, MEDITATING, MEDITATION]
Jos 1: 8 you shall **m** on it day and night,
Ps 1: 2 and on his law they **m** day and night.
38:12 and **m** treachery all day long.
63: 6 and **m** on you in the watches of the night;
77: 3 I think of God, and I moan; I **m**,
77: 6 I **m** and search my spirit:
77:12 I will **m** on all your work,
119:15 I will **m** on your precepts,
119:23 your servant will **m** on your statutes.
119:27 and I will **m** on your wondrous works.
119:48 which I love, and I will **m** on your statutes.
119:78 as for me, I will **m** on your precepts.
119:148 that I may **m** on your promise.
143: 5 I **m** on the works of your hands.
145: 5 and on your wondrous works, I will **m**.
Wis 12:22 when we judge, we may **m** upon your goodness,
Sir 6:37 and **m** at all times on his commandments.

MEDITATES (2) [MEDITATE]
Sir 14:20 Happy is the person who **m** on wisdom
39: 7 as he **m** on his mysteries.

MEDITATING (1) [MEDITATE]
1Ki 18:27 either he is **m**, or he has wandered away,

MEDITATION (6) [MEDITATE]
Job 15: 4 and hindering **m** before God.
Ps 19:14 Let the words of my mouth and the **m** of my heart
49: 3 the **m** of my heart shall be understanding.
104:34 May my **m** be pleasing to him,
119:97 Oh, how I love your law! It is my **m** all day long.
119:99 for your decrees are my **m**.

MEDITERRANEAN (1)
Jos 15:12 And the west boundary was the **M** with its coast.

MEDIUM (4) [MEDIUMS]
Lev 20:27 A man or a woman who is a **m** or a wizard shall
1Sa 28: 7 "Seek out for me a woman who is a **m**,
28: 7 His servants said to him, "There is a **m** at Endor."
1Ch 10:13 moreover, he had consulted a **m**, seeking guidance,

MEDIUMS (7) [MEDIUM]
Lev 19:31 Do not turn to **m** or wizards;
20: 6 If any turn to **m** and wizards,
1Sa 28: 3 Saul had expelled the **m** and the wizards from
28: 9 he has cut off the **m** and the wizards from the land.
2Ki 21: 6 and dealt with **m** and with wizards.
23:24 Moreover Josiah put away the **m**, wizards,
2Ch 33: 6 and dealt with **m** and with wizards.

MEEK (6) [MEEKNESS]
Ps 10:17 O LORD, you will hear the desire of the **m**;
37:11 But the **m** shall inherit the land,
Isa 11: 4 and decide with equity for the **m** of the earth;
29:19 The **m** shall obtain fresh joy in the LORD,
Mt 5: 5 "Blessed are the **m**, for they will inherit the earth.
2Es 11:42 for you have oppressed the **m** and injured

MEEKNESS[‡] (4) [MEEK]
2Co 10: 1 appeal to you by the **m** and gentleness of Christ—
Col 3:12 kindness, humility, **m**, and patience.
Jas 1:21 and welcome with **m** the implanted word that has
Sir 45: 4 For his faithfulness and **m** he consecrated him,

MEET[‡] (170) [MEETING, MEETS, MET]
Ge 14:17 the king of Sodom went out to **m** him at the Valley
18: 2 he ran from the tent entrance to **m** them,
19: 1 When Lot saw them, he rose to **m** them,
24:17 Then the servant ran to **m** her and said,
24:65 walking in the field to **m** us?"
29:13 about his sister's son Jacob, he ran to **m** him;
30:16 Leah went out to **m** him, and said,
32: 6 and he is coming to **m** you,
32:19 the same thing to Esau when you **m** him,
33: 4 But Esau ran to **m** him, and embraced him,
46:29 and went up to **m** his father Israel in Goshen.
Ex 4:14 even now he is coming out to **m** you,
4:27 "Go into the wilderness to **m** Moses."
5:20 and Aaron who were waiting to **m** them.
7:15 stand by at the river bank to **m** him,
18: 7 Moses went out to **m** his father-in-law;
19:17 the people out of the camp to **m** God.
25:22 There I will **m** with you,
29:42 where I will **m** with you, to speak to you there.
29:43 I will **m** with the Israelites there,
30: 6 where I will **m** with you.
30:36 the covenant in the tent of meeting where I shall **m**
Nu 17: 4 the tent of meeting before the covenant, where I **m**
22:36 he went out to **m** him at Ir-moab,
23: 3 Perhaps the LORD will come to **m** me.
23:15 while I **m** the LORD over there.
31:13 the congregation went to **m** them outside the camp.
35:19 when they **m**, the avenger of blood shall execute
35:21 the murderer to death, when they **m**.
Dt 15: 8 willingly lending enough to **m** the need,
23: 4 not **m** you with food and water on your journey out
Jos 8:14 to the meeting place facing the Arabah to **m** Israel
9:11 go to **m** them, and say to them,
Jdg 4: 7 to **m** you by the Wadi Kishon with his chariots
4:18 Jael came out to **m** Sisera, and said to him,
4:22 Jael went out to **m** him, and said to him, "Come,
6:35 and Naphtali, and they went up to **m** them.
11:31 of the doors of my house to **m** me,
11:34 and there was his daughter coming out to **m** him
15:14 the Philistines came shouting to **m** him;
19: 3 girl's father saw him and came with joy to **m** him.
1Sa 6:13 they went with rejoicing to **m** it.
9:13 Now go up, for you will **m** him immediately."
10: 2 from me today you will **m** two men
10: 3 up to God at Bethel will **m** you there,
10: 5 to the town, you will **m** a band of prophets coming
10: 7 Now when these signs **m** you,
13:10 and Saul went out to **m** him and salute him.
15:12 Samuel rose early in the morning to **m** Saul,
16: 4 The elders of the city came to **m** him trembling,
17:48 When the Philistine drew nearer to **m** David,
17:48 David ran quickly toward the battle line to **m**
18: 6 singing and dancing, to **m** King Saul,
21: 1 Ahimelech came trembling to **m** David,
25:32 the God of Israel, who sent you to **m** me today!
25:34 unless you had hurried and come to **m** me,
30:21 to **m** David and to **m** the people who were
2Sa 6:20 Michal the daughter of Saul came out to **m** David,
10: 5 When David was told, he sent to **m** them,
15:32 to **m** him with his coat torn and earth on his head.
18: 9 Absalom happened to **m** the servants of David.
19:15 to **m** the king and to bring him over the Jordan.
19:16 down with the people of Judah to **m** King David;
19:20 of Joseph to come down to **m** my lord the king."
19:24 Mephibosheth grandson of Saul came down to **m**
19:25 When he came from Jerusalem to **m** the king,
20: 8 that is in Gibeon, Amasa came to **m** them.
1Ki 2: 8 but when he came down to **m** me at the Jordan,
2:19 The king rose to **m** her, and bowed down to her;
5: 9 And you shall **m** my needs by providing food
18:16 So Obadiah went to **m** Ahab, and told him;
18:16 and Ahab went to **m** Elijah.
21:18 to **m** King Ahab of Israel, who rules in Samaria;
2Ki 1: 3 go to **m** the messengers of the king of Samaria,

2Ki 1: 6 They answered him, "There came a man to **m** us,
1: 7 "What sort of man was he who came to **m** you
2:15 to **m** him and bowed to the ground before him.
4:26 run at once to **m** her,
4:29 If you **m** anyone, give no greeting,
4:31 He came back to **m** him and told him,
5:21 he jumped down from the chariot to **m** him
5:26 in spirit when someone left his chariot to **m** you?
8: 8 a present with you and go to **m** the man of God.
8: 9 So Hazael went to **m** him,
9:17 send him to **m** them, and let him say,
9:18 So the horseman went to **m** him;
9:21 each in his chariot, and went to **m** Jehu;
10:15 he met Jehonadab son of Rechab coming to **m** him;
16:10 to Damascus to **m** King Tiglath-pileser of Assyria,
23:29 King Josiah went to **m** him;
23:35 in order to **m** Pharaoh's demand for money.
1Ch 12:17 David went out to **m** them and said to them,
2Ch 14:10 Asa went out to **m** him,
15: 2 He went out to **m** Asa and said to him, "Hear me,
19: 2 Jehu son of Hanani the seer went out to **m** him
22: 7 with Jehoram to **m** Jehu son of Nimshi,
28: 9 he went out to **m** the army that came to Samaria,
Ne 6: 2 "Come and let us **m** together in one of the villages
6:10 he said, "Let us **m** together in the house of God,
13: 2 because they did not **m** the Israelites with bread
Job 5:14 They **m** with darkness in the daytime,
30:27 days of affliction come to **m** me.
39:21 it goes out to **m** the weapons.
Ps 10: 6 all generations we shall not **m** adversity."
21: 3 For you **m** him with rich blessings;
59:10 My God in his steadfast love will **m** me;
79: 8 let your compassion come speedily to **m** us,
85:10 Steadfast love and faithfulness will **m**;
Pr 7:15 so now I have come out to **m** you,
17:12 to **m** a she-bear robbed of its cubs than to confront
Ecc 8: 5 Whoever obeys a command will **m** no harm,
Isa 7: 3 Then the LORD said to Isaiah, Go out to **m** Ahaz,
14: 9 Sheol beneath is stirred up to **m** you
21:14 the thirsty, **m** the fugitive with bread, O inhabitants
34:14 Wildcats shall **m** with hyenas,
64: 5 You **m** those who gladly do right,
Jer 18:21 May their men **m** death by pestilence,
41: 6 of Nethaniah came out from Mizpah to **m** them,
51:31 One runner runs to **m** another,
51:31 and one messenger to **m** another,
Am 4:12 I will do this to you, prepare to **m** your God,
9:10 who say, "Evil shall not overtake or **m** us."
Zec 2: 3 and another angel came forward to **m** him,
Mt 8:34 Then the whole town came out to **m** Jesus;
25: 1 Ten bridesmaids took their lamps and went to **m**
25: 6 Come out to **m** him.'
Mk 14:13 and a man carrying a jar of water will **m** you;
Lk 22:10 a man carrying a jar of water will **m** you;
Jn 12:13 of palm trees and went out to **m** him,
12:18 that the crowd went to **m** him.
Ac 20:17 asking the elders of the church to **m** him.
22:30 the chief priests and the entire council to **m**.
28:15 the Forum of Appius and Three Taverns to **m** us.
28:23 After they had set a day to **m** with him,
2Co 13: 5 unless, indeed, you fail to **m** the test!
1Th 4:17 be caught up in the clouds together with them to **m**
Tit 3:14 to good works in order to **m** urgent needs,
Heb 10:25 not neglecting to **m** together,
Tob 11:16 to **m** his daughter-in-law at the gate of Nineveh.
Jdt 5: 4 refused to come out and **m** me?"
Wis 19: 5 but they themselves might **m** a strange death.
Sir 15: 2 She will come to **m** him like a mother,
36:11 may those who harm your people **m** destruction.
42:23 each creature is preserved to **m** a particular need.
1Mc 3:11 When Judas learned of it, he went out to **m** him,
3:16 Judas went out to **m** him with a small company.
3:17 But when they saw the army coming to **m** them,
5:39 And Judas went to **m** them.
5:59 and his men came out of the town to **m** them
7:30 he was afraid of him and would not **m** him again.
7:31 to **m** Judas in battle near Caphar-salama.
9:39 and his brothers to **m** them with tambourines
10: 2 a very large army and marched out to **m** him
10:39 to **m** the necessary expenses of the sanctuary.
10:56 And now I will do for you as you wrote, but **m** me
10:59 to Jonathan to come and **m** him.
10:71 come down to the plain to **m** us,
10:86 of the city came out to **m** him with great pomp.
11: 2 to him and went to **m** him,
11: 2 King Alexander had commanded them to **m** him,
11:22 to **m** him for a conference at Ptolemais as quickly
11:64 He went to **m** them, but left his brother Simon in
12:41 to **m** him with forty thousand picked warriors,
16: 5 of infantry and cavalry was coming to **m** them;
2Mc 14:21 The leaders set a day on which to **m** by themselves.
1Es 9: 4 if any did not **m** there within two or three days,
Pm 151: 6 I went out to **m** the Philistine,
3Mc 5: 2 so that the Jews might **m** their doom.
6:30 in which they had expected to **m** their destruction.

MEETING (154) [MEET]

Ex 27:21 In the tent of **m,** outside the curtain that is before
28:43 into the tent of **m,** or when they come near the altar
29: 4 and his sons to the entrance of the tent of **m,**
29:10 You shall bring the bull in front of the tent of **m.**
29:11 at the entrance of the tent of **m,**
29:30 when he comes into the tent of **m** to minister in
29:32 at the entrance of the tent of **m.**
29:42 at the entrance of the tent of **m** before the LORD,
29:44 I will consecrate the tent of **m** and the altar;
Ex 30:16 for the service of the tent of **m;**
30:18 You shall put it between the tent of **m** and the altar,
30:20 When they go into the tent of **m,**
30:26 With it you shall anoint the tent of **m** and the ark of
30:36 the covenant in the tent of **m** where I shall meet
31: 7 the tent of **m,** and the ark of the covenant,
33: 7 he called it the tent of **m.**
33: 7 the LORD would go out to the tent of **m,**
35:21 the LORD's offering to be used for the tent of **m,**
38: 8 at the entrance to the tent of **m.**
38:30 the bases for the entrance of the tent of **m,**
39:32 of the tabernacle of the tent of **m** was finished;
39:40 for the service of the tabernacle, for the tent of **m;**
40: 2 up the tabernacle of the tent of **m.**
40: 6 the entrance of the tabernacle of the tent of **m,**
40: 7 place the basin between the tent of **m** and the altar,
40:12 and his sons to the entrance of the tent of **m,**
40:22 He put the table in the tent of **m,**
40:24 He put the lampstand in the tent of **m,**
40:26 the golden altar in the tent of **m** before the curtain,
40:29 at the entrance of the tabernacle of the tent of **m,**
40:30 the basin between the tent of **m** and the altar,
40:32 When they went into the tent of **m,**
40:34 Then the cloud covered the tent of **m,**
40:35 Moses was not able to enter the tent of **m** because
Lev 1: 1 and spoke to him from the tent of **m,** saying:
1: 3 you shall bring it to the entrance of the tent of **m,**
1: 5 of the altar that is at the entrance of the tent of **m.**
3: 2 and slaughter it at the entrance of the tent of **m;**
3: 8 It shall be slaughtered before the tent of **m,**
3:13 it shall be slaughtered before the tent of **m;**
4: 4 of the tent of **m** before the LORD and lay his hand
4: 5 the blood of the bull and bring it into the tent of **m.**
4: 7 the altar of fragrant incense that is in the tent of **m**
4: 7 which is at the entrance of the tent of **m.**
4:14 for a sin offering and bring it before the tent of **m.**
4:16 of the blood of the bull into the tent of **m,**
4:18 the altar that is before the LORD in the tent of **m;**
4:18 that is at the entrance of the tent of **m.**
6:16 in the court of the tent of **m** they shall eat it.
6:26 in the court of the tent of **m.**
6:30 from which any blood is brought into the tent of **m**
8: 3 at the entrance of the tent of **m.**
8: 4 at the entrance of the tent of **m,**
8:31 "Boil the flesh at the entrance of the tent of **m,**
8:33 the entrance of the tent of **m** for seven days,
8:35 the tent of **m** day and night for seven days, keeping
9: 5 to the front of the tent of **m;**
9:23 Moses and Aaron entered the tent of **m,**
10: 7 the entrance of the tent of **m,** or you will die;
10: 9 when you enter the tent of **m,** that you may not die;
12: 6 the entrance of the tent of **m** a lamb in its first year
14:11 before the LORD, at the entrance of the tent of **m.**
14:23 to the entrance of the tent of **m,** before the LORD;
15:14 before the LORD to the entrance of the tent of **m**
15:29 to the priest to the entrance of the tent of **m.**
16: 7 before the LORD at the entrance of the tent of **m;**
16:16 and so he shall do for the tent of **m,**
16:17 of **m** from the time he enters to make atonement in
16:20 for the holy place and the tent of **m** and the altar,
16:23 Then Aaron shall enter the tent of **m,**
16:33 and he shall make atonement for the tent of **m** and
17: 4 of **m,** to present it as an offering to the LORD
17: 5 to the priest at the entrance of the tent of **m,**
17: 6 of the LORD at the entrance of the tent of **m,**
17: 9 does not bring it to the entrance of the tent of **m,**
19:21 at the entrance of the tent of **m,**
24: 3 Aaron shall set it up in the tent of **m,**
Nu 1: 1 the tent of **m,** on the first day of the second month,
2: 2 they shall camp facing the tent of **m** on every side.
2:17 The tent of **m,** with the camp of the Levites,
3: 7 the whole congregation in front of the tent of **m,**
3: 8 be in charge of all the furnishings of the tent of **m,**
3:25 of the sons of Gershon in the tent of **m** was to be
3:25 the screen for the entrance of the tent of **m,**
3:38 in front of the tent of **m** toward the east—
4: 3 all who qualify to do work relating to the tent of **m.**
4: 4 of the Kohathites relating to the tent of **m** concerns
4:15 the things of the tent of **m** that the Kohathites are
4:23 all who qualify to do work in the tent of **m.**
4:25 and the tent of **m** with its covering,
4:25 and the screen for the entrance of the tent of **m,**
4:28 of the Gershonites relating to the tent of **m,**
4:30 to do the work of the tent of **m.**
4:31 as the whole of their service in the tent of **m:**
4:33 the whole of their service relating to the tent of **m,**
4:35 for work relating to the tent of **m;**
4:37 all who served at the tent of **m,**
4:39 for work relating to the tent of **m—**
4:41 all who served at the tent of **m,**
4:43 for work relating to the tent of **m—**
4:47 of bearing burdens relating to the tent of **m,**
6:10 to the priest at the entrance of the tent of **m,**
6:13 be brought to the entrance of the tent of **m,**
6:18 at the entrance of the tent of **m,**
7: 5 be used in doing the service of the tent of **m,**
7:89 When Moses went into the tent of **m** to speak with
8: 9 You shall bring the Levites before the tent of **m,**
8:15 in to do service at the tent of **m,**
8:19 to do the service for the Israelites at the tent of **m,**
8:22 in to do their service in the tent of **m** in attendance
8:24 to do duty in the service of the tent of **m;**
8:26 They may assist their brothers in the tent of **m**
10: 3 before you at the entrance of the tent of **m.**
11:16 bring them to the tent of **m,**
12: 4 "Come out, you three, to the tent of **m.**"
14:10 the glory of the LORD appeared at the tent of **m**
Nu 16:18 and they stood at the entrance of the tent of **m**
16:19 against them at the entrance of the tent of **m.**
16:42 Moses and Aaron turned toward the tent of **m;**
16:43 and Aaron came to the front of the tent of **m,**
16:50 to Moses at the entrance of the tent of **m.**
17: 4 Place them in the tent of **m** before the covenant,
18: 4 the duties of the tent of **m,** for all the service of
18: 6 to perform the service of the tent of **m.**
18:21 the service in the tent of **m.**
18:22 the tent of **m,** or else they will incur guilt
18:23 Levites shall perform the service of the tent of **m,**
18:31 it is your payment for your service in the tent of **m.**
19: 4 the front of the tent of **m.**
20: 6 from the assembly to the entrance of the tent of **m;**
25: 6 they were weeping at the entrance of the tent of **m.**
27: 2 at the entrance of the tent of **m,** and they said,
31:54 the tent of **m** as a memorial for the Israelites before
Dt 31:14 call Joshua and present yourselves in the tent of **m,**
31:14 and presented themselves in the tent of **m,**
Jos 8:14 in the morning to the **m** place facing the Arabah
18: 1 and set up the tent of **m** there.
19:51 at the entrance of the tent of **m.**
1Sa 2:22 at the entrance to the tent of **m.**
1Ki 8: 4 of **m,** and all the holy vessels that were in the tent;
1Ch 6:32 the tent of **m,** until Solomon had built the house of
9:21 at the entrance of the tent of **m.**
23:32 Thus they shall keep charge of the tent of **m** and
2Ch 1: 3 for God's tent of **m,** which Moses the servant of
1: 6 which was at the tent of **m,**
1:13 from the tent of **m,** to Jerusalem.
5: 5 So they brought up the ark, the tent of **m,**
Ps 74: 8 they burned all the **m** places of God in the land.
Jn 11:47 So the chief priests and the Pharisees called a **m** of
Ac 13:43 When the **m** of the synagogue broke up,
20: 8 in the room upstairs where we were **m.**
Gal 2: 2 in a private **m** with the acknowledged leaders)
2Mc 14: 5 a **m** of the council and was asked about the attitude
14:30 was **m** him more rudely than had been his custom,

MEETS (7) [MEET]

Ge 4:14 and anyone who **m** me may kill me."
32:17 "When Esau my brother **m** you, and asks you,
Dt 22:23 and a man **m** her in the town and lies with her,
22:25 man **m** the engaged woman in the open country,
22:28 If a man **m** a virgin who is not engaged,
Ecc 10:19 wine gladdens life, and money **m** every need.
Wis 6:16 and **m** them in every thought.

MEGIDDO (13)

Jos 12:21 the king of Taanach one the king of **M** one
17:11 of **M** and its villages (the third is Naphath).
Jdg 1:27 or the inhabitants of **M** and its villages;
5:19 by the waters of **M;** they got no spoils of silver.
1Ki 4:12 in Taanach, **M,** and all Beth-shean,
9:15 the Millo and the wall of Jerusalem, Hazor, **M,**
2Ki 9:27 Then he fled to **M,** and died there.
23:29 when Pharaoh Neco met him at **M,** he killed him.
23:30 His servants carried him dead in a chariot from **M,**
1Ch 7:29 Taanach and its towns, **M** and its towns,
2Ch 35:22 but joined battle in the plain of **M.**
Zec 12:11 the mourning for Hadad-rimmon in the plain of **M.**
1Es 1:29 He joined battle with him in the plain of **M,**

MEGIDDON (KJV) See MEGIDDO

MEHEBEL See Index to Footnotes

MEHETABEL (3)

Ge 36:39 his wife's name was **M,** the daughter of Matred,
1Ch 1:50 and his wife's name **M** daughter of Matred,
Ne 6:10 the house of Shemaiah son of Delaiah son of **M,**

MEHIDA (3)

Ezr 2:52 Bazluth, **M,** Harsha,
Ne 7:54 of Bazlith, of **M,** of Harsha,
1Es 5:32 the descendants of **M,** the descendants of Cutha,

MEHIR (1)

1Ch 4:11 the brother of Shuhah became the father of **M,**

MEHOLATHITE (2)

1Sa 18:19 she was given to Adriel the **M** as a wife.
2Sa 21: 8 whom she bore to Adriel son of Barzillai the **M;**

MEHUJAEL (2)

Ge 4:18 and Irad was the father of **M,** and **M** the father of Methushael,

MEHUMAN (1)

Est 1:10 he commanded **M,** Biztha, Harbona,

MEHUNIM (KJV) See MEUNIM

MEHUNIMS (KJV) See MEUNITES

MEKONAH (KJV) See MECONAH

MELATIAH (1)

Ne 3: 7 by **M** the Gibeonite and Jadon the Meronothite—

MELCHI (2)
Lk 3:24 son of **M,** son of Jannai, son of Joseph,
3:28 son of **M,** son of Addi, son of Cosam, son

MELCHI-SHUA (KJV) See MALCHISHUA

MELCHIAS (1)
1Es 9:32 and **M** and Sabbaias and Simon Chosamaeus.

MELCHIEL (1)
Jdt 6:15 of Gothoniel, and Charmis son of **M.**

MELCHISEDEC (KJV) See MELCHIZEDEK

MELCHIZEDEK (10)
Ge 14:18 And King **M** of Salem brought out bread and wine;
Ps 110: 4 a priest forever according to the order of **M."**
Heb 5: 6 according to the order of **M."**
5:10 by God a high priest according to the order of **M.**
6:20 a high priest forever according to the order of **M.**
7: 1 This "King **M** of Salem, priest of the Most High
7:10 in the loins of his ancestor when **M** met him.
7:11 priest arising according to the order of **M,**
7:15 when another priest arises, resembling **M,**
7:17 priest forever, according to the order of **M."**

MELEA (1)
Lk 3:31 son of **M,** son of Menna, son of Mattatha, son

MELECH (2)
1Ch 8:35 The sons of Micah: Pithon, **M,** Tarea, and Ahaz.
9:41 The sons of Micah: Pithon, **M,** Tahrea, and Ahaz;

MELICU (KJV) See MALLUCHI

MELITA (KJV) See MALTA

MELODIES (1) [MELODY]
4Mc 15:21 the **m** of sirens nor the songs of swans attract

MELODIOUS (3) [MELODY]
Wis 17:18 or a **m** sound of birds in wide-spreading branches,
3Mc 7:16 in words of praise and all kinds of **m** songs.
4Mc 10:21 for you are cutting out a tongue that has been **m**

MELODY (16) [MELODIES, MELODIOUS]
Jdg 5: 3 I will make **m** to the LORD, the God of Israel.
Ps 27: 6 I will sing and make **m** to the LORD.
33: 2 make **m** to him with the harp of ten strings.
57: 7 I will sing and make **m.**
92: 3 to the **m** of the lyre.
98: 5 with the lyre and the sound of **m.**
108: 1 I will sing and make **m.**
147: 7 make **m** to our God on the lyre.
149: 3 making **m** to him with tambourine and lyre.
Isa 23:16 Make sweet **m,** sing many songs,
Am 5:23 I will not listen to the **m** of your harps.
Eph 5:19 singing and making **m** to the Lord in your hearts,
Sir 32: 6 A seal of emerald in a rich setting of gold is the **m**
40:21 The flute and the harp make sweet **m,**
47: 9 to make sweet **m** with their voices.
50:18 with their voices in sweet and full-toned **m.**

MELONS (1)
Nu 11: 5 the cucumbers, the **m,** the leeks, the onions,

MELT (27) [MELTED, MELTING, MELTS, QUICK-MELTING]
Dt 1:28 Our kindred have made our hearts **m** by reporting,
20: 8 or he might cause the heart of his comrades to **m**
Jos 2: 9 all the inhabitants of the land **m** in fear before you.
2:24 all the inhabitants of the land **m** in fear before us."
14: 8 up with me made the heart of the people **m;**
2Sa 17:10 like the heart of a lion, will utterly **m** with fear;
Ps 97: 5 The mountains **m** like wax before the LORD,
112:10 they gnash their teeth and **m** away;
Isa 8: 6 **m** in fear before Rezin and the son of Remaliah;
13: 7 and every human heart will **m,**
14:31 **m** in fear, O Philistia, all of you!
19: 1 and the heart of the Egyptians will **m** within them.
Jer 49:23 they **m** in fear, they are troubled like the sea
Eze 21: 7 Every heart will **m** and all hands will be feeble,
21:15 therefore hearts **m** and many stumble.
22:20 to blow the fire upon them in order to **m** them;
22:20 and I will put you in and **m** you.
24:11 its filth **m** in it, its rust be consumed.
Mic 1: 4 Then the mountains will **m** under him and
Na 1: 5 The mountains quake before him, and the hills **m;**
2Pe 3:12 and the elements will **m** with fire?
Jdt 16:15 before your glance the rocks shall **m** like wax.
Wis 16:29 of an ungrateful person will **m** like wintry frost,
19:21 nor did they **m** the crystalline,
Sir 3:15 like frost in fair weather, your sins will **m** away.
1Mc 4:32 **m** the boldness of their strength;
2Es 8:23 whose indignation makes the mountains **m** away,

MELTED‡ (13) [MELT]
Ex 15:15 all the inhabitants of Canaan **m** away.
16:21 but when the sun grew hot, it **m.**
Jos 2:11 As soon as we heard it, our hearts **m,**
5: 1 their hearts **m,** and there was no longer any spirit
7: 5 The hearts of the people **m** and turned to water.
Jdg 15:14 and his bonds **m** off his hands.
Ps 22:14 it is **m** within my breast;
107:26 their courage **m** away in their calamity;
Eze 22:21 and you shall be **m** within it.
22:22 As silver is **m** in a smelter, so you shall be **m** in it;
Wis 16:27 not destroyed by fire was **m** when simply warmed
2Es 13: 4 all who heard his voice **m** as wax melts

MELTING (2) [MELT]
Job 6:16 that run dark with ice, turbid with **m** snow.
Wis 16:22 Snow and ice withstood fire without **m,**

MELTS (8) [MELT]
Ps 46: 6 he utters his voice, the earth **m.**
68: 2 as wax **m** before the fire,
119:28 My soul **m** away for sorrow;
147:18 He sends out his word, and **m** them;
Isa 15: 3 and in the squares everyone wails and **m** in tears.
Am 9: 5 GOD of hosts, he who touches the earth and it **m,**
Sir 38:28 the breath of the fire **m** his flesh,
2Es 13: 4 all who heard his voice melted as wax **m**

MELZAR (KJV) See GUARD

MEMBER (30) [MEMBERS]
Lev 15: 2 When any man has a discharge from his **m,**
15: 3 whether his **m** flows with his discharge,
15: 3 or his **m** is stopped from discharging,
Nu 27: 1 a **m** of the Manassite clans.
Dt 15: 2 of a neighbor who is a **m** of the community,
15: 3 but you must remit your claim on whatever any **m**
15: 7 a **m** of your community in any of your towns
15:12 If a **m** of your community,
1Sa 22:15 the king impute anything to his servant or to any **m**
1Ki 20:35 At the command of the LORD a certain **m** of
2Ki 4: 1 of a **m** of the company of prophets cried to Elisha,
9: 1 Then the prophet Elisha called a **m** of the company
Isa 3: 6 Someone will even seize a relative, a **m** of the clan,
Mt 18:15 "If another **m** of the church sins against you,
18:15 If the **m** listens to you, you have regained that one.
18:17 the **m** refuses to listen to them, tell it to the church;
18:21 "Lord, if another **m** of the church sins against me,
Mk 15:43 a respected **m** of the council,
Lk 23:50 who, though a **m** of the council,
Ac 13: 1 Manaen a **m** of the court of Herod the ruler,
Ro 11: 1 a **m** of the tribe of Benjamin.
1Co 12:14 the body does not consist of one **m** but of many.
12:19 If all were a single **m,** where would the body be?
12:24 giving the greater honor to the inferior **m,**
12:26 If one **m** suffers, all suffer together with it;
12:26 if one **m** is honored, all rejoice together with it.
Php 3: 5 a **m** of the people of Israel,
Jas 3: 5 tongue is a small **m,** yet it boasts of great exploits.
Tob 1: 9 a **m** of our own family,
4Mc 9:14 with every **m** disjointed he denounced the tyrant,

MEMBERS (59) [MEMBER]
Ge 36: 6 his daughters, and all the **m** of his household,
39:14 she called out to the **m** of her household and said
Dt 1:16 "Give the **m** of your community a fair hearing,
17:20 above other **m** of the community nor turning aside
18: 2 among the other **m** of the community;
1Sa 2:33 all the **m** of your household shall die by the sword.
2Ki 5:22 'Two **m** of a company of prophets have just come
1Ch 5:23 **m** of the half-tribe of Manasseh lived in the land;
2Ch 21:13 and because you also have killed your brothers, **m**
Job 17: 7 and all my **m** are like a shadow.
Eze 23:20 whose **m** were like those of donkeys,
Mic 7: 6 your enemies are **m** of your own household.
Mt 5:29 to lose one of your **m** than for your whole body to
5:30 of your **m** than for your whole body to go into hell.
10:36 and one's foes will be **m** of one's own household.
25:40 as you did it to one of the least of these who are **m**
Ac 15:22 from among their **m** and to send them to Antioch
15:31 When its **m** read it, they rejoiced at the exhortation.
Ro 6:13 No longer present your **m** to sin as instruments
6:13 and present your **m** to God as instruments
6:19 as you once presented your **m** as slaves to impurity
6:19 so now present your **m** as slaves to righteousness
7: 5 were at work in our **m** to bear fruit for death.
7:23 but I see in my **m** another law at war with the law
7:23 to the law of sin that dwells in my **m.**
12: 4 For as in one body we have many **m,** and not all the **m** have the same function,
12: 5 and individually we are **m** one of another.
1Co 6:15 Do you not know that your bodies are **m** of Christ?
6:15 the **m** of Christ and make them **m** of a prostitute?
8:12 But when you thus sin against **m** of your family,
12:12 For just as the body is one and has many **m,** and all the **m** of the body, though many, are one body,
12:18 But as it is, God arranged the **m** in the body,
12:20 As it is, there are many **m,** yet one body.
12:22 the **m** of the body that seem to be weaker
12:23 and those **m** of the body that we think less
12:23 and our less respectable **m** are treated with greater
12:24 whereas our more respectable **m** do not need this.
12:25 but the **m** may have the same care for one another.
12:27 you are the body of Christ and individually **m** of it.
16:15 that **m** of the household of Stephanas were
Gal 1: 2 and all the **m** of God's family who are with me,
Eph 2:19 with the saints and also **m** of the household of God,
3: 6 that is, the Gentiles have become fellow heirs, **m** of
4:25 for we are **m** of one another.
5:30 because we are **m** of his body.
1Ti 5: 8 and especially for family **m,**
6: 2 on the ground that they are **m** of the church;
Jas 3: 6 The tongue is placed among our **m** as a world
Rev 11: 9 and a half days **m** of the peoples and tribes
Sir 10:20 Among family **m** their leader is worthy of honor,
1Es 2:17 and the other **m** of their council, and the judges
3Mc 1:11 even **m** of their own nation were allowed to enter,
2Es 8: 8 now fashioned in the womb, and furnish it with **m,**
8:10 you have commanded that from the **m** themselves
4Mc 10:20 we let our bodily **m** be mutilated.
11:10 and all his **m** were disjointed.

MEMMIUS (1)
2Mc 11:34 "Quintus **M** and Titus Manius,

MEMOIRS (1)
2Mc 2:13 in the records and in the **m** of Nehemiah,

MEMORANDUM (1)
AdE 2:23 a **m** to be deposited in the royal library in praise of

MEMORIAL‡ (18) [MEMORY]
Lev 5:12 of it as its **m** portion, and turn this into smoke on
6:15 and they shall turn its **m** portion into smoke on
Nu 5:26 as its **m** portion, and turn it into smoke on the altar,
31:54 the tent of meeting as a **m** for the Israelites before
Jos 4: 7 these stones shall be to the Israelites a **m** forever."
Ps 38: T *A Psalm of David, for the **m** offering.*
70: T *To the leader. Of David, for the **m** offering.*
Isa 55:13 and it shall be to the LORD for a **m,**
66: 3 whoever makes a **m** offering of frankincense,
Zec 6:14 as a **m** in the temple of the LORD.
Ac 10: 4 "Your prayers and your alms have ascended as a **m**
AdE 9:27 of Purim should be a **m** and kept from generation
9:32 and it was written for a **m.**
Sir 38:11 and a **m** portion of choice flour,
45:16 incense and a pleasing odor as a **m** portion,
1Mc 8:22 to Jerusalem to remain with them there as a **m**
13:29 of armor for a permanent **m,**
2Mc 6:31 leaving in his death an example of nobility and a **m**

MEMORIZE (1) [MEMORY]
2Mc 2:25 to make it easy for those who are inclined to **m,**

MEMORY‡ (25) [MEMORIAL, MEMORIZE]
Dt 32:26 and blot out the **m** of them from humankind;
Job 18:17 Their **m** perishes from the earth,
Ps 9: 6 the very **m** of them has perished.
109:15 and may his **m** be cut off from the earth.
Pr 10: 7 The **m** of the righteous is a blessing,
Ecc 9: 5 and even the **m** of them is lost.
Isa 26:14 and wiped out all **m** of them.
2Pe 1:13 as long as I am in this body, to refresh your **m,**
Wis 4: 1 for in the **m** of virtue is immortality,
4:19 and the **m** of them will perish.
11:12 and a groaning at the **m** of what had occurred.
Sir 10:17 and erases the **m** of them from the earth.
23:26 behind an accursed **m** and her disgrace will never
24:20 For the **m** of me is sweeter than honey,
39: 9 His **m** will not disappear, and his name will live
44: 9 But of others there is no **m;**
45: 1 Moses, whose **m** is blessed.
46:11 from the Lord—may their **m** be blessed!
49: 1 his **m** is as sweet as honey to every mouth,
49:13 The **m** of Nehemiah also is lasting;
1Mc 3: 7 and his **m** is blessed forever.
3:35 he was to banish the **m** of them from the place,
12:53 and blot out the **m** of them from humankind."
2Mc 7:20 and worthy of honorable **m.**
2Es 14:40 for my spirit retained its **m,**

MEMPHIS (9)
Isa 19:13 and the princes of **M** are deluded;
Jer 2:16 the people of **M** and Tahpanhes have broken
44: 1 at Tahpanhes, at **M,** and in the land of Pathros,
46:14 proclaim in **M** and Tahpanhes;
46:19 **M** shall become a waste, a ruin, without inhabitant.
Eze 30:13 the idols and put an end to the images in **M;**
30:16 and **M** face adversaries by day.
Hos 9: 6 Egypt shall gather them, **M** shall bury them.
Jdt 1:10 even beyond Tanis and **M,**

MEMUCAN (3)
Est 1:14 and **M,** the seven officials of Persia and Media,
1:16 Then **M** said in the presence of the king and
1:21 and the king did as **M** proposed;

MEN‡ (843) [MAN]
A. YOUNG MEN (108)
B. MEN AND WOMEN (29)
C. MEN OF ISRAEL (24)
D. ALL THE MEN (21)
E. WISE MEN (20)
F. OLD MEN (9)

Ge 12:20 And Pharaoh gave his **m** orders concerning him;
14:14 he led forth his trained **m,** born in his house,
14:24 but what the young **m** have eaten, and the share A
14:24 and the share of the **m** who went with me—

Ge 17:23 every male among the **m** of Abraham's house,
17:27 and all the **m** of his house, D
18: 2 He looked up and saw three **m** standing near him.
18:16 Then the **m** set out from there,
18:22 So the **m** turned from there,
19: 4 But before they lay down, the **m** of the city,
19: 4 the **m** of Sodom, both young and old,
19: 5 "Where are the **m** who came to you tonight?
19: 6 Lot went out of the door to the **m,**
19: 8 only do nothing to these **m,**
19:10 But the **m** inside reached out their hands
19:11 And they struck with blindness the **m** who were at
19:12 the **m** said to Lot, "Have you anyone else here?
19:16 so the **m** seized him and his wife
20: 8 and the **m** were very much afraid.
21:27 and the two **m** made a covenant.
22: 3 and took two of his young **m** with him, A
22: 5 Then Abraham said to his young **m,** A
22:19 So Abraham returned to his young **m,** A
24:32 to wash his feet and the feet of the **m** who were
24:54 he and the **m** who were with him ate and drank,
24:59 along with Abraham's servant and his **m.**
26: 7 When the **m** of the place asked him about his wife,
26: 7 to say, "My wife," thinking, "or else the **m** of
32: 6 and four hundred **m** are with him."
33: 1 and four hundred **m** with him.
34: 7 the **m** were indignant and very angry,
34:20 of their city and spoke to the **m** of their city,
41: 8 for all the magicians of Egypt and all its wise **m.** E
42:11 We are all sons of one man; we are honest **m;**
42:19 if you are honest **m,** let one
42:31 But we said to him, 'We are honest **m,**
42:33 'By this I shall know that you are honest **m:**
42:34 I shall know that you are not spies but honest **m.**
43:15 So the **m** took the present,
43:16 "Bring the **m** into the house,
43:16 for the **m** are to dine with me at noon."
43:17 and brought the **m** to Joseph's house.
43:18 Now the **m** were afraid because they were brought
43:24 the steward had brought the **m** into Joseph's house,
43:33 the **m** looked at one another in amazement.
44: 3 the **m** were sent away with their donkeys.
44: 4 to his steward, "Go, follow after the **m;**
46:32 The **m** are shepherds, for they have been keepers
47: 2 From among his brothers he took five **m**
47: 6 if you know that there are capable **m** among them,
49: 6 for in their anger they killed **m,**
Ex 7:11 Pharaoh summoned the wise **m** and the E
10:11 Your **m** may go and worship the LORD,
12:37 about six hundred thousand **m** on foot,
17: 9 "Choose some **m** for us and go out,
18:21 You should also look for able **m** among all
18:21 **m** who fear God, are trustworthy,
18:21 set such **m** over them as officers over thousands,
18:25 Moses chose able **m** from all Israel
24: 5 He sent young **m** of the people of Israel, A
24:11 not lay his hand on the chief **m** of the people
35:22 So they came, both **m** and women; B
35:29 All the Israelite **m** and women whose hearts B
38:26 six hundred three thousand, five hundred fifty **m.**
Nu 1: 5 These are the names of the **m** who shall assist you:
1:17 and Aaron took these **m** who had been designated
1:44 twelve **m,** each representing his ancestral house.
6: 2 When either **m** or women make a special vow,
11:26 Two **m** remained in the camp, one named Eldad,
11:28 the assistant of Moses, one of his chosen **m,** said,
13: 2 "Send **m** to spy out the land of Canaan,
13: 3 all of them leading **m** among the Israelites.
13:16 These were the names of the **m** whom Moses sent
13:31 Then the **m** who had gone up with him said,
14:36 And the **m** whom Moses sent to spy out the land,
14:37 the **m** who brought an unfavorable report about
14:38 of those **m** who went to spy out the land.
16: 2 two hundred fifty Israelite **m,**
16: 2 well-known **m,** and they confronted Moses.
16:14 Would you put out the eyes of these **m?**
16:26 "Turn away from the tents of these wicked **m,**
16:30 then you shall know that these **m** have despised
16:35 and consumed the two hundred fifty **m** offering
22: 9 "Who are these **m** with you?"
22:20 "If the **m** have come to summon you,
22:35 of the LORD said to Balaam, "Go with the **m;**
26:10 when the fire devoured two hundred fifty **m;**
34:17 These are the names of the **m** who shall apportion
34:19 These are the names of the **m:**
Dt 1:22 "Let us send **m** ahead of us to explore the land
2:34 and in each town we utterly destroyed **m,** women,
3: 6 in each city utterly destroying **m,** women,
21:21 all the **m** of the town shall stone him to death. D
22:21 to the entrance of her father's house and the **m**
25:11 If **m** get into a fight with one another,
28:54 and gentle of **m** among you will begrudge food
29:10 elders, and your officials, all the **m** of Israel, CD
31:12 Assemble the people—**m,** women, and children,
Jos 2: 1 of Nun sent two **m** secretly from Shittim as spies,
2: 3 "Bring out the **m** who have come to you,
2: 4 But the woman took the two **m** and hid them.
2: 4 Then she said, "True, the **m** came to me,
2: 5 to close the gate at dark, the **m** went out.
2: 5 Where the **m** went I do not know.
2: 7 the **m** pursued them on the way to the Jordan as far
2: 9 and said to the **m:** "I know that the LORD has
2:14 The **m** said to her, "Our life for yours!
2:17 The **m** said to her, "We will be released
2:23 the two **m** came down again from the hill country.
3:12 So now select twelve **m** from the tribes of Israel,
4: 2 "Select twelve **m** from the people,
Jos 4: 4 Joshua summoned the twelve **m** from the Israelites,
6: 7 have the armed **m** pass on before the ark of
6: 9 And the armed **m** went before the priests who blew
6:13 The armed **m** went before them,
6:21 both **m** and women, young and old, oxen, sheep, B
6:22 Joshua said to the two **m** who had spied out
6:23 So the young **m** who had been spies went in A
7: 2 Joshua sent **m** from Jericho to Ai,
7: 2 And the **m** went up and spied out Ai.
7: 3 or three thousand **m** should go up and attack Ai.
7: 4 and they fled before the **m** of Ai.
7: 5 The **m** of Ai killed about thirty-six of them,
8: 1 take all the fighting **m** with you,
8: 3 and all the fighting **m** set out to go up against Ai.
8:11 All the fighting **m** who were with him went up,
8:12 Taking about five thousand **m,**
8:20 So when the **m** of Ai looked back,
8:21 then they turned back and struck down the **m** of Ai.
8:25 both **m** and women, was twelve thousand— B
10: 2 and was larger than Ai, and all its **m** were warriors.
10:18 and set **m** by it to guard them;
18: 4 Provide three **m** from each tribe,
18: 8 So the **m** started on their way;
18: 9 So the **m** went and traversed the land and set down
Jdg 3:29 all strong, able-bodied **m;** no one escaped.
7:11 the outposts of the armed **m** that were in the camp.
7:16 the three hundred **m** into three companies,
7:21 all the **m** in camp ran; they cried out and fled. D
7:23 the **m** of Israel were called out from Naphtali C
7:24 So all the **m** of Ephraim were called out, D
8:10 about fifteen thousand **m,** all who were left of all
8:10 one hundred twenty thousand **m** bearing arms
8:17 and killed the **m** of the city.
8:18 "What about the **m** whom you killed at Tabor?"
9: 5 the sons of Jerubbaal, seventy **m,** on one stone;
9:18 and have killed his sons, seventy **m** on one stone,
9:28 and Zebul his officer serve the **m** of Hamor father
9:49 about a thousand **m** and women.
9:51 all the **m** and women and all the lords of BD
12: 1 The **m** of Ephraim were called to arms,
12: 4 Then Jephthah gathered all the **m** of Gilead D
12: 4 and the **m** of Gilead defeated Ephraim,
12: 5 the **m** of Gilead would say to him,
14:10 a feast there as the young **m** were accustomed A
14:18 The **m** of the town said to him on the seventh day
14:19 He killed thirty **m** of the town, took their spoil,
15:10 The **m** of Judah said, "Why have you come up
15:11 Then three thousand **m** of Judah went down to
15:15 and with it he killed a thousand **m.**
15:16 jawbone of a donkey I have slain a thousand **m."**
16: 9 While **m** were lying in wait in an inner chamber,
16:12 (The **m** lying in wait were in an inner chamber.)
16:27 Now the house was full of **m** and women; B
16:27 about three thousand **m** and women, B
18: 2 So the Danites sent five valiant **m** from
18: 7 The five **m** went on, and when they came to Laish,
18:11 Six hundred **m** of the Danite clan,
18:14 five **m** who had gone to spy out the land (that is,
18:16 While the six hundred **m** of the Danites,
18:17 the five **m** who had gone to spy out
18:17 the six hundred **m** armed with weapons of war.
18:18 the **m** went into Micah's house and took the idol
18:22 the **m** who were in the houses
19: 6 So the two **m** sat and ate and drank together;
19:22 they were enjoying themselves, the **m** of the city,
19:25 But the **m** would not listen to him.
19:30 Then he commanded the **m** whom he sent, saying,
20:10 We will take ten **m** of a hundred throughout all
20:11 So all the **m** of Israel gathered against the city, CD
20:12 of Israel sent **m** through all the tribe of Benjamin,
20:15 mustered twenty-six thousand armed **m**
20:16 seven hundred picked **m** who were left-handed;
20:17 mustered four hundred thousand armed **m,**
20:25 of the Israelites, all of them armed **m.**
20:29 So Israel stationed **m** in ambush around Gibeah.
20:31 killing about thirty **m** of Israel. C
20:34 against Gibeah ten thousand picked **m** out
20:35 destroyed twenty-five thousand one hundred **m**
20:38 the main body of Israel and the **m** in ambush was
20:46 were twenty-five thousand arms-bearing **m,**
Ru 2: 9 I have ordered the young **m** not to bother you. A
2: 9 and drink from what the young **m** have drawn." A
2:15 got up to glean, Boaz instructed his young **m,** A
3:10 you have not gone after young **m,** A
4: 2 Then Boaz took ten **m** of the elders of the city,
1Sa 2:17 sin of the young **m** was very great in the sight A
4: 2 who killed about four thousand **m** on the field
4: 9 Take courage, and be **m,** O Philistines,
4: 9 as they have been to you; be **m** and fight."
6:10 The **m** did so; they took two milch cows
6:19 and he killed seventy **m** of them.
7:11 the **m** of Israel went out of Mizpah and pursued C
10: 2 from me today you will meet two **m**
10: 3 three **m** going up to God
10:27 But there were seven thousand **m** who had escaped
11: 1 and all the **m** of Jabesh said to Nahash, D
13:15 with him, about six hundred **m.**
14: 2 that were with him were about six hundred **m,**
14: 8 over to those **m** and will show ourselves to them.
14:12 The **m** of the garrison hailed Jonathan
14:14 and his armor-bearer killed about twenty **m** within
14:23 Saul numbered altogether about ten thousand **m.**
16:18 One of the young **m** answered, A
17:19 Now Saul, and they, and all the **m** of Israel, CD
17:26 David said to the **m** who stood by him,
17:28 eldest brother Eliab heard him talking to the **m;**
18:27 along with his **m,** and killed one hundred of
1Sa 21: 2 I have made an appointment with the young **m** A
21: 4 young **m** have kept themselves from women." A
21: 5 the vessels of the young **m** are holy even when A
22:19 **m** and women, children and infants, oxen, B
23: 3 But David's **m** said to him, "Look,
23: 5 So David and his **m** went to Keilah,
23: 8 to go down to Keilah, to besiege David and his **m.**
23:12 "Will the **m** of Keilah surrender me and my men
23:12 "Will the men of Keilah surrender me and my **m**
23:13 and his **m,** who were about six hundred, set out
23:24 David and his **m** were in the wilderness of Maon,
23:25 Saul and his **m** went to search for him.
23:26 David and his **m** on the other side of the mountain.
23:26 and his **m** were closing in on David and his **m**
24: 2 Saul took three thousand chosen **m** out of all Israel,
24: 2 for David and his **m** in the direction of the Rocks
24: 3 and his **m** were sitting in the innermost parts of
24: 4 The **m** of David said to him,
24: 6 He said to his **m,** "The LORD forbid
24: 7 So David scolded his **m** severely and did
24:22 but David and his **m** went up to the stronghold.
25: 5 So David sent ten young **m;** A
25: 5 David said to the young **m,** "Go up to Carmel, A
25: 8 Ask your young **m,** and they will tell you. A
25: 8 let my young **m** find favor in your sight; A
25: 9 When David's young **m** came, A
25:11 to **m** who come from I do not know where?"
25:12 So David's young **m** turned away, A
25:13 David said to his **m,** "Every man strap
25:13 and about four hundred **m** went up after David,
25:14 one of the young **m** told Abigail, Nabal's wife, A
25:15 Yet the **m** were very good to us,
25:19 and said to her young **m,** "Go on ahead of me; A
25:20 David and his **m** came down toward her;
25:25 servant, did not see the young **m** of my lord, A
25:27 be given to the young **m** who follow my lord. A
26: 2 with three thousand chosen **m** of Israel, C
26:22 Let one of the young **m** come over and get it. A
27: 2 he and the six hundred **m** who were with him,
27: 8 Now David and his **m** went up and made raids on
28: 1 you and your **m** are to go out with me in the army."
28: 8 he and two **m** with him.
29: 2 and his **m** were passing on in the rear with Achish,
29: 4 Would it not be with the heads of the **m** here?
29:11 So David set out with his **m** early in the morning,
30: 1 David and his **m** came to Ziklag on the third day,
30: 3 When David and his **m** came to the city,
30: 9 he and the six hundred **m** who were with him.
30:10 on with the pursuit, he and four hundred **m;**
30:17 except four hundred young **m,** A
30:21 to the two hundred **m** who had been too exhausted
30:22 and worthless fellows among the **m** who had gone
30:31 all the places where David and his **m** had roamed.
31: 1 and the **m** of Israel fled before the Philistines, C
31: 6 and his armor-bearer and all his **m** died together on
31: 7 the **m** of Israel who were on the other side C
31: 7 the Jordan saw that the **m** of Israel had fled C
31:12 all the valiant **m** set out,
2Sa 1:11 and all the **m** who were with him did the same. D
1:15 Then David called one of the young **m** and said, A
2: 3 David brought up the **m** who were with him,
2:14 the young **m** come forward and have a contest A
2:17 and the **m** of Israel were beaten by the servants C
2:21 seize one of the young **m,** and take his spoil." A
2:29 Abner and his **m** traveled all that night through
2:30 of David's servants nineteen **m** besides Asahel.
2:31 of Benjamin three hundred sixty of Abner's **m.**
2:32 Joab and his **m** marched all night,
3:20 Abner came with twenty **m** to David at Hebron,
3:20 David made a feast for Abner and the **m** who were
3:39 these **m,** the sons of Zeruiah,
4:11 when wicked **m** have killed a righteous man
4:12 So David commanded the young **m,** A
5: 6 The king and his **m** marched to Jerusalem against
5:21 and David and his **m** carried them away.
6: 1 David again gathered all the chosen **m** of Israel, C
6:19 whole multitude of Israel, both **m** and women, B
8: 5 David killed twenty-two thousand **m** of
10: 5 for the **m** were greatly ashamed.
10: 6 as well as the king of Maacah, one thousand **m,**
10: 6 and the **m** of Tob, twelve thousand **m.**
10: 8 and the **m** of Tob and Maacah,
10: 9 he chose some of the picked **m** of Israel, C
10:10 the rest of his **m** he put in the charge
11:17 The **m** of the city came out and fought with Joab;
11:23 "The **m** gained an advantage over us,
12: 1 "There were two **m** in a certain city,
13:32 that they have killed all the young **m** A
15: 1 and fifty **m** to run ahead of him.
15:11 Two hundred **m** from Jerusalem went
15:22 with all his **m** and all the little ones who were
16: 2 bread and summer fruit for the young **m** to eat, A
16:13 So David and his **m** went on the road,
17: 1 "Let me choose twelve thousand **m,**
17: 8 "You know that your father and his **m** are warriors,
17:14 Absalom and all the **m** of Israel said, CD
17:21 they had gone, the **m** came up out of the well,
17:24 crossed the Jordan with all the **m** of Israel. CD
18: 1 Then David mustered the **m** who were with him,
18: 2 The king said to the **m,**
18: 3 But the **m** said, "You shall not go out.
18: 7 The **m** of Israel were defeated there by the C
18: 7 was great on that day, twenty thousand **m.**
18:15 And ten young **m,** Joab's armor-bearers, A
18:28 who has delivered up the **m** who raised their hand
19:35 to the voice of singing **m** and singing women?
19:41 and all David's **m** with him?"

2Sa 20: 4 the **m** of Judah together to me within three days,
20: 7 Joab's **m** went out after him,
20:11 And one of Joab's **m** took his stand by Amasa,
21:17 Then David's **m** swore to him,
23:17 Can I drink the blood of the **m** who went at the risk
23:18 With his spear he fought against three hundred **m**
1Ki 1: 5 and fifty **m** to run before him.
2:32 and killed with the sword two **m** more righteous
5:13 the levy numbered thirty thousand **m.**
12: 6 the older **m** who had attended his father Solomon
12: 8 the advice that the older **m** gave him,
12: 8 consulted with the young **m** who had grown up A
12:10 young **m** who had grown up with him A
12:13 the advice that the older **m** had given him
12:14 young **m,** "My father made your yoke heavy, A
20:12 he said to his **m,** "Take your positions!"
20:14 the young **m** who serve the district governors." A
20:15 the young **m** who serve the district governors, A
20:17 The young **m** who serve the district governors A
20:17 "**M** have come out from Samaria."
20:19 the young **m** who serve the district governors, A
20:30 and the wall fell on twenty-seven thousand **m**
20:33 Now the **m** were watching for an omen;
21:11 The **m** of his city, the elders and
2Ki 1: 9 king sent to him a captain of fifty with his fifty **m.**
1:14 the two former captains of fifty **m** with their fifties;
2: 7 Fifty **m** of the company of prophets also went,
2:16 we have fifty strong **m** among your servants;
2:17 So they sent fifty **m** who searched for three days
4:40 They served some for the **m** to eat.
5:24 he dismissed the **m,** and they left.
6:20 open the eyes of these **m** so that they may see."
7: 3 there were four leprous **m** outside the city gate,
7: 8 these leprous **m** had come to the edge of the camp,
7:13 "Let some **m** take five of the remaining horses,
7:14 So they took two mounted **m,**
8:12 you will kill their young **m** with the sword, A
10:24 Now Jehu had stationed eighty **m** outside, saying,
11: 9 each brought his **m** who were to go off duty on
20:14 and said to him, "What did these **m** say?
24:16 brought captive to Babylon all the **m** of valor, D
25:19 and five **m** of the king's council who were found
25:19 and sixty **m** of the people of the land
25:23 the captains of the forces and their **m** heard that
25:23 they came with their **m** to Gedaliah at Mizpah,
25:24 Gedaliah swore to them and their **m,** saying,
25:25 of the royal family, came with ten **m;**
1Ch 4:12 These are the **m** of Recah.
4:22 and the **m** of Cozeba, and Joash, and Saraph,
4:42 some of them, five hundred **m** of the Simeonites,
5:24 mighty warriors, famous **m,** heads of their clans.
6:31 the **m** whom David put in charge of the service
6:33 These are the **m** who served;
7:40 All of these were **m** of Asher,
7:40 for service in war, was twenty-six thousand **m.**
10: 1 and the **m** of Israel fled before the Philistines, C
10: 7 all the **m** of Israel who were in the valley saw CD
11:19 Can I drink the blood of these **m?**
12:15 the **m** who crossed the Jordan in the first month,
19: 5 When David was told about the **m,**
19:10 some of the picked **m** of Israel and arrayed C
21: 5 there were one million one hundred thousand **m**
24: 4 Since more chief **m** were found among the sons
26: 6 for they were **m** of great ability.
26: 7 whose brothers were able **m,** Elihu and Semachiah.
26: 8 were able **m** qualified for the service;
26: 9 Meshelemiah had sons and brothers, able **m,**
26:30 one thousand seven hundred **m** of ability,
26:31 and **m** of great ability among them were found
26:32 two thousand seven hundred **m** of ability,
2Ch 10: 6 the older **m** who had attended his father Solomon
10: 8 he rejected the advice that the older **m** gave him,
10: 8 and consulted the young **m** who had grown up A
10:10 young **m** who had grown up with him said A
10:13 the advice of the older **m;**
10:14 young **m,** "My father made your yoke heavy, A
13: 3 four hundred thousand picked **m;**
13:17 five hundred thousand picked **m** of Israel fell C
14: 9 an army of a million **m** and three hundred chariots,
23: 8 each brought his **m,** who were to come on duty on
24:24 Although the army of Aram had come with few **m,**
25:11 and struck down ten thousand **m** of Seir.
25:13 But the **m** of the army whom Amaziah sent back,
26:17 with eighty priests of the LORD who were **m**
35:25 the singing **m** and singing women have spoken
Ezr 5: 4 of the **m** who are building this building?"
5:10 so that we might write down the names of the **m**
10: 1 a very great assembly of **m,** women,
10:16 Ezra the priest selected **m,** heads of families,
10:17 of all the **m** who had married foreign women. D
Ne 1: 2 Hanani, came with certain **m** from Judah;
2:12 I got up during the night, I and a few **m** with me;
3: 2 And the **m** of Jericho built next to him.
3: 7 the **m** of Gibeon and of Mizpah—
3:22 him the priests, the **m** of the surrounding area,
4:23 nor my brothers nor my servants nor the **m** of
8: 2 both **m** and women and all who could hear B
8: 3 in the presence of the **m** and the women
12:44 On that day **m** were appointed over the chambers
Est 2:23 both the **m** were hanged on the gallows.
7: 4 had been sold merely as slaves, **m** and women, B
Job 29: 8 the young **m** saw me and withdrew, A
31:10 and let other **m** kneel over her.
32: 1 So these three **m** ceased to answer Job,
32: 5 in the mouths of these three **m,**
34: 2 you wise **m,** and give ear to me, you who know; E
34:18 and to princes, 'You wicked **m!**';

Ps 45: 2 You are the most handsome of **m;**
78:63 Fire devoured their young **m,** A
148:12 Young **m** and women alike, AB
Ecc 2: 8 I got singers, both **m** and women, B
12: 3 and the strong **m** are bent,
SS 2: 3 so is my beloved among young **m.** A
3: 7 Around it are sixty mighty **m** of the mighty men
3: 7 mighty men of the mighty **m** of Israel, C
Isa 3:25 Your **m** shall fall by the sword and your warriors
13:18 Their bows will slaughter the young **m;** A
23: 4 nor given birth, I have neither reared young **m** A
31: 8 and his young **m** shall be put to forced labor. A
39: 3 and said to him, "What did these **m** say?
Jer 6:11 and on the gatherings of young **m** as well; A
9:21 the children from the streets and the young **m** A
11:22 the young **m** shall die by the sword; A
18:21 May their **m** meet death by pestilence,
26:22 of Achbor and **m** with him to Egypt,
31:13 and the young **m** and the old shall be merry. A
37:10 and there remained of them only wounded **m**
38: 9 these **m** have acted wickedly in all they did to
38:10 "Take three **m** with you from here,
38:11 the **m** with him and went to the house of the king,
38:16 or hand you over to these **m** who seek your life."
40: 7 and had committed to him **m,** women,
41: 1 came with ten **m** to Gedaliah son of Ahikam,
41: 2 of Nethaniah and the ten **m** with him got up
41: 5 eighty **m** arrived from Shechem and Shiloh
41: 7 of Nethaniah and the **m** with him slaughtered them,
41: 8 there were ten **m** among them who said to Ishmael,
41: 9 the bodies of the **m** whom he had struck down was
41:12 they took all their **m** and went to fight
41:15 of Nethaniah escaped from Johanan with eight **m,**
43: 2 and all the other insolent **m** said to Jeremiah,
43: 6 the **m,** the women, the children, the princesses,
44:15 Then all the **m** who were aware D
44:20 Jeremiah said to all the people, **m** and women, B
48:15 the choicest of his young **m** have gone down A
49:26 Therefore her young **m** shall fall in her squares, A
50:30 Therefore her young **m** shall fall in her squares, A
51: 3 Do not spare her young **m;** A
52:25 seven **m** of the king's council who were found
52:25 and sixty **m** of the people of the land
La 1:15 a time against me to crush my young **m;** A
1:18 my young women and young **m** have gone A
2:21 my young women and my young **m** have fallen A
5:13 Young **m** are compelled to grind, A
5:14 The old **m** have left the city gate, F
5:14 the city gate, the young **m** their music. A
Eze 8:16 were about twenty-five **m,**
9: 2 six **m** came from the direction of the upper gate,
9: 6 Cut down old **m,** young men and young women, F
9: 6 Cut down old men, young **m** and young women, A
11: 1 the entrance of the gateway, were twenty-five **m;**
11: 2 these are the **m** who devise iniquity
14: 3 these **m** have taken their idols into their hearts,
14:16 even if these three **m** were in it, as I live, says
14:18 though these three **m** were in it,
17:13 under oath (he had taken away the chief **m** of
23: 6 all of them handsome young **m,** A
23: 7 the choicest **m** of Assyria all of them;
23: 8 for in her youth **m** had lain with her
23:12 all of them handsome young **m.** A
23:23 the Assyrians with them, handsome young **m,** A
23:40 They even sent for **m** to come from far away,
27: 8 skilled **m** of Zemer were within you,
27:11 **M** of Arvad and Helech were
27:11 **m** of Gamad were at your towers.
30:17 The young **m** of On and of Pi-beseth shall fall A
39:14 They will set apart **m** to pass through
Da 1: 4 young **m** without physical defect and handsome, A
1:10 in poorer condition than the other young **m** A
1:13 with the appearance of the young **m** who eat A
1:15 young **m** who had been eating the royal rations. A
1:17 To these four young **m** God gave knowledge A
2:12 violent rage and commanded that all the wise **m** E
2:13 and the wise **m** were about to be executed; E
2:14 who had gone out to execute the wise **m** E
2:18 rest of the wise **m** of Babylon might not perish. E
2:24 the king had appointed to destroy the wise **m** E
2:24 "Do not destroy the wise **m** of Babylon; E
2:27 Daniel answered the king, "No wise **m,** E
2:48 chief prefect over all the wise **m** of Babylon. E
3:13 so they brought those **m** before the king.
3:21 So the **m** were bound, still wearing their tunics,
3:22 the raging flames killed the **m** who lifted Shadrach,
3:23 But the three **m,** Shadrach, Meshach,
3:24 not three **m** that we threw bound into the fire?"
3:25 He replied, "But I see four **m** unbound,
3:27 not had any power over the bodies of those **m;**
4: 6 all the wise **m** of Babylon should be brought E
4:18 the wise **m** of my kingdom are unable to tell me E
5: 7 and the king said to the wise **m** of Babylon, E
5: 8 Then all the king's wise **m** came in, E
5:15 Now the wise **m,** the enchanters, E
6: 5 The **m** said, "We shall not find any ground
Hos 4:14 for the **m** themselves go aside with whores,
Joel 2:28 your old **m** shall dream dreams, F
2:28 and your young **m** shall see visions. A
Am 4:10 I killed your young **m** with the sword; A
8:13 and the young **m** shall faint for thirst. A
Jnh 1:10 Then the **m** were even more afraid,
1:10 the **m** knew that he was fleeing from the presence
1:13 the **m** rowed hard to bring the ship back to land,
1:16 Then the **m** feared the LORD even more,
Zec 7: 2 and Regem-melech and their **m,**
8: 4 Old **m** and old women shall again sit in the F

Zec 8:23 In those days ten **m** from nations
9:17 Grain shall make the young **m** flourish, A
Mt 2: 1 wise **m** from the East came to Jerusalem, E
2: 7 wise **m** and learned from them the exact time E
2:16 saw that he had been tricked by the wise **m,** E
2:16 to the time that he had learned from the wise **m.** E
9:27 two blind **m** followed him, crying loudly,
9:28 he entered the house, the blind **m** came to him;
14:21 And those who ate were about five thousand **m,**
15:38 Those who had eaten were four thousand **m,**
20:30 There were two blind **m** sitting by the roadside.
28: 4 of him the guards shook and became like dead **m.**
Mk 1:20 in the boat with the hired **m,**
6:17 For Herod himself had sent **m** who arrested John,
6:44 the loaves numbered five thousand **m.**
Lk 5:18 Just then some **m** came, carrying a paralyzed man
7:20 When the **m** had come to him, they said,
9:14 For there were about five thousand **m.**
9:30 Suddenly they saw two **m,** Moses and Elijah,
9:32 they saw his glory and the two **m** who stood
12:45 **m** and women, and to eat and drink and B
18:10 "Two **m** went up to the temple to pray,
22:63 the **m** who were holding Jesus began to mock him
24: 4 suddenly two **m** in dazzling clothes stood
24: 5 but the **m** said to them,
Jn 18: 8 So if you are looking for me, let these **m** go."
19:31 of the crucified **m** broken and the bodies removed.
Ac 1:10 suddenly two **m** in white robes stood by them.
1:11 "**M** of Galilee, why do you stand looking up
1:21 of the **m** who have accompanied us during all
2:14 "**M** of Judea and all who live in Jerusalem,
2:17 and your young **m** shall see visions, A
2:17 and your old **m** shall dream dreams. F
2:18 Even upon my slaves, both **m** and women, B
4:13 that they were uneducated and ordinary **m,**
5: 6 The young **m** came and wrapped up his body, A
5:10 the young **m** came in they found her dead, A
5:14 great numbers of both **m** and women, B
5:25 the **m** whom you put in prison are standing in
5:34 stood up and ordered the **m** to be put outside for
5:35 carefully what you propose to do to these **m.**
5:36 claiming to be somebody, and a number of **m,**
5:38 keep away from these **m** and let them alone;
6: 3 from among yourselves seven **m** of good standing,
6: 6 They had these **m** stand before the apostles,
6:11 Then they secretly instigated some **m** to say,
7:26 saying, '**M,** you are brothers;
8: 2 Devout **m** buried Stephen
8: 3 dragging off both **m** and women, B
8:12 they were baptized, both **m** and women. B
9: 2 the Way, **m** or women, he might bring them bound
9: 7 The **m** who were traveling
9:38 sent two **m** to him with the request,
10: 5 Now send **m** to Joppa for a certain Simon
10:17 suddenly the **m** sent by Cornelius appeared.
10:19 "Look, three **m** are searching for you.
10:21 So Peter went down to the **m** and said,
11: 3 "Why did you go to uncircumcised **m** and eat
11:11 At that very moment three **m,**
11:20 But among them were some **m** of Cyprus
13:50 of high standing and the leading **m** of the city,
15:22 decided to choose **m** from among their members
16:17 "These **m** are slaves of the Most High God,
16:20 they said, "These **m** are disturbing our city;
16:35 the police, saying, "Let those **m** go."
16:37 uncondemned, **m** who are Roman citizens,
17:12 not a few Greek women and **m** of high standing.
19:25 with the workers of the same trade, and said, "**M,**
19:37 You have brought these **m** here who are neither
21:23 We have four **m** who are under a vow.
21:24 Join these **m,** go through the rite of purification
21:26 Then Paul took the **m,** and the next day,
22: 4 point of death by binding both **m** and women B
23:21 for more than forty of their **m** are lying in ambush
24:20 Or let these **m** here tell what crime they had found
25:23 with the military tribunes and the prominent **m** of
27:21 Paul then stood up among them and said, "**M,**
27:25 So keep up your courage, **m,**
27:31 "Unless these **m** stay in the ship,
Ro 1:27 and in the same way also the **m,**
1:27 **M** committed shameless acts with **m** and received
Eph 6: 7 as to the Lord and not to **m** and women, B
1Ti 2: 8 then, that in every place the **m** should pray,
5: 1 to him as to a father, to younger **m** as brothers,
2Ti 3: 9 because, as in the case of those two **m,**
Tit 2: 2 Tell the older **m** to be temperate, serious, prudent,
2: 6 Likewise, urge the younger **m** to be self-controlled.
2Pe 1:21 **m** and women moved by the Holy Spirit spoke B
Tob 6:12 have before all other **m** a hereditary claim on her.
7:11 I have given her to seven **m** of our kinsmen,
Jdt 2: 5 Leave my presence and take with you **m** confident
2:27 ravaged their lands and put all their young **m** A
3: 5 The **m** came to Holofernes and told him all this.
3: 6 in the fortified towns and took picked **m** from them
4:11 And all the Israelite **m,** women,
6:12 When the **m** of the town saw them,
6:16 all their young **m** and women ran to the AB
7:12 and keep all the **m** in your forces with you; D
7:18 and they sent some of their **m** toward the south
7:22 and the women and young **m** fainted from thirst A
7:23 Then all the people, the young **m,** the women, A
8: 7 **m** and women slaves, livestock, and fields; B
10: 4 entice the eyes of all the **m** who might see her. D
10: 9 ordered the young **m** to open the gate for her, A
10:10 The **m** of the town watched her until she had gone
10:13 the hill country without losing one of his **m,**
10:14 the **m** heard her words, and observed her face—

Jdt 10:17 from their number a hundred **m** to accompany her
10:19 It is not wise to leave one of their **m** alive,
14: 6 the head of Holofernes in the hand of one of the **m**
15: 1 When the **m** in the tents heard it,
15: 4 Uzziah sent **m** to Betomasthaim and Choba
15: 5 The **m** in Gilead and in Galilee outflanked them
15:13 while all the **m** of Israel followed, CD
16: 4 and kill my young **m** with the sword, A
16: 6 by the hands of the young **m**, nor did the sons A
Sir 19: 2 Wine and women lead intelligent **m** astray,
26:28 intelligent **m** who are treated contemptuously,
36:28 her husband is more fortunate than other **m**.
44: 1 now sing the praises of famous **m**,
44: 6 rich **m** endowed with resources, living peacefully
44:10 But these also were godly **m**,
48: 6 and famous **m**, from their sickbeds.
Sus 1: 6 These **m** were frequently at Joakim's house,
1:43 that these **m** have given false evidence against me.
1:49 for these **m** have given false evidence against her."
Bel 1:20 the footprints of **m** and women and children." B
1Mc 1:26 young women and young **m** became faint, A
1:34 a sinful people, **m** who were renegades.
3:15 Once again a strong army of godless **m** went up
3:38 able **m** among the Friends of the king,
4: 2 **M** from the citadel were his guides.
4: 5 "These **m** are running away from us."
4: 6 in the plain with three thousand **m**,
4: 7 and these **m** were trained in war.
4:13 Then the **m** with Judas blew their trumpets
4:29 and Judas met them with ten thousand **m**.
4:34 there fell of the army of Lysias five thousand **m**;
4:41 Then Judas detailed **m** to fight against those in
5:17 "Choose your **m** and go and rescue your kindred
5:20 Then three thousand **m** were assigned to Simon
5:32 and he said to the **m** of his forces,
5:38 Judas sent **m** to spy out the camp,
5:50 So the **m** of the forces encamped,
5:58 So they issued orders to the **m** of the forces
5:59 and his **m** came out of the town to meet them
5:62 of those **m** through whom deliverance was given
6:35 a thousand **m** armed with coats of mail,
6:37 on each were four armed **m** who fought from there,
6:45 he killed **m** right and left,
6:54 Only a few **m** were left in the sanctuary;
6:57 and to the troops, **m**, "Daily we grow weaker,
7: 1 sailed with a few **m** to a town by the sea,
7: 5 to him all the renegade and godless **m** of Israel; C
7:19 and seized many of the **m** who had deserted to him,
7:28 I shall come with a few **m** to see you face to face
7:40 Judas encamped in Adasa with three thousand **m**.
9: 5 and with him were three thousand picked **m**.
9:12 and the **m** with Judas also blew their trumpets.
9:14 then all the stouthearted **m** went with him,
9:16 and followed close behind Judas and his **m**.
9:48 the **m** with him leaped into the Jordan and swam
9:49 about one thousand of Bacchides' **m** fell that day.
9:53 the leading **m** of the land as hostages and put them
9:58 and his **m** are living in quiet and confidence.
9:60 telling them to seize Jonathan and his **m**;
9:61 And Jonathan's **m** seized about fifty of the **m** of
9:62 Then Jonathan with his **m**, and Simon,
9:63 and sent orders to the **m** of Judea.
9:65 and he went with only a few **m**.
9:67 and his **m** sallied out from the town and set fire to
10:32 so that he may station in it **m** of his own choice
10:36 to the number of thirty thousand **m**,
10:74 He chose ten thousand **m** and set out
10:80 at his **m** from early morning until late afternoon.
10:81 But his **m** stood fast, as Jonathan had commanded,
11:43 you will do well to send me **m** who will help me,
11:44 So Jonathan sent three thousand stalwart **m** to him
11:69 Then the **m** in ambush emerged from their places
11:70 All the **m** with Jonathan fled; D
11:73 When his **m** who were fleeing saw this,
12: 1 he chose **m** and sent them to Rome to confirm
12:45 and choose for yourself a few **m** to stay with you,
12:47 He kept with himself three thousand **m**,
12:50 and had perished along with his **m**,
13:21 Now the **m** in the citadel kept sending envoys
13:44 The **m** in the siege engine leaped out into the city,
13:45 The **m** in the city, with their wives and children,
13:52 and he and his **m** lived there.
14: 9 Old **m** sat in the streets; F
14:23 to receive these **m** with honor and to put a copy
16:15 he gave them a great banquet, and hid **m** there.
16:16 Ptolemy and his **m** rose up, took their weapons,
16:21 and that "he has sent **m** to kill you also."
16:22 the **m** who came to destroy him and killed them,
2Mc 1:15 with a few **m** inside the wall of the sacred precinct,
1:16 and struck down the leader and his **m**;
3:26 Two young **m** also appeared to him, A
3:27 his **m** took him up, put him on a stretcher,
3:33 the same young **m** appeared again A
4:12 he induced the noblest of the young **m** to wear A
4:40 Lysimachus armed about three thousand **m**
4:41 in wild confusion at Lysimachus and his **m**.
4:44 three **m** sent by the senate presented the case
4:47 while he sentenced to death those unfortunate **m**,
5: 5 a thousand **m** and suddenly made an assault on
5:24 and commanded him to kill all the grown **m** and
8:22 putting fifteen hundred **m** under each.
10:21 and accused these **m** of having sold their kindred
10:22 Then he killed these **m** who had turned traitor,
10:25 Maccabeus and his **m** sprinkled dust on their heads
10:29 to the enemy from heaven five resplendent **m**
10:33 Then Maccabeus and his **m** were glad,
10:34 The **m** within, relying on the strength of the place,
2Mc 10:35 twenty young **m** in the army of Maccabeus, A
11: 6 and his **m** got word that Lysias was besieging
11:20 I have ordered these **m** and my representatives
12: 5 he gave orders to his **m**
12:14 behaved most insolently toward Judas and his **m**,
12:15 and his **m**, calling against the great Sovereign of
12:19 more than ten thousand **m**.
12:20 set **m** in command of the divisions,
12:22 so that often they were injured by their own **m**
12:24 the hands of Dositheus and Sosipater and their **m**.
12:27 young **m** took their stand before the walls A
12:35 But a certain Dositheus, one of Bacenor's **m**,
12:36 and his **m** had been fighting for a long time
12:39 and his **m** went to take up the bodies of the fallen
12:40 to all that this was the reason these **m** had fallen.
13: 1 and his **m** that Antiochus Eupator was coming with
13:15 and with a picked force of the bravest young **m**, A
13:15 and killed as many as two thousand **m** in the camp.
13:22 withdrew, attacked Judas and his **m**, was defeated;
14: 1 word came to Judas and his **m** that Demetrius son
14:22 Judas posted armed **m** in readiness at key places
14:30 So he gathered not a few of his **m**,
1Es 1:32 and the principal **m**, with the women,
1:34 The **m** of the nation took Jeconiah son of Josiah,
1:53 These killed their young **m** with the sword A
3: 4 Then the three young **m** of the bodyguard, A
3:16 He said, "Call the young **m**, A
4: 2 not **m** strongest, who rule over land and sea and
4:14 and are not **m** many, and is not wine strong?
4:16 and women brought up the very **m** who plant
4:17 Women make men's clothes; they bring **m** glory;
4:17 **m** cannot exist without women.
4:18 If **m** gather gold and silver
4:26 Many **m** have lost their minds because of women,
5: 4 These are the names of the **m** who went up,
5:39 in the register and the genealogy of these **m** was
5:63 old **m** who had seen the former house, F
6:29 a portion be scrupulously given to these **m**,
8:27 and I gathered **m** from Israel to go up with me."
8:30 and with him a hundred fifty **m** enrolled.
8:31 and with him two hundred **m**.
8:32 and with him three hundred **m**.
8:32 and with him two hundred fifty **m**.
8:33 of Gotholiah, and with him seventy **m**.
8:34 Zeraiah son of Michael, and with him seventy **m**.
8:35 and with him two hundred twelve **m**.
8:36 and with him a hundred sixty **m**.
8:37 and with him twenty-eight **m**.
8:38 and with him a hundred ten **m**.
8:39 Jeuel, and Shemaiah, and with them seventy **m**.
8:40 Uthai son of Istalcurus, and with him seventy **m**.
8:44 who were leaders and **m** of understanding;
8:46 the treasurers at that place to send us **m** to serve
8:47 of our Lord they brought us competent **m** of
8:48 and their descendants, twenty **m**;
8:50 There I proclaimed a fast for the young **m** A
8:91 around him a very great crowd of **m** and women B
8:92 Shecaniah son of Jehiel, one of the **m** of Israel, C
9: 4 and the **m** themselves expelled from the multitude
9: 5 Then the **m** of the tribe of Judah
9:16 for himself the leading **m** of their ancestral houses,
9:17 of the **m** who had foreign wives were brought to
9:40 **m** and women, and all the priests to hear the law, B
9:41 in the presence of both **m** and women; B
3Mc 1:12 "Even if those **m** are deprived of this honor,
1:23 barely restrained by the old **m** and the elders, F
2:17 for the defilement committed by these **m**,
4: 5 For a multitude of gray-headed old **m**, F
7:15 to death more than three hundred **m**;
2Es 10:22 our righteous **m** have been carried off,
10:22 our young **m** have been enslaved A
10:22 and our strong **m** made powerless.
14:37 So I took the five **m**, as he commanded me,
14:42 the Most High gave understanding to the five **m**,
4Mc 8: 5 "Young **m**, with favorable feelings I admire A
8:19 O **m** and brothers, should we not fear
9: 6 And if the aged **m** of the Hebrews because
9: 6 we young **m** should die despising your coercive A
12:13 of **m** who have feelings like yours and are made
14: 9 as we hear of the suffering of these young **m**; A
14:11 that reason had full command over these **m**
14:12 the mother of the seven young **m** bore up under A
14:20 not sway the mother of the young **m**; A
15:30 and more courageous than **m** in endurance!
16: 2 not only that **m** have ruled over the emotions,
16:17 you young **m** were to be terrified by tortures. A

MEN'S (2) [MAN]

Ge 44: 1 "Fill the **m** sacks with food,
1Es 4:17 Women make **m** clothes; they bring men glory;

MENACE (1) [MENACING]

1Mc 1:35 they stored them there, and became a great **m**,

MENACING (1) [MENACE]

Hab 1: 8 more **m** than wolves at dusk; their horses charge.

MENAHEM (8)

2Ki 15:14 Then **M** son of Gadi came up from Tirzah
15:16 At that time **M** sacked Tiphsah,
15:17 **M** son of Gadi began to reign over Israel;
15:19 **M** gave Pul a thousand talents of silver,
15:20 **M** exacted the money from Israel, that is,
15:21 Now the rest of the deeds of **M**, and all that he did,
15:22 **M** slept with his ancestors,
2Ki 15:23 Pekahiah son of **M** began to reign over Israel

MENAN (KJV) See MENNA

MENCHILDREN (KJV) See MALES

MENDED (2) [MENDING]

Jos 9: 4 and wineskins, worn-out and torn and **m**,
Jer 19:11 so that it can never be **m**.

MENDING (2) [MENDED]

Mt 4:21 in the boat with their father Zebedee, **m** their nets,
Mk 1:19 who were in their boat **m** the nets.

MENE (3)

Da 5:25 this is the writing that was inscribed: **M**, **M**, TEKEL,
5:26 This is the interpretation of the matter: **M**,

MENELAUS (17)

2Mc 4:23 After a period of three years Jason sent **M**,
4:27 Although **M** continued to hold the office,
4:29 **M** left his own brother Lysimachus as deputy in
4:32 But **M**, thinking he had obtained
4:34 Therefore **M**, taking Andronicus aside,
4:39 the city by Lysimachus with the connivance of **M**,
4:43 Charges were brought against **M**
4:45 But **M**, already as good as beaten,
4:47 **M**, the cause of all the trouble,
4:50 But **M**, because of the greed of those in power,
5: 5 **M** took refuge in the citadel.
5:15 the world, guided by **M**, who had become a traitor
5:23 and besides these **M**, who lorded it
11:29 **M** has informed us that you wish to return home
11:32 And I have also sent **M** to encourage you.
13: 3 **M** also joined them and with utter
13: 7 a fate it came about that **M** the lawbreaker died,

MENESTHEUS (2)

2Mc 4: 4 and that Apollonius son of **M**, and governor of
4:21 When Apollonius son of **M** was sent to Egypt for

MENNA (1)

Lk 3:31 son of **M**, son of Mattatha, son of Nathan,

MENPLEASERS (KJV) See PLEASE THEM

MENSTEALERS (KJV) See SLAVE TRADERS

MENSTRUAL (4) [MENSTRUATION]

Lev 18:19 while she is in her **m** uncleanness.
Eze 18: 6 or approach a woman during her **m** period,
22:10 in you they violate women in their **m** periods.
36:17 like the uncleanness of a woman in her **m** period.

MENSTRUATION (2) [MENSTRUAL, MENSTRUOUS]

Lev 12: 2 as at the time of her **m**, she shall be unclean.
12: 5 she shall be unclean two weeks, as in her **m**;

MENSTRUOUS (1) [MENSTRUATION]

2Es 5: 8 and **m** women shall bring forth monsters.

MENTAL (2)

4Mc 1:32 Some desires are **m**, others are physical,
2: 2 because by **m** effort he overcame sexual desire.

MENTION (10) [AFOREMENTIONED, MENTIONED]

Ge 40:14 please do me the kindness to make **m** of me
Jos 23: 7 or make **m** of the names of their gods,
Job 28:18 No **m** shall be made of coral or of crystal;
Ps 87: 4 Among those who know me I **m** Rahab
Jer 20: 9 If I say, "I will not **m** him,
23:36 "the burden of the LORD" you shall **m** no more,
Am 6:10 We must not **m** the name of the LORD."
Eph 5:12 even to **m** what such people do secretly;
1Th 1: 2 to God for all of you and **m** you in our prayers,
Heb 11:22 made **m** of the exodus of the Israelites

MENTIONED (24) [MENTION]

Jos 21: 9 of Simeon they gave the following towns **m**
1Sa 4:18 When he **m** the ark of God,
1Ch 4:38 these **m** by name were leaders in their families,
6:65 and Benjamin these towns that are **m** by name.
2Ch 28:15 Then those who were **m** by name got up and took
Ezr 8:20 These were all **m** by name.
Est 6:10 Leave out nothing that you have **m**."
Isa 19:17 to whom it is **m** will fear because of the plan that
Hos 2:17 and they shall be **m** by name no more.
Eph 5: 3 or greed, must not even be **m** among you,
2Ti 2:21 of the things I have **m** will become special utensils,
Sir 49: 9 also **m** Job who held fast to all the ways of justice.
2Mc 2: 1 to take some of the fire, as has been **m**,
4: 1 The previously **m** Simon, who had informed about
4:23 the brother of the previously **m** Simon,
14: 8 of those whom I have **m** our whole nation is now

3Mc 2:25 abetted by the previously **m** drinking companions
4:14 for the hard labor that has been briefly **m** before,
4:17 But after the previously **m** interval of time
2Es 5:40 as you cannot do one of the things that were **m**,
7:*87* which is worse than all the ways that have been **m**,
7:*98* which is greater than all that have been **m**,
7:*99* and the previously **m** are the ways of torment
13:21 also explain to you the things that you have **m**.

MENUHOTH (1)

1Ch 2:52 had other sons: Haroeh, half of the **M**.

MEONENIM (KJV) See ELON-MEONENIM

MEONOTHAI‡ (2)

1Ch 4:13 of Othniel: Hathath and **M**.
4:14 **M** became the father of Ophrah;

MEPHAATH (4)

Jos 13:18 and Jahaz, and Kedemoth, and **M**,
21:37 and **M** with its pasture lands—four towns.
1Ch 6:79 and **M** with its pasture lands;
Jer 48:21 upon Holon, and Jahzah, and **M**,

MEPHIBOSHETH (14) [MEPHIBOSHETH'S, =MERIB-BAAL]

2Sa 4:4 and became lame. His name was **M**.
9:6 **M** son of Jonathan son of Saul came to David,
9:6 and did obeisance. David said, "**M!**"
9:10 but your master's grandson **M** shall always eat
9:11 **M** ate at David's table, like one of the king's sons.
9:12 **M** had a young son whose name was Mica.
9:13 **M** lived in Jerusalem, for he always ate at
16:1 Ziba the servant of **M** met him,
16:4 "All that belonged to **M** is now yours."
19:24 **M** grandson of Saul came down to meet the king;
19:25 "Why did you not go with me, **M?**"
19:30 **M** said to the king, "Let him take it all,
21:7 the king spared **M**, the son of Saul's son Jonathan,
21:8 whom she bore to Saul, Armoni and **M**;

MEPHIBOSHETH'S (1) [MEPHIBOSHETH]

2Sa 9:12 all who lived in Ziba's house became **M** servants.

MERAB (4)

1Sa 14:49 the name of the firstborn was **M**,
18:17 Saul said to David, "Here is my elder daughter **M**;
18:19 when Saul's daughter **M** should have been given
2Sa 21:8 and the five sons of **M** daughter of Saul,

MERAIAH (1)

Ne 12:12 of ancestral houses, were: of Seraiah, **M**;

MERAIMOTH (1)

2Es 1:2 of Eli son of Amariah son of Azariah son of **M** son

MERAIOTH (7)

1Ch 6:6 Uzzi of Zerahiah, Zerahiah of **M**,
6:7 **M** of Amariah, Amariah of Ahitub,
6:52 **M** his son, Amariah his son, Ahitub his son,
9:11 son of Meshullam, son of Zadok, son of **M**,
Ezr 7:3 son of Amariah, son of Azariah, son of **M**,
Ne 11:11 of Meshullam son of Zadok son of **M** son
12:15 of Harim, Adna; of **M**, Helkai;

MERARI (30) [MERARITE, MERARITES]

Ge 46:11 The children of Levi: Gershon, Kohath, and **M**.
Ex 6:16 Gershon, Kohath, and **M**, and the length
6:19 The sons of **M**: Mahli and Mushi.
Nu 3:17 by their names: Gershon, Kohath, and **M**.
3:20 The sons of **M** by their clans: Mahli and Mushi.
3:33 To **M** belonged the clan of the Mahlites and
3:33 these are the clans of **M**.
3:35 of the clans of **M** was Zuriel son of Abihail;
3:36 The responsibility assigned to the sons of **M** was
26:57 of **M**, the clan of the Merarites.
1Ch 6:1 The sons of Levi: Gershon, Kohath, and **M**.
6:16 The sons of Levi: Gershom, Kohath, and **M**.
6:19 The sons of **M**: Mahli and Mushi.
6:29 The sons of **M**: Mahli, Libni his son,
6:44 On the left were their kindred the sons of **M**:
6:47 son of Mahli, son of Mushi, son of **M**, son of Levi;
9:14 son of Hashabiah, of the sons of **M**;
15:6 of **M**, Asaiah the chief, with two hundred twenty
15:17 and of the sons of **M**, their kindred,
23:6 of Levi: Gershon, Kohath, and **M**.
23:21 The sons of **M**: Mahli and Mushi.
24:26 The sons of **M**: Mahli and Mushi.
24:27 The sons of **M**: of Jaaziah,
26:10 Hosah, of the sons of **M**, had sons:
26:19 among the Korahites and the sons of **M**.
2Ch 29:12 and of the sons of **M**, Kish son of Abdi,
34:12 the Levites Jahath and Obadiah, of the sons of **M**,
Ezr 8:19 and with him Jeshaiah of the descendants of **M**,
Jdt 8:1 the daughter of **M** son of Ox son of Joseph son
16:6 but Judith daughter of **M** with the beauty of her

MERARITE (2) [MERARI]

Jos 21:34 To the rest of the Levites—the **M** families—
21:40 As for the towns of the several **M** families, that is,

MERARITES (10) [MERARI]

Nu 4:29 As for the **M**, you shall enroll them by their clans
4:33 This is the service of the clans of the **M**,
4:42 The enrollment of the clans of the **M**,
4:45 This is the enrollment of the clans of the **M**,
7:8 and four wagons and eight oxen he gave to the **M**,
10:17 and the Gershonites and the **M**,
26:57 of Merari, the clan of the **M**.
Jos 21:7 The **M** according to their families received twelve
1Ch 6:63 To the **M** according to their
6:77 To the rest of the **M** out of the tribe of Zebulun:

MERATHAIM (1)

Jer 50:21 Go up to the land of **M**;

MERCENARIES (5) [MERCENARY]

Jer 46:21 Even her **m** in her midst are like fatted calves;
Jdt 6:2 Achior and you **m** of Ephraim,
1Mc 4:35 and enlisted **m** in order to invade Judea again with
2Mc 10:14 he maintained a force of **m**,
10:24 a tremendous force of **m** and collected the cavalry

MERCENARY (3) [MERCENARIES]

Jdt 6:5 "As for you, Achior, you Ammonite **m**,
1Mc 6:29 **M** forces also came to him from other kingdoms
15:3 a host of **m** troops and have equipped warships,

MERCHANDISE (15) [MERCHANT]

Ne 10:31 the land bring in **m** or any grain on the sabbath day
13:16 brought in fish and all kinds of **m** and sold them on
13:20 the merchants and sellers of all kinds of **m** spent
Pr 31:18 She perceives that her **m** is profitable.
Isa 23:18 Her **m** and her wages will be dedicated to
23:18 but her **m** will supply abundant food
45:14 The wealth of Egypt and the **m** of Ethiopia,
Eze 26:12 They will plunder your riches and loot your **m**;
27:13 and vessels of bronze for your **m**.
27:17 they exchanged for your **m** wheat from Minnith,
27:19 cassia, and sweet cane were bartered for your **m**.
27:27 Your riches, your wares, your **m**,
27:27 your caulkers, your dealers in **m**,
27:33 with your abundant wealth and **m** you enriched
27:34 your **m** and all your crew have sunk with you.

MERCHANT (8) [MERCHANDISE, MERCHANTS]

Pr 31:14 She is like the ships of the **m**,
31:24 she supplies the **m** with sashes.
SS 3:6 with all the fragrant powders of the **m**?
Isa 23:3 you were the **m** of the nations.
Eze 27:3 **m** of the peoples on many coastlands,
Mt 13:45 of heaven is like a **m** in search of fine pearls;
Sir 26:29 A **m** can hardly keep from wrongdoing,
37:11 with a **m** about business or with a buyer about

MERCHANTMEN (KJV) See MERCHANTS, TRADERS

MERCHANTS (25) [MERCHANT]

Ge 23:16 according to the weights current among the **m**.
1Ki 10:15 from the traders and from the business of the **m**,
2Ch 9:14 besides that which the traders and **m** brought;
Ne 3:31 as the house of the temple servants and of the **m**,
3:32 the goldsmiths and the **m** made repairs.
13:20 the **m** and sellers of all kinds of merchandise spent
Job 41:6 Will they divide it up among the **m**?
Isa 23:2 Be still, O inhabitants of the coast, O **m** of Sidon,
23:8 whose **m** were princes, whose traders were the
Eze 16:29 with Chaldea, the land of **m**;
17:4 He carried it to a land of trade, set it in a city of **m**.
27:22 The **m** of Sheba and Raamah traded with you;
27:23 Haran, Canneh, Eden, the **m** of Sheba, Asshur,
27:36 The **m** among the peoples hiss at you;
38:13 Sheba and Dedan and the **m** of Tarshish
Na 3:16 You increased your **m** more than the stars of
Zec 11:7 So, on behalf of the sheep **m**,
11:11 So it was annulled on that day, and the sheep **m**,
Rev 18:3 the **m** of the earth have grown rich from the power
18:11 And the **m** of the earth weep and mourn for her,
18:15 The **m** of these wares, who gained wealth from her,
18:23 for your **m** were the magnates of the earth,
Sir 42:5 of profit from dealing with **m**,
Bar 3:23 the **m** of Merran and Teman,
2Mc 8:34 who had brought the thousand **m** to buy the Jews,

MERCIES (11) [MERCY]

Ne 9:19 you in your great **m** did not forsake them in
9:27 to your great **m** you gave them saviors who saved
9:28 many times you rescued them according to your **m**.
9:31 in your great **m** you did not make an end of them
La 3:22 his **m** never come to an end;
Da 9:18 but on the ground of your great **m**.
Ro 12:1 brothers and sisters, by the **m** of God,
2Co 1:3 the Father of **m** and the God of all consolation,
Sir 18:5 And who can fully recount his **m**?
Man 1:7 of your **m** you have appointed repentance
3Mc 2:20 Speedily let your **m** overtake us,

MERCIFUL (53) [MERCY]

Ge 19:16 the LORD being **m** to him,
Ex 34:6 the LORD, a God **m** and gracious, slow to anger,
Dt 4:31 Because the LORD your God is a **m** God,
1Ki 20:31 that the kings of the house of Israel are **m** kings;
2Ch 30:9 For the LORD your God is gracious and **m**,
Ne 9:17 you are a God ready to forgive, gracious and **m**,
9:31 for you are a gracious and **m** God.
Ps 57:1 Be **m** to me, O God, be merciful to me,
57:1 be **m** to me, for in you my soul takes refuge;
86:15 But you, O Lord, are a God **m** and gracious,
103:8 The LORD is **m** and gracious,
111:4 the LORD is gracious and **m**.
112:4 they are gracious, **m**, and righteous.
116:5 and righteous; our God is **m**.
145:8 The LORD is gracious and **m**,
Jer 3:12 I will not look on you in anger, for I am **m**,
Joel 2:13 your God, for he is gracious and **m**, slow to anger,
Jnh 4:2 for I knew that you are a gracious God and **m**,
Mt 5:7 "Blessed are the **m**, for they will receive mercy.
Lk 6:36 Be **m**, just as your Father is **m**.
18:13 'God, be **m** to me, a sinner!'
Ro 11:32 in disobedience so that he may be **m** to all.
Heb 2:17 so that he might be a **m** and faithful high priest in
8:12 For I will be **m** toward their iniquities,
Jas 5:11 how the Lord is compassionate and **m**.
Tob 3:11 "Blessed are you, **m** God! Blessed is your name
8:17 Be **m** to them, O Master, and keep them safe;
11:17 Tobit acknowledged that God had been **m** to him
Wis 11:23 But you are **m** to all, for you can do all things,
Sir 2:11 For the Lord is compassionate and **m**;
29:1 The **m** lend to their neighbors;
48:20 But they called upon the Lord who is **m**,
50:19 before the **M** One, until the order of worship of
1Mc 2:57 David, because he was **m**,
2Mc 1:24 you are awe-inspiring and strong and just and **m**,
8:29 and implored the **m** Lord to be wholly reconciled
11:9 And together they all praised the **m** God,
13:12 in the same petition and had implored the **m** Lord
1Es 8:53 and we found him very **m**.
Man 1:7 of great compassion, long-suffering, and very **m**,
3Mc 5:7 and Ruler of all power, their **m** God and Father,
5:51 over every power to manifest himself and be **m**
2Es 2:31 for I am **m**, says the Lord Almighty.
7:*132* [62] O Lord, that the Most High is now called **m**,
8:31 it is because of us sinners that you are called **m**.
8:32 then you will be called **m**.
8:36 when you are **m** to those who have no store
10:24 so that the Mighty One may be **m** to you again,
4Mc 6:28 Be **m** to your people, and let our punishment
8:14 whatever justice you revere will be **m** to you
9:24 of our ancestors may become **m** to our nation
12:17 on the God of our ancestors to be **m** to our nation;

MERCIFULLY See Index to Footnotes

MERCILESS (4) [MERCY]

Pr 5:9 and your years to the **m**,
Jer 30:14 the punishment of a **m** foe,
Wis 12:5 their **m** slaughter of children,
Sir 37:11 the **m** about kindness, with an idler about any work

MERCURIUS (KJV) See HERMES

MERCY‡ (246) [ALL-MERCIFUL, MERCIES, MERCIFUL, MERCILESS]

A. HIS MERCY ENDURES FOREVER (17)

Ge 43:14 may God Almighty grant you **m** before the man,
Ex 25:17 Then you shall make a **m** seat of pure gold;
25:18 at the two ends of the **m** seat.
25:19 with the **m** seat you shall make the cherubim
25:20 overshadowing the **m** seat with their wings.
25:20 of the cherubim shall be turned toward the **m** seat.
25:21 You shall put the **m** seat on the top of the ark;
25:22 and from above the **m** seat,
26:34 You shall put the **m** seat on the ark of the covenant
30:6 in front of the **m** seat that is over the covenant,
31:7 and the **m** seat that is on it,
33:19 and will show **m** on whom I will show **m**.
35:12 the **m** seat, and the curtain for the screen;
37:6 He made a **m** seat of pure gold;
37:7 at the two ends of the **m** seat he made them,
37:8 of one piece with the **m** seat he made the cherubim
37:9 overshadowing the **m** seat with their wings.
37:9 of the cherubim were turned toward the **m** seat.
39:35 ark of the covenant with its poles and the **m** seat;
40:20 and set the **m** seat above the ark;
Lev 16:2 the sanctuary inside the curtain before the **m** seat
16:2 for I appear in the cloud upon the **m** seat.
16:13 that the cloud of the incense may cover the **m** seat
16:14 with his finger on the front of the **m** seat,
16:14 and before the **m** seat he shall sprinkle the blood
16:15 upon the **m** seat and before the **m** seat.
Nu 7:89 the **m** seat that was on the ark of the covenant from
Dt 7:2 Make no covenant with them and show them no **m**.
Jos 11:20 and might receive no **m**, but be exterminated,
2Sa 24:14 into the hand of the LORD, for his **m** is great;
1Ch 21:13 the hand of the LORD, for his **m** is very great;
28:11 and of the room for the **m** seat;
Ne 1:11 and grant him **m** in the sight of this man!"
Job 9:15 I must appeal for **m** to my accuser.
16:13 He slashes open my kidneys, and shows no **m**;
Ps 23:6 Surely goodness and **m** shall follow me all the days
25:6 Be mindful of your **m**, O LORD,
40:11 Do not, O LORD, withhold your **m** from me;
51:1 Have **m** on me, O God,

Ps 51: 1 to your abundant **m** blot out my transgressions.
69:16 according to your abundant **m,** turn to me.
103: 4 who crowns you with steadfast love and **m,**
119:77 Let your **m** come to me, that I may live;
119:156 Great is your **m,** O LORD;
123: 2 until he has **m** upon us.
123: 3 Have **m** upon us, O LORD, have **m** upon us,
Pr 12:10 but the **m** of the wicked is cruel.
21:10 their neighbors find no **m** in their eyes.
28:13 and forsakes them will obtain **m.**
Isa 13:18 they will have no **m** on the fruit of the womb;
30:18 therefore he will rise up to show **m** to you.
47: 6 into your hand, you showed them no **m;**
55: 7 that he may have **m** on them, and to our God,
60:10 but in my favor I have had **m** on you.
63: 7 that he has shown them according to his **m,**
Jer 6:23 they are cruel and have no **m,**
16: 5 says the LORD, my steadfast love and **m.**
31:20 I will surely have **m** on him, says the LORD.
33:26 and will have **m** upon them.
42:12 I will grant you **m,** and he will have **m** on you
50:42 they are cruel and have no **m.**
La 2: 2 The Lord has destroyed without **m** all
2:21 you have killed them, slaughtering without **m.**
Eze 39:25 and have **m** on the whole house of Israel;
Da 2:18 and told them to seek **m** from the God of heaven
4:27 and your iniquities with **m** to the oppressed,
6:11 and found Daniel praying and seeking **m**
9: 9 To the Lord our God belong **m** and forgiveness,
Hos 2:19 in steadfast love, and in **m.**
14: 3 In you the orphan finds **m.**"
Hab 1:17 and destroying nations without **m?**
3: 2 in wrath may you remember **m.**
Zec 1:12 how long will you withhold **m** from Jerusalem and
7: 9 show kindness and **m** to one another;
Mt 5: 7 "Blessed are the merciful, for they will receive **m.**
9:13 Go and learn what this means, 'I desire **m,**
9:27 crying loudly, "Have **m** on us, Son of David!"
12: 7 'I desire **m** and not sacrifice,'
15:22 "Have **m** on me, Lord, Son of David;
17:15 "Lord, have **m** on my son,
18:33 Should you not have had **m** on your fellow slave,
as I had **m** on you?'
20:30 they shouted, "Lord, have **m** on us, Son of David!"
20:31 but they shouted even more loudly, "Have **m** on us,
23:23 of the law: justice and **m** and faith.
Mk 5:19 and what **m** he has shown you."
10:47 "Jesus, Son of David, have **m** on me!"
10:48 "Son of David, have **m** on me!"
Lk 1:50 His **m** is for those who fear him from generation
1:54 helped his servant Israel, in remembrance of his **m,**
1:58 that the Lord had shown his great **m** to her,
1:72 Thus he has shown the **m** promised
1:78 By the tender **m** of our God,
10:37 He said, "The one who showed him **m.**"
16:24 He called out, 'Father Abraham, have **m** on me,
17:13 saying, "Jesus, Master, have **m** on us!"
18:38 he shouted, "Jesus, Son of David, have **m** on me!"
18:39 "Son of David, have **m** on me!"
Ro 9:15 "I will have **m** on whom I have **m,**
9:16 but on God who shows **m.**
9:18 So then he has **m** on whomever he chooses,
9:23 the riches of his glory for the objects of **m,**
11:30 now received **m** because of their disobedience,
11:31 the **m** shown to you, they too may now receive **m.**
15: 9 that the Gentiles might glorify God for his **m.**
1Co 7:25 as one who by the Lord's **m** is trustworthy.
2Co 4: 1 by God's **m** that we are engaged in this ministry,
Gal 6:16 peace be upon them, and **m,**
Eph 2: 4 But God, who is rich in **m,** out of the great love
Php 2:27 But God had **m** on him, and not only on him
1Ti 1: 2 Grace, **m,** and peace from God the Father
1:13 But I received **m** because I had acted ignorantly
1:16 But for that very reason I received **m,**
2Ti 1: 2 Grace, **m,** and peace from God the Father
1:16 the Lord grant **m** to the household of Onesiphorus,
1:18 the Lord grant that he will find **m** from the Lord on
Tit 3: 5 but according to his **m,** through the water of rebirth
Heb 4:16 so that we may receive **m** and find grace to help
9: 5 the cherubim of glory overshadowing the **m** seat.
10:28 the law of Moses dies without **m** "on the testimony
Jas 2:13 be without **m** to anyone who has shown no **m;**
2:13 **m** triumphs over judgment.
3:17 gentle, willing to yield, full of **m** and good fruits,
1Pe 1: 3 By his great **m** he has given us a new birth into
2:10 once you had not received **m,** but now you have
received **m.**
2Jn 1: 3 **m,** and peace will be with us from God the Father
Jude 1: 2 May **m,** peace, and love be yours in abundance.
1:21 look forward to the **m** of our Lord Jesus Christ
1:22 And have **m** on some who are wavering;
1:23 and have **m** on still others with fear,
Tob 3: 2 all your ways are **m** and truth; you judge the world.
6:18 of heaven that **m** and safety may be granted to you.
7:11 and prosper you both this night and grant you **m**
8: 4 and implore our Lord that he grant us **m**
8: 7 Grant that she and I may find **m** and
8:16 you have dealt with us according to your great **m.**
8:17 bring their lives to fulfillment in happiness and **m.**"
11:15 Though he afflicted me, he has had **m** upon me.
13: 2 For he afflicts, and he shows **m;**
13: 5 but he will again show **m** on all of you.
13: 6 with favor upon you and show you **m.**'
13: 9 will again have **m** on the children of the righteous.
14: 5 "But God will again have **m** on them,
Jdt 2:11 But to those who resist show no **m,**
7:30 by that time the Lord our God will turn his **m**
Jdt 13:14 not withdrawn his **m** from the house of Israel,
16:15 But to those who fear you you show **m.**
AdE 13:17 and have **m** upon your inheritance;
Wis 3: 9 because grace and **m** are upon his holy ones,
4:15 that God's grace and **m** are with his elect,
6: 6 For the lowliest may be pardoned in **m,**
9: 1 "O God of my ancestors and Lord of **m,**
11: 9 though they were being disciplined in **m,**
12:22 and when we are judged, we may expect **m.**
15: 1 patient, and ruling all things in **m.**
16:10 for your **m** came to their help and healed them.
Sir 2: 7 You who fear the Lord, wait for his **m;**
2: 9 hope for good things, for lasting joy and **m.**
2:17 for equal to his majesty is his **m,**
5: 6 Do not say, "His **m** is great,
5: 6 for both **m** and wrath are with him,
16:11 For **m** and wrath are with the Lord;
16:12 Great as his **m,** so also is his chastisement;
16:14 He makes room for every act of **m;**
17:29 How great is the **m** of the Lord,
18:11 the Lord is patient with them and pours out his **m**
28: 4 If one has no **m** toward another like himself,
35:25 of his people and makes them rejoice in his **m.**
35:26 His **m** is as welcome in time of distress as clouds
36: 1 Have **m** upon us, O God of all,
36:17 Have **m,** O Lord, on the people called
47:22 But the Lord will never give up his **m,**
50:22 and deals with us according to his **m.**
50:24 May he entrust to us his **m,**
51: 3 in the greatness of your **m** and of your name,
51: 8 Then I remembered your **m,** O Lord,
51:12 *for his* **m** *endures forever;* A
51:12 *for his* **m** *endures forever;* A
51:12 *for his* **m** *endures forever;* A
51:12 *for his* **m** *endures forever;* A
51:12 *for his* **m** *endures forever;* A
51:12 *for his* **m** *endures forever;* A
51:12 *for his* **m** *endures forever;* A
51:12 *for his* **m** *endures forever;* A
51:12 *for his* **m** *endures forever;* A
51:12 *for his* **m** *endures forever;* A
51:12 *for his* **m** *endures forever;* A
51:12 *for his* **m** *endures forever;* A
51:12 *for his* **m** *endures forever;* A
51:12 *for his* **m** *endures forever;* A
51:12 *for his* **m** *endures forever;* A
51:12 *for his* **m** *endures forever;* A
51:29 May your soul rejoice in God's **m,**
Bar 2:19 that we bring before you our prayer for **m,**
3: 2 Hear, O Lord, and have **m,**
4:22 because of the **m** that will soon come to you
5: 9 with the **m** and righteousness that come from him.
Aza 1:12 Do not withdraw your **m** from us,
1:15 to make an offering before you and to find **m.**
1:19 with us in your patience and in your abundant **m.**
1:67 for he is good, for his **m** endures forever. A
1:68 for his **m** endures forever." A
1Mc 3:44 and to pray and ask for **m** and compassion.
4:24 "For he is good, for his **m** endures forever." A
13:46 to our wicked acts but according to your **m.**"
16: 3 and you by Heaven's **m** are mature in years.
2Mc 2: 7 gathers his people together again and shows his **m.**
2:18 that he will soon have **m** on us and will gather us
6:16 Therefore he never withdraws his **m** from us.
7:23 in his **m** give life and breath back to you again,
7:29 so that in God's **m** I may get you back again along
7:37 appealing to God to show **m** soon to our nation and
8: 3 to have **m** on the city that was being destroyed and
8: 5 for the wrath of the Lord had turned to **m.**
8:27 and allotted it to them as the beginning of **m.**
9:13 who would no longer have **m** on him,
11:10 for the Lord had **m** on them.
1Es 8:78 now in some measure **m** has come to us from you,
Man 1: 6 and unsearchable is your promised **m,**
1:14 you will save me according to your great **m,**
3Mc 2:19 and reveal your **m** at this hour.
6: 2 governing all creation with **m,**
6: 4 manifesting the light of your **m** on the nation
6:12 and have **m** on us who by the senseless insolence
6:39 the Lord of all most gloriously revealed his **m**
2Es 1:25 When you beg **m** of me, I will show you no **m.**
2: 4 Go, my children, and ask for **m** from the Lord.'
2:31 and will show **m** to them;
2:32 until I come, and proclaim **m** to them;
4:24 and we are not worthy to obtain **m.**
7:*115* [45] have **m** on someone who has been condemned
7:*132* [62] he has **m** on those who have not yet come
8:11 and afterwards you will still guide it in your **m.**
8:45 spare your people and have **m** on your inheritance,
8:45 for you have **m** on your own creation."
11:46 for the judgment and **m** of him who made it.' "
12:34 But in **m** he will set free the remnant of my people,
12:48 the desolation of Zion, and to seek **m** on account of
14:34 and after death you shall obtain **m.**

MERCYSEAT (KJV) See MERCY SEAT

MERE (21) [MERELY]

2Ki 8:13 "What is your servant, who is a **m** dog,
18:20 Do you think that **m** words are strategy and power
Ps 39: 5 Surely everyone stands as a **m** breath.
39:11 surely everyone is a **m** breath.
56:11 What can a **m** mortal do to me?
Pr 14:23 but **m** talk leads only to poverty.
29:19 By **m** words servants are not disciplined,
Isa 5:10 and a homer of seed shall yield a **m** ephah.
36: 5 Do you think that **m** words are strategy and power
51:12 then are you afraid of a **m** mortal who must die,
Jer 17: 5 in **m** mortals and make **m** flesh their strength,
Hos 10: 4 They utter **m** words; with empty
2Th 3:11 **m** busybodies, not doing any work.
Heb 9:24 a **m** copy of the true one,
2Pe 2:12 are like irrational animals, **m** creatures of instinct,
Jdt 8:16 or like a **m** mortal, to be won over by pleading.
Wis 2: 2 For we were born by **m** chance,
11:19 but the **m** sight of them could kill by fright.
Sir 28: 5 If a **m** mortal harbors wrath,
4Mc 11:13 he too had died, the sixth, a **m** boy, was led in.

MERED (2)

1Ch 4:17 The sons of Ezrah: Jether, **M,** Epher, and Jalon.
4:17 daughter of Pharaoh, whom **M** married;

MERELY (14) [MERE]

Est 7: 4 If we had been sold **m** as slaves, men and women,
Job 30:20 I stand, and you **m** look at me.
Isa 44:11 the artisans too are **m** human.
Jn 11:13 but they thought that he was referring **m** to sleep.
1Co 3: 4 "I belong to Apollos," are you not **m** human?
15:32 If with **m** human hopes I fought with wild animals
2Co 8: 5 and this, not **m** as we expected;
10: 4 for the weapons of our warfare are not **m** human,
1Ti 5:13 and they are not **m** idle,
Jas 1:22 and not **m** hearers who deceive themselves.
Wis 16: 4 while to these others it was **m** shown
18:25 for **m** to test the wrath was enough.
Sir 19:23 and there is a fool who **m** lacks wisdom.
2Es 7:*48* and that not **m** for a few but

MEREMOTH (7)

Ezr 8:33 into the hands of the priest **M** son of Uriah,
10:36 Vaniah, **M,** Eliashib,
Ne 3: 4 Next to them **M** son of Uriah son
3:21 After him **M** son of Uriah son
10: 5 Harim, **M,** Obadiah,
12: 3 Shecaniah, Rehum, **M,**
1Es 8:62 the house of our Lord to the priest **M** son of Uriah;

MERES (1)

Est 1:14 Admatha, Tarshish, **M,** Marsena, and Memucan,

MERIB-BAAL[‡] (4) [=MEPHIBOSHETH]

1Ch 8:34 and the son of Jonathan was **M;** and **M** became
the father of Micah.
9:40 and the son of Jonathan was **M;** and **M** became
the father of Micah.

MERIB-BAAL'S See Index to Footnotes

MERIBAH (7) [MERIBATH-KADESH]

Ex 17: 7 He called the place Massah and **M,**
Nu 20:13 These are the waters of **M,**
20:24 against my command at the waters of **M.**
Dt 33: 8 with whom you contended at the waters of **M;**
Ps 81: 7 I tested you at the waters of **M.**
95: 8 Do not harden your hearts, as at **M,**
106:32 They angered the LORD at the waters of **M,**

MERIBATH-KADESH (4) [MERIBAH]

Nu 27:14 (These are the waters of **M** in the wilderness
Dt 32:51 with me among the Israelites at the waters of **M** in
Eze 47:19 it shall run from Tamar as far as the waters of **M,**
48:28 boundary shall run from Tamar to the waters of **M,**

MERODACH (1)

Jer 50: 2 Bel is put to shame, **M** is dismayed.

MERODACH-BALADAN (2) [BALADAN]

2Ki 20:12 At that time King **M** son of Baladan
Isa 39: 1 At that time King **M** son of Baladan

MEROM (2)

Jos 11: 5 and came and camped together at the waters of **M,**
11: 7 by the waters of **M,** and fell upon them.

MERONOTHITE (2)

1Ch 27:30 Over the donkeys was Jehdeiah the **M.**
Ne 3: 7 by Melatiah the Gibeonite and Jadon the **M**—

MEROZ (1)

Jdg 5:23 "Curse **M,** says the angel of the LORD,

MERRAN (1)

Bar 3:23 the merchants of **M** and Teman,

MERRILY (1) [MERRY]

AdE 5:14 Then, go **m** with the king to the dinner."

MERRIMENT (1) [MERRY]

Tob 11:18 With **m** they celebrated Tobias's wedding feast

MERRY (16) [MERRILY, MERRIMENT, MERRY-HEARTED, MERRYMAKERS, MERRYMAKING]

Ge 43:34 So they drank and were **m** with him.
Jdg 16:25 And when their hearts were **m,** they said,

1Sa 18: 7 the women sang to one another as they made **m,**
25:36 Nabal's heart was **m** within him,
2Sa 13:28 "Watch when Amnon's heart is **m** with wine,
Est 1:10 when the king was **m** with wine,
Ecc 9: 7 and drink your wine with a **m** heart;
Jer 31:13 and the young men and the old shall be **m.**
51:39 until they become **m** and then sleep
Eze 21:10 How can we make **m?** You have despised the rod,
Lk 12:19 for many years; relax, eat, drink, be **m.'**
Tob 7:10 "Eat and drink, and be **m** tonight.
Jdt 12:17 "Have a drink and be **m** with us!"
Sir 30:25 Those who are cheerful and **m** at table will benefit
32: 2 so that you may be **m** along with them and receive
1Es 5: 3 all their kindred were making **m.**

MERRY-HEARTED (1) [HEART, MERRY]

Isa 24: 7 wine dries up, the vine languishes, all the **m** sigh.

MERRYMAKERS (3) [MAKE, MERRY]

Jer 15:17 I did not sit in the company of **m,** nor did I rejoice;
30:19 shall come thanksgiving, and the sound of **m.**
31: 4 and go forth in the dance of the **m.**

MERRYMAKING (1) [MAKE, MERRY]

Sir 31:31 and do not despise him in his **m;**

MESALOTH (1)

1Mc 9: 2 to Gilgal and encamped against **M** in Arbela,

MESECH (KJV) See MESHECH

MESHA (4)

Ge 10:30 The territory in which they lived extended from **M**
2Ki 3: 4 Now King **M** of Moab was a sheep breeder,
1Ch 2:42 **M** his firstborn, who was father of Ziph.
8: 9 He had sons by his wife Hodesh: Jobab, Zibia, **M,**

MESHACH (15) [=MISHAEL]

Da 1: 7 Hananiah he called Shadrach, Mishael he called **M,**
2:49 and he appointed Shadrach, **M,** and Abednego
3:12 Shadrach, **M,** and Abednego.
3:13 Shadrach, **M,** and Abednego be brought in;
3:14 "Is it true, O Shadrach, **M,** and Abednego,
3:16 Shadrach, **M,** and Abednego answered the king,
3:19 **M,** and Abednego that his face was distorted.
3:20 in his army to bind Shadrach, **M,** and Abednego
3:22 the men who lifted Shadrach, **M,** and Abednego.
3:23 But the three men, Shadrach, **M,** and Abednego,
3:26 **M,** and Abednego, servants of the Most High God,
3:26 **M,** and Abednego came out from the fire.
3:28 "Blessed be the God of Shadrach, **M,**
3:29 **M,** and Abednego shall be torn limb from limb,
3:30 the king promoted Shadrach, **M,** and Abednego

MESHECH (9)

Ge 10: 2 Gomer, Magog, Madai, Javan, Tubal, **M,**
1Ch 1: 5 Gomer, Magog, Madai, Javan, Tubal, **M,**
1:17 Arpachshad, Lud, Aram, Uz, Hul, Gether, and **M.**
Ps 120: 5 Woe is me, that I am an alien in **M,**
Eze 27:13 Javan, Tubal, and **M** traded with you;
32:26 **M** and Tubal are there, and all their multitude,
38: 2 the chief prince of **M** and Tubal.
38: 3 O Gog, chief prince of **M** and Tubal;
39: 1 O Gog, chief prince of **M** and Tubal!

MESHELEMIAH (4)

1Ch 9:21 Zechariah son of **M** was gatekeeper at the entrance
26: 1 of the Korahites, **M** son of Kore,
26: 2 **M** had sons: Zechariah the firstborn,
26: 9 **M** had sons and brothers, able men, eighteen.

MESHEZABEL (3)

Ne 3: 4 of Berechiah son of **M** made repairs.
10:21 **M,** Zadok, Jaddua,
11:24 And Pethahiah son of **M,** of the descendants

MESHILLEMITH (1)

1Ch 9:12 son of Jahzerah, son of Meshullam, son of **M,**

MESHILLEMOTH (2)

2Ch 28:12 Berechiah son of **M,** Jehizkiah son of Shallum,
Ne 11:13 of Azarel son of Ahzai son of **M** son of Immer,

MESHOBAB (1)

1Ch 4:34 **M,** Jamlech, Joshah son of Amaziah,

MESHULLAM (27)

2Ki 22: 3 the king sent Shaphan son of Azaliah, son of **M,**
1Ch 3:19 **M** and Hananiah, and Shelomith was their sister;
5:13 Michael, **M,** Sheba, Jorai, Jacan, Zia, and Eber,
8:17 Zebadiah, **M,** Hizki, Heber,
9: 7 Of the Benjaminites: Sallu son of **M,**
9: 8 son of Michri, and **M** son of Shephatiah,
9:11 son of **M,** son of Zadok, son of Meraioth,
9:12 son of Jahzerah, son of **M,** son of Meshillemith,
2Ch 34:12 along with Zechariah and **M,**
Ezr 8:16 Nathan, Zechariah, and **M,** who were leaders,
10:15 and **M** and Shabbethai the Levites supported them.
10:29 **M,** Malluch, Adaiah, Jashub, Sheal, and Jeremoth.
Ne 3: 4 Next to them **M** son of Berechiah son
3: 6 and **M** son of Besodeiah repaired the Old Gate;
3:30 After him **M** son of Besodeiah made repairs
6:18 the daughter of **M** son of Berechiah.
8: 4 Zechariah, and **M** on his left hand.
10: 7 **M,** Abijah, Mijamin,
10:20 Magpiash, **M,** Hezir,
11: 7 Sallu son of **M** son of Joed son of Pedaiah son
11:11 of **M** son of Zadok son of Meraioth son of Ahitub,
12:13 of Ezra, **M;** of Amariah, Jehohanan;
12:16 of Iddo, Zechariah; of Ginnethon, **M;**
12:25 Mattaniah, Bakbukiah, Obadiah, **M,** Talmon,
12:33 and Azariah, Ezra, **M,**
1Es 8:44 Jarib, Nathan, Elnathan, Zechariah, and **M,**
9:14 and **M** and Levi and Shabbethai served with them

MESHULLEMETH (1)

2Ki 21:19 His mother's name was **M** daughter of Haruz

MESOBAITE (KJV) See MEZOBAITE

MESOPOTAMIA (8)

Dt 23: 4 from Pethor of **M,** to curse you.
1Ch 19: 6 of silver to hire chariots and cavalry from **M,**
Ac 2: 9 Parthians, Medes, Elamites, and residents of **M,**
7: 2 to our ancestor Abraham when he was in **M,**
Jdt 2:24 through **M** and destroyed all the fortified towns
5: 7 At one time they lived in **M,**
5: 8 So they fled to **M,** and lived there for a long time.
8:26 and what happened to Jacob in Syrian **M,**

MESS (KJV) See PORTION, PRESENT

MESSAGE (72) [MESSAGES, MESSENGER, MESSENGERS]

Nu 22: 7 they came to Balaam, and gave him Balak's **m.**
22:10 of Zippor of Moab, has sent me this **m:**
Jos 10: 3 of Jerusalem sent a **m** to King Hoham of Hebron,
Jdg 3:19 and said, "I have a secret **m** for you, O king."
3:20 and said, "I have a **m** from God for you."
11:28 But the king of the Ammonites did not heed the **m**
1Sa 11: 5 they told him the **m** from the inhabitants of Jabesh.
2Sa 12:25 and sent a **m** by the prophet Nathan;
19:11 King David sent this **m** to the priests Zadok
1Ki 5: 8 "I have heard the **m** that you have sent to me;
20:12 When Ben-hadad heard this **m—**
2Ki 5: 8 he sent a **m** to the king,
9: 5 and he announced, "I have a **m** for you,
22:20 They took the **m** back to the king.
2Ch 34:28 They took the **m** back to the king.
Est 4:10 Then Esther spoke to Hathach and gave him a **m**
Pr 26: 6 to send a **m** by a fool.
Isa 28: 9 and to whom will he explain the **m?**
28:19 and it will be sheer terror to understand the **m.**
Jnh 3: 2 and proclaim to it the **m** that I tell you."
Hag 1:13 spoke to the people with the LORD's **m,** saying,
Zec 1:14 with me said to me, Proclaim this **m:**
Mt 11: 1 he went on from there to teach and proclaim his **m**
28: 7 This is my **m** for you."
Mk 1:38 so that I may proclaim the **m** there also;
1:39 the **m** in their synagogues and casting out demons.
3:14 and to be sent out to proclaim the **m,**
16:20 ⟦the Lord worked with them and confirmed the **m**⟧
Lk 4:44 So he continued proclaiming the **m** in
Jn 11: 3 So the sisters sent a **m** to Jesus, "Lord,
12:38 "Lord, who has believed our **m,**
Ac 2:41 So those who welcomed his **m** were baptized,
5:20 stand in the temple and tell the people the whole **m**
10:36 You know the **m** he sent to the people of Israel,
10:37 That **m** spread throughout Judea,
11:14 a **m** by which you and your entire household will
13:15 the officials of the synagogue sent them a **m,**
13:26 to us the **m** of this salvation has been sent.
15: 7 through whom the Gentiles would hear the **m** of
16:36 And the jailer reported the **m** to Paul, saying,
17:11 for they welcomed the **m** very eagerly
19:31 a **m** urging him not to venture into the theater.
20:17 From Miletus he sent a **m** to Ephesus,
20:20 the **m** to you and teaching you publicly and
20:32 I commend you to God and to the **m** of his grace,
20:32 a **m** that is able to build you up and to give you
Ro 10:16 for Isaiah says, "Lord, who has believed our **m?"**
1Co 1:18 For the **m** about the cross is foolishness
15: 2 if you hold firmly to the **m** that I proclaimed
2Co 5:19 and entrusting the **m** of reconciliation to us.
Eph 6:19 a **m** may be given to me to make known
1Th 1: 5 because our **m** of the gospel came to you not
2: 4 by God to be entrusted with the **m** of the gospel,
2Ti 4: 2 proclaim the **m;** be persistent
4:15 for he strongly opposed our **m.**
4:17 that through me the **m** might be fully proclaimed
Heb 2: 2 For if the **m** declared through angels was valid,
4: 2 but the **m** they heard did not benefit them,
2Pe 1:19 So we have the prophetic **m** more fully confirmed.
1Jn 1: 5 the **m** we have heard from him and proclaim
3:11 this is the **m** you have heard from the beginning,
Jdt 12: 6 and sent this **m** to Holofernes:
AdE 4:12 Hachratheus delivered her entire **m** to Mordecai,
LtJ 6: 1 to give them the **m** that God had commanded him.
1Mc 5:48 Judas sent them this friendly **m,**
7:27 to Judas and his brothers this peaceable **m,**
10:25 So he sent a **m** to them in the following words:
10:51 to Ptolemy king of Egypt with the following **m:**
10:69 he sent the following **m** to the high priest Jonathan:
11:42 And Demetrius sent this **m** back to Jonathan:
1Mc 15:32 When he reported to him the king's **m,**
2Mc 14:28 When this **m** came to Nicanor,

MESSAGES (1) [MESSAGE]

1Mc 5:16 When Judas and the people heard these **m,**

MESSENGER‡ (40) [MESSAGE]

1Sa 4:17 The **m** replied, "Israel has fled before
23:27 Then a **m** came to Saul, saying, "Hurry and come;
2Sa 11:19 the **m,** "When you have finished telling the king all
11:22 So the **m** went, and came and told David all
11:23 The **m** said to David, "The men gained
11:25 David said to the **m,** "Thus you shall say to Joab,
15:13 A **m** came to David, saying,
1Ki 19: 2 Then Jezebel sent a **m** to Elijah, saying,
22:13 **m** who had gone to summon Micaiah said to him,
2Ki 5:10 Elisha sent a **m** to him, saying, "Go,
6:32 Before the **m** arrived, Elisha said to the elders,
6:32 When the **m** comes, see that you shut the door
9:18 sentinel reported, saying, "The **m** reached them,
10: 8 When the **m** came and told him,
2Ch 18:12 **m** who had gone to summon Micaiah said to him,
Job 1:14 a **m** came to Job and said,
Pr 13:17 bad **m** brings trouble, but a faithful envoy, healing.
16:14 A king's wrath is a **m** of death,
17:11 but a cruel **m** will be sent against them.
Ecc 5: 6 and do not say before the **m** that it was a mistake;
Isa 42:19 or deaf like my **m** whom I send?
52: 7 the feet of the **m** who announces peace,
63: 9 It was no **m** or angel but his presence that saved
Jer 49:14 and a **m** has been sent among the nations:
51:31 and one **m** to meet another,
Eze 23:40 to whom a **m** was sent, and they came.
Ob 1: 1 and a **m** has been sent among the nations:
Hag 1:13 Then Haggai, the **m** of the LORD,
Mal 2: 7 for he is the **m** of the LORD of hosts.
3: 1 I am sending my **m** to prepare the way before me,
3: 1 The **m** of the covenant in whom you delight—
Mt 11:10 'See, I am sending my **m** ahead of you,
Mk 1: 2 "See, I am sending my **m** ahead of you,
Lk 7:27 'See, I am sending my **m** ahead of you,
2Co 12: 7 in the flesh, a **m** of Satan to torment me,
Php 2:25 your **m** and minister to my need;
AdE 4:15 Then Esther gave the **m** this answer to take back
1Es 1:50 God of their ancestors sent his **m** to call them back,
Pm 151: 4 It was he who sent his **m** and took me
2Es 1:40 who is also called the **m** of the Lord.

MESSENGERS (100) [MESSAGE]

Ge 32: 3 Jacob sent **m** before him to his brother Esau in
32: 6 The **m** returned to Jacob, saying,
Nu 20:14 Moses sent **m** from Kadesh to the king of Edom,
21:21 Then Israel sent **m** to King Sihon of the Amorites,
22: 5 He sent **m** to Balaam son of Beor at Pethor,
24:12 "Did I not tell your **m** whom you sent to me,
Dt 2:26 So I sent **m** from the wilderness of Kedemoth
Jos 6:17 because she hid the **m** we sent.
6:25 she hid the **m** whom Joshua sent to spy out Jericho.
7:22 So Joshua sent **m,** and they ran to the tent;
Jdg 6:35 He sent **m** throughout all Manasseh,
6:35 He also sent **m** to Asher, Zebulun, and Naphtali,
7:24 Then Gideon sent **m** throughout all the hill country
9:31 He sent **m** to Abimelech at Arumah, saying,
11:12 Then Jephthah sent **m** to the king of
11:13 of the Ammonites answered the **m** of Jephthah,
11:14 Once again Jephthah sent **m** to the king of
11:17 Israel then sent **m** to the king of Edom, saying,
11:19 Israel then sent **m** to King Sihon of the Amorites,
1Sa 6:21 So they sent **m** to the inhabitants of Kiriath-jearim,
11: 3 "Give us seven days' respite that we may send **m**
11: 4 When the **m** came to Gibeah of Saul,
11: 7 throughout all the territory of Israel by **m,**
11: 9 They said to the **m** who had come,
11: 9 the **m** came and told the inhabitants of Jabesh,
16:19 So Saul sent **m** to Jesse, and said,
19:11 Saul sent **m** to David's house to keep watch
19:14 Saul sent **m** to take David, she said, "He is sick."
19:15 Then Saul sent the **m** to see David for themselves
19:16 When the **m** came in, the idol was in the bed,
19:20 Then Saul sent **m** to take David.
19:20 the spirit of God came upon the **m** of Saul,
19:21 When Saul was told, he sent other **m,**
19:21 Saul sent **m** again the third time,
25:14 "David sent **m** out of the wilderness
25:42 after the **m** of David and became his wife.
31: 9 and sent **m** throughout the land of the Philistines
2Sa 2: 5 David sent **m** to the people of Jabesh-gilead,
3:12 Abner sent **m** to David at Hebron, saying,
3:14 Then David sent **m** to Saul's son Ishbaal, saying,
3:26 he sent **m** after Abner, and they brought him back
5:11 King Hiram of Tyre sent **m** to David,
10: 3 because he has sent **m** with condolences to you?
11: 4 So David sent **m** to get her, and she came to him,
12:27 Joab sent **m** to David, and said,
15:10 But Absalom sent secret **m** throughout all
1Ki 20: 2 he sent **m** into the city to King Ahab of Israel,
20: 5 The **m** came again and said:
20: 9 So he said to the **m** of Ben-hadad,
20: 9 The **m** left and brought him word again.
2Ki 1: 2 so he sent **m,** telling them, "Go,
1: 3 "Get up, go to meet the **m** of the king of Samaria,
1: 5 The **m** returned to the king, who said to them,
1:16 Because you have sent **m** to inquire of Baal-zebub,
7:15 So the **m** returned, and told the king.
14: 8 Amaziah sent **m** to King Jehoash son of Jehoahaz,

2Ki 16: 7 Ahaz sent **m** to King Tiglath-pileser of Assyria,
17: 4 for he had sent **m** to King So of Egypt,
19: 9 he sent **m** again to Hezekiah, saying,
19:14 the letter from the hand of the **m** and read it;
19:23 By your **m** you have mocked the Lord,
1Ch 10: 9 and sent **m** throughout the land of the Philistines
14: 1 King Hiram of Tyre sent **m** to David,
19: 2 David sent **m** to console him concerning his father.
19: 5 David was told about the men, he sent **m** to them,
19:16 they sent **m** and brought out
2Ch 20: 2 **M** came and told Jehoshaphat,
36:15 sent persistently to them by his **m,**
36:16 but they kept mocking the **m** of God,
Ne 6: 3 So I sent **m** to them, saying,
Ps 104: 4 you make the winds your **m,**
Pr 25:13 of harvest are faithful **m** to those who send them;
Isa 14:32 What will one answer the **m** of the nation?
18: 2 Go, you swift **m,** to a nation tall and smooth,
23: 2 your **m** crossed over the sea
37: 9 When he heard it, he sent **m** to Hezekiah, saying,
37:14 the letter from the hand of the **m** and read it;
44:26 and fulfills the prediction of his **m;**
Eze 23:16 and sent **m** to them in Chaldea.
30: 9 **m** shall go out from me in ships to terrify
Na 2:13 and the voice of your **m** shall be heard no more.
Lk 7:24 When John's **m** had gone, Jesus began to speak to
9:52 And he sent **m** ahead of him.
Jn 5:33 You sent **m** to John, and he testified to the truth.
13:16 nor are **m** greater than the one who sent them.
2Co 8:23 as for our brothers, they are **m** of the churches,
Jas 2:25 also justified by works when she welcomed the **m**
Tob 10: 8 I will send **m** to your father Tobit
Jdt 1: 7 sent **m** to all who lived in Persia and
1:11 So they sent back his **m** empty-handed and
3: 1 They therefore sent **m** to him to sue for peace
11:14 they have sent **m** there in order
AdE 8:14 So the **m** on horseback set out with all speed
Sir 43:26 Because of him each of his **m** succeeds,
1Mc 1:44 And the king sent letters by **m** to Jerusalem and
5:14 While the letter was still being read, other **m,**
7:10 and he sent **m** to Judas and his brothers
7:41 "When the **m** from the king spoke blasphemy,
2Mc 11:37 and send **m** so that we may have your judgment.
1Es 1:51 But they mocked his **m,** and whenever

MESSIAH‡ (69) [CHRIST, MESSIAHS]

Mt 1: 1 An account of the genealogy of Jesus the **M,**
1:16 of whom Jesus was born, who is called the **M.**
1:17 and from the deportation to Babylon to the **M,**
1:18 the birth of Jesus the **M** took place in this way.
2: 4 he inquired of them where the **M** was to be born.
11: 2 When John heard in prison what the **M** was doing,
16:16 Simon Peter answered, "You are the **M,**
16:20 the disciples not to tell anyone that he was the **M.**
22:42 "What do you think of the **M?**
23:10 for you have one instructor, the **M.**
24: 5 many will come in my name, saying, 'I am the **M!'**
24:23 says to you, 'Look! Here is the **M!'**
26:63 tell us if you are the **M,** the Son of God."
26:68 "Prophesy to us, you **M!** Who is it that struck you?
27:17 Jesus Barabbas or Jesus who is called the **M?"**
27:22 what should I do with Jesus who is called the **M?"**
Mk 8:29 Peter answered him, "You are the **M."**
12:35 can the scribes say that the **M** is the son of David?
13:21 that time, 'Look! Here is the **M!'**
14:61 Again the high priest asked him, "Are you the **M,**
15:32 Let the **M,** the King of Israel,
Lk 2:11 in the city of David a Savior, who is the **M,**
2:26 not see death before he had seen the Lord's **M.**
3:15 whether he might be the **M,**
4:41 because they knew that he was the **M.**
9:20 Peter answered, "The **M** of God."
20:41 "How can they say that the **M** is David's son?
22:67 They said, "If you are the **M,** tell us."
23: 2 and saying that he himself is the **M,** a king."
23:35 let him save himself if he is the **M** of God,
23:39 and saying, "Are you not the **M?**
24:26 necessary that the **M** should suffer these things
24:46 that the **M** is to suffer and to rise from the dead on
Jn 1:20 but confessed, "I am not the **M."**
1:25 then are you baptizing if you are neither the **M,**
1:41 the **M"** (which is translated Anointed).
3:28 that I said, 'I am not the **M,** but I have been sent
4:25 "I know that **M** is coming" (who is called Christ).
4:29 He cannot be the **M,** can he?"
7:26 that the authorities really know that this is the **M?**
7:27 the **M** comes, no one will know where he is from."
7:31 in him and were saying, "When the **M** comes,
7:41 Others said, "This is the **M."**
7:41 "Surely the **M** does not come from Galilee,
7:42 Has not the scripture said that the **M** is descended
9:22 to be the **M** would be put out of the synagogue.
10:24 If you are the **M,** tell us plainly."
11:27 Lord, I believe that you are the **M,** the Son of God,
12:34 from the law that the **M** remains forever.
20:31 that you may come to believe that Jesus is the **M,**
Ac 2:31 David spoke of the resurrection of the **M,** saying,
2:36 that God has made him both Lord and **M,**
3:18 through all the prophets, that his **M** would suffer.
3:20 and that he may send the **M** appointed for you,
4:26 against the Lord and against his **M.'**
5:42 not cease to teach and proclaim Jesus as the **M.**
8: 5 the city of Samaria and proclaimed the **M** to them.
9:22 in Damascus by proving that Jesus was the **M.**
17: 3 that it was necessary for the **M** to suffer and to rise
17: 3 and saying, "This is the **M,**
Ac 18: 5 testifying to the Jews that the **M** was Jesus.
18:28 showing by the scriptures that the **M** is Jesus.
26:23 that the **M** must suffer, and that, by being the first
Ro 9: 5 comes the **M,** who is over all, God blessed forever.
Rev 11:15 the kingdom of our Lord and of his **M,**
12:10 of our God and the authority of his **M,**
2Es 7:28 the **M** shall be revealed with those who are
7:29 After those years my son the **M** shall die,
12:32 the **M** whom the Most High has kept until the end

MESSIAHS (2) [MESSIAH]

Mt 24:24 For false **m** and false prophets will appear
Mk 13:22 False **m** and false prophets will appear

MESSIAS (KJV) See MESSIAH

MET (76) [MEET]

Ge 32: 1 on his way and the angels of God **m** him;
33: 8 "What do you mean by all this company that I **m?"**
Ex 3:18 the God of the Hebrews, has **m** with us;
4:24 the LORD **m** him and tried to kill him.
4:27 he **m** him at the mountain of God and kissed him.
Nu 23: 4 Then God **m** Balaam; and Balaam said to him,
23:16 The LORD **m** Balaam, put a word into his mouth,
1Sa 9:11 they **m** some girls coming out to draw water,
10:10 a band of prophets **m** him;
25:20 toward her; and she **m** them.
2Sa 2:13 went out and **m** them at the pool of Gibeon.
16: 1 Ziba the servant of Mephibosheth **m** him,
1Ki 2: 7 for with such loyalty they **m** me when I fled
13:24 a lion **m** him on the road and killed him.
18: 7 As Obadiah was on the way, Elijah **m** him;
20:36 when he had left him, a lion **m** him and killed him.
2Ki 9:21 they **m** him at the property of Naboth
10:13 Jehu **m** relatives of King Ahaziah of Judah
10:15 he **m** Jehonadab son of Rechab coming
23:29 Pharaoh Neco **m** him at Megiddo, he killed him.
2Ch 22: 8 he **m** the officials of Judah and the sons
Job 2:11 They **m** together to go and console
SS 8: 1 If I **m** you outside, I would kiss you,
Jer 41: 6 As he **m** them, he said to them,
Hos 12: 4 he **m** him at Bethel, and there he spoke with him.
Am 5:19 and was **m** by a bear;
Mt 8:28 two demoniacs coming out of the tombs **m** him.
28: 9 Suddenly Jesus **m** them and said, "Greetings!"
Mk 5: 2 of the tombs with an unclean spirit **m** him.
Lk 8:27 a man of the city who had demons **m** him.
9:37 down from the mountain, a great crowd **m** him.
Jn 4:51 his slaves **m** him and told him
11:20 she went and **m** him, while Mary stayed at home.
11:30 but was still at the place where Martha had **m** him.
18: 2 because Jesus often **m** there with his disciples.
20:19 where the disciples had **m** were locked for fear of
Ac 10:25 On Peter's arrival Cornelius **m** him,
11:26 an entire year they **m** with the church and taught
13: 6 they **m** a certain magician, a Jewish false prophet,
15: 6 and the elders **m** together to consider this matter.
16:16 we **m** a slave-girl who had a spirit of divination
20: 7 when we **m** to break bread,
20:14 When he **m** us in Assos,
25:16 before the accused had **m** the accusers face to face
25:17 So when they **m** here, I lost no time,
2Co 13: 7 not that we may appear to have **m** the test,
Heb 7: 1 **m** Abraham as he was returning from defeating
7:10 the loins of his ancestor when Melchizedek **m** him.
Tob 11:17 When Tobit **m** Sarah the wife of his son Tobias,
Jdt 10:11 on through the valley, an Assyrian patrol **m** her
15: 9 When they **m** her, they all blessed her
Sir 19:29 and a sensible person is known when first **m,**
31: 6 and their destruction has **m** them face to face.
Sus 1:14 But turning back, they **m** again;
1Mc 4:29 and Judas **m** them with ten thousand men.
5:25 who **m** them peaceably and told them all
7:43 So the armies **m** in battle on the thirteenth day of
10:49 The two kings **m** in battle,
10:53 I **m** him in battle, and he and his army were
10:58 King Alexander **m** him,
10:60 with pomp to Ptolemais and **m** the two kings;
10:74 and his brother Simon **m** him to help him.
11: 6 Jonathan **m** the king at Joppa with pomp,
11:15 Ptolemy marched out and **m** him with
11:60 the people of the city **m** him and paid him honor.
11:68 there in the plain the army of the foreigners **m** him;
11:68 but they themselves **m** him face to face.
12:25 So he marched away from Jerusalem and **m** them
2Mc 3: 7 When Apollonius **m** the king,
5: 8 Finally he **m** a miserable end.
5:12 to cut down relentlessly everyone they **m** and
8:14 by the ungodly Nicanor before he ever **m** them,
10:35 and with savage fury cut down everyone they **m.**
13: 8 and ashes were holy, he **m** his death in ashes.
15:26 but Judas and his troops **m** the enemy in battle
3Mc 7:14 to a public and shameful death any whom they **m**

METAL (7)

Jdg 17: 3 to make an idol of cast **m."**
17: 4 who made it into an idol of cast **m;**
18:14 teraphim, and an idol of cast **m?**
18:17 to enter and take the idol of cast **m,**
18:18 into Micah's house and took the idol of cast **m,**
Na 2: 3 The **m** on the chariots flashes on the day
Sir 50:16 they blew their trumpets of hammered **m;**

METEYARD (KJV) See MEASURING

METHEG-AMMAH (1)

2Sa 8: 1 David took **M** out of the hand of the Philistines.

METHOD (1) [METHODS]

2Mc 13: 4 and to put him to death by the **m** that is customary

METHODS (2) [METHOD]

AdE 16: 9 by changing our **m** and always judging what comes
16:14 that by these **m** he would catch us undefended

METHUSELAH (7)

Ge 5:21 he became the father of **M.**
5:22 Enoch walked with God after the birth of **M**
5:25 **M** had lived one hundred eighty-seven years,
5:26 **M** lived after the birth of Lamech
5:27 the days of **M** were nine hundred sixty-nine years;
1Ch 1: 3 Enoch, **M,** Lamech;
Lk 3:37 son of **M,** son of Enoch, son of Jared,

METHUSHAEL (2)

Ge 4:18 and Mehujael the father of **M,** and **M** the father of Lamech.

MEUNIM (3)

1Ch 4:41 and the **M** who were found there,
Ezr 2:50 Asnah, **M,** Nephisim,
Ne 7:52 of Besai, of **M,** of Nephushesim,

MEUNITES (2)

2Ch 20: 1 and with them some of the **M,**
26: 7 in Gur-baal, and against the **M.**

MEZOBAITE (1)

1Ch 11:47 Eliel, and Obed, and Jaasiel the **M.**

MIAMIN (KJV) See MIJAMIN

MIBHAR (1)

1Ch 11:38 Joel the brother of Nathan, **M** son of Hagri,

MIBSAM (3)

Ge 25:13 of Ishmael; and Kedar, Adbeel, **M,**
1Ch 1:29 Nebaioth; and Kedar, Adbeel, **M,**
4:25 Shallum was his son, **M** his son, Mishma his son.

MIBZAR (2)

Ge 36:42 Kenaz, Teman, **M,**
1Ch 1:53 Kenaz, Teman, **M,**

MICA (5)

2Sa 9:12 a young son whose name was **M.**
1Ch 9:15 Galal, and Mattaniah son of **M,** son of Zichri,
Ne 10:11 **M,** Rehob, Hashabiah,
11:17 of **M** son of Zabdi son of Asaph, who was
11:22 of Hashabiah son of Mattaniah son of **M,**

MICAH (31) [MICAH'S]

Jdg 17: 1 in the hill country of Ephraim whose name was **M.**
17: 4 and it was in the house of **M.**
17: 5 This man **M** had a shrine,
17: 8 to the house of **M** in the hill country of Ephraim
17: 9 **M** said to him, "From where do you come?"
17:10 Then **M** said to him, "Stay with me,
17:12 So **M** installed the Levite,
17:12 and was in the house of **M.**
17:13 Then **M** said, "Now I know that
18: 2 to the house of **M,** they stayed there.
18: 4 He said to them, **"M** did such and such for me,
18:13 and came to the house of **M.**
18:15 at the home of **M,** and greeted him.
18:22 they were some distance from the home of **M,**
18:23 who turned around and said to **M,**
18:26 When **M** saw that they were too strong for him,
18:27 The Danites, having taken what **M** had made,
1Ch 5: 5 **M** his son, Reaiah his son, Baal his son,
8:34 and Merib-baal became the father of **M.**
8:35 The sons of **M:** Pithon, Melech, Tarea, and Ahaz.
9:40 and Merib-baal became the father of **M.**
9:41 The sons of **M:** Pithon, Melech, Tahrea, and Ahaz;
23:20 sons of Uzziel: **M** the chief and Isshiah the second.
24:24 sons of Uzziel, **M;** of the sons of **M,** Shamir.
24:25 The brother of **M,** Isshiah;
2Ch 34:20 Ahikam son of Shaphan, Abdon son of **M,**
Jer 26:18 **"M** of Moresheth, who prophesied during the days
Mic 1: 1 to **M** of Moresheth in the days of Kings Jotham,
Jdt 6:15 who in those days were Uzziah son of **M,**
2Es 1:39 and Hosea and Amos and **M** and Joel and Obadiah

MICAH'S (4) [MICAH]

Jdg 18: 3 While they were at **M** house,
18:18 the men went into **M** house and took the idol
18:22 in the houses near **M** house were called out,
18:31 So they maintained as their own **M** idol

MICAIAH (29)

1Ki 22: 8 by whom we may inquire of the LORD, **M** son
22: 9 "Bring quickly **M** son of Imlah."
22:13 The messenger who had gone to summon **M** said
22:14 But **M** said, "As the LORD lives,

1Ki 22:15 he had come to the king, the king said to him, “**M**,
22:17 Then **M** said, “I saw all Israel scattered on
22:19 **M** said, “Therefore hear the word of the LORD:
22:24 Then Zedekiah son of Chenaanah came up to **M**,
22:25 **M** replied, “You will find out on that day
22:26 The king of Israel then ordered, “Take **M**,
22:28 **M** said, “If you return in peace,
2Ki 22:12 Ahikam son of Shaphan, Achbor son of **M**,
2Ch 13: 2 His mother's name was **M** daughter of Uriel
17: 7 Ben-hail, Obadiah, Zechariah, Nethanel, and **M**,
18: 7 by whom we may inquire of the LORD, **M** son
18: 8 “Bring quickly **M** son of Imlah.”
18:12 The messenger who had gone to summon **M** said
18:13 But **M** said, “As the LORD lives,
18:14 he had come to the king, the king said to him, “**M**,
18:16 Then **M** said, “I saw all Israel scattered on
18:18 **M** said, “Therefore hear the word of the LORD:
18:23 Then Zedekiah son of Chenaanah came up to **M**,
18:24 **M** replied, “You will find out on that day
18:25 The king of Israel then ordered, “Take **M**,
18:27 **M** said, “If you return in peace,
Ne 12:35 of Shemaiah son of Mattaniah son of **M** son
12:41 Miniamin, **M**, Elioenai, Zechariah, and Hananiah,
Jer 36:11 When **M** son of Gemariah son
36:13 And **M** told them all the words that he had heard,

MICE (4) [MOUSE]

1Sa 6: 4 “Five gold tumors and five gold **m**,
6: 5 of your tumors and images of your **m** that ravage
6:11 with the gold **m** and the images of their tumors.
6:18 also the gold **m**, according to the number of all

MICHA (KJV) See MICA

MICHAEL (16)

Nu 13:13 from the tribe of Asher, Sethur son of **M**;
1Ch 5:13 **M**, Meshullam, Sheba, Jorai, Jacan, Zia, and Eber,
5:14 son of Gilead, son of **M**, son of Jeshishai,
6:40 son of **M**, son of Baaseiah, son of Malchijah,
7: 3 And the sons of Izrahiah: **M**, Obadiah, Joel,
8:16 **M**, Ishpah, and Joha were sons of Beriah.
12:20 Adnah, Jozabad, Jediael, **M**, Jozabad, Elihu,
27:18 for Issachar, Omri son of **M**;
2Ch 21: 2 Azariah, Jehiel, Zechariah, Azariah, **M**,
Ezr 8: 8 Zebadiah son of **M**, and with him eighty males.
Da 10:13 So **M**, one of the chief princes, came to help me,
10:21 against these princes except **M**,
12: 1 “At that time **M**, the great prince,
Jude 1: 9 when the archangel **M** contended with the devil
Rev 12: 7 **M** and his angels fought against the dragon.
1Es 8:34 Zeraiah son of **M**, and with him seventy men.

MICHAIAH (KJV) See MICAIAH

MICHAL‡ (17)

1Sa 14:49 and the name of the younger, **M**.
18:20 Now Saul's daughter **M** loved David.
18:27 Saul gave him his daughter **M** as a wife.
18:28 and that Saul's daughter **M** loved him,
19:11 David's wife **M** told him, “If you do
19:12 So **M** let David down through the window;
19:13 **M** took an idol and laid it on the bed;
19:17 Saul said to **M**, “Why have you deceived me
19:17 **M** answered Saul, “He said to me, ‘Let me go;
25:44 Saul had given his daughter **M**, David's wife,
2Sa 3:13 unless you bring Saul's daughter **M**
3:14 saying, “Give me my wife **M**,
6:16 **M** daughter of Saul looked out of the window,
6:20 **M** the daughter of Saul came out to meet David,
6:21 David said to **M**, “It was before the LORD,
6:23 And **M** the daughter of Saul had no child to
1Ch 15:29 **M** daughter of Saul looked out of the window,

MICHMAS (2)

Ezr 2:27 The people of **M**, one hundred twenty-two.
Ne 7:31 Of **M**, one hundred twenty-two.

MICHMASH (10)

1Sa 13: 2 with Saul in **M** and the hill country of Bethel,
13: 5 they came up and encamped at **M**,
13:11 and that the Philistines were mustering at **M**,
13:16 but the Philistines encamped at **M**.
13:23 of the Philistines had gone out to the pass of **M**.
14: 5 One crag rose on the north in front of **M**,
14:31 down the Philistines that day from **M** to Aijalon,
Ne 11:31 at **M**, Aija, Bethel and its villages,
Isa 10:28 at **M** he stores his baggage;
1Mc 9:73 Jonathan settled in **M** and began to judge

MICHMETHATH (2)

Jos 16: 6 to the sea; on the north is **M**;
17: 7 territory of Manasseh reached from Asher to **M**,

MICHRI (1)

1Ch 9: 8 son of **M**, and Meshullam son of Shephatiah,

MID-LIFE (1) [LIVE]

Jer 17:11 amass wealth unjustly; in **m** it will leave them,

MID-POINT (1) [POINT]

Ps 102:24 I say, “do not take me away at the **m** of my life,

MIDCOURSE (1) [COURSE]

Ps 102:23 He has broken my strength in **m**;

MIDDAY (4) [DAY]

1Ki 18:29 As **m** passed, they raved on until the time of
Ne 8: 3 before the Water Gate from early morning until **m**,
Ac 26:13 when at **m** along the road,
1Es 9:41 the gate of the temple from early morning until **m**,

MIDDIN (1)

Jos 15:61 In the wilderness, Beth-arabah, **M**, Secacah,

MIDDLE (69) [AMID, MIDST]

Ge 3: 3 of the fruit of the tree that is in the **m** of the garden,
Ex 26:28 The **m** bar, halfway up the frames,
28:32 It shall have an opening for the head in the **m** of it,
36:33 the **m** bar to pass through from end to end halfway
39:23 and the opening of the robe in the **m** of it was like
Nu 16:47 and ran into the **m** of the assembly,
35: 5 with the town in the **m**;
Dt 3:16 with the **m** of the wadi as a boundary,
Jos 3:17 of the LORD stood on dry ground in the **m** of
4: 3 ‘Take twelve stones from here out of the **m** of
4: 5 before the ark of the LORD your God into the **m**
4: 8 up twelve stones out of the **m** of the Jordan,
4: 9 (Joshua set up twelve stones in the **m** of the Jordan,
4:10 the ark remained standing in the **m** of the Jordan,
4:18 the covenant of the LORD came up from the **m** of
12: 2 from the **m** of the valley as far as the river Jabbok,
13: 9 and the town that is in the **m** of the valley,
13:16 and the town that is in the **m** of the valley,
Jdg 7:19 of the **m** watch, when they had just set the watch;
16:29 And Samson grasped the two **m** pillars on which
2Sa 10: 4 cut off their garments in the **m** at their hips,
23:12 But he took his stand in the **m** of the plot,
24: 5 from Aroer and from the city that is in the **m** of
1Ki 3:20 the **m** of the night and took my son from beside me
6: 6 the **m** one was six cubits wide,
6: 8 The entrance for the **m** story was on the south side
6: 8 one went up by winding stairs to the **m** story,
6: 8 and from the **m** story to the third.
8:64 the **m** of the court that was in front of the house of
2Ki 20: 4 Before Isaiah had gone out of the **m** court,
1Ch 11:14 and David took their stand in the **m** of the plot,
19: 4 cut off their garments in the **m** at their hips,
2Ch 7: 7 the **m** of the court that was in front of the house of
20:14 in the **m** of the assembly.
Jer 39: 3 of the king of Babylon came and sat in the **m** gate:
41: 7 When they reached the **m** of the city,
51:63 and throw it into the **m** of the Euphrates,
Eze 1: 4 and in the **m** of the fire,
1: 5 In the **m** of it was something
1:13 the **m** of the living creatures there was something
11:23 And the glory of the LORD ascended from the **m**
15: 4 the fire has consumed both ends of it and the **m**
37: 1 the spirit of the LORD and set me down in the **m**
41: 7 to the uppermost story by way of the **m** one.
42: 5 from them than from the lower and **m** chambers in
42: 6 the ground more than the lower and the **m** ones.
48: 8 with the sanctuary in the **m** of it.
48:10 with the sanctuary of the LORD in the **m** of it.
48:15 In the **m** of it shall be the city;
48:21 with the sanctuary of the temple in the **m** of it,
48:22 be in the **m** of that which belongs to the prince.
Da 2:32 its **m** and thighs of bronze,
3:25 walking in the **m** of the fire, and they are not hurt;
Lk 5:19 the tiles into the **m** of the crowd in front of Jesus.
12:38 If he comes during the **m** of the night,
22:55 in the **m** of the courtyard and sat down together,
Jn 7:14 the **m** of the festival Jesus went up into the temple
Ac 1:18 and falling headlong, he burst open in the **m**
Rev 22: 2 through the **m** of the street of the city.
Tob 5: 6 while Ecbatana is in the **m** of the plain.”
Wis 7:18 the beginning and end and **m** of times,
1Mc 10:63 into the **m** of the city and proclaim that no one is
2Mc 14:44 and he fell in the **m** of the empty space.
3Mc 5:14 now, since it was nearly the **m** of the tenth hour,
2Es 11: 4 the **m** head was larger than the other heads,
11:10 but from the **m** of its body.
11:29 at rest (the one that was in the **m**) suddenly awoke;
11:33 and saw the head in the **m** suddenly disappear,
12:21 two of them shall perish when the **m**

MIDHEAVEN (4) [HEAVEN]

Jos 10:13 The sun stopped in **m**, and did not hurry to set for
Rev 8:13 an eagle crying with a loud voice as it flew in **m**,
14: 6 Then I saw another angel flying in **m**,
19:17 a loud voice he called to all the birds that fly in **m**,

MIDIAN (48) [MIDIANITE, MIDIANITES]

Ge 25: 2 She bore him Zimran, Jokshan, Medan, **M**, Ishbak,
25: 4 The sons of **M** were Ephah, Epher, Hanoch,
36:35 who defeated **M** in the country of Moab,
Ex 2:15 He settled in the land of **M**,
2:16 The priest of **M** had seven daughters.
3: 1 of his father-in-law Jethro, the priest of **M**;
4:19 LORD said to Moses in **M**, “Go back to Egypt;
18: 1 Jethro, the priest of **M**, Moses' father-in-law,
Nu 22: 4 And Moab said to the elders of **M**,
22: 7 the elders of Moab and the elders of **M** departed
25:15 the head of a clan, an ancestral house in **M**.
25:18 the daughter of a leader of **M**, their sister;
31: 3 so that they may go against **M**,
31: 3 to execute the LORD's vengeance on **M**.
31: 7 They did battle against **M**,
31: 8 They killed the kings of **M**:
31: 8 Rekem, Zur, Hur, and Reba, the five kings of **M**,
31: 9 the women of **M** and their little ones captive;
Jos 13:21 whom Moses defeated with the leaders of **M**,
Jdg 6: 1 LORD gave them into the hand of **M** seven years.
6: 2 The hand of **M** prevailed over Israel;
6: 2 and because of **M** the Israelites provided
6: 6 Israel was greatly impoverished because of **M**;
6:13 and given us into the hand of **M**.”
6:14 of yours and deliver Israel from the hand of **M**;
7: 1 and the camp of **M** was north of them,
7: 8 The camp of **M** was below him in the valley.
7:13 the camp of **M**, and came to the tent, and struck it
7:14 into his hand God has given **M** and all the army.”
7:15 LORD has given the army of **M** into your hand.”
7:25 They captured the two captains of **M**,
8: 3 God has given into your hands the captains of **M**,
8: 5 and Zalmunna, the kings of **M**.”
8:12 and he pursued them and took the two kings of **M**,
8:22 for you have delivered us out of the hand of **M**.”
8:26 and the purple garments worn by the kings of **M**,
8:28 So **M** was subdued before the Israelites,
9:17 and rescued you from the hand of **M**;
1Ki 11:18 They set out from **M** and came to Paran;
1Ch 1:32 she bore Zimran, Jokshan, Medan, **M**, Ishbak,
1:33 The sons of **M**: Ephah, Epher,
1:46 who defeated **M** in the country of Moab,
Ps 83: 9 Do to them as you did to **M**,
Isa 9: 4 you have broken as on the day of **M**.
10:26 as when he struck **M** at the rock of Oreb;
60: 6 the young camels of **M** and Ephah;
Hab 3: 7 the tent-curtains of the land of **M** trembled.
Ac 7:29 and became a resident alien in the land of **M**.

MIDIANITE (5) [MIDIAN]

Ge 37:28 When some **M** traders passed by,
Nu 10:29 Moses said to Hobab son of Reuel the **M**,
25: 6 of the Israelites came and brought a **M** woman
25:14 who was killed with the **M** woman,
25:15 the **M** woman who was killed was Cozbi daughter

MIDIANITES (16) [MIDIAN]

Ge 37:36 the **M** had sold him in Egypt to Potiphar,
Nu 25:17 “Harass the **M**, and defeat them;
31: 2 “Avenge the Israelites on the **M**;
Jdg 6: 3 the **M** and the Amalekites and the people of
6: 7 Israelites cried to the LORD on account of the **M**,
6:11 to hide it from the **M**.
6:16 and you shall strike down the **M**,
6:33 Then all the **M** and the Amalekites and the people
7: 2 with you are too many for me to give the **M**
7: 7 and give the **M** into your hand.
7:12 The **M** and the Amalekites and all the people of
7:23 and they pursued after the **M**.
7:24 against the **M** and seize the waters against them,
7:25 at the wine press of Zeeb, as they pursued the **M**.
8: 1 to call us when you went to fight against the **M**?”
Jdt 2:26 He surrounded all the **M**, and burned their tents

MIDIANITISH (KJV) See MIDIANITE

MIDNIGHT (14) [NIGHT]

Ex 11: 4 About **m** I will go out through Egypt.
12:29 At **m** the LORD struck down all the firstborn in
Jdg 16: 3 But Samson lay only until **m**. Then at **m** he rose
Ru 3: 8 At **m** the man was startled, and turned over,
Job 34:20 at **m** the people are shaken and pass away,
Ps 119:62 At **m** I rise to praise you,
Mt 25: 6 But at **m** there was a shout, ‘Look!
Mk 13:35 in the evening, or at **m**, or at cockcrow, or at dawn,
Lk 11: 5 and you go to him at **m** and say to him, ‘Friend,
Ac 16:25 About **m** Paul and Silas were praying
20: 7 he continued speaking until **m**.
27:27 about **m** the sailors suspected
Jdt 12: 5 into the tent, and she slept until **m**.

MIDST‡ (125) [MIDDLE]

Ge 1: 6 “Let there be a dome in the **m** of the waters,
2: 9 the tree of life also in the **m** of the garden,
19:29 and sent Lot out of the **m** of the overthrow,
Ex 9:24 with fire flashing continually in the **m** of it,
Lev 15:31 by defiling my tabernacle that is in their **m**.
16:16 of meeting, which remains with them in the **m**
23:30 such a one I will destroy from the **m** of the people.
26:11 I will place my dwelling in your **m**,
Nu 14:14 O LORD, are in the **m** of this people;
16:33 and they perished from the **m** of the assembly.
Dt 1:42 for I am not in the **m** of you;
4:34 a nation for himself from the **m** of another nation,
11: 6 in the **m** of all Israel the earth opened its mouth
13: 5 So you shall purge the evil from your **m**.
17: 7 So you shall purge the evil from your **m**.
19:19 So you shall purge the evil from your **m**.
21: 8 not let the guilt of innocent blood remain in the **m**
21: 9 the guilt of innocent blood from your **m**,
21:21 So you shall purge the evil from your **m**;
22:21 So you shall purge the evil from your **m**.
22:24 So you shall purge the evil from your **m**.
23:16 They shall reside with you, in your **m**,
24: 7 So you shall purge the evil from your **m**.
29:16 the **m** of the nations through which you passed.
31:16 to the foreign gods in their **m**, the gods of the land
31:17 upon us because our God is not in our **m**?’

Jos 24: 5 and I plagued Egypt with what I did in its **m;**
2Sa 1:25 How the mighty have fallen in the **m** of the battle!
1Ki 3: 8 in the **m** of the people whom you have chosen,
8:51 from the **m** of the iron-smelter).
Ps 22:22 in the **m** of the congregation I will praise you:
46: 5 God is in the **m** of the city;
48: 9 O God, in the **m** of your temple.
55:11 ruin is in its **m;** oppression
82: 1 in the **m** of the gods he holds judgment:
109:30 I will praise him in the **m** of the throng.
110: 2 Rule in the **m** of your foes.
116:19 the courts of the house of the LORD, in your **m,**
135: 9 he sent signs and wonders into your **m,**
136:14 the **m** of it, for his steadfast love endures forever;
138: 7 Though I walk in the **m** of trouble,
Pr 23:34 You will be like one who lies down in the **m** of
Isa 4: 4 of Jerusalem from its **m** by a spirit of judgment and
5: 2 he built a watchtower in the **m** of it,
5: 8 and you are left to live alone in the **m** of the land!
6:12 and vast is the emptiness in the **m** of the land.
12: 6 for great in your **m** is the Holy One of Israel.
19:24 a blessing in the **m** of the earth,
25:11 Though they spread out their hands in the **m** of it,
29:23 in his **m,** they will sanctify my name;
41:18 and fountains in the **m** of the valleys;
52:11 Touch no unclean thing; go out from the **m** of it,
Jer 6: 1 O children of Benjamin, from the **m** of Jerusalem!
12:16 then they shall be built up in the **m** of my people.
14: 9 Yet you, O LORD, are in the **m** of us,
30:21 their ruler shall come from their **m;**
44: 7 child and infant, from the **m** of Judah,
46:21 her mercenaries in her **m** are like fatted calves;
50:37 and against all the foreign troops in her **m,**
51: 6 Flee from the **m** of Babylon, save your lives,
51:47 and all her slain shall fall in her **m.**
La 1: 3 her pursuers have all overtaken her in the **m**
1:15 The LORD has rejected all my warriors in the **m**
4:13 who shed the blood of the righteous in the **m**
Eze 5:10 Surely, parents shall eat their children in your **m,**
6: 7 The slain shall fall in your **m;**
12: 2 you are living in the **m** of a rebellious house,
14: 8 a sign and a byword and cut them off from the **m**
14: 9 will destroy him from the **m** of my people Israel.
20: 8 and spend my anger against them in the **m** of
22: 9 who commit lewdness in your **m.**
22:19 I will gather you into the **m** of Jerusalem.
25: 4 among you and pitch their tents in your **m;**
26: 5 It shall become, in the **m** of the sea,
27:32 "Who was ever destroyed like Tyre in the **m** of
28:22 O Sidon, and I will gain glory in your **m.**
28:23 and the dead shall fall in its **m,**
29: 3 the great dragon sprawling in the **m** of its channels,
32:21 with their helpers, out of the **m** of Sheol:
Hos 11: 9 I am God and no mortal, the Holy One in your **m,**
Joel 2:27 You shall know that I am in the **m** of Israel,
Am 2: 3 I will cut off the ruler from its **m,**
3: 9 and what oppressions are in its **m."**
5:17 for I will pass through the **m** of you,
7: 8 a plumb line in the **m** of my people Israel;
Mic 7:14 which lives alone in a forest in the **m** of
Na 3:13 Look at your troops: they are women in your **m.**
Zep 3:11 from your **m** your proudly exultant ones,
3:12 For I will leave in the **m** of you a people humble
3:15 The king of Israel, the LORD, is in your **m;**
3:17 The LORD, your God, is in your **m,**
Zec 2:10 For lo, I will come and dwell in your **m,**
2:11 and I will dwell in your **m.**
8: 3 and will dwell in the **m** of Jerusalem;
14: 1 plunder taken from you will be divided in your **m.**
Mt 10:16 I am sending you out like sheep into the **m**
Lk 4:30 But he passed through the **m** of them and went
10: 3 I am sending you out like lambs into the **m**
Ac 4: 7 they had made the prisoners stand in their **m,**
Php 2:15 in the **m** of a crooked and perverse generation,
Heb 2:12 in the **m** of the congregation I will praise you."
Jas 1:11 in the **m** of a busy life, they will wither away.
Rev 1:13 in the **m** of the lampstands I saw one like the Son
6: 6 a voice in the **m** of the four living creatures saying,
Jdt 6:16 They set Achior in the **m** of all their people,
Wis 4:14 he took them quickly from the **m** of wickedness.
12: 5 These initiates from the **m** of a heathen cult,
16:19 the **m** of water it burned more intensely than fire,
18:15 into the **m** of the land that was doomed,
Sir 14:27 and dwells in the **m** of her glory.
15: 5 and will open his mouth in the **m** of the assembly.
24: 1 and tells of her glory in the **m** of her people.
48:17 and brought water into its **m;**
51: 4 and from the **m** of fire that I had not kindled,
Aza 1: 1 They walked around in the **m** of the flames,
1:66 from the **m** of the burning fiery furnace;
1:66 from the **m** of the fire he has delivered us.
1Mc 6:45 He courageously ran into the **m** of the phalanx
2Es 2:43 In their **m** was a young man of great stature,
12:17 the eagle's heads but from the **m** of its body, this is
12:18 In the **m** of the time of
16:40 prepare for battle, and in the **m** of the calamities be
16:58 he has confined the sea in the **m** of the waters;
16:61 He formed human beings and put a heart in the **m** of
4Mc 15:23 a man's courage in the very **m** of her emotions,

MIDWIFE (3) [MIDWIVES]

Ge 35:17 When she was in her hard labor, the **m** said to her,
38:28 **m** took and bound on his hand a crimson thread,
Ex 1:19 and give birth before the **m** comes to them."

MIDWIVES (7) [MIDWIFE]

Ex 1:15 The king of Egypt said to the Hebrew **m,**
1:16 "When you act as **m** to the Hebrew women,
1:17 But the **m** feared God; they did not do as the king
1:18 king of Egypt summoned the **m** and said to them,
1:19 The **m** said to Pharaoh,
1:20 So God dealt well with the **m;**
1:21 because the **m** feared God, he gave them families.

MIEN (1)

2Mc 3:25 caparisoned horse, with a rider of frightening **m;**

MIGDAL-EL (1)

Jos 19:38 **M,** Horem, Beth-anath, and Beth-shemesh—

MIGDAL-GAD (1)

Jos 15:37 Zenan, Hadashah, **M,**

MIGDOL (6)

Ex 14: 2 between **M** and the sea, in front of Baal-zephon;
Nu 33: 7 and they camped before **M.**
Jer 44: 1 at **M,** at Tahpanhes, at Memphis,
46:14 in Egypt, and proclaim in **M;**
Eze 29:10 from **M** to Syene, as far as the border of Ethiopia.
30: 6 from **M** to Syene they shall fall within it by the

MIGHT‡ (413) [ALMIGHTY, MIGHTIER, MIGHTIEST, MIGHTILY, MIGHTY]

Ge 3:22 he **m** reach out his hand and take also from the tree
14:23 so that you **m** not say, 'I have made Abram rich.'
17:18 "O that Ishmael **m** live in your sight!"
26: 7 "or else the men of the place **m** kill me for the sake
26: 9 "Because I thought I **m** die because of her."
26:10 of the people **m** easily have lain with your wife,
30:41 that they **m** breed among the rods,
37:22 that he **m** rescue him out of their hand
42: 4 for he feared that harm **m** come to him.
49: 3 my **m** and the first fruits of my vigor,
Ex 13:21 so that they **m** travel by day and by night.
15: 2 The LORD is my strength and my **m,**
15:16 by the **m** of your arm,
29:46 of the land of Egypt that I **m** dwell among them;
36:18 to join the tent together so that it **m** be one whole.
39:23 so that it **m** not be torn.
Nu 14:13 for in your **m** you brought up this people from
Dt 3:24 to show your servant your greatness and your **m;**
5:29 so that it **m** go well with them and
6: 5 and with all your soul, and with all your **m.**
8:17 not say to yourself, "My power and the **m**
9:28 the land from which you have brought us **m** say,
15: 9 your neighbor **m** cry to the LORD against you,
19: 4 the case of a homicide who **m** flee there and live,
19: 6 of blood in hot anger **m** pursue and overtake
20: 5 or he **m** die in the battle and another dedicate it.
20: 6 or he **m** die in the battle and another be first
20: 7 or he **m** die in the battle and another marry her."
20: 8 or he **m** cause the heart of his comrades to melt
22: 8 otherwise you **m** have bloodguilt on your house,
24:15 otherwise they **m** cry to the LORD against you,
32:27 for their adversaries **m** misunderstand and say,
Jos 11:20 in order that they **m** be utterly destroyed,
11:20 and **m** receive no mercy, but be exterminated,
22:24 from fear that in time to come your children **m** say
22:25 So your children **m** make our children cease
Jdg 3: 2 successive generations of Israelites **m** know war,
5:21 March on, my soul, with **m!**
5:31 your friends be like the sun as it rises in its **m."**
6:14 in this **m** of yours and deliver Israel from the hand
9:24 of Jerubbaal **m** be avenged and their blood be laid
14: 6 the lion apart barehanded as one **m** tear apart a kid.
16:30 He strained with all his **m;**
Ru 2:22 otherwise you **m** be bothered in another field."
1Sa 2: 9 for not by **m** does one prevail.
9:24 so that you **m** eat with the guests."
18:27 that he **m** become the king's son-in-law.
27:11 thinking, "They **m** tell about us, and say,
2Sa 6: 5 before the LORD with all their **m,**
6:14 David danced before the LORD with all his **m;**
6:20 any vulgar fellow **m** shamelessly uncover himself!
15: 4 Then all who had a suit or cause **m** come to me,
17:14 so that the LORD **m** bring ruin on Absalom.
1Ki 6:22 in order that the whole house **m** be perfect;
8:16 that my name **m** be there;
12:15 about by the LORD that he **m** fulfill his word,
19: 4 He asked that he **m** die:
2Ki 13: 8 that he did, including his **m,** are they not written in
13:12 the **m** with which he fought against King Amaziah
14:15 Now the rest of the acts that Jehoash did, his **m,**
14:28 and all that he did, and his **m,** how he fought,
15:19 so that he **m** help him confirm his hold on the
23:25 with all his soul, and with all his **m,**
23:33 so that he **m** not reign in Jerusalem,
1Ch 4:10 and that your hand **m** be with me,
13: 8 before God with all their **m,**
29:12 In your hand are power and **m;**
29:30 with accounts of all his rule and his **m** and of
2Ch 6: 5 so that my name **m** be there,
6:41 you and the ark of your **m.**
10:15 by God so that the LORD **m** fulfill his word,
20: 6 In your hand are power and **m,**
31: 4 so that they **m** devote themselves to the law of
32:18 in order that they **m** take the city.
35:12 the burnt offerings so that they **m** distribute them
Ezr 1: 1 of Jeremiah **m** be accomplished, the LORD stirred
5:10 so that we **m** write down the names of the men
8:21 that we **m** deny ourselves before our God,
Est 4: 2 for no one **m** enter the king's gate clothed
4: 4 so that he **m** take off his sackcloth;
4: 8 that he **m** show it to Esther, explain it to her,
8:11 of any people or province that **m** attack them,
10: 2 All the acts of his power and **m,**
Job 6: 8 "O that I **m** have my request,
9:32 he is not a mortal, as I am, that I **m** answer him,
9:33 who **m** lay his hand on us both.
23: 3 Oh, that I knew where I **m** find him,
23: 3 that I **m** come even to his dwelling!
30:21 with the **m** of your hand you persecute me.
31:31 'O that we **m** be sated with his flesh!'—
38:13 so that it **m** take hold of the skirts of the earth,
39:19 "Do you give the horse its **m?**
Ps 4: 6 "O that we **m** see some good!
10:10 they crouch, and the helpless fall by their **m.**
33:17 and by its great **m** it cannot save.
54: 1 by your name, and vindicate me by your **m.**
59:16 But I will sing of your **m;**
65: 6 established the mountains; you are girded with **m.**
66: 7 by his **m** forever, whose eyes keep watch on
68:28 Summon your **m,** O God; show your strength,
71:18 I proclaim your **m** to all the generations to come.
74:13 You divided the sea by your **m;**
77:14 you have displayed your **m** among the peoples.
78: 4 and his **m,** and the wonders that he has done.
78: 6 that the next generation **m** know them,
80: 2 Stir up your **m,** and come to save us!
104: 9 so that they **m** not again cover the earth.
105:45 that they **m** keep his statutes and observe his laws.
106: 8 so that he **m** make known his mighty power.
118:14 The LORD is my strength and my **m;**
119:71 so that I **m** learn your statutes.
125: 3 so that the righteous **m** not stretch out their hands
132: 8 you and the ark of your **m.**
145: 6 The **m** of your awesome deeds shall be proclaimed,
Pr 8:29 so that the waters **m** not transgress his command,
Ecc 2: 3 on folly, until I **m** see what was good for mortals
4:12 And though one **m** prevail against another,
9:10 Whatever your hand finds to do, do with your **m;**
9:16 So I said, "Wisdom is better than **m;**
Isa 11: 2 the spirit of counsel and **m,**
12: 2 for the LORD GOD is my strength and my **m;**
25: 9 we have waited for him, so that he **m** save us.
33:13 and you who are near, acknowledge my **m.**
40:10 See, the Lord GOD comes with **m,**
41:26 from the beginning, so that we **m** know,
41:26 and beforehand, so that we **m** say, "He is right"?
43:21 for myself so that they **m** declare my praise.
49: 5 and that Israel **m** be gathered to him,
60:21 the work of my hands, so that I **m** be glorified.
63: 1 so splendidly robed, marching in his great **m?"**
63:15 Where are your zeal and your **m?**
64: 2 so that the nations **m** tremble at your presence!
Jer 9: 1 so that I **m** weep day and night for the slain
9: 2 that I **m** leave my people and go away from them!
9:23 do not let the mighty boast in their **m,**
10: 6 you are great, and your name is great in **m.**
13:11 in order that they **m** be for me a people, a name,
16:21 to teach them my power and my **m,**
23:10 Their course has been evil, and their **m** is not right.
38:19 for I **m** be handed over to them
49:35 to break the bow of Elam, the mainstay of their **m;**
La 2: 3 He has cut down in fierce anger all the **m** of Israel;
2:17 and exalted the **m** of your foes.
Eze 13: 5 that it **m** stand in battle on the day of the LORD.
17: 7 toward him, so that he **m** water it.
17: 8 so that it **m** produce branches and bear fruit
17:14 the kingdom **m** be humble and not lift itself up,
17:14 and that by keeping his covenant it **m** stand.
17:15 that they **m** give him horses and a large army.
20:12 that they **m** know that I the LORD sanctify them.
20:26 in order that I **m** horrify them,
20:26 so that they **m** know that I am the LORD.
30: 6 and its proud **m** shall come down;
30:18 and its proud **m** shall come to an end;
32:29 for all their **m** are laid with those who are killed by
32:30 for all the terror that they caused by their **m;**
33:28 and its proud **m** shall come to an end;
40: 4 for you were brought here in order that I **m** show it
Da 2:18 the rest of the wise men of Babylon **m** not perish.
2:37 the power, the **m,** and the glory,
4: 6 that they **m** tell me the interpretation of the dream.
5: 2 his wives, and his concubines **m** drink from them.
6: 2 so that the king **m** suffer no loss.
6:17 so that nothing **m** be changed concerning Daniel.
Jnh 4: 8 so that he was faint and asked that he **m** die.
Mic 3: 8 of the LORD, and with justice and **m,** to declare
7:16 nations shall see and be ashamed of all their **m;**
Hab 1:11 their own **m** is their god!
Zec 4: 6 Not by **m,** nor by power, but by my spirit,
Mt 2:23 that what had been spoken through the prophets **m**
4:14 through the prophet Isaiah **m** be fulfilled:
12:10 so that they **m** accuse him.
13:15 so that they **m** not look with their eyes,
14: 7 on oath to grant her whatever she **m** ask.
14:36 and begged him that they **m** touch even the fringe
15: 5 'Whatever support you **m** have had
15:32 for they **m** faint on the way."
19:13 in order that he **m** lay his hands on them and pray.
26:59 against Jesus so that they **m** put him to death,
Mk 3: 2 so that they **m** accuse him.
5:18 by demons begged him that he **m** be with him.
6:56 and begged him that they **m** touch even the fringe

Mk 7:11 'Whatever support you **m** have had
10:13 to him in order that he **m** touch them;
14:35 if it were possible, the hour **m** pass from him.
16: 1 so that they **m** go and anoint him.
Lk 1:29 and pondered what sort of greeting this **m** be.
1:74 from the hands of our enemies, **m** serve him
3:15 whether he **m** be the Messiah,
4:29 so that they **m** hurl him off the cliff.
6: 7 so that they **m** find an accusation against him.
6:11 and discussed with one another what they **m** do
8:38 from whom the demons had gone begged that he **m**
11:54 to catch him in something he **m** say.
15:29 a young goat so that I **m** celebrate with my friends.
16:26 so that those who **m** want to pass from here
18:15 even infants to him that he **m** touch them;
19:15 that he **m** find out what they had gained by trading.
20:10 the tenants in order that they **m** give him his share
22: 4 of the temple police about how he **m** betray him
Jn 1: 7 so that all **m** believe through him.
1:31 that he **m** be revealed to Israel."
3:17 in order that the world **m** be saved through him.
8: 6 ⟦they **m** have some charge to bring against him.⟧
9: 3 so that God's works **m** be revealed in him.
11:57 so that they **m** arrest him.
12: 7 She bought it so that she **m** keep it for the day
12:40 so that they **m** not look with their eyes,
17:12 so that the scripture **m** be fulfilled.
19:36 These things occurred so that the scripture **m**
Ac 5:15 in order that Peter's shadow **m** fall on some
5:24 wondering what **m** be going on.
5:31 that he **m** give repentance to Israel and forgiveness
7:46 and asked that he **m** find a dwelling place for
8:15 down and prayed for them that they **m** receive
9: 2 he **m** bring them bound to Jerusalem.
9:12 on him so that he **m** regain his sight."
9:24 the gates day and night so that they **m** kill him;
20:16 so that he **m** not have to spend time in Asia;
26:29 to me today **m** become such as I am—
27:29 Fearing that we **m** run on the rocks,
27:42 so that none **m** swim away and escape;
28:27 so that they **m** not look with their eyes,
Ro 5: 7 for a good person someone **m** actually dare to die.
5:21 so grace **m** also exercise dominion
6: 4 so we too **m** walk in newness of life.
6: 6 with him so that the body of sin **m** be destroyed,
6: 6 and we **m** no longer be enslaved to sin.
7:13 in order that sin **m** be shown to be sin,
7:13 commandment **m** become sinful beyond measure.
8: 4 the just requirement of the law **m** be fulfilled in us,
8:29 that he **m** be the firstborn within a large family.
9:11 (so that God's purpose of election **m** continue,
11:19 "Branches were broken off so that I **m** be grafted
14: 9 that he **m** be Lord of both the dead and the living.
15: 4 of the scriptures we **m** have hope.
15: 8 in order that he **m** confirm the promises given to
15: 9 that the Gentiles **m** glorify God for his mercy.
1Co 1:17 the cross of Christ **m** not be emptied of its power.
1:29 so that no one **m** boast in the presence of God.
2: 5 that your faith **m** rest not on human wisdom but on
4: 8 so that we **m** be kings with you!
4:15 you **m** have ten thousand guardians in Christ,
7:16 Wife, for all you know, you **m** save your husband.
7:16 Husband, for all you know, you **m** save your wife.
8:10 **m** they not, since their conscience is weak,
9:19 so that I **m** win more of them.
9:20 under the law) so that I **m** win those under the law.
9:21 so that I **m** win those outside the law.
9:22 so that I **m** win the weak.
9:22 that I **m** by all means save some.
10: 6 so that we **m** not desire evil as they did.
2Co 1:15 so that you **m** have a double favor;
2: 3 as I did, so that when I came, I **m** not suffer pain
5:15 those who live **m** live no longer for themselves,
5:21 in him we **m** become the righteousness of God.
7:12 but in order that your zeal for us **m** be made known
8: 6 so that we **m** urge Titus that,
8: 9 so that by his poverty you **m** become rich.
11: 7 a sin by humbling myself so that you **m** be exalted,
Gal 1:16 so that I **m** proclaim him among the Gentiles,
2: 4 so that they **m** enslave us—
2: 5 the truth of the gospel **m** always remain with you.
2:16 so that we **m** be justified by faith in Christ,
2:19 the law I died to the law, so that I **m** live to God.
3:14 in Christ Jesus the blessing of Abraham **m** come to
3:14 so that we **m** receive the promise of the Spirit
3:22 in Jesus Christ **m** be given to those who believe.
3:24 so that we **m** be justified by faith.
4: 5 so that we **m** receive adoption as children.
Eph 1:12 **m** live for the praise of his glory.
2: 7 to come he **m** show the immeasurable riches
2:15 that he **m** create in himself one new humanity
2:16 and **m** reconcile both groups to God in one body
3:10 of God in its rich variety **m** now be made known to
4:10 so that he **m** fill all things.)
Col 1:18 so that he **m** come to have first place in everything.
1Th 2: 7 we **m** have made demands as apostles of Christ.
2: 9 and day, so that we **m** not burden any of you
2Th 1: 9 of the Lord and from the glory of his **m**,
3: 8 so that we **m** not burden any of you.
1Ti 1:16 Jesus Christ **m** display the utmost patience,
2Ti 4:17 that through me the message **m** be fully
proclaimed and all the Gentiles **m** hear it.
Tit 2:14 that he **m** redeem us from all iniquity and purify
3: 7 we **m** become heirs according to the hope
Phm 1:13 so that he **m** be of service to me in your place
1:14 in order that your good deed **m** be voluntary and
1:15 so that you **m** have him back forever,

Heb 2: 9 by the grace of God he **m** taste death for everyone.
2:14 so that through death he **m** destroy the one who has
2:17 so that he **m** be a merciful and faithful high priest
6:18 we who have taken refuge **m**
7: 9 One **m** even say that Levi himself,
Jas 5:17 and he prayed fervently that it **m** not rain,
1Pe 2:24 so that, free from sins, we **m** live for righteousness;
3: 9 that you **m** inherit a blessing.
4: 6 they **m** live in the spirit as God does.
2Pe 2:11 though greater in **m** and power,
1Jn 4: 9 into the world so that we **m** live through him.
Rev 5:12 and wealth and wisdom and **m** and honor and glory
5:13 be blessing and honor and glory and **m** forever
7:12 and honor and power and **m** be to our God forever
12: 4 that he **m** devour her child as soon as it was born.
Tob 2: 4 in one of the rooms until sunset when I **m** bury it.
3:17 so that he **m** see God's light with his eyes;
8: 5 and they began to pray and implore that they **m**
Jdt 4:15 they cried out to the Lord with all their **m** to look
5:15 and by their **m** destroyed all the inhabitants
6: 3 They cannot resist the **m** of our cavalry.
9: 8 Break their strength by your **m**,
9:11 nor your **m** on the powerful.
9:14 the God of all power and **m**,
10: 4 to entice the eyes of all the men who **m** see her.
13: 4 said in her heart, "O Lord God of all **m**,
13: 8 Then she struck his neck twice with all her **m**,
AdE 13: 3 "When I asked my counselors how this **m**
13:14 so that I **m** not set human glory above the glory
14:19 O God, whose **m** is over all,
Wis 1:14 For he created all things so that they **m** exist;
2:11 But let our **m** be our law of right,
4:11 up so that evil **m** not change their understanding
10:12 the victory, so that he **m** learn
11:16 so that they **m** learn that one is punished by
11:21 and who can withstand the **m** of your arm?
12: 7 that the land most precious of all to you **m** receive
14:17 so that by their zeal they **m** flatter the absent one as
16: 3 **m** lose the least remnant of appetite because of
16: 3 after suffering want a short time, **m** partake
16:18 so that it **m** not consume the creatures sent against
16:18 but that seeing this they **m** know
16:22 so that they **m** know that the crops
16:23 in order that the righteous **m** be fed,
16:26 **m** learn that it is not the production of crops
18: 6 that they **m** rejoice in sure knowledge of the oaths
18:19 so that they **m** not perish
19: 4 in order that they **m** fill up the punishment
19: 5 your people **m** experience an incredible journey,
19: 5 but they themselves **m** meet a strange death.
19: 6 so that your children **m** be kept unharmed.
Sir Pr: 1 also with his book those who love learning **m** make
3:20 For great is the **m** of the Lord;
6:26 and keep her ways with all your **m**.
7:30 With all your **m** love your Maker,
12: 5 for by means of it they **m** subdue you;
16: 7 the ancient giants who revolted in their **m**.
36: 3 against foreign nations and let them see your **m**.
38: 5 with a tree in order that its power **m** be known?
38: 6 that he **m** be glorified in his marvelous works.
45: 5 so that he **m** teach Jacob the covenant,
46: 1 so that he **m** give Israel its inheritance.
46: 6 so that the nations **m** know his armament,
46:10 that all the Israelites **m** see how good it is to follow
47:13 so that he **m** build a house in his name and provide
LtJ 6: 9 as they **m** for a girl who loves ornaments.
Sus 1:32 so that they **m** feast their eyes on her beauty.
1Mc 1:16 in order that he **m** reign over both kingdoms.
3:30 He feared that he **m** not have such funds as he had
4:61 the people **m** have a stronghold that faced Idumea.
6:15 that he **m** guide his son Antiochus and bring him
6:47 the Jews saw the royal **m** and the fierce attack of
12:40 He feared that Jonathan **m** not permit him to do so,
12:40 but **m** make war on him,
13:17 among the people, who **m** say,
13:27 he made it high so that it **m** be seen,
14:29 that their sanctuary and the law **m** be preserved;
14:49 so that Simon and his sons **m** have them.
15:41 so that they **m** go out and make raids along
16:19 so that he **m** give them silver and gold and gifts;
2Mc 3:32 fearing that the king **m** get the notion
5: 4 the apparition **m** prove to have been a good omen.
5:27 so that they **m** not share in the defilement.
6:22 so that by doing this he **m** be saved from death,
6:24 "for many of the young **m** suppose that Eleazar
6:30 though I **m** have been saved from death,
10: 4 and implored the Lord that they **m** never again fall
10: 4 they **m** be disciplined by him with forbearance and
12:12 that they **m** indeed be useful in many ways, agreed
12:28 upon the Sovereign who with power shatters the **m**
12:42 that had been committed **m** be wholly blotted out.
12:45 so that they **m** be delivered from their sin.
15:24 By the **m** of your arm may these blasphemers who
1Es 2: 1 the word of the Lord by the mouth of Jeremiah **m**
6:12 In order that we **m** inform you in writing who
3Mc 2:30 In order that he **m** not appear to be an enemy of all,
3:11 and not considering the **m** of the supreme God,
5: 2 so that the Jews **m** meet their doom.
5:13 to show the **m** of his all-powerful hand to
6:12 you, O Eternal One, who have all **m** and all power,
6:13 in fear of your invincible **m**,
7:12 they **m** destroy those everywhere
2Es 3:20 so that your law **m** produce fruit in them.
5:43 so that you **m** show your judgment the sooner?"
5:45 it **m** even now be able to support all
6:41 so that one part **m** move upward and
6:42 that some of them **m** be planted and cultivated and

2Es 6:48 the nations **m** declare your wondrous works.
7:*63* so that the mind **m** not have been made from it.
7:*89* that they **m** keep the law of the Lawgiver perfectly.
7:*92* that it **m** not lead them astray from life into death.
7:*109* [39] and for the one who was dead, that he **m** live,
7:*138* [68] so that those who have committed iniquities **m**
11:39 so that the end of my times **m** come through them?
13:42 at least they **m** keep their statutes that they had
15:16 they shall in their **m** have no respect for their king
4Mc 1: 5 Some **m** perhaps ask, "If reason rules the emotions,
2:24 How is it then, one **m** say,
6:27 O God, that though I **m** have saved myself,
7:17 Some perhaps **m** say, "Not all have full command
8:16 what arguments **m** have been used if some
15: 4 In what manner **m** I express the emotions
17: 1 into the flames so that no one **m** touch her body.
17: 7 to paint the history of your religion as an artist **m**,

MIGHTIER (8) [MIGHT]

Nu 14:12 of you a nation greater and **m** than they."
Dt 4:38 before you nations greater and **m** than yourselves,
7: 1 seven nations **m** and more numerous than you—
9: 1 in and dispossess nations larger and **m** than you,
9:14 of you a nation **m** and more numerous than they."
11:23 dispossess nations larger and **m** than yourselves.
Pr 24: 5 Wise warriors are **m** than strong ones,
Sir 13: 2 or associate with one **m** and richer than you.

MIGHTIEST (1) [MIGHT]

Pr 30:30 which is **m** among wild animals and does

MIGHTILY‡ (9) [MIGHT]

Ge 7:19 so **m** on the earth that all the high mountains under
1Sa 16:13 the spirit of the LORD came **m** upon David from
Job 39:21 It paws violently, exults **m**;
Jer 25:30 he will roar **m** against his fold, and shout,
Jnh 3: 8 and they shall cry **m** to God.
Ac 19:20 So the word of the Lord grew **m** and prevailed.
AdE 13:18 And all Israel cried out **m**,
Wis 6: 6 but the mighty will be **m** tested.
8: 1 She reaches **m** from one end of the earth to

MIGHTY‡ (252) [MIGHT]

A. MIGHTY WARRIORS (27)
B. MIGHTY HAND (22)
C. MIGHTY ONE (21)
D. MIGHTY WATERS (20)
E. MIGHTY WARRIOR (11)
F. MIGHTY DEEDS (7)

Ge 10: 8 he was the first on earth to become a **m** warrior. E
10: 9 He was a **m** hunter before the LORD;
10: 9 "Like Nimrod a **m** hunter before the LORD."
18:18 that Abraham shall become a great and **m** nation,
23: 6 you are a **m** prince among us.
30: 8 "With **m** wrestlings I have wrestled with my sister,
49:24 by the hands of the **M** One of Jacob, C
Ex 3:19 not let you go unless compelled by a **m** hand. B
6: 1 Indeed, by a **m** hand he will let them go; B
6: 1 by a **m** hand he will drive them out of his land." B
6: 6 an outstretched arm and with **m** acts of judgment.
15:10 they sank like lead in the **m** waters. D
32:11 of Egypt with great power and with a **m** hand? B
Dt 3:24 on earth can perform deeds and **m** acts like yours!
4:34 by war, by a **m** hand and by an outstretched arm, B
5:15 there with a **m** hand and an outstretched arm; B
6:21 the LORD brought us out of Egypt with a **m** hand. B
7: 8 the LORD has brought you out with a **m** hand, B
7:19 the **m** hand and the outstretched arm by which B
9:26 whom you brought out of Egypt with a **m** hand. B
10:17 the great God, **m** and awesome,
11: 2 his **m** hand and his outstretched arm, B
26: 5 there he became a great nation, **m** and populous.
26: 8 LORD brought us out of Egypt with a **m** hand B
34:12 **m** deeds and all the terrifying displays of power F
Jos 4:24 that the hand of the LORD is **m**,
10: 7 the fighting force with him, all the **m** warriors. A
Jdg 5:13 the LORD marched down for him against the **m**.
5:23 to the help of the LORD against the **m**.
6:12 "The LORD is with you, you **m** warrior." E
11: 1 the son of a prostitute, was a **m** warrior. E
1Sa 2: 4 The bows of the **m** are broken,
4: 5 all Israel gave a **m** shout,
4: 8 from the power of these **m** gods?
7:10 but the LORD thundered with a **m** voice that day
2Sa 1:19 How the **m** have fallen!
1:21 For there the shield of the **m** was defiled,
1:22 From the blood of the slain, from the fat of the **m**,
1:25 How the **m** have fallen in the midst of the battle!
1:27 **m** have fallen, and the weapons of war perished!
22:17 he took me, he drew me out of **m** waters. D
22:18 for they were too **m** for me.
1Ki 8:42 your **m** hand, and your outstretched arm— B
2Ki 5: 1 man, though a **m** warrior, suffered from leprosy. E
1Ch 1:10 he was the first to be a **m** one on the earth. C
5:24 Hodaviah, and Jahdiel, **m** warriors, famous men, A
7: 2 namely of Tola, **m** warriors of their generations, A
7: 5 in all eighty-seven thousand **m** warriors, A
7: 7 five, heads of ancestral houses, **m** warriors; A
7: 9 **m** warriors, was twenty thousand two hundred. A
7:11 **m** warriors, seventeen thousand two hundred, A
7:40 heads of ancestral houses, select **m** warriors, A
8:40 The sons of Ulam were **m** warriors, archers, A
11:11 This is an account of David's **m** warriors: A
12: 1 were among the **m** warriors who helped him A

1Ch 12: 8 to David at the stronghold in the wilderness **m** and
12:25 Of the Simeonites, **m** warriors, A
12:30 **m** warriors, notables in their ancestral houses. A
27: 6 the Benaiah who was a **m** man of the Thirty
28: 1 with the palace officials, the **m** warriors, A
29:24 All the leaders and the **m** warriors, A
2Ch 6:32 and your **m** hand, and your outstretched arm, B
13: 3 with eight hundred thousand picked **m** warriors. A
14: 8 and drew bows; all these were **m** warriors. A
14:11 for you between helping the **m** and the weak.
17:13 He had soldiers, **m** warriors, in Jerusalem. A
17:14 with three hundred thousand **m** warriors, A
17:16 with two hundred thousand **m** warriors. A
17:17 Of Benjamin: Eliada, a **m** warrior, E
25: 6 He also hired one hundred thousand **m** warriors A
26:12 of **m** warriors was two thousand six hundred. A
26:13 who could make war with **m** power,
28: 7 And Zichri, a **m** warrior of Ephraim, E
32:21 the **m** warriors and commanders and officers in A
Ezr 4:20 Jerusalem has had **m** kings who ruled over
7:28 and before all the king's **m** officers.
Ne 9:11 like a stone into **m** waters. D
9:32 the great and **m** and awesome God,
Job 5:15 from the hand of the **m**.
9: 4 and **m** in strength—who has resisted him,
12:19 leads priests away stripped, and overthrows the **m**.
21: 7 reach old age, and grow **m** in power?
24:22 Yet God prolongs the life of the **m** by his power;
34:17 Will you condemn one who is righteous and **m**,
34:20 and the **m** are taken away by no human hand.
34:24 He shatters the **m** without investigation,
35: 9 they call for help because of the arm of the **m**.
36: 5 "Surely God is **m** and does not despise any;
36: 5 he is **m** in strength of understanding.
41:12 or its **m** strength, or its splendid frame.
Ps 18:16 he drew me out of **m** waters. D
18:17 for they were too **m** for me.
20: 6 from his holy heaven with **m** victories
24: 8 The LORD, strong and **m**, the LORD, **m** in battle.
29: 3 God of glory thunders, the LORD, over **m** waters. D
32: 6 the rush of **m** waters shall not reach them. D
35:18 in the **m** throng I will praise you.
36: 6 Your righteousness is like the **m** mountains,
38:19 Those who are my foes without cause are **m**,
45: 3 Gird your sword on your thigh, O **m** one, C
50: 1 The **m** one, God the LORD, speaks and C
50: 3 and a **m** tempest all around him.
52: 1 O **m** one, of mischief done against the godly? C
59: 3 the **m** stir up strife against me.
62: 7 my **m** rock, my refuge is in God.
68:15 O **m** mountain, mountain of Bashan;
68:17 With **m** chariotry, twice ten thousand,
68:33 listen, he sends out his voice, his **m** voice.
71:16 I will come praising the **m** deeds of F
77:12 and muse on your **m** deeds. F
77:19 your path, through the **m** waters; D
80:10 the **m** cedars with its branches;
89: 8 O LORD God of hosts, who is as **m** as you,
89:10 you scattered your enemies with your **m** arm.
89:13 You have a **m** arm; strong is your hand,
89:19 "I have set the crown on one who is **m**,
93: 4 More majestic than the thunders of **m** waters, D
99: 4 **M** King, lover of justice, you have established
103:20 O you his angels, you **m** ones who do his bidding,
106: 2 Who can utter the **m** doings of the LORD,
106: 8 so that he might make known his **m** power.
107:23 doing business on the **m** waters; D
110: 2 The LORD sends out from Zion your **m** scepter.
112: 2 Their descendants will be **m** in the land;
132: 2 to the LORD and vowed to the **M** One of Jacob, C
132: 5 a dwelling place for the **M** One of Jacob." C
135:10 down many nations and killed **m** kings—
144: 7 set me free and rescue me from the **m** waters, D
145: 4 and shall declare your **m** acts.
145:12 to make known to all people your **m** deeds, F
150: 1 praise him in his **m** firmament!
150: 2 Praise him for his **m** deeds; F
Pr 16:32 One who is slow to anger is better than the **m**,
SS 3: 7 Around it are sixty **m** men of the **m** men
Isa 1:24 the LORD of hosts, the **M** One of Israel: C
8: 7 against it the **m** flood waters of the River,
9: 6 and he is named Wonderful Counselor, **M** God,
10:21 the remnant of Jacob, to the **m** God.
17:12 they roar like the roaring of **m** waters! D
18: 2 a nation **m** and conquering,
18: 7 a nation **m** and conquering,
23: 3 and were on the **m** waters; D
28: 2 See, the Lord has one who is **m** and strong;
28: 2 a destroying tempest, like a storm of **m**,
34: 7 and young steers with the **m** bulls.
40:26 because he is great in strength, **m** in power,
42:13 he shows himself **m** against his foes.
43:16 a path in the **m** waters, D
49:24 Can the prey be taken from the **m**,
49:25 Even the captives of the **m** shall be taken,
49:26 and your Redeemer, the **M** One of Jacob. C
56:11 dogs have a **m** appetite; they never have enough.
60:16 and your Redeemer, the **M** One of Jacob. C
60:22 and the smallest one a **m** nation;
62: 8 by his right hand and by his **m** arm:
63: 1 "It is I, announcing vindication, **m** to save."
Jer 5:16 all of them are **m** warriors. A
9:23 do not let the **m** boast in their might,
14: 9 like a **m** warrior who cannot give help? E
21: 5 against you with outstretched hand and **m** arm,
32:18 and **m** God whose name is the LORD of hosts,
32:19 great in counsel and **m** in deed;

Jer 48:14 can you say, "We are heroes and **m** warriors"? A
48:17 say, "How the **m** scepter is broken,
50:41 a **m** nation and many kings are stirring from
51:13 You who live by **m** waters, rich in treasures, D
51:55 Their waves roar like **m** waters, D
Eze 1:24 like the sound of **m** waters, like the thunder of D
17: 9 No strong arm or **m** army will be needed to pull it
17:17 Pharaoh with his **m** army and great company will
20:33 surely with a **m** hand and an outstretched arm, B
20:34 with a **m** hand and an outstretched arm, B
26:17 once **m** on the sea, you and your inhabitants,
27:10 and Put were in your army, your **m** warriors; A
31:15 and its **m** waters were checked. D
32:12 to fall by the swords of **m** ones,
32:21 The **m** chiefs shall speak of them,
38:15 of them riding on horses, a great horde, a **m** army;
39:18 You shall eat the flesh of the **m**,
43: 2 the sound was like the sound of **m** waters; D
Da 4: 3 How great are his signs, how **m** his wonders!
4:30 by my **m** power and for my glorious majesty?"
9:15 a **m** hand and made your name renowned even B
Am 2:14 nor shall the **m** save their lives;
2:16 among the **m** shall flee away naked in that day,
Jnh 1: 4 and such a **m** storm came upon the sea that
Hab 3:15 sea with your horses, churning the **m** waters. D
Lk 1:49 for the **M** One has done great things for me, C
1:69 a **m** savior for us in the house of his servant David,
24:19 who was a prophet **m** in deed and word before God
2Co 12:12 signs and wonders and **m** works.
2Th 1: 7 from heaven with his **m** angels
Heb 11:34 won strength out of weakness, became **m** in war,
1Pe 2: 9 the **m** acts of him who called you out of darkness
5: 6 Humble yourselves therefore under the **m** hand B
Rev 5: 2 and I saw a **m** angel proclaiming with a loud voice,
10: 1 I saw another **m** angel coming down from heaven,
18: 2 He called out with a **m** voice, "Fallen,
18: 8 for **m** is the Lord God who judges her."
18:10 "Alas, alas, the great city, Babylon, the **m** city!
18:21 a **m** angel took up a stone like a great millstone
19: 6 and like the sound of **m** thunderpeals,
19:18 the flesh of captains, the flesh of the **m**,
Jdt 16: 6 For their **m** one did not fall by the hands of C
AdE 16:16 most **m**, who has directed the kingdom both for us
Wis 5:23 a **m** wind will rise against them,
6: 6 but the **m** will be mightily tested.
6: 8 But a strict inquiry is in store for the **m**.
18: 5 and you destroyed them all together by a **m** flood.
Sir 15:18 he is **m** in power and sees everything;
16:11 he is **m** to forgive—but he also pours out wrath.
18: 4 and who can search out his **m** deeds? F
21: 7 The **m** in speech are widely known;
34:19 a **m** shield and strong support,
36:10 and let people recount your **m** deeds. F
46: 1 Joshua son of Nun was **m** in war,
46: 5 He called upon the Most High, the **M** One, C
46: 5 with hailstones of **m** power.
46: 6 for he was a devoted follower of the **M** One. C
46:16 He called upon the Lord, the **M** One, C
46:17 and made his voice heard with a **m** sound;
47: 5 to his right arm to strike down a **m** warrior, E
50:16 they sounded a **m** fanfare as a reminder before
51:12 *Give thanks to the **m** one of Jacob,* C
Bar 2:11 the land of Egypt with a **m** hand and with signs B
1Mc 2:42 with them a company of Hasideans, **m** warriors A
2:66 Judas Maccabeus has been a **m** warrior E
4:30 the **m** warrior by the hand of your servant David, E
9:21 "How is the **m** fallen, the savior of Israel!"
10:19 you are a **m** warrior and worthy to be our friend. E
2Mc 7:17 and see how his **m** power will torture you
11:13 because the **m** God fought on their side.
1Es 2:27 and that **m** and cruel kings ruled in Jerusalem
8:47 And by the **m** hand of our Lord B
8:61 arrived in Jerusalem by the **m** hand of our Lord, B
3Mc 2: 6 You made known your **m** power
2Es 2:19 seven **m** mountains on which roses and lilies grow;
6:17 and its sound was like the sound of **m** waters. D
6:32 for the **M** One has seen your uprightness and C
9: 6 beginnings are manifest in wonders and **m** works,
9:45 and we gave great glory to the **M** One. C
10:24 so that the **M** One may be merciful to you again, C
11:43 and your pride to the **M** One. C
12:47 **M** One has not forgotten you in your struggle. C
15:11 but I will bring them out with a **m** hand and B
15:40 Great and **m** clouds, full of wrath and tempest,
15:51 so that you cannot receive your **m** lovers.
16:16 Just as an arrow shot by a **m** archer does not return,
4Mc 7: 2 of the tyrant and overwhelmed by the **m** waves
15:25 of her own soul she saw **m** advocates—

MIGRATED (1)

Ge 11: 2 And as they **m** from the east,

MIGRON (2)

1Sa 14: 2 of Gibeah under the pomegranate tree that is at **M**;
Isa 10:28 he has passed through **M**, at Michmash he stores

MIJAMIN (5) [=MINIAMIN]

1Ch 24: 9 the fifth to Malchijah, the sixth to **M**,
Ezr 10:25 Ramiah, Izziah, Malchijah, **M**, Eleazar,
Ne 10: 7 Meshullam, Abijah, **M**,
12: 5 **M**, Maadiah, Bilgah,
1Es 9:26 Ramiah, Izziah, Malchijah, **M**, and Eleazar,

MIKLOTH (4)

1Ch 8:32 and **M**, who became the father
9:37 Gedor, Ahio, Zechariah, and **M**;
9:38 and **M** became the father of Shimeam;
27: 4 **M** was the chief officer of his division.

MIKNEIAH (2)

1Ch 15:18 and **M**, and the gatekeepers Obed-edom and Jeiel.
15:21 Eliphelehu, **M**, Obed-edom, Jeiel,

MIKTAM (6)

Ps 16: T *A **M** of David.*
56: T *Of David. A **M**, when the Philistines seized him*
57: T *To the leader: Do Not Destroy. Of David. A **M**,*
58: T *To the leader: Do Not Destroy. Of David. A **M**.*
59: T *To the leader: Do Not Destroy. Of David. A **M**,*
60: T *A **M** of David; for instruction;*

MILALAI (1)

Ne 12:36 **M**, Gilalai, Maai, Nethanel, Judah, and Hanani,

MILCAH (11)

Ge 11:29 and the name of Nahor's wife was **M**.
11:29 the daughter of Haran the father of **M** and Iscah.
22:20 "**M** also has borne children, to your brother Nahor:
22:23 These eight **M** bore to Nahor, Abraham's brother.
24:15 who was born to Bethuel son of **M**,
24:24 "I am the daughter of Bethuel son of **M**,
24:47 Nahor's son, whom **M** bore to him.'
Nu 26:33 Noah, Hoglah, **M**, and Tirzah.
27: 1 Mahlah, Noah, Hoglah, **M**, and Tirzah.
36:11 Mahlah, Tirzah, Hoglah, **M**, and Noah,
Jos 17: 3 Mahlah, Noah, Hoglah, **M**, and Tirzah.

MILCH (3)

Ge 32:15 thirty **m** camels and their colts,
1Sa 6: 7 a new cart and two **m** cows that have never borne
6:10 they took two **m** cows and yoked them to the cart,

MILCOM (8) [=MOLECH]

2Sa 12:30 He took the crown of **M** from his head;
1Ki 11: 5 and **M** the abomination of the Ammonites.
11:33 and **M** the god of the Ammonites,
2Ki 23:13 and for **M** the abomination of the Ammonites.
1Ch 20: 2 David took the crown of **M** from his head;
Jer 49: 1 Why then has **M** dispossessed Gad,
49: 3 For **M** shall go into exile, with his priests and
Zep 1: 5 and swear to the LORD, but also swear by **M**;

MILD (1) [MILDNESS]

Wis 12:26 the warning of **m** rebukes will experience

MILDEW (5)

Dt 28:22 and drought, and with blight and **m**;
1Ki 8:37 if there is plague, blight, **m**, locust, or caterpillar;
2Ch 6:28 if there is plague, blight, **m**, locust, or caterpillar;
Am 4: 9 I struck you with blight and **m**;
Hag 2:17 and all the products of your toil with blight and **m**

MILDNESS (1) [MILD]

Wis 12:18 you are sovereign in strength, you judge with **m**,

MILE (4) [MILES]

Mt 5:41 and if anyone forces you to go one **m**, go also the second **m**.
2Mc 12:10 When they had gone more than a **m** from there,
12:16 so that the adjoining lake, a quarter of a **m** wide,

MILES (8) [MILE]

Lk 24:13 about seven **m** from Jerusalem,
Jn 6:19 When they had rowed about three or four **m**,
11:18 Bethany was near Jerusalem, some two **m** away,
Rev 14:20 for a distance of about two hundred **m**.
21:16 the city with his rod, fifteen hundred **m**;
2Mc 12: 9 of the light was seen in Jerusalem, thirty **m** distant.
12:17 When they had gone ninety-five **m** from there,
12:29 which is seventy-five **m** from Jerusalem.

MILETUS (3)

Ac 20:15 and the day after that we came to **M**.
20:17 From **M** he sent a message to Ephesus,
2Ti 4:20 Trophimus I left ill in **M**.

MILITARY (8)

Nu 33: 1 in **m** formation under the leadership of Moses
Ac 25:23 the **m** tribunes and the prominent men of the city.
1Co 9: 7 at any time pays the expenses for doing **m** service?
Jdt 11: 8 and the most astounding in **m** strategy.
1Mc 14: 9 and the youths put on splendid **m** attire.
15:26 and gold and a large amount of **m** equipment.
2Mc 8: 9 a general and a man of experience in **m** service.
4Mc 4: 5 by the accursed Simon and a very strong **m** force.

MILK (55)

A. LAND FLOWING WITH MILK AND HONEY (20)

Ge 18: 8 and **m** and the calf that he had prepared, and set it
49:12 and his teeth whiter than **m**.
Ex 3: 8 a land flowing with **m** and honey, A
3:17 a land flowing with **m** and honey.' A
13: 5 a land flowing with **m** and honey, A
23:19 You shall not boil a kid in its mother's **m**.

Ex 33: 3 Go up to a land flowing with **m** and honey; A
34:26 You shall not boil a kid in its mother's **m.**
Lev 20:24 a land flowing with **m** and honey. A
Nu 13:27 it flows with **m** and honey, and this is its fruit.
14: 8 a land that flows with **m** and honey.
16:13 of a land flowing with **m** and honey to kill us in A
16:14 into a land flowing with **m** and honey, A
Dt 6: 3 in a land flowing with **m** and honey, A
11: 9 a land flowing with **m** and honey. A
14:21 You shall not boil a kid in its mother's **m.**
26: 9 a land flowing with **m** and honey. A
26:15 a land flowing with **m** and honey." A
27: 3 a land flowing with **m** and honey, as the LORD, A
31:20 into the land flowing with **m** and honey, A
32:14 and **m** from the flock, with fat of lambs and rams;
Jos 5: 6 a land flowing with **m** and honey. A
Jdg 4:19 a skin of **m** and gave him a drink and covered him.
5:25 He asked water and she gave him **m,**
Job 10:10 not pour me out like **m** and curdle me like cheese?
21:24 of **m** and the marrow of his bones moist.
29: 6 when my steps were washed with **m,**
Pr 27:27 there will be enough goats' **m** for your food,
30:33 For as pressing **m** produces curds,
SS 4:11 honey and **m** are under your tongue;
5: 1 I drink my wine with my **m.**
5:12 bathed in **m,** fitly set.
Isa 7:22 and will eat curds because of the abundance of **m**
28: 9 Those who are weaned from **m,**
55: 1 Come, buy wine and **m** without money and
60:16 You shall suck the **m** of nations,
Jer 11: 5 to give them a land flowing with **m** and honey, A
32:22 a land flowing with **m** and honey; A
La 4: 7 Her princes were purer than snow, whiter than **m;**
Eze 20: 6 a land flowing with **m** and honey, A
20:15 a land flowing with **m** and honey, A
25: 4 and they shall drink your **m.**
Joel 3:18 the hills shall flow with **m,**
1Co 3: 2 I fed you with **m,** not solid food,
9: 7 who tends a flock and does not get any of its **m?**
Heb 5:12 You need **m,** not solid food;
5:13 for everyone who lives on **m,**
1Pe 2: 2 long for the pure, spiritual **m,**
Sir 39:26 and iron and salt and wheat flour and **m** and honey,
46: 8 the land flowing with **m** and honey. A
Bar 1:20 to give to us a land flowing with **m** and honey. A
3Mc 5:49 at their breasts who were drawing their last **m.**
2Es 2:19 with **m** and honey, and seven mighty mountains
8:10 from the breasts) **m,** the fruit of the breasts,
4Mc 13:21 they drank **m** from the same fountains.

MILL (2) [HANDMILL, MILLS, MILLSTONE, MILLSTONES]

Dt 24: 6 No one shall take a **m** or an upper millstone
Jdg 16:21 and he ground at the **m** in the prison.

MILLET (2)

Eze 4: 9 beans and lentils, **m** and spelt;
27:17 for your merchandise wheat from Minnith, **m,**

MILLION (4) [MILLIONS]

1Ch 21: 5 all Israel there were one **m** one hundred thousand
22:14 one **m** talents of silver, and bronze and iron
2Ch 14: 9 an army of a **m** men and three hundred chariots,
Rev 9:16 of the troops of cavalry was two hundred **m;**

MILLIONS (1) [MILLION]

1Es 3:21 and makes everyone talk in **m.**

MILLO (7)

2Sa 5: 9 David built the city all around from the **M** inward.
1Ki 9:15 the **M** and the wall of Jerusalem, Hazor, Megiddo,
9:24 for her; then he built the **M.**
11:27 the **M,** and closed up the gap in the wall of the city
2Ki 12:20 and killed Joash in the house of **M,**
1Ch 11: 8 from the **M** in complete circuit;
2Ch 32: 5 he also strengthened the **M** in the city of David,

MILLS (1) [MILL]

Nu 11: 8 ground it in **m** or beat it in mortars,

MILLSTONE (9) [MILL, STONE]

Dt 24: 6 No one shall take a mill or an upper **m** in pledge,
Jdg 9:53 But a certain woman threw an upper **m**
2Sa 11:21 a woman throw an upper **m** on him from the wall,
Job 41:24 Its heart is as hard as stone, as hard as the lower **m.**
Mt 18: 6 if a great **m** were fastened around your neck
Mk 9:42 it would be better for you if a great **m** were hung
Lk 17: 2 It would be better for you if a **m** were hung
Rev 18:21 Then a mighty angel took up a stone like a great **m**
18:22 the sound of the **m** will be heard in you no more;

MILLSTONES (2) [MILL, STONE]

Isa 47: 2 Take the **m** and grind meal, remove your veil,
Jer 25:10 the sound of the **m** and the light of the lamp.

MINA (1) [MINAS]

Eze 45:12 and fifteen shekels shall make a **m** for you.

MINAS (9) [MINA]

1Ki 10:17 three **m** of gold went into each shield;
Ezr 2:69 of gold, five thousand **m** of silver,
Ne 7:71 of gold and two thousand two hundred **m** of silver.
7:72 of gold, two thousand **m** of silver,
1Mc 14:24 with a large gold shield weighing one thousand **m,**
15:18 a gold shield weighing one thousand **m.**
1Es 5:45 to the sacred treasury for the work a thousand **m**
of gold, five thousand **m** of silver,
3Mc 1: 4 to give them each two **m** of gold if they won

MINCING (1)

Isa 3:16 **m** along as they go, tinkling with their feet;

MIND‡ (267) [DOUBLE-MINDED, HOLY-MINDED, LIKE-MINDED, MINDED, MINDFUL, MINDS, SIMPLE-MINDED, SMALL-MINDED, VAIN-MINDED]

Ge 37:11 but his father kept the matter in **m.**
Ex 10:10 Plainly, you have some evil purpose in **m.**
32:12 change your **m** and do not bring disaster
32:14 And the LORD changed his **m** about the disaster
Nu 23:19 or a mortal, that he should change his **m.**
Dt 4: 9 nor to let them slip from your **m** all the days
5:29 If only they had such a **m** as this,
28:28 blindness, and confusion of **m;**
29: 4 But to this day the LORD has not given you a **m**
30: 1 if you call them to **m** among all the nations where
1Sa 2:35 according to what is in my heart and in my **m.**
9:19 and will tell you all that is on your **m.**
14: 7 "Do all that your **m** inclines to.
14: 7 I am with you; as your **m** is, so is mine."
15:29 the Glory of Israel will not recant or change his **m;**
15:29 for he is not a mortal, that he should change his **m.**
2Sa 7: 3 "Go, do all that you have in **m;**
14: 1 of Zeruiah perceived that the king's **m** was
14:11 may the king keep the LORD your God in **m,**
19:19 may the king not bear it in **m.**
1Ki 3: 9 Give your servant therefore an understanding **m**
3:12 Indeed I give you a wise and discerning **m;**
8:17 in **m** to build a house for the name of the LORD,
10: 2 she told him all that was on her **m.**
10:24 which God had put into his **m.**
11:11 "Since this has been your **m** and you have
2Ki 6:11 The **m** of the king of Aram was greatly perturbed
1Ch 12:38 of Israel were of a single **m** to make David king.
17: 2 Nathan said to David, "Do all that you have in **m,**
22:19 set your **m** and heart to seek the LORD your God.
28: 9 and serve him with single **m** and willing heart;
28: 9 for the LORD searches every **m,**
28:12 and the plan of all that he had in **m:**
29: 9 for with single **m** they had offered freely to
29:19 with single **m** he may keep your commandments,
2Ch 6: 7 in **m** to build a house for the name of the LORD,
9: 1 she discussed with him all that was on her **m.**
9:23 which God had put into his **m.**
Ne 4: 6 for the people had a **m** to work.
6: 8 you are inventing them out of your own **m"**
7: 5 into my **m** to assemble the nobles and the officials
Job 7:17 that you set your **m** on them,
23:14 and many such things are in his **m.**
38:36 or given understanding to the **m?**
Ps 26: 2 and try me; test my heart and **m.**
31:12 I have passed out of **m** like one who is dead;
64: 6 For the human heart and **m** are deep.
77:11 I will call to **m** the deeds of the LORD;
78:42 They did not keep in **m** his power,
110: 4 The LORD has sworn and will not change his **m,**
Pr 6:14 with perverted **m** devising evil,
10:20 the **m** of the wicked is of little worth.
12: 8 but a perverse **m** is despised.
12:20 Deceit is in the **m** of those who plan evil,
12:23 but the **m** of a fool broadcasts folly.
14:30 A tranquil **m** gives life to the flesh,
14:33 at home in the **m** of one who has understanding,
15:14 **m** of one who has understanding seeks knowledge,
15:28 The **m** of the righteous ponders how to answer,
16: 1 The plans of the **m** belong to mortals,
16: 9 The human **m** plans the way,
16:23 The **m** of the wise makes their speech judicious,
17:16 when they have no **m** to learn?
17:20 The crooked of **m** do not prosper,
18:15 An intelligent **m** acquires knowledge,
19:21 The human **m** may devise many plans,
20: 5 The purposes in the human **m** are like deep water,
22:17 and apply your **m** to my teaching;
23:12 Apply your **m** to instruction and your ear to words
23:19 and be wise, and direct your **m** in the way.
23:33 and your **m** utter perverse things.
25: 3 so the **m** of kings is unsearchable.
Ecc 1:13 applied my **m** to seek and to search out
1:16 and my **m** has had great experience of wisdom
1:17 And I applied my **m** to know wisdom and
2: 3 with my **m** how to cheer my body with wine—
2: 3 my **m** still guiding me with wisdom—
7:25 I turned my **m** to know and to search out and
7:28 which my **m** has sought repeatedly,
8: 5 and the wise **m** will know the time and way.
8: 9 applying my **m** to all that is done under the sun,
8:16 When I applied my **m** to know wisdom,
11:10 Banish anxiety from your **m,**
Isa 6:10 Make the **m** of this people dull, and stop their ears,
10: 7 nor does he have this in **m;**
21: 4 My **m** reels, horror has appalled me;
26: 3 Those of steadfast **m** you keep in peace—
33:18 Your **m** will muse on the terror:
44:20 He feeds on ashes; a deluded **m** has led him astray,
46: 8 Remember this and consider, recall it to **m,**
65:17 not be remembered or come to **m.**
Jer 3:16 It shall not come to **m,** or be remembered,
7:31 nor did it come into my **m.**
11:20 who try the heart and the **m,**
17:10 I the LORD test the **m** and search the heart,
18: 8 I will change my **m** about the disaster
18:10 then I will change my **m** about the good
19: 5 nor did it enter my **m.**
20:12 you test the righteous, you see the heart and the **m;**
23:20 and accomplished the intents of his **m.**
26: 3 that I may change my **m** about the disaster
26:13 the LORD will change his **m** about the disaster
26:19 not the LORD change his **m** about the disaster
30:24 and accomplished the intents of his **m.**
32:35 nor did it enter my **m**
44:21 Did it not come into his **m?**
51:50 and let Jerusalem come into your **m:**
La 3:21 But this I call to **m,** and therefore I have hope:
Eze 11: 5 I know the things that come into your **m.**
20:32 What is in your **m** shall never happen—
28: 2 you compare your **m** with the **m** of a god.
28: 6 you compare your **m** with the **m** of a god,
38:10 On that day thoughts will come into your **m,**
40: 4 and set your **m** upon all that I shall show you,
Da 2:30 that you may understand the thoughts of your **m.**
4:16 Let his **m** be changed from that of a human, and
let the **m** of an animal be given to him.
5:21 and his **m** was made like that of an animal.
7: 4 and a human **m** was given to it.
7:28 but I kept the matter in my **m.**
8:25 and in his own **m** he shall be great.
10:12 that you set your **m** to gain understanding and
11:17 He shall set his **m** to come with the strength
Jnh 3: 9 God may relent and change his **m;**
3:10 God changed his **m** about the calamity
Mt 16:23 for you are setting your **m** not on divine things but
21:29 but later he changed his **m** and went.
22:37 and with all your soul, and with all your **m.'**
Mk 3:21 people were saying, "He has gone out of his **m."**
5:15 clothed and in his right **m,**
8:33 For you are setting your **m** not on divine things but
12:30 and with all your **m,** and with all your strength.'
Lk 8:35 clothed and in his right **m.**
10:27 and with all your strength, and with all your **m;**
Jn 10:20 "He has a demon and is out of his **m.**
Ac 12:15 They said to her, "You are out of your **m!"**
26:12 "With this in **m,** I was traveling to Damascus with
26:24 Festus exclaimed, "You are out of your **m,** Paul!
26:25 But Paul said, "I am not out of my **m,**
Ro 1:28 a debased **m** and to things that should not be done.
7:23 at war with the law of my **m,**
7:25 So then, with my **m** I am a slave to the law of God,
8: 6 To set the **m** on the flesh is death, but to set the **m**
on the Spirit is life and peace.
8: 7 the **m** that is set on the flesh is hostile to God;
8:27 knows what is the **m** of the Spirit,
11:34 "For who has known the **m** of the Lord?
1Co 1:10 you be united in the same **m** and the same purpose.
2:16 "For who has known the **m** of the Lord so as
2:16 But we have the **m** of Christ.
7:37 and has determined in his own **m** to keep her
14:14 my spirit prays but my **m** is unproductive.
14:15 but I will pray with the **m** also;
14:15 but I will sing praise with the **m** also.
14:19 with my **m,** in order to instruct others
14:23 will they not say that you are out of your **m?**
15:34 Come to a sober and right **m,** and sin no more;
2Co 2: 1 up my **m** not to make you another painful visit.
2:13 but my **m** could not rest because I did
5:13 if we are in our right **m,** it is for you.
7:13 because his **m** has been set at rest by all of you.
9: 7 of you must give as you have made up your **m,**
Php 1:27 striving side by side with one **m** for the faith of
2: 2 be of the same **m,** having the same love, being in
full accord and of one **m.**
2: 5 Let the same **m** be in you that was in Christ Jesus,
3:15 of us then who are mature be of the same **m;**
4: 2 and I urge Syntyche to be of the same **m** in
Col 1:21 you who were once estranged and hostile in **m,**
1Th 4:11 to aspire to live quietly, to **m** your own affairs,
2Th 2: 2 not to be quickly shaken in **m** or alarmed,
1Ti 6: 5 and wrangling among those who are depraved in **m**
2Ti 3: 8 so these people, of corrupt **m** and counterfeit faith,
Heb 7:21 "The Lord has sworn and will not change his **m,**
1Pe 3: 8 a tender heart, and a humble **m.**
Rev 17: 9 "This calls for a **m** that has wisdom:
Jdt 8:14 or understand the workings of the human **m;**
8:14 and find out his **m** or comprehend his thought?
9: 5 What you had in **m** has happened;
11:10 but keep it in your **m,** for it is true.
16: 9 her beauty captivated his **m,**
AdE 11:12 and after he awoke he had it on his **m,**
Wis 4:12 and roving desire perverts the innocent **m.**
9:15 and this earthy tent burdens the thoughtful **m.**
Sir 1:28 do not approach him with a divided **m.**
3:13 even if his **m** fails, be patient with him;
3:26 A stubborn **m** will fare badly at the end,
3:27 A stubborn **m** will be burdened by troubles,
3:29 The **m** of the intelligent appreciates proverbs,
6:37 It is he who will give insight to your **m,**
11:30 so is the **m** of the proud,
16:17 and who from on high has me in **m?**
16:20 But no human **m** can grasp this,
17: 6 ears and a **m** for thinking he gave them.
19: 4 One who trusts others too quickly has a shallow **m,**
21:14 The **m** of a fool is like a broken jar;
21:26 The **m** of fools is in their mouth,
21:26 but the mouth of the wise is in their **m.**

Sir 22:16 the **m** firmly resolved after due reflection will not
22:17 A **m** settled on an intelligent thought is
22:18 a timid **m** with a fool's resolve will not stand firm
23: 2 and the discipline of wisdom over my **m,**
25:23 Dejected **m,** gloomy face,
27: 6 person's speech discloses the cultivation of his **m.**
33:20 in case you change your **m** and must ask for it.
34: 5 and like a woman in labor, the **m** has fantasies.
36:24 so an intelligent **m** detects false words.
36:25 A perverse **m** will cause grief,
37:14 our own **m** sometimes keeps us better informed
37:17 The **m** is the root of all conduct;
39:12 I have more on my **m** to express;
40: 5 his sleep at night confuses his **m.**
40: 6 the visions of his **m** like one who has escaped from
42:15 I will now call to **m** the works of the Lord,
43:18 and the **m** is amazed as it falls.
45:26 May the Lord grant you wisdom of **m**
50:27 whose **m** poured forth wisdom.
1Mc 3:31 He was greatly perplexed in **m;**
2Mc 4:46 induced the king to change his **m.**
5:21 and walk on the sea, because his **m** was elated.
14:20 and it had appeared that they were of one **m,**
15: 8 in **m** the former times when help had come to them
1Es 3:19 It makes equal the **m** of the king and the orphan,
3Mc 1:25 in various ways to change his arrogant **m** from
4:16 a **m** alienated from truth and with a profane mouth,
5:28 for he had implanted in the king's **m**
5:30 of God his whole **m** had been deranged
5:39 wondering at his instability of **m,**
5:42 took no account of the changes of **m** that had come
5:47 when he had filled his impious **m** with a deep rage,
2Es 4:11 how then can your **m** comprehend the way of
5:33 "Are you greatly disturbed in **m** over Israel?
7:16 Why have you not considered in your **m** what is
7:*62* if the **m** is made out of the dust like
7:*63* so that the **m** might not have been made from it.
7:*64* But now the **m** grows with us,
7:*71* for you have said that the **m** grows with us.
9: 1 "Measure carefully in your **m,**
10:31 and the thoughts of your **m** troubled?"
10:36 —or is my **m** deceived, and my soul dreaming?
12: 3 I woke up in great perplexity of **m** and great fear,
12: 5 I am still weary in **m** and very weak in my spirit,
13:16 For as I consider it in my **m,**
13:30 of **m** shall come over those who inhabit the earth.
4Mc 1:15 Now reason is the **m** that with sound logic prefers
1:35 checked by the temperate **m,**
2: 1 And why is it amazing that the desires of the **m** for
2:16 temperate **m** repels all these malicious emotions,
2:18 the temperate **m** is able to get the better of
2:22 but at the same time he enthroned the **m** among
2:23 To the **m** he gave the law;
3: 3 No one of us can eradicate anger from the **m,**
3:17 For the temperate **m** can conquer the drives of
5:11 adopt a **m** appropriate to your years,
7: 5 For in setting his **m** firm like a jutting cliff,
8:29 all with one voice together, as from one **m,** said:
9:15 savage of **m,** you are mangling me in this manner,
11:14 but I am their equal in **m.**
11:25 to change our **m** or to force us to eat defiling foods,
13: 4 The supremacy of the **m** over these cannot
14: 6 in harmony with the guidance of the **m,**
14:11 **m** of woman despised even more diverse agonies,
14:20 she was of the same **m** as Abraham.
15: 4 of a small child a wondrous likeness both of **m** and
16:13 though having a **m** like adamant and giving rebirth

MINDED (1) [MIND]

1Es 8:16 Whatever you and your kindred are **m** to do with

MINDFUL (14) [MIND]

Ne 9:17 and were not **m** of the wonders that you performed
Ps 8: 4 what are human beings that you are **m** of them,
9:12 For he who avenges blood is **m** of them;
25: 6 Be **m** of your mercy, O LORD,
105: 8 He is **m** of his covenant forever,
111: 5 he is ever **m** of his covenant.
115:12 The LORD has been **m** of us;
Zep 2: 7 For the LORD their God will be **m** of them
Heb 2: 6 "What are human beings that you are **m** of them,
Tob 1:12 Because I was **m** of God with all my heart,
2: 2 who is wholeheartedly **m** of God,
14: 7 and are truly **m** of God will be gathered together;
14:8,9 to be **m** of God and to bless his name at all times
2Es 16:20 or ever be **m** of the scourges.

MINDS‡ (49) [MIND]

Ex 13:17 they may change their **m** and return to Egypt."
14: 5 the **m** of Pharaoh and his officials were changed
Job 17: 4 Since you have closed their **m** to understanding,
Ps 7: 9 you who test the **m** and hearts, O righteous God.
140: 2 who plan evil things in their **m** and stir
Pr 11:20 Crooked **m** are an abomination to the LORD,
15: 7 not so the **m** of fools.
24: 2 for their **m** devise violence,
Ecc 2:23 even at night their **m** do not rest.
3:11 he has put a sense of past and future into their **m,**
Isa 6:10 and comprehend with their **m,**
32: 4 The **m** of the rash will have good judgment,
32: 6 For fools speak folly, and their **m** plot iniquity:
44:18 and their **m** as well, so that they cannot understand.
Jer 14:14 and the deceit of their own **m.**
23:16 They speak visions of their own **m,**
25:16 They shall drink and stagger and go out of their **m**
Da 11:27 The two kings, their **m** bent on evil,
Mt 21:32 you did not change your **m** and believe him.
Lk 21:14 up your **m** not to prepare your defense in advance;
24:45 he opened their **m** to understand the scriptures,
Ac 14: 2 up the Gentiles and poisoned their **m** against
15:24 to disturb you and have unsettled your **m,**
28: 6 they changed their **m** and began to say that he was
Ro 1:21 and their senseless **m** were darkened.
8: 5 according to the flesh set their **m** on the things of
8: 5 to the Spirit set their **m** on the things of the Spirit.
12: 2 but be transformed by the renewing of your **m,**
14: 5 Let all be fully convinced in their own **m.**
2Co 3:14 But their **m** were hardened.
3:15 a veil lies over their **m;**
4: 4 of this world has blinded the **m** of the unbelievers,
Eph 4:17 as the Gentiles live, in the futility of their **m.**
4:23 and to be renewed in the spirit of your **m,**
Php 3:19 their **m** are set on earthly things.
4: 7 will guard your hearts and your **m** in Christ Jesus.
Col 3: 2 Set your **m** on things that are above,
Tit 1:15 Their very **m** and consciences are corrupted.
Heb 8:10 I will put my laws in their **m,**
10:16 and I will write them on their **m,"**
1Pe 1:13 Therefore prepare your **m** for action;
Rev 2:23 that I am the one who searches **m** and hearts,
Wis 19: 2 they would change their **m** and pursue them.
Sir 8: 2 and has perverted the **m** of kings.
21:17 and they ponder his words in their **m.**
1Es 3:18 It leads astray the **m** of all who drink it.
4:26 Many men have lost their **m** because of women,
3Mc 4: 1 in their **m** was now made evident and outspoken.
2Es 14:34 will rule over your **m** and discipline your hearts,

MINE‡ (2 of 85) [I, MINERS, MINES] See Index of Articles Etc. for an Exhaustive Listing (See Introduction, page xi)

Dt 8: 9 and from whose hills you may **m** copper.
Job 28: 1 "Surely there is a **m** for silver, and a place for gold

MINERS (1) [MINE]

Job 28: 3 **M** put an end to darkness, and search out to the

MINES (1) [MINE]

1Mc 8: 3 to get control of the silver and gold **m** there,

MINGLE (1) [MINGLED, MINGLING]

Ps 102: 9 I eat ashes like bread, and **m** tears with my drink,

MINGLED (3) [MINGLE]

Ps 106:35 but they **m** with the nations and learned to do
Lk 13: 1 about the Galileans whose blood Pilate had **m**
2Es 13:11 All these were **m** together,

MINGLING (1) [MINGLE]

2Mc 14:38 when there was no **m** with the Gentiles,

MINIAMIN (3) [=MIJAMIN]

2Ch 31:15 Eden, **M,** Jeshua, Shemaiah, Amariah,
Ne 12:17 of Abijah, Zichri; of **M,** of Moadiah, Piltai;
12:41 **M,** Micaiah, Elioenai, Zechariah, and Hananiah,

MINIATURE (1)

AdE 1: 7 and a **m** cup was displayed, made of ruby,

MINISH, MINISHED (KJV) See LESSEN, DIMINISHED

MINISTER‡ (48) [MINISTERED, MINISTERING, MINISTERS, MINISTRY]

Ex 28:43 they come near the altar to **m** in the holy place;
29:30 when he comes into the tent of meeting to **m** in
30:20 or when they come near the altar to **m,**
Nu 3: 3 whom he ordained to **m** as priests.
3:31 vessels of the sanctuary with which the priests **m,**
Dt 10: 8 to stand before the LORD to **m** to him,
17:12 to disobey the priest appointed to **m** there to
18: 5 to stand and **m** in the name of the LORD,
18: 7 then he may **m** in the name of the LORD his God,
18: 7 like all his fellow-Levites who stand to **m** there
21: 5 the LORD your God has chosen them to **m** to him
1Sa 2:11 while the boy remained to **m** to the LORD,
1Ki 8:11 priests could not stand to **m** because of the cloud;
1Ch 15: 2 the ark of the LORD and to **m** to him forever.
16:37 to **m** regularly before the ark as each day required,
23:13 and **m** to him and pronounce blessings
2Ch 5:14 priests could not stand to **m** because of the cloud;
29:11 to stand in his presence to **m** to him,
31: 2 to **m** in the gates of the camp of the LORD and
Ne 10:36 to the priests who **m** in the house of our God,
10:39 and where the priests that **m,**
Ps 101: 6 whoever walks in the way that is blameless shall **m**
Isa 56: 6 to **m** to him, to love the name of the LORD,
60: 7 the rams of Nebaioth shall **m** to you;
60:10 and their kings shall **m** to you;
Jer 33:22 and the Levites who **m** to me.
Eze 40:46 of Levi may come near to the LORD to **m**
42:14 the vestments in which they **m,** for these are holy;
43:19 who draw near to me to **m** to me,
44:15 shall come near to me to **m** to me;
44:16 it is they who shall approach my table, to **m** to me,
Eze 44:17 while they **m** at the gates of the inner court,
44:27 into the inner court, to **m** in the holy place,
45: 4 who **m** in the sanctuary and approach the LORD
45: 4 in the sanctuary and approach the LORD to **m**
45: 5 shall be for the Levites who **m** at the temple,
Ro 15:16 to be a **m** of Christ Jesus to the Gentiles in
Eph 6:21 He is a dear brother and a faithful **m** in the Lord.
Php 2:25 your messenger and **m** to my need;
Col 1: 7 He is a faithful **m** of Christ on your behalf,
4: 7 he is a beloved brother, a faithful **m,**
Heb 8: 2 a **m** in the sanctuary and the true tent that the Lord,
Jdt 11:13 and set aside for the priests who **m** in the presence
Sir 4:14 Those who serve her **m** to the Holy One;
45:15 as the heavens endure, to **m** to the Lord and serve
1Mc 10:42 because it belongs to the priests who **m** there.
1Es 1: 5 who **m** before your kindred the people of Israel,
4:54 and the priests' vestments in which they were to **m.**

MINISTERED (7) [MINISTER]

Jdg 20:28 son of Aaron, **m** before it in those days), saying,
1Ch 6:32 They **m** with song before the tabernacle of the tent
Ne 12:44 over the priests and the Levites who **m.**
Eze 44:12 Because they **m** to them before their idols
Tob 1: 7 and the rest of the fruits to the sons of Levi who **m**
Jdt 4:14 the priests who stood before the Lord and **m** to
Sir 24:10 In the holy tent I **m** before him,

MINISTERING (12) [MINISTER]

Ex 35:19 finely worked vestments for **m** in the holy place,
39: 1 for **m** in the holy place;
39:26 around on the lower hem of the robe for **m;**
39:41 finely worked vestments for **m** in the holy place,
1Sa 2:18 Samuel was **m** before the LORD,
3: 1 the boy Samuel was **m** to the LORD under Eli.
1Ch 26:12 **m** in the house of the LORD;
2Ch 13:10 priests **m** to the LORD who are descendants of
23: 6 of the LORD except the priests and **m** Levites;
Eze 44:19 in which they have been **m,** and lay them in
Ro 12: 7 ministry, in **m;** the teacher, in teaching;
Wis 16:21 the bread, **m** to the desire of the one who took it,

MINISTERS (22) [MINISTER]

Ex 28:35 Aaron shall wear it when he **m,**
1Ch 16: 4 of the Levites as **m** before the ark of the LORD,
2Ch 29:11 and to be his **m** and make offerings to him."
Ezr 8:17 namely, to send us **m** for the house of our God.
Est 1: 3 he gave a banquet for all his officials and **m.**
2:18 king gave a great banquet to all his officials and **m**
5:11 above the officials and the **m** of the king.
Ps 103:21 all his hosts, his **m** that do his will.
104: 4 the winds your messengers, fire and flame your **m.**
Isa 61: 6 you shall be named **m** of our God;
Jer 33:21 and my covenant with my **m** the Levites.
Eze 44:11 They shall be **m** in my sanctuary,
Joel 1: 9 The priests mourn, the **m** of the LORD.
1:13 wail, you **m** of the altar.
1:13 pass the night in sackcloth, you **m** of my God!
2:17 the **m** of the LORD, weep.
2Co 3: 6 be **m** of a new covenant, not of letter but of spirit;
11:15 if his **m** also disguise themselves as **m** of
righteousness.
11:23 Are they **m** of Christ?
Jdt 2: 2 He summoned all his **m** and all his nobles and set
Sir 7:30 and do not neglect his **m.**

MINISTRATION (KJV) See DISTRIBUTION, MINISTRY, SERVICE

MINISTRY (26) [MINISTER]

2Ch 7: 6 whenever David offered praises by their **m.**
8:14 of praise and **m** alongside the priests as the duty
Ac 1:17 among us and was allotted his share in this **m."**
1:25 to take the place in this **m** and apostleship
20:24 and the **m** that I received from the Lord Jesus,
21:19 among the Gentiles through his **m.**
Ro 11:13 as I am an apostle to the Gentiles, I glorify my **m**
12: 7 **m,** in ministering; the teacher, in teaching;
15:25 I am going to Jerusalem in a **m** to the saints;
15:31 my **m** to Jerusalem may be acceptable to the saints,
2Co 3: 7 Now if the **m** of death,
3: 8 much more will the **m** of the Spirit come in glory?
3: 9 For if there was glory in the **m** of condemnation,
3: 9 much more does the **m** of justification abound
4: 1 it is by God's mercy that we are engaged in this **m,**
5:18 and has given us the **m** of reconciliation;
6: 3 so that no fault may be found with our **m,**
8: 4 for the privilege of sharing in this **m** to the saints—
9: 1 not necessary for me to write you about the **m** to
9:12 the rendering of this **m** not only supplies the needs
9:13 of this **m** you glorify God by your obedience to
Eph 4:12 to equip the saints for the work of **m,**
2Ti 4: 5 the work of an evangelist, carry out your **m** fully.
4:11 for he is useful in my **m.**
Heb 8: 6 But Jesus has now obtained a more excellent **m,**
Wis 18:21 he brought forward the shield of his **m,**

MINNI (1)

Jer 51:27 summon against her the kingdoms, Ararat, **M,**

MINNITH (2)

Jdg 11:33 on them from Aroer to the neighborhood of **M,**
Eze 27:17 for your merchandise wheat from **M,**

MINOR (2) [MINORS]
Ex 18:22 but decide every **m** case themselves.
18:26 but any **m** case they decided themselves.

MINORS (2) [MINOR]
Gal 4: 1 My point is this: heirs, as long as they are **m,**
4: 3 So with us; while we were **m,**

MINSTREL (KJV) See MUSICIAN

MINSTRELS (1)
Rev 18:22 and **m** and of flutists and trumpeters will be heard

MINT (3)
Mt 23:23 For you tithe the **m,** dill, and cummin,
Lk 11:42 For you tithe the **m** and rue and herbs of all kinds,
1Mc 15: 6 to **m** your own coinage as money for your country,

MINUS (1)
2Co 11:24 from the Jews the forty lashes **m** one.

MIPHKAD (KJV) See MUSTER GATE

MIRACLE[S] (KJV) See also DEED[S] OF POWER, SIGN[S], WONDER[S], WONDERFUL DEEDS

MIRACLES (12)
1Ch 16:12 his **m,** and the judgments he uttered,
Ps 78:11 and the **m** that he had shown them.
78:43 and his **m** in the fields of Zoan.
105: 5 his **m,** and the judgments he uttered,
105:27 and **m** in the land of Ham.
Ac 8:13 when he saw the signs and great **m** that took place.
19:11 God did extraordinary **m** through Paul,
1Co 12:10 to another the working of **m,**
12:29 Are all teachers? Do all work **m?**
Gal 3: 5 and work **m** among you by your doing the works
Heb 2: 4 by signs and wonders and various **m,**
Sir 45: 3 By his words he performed swift **m;**

MIRE (9) [MIRY]
2Sa 22:43 I crushed them and stamped them down like the **m**
Job 30:19 He has cast me into the **m,**
41:30 it spreads itself like a threshing sledge on the **m.**
Ps 18:42 I cast them out like the **m** of the streets.
69: 2 I sink in deep **m,** where there is no foothold;
69:14 rescue me from sinking in the **m;**
Isa 10: 6 and to tread them down like the **m** of the streets.
57:20 its waters toss up **m** and mud.
Mic 7:10 she will be trodden down like the **m** of the streets.

MIRIAM (15)
Ex 15:20 Then the prophet **M,** Aaron's sister,
15:21 And **M** sang to them: "Sing to the
Nu 12: 1 **M** and Aaron spoke against Moses because of
12: 4 Aaron, and **M,** "Come out, you three,
12: 5 the entrance of the tent, and called Aaron and **M;**
12:10 **M** had become leprous, as white as snow.
12:10 And Aaron turned towards **M** and saw
12:15 So **M** was shut out of the camp for seven days;
12:15 not set out on the march until **M** had been brought
20: 1 **M** died there, and was buried there.
26:59 Aaron, Moses, and their sister **M.**
Dt 24: 9 the LORD your God did to **M** on your journey out
1Ch 4:17 and she conceived and bore **M,** Shammai,
6: 3 The children of Amram: Aaron, Moses, and **M.**
Mic 6: 4 and I sent before you Moses, Aaron, and **M.**

MIRMAH (1)
1Ch 8:10 Sachia, and **M.** These were his sons,

MIRROR (6) [MIRRORS]
Job 37:18 spread out the skies, hard as a molten **m?**
1Co 13:12 For now we see in a **m,** dimly, but then we will see
2Co 3:18 though reflected in a **m,** are being transformed into
Jas 1:23 they are like those who look at themselves in a **m;**
Wis 7:26 a spotless **m** of the working of God,
Sir 12:11 Be to him like one who polishes a **m,**

MIRRORS (1) [MIRROR]
Ex 38: 8 the **m** of the women who served at the entrance to

MIRTH (12)
Ge 31:27 I would have sent you away with **m** and songs,
Ps 137: 3 and our tormentors asked for **m,** saying,
Ecc 7: 4 but the heart of fools is in the house of **m.**
Isa 24: 8 The **m** of the timbrels is stilled,
24: 8 the **m** of the lyre is stilled.
Jer 7:34 I will bring to an end the sound of **m** and gladness,
16: 9 the voice of **m** and the voice of gladness,
25:10 And I will banish from them the sound of **m** and
33:11 the voice of **m** and the voice of gladness, the voice
Hos 2:11 I will put an end to all her **m,** her festivals,
Bar 2:23 from the region around Jerusalem the voice of **m**
1Es 3:20 It turns every thought to feasting and **m,**

MIRY (1) [MIRE]
Ps 40: 2 out of the **m** bog, and set my feet upon a rock,

MISCARRIAGE (2) [MISCARRY]
Ex 21:22 a pregnant woman so that there is a **m,**
2Ki 2:21 now on neither death nor **m** shall come from it."

MISCARRIED (1) [MISCARRY]
Ge 31:38 your ewes and your female goats have not **m,**

MISCARRIES (1) [MISCARRY]
Job 21:10 their cow calves and never **m.**

MISCARRY (1) [MISCARRIAGE, MISCARRIED, MISCARRIES, MISCARRYING]
Ex 23:26 No one shall **m** or be barren in your land;

MISCARRYING (1) [MISCARRY]
Hos 9:14 Give them a **m** womb and dry breasts.

MISCHIEF (17) [MISCHIEF-MAKER, MISCHIEVOUS]
Jdg 15: 3 "This time, when I do **m** to the Philistines,
Job 15:35 They conceive **m** and bring forth evil
Ps 7:14 and are pregnant with **m,** and bring forth lies.
7:16 Their **m** returns upon their own heads,
10: 7 under their tongues are **m** and iniquity.
21:11 If they plan evil against you, if they devise **m,**
28: 3 while **m** is in their hearts.
36: 3 The words of their mouths are **m** and deceit;
36: 4 They plot **m** while on their beds;
41: 6 while their hearts gather **m;**
52: 1 O mighty one, of **m** done against the godly?
94:20 those who contrive **m** by statute?
140: 9 let the **m** of their lips overwhelm them!
Pr 24: 2 and their lips talk of **m.**
Isa 59: 4 conceiving **m** and begetting iniquity.
1Pe 4:15 a thief, a criminal, or even as a **m** maker.
Sir 27:22 Whoever winks the eye plots **m,**

MISCHIEF[S] (KJV) See also ASSAIL, CALAMITY, DESTRUCTION, DISASTER, EVIL, EVIL DESIGN, VILLAINY, WRONG

MISCHIEF-MAKER (1) [MAKE, MISCHIEF]
Pr 24: 8 Whoever plans to do evil will be called a **m.**

MISCHIEVOUS (1) [MISCHIEF]
Pr 17: 4 and a liar gives heed to a **m** tongue.

MISDEEDS (1)
4Mc 2:12 so that one punishes them for **m.**

MISER (5)
Pr 28:22 The **m** is in a hurry to get rich and does not know
Sir 14: 3 and of what use is wealth to a **m?**
14: 8 The **m** is an evil person;
14:10 A **m** begrudges bread, and it is lacking at his table.
37:11 with a **m** about generosity or with the merciless

MISERABLE (13) [MISERY]
Nu 21: 5 and we detest this **m** food."
Job 16: 2 heard many such things; **m** comforters are you all.
Mt 21:41 "He will put those wretches to a **m** death,
Tob 7: 7 "O most **m** of calamities that such an upright
Wis 3:11 those who despise wisdom and instruction are **m.**
13:10 But **m,** with their hopes set on dead things,
15:14 But most foolish, and more **m** than an infant,
Sir 18:12 He sees and recognizes that their end is **m;**
29:24 It is a **m** life to go from house to house;
2Mc 5: 8 Finally he met a **m** end.
3Mc 4: 4 of life and shed tears at the most **m** expulsion
5:49 the end of their most **m** suspense,
2Es 15:47 woe to you, **m** wretch!

MISERABLY (2) [MISERY]
2Es 7:*120* [50] to us, but we have **m** failed?
4Mc 12: 4 will be **m** tortured and die before your time,

MISERIES (3) [MISERY]
Jas 5: 1 weep and wail for the **m** that are coming to you.
2Es 8:50 for many **m** will affect those who inhabit the world
15:59 you shall come and suffer fresh **m.**

MISERY (22) [MISERABLE, MISERABLY, MISERIES]
Ex 3: 7 "I have observed the **m** of my people who are
3:17 that I will bring you up out of the **m** of Egypt,
4:31 to the Israelites and that he had seen their **m,**
Nu 11:15 and do not let me see my **m."**
1Sa 1:11 if only you will look on the **m** of your servant,
Job 3:20 "Why is light given to one in **m,**
5: 6 For **m** does not come from the earth,
7: 3 and nights of **m** are apportioned to me.
11:16 You will forget your **m;** you will remember it
20:22 all the force of **m** will come upon them.
Ps 31:10 my strength fails because of my **m,**
107:10 prisoners in **m** and in irons,
119:92 I would have perished in my **m.**
119:153 Look on my **m** and rescue me,
Pr 31: 7 and remember their **m** no more.
Ro 3:16 ruin and **m** are in their paths,
Jdt 7:32 In the town they were in great **m.**
Sir 11:27 An hour's **m** makes one forget past delights,
30:17 Death is better than a life of **m,**
Bar 2:25 They perished in great **m,** by famine and sword
2Mc 6: 9 therefore, the **m** that had come upon them.
2Es 15:15 For the sword and **m** draw near them,

MISFORTUNE (15) [MISFORTUNES]
Nu 23:21 He has not beheld **m** in Jacob;
Jdg 2:15 hand of the LORD was against them to bring **m,**
1Ki 5: 4 there is neither adversary nor **m.**
Job 12: 5 Those at ease have contempt for **m,**
Pr 13:21 **M** pursues sinners, but prosperity rewards
Jer 44:17 and prospered, and saw no **m.**
Ob 1:12 over your brother on the day of his **m;**
Wis 14:21 in bondage to **m** or to royal authority,
2Mc 4: 1 and had been the real cause of the **m.**
5: 6 at the cost of one's kindred is the greatest **m,**
12:30 and their kind treatment of them in times of **m,**
14: 8 our whole nation is now in no small **m.**
3Mc 4:12 to lament bitterly the ignoble **m** of their kindred,
2Es 10:43 and who told you about the **m** of her son—
10:48 and that **m** had overtaken her,

MISFORTUNES‡ (8) [MISFORTUNE]
Ge 41:52 God has made me fruitful in the land of my **m."**
Nu 11: 1 in the hearing of the LORD about their **m,**
1Mc 3:42 and his brothers saw that **m** had increased and that
3:59 to die in battle than to see the **m** of our nation and
6:13 because of this that these **m** have come upon me;
2Mc 5:20 the place itself shared in the **m** that befell
10: 4 that they might never again fall into such **m,**
14:14 thinking that the **m** and calamities of

MISGUIDED (1)
Sir 16:23 a senseless and **m** person thinks foolishly.

MISHAEL (14) [=MESHACH]
Ex 6:22 The sons of Uzziel: **M,** Elzaphan, and Sithri.
Lev 10: 4 Moses summoned **M** and Elzaphan,
Ne 8: 4 and Pedaiah, **M,** Malchijah, Hashum,
Da 1: 6 Among them were Daniel, Hananiah, **M,**
1: 7 he called Shadrach, **M** he called Meshach,
1:11 Hananiah, **M,** and Azariah:
1:19 Hananiah, **M,** and Azariah;
2:17 Hananiah, **M,** and Azariah,
Aza 1:66 "Bless the Lord, Hananiah, Azariah, and **M;**
1Mc 2:59 and **M** believed and were saved from the flame.
1Es 9:44 **M,** Malchijah, Lothasubus, Nabariah,
4Mc 16: 3 was the raging fiery furnace of **M** so intensely hot,
16:21 and **M** were hurled into the fiery furnace
18:12 about Hananiah, Azariah, and **M** in the fire.

MISHAL (2)
Jos 19:26 Amad, and **M;** on the west it touches Carmel
21:30 **M** with its pasture lands, Abdon

MISHAM (1)
1Ch 8:12 The sons of Elpaal: Eber, **M,** and Shemed,

MISHMA (4)
Ge 25:14 **M,** Dumah, Massa,
1Ch 1:30 **M,** Dumah, Massa, Hadad, Tema,
4:25 Shallum was his son, Mibsam his son, **M** his son.
4:26 The sons of **M:** Hammuel his son,

MISHMANNAH (1)
1Ch 12:10 **M** fourth, Jeremiah fifth,

MISHRAITES (1)
1Ch 2:53 Ithrites, the Puthites, the Shumathites, and the **M;**

MISLEAD (5) [MISLEADING, MISLEADS, MISLED]
2Ki 4:28 Did I not say, Do not **m** me?"
2Ch 32:15 therefore do not let Hezekiah deceive you or **m** you
Pr 28:10 Those who **m** the upright into evil ways will fall
Isa 3:12 O my people, your leaders **m** you,
36:18 Do not let Hezekiah **m** you by saying,

MISLEADING (3) [MISLEAD]
2Ch 32:11 Is not Hezekiah **m** you, handing you over to die
La 2:14 but have seen oracles for you that are false and **m.**
Da 2: 9 You have agreed to speak lying and **m** words to me

MISLEADS (3) [MISLEAD]
Dt 27:18 be anyone who **m** a blind person on the road."
2Ki 18:32 not listen to Hezekiah when he **m** you by saying,
Pr 14: 8 but the folly of fools **m.**

MISLED (5) [MISLEAD]
2Ki 21: 9 Manasseh **m** them to do more evil than
2Ch 33: 9 Manasseh **m** Judah and the inhabitants
Eze 13:10 Because, in truth, because they have **m** my people,

Wis 15: 4 For neither has the evil intent of human art **m** us,
1Mc 1: 11 from Israel and **m** many, saying, "Let us go

MISMATCHED (1)
2Co 6: 14 Do not be **m** with unbelievers.

MISPAR (1)
Ezr 2: 2 Seraiah, Reelaiah, Mordecai, Bilshan, **M,** Bigvai,

MISPERETH (1)
Ne 7: 7 Nahamani, Mordecai, Bilshan, **M,** Bigvai, Nehum,

MISREPHOTH-MAIM (2)
Jos 11: 8 and chased them as far as Great Sidon and **M,**
13: 6 of the hill country from Lebanon to **M,**

MISREPRESENTED (1) [MISREPRESENTING]
2Mc 3: 11 an extent the impious Simon had **m** the facts.

MISREPRESENTING (1) [MISREPRESENTED]
1Co 15: 15 We are even found to be **m** God,

MISS (4) [MISSED, MISSES, MISSING]
Jdg 20: 16 every one could sling a stone at a hair, and not **m.**
Job 5: 24 you shall inspect your fold and **m** nothing.
Pr 8: 36 but those who **m** me injure themselves;
2Es 16: 13 to the ends of the world will not **m** once.

MISSED (7) [MISS]
1Sa 20: 18 you will be **m,** because your place will be empty.
25: 7 and we did them no harm, and they **m** nothing,
25: 15 we never **m** anything when we were in the fields,
25: 21 so that nothing was **m** of all that belonged to him;
Jer 3: 16 or **m;** nor shall another one be made.
46: 17 the name "Braggart who **m** his chance."
1Ti 6: 21 by professing it some have **m** the mark as regards

MISSES (3) [MISS]
1Sa 20: 6 If your father **m** me at all, then say,
Pr 19: 2 and one who moves too hurriedly **m** the way.
Sir 20: 7 but a boasting fool **m** the right moment.

MISSILES (2)
2Mc 5: 3 hurling of **m,** the flash of golden trappings,
12: 27 and great stores of war engines and **m** were there.

MISSING (11) [MISS]
Nu 31: 49 and not one of us is **m.**
1Sa 30: 19 Nothing was **m,** whether small or great,
2Sa 2: 30 the people together, there were **m**
1Ki 20: 39 if he is **m,** your life shall be given for his life,
2Ki 10: 19 let none be **m,** for I have a great sacrifice to offer
10: 19 whoever is **m** shall not live."
Isa 34: 16 Not one of these shall be **m;**
40: 26 mighty in power, not one is **m.**
Jer 23: 4 nor shall any be **m,** says the LORD.
Jdt 14: 15 on the floor dead, with his head **m.**
14: 18 on the ground, and his head is **m!"**

MISSION (7)
Jdg 18: 5 the **m** we are undertaking will succeed."
18: 6 The **m** you are on is under the eye of the LORD."
1Sa 15: 18 And the LORD sent you on a **m,** and said, 'Go,
15: 20 on the **m** on which the LORD sent me,
Ac 12: 25 Then after completing their **m** Barnabas
2Mc 3: 37 of person would be suitable to send on another **m**
4: 11 on the **m** to establish friendship and alliance with

MISSPENT (1)
Wis 15: 8 With **m** toil, these workers form a futile god from

MISSTEP (1)
Sir 9: 13 But if you approach them, make no **m,**

MIST (13) [MISTS]
Job 36: 27 he distills his **m** in rain,
Isa 44: 22 like a cloud, and your sins like **m;**
Jer 10: 13 and he makes the **m** rise from the ends of the earth.
51: 16 and he makes the **m** rise from the ends of the earth.
Hos 13: 3 Therefore they shall be like the morning **m** or like
Ac 2: 19 blood, and fire, and smoky **m.**
13: 11 Immediately **m** and darkness came over him,
Jas 4: 14 For you are a **m** that appears for a little while and
Wis 2: 4 and be scattered like **m** that is chased by the rays of
Sir 24: 3 and covered the earth like a **m.**
43: 22 A **m** quickly heals all things;
2Es 4: 24 and our life is like a **m,**
7: *61* for it is they who are now like a **m,**

MISTAKE (6) [MISTAKES]
Jos 20: 3 a person without intent or by **m** may flee there;
20: 5 because the neighbor was killed by **m,**
1Sa 26: 21 I have been a fool, and have made a great **m."**
Ecc 5: 6 do not say before the messenger that it was a **m;**
Jer 42: 20 that you have made a fatal **m.**
Sir 14: 7 If ever he does good, it is by **m;**

MISTAKES (4) [MISTAKE]
Jas 3: 2 For all of us make many **m.**
3: 2 Anyone who makes no **m** in speaking is perfect,
Sir 23: 3 Otherwise my **m** may be multiplied,
1Es 8: 75 and our **m** have mounted up to heaven

MISTREAT (2) [MISTREATED, MISTREATMENT]
Ac 7: 6 and **m** them during four hundred years.
14: 5 with their rulers, to **m** them and to stone them,

MISTREATED (7) [MISTREAT]
Ex 5: 22 "O LORD, why have you **m** this people?
5: 23 he has **m** this people, and you have done nothing
Mt 22: 6 while the rest seized his slaves, **m** them,
1Th 2: 2 and been shamefully **m** at Philippi,
Sir 49: 7 For they had **m** him, who even in
Bar 4: 31 be those who **m** you and who rejoiced at your fall.
4Mc 17: 22 that previously had been **m.**

MISTREATMENT (1) [MISTREAT]
Ac 7: 34 surely seen the **m** of my people who are in Egypt

MISTRESS (11)
Ge 16: 4 she looked with contempt on her **m.**
16: 8 She said, "I am running away from my **m** Sarai."
16: 9 "Return to your **m,** and submit to her."
1Ki 17: 17 this the son of the woman, the **m** of the house,
2Ki 5: 3 She said to her **m, "**If only my lord were with
Ps 123: 2 as the eyes of a maid to the hand of her **m,**
Pr 30: 23 and a maid when she succeeds her **m.**
Isa 24: 2 as with the maid, so with her **m;**
47: 5 you shall no more be called the **m** of kingdoms.
47: 7 You said, "I shall be **m** forever,"
Na 3: 4 gracefully alluring, **m** of sorcery,

MISTS (1) [MIST]
2Pe 2: 17 These are waterless springs and **m** driven by

MISUNDERSTAND (1)
Dt 32: 27 for their adversaries might **m** and say,

MISUSES (2)
Ex 20: 7 LORD will not acquit anyone who **m** his name.
Dt 5: 11 LORD will not acquit anyone who **m** his name.

MITE[S] (KJV) See PENNY, SMALL COPPER COINS

MITHKAH (2)
Nu 33: 28 They set out from Terah and camped at **M.**
33: 29 They set out from **M** and camped at Hashmonah.

MITHNITE (1)
1Ch 11: 43 Hanan son of Maacah, and Joshaphat the **M,**

MITHREDATH (2)
Ezr 1: 8 of Persia had them released into the charge of **M**
4: 7 Bishlam and **M** and Tabeel and the rest

MITHRIDATES (2)
1Es 2: 11 he gave them to **M,** his treasurer,
2: 16 Bishlam, **M,** Tabeel, Rehum, Beltethmus,

MITRE (KJV) See TURBAN

MITYLENE (1)
Ac 20: 14 we took him on board and went to **M.**

MIX (5) [MIXED, MIXES, MIXING, MIXTURE]
Eze 24: 10 boil the meat well, **m** in the spices,
Da 2: 43 so will they **m** with one another in marriage,
2: 43 just as iron does not **m** with clay.
Rev 18: 6 **m** a double draught for her in the cup she mixed.
Sir 18: 15 My child, do not **m** reproach with your good deeds,

MIXED (63) [MIX]
Ex 12: 38 A **m** crowd also went up with them,
29: 2 unleavened cakes **m** with oil,
29: 40 of a measure of choice flour **m** with one-fourth of
Lev 2: 4 unleavened cakes **m** with oil,
2: 5 it shall be of choice flour **m** with oil, unleavened;
7: 10 But every other grain offering, **m** with oil or dry,
7: 12 the thank offering unleavened cakes **m** with oil,
9: 4 and a grain offering **m** with oil.
14: 10 of three-tenths of an ephah of choice flour **m**
14: 21 of choice flour **m** with oil for a grain offering and
23: 13 of an ephah of choice flour **m** with oil, an offering
Nu 6: 15 cakes of choice flour **m** with oil
7: 13 both of them full of choice flour **m** with oil for
7: 19 both of them full of choice flour **m** with oil for
7: 25 both of them full of choice flour **m** with oil for
7: 31 both of them full of choice flour **m** with oil for
7: 37 both of them full of choice flour **m** with oil for
7: 43 both of them full of choice flour **m** with oil for
7: 49 both of them full of choice flour **m** with oil for
7: 55 both of them full of choice flour **m** with oil for
7: 61 both of them full of choice flour **m** with oil for
Nu 7: 67 both of them full of choice flour **m** with oil for
7: 73 both of them full of choice flour **m** with oil for
7: 79 both of them full of choice flour **m** with oil for
8: 8 and its grain offering of choice flour **m** with oil,
15: 4 **m** with one-fourth of a hin of oil.
15: 6 an ephah of choice flour **m** with one-third of a hin
15: 9 **m** with half a hin of oil,
28: 5 **m** with one-fourth of a hin of beaten oil.
28: 9 **m** with oil, and its drink offering—
28: 12 **m** with oil, for each bull;
28: 12 **m** with oil, for the one ram;
28: 13 of choice flour **m** with oil as a grain offering
28: 20 Their grain offering shall be of choice flour **m**
28: 28 Their grain offering shall be of choice flour **m**
29: 3 Their grain offering shall be of choice flour **m**
29: 9 Their grain offering shall be of choice flour **m**
29: 14 Their grain offering shall be of choice flour **m**
Jos 23: 7 that you may not be **m** with these nations left here
1Ch 23: 29 the baked offering, the offering **m** with oil,
Ezr 9: 2 Thus the holy seed has **m** itself with the peoples of
Ps 75: 8 a cup with foaming wine, well **m;**
Pr 9: 2 she has **m** her wine, she has also set her table.
9: 5 eat of my bread and drink of the wine I have **m.**
23: 30 those who keep trying **m** wines.
SS 7: 2 a rounded bowl that never lacks **m** wine.
Isa 1: 22 your wine is **m** with water.
65: 11 who set a table for Fortune and fill cups of **m** wine
Jer 25: 20 all the **m** people; all the kings of the
25: 24 the kings of the **m** peoples that live in the desert;
Da 2: 41 as you saw the iron **m** with the clay.
2: 43 As you saw the iron **m** with clay,
Mt 13: 33 of heaven is like yeast that a woman took and **m** in
27: 34 they offered him wine to drink, **m** with gall;
Mk 15: 23 And they offered him wine **m** with myrrh;
Lk 13: 21 that a woman took and **m** in with three measures
Rev 8: 7 **m** with blood, and they were hurled to the earth;
15: 2 And I saw what appeared to be a sea of glass **m**
18: 6 mix a double draught for her in the cup she **m.**
Jdt 2: 20 with them went a **m** crowd like a swarm of locusts,
2Mc 15: 39 while wine **m** with water is sweet and delicious
1Es 8: 70 the holy race has been **m** with the alien peoples of
3Mc 5: 45 by the very fragrant draughts of wine **m**

MIXES (1) [MIX]
Hos 7: 8 Ephraim **m** himself with the peoples;

MIXING‡ (3) [MIX]
1Ch 9: 30 prepared the **m** of the spices,
Isa 5: 22 in drinking wine and valiant at **m** drink,
1Es 8: 87 to transgress your law by **m** with the uncleanness

MIXTURE (2) [MIX]
Jn 19: 39 also came, bringing a **m** of myrrh and aloes,
Sir 38: 8 the pharmacist makes a **m** from them.

MIZAR (1)
Ps 42: 6 the land of Jordan and of Hermon, from Mount **M.**

MIZPAH (44)
Ge 31: 49 and the pillar **M,** for he said, "The LORD watch
Jos 11: 3 and the Hivites under Hermon in the land of **M.**
Jdg 10: 17 Israelites came together, and they encamped at **M.**
11: 11 Jephthah spoke all his words before the LORD at **M**
11: 29 He passed on to **M** of Gilead,
11: 29 from **M** of Gilead he passed on to the Ammonites.
11: 34 Then Jephthah came to his home at **M;**
20: 1 in one body before the LORD at **M.**
20: 3 that the people of Israel had gone up to **M.)**
21: 1 Now the Israelites had sworn at **M,**
21: 5 not come up to the LORD to **M,**
21: 8 not come up to the LORD to **M?"**
1Sa 7: 5 Then Samuel said, "Gather all Israel at **M,**
7: 6 at **M,** and drew water and poured it out before
7: 6 And Samuel judged the people of Israel at **M.**
7: 7 that the people of Israel had gathered at **M,**
7: 11 And the men of Israel went out of **M** and pursued
7: 12 Then Samuel took a stone and set it up between **M**
7: 16 and **M;** and he judged Israel in all these places.
10: 17 Samuel summoned the people to the LORD at **M**
1Ki 15: 22 King Asa built Geba of Benjamin and **M.**
2Ki 25: 23 they came with their men to Gedaliah at **M,**
25: 25 and Chaldeans who were with him at **M.**
2Ch 16: 6 and with them he built up Geba and **M.**
Ne 3: 7 the men of Gibeon and of **M—**
3: 15 of the district of **M,** repaired the Fountain Gate;
3: 19 of **M,** repaired another section opposite the ascent
Jer 40: 6 Jeremiah went to Gedaliah son of Ahikam at **M,**
40: 8 they went to Gedaliah at **M—**
40: 10 I am staying at **M** to represent you before
40: 12 and came to the land of Judah, to Gedaliah at **M;**
40: 13 in the open country came to Gedaliah at **M**
40: 15 of Kareah spoke secretly to Gedaliah at **M,**
41: 1 with ten men to Gedaliah son of Ahikam, at **M.**
41: 1 As they ate bread together there at **M,**
41: 3 the Judeans who were with Gedaliah at **M,**
41: 6 And Ishmael son of Nethaniah came out from **M**
41: 10 the rest of the people who were in **M,**
41: 10 and all the people who were left at **M,**
41: 14 from **M** turned around and came back,
41: 16 of Nethaniah had carried away captive from **M**
Hos 5: 1 for you have been a snare at **M,**
1Mc 3: 46 Then they gathered together and went to **M,**
3: 46 because Israel formerly had a place of prayer in **M.**

MIZPAR (KJV) See MISPAR

MIZPEH (4)

Jos 11: 8 and eastward as far as the valley of **M.**
15:38 Dilan, **M,** Jokthe-el,
18:26 **M,** Chephirah, Mozah,
1Sa 22: 3 David went from there to **M** of Moab.

MIZPEH (KJV) See also MIZPAH

MIZZAH (3)

Ge 36:13 Nahath, Zerah, Shammah, and **M.**
36:17 the clans Nahath, Zerah, Shammah, and **M;**
1Ch 1:37 sons of Reuel: Nahath, Zerah, Shammah, and **M.**

MNASON (1)

Ac 21:16 along and brought us to the house of **M** of Cyprus,

MOAB (170) [MOABITE, MOABITES]

Ge 19:37 The firstborn bore a son, and named him **M;**
36:35 who defeated Midian in the country of **M,**
Ex 15:15 trembling seized the leaders of **M;**
Nu 21:11 in the wilderness bordering **M** toward the sunrise.
21:13 for the Arnon is the boundary of **M,**
21:13 between **M** and the Amorites.
21:15 and lie along the border of **M."**
21:20 the region of **M** by the top of Pisgah that overlooks
21:26 of **M** and captured all his land as far as the Arnon.
21:28 It devoured Ar of **M,** and swallowed up the heights
21:29 Woe to you, O **M!**
22: 1 in the plains of **M** across the Jordan from Jericho.
22: 3 **M** was in great dread of the people,
22: 3 **M** was overcome with fear of the people of Israel.
22: 4 And **M** said to the elders of Midian,
22: 4 Balak son of Zippor was king of **M** at that time.
22: 7 the elders of **M** and the elders of Midian departed
22: 8 so the officials of **M** stayed with Balaam.
22:10 "King Balak son of Zippor of **M,**
22:14 So the officials of **M** rose and went to Balak,
22:21 and went with the officials of **M.**
23: 6 with all the officials of **M.**
23: 7 the king of **M** from the eastern mountains:
23:17 beside his burnt offerings with the officials of **M.**
24:17 it shall crush the borderlands of **M,**
25: 1 to have sexual relations with the women of **M.**
26: 3 in the plains of **M** by the Jordan opposite Jericho,
26:63 in the plains of **M** by the Jordan opposite Jericho.
31:12 at the camp on the plains of **M** by the Jordan
33:44 and camped at Iye-abarim, in the territory of **M.**
33:48 and camped in the plains of **M** by the Jordan
33:49 as far as Abel-shittim in the plains of **M.**
33:50 In the plains of **M** by the Jordan at Jericho,
35: 1 In the plains of **M** by the Jordan at Jericho,
36:13 through Moses to the Israelites in the plains of **M**
Dt 1: 5 Beyond the Jordan in the land of **M,**
2: 8 along the route of the wilderness of **M,**
2: 9 "Do not harass **M** or engage them in battle,
2:18 "Today you are going to cross the boundary of **M**
29: 1 to make with the Israelites in the land of **M,**
32:49 which is in the land of **M,** across from Jericho,
34: 1 up from the plains of **M** to Mount Nebo, to the top
34: 5 died there in the land of **M,**
34: 6 He was buried in a valley in the land of **M,**
34: 8 for Moses in the plains of **M** thirty days;
Jos 13:32 that Moses distributed in the plains of **M,**
24: 9 Then King Balak son of Zippor of **M,**
Jdg 3:12 and the LORD strengthened King Eglon of **M**
3:14 Israelites served King Eglon of **M** eighteen years.
3:15 Israelites sent tribute by him to King Eglon of **M.**
3:17 Then he presented the tribute to King Eglon of **M.**
3:30 **M** was subdued that day under the hand of Israel.
10: 6 the gods of **M,** the gods of the Ammonites,
11:15 Israel did not take away the land of **M** or the land
11:17 They also sent to the king of **M,**
11:18 went around the land of Edom and the land of **M,**
11:18 arrived on the east side of the land of **M,**
11:18 They did not enter the territory of **M,**
11:18 for the Arnon was the boundary of **M.**
11:25 any better than King Balak son of Zippor of **M?**
Ru 1: 1 in Judah went to live in the country of **M,**
1: 2 into the country of **M** and remained there.
1: 6 with her daughters-in-law from the country of **M,**
1: 6 of **M** that the LORD had considered his people
1:22 who came back with her from the country of **M.**
2: 6 with Naomi from the country of **M.**
4: 3 who has come back from the country of **M,**
1Sa 12: 9 and into the hand of the king of **M;**
14:47 against **M,** against the Ammonites, against Edom,
22: 3 David went from there to Mizpeh of **M.**
22: 3 He said to the king of **M,**
22: 4 He left them with the king of **M,**
2Sa 8:12 **M,** the Ammonites, the Philistines, Amalek,
23:20 he struck down two sons of Ariel of **M.**
1Ki 11: 7 a high place for Chemosh the abomination of **M,**
11:33 Chemosh the god of **M,** and Milcom the god of
2Ki 1: 1 After the death of Ahab, **M** rebelled against Israel.
3: 4 Now King Mesha of **M** was a sheep breeder,
3: 5 the king of **M** rebelled against the king of Israel.
3: 7 "The king of **M** has rebelled against me;
3: 7 will you go with me to battle against **M?"**
3:10 three kings, only to be handed over to **M."**
3:13 three kings, only to be handed over to **M."**
3:18 for he will also hand **M** over to you.
3:23 Now then, **M,** to the spoil!"
3:24 as they entered **M** they continued the attack.
3:26 When the king of **M** saw that the battle was going
23:13 for Chemosh the abomination of **M,**
1Ch 1:46 who defeated Midian in the country of **M,**
4:22 who married into **M** but returned to Lehem (now
8: 8 of **M** after he had sent away his wives Hushim
11:22 he struck down two sons of Ariel of **M.**
18: 2 He defeated **M,** and the Moabites became subject
18:11 **M,** the Ammonites, the Philistines, and Amalek.
2Ch 20:10 See now, the people of Ammon, **M,**
20:22 **M,** and Mount Seir, who had come against Judah,
20:23 For the Ammonites and **M** attacked the inhabitants
Ne 13:23 of Ashdod, Ammon, and **M;**
Ps 60: 8 **M** is my washbasin; on Edom I hurl my shoe;
83: 6 of Edom and the Ishmaelites, **M** and the Hagrites,
108: 9 **M** is my washbasin; on Edom I hurl my shoe;
Isa 11:14 put forth their hand against Edom and **M,**
15: 1 An oracle concerning **M.**
15: 1 Because Ar is laid waste in a night, **M** is undone;
15: 1 because Kir is laid waste in a night, **M** is undone.
15: 2 over Nebo and over Medeba **M** wails.
15: 4 therefore the loins of **M** quiver; his soul trembles.
15: 5 My heart cries out for **M;**
15: 8 For a cry has gone around the land of **M;**
15: 9 a lion for those of **M** who escape,
16: 2 so are the daughters of **M** at the fords of the Arnon.
16: 4 let the outcasts of **M** settle among you;
16: 6 of the pride of **M**—how proud he is!—
16: 7 Therefore let **M** wail, let everyone wail for Moab.
16: 7 Therefore let Moab wail, let everyone wail for **M.**
16:11 Therefore my heart throbs like a harp for **M,**
16:12 When **M** presents himself,
16:13 the word that the LORD spoke concerning **M** in
16:14 the glory of **M** will be brought into contempt,
Jer 9:26 Judah, Edom, the Ammonites, **M,**
25:21 Edom, **M,** and the Ammonites;
27: 3 Send word to the king of Edom, the king of **M,**
40:11 in **M** and among the Ammonites and in Edom and
48: 1 Concerning **M.** Thus says the LORD of hosts,
48: 2 the renown of **M** is no more.
48: 4 **"M** is destroyed!" her little ones cry out.
48: 9 Set aside salt for **M,** for she will surely fall;
48:11 **M** has been at ease from his youth,
48:13 Then **M** shall be ashamed of Chemosh,
48:15 The destroyer of **M** and his towns has come up,
48:16 The calamity of **M** is near at hand
48:18 For the destroyer of **M** has come up against you;
48:20 **M** is put to shame, for it is broken down;
48:20 Tell it by the Arnon, that **M** is laid waste.
48:24 and all the towns of the land of **M,** far and near.
48:25 The horn of **M** is cut off, and his arm is broken,
48:26 let **M** wallow in his vomit;
48:28 and live on the rock, O inhabitants of **M!**
48:29 We have heard of the pride of **M**—
48:31 Therefore I wail for **M;** I cry out for all **M;**
48:33 from the fruitful land of **M;**
48:35 And I will bring to an end in **M,** says the LORD,
48:36 Therefore my heart moans for **M** like a flute,
48:38 of **M** and in the squares there is nothing
48:38 I have broken **M** like a vessel that no one wants,
48:39 How **M** has turned his back in shame!
48:39 So **M** has become a derision and a horror
48:40 and spread his wings against **M;**
48:41 The hearts of the warriors of **M,** on that day,
48:42 **M** shall be destroyed as a people,
48:43 pit, and trap are before you, O inhabitants of **M!**
48:44 For I will bring these things upon **M** in the year
48:45 it has destroyed the forehead of **M,**
48:46 Woe to you, O **M!**
48:47 I will restore the fortunes of **M** in the latter days,
48:47 Thus far is the judgment on **M.**
Eze 25: 8 Thus says the Lord GOD: Because **M** said,
25: 9 the flank of **M** from the towns on its frontier,
25:11 and I will execute judgments upon **M.**
Da 11:41 but Edom and **M** and the main part of
Am 2: 1 For three transgressions of **M,** and for four,
2: 2 So I will send a fire on **M,**
2: 2 and **M** shall die amid uproar,
Mic 6: 5 remember now what King Balak of **M** devised,
Zep 2: 8 I have heard the taunts of **M** and the revilings of
2: 9 **M** shall become like Sodom and the Ammonites
Jdt 1:12 also all the inhabitants of the land of **M,**
5: 2 the princes of **M** and the commanders of Ammon
5:22 the seacoast and **M** insisted that he should be cut

MOABITE (12) [MOAB]

Dt 23: 3 or **M** shall be admitted to the assembly of
Ru 1: 4 These took **M** wives; the name of the
1:22 So Naomi returned together with Ruth the **M,**
2: 2 And Ruth the **M** said to Naomi,
2: 6 "She is the **M** who came back with Naomi from
2:21 Then Ruth the **M** said, "He even said to me,
4: 5 you are also acquiring Ruth the **M,**
4:10 I have also acquired Ruth the **M,**
1Ki 11: 1 **M,** Ammonite, Edomite, Sidonian,
1Ch 11:46 and Joshaviah sons of Elnaam, and Ithmah the **M,**
2Ch 24:26 and Jehozabad son of Shimrith the **M.**
Ne 13: 1 or **M** should ever enter the assembly of God,

MOABITES‡ (19) [MOAB]

Ge 19:37 he is the ancestor of the **M** to this day.
Dt 2:11 though the **M** call them Emim.
2:29 for me and likewise the **M** who live in Ar—
Jdg 3:28 for the LORD has given your enemies the **M**
3:28 and seized the fords of the Jordan against the **M,**
3:29 that time they killed about ten thousand of the **M,**
2Sa 8: 2 He also defeated the **M** and,
8: 2 **M** became servants to David and brought tribute.
2Ki 3:21 When all the **M** heard that the kings had come up
3:22 the **M** saw the water opposite them as red as blood.
3:24 the Israelites rose up and attacked the **M,**
13:20 of **M** used to invade the land in the spring of
24: 2 bands of the **M,** and bands of the Ammonites;
1Ch 18: 2 **M** became subject to David and brought tribute.
2Ch 20: 1 After this the **M** and Ammonites,
Ezr 9: 1 the **M,** the Egyptians, and the Amorites.
Isa 25:10 The **M** shall be trodden down in their place
Jdt 7: 8 the **M** and the commanders of the coastland came
1Es 8:69 the Perizzites, the Jebusites, the **M,** the Egyptians,

MOABITISH (KJV) See MOABITE

MOADIAH (1) [=MAADIAH]

Ne 12:17 of Abijah, Zichri; of Miniamin, of **M,** Piltai;

MOAN (7) [BEMOAN, MOANING, MOANS]

Ps 55:17 and at noon I utter my complaint and **m,**
77: 3 I think of God, and I **m;**
Isa 38:14 a swallow or a crane I clamor, I **m** like a dove.
59:11 like doves we **m** mournfully.
Eze 21: 6 **M** therefore, mortal; moan with breaking
21: 6 **m** with breaking heart and bitter grief
21: 7 And when they say to you, "Why do you **m?"**

MOANING (4) [MOAN]

Ps 6: 6 I am weary with my **m;**
Isa 29: 2 and there shall be **m** and lamentation,
Eze 7:16 all of them **m** over their iniquity.
Na 2: 7 **m** like doves and beating their breasts.

MOANS (2) [MOAN]

Jer 48:36 Therefore my heart **m** for Moab like a flute,
48:36 my heart **m** like a flute for the people of Kir-heres;

MOAT (1)

Da 9:25 be built again with streets and **m,**

MOB (4)

Eze 16:40 They shall bring up a **m** against you,
Ac 17: 5 the marketplaces they formed a **m** and set the city
21:35 of the **m** was so great that he had to be carried by
Sir 26: 5 Slander in the city, the gathering of a **m,**

MOBILE (2)

Wis 7:22 subtle, **m,** clear, unpolluted, distinct, invulnerable,
7:24 For wisdom is more **m** than any motion;

MOCHMUR (1)

Jdt 7:18 which is near Chusi beside the Wadi **M.**

MOCK (16) [MOCKED, MOCKER, MOCKERS, MOCKERY, MOCKING, MOCKINGLY, MOCKS]

2Ki 19: 4 to **m** the living God, and will rebuke the words that
19:16 which he has sent to **m** the living God.
Job 11: 3 and when you **m,** shall no one shame you?
21: 3 then after I have spoken, **m** on.
30: 9 now they **m** me in song; I am a byword to them.
Ps 22: 7 All who see me **m** at me;
Pr 1:26 I will **m** when panic strikes you,
14: 9 Fools **m** at the guilt offering,
17: 5 Those who **m** the poor insult their Maker;
Isa 37: 4 to **m** the living God, and will rebuke the words that
37:17 which he has sent to **m** the living God.
66: 4 to **m** them, and bring upon them what they fear;
Eze 22: 5 near and those who are far from you will **m** you,
Mk 10:34 they will **m** him, and spit upon him, and flog him,
Lk 22:63 the men who were holding Jesus began to **m** him
Wis 12:25 you sent your judgment to **m** them

MOCKED (21) [MOCK]

Jdg 16:10 "You have **m** me and told me lies;
16:13 "Until now you have **m** me and told me lies;
16:15 You have **m** me three times now and have
1Ki 18:27 At noon Elijah **m** them, saying, "Cry aloud!
2Ki 19:22 Whom have you **m** and reviled?
19:23 By your messengers you have **m** the Lord,
2Ch 30:10 but they laughed them to scorn, and **m** them.
Ne 2:19 they **m** and ridiculed us, saying,
4: 1 and greatly enraged, and he **m** the Jews.
Ps 35:16 they impiously **m** more and more,
79: 4 **m** and derided by those around us.
Isa 37:23 Whom have you **m** and reviled?
37:24 By your servants you have **m** the Lord,
Mt 20:19 to the Gentiles to be **m** and flogged and crucified;
27:29 in his right hand and knelt before him and **m** him,
Lk 18:32 and he will be **m** and insulted and spat upon.
23:11 soldiers treated him with contempt and **m** him;
23:36 The soldiers also **m** him, coming up
Gal 6: 7 God is not **m,** for you reap whatever you sow.
1Mc 7:34 But he **m** them and derided them and defiled them
1Es 1:51 But they **m** his messengers,

MOCKER (1) [MOCK]

Pr 20: 1 Wine is a **m,** strong drink a brawler,

MOCKERIES See Index to Footnotes

MOCKERS‡ (2) [MOCK]
Job 17: 2 Surely there are **m** around me,
Hos 7: 5 he stretched out his hand with **m.**

MOCKERY‡ (7) [MOCK]
La 1: 8 so she has become a **m;**
Eze 5:15 You shall be a **m** and a taunt,
16:57 Now you are a **m** to the daughters of Aram
22: 4 and a **m** to all the countries.
Joel 2:17 O LORD, and do not make your heritage a **m,**
2:19 I will no more make you a **m** among the nations.
Sir 27:28 **M** and abuse issue from the proud,

MOCKING (12) [MOCK]
Ge 27:12 and I shall seem to be **m** him,
2Ch 36:16 but they kept **m** the messengers of God,
Isa 57: 4 Whom are you **m?** Against whom do you open
La 1: 7 the foe looked on **m** over her downfall.
Eze 5:14 a desolation and an object of **m** among the nations
Hab 2: 6 with **m** riddles, say about them,
Mt 27:31 After **m** him, they stripped him of the robe
27:41 along with the scribes and elders, were **m** him,
Mk 15:20 After **m** him, they stripped him of the purple cloak
15:31 were also **m** him among themselves and saying,
Heb 11:36 Others suffered **m** and flogging,
Sir 33: 6 A **m** friend is like a stallion

MOCKINGLY (1) [MOCK]
Wis 11:14 For though they had **m** rejected him who long

MOCKS (4) [MOCK]
Job 9:23 he **m** at the calamity of the innocent.
Pr 19:28 A worthless witness **m** at justice,
30:17 that **m** a father and scorns to obey a mother will
Jer 20: 7 a laughingstock all day long; everyone **m** me.

MODE (1)
AdE 2:20 So Esther did not change her **m** of life.

MODEIN (9)
1Mc 2: 1 moved from Jerusalem and settled in **M.**
2:15 to the town of **M** to make them offer sacrifice.
2:23 the sight of all to offer sacrifice on the altar in **M,**
2:70 and was buried in the tomb of his ancestors at **M.**
9:19 and buried him in the tomb of their ancestors at **M,**
13:25 and buried him in **M,** the city of his ancestors.
13:30 This is the tomb that he built in **M;**
16: 4 against Cendebeus and camped for the night in **M.**
2Mc 13:14 and commonwealth, he pitched his camp near **M.**

MODEL (2)
2Ki 16:10 King Ahaz sent to the priest Uriah a **m** of the altar,
Tit 2: 7 Show yourself in all respects a **m** of good works,

MODERATE (3) [MODERATION]
Ac 27:13 When a **m** south wind began to blow,
Sir 31:20 Healthy sleep depends on **m** eating;
31:22 In everything you do be **m,**

MODERATION (4) [MODERATE]
Sir 31:27 Wine is very life to human beings if taken in **m.**
31:28 Wine drunk at the proper time and in **m** is rejoicing
2Mc 4:37 and wept because of the **m** and good conduct of
9:27 and will treat you with **m** and kindness."

MODERATION (KJV) See also GENTLENESS

MODEST (5) [MODESTLY, MODESTY]
Sir 26:15 A **m** wife adds charm to charm,
26:24 *a* **m** *daughter will even be embarrassed before her*
32:10 and approval goes before one who is **m.**
2Mc 15:12 of **m** bearing and gentle manner,
4Mc 8: 3 **m,** noble, and accomplished in every way—

MODESTLY (1) [MODEST]
1Ti 2: 9 also that the women should dress themselves **m**

MODESTY (2) [MODEST]
1Ti 2:15 in faith and love and holiness, with **m.**
3Mc 1:19 for wedded union, and, neglecting proper **m,** in

MOETH (1)
1Es 8:63 with them were Jozabad son of Jeshua and **M** son

MOIST (3) [MOISTEN, MOISTENING, MOISTURE]
Dt 29:19 (thus bringing disaster on **m** and dry alike)—
Job 21:24 of milk and the marrow of his bones **m.**
Aza 1:27 of the furnace as though a **m** wind were whistling

MOISTEN (1) [MOIST]
Eze 46:14 and one-third of a hin of oil to **m** the choice flour,

MOISTENING (1) [MOIST]
3Mc 6: 6 **m** the fiery furnace with dew and turning the flame

MOISTURE (2) [MOIST]
Job 37:11 He loads the thick cloud with **m;**
Lk 8: 6 and as it grew up, it withered for lack of **m.**

MOLADAH (4)
Jos 15:26 Amam, Shema, **M,**
19: 2 It had for its inheritance Beer-sheba, Sheba, **M,**
1Ch 4:28 They lived in Beer-sheba, **M,** Hazar-shual,
Ne 11:26 and in Jeshua and in **M** and Beth-pelet,

MOLD (3) [MOLDED, MOLDING, MOLDS]
Ex 32: 4 He took the gold from them, formed it in a **m,**
Na 3:14 tread the mortar, take hold of the brick **m!**
Wis 15: 9 they count it a glorious thing to **m** counterfeit gods.

MOLDED (3) [MOLD]
Ro 9:20 Will what is **m** say to the one who molds it,
Wis 7: 1 and in the womb of a mother I was **m** into flesh,
Sir 33:13 to be **m** as he pleases,

MOLDING (10) [MOLD]
Ex 25:11 and you shall make a **m** of gold upon it all around.
25:24 and make a **m** of gold around it.
25:25 and a **m** of gold around the rim.
30: 3 and you shall make for it a **m** of gold all around.
30: 4 under its **m** on two opposite sides
37: 2 and made a **m** of gold around it.
37:11 and made a **m** of gold around it.
37:12 and made a **m** of gold around the rim.
37:26 and he made for it a **m** of gold all around,
37:27 and made two golden rings for it under its **m,**

MOLDS (3) [MOLD]
Ro 9:20 Will what is molded say to the one who **m** it,
Wis 15: 7 and laboriously **m** each vessel for our service,
Sir 38:30 He **m** the clay with his arm and makes it pliable

MOLDY (2)
Jos 9: 5 and all their provisions were dry and **m.**
9:12 but now, see, it is dry and **m;**

MOLE[S] (KJV) See CHAMELEON

MOLECH‡ (9) [=MILCOM, =MOLOCH]
Lev 18:21 to sacrifice them to **M,** and so profane the name
20: 2 who give any of their offspring to **M** shall be put
20: 3 because they have given of their offspring to **M,**
20: 4 when they give of their offspring to **M,**
20: 5 in prostituting themselves to **M.**
1Ki 11: 7 and for **M** the abomination of the Ammonites,
2Ki 23:10 or a daughter pass through fire as an offering to **M.**
Isa 57: 9 You journeyed to **M** with oil,
Jer 32:35 to offer up their sons and daughters to **M,**

MOLES (1)
Isa 2:20 On that day people will throw away to the **m** and

MOLESTED (1)
2Mc 11:31 be **m** in any way for what may have been done

MOLID (1)
1Ch 2:29 and she bore him Ahban and **M.**

MOLLIFIED (KJV) See SOFTENED

MOLOCH (1) [=MOLECH]
Ac 7:43 No; you took along the tent of **M,**

MOLOCH (KJV) See also SAKKUTH

MOLTEN (4)
1Ki 7:16 He also made two capitals of **m** bronze,
7:23 Then he made the **m** sea;
2Ch 4: 2 Then he made the **m** sea;
Job 37:18 like him, spread out the skies, hard as a **m** mirror?

MOLTEN (KJV) See also CAST, CAST AN IMAGE, GOLD-PLATED, MELT, SMELTED

MOMDIUS (1)
1Es 9:34 Of the descendants of Bani: Jeremai, **M,** Maerus,

MOMENT (52) [MOMENT'S, MOMENTARY]
Ex 33: 5 if for a single **m** I should go up among you,
Nu 4:20 not go in to look on the holy things even for a **m;**
16:21 so that I may consume them in a **m.**
16:45 so that I may consume them in a **m."**
Ru 2: 7 without resting even for a **m."**
Ezr 9: 8 But now for a brief **m** favor has been shown by
Job 7:18 visit them every morning, test them every **m?**
20: 5 and the joy of the godless is but for a **m?**
34:20 In a **m** they die; at midnight
Ps 6:10 they shall turn back, and in a **m** be put to shame.
30: 5 his anger is but for a **m;** his favor is for a lifetime.
73:19 How they are destroyed in a **m,**
Pr 6:15 in a **m,** damage beyond repair.
12:19 but a lying tongue lasts only a **m.**
Isa 27: 3 I, the LORD, am its keeper; every **m** I water it.
47: 9 both these things shall come upon you in a **m,**
54: 7 For a brief **m** I abandoned you,
54: 8 In overflowing wrath for a **m** I hid my face
66: 8 Shall a nation be delivered in one **m?**
Jer 4:20 my tents are destroyed, my curtains in a **m.**
18: 7 At one **m** I may declare concerning a nation or
18: 9 at another **m** I may declare concerning a nation or
La 4: 6 which was overthrown in a **m,**
Eze 26:16 they shall tremble every **m,** and be appalled at you.
32:10 they shall tremble every **m** for their lives,
Mt 26:16 from that **m** he began to look for an opportunity
26:74 At that **m** the cock crowed.
27:51 At that **m** the curtain of the temple was torn in two,
Mk 14:72 At that **m** the cock crowed for the second time.
Lk 2:38 At that **m** she came, and began to praise God and
22:60 At that **m,** while he was still speaking,
Jn 18:27 and at that **m** the cock crowed.
Ac 9:11 At this **m** he is praying,
11:11 At that very **m** three men,
Ro 13:11 how it is now the **m** for you to wake from sleep.
1Co 15:52 in a **m,** in the twinkling of an eye,
Gal 2: 5 we did not submit to them even for a **m,**
Rev 11:13 At that **m** there was a great earthquake,
Tob 3:16 At that very **m,** the prayers of both
Jdt 6: 5 you have said these words in a **m** of perversity;
14: 8 the day she left until the **m** she began speaking
AdE 10:11 the hour and **m** and day of decision before God and
Sir 1:23 Those who are patient stay calm until the right **m,**
1:24 They hold back their words until the right **m;**
4:23 Do not refrain from speaking at the proper **m,**
18:24 the **m** of vengeance when he turns away his face.
20: 7 The wise remain silent until the right **m,**
20: 7 but a boasting fool misses the right **m.**
40: 7 At the **m** he reaches safety he wakes up,
2Mc 6:25 for the sake of living a brief **m** longer,
9:11 for he was tortured with pain every **m.**
3Mc 5:49 they thought that this was their last **m** of life,

MOMENT'S (1) [MOMENT]
2Es 16:38 there will not be a **m** delay,

MOMENTARY (1) [MOMENT]
2Co 4:17 For this slight **m** affliction is preparing us for

MONARCH (1) [MONARCHS]
Wis 12:14 nor can any king or **m** confront you

MONARCHS (5) [MONARCH]
Wis 6: 9 To you then, O **m,** my words are directed,
6:21 O **m** over the peoples, honor wisdom,
8:15 dread **m** will be afraid of me when they hear of me;
14:16 the command of **m** carved images were worshiped.
14:17 When people could not honor **m** in their presence,

MONEY‡ (200) [MONEY-HUNGRY, MONEY-MAKER, MONEYLENDER]
Ge 17:12 in your house and the one bought with your **m**
17:13 the one bought with your **m** must be circumcised.
17:23 the slaves born in his house or bought with his **m,**
17:27 slaves born in the house and those bought with **m**
31:15 and he has been using up the **m** given for us.
33:19 he bought for one hundred pieces of **m** the plot
42:25 to return every man's **m** to his sack,
42:27 he saw his **m** at the top of the sack.
42:28 He said to his brothers, "My **m** has been put back;
42:35 there in each one's sack was his bag of **m.**
42:35 When they and their father saw their bundles of **m,**
43:12 Take double the **m** with you.
43:12 the **m** that was returned in the top of your sacks;
43:15 and they took double the **m** with them,
43:18 and they said, "It is because of the **m,**
43:21 and there was each one's **m** in the top of his sack,
43:21 in the top of his sack, our **m** in full weight.
43:22 down with us additional **m** to buy food.
43:22 We do not know who put our **m** in our sacks."
43:23 for you; I received your **m."**
44: 1 and put each man's **m** in the top of his sack.
44: 2 with his **m** for the grain."
44: 8 Look, the **m** that we found at the top of our sacks,
47:14 Joseph collected all the **m** to be found in the land
47:14 and Joseph brought the **m** into Pharaoh's house.
47:15 the **m** from the land of Egypt and from the land
47:15 For our **m** is gone."
47:16 in exchange for your livestock, if your **m** is gone."
47:18 not hide from my lord that our **m** is all spent;
Ex 21:11 without debt, without payment of **m.**
21:34 giving **m** to its owner, but keeping the dead animal.
22: 7 When someone delivers to a neighbor **m** or goods
22:25 If you lend **m** to my people,
30:16 You shall take the atonement **m** from the Israelites
Lev 25:37 not lend them your **m** at interest taken in advance,
Nu 3:48 and his sons the **m** by which the excess number
3:49 the redemption **m** from those who were over and
3:50 from the firstborn of the Israelites he took the **m,**
3:51 and Moses gave the redemption **m** to Aaron
Dt 2: 6 You shall purchase food from them for **m,**
2: 6 and you shall also buy water from them for **m,**
2:28 You shall sell me food for **m,** so that I may eat,
2:28 and supply me water for **m,** so that I may drink.
14:25 then you may turn it into **m.**

Dt 14:25 With the **m** secure in hand,
14:26 spend the **m** for whatever you wish—
21:14 you shall let her go free and not sell her for **m.**
23:19 interest on **m,** interest on provisions,
Jos 24:32 for one hundred pieces of **m;**
Jdg 16:18 and brought the **m** in their hands.
17: 4 So when he returned the **m** to his mother,
1Ki 21: 2 seems good to you, I will give you its value in **m."**
21: 6 'Give me your vineyard for **m;**
21:15 which he refused to give you for **m;**
2Ki 5:26 Is this a time to accept **m** and to accept clothing,
12: 4 the **m** offered as sacred donations that is brought
12: 4 the **m** for which each person is assessed—
12: 4 the **m** from the assessment of persons—
12: 4 the **m** from the voluntary offerings brought into
12: 7 Now therefore do not accept any more **m**
12: 8 that they would neither accept more **m** from
12: 9 the threshold put in it all the **m** that was brought
12:10 that there was a great deal of **m** in the chest,
12:10 the **m** that was found in the house of the LORD,
12:11 They would give the **m** that was weighed out into
12:13 from the **m** that was brought into the house of
12:15 into whose hand they delivered the **m** to pay out to
12:16 The **m** from the guilt offerings and the **m** from
15:20 Menahem exacted the **m** from Israel, that is,
22: 4 the entire sum of the **m** that has been brought into
22: 7 be asked from them for the **m** that is delivered
22: 9 "Your servants have emptied out the **m**
23:35 the land in order to meet Pharaoh's demand for **m.**
2Ch 24: 5 to the cities of Judah and gather **m** from all Israel
24:11 they saw that there was a large amount of **m** in it,
24:11 and collected **m** in abundance.
24:14 the rest of the **m** to the king and Jehoiada,
34: 9 the **m** that had been brought into the house of God,
34:14 the **m** that had been brought into the house of
34:17 the **m** that was found in the house of the LORD
Ezr 3: 7 So they gave **m** to the masons and the carpenters,
7:17 With this **m,** then, you shall
Ne 5: 4 to borrow **m** on our fields and vineyards to pay
5:10 and my servants are lending them **m** and grain.
5:11 and their houses, and the interest on **m,** grain,
Est 3:11 The king said to Haman, "The **m** is given to you,
4: 7 and the exact sum of **m** that Haman had promised
Job 42:11 of them gave him a piece of **m** and a gold ring.
Ps 15: 5 who do not lend **m** at interest,
Pr 7:20 He took a bag of **m** with him;
Ecc 5:10 The lover of **m** will not be satisfied with **m;**
7:12 protection of wisdom is like the protection of **m,**
10:19 wine gladdens life, and **m** meets every need.
Isa 43:24 You have not bought me sweet cane with **m,**
52: 3 and you shall be redeemed without **m.**
55: 1 and you that have no **m,** come, buy and eat!
55: 1 buy wine and milk without **m** and without price.
55: 2 Why do you spend your **m** for that which is
Jer 32: 9 and weighed out the **m** to him,
32:10 got witnesses, and weighed the **m** on scales.
32:25 "Buy the field for **m** and get witnesses"—
32:44 Fields shall be bought for **m,**
Mic 3:11 its prophets give oracles for **m;**
Mt 19:21 sell your possessions, and give the **m** to the poor,
21:12 and he overturned the tables of the **m** changers and
25:18 a hole in the ground and hid his master's **m.**
25:27 you ought to have invested my **m** with the bankers,
26: 9 and the **m** given to the poor."
27: 6 into the treasury, since they are blood **m."**
28:12 they devised a plan to give a large sum of **m** to
28:15 So they took the **m** and did as they were directed.
Mk 6: 8 no bread, no bag, no **m** in their belts;
10:21 go, sell what you own, and give the **m** to the poor,
11:15 and he overturned the tables of the **m** changers and
12:41 and watched the crowd putting **m** into the treasury.
14: 5 and the **m** given to the poor."
14:11 and promised to give him **m.**
Lk 3:14 "Do not extort **m** from anyone by threats
9: 3 nor bag, nor bread, nor **m**—not even an extra tunic.
16:14 The Pharisees, who were lovers of **m,**
18:22 that you own and distribute the **m** to the poor,
19:15 to whom he had given the **m,**
19:23 Why then did you not put my **m** into the bank?
22: 5 and agreed to give him **m.**
Jn 2:14 and the **m** changers seated at their tables.
2:15 He also poured out the coins of the **m** changers
12: 5 not sold for three hundred denarii and the **m** given
Ac 4:37 then brought the **m,** and laid it at the apostles' feet.
8:18 on of the apostles' hands, he offered them **m,**
8:20 you thought you could obtain God's gift with **m!**
16:16 and brought her owners a great deal of **m**
16:19 that their hope of making **m** was gone,
22:28 a large sum of **m** to get my citizenship."
24:26 the same time he hoped that **m** would be given him
1Ti 3: 3 not quarrelsome, and not a lover of **m.**
3: 8 not indulging in much wine, not greedy for **m;**
6:10 For the love of **m** is a root of all kinds of evil,
2Ti 3: 2 people will be lovers of themselves, lovers of **m,**
Heb 13: 5 Keep your lives free from the love of **m,**
Jas 4:13 doing business and making **m."**
Tob 1: 7 for six years I would save up a second tenth in **m**
2:11 also, my wife Anna earned **m** at women's work.
4: 1 the **m** that he had left in trust with Gabael at Rages
4: 2 and explain to him about the **m** before I die?"
5: 2 but how can I obtain the **m** from him,
5: 2 and trust me, and give me the **m?**
5: 3 we each took one part, and I put one with the **m.**
5: 3 now twenty years have passed since I left this **m**
5: 3 But get back the **m** from Gabael."
5:19 Do not heap **m** upon **m,**
9: 2 give him the bond, get the **m,**
Tob 9: 5 Gabael got up and counted out to him the **m** bags,
10: 2 and there is no one to give him the **m?"**
10:10 oxen and sheep, donkeys and camels, clothing, **m,**
11:15 that he had brought the **m,**
12: 3 he brought the **m** back with me, and he healed you.
AdE 3:11 The king told Haman, "Keep the **m,**
Wis 15:12 for they say one must get **m** however one can,
Sir 7:18 Do not exchange a friend for **m,**
18:33 not become a beggar by feasting with borrowed **m,**
21: 8 Whoever builds his house with other people's **m** is
29: 5 and is deferential in speaking of his neighbor's **m;**
29: 6 the borrower has robbed the other of his **m,**
31: 5 one who pursues **m** will be led astray by it.
51:25 Acquire wisdom for yourselves without **m.**
Bar 1: 6 they collected as much **m** as each could give,
1:10 They said: Here we send you **m;**
1:10 so buy with the **m** burnt offerings and sin offerings
LtJ 6:28 to these gods and use the **m** themselves.
6:35 not able to give either wealth or **m;**
1Mc 3:29 he saw that the **m** in the treasury was exhausted,
8:26 arms, **m,** or ships, just as Rome has decided;
8:28 arms, **m,** or ships, just as Rome has decided;
10:43 because they owe **m** to the king or are in debt,
13:15 "It is for the **m** that your brother Jonathan owed
13:17 but he sent to get the **m** and the sons,
13:18 "It was because Simon did not send him the **m** and
14:32 He spent great sums of his own **m;**
15: 6 to mint your own coinage as **m** for your country,
15:30 that you have seized and the tribute **m** of the places
15:31 and five hundred talents more for the tribute **m** of
2Mc 3: 6 in Jerusalem was full of untold sums of **m,**
3: 7 of the **m** about which he had been informed.
3:11 and also some **m** of Hyrcanus son of Tobias,
3:13 said that this **m** must in any case be confiscated for
4: 1 about the **m** against his own country,
4:19 Those who carried the **m,** however,
4:20 So this **m** was intended by the sender for
4:23 the **m** to the king and to complete the records
4:27 he did not pay regularly any of the **m** promised to
8:25 They captured the **m** of those who had come
10:21 for **m** by setting their enemies free to fight
1Es 5:54 They gave **m** to the masons and the carpenters,
3Mc 2:32 and by paying **m** in exchange
4Mc 2: 8 even though a lover of **m,**
3:20 both appropriated **m** to them for the temple service
4:10 up with his armed forces to seize the **m,**

MONEY-HUNGRY (1) [HUNGRY, MONEY]

2Mc 10:20 But those with Simon, who were **m,**

MONEY-MAKING (1) [MAKE, MONEY]

Wis 13:19 for **m** and work and success with his hands

MONEYLENDER (1) [LEND, MONEY]

Sir 29:28 about lodging and the insults of the **m.**

MONGREL (1)

Zec 9: 6 a **m** people shall settle in Ashdod,

MONSTER (3) [MONSTERS, MONSTROUS, SEA-MONSTERS]

Jer 51:34 he has swallowed me like a **m;**
Mt 12:40 and three nights in the belly of the sea **m,**
3Mc 6: 8 wasting away in the belly of a huge, sea-born **m,**

MONSTERS (3) [MONSTER]

Ge 1:21 the great sea **m** and every living creature
Ps 148: 7 you sea **m** and all deeps,
2Es 5: 8 and menstruous women shall bring forth **m.**

MONSTERS (KJV) See also JACKALS

MONSTROUS (3) [MONSTER]

Hos 6: 9 on the road to Shechem, they commit a **m** crime.
Wis 17:15 and now were driven by **m** specters,
3Mc 4:11 that had been built with a **m** perimeter wall in front

MONTH‡ (297) [MONTHLY, MONTHS, MONTHS']

A. THE FIRST MONTH (42)
B. SEVENTH MONTH (31)

Ge 7:11 in the second **m,** on the seventeenth day of
7:11 on the seventeenth day of the **m,**
8: 4 and in the seventh **m,** on the seventeenth day of B
8: 4 on the seventeenth day of the **m,**
8: 5 The waters continued to abate until the tenth **m;**
8: 5 in the tenth **m,** on the first day of the **m,**
8:13 In the six hundred first year, in the first **m,** A
8:13 in the first month, the first day of the **m,**
8:14 the second **m,** on the twenty-seventh day of the **m,**
29:14 And he stayed with him a **m.**
Ex 12: 2 This **m** shall mark for you the beginning
12: 2 it shall be the first **m** of the year for you. A
12: 3 of Israel that on the tenth of this **m** they are to take
12: 6 until the fourteenth day of this **m;**
12:18 first **m,** from the evening of the fourteenth day A
13: 4 Today, in the **m** of Abib, you are going out.
13: 5 you shall keep this observance in this **m.**
16: 1 the second **m** after they had departed from the land
23:15 for seven days at the appointed time in the **m**
34:18 at the time appointed in the **m** of Abib;
Ex 34:18 for in the **m** of Abib you came out from Egypt.
40: 2 of the first **m** you shall set up the tabernacle of A
40:17 In the first **m** in the second year, A
40:17 on the first day of the **m,** the tabernacle was set up.
Lev 16:29 In the seventh **m,** on the tenth day of the month, B
16:29 In the seventh month, on the tenth day of the **m,**
23: 5 In the first **m,** on the fourteenth day of the A
23: 5 In the first month, on the fourteenth day of the **m,**
23: 6 of the same **m** is the festival of unleavened bread
23:24 In the seventh **m,** on the first day of the month, B
23:24 In the seventh month, on the first day of the **m,**
23:27 of this seventh **m** is the day of atonement; B
23:32 on the ninth day of the **m** at evening,
23:34 On the fifteenth day of this seventh **m,** B
23:39 Now, the fifteenth day of the seventh **m,** B
23:41 you shall keep it in the seventh **m** as B
25: 9 on the tenth day of the seventh **m**— B
27: 6 If the age is from one **m** to five years,
Nu 1: 1 on the first day of the second **m,**
1:18 on the first day of the second **m** they assembled
3:15 You shall enroll every male from a **m** old
3:22 counting all the males from a **m** old and upward,
3:28 Counting all the males, from a **m** old and upward,
3:34 counting all the males from a **m** old and upward,
3:39 all the males from a **m** old and upward,
3:40 from a **m** old and upward, and count their names.
3:43 all the firstborn males from a **m** old and upward,
9: 1 in the first **m** of the second year A
9: 3 On the fourteenth day of this **m,** at twilight,
9: 5 They kept the passover in the first **m,** A
9: 5 on the fourteenth day of the **m,** at twilight,
9:11 In the second **m** on the fourteenth day, at twilight,
9:22 Whether it was two days, or a **m,** or a longer time,
10:11 in the second **m,** on the twentieth day of the **m,**
11:20 for a whole **m**—until it comes out of your
11:21 that they may eat for a whole **m'!**
18:16 reckoned from one **m** of age,
20: 1 came into the wilderness of Zin in the first **m,** A
26:62 every male one **m** old and up;
28:14 This is the burnt offering of every **m** throughout
28:16 On the fourteenth day of the first **m** there shall A
28:17 And on the fifteenth day of this **m** is a festival;
29: 1 seventh **m** you shall have a holy convocation; B
29: 7 seventh **m** you shall have a holy convocation, B
29:12 seventh **m** you shall have a holy convocation; B
33: 3 They set out from Rameses in the first **m,** A
33: 3 on the fifteenth day of the first **m;** A
33:38 on the first day of the fifth **m.**
Dt 1: 3 on the first day of the eleventh **m,**
16: 1 Observe the **m** of Abib by keeping the passover for
16: 1 for in the **m** of Abib the LORD you God brought
21:13 and shall remain in your house a full **m,**
Jos 4:19 out of the Jordan on the tenth day of the first **m,** A
5:10 the fourteenth day of the **m** in the plains of Jericho.
1Sa 11: 1 About a **m** later, Nahash the Ammonite went up
20:34 and ate no food on the second day of the **m,**
1Ki 4: 7 each one had to make provision for one **m** in
4:27 each one in his **m;** they let nothing be lacking.
5:14 ten thousand a **m** in shifts;
5:14 they would be a **m** in the Lebanon and two months
6: 1 in the **m** of Ziv, which is the second **m,**
6:37 the house of the LORD was laid, in the **m** of Ziv.
6:38 in the **m** of Bul, which is the eighth **m,**
8: 2 to King Solomon at the festival in the **m** Ethanim,
8: 2 in the month Ethanim, which is the seventh **m.** B
12:32 on the fifteenth day of the eighth **m** like the festival
12:33 on the fifteenth day in the eighth **m,** in the month
12:33 in the **m** that he alone had devised;
2Ki 15:13 he reigned one **m** in Samaria.
25: 1 in the tenth **m,** on the tenth day of the **m,**
25: 3 the ninth day of the fourth **m** the famine became
25: 8 In the fifth **m,** on the seventh day of the **m**—
25:25 in the seventh **m,** Ishmael son of Nethaniah son B
25:27 the twelfth **m,** on the twenty-seventh day of the **m,**
1Ch 12:15 the men who crossed the Jordan in the first **m,** A
27: 1 **m** after **m** throughout the year,
27: 2 in charge of the first division in the first **m;** A
27: 3 all the commanders of the army for the first **m.** A
27: 4 in charge of the division of the second **m;**
27: 5 The third commander, for the third **m,**
27: 7 for the fourth **m,** and his son Zebadiah after him;
27: 8 The fifth commander, for the fifth **m,**
27: 9 for the sixth **m,** was Ira son of Ikkesh the Tekoite;
27:10 Seventh, for the seventh **m,** B
27:11 for the eighth **m,** was Sibbecai the Hushathite,
27:12 Ninth, for the ninth **m,** was Abiezer of Anathoth,
27:13 Tenth, for the tenth **m,** was Maharai of Netophah,
27:14 Eleventh, for the eleventh **m,**
27:15 Twelfth, for the twelfth **m,**
2Ch 3: 2 the second day of the second **m** of the fourth year
5: 3 the king at the festival that is in the seventh **m.** B
7:10 the twenty-third day of the seventh **m** he sent B
15:10 the third **m** of the fifteenth year of the reign of Asa.
29: 3 In the first year of his reign, in the first **m,** A
29:17 first day of the first **m,** and on the eighth day A
29:17 of the **m** they came to the vestibule of the LORD;
29:17 on the sixteenth day of the first **m** they finished. A
30: 2 to keep the passover in the second **m**
30:13 the festival of unleavened bread in the second **m,**
30:15 on the fourteenth day of the second **m.**
31: 7 In the third **m** they began to pile up the heaps,
31: 7 and finished them in the seventh **m.** B
35: 1 on the fourteenth day of the first **m.** A
Ezr 3: 1 When the seventh **m** came, B
3: 6 seventh **m** they began to offer burnt offerings B
3: 8 at the house of God at Jerusalem, in the second **m,**
6:15 on the third day of the **m** of Adar,

Ezr 6:19 the first **m** the returned exiles kept the passover. A
7:8 They came to Jerusalem in the fifth **m,**
7:9 On the first day of the first **m** the journey up A
7:9 the first day of the fifth **m** he came to Jerusalem,
8:31 twelfth day of the first **m,** to go to Jerusalem; A
10:9 the ninth **m,** on the twentieth day of the **m.**
10:16 of the tenth **m** they sat down to examine the matter.
10:17 first day of the first **m** they had come to the end A
Ne 1:1 In the **m** of Chislev, in the twentieth year,
2:1 In the **m** of Nisan, in the twentieth year
6:15 on the twenty-fifth day of the **m** Elul,
7:73 When the seventh **m** came— B
8:2 This was on the first day of the seventh **m.** B
8:14 in booths during the festival of the seventh **m,** B
9:1 Now on the twenty-fourth day of this **m** the people
Est 2:16 in his royal palace in the tenth **m,**
2:16 which is the **m** of Tebeth,
3:7 In the first **m,** which is the month of Nisan, A
3:7 In the first month, which is the **m** of Nisan,
3:7 before Haman for the day and for the **m,**
3:7 of the twelfth **m,** which is the **m** of Adar.
3:12 on the thirteenth day of the first **m,** and an edict, A
3:13 of the twelfth **m,** which is the **m** of Adar,
8:9 in the third **m,** which is the **m** of Sivan,
8:12 of the twelfth **m,** which is the **m** of Adar.
9:1 Now in the twelfth **m,** which is the **m** of Adar,
9:15 also on the fourteenth day of the **m** of Adar
9:17 This was on the thirteenth day of the **m** of Adar,
9:19 hold the fourteenth day of the **m** of Adar as a day
9:21 **m** Adar and also the fifteenth day of the same **m,**
9:22 the **m** that had been turned for them from sorrow
Jer 1:3 until the captivity of Jerusalem in the fifth **m.**
2:24 in her **m** they will find her.
28:1 in the fifth **m** of the fourth year,
28:17 In that same year, in the seventh **m,** B
36:9 in the ninth **m,** all the people in Jerusalem and all
36:22 in his winter apartment (it was the ninth **m**),
39:1 in the tenth **m,** King Nebuchadrezzar of Babylon
39:2 in the fourth **m,** on the ninth day of the **m,**
41:1 In the seventh **m,** Ishmael son of Nethaniah son B
52:4 in the tenth **m,** on the tenth day of the **m,**
52:6 the ninth day of the fourth **m** the famine became
52:12 In the fifth **m,** on the tenth day of the **m**—
52:31 in the twelfth **m,** on the twenty-fifth day of the **m,**
Eze 1:1 in the fourth **m,** on the fifth day of the **m,**
1:2 On the fifth day of the **m** (it was the fifth year of
8:1 in the sixth **m,** on the fifth day of the **m,**
20:1 in the fifth **m,** on the tenth day of the **m,**
24:1 in the tenth **m,** on the tenth day of the **m,**
26:1 In the eleventh year, on the first day of the **m,**
29:1 in the tenth **m,** on the twelfth day of the **m,**
29:17 In the twenty-seventh year, in the first **m,** A
29:17 in the first month, on the first day of the **m,**
30:20 In the eleventh year, in the first **m,** A
30:20 in the first month, on the seventh day of the **m,**
31:1 in the third **m,** on the first day of the **m,**
32:1 in the twelfth **m,** on the first day of the **m,**
32:17 In the twelfth year, in the first **m,** A
32:17 in the first month, on the fifteenth day of the **m,**
33:21 our exile, in the tenth **m,** on the fifth day of the **m,**
40:1 on the tenth day of the **m,**
45:18 In the first **m,** on the first day of the month, A
45:18 In the first month, on the first day of the **m,**
45:20 You shall do the same on the seventh day of the **m**
45:21 In the first **m,** on the fourteenth day of the A
45:21 In the first month, on the fourteenth day of the **m,**
45:25 In the seventh **m,** on the fifteenth day of the B
45:25 the fifteenth day of the **m** and for the seven days
47:12 but they will bear fresh fruit every **m,**
Da 10:4 On the twenty-fourth day of the first **m,** A
Hag 1:1 Darius, in the sixth **m,** on the first day of the **m,**
1:15 on the twenty-fourth day of the **m,**in the sixth **m.**
2:1 in the seventh **m,** on the twenty-first day of B
2:1 on the twenty-first day of the **m,**
2:10 On the twenty-fourth day of the ninth **m,**
2:18 from the twenty-fourth day of the ninth **m.**
2:20 to Haggai on the twenty-fourth day of the **m:**
Zec 1:1 In the eighth **m,** in the second year of Darius,
1:7 the eleventh **m,** the **m** of Shebat, in the second year
7:1 to Zechariah on the fourth day of the ninth **m,**
7:3 and practice abstinence in the fifth **m,**
7:5 When you fasted and lamented in the fifth **m** and
8:19 The fast of the fourth **m,** and the fast of the fifth,
11:8 In one **m** I disposed of the three shepherds,
Lk 1:26 In the sixth **m** the angel Gabriel was sent by God to
1:36 and this is the sixth **m** for her who was said to
Rev 9:15 the **m,** and the year, to kill a third of humankind.
22:2 producing its fruit each **m;**
Jdt 2:1 on the twenty-second day of the first **m,** A
3:10 and remained for a whole **m** in order to collect all
AdE 2:16 in to King Artaxerxes in the twelfth **m,**
3:7 The lot fell on the fourteenth day of the **m** of Adar.
3:12 first **m** the king's secretaries were summoned, A
3:13 the Jewish people on a given day of the twelfth **m,**
8:9 twenty-third day of the first **m,** that is, Nisan, A
8:12 the thirteenth of the twelfth **m,** which is Adar,
9:1 Now on the thirteenth day of the twelfth **m,**
9:22 The whole **m** (namely, Adar),
10:13 So they will observe these days in the **m** of Adar,
10:13 on the fourteenth and fifteenth of that **m,**
13:6 on the fourteenth day of the twelfth **m,** Adar,
16:20 so that on the thirteenth day of the twelfth **m,**
Bar 1:2 on the seventh day of the **m,**
1Mc 1:58 against those who were found **m** after **m** in
1:59 of the **m** they offered sacrifice on the altar that was
4:52 of the ninth **m,** which is the **m** of Chislev,
4:59 with the twenty-fifth day of the **m** of Chislev.
1Mc 7:43 in battle on the thirteenth day of the **m** of Adar.
9:3 In the first **m** of the one hundred fifty-second A
9:54 in the second **m,** Alcimus gave orders to tear down
10:21 the seventh **m** of the one hundred sixtieth year, B
13:51 On the twenty-third day of the second **m,**
16:14 in the eleventh **m,** which is the **m** of Shebat.
2Mc 1:9 that you keep the festival of booths in the **m**
10:5 that is, on the twenty-fifth day of the same **m,**
15:36 to celebrate the thirteenth day of the twelfth **m**—
1Es 1:1 on the fourteenth day of the first **m,** A
5:6 in the second year of his reign, in the **m** of Nisan,
5:6 in the month of Nisan, the first **m.** A
5:47 When the seventh **m** came, B
5:53 from the new moon of the seventh **m,** B
5:56 in the second **m,** Zerubbabel son of Shealtiel
5:57 of the second **m** in the second year after they came
7:5 by the twenty-third day of the **m** of Adar,
7:10 the passover on the fourteenth day of the first **m,** A
8:6 in the fifth **m** (this was the king's seventh year);
8:6 on the new moon of the first **m** and arrived A
8:6 in Jerusalem on the new moon of the fifth **m,**
8:61 river Theras on the twelfth day of the first **m;** A
9:5 was the ninth **m,** on the twentieth day of the **m.**
9:16 tenth **m** they began their sessions to investigate
9:17 to an end by the new moon of the first **m.** A
9:37 On the new moon of the seventh **m,** B
9:40 on the new moon of the seventh **m.** B
2Es 16:38 in the ninth **m** when the time of her delivery draws

MONTHLY (1) [MONTH]

2Mc 6:7 On the **m** celebration of the king's birthday,

MONTHS‡ (71) [MONTH]

A. THREE MONTHS (20)

Ge 38:24 About three **m** later Judah was told, A
Ex 2:2 that he was a fine baby, she hid him three **m.** A
12:2 This month shall mark for you the beginning of **m;**
Nu 10:10 and at the beginnings of your **m,**
28:11 of your **m** you shall offer a burnt offering to
28:14 the burnt offering of every month throughout the **m**
Dt 33:14 and the rich yield of the **m;**
Jdg 11:37 Grant me two **m,** so that I may go and wander on
11:38 "Go," he said and sent her away for two **m.**
11:39 At the end of two **m,** she returned to her father,
19:2 and was there some four **m.**
20:47 and remained at the rock of Rimmon for four **m.**
1Sa 6:1 in the country of the Philistines seven **m.**
27:7 of the Philistines was one year and four **m.**
2Sa 2:11 the house of Judah was seven years and six **m.**
5:5 over Judah seven years and six **m;**
6:11 in the house of Obed-edom the Gittite three **m;** A
24:8 to Jerusalem at the end of nine **m** and twenty days.
24:13 Or will you flee three **m** before your foes A
1Ki 5:14 they would be a month in the Lebanon and two **m**
11:16 (for Joab and all Israel remained there six **m,**
2Ki 15:8 of Jeroboam reigned over Israel in Samaria six **m.**
23:31 he reigned three **m** in Jerusalem. A
24:8 he reigned three **m** in Jerusalem. A
1Ch 3:4 where he reigned for seven years and six **m.**
13:14 household of Obed-edom in his house three **m,** A
21:12 or three **m** of devastation by your foes, A
2Ch 36:2 he reigned three **m** in Jerusalem. A
36:9 he reigned three **m** and ten days in Jerusalem. A
Est 2:12 after being twelve **m** under the regulations for
2:12 six **m** with oil of myrrh and six months
2:12 of myrrh and six **m** with perfumes and cosmetics
Job 3:6 let it not come into the number of the **m.**
7:3 so I am allotted **m** of emptiness,
14:5 and the number of their **m** is known to you,
21:21 when the number of their **m** is cut off?
29:2 that I were as in the **m** of old,
39:2 Can you number the **m** that they fulfill,
Eze 39:12 Seven **m** the house of Israel
39:14 for seven **m** they shall make their search.
Da 4:29 At the end of twelve **m** he was walking on the roof
Am 4:7 the rain from you when there were still three **m** A
Lk 1:24 and for five **m** she remained in seclusion.
1:56 And Mary remained with her about three **m** and A
4:25 the heaven was shut up three years and six **m,**
Jn 4:35 Do you not say, 'Four **m** more,
Ac 7:20 three **m** he was brought up in his father's house; A
18:11 He stayed there a year and six **m,**
19:8 the synagogue and for three **m** spoke out boldly, A
20:3 where he stayed for three **m.** A
28:11 Three **m** later we set sail on a ship A
Gal 4:10 You are observing special days, and **m,**
Heb 11:23 for three **m** after his birth, because they saw A
Jas 5:17 three years and six **m** it did not rain on the earth.
Rev 9:5 They were allowed to torture them for five **m,**
9:10 to harm people for five **m.**
11:2 over the holy city for forty-two **m.**
13:5 to exercise authority for forty-two **m.**
Jdt 8:4 as a widow for three years and four **m**
16:20 For three **m** the people continued feasting A
AdE 2:12 a girl was to go to the king was twelve **m.**
2:12 six **m** while they are anointing themselves with oil
2:12 and six **m** with spices and ointments for women.
3:7 taking the days and the **m** one by one,
Wis 7:2 within the period of ten **m,**
2Mc 7:27 I carried you nine **m** in my womb,
1Es 1:35 He reigned three **m** in Judah and Jerusalem. A
1:44 he reigned three **m** and ten days in Jerusalem. A
2Es 4:40 when her nine **m** have been completed,
6:21 to premature children at three and four **m,**
8:8 and for nine **m** the womb endures your creature

MONTHS' (1) [MONTH]

Jn 6:7 "Six **m** wages would not buy enough bread

MONUMENT (9)

1Sa 15:12 where he set up a **m** for himself,
2Sa 8:3 as he went to restore his **m** at the river Euphrates.
18:18 It is called Absalom's **M** to this day.
2Ki 23:17 Then he said, "What is that **m** that I see?"
1Ch 18:3 as he went to set up a **m** at the river Euphrates.
Isa 56:5 a **m** and a name better than sons and daughters;
Wis 10:7 not ripen, and a pillar of salt standing as a **m** to
1Mc 13:27 And Simon built a **m** over the tomb of his father
2Mc 15:6 and arrogance had determined to erect a public **m**

MOOD (1)

Ru 3:7 had eaten and drunk, and he was in a contented **m,**

MOON‡ (82) [MOONS]

A. NEW MOON (28)

Ge 37:9 the **m,** and eleven stars were bowing down to me."
Ex 19:1 The third new **m** after the Israelites had gone out A
Nu 29:6 in addition to the burnt offering of the new **m** A
Dt 4:19 you look up to the heavens and see the sun, the **m,**
17:3 the sun or the **m** or any of the host of heaven,
Jos 10:12 "Sun, stand still at Gibeon, and **M,**
10:13 And the sun stood still, and the **m** stopped,
1Sa 20:5 said to Jonathan, "Tomorrow is the new **m,** A
20:18 Jonathan said to him, "Tomorrow is the new **m;** A
20:24 the new **m** came, the king sat at the feast to eat. A
20:27 But on the second day, the day after the new **m,** A
2Ki 4:23 It is neither new **m** nor sabbath." A
23:5 to the sun, the **m,** the constellations,
Ezr 3:5 at the new **m** and at all the sacred festivals of A
Job 25:5 even the **m** is not bright and the stars are not pure
26:9 He covers the face of the full **m,**
31:26 or the **m** moving in splendor,
Ps 8:3 the **m** and the stars that you have established;
72:5 and as long as the **m,** throughout all generations.
72:7 until the **m** is no more.
81:3 Blow the trumpet at the new **m,** at the full moon, A
81:3 Blow the trumpet at the new moon, at the full **m,**
89:37 It shall be established forever like the **m,**
104:19 You have made the **m** to mark the seasons;
121:6 sun shall not strike you by day, nor the **m** by night.
136:9 the **m** and stars to rule over the night,
148:3 sun and **m;** praise him, all you shining stars!
Pr 7:20 he will not come home until full **m.**"
Ecc 12:2 the light and the **m** and the stars are darkened and
SS 6:10 fair as the **m,** bright as the sun,
Isa 1:13 New **m** and sabbath and calling of convocation A
13:10 and the **m** will not shed its light.
24:23 Then the **m** will be abashed, and the sun ashamed;
30:26 the light of the **m** will be like the light of the sun,
47:13 and at each new **m** predict what shall befall you. A
60:19 brightness shall the **m** give light to you by night;
60:20 or your **m** withdraw itself;
66:23 From new **m** to new moon, A
66:23 From new moon to new **m,** A
Jer 8:2 be spread before the sun and the **m** and all the host
31:35 the **m** and the stars for light by night, who stirs up
Eze 32:7 and the **m** shall not give its light.
46:1 and on the day of the new **m** it shall be opened. A
46:6 the day of the new **m** he shall offer a young bull A
Hos 5:7 new **m** shall devour them along with their fields. A
Joel 2:10 The sun and the **m** are darkened,
2:31 sun shall be turned to darkness, and the **m** to blood,
3:15 The sun and the **m** are darkened,
Am 8:5 the new **m** be over so that we may sell grain; A
Hab 3:11 the **m** stood still in its exalted place,
Mt 24:29 and the **m** will not give its light;
Mk 13:24 and the **m** will not give its light,
Lk 21:25 "There will be signs in the sun, the **m,**
Ac 2:20 sun shall be turned to darkness and the **m** to blood,
1Co 15:41 and another glory of the **m,**
Rev 6:12 the full **m** became like blood,
8:12 and a third of the **m,** and a third of the stars,
12:1 a woman clothed with the sun, with the **m**
21:23 And the city has no need of sun or **m** to shine on it,
Jdt 8:6 before the new **m** and the day of the new moon, A
8:6 before the new moon and the day of the new **m,** A
Sir 27:11 but the fool changes like the **m.**
39:12 I am full like the full **m.**
43:6 It is the **m** that marks the changing seasons,
43:7 From the **m** comes the sign for festal days,
43:8 The new **m,** as its name suggests, renews itself; A
50:6 like the full **m** at the festal season;
LtJ 6:60 For sun and **m** and stars are bright,
6:67 or shine like the sun or give light like the **m.**
Aza 1:40 Bless the Lord, sun and **m;**
1Es 5:53 from the new **m** of the seventh month, A
5:57 foundation of the temple of God on the new **m** A
8:6 on the new **m** of the first month and arrived A
8:6 in Jerusalem on the new **m** of the fifth month, A
9:16 and on the new **m** of the tenth month A
9:17 to an end by the new **m** of the first month. A
9:37 On the new **m** of the seventh month, A
9:40 on the new **m** of the seventh month. A
2Es 5:4 to shine at night, and the **m** during the day.
6:45 the light of the **m,** and the arrangement of the stars
7:39 a day that has no sun or **m** or stars,
4Mc 17:5 The **m** in heaven, with the stars,

MOONS (13) [MOON]

1Ch 23:31 new **m,** and appointed festivals,
2Ch 2: 4 and the new **m** and the appointed festivals of
8:13 the new **m,** and the three annual festivals—
31: 3 the new **m,** and the appointed festivals,
Ne 10:33 the regular burnt offering, the sabbaths, the new **m,**
Isa 1:14 new **m** and your appointed festivals my soul hates;
Eze 45:17 and drink offerings, at the festivals, the new **m,**
46: 3 the LORD on the sabbaths and on the new **m.**
Hos 2:11 her festivals, her new **m,** her sabbaths,
Col 2:16 of food and drink or of observing festivals, new **m,**
1Mc 10:34 and new **m** and appointed days, and the three days
1Es 5:52 and sacrifices on sabbaths and at new **m** and at all
2Es 1:31 for I have rejected your festal days, and new **m,**

MOONSTONE (3) [STONE]

Ex 28:18 the second row a turquoise, a sapphire and a **m;**
39:11 a turquoise, a sapphire, and a **m;**
Eze 28:13 and **m,** beryl, onyx, and jasper, sapphire, turquoise,

MOORED (1)

Mk 6:53 they came to land at Gennesaret and **m** the boat.

MOOSSIAS (1)

1Es 9:31 Of the descendants of Addi: Naathus and **M,**

MORALE (2)

Col 2: 5 to see your **m** and the firmness of your faith
3Mc 1: 7 he strengthened the **m** of his subjects.

MORALS (1)

1Co 15:33 Do not be deceived: "Bad company ruins good **m.**"

MORASTHITE (KJV) See MORESHETH

MORBID (1)

1Ti 6: 4 a **m** craving for controversy and for disputes

MORDECAI‡ (118) [MORDECAI'S]

Ezr 2: 2 Nehemiah, Seraiah, Reelaiah, **M,** Bilshan, Mispar,
Ne 7: 7 **M,** Bilshan, Mispereth, Bigvai, Nehum, Baanah.
Est 2: 5 in the citadel of Susa whose name was **M** son
2: 7 **M** had brought up Hadassah, that is Esther,
2: 7 **M** adopted her as his own daughter.
2:10 for **M** had charged her not to tell.
2:11 Every day **M** would walk around in front of
2:15 for Esther daughter of Abihail the uncle of **M,**
2:19 **M** was sitting at the king's gate.
2:20 or her people, as **M** had charged her;
2:20 for Esther obeyed **M** just as when she was brought
2:21 while **M** was sitting at the king's gate,
2:22 But the matter came to the knowledge of **M,**
2:22 and Esther told the king in the name of **M.**
3: 2 But **M** did not bow down or do obeisance.
3: 3 at the king's gate said to **M,**
3: 5 that **M** did not bow down or do obeisance to him,
3: 6 he thought it beneath him to lay hands on **M** alone.
3: 6 the people of **M,** throughout the whole kingdom
4: 1 When **M** learned all that had been done,
4: 1 **M** tore his clothes and put on sackcloth and ashes,
4: 4 she sent garments to clothe **M,**
4: 5 to go to **M** to learn what was happening and why.
4: 6 to **M** in the open square of the city in front of
4: 7 and **M** told him all that had happened to him,
4: 8 **M** also gave him a copy of
4: 9 Hathach went and told Esther what **M** had said.
4:10 to Hathach and gave him a message for **M,**
4:12 When they told **M** what Esther had said,
4:13 **M** told them to reply to Esther,
4:15 Then Esther said in reply to **M,**
4:17 **M** then went away and did everything
5: 9 But when Haman saw **M** in the king's gate,
5: 9 he was infuriated with **M;**
5:13 as I see the Jew **M** sitting at the king's gate."
5:14 and in the morning tell the king to have **M** hanged
6: 2 how **M** had told about Bigthana and Teresh,
6: 3 or distinction has been bestowed on **M** for this?"
6: 4 to the king about having **M** hanged on the gallows
6:10 and do so to the Jew **M** who sits at the king's gate.
6:11 the horse and robed **M** and led him riding through
6:12 Then **M** returned to the king's gate,
6:13 "If **M,** before whom your downfall has begun,
7: 9 the very gallows that Haman has prepared for **M,**
7:10 on the gallows that he had prepared for **M.**
8: 1 and **M** came before the king,
8: 2 which he had taken from Haman, and gave it to **M.**
8: 2 So Esther set **M** over the house of Haman.
8: 7 to Queen Esther and to the Jew **M,**
8: 9 according to all that **M** commanded,
8:15 Then **M** went out from the presence of the king,
9: 3 because the fear of **M** had fallen upon them.
9: 4 For **M** was powerful in the king's house,
9: 4 as the man **M** grew more and more powerful.
9:20 **M** recorded these things, and sent letters to all
9:23 as **M** had written to them.
9:29 along with the Jew **M,** gave full written authority,
9:31 the Jew **M** and Queen Esther enjoined on the Jews,
10: 2 and the full account of the high honor of **M,**
10: 3 **M** the Jew was next in rank to King Ahasuerus,
AdE 2: 5 a Jew in Susa the capital whose name was **M** son
2:10 for **M** had commanded her not to make it known.
2:11 every day **M** walked in the courtyard of the harem,
AdE 2:19 Meanwhile **M** was serving in the courtyard.
2:20 such were the instructions of **M;**
2:22 The matter became known to **M,**
2:23 in praise of the goodwill shown by **M.**
3: 2 **M,** however, did not do obeisance.
3: 3 Then the king's courtiers said to **M,** "**M,**
3: 4 Then they informed Haman that **M** was resisting
3: 4 **M** had told them that he was a Jew.
3: 5 that **M** was not doing obeisance to him,
3: 7 to fix on one day to destroy the whole race of **M.**
4: 1 When **M** learned of all that had been done,
4: 4 and sent some clothes to **M** to put on instead
4: 5 to get accurate information for her from **M.**
4: 7 So **M** told him what had happened and
4:10 And she said to him, "Go to **M** and say,
4:12 Hachratheus delivered her entire message to **M,**
4:13 **M** told him to go back and say to her,
4:15 the messenger this answer to take back to **M:**
4:17 So **M** went away and did what Esther had told him
5: 9 But when he saw **M** the Jew in the courtyard,
5:13 as long as I see **M** the Jew in the courtyard."
5:14 and in the morning tell the king to have **M** hanged
6: 2 He found the words written about **M,**
6: 3 "What honor or dignity did we bestow on **M?**"
6: 4 about the goodwill shown by **M,**
6: 4 to the king about hanging **M** on the gallows
6:10 Do just as you have said for **M** the Jew,
6:11 on **M** and made him ride through the open square
6:12 Then **M** returned to the courtyard,
6:13 "If **M** is of the Jewish people,
7: 9 "Look, Haman has even prepared a gallows for **M,**
7:10 on the gallows he had prepared for **M.**
8: 1 **M** was summoned by the king,
8: 2 from Haman, and gave it to **M;**
8: 2 and Esther set **M** over everything
8:15 **M** went out dressed in the royal robe and wearing
9: 3 because fear of **M** weighed upon them.
9:20 **M** recorded these things in a book,
9:23 So the Jews accepted what **M** had written to them
9:25 how he went in to the king, telling him to hang **M;**
9:26 **M** established this festival,
9:29 with **M** the Jew wrote down what they had done,
9:31 And **M** and Queen Esther established this decision
10: 3 **M** acted with authority on behalf
10: 4 And **M** said, "These things have come from God;
11: 2 **M** son of Jair son of Shimei son of Kish,
11:12 **M** saw in this dream what God had determined
12: 1 Now **M** took his rest in the courtyard with Gabatha
12: 4 and **M** wrote an account of them.
12: 5 And the king ordered **M** to serve in the court,
12: 6 determined to injure **M** and his people because of
13: 8 Then **M** prayed to the Lord,
16:13 and deceit asked for the destruction of **M,**
1Es 5: 8 Resaiah, Eneneus, **M,** Beelsarus, Aspharasus,

MORDECAI'S (6) [MORDECAI]

Est 3: 4 in order to see whether **M** words would avail;
3: 6 So, having been told who **M** people were,
AdE 2:15 the brother of **M** father, to go in to the king,
2:21 were angry because of **M** advancement,
9: 4 The king's decree required that **M** name be held
2Mc 15:36 in the Aramaic language—the day before **M** day.

MORE‡ (744) [MOST]

Ge 3: 1 serpent was **m** crafty than any other wild animal
5:24 then he was no **m,** because God took him.
8:12 and it did not return to him any **m.**
18:32 not let the Lord be angry if I speak just once **m.**
26:13 prospered **m** and **m** until he became very wealthy.
29:30 and he loved Rachel **m** than Leah.
37: 3 Now Israel loved Joseph **m** than any other
37: 4 that their father loved him **m** than all his brothers,
37: 5 to his brothers, they hated him even **m.**
37: 8 So they hated him even **m** because of his dreams
38:26 "She is **m** in the right than I,
42:13 however, is now with our father, and one is no **m.**"
42:32 one is no **m,** and the youngest is now
42:36 Joseph is no **m,** and Simeon is no **m,**
43: 2 "Go again, buy us a little **m** food."
44:23 you shall see my face no **m.**'
45: 6 and there are five **m** years in which there will
45:11 since there are five **m** years of famine to come—
48:22 to you one portion **m** than to your brothers,
Ex 1: 9 the Israelite people are **m** numerous and **m** powerful than we.
1:12 But the **m** they were oppressed, the **m** they multiplied and spread,
5: 5 "Now they are **m** numerous than the people of
9:29 the thunder will cease, and there will be no **m** hail,
9:34 he sinned once **m** and hardened his heart,
11: 1 "I will bring one **m** plague upon Pharaoh and
16:17 The Israelites did so, some gathering **m,** some less.
30:15 The rich shall not give **m,**
36: 5 "The people are bringing much **m** than enough
36: 7 what they had already brought was **m** than enough
Lev 13: 5 then the priest shall confine him seven days **m.**
13:33 the person with the itch for seven days **m.**
13:54 and he shall put it aside seven days **m.**
25:16 If the years are **m,** you shall increase the price,
26:13 to be their slaves no **m;**
Nu 8:25 from the duty of the service and serve no **m.**
12: 3 **m** so than anyone else on the face of the earth.
14: 9 for they are no **m** than bread for us;
22:15 **m** numerous and **m** distinguished than these.
22:18 of the LORD my God, to do less or **m.**
22:19 I may learn what **m** the LORD may say to me."
Dt 1:11 increase you a thousand times **m** and bless you,
5:22 and the thick darkness, and he added no **m.**
7: 1 and **m** numerous than you—
7: 7 you were **m** numerous than any other people
7:17 "These nations are **m** numerous than I;
9:14 a nation mightier and **m** numerous than they."
17:16 the people to Egypt in order to acquire **m** horses,
18:16 "If I hear the voice of the LORD my God any **m,**
19: 9 then you shall add three **m** cities to these three,
25: 3 Forty lashes may be given but not **m;**
25: 3 if **m** lashes than these are given,
30: 5 he will make you **m** prosperous
31:27 how much **m** after my death!
Jos 7:12 I will be with you no **m,**
10:11 there were **m** who died because of
22:33 and the Israelites blessed God and spoke no **m**
Jdg 6:39 let me speak one **m** time;
6:39 please, make trial with the fleece just once **m;**
8:28 and they lifted up their heads no **m.**
10:13 therefore I will deliver you no **m.**
16:30 at his death were **m** than those he had killed
19:19 with us. We need nothing **m.**"
20:28 "Shall we go out once **m** to battle
Ru 1:13 it has been far **m** bitter for me than for you,
1:17 and **m** as well, if even death parts me from you!"
1:18 she said no **m** to her.
3:12 there is another kinsman **m** closely related than I.
4:15 who is **m** to you than seven sons, has borne him."
1Sa 1: 8 Am I not **m** to you than ten sons?"
2: 3 Talk no **m** so very proudly,
2:29 and honor your sons **m** than me
3:17 May God do so to you and **m** also,
9: 2 among the people of Israel **m** handsome than he;
14:19 the camp of the Philistines increased **m** and **m;**
14:44 Saul said, "God do so to me and **m** also;
18: 8 what **m** can he have but the kingdom?"
18:29 Saul was still **m** afraid of David.
18:30 David had **m** success than all the servants of Saul,
20:13 the LORD do so to Jonathan, and **m** also,
20:41 with each other; David wept the **m.**
21: 5 how much **m** today will their vessels be holy?"
23: 3 how much **m** then if we go to Keilah against
23:22 Go and make sure once **m;**
24:17 He said to David, "You are **m** righteous than I;
25:22 God do so to David and **m** also,
28:15 from me and answers me no **m,** either by prophets
30: 4 until they had no **m** strength to weep.
2Sa 1:21 the shield of Saul, anointed with oil no **m.**
3:35 saying, "So may God do to me, and **m,**
4:11 How much **m** then, when wicked men have killed
5:13 David took **m** concubines and wives;
5:13 and **m** sons and daughters were born to David.
6:22 I will make myself yet **m** contemptible than this,
7:10 in their own place, and be disturbed no **m;**
7:10 and evildoers shall afflict them no **m,** as formerly,
7:20 And what **m** can David say to you?
10:19 to help the Ammonites any **m.**
12: 8 had been too little, I would have added as much **m.**
14:11 so that the avenger of blood may kill no **m,**
16:11 how much **m** now may this Benjaminite!
18: 8 forest claimed **m** victims that day than the sword.
19:13 So may God do to me, and **m,**
19:29 "Why speak any **m** of your affairs?
19:43 and in David also we have **m** than you.
20: 6 of Bichri will do us **m** harm than Absalom;
1Ki 1:47 the name of Solomon **m** famous than yours,
2:23 "So may God do to me, and **m** also,
2:32 and killed with the sword two men **m** righteous
10: 5 there was no **m** spirit in her.
14:22 **m** than all that their ancestors had done.
16:25 he did **m** evil than all who were before him.
16:30 of the LORD **m** than all who were before him.
16:33 Ahab did **m** to provoke the anger of the LORD,
19: 2 saying, "So may the gods do to me, and **m** also,
20:10 "The gods do so to me, and **m** also,
2Ki 4: 6 But he said to her, "There are no **m.**"
5:13 How much **m,** when all he said to you was, 'Wash,
6:10 **M** than once or twice he warned such a place so
6:16 for there are **m** with us than there are with them."
6:31 "So may God do to me, and **m,**
9:35 they found no **m** of her than the skull and the feet
10:18 but Jehu will offer much **m.**
12: 7 Now therefore do not accept any **m** money
12: 8 that they would neither accept **m** money from
13: 7 an army of not **m** than fifty horsemen, ten chariots
21: 8 not cause the feet of Israel to wander any **m** out of
21: 9 to do **m** evil than the nations had done
21:11 has done things **m** wicked than all that
1Ch 4: 9 Jabez was honored **m** than his brothers;
14: 3 David took **m** wives in Jerusalem,
14: 3 David became the father of **m** sons and daughters.
17: 9 in their own place, and be disturbed no **m;**
17: 9 and evildoers shall wear them down no **m,**
17:18 And what **m** can David say to you
19:19 not willing to help the Ammonites any **m.**
22:14 To these you must add **m.**
24: 4 Since **m** chief men were found among the sons
2Ch 9: 4 there was no **m** spirit left in her.
11:21 of Absalom **m** than all his other wives
15:19 And there was no **m** war until the thirty-fifth year
20:25 for themselves until they could carry no **m.**
25: 9 LORD is able to give you much **m** than this."
28:22 the time of his distress he became yet **m** faithless
29:34 the Levites were **m** conscientious than the priests
32:16 His servants said still **m** against the Lord GOD
33: 9 so that they did **m** evil than the nations whom
33:23 but this Amon incurred **m** and **m** guilt.

Ne 5:12 “We will restore everything and demand nothing **m**
7: 2 a faithful man and feared God **m** than many.
13:18 Yet you bring **m** wrath on Israel by profaning
Est 2:17 the king loved Esther **m** than all the other women;
4:13 in the king’s palace you will escape any **m** than all
6: 6 “Whom would the king wish to honor **m** than me?”
9: 4 as the man Mordecai grew **m** and **m** powerful.
Job 3:21 and dig for it **m** than for hidden treasures;
4:19 how much **m** those who live in houses of clay,
7: 8 The eye that beholds me will see me no **m;**
7:10 they return no **m** to their houses,
7:10 nor do their places know them any **m.**
8:22 and the tent of the wicked will be no **m.”**
14:12 until the heavens are no **m,**
20: 9 The eye that saw them will see them no **m,**
27:19 They go to bed with wealth, but will do so no **m;**
32:15 “They are dismayed, they answer no **m;**
32:16 because they stand there, and answer no **m?**
34:19 nor regards the rich **m** than the poor,
34:31 I will not offend any **m;**
34:32 if I have done iniquity, I will do it no **m’?**
35:11 who teaches us **m** than the animals of the earth,
42:12 the latter days of Job **m** than his beginning;
Ps 4: 7 You have put gladness in my heart **m** than
10:18 so that those from earth may strike terror no **m.**
17:14 may their children have **m** than enough;
19:10 **M** to be desired are they than gold,
28: 5 he will break them down and build them up no **m.**
35:16 they impiously mocked **m** and **m,**
37:10 Yet a little while, and the wicked will be no **m;**
37:36 Again I passed by, and they were no **m;**
39:13 before I depart and am no **m.”**
40: 5 they would be **m** than can be counted.
40:12 they are **m** than the hairs of my head,
52: 3 You love evil **m** than good,
52: 3 and lying **m** than speaking the truth.
59:13 consume them until they are no **m.**
69: 4 **M** in number than the hairs
69:26 those whom you have wounded, they attack still **m.**
69:31 This will please the LORD **m** than an ox or a bull
71:14 and will praise you yet **m** and **m.**
72: 7 until the moon is no **m.**
76: 4 **m** majestic than the everlasting mountains.
78:17 Yet they sinned still **m** against him,
83: 4 let the name of Israel be remembered no **m.”**
87: 2 the gates of Zion **m** than all the dwellings of Jacob.
88: 5 like those whom you remember no **m,**
93: 4 **M** majestic than the thunders of mighty waters,
93: 4 **m** majestic than the waves of the sea,
103:16 and it is gone, and its place knows it no **m.**
104:35 and let the wicked be no **m.**
119:99 I have **m** understanding than all my teachers,
119:100 I understand **m** than the aged,
119:127 Truly I love your commandments **m** than gold, **m** than fine gold.
120: 3 what **m** shall be done to you, you deceitful tongue?
123: 3 for we have had **m** than enough of contempt.
123: 4 Our soul has had **m** than its fill of the scorn
130: 6 the Lord **m** than those who watch for the morning,
130: 6 **m** than those who watch for the morning.
139:18 I try to count them—they are **m** than the sand;
140:10 Let them be flung into pits, no **m** to rise!
Pr 3:15 She is **m** precious than jewels,
10:25 When the tempest passes, the wicked are no **m,**
11:31 how much **m** the wicked and the sinner!
12: 7 The wicked are overthrown and are no **m,**
15:11 how much **m** human hearts!
19: 7 how much **m** are they shunned by their friends!
21: 3 To do righteousness and justice is **m** acceptable to
21:27 how much **m** when brought with evil intent.
26:12 There is **m** hope for fools than for them.
28:23 will afterward find **m** favor than one who flatters
29:20 There is **m** hope for a fool than for anyone
31: 7 and remember their misery no **m.**
31:10 She is far **m** precious than jewels.
Ecc 1: 8 All things are wearisome; **m** than one can express;
2: 7 **m** than any who had been before me in Jerusalem.
4: 2 who have already died, **m** fortunate than the living,
6:11 The **m** words, the **m** vanity,
7:19 to the wise **m** than ten rulers that are in a city.
7:26 I found **m** bitter than death the woman who is
9: 5 they have no **m** reward, and even the memory
9:17 of the wise are **m** to be heeded than the shouting of
10:10 then **m** strength must be exerted;
SS 1: 4 we will extol your love **m** than wine;
5: 9 What is your beloved **m** than another beloved,
5: 9 What is your beloved **m** than another beloved,
Isa 1:12 Trample my courts no **m;**
2: 4 neither shall they learn war any **m.**
5: 4 What **m** was there to do for my vineyard
10:20 the survivors of the house of Jacob will no **m** lean
13:12 I will make mortals **m** rare than fine gold,
15: 6 the new growth fails, the verdure is no **m.**
15: 9 yet I will bring upon Dibon even **m—**
16: 4 When the oppressor is no **m,**
17:14 Before morning, they are no **m.**
19: 7 be driven away, and be no **m.**
23:10 this is a harbor no **m.**
25: 2 the palace of aliens is a city no **m,**
29:20 For the tyrant shall be no **m,**
30:11 let us hear no **m** about the Holy One of Israel.”
30:19 inhabitants of Jerusalem, you shall weep no **m.**
30:20 yet your Teacher will not hide himself any **m,**
32:10 In little **m** than a year you will shudder,
38:11 upon mortals no **m** among the inhabitants of
47: 1 For you shall no **m** be called tender and delicate.
47: 5 you shall no **m** be called the mistress of kingdoms.
Isa 51:22 you shall drink no **m** from the bowl of my wrath.
52: 1 and the unclean shall enter you no **m.**
54: 1 of the desolate woman will be **m** than the children
54: 4 of your widowhood you will remember no **m.**
60:18 Violence shall no **m** be heard in your land,
60:20 Your sun shall no **m** go down,
62: 4 You shall no **m** be termed Forsaken,
62: 4 and your land shall no **m** be termed Desolate;
65:19 no **m** shall the sound of weeping be heard in it,
65:20 No **m** shall there be in it an infant that lives but
Jer 2: 9 Therefore once **m** I accuse you, says the LORD,
2:31 “We are free, we will come to you no **m”?**
7:32 when it will no **m** be called Topheth,
7:32 they will bury in Topheth until there is no **m** room.
10:20 from me, and they are no **m;**
15: 8 Their widows became **m** numerous than the sand
19: 6 when this place shall no **m** be called Topheth,
19:11 In Topheth they shall bury until there is no **m** room
20: 9 or speak any **m** in his name,”
22:10 for he shall return no **m** to see his native land.
22:11 He shall return here no **m,**
23:14 of Jerusalem I have seen a **m** shocking thing:
23:36 burden of the LORD” you shall mention no **m,**
25:27 Drink, get drunk and vomit, fall and rise no **m,**
30: 8 and strangers shall no **m** make a servant of him.
31:15 for her children, because they are no **m.**
31:23 Once **m** they shall use these words in the land
31:34 and remember their sin no **m.**
33:10 or animal, there shall once **m** be heard
42:18 You shall see this place no **m.**
46:23 because they are **m** numerous than locusts;
48: 2 the renown of Moab is no **m.**
48:32 **M** than for Jazer I weep for you,
49:10 and his neighbors; and he is no **m.**
51:64 ‘Thus shall Babylon sink, to rise no **m,**
La 2: 9 among the nations; guidance is no **m,**
4: 7 their bodies were **m** ruddy than coral,
4:16 he will regard them no **m;**
5: 7 they are no **m,** and we bear their iniquities.
Eze 5: 6 becoming **m** wicked than the nations and
5: 7 Because you are **m** turbulent than the nations
5:16 and when I bring **m** and **m** famine upon you,
12:23 and they shall use it no **m** as a proverb in Israel.”
13:15 and I will say to you, The wall is no **m,**
14:11 nor defile themselves any **m**
14:21 How much **m** when I send
16:41 and you shall also make no **m** payments.
16:47 a very little time you were **m** corrupt than they
16:51 you have committed **m** abominations than they,
16:52 about for your sisters a **m** favorable judgment;
16:52 in which you acted **m** abominably than they,
16:52 they are **m** in the right than you.
18: 3 this proverb shall no **m** be used by you in Israel.
19: 9 be heard no **m** on the mountains of Israel.
20:39 but my holy name you shall no **m** profane
21:32 You shall be remembered no **m,**
23:11 yet she was **m** corrupt than she in her lusting and
23:27 or remember Egypt any **m.**
25:10 Thus Ammon shall be remembered no **m** among
26:13 the sound of your lyres shall be heard no **m.**
26:21 and you shall be no **m;**
27:36 to a dreadful end and shall be no **m** forever.”
28:19 to a dreadful end and shall be no **m** forever.
32:13 and no human foot shall trouble them any **m,**
34:28 They shall no **m** be plunder for the nations,
34:29 so that they shall no **m** be consumed with hunger
36:11 and will do **m** good to you than ever before.
39: 7 I will not let my holy name be profaned any **m;**
42: 5 for the galleries took **m** away from them than from
42: 6 the ground **m** than the lower and the middle ones.
43: 7 house of Israel shall no **m** defile my holy name,
Da 2:30 that I have **m** than any other living being,
3:19 up seven times **m** than was customary,
4:36 and still **m** greatness was added to me.
11: 2 Three **m** kings shall arise in Persia.
11:39 who acknowledge him he shall make **m** wealthy,
Hos 2:17 and they shall be mentioned by name no **m.**
4: 7 **m** they increased, the **m** they sinned against me;
4:18 they love lewdness **m** than their glory.
9:15 I will love them no **m;** all their officials are rebels.
10: 1 The **m** his fruit increased the **m** altars he built;
11: 2 The **m** I called them, the **m** they went from me;
14: 3 we will say no **m,** ‘Our God,’
Joel 2:19 will no **m** make you a mockery among the nations.
Am 5: 2 no **m** to rise, is maiden Israel;
Jnh 1:10 Then the men were even **m** afraid, and said to him,
1:11 For the sea was growing **m** and **m** tempestuous.
1:13 for the sea grew **m** and **m** stormy against them.
1:16 Then the men feared the LORD even **m,**
3: 4 And he cried out, “Forty days **m,**
4:11 in which there are **m** than a hundred
Mic 4: 3 neither shall they learn war any **m;**
5:12 and you shall have no **m** soothsayers;
5:13 and you shall bow down no **m** to the work
Na 1:12 I have afflicted you, I will afflict you no **m.**
2:13 the voice of your messengers shall be heard no **m.**
3:16 You increased your merchants **m** than the stars of
Hab 1: 8 **m** menacing than wolves at dusk;
1:13 the wicked swallow those **m** righteous than they?
Zep 3: 7 the **m** eager to make all their deeds corrupt.
3:15 you shall fear disaster no **m.**
Zec 11:15 Take once **m** the implements of
13: 2 so that they shall be remembered no **m;**
Mal 3:18 Then once **m** you shall see the difference between
Mt 2:18 she refused to be consoled, because they are no **m.**
3:11 one who is **m** powerful than I is coming after me;
5:37 anything **m** than this comes from the evil one.
Mt 5:47 what **m** are you doing than others?
6:25 is not life **m** than food, and the body **m** than clothing?
6:26 Are you not of **m** value than they?
6:30 will he not much **m** clothe you—
7:11 how much **m** will your Father
10:15 it will be **m** tolerable for the land of Sodom
10:25 much **m** will they malign those of his household!
10:31 you are of **m** value than many sparrows.
10:37 Whoever loves father or mother **m** than me is
10:37 and whoever loves son or daughter **m** than me is
11: 9 Yes, I tell you, and **m** than a prophet.
11:22 the day of judgment it will be **m** tolerable for Tyre
11:24 be **m** tolerable for the land of Sodom than for you.”
12:12 much **m** valuable is a human being than a sheep!
12:45 along seven other spirits **m** evil than itself,
13:12 For to those who have, **m** will be given,
18:13 he rejoices over it **m** than over the ninety-nine
20:10 the first came, they thought they would receive **m;**
20:31 but they shouted even **m** loudly,
21:36 Again he sent other slaves, **m** than the first;
22: 1 Once **m** Jesus spoke to them in parables, saying:
22:46 to ask him any **m** questions.
25:16 and traded with them, and made five **m** talents.
25:17 one who had the two talents made two **m** talents.
25:20 bringing five **m** talents, saying, ‘Master,
25:20 see, I have made five **m** talents.’
25:22 see, I have made two **m** talents.’
25:29 For to all those who have, **m** will be given,
26:53 and he will at once send me **m** than twelve legions
27:23 But they shouted all the **m,** “Let him be crucified!”
Mk 1: 7 one who is **m** powerful than I is coming after me;
4:24 and still **m** will be given you.
4:25 For to those who have, **m** will be given;
5: 3 and no one could restrain him any **m,**
7:36 but the **m** he ordered them, the **m** zealously they proclaimed it.
9: 8 they saw no one with them any **m,** but only Jesus.
10:48 but he cried out even **m** loudly, “Son of David,
12:33 much **m** important than all whole burnt offerings
12:43 in **m** than all those who are contributing to
14: 5 for **m** than three hundred denarii,
14:40 And once **m** he came and found them sleeping,
15:14 But they shouted all the **m,** “Crucify him!”
Lk 3:13 “Collect no **m** than the amount prescribed for you.”
3:16 but one who is **m** powerful than I is coming;
5:15 **m** than ever the word about Jesus spread abroad;
7:26 Yes, I tell you, and **m** than a prophet.
7:42 Now which of them will love him **m?”**
8:18 for to those who have, **m** will be given;
9:13 “We have no **m** than five loaves and two fish—
10:12 that day it will be **m** tolerable for Sodom than for
10:14 But at the judgment it will be **m** tolerable for Tyre
10:35 I will repay you whatever **m** you spend.’
11:13 how much **m** will the heavenly Father give
11:26 and brings seven other spirits **m** evil than itself,
12: 4 and after that can do nothing **m.**
12: 7 you are of **m** value than many sparrows.
12:23 life is **m** than food, and the body **m** than clothing.
12:24 Of how much **m** value are you than the birds!
12:28 how much **m** will he clothe you—
12:48 even **m** will be demanded.
13: 8 He replied, ‘Sir, let it alone for one **m** year,
14: 8 in case someone **m** distinguished than you has
15: 7 there will be **m** joy in heaven over one sinner who
16: 8 for the children of this age are **m** shrewd in dealing
18:30 who will not get back very much **m** in this age,
18:39 but he shouted even **m** loudly, “Son of David,
19:16 ‘Lord, your pound has made ten **m** pounds.’
19:26 ‘I tell you, to all those who have, **m** will be given;
21: 3 this poor widow has put in **m** than all of them;
22:44 ⟦In his anguish he prayed **m** earnestly,⟧
22:51 But Jesus said, “No **m** of this!”
Jn 4: 1 and baptizing **m** disciples than John”
4:35 Do you not say, ‘Four months **m,**
4:41 And many **m** believed because of his word.
5:14 Do not sin any **m,** so that nothing worse happens
5:18 For this reason the Jews were seeking all the **m**
7:31 will he do **m** signs than this man has done?”
12:43 for they loved human glory **m** than the glory
15: 2 that bears fruit he prunes to make it bear **m** fruit.
19: 8 when Pilate heard this, he was **m** afraid than ever.
21:15 do you love me **m** than these?”
Ac 4:17 let us warn them to speak no **m** to anyone
4:22 healing had been performed was **m** than forty
5:14 Yet **m** than ever believers were added to the Lord,
8:39 the eunuch saw him no **m,**
9:22 Saul became increasingly **m** powerful
13:34 no **m** to return to corruption,
17:11 These Jews were **m** receptive than those
18:26 the Way of God to him **m** accurately.
20:35 ‘It is **m** blessed to give than to receive.’ ”
21:28 **m** than that, he has actually brought Greeks into
22: 2 they became even **m** quiet.
23:13 There were **m** than forty who joined
23:15 that you want to make a **m** thorough examination
23:20 as though they were going to inquire **m** thoroughly
23:21 for **m** than forty of their men are lying in ambush
24:11 not **m** than twelve days since I went up to worship
25: 6 among them not **m** than eight or ten days, he went
27:11 But the centurion paid **m** attention to the pilot and
Ro 5: 9 Much **m** surely then, now that we have been
5:10 much **m** surely, having been reconciled,
5:11 But **m** than that, we even boast in God
5:15 much **m** surely have the grace of God and
5:17 much **m** surely will those who receive
5:20 but where sin increased, grace abounded all the **m,**

Ro 8:37 in all these things we are **m** than conquerors
11:12 how much **m** will their full inclusion mean!
11:24 how much **m** will these natural branches
12: 3 not to think of yourself **m** highly than you ought
1Co 7:21 of your present condition now **m** than ever.
7:40 in my judgment she is **m** blessed if she remains
9:12 on you, do not we still **m?**
9:19 so that I might win **m** of them.
12:24 whereas our **m** respectable members do
12:31 And I will show you a still **m** excellent way.
14: 5 like all of you to speak in tongues, but even **m**
14:18 I thank God that I speak in tongues **m** than all
15: 6 Then he appeared to **m** than five hundred brothers
15:34 Come to a sober and right mind, and sin no **m;**
2Co 1:12 and all the **m** toward you.
3: 8 how much **m** will the ministry of the Spirit come
3: 9 much **m** does the ministry of justification abound
3:11 much **m** has the permanent come in glory!
4:15 so that grace, as it extends to **m** and **m** people,
7: 7 your zeal for me, so that I rejoiced still **m.**
7:13 we rejoiced still **m** at the joy of Titus,
7:15 And his heart goes out all the **m** to you,
8:17 but since he is **m** eager than ever,
8:22 but who is now **m** eager than ever because
11:23 with far greater labors, far **m** imprisonments,
12: 9 So, I will boast all the **m** gladly of my weaknesses,
12:15 If I love you **m,** am I to be loved less?
Gal 1:14 for I was far **m** zealous for the traditions
3:20 Now a mediator involves **m** than one party;
4:27 of the desolate woman are **m** numerous than
Eph 3:20 to accomplish abundantly far **m** than all we can ask
Php 1: 9 that your love may overflow **m** and **m**
1:24 but to remain in the flesh is **m** necessary for you.
2:12 but much **m** now in my absence,
2:28 I am the **m** eager to send him, therefore,
3: 4 to be confident in the flesh, I have **m:**
3: 8 **M** than that, I regard everything as loss because of
4:16 you sent me help for my needs **m** than once.
4:18 I have been paid in full and have **m** than enough;
1Th 4: 1 you are doing), you should do so **m** and **m.**
4:10 But we urge you, beloved, to do so **m** and **m,**
1Ti 6: 2 rather they must serve them all the **m,**
2Ti 2:16 for it will lead people into **m** and **m** impiety,
Tit 3:10 a first and second admonition, have nothing **m**
Phm 1:16 as a slave but **m** than a slave, a beloved brother—
1:16 especially to me but how much **m** to you,
1:21 knowing that you will do even **m** than I say.
1:22 One thing **m**—prepare a guest room
Heb 1: 4 name he has inherited is **m** excellent than theirs.
3: 3 Yet Jesus is worthy of **m** glory than Moses,
3: 3 just as the builder of a house has **m** honor than
6:17 to show even **m** clearly to the heirs of the promise
7:15 It is even **m** obvious when another priest arises,
8: 6 But Jesus has now obtained a **m** excellent ministry,
8:12 and I will remember their sins no **m.**"
9:14 how much **m** will the blood of Christ,
10:17 and their lawless deeds no **m.**"
10:25 and all the **m** as you see the Day approaching.
10:34 possessed something better and **m** lasting.
11: 4 to God a **m** acceptable sacrifice than Cain's.
11:32 And what **m** should I say?
12: 9 even **m** willing to be subject to the Father of spirits
12:26 but now he has promised, "Yet once **m** I will shake
12:27 This phrase, "Yet once **m,**"
13:19 I urge you all the **m** to do this,
Jas 3:12 No **m** can salt water yield fresh.
4: 6 But he gives all the **m** grace;
1Pe 1: 7 being **m** precious than gold that, though perishable,
2Pe 1:10 the **m** eager to confirm your call and election,
1:19 we have the prophetic message **m** fully confirmed.
Rev 7:16 They will hunger no **m,** and thirst no more;
7:16 They will hunger no more, and thirst no **m;**
10: 6 "There will be no **m** delay,
18:21 and will be found no **m;**
18:22 and trumpeters will be heard in you no **m;**
18:22 an artisan of any trade will be found in you no **m;**
18:22 sound of the millstone will be heard in you no **m;**
18:23 and the light of a lamp will shine in you no **m;**
18:23 and bride will be heard in you no **m;**
19: 3 Once **m** they said, "Hallelujah!
20: 3 so that he would deceive the nations no **m,**
21: 1 and the sea was no **m.**
21: 4 from their eyes. Death will be no **m;**
21: 4 mourning and crying and pain will be no **m,**
22: 3 Nothing accursed will be found there any **m.**
22: 5 And there will be no **m** night;
Tob 2:10 but the **m** they treated me with ointments
2:10 the **m** my vision was obscured by the white films,
3:13 the earth and not listen to such reproaches any **m.**
5:10 Tobit retorted, "What joy is left for me any **m?**
5:21 to you in good health. Say no **m!**
6:16 brother, and say no **m** about this demon.
6:18 and will never be seen near her any **m.**
6:18 as brothers to you. Now say no **m!**"
7:10 But let me explain to you the true situation **m** fully,
12:21 Then they stood up, and could see him no **m.**
Jdt 7:30 Let us hold out for five days **m;**
12: 3 where can we get you **m** of the same?
12:20 much **m** than he had ever drunk in any one day
16:23 She became **m** and **m** famous,
AdE 6: 6 "Whom would the king wish to honor **m** than me?"
9:12 Whatever **m** you ask will be done for you."
16: 2 the **m** they are honored with the most generous
16: 2 the **m** proud do they become,
16: 7 much from the **m** ancient records that we hand on,
16: 9 before our eyes with **m** equitable consideration.
Wis 7:10 I loved her **m** than health and beauty,
Wis 7:24 For wisdom is **m** mobile than any motion;
7:29 She is **m** beautiful than the sun,
8: 6 who **m** than she is fashioner of what exists?
8: 7 in life is **m** profitable for mortals than these.
10:12 that godliness is **m** powerful than anything else.
12:22 you scourge our enemies ten thousand times **m,**
13: 4 from them how much **m** powerful is
14: 1 of wood **m** fragile than the ship that carries him.
14:19 the likeness to take **m** beautiful form,
15:13 For these persons, **m** than all others,
15:14 But most foolish, and **m** miserable than an infant,
16:19 the midst of water it burned **m** intensely than fire,
19:13 for they practiced a **m** bitter hatred of strangers.
Sir 3:18 greater you are, the **m** you must humble yourself;
3:23 **m** than you can understand has been shown you.
4:10 and he will love you **m** than does your mother.
7:19 for her charm is worth **m** than gold.
10:31 in poverty, how much **m** in wealth!
10:31 one dishonored in wealth, how much **m** in poverty!
11:11 but are so much the **m** in want.
13: 9 be reserved, and he will invite you **m** insistently.
13:17 No **m** has a sinner with the devout.
16: 5 and my ear has heard things **m** striking than these.
18:12 therefore he grants them forgiveness all the **m.**
21: 1 Do so no **m,** but ask forgiveness for your past sins.
24:21 Those who eat of me will hunger for **m,**
24:21 and those who drink of me will thirst for **m.**
24:29 For her thoughts are **m** abundant than the sea,
29:11 and it will profit you **m** than gold.
31:13 What has been created **m** greedy than the eye?
32: 7 if you are obliged to, but no **m** than twice,
33: 7 Why is one day **m** important than another,
34:12 and I understand **m** than I can express.
36:27 and there is nothing he desires **m.**
36:28 her husband is **m** fortunate than other men.
37:13 for no one is **m** faithful to you than it is.
39:12 I have **m** on my mind to express;
40: 8 human and animal, but to sinners seven times **m,**
40:22 but the green shoots of grain **m** than either.
40:25 but good counsel is esteemed **m** than either.
43:27 We could say **m** but could never say enough;
47:24 Their sins increased **m** and **m,**
48:16 but others sinned **m** and **m.**
LtJ 6:19 They light **m** lamps for them than they light
1Mc 3:30 to give **m** lavishly than preceding kings.
7:23 it was **m** than the Gentiles had done.
9: 6 until no **m** than eight hundred of them were left.
10:88 he honored Jonathan still **m;**
15:31 and five hundred talents **m** for the tribute money of
2Mc 2:32 let us begin our narrative, without adding any **m**
4: 9 to this he promised to pay one hundred fifty **m**
5:22 a Phrygian and in character **m** barbarous than
8: 8 he was pushing ahead with **m** frequent successes,
8:24 they killed **m** than nine thousand of the enemy,
8:30 and Bacchides they killed **m** than twenty thousand
9: 7 but was even **m** filled with arrogance,
9:28 having endured the **m** intense suffering,
10:19 for places where he was **m** urgently needed.
10:23 he destroyed **m** than twenty thousand in
12:10 When they had gone **m** than a mile from there,
12:19 in the stronghold, **m** than ten thousand men.
14:11 quickly inflamed Demetrius still **m.**
14:30 noticing that Nicanor was **m** austere in his dealings
14:30 meeting him **m** rudely than had been his custom,
14:39 sent **m** than five hundred soldiers to arrest him;
15: 9 he made them the **m** eager.
1Es 2:28 the city and to take care that nothing **m** be done
4:25 man loves his wife **m** than his father or his mother.
5:41 All those of Israel, twelve or **m** years of age,
5:58 or **m** years of age to have charge of the work of
Man 1: 9 the sins I have committed are **m** in number than
3Mc 1: 8 the **m** eager to visit them as soon as possible.
3: 1 but was still **m** bitterly hostile toward those in
3:10 and to exert **m** earnest efforts for their assistance.
5:17 of the banquet joyful by celebrating all the **m.**
5:38 the elephants now once **m** for the destruction of
7: 5 a cruelty **m** savage than that of Scythian custom,
7:15 to death **m** than three hundred men;
2Es 1:21 What **m** can I do for you?
2:43 but he was **m** exalted than they.
3:12 to be **m** ungodly than were their ancestors.
4:14 and so that we may make for ourselves **m** forests.'
4:15 the plain so that there also we may gain **m** territory
4:45 whether **m** time is to come than has passed,
4:50 for just as the rain is **m** than the drops,
5:22 and I began once **m** to speak words in the presence
5:32 pay attention to me, and I will tell you **m.**"
5:33 Or do you love him **m** than his Maker does?"
7:*49* and will admonish you once **m.**
7:*56* but silver is **m** abundant than gold,
7:*58* for what is **m** rare is **m** precious."
7:*59* the person who has what is hard to get rejoices **m**
7:*125* [55] those who practiced self-control shall shine **m**
7:*136* [66] because he makes his compassions abound **m**
7:*136* [66] and **m** to those now living and
8:47 of being able to love my creation **m** than I love it.
8:55 not ask any **m** questions about the great number
9:15 there are **m** who perish than those who will
9:23 "Now, if you will let seven days **m** pass—
10:11 Who then ought to mourn the **m,**
10:57 For you are **m** blessed than many,
11:27 and this disappeared **m** quickly than the first.
12:13 and it shall be **m** terrifying than all the kingdoms
12:24 its inhabitants **m** oppressively than all who were
12:39 But as for you, wait here seven days **m,**
13:16 And still **m,** alas for those who are not left!
13:24 are left are **m** blessed than those who have died.
2Es 13:41 of the nations and go to a **m** distant region,
13:56 that after three **m** days I will tell you other things,
14:17 the **m** shall evils be increased upon its inhabitants.
16:47 the **m** they adorn their cities,
16:48 the **m** angry I will be with them for their sins,
4Mc 2: 6 I could prove to you all the **m** that reason is able
2:15 that reason rules even the **m** violent emotions:
3: 6 Now this can be explained **m** clearly by the story
5:10 to me that you will do something even **m** senseless
5:16 no compulsion **m** powerful than our obedience
5:32 and fan the fire **m** vehemently!
6:16 as though **m** bitterly tormented by this counsel,
7:10 O aged man, **m** powerful than tortures;
8: 2 they would be tortured even **m** cruelly.
9: 3 for us do not pity us **m** than we pity ourselves.
9: 4 to be **m** grievous than death itself.
9: 6 it would be even **m** fitting
9:30 that you are being tortured **m** than I,
11: 3 from the heavenly justice for even **m** crimes.
13:23 brothers were the **m** sympathetic to one another.
13:24 they loved one another all the **m.**
13:26 they could make their brotherly love **m** fervent
14: 2 **m** royal than kings and freer than the free!
14:10 What could be **m** excruciatingly painful than this?
14:11 mind of woman despised even **m** diverse agonies,
15: 1 **m** desirable to the mother than her children!
15: 3 She loved religion **m,** the religion
15: 5 they are **m** devoted to their children.
15: 6 **m** than any other mother, loved her children.
15:16 tried now by **m** bitter pains than even
15:30 O **m** noble than males in steadfastness,
15:30 and **m** courageous than men in endurance!
16: 8 and the **m** grievous anxieties of your upbringing.
16:14 and deed you have proved **m** powerful than a man.
18:20 to the catapult and back again to **m** tortures,

MOREH (3)

Ge 12: 6 the land to the place at Shechem, to the oak of **M.**
Dt 11:30 opposite Gilgal, beside the oak of **M.**
Jdg 7: 1 below the hill of **M,** in the valley.

MOREOVER (98)

Ge 17:16 I will bless her, and **m** I will give you a son by her.
22:24 **M,** his concubine, whose name was Reumah,
32:18 and **m** he is behind us.'"
32:20 '**M** your servant Jacob is behind us.'"
38:22 not found her; **m** the townspeople said,
38:24 **m** she is pregnant as a result of whoredom."
41:44 **M** Pharaoh said to Joseph, "I am Pharaoh,
41:57 **M,** all the world came to Joseph in Egypt
43:22 **M** we have brought down with us
44: 9 **m** the rest of us will become my lord's slaves."
Ex 11: 3 **M,** Moses himself was a man of great importance
26: 1 **M** you shall make the tabernacle with ten curtains
31: 6 **M,** I have appointed with him Oholiab son
Lev 26:40 **m,** that they continued hostile to me—
Nu 8:19 **M,** I have given the Levites as a gift to Aaron
10:32 **M,** if you go with us, whatever good
15: 5 **M,** you shall offer one-fourth of a hin of wine as
35:31 **M** you shall accept no ransom for the life of
Dt 2:12 **M,** the Horim had formerly inhabited Seir,
7:20 **M,** the LORD your God will send the pestilence
30: 6 **M,** the LORD your God will circumcise your heart
Jos 2:24 **m** all the inhabitants of the land melt in fear
Jdg 2:10 **M,** that whole generation was gathered
1Sa 2:15 **M,** before the fat was burned,
12:23 **M** as for me, far be it from me that I should sin
15:29 **M** the Glory of Israel will not recant
28:19 **M** the LORD will give Israel along with you into
2Sa 7:11 **M** the LORD declares to you that
12:27 **m,** I have taken the water city.
15: 4 Absalom said **m,** "If only I were judge in the land!
16:19 **M,** whom should I serve?
17: 1 **M** Ahithophel said to Absalom,
1Ki 1:47 **M** the king's servants came
2: 5 "**M** you know also what Joab son of Zeruiah did
10:11 **M,** the fleet of Hiram, which carried gold
14:14 **M** the LORD will raise up for himself a king
16: 7 **M** the word of the LORD came by
2Ki 18:25 **M,** is it without the LORD that I have come up
21:16 **M** Manasseh shed very much innocent blood,
23:15 **M,** the altar at Bethel, the high place erected
23:19 **M,** Josiah removed all the shrines of
23:24 **M** Josiah put away the mediums, wizards,
1Ch 10:13 **m,** he had consulted a medium, seeking guidance,
17:10 **M** I declare to you that the LORD will build you
29: 3 **M,** in addition to all that I have provided for
2Ch 1: 5 **M** the bronze altar that Bezalel son of Uri,
9:10 **M** the servants of Huram and the servants
12:12 **m,** conditions were good in Judah.
19: 8 **M** in Jerusalem Jehoshaphat appointed certain
21:11 **M** he made high places in the hill country
26: 9 **M** Uzziah built towers in Jerusalem at
26:11 **M** Uzziah had an army of soldiers, fit for war,
27: 4 **M** he built cities in the hill country of Judah,
28:12 **M,** certain chiefs of the Ephraimites,
Ezr 4:22 **M,** take care not to be slack in this matter;
5:14 **M,** the gold and silver vessels of the house of God,
6: 5 **M,** let the gold and silver vessels of the house
6: 8 **M** I make a decree regarding what you shall do
Ne 5:10 **M** I and my brothers and my servants are lending
5:14 **M** from the time that I was appointed to
5:17 **M** there were at my table one hundred fifty people,
6:17 **M** in those days the nobles
9:12 **M,** you led them by day with a pillar of cloud,
Ps 19:11 **M** by them is your servant warned;

Ps 89:43 **M,** you have turned back the edge of his sword,
Ecc 3:11 **m** he has put a sense of past and future
3:13 **m,** it is God's gift that all should eat and drink
3:16 **M** I saw under the sun that in the place of justice,
6: 5 **m** it has not seen the sun or known anything;
9: 3 **M,** the hearts of all are full of evil;
Isa 30:26 **M** the light of the moon will be like the light of
36:10 **M,** is it without the LORD that I have come up
Jer 2:16 **M,** the people of Memphis
Eze 5:14 **M** I will make you a desolation and an object
20:12 **M** I gave them my sabbaths,
20:15 **M** I swore to them in the wilderness that I would
20:23 **M** I swore to them in the wilderness
20:25 **M** I gave them statutes that were not good
23:38 **M** this they have done to me:
28:11 **M** the word of the LORD came to me:
Hab 2: 5 **M,** wealth is treacherous; the arrogant do
Zec 4: 8 **M** the word of the LORD came to me, saying,
Lk 24:22 **M,** some women of our group astounded us.
Ac 2:26 **m** my flesh will live in hope.
1Co 4: 2 **M,** it is required of stewards that they
1Ti 3: 7 **M,** he must be well thought of by outsiders,
Heb 12: 9 **M,** we had human parents to discipline us,
Tob 6:12 **M,** the girl is sensible, brave, and very beautiful,
Wis 15:18 **M,** they worship even the most hateful animals,
1Mc 6:24 **m,** they have put to death as many of us
10:42 **M,** the five thousand shekels of silver
2Mc 6:23 and **m** according to the holy God-given law,
8:19 **M,** he told them of the occasions when help came
9:25 **M,** I understand how the princes along the borders
2Es 2:11 **M,** I will take back to myself their glory,
8:57 **M,** they have even trampled on his righteous ones,
11:32 **M** this head gained control of the whole earth,
14:42 **M,** the Most High gave understanding to

MORESHETH (2) [MORESHETH-GATH]

Jer 26:18 "Micah of **M,** who prophesied during the days
Mic 1: 1 of the LORD that came to Micah of **M** in the days

MORESHETH-GATH (1) [MORESHETH]

Mic 1:14 Therefore you shall give parting gifts to **M;**

MORIAH (2)

Ge 22: 2 whom you love, and go to the land of **M,**
2Ch 3: 1 of the LORD in Jerusalem on Mount **M,**

MORNING‡ (262) [MORNINGS]

A. IN THE MORNING (115)
B. UNTIL [THE] MORNING (31)
C. MORNING ... EVENING (16)
D. EVENING ... MORNING (12)
E. EVERY MORNING (12)

Ge 1: 5 was evening and there was **m,** the first day. D
1: 8 And there was evening and there was **m,** D
1:13 was evening and there was **m,** the third day. D
1:19 was evening and there was **m,** the fourth day. D
1:23 was evening and there was **m,** the fifth day. D
1:31 was evening and there was **m,** the sixth day. D
19:15 When **m** dawned, the angels urged Lot, saying,
19:27 in the **m** to the place where he had stood before A
20: 8 So Abimelech rose early in the **m,** A
21:14 So Abraham rose early in the **m,** A
22: 3 So Abraham rose early in the **m,** A
24:54 When they rose in the **m,** he said, A
26:31 In the **m** they rose early and exchanged oaths; A
28:18 So Jacob rose early in the **m,** A
29:25 When **m** came, it was Leah!
31:55 Early in the **m** Laban rose up, A
40: 6 When Joseph came to them in the **m,** A
41: 8 In the **m** his spirit was troubled; A
44: 3 As soon as the **m** was light,
49:27 in the **m** devouring the prey, A
Ex 7:15 Go to Pharaoh in the **m,** as he is going out to A
8:20 in the **m** and present yourself before Pharaoh, A
9:13 in the **m** and present yourself before Pharaoh, A
10:13 **m** came, the east wind had brought the locusts.
12:10 You shall let none of it remain until the **m;** B
12:10 anything that remains until the **m** you shall burn. B
12:22 the door of your house until **m.** B
14:24 At the **m** watch the LORD in the pillar of fire
16: 7 and in the **m** you shall see the glory of the LORD, A
16: 8 of bread in the **m,** because the LORD has heard A
16:12 and in the **m** you shall have your fill of bread; A
16:13 in the **m** there was a layer of dew around the A
16:19 "Let no one leave any of it over until **m.**" B
16:20 some left part of it until **m,** B
16:21 **M** by **m** they gathered it,
16:23 that is left over put aside to be kept until **m.'** " B
16:24 So they put it aside until **m,** B
18:13 people stood around him from **m** until evening. C
18:14 people stand around you from **m** until evening?" C
19:16 On the **m** of the third day there was thunder
23:18 or let the fat of my festival remain until the **m.** B
24: 4 He rose early in the **m,** A
27:21 and his sons shall tend it from evening to **m** D
29:34 or of the bread, remains until the **m,** B
29:39 One lamb you shall offer in the **m,** A
29:41 as in the **m,** for a pleasing odor, A
30: 7 every **m** when he dresses the lamps he shall E
34: 2 in the **m,** and come up in the morning to A
34: 2 in the **m** to Mount Sinai and present yourself A
34: 4 rose early in the **m** and went up on Mount Sinai, A
34:25 of the passover shall not be left until the **m.** B
36: 3 kept bringing him freewill offerings every **m,** E
Lev 6: 9 on the hearth upon the altar all night until the **m,** B
6:12 Every **m** the priest shall add wood to it, E
6:20 half of it in the **m** and half in the evening. AC
7:15 you shall not leave any of it until **m.** B
9:17 in addition to the burnt offering of the **m.**
19:13 for yourself the wages of a laborer until **m.** B
22:30 you shall not leave any of it until **m:** B
24: 3 from evening to **m** before the LORD regularly; D
Nu 9:12 They shall leave none of it until **m,** B
9:15 evening until **m** it was over the tabernacle, BD
9:21 the cloud would remain from evening until **m;** BD
9:21 and when the cloud lifted in the **m,** A
14:40 rose early in the **m** and went up to the heights A
16: 5 In the **m** the LORD will make known who is his, A
22:13 So Balaam rose in the **m,** A
22:21 So Balaam got up in the **m,** saddled his donkey, A
28: 4 One lamb you shall offer in the **m,** A
28: 8 and a drink offering like the one in the **m;** A
28:23 in addition to the burnt offering of the **m,**
Dt 16: 4 the evening of the first day shall remain until **m.** B
16: 7 the next **m** you may go back to your tents.
28:67 In the **m** you shall say, "If only it were evening!" A
28:67 at evening you shall say, "If only it were **m!**"—
Jos 3: 1 Early in the **m** Joshua rose and set out from A
6:12 Then Joshua rose early in the **m,** A
7:14 In the **m** therefore you shall come forward tribe A
7:16 So Joshua rose early in the **m,** A
8:10 In the **m** Joshua rose early and mustered A
8:14 in the **m** to the meeting place facing the Arabah A
Jdg 6:28 When the townspeople rose early in the **m,** A
6:31 for him shall be put to death by **m.**
6:38 he rose early next **m** and squeezed the fleece,
9:33 Then early in the **m,** as soon as the sun rises, A
16: 2 thinking, "Let us wait until the light of the **m;**
19: 5 On the fourth day they got up early in the **m,** A
19: 8 the fifth day he got up early in the **m** to leave; A
19: 9 Tomorrow you can get up early in the **m** A
19:25 abused her all through the night until the **m.** B
19:26 As **m** appeared, the woman came and fell down
19:27 In the **m** her master got up, A
20:19 Then the Israelites got up in the **m,** A
Ru 2: 7 she has been on her feet from early this **m** until
3:13 Remain this night, and in the **m,** A
3:13 Lie down until the **m."** B
3:14 So she lay at his feet until **m,** B
1Sa 1:19 They rose early in the **m** and worshiped before A
3:15 Samuel lay there until **m;** B
5: 4 But when they rose early on the next **m,**
9:19 and in the **m** I will let you go and will tell you A
11:11 the **m** watch they came into the camp and
14:36 by night and despoil them until the **m** light; B
15:12 Samuel rose early in the **m** to meet Saul, A
17:16 and took his stand, **m** and evening. C
17:20 David rose early in the **m,** A
19: 2 therefore be on guard tomorrow **m;**
19:11 planning to kill him in the **m.** A
20:35 In the **m** Jonathan went out into the field to A
25:22 if by **m** I leave so much as one male
25:34 truly by **m** there would not have been left to Nabal
25:36 so she told him nothing at all until the **m** light. B
25:37 In the **m,** when the wine had gone out of Nabal, A
29:10 Now then rise early in the **m,** A
29:10 Start early in the **m,** and leave as soon A
29:11 So David set out with his men early in the **m,** A
2Sa 2:27 to pursue their kinsmen, not stopping until **m."** B
11:14 In the **m** David wrote a letter to Joab, A
13: 4 why are you so haggard **m** after **m?**
23: 4 is like the light of **m,** like the sun rising
23: 4 like the sun rising on a cloudless **m,**
24:11 When David rose in the **m,** A
24:15 the LORD sent a pestilence on Israel from that **m**
1Ki 3:21 When I rose in the **m** to nurse my son, A
3:21 but when I looked at him closely in the **m,** A
17: 6 ravens brought him bread and meat in the **m,** A
18:26 and called on the name of Baal from **m** until noon,
2Ki 3:20 The next day, about the time of the **m** offering,
3:22 When they rose early in the **m,** A
6:15 attendant of the man of God rose early in the **m** A
7: 9 if we are silent and wait until the **m** light, B
10: 8 heaps at the entrance of the gate until the **m."** B
10: 9 Then in the **m** when he went out, A
16:15 "Upon the great altar offer the **m** burnt offering,
19:35 when **m** dawned, they were all dead bodies.
1Ch 9:27 and they had charge of opening it every **m.** E
16:40 **m** and evening, according to all that is written C
23:30 And they shall stand every **m,** E
2Ch 2: 4 and for burnt offerings **m** and evening, C
13:11 offer to the LORD every **m** and every evening CE
20:20 in the **m** and went out into the wilderness A
31: 3 the burnt offerings of **m** and evening, C
Ezr 3: 3 upon it to the LORD, **m** and evening. C
Ne 8: 3 before the Water Gate from early **m** until midday,
Est 2:14 in the **m** she came back to the second harem A
5:14 in the **m** tell the king to have Mordecai hanged A
Job 1: 5 in the **m** and offer burnt offerings according to A
3: 9 may it not see the eyelids of the **m**—
4:20 Between **m** and evening they are destroyed; C
7:18 visit them every **m,** test them every moment? E
11:17 its darkness will be like the **m.**
24:17 For deep darkness is **m** to all of them;
38: 7 when the **m** stars sang together and all
38:12 "Have you commanded the **m** since your days
Ps 5: 3 O LORD, in the **m** you hear my voice; A
5: 3 in the **m** I plead my case to you, and watch. A
30: 5 but joy comes with the **m.**
46: 5 God will help it when the **m** dawns.
55:17 Evening and **m** and at noon I utter my complaint D
Ps 59:16 I will sing aloud of your steadfast love in the **m.** A
65: 8 the gateways of the **m** and the evening shout C
73:14 and am punished every **m.** E
88:13 in the **m** my prayer comes before you. A
90: 5 like grass that is renewed in the **m;** A
90: 6 in the **m** it flourishes and is renewed; A
90:14 Satisfy us in the **m** with your steadfast love, A
92: 2 to declare your steadfast love in the **m,** A
101: 8 **M** by **m** I will destroy all the wicked in
110: 3 From the womb of the **m,** like dew, your youth
130: 6 for the Lord more than those who watch for the **m,**
130: 6 more than those who watch for the **m.**
139: 9 of the **m** and settle at the farthest limits of the sea,
143: 8 Let me hear of your steadfast love in the **m,** A
Pr 7:18 Come, let us take our fill of love until **m;** B
27:14 rising early in the **m,** will be counted as cursing. A
Ecc 10:16 and your princes feast in the **m!** A
11: 6 In the **m** sow your seed, and at evening do A
Isa 5:11 you who rise early in the **m** in pursuit A
17:11 and make them blossom in the **m** that you sow; A
17:14 Before **m,** they are no more.
21:12 The sentinel says: "**M** comes, and also the night.
28:19 for **m** by **m** it will pass through,
33: 2 Be our arm every **m,** our salvation in the time E
37:36 when **m** dawned, they were all dead bodies.
38:13 I cry for help until **m;** B
50: 4 **M** by **m** he wakens—
Jer 20: 3 The next **m** when Pashhur released Jeremiah from
20:16 let him hear a cry in the **m** and an alarm at noon, A
21:12 Execute justice in the **m,** and deliver from the A
La 3:23 they are new every **m;** great is your faithfulness. E
Eze 12: 8 In the **m** the word of the LORD came to me: A
24:18 people in the **m,** and at evening my wife died. AC
24:18 And on the next **m** I did as I was commanded.
33:22 by the time the fugitive came to me in the **m;** A
46:13 **m** by **m** he shall provide it.
46:14 a grain offering with it **m** by **m** regularly,
46:15 **m** by **m,** as a regular burnt offering.
Hos 6: 4 Your love is like a **m** cloud,
7: 6 in the **m** it blazes like a flaming fire. A
13: 3 the **m** mist or like the dew that goes away early,
Am 4: 4 bring your sacrifices every **m,** E
4:13 makes the **m** the darkness, and treads on the heights
5: 8 and turns deep darkness into the **m,**
Mic 2: 1 When the **m** dawns, they perform it,
Zep 3: 3 that leave nothing until the **m.** B
3: 5 Every **m** he renders his judgment, E
Mt 14:25 in the **m** he came walking toward them on the A
16: 3 And in the **m,** 'It will be stormy today, A
20: 1 like a landowner who went out early in the **m** A
21:18 In the **m,** when he returned to the city, A
27: 1 When **m** came, all the chief priests and the elders
Mk 1:35 In the **m,** while it was still very dark, A
6:48 he came towards them early in the **m,** A
11:20 In the **m** as they passed by, A
15: 1 As soon as it was **m,**
15:25 in the **m** when they crucified him. A
Lk 21:38 the people would get up early in the **m** to listen A
24:22 They were at the tomb early this **m,**
Jn 8: 2 ⟦Early in the **m** he came again to the temple.⟧ A
18:28 It was early in the **m.** A
Ac 2:15 for it is only nine o'clock in the **m.** A
12:18 When **m** came, there was no small commotion
16:35 When **m** came, the magistrates sent the police,
23:12 In the **m** the Jews joined in a conspiracy A
27:39 In the **m** they did not recognize the land, A
28:23 From **m** until evening he explained the matter C
2Pe 1:19 the day dawns and the **m** star rises in your hearts.
Rev 2:28 the one who conquers I will also give the **m** star.
22:16 and the descendant of David, the bright **m** star."
Tob 9: 6 In the **m** they both got up early and went to A
Jdt 12: 5 Toward the **m** watch she got up
AdE 2:14 the evening she enters and in the **m** she departs A
5:14 in the **m** tell the king to have Mordecai hanged A
Wis 11:22 and like a drop of **m** dew that falls on the ground.
Sir 4:12 and those who seek her from early **m** are filled
18:26 From **m** to evening conditions change; C
47:10 and the sanctuary resounded from early **m.**
50: 6 Like the **m** star among the clouds,
Bel 1:12 When you return in the **m,** A
1:16 Early in the **m** the king rose and came, A
1Mc 3:58 Be ready early in the **m** to fight A
4:52 Early in the **m** on the twenty-fifth day of A
6:33 Early in the **m** the king set out and took his A
9:13 and the battle raged from **m** until evening. C
10:80 at his men from early **m** until late afternoon.
11:67 Early in the **m** they marched to the plain of A
12:29 Jonathan and his troops did not know it until **m,** B
16: 5 Early in the **m** they started out and marched A
1Es 1:11 this they did in the **m.** A
5:50 burnt offerings to the Lord **m** and evening. C
9:41 the gate of the temple from early **m** until midday,
3Mc 5:10 the courtyard early in the **m** to report to the king A
5:23 as soon as the cock had crowed in the early **m,**
2Es 7:*40* or darkness or evening or **m,** D

MORNINGS (2) [MORNING]

Da 8:14 "For two thousand three hundred evenings and **m;**
8:26 of the evenings and the **m** that has been told is true.

MORROW (KJV) See DAY AFTER, FOLLOWING DAY, MORNING, NEXT DAY, NEXT MORNING, TOMORROW

MORSEL (6) [MORSELS]

Ru 2:14 and dip your **m** in the sour wine."
1Sa 2:36 that I may eat a **m** of bread.' "
28:22 let me set a **m** of bread before you.
1Ki 17:11 "Bring me a **m** of bread in your hand."
Job 31:17 or have eaten my **m** alone, and the orphan has
Pr 17: 1 a dry **m** with quiet than a house full of feasting

MORSELS (2) [MORSEL]

Pr 18: 8 The words of a whisperer are like delicious **m;**
26:22 The words of a whisperer are like delicious **m;**

MORTAL‡ (147) [MORTALLY, MORTALS]

Nu 23:19 or a **m,** that he should change his mind.
1Sa 15:29 for he is not a **m,** that he should change his mind."
2Ch 14:11 let no **m** prevail against you."
Job 9: 2 but how can a **m** be just before God?
9:32 For he is not a **m,** as I am, that I might answer him,
14: 1 "A **m,** born of woman, few of days and full
16:21 that he would maintain the right of a **m** with God,
22: 2 "Can a **m** be of use to God?
25: 4 How then can a **m** be righteous before God?
25: 6 a **m,** who is a maggot, and a human being, who is
32: 8 But truly it is the spirit in a **m,**
33:12 I will answer you: God is greater than any **m.**
Ps 56:11 What can a mere **m** do to me?
Isa 51:12 why then are you afraid of a mere **m** who must die,
56: 2 Happy is the **m** who does this,
Jer 51:43 and through which no **m** passes.
Eze 2: 1 He said to me: O **m,** stand up on your feet,
2: 3 **M,** I am sending you to the people of Israel,
2: 6 And you, O **m,** do not be afraid of them,
2: 8 But you, **m,** hear what I say to you;
3: 1 He said to me, O **m,** eat what is offered to you;
3: 3 to me, **M,** eat this scroll that I give you
3: 4 **M,** go to the house of Israel
3:10 **M,** all my words that I shall speak to you receive
3:17 **M,** I have made you a sentinel for the house
3:25 As for you, **m,** cords shall be placed on you,
4: 1 And you, O **m,** take a brick and set it before you.
4:16 **M,** I am going to break the staff of bread
5: 1 And you, O **m,** take a sharp sword;
6: 2 O **m,** set your face toward the mountains of Israel,
7: 2 O **m,** thus says the Lord GOD to the land
8: 5 Then God said to me, "O **m,**
8: 6 "**M,** do you see what they are doing,
8: 8 Then he said to me, "**M,** dig through the wall";
8:12 "**M,** have you seen what the elders of the house
8:15 Then he said to me, "Have you seen this, O **m?**
8:17 Then he said to me, "Have you seen this, O **m?**
11: 2 "**M,** these are the men who devise iniquity
11: 4 Therefore prophesy against them; prophesy, O **m.**"
11:15 **M,** your kinsfolk, your own kin,
12: 2 **M,** you are living in the midst of
12: 3 **m,** prepare for yourself an exile's baggage,
12: 9 **M,** has not the house of Israel,
12:18 **M,** eat your bread with quaking,
12:22 **M,** what is this proverb of yours about the land
12:27 **M,** the house of Israel is saying, "The vision
13: 2 **M,** prophesy against the prophets
13:17 **m,** set your face against the daughters
14: 3 **M,** these men have taken their idols
14:13 **M,** when a land sins against me
15: 2 O **m,** how does the wood of the vine surpass all
16: 2 **M,** make known to Jerusalem her abominations,
17: 2 O **m,** propound a riddle, and speak an allegory to
20: 3 **M,** speak to the elders of Israel, and say to them:
20: 4 Will you judge them, **m,** will you judge them?
20:27 **m,** speak to the house of Israel and say to them,
20:46 **M,** set your face toward the south, preach against
21: 2 **M,** set your face toward Jerusalem and preach
21: 6 Moan therefore, **m;** moan with breaking
21: 9 **M,** prophesy and say: Thus says the Lord;
21:12 Cry and wail, O **m,** for it is against my people;
21:14 And you, **m,** prophesy; Strike hand to hand.
21:19 **M,** mark out two roads for the sword of the king
21:28 As for you, **m,** prophesy, and say,
22: 2 **m,** will you judge, will you judge the bloody city?
22:18 **M,** the house of Israel has become dross to me;
22:24 **M,** say to it: You are a land
23: 2 **M,** there were two women, the daughters
23:36 **M,** will you judge Oholah and Oholibah?
24: 2 **M,** write down the name of this
24:16 **M,** with one blow I am about to take away
24:25 And you, **m,** on the day when I take
25: 2 **M,** set your face toward the Ammonites
26: 2 **M,** because Tyre said concerning Jerusalem,
27: 2 Now you, **m,** raise a lamentation over Tyre,
28: 2 **M,** say to the prince of Tyre, Thus says
28: 2 in the heart of the seas," yet you are but a **m,**
28: 9 though you are but a **m,** and no god,
28:12 **M,** raise a lamentation over the king of Tyre,
28:21 **M,** set your face toward Sidon, and prophesy
29: 2 **M,** set your face against Pharaoh king of Egypt,
29:18 **M,** King Nebuchadrezzar of Babylon
30: 2 **M,** prophesy, and say, Thus says the Lord GOD:
30:21 **M,** I have broken the arm of Pharaoh king
31: 2 **M,** say to Pharaoh king of Egypt and to his hordes:
32: 2 **M,** raise a lamentation over Pharaoh king
32:18 **M,** wail over the hordes of Egypt, and send them
33: 2 O **M,** speak to your people and say to them,
33: 7 **m,** I have made a sentinel for the house of Israel;
33:10 Now you, **m,** say to the house of Israel,
33:12 And you, **m,** say to your people,
33:24 **M,** the inhabitants of these waste places in the land
Eze 33:30 **m,** your people who talk together about you by
34: 2 **M,** prophesy against the shepherds of Israel:
35: 2 **M,** set your face against Mount Seir, and prophesy
36: 1 And you, **m,** prophesy to the mountains of Israel,
36:17 **M,** when the house of Israel lived
37: 3 He said to me, "**M,** can these bones live?"
37: 9 "Prophesy to the breath, prophesy, **m,**
37:11 "**M,** these bones are the whole house of Israel.
37:16 **M,** take a stick and write on it, "For Judah,
38: 2 **M,** set your face toward Gog, of the land
38:14 Therefore, **m,** prophesy, and say to Gog:
39: 1 And you, **m,** prophesy against Gog, and say:
39:17 As for you, **m,** thus says the Lord GOD:
40: 4 "**M,** look closely and listen attentively,
43: 7 **M,** this is the place of my throne and the place for
43:10 **m,** describe the temple to the house of Israel,
43:18 Then he said to me: **M,** thus says the Lord GOD:
44: 5 The LORD said to me: **M,** mark well,
47: 6 He said to me, "**M,** have you seen this?"
Da 8:17 But he said to me, "Understand, O **m,**
Hos 11: 9 I am God and no **m,** the Holy One in your midst,
Mic 5: 7 not depend upon people or wait for any **m.**
6: 8 He has told you, O **m,** what is good;
Na 3:19 There is no assuaging your hurt, your wound is **m.**
Ac 10:26 "Stand up; I am only a **m.**"
12:22 "The voice of a god, and not of a **m!**"
Ro 1:23 a **m** human being or birds or four-footed animals
6:12 do not let sin exercise dominion in your **m** bodies,
8:11 to your **m** bodies also through his Spirit that dwells
1Co 15:53 and this **m** body must put on immortality.
15:54 and this **m** body puts on immortality,
2Co 4:11 life of Jesus may be made visible in our **m** flesh.
5: 4 so that what is **m** may be swallowed up by life.
12: 4 that no **m** is permitted to repeat.
Heb 7: 8 tithes are received by those who are **m;**
8: 2 and not any **m,** has set up.
1Jn 5:16 not a **m** sin, you will ask, and God will give life
5:16 to those whose sin is not **m.**
5:16 There is sin that is **m;**
5:17 All wrongdoing is sin, but there is sin that is not **m.**
Rev 13: 3 but its **m** wound had been healed.
13:12 whose **m** wound had been healed.
Jdt 8:16 or like a mere **m,** to be won over by pleading.
AdE 14:10 and to magnify forever a **m** king.
Wis 7: 1 I also am **m,** like everyone else,
15:17 People are **m,** and what they make
Sir 28: 5 If a mere **m** harbors wrath,
2Mc 7:16 though you also are **m,** you do what you please.
3Mc 3:29 for all time to any **m** creature."
7: 9 we always shall have not a **m** but the Ruler
2Es 2:45 "These are they who have put off **m** clothing
7:15 Why are you moved, seeing that you are **m?**
7:*88* when they shall be separated from their **m** body.
8: 6 by which every **m** who bears the likeness of
14:14 and put away from you **m** thoughts;

MORTALLY (2) [MORTAL]

Ex 21:12 Whoever strikes a person **m** shall be put to death.
Eze 30:24 before him with the groans of one **m** wounded.

MORTALS‡ (112) [MORTAL]

Ge 6: 3 "My spirit shall not abide in **m** forever,
11: 5 to see the city and the tower, which **m** had built.
Ex 4:11 the LORD said to him, "Who gives speech to **m?**
Jdg 9: 9 by which gods and **m** are honored,
9:13 that cheers gods and **m,** and go to sway over
1Sa 16: 7 for the LORD does not see as **m** see;
26:19 if it is **m,** may they be cursed before the LORD,
2Sa 7:14 I will punish him with a rod such as **m** use,
1Ch 29: 1 temple will not be for **m** but for the LORD God.
2Ch 6:18 "But will God indeed reside with **m** on earth?
Job 4:13 when deep sleep falls on **m,**
4:17 'Can **m** be righteous before God?
10: 5 Are your days like the days of **m,**
14:10 But **m** die, and are laid low;
14:12 so **m** lie down and do not rise again;
14:14 If **m** die, will they live again?
14:19 so you destroy the hope of **m.**
15:14 What are **m,** that they can be clean?
20: 4 ever since **m** were placed on earth,
21: 4 As for me, is my complaint addressed to **m?**
28:13 **M** do not know the way to it,
33:15 when deep sleep falls on **m,**
33:29 twice, three times, with **m,**
34:15 and all **m** return to dust.
34:21 "For his eyes are upon the ways of **m,**
36:24 to extol his work, of which **m** have sung.
36:28 the skies pour down and drop upon **m** abundantly.
37:24 Therefore **m** fear him; he does
Ps 8: 4 **m** that you care for them?
9:19 O LORD! Do not let **m** prevail;
17:14 from **m**—by your hand, O LORD—
17:14 from **m** whose portion in life is in this world.
39:11 "You chastise **m** in punishment for sin,
49:12 **M** cannot abide in their pomp;
49:20 **M** cannot abide in their pomp;
66: 5 he is awesome in his deeds among **m.**
78:25 **M** ate of the bread of angels;
78:60 the tent where he dwelt among **m,**
82: 7 you shall die like **m,** and fall like any prince."
89:47 for what vanity you have created all **m!**
90: 3 and say, "Turn back, you **m.**"
103:15 As for **m,** their days are like grass;
118: 6 What can **m** do to me?
118: 8 in the LORD than to put confidence in **m.**
144: 3 or **m** that you think of them?
Ps 146: 3 Do not put your trust in princes, in **m,**
Pr 16: 1 The plans of the mind belong to **m,**
30:14 from off the earth, the needy from among **m.**
Ecc 2: 3 on folly, until I might see what was good for **m**
2:22 What do **m** get from all the toil and strain
2:24 There is nothing better for **m** than to eat and drink,
6:12 For who knows what is good for **m** while they live
7:14 so that **m** may not find out anything that will come
8: 6 although the troubles of **m** lie heavy upon them.
9:12 so **m** are snared at a time of calamity,
Isa 2:22 from **m,** who have only breath in their nostrils,
7:13 Is it too little for you to weary **m,**
13:12 I will make **m** more rare than fine gold,
31: 8 "Then the Assyrian shall fall by a sword, not of **m;**
38:11 I shall look upon **m** no more among the inhabitants
52:14 and his form beyond that of **m**—
Jer 10:23 that **m** as they walk cannot direct their steps.
16:20 Can **m** make for themselves gods?
17: 5 in mere **m** and make mere flesh their strength,
32:19 whose eyes are open to all the ways of **m,**
Eze 31:14 with all **m,** with those who go down to the Pit.
Da 2:11 whose dwelling is not with **m.**"
4:17 the Most High is sovereign over the kingdom of **m;**
4:25 over the kingdom of **m,** and gives it
4:32 the kingdom of **m** and gives it to whom he will."
5:21 over the kingdom of **m,** and sets
Am 4:13 creates the wind, reveals his thoughts to **m,**
Mt 19:26 at them and said, "For **m** it is impossible,
Mk 10:27 "For **m** it is impossible, but not for God;
Lk 18:27 "What is impossible for **m** is possible for God."
Ac 4:12 under heaven given among **m** by which we must
14:15 We are **m** just like you,
17:25 since he himself gives to all **m** life and breath
17:29 an image formed by the art and imagination of **m.**
1Co 4: 9 a spectacle to the world, to angels and to **m.**
13: 1 If I speak in the tongues of **m** and of angels,
1Th 2: 4 even so we speak, not to please **m,**
2: 6 nor did we seek praise from **m,**
Heb 2: 6 or **m,** that you care for them?
5: 1 from among **m** is put in charge of things pertaining
9:27 And just as it is appointed for **m** to die once,
1Pe 2: 4 though rejected by **m** yet chosen and precious
Rev 21: 3 "See, the home of God is among **m.**
Wis 4: 1 because it is known both by God and by **m.**
7:14 for it is an unfailing treasure for **m;**
8: 7 nothing in life is more profitable for **m** than these.
9:14 For the reasoning of **m** is worthless,
12: 8 But even these you spared, since they were but **m,**
15: 8 these **m** who were made of earth a short time
15: 8 while go to the earth from which all **m** are taken,
15: 9 that **m** are destined to die or that their life is brief,
16:13 you lead **m** down to the gates of Hades
Sir 1:16 she inebriates **m** with her fruits;
2:17 but not into the hands of **m;**
5:13 and the tongue of **m** may be their downfall.
10: 7 Arrogance is hateful to the Lord and to **m,**
25: 1 and they are beautiful in the sight of God and of **m:**
35:24 until he repays **m** according to their deeds,
2Mc 6:26 for the present I would avoid the punishment of **m,**
7:14 but choose to die at the hands of **m** and to cherish
7:16 and said, "Because you have authority among **m,**
7:34 But you, unholy wretch, you most defiled of all **m,**
9:12 **m** should not think that they are equal to God."
2Es 5:38 except he whose dwelling is not with **m?**
7:*46* among **m** that has not transgressed your covenant?
8:34 But what are **m,** that you are angry with them;
4Mc 18: 3 the sake of religion were not only admired by **m,**

MORTAR (6) [MORTARS]

Ge 11: 3 And they had brick for stone, and bitumen for **m.**
Ex 1:14 with hard service in **m** and brick and in every kind
Pr 27:22 in a **m** with a pestle along with crushed grain,
Isa 41:25 He shall trample on rulers as on **m,**
Na 3:14 trample the clay, tread the **m,**
Zep 1:11 The inhabitants of the **M** wail,

MORTARS (1) [MORTAR]

Nu 11: 8 ground it in mills or beat it in **m,**

MORTER (KJV) MORTAR, PLASTER, WHITEWASH

MORTIFY (KJV) See PUT TO DEATH

MOSAIC (2)

Est 1: 6 of gold and silver on a **m** pavement of porphyry,
AdE 1: 6 Gold and silver couches were placed on a **m** floor

MOSERAH (1)

Dt 10: 6 from Beeroth-bene-jaakan to **M.**

MOSEROTH (2)

Nu 33:30 They set out from Hashmonah and camped at **M.**
33:31 They set out from **M** and camped at Bene-jaakan.

MOSES‡ (870) [MOSES']

A. LAW OF MOSES (28)
B. MOSES THE SERVANT (23)
C. SERVANT MOSES (16)
D. BOOK OF MOSES (12)

Ex 2:10 She named him **M,** "because," she said,
2:11 One day, after **M** had grown up,

Ex 2:14 Then **M** was afraid and thought,
2:15 When Pharaoh heard of it, he sought to kill **M.**
2:15 But **M** fled from Pharaoh.
2:17 **M** got up and came to their defense
2:21 **M** agreed to stay with the man, and he gave **M** his daughter Zipporah in marriage.
3: 1 **M** was keeping the flock of his
3: 3 Then **M** said, "I must turn aside and look
3: 4 God called to him out of the bush, **"M, M!"**
3: 6 **M** hid his face, for he was afraid to look at God.
3:11 But **M** said to God, "Who am I that I should go
3:13 But **M** said to God, "If I come to the Israelites
3:14 God said to **M,** "I AM WHO I AM."
3:15 God also said to **M,** "Thus you shall say to
4: 1 Then **M** answered, "But suppose they do
4: 3 and **M** drew back from it.
4: 4 Then the LORD said to **M,** "Reach out your hand,
4:10 But **M** said to the LORD, "O my Lord,
4:14 of the LORD was kindled against **M** and he said,
4:18 **M** went back to his father-in-law Jethro and said
4:18 And Jethro said to **M,** "Go in peace."
4:19 LORD said to **M** in Midian, "Go back to Egypt;
4:20 So **M** took his wife and his sons,
4:20 and **M** carried the staff of God in his hand.
4:21 And the LORD said to **M,**
4:27 "Go into the wilderness to meet **M."**
4:28 **M** told Aaron all the words of the LORD
4:29 Then **M** and Aaron went and assembled all
4:30 the words that the LORD had spoken to **M,**
5: 1 Afterward **M** and Aaron went to Pharaoh and said,
5: 4 But the king of Egypt said to them, **"M** and Aaron,
5:20 they came upon **M** and Aaron who were waiting
5:22 Then **M** turned again to the LORD and said,
6: 1 Then the LORD said to **M,**
6: 2 God also spoke to **M** and said to him:
6: 9 **M** told this to the Israelites;
6: 9 but they would not listen to **M,**
6:10 Then the LORD spoke to **M,**
6:12 But **M** spoke to the LORD,
6:13 Thus the LORD spoke to **M** and Aaron,
6:20 and she bore him Aaron and **M,**
6:26 It was this same Aaron and **M** to whom
6:27 the Israelites out of Egypt, the same **M** and Aaron.
6:28 when the LORD spoke to **M** in the land of Egypt,
6:30 But **M** said in the LORD's presence,
7: 1 The LORD said to **M,** "See,
7: 6 **M** and Aaron did so; they did just
7: 7 **M** was eighty years old and Aaron eighty-three
7: 8 The LORD said to **M** and Aaron,
7:10 So **M** and Aaron went to Pharaoh and did as
7:14 LORD said to **M,** "Pharaoh's heart is hardened;
7:19 The LORD said to **M,** "Say to Aaron,
7:20 **M** and Aaron did just as the LORD commanded.
8: 1 Then the LORD said to **M,**
8: 5 And the LORD said to **M,** "Say to Aaron,
8: 8 Then Pharaoh called **M** and Aaron, and said,
8: 9 **M** said to Pharaoh, "Kindly tell me when I am
8:10 **M** said, "As you say!
8:12 Then **M** and Aaron went out from Pharaoh;
8:12 and **M** cried out to the LORD concerning
8:13 And the LORD did as **M** requested:
8:16 Then the LORD said to **M,** "Say to Aaron,
8:20 Then the LORD said to **M,**
8:25 Then Pharaoh summoned **M** and Aaron, and said,
8:26 But **M** said, "It would not be right to do so;
8:29 Then **M** said, "As soon as I leave you,
8:30 So **M** went out from Pharaoh and prayed to
8:31 And the LORD did as **M** asked:
9: 1 Then the LORD said to **M,** "Go to Pharaoh,
9: 8 Then the LORD said to **M** and Aaron,
9: 8 let **M** throw it in the air in the sight of Pharaoh.
9:10 and **M** threw it in the air,
9:11 The magicians could not stand before **M** because
9:12 just as the LORD had spoken to **M.**
9:13 Then the LORD said to **M,**
9:22 to **M,** "Stretch out your hand toward heaven so
9:23 Then **M** stretched out his staff toward heaven,
9:27 Then Pharaoh summoned **M** and Aaron,
9:29 **M** said to him, "As soon as I have gone out of
9:33 So **M** left Pharaoh, went out of the city,
9:35 just as the LORD had spoken through **M.**
10: 1 Then the LORD said to **M,** "Go to Pharaoh;
10: 3 So **M** and Aaron went to Pharaoh, and said to him,
10: 8 So **M** and Aaron were brought back to Pharaoh,
10: 9 **M** said, "We will go with our young and our old;
10:12 Then the LORD said to **M,**
10:13 So **M** stretched out his staff over the land of Egypt,
10:16 Pharaoh hurriedly summoned **M** and Aaron
10:21 Then the LORD said to **M,**
10:22 So **M** stretched out his hand toward heaven,
10:24 Then Pharaoh summoned **M,** and said, "Go,
10:25 But **M** said, "You must also let us have sacrifices
10:29 **M** said, "Just as you say!
11: 1 to **M,** "I will bring one more plague upon Pharaoh
11: 3 **M** himself was a man of great importance in
11: 4 **M** said, "Thus says the LORD:
11: 9 The LORD said to **M,** "Pharaoh will not listen
11:10 **M** and Aaron performed all these wonders
12: 1 LORD said to **M** and Aaron in the land of Egypt:
12:21 **M** called all the elders of Israel and said to them,
12:28 and did just as the LORD had commanded **M**
12:31 Then he summoned **M** and Aaron in the night,
12:35 The Israelites had done as **M** told them;
12:43 The LORD said to **M** and Aaron:
12:50 as the LORD had commanded **M** and Aaron.
13: 1 The LORD said to **M:**
13: 3 **M** said to the people, "Remember this day

Ex 13:19 And **M** took with him the bones
14: 1 Then the LORD said to **M:**
14:11 to **M,** "Was it because there were no graves
14:13 But **M** said to the people, "Do not be afraid,
14:15 LORD said to **M,** "Why do you cry out to me?
14:21 Then **M** stretched out his hand over the sea.
14:26 Then the LORD said to **M,**
14:27 So **M** stretched out his hand over the sea,
14:31 and believed in the LORD and in his servant **M.** C
15: 1 **M** and the Israelites sang this song to the LORD:
15:22 Then **M** ordered Israel to set out from the Red Sea,
15:24 And the people complained against **M,** saying,
16: 2 of the Israelites complained against **M** and Aaron
16: 4 Then the LORD said to **M,**
16: 6 So **M** and Aaron said to all the Israelites,
16: 8 And **M** said, "When the LORD gives you meat
16: 9 Then **M** said to Aaron, "Say to
16:11 The LORD spoke to **M** and said,
16:15 **M** said to them, "It is the bread that
16:19 And **M** said to them, "Let no one leave any of it
16:20 But they did not listen to **M;**
16:20 And **M** was angry with them.
16:22 the leaders of the congregation came and told **M,**
16:24 until morning, as **M** commanded them;
16:25 **M** said, "Eat it today, for today is a sabbath to
16:28 The LORD said to **M,** "How long will you refuse
16:32 **M** said, "This is what the LORD has commanded:
16:33 And **M** said to Aaron, "Take a jar,
16:34 As the LORD commanded **M,**
17: 2 The people quarreled with **M,** and said,
17: 2 **M** said to them, "Why do you quarrel with me?
17: 3 and the people complained against **M** and said,
17: 4 So **M** cried out to the LORD,
17: 5 to **M,** "Go on ahead of the people, and take some
17: 6 **M** did so, in the sight of the elders of Israel.
17: 9 **M** said to Joshua, "Choose some men for us
17:10 So Joshua did as **M** told him,
17:10 and fought with Amalek, while **M,** Aaron,
17:11 Whenever **M** held up his hand, Israel prevailed;
17:14 Then the LORD said to **M,**
17:15 And **M** built an altar and called it,
18: 1 that God had done for **M** and for his people Israel,
18: 2 After **M** had sent away his wife Zipporah,
18: 5 came into the wilderness where **M** was encamped
18: 6 He sent word to **M,** "I, your father-in-law Jethro,
18: 7 **M** went out to meet his father-in-law;
18: 8 Then **M** told his father-in-law all that
18:13 The next day **M** sat as judge for the people,
18:15 **M** said to his father-in-law,
18:24 So **M** listened to his father-in-law and did all
18:25 **M** chose able men from all Israel
18:26 hard cases they brought to **M,**
18:27 Then **M** let his father-in-law depart,
19: 3 Then **M** went up to God;
19: 7 So **M** came, summoned the elders of the people,
19: 8 **M** reported the words of the people to the LORD.
19: 9 Then the LORD said to **M,**
19: 9 **M** had told the words of the people to the LORD,
19:10 the LORD said to **M:** "Go to the
19:14 So **M** went down from the mountain to the people.
19:17 **M** brought the people out of the camp
19:19 **M** would speak and God would answer him
19:20 LORD summoned **M** to the top of the mountain,
19:20 to the top of the mountain, and **M** went up.
19:21 Then the LORD said to **M,**
19:23 **M** said to the LORD, "The people are
19:25 So **M** went down to the people and told them.
20:19 said to **M,** "You speak to us, and we will listen;
20:20 **M** said to the people, "Do not be afraid;
20:21 **M** drew near to the thick darkness where God was.
20:22 The LORD said to **M:** Thus you shall say to the
24: 1 Then he said to **M,** "Come up to the LORD,
24: 2 **M** alone shall come near the LORD;
24: 3 **M** came and told the people all the words of
24: 4 And **M** wrote down all the words of the LORD.
24: 6 **M** took half of the blood and put it in basins,
24: 8 **M** took the blood and dashed it on the people,
24: 9 Then **M** and Aaron, Nadab, and Abihu,
24:12 The LORD said to **M,** "Come up to me on
24:13 So **M** set out with his assistant Joshua,
24:13 and **M** went up into the mountain of God.
24:15 Then **M** went up on the mountain,
24:16 on the seventh day he called to **M** out of the cloud.
24:18 **M** entered the cloud, and went up on the mountain.
24:18 **M** was on the mountain for forty days
25: 1 The LORD said to **M:**
30:11 The LORD spoke to **M:**
30:17 The LORD spoke to **M:**
30:22 The LORD spoke to **M:**
30:34 The LORD said to **M:** Take sweet spices,
31: 1 The LORD spoke to **M:**
31:12 The LORD said to **M:**
31:18 God finished speaking with **M** on Mount Sinai,
32: 1 the people saw that **M** delayed to come down from
32: 1 as for this **M,** the man who brought us up out of
32: 7 The LORD said to **M,** "Go down at once!
32: 9 The LORD said to **M,** "I have seen this people,
32:11 But **M** implored the LORD his God, and said,
32:15 Then **M** turned and went down from the mountain,
32:17 the people as they shouted, he said to **M,** "There is
32:21 **M** said to Aaron, "What did this people do to you
32:23 as for this **M,** the man who brought us up out of
32:25 When **M** saw that the people were running wild
32:26 then **M** stood in the gate of the camp,
32:28 The sons of Levi did as **M** commanded,
32:29 **M** said, "Today you have ordained yourselves for
32:30 On the next day **M** said to the people,

Ex 32:31 So **M** returned to the LORD and said, "Alas,
32:33 But the LORD said to **M,**
33: 1 The LORD said to **M,** "Go, leave this place,
33: 5 For the LORD had said to **M,**
33: 7 Now **M** used to take the tent and pitch it outside
33: 8 Whenever **M** went out to the tent,
33: 8 of their tents and watch **M** until he had gone into
33: 9 When **M** entered the tent, the pillar
33: 9 and the LORD would speak with **M.**
33:11 Thus the LORD used to speak to **M** face to face,
33:12 **M** said to the LORD, "See, you have said to me,
33:17 The LORD said to **M,** "I will do the very thing
33:18 **M** said, "Show me your glory, I pray."
34: 1 The LORD said to **M,** "Cut two tablets of stone
34: 4 So **M** cut two tablets of stone like the former ones;
34: 8 And **M** quickly bowed his head toward the earth,
34:27 The LORD said to **M:** Write these words;
34:29 **M** came down from Mount Sinai.
34:29 **M** did not know that the skin of his face shone
34:30 When Aaron and all the Israelites saw **M,**
34:31 But **M** called to them;
34:31 of the congregation returned to him, and **M** spoke
34:33 When **M** had finished speaking with them,
34:34 but whenever **M** went in before the LORD
34:35 the Israelites would see the face of **M,** that the skin
34:35 and **M** would put the veil on his face again,
35: 1 **M** assembled all the congregation of the Israelites
35: 4 **M** said to all the congregation of the Israelites:
35:20 of the Israelites withdrew from the presence of **M.**
35:29 the work that the LORD had commanded by **M** to
35:30 Then **M** said to the Israelites:
36: 2 **M** then called Bezalel and Oholiab
36: 3 and they received from **M** all the freewill offerings
36: 5 said to **M,** "The people are bringing much more
36: 6 So **M** gave command, and word was proclaimed
38:21 which were drawn up at the commandment of **M,**
38:22 made all that the LORD commanded **M;**
39: 1 as the LORD had commanded **M.**
39: 5 as the LORD had commanded **M.**
39: 7 as the LORD had commanded **M.**
39:21 as the LORD had commanded **M.**
39:26 as the LORD had commanded **M.**
39:29 as the LORD had commanded **M.**
39:31 as the LORD had commanded **M.**
39:32 as the LORD had commanded **M.**
39:33 Then they brought the tabernacle to **M,**
39:42 of the work just as the LORD had commanded **M.**
39:43 When **M** saw that they had done all the work just
40: 1 The LORD spoke to **M:**
40:16 **M** did everything just as the LORD had commanded
40:18 **M** set up the tabernacle; he laid its bases,
40:19 as the LORD had commanded **M.**
40:21 as the LORD had commanded **M.**
40:23 as the LORD had commanded **M.**
40:25 as the LORD had commanded **M.**
40:27 as the LORD had commanded **M.**
40:29 as the LORD had commanded **M.**
40:31 with which **M** and Aaron
40:32 as the LORD had commanded **M.**
40:33 So **M** finished the work.
40:35 **M** was not able to enter the tent of meeting

Lev 1: 1 The LORD summoned **M** and spoke to him from
4: 1 The LORD spoke to **M,** saying,
5:14 The LORD spoke to **M,** saying:
6: 1 The LORD spoke to **M,** saying:
6: 8 The LORD spoke to **M,** saying:
6:19 The LORD spoke to **M,** saying:
6:24 The LORD spoke to **M,** saying:
7:22 The LORD spoke to **M,** saying:
7:28 The LORD spoke to **M,** saying:
7:38 which the LORD commanded **M** on Mount Sinai,
8: 1 The LORD spoke to **M,** saying:
8: 4 And **M** did as the LORD commanded him.
8: 5 **M** said to the congregation,
8: 6 Then **M** brought Aaron and his sons forward,
8: 9 the holy crown, as the LORD commanded **M.**
8:10 Then **M** took the anointing oil and anointed
8:13 And **M** brought forward Aaron's sons,
8:13 as the LORD commanded **M.**
8:15 **M** took the blood and with his finger put some
8:16 **M** took all the fat that was around the entrails,
8:17 as the LORD commanded **M.**
8:19 **M** dashed the blood against all sides of the altar.
8:20 and **M** turned into smoke the head and the parts
8:21 **M** turned into smoke the whole ram on the altar;
8:21 as the LORD commanded **M.**
8:23 **M** took some of its blood and put it on the lobe
8:24 **M** put some of the blood on the lobes
8:24 and **M** dashed the rest of the blood against all sides
8:28 Then **M** took them from their hands
8:29 **M** took the breast and raised it as
8:29 as the LORD commanded **M.**
8:30 Then **M** took some of the anointing oil and some
8:31 And **M** said to Aaron and his sons,
8:36 the things that the LORD commanded through **M.**
9: 1 the eighth day **M** summoned Aaron and his sons
9: 5 They brought what **M** commanded to the front of
9: 6 And **M** said, "This is the thing that
9: 7 Then **M** said to Aaron, "Draw near to the altar
9:10 as the LORD commanded **M;**
9:21 before the LORD, as **M** had commanded.
9:23 **M** and Aaron entered the tent of meeting,
10: 3 Then **M** said to Aaron, "This is what
10: 4 **M** summoned Mishael and Elzaphan,
10: 5 by their tunics out of the camp, as **M** had ordered.
10: 6 And **M** said to Aaron and to his sons Eleazar
10: 7 And they did as **M** had ordered.

Lev 10:11 that the LORD has spoken to them through **M.**
10:12 **M** spoke to Aaron and to his remaining sons,
10:16 **M** made inquiry about the goat of the sin offering,
10:19 And Aaron spoke to **M,** "See,
10:20 And when **M** heard that, he agreed.
11: 1 LORD spoke to **M** and Aaron, saying to them:
12: 1 The LORD spoke to **M,** saying:
13: 1 The LORD spoke to **M** and Aaron, saying:
14: 1 The LORD spoke to **M,** saying:
14:33 The LORD spoke to **M** and Aaron, saying:
15: 1 The LORD spoke to **M** and Aaron, saying:
16: 1 to **M** after the death of the two sons of Aaron,
16: 2 The LORD said to **M:** Tell your brother Aaron
16:34 And **M** did as the LORD had commanded him.
17: 1 The LORD spoke to **M:**
18: 1 The LORD spoke to **M,** saying:
19: 1 The LORD spoke to **M,** saying:
20: 1 The LORD spoke to **M,** saying:
21: 1 The LORD said to **M:** Speak to the
21:16 The LORD spoke to **M,** saying:
21:24 Thus **M** spoke to Aaron and to his sons and to all
22: 1 The LORD spoke to **M,** saying:
22:17 The LORD spoke to **M,** saying:
22:26 The LORD spoke to **M,** saying:
23: 1 The LORD spoke to **M,** saying:
23: 9 The LORD spoke to **M:**
23:23 The LORD spoke to **M,** saying:
23:26 The LORD spoke to **M,** saying:
23:33 The LORD spoke to **M,** saying:
23:44 Thus **M** declared to the people of Israel
24: 1 The LORD spoke to **M,** saying:
24:11 And they brought him to **M—**
24:13 The LORD said to **M,** saying:
24:23 **M** spoke thus to the people of Israel;
24:23 of Israel did as the LORD had commanded **M.**
25: 1 The LORD spoke to **M** on Mount Sinai, saying:
26:46 the people of Israel on Mount Sinai through **M.**
27: 1 The LORD spoke to **M,** saying:
27:34 the commandments that the LORD gave to **M** for
Nu 1: 1 The LORD spoke to **M** in the wilderness of Sinai,
1:17 **M** and Aaron took these men who had been
1:19 as the LORD commanded **M.**
1:44 whom **M** and Aaron enrolled with the help of
1:48 The LORD had said to **M:**
1:54 they did just as the LORD commanded **M.**
2: 1 The LORD spoke to **M** and Aaron, saying:
2:33 Just as the LORD had commanded **M,**
2:34 as the LORD had commanded **M:**
3: 1 This is the lineage of Aaron and **M** at the time
3: 1 when the LORD spoke with **M** on Mount Sinai.
3: 5 Then the LORD spoke to **M,** saying:
3:11 Then the LORD spoke to **M,** saying:
3:14 the LORD spoke to **M** in the wilderness of Sinai,
3:16 So **M** enrolled them according to the word of
3:38 were **M** and Aaron and Aaron's sons,
3:39 of the Levites whom **M** and Aaron enrolled at
3:40 Then the LORD said to **M:**
3:42 **M** enrolled all the firstborn among the Israelites,
3:44 Then the LORD spoke to **M,** saying:
3:49 So **M** took the redemption money
3:51 and **M** gave the redemption money to Aaron
3:51 as the LORD had commanded **M.**
4: 1 The LORD spoke to **M** and Aaron, saying:
4:17 Then the LORD spoke to **M** and Aaron, saying:
4:21 Then the LORD spoke to **M,** saying:
4:34 So **M** and Aaron and the leaders of
4:37 whom **M** and Aaron enrolled according to the
commandment of the LORD by **M.**
4:41 whom **M** and Aaron enrolled according to
4:45 whom **M** and Aaron enrolled according to the
commandment of the LORD by **M.**
4:46 whom **M** and Aaron and the leaders
4:49 of the LORD through **M** they were appointed
4:49 as the LORD commanded **M.**
5: 1 The LORD spoke to **M,** saying:
5: 4 the LORD had spoken to **M,** so the Israelites did.
5: 5 The LORD spoke to **M,** saying:
5:11 The LORD spoke to **M,** saying:
6: 1 The LORD spoke to **M,** saying:
6:22 The LORD spoke to **M,** saying:
7: 1 when **M** had finished setting up the tabernacle,
7: 4 Then the LORD said to **M:**
7: 6 So **M** took the wagons and the oxen,
7:11 The LORD said to **M:** They shall present their
7:89 When **M** went into the tent of meeting to speak
8: 1 The LORD spoke to **M,** saying:
8: 3 as the LORD had commanded **M.**
8: 4 to the pattern that the LORD had shown **M,**
8: 5 The LORD spoke to **M,** saying:
8:20 **M** and Aaron and the whole congregation of
8:20 the Levites just as the LORD had commanded **M**
8:22 As the LORD had commanded **M** concerning
8:23 The LORD spoke to **M,** saying:
9: 1 The LORD spoke to **M** in the wilderness of Sinai,
9: 4 So **M** told the Israelites that they should keep
9: 5 Just as the LORD had commanded **M,**
9: 6 They came before **M** and Aaron on that day,
9: 8 **M** spoke to them, "Wait, so that I may hear what
9: 9 The LORD spoke to **M,** saying:
9:23 at the command of the LORD by **M.**
10: 1 The LORD spoke to **M,** saying:
10:13 the first time at the command of the LORD by **M.**
10:29 **M** said to Hobab son of Reuel the Midianite,
10:35 Whenever the ark set out, **M** would say, "Arise,
11: 2 But the people cried out to **M;**
11: 2 and **M** prayed to the LORD, and the fire abated.
11:10 **M** heard the people weeping

Nu 11:10 LORD became very angry, and **M** was displeased.
11:11 So **M** said to the LORD,
11:16 So the LORD said to **M,** "Gather for me seventy
11:21 But **M** said, "The people I am
11:23 The LORD said to **M,** "Is
11:24 So **M** went out and told the people the words of
11:27 And a young man ran and told **M,**
11:28 And Joshua son of Nun, the assistant of **M,**
11:28 one of his chosen men, said, "My lord **M,**
11:29 But **M** said to him, "Are you jealous for my sake?
11:30 **M** and the elders of Israel returned to the camp.
12: 1 Miriam and Aaron spoke against **M** because of
12: 2 "Has the LORD spoken only through **M?**
12: 3 Now the man **M** was very humble,
12: 4 Suddenly the LORD said to **M,** Aaron,
12: 7 Not so with my servant **M;** C
12: 8 not afraid to speak against my servant **M?"** C
12:11 Then Aaron said to **M,** "Oh, my lord,
12:13 **M** cried to the LORD, "O God, please heal her."
12:14 But the LORD said to **M,**
13: 1 The LORD said to **M,**
13: 3 So **M** sent them from the wilderness of Paran,
13:16 These were the names of the men whom **M** sent
13:16 And **M** changed the name of Hoshea son of Nun
13:17 **M** sent them to spy out the land of Canaan,
13:26 to **M** and Aaron and to all the congregation of
13:30 But Caleb quieted the people before **M,** and said,
14: 2 all the Israelites complained against **M** and Aaron;
14: 5 Then **M** and Aaron fell on their faces before all
14:11 And the LORD said to **M,**
14:13 But **M** said to the LORD,
14:26 And the LORD spoke to **M** and to Aaron, saying:
14:36 And the men whom **M** sent to spy out the land,
14:39 When **M** told these words to all the Israelites,
14:41 But **M** said, "Why do you continue to transgress
14:44 and **M,** had not left the camp.
15: 1 The LORD spoke to **M,** saying:
15:17 The LORD spoke to **M,** saying:
15:22 that the LORD has spoken to **M—**
15:23 that the LORD has commanded you by **M,** from
15:33 found him gathering sticks brought him to **M,**
15:35 LORD said to **M,** "The man shall be put to death;
15:36 just as the LORD had commanded **M.**
15:37 The LORD said to **M:**
16: 2 well-known men, and they confronted **M.**
16: 3 They assembled against **M** and against Aaron,
16: 4 When **M** heard it, he fell on his face.
16: 8 Then **M** said to Korah, "Hear now, you Levites!
16:12 **M** sent for Dathan and Abiram sons of Eliab;
16:15 **M** was very angry and said to the LORD,
16:16 And **M** said to Korah, "As for you
16:18 at the entrance of the tent of meeting with **M**
16:20 Then the LORD spoke to **M** and to Aaron, saying:
16:23 And the LORD spoke to **M,** saying:
16:25 So **M** got up and went to Dathan and Abiram;
16:28 And **M** said, "This is how you shall know that
16:36 Then the LORD spoke to **M,** saying:
16:40 just as the LORD had said to him through **M.**
16:41 of the Israelites rebelled against **M** and
16:42 **M** and Aaron turned toward the tent of meeting;
16:43 Then **M** and Aaron came to the front of the tent
16:44 and the LORD spoke to **M,** saying,
16:46 **M** said to Aaron, "Take your censer,
16:47 So Aaron took it as **M** had ordered,
16:50 Aaron returned to **M** at the entrance of the tent
17: 1 The LORD spoke to **M,** saying:
17: 6 **M** spoke to the Israelites;
17: 7 So **M** placed the staffs before the LORD in
17: 8 When **M** went into the tent of the covenant on
17: 9 Then **M** brought out all the staffs from before
17:10 And the LORD said to **M,**
17:11 **M** did so; just as the LORD commanded him,
17:12 The Israelites said to **M,** "We are perishing;
18:25 Then the LORD spoke to **M,** saying:
19: 1 The LORD spoke to **M** and Aaron, saying:
20: 2 so they gathered together against **M** and
20: 3 The people quarreled with **M** and said,
20: 6 Then **M** and Aaron went away from the assembly
20: 7 The LORD spoke to **M,** saying:
20: 9 So **M** took the staff from before the LORD,
20:10 **M** and Aaron gathered the assembly together
20:11 Then **M** lifted up his hand and struck
20:12 But the LORD said to **M** and Aaron,
20:14 **M** sent messengers from Kadesh to the king
20:23 the LORD said to **M** and Aaron at Mount Hor,
20:27 **M** did as the LORD had commanded;
20:28 **M** stripped Aaron of his vestments,
20:28 **M** and Eleazar came down from the mountain.
21: 5 The people spoke against God and against **M,**
21: 7 The people came to **M** and said,
21: 7 So **M** prayed for the people.
21: 8 And the LORD said to **M,**
21: 9 So **M** made a serpent of bronze,
21:16 that is the well of which the LORD said to **M,**
21:32 **M** sent to spy out Jazer;
21:34 the LORD said to **M,** "Do not be afraid of him;
25: 4 The LORD said to **M,** "Take all the chiefs of
25: 5 And **M** said to the judges of Israel,
25: 6 of **M** and in the sight of the whole congregation of
25:10 The LORD spoke to **M,** saying:
25:16 The LORD said to **M,**
26: 1 the LORD said to **M** and to Eleazar son of Aaron
26: 3 **M** and Eleazar the priest spoke with them in
26: 4 as the LORD commanded **M.**
26: 9 who rebelled against **M** and Aaron in the company
26:52 The LORD spoke to **M,** saying:
26:59 Aaron, **M,** and their sister Miriam.

Nu 26:63 These were those enrolled by **M** and Eleazar
26:64 of those enrolled by **M** and Aaron the priest,
27: 2 They stood before **M,** Eleazar the priest,
27: 5 **M** brought their case before the LORD.
27: 6 And the LORD spoke to **M,** saying:
27:11 as the LORD commanded **M."**
27:12 to **M,** "Go up this mountain of the Abarim range,
27:15 **M** spoke to the LORD, saying,
27:18 to **M,** "Take Joshua son of Nun, a man in whom is
27:22 So **M** did as the LORD commanded him.
27:23 as the LORD had directed through **M.**
28: 1 The LORD spoke to **M,** saying:
29:40 So **M** told the Israelites everything just as the
LORD had commanded **M.**
30: 1 **M** said to the heads of the tribes of the Israelites:
30:16 the LORD commanded **M** concerning a husband
31: 1 The LORD spoke to **M,** saying,
31: 3 So **M** said to the people,
31: 6 **M** sent them to the war,
31: 7 as the LORD had commanded **M,**
31:12 the captives and the booty and the spoil to **M,**
31:13 **M,** Eleazar the priest, and all the leaders of
31:14 **M** became angry with the officers of the army,
31:15 **M** said to them, "Have you allowed all the women
31:21 of the law that the LORD has commanded **M:**
31:25 The LORD spoke to **M,** saying,
31:31 Then **M** and Eleazar the priest did as the LORD had
commanded **M:**
31:41 **M** gave the tribute, the offering for the LORD,
31:41 as the LORD had commanded **M.**
31:42 which **M** separated from that of the troops,
31:47 From the Israelites' half **M** took one of every fifty,
31:47 as the LORD had commanded **M.**
31:48 and the commanders of hundreds, approached **M,**
31:49 and said to **M,** "Your servants have counted
31:51 **M** and Eleazar the priest received the gold
31:54 So **M** and Eleazar the priest received the gold from
32: 2 Gadites and the Reubenites came and spoke to **M,**
32: 6 But **M** said to the Gadites and to the Reubenites,
32:20 So **M** said to them, "If you do this—
32:25 Then the Gadites and the Reubenites said to **M,**
32:28 So **M** gave command concerning them to Eleazar
32:29 And **M** said to them, "If the Gadites and
32:33 **M** gave to them—to the Gadites
32:40 so **M** gave Gilead to Machir son of Manasseh,
33: 1 in military formation under the leadership of **M**
33: 2 **M** wrote down their starting points, stage by stage,
33:50 the LORD spoke to **M,** saying:
34: 1 The LORD spoke to **M,** saying:
34:13 **M** commanded the Israelites, saying:
34:16 The LORD spoke to **M,** saying:
35: 1 the LORD spoke to **M,** saying:
35: 9 The LORD spoke to **M,** saying:
36: 1 came forward and spoke in the presence of **M** and
36: 5 Then **M** commanded the Israelites according to
36:10 as the LORD had commanded **M.**
36:13 through **M** to the Israelites in the plains of Moab
Dt 1: 1 that **M** spoke to all Israel beyond the Jordan—
1: 3 **M** spoke to the Israelites just as the LORD
1: 5 **M** undertook to expound this law as follows:
4:41 Then **M** set apart on the east side of
4:44 This is the law that **M** set before the Israelites.
4:45 and the statutes and ordinances that **M** spoke to
4:46 whom **M** and the Israelites defeated
5: 1 **M** convened all Israel, and said to them:
27: 1 Then **M** and the elders of Israel charged all
27: 9 Then **M** and the levitical priests spoke to all Israel,
27:11 The same day **M** charged the people as follows:
29: 1 of the covenant that the LORD commanded **M**
29: 2 **M** summoned all Israel and said to them:
31: 1 When **M** had finished speaking all these words
31: 7 Then **M** summoned Joshua and said to him in
31: 9 Then **M** wrote down this law,
31:10 **M** commanded them: "Every seventh year,
31:14 The LORD said to **M,** "Your time to die is near;
31:14 So **M** and Joshua went and presented themselves
31:16 The LORD said to **M,** "Soon you will lie down
31:22 That very day **M** wrote this song and taught it to
31:24 When **M** had finished writing down in a book
31:25 **M** commanded the Levites who carried the ark of
31:30 Then **M** recited the words of this song,
32:44 **M** came and recited all the words of this song in
32:45 When **M** had finished reciting all these words
32:48 that very day the LORD addressed **M** as follows:
33: 1 This is the blessing with which **M,**
33: 4 **M** charged us with the law,
34: 1 Then **M** went up from the plains of Moab
34: 5 Then **M,** the servant of the LORD, died there B
34: 7 **M** was one hundred twenty years old
34: 8 for **M** in the plains of Moab thirty days;
34: 8 then the period of mourning for **M** was ended.
34: 9 because **M** had laid his hands on him;
34: 9 doing as the LORD had commanded **M.**
34:10 since has there arisen a prophet in Israel like **M,**
34:12 the terrifying displays of power that **M** performed
Jos 1: 1 After the death of **M** the servant of the LORD, B
1: 2 "My servant **M** is dead. C
1: 3 upon I have given to you, as I promised to **M.**
1: 5 As I was with **M,** so I will be with you;
1: 7 the law that my servant **M** commanded you; C
1:13 that **M** the servant of the LORD commanded you, B
1:14 in the land that **M** gave you beyond the Jordan.
1:15 land that **M** the servant of the LORD gave you B
1:17 Just as we obeyed **M** in all things,
1:17 LORD your God be with you, as he was with **M!**
3: 7 that I will be with you as I was with **M.**
4:10 according to all that **M** had commanded Joshua.

Jos 4:12 before the Israelites, as M had ordered them.
4:14 as they had stood in awe of M,
8:31 as M the servant of the LORD had commanded B
8:31 as it is written in the book of the law of M, A
8:32 wrote on the stones a copy of the law of M, A
8:33 as M the servant of the LORD had commanded B
8:35 all that M commanded that Joshua did
9:24 LORD your God had commanded his servant M C
11:12 as M the servant of the LORD had commanded. B
11:15 As the LORD had commanded his servant M, C
11:15 so M commanded Joshua, and so Joshua did;
11:15 of all that the LORD had commanded M.
11:20 just as the LORD had commanded M.
11:23 according to all that the LORD had spoken to M;
12: 6 M, the servant of the LORD, B
12: 6 and M the servant of the LORD gave their land B
13: 8 which M gave them, beyond the Jordan eastward,
13: 8 as M the servant of the LORD gave them: B
13:12 these M had defeated and driven out.
13:14 To the tribe of Levi alone M gave no inheritance;
13:15 M gave an inheritance to the tribe of
13:21 whom M defeated with the leaders of Midian,
13:24 M gave an inheritance also to the tribe of
13:29 M gave an inheritance to the half-tribe
13:32 the inheritances that M distributed in the plains
13:33 But to the tribe of Levi M gave no inheritance;
14: 2 as the LORD had commanded M for the nine
14: 3 For M had given an inheritance to the two
14: 5 The Israelites did as the LORD commanded M;
14: 6 "You know what the LORD said to M the man
14: 7 forty years old when M the servant of the LORD B
14: 9 And M swore on that day, saying,
14:10 the time that the LORD spoke this word to M,
14:11 as strong today as I was on the day that M sent me;
17: 4 "The LORD commanded M to give us
18: 7 which M the servant of the LORD gave them." B
20: 2 of which I spoke to you through M,
21: 2 "The LORD commanded through M that we
21: 8 as the LORD had commanded through M.
22: 2 that M the servant of the LORD commanded you, B
22: 4 which M the servant of the LORD gave you B
22: 5 that M the servant of the LORD commanded you, B
22: 7 of the tribe of Manasseh M had given a possession
22: 9 by command of the LORD through M.
23: 6 that is written in the book of the law of M, A
24: 5 Then I sent M and Aaron,
Jdg 1:20 Hebron was given to Caleb, as M had said;
3: 4 which he commanded their ancestors by M.
4:11 the descendants of Hobab the father-in-law of M,
18:30 Jonathan son of Gershom, son of M,
1Sa 12: 6 who appointed M and Aaron
12: 8 to the LORD and the LORD sent M and Aaron,
1Ki 2: 3 as it is written in the law of M, A
8: 9 the two tablets of stone that M had placed there
8:53 just as you promised through M, your servant,
8:56 which he spoke through his servant M. C
2Ki 14: 6 of the law of M, where the LORD commanded, A
18: 4 in pieces the bronze serpent that M had made,
18: 6 that the LORD commanded M.
18:12 that M the servant of the LORD had commanded; B
21: 8 the law that my servant M commanded them." C
23:25 according to all the law of M; A
1Ch 6: 3 The children of Amram: Aaron, M, and Miriam.
6:49 all that M the servant of God had commanded. B
15:15 as M had commanded according to the word of
21:29 which M had made in the wilderness,
22:13 and the ordinances that the LORD commanded M
23:13 The sons of Amram: Aaron and M.
23:14 but as for M the man of God,
23:15 The sons of M: Gershom and Eliezer.
26:24 of Gershom, son of M, was chief officer in charge
2Ch 1: 3 which M the servant of the LORD had made B
5:10 in the ark except the two tablets that M put there
8:13 offering according to the commandment of M for
23:18 as it is written in the law of M, A
24: 6 the tax levied by M, the servant of the LORD, B
24: 9 the LORD the tax that M the servant of God laid B
25: 4 in the book of M, where the LORD commanded, D
30:16 according to the law of M the man of God; A
33: 8 the statutes, and the ordinances given through M." B
34:14 of the law of the LORD given through M.
35: 6 acting according to the word of the LORD by M."
35:12 as it is written in the book of M. D
Ezr 3: 2 as prescribed in the law of M the man of God. A
6:18 as it is written in the book of M. D
7: 6 the law of M that the LORD the God of Israel A
Ne 1: 7 ordinances that you commanded your servant M. C
1: 8 the word that you commanded your servant M, C
8: 1 scribe Ezra to bring the book of the law of M, A
8:14 which the LORD had commanded by M,
9:14 and statutes and a law through your servant M. C
10:29 which was given by M the servant of God, B
13: 1 from the book of M in the hearing of the people; D
Ps 77:20 You led your people like a flock by the hand of M
90: T *A Prayer of M, the man of God.*
99: 6 M and Aaron were among his priests,
103: 7 He made known his ways to M,
105:26 He sent his servant M, C
106:16 They were jealous of M in the camp,
106:23 had not M, his chosen one, stood in the breach
106:32 and it went ill with M on their account;
Isa 63:11 they remembered the days of old, of M his servant.
63:12 to march at the right hand of M,
Jer 15: 1 Though M and Samuel stood before me,
Da 9:11 written in the law of M, the servant of God, AB
9:13 Just as it is written in the law of M, A
Mic 6: 4 and I sent before you M, Aaron, and Miriam.
Mal 4: 4 Remember the teaching of my servant M, C
Mt 8: 4 and offer the gift that M commanded,
17: 3 Suddenly there appeared to them M and Elijah,
17: 4 one for you, one for M, and one for Elijah."
19: 7 "Why then did M command us to give a certificate
19: 8 that M allowed you to divorce your wives,
22:24 M said, 'If a man dies childless,
Mk 1:44 and offer for your cleansing what M commanded,
7:10 For M said, 'Honor your father and your mother';
9: 4 And there appeared to them Elijah with M,
9: 5 one for you, one for M, and one for Elijah."
10: 3 He answered them, "What did M command you?"
10: 4 "M allowed a man to write a certificate
12:19 M wrote for us that 'if a man's brother dies,
12:26 have you not read in the book of M, D
Lk 2:22 for their purification according to the law of M, A
5:14 to the priest, and, as M commanded, make
9:30 Suddenly they saw two men, M and Elijah,
9:33 one for you, one for M, and one for Elijah"—
16:29 Abraham replied, 'They have M and the prophets;
16:31 'If they do not listen to M and the prophets,
20:28 M wrote for us that if a man's brother dies,
20:37 the fact that the dead are raised M himself showed,
24:27 Then beginning with M and all the prophets,
24:44 everything written about me in the law of M, A
Jn 1:17 The law indeed was given through M;
1:45 "We have found him about whom M in the law
3:14 just as M lifted up the serpent in the wilderness,
5:45 before the Father; your accuser is M,
5:46 If you believed M, you would believe me,
6:32 it was not M who gave you the bread from heaven,
7:19 "Did not M give you the law?
7:22 M gave you circumcision (it is, of course, not
from M, but from the patriarchs),
7:23 the sabbath in order that the law of M may not A
8: 5 [[the law M commanded us to stone such women.]]
9:28 "You are his disciple, but we are disciples of M.
9:29 We know that God has spoken to M,
Ac 3:22 M said, 'The Lord your God will raise up for you
6:11 speak blasphemous words against M and God."
6:14 and will change the customs that M handed on
7:20 At this time M was born,
7:22 So M was instructed in all the wisdom of
7:27 who was wronging his neighbor pushed M aside,
7:29 M fled and became a resident alien in the land
7:31 When M saw it, he was amazed at the sight;
7:32 M began to tremble and did not dare to look.
7:35 "It was this M whom they rejected when they said,
7:37 This is the M who said to the Israelites,
7:40 for this M who led us out from the land of Egypt,
7:44 as God directed when he spoke to M,
13:39 not be freed by the law of M. A
15: 1 circumcised according to the custom of M,
15: 5 circumcised and ordered to keep the law of M." A
15:21 M has had those who proclaim him,
21:21 the Jews living among the Gentiles to forsake M,
26:22 the prophets and M said would take place:
28:23 both from the law of M and from the prophets. A
Ro 5:14 Yet death exercised dominion from Adam to M,
9:15 to M, "I will have mercy on whom I have mercy,
10: 5 M writes concerning the righteousness that comes
10:19 First M says, "I will make you jealous
1Co 9: 9 For it is written in the law of M, A
10: 2 and all were baptized into M in the cloud and in
2Co 3:13 not like M, who put a veil over his face to keep
3:15 Indeed, to this very day whenever M is read,
2Ti 3: 8 As Jannes and Jambres opposed M,
Heb 3: 2 just as M also "was faithful in all God's house."
3: 3 Yet Jesus is worthy of more glory than M,
3: 5 M was faithful in all God's house as a servant,
3:16 who left Egypt under the leadership of M?
7:14 and in connection with that tribe M said nothing
8: 5 for M, when he was about to erect the tent,
9:19 to all the people by M in accordance with the law,
10:28 has violated the law of M dies without mercy A
11:23 By faith M was hidden by his parents
11:24 By faith M, when he was grown up,
12:21 Indeed, so terrifying was the sight that M said,
Jude 1: 9 with the devil and disputed about the body of M,
Rev 15: 3 they sing the song of M, the servant of God, B
Tob 1: 8 law of M and according to the instructions A
6:13 death according to the decree of the book of M. D
7:11 in accordance with the decree in the book of M, D
7:12 the law and decree written in the book of M. D
7:13 as wife according to the decree of the law of M. A
Sir 24:23 the law that M commanded us as an inheritance
45: 1 M, whose memory is blessed.
45: 6 a holy man like M who was his brother,
45:15 M ordained him, and anointed him with holy oil;
46: 1 and was the successor of M in the prophetic office.
46: 7 And in the days of M he proved his loyalty,
Bar 1:20 that the Lord declared through his servant M C
2: 2 the threats that were written in the law of M. A
2:28 as you spoke by your servant M on the day C
Sus 1: 3 according to the law of M. A
1:62 Acting in accordance with the law of M, A
2Mc 1:29 in your holy place, as M promised."
2: 4 where M had gone up and had seen the inheritance
2: 8 as they were shown in the case of M,
2:10 Just as M prayed to the Lord,
2:11 And M said, "They were consumed because
7: 6 as M declared in his song that bore witness against
7:30 the law that was given to our ancestors through M.
1Es 1: 6 of the Lord that was given to M."
1:11 to the Lord as it is written in the book of M; D
5:49 accordance with the directions in the book of M D
7: 6 according to what was written in the book of M. D
1Es 7: 9 of Israel in accordance with the book of M; D
8: 3 scribe skilled in the law of M, which was given A
9:39 the law of M that had been given by the Lord A
2Es 1:13 I gave you M as leader and Aaron as priest;
7:*106* [36] M for our ancestors who sinned in the desert,
7:*129* [59] For this is the way of which M,
14: 3 and spoke to M when my people were in bondage
4Mc 2:17 When M was angry with Dathan and Abiram,
9: 2 to the law and to M our counselor.
17:19 For M says, "All who are consecrated are
18:18 not forget to teach you the song that M taught,

MOSES' (16) [MOSES]

Ex 4:25 and touched M feet with it, and said,
17:12 But M hands grew weary;
18: 1 Jethro, the priest of Midian, M father-in-law,
18: 5 M father-in-law, came into the wilderness
18: 5 bringing M sons and wife to him.
18:12 And Jethro, M father-in-law,
18:12 to eat bread with M father-in-law in the presence
18:14 When M father-in-law saw all that he was doing
18:17 M father-in-law said to him,
32:19 the dancing, M anger burned hot, and he threw
Lev 8:29 it was M portion of the ram of ordination,
Nu 10:29 M father-in-law, "We are setting out for the place
Jos 1: 1 to Joshua son of Nun, M assistant,
Jdg 1:16 M father-in-law, went up with the people of Judah
Mt 23: 2 "The scribes and the Pharisees sit on M seat;
2Co 3: 7 that the people of Israel could not gaze at M face

MOSHEH See Index to Footnotes

MOST‡ (349) [MORE]

A. MOST HIGH (187)
B. MOST HOLY (50)
C. MOST HIGH *GOD (18)
D. MOST HOLY PLACE (13)
E. *GOD MOST HIGH (8)

Ge 14:18 he was priest of God M High. AE
14:19 "Blessed be Abram by God M High, AE
14:20 and blessed be God M High, AE
14:22 "I have sworn to the LORD, God M High, AE
34:19 Now he was the m honored of all his family.
Ex 26:33 for you the holy place from the m holy. B
26:34 on the ark of the covenant in the m holy place. BD
29:37 and consecrate it, and the altar shall be m holy; B
30:10 It is m holy to the LORD. B
30:29 so that they may be m holy; B
30:36 it shall be for you m holy. B
40:10 so that the altar shall be m holy. B
Lev 2: 3 m holy part of the offerings by fire to the LORD. B
2:10 it is a m holy part of the offerings by fire to B
6:17 it is m holy, like the sin offering and B
6:25 the burnt offering is slaughtered; it is m holy. B
6:29 among the priests shall eat of it; it is m holy. B
7: 1 the ritual of the guilt offering. It is m holy; B
7: 6 in a holy place; it is m holy. B
10:12 beside the altar, for it is m holy; B
10:17 For it is m holy, and God has given it to you B
14:13 to the priest: it is m holy. B
21:22 of the m holy as well as of the holy. B
24: 9 for they are m holy portions for him from B
27:28 every devoted thing is m holy to the LORD. B
Nu 4: 4 the tent of meeting concerns the m holy things. B
4:19 when they come near to the m holy things: B
18: 9 This shall be yours from the m holy things, B
18: 9 theirs that they render to me as a m holy thing, B
18:10 As a m holy thing you shall eat it; B
24:16 and knows the knowledge of the M High, A
Dt 7:14 You shall be the m blessed of peoples,
13: 6 or your m intimate friend—
28:54 Even the m refined and gentle of men
28:56 She who is the m refined and gentle among you,
32: 8 When the M High apportioned the nations, A
33:24 And of Asher he said: M blessed of sons be Asher;
Jdg 5:24 "M blessed of women be Jael,
5:24 of tent-dwelling women m blessed.
13: 6 like that of an angel of God, m awe-inspiring;
1Sa 2:10 the M High will thunder in heaven. A
2Sa 22:14 the M High uttered his voice. A
23:19 He was the m renowned of the Thirty,
1Ki 6:16 as an inner sanctuary, as the m holy place. BD
7:50 innermost part of the house, the m holy place, BD
8: 6 of the house, in the m holy place, underneath BD
21:26 He acted m abominably in going after idols,
1Ch 6:49 doing all the work of the m holy place, BD
11:21 He was the m renowned of the Thirty,
23:13 to consecrate the m holy things, so that he B
2Ch 3: 8 He made the m holy place; BD
3:10 In the m holy place he made two carved BD
4:22 inner doors to the m holy place and the doors BD
5: 7 of the house, in the m holy place, underneath BD
31:14 for the LORD and the m holy offerings. B
Ezr 2:63 that they were not to partake of the m holy food, B
Ne 7:65 that they were not to partake of the m holy food, B
Est 4: 3 and m of them lay in sackcloth and ashes.
6: 9 over to one of the king's m noble officials;
Ps 7:17 to the name of the LORD, the M High. A
9: 2 I will sing praise to your name, O M High. A
18:13 and the M High uttered his voice. A
21: 7 through the steadfast love of the M High A
28: 2 lift up my hands toward your m holy sanctuary. B
45: 2 You are the m handsome of men;
46: 4 the holy habitation of the M High. A

Ps 47: 2 For the LORD, the **M** High, is awesome, A
50:14 and pay your vows to the **M** High. A
56: 2 for many fight against me. O **M** High, A
57: 2 I cry to God **M** High, AE
73:11 Is there knowledge in the **M** High?" A
77:10 that the right hand of the **M** High has changed." A
78:17 rebelling against the **M** High in the desert. A
78:35 the **M** High God their redeemer. AC
78:56 Yet they tested the **M** High God, AC
82: 6 I say, "You are gods, children of the **M** High, A
83:18 are the **M** High over all the earth. A
87: 5 for the **M** High himself will establish it. A
91: 1 You who live in the shelter of the **M** High, A
91: 9 the **M** High your dwelling place, A
92: 1 to sing praises to your name, O **M** High; A
97: 9 For you, O LORD, are **m** high over all the earth; A
106: 7 but rebelled against the **M** High at the Red Sea. A
107:11 and spurned the counsel of the **M** High. A
SS 5:16 His speech is **m** sweet,
Isa 14:14 I will make myself like the **M** High." A
Jer 3:19 the **m** beautiful heritage of all the nations.
6:26 as for an only child, **m** bitter lamentation:
18:13 The virgin Israel has done a **m** horrible thing.
La 3:35 in the presence of the **M** High, A
3:38 mouth of the **M** High that good and bad come? A
Eze 20: 6 the **m** glorious of all lands,
20:15 the **m** glorious of all lands,
28: 7 the **m** terrible of the nations;
29:15 It shall be the **m** lowly of the kingdoms,
30:11 the **m** terrible of the nations,
31:12 from the **m** terrible of the nations have cut it down
32:12 all of them **m** terrible among the nations.
41: 4 And he said to me, This is the **m** holy place. BD
42:13 the LORD shall eat the **m** holy offerings; B
42:13 there they shall deposit the **m** holy offerings— B
43:12 top of the mountain all around shall be **m** holy. B
44:13 the things that are **m** sacred;
45: 3 which shall be the sanctuary, the **m** holy place. BD
48:12 a **m** holy place, adjoining the territory of BD
Da 3:26 and Abednego, servants of the **M** High God, AC
4: 2 the **M** High God has worked for me AC
4:17 the **M** High is sovereign over the kingdom A
4:24 the **M** High that has come upon my lord A
4:25 the **M** High has sovereignty over the kingdom A
4:32 the **M** High has sovereignty over the kingdom A
4:34 I blessed the **M** High, and praised and honored A
5:18 the **M** High God gave your father AC
5:21 the **M** High God has sovereignty over AC
7:18 the **M** High shall receive the kingdom and A
7:22 for the holy ones of the **M** High, A
7:25 He shall speak words against the **M** High, A
7:25 shall wear out the holy ones of the **M** High, A
7:27 to the people of the holy ones of the **M** High; A
9:24 and to anoint a **m** holy place. BD
Hos 11: 7 To the **M** High they call, A
Mic 7: 4 the **m** upright of them a thorn hedge.
Mt 11:20 in which **m** of his deeds of power had been done,
Mk 5: 7 Jesus, Son of the **M** High God? AC
9:26 so that **m** of them said, "He is dead."
Lk 1: 3 for you, **m** excellent Theophilus,
1:32 and will be called the Son of the **M** High, A
1:35 the power of the **M** High will overshadow you; A
1:76 child, will be called the prophet of the **M** High; A
6:35 and you will be children of the **M** High; A
8:28 Jesus, Son of the **M** High God? AC
Ac 7:48 Yet the **M** High does not dwell in houses made A
16:17 "These men are slaves of the **M** High God, AC
19:32 the assembly was in confusion, and **m** of them did
26:25 "I am not out of my mind, **m** excellent Festus,
1Co 10: 5 God was not pleased with **m** of them,
14:27 let there be only two or at **m** three,
15: 6 **m** of whom are still alive, though some have died.
15:19 we are of all people **m** to be pitied.
2Co 9: 2 and your zeal has stirred up **m** of them.
12:15 I will **m** gladly spend and be spent for you.
Eph 5:16 making the **m** of the time,
Php 1:14 and **m** of the brothers and sisters,
Col 4: 5 making the **m** of the time.
1Th 3:10 Night and day we pray **m** earnestly
Heb 7: 1 priest of the **M** High God, AC
Jude 1:20 build yourselves up on your **m** holy faith; B
Tob 1:13 the **M** High gave me favor and good standing A
4:11 in the presence of the **M** High. A
7: 7 "O **m** miserable of calamities that such an upright
Jdt 11: 8 the **m** informed and the **m** astounding in military
13:18 by the **M** High God above all other women AC
AdE 15: 6 and precious stones. He was **m** terrifying.
16: 2 with the **m** generous kindness of their benefactors,
16:15 but are governed by **m** righteous laws
16:16 and are children of the living God, **m** high, A
16:16 **m** mighty, who has directed the kingdom both
16:16 and for our ancestors in the **m** excellent order.
16:24 **m** hateful to wild animals and birds for all time.
Wis 5:15 the **M** High takes care of them. A
6: 3 and your sovereignty from the **M** High; A
6:17 of wisdom is the **m** sincere desire for instruction,
12: 7 that the land **m** precious of all to you might receive
15:14 But **m** foolish, and more miserable than an infant,
15:18 they worship even the **m** hateful animals,
16:17 For—**m** incredible of all—in water,
17:19 or the sound of the **m** savage roaring beasts,
18:12 instant their **m** valued children had been destroyed.
Sir 4:10 you will then be like a son of the **M** High, A
7: 9 when I make an offering to the **M** High God, AC
7:15 which was created by the **M** High. A
9:15 be about the law of the **M** High. A
12: 2 if not by them, certainly by the **M** High. A
Sir 12: 6 For the **M** High also hates sinners A
16:21 so **m** of his works are concealed.
17:26 to the **M** High and turn away from iniquity, A
17:27 Who will sing praises to the **M** High in Hades A
19:17 and let the law of the **M** High take its course. A
23:18 The **M** High will not remember sins." A
23:23 she has disobeyed the law of the **M** High; A
24: 2 assembly of the **M** High she opens her mouth, A
24: 3 "I came forth from the mouth of the **M** High, A
24:23 the book of the covenant of the **M** High God, AC
28: 7 remember the covenant of the **M** High, A
29:11 according to the commandments of the **M** High, A
33:15 Look at all the works of the **M** High; A
34: 6 they are sent by intervention from the **M** High, A
34:23 The **M** High is not pleased with the offerings of A
35: 8 and its pleasing odor rises before the **M** High. A
35:12 Give to the **M** High as he has given to you, A
35:21 it will not desist until the **M** High responds A
37:15 the **M** High that he may direct your way in truth. A
38: 2 for their gift of healing comes from the **M** High, A
38:34 to the study of the law of the **M** High! A
39: 5 and to petition the **M** High; A
41: 4 then should you reject the will of the **M** High? A
41: 8 have forsaken the law of the **M** High God! AC
42: 2 of the law of the **M** High and his covenant, A
42:18 For the **M** High knows all that may be known; A
43: 2 the work of the **M** High. A
43:12 the hands of the **M** High have stretched it out. A
44:20 He kept the law of the **M** High, A
46: 5 He called upon the **M** High, the Mighty One, A
47: 5 For he called on the Lord, the **M** High, A
47: 8 the **M** High, proclaiming his glory; A
48: 5 by the word of the **M** High. A
49: 4 for they abandoned the law of the **M** High; A
50: 7 the sun shining on the temple of the **M** High, A
50:14 and arranging the offering to the **M** High, A
50:15 a pleasing odor to the **M** High, the king of all. A
50:16 fanfare as a reminder before the **M** High. A
50:17 the Almighty, God **M** High. AE
50:19 people of the Lord **M** High offered their prayers A
50:21 to receive the blessing from the **M** High. A
Aza 1: 9 the **m** wicked in all the world.
Sus 1: 4 to him because he was the **m** honored of them all.
Bel 1: 2 and was the **m** honored of all his friends.
1Mc 1: 6 So he summoned his **m** honored officers,
2Mc 1:14 to secure **m** of its treasures as a dowry.
1:36 but by **m** people it is called naphtha.
3:31 to call upon the **M** High to grant life A
5:15 Antiochus dared to enter the **m** holy temple B
6:11 in view of their regard for that **m** holy day. B
7:34 you, unholy wretch, you **m** defiled of all mortals,
8: 7 the nights **m** advantageous for such attacks.
8:24 and wounded and disabled **m** of Nicanor's army,
8:32 a **m** wicked man, and one who had greatly troubled
9:25 whom I have often entrusted and commended to **m**
9:28 came to the end of his life by a **m** pitiable fate,
11:12 **M** of them got away stripped and wounded,
12:14 behaved **m** insolently toward Judas and his men,
12:24 because he held the parents of **m** of them,
14:38 and he had **m** zealously risked body and life
1Es 2: 3 The Lord of Israel, the Lord **M** High, A
6:31 libations may be made to the **M** High God AC
8:19 and reader of the law of the **M** High God AC
8:21 be scrupulously fulfilled for the **M** High God, AC
9:46 And Ezra blessed the Lord God **M** High, AE
Man 1: 7 for you are the Lord **M** High, A
3Mc 1:20 they crowded together at the **m** high temple. A
3: 1 and put to death by the **m** cruel means.
3:17 with magnificent and **m** beautiful offerings,
3:27 be tortured to death with the **m** hateful torments,
4: 4 of life and shed tears at the **m** miserable expulsion
4:18 though **m** of them were still in the country,
5:24 for this **m** pitiful spectacle
5:25 toward heaven and with **m** tearful supplication
5:44 in the city **m** favorable for keeping guard.
5:49 the end of their **m** miserable suspense,
6: 2 Almighty God **M** High, governing all creation AE
6:18 Then the **m** glorious, almighty,
6:39 the Lord of all **m** gloriously revealed his mercy
7: 9 Ruler over every power, the **M** High God, AC
2Es 3: 3 I began to speak anxious words to the **M** High, A
4: 2 the way of the **M** High?" A
4:11 the way of the **M** High? A
4:34 "Do not be in a greater hurry than the **M** High. A
5: 4 But if the **M** High grants that you live, A
5:22 to speak words in the presence of the **M** High. A
5:34 the way of the **M** High and to search out A
6:32 voice has surely been heard by the **M** High; A
6:36 I began to speak in the presence of the **M** High. A
6:58 and **m** dear, have been given into their hands.
7:19 or wiser than the **M** High!
7:23 even declared that the **M** High does not exist, A
7:*33* The **M** High shall be revealed on the seat of A
7:*37* Then the **M** High will say to the nations A
7:*42* only the splendor of the glory of the **M** High, A
7:*50* the **M** High has made not one world but two. A
7:*70* "When the **M** High made the world and Adam A
7:*74* How long the **M** High has been patient A
7:*77* a treasure of works stored up with the **M** High, A
7:*78* decisive decree has gone out from the **M** High A
7:*78* first of all it adores the glory of the **M** High. A
7:*79* way of the **M** High, who have despised his law A
7:*81* they have scorned the law of the **M** High. A
7:*83* the covenants of the **M** High. A
7:*87* of the **M** High in whose presence they sinned A
7:*88* of those who have kept the ways of the **M** High, A
7:*89* they laboriously served the **M** High, A
2Es 7:*102* the ungodly or to entreat the **M** High for them— A
7:*103* or friends for those who are **m** dear."
7:*122* [52] the **M** High will defend those who have led A
7:*122* [52] but we have walked in the **m** wicked ways?
7:*132* [62] that the **M** High is now called merciful, A
8: 1 **M** High made this world for the sake of many, A
8:48 be praiseworthy before the **M** High, A
8:56 they despised the **M** High, A
8:59 For the **M** High did not intend that anyone A
9: 2 it is the very time when the **M** High is about A
9: 4 **M** High spoke from the days that were of old, A
9: 6 so also are the times of the **M** High: A
9:25 and pray to the **M** High continually. A
9:28 I began to speak before the **M** High, and said, A
9:44 during those thirty years I prayed to the **M** High, A
10: 6 "You **m** foolish of women,
10: 8 It is **m** appropriate to mourn now,
10:24 and the **M** High may give you rest, A
10:38 the **M** High has revealed many secrets to you. A
10:50 **M** High, seeing that you are sincerely grieved A
10:52 the **M** High would reveal these things to you. A
10:54 where the city of the **M** High was to be revealed. A
10:57 and you have been called to be with the **M** High A
10:59 and the **M** High will show you A
10:59 **M** High will do to those who inhabit the earth A
11:38 The **M** High says to you, A
11:43 Your insolence has come up before the **M** High, A
11:44 The **M** High has looked at his times; A
11:45 your **m** evil little wings, your malicious heads,
11:45 your **m** evil talons, and your whole worthless body,
12: 4 because you search out the ways of the **M** High. A
12: 6 entreat the **M** High that he may strengthen me A
12:23 the **M** High will raise up three kings, A
12:30 It is these whom the **M** High has kept for A
12:32 this is the Messiah whom the **M** High has kept A
12:36 to learn this secret of the **M** High. A
12:39 be shown whatever it pleases the **M** High A
12:47 for the **M** High has you in remembrance, A
13:13 and prayed to the **M** High, and said, A
13:26 this is he whom the **M** High has been keeping A
13:29 **M** High will deliver those who are on the earth. A
13:44 at that time the **M** High performed signs A
13:47 **M** High will stop the channels of the river again, A
13:56 for there is a reward laid up with the **M** High. A
13:57 the **M** High for the wonders that he does from A
14:15 to one side the thoughts that are **m** grievous to you,
14:31 the ways that the **M** High commanded you. A
14:42 the **M** High gave understanding to the five men, A
14:45 forty days were ended, the **M** High spoke to me, A
4Mc 1: 1 that I am about to discuss is **m** philosophical,
1:20 The two **m** comprehensive types of emotions
1:25 which is the **m** complex of all the emotions.
2:19 Why else did Jacob, our **m** wise father,
5:26 He has permitted us to eat what will be **m** suitable
5:27 which are **m** hateful to us.
7: 1 For like a **m** skillful pilot,
7: 4 has ever held out as did that **m** holy man. B
7:13 **M** amazing, indeed, though he was an old man,
7:16 **m** certainly devout reason is governor of
8: 1 have prevailed over the **m** painful instruments
8:23 from this **m** pleasant life and deprive ourselves
9:15 "**M** abominable tyrant, enemy
9:30 "Do you not think, you **m** savage tyrant,
9:32 You will not escape, you **m** abominable tyrant,
10:10 **m** abominable tyrant, are suffering because
12:11 "You profane tyrant, **m** impious of all the wicked,
12:13 a man, were you not ashamed, you **m** savage beast,
14: 7 O **m** holy seven, brothers in harmony! B

MOTE (KJV) See SPECK

MOTH‡ (9) [MOTH-EATEN]

Job 4:19 who are crushed like a **m.**
Ps 39:11 consuming like a **m** what is dear to them;
Pr 25:20 Like a **m** in clothing or a worm in wood,
Isa 50: 9 the **m** will eat them up.
51: 8 For the **m** will eat them up like a garment,
Mt 6:19 where **m** and rust consume and
6:20 where neither **m** nor rust consumes and
Lk 12:33 where no thief comes near and no **m** destroys.
Sir 42:13 for from garments comes the **m,**

MOTH-EATEN (2) [EAT, MOTH]

Job 13:28 like a garment that is **m.**
Jas 5: 2 Your riches have rotted, and your clothes are **m.**

MOTHER‡ (302) [GRANDMOTHER, MOTHER'S, MOTHER-IN-LAW, MOTHERS, MOTHERS']

A. FATHER ... MOTHER (69)

Ge 2:24 a man leaves his father and his **m** and clings
3:20 because she was the **m** of all living.
20:12 of my father but not the daughter of my **m;**
21:21 his **m** got a wife for him from the land of Egypt.
24:53 to her brother and to her **m** costly ornaments.
24:55 Her brother and her **m** said,
24:67 Then Isaac brought her into his **m** Sarah's tent.
27:11 But Jacob said to his **m** Rebekah, "Look,
27:13 His **m** said to him, "Let your curse be on me,
27:14 he went and got them and brought them to his **m;**
27:14 and his **m** prepared savory food,
28: 5 the brother of Rebekah, Jacob's and Esau's **m.**
28: 7 and that Jacob had obeyed his father and his **m**

Ge 30:14 and brought them to his **m** Leah.
37:10 I and your **m** and your brothers,
Ex 2: 8 So the girl went and called the child's **m.**
20:12 Honor your father and your **m,** A
21:15 strikes father or **m** shall be put to death. A
21:17 curses father or **m** shall be put to death. A
22:30 seven days it shall remain with its **m;**
Lev 18: 7 which is the nakedness of your **m;**
18: 7 is your **m,** you shall not uncover her nakedness.
19: 3 You shall each revere your **m** and father,
20: 9 All who curse father or **m** shall be put to death; A
20: 9 having cursed father or **m,** A
20:14 a man takes a wife and her **m** also, it is depravity;
20:17 a daughter of his father or a daughter of his **m,**
21: 2 his **m,** his father, his son, his daughter, his brother;
21:11 shall not defile himself even for his father or **m.** A
22:27 it shall remain seven days with its **m,**
24:10 A man whose **m** was an Israelite
Nu 6: 7 Even if their father or **m,** brother or sister, A
Dt 5:16 Honor your father and your **m,** A
21:13 mourning for her father and **m;** A
21:18 not obey his father and **m,** A
21:19 his father and his **m** shall take hold of him A
22: 6 with the **m** sitting on the fledglings or on the eggs,
22: 6 you shall not take the **m** with the young.
22: 7 Let the **m** go, taking only the young for yourself,
22:15 of the young woman and her **m** shall then submit
27:16 "Cursed be anyone who dishonors father or **m.**" A
27:22 daughter of his father or the daughter of his **m.**"
33: 9 said of his father and **m,** "I regard them not"; A
Jos 2:13 that you will spare my father and **m,** A
2:18 not gather into your house your father and **m,** A
6:23 with her father, her **m,** her brothers, and all who A
Jdg 5: 7 because you arose, Deborah, arose as a **m** in Israel.
5:28 the **m** of Sisera gazed through the lattice:
8:19 "They were my brothers, the sons of my **m;**
14: 2 Then he came up, and told his father and **m,** A
14: 3 But his father and **m** said to him, A
14: 4 father and **m** did not know that this was from A
14: 5 Then Samson went down with his father and **m** A
14: 6 not tell his father or his **m** what he had done. A
14: 9 When he came to his father and **m,** A
14:16 "Look, I have not told my father or my **m.** A
17: 2 to his **m,** "The eleven hundred pieces of silver
17: 2 And his **m** said, "May my son be blessed by
17: 3 the eleven hundred pieces of silver to his **m;**
17: 3 and his **m** said, "I consecrate the silver to
17: 4 So when he returned the money to his **m,**
17: 4 his **m** took two hundred pieces of silver,
Ru 2:11 left your father and **m** and your native land A
1Sa 2:19 His **m** used to make for him a little robe and take
15:33 so your **m** shall be childless among women."
22: 3 "Please let my father and **m** come to you, A
2Sa 17:25 sister of Zeruiah, Joab's **m.**
19:37 near the graves of my father and my **m.** A
20:19 you seek to destroy a city that is a **m** in Israel;
1Ki 1:11 Then Nathan said to Bathsheba, Solomon's **m,**
2:13 of Haggith came to Bathsheba, Solomon's **m.**
2:19 and had a throne brought for the king's **m,**
2:20 the king said to her, "Make your request, my **m;**
2:22 King Solomon answered his **m,**
3:27 do not kill him. She is his **m.**"
15:13 also removed his **m** Maacah from being queen **m,**
17:23 and gave him to his **m;**
19:20 and said, "Let me kiss my father and my **m,** A
22:52 and walked in the way of his father and **m,** A
2Ki 3: 2 though not like his father and **m,** A
4:19 father said to his servant, "Carry him to his **m.**"
4:20 He carried him and brought him to his **m;**
4:30 Then the **m** of the child said, "As the LORD lives,
9:22 and sorceries of your **m** Jezebel continue?"
10:13 the royal princes and the sons of the queen **m.**"
11: 1 Now when Athaliah, Ahaziah's **m,**
24:12 himself, his **m,** his servants, his officers,
24:15 the king's **m,** the king's wives, his officials,
1Ch 2:26 she was the **m** of Onam.
4: 9 and his **m** named him Jabez, saying,
2Ch 15:16 even removed his **m** Maacah from being queen **m**
22: 3 for his **m** was his counselor in doing wickedly.
22:10 Now when Athaliah, Ahaziah's **m,**
Est 2: 7 his cousin, for she had neither father nor **m;** A
2: 7 and when her father and her **m** died, A
Job 17:14 'You are my father,' and to the worm, 'My **m,**'
Ps 22:10 and since my **m** bore me you have been my God.
27:10 If my father and **m** forsake me, A
35:14 I went about as one who laments for a **m,**
51: 5 a sinner when my **m** conceived me.
109:14 and do not let the sin of his **m** be blotted out.
113: 9 making her the joyous **m** of children.
131: 2 like a weaned child with its **m;**
Pr 19:26 violence to their father and chase away their **m** A
20:20 If you curse father or **m,** A
23:22 and do not despise your **m** when she is old.
23:25 Let your father and **m** be glad; A
28:24 Anyone who robs father or **m** and says, A
29:15 but a **m** is disgraced by a neglected child.
30:17 and scorns to obey a **m** will be pecked out
31: 1 An oracle that his **m** taught him:
SS 3:11 at the crown with which his **m** crowned him on
6: 9 the darling of her **m,** flawless to her that bore her.
8: 2 and bring you into the house of my **m,**
8: 5 There your **m** was in labor with you;
Isa 8: 4 child knows how to call "My father" or "My **m,**"
40:11 and gently lead the **m** sheep.
50: 1 and for your transgressions your **m** was put away.
66:13 As a **m** comforts her child, so I will comfort you;
Jer 13:18 Say to the king and the queen **m;**
Jer 15:10 Woe is me, my **m,** that you ever bore me,
20:14 The day when my **m** bore me, let it not be blessed!
20:17 so my **m** would have been my grave,
22:26 and the **m** who bore you into another country,
29: 2 This was after King Jeconiah, and the queen **m,**
50:12 your **m** shall be utterly shamed,
Eze 16: 3 your father was an Amorite, and your **m** a Hittite.
16:44 will use this proverb about you, "Like **m,**
16:45 You are the daughter of your **m,**
16:45 Your **m** was a Hittite and your father an Amorite.
19: 2 What a lioness was your **m** among lions!
19:10 Your **m** was like a vine in a vineyard transplanted
22: 7 Father and **m** are treated with contempt in you; A
23: 2 there were two women, the daughters of one **m;**
44:25 father or **m,** however, and for son or daughter, A
Hos 2: 2 Plead with your **m,** plead—
2: 5 For their **m** has played the whore;
4: 5 with you by night, and I will destroy your **m.**
Mic 7: 6 the daughter rises up against her **m,**
Mt 1:18 When his **m** Mary had been engaged to Joseph,
2:11 they saw the child with Mary his **m;**
2:13 take the child and his **m,** and flee to Egypt,
2:14 Joseph got up, took the child and his **m** by night,
2:20 take the child and his **m,**
2:21 Then Joseph got up, took the child and his **m,**
10:35 and a daughter against her **m,**
10:37 Whoever loves father or **m** more than me is A
12:46 his **m** and his brothers were standing outside,
12:47 your **m** and your brothers are standing outside,
12:48 "Who is my **m,** and who are my brothers?"
12:49 he said, "Here are my **m** and my brothers!
12:50 in heaven is my brother and sister and **m.**"
13:55 Is not his **m** called Mary?
14: 8 Prompted by her **m,** she said,
14:11 who brought it to her **m.**
15: 4 For God said, 'Honor your father and your **m,**' A
15: 4 'Whoever speaks evil of father or **m** must A
15: 5 But you say that whoever tells father or **m,** A
19: 5 this reason a man shall leave his father and **m** A
19:19 Honor your father and **m;** A
19:29 or brothers or sisters or father or **m** or children A
20:20 Then the **m** of the sons of Zebedee came to him
27:56 and Mary the **m** of James and Joseph,
27:56 and the **m** of the sons of Zebedee.
Mk 3:31 Then his **m** and his brothers came;
3:32 "Your **m** and your brothers and sisters are outside,
3:33 And he replied, "Who are my **m** and my brothers?"
3:34 he said, "Here are my **m** and my brothers!
3:35 the will of God is my brother and sister and **m.**"
5:40 the child's father and **m** and those who were A
6:24 She went out and said to her **m,**
6:28 Then the girl gave it to her **m.**
7:10 Moses said, 'Honor your father and your **m**'; A
7:10 and, 'Whoever speaks evil of father or **m** must A
7:11 But you say that if anyone tells father or **m,** A
7:12 permit doing anything for a father or **m,** A
10: 7 this reason a man shall leave his father and **m** A
10:19 Honor your father and **m.**' " A
10:29 or brothers or sisters or **m** or father or children
15:40 and Mary the **m** of James the younger and of Joses,
15:47 Mary Magdalene and Mary the **m** of Joses saw
16: 1 Mary Magdalene, and Mary the **m** of James,
Lk 1:43 that the **m** of my Lord comes to me?
1:60 But his **m** said, "No; he is to be called John."
2:33 the child's father and **m** were amazed at what A
2:34 Then Simeon blessed them and said to his **m** Mary,
2:48 and his **m** said to him, "Child,
2:51 His **m** treasured all these things in her heart.
7:15 and Jesus gave him to his **m.**
8:19 Then his **m** and his brothers came to him,
8:20 "Your **m** and your brothers are standing outside,
8:21 "My **m** and my brothers are those who hear
8:51 John, and James, and the child's father and **m.** A
12:53 **m** against daughter and daughter against **m,**
14:26 to me and does not hate father and **m,** A
18:20 Honor your father and **m.**' " A
24:10 Joanna, Mary the **m** of James,
Jn 2: 1 and the **m** of Jesus was there.
2: 3 the wine gave out, the **m** of Jesus said to him,
2: 5 His **m** said to the servants,
2:12 After this he went down to Capernaum with his **m,**
6:42 the son of Joseph, whose father and **m** we know? A
19:25 standing near the cross of Jesus were his **m,**
19:26 When Jesus saw his **m** and the disciple whom he
19:26 he said to his **m,** "Woman, here is your son."
19:27 Then he said to the disciple, "Here is your **m.**"
Ac 1:14 including Mary the **m** of Jesus,
12:12 the **m** of John whose other name was Mark,
Ro 16:13 and greet his **m**—a **m** to me also.
Gal 4:26 she is free, and she is our **m.**
Eph 5:31 this reason a man will leave his father and **m** A
6: 2 "Honor your father and **m**"—this is the first A
1Ti 1: 9 those who kill their father or **m,** for murderers, A
2Ti 1: 5 in your grandmother Lois and your **m** Eunice and
Heb 7: 3 Without father, without **m,** without genealogy,
Rev 17: 5 **m** of whores and of earth's abominations."
Tob 1: 8 the **m** of my father Tobiel,
4: 3 Honor your **m** and do not abandon her all the days
4:13 because idleness is the **m** of famine.
5:17 he kissed his father and **m.** A
5:18 But his **m** began to weep, and said to Tobit,
7:13 Then he called her **m** and told her
8:21 I am your father and Edna is your **m,**
9: 6 and to your wife's father and **m.** A
10: 7 father and **m** do not believe that they will see A
10:12 on I am your **m** and Sarah is your beloved wife.
11:17 Blessed be your father and your **m,** A
Tob 14:10 On whatever day you bury your **m** beside me,
14:12 Tobias's **m** died, he buried her beside his father.
Wis 7: 1 and in the womb of a **m** I was molded into flesh,
7:12 but I did not know that she was their **m.**
Sir 3: 4 and those who respect their **m** are
3: 6 and those who honor their **m** obey the Lord;
3:11 it is a disgrace for children not to respect their **m.**
3:16 and whoever angers a **m** is cursed by the Lord.
4:10 and be like a husband to their **m;**
4:10 and he will love you more than does your **m.**
7:27 and do not forget the birth pangs of your **m.**
15: 2 She will come to meet him like a **m,**
23:14 Remember your father and **m** when you sit A
40: 1 until the day they return to the **m** of all the living.
41:17 of sexual immorality, before your father or **m;** A
1Mc 13:28 for his father and **m** and four brothers. A
2Mc 7: 1 also that seven brothers and their **m** were arrested
7: 4 while the rest of the brothers and the **m** looked on.
7: 5 and their **m** encouraged one another to die nobly,
7:20 The **m** was especially admirable and worthy
7:25 the **m** to him and urged her to advise the youth
7:41 Last of all, the **m** died, after her sons.
1Es 4:21 with no thought of his father or his **m** A
4:25 loves his wife more than his father or his **m.** A
2Es 1:28 as a father entreats his sons or a **m** her daughters
2: 2 The **m** who bore them says to them, 'Go,
2: 5 as a witness in addition to the **m** of the children,
2: 6 on them and bring their **m** to ruin,
2:15 "**M,** embrace your children;
2:17 Do not fear, **m** of children, for I have chosen you,
2:30 "Rejoice, O **m,** with your children,
5:50 Is our **m,** of whom you have told me, still young?
10: 7 For Zion, the **m** of us all,
10: 8 but we, the whole world, for our **m.**
13:55 and called understanding your **m.**
4Mc 1: 8 Eleazar and the seven brothers and their **m.**
1:10 to praise for their virtues those who, with their **m,**
8: 3 were brought before him along with their aged **m.**
8: 4 grouped about their **m** as though a chorus,
10: 2 and the same **m** bore me,
12: 6 he sent for the boy's **m** to show compassion
12: 7 his **m** had exhorted him in the Hebrew language,
14:12 for the **m** of the seven young men bore up under
14:20 But sympathy for her children did not sway the **m**
15: 1 more desirable to the **m** than her children!
15: 2 Two courses were open to this **m,** that of religion,
15: 6 The **m** of the seven boys, more than any other **m,**
15:10 and loved their brothers and their **m,**
15:11 though so many factors influenced the **m** to suffer
15:12 and all of them together the **m** urged on to death
15:14 This **m,** who saw them tortured and burned one
15:16 O **m,** tried now by more bitter pains than even
15:21 of the children in torture calling to their **m.**
15:22 the **m** then suffered as her sons were tortured on
15:24 this noble **m** disregarded all these because of faith
15:26 this **m** held two ballots, one bearing death and
15:29 O **m** of the nation, vindicator of the law
16: 1 a woman, advanced in years and **m** of seven sons,
16: 4 the **m** quenched so many and such great emotions
16: 5 If this woman, though a **m,** had been fainthearted,
16: 6 bearing seven children, I am now the **m** of none!
16:12 that holy and God-fearing **m** did not wail with such
16:14 O **m,** soldier of God in the cause of religion,
16:24 the **m** of the seven encouraged and persuaded each
17: 2 O **m,** who with your seven sons nullified
17: 4 Take courage, therefore, O holy-minded **m,**
17: 7 as they saw the **m** of the seven children enduring
17:13 the **m** of the seven sons entered the competition,
18: 6 The **m** of seven sons expressed
18:23 with their victorious **m** are gathered together into

MOTHER'S (87) [MOTHER]

A. MOTHER'S NAME (30)

Ge 24:28 and told her **m** household about these things.
24:67 So Isaac was comforted after his **m** death.
27:29 and may your **m** sons bow down to you.
28: 2 to the house of Bethuel, your **m** father;
28: 2 of the daughters of Laban, your **m** brother.
29:10 the daughter of his **m** brother Laban,
29:10 and the sheep of his **m** brother Laban,
29:10 and watered the flock of his **m** brother Laban.
43:29 his **m** son, and said, "Is this your youngest brother,
44:20 he alone is left of his **m** children,
Ex 23:19 You shall not boil a kid in its **m** milk.
34:26 You shall not boil a kid in its **m** milk.
Lev 18: 9 your father's daughter or your **m** daughter,
18:13 not uncover the nakedness of your **m** sister,
18:13 for she is your **m** flesh.
20:19 of your **m** sister or of your father's sister,
24:11 his **m** name was Shelomith, daughter of Dibri, A
Nu 12:12 when it comes out of its **m** womb."
Dt 13: 6 it is your brother, your father's son or your **m** son,
14:21 You shall not boil a kid in its **m** milk.
Jdg 9: 1 to Shechem to his **m** kinsfolk and said to them and
to the whole clan of his **m** family,
9: 3 So his **m** kinsfolk spoke all these words
16:17 I have been a nazirite to God from my **m** womb.
Ru 1: 8 "Go back each of you to your **m** house.
1Sa 20:30 and to the shame of your **m** nakedness?
1Ki 11:26 servant of Solomon, whose **m** name was Zeruah, A
14:21 His **m** name was Naamah the Ammonite. A
14:31 His **m** name was Naamah the Ammonite. A
15: 2 **m** name was Maacah daughter of Abishalom. A
15:10 **m** name was Maacah daughter of Abishalom. A
22:42 His **m** name was Azubah daughter of Shilhi. A

2Ki 3:13 Go to your father's prophets or to your **m.**"
8:26 His **m** name was Athaliah, A
12: 1 His **m** name was Zibiah of Beer-sheba. A
14: 2 His **m** name was Jehoaddin of Jerusalem. A
15: 2 His **m** name was Jecoliah of Jerusalem. A
15:33 His **m** name was Jerusha daughter of Zadok. A
18: 2 His **m** name was Abi daughter of Zechariah. A
21: 1 His **m** name was Hephzibah. A
21:19 His **m** name was Meshullemeth daughter of A
22: 1 His **m** name was Jedidah daughter of Adaiah A
23:31 His **m** name was Hamutal daughter of Jeremiah A
23:36 His **m** name was Zebidah daughter of Pedaiah A
24: 8 His **m** name was Nehushta daughter of Elnathan A
24:18 His **m** name was Hamutal daughter of Jeremiah A
2Ch 12:13 His **m** name was Naamah the Ammonite. A
13: 2 His **m** name was Micaiah daughter of Uriel A
20:31 His **m** name was Azubah daughter of Shilhi. A
22: 2 His **m** name was Athaliah, A
24: 1 his **m** name was Zibiah of Beer-sheba. A
25: 1 His **m** name was Jehoaddan of Jerusalem. A
26: 3 His **m** name was Jecoliah of Jerusalem. A
27: 1 His **m** name was Jerushah daughter of Zadok. A
29: 1 His **m** name was Abijah daughter of Zechariah. A
Job 1:21 He said, "Naked I came from my **m** womb,
3:10 because it did not shut the doors of my **m** womb,
31:18 and from my **m** womb I guided the widow—
Ps 22: 9 you kept me safe on my **m** breast.
50:20 you slander your own **m** child.
69: 8 an alien to my **m** children.
71: 6 it was you who took me from my **m** womb.
139:13 you knit me together in my **m** womb.
Pr 1: 8 and do not reject your **m** teaching;
4: 3 tender, and my **m** favorite,
6:20 and do not forsake your **m** teaching.
10: 1 but a foolish child is a **m** grief.
Ecc 5:15 As they came from their **m** womb,
11: 5 how the breath comes to the bones in the **m** womb,
SS 1: 6 My **m** sons were angry with me;
3: 4 until I brought him into my **m** house,
8: 1 who nursed at my **m** breast!
Isa 49: 1 while I was in my **m** womb he named me.
50: 1 Where is your **m** bill of divorce
Jer 52: 1 His **m** name was Hamutal daughter of Jeremiah A
Lk 7:12 He was his **m** only son, and she was a widow;
Jn 3: 4 Can one enter a second time into the **m** womb and
19:25 and his **m** sister, Mary the wife of Clopas,
Tob 6:15 and my **m** life down to their grave, grieving for me—
Jdt 8:26 the sheep of Laban, his **m** brother.
Sir 3: 2 and he confirms a **m** right over her children.
3: 9 but a **m** curse uproots their foundations.
40: 1 from the day they come forth from their **m** womb
2Es 5:35 Or why did not my **m** womb become my grave,
4Mc 8:20 on our youth and have compassion on our **m** age;
13:19 and which was implanted in the **m** womb.
14:13 Observe how complex is a **m** love for her children,

MOTHER-IN-LAW‡ (19) [MOTHER]

Dt 27:23 "Cursed be anyone who lies with his **m.**"
Ru 1:14 Orpah kissed her **m,** but Ruth clung to her.
2:11 "All that you have done for your **m** since the death
2:18 and her **m** saw how much she had gleaned.
2:19 Her **m** said to her, "Where did you glean today?
2:19 So she told her **m** with whom she had worked,
2:23 and she lived with her **m.**
3: 1 Naomi her **m** said to her, "My daughter,
3: 6 and did just as her **m** had instructed her.
3:16 She came to her **m,** who said,
3:17 'Do not go back to your **m** empty-handed.' "
Mic 7: 6 the daughter-in-law against her **m;**
Mt 8:14 he saw his **m** lying in bed with a fever;
10:35 and a daughter-in-law against her **m;**
Mk 1:30 Now Simon's **m** was in bed with a fever,
Lk 4:38 Now Simon's **m** was suffering from a high fever,
12:53 **m** against her daughter-in-law and daughter-in-law
12:53 and daughter-in-law against **m.**"
Tob 10:12 honor your father-in-law and your **m,**

MOTHER-OF-PEARL (2) [PEARL]

Est 1: 6 of porphyry, marble, **m,** and colored stones.
AdE 1: 6 on a mosaic floor of emerald, **m,** and marble.

MOTHERS (20) [MOTHER]

Ge 32:11 he may come and kill us all, the **m** with
Pr 15:20 but the foolish despise their **m.**
30:11 and do not bless their **m.**
Isa 49:23 and their queens your nursing **m.**
Jer 15: 8 I have brought against the **m** of youths a destroyer
16: 3 and concerning the **m** who bear them and
16: 7 of consolation to drink for their fathers or their **m.**
La 2:12 They cry to their **m,** "Where is bread and wine?"
5: 3 fatherless; our **m** are like widows.
Hos 10:14 on the day of battle when **m** were dashed in pieces
Zec 13: 3 and **m** who bore them will say to them, "You shall
13: 3 and their **m** who bore them shall pierce them
Mk 10:30 houses, brothers and sisters, **m** and children,
1Ti 5: 2 to older women as **m,** to younger women
3Mc 1:18 in their chambers rushed out with their **m,**
1:20 **M** and nurses abandoned
5:49 parents and children, **m** and daughters,
4Mc 15: 4 Especially is this true of **m,**
15: 5 that **m** are the weaker sex and give birth to many,
15:13 nurture and indomitable suffering by **m!**

MOTHERS' (2) [MOTHER]

La 2:12 as their life is poured out on their **m** bosom.
1Mc 1:61 and they hung the infants from their **m** necks.

MOTION (1) [MOTIONED, MOTIONING]

Wis 7:24 For wisdom is more mobile than any **m;**

MOTIONED (5) [MOTION]

Jn 13:24 Simon Peter therefore **m** to him to ask Jesus
Ac 12:17 He **m** to them with his hand to be silent,
19:33 And Alexander **m** for silence and tried to make
21:40 on the steps and **m** to the people for silence;
24:10 the governor **m** to him to speak, Paul replied:

MOTIONING (2) [MOTION]

Lk 1:22 He kept **m** to them and remained unable to speak.
1:62 Then they began **m** to his father

MOTIVES (3)

Php 1:18 whether out of false **m** or true; and in that I rejoice.
1Th 2: 3 not spring from deceit or impure **m** or trickery,
2Mc 14:30 that this austerity did not spring from the best **m.**

MOTTLED (2)

Ge 31:10 upon the flock were striped, speckled, and **m.**
31:12 that leap on the flock are striped, speckled, and **m;**

MOULDY (KJV) See MOLDY

MOUND (3) [MOUNDS]

Jer 30:18 the city shall be rebuilt upon its **m,**
49: 2 it shall become a desolate **m,**
Sir 21: 8 like one who gathers stones for his burial **m.**

MOUNDS (1) [MOUND]

Jos 11:13 of the towns that stood on **m** except Hazor,

MOUNT‡ (174) [MOUNTAIN, MOUNTAIN-SHEEP, MOUNTAINOUS, MOUNTAINS, MOUNTED, MOUNTS]

A. MOUNT ZION (32)
B. MOUNT SINAI (23)
C. MOUNT HOR (12)
D. MOUNT SEIR (12)

Ge 22:14 "On the **m** of the LORD it shall be provided."
Ex 19:11 the LORD will come down upon **M** Sinai B
19:18 Now **M** Sinai was wrapped in smoke, B
19:20 When the LORD descended upon **M** Sinai, B
19:23 people are not permitted to come up to **M** Sinai; B
24:16 The glory of the LORD settled on **M** Sinai, B
28:11 you shall **m** them in settings of gold filigree.
31:18 God finished speaking with Moses on **M** Sinai, B
33: 6 of their ornaments, from **M** Horeb onward.
34: 2 morning to **M** Sinai and present yourself there B
34: 4 in the morning and went up on **M** Sinai, B
34:29 Moses came down from **M** Sinai. B
34:32 that the LORD had spoken with him on **M** Sinai. B
Lev 7:38 which the LORD commanded Moses on **M** Sinai, B
25: 1 The LORD spoke to Moses on **M** Sinai, saying: B
26:46 the people of Israel on **M** Sinai through Moses. B
27:34 to Moses for the people of Israel on **M** Sinai. B
Nu 3: 1 when the LORD spoke with Moses on **M** Sinai. B
10:33 from the **m** of the LORD three days' journey with
20:22 the whole congregation, came to **M** Hor. C
20:23 the LORD said to Moses and Aaron at **M** Hor, C
20:25 and bring them up **M** Hor; C
20:27 **M** Hor in the sight of the whole congregation. C
21: 4 From **M** Hor they set out by the way to C
28: 6 ordained at **M** Sinai for a pleasing odor, B
33:23 from Kehelathah and camped at **M** Shepher.
33:24 They set out from **M** Shepher and camped
33:37 They set out from Kadesh and camped at **M** Hor, C
33:38 Aaron the priest went up **M** Hor at the command C
33:39 when he died on **M** Hor. C
33:41 from **M** Hor and camped at Zalmonah. C
34: 7 you shall mark out your line to **M** Hor, C
34: 8 **M** Hor you shall mark it out to Lebo-hamath, C
Dt 1: 2 (By the way of **M** Seir it takes eleven days D
2: 1 as the LORD had told me and skirted **M** Seir D
2: 5 I have given **M** Seir to Esau as a possession. D
3: 8 from the Wadi Arnon to **M** Hermon
4:48 as far as **M** Sirion (that is, Hermon),
11:29 on **M** Gerizim and the curse on **M** Ebal.
27: 4 on **M** Ebal, and you shall cover them with plaster.
27:12 these shall stand on **M** Gerizim for the blessing of
27:13 And these shall stand on **M** Ebal for the curse:
32:49 **M** Nebo, which is in the land of Moab,
32:50 on **M** Hor and was gathered to his kin; C
33: 2 he shone forth from **M** Paran.
34: 1 up from the plains of Moab to **M** Nebo, to the top
Jos 8:30 Joshua built on **M** Ebal an altar to the LORD,
8:33 half of them in front of **M** Gerizim and half of them in front of **M** Ebal,
11:17 from **M** Halak, which rises toward Seir, as far
11:17 in the valley of Lebanon below **M** Hermon.
12: 1 from the Wadi Arnon to **M** Hermon,
12: 5 over **M** Hermon and Salecah and all Bashan to
12: 7 in the valley of Lebanon to **M** Halak,
13: 5 from Baal-gad below **M** Hermon to Lebo-hamath,
13:11 and all **M** Hermon, and all Bashan to Salecah;
15: 9 and from there to the towns of **M** Ephron;
15:10 the boundary circles west of Baalah to **M** Seir, D
15:10 the northern slope of **M** Jearim (that is, Chesalon),
15:11 and passes along to **M** Baalah,
24:30 in the hill country of Ephraim, north of **M** Gaash.
Jdg 2: 9 in the hill country of Ephraim, north of **M** Gaash.
3: 3 and the Hivites who lived on **M** Lebanon,
3: 3 from **M** Baal-hermon as far as Lebo-hamath.
4: 6 commands you, 'Go, take position at **M** Tabor,
4:12 of Abinoam had gone up to **M** Tabor,
4:14 So Barak went down from **M** Tabor
9: 7 he went and stood on the top of **M** Gerizim,
9:48 So Abimelech went up to **M** Zalmon,
1Sa 31: 1 and many fell on **M** Gilboa.
31: 8 and his three sons fallen on **M** Gilboa.
2Sa 1: 6 "I happened to be on **M** Gilboa;
15:30 But David went up the ascent of the **M** of Olives,
1Ki 18:19 have all Israel assemble for me at **M** Carmel,
18:20 and assembled the prophets at **M** Carmel.
19: 8 and forty nights to Horeb the **m** of God.
2Ki 2:25 From there he went on to **M** Carmel,
4:25 and came to the man of God at **M** Carmel.
19:31 and from **M** Zion a band of survivors. A
23:13 to the south of the **M** of Destruction,
23:16 Josiah turned, he saw the tombs there on the **m;**
1Ch 4:42 went to **M** Seir, having as their leaders Pelatiah, D
5:23 to Baal-hermon, Senir, and **M** Hermon.
10: 1 and fell slain on **M** Gilboa.
10: 8 they found Saul and his sons fallen on **M** Gilboa.
2Ch 3: 1 of the LORD in Jerusalem on **M** Moriah,
13: 4 the slope of **M** Zemaraim that is in the hill country
20:10 the people of Ammon, Moab, and **M** Seir, D
20:22 Moab, and **M** Seir, who had come against Judah, D
20:23 inhabitants of **M** Seir, destroying them utterly; D
Ne 9:13 You came down also upon **M** Sinai, B
Job 20: 6 Even though they **m** up high as the heavens,
Ps 42: 6 the land of Jordan and of Hermon, from **M** Mizar.
48: 2 **M** Zion, in the far north, the city of the great A
48:11 **M** Zion be glad, let the towns of Judah rejoice A
68:16 at the **m** that God desired for his abode,
68:18 You ascended the high **m,**
74: 2 Remember **M** Zion, where you came to dwell. A
78:68 but he chose the tribe of Judah, **M** Zion, A
87: 1 On the holy **m** stands the city he founded;
125: 1 Those who trust in the LORD are like **M** Zion, A
Isa 4: 5 **M** Zion and over its places of assembly a cloud A
7: 1 but could not **m** an attack against it.
8:18 from the LORD of hosts, who dwells on **M** Zion. A
10:12 the Lord has finished all his work on **M** Zion A
10:32 he will shake his fist at the **m** of daughter Zion,
14:13 on the **m** of assembly on the heights of Zaphon;
16: 1 by way of the desert, to the **m** of daughter Zion.
18: 7 whose land the rivers divide, to **M** Zion, A
24:23 for the LORD of hosts will reign on **M** Zion and A
28:21 For the LORD will rise up as on **M** Perazim,
29: 8 of all the nations be that fight against **M** Zion. A
31: 4 of hosts will come down to fight upon **M** Zion A
37:32 and from **M** Zion a band of survivors. A
40:31 they shall **m** up with wings like eagles,
Jer 4:15 from Dan and proclaims disaster from **M** Ephraim.
46: 4 Harness the horses; **m** the steeds!
49:22 Look, he shall **m** up and swoop down like an eagle,
51:53 Though Babylon should **m** up to heaven,
La 5:18 because of **M** Zion, which lies desolate; A
Eze 35: 2 set your face against **M** Seir, D
35: 3 I am against you, **M** Seir; I stretch out my hand D
35: 7 I will make **M** Seir a waste and a desolation; D
35:15 you shall be desolate, **M** Seir, and all Edom, D
Joel 2:32 for in **M** Zion and in Jerusalem there shall A
Am 3: 9 and say, "Assemble yourselves on **M** Samaria,
4: 1 you cows of Bashan who are on **M** Samaria,
6: 1 and for those who feel secure on **M** Samaria,
Ob 1: 8 and understanding out of **M** Esau.
1: 9 so that everyone from **M** Esau will be cut off.
1:17 But on **M** Zion there shall be those that escape, A
1:19 Those of the Negeb shall possess **M** Esau,
1:21 who have been saved shall go up to **M** Zion A
1:21 up to Mount Zion to rule **M** Esau;
Mic 4: 7 the LORD will reign over them in **M** Zion now A
Hab 3: 3 the Holy One from **M** Paran.
Zec 14: 4 On that day his feet shall stand on the **M** of Olives,
14: 4 and the **M** of Olives shall be split in two from east
14: 4 that one half of the **M** shall withdraw northward,
Mt 21: 1 at the **M** of Olives, Jesus sent two disciples,
24: 3 When he was sitting on the **M** of Olives,
26:30 they went out to the **M** of Olives.
Mk 11: 1 at Bethphage and Bethany, near the **M** of Olives,
13: 3 When he was sitting on the **M** of Olives opposite
14:26 they went out to the **M** of Olives.
Lk 19:29 at the place called the **M** of Olives,
19:37 now approaching the path down from the **M**
21:37 and spend the night on the **M** of Olives,
22:39 to the **M** of Olives; and the disciples followed him.
Jn 8: 1 ⟦while Jesus went to the **M** of Olives.⟧
Ac 1:12 to Jerusalem from the **m** called Olivet,
7:30 to him in the wilderness of **M** Sinai, B
7:38 with the angel who spoke to him at **M** Sinai, B
Gal 4:24 One woman, in fact, is Hagar, from **M** Sinai, B
4:25 Hagar is **M** Sinai in Arabia and corresponds B
Heb 12:22 But you have come to **M** Zion and to the city A
Rev 14: 1 and there was the Lamb, standing on **M** Zion! A
Jdt 9:13 against your sacred house, and against **M** Zion, A
AdE 6: 9 the person whom the king loves and **m** him on
1Mc 4:37 all the army assembled and went up to **M** Zion. A
4:60 that time they fortified **M** Zion with high walls A
5:54 they went up to **M** Zion with joy and gladness, A
6:48 and the king encamped in Judea and at **M** Zion. A
6:62 But when the king entered **M** Zion and saw A
7:33 After these events Nicanor went up to **M** Zion. A
9:15 and he pursued them as far as **M** Azotus.

1Mc 10:11 walls and encircle **M** Zion with squared stones, A
14:27 bronze tablets and put it on pillars on **M** Zion. A
2Es 2:33 received a command from the Lord on **M** Horeb
2:42 saw on **M** Zion a great multitude that I could A
3:17 you brought them to **M** Sinai. B
13:35 But he shall stand on the top of **M** Zion. A
14: 4 and I led him up on **M** Sinai, B

MOUNTAIN‡ (196) [MOUNT]

A. HOLY MOUNTAIN (22)

Ex 3: 1 and came to Horeb, the **m** of God.
3:12 you shall worship God on this **m."**
4:27 and he met him at the **m** of God and kissed him.
15:17 and planted them on the **m** of your own possession,
18: 5 where Moses was encamped at the **m** of God,
19: 2 Israel camped there in front of the **m.**
19: 3 the LORD called to him from the **m,** saying,
19:12 'Be careful not to go up the **m** or to touch the edge
19:12 Any who touch the **m** shall be put to death.
19:13 they may go up on the **m."**
19:14 So Moses went down from the **m** to the people.
19:16 as well as a thick cloud on the **m,**
19:17 They took their stand at the foot of the **m.**
19:18 while the whole **m** shook violently.
19:20 upon Mount Sinai, to the top of the **m,**
19:20 the LORD summoned Moses to the top of the **m,**
19:23 'Set limits around the **m** and keep it holy.' "
20:18 the sound of the trumpet, and the **m** smoking,
24: 4 and built an altar at the foot of the **m,**
24:12 LORD said to Moses, "Come up to me on the **m,**
24:13 and Moses went up into the **m** of God.
24:15 Then Moses went up on the **m,**
24:15 and the cloud covered the **m.**
24:17 the top of the **m** in the sight of the people of Israel.
24:18 Moses entered the cloud, and went up on the **m.**
24:18 Moses was on the **m** for forty days and forty nights.
25:40 which is being shown you on the **m.**
26:30 to the plan for it that you were shown on the **m.**
27: 8 be made just as you were shown on the **m.**
32: 1 the **m,** the people gathered around Aaron, and said
32:15 Then Moses turned and went down from the **m,**
32:19 from his hands and broke them at the foot of the **m.**
34: 2 present yourself there to me, on the top of the **m.**
34: 3 do not let anyone be seen throughout all the **m;**
34: 3 do not let flocks or herds graze in front of that **m."**
34:29 As he came down from the **m** with the two tablets
Nu 20:28 and Aaron died there on the top of the **m.**
20:28 Moses and Eleazar came down from the **m.**
27:12 "Go up this **m** of the Abarim range,
Dt 1: 6 saying, "You have stayed long enough at this **m.**
4:11 the foot of the **m** while the **m** was blazing
5: 4 The LORD spoke with you face to face at the **m,**
5: 5 because of the fire and did not go up the **m.)**
5:22 with a loud voice to your whole assembly at the **m,**
5:23 while the **m** was burning with fire,
9: 9 When I went up the **m** to receive the stone tablets,
9: 9 I remained on the **m** forty days and forty nights;
9:10 at the **m** out of the fire on the day of the assembly.
9:15 So I turned and went down from the **m,**
9:15 down from the mountain, while the **m** was ablaze;
9:21 the dust of it into the stream that runs down the **m.**
10: 1 and come up to me on the **m,**
10: 3 and went up the **m** with the two tablets in my hand.
10: 4 on the **m** out of the fire on the day of the assembly;
10: 5 So I turned and came down from the **m,**
10:10 I stayed on the **m** forty days and forty nights,
12: 2 on the **m** heights, on the hills,
32:49 "Ascend this **m** of the Abarim,
32:50 on the **m** that you ascend and shall be gathered
33:19 They call peoples to the **m;**
Jos 15: 8 to the top of the **m** that lies over against the valley
15: 9 then the boundary extends from the top of the **m** to
18:13 on the **m** that lies south of Lower Beth-horon.
18:14 on the western side southward from the **m** that lies
18:16 to the border of the **m** that overlooks the valley of
Jdg 9:25 the lords of Shechem set ambushes on the **m** tops.
9:36 "Look, people are coming down from the **m** tops!"
1Sa 13:18 the **m** that looks down upon the valley of Zeboim
17: 3 The Philistines stood on the **m** on the one side,
17: 3 and Israel stood on the **m** on the other side,
23:26 Saul went on one side of the **m,**
23:26 and David and his men on the other side of the **m.**
25:20 the **m,** David and his men came down toward her;
2Sa 13:34 from the Horonaim road by the side of the **m.**
21: 6 the LORD at Gibeon on the **m** of the LORD."
21: 9 they impaled them on the **m** before the LORD.
1Ki 11: 7 on the **m** east of Jerusalem.
19:11 "Go out and stand on the **m** before the LORD,
2Ki 2:16 up and thrown him down on some **m** or
4:27 When she came to the man of God at the **m,**
6:17 the **m** was full of horses and chariots of fire all
2Ch 33:15 the **m** of the house of the LORD and in Jerusalem,
Job 14:18 "But the **m** falls and crumbles away,
39: 1 "Do you know when the **m** goats give birth?
Ps 30: 7 O LORD, you had established me as a strong **m;**
48: 1 in the city of our God. His holy **m,** A
68:15 O mighty **m, m** of Bashan; O many-peaked **m, m** of Bashan!
68:16 Why do you look with envy, O many-peaked **m,**
78:54 to the **m** that his right hand had won.
99: 9 and worship at his holy **m;** A
SS 4: 6 to the **m** of myrrh and the hill of frankincense.
Isa 2: 2 In days to come the **m** of the LORD's house shall
2: 3 "Come, let us go up to the **m** of the LORD,
Isa 11: 9 They will not hurt or destroy on all my holy **m;** A
25: 6 On this **m** the LORD of hosts will make
25: 7 on this **m** the shroud that is cast over all peoples,
25:10 For the hand of the LORD will rest on this **m.**
27:13 the LORD on the holy **m** at Jerusalem. A
30:17 until you are left like a flagstaff on the top of a **m,**
30:25 On every lofty **m** and every high hill there will
30:29 the sound of the flute to go to the **m** of the LORD,
40: 4 and every **m** and hill be made low;
40: 9 Get you up to a high **m,** O Zion,
56: 7 my holy **m,** and make them joyful in my house A
57: 7 Upon a high and lofty **m** you have set your bed,
57:13 shall possess the land and inherit my holy **m.** A
65:11 forget my holy **m,** who set a table for Fortune A
65:25 They shall not hurt or destroy on all my holy **m,** A
66:20 and on dromedaries, to my holy **m** Jerusalem, A
Jer 16:16 they shall hunt them from every **m** and every hill,
18:14 Do the **m** waters run dry, the cold flowing streams?
26:18 and the **m** of the house a wooded height.'
50: 6 from **m** to hill they have gone,
51:25 I am against you, O destroying **m,**
51:25 and make you a burned-out **m.**
Eze 6:13 on all the **m** tops, under every green tree,
11:23 and stopped on the **m** east of the city.
17:22 I myself will plant it on a high and lofty **m.**
17:23 On the **m** height of Israel I will plant it,
20:40 For on my holy **m,** the mountain height of Israel, A
20:40 For on my holy mountain, the **m** height of Israel,
28:14 you were on the holy **m** of God; A
28:16 I cast you as a profane thing from the **m** of God,
34:14 and the **m** heights of Israel shall be their pasture;
40: 2 and set me down upon a very high **m,**
43:12 on the top of the **m** all around shall be most holy.
Da 2:35 that struck the statue became a great **m** and filled
2:45 just as you saw that a stone was cut from the **m**
9:16 away from your city Jerusalem, your holy **m;** A
9:20 the LORD my God on behalf of the holy **m** A
11:45 between the sea and the beautiful holy **m.** A
Joel 2: 1 sound the alarm on my holy **m!** A
3:17 the LORD your God, dwell in Zion, my holy **m.** A
Ob 1:16 For as you have drunk on my holy **m,** A
Mic 3:12 and the **m** of the house a wooded height.
4: 1 In days to come the **m** of the LORD's house shall
4: 2 "Come, let us go up to the **m** of the LORD,
7:12 from sea to sea and from **m** to **m.**
Zep 3:11 you shall no longer be haughty in my holy **m.** A
Zec 4: 7 What are you, O great **m?**
8: 3 be called the faithful city, and the **m** of the LORD
8: 3 of the LORD of hosts shall be called the holy **m.** A
14: 5 you shall flee by the valley of the LORD's **m,**
Mt 4: 8 a very high **m** and showed him all the kingdoms of
5: 1 When Jesus saw the crowds, he went up the **m;**
8: 1 When Jesus had come down from the **m,**
14:23 he went up the **m** by himself to pray.
15:29 and he went up the **m,** where he sat down.
17: 1 and his brother John and led them up a high **m,**
17: 9 As they were coming down the **m,**
17:20 you will say to this **m,** 'Move from here to there,'
21:21 but even if you say to this **m,**
28:16 to the **m** to which Jesus had directed them.
Mk 3:13 up the **m** and called to him those whom he wanted,
6:46 he went up on the **m** to pray.
9: 2 and led them up a high **m** apart, by themselves.
9: 9 As they were coming down the **m,**
11:23 Truly I tell you, if you say to this **m,**
Lk 3: 5 and every **m** and hill shall be made low,
6:12 during those days he went out to the **m** to pray;
9:28 and went up on the **m** to pray.
9:37 when they had come down from the **m,**
Jn 4:20 Our ancestors worshiped on this **m,**
4:21 when you will worship the Father neither on this **m**
6: 3 up the **m** and sat down there with his disciples.
6:15 he withdrew again to the **m** by himself.
Heb 8: 5 to the pattern that was shown you on the **m."**
12:20 "If even an animal touches the **m,**
2Pe 1:18 while we were with him on the holy **m.** A
Rev 6:14 every **m** and island was removed from its place.
8: 8 and something like a great **m,** burning with fire,
21:10 in the spirit he carried me away to a great, high **m**
Jdt 2:21 and camped opposite Bectileth near the **m** that is to
4: 7 to seize the **m** passes, since by them Judea could
5: 1 the **m** passes and fortified all the high hilltops
5: 5 about this people that lives in the **m** district
7:12 of water that flows from the foot of the **m,**
10:10 until she had gone down the **m** and passed through
13:10 and went up the **m** to Bethulia,
14:11 and they went out in companies to the **m** passes.
Wis 9: 8 to build a temple on your holy **m,** A
Bar 5: 7 For God has ordered that every high **m** and
LtJ 6:39 with gold and silver are like stones from the **m,**
1Mc 9:38 they went up and hid under cover of the **m.**
9:40 and the rest fled to the **m;**
11:37 put up in a conspicuous place on the holy **m.' "** A
2Mc 2: 4 that he went out to the **m** where Moses had gone
2Es 13: 6 and saw that he carved out for himself a great **m,**
13: 7 the region or place from which the **m** was carved,
13:12 from the **m** and call to himself another multitude
13:36 as you saw the **m** carved out without hands.

MOUNTAIN-SHEEP (1) [MOUNT, SHEEP]

Dt 14: 5 the wild goat, the ibex, the antelope, and the **m.**

MOUNTAINOUS (1) [MOUNT]

Tob 5: 6 for it lies in a **m** area,

MOUNTAINS‡ (193) [MOUNT]

A. MOUNTAINS OF ISRAEL (16)

Ge 7:19 the high **m** under the whole heaven were covered;
7:20 the waters swelled above the **m,**
8: 4 the ark came to rest on the **m** of Ararat.
8: 5 the tops of the **m** appeared.
22: 2 on one of the **m** that I shall show you."
49:26 the eternal **m,** the bounties of the everlasting hills;
Ex 32:12 that he brought them out to kill them in the **m,**
Nu 23: 7 the king of Moab from the eastern **m:**
33:47 from Almon-diblathaim and camped in the **m**
33:48 the **m** of Abarim and camped in the plains of Moab
Dt 32:22 and sets on fire the foundations of the **m.**
33:15 with the finest produce of the ancient **m,** and
Jdg 5: 5 The **m** quaked before the LORD,
6: 2 for themselves hiding places in the **m,**
9:36 "The shadows on the **m** look like people to you."
11:37 so that I may go and wander on the **m,**
11:38 and bewailed her virginity on the **m.**
1Sa 26:20 like one who hunts a partridge in the **m."**
2Sa 1:21 You **m** of Gilboa, let there be no dew or rain
1Ki 19:11 so strong that it was splitting **m** and breaking rocks
22:17 Micaiah said, "I saw all Israel scattered on the **m,**
2Ki 19:23 up the heights of the **m,** to the far recesses
1Ch 12: 8 and who were swift as gazelles on the **m:**
2Ch 18:16 Micaiah said, "I saw all Israel scattered on the **m,**
Job 9: 5 he who removes **m,** and they do not know it,
24: 8 They are wet with the rain of the **m,**
28: 9 and overturn **m** by the roots.
39: 8 It ranges the **m** as its pasture,
40:20 **m** yield food for it where all the wild animals play.
Ps 11: 1 how can you say to me, "Flee like a bird to the **m;**
18: 7 the foundations also of the **m** trembled and quaked,
36: 6 Your righteousness is like the mighty **m,**
46: 2 though the **m** shake in the heart of the sea;
46: 3 though the **m** tremble with its tumult.
65: 6 By your strength you established the **m;**
72: 3 May the **m** yield prosperity for the people,
72:16 may it wave on the tops of the **m;**
76: 4 more majestic than the everlasting **m.**
80:10 The **m** were covered with its shade,
83:14 as the flame sets the **m** ablaze,
90: 2 Before the **m** were brought forth,
95: 4 the heights of the **m** are his also.
97: 5 The **m** melt like wax before the LORD,
104: 6 the waters stood above the **m.**
104: 8 They rose up to the **m,**
104:13 From your lofty abode you water the **m;**
104:18 The high **m** are for the wild goats;
104:32 who touches the **m** and they smoke.
110: 3 on the day you lead your forces on the holy **m.** A
114: 4 The **m** skipped like rams, the hills like lambs.
114: 6 O **m,** that you skip like rams? O hills, like lambs?
125: 2 As the **m** surround Jerusalem,
133: 3 which falls on the **m** of Zion.
144: 5 touch the **m** so that they smoke.
148: 9 **M** and all hills, fruit trees and all cedars!
Pr 8:25 Before the **m** had been shaped, before the hills,
27:25 and the herbage of the **m** is gathered,
SS 2: 8 leaping upon the **m,** bounding over the hills.
2:17 be like a gazelle or a young stag on the cleft **m.**
4: 8 from the dens of lions, from the **m** of leopards.
8:14 like a gazelle or a young stag upon the **m** of spices!
Isa 2: 2 as the highest of the **m,** and shall be raised above
2:14 the high **m,** and against all the lofty hills;
5:25 the **m** quaked, and their corpses were like refuse in
13: 4 Listen, a tumult on the **m** as of a great multitude!
14:25 and on my **m** trample him under foot;
17:13 on the **m** before the wind and whirling dust before
18: 3 when a signal is raised on the **m,** look!
18: 6 to the birds of prey of the **m** and to the animals of
22: 5 battering down of walls and a cry for help to the **m.**
34: 3 the **m** shall flow with their blood.
37:24 up the heights of the **m,** to the far recesses
40:12 weighed the **m** in scales and the hills in a balance?
41:15 you shall thresh the **m** and crush them,
42:11 let them shout from the tops of the **m.**
42:15 I will lay waste **m** and hills,
44:23 break forth into singing, O **m,** O forest,
45: 2 I will go before you and level the **m,**
49:11 And I will turn all my **m** into a road,
49:13 break forth, O **m,** into singing!
52: 7 How beautiful upon the **m** are the feet of
54:10 For the **m** may depart and the hills be removed,
55:12 the **m** and the hills before you shall burst into song,
64: 1 so that the **m** would quake at your presence—
64: 3 you came down, the **m** quaked at your presence.
65: 7 because they offered incense on the **m**
65: 9 and from Judah inheritors of my **m;**
Jer 3:23 Truly the hills are a delusion, the orgies on the **m.**
4:24 I looked on the **m,** and lo, they were quaking,
9:10 Take up weeping and wailing for the **m,**
13:16 and before your feet stumble on the **m** at twilight;
17: 3 on the **m** in the open country.
31: 5 Again you shall plant vineyards on the **m**
46:18 one is coming like Tabor among the **m,**
50: 6 turning them away on the **m;**
La 4:19 they chased us on the **m,** they lay in wait for us
Eze 6: 2 set your face toward the **m** of Israel, A
6: 3 You **m** of Israel, hear the word of the Lord GOD! A
6: 3 Thus says the Lord GOD to the **m** and the hills,
7: 7 of tumult, not of reveling on the **m.**
7:16 be found on the **m** like doves of the valleys,
18: 6 not eat upon the **m** or lift up his eyes to the idols of
18:11 who eats upon the **m,** defiles his neighbor's wife,

Eze 18:15 not eat upon the **m** or lift up his eyes to the idols of
19: 9 should be heard no more on the **m** of Israel. A
22: 9 those in you who eat upon the **m**,
31:12 On the **m** and in all
32: 5 I will strew your flesh on the **m**,
32: 6 the land with your flowing blood up to the **m**,
33:28 and the **m** of Israel shall be so desolate A
34: 6 over all the **m** and on every high hill;
34:13 and I will feed them on the **m** of Israel, A
34:14 shall feed on rich pasture on the **m** of Israel. A
35: 8 I will fill its **m** with the slain;
35:12 speech that you uttered against the **m** of Israel, A
36: 1 mortal, prophesy to the **m** of Israel, and say: A
36: 1 O **m** of Israel, hear the word of the LORD. A
36: 4 O **m** of Israel, hear the word of the Lord GOD: A
36: 4 Thus says the Lord GOD to the **m** and the hills,
36: 6 and say to the **m** and hills,
36: 8 O **m** of Israel, shall shoot out your branches, A
37:22 in the land, on the **m** of Israel; A
38: 8 on the **m** of Israel, which had long lain waste; A
38:20 and the **m** shall be thrown down,
38:21 I will summon the sword against Gog in all my **m**,
39: 2 and lead you against the **m** of Israel. A
39: 4 You shall fall upon the **m** of Israel, A
39:17 a great sacrificial feast on the **m** of Israel, A
Hos 4:13 They sacrifice on the tops of the **m**,
10: 8 They shall say to the **m**, Cover us, and to the hills,
Joel 2: 2 upon the **m** a great and powerful army comes;
2: 5 they leap on the tops of the **m**,
3:18 In that day the **m** shall drip sweet wine,
Am 4:13 For lo, the one who forms the **m**, creates the wind,
9:13 the **m** shall drip sweet wine,
Jnh 2: 6 at the roots of the **m**.
Mic 1: 4 Then the **m** will melt under him and
4: 1 be established as the highest of the **m**,
6: 1 Rise, plead your case before the **m**,
6: 2 Hear, you **m**, the controversy of the LORD,
Na 1: 5 The **m** quake before him, and the hills melt;
1:15 On the **m** the feet of one who brings good tidings,
3:18 Your people are scattered on the **m** with no one
Hab 3: 6 The eternal **m** were shattered;
3:10 The **m** saw you, and writhed;
Zec 6: 1 coming out from between two **m**—**m** of bronze.
14: 5 for the valley between the **m** shall reach to Azal;
Mt 18:12 not leave the ninety-nine on the **m** and go in search
24:16 then those in Judea must flee to the **m**;
Mk 5: 5 the **m** he was always howling and bruising himself
13:14 then those in Judea must flee to the **m**;
Lk 21:21 Then those in Judea must flee to the **m**,
23:30 Then they will begin to say to the **m**, 'Fall on us';
1Co 13: 2 and if I have all faith, so as to remove **m**,
Heb 11:38 They wandered in deserts and **m**,
Rev 6:15 hid in the caves and among the rocks of the **m**,
6:16 calling to the **m** and rocks, "Fall on us and hide us
16:20 every island fled away, and no **m** were to be found;
17: 9 the seven heads are seven **m** on which
Tob 1: 5 of Israel had erected in Dan and on all the **m**
1:21 and they fled to the **m** of Ararat,
5:10 and I am familiar with its **m** and all of its roads."
Jdt 1:15 He captured Arphaxad in the **m** of Ragau
6: 4 their **m** will be drunk with their blood,
7: 4 neither the high **m** nor the valleys nor
7:10 not rely on their spears but on the height of the **m**
7:10 for it is not easy to reach the tops of their **m**.
7:13 the nearby **m** and camp there to keep watch to see
16: 3 The Assyrian came down from the **m** of the north;
16:15 For the **m** shall be shaken to their foundations with
Wis 17:19 or an echo thrown back from a hollow of the **m**,
Sir 16:19 The very **m** and the foundations of the earth quiver
39:28 and in their anger they can dislodge **m**;
43: 4 but three times as hot is the sun scorching the **m**;
43:16 when he appears, the **m** shake.
43:21 He consumes the **m** and burns up the wilderness,
LtJ 6:63 to consume **m** and woods does what it is ordered.
Aza 1:53 Bless the Lord, **m** and hills;
1Mc 4:38 or as on one of the **m**.
11:68 they had set an ambush against him in the **m**,
2Mc 5:27 and kept himself and his companions alive in the **m**
9: 8 and had imagined that he could weigh the high **m**
9:28 among the **m** in a strange land.
10: 6 they had been wandering in the **m** and caves
1Es 4: 4 they go, and conquer **m**, walls, and towers.
2Es 2:19 seven mighty **m** on which roses and lilies grow;
6:51 to live in it, where there are a thousand **m**;
8:23 and whose indignation makes the **m** melt away,
15:42 They shall destroy cities and walls, **m** and hills,
15:58 Those who are in the **m** and highlands shall perish
15:62 and your cities, your land and your **m**;
16:60 and pools on the tops of the **m**,

MOUNTED (17) [MOUNT]

Ge 24:61 Rebekah and her maids rose up, **m** the camels,
1Sa 30:17 four hundred young men, who **m** camels and fled.
2Sa 13:29 and each **m** his mule and fled.
1Ki 12:18 then hurriedly **m** his chariot to flee to Jerusalem.
13:13 So they saddled a donkey for him, and he **m** it.
2Ki 7:14 So they took two **m** men,
9:16 Then Jehu **m** his chariot and went to Jezreel,
2Ch 10:18 King Rehoboam hurriedly **m** his chariot to flee
Ezr 9: 6 and our guilt has **m** up to the heavens.
Est 8:10 by **m** couriers riding on fast steeds bred from
8:14 So the couriers, **m** on their swift royal steeds,
Ps 78:21 his anger **m** against Israel,
107:26 They **m** up to heaven, they went down to
Eze 23: 6 all of them handsome young men, **m** horsemen.
23:12 **m** horsemen, all of them handsome young men.
Mt 21: 5 humble, and **m** on a donkey, and on a colt,
1Es 8:75 and our mistakes have **m** up to heaven

MOUNTING (KJV) See ASCENT

MOUNTS (2) [MOUNT]

Job 39:27 that the eagle **m** up and makes its nest on high?
Ac 23:24 Also provide **m** for Paul to ride,

MOURN‡ (60) [MOURNED, MOURNER, MOURNERS, MOURNERS', MOURNFUL, MOURNFULLY, MOURNING, MOURNS]

Ge 23: 2 and Abraham went in to **m** for Sarah and to weep
Lev 10: 6 may **m** the burning that the LORD has sent.
2Sa 3:31 and put on sackcloth, and **m** over Abner."
1Ki 13:29 to **m** and to bury him.
14:13 All Israel shall **m** for him and bury him;
Ne 8: 9 to the LORD your God; do not **m** or weep."
Job 5:11 and those who **m** are lifted to safety.
14:22 and **m** only for themselves."
Ecc 3: 4 a time to **m**, and a time to dance;
Isa 3:26 And her gates shall lament and **m**;
16: 7 **M**, utterly stricken, for the raisin cakes of
19: 8 Those who fish will **m**; all who cast hooks in the
61: 2 of our God; to comfort all who **m**;
61: 3 to provide for those who **m** in Zion—
66:10 rejoice with her in joy, all you who **m** over her—
Jer 4:28 Because of this the earth shall **m**,
8:21 For the hurt of my poor people I am hurt, I **m**,
12: 4 How long will the land **m**,
48:17 **M** over him, all you his neighbors,
48:31 for the people of Kir-heres I **m**.
La 1: 4 roads to Zion **m**, for no one comes to the festivals;
Eze 7:12 let not the buyer rejoice, nor the seller **m**,
7:27 The king shall **m**, the prince shall be wrapped
24:16 yet you shall not **m** or weep,
24:23 you shall not **m** or weep,
Hos 10: 5 Its people shall **m** for it, and its idolatrous priests
Joel 1: 9 The priests **m**, the ministers of the LORD.
Am 8: 8 and everyone **m** who lives in it,
9: 5 and all who live in it **m**,
Zec 7: 3 "Should I **m** and practice abstinence in
12:10 on the one whom they have pierced, they shall **m**
12:12 The land shall **m**, each family by itself;
Mt 5: 4 "Blessed are those who **m**,
9:15 "The wedding guests cannot **m** as long as
11:17 we wailed, and you did not **m**.'
24:30 and then all the tribes of the earth will **m**,
Lk 6:25 for you will **m** and weep.
Jn 16:20 Very truly, I tell you, you will weep and **m**,
1Co 7:30 those who **m** as though they were not mourning,
2Co 12:21 to **m** over many who previously sinned and have
Jas 4: 9 Lament and **m** and weep.
Rev 18:11 the merchants of the earth weep and **m** for her,
Tob 10: 4 And she began to weep and **m** for her son, saying,
10: 7 When the sun had set she would go in and **m**
Sir 7:34 but **m** with those who **m**.
Bel 1:40 On the seventh day the king came to **m** for Daniel.
1Mc 3:51 and your priests **m** in humiliation.
2Mc 5:10 to lie unburied had no one to **m** for him;
2Es 9:41 so that I may weep for myself and continue to **m**,
10: 4 but will **m** and fast continually until I die."
10: 8 It is most appropriate to **m** now,
10: 9 and she will tell you that it is she who ought to **m**
10:11 Who then ought to **m** the more,
15:12 Let Egypt **m**, and its foundations,
15:13 Let the farmers that till the ground **m**,
15:44 and all who are around it shall **m** for it.
16:33 Virgins shall **m** because they have no bridegrooms;
16:33 women shall **m** because they have no husbands;
16:33 their daughters shall **m**, because they have no help.

MOURNED (31) [MOURN]

Ge 37:34 and **m** for his son many days.
Ex 33: 4 When the people heard these harsh words, they **m**,
Nu 14:39 to all the Israelites, the people **m** greatly.
20:29 all the house of Israel **m** for Aaron thirty days.
1Sa 6:19 The people **m** because the LORD had made
25: 1 and all Israel assembled and **m** for him.
28: 3 all Israel had **m** for him and buried him in Ramah,
2Sa 1:12 They **m** and wept, and fasted until evening for Saul
13:37 David **m** for his son day after day.
1Ki 13:30 and they **m** over him, saying, "Alas, my brother!"
14:18 All Israel buried him and **m** for him,
1Ch 7:22 And their father Ephraim **m** many days,
2Ch 35:24 All Judah and Jerusalem **m** for Josiah.
Ne 1: 4 and **m** for days, fasting and praying before the God
1Co 5: 2 Should you not rather have **m**,
Rev 18:19 they threw dust on their heads, as they wept and **m**,
Jdt 16:24 and the house of Israel **m** her for seven days.
1Mc 1:25 Israel **m** deeply in every community,
2:14 put on sackcloth, and **m** greatly.
2:39 and his friends learned of it, they **m**
2:70 And all Israel **m** for him with great lamentation.
4:39 Then they tore their clothes and **m**
9:20 they **m** many days and said,
12:52 and they **m** for Jonathan and his companions
12:52 in great fear; and all Israel **m** deeply.
13:26 and **m** for him many days.
1Es 1:32 In all Judea they **m** for Josiah.
8:72 as I **m** over this iniquity,
2Es 10:39 for your people and **m** greatly over Zion.
10:49 So you saw her likeness, how she **m** for her son,
4Mc 16: 5 a mother, had been fainthearted, she would have **m**

MOURNER (2) [MOURN]

2Sa 14: 2 He said to her, "Pretend to be a **m**;
Jer 16: 7 No one shall break bread for the **m**,

MOURNERS (7) [MOURN]

Job 29:25 a king among his troops, like one who comforts **m**.
Ecc 12: 5 and the **m** will go about the streets;
Isa 57:18 creating for their **m** the fruit of the lips.
Eze 24:17 do not cover your upper lip or eat the bread of **m**.
24:22 not cover your upper lip or eat the bread of **m**.
Mal 3:14 by going about as **m** before the LORD of hosts?
Sir 48:24 and comforted the **m** in Zion.

MOURNERS' (1) [MOURN]

Hos 9: 4 Such sacrifices shall be like **m** bread;

MOURNFUL (1) [MOURN]

3Mc 5:25 and **m** dirges implored the supreme God

MOURNFULLY (3) [MOURN]

Ps 42: 9 Why must I walk about **m** because the enemy
43: 2 Why must I walk about **m** because of the
Isa 59:11 We all growl like bears; like doves we moan **m**.

MOURNING‡ (75) [MOURN]

Ge 27:41 "The days of **m** for my father are approaching;
37:35 "No, I shall go down to Sheol to my son, **m**."
38:12 when Judah's time of **m** was over,
50:10 he observed a time of **m** for his father seven days.
50:11 the Canaanite inhabitants of the land saw the **m** on
50:11 "This is a grievous **m** on the part of the Egyptians."
Dt 21:13 **m** for her father and mother;
26:14 I have not eaten of it while in **m**;
34: 8 then the period of **m** for Moses was ended.
2Sa 11:27 When the **m** was over, David sent and brought her
14: 2 put on **m** garments, do not anoint yourself with oil,
14: 2 a woman who has been **m** many days for the dead.
19: 1 "The king is weeping and **m** for Absalom."
19: 2 So the victory that day was turned into **m** for all
Ezr 10: 6 for he was **m** over the faithlessness of the exiles.
Est 4: 3 there was great **m** among the Jews,
6:12 **m** and with his head covered.
9:22 for them from sorrow into gladness and from **m**
Job 30:31 My lyre is turned to **m**,
Ps 30:11 You have turned my **m** into dancing;
35:14 for a mother, bowed down and in **m**.
38: 6 all day long I go around **m**.
Ecc 7: 2 the house of **m** than to go to the house of feasting;
7: 4 The heart of the wise is in the house of **m**;
Isa 22:12 the Lord GOD of hosts called to weeping and **m**,
60:20 and your days of **m** shall be ended.
61: 3 the oil of gladness instead of **m**,
Jer 6:26 make **m** as for an only child,
9:17 Consider, and call for the **m** women to come;
16: 5 Do not enter the house of **m**, or go to lament,
31:13 I will turn their **m** into joy, I will comfort them,
La 2: 5 multiplied in daughter Judah **m** and lamentation.
5:15 our dancing has been turned to **m**.
Eze 2:10 and written on it were words of lamentation and **m**
24:17 Sigh, but not aloud; make no **m** for the dead.
27:31 over you in bitterness of soul, with bitter **m**.
Da 10: 2 At that time I, Daniel, had been **m** for three weeks.
Joel 2:12 with fasting, with weeping, and with **m**;
Am 5:16 They shall call the farmers to **m**,
8:10 I will turn your feasts into **m**,
8:10 I will make it like the **m** for an only son,
Mic 1: 8 I will make lamentation like the jackals, and **m** like
Zec 12:11 the **m** in Jerusalem will be as great as the **m** for
Mk 16:10 ⟦while they were **m** and weeping.⟧
1Co 7:30 and those who mourn as though they were not **m**,
2Co 7: 7 as he told us of your longing, your **m**,
Jas 4: 9 Let your laughter be turned into **m** and your joy
Rev 18: 8 pestilence and **m** and famine—
18:15 in fear of her torment, weeping and **m** aloud,
21: 4 **m** and crying and pain will be no more,
Tob 2: 6 "Your festivals shall be turned into **m**,
AdE 4: 3 a loud cry of **m** and lamentation among the Jews,
6:12 **m** and with his head covered.
13:17 turn our **m** into feasting that we may live
14: 2 on the garments of distress and **m**, and instead
Wis 19: 3 For while they were still engaged in **m**,
Sir 19:26 There is the villain bowed down in **m**,
22: 6 Like music in time of **m** is ill-timed conversation,
22:12 **M** for the dead lasts seven days,
38:17 make your **m** worthy of the departed, for one day,
1Mc 1:27 she who sat in the bridal chamber was **m**.
1:39 her feasts were turned into **m**,
1:40 her exaltation was turned into **m**.
9:41 So the wedding was turned into **m** and the voice
1Es 9: 2 he was **m** over the great iniquities of the multitude.
3Mc 4: 2 But among the Jews there was incessant **m**,
4: 3 or what streets were not filled with **m** and wailing
6:32 Putting an end to all **m** and wailing,
2Es 2: 3 but with **m** and sorrow I have lost you,
5:20 So I fasted seven days, **m** and weeping,
9:38 she was **m** and weeping with a loud voice,
10: 6 do you not see our **m**,
10: 8 because we are all **m**, and to be sorrowful,
10:41 whom you saw **m** and whom you began to console

MOURNS (7) [MOURN]

Isa 33: 9 The land **m** and languishes;
Jer 12:11 have made it a desolation; desolate, it **m** to me.

Jer 14: 2 Judah **m** and her gates languish;
23:10 because of the curse the land **m,**
Hos 4: 3 the land **m,** and all who live in it languish;
Joel 1:10 The fields are devastated, the ground **m;**
Zec 12:10 as one **m** for an only child,

MOUSE (1) [MICE]

Lev 11:29 the **m,** the great lizard according to its kind,

MOUSE (KJV) See also RODENTS

MOUTH‡ (333) [MOUTHS]

Ge 4:11 from the ground, which has opened its **m**
29: 2 The stone on the well's **m** was large,
29: 3 the shepherds would roll the stone from the **m** of
29: 3 put the stone back in its place on the **m** of the well.
29: 8 and the stone is rolled from the **m** of the well;
29:10 up and rolled the stone from the well's **m,**
45:12 of my brother Benjamin see that it is my own **m**
Ex 4:12 with your **m** and teach you what you are to speak."
4:15 and put the words in his **m;** and I will be with your **m** and with his **m,**
4:16 he shall serve as a **m** for you,
Nu 16:30 and the ground opens its **m** and swallows them up,
16:32 The earth opened its **m** and swallowed them up,
22:28 Then the LORD opened the **m** of the donkey,
22:38 word God puts in my **m,** that is what I must say."
23: 5 The LORD put a word in Balaam's **m,** and said,
23:12 to say what the LORD puts into my **m?"**
23:16 The LORD met Balaam, put a word into his **m,**
26:10 and the earth opened its **m** and swallowed them up
30: 2 according to all that proceeds out of his **m.**
Dt 8: 3 but by every word that comes from the **m** of
11: 6 how in the midst of all Israel the earth opened its **m**
18:18 I will put my words in the **m** of the prophet,
23:23 to the LORD your God with your own **m.**
30:14 it is in your **m** and in your heart for you to observe.
32: 1 let the earth hear the words of my **m.**
Jos 1: 8 of the law shall not depart out of your **m;**
10:18 "Roll large stones against the **m** of the cave,
10:22 Then Joshua said, "Open the **m** of the cave,
10:27 they set large stones against the **m** of the cave,
15: 5 to the **m** of the Jordan.
15: 5 the north side runs from the bay of the sea at the **m**
Jdg 11:35 For I have opened my **m** to the LORD,
11:36 if you have opened your **m** to the LORD,
11:36 to me according to what has gone out of your **m,**
18:19 Put your hand over your **m,** and come with us,
1Sa 1:12 before the LORD, Eli observed her **m.**
2: 1 My **m** derides my enemies,
2: 3 let not arrogance come from your **m;**
14:27 and put his hand to his **m;** and his eyes brightened.
17:35 rescuing the lamb from its **m;**
2Sa 1:16 for your own **m** has testified against you, saying,
14: 3 And Joab put the words into her **m.**
14:19 it was he who put all these words into the **m**
17:19 stretched it over the well's **m,**
18:25 said, "If he is alone, there are tidings in his **m."**
22: 9 and devouring fire from his **m;**
1Ki 8:15 with his **m** to my father David,
8:24 with your **m** and have this day fulfilled
17:24 that the word of the LORD in your **m** is truth."
19:18 and every **m** that has not kissed him."
22:22 and be a lying spirit in the **m** of all his prophets.'
22:23 a lying spirit in the **m** of all these your prophets;
2Ki 4:34 putting his **m** upon his **m,**
19:28 in your nose and my bit in your **m;**
2Ch 6: 4 with his **m** to my father David,
6:15 with your **m** and this day have fulfilled
18:21 and be a lying spirit in the **m** of all his prophets.'
18:22 a lying spirit in the **m** of these your prophets;
35:22 not listen to the words of Neco from the **m** of God,
36:12 before the prophet Jeremiah who spoke from the **m**
36:21 the word of the LORD by the **m** of Jeremiah,
Ezr 1: 1 in order that the word of the LORD by the **m**
Est 7: 8 As the words left the **m** of the king,
Job 3: 1 After this Job opened his **m** and cursed the day
5:15 But he saves the needy from the sword of their **m,**
5:16 So the poor have hope, and injustice shuts its **m.**
7:11 "Therefore I will not restrain my **m;**
8: 2 and the words of your **m** be a great wind?
8:21 He will yet fill your **m** with laughter,
9:20 I am innocent, my own **m** would condemn me;
15: 5 For your iniquity teaches your **m,**
15: 6 Your own **m** condemns you, and not I;
15:13 and let such words go out of your **m?**
16: 5 I could encourage you with my **m,**
20:12 "Though wickedness is sweet in their **m,**
21: 5 and be appalled, and lay your hand upon your **m.**
22:22 Receive instruction from his **m,**
23: 4 and fill my **m** with arguments.
23:12 I have treasured in my bosom the words of his **m.**
31:27 and my **m** has kissed my hand;
31:30 I have not let my **m** sin by asking for their lives
33: 2 See, I open my **m;** the tongue in my **m** speaks.
35:16 Job opens his **m** in empty talk,
37: 2 and the rumbling that comes from his **m.**
40: 4 I lay my hand on my **m.**
40:23 it is confident though Jordan rushes against its **m.**
41:19 From its **m** go flaming torches;
41:21 and a flame comes out of its **m.**
Ps 17: 3 in me; my **m** does not transgress.
18: 8 and devouring fire from his **m;**
19:14 the words of my **m** and the meditation of my heart
22:15 my **m** is dried up like a potsherd,
Ps 22:21 Save me from the **m** of the lion!
33: 6 and all their host by the breath of his **m.**
34: 1 his praise shall continually be in my **m.**
38:14 and in whose **m** is no retort.
39: 1 a muzzle on my **m** as long as the wicked are
39: 9 I do not open my **m,** for it is you who have done it.
40: 3 He put a new song in my **m,**
49: 3 My **m** shall speak wisdom;
50:19 "You give your **m** free rein for evil,
51:15 open my lips, and my **m** will declare your praise.
54: 2 give ear to the words of my **m.**
63: 5 and my **m** praises you with joyful lips
66:14 those that my lips uttered and my **m** promised
69:15 or the Pit close its **m** over me.
71: 8 My **m** is filled with your praise,
71:15 My **m** will tell of your righteous acts,
78: 1 incline your ears to the words of my **m.**
78: 2 I will open my **m** in a parable;
81:10 Open your **m** wide and I will fill it.
89: 1 with my **m** I will proclaim your faithfulness
107:42 and all wickedness stops its **m.**
109:30 With my **m** I will give great thanks to the LORD;
119:13 my lips I declare all the ordinances of your **m.**
119:43 Do not take the word of truth utterly out of my **m,**
119:72 The law of your **m** is better to me than thousands
119:88 so that I may keep the decrees of your **m.**
119:103 sweeter than honey to my **m!**
119:131 With open **m** I pant, because I long
126: 2 Then our **m** was filled with laughter,
137: 6 Let my tongue cling to the roof of my **m,**
138: 4 for they have heard the words of your **m.**
141: 3 Set a guard over my **m,** O LORD;
141: 7 so shall their bones be strewn at the **m** of Sheol.
145:21 My **m** will speak the praise of the LORD,
Pr 2: 6 from his **m** come knowledge and understanding;
4: 5 nor turn away from the words of my **m.**
5: 7 and do not depart from the words of my **m.**
6: 2 caught by the words of your **m.**
7:24 and be attentive to the words of my **m.**
8: 7 for my **m** will utter truth;
8: 8 All the words of my **m** are righteous;
10: 6 but the **m** of the wicked conceals violence.
10:11 The **m** of the righteous is a fountain of life,
10:11 but the **m** of the wicked conceals violence.
10:31 The **m** of the righteous brings forth wisdom,
10:32 but the **m** of the wicked what is perverse.
11:11 but it is overthrown by the **m** of the wicked.
12:14 the fruit of the **m** one is filled with good things,
15:28 but the **m** of the wicked pours out evil.
16:10 his **m** does not sin in judgment.
18: 4 The words of the **m** are deep waters;
18: 6 and a fool's **m** invites a flogging.
18:20 From the fruit of the **m** one's stomach is satisfied;
19:24 and will not even bring it back to the **m.**
19:28 and the **m** of the wicked devours iniquity.
20:17 but afterward the **m** will be full of gravel.
21:23 over **m** and tongue is to keep out of trouble.
22:14 The **m** of a loose woman is a deep pit;
26: 7 so does a proverb in the **m** of a fool.
26: 9 by the hand of a drunkard is a proverb in the **m** of
26:15 and is too tired to bring it back to the **m.**
26:28 and a flattering **m** works ruin.
27: 2 Let another praise you, and not your own **m—**
30:20 she eats, and wipes her **m,** and says,
30:32 put your hand on your **m.**
31:26 She opens her **m** with wisdom,
Ecc 5: 2 Never be rash with your **m,**
5: 6 Do not let your **m** lead you into sin,
6: 7 All human toil is for the **m,**
SS 1: 2 Let him kiss me with the kisses of his **m!**
4: 3 like a crimson thread, and your **m** is lovely.
Isa 1:20 for the **m** of the LORD has spoken.
5:14 and opened its **m** beyond measure;
6: 7 The seraph touched my **m** with it and said:
9:12 and they devoured Israel with open **m.**
9:17 and an evildoer, and every **m** spoke folly.
10:14 or opened its **m,** or chirped."
11: 4 he shall strike the earth with the rod of his **m,**
34:16 For the **m** of the LORD has commanded,
37:29 in your nose and my bit in your **m;**
40: 5 for the **m** of the LORD has spoken."
45:23 from my **m** has gone forth in righteousness a word
48: 3 they went out from my **m** and I made them known;
49: 2 He made my **m** like a sharp sword,
51:16 I have put my words in your **m,**
53: 7 and he was afflicted, yet he did not open his **m;**
53: 7 so he did not open his **m.**
53: 9 and there was no deceit in his **m.**
55:11 so shall my word be that goes out from my **m;**
57: 4 Against whom do you open your **m** wide
58:14 for the **m** of the LORD has spoken.
59:21 and my words that I have put in your **m,**
59:21 shall not depart out of your **m,**
62: 2 by a new name that the **m** of the LORD will give.
Jer 1: 9 the LORD put out his hand and touched my **m;**
1: 9 "Now I have put my words in your **m.**
5:14 I am now making my words in your **m** a fire,
9: 8 it speaks deceit through the **m.**
9:12 To whom has the **m** of the LORD spoken,
9:20 and let your ears receive the word of his **m;**
15:19 and not what is worthless, you shall serve as my **m.**
23:16 not from the **m** of the LORD.
48:28 the dove that nests on the sides of the **m** of a gorge.
La 3:29 to put one's **m** to the dust (there may yet be hope),
3:38 the **m** of the Most High that good and bad come?
4: 4 The tongue of the infant sticks to the roof of its **m**
Eze 2: 8 open your **m** and eat what I give you.
Eze 3: 2 I opened my **m,** and he gave me the scroll to eat.
3: 3 I ate it; and in my **m** it was as sweet as honey.
3:17 whenever you hear a word from my **m,**
3:26 the roof of your **m,** so that you shall be speechless
3:27 But when I speak with you, I will open your **m,**
4:14 nor has carrion flesh come into my **m."**
16:56 Was not your sister Sodom a byword in your **m** in
16:63 never open your **m** again because of your shame,
24:27 On that day your **m** shall be opened to
33: 7 whenever you hear a word from my **m,**
33:22 but he had opened my **m** by the time
33:22 so my **m** was opened, and I was no longer unable
35:13 you magnified yourselves against me with your **m,**
Da 4:31 While the words were still in the king's **m,**
6:17 A stone was brought and laid on the **m** of the den,
7: 5 had three tusks in its **m** among its teeth
7: 8 and a **m** speaking arrogantly.
7:20 horn that had eyes and a **m** that spoke arrogantly,
10: 3 no meat or wine had entered my **m,**
10:16 and I opened my **m** to speak,
Hos 2:17 I will remove the names of the Baals from her **m,**
6: 5 I have killed them by the words of my **m,**
13:13 not present himself at the **m** of the womb.
Joel 1: 5 over the sweet wine, for it is cut off from your **m.**
Am 3:12 shepherd rescues from the **m** of the lion two legs,
Mic 4: 4 for the **m** of the LORD of hosts has spoken.
7: 5 of your **m** from her who lies in your embrace;
Na 3:12 if shaken they fall into the **m** of the eater.
Zec 5: 8 and pressed the leaden weight down on its **m.**
9: 7 I will take away its blood from its **m,**
Mal 2: 6 True instruction was in his **m,**
2: 7 and people should seek instruction from his **m,**
Mt 4: 4 by every word that comes from the **m** of God.' "
12:34 For out of the abundance of the heart the **m** speaks.
13:35 "I will open my **m** to speak in parables;
15:11 it is not what goes into the **m** that defiles a person,
15:11 but it is what comes out of the **m** that defiles."
15:17 that whatever goes into the **m** enters the stomach,
15:18 what comes out of the **m** proceeds from the heart,
17:27 and when you open its **m,** you will find a coin;
Mk 9:20 on the ground and rolled about, foaming at the **m.**
Lk 1:64 Immediately his **m** was opened
1:70 through the **m** of his holy prophets from of old,
4:22 at the gracious words that came from his **m.**
6:45 of the abundance of the heart that the **m** speaks.
9:39 It convulses him until he foams at the **m;**
Jn 19:29 on a branch of hyssop and held it to his **m.**
Ac 8:32 so he does not open his **m.**
11: 8 or unclean has ever entered my **m.'**
15:27 the same things by word of **m.**
23: 2 near him to strike him on the **m.**
Ro 3:19 so that every **m** may be silenced,
10:10 and one confesses with the **m** and so is saved.
Col 3: 8 slander, and abusive language from your **m.**
2Th 2: 8 with the breath of his **m,**
2:15 either by word of **m** or by our letter.
2Ti 4:17 So I was rescued from the lion's **m.**
Jas 3:10 From the same **m** come blessing and cursing.
1Pe 2:22 and no deceit was found in his **m."**
Rev 1:16 and from his **m** came a sharp, two-edged sword,
2:16 against them with the sword of my **m.**
3:16 I am about to spit you out of my **m.**
10: 9 but sweet as honey in your **m."**
10:10 it was sweet as honey in my **m,**
11: 5 fire pours from their **m** and consumes their foes;
12:15 from his **m** the serpent poured water like a river
12:16 it opened its **m** and swallowed the river that the dragon had poured from his **m.**
13: 2 and its **m** was like a lion's **m.**
13: 5 a **m** uttering haughty and blasphemous words,
13: 6 It opened its **m** to utter blasphemies against God,
14: 5 and in their **m** no lie was found;
16:13 coming from the **m** of the dragon, from the **m** of the beast, and from the **m** of the false prophet.
19:15 From his **m** comes a sharp sword with which
19:21 the sword that came from his **m;**
Jdt 5: 5 "May my lord please listen to a report from the **m**
5: 5 No falsehood shall come from your servant's **m.**
AdE 14: 9 to abolish what your **m** has ordained,
14:13 Put eloquent speech in my **m** before the lion,
Wis 1:11 and a lying **m** destroys the soul.
Sir 5:12 but if not, put your hand over your **m.**
8: 3 Do not argue with the loud of **m,**
9:18 The loud of **m** are feared in their city,
15: 5 and will open his **m** in the midst of the assembly.
20:15 he opens his **m** like a town crier.
20:29 like a muzzle on the **m** they stop reproofs.
21:26 The mind of fools is in their **m,**
21:26 but the **m** of the wise is in their mind.
22:22 If you open your **m** against your friend,
22:27 Who will set a guard over my **m,**
23: 7 my children, to instruction concerning the **m;**
23: 9 Do not accustom your **m** to oaths,
23:13 Do not accustom your **m** to coarse, foul language,
24: 2 In the assembly of the Most High she opens her **m,**
24: 3 "I came forth from the **m** of the Most High,
26:12 As a thirsty traveler opens his **m** and drinks
27:23 In your presence his **m** is all sweetness,
28:12 yet both come out of your **m.**
28:25 so make a door and a bolt for your **m.**
29:24 as a guest you should not open your **m;**
30:18 a **m** that is closed are like offerings of food placed
34: 8 and wisdom is complete in the **m** of the faithful.
39: 5 opens his **m** in prayer and asks pardon for his sins.
39:17 and the reservoirs of water at the word of his **m.**
40:30 In the **m** of the shameless begging is sweet,
48:12 and marvels with every utterance of his **m.**

Sir 49: 1 his memory is as sweet as honey to every **m,**
51:25 I opened my **m** and said,
1Mc 2:60 was delivered from the **m** of the lions.
9:55 his **m** was stopped and he was paralyzed,
2Mc 6:18 to open his **m** to eat swine's flesh.
1Es 1:28 the words of the prophet Jeremiah from the **m** of
1:47 by the prophet Jeremiah from the **m** of the Lord.
1:57 in fulfillment of the word of the Lord by the **m**
2: 1 the word of the Lord by the **m** of Jeremiah might
4:31 At this the king would gaze at her with **m** agape.
3Mc 2:20 and put praises in the **m** of those who are downcast
4:16 a mind alienated from truth and with a profane **m,**
2Es 9:28 Then my **m** was opened, and I began to speak
13: 4 and whenever his voice issued from his **m,**
13:10 how he sent forth from his **m** something like
13:27 and fire and a storm coming out of his **m,**
14:38 open your **m** and drink what I give you to drink."
14:39 I opened my **m,** and a full cup was offered to me;
14:41 and my **m** was opened and was no longer closed.
15: 1 the words of the prophecy that I will put in your **m,**
4Mc 5:36 shall not defile the honorable **m** of my old age,

MOUTHS‡ (71) [MOUTH]

Dt 31:19 in their **m,** in order that this song may be a witness
31:21 it will not be lost from the **m** of their descendants.
Jdg 7: 5 putting their hands to their **m,**
1Sa 14:26 but they did not put their hands to their **m,**
Ne 9:20 and did not withhold your manna from their **m,**
Job 16:10 They have gaped at me with their **m;**
20:13 and hold it in their **m,**
29: 9 and laid their hands on their **m;**
29:10 and their tongues stuck to the roof of their **m.**
29:23 they opened their **m** as for the spring rain.
32: 5 when Elihu saw that there was no answer in the **m**
Ps 5: 9 For there is no truth in their **m;**
8: 2 of the **m** of babes and infants you have founded
10: 7 Their **m** are filled with cursing and deceit
17:10 with their **m** they speak arrogantly.
22: 7 they make **m** at me, they shake their heads;
22:13 they open wide their **m** at me,
35:21 They open wide their **m** against me;
36: 3 The words of their **m** are mischief and deceit;
37:30 The **m** of the righteous utter wisdom,
58: 6 O God, break the teeth in their **m;**
59: 7 There they are, bellowing with their **m,**
59:12 For the sin of their **m,** the words of their lips,
62: 4 they bless with their **m,**
63:11 for the **m** of liars will be stopped.
73: 9 They set their **m** against heaven,
78:30 while the food was still in their **m,**
78:36 But they flattered him with their **m;**
109: 2 For wicked and deceitful **m** are opened against me,
115: 5 They have **m,** but do not speak;
135:16 They have **m,** but they do not speak;
135:17 and there is no breath in their **m.**
144: 8 whose **m** speak lies, and whose right hands are
144:11 whose **m** speak lies, and whose right hands are
Pr 11: 9 their **m** the godless would destroy their neighbors,
13: 3 Those who guard their **m** preserve their lives;
15: 2 but the **m** of fools pour out folly.
15:14 but the **m** of fools feed on folly.
18: 7 The **m** of fools are their ruin,
24: 7 in the gate they do not open their **m.**
Ecc 10:13 The words of their **m** begin in foolishness,
Isa 29:13 near with their **m** and honor me with their lips,
52:15 kings shall shut their **m** because of him;
59:21 or out of the **m** of your children,
59:21 or out of the **m** of your children's children,
Jer 12: 2 you are near in their **m** yet far from their hearts.
La 2:16 All your enemies open their **m** against you;
3:46 All our enemies have opened their **m** against us;
Eze 34:10 I will rescue my sheep from their **m,**
Da 6:22 My God sent his angel and shut the lions' **m** so
Mic 3: 5 against those who put nothing into their **m.**
6:12 with tongues of deceit in their **m.**
7:16 they shall lay their hands on their **m;**
Zep 3:13 nor shall a deceitful tongue be found in their **m.**
Zec 8: 9 from the **m** of the prophets who were present when
14:12 and their tongues shall rot in their **m.**
Mt 21:16 have you never read, 'Out of the **m** of infants
Ro 3:14 "Their **m** are full of cursing and bitterness."
Eph 4:29 Let no evil talk come out of your **m,**
Heb 11:33 obtained promises, shut the **m** of lions,
Jas 3: 3 into the **m** of horses to make them obey us,
Rev 9:17 and fire and smoke and sulfur came out of their **m.**
9:18 and smoke and sulfur coming out of their **m.**
9:19 power of the horses is in their **m** and in their tails;
AdE 14: 9 to stop the **m** of those who praise you and
14:10 the **m** of the nations for the praise of vain idols,
Wis 8:12 they will put their hands on their **m.**
10:21 for wisdom opened the **m** of those who were mute,
Aza 1:10 And now we cannot open our **m;**
Sus 1:61 of their own **m** Daniel had convicted them
1Es 4:19 and gape at her, and with open **m** stare at her,

MOVE (22) [MOVED, MOVEMENT, MOVEMENTS, MOVES, MOVING]

Ex 10:23 three days they could not **m** from where they were;
Dt 19:14 You must not **m** your neighbor's boundary marker,
2Ki 23:18 He said, "Let him rest; let no one **m** his bones."
1Ch 12: 1 not **m** about freely because of Saul son of Kish;
Ps 80:13 and all that **m** in the field feed on it.
Isa 46: 7 it cannot **m** from its place.
Jer 10: 4 with hammer and nails so that it cannot **m.**
Mt 17:20 **'M** from here to there,' and it will **m;**
23: 4 to lift a finger to **m** them.
Lk 10: 7 Do not **m** about from house to house.
14:10 he may say to you, 'Friend, **m** up higher';
Ac 7: 4 God had him **m** from there to this country
17:28 For 'In him we live and **m** and have our being';
Jdt 7: 1 to break camp and **m** against Bethulia,
Sir 18:26 all things **m** swiftly before the Lord.
LtJ 6:27 If anyone sets it upright, it cannot **m** itself;
3Mc 5:23 began to **m** them along in the great colonnade.
2Es 4:37 and he will not **m** or arouse them until
5:44 "The creation cannot **m** faster than the Creator,
6:41 so that one part might **m** upward and
4Mc 14: 7 as the seven days of creation **m** in choral dance

MOVEABLE (KJV) See WANDER

MOVED‡ (74) [MOVE]

Ge 7:21 And all flesh died that **m** on the earth, birds,
12: 8 From there he **m** on to the hill country on the east
13:12 among the cities of the Plain and **m** his tent as far
13:18 So Abram **m** his tent, and came and settled by
26:22 He **m** from there and dug another well,
36: 6 and he **m** to a land some distance
Ex 14:19 before the Israelite army **m** and went behind them;
14:19 of cloud **m** from in front of them and took its place
35:26 all the women whose hearts **m** them
Jdg 2:18 the LORD would be **m** to pity by their groaning
9:26 of Ebed **m** into Shechem with his kinsfolk,
20:25 Benjamin **m** out against them from Gibeah
1Sa 1:13 only her lips **m,** but her voice was not heard;
5: 8 "Let the ark of God be **m** on to us."
5: 8 So they **m** the ark of the God of Israel to Gath.
2Sa 7: 7 Wherever I have **m** about among all the people
10:13 and the people who were with him **m** forward
15:23 and all the people **m** on toward the wilderness.
18:33 The king was deeply **m,** and went up to
1Ch 16:30 world is firmly established; it shall never be **m.**
17: 6 Wherever I have **m** about among all Israel,
Ps 10: 6 They think in their heart, "We shall not be **m;**
15: 5 Those who do these things shall never be **m.**
16: 8 because he is at my right hand, I shall not be **m.**
21: 7 steadfast love of the Most High he shall not be **m.**
30: 6 I said in my prosperity, "I shall never be **m."**
46: 5 God is in the midst of the city; it shall not be **m;**
55:22 he will never permit the righteous to be **m.**
78:58 they **m** him to jealousy with their idols.
93: 1 He has established the world; it shall never be **m;**
96:10 world is firmly established; it shall never be **m.**
112: 6 For the righteous will never be **m;**
121: 3 He will not let your foot be **m;**
125: 1 which cannot be **m,** but abides forever.
Pr 12: 3 but the root of the righteous will never be **m.**
Isa 10:14 and there was none that **m** a wing,
41: 7 and they fasten it with nails so that it cannot be **m.**
Jer 4:24 they were quaking, and all the hills **m** to and fro.
31:20 Therefore I am deeply **m** for him;
Eze 1: 9 them **m** straight ahead, without turning as they **m.**
1:12 Each **m** straight ahead; wherever the spirit would
1:17 When they **m,** they **m** in any of the four directions without veering as they **m.**
1:19 living creatures **m,** the wheels **m** beside them;
1:21 When they **m,** the others **m;**
1:24 When they **m,** I heard the sound of their wings like
10:11 When they **m,** they **m** in any of the four directions without veering as they **m;**
10:11 the others followed without veering as they **m.**
10:16 the cherubim **m,** the wheels **m** beside them;
10:22 Each one **m** straight ahead.
Da 11:11 **M** with rage, the king of the south shall go out
Mt 20:34 **M** with compassion, Jesus touched their eyes.
Mk 1:41 **M** with pity, Jesus stretched out his hand
Lk 10:33 and when he saw him, he was **m** with pity.
Jn 11:33 he was greatly disturbed in spirit and deeply **m.**
2Pe 1:21 and women **m** by the Holy Spirit spoke from God.
Jdt 7:17 So the army of the Ammonites **m** forward,
Wis 19:19 and creatures that swim **m** over to the land.
1Mc 2: 1 **m** from Jerusalem and settled in Modein.
4: 1 and this division **m** out by night
4: 3 and his warriors **m** out to attack the king's force
1Es 8:72 And all who were ever **m** at the word of the Lord
2Es 3:18 and **m** the world, and caused the depths to tremble,
7:15 Why are you **m,** seeing that you are mortal?
4Mc 4:13 **M** by these words, the high priest Onias,
14: 6 Just as the hands and feet are **m** in harmony with
14: 6 as though **m** by an immortal spirit of devotion,

MOVEMENT (1) [MOVE]

Wis 5:11 is traversed by the **m** of its wings,

MOVEMENTS (1) [MOVE]

2Es 6: 3 and before the powers of **m** were established,

MOVER (KJV) See AGITATOR

MOVES (12) [MOVE]

Ge 1:21 and every living creature that **m,**
1:28 and over every living thing that **m** upon the earth."
8:19 and every bird, everything that **m** on the earth,
Lev 11:42 Whatever **m** on its belly, and whatever **m** on all fours,
11:44 with any swarming creature that **m** on the earth.
11:46 and every living creature that **m** through the waters
Dt 27:17 be anyone who **m** a neighbor's boundary marker."
Job 9:11 he **m** on, but I do not perceive him.
Ps 50:11 and all that **m** in the field is mine.
69:34 the seas and everything that **m** in them.
Pr 19: 2 and one who **m** too hurriedly misses the way.

MOVING (7) [MOVE]

Ge 9: 3 Every **m** thing that lives shall be food for you;
2Sa 7: 6 but I have been **m** about in a tent and a tabernacle.
Job 31:26 or the moon **m** in splendor,
Ecc 4:15 I saw all the living who, **m** about under the sun,
SS 4: 1 **m** down the slopes of Gilead.
6: 5 **m** down the slopes of Gilead.
Eze 1:13 like torches **m** to and fro among

MOWED (1) [MOWINGS, MOWN]

Jas 5: 4 The wages of the laborers who **m** your fields,

MOWINGS (1) [MOWED]

Am 7: 1 the latter growth after the king's **m).**

MOWN (1) [MOWED]

Ps 72: 6 May he be like rain that falls on the **m** grass,

MOZA (5)

1Ch 2:46 Ephah also, Caleb's concubine, bore Haran, **M,**
8:36 Zimri became the father of **M.**
8:37 **M** became the father of Binea;
9:42 and Zimri became the father of **M.**
9:43 **M** became the father of Binea;

MOZAH (1)

Jos 18:26 Mizpeh, Chephirah, **M,**

MUCH‡ (261)

Ge 20: 8 and the men were very **m** afraid.
43:34 but Benjamin's portion was five times as **m** as any
44: 1 as **m** as they can carry,
Ex 16: 5 it will be twice as **m** as they gather on other days."
16:16 'Gather as **m** of it as each of you needs,
16:18 those who gathered **m** had nothing over,
16:18 they gathered as **m** as each of them needed.
16:21 by morning they gathered it, as **m** as each needed;
16:22 On the sixth day they gathered twice as **m** food,
21:22 paying as **m** as the judges determine.
30:23 and of sweet-smelling cinnamon half as **m,** that is,
36: 5 "The people are bringing **m** more than enough
Lev 14:21 But if he is poor and cannot afford so **m,**
Dt 2: 5 for I will not give you even so **m** as a foot's length
3:19 I know that you have **m** livestock—
28:38 You shall carry **m** seed into the field
31:27 how **m** more after my death!
Jos 13: 1 very **m** of the land still remains to be possessed.
22: 8 "Go back to your tents with **m** wealth,
22: 8 and with very **m** livestock, with silver, gold,
Ru 2:18 her mother-in-law saw how **m** she had gleaned.
1Sa 14:30 How **m** better if today the troops had eaten freely
17:24 fled from him and were very **m** afraid.
21: 5 how **m** more today will their vessels be holy?"
21:12 and was very **m** afraid of King Achish of Gath.
22:15 for your servant has known nothing of all this, **m**
23: 3 how **m** more then if we go to Keilah against
25:22 so **m** as one male of all who belong to him."
25:34 not have been left to Nabal so **m** as one male."
2Sa 3:22 bringing **m** spoil with them.
4:11 How **m** more then, when wicked men have killed
12: 8 had been too little, I would have added as **m** more.
14:25 in all Israel there was no one to be praised so **m**
16:11 how **m** more now may this Benjaminite!
1Ki 8:27 **m** less this house that I have built!
9:11 and gold, as **m** as he desired, King Solomon gave
10: 2 with camels bearing spices, and very **m** gold,
10:25 spices, horses, and mules, so **m** year by year.
19: 7 otherwise the journey will be too **m** for you."
2Ki 5:13 How **m** more, when all he said to you was, 'Wash,
10:18 but Jehu will offer **m** more.
21: 6 He did **m** evil in the sight of the LORD,
21:16 Moreover Manasseh shed very **m** innocent blood,
1Ch 22: 8 to me, saying, 'You have shed **m** blood
22: 8 you have shed so **m** blood in my sight on the earth.
22:14 for there is so **m** of it;
2Ch 6:18 how **m** less this house that I have built!
9: 1 and camels bearing spices and very **m** gold
9:24 spices, horses, and mules, so **m** year by year.
14:14 for there was **m** plunder in them.
25: 9 LORD is able to give you **m** more than this."
25:13 in them, and took **m** booty.
28: 8 they also took **m** booty from them and brought
32:15 **m** less will your God save you out of my hand!"
33: 6 He did **m** evil in the sight of the LORD,
Ne 2: 2 Then I was very **m** afraid.
4:10 and there is too **m** rubbish so that we are unable
Job 4:19 how **m** more those who live in houses of clay,
7:17 that you make so **m** of them,
15:16 how **m** less one who is abominable and corrupt,
16: 6 and if I forbear, how **m** of it leaves me?
25: 6 how **m** less a mortal, who is a maggot,
26: 3 one who has no wisdom, and given **m** good advice!
31:25 or because my hand had gotten **m;**
35:14 How **m** less when you say that you do not see him,
42:10 the LORD gave Job twice as **m** as he had before.
Ps 19:10 to be desired are they than gold, even **m** fine gold;
119:14 in the way of your decrees as **m** as in all riches.
Pr 7:21 With **m** seductive speech she persuades him;
11:31 how **m** more the wicked and the sinner!

Pr 13:23 The field of the poor may yield **m** food,
15: 6 In the house of the righteous there is **m** treasure,
15:11 how **m** more human hearts!
16:16 How **m** better to get wisdom than gold!
19: 7 how **m** more are they shunned by their friends!
19:10 **m** less for a slave to rule over princes.
21:27 how **m** more when brought with evil intent.
25:16 eat only enough for you, or else, having too **m,**
25:27 It is not good to eat **m** honey,
29:22 and the hothead causes **m** transgression.
Ecc 1:18 For in **m** wisdom is **m** vexation,
5:12 whether they eat little or **m;**
5:17 in **m** vexation and sickness and resentment.
8:17 However **m** they may toil in seeking,
9:18 but one bungler destroys **m** good.
12:12 and **m** study is a weariness of the flesh.
SS 4:10 how **m** better is your love than wine,
Jer 2:22 you wash yourself with lye and use **m** soap,
Eze 14:21 How **m** more when I send
15: 5 how **m** less—when the fire has consumed it,
17: 7 with great wings and **m** plumage.
23:32 you shall be scorned and derided, it holds so **m.**
46: 5 and the grain offering with the lambs shall be as **m**
46: 7 and with the lambs as **m** as he wishes,
46:11 and with the lambs as **m** as one wishes to give,
Da 6:14 king heard the charge, he was very **m** distressed.
11:25 of the south shall wage war with a **m** greater
Hos 7:16 So **m** for their babbling in the land of Egypt.
Hag 1: 6 You have sown **m,** and harvested little;
1: 9 You have looked for **m,** and, lo, it came to little;
Mt 6:30 will he not **m** more clothe you—you of little faith?
7:11 how **m** more will your Father
10:25 **m** more will they malign those of his household!
12:12 **m** more valuable is a human being than a sheep!
13: 5 where they did not have **m** soil,
14: 7 so **m** that he promised on oath
17:17 how **m** longer must I be with you?
17:17 How **m** longer must I put up with you?
23:15 and you make the new convert twice as **m** a child
Mk 4: 5 where it did not have **m** soil,
5:19 and tell them how **m** the Lord has done for you,
5:20 to proclaim in the Decapolis how **m** Jesus had done
5:26 She had endured **m** under many physicians,
9:19 how **m** longer must I be among you?
9:19 How **m** longer must I put up with you?
12:33 is **m** more important than all whole burnt offerings
Lk 1:29 But she was **m** perplexed by his words
6:34 Even sinners lend to sinners, to receive as **m** again.
8:39 and declare how **m** God has done for you."
8:39 throughout the city how **m** Jesus had done for him.
9:41 **m** longer must I be with you and bear with you?
11:13 how **m** more will the heavenly Father give
12:24 Of how **m** more value are you than the birds!
12:28 how **m** more will he clothe you—
12:48 to whom **m** has been given, **m** will be required;
12:48 and from the one to whom **m** has been entrusted,
16: 5 'How **m** do you owe my master?'
16: 7 Then he asked another, 'And how **m** do you owe?'
16:10 faithful in a very little is faithful also in **m;**
16:10 dishonest in a very little is dishonest also in **m.**
17:25 But first he must endure **m** suffering and
18:30 who will not get back very **m** more in this age,
19: 8 I will pay back four times as **m."**
Jn 6:11 so also the fish, as **m** as they wanted.
8:26 I have **m** to say about you and **m** to condemn;
12:24 but if it dies, it bears **m** fruit.
14:30 I will no longer talk **m** with you,
15: 5 Those who abide in me and I in them bear **m** fruit,
15: 8 that you bear **m** fruit and become my disciples.
Ac 2:46 as they spent **m** time together in the temple,
4: 2 **m** annoyed because they were teaching the people
9:13 **m** evil he has done to your saints in Jerusalem;
9:16 I myself will show him how **m** he must suffer for
15: 7 After there had been **m** debate,
15:32 said **m** to encourage and strengthen the believers.
16:18 But Paul, very **m** annoyed,
20: 2 and had given the believers **m** encouragement,
20:37 There was **m** weeping among them all;
26:24 Too **m** learning is driving you insane!"
27: 9 Since **m** time had been lost and sailing was
27:10 the voyage will be with danger and **m** heavy loss,
Ro 3: 2 **M,** in every way. For in the first place the Jews
5: 9 **M** more surely then, now that we have been
5:10 **m** more surely, having been reconciled,
5:15 **m** more surely have the grace of God and
5:17 **m** more surely will those who receive
9:22 with **m** patience the objects of wrath that are made
11:12 how **m** more will their full inclusion mean!
11:24 how **m** more will these natural branches
1Co 2: 3 to you in weakness and in fear and in **m** trembling.
9:11 is it too **m** if we reap your material benefits?
2Co 2: 4 For I wrote you out of **m** distress and anguish
3: 8 how **m** more will the ministry of the Spirit come
3: 9 **m** more does the ministry of justification abound
3:11 **m** more has the permanent come in glory!
8:15 "The one who had **m** did not have too **m,**
10: 8 Now, even if I boast a little too **m** of our authority,
Gal 3: 4 Did you experience so **m** for nothing?—
4:17 They make **m** of you, but for no good purpose;
4:17 so that you may make **m** of them.
4:18 to be made **m** of for a good purpose at all times,
Php 2:12 but **m** more now in my absence,
Col 2: 1 I want you to know how **m** I am struggling for you,
1Ti 3: 8 not indulging in **m** wine, not greedy for money;
2Ti 1:18 how **m** service he rendered in Ephesus.
3: 9 But they will not make **m** progress, because,
Phm 1: 7 I have indeed received **m** joy and encouragement
Phm 1:16 especially to me but how **m** more to you,
Heb 1: 4 having become as **m** superior to angels as
4: 7 "today"—saying through David **m** later,
5:11 About this we have **m** to say that is hard to explain,
9:14 how **m** more will the blood of Christ,
10:29 How **m** worse punishment do you think will
12:25 on earth, how **m** less will we escape if we reject
1Jn 4:11 Beloved, since God loved us so **m,**
2Jn 1:12 Although I have **m** to write to you,
3Jn 1:13 I have **m** to write to you,
Tob 3: 1 Then with **m** grief and anguish of heart I wept,
3: 6 for me to die than to see so **m** distress in my life
6:18 through his father's lineage, he loved her very **m,**
7: 2 **m** the young man resembles my kinsman Tobit!"
9: 4 if I delay even one day I will upset him very **m.**
10:12 as **m** your parents as those who gave you birth.
12: 2 He replied, "Father, how **m** shall I pay him?
12: 3 How **m** extra shall I give him as a bonus?"
14:10 For I see that there is **m** wickedness within it,
14:10 and that **m** deceit is practiced within it,
Jdt 4: 9 and they humbled themselves with **m** fasting.
5: 9 in gold and silver and very **m** livestock.
11:19 and no dog will so **m** as growl at you.
12:20 **m** more than he had ever drunk in any one day
AdE 16: 7 **m** from the more ancient records that we hand on,
Wis 7:28 for God loves nothing so **m** as the person who lives
13: 3 how **m** better than these is their Lord,
13: 4 from them how **m** more powerful is
13: 9 to know so **m** that they could investigate the world,
Sir 9:14 As **m** as you can, aim to know your neighbors,
10:31 honored in poverty, how **m** more in wealth!
10:31 one dishonored in wealth, how **m** more in poverty!
11:11 but are so **m** the more in want.
12: 5 as **m** evil for all the good you have done to them.
12:18 and whisper **m,** and show his true face.
14:13 and reach out and give to them as **m** as you can.
20: 2 How **m** better it is to rebuke than to fume!
20: 8 Whoever talks too **m** is detested,
20:12 Some buy **m** for little, but pay
20:15 He gives little and upbraids **m;**
22:13 Do not talk **m** with a senseless person or visit
29:23 Be content with little or **m,**
31:12 and do not say, "How **m** food there is here!"
32: 8 Be brief; say **m** in few words;
33:29 for idleness teaches **m** evil.
34: 9 with **m** experience knows what he is talking about.
34:11 but he that has traveled acquires **m** cleverness.
38:11 as **m** as you can afford.
42: 4 and of acquiring **m** or little;
43:30 Glorify the Lord and exalt him as **m** as you can,
46:19 "No property, not so **m** as a pair of shoes,
51:16 and I found for myself **m** instruction.
51:27 but little and found for myself **m** serenity.
Bar 1: 6 they collected as **m** money as each could give,
Sus 1:27 the servants felt very **m** ashamed,
Bel 1: 6 not see how **m** he eats and drinks every day?"
1Mc 1:24 He shed **m** blood, and spoke with great arrogance.
6:54 for the famine proved too **m** for them.
10:46 in Israel and how **m** he had oppressed them.
12:44 "Why have you put all these people to so **m** trouble
2Mc 6: 6 nor so **m** as confess themselves to be Jews.
7:26 After **m** urging on his part,
9:11 he began to lose **m** of his arrogance and to come
15:11 so **m** with confidence in shields and spears as with
15:14 the family of Israel and prays **m** for the people and
1Es 9:11 for we have sinned too **m** in these things.
3Mc 5:22 not so **m** employ the duration of the night in sleep
2Es 4:30 how **m** ungodliness it has produced until now—
4:31 for yourself how **m** fruit of ungodliness a grain
7:*66* It is **m** better with them than with us;
7:*131* [61] so **m** as joy over those to whom salvation is
8:43 or if it has been ruined by too **m** rain, it perishes.
9:22 because with **m** labor I have perfected them.
9:46 And I brought him up with **m** care.
10:47 that she brought him up with **m** care,
10:56 afterward you will hear as **m** as your ears can hear.
11:32 and with **m** oppression dominated its inhabitants;
12:44 how **m** better it would have been for us if we
13:19 For they shall see great dangers and **m** distress,
16:18 when there shall be **m** lamentation;

MUCHAEUS (2)

AdE 1:16 Then **M** said to the king and the governors,
1:21 and the king did as **M** had recommended.

MUD (11) [MUDDIED]

Isa 57:20 its waters toss up mire and **m.**
Jer 38: 6 cistern, but only **m,** and Jeremiah sank in the **m.**
38:22 that your feet are stuck in the **m,** they desert you.'
Zec 10: 5 trampling the foe in the **m** of the streets;
Jn 9: 6 and made **m** with the saliva and spread the **m** on the man's eyes,
9:11 He answered, "The man called Jesus made **m,**
9:14 Now it was a sabbath day when Jesus made the **m**
9:15 He said to them, "He put **m** on my eyes.
2Pe 2:22 and, "The sow is washed only to wallow in the **m."**

MUDDIED (1) [MUD]

Pr 25:26 Like a **m** spring or a polluted fountain are

MUFFLERS (KJV) See SCARFS

MULBERRIES (1) [MULBERRY]

1Mc 6:34 the elephants the juice of grapes and **m,**

MULBERRY (2) [MULBERRIES]

Isa 40:20 As a gift one chooses **m** wood—wood that will
Lk 17: 6 you could say to this **m** tree,

MULE (8) [MULE-LOADS, MULES]

2Sa 13:29 and each mounted his **m** and fled.
18: 9 Absalom was riding on his **m,**
18: 9 the **m** went under the thick branches of a great oak.
18: 9 while the **m** that was under him went on.
1Ki 1:33 and have my son Solomon ride on my own **m,**
1:38 down and had Solomon ride on King David's **m,**
1:44 and they had him ride on the king's **m;**
Ps 32: 9 Do not be like a horse or a **m,**

MULE-LOADS (1) [LOAD, MULE]

2Ki 5:17 please let two **m** of earth be given to your servant;

MULES‡ (12) [MULE]

1Ki 10:25 spices, horses, and **m,** so much year by year.
18: 5 to keep the horses and **m** alive,
1Ch 12:40 came bringing food on donkeys, camels, **m,**
2Ch 9:24 spices, horses, and **m,** so much year by year.
Ezr 2:66 two hundred forty-five **m,**
Ne 7:68 two hundred forty-five **m,**
Isa 66:20 on horses, and in chariots, and in litters, and on **m,**
Eze 27:14 for your wares horses, war horses, and **m.**
Zec 14:15 the **m,** the camels, the donkeys,
Jdt 2:17 along a vast number of camels and donkeys and **m**
15:11 She took them and loaded her **m** and hitched
1Es 5:43 two hundred forty-five **m,**

MULTIPLIED (31) [MULTIPLY]

Ge 47:27 and were fruitful and **m** exceedingly.
Ex 1: 7 they **m** and grew exceedingly strong,
1:12 the more they **m** and spread,
1:20 and the people **m** and became very strong.
11: 9 that my wonders may be **m** in the land of Egypt."
Dt 1:10 The LORD your God has **m** you,
8:13 and when your herds and flocks have **m,** and your silver and gold is **m,** and all that you have is **m,**
11:21 the days of your children may be **m** in the land that
1Ch 5: 9 because their cattle had **m** in the land of Gilead.
Ne 9:23 You **m** their descendants like the stars of heaven,
Job 27:14 If their children are **m,** it is for the sword;
35: 6 your transgressions are **m,** what do you do to him?
Ps 40: 5 You have **m,** O LORD my God,
Pr 9:11 For by me your days will be **m,**
Isa 9: 3 You have **m** the nation, you have increased its joy;
57: 9 to Molech with oil, and **m** your perfumes;
Jer 3:16 And when you have **m** and increased in the land,
La 2: 5 **m** in daughter Judah mourning and lamentation.
Eze 16:29 You **m** your whoring with Chaldea,
35:13 and **m** your words against me; I heard it.
Hos 8:11 When Ephraim **m** altars to expiate sin,
8:14 and Judah has **m** fortified cities;
12:10 I spoke to the prophets; it was I who **m** visions,
Ac 7:17 our people in Egypt increased and **m**
Ro 5:20 law came in, with the result that the trespass **m;**
Sir 23: 3 Otherwise my mistakes may be **m,**
Man 1: 9 my transgressions are **m,** O Lord, they are **m!**
2Es 7:*111* [41] and unrighteousness has **m,**

MULTIPLIES (5) [MULTIPLY]

Job 9:17 and **m** my wounds without cause;
34:37 and **m** his words against God."
35:16 he **m** words without knowledge."
Sir 6: 5 Pleasant speech **m** friends, and a gracious tongue **m** courtesies.

MULTIPLY (38) [MULTIPLIED, MULTIPLIES, MULTIPLYING]

Ge 1:22 "Be fruitful and **m** and fill the waters in the seas, and let birds **m** on the earth."
1:28 "Be fruitful and **m,** and fill the earth and subdue it;
6: 1 When people began to **m** on the face of the ground,
8:17 and be fruitful and **m** on the earth."
9: 1 and said to them, "Be fruitful and **m,**
9: 7 be fruitful and **m,** abound on the earth and **m** in it."
16:10 "I will so greatly **m** your offspring that they cannot
35:11 "I am God Almighty: be fruitful and **m;**
Ex 7: 3 and I will **m** my signs and wonders in the land
23:29 and the wild animals would **m** against you.
32:13 'I will **m** your descendants like the stars of heaven,
Lev 26: 9 upon you and make you fruitful and **m** you;
Dt 6: 3 that you may **m** greatly in a land flowing with milk
7:13 he will love you, bless you, and **m** you;
13:17 and in his compassion **m** you,
1Ch 4:27 nor did all their family **m** like the Judeans.
Job 29:18 and I shall **m** my days like the phoenix;
Ps 16: 4 Those who choose another god **m** their sorrows;
107:38 By his blessing they **m** greatly,
Jer 23: 3 and they shall be fruitful and **m.**
29: 6 **m** there, and do not decrease.
Eze 36:10 and I will **m** your population, the whole house
36:11 and I will **m** human beings and animals upon you.
37:26 and I will bless them and **m** them,
Hos 4:10 they shall play the whore, but not **m;**
12: 1 they **m** falsehood and violence;
Am 4: 4 to Gilgal—and **m** transgression;
Na 3:15 **M** yourselves like the locust,
3:15 like the locust, **m** like the grasshopper!
2Co 9:10 for food will supply and **m** your seed for sowing
Heb 6:14 saying, "I will surely bless you and **m** you."

Sir 11:10 if you **m** activities, you will not be held blameless.
16:2 If they **m**, do not rejoice in them,
23:16 Two kinds of individuals **m** sins,
Aza 1:13 to whom you promised to **m** their descendants like
2Es 3:12 "When those who lived on earth began to **m**,

MULTIPLYING (3) [MULTIPLY]
Eze 16:25 to every passer-by, and **m** your whoring.
16:26 **m** your whoring, to provoke me to anger.
Man 1:10 setting up abominations and **m** offenses.

MULTITUDE‡ (129) [MULTITUDES]
Ge 2:1 and the earth were finished, and all their **m**.
16:10 that they cannot be counted for **m**."
17:4 You shall be the ancestor of a **m** of nations.
17:5 for I have made you the ancestor of a **m** of nations.
48:16 and let them grow into a **m** on the earth."
48:19 and his offspring shall become a **m** of nations."
1Sa 13:5 and troops like the sand on the seashore in **m**;
14:16 as the **m** was surging back and forth.
2Sa 6:19 the whole **m** of Israel, both men and women,
17:11 like the sand by the sea for **m**,
1Ki 20:13 Have you seen all this great **m**?
20:28 therefore I will give all this great **m** into your hand,
2Ki 7:13 of the whole **m** of Israel that have perished already;
2Ch 13:8 a great **m** and have with you the golden calves
14:11 and in your name we have come against this **m**.
20:2 "A great **m** is coming against you from Edom,
20:12 against this great **m** that is coming against us.
20:15 'Do not fear or be dismayed at this great **m**;
20:24 they looked toward the **m**;
30:18 For a **m** of the people,
31:18 their sons, and their daughters, the whole **m**;
Job 11:2 "Should a **m** of words go unanswered,
31:34 of the **m**, and the contempt of families terrified me,
35:9 "Because of the **m** of oppressions people cry out;
Ps 42:4 and songs of thanksgiving, a **m** keeping festival.
Pr 14:28 The glory of a king is a **m** of people;
Ecc 5:7 With many dreams come vanities and a **m**
Isa 1:11 What to me is the **m** of your sacrifices?
5:13 and their **m** is parched with thirst.
5:14 the nobility of Jerusalem and her **m** go down,
13:4 Listen, a tumult on the mountains as of a great **m**!
16:14 in spite of all its great **m**;
29:5 But the **m** of your foes shall be like small dust,
29:5 and the **m** of tyrants like flying chaff.
29:7 the **m** of all the nations that fight against Ariel,
29:8 so shall the **m** of all the nations be that fight
60:6 A **m** of camels shall cover you,
Jer 46:16 Your **m** stumbled and fell, and one said to another,
La 1:5 because the LORD has made her suffer for the **m**
Eze 7:12 nor the seller mourn, for wrath is upon all their **m**.
7:13 vision concerns all their **m**; it shall not be revoked.
7:14 for my wrath is upon all their **m**.
14:4 with the **m** of their idols,
23:42 The sound of a raucous **m** was around her,
28:18 By the **m** of your iniquities,
32:26 Meshech and Tubal are there, and all their **m**,
32:32 Pharaoh and all his **m**, says the Lord GOD.
37:10 and they lived, and stood on their feet, a vast **m**.
Da 10:6 and the sound of his words like the roar of a **m**.
11:10 "His sons shall wage war and assemble a **m**
11:11 who shall muster a great **m**, which shall, however,
11:12 When the **m** has been carried off,
11:13 For the king of the north shall again raise a **m**,
Hos 8:12 Though I write for him the **m** of my instructions,
10:13 in your power and in the **m** of your warriors,
Zec 2:4 because of the **m** of people and animals in it.
Mk 3:7 and a great **m** from Galilee followed him;
Lk 2:13 And suddenly there was with the angel a **m** of
6:17 with a great crowd of his disciples and a great **m**
19:37 the whole **m** of the disciples began
Jas 5:20 the sinner's soul from death and will cover a **m**
1Pe 4:8 for love covers a **m** of sins.
Rev 7:9 and there was a great **m** that no one could count,
19:1 to be the loud voice of a great **m** in heaven,
19:6 I heard what seemed to be the voice of a great **m**,
Jdt 2:20 a **m** that could not be counted,
5:10 so great a **m** that their race could not be counted.
7:2 and the foot soldiers handling it, a very great **m**.
7:18 and they formed a vast **m**.
Wis 6:24 The **m** of the wise is the salvation of the world,
11:15 you sent upon them a **m** of irrational creatures
11:17 not lack the means to send upon them a **m** of bears,
14:20 and the **m**, attracted by the charm of his work,
16:1 and were tormented by a **m** of animals.
18:5 you in punishment took away a **m** of their children;
18:20 and a plague came upon the **m** in the desert,
Sir 5:6 he will forgive the **m** of my sins,"
16:1 Do not desire a **m** of worthless children,
34:23 nor for a **m** of sacrifices does he forgive sins.
35:23 until he destroys the **m** of the insolent,
44:19 Abraham was the great father of a **m** of nations,
Bar 2:29 this very great **m** will surely turn into
LtJ 6:6 the **m** before and behind them worshiping them.
1Mc 3:17 fight against so great and so strong a **m**?
6:41 All who heard the noise made by their **m**,
6:41 by the marching of the **m** and the clanking
9:35 So Jonathan sent his brother as leader of the **m**
2Mc 8:16 the great **m** of Gentiles who were wickedly coming
1Es 5:65 For the **m** sounded the trumpets loudly,
8:91 for there was great weeping among the **m**.
9:2 he was mourning over the great iniquities of the **m**.
9:4 and the men themselves expelled from the **m**
9:6 All the **m** sat in the open square before the temple,
9:10 Then all the **m** shouted and said with a loud voice,
1Es 9:11 But the **m** is great and it is winter,
9:12 So let the leaders of the **m** stay,
9:38 the whole **m** gathered with one accord in
9:40 Ezra the chief priest brought the law, for all the **m**,
9:41 and all the **m** gave attention to the law.
9:45 up the book of the law in the sight of the **m**,
9:47 and the **m** answered, "Amen."
9:49 and to the Levites who were teaching the **m**,
Man 1:7 to those who have sinned against you, and in the **m**
1:9 up and see the height of heaven because of the **m**
3Mc 4:5 For a **m** of gray-headed old men,
7:13 and the whole **m** shouted the Hallelujah
2Es 2:42 on Mount Zion a great **m** that I could not number,
3:16 and Jacob became a great **m**.
5:27 and from all the **m** of peoples you have gotten
7:*139* [69] by his word and blot out the **m** of their sins,
7:*140* [70] be left only very few of the innumerable **m**."
8:41 in the ground and plants a **m** of seedlings,
9:22 So let the **m** perish that has been born in vain,
10:10 and a **m** of them will come to doom.
10:11 she who lost so great a **m**,
10:13 the **m** that is now in it goes as it came';
13:5 After this I looked and saw that an innumerable **m**
13:9 When he saw the onrush of the approaching **m**,
13:11 fell on the onrushing **m** that was prepared to fight,
13:11 the innumerable **m** but only the dust of ashes and
13:12 and call to himself another **m** that was peaceable.
13:28 the onrushing **m** that came to conquer him, this is
13:34 and an innumerable **m** shall be gathered together,
13:39 as for your seeing him gather to himself another **m**
13:41 that they would leave the **m** of the nations and go
13:47 you saw the **m** gathered together in peace.
13:49 Therefore when he destroys the **m** of the nations
16:68 burning wrath of a great **m** is kindled over you;
4Mc 7:11 the **m** of the people and conquered the fiery angel,

MULTITUDES (6) [MULTITUDE]
Joel 3:14 **M**, **m**, in the valley of decision!
Rev 17:15 are peoples and **m** and nations and languages.
Wis 6:2 Give ear, you that rule over **m**,
8:10 I shall have glory among the **m** and honor in
2Mc 12:27 a fortified town where Lysias lived with **m**

MUNITION (KJV) See RAMPARTS, STRONGHOLD

MUPPIM (1)
Ge 46:21 Ashbel, Gera, Naaman, Ehi, Rosh, **M**, Huppim,

MURDER‡ (31) [MURDERED, MURDERER, MURDERERS, MURDERING, MURDEROUS, MURDERS]
Ex 20:13 You shall not **m**.
Dt 5:17 You shall not **m**.
Ps 10:8 in hiding places they **m** the innocent.
94:6 the widow and the stranger, they **m** the orphan,
Jer 7:9 Will you steal, **m**, commit adultery, swear falsely,
41:4 On the day after the **m** of Gedaliah,
Hos 4:2 lying, and **m**, and stealing and adultery break out;
6:9 they **m** on the road to Shechem,
Mt 5:21 to those of ancient times, 'You shall not **m**';
15:19 For out of the heart come evil intentions, **m**,
19:18 And Jesus said, "You shall not **m**;
Mk 7:21 that evil intentions come: fornication, theft, **m**,
10:19 You know the commandments: 'You shall not **m**;
15:7 in prison with the rebels who had committed **m**
Lk 18:20 not commit adultery; You shall not **m**;
23:19 that had taken place in the city, and for **m**.)
23:25 in prison for insurrection and **m**,
Ac 9:1 still breathing threats and **m** against the disciples of
Ro 1:29 Full of envy, **m**, strife, deceit, craftiness,
13:9 not commit adultery; You shall not **m**;
Jas 2:11 also said, "You shall not **m**."
2:11 Now if you do not commit adultery but if you **m**,
4:2 not have it; so you commit **m**.
1Jn 3:12 And why did he **m** him?
Wis 12:6 these parents who **m** helpless lives,
14:25 and all is a raging riot of blood and **m**,
Sir 34:26 To take away a neighbor's living is to commit **m**;
2Mc 4:35 were grieved and displeased at the unjust **m** of
4:36 to him with regard to the unreasonable **m** of Onias,
2Es 1:26 and your feet are swift to commit **m**.
4Mc 12:11 were you not ashamed to **m** his servants and torture

MURDERED (11) [MURDER]
Jdg 20:4 The Levite, the husband of the woman who was **m**,
2Sa 3:30 So Joab and his brother Abishai **m** Abner
14:7 for the life of his brother whom he **m**,
1Ki 2:5 and Amasa son of Jether, whom he **m**,
2Ki 14:5 he killed his servants who had **m** his father
2Ch 25:3 he killed his servants who had **m** his father
Mt 23:31 that you are descendants of those who **m**
23:35 whom you **m** between the sanctuary and the altar.
Jas 5:6 You have condemned and **m** the righteous one,
1Jn 3:12 from the evil one and **m** his brother.
Tob 2:3 one of our own people has been **m** and thrown into

MURDERER (23) [MURDER]
Nu 35:16 death ensues, is a **m**; the **m** shall be put to death.
35:17 death ensues, is a **m**; the **m** shall be put to death.
35:18 death ensues, is a **m**; the **m** shall be put to death.
35:19 of blood is the one who shall put the **m** to death;
35:21 a **m**; the avenger of blood shall put the **m** to death,
Nu 35:30 the **m** shall be put to death on the evidence
35:31 accept no ransom for the life of a **m**
35:31 a **m** must be put to death.
2Sa 16:7 while he cursed, "Out! Out! **M**!
2Ki 6:32 that this **m** has sent someone to take off my head?
9:31 she said, "Is it peace, Zimri, **m** of your master?"
Job 24:14 The **m** rises at dusk to kill the poor and needy,
Jn 8:44 He was a **m** from the beginning and does not stand
Ac 3:14 and Righteous One and asked to have a **m** given
28:4 they said to one another, "This man must be a **m**;
1Pe 4:15 But let none of you suffer as a **m**, a thief,
Sir 34:25 whoever deprives them of it is a **m**.
2Mc 9:28 So the **m** and blasphemer, having endured
4Mc 9:15 not because I am a **m**,

MURDERERS (10) [MURDER]
2Ki 14:6 But he did not put to death the children of the **m**;
Isa 1:21 righteousness lodged in her—but now **m**!
Mt 22:7 He sent his troops, destroyed those **m**,
Ac 7:52 and now you have become his betrayers and **m**.
1Ti 1:9 for those who kill their father or mother, for **m**,
1Jn 3:15 All who hate a brother or sister are **m**,
3:15 that **m** do not have eternal life abiding in them.
Rev 21:8 for the cowardly, the faithless, the polluted, the **m**,
22:15 and sorcerers and fornicators and **m** and idolaters,
2Mc 12:6 the righteous judge, attacked the **m** of his kindred.

MURDERING (1) [MURDER]
4Mc 11:3 so that by **m** me you will incur punishment from

MURDEROUS (1) [MURDER]
4Mc 10:17 When he heard this, the bloodthirsty, **m**,

MURDERS (4) [MURDER]
Dt 22:26 that of someone who attacks and **m** a neighbor.
Mt 5:21 and 'whoever **m** shall be liable to judgment.'
Rev 9:21 of their **m** or their sorceries or their fornication
2Mc 4:3 to such a degree that even **m** were committed

MURMUR, MURMURED, MURMURS, MURMURING, MURMURINGS (KJV)
See also COMPLAIN, COMPLAINED, COMPLAINING, COMPLAINTS, GRUMBLE, GRUMBLED, GRUMBLERS, GRUMBLING, MUTTERING, RAIL, REBELLED, SCOLDED

MURMURED (1) [MURMURING]
Jos 9:18 Then all the congregation **m** against the leaders.

MURMURING (1) [MURMURED, MURMURS]
Php 2:14 Do all things without **m** and arguing,

MURMURS (1) [MURMURING]
La 3:62 and **m** of my assailants are against me all day long.

MURRAIN (KJV) See PESTILENCE

MUSCLE (2) [MUSCLES]
Ge 32:32 to this day the Israelites do not eat the thigh **m**
32:32 he struck Jacob on the hip socket at the thigh **m**.

MUSCLES (2) [MUSCLE]
Job 40:16 and its power in the **m** of its belly.
4Mc 7:13 his body no longer tense and firm, his **m** flabby,

MUSE (2) [MUSED]
Ps 77:12 and **m** on your mighty deeds.
Isa 33:18 Your mind will **m** on the terror:

MUSED (1) [MUSE]
Ps 39:3 While I **m**, the fire burned;

MUSHI (8) [MUSHITES]
Ex 6:19 The sons of Merari: Mahli and **M**.
Nu 3:20 The sons of Merari by their clans: Mahli and **M**.
1Ch 6:19 The sons of Merari: Mahli and **M**.
6:47 son of **M**, son of Merari, son of Levi;
23:21 The sons of Merari: Mahli and **M**.
23:23 The sons of **M**: Mahli, Eder, and Jeremoth, three.
24:26 The sons of Merari: Mahli and **M**.
24:30 The sons of **M**: Mahli, Eder, and Jerimoth.

MUSHITES (2) [MUSHI]
Nu 3:33 the clan of the Mahlites and the clan of the **M**:
26:58 the clan of the **M**, the clan of the Korahites.

MUSIC‡ (23) [MUSICAL, MUSICIAN, MUSICIANS]
1Sa 19:9 while David was playing **m**.
1Ch 15:22 leader of the Levites in **m**, was to direct the **m**,
15:27 and Chenaniah the leader of the **m** of the singers;
15:28 and cymbals, and made loud **m** on harps and lyres.
16:42 with them trumpets and cymbals for the **m**,
25:6 for the **m** in the house of the LORD with cymbals,

2Ch 7: 6 for **m** to the LORD that King David had made
34:12 Other Levites, all skillful with instruments of **m,**
Ps 49: 4 I will solve my riddle to the **m** of the harp.
92: 3 to the **m** of the lute and the harp,
La 5:14 the city gate, the young men their **m.**
Eze 26:13 I will silence the **m** of your songs;
Am 6: 5 and like David improvise on instruments of **m;**
Lk 15:25 and approached the house, he heard **m**
Sir 22: 6 Like **m** in time of mourning
32: 3 and do not interrupt the **m.**
32: 5 A ruby seal in a setting of gold is a concert of **m** at
32: 6 of gold is the melody of **m** with good wine.
40:20 Wine and **m** gladden the heart,
49: 1 and like **m** at a banquet of wine.
1Es 4:63 they feasted, with **m** and rejoicing, for seven days.
5: 2 with the **m** of drums and flutes;

MUSICAL (11) [MUSIC]

1Sa 18: 6 with songs of joy, and with **m** instruments.
1Ch 15:16 as the singers to play on **m** instruments,
2Ch 5:13 and cymbals and other **m** instruments,
23:13 with their **m** instruments leading in the celebration.
Ne 12:36 with the **m** instruments of David the man of God;
Da 3: 5 lyre, trigon, harp, drum, and entire **m** ensemble,
3: 7 harp, drum, and entire **m** ensemble, all the peoples,
3:10 lyre, trigon, harp, drum, and entire **m** ensemble,
3:15 and entire **m** ensemble to fall down and worship
Sir 44: 5 those who composed **m** tunes, or put verses
1Es 5:59 with **m** instruments and trumpets, and the Levites,

MUSICIAN (2) [MUSIC]

2Ki 3:15 But get me a **m."**
3:15 And then, while the **m** was playing,

MUSICIANS (5) [MUSIC]

Jdg 5:11 To the sound of **m** at the watering places,
Ps 68:25 **m** last, between them girls playing tambourines:
1Mc 9:39 with tambourines and **m** and many weapons.
9:41 and the voice of their **m** into a funeral dirge.
1Es 5:42 there were two hundred forty-five **m** and singers.

MUST‡ (384)

Ge 4: 7 its desire is for you, but you **m** master it."
17:13 the one bought with your money **m** be circumcised.
18:21 I **m** go down and see whether they have done
20:13 I said to her, 'This is the kindness you **m** do me:
24: 5 **m** I then take your son back to the land
24: 8 only you **m** not take my son back there."
30:16 and said, "You **m** come in to me;
43:11 Then their father Israel said to them, "If it **m** be so,
43:23 of your father **m** have put treasure in your sacks
45:13 You **m** tell my father how greatly I am honored
45:28 I **m** go and see him before I die."
Ex 2: 6 "This **m** be one of the Hebrews' children,"
3: 3 "I **m** turn aside and look at this great sight,
8:27 We **m** go a three days' journey into the wilderness
10:25 "You **m** also let us have sacrifices
10:26 Our livestock also **m** go with us;
10:26 for we **m** choose some of them for the worship of
12:16 only what everyone **m** eat,
13:13 if you do not redeem it, you **m** break its neck.
13:19 then you **m** carry my bones with you from here."
19:22 the LORD **m** consecrate themselves or
23: 5 you **m** help to set it free.
Lev 2:11 for you **m** not turn any leaven or honey into smoke
3:17 you **m** not eat any fat or any blood.
7:24 but you **m** not eat it.
7:26 You **m** not eat any blood whatever,
7:29 of well-being **m** yourself bring to
19:23 three years it shall be forbidden to you, it **m** not
22:21 to be acceptable it **m** be perfect;
27:13 one-fifth **m** be added to the assessment.
27:31 they **m** add one-fifth to them.
Nu 4:15 but they **m** not touch the holy things,
4:18 You **m** not let the tribe of the clans of
4:19 This is how you **m** deal with them in order
4:20 But the Kohathites **m** not go in to look on
5: 3 they **m** not defile their camp,
6:21 Their offering to the LORD **m** be in accordance
9: 7 why **m** we be kept from presenting
16:13 that you **m** also lord it over us?
18: 3 But they **m** not approach either the utensils of
22:38 word God puts in my mouth, that is what I **m** say."
23: 5 "Return to Balak, and this is what you **m** say."
23:12 **"M** I not take care to say what the LORD puts
23:26 'Whatever the LORD says, that is what I **m** do'?"
31:24 You **m** wash your clothes on the seventh day,
35:28 For the slayer **m** remain in the city of refuge until
35:31 a murderer **m** be put to death.
36: 6 only it **m** be into a clan of their father's tribe
Dt 1:17 You **m** not be partial in judging:
4: 2 You **m** neither add anything to what I command
4: 6 You **m** observe them diligently,
5:32 You **m** therefore be careful to do as
5:33 You **m** follow exactly the path that
6:17 You **m** diligently keep the commandments of
7: 2 then you **m** utterly destroy them.
7: 5 But this is how you **m** deal with them:
7:26 You **m** utterly detest and abhor it,
8: 1 I command you today you **m** diligently observe,
11: 2 but it is you who **m** acknowledge his greatness,
11:32 you **m** diligently observe all the statutes
12: 1 and ordinances that you **m** diligently observe in
12: 2 You **m** demolish completely all the places where
12:16 The blood, however, you **m** not eat;
Dt 12:31 You **m** not do the same for the LORD your God,
12:32 You **m** diligently observe everything
13: 3 you **m** not heed the words of those prophets
13: 8 you **m** not yield to or heed any such persons.
14: 1 You **m** not lacerate yourselves
15: 3 but you **m** remit your claim
15:23 Its blood, however, you **m** not eat;
16: 3 You **m** not eat with it anything leavened.
16:19 **m** not distort justice; you **m** not show partiality;
16:19 and you **m** not accept bribes,
17: 1 You **m** not sacrifice to the LORD your God an ox
17: 6 a person **m** not be put to death on the evidence
17:11 You **m** carry out fully the law that they interpret
17:16 Even so, he **m** not acquire many horses for himself,
17:16 "You **m** never return that way again."
17:17 And he **m** not acquire many wives for himself,
17:17 and gold he **m** not acquire in great quantity
18: 9 you **m** not learn to imitate the abhorrent practices
18:13 You **m** remain completely loyal to
19:14 You **m** not move your neighbor's boundary
20:16 you **m** not let anything that breathes remain alive.
20:19 you **m** not destroy its trees by wielding an ax
20:19 you **m** not cut them down.
21: 9 you **m** do what is right in the sight of the LORD.
21:14 You **m** not treat her as a slave,
21:17 He **m** acknowledge as firstborn the son of
21:23 his corpse **m** not remain all night upon the tree;
21:23 You **m** not defile the land that
23:10 he **m** not come within the camp.
23:14 therefore your camp **m** be holy,
23:23 Whatever your lips utter you **m** diligently perform,
27: 6 You **m** build the altar of the LORD your God
Jos 9:19 the God of Israel, and now we **m** not touch them.
22:18 that you **m** turn away today from following
Jdg 3:24 "He **m** be relieving himself in the cool chamber."
14: 3 that you **m** go to take a wife from
21:17 "There **m** be heirs for the survivors of Benjamin,
Ru 2:16 You **m** also pull out some handfuls for her from
3:14 "It **m** not be known that the woman came to
1Sa 2:16 you **m** give it now; if not, I will take it by force."
5: 7 ark of the God of Israel **m** not remain with us;
6: 5 So you **m** make images of your tumors and images
9:13 since he **m** bless the sacrifice;
13:19 "The Hebrews **m** not make swords or spears
21: 2 'No one **m** know anything of the matter
2Sa 14:14 We **m** all die; we are like water
1Ki 2: 9 to do to him, and you **m** bring his gray head down
12:10 but you **m** lighten it for us';
18:27 or perhaps he is asleep and **m** be awakened."
22:16 "How many times **m** I make you swear
2Ki 3:23 the kings **m** have fought together,
1Ch 22: 5 the LORD **m** be exceedingly magnificent, famous
22:14 To these you **m** add more.
2Ch 10:10 but you **m** lighten it for us';
18:15 "How many times **m** I make you swear
Ezr 10:12 we **m** do as you have said.
Ne 5: 2 we **m** get grain, so that we may eat and stay alive."
5: 8 who **m** then be bought back by us!"
Job 9:15 I **m** appeal for mercy to my accuser.
19:16 I **m** myself plead with him.
30: 6 In the gullies of wadis they **m** live,
32:20 I **m** speak, so that I may find relief;
32:20 I **m** open my lips and answer.
34:33 For you **m** choose, and not I;
40: 2 Anyone who argues with God **m** respond."
Ps 13: 2 How long **m** I bear pain in my soul,
32: 9 whose temper **m** be curbed with bit and bridle,
42: 9 Why **m** I walk about mournfully because
43: 2 Why **m** I walk about mournfully because of
56:12 My vows to you I **m** perform, O God;
69: 4 What I did not steal **m** I now restore?
119:84 How long **m** your servant endure?
120: 5 that I **m** live among the tents of Kedar.
Ecc 2:18 seeing that I **m** leave it to those who come after me
2:21 and knowledge and skill **m** leave all to be enjoyed
10:10 then more strength **m** be exerted;
12: 5 because all **m** go to their eternal home,
Isa 38:10 In the noontide of my days I **m** depart;
51:12 then are you afraid of a mere mortal who **m** die,
Jer 4:21 How long **m** I see the standard,
6: 6 This is the city that **m** be punished;
10:19 "Truly this is my punishment, and I **m** bear it."
20: 8 For whenever I speak, I **m** cry out, I **m** shout,
25:28 Thus says the LORD of hosts: You **m** drink!
27: 9 You, therefore, **m** not listen to your prophets,
34:14 of you **m** set free any Hebrews who have been sold
34:14 you **m** set them free from your service."
36:16 "We certainly **m** report all these words to
49:12 You shall not go unpunished; you **m** drink it.
51:49 Babylon **m** fall for the slain of Israel,
La 5: 4 We **m** pay for the water we drink;
5: 4 the wood we get **m** be bought.
Eze 8:17 **M** they fill the land with violence,
16:58 You **m** bear the penalty of your lewdness
34:18 but you **m** tread down with your feet the rest
34:18 **m** you foul the rest with your feet?
34:19 And **m** my sheep eat what you have trodden
Da 9: 2 **m** be fulfilled for the devastation of Jerusalem,
10:20 I **m** return to fight against the prince of Persia,
Hos 3: 3 "You **m** remain as mine for many days;
9:13 now Ephraim **m** lead out his children for slaughter.
10: 2 Their heart is false; now they **m** bear their guilt.
10:11 Judah **m** plow; Jacob **m** harrow for himself.
Am 6:10 We **m** not mention the name of the LORD."
7:11 and Israel **m** go into exile away from his land.' "
Mic 7: 9 I **m** bear the indignation of the LORD,
Mt 15: 4 'Whoever speaks evil of father or mother **m**
Mt 16:21 to show his disciples that he **m** go to Jerusalem
16:22 This **m** never happen to you."
17:10 then, do the scribes say that Elijah **m** come first?"
17:17 how much longer **m** I be with you?
17:17 How much longer **m** I put up with you?
19:16 what good deed **m** I do to have eternal life?"
20:26 but whoever wishes to be great among you **m**
20:27 and whoever wishes to be first among you **m**
24: 6 for this **m** take place, but the end is not yet.
24:16 then those in Judea **m** flee to the mountains;
24:17 on the housetop **m** not go down to take what is in
24:18 the one in the field **m** not turn back to get a coat.
24:44 Therefore you also **m** be ready,
26:35 Peter said to him, "Even though I **m** die with you,
26:54 which say it **m** happen in this way?"
28:13 "You **m** say, 'His disciples came by night
Mk 7:10 and, 'Whoever speaks evil of father or mother **m**
8:31 that the Son of Man **m** undergo great suffering,
9:11 "Why do the scribes say that Elijah **m** come first?"
9:19 how much longer **m** I be among you?
9:19 How much longer **m** I put up with you?
9:35 to be first **m** be last of all and servant of all."
10:17 what **m** I do to inherit eternal life?"
10:43 but whoever wishes to become great among you **m**
10:44 and whoever wishes to be first among you **m**
13: 7 this **m** take place, but the end is still to come.
13:10 the good news **m** first be proclaimed to all nations.
13:14 then those in Judea **m** flee to the mountains;
13:15 on the housetop **m** not go down or enter the house
13:16 the one in the field **m** not turn back to get a coat.
14:31 "Even though I **m** die with you,
Lk 1:15 He **m** never drink wine or strong drink;
2:49 not know that I **m** be in my Father's house?"
3:11 "Whoever has two coats **m** share
3:11 and whoever has food **m** do likewise."
4:43 "I **m** proclaim the good news of the kingdom
5:38 But new wine **m** be put into fresh wineskins.
9:22 "The Son of Man **m** undergo great suffering,
9:41 much longer **m** I be with you and bear with you?
10:25 he said, "what **m** I do to inherit eternal life?"
12:40 You also **m** be ready, for the Son of Man is coming
13:33 tomorrow, and the next day I **m** be on my way,
14:18 and I **m** go out and see it;
17: 3 If another disciple sins, you **m** rebuke the offender,
17: 3 and if there is repentance, you **m** forgive.
17: 4 'I repent,' you **m** forgive."
17:25 But first he **m** endure much suffering and
17:31 in the house **m** not come down to take them away;
17:31 and likewise anyone in the field **m** not turn back.
18:18 what **m** I do to inherit eternal life?"
19: 5 for I **m** stay at your house today."
21: 9 for these things **m** take place first,
21:21 Then those in Judea **m** flee to the mountains,
21:21 and those inside the city **m** leave it,
21:21 and those out in the country **m** not enter it;
22:26 rather the greatest among you **m** become like
22:36 "But now, the one who has a purse **m** take it,
22:36 And the one who has no sword **m** sell his cloak
22:37 For I tell you, this scripture **m** be fulfilled in me,
24: 7 that the Son of Man **m** be handed over to sinners,
24:44 the prophets, and the psalms **m** be fulfilled."
Jn 3: 7 'You **m** be born from above.'
3:14 so **m** the Son of Man be lifted up,
3:30 He **m** increase, but I **m** decrease."
3:36 but **m** endure God's wrath.
4:20 the place where people **m** worship is in Jerusalem."
4:24 and those who worship him **m** worship in spirit
6:28 "What **m** we do to perform the works of God?"
9: 4 We **m** work the works of him who sent me
10:16 I **m** bring them also, and they will listen
12:26 Whoever serves me **m** follow me, and where I am,
12:34 can you say that the Son of Man **m** be lifted up?
20: 9 that he **m** rise from the dead.
Ac 1:22 one of these **m** become a witness with us
3:21 who **m** remain in heaven until the time
3:22 You **m** listen to whatever he tells you.
4:12 under heaven given among mortals by which we **m**
4:19 to listen to you rather than to God, you **m** judge;
5:29 "We **m** obey God rather than any human authority.
9:16 I myself will show him how much he **m** suffer for
10:15 a second time, "What God has made clean, you **m**
11: 9 from heaven, 'What God has made clean, you **m**
14:22 "It is through many persecutions that we **m** enter
16:30 "Sirs, what **m** I do to be saved?"
19:21 "After I have gone there, I **m** also see Rome."
19:39 it **m** be settled in the regular assembly.
20:35 an example that by such work we **m** support
23:11 so you **m** bear witness also in Rome."
23:15 the council **m** notify the tribune to bring him down
26:23 the Messiah **m** suffer, and that, by being the first
27:24 you **m** stand before the emperor;
28: 4 "This man **m** be a murderer;
Ro 6:11 also **m** consider yourselves dead to sin and alive
13: 5 Therefore one **m** be subject,
14: 3 Those who eat **m** not despise those who abstain,
14: 3 and those who abstain **m** not pass judgment
15: 2 of us **m** please our neighbor for the good purpose
1Co 3:10 Each builder **m** choose with care how to build
10: 8 We **m** not indulge in sexual immorality as some
10: 9 We **m** not put Christ to the test,
14:37 **m** acknowledge that what I am writing to you is
15:25 For he **m** reign until he has put all his enemies
15:53 For this perishable body **m** put on imperishability,
15:53 and this mortal body **m** put on immortality.
2Co 5:10 of us **m** appear before the judgment seat of Christ,
9: 7 of you **m** give as you have made up your mind,
11:21 To my shame, I **m** say, we were too weak for that!

2Co 11:30 If I **m** boast, I will boast of the things
13: 1 "Any charge **m** be sustained by the evidence
Gal 6: 4 All **m** test their own work;
6: 5 For all **m** carry their own loads.
6: 6 Those who are taught the word **m** share
Eph 4:14 We **m** no longer be children,
4:15 we **m** grow up in every way into him who is
4:17 you **m** no longer live as the Gentiles live,
4:28 Thieves **m** give up stealing;
5: 3 or greed, **m** not even be mentioned among you,
6:20 Pray that I may declare it boldly, as I **m** speak.
Php 2:18 in the same way you also **m** be glad and rejoice
Col 3: 8 But now you **m** get rid of all such things—
3:13 the Lord has forgiven you, so you also **m** forgive.
2Th 1: 3 We **m** always give thanks to God for you,
2:13 But we **m** always give thanks to God for you,
1Ti 3: 2 Now a bishop **m** be above reproach,
3: 4 He **m** manage his own household well,
3: 6 He **m** not be a recent convert,
3: 7 Moreover, he **m** be well thought of by outsiders,
3: 8 Deacons likewise **m** be serious,
3: 9 they **m** hold fast to the mystery of the faith with
3:11 Women likewise **m** be serious, not slanderers,
4:11 These are the things you **m** insist on and teach.
5:10 she **m** be well attested for her good works,
6: 2 Those who have believing masters **m** not
6: 2 rather they **m** serve them all the more,
2Ti 2:24 the Lord's servant **m** not be quarrelsome but kindly
3: 1 You **m** understand this,
4:15 You also **m** beware of him,
Tit 1: 7 For a bishop, as God's steward, **m** be blameless;
1: 7 he **m** not be arrogant or quick-tempered
1: 8 but he **m** be hospitable, a lover
1: 9 He **m** have a firm grasp of the word
1:11 they **m** be silenced, since they are upsetting whole
Heb 2: 1 we **m** pay greater attention to what we have heard,
4:13 of the one to whom we **m** render an account.
5: 3 of this he **m** offer sacrifice for his own sins as well
9:16 the death of the one who made it **m** be established.
11: 6 for whoever would approach him **m** believe
Jas 1:7,8 **m** not expect to receive anything from the Lord.
1:19 You **m** understand this, my beloved:
5: 8 You also **m** be patient.
1Pe 4:11 Whoever speaks **m** do so as one speaking
4:11 whoever serves **m** do so with the strength
5: 5 you who are younger **m** accept the authority of
5: 5 And all of you **m** clothe yourselves with humility
2Pe 1: 5 you **m** make every effort to support your faith
1:20 First of all you **m** understand this,
3: 3 First of all you **m** understand this,
1Jn 3:12 We **m** not be like Cain who was from the evil one
4:21 those who love God **m** love their brothers
2Jn 1: 6 from the beginning—you **m** walk in it.
Jude 1:17 **m** remember the predictions of the apostles
Rev 1: 1 to show his servants what **m** soon take place;
4: 1 and I will show you what **m** take place after this."
10:11 "You **m** prophesy again about many peoples
11: 5 anyone who wants to harm them **m** be killed
13:10 with the sword you **m** be killed.
17:10 when he comes, he **m** remain only a little while.
19:10 but he said to me, "You **m** not do that!
20: 3 After that he **m** be let out for a little while.
22: 6 to show his servants what **m** soon take place."
22: 9 but he said to me, "You **m** not do that!
Tob 6: 8 you **m** burn them to make a smoke in the presence
6:11 "We **m** stay this night in the home of Raguel.
6:18 both of you **m** first stand up and pray,
9: 4 you know that my father **m** be counting the days,
Jdt 2:10 They **m** yield themselves to you,
AdE 1:15 and told him what **m** be done to Queen Vashti for
4:16 contrary to the law, even if I **m** die."
Wis 12:19 that the righteous **m** be kind,
15:12 for they say one **m** get money however one can,
16:28 that one **m** rise before the sun to give you thanks,
16:28 and **m** pray to you at the dawning of the light;
Sir Pr: 1 who read the scriptures **m** not only themselves
Pr: 1 but **m** also as lovers of learning be able through
3:18 greater you are, the more you **m** humble yourself;
8: 7 remember that we **m** all die.
13: 3 a poor person suffers wrong, and **m** add apologies.
14:17 for the decree from of old is, "You **m** die!"
15:10 For in wisdom **m** praise be uttered,
16:30 and into it they **m** return.
33:20 in case you change your mind and **m** ask for it.
LtJ 6: 6 "It is you, O Lord, whom we **m** worship."
6:27 they themselves **m** pick it up.
6:40 Why then **m** anyone think that they are gods,
6:44 Why then **m** anyone think that they are gods,
6:56 then **m** anyone admit or think that they are gods?
6:64 Therefore one **m** not think that they are gods,
2Mc 2:29 the master builder of a new house **m** be concerned
3:13 said that this money **m** in any case be confiscated
6:17 we **m** go on briefly with the story.
1Es 4:22 Therefore you **m** realize that women rule over you!
3Mc 5:37 **m** I give you orders about these things?
2Es 6:16 for they know that their end **m** be changed."
8:58 though they knew well that they **m** die.
9:12 these **m** in torment acknowledge it after death.
16:53 Sinners **m** not say that they have not sinned;
16:76 **m** not let your sins weigh you down,
4Mc 13: 1 even unto death, everyone **m** concede
16: 1 it **m** be admitted that devout reason is sovereign
16:22 You too **m** have the same faith in God and not

MUSTARD (5)

Mt 13:31 a **m** seed that someone took and sowed in his field;
Mt 17:20 if you have faith the size of a **m** seed,
Mk 4:31 It is like a **m** seed, which,
Lk 13:19 It is like a **m** seed that someone took and sowed in
17: 6 Lord replied, "If you had faith the size of a **m** seed,

MUSTER (5) [MUSTERED, MUSTERING, MUSTERS]

1Ki 20:25 and **m** an army like the army that you have lost,
2Ch 17:14 This was the **m** of them by ancestral houses:
26:11 to the numbers in the **m** made by the secretary Jeiel
Ne 3:31 and of the merchants, opposite the **M** Gate,
Da 11:11 who shall **m** a great multitude, which shall,

MUSTERED‡ (21) [MUSTER]

Jos 8:10 In the morning Joshua rose early and **m** the people,
Jdg 20:15 Benjaminites **m** twenty-six thousand armed men
20:17 **m** four hundred thousand armed men,
1Sa 4: 1 the Philistines **m** for war against Israel,
11: 8 When he **m** them at Bezek,
13: 5 The Philistines **m** to fight with Israel,
2Sa 18: 1 Then David **m** the men who were with him,
1Ki 20:15 Then he **m** the young men who serve
20:15 them he **m** all the people of Israel, seven thousand.
20:26 the spring Ben-hadad **m** the Arameans and went up
20:27 After the Israelites had been **m** and provisioned,
2Ki 3: 6 of Samaria at that time and **m** all Israel.
6:24 of Aram **m** his entire army;
25:19 the commander of the army who **m** the people of
1Ch 19: 7 the Ammonites were **m** from their cities and came
2Ch 25: 5 He **m** those twenty years old and upward,
Jer 52:25 the secretary of the commander of the army who **m**
Eze 38: 8 After many days you shall be **m**;
Jdt 2:15 He **m** the picked troops by divisions
1Mc 4:28 the next year he **m** sixty thousand picked infantry
10:77 he **m** three thousand cavalry and a large army,

MUSTERING (2) [MUSTER]

1Sa 13:11 and that the Philistines were **m** at Michmash,
Isa 13: 4 The LORD of hosts is **m** an army for battle.

MUSTERS (1) [MUSTER]

Na 2: 3 on the chariots flashes on the day when he **m** them;

MUTE (15)

Ex 4:11 Who makes them **m** or deaf, seeing or blind?
Ps 38:13 like the **m**, who cannot speak.
Mt 9:32 a demoniac who was **m** was brought to him.
9:33 the one who had been **m** spoke;
12:22 to him a demoniac who was blind and **m**;
12:22 that the one who had been **m** could speak and see.
15:30 the maimed, the blind, the **m**, and many others.
15:31 crowd was amazed when they saw the **m** speaking,
Mk 7:37 even makes the deaf to hear and the **m** to speak."
Lk 1:20 you will become **m**, unable to speak,
11:14 Now he was casting out a demon that was **m**;
11:14 the one who had been **m** spoke,
Wis 10:21 wisdom opened the mouths of those who were **m**,
LtJ 6:40 they bring Bel and pray that the **m** may speak,
4Mc 10:18 God hears also those who are **m**.

MUTH-LABBEN (1)

Ps 9: T *To the leader: according to* ***M****. A Psalm of David.*

MUTILATE (1) [MUTILATED]

Php 3: 2 beware of those who **m** the flesh!

MUTILATED (3) [MUTILATE]

Lev 21:18 or one who has a **m** face or a limb too long,
22:25 since they are **m**, with a blemish in them,
4Mc 10:20 we let our bodily members be **m**.

MUTILATION See Index to Footnotes

MUTTER (1) [MUTTERING, MUTTERS]

Isa 8:19 and the familiar spirits that chirp and **m**;

MUTTERING (1) [MUTTER]

Jn 7:32 The Pharisees heard the crowd **m** such things

MUTTERS (1) [MUTTER]

Isa 59: 3 your tongue **m** wickedness.

MUTUAL (7) [MUTUALLY]

Ro 12:10 love one another with **m** affection;
14:19 for peace and for **m** upbuilding.
Heb 13: 1 Let **m** love continue.
1Pe 1:22 to the truth so that you have genuine **m** love,
2Pe 1: 7 with **m** affection, and **m** affection with love.
3Mc 2:33 and depriving them of companionship and **m** help.

MUTUALLY (1) [MUTUAL]

Ro 1:12 or rather so that we may be **m** encouraged

MUZZLE (5)

Dt 25: 4 You shall not **m** an ox while it is treading out
Ps 39: 1 a **m** on my mouth as long as the wicked are
1Co 9: 9 "You shall not **m** an ox while it is treading out
1Ti 5:18 "You shall not **m** an ox while it is treading out
Sir 20:29 like a **m** on the mouth they stop reproofs.

MY (5481) [I] See Index of Articles Etc.

MYNDOS (1)

1Mc 15:23 and to the Spartans, and to Delos, and to **M**,

MYRA‡ (1)

Ac 27: 5 we came to **M** in Lycia.

MYRIAD‡ (2) [MYRIADS]

Dt 32:30 and two put a **m** to flight,
3Mc 3:21 and the **m** affairs liberally entrusted to them from

MYRIADS (6) [MYRIAD]

Ge 24:60 "May you, our sister, become thousands of **m**;
Dt 33: 2 With him were **m** of holy ones;
33:17 such are the **m** of Ephraim,
Rev 5:11 they numbered **m** of **m** and thousands
Jdt 16: 3 he came with **m** of his warriors;

MYRRH (18) [MYRRH-PERFUMED]

Ex 30:23 of liquid **m** five hundred shekels,
Est 2:12 of **m** and six months with perfumes and cosmetics
Ps 45: 8 your robes are all fragrant with **m** and aloes
Pr 7:17 I have perfumed my bed with **m**,
SS 1:13 to me a bag of **m** that lies between my breasts.
3: 6 perfumed with **m** and frankincense,
4: 6 to the mountain of **m** and the hill of frankincense.
4:14 **m** and aloes, with all chief spices—
5: 1 I gather my **m** with my spice,
5: 5 and my hands dripped with **m**,
5: 5 fingers with liquid **m**, upon the handles of the bolt.
5:13 His lips are lilies, distilling liquid **m**.
Mt 2:11 of gold, frankincense, and **m**.
Mk 15:23 And they offered him wine mixed with **m**;
Jn 19:39 also came, bringing a mixture of **m** and aloes,
Rev 18:13 spice, incense, **m**, frankincense, wine, olive oil,
AdE 2:12 while they are anointing themselves with oil of **m**,
Sir 24:15 and like choice **m** I spread my fragrance,

MYRRH-PERFUMED (1) [MYRRH, PERFUME]

3Mc 4: 6 their **m** hair sprinkled with ashes,

MYRTLE (6)

Ne 8:15 **m**, palm, and other leafy trees to make booths,
Isa 41:19 the acacia, the **m**, and the olive;
55:13 instead of the brier shall come up the **m**;
Zec 1: 8 He was standing among the **m** trees in the glen;
1:10 among the **m** trees answered,
1:11 the LORD who was standing among the **m** trees,

MYSELF (180) [I] See Index of Articles Etc.

MYSIA (2) [MYSIANS]

Ac 16: 7 When they had come opposite **M**,
16: 8 so, passing by **M**, they went down to Troas.

MYSIANS (1) [MYSIA]

2Mc 5:24 of the **M**, with an army of twenty-two thousand,

MYSTERIES‡ (9) [MYSTERY]

Da 2:28 but there is a God in heaven who reveals **m**,
2:29 the revealer of **m** disclosed to you what is to be.
2:47 of gods and Lord of kings and a revealer of **m**,
1Co 4: 1 as servants of Christ and stewards of God's **m**.
13: 2 and understand all **m** and all knowledge,
14: 2 since they are speaking **m** in the Spirit.
Wis 14:23 or celebrate secret **m**, or hold frenzied revels
Sir 39: 7 as he meditates on his **m**.
3Mc 2:30 to join those who have been initiated into the **m**,

MYSTERIOUS (1) [MYSTERY]

3Mc 1:17 supposing that something **m** was occurring.

MYSTERY‡ (28) [MYSTERIES, MYSTERIOUS]

Da 2:18 from the God of heaven concerning this **m**,
2:19 **m** was revealed to Daniel in a vision of the night,
2:27 or diviners can show to the king the **m** that
2:30 this **m** has not been revealed to me because
2:47 for you have been able to reveal this **m**!"
4: 9 the holy gods and that no **m** is too difficult for you.
Ro 11:25 I want you to understand this **m**:
16:25 to the revelation of the **m** that was kept secret
1Co 2: 1 I did not come proclaiming the **m** of God to you
15:51 Listen, I will tell you a **m**!
Eph 1: 9 he has made known to us the **m** of his will,
3: 3 how the **m** was made known to me by revelation,
3: 4 to perceive my understanding of the **m** of Christ.
3: 5 In former generations this **m** was not made known
3: 9 the plan of the **m** hidden for ages
5:32 This is a great **m**, and I am applying it to Christ
6:19 to make known with boldness the **m** of the gospel,
Col 1:26 the **m** that has been hidden throughout the ages
1:27 the Gentiles are the riches of the glory of this **m**,
2: 2 and have the knowledge of God's **m**,
4: 3 that we may declare the **m** of Christ,
2Th 2: 7 For the **m** of lawlessness is already at work,
1Ti 3: 9 they must hold fast to the **m** of the faith with

1Ti 3:16 Without any doubt, the m of our religion is great:
Rev 1:20 m of the seven stars that you saw in my right hand,
10: 7 the m of God will be fulfilled,
17: 5 and on her forehead was written a name, a m:
17: 7 I will tell you the m of the woman,

MYTHS (5)
1Ti 1: 4 and not to occupy themselves with m
4: 7 to do with profane m and old wives' tales.
2Ti 4: 4 from listening to the truth and wander away to m.
Tit 1:14 not paying attention to Jewish m or
2Pe 1:16 For we did not follow cleverly devised m

N

NAAM (1)
1Ch 4:15 Iru, Elah, and N; and the son of Elah: Kenaz.

NAAMAH (5)
Ge 4:22 The sister of Tubal-cain was N.
Jos 15:41 Beth-dagon, N, and Makkedah:
1Ki 14:21 His mother's name was N the Ammonite.
14:31 His mother's name was N the Ammonite.
2Ch 12:13 His mother's name was N the Ammonite.

NAAMAN (18) [NAAMAN'S]
Ge 46:21 Bela, Becher, Ashbel, Gera, N, Ehi, Rosh,
Nu 26:40 And the sons of Bela were Ard and N:
26:40 of N, the clan of the Naamites.
2Ki 5: 1 N, commander of the army of the king of Aram,
5: 4 So N went in and told his lord just what the girl
5: 6 know that I have sent to you my servant N,
5: 9 So N came with his horses and chariots,
5:11 But N became angry and went away, saying,
5:17 Then N said, "If not, please let two mule-loads
5:19 But when N had gone from him a short distance,
5:20 "My master has let that Aramean N off too lightly
5:21 So Gehazi went after N.
5:21 When N saw someone running after him,
5:23 N said, "Please accept two talents."
5:27 Therefore the leprosy of N shall cling to you,
1Ch 8: 4 Abishua, N, Ahoah,
8: 7 N, Ahijah, and Gera, that is, Heglam, who became
Lk 4:27 none of them was cleansed except N the Syrian."

NAAMAN'S (1) [NAAMAN]
2Ki 5: 2 from the land of Israel, and she served N wife.

NAAMATHITE (4)
Job 2:11 Bildad the Shuhite, and Zophar the N.
11: 1 Then Zophar the N answered:
20: 1 Then Zophar the N answered:
42: 9 the Shuhite and Zophar the N went and did what

NAAMITES (1)
Nu 26:40 of Naaman, the clan of the N.

NAARAH (4)
Jos 16: 7 it goes down from Janoah to Ataroth and to N,
1Ch 4: 5 of Tekoa had two wives, Helah and N;
4: 6 N bore him Ahuzzam, Hepher, Temeni,
4: 6 These were the sons of N.

NAARAI (1)
1Ch 11:37 Hezro of Carmel, N son of Ezbai,

NAARAN (1)
1Ch 7:28 and eastward N, and westward Gezer

NAARATH (KJV) See NAARAH

NAASHON, NAASSON (KJV) See NAHSHON

NAATHUS (1)
1Es 9:31 Of the descendants of Addi: N and Moossias,

NABAL (18) [NABAL'S]
1Sa 25: 3 Now the name of the man was N,
25: 4 in the wilderness that N was shearing his sheep.
25: 5 and go to N, and greet him in my name.
25: 9 they said all this to N in the name of David;
25:10 N answered David's servants, "Who is David?
25:19 But she did not tell her husband N.
25:25 do not take seriously this ill-natured fellow, N;
25:25 N is his name, and folly is with him;
25:26 to do evil to my lord be like N.
25:34 by morning there would not have been left to N
25:36 Abigail came to N; he was holding a feast in his
25:37 In the morning, when the wine had gone out of N,
1Sa 25:38 About ten days later the LORD struck N,
25:39 When David heard that N was dead, he said,
25:39 the LORD has returned the evildoing of N
30: 5 and Abigail the widow of N of Carmel.
2Sa 2: 2 and Abigail the widow of N of Carmel.
3: 3 Chileab, of Abigail the widow of N of Carmel;

NABAL'S (4) [NABAL]
1Sa 25:14 But one of the young men told Abigail, N wife,
25:36 N heart was merry within him,
25:39 be the LORD who has judged the case of N insult
27: 3 and Abigail of Carmel, N widow.

NABARIAH (1)
1Es 9:44 Malchijah, Lothasubus, N, and Zechariah.

NABATEANS (2)
1Mc 5:25 They encountered the N, who met them peaceably
9:35 as leader of the multitude and begged the N,

NABOTH (22)
1Ki 21: 1 N the Jezreelite had a vineyard in Jezreel,
21: 2 And Ahab said to N, "Give me your vineyard,
21: 3 But N said to Ahab, "The LORD forbid
21: 4 because of what N the Jezreelite had said to him;
21: 6 I spoke to N the Jezreelite and said to him,
21: 7 I will give you the vineyard of N the Jezreelite."
21: 8 to the elders and the nobles who lived with N
21: 9 and seat N at the head of the assembly;
21:12 they proclaimed a fast and seated N at the head of
21:13 and the scoundrels brought a charge against N,
21:13 saying, "N cursed God and the king."
21:14 they sent to Jezebel, saying, "N has been stoned;
21:15 that N had been stoned and was dead, Jezebel said
21:15 take possession of the vineyard of N the Jezreelite,
21:15 for N is not alive, but dead."
21:16 As soon as Ahab heard that N was dead,
21:16 to go down to the vineyard of N the Jezreelite,
21:18 he is now in the vineyard of N,
21:19 In the place where dogs licked up the blood of N,
2Ki 9:21 they met him at the property of N the Jezreelite.
9:25 the plot of ground belonging to N the Jezreelite;
9:26 the blood of N and for the blood of his children

NACHON'S (KJV) See NACON

NACHOR (KJV) See NAHOR

NACON (1)
2Sa 6: 6 When they came to the threshing floor of N,

NADAB (26)
Ex 6:23 and she bore him N, Abihu, Eleazar, and Ithamar.
24: 1 N, and Abihu, and seventy of the elders of Israel,
24: 9 Then Moses and Aaron, N, and Abihu,
28: 1 Aaron and Aaron's sons, N and Abihu,
Lev 10: 1 Now Aaron's sons, N and Abihu,
Nu 3: 2 N the firstborn, and Abihu, Eleazar, and Ithamar;
3: 4 N and Abihu died before the LORD
26:60 To Aaron were born N, Abihu, Eleazar,
26:61 But N and Abihu died
1Ki 14:20 and his son N succeeded him.
15:25 N son of Jeroboam began to reign over Israel in
15:27 N and all Israel were laying siege to Gibbethon.
15:28 So Baasha killed N in the third year of King Asa
15:31 Now the rest of the acts of N, and all that he did,
1Ch 2:28 The sons of Shammai: N and Abishur.
2:30 The sons of N: Seled and Appaim;
6: 3 sons of Aaron: N, Abihu, Eleazar, and Ithamar.
8:30 His firstborn son: Abdon, then Zur, Kish, Baal, N,
9:36 then Zur, Kish, Baal, Ner, N,
24: 1 sons of Aaron: N, Abihu, Eleazar, and Ithamar.
24: 2 But N and Abihu died before their father,
Tob 11:18 Ahikar and his nephew N were also present
14:10 what N did to Ahikar who had reared him.
14:10 but N went into the eternal darkness,
14:10 Ahikar escaped the fatal trap that N had set
14:10 but N fell into it himself, and was destroyed.

NADABATH (1)
1Mc 9:37 nobles of Canaan, from N with a large escort."

NAGGAI (1)
Lk 3:25 son of Nahum, son of Esli, son of N,

NAGGED (2)
Jdg 14:17 because she n him, on the seventh day he told her.
16:16 after she had n him with her words day after day,

NAHALAL (2)
Jos 19:15 N, Shimron, Idalah, and Bethlehem—
21:35 N with its pasture lands—four towns.

NAHALIEL (2)
Nu 21:19 from Mattanah to N, from from N to Bamoth,

NAHALOL (1)
Jdg 1:30 the inhabitants of Kitron, or the inhabitants of N;

NAHAM (1)
1Ch 4:19 The sons of the wife of Hodiah, the sister of N,

NAHAMANI (1)
Ne 7: 7 N, Mordecai, Bilshan, Mispereth, Bigvai, Nehum,

NAHARAI (2)
2Sa 23:37 N of Beeroth, the armor-bearer of Joab son
1Ch 11:39 the Ammonite, N of Beeroth, the armor-bearer

NAHASH‡ (11)
1Sa 10:27 Now N, king of the Ammonites,
10:27 the Israelites across the Jordan whose right eye N,
11: 1 N the Ammonite went up
11: 1 and all the men of Jabesh said to N,
11: 2 But N the Ammonite said to them,
12:12 that King N of the Ammonites came against you,
2Sa 10: 2 "I will deal loyally with Hanun son of N,
17:25 who had married Abigal daughter of N,
17:27 Shobi son of N from Rabbah of the Ammonites,
1Ch 19: 1 King N of the Ammonites died,
19: 2 "I will deal loyally with Hanun son of N,

NAHATH (5)
Ge 36:13 N, Zerah, Shammah, and Mizzah.
36:17 the clans N, Zerah, Shammah, and Mizzah;
1Ch 1:37 sons of Reuel: N, Zerah, Shammah, and Mizzah.
6:26 Elkanah his son, Zophai his son, N his son,
2Ch 31:13 N, Asahel, Jerimoth, Jozabad, Eliel, Ismachiah,

NAHBI (1)
Nu 13:14 from the tribe of Naphtali, N son of Vophsi;

NAHOR (17) [NAHOR'S]
Ge 11:22 he became the father of N;
11:23 Serug lived after the birth of N two hundred years,
11:24 When N had lived twenty-nine years,
11:25 and N lived after the birth
11:26 he became the father of Abram, N, and Haran.
11:27 Terah was the father of Abram, N, and Haran;
11:29 Abram and N took wives;
22:20 also has borne children, to your brother N:
22:23 These eight Milcah bore to N, Abraham's brother.
24:10 and went to Aram-naharaim, to the city of N.
24:15 the wife of N, Abraham's brother,
24:24 of Bethuel son of Milcah, whom she bore to N."
29: 5 He said to them, "Do you know Laban son of N?"
31:53 May the God of Abraham and the God of N"—
Jos 24: 2 Terah and his sons Abraham and N—
1Ch 1:26 Serug, N, Terah;
Lk 3:34 son of Abraham, son of Terah, son of N,

NAHOR'S (2) [NAHOR]
Ge 11:29 and the name of N wife was Milcah.
24:47 She said, 'The daughter of Bethuel, N son,

NAHSHON (13)
Ex 6:23 daughter of Amminadab and sister of N,
Nu 1: 7 From Judah, N son of Amminadab.
2: 3 the people of Judah shall be N son of Amminadab,
7:12 the first day was N son of Amminadab,
7:17 This was the offering of N son of Amminadab.
10:14 the whole company was N son of Amminadab.
Ru 4:20 Amminadab of N, N of Salmon,
1Ch 2:10 and Amminadab became the father of N,
2:11 N became the father of Salma, Salma of Boaz,
Mt 1: 4 Aminadab the father of N, and N the father of Salmon,
Lk 3:32 son of Obed, son of Boaz, son of Sala, son of N,

NAHUM (4)
Na 1: 1 The book of the vision of N of Elkosh.
Lk 3:25 son of Amos, son of N, son of Esli, son of Naggai,
Tob 14: 4 the word of God that N spoke about Nineveh,
2Es 1:40 and N and Habakkuk, Zephaniah,

NAIDUS (1)
1Es 9:31 Naathus and Moossias, Laccunus and N,

NAILING (1) [NAILS]
Col 2:14 He set this aside, n it to the cross.

NAILS (9) [NAILING]
Dt 21:12 she shall shave her head, pare her n,
1Ch 22: 3 David also provided great stores of iron for n for
2Ch 3: 9 The weight of the n was fifty shekels of gold.
Ecc 12:11 and like n firmly fixed are the collected sayings
Isa 41: 7 they fasten it with n so that it cannot be moved.
Jer 10: 4 with hammer and n so that it cannot move.
Da 4:33 as long as eagles' feathers and his n became
Jn 20:25 "Unless I see the mark of the n in his hands,
20:25 in the mark of the n and my hand in his side,

NAIN (1)
Lk 7:11 Soon afterwards he went to a town called N,

NAIOTH (6)
1Sa 19:18 He and Samuel went and settled at N.
19:19 Saul was told, "David is at N in Ramah."
19:22 And someone said, "They are at N in Ramah."

1Sa 19:23 He went there, toward **N** in Ramah;
19:23 until he came to **N** in Ramah.
20: 1 David fled from **N** in Ramah.

NAKED (45) [NAKEDNESS]

Ge 2:25 And the man and his wife were both **n**,
3: 7 and they knew that they were **n;**
3:10 because I was **n;** and I hid myself."
3:11 He said, "Who told you that you were **n?**
Ex 28:42 linen undergarments to cover their **n** flesh;
1Sa 19:24 He lay **n** all that day and all that night.
2Ch 28:15 and with the booty they clothed all that were **n**
Job 1:21 He said, "**N** I came from my mother's womb,
1:21 and **n** shall I return there;
22: 6 and stripped the **n** of their clothing.
24: 7 They lie all night **n**, without clothing,
24:10 They go about **n**, without clothing;
26: 6 Sheol is **n** before God,
Ecc 5:15 so they shall go again, **n** as they came;
Isa 20: 2 and he had done so, walking **n** and barefoot.
20: 3 as my servant Isaiah has walked **n** and barefoot
20: 4 both the young and the old, **n** and barefoot,
58: 7 when you see the **n**, to cover them,
Eze 16: 7 yet you were **n** and bare.
16:22 when you were **n** and bare,
16:39 and take your beautiful objects and leave you **n**
18: 7 to the hungry and covers the **n** with a garment,
18:16 but gives his bread to the hungry and covers the **n**
23:29 and leave you **n** and bare,
Hos 2: 3 or I will strip her **n** and expose her as in
Am 2:16 among the mighty shall flee away **n** in that day,
Mic 1: 8 I will go barefoot and **n;**
Hab 3: 9 You brandished your **n** bow,
Mt 25:36 I was **n** and you gave me clothing,
25:38 or **n** and gave you clothing?
25:43 **n** and you did not give me clothing,
25:44 or thirsty or a stranger or **n** or sick or in prison,
Mk 14:52 but he left the linen cloth and ran off **n**.
Jn 21: 7 for he was **n**, and jumped into the sea.
Ac 19:16 that they fled out of the house **n** and wounded.
2Co 5: 3 when we have taken it off we will not be found **n**.
11:27 hungry and thirsty, often without food, cold and **n**.
Heb 4:13 but all are **n** and laid bare to the eyes of the one
Jas 2:15 If a brother or sister is **n** and lacks daily food,
Rev 3:17 pitiable, poor, blind, and **n**.
16:15 not going about **n** and exposed to shame.")
17:16 they will make her desolate and **n;**
Tob 1:17 to the hungry and my clothing to the **n;**
4:16 and some of your clothing to the **n**.
2Es 2:20 give to the needy, defend the orphan, clothe the **n**,

NAKEDNESS (55) [NAKED]

Ge 9:22 Ham, the father of Canaan, saw the **n** of his father,
9:23 and walked backward and covered the **n**
9:23 and they did not see their father's **n**.
42: 9 you have come to see the **n** of the land!"
42:12 "No, you have come to see the **n** of the land!"
Ex 20:26 so that your **n** may not be exposed on it."
Lev 18: 6 near of kin to uncover **n:**
18: 7 You shall not uncover the **n** of your father, which is the **n** of your mother; she is your mother, you shall not uncover her **n**.
18: 8 You shall not uncover the **n** of your father's wife; it is the **n** of your father.
18: 9 You shall not uncover the **n** of your sister,
18:10 not uncover the **n** of your son's daughter or
18:10 for their **n** is your own **n**.
18:11 not uncover the **n** of your father's wife's daughter,
18:12 You shall not uncover the **n** of your father's sister;
18:13 not uncover the **n** of your mother's sister,
18:14 the **n** of your father's brother, that is, you shall
18:15 not uncover the **n** of your daughter-in-law: she is your son's wife; you shall not uncover her **n**.
18:16 not uncover the **n** of your brother's wife; it is your brother's **n**.
18:17 not uncover the **n** of a woman and her daughter,
18:17 or her daughter's daughter to uncover her **n**,
18:18 uncovering her **n** while her sister is still alive.
18:19 You shall not approach a woman to uncover her **n**
20:11 with his father's wife has uncovered his father's **n;**
20:17 and sees her **n**, and she sees his **n**,
20:17 he has uncovered his sister's **n**,
20:18 a woman having her sickness and uncovers her **n**,
20:19 not uncover the **n** of your mother's sister or
20:20 he has uncovered his uncle's **n;**
20:21 he has uncovered his brother's **n;**
Dt 28:48 in hunger and thirst, in **n** and lack of everything.
1Sa 20:30 and to the shame of your mother's **n?**
Isa 47: 3 Your **n** shall be uncovered,
57: 8 you have gazed on their **n**.
La 1: 8 for they have seen her **n;**
Eze 16: 8 of my cloak over you, and covered your **n:**
16:36 and your **n** uncovered in your whoring
16:37 your **n** to them, so that they may see all your **n**.
22:10 In you they uncover their fathers' **n;**
23:10 These uncovered her **n;** they seized her sons
23:18 on her whorings so openly and flaunted her **n**,
23:29 and the **n** of your whorings shall be exposed.
Hos 2: 9 which were to cover her **n**.
Mic 1:11 inhabitants of Shaphir, in **n** and shame;
Na 3: 5 and I will let nations look on your **n** and kingdoms
Hab 2:15 in order to gaze on their **n!"**
Ro 8:35 or persecution, or famine, or **n**, or peril, or sword?
Rev 3:18 and to keep the shame of your **n** from being seen;

NAME[‡] (939) [NAME'S, NAMED, NAMELY, NAMES, RENAMED, SURNAME, SURNAMED]

A. NAME OF THE †LORD (83)
B. HOLY NAME (30)
C. MOTHER'S NAME (30)
D. NAME OF THE *LORD (26)
E. NAME [BE] FOREVER (16)
F. NAME OF JESUS (11)
G. GLORIOUS NAME (8)

Ge 2:11 The **n** of the first is Pishon;
2:13 The **n** of the second river is Gihon;
2:14 The **n** of the third river is Tigris,
2:19 the man called every living creature, that was its **n**.
4:19 the **n** of the one was Adah, and the **n** of the other Zillah.
4:21 His brother's **n** was Jubal;
4:26 people began to invoke the **n** of the LORD. A
10:25 the **n** of the one was Peleg,
10:25 and his brother's **n** was Joktan.
11: 4 and let us make a **n** for ourselves;
11:29 the **n** of Abram's wife was Sarai,
11:29 and the **n** of Nahor's wife was Milcah.
12: 2 and I will bless you, and make your **n** great,
12: 8 to the LORD and invoked the **n** of the LORD. A
13: 4 and there Abram called on the **n** of the LORD. A
16: 1 an Egyptian slave-girl whose **n** was Hagar,
17: 5 No longer shall your **n** be Abram, but your **n** shall be Abraham;
17:15 shall not call her Sarai, but Sarah shall be her **n**.
17:19 and you shall **n** him Isaac.
21: 3 the **n** Isaac to his son whom Sarah bore him.
21:33 and called there on the **n** of the LORD, A
22:24 Moreover, his concubine, whose **n** was Reumah,
24:29 Rebekah had a brother whose **n** was Laban;
25: 1 Abraham took another wife, whose **n** was Keturah.
26:25 called on the **n** of the LORD, A
26:33 the **n** of the city is Beer-sheba to this day.
28:19 but the **n** of the city was Luz at the first.
29:16 the **n** of the elder was Leah, and the **n** of the younger was Rachel.
30:28 **n** your wages, and I will give it."
32:27 So he said to him, "What is your **n?"**
32:29 Then Jacob asked him, "Please tell me your **n**."
32:29 But he said, "Why is it that you ask my **n?"**
35:10 God said to him, "Your **n** is Jacob;
35:10 but Israel shall be your **n**."
36:32 the **n** of his city being Dinhabah.
36:35 the **n** of his city being Avith.
36:39 the **n** of his city being Pau;
36:39 his wife's **n** was Mehetabel,
38: 1 near a certain Adullamite whose **n** was Hirah.
38: 2 of a certain Canaanite whose **n** was Shua;
38: 6 for Er his firstborn; her **n** was Tamar.
41:45 Pharaoh gave Joseph the **n** Zaphenath-paneah;
48:16 and in them let my **n** be perpetuated,
48:16 and the **n** of my ancestors Abraham and Isaac;
49:24 by the **n** of the Shepherd, the Rock of Israel,
Ex 3:13 and they ask me, 'What is his **n?'**
3:15 This is my **n** forever, and this my title E
5:23 Since I first came to Pharaoh to speak in your **n**,
6: 3 but by my **n** 'The LORD' I did
9:16 and to make my **n** resound through all the earth.
15: 3 The LORD is a warrior; the LORD is his **n**.
18: 3 The **n** of the one was Gershom (for he said,
18: 4 and the **n** of the other,
20: 7 not make wrongful use of the **n** of the LORD A
20: 7 LORD will not acquit anyone who misuses his **n**.
20:24 where I cause my **n** to be remembered I will come
23:21 for my **n** is in him.
28:21 each engraved with its **n**, for the twelve tribes.
31: 2 I have called by **n** Bezalel son of Uri son of Hur,
33:12 Yet you have said, 'I know you by **n**,
33:17 in my sight, and I know you by **n**."
33:19 and will proclaim before you the **n**, 'The LORD';
34: 5 and proclaimed the **n**, "The LORD."
34:14 because the LORD, whose **n** is Jealous,
35:30 the LORD has called by **n** Bezalel son of Uri son
39:14 they were like signets, each engraved with its **n**,
Lev 18:21 and so profane the **n** of your God:
19:12 And you shall not swear falsely by my **n**,
19:12 profaning the **n** of your God: I am the LORD.
20: 3 defiling my sanctuary and profaning my holy **n**. B
21: 6 and not profane the **n** of their God;
22: 2 so that they may not profane my holy **n;** B
22:32 You shall not profane my holy **n**, B
24:11 The Israelite woman's son blasphemed the **N** in
24:11 now his mother's **n** was Shelomith, C
24:16 One who blasphemes the **n** of the LORD shall A
24:16 when they blaspheme the **N**, shall be put to death.
Nu 1:17 took these men who had been designated by **n**,
4:32 by **n** the objects that they are required to carry.
6:27 So they shall put my **n** on the Israelites,
13:16 And Moses changed the **n** of Hoshea son of Nun
17: 2 Write each man's **n** on his staff,
17: 3 and write Aaron's **n** on the staff of Levi.
25:14 The **n** of the slain Israelite man,
25:15 The **n** of the Midianite woman who was killed
26:46 And the **n** of the daughter of Asher was Serah.
26:59 The **n** of Amram's wife was Jochebed daughter
27: 4 the **n** of our father be taken away from his clan
Dt 5:11 not make wrongful use of the **n** of the LORD A
5:11 LORD will not acquit anyone who misuses his **n**.
6:13 and by his **n** alone you shall swear.
7:24 and you shall blot out their **n** from under heaven;
9:14 that I may destroy them and blot out their **n** from
10: 8 and to bless in his **n**, to this day.
10:20 and by his **n** you shall swear.
12: 3 and thus blot out their **n** from their places.
12: 5 as his habitation to put his **n** there.
12:11 as a dwelling for his **n:**
12:21 to put his **n** is too far from you,
14:23 that he will choose as a dwelling for his **n**,
14:24 to set his **n** is too far away from you,
16: 2 the LORD will choose as a dwelling for his **n**.
16: 6 as a dwelling for his **n**,
16:11 as a dwelling for his **n**.
18: 5 to stand and minister in the **n** of the LORD, A
18: 7 he may minister in the **n** of the LORD his God, A
18:19 the words that the prophet shall speak in my **n**,
18:20 any prophet who speaks in the **n** of other gods,
18:20 in my **n** a word that I have not commanded
18:22 If a prophet speaks in the **n** of the LORD but A
21: 5 and to pronounce blessings in the **n** of the LORD, A
25: 6 to the **n** of the deceased brother,
25: 6 so that his **n** may not be blotted out of Israel.
25: 7 to perpetuate his brother's **n** in Israel;
26: 2 as a dwelling for his **n**.
28:10 see that you are called by the **n** of the LORD, A
28:58 fearing this glorious and awesome **n**,
32: 3 For I will proclaim the **n** of the LORD; A
Jos 2: 1 the house of a prostitute whose **n** was Rahab,
7: 9 and surround us, and cut off our **n** from the earth.
7: 9 Then what will you do for your great **n?"**
9: 9 because of the **n** of the LORD your God; A
14:15 Now the **n** of Hebron formerly was Kiriath-arba;
15:15 now the **n** of Debir formerly was Kiriath-sepher.
21: 9 the following towns mentioned by **n**,
Jdg 1:10 against the Canaanites who lived in Hebron (the **n**
1:11 (the **n** of Debir was formerly Kiriath-sepher).
1:23 The house of Joseph sent out spies to Bethel (the **n**
1:26 that is its **n** to this day.
13: 2 of the tribe of the Danites, whose **n** was Manoah.
13: 6 and he did not tell me his **n;**
13:17 to the angel of the LORD, "What is your **n**, so
13:18 "Why do you ask my **n?**
16: 4 in the valley of Sorek, whose **n** was Delilah.
17: 1 the hill country of Ephraim whose **n** was Micah.
18:29 but the **n** of the city was formerly Laish.
Ru 1: 2 The **n** of the man was Elimelech and the **n** of his
1: 4 **n** of the one was Orpah and the **n** of the other Ruth.
2: 1 of the family of Elimelech, whose **n** was Boaz.
2:19 **n** of the man with whom I worked today is Boaz."
4: 5 to maintain the dead man's **n** on his inheritance."
4:10 to maintain the dead man's **n** on his inheritance,
4:10 in order that the **n** of the dead may not be cut off
4:11 in Ephrathah and bestow a **n** in Bethlehem;
4:14 and may his **n** be renowned in Israel!
4:17 The women of the neighborhood gave him a **n**,
1Sa 1: 1 whose **n** was Elkanah son of Jeroham son
1: 2 He had two wives; the **n** of the one was Hannah, and the **n** of the other Peninnah.
8: 2 The **n** of his firstborn son was Joel, and the **n** of his second, Abijah;
9: 1 of Benjamin whose **n** was Kish son of Abiel son
9: 2 He had a son whose **n** was Saul,
14: 4 the **n** of the one was Bozez, and the **n** of the other Seneh.
14:49 the **n** of the firstborn was Merab, and the **n** of the younger, Michal.
14:50 The **n** of Saul's wife was Ahinoam daughter
14:50 And the **n** of the commander of his army
16: 3 you shall anoint for me the one whom I **n** to you."
17:23 the champion, the Philistine of Gath, Goliath by **n**,
17:45 but I come to you in the **n** of the LORD of hosts, A
20:42 both of us have sworn in the **n** of the LORD, A
21: 7 his **n** was Doeg the Edomite,
24:21 not wipe out my **n** from my father's house."
25: 3 Now the **n** of the man was Nabal, and the **n** of his wife Abigail.
25: 5 and go to Nabal, and greet him in my **n**.
25: 9 they said all this to Nabal in the **n** of David;
25:25 for as his **n** is, so is he; Nabal is his **n**, and folly
28: 8 and bring up for me the one whom I **n** to you."
2Sa 3: 7 a concubine whose **n** was Rizpah daughter
4: 2 the **n** of the one was Baanah, and the **n** of the other Rechab.
4: 4 His **n** was Mephibosheth.
6: 2 the **n** of the LORD of hosts who is enthroned on A
6:18 he blessed the people in the **n** of the LORD A
7: 9 and I will make for you a great **n**, like the **n** of the great ones of the earth.
7:13 He shall build a house for my **n**,
7:23 and to make a **n** for himself,
7:26 Thus your **n** will be magnified forever in
8:13 David won a **n** for himself.
9: 2 a servant of the house of Saul whose **n** was Ziba,
9:12 a young son whose **n** was Mica.
12:28 and it will be called by my **n**."
13: 1 a beautiful sister whose **n** was Tamar;
13: 3 But Amnon had a friend whose **n** was Jonadab,
14: 7 and leave to my husband neither **n** nor remnant on
14:27 and one daughter whose **n** was Tamar;
16: 5 of Saul came out whose **n** was Shimei son
18:18 "I have no son to keep my **n** in remembrance";
18:18 he called the pillar by his own **n**.
22:50 among the nations, and sing praises to your **n**.
23:18 and won a **n** beside the Three.
23:22 and won a **n** beside the three warriors.
1Ki 1:47 the **n** of Solomon more famous than yours,
3: 2 house had yet been built for the **n** of the LORD. A

1Ki 5: 3 not build a house for the **n** of the LORD his God A
5: 5 to build a house for the **n** of the LORD my God, A
5: 5 shall build the house for my **n.'**
8:16 that my **n** might be there;
8:17 in mind to build a house for the **n** of the LORD, A
8:18 to consider building a house for my **n;**
8:19 be born to you shall build the house for my **n.'**
8:20 and have built the house for the **n** of the LORD, A
8:29 the place of which you said, 'My **n** shall be there,'
8:33 to you, confess your **n,** pray and plead with you
8:35 confess your **n,** and turn from their sin,
8:41 comes from a distant land because of your **n**
8:42 —for they shall hear of your great **n,**
8:43 that all the peoples of the earth may know your **n**
8:43 that they may know that your **n** has been invoked
8:44 and the house that I have built for your **n,**
8:48 and the house that I have built for your **n;**
9: 3 and put my **n** there forever;
9: 7 that I have consecrated for my **n** I will cast out
10: 1 (fame due to the **n** of the LORD), A
11:26 whose mother's **n** was Zeruah, a widow, C
11:36 the city where I have chosen to put my **n.**
13: 2 be born to the house of David, Josiah by **n;**
14:21 of all the tribes of Israel, to put his **n** there.
14:21 His mother's **n** was Naamah the Ammonite. C
14:31 His mother's **n** was Naamah the Ammonite. C
15: 2 His mother's **n** was Maacah daughter C
15:10 His mother's **n** was Maacah daughter C
16:24 after the **n** of Shemer, the owner of the hill.
18:24 on the **n** of your god and I will call on the name
18:24 of your god and I will call on the **n** of the LORD; A
18:25 call on the **n** of your god, but put no fire to it."
18:26 called on the **n** of Baal from morning until noon,
18:31 saying, "Israel shall be your **n";**
18:32 the stones he built an altar in the **n** of the LORD. A
21: 8 So she wrote letters in Ahab's **n** and sealed them
22:16 nothing but the truth in the **n** of the LORD?" A
22:42 His mother's **n** was Azubah daughter of Shilhi. C
2Ki 2:24 he cursed them in the **n** of the LORD. A
5:11 and stand and call on the **n** of the LORD his God, A
8:26 His mother's **n** was Athaliah, C
12: 1 His mother's **n** was Zibiah of Beer-sheba. C
14: 2 His mother's **n** was Jehoaddin of Jerusalem. C
14: 7 he called it Jokthe-el, which is its **n** to this day.
14:27 not said that he would blot out the **n** of Israel from
15: 2 His mother's **n** was Jecoliah of Jerusalem. C
15:33 His mother's **n** was Jerusha daughter of Zadok. C
18: 2 His mother's **n** was Abi daughter of Zechariah. C
21: 1 His mother's **n** was Hephzibah. C
21: 4 "In Jerusalem I will put my **n."**
21: 7 I will put my **n** forever; E
21:19 His mother's **n** was Meshullemeth daughter C
22: 1 His mother's **n** was Jedidah daughter of Adaiah C
23:27 the house of which I said, My **n** shall be there."
23:31 His mother's **n** was Hamutal daughter of C
23:34 and changed his **n** to Jehoiakim.
23:36 His mother's **n** was Zebidah daughter of Pedaiah C
24: 8 His mother's **n** was Nehushta daughter C
24:17 king in his place, and changed his **n** to Zedekiah.
24:18 His mother's **n** was Hamutal daughter of C
1Ch 1:19 the **n** of the one was Peleg (for in his days
1:19 and the **n** of his brother Joktan.
1:46 and the **n** of his city was Avith.
1:50 the **n** of his city was Pai,
1:50 and his wife's **n** Mehetabel daughter of Matred,
2:26 also had another wife, whose **n** was Atarah;
2:29 The **n** of Abishur's wife was Abihail,
2:34 an Egyptian slave, whose **n** was Jarha.
4: 3 and the **n** of their sister was Hazzelelponi,
4:38 by **n** were leaders in their families,
4:41 by **n,** came in the days of King Hezekiah of Judah,
6:65 Benjamin these towns that are mentioned by **n.**
7:15 The **n** of his sister was Maacah.
7:15 And the **n** of the second was Zelophehad;
7:16 the **n** of his brother was Sheresh;
8:29 and the **n** of his wife was Maacah.
9:35 Jeiel, and the **n** of his wife was Maacah.
11:20 and won a **n** beside the Three.
11:24 and he won a **n** beside the three warriors.
13: 6 which is called by his **n.**
16: 2 he blessed the people in the **n** of the LORD; A
16: 8 O give thanks to the LORD, call on his **n,**
16:10 Glory in his holy **n;** let the hearts of those B
16:29 Ascribe to the LORD the glory due his **n;**
16:35 that we may give thanks to your holy **n,** B
17: 8 and I will make for you a **n,**
17: 8 like the **n** of the great ones of the earth.
17:21 for yourself a **n** for great and terrible things,
17:24 Thus your **n** will be established
21:19 which he had spoken in the **n** of the LORD. A
22: 7 to build a house to the **n** of the LORD my God. A
22: 8 you shall not build a house to my **n,**
22: 9 for his **n** shall be Solomon,
22:10 He shall build a house for my **n.**
22:19 brought into a house built for the **n** of the LORD." A
23:13 to him and pronounce blessings in his **n** forever; E
28: 3 'You shall not build a house for my **n,**
29:13 give thanks to you and praise your glorious **n.** G
29:16 for building you a house for your holy **n** comes B
2Ch 2: 1 decided to build a temple for the **n** of the LORD, A
2: 4 build a house for the **n** of the LORD my God A
6: 5 so that my **n** might be there,
6: 6 in order that my **n** may be there,
6: 7 in mind to build a house for the **n** of the LORD, A
6: 8 to consider building a house for my **n;**
6: 9 be born to you shall build the house for my **n.'**
6:10 and have built the house for the **n** of the LORD, A

2Ch 6:20 the place where you promised to set your **n,**
6:24 to you, confess your **n,** pray and plead with you
6:26 confess your **n,** and turn from their sin,
6:32 come from a distant land because of your great **n,**
6:33 that all the peoples of the earth may know your **n**
6:33 that they may know that your **n** has been invoked
6:34 and the house that I have built for your **n,**
6:38 and the house that I have built for your **n,**
7:14 by my **n** humble themselves,
7:16 and consecrated this house so that my **n** may
7:20 this house, which I have consecrated for my **n,**
12:13 of all the tribes of Israel to put his **n** there.
12:13 His mother's **n** was Naamah the Ammonite. C
13: 2 His mother's **n** was Micaiah daughter of Uriel C
14:11 in your **n** we have come against this multitude.
18:15 nothing but the truth in the **n** of the LORD?" A
20: 8 and in it have built you a sanctuary for your **n,**
20: 9 and before you, for your **n** is in this house,
20:31 His mother's **n** was Azubah daughter of Shilhi. C
22: 2 His mother's **n** was Athaliah, C
24: 1 his mother's **n** was Zibiah of Beer-sheba. C
25: 1 His mother's **n** was Jehoaddan of Jerusalem. C
26: 3 His mother's **n** was Jecoliah of Jerusalem. C
27: 1 His mother's **n** was Jerushah daughter of Zadok. C
28: 9 of the LORD was there, whose **n** was Oded;
28:15 Then those who were mentioned by **n** got up
29: 1 His mother's **n** was Abijah daughter of C
31:19 by **n** were to distribute portions to every male
33: 4 "In Jerusalem shall my **n** be forever." E
33: 7 I will put my **n** forever; E
33:18 the seers who spoke to him in the **n** of the LORD A
36: 4 and changed his **n** to Jehoiakim;
Ezr 2:61 and was called by their **n).**
5: 1 in the **n** of the God of Israel who was over them.
6:12 God who has established his **n** there
8:20 These were all mentioned by **n.**
10:16 each of them designated by **n.**
Ne 1: 9 at which I have chosen to establish my **n.'**
1:11 of your servants who delight in revering your **n.**
6:13 and so they could give me a bad **n,**
7:63 the Gileadite and was called by their **n).**
9: 5 Blessed be your glorious **n,** G
9: 7 of the Chaldeans and gave him the **n** Abraham;
9:10 You made a **n** for yourself,
13:25 and I made them take an oath in the **n** of God,
Est 2: 5 in the citadel of Susa whose **n** was Mordecai son
2:14 king delighted in her and she was summoned by **n.**
2:22 and Esther told the king in the **n** of Mordecai.
3:12 in the **n** of King Ahasuerus and sealed with
8: 8 the **n** of the king, and seal it with the king's ring;
8: 8 for an edict written in the **n** of the king and sealed
8:10 He wrote letters in the **n** of King Ahasuerus,
Job 1: 1 a man in the land of Uz whose **n** was Job.
1:21 blessed be the **n** of the LORD." A
18:17 and they have no **n** in the street.
Ps 5:11 so that those who love your **n** may exult in you.
7:17 and sing praise to the **n** of the LORD, A
8: 1 how majestic is your **n** in all the earth!
8: 9 how majestic is your **n** in all the earth!
9: 2 I will sing praise to your **n,** O Most High.
9: 5 you have blotted out their **n** forever and ever. E
9:10 And those who know your **n** put their trust in you,
18:49 among the nations, and sing praises to your **n.**
20: 1 The **n** of the God of Jacob protect you!
20: 5 and in the **n** of our God set up our banners.
20: 7 but our pride is in the **n** of the LORD our God. A
22:22 I will tell of your **n** to my brothers and sisters;
29: 2 Ascribe to the LORD the glory of his **n;**
30: 4 and give thanks to his holy **n.** B
33:21 because we trust in his holy **n.** B
34: 3 and let us exalt his **n** together.
41: 5 in malice when I will die, and my **n** perish.
44: 5 through your **n** we tread down our assailants.
44: 8 and we will give thanks to your **n** forever. E
44:20 If we had forgotten the **n** of our God,
45:17 I will cause your **n** to be celebrated
48:10 Your **n,** O God, like your praise,
52: 9 the presence of the faithful I will proclaim your **n,**
54: 1 by your **n,** and vindicate me by your might.
54: 6 I will give thanks to your **n,** O LORD,
61: 5 the heritage of those who fear your **n.**
61: 8 So I will always sing praises to your **n,**
63: 4 I will lift up my hands and call on your **n.**
66: 2 sing the glory of his **n;**
66: 4 they sing praises to you, sing praises to your **n."**
68: 4 Sing to God, sing praises to his **n;**
68: 4 his **n** is the LORD—be exultant before him.
69:30 I will praise the **n** of God with a song;
69:36 and those who love his **n** shall live in it.
72:17 May his **n** endure forever,
72:19 Blessed be his glorious **n** forever; EG
74: 7 they desecrated the dwelling place of your **n,**
74:10 Is the enemy to revile your **n** forever? E
74:18 and an impious people reviles your **n.**
74:21 let the poor and needy praise your **n.**
75: 1 we give thanks; your **n** is near.
76: 1 In Judah God is known, his **n** is great in Israel.
79: 6 and on the kingdoms that do not call on your **n.**
79: 9 O God of our salvation, for the glory of your **n;**
80:18 give us life, and we will call on your **n.**
83: 4 let the **n** of Israel be remembered no more."
83:16 so that they may seek your **n,** O LORD.
83:18 whose **n** is the LORD, are the Most High over all
86: 9 O Lord, and shall glorify your **n.**
86:11 give me an undivided heart to revere your **n.**
86:12 and I will glorify your **n** forever. E
89:12 Tabor and Hermon joyously praise your **n.**

Ps 89:16 they exult in your **n** all day long,
89:24 and in my **n** his horn shall be exalted.
91:14 I will protect those who know my **n.**
92: 1 to sing praises to your **n,** O Most High;
96: 2 Sing to the LORD, bless his **n;**
96: 8 Ascribe to the LORD the glory due his **n;**
97:12 O you righteous, and give thanks to his holy **n!** B
99: 3 Let them praise your great and awesome **n.**
99: 6 Samuel also was among those who called on his **n.**
100: 4 Give thanks to him, bless his **n.**
102: 8 those who deride me use my **n** for a curse.
102:12 your **n** endures to all generations.
102:15 The nations will fear the **n** of the LORD, A
102:21 that the **n** of the LORD may be declared in Zion, A
103: 1 and all that is within me, bless his holy **n.** B
105: 1 O give thanks to the LORD, call on his **n,**
105: 3 Glory in his holy **n;** let the hearts of those B
106:47 that we may give thanks to your holy **n** and B
109:13 may his **n** be blotted out in the second generation.
111: 9 Holy and awesome is his **n.**
113: 1 praise the **n** of the LORD. A
113: 2 Blessed be the **n** of the LORD from this time on A
113: 3 to its setting the **n** of the LORD is to be praised. A
115: 1 O LORD, not to us, but to your **n** give glory,
116: 4 Then I called on the **n** of the LORD: A
116:13 cup of salvation and call on the **n** of the LORD, A
116:17 sacrifice and call on the **n** of the LORD. A
118:10 in the **n** of the LORD I cut them off! A
118:11 in the **n** of the LORD I cut them off! A
118:12 in the **n** of the LORD I cut them off! A
118:26 the one who comes in the **n** of the LORD. A
119:55 I remember your **n** in the night, O LORD,
119:132 as is your custom toward those who love your **n.**
122: 4 to give thanks to the **n** of the LORD. A
124: 8 Our help is in the **n** of the LORD, A
129: 8 We bless you in the **n** of the LORD!" A
135: 1 Praise the **n** of the LORD; A
135: 3 sing to his **n,** for he is gracious.
135:13 Your **n,** O LORD, endures forever, your renown,
138: 2 toward your holy temple and give thanks to your **n**
138: 2 for you have exalted your **n** and your word
140:13 Surely the righteous shall give thanks to your **n;**
142: 7 so that I may give thanks to your **n.**
145: 1 and bless your **n** forever and ever. E
145: 2 and praise your **n** forever and ever. E
145:21 and all flesh will bless his holy **n** forever BE
148: 5 Let them praise the **n** of the LORD, A
148:13 Let them praise the **n** of the LORD, A
148:13 for his **n** alone is exalted;
149: 3 Let them praise his **n** with dancing,
Pr 10: 7 but the **n** of the wicked will rot.
18:10 The **n** of the LORD is a strong tower; A
22: 1 A good **n** is to be chosen rather than great riches,
30: 4 What is the person's **n?** And what is the **n** of the person's child?
30: 9 and steal, and profane the **n** of my God.
Ecc 6: 4 and in darkness its **n** is covered;
7: 1 A good **n** is better than precious ointment,
SS 1: 3 your **n** is perfume poured out;
Isa 4: 1 just let us be called by your **n;**
7:14 and shall **n** him Immanuel.
8: 3 LORD said to me, **N** him Maher-shalal-hash-baz;
12: 4 Give thanks to the LORD, call on his **n;**
12: 4 proclaim that his **n** is exalted.
14:22 and will cut off from Babylon **n** and remnant,
18: 7 the place of the **n** of the LORD of hosts. A
24:15 coastlands of the sea glorify the **n** of the LORD, A
25: 1 I will exalt you, I will praise your **n;**
26: 8 your **n** and your renown are the soul's desire.
26:13 but we acknowledge your **n** alone.
29:23 in his midst, they will sanctify my **n;**
30:27 See, the **n** of the LORD comes from far away, A
34:12 They shall **n** it No Kingdom There,
40:26 and numbers them, calling them all by **n;**
41:25 from the rising of the sun he was summoned by **n.**
42: 8 I am the LORD, that is my **n;**
43: 1 I have called you by **n,** you are mine.
43: 7 everyone who is called by my **n,**
44: 5 another will be called by the **n** of Jacob,
44: 5 "The LORD's," and adopt the **n** of Israel.
45: 3 the God of Israel, who call you by your **n.**
45: 4 I call you by your **n,** I surname you, though you
47: 4 Our Redeemer—the LORD of hosts is his **n—**
48: 1 who are called by the **n** of Israel,
48: 1 who swear by the **n** of the LORD, A
48: 2 the LORD of hosts is his **n.**
48:11 I do it, for why should my **n** be profaned?
48:19 their **n** would never be cut off or destroyed from
50:10 in the **n** of the LORD and relies upon his God? A
51:15 the LORD of hosts is his **n.**
52: 5 and continually, all day long, my **n** is despised.
52: 6 Therefore my people shall know my **n;**
54: 5 the LORD of hosts is his **n;**
56: 5 monument and a **n** better than sons and daughters;
56: 5 I will give them an everlasting **n** that shall not
56: 6 to love the **n** of the LORD, and to be his servants, A
57:15 lofty one who inhabits eternity, whose **n** is Holy:
59:19 So those in the west shall fear the **n** of the LORD, A
60: 9 for the **n** of the LORD your God, A
62: 2 by a new **n** that the mouth of the LORD will give.
63:12 before them to make for himself an everlasting **n,**
63:14 to make for yourself a glorious **n.** G
63:16 our Redeemer from of old is your **n.**
63:19 like those not called by your **n.**
64: 2 to make your **n** known to your adversaries,
64: 7 There is no one who calls on your **n,**
65: 1 here I am," to a nation that did not call on my **n.**

Isa 65:15 You shall leave your **n** to my chosen to use as
65:15 but to his servants he will give a different **n.**
66:22 so shall your descendants and your **n** remain.
Jer 7:10 which is called by my **n,** and say,
7:11 Has this house, which is called by my **n,**
7:12 where I made my **n** dwell at first,
7:14 I will do to the house that is called by my **n,**
7:30 in the house that is called by my **n,**
10: 6 you are great, and your **n** is great in might.
10:16 the LORD of hosts is his **n.**
10:25 and on the peoples that do not call on your **n;**
11:19 so that his **n** will no longer be remembered!"
11:21 "You shall not prophesy in the **n** of the LORD, A
12:16 to swear by my **n,** "As the LORD lives,"
13:11 in order that they might be for me a people, a **n,**
14: 9 and we are called by your **n;** do not forsake us!
14:14 The prophets are prophesying lies in my **n;**
14:15 the prophets who prophesy in my **n** though I did
15:16 I am called by your **n,** O LORD, God of hosts.
16:21 and they shall know that my **n** is the LORD."
20: 9 or speak any more in his **n,"**
23: 6 And this is the **n** by which he will be called:
23:25 the prophets have said who prophesy lies in my **n,**
23:27 to make my people forget my **n** by their dreams
23:27 just as their ancestors forgot my **n** for Baal.
25:29 to bring disaster on the city that is called by my **n,**
26: 9 Why have you prophesied in the **n** of the LORD, A
26:16 to us in the **n** of the LORD our God." A
26:20 another man prophesying in the **n** of the LORD, A
27:15 but they are prophesying falsely in my **n,**
29: 9 a lie that they are prophesying to you in my **n;**
29:21 who are prophesying a lie to you in my **n:**
29:23 in my **n** lying words that I did not command them;
29:25 In your own **n** you sent a letter to all
31:35 the LORD of hosts is his **n:**
32:18 and mighty God whose **n** is the LORD of hosts,
32:20 and have made yourself a **n** that continues
32:34 in the house that bears my **n,**
33: 2 to establish it—the LORD is his **n:**
33: 9 And this city shall be to me a **n** of joy,
33:16 And this is the **n** by which it will be called:
34:15 before me in the house that is called by my **n;**
34:16 but then you turned around and profaned my **n**
44:16 you have spoken to us in the **n** of the LORD, A
44:26 Lo, I swear by my great **n,** says the LORD,
44:26 that my **n** shall no longer be pronounced on
46:17 the **n** "Braggart who missed his chance."
46:18 says the King, whose **n** is the LORD of hosts,
48:15 says the King, whose **n** is the LORD of hosts.
48:17 all you his neighbors, and all who know his **n;**
50:34 the LORD of hosts is his **n.**
51:19 the LORD of hosts is his **n.**
51:57 says the King, whose **n** is the LORD of hosts.
52: 1 His mother's **n** was Hamutal daughter of C
La 3:55 I called on your **n,** O LORD,
Eze 20: 9 But I acted for the sake of my **n,**
20:14 But I acted for the sake of my **n,**
20:22 and acted for the sake of my **n,**
20:39 but my holy **n** you shall no more profane B
23: 4 Oholah was the **n** of the elder and Oholibah the **n**
of her sister.
24: 2 write down the **n** of this day, this very day.
36:20 wherever they came, they profaned my holy **n,** B
36:21 But I had concern for my holy **n,** B
36:22 but for the sake of my holy **n,** B
36:23 I will sanctify my great **n,**
39: 7 My holy **n** I will make known B
39: 7 I will not let my holy **n** be profaned any more; B
39:25 and I will be jealous for my holy **n.** B
43: 7 house of Israel shall no more defile my holy **n,** B
43: 8 they were defiling my holy **n** B
48:35 And the **n** of the city from that time on shall be,
Da 2:20 "Blessed be the **n** of God from age to age,
2:26 king said to Daniel, whose **n** was Belteshazzar,
4: 8 the **n** of my god, and who is endowed with a spirit
9: 6 who spoke in your **n** to our kings, our princes,
9:15 a mighty hand and made your **n** renowned even
9:18 at our desolation and the city that bears your **n.**
9:19 because your city and your people bear your **n!"**
Hos 1: 4 And the LORD said to him, "**N** him Jezreel;
1: 6 Then the LORD said to him, "**N** her Lo-ruhamah,
1: 9 Then the LORD said, "**N** him Lo-ammi,
2:17 and they shall be mentioned by **n** no more.
12: 5 The LORD the God of hosts, the LORD is his **n!**
Joel 2:26 and praise the **n** of the LORD your God, A
2:32 on the **n** of the LORD shall be saved; A
Am 2: 7 so that my holy **n** is profaned; B
4:13 the LORD, the God of hosts, is his **n!**
5: 8 on the surface of the earth, the LORD is his **n,**
5:27 says the LORD, whose **n** is the God of hosts.
6:10 We must not mention the **n** of the LORD." A
9: 6 of the earth—the LORD is his **n.**
9:12 and all the nations who are called by my **n,**
Mic 4: 5 For all the peoples walk, each in the **n** of its god,
4: 5 in the **n** of the LORD our God forever and ever. A
5: 4 in the majesty of the **n** of the LORD his God. A
6: 9 to the city (it is sound wisdom to fear your **n**):
Na 1:14 "Your **n** shall be perpetuated no longer;
Zep 1: 4 from this place every remnant of Baal and the **n** of
3: 9 that all of them may call on the **n** of the LORD A
3:12 They shall seek refuge in the **n** of the LORD— A
Zec 5: 4 the house of anyone who swears falsely by my **n;**
6:12 Here is a man whose **n** is Branch:
10:12 and they shall walk in his **n,** says the LORD.
13: 3 for you speak lies in the **n** of the LORD"; A
13: 9 They will call on my **n,** and I will answer them.
14: 9 on that day the LORD will be one and his **n** one.

Mal 1: 6 O priests, who despise my **n.**
1: 6 You say, "How have we despised your **n?"**
1:11 to its setting my **n** is great among the nations,
1:11 and in every place incense is offered to my **n,**
1:11 for my **n** is great among the nations,
1:14 and my **n** is reverenced among the nations.
2: 2 if you will not lay it to heart to give glory to my **n,**
2: 5 and he revered me and stood in awe of my **n.**
3:16 the LORD and thought on his **n.**
4: 2 But for you who revere my **n** the sun
Mt 1:21 She will bear a son, and you are to **n** him Jesus,
1:23 and they shall **n** him Emmanuel," which means,
6: 9 Our Father in heaven, hallowed be your **n.**
7:22 'Lord, Lord, did we not prophesy in your **n,**
7:22 and cast out demons in your **n,**
7:22 and do many deeds of power in your **n?'**
10:22 and you will be hated by all because of my **n.**
10:41 the **n** of a prophet will receive a prophet's reward;
10:41 and whoever welcomes a righteous person in the **n**
10:42 of cold water to one of these little ones in the **n** of
12:21 And in his **n** the Gentiles will hope."
18: 5 welcomes one such child in my **n** welcomes me.
18:20 For where two or three are gathered in my **n,**
21: 9 is the one who comes in the **n** of the Lord! D
23:39 the one who comes in the **n** of the Lord.' " D
24: 5 For many will come in my **n,** saying,
24: 9 you will be hated by all nations because of my **n.**
28:19 baptizing them in the **n** of the Father and of
Mk 3:16 Simon (to whom he gave the **n** Peter);
3:17 (to whom he gave the **n** Boanerges, that is, Sons
5: 9 Then Jesus asked him, "What is your **n?"**
5: 9 He replied, "My **n** is Legion; for we are many."
6:14 for Jesus' **n** had become known.
9:37 welcomes one such child in my **n** welcomes me,
9:38 we saw someone casting out demons in your **n,**
9:39 for no one who does a deed of power in my **n** will
9:41 the **n** of Christ will by no means lose the reward.
11: 9 is the one who comes in the **n** of the Lord! D
13: 6 Many will come in my **n** and say, 'I am he!'
13:13 and you will be hated by all because of my **n.**
16:17 ⟦by using my **n** they will cast out demons;⟧
Lk 1: 5 a descendant of Aaron, and her **n** was Elizabeth.
1:13 and you will **n** him John.
1:27 to a virgin engaged to a man whose **n** was Joseph,
1:27 The virgin's **n** was Mary.
1:31 and you will **n** him Jesus.
1:49 for me, and holy is his **n.**
1:59 and they were going to **n** him Zechariah
1:61 "None of your relatives has this **n."**
1:62 to find out what **n** he wanted to give him.
1:63 for a writing tablet and wrote, "His **n** is John."
2:21 the **n** given by the angel before he was conceived
2:25 a man in Jerusalem whose **n** was Simeon;
8:30 Jesus then asked him, "What is your **n?"**
9:48 welcomes this child in my **n** welcomes me,
9:49 we saw someone casting out demons in your **n,**
10:17 "Lord, in your **n** even the demons submit to us!"
11: 2 Father, hallowed be your **n.**
13:35 the one who comes in the **n** of the Lord.' " D
19:38 is the king who comes in the **n** of the Lord! D
21: 8 for many will come in my **n** and say, 'I am he!'
21:12 before kings and governors because of my **n.**
21:17 You will be hated by all because of my **n.**
24:18 Then one of them, whose **n** was Cleopas,
24:47 and forgiveness of sins is to be proclaimed in his **n**
Jn 1: 6 a man sent from God, whose **n** was John.
1:12 to all who received him, who believed in his **n,**
2:23 many believed in his **n** because they saw the signs
3:18 not believed in the **n** of the only Son of God.
5:43 I have come in my Father's **n,** and you do not
5:43 another comes in his own **n,** you will accept him.
10: 3 He calls his own sheep by **n** and leads them out.
10:25 The works that I do in my Father's **n** testify to me;
12:13 the one who comes in the **n** of the Lord— D
12:28 glorify your **n."** Then a voice came from heaven,
14:13 I will do whatever you ask in my **n,**
14:14 If in my **n** you ask me for anything, I will do it.
14:26 whom the Father will send in my **n,**
15:16 will give you whatever you ask him in my **n.**
15:21 to you on account of my **n,**
16:23 if you ask anything of the Father in my **n,**
16:24 now you have not asked for anything in my **n.**
16:26 On that day you will ask in my **n.**
17: 6 "I have made your **n** known
17:11 protect them in your **n** that you have given me,
17:12 I protected them in your **n** that you have given me.
17:26 I made your **n** known to them,
18:10 The slave's **n** was Malchus.
20:31 that through believing you may have life in his **n.**
Ac 2:21 Then everyone who calls on the **n** of the Lord D
2:38 in the **n** of Jesus Christ so that your sins may F
3: 6 in the **n** of Jesus Christ of Nazareth, F
3:16 And by faith in his **n,**
3:16 his **n** itself has made this man strong,
4: 7 "By what power or by what **n** did you do this?"
4:10 in good health by the **n** of Jesus Christ F
4:12 for there is no other **n** under heaven given
4:17 to speak no more to anyone in this **n."**
4:18 not to speak or teach at all in the **n** of Jesus. F
4:30 through the **n** of your holy servant Jesus."
4:36 the **n** Barnabas (which means "son
5:28 "We gave you strict orders not to teach in this **n,**
5:40 they ordered them not to speak in the **n** of Jesus, F
5:41 to suffer dishonor for the sake of the **n.**
8:12 the kingdom of God and the **n** of Jesus Christ, F
8:16 only been baptized in the **n** of the Lord Jesus). D
9:14 the chief priests to bind all who invoke your **n."**

Ac 9:15 an instrument whom I have chosen to bring my **n**
9:16 how much he must suffer for the sake of my **n."**
9:21 in Jerusalem among those who invoked this **n?**
9:27 he had spoken boldly in the **n** of Jesus. F
9:28 speaking boldly in the **n** of the Lord. D
9:36 a disciple whose **n** was Tabitha,
10:43 in him receives forgiveness of sins through his **n."**
10:48 ordered them to be baptized in the **n** of Jesus F
12:12 the mother of John whose other **n** was Mark,
12:25 with them John, whose other **n** was Mark.
13: 8 (for that is the translation of his **n**) opposed them
15:14 to take from among them a people for his **n.**
15:17 all the Gentiles over whom my **n** has been called.
16:18 "I order you in the **n** of Jesus Christ to come out F
19: 5 they were baptized in the **n** of the Lord Jesus. D
19:13 to use the **n** of the Lord Jesus D
19:17 and the **n** of the Lord Jesus was praised. D
21:13 to die in Jerusalem for the **n** of the Lord Jesus." D
22:16 and have your sins washed away, calling on his **n.'**
26: 9 ought to do many things against the **n** of Jesus F
Ro 1: 5 among all the Gentiles for the sake of his **n,**
2:24 "The **n** of God is blasphemed among the Gentiles
9:17 so that my **n** may be proclaimed in all the earth."
10:13 "Everyone who calls on the **n** of the Lord shall D
15: 9 and sing praises to your **n";**
1Co 1: 2 on the **n** of our Lord Jesus Christ, both their Lord
1:10 by the **n** of our Lord Jesus Christ,
1:13 Or were you baptized in the **n** of Paul?
1:15 no one can say that you were baptized in my **n.**
5: 4 in the **n** of the Lord Jesus on the man D
5:11 the **n** of brother or sister who is sexually immoral
6:11 were justified in the **n** of the Lord Jesus Christ D
Eph 1:21 and above every **n** that is named,
3:15 in heaven and on earth takes its **n.**
5:20 the Father at all times and for everything in the **n**
Php 2: 9 also highly exalted him and gave him the **n** that is
2: 9 and gave him the name that is above every **n,**
2:10 so that at the **n** of Jesus every knee should bend, F
Col 3:17 do everything in the **n** of the Lord Jesus, D
2Th 1:12 the **n** of our Lord Jesus may be glorified in you,
3: 6 beloved, in the **n** of our Lord Jesus Christ,
1Ti 6: 1 so that the **n** of God and the teaching may not
2Ti 2:19 the **n** of the Lord turn away from wickedness." D
Heb 1: 4 **n** he has inherited is more excellent than theirs.
2:12 "I will proclaim your **n** to my brothers and sisters,
7: 2 His **n,** in the first place, means "king
13:15 that is, the fruit of lips that confess his **n.**
Jas 2: 7 Is it not they who blaspheme the excellent **n**
5:10 the prophets who spoke in the **n** of the Lord. D
5:14 anointing them with oil in the **n** of the Lord. D
1Pe 4:14 If you are reviled for the **n** of Christ,
4:16 but glorify God because you bear this **n.**
1Jn 2:12 because your sins are forgiven on account of his **n.**
3:23 the **n** of his Son Jesus Christ and love one another,
5:13 I write these things to you who believe in the **n** of
3Jn 1:15 Greet the friends there, each by **n.**
Rev 2: 3 and bearing up for the sake of my **n,**
2:13 Yet you are holding fast to my **n,**
2:17 and on the white stone is written a new **n**
3: 1 you have a **n** of being alive, but you are dead.
3: 5 and I will not blot your **n** out of the book of life;
I will confess your **n** before my Father and
3: 8 you have kept my word and have not denied my **n.**
3:12 I will write on you the **n** of my God, and the **n** of
the city of my God,
3:12 from my God out of heaven, and my own new **n.**
6: 8 Its rider's **n** was Death, and Hades followed
8:11 The **n** of the star is Wormwood.
9:11 his **n** in Hebrew is Abaddon,
11:18 the prophets and saints and all who fear your **n,**
13: 6 blaspheming his **n** and his dwelling, that is,
13: 8 everyone whose **n** has not been written from
13:17 the **n** of the beast or the number of its **n.**
14: 1 one hundred forty-four thousand who had his **n**
and his Father's **n** written on their foreheads.
14:11 and for anyone who receives the mark of its **n."**
15: 2 the beast and its image and the number of its **n,**
15: 4 Lord, who will not fear and glorify your **n?**
16: 9 but they cursed the **n** of God,
17: 5 and on her forehead was written a **n,** a mystery;
19:12 a **n** inscribed that no one knows but himself.
19:13 and his **n** is called The Word of God.
19:16 On his robe and on his thigh he has a **n** inscribed,
20:15 and anyone whose **n** was not found written in
22: 4 and his **n** will be on their foreheads.
Tob 3: 8 and have not borne the **n** of a single one of them.
3:11 Blessed is your **n** forever; E
3:15 not disgraced my **n** or the **n** of my father in
5:12 brother, whose son you are and what your **n** is."
8: 5 and blessed is your **n** in all generations forever.
11:14 "Blessed be God, and blessed be his great **n,**
11:14 his holy **n** be blessed throughout all the ages. B
12: 6 Bless and sing praise to his **n.**
13:11 of the remotest parts of the earth to your holy **n,** B
13:11 the **n** of the chosen city will endure forever.
13:17 blessed will bless the holy **n** forever and ever." BE
14:8,9 of God and to bless his **n** at all times with sincerity
Jdt 9: 7 the Lord who crushes wars; the Lord is your **n.**
9: 8 the tabernacle where your glorious **n** resides, G
14: 7 In every nation those who hear your **n** will
16: 1 exalt him, and call upon his **n.**
AdE 2: 5 the capital whose **n** was Mordecai son of Jair son
2: 7 Aminadab, and her **n** was Esther.
2:14 in to the king again unless she is summoned by **n.**
3:12 in the **n** of King Artaxerxes to the magistrates and
8: 8 Write in my **n** what you think best and seal it
9: 4 that Mordecai's **n** be held in honor throughout

AdE 10: 8 that gathered to destroy the **n** of the Jews.
13:17 that we may live and sing praise to your **n,**
Wis 2: 4 Our **n** will be forgotten in time,
10:20 they sang hymns, O Lord, to your holy **n,** B
13:10 are those who give the **n** "gods" to the works
14:21 on objects of stone or wood the **n** that ought not to
Sir 2:17 and equal to his **n** are his works.
6: 1 for a bad **n** incurs shame and reproach;
6:22 For wisdom is like her **n;**
15: 6 and will inherit an everlasting **n.**
17:10 And they will praise his holy **n,** B
22:14 And what is its **n** except "Fool"?
23: 9 nor habitually utter the **n** of the Holy One;
23:10 and utters the **N** will never be cleansed from sin.
36:17 O Lord, on the people called by your **n,** on Israel,
36:20 and fulfill the prophecies spoken in your **n.**
37: 1 but some friends are friends only in **n.**
37:26 and his **n** will live forever.
39: 9 and his **n** will live through all generations.
39:11 he will leave a **n** greater than a thousand,
39:15 Ascribe majesty to his **n** and give thanks to him
39:35 and bless the **n** of the Lord. D
40:19 and the building of a city establish one's **n,**
41:11 but a virtuous **n** will never be blotted out.
41:12 for your **n,** since it will outlive you longer than
41:13 but a good **n** lasts forever.
43: 8 The new moon, as its **n** suggests, renews itself;
44: 3 and made a **n** for themselves by their valor;
44: 8 Some of them have left behind a **n,**
44:14 but their **n** lives on generation after generation.
45:15 and serve as priest and bless his people in his **n.**
46: 1 He became, as his **n** implies,
47:10 while they praised God's holy **n,** B
47:13 so that he might build a house in his **n** and provide
47:18 In the **n** of the Lord God, D
49: 1 The **n** of Josiah is like blended incense prepared
50:20 and to glory in his **n;**
51: 1 I give thanks to your **n,**
51: 3 in the greatness of your mercy and of your **n,**
51:11 I will praise your **n** continually,
51:12 and I bless the **n** of the Lord. D
Bar 2:11 and made yourself a **n** that continues to this day,
2:15 for Israel and his descendants are called by your **n.**
2:26 the house that is called by your **n** you have made
2:32 in the land of their exile, and will remember my **n**
3: 5 but in this crisis remember your power and your **n.**
3: 7 in our hearts so that we would call upon your **n;**
4: 5 my people, who perpetuate Israel's **n!**
5: 4 For God will give you evermore the **n,**
Aza 1: 3 and glorious is your **n** forever! E
1:20 and bring glory to your **n,** O Lord.
1:30 And blessed is your glorious, holy **n,** and to B
Sus 1: 1 a man living in Babylon whose **n** was Joakim.
1Mc 2:51 you will receive great honor and an everlasting **n.**
3:14 a **n** for myself and win honor in the kingdom.
4:33 let all who know your **n** praise you with hymns."
5:57 So they said, "Let us also make a **n** for ourselves;
5:63 wherever their **n** was heard.
6:44 and to win for himself an everlasting **n.**
7:37 "You chose this house to be called by your **n,**
14:43 in the country should be written in his **n,**
2Mc 8: 4 and the blasphemies committed against his **n;**
8:15 he had called them by his holy and glorious **n.** G
12:13 of Gentiles. Its **n** was Caspin.
1Es 1:48 the **n** of the Lord, he broke his oath and rebelled; D
4:63 and the temple that is called by his **n;**
5:38 the daughters of Barzillai, and was called by his **n.**
6: 1 prophesied to them in the **n** of the Lord God D
6:33 may the Lord, whose **n** is there called upon,
8:78 to leave to us a root and a **n** in your holy place,
8:88 to destroy us without leaving a root or seed or **n?**
9:16 of their ancestral houses, all of them by **n;**
Man 1: 3 and sealed it with your terrible and glorious **n;** G
3Mc 2: 9 chose this city and sanctified this place for your **n,**
2: 9 for the glory of your great and honored **n.**
2:14 on earth dedicated to your glorious **n.** G
2Es 1:16 You have not exulted in my **n** at the destruction
1:22 at the bitter stream, thirsty and blaspheming my **n,**
1:24 to other nations and will give them my **n,**
2:16 because I recognize my **n** in them.
2:45 and have confessed the **n** of God.
2:47 who had stood valiantly for the **n** of the Lord. D
3:13 for yourself one of them, whose **n** was Abraham;
3:24 You commanded him to build a city for your **n,**
4: 1 angel that had been sent to me, whose **n** was Uriel,
4:25 what will he do for his **n** that is invoked over us?
6:49 the one you called Behemoth and the **n** of
7:*60* and through them my **n** has now been honored.
8:60 the **n** of him who made them,
10:22 our holy things have been polluted, and the **n**
4Mc 5: 4 one man, Eleazar by **n,** leader of the flock,

NAME'S (15) [NAME]

1Sa 12:22 not cast away his people, for his great **n** sake,
Ps 23: 3 He leads me in right paths for his **n** sake.
25:11 For your **n** sake, O LORD, pardon my guilt,
31: 3 for your **n** sake lead me and guide me,
79: 9 deliver us, and forgive our sins, for your **n** sake.
106: 8 Yet he saved them for his **n** sake,
109:21 act on my behalf for your **n** sake;
143:11 For your **n** sake, O LORD, preserve my life.
Isa 48: 9 For my **n** sake I defer my anger,
66: 5 and reject you for my **n** sake have said, "Let
Jer 14: 7 act, O LORD, for your **n** sake;
14:21 Do not spurn us, for your **n** sake;
Eze 20:44 when I deal with you for my **n** sake,
Mt 19:29 for my **n** sake, will receive a hundredfold,
Aza 1:11 For your **n** sake do not give us up forever,

NAMED‡ (143) [NAME]

Ge 3:20 The man **n** his wife Eve,
4:17 he built a city, and **n** it Enoch after his son Enoch.
4:25 and she bore a son and **n** him Seth, for she said,
4:26 To Seth also a son was born, and he **n** him Enosh.
5: 2 and **n** them "Humankind" when they were created.
5: 3 according to his image, and **n** him Seth.
5:29 he **n** him Noah, saying, "Out of the ground that
16:13 So she **n** the LORD who spoke to her,
16:15 and Abram **n** his son, whom Hagar bore, Ishmael.
19:37 The firstborn bore a son, and **n** him Moab;
19:38 The younger also bore a son and **n** him Ben-ammi;
21:12 it is through Isaac that offspring shall be **n** for you.
23:16 for Ephron the silver that he had **n** in the hearing
25:13 **n** in the order of their birth:
25:25 like a hairy mantle; so they **n** him Esau.
25:26 his hand gripping Esau's heel; so he was **n** Jacob.
27:36 Esau said, "Is he not rightly **n** Jacob?
29:32 and bore a son, and she **n** him Reuben;
29:33 given me this son also"; and she **n** him Simeon.
29:34 borne him three sons"; therefore he was **n** Levi.
29:35 therefore she **n** him Judah;
30: 6 and given me a son"; therefore she **n** him Dan.
30: 8 and have prevailed"; so she **n** him Naphtali.
30:11 so she **n** him Gad.
30:13 women will call me happy"; so she **n** him Asher.
30:18 to my husband"; so she **n** him Issachar.
30:20 I have borne him six sons"; so she **n** him Zebulun.
30:21 Afterwards she bore a daughter, and **n** her Dinah.
30:24 and she **n** him Joseph, saying, "May the LORD
35:18 (for she died), she **n** him Ben-oni;
38: 3 She conceived and bore a son; and he **n** him Er.
38: 4 and bore a son whom she **n** Onan.
38: 5 Yet again she bore a son, and she **n** him Shelah.
38:29 Therefore he was **n** Perez.
38:30 on his hand; and he was **n** Zerah.
41:51 Joseph **n** the firstborn Manasseh, "For," he said,
41:52 The second he **n** Ephraim,
50:11 Therefore the place was **n** Abel-mizraim;
Ex 1:15 one of whom was **n** Shiphrah and the other Puah,
2:10 She **n** him Moses, "because," she said,
2:22 She bore a son, and he **n** him Gershom;
Nu 11:26 in the camp, one **n** Eldad, and the other **n** Medad,
Dt 3:14 and the Maacathites, and he **n** them—
Jdg 1:26 and **n** it Luz; that is its name to this day.
2: 5 So they **n** that place Bochim,
8:31 also bore him a son, and he **n** him Abimelech.
13:24 The woman bore a son, and **n** him Samson.
15:19 it was **n** En-hakkore, which is at Lehi to this day.
18:29 They **n** the city Dan, after their ancestor Dan,
Ru 4:17 to Naomi." They **n** him Obed;
1Sa 1:20 She **n** him Samuel, for she said,
4:21 She **n** the child Ichabod, meaning,
7:12 between Mizpah and Jeshanah, and **n** it Ebenezer;
17: 4 the camp of the Philistines a champion **n** Goliath,
17:12 **n** Jesse, who had eight sons.
22:20 **n** Abiathar, escaped and fled after David.
2Sa 5: 9 and **n** it the city of David.
12:24 and she bore a son, and he **n** him Solomon.
12:25 so he **n** him Jedidiah, because of the LORD.
17:25 the son of a man **n** Ithra the Ishmaelite,
20: 1 Now a scoundrel **n** Sheba son of Bichri,
2Ki 17:34 the children of Jacob, whom he **n** Israel.
1Ch 4: 9 and his mother **n** him Jabez, saying,
7:16 of Machir bore a son, and she **n** him Peresh;
7:23 and bore a son; and he **n** him Beriah,
12:31 who were expressly **n** to come
16:41 of those chosen and expressly **n** to render thanks
Ezr 5:14 and they were delivered to a man **n** Sheshbazzar,
Job 42:14 He **n** the first Jemimah, the second Keziah,
Ps 49:11 though they **n** lands their own.
Pr 21:24 The proud, haughty person, **n** "Scoffer,"
Ecc 6:10 Whatever has come to be has already been **n,**
Isa 9: 6 and he is **n** Wonderful Counselor, Mighty God,
14:20 May the descendants of evildoers nevermore be **n!**
49: 1 while I was in my mother's womb he **n** me.
61: 6 you shall be **n** ministers of our God;
Jer 20: 3 The LORD has **n** you not Pashhur
37:13 a sentinel there **n** Irijah son of Shelemiah son
Eze 48:31 gates of the city being **n** after the tribes of Israel.
Da 4: 8 he who was **n** Belteshazzar after the name
5:12 whom the king **n** Belteshazzar.
10: 1 to Daniel, who was **n** Belteshazzar.
Zec 11: 7 one I **n** Favor, the other I **n** Unity,
Mt 1:25 until she had borne a son; and he **n** him Jesus.
27:32 they came upon a man from Cyrene **n** Simon;
27:57 there came a rich man from Arimathea, **n** Joseph,
Mk 3:14 he appointed twelve, whom he also **n** apostles,
5:22 of the leaders of the synagogue **n** Jairus came and,
Lk 1: 5 there was a priest **n** Zechariah,
5:27 this he went out and saw a tax collector **n** Levi,
6:13 of them, whom he also **n** apostles:
6:14 whom he **n** Peter, and his brother Andrew,
8:41 Just then there came a man **n** Jairus,
10:38 a woman **n** Martha welcomed him into her home.
10:39 She had a sister **n** Mary,
16:20 And at his gate lay a poor man **n** Lazarus,
19: 2 A man was there **n** Zacchaeus;
23:50 there was a good and righteous man **n** Joseph,
Jn 3: 1 Now there was a Pharisee **n** Nicodemus,
Ac 5: 1 But a man **n** Ananias, with the consent
5:34 But a Pharisee in the council **n** Gamaliel,
7:58 at the feet of a young man **n** Saul.
Ac 8: 9 man **n** Simon had previously practiced magic
9:10 Now there was a disciple in Damascus **n** Ananias.
9:11 of Judas look for a man of Tarsus **n** Saul.
9:12 and he has seen in a vision a man **n** Ananias come
9:33 There he found a man **n** Aeneas,
10: 1 In Caesarea there was a man **n** Cornelius,
11:28 One of them **n** Agabus stood up and predicted by
12:13 a maid **n** Rhoda came to answer.
13: 6 a Jewish false prophet, **n** Bar-Jesus.
16: 1 where there was a disciple **n** Timothy,
16:14 A certain woman **n** Lydia, a worshiper of God,
17: 7 saying that there is another king **n** Jesus."
17:34 the Areopagite and a woman **n** Damaris,
18: 2 There he found a Jew **n** Aquila, a native of Pontus,
18: 7 to the house of a man **n** Titius Justus, a worshiper
18:24 Now there came to Ephesus a Jew **n** Apollos,
19:14 of a Jewish high priest **n** Sceva were doing this.
19:24 A man **n** Demetrius, a silversmith who made
20: 9 A young man **n** Eutychus,
21:10 a prophet **n** Agabus came down from Judea.
27: 1 to a centurion of the Augustan Cohort, **n** Julius.
28: 7 to the leading man of the island, **n** Publius,
Ro 9: 7 through Isaac that descendants shall be **n** for you."
15:20 not where Christ has already been **n,**
Eph 1:21 and above every name that is **n,**
Heb 11:18 through Isaac that descendants shall be **n** for you."
Tob 1: 9 the father of a son whom I **n** Tobias.
6:11 He is your relative, and he has a daughter **n** Sarah.
Wis 14: 8 and the perishable thing because it was **n** a god.
14:27 the worship of idols not to be **n** is the beginning
Sir 36:17 on Israel, whom you have **n** your firstborn,
Bar 4:30 for the one who **n** you will comfort you.
Sus 1: 2 He married the daughter of Hilkiah, **n** Susanna,
1:45 up the holy spirit of a young lad **n** Daniel,
1Mc 6:17 from boyhood; he **n** him Eupator.
2Mc 3: 4 But a man **n** Simon, of the tribe of Benjamin,
2Es 3:23 and you raised up for yourself a servant, **n** David.
5:26 the birds that have been created you have **n**
6: 4 before the measures of the firmaments were **n,**

NAMELY‡ (21) [NAME]

Nu 1:32 The descendants of Joseph, **n,**
1Sa 11: 2 **n** that I gouge out everyone's right eye,
2Ki 25:23 **n,** Ishmael son of Nethaniah,
1Ch 5:26 and he carried them away, **n,** the Reubenites,
6:39 **n,** Asaph son of Berechiah, son of Shimea,
7: 2 **n** of Tola, mighty warriors of their generations,
Ezr 2: 6 **n** the descendants of Jeshua and Joab,
2:16 Of Ater, **n** of Hezekiah, ninety-eight.
8:17 **n,** to send us ministers for the house of our God.
8:18 **n** Sherebiah, with his sons and kin, eighteen;
Ne 7:11 **n** the descendants of Jeshua and Joab,
7:21 Of Ater, **n** of Hezekiah, ninety-eight.
7:39 the descendants of Jedaiah, **n** the house of Jeshua,
7:43 **n** of Kadmiel of the descendants of Hodevah,
Da 9: 2 be fulfilled for the devastation of Jerusalem, **n,**
3Jn 1: 3 **n** how you walk in the truth.
AdE 9:22 The whole month (**n,** Adar),
1Es 5:15 descendants of Ater, **n** of Hezekiah, ninety-two.
8:47 **n** Sherebiah with his descendants and kinsmen,
4Mc 1: 3 over those emotions that hinder self-control, **n,**
1: 4 that stand in the way of courage, **n** anger, fear,

NAMES (98) [NAME]

Ge 2:20 The man gave **n** to all cattle,
25:13 These are the **n** of the sons of Ishmael,
25:16 the sons of Ishmael and these are their **n,**
26:18 he gave them the **n** that his father had given them.
36:10 These are the **n** of Esau's sons:
36:40 These are the **n** of the clans of Esau,
36:40 to their families and their localities by their **n:**
46: 8 Now these are the **n** of the Israelites,
48: 6 be recorded under the **n** of their brothers
Ex 1: 1 These are the **n** of the sons of Israel who came
6:16 The following are the **n** of the sons of Levi
23:13 Do not invoke the **n** of other gods;
28: 9 and engrave on them the **n** of the sons of Israel,
28:10 six of their **n** on the one stone,
28:10 and the **n** of the remaining six on the other stone,
28:11 so you shall engrave the two stones with the **n** of
28:12 and Aaron shall bear their **n** before the LORD
28:21 There shall be twelve stones with **n** corresponding
to the **n** of the sons of Israel;
28:29 So Aaron shall bear the **n** of the sons of Israel in
39: 6 according to the **n** of the sons of Israel.
39:14 There were twelve stones with **n** corresponding to
39:14 with names corresponding to the **n** of the sons
Nu 1: 2 by ancestral houses, according to the number of **n,**
1: 5 These are the **n** of the men who shall assist you:
1:18 to the number of **n** from twenty years old
1:20 according to the number of **n,**
1:22 according to the number of **n,**
1:24 according to the number of the **n,**
1:26 according to the number of **n,**
1:28 according to the number of **n,**
1:30 according to the number of **n,**
1:32 according to the number of **n,**
1:34 according to the number of **n,**
1:36 according to the number of **n,**
1:38 according to the number of **n,**
1:40 according to the number of **n,**
1:42 according to the number of **n,**
3: 2 These are the **n** of the sons of Aaron:
3: 3 these are the **n** of the sons of Aaron,
3:17 The following were the sons of Levi, by their **n:**
3:18 the **n** of the sons of Gershon by their clans:

Nu 3:40 from a month old and upward, and count their **n.**
3:43 counting the number of **n,**
13: 4 These were their **n:** From the
13:16 These were the **n** of the men whom Moses sent
26:33 **n** of the daughters of Zelophehad were Mahlah,
26:53 for inheritance according to the number of **n.**
26:55 to the **n** of their ancestral tribes they shall inherit.
27: 1 The **n** of his daughters were:
32:38 and Baal-meon (some **n** being changed),
32:38 and they gave **n** to the towns that they rebuilt.
34:17 These are the **n** of the men who shall apportion
34:19 These are the **n** of the men:
Dt 29:20 LORD will blot out their **n** from under heaven.
Jos 17: 3 and these are the **n** of his daughters:
23: 7 or make mention of the **n** of their gods,
Ru 1: 2 the **n** of his two sons were Mahlon and Chilion;
1Sa 14:49 and the **n** of his two daughters were these:
17:13 the **n** of his three sons who went to
2Sa 5:14 the **n** of those who were born to him in Jerusalem:
23: 8 These are the **n** of the warriors whom David had:
1Ki 4: 8 These were their **n:** Ben-hur,
1Ch 6:17 These are the **n** of the sons of Gershom:
8:38 Azel had six sons, and these are their **n:**
9:44 Azel had six sons, and these are their **n:**
14: 4 the **n** of the children whom he had in Jerusalem:
23:24 according to the number of the **n** of the individuals
Ezr 5: 4 the **n** of the men who are building this building?"
5:10 We also asked them their **n,** for your information,
5:10 so that we might write down the **n** of the men
8:13 those who came later, their **n** being Eliphelet,
Ne 9:38 and on that sealed document are inscribed the **n**
10: 1 Upon the sealed document are the **n** of Nehemiah
Ps 16: 4 of blood I will not pour out or take their **n**
147: 4 he gives to all of them their **n.**
Eze 23: 4 As for their **n,** Oholah is Samaria,
48: 1 These are the **n** of the tribes:
Da 1: 7 The palace master gave them other **n:**
Hos 2:17 I will remove the **n** of the Baals from her mouth,
Zec 13: 2 I will cut off the **n** of the idols from the land,
Mt 10: 2 These are the **n** of the twelve apostles:
Lk 10:20 but rejoice that your **n** are written in heaven."
Ac 18:15 of questions about words and **n** and your own law,
Php 4: 3 whose **n** are in the book of life.
Rev 13: 1 and on its heads were blasphemous **n.**
17: 3 on a scarlet beast that was full of blasphemous **n,**
17: 8 whose **n** have not been written in the book of life
21:12 the gates are inscribed the **n** of the twelve tribes of
21:14 on them are the twelve **n** of the twelve apostles of
Sir 46:11 The judges also, with their respective **n,**
46:12 the **n** of those who have been honored live again
1Es 5: 4 These are the **n** of the men who went up,
6:12 and asked them for a list of the **n** of those who are
8:39 their **n** being Eliphelet, Jeuel, and Shemaiah,
8:49 the list of all their **n** was reported.
2Es 2: 7 let their **n** be blotted out from the earth,
14:35 then the **n** of the righteous shall become manifest,

NANEA (3)

2Mc 1:13 in the temple of **N** by a deception employed by
1:13 by the priests of the goddess **N.**
1:15 When the priests of the temple of **N** had set out

NAOMI (22) [=MARA]

Ru 1: 2 and the name of his wife **N,** and the names
1: 3 But Elimelech, the husband of **N,** died,
1: 8 But **N** said to her two daughters-in-law,
1:11 But **N** said, "Turn back, my daughters,
1:18 **N** saw that she was determined to go with her,
1:19 and the women said, "Is this **N?"**
1:20 "Call me no longer **N,** call me Mara,
1:21 why call me **N** when the LORD has dealt harshly
1:22 So **N** returned together with Ruth the Moabite,
2: 1 Now **N** had a kinsman on her husband's side,
2: 2 And Ruth the Moabite said to **N,**
2: 6 "She is the Moabite who came back with **N** from
2:20 Then **N** said to her daughter-in-law,
2:20 **N** also said to her, "The man is a relative of ours,
2:22 **N** said to Ruth, her daughter-in-law, "It is better,
3: 1 **N** her mother-in-law said to her, "My daughter,
4: 3 He then said to the next-of-kin, "**N,**
4: 5 day you acquire the field from the hand of **N,**
4: 9 from the hand of **N** all that belonged to Elimelech
4:14 Then the women said to **N,**
4:16 Then **N** took the child and laid him in her bosom,
4:17 saying, "A son has been born to **N."**

NAPE (1)

Lev 5: 8 wringing its head at the **n** without severing it.

NAPHATH (1) [NAPHATH-DOR, NAPHOTH-DOR]

Jos 17:11 of Megiddo and its villages (the third is **N).**

NAPHATH-DOR (2) [DOR, NAPHATH]

Jos 12:23 king of Dor in **N** one the king of Goiim in Galilee,
1Ki 4:11 in all **N** (he had Taphath, Solomon's daughter,

NAPHISH (3)

Ge 25:15 Hadad, Tema, Jetur, **N,** and Kedemah.
1Ch 1:31 **N,** and Kedemah. These are the sons of Ishmael.
5:19 They made war on the Hagrites, Jetur, **N,**

NAPHOTH-DOR (1) [DOR, NAPHATH]

Jos 11: 2 and in the lowland, and in **N** on the west,

NAPHTALI‡ (55) [NAPHTALITES]

Ge 30: 8 and have prevailed"; so she named him **N.**
35:25 The sons of Bilhah, Rachel's maid: Dan and **N.**
46:24 The children of **N:** Jahzeel,
49:21 **N** is a doe let loose that bears lovely fawns.
Ex 1: 4 Dan and **N,** Gad and Asher.
Nu 1:15 From **N,** Ahira son of Enan.
1:42 The descendants of **N,** their lineage, in their clans,
1:43 of **N** were fifty-three thousand four hundred.
2:29 Then the tribe of **N:** The leader of the
10:27 over the company of the tribe of **N** was Ahira son
13:14 from the tribe of **N,** Nahbi son of Vophsi;
26:48 The descendants of **N** by their clans:
Dt 27:13 Reuben, Gad, Asher, Zebulun, Dan, and **N.**
33:23 And of **N** he said: O **N,** sated with favor,
34: 2 all **N,** the land of Ephraim and Manasseh, all
Jos 19:32 The sixth lot came out for the tribe of **N,**
19:32 for the tribe of **N,** according to its families.
19:39 This is the inheritance of the tribe of **N** according
20: 7 in Galilee in the hill country of **N,**
21: 6 from the tribe of Asher, from the tribe of **N,**
21:32 Out of the tribe of **N:**
Jdg 1:33 **N** did not drive out the inhabitants
4: 6 of Abinoam from Kedesh in **N,**
4: 6 bringing ten thousand from the tribe of **N** and
4:10 Barak summoned Zebulun and **N** to Kedesh;
5:18 **N** too, on the heights of the field.
6:35 Zebulun, and **N,** and they went up to meet them.
7:23 And the men of Israel were called out from **N** and
1Ki 4:15 in **N** (he had taken Basemath,
7:14 He was the son of a widow of the tribe of **N,**
15:20 and all Chinneroth, with all the land of **N.**
2Ki 15:29 Hazor, Gilead, and Galilee, all the land of **N;**
1Ch 2: 2 Dan, Joseph, Benjamin, **N,** Gad, and Asher.
6:62 Asher, **N,** and Manasseh in Bashan.
6:76 and out of the tribe of **N:**
7:13 The descendants of **N:** Jahziel,
12:34 Of **N,** a thousand commanders,
12:40 from as far away as Issachar and Zebulun and **N,**
27:19 for **N,** Jerimoth son of Azriel;
2Ch 16: 4 Dan, Abel-maim, and all the store-cities of **N.**
34: 6 and as far as **N,** in their ruins all around,
Ps 68:27 the princes of Zebulun, the princes of **N.**
Isa 9: 1 the land of Zebulun and the land of **N,**
Eze 48: 3 from the east side to the west, **N,** one portion.
48: 4 Adjoining the territory of **N,**
48:34 the gate of Asher, and the gate of **N.**
Mt 4:13 in the territory of Zebulun and **N,**
4:15 land of **N,** on the road by the sea,
Rev 7: 6 from the tribe of **N** twelve thousand,
Tob 1: 1 of the descendants of Asiel, of the tribe of **N,**
1: 2 to the south of Kedesh **N** in Upper Galilee,
1: 4 of my ancestor **N** deserted the house of David
1: 5 and our ancestral house of **N** sacrificed to the calf
7: 3 the descendants of **N** who are exiles in Nineveh."

NAPHTALITES (4) [NAPHTALI]

Nu 2:29 The leader of the **N** shall be Ahira son of Enan,
7:78 of Enan, the leader of the **N:**
26:50 These are the **N** by their clans:
34:28 Of the tribe of the **N** a leader,

NAPHTHA (2)

Aza 1:23 in kept stoking the furnace with **n,**
2Mc 1:36 but by most people it is called **n.**

NAPHTUHIM (2)

Ge 10:13 the father of Ludim, Anamim, Lehabim, **N,**
1Ch 1:11 the father of Ludim, Anamim, Lehabim, **N,**

NAPKIN (KJV) See CLOTH

NARCISSUS (1)

Ro 16:11 in the Lord who belong to the family of **N.**

NARD (5)

SS 1:12 my **n** gave forth its fragrance.
4:13 with all choicest fruits, henna with **n,**
4:14 **n** and saffron, calamus and cinnamon,
Mk 14: 3 with an alabaster jar of very costly ointment of **n,**
Jn 12: 3 a pound of costly perfume made of pure **n,**

NARRATIVE (3) [NARRATIVES]

2Mc 2:31 but the one who recasts the **n** should be allowed
2:32 At this point therefore let us begin our **n,**
4Mc 3:19 to a **n** demonstration of temperate reason.

NARRATIVES (1) [NARRATIVE]

2Mc 2:24 to enter upon the **n** of history because of the mass

NARROW (14) [NARROWER, NARROWNESS]

Nu 22:24 the angel of the LORD stood in a **n** path between
22:26 and stood in a **n** place,
Jos 17:15 since the hill country of Ephraim is too **n** for you."
Pr 23:27 a prostitute is a deep pit; an adulteress is a **n** well.
Isa 28:20 and the covering too **n** to wrap oneself in it.
Mt 7:13 "Enter through the **n** gate;
Mt 7:14 the gate is **n** and the road is hard that leads to life,
Lk 13:24 "Strive to enter through the **n** door;
Jdt 4: 7 to enter, for the approach was **n,**
2Es 7: 4 but it has an entrance set in a **n** place,
7: 5 the broad part unless they pass through the **n** part?
7: 7 entrance to it is **n** and set in a precipitous place,
7:12 And so the entrances of this world were made **n**
13:43 in by the **n** passages of the Euphrates river.

NARROWER (1) [NARROW]

Eze 42: 5 Now the upper chambers were **n,**

NARROWNESS (1) [NARROW]

2Mc 12:21 to besiege and difficult of access because of the **n**

NATHAMIAH See Index to Footnotes

NATHAN (46)

2Sa 5:14 Shammua, Shobab, **N,** Solomon,
7: 2 the king said to the prophet **N,**
7: 3 **N** said to the king, "Go, do all that you have
7: 4 same night the word of the LORD came to **N:**
7:17 and with all this vision, **N** spoke to David.
12: 1 and the LORD sent **N** to David.
12: 5 He said to **N,** "As the LORD lives,
12: 7 **N** said to David, "You are the man!
12:13 David said to **N,** "I have sinned against
12:13 **N** said to David, "Now the LORD has put away
12:15 Then **N** went to his house.
12:25 and sent a message by the prophet **N;**
23:36 Igal son of **N** of Zobah; Bani the Gadite;
1Ki 1: 8 and Benaiah son of Jehoiada, and the prophet **N,**
1:10 not invite the prophet **N** or Benaiah or the warriors
1:11 Then **N** said to Bathsheba, Solomon's mother,
1:22 with the king, the prophet **N** came in.
1:23 The king was told, "Here is the prophet **N."**
1:24 **N** said, "My lord the king, have you said,
1:32 "Summon to me the priest Zadok, the prophet **N,**
1:34 and the prophet **N** anoint him king over Israel;
1:38 So the priest Zadok, the prophet **N,**
1:44 the prophet **N,** and Benaiah son of Jehoiada,
1:45 the prophet **N** have anointed him king at Gihon;
4: 5 Azariah son of **N** was over the officials;
4: 5 Zabud son of **N** was priest and king's friend;
1Ch 2:36 Attai became the father of **N,**
2:36 the father of Nathan, and **N** of Zabad.
3: 5 Shimea, Shobab, **N,** and Solomon,
11:38 Joel the brother of **N,** Mibhar son of Hagri,
14: 4 Shammua, Shobab, and **N;**
17: 1 David said to the prophet **N,**
17: 2 **N** said to David, "Do all that you have in mind,
17: 3 same night the word of the LORD came to **N,**
17:15 with all these words and all this vision, **N** spoke
29:29 and in the records of the prophet **N,**
2Ch 9:29 not written in the history of the prophet **N,**
29:25 and of Gad the king's seer and of the prophet **N,**
Ezr 8:16 **N,** Zechariah, and Meshullam, who were leaders,
10:39 Shelemiah, **N,** Adaiah,
Ps 51: T *of David, when the prophet N came to him,*
Zec 12:12 the family of the house of **N** by itself,
Lk 3:31 son of Menna, son of Mattatha, son of **N,**
Tob 5:14 For I knew Hananiah and **N,**
Sir 47: 1 him **N** rose up to prophesy in the days of David.
1Es 8:44 Jarib, **N,** Elnathan, Zechariah, and Meshullam,

NATHAN-MELECH (1)

2Ki 23:11 by the chamber of the eunuch **N,**

NATHANAEL (8) [=BARTHOLOMEW?]

Jn 1:45 Philip found **N** and said to him,
1:46 **N** said to him, "Can anything good come out
1:47 When Jesus saw **N** coming toward him,
1:48 **N** asked him, "Where did you get to know me?"
1:49 **N** replied, "Rabbi, you are the Son of God!
21: 2 Thomas called the Twin, **N** of Cana in Galilee,
Jdt 8: 1 of Elijah son of Hilkiah son of Eliab son of **N** son
1Es 9:22 Elioenai, Maaseiah, Ishmael, and **N,**

NATION‡ (269) [NATION'S, NATIONAL, NATIONALITIES, NATIONS]

A. EVERY NATION (13)
B. WHOLE NATION (10)
C. NATION OF THE JEWS (9)

Ge 12: 2 I will make of you a great **n,** and I will bless you,
15:14 but I will bring judgment on the **n** that they serve,
17:20 and I will make him a great **n.**
18:18 that Abraham shall become a great and mighty **n,**
21:13 I will make a **n** of him also,
21:18 for I will make a great **n** of him."
35:11 **n** and a company of nations shall come from you,
46: 3 for I will make of you a great **n** there.
Ex 9:24 in all the land of Egypt since it became a **n.**
19: 6 be for me a priestly kingdom and a holy **n.**
32:10 and of you I will make a great **n."**
33:13 Consider too that this **n** is your people."
34:10 not been performed in all the earth or in any **n;**
Lev 18:28 as it vomited out the **n** that was before you.
20:23 You shall not follow the practices of the **n**
Nu 14:12 of you a **n** greater and mightier than they."
Dt 4: 6 this great **n** is a wise and discerning people!"
4: 7 For what other great **n** has a god so near to it as
4: 8 And what other great **n** has statutes

Dt 4:34 Or has any god ever attempted to go and take a **n**
for himself from the midst of another **n,**
9:14 a **n** mightier and more numerous than they."
26: 5 few in number, and there he became a great **n,**
28:36 to a **n** that neither you
28:49 The LORD will bring a **n** from far away,
28:49 a **n** whose language you do not understand,
28:50 a grim-faced **n** showing no respect to the old
32:21 provoke them with a foolish **n.**
32:28 They are a **n** void of sense;
Jos 3:17 until the entire **n** finished crossing over the Jordan.
4: 1 the entire **n** had finished crossing over the Jordan,
5: 6 until all the **n,** the warriors who came out
5: 8 When the circumcising of all the **n** was done,
10:13 until the **n** took vengeance on their enemies.
2Sa 7:23 Is there another **n** on earth whose God went
1Ki 18:10 there is no **n** or kingdom to which my lord has
18:10 he would require an oath of the kingdom or **n,**
2Ki 17:29 But every **n** still made gods of its own A
17:29 every **n** in the cities in which they lived; A
1Ch 16:20 wandering from **n** to **n,**
17:21 one **n** on the earth whom God went to redeem to
2Ch 15: 6 **n** against **n** and city against city,
32:15 for no god of any **n** or kingdom has been able
Job 34:29 whether it be a **n** or an individual?—
Ps 33:12 Happy is the **n** whose God is the LORD,
83: 4 They say, "Come, let us wipe them out as a **n;**
105:13 wandering from **n** to **n,**
106: 5 that I may rejoice in the gladness of your **n,**
147:20 He has not dealt thus with any other **n;**
Pr 11:14 Where there is no guidance, a **n** falls,
14:34 Righteousness exalts a **n,** but sin is a reproach
Isa 1: 4 Ah, sinful **n,** people laden with iniquity,
2: 4 **n** shall not lift up sword against **n,**
5:26 He will raise a signal for a **n** far away,
9: 3 You have multiplied the **n,**
10: 6 Against a godless **n** I send him,
14:32 What will one answer the messengers of the **n?**
18: 2 Go, you swift messengers, to a **n** tall and smooth,
18: 2 a **n** mighty and conquering,
18: 7 a **n** mighty and conquering,
26: 2 that the righteous **n** that keeps faith may enter in.
26:15 But you have increased the **n,** O LORD,
26:15 O LORD, you have increased the **n;**
51: 4 my people, and give heed to me, my **n;**
58: 2 as if they were a **n** that practiced righteousness
60:12 **n** and kingdom that will not serve you shall perish;
60:22 and the smallest one a mighty **n;**
65: 1 here I am," to a **n** that did not call on my name.
66: 8 Shall a **n** be delivered in one moment?
Jer 2:11 Has a **n** changed its gods,
5: 9 shall I not bring retribution on a **n** such as this?
5:15 I am going to bring upon you a **n** from far away,
5:15 It is an enduring **n,** it is an ancient **n,**
5:15 a **n** whose language you do not know,
5:29 shall I not bring retribution on a **n** such as this?
6:22 the land of the north, a great **n** is stirring from
7:28 This is the **n** that did not obey the voice of
9: 9 shall I not bring retribution on a **n** such as this?
12:17 But if any **n** will not listen,
18: 7 At one moment I may declare concerning a **n** or
18: 8 if that **n,** concerning which I have spoken, turns
18: 9 at another moment I may declare concerning a **n**
25:12 I will punish the king of Babylon and that **n,**
25:32 See, disaster is spreading from **n** to **n,**
27: 8 But if any **n** or kingdom will not serve this king,
27: 8 then I will punish that **n** with the sword,
27:11 But any **n** that will bring its neck under the yoke
27:13 the LORD has spoken concerning any **n** that will
31:36 of Israel would cease to be a **n** before me forever.
33:24 that they no longer regard them as a **n?**
48: 2 "Come, let us cut her off from being a **n!**"
49:31 Rise up, advance against a **n** at ease,
49:36 to all these winds, and there shall be no **n** to which
50: 3 For out of the north a **n** has come up against her;
50:41 a mighty **n** and many kings are stirring from
La 4:17 we were watching eagerly for a **n** that could
Eze 2: 3 to a **n** of rebels who have rebelled against me;
36:13 and you bereave your **n** of children,"
36:14 and no longer bereave your **n** of children, says
36:15 and no longer shall you cause your **n** to stumble,
37:22 I will make them one **n** in the land,
Da 3:29 Therefore I make a decree: Any people, **n,**
8:22 four kingdoms shall arise from his **n,**
Joel 1: 6 For a **n** has invaded my land,
3: 8 to a **n** far away; for the LORD has spoken.
Am 6:14 Indeed, I am raising up against you a **n,**
Mic 4: 3 **n** shall not lift up sword against **n,**
4: 7 and those who were cast off, a strong **n;**
Hab 1: 6 that fierce and impetuous **n,**
Zep 2: 1 Gather together, gather, O shameless **n,**
2: 5 of the seacoast, you **n** of the Cherethites!
2: 9 and the survivors of my **n** shall possess them.
Hag 2:14 and with this **n** before me, says the LORD;
Mal 3: 9 for you are robbing me—the whole **n** of you! B
Mt 24: 7 For **n** will rise against **n,**
Mk 13: 8 For **n** will rise against **n,**
Lk 21:10 Then he said to them, "**N** will rise against **n,**
23: 2 saying, "We found this man perverting our **n,**
Jn 11:48 and destroy both our holy place and our **n.**"
11:50 the people than to have the whole **n** destroyed." B
11:51 that Jesus was about to die for the **n,**
11:52 and not for the **n** only,
18:35 Your own **n** and the chief priests have handed you
Ac 2: 5 from every **n** under heaven living in Jerusalem. A
7: 7 'But I will judge the **n** that they serve,' said God,
10:22 who is well spoken of by the whole Jewish **n,**

Ac 10:35 but in every **n** anyone who fears him A
24:10 for many years you have been a judge over this **n.**
24:17 after some years I came to bring alms to my **n** and
28:19 though I had no charge to bring against my **n.**
Ro 10:19 "I will make you jealous of those who are not a **n;**
10:19 with a foolish **n** I will make you angry."
1Pe 2: 9 a royal priesthood, a holy **n,** God's own people,
Rev 5: 9 from every tribe and language and people and **n;**
7: 9 from every **n,** from all tribes and peoples A
13: 7 over every tribe and people and language and **n,**
14: 6 to every **n** and tribe and language and people. A
Tob 13: 6 and show his power and majesty to a **n** of sinners:
Jdt 5:21 But if they are not a guilty **n,**
8:20 that he will not disdain us or any of our **n.**
9:14 Let your whole **n** and every tribe know B
11:10 Indeed our **n** cannot be punished,
13:20 when our **n** was brought low,
14: 7 In every **n** those who hear your name will A
15: 9 you are the great pride of our **n!**
AdE 3: 8 a certain **n** scattered among the other nations
3: 8 different from those of every other **n,**
3:11 and do whatever you want with that **n.**"
4: 1 "An innocent **n** is being destroyed!"
8: 6 How can I be safe if my ancestral **n** is destroyed?"
10: 3 as to make him beloved to his whole **n.** B
10: 9 And my **n,** this is Israel, who cried out to God
11: 7 At their roaring every **n** prepared for war, A
11: 7 to fight against the righteous **n.**
11: 9 And the whole righteous **n** was troubled;
13: 4 to those of every **n** and continually disregard A
13: 5 stands constantly in opposition to every **n,** A
16:11 so fully the goodwill that we have for every **n** A
16:13 together with their whole **n.** B
Wis 10:15 and blameless race wisdom delivered from a **n**
17: 2 that they held the holy **n** in their power,
19: 8 by your hand passed through as one **n,**
Sir 10: 8 Sovereignty passes from **n** to **n** on account
16: 6 and in a disobedient **n** wrath blazes up.
16: 9 He showed no pity on the doomed **n,**
17:17 He appointed a ruler for every **n,** A
24: 6 and over every people and **n** I have held sway.
28:14 and scattered them from **n** to **n;**
46: 6 He overwhelmed that **n** in battle,
49: 5 and their glory to a foreign **n,**
Bar 2: 5 because our **n** sinned against the Lord our God,
4:15 For he brought a distant **n** against them,
4:15 a **n** ruthless and of a strange language,
Aza 1:14 we, O Lord, have become fewer than any other **n,**
1Mc 2:10 What **n** has not inherited her palaces and has
3:59 to die in battle than to see the misfortunes of our **n**
6:58 and make peace with them and with all their **n.**
8:23 the Romans and with the **n** of the Jews at sea C
8:25 the **n** of the Jews shall act C
8:27 if war comes first to the **n** of the Jews, C
9:29 and to deal with those of our **n** who hate us.
10: 5 that we did to him and to his brothers and his **n.**"
10:20 to be the high priest of your **n;**
10:25 "King Demetrius to the **n** of the Jews, greetings. C
11:21 But certain renegades who hated their **n** went to
11:25 of his **n** kept making complaints against him,
11:30 to his brother Jonathan and to the **n** of the Jews, C
11:33 determined to do good to the **n** of the Jews, C
11:42 only will I do these things for you and your **n,**
11:42 but I will confer great honor on you and your **n,**
12: 3 and the Jewish **n** have sent us to renew
12: 6 the senate of the **n,** the priests,
13: 6 But I will avenge my **n** and the sanctuary
13:36 and to the elders and **n** of the Jews, greetings. C
14: 4 He sought the good of his **n;**
14: 6 He extended the borders of his **n,**
14:28 of the priests and the people and the rulers of the **n**
14:29 the enemies of their **n,** in order that their sanctuary
14:29 and they brought great glory to their **n.**
14:30 Jonathan rallied the **n,** became their high priest,
14:32 then Simon rose up and fought for his **n.**
14:32 the soldiers of his **n** and paid them wages.
14:35 and the glory that he had resolved to win for his **n,**
14:35 and loyalty that he had maintained toward his **n.**
15: 1 and ethnarch of the Jews, and to all the **n;**
15: 2 and ethnarch and to the **n** of the Jews, greetings. C
15: 9 we will bestow great honor on you and your **n** and
16: 3 and go out and fight for our **n,**
2Mc 5:19 But the Lord did not choose the **n** for the sake of
5:19 but the place for the sake of the **n.**
5:20 the **n** and afterward participated in its benefits;
6:31 only to the young but to the great body of his **n.**
7:37 appealing to God to show mercy soon to our **n** and
7:38 that has justly fallen on our whole **n.**" B
10: 8 ratified by vote, that the whole **n** of the Jews BC
11:25 that this **n** also should be free from disturbance,
11:27 To the **n** the king's letter was as follows:
14: 8 our whole **n** is now in no small misfortune. B
14: 9 and our hard-pressed **n** with the gracious kindness
14:34 and called upon the constant Defender of our **n,**
1Es 1:32 be done throughout the whole **n** of Israel. B
1:34 The men of the **n** took Jeconiah son of Josiah,
1:36 the **n** one hundred talents of silver and one talent
5: 9 The number of those of the **n** and their leaders:
6:33 and **n** that shall stretch out their hands to hinder
8:10 I have given orders that those of the Jewish **n** and
8:14 together with what is given by the **n** for the temple
3Mc 1:11 members of their own **n** were allowed to enter,
2:33 considering them to be enemies of the Jewish **n,**
3: 2 against the Jewish **n** by some who conspired
3: 6 to their **n,** which was common talk among all;
5: 5 whole **n** would experience its final destruction. B
6: 4 manifesting the light of your mercy on the **n**

3Mc 6: 9 reveal yourself quickly to those of the **n**
6:13 who have power to save the **n** of Jacob.
7:10 of the Jewish **n** who had willfully transgressed
2Es 2: 8 O wicked **n,** remember what I did to Sodom
3: 8 And every **n** walked after its own will; A
3:32 Or has another **n** known you besides Israel?
3:35 Or what **n** has kept your commandments so well?
15:15 and **n** shall rise up to fight against **n,**
4Mc 1:11 the cause of the downfall of tyranny over their **n.**
3: 7 with the soldiers of his **n** had killed many of them.
4: 1 to injure Onias in the eyes of the **n,**
4:18 king appointed him high priest and ruler of the **n.**
4:26 to compel everyone in the **n** to eat defiling foods
9:24 of our ancestors may become merciful to our **n**
12:17 the God of our ancestors to be merciful to our **n;**
15:29 of the **n,** vindicator of the law and champion
16:16 to which you are called to bear witness for the **n.**
16:20 to sacrifice his son Isaac, the ancestor of our **n;**
17: 8 as a reminder to the people of our **n:**
17:10 They vindicated their **n,** looking to God
17:20 of them our enemies did not rule over our **n,**
17:21 as it were, a ransom for the sin of our **n.**
18: 4 Because of them the **n** gained peace,

NATION'S (1) [NATION]

4Mc 4:19 the **n** way of life and altered its form

NATIONAL (1) [NATION]

4Mc 8: 7 the ancestral tradition of your **n** life.

NATIONALITIES (1) [NATION]

2Mc 12:27 with multitudes of people of all **n.**

NATIONS‡ (582) [NATION]

A. ALL ... NATIONS (118)
B. OTHER NATIONS (11)

Ge 10: 5 by their families, in their **n.**
10:20 their languages, their lands, and their **n.**
10:31 their languages, their lands, and their **n.**
10:32 according to their genealogies, in their **n;**
10:32 from these the **n** spread abroad on the earth after
17: 4 You shall be the ancestor of a multitude of **n.**
17: 5 I have made you the ancestor of a multitude of **n.**
17: 6 and I will make **n** of you,
17:16 I will bless her, and she shall give rise to **n;**
18:18 and all the **n** of the earth shall be blessed in him? A
22:18 all the **n** of the earth gain blessing for A
25:23 the LORD said to her, "Two **n** are in your womb,
26: 4 and all the **n** of the earth shall gain blessing A
27:29 Let peoples serve you, and **n** bow down to you.
35:11 a nation and a company of **n** shall come from you,
48:19 and his offspring shall become a multitude of **n.**"
Ex 34:24 For I will cast out **n** before you,
Lev 18:24 for by all these practices the **n** I am casting out
25:44 from the **n** around you that you may acquire male
26:33 And you I will scatter among the **n,**
26:38 You shall perish among the **n,**
26:45 of Egypt in the sight of the **n,** to be their God:
Nu 14:15 then the **n** who have heard about you will say,
23: 9 and not reckoning itself among the **n!**
24: 8 the **n** that are his foes and break their bones.
24:20 "First among the **n** was Amalek,
Dt 4:27 only a few of you will be left among the **n** where
4:38 before you **n** greater and mightier than yourselves,
7: 1 and he clears away many **n** before you—
7: 1 seven **n** mightier and more numerous than you—
7:17 "These **n** are more numerous than I;
7:22 The LORD your God will clear away these **n**
8:20 the **n** that the LORD is destroying before you,
9: 1 in and dispossess **n** larger and mightier than you,
9: 4 of these **n** that the LORD is dispossessing them
9: 5 but because of the wickedness of these **n**
11:23 the LORD will drive out all these **n** before you, A
11:23 and you will dispossess **n** larger
12: 2 the places where the **n** whom you are about
12:29 before you the **n** whom you are about to enter
12:30 saying, "How did these **n** worship their gods?
15: 6 you will lend to many **n,** but you will not borrow;
15: 6 you will rule over many **n,**
17:14 like all the **n** that are around me," A
18: 9 to imitate the abhorrent practices of those **n.**
18:14 Although these **n** that you are about
19: 1 the LORD your God has cut off the **n** whose land
20:15 which are not towns of the **n** here.
26:19 above all **n** that he has made, in praise and in A
28: 1 above all the **n** of the earth; A
28:12 You will lend to many **n,** but you will not borrow.
28:65 Among those **n** you shall find no ease,
29:16 the midst of the **n** through which you passed.
29:18 the LORD our God to serve the gods of those **n.**
29:24 they and indeed all the **n** will wonder, A
30: 1 among all the **n** where the LORD your God has A
31: 3 He will destroy these **n** before you,
32: 8 When the Most High apportioned the **n,**
Jos 23: 3 that the LORD your God has done to all these **n** A
23: 4 an inheritance for your tribes those **n** that remain,
23: 4 along with all the **n** that I have already cut off, A
23: 7 that you may not be mixed with these **n** left here
23: 9 before you great and strong **n;**
23:12 join the survivors of these **n** left here among you,
23:13 not continue to drive out these **n** before you;
Jdg 2:21 I will no longer drive out before them any of the **n**
2:23 the LORD had left those **n,**
3: 1 the **n** that the LORD left to test all those

1Sa 8: 5 then, a king to govern us, like other **n**." B
8:20 so that we also may be like other **n**, B
2Sa 7:23 by driving out before his people **n** and their gods?
8:11 that he dedicated from all the **n** he subdued, A
22:44 you kept me as the head of the **n**;
22:50 For this I will extol you, O LORD, among the **n**,
1Ki 4:31 his fame spread throughout all the surrounding **n**.
4:34 People came from all the **n** to hear the wisdom A
11: 2 from the **n** concerning which the LORD had said
14:24 They committed all the abominations of the **n** that
2Ki 16: 3 of the **n** whom the LORD drove out before
17: 8 the customs of the **n** whom the LORD drove out
17:11 **n** did whom the LORD carried away before them.
17:15 they followed the **n** that were around them,
17:26 "The **n** that you have carried away and placed in
17:33 after the manner of the **n** from
17:41 So these **n** worshiped the LORD,
18:33 of the **n** ever delivered its land out of the hand of
19:12 Have the gods of the **n** delivered them,
19:12 the **n** that my predecessors destroyed, Gozan,
19:17 of Assyria have laid waste the **n** and their lands,
21: 2 the **n** that the LORD drove out before the people
21: 9 the **n** had done that the LORD destroyed before
1Ch 14:17 and the LORD brought the fear of him on all **n**. A
16:24 Declare his glory among the **n**,
16:31 and let them say among the **n**,
16:35 and gather and rescue us from among the **n**,
17:21 for great and terrible things, in driving out **n**
18:11 and gold that he had carried off from all the **n**, A
2Ch 20: 6 Do you not rule over all the kingdoms of the **n**?
28: 3 of the **n** whom the LORD drove out before
32:13 Were the gods of the **n** of those lands at all able
32:14 Who among all the gods of those **n**
32:17 of the **n** in other lands did not rescue their people
32:23 so that he was exalted in the sight of all **n** from A
33: 2 of the **n** whom the LORD drove out before
33: 9 the **n** whom the LORD had destroyed before
36:14 following all the abominations of the **n**;
Ezr 4:10 and the rest of the **n** whom the great
6:21 from the pollutions of the **n** of the land to worship
Ne 5: 8 Jewish kindred who had been sold to other **n**; B
5: 9 to prevent the taunts of the **n** our enemies?
5:17 besides those who came to us from the **n**
6: 6 In it was written, "It is reported among the **n**—
6:16 all the **n** around us were afraid and fell greatly A
13:26 Among the many **n** there was no king like him,
Job 12:23 He makes **n** great, then destroys them;
12:23 he enlarges **n**, then leads them away.
Ps 2: 1 Why do the **n** conspire, and the peoples plot
2: 8 Ask of me, and I will make the **n** your heritage,
9: 5 You have rebuked the **n**, you have destroyed
9:15 The **n** have sunk in the pit that they made;
9:17 all the **n** that forget God. A
9:19 let the **n** be judged before you.
9:20 let the **n** know that they are only human.
10:16 the **n** shall perish from his land.
18:43 you made me head of the **n**;
18:49 For this I will extol you, O LORD, among the **n**,
22:27 all the families of the **n** shall worship before him.
22:28 and he rules over the **n**.
33:10 LORD brings the counsel of the **n** to nothing;
44: 2 you with your own hand drove out the **n**,
44:11 and have scattered us among the **n**.
44:14 You have made us a byword among the **n**,
46: 6 The **n** are in an uproar, the kingdoms totter;
46:10 I am exalted among the **n**,
47: 3 peoples under us, and **n** under our feet.
47: 8 God is king over the **n**;
57: 9 I will sing praises to you among the **n**.
59: 5 Awake to punish all the **n**; A
59: 8 you hold all the **n** in derision. A
66: 7 whose eyes keep watch on the **n**—
67: 2 your saving power among all **n**. A
67: 4 Let the **n** be glad and sing for joy,
67: 4 the peoples with equity and guide the **n**
72:11 down before him, all **n** give him service. A
72:17 May all **n** be blessed in him; A
78:55 He drove out **n** before them;
79: 1 the **n** have come into your inheritance;
79: 6 Pour out your anger on the **n** that do
79:10 Why should the **n** say, "Where is their God?
79:10 of your servants be known among the **n**
80: 8 you drove out the **n** and planted it.
82: 8 for all the **n** belong to you! A
86: 9 All the **n** you have made shall come and bow A
94:10 He who disciplines the **n**,
96: 3 Declare his glory among the **n**,
96:10 Say among the **n**, "The LORD is king!
98: 2 in the sight of the **n**.
102:15 The **n** will fear the name of the LORD,
105:44 He gave them the lands of the **n**,
106:27 would disperse their descendants among the **n**,
106:35 but they mingled with the **n** and learned to do
106:41 he gave them into the hand of the **n**,
106:47 and gather us from among the **n**,
108: 3 and I will sing praises to you among the **n**.
110: 6 He will execute judgment among the **n**,
111: 6 in giving them the heritage of the **n**.
113: 4 The LORD is high above all **n**, A
115: 2 Why should the **n** say, "Where is their God?"
117: 1 Praise the LORD, all you **n**! A
118:10 All **n** surrounded me; A
126: 2 then it was said among the **n**,
135:10 He struck down many **n** and killed mighty kings—
135:15 The idols of the **n** are silver and gold,
149: 7 to execute vengeance on the **n** and punishment on
Pr 24:24 will be cursed by peoples, abhorred by **n**;

Isa 2: 2 all the **n** shall stream to it. A
2: 4 He shall judge between the **n**,
9: 1 the land beyond the Jordan, Galilee of the **n**.
10: 7 and to cut off **n** not a few.
11:10 the **n** shall inquire of him,
11:12 He will raise a signal for the **n**,
12: 4 make known his deeds among the **n**;
13: 4 an uproar of kingdoms, of **n** gathering together!
14: 2 the **n** will take them and bring them to their place,
14: 2 and the house of Israel will possess the **n** as male
14: 6 ruled the **n** in anger with unrelenting persecution.
14: 9 from their thrones all who were kings of the **n**.
14:12 you who laid the **n** low!
14:18 All the kings of the **n** lie in glory,
14:26 the hand that is stretched out over all the **n**. A
16: 8 the lords of the **n**, reached to Jazer and strayed to
17:12 Ah, the roar of **n**, they roar like the roaring of
17:13 The **n** roar like the roaring of many waters,
23: 3 you were the merchant of the **n**.
24:13 For thus it shall be on the earth and among the **n**,
25: 3 cities of ruthless **n** will fear you.
25: 7 the sheet that is spread over all **n**; A
29: 7 the multitude of all the **n** that fight against Ariel, A
29: 8 so shall the multitude of all the **n** be that fight A
30:28 to sift the **n** with the sieve of destruction,
33: 3 before your majesty, **n** scattered.
34: 1 Draw near, O **n**, to hear; O peoples, give heed!
34: 2 For the LORD is enraged against all the **n**, A
36:18 the gods of the **n** saved their land out of the hand
37:12 Have the gods of the **n** delivered them,
37:12 the **n** that my predecessors destroyed, Gozan,
37:18 the kings of Assyria have laid waste all the **n** A
40:15 Even the **n** are like a drop from a bucket,
40:17 All the **n** are as nothing before him; A
41: 2 He delivers up **n** to him, and tramples kings
42: 1 he will bring forth justice to the **n**.
42: 6 as a covenant to the people, a light to the **n**,
43: 4 **n** in exchange for your life.
43: 9 Let all the **n** gather together, A
45: 1 subdue **n** before him and strip kings of their robes,
45:20 draw near, you survivors of the **n**!
49: 6 I will give you as a light to the **n**,
49: 7 to one deeply despised, abhorred by the **n**,
49:22 I will soon lift up my hand to the **n**,
52:10 before the eyes of all the **n**; A
52:15 so he shall startle many **n**;
54: 3 and your descendants will possess the **n**
55: 5 See, you shall call **n** that you do not know,
55: 5 and **n** that do not know you shall run to you,
60: 3 **N** shall come to your light,
60: 5 the wealth of the **n** shall come to you.
60:11 so that **n** shall bring you their wealth,
60:12 those **n** shall be utterly laid waste.
60:16 You shall suck the milk of **n**,
61: 6 you shall enjoy the wealth of the **n**,
61: 9 Their descendants shall be known among the **n**,
61:11 and praise to spring up before all the **n**. A
62: 2 The **n** shall see your vindication,
64: 2 so that the **n** might tremble at your presence!
66:12 the wealth of the **n** like an overflowing stream;
66:18 and I am coming to gather all **n** and tongues; A
66:19 From them I will send survivors to the **n**,
66:19 and they shall declare my glory among the **n**.
66:20 They shall bring all your kindred from all the **n** A
Jer 1: 5 I appointed you a prophet to the **n**."
1:10 today I appoint you over **n** and over kingdoms,
3:17 and all **n** shall gather to it, A
3:19 the most beautiful heritage of all the **n**. A
4: 2 and in uprightness, then **n** shall be blessed by him,
4: 7 a destroyer of **n** has set out;
4:16 Tell the **n**, "Here they are!"
6:18 Therefore hear, O **n**, and know, O congregation,
9:16 I will scatter them among **n** that neither they
9:26 For all these **n** are uncircumcised, A
10: 2 Do not learn the way of the **n**,
10: 2 for the **n** are dismayed at them.
10: 7 Who would not fear you, O King of the **n**?
10: 7 of the **n** and in all their kingdoms there is no one
10:10 and the **n** cannot endure his indignation.
10:25 on the **n** that do not know you, and on the peoples
14:22 Can any idols of the **n** bring rain?
16:19 to you shall the **n** come from the ends of the earth
18:13 Ask among the **n**: Who has heard the like of this?
22: 8 And many **n** will pass by this city,
25: 9 and against all these **n** around; A
25:11 and these **n** shall serve the king
25:13 which Jeremiah prophesied against all the **n**. A
25:14 For many **n** and great kings shall make slaves
25:15 and make all the **n** to whom I send you drink it. A
25:17 all the **n** to whom the LORD sent me drink it: A
25:31 for the LORD has an indictment against the **n**;
26: 6 and I will make this city a curse for all the **n** of A
27: 7 All the **n** shall serve him and his son and A
27: 7 of his own land comes; then many **n**
28:11 from the neck of all the **n** within two years." A
28:14 have put an iron yoke on the neck of all these **n** A
29:14 from all the **n** and all the places where I have A
29:18 among all the **n** where I have driven them, A
30:11 an end of all the **n** among which I scattered you, A
31: 7 and raise shouts for the chief of the **n**;
31:10 Hear the word of the LORD, O **n**,
33: 9 glory before all the **n** of the earth who shall hear A
36: 2 to you against Israel and Judah and all the **n**, A
43: 5 from all the **n** to which they had been driven— A
44: 8 object of cursing and ridicule among all the **n** A
46: 1 to the prophet Jeremiah concerning the **n**.
46:12 The **n** have heard of your shame,

Jer 46:28 of all the **n** among which I have banished you, A
49:14 and a messenger has been sent among the **n**:
49:15 For I will make you least among the **n**,
50: 2 among the **n** and proclaim, set up a banner
50: 9 a company of great **n** from the land of the north;
50:12 Lo, she shall be the last of the **n**, a wilderness,
50:23 How Babylon has become a horror among the **n**!
50:46 and her cry shall be heard among the **n**.
51: 7 the **n** drank of her wine, and so the **n** went mad.
51:20 with you I smash **n**; with you I destroy kingdoms;
51:27 blow the trumpet among the **n**;
51:27 prepare the **n** for war against her,
51:28 Prepare the **n** for war against her,
51:41 an object of horror among the **n**!
51:44 The **n** shall no longer stream to him;
51:58 and the **n** weary themselves only for fire.
La 1: 1 she that was great among the **n**!
1: 3 she lives now among the **n**,
1:10 she has even seen the **n** invade her sanctuary,
2: 9 her king and princes are among the **n**;
4:15 it was said among the **n**,
4:20 "Under his shadow we shall live among the **n**."
Eze 4:13 unclean, among the **n** to which I will drive them."
5: 5 I have set her in the center of the **n**,
5: 6 becoming more wicked than the **n** and
5: 7 Because you are more turbulent than the **n**
5: 7 to the ordinances of the **n** that are all around you;
5: 8 among you in the sight of the **n**.
5:14 an object of mocking among the **n** around you,
5:15 a warning and a horror, to the **n** around you,
6: 8 Some of you shall escape the sword among the **n**
6: 9 among the **n** where they are carried captive,
7:24 I will bring the worst of the **n** to take possession
11:12 to the ordinances of the **n** that are around you."
11:16 Though I removed them far away among the **n**,
12:15 the **n** and scatter them through the countries.
12:16 of all their abominations among the **n**
16:14 Your fame spread among the **n** on account
19: 4 The **n** sounded an alarm against him;
19: 8 The **n** set upon him from the provinces all around;
20: 9 that it should not be profaned in the sight of the **n**
20:14 that it should not be profaned in the sight of the **n**
20:22 that it should not be profaned in the sight of the **n**,
20:23 the **n** and disperse them through the countries,
20:32 the thought, "Let us be like the **n**,
20:41 among you in the sight of the **n**.
22: 4 I have made you a disgrace before the **n**,
22:15 I will scatter you among the **n** and disperse you
22:16 be profaned through you in the sight of the **n**;
23:30 because you played the whore with the **n**,
25: 7 and will hand you over as plunder to the **n**.
25: 8 The house of Judah is like all the other **n**, AB
25:10 be remembered no more among the **n**,
26: 3 I will hurl many **n** against you,
26: 5 It shall become plunder for the **n**,
28: 7 the most terrible of the **n**;
28:25 manifest my holiness in them in the sight of the **n**,
29:12 I will scatter the Egyptians among the **n**,
29:15 and never again exalt itself above the **n**;
29:15 so small that they will never again rule over the **n**.
30: 3 a time of doom for the **n**.
30:11 the most terrible of the **n**,
30:23 I will scatter the Egyptians among the **n**,
30:26 the **n** and disperse them throughout the countries.
31: 6 and in its shade all great **n** lived. A
31:11 I gave it into the hand of the prince of the **n**;
31:12 from the most terrible of the **n** have cut it down
31:16 I made the **n** quake at the sound of its fall,
31:17 those who lived in its shade among the **n**.
32: 2 You consider yourself a lion among the **n**,
32: 9 as I carry you captive among the **n**,
32:12 all of them most terrible among the **n**.
32:16 The women of the **n** shall chant it.
32:18 with Egypt and the daughters of majestic **n**,
34:28 They shall no more be plunder for the **n**,
34:29 and no longer suffer the insults of the **n**.
35:10 "These two **n** and these two countries shall
36: 3 you became the possession of the rest of the **n**,
36: 4 an object of derision to the rest of the **n** all around;
36: 5 in my hot jealousy against the rest of the **n**,
36: 6 because you have suffered the insults of the **n**;
36: 7 I swear that the **n** that are all
36:15 of the **n**, no longer shall you bear the disgrace of
36:19 I scattered them among the **n**,
36:20 But when they came to the **n**,
36:21 the house of Israel had profaned among the **n**
36:22 which you have profaned among the **n**
36:23 which has been profaned among the **n**,
36:23 and the **n** shall know that I am the LORD,
36:24 I will take you from the **n**,
36:30 the disgrace of famine among the **n**.
36:36 the **n** that are left all around you shall know that I,
37:21 of Israel from the **n** among which they have gone,
37:22 Never again shall they be two **n**,
37:28 the **n** shall know that I the LORD sanctify Israel,
38: 8 a land where people were gathered from many **n**
38: 8 its people were brought out from the **n** and
38:12 and the people who were gathered from the **n**,
38:16 so that the **n** may know me, when through you,
38:23 and make myself known in the eyes of many **n**.
39: 7 and the **n** shall know that I am the LORD,
39:21 I will display my glory among the **n**;
39:21 and all the **n** shall see my judgment that I A
39:23 And the **n** shall know that the house of Israel went
39:27 in the sight of many **n**.
39:28 because I sent them into exile among the **n**,
Da 3: 4 "You are commanded, O peoples, **n**,

Da 3: 7 and entire musical ensemble, all the peoples, **n**,
4: 1 King Nebuchadnezzar to all peoples, **n**,
5:19 of the greatness that he gave him, all peoples, **n**,
6:25 to all peoples and **n** of every language throughout
7:14 **n**, and languages should serve him.
12: 1 such as has never occurred since **n** first came
Hos 8: 8 now they are among the **n** as a useless vessel.
8:10 Though they bargain with the **n**,
9: 1 Do not exult as other **n** do; B
9:17 they shall become wanderers among the **n**.
10:10 and **n** shall be gathered against them
Joel 2:17 a mockery, a byword among the **n**.
2:19 I will no more make you a mockery among the **n**.
3: 2 I will gather all the **n** and bring them down to A
3: 2 because they have scattered them among the **n**.
3: 9 Proclaim this among the **n**:
3:11 Come quickly, all you **n** all around, A
3:12 Let the **n** rouse themselves,
3:12 for there I will sit to judge all the neighboring **n**. A
Am 6: 1 the notables of the first of the **n**,
9: 9 and shake the house of Israel among all the **n** A
9:12 and all the **n** who are called by my name, A
Ob 1: 1 and a messenger has been sent among the **n**:
1: 2 I will surely make you least among the **n**;
1:15 For the day of the LORD is near against all the **n**. A
1:16 all the **n** around you shall drink; A
Mic 4: 2 and many **n** shall come and say:
4: 3 and shall arbitrate between strong **n** far away;
4:11 Now many **n** are assembled against you, saying,
5: 8 And among the **n** the remnant of Jacob,
5:15 and wrath I will execute vengeance on the **n**
7:16 The **n** shall see and be ashamed of all their might;
Na 3: 4 who enslaves **n** through her debaucheries,
3: 5 and I will let **n** look on your nakedness
Hab 1: 5 Look at the **n**, and see!
1:17 and destroying **n** without mercy?
2: 5 They gather all **n** for themselves, A
2: 8 Because you have plundered many **n**,
2:13 and **n** weary themselves for nothing?
3: 6 he looked and made the **n** tremble.
3:12 the earth, in anger you trampled **n**.
Zep 2:11 all the coasts and islands of the **n**.
3: 6 I have cut off **n**; their battlements are in ruins;
3: 8 For my decision is to gather **n**,
Hag 2: 7 and I will shake all the **n**, A
2: 7 so that the treasure of all **n** shall come, A
2:22 the kingdoms of the **n**, and overthrow the chariots
Zec 1:15 I am extremely angry with the **n** that are at ease;
1:21 the horns of the **n** that lifted up their horns against
2: 8 of hosts (after his glory sent me) regarding the **n**
2:11 Many **n** shall join themselves to the LORD on
7:14 with a whirlwind among all the **n** that they had A
8:13 Just as you have been a cursing among the **n**,
8:22 Many peoples and strong **n** shall come to seek
8:23 from **n** of every language shall take hold of a Jew,
9:10 and he shall command peace to the **n**;
10: 9 Though I scattered them among the **n**,
12: 3 all the **n** of the earth shall come together against A
12: 9 day I will seek to destroy all the **n** that come A
14: 2 I will gather all the **n** against Jerusalem to battle, A
14: 3 the LORD will go forth and fight against those **n**
14:14 And the wealth of all the surrounding **n** shall A
14:16 of the **n** that have come against Jerusalem shall go
14:18 the plague that the LORD inflicts on the **n** that do
14:19 the punishment of all the **n** that do not go up A
Mal 1:11 among the **n**, and in every place incense is offered
1:11 for my name is great among the **n**,
1:14 and my name is reverenced among the **n**.
3:12 Then all **n** will count you happy, A
Mt 24: 9 you will be hated by all **n** because of my name. A
24:14 as a testimony to all the **n**; A
25:32 All the **n** will be gathered before him, A
28:19 Go therefore and make disciples of all **n**, A
Mk 11:17 be called a house of prayer for all the **n**'? A
13:10 the good news must first be proclaimed to all **n**. A
Lk 12:30 the **n** of the world that strive after all these things,
21:24 and be taken away as captives among all **n**; A
21:25 the earth distress among **n** confused by the roaring
24:47 of sins is to be proclaimed in his name to all **n**, A
Ac 7:45 when they dispossessed the **n** that God drove out
13:19 he had destroyed seven **n** in the land of Canaan,
14:16 In past generations he allowed all the **n** A
17:26 From one ancestor he made all **n** to inhabit A
Ro 4:17 "I have made you the father of many **n**")—
4:18 that he would become "the father of many **n**,"
Rev 2:26 I will give authority over the **n**;
10:11 about many peoples and **n** and languages
11: 2 leave that out, for it is given over to the **n**,
11: 9 and languages and **n** will gaze at their dead bodies
11:18 The **n** raged, but your wrath has come,
12: 5 who is to rule all the **n** with a rod of iron. A
14: 8 has made all **n** drink of the wine of the wrath A
15: 3 Just and true are your ways, King of the **n**!
15: 4 All **n** will come and worship before you, A
16:19 and the cities of the **n** fell.
17:15 are peoples and multitudes and **n** and languages.
18: 3 all the **n** have drunk of the wine of the wrath A
18:23 and all **n** were deceived by your sorcery. A
19:15 to strike down the **n**, and he will rule them with
20: 3 so that he would deceive the **n** no more,
20: 8 to deceive the **n** at the four corners of the earth,
21:24 The **n** will walk by its light,
21:26 into it the glory and the honor of the **n**.
22: 2 the leaves of the tree are for the healing of the **n**.
Tob 3: 4 all the **n** among whom you have dispersed us. A
4:19 For none of the **n** has understanding,
13: 3 Acknowledge him before the **n**,
Tob 13: 5 all the **n** among whom you have been scattered. A
13:11 many **n** will come to you from far away,
14: 6 the **n** in the whole world will all be converted
Jdt 1: 6 Thus, many **n** joined the forces of the Chaldeans.
1: 8 and those among the **n** of Carmel and Gilead,
3: 8 that all **n** should worship Nebuchadnezzar A
4: 1 the king of the Assyrians, had done to the **n**,
16:17 Woe to the **n** that rise up against my people!
AdE 1: 3 for his Friends and other persons of various **n**,
1: 5 for the people of various **n** who lived in the city.
1:11 to all the governors and the people of various **n**,
3: 8 a certain nation scattered among the other **n** B
3:14 all the **n** were ordered to be prepared for that A
4:11 'All **n** of the empire know that if any man A
10: 8 The **n** are those that gathered to destroy the name
10: 9 wonders that have never happened among the **n**.
10:10 one for the people of God and one for all the **n**, A
10:11 of decision before God and among all the **n**. A
13: 2 "Having become ruler of many **n** and master of
13: 4 among all the **n** in the world there is scattered A
14: 5 O Lord, took Israel out of all the **n**, A
14:10 the mouths of the **n** for the praise of vain idols,
Wis 3: 8 They will govern **n** and rule over peoples,
6: 2 that rule over multitudes, and boast of many **n**.
8:14 and **n** will be subject to me;
10: 5 **n** in wicked agreement had been put to confusion,
12:12 Who will accuse you for the destruction of **n**
Sir 4:15 Those who obey her will judge the **n**,
10:15 The Lord plucks up the roots of the **n**,
10:16 The Lord lays waste the lands of the **n**,
29:18 and they have wandered among foreign **n**.
35:23 and repays vengeance on the **n**;
36: 2 and put all the **n** in fear of you. A
36: 3 against foreign **n** and let them see your might.
39:10 **N** will speak of his wisdom,
39:23 But his wrath drives out the **n**,
44:19 Abraham was the great father of a multitude of **n**,
44:21 that the **n** would be blessed through his offspring;
46: 6 so that the **n** might know his armament,
47:17 and the answers you gave astounded the **n**.
50:25 Two **n** my soul detests, and the third is not even
Bar 2:13 among the **n** where you have scattered us.
2:29 surely turn into a small number among the **n**,
3:16 Where are the rulers of the **n**,
4: 6 not for destruction that you were sold to the **n**,
LtJ 6:51 to all the **n** and kings that they are not gods A
6:67 they cannot show signs in the heavens for the **n**,
1Mc 1: 3 to the ends of the earth, and plundered many **n**.
1: 4 **n**, and princes, and they became tributary to him.
2:19 all the **n** that live under the rule of the king A
11:38 that he had recruited from the islands of the **n**.
12:53 All the **n** around them tried to destroy them, A
13: 6 for all the **n** have gathered together out of hatred A
2Mc 4:35 but many also of other **n**, B
6:14 the other **n** the Lord waits patiently to punish B
8: 9 Gentiles of all **n**, to wipe out the whole race A
10: 4 be handed over to blasphemous and barbarous **n**.
11: 3 as he did on the sacred places of the other **n**, B
1Es 1:49 of all the **n**, and polluted the temple of the Lord A
3Mc 3:15 that we should not rule the **n** inhabiting Coelesyria
3:19 all **n** who hold their heads high in defiance A
3:20 since we treat all **n** with benevolence. A
6: 5 broke in pieces, showing your power to many **n**.
6:26 differed from all **n** in their goodwill toward us A
7: 4 of the ill-will that these people had toward all **n**. A
2Es 1:11 I destroyed all **n** before them, A
1:24 will turn to other **n** and will give them my name, B
2: 7 Let them be scattered among the **n**;
2:28 The **n** shall envy you, but they shall not be able
2:34 I say to you, O **n** that hear and understand,
3: 7 From him there sprang **n** and tribes,
3:12 they produced children and peoples and many **n**,
3:33 the **n** and have seen that they abound in wealth,
3:36 but **n** you will not find."
6:48 the **n** might declare your wondrous works.
6:56 for the other **n** that have descended from Adam, B
6:57 And now, O Lord, these **n**,
7:37 to the **n** that have been raised from the dead,
9: 3 intrigues of **n**, wavering of leaders,
13:33 "Then, when all the **n** hear his voice, A
13:33 all the **n** shall leave their own lands and A
13:37 will reprove the assembled **n**
13:41 that they would leave the multitude of the **n**
13:49 Therefore when he destroys the multitude of the **n**
15:29 The **n** of the dragons of Arabia shall come out

NATIVE (22) [NATIVES]

Ex 12:19 whether an alien or a **n** of the land.
12:48 he shall be regarded as a **n** of the land.
12:49 for the **n** and for the alien who resides among you.
Nu 9:14 for both the resident alien and the **n**.
15:13 Every **n** Israelite shall do these things in this way,
15:29 the **n** among the Israelites and the alien residing
15:30 whether a **n** or an alien, affronts the LORD,
Ru 2:11 and your **n** land and came to a people that you did
4:10 from his kindred and from the gate of his **n** place;
Jer 22:10 for he shall return no more to see his **n** land.
42:12 on you and restore you to your **n** soil.
Eze 23:15 picture of Babylonians whose **n** land was Chaldea.
Ac 2: 6 in the **n** language of each.
2: 8 each of us, in our own **n** language?
4:36 There was a Levite, a **n** of Cyprus, Joseph,
18: 2 a **n** of Pontus, who had recently come from Italy
18:24 a Jew named Apollos, a **n** of Alexandria.
Wis 16:23 be fed, even forgot its **n** power.
2Mc 7:27 she spoke in their **n** language as follows,
1Es 6:25 of hewn stone and one course of new **n** timber;
4Mc 1:11 and thus their **n** land was purified through them.
4:20 at the very citadel of our **n** land,

NATIVES (2) [NATIVE]

Ac 28: 2 The **n** showed us unusual kindness.
28: 4 the **n** saw the creature hanging from his hand,

NATIVITY (KJV) See BIRTH, NATIVE, ORIGIN

NATURAL‡ (9) [NATURE]

Nu 16:29 If these people die a **n** death, or if a **n** fate comes
Ro 1:26 Their women exchanged **n** intercourse
1:27 giving up **n** intercourse with women,
6:19 in human terms because of your **n** limitations.
11:21 For if God did not spare the **n** branches,
11:24 how much more will these **n** branches
2Mc 6:20 even for the **n** love of life.
4Mc 2: 8 to **n** ways and to lend without interest to the needy

NATURALLY‡ (2) [NATURE]

Nu 19:16 or who has died **n**, or a human bone, or a grave,
Wis 8:19 child I was **n** gifted, and a good soul fell to my lot;

NATURE‡ (23) [ILL-NATURED, NATURAL, NATURALLY, NATURES]

Jn 8:44 When he lies, he speaks according to his own **n**,
Ro 1:20 of the world his eternal power and divine **n**,
11:24 from what is by **n** a wild olive tree and grafted,
contrary to **n**, into a cultivated olive tree,
1Co 11:14 Does not **n** itself teach you that if
2Co 4:16 Even though our outer **n** is wasting away, our
inner **n** is being renewed day by day.
Gal 4: 8 you were enslaved to beings that by **n** are
Eph 2: 3 and we were by **n** children of wrath,
Jas 3: 6 sets on fire the cycle of **n**,
2Pe 1: 4 and may become participants of the divine **n**.
Wis 13: 1 of God were foolish by **n**;
19: 6 the whole creation in its **n** was fashioned anew,
19:18 as on a harp the notes vary the **n** of the rhythm,
19:20 and water forgot its fire-quenching **n**.
2Es 14:14 and divest yourself now of your weak **n**;
4Mc 1:20 of these is by **n** concerned with both body
5: 8 When **n** has granted it to us,
5: 9 and wrong to spurn the gifts of **n**.
5:25 that in the **n** of things the Creator of the world
13:27 But although **n** and companionship
15:13 O sacred **n** and affection of parental love,
15:25 **n**, family, parental love, and the rackings

NATURES (2) [NATURE]

AdE 16: 6 of their evil **n** beguile the sincere goodwill
Wis 7:20 the **n** of animals and the tempers of wild animals,

NAUGHT (2) [NO]

Isa 8:10 but it shall be brought to **n**;
40:23 who brings princes to **n**, and makes the rulers of

NAUGHTINESS, NAUGHTY (KJV) See BAD, EVIL, MISCHIEVOUS, SCHEMES, SCOUNDREL, WICKEDNESS

NAUM (KJV) See NAHUM

NAUSEA (2)

Sir 31:20 The distress of sleeplessness and of **n** and colic are
37:30 overeating brings sickness, and gluttony leads to **n**.

NAVE (17)

1Ki 6: 3 of the **n** of the house was twenty cubits wide,
6: 5 both the **n** and the inner sanctuary;
6:17 house, that is, the **n** in front of the inner sanctuary,
6:33 for the entrance to the **n** doorposts of olivewood,
7:50 and for the doors of the **n** of the temple, of gold.
2Ch 3: 4 the **n** of the house was twenty cubits long,
3: 5 The **n** he lined with cypress,
3:13 the cherubim stood on their feet, facing the **n**.
4:22 and the doors of the **n** of the temple were of gold.
Eze 41: 1 Then he brought me to the **n**,
41: 2 He measured the length of the **n**, forty cubits,
41: 4 and its width, twenty cubits, beyond the **n**.
41:15 The **n** of the temple and the inner room and
41:17 in the inner room and the **n** there was a pattern.
41:21 The doorposts of the **n** were square.
41:23 The **n** and the holy place had each a double door.
41:25 the **n** were carved cherubim and palm trees, such

NAVEL‡ (2)

SS 7: 2 Your **n** is a rounded bowl
Eze 16: 4 on the day you were born your **n** cord was not cut,

NAVES (KJV) See HUB

NAVIGATE (1)

2Es 7: 5 who wish to reach the sea, to look at it or to **n** it,

NAVY (KJV) See FLEET OF SHIPS, SHIPS

NAY (KJV) See NO

NAZARENES (1) [NAZARETH]

Ac 24: 5 and a ringleader of the sect of the N.

NAZARETH (29) [NAZARENES]

A. JESUS OF NAZARETH (15)

Mt 2:23 There he made his home in a town called N,
4:13 He left N and made his home in Capernaum by
21:11 "This is the prophet Jesus from N in Galilee."
26:71 "This man was with Jesus of N." A
Mk 1: 9 from N of Galilee and was baptized by John in
1:24 "What have you to do with us, Jesus of N? A
10:47 When he heard that it was Jesus of N, A
14:67 "You also were with Jesus, the man from N."
16: 6 are looking for Jesus of N, who was crucified. A
Lk 1:26 by God to a town in Galilee called N,
2: 4 also went from the town of N in Galilee to Judea,
2:39 they returned to Galilee, to their own town of N.
2:51 Then he went down with them and came to N,
4:16 When he came to N, where he had been brought
4:34 What have you to do with us, Jesus of N? A
18:37 They told him, "Jesus of N is passing by." A
24:19 They replied, "The things about Jesus of N, A
Jn 1:45 Jesus son of Joseph from N."
1:46 "Can anything good come out of N?"
18: 5 They answered, "Jesus of N." A
18: 7 And they said, "Jesus of N." A
19:19 It read, "Jesus of N, the King of the Jews." A
Ac 2:22 Jesus of N, a man attested to you by God A
3: 6 in the name of Jesus Christ of N,
4:10 in good health by the name of Jesus Christ of N,
6:14 this Jesus of N will destroy this place and A
10:38 God anointed Jesus of N with the Holy Spirit A
22: 8 'I am Jesus of N whom you are persecuting.' A
26: 9 do many things against the name of Jesus of N. A

NAZARITE (KJV) See NAZIRITE

NAZIRITE‡ (8) [NAZIRITES]

Nu 6: 2 or women make a special vow, the vow of a n,
6: 5 of their n vow no razor shall come upon the head;
6:21 the LORD must be in accordance with the n vow,
Jdg 13: 5 for the boy shall be a n to God from birth.
13: 7 be a n to God from birth to the day of his death.' "
16:17 I have been a n to God from my mother's womb.
1Sa 1:11 a male child, then I will set him before you as a n
1:22 I will offer him as a n for all time."

NAZIRITES (11) [NAZIRITE]

Nu 6: 4 as n they shall eat nothing that is produced by
6: 8 All their days as n they are holy to the LORD.
6:12 to the LORD for their days as n,
6:13 This is the law for the n when the time
6:18 Then the n shall shave the consecrated head at
6:19 and shall put them in the palms of the n,
6:20 After that the n may drink wine.
6:21 This is the law for the n who take a vow.
Am 2:11 to be prophets and some of your youths to be n.
2:12 But you made the n drink wine,
1Mc 3:49 up the n who had completed their days;

NAZOREAN‡ (1)

Mt 2:23 "He will be called a N."

NAZOREANS See Index to Footnotes

NEAH (1)

Jos 19:13 and going on to Rimmon it bends toward N;

NEAPOLIS (1)

Ac 16:11 to Samothrace, the following day to N,

NEAR‡ (318) [NEARBY, NEARER, NEAREST, NEARING, NEARLY, NEARSIGHTED]

Ge 18: 2 He looked up and saw three men standing n him.
18:23 Then Abraham came n and said,
19: 9 and came n the door to break it down.
19:20 Look, that city is n enough to flee to,
27:21 Then Isaac said to Jacob, "Come n,
27:26 his father Isaac said to him, "Come n and kiss me,
27:27 So he came n and kissed him;
33: 3 until he came n his brother.
33: 6 Then the maids drew n, they and their children,
33: 7 and her children drew n and bowed down;
33: 7 and finally Joseph and Rachel drew n,
35: 4 Jacob hid them under the oak that was n Shechem.
37:12 to pasture their father's flock n Shechem.
37:18 and before he came n to them,
38: 1 down from his brothers and settled n
45:10 and you shall be n me,
47:29 When the time of Israel's death drew n,
48:10 So Joseph brought them n him;
48:13 toward Israel's right, and brought them n him.
49:30 n Mamre, in the land of Canaan,
50:13 in the cave of the field at Machpelah, the field n
Ex 12:48 then he may draw n to celebrate it;
14:10 As Pharaoh drew n, the Israelites looked back,
14:20 one did not come n the other all night.
Ex 16: 9 the whole congregation of the Israelites, 'Draw n
19:15 do not go n a woman."
20:21 while Moses drew n to the thick darkness
24: 2 Moses alone shall come n the LORD; but the others shall not come n,
28: 1 Then bring n to you your brother Aaron,
28:43 they come n the altar to minister in the holy place;
30:20 or when they come n the altar to minister,
32:19 As soon as he came n the camp and saw the calf
34:30 and they were afraid to come n him.
34:32 Afterward all the Israelites came n,
Lev 9: 5 the whole congregation drew n and stood before
9: 7 "Draw n to the altar and sacrifice your sin offering
9: 8 Aaron drew n to the altar,
10: 3 those who are n me I will show myself holy,
16: 1 when they drew n before the LORD and died.
18: 6 None of you shall approach anyone n of kin
21:18 For no one who has a blemish shall draw n,
21:21 the priest who has a blemish shall come n to offer
21:21 he shall not come n to offer the food of his God.
21:23 But he shall not come n the curtain or approach
22: 3 throughout your generations comes n
Nu 1:51 any outsider who comes n shall be put to death.
3: 6 Bring the tribe of Levi n,
3:10 any outsider who comes n shall be put to death.
3:38 any outsider who came n was to be put to death.
4:19 not die when they come n to the most holy things:
5:16 Then the priest shall bring her n,
6: 6 to the LORD they shall not go n a corpse.
13:21 the wilderness of Zin to Rehob, n Lebo-hamath.
24:17 I behold him, but not n—
Dt 4: 7 For what other great nation has a god so n to it as
5:27 Go n, you yourself, and hear all that
13: 7 whether n you or far away from you,
15: 9 "The seventh year, the year of remission, is n,"
20: 3 Today you are drawing n to do battle
20:10 When you draw n to a town to fight against it,
21: 2 to measure the distances to the towns that are n
22: 2 If the owner does not reside n you or you do
30:14 No, the word is very n to you;
31:14 LORD said to Moses, "Your time to die is n;
Jos 3: 9 "Draw n and hear the words of
7: 2 which is n Beth-aven, east of Bethel,
7:14 tribe that the LORD takes shall come n by clans,
7:14 that the LORD takes shall come n by households,
7:14 the household that the LORD takes shall come n
7:16 and brought Israel n tribe by tribe,
7:17 He brought n the clans of Judah,
7:17 and he brought n the clan of the Zerahites,
7:18 And he brought n his household one by one,
8:11 and drew n before the city,
10:24 of the warriors who had gone with him, "Come n,
10:24 Then they came n and put their feet on their necks.
15:46 all that were n Ashdod, with their villages.
22:10 to the region n the Jordan that lies in the land
22:11 in the region n the Jordan,
Jdg 1:16 which lies in the Negeb n Arad.
3:19 at the sculptured stones n Gilgal,
4:11 as far away as Elon-bezaanannim, which is n
9:52 and came n to the entrance of the tower to burn it
18:22 in the houses n Micah's house were called out,
19:11 When they were n Jebus, the day was far spent,
19:14 and the sun went down on them n Gibeah,
20:23 of the LORD, "Shall we again draw n to battle
Ru 3:12 But now, though it is true that I am a n kinsman,
1Sa 7:10 the Philistines drew n to attack Israel;
10:20 Then Samuel brought all the tribes of Israel n,
10:21 He brought the tribe of Benjamin n by its families,
10:21 Finally he brought the family of the Matrites n
14:36 But the priest said, "Let us draw n to God here."
17:40 and he drew n to the Philistine.
17:41 The Philistine came on and drew n to David,
30:21 When David drew n to the people he saluted them.
2Sa 11:20 'Why did you go so n the city to fight?
11:21 Why did you go so n the wall?'
13:11 But when she brought them n him to eat,
13:23 which is n Ephraim, and Absalom invited all
15: 5 Whenever people came n to do obeisance to him,
18:25 He kept coming, and drew n.
19:37 n the graves of my father and my mother.
19:42 Because the king is n of kin to us.
20:17 He came n her; and the woman said,
1Ki 2: 1 When David's time to die drew n,
2:34 he was buried at his own house n the wilderness.
8:46 to the land of the enemy, far off or n;
8:59 be n to the LORD our God day and night,
9:26 which is n Eloth on the shore of the Red Sea,
18:21 Elijah then came n to all the people, and said,
18:36 the prophet Elijah came n and said, "O LORD,
21: 2 because it is n my house;
2Ki 2: 5 of prophets who were at Jericho drew n to Elisha,
16:12 Then the king drew n to the altar, went up on it,
1Ch 9:27 they would spend the night n the house of God;
2Ch 6:36 they are carried away captive to a land far or n;
21:16 of the Philistines and of the Arabs who are n
26:23 they buried him n his ancestors in the burial field
29:31 come n, bring sacrifices and thank offerings to
Ne 4:12 When the Jews who lived n them came,
Est 9:20 the provinces of King Ahasuerus, both n and far,
Job 17:12 'The light,' they say, 'is n to the darkness.'
33:22 Their souls draw n the Pit,
41:16 One is so n to another that no air can come
Ps 22:11 for trouble is n and there is no one to help.
32: 9 else it will not stay n you.
34:18 The LORD is n to the brokenhearted,
65: 4 Happy are those whom you choose and bring n
69:18 Draw n to me, redeem me,
Ps 73:28 But for me it is good to be n God;
75: 1 we give thanks; your name is n.
88: 3 and my life draws n to Sheol.
91: 7 but it will not come n you.
91:10 no scourge come n your tent.
107:18 and they drew n to the gates of death.
119:150 with evil purpose draw n;
119:151 Yet you are n, O LORD,
145:18 The LORD is n to all who call on him,
Pr 5: 8 and do not go n the door of her house;
7: 8 passing along the street n her corner,
10:14 but the babbling of a fool brings ruin n.
Ecc 5: 1 to draw n to listen is better than
12: 1 and the years draw n when you will say,
Isa 13: 6 Wail, for the day of the LORD is n;
18: 2 to a people feared n and far,
18: 7 from a people feared n and far,
26:17 and cries out in her pangs when she is n her time,
29:13 Because these people draw n with their mouths
33:13 and you who are n, acknowledge my might.
34: 1 Draw n, O nations, to hear; O peoples, give heed!
41: 1 let us together draw n for judgment.
41: 5 they have drawn n and come.
45:20 Assemble yourselves and come together, draw n,
46:13 I bring n my deliverance, it is not far off,
48:16 Draw n to me, hear this!
50: 8 he who vindicates me is n.
51: 5 I will bring n my deliverance swiftly,
54:14 and from terror, for it shall not come n you.
55: 6 call upon him while he is n;
57:19 Peace, peace, to the far and the n,
58: 2 they delight to draw n to God.
65: 5 do not come n me, for I am too holy for you."
Jer 12: 2 you are n in their mouths yet far from their hearts.
23:23 Am I a God n by, says the LORD,
25:26 far and n, one after another,
30:21 I will bring him n, and he shall approach me,
35: 4 which was n the chamber of the officials,
41:17 and stopped at Geruth Chimham n Bethlehem,
48:16 The calamity of Moab is n at hand
48:24 and all the towns of the land of Moab, far and n.
La 3:57 You came n when I called on you;
4:18 in our streets; our end drew n;
Eze 7: 7 The time has come, the day is n—
7:12 The time has come, the day draws n;
9: 1 saying, "Draw n, you executioners of the city,
11: 3 'The time is not n to build houses;
12:23 But say to them, The days are n,
22: 4 you have brought your day n,
22: 5 Those who are n and those who are far
30: 3 For a day is n, the day of the LORD is n;
40:46 among the descendants of Levi may come n to
42:14 they shall put on other garments before they go n
43:19 who draw n to me to minister to me,
44:13 They shall not come n to me, to serve me as priest,
44:13 nor come n any of my sacred offerings,
44:15 shall come n to me to minister to me;
44:25 not defile themselves by going n to a dead person;
Da 6:20 When he came n the den where Daniel was,
8:17 So he came n where I stood;
9: 7 those who are n and those who are far away,
Joel 1:15 For the day of the LORD is n,
2: 1 for the day of the LORD is coming, it is n—
3: 9 Let all the soldiers draw n, let them come up.
3:14 day of the LORD is n in the valley of decision.
Am 6: 3 and bring n a reign of violence?
Ob 1:15 the day of the LORD is n against all the nations.
Mic 1: 4 like wax n the fire, like waters poured down a
Zep 1:14 The great day of the LORD is n,
1:14 of the LORD is near, n and hastening fast;
3: 2 it has not drawn n to its God.
Mal 3: 5 Then I will draw n to you for judgment;
Mt 3: 2 "Repent, for the kingdom of heaven has come n."
4:17 "Repent, for the kingdom of heaven has come n."
10: 7 'The kingdom of heaven has come n.'
21: 1 When they had come n Jerusalem
24:32 you know that summer is n.
24:33 you see all these things, you know that he is n,
26:18 and say to him, 'The Teacher says, My time is n;
Mk 1:15 and the kingdom of God has come n;
11: 1 at Bethphage and Bethany, n the Mount of Olives,
11: 4 They went away and found a colt tied n a door,
12:28 of the scribes came n and heard them disputing
13:28 you know that summer is n.
13:29 you know that he is n, at the very gates.
14:47 of those who stood n drew his sword and struck
Lk 5:17 Pharisees and teachers of the law were sitting n
9:18 with only the disciples n him, he asked them,
9:51 When the days drew n for him to be taken up,
10: 9 'The kingdom of God has come n to you.'
10:11 Yet know this: the kingdom of God has come n.'
10:33 But a Samaritan while traveling came n him;
12:33 where no thief comes n and no moth destroys.
12:38 or n dawn, and finds them so,
15: 1 the tax collectors and sinners were coming n
18:40 and when he came n, he asked him,
19:11 because he was n Jerusalem,
19:29 When he had come n Bethphage and Bethany,
19:41 As he came n and saw the city, he wept over it,
21: 8 and, 'The time is n!'
21:20 then know that its desolation has come n.
21:28 because your redemption is drawing n."
21:30 for yourselves and know that summer is already n.
21:31 you know that the kingdom of God is n.
22: 1 which is called the Passover, was n.
24:15 Jesus himself came n and went with them,
24:28 they came n the village to which they were going,

Jn 2:13 The Passover of the Jews was n,
3:23 John also was baptizing at Aenon n Salim
4: 5 n the plot of ground that Jacob had given
6: 4 Now the Passover, the festival of the Jews, was n.
6:19 they saw Jesus walking on the sea and coming n
6:23 Then some boats from Tiberias came n the place
7: 2 Now the Jewish festival of Booths was n.
9:40 of the Pharisees n him heard this and said to him,
11:18 Now Bethany was n Jerusalem,
11:54 to a town called Ephraim in the region n
11:55 Now the Passover of the Jews was n,
19:20 the place where Jesus was crucified was n the city;
19:25 standing n the cross of Jesus were his mother,
Ac 1:12 the mount called Olivet, which is n Jerusalem,
7:17 the time drew n for the fulfillment of the promise
9:38 Since Lydda was n Joppa, the disciples,
23: 2 the high priest Ananias ordered those standing n
23:11 That night the Lord stood n him and said,
27: 8 to a place called Fair Havens, n the city of Lasea.
Ro 10: 8 "The word is n you, on your lips and in your heart"
13:12 the night is far gone, the day is n.
2Co 11:23 with countless floggings, and often n death.
Eph 2:13 in Christ Jesus you who once were far off have been brought n
2:17 and peace to those who were n;
Php 4: 5 be known to everyone. The Lord is n.
Jas 4: 8 Draw n to God, and he will draw n to you.
5: 8 for the coming of the Lord is n.
1Pe 4: 7 The end of all things is n;
Rev 1: 3 what is written in it; for the time is n.
22:10 of the prophecy of this book, for the time is n.
Tob 5:10 the time is n for God to heal you; take courage."
6: 6 on their way together until they were n Media.
6:18 and will never be seen n her any more.
11: 1 When they came n to Kaserin,
11:15 on her way there, very n to the gate of Nineveh.
Jdt 2:21 and camped opposite Bectileth n the mountain
3: 9 Then he came toward Esdraelon, n Dothan,
4: 6 which faces Esdraelon opposite the plain n
5: 5 that lives in the mountain district n you.
7: 3 They encamped in the valley n Bethulia,
7:18 which is n Chusi beside the Wadi Mochmur.
13: 6 She went up to the bedpost n Holofernes' head,
AdE 9:20 to the Jews in the kingdom of Artaxerxes both n
15:10 for our law applies only to our subjects. Come n."
Wis 6:19 and immortality brings one n to God;
Sir 9: 3 Do not go n a loose woman,
12:13 or all those who go n wild animals?
14:24 who camps n her house and fastens his tent peg
14:25 who pitches his tent n her, and so occupies
23:16 one who commits fornication with his n
26:12 and drinks from any water n him,
33:12 and some he made holy and brought n to himself;
51: 6 My soul drew n to death, and my life was on the
51:23 Draw n to me, you who are uneducated,
Aza 1:25 and burned those Chaldeans who were caught n
1Mc 2:49 Now the days drew n for Mattathias to die,
3:40 and when they arrived they encamped n Emmaus
4:18 Gorgias and his force are n us in the hills.
5:40 Judas and his army drew n to the stream of water,
7:31 to meet Judas in battle n Caphar-salama.
8:12 They have subdued kings far and n,
2Mc 4:33 to a place of sanctuary at Daphne n Antioch.
7:14 When he was n death, he said,
10:25 As he drew n, Maccabeus
10:27 and when they came n the enemy they halted.
11: 8 And there, while they were still n Jerusalem,
13:14 he pitched his camp n Modein.
3Mc 1: 1 and marched out to the region n Raphia,
1:25 while the elders n the king tried in various ways
6:31 those disgracefully treated and n to death,
2Es 5:19 from me and do not come n me for seven days;
6:18 when I draw n to visit the inhabitants of the earth,
8:61 Therefore my judgment is now drawing n;
12:21 when the middle of its time draws n;
14:18 and falsehood shall come n.
15:15 For the sword and misery draw n them,
16:37 The calamities draw n, and are not delayed.
16:38 when the time of her delivery draws n,

NEARBY (10) [NEAR]

Nu 6: 9 If someone dies very suddenly n,
Pr 27:10 neighbor who is n than kindred who are far away.
Eze 6:12 those n shall fall by the sword;
Jn 18:22 of the police standing n struck Jesus on the face,
19:42 and the tomb was n, they laid Jesus there.
Ac 23: 4 Those standing n said, "Do you dare
1Co 14:30 If a revelation is made to someone else sitting n,
Jdt 7:13 of the n mountains and camp there to keep watch
2Mc 6:11 Others who had assembled in the caves n,
3Mc 6:17 the n valleys resounded with them and brought

NEARER (6) [NEAR]

Ex 13:17 of the land of the Philistines, although that was n;
Jos 3: 4 do not come any n to it."
1Sa 17:48 When the Philistine drew n to meet David,
Ro 13:11 For salvation is n to us now than
4Mc 8: 4 and summoned them n and said,
12: 2 He summoned him to come n and tried

NEAREST (9) [NEAR]

Lev 21: 2 except for his n kin: his mother,
Nu 27:11 to the n kinsman of his clan,
Dt 21: 3 The elders of the town n the body shall take
21: 6 that town n the body shall wash their hands over
Ru 2:20 "The man is a relative of ours, one of our n kin."
Pr 18:24 but a true friend sticks closer than one's n kin.
Tob 7:10 because you are my n relative.
Jdt 16:24 and to her own n kindred.
4Mc 12:10 Running to the n of the braziers,

NEARIAH (3)

1Ch 3:22 Hattush, Igal, Bariah, N, and Shaphat, six.
3:23 sons of N: Elioenai, Hizkiah, and Azrikam, three.
4:42 having as their leaders Pelatiah, N, Rephaiah,

NEARING (1) [NEAR]

Ac 27:27 the sailors suspected that they were n land.

NEARLY (4) [NEAR]

Ps 73: 2 feet had almost stumbled; my steps had n slipped.
Lk 24:29 it is almost evening and the day is now n over."
Php 2:27 He was indeed so ill that he n died.
3Mc 5:14 now, since it was n the middle of the tenth hour,

NEARSIGHTED (1) [NEAR, SEE]

2Pe 1: 9 For anyone who lacks these things is n and blind,

NEBAI (1)

Ne 10:19 Hariph, Anathoth, N,

NEBAIOTH (5)

Ge 25:13 N, the firstborn of Ishmael;
28: 9 of Abraham's son Ishmael, and sister of N, to
36: 3 and Basemath, Ishmael's daughter, sister of N.
1Ch 1:29 the firstborn of Ishmael, N;
Isa 60: 7 the rams of N shall minister to you;

NEBAJOTH (KJV) See NEBAIOTH

NEBALLAT (1)

Ne 11:34 Hadid, Zeboim, N,

NEBAT (26)

1Ki 11:26 Jeroboam son of N, an Ephraimite of Zeredah,
12: 2 son of N heard of it (for he was still in Egypt,
12:15 by Ahijah the Shilonite to Jeroboam son of N.
15: 1 in the eighteenth year of King Jeroboam son of N,
16: 3 like the house of Jeroboam son of N.
16:26 he walked in all the way of Jeroboam son of N,
16:31 for him to walk in the sins of Jeroboam son of N,
21:22 like the house of Jeroboam son of N,
22:52 and in the way of Jeroboam son of N,
2Ki 3: 3 he clung to the sin of Jeroboam son of N,
9: 9 of Ahab like the house of Jeroboam son of N,
10:29 not turn aside from the sins of Jeroboam son of N,
13: 2 and followed the sins of Jeroboam son of N,
13:11 not depart from all the sins of Jeroboam son of N,
14:24 not depart from all the sins of Jeroboam son of N,
15: 9 not depart from the sins of Jeroboam son of N,
15:18 from any of the sins of Jeroboam son of N,
15:24 not turn away from the sins of Jeroboam son of N,
15:28 not depart from the sins of Jeroboam son of N,
17:21 they made Jeroboam son of N king.
23:15 the high place erected by Jeroboam son of N,
2Ch 9:29 of the seer Iddo concerning Jeroboam son of N?
10: 2 When Jeroboam son of N heard of it (for he was
10:15 by Ahijah the Shilonite to Jeroboam son of N.
13: 6 Yet Jeroboam son of N, a servant of Solomon son
Sir 47:23 Then Jeroboam son of N led Israel into sin

NEBO (13)

Nu 32: 3 Jazer, Nimrah, Heshbon, Elealeh, Sebam, N,
32:38 N, and Baal-meon (some names being changed),
33:47 in the mountains of Abarim, before N.
Dt 32:49 Mount N, which is in the land of Moab,
34: 1 up from the plains of Moab to Mount N, to the top
1Ch 5: 8 who lived in Aroer, as far as N and Baal-meon.
Ezr 2:29 The descendants of N, fifty-two.
10:43 Of the descendants of N: Jeiel,
Ne 7:33 Of the other N, fifty-two.
Isa 15: 2 over N and over Medeba Moab wails.
46: 1 Bel bows down, N stoops,
Jer 48: 1 Alas for N, it is laid waste!
48:22 and Dibon, and N, and Beth-diblathaim,

NEBUCHADNEZZAR‡ (92) [NEBUCHADNEZZAR'S, =NEBUCHADREZZAR]

2Ki 24: 1 In his days King N of Babylon came up;
24:10 that time the servants of King N of Babylon came
24:11 King N of Babylon came to the city,
25: 1 King N of Babylon came with all his army
25: 8 which was the nineteenth year of King N,
25:22 whom King N of Babylon had left.
1Ch 6:15 and Jerusalem into exile by the hand of N.
2Ch 36: 6 Against him King N of Babylon came up,
36: 7 N also carried some of the vessels of the house of
36:10 the year King N sent and brought him to Babylon,
36:13 He also rebelled against King N,
Ezr 1: 7 the house of the LORD that N had carried away
2: 1 from those captive exiles whom King N
5:12 he gave them into the hand of King N of Babylon,
5:14 which N had taken out of the temple in Jerusalem
6: 5 which N took out of the temple in Jerusalem
Ne 7: 6 of the captivity of those exiles whom King N
Est 2: 6 whom King N of Babylon had carried away.
Jer 27: 6 into the hand of King N of Babylon,
27: 8 or kingdom will not serve this king, N of Babylon,
27:20 which King N of Babylon did not take away
28: 3 which King N of Babylon took away
28:11 how I will break the yoke of King N of Babylon
28:14 of all these nations so that they may serve King N
29: 1 whom N had taken into exile from Jerusalem
29: 3 of Judah sent to Babylon to King N of Babylon.
Da 1: 1 King N of Babylon came to Jerusalem
1:18 palace master brought them into the presence of N,
2: 1 N dreamed such dreams that his spirit was troubled
2:28 and he has disclosed to King N what will happen
2:46 Then King N fell on his face, worshiped Daniel,
3: 1 King N made a golden statue whose height was
3: 2 Then King N sent for the satraps, the prefects,
3: 2 the dedication of the statue that King N had set up.
3: 3 the dedication of the statue that King N had set up.
3: 3 before the statue that N had set up,
3: 5 the golden statue that King N has set up.
3: 7 the golden statue that King N had set up.
3: 9 They said to King N, "O king, live forever!
3:13 Then N in furious rage commanded that Shadrach,
3:14 N said to them, "Is it true, O Shadrach, Meshach,
3:16 and Abednego answered the king, "O N,
3:19 Then N was so filled with rage against Shadrach,
3:24 Then King N was astonished and rose up quickly.
3:26 N then approached the door of the furnace
3:28 N said, "Blessed be the God of Shadrach,
4: 1 King N to all peoples, nations,
4: 4 N, was living at ease in my home and prospering
4:18 This is the dream that I, King N, saw.
4:28 All this came upon King N.
4:31 "O King N, to you it is declared:
4:33 Immediately the sentence was fulfilled against N.
4:34 When that period was over, I, N,
4:37 N, praise and extol and honor the King of heaven,
5: 2 of gold and silver that his father N had taken out
5:11 King N, made him chief of the magicians,
5:18 the Most High God gave your father N kingship,
Jdt 1: 1 It was the twelfth year of the reign of N,
1: 5 Then King N made war against King Arphaxad in
1: 7 Then N, king of the Assyrians,
1:11 the whole region disregarded the summons of N,
1:12 N became very angry with this whole region,
2: 1 there was talk in the palace of N,
2: 4 When he had completed his plan, N,
2:19 to go ahead of King N and to cover the whole face
3: 2 the servants of N, the Great King,
3: 8 so that all nations should worship N alone,
4: 1 the general of N, the king of the Assyrians,
6: 2 What god is there except N?
6: 4 So says King N, lord of the whole earth.
11: 1 I have never hurt anyone who chose to serve N,
11: 4 as they do the servants of my lord King N."
11: 7 By the life of N, king of the whole earth,
11: 7 because of your power, under N and all his house.
11:23 the palace of King N and be renowned throughout
12:13 Assyrian women who serve in the palace of N."
14:18 on the house of King N.
AdE 2: 6 from Jerusalem among those whom King N
11: 4 He was one of the captives whom King N
Bar 1: 9 after King N of Babylon had carried away
1:11 and pray for the life of King N of Babylon,
1:12 we shall live under the protection of King N
LtJ 6: 2 you will be taken to Babylon as exiles by N,
1Es 1:40 King N of Babylon came up against him;
1:41 N also took some holy vessels of the Lord,
1:45 A year later N sent and removed him to Babylon,
1:48 Although King N had made him swear by
2:10 the Lord that N had carried away from Jerusalem
5: 7 whom King N of Babylon had carried away
6:15 over into the hands of King N of Babylon, king of
6:18 which N had taken out of the house in Jerusalem
6:26 which N took out of the house in Jerusalem

NEBUCHADNEZZAR'S (1) [NEBUCHADNEZZAR]

Da 2: 1 In the second year of N reign,

NEBUCHADREZZAR (33) [=NEBUCHADNEZZAR]

Jer 21: 2 for King N of Babylon is making war against us;
21: 7 into the hands of King N of Babylon,
22:25 even into the hands of King N of Babylon and into
24: 1 after King N of Babylon had taken into exile
25: 1 (that was the first year of King N of Babylon),
25: 9 says the LORD, even for King N of Babylon,
29:21 to deliver them into the hand of King N
32: 1 which was the eighteenth year of N.
32:28 of the Chaldeans and into the hand of King N
34: 1 when King N of Babylon and all his army and all
35:11 King N of Babylon came up against the land,
37: 1 whom King N of Babylon made king in the land
39: 1 King N of Babylon and all his army came
39: 5 they brought him up to King N of Babylon,
39:11 King N of Babylon gave command
43:10 to send and take my servant King N of Babylon,
44:30 of Judah into the hand of King N of Babylon,
46: 2 and which King N of Babylon defeated in
46:13 of King N of Babylon to attack the land of Egypt:
46:26 to King N of Babylon and his officers.
49:28 of Hazor that King N of Babylon defeated.
49:30 King N of Babylon has made a plan against you
50:17 the end King N of Babylon has gnawed its bones.

Jer 51:34 "King **N** of Babylon has devoured me,
52: 4 King **N** of Babylon came with all his army
52:12 which was the nineteenth year of King **N**,
52:28 the number of the people whom **N** took into exile:
52:29 in the eighteenth year of **N** he took into exile
52:30 of **N**, Nebuzaradan the captain of the guard took
Eze 26: 7 against Tyre from the north King **N** of Babylon,
29:18 King **N** of Babylon made his army labor hard
29:19 the land of Egypt to King **N** of Babylon;
30:10 by the hand of King **N** of Babylon.

NEBUSHAZBAN (1)

Jer 39:13 **N** the Rabsaris, Nergal-sharezer the Rabmag,

NEBUZARADAN (15)

2Ki 25: 8 **N**, the captain of the bodyguard,
25:11 **N** the captain of the guard carried into exile
25:20 **N** the captain of the guard took them,
Jer 39: 9 Then **N** the captain of the guard exiled to Babylon
39:10 **N** the captain of the guard left in the land
39:11 concerning Jeremiah through **N**,
39:13 So **N** the captain of the guard,
40: 1 to Jeremiah from the LORD after **N** the captain
41:10 whom **N**, the captain of the guard,
43: 6 and everyone whom **N** the captain of
52:12 **N** the captain of the bodyguard who served
52:15 **N** the captain of the guard carried into exile some
52:16 But **N** the captain of the guard left some of
52:26 Then **N** the captain of the guard took them,
52:30 **N** the captain of the guard took into exile of

NECESSARILY (1) [NECESSARY]

Heb 7:12 there is **n** a change in the law as well.

NECESSARY‡ (24) [NECESSARILY, NECESSITIES, NECESSITY]

Lk 24:26 not **n** that the Messiah should suffer these things
Ac 13:46 "It was **n** that the word of God should
15: 5 "It is **n** for them to be circumcised and ordered
17: 3 and proving that it was **n** for the Messiah to suffer
1Co 8: 2 not yet have the **n** knowledge;
2Co 9: 1 not **n** for me to write you about the ministry to
9: 5 So I thought it **n** to urge the brothers to go on
12: 1 It is **n** to boast; nothing is to be
Php 1:24 but to remain in the flesh is more **n** for you.
2:25 Still, I think it **n** to send to you Epaphroditus—
Heb 8: 3 hence it is **n** for this priest also to have something
9:23 Thus it was **n** for the sketches of
Jude 1: 3 I find it **n** to write and appeal to you to contend for
Wis 16: 4 For it was **n** that upon those
Sir Pr: 3 highly **n** that I should myself devote some
1Mc 10:39 to meet the **n** expenses of the sanctuary.
14:34 and provided in those towns whatever was **n**
2Mc 1:18 we thought it **n** to notify you,
8:18 and even, if **n**, the whole world."
9:21 and I have deemed it **n** to take thought for
12:39 On the next day, as had now become **n**,
13:20 Judas sent in to the garrison whatever was **n**.
1Es 8:18 And whatever else occurs to you as **n** for
4Mc 14:18 And why is it **n** to demonstrate sympathy

NECESSITIES (2) [NECESSARY]

Sir 29:21 The **n** of life are water, bread, and clothing,
39:26 The basic **n** of human life are water and fire

NECESSITY (3) [NECESSARY]

1Co 7:37 being under no **n** but having his own desire
Tob 4: 9 a good treasure for yourself against the day of **n**.
AdE 14:16 You know my **n**—that I abhor the sign of my

NECHO (KJV) See NECO

NECK (65) [NECKLACE, NECKS, STIFF-NECKED]

Ge 27:16 on his hands and on the smooth part of his **n**.
27:40 you shall break his yoke from your **n**."
33: 4 and fell on his **n** and kissed him, and they wept.
41:42 and put a gold chain around his **n**.
45:14 he fell upon his brother Benjamin's **n** and wept,
45:14 while Benjamin wept upon his **n**.
46:29 fell on his **n**, and wept on his **n** a good while.
49: 8 your hand shall be on the **n** of your enemies;
Ex 13:13 if you do not redeem it, you must break its **n**.
34:20 or if you will not redeem it you shall break its **n**.
Dt 21: 4 and shall break the heifer's **n** there in the wadi.
21: 6 over the heifer whose **n** was broken in the wadi,
28:48 an iron yoke on your **n** until he has destroyed you.
Jdg 5:30 two pieces of dyed work embroidered for my **n**
1Sa 4:18 and his **n** was broken and he died,
2Ch 36:13 he stiffened his **n** and hardened his heart
Ne 9:29 and stiffened their **n** and would not obey.
Job 16:12 he seized me by the **n** and dashed me to pieces;
39:19 Do you clothe its **n** with mane?
41:22 In its **n** abides strength, and terror dances before it.
Ps 69: 1 O God, for the waters have come up to my **n**.
75: 5 up your horn on high, or speak with insolent **n**."
105:18 his **n** was put in a collar of iron;
Pr 1: 9 for your head, and pendants for your **n**.
3: 3 bind them around your **n**,
3:22 be life for your soul and adornment for your **n**.
6:21 upon your heart always; tie them around your **n**.
SS 1:10 your **n** with strings of jewels.
SS 4: 4 Your **n** is like the tower of David, built in courses;
7: 4 Your **n** is like an ivory tower.
Isa 8: 8 and, pouring over, it will reach up to the **n**;
10:27 and his yoke will be destroyed from your **n**.
30:28 an overflowing stream that reaches up to the **n**—
48: 4 your **n** is an iron sinew and your forehead brass,
52: 2 loose the bonds from your **n**,
66: 3 like one who breaks a dog's **n**;
Jer 27: 2 a yoke of straps and bars, and put them on your **n**.
27: 8 put its **n** under the yoke of the king of Babylon,
27:11 But any nation that will bring its **n** under the yoke
28:10 the prophet Hananiah took the yoke from the **n** of
28:11 of King Nebuchadnezzar of Babylon from the **n**
28:12 from the **n** of the prophet Jeremiah, the word of
28:14 an iron yoke on the **n** of all these nations so
30: 8 I will break the yoke from off his **n**,
La 1:14 they weigh on my **n**, sapping my strength;
Eze 16:11 I put bracelets on your arms, a chain on your **n**,
Da 5: 7 have a chain of gold around his **n**,
5:16 have a chain of gold around your **n**,
5:29 a chain of gold was put around his **n**,
Hos 10:11 and I spared her fair **n**;
Mt 18: 6 around your **n** and you were drowned in the depth
Mk 9:42 around your **n** and you were thrown into the sea.
Lk 17: 2 for you if a millstone were hung around your **n**
Ac 15:10 the test by placing on the **n** of the disciples a yoke
Jdt 13: 8 Then she struck his **n** twice with all her might,
16: 9 and the sword severed his **n**!
AdE 15:11 the golden scepter and touched her **n** with it;
Sir 6:24 and your **n** into her collar.
30:12 Bow down his **n** in his youth,
33:27 Yoke and thong will bow the **n**,
51:26 Put your **n** under her yoke,
1Es 1:48 he stiffened his **n** and hardened his heart
3: 6 and a necklace around his **n**;
3Mc 4: 9 some were fastened by the **n** to the benches of

NECKLACE (3) [NECK]

Ps 73: 6 Therefore pride is their **n**;
SS 4: 9 with one jewel of your **n**.
1Es 3: 6 and a **n** around his neck;

NECKS‡ (18) [NECK]

Jos 10:24 put your feet on the **n** of these kings."
10:24 Then they came near and put their feet on their **n**.
Jdg 8:21 the crescents that were on the **n** of their camels.
8:26 and the collars that were on the **n** of their camels).
Ne 9:16 and stiffened their **n** and did
9:17 but they stiffened their **n** and determined to return
Isa 3:16 of Zion are haughty and walk with outstretched **n**,
Jer 7:26 or pay attention, but they stiffened their **n**.
17:23 they stiffened their **n** and would not hear
19:15 because they have stiffened their **n**,
27:12 Bring your **n** under the yoke of the king
La 5: 5 With a yoke on our **n** we are hard driven;
Eze 21:29 they place you over the **n** of the vile, wicked ones
Mic 2: 3 an evil from which you cannot remove your **n**;
Ro 16: 4 and who risked their **n** for my life,
Bar 4:25 and will tread upon their **n**.
1Mc 1:61 and they hung the infants from their mothers' **n**.
3Mc 4: 8 their **n** encircled with ropes instead of garlands,

NECO (10)

2Ki 23:29 In his days Pharaoh **N** king of Egypt went up to
23:29 Pharaoh **N** met him at Megiddo, he killed him.
23:33 Pharaoh **N** confined him at Riblah in the land
23:34 Pharaoh **N** made Eliakim son of Josiah king
23:35 to give it to Pharaoh **N**.
2Ch 35:20 King **N** of Egypt went up to fight at Carchemish
35:21 But **N** sent envoys to him, saying,
35:22 not listen to the words of **N** from the mouth
36: 4 but **N** took his brother Jehoahaz and carried him
Jer 46: 2 Concerning Egypt, about the army of Pharaoh **N**,

NECROMANCER (KJV) See ORACLES FROM THE DEAD

NECTAR (1)

SS 4:11 Your lips distill **n**, my bride;

NEDABIAH (1)

1Ch 3:18 Pedaiah, Shenazzar, Jekamiah, Hoshama, and **N**;

NEED (112) [NEEDED, NEEDIEST, NEEDLESSLY, NEEDS, NEEDY]

Ex 9:28 I will let you go; you **n** stay no longer."
20:24 You **n** make for me only an altar of earth
Lev 13:36 the priest **n** not seek for the yellow hair;
Dt 15: 4 There will, however, be no one in **n** among you,
15: 7 If there is among you anyone in **n**,
15: 8 willingly lending enough to meet the **n**,
15:11 there will never cease to be some in **n** on the earth,
Jos 7: 3 "Not all the people **n** go up;
Jdg 19:19 with us. We **n** nothing more."
Ru 3: 1 "My daughter, I **n** to seek some security for you,
1Ki 5:10 So Hiram supplied Solomon's every **n** for timber
2Ki 12: 5 and let them repair the house wherever any **n**
1Ch 23:26 so the Levites no longer **n** to carry the tabernacle
2Ch 2:16 We will cut whatever timber you **n** from Lebanon,
35: 3 you **n** no longer carry it on your shoulders.
35:15 they did not **n** to interrupt their service,
Job 33: 7 No fear of me **n** terrify you;
Pr 30: 8 feed me with the food that I **n**,
Ecc 10:19 wine gladdens life, and money meets every **n**.
Jer 2:24 None who seek her **n** weary themselves;
40: 4 to come with me to Babylon, you **n** not come.
Eze 39:10 They will not **n** to take wood out of the field or cut
Da 3:16 we have no **n** to present a defense to you
Hos 7: 4 whose baker does not **n** to stir the fire,
Mt 3:14 saying, "I **n** to be baptized by you,
6: 8 for your Father knows what you **n**
6:32 that you **n** all these things.
9:12 "Those who are well have no **n** of a physician,
14:16 Jesus said to them, "They **n** not go away;
15: 5 then that person **n** not honor the father.
26:65 Why do we still **n** witnesses?
Mk 2:17 "Those who are well have no **n** of a physician,
2:25 and his companions were hungry and in **n** of food?
14:63 "Why do we still **n** witnesses?
Lk 5:31 "Those who are well have no **n** of a physician,
10:42 there is **n** of only one thing.
12:30 and your Father knows that you **n** them.
15: 7 righteous persons who **n** no repentance.
15:14 and he began to be in **n**.
18: 1 about their **n** to pray always and not to lose heart.
22:71 they said, "What further testimony do we **n**?
Jn 13:10 "One who has bathed does not **n** to wash,
13:29 "Buy what we **n** for the festival";
16:30 and do not **n** to have anyone question you;
Ac 2:45 and distribute the proceeds to all, as any had **n**.
4:35 and it was distributed to each as any had **n**.
1Co 5:10 since you would then **n** to go out of the world.
12:21 eye cannot say to the hand, "I have no **n** of you,"
12:21 nor again the head to the feet, "I have no **n** of you."
12:24 our more respectable members do not **n** this.
16: 2 so that collections **n** not be taken when I come.
2Co 3: 1 Surely we do not **n**, as some do,
8:14 your present abundance and their **n**,
8:14 so that their abundance may be for your **n**,
10: 2 I ask that when I am present I **n** not show boldness
11: 9 And when I was with you and was in **n**,
Eph 4:29 as there is **n**, so that your words may give grace
Php 2:25 your messenger and minister to my **n**;
4:11 Not that I am referring to being in **n**;
4:12 of having plenty and of being in **n**.
4:19 And my God will fully satisfy every **n** of yours
1Th 1: 8 so that we have no **n** to speak about it.
4: 9 you do not **n** to have anyone write to you,
5: 1 you do not **n** to have anything written to you.
2Ti 2:15 a worker who has no **n** to be ashamed,
Heb 4:16 and find grace to help in time of **n**.
5:12 you **n** someone to teach you again
5:12 You **n** milk, not solid food;
7:11 what further **n** would there have been to speak
7:27 he has no **n** to offer sacrifices day after day,
8: 7 there would have been no **n** to look for
9:23 heavenly things themselves **n** better sacrifices than
10:36 For you **n** endurance, so that when you have done
1Jn 2:27 and so you do not **n** anyone to teach you.
3:17 the world's goods and sees a brother or sister in **n**
Rev 3:17 'I am rich, I have prospered, and I **n** nothing.'
21:23 the city has no **n** of sun or moon to shine on it,
22: 5 they **n** no light of lamp or sun,
Tob 5: 7 for I do **n** you to travel with me,
5:12 He replied, "Why do you **n** to know my tribe?"
10: 1 how many days Tobias would **n** for going and
AdE 2: 3 and let ointments and whatever else they **n**
Wis 11: 5 they themselves received benefit in their **n**.
13:16 for it is only an image and has **n** of help.
16:25 according to the desire of those who had **n**,
Sir 4: 2 Do not grieve the hungry, or anger one in **n**.
8: 9 and to give an answer when the **n** arises.
10:26 and do not boast when you are in **n**.
11:12 There are others who are slow and **n** help,
11:23 Do not say, "What do I **n**,
13: 4 but if you are in **n** he will abandon you.
13: 6 to you kindly and say, "What do you **n**?"
14: 1 and **n** not suffer remorse for sin.
15:12 for he has no **n** of the sinful.
18:25 in days of wealth think of poverty and **n**.
29: 2 Lend to your neighbor in his time of **n**;
29: 3 and on every occasion you will find what you **n**.
29: 9 in their **n** do not send them away empty-handed
29:27 my brother has come for a visit, and I **n**
33:31 for you will **n** him as you **n** your life.
38:12 do not let him leave you, for you **n** him.
39:33 and he will supply every **n** in its time.
40:26 and with it there is no **n** to seek for help.
42:23 each creature is preserved to meet a particular **n**.
LtJ 6:59 or a household utensil that serves its owner's **n**,
1Mc 3:28 and ordered them to be ready for any **n**.
12: 9 Therefore, though we have no **n** of these things,
2Mc 2:15 So if you have **n** of them,
14:35 though you have **n** of nothing,
1Es 1: 4 "You **n** no longer carry it on your shoulders.
3Mc 2: 9 though you have no **n** of anything;

NEEDED (14) [NEED]

Ex 16:18 they gathered as much as each of them **n**.
16:21 by morning they gathered it, as much as each **n**;
Ezr 6: 9 Whatever is **n**—young bulls,
Eze 17: 9 No strong arm or mighty army will be **n** to pull it
Lk 9:11 and healed those who **n** to be cured.
Jn 2:25 and **n** no one to testify about anyone;
Ac 17:25 as though he **n** anything, since he himself gives
28:10 they put on board all the provisions we **n**.
2Pe 1: 3 His divine power has given us everything **n**
Tob 1:13 and I used to buy everything he **n**.
2Mc 10:19 for places where he was more urgently **n**.

2Mc 11:18 I have informed the king of everything that n to
1Es 1:16 no one n to interrupt his daily duties,
3Mc 6:30 and everything else n for a festival of seven days,

NEEDIEST (1) [NEED]

Isa 29:19 the n people shall exult in the Holy One of Israel.

NEEDLE (3) [NEEDLEWORK]

Mt 19:24 for a camel to go through the eye of a n than
Mk 10:25 for a camel to go through the eye of a n than
Lk 18:25 for a camel to go through the eye of a n than

NEEDLESSLY (2) [NEED]

Sir 29: 6 and he has n made him an enemy;
29: 7 but from fear of being defrauded n.

NEEDLEWORK (6) [NEEDLE]

Ex 26:36 and of fine twisted linen, embroidered with n.
27:16 and of fine twisted linen, embroidered with n;
28:39 and you shall make a sash embroidered with n.
36:37 and fine twisted linen, embroidered with n;
38:18 the entrance to the court was embroidered with n
39:29 purple, and crimson yarns, embroidered with n;

NEEDS (23) [NEED]

Ex 16:16 'Gather as much of it as each of you n,
Nu 4:26 and they shall do all that n to be done with regard
1Ki 5: 8 I will fulfill all your n in the matter of cedar
5: 9 And you shall meet my n by providing food
Pr 12:10 The righteous know the n of their animals,
Isa 58:10 to the hungry and satisfy the n of the afflicted,
58:11 and satisfy your n in parched places,
Mt 21: 3 just say this, 'The Lord n them.'
Mk 11: 3 just say this, 'The Lord n it
Lk 11: 8 up and give him whatever he n.
19:31 just say this, 'The Lord n it.' "
19:34 They said, "The Lord n it."
Ac 24:23 of his friends from taking care of his n.
Ro 12:13 Contribute to the n of the saints;
2Co 9:12 of this ministry not only supplies the n of
11: 9 for my n were supplied by the friends who came
Php 4:16 you sent me help for my n more than once.
Tit 3:14 to good works in order to meet urgent n,
Jas 2:16 and yet you do not supply their bodily n,
Wis 13:11 a useful vessel that serves life's n,
Sir 13: 6 When he n you he will deceive you,
42:21 and he n no one to be his counselor.
1Mc 16:14 the towns of the country and attending to their n,

NEEDY (63) [NEED]

Dt 15: 7 or tight-fisted toward your n neighbor.
15: 9 and therefore view your n neighbor with hostility
15:11 "Open your hand to the poor and n neighbor
24:14 not withhold the wages of poor and n laborers,
1Sa 2: 8 he lifts the n from the ash heap,
Job 5:15 But he saves the n from the sword of their mouth,
24: 4 They thrust the n off the road;
24:14 The murderer rises at dusk to kill the poor and n,
29:16 I was a father to the n,
30:24 "Surely one does not turn against the n,
Ps 9:18 For the n shall not always be forgotten,
12: 5 the poor are despoiled, because the n groan,
35:10 the weak and n from those who despoil them."
37:14 and bend their bows to bring down the poor and n,
40:17 As for me, I am poor and n,
68:10 in your goodness, O God, you provided for the n.
69:33 For the LORD hears the n,
70: 5 But I am poor and n; hasten to me, O God!
72: 4 give deliverance to the n, and crush the oppressor.
72:12 For he delivers the n when they call,
72:13 He has pity on the weak and the n,
72:13 and saves the lives of the n.
74:21 let the poor and n praise your name.
82: 4 Rescue the weak and the n;
86: 1 O LORD, and answer me, for I am poor and n.
107:41 but he raises up the n out of distress,
109:16 but pursued the poor and n and the brokenhearted
109:22 For I am poor and n,
109:31 For he stands at the right hand of the n,
113: 7 and lifts the n from the ash heap,
140:12 that the LORD maintains the cause of the n,
Pr 14:31 but those who are kind to the n honor him.
30:14 the n from among mortals.
31: 9 defend the rights of the poor and n.
31:20 and reaches out her hands to the n.
Isa 10: 2 to turn aside the n from justice and to rob the poor
14:30 and the n lie down in safety;
14:32 the n among his people will find refuge in her."
25: 4 a refuge to the n in their distress,
26: 6 the feet of the poor, the steps of the n.
32: 7 even when the plea of the n is right.
41:17 When the poor and n seek water,
Jer 5:28 and they do not defend the rights of the n.
20:13 the life of the n from the hands of evildoers.
22:16 He judged the cause of the poor and n;
Eze 16:49 but did not aid the poor and n.
18:12 oppresses the poor and n,
22:29 they have oppressed the poor and n,
Am 2: 6 and the n for a pair of sandals—
4: 1 who crush the n, who say to their husbands,
5:12 who take a bribe, and push aside the n in the gate.
8: 4 Hear this, you that trample on the n,
8: 6 the poor for silver and the n for a pair of sandals,
Ac 4:34 There was not a n person among them,
Eph 4:28 so as to have something to share with the n.
Sir 4: 1 and do not keep n eyes waiting.
4: 3 or delay giving to the n.
4: 5 Do not avert your eye from the n,
31: 4 and if ever he rests he becomes n.
34:25 The bread of the n is the life of the poor;
41: 2 to one who is n and failing in strength, worn down
2Es 2:20 give to the n, defend the orphan, clothe the naked,
4Mc 2: 8 and to lend without interest to the n and to cancel

NEESINGS (KJV) See SNEEZES

NEGEB (41)

Ge 12: 9 And Abram journeyed on by stages toward the N.
13: 1 and all that he had, and Lot with him, into the N.
13: 3 He journeyed on by stages from the N as far
20: 1 toward the region of the N,
24:62 and was settled in the N.
Nu 13:17 and said to them, "Go up there into the N,
13:22 They went up into the N, and came to Hebron;
13:29 The Amalekites live in the land of the N;
21: 1 Canaanite, the king of Arad, who lived in the N,
33:40 who lived in the N in the land of Canaan,
Dt 1: 7 the Arabah, the hill country, the Shephelah, the N,
34: 3 the N, and the Plain—that is, the valley of Jericho,
Jos 10:40 the hill country and the N and the lowland and
11:16 the N and all the land of Goshen and the lowland
12: 8 and in the N, the land of the Hittites, Amorites,
15:19 since you have set me in the land of the N,
19: 8 as far as Baalath-beer, Ramah of the N.
Jdg 1: 9 in the N, and in the lowland.
1:15 since you have set me in the land of the N,
1:16 which lies in the N near Arad.
1Sa 27:10 David would say, "Against the N of Judah,"
27:10 or "Against the N of the Jerahmeelites," or,
27:10 or, "Against the N of the Kenites."
30: 1 the Amalekites had made a raid on the N and
30:14 the N of the Cherethites and on that which belongs
30:14 and on that which belongs to Judah and on the N
30:27 in Ramoth of the N, in Jattir,
2Sa 24: 7 and they went out to the N of Judah at Beer-sheba.
2Ch 28:18 on the cities in the Shephelah and the N of Judah,
Ps 126: 4 O LORD, like the watercourses in the N.
Isa 21: 1 As whirlwinds in the N sweep on,
30: 6 An oracle concerning the animals of the N.
Jer 13:19 of the N are shut up with no one to open them;
17:26 from the hill country, and from the N,
32:44 of the Shephelah, and of the N;
33:13 and of the N, in the land of Benjamin,
Eze 20:46 and prophesy against the forest land in the N;
20:47 the forest of the N, Hear the word of the LORD:
Ob 1:19 Those of the N shall possess Mount Esau,
1:20 in Sepharad shall possess the towns of the N.
Zec 7: 7 when the N and the Shephelah were inhabited?

NEGLECT‡ (16) [NEGLECTED, NEGLECTING, NEGLIGENCE, NEGLIGENT]

Dt 12:19 not n the Levite as long as you live in your land.
14:27 the Levites resident in your towns, do not n them,
Ne 10:39 We will not n the house of our God.
Pr 8:33 Hear instruction and be wise, and do not n it.
Lk 11:42 and n justice and the love of God;
Ac 6: 2 that we should n the word of God in order to wait
1Ti 4:14 Do not n the gift that is in you,
Heb 2: 3 how can we escape if we n so great a salvation?
13: 2 Do not n to show hospitality to strangers,
13:16 Do not n to do good and to share what you have,
AdE 13:16 Do not n your portion, which you redeemed
Sir 7:10 do not n to give alms.
7:30 and do not n his ministers.
38:16 and do not n the burial.
1Es 2:20 we think it best not to n such a matter,
3Mc 6:15 in the land of their enemies did I n them,'

NEGLECTED (7) [NEGLECT]

Pr 29:15 but a mother is disgraced by a n child.
Mt 23:23 and have n the weightier matters of the law:
Ac 6: 1 the Hebrews because their widows were being n
AdE 2:15 she n none of the things that Gai,
Wis 19:22 and you have not n to help them at all times and
Sir 2:10 Or has anyone called upon him and been n?
2Es 1:34 because with you they have n my commandment

NEGLECTING (5) [NEGLECT]

Mt 23:23 It is these you ought to have practiced without n
Lk 11:42 it is these you ought to have practiced, without n
Heb 10:25 not n to meet together, as is the habit of some,
2Mc 4:14 Despising the sanctuary and n the sacrifices,
3Mc 1:19 for wedded union, and, n proper modesty,

NEGLIGENCE (1) [NEGLECT]

Da 6: 4 and no n or corruption could be found in him.

NEGLIGENT (2) [NEGLECT]

2Ch 29:11 My sons, do not now be n,
Bar 1:19 and we have been n, in not heeding his voice.

NEGOTIATED (1)

2Mc 13:22 king n a second time with the people in Beth-zur,

NEHELAM (3)

Jer 29:24 To Shemaiah of N you shall say:
29:31 Thus says the LORD concerning Shemaiah of N:
29:32 to punish Shemaiah of N and his descendants;

NEHEMIAH (19)

Ezr 2: 2 They came with Zerubbabel, Jeshua, N, Seraiah,
Ne 1: 1 The words of N son of Hacaliah.
3:16 After him N son of Azbuk,
7: 7 They came with Zerubbabel, Jeshua, N, Azariah,
8: 9 And N, who was the governor,
10: 1 of N the governor, son of Hacaliah, and Zedekiah;
12:26 the days of the governor N and of the priest Ezra,
12:47 the days of N all Israel gave the daily portions for
Sir 49:13 The memory of N also is lasting;
2Mc 1:18 and the festival of the fire given when N,
1:20 many years had passed, when it pleased God, N,
1:21 N ordered the priests to sprinkle the liquid on
1:23 Jonathan led, and the rest responded, as did N.
1:31 N ordered that the liquid that was left should
1:33 with which N and his associates had burned
1:36 N and his associates called this "nephthar,"
2:13 in the records and in the memoirs of N,
1Es 5: 8 They came with Zerubbabel and Jeshua, N,
5:40 And N and Attharias told them not to share in

NEHUM (1)

Ne 7: 7 Mordecai, Bilshan, Mispereth, Bigvai, N, Baanah.

NEHUSHTA (1)

2Ki 24: 8 His mother's name was N daughter of Elnathan

NEHUSHTAN (1)

2Ki 18: 4 of Israel had made offerings to it; it was called N.

NEIEL (1)

Jos 19:27 of Iphtah-el northward to Beth-emek and N;

NEIGH (1) [NEIGHING, NEIGHINGS, NEIGHS]

Jer 50:11 like a heifer on the grass, and n like stallions,

NEIGHBOR (102) [NEIGHBOR'S, NEIGHBORHOOD, NEIGHBORING, NEIGHBORS, NEIGHBORS']

A. LOVE YOUR/ONE'S NEIGHBOR (9)

Ex 3:22 each woman shall ask her n and any woman living
11: 2 that every man is to ask his n and every woman is
to ask her n for objects
12: 4 it shall join its closest n in obtaining one;
20:16 You shall not bear false witness against your n.
20:17 or donkey, or anything that belongs to your n.
22: 7 When someone delivers to a n money or goods
22:27 And if your n cries out to me, I will listen,
32:27 of you kill your brother, your friend, and your n.' "
Lev 6: 2 against the LORD by deceiving a n in a matter of
6: 2 or by robbery, or if you have defrauded a n,
19:13 You shall not defraud your n;
19:15 with justice you shall judge your n.
19:16 and you shall not profit by the blood of your n:
19:17 of your kin; you shall reprove your n,
19:18 but you shall love your n as yourself: A
20:10 If a man commits adultery with the wife of his n,
25:14 a sale to your n or buy from your n,
25:15 When you buy from your n,
Dt 5:20 Neither shall you bear false witness against your n.
5:21 or donkey, or anything that belongs to your n.
15: 2 the claim that is held against a n, not exacting it of
a n who is a member of the community,
15: 7 or tight-fisted toward your needy n.
15: 9 view your needy n with hostility and give nothing;
15: 9 your n might cry to the LORD against you,
15:11 "Open your hand to the poor and needy n
22: 3 with anything else that your n loses and you find.
22:26 like that of someone who attacks and murders a n.
24:10 When you make your n a loan of any kind,
24:13 that your n may sleep in the cloak and bless you;
25: 3 your n will be degraded in your sight.
27:24 be anyone who strikes down a n in secret."
Jos 20: 5 because the n was killed by mistake,
1Sa 15:28 and has given it to a n of yours,
28:17 and given it to your n, David.
2Sa 12:11 before your eyes, and give them to your n,
1Ki 8:31 "If someone sins against a n and is given an oath
Job 16:21 as one does for a n.
Ps 88:18 You have caused friend and n to shun me;
101: 5 One who secretly slanders a n I will destroy.
Pr 3:28 Do not say to your n, "Go, and come again,
3:29 not plan harm against your n who lives trustingly
6: 1 My child, if you have given your pledge to your n,
6: 3 go, hurry, and plead with your n.
17:18 to become surety for a n.
24:28 Do not be a witness against your n without cause,
25: 8 when your n puts you to shame?
25: 9 Argue your case with your n directly,
25:17 the n will become weary of you and hate you.
25:18 arrow is one who bears false witness against a n.
26:19 so is one who deceives a n and says,
27:10 a n who is nearby than kindred who are far away.
27:14 Whoever blesses a n with a loud voice,
29: 5 a n is spreading a net for the neighbor's feet.

Isa 3: 5 everyone by another and everyone by a **n**;
19: 2 one against the other, **n** against **n**,
Jer 6:21 and children together, **n** and friend shall perish.
9: 4 and every **n** goes around like a slanderer.
9:20 and each to her **n** a lament.
Eze 33:30 say to one another, each to a **n**,
Zec 11: 6 every one, to fall each into the hand of a **n**,
14:13 so that each will seize the hand of a **n**,
Mt 5:43 'You shall love your **n** and hate your enemy.' A
7: 4 Or how can you say to your **n**,
19:19 also, You shall love your **n** as yourself." A
22:39 'You shall love your **n** as yourself.' A
Mk 12:31 'You shall love your **n** as yourself.' A
12:33 and 'to love one's **n** as oneself,'— A
Lk 6:42 Or how can you say to your **n**, 'Friend,
10:27 with all your mind; and your **n** as yourself."
10:29 he asked Jesus, "And who is my **n**?"
10:36 was a **n** to the man who fell into the hands of
Ac 7:27 man who was wronging his **n** pushed Moses aside,
Ro 13: 9 "Love your **n** as yourself." A
13:10 Love does no wrong to a **n**;
15: 2 Each of us must please our **n** for the good purpose
15: 2 for the good purpose of building up the **n**.
Gal 5:14 "You shall love your **n** as yourself." A
Jas 2: 8 "You shall love your **n** as yourself." A
4:12 So who, then, are you to judge your **n**?
Sir 5:12 If you know what to say, answer your **n**;
10: 6 Do not get angry with your **n** for every injury,
13:15 like, and every person the **n**.
17:14 to each of them concerning the **n**.
19:14 Question a **n**; perhaps he did not say it;
19:17 Question your **n** before you threaten him;
22:23 Gain the trust of your **n** in his poverty,
27:18 so you have destroyed the friendship of your **n**.
27:19 so you have let your **n** go,
28: 2 Forgive your **n** the wrong he has done,
28: 7 and do not be angry with your **n**;
29: 2 Lend to your **n** in his time of need;
29: 2 repay your **n** when a loan falls due.
29:14 A good person will be surety for his **n**,
29:20 Assist your **n** to the best of your ability,
31:14 and do not crowd your **n** at the dish.
31:31 Do not reprove your **n** at a banquet of wine,
Sus 1:61 as they had wickedly planned to do to their **n**.
2Es 5:11 One country shall ask its **n**, 'Has righteousness,

NEIGHBOR'S (40) [NEIGHBOR]

Ex 3:22 and any woman living in the **n** house for jewelry
20:17 You shall not covet your **n** house;
20:17 you shall not covet your **n** wife,
22: 7 and they are stolen from the **n** house,
22: 8 or not the owner had laid hands on the **n** goods.
22:26 If you take your **n** cloak in pawn,
22:27 for it may be your **n** only clothing to use as cover;
Dt 5:21 Neither shall you covet your **n** wife.
5:21 Neither shall you desire your **n** house, or field,
19:14 You must not move your **n** boundary marker,
22: 1 not watch your **n** ox or sheep straying away
22: 3 You shall do the same with a **n** donkey;
22: 3 you shall do the same with a **n** garment;
22: 4 You shall not see your **n** donkey or ox fallen on
22:24 and the man because he violated his **n** wife.
23:24 If you go into your **n** vineyard,
23:25 If you go into your **n** standing grain,
23:25 you shall not put a sickle to your **n** standing grain.
27:17 be anyone who moves a **n** boundary marker."
Job 31: 9 and I have lain in wait at my **n** door;
Pr 6: 3 for you have come into your **n** power:
6:29 So is he who sleeps with his **n** wife;
25:17 Let your foot be seldom in your **n** house,
29: 5 a neighbor is spreading a net for the **n** feet.
Jer 5: 8 each neighing for his **n** wife.
Eze 18: 6 does not defile his **n** wife or approach a woman
18:11 who eats upon the mountains, defiles his **n** wife,
18:15 does not defile his **n** wife,
22:11 One commits abomination with his **n** wife;
33:26 and each of you defiles his **n** wife;
Mt 7: 3 Why do you see the speck in your **n** eye,
7: 5 to take the speck out of your **n** eye.
Lk 6:41 Why do you see the speck in your **n** eye,
6:42 to take the speck out of your **n** eye.
Gal 6: 4 then that work, rather than their **n** work,
Sir 29: 5 and is deferential in speaking of his **n** money;
31:15 Judge your **n** feelings by your own,
34:26 To take away a **n** living is to commit murder;
4Mc 2: 5 not covet your **n** wife or anything that is your **n**."

NEIGHBORHOOD (7) [NEIGHBOR]

Jdg 6: 4 as far as the **n** of Gaza,
11:33 a massive defeat on them from Aroer to the **n**
Ru 4:17 The women of the **n** gave him a name, saying,
Mt 8:34 they saw him, they begged him to leave their **n**.
Mk 5:17 Then they began to beg Jesus to leave their **n**.
Ac 28: 7 Now in the **n** of that place were lands belonging to
Sir 21:28 whisperer degrades himself and is hated in his **n**.

NEIGHBORING (9) [NEIGHBOR]

Dt 1: 7 of the Amorites as well as into the **n** regions—
Ezr 3: 3 because they were in dread of the **n** peoples,
Joel 3:12 for there I will sit to judge all the **n** nations.
Mk 1:38 He answered, "Let us go on to the **n** towns,
1Mc 12:33 as far as Askalon and the **n** strongholds.
2Mc 4:32 he had sold to Tyre and the **n** cities.
6: 8 to the **n** Greek cities that they should adopt
3Mc 1: 6 to visit the **n** cities and encourage them.

2Es 16:70 For in many places and in **n** cities there shall be

NEIGHBORS (65) [NEIGHBOR]

Jos 9:16 they heard that they were their **n** and were living
2Ki 4: 3 "Go outside, borrow vessels from all your **n**,
1Ch 12:40 And also their **n**, from as far away as Issachar
Ezr 1: 6 All their **n** aided them with silver vessels,
Ps 15: 3 nor take up a reproach against their **n**;
28: 3 who speak peace with their **n**,
31:11 to my **n**, an object of dread to my acquaintances;
38:11 and my **n** stand far off.
44:13 You have made us the taunt of our **n**,
79: 4 We have become a taunt to our **n**,
79:12 of our **n** the taunts with which they taunted you,
80: 6 You make us the scorn of our **n**;
89:41 he has become the scorn of his **n**.
Pr 11: 9 the godless would destroy their **n**,
14:20 The poor are disliked even by their **n**,
14:21 Those who despise their **n** are sinners,
16:29 The violent entice their **n**,
21:10 their **n** find no mercy in their eyes.
Jer 9: 4 of your **n**, and put no trust in any of your kin;
9: 5 They all deceive their **n**, and no one speaks
9: 8 They all speak friendly words to their **n**,
12:14 concerning all my evil **n** who touch the heritage
19: 9 and all shall eat the flesh of their **n** in the siege,
22:13 who makes his **n** work for nothing,
34:17 not obeyed me by granting a release to your **n**
48:17 Mourn over him, all you his **n**,
48:39 a derision and a horror to all his **n**.
49: 5 says the Lord GOD of hosts, from all your **n**,
49:10 his kinsfolk and his **n**; and he is no more.
49:18 and Gomorrah and their **n** were overthrown,
50:40 God overthrew Sodom and Gomorrah and their **n**,
La 1:17 against Jacob that his **n** should become his foes;
Eze 16:26 your lustful **n**, multiplying your whoring,
16:57 a mockery to the daughters of Aram and all her **n**,
22:12 and make gain of your **n** by extortion;
28:24 among all their **n** who have treated them
28:26 upon all their **n** who have treated them
Da 9:16 a disgrace among all our **n**.
Hab 2:15 "Alas for you who make your **n** drink,
Lk 1:58 Her **n** and relatives heard that
1:65 Fear came over all their **n**,
14:12 or your brothers or your relatives or rich **n**,
15: 6 he calls together his friends and **n**, saying to them,
15: 9 she calls together her friends and **n**, saying,
Jn 9: 8 The **n** and those who had seen him before as
Eph 4:25 let all of us speak the truth to our **n**,
Tob 2: 8 And my **n** laughed and said, "Is he still not afraid?
Sir 6:17 for as they are, so are their **n** also.
9:14 As much as you can, aim to know your **n**,
15: 5 She will exalt him above his **n**,
16: 8 He did not spare the **n** of Lot,
18:13 The compassion of human beings is for their **n**,
25: 1 among brothers and sisters, friendship among **n**,
25:18 Her husband sits among the **n**,
29: 1 The merciful lend to their **n**;
Bar 4: 9 you **n** of Zion, God has brought great sorrow upon
4:14 Let the **n** of Zion come;
4:24 For as the **n** of Zion have now seen your capture,
1Mc 2:40 And all said to their **n**:
2Mc 9:25 how the princes along the borders and the **n**
1Es 2: 9 their **n** helped them with everything,
3Mc 3:10 And already some of their **n** and friends
2Es 9:45 I and my husband and all my **n**;
10: 2 and all my **n** attempted to console me;
15:19 People shall have no pity for their **n**,

NEIGHBORS' (1) [NEIGHBOR]

Jer 29:23 and have committed adultery with their **n** wives,

NEIGHING (2) [NEIGH]

Jer 5: 8 each **n** for his neighbor's wife.
8:16 of the **n** of their stallions the whole land quakes.

NEIGHINGS (1) [NEIGH]

Jer 13:27 and **n**, your shameless prostitutions on the hills of

NEIGHS (1) [NEIGH]

Sir 33: 6 like a stallion that **n** no matter who the rider is.

NEITHER‡ (181)

Ge 31:29 'Take heed that you speak to Jacob **n** good
45: 6 in which there will be **n** plowing nor harvest.
Ex 4:10 **n** in the past nor even now that you have spoken
10: 6 something that **n** your parents
13:22 **N** the pillar of cloud by day nor the pillar of fire
34:28 he **n** ate bread nor drank water.
Lev 10: 9 **n** you nor your sons, when you enter the tent
16:29 **n** the citizen nor the alien who resides among you.
21: 7 **n** shall they marry a woman divorced
Dt 1:45 the LORD would **n** heed your voice
2:27 I will turn aside **n** to the right nor to the left.
4: 2 You must **n** add anything to what I command you
4: 9 as **n** to forget the things that your eyes have seen
4:28 objects of wood and stone that **n** see, nor hear,
4:31 he will **n** abandon you nor destroy you;
5:18 **N** shall you commit adultery.
5:19 **N** shall you steal.
5:20 **N** shall you bear false witness
5:21 **N** shall you covet your neighbor's wife.
5:21 **N** shall you desire your neighbor's house, or field,
7:14 with **n** sterility nor barrenness among you

Dt 8: 3 by feeding you with manna, with which **n** you
9: 9 I **n** ate bread nor drank water.
9:18 I **n** ate bread nor drank water,
9:23 **n** trusting him nor obeying him.
13: 6 whom **n** you nor your ancestors have known,
17:20 **n** exalting himself above other members of
21: 4 which is **n** plowed nor sown,
26:13 I have **n** transgressed nor forgotten any
28:36 that **n** you nor your ancestors have known,
28:39 you shall **n** drink the wine nor gather the grapes,
28:51 leaving you **n** grain, wine, and oil,
28:64 which **n** you nor your ancestors have known.
30:13 **N** is it beyond the sea, that you should say,
32:36 **n** bond nor free remaining.
Jos 5:14 He replied, "**N**; but as commander of the
23: 6 turning aside from it **n** to the right nor to the left,
Jdg 6: 5 **n** they nor their camels could be counted;
21:22 But **n** did you incur guilt by giving your daughters
1Sa 1:11 He shall drink **n** wine nor intoxicants,
1:15 I have drunk **n** wine nor strong drink,
6:12 they turned **n** to the right nor to the left,
13:22 of the battle **n** sword nor spear was to be found in
16: 8 He said, "**N** has the LORD chosen this one."
16: 9 And he said, "**N** has the LORD chosen this one."
20:31 **n** you nor your kingdom shall be established.
27: 9 leaving **n** man nor woman alive,
27:11 David left **n** man nor woman alive to
2Sa 2:19 turning **n** to the right nor to the left
13:22 But Absalom spoke to Amnon **n** good nor bad;
14: 7 to my husband **n** name nor remnant on the face of
21: 4 **n** is it for us to put anyone to death in Israel."
1Ki 3:26 The other said, "It shall be **n** mine nor yours;
5: 4 there is **n** adversary nor misfortune.
6: 7 so that **n** hammer nor ax nor any tool
11: 2 into marriage with them, **n** shall they with you;
17: 1 there shall be **n** dew nor rain these years,
17:16 **n** did the jug of oil fail,
2Ki 2:21 from now on **n** death nor miscarriage shall come
3:14 I would give you **n** a look nor a glance.
3:17 'You shall see **n** wind nor rain,
4:23 It is **n** new moon nor sabbath."
12: 8 that they would **n** accept more money from
18:12 they **n** listened nor obeyed.
Ezr 9:12 **n** take their daughters for your sons,
Ne 4:23 So **n** I nor my brothers nor my servants nor
5:14 **n** I nor my brothers ate the food allowance of
Est 2: 7 his cousin, for she had **n** father nor mother;
4:16 and **n** eat nor drink for three days, night or day.
5: 9 observed that he **n** rose nor trembled before him,
Ps 82: 5 They have **n** knowledge nor understanding,
121: 4 He who keeps Israel will **n** slumber nor sleep.
Pr 30: 8 give me **n** poverty nor riches;
Ecc 8:13 **n** will they prolong their days like a shadow,
8:16 how one's eyes see sleep **n** day nor night,
SS 8: 7 waters cannot quench love, **n** can floods drown it.
Isa 2: 4 **n** shall they learn war any more.
3: 7 in my house there is **n** bread nor cloak;
19:15 **N** head nor tail, palm branch or reed,
23: 4 "I have **n** labored nor given birth, I have **n** reared
30: 5 that brings **n** help nor profit,
44: 9 their witnesses **n** see nor know.
49:10 **n** scorching wind nor sun shall strike them down,
Jer 9:16 I will scatter them among nations that **n** they
16:13 a land that **n** you nor your ancestors have known,
19: 4 in it to other gods whom **n** they nor their ancestors
25: 4 you have **n** listened nor inclined your ears to hear
35: 6 shall never drink wine, **n** you nor your children;
36:24 Yet **n** the king, nor any of his
37: 2 But **n** he nor his servants nor the people of
44: 3 **n** they, nor you, nor your ancestors.
51:62 so that **n** human beings nor animals shall live in it,
Eze 14:16 they would save **n** sons nor daughters;
14:18 they would save **n** sons nor daughters,
14:20 they would save **n** son nor daughter;
22:26 and the common, **n** have they taught the difference
29:18 yet **n** he nor his army got anything from Tyre
43: 7 **n** they nor their kings, by their whoring,
Hos 1:10 which can be **n** measured nor numbered;
Mic 4: 3 **n** shall they learn war any more;
Zep 1:18 **N** their silver nor their gold will be able
Mal 4: 1 so that it will leave them **n** root nor branch.
Mt 6:15 **n** will your Father forgive your trespasses.
6:20 where **n** moth nor rust consumes and
6:26 they **n** sow nor reap nor gather into barns,
6:28 how they grow; they **n** toil nor spin,
9:17 **N** is new wine put into old wineskins;
11:18 For John came **n** eating nor drinking, and they say,
21:27 And he said to them, "**N** will I tell you
22:29 you know **n** the scriptures nor the power of God.
22:30 For in the resurrection they **n** marry nor are given
24:36 **n** the angels of heaven, nor the Son,
25:13 for you know **n** the day nor the hour.
Mk 11:33 And Jesus said to them, "**N** will I tell you
12:24 you know **n** the scriptures nor the power of God?
12:25 they **n** marry nor are given in marriage,
13:32 **n** the angels in heaven, nor the Son,
Lk 12:24 Consider the ravens: they **n** sow nor reap,
12:24 they have **n** storehouse nor barn,
12:27 how they grow: they **n** toil nor spin;
14:35 It is fit **n** for the soil nor for the manure pile;
16:31 **n** will they be convinced even if someone rises
18: 2 a certain city there was a judge who **n** feared God
20: 8 Then Jesus said to them, "**N** will I tell you
20:35 from the dead **n** marry nor are given in marriage.
23:15 **N** has Herod, for he sent him back to us.
Jn 1:25 then are you baptizing if you are **n** the Messiah,
4:21 the Father **n** on this mountain nor in Jerusalem.

Jn 6:24 that **n** Jesus nor his disciples were there,
8:11 ⟦And Jesus said, "**N** do I condemn you.⟧
8:19 Jesus answered, "You know **n** me nor my Father.
9: 3 "**N** this man nor his parents sinned;
14:17 because it **n** sees him nor knows him.
15: 4 **n** can you unless you abide in me.
Ac 9: 9 For three days he was without sight, and **n** ate
15:10 a yoke that **n** our ancestors nor we have been able
19:37 brought these men here who are **n** temple robbers
23:12 a conspiracy and bound themselves by an oath **n**
23:21 They have bound themselves by an oath **n** to eat
24:13 **N** can they prove to you the charge that they
27:20 When **n** sun nor stars appeared for many days,
Ro 4:15 but where there is no law, **n** is there violation.
8:38 For I am convinced that **n** death, nor life,
1Co 3: 7 So **n** the one who plants nor
11: 9 **N** was man created for the sake of woman,
Gal 1: 1 sent **n** by human commission nor
5: 6 For in Christ Jesus **n** circumcision
6:15 **n** circumcision nor uncircumcision is anything;
Heb 7: 3 having **n** beginning of days nor end of life,
10: 8 "You have **n** desired nor taken pleasure
Rev 3:15 you are **n** cold nor hot.
3:16 So, because you are lukewarm, and **n** cold nor hot,
Tob 7:11 "I will **n** eat nor drink anything until you settle
Jdt 7: 4 **n** the high mountains nor the valleys nor
Wis 7: 9 **N** did I liken to her any priceless gem,
12:13 For **n** is there any god besides you,
15: 4 For **n** has the evil intent of human art misled us,
15:15 these have **n** the use of their eyes to see with,
16:12 For **n** herb nor poultice cured them,
Sir 3:21 **N** seek what is too difficult for you,
16:27 They **n** hunger nor grow weary,
23: 6 Let **n** gluttony nor lust overcome me,
30:19 For it can **n** eat nor smell.
LtJ 6:66 They can **n** curse nor bless kings;
1Mc 12:36 to isolate it so that its garrison could **n** buy
15:33 "We have **n** taken foreign land
2Mc 6: 6 People could **n** keep the sabbath,
3Mc 3: 7 alleging that these people were loyal **n** to the king
4:11 so that they could **n** communicate with
2Es 2:12 and they shall **n** toil nor become weary.
4: 8 **n** did I ever ascend into heaven.'
7:*105* **n** shall anyone lay a burden on another;
10: 4 I will **n** eat nor drink,
12:48 I have **n** forsaken you nor withdrawn from you;
13: 9 he **n** lifted his hand nor held a spear
15: 8 **n** will I tolerate their wicked practices.
4Mc 2: 9 through reason so that one **n** gleans the harvest
7: 6 you **n** defiled your sacred teeth
8:27 **n** said any of these things nor
15:21 **N** the melodies of sirens nor the songs

NEKODA (5)

Ezr 2:48 Rezin, **N**, Gazzam,
2:60 Tobiah, and **N**, six hundred fifty-two.
Ne 7:50 of Reaiah, of Rezin, of **N**,
7:62 of Tobiah, of **N**, six hundred forty-two.
1Es 5:37 and the descendants of **N**, six hundred fifty-two.

NEMUEL (3) [NEMUELITES]

Nu 26: 9 The descendants of Eliab: **N**, Dathan, and Abiram.
26:12 of **N**, the clan of the Nemuelites;
1Ch 4:24 **N**, Jamin, Jarib, Zerah, Shaul;

NEMUELITES (1) [NEMUEL]

Nu 26:12 of Nemuel, the clan of the **N**;

NEPHEG (4)

Ex 6:21 The sons of Izhar: Korah, **N**, and Zichri.
2Sa 5:15 Ibhar, Elishua, **N**, Japhia,
1Ch 3: 7 Nogah, **N**, Japhia,
14: 6 Nogah, **N**, and Japhia;

NEPHEW (4)

Ge 14:14 Abram heard that his **n** had been taken captive,
14:16 and also brought back his **n** Lot with his goods,
Tob 1:22 He was my **n** and so a close relative.
11:18 Ahikar and his **n** Nadab were also present

NEPHILIM (3)

Ge 6: 4 The **N** were on the earth in those days—
Nu 13:33 the **N** (the Anakites come from the **N**);

NEPHISH (KJV) See NAPHISH

NEPHISHESIM (KJV) See NEPHUSHESIM

NEPHISIM (2) [=NEPHUSHESIM]

Ezr 2:50 Asnah, Meunim, **N**,
1Es 5:31 the descendants of **N**, the descendants of Acuph,

NEPHTHAI See Index to Footnotes

NEPHTHALIM (KJV) See NAPHTALI

NEPHTHAR (1)

2Mc 1:36 Nehemiah and his associates called this "**n**,"

NEPHTOAH (2)

Jos 15: 9 the mountain to the spring of the Waters of **N**, and
Jos 18:15 to the spring of the Waters of **N**;

NEPHUSHESIM (1) [=NEPHISIM]

Ne 7:52 of Besai, of Meunim, of **N**,

NEPHUSIM (KJV) See NEPHISIM

NEPTHALIM (KJV) See NAPHTALI

NER‡ (16)

1Sa 14:50 the commander of his army was Abner son of **N**,
14:51 and **N** the father of Abner was the son of Abiel.
26: 5 with Abner son of **N**, the commander of his army.
26:14 David called to the army and to Abner son of **N**,
2Sa 2: 8 But Abner son of **N**, commander of Saul's army,
2:12 Abner son of **N**, and the servants of Ishbaal son
3:23 "Abner son of **N** came to the king,
3:25 that Abner son of **N** came to deceive you,
3:28 the LORD for the blood of Abner son of **N**.
3:37 in the killing of Abner son of **N**.
1Ki 2: 5 Abner son of **N**, and Amasa son of Jether,
2:32 Abner son of **N**, commander of the army of Israel,
1Ch 8:33 **N** became the father of Kish, Kish of Saul,
9:36 then Zur, Kish, Baal, **N**, Nadab,
9:39 **N** became the father of Kish, Kish of Saul,
26:28 and Saul son of Kish, and Abner son of **N**,

NEREUS (1)

Ro 16:15 Greet Philologus, Julia, **N** and his sister,

NERGAL (1)

2Ki 17:30 the people of Cuth made **N**,

NERGAL-SHAREZER (3)

Jer 39: 3 **N**, Samgar-nebo, Sarsechim the Rabsaris, **N** the
39:13 Nebushazban the Rabsaris, **N** the Rabmag,

NERI (1)

Lk 3:27 son of Zerubbabel, son of Shealtiel, son of **N**,

NERIAH (11)

Jer 32:12 of purchase to Baruch son of **N** son of Mahseiah,
32:16 the deed of purchase to Baruch son of **N**, I prayed
36: 4 Then Jeremiah called Baruch son of **N**,
36: 8 of **N** did all that the prophet Jeremiah ordered him
36:14 of **N** took the scroll in his hand and came to them.
36:32 to the secretary Baruch son of **N**, who wrote on it
43: 3 but Baruch son of **N** is inciting you against us,
43: 6 also the prophet Jeremiah and Baruch son of **N**.
45: 1 to Baruch son of **N**, when he wrote these words in
51:59 Seraiah son of **N** son of Mahseiah, when he went
Bar 1: 1 the words of the book that Baruch son of **N** son

NERVE (1)

Sir 2:14 Woe to you who have lost your **n**!

NEST‡ (14) [NESTED, NESTLINGS, NESTS]

Nu 24:21 and your **n** is set in the rock;
Dt 22: 6 If you come on a bird's **n**,
32:11 an eagle stirs up its **n**, and hovers over its young;
Job 29:18 Then I thought, 'I shall die in my **n**,
39:27 that the eagle mounts up and makes its **n** on high?
Ps 84: 3 and the swallow a **n** for herself,
Pr 27: 8 that strays from its **n** is one who strays from home.
Isa 10:14 My hand has found, like a **n**,
34:15 There shall the owl **n** and lay and hatch and brood
Jer 49:16 Although you make your **n** as high as the eagle's,
Eze 17:23 the shade of its branches will **n** winged creatures
Ob 1: 4 though your **n** is set among the stars,
Hab 2: 9 setting your **n** on high to be safe from the reach
Sir 36:31 So who will trust a man that has no **n**,

NESTED (2) [NEST]

Jer 22:23 O inhabitant of Lebanon, **n** among the cedars,
Da 4:12 the birds of the air **n** in its branches,

NESTLINGS (2) [NEST]

Isa 16: 2 Like fluttering birds, like scattered **n**,
4Mc 14:16 hatch the **n** and ward off the intruder.

NESTS (10) [NEST]

Job 27:18 They build their houses like **n**,
Ps 104:17 In them the birds build their **n**;
Jer 48:28 Be like the dove that **n** on the sides of the mouth
Eze 31: 6 All the birds of the air made their **n** in its boughs;
Da 4:21 and in whose branches the birds of the air had **n**—
Mt 8:20 "Foxes have holes, and birds of the air have **n**;
13:32 birds of the air come and make **n** in its branches."
Mk 4:32 that the birds of the air can make **n** in its shade."
Lk 9:58 "Foxes have holes, and birds of the air have **n**;
13:19 and the birds of the air made **n** in its branches."

NET‡ (35) [DRAGNET, NETS, NETWORK]

Ex 27: 4 and on the **n** you shall make four bronze rings
27: 5 so that the **n** shall extend halfway down the altar.
1Sa 19:13 she put a **n** of goats' hair on its head,
Job 18: 8 For they are thrust into a **n** by their own feet,
19: 6 and closed his **n** around me.
Ps 9:15 the **n** that they hid has their own foot been caught.
10: 9 they seize the poor and drag them off in their **n**.
25:15 for he will pluck my feet out of the **n**.
31: 4 take me out of the **n** that is hidden for me,
35: 7 For without cause they hid their **n** for me;
35: 8 And let the **n** that they hid ensnare them;
57: 6 They set a **n** for my steps;
66:11 You brought us into the **n**;
140: 5 and with cords they have spread a **n**,
Pr 1:17 in vain is the **n** baited while the bird is looking on;
29: 5 a neighbor is spreading a **n** for the neighbor's feet.
Ecc 9:12 Like fish taken in a cruel **n**,
Isa 51:20 at the head of every street like an antelope in a **n**;
La 1:13 he spread a **n** for my feet;
Eze 12:13 I will spread my **n** over him,
17:20 I will spread my **n** over him,
19: 8 they spread their **n** over him;
32: 3 In an assembly of many peoples I will throw my **n**
Hos 5: 1 and a **n** spread upon Tabor,
7:12 As they go, I will cast my **n** over them;
Hab 1:15 he drags them out with his **n**,
1:16 to his **n** and makes offerings to his seine;
1:17 Is he then to keep on emptying his **n**,
Mt 4:18 casting a **n** into the sea—for they were fishermen.
13:47 the kingdom of heaven is like a **n** that was thrown
Mk 1:16 he saw Simon and his brother Andrew casting a **n**
Jn 21: 6 "Cast the **n** to the right side of the boat,
21: 8 dragging the **n** full of fish,
21:11 Simon Peter went aboard and hauled the **n** ashore,
21:11 though there were so many, the **n** was not torn.

NETAIM (1)

1Ch 4:23 the potters and inhabitants of **N** and Gederah;

NETHANEL (15)

Nu 1: 8 From Issachar, **N** son of Zuar.
2: 5 leader of the Issacharites shall be **N** son of Zuar,
7:18 On the second day **N** son of Zuar,
7:23 This was the offering of **N** son of Zuar.
10:15 the company of the tribe of Issachar was **N** son
1Ch 2:14 **N** the fourth, Raddai the fifth,
15:24 Shebaniah, Joshaphat, **N**, Amasai, Zechariah,
24: 6 The scribe Shemaiah son of **N**, a Levite,
26: 4 Joah the third, Sachar the fourth, **N** the fifth,
2Ch 17: 7 Ben-hail, Obadiah, Zechariah, **N**, and Micaiah,
35: 9 Conaniah also, and his brothers Shemaiah and **N**,
Ezr 10:22 Elioenai, Maaseiah, Ishmael, **N**, Jozabad,
Ne 12:21 of Hilkiah, Hashabiah; of Jedaiah, **N**.
12:36 Milalai, Gilalai, Maai, **N**, Judah, and Hanani,
1Es 1: 9 And Jeconiah and Shemaiah and his brother **N**,

NETHANIAH (21)

2Ki 25:23 namely, Ishmael son of **N**, Johanan son of Kareah,
25:25 Ishmael son of **N** son of Elishama,
1Ch 25: 2 Zaccur, Joseph, **N**, and Asarelah, sons of Asaph,
25:12 the fifth to **N**, his sons and his brothers, twelve;
2Ch 17: 8 With them were the Levites, Shemaiah, **N**,
Jer 36:14 Then all the officials sent Jehudi son of **N** son
40: 8 Ishmael son of **N**, Johanan son of Kareah,
40:14 of the Ammonites has sent Ishmael son of **N**
40:15 "Please let me go and kill Ishmael son of **N**,
41: 1 Ishmael son of **N** son of Elishama,
41: 2 Ishmael son of **N** and the ten men with him got up
41: 6 And Ishmael son of **N** came out from Mizpah
41: 7 of **N** and the men with him slaughtered them,
41: 9 Ishmael son of **N** filled that cistern
41:10 of **N** took them captive and set out to cross over to
41:11 of all the crimes that Ishmael son of **N** had done,
41:12 and went to fight against Ishmael son of **N**.
41:15 But Ishmael son of **N** escaped from Johanan
41:16 of **N** had carried away captive from Mizpah
41:18 because Ishmael son of **N** had killed Gedaliah son
1Es 9:34 Eliasis, Binnui, Elialis, Shimei, Shelemiah, **N**.

NETHER, NETHERMOST (KJV) See BELOW, FOOT, LOWER, LOWEST

NETHINIMS (KJV) See TEMPLE SERVANTS

NETOPHAH (8) [NETOPHATHITE, NETOPHATHITES]

2Sa 23:28 Zalmon the Ahohite; Maharai of **N**;
23:29 Heleb son of Baanah of **N**;
1Ch 11:30 Maharai of **N**, Heled son of Baanah of **N**,
27:13 Tenth, for the tenth month, was Maharai of **N**,
Ezr 2:22 The people of **N**, fifty-six.
Ne 7:26 The people of Bethlehem and **N**,
1Es 5:18 Those from **N**, fifty-five. Those from Anathoth,

NETOPHATHITE (3) [NETOPHAH]

2Ki 25:23 Seraiah son of Tanhumeth the **N**,
1Ch 27:15 Twelfth, for the twelfth month, was Heldai the **N**,
Jer 40: 8 of Tanhumeth, the sons of Ephai the **N**,

NETOPHATHITES (3) [NETOPHAH]

1Ch 2:54 The sons of Salma: Bethlehem, the **N**,
9:16 son of Elkanah, who lived in the villages of the **N**.
Ne 12:28 around Jerusalem and from the villages of the **N**;

NETS (16) [NET]

1Ki 7:17 There were **n** of checker work with wreaths
Ps 141:10 Let the wicked fall into their own **n**,
Ecc 7:26 whose heart is snares and **n**,
Isa 19: 8 and those who spread **n** on the water will languish.

Eze 26: 5 in the midst of the sea, a place for spreading **n.**
26:14 you shall be a place for spreading **n.**
47:10 it will be a place for the spreading of **n;**
Mic 7: 2 and they hunt each other with **n.**
Mt 4:20 Immediately they left their **n** and followed him.
4:21 mending their **n,** and he called them.
Mk 1:18 immediately they left their **n** and followed him.
1:19 who were in their boat mending the **n.**
Lk 5: 2 of them and were washing their **n.**
5: 4 "Put out into the deep water and let down your **n**
5: 5 Yet if you say so, I will let down the **n."**
5: 6 so many fish that their **n** were beginning to break.

NETTLES (5)

Job 30: 7 under the **n** they huddle together.
Pr 24:31 the ground was covered with **n,**
Isa 34:13 **n** and thistles in its fortresses.
Hos 9: 6 **N** shall possess their precious things of silver;
Zep 2: 9 a land possessed by **n** and salt pits,

NETWORK (2) [NET]

Ex 27: 4 You shall also make for it a grating, a **n** of bronze;
38: 4 He made for the altar a grating, a **n** of bronze,

NETWORKS (KJV) See LATTICEWORKS

NEVER‡ (325) [NEVERMORE, NEVERTHELESS]

Ge 8:21 "I will **n** again curse the ground because
9:11 that **n** again shall all flesh be cut off by the waters
9:11 **n** again shall there be a flood to destroy the earth."
9:15 and the waters shall **n** again become a flood
41:19 **N** had I seen such ugly ones in all the land
42:11 your servants have **n** been spies."
44:28 and I have **n** seen him since.
49: 6 May I **n** come into their council;
Ex 4:10 "O my Lord, I have **n** been eloquent,
9:24 such heavy hail as had **n** fallen in all the land
10:11 **n!** Your men may go and worship the LORD,
10:14 a dense swarm of locusts as had **n** been before,
10:29 I will **n** see your face again."
11: 6 such as has **n** been or will ever be again.
14:13 whom you see today you shall **n** see again.
Nu 18: 5 that wrath may **n** again come upon the Israelites.
Dt 3:26 **N** speak to me of this matter again!
13:11 and **n** again do any such wickedness.
13:16 It shall remain a perpetual ruin, **n** to be rebuilt.
15:11 there will **n** cease to be some in need on the earth,
17:16 "You must **n** return that way again."
19:20 a crime such as this shall **n** again be committed
21: 3 that has **n** been worked, one that has not pulled in
23: 6 You shall **n** promote their welfare
28:68 by a route that I promised you would **n** see again;
32:17 not God, to deities they had **n** known,
34:10 **N** since has there arisen a prophet in Israel
Jos 22:27 so that your children may **n** say to our children
Jdg 2: 1 I said, 'I will **n** break my covenant with you.
11:39 She had **n** slept with a man.
16:17 "A razor has **n** come upon my head;
21:12 four hundred young virgins who had **n** slept with
1Sa 6: 7 a new cart and two milch cows that have **n** borne
20: 2 and why should my father hide this from me? **N!"**
20:15 **n** cut off your faithful love from my house,
25:15 we **n** missed anything when we were in the fields,
26:21 my son David, for I will **n** harm you again,
2Sa 3:13 you shall **n** appear in my presence
3:29 of Joab **n** be without one who has a discharge,
12:10 the sword shall **n** depart from your house,
14:10 bring him to me, and he shall **n** touch you again."
1Ki 1: 6 His father had **n** at any time displeased him
8:25 'There shall **n** fail you a successor before me to sit
10:10 **n** again did spices come in such quantity as
22: 8 for he **n** prophesies anything favorable about me,
1Ch 16:30 world is firmly established; it shall **n** be moved.
2Ch 6:16 'There shall **n** fail you a successor before me to sit
7:18 'You shall **n** lack a successor to rule over Israel.'
9:11 there **n** was seen the like of them before in
9:19 The like of it was **n** made in any kingdom.
18: 7 for he **n** prophesies anything favorable about me,
33: 8 I will **n** again remove the feet of Israel from
Ezr 9:12 and **n** seek their peace or prosperity,
Ne 2: 1 Now, I had **n** been sad in his presence before.
Est 1:19 Vashti is **n** again to come before King Ahasuerus;
9:28 of Purim should **n** fall into disuse among the Jews,
Job 3:16 like an infant that **n** sees the light?
7: 7 my eye will **n** again see good.
8:18 then it will deny them, saying, 'I have **n** seen you.'
10:21 before I go, **n** to return, to the land of gloom
19:22 like God, pursue me, **n** satisfied with my flesh?
21:10 their cow calves and **n** miscarries.
21:25 in bitterness of soul, **n** having tasted of good.
24: 1 and why do those who know him **n** see his days?
30:27 My inward parts are in turmoil, and are **n** still;
Ps 10:11 he has hidden his face, he will **n** see it."
15: 5 Those who do these things shall **n** be moved.
30: 6 me, I said in my prosperity, "I shall **n** be moved."
34: 5 so your faces shall **n** be ashamed.
49: 8 For the ransom of life is costly, and can **n** suffice
49: 9 one should live on forever and **n** see the grave.
49:19 who will **n** again see the light.
55:22 he will **n** permit the righteous to be moved.
58: 8 like the untimely birth that **n** sees the sun.
62: 2 my fortress; I shall **n** be shaken.
71: 1 let me **n** be put to shame.
Ps 77: 7 and **n** again be favorable?
80:18 Then we will **n** turn back from you;
89:48 Who can live and **n** see death?
93: 1 He has established the world; it shall **n** be moved;
96:10 world is firmly established; it shall **n** be moved.
104: 5 so that it shall **n** be shaken.
112: 6 For the righteous will **n** be moved;
119:93 I will **n** forget your precepts,
119:133 and **n** let iniquity have dominion over me.
141: 5 **N** let the oil of the wicked anoint my head,
Pr 2:19 those who go to her **n** come back,
10:30 The righteous will **n** be removed,
12: 3 but the root of the righteous will **n** be moved.
25:14 without rain is one who boasts of a gift **n** given.
27:20 Sheol and Abaddon are **n** satisfied,
27:20 and human eyes are **n** satisfied.
28:14 Happy is the one who is **n** without fear,
30:15 Three things are **n** satisfied; four **n** say, "Enough":
30:16 and the fire that **n** says, "Enough."
Ecc 4: 8 and their eyes are **n** satisfied with riches.
5: 2 **N** be rash with your mouth,
9: 6 **n** again will they have any share in all
SS 7: 2 a rounded bowl that **n** lacks mixed wine.
Isa 13:20 It will **n** be inhabited or lived in
14:21 Let them **n** rise to possess the earth or cover
25: 2 of aliens is a city no more, it will **n** be rebuilt.
33:20 whose stakes will **n** be pulled up,
48: 7 before today you have **n** heard of them,
48: 8 You have **n** heard, you have **n** known,
48:19 their name would **n** be cut off or destroyed from
51: 6 and my deliverance will **n** be ended.
54: 9 that the waters of Noah would **n** again go over
56:11 dogs have a mighty appetite; they **n** have enough.
58:11 like a spring of water, whose waters **n** fail.
62: 6 all day and all night they shall **n** be silent.
Jer 11:12 they will **n** save them in the time of their trouble.
19:11 so that it can **n** be mended.
20:11 Their eternal dishonor will **n** be forgotten.
22:12 and he shall **n** see this land again.
31:12 and they shall **n** languish again.
31:40 It shall **n** again be uprooted or overthrown.
32:40 **n** to draw back from doing good to them;
33:17 David shall **n** lack a man to sit on the throne of
33:18 and the levitical priests shall **n** lack a man
35: 6 'You shall **n** drink wine, neither you
50: 5 the LORD by an everlasting covenant that will **n**
50:39 she shall **n** again be peopled,
51:39 and then sleep a perpetual sleep and **n** wake,
51:57 they shall sleep a perpetual sleep and **n** wake,
La 3:22 love of the LORD **n** ceases, his mercies **n** come to
Eze 4:14 "Ah Lord GOD! I have **n** defiled myself;
4:14 now I have **n** eaten what died of itself or was torn
5: 9 I will do to you what I have **n** yet done,
5: 9 and the like of which I will **n** do again.
16:63 **n** open your mouth again because of your shame,
20:32 What is in your mind shall **n** happen—
21:27 I will make it! (Such has **n** occurred.)
26:14 You shall **n** again be rebuilt,
26:21 though sought for, you will **n** be found again,
29:15 and **n** again exalt itself above the nations;
29:15 that they will **n** again rule over the nations.
29:16 The Egyptians shall **n** again be the reliance of
35: 9 and your cities shall **n** be inhabited.
36:30 that you may **n** again suffer the disgrace of famine
37:22 **N** again shall they be two nations,
37:22 **n** again shall they be divided into two kingdoms.
37:23 They shall **n** again defile themselves
39:29 and I will **n** again hide my face from them,
Da 2:44 of heaven will set up a kingdom that shall **n**
6:26 His kingdom shall **n** be destroyed,
7:14 and his kingship is one that shall **n** be destroyed.
9:12 that what has been done against Jerusalem has **n**
12: 1 such as has **n** occurred since nations first came
Joel 2: 2 their like has **n** been from of old,
2:26 And my people shall **n** again be put to shame.
2:27 And my people shall **n** again be put to shame.
3:17 and strangers shall **n** again pass through it.
Am 7: 8 I will **n** again pass them by;
7:13 but **n** again prophesy at Bethel,
8: 2 I will **n** again pass them by.
8: 7 Surely I will **n** forget any of their deeds.
8:14 they shall fall, and **n** rise again.
9:15 and they shall **n** again be plucked up out of
Ob 1:16 and shall be as though they had **n** been.
Na 1:15 for **n** again shall the wicked invade you;
Hab 1: 4 So the law becomes slack and justice **n** prevails.
2: 5 like Death they **n** have enough.
Hag 1: 6 you eat, but you **n** have enough;
1: 6 you drink, but you **n** have your fill;
Zec 14:11 for **n** again shall it be doomed to destruction;
Mt 5:20 you will **n** enter the kingdom of heaven.
5:26 you will **n** get out until you have paid
7:23 Then I will declare to them, 'I **n** knew you;
9:33 **"N** has anything like this been seen in Israel."
13:14 'You will indeed listen, but **n** understand,
13:14 and you will indeed look, but **n** perceive.
16:22 This must **n** happen to you."
18: 3 you will **n** enter the kingdom of heaven.
18:13 over the ninety-nine that **n** went astray.
21:16 Jesus said to them, "Yes; have you **n** read,
21:42 "Have you **n** read in the scriptures:
24:21 of the world until now, no, and **n** will be.
26:29 I will **n** again drink of this fruit of the vine until
26:33 because of you, I will **n** desert you."
Mk 2:12 saying, "We have **n** seen anything like this!"
2:25 "Have you **n** read what David did when he
3:29 against the Holy Spirit can **n** have forgiveness,
Mk 9:25 come out of him, and **n** enter him again!"
9:48 their worm **n** dies, and the fire is **n** quenched.
10:15 of God as a little child will **n** enter it."
11: 2 a colt that has **n** been ridden;
13:19 that God created until now, no, and **n** will be.
14:25 I will **n** again drink of the fruit of the vine until
Lk 1:15 He must **n** drink wine or strong drink;
2:37 She **n** left the temple but worshiped there
12:59 you will **n** get out until you have paid
15:29 and I have **n** disobeyed your command;
15:29 yet you have **n** given me even a young goat
18:17 of God as a little child will **n** enter it."
19:30 a colt that has **n** been ridden.
23:29 wombs that **n** bore, and the breasts that **n** nursed.'
Jn 4:14 of the water that I will give them will **n** be thirsty.
4:15 so that I may **n** be thirsty or have
5:37 You have **n** heard his voice or seen his form,
6:35 Whoever comes to me will **n** be hungry, and whoever believes in me will **n** be thirsty.
6:37 and anyone who comes to me I will **n** drive away;
7:15 when he has **n** been taught?"
7:46 police answered, **"N** has anyone spoken like this!"
8:12 Whoever follows me will **n** walk in darkness
8:33 of Abraham and have **n** been slaves to anyone.
8:51 whoever keeps my word will **n** see death."
8:52 'Whoever keeps my word will **n** taste death.'
9:32 **N** since the world began has it been heard
10:28 I give them eternal life, and they will **n** perish.
11:26 everyone who lives and believes in me will **n** die.
13: 8 Peter said to him, "You will **n** wash my feet."
Ac 6:13 "This man **n** stops saying things
10:14 for I have **n** eaten anything that is profane
13:41 a work that you will **n** believe,
14: 8 not use his feet and had **n** walked,
28:26 but **n** understand, and you will indeed look,
28:26 and you will indeed look, but **n** perceive.
Ro 6: 9 being raised from the dead, will **n** die again;
10:14 to believe in one of whom they have **n** heard?
12:19 Beloved, **n** avenge yourselves,
14:13 but resolve instead **n** to put a stumbling block
15:21 "Those who have **n** been told of him shall see,
15:21 those who have **n** heard of him shall understand."
1Co 6:15 and make them members of a prostitute? **N!**
8:13 if food is a cause of their falling, I will **n** eat meat,
13: 8 Love **n** ends. But as for prophecies,
Gal 6:14 May I **n** boast of anything except the cross
Col 3:19 love your wives and **n** treat them harshly.
1Th 2: 5 we **n** came with words of flattery or with a pretext
1Ti 5:19 **N** accept any accusation against an elder except
2Ti 3: 7 who are always being instructed and can **n** arrive
Tit 1: 2 who **n** lies, promised before the ages began—
Heb 1:12 But you are the same, and your years will **n** end."
10: 1 and not the true form of these realities, it can **n,**
10:11 the same sacrifices that can **n** take away sins.
13: 5 he has said, "I will **n** leave you or forsake you."
Jas 1: 6 But ask in faith, **n** doubting,
1Pe 3: 6 as you do what is good and **n** let fears alarm you.
5: 4 you will win the crown of glory that **n** fades away.
2Pe 1:10 for if you do this, you will **n** stumble.
2:21 For it would have been better for them **n**
Rev 3:12 you will **n** go out of it.
18: 7 I am no widow, and I will **n** see grief,'
18:14 and your splendor are lost to you, **n** to
21:25 Its gates will **n** be shut by day—
Tob 3: 9 May we **n** see a son or daughter of yours!"
3:10 **"N** shall they reproach my father, saying to him,
6: 8 and every affliction will flee away and **n** remain
6:18 and will **n** be seen near her any more.
Jdt 8:13 but you will **n** learn anything!
8:18 "For **n** in our generation, nor in these present days,
11: 1 for I have **n** hurt anyone who chose
11: 2 I would **n** have lifted my spear against them.
13:19 Your praise will **n** depart from the hearts
AdE 9:28 of them was **n** to cease among their descendants.
10: 9 wonders that have **n** happened among the nations.
Wis 2: 2 hereafter we shall be as though we had **n** been,
7:10 because her radiance **n** ceases.
10: 8 so that their failures could **n** go unnoticed.
12:10 and that their way of thinking would **n** change.
15:17 since they have life, but the idols **n** had.
Sir 4:25 **N** speak against the truth,
7: 1 Do no evil, and evil will **n** overtake you.
7:36 and then you will **n** sin.
9: 9 **N** dine with another man's wife,
11: 5 but one who was **n** thought of has worn a crown.
12:10 **N** trust your enemy, for like corrosion in copper,
12:16 if he finds an opportunity he will **n** have enough
15: 8 and liars will **n** think of her.
16:28 and they **n** disobey his word.
19: 7 **N** repeat a conversation, and you will lose nothing
22:13 and you will **n** be wearied by his lack of sense.
23: 7 the one who observes it will **n** be caught.
23:10 and utters the Name will **n** be cleansed from sin.
23:12 may it **n** be found in the inheritance of Jacob!
23:14 then you will wish that you had **n** been born,
23:15 using abusive language will **n** become disciplined
23:16 near of kin will **n** cease until the fire burns him up.
23:17 he will **n** weary until he dies.
23:26 an accursed memory and her disgrace will **n**
27:16 and will **n** find a congenial friend.
35: 9 and it will **n** be forgotten.
38: 8 God's works will **n** be finished;
39: 9 it will **n** be blotted out.
39:31 their time comes they **n** disobey his command."
41:11 but a virtuous name will **n** be blotted out.
43:10 they **n** relax in their watches.
43:27 We could say more but could **n** say enough;

Sir 44: 9 they have perished as though they had **n** existed;
44: 9 they have become as though they had **n** been born,
44:13 and their glory will **n** be blotted out.
44:18 that all flesh should **n** again be blotted out by
47:22 But the Lord will **n** give up his mercy,
47:22 he will **n** blot out the descendants
48:12 **N** in his lifetime did he tremble before any ruler,
51:18 and I shall **n** be disappointed.
51:20 therefore I will **n** be forsaken.
51:29 and may you **n** be ashamed to praise him.
Bar 2:35 and I will **n** again remove my people Israel from
Bel 1: 7 and it **n** ate or drank anything."
1:35 Habakkuk said, "Sir, I have **n** seen Babylon,
1Mc 2:48 and they **n** let the sinner gain the upper hand.
6:36 they went with it, and they **n** left it.
2Mc 6:16 Therefore he **n** withdraws his mercy from us.
10: 4 and implored the Lord that they might **n** again fall
15:36 by public vote **n** to let this day go unobserved,
3Mc 3:16 who **n** cease from their folly.
7: 4 that our government would **n** be firmly established
7:11 the divine commandments would **n**
2Es 3:15 that you would **n** forsake his descendants;
4: 8 'I **n** went down into the deep,
7:14 they can **n** receive those things
7:18 the difficult circumstances and will **n** see
8:47 to the unrighteous. **N** do so!
11:19 after another and then were **n** seen again.
16:67 from your sins, and forget your iniquities, **n**
4Mc 6:17 "**N** may we, the children of Abraham, think
12:12 and these throughout all time will **n** let you go.

NEVERMORE (1) [NEVER]

Isa 14:20 May the descendants of evildoers **n** be named!

NEVERTHELESS (57) [NEVER]

Ge 48:19 **N** his younger brother shall be greater than he,
Ex 32:34 **N,** when the day comes for punishment,
Nu 14:21 **n**—as I live, and as all the earth shall be filled
25: 9 **N** those that died by the plague were twenty-four thousand.
31:23 **N** it shall also be purified with the water
Jdg 1:33 **n** the inhabitants of Beth-shemesh and
4: 9 And she said, "I will surely go with you; **n,**
11: 8 The elders of Gilead said to Jephthah, "**N,**
1Sa 29: 6 **N** the lords do not approve of you.
29: 9 **n,** the commanders of the Philistines have said,
2Sa 5: 7 **N** David took the stronghold of Zion,
12:14 **N,** because by this deed you have utterly scorned
1Ki 8:19 **n** you shall not build the house,
11:34 **N** I will not take the whole kingdom away
15: 4 **N** for David's sake the LORD his God gave him
15:14 **N** the heart of Asa was true to the LORD
20: 6 **n** I will send my servants to you tomorrow
2Ki 3: 3 **N** he clung to the sin of Jeroboam son of Nebat,
12: 3 **N** the high places were not taken away;
13: 6 **N** they did not depart from the sins of the house
15: 4 **N** the high places were not taken away;
15:35 **N** the high places were not removed;
1Ch 11: 5 **N** David took the stronghold of Zion,
2Ch 6: 9 **n** you shall not build the house,
12: 8 **N** they shall be his servants,
15:17 **N** the heart of Asa was true all his days.
19: 3 **N,** some good is found in you,
Ne 9:26 "**N** they were disobedient and rebelled against you
9:31 **N,** in your great mercies you did not make an end
13:26 **n,** foreign women made even him to sin.
Est 5:10 **n** Haman restrained himself and went home.
Ps 73:23 **N** I am continually with you;
82: 7 **n,** you shall die like mortals, and fall
106:44 **N** he regarded their distress
Eze 20:17 **N** my eye spared them, and I did not destroy them
Da 5:17 **N** I will read the writing to the king
Jnh 1:13 **N** the men rowed hard to bring the ship back
Lk 7:35 **N,** wisdom is vindicated by all her children."
10:20 **N,** do not rejoice at this, that the spirits submit
Jn 12:42 **N** many, even of the authorities, believed in him.
16: 7 **N** I tell you the truth:
Ro 15:15 **N** on some points I have written
1Co 9:12 **N,** we have not made use of this right,
10: 5 **N,** God was not pleased with most of them,
11:11 **N,** in the Lord woman is not independent of man
14:19 **n,** in church I would rather speak five words
2Co 12:16 **N** (you say) since I was crafty,
AdE 5:10 **N,** he went home and summoned his friends
Sir 19:28 he will **n** do evil when he finds the opportunity.
29: 8 **N,** be patient with someone
2Mc 2:27 **N,** to secure the gratitude
14:18 **N** Nicanor, hearing of the valor of Judas
15: 5 **N,** he did not succeed in carrying
3Mc 3: 6 **N** those of other races paid no heed
2Es 7:22 **N** they were not obedient, and spoke against him;
12:18 **n** it shall not fall then,
4Mc 15:11 **N,** though so many factors influenced the mother

NEW‡ (176) [ANEW, NEWBORN, NEWLY, NEWLY-CREATED, NEWNESS]

A. NEW MOON (28)
B. NEW WINE (14)
C. NEW MOONS (13)
D. NEW SONG (10)
E. NEW COVENANT (8)

Ex 1: 8 Now a **n** king arose over Egypt,
19: 1 the third **n** moon after the Israelites had gone A
Lev 2:14 the grain offering of your first fruits coarse **n** grain
Lev 23:16 then you shall present an offering of **n** grain to
26:10 to clear out the old to make way for the **n.**
Nu 16:30 But if the LORD creates something **n,**
28:26 of **n** grain to the LORD at your festival of weeks,
29: 6 in addition to the burnt offering of the **n** moon A
Dt 20: 5 "Has anyone built a **n** house but not dedicated it?
22: 8 When you build a **n** house,
32: 2 like showers on **n** growth.
32:17 to **n** ones recently arrived,
Jos 9:13 these wineskins were **n** when we filled them,
Jdg 5: 8 **n** gods were chosen, then war was in the gates.
15:13 So they bound him with two **n** ropes,
16:11 they bind me with **n** ropes that have not been used,
16:12 So Delilah took **n** ropes and bound him with them,
1Sa 6: 7 a **n** cart and two milch cows that have never borne
20: 5 said to Jonathan, "Tomorrow is the **n** moon, A
20:18 Jonathan said to him, "Tomorrow is the **n** moon; A
20:24 the **n** moon came, the king sat at the feast to eat. A
20:27 But on the second day, the day after the **n** moon, A
2Sa 6: 3 They carried the ark of God on a **n** cart,
6: 3 the sons of Abinadab, were driving the **n** cart
21:16 and who was fitted out with **n** weapons,
1Ki 11:29 Ahijah had clothed himself with a **n** garment.
11:30 of the **n** garment he was wearing and tore it
2Ki 2:20 He said, "Bring me a **n** bowl, and put salt in it."
4:23 It is neither **n** moon nor sabbath." A
1Ch 13: 7 They carried the ark of God on a **n** cart,
23:31 **n** moons, and appointed festivals, C
2Ch 2: 4 and the **n** moons and the appointed festivals of C
8:13 the **n** moons, and the three annual festivals— C
20: 5 in the house of the LORD, before the **n** court,
31: 3 the **n** moons, and the appointed festivals, C
Ezr 3: 5 at the **n** moon and at all the sacred festivals of A
9: 9 to give us **n** life to set up the house of our God,
Ne 10:33 sabbaths, the **n** moons, the appointed festivals, C
Job 29:20 and my bow ever **n** in my hand.'
32:19 like **n** wineskins, it is ready to burst.
Ps 33: 3 Sing to him a **n** song; D
40: 3 He put a **n** song in my mouth, D
51:10 O God, and put a **n** and right spirit within me.
81: 3 the trumpet at the **n** moon, at the full moon, A
96: 1 O sing to the LORD a **n** song; D
98: 1 O sing to the LORD a **n** song, D
144: 9 I will sing a **n** song to you, O God; D
149: 1 Sing to the LORD a **n** song, D
Pr 27:25 When the grass is gone, and **n** growth appears,
Ecc 1: 9 there is nothing **n** under the sun.
1:10 Is there a thing of which it is said, "See, this is **n**"?
SS 7:13 **n** as well as old, which I have laid up for you,
Isa 1:13 **N** moon and sabbath and calling of convocation A
1:14 Your **n** moons and your appointed festivals C
15: 6 the grass is withered, the **n** growth fails,
41:15 I will make of you a threshing sledge, sharp, **n,**
42: 9 and **n** things I now declare;
42:10 Sing to the LORD a **n** song, D
43:19 I am about to do a **n** thing;
47:13 at each **n** moon predict what shall befall you. A
48: 6 From this time forward I make you hear **n** things,
62: 2 and you shall be called by a **n** name that the mouth
65:17 I am about to create **n** heavens and a **n** earth;
66:22 For as the **n** heavens and the **n** earth,
66:23 From **n** moon to new moon, A
66:23 From new moon to **n** moon, A
Jer 26:10 and took their seat in the entry of the **N** Gate of
31:22 For the LORD has created a **n** thing on the earth:
31:31 when I will make a **n** covenant with the house E
36:10 at the entry of the **N** Gate of the LORD's house.
La 3:23 they are **n** every morning;
Eze 11:19 and put a **n** spirit within them;
18:31 and get yourselves a **n** heart and a **n** spirit!
36:26 A **n** heart I will give you, and a **n** spirit I will put
45:17 drink offerings, at the festivals, the **n** moons, C
46: 1 and on the day of the **n** moon it shall be opened. A
46: 3 the LORD on the sabbaths and on the **n** moons. C
46: 6 day of the **n** moon he shall offer a young bull A
Hos 2:11 her festivals, her **n** moons, her sabbaths, C
4:11 Wine and **n** wine take away the understanding. B
5: 7 **n** moon shall devour them along with their A
9: 2 and the **n** wine shall fail them. B
Am 8: 5 the **n** moon be over so that we may sell grain; A
Hag 1:11 the **n** wine, the oil, on what the soil produces, B
Zec 9:17 and **n** wine the young women. B
Mt 9:17 Neither is **n** wine put into old wineskins; B
9:17 but **n** wine is put into fresh wineskins, B
13:52 of his treasure what is **n** and what is old."
23:15 and you make the **n** convert twice as much a child
26:29 the vine until that day when I drink it **n** with you
27:60 and laid it in his own **n** tomb,
Mk 1:27 A **n** teaching—with authority!
2:21 the patch pulls away from it, the **n** from the old,
2:22 And no one puts **n** wine into old wineskins; B
2:22 but one puts **n** wine into fresh wineskins." B
14:25 that day when I drink it **n** in the kingdom of God."
16:17 ⟦they will speak in **n** tongues;⟧
Lk 5:36 from a **n** garment and sews it on an old garment;
5:36 otherwise the **n** will be torn,
5:36 and the piece from the **n** will not match the old.
5:37 And no one puts **n** wine into old wineskins; B
5:37 **n** wine will burst the skins and will be spilled, B
5:38 But **n** wine must be put into fresh wineskins. B
5:39 no one after drinking old wine desires **n** wine, B
22:20 that is poured out for you is the **n** covenant E
Jn 13:34 I give you a **n** commandment,
19:41 a **n** tomb in which no one had ever been laid.
Ac 2:13 "They are filled with **n** wine." B
17:19 "May we know what this **n** teaching is
17:21 in nothing but telling or hearing something **n.**
Ro 7: 6 the old written code but in the **n** life of the Spirit.
1Co 5: 7 the old yeast so that you may be a **n** batch,
11:25 saying, "This cup is the **n** covenant in my blood. E
2Co 3: 6 to be ministers of a **n** covenant, not of letter but E
5:17 So if anyone is in Christ, there is a **n** creation:
5:17 see, everything has become **n!**
Gal 6:15 but a **n** creation is everything!
Eph 2:15 that he might create in himself one **n** humanity
4:24 and to clothe yourselves with the **n** self,
Col 2:16 and drink or of observing festivals, **n** moons, C
3:10 and have clothed yourselves with the **n** self,
Heb 8: 8 I will establish a **n** covenant with the house E
8:13 In speaking of "a **n** covenant," E
9:15 this reason he is the mediator of a **n** covenant, E
10:20 the **n** and living way that he opened for us through
12:24 Jesus, the mediator of a **n** covenant, E
1Pe 1: 3 By his great mercy he has given us a **n** birth into
2Pe 3:13 we wait for **n** heavens and a **n** earth,
1Jn 2: 7 Beloved, I am writing you no **n** commandment,
2: 8 a **n** commandment that is true in him and in you,
2Jn 1: 5 as though I were writing you a **n** commandment,
Rev 2:17 and on the white stone is written a **n** name
3:12 the **n** Jerusalem that comes down from my God out of heaven, and my own **n** name.
5: 9 They sing a **n** song: "You are worthy to take D
14: 3 and they sing a **n** song before the throne and D
21: 1 Then I saw a **n** heaven and a **n** earth;
21: 2 And I saw the holy city, the **n** Jerusalem,
21: 5 "See, I am making all things **n.**"
Jdt 8: 6 before the **n** moon and the day of the new moon, A
8: 6 before the new moon and the day of the **n** moon, A
16: 1 Raise to him a **n** psalm; exalt him, and call upon
16:13 I will sing to my God a **n** song: D
Wis 14: 6 to the world the seed of a **n** generation.
19:11 Afterward they saw also a **n** kind of birds,
Sir 9:10 for **n** ones cannot equal them.
9:10 A **n** friend is like new wine;
9:10 A new friend is like **n** wine; B
36: 6 Give **n** signs, and work other wonders;
43: 8 The **n** moon, as its name suggests, renews itself; A
46:12 May their bones send forth **n** life from
49:10 the bones of the Twelve Prophets send forth **n** life
1Mc 4:47 and built a **n** altar like the former one.
4:49 They made **n** holy vessels,
4:53 on the **n** altar of burnt offering that they had built.
10:34 and sabbaths and **n** moons and appointed days, C
2Mc 2:29 the master builder of a **n** house must be concerned
4:11 of living and introduced **n** customs contrary to
1Es 5:52 and at **n** moons and at all the consecrated feasts. C
5:53 from the **n** moon of the seventh month, A
5:57 of God on the **n** moon of the second month in A
6: 9 the city of Jerusalem a great **n** house for the Lord,
6:25 of hewn stone and one course of **n** native timber;
8: 6 on the **n** moon of the first month and arrived A
8: 6 in Jerusalem on the **n** moon of the fifth month, A
9:16 and on the **n** moon of the tenth month A
9:17 to an end by the **n** moon of the first month. A
9:37 On the **n** moon of the seventh month, A
9:40 on the **n** moon of the seventh month. A
2Es 1:31 I have rejected your festal days, and **n** moons, C

NEWBORN (3) [BEAR, NEW]

Jer 14: 5 Even the doe in the field forsakes her **n** fawn
1Pe 2: 2 Like **n** infants, long for the pure, spiritual milk,
3Mc 1:20 and nurses abandoned even **n** children here

NEWLY (1) [NEW]

Dt 24: 5 When a man is **n** married, he shall not go out with

NEWLY-CREATED (1) [CREATE, NEW]

Wis 11:18 or **n** unknown beasts full of rage, or such

NEWNESS (1) [NEW]

Ro 6: 4 so we too might walk in **n** of life.

NEWS (89)

A. GOOD NEWS (61)

Ge 29:13 Laban heard the **n** about his sister's son Jacob,
1Sa 4:13 When the man came into the city and told the **n,**
4:19 she heard the **n** that the ark of God was captured,
31: 9 to carry the good **n** to the houses of their idols A
2Sa 4: 4 the **n** about Saul and Jonathan came from Jezreel.
4:10 Saul is dead,' thought he was bringing good **n,** A
4:10 this was the reward I gave him for his **n.**
11:18 Then Joab sent and told David all the **n** about
11:19 "When you have finished telling the king all the **n**
1Ki 1:42 a worthy man and surely you bring good **n.**" A
2:28 When the **n** came to Joab—
2Ki 7: 9 This is a day of good **n;** A
9:15 of the city to go and tell the **n** in Jezreel."
1Ch 10: 9 to carry the good **n** to their idols and to the A
Ps 40: 9 I have told the glad **n** of deliverance in
Pr 15:30 and good **n** refreshes the body. A
25:25 so is good **n** from a far country. A
Isa 52: 7 who brings good **n,** who announces salvation, A
61: 1 he has sent me to bring good **n** to the oppressed, A
Jer 6:24 "We have heard **n** of them, our hands fall helpless;
20:15 be the man who brought the **n** to my father,
37: 5 Chaldeans who were besieging Jerusalem heard **n**
49:23 for they have heard bad **n;**
50:43 The king of Babylon heard **n** of them,
Eze 21: 7 you shall say, "Because of the **n** that has come.
24:26 to you to report to you the **n.**

Jnh 3:6 When the **n** reached the king of Nineveh,
Na 3:19 All who hear the **n** about you clap their hands
Mt 4:23 in their synagogues and proclaiming the good **n** A
9:31 But they went away and spread the **n** about him
9:35 and proclaiming the good **n** of the kingdom, A
10:7 As you go, proclaim the good **n,** A
11:5 and the poor have good **n** brought to them. A
24:14 And this good **n** of the kingdom will A
26:13 wherever this good **n** is proclaimed in A
Mk 1:1 The beginning of the good **n** of Jesus Christ, A
1:14 proclaiming the good **n** of God, A
1:15 repent, and believe in the good **n."** A
10:29 for my sake and for the sake of the good **n,** A
13:10 good **n** must first be proclaimed to all nations. A
14:9 the good **n** is proclaimed in the whole world, A
16:15 ⟦Go into all the world and proclaim the good **n**⟧ A
16:20 ⟦and proclaimed the good **n** everywhere,⟧ A
Lk 1:19 to speak to you and to bring you this good **n.** A
2:10 I am bringing you good **n** of great joy for all A
3:18 he proclaimed the good **n** to the people. A
4:18 he has anointed me to bring good **n** to the poor. A
4:43 "I must proclaim the good **n** of the kingdom A
7:22 the poor have good **n** brought to them. A
8:1 and bringing the good **n** of the kingdom of God. A
9:6 the good **n** and curing diseases everywhere. A
16:16 the good **n** of the kingdom of God is proclaimed, A
20:1 the people in the temple and telling the good **n,** A
Ac 8:12 the good **n** about the kingdom of God and A
8:25 the good **n** to many villages of the Samaritans. A
8:35 he proclaimed to him the good **n** about Jesus. A
8:40 he proclaimed the good **n** to all the towns A
11:22 **N** of this came to the ears of the church
13:32 the good **n** that what God promised A
14:7 there they continued proclaiming the good **n.** A
14:15 and we bring you good **n,** A
14:21 they had proclaimed the good **n** to that city A
15:7 Gentiles would hear the message of the good **n** A
16:10 that God had called us to proclaim the good **n** A
17:18 because he was telling the good **n** about Jesus A
20:24 to testify to the good **n** of God's grace. A
Ro 10:15 are the feet of those who bring good **n!"** A
10:16 But not all have obeyed the good **n;** A
15:19 as Illyricum I have fully proclaimed the good **n** A
15:20 to proclaim the good **n,** not A
1Co 15:1 of the good **n** that I proclaimed to you, A
2Co 2:12 came to Troas to proclaim the good **n** of Christ, A
8:18 the churches for his proclaiming the good **n;** A
10:14 to come all the way to you with the good **n** A
10:16 we may proclaim the good **n** in lands beyond A
11:7 proclaimed God's good **n** to you free of charge? A
Eph 3:8 to the Gentiles the **n** of the boundless riches
Php 2:19 so that I may be cheered by **n** of you.
Col 4:7 Tychicus will tell you all the **n** about me;
1Th 3:6 brought us the good **n** of your faith and love. A
2Th 2:14 through our proclamation of the good **n,** A
Heb 2:2 indeed the good **n** came to us just as to them; A
4:6 good **n** failed to enter because of disobedience, A
1Pe 1:12 through those who brought you good **n** by A
1:25 word is the good **n** that was announced to you. A
1Mc 6:8 When the king heard this **n,**
2Mc 5:11 When **n** of what had happened reached the king,
9:3 **n** came to him of what had happened to Nicanor
9:24 or any unwelcome **n** came,

NEXT‡ (148) [NEXT-OF-KIN]

Ge 4:2 **N** she bore his brother Abel.
17:21 to you at this season **n** year."
19:34 On the **n** day, the firstborn said to the younger,
Ex 2:13 When he went out the **n** day,
9:6 And on the **n** day the LORD did so;
18:13 The **n** day Moses sat as judge for the people,
25:35 of one piece with it under the **n** pair of branches,
26:19 and two bases under the **n** frame for its two pegs;
26:21 and two bases under the **n** frame;
26:25 and two bases under the **n** frame.
28:26 on its inside edge **n** to the ephod.
32:6 They rose early the **n** day,
32:30 On the **n** day Moses said to the people,
36:24 and two bases under the **n** frame for its two pegs;
36:26 the first frame and two bases under the **n** frame.
37:21 of one piece with it under the **n** pair of branches,
39:19 on its inside edge **n** to the ephod.
Lev 6:10 after putting on his linen undergarments **n**
7:16 and what is left of it shall be eaten the **n** day;
9:15 **N** he presented the people's offering.
16:4 shall have the linen undergarments **n** to his body,
19:6 on the same day you offer it, or on the **n** day;
25:25 then the **n** of kin shall come and redeem what
Nu 2:5 to camp **n** to him shall be the tribe of Issachar.
2:12 to camp **n** to him shall be the tribe of Simeon.
2:20 **N** to him shall be the tribe of Manasseh.
2:27 to camp **n** to him shall be the tribe of Asher.
5:8 If the injured party has no **n** of kin
10:18 **N** the standard of the camp of Reuben set out,
10:22 **N** the standard of the Ephraimite camp set out,
11:32 and night and all the **n** day, gathering the quails;
16:41 On the **n** day, however, the whole congregation of
17:8 into the tent of the covenant on the **n** day,
22:5 and they have settled **n** to me.
22:41 On the **n** day Balak took Balaam and brought him
Dt 16:7 the **n** morning you may go back to your tents.
29:22 The **n** generation, your children who rise up
Jos 10:31 **N** Joshua passed on from Libnah,
12:9 the king of Ai, which is **n** to Bethel one
Jdg 6:38 he rose early **n** morning and squeezed the fleece,
21:4 On the **n** day, the people got up early,

1Sa 5:3 When the people of Ashdod rose early the **n** day,
5:4 But when they rose early on the **n** morning,
11:11 The **n** day Saul put the people in three companies.
17:13 and **n** to him Abinadab, and the third Shammah.
18:10 **n** day an evil spirit from God rushed upon Saul,
30:17 from twilight until the evening of the **n** day.
31:8 The **n** day, when the Philistines came to strip
2Sa 11:12 in Jerusalem that day. On the **n** day,
14:30 Joab's field is **n** to mine, and he has barley there;
23:9 **N** to him among the three warriors was Eleazar
23:11 **N** to him was Shammah son of Agee, the Hararite.
1Ki 1:6 and he was born **n** after Absalom.
6:22 **N** he overlaid the whole house with gold,
18:33 **N** he put the wood in order, cut the bull in pieces,
2Ki 3:20 The **n** day, about the time of the morning offering,
6:29 The **n** day I said to her,
8:15 But the **n** day he took the bed-cover and dipped it
1Ch 10:8 **n** day when the Philistines came to strip the dead,
11:12 **n** to him among the three warriors was Eleazar
29:21 On the **n** day they offered sacrifices
2Ch 17:15 and **n** to him Jehohanan the commander,
17:16 and **n** to him Amasiah son of Zichri,
17:18 and **n** to him Jehozabad with one
28:7 and Elkanah the **n** in authority to the king.
Ne 3:2 And the men of Jericho built **n** to him.
3:2 And **n** to them Zaccur son of Imri built.
3:4 **N** to them Meremoth son of Uriah son
3:4 **N** to them Meshullam son of Berechiah son
3:4 **N** to them Zadok son of Baana made repairs.
3:5 **N** to them the Tekoites made repairs;
3:7 **N** to them repairs were made by Melatiah
3:8 **N** to them Uzziel son of Harhaiah,
3:8 **N** to him Hananiah, one of the perfumers,
3:9 **N** to them Rephaiah son of Hur,
3:10 **N** to them Jedaiah son of Harumaph
3:10 and **n** to him Hattush son
3:12 **N** to him Shallum son of Hallohesh,
3:17 **n** to him Hashabiah, ruler of half the district
3:19 **n** to him Ezer son of Jeshua,
Est 1:14 and those **n** to him were Carshena,
10:3 the Jew was **n** in rank to King Ahasuerus,
Ps 48:13 that you may tell the **n** generation
78:6 that the **n** generation might know them,
Jer 20:3 The **n** morning when Pashhur released Jeremiah
51:46 one year one rumor comes, the **n** year another,
Eze 24:18 And on the **n** morning I did as I was commanded.
40:14 the gate **n** to the pilaster on every side of the court.
Da 5:5 of the wall of the royal palace, **n** to the lampstand.
Jnh 4:7 But when dawn came up the **n** day,
Mt 10:23 they persecute you in one town, flee to the **n;**
27:62 The **n** day, that is, after the day of Preparation,
Lk 9:37 On the **n** day, when they had come down from
10:35 The **n** day he took out two denarii,
13:9 If it bears fruit **n** year, well and good;
13:33 tomorrow, and the **n** day I must be on my way,
20:11 **N** he sent another slave;
Jn 1:29 The **n** day he saw Jesus coming toward him
1:35 The **n** day John again was standing with two
1:43 The **n** day Jesus decided to go to Galilee.
6:22 The **n** day the crowd that had stayed on
12:12 The **n** day the great crowd that had come to
13:23 one whom Jesus loved—was reclining **n** to him;
13:25 So while reclining **n** to Jesus, he asked him,
21:20 the one who had reclined **n** to Jesus at the supper
Ac 4:3 and put them in custody until the **n** day,
4:5 The **n** day their rulers, elders,
7:26 The **n** day he came to some of them
10:9 the **n** day, as they were on their journey
10:23 The **n** day he got up and went with them,
13:42 to speak about these things again the **n** sabbath.
13:44 The **n** sabbath almost the whole city gathered
14:20 The **n** day he went on with Barnabas to Derbe.
18:7 his house was **n** door to the synagogue.
20:7 since he intended to leave the **n** day,
20:15 The **n** day we touched at Samos,
21:1 and the **n** day to Rhodes, and from there to Patara.
21:8 The **n** day we left and came to Caesarea;
21:18 The **n** day Paul went with us to visit James;
21:26 Then Paul took the men, and the **n** day,
22:30 the **n** day he released him and ordered
23:32 The **n** day they let the horsemen go on with him,
25:6 the **n** day he took his seat on the tribunal
25:17 the **n** day took my seat on the tribunal and ordered
25:23 So on the **n** day Agrippa and Bernice came
27:3 The **n** day we put in at Sidon;
27:18 the storm so violently that on the **n** day they began
Heb 7:2 **n** he is also king of Salem, that is, "king of peace."
Tob 4:14 over until the **n** day the wages of those who work
6:12 and you, as **n** of kin to her,
11:13 **N,** with both his hands he peeled off
Jdt 7:1 The **n** day Holofernes ordered his whole army,
13:9 **N** she rolled his body off the bed and pulled down
16:24 to all those who were **n** of kin
AdE 4:8 for Haman, who stands **n** to the king,
Sir 12:12 Do not put him **n** to you,
LtJ 6:43 she derides the woman **n** to her,
Sus 1:28 The **n** day, when the people gathered at the house
1Mc 4:28 **n** year he mustered sixty thousand picked infantry
5:35 **N** he turned aside to Maapha,
2Mc 7:15 **N** they brought forward the fifth
12:39 On the **n** day, as had now become necessary,
1Es 3:7 and because of his wisdom he shall sit **n** to Darius
4:42 You shall sit **n** to me, and be called my Kinsman."
2Es 11:13 Then the **n** wing rose up and reigned,
14:38 And on the **n** day a voice called me, saying, "Ezra,
4Mc 1:16 **n,** is the knowledge of divine and human matters
9:26 the guards brought in the **n** eldest,

NEXT-OF-KIN (9) [KIN, NEXT]

Ru 3:9 your cloak over your servant, for you are **n."**
3:13 and in the morning, if he will act as **n** for you,
3:13 If he is not willing to act as **n** for you, then, as the LORD lives, I will act as **n** for you.
4:1 up to the gate and sat down there than the **n,**
4:3 He then said to the **n,** "Naomi,
4:6 At this, the **n** said, "I cannot redeem it for myself
4:8 So when the **n** said to Boaz,
4:14 who has not left you this day without **n;**

NEZIAH (3)

Ezr 2:54 **N,** and Hatipha.
Ne 7:56 of **N,** of Hatipha.
1Es 5:32 the descendants of **N,** the descendants of Hatipha.

NEZIB (1)

Jos 15:43 Iphtah, Ashnah, **N,**

NIBHAZ (1)

2Ki 17:31 the Avvites made **N** and Tartak;

NIBSHAN (1)

Jos 15:62 **N,** the City of Salt, and En-gedi:

NICANOR (39) [NICANOR'S]

Ac 6:5 Prochorus, **N,** Timon, Parmenas, and Nicolaus,
1Mc 3:38 and **N** and Gorgias, able men among the Friends
7:26 Then the king sent **N,** one of his honored princes,
7:27 So **N** came to Jerusalem with a large force,
7:30 It became known to Judas that **N** had come to him
7:31 When **N** learned that his plan had been disclosed,
7:32 About five hundred of the army of **N** fell,
7:33 After these events **N** went up to Mount Zion.
7:39 Now **N** went out from Jerusalem and encamped
7:42 that **N** has spoken wickedly against the sanctuary,
7:43 The army of **N** was crushed,
7:44 When his army saw that **N** had fallen,
9:1 that **N** and his army had fallen in battle,
2Mc 8:9 Ptolemy promptly appointed **N** son of Patroclus,
8:10 **N** determined to make up for the king
8:14 by the ungodly **N** before he ever met them,
8:23 the first division himself, he joined battle with **N.**
8:34 The thrice-accursed **N,** who had brought
9:3 news came to him of what had happened to **N** and
12:2 and in addition to these **N** the governor of Cyprus,
14:12 He immediately chose **N,**
14:14 who had fled before Judas, flocked to join **N,**
14:17 Simon, the brother of Judas, had encountered **N,**
14:18 Nevertheless **N,** hearing of the valor of Judas
14:23 **N** stayed on in Jerusalem and did nothing out of
14:26 that **N** was disloyal to the government,
14:27 wrote to **N,** stating that he was displeased with
14:28 When this message came to **N,**
14:30 that **N** was more austere in his dealings with him
14:30 and went into hiding from **N.**
14:37 to **N** as a man who loved his compatriots
14:39 **N,** wishing to exhibit the enmity that he had for
15:1 When **N** heard that Judas and his troops were in
15:6 This **N** in his utter boastfulness
15:25 **N** and his troops advanced with trumpets
15:28 they recognized **N,** lying dead, in full armor.
15:33 He cut out the tongue of the ungodly **N** and said
15:37 This, then, is how matters turned out with **N,**
4Mc 3:20 so that even Seleucus **N,** king of Asia,

NICANOR'S (7) [NICANOR]

1Mc 7:47 they cut off **N** head and the right hand that he had
2Mc 8:12 Word came to Judas concerning **N** invasion;
8:24 and wounded and disabled most of **N** army,
14:15 the Jews heard of **N** coming and the gathering of
15:30 to cut off **N** head and arm and carry them
15:32 the vile **N** head and that profane man's arm,
15:35 Judas hung **N** head from the citadel,

NICHE (1)

Wis 13:15 then he makes a suitable **n** for it,

NICODEMUS (5)

Jn 3:1 Now there was a Pharisee named **N,**
3:4 **N** said to him, "How can anyone be born
3:9 **N** said to him, "How can these things be?"
7:50 **N,** who had gone to Jesus before,
19:39 **N,** who had at first come to Jesus by night,

NICOLAITANS (2)

Rev 2:6 you hate the works of the **N,** which I also hate.
2:15 also have some who hold to the teaching of the **N.**

NICOLAUS (1)

Ac 6:5 Timon, Parmenas, and **N,** a proselyte of Antioch.

NICOPOLIS (1)

Tit 3:12 or Tychicus, do your best to come to me at **N,**

NIGER (1)

Ac 13:1 Barnabas, Simeon who was called **N,**

NIGH (KJV) See ADVANCED, ALONG, AT HAND, APPROACH, APPROACHED, APPROACHES, BY, CLOSE, FORWARD, HASTEN TO FULFILLMENT, NEAR, NEARBY, NEARER, NEARLY, NEIGHBORS, ON, ON THE VERGE OF, OWN FLESH

NIGHT‡ (377) [MIDNIGHT, NIGHTFALL, NIGHTS, OVERNIGHT]

Ge 1: 5 and the darkness he called **N.**
1:14 of the sky to separate the day from the **n;**
1:16 to rule the day and the lesser light to rule the **n**—
1:18 to rule over the day and over the **n,**
8:22 summer and winter, day and **n,** shall not cease."
14:15 He divided his forces against them by **n,**
19: 2 turn aside to your servant's house and spend the **n,**
19: 2 we will spend the **n** in the square."
19:33 So they made their father drink wine that **n;**
19:34 "Look, I lay last **n** with my father;
19:35 So they made their father drink wine that **n** also;
20: 3 But God came to Abimelech in a dream by **n,**
24:23 in your father's house for us to spend the **n?"**
24:25 of straw and fodder and a place to spend the **n."**
24:54 and they spent the **n** there.
26:24 that very **n** the LORD appeared to him and said,
28:11 to a certain place and stayed there for the **n,**
30:16 So he lay with her that **n.**
31:24 God came to Laban the Aramean in a dream by **n,**
31:29 but the God of your father spoke to me last **n,**
31:39 whether stolen by day or stolen by **n.**
31:40 by day the heat consumed me, and the cold by **n,**
31:42 the labor of my hands, and rebuked you last **n."**
31:54 they ate bread and tarried all **n** in the hill country.
32:13 So he spent that **n** there,
32:21 and he himself spent that **n** in the camp.
32:22 The same **n** he got up and took his two wives,
40: 5 One **n** they both dreamed—
41:11 We dreamed on the same **n,** he and I,
46: 2 God spoke to Israel in visions of the **n,** and said,
Ex 4:24 On the way, at a place where they spent the **n,**
10:13 upon the land all that day and all that **n;**
12: 8 They shall eat the lamb that same **n;**
12:12 For I will pass through the land of Egypt that **n,**
12:30 Pharaoh arose in the **n,** he and all his officials
12:31 Then he summoned Moses and Aaron in the **n,**
12:42 That was for the LORD a **n** of vigil,
12:42 That same **n** is a vigil to be kept for the LORD
13:21 and in a pillar of fire by **n,** to give them light,
13:21 so that they might travel by day and by **n.**
13:22 nor the pillar of fire by **n** left its place in front of
14:20 and it lit up the **n;**
14:20 one did not come near the other all **n.**
14:21 by a strong east wind all **n,** and turned the sea
40:38 and fire was in the cloud by **n,**
Lev 6: 9 the hearth upon the altar all **n** until the morning,
8:35 of the tent of meeting day and **n** for seven days,
Nu 9:16 by day and the appearance of fire by **n.**
9:21 or if it continued for a day and a **n,**
11: 9 When the dew fell on the camp in the **n,**
11:32 and **n** and all the next day, gathering the quails;
14: 1 and the people wept that **n.**
14:14 a pillar of cloud by day and in a pillar of fire by **n.**
22:20 That **n** God came to Balaam and said to him,
Dt 1:33 in fire by **n,** and in the cloud by day,
16: 1 the LORD your God brought you out of Egypt by **n.**
21:23 his corpse must not remain all **n** upon the tree;
28:66 **n** and day you shall be in dread,
Jos 1: 8 you shall meditate on it day and **n,**
2: 1 whose name was Rahab, and spent the **n** there.
6:11 and spent the **n** in the camp.
8: 3 and sent them out by **n**
8: 9 but Joshua spent that **n** in the camp.
8:13 But Joshua spent that **n** in the valley.
10: 9 having marched up all **n** from Gilgal.
Jdg 6:25 That **n** the LORD said to him,
6:27 and the townspeople to do it by day, he did it by **n.**
6:40 And God did so that **n.**
7: 9 That same **n** the LORD said to him, "Get up,
9:32 go by **n,** you and the troops that are with you,
9:34 the troops with him got up by **n** and lay in wait
16: 2 and lay in wait for him all **n** at the city gate.
16: 2 They kept quiet all **n,** thinking,
19: 6 "Why not spend the **n** and enjoy yourself?"
19: 7 until he spent the **n** there again.
19: 9 until it is almost evening. Spend the **n.**
19: 9 Spend the **n** here and enjoy yourself.
19:10 But the man would not spend the **n;**
19:11 and spend the **n** in it."
19:13 and spend the **n** at Gibeah or at Ramah."
19:15 to go in and spend the **n** at Gibeah.
19:15 but no one took them in to spend the **n.**
19:20 only do not spend the **n** in the square."
19:25 and abused her all through the **n** until the morning.
20: 4 I and my concubine, to spend the **n.**
20: 5 and surrounded the house at **n.**
Ru 3:13 Remain this **n,** and in the morning,
1Sa 14:34 of the troops brought their oxen with them that **n,**
14:36 down after the Philistines by **n** and despoil them
15:11 and he cried out to the LORD all **n.**
15:16 I will tell you what the LORD said to me last **n."**
19:10 David fled and escaped that **n.**
19:24 He lay naked all that day and all that **n.**
1Sa 25:16 they were a wall to us both by **n** and by day,
26: 7 So David and Abishai went to the army by **n;**
28: 8 They came to the woman by **n.**
28:20 for he had eaten nothing all day and all **n.**
28:25 Then they rose and went away that **n.**
31:12 traveled all **n** long, and took the body of Saul and
2Sa 2:29 Abner and his men traveled all that **n** through
2:32 Joab and his men marched all **n,**
4: 7 and traveled by way of the Arabah all **n** long.
7: 4 same **n** the word of the LORD came to Nathan:
12:16 and went in and lay all **n** on the ground.
17: 8 he will not spend the **n** with the troops.
19: 7 not a man will stay with you this **n;**
21:10 on the bodies by day, or the wild animals by **n.**
1Ki 3: 5 to Solomon in a dream by **n;**
3:19 Then this woman's son died in the **n,**
3:20 She got up in the middle of the **n** and took my son
8:29 that your eyes may be open **n** and day
8:59 be near to the LORD our God day and **n,**
19: 9 that place he came to a cave, and spent the **n** there.
2Ki 6:14 they came by **n,** and surrounded the city.
7:12 The king got up in the **n,** and said to his servants,
8:21 He set out by **n** and attacked the Edomites
19:35 That very **n** the angel of the LORD set out
25: 4 by **n** by the way of the gate between the two walls,
1Ch 9:27 they would spend the **n** near the house of God;
9:33 for they were on duty day and **n.**
17: 3 same **n** the word of the LORD came to Nathan,
2Ch 1: 7 That **n** God appeared to Solomon, and said to him,
6:20 be open day and **n** toward this house,
7:12 the LORD appeared to Solomon in the **n** and said
21: 9 He set out by **n** and attacked the Edomites,
35:14 the burnt offerings and the fat parts until **n;**
Ezr 10: 6 of Eliashib, where he spent the **n.**
Ne 1: 6 now pray before you day and **n** for your servants,
2:12 I got up during the **n,** I and a few men with me;
2:13 by **n** by the Valley Gate past the Dragon's Spring
2:15 by way of the valley by **n** and inspected the wall.
4: 9 set a guard as a protection against them day and **n.**
4:22 and his servant pass the **n** inside Jerusalem,
4:22 be a guard for us by **n** and may labor by day."
9:12 and by **n** with a pillar of fire,
9:19 nor the pillar of fire by **n** that gave them light on
13:20 of merchandise spent the **n** outside Jerusalem once
13:21 "Why do you spend the **n** in front of the wall?
Est 4:16 and neither eat nor drink for three days, **n** or day.
6: 1 On that **n** the king could not sleep,
Job 3: 3 and the **n** that said, 'A man-child is conceived.'
3: 6 That **n**—let thick darkness seize it!
3: 7 let that **n** be barren; let no joyful cry be heard in it.
4:13 Amid thoughts from visions of the **n,**
5:14 and grope at noonday as in the **n.**
7: 4 the **n** is long, and I am full of tossing until dawn.
17:12 They make **n** into day; 'The light,'
20: 8 they will be chased away like a vision of the **n.**
24: 7 They lie all **n** naked, without clothing,
24:14 and in the **n** is like a thief.
27:20 in the **n** a whirlwind carries them off.
29:19 with the dew all **n** on my branches;
30:17 The **n** racks my bones, and the pain
33:15 In a dream, in a vision of the **n,**
34:25 knowing their works, he overturns them in the **n,**
35:10 who gives strength in the **n,**
36:20 Do not long for the **n,**
39: 9 Will it spend the **n** at your crib?
Ps 1: 2 and on his law they meditate day and **n.**
6: 6 every **n** I flood my bed with tears;
16: 7 in the **n** also my heart instructs me.
17: 3 If you try my heart, if you visit me by **n,**
19: 2 and **n** to **n** declares knowledge.
22: 2 and by **n,** but find no rest.
30: 5 Weeping may linger for the **n,**
32: 4 For day and **n** your hand was heavy upon me;
42: 3 My tears have been my food day and **n,**
42: 8 and at **n** his song is with me,
55:10 Day and **n** they go around it on its walls,
63: 6 and meditate on you in the watches of the **n;**
74:16 Yours is the day, yours also the **n;**
77: 2 the **n** my hand is stretched out without wearying;
77: 6 I commune with my heart in the **n;**
78:14 and all **n** long with a fiery light.
88: 1 when, at **n,** I cry out in your presence,
90: 4 or like a watch in the **n.**
91: 5 You will not fear the terror of the **n,**
92: 2 and your faithfulness by **n,**
104:20 You make darkness, and it is **n,**
105:39 and fire to give light by **n.**
119:55 I remember your name in the **n,** O LORD,
119:148 My eyes are awake before each watch of the **n,**
121: 6 not strike you by day, nor the moon by **n.**
134: 1 who stand by **n** in the house of the LORD!
136: 9 over the **n,** for his steadfast love endures forever;
139:11 and the light around me become **n,"**
139:12 the **n** is as bright as the day,
Pr 7: 9 in the evening, at the time of **n** and darkness.
31:15 She rises while it is still **n** and provides food
31:18 Her lamp does not go out at **n.**
Ecc 2:23 even at **n** their minds do not rest.
8:16 how one's eyes see sleep neither day nor **n,**
SS 3: 1 at **n** I sought him whom my soul loves;
3: 8 with his sword at his thigh because of alarms by **n.**
5: 2 my locks with the drops of the **n."**
Isa 4: 5 and smoke and the shining of a flaming fire by **n.**
10:29 at Geba they lodge for the **n;**
15: 1 Because Ar is laid waste in a **n,** Moab is undone;
15: 1 because Kir is laid waste in a **n,** Moab is undone.
16: 3 make your shade like **n** at the height of noon;
Isa 21: 8 and at my post I am stationed throughout the **n.**
21:11 "Sentinel, what of the **n?** Sentinel, what of the **n?"**
21:12 sentinel says: "Morning comes, and also the **n.**
26: 9 My soul yearns for you in the **n,**
27: 3 I guard it **n** and day so that no one can harm it;
28:19 by morning it will pass through, by day and by **n;**
29: 7 shall be like a dream, a vision of the **n.**
30:29 a song as in the **n** when a holy festival is kept;
34:10 **N** and day it shall not be quenched;
38:12 from day to **n** you bring me to an end;
38:13 from day to **n** you bring me to an end.
60:11 day and **n** they shall not be shut,
60:19 brightness shall the moon give light to you by **n;**
62: 6 all day and all **n** they shall never be silent.
65: 4 and spend the **n** in secret places;
Jer 6: 5 "Up, and let us attack by **n,**
9: 1 so that I might weep day and **n** for the slain
14: 8 like a traveler turning aside for the **n?**
14:17 Let my eyes run down with tears **n** and day,
16:13 and there you shall serve other gods day and **n,**
31:35 and the stars for light by **n,** who stirs up the sea so
33:20 with the day and my covenant with the **n,**
33:20 day and **n** would not come at their appointed time,
33:25 not established my covenant with day and **n** and
36:30 be cast out to the heat by day and the frost by **n.**
39: 4 at **n** by way of the king's garden through the gate
49: 9 If thieves came by **n,** even they would pillage only
52: 7 by **n** by the way of the gate between the two walls,
La 1: 2 She weeps bitterly in the **n,**
2:18 Let tears stream down like a torrent day and **n!**
2:19 cry out in the **n,** at the beginning of the watches!
Da 2:19 to Daniel in a vision of the **n,**
5:30 very **n** Belshazzar, the Chaldean king, was killed.
6:18 the king went to his palace and spent the **n** fasting;
7: 2 by **n** the four winds of heaven stirring up
7: 7 After this I saw in the visions by **n** a fourth beast,
7:13 As I watched in the **n** visions,
Hos 4: 5 the prophet also shall stumble with you by **n,**
7: 6 all **n** their anger smolders;
Joel 1:13 Come, pass the **n** in sackcloth,
Am 5: 8 and darkens the day into **n,**
Ob 1: 5 by **n**—how you have been destroyed!—
Jnh 4:10 it came into being in a **n** and perished in a **n.**
Mic 3: 6 Therefore it shall be **n** to you, without vision,
Zec 1: 8 In the **n** I saw a man riding on a red horse!
14: 7 not day and not **n,** for at evening time there shall
Mt 2:14 Joseph got up, took the child and his mother by **n,**
21:17 of the city to Bethany, and spent the **n** there.
24:43 of the house had known in what part of the **n**
26:31 will all become deserters because of me this **n;**
26:34 Jesus said to him, "Truly I tell you, this very **n,**
28:13 by **n** and stole him away while we were asleep.'
Mk 4:27 and would sleep and rise **n** and day,
5: 5 **N** and day among the tombs and on
14:30 this day, this very **n,** before the cock crows twice,
Lk 2: 8 keeping watch over their flock by **n.**
2:37 but worshiped there with fasting and prayer **n**
5: 5 we have worked all **n** long
6:12 and he spent the **n** in prayer to God.
12:20 This very **n** your life is being demanded of you.
12:38 If he comes during the middle of the **n,**
17:34 I tell you, on that **n** there will be two in one bed;
18: 7 to his chosen ones who cry to him day and **n?**
21:37 and at **n** he would go out and spend the **n** on
Jn 3: 2 He came to Jesus by **n** and said to him, "Rabbi,
9: 4 **n** is coming when no one can work.
11:10 But those who walk at **n** stumble,
13:30 he immediately went out. And it was **n.**
19:39 Nicodemus, who had at first come to Jesus by **n,**
21: 3 but that **n** they caught nothing.
Ac 5:19 But during the **n** an angel of the Lord opened
9:24 the gates day and **n** so that they might kill him;
9:25 but his disciples took him by **n** and let him down
12: 6 very **n** before Herod was going to bring him out,
16: 9 During the **n** Paul had a vision:
16:33 of the **n** he took them and washed their wounds;
17:10 That very **n** the believers sent Paul and Silas off
18: 9 One **n** the Lord said to Paul in a vision,
20:31 remembering that for three years I did not cease **n**
23:11 That **n** the Lord stood near him and said,
23:31 and brought him during the **n** to Antipatris.
26: 7 as they earnestly worship day and **n.**
27:23 For last **n** there stood by me an angel of the God
27:27 When the fourteenth **n** had come,
Ro 13:12 the **n** is far gone, the day is near.
1Co 11:23 the **n** when he was betrayed took a loaf of bread,
2Co 11:25 for a **n** and a day I was adrift at sea;
11:27 through many a sleepless **n,** hungry and thirsty,
1Th 2: 9 we worked **n** and day, so that we might
3:10 **N** and day we pray most earnestly
5: 2 the day of the Lord will come like a thief in the **n.**
5: 5 we are not of the **n** or of darkness.
5: 7 for those who sleep sleep at **n,**
5: 7 and those who are drunk get drunk at **n.**
2Th 3: 8 but with toil and labor we worked **n** and day,
1Ti 5: 5 and continues in supplications and prayers **n**
2Ti 1: 3 when I remember you constantly in my prayers **n**
Rev 4: 8 Day and **n** without ceasing they sing, "Holy, holy,
7:15 and worship him day and **n** within his temple,
8:12 the day was kept from shining, and likewise the **n.**
12:10 who accuses them day and **n** before our God.
14:11 or **n** for those who worship the beast and its image
20:10 they will be tormented day and **n** forever and ever.
21:25 and there will be no **n** there.
22: 5 And there will be no more **n;**
Tob 2: 9 That same **n** I washed myself and went
6: 2 and when the first **n** overtook them they camped

Tob 6:11 "We must stay this **n** in the home of Raguel.
6:14 On the **n** when they went in to her, they would die.
6:16 I know that this very **n** she will be given to you
7:11 and all died on the **n** when they went in to her.
7:11 and prosper you both this **n** and grant you mercy
8: 9 Then they went to sleep for the **n.**
10: 7 in and mourn and weep all **n** long,
Jdt 6:21 all that **n** they called on the God of Israel for help.
7: 5 they remained on guard all that **n.**
11: 5 I will say nothing false to my lord this **n.**
11:17 and serves the God of heaven **n** and day.
11:17 but every **n** your servant will go out into the valley
12: 7 She went out each **n** to the valley of Bethulia,
13:14 by my hand this very **n!"**
AdE 6: 1 That **n** the Lord took sleep from the king,
Wis 7:30 for it is succeeded by the **n,**
10:17 and a starry flame through the **n.**
17: 2 as captives of darkness and prisoners of long **n,**
17: 5 of the stars avail to illumine that hateful **n.**
17:14 But throughout the **n,** which was really powerless
17:21 while over those people alone heavy **n** was spread,
18: 6 **n** was made known beforehand to our ancestors,
18:14 and **n** in its swift course was now half gone,
Sir Pr: 3 During that time I have applied my skill day and **n**
36:31 but lodges wherever **n** overtakes him?
38:27 and master artisan who labors by **n** as well as
40: 5 his sleep at **n** confuses his mind.
Bar 2:25 to the heat of day and the frost of **n.**
Bel 1:15 During the **n** the priests came as usual,
1Mc 4: 1 and this division moved out by **n**
4: 5 When Gorgias entered the camp of Judas by **n,**
5:29 He left the place at **n,**
5:50 against the town all that day and all the **n,**
9:58 and he will capture them all in one **n."**
11: 6 they greeted one another and spent the **n** there.
12:26 up in formation to attack the Jews by **n.**
12:27 to keep their arms at hand so as to be ready all **n**
13:22 but that **n** a very heavy snow fell,
16: 4 against Cendebeus and camped for the **n**
2Mc 12: 6 He set fire to the harbor by **n,** burned the boats,
12: 9 the Jamnites by **n** and set fire to the harbor and
13:10 the people to call upon the Lord day and **n,**
13:15 at **n** and killed as many as two thousand men in
1Es 9: 2 and spent the **n** there;
3Mc 1: 2 and crossed over by **n** to the tent of Ptolemy,
5: 5 for their continued custody through the **n,**
5:11 that from the beginning, **n** and day, is bestowed
5:19 while it was still **n** he had carried out completely
5:22 not so much employ the duration of the **n** in sleep
2Es 3:14 the end of the times, secretly by **n.**
5: 4 and the sun shall suddenly begin to shine at **n,**
5: 7 not know shall make his voice heard by **n,**
5:16 Now on the second **n** Phaltiel,
5:31 to me on a previous **n** was sent to me.
6:12 of which you showed me a part on a previous **n."**
6:30 "I have come to show you these things this **n.**
6:36 Then on the eighth **n** my heart was troubled
7:42 or **n,** or dawn or shining or brightness or light,
9:44 to the Most High, **n** and day.
10: 3 I got up in the **n** and fled, and I came to this field,
10:58 But tomorrow **n** you shall remain here,
10:59 So I slept that **n** and the following one,
11: 1 On the second **n** I had a dream:
13: 1 After seven days I dreamed a dream in the **n.**
14:42 during the daytime, and ate their bread at **n.**
14:43 me, I spoke in the daytime and was not silent at **n.**

NIGHTFALL (1) [NIGHT]

1Es 1:14 because the priests were offering the fat until **n;**

NIGHTHAWK (2)

Lev 11:16 the **n,** the sea gull, the hawk of any kind;
Dt 14:15 the **n,** the sea gull, the hawk, of any kind;

NIGHTS (22) [NIGHT]

A. FORTY NIGHTS (11)

Ge 7: 4 on the earth for forty days and forty **n;** A
7:12 The rain fell on the earth forty days and forty **n.** A
Ex 24:18 on the mountain for forty days and forty **n.** A
34:28 with the LORD forty days and forty **n;** A
Dt 9: 9 on the mountain forty days and forty **n;** A
9:11 of forty days and forty **n** the LORD gave me A
9:18 the LORD as before, forty days and forty **n;** A
9:25 and forty **n** that I lay prostrate before the LORD A
10:10 I stayed on the mountain forty days and forty **n,** A
1Sa 30:12 or drunk water for three days and three **n.**
1Ki 19: 8 the strength of that food forty days and forty **n** A
Job 2:13 with him on the ground seven days and seven **n,**
7: 3 and **n** of misery are apportioned to me.
Jnh 1:17 in the belly of the fish three days and three **n.**
Mt 4: 2 He fasted forty days and forty **n,** A
12:40 as Jonah was three days and three **n** in the belly of
12:40 and three **n** the Son of Man will be in the heart of
2Co 6: 5 imprisonments, riots, labors, sleepless **n,** hunger;
AdE 4:16 for three days and **n** do not eat or drink,
Aza 1:47 Bless the Lord, **n** and days;
2Mc 8: 7 the **n** most advantageous for such attacks.
2Es 7: 1 to me on the former **n** was sent to me again.

NILE‡ (37)

Ge 41: 1 Pharaoh dreamed that he was standing by the **N,**
41: 2 and there came up out of the **N** seven sleek
41: 3 ugly and thin, came up out of the **N** after them,
41: 3 and stood by the other cows on the bank of the **N.**
41:17 on the banks of the **N;**
41:18 came up out of the **N** and fed in the reed grass.
Ex 1:22 to the Hebrews you shall throw into the **N,**
4: 9 you shall take some water from the **N** and pour it
4: 9 from the **N** will become blood on the dry ground."
7:17 in my hand I will strike the water that is in the **N,**
7:18 be unable to drink water from the **N.'"**
7:24 the Egyptians had to dig along the **N** for water
7:25 after the LORD had struck the **N.**
8: 9 and your houses and be left only in the **N."**
8:11 they shall be left only in the **N."**
17: 5 the staff with which you struck the **N,**
Isa 18: 2 by the **N** in vessels of papyrus on the waters!
19: 5 The waters of the **N** will be dried up,
19: 6 branches of Egypt's **N** will diminish and dry up,
19: 7 There will be bare places by the **N,** on the brink of
the **N;** and all that is sown by the **N** will dry up,
19: 8 all who cast hooks in the **N** will lament,
23: 3 the grain of Shihor, the harvest of the **N;**
Jer 2:18 to drink the waters of the **N?**
46: 7 Who is this, rising like the **N,**
46: 8 Egypt rises like the **N,** like rivers
Eze 29: 3 saying, "My **N** is my own; I made it for myself."
29: 9 Because you said, "The **N** is mine, and I made it,"
Am 8: 8 and all of it rise like the **N,** and be tossed about
and sink again, like the **N** of Egypt?
9: 5 and all of it rises like the **N,** and sinks again, like
the **N** of Egypt;
Na 3: 8 Are you better than Thebes that sat by the **N,**
Zec 10:11 and all the depths of the **N** dried up.
Sir 24:27 It pours forth instruction like the **N,**
47:14 You overflowed like the **N** with understanding.

NIMBLE (1)

Sir 36:31 For who will trust a **n** robber that skips from city

NIMRAH (1) [BETH-NIMRAH]

Nu 32: 3 Dibon, Jazer, **N,** Heshbon, Elealeh, Sebam, Nebo,

NIMRIM (2)

Isa 15: 6 the waters of **N** are a desolation;
Jer 48:34 For even the waters of **N** have become desolate.

NIMROD (4)

Ge 10: 8 Cush became the father of **N;**
10: 9 "Like **N** a mighty hunter before the LORD."
1Ch 1:10 Cush became the father of **N;**
Mic 5: 6 and the land of **N** with the drawn sword;

NIMSHI (5)

1Ki 19:16 you shall anoint Jehu son of **N** as king over Israel;
2Ki 9: 2 look there for Jehu son of Jehoshaphat, son of **N;**
9:14 of Jehoshaphat son of **N** conspired against Joram.
9:20 It looks like the driving of Jehu son of **N;**
2Ch 22: 7 with Jehoram to meet Jehu son of **N,**

NINE‡ (43) [NINTH]

Ge 5: 5 that Adam lived were **n** hundred thirty years;
5: 8 the days of Seth were **n** hundred twelve years;
5:11 the days of Enosh were **n** hundred five years;
5:14 the days of Kenan were **n** hundred and ten years;
5:20 the days of Jared were **n** hundred sixty-two years;
5:27 of Methuselah were **n** hundred sixty-nine years;
9:29 All the days of Noah were **n** hundred fifty years;
11:19 after the birth of Reu two hundred **n** years,
Nu 29:26 On the fifth day: **n** bulls, two rams,
34:13 the LORD has commanded to give to the **n** tribes
Dt 3:11 By the common cubit it is **n** cubits long
Jos 13: 7 for an inheritance to the **n** tribes and the half-tribe
14: 2 as the LORD had commanded Moses for the **n**
15:44 **n** towns with their villages.
15:54 **n** towns with their villages.
21:16 **n** towns out of these two tribes.
Jdg 4: 3 for he had **n** hundred chariots of iron,
4:13 **n** hundred chariots of iron,
2Sa 24: 8 at the end of **n** months and twenty days,
2Ki 17: 1 over Israel; he reigned **n** years.
1Ch 3: 8 Elishama, Eliada, and Eliphelet, **n.**
9: 9 according to their generations, **n** hundred fifty-six.
Ezr 2: 8 Of Zattu, **n** hundred forty-five.
2:36 of the house of Jeshua, **n** hundred seventy-three.
Ne 7:38 Of Senaah, three thousand **n** hundred thirty.
7:39 the house of Jeshua, **n** hundred seventy-three.
11: 8 Sallai: **n** hundred twenty-eight.
Mt 20: 3 When he went out about **n** o'clock,
Mk 15:25 It was **n** o'clock in the morning
Lk 17:17 But the other **n,** where are they?
Ac 2:15 for it is only **n** o'clock in the morning.
23:23 to leave by **n** o'clock tonight for Caesarea
Sir 25: 7 I can think of **n** whom I would call blessed,
2Mc 5:27 But Judas Maccabeus, with about **n** others,
7:27 I carried you **n** months in my womb,
8:24 they killed more than **n** thousand of the enemy,
10:18 When at least **n** thousand took refuge
1Es 5:12 The descendants of Zattu, **n** hundred forty-five.
5:24 of Anasib, **n** hundred seventy-two.
2Es 4:40 when her **n** months have been completed,
8: 8 and for **n** months the womb endures your creature
13:40 these are the **n** tribes that were taken away
14:11 and **n** of its parts have already passed,

NINE-TENTHS (1) [TEN]

Ne 11: 1 while **n** remained in the other towns.

NINETEEN (3) [NINETEENTH]

Ge 11:25 after the birth of Terah one hundred **n** years,
Jos 19:38 **n** towns with their villages.
2Sa 2:30 of David's servants **n** men besides Asahel.

NINETEENTH (4) [NINETEEN]

2Ki 25: 8 which was the **n** year of King Nebuchadnezzar,
1Ch 24:16 the **n** to Pethahiah, the twentieth to Jehezkel,
25:26 to the **n,** to Mallothi, his sons
Jer 52:12 which was the **n** year of King Nebuchadrezzar,

NINETIETH (1) [NINETY]

2Mc 6:24 in his **n** year had gone over to an alien religion,

NINETY (8) [NINETIETH]

Ge 5: 9 When Enosh had lived **n** years,
17:17 Can Sarah, who is **n** years old, bear a child?"
1Ch 9: 6 Jeuel and their kin, six hundred **n.**
Eze 4: 5 three hundred **n** days, equal to the number of
4: 9 three hundred **n** days, you shall eat it.
41:12 around, and its depth **n** cubits.
Da 12:11 there shall be one thousand two hundred **n** days.
2Mc 8:11 and promising to hand over **n** slaves for a talent,

NINETY-EIGHT (3)

1Sa 4:15 Now Eli was **n** years old and his eyes were set,
Ezr 2:16 Of Ater, namely of Hezekiah, **n.**
Ne 7:21 Of Ater, namely of Hezekiah, **n.**

NINETY-FIVE (5)

Ge 5:17 the days of Mahalalel were eight hundred **n** years;
5:30 after the birth of Noah five hundred **n** years,
Ezr 2:20 Of Gibbar, **n.**
Ne 7:25 Of Gibeon, **n.**
2Mc 12:17 When they had gone **n** miles from there,

NINETY-FOUR (1)

2Es 14:44 So during the forty days, **n** books were written.

NINETY-NINE (6)

Ge 17: 1 When Abram was **n** years old,
17:24 Abraham was **n** years old
Mt 18:12 the **n** on the mountains and go in search of the one
18:13 he rejoices over it more than over the **n**
Lk 15: 4 does not leave the **n** in the wilderness and go after
15: 7 over **n** righteous persons who need no repentance.

NINETY-SIX (3)

Ezr 8:35 twelve bulls for all Israel, **n** rams,
Jer 52:23 There were **n** pomegranates on the sides;
1Es 8:65 twelve bulls for all Israel, **n** rams,

NINETY-TWO (3)

Ezr 2:58 of Solomon's servants were three hundred **n.**
Ne 7:60 of Solomon's servants were three hundred **n.**
1Es 5:15 The descendants of Ater, namely of Hezekiah, **n.**

NINEVEH (41) [NINEVITES]

Ge 10:11 From that land he went into Assyria, and built **N,**
10:12 Resen between **N** and Calah; that is the great city.
2Ki 19:36 left, went home, and lived at **N.**
Isa 37:37 left, went home, and lived at **N.**
Jnh 1: 2 at once to **N,** that great city, and cry out against it;
3: 2 up, go to **N,** that great city, and proclaim to it
3: 3 So Jonah set out and went to **N,**
3: 3 Now **N** was an exceedingly large city,
3: 4 "Forty days more, and **N** shall be overthrown!"
3: 5 And the people of **N** believed God;
3: 6 When the news reached the king of **N,**
3: 7 Then he had a proclamation made in **N:**
4:11 And should I not be concerned about **N,**
Na 1: 1 An oracle concerning **N.** The book of the
2: 8 **N** is like a pool whose waters run away.
3: 7 "**N** is devastated; who will bemoan her?"
Zep 2:13 and he will make **N** a desolation,
Mt 12:41 The people of **N** will rise up at the judgment
Lk 11:30 just as Jonah became a sign to the people of **N,**
11:32 The people of **N** will rise up at the judgment
Tob 1: 3 with me in exile to **N** in the land of the Assyrians.
1:10 to Assyria and came as a captive to **N,**
1:17 of my people thrown out behind the wall of **N,**
1:22 Ahikar interceded for me, and I returned to **N.**
2: 2 of our people among the exiles in **N,**
7: 3 the descendants of Naphtali who are exiles in **N."**
11: 1 they came near to Kaserin, which is opposite **N,**
11:15 on her way there, very near to the gate of **N.**
11:16 to meet his daughter-in-law at the gate of **N.**
11:16 When the people of **N** saw him coming,
11:17 among all the Jews who were in **N.**
14: 2 and was buried with great honor in **N.**
14: 4 the word of God that Nahum spoke about **N,**
14: 4 and overtake Assyria and **N.**
14:8,9 So now, my son, leave **N;** do not remain here.
14:15 Before he died he heard of the destruction of **N,**
14:15 for all he had done to the people of **N** and Assyria;
14:15 before he died he rejoiced over **N,**
Jdt 1: 1 over the Assyrians in the great city of **N.**
1:16 to **N,** he and all his combined forces, a vast body
2:21 They marched for three days from **N** to the plain

NINEVITES (1) [NINEVEH]

Tob 1:19 of the **N** went and informed the king about me,

NINTH‡ (27) [NINE]

Lev 23:32 on the **n** day of the month at evening,
25:22 until the **n** year, when its produce comes in,
Nu 7:60 On the **n** day Abidan son of Gideoni,
2Ki 17: 6 In the **n** year of Hoshea the king
18:10 which was the **n** year of King Hoshea of Israel,
25: 1 And in the **n** year of his reign, in the tenth month,
25: 3 the **n** day of the fourth month the famine became
1Ch 12:12 Johanan eighth, Elzabad **n**,
24:11 the **n** to Jeshua, the tenth to Shecaniah,
25:16 **n** to Mattaniah, his sons and his brothers, twelve;
27:12 **N**, for the **n** month, was Abiezer of Anathoth,
Ezr 10: 9 it was the **n** month, on the twentieth day of
Jer 36: 9 in the **n** month, all the people in Jerusalem and all
36:22 in his winter apartment (it was the **n** month),
39: 1 In the **n** year of King Zedekiah of Judah,
39: 2 in the fourth month, on the **n** day of the month,
52: 4 And in the **n** year of his reign, in the tenth month,
52: 6 the **n** day of the fourth month the famine became
Eze 24: 1 In the **n** year, in the tenth month,
Hag 2:10 On the twenty-fourth day of the **n** month,
2:18 from the twenty-fourth day of the **n** month.
Zec 7: 1 to Zechariah on the fourth day of the **n** month,
Rev 21:20 the **n** topaz, the tenth chrysoprase,
1Mc 4:52 on the twenty-fifth day of the **n** month,
1Es 9: 5 this was the **n** month, on the twentieth day of
2Es 16:38 the **n** month when the time of her delivery draws

NIPHISH (1)

1Es 5:21 The descendants of **N**, one hundred fifty-six.

NIPHTAL See Index to Footnotes

NISAN (5)

Ne 2: 1 of **N**, in the twentieth year of King Artaxerxes,
Est 3: 7 In the first month, which is the month of **N**,
AdE 8: 9 that is, **N**, in the same year;
11: 2 on the first day of **N**,
1Es 5: 6 in the second year of his reign, in the month of **N**,

NISROCH (2)

2Ki 19:37 As he was worshiping in the house of his god **N**,
Isa 37:38 As he was worshiping in the house of his god **N**,

NITRE (KJV) See LYE

NO (2336) [CANNOT, NAUGHT, NONE, NOT] See Index of Articles Etc.

NO [THE CITY] (KJV) See THEBES

NO-AMON See Index to Footnotes

NOADIAH (2)

Ezr 8:33 Jozabad son of Jeshua and **N** son of Binnui.
Ne 6:14 and also the prophetess **N** and the rest of

NOAH (56) [NOAH'S]

Ge 5:29 he named him **N**, saying, "Out of the ground that
5:30 after the birth of **N** five hundred ninety-five years,
5:32 After **N** was five hundred years old,
5:32 **N** became the father of Shem, Ham, and Japheth.
6: 8 But **N** found favor in the sight of the LORD.
6: 9 These are the descendants of **N**.
6: 9 **N** was a righteous man, blameless in his generation; **N** walked with God.
6:10 And **N** had three sons, Shem, Ham, and Japheth.
6:13 And God said to **N**, "I have determined to make
6:22 **N** did this; he did all that God commanded him.
7: 1 Then the LORD said to **N**, "Go into the ark,
7: 5 **N** did all that the LORD had commanded him.
7: 6 **N** was six hundred years old when the flood
7: 7 And **N** with his sons and his wife
7: 9 into the ark with **N**, as God had commanded **N**.
7:13 On the very same day **N** with his sons,
7:15 They went into the ark with **N**,
7:23 Only **N** was left, and those that were with him in
8: 1 But God remembered **N** and all the wild animals
8: 6 At the end of forty days **N** opened the window of
8:11 so **N** knew that the waters had subsided from
8:13 and **N** removed the covering of the ark,
8:15 Then God said to **N**,
8:18 So **N** went out with his sons and his wife
8:20 Then **N** built an altar to the LORD,
9: 1 God blessed **N** and his sons, and said to them,
9: 8 Then God said to **N** and to his sons with him,
9:17 God said to **N**, "This is the sign of the covenant
9:18 sons of **N** who went out of the ark were Shem,
9:19 These three were the sons of **N**;
9:20 **N**, a man of the soil, was the first to plant
9:24 When **N** awoke from his wine
9:28 After the flood **N** lived three hundred fifty years.
9:29 All the days of **N** were nine hundred fifty years;
Nu 26:33 **N**, Hoglah, Milcah, and Tirzah.
27: 1 Mahlah, **N**, Hoglah, Milcah, and Tirzah.
36:11 Mahlah, Tirzah, Hoglah, Milcah, and **N**,
Jos 17: 3 Mahlah, **N**, Hoglah, Milcah, and Tirzah.
1Ch 1: 4 **N**, Shem, Ham, and Japheth.
Isa 54: 9 This is like the days of **N** to me:
54: 9 that the waters of **N** would never again go over
Eze 14:14 even if **N**, Daniel, and Job, these three, were
14:20 if **N**, Daniel, and Job were in it, as I live, says
Mt 24:37 For as the days of **N** were, so will be the coming of
24:38 until the day **N** entered the ark,
Lk 3:36 son of Arphaxad, son of Shem, son of **N**,
17:26 Just as it was in the days of **N**, so too it will be
17:27 until the day **N** entered the ark,
Heb 11: 7 By faith **N**, warned by God about events as
1Pe 3:20 when God waited patiently in the days of **N**,
2Pe 2: 5 though he saved **N**, a herald of righteousness,
Tob 4:12 Remember, my son, that **N**, Abraham, Isaac,
Sir 44:17 **N** was found perfect and righteous;
2Es 3:11 But you left one of them, **N** with his household,

NOAH'S (5) [NOAH]

Ge 7:11 In the six hundredth year of **N** life,
7:13 and **N** wife and the three wives of his sons entered
10: 1 These are the descendants of **N** sons, Shem, Ham,
10:32 These are the families of **N** sons,
4Mc 15:31 Just as **N** ark, carrying the world in the universal

NOB (6)

1Sa 21: 1 David came to **N** to the priest Ahimelech.
22: 9 answered, "I saw the son of Jesse coming to **N**,
22:11 the priests who were at **N**;
22:19 **N**, the city of the priests, he put to the sword;
Ne 11:32 Anathoth, **N**, Ananiah,
Isa 10:32 This very day he will halt at **N**,

NOBAH (3)

Nu 32:42 And **N** went and captured Kenath and its villages,
32:42 and renamed it **N** after himself.
Jdg 8:11 So Gideon went up by the caravan route east of **N**

NOBILITY‡ (9) [NOBLE]

Isa 5:14 the **n** of Jerusalem and her multitude go down,
Da 1: 3 of the Israelites of the royal family and of the **n**,
2Mc 6:31 in his death an example of **n** and a memorial
4Mc 1:10 died for the sake of **n** and goodness,
3:18 and by **n** of reason spurn all domination by
8: 4 And struck by their appearance and **n**,
11:22 I also, equipped with **n**, will die with my brothers,
13:25 A common zeal for **n** strengthened their goodwill
15: 9 of the **n** of her sons and their ready obedience to

NOBLE‡ (45) [NOBILITY, NOBLEMAN, NOBLES, NOBLEST, NOBLY]

Jdg 5:13 Then down marched the remnant of the **n**;
Ezr 4:10 and **n** Osnappar deported and settled in the cities
Est 1:18 the **n** ladies of Persia and Media who have heard
6: 9 over to one of the king's most **n** officials;
Ps 16: 3 As for the holy ones in the land, they are the **n**,
Pr 8: 6 Hear, for I will speak **n** things,
17:26 or to flog the **n** for their integrity.
25: 7 than to be put lower in the presence of a **n**.
Isa 32: 5 A fool will no longer be called **n**,
32: 8 But those who are **n** plan **n** things, and by **n** things they stand.
Eze 17: 8 and bear fruit and become a **n** vine.
17:23 and bear fruit, and become a **n** cedar.
Ro 12:17 but take thought for what is **n** in the sight of all.
1Co 1:26 not many were of **n** birth.
1Ti 3: 1 to the office of bishop desires a **n** task.
Tob 5:14 and of good and **n** lineage.
7: 7 my child, son of a good and **n** father!"
9: 6 "Good and **n** son of a father good and **n**,
Wis 8: 3 She glorifies her **n** birth by living with God,
Sir 45:23 in the **n** courage of his soul;
2Mc 6:18 a man now advanced in age and of **n** presence,
6:28 and leave to the young a **n** example of how to die
7:21 a **n** spirit, she reinforced her woman's reasoning
12:42 The **n** Judas exhorted the people
14:42 and suffer outrages unworthy of his **n** birth.
15:12 who had been high priest, a **n** and good man,
15:17 so **n** and so effective in arousing valor
4Mc 1: 8 from the **n** bravery of those who died for the sake
4: 1 a political opponent of the **n** and good man, Onias,
6: 5 But the courageous and **n** man, like a true Eleazar,
6:10 Like a **n** athlete the old man, while being beaten,
7: 8 with their own blood and **n** sweat in sufferings
8: 3 modest, **n**, and accomplished in every way—
9:13 When the **n** youth was stretched out around this,
9:24 Fight the sacred and **n** battle for religion.
9:27 and they heard his **n** decision.
10: 3 I do not renounce the **n** kinship that binds me
10:15 I will not renounce our **n** family ties.
11:12 because through these **n** sufferings you give us
15:24 this **n** mother disregarded all these because
15:30 O more **n** than males in steadfastness,
16:16 **n** is the contest to which you are called

NOBLEMAN (2) [MAN, NOBLE]

Ecc 10:17 Happy are you, O land, when your king is a **n**,
Lk 19:12 "A **n** went to a distant country to get royal power

NOBLES (41) [NOBLE]

Nu 21:18 that the **n** of the people dug, with the scepter,
1Ki 21: 8 to the elders and the **n** who lived with Naboth
21:11 the elders and the **n** who lived in his city,
2Ch 23:20 And he took the captains, the **n**,
Ne 2:16 I had not yet told the Jews, the priests, the **n**,
Ne 3: 5 but their **n** would not put their shoulders to
4:14 to the **n** and the officials and the rest of the people,
4:19 And I said to the **n**, the officials,
5: 7 I brought charges against the **n** and the officials;
6:17 in those days the **n** of Judah sent many letters
7: 5 to assemble the **n** and the officials and the people
10:29 their **n**, and enter into a curse and an oath to walk
13:17 Then I remonstrated with the **n** of Judah and said
Est 1: 3 the **n** and governors of the provinces were present,
Job 29: 9 the **n** refrained from talking, and laid their hands
34:19 who shows no partiality to **n**,
Ps 83:11 Make their **n** like Oreb and Zeeb,
149: 8 with fetters and their **n** with chains of iron,
Pr 8:16 by me rulers rule, and **n**, all who govern rightly.
Isa 5:13 their **n** are dying of hunger,
13: 2 wave the hand for them to enter the gates of the **n**.
34:11 and the plummet of chaos over its **n**.
Jer 14: 3 Her **n** send their servants for water;
27:20 and all the **n** of Judah and Jerusalem—
39: 6 the king of Babylon slaughtered all the **n** of Judah.
Jnh 3: 7 "By the decree of the king and his **n**:
Na 3:10 lots were cast for her **n**, all her dignitaries were
3:18 of Assyria; your **n** slumber.
Jdt 2: 2 and all his **n** and set before them his secret plan
AdE 1: 3 the Persians and Median **n**,
Bar 1: 4 and to the **n** and the princes,
1: 9 the prisoners and the **n** and the people of the land,
1Mc 9:37 a daughter of one of the great **n** of Canaan,
1Es 1:38 Jehoiakim put the **n** in prison,
3: 1 and all the **n** of Media and Persia,
3: 9 the one whose statement the king and the three **n**
3:14 and summoned all the **n** of Persia and Media and
4:33 Then the king and the **n** looked at one another;
8:26 and his counselors and all his Friends and **n**.
8:55 the king himself and his counselors and the **n**
8:70 and the **n** have been sharing in this iniquity."

NOBLEST (1) [NOBLE]

2Mc 4:12 and he induced the **n** of the young men to wear

NOBLY (13) [NOBLE]

1Mc 4:35 and how ready they were either to live or to die **n**,
2Mc 6:28 to die a good death willingly and **n** for the revered
7: 5 and their mother encouraged one another to die **n**,
7:11 and said **n**, "I got these from Heaven,
8:16 against them, but to fight **n**,
14:42 preferring to die **n** rather than to fall into the hands
4Mc 6:22 O children of Abraham, die **n** for your religion!
6:30 he said this, the holy man died **n** in his tortures;
9:22 he **n** endured the rackings.
12:14 they by dying **n** fulfilled their service to God,
13:11 "Courage, brother," another said, "Bear up **n**,"
15:32 endured **n** and withstood the wintry storms
17: 3 **N** set like a roof on the pillars of your sons,

NOBODY (2)

Jdg 19:18 **N** has offered to take me in.
1Co 14: 2 for **n** understands them, for they are speaking

NOCTURNAL (1)

Dt 23:10 of a **n** emission, then he shall go outside the camp;

NOD (2)

Ge 4:16 and settled in the land of **N**, east of Eden.
2Mc 8:18 a single **n** to strike down those who are coming

NODAB (1)

1Ch 5:19 on the Hagrites, Jetur, Naphish, and **N**;

NOE (KJV) See NOAH

NOEBA (1)

1Es 5:31 the descendants of **N**, the descendants of Chezib,

NOGAH (2)

1Ch 3: 7 **N**, Nepheg, Japhia,
14: 6 **N**, Nepheg, and Japhia;

NOHAH (2)

Jdg 20:43 from **N** and trod them down as far as a place east
1Ch 8: 2 **N** the fourth, and Rapha the fifth.

NOISE (34) [NOISES, NOISY]

Ex 32:17 Joshua heard the **n** of the people as they shouted,
32:17 "There is a **n** of war in the camp."
1Sa 4: 6 When the Philistines heard the **n** of the shouting,
1Ki 1:40 so that the earth quaked at their **n**.
1:45 This is the **n** that you heard.
2Ki 11:13 the **n** of the guard and of the people, she went into
2Ch 23:12 the **n** of the people running and praising the king,
Ps 55: 3 by the **n** of the enemy,
66: 1 Make a joyful **n** to God, all the earth;
95: 1 let us make a joyful **n** to the rock of our salvation!
95: 2 let us make a joyful **n** to him with songs of praise!
98: 4 Make a joyful **n** to the LORD, all the earth;
98: 6 and the sound of the horn make a joyful **n** before
100: 1 Make a joyful **n** to the LORD, all the earth.
Isa 24: 8 the **n** of the jubilant has ceased,
25: 5 the **n** of aliens like heat in a dry place,
29: 6 of hosts with thunder and earthquake and great **n**,
31: 4 by their shouting or daunted at their **n**,
Jer 4:29 At the **n** of horseman and archer every town takes

Jer 10:22 a **n**! Listen, it is coming—
47: 3 the **n** of the stamping of the hoofs of his stallions,
50:22 **n** of battle is in the land, and great destruction!
Eze 26:10 At the **n** of cavalry, wheels,
37: 7 and as I prophesied, suddenly there was a **n**,
Da 7:11 then because of the **n** of the arrogant words that
Am 5:23 Take away from me the **n** of your songs;
2Pe 3:10 then the heavens will pass away with a loud **n**,
Rev 9: 9 and the **n** of their wings was like the **n** of many
chariots with horses rushing
Jdt 14: 9 a great shout and made a joyful **n** in their town.
1Mc 6:41 All who heard the **n** made by their multitude,
9:13 The earth was shaken by the **n** of the armies,
1Es 5:64 while many came with trumpets and a joyful **n**,
3Mc 5:48 and heard the loud and tumultuous **n**,

NOISED (KJV) See REPORTED, SOUND, TALKED ABOUT

NOISES (1) [NOISE]
AdE 11: 5 **N** and confusion, thunders and earthquake, tumult

NOISOME (KJV) See DEADLY, FOUL, WILD

NOISY (1) [NOISE]
1Co 13: 1 I am a **n** gong or a clanging cymbal.

NOMAD (1) [NOMADS]
Jer 3: 2 like a **n** in the wilderness.

NOMADS (1) [NOMAD]
2Mc 12:11 The defeated **n** begged Judas

NON (KJV) See NUN; See also Index to Footnotes

NON-BELIEVERS (1) [UNBELIEVERS]
3Jn 1: 7 the sake of Christ, accepting no support from **n**.

NONE (155) [NO]
Ge 23: 6 **n** of us will withhold from you any burial ground
28:17 This is **n** other than the house of God,
Ex 12:10 You shall let **n** of it remain until the morning;
12:22 **N** of you shall go outside the door of your house
16:26 which is a sabbath, there will be **n**."
16:27 of the people went out to gather, and they found **n**.
Lev 18: 6 **N** of you shall approach anyone near of kin
18:26 and commit **n** of these abominations,
Nu 7: 9 But to the Kohathites he gave **n**,
9:12 They shall leave **n** of it until morning,
14:22 **n** of the people who have seen my glory and
14:23 **n** of those who despised me shall see it.
32:11 'Surely **n** of the people who came up out of Egypt,
32:12 **n** except Caleb son of Jephunneh the Kenizzite
Dt 16: 4 and **n** of the meat of what you slaughter on
23: 2 **n** of their descendants shall be admitted to
23: 3 **n** of their descendants shall be admitted to
23:17 **N** of the daughters of Israel shall be
23:17 **n** of the sons of Israel shall be a temple prostitute.
28:55 giving to **n** of them any of the flesh
33:26 There is **n** like God, O Jeshurun,
Jos 11:13 But Israel burned **n** of the towns that stood
11:22 **N** of the Anakim was left in the land of
1Sa 3:19 with him and let **n** of his words fall to the ground.
14:24 So **n** of the troops tasted food.
21: 9 take it, for there is **n** here except that one."
21: 9 David said, "There is **n** like it; give it to me."
22: 8 **n** of you is sorry for me or discloses to me
30: 2 they killed **n** of them, but carried them off,
1Ki 10:21 of pure gold; **n** were of silver—
15:22 a proclamation to all Judah, **n** was exempt:
2Ki 10:14 in all; he spared **n** of them.
10:19 let **n** be missing, for I have a great sacrifice
17:18 **n** was left but the tribe of Judah alone.
2Ch 1:12 such as **n** of the kings had who were before you,
and **n** after you shall have the like."
35:18 **n** of the kings of Israel had kept such a passover
Ezr 8:15 I found there **n** of the descendants of Levi.
Job 3: 9 let it hope for light, but have **n**;
33:13 saying, 'He will answer **n** of my words'?
Ps 10:15 seek out their wickedness until you find **n**.
34:22 **n** of those who take refuge in him will
40: 5 toward us; **n** can compare with you.
59: 5 spare **n** of those who treacherously plot evil.
69:20 I looked for pity, but there was **n**;
69:20 and for comforters, but I found **n**.
76: 5 **n** of the troops was able to lift a hand.
86: 8 There is **n** like you among the gods, O Lord,
139:16 when **n** of them as yet existed.
Pr 1:25 and would have **n** of my reproof,
1:30 would have **n** of my counsel,
Isa 5:27 **N** of them is weary, **n** stumbles,
5:27 **n** slumbers or sleeps, not a loincloth is loose,
10:14 and there was **n** that moved a wing,
33:20 and **n** of whose ropes will be broken.
34:16 **n** shall be without its mate.
41:17 the poor and needy seek water, and there is **n**,
41:26 **n** who proclaimed, **n** who heard your words.
59:11 We wait for justice, but there is **n**;
Jer 2:24 **N** who seek her need weary themselves;
10: 6 There is **n** like you, O LORD;
22:30 for **n** of his offspring shall succeed in sitting on
Jer 30: 7 that day is so great there is **n** like it;
35:14 and they drink **n** to this day,
44:14 so that **n** of the remnant of Judah who have come
50:20 of Israel shall be sought, and there shall be **n**;
50:20 and the sins of Judah, and **n** shall be found;
La 1: 9 her downfall was appalling, with **n** to comfort her.
Eze 7:11 **N** of them shall remain, not their abundance, not
7:25 they will seek peace, but there shall be **n**.
12:28 **N** of my words will be delayed any longer,
18:11 of these things (though his father does **n** of them),
18:22 **N** of the transgressions
18:24 **N** of the righteous deeds that they have done shall
33:13 **n** of their righteous deeds shall be remembered;
33:16 **N** of the sins that they have committed shall
39:28 I will leave **n** of them behind;
46:18 of his own holding, so that **n** of my people shall
Da 11:24 and do what **n** of his predecessors had ever done,
12:10 **N** of the wicked shall understand,
Hos 4: 4 Yet let no one contend, and let **n** accuse,
7: 7 **n** of them calls upon me.
Mt 10:42 truly I tell you, **n** of these will lose their reward."
12:43 for a resting place, but it finds **n**.
26:60 but they found **n**, though many false witnesses
Mk 12:22 **n** of the seven left children.
14:55 to put him to death; but they found **n**.
Lk 1:61 "**N** of your relatives has this name."
3:11 has two coats must share with anyone who has **n**;
4:26 yet Elijah was sent to **n** of them except to a widow
4:27 and **n** of them was cleansed except Naaman
13: 6 and he came looking for fruit on it and found **n**.
13: 7 for fruit on this fig tree, and still I find **n**.
14:24 For I tell you, **n** of those
14:33 **n** of you can become my disciple if you do
17:18 Was **n** of them found to return and give praise
21:15 that **n** of your opponents will be able to withstand
Jn 7:19 Yet **n** of you keeps the law.
16: 5 yet **n** of you asks me, 'Where are you going?'
19:36 "**N** of his bones shall be broken."
21:12 Now **n** of the disciples dared to ask him,
Ac 5:13 **N** of the rest dared to join them,
20:25 "And now I know that **n** of you,
26:26 that **n** of these things has escaped his notice,
27:34 for **n** of you will lose a hair from your heads."
27:42 so that **n** might swim away and escape;
28:21 and **n** of the brothers coming here has reported
1Co 1:14 that I baptized **n** of you except Crispus and Gaius,
2: 8 **N** of the rulers of this age understood this;
4: 6 so that **n** of you will be puffed up in favor of one
6:10 **n** of these will inherit the kingdom of God.
7:29 be as though they had **n**,
1Th 5:15 See that **n** of you repays evil for evil,
Heb 3:12 that **n** of you may have an evil,
3:13 so that **n** of you may be hardened by
4: 1 let us take care that **n** of you should seem
1Pe 4:15 But let **n** of you suffer as a murderer, a thief,
1Jn 2:19 But by going out they made it plain that **n**
Tob 4:17 the grave of the righteous, but give **n** to sinners.
4:19 For **n** of the nations has understanding,
14: 4 **N** of all their words will fail,
Jdt 6: 4 For he has spoken; **n** of his words shall be in vain.
6: 9 and **n** of my words shall fail to come true."
12: 3 For **n** of your people are here with us."
16:14 there is **n** that can resist your voice.
AdE 2:15 she neglected **n** of the things that Gai,
10: 5 and **n** of them has failed to be fulfilled.
Wis 2: 9 Let **n** of us fail to share in our revelry;
4: 3 and **n** of their illegitimate seedlings will strike
11:24 and detest **n** of the things that you have made,
15:16 for **n** can form gods that are like themselves.
Sir 10:24 but **n** of them is greater than the one who fears
18: 4 To **n** has he given power to proclaim his works;
25:10 But **n** is superior to the one who fears the Lord.
39:18 and **n** can limit his saving power.
51: 7 I looked for human assistance, and there was **n**.
LtJ 6:19 though their gods can see **n** of them.
6:28 but give **n** to the poor or helpless.
Sus 1:43 though I have done **n** of the wicked things
1Mc 2:61 that **n** of those who put their trust
14: 7 and there was **n** to oppose him.
14:12 and there was **n** to make them afraid.
14:44 "**N** of the people or priests shall be permitted
2Mc 11:31 and **n** of them shall be molested in any way
1Es 1:21 **n** of the kings of Israel had kept such a passover
8:42 When I found there **n** of the descendants of
9:51 and send portions to those who have **n**;
9:54 and to give portions to those who had **n**,
3Mc 2:28 "**N** of those who do not sacrifice shall enter their
4Mc 14: 4 **N** of the seven youths proved coward or shrank
15:11 in the case of **n** of them were
16: 6 bearing seven children, I am now the mother of **n**!
16:11 when I die, I shall have **n** of my sons to bury me."

NONSENSE (2)
Zec 10: 2 For the teraphim utter **n**, and the diviners see lies;
2Pe 2:18 For they speak bombastic **n**,

NOOMA (1)
1Es 9:35 Of the descendants of **N**: Mazitias,

NOON‡ (26) [AFTERNOON, FORENOON, NOONDAY, NOONTIDE]
Ge 43:16 for the men are to dine with me at **n**."
43:25 the present ready for Joseph's coming at **n**,
Dt 28:29 you shall grope about at **n** as blind people grope
1Ki 18:26 called on the name of Baal from morning until **n**,
1Ki 18:27 At **n** Elijah mocked them, saying, "Cry aloud!
20:16 at **n**, while Ben-hadad was drinking himself drunk
2Ki 4:20 the child sat on her lap until **n**, and he died.
Ps 55:17 and morning and at **n** I utter my complaint
SS 1: 7 where you make it lie down at **n**;
Isa 16: 3 make your shade like night at the height of **n**;
59:10 we stumble at **n** as in the twilight,
Jer 6: 4 up, and let us attack at **n**!"
20:16 a cry in the morning and an alarm at **n**,
Am 8: 9 I will make the sun go down at **n**,
Zep 2: 4 Ashdod's people shall be driven out at **n**,
Mt 20: 5 he went out again about **n** and about three o'clock,
27:45 From **n** on, darkness came over the whole land
Mk 15:33 When it was **n**, darkness came over
Lk 23:44 about **n**, and darkness came over the whole land
Jn 4: 6 by the well. It was about **n**.
19:14 for the Passover; and it was about **n**.
Ac 10: 9 About **n** the next day, as they were
22: 6 about **n** a great light from heaven suddenly shone
Sir 43: 3 At **n** it parches the land,
Sus 1: 7 When the people left at **n**,
2Es 7:*42* or **n** or night, or dawn or shining or brightness

NOONDAY (8) [DAY, NOON]
2Sa 4: 5 while he was taking his **n** rest.
Job 5:14 and grope at **n** as in the night.
11:17 And your life will be brighter than the **n**;
Ps 37: 6 and the justice of your cause like the **n**.
91: 6 or the destruction that wastes at **n**.
Isa 58:10 in the darkness and your gloom be like the **n**.
Jer 15: 8 against the mothers of youths a destroyer at **n**;
Sir 34:19 from scorching wind and a shade from **n** sun,

NOONTIDE (1) [NOON]
Isa 38:10 In the **n** of my days I must depart;

NOR (418) See Index of Articles Etc.

NORMAL (3)
Ex 14:27 and at dawn the sea returned to its **n** depth.
2Ki 20:10 "It is **n** for the shadow to lengthen ten intervals;
Wis 19:20 Fire even in water retained its **n** power,

NORTH‡ (153) [NORTHEASTER, NORTHERLY, NORTHERN, NORTHWARD, NORTHWEST]
Ge 14:15 and pursued them to Hobah, **n** of Damascus.
28:14 to the west and to the east and to the **n** and to
Ex 26:20 on the **n** side twenty frames,
26:35 and you shall put the table on the **n** side.
27:11 Likewise for its length on the **n** side there shall
36:25 the second side of the tabernacle, on the **n** side,
38:11 **n** side there were hangings one hundred cubits
40:22 on the **n** side of the tabernacle, outside the curtain,
Lev 1:11 It shall be slaughtered on the **n** side of the altar
Nu 2:25 On the **n** side shall be the regimental encampment
3:35 they were to camp on the **n** side of the tabernacle.
35: 5 and for the **n** side two thousand cubits,
Dt 2: 3 skirting this hill country long enough. Head **n**,
3:12 to the Reubenites and Gadites the territory **n**
3:27 to the **n**, to the south, and to the east.
Jos 8:11 and camped on the **n** side of Ai,
8:13 that was **n** of the city and its rear guard west of
15: 5 And the boundary on the **n** side runs from the bay
15: 6 and passes along **n** of Beth-arabah;
15:11 of the hill **n** of Ekron, then the boundary bends
16: 6 to the sea; on the **n** is Michmethath;
17: 9 the boundary of Manasseh goes along the **n** side of
17:10 and that to the **n** is Manasseh's,
17:10 on the **n** Asher is reached,
18: 5 and the house of Joseph in their territory on the **n**.
18:12 On the **n** side their boundary began at the Jordan;
18:12 boundary goes up to the slope of Jericho on the **n**,
18:16 which is at the **n** end of the valley of Rephaim;
18:18 the **n** of the slope of Beth-arabah it goes down to
18:19 then the boundary passes on to the **n** of the slope
19:14 on the **n** the boundary makes a turn to Hannathon,
19:27 then it continues in the **n** to Cabul,
24:30 in the hill country of Ephraim, **n** of Mount Gaash.
Jdg 2: 9 in the hill country of Ephraim, **n** of Mount Gaash.
7: 1 and the camp of Midian was **n** of them,
21:19 of the LORD is taking place at Shiloh, which is **n**
1Sa 14: 5 One crag rose on the **n** in front of Michmash,
1Ki 7:21 and he set up the pillar on the **n** and called it Boaz.
7:25 It stood on twelve oxen, three facing **n**,
7:39 and five on the **n** side of the house;
7:49 five on the south side and five on the **n**,
2Ki 11:11 from the south side of the house to the **n** side of
16:14 and put it on the **n** side of his altar.
1Ch 9:24 gatekeepers were on the four sides, east, west, **n**,
26:14 and his lot came out for the **n**.
26:17 on the **n** four each day, on the south four each day,
2Ch 4: 4 It stood on twelve oxen, three facing **n**,
4: 7 five on the south side and five on the **n**.
23:10 from the south side of the house to the **n** side of
Job 37:22 Out of the **n** comes golden splendor;
Ps 48: 2 Mount Zion, in the far **n**, the city of the great King.
89:12 The **n** and the south—you created them;
107: 3 from the **n** and from the south.
Pr 25:23 The **n** wind produces rain,
Ecc 1: 6 and goes around to the **n**;
11: 3 whether a tree falls to the south or to the **n**,
SS 4:16 Awake, O **n** wind, and come, O south wind!
Isa 14:31 For smoke comes out of the **n**,

Isa 41:25 I stirred up one from the **n**, and he has come,
43: 6 to the **n**, "Give them up," and to the south, "Do
49:12 and lo, these from the **n** and from the west,
Jer 1:13 I said, "I see a boiling pot, tilted away from the **n**."
1:14 the **n** disaster shall break out on all the inhabitants
1:15 of the kingdoms of the **n**, says the LORD;
3:12 Go, and proclaim these words toward the **n**,
3:18 of the **n** to the land that I gave your ancestors for
4: 6 do not delay, for I am bringing evil from the **n**,
6: 1 for evil looms out of the **n**, and great destruction.
6:22 See, a people is coming from the land of the **n**,
10:22 a great commotion from the land of the **n** to make
13:20 up your eyes and see those who come from the **n**.
15:12 Can iron and bronze break iron from the **n**?
16:15 up out of the land of the **n** and out of all the lands
23: 8 the house of Israel out of the land of the **n** and out
25: 9 to send for all the tribes of the **n**, says the LORD,
25:26 all the kings of the **n**,
31: 8 I am going to bring them from the land of the **n**,
46: 6 in the **n** by the river Euphrates they have stumbled
46:10 of hosts holds a sacrifice in the land of the **n** by
46:20 a gadfly from the **n** lights upon her.
46:24 she shall be handed over to a people from the **n**.
47: 2 of the **n** and shall become an overflowing torrent;
50: 3 For out of the **n** a nation has come up against her;
50: 9 of great nations from the land of the **n**;
50:41 Look, a people is coming from the **n**;
51:48 destroyers shall come against them out of the **n**,
Eze 1: 4 As I looked, a stormy wind came out of the **n**:
8: 3 of the gateway of the inner court that faces **n**,
8: 5 lift up your eyes now in the direction of the **n**."
8: 5 So I lifted up my eyes toward the **n**, and there,
8: 5 and there, **n** of the altar gate, in the entrance,
8:14 Then he brought me to the entrance of the **n** gate
9: 2 which faces **n**, each with his weapon for slaughter
16:46 who lived with her daughters to the **n** of you;
20:47 all faces from south to **n** shall be scorched by it.
21: 4 of its sheath against all flesh from south to **n**;
23:24 against you from the **n** with chariots and wagons
26: 7 against Tyre from the **n** King Nebuchadrezzar
32:30 The princes of the **n** are there, all of them,
38: 6 Beth-togarmah from the remotest parts of the **n**
38:15 from your place out of the remotest parts of the **n**,
39: 2 and bring you up from the remotest parts of the **n**,
40:20 the gate of the outer court that faced **n**—
40:23 Opposite the gate on the **n**, as on the east,
40:35 he brought me to the **n** gate, and he measured it;
40:40 at the entrance of the **n** gate were two tables;
40:44 one at the side of the **n** gate facing south,
40:44 the other at the side of the east gate facing **n**.
40:46 that faces **n** is for the priests who have charge of
41:11 toward the **n**, and another door toward the south;
42: 1 he led me out into the outer court, toward the **n**,
42: 1 and opposite the building on the **n**.
42: 2 that was on the **n** side was one hundred cubits,
42: 4 and its entrances were on the **n**.
42:11 they were similar to the chambers on the **n**,
42:13 "The **n** chambers and the south chambers opposite
42:17 Then he turned and measured the **n** side,
44: 4 by way of the **n** gate to the front of the temple;
46: 9 by the **n** gate to worship shall go out by
46: 9 by the south gate shall go out by the **n** gate:
46:19 to the **n** row of the holy chambers for the priests;
47: 2 Then he brought me out by way of the **n** gate,
47:15 the **n** side, from the Great Sea by way of Hethlon
47:17 which is **n** of the border of Damascus,
47:17 with the border of Hamath to the **n**.
47:17 This shall be the **n** side.
48: 1 the border of Damascus, with Hamath to the **n**),
48:16 the **n** side four thousand five hundred cubits,
48:17 on the **n** two hundred fifty cubits,
48:30 These shall be the exits of the city: On the **n** side,
Da 11: 6 the south shall come to the king of the **n** to ratify
11: 7 and enter the fortress of the king of the **n**,
11: 8 from attacking the king of the **n**;
11:11 and do battle against the king of the **n**,
11:13 For the king of the **n** shall again raise a multitude,
11:15 king of the **n** shall come and throw up siegeworks,
11:40 king of the **n** shall rush upon him like a whirlwind,
11:44 reports from the east and the **n** shall alarm him,
Am 8:12 from sea to sea, and from **n** to east;
Zep 2:13 And he will stretch out his hand against the **n**,
Zec 2: 6 Flee from the land of the **n**, says the LORD;
6: 6 with the black horses goes toward the **n** country,
6: 8 toward the **n** country have set my spirit at rest in
the **n** country."
Lk 13:29 Then people will come from east and west, from **n**
Rev 21:13 on the **n** three gates, on the south three gates,
Tob 1: 2 above Asher toward the west, and **n** of Phogor.
Jdt 2:21 near the mountain that is to the **n** of Upper Cilicia.
16: 3 down from the mountains of the **n**;
Sir 43:17 so do the storm from the **n** and the whirlwind.
43:20 cold **n** wind blows, and ice freezes on the water;
2Es 15:34 and from the **n** to the south!
15:38 and from the **n**, and another part from the west.

NORTHEASTER (1) [EAST, NORTH]

Ac 27:14 But soon a violent wind, called the **n**,

NORTHERLY (1) [NORTH]

Jos 18:17 in a **n** direction going on to En-shemesh,

NORTHERN (9) [NORTH]

Nu 34: 7 This shall be your **n** boundary:
34: 9 this shall be your **n** boundary.
Jos 11: 2 and to the kings who were in the **n** hill country,
15: 8 on the west, at the **n** end of the valley of Rephaim;
15:10 to the **n** slope of Mount Jearim (that is, Chesalon),
18:19 the boundary ends at the **n** bay of the Dead Sea,
Eze 48: 1 Beginning at the **n** border, on the Hethlon road,
48:10 on the **n** side, ten thousand cubits in width on
Joel 2:20 I will remove the **n** army far from you,

NORTHWARD (6) [NORTH]

Ge 13:14 **n** and southward and eastward and westward;
Jos 13: 3 **n** to the boundary of Ekron,
15: 7 and so **n**, turning toward Gilgal,
19:27 and touches Zebulun and the valley of Iphtah-el **n**
Da 8: 4 the ram charging westward and **n** and southward.
Zec 14: 4 so that one half of the Mount shall withdraw **n**,

NORTHWEST (1) [NORTH, WEST]

Ac 27:12 It was a harbor of Crete, facing southwest and **n**.

NOSE (11) [NOSE-RING, NOSES]

Ge 24:47 So I put the ring on her **n**,
2Ki 19:28 I will put my hook in your **n** and my bit
Job 40:24 Can one take it with hooks or pierce its **n** with
41: 2 Can you put a rope in its **n**,
Pr 30:33 and pressing the **n** produces blood,
SS 7: 4 Your **n** is like a tower of Lebanon,
Isa 3:21 the signet rings and **n** rings;
37:29 I will put my hook in your **n** and my bit
Eze 8:17 See, they are putting the branch to their **n**!
16:12 a ring on your **n**, earrings in your ears,
23:25 They shall cut off your **n** and your ears,

NOSE-RING (2) [NOSE, RING]

Ge 24:22 the man took a gold **n** weighing a half shekel,
24:30 As soon as he had seen the **n**,

NOSES (1) [NOSE]

Ps 115: 6 They have ears, but do not hear; **n**,

NOSTRILS (17)

Ge 2: 7 and breathed into his **n** the breath of life;
7:22 on dry land in whose **n** was the breath of life died.
Ex 15: 8 At the blast of your **n** the waters piled up,
Nu 11:20 of your **n** and becomes loathsome to you—
2Sa 22: 9 Smoke went up from his **n**,
22:16 at the blast of the breath of his **n**.
Job 27: 3 in me and the spirit of God is in my **n**,
41:20 Out of its **n** comes smoke,
Ps 18: 8 Smoke went up from his **n**,
18:15 O LORD, at the blast of the breath of your **n**.
Isa 2:22 who have only breath in their **n**,
65: 5 These are a smoke in my **n**,
Am 4:10 I made the stench of your camp go up into your **n**;
Wis 2: 2 for the breath in our **n** is smoke,
15:15 nor **n** with which to draw breath,
4Mc 6:25 and poured stinking liquids into his **n**.
15:19 saw in their **n** the signs of the approach of death.

NOT (7614) [NO] See Index of Articles Etc.

NOTABLE (3) [NOTE]

Ac 4:16 that a **n** sign has been done through them;
AdE 16:22 as a **n** day among your commemorative festivals,
3Mc 6:28 an unimpeded and **n** stability to our government."

NOTABLES (2) [NOTE]

1Ch 12:30 mighty warriors, **n** in their ancestral houses.
Am 6: 1 the **n** of the first of the nations,

NOTE (11) [NOTABLE, NOTABLES, NOTES]

Ge 38:25 And she said, "Take **n**, please, whose these are,
1Sa 2:21 And the LORD took **n** of Hannah;
1Ch 21:15 about to destroy it, the LORD took **n** and relented
Ps 10:14 Indeed you **n** trouble and grief,
Jer 5: 1 the streets of Jerusalem, look around and take **n**!
Mal 3:16 The LORD took **n** and listened,
Mt 24:25 Take **n**, I have told you beforehand.
Ro 11:22 **N** then the kindness and the severity of God:
2Th 3:14 Take **n** of those who do not obey what we say
Wis 19:18 while each **n** remains the same.
2Es 8:27 Do not take **n** of the endeavors

NOTES (2) [NOTE]

1Co 14: 7 If they do not give distinct **n**,
Wis 19:18 as on a harp the **n** vary the nature of the rhythm,

NOTHING‡ (372) [NOTHINGS]

Ge 11: 6 **n** that they propose to do will now be impossible
14:24 I will take **n** but what the young men have eaten,
19: 8 only do **n** to these men,
19:22 escape there, for I can do **n** until you arrive there."
26:29 not touched you and have done to you **n** but good
29:15 should you therefore serve me for **n**?
40:15 also I have done **n** that they should have put me
47:18 There is **n** left in the sight of my lord
Ex 5:23 and you have done **n** at all to deliver your people."
9: 4 **n** shall die of all that belongs to the Israelites.' "
10:15 **n** green was left, no tree, no plant in the field,
12:20 You shall eat **n** leavened;
16:18 those who gathered much had **n** over,
Lev 27:28 **N** that a person owns that has been devoted
Nu 6: 4 as nazirites they shall eat **n** that is produced by
11: 5 to eat in Egypt for **n**, the cucumbers, the melons,
11: 6 and there is **n** at all but this manna to look at."
16:26 and touch **n** of theirs, or you will be swept away
23:11 but now you have done **n** but bless them."
30: 4 by which she has bound herself, and says **n** to her;
30: 7 and her husband hears of it and says **n** to her at
30:11 and her husband heard it and said **n** to her,
30:14 But if her husband says **n** to her from day to day,
30:14 he said **n** to her at the time that he heard of them.
Dt 2: 7 with you; you have lacked **n**."
8: 9 without scarcity, where you will lack **n**,
15: 9 with hostility and give **n**;
22:26 You shall do **n** to the young woman;
28:55 because **n** else remains to him,
29:23 **n** planted,**n** sprouting, unable to support any
Jos 2:22 along the way and found **n**.
11:15 he left **n** undone of all that
Jdg 13: 7 drink no wine or strong drink, and eat **n** unclean,
18: 7 quiet and unsuspecting, lacking **n** on earth,
18: 9 and it is very good. Will you do **n**?
19:19 with us. We need **n** more."
1Sa 3:18 Samuel told him everything and hid **n** from him.
4: 7 For **n** like this has happened before.
14: 6 for **n** can hinder the LORD from saving by many
20: 2 My father does **n** either great or small
20:39 But the boy knew **n**; only Jonathan
22:15 for your servant has known **n** of all this,
25: 7 and we did them no harm, and they missed **n**,
25:21 so that **n** was missed of all that belonged to him;
25:36 so she told him **n** at all until the morning light.
27: 1 there is **n** better for me than to escape to the land
28:20 for he had eaten **n** all day and all night.
29: 6 for I have found **n** wrong in you from the day
29: 7 do **n** to displease the lords of the Philistines."
30:19 **N** was missing, whether small or great,
2Sa 12: 3 but the poor man had **n** but one little ewe lamb,
15:11 and they went in their innocence, knowing **n** of
17:19 and **n** was known of it.
18:13 against his life (and there is **n** hidden from
19: 6 that commanders and officers are **n** to you;
19:10 why do you say **n** about bringing the king back?"
24:24 to the LORD my God that cost me **n**."
1Ki 4:27 in his month; they let **n** be lacking.
8: 9 There was **n** in the ark except the two tablets
10: 3 there was **n** hidden from the king that he could
10:20 **N** like it was ever made in any kingdom.
17:12 "As the LORD your God lives, I have **n** baked,
18:43 He went up and looked, and said, "There is **n**."
22: 3 yet we are doing **n** to take it out of the hand of
22:16 to tell me **n** but the truth in the name of
2Ki 4: 2 She answered, "Your servant has **n** in the house,
4:41 And there was **n** harmful in the pot.
5:16 whom I serve, I will accept **n**!"
7:10 **n** but the horses tied, the donkeys tied,
10:10 then that there shall fall to the earth **n** of the word
20:13 there was **n** in his house or in all his realm
20:15 there is **n** in my storehouses that I did
20:17 **n** shall be left, says the LORD.
1Ch 21:24 nor offer burnt offerings that cost me **n**."
2Ch 5:10 There was **n** in the ark except the two tablets
9: 2 there was **n** hidden from Solomon that he could
18:15 to tell me **n** but the truth in the name of
30:26 of King David of Israel there had been **n** like this
Ne 5:12 "We will restore everything and demand **n** more
8:10 for whom **n** is prepared, for this day is holy
9:21 in the wilderness so that they lacked **n**;
Est 2:15 for **n** except what Hegai the king's eunuch,
6: 3 "**N** has been done for him."
6:10 Leave out **n** that you have mentioned."
Job 1: 9 "Does Job fear God for **n**?
5:24 you shall inspect your fold and miss **n**.
8: 9 but of yesterday, and we know **n**, for our days
18:15 In their tents **n** remains; sulfur is scattered upon
20:20 in their greed they let **n** escape.
20:21 There was **n** left after they had eaten;
21:34 There is **n** left of your answers but falsehood."
24:25 and show that there is **n** in what I say?"
26: 7 and hangs the earth upon **n**.
34: 9 'It profits one **n** to take delight in God.'
Ps 19: 6 and **n** is hid from its heat.
33:10 LORD brings the counsel of the nations to **n**;
39: 5 and my lifetime is as **n** in your sight.
39: 6 Surely for **n** they are in turmoil;
49:17 For when they die they will carry **n** away;
73:25 there is **n** on earth that I desire other than you.
101: 4 I will know **n** of evil.
112:10 the desire of the wicked comes to **n**.
119:165 **n** can make them stumble.
Pr 3:15 and **n** you desire can compare with her.
8: 8 there is **n** twisted or crooked in them.
9:13 she is ignorant and knows **n**.
10:28 but the expectation of the wicked comes to **n**.
11: 7 and the expectation of the godless comes to **n**.
13: 4 The appetite of the lazy craves, and gets **n**,
13: 7 Some pretend to be rich, yet have **n**;
20: 4 harvest comes, and there is **n** to be found.
22:27 If you have **n** with which to pay,
28:27 Whoever gives to the poor will lack **n**,
29:24 one hears the victim's curse, but discloses **n**.
Ecc 1: 9 there is **n** new under the sun.
2:11 and there was **n** to be gained under the sun.
2:24 There is **n** better for mortals than to eat and drink,
3:12 that there is **n** better for them than to be happy
3:14 **n** can be added to it, nor anything taken from it;
3:22 So I saw that there is **n** better than
5:14 they have **n** in their hands.

Ecc 5:15 they shall take **n** for their toil,
6: 2 so that they lack **n** of all that they desire,
8:15 for there is **n** better for people under the sun than
9: 5 that they will die, but the dead know **n;**
Isa 34:12 and all its princes shall be **n.**
39: 2 There was **n** in his house or in all his realm
39: 4 there is **n** in my storehouses that I did
39: 6 **n** shall be left, says the LORD.
40:17 All the nations are as **n** before him;
40:17 they are accounted by him as less than **n**
40:23 and makes the rulers of the earth as **n.**
41:11 those who strive against you shall be as **n**
41:12 those who war against you shall be as **n** at all.
41:24 You, indeed, are **n** and your work is **n** at all;
41:29 their works are **n;** their images are empty wind.
44: 9 All who make idols are **n,**
47:11 on you suddenly, of which you know **n.**
49: 4 I have spent my strength for **n** and vanity;
52: 3 For thus says the LORD: You were sold for **n,**
53: 2 **n** in his appearance that we should desire him.
Jer 5:12 and have said, "He will do **n.**
5:13 The prophets are **n** but wind,
6: 6 there is **n** but oppression within her.
10:24 not in your anger, or you will bring me to **n.**
12:13 they have tired themselves out but profit **n.**
13: 7 now the loincloth was ruined; it was good for **n.**
13:10 shall be like this loincloth, which is good for **n.**
16:19 Our ancestors have inherited **n** but lies,
22:13 who makes his neighbors work for **n,**
30:14 lovers have forgotten you; they care **n** for you;
32:17 **N** is too hard for you.
32:23 of all you commanded them to do, they did **n.**
32:30 of Israel and the people of Judah have done **n**
32:30 of Israel have done **n** but provoke me to anger by
39:10 of Judah some of the poor people who owned **n,**
42: 4 I will keep **n** back from you."
48:38 and in the squares there is **n** but lamentation;
50:26 let **n** be left of her.
51:58 The peoples exhaust themselves for **n,**
La 1:12 Is it **n** to you, all you who pass by?
Eze 12:22 and every vision comes to **n"?**
13: 3 who follow their own spirit, and have seen **n!**
15: 5 When it was whole it was used for **n;**
16:16 **n** like this has ever been or ever shall be.
31: 8 plane trees were as **n** compared with its branches;
44:17 they shall have **n** of wool on them,
Da 4:35 All the inhabitants of the earth are accounted as **n,**
6:17 so that **n** might be changed concerning Daniel.
9:26 an anointed one shall be cut off and shall have **n,**
Hos 12:11 they shall surely come to **n.**
Joel 2: 3 a desolate wilderness, and **n** escapes them.
Am 3: 4 from its den, if it has caught **n?**
3: 5 up from the ground, when it has taken **n?**
3: 7 Surely the Lord GOD does **n,**
5: 5 and Bethel shall come to **n.**
Mic 3: 5 against those who put **n** into their mouths.
Hab 2:13 and nations weary themselves for **n?**
Zep 3: 3 its judges are evening wolves that leave **n** until
Hag 2: 3 Is it not in your sight as **n?**
2:19 the pomegranate, and the olive tree still yield **n?**
Mt 8: 4 Jesus said to him, "See that you say **n** to anyone;
10:26 for **n** is covered up that will not be uncovered,
10:26 and **n** secret that will not become known.
13:12 but from those who have **n,**
13:22 the lure of wealth choke the word, and it yields **n.**
13:34 without a parable he told them **n.**
14:17 "We have **n** here but five loaves and two fish."
15:32 with me now for three days and have **n** to eat;
17:20 and **n** will be impossible for you."
21:19 he went to it and found **n** at all on it but leaves.
23:16 'Whoever swears by the sanctuary is bound by **n,**
23:18 'Whoever swears by the altar is bound by **n,**
24:39 and they knew **n** until the flood came
25:29 but from those who have **n,**
25:42 I was thirsty and you gave me **n** to drink,
27:19 "Have **n** to do with that innocent man,
27:24 So when Pilate saw that he could do **n,**
Mk 1:44 "See that you say **n** to anyone;
4:19 in and choke the word, and it yields **n.**
4:22 For there is **n** hidden, except to be disclosed;
4:25 and from those who have **n,**
6: 8 He ordered them to take **n** for their journey except
7:15 there is **n** outside a person that by going
8: 2 with me now for three days and have **n** to eat.
11:13 When he came to it, he found **n** but leaves,
14:51 wearing **n** but a linen cloth.
16: 8 and they said **n** to anyone, for they were afraid.
Lk 1:37 For **n** will be impossible with God."
4: 2 He ate **n** at all during those days,
5: 5 we have worked all night long but have caught **n.**
6:35 do good, and lend, expecting **n** in return.
8:17 For **n** is hidden that will not be disclosed,
9: 3 He said to them, "Take **n** for your journey,
10:19 of the enemy; and **n** will hurt you.
11: 6 and I have **n** to set before him.'
12: 2 **N** is covered up that will not be uncovered,
12: 2 and **n** secret that will not become known.
12: 4 and after that can do **n** more.
18:34 But they understood **n** about all these things;
19:26 but from those who have **n,**
23:15 Indeed, he has done **n** to deserve death.
23:41 but this man has done **n** wrong."
Jn 5:14 so that **n** worse happens to you."
5:19 I tell you, the Son can do **n** on his own,
5:30 "I can do **n** on my own.
6:12 so that **n** may be lost."
6:39 that I should lose **n** of all that he has given me,
Jn 7:18 and there is **n** false in him.
7:26 here he is, speaking openly, but they say **n** to him!
8:28 and that I do **n** on my own,
8:54 "If I glorify myself, my glory is **n.**
9:33 If this man were not from God, he could do **n."**
11:49 said to them, "You know **n** at all!
12:19 then said to one another, "You see, you can do **n.**
15: 5 because apart from me you can do **n.**
16:23 On that day you will ask **n** of me.
18:20 I have said **n** in secret.
21: 3 but that night they caught **n.**
Ac 4:14 they had **n** to say in opposition.
8:24 that **n** of what you have said may happen to me."
9: 8 and though his eyes were open, he could see **n;**
11: 8 **n** profane or unclean has ever entered my mouth.'
17:21 in **n** but telling or hearing something new.
19:36 you ought to be quiet and do **n** rash.
21:24 that there is **n** in what they have been told
23: 9 "We find **n** wrong with this man.
23:29 with **n** deserving death or imprisonment.
25:11 but if there is **n** to their charges against me,
25:25 But I found that he had done **n** deserving death;
25:26 But I have **n** definite to write to our sovereign
26:22 saying **n** but what the prophets
26:31 "This man is doing **n** to deserve death
27:33 and remaining without food, having eaten **n.**
28: 6 a long time and saw that **n** unusual had happened
28:17 though I had done **n** against our people or
Ro 7:18 For I know that **n** good dwells within me, that is,
14:14 in the Lord Jesus that **n** is unclean in itself;
1Co 1:28 things that are not, to reduce to **n** things that are,
2: 2 to know **n** among you except Jesus Christ,
4: 6 "**N** beyond what is written,"
6: 3 to say **n** of ordinary matters?
7:19 Circumcision is **n,** and uncircumcision is **n;**
11:22 of God and humiliate those who have **n?**
13: 2 but do not have love, I am **n.**
13: 3 but do not have love, I gain **n.**
14:10 of sounds in the world, and **n** is without sound.
16:10 see that he has **n** to fear among you,
2Co 1:13 For we write you **n** other than what you can read
6:10 as having **n,** and yet possessing everything.
6:17 and touch **n** unclean; then I will welcome you,
9: 4 to say **n** of you—in this undertaking.
12: 1 It is necessary to boast; **n** is to be gained by it,
12:11 to these super-apostles, even though I am **n.**
Gal 2: 6 those leaders contributed **n** to me.
2:21 through the law, then Christ died for **n.**
3: 4 Did you experience so much for **n?**—if it really
was for **n.**
6: 3 For if those who are **n** think they are something,
Php 2: 3 Do **n** from selfish ambition or conceit,
2Th 3:14 have **n** to do with them,
1Ti 4: 4 and **n** is to be rejected, provided it is received
4: 7 Have **n** to do with profane myths
5:21 doing **n** on the basis of partiality.
6: 4 understanding **n,** and has a morbid craving
6: 7 for we brought **n** into the world, so that we can
take **n** out of it;
2Ti 2:23 Have **n** to do with stupid
Tit 1:15 but to the corrupt and unbelieving **n** is pure.
2: 8 having **n** evil to say of us.
3:10 After a first and second admonition, have **n** more
3:13 and see that they lack **n.**
Phm 1:14 but I preferred to do **n** without your consent,
1:19 I say **n** about your owing me even your own self.
Heb 2: 8 God left **n** outside their control.
7:14 and in connection with that tribe Moses said **n**
7:19 (for the law made **n** perfect);
Jas 1: 2 of any kind, consider it **n** but joy,
1: 4 be mature and complete, lacking in **n.**
4: 5 Or do you suppose that it is for **n** that
1Pe 3: 7 so that **n** may hinder your prayers.
Rev 3:17 'I am rich, I have prospered, and I need **n.'**
21:27 But **n** unclean will enter it,
22: 3 **N** accursed will be found there any more.
Tob 1:20 **n** was left to me that was not taken into
8:14 that he was alive and that **n** was wrong.
10:12 do **n** to grieve her all the days of your life.
12:11 the whole truth to you and will conceal **n**
13: 2 and there is **n** that can escape his hand.
Jdt 11: 5 I will say **n** false to my lord this night.
AdE 6:10 let **n** be omitted from what you have proposed."
16: 4 carried away by the boasts of those who know **n**
Wis 4: 5 not ripe enough to eat, and good for **n.**
7: 8 I accounted wealth as **n** in comparison with her.
7:25 therefore **n** defiled gains entrance into her.
7:28 for God loves **n** so much as the person who lives
8: 7 **n** in life is more profitable for mortals than these.
9: 6 be regarded as **n** without the wisdom that comes
13:13 a cast-off piece from among them, useful for **n,**
17: 6 **N** was shining through to them except a dreadful,
17: 9 For even if **n** disturbing frightened them, yet,
17:12 For fear is **n** but a giving up of the helps that come
Sir 8:16 because bloodshed means **n** to them,
8:18 In the presence of strangers do **n** that is to
18:22 Let **n** hinder you from paying a vow promptly,
18:33 when you have **n** in your purse.
19: 7 and you will lose **n** at all.
20: 6 Some people keep silent because they have **n**
20:10 There is the gift that profits you **n,**
20:14 A fool's gift will profit you **n,**
20:23 and so makes an enemy for **n.**
23:27 that **n** is better than the fear of the Lord,
23:27 and **n** sweeter than to heed the commandments of
25: 3 If you gathered **n** in your youth,
26:14 and **n** is so precious as her self-discipline.
Sir 32:19 Do **n** without deliberation,
33:30 be overbearing toward anyone, and do **n** unjust.
36:27 and there is **n** he desires more.
39:19 and **n** can be hidden from his eyes.
39:20 and **n** is too marvelous for him.
41: 1 who has **n** to worry about and is prosperous
42:20 and **n** is hidden from him.
42:21 **N** can be added or taken away,
42:24 and he has made **n** incomplete.
48:13 **N** was too hard for him, and when he was dead,
LtJ 6:45 they can be **n** but what the artisans wish them
6:70 which guards **n,** so are their gods of wood,
Sus 1:27 for **n** like this had ever been said about Susanna.
Bel 1:32 but now they were given **n,**
1:35 and I know **n** about the den."
1Mc 3:17 And we are faint, for we have eaten **n** today."
2Mc 7:12 for he regarded his sufferings as **n.**
12: 4 they wished to live peaceably and suspected **n,**
14:23 Nicanor stayed on in Jerusalem and did **n** out of
14:35 though you have need of **n,**
1Es 2:28 from building the city and to take care that **n** more
4:36 and with him there is **n** unrighteous.
4:40 and there is **n** unrighteous in its judgment.
5:70 "You have **n** to do with us in building the house
8: 7 so that he omitted **n** from the law of the Lord or
3Mc 1:26 But he, in his arrogance, took heed of **n,**
2Es 6:10 seek for **n** else, Ezra, between the heel and
6:56 you have said that they are **n,**
6:57 these nations, which are reputed to be as **n,**
11:23 and **n** remained on the eagle's body except
13:11 so that suddenly **n** was seen of
4Mc 2:17 he did **n** against them in anger,
8:11 **n** remains for you but to die on the rack?"
9: 5 a short time ago you learned **n** from Eleazar.

NOTHINGNESS See Index to Footnotes

NOTHINGS (1) [NOTHING]

Job 21:34 How then will you comfort me with empty **n?**

NOTICE (17) [NOTICED, NOTICES, NOTICING]

Ex 2:25 and God took **n** of them.
13:19 saying, "God will surely take **n** of you,
Lev 4:13 the **n** of the assembly, and they do any one of
Ru 2:10 that you should take **n** of me,
2:19 Blessed be the man who took **n** of you."
2Sa 3:36 All the people took **n** of it, and it pleased them;
20:10 But Amasa did not **n** the sword in Joab's hand;
Ps 142: 4 there is no one who takes **n** of me;
Isa 58: 3 Why humble ourselves, but you do not **n?"**
Mt 7: 3 but do not **n** the log in your own eye?
Mk 7:24 Yet he could not escape **n,**
Lk 6:41 but do not **n** the log in your own eye?
Ac 26:26 that none of these things has escaped his **n,**
Jas 2: 3 if you take **n** of the one wearing the fine clothes
Wis 1: 8 not escape **n,** and justice, when it punishes, will
LtJ 6:20 their robes. They do not **n**
Bel 1:19 he said, "and **n** whose footprints these are."

NOTICED (8) [NOTICE]

Mt 14:30 But when he **n** the strong wind,
22:11 he **n** a man there who was not wearing
Mk 7: 2 they **n** that some of his disciples were eating
Lk 8:46 for I **n** that power had gone out from me."
14: 7 he **n** how the guests chose the places of honor,
Ac 23: 6 When Paul **n** that some were Sadducees
27:39 but they **n** a bay with a beach,
2Mc 14:26 when Alcimus **n** their goodwill for one another,

NOTICES (1) [NOTICE]

Sir 19:27 but when no one **n,** he will take advantage of you.

NOTICING (1) [NOTICE]

2Mc 14:30 **n** that Nicanor was more austere in his dealings

NOTIFY (3)

Ezr 7:24 We also **n** you that it shall not be lawful
Ac 23:15 the council must **n** the tribune to bring him down
2Mc 1:18 we thought it necessary to **n** you,

NOTION (1)

2Mc 3:32 the **n** that some foul play had been perpetrated by

NOTORIOUS (3)

Mt 27:16 At that time they had a **n** prisoner,
2Mc 13: 6 to destruction anyone guilty of sacrilege or **n**
3Mc 2: 5 who were **n** for their vices;

NOTWITHSTANDING (1)

Nu 26:11 **N,** the sons of Korah did not die.

NOTWITHSTANDING (KJV) See also AS FOR, BUT, HOWEVER, IN ANY CASE, JUST THIS, NEVERTHELESS, STILL, THEN, YET

NOUGHT (KJV) See ANYTHING, BAD, CONTEMPT, CRUMBLES, DESPISE, DISAPPEAR, DISREPUTE, FAIL, FRUSTRATED, IGNORED, IN VAIN, LO DEBAR, NO MORE, NO REASON, NOTHING, PERISH, REJECTED, RIDICULED, RUIN, TRIFLE, WASTE, WITHOUT A CAUSE, WITHOUT GROUNDS, WITHOUT PAYING

NOURISH‡ (2) [ALL-NOURISHING, NOURISHED, NOURISHER, NOURISHES, NOURISHMENT]

Zec 11:16 or heal the maimed, or **n** the healthy,
2Es 2:25 "Good nurse, **n** your children;

NOURISHED‡ (7) [NOURISH]

Eze 31: 4 The waters **n** it, the deep made it grow tall,
Col 2:19 **n** and held together by its ligaments and sinews,
1Ti 4: 6 **n** on the words of the faith and of
Rev 12: 6 be **n** for one thousand two hundred sixty days.
12:14 to her place where she is **n** for a time, and times,
2Es 8:11 that what has been fashioned may be **n** for a time;
4Mc 13:21 From such embraces brotherly-loving souls are **n**;

NOURISHER (1) [NOURISH]

Ru 4:15 be to you a restorer of life and a **n** of your old age;

NOURISHES (2) [NOURISH]

Isa 44:14 He plants a cedar and the rain **n** it.
Eph 5:29 but he **n** and tenderly cares for it,

NOURISHMENT (2) [NOURISH]

Pr 27:27 of your household and **n** for your servant-girls.
2Es 9:26 and the **n** they afforded satisfied me.

NOVICE (KJV) See RECENT CONVERT

NOW‡ (1703)

Ge 3: 1 **N** the serpent was more crafty than any other wild
3:22 and **n**, he might reach out his hand and take also
4: 1 **N** the man knew his wife Eve,
4: 2 **N** Abel was a keeper of sheep,
4:11 And **n** you are cursed from the ground,
6:11 **N** the earth was corrupt in God's sight,
6:13 **n** I am going to destroy them along with the earth.
11: 1 **N** the whole earth had one language and
11: 6 that they propose to do will **n** be impossible
11:27 **N** these are the descendants of Terah.
11:30 **N** Sarai was barren; she had no child.
12: 1 **N** the LORD said to Abram,
12:10 **N** there was a famine in the land.
12:19 **N** then, here is your wife, take her, and be gone."
13: 2 **N** Abram was very rich in livestock, in silver,
13: 5 **N** Lot, who went with Abram,
13:13 **N** the people of Sodom were wicked,
13:14 "Raise your eyes **n**, and look from the place
14:10 **N** the Valley of Siddim was full of bitumen pits;
16: 1 **N** Sarai, Abram's wife, bore him no children.
16:11 "**N** you have conceived and shall bear a son;
17: 8 the land where you are **n** an alien,
18:11 **N** Abraham and Sarah were old, advanced in age;
18:13 'Shall I indeed bear a child, **n** that I am old?'
19: 9 **N** we will deal worse with you than with them."
19:30 **N** Lot went up out of Zoar and settled in the hills
20: 4 **N** Abimelech had not approached her;
20: 7 **N** then, return the man's wife;
21: 6 **N** Sarah said, "God has brought laughter for me;
21:23 **n** therefore swear to me here by God that you will
22:12 for **n** I know that you fear God,
22:20 **N** after these things it was told Abraham,
23:10 **N** Ephron was sitting among the Hittites;
24: 1 **N** Abraham was old, well advanced in years;
24:42 if **n** you will only make successful
24:49 **N** then, if you will deal loyally and truly
24:62 **N** Isaac had come from Beer-lahai-roi,
26: 1 **N** there was a famine in the land,
26:15 (**N** the Philistines had stopped up and filled
26:22 saying, "**N** the LORD has made room for us,
26:29 You are **n** the blessed of the LORD."
27: 3 **N** then, take your weapons,
27: 5 **N** Rebekah was listening when Isaac spoke
27: 8 **N** therefore, my son, obey my word
27:19 **n** sit up and eat of my game,
27:36 and look, **n** he has taken away my blessing."
27:41 **N** Esau hated Jacob because of the blessing
27:43 **N** therefore, my son, obey my voice;
28: 4 of the land where you **n** live as an alien—
28: 6 **N** Esau saw that Isaac had blessed Jacob
29:10 **N** when Jacob saw Rachel,
29:16 **N** Laban had two daughters;
29:32 surely **n** my husband will love me."
29:34 "**N** this time my husband will be joined to me,
30:20 **n** my husband will honor me,
30:30 But **n** when shall I provide
31: 1 **N** Jacob heard that the sons of Laban were saying,
31:13 **N** leave this land at once and return to the land
31:16 **n** then, do whatever God has said to you."
31:19 **N** Laban had gone to shear his sheep,
Ge 31:25 **N** Jacob had pitched his tent in the hill country,
31:32 **N** Jacob did not know that Rachel had stolen
31:34 **N** Rachel had taken the household gods
31:42 **n** you would have sent me away empty-handed.
31:44 Come **n**, let us make a covenant, you and I;
32: 4 with Laban as an alien, and stayed until **n**;
32:10 and **n** I have become two companies.
33: 1 **N** Jacob looked up and saw Esau coming,
34: 1 **N** Dinah the daughter of Leah,
34: 5 **N** Jacob heard that Shechem had defiled his
34:19 **N** he was the most honored of all his family.
35:17 for **n** you will have another son."
35:22 **N** the sons of Jacob were twelve.
35:28 **N** the days of Isaac were one hundred eighty years.
37: 3 **N** Israel loved Joseph more than any other
37:12 **N** his brothers went to pasture their father's flock
37:14 So he said to him, "Go **n**,
37:20 Come **n**, let us kill him and throw him into one of
37:32 see **n** whether it is your son's robe or not."
39: 1 **N** Joseph was taken down to Egypt, and Potiphar,
39: 6 **N** Joseph was handsome and good-looking.
41:33 **N** therefore let Pharaoh select
42: 6 **N** Joseph was governor over the land;
42:13 the youngest, however, is **n** with our father,
42:22 So **n** there comes a reckoning for his blood."
42:32 and the youngest is **n** with our father in the land
42:36 and **n** you would take Benjamin.
43: 1 **N** the famine was severe in the land.
43:10 we would **n** have returned twice."
43:18 **N** the men were afraid because they were brought
44:30 **N** therefore, when I come
44:33 **N** therefore, please let your servant remain as
45: 5 And **n** do not be distressed,
45:12 And **n** your eyes and the eyes
46: 8 **N** these are the names of the Israelites,
46:30 Israel said to Joseph, "I can die **n**,
46:34 of livestock from our youth even until **n**, both we
47: 1 they are **n** in the land of Goshen."
47: 4 **N**, we ask you, let your servants settle in the land
47:13 **N** there was no food in all the land,
47:23 "**N** that I have this day bought you and your land
48: 5 of Egypt before I came to you in Egypt, are **n**
48:10 **N** the eyes of Israel were dim with age,
48:22 I **n** give to you one portion more than
50: 4 "If **n** I have found favor with you,
50: 5 **N** therefore let me go up,
50:17 **N** therefore please forgive the crime of
Ex 1: 8 **N** a new king arose over Egypt,
2: 1 **N** a man from the house of Levi went and married
3: 9 The cry of the Israelites has **n** come to me;
3:18 let us **n** go a three days' journey into
4:10 nor even **n** that you have spoken to your servant;
4:12 **N** go, and I will be with your mouth
4:14 even **n** he is coming out to meet you,
4:23 **n** I will kill your firstborn son.'"
5: 5 "**N** they are more numerous than the people of
5:18 Go **n**, and work; for no straw shall be given
6: 1 "**N** you shall see what I will do to Pharaoh:
7:16 But until **n** you have not listened.'
9:15 For by **n** I could have stretched out my hand
9:18 in Egypt from the day it was founded until **n**.
9:31 (**N** the flax and the barley were ruined,
18:11 **N** I know that the LORD is greater than all gods,
18:19 **N** listen to me. I will give you counsel,
19: 5 **N** therefore, if you obey my voice
19:18 **N** Mount Sinai was wrapped in smoke,
24:17 **N** the appearance of the glory of the LORD was
29: 1 **N** this is what you shall do to them
29:38 **N** this is what you shall offer on the altar:
32:10 **N** let me alone, so that my wrath may burn hot
32:30 But **n** I will go up to the LORD;
32:32 But **n**, if you will only forgive their sin—
32:34 But **n** go, lead the people to the place
33: 5 So **n** take off your ornaments,
33: 7 **N** Moses used to take the tent and pitch it outside
33:13 **N** if I have found favor in your sight,
34: 9 He said, "If **n** I have found favor in your sight,
Lev 10: 1 **N** Aaron's sons, Nadab and Abihu,
23:27 **N**, the tenth day of this seventh month is the day
23:39 **N**, the fifteenth day of the seventh month,
24:11 **n** his mother's name was Shelomith,
Nu 5:22 **n** may this water that brings
8: 4 **N** this was how the lampstand was made,
9: 6 **N** there were certain people who were unclean
11: 1 **N** when the people complained in the hearing of
11: 6 but **n** our strength is dried up,
11: 7 **N** the manna was like coriander seed,
11:23 **N** you shall see whether my word will come true
12: 3 **N** the man Moses was very humble,
13:20 **N** it was the season of the first ripe grapes.
14:15 **N** if you kill this people all at one time,
14:17 And **n**, therefore, let the power of the LORD
14:19 pardoned this people, from Egypt even until **n**."
14:25 **N**, since the Amalekites and the Canaanites live in
16: 1 **N** Korah son of Izhar son of Kohath son of Levi,
16: 8 Then Moses said to Korah, "Hear **n**, you Levites!
18: 6 It is I who **n** take your brother Levites from
18: 6 they are **n** yours as a gift, dedicated to the LORD,
18:22 From **n** on the Israelites shall no longer approach
20: 2 **N** there was no water for the congregation;
20:17 **N** let us pass through your land.
22: 2 **N** Balak son of Zippor saw all that Israel had done
22: 4 "This horde will **n** lick up all that is around us,
22: 4 **N** Balak son of Zippor was king of Moab at
22: 6 Come **n**, curse this people for me,
22:11 **n** come, curse them for me;
22:22 **N** he was riding on the donkey,
Nu 22:29 I would kill you right **n**!"
22:33 just **n** I would have killed you and let it live."
22:34 **N** therefore, if it is displeasing to you,
22:38 Balaam said to Balak, "I have come to you **n**,
23:11 but **n** you have done nothing but bless them."
23:23 **n** it shall be said of Jacob and Israel,
23:27 So Balak said to Balaam, "Come **n**,
24: 1 **N** Balaam saw that it pleased the LORD
24:11 **N** be off with you!
24:14 So **n**, I am going to my people;
24:17 I see him, but not **n**; I behold him,
26:33 **N** Zelophehad son of Hepher had no sons,
26:58 **N** Kohath was the father of Amram.
31:17 **N** therefore, kill every male among the little ones,
32: 1 **N** the Reubenites and the Gadites owned
32:14 And **n** you, a brood of sinners,
Dt 2:13 "**N** then, proceed to cross over the Wadi Zered."
2:30 in order to hand him over to you, as he has **n** done.
2:31 Begin **n** to take possession of his land."
3:11 (**N** only King Og of Bashan was left of
4: 1 So **n**, Israel, give heed to the statutes
4: 5 I **n** teach you statutes and ordinances for you
4:20 a people of his very own possession, as you are **n**.
4:32 For ask **n** about former ages,
5:25 So **n** why should we die?
6: 1 **N** this is the commandment—
6:24 so as to keep us alive, as is **n** the case.
10:12 So **n**, O Israel, what does the LORD your God
10:22 and **n** the LORD your God has made you
19: 4 **N** this is the case of
22:17 **n** he has made up charges against her,
26:10 So **n** I bring the first of the fruit of the ground
29:28 and cast them into another land, as is **n** the case."
31: 2 "I am **n** one hundred twenty years old.
31:19 **N** therefore write this song,
31:21 For I know what they are inclined to do even **n**,
32:39 See **n** that I, even I, am he;
Jos 1: 2 **N** proceed to cross the Jordan,
2:12 **N** then, since I have dealt kindly with you,
3:12 So **n** select twelve men from the tribes of Israel,
3:15 **N** the Jordan overflows all its banks throughout
5:14 as commander of the army of the LORD I have **n**
6: 1 **N** Jericho was shut up inside and out because of
7: 8 **n** that Israel has turned their backs
7:19 Tell me **n** what you have done;
7:21 They **n** lie hidden in the ground inside my tent,
8: 1 take all the fighting men with you, and go up **n**
9: 1 **N** when all the kings who were beyond the Jordan
9: 6 so **n** make a treaty with us."
9:11 come **n**, make a treaty with us."'
9:12 on the day we set out to come to you, but **n**, see,
9:17 **N** their cities were Gibeon, Chephirah, Beeroth,
9:19 the God of Israel, and **n** we must not touch them.
9:23 **N** therefore you are cursed,
9:25 And **n** we are in your hand:
12: 1 **N** these are the kings of the land,
13: 1 **N** Joshua was old and advanced in years;
13: 7 **N** therefore divide this land for an inheritance to
14:10 And **n**, as you see, the LORD has kept me alive,
14:11 my strength **n** is as my strength was then, for war,
14:12 So **n** give me this hill country of which
14:15 **N** the name of Hebron formerly was Kiriath-arba;
15:15 **n** the name of Debir formerly was Kiriath-sepher.
17: 3 **N** Zelophehad son of Hepher son of Gilead son
18:21 **N** the towns of the tribe of Benjamin according
22: 4 And **n** the LORD your God has given rest
22: 7 **N** to the one half of the tribe
22:19 But **n**, if your land is unclean,
22:19 where the LORD's tabernacle **n** stands, and take
22:26 Therefore we said, 'Let us **n** build an altar,
22:31 **n** you have saved the Israelites from the hand of
23: 2 "I am **n** old and well advanced in years;
23:14 "And **n** I am about to go the way of all the earth,
24:14 "**N** therefore revere the LORD,
24:15 **N** if you are unwilling to serve the LORD,
Jdg 2: 1 **N** the angel of the LORD went up from Gilgal
2: 3 So **n** I say, I will not drive them out before you;
3: 1 **N** these are the nations that the LORD left
3:17 **N** Eglon was a very fat man.
4:11 **N** Heber the Kenite had separated from
4:17 **N** Sisera had fled away on foot to the tent
6:11 **N** the angel of the LORD came and sat under
6:13 But **n** the LORD has cast us off,
6:17 he said to him, "If **n** I have found favor with you,
7: 3 **N** therefore proclaim this in the hearing of
8: 2 "What have I done **n** in comparison with you?
8:10 **N** Zebah and Zalmunna were in Karkor
8:30 **N** Gideon had seventy sons, his own offspring,
9: 1 **N** Abimelech son of Jerubbaal went to Shechem
9:16 "**N** therefore, if you acted in good faith and honor
9:32 **N** therefore, go by night, you and the troops
9:38 Then Zebul said to him, "Where is your boast **n**,
9:38 Go out **n** and fight with them."
11: 1 **N** Jephthah the Gileadite, the son of a prostitute,
11: 7 So why do you come to me **n** when you are
11: 8 "Nevertheless, we have **n** turned back to you,
11:13 **n** therefore restore it peaceably."
11:23 So **n** the LORD, the God of Israel,
11:25 **N** are you any better than King Balak son
11:36 **n** that the LORD has given you vengeance
13: 4 **N** be careful not to drink wine or strong drink,
13:12 Manoah said, "**N** when your words come true,
13:23 or **n** announced to us such things as these."
14: 2 **n** get her for me as my wife."
14:12 "Let me **n** put a riddle to you.
15:18 Am I **n** to die of thirst,
16:13 "Until **n** you have mocked me and told me lies;

Jdg 16:15 You have mocked me three times **n** and have
16:23 **N** the lords of the Philistines gathered to offer
16:27 **N** the house was full of men and women;
17: 2 but **n** I will return it to you."
17: 7 **N** there was a young man of Bethlehem in Judah,
17:13 "**N** I know that the LORD will prosper me,
18:14 **N** therefore consider what you will do."
19:11 and the servant said to his master, "Come **n**,
19:24 let me bring them out **n**.
20: 3 (**N** the Benjaminites heard that the people
20: 7 So **n**, you Israelites, all of you,
20: 9 But **n** this is what we will do to Gibeah:
20:13 **N** then, hand over those scoundrels in Gibeah,
20:38 **N** the agreement between the main body of Israel
21: 1 **N** the Israelites had sworn at Mizpah,
Ru 2: 1 **N** Naomi had a kinsman on her husband's side,
2: 7 on her feet from early this morning until **n**,
2: 8 Then Boaz said to Ruth, "**N** listen, my daughter,
3: 2 **N** here is our kinsman Boaz,
3: 3 **N** wash and anoint yourself,
3:11 And **n**, my daughter, do not be afraid,
3:12 But **n**, though it is true that I am a near kinsman,
4: 7 **N** this was the custom in former times in Israel
4:18 **N** these are the descendants of Perez:
1Sa 1: 3 **N** this man used to go up year by year
1: 9 **N** Eli the priest was sitting on the seat beside
2:12 **N** the sons of Eli were scoundrels;
2:16 you must give it **n**; if not, I will take it by force."
2:22 **N** Eli was very old.
2:26 **N** the boy Samuel continued to grow both
2:30 but **n** the LORD declares:
3: 1 **N** the boy Samuel was ministering to the LORD
3: 7 **N** Samuel did not yet know the LORD,
3:10 **N** the LORD came and stood there,
4:15 **N** Eli was ninety-eight years old
4:19 **N** his daughter-in-law, the wife of Phinehas,
6: 7 **N** then, get ready a new cart and two milch cows
6:13 **N** the people of Beth-shemesh
8: 9 **N** then, listen to their voice;
9: 3 **N** the donkeys of Kish, Saul's father, had strayed.
9: 6 Let us go there **n**;
9: 9 for the one who is **n** called a prophet was formerly
9:12 Hurry; he has come just **n** to the town,
9:13 **N** go up, for you will meet him immediately."
9:15 **N** the day before Saul came,
10: 1 **N** this shall be the sign to you that
10: 2 and **n** your father has stopped worrying
10: 7 **N** when these signs meet you,
10:19 **N** therefore present yourselves before the LORD
10:27 **N** Nahash, king of the Ammonites,
11: 5 **N** Saul was coming from the field behind
12: 2 See, it is the king who leads you **n**;
12: 7 **N** therefore take your stand,
12:10 but **n** rescue us out of the hand of our enemies,
12:16 **N** therefore take your stand
13:12 '**N** the Philistines will come down upon me
13:14 but **n** your kingdom will not continue;
13:19 **N** there was no smith to be found throughout all
13:23 **N** a garrison of the Philistines had gone out to
14: 3 **N** the people did not know
14: 8 "**N** we will cross over to those men
14:21 **N** the Hebrews who previously had been with
14:24 **N** Saul committed a very rash act on that day.
14:30 for **n** the slaughter among the Philistines has
14:49 **N** the sons of Saul were Jonathan, Ishvi,
15: 1 **n** therefore listen to the words of the LORD.
15: 3 **N** go and attack Amalek, and utterly destroy all
15:25 **N** therefore, I pray, pardon my sin,
15:30 yet honor me **n** before the elders of my people and
16: 6 the LORD's anointed is **n** before the LORD."
16:12 **N** he was ruddy, and had beautiful eyes,
16:14 **N** the spirit of the LORD departed from Saul,
16:15 And Saul's servants said to him, "See **n**,
16:16 Let our lord **n** command the servants who attend
17: 1 **N** the Philistines gathered their armies for battle;
17:12 **N** David was the son of an Ephrathite
17:19 **N** Saul, and they, and all the men of Israel,
17:29 David said, "What have I done **n**?
18:20 **N** Saul's daughter Michal loved David.
18:21 "You shall **n** be my son-in-law."
18:22 **n** then, become the king's son-in-law.' "
18:25 **N** Saul planned to make David fall by the hand of
19:18 **N** David fled and escaped;
20:29 So **n**, if I have found favor in your sight,
20:31 **N** send and bring him to me,
21: 3 **N** then, what have you at hand?
21: 7 **N** a certain man of the servants of Saul was there
22: 7 "Hear **n**, you Benjaminites;
22:12 Saul said, "Listen **n**, son of Ahitub."
23: 1 **N** they told David, "The Philistines are fighting
23: 7 **N** it was told Saul that David had come to Keilah.
23:11 And **n**, will Saul come down
23:20 **N**, O king, whenever you wish to come down,
24: 3 **N** David and his men were sitting in
24:20 **N** I know that you shall surely be king,
25: 1 **N** Samuel died; and all Israel assembled
25: 3 **N** the name of the man was Nabal,
25: 7 **n** your shepherds have been with us,
25:17 **N** therefore know this
25:21 **N** David had said, "Surely it was in vain
25:26 **N** then, my lord, as the LORD lives,
25:26 **n** let your enemies and those who seek to do evil
25:27 And **n** let this present
26: 8 **n** therefore let me pin him to the ground
26:11 but **n** take the spear that is at his head,
26:16 See **n**, where is the king's spear,
26:19 **N** therefore let my lord the king hear the words
1Sa 26:20 **N** therefore, do not let my blood fall to
27: 1 "I shall **n** perish one day by the hand of Saul;
27: 8 **N** David and his men went up and made raids on
28: 3 **N** Samuel had died, and all Israel had mourned
28:22 **N** therefore, you also listen to your servant;
28:24 **N** the woman had a fatted calf in the house.
29: 1 **N** the Philistines gathered all their forces
29: 3 who has been with me **n** for days and years?
29: 7 So go back **n**; and go peaceably;
29: 8 from the day I entered your service until **n**,
29:10 **N** then rise early in the morning,
30: 1 **N** when David and his men came to Ziklag on
31: 1 **N** the Philistines fought against Israel;
2Sa 2: 6 **N** may the LORD show steadfast love
2:18 **N** Asahel was as swift of foot as a wild gazelle.
3: 7 **N** Saul had a concubine whose name was Rizpah
3: 8 and yet you charge me **n** with a crime
3:18 **N** then bring it about; for the LORD has promised
4: 3 (**N** the people of Beeroth had fled to Gittaim
4: 5 **N** the sons of Rimmon the Beerothite,
4: 7 **N** they had come into the house
4:11 And **n** shall I not require his blood at your hand,
5: 7 which is **n** the city of David.
5:18 **N** the Philistines had come and spread out in
7: 1 **N** when the king was settled in his house,
7: 2 "See **n**, I am living in a house of cedar,
7: 8 **N** therefore thus you shall say
7:25 And **n**, O LORD God, as for the word
7:28 And **n**, O Lord GOD, you are God,
7:29 **n** therefore may it please you to bless the house
8:10 **N** Hadadezer had often been at war with Toi.
9: 2 **N** there was a servant of the house
9:10 **N** Ziba had fifteen sons and twenty servants.
9:13 **N** he was lame in both his feet.
11: 4 (**N** she was purifying herself after her period.)
11:25 for the sword devours **n** one and now another;
11:25 for the sword devours now one and **n** another;
12: 4 **N** there came a traveler to the rich man,
12:10 **N** therefore the sword shall never depart
12:13 "**N** the LORD has put away your sin;
12:23 But **n** he is dead; why should I fast?
12:26 **N** Joab fought against Rabbah of the Ammonites,
12:28 **N**, then, gather the rest of the people together,
13:13 **N** therefore, I beg you, speak to the king;
13:18 (**N** she was wearing a long robe with sleeves;
13:20 Be quiet for **n**, my sister;
13:33 **N** therefore, do not let my lord the king take it
13:39 for he was **n** consoled over the death of Amnon.
14: 1 **N** Joab son of Zeruiah perceived that
14: 7 **N** the whole family has risen against your servant.
14:15 **N** I have come to say this to my lord the king
14:25 **N** in all Israel there was no one to be praised
14:32 **N** let me go into the king's presence;
15:34 so **n** I will be your servant,'
16: 4 "All that belonged to Mephibosheth is **n** yours."
16: 6 **n** all the people and all the warriors were
16:11 how much more **n** may this Benjaminite!
16:15 **N** Absalom and all the Israelites came
16:23 **N** in those days the counsel
17: 9 Even **n** he has hidden himself in one of the pits,
17:25 **N** Absalom had set Amasa over the army in
18:18 **N** Absalom in his lifetime had taken and set up
18:24 **N** David was sitting between the two gates.
19: 7 that has come upon you from your youth until **n**."
19: 9 **n** he has fled out of the land because of Absalom.
19:10 **N** therefore why do you say nothing
19:13 you are not the commander of my army from **n** on,
19:31 **N** Barzillai the Gileadite had come down
20: 1 **N** a scoundrel named Sheba son of Bichri,
20: 6 David said to Abishai, "**N** Sheba son
20: 8 **N** Joab was wearing a soldier's garment and
20:23 **N** Joab was in command of all the army of Israel;
21: 1 **N** there was a famine in the days of David
21: 2 (**N** the Gibeonites were not of the people of Israel,
23: 1 **N** these are the last words of David:
23:18 **N** Abishai son of Zeruiah, the brother of Joab,
24:10 But **n**, O LORD, I pray you,
24:13 **N** consider, and decide what answer I shall return
24:16 "It is enough; **n** stay your hand."
1Ki 1: 5 **N** Adonijah son of Haggith exalted himself,
1:12 **N** therefore come, let me give you advice,
1:18 But **n** suddenly Adonijah has become king,
1:25 who are **n** eating and drinking before him,
1:46 Solomon **n** sits on the royal throne.
2:16 And **n** I have one request to make of you;
2:24 **N** therefore as the LORD lives,
2:29 to the tent of the LORD and **n** is beside the altar,"
3: 7 And **n**, O LORD my God,
3:12 I **n** do according to your word.
5: 1 **N** King Hiram of Tyre sent his servants
5: 4 But **n** the LORD my God has given me rest
6:11 **N** the word of the LORD came to Solomon,
7:13 **N** King Solomon invited and received Hiram
7:19 **N** the capitals that were on the tops of the pillars
8:20 **N** the LORD has upheld the promise
8:54 **N** when Solomon finished offering all this prayer
11:22 "What do you lack with me that you **n** seek to go
11:41 **N** the rest of the acts of Solomon,
12: 4 **N** therefore lighten the hard service of your father
12: 8 the young men who had grown up with him and **n**
12:11 **N**, whereas my father laid on you a heavy yoke,
12:16 Look **n** to your own house, O David."
12:26 "**N** the kingdom may well revert to the house
13: 6 "Entreat **n** the favor of the LORD your God,
13:11 **N** there lived an old prophet in Bethel.
14: 4 **N** Ahijah could not see, for his eyes were dim
14:14 the house of Jeroboam today, even right **n**!
1Ki 14:19 **N** the rest of the acts of Jeroboam,
14:21 **N** Rehoboam son of Solomon reigned in Judah.
14:29 **N** the rest of the acts of Rehoboam,
15: 1 **N** in the eighteenth year of King Jeroboam son
15:23 **N** the rest of all the acts of Asa, all his power,
15:31 **N** the rest of the acts of Nadab, and all that he did,
16: 5 **N** the rest of the acts of Baasha, what he did,
16:14 **N** the rest of the acts of Elah, and all that he did,
16:15 **N** the troops were encamped against Gibbethon,
16:20 **N** the rest of the acts of Zimri,
16:27 **N** the rest of the acts of Omri that he did,
17: 1 **N** Elijah the Tishbite, of Tishbe in Gilead,
17: 9 "Go **n** to Zarephath, which belongs to Sidon,
17:12 I am **n** gathering a couple of sticks,
17:24 "**N** I know that you are a man of God,
18: 3 (**N** Obadiah revered the LORD greatly;
18:11 **n** you say, 'Go, tell your lord that Elijah is here.'
18:14 **n** you say, 'Go, tell your lord that Elijah is here';
18:19 **N** therefore have all Israel assemble for me
18:43 He said to his servant, "Go up **n**,
19: 4 He asked that he might die: "It is enough; **n**,
19:11 **N** there was a great wind,
20: 7 the elders of the land, and said, "Look **n**!
20:12 **n** he had been drinking with the kings in
20:33 **N** the men were watching for an omen;
21: 7 to him, "Do you **n** govern Israel?
21:18 he is **n** in the vineyard of Naboth,
22:10 **N** the king of Israel and King Jehoshaphat
22:31 **N** the king of Aram had commanded
22:39 **N** the rest of the acts of Ahab, and all that he did,
22:45 **N** the rest of the acts of Jehoshaphat,
2Ki 1: 4 **N** therefore thus says the LORD,
1:14 but **n** let my life be precious in your sight."
1:18 **N** the rest of the acts of Ahaziah that he did,
2: 1 **N** when the LORD was about to take Elijah up
2:16 They said to him, "See **n**,
2:19 **N** the people of the city said to Elisha,
2:21 **n** on neither death nor miscarriage shall come from
3: 4 **N** King Mesha of Moab was a sheep breeder,
3:23 **N** then, Moab, to the spoil!"
4: 1 **N** the wife of a member of the company
5: 2 **N** the Arameans on one of their raids had taken
5:15 he came and stood before him and said, "**N** I know
6: 1 **N** the company of prophets said to Elisha,
6:11 and said to them, "**N** tell me who among us sides
6:26 **N** as the king of Israel was walking on
6:30 **n** since he was walking on the city wall,
6:32 **N** Elisha was sitting in his house,
7: 3 **N** there were four leprous men outside
7:17 **N** the king had appointed the captain
8: 1 **N** Elisha had said to the woman whose son he had
8: 4 **N** the king was talking with Gehazi the servant of
8: 6 from the day that she left the land until **n**."
8:23 **N** the rest of the acts of Joram, and all that he did,
9:26 **N** therefore lift him out and throw him on the plot
10: 1 **N** Ahab had seventy sons in Samaria.
10: 6 **N** the king's sons, seventy persons,
10:19 **N** therefore summon to me all the prophets
10:24 **N** Jehu had stationed eighty men outside, saying,
10:34 **N** the rest of the acts of Jehu, all that he did,
11: 1 **N** when Athaliah, Ahaziah's mother,
12: 7 **N** therefore do not accept any more money
12:19 **N** the rest of the acts of Joash, and all that he did,
13: 8 **N** the rest of the acts of Jehoahaz and all
13:12 **N** the rest of the acts of Joash, and all that he did,
13:14 **N** when Elisha had fallen sick with the illness
13:19 **n** you will strike down Aram only three times."
13:20 **N** bands of Moabites used to invade the land in
13:22 **N** King Hazael of Aram oppressed Israel all
13:23 has he banished them from his presence until **n**.
14:15 **N** the rest of the acts that Jehoash did, his might,
14:18 **N** the rest of the deeds of Amaziah,
14:28 **N** the rest of the acts of Jeroboam,
15: 6 **N** the rest of the acts of Azariah,
15:11 **N** the rest of the deeds of Zechariah are written in
15:15 **N** the rest of the deeds of Shallum,
15:21 **N** the rest of the deeds of Menahem,
15:26 **N** the rest of the deeds of Pekahiah,
15:31 **N** the rest of the acts of Pekah, and all that he did,
15:36 **N** the rest of the acts of Jotham,
16:19 **N** the rest of the acts of Ahaz that he did,
18:20 On whom do you **n** rely,
18:21 See, you are relying **n** on Egypt,
18:23 Come **n**, make a wager with my master the king
19:19 So **n**, O LORD our God, save us, I pray you,
19:25 I planned from days of old what **n** I bring to pass,
20: 3 "Remember **n**, O LORD, I implore you,
20: 9 the shadow has **n** advanced ten intervals;
21:17 **N** the rest of the acts of Manasseh, all that he did,
21:25 **N** the rest of the acts of Amon that he did,
23:28 **N** the rest of the acts of Josiah, and all that he did,
24: 5 **N** the rest of the deeds of Jehoiakim,
25:23 **N** when all the captains of the forces
1Ch 2: 3 **N** Er, Judah's firstborn, was wicked in the sight of
2:34 **N** Sheshan had no sons, only daughters;
4:22 but returned to Lehem (**n** the records are ancient).
7:21 **N** the people of Gath, who were born in the land,
8:32 **N** these also lived opposite their kindred
9: 2 **N** the first to live again in their possessions
9:33 **N** these are the singers, the heads
10: 1 **N** the Philistines fought against Israel;
11: 2 For some time **n**, even while Saul was king,
11: 5 Nevertheless David took the stronghold of Zion, **n**
11:10 **N** these are the chiefs of David's warriors,
11:13 **N** the people had fled from the Philistines,
11:20 **N** Abishai, the brother of Joab,
14: 9 **N** the Philistines had come and made a raid in

1Ch 17: 1 **N** when David settled in his house,
17: 7 **N** therefore thus you shall say
17:23 "And **n,** O LORD, as for the word
17:26 And **n,** O LORD, you are God,
18:10 **N** Hadadezer had often been at war with Tou.
21: 8 **n,** I pray you, take away the guilt of your servant;
21:12 **N** decide what answer I shall return to
22:11 **N,** my son, the LORD be with you,
22:16 **N** begin the work, and the LORD be with you."
22:19 **N** set your mind and heart to seek
28: 8 **N** therefore in the sight of all Israel,
28:10 Take heed **n,** for the LORD has chosen you
29:13 And **n,** our God, we give thanks to you
29:17 and **n** I have seen your people,
29:29 **N** the acts of King David, from first to last,
2Ch 1: 9 let your promise to my father David **n** be fulfilled,
1:10 Give me **n** wisdom and knowledge to go out
2: 4 I am **n** about to build a house for the name of
2: 7 So **n** send me an artisan skilled to work in gold,
2:15 **N,** as for the wheat, barley, oil, and wine,
5:11 **N** when the priests came out of the holy place
6:10 **N** the LORD has fulfilled his promise
6:40 **N,** O my God, let your eyes be open
6:41 "**N** rise up, O LORD God,
7:15 **N** my eyes will be open and my ears attentive to
7:16 For **n** I have chosen and consecrated this house so
7:21 And regarding this house, **n** exalted,
9:29 **N** the rest of the acts of Solomon,
10: 4 **N** therefore lighten the hard service of your father
10: 8 the young men who had grown up with him and **n**
10:11 **N,** whereas my father laid on you a heavy yoke,
10:16 Look **n** to your own house, O David."
12:15 **N** the acts of Rehoboam, from first to last,
13: 2 **N** there was war between Abijah and Jeroboam.
13: 8 "And **n** you think that you can withstand
16: 9 for from **n** on you will have wars."
18: 1 **N** Jehoshaphat had great riches and honor;
18: 9 **N** the king of Israel and King Jehoshaphat
18:30 **N** the king of Aram had commanded the captains
19: 7 **N,** let the fear of the LORD be upon you;
20:10 See **n,** the people of Ammon, Moab,
20:34 **N** the rest of the acts of Jehoshaphat,
22:10 **N** when Athaliah, Ahaziah's mother,
24:17 **N** after the death of Jehoiada the officials
25:14 **N** after Amaziah came from the slaughter of
25:19 in boastfulness. **N** stay at home;
25:26 **N** the rest of the deeds of Amaziah,
26:19 **N** he had a censer in his hand to make offering,
26:22 **N** the rest of the acts of Uzziah, from first to last,
27: 7 **N** the rest of the acts of Jotham,
28:10 **N** you intend to subjugate the people of Judah
28:11 **N** hear me, and send back
28:26 **N** the rest of his acts and all his ways,
29:10 **N** it is in my heart to make a covenant with
29:11 My sons, do not **n** be negligent,
29:31 "You have **n** consecrated yourselves to
30: 8 Do not **n** be stiff-necked as your ancestors were,
31: 1 **N** when all this was finished,
32:15 **N** therefore do not let Hezekiah deceive you
32:32 **N** the rest of the acts of Hezekiah,
33:18 **N** the rest of the acts of Manasseh,
35: 3 **N** serve the LORD your God
35:26 **N** the rest of the acts of Josiah
36: 8 **N** the rest of the acts of Jehoiakim,
Ezr 1: 3 are **n** permitted to go up to Jerusalem in Judah,
2: 1 **N** these were the people of the province who came
4:10 Beyond the River wrote—and **n**
4:11 Beyond the River, send greeting. And **n**
4:13 **N** may it be known to the king that,
4:14 **N** because we share the salt of the palace and it is
4:17 Beyond the River, greeting. And **n**
5: 1 **N** the prophets, Haggai and Zechariah son of Iddo,
5:16 that time until **n** it has been under construction,
5:17 And **n,** if it seems good to the king,
6: 6 "**N** you, Tattenai, governor of the province
7:12 God of heaven: Peace. And **n**
9: 7 to plundering, and to utter shame, as is **n** the case.
9: 8 But **n** for a brief moment favor has been shown by
9:10 "And **n,** our God, what shall we say after this?
9:15 but we have escaped as a remnant, as is **n** the case.
10: 2 but even **n** there is hope for Israel in spite of this.
10: 3 So **n** let us make a covenant with our God
10:11 **N** make confession to the LORD the God
Ne 1: 6 to hear the prayer of your servant that I **n** pray
2: 1 **N,** I had never been sad in his presence before.
2: 9 **N** the king had sent officers of the army
4: 1 **N** when Sanballat heard that we were building
5: 1 **N** there was a great outcry of the people and
5: 5 **N** our flesh is the same as that of our kindred;
5: 5 and our fields and vineyards **n** belong to others."
5: 8 but **n** you are selling your own kin,
5:18 **N** that which was prepared for one day was one ox
6: 1 **N** when it was reported to Sanballat and Tobiah
6: 7 And **n** it will be reported to the king according
6: 9 But **n,** O God, strengthen my hands.
7: 1 **N** when the wall had been built and I had set up
7:70 **N** some of the heads of ancestral
9: 1 **N** on the twenty-fourth day of this month
9:32 "**N** therefore, our God—the great
11: 1 **N** the leaders of the people lived in Jerusalem;
12:27 **N** at the dedication of the wall
13: 4 **N** before this, the priest Eliashib,
Est 2: 5 **N** there was a Jew in the citadel
2:15 **N** Esther was admired by all who saw her.
2:20 **N** Esther had not revealed her kindred
6: 4 **N** Haman had just entered the outer court of
9: 1 **N** in the twelfth month, which is the month

Est 9:12 **N** what is your petition?
9:16 **N** the other Jews who were in the king's provinces
Job 1:11 But stretch out your hand **n,**
2: 5 But stretch out your hand **n** and touch his bone
2:11 **N** when Job's three friends heard
3:13 **N** I would be lying down and quiet;
4: 5 But **n** it has come to you, and you are impatient;
4: 7 "Think **n,** who that was innocent ever perished?
4:12 "**N** a word came stealing to me,
5: 1 "Call **n;** is there anyone who will answer you?
6:21 Such you have **n** become to me;
6:28 "But **n,** be pleased to look at me;
6:29 Turn **n,** my vindication is at stake.
7:21 For **n** I shall lie in the earth;
8: 8 "For inquire **n** of bygone generations,
10: 8 and **n** you turn and destroy me.
13: 6 Hear **n** my reasoning, and listen to the pleadings
16: 7 Surely **n** God has worn me out;
16:19 Even **n,** in fact, my witness is in heaven,
17:10 But you, come back **n,** all of you,
30: 1 "But **n** they make sport of me,
30: 9 **n** they mock me in song; I am a byword to them.
30:16 "And **n** my soul is poured out within me;
32: 4 **N** Elihu had waited to speak to Job,
33: 1 "But **n,** hear my speech, O Job,
33:21 and their bones, once invisible, **n** stick out.
35:15 And **n,** because his anger does not punish,
37:21 **N,** no one can look on the light when it is bright in
42: 5 but **n** my eye sees you;
42: 8 **N** therefore take seven bulls and seven rams,
Ps 2:10 **N** therefore, O kings, be wise;
12: 5 because the needy groan, I will **n** rise up,"
17:11 They track me down; **n** they surround me;
20: 6 **N** I know that the LORD will help his anointed;
27: 6 **N** my head is lifted up above my enemies all
37:25 I have been young, and **n** am old,
39: 7 "And **n,** O Lord, what do I wait for?
50:21 But **n** I rebuke you, and lay the charge before you.
59: 3 Even **n** they lie in wait for my life;
60: 1 you have been angry; **n** restore us!
69: 4 What I did not steal must I **n** restore?
83: 2 Even **n** your enemies are in tumult;
89:38 But **n** you have spurned and rejected him;
119:67 but **n** I keep your word.
124: 1 the LORD who was on our side—let Israel **n**
129: 1 from my youth"—let Israel **n** say—
Pr 5: 7 And **n,** my child, listen to me,
5:14 **N** I am at the point of utter ruin in
7:12 **n** in the street, now in the squares,
7:12 **n** in the squares, and at every corner she lies
7:15 so **n** I have come out to meet you,
7:24 And **n,** my children, listen to me,
8:32 And **n,** my children, listen to me:
Ecc 2: 1 I said to myself, "Come **n,**
9:15 **N** there was found in it a poor wise man,
SS 2:11 for **n** the winter is past, the rain is over and gone.
3: 2 "I will rise **n** and go about the city,
Isa 1:18 Come **n,** let us argue it out, says the LORD:
1:21 in her—but **n** murderers!
3: 1 For **n** the Sovereign, the LORD of hosts,
5: 3 And **n,** inhabitants of Jerusalem and people
5: 5 **n** I will tell you what I will do to my vineyard.
6: 7 "**N** that this has touched your lips,
8:19 **N** if people say to you, "Consult the ghosts and
16:14 But **n** the LORD says, In three years,
19:12 Where **n** are your sages?
24: 1 **N** the LORD is about to lay waste the earth
28:22 **N** therefore do not scoff, or your bonds will
30: 8 Go **n,** write it before them on a tablet,
33:10 "**N** I will arise," says the LORD,
33:10 "**n** I will lift myself up; now I will be exalted.
33:10 "now I will lift myself up; **n** I will be exalted.
36: 5 On whom do you **n** rely,
36: 8 Come **n,** make a wager with my master the king
37: 9 **N** the king heard concerning King Tirhakah
37:20 So **n,** O LORD our God, save us from his hand,
37:26 I planned from days of old what **n** I bring to pass,
38: 3 "Remember **n,** O LORD, I implore you,
38:21 **N** Isaiah had said, "Let them take a lump of figs,
41:15 **N,** I will make of you a threshing sledge, sharp,
42: 9 and new things I **n** declare;
42:14 **n** I will cry out like a woman in labor,
43: 1 But **n** thus says the LORD, he who created you,
43:19 **n** it springs forth, do you not perceive it?
44: 1 But **n** hear, O Jacob my servant,
44:19 **N** shall I make the rest of it an abomination?
47: 8 **N** therefore hear this, you lover of pleasures,
48: 6 **n** see all this; and will you not declare it?
48: 7 They are created **n,** not long ago;
48:16 And **n** the Lord GOD has sent me and his spirit.
49: 5 And **n** the LORD says, who formed me in
49:19 **n** you will be too crowded for your inhabitants,
52: 5 **N** therefore what am I doing here,
59:21 says the LORD, from **n** on and forever.
63:18 but **n** our adversaries have trampled
64: 9 **N** consider, we are all your people.
Jer 1: 4 **N** the word of the LORD came to me saying,
1: 9 "**N** I have put my words in your mouth.
1:15 For **n** I am calling all the tribes of the kingdoms of
2:35 **N** I am bringing you to judgment for saying,
3: 4 Have you not just **n** called to me, "My Father,
4:12 **N** it is I who speak in judgment against them.
5:14 I am **n** making my words in your mouth a fire,
7:12 Go **n** to my place that was in Shiloh,
7:13 And **n,** because you have done all these things,
9: 7 I will **n** refine and test them,
13: 4 and go **n** to the Euphrates,

Jer 13: 6 to me, "Go **n** to the Euphrates, and take from there
13: 7 But **n** the loincloth was ruined;
14:10 not accept them, **n** he will remember their iniquity
16:16 I am **n** sending for many fishermen,
18:11 **N,** therefore, say to the people of Judah and
18:11 Turn **n,** all of you from your evil way,
19:15 I am **n** bringing upon this city and
20: 1 **N** the priest Pashhur son of Immer,
25: 5 "Turn **n,** everyone of you,
26:13 **N** therefore amend your ways and your doings,
27: 6 **N** I have given all these lands into the hand
28: 7 But listen **n** to this word that I speak
29:20 But **n,** all you exiles whom I sent away
29:27 So **n** why have you not rebuked Jeremiah
30: 6 Ask **n,** and see, can a man bear a child?
32:36 **N** therefore thus says the LORD,
32:42 the good fortune that I **n** promise them.
35:15 'Turn **n** everyone of you from your evil way,
36:17 Then they questioned Baruch, "Tell us **n,**
36:22 **N** the king was sitting in his
36:27 **N,** after the king had burned the scroll with
37: 4 **N** Jeremiah was still going in and out among
37:11 **N** when the Chaldean army had withdrawn
37:20 **N** please hear me, my lord king:
38: 1 **N** Shephatiah son of Mattan,
38: 6 **N** there was no water in the cistern, but only mud,
38:22 **N** that your feet are stuck in the mud,
40: 3 and **n** the LORD has brought it about,
40: 4 **N** look, I have just released you today from
40:13 **N** Johanan son of Kareah and all the leaders of
41: 9 **N** the cistern into which Ishmael had thrown all
44: 7 And **n** thus says the LORD God of hosts,
50:17 and **n** at the end King Nebuchadrezzar
La 1: 3 she lives **n** among the nations,
4: 8 **N** their visage is blacker than soot;
Eze 4:14 up until **n** I have never eaten what died of itself
7: 3 **N** the end is upon you, I will let loose my anger
7: 8 Soon **n** I will pour out my wrath upon you;
8: 5 lift up your eyes **n** in the direction of the north."
9: 3 **N** the glory of the God of Israel had gone up from
10: 3 **N** the cherubim were standing on the south side of
11:13 **N,** while I was prophesying,
16:57 **N** you are a mockery to the daughters of Aram
17:12 Say **n** to the rebellious house:
18:25 Hear **n,** O house of Israel: Is my way unfair?
19:13 **N** it is transplanted into the wilderness,
20:39 everyone of you **n** and hereafter,
26: 2 I shall be replenished, **n** that it is wasted."
26:18 **N** the coastlands tremble on the day of your fall;
27: 2 **N** you, mortal, raise a lamentation over Tyre,
27:34 **N** you are wrecked by the seas,
31:18 **N** you shall be brought down with the trees
33:10 **N** you, mortal, say to the house of Israel,
33:22 **N** the hand of the LORD had been upon me
36: 9 See **n,** I am for you;
36:35 and the waste and desolate and ruined towns are **n**
38: 8 its people were brought out from the nations and **n**
38:12 to assail the waste places that are **n** inhabited,
39:25 **N** I will restore the fortunes of Jacob,
40: 5 **N** there was a wall all around the outside of
41:16 up to the windows (**n** the windows were covered),
42: 5 **N** the upper chambers were narrower,
43: 9 **N** let them put away their idolatry and the corpses
Da 1: 9 **N** God allowed Daniel to receive favor
2:23 and have **n** revealed to me what we asked of you,
2:36 **n** we will tell the king its interpretation.
3:15 **N** if you are ready when you hear the sound of
4:18 **N** you, Belteshazzar, declare the interpretation,
4:37 **N** I, Nebuchadnezzar, praise and extol and honor
5:12 **N** let Daniel be called, and he will give
5:15 **N** the wise men, the enchanters,
5:16 **N** if you are able to read the writing
6: 8 **N,** O king, establish the interdict and sign
8:26 for it refers to many days from **n."**
9:15 "And **n,** O Lord our God,
9:17 **N** therefore, O our God, listen to the prayer
9:22 I have **n** come out to give you wisdom
10:11 Stand on your feet, for I have **n** been sent to you."
10:20 **N** I must return to fight against the prince
11: 2 "**N** I will announce the truth to you.
Hos 2: 7 for it was better with me then than **n."**
2:10 **N** I will uncover her shame in the sight
2:14 Therefore, I will **n** allure her,
4:16 can the LORD **n** feed them like a lamb in
5: 3 for **n,** O Ephraim, you have played the whore;
5: 7 **N** the new moon shall devour them along
7: 2 **N** their deeds surround them,
8: 8 **n** they are among the nations as a useless vessel.
8:10 I will **n** gather them up.
8:13 **N** he will remember their iniquity,
9:13 but **n** Ephraim must lead out his children
10: 2 Their heart is false; **n** they must bear their guilt.
10: 3 For **n** they will say: "We have no king,
13: 2 And **n** they keep on sinning and make
13:10 Where **n** is your king, that he may save you?
Joel 2:12 Yet even **n,** says the LORD,
3: 7 But **n** I will rouse them to leave the places
Am 6: 7 Therefore they shall **n** be the first to go into exile,
7:16 "**N** therefore hear the word of the LORD.
Jnh 1: 1 **N** the word of the LORD came to Jonah son
3: 3 **N** Nineveh was an exceedingly large city,
4: 3 And **n,** O LORD, please take my life from me,
Mic 2: 3 Therefore thus says the LORD: **N,** I am devising
4: 7 the LORD will reign over them in Mount Zion **n**
4: 9 **N** why do you cry aloud?
4:10 for **n** you shall go forth from the city and camp in
4:11 **N** many nations are assembled against you,

Mic 5: 1 **N** you are walled around with a wall;
5: 4 for **n** he shall be great to the ends of the earth;
6: 5 remember **n** what King Balak of Moab devised,
7: 4 **n** their confusion is at hand.
7:10 **n** she will be trodden down like the mire of
Na 1:13 And **n** I will break off his yoke from you and snap
Hag 1: 5 **N** therefore thus says the LORD of hosts:
2: 2 Speak **n** to Zerubbabel son of Shealtiel,
2: 3 How does it look to you **n?**
2: 4 **n** take courage, O Zerubbabel, says the LORD;
2:15 But **n,** consider what will come to pass
Zec 2: 9 See **n,** I am going to raise my hand against them,
3: 3 **N** Joshua was dressed with filthy clothes
3: 8 **N** listen, Joshua, high priest,
7: 2 **N** the people of Bethel had sent Sharezer
8:11 But **n** I will not deal with the remnant
9: 4 But **n,** the Lord will strip it of its possessions
9: 8 for **n** I have seen with my own eyes.
11:16 For I am **n** raising up in the land
Mal 1: 9 And **n** implore the favor of God,
2: 1 And **n,** O priests, this command is for you.
3:15 **N** we count the arrogant happy;
Mt 1:18 **N** the birth of Jesus the Messiah took place
2:13 **N** after they had left, an angel of
3: 4 **N** John wore clothing of camel's hair with
3:10 Even **n** the ax is lying at the root of the trees;
3:15 But Jesus answered him, "Let it be so **n;**
4:12 **N** when Jesus heard that John had been arrested,
7:28 **N** when Jesus had finished saying these things,
8:18 **N** when Jesus saw great crowds around him,
8:30 **N** a large herd of swine was feeding
11: 1 **N** when Jesus had finished instructing his twelve
11:12 the days of John the Baptist until **n** the kingdom
14:13 **N** when Jesus heard this, he withdrew from there
14:15 "This is a deserted place, and the hour is **n** late;
15:32 with me **n** for three days and have nothing to eat;
16:13 **N** when Jesus came into the district
20:10 **N** when the first came, they thought they would
21:40 **N** when the owner of the vineyard comes,
22:25 **N** there were seven brothers among us;
22:41 **N** while the Pharisees were gathered together,
24:21 not been from the beginning of the world until **n,**
26: 6 **N** while Jesus was at Bethany in the house
26:48 **N** the betrayer had given them a sign, saying,
26:59 **N** the chief priests and the whole council were
26:64 From **n** on you will see the Son of Man seated at
26:65 You have **n** heard his blasphemy.
26:69 **N** Peter was sitting outside in the courtyard.
27:11 **N** Jesus stood before the governor;
27:15 **N** at the festival the governor was accustomed
27:20 **N** the chief priests and the elders persuaded
27:42 let him come down from the cross **n,**
27:43 let God deliver him **n,** if he wants to;
27:54 **N** when the centurion and those with him,
28:16 **N** the eleven disciples went to Galilee,
Mk 1: 6 **N** John was clothed with camel's hair,
1:14 **N** after John was arrested, Jesus came to Galilee,
1:30 **N** Simon's mother-in-law was in bed with a fever,
2: 6 **N** some of the scribes were sitting there,
2:18 **N** John's disciples and the Pharisees were fasting;
5:11 **N** there on the hillside a great herd
5:25 **N** there was a woman who had been suffering
6:33 **N** many saw them going and recognized them,
6:35 and the hour is **n** very late;
7: 1 **N** when the Pharisees and some of
7:26 **N** the woman was a Gentile,
8: 2 with me **n** for three days and have nothing to eat.
8: 9 **N** there were about four thousand people.
8:14 **N** the disciples had forgotten to bring any bread;
10:30 who will not receive a hundredfold **n** in this age—
13:19 of the creation that God created until **n,**
14:44 **N** the betrayer had given them a sign, saying,
14:55 **N** the chief priests and the whole council were
15: 6 **N** at the festival he used to release a prisoner
15: 7 **N** a man called Barabbas was in prison with
15:32 the King of Israel, come down from the cross **n,**
15:39 **N** when the centurion, who stood facing him,
16: 9 ⟦**N** after he rose early on the first day of the week,⟧
Lk 1:10 **N** at the time of the incense offering,
1:20 But **n,** because you did not believe my words,
1:31 And **n,** you will conceive in your womb and bear
1:36 And **n,** your relative Elizabeth in her old age has
1:48 from **n** on all generations will call me blessed;
1:57 **N** the time came for Elizabeth to give birth,
2:15 "Let us go **n** to Bethlehem and see this thing
2:25 **N** there was a man in Jerusalem
2:29 **n** you are dismissing your servant in peace,
2:41 **N** every year his parents went to Jerusalem for
3: 9 Even **n** the ax is lying at the root of the trees;
3:21 **N** when all the people were baptized,
4:38 **N** Simon's mother-in-law was suffering from
5:10 from **n** on you will be catching people."
5:15 But **n** more than ever the word
6:12 **N** during those days he went out to the mountain
6:21 "Blessed are you who are hungry **n,**
6:21 "Blessed are you who weep **n,** for you will laugh.
6:25 "Woe to you who are full **n,**
6:25 "Woe to you who are laughing **n,**
7:39 **N** when the Pharisee who had invited him saw it,
7:42 **N** which of them will love him more?"
8:11 "**N** the parable is this: The seed is the word of God.
8:32 **N** there on the hillside a large herd
8:40 **N** when Jesus returned, the crowd welcomed him,
8:43 **N** there was a woman who had been suffering
9: 7 **N** Herod the ruler heard about all
9:28 **N** about eight days after these sayings Jesus took
9:32 **N** Peter and his companions were weighed down
Lk 10:31 **N** by chance a priest was going down that road;
10:38 **N** as they went on their way,
11:14 **N** he was casting out a demon that was mute;
11:19 **N** if I cast out the demons by Beelzebul,
11:39 "**N** you Pharisees clean the outside of the cup and
12:52 From **n** on five in one household will be divided,
13:10 **N** he was teaching in one of the synagogues on
14:17 for everything is ready **n.'**
14:25 **N** large crowds were traveling with him;
15: 1 **N** all the tax collectors and sinners were coming
15:25 "**N** his elder son was in the field;
16: 3 **n** that my master is taking the position away
16:25 but **n** he is comforted here, and you are in agony.
19:37 As he was **n** approaching the path down from
19:42 But **n** they are hidden from your eyes.
20:29 **N** there were seven brothers;
20:38 **N** he is God not of the dead, but of the living;
21:28 **N** when these things begin to take place,
22: 1 **N** the festival of Unleavened Bread,
22:18 from **n** on I will not drink of the fruit of the vine
22:36 "But **n,** the one who has a purse must take it,
22:63 **N** the men who were holding Jesus began
22:69 But from **n** on the Son of Man will be seated at
23:44 It was **n** about noon, and darkness came over
23:50 **N** there was a good and righteous man named
24:10 **N** it was Mary Magdalene, Joanna,
24:13 **N** on that same day two of them were going to
24:21 it is **n** the third day since these things took place.
24:29 it is almost evening and the day is **n** nearly over."
Jn 1:24 **N** they had been sent from the Pharisees.
1:44 **N** Philip was from Bethsaida,
2: 6 **N** standing there were six stone water jars for
2: 8 He said to them, "**N** draw some out,
2:10 But you have kept the good wine until **n."**
3: 1 **N** there was a Pharisee named Nicodemus,
3:25 **N** a discussion about purification arose
4: 1 **N** when Jesus learned that
4:18 and the one you have **n** is not your husband.
4:23 But the hour is coming, and is **n** here,
4:46 **N** there was a royal official whose son lay ill
4:54 **N** this was the second sign that Jesus did
5: 2 **N** in Jerusalem by the Sheep Gate there is a pool,
5: 9 **N** that day was a sabbath.
5:13 **N** the man who had been healed did
5:25 I tell you, the hour is coming, and is **n** here,
6: 4 **N** the Passover, the festival of the Jews, was near.
6:10 **N** there was a great deal of grass in the place;
6:17 It was **n** dark, and Jesus had not yet come to them.
6:42 can he **n** say, 'I have come down from heaven'?"
7: 2 **N** the Jewish festival of Booths was near.
7:25 **N** some of the people of Jerusalem were saying,
7:39 **N** he said this about the Spirit,
8: 5 ⟦**N** in the law Moses commanded us⟧
8: 5 ⟦**N** what do you say?"⟧
8:11 ⟦Go your way, and from **n** on do not sin again."⟧
8:40 but **n** you are trying to kill me,
8:42 for I came from God and **n** I am here.
8:52 "**N** we know that you have a demon.
9:14 **N** it was a sabbath day when Jesus made the mud
9:15 Then I washed, and **n** I see."
9:19 How then does he **n** see?"
9:21 but we do not know how it is that **n** he sees,
9:25 that though I was blind, **n** I see."
9:41 But **n** that you say, 'We see,' your sin remains.
11: 1 **N** a certain man was ill, Lazarus of Bethany,
11: 8 "Rabbi, the Jews were just **n** trying to stone you,
11:18 **N** Bethany was near Jerusalem,
11:22 even **n** I know that God will give you whatever
11:30 **N** Jesus had not yet come to the village,
11:55 **N** the Passover of the Jews was near,
11:57 **N** the chief priests and the Pharisees had given
12:20 **N** among those who went up to worship at
12:27 "**N** my soul is troubled.
12:31 **N** is the judgment of this world;
12:31 **n** the ruler of this world will be driven out.
13: 1 **N** before the festival of the Passover,
13: 7 "You do not know **n** what I am doing,
13:19 I tell you this **n,** before it occurs,
13:28 **N** no one at the table knew why he said this
13:31 Jesus said, "**N** the Son of Man has been glorified,
13:33 and as I said to the Jews so **n** I say to you,
13:36 "Where I am going, you cannot follow me **n;**
13:37 "Lord, why can I not follow you **n?**
14: 7 From **n** on you do know him and have seen him."
14:29 And **n** I have told you this before it occurs,
15:22 but **n** they have no excuse for their sin.
15:24 But **n** they have seen and hated both me
16: 5 But **n** I am going to him who sent me;
16:12 but you cannot bear them **n.**
16:22 So you have pain **n;** but I will see you again,
16:24 Until **n** you have not asked for anything
16:29 "Yes, **n** you are speaking plainly,
16:30 **N** we know that you know all things,
16:31 Jesus answered them, "Do you **n** believe?
17: 5 So **n,** Father, glorify me in your own presence
17: 7 **N** they know that everything you have given me is
17:11 And **n** I am no longer in the world,
17:13 But **n** I am coming to you,
18: 2 **N** Judas, who betrayed him, also knew the place,
18:18 **N** the slaves and the police had made
18:25 **N** Simon Peter was standing
18:40 **N** Barabbas was a bandit.
19: 8 **N** when Pilate heard this, he was more afraid than
19:14 **N** it was the day of Preparation for the Passover;
19:23 They also took his tunic; **n** the tunic was seamless,
19:28 this, when Jesus knew that all was **n** finished,
19:41 **N** there was a garden in the place
Jn 20:30 **N** Jesus did many other signs in the presence
21: 6 and **n** they were not able to haul it in
21:12 **N** none of the disciples dared to ask him,
21:14 This was **n** the third time that Jesus appeared to
Ac 1: 5 with the Holy Spirit not many days from **n."**
1:18 (**N** this man acquired a field with the reward
2: 5 **N** there were devout Jews from every nation
2:37 **N** when they heard this, they were cut to the heart
3:17 "And **n,** friends, I know that you acted
4:13 **N** when they saw the boldness of Peter and John
4:29 And **n,** Lord, look at their threats,
4:32 **N** the whole group of those who believed were
5: 5 **N** when Ananias heard these words,
5:12 **N** many signs and wonders were done among
5:24 **N** when the captain of the temple and
6: 1 **N** during those days,
7: 4 from there to this country in which you are **n**
7:11 **N** there came a famine throughout Egypt
7:30 "**N** when forty years had passed,
7:34 Come **n,** I will send you to Egypt.'
7:35 and whom God **n** sent as both ruler and liberator
7:52 **n** you have become his betrayers and murderers.
8: 4 **N** those who were scattered went from place
8: 9 **N** a certain man named Simon had previously
8:14 **N** when the apostles at Jerusalem heard
8:18 **N** when Simon saw that the Spirit was given
8:25 **N** after Peter and John had testified and spoken
8:27 **N** there was an Ethiopian eunuch,
8:32 **N** the passage of the scripture
9: 3 **N** as he was going along
9:10 **N** there was a disciple in Damascus
9:32 **N** as Peter went here and there among all
9:36 **N** in Joppa there was a disciple whose name was
10: 5 **N** send men to Joppa for
10:17 **N** while Peter was greatly puzzled about what
10:20 **N** get up, go down, and go with them
10:29 **N** may I ask why you sent for me?"
10:33 So **n** all of us are here in the presence of God
11: 1 **N** the apostles and the believers who were
11:19 **N** those who were scattered because of
12:11 "**N** I am sure that the Lord has sent his angel
12:20 **N** Herod was angry with the people of Tyre
13: 1 **N** in the church at Antioch there were prophets
13:11 And **n** listen—the hand of the Lord
13:31 and they are **n** his witnesses to the people.
13:46 we are **n** turning to the Gentiles.
15:10 **N** therefore why are you putting God to the test
16:36 therefore come out **n** and go in peace."
16:37 and **n** are they going to discharge us in secret?
17:21 **N** all the Athenians and the foreigners living there
17:30 **n** he commands all people everywhere to repent,
18: 6 From **n** on I will go to the Gentiles."
18:24 **N** there came to Ephesus a Jew named Apollos,
19:21 **N** after these things had been accomplished,
20:22 And **n,** as a captive to the Spirit,
20:25 "And **n** I know that none of you,
20:32 And **n** I commend you to God and to the message
22: 1 listen to the defense that I **n** make before you."
22: 9 **N** those who were with me saw the light but did
22:16 And **n** why do you delay?
23:15 **N** then, you and the council must notify
23:16 **N** the son of Paul's sister heard about the ambush;
23:21 They are ready **n** and are waiting
24:13 to you the charge that they **n** bring against me.
24:17 **N** after some years I came to bring alms
25:11 **N** if I am in the wrong
26: 6 And **n** I stand here on trial on account of my hope
27: 9 Since much time had been lost and sailing was **n**
27:22 I urge you **n** to keep up your courage,
28: 7 **N** in the neighborhood of
Ro 3:19 **N** we know that whatever the law says,
3:21 But **n,** apart from law, the righteousness
3:24 they are **n** justified by his grace as a gift,
4: 4 **N** to one who works, wages are not reckoned as
4:23 **N** the words, "it was reckoned to him,"
5: 9 **n** that we have been justified by his blood,
5:11 through whom we have **n** received reconciliation.
6:19 so **n** present your members as slaves
6:21 from the things of which you **n** are ashamed?
6:22 But **n** that you have been freed from sin
7: 6 But **n** we are discharged from the law,
7:16 **N** if I do what I do not want,
7:20 **N** if I do what I do not want,
8: 1 therefore **n** no condemnation for those who are
8:22 creation has been groaning in labor pains until **n;**
8:24 **N** hope that is seen is not hope.
11:12 **N** if their stumbling means riches for the world,
11:13 **N** I am speaking to you Gentiles.
11:30 as you were once disobedient to God but have **n**
11:31 so they have **n** been disobedient in order that,
11:31 they too may **n** receive mercy.
13:11 it is **n** the moment for you to wake from sleep.
13:11 to us **n** than when we became believers;
15:23 But **n,** with no further place for me
16:25 **N** to God who is able to strengthen you according
16:26 but is **n** disclosed,
1Co 1:10 **N** I appeal to you, brothers and sisters,
2:12 **N** we have received not the spirit of the world,
3: 2 Even **n** you are still not ready,
3:12 **N** if anyone builds on the foundation with gold,
4: 5 the things **n** hidden in darkness and will disclose
5:11 But **n** I am writing to you not to associate
7: 1 **N** concerning the matters about which you wrote:
7:21 of your present condition **n** more than ever.
7:25 **N** concerning virgins, I have no command of
7:29 from **n** on, let even those who have wives be as
8: 1 **N** concerning food sacrificed to idols:

1Co 8: 7 some have become so accustomed to idols until **n**,
10: 6 **N** these things occurred as examples for us,
11:17 **N** in the following instructions I do
12: 1 **N** concerning spiritual gifts, brothers and sisters,
12: 4 **N** there are varieties of gifts, but the same Spirit;
12:27 **N** you are the body of Christ
13:12 For **n** we see in a mirror, dimly,
13:12 **N** I know only in part;
13:13 And **n** faith, hope, and love abide, these three;
14: 5 **N** I would like all of you to speak in tongues,
14: 6 **N**, brothers and sisters, if I come to you speaking
15: 1 **N** I would remind you, brothers and sisters,
15:12 **N** if Christ is proclaimed as raised from the dead,
16: 1 **N** concerning the collection for the saints:
16: 7 I do not want to see you **n** just in passing,
16:12 **N** concerning our brother Apollos,
16:12 but he was not at all willing to come **n**.
16:15 **N**, brothers and sisters, you know that members of
2Co 2: 7 so **n** instead you should forgive and console him,
3: 7 **N** if the ministry of death,
3: 7 of the glory of his face, a glory **n** set aside,
3:17 **N** the Lord is the Spirit,
5:16 From **n** on, therefore, we regard no one from
6: 2 See, **n** is the acceptable time;
6: 2 see, **n** is the day of salvation!
7: 9 **N** I rejoice, not because you were grieved,
8: 7 **N** as you excel in everything—
8:11 **n** finish doing it, so that your eagerness may
8:22 but who is **n** more eager than ever because
9: 1 **N** it is not necessary for me to write you about
10: 8 **N**, even if I boast a little too much
13: 2 and I warn them **n** while absent,
Gal 1: 9 As we have said before, so **n** I repeat,
1:10 Am I **n** seeking human approval,
1:23 "The one who formerly was persecuting us is **n**
2:20 And the life I **n** live in the flesh I live by faith in
3: 3 are you **n** ending with the flesh?
3:11 **N** it is evident that no one is justified before God
3:16 **N** the promises were made to Abraham and
3:20 **N** a mediator involves more than one party;
3:23 **N** before faith came, we were imprisoned
3:25 But **n** that faith has come,
4: 9 **N**, however, that you have come to know God,
4:16 Have I **n** become your enemy by telling you
4:20 with you **n** and could change my tone,
4:24 **N** this is an allegory: these women are two
4:25 **N** Hagar is Mount Sinai in Arabia
4:28 **N** you, my friends, are children of the promise,
4:29 according to the Spirit, so it is **n** also.
5:19 **N** the works of the flesh are obvious:
6:17 From **n** on, let no one make trouble for me;
Eph 2: 2 the spirit that is **n** at work
2:13 But **n** in Christ Jesus you who once were far off
3: 5 as it has **n** been revealed to his holy apostles
3:10 of God in its rich variety might **n** be made known
3:20 **N** to him who by the power at work
4:17 **N** this I affirm and insist on in the Lord:
5: 8 but **n** in the Lord you are light.
Php 1: 5 in the gospel from the first day until **n**.
1:20 Christ will be exalted **n** as always in my body,
1:30 the same struggle that you saw I had and **n** hear
2:12 but much more **n** in my absence,
3:18 and **n** I tell you even with tears.
4:10 that **n** at last you have revived your concern
4:18 I am fully satisfied, **n** that I have received
Col 1:22 he has **n** reconciled in his fleshly body
1:24 I am **n** rejoicing in my sufferings for your sake,
1:26 the ages and generations but has **n** been revealed
3: 8 But **n** you must get rid of all such things—
1Th 3: 6 But Timothy has just **n** come to us from you,
3: 8 For we **n** live, if you continue to stand firm in
3:11 **N** may our God and Father himself
4: 9 **N** concerning love of the brothers and sisters,
5: 1 **N** concerning the times and the seasons,
2Th 2: 6 And you know what is **n** restraining him,
2: 7 only until the one who **n** restrains it is removed.
2:16 **N** may our Lord Jesus Christ himself
3: 6 **N** we command you, beloved,
3:12 **N** such persons we command and exhort in
3:16 **N** may the Lord of peace himself give you peace
1Ti 1: 8 **N** we know that the law is good,
3: 2 **N** a bishop must be above reproach,
4: 1 **N** the Spirit expressly says that
2Ti 1: 5 and your mother Eunice and **n**,
1:10 but it has **n** been revealed through the appearing
3:10 **N** you have observed my teaching, my conduct,
4: 8 From **n** on there is reserved for me the crown
Phm 1: 9 and **n** also as a prisoner of Christ Jesus.
1:11 but **n** he is indeed useful both to you and to me.
Heb 2: 5 **N** God did not subject the coming world,
2: 8 **N** in subjecting all things to them,
2: 9 **n** crowned with glory and honor because of
3: 5 **N** Moses was faithful in all God's house as
3:16 **N** who were they who heard and
7:11 **N** if perfection had been attainable through
7:13 **N** the one of whom these things are spoken
8: 1 **N** the main point in what we are saying is this:
8: 4 **N** if he were on earth,
8: 6 Jesus has **n** obtained a more excellent ministry,
9: 1 **N** even the first covenant had regulations
9: 5 Of these things we cannot speak **n** in detail.
9:24 **n** to appear in the presence of God on our behalf.
11: 1 **N** faith is the assurance of things hoped for,
12:11 **N**, discipline always seems painful rather than
12:26 his voice shook the earth; but **n** he has promised,
13:20 **N** may the God of peace,
Jas 2:11 **N** if you do not commit adultery but
Jas 4:13 Come **n**, you who say, "Today
5: 1 Come **n**, you rich people,
1Pe 1: 6 even if **n** for a little while you have had
1: 8 and even though you do not see him **n**,
1:12 in regard to the things that have **n** been announced
1:22 **N** that you have purified your souls
2:10 but **n** you are God's people;
2:10 but **n** you have received mercy.
2:25 but **n** you have returned to the shepherd
3:13 **N** who will harm you if you are eager
3:21 baptism, which this prefigured, **n** saves you—
5: 1 **N** as an elder myself and a witness of
2Pe 3: 1 This is **n**, beloved, the second letter I am writing
3:18 be the glory both **n** and to the day of eternity.
1Jn 2: 3 **N** by this we may be sure that we know him,
2:18 so **n** many antichrists have come.
2:28 And **n**, little children, abide in him,
3: 2 Beloved, we are God's children **n**;
4: 3 and **n** it is already in the world.
2Jn 1: 5 But **n**, dear lady, I ask you,
Jude 1: 5 **N** I desire to remind you,
1:24 **N** to him who is able to keep you from falling,
1:25 and authority, before all time and **n** and forever.
Rev 1:19 **N** write what you have seen, what is,
8: 6 **N** the seven angels who had
12:10 "**N** have come the salvation and the power and
14:13 Blessed are the dead who from **n** on die in
Tob 1:22 **N** Ahikar was chief cupbearer,
2: 3 and **n** he lies there strangled."
3: 3 And **n**, O Lord, remember me and look favorably
3: 5 And **n** your many judgments are true
3: 6 So **n** deal with me as you will;
3:12 And **n**, Lord, I turn my face to you,
4: 2 "**N** I have asked for death.
4:13 So **n**, my son, love your kindred,
4:19 So **n**, my child, remember these commandments,
4:20 "And **n**, my son, let me explain to you
5: 3 And **n** twenty years have passed
5: 3 So **n**, my son, find yourself a trustworthy man
6:13 So **n** listen to me, brother,
6:15 So **n**, since I am the only son my father has,
6:16 **N** listen to me, brother, and say no more
6:18 **N** when you are about to go to bed with her,
6:18 as brothers to you. **N** say no more!"
7: 1 **N** when they entered Ecbatana,
7:11 But **n**, my child, eat and drink,
7:11 from **n** on you are her brother
8: 7 I **n** am taking this kinswoman of mine,
8:21 and we belong to you as well as to your wife **n**
10: 1 **N**, day by day, Tobit kept counting
10: 7 **N** when the fourteen days of
10:12 since from **n** on they are as much your parents
10:12 From **n** on I am your mother
11: 9 saying, "**N** that I have seen you, my child,
11:15 **N** I see my son Tobias!"
11:17 Come in **n** to your home, and welcome,
12:11 "I will **n** declare the whole truth to you
12:12 So **n** when you and Sarah prayed,
12:20 **n** get up from the ground, and acknowledge God.
13: 6 So **n** see what he has done for you;
14:8,9 So **n**, my children, I command you,
14:8,9 So **n**, my son, leave Nineveh; do not remain here.
14:11 **n**, my children, see what almsgiving accomplishes,
14:11 But **n** my breath fails me."
Jdt 4: 3 the people of Judea had just **n** gathered together,
5:19 But **n** they have returned to their God,
5:20 "So **n**, my master and lord,
6: 7 **N** my slaves are going to take you back into
7: 4 "They will **n** strip clean the whole land;
7:25 For **n** we have no one to help us;
7:26 **N** summon them and surrender the whole town
8: 1 **N** in those days Judith heard about these things:
8:31 **N** since you are a God-fearing woman,
9: 5 You have designed the things that are **n**,
9: 7 "Here **n** are the Assyrians,
11: 2 Even **n**, if your people who live in
11: 3 But **n** tell me why you have fled from them
11: 9 "**N** as for Achior's speech in your council,
11:11 "But **n**, in order that my lord may not be defeated
12: 6 "Let my lord **n** give orders to allow your servant
13: 3 **N** Judith had told her maid to stand outside
13: 11 **N** indeed is the time to help your heritage and
14: 8 **N** tell me what you have done during these days."
AdE 1:18 so **n** the other ladies who are wives of the Persian
2: 5 **N** there was a Jew in Susa
2:10 **N** Esther had not disclosed her people or country,
2:12 **N** the period after which a girl was to go to
2:15 **N** Esther found favor in the eyes
2:21 **N** the king's eunuchs, who were chief bodyguards,
4:11 and it is **n** thirty days since I was called to go to
6: 4 **N** Haman had come to speak to the king
8: 7 "**N** that I have granted all of Haman's property
9: 1 **N** on the thirteenth day of the twelfth month,
9: 6 **N** in the city of Susa
9:16 **N** the other Jews in the kingdom gathered
12: 1 **N** Mordecai took his rest in the courtyard
13:15 And **n**, O Lord God and King, God of Abraham,
14: 6 And **n** we have sinned before you,
14: 8 And **n** they are not satisfied that we are
14:18 since the day that I was brought here until **n**,
16:23 both **n** and hereafter it may represent deliverance
Wis 14:15 he **n** honored as a god what was once
14:20 **n** regarded as an object of worship
17:15 and **n** were driven by monstrous specters,
17:15 and **n** were paralyzed by their souls' surrender;
18:14 and night in its swift course was **n** half gone,
Sir Pr: 1 **N**, those who read the scriptures must
Sir 11:19 and **n** I shall feast on my goods!"
11:24 and what harm can come to me **n**?"
33:16 **N** I was the last to keep vigil;
39:35 So **n** sing praise with all your heart and voice,
42:15 I will **n** call to mind the works of the Lord,
44: 1 Let us **n** sing the praises of famous men,
45:26 **n** bless the Lord who has crowned you with glory.
50:22 And **n** bless the God of all,
Bar 2:11 And **n**, O Lord God of Israel,
3: 4 hear **n** the prayer of the people of Israel,
4:24 as the neighbors of Zion have **n** seen your capture,
LtJ 6: 4 **N** in Babylon you will see gods made of silver
Aza 1:10 And **n** we cannot open our mouths;
1:18 And **n** with all our heart we follow you;
1:23 **N** the king's servants who threw them
Sus 1:31 **N** Susanna was a woman of great refinement
1:43 And **n** I am to die,
1:52 your sins have **n** come home,
1:54 **N** then, if you really saw this woman, tell me this:
1:58 **N** then, tell me: Under what
Bel 1: 3 **N** the Babylonians had an idol called Bel,
1:10 **N** there were seventy priests of Bel,
1:11 priests of Bel said, "See, we are **n** going outside;
1:23 **N** in that place there was a great dragon,
1:32 but **n** they were given nothing,
1:33 **N** the prophet Habakkuk was in Judea;
1Mc 1:40 Her dishonor **n** grew as great as her glory;
1:54 **N** on the fifteenth day of Chislev,
2:18 **N** be the first to come and do what
2:49 **N** the days drew near for Mattathias to die,
2:49 "Arrogance and scorn have **n** become strong;
2:50 **N**, my children, show zeal for the law,
3:10 Apollonius **n** gathered together Gentiles and
3:42 **N** Judas and his brothers saw
4: 1 **N** Gorgias took five thousand infantry
4:10 And **n**, let us cry to Heaven,
4:18 But stand **n** against our enemies and fight them,
5: 9 **N** the Gentiles in Gilead gathered together against
5:12 **N** then, come and rescue us from their hands,
5:40 **N** as Judas and his army drew near to the stream
5:55 **N** while Judas and Jonathan were in Gilead
6:11 And into what a great flood I **n** am plunged!
6:12 But **n** I remember the wrong I did in Jerusalem.
6:40 **N** a part of the king's army was spread out on
6:43 **N** Eleazar, called Avaran,
6:58 **N** then let us come to terms with these people,
7: 7 **N** then send a man whom you trust;
7:39 **N** Nicanor went out from Jerusalem
8: 1 **N** Judas heard of the fame of the Romans,
8:32 If **n** they appeal again for help against you,
9: 5 **N** Judas was encamped in Elasa,
9: 9 Let us rather save our own lives **n**,
9:22 **N** the rest of the acts of Judas,
9:30 **N** therefore we have chosen you today
9:44 "Let us get up **n** and fight for our lives,
9:46 Cry out **n** to Heaven that you may be delivered
9:58 So **n** let us bring Bacchides back,
10:15 **N** King Alexander heard of all the promises
10:16 Come **n**, we will make him our friend and ally."
10:27 **N** continue still to keep faith with us,
10:29 "I **n** free you and exempt all the Jews
10:41 they shall give from **n** on for the service of
10:48 **N** King Alexander assembled large forces
10:54 **n** therefore let us establish friendship
10:54 give me **n** your daughter as my wife,
10:56 And **n** I will do for you as you wrote,
10:71 If you **n** have confidence in your forces,
10:73 And **n** you will not be able
10:79 **N** Apollonius had secretly left a thousand cavalry
11:10 I **n** regret that I gave him my daughter,
11:14 **N** King Alexander was in Cilicia at that time,
11:37 **N** therefore take care to make a copy of this,
11:41 **N** Jonathan sent to King Demetrius the request
11:43 **N** then you will do well
12: 1 **N** when Jonathan saw that the time was favorable
12:18 And **n** please send us a reply to this."
12:22 And **n** that we have learned this,
12:24 **N** Jonathan heard that the commanders
12:45 Dismiss them **n** to their homes and choose
12:53 **N** therefore let us make war on them and blot out
13: 5 And **n**, far be it from me to spare my life
13:16 Send **n** one hundred talents of silver and two
13:21 **N** the men in the citadel kept sending envoys
15: 5 **n** therefore I confirm to you all the tax remissions
15: 7 that you have built and **n** hold shall remain yours.
15:30 **N** then, hand over the cities that you have seized
15:34 **N** that we have the opportunity,
16: 3 But **n** I have grown old,
16:11 **N** Ptolemy son of Abubus
16:14 **N** Simon was visiting the towns of the country
2Mc 1: 6 We are **n** praying for you here.
1: 9 And **n** see that you keep the festival of booths in
3:28 a great retinue and all his bodyguard but was **n**
3:30 **n** that the Almighty Lord had appeared.
6:12 **N** I urge those who read this book not to
6:18 a man **n** advanced in age and of noble presence,
6:27 Therefore, by bravely giving up my life **n**,
6:29 toward him with goodwill **n** changed to ill will,
7:23 you **n** forget yourselves for the sake of his laws."
9:14 he was **n** declaring to be free;
10: 1 **N** Maccabeus and his followers,
10:10 **N** we will tell what took place
10:24 **N** Timothy, who had been defeated by the Jews
11:23 **N** that our father has gone on to the gods,
12:39 On the next day, as had **n** become necessary,
13:10 **n** if ever to help those who were on the point
14: 3 **N** a certain Alcimus, who had formerly been

2Mc 14: 7 I mean the high priesthood—and have **n** come
14: 8 whole nation is **n** suffering no small misfortune.
14:36 so **n**, O holy One, Lord of all
14:43 and the crowd was **n** rushing in through the doors.
14:46 with his blood **n** completely drained from him,
15:20 all were **n** looking forward to the coming issue,
15:23 So **n**, O Sovereign of the heavens,
1Es 1: 4 **N** worship the Lord your God
1:27 And **n** the Lord is with me!
1:33 that he had done before, and these that are **n** told,
2:18 Let it **n** be known to our lord the king that
2:19 **N** if this city is built and the walls finished,
2:20 Since the building of the temple is **n** going on,
2:24 Therefore we **n** make known to you,
2:28 Therefore I have **n** issued orders
3: 1 **N** King Darius gave a great banquet for all
4:28 And **n** do you not believe me?
4:46 And **n**, O lord the king, this is what I ask
6: 1 **N** in the second year of the reign of Darius,
6:20 in process of construction from that time until **n**,
6:21 **N** therefore, O king, if it seems wise to do so,
8:78 And **n** in some measure mercy has come to us
8:82 "And **n**, O Lord, what shall we say,
8:90 See, we are **n** before you in our iniquities;
8:92 but even **n** there is hope for Israel.
9: 8 **N** then make confession and give glory to
9:50 **n** they were all weeping as they heard the law—
Man 1:11 And **n** I bend the knee of my heart,
3Mc 1: 6 **N** that he had foiled the plot,
1:26 took heed of nothing, and began **n** to approach,
2:13 see **n**, O holy King, that because of our many
2:31 **N** some, however, with an obvious abhorrence of
4: 1 in their minds was **n** made evident and outspoken.
5: 8 from the fate **n** prepared for them.
5:14 But **n**, since it was nearly the middle of
5:38 the elephants **n** once more for the destruction of
5:40 ordering **n** for a third time that they be destroyed,
5:45 **N** when the animals had been brought virtually to
5:46 the city **n** being filled with countless masses
5:51 as they stood **n** at the gates of death.
6: 9 And **n**, you who hate insolence,
6:12 watch over us **n** and have mercy on us who by
6:24 even me, your benefactor, you are **n** attempting
6:28 of our ancestors until **n** has granted an unimpeded
6:29 since they **n** had escaped death.
2Es 1: 8 **N** you, pull out the hair of your head
1:30 But **n**, what shall I do to you?
1:38 "And **n**, father, look with pride and see
2: 4 But **n** what can I do for you?
2: 5 **N** I call upon you, father, as a witness in addition
2:41 whom you desired, is **n** complete;
2:45 **N** they are being crowned, and receive palms."
3:34 **N** therefore weigh in a balance our iniquities
4: 9 But **n** I have asked you only about fire and wind
4:18 If **n** you were a judge between them,
4:30 how much ungodliness it has produced until **n**—
4:31 Consider **n** for yourself how much fruit
5: 1 "**N** concerning the signs: lo,
5: 3 that you **n** see ruling shall be a trackless waste,
5:13 and weep as you do **n**, and fast for seven days,
5:16 **N** on the second night Phaltiel,
5:28 And **n**, O Lord, why have you handed the one
5:45 even **n** be able to support all of them present
5:50 "Since you have **n** given me the opportunity,
5:50 Or is she **n** approaching old age?"
6: 5 and before the imaginations of those who **n**
6: 9 **N** Esau is the end of this age,
6:35 **N** after this I wept again and fasted seven days in
6:57 And **n**, O Lord, these nations,
7: 9 If **n** the city is given to someone as an inheritance,
7:15 **N** therefore why are you disturbed,
7:16 rather than what is **n** present?"
7:20 Let many perish who are **n** living,
7:26 that the city that **n** is not seen shall appear,
7:26 and the land that **n** is hidden shall be disclosed.
7:*37* 'Look **n**, and understand whom you have denied,
7:*45* "O sovereign Lord, I said then and I say **n**:
7:*47* And **n** I see that the world
7:*60* it is they who have made my glory to prevail **n**,
7:*60* and through them my name has **n** been honored
7:*61* for it is they who are **n** like a mist,
7:*64* But **n** the mind grows with us,
7:*71* But **n**, understand from your own words—
7:*78* **N** concerning death, the teaching is:
7:*82* because they cannot **n** make a good repentance so
7:*88* "**N** this is the order of those who have kept
7:*95* they understand the rest that they **n** enjoy,
7:*96* that they have **n** escaped what is corruptible
7:*104* Just as **n** a father does not send his son,
7:*111* [41] So if **n**, when corruption has increased
7:*117* [47] what good is it to all that they live in sorrow **n**
7:*132* [62] Lord, that the Most High is **n** called merciful,
7:*136* [66] to those **n** living and to those who are gone
8: 8 And because you give life to the body that is **n**
8:15 And **n** I will speak out:
8:18 and **n** also I have heard of the swiftness of
8:46 "Things that are present are for those who live **n**,
8:60 to him who prepared life for them **n**.
8:61 Therefore my judgment is **n** drawing near;
9: 9 Then those who have **n** abused my ways shall
9:15 and I say **n**, and will say it again:
9:18 for those who **n** exist, before the world was made
9:19 but **n** those who have been created in this world,
9:23 "**N**, if you will let seven days more pass—
9:34 **N** this is the general rule that,
10: 4 And **n** I intend not to return to the town,
10: 8 It is most appropriate to mourn **n**,
2Es 10: 9 **N** ask the earth, and she will tell you
10:13 the multitude that is **n** in it goes as it came';
10:15 **N**, therefore, keep your sorrow to yourself,
10:37 **N** therefore I beg you to give your servant
10:42 (you do not **n** see the form of a woman,
10:44 which you **n** behold as a city being built.
10:50 For **n** the Most High, seeing
11:44 at his times; **n** they have ended,
12: 6 Therefore I will **n** entreat the Most High
12:12 to him as I **n** explain to you or have explained it.
12:49 **N** go to your homes, every one of you,
13:15 **n** show me the interpretation of this dream also.
13:46 "Then they lived there until the last times; and **n**,
14: 7 And **n** I say to you:
14:13 **N** therefore, set your house in order,
14:13 And **n** renounce the life that is corruptible,
14:14 and divest yourself **n** of your weak nature;
14:16 For evils worse than those that you have **n**
14:20 and I will reprove the people who are **n** living;
14:33 And **n** you are here, and your people are farther in
14:36 But let no one come to me **n**,
16:35 Listen **n** to these things, and understand them,
4Mc 1:15 **N** reason is the mind that with sound logic prefers
1:18 **N** the kinds of wisdom are rational judgment,
1:30 Observe **n**, first of all, that rational judgment
2:21 **N** when God fashioned human beings,
3: 6 **N** this can be explained more clearly by the story
3: 9 **N** all the rest were at supper,
3:19 The present occasion **n** invites us to
4: 1 **N** there was a certain Simon,
6:18 we should **n** change our course
6:26 When he was **n** burned to his very bones and
6:33 But **n** that reason has conquered the emotions,
10:16 a brother to those who have just **n** been tortured."
14: 9 Even **n**, we ourselves shudder as we hear of
15:16 tried **n** by more bitter pains than even
16: 6 bearing seven children, I am **n** the mother of none!
17:18 of which they **n** stand before the divine throne

NOWHERE (5) [WHERE]

Pr 26: 2 an undeserved curse goes **n**.
Mt 8:20 but the Son of Man has **n** to lay his head."
10: 5 "Go **n** among the Gentiles,
Lk 9:58 but the Son of Man has **n** to lay his head."
Wis 17:10 though it **n** could be avoided.

NUBIA, NUBIAN, NUBIANS See Index to Footnotes

NUDGED (1)

3Mc 5:14 were assembled, approached the king and **n** him.

NULL (1) [NULLIFY]

Ro 4:14 faith is **n** and the promise is void.

NULLIFIED (4) [NULLIFY]

Nu 30:12 Her husband has **n** them,
4Mc 2: 3 by his reason he **n** the frenzy of the passions.
8:15 and by their right reasoning **n** his tyranny.
17: 2 with your seven sons **n** the violence of the tyrant,

NULLIFIES (2) [NULLIFY]

Nu 30:12 her husband **n** them at the time that he hears them,
30:15 if he **n** them some time after he has heard of them,

NULLIFY (7) [NULL, NULLIFIED, NULLIFIES]

Nu 30: 8 he shall **n** the vow by which she was obligated,
30:13 to stand, or her husband may **n**.
Ro 3: 3 Will their faithlessness **n** the faithfulness of God?
Gal 2:21 I do not **n** the grace of God;
3:17 a covenant previously ratified by God, so as to **n**
1Mc 14:44 of the people or priests shall be permitted to **n** any
1Es 6:32 that if anyone should transgress or **n** any of

NUMBER (210) [NUMBERED, NUMBERING, NUMBERLESS, NUMBERS, NUMEROUS]

Ge 32:12 which cannot be counted because of their **n**.' "
47:12 according to the **n** of their dependents.
Ex 1: 5 The total **n** of people born to Jacob was seventy.
5:18 but you shall still deliver the same **n** of bricks."
5:19 "You shall not lessen your daily **n** of bricks."
12: 4 the lamb shall be divided in proportion to the **n**
16:16 an omer to a person according to the **n** of persons,
23:26 I will fulfill the **n** of your days.
Lev 25:15 you shall pay only for the **n** of years since
25:16 for it is a certain **n** of harvests that are being sold
25:50 price of the sale shall be applied to the **n** of years:
26:22 they shall make you few in **n**,
Nu 1: 2 by ancestral houses, according to the **n** of names,
1:18 according to the **n** of names from twenty years old
1:20 according to the **n** of names, individually,
1:22 according to the **n** of names, individually,
1:24 according to the **n** of the names,
1:26 according to the **n** of names,
1:28 according to the **n** of names,
1:30 according to the **n** of names,
1:32 according to the **n** of names,
1:34 according to the **n** of names,
1:36 according to the **n** of names,
Nu 1:38 according to the **n** of names,
1:40 according to the **n** of names,
1:42 according to the **n** of names,
1:45 So the whole **n** of the Israelites,
1:46 their whole **n** was six hundred three thousand five hundred fifty.
3:43 a month old and upward, counting the **n** of names,
3:46 over and above the **n** of the Levites,
3:48 and his sons the money by which the excess **n**
11:21 people I am with **n** six hundred thousand on foot;
14:29 and of all your **n**, included in the census,
14:34 the **n** of the days in which you spied out the land,
15:12 According to the **n** that you offer,
23:10 or **n** the dust-cloud of Israel?
26: 7 of the Reubenites; the **n** of those enrolled
26:18 of the Gadites: the **n** of those enrolled
26:22 of Judah: the **n** of those enrolled
26:27 of the Zebulunites; the **n** of those enrolled
26:34 of Manasseh; the **n** of those enrolled
26:37 of the Ephraimites: the **n** of those enrolled
26:41 of Benjamin by their clans; the **n** of those enrolled
26:47 of the Asherites: the **n** of those enrolled
26:50 Naphtalites by their clans: the **n** of those enrolled
26:51 This was the **n** of the Israelites enrolled:
26:53 be apportioned for inheritance according to the **n**
26:62 **n** of those enrolled was twenty-three thousand,
29:18 as prescribed in accordance with their **n**;
29:21 as prescribed in accordance with their **n**;
29:24 as prescribed in accordance with their **n**;
29:27 as prescribed in accordance with their **n**;
29:30 as prescribed in accordance with their **n**;
29:33 as prescribed in accordance with their **n**;
29:37 as prescribed in accordance with their **n**;
31: 3 "Arm some of your **n** for the war,
31:36 in **n** three hundred thirty-seven thousand five
32: 1 and the Gadites owned a very great **n** of cattle.
Dt 25: 2 in his presence with the **n** of lashes proportionate
26: 5 few in **n**, and there he became a great nation,
28:62 you shall be left few in **n**,
32: 8 the boundaries of the peoples according to the **n** of
Jos 4: 8 according to the **n** of the tribes of the Israelites,
11: 4 a great army, in **n** like the sand on the seashore,
Jdg 7: 6 The **n** of those that lapped was three hundred;
7:12 and their camels were without **n**,
18: 2 the Danites sent five valiant men from the whole **n**
1Sa 6: 4 according to the **n** of the lords of the Philistines;
6:18 the **n** of all the cities of the Philistines belonging
18:27 which were given in full **n** to the king,
2Sa 21:20 and six toes on each foot, twenty-four in **n**;
24: 3 the LORD your God increase the **n** of the people
24: 9 to the king the **n** of those who had been recorded:
1Ki 18:22 but Baal's prophets **n** four hundred fifty.
18:31 to the **n** of the tribes of the sons of Jacob, to whom
1Ch 7: 2 of their generations, their **n** in the days
7:40 Their **n** enrolled by genealogies,
16:19 When they were few in **n**, of little account,
20: 6 and six toes on each foot, twenty-four in **n**;
21: 2 "Go, **n** Israel, from Beer-sheba to Dan,
21: 2 and bring me a report, so that I may know their **n**."
21: 3 "May the LORD increase the **n** of his people
22: 4 and cedar logs without **n**—
22:15 carpenters, and all kinds of artisans without **n**,
23:24 according to the **n** of the names of the individuals
23:27 to the last words of David these were the **n** of
23:31 according to the **n** required of them,
27:24 for this, and the **n** was not entered into the account
2Ch 26:12 The whole **n** of the heads of ancestral houses
28: 5 who defeated him and took captive a great **n**
29:32 The **n** of the burnt offerings that
29:35 the great **n** of burnt offerings there was the fat of
30: 3 not sanctified themselves in sufficient **n**,
35: 7 and kids from the flock to the **n** of thirty thousand,
Ezr 2: 2 The **n** of the Israelite people:
3: 4 the daily burnt offerings by **n** according to
6:17 according to the **n** of the tribes of Israel.
Ne 7: 7 The **n** of the Israelite people:
Est 5:11 of his riches, the **n** of his sons, all the promotions
9:11 That very day the **n** of those killed in the citadel
Job 1: 5 and offer burnt offerings according to the **n**
3: 6 let it not come into the **n** of the months.
5: 9 marvelous things without **n**.
9:10 and marvelous things without **n**.
14: 5 and the **n** of their months is known to you,
14:16 For then you would not **n** my steps,
21:21 when the **n** of their months is cut off?
25: 3 Is there any **n** to his armies?
31: 4 Does he not see my ways, and **n** all my steps?
36:26 the **n** of his years is unsearchable.
38:21 and the **n** of your days is great!
38:37 Who has the wisdom to **n** the clouds?
39: 2 Can you **n** the months that they fulfill,
Ps 40:12 For evils have encompassed me without **n**;
69: 4 More in **n** than the hairs
71:15 though their **n** is past my knowledge.
105:12 When they were few in **n**, of little account,
105:34 and young locusts without **n**;
147: 4 He determines the **n** of the stars;
Pr 23:28 She lies in wait like a robber and increases the **n**
SS 6: 8 and eighty concubines, and maidens without **n**.
Jer 2:32 Yet my people have forgotten me, days without **n**.
44:28 the land of Egypt to the land of Judah, few in **n**;
46:23 more numerous than locusts; they are without **n**.
52:28 the **n** of the people whom Nebuchadrezzar took
Eze 4: 4 you shall bear their punishment for the **n** of
4: 5 For I assign to you a **n** of days,
4: 5 equal to the **n** of the years of their punishment;
4: 9 During the **n** of days that you lie on your side,

Eze 5: 3 Then you shall take from these a small **n**,
33: 2 of the land take one of their **n** as their sentinel;
Da 9: 2 Daniel, perceived in the books the **n** of years that,
Hos 1:10 the **n** of the people of Israel shall be like the sand
Lk 23:27 A great **n** of the people followed him,
Ac 2:47 to their **n** those who were being saved.
5:16 A great **n** of people would also gather from
5:36 and a **n** of men, about four hundred, joined him;
6: 1 when the disciples were increasing in **n**,
6: 7 **n** of the disciples increased greatly in Jerusalem,
11:21 a great **n** became believers and turned to the Lord.
14: 1 and spoke in such a way that a great **n** of
19:19 A **n** of those who practiced magic collected their
19:26 and drawn away a considerable **n** of people
27: 7 a **n** of days and arrived with difficulty off Cnidus,
Ro 9:27 the **n** of the children of Israel were like the sand of
11:25 until the full **n** of the Gentiles has come in.
Heb 7:23 Furthermore, the former priests were many in **n**,
Rev 6:11 until the **n** would be complete both
7: 4 And I heard the **n** of those who were sealed,
9:16 The **n** of the troops of cavalry was two hundred million; I heard their **n**.
13:17 that is, the name of the beast or the **n** of its name.
13:18 let anyone with understanding calculate the **n** of the beast, for it is the **n** of a person. Its **n** is six hundred sixty-six.
15: 2 the beast and its image and the **n** of its name,
Jdt 2:17 along a vast **n** of camels and donkeys and mules
7:18 Their tents and supply trains spread out in great **n**,
10:17 from their **n** a hundred men to accompany her
AdE 9:11 the **n** of those killed in Susa was reported to
Wis 4: 8 or measured by **n** of years;
11:20 But you have arranged all things by measure and **n**
Sir 7: 9 "He will consider the great **n** of my gifts,
17: 2 He gave them a fixed **n** of days,
18: 9 The **n** of days in their life is great
26: 1 the **n** of his days will be doubled.
26:26 *for the **n** of his years will be doubled.*
32: 1 be among them as one of their **n**.
37:25 but the days of Israel are without **n**.
48: 2 and by his zeal he made them few in **n**.
48:15 The people were left very few in **n**,
Bar 2:13 for we are left, few in **n**,
2:29 surely turn into a small **n** among the nations,
1Mc 2:38 to the **n** of a thousand persons.
6:30 The **n** of his forces was one hundred thousand
9: 6 When they saw the huge **n** of the enemy forces,
10:36 "Let Jews be enrolled in the king's forces to the **n**
10:37 Let their officers and leaders be of their own **n**,
10:85 The **n** of those who fell by the sword,
11:45 to the **n** of a hundred and twenty thousand,
2Mc 2:21 so that though few in **n** they seized the whole land
8:16 to the **n** six thousand, and exhorted them not to
10:24 and collected the cavalry from Asia in no small **n**.
1Es 2: 9 and with a very great **n** of votive offerings
2:13 The **n** of these was: one thousand gold cups,
2:30 with cavalry and a large **n** of armed troops,
5: 9 The **n** of those of the nation and their leaders:
7: 8 the **n** of the twelve leaders of the tribes of Israel;
Man 1: 9 For the sins I have committed are more in **n** than
Pm 151: T *as his own composition (though it is outside the **n**),*
3Mc 4:17 of the Jews because of their immense **n**,
5: 2 to drug all the elephants—five hundred in **n**—
2Es 2:19 and the same **n** of springs flowing with milk
2:26 for I will require them from among your **n**.
2:38 the **n** of those who have been sealed at the feast of
2:40 Take again your full **n**, O Zion,
2:41 The **n** of your children, whom you desired,
2:42 a great multitude that I could not **n**,
3: 7 peoples and clans without **n**.
3:29 when I came here I saw ungodly deeds without **n**,
4:32 When heads of grain without **n** are sown,
4:36 'When the **n** of those like yourselves is completed;
4:37 and numbered the times by **n**;
7:*61* not grieve over the great **n** of those who perish;
7:*76* or **n** yourself among those who are tormented.
8:55 not ask any more questions about the great **n**
8:63 you have already shown me a great **n** of the signs
16:56 and he knows the **n** of the stars.
4Mc 8: 5 and greatly respect the beauty and the **n**
16:13 and giving rebirth for immortality to the whole **n**

NUMBERED (31) [NUMBER]

Ge 46:15 in all his sons and his daughters **n** thirty-three).
Nu 1:22 those of them that were **n**,
1:47 not **n** by their ancestral tribe along with them.
1Sa 14:23 with Saul **n** altogether about ten thousand men.
15: 4 Saul summoned the people, and **n** them in Telaim,
22: 2 Those who were with him **n** about four hundred.
2Sa 24:10 David was stricken to the heart because he had **n**
1Ki 3: 8 so numerous they cannot be **n** or counted.
4:32 and his songs **n** a thousand and five.
5:13 the levy **n** thirty thousand men.
8: 5 and oxen that they could not be counted or **n**.
1Ch 12:24 spear **n** six thousand eight hundred armed troops.
25: 7 **n** two hundred eighty-eight.
2Ch 5: 6 so many sheep and oxen that they could not be **n**
Isa 53:12 and was **n** with the transgressors;
Jer 33:22 as the host of heaven cannot be **n** and the sands of
52:23 the latticework **n** one hundred.
La 4:18 our days were **n**; for our end had come.
Da 5:26 God has **n** the days of your kingdom
Hos 1:10 which can be neither measured nor **n**;
Mk 6:44 the loaves **n** five thousand men.
Ac 1:15 the crowd **n** about one hundred twenty persons)
1:17 for he was **n** among us and was allotted his share
Ac 4: 4 and they **n** about five thousand.
Rev 5:11 they **n** myriads of myriads and thousands
Jdt 7: 2 fighting forces **n** one hundred seventy thousand
Wis 5: 5 Why have they been **n** among the children
Sir 37:25 The days of a person's life are **n**,
41:13 The days of a good life are **n**,
1Mc 2:18 and your sons will be **n** among the Friends of
2Es 4:37 and **n** the times by number;

NUMBERING (3) [NUMBER]

1Ch 21: 6 he did not include Levi and Benjamin in the **n**,
27: 1 each division **n** twenty-four thousand:
Mk 5:13 and the herd, **n** about two thousand,

NUMBERLESS (1) [NUMBER]

Joel 2:11 **N** are those who obey his command.

NUMBERS (24) [NUMBER]

Ge 34:30 my **n** are few, and if they gather themselves
48: 4 to make you fruitful and increase your **n**;
Ex 12:38 and livestock in great **n**, both flocks and herds.
Dt 33: 6 and not die out, even though his **n** are few.
1Ch 12:23 These are the **n** of the divisions of
2Ch 15: 9 for great **n** had deserted to him from Israel
20:25 they found livestock in great **n**, goods, clothing,
26:11 the **n** in the muster made by the secretary Jeiel and
30: 5 for they had not kept it in great **n** as prescribed.
30:24 The priests sanctified themselves in great **n**.
Isa 40:26 He who brings out their host and **n** them,
Mk 3: 8 they came to him in great **n** from Judea,
Ac 5:14 great **n** of both men and women,
9:31 in the comfort of the Holy Spirit, it increased in **n**.
16: 5 in the faith and increased in **n** daily.
28:23 they came to him at his lodgings in great **n**.
Jdt 7: 4 When the Israelites saw their vast **n**,
9:11 "For your strength does not depend on **n**,
16: 3 their **n** blocked up the wadis,
Wis 19:10 instead of fish the river spewed out vast **n** of frogs.
Sir 16: 3 Do not trust in their survival, or rely on their **n**;
1Mc 4: 8 "Do not fear their **n** or be afraid when they charge.
2Mc 5:26 the city with his armed warriors and killed great **n**
12:16 and slaughtered untold **n**,

NUMENIUS (4)

1Mc 12:16 We therefore have chosen **N** son of Antiochus
14:22 '**N** son of Antiochus and Antipater son of Jason,
14:24 After this Simon sent **N** to Rome with
15:15 Then **N** and his companions arrived from Rome,

NUMEROUS (46) [NUMBER]

Ge 17: 2 and will make you exceedingly **n**."
17:20 and make him fruitful and exceedingly **n**;
22:17 as **n** as the stars of heaven and as the sand that is
26: 4 I will make your offspring as **n** as the stars
26:24 and will bless you and make your offspring **n**
28: 3 and make you fruitful and **n**,
50:20 in order to preserve a **n** people,
Ex 1: 9 the Israelite people are more **n**
5: 5 "Now they are more **n** than the people of the land
Nu 22: 3 of the people, because they were so **n**;
22:15 more **n** and more distinguished than these.
Dt 1:10 so that today you are as **n** as the stars of heaven.
2:10 a large and **n** people, as tall as the Anakim—
2:21 a strong and **n** people, as tall as
7: 1 seven nations mightier and more **n** than you—
7: 7 because you were more **n** than any other people
7:17 "These nations are more **n** than I;
7:22 otherwise the wild animals would become too **n**
9:14 of you a nation mightier and more **n** than they."
10:22 and now the LORD your God has made you as **n**
28:62 once you were as **n** as the stars in heaven,
28:63 and **n**, so the LORD will take delight
30: 5 and **n** than your ancestors.
30:16 and ordinances, then you shall live and become **n**,
Jos 17:14 since we are a **n** people,
17:15 And Joshua said to them, "If you are a **n** people,
17:17 "You are indeed a **n** people, and have great power;
1Ki 3: 8 so **n** they cannot be numbered or counted.
4:20 Judah and Israel were as **n** as the sand by the sea;
10:27 and he made cedars as **n** as the sycamores of
1Ch 5:23 they were very **n** from Bashan to Baal-hermon,
23:17 but the sons of Rehabiah were very **n**.
27:23 for the LORD had promised to make Israel as **n**
2Ch 1: 9 for you have made me king over a people as **n** as
Pr 7:26 are those she has laid low, and **n** are her victims.
Jer 15: 8 Their widows became more **n** than the sand of
30:14 because your sins are so **n**.
30:15 your guilt is great, because your sins are so **n**,
46:23 because they are more **n** than locusts;
Zec 10: 8 and they shall be as **n** as they were before.
Ro 4:18 "So **n** shall your descendants be."
Gal 4:27 the desolate woman are more **n** than the children
Rev 20: 8 they are as **n** as the sands of the sea.
Sir 44:21 he would make him as **n** as the dust of the earth,
1Mc 11:24 and gold and clothing and **n** other gifts.
16: 7 for the cavalry of the enemy were very **n**.

NUN (31)

Ex 33:11 but his young assistant, Joshua son of **N**,
Nu 11:28 And Joshua son of **N**, the assistant of Moses,
13: 8 from the tribe of Ephraim, Hoshea son of **N**;
13:16 And Moses changed the name of Hoshea son of **N**
14: 6 And Joshua son of **N** and Caleb son of Jephunneh,
14:30 of Jephunneh and Joshua son of **N**.
Nu 14:38 But Joshua son of **N** and Caleb son
26:65 of Jephunneh and Joshua son of **N**.
27:18 the LORD said to Moses, "Take Joshua son of **N**,
32:12 of Jephunneh the Kenizzite and Joshua son of **N**,
32:28 the priest, to Joshua son of **N**, and to the heads of
34:17 the priest Eleazar and Joshua son of **N**.
Dt 1:38 Joshua son of **N**, your assistant, shall enter there;
31:23 LORD commissioned Joshua son of **N** and said,
32:44 he and Joshua son of **N**.
34: 9 Joshua son of **N** was full of the spirit of wisdom,
Jos 1: 1 the LORD spoke to Joshua son of **N**,
2: 1 of **N** sent two men secretly from Shittim as spies,
2:23 They crossed over, came to Joshua son of **N**,
6: 6 So Joshua son of **N** summoned the priests and said
14: 1 which the priest Eleazar, and Joshua son of **N**,
17: 4 before the priest Eleazar and Joshua son of **N** and
19:49 an inheritance among them to Joshua son of **N**.
19:51 and Joshua son of **N** and the heads of the families
21: 1 to Joshua son of **N** and to the heads of the families
24:29 After these things Joshua son of **N**,
Jdg 2: 8 Joshua son of **N**, the servant of the LORD,
1Ki 16:34 which he spoke by Joshua son of **N**.
1Ch 7:27 **N** his son, Joshua his son.
Ne 8:17 the days of Jeshua son of **N** to that day the people
Sir 46: 1 Joshua son of **N** was mighty in war,

NURSE (18) [NURSED, NURSES, NURSES', NURSING, NURSINGS]

Ge 21: 7 to Abraham that Sarah would **n** children?
24:59 So they sent away their sister Rebekah and her **n**
35: 8 And Deborah, Rebekah's **n**, died,
Ex 2: 7 get you a **n** from the Hebrew women to **n** the child
2: 9 "Take this child and **n** it for me,
Nu 11:12 as a **n** carries a sucking child,'
Ru 4:16 and laid him in her bosom, and became his **n**.
2Sa 4: 4 His **n** picked him up and fled;
1Ki 3:21 When I rose in the morning to **n** my son,
2Ki 11: 2 she put him and his **n** in a bedroom.
2Ch 22:11 she put him and his **n** in a bedroom.
Isa 66:11 that you may **n** and be satisfied
66:12 and you shall **n** and be carried on her arm,
La 4: 3 the jackals offer the breast and **n** their young,
1Th 2: 7 like a **n** tenderly caring for her own children.
2Es 1:28 or a mother her daughters or a **n** her children,
2:25 "Good **n**, nourish your children;

NURSED (8) [NURSE]

Ex 2: 9 So the woman took the child and **n** it.
Dt 32:13 he **n** him with honey from the crags,
1Sa 1:23 So the woman remained and **n** her son,
SS 8: 1 who **n** at my mother's breast!
Lk 11:27 that bore you and the breasts that **n** you!"
23:29 and the breasts that never **n**.'
Wis 7: 4 I was **n** with care in swaddling cloths.
2Mc 7:27 and **n** you for three years,

NURSES (1) [NURSE]

3Mc 1:20 and **n** abandoned even newborn children here

NURSES' (1) [NURSE]

Isa 60: 4 your daughters shall be carried on their **n'** arms.

NURSING (10) [NURSE]

Ge 33:13 which are **n**, are a care to me;
Dt 32:25 **n** child and old gray head.
Ps 78:71 from tending the **n** ewes he brought him to be
Isa 11: 8 The **n** child shall play over the hole of the asp,
49:15 Can a woman forget her **n** child,
49:23 and their queens your **n** mothers.
Mt 21:16 of infants and **n** babies you have prepared praise
24:19 and to those who are **n** infants in those days!
Mk 13:17 and to those who are **n** infants in those days!
Lk 21:23 and to those who are **n** infants in those days!

NURSINGS (1) [NURSE]

4Mc 16: 7 fruitless nurturings and wretched **n**!

NURTURE (3) [NURTURED, NURTURINGS]

3Mc 5:32 not for an affection arising from our **n** in common
4Mc 13:22 from this common **n** and daily companionship,
15:13 **n** and indomitable suffering by mothers!

NURTURED (2) [NURTURE]

Bar 4:11 With joy I **n** them, but I sent them away
2Es 8:12 You have **n** it in your righteousness,

NURTURINGS (1) [NURTURE]

4Mc 16: 7 fruitless **n** and wretched nursings!

NUT (1) [NUTS]

SS 6:11 I went down to the **n** orchard,

NUTS (1) [NUT]

Ge 43:11 gum, resin, pistachio **n**, and almonds.

NYMPHA (1)

Col 4:15 and to **N** and the church in her house.

O

O (1304) [OH] See Index of Articles Etc.

O'CLOCK‡ (13)

Mt 20: 3 When he went out about nine **o**,
20: 5 he went out again about noon and about three **o**,
20: 6 And about five **o** he went out
20: 9 When those hired about five **o** came,
27:46 And about three **o** Jesus cried with a loud voice,
Mk 15:25 It was nine **o** in the morning
15:34 At three **o** Jesus cried out with a loud voice, "Eloi,
Jn 1:39 It was about four **o** in the afternoon.
Ac 2:15 for it is only nine **o** in the morning.
3: 1 at three **o** in the afternoon.
10: 3 One afternoon at about three **o** he had a vision
10:30 "Four days ago at this very hour, at three **o**,
23:23 "Get ready to leave by nine **o** tonight for Caesarea

OAK‡ (23) [OAKS]

Ge 12: 6 through the land to the place at Shechem, to the **o**
35: 4 and Jacob hid them under the **o** that was
35: 8 died, and she was buried under an **o** below Bethel.
Dt 11:30 opposite Gilgal, beside the **o** of Moreh.
Jos 19:33 from the **o** in Zaanannim, and Adami-nekeb,
24:26 and set it up there under the **o** in the sanctuary of
Jdg 6:11 of the LORD came and sat under the **o** at Ophrah,
6:19 in a pot, and brought them to him under the **o**
9: 6 by the **o** of the pillar at Shechem.
1Sa 10: 3 on from there further and come to the **o** of Tabor;
2Sa 18: 9 mule went under the thick branches of a great **o**.
18: 9 His head caught fast in the **o**,
18:10 and told Joab, "I saw Absalom hanging in an **o**."
18:14 while he was still alive in the **o**.
1Ki 13:14 and found him sitting under an **o** tree.
1Ch 10:12 they buried their bones under the **o** in Jabesh,
Isa 1:30 For you shall be like an **o** whose leaf withers,
6:13 like a terebinth or an **o** whose stump remains
44:14 a holm tree or an **o** and lets it grow strong among
Eze 6:13 under every green tree, and under every leafy **o**,
Hos 4:13 and make offerings upon the hills, under **o**,
Sus 1:58 He answered, "Under an evergreen **o**."
2Es 14: 1 On the third day, while I was sitting under an **o**,

OAKS‡ (11) [OAK]

Ge 13:18 and came and settled by the **o** of Mamre,
14:13 who was living by the **o** of Mamre the Amorite,
18: 1 LORD appeared to Abraham by the **o** of Mamre,
Ps 29: 9 The voice of the LORD causes the **o** to whirl,
Isa 1:29 be ashamed of the **o** in which you delighted;
2:13 and against all the **o** of Bashan;
57: 5 with lust among the **o**, under every green tree;
61: 3 They will be called **o** of righteousness,
Eze 27: 6 From **o** of Bashan they made your oars;
Am 2: 9 and who was as strong as **o**;
Zec 11: 2 Wail, **o** of Bashan, for the thick forest has been

OAR (1) [OARS, STEERING-OARS]

Eze 27:29 down from their ships come all that handle the **o**.

OARS (3) [OAR]

Isa 33:21 where no galley with **o** can go,
Eze 27: 6 From oaks of Bashan they made your **o**;
Mk 6:48 When he saw that they were straining at the **o**

OATH‡ (104) [OATHS]

Ge 21:31 because there both of them swore an **o**.
24: 8 then you will be free from this **o** of mine;
24:41 Then you will be free from my **o**;
24:41 you will be free from my **o**.'
26: 3 the **o** that I swore to your father Abraham.
26:28 so we say, let there be an **o** between you and us,
50: 5 My father made me swear an **o**;
Ex 13:19 the bones of Joseph who had required a solemn **o**
22:11 an **o** before the LORD shall decide between
22:11 the owner shall accept the **o**,
Lev 5: 4 Or when any of you utter aloud a rash **o** for a bad
5: 4 whatever people utter in an **o**,
Nu 5:19 Then the priest shall make her take an **o**, saying,
5:21 the priest make the woman take the **o** of the curse
5:21 an execration and an **o** among your people,
11:12 the land that you promised on **o** to their ancestors?
30: 2 or swears an **o** to bind himself by a pledge,
30:10 or bound herself by a pledge with an **o**,
30:13 Any vow or any binding **o** to deny herself,
Dt 6:23 the land that he promised on **o** to our ancestors.
7: 8 the LORD loved you and kept the **o** that he swore
8: 1 that the LORD promised on **o** to your ancestors.
9: 5 to fulfill the promise that the LORD made on **o**
29:12 by an **o**, which the LORD your God is making
29:14 I am making this covenant, sworn by an **o**,
29:19 the words of this **o** and bless themselves, thinking
31:20 which I promised on **o** to their ancestors,
31:21 into the land that I promised them on **o**."
Jos 2:17 from this **o** that you have made us swear to you
2:20 be released from this **o** that you made us swear
Jos 6:26 Joshua then pronounced this **o**, saying,
9:15 leaders of the congregation swore an **o** to them.
9:20 because of the **o** that we swore to them."
Jdg 21: 5 For a solemn **o** had been taken
1Sa 14:24 He had laid an **o** on the troops, saying,
14:26 to their mouths, for they feared the **o**.
14:27 not heard his father charge the troops with the **o**;
14:28 "Your father strictly charged the troops with an **o**,
2Sa 19:23 And the king gave him his **o**.
21: 7 of the **o** of the LORD that was between them,
1Ki 2:43 Why then have you not kept your **o** to the LORD
8:31 against a neighbor and is given an **o** to swear,
18:10 he would require an **o** of the kingdom or nation,
2Ki 11: 4 and put them under **o** in the house of the LORD;
2Ch 6:22 and is required to take an **o** and comes and swears
15:14 They took an **o** to the LORD with a loud voice,
15:15 All Judah rejoiced over the **o**;
Ne 5:12 made them take an **o** to do as they had promised.
6:18 For many in Judah were bound by **o** to him,
10:29 enter into a curse and an **o** to walk in God's law,
13:25 and I made them take an **o** in the name of God,
Ps 15: 4 who stand by their **o** even to their hurt;
119:106 I have sworn an **o** and confirmed it,
132:11 a sure **o** from which he will not turn back:
Ecc 8: 2 the king's command because of your sacred **o**.
9: 2 those who swear are like those who shun an **o**.
Isa 65:16 and whoever takes an **o** in the land shall swear by
Jer 11: 5 I may perform the **o** that I swore to your ancestors,
38:16 King Zedekiah swore an **o** in secret to Jeremiah,
Eze 16:59 you who have despised the **o**,
17:13 under **o** (he had taken away the chief men of
17:16 whose **o** he despised, and whose covenant
17:18 Because he despised the **o** and broke the covenant,
17:19 surely return upon his head my **o** that he despised,
Da 9:11 So the curse and the **o** written in the law of Moses,
Zec 8:17 against one another, and love no false **o**;
Mt 14: 7 on **o** to grant her whatever she might ask.
23:16 by the gold of the sanctuary is bound by the **o**.'
23:18 by the gift that is on the altar is bound by the **o**.'
26:63 "I put you under **o** before the living God,
26:72 Again he denied it with an **o**,
26:74 Then he began to curse, and he swore an **o**,
Mk 14:71 But he began to curse, and he swore an **o**,
Lk 1:73 the **o** that he swore to our ancestor Abraham,
Ac 2:30 he knew that God had sworn with an **o** to him
23:12 and bound themselves by an **o** neither to eat
23:14 by an **o** to taste no food until we have killed Paul.
23:21 They have bound themselves by an **o** neither to eat
Heb 6:16 **o** given as confirmation puts an end to all dispute.
6:17 he guaranteed it by an **o**,
7:20 This was confirmed with an **o**;
7:20 who became priests took their office without an **o**,
7:21 but this one became a priest with an **o**, because of
7:28 but the word of the **o**,
Jas 5:12 either by heaven or by earth or by any other **o**,
Tob 8:20 for Tobias and swore on **o** to him in these words:
9: 3 You are witness to the **o** Raguel has sworn,
9: 3 and I cannot violate his **o**."
Jdt 8: 9 and how he promised them under **o** to surrender
8:11 even sworn and pronounced this **o** between God
8:30 and made us take an **o** that we cannot break.
Sir 23:11 if he swears a false **o**, he will not be justified,
41:19 Be ashamed of breaking an **o** or agreement,
44:21 Therefore the Lord assured him with an **o** that
1Mc 6:61 the king and the commanders gave them their **o**.
6:62 the **o** he had sworn and gave orders to tear down
7:15 to them and swore this **o** to them,
7:18 for they have violated the agreement and the **o**
7:35 and in anger he swore this **o**,
2Mc 14:32 When they declared on **o** that they did not know
14:33 toward the sanctuary, and swore this **o**:
1Es 1:48 he broke his **o** and rebelled;
8:93 Let us take an **o** to the Lord about this,
3Mc 5:42 an irrevocable **o** that he would send them to death

OATHS‡ (15) [OATH]

Ge 26:31 In the morning they rose early and exchanged **o**;
Isa 33: 8 The treaty is broken, its **o** are despised,
Eze 21:23 they have sworn solemn **o**;
Hos 10: 4 with empty **o** they make covenants,
Mt 14: 9 yet out of regard for his **o** and for the guests,
Mk 6:26 yet out of regard for his **o** and for the guests,
Wis 12:21 to whose ancestors you gave **o** and covenants full
14:29 in lifeless idols they swear wicked **o** and expect
18: 6 that they might rejoice in sure knowledge of the **o**
18:22 to the **o** and covenants given to our ancestors.
Sir 23: 9 Do not accustom your mouth to **o**,
23:11 The one who swears many **o** is full of iniquity,
2Mc 7:24 but promised with **o** that he would make him rich
15:10 the perfidy of the Gentiles and their violation of **o**.
4Mc 5:29 nor will I transgress the sacred **o** of my ancestors

OBADIAH (23)

1Ki 18: 3 Ahab summoned **O**, who was in charge of
18: 3 (Now **O** revered the LORD greatly;
18: 4 **O** took a hundred prophets,
18: 5 Then Ahab said to **O**, "Go through the land to all
18: 6 and **O** went in another direction by himself.
18: 7 As **O** was on the way, Elijah met him;
18: 7 **O** recognized him, fell on his face, and said,
18:16 So **O** went to meet Ahab, and told him;
1Ch 3:21 his son Arnan, his son **O**, his son Shecaniah.
7: 3 And the sons of Izrahiah: Michael, **O**, Joel,
8:38 Azrikam, Bocheru, Ishmael, Sheariah, **O**,
9:16 and **O** son of Shemaiah, son of Galal, son
9:44 Azrikam, Bocheru, Ishmael, Sheariah, **O**,
1Ch 12: 9 Ezer the chief, **O** second, Eliab third,
27:19 for Zebulun, Ishmaiah son of **O**;
2Ch 17: 7 Ben-hail, **O**, Zechariah, Nethanel, and Micaiah,
34:12 and **O**, of the sons of Merari, along with Zechariah
Ezr 8: 9 Of the descendants of Joab, **O** son of Jehiel,
Ne 10: 5 Harim, Meremoth, **O**,
12:25 Mattaniah, Bakbukiah, **O**, Meshullam, Talmon,
Ob 1: 1 The vision of **O**. Thus says the Lord GOD
1Es 8:35 Of the descendants of Joab, **O** son of Jehiel,
2Es 1:39 and Hosea and Amos and Micah and Joel and **O**

OBAL (1)

Ge 10:28 **O**, Abimael, Sheba,

OBDURACY See Index to Footnotes

OBED (14)

Ru 4:17 They named him **O**; he became the father of Jesse,
4:21 Salmon of Boaz, Boaz of **O**,
4:22 **O** of Jesse, and Jesse of David.
1Ch 2:12 Boaz of **O**, **O** of Jesse.
2:37 the father of Ephlal, and Ephlal of **O**.
2:38 **O** became the father of Jehu, and Jehu of Azariah.
11:47 Eliel, and **O**, and Jaasiel the Mezobaite.
26: 7 The sons of Shemaiah: Othni, Rephael, **O**,
2Ch 23: 1 Ishmael son of Jehohanan, Azariah son of **O**,
Mt 1: 5 Boaz the father of **O** by Ruth, and **O** the father of
Lk 3:32 son of **O**, son of Boaz, son of Sala,
1Es 8:32 Of the descendants of Adin, **O** son of Jonathan,

OBED-EDOM (19) [OBED-EDOM'S]

2Sa 6:10 instead David took it to the house of **O** the Gittite.
6:11 The ark of the LORD remained in the house of **O**
6:11 and the LORD blessed **O** and all his household.
6:12 the household of **O** and all that belongs to him,
6:12 and brought up the ark of God from the house of **O**
1Ch 13:13 he took it instead to the house of **O** the Gittite.
13:14 with the household of **O** in his house three months,
13:14 and the LORD blessed the household of **O** and all
15:18 and Mikneiah, and the gatekeepers **O** and Jeiel.
15:21 Eliphelehu, Mikneiah, **O**, Jeiel,
15:24 **O** and Jehiah also were to be gatekeepers for
15:25 of the covenant of the LORD from the house of **O**
16: 5 Eliab, Benaiah, **O**, and Jeiel, with harps and lyres;
16:38 and also **O** and his sixty-eight kinsfolk;
16:38 while **O** son of Jeduthun and Hosah were to
26: 4 **O** had sons: Shemaiah the firstborn,
26: 8 All these, sons of **O** with their sons and brothers,
26: 8 for the service; sixty-two of **O**.
2Ch 25:24 that were found in the house of God, and **O**

OBED-EDOM'S (1) [OBED-EDOM]

1Ch 26:15 **O** came out for the south,

OBEDIENCE (16) [OBEY]

Ge 49:10 and the **o** of the peoples is his.
Ro 1: 5 to bring about the **o** of faith among all the Gentiles
5:19 the one man's **o** the many will be made righteous.
6:16 either of sin, which leads to death, or of **o**,
15:18 through me to win **o** from the Gentiles,
16:19 For while your **o** is known to all,
16:26 to bring about the **o** of faith—
2Co 7:15 as he remembers the **o** of all of you,
9:13 by your **o** to the confession of the gospel of Christ
10: 6 every disobedience when your **o** is complete.
Phm 1:21 Confident of your **o**, I am writing to you,
Heb 5: 8 he learned **o** through what he suffered;
1Pe 1:22 Now that you have purified your souls by your **o**
4Mc 5:16 there is no compulsion more powerful than our **o**
9: 2 unless we should practice ready **o** to the law and
15: 9 of the nobility of her sons and their ready **o** to

OBEDIENT‡ (15) [OBEY]

Ex 24: 7 LORD has spoken we will do, and we will be **o**."
Ps 103:20 ones who do his bidding, **o** to his spoken word.
Isa 1:19 If you are willing and **o**, you shall eat the good of
Lk 2:51 and came to Nazareth, and was **o** to them
Ac 6: 7 a great many of the priests became **o** to the faith.
Ro 6:16 if you present yourselves to anyone as **o** slaves,
6:17 have become **o** from the heart to the form
2Co 2: 9 and to know whether you are **o** in everything.
Php 2: 8 he humbled himself and became **o** to the point
Tit 3: 1 to be **o**, to be ready for every good work,
1Pe 1: 2 and sanctified by the Spirit to be **o** to Jesus Christ
1:14 Like **o** children, do not be conformed to the desires
Sir 7:23 and make them **o** from their youth.
LtJ 6:60 and when sent to do a service, they are **o**.
2Es 7:22 they were not **o**, and spoke against him;

OBEISANCE (24)

Ge 43:28 And they bowed their heads and did **o**.
1Sa 24: 8 with his face to the ground, and did **o**.
28:14 with his face to the ground, and did **o**.
2Sa 1: 2 he came to David, he fell to the ground and did **o**.
9: 6 and fell on his face and did **o**.
9: 8 He did **o** and said, "What is your servant,
14: 4 she fell on her face to the ground and did **o**,
14:22 with his face to the ground and did **o**, and blessed
15: 5 Whenever people came near to do **o** to him,
16: 4 now yours." Ziba said, "I do **o**;
1Ki 1:16 Bathsheba bowed and did **o** to the king,
1:23 he came in before the king, he did **o** to the king,
1:31 and did **o** to the king, and said,

1Ki 1:53 He came to do o to King Solomon;
1Ch 21:21 and did o to David with his face to the ground.
2Ch 24:17 of Jehoiada the officials of Judah came and did o
Est 3: 2 the king's gate bowed down and did o to Haman;
3: 2 But Mordecai did not bow down or do o.
3: 5 that Mordecai did not bow down or do o to him,
Jdt 10:23 She prostrated herself and did o to him,
14: 7 and did o to her, and said,
AdE 3: 2 So all who were at court used to do o to Haman,
3: 2 Mordecai, however, did not do o.
3: 5 that Mordecai was not doing o to him,

OBEISANCE (KJV) See also BOWED, BOWING

OBELISKS (1)

Jer 43:13 He shall break the o of Heliopolis,

OBEY‡ (140) [OBEDIENCE, OBEDIENT, OBEYED, OBEYING, OBEYS]

Ge 27: 8 therefore, my son, o my word as I command you.
27:13 only o my word, and go, get them for me."
27:43 Now therefore, my son, o my voice;
Ex 19: 5 if you o my voice and keep my covenant,
Lev 26:14 But if you will not o me,
26:18 And if in spite of this you will not o me,
26:21 If you continue hostile to me, and will not o me,
Nu 27:20 so that all the congregation of the Israelites may o.
Dt 8:20 not o the voice of the LORD your God.
11:27 if you o the commandments of the LORD your God
11:28 not o the commandments of the LORD your God,
12:28 to o all these words that I command you today,
13: 4 his voice you shall o, him you shall serve,
13:18 if you o the voice of the LORD your God
15: 5 if only you will o the LORD your God
21:18 and rebellious son who will not o his father
21:20 He will not o us.
26:17 and his ordinances, and to o him.
27:10 Therefore o the LORD your God,
28: 1 If you will only o the LORD your God,
28: 2 if you o the LORD your God:
28:13 if you o the commandments of
28:15 But if you will not o the LORD your God
28:45 because you did not o the LORD your God,
28:62 because you did not o the LORD your God.
30: 2 and your children o him with all your heart and
30: 8 Then you shall again o the LORD,
30:10 when you o the LORD your God
30:16 If you o the commandments of the LORD your God
Jos 1:17 in all things, so we will o you.
24:24 LORD our God we will serve, and him we will o."
Jdg 3: 4 know whether Israel would o the commandments
1Sa 15:19 Why then did you not o the voice of the LORD?
15:22 Surely, to o is better than sacrifice,
28:18 Because you did not o the voice of the LORD,
1Ki 6:12 if you will walk in my statutes, o my ordinances,
2Ki 10: 6 and if you are ready to o me,
18:12 not o the voice of the LORD their God
22:13 our ancestors did not o the words of this book,
Ezr 7:26 not o the law of your God and the law of the king,
Ne 9:16 and did not o your commandments;
9:17 they refused to o, and were not mindful of
9:29 and did not o your commandments,
9:29 and stiffened their neck and would not o.
Ps 106:25 and did not o the voice of the LORD.
Pr 30:17 scorns to o a mother will be pecked out by the
Isa 11:14 and the Ammonites shall o them.
42:24 and whose law they would not o?
Jer 7:23 But this command I gave them, "O my voice,
7:24 Yet they did not o or incline their ear, but,
7:28 that did not o the voice of the LORD their God,
11: 7 even to this day, saying, O my voice.
11: 8 Yet they did not o or incline their ear,
22: 4 For if you will indeed o this word,
26:13 and o the voice of the LORD your God,
32:23 But they did not o your voice or follow your law;
35:13 Can you not learn a lesson and o my words?
35:15 But you did not incline your ear or o me.
38:20 Just o the voice of the LORD in what I say
40: 3 against the LORD and did not o his voice.
42: 6 we will o the voice of the LORD our God
42: 6 that it may go well with us when we o the voice of
43: 4 the forces and all the people did not o the voice of
43: 7 for they did not o the voice of the LORD.
44:23 the LORD and did not o the voice of the LORD
Eze 11:20 and keep my ordinances and o them.
33:31 but they will not o them.
Da 7:27 and all dominions shall serve and o them."
9:11 and turned aside, refusing to o your voice.
Joel 2:11 Numberless are those who o his command.
Mic 5:15 on the nations that did not o.
Zec 6:15 This will happen if you diligently o the voice of
Mt 8:27 that even the winds and the sea o him?"
28:20 to o everything that I have commanded you.
Mk 1:27 even the unclean spirits, and they o him."
4:41 that even the wind and the sea o him?"
Lk 8:25 even the winds and the water, and they o him?"
11:28 the word of God and o it!"
17: 6 and planted in the sea,' and it would o you.
Ac 5:29 "We must o God rather than any human authority.
5:32 Holy Spirit whom God has given to those who o
7:39 Our ancestors were unwilling to o him;
Ro 2: 8 while for those who are self-seeking and who o
2:25 Circumcision indeed is of value if you o the law;
Ro 6:12 to make you o their passions.
6:16 you are slaves of the one whom you o,
2Co 10: 5 and we take every thought captive to o Christ.
Gal 3:10 not observe and o all the things written in
5: 3 be circumcised that he is obliged to o
6:13 Even the circumcised do not themselves o the law,
Eph 6: 1 Children, o your parents in the Lord,
6: 5 o your earthly masters with fear and trembling,
6: 5 in singleness of heart, as you o Christ;
Col 3:20 Children, o your parents in everything,
3:22 Slaves, o your earthly masters in everything,
2Th 1: 8 not know God and on those who do not o
3:14 of those who do not o what we say in this letter;
Heb 5: 9 the source of eternal salvation for all who o him,
13:17 O your leaders and submit to them,
Jas 3: 3 into the mouths of horses to make them o us,
1Pe 3: 1 so that, even if some of them do not o the word,
3:20 who in former times did not o,
4:17 the end for those who do not o the gospel of God?
1Jn 2: 3 if we o his commandments.
2: 4 but does not o his commandments, is a liar,
3:22 we o his commandments and do what pleases him.
3:24 All who o his commandments abide in him,
5: 2 when we love God and o his commandments.
5: 3 love of God is this, that we o his commandments.
Rev 3: 3 Remember then what you received and heard; o it,
AdE 1:12 to o him and would not come with the eunuchs.
Sir 3: 6 and those who honor their mother o the Lord;
4:15 Those who o her will judge the nations,
33:30 and if he does not o, make his fetters heavy.
Bar 2:22 But if you will not o the voice of the Lord and will
2:24 But we did not o your voice,
2:29 "If you will not o my voice,
2:30 For I know that they will not o me,
1Mc 1:50 "And whoever does not o the command of
2:19 that live under the rule of the king o him,
2:19 and have chosen to o his commandments,
2:22 We will not o the king's words by turning aside
2:68 and o the commands of the law."
10:38 to be under one ruler and o no other authority than
12:43 and his troops to o him as they would himself.
2Mc 7:30 I will not o the king's command,
7:30 but I o the command of the law that was given
1Es 4: 3 and whatever he says to them they o.
4:10 All his people and his armies o him.
5:69 For we o your Lord just as you do
8:94 as seems good to you and to all who o the law of
2Es 1:24 You, Judah, would not o me.
4Mc 6: 4 "O the king's commands!"
8: 6 so I can be a benefactor to those who o me.
8:17 to accept kind treatment if we o him,
8:26 when we can live in peace if we o the king?"
10:13 but o the king and save yourself."
12: 4 You too, if you do not o,
12: 6 to influence her to persuade the surviving son to o
18: 1 o this law and exercise piety in every way,

OBEYED‡ (48) [OBEY]

Ge 22:18 because you have o my voice."
26: 5 because Abraham o my voice and kept my charge,
28: 7 and that Jacob had o his father and his mother
Nu 14:22 and have not o my voice,
Dt 26:14 I have o the LORD my God,
34: 9 and the Israelites o him, doing as the LORD
Jos 1:17 Just as we o Moses in all things,
22: 2 and have o me in all that I have commanded you;
Jdg 2: 2 But you have not o my command.
2:17 who had o the commandments of the LORD;
2:20 and have not o my voice,
1Sa 15:20 "I have o the voice of the LORD,
15:24 because I feared the people and o their voice.
2Sa 22:45 as soon as they heard of me, they o me.
1Ki 20:36 "Because you have not o the voice of the LORD,
2Ki 18:12 they neither listened nor o.
1Ch 29:23 he prospered, and all Israel o him.
Est 2:20 for Esther o Mordecai just as
Ps 18:44 As soon as they heard of me they o me;
Jer 3:13 and have not o my voice, says the LORD.
3:25 we have not o the voice of the LORD our God."
9:13 that I set before them, and have not o my voice,
22:21 for you have not o my voice.
25: 8 Because you have not o my words,
34:10 And they o, all the officials and all
34:10 they o and set them free.
34:17 not o me by granting a release to your neighbors
35: 8 We have o the charge of our ancestor Jonadab son
35:10 and have o and done all that our ancestor
35:14 for they have o their ancestor's command.
35:14 and you have not o me.
35:16 but this people has not o me.
35:18 Because you have o the command
42:21 not o the voice of the LORD your God
Da 9:10 and have not o the voice of the LORD our God
Hag 1:12 o the voice of the LORD their God,
Ro 10:16 But not all have o the good news;
Php 2:12 my beloved, just as you have always o me,
Heb 11: 8 By faith Abraham o when he was called to set out
1Pe 3: 6 Thus Sarah o Abraham and called him lord.
Jdt 2: 3 that every one who had not o his command should
Bar 2:10 Yet we have not o his voice,
3:33 he called it, and it o him, trembling;
Aza 1: 7 We have not o your commandments,
1Mc 14:43 and that he should be o by all,
1Es 4:12 since he is to be o in this fashion?"
2Es 1: 8 for they have not o my law—
4Mc 15:10 so that they o her even to death in keeping

OBEYING (6) [OBEY]

Dt 9:23 neither trusting him nor o him.
30:20 o him, and holding fast to him;
1Sa 15:22 as in o the voice of the LORD?
1Co 7:19 but o the commandments of God is everything.
Gal 5: 7 who prevented you from o the truth?
AdE 1:15 be done to Queen Vashti for not o the order that

OBEYS (6) [OBEY]

Ecc 8: 5 Whoever o a command will meet no harm,
Isa 50:10 Who among you fears the LORD and o the voice
Jn 9:31 to one who worships him and o his will.
1Jn 2: 5 but whoever o his word, truly in this person
Sir 24:22 Whoever o me will not be put to shame,
Bar 2:31 I will give them a heart that o and ears that hear;

OBIL (1)

1Ch 27:30 Over the camels was O the Ishmaelite.

OBJECT (38) [OBJECTED, OBJECTION, OBJECTIONABLE, OBJECTS]

Nu 35:16 But anyone who strikes another with an iron o,
35:22 or hurls any o without lying in wait,
Dt 28:25 an o of horror to all the kingdoms of the earth.
28:37 You shall become an o of horror, a proverb,
Jos 6:18 and make the camp of Israel an o for destruction,
2Ch 29: 8 and he has made them an o of horror,
Ps 31:11 an o of dread to my acquaintances;
109:25 I am an o of scorn to my accusers;
Jer 6:10 The word of the LORD is to them an o of scorn;
25: 9 and make them an o of horror and of hissing,
25:18 an o of hissing and of cursing, as they are today;
29:18 to be an o of cursing, and horror, and hissing,
42:18 You shall become an o of execration and horror,
44: 8 and become an o of cursing and ridicule among all
44:12 they shall become an o of execration and horror,
49:13 Bozrah shall become an o of horror and ridicule,
49:13 a waste, and an o of cursing;
49:17 Edom shall become an o of horror;
51:37 an o of horror and of hissing, without inhabitant.
51:41 How Babylon has become an o of horror among
51:43 Her cities have become an o of horror,
La 3:14 the o of their taunt-songs all day long.
3:63 see, I am the o of their taunt-songs.
Eze 5:14 Moreover I will make you a desolation and an o
15: 3 a peg from it on which to hang any o?
23:46 and make them an o of terror and of plunder.
36: 3 and you became an o of gossip and slander among
36: 4 a source of plunder and an o of derision to the rest
Mic 6:16 and your inhabitants an o of hissing;
Ro 9:21 the same lump one o for special use and another
2Th 2: 4 and exalts himself above every so-called god or o
Tob 3: 4 and an o of reproach among all the nations
8:10 and we will become an o of ridicule and derision."
Wis 14:20 as an o of worship the one whom shortly
Sir 38:28 and his eyes are on the pattern of the o.
Bar 2: 4 to be an o of scorn and a desolation among all
3Mc 2:28 Those who o to this are to be taken by force
4: 4 perceiving the common o of pity before their eyes,

OBJECTED (1) [OBJECT]

Ac 28:19 But when the Jews o, I was compelled to appeal

OBJECTION (1) [OBJECT]

Ac 10:29 So when I was sent for, I came without o.

OBJECTIONABLE (1) [OBJECT]

Dt 24: 1 not please him because he finds something o

OBJECTS (15) [OBJECT]

Ex 11: 2 and every woman is to ask her neighbor for o
35:22 and signet rings and pendants, all sorts of gold o,
Nu 4:32 by name the o that they are required to carry.
Dt 4:28 o of wood and stone that neither see, nor hear,
1Sa 6:15 in which were the gold o,
1Ki 10:25 o of silver and gold, garments, weaponry, spices,
2Ch 9:24 o of silver and gold, garments, weaponry, spices,
32:27 for shields, and for all kinds of costly o;
Eze 16:39 and take your beautiful o and leave you naked
Ac 17:23 and looked carefully at the o of your worship,
Ro 9:22 with much patience the o of wrath that are made
9:23 the o of mercy, which he has prepared beforehand
Wis 14:21 on o of stone or wood the name that ought not to
15: 6 for such o of hope are those who either make
15:17 for they are better than the o they worship,

OBLATION (3)

1Ki 18:29 on until the time of the offering of the o,
18:36 At the time of the offering of the o,
Aza 1:15 no burnt offering, or sacrifice, or o, or incense,

OBLATION[S] (KJV) See also GIFT, OFFERING[S], PORTION[S], SACRIFICE

OBLATIONS (2) [OBLIGATE]

2Es 1:31 you offer o to me, I will turn my face from you;
3:24 and there to offer you o from what is yours.

OBLIGATE (1) [OBLIGATIONS, OBLIGATED, OBLIGATION, OBLIGATIONS, OBLIGED]
Ne 10:35 We **o** ourselves to bring the first fruits of our soil

OBLIGATED (3) [OBLIGATE]
Nu 30: 6 while **o** by her vows or any thoughtless utterance
30: 8 then he shall nullify the vow by which she was **o**,
30:14 or all her pledges, by which she is **o**;

OBLIGATION (5) [OBLIGATE]
Nu 32:22 that you may return and be free of **o** to the LORD
Ne 10:32 the **o** to charge ourselves yearly one-third of
Isa 33: 8 its oaths are despised, its **o** is disregarded.
Eze 45:17 the **o** of the prince regarding the burnt offerings,
1Co 9:16 for an **o** is laid on me,

OBLIGATIONS (3) [OBLIGATE]
1Mc 8:26 and they shall keep their **o**
8:28 they shall keep these **o** and do so without deceit.
11:33 who are our friends and fulfill their **o** to us,

OBLIGED‡ (4) [OBLIGATE]
1Ch 9:25 in their villages were **o** to come
Gal 5: 3 be circumcised that he is **o** to obey the entire law.
Sir 32: 7 Speak, you who are young, if you are **o** to,
2Mc 8:25 they were **o** to return because the hour was late.

OBLIVION See Index to Footnotes

OBOTH (4)
Nu 21:10 The Israelites set out, and camped in **O**.
21:11 They set out from **O**, and camped at Iye-abarim,
33:43 They set out from Punon and camped at **O**.
33:44 They set out from **O** and camped at Iye-abarim,

OBSCENE (1)
Eph 5: 4 Entirely out of place is **o**, silly, and vulgar talk;

OBSCURE (3) [OBSCURED, OBSCURES, OBSCURITIES]
Isa 33:19 of an **o** speech that you cannot comprehend,
Eze 3: 5 a people of **o** speech and difficult language,
3: 6 of **o** speech and difficult language,

OBSCURED (1) [OBSCURE]
Tob 2:10 the more my vision was **o** by the white films,

OBSCURES (1) [OBSCURE]
Wis 4:12 For the fascination of wickedness **o** what is good,

OBSCURITIES (1) [OBSCURE]
Sir 39: 3 of proverbs and is at home with the **o** of parables.

OBSERVANCE (13) [OBSERVE]
Ex 12:25 as he has promised, you shall keep this **o**.
12:26 'What do you mean by this **o**?'
13: 5 you shall keep this **o** in this month.
Ne 9:29 by the **o** of which a person shall live.
Eze 20:11 by whose **o** everyone shall live.
20:13 by whose **o** everyone shall live;
20:21 by whose **o** everyone shall live;
Ac 16: 4 to them for **o** the decisions that had been reached
3Mc 3: 2 by a report that they hindered others from the **o**
6:36 they instituted the **o** of the aforesaid days as
4Mc 3:20 because of their **o** of the law and were prospering,
4:24 in any way to put an end to the people's **o** of
18: 4 and by reviving **o** of the law in the homeland

OBSERVE (123) [OBSERVANCE, OBSERVED, OBSERVER, OBSERVES, OBSERVING]
Ex 12:14 throughout your generations you shall **o** it as
12:17 You shall **o** the festival of unleavened bread,
12:17 you shall **o** this day throughout your generations
12:24 You shall **o** this rite as a perpetual ordinance
23:15 You shall **o** the festival of unleavened bread;
23:16 You shall **o** the festival of harvest,
23:16 You shall **o** the festival of ingathering at the end
34:11 **O** what I command you today.
34:22 You shall **o** the festival of weeks,
Lev 18: 4 My ordinances you shall **o**
19:37 and **o** them: I am the LORD.
20: 8 Keep my statutes, and **o** them;
20:22 and **o** them, so that the land to which I bring you
22:31 Thus you shall keep my commandments and **o**
23:24 you shall **o** a day of complete rest,
23:36 on the eighth day you shall **o** a holy convocation
25: 2 the land shall **o** a sabbath for the LORD.
25:18 You shall **o** my statutes
26: 3 and keep my commandments and **o** them faithfully,
26:14 and do not **o** all these commandments,
26:15 so that you will not **o** all my commandments,
Nu 15:22 to **o** all these commandments that
Dt 4: 1 and ordinances that I am teaching you to **o**,
4: 5 now teach you statutes and ordinances for you to **o**
4: 6 You must **o** them diligently,
4:13 which he charged you to **o**, that is,
4:14 for you to **o** in the land that you are about to cross
5: 1 you shall learn them and **o** them diligently.
Dt 5:12 **O** the sabbath day and keep it holy,
6: 1 to **o** in the land that you are about to cross into
6: 3 Hear therefore, O Israel, and **o** them diligently,
6:24 the LORD commanded us to **o** all these statutes,
6:25 If we diligently **o** this entire commandment before
7:11 Therefore, **o** diligently the commandment—
8: 1 that I command you today you must diligently **o**,
11:22 If you will diligently **o** this entire commandment
11:32 you must diligently **o** all the statutes
12: 1 and ordinances that you must diligently **o** in
12:32 You must diligently **o** everything
16: 1 **O** the month of Abib by keeping the passover for
16:12 and diligently **o** these statutes.
19: 9 provided you diligently **o** this entire commandment
24: 8 you shall carefully **o** whatever the levitical priests
26:16 to **o** these statutes and ordinances;
26:16 so **o** them diligently with all your heart and
28:58 If you do not diligently **o** all the words of this law
29: 9 Therefore diligently **o** the words of this covenant,
29:29 to **o** all the words of this law.
30:12 and get it for us so that we may hear it and **o** it?"
30:13 and get it for us so that we may hear it and **o** it?"
30:14 it is in your mouth and in your heart for you to **o**.
31:12 to fear the LORD your God and to **o** diligently all
32:46 they may diligently **o** all the words of this law.
Jos 22: 5 to **o** the commandment and instruction that Moses
23: 6 be very steadfast to **o** and do all that is written in
Jdg 13:14 She is to **o** everything that I commanded her."
Ru 3: 4 When he lies down, **o** the place where he lies;
1Ki 11:10 but he did not **o** what the LORD commanded.
2Ki 17:37 you shall always be careful to **o**.
1Ch 22:13 Then you will prosper if you are careful to **o**
28: 8 **o** and search out all the commandments of
2Ch 23: 6 but all the other people shall **o** the instructions of
Ne 10:29 and to **o** and do all the commandments of
Est 9:27 to **o** these two days every year,
Job 35: 5 **o** the clouds, which are higher than you.
39: 1 Do you **o** the calving of the deer?
Ps 78:56 They did not **o** his decrees,
105:45 that they might keep his statutes and **o** his laws.
106: 3 Happy are those who **o** justice,
119: 8 I will **o** your statutes; do not utterly forsake me.
119:17 so that I may live and **o** your word.
119:33 the way of your statutes, and I will **o** it to the end.
119:34 I may keep your law and **o** it with my whole heart.
119:106 to **o** your righteous ordinances.
119:146 I cry to you; save me, that I may **o** your decrees.
Pr 23: 1 **o** carefully what is before you,
23:26 give me your heart, and let your eyes **o** my ways.
Isa 42:20 He sees many things, but does not **o** them;
Jer 8: 7 swallow, and crane **o** the time of their coming;
Eze 18: 9 and is careful to **o** my ordinances,
18:19 and has been careful to **o** all my statutes,
20:13 not **o** my statutes but rejected my ordinances,
20:16 not **o** my statutes, and profaned my sabbaths;
20:18 the statutes of your parents, nor **o** their ordinances,
20:19 and be careful to **o** my ordinances,
20:21 and were not careful to **o** my ordinances,
36:27 and be careful to **o** my ordinances.
37:24 and be careful to **o** my statutes.
43:11 and write it down in their sight, so that they may **o**
Da 1:13 deal with your servants according to what you **o**."
Mk 7: 4 there are also many other traditions that they **o**,
Jn 9:16 for he does not **o** the sabbath."
Ac 16:21 that are not lawful for us as Romans to adopt or **o**."
21:21 not to circumcise their children or **o** the customs.
21:24 but that you yourself **o** and guard the law.
Ro 14: 6 Those who **o** the day, **o** it in honor of the Lord.
Gal 3:10 not **o** and obey all the things written in the book of
Php 3:17 and **o** those who live according to
Heb 13: 9 which have not benefited those who **o** them.
Tob 10: 7 that Raguel had sworn to **o** for his daughter,
AdE 8:11 the Jews in every city to **o** their own laws,
9:27 upon all who would join them, to **o** it without fail.
10:13 So they will **o** these days in the month of Adar,
16:22 "Therefore you shall **o** this with all good cheer as
Wis 6:10 For they will be made holy who **o** holy things
Sir 11:30 and like spies they **o** your weakness;
24:34 **O** that I have not labored for myself alone,
1Mc 1:13 who authorized them to **o** the ordinances of
2:61 "And so **o**, from generation to generation,
2:67 You shall rally around you all who **o** the law,
2Mc 6: 6 nor **o** the festivals of their ancestors,
6:11 in order to **o** the seventh day secretly,
10: 8 of the Jews should **o** these days every year.
13:23 yielded and swore to **o** all their rights,
15: 4 who ordered us to **o** the seventh day,"
3Mc 7:19 to **o** these days as a joyous festival during the time
2Es 7:21 and what they should do to avoid punishment.
9:32 they did not keep it and did not **o** the statutes;
15:24 and do not **o** my commandments, says the Lord;
4Mc 1:30 **O** now, first of all, that rational judgment
5: 7 a philosopher when you **o** the religion of the Jews.
14:13 **O** how complex is a mother's love

OBSERVED‡ (29) [OBSERVE]
Ge 50:10 he **o** a time of mourning for his father seven days.
Ex 3: 7 "I have **o** the misery of my people who are
27:21 be **o** throughout their generations by the Israelites.
Dt 33: 9 For they **o** your word, and kept your covenant.
Jos 22: 2 "You have **o** all that Moses the servant of
Jdg 18: 7 they **o** the people who were there living securely,
1Sa 1:12 before the LORD, Eli **o** her mouth.
1Ki 10: 4 queen of Sheba had **o** all the wisdom of Solomon,
2Ch 7: 9 for they had **o** the dedication of
9: 3 the queen of Sheba had **o** the wisdom of Solomon,
Est 5: 9 **o** that he neither rose nor trembled before him,
9:31 of Purim should be **o** at their appointed seasons,
Pr 7: 7 I **o** among the youths, a young man without sense,
Ecc 8: 9 All this I **o**, applying my mind to all that is done
Jer 33:24 Have you not **o** how these people say,
Da 1:15 of ten days it was **o** that they appeared better
Mt 2: 2 For we **o** his star at its rising,
Lk 17:20 of God is not coming with things that can be **o**;
2Ti 3:10 Now you have **o** my teaching, my conduct,
Jdt 10:14 When the men heard her words, and **o** her face—
AdE 9:28 These days of Purim were to be **o** for all time,
1Mc 4:35 of his troops and **o** the boldness that inspired those
4:59 of dedication of the altar should be **o** with joy
13:48 and settled in it those who **o** the law.
2Mc 3: 1 and the laws were strictly **o** because of the piety of
9:23 but I **o** that my father,
3Mc 1:27 When those who were around him **o** this,
6:17 the Jews **o** this they raised great cries to heaven so
2Es 6:32 and has also **o** the purity that you have maintained

OBSERVER (1) [OBSERVE]
Wis 1: 6 and a true **o** of their hearts,

OBSERVES (5) [OBSERVE]
Ps 33:15 the hearts of them all, and **o** all their deeds.
Pr 21:12 The Righteous One **o** the house of the wicked;
Ecc 11: 4 Whoever **o** the wind will not sow;
Eze 18:17 **o** my ordinances, and follows my statutes;
Sir 23: 7 the one who **o** it will never be caught.

OBSERVING (20) [OBSERVE]
Ex 31:16 **o** the sabbath throughout their generations,
Dt 7:12 If you heed these ordinances, by diligently **o** them,
15: 5 by diligently **o** this entire commandment
17:10 diligently **o** everything they instruct you.
17:19 diligently **o** all the words of this law
27:10 **o** his commandments and his statutes
27:26 not uphold the words of this law by **o** them."
28: 1 by diligently **o** all his commandments
28:13 I am commanding you today, by diligently **o** them,
28:15 by diligently **o** all his commandments and decrees,
28:45 by **o** the commandments and the decrees
30: 8 the LORD, **o** all his commandments
30:10 the LORD your God by **o** his commandments
30:16 walking in his ways, and **o** his commandments,
Mk 7: 3 thus **o** the tradition of the elders;
Gal 4:10 You are **o** special days, and months, and seasons,
Col 2:16 in matters of food and drink or of **o** festivals,
2Mc 15:21 **o** the masses that were in front of him and
3Mc 2:26 many of his friends, intently **o** the king's purpose,
4Mc 4:23 a decree that if any of them were found **o**

OBSESSED (1)
Job 36:17 "But you are **o** with the case of the wicked;

OBSOLETE (2)
Heb 8:13 he has made the first one **o**.
8:13 what is **o** and growing old will soon disappear.

OBSTACLE (4)
1Co 9:12 but we endure anything rather than put an **o** in
2Co 6: 3 We are putting no **o** in anyone's way,
10: 5 and every proud **o** raised up against
Sir 32:20 and do not stumble at an **o** twice.

OBSTINACY (1) [OBSTINATE]
Sir 28:10 and in proportion to the **o**, so will strife increase;

OBSTINATE (1) [OBSTINACY]
Isa 48: 4 Because I know that you are **o**,

OBSTRUCTION (1)
Isa 57:14 remove every **o** from my people's way."

OBTAIN (29) [OBTAINED, OBTAINING, OBTAINS]
Ge 16: 2 it may be that I shall **o** children by her."
24:48 who had led me by the right way to **o** the daughter
Pr 12: 2 The good **o** favor from the LORD,
12:27 but the diligent **o** precious wealth.
28:13 and forsakes them will **o** mercy.
29:23 but one who is lowly in spirit will **o** honor.
Isa 29:19 The meek shall **o** fresh joy in the LORD,
35:10 they shall **o** joy and gladness,
51:11 they shall **o** joy and gladness,
La 2: 9 and her prophets **o** no vision from the LORD.
Da 11:21 he shall come in without warning and **o**
Ac 8:20 you thought you could **o** God's gift with money!
Ro 8:21 and will **o** the freedom of the glory of the children
11: 7 Israel failed to **o** what it was seeking.
2Th 2:14 that you may **o** the glory of our Lord Jesus Christ.
2Ti 2:10 so that they may also **o** the salvation that is
Heb 11:35 in order to **o** a better resurrection.
12:15 See to it that no one fails to **o** the grace of God;
Jas 4: 2 And you covet something and cannot **o** it;
Tob 5: 2 but how can I **o** the money from him,
Wis 7:14 those who get it **o** friendship with God,
Sir 4:16 their descendants will also **o** her.
15: 1 and whoever holds to the law will **o** wisdom.
15: 7 foolish will not **o** her, and sinners will not see her.
1Mc 9:70 to him to make peace with him and **o** release of
14: 1 and marched into Media to **o** help,

2Es 4:24 and we are not worthy to **o** mercy.
5:12 At that time people shall hope but not **o;**
14:34 and after death you shall **o** mercy.

OBTAINED‡ (17) [OBTAIN]

Nu 32:18 until all the Israelites have **o** their inheritance.
Dt 26:17 Today you have **o** the LORD's agreement:
26:18 Today the LORD has **o** your agreement:
Jos 19: 9 for them, the tribe of Simeon **o** an inheritance
Ac 20:28 of God that he **o** with the blood of his own Son.
Ro 5: 2 through whom we have **o** access to this grace
11: 7 The elect **o** it, but the rest were hardened,
Eph 1:11 In Christ we have also **o** an inheritance,
Php 3:12 that I have already **o** this or have already reached
Heb 6:15 having patiently endured, **o** the promise.
8: 6 But Jesus has now **o** a more excellent ministry,
11:33 **o** promises, shut the mouths of lions,
1Jn 5:15 we know that we have **o** the requests made of him.
Sir 46: 9 and his children **o** it for an inheritance,
2Mc 4: 7 Jason the brother of Onias **o** the high priesthood
4:32 thinking he had **o** a suitable opportunity,
2Es 7:72 and though they **o** the law,

OBTAINING (4) [OBTAIN]

Ex 12: 4 it shall join its closest neighbor in **o** one;
1Th 5: 9 but for **o** salvation through our Lord Jesus Christ,
Heb 9:12 but with his own blood, thus **o** eternal redemption.
3Mc 2:33 They remained resolutely hopeful of **o** help,

OBTAINS‡ (4) [OBTAIN]

Nu 35: 8 each, in proportion to the inheritance that it **o,**
Pr 8:35 For whoever finds me finds life and **o** favor from
18:22 and **o** favor from the LORD.
Sir 22: 4 A sensible daughter **o** a husband of her own,

OBVIOUS (5) [OBVIOUSLY]

Ac 4:16 For it is **o** to all who live in Jerusalem that
Gal 5:19 Now the works of the flesh are **o:**
Heb 7:15 It is even more **o** when another priest arises,
3Mc 2:31 with an **o** abhorrence of the price to be exacted
4:11 an **o** spectacle to all coming back into the city and

OBVIOUSLY (2) [OBVIOUS]

4Mc 1:32 others are physical, and reason **o** rules over both.
9: 2 we are **o** putting our forebears to shame

OCCASION (8) [OCCASIONS]

Lk 14: 1 On one **o** when Jesus was going to the house of
1Ti 5:14 so as to give the adversary no **o** to revile us.
Sir 29: 3 and on every **o** you will find what you need.
1Mc 8:25 as the **o** may indicate to them.
8:27 as the **o** may indicate to them.
12:11 therefore remember you constantly on every **o,**
4Mc 3:19 The present **o** now invites us to
5:28 But you shall have no such **o** to laugh at me,

OCCASIONED (KJV) See RESPONSIBLE

OCCASIONS (5) [OCCASION]

Job 33:10 Look, he finds **o** against me,
Mt 18: 7 **O** for stumbling are bound to come,
Lk 17: 1 **"O** for stumbling are bound to come,
2Mc 8:19 of the **o** when help came to their ancestors;
9:23 on the **o** when he made expeditions into

OCCUPANTS (1) [OCCUPY]

1Mc 13:11 he drove out its **o** and remained there.

OCCUPATION (3) [OCCUPATIONS]

Ge 46:33 Pharaoh calls you, and says, 'What is your **o?'**
47: 3 Pharaoh said to his brothers, "What is your **o?"**
Jnh 1: 8 upon us. What is your **o?**

OCCUPATIONS (13) [OCCUPATION]

Lev 23: 7 you shall not work at your **o.**
23: 8 you shall not work at your **o.**
23:21 you shall not work at your **o.**
23:25 You shall not work at your **o;**
23:35 you shall not work at your **o.**
23:36 you shall not work at your **o.**
Nu 28:18 You shall not work at your **o.**
28:25 you shall not work at your **o.**
28:26 you shall not work at your **o.**
29: 1 you shall not work at your **o.**
29:12 you shall not work at your **o.**
29:35 you shall not work at your **o.**
3Mc 5:34 the assembled people to their own **o.**

OCCUPIED (16) [OCCUPY]

Dt 3:20 and they too have **o** the land that the LORD
4:47 They **o** his land and the land of King Og
Jos 12: 1 whose land they **o** beyond the Jordan toward
Jdg 11:21 so Israel **o** all the land of the Amorites,
11:22 They **o** all the territory of the Amorites from
1Sa 31: 7 and the Philistines came and **o** them.
2Sa 5: 9 David **o** the stronghold, and named it the city
1Ch 10: 7 and the Philistines came and **o** them.
2Ch 35:14 of Aaron were **o** in offering the burnt offerings
Ecc 5:20 God keeps them **o** with the joy of their hearts.
Ac 18: 5 Paul was **o** with proclaiming the word,
Jdt 5:18 and their towns were **o** by their enemies.
Jdt 5:19 and have **o** Jerusalem, where their sanctuary is,
Sir 38:25 who drives oxen and is **o** with their work,
1Mc 10: 1 son of Antiochus, landed and **o** Ptolemais.
2Mc 10:36 the gates and let in the rest of the force, and they **o**

OCCUPIES (1) [OCCUPY]

Sir 14:25 and so **o** an excellent lodging place;

OCCUPY (31) [OCCUPANTS, OCCUPIED, OCCUPIES]

Nu 13:30 and said, "Let us go up at once and **o** it,
Dt 3:18 the LORD your God has given you this land to **o,**
4: 1 so that you may live to enter and **o** the land that
4: 5 in the land that you are about to enter and **o.**
4:14 in the land that you are about to cross into and **o.**
4:26 the land that you are crossing the Jordan to **o;**
6: 1 in the land that you are about to cross into and **o,**
6:18 and so that you may go in and **o** the good land that
7: 1 to enter and **o,** and he clears away many nations
8: 1 and go in and **o** the land that the LORD promised
9: 4 that the LORD has brought me in to **o** this land";
9: 5 of your heart that you are going in to **o** their land;
9: 6 not giving you this good land to **o** because
9:23 "Go up and **o** the land that I have given you,"
10:11 in and **o** the land that I swore to their ancestors
11: 8 that you may have strength to go in and **o** the land
11: 8 the land that you are crossing over to **o,**
11:10 that you are about to enter to **o** is not like the land
11:11 the land that you are crossing over to **o** is a land
11:29 into the land that you are entering to **o,**
11:31 When you cross the Jordan to go in to **o** the land
11:31 and when you **o** it and live in it,
12: 1 has given you to **o** all the days that you live on
15: 4 LORD your God is giving you as a possession to **o,**
16:20 so that you may live and **o** the land that
Ne 2: 8 and for the house that I shall **o."**
Ps 131: 1 I do not **o** myself with things too great
Da 11:31 Forces sent by him shall **o** and profane the temple
1Ti 1: 4 and not to **o** themselves with myths
2Mc 2:30 the duty of the original historian to **o** the ground,
1Es 4:50 that they would **o** should be theirs without tribute;

OCCUR (7) [OCCURRED, OCCURRING, OCCURS]

Lk 1:20 unable to speak, until the day these things **o."**
Jn 13:19 before it occurs, so that when it does **o,**
14:29 so that when it does **o,** you may believe.
Tob 14: 4 by the prophets of Israel, whom God sent, will **o.**
Sir 20:18 the downfall of the wicked will **o** just as speedily.
48:25 He revealed what was to **o** to the end of time,
2Es 13:32 When these things take place and the signs **o**

OCCURRED (15) [OCCUR]

Ge 26: 1 besides the former famine that had **o** in the days
Dt 17: 4 that such an abhorrent thing has **o** in Israel,
2Ki 17: 7 This **o** because the people of Israel had sinned
Eze 21:27 a ruin—I will make it! (Such has never **o.)**
Da 12: 1 such as has never **o** since nations first came
Jn 19:36 These things **o** so that the scripture might
Ac 14: 1 The same thing **o** in Iconium,
1Co 10: 6 Now these things **o** as examples for us,
Heb 9:15 because a death has **o** that redeems them from
Rev 16:18 as had not **o** since people were upon the earth,
Wis 11:12 and a groaning at the memory of what had **o.**
1Mc 9:24 In those days a very great famine **o,**
14:29 "Since wars often **o** in the country,
2Es 9: 1 you see that some of the predicted signs have **o,**
9: 5 For just as with everything that has **o** in the world,

OCCURRING (1) [OCCUR]

3Mc 1:17 supposing that something mysterious was **o.**

OCCURS (4) [OCCUR]

Lk 21:12 all this **o,** they will arrest you and persecute you;
Jn 13:19 I tell you this now, before it **o,**
14:29 And now I have told you this before it **o,**
1Es 8:18 And whatever else **o** to you as necessary for

OCHIEL (1)

1Es 1: 9 and Hashabiah and **O** and Joram,

OCHRAN (5)

Nu 1:13 From Asher, Pagiel son of **O.**
2:27 leader of the Asherites shall be Pagiel son of **O,**
7:72 On the eleventh day Pagiel son of **O,**
7:77 This was the offering of Pagiel son of **O.**
10:26 of the tribe of Asher was Pagiel son of **O,**

OCINA (1)

Jdt 2:28 in Sur and **O** and all who lived in Jamnia.

ODD (KJV) See EXCESS NUMBER

ODDS (1)

Ge 16:12 and he shall live at **o** with all his kin."

ODED (3)

2Ch 15: 1 The spirit of God came upon Azariah son of **O.**
15: 8 the prophecy of Azariah son of **O,**
28: 9 of the LORD was there, whose name was **O;**

ODIOUS (6)

Ge 34:30 "You have brought trouble on me by making me **o**
1Sa 13: 4 also that Israel had become **o** to the Philistines,
2Sa 10: 6 Ammonites saw that they had become **o** to David,
16:21 that you have made yourself **o** to your father,
1Ch 19: 6 that they had made themselves **o** to David,
Wis 16: 3 of appetite because of the **o** creatures sent to them,

ODOMERA (1)

1Mc 9:66 He struck down **O** and his kindred and the people

ODOR (50) [ODORS]

Ge 8:21 And when the LORD smelled the pleasing **o,**
Ex 5:21 You have brought us into bad **o** with Pharaoh
29:18 it is a pleasing **o,** an offering by fire to the LORD.
29:25 the altar on top of the burnt offering of pleasing **o**
29:41 for a pleasing **o,** an offering by fire to the LORD.
Lev 1: 9 an offering by fire of pleasing **o** to the LORD.
1:13 an offering by fire of pleasing **o** to the LORD.
1:17 an offering by fire of pleasing **o** to the LORD.
2: 2 an offering by fire of pleasing **o** to the LORD.
2: 9 an offering by fire of pleasing **o** to the LORD.
2:12 not be offered on the altar for a pleasing **o.**
3: 5 as an offering by fire of pleasing **o** to the LORD.
3:16 the altar as a food offering by fire for a pleasing **o.**
4:31 on the altar for a pleasing **o** to the LORD.
6:15 on the altar as a pleasing **o** to the LORD.
6:21 you shall present it as a pleasing **o** to the LORD.
8:21 it was a burnt offering for a pleasing **o,**
8:28 This was an ordination offering for a pleasing **o,**
17: 6 the fat into smoke as a pleasing **o** to the LORD,
23:13 an offering by fire of pleasing **o** to the LORD;
23:18 an offering by fire of pleasing **o** to the LORD.
Nu 15: 3 to make a pleasing **o** for the LORD,
15: 7 a pleasing **o** to the LORD.
15:10 as an offering by fire, a pleasing **o** to the LORD.
15:13 an offering by fire, a pleasing **o** to the LORD.
15:14 a pleasing **o** to the LORD, shall do as you do.
15:24 a burnt offering, a pleasing **o** to the LORD,
18:17 an offering by fire for a pleasing **o** to the LORD;
28: 2 the food for my offerings by fire, my pleasing **o,**
28: 6 ordained at Mount Sinai for a pleasing **o,**
28: 8 an offering by fire, a pleasing **o** to the LORD.
28:13 a burnt offering of pleasing **o,**
28:24 an offering by fire, a pleasing **o** to the LORD;
28:27 a burnt offering, a pleasing **o** to the LORD:
29: 2 a burnt offering, a pleasing **o** to the LORD:
29: 6 according to the ordinance for them, a pleasing **o,**
29: 8 a burnt offering to the LORD, a pleasing **o:**
29:13 an offering by fire, a pleasing **o** to the LORD:
29:36 an offering by fire, a pleasing **o** to the LORD:
Ecc 10: 1 the perfumer's ointment give off a foul **o;**
Eze 6:13 wherever they offered pleasing **o** to all their idols.
16:19 you set it before them as a pleasing **o;**
20:41 As a pleasing **o** I will accept you,
Tob 6:17 An **o** will be given off;
8: 3 The **o** of the fish so repelled the demon
Sir 24:15 and stacte, and like the **o** of incense in the tent.
35: 8 and its pleasing **o** rises before the Most High.
45:16 incense and a pleasing **o** as a memorial portion,
50:15 a pleasing **o** to the Most High, the king of all.
1Es 1:12 in bronze pots and caldrons, with a pleasing **o,**

ODORS (3) [ODOR]

Lev 26:31 and I will not smell your pleasing **o.**
Eze 20:28 there they sent up their pleasing **o,**
2Es 6:44 and **o** of inexpressible fragrance.

ODOUR (KJV) See FRAGRANCE

OF (35325) See Index of Articles Etc.

OFF‡ (477) [OFFSETS, OFFSHOOTS]

Ge 9:11 that never again shall all flesh be cut **o** by
11: 8 and they left **o** building the city.
17:14 of his foreskin shall be cut **o** from his people;
21:16 and sat down opposite him a good way **o,** about
38:14 she put **o** her widow's garments,
38:19 and taking **o** her veil she put on the garments
Ex 4:25 Zipporah took a flint and cut **o** her son's foreskin,
9:15 and you would have been cut **o** from the earth.
9:20 of the LORD hurried their slaves and livestock **o**
12:15 the first day until the seventh day shall be cut **o**
12:19 for whoever eats what is leavened shall be cut **o**
18:27 and he went **o** to his own country.
22:10 and it dies or is injured or is carried **o,**
30:33 of it on an unqualified person shall be cut **o** from
30:38 to use as perfume shall be cut **o** from the people.
31:14 whoever does any work on it shall be cut **o** from
32: 2 "Take **o** the gold rings that are on the ears
32: 3 all the people took **o** the gold rings from their ears,
32:24 So I said to them, 'Whoever has gold, take it **o';**
33: 5 So now take **o** your ornaments,
33: 7 and pitch it outside the camp, far **o** from the camp;
34:34 he would take the veil **o,** until he came out;
Lev 1:15 and wring **o** its head, and turn it into smoke on
6:11 Then he shall take **o** his vestments and put
7:20 a state of uncleanness shall be cut **o** from their kin.
7:21 you shall be cut **o** from your kin.
7:25 you who eat it shall be cut **o** from your kin.
7:27 Any one of you who eats any blood shall be cut **o**
14: 8 and shave **o** all his hair,
14:41 and the plaster that is scraped **o** shall be dumped

Lev 16:23 and shall take **o** the linen vestments that he put on
17: 4 and he shall be cut **o** from the people.
17: 9 shall be cut **o** from the people.
17:10 and will cut that person **o** from the people.
17:14 whoever eats it shall be cut **o.**
18:29 of these abominations shall be cut **o**
19: 8 any such person shall be cut **o** from the people.
19:27 You shall not round **o** the hair on your temples
20: 3 and will cut them **o** from the people,
20: 5 and will cut them **o** from among their people,
20: 6 and will cut them **o** from the people.
20:17 and they shall be cut **o** in the sight of their people;
20:18 both of them shall be cut **o** from their people.
21: 5 or shave **o** the edges of their beards,
22: 3 that person shall be cut **o** from my presence:
23:15 you shall count **o** seven weeks;
23:29 that entire day shall be cut **o** from the people.
25: 8 You shall count **o** seven weeks of years,
Nu 5:23 and wash them **o** into the water of bitterness.
9:13 shall be cut **o** from the people for not presenting
15:30 and shall be cut **o** from among the people.
15:31 a person shall be utterly cut **o** and bear the guilt.
19:13 such persons shall be cut **o** from Israel.
19:20 those persons shall be cut **o** from the assembly,
22:23 donkey turned **o** the road, and went into the field;
24:11 Now be **o** with you!
Dt 2:16 as soon as all the warriors had died **o** from among
11:17 then you will perish quickly **o** the good land that
12:29 When the LORD your God has cut **o** before you
15:16 since he is well **o** with you,
19: 1 When the LORD your God has cut **o**
23: 1 or whose penis is cut **o** shall be admitted to
24: 2 and goes **o** to become another man's wife.
25: 9 pull his sandal **o** his foot, spit in his face,
25:10 as "the house of him whose sandal was pulled **o.**"
25:12 you shall cut **o** her hand; show no pity.
28:21 to you until it has consumed you **o** the land
28:40 for your olives shall drop **o.**
28:63 be plucked **o** the land that you are entering
Jos 3:13 of the Jordan flowing from above shall be cut **o;**
3:16 rising up in a single heap far **o** at Adam,
3:16 the Dead Sea, were wholly cut **o.**
4: 7 that the waters of the Jordan were cut **o** in front of
4: 7 the waters of the Jordan were cut **o.**
7: 9 and cut **o** our name from the earth.
23: 4 with all the nations that I have already cut **o,**
Jdg 1: 6 and caught him, and cut **o** his thumbs and big toes.
1: 7 with their thumbs and big toes cut **o** used to pick
6:13 But now the LORD has cast us **o,**
8:11 for the army was **o** its guard.
15:14 and his bonds melted **o** his hands.
16:12 But he snapped the ropes **o** his arms like a thread.
16:19 and had him shave **o** the seven locks of his head.
21: 6 and said, "One tribe is cut **o** from Israel this day.
21:21 and each of you carry **o** a wife for himself from
Ru 4: 7 the one took **o** a sandal and gave it to the other;
4: 8 "Acquire it for yourself," he took **o** his sandal.
4:10 of the dead may not be cut **o** from his kindred and
1Sa 2: 9 but the wicked shall be cut **o** in darkness;
2:31 a time is coming when I will cut **o** your strength
2:33 of you whom I shall not cut **o** from my altar shall
5: 4 of Dagon and both his hands were lying cut **o**
6: 8 Then send it **o,** and let it go its way.
17:46 and I will strike you down and cut **o** your head;
17:51 then he cut **o** his head with it.
19:24 He too stripped **o** his clothes,
20:15 never cut **o** your faithful love from my house,
20:15 the LORD were to cut **o** every one of the enemies
24: 4 Then David went and stealthily cut **o** a corner
24: 5 because he had cut **o** a corner of Saul's cloak.
24:11 for by the fact that I cut **o** the corner of your cloak,
24:21 the LORD that you will not cut **o** my descendants
28: 9 how he has cut **o** the mediums and the wizards
30: 2 they killed none of them, but carried them **o,**
31: 9 They cut **o** his head, stripped **o** his armor,
2Sa 4:12 they cut **o** their hands and feet,
7: 9 and have cut **o** all your enemies from before you;
8: 2 measured them **o** with a cord;
10: 4 shaved **o** half the beard of each
10: 4 cut **o** their garments in the middle at their hips,
14:16 both me and my son **o** from the heritage of God.'
14:23 So Joab set **o,** went to Geshur,
16: 9 Let me go over and take **o** his head."
17:23 he saddled his donkey and went **o** home
20:22 And they cut **o** the head of Sheba son of Bichri,
1Ki 8:46 to the land of the enemy, far **o** or near;
9: 7 then I will cut Israel **o** from the land
13:34 so as to cut it **o** and to destroy it from the face of
14:10 I will cut **o** from Jeroboam every male,
14:14 who shall cut **o** the house of Jeroboam today,
18: 4 Jezebel was killing **o** the prophets of the LORD,
18:45 Ahab rode **o** and went to Jezreel.
20:11 on armor should not brag like one who takes it **o.**"
21:21 and will cut **o** from Ahab every male,
2Ki 5:20 that Aramean Naaman **o** too lightly by
6: 6 When he showed him the place, he cut **o** a stick,
6:32 this murderer has sent someone to take **o** my head?
7: 8 ate and drank, carried **o** silver, gold, and clothing,
7: 8 carried **o** things from it, and went and hid them.
9: 8 I will cut **o** from Ahab every male, bond or free,
10:32 In those days the LORD began to trim **o** parts
11: 5 those who go **o** duty on the sabbath and guard
11: 9 each brought his men who were to go **o** duty on
16:17 Then King Ahaz cut **o** the frames of the stands,
21:14 I will cast **o** the remnant of my heritage,
24:13 He carried **o** all the treasures of the house of
1Ch 17: 8 and have cut **o** all your enemies before you;
1Ch 18:11 and gold that he had carried **o** from all the nations,
19: 4 cut **o** their garments in the middle at their hips,
2Ch 23: 8 with those who were to go **o** duty on the sabbath;
32:21 And the LORD sent an angel who cut **o** all
Ne 4:23 guard who followed me ever took **o** our clothes;
Est 4: 4 so that he might take **o** his sackcloth;
6:14 the king's eunuchs arrived and hurried Haman **o**
8: 2 Then the king took **o** his signet ring,
Job 1:15 and the Sabeans fell on them and carried them **o,**
1:17 made a raid on the camels and carried them **o,**
4: 7 Or where were the upright cut **o?**
6: 9 that he would let loose his hand and cut me **o!**
9:27 I will put **o** my sad countenance and be
15:33 They will shake **o** their unripe grape, like the vine,
15:33 and cast **o** their blossoms, like the olive tree.
17:11 My days are past, my plans are broken **o,**
20:28 dragged **o** in the day of God's wrath.
21:21 when the number of their months is cut **o?**
22:20 'Surely our adversaries are cut **o,**
24: 4 They thrust the needy **o** the road;
24:24 they are cut **o** like the heads of grain.
27: 8 the hope of the godless when God cuts them **o,**
27:20 in the night a whirlwind carries them **o.**
30:11 they have cast **o** restraint in my presence.
35: 3 How am I better **o** than if I had sinned?'
36:20 when peoples are cut **o** in their place.
41:13 Who can strip **o** its outer garment?
Ps 10: 1 O LORD, do you stand far **o?**
10: 9 they seize the poor and drag them **o** in their net.
12: 3 May the LORD cut **o** all flattering lips,
27: 9 Do not cast me **o,** do not forsake me,
30:11 you have taken **o** my sackcloth and clothed me
34:16 to cut **o** the remembrance of them from the earth.
37: 9 For the wicked shall be cut **o,**
37:22 but those cursed by him shall be cut **o.**
37:28 but the children of the wicked shall be cut **o.**
37:38 the posterity of the wicked shall be cut **o.**
38:11 and my neighbors stand far **o.**
43: 2 why have you cast me **o?**
44:23 Awake, do not cast us **o** forever!
71: 9 Do not cast me **o** in the time of old age;
74: 1 why do you cast us **o** forever?
75:10 All the horns of the wicked I will cut **o,**
76:12 who cuts **o** the spirit of princes,
88: 5 for they are cut **o** from your hand.
88:14 O LORD, why do you cast me **o?**
101: 8 cutting **o** all evildoers from the city of the LORD.
109:13 May his posterity be cut **o;**
109:15 and may his memory be cut **o** from the earth.
109:23 I am shaken **o** like a locust.
118:10 in the name of the LORD I cut them **o!**
118:11 in the name of the LORD I cut them **o!**
118:12 in the name of the LORD I cut them **o!**
143:12 In your steadfast love cut **o** my enemies,
Pr 2:22 but the wicked will be cut **o** from the land,
10:31 but the perverse tongue will be cut **o.**
14:16 but the fool throws **o** restraint and is careless.
23:18 there is a future, and your hope will not be cut **o.**
24:14 and your hope will not be cut **o.**
26: 6 It is like cutting **o** one's foot and drinking
29:18 there is no prophecy, the people cast **o** restraint,
30:14 to devour the poor from **o** the earth,
Ecc 6: 3 I say that a stillborn child is better **o** than he.
7:24 That which is, is far **o,** and deep, very deep;
10: 1 Dead flies make the perfumer's ointment give **o**
SS 5: 3 I had put **o** my garment;
Isa 5:29 they growl and seize their prey, they carry it **o,**
7: 6 against Judah and cut **o** Jerusalem and conquer it
7:20 and it will take **o** the beard as well.
9:14 So the LORD cut **o** from Israel head and tail,
10: 7 and to cut **o** nations not a few.
11:13 the hostility of Judah shall be cut **o;**
14:22 and will cut **o** from Babylon name and remnant,
18: 5 he will cut **o** the shoots with pruning hooks,
20: 2 and take your sandals **o** your feet,"
29:20 all those alert to do evil shall be cut **o**—
33: 9 and Bashan and Carmel shake **o** their leaves.
38:12 he cuts me **o** from the loom;
40:12 of his hand and marked **o** the heavens with a span,
40:24 and the tempest carries them **o** like stubble.
41: 9 I have chosen you and not cast you **o";**
46:13 it is not far **o,** and my salvation will not tarry;
47: 2 strip **o** your robe, uncover your legs,
47:11 which you will not be able to ward **o;**
48: 9 so that I may not cut you **o.**
48:19 their name would never be cut **o** or destroyed from
53: 8 For he was cut **o** from the land of the living,
54: 6 like the wife of a man's youth when she is cast **o,**
55:13 for an everlasting sign that shall not be cut **o.**
56: 5 an everlasting name that shall not be cut **o.**
57:13 The wind will carry them **o,**
Jer 7:28 it is cut **o** from their lips.
7:29 Cut **o** your hair and throw it away;
9:21 to cut **o** the children from the streets and
11:19 let us cut him **o** from the land of the living,
22:19 dragged **o** and thrown out beyond the gates
22:24 even from there I would tear you **o**
23:23 says the LORD, and not a God far **o?**
23:33 "You are the burden, and I will cast you **o,**
28:16 I am going to send you **o** the face of the earth.
30: 8 I will break the yoke from **o** his neck,
36:23 the king would cut them **o** with a penknife
36:29 and will cut **o** from it human beings and animals?
44: 7 to cut **o** man and woman, child and infant,
44: 8 Will you be cut **o** and become an object of cursing
47: 4 to cut **o** from Tyre and Sidon every helper
48: 2 "Come, let us cut her **o** from being a nation!"
Jer 48:25 The horn of Moab is cut **o,** and his arm is broken,
48:37 For every head is shaved and every beard cut **o;**
49:29 carry **o** their camels for yourselves,
50:16 Cut **o** from Babylon the sower,
La 3:11 he led me **o** my way and tore me to pieces;
Eze 6:12 Those far **o** shall die of pestilence;
13:21 I will tear **o** your veils, and save my people
14: 8 and cut them **o** from the midst of my people;
14:13 and cut **o** from it human beings and animals,
14:17 and I cut **o** human beings and animals from it;
14:19 to cut **o** humans and animals from it;
14:21 to cut **o** humans and animals from it!
16: 9 with water and washed **o** the blood from you,
17: 4 broke **o** its topmost shoot;
17:17 up and siege walls built to cut **o** many lives.
17:22 I will break **o** a tender one from the topmost
19:12 the east wind dried it up; its fruit was stripped **o,**
21: 3 will cut **o** from you both righteous and wicked.
21: 4 I will cut **o** from you both righteous and wicked,
21:26 Remove the turban, take **o** the crown;
23:25 They shall cut **o** your nose and your ears,
25: 7 I will cut you **o** from the peoples
25:13 and cut **o** from it humans and animals,
25:16 the Philistines, cut **o** the Cherethites, and destroy
26:16 and strip **o** their embroidered garments.
29: 8 and will cut **o** from you human being and animal;
29:19 and he shall carry **o** its wealth and despoil it
30:15 and cut **o** the hordes of Thebes.
35: 7 and I will cut **o** from it all who come and go.
37:11 and our hope is lost; we are cut **o** completely.'
38:12 to seize spoil and carry **o** plunder;
38:13 to carry **o** plunder, to carry away silver and gold,
45: 3 In the holy district you shall measure **o**
Da 4:14 'Cut down the tree and chop **o** its branches,
4:14 strip **o** its foliage and scatter its fruit.
7: 4 Then, as I watched, its wings were plucked **o,**
9:26 anointed one shall be cut **o** and shall have nothing,
11: 8 he shall carry **o** to Egypt as spoils of war.
11:12 When the multitude has been carried **o,**
Hos 5:14 I will carry **o,** and no one shall rescue.
10:15 At dawn the king of Israel shall be utterly cut **o.**
Joel 1: 5 for it is cut **o** from your mouth.
1: 7 it has stripped **o** their bark and thrown it down;
1: 9 The grain offering and the drink offering are cut **o**
1:16 Is not the food cut **o** before our eyes,
Am 1: 5 and cut **o** the inhabitants from the Valley of Aven,
1: 8 I will cut **o** the inhabitants from Ashdod,
1:11 with the sword and cast **o** all pity;
2: 3 I will cut **o** the ruler from its midst,
3:14 and the horns of the altar shall be cut **o** and fall to
Ob 1: 9 so that everyone from Mount Esau will be cut **o.**
1:10 and you shall be cut **o** forever.
1:11 on the day that strangers carried **o** his wealth,
1:14 at the crossings to cut **o** his fugitives;
Mic 1:16 and cut **o** your hair for your pampered children;
3: 2 who tear the skin **o** my people,
3: 2 and the flesh **o** their bones;
3: 3 flay their skin **o** them, break their bones in pieces,
4: 7 and those who were cast **o,** a strong nation;
5: 9 and all your enemies shall be cut **o.**
5:10 I will cut **o** your horses from among you
5:11 and I will cut **o** the cities of your land and throw
5:12 and I will cut **o** sorceries from your hand,
5:13 and I will cut **o** your images and your pillars from
Na 1:12 they will be cut **o** and pass away.
1:13 now I will break **o** his yoke from you and snap
1:14 of your gods I will cut **o** the carved image and
1:15 shall the wicked invade you; they are utterly cut **o.**
2:13 I will cut **o** your prey from the earth,
3:15 the sword will cut you **o.**
Hab 2:10 for your house by cutting **o** many peoples;
3:17 though the flock is cut **o** from the fold
Zep 1: 3 I will cut **o** humanity from the face of the earth,
1: 4 and I will cut **o** from this place every remnant
1:11 all who weigh out silver are cut **o.**
3: 6 I have cut **o** nations; their battlements are in ruins;
Hag 1: 9 while all of you hurry **o** to your own houses.
Zec 3: 4 "Take **o** his filthy clothes."
5: 3 for everyone who steals shall be cut **o** according to
5: 3 be cut **o** according to the writing on the other side.
6: 7 they were impatient to get **o** and patrol the earth.
6:15 Those who are far **o** shall come and help to build
9:10 He will cut **o** the chariot from Ephraim and
9:10 and the battle bow shall be cut **o,**
11:16 tearing **o** even their hoofs.
13: 2 I will cut **o** the names of the idols from the land,
13: 8 two-thirds shall be cut **o** and perish,
14: 2 rest of the people shall not be cut **o** from the city.
Mal 2:12 May the LORD cut **o** from the tents
Mt 5:30 cut it **o** and throw it away;
8:33 The swineherds ran **o,** and on going into the town,
10:14 shake **o** the dust from your feet as you leave
18: 8 cut it **o** and throw it away;
25:16 The one who had received the five talents went **o**
25:18 the one talent went **o** and dug a hole in the ground
26:51 the slave of the high priest, cutting **o** his ear.
Mk 5:14 The swineherds ran **o** and told it in the city and in
6:11 shake **o** the dust that is on your feet as a testimony
9:43 If your hand causes you to stumble, cut it **o;**
9:45 And if your foot causes you to stumble, cut it **o;**
10:50 So throwing **o** his cloak, he sprang up and came
14:47 the slave of the high priest, cutting **o** his ear.
14:52 but he left the linen cloth and ran **o** naked.
Lk 4:29 so that they might hurl him **o** the cliff.
8:34 they ran **o** and told it in the city and in the country.
9: 5 that town shake the dust **o** your feet as a testimony
10:11 we wipe **o** in protest against you.

Lk 15:20 So he set **o** and went to his father.
15:20 But while he was still far **o,**
17:23 Do not go, do not set **o** in pursuit.
18:13 But the tax collector, standing far **o,**
22:50 the slave of the high priest and cut **o** his right ear.
23: 7 he sent him **o** to Herod,
Jn 13: 4 up from the table, took **o** his outer robe, and tied
18:10 and cut **o** his right ear.
18:26 a relative of the man whose ear Peter had cut **o,**
21: 8 only about a hundred yards **o.**
Ac 7:33 'Take **o** the sandals from your feet,
8: 3 dragging **o** both men and women,
9:30 down to Caesarea and sent him **o** to Tarsus.
12: 7 And the chains fell **o** his wrists.
13: 3 on them and sent them **o.**
13:51 So they shook the dust **o** their feet in protest
15:30 So they were sent **o** and went down to Antioch.
15:33 they were sent **o** in peace by the believers
17:10 That very night the believers sent Paul and Silas **o**
20: 9 began to sink **o** into a deep sleep
22:23 while they were shouting, throwing **o** their cloaks,
27: 5 After we had sailed across the sea that is **o** Cilicia
27: 7 of days and arrived with difficulty **o** Cnidus,
27: 7 we sailed under the lee of Crete **o** Salmone.
27:40 So they cast **o** the anchors and left them in the sea.
28: 5 shook **o** the creature into the fire
Ro 3: 9 Are we any better **o?**
9: 3 that I myself were accursed and cut **o** from Christ
11:17 But if some of the branches were broken **o,**
11:19 "Branches were broken **o** so that I might
11:20 They were broken **o** because of their unbelief,
11:22 otherwise you also will be cut **o.**
1Co 8: 8 We are no worse **o** if we do not eat, and no better **o** if we do.
11: 6 then she should cut **o** her hair;
11: 6 a woman to have her hair cut **o** or to be shaved,
2Co 5: 3 we have taken it **o** we will not be found naked.
12:13 have you been worse **o** than the other churches,
Gal 5: 4 to be justified by the law have cut yourselves **o**
Eph 2:13 in Christ Jesus you who once were far **o** have been
2:17 and proclaimed peace to you who were far **o**
Col 2:11 by putting **o** the body of the flesh in
3: 9 seeing that you have stripped **o** the old self
Rev 12:17 went **o** to make war on the rest of her children,
18:10 they will stand far **o,** in fear of her torment,
18:15 who gained wealth from her, will stand far **o,**
18:17 and all whose trade is on the sea, stood far **o**
Tob 1: 6 I would hurry **o** to Jerusalem with the first fruits
2:12 when she cut **o** a piece she had woven and sent it
6:17 An odor will be given **o;**
10:11 Then he saw them safely **o;**
10:12 Then she kissed them both and saw them safely **o.**
11: 8 the white films shrink and peel **o** from his eyes,
11:13 both his hands he peeled **o** the white films from
14: 4 and hurry **o** to Media, for I believe the word
Jdt 4:12 be carried **o** and their wives to be taken as booty,
7: 2 So all their warriors marched **o** that day;
9: 2 to take revenge on those strangers who had torn **o**
9: 8 to break **o** the horns of your altar with the sword.
10: 3 took **o** her widow's garments,
13: 8 with all her might, and cut **o** his head.
13: 9 Next she rolled his body **o** the bed and pulled
13:18 who has guided you to cut **o** the head of the leader
AdE 3:10 So the king took **o** his signet ring and gave it
14: 2 She took **o** her splendid apparel and put on
15: 1 when she ended her prayer, she took **o**
Wis 4: 5 The branches will be broken **o** before they come
11: 3 withstood their enemies and fought **o** their foes.
13:11 to handle and skillfully strip **o** all its bark,
17: 8 For those who promised to drive **o** the fears
18:23 and cut **o** its way to the living.
Sir 16:22 For his decree is far **o.**"
22: 2 anyone that picks it up will shake it **o** his hand.
22:13 and be spattered when he shakes himself **o.**
27:20 Do not go after him, for he is too far **o,**
29:27 "Be **o,** stranger, for an honored guest is here;
30:14 Better **o** poor, healthy, and fit than rich
31: 2 and a severe illness carries **o** sleep.
48:15 until they were carried **o** as plunder
Bar 4:20 I have taken **o** the robe of peace and put
4:26 they were taken away like a flock carried **o** by
5: 1 Take **o** the garment of your sorrow and affliction,
LtJ 6:24 not shine unless someone wipes **o** the tarnish;
6:43 of them is led **o** by one of the passers-by
6:58 and go **o** with this booty,
Sus 1:45 Just as she was being led **o** to execution,
1Mc 1:22 on the front of the temple; he stripped it all **o.**
5:66 he marched **o** to go into the land of the Philistines,
6:63 Then he set **o** in haste and returned to Antioch.
7:47 they cut **o** Nicanor's head and the right hand
9: 4 then they marched **o** and went to Berea
10:62 to take **o** Jonathan's garments and to clothe him
11:17 the Arab cut **o** the head of Alexander and sent it
13:22 He marched **o** and went into the land of Gilead.
2Mc 1:16 they dismembered them and cut **o** their heads
3:35 he marched **o** with his forces to the king.
4:38 he immediately stripped **o** the purple robe
4:38 tore **o** his purple robe, and led him around
5:21 So Antiochus carried **o** eighteen hundred talents
7: 4 that they scalp him and cut **o** his hands and feet,
7: 7 They tore **o** the skin of his head with the hair,
8:13 cowardly and distrustful of God's justice ran **o**
8:35 took **o** his splendid uniform
9:25 and commended to most of you when I hurried **o**
10:17 and beat **o** all who fought upon the wall,
10:19 and he himself set **o** for places
11: 7 Then they eagerly rushed **o** together.
2Mc 12:21 he sent **o** the women and the children and also
12:35 and grasping his cloak was dragging him **o**
12:35 down on him and cut **o** his arm;
14:12 appointed him governor of Judea, and sent him **o**
15:30 to cut **o** Nicanor's head and arm and carry them
1Es 5:72 cut **o** their supplies, and hindered their building;
3Mc 4: 4 a harsh and ruthless spirit were they being sent **o,**
2Es 2:45 "These are they who have put **o** mortal clothing
7:*114* [44] to an end, unbelief has been cut **o,**
10: 5 Then I broke **o** the reflections
10:22 our righteous men have been carried **o,**
10:24 Therefore shake **o** your great sadness
16: 6 Can one drive **o** a hungry lion in the forest,
16:78 It is shut **o** and given up to be consumed by fire.
4Mc 9:11 and having torn **o** his tunic,
9:20 of flesh were falling **o** the axles of the machine.
10:19 See, here is my tongue; cut it **o,**
14:16 hatch the nestlings and ward **o** the intruder.

OFFEND (2) [OFFENDED, OFFENDER, OFFENDERS, OFFENDS, OFFENSE, OFFENSES, OFFENSIVE]

Job 34:31 'I have endured punishment; I will not **o** any more;
Jn 6:61 said to them, "Does this **o** you?

OFFENDED (9) [OFFEND]

Ge 40: 1 of the king of Egypt and his baker **o** their lord
Ne 1: 7 We have **o** you deeply, failing to keep
Job 4: 2 "If one ventures a word with you, will you be **o?**
Pr 18:19 An ally **o** is stronger than a city;
Eze 25:12 of Judah and has grievously **o** in taking vengeance
AdE 1:12 This **o** the king and he became furious.
Sir 30:13 so that you may not be **o** by his shamelessness.
LtJ 6:18 on every side against anyone who has **o** a king,
2Es 12:41 "How have we **o** you,

OFFENDER (2) [OFFEND]

Mt 18:17 and if the **o** refuses to listen even to the church,
Lk 17: 3 If another disciple sins, you must rebuke the **o,**

OFFENDERS (2) [OFFEND]

1Ki 1:21 that my son Solomon and I will be counted **o.**"
Lk 13: 4 that they were worse **o** than all the others living

OFFENDS (1) [OFFEND]

LtJ 6:14 but is unable to destroy anyone who **o** it.

OFFENSE (26) [OFFEND]

Ge 31:36 Jacob said to Laban, "What is my **o?**
Dt 19:15 or wrongdoing in connection with any **o** that may
22:26 not committed an **o** punishable by death,
25: 2 with the number of lashes proportionate to the **o.**
Job 31:11 that would be a criminal **o;**
Pr 19:11 and it is their glory to overlook an **o.**
Hos 12: 8 of my gain no **o** has been found in me that would
12:14 Ephraim has given bitter **o,**
Mt 11: 6 And blessed is anyone who takes no **o** at me."
13:57 And they took **o** at him.
15:12 "Do you know that the Pharisees took **o**
17:27 However, so that we do not give **o** to them,
Mk 6: 3 And they took **o** at him.
Lk 7:23 And blessed is anyone who takes no **o** at me."
Ac 25: 8 "I have in no way committed an **o** against the law
1Co 10:32 Give no **o** to Jews or to Greeks or to the church
Gal 5:11 In that case the **o** of the cross has been removed.
Jdt 5:20 against their God and we find out their **o,**
8:22 and we shall be an **o** and a disgrace in the eyes
12: 2 "I cannot partake of them, or it will be an **o;**
Sir 7: 7 Commit no **o** against the public,
17:25 pray in his presence and lessen your **o.**
23:23 she has committed an **o** against her husband;
31:16 and do not chew greedily, or you will give **o.**
31:17 and do not be insatiable, or you will give **o.**
3Mc 3: 9 not be left to its fate when it had committed no **o.**

OFFENSES (9) [OFFEND]

Nu 18: 1 with you shall bear responsibility for **o** connected
18: 1 for **o** connected with the priesthood.
18:23 and they shall bear responsibility for their own **o;**
Pr 10:12 Hatred stirs up strife, but love covers all **o.**
Ecc 10: 4 for calmness will undo great **o.**
Ro 16:17 an eye on those who cause dissensions and **o,**
Tob 3: 3 not punish me for my sins and for my unwitting **o**
1Mc 13:39 and **o** committed to this day, and cancel
Man 1:10 setting up abominations and multiplying **o.**

OFFENSIVE (3) [OFFEND]

Ex 8:26 to the LORD our God are **o** to the Egyptians.
8:26 in the sight of the Egyptians sacrifices that are **o**
Sir 27:13 The talk of fools is **o,**

OFFER‡ (230) [OFFERED, OFFERING, OFFERINGS, OFFERS]

Ge 22: 2 and **o** him there as a burnt offering on one of
24:14 'Please **o** your jar that I may drink,'
Ex 5: 8 'Let us go and **o** sacrifice to our God.'
8:26 that we **o** to the LORD our God are offensive to
8:26 If we **o** in the sight of the Egyptians sacrifices
23:18 You shall not **o** the blood of my sacrifice
29:36 Also every day you shall **o** a bull as a sin offering
29:36 Also you shall **o** a sin offering for the altar,
Ex 29:38 Now this is what you shall **o** on the altar:
29:39 One lamb you shall **o** in the morning,
29:39 and the other lamb you shall **o** in the evening;
29:41 And the other lamb you shall **o** in the evening,
29:41 and shall **o** with it a grain offering
30: 1 You shall make an altar on which to **o** incense;
30: 7 Aaron shall **o** fragrant incense on it;
30: 7 when he dresses the lamps he shall **o** it,
30: 8 he shall **o** it, a regular incense offering before
30: 9 You shall not **o** unholy incense on it,
34:25 not **o** the blood of my sacrifice with leaven,
Lev 1: 3 you shall **o** a male without blemish;
1: 5 and Aaron's sons the priests shall **o** the blood,
1:13 the priest shall **o** the whole and turn it into smoke
2:13 with all your offerings you shall **o** salt.
3: 1 if you **o** an animal of the herd,
3: 1 you shall **o** one without blemish before
3: 3 You shall **o** from the sacrifice of well-being,
3: 6 male or female, you shall **o** one without blemish.
4: 3 he shall **o** for the sin that he has committed a bull
4:14 the assembly shall **o** a bull of the herd for
5: 8 who shall **o** first the one for the sin offering,
5:10 And the second he shall **o** for a burnt offering
6:14 The sons of Aaron shall **o** it before the LORD,
6:20 This is the offering that Aaron and his sons shall **o**
7:11 of the offering of well-being that one may **o** to
7:12 If you **o** it for thanksgiving, you shall **o** with
7:14 From this you shall **o** one cake from each offering,
7:16 But if the sacrifice you **o** is a votive offering or
7:16 the day that you **o** your sacrifice, and what is left
7:29 of you who would **o** to the LORD your sacrifice
9: 2 without blemish, and **o** them before the LORD.
12: 7 He shall **o** it before the LORD,
14:12 and **o** it as a guilt offering,
14:19 the priest shall **o** the sin offering,
14:20 and the priest shall **o** the burnt offering and
14:30 And he shall **o,** of the turtledoves or pigeons such
15:15 The priest shall **o** them, one for a sin offering and
15:30 The priest shall **o** one for a sin offering and
16: 6 Aaron shall **o** the bull as a sin offering for himself,
16: 9 and **o** it as a sin offering;
16:24 and **o** his burnt offering and the burnt offering of
17: 5 of Israel may bring their sacrifices that they **o** in
17: 5 **o** them as sacrifices of well-being to the LORD.
17: 7 so that they may no longer **o** their sacrifices
19: 5 you **o** a sacrifice of well-being to the LORD,
19: 5 **o** it in such a way that it is acceptable
19: 6 It shall be eaten on the same day you **o** it,
21: 6 for they **o** the LORD's offerings by fire,
21: 8 since they **o** the food of your God;
21:17 a blemish may approach to **o** the food of his God.
21:21 the priest who has a blemish shall come near to **o**
21:21 he shall not come near to **o** the food of his God.
22:15 which they **o** to the LORD,
22:20 You shall not **o** anything that has a blemish,
22:22 not **o** to the LORD or put any of them on the altar
22:24 you shall not **o** to the LORD;
22:25 from a foreigner to **o** as food to your God;
23:12 you shall **o** a lamb a year old, without blemish,
23:19 You shall also **o** one male goat for a sin offering,
Nu 6:11 and the priest shall **o** one as a sin offering and
6:14 and they shall **o** their gift to the LORD,
6:16 and **o** their sin offering and burnt offering,
6:17 and shall **o** the ram as a sacrifice of well-being to
8:12 and he shall **o** the one for a sin offering and
15: 5 you shall **o** one-fourth of a hin of wine as
15: 6 For a ram, you shall **o** a grain offering,
15: 7 as a drink offering you shall **o** one-third of a hin
15: 8 you **o** a bull as a burnt offering or a sacrifice,
15:12 According to the number that you **o,**
15:14 and wishes to **o** an offering by fire,
15:24 the whole congregation shall **o** one young bull for
16:40 shall approach to **o** incense before the LORD,
28: 2 by fire, my pleasing odor, you shall take care to **o**
28: 3 the offering by fire that you shall **o** to the LORD:
28: 4 One lamb you shall **o** in the morning,
28: 4 and the other lamb you shall **o** at twilight
28: 8 The other lamb you shall **o** at twilight with
28: 8 you shall **o** it as an offering by fire,
28:11 of your months you shall **o** a burnt offering to
28:19 You shall **o** an offering by fire,
28:20 three-tenths of an ephah shall you **o** for a bull,
28:21 one-tenth shall you **o** for each of the seven lambs;
28:23 You shall **o** these in addition to the burnt offering
28:24 In the same way you shall **o** daily, for seven days,
28:26 when you **o** a grain offering of new grain to
28:27 You shall **o** a burnt offering,
28:31 you shall **o** them and their drink offering.
29: 2 and you shall **o** a burnt offering, a pleasing odor to
29: 8 You shall **o** a burnt offering to the LORD,
29:13 You shall **o** a burnt offering, an offering by fire,
29:36 You shall **o** a burnt offering, an offering by fire,
29:39 These you shall **o** to the LORD
Dt 12:13 not **o** your burnt offerings at any place you happen
12:14 there you shall **o** your burnt offerings
16: 2 You shall **o** the passover sacrifice for
16: 5 You are not permitted to **o** the passover sacrifice
16: 6 only there shall you **o** the passover sacrifice,
20:10 to a town to fight against it, **o** it terms of peace.
27: 6 **o** up burnt offerings on it to the LORD your God,
28:68 and there you shall **o** yourselves for sale
33:19 there they **o** the right sacrifices;
Jos 22:23 if we did so to **o** burnt offerings or grain offerings
Jdg 5: 2 when the people **o** themselves willingly—
6:26 the second bull, and **o** it as a burnt offering with
13:16 if you want to prepare a burnt offering, then **o** it to
16:23 of the Philistines gathered to **o** a great sacrifice

Jdg 18:20 Then the priest accepted the **o**.
1Sa 1:21 and all his household went up to **o** to the LORD
1:22 I will **o** him as a nazirite for all time."
2:19 up with her husband to **o** the yearly sacrifice.
2:28 to **o** incense, to wear an ephod before me;
10: 8 to you to present burnt offerings and **o** sacrifices
2Sa 24:12 Thus says the LORD: Three things I **o** you;
24:22 the king take and **o** up what seems good to him;
24:24 I will not **o** burnt offerings to the LORD my God
1Ki 3: 4 Solomon used to **o** a thousand burnt offerings on
9:25 a year Solomon used to **o** up burnt offerings
12:27 to go up to **o** sacrifices in the house of the LORD
12:33 and he went up to the altar to **o** incense.
13: 1 Jeroboam was standing by the altar to **o** incense,
13: 2 the priests of the high places who **o** incense
2Ki 5:17 for your servant will no longer **o** burnt offering
10:18 but Jehu will **o** much more.
10:19 for I have a great sacrifice to **o** to Baal;
10:24 they proceeded to **o** sacrifices and burnt offerings.
16:15 the great altar **o** the morning burnt offering,
1Ch 16:40 to **o** burnt offerings to the LORD on the altar
21:10 'Thus says the LORD: Three things I **o** you;
21:24 nor **o** burnt offerings that cost me nothing."
23: 5 and four thousand shall **o** praises to the LORD
29: 5 Who then will **o** willingly,
2Ch 13:11 They **o** to the LORD every morning
23:18 to **o** burnt offerings to the LORD,
29:21 the descendants of Aaron to **o** them on the altar of
35:12 of the people, to **o** to the LORD, as it is written in
35:16 the passover and to **o** burnt offerings on the altar
Ezr 3: 2 to **o** burnt offerings on it,
3: 6 the seventh month they began to **o** burnt offerings
6:10 so that they may **o** pleasing sacrifices to the God
7:17 and you shall **o** them on the altar of the house
Job 1: 5 in the morning and **o** burnt offerings according to
6:22 Or, 'From your wealth **o** a bribe for me'?
42: 8 and **o** up for yourselves a burnt offering;
Ps 4: 5 **O** right sacrifices, and put your trust in
27: 6 and I will **o** in his tent sacrifices with shouts of joy;
32: 6 Therefore let all who are faithful **o** prayer to you;
50:14 **O** to God a sacrifice of thanksgiving,
66:15 I will **o** to you burnt offerings of fatlings,
107:22 And let them **o** thanksgiving sacrifices,
110: 3 Your people will **o** themselves willingly on
116:17 I will **o** to you a thanksgiving sacrifice and call on
Pr 7:14 to **o** sacrifices, and today I have paid my vows;
28:17 until death; let no one **o** assistance.
Isa 57: 7 and there you went up to **o** sacrifice.
58:10 if you **o** your food to the hungry and satisfy
Jer 14:12 although they **o** burnt offering and grain offering,
16: 7 to **o** comfort for the dead;
32:35 to **o** up their sons and daughters to Molech,
33:18 a man in my presence to **o** burnt offerings,
35: 2 then **o** them wine to drink.
48:35 those who **o** sacrifice at a high place
La 4: 3 the jackals **o** the breast and nurse their young,
Eze 20:31 When you **o** your gifts
43:22 On the second day you shall **o** a male goat
43:23 you shall **o** a bull without blemish and a ram from
43:24 the priests shall throw salt on them and **o** them up
43:27 then from the eighth day onward the priests shall **o**
44: 7 profaning my temple when you **o** to me my food,
44:15 they shall attend me to **o** me the fat and the blood,
44:27 he shall **o** his sin offering, says the Lord GOD.
46: 2 The priests shall **o** his burnt offering
46: 6 the day of the new moon he shall **o** a young bull
46:12 and he shall **o** his burnt offering or his offerings
Hos 8:13 Though they **o** choice sacrifices,
14: 2 and we will **o** the fruit of our lips.
Am 5:22 you **o** me your burnt offerings and grain offerings,
8: 5 and the sabbath, so that we may **o** wheat for sale?
Hag 2:14 and what they **o** there is unclean.
Mal 1: 8 you **o** blind animals in sacrifice, is that not wrong?
1: 8 And when you **o** those that are lame or sick,
Mt 5:24 and then come and **o** your gift.
8: 4 and **o** the gift that Moses commanded,
Mk 1:44 and **o** for your cleansing what Moses commanded,
Lk 1: 9 to enter the sanctuary of the Lord and **o** incense.
6:29 anyone strikes you on the cheek, **o** the other also;
Ac 7:42 'Did you **o** to me slain victims
14:13 he and the crowds wanted to **o** sacrifice.
24:17 to bring alms to my nation and to **o** sacrifices.
Heb 5: 1 to **o** gifts and sacrifices for sins.
5: 3 of this he must **o** sacrifice for his own sins as well
7:27 he has no need to **o** sacrifices day after day,
8: 3 For every high priest is appointed to **o** gifts
8: 3 for this priest also to have something to **o**.
8: 4 there are priests who **o** gifts according to the law.
8: 5 They **o** worship in a sanctuary that is a sketch
9:25 Nor was it to **o** himself again and again,
11:17 He who had received the promises was ready to **o**
12:28 by which we **o** to God an acceptable worship
13:15 let us continually **o** a sacrifice of praise to God,
1Pe 2: 5 to **o** spiritual sacrifices acceptable to God
Rev 8: 3 of incense to **o** with the prayers of all the saints on
Tob 1: 4 where all the tribes of Israel should **o** sacrifice and
Sir 35: 7 that you **o** is in fulfillment of the commandment.
35:14 Do not **o** him a bribe, for he will not accept it;
38:11 **O** a sweet-smelling sacrifice,
45:16 He chose him out of all the living to **o** sacrifice to
Bar 1:10 and **o** them on the altar of the Lord our God;
LtJ 6:56 they can **o** no resistance to king or enemy.
1Mc 1:51 and commanded the towns of Judah to **o** sacrifice,
2:15 to the town of Modein to make them **o** sacrifice.
2:23 in the sight of all to **o** sacrifice on the altar
6:60 and he sent to the Jews an **o** of peace,
11:34 To all those who **o** sacrifice
1Mc 12:11 at the sacrifices that we **o** and in our prayers,
1Es 5:49 to **o** burnt offerings upon it,
5:53 to God began to **o** sacrifices to God,
8:15 as to **o** sacrifices on the altar of their Lord that is
9:20 and to **o** rams in expiation of their error.
2Es 1:31 When you **o** oblations to me,
3:24 and there to **o** you oblations from what is yours.

OFFERED (163) [OFFER]

Ge 8:20 and **o** burnt offerings on the altar.
22:13 and **o** it up as a burnt offering instead of his son.
31:54 and Jacob **o** a sacrifice on the height
46: 1 he **o** sacrifices to the God of his father Isaac.
Ex 24: 5 who **o** burnt offerings and sacrificed oxen
32: 6 and **o** burnt offerings and brought sacrifices
40:27 and **o** fragrant incense on it;
40:29 and **o** on it the burnt offering and
Lev 2:12 they shall not be **o** on the altar for a pleasing odor.
7: 3 All its fat shall be **o**:
7: 8 the skin of the burnt offering that he has **o**.
7:15 of well-being shall be eaten on the day it is **o**;
7:34 and the thigh that is **o**, from the people of Israel,
10: 1 and they **o** unholy fire before the LORD,
10:19 today they **o** their sin offering
22:18 or as a freewill offering that is **o** to the LORD as
Nu 3: 4 before the LORD when they **o** illicit fire before
6:20 the breast that is elevated and the thigh that is **o**.
18:15 human and animal, which is **o** to the LORD,
18:32 when you have **o** the best of it.
23: 2 and Balaam **o** a bull and a ram on each altar.
23: 4 and have **o** a bull and a ram on each altar."
23:14 and **o** a bull and a ram on each altar.
23:30 and **o** a bull and a ram on each altar.
26:61 But Nadab and Abihu died when they **o** illicit fire
28:15 be **o** in addition to the regular burnt offering
28:24 be **o** in addition to the regular burnt offering
31:52 the gold of the offering that they **o** to the LORD,
Dt 26:14 and I have not **o** any of it to the dead.
Jos 8:31 and they **o** on it burnt offerings to the LORD,
Jdg 5: 9 of Israel who **o** themselves willingly among
6:28 second bull was **o** on the altar that had been built.
11:31 to be **o** up by me as a burnt offering."
13:19 and **o** it on the rock to the LORD,
19:18 Nobody has **o** to take me in.
20:26 Then they **o** burnt offerings and sacrifices
21: 4 and **o** burnt offerings and sacrifices of well-being.
1Sa 2:13 When anyone **o** sacrifice,
6:14 and **o** the cows as a burnt offering to the LORD.
6:15 the people of Beth-shemesh **o** burnt offerings
7: 9 a sucking lamb and **o** it as a whole burnt offering
13: 9 And he **o** the burnt offering.
13:12 so I forced myself, and **o** the burnt offering."
2Sa 6:17 and David **o** burnt offerings and offerings
24:25 and **o** burnt offerings and offerings of well-being.
1Ki 3: 3 he sacrificed and **o** incense at the high places.
3:15 He **o** up burnt offerings and offerings
8:62 **o** sacrifice before the LORD.
8:63 Solomon **o** as sacrifices of well-being to
8:64 for there he **o** the burnt offerings and
10: 5 and his burnt offerings that he **o** at the house of
11: 8 who **o** incense and sacrificed to their gods.
12:32 and he **o** sacrifices on the altar;
22:43 and the people still sacrificed and **o** incense on
2Ki 3:27 and **o** him as a burnt offering on the wall.
5:20 by not accepting from him what he **o**.
10:18 "Ahab **o** Baal small service;
12: 4 the money **o** as sacred donations that is brought
16:13 and **o** his burnt offering and his grain offering,
17: 4 and **o** no tribute to the king of Assyria,
1Ch 16: 1 and they **o** burnt offerings and offerings
23:31 and whenever burnt offerings are **o** to the LORD
29: 9 with single mind they had **o** freely to the LORD;
29:17 of my heart I have freely **o** all these things,
29:21 the next day they **o** sacrifices and burnt offerings
2Ch 1: 6 and **o** a thousand burnt offerings on it.
7: 4 Then the king and all the people **o** sacrifice before
7: 5 Solomon **o** as a sacrifice twenty-two thousand oxen
7: 6 whenever David **o** praises by their ministry.
7: 7 for there he **o** the burnt offerings and the fat of
8:12 Then Solomon **o** up burnt offerings to the LORD
9: 4 and his burnt offerings that he **o** at the house of
24:14 They **o** burnt offerings in the house of
29: 7 and have not **o** incense or made burnt offerings in
29:27 that the burnt offering be **o** on the altar.
33:16 of the LORD and **o** on it sacrifices of well-being
Ezr 1: 6 besides all that was freely **o**.
3: 3 and they **o** burnt offerings upon it to the LORD,
3: 4 and **o** the daily burnt offerings by number
6: 3 be rebuilt, the place where sacrifices are **o**
6:17 They **o** at the dedication of this house
7:15 that the king and his counselors have freely **o** to
8:25 his lords, and all Israel there present had **o**;
8:35 **o** burnt offerings to the God of Israel,
Ne 11: 2 the people blessed all those who willingly **o** to live
12:43 They **o** great sacrifices that day and rejoiced,
Ps 51:19 then bulls will be **o** on your altar.
106:28 and ate sacrifices **o** to the dead;
Ecc 5: 1 to listen is better than the sacrifice **o** by fools;
SS 8: 7 If one **o** for love all the wealth of his house,
Isa 65: 7 because they **o** incense on the mountains
Eze 3: 1 He said to me, O mortal, eat what is **o** to you;
6:13 wherever they **o** pleasing odor to all their idols.
20:28 there they **o** their sacrifices and presented
23:37 and they have even **o** up to them for food
Da 2:46 that a grain offering and incense be **o** to him.
Hos 2:13 when she **o** incense to them and decked herself
Jnh 1:16 they **o** a sacrifice to the LORD and made vows.
Mal 1:11 and in every place incense is **o** to my name,
Mt 2:11 they **o** him gifts of gold, frankincense, and myrrh.
27:34 they **o** him wine to drink, mixed with gall;
Mk 15:23 And they **o** him wine mixed with myrrh;
Lk 2:24 and they **o** a sacrifice according to what is stated
Ac 7:41 **o** a sacrifice to the idol,
8:18 on of the apostles' hands, he **o** them money,
Ro 11:16 If the part of the dough **o** as first fruits is holy,
1Co 8: 4 Hence, as to the eating of food **o** to idols,
8: 7 they still think of the food they eat as food **o** to
10:28 "This has been **o** in sacrifice," then do not eat it,
Heb 5: 7 Jesus **o** up prayers and supplications,
7:27 this he did once for all when he **o** himself.
9: 9 and sacrifices are **o** that cannot perfect
9:14 the eternal Spirit **o** himself without blemish
9:28 having been **o** once to bear the sins of many,
10: 1 by the same sacrifices that are continually **o** year
10: 2 Otherwise, would they not have ceased being **o**,
10: 8 and burnt offerings and sin offerings" (these are **o**
10:12 Christ had **o** for all time a single sacrifice for sins,
11: 4 By faith Abel **o** to God
11:17 when put to the test, **o** up Isaac.
Jas 2:21 by works when he **o** his son Isaac on the altar?
Jdt 4:14 **o** the daily burnt offerings, the votive offerings,
9: 1 the evening incense was being **o** in the house
16:18 they **o** their burnt offerings,
Wis 18: 9 the holy children of good people **o** sacrifices,
Sir 46:16 and he **o** in sacrifice a suckling lamb.
50:19 the people of the Lord Most High **o** their prayers
LtJ 6:28 the sacrifices that are **o** to these gods and use
1Mc 1:55 and **o** incense at the doors of the houses and in
1:59 of the month they **o** sacrifice on the altar that was
2:42 all who **o** themselves willingly for the law.
4:50 Then they **o** incense on the altar and lit the lamps
4:53 and **o** sacrifice, as the law directs, on the new altar
4:56 and joyfully **o** burnt offerings;
4:56 they **o** a sacrifice of well-being and
5:54 and **o** burnt offerings, because they had returned
6:34 They **o** the elephants the juice of grapes
7:33 to show him the burnt offering that was being **o**
2Mc 1: 8 and we **o** sacrifice and grain offering,
1:18 who built the temple and the altar, **o** sacrifices.
1:23 the priests **o** prayer—the priests and everyone.
2: 9 of wisdom Solomon **o** sacrifice for the dedication
3:32 **o** sacrifice for the man's recovery.
3:35 Then Heliodorus **o** sacrifice to the Lord
4:34 **o** him sworn pledges and gave him his right hand;
10: 3 then, striking fire out of flint, they **o** sacrifices,
10: 3 of two years, and they **o** incense and lighted lamps
10: 7 they **o** hymns of thanksgiving
13:23 settled with them and **o** sacrifice,
1Es 1:18 and the sacrifices were **o** on the altar of the Lord,
4:52 to be **o** on the altar every day, in accordance with
5:50 and they **o** sacrifices at the proper times
5:51 and **o** the proper sacrifices every day,
6:31 and prayers be **o** for their lives."
7: 7 They **o** at the dedication of the temple of
8:65 from exile **o** sacrifices to the Lord,
3Mc 1: 9 he **o** sacrifice to the supreme God
5:43 of those who **o** sacrifices there.
2Es 1: 6 for they have forgotten me and have **o** sacrifices
10:45 in the world before any offering was **o** in it.
10:46 Solomon built the city, and **o** offerings;
14:39 I opened my mouth, and a full cup was **o** to me;
4Mc 18:11 and Isaac who was **o** as a burnt offering,

OFFERING‡ (820) [OFFER]

A. BURNT OFFERING (201)
B. GRAIN OFFERING (125)
C. SIN OFFERING (123)
D. OFFERING BY FIRE (43)
E. GUILT OFFERING (39)
F. DRINK OFFERING (32)
G. ELEVATION OFFERING (20)
H. FREEWILL OFFERING (13)
I. †LORD'S OFFERING (12)
J. OFFERING OF WELL-BEING (10)

Ge 4: 3 to the LORD an **o** of the fruit of the ground,
4: 4 And the LORD had regard for Abel and his **o**,
4: 5 but for Cain and his **o** he had no regard.
22: 2 and offer him there as a burnt **o** on one of A
22: 3 he cut the wood for the burnt **o**, A
22: 6 Abraham took the wood of the burnt **o** and laid A
22: 7 but where is the lamb for a burnt **o**?" A
22: 8 God himself will provide the lamb for a burnt **o**, A
22:13 and offered it up as a burnt **o** instead of his son. A
35:14 poured out a drink **o** on it, and poured oil on it. F
Ex 18:12 brought a burnt **o** and sacrifices to God; A
25: 2 Tell the Israelites to take for me an **o**;
25: 2 to give you shall receive the **o** for me.
25: 3 This is the **o** that you shall receive from them:
28:38 on himself any guilt incurred in the holy **o** that
29:14 with fire outside the camp; it is a sin **o**. C
29:18 it is a burnt **o** to the LORD; A
29:18 it is a pleasing odor, an **o** by fire to the LORD. D
29:24 raise them as an elevation **o** before the LORD. G
29:25 of the burnt **o** of pleasing odor before the LORD; A
29:25 it is an **o** by fire to the LORD. D
29:26 Aaron's ordination and raise it as an elevation **o** G
29:27 as an elevation **o** and the thigh that was raised G
29:27 the thigh that was raised as an elevation **o** from G
29:28 and his sons from the Israelites, for this is an **o**;
29:28 be an **o** by the Israelites from their sacrifice
29:28 of offerings of well-being, their **o** to the LORD.

Ex 29:36 Also every day you shall offer a bull as a sin **o** C
29:36 Also you shall offer a sin **o** for the altar, C
29:40 and one-fourth of a hin of wine for a drink **o.** F
29:41 offer with it a grain **o** and its drink offering, B
29:41 offer with it a grain offering and its drink **o,** F
29:41 for a pleasing odor, an **o** by fire to the LORD. D
29:42 a regular burnt **o** throughout your generations A
30: 8 a regular incense **o** before the LORD
30: 9 or a burnt **o,** or a grain offering; A
30: 9 or a burnt offering, or a grain **o;** B
30: 9 and you shall not pour a drink **o** on it. F
30:10 a year with the blood of the atoning sin **o.** C
30:13 half a shekel as an **o** to the LORD.
30:14 shall give the LORD's **o.** I
30:15 when you bring this **o** to the LORD
30:20 to make an **o** by fire to the LORD, D
30:28 and the altar of burnt **o** with all its utensils, A
31: 9 and the altar of burnt **o** with all its utensils, A
35: 5 Take from among you an **o** to the LORD;
35: 5 of a generous heart bring the LORD's **o:** I
35:16 of burnt **o,** with its grating of bronze, its poles, A
35:21 and brought the LORD's **o** to be used for the tent I
35:22 everyone bringing an **o** of gold to the LORD.
35:24 Everyone who could make an **o** of silver
35:24 of silver or bronze brought it as the LORD's **o;** I
35:29 brought it as a freewill **o** to the LORD. H
36: 6 to make anything else as an **o** for the sanctuary."
38: 1 made the altar of burnt **o** also of acacia wood; A
38:24 the gold from the **o,** was twenty-nine talents
40: 6 of burnt **o** before the entrance of the tabernacle A
40:10 anoint the altar of burnt **o** and all its utensils, A
40:29 of burnt **o** at the entrance of the tabernacle of A
40:29 offered on it the burnt **o** and the grain offering A
40:29 offered on it the burnt offering and the grain **o** B
Lev 1: 2 any of you bring an **o** of livestock to the LORD,
1: 2 of livestock to the LORD, you shall bring your **o**
1: 3 If the **o** is a burnt offering from the herd,
1: 3 If the offering is a burnt **o** from the herd, A
1: 4 on the head of the burnt **o,** A
1: 6 burnt **o** shall be flayed and cut up into its parts. A
1: 9 the whole into smoke on the altar as a burnt **o,** A
1: 9 an **o** by fire of pleasing odor to the LORD. D
1:10 If your gift for a burnt **o** is from the flock, A
1:10 your **o** shall be a male without blemish.
1:13 a burnt **o,** an offering by fire of pleasing odor A
1:13 an **o** by fire of pleasing odor to the LORD. D
1:14 your **o** to the LORD is a burnt offering of birds,
1:14 your offering to the LORD is a burnt **o** of birds, A
1:14 you shall choose your **o** from turtledoves
1:17 a burnt **o,** an offering by fire of pleasing odor A
1:17 an **o** by fire of pleasing odor to the LORD. D
2: 1 When anyone presents a grain **o** to the LORD, B
2: 1 the **o** shall be of choice flour;
2: 2 an **o** by fire of pleasing odor to the LORD. D
2: 3 what is left of the grain **o** shall be for Aaron B
2: 4 When you present a grain **o** baked in the oven, B
2: 5 If your **o** is grain prepared on a griddle,
2: 6 in pieces, and pour oil on it; it is a grain **o.** B
2: 7 If your **o** is grain prepared in a pan,
2: 8 the grain **o** that is prepared in any of these ways; B
2: 9 from the grain **o** its token portion and turn this B
2: 9 an **o** by fire of pleasing odor to the LORD. D
2:10 what is left of the grain **o** shall be for Aaron B
2:11 No grain **o** that you bring to the LORD shall B
2:11 or honey into smoke as an **o** by fire to the LORD. D
2:12 You may bring them to the LORD as an **o**
2:14 If you bring a grain **o** of first fruits to the LORD, B
2:14 the grain **o** of your first fruits coarse new grain B
2:15 lay frankincense on it; it is a grain **o.** B
2:16 it is an **o** by fire to the LORD. D
3: 1 If the **o** is a sacrifice of well-being,
3: 2 the head of the **o** and slaughter it at the entrance
3: 3 as an **o** by fire to the LORD, D
3: 5 with the burnt **o** that is on the wood on the fire, A
3: 5 as an **o** by fire of pleasing odor to the LORD. D
3: 6 If your **o** for a sacrifice of well-being to
3: 7 If you present a sheep as your **o,**
3: 8 and lay your hand on the head of the **o.**
3: 9 as an **o** by fire to the LORD: D
3:11 on the altar as a food **o** by fire to the LORD. D
3:12 If your **o** is a goat,
3:14 You shall present as your **o** from it,
3:14 as an **o** by fire to the LORD, D
3:16 the altar as a food **o** by fire for a pleasing odor. D
4: 3 the herd without blemish as a sin **o** to the LORD. C
4: 7 at the base of the altar of burnt **o,** A
4: 8 shall remove all the fat from the bull of sin **o:** C
4:10 into smoke upon the altar of burnt **o.** A
4:14 a sin **o** and bring it before the tent of meeting. C
4:18 of the altar of burnt **o** that is at the entrance of A
4:20 the bull just as is done with the bull of sin **o;** C
4:21 it is the sin **o** for the assembly. C
4:23 as his **o** a male goat without blemish.
4:24 at the spot where the burnt **o** is slaughtered A
4:24 before the LORD; it is a sin **o.** C
4:25 priest shall take some of the blood of the sin **o** C
4:25 and put it on the horns of the altar of burnt **o,** A
4:25 of its blood at the base of the altar of burnt **o.** A
4:28 a female goat without blemish as your **o,**
4:29 You shall lay your hand on the head of the sin **o;** C
4:29 and the sin **o** shall be slaughtered at the place of C
4:29 be slaughtered at the place of the burnt **o.** A
4:30 and put it on the horns of the altar of burnt **o,** A
4:31 as the fat is removed from the **o** of well-being, J
4:32 If the **o** you bring as a sin offering is a sheep,
4:32 If the offering you bring as a sin **o** is a sheep, C
4:33 shall lay your hand on the head of the sin **o;** C

Lev 4:33 and it shall be slaughtered as a sin **o** at the spot C
4:33 at the spot where the burnt **o** is slaughtered. A
4:34 priest shall take some of the blood of the sin **o** C
4:34 and put it on the horns of the altar of burnt **o,** A
5: 6 a sheep or a goat, as a sin **o;** C
5: 7 one for a sin **o** and the other for a burnt offering. C
5: 7 one for a sin offering and the other for a burnt **o.** A
5: 8 who shall offer first the one for the sin **o,** C
5: 9 He shall sprinkle some of the blood of the sin **o** C
5: 9 the base of the altar; it is a sin **o.** C
5:10 he shall offer for a burnt **o** according to A
5:11 you shall bring as your **o** for the sin
5:11 of an ephah of choice flour for a sin **o;** C
5:11 on it or lay frankincense on it, for it is a sin **o.** C
5:12 to the LORD; it is a sin **o.** C
5:13 Like the grain **o,** the rest shall be for the priest. B
5:15 you shall bring, as your guilt **o** to the LORD, E
5:15 by the sanctuary shekel; it is a guilt **o.** E
5:16 on your behalf with the ram of the guilt **o,** E
5:18 or the equivalent, as a guilt **o;** E
5:19 It is a guilt **o;** you have incurred guilt E
6: 6 as your guilt **o** to the LORD, E
6: 6 or its equivalent, for a guilt **o.** E
6: 9 This is the ritual of the burnt **o.** A
6: 9 The burnt **o** itself shall remain on the hearth A
6:10 ashes to which the fire has reduced the burnt **o** A
6:12 lay out the burnt **o** on it, A
6:14 This is the ritual of the grain **o:** B
6:15 handful of the choice flour and oil of the grain **o,** B
6:15 with all the frankincense that is on the **o,**
6:17 most holy, like the sin **o** and the guilt offering. C
6:17 like the sin offering and the guilt **o.** E
6:20 This is the **o** that Aaron and his sons shall offer to
6:20 of an ephah of choice flour as a regular **o,**
6:21 as a grain **o** of baked pieces, B
6:23 Every grain **o** of a priest shall be wholly burned; B
6:25 This is the ritual of the sin **o.** C
6:25 The sin **o** shall be slaughtered before the LORD C
6:25 at the spot where the burnt **o** is slaughtered; A
6:26 The priest who offers it as a sin **o** shall eat of it; C
6:30 But no sin **o** shall be eaten C
7: 1 This is the ritual of the guilt **o.** It is most holy; E
7: 2 at the spot where the burnt **o** is slaughtered, A
7: 2 they shall slaughter the guilt **o,** E
7: 5 on the altar as an **o** by fire to the LORD; D
7: 5 to the LORD; it is a guilt **o.** E
7: 7 The guilt **o** is like the sin offering, E
7: 7 The guilt offering is like the sin **o,** C
7: 8 priest who offers anyone's burnt **o** shall keep A
7: 8 the skin of the burnt **o** that he has offered. A
7: 9 And every grain **o** baked in the oven, B
7:10 But every other grain **o,** mixed with oil or dry, B
7:11 the ritual of the sacrifice of the **o** of well-being J
7:12 with the thank **o** unleavened cakes mixed with oil,
7:13 of well-being you shall bring your **o** with cakes
7:14 From this you shall offer one cake from each **o,**
7:14 who dashes the blood of the **o** of well-being. J
7:16 a votive **o** or a freewill offering, it shall be eaten
7:16 a votive offering or a freewill **o,** it shall be eaten H
7:25 an animal of which an **o** by fire may be made D
7:29 to the LORD your **o** from your sacrifice
7:30 own hands shall bring the LORD's **o** by fire; DI
7:30 that the breast may be raised as an elevation **o** G
7:32 of well-being you shall give to the priest as an **o;**
7:33 of the **o** of well-being shall have the right thigh J
7:34 For I have taken the breast of the elevation **o,** G
7:37 the ritual of the burnt **o,** the grain offering, A
7:37 the ritual of the burnt offering, the grain **o,** B
7:37 the grain offering, the sin **o,** the guilt offering, C
7:37 the grain offering, the sin offering, the guilt **o,** E
7:37 the guilt offering, the **o** of ordination,
8: 2 vestments, the anointing oil, the bull of sin **o,** C
8:14 He led forward the bull of sin **o;** C
8:14 upon the head of the bull of sin **o,** C
8:18 Then he brought forward the ram of burnt **o.** A
8:21 it was a burnt **o** for a pleasing odor, A
8:21 an **o** by fire to the LORD, D
8:27 raised them as an elevation **o** before the LORD. G
8:28 into smoke on the altar with the burnt **o.** A
8:28 This was an ordination **o** for a pleasing odor,
8:28 an **o** by fire to the LORD. D
8:29 and raised it as an elevation **o** before the LORD; G
9: 2 "Take a bull calf for a sin **o** and a ram for C
9: 2 for a sin offering and a ram for a burnt **o,** A
9: 3 'Take a male goat for a sin **o;** C
9: 3 yearlings without blemish, for a burnt **o;** A
9: 4 an ox and a ram for an **o** of well-being J
9: 4 and a grain **o** mixed with oil. B
9: 7 and sacrifice your sin **o** and your burnt offering, C
9: 7 and sacrifice your sin offering and your burnt **o,** A
9: 7 and sacrifice the **o** of the people,
9: 8 and slaughtered the calf of the sin **o,** C
9:10 the appendage of the liver from the sin **o** C
9:12 Then he slaughtered the burnt **o.** A
9:13 they brought him the burnt **o** piece by piece, A
9:14 with the burnt **o,** turned them into smoke on A
9:15 Next he presented the people's **o.**
9:15 the goat of the sin **o** that was for the people, C
9:15 and presented it as a sin **o** like the first one. C
9:16 He presented the burnt **o,** A
9:17 He presented the grain **o,** and, B
9:17 in addition to the burnt **o** of the morning. A
9:21 the right thigh Aaron raised as an elevation **o** G
9:22 and he came down after sacrificing the sin **o,** C
9:22 the burnt **o,** and the offering of well-being. A
9:22 the burnt offering, and the **o** of well-being. J
9:24 consumed the burnt **o** and the fat on the altar; A

Lev 10:12 the grain **o** that is left from the LORD's offerings B
10:15 to raise for an elevation **o** before the LORD; G
10:16 Moses made inquiry about the goat of the sin **o,** C
10:17 Why did you not eat the sin **o** in the sacred area? C
10:19 today they offered their sin **o** C
10:19 and their burnt **o** before the LORD; A
10:19 If I had eaten the sin **o** today, C
12: 6 of meeting a lamb in its first year for a burnt **o,** A
12: 6 and a pigeon or a turtledove for a sin **o.** C
12: 8 one for a burnt **o** and the other for a sin offering; A
12: 8 one for a burnt offering and the other for a sin **o;** C
14:10 and a grain **o** of three-tenths of an ephah B
14:12 and offer it as a guilt **o,** along with the log of oil, E
14:12 raise them as an elevation **o** before the LORD. G
14:13 the sin **o** and the burnt offering are slaughtered C
14:13 the sin offering and the burnt **o** are slaughtered A
14:13 the guilt **o,** like the sin offering, belongs to the E
14:13 offering, like the sin **o,** belongs to the priest: C
14:14 the blood of the guilt **o** and put it on the lobe of E
14:17 on top of the blood of the guilt **o.** E
14:19 the priest shall offer the sin **o,** C
14:19 Afterward he shall slaughter the burnt **o;** A
14:20 the burnt **o** and the grain offering on the altar. A
14:20 the burnt offering and the grain **o** on the altar. B
14:21 for a guilt **o** to be elevated, to make atonement E
14:21 of choice flour mixed with oil for a grain **o** and B
14:22 one for a sin **o** and the other for a burnt offering. C
14:22 one for a sin offering and the other for a burnt **o.** A
14:24 and the priest shall take the lamb of the guilt **o** E
14:24 the priest shall raise them as an elevation **o** G
14:25 of the guilt **o** and shall take some of the blood E
14:25 and shall take some of the blood of the guilt **o,** E
14:28 where the blood of the guilt **o** was placed. E
14:31 for a sin **o** and the other for a burnt offering, C
14:31 for a sin offering and the other for a burnt **o,** A
14:31 for a burnt offering, along with a grain **o;** B
15:15 one for a sin **o** and the other for a burnt offering; C
15:15 one for a sin offering and the other for a burnt **o;** A
15:30 priest shall offer one for a sin **o** and the other C
15:30 for a sin offering and the other for a burnt **o;** A
16: 3 with a young bull for a sin **o** and a ram for C
16: 3 for a sin offering and a ram for a burnt **o.** A
16: 5 the people of Israel two male goats for a sin **o,** C
16: 5 and one ram for a burnt **o.** A
16: 6 Aaron shall offer the bull as a sin **o** for himself, C
16: 9 and offer it as a sin **o;** C
16:11 shall present the bull as a sin **o** for himself, C
16:11 he shall slaughter the bull as a sin **o** for himself. C
16:15 sin **o** that is for the people and bring its blood C
16:24 then he shall come out and offer his burnt **o** and A
16:24 and offer his burnt offering and the burnt **o** of A
16:25 of the sin **o** he shall turn into smoke on the altar. C
16:27 bull of the sin **o** and the goat of the sin offering, C
16:27 bull of the sin offering and the goat of the sin **o,** C
17: 4 as an **o** to the LORD before the tabernacle of
17: 8 among them who offers a burnt **o** or sacrifice, A
19:21 he shall bring a guilt **o** for himself to the LORD, E
19:21 of the tent of meeting, a ram as guilt **o.** E
19:22 for him with the ram of guilt **o** before the LORD E
22:12 she shall not eat of the **o** of the sacred donations;
22:16 causing them to bear guilt requiring a guilt **o,** E
22:18 or of the aliens residing in Israel presents an **o,**
22:18 or as a freewill **o** that is offered to the LORD as H
22:18 that is offered to the LORD as a burnt **o,** A
22:21 in fulfillment of a vow or as a freewill **o,** H
22:23 or too short you may present for a freewill **o;** H
22:27 shall be acceptable as the LORD's **o** by fire. DI
22:29 you sacrifice a thanksgiving **o** to the LORD,
23: 5 there shall be a passover **o** to the LORD,
23:12 without blemish, as a burnt **o** to the LORD. A
23:13 grain **o** with it shall be two-tenths of an ephah B
23:13 an **o** by fire of pleasing odor to the LORD; D
23:13 and the drink **o** with it shall be of wine, F
23:14 until you have brought the **o** of your God:
23:15 the elevation **o,** you shall count off seven weeks; G
23:16 you shall present an **o** of new grain to the LORD.
23:17 as an elevation **o,** each made of two-tenths of G
23:18 they shall be a burnt **o** to the LORD, A
23:18 with their grain **o** and their drink offerings, B
23:18 an **o** by fire of pleasing odor to the LORD. D
23:19 You shall also offer one male goat for a sin **o,** C
23:20 first fruits as an elevation **o** before the LORD, G
23:25 and you shall present the LORD's **o** by fire. DI
23:27 and present the LORD's **o** by fire; DI
24: 7 to be a token **o** for the bread,
24: 7 as an **o** by fire to the LORD. D
27: 9 that may be brought as an **o** to the LORD,
27:11 that may not be brought as an **o** to the LORD,
Nu 4: 7 the bowls, and the flagons for the drink **o;** F
4:16 the regular grain **o,** and the anointing oil, B
5:15 And he shall bring the **o** required for her,
5:15 for it is a grain **o** of jealousy, B
5:15 a grain **o** of remembrance, B
5:18 place in her hands the grain **o** of remembrance, B
5:18 which is the grain **o** of jealousy. B
5:25 The priest shall take the grain **o** of jealousy B
5:25 and shall elevate the grain **o** before the LORD B
5:26 and the priest shall take a handful of the grain **o,** B
6:11 the priest shall offer one as a sin **o** and the other C
6:11 as a sin offering and the other as a burnt **o,** A
6:12 and bring a male lamb a year old as a guilt **o.** E
6:14 a year old without blemish as a burnt **o,** A
6:14 a year old without blemish as a sin **o,** C
6:14 one ram without blemish as an **o** of well-being, J
6:15 with their grain **o** and their drink offerings. B
6:16 and offer their sin **o** and burnt offering, C
6:16 and offer their sin offering and burnt **o,** A

Nu 6:17 the accompanying grain **o** and drink offering. B
6:17 the accompanying grain offering and drink **o.** F
6:20 the priest shall elevate them as an elevation **o** G
6:21 Their **o** to the LORD must be in accordance with
7:10 the leaders presented their **o** before the altar.
7:12 The one who presented his **o**
7:13 his **o** was one silver plate weighing one hundred
7:13 of choice flour mixed with oil for a grain **o;** B
7:15 one male lamb a year old, for a burnt **o;** A
7:16 one male goat for a sin **o;** C
7:17 This was the **o** of Nahshon son of Amminadab.
7:18 the leader of Issachar, presented an **o;**
7:19 his **o** one silver plate weighing one hundred
7:19 of choice flour mixed with oil for a grain **o;** B
7:21 one ram, one male lamb a year old, as a burnt **o;** A
7:22 one male goat as a sin **o;** C
7:23 This was the **o** of Nethanel son of Zuar.
7:25 his **o** was one silver plate weighing one hundred
7:25 of choice flour mixed with oil for a grain **o;** B
7:27 one male lamb a year old, for a burnt **o;** A
7:28 one male goat for a sin **o;** C
7:29 This was the **o** of Eliab son of Helon.
7:31 his **o** was one silver plate weighing one hundred
7:31 of choice flour mixed with oil for a grain **o;** B
7:33 one male lamb a year old, for a burnt **o;** A
7:34 one male goat for a sin **o;** C
7:35 This was the **o** of Elizur son of Shedeur.
7:37 his **o** was one silver plate weighing one hundred
7:37 of choice flour mixed with oil for a grain **o;** B
7:39 one male lamb a year old, for a burnt **o;** A
7:40 one male goat for a sin **o;** C
7:41 This was the **o** of Shelumiel son of Zurishaddai.
7:43 his **o** was one silver plate weighing one hundred
7:43 of choice flour mixed with oil for a grain **o;** B
7:45 one male lamb a year old, for a burnt **o;** A
7:46 one male goat for a sin **o;** C
7:47 This was the **o** of Eliasaph son of Deuel.
7:49 his **o** was one silver plate weighing one hundred
7:49 of choice flour mixed with oil for a grain **o;** B
7:51 one male lamb a year old, for a burnt **o;** A
7:52 one male goat for a sin **o;** C
7:53 This was the **o** of Elishama son of Ammihud.
7:55 his **o** was one silver plate weighing one hundred
7:55 of choice flour mixed with oil for a grain **o;** B
7:57 one male lamb a year old, for a burnt **o;** A
7:58 one male goat for a sin **o;** C
7:59 This was the **o** of Gamaliel son of Pedahzur.
7:61 his **o** was one silver plate weighing one hundred
7:61 of choice flour mixed with oil for a grain **o;** B
7:63 one male lamb a year old, for a burnt **o;** A
7:64 one male goat for a sin **o;** C
7:65 This was the **o** of Abidan son of Gideoni.
7:67 his **o** was one silver plate weighing one hundred
7:67 of choice flour mixed with oil for a grain **o;** B
7:69 one male lamb a year old, for a burnt **o;** A
7:70 one male goat for a sin **o;** C
7:71 This was the **o** of Ahiezer son of Ammishaddai.
7:73 his **o** was one silver plate weighing one hundred
7:73 of choice flour mixed with oil for a grain **o;** B
7:75 one male lamb a year old, for a burnt **o;** A
7:76 one male goat for a sin **o;** C
7:77 This was the **o** of Pagiel son of Ochran.
7:79 his **o** was one silver plate weighing one hundred
7:79 of choice flour mixed with oil for a grain **o;** B
7:81 one male lamb a year old, for a burnt **o;** A
7:82 one male goat for a sin **o;** C
7:83 This was the **o** of Ahira son of Enan.
7:84 This was the dedication **o** for the altar,
7:87 all the livestock for the burnt **o** twelve bulls, A
7:87 twelve male lambs a year old, with their grain **o;** B
7:87 and twelve male goats for a sin **o;** C
7:88 This was the dedication **o** for the altar,
8:8 a young bull and its grain **o** of choice flour B
8:8 and you shall take another young bull for a sin **o.** C
8:11 the LORD as an elevation **o** from the Israelites, G
8:12 he shall offer the one for a sin **o** and the other C
8:12 for a sin offering and the other for a burnt **o** to A
8:13 and you shall present them as an elevation **o** to G
8:15 and presented them as an elevation **o.** G
8:21 then Aaron presented them as an elevation **o** G
9:7 the LORD's **o** at its appointed time among I
9:13 from the people for not presenting the LORD's **o** I
15:3 an **o** by fire to the LORD from the herd or from D
15:3 whether a burnt **o** or a sacrifice, A
15:3 a sacrifice, to fulfill a vow or as a freewill **o** H
15:4 an **o** to the LORD shall present also
15:4 to the LORD shall present also a grain **o,** B
15:5 hin of wine as a drink **o** with the burnt offering F
15:5 hin of wine as a drink offering with the burnt **o** A
15:6 For a ram, you shall offer a grain **o,** B
15:7 drink **o** you shall offer one-third of a hin of wine, F
15:8 When you offer a bull as a burnt **o** or a sacrifice, A
15:8 a vow or as an **o** of well-being to the LORD, J
15:9 then you shall present with the bull a grain **o,** B
15:10 you shall present as a drink **o** half a hin of wine, F
15:10 as an **o** by fire, a pleasing odor to the LORD. D
15:13 in presenting an **o** by fire, D
15:14 and wishes to offer an **o** by fire, D
15:24 a burnt **o,** a pleasing odor to the LORD, A
15:24 together with its grain **o** and its drink offering, B
15:24 together with its grain offering and its drink **o,** F
15:24 and one male goat for a sin **o.** C
15:25 and they have brought their **o,**
15:25 an **o** by fire to the LORD, D
15:25 and their sin **o** before the LORD, for their error. C
15:27 a female goat a year old for a sin **o.** C
16:15 "Pay no attention to their **o.**

Nu 16:35 and consumed the two hundred fifty men **o**
18:9 every **o** of theirs that they render to me as
18:9 whether grain **o,** sin offering, or guilt offering, B
18:9 whether grain offering, sin **o,** or guilt offering, C
18:9 whether grain offering, sin offering, or guilt **o,** E
18:17 as an **o** by fire for a pleasing odor to the LORD; D
18:24 which they set apart as an **o** to the LORD.
18:26 you shall set apart an **o** from it to the LORD,
18:28 Thus you also shall set apart an **o** to the LORD
18:28 and from them you shall give the LORD's **o** to I
18:29 you shall set apart every **o** due to the LORD;
19:9 It is a purification **o.**
19:17 the burnt purification **o,** and running water shall
28:2 My **o,** the food for my offerings by fire,
28:3 the **o** by fire that you shall offer to the LORD: D
28:3 a year old without blemish, daily, as a regular **o.**
28:5 of an ephah of choice flour for a grain **o,** B
28:6 It is a regular burnt **o,** A
28:6 an **o** by fire to the LORD. D
28:7 Its drink **o** shall be one-fourth of a hin F
28:7 in the sanctuary you shall pour out a drink **o** F
28:8 at twilight with a grain **o** and a drink offering B
28:8 at twilight with a grain offering and a drink **o** F
28:8 you shall offer it as an **o** by fire, D
28:9 a grain **o,** mixed with oil, and its drink offering B
28:9 mixed with oil, and its drink **o—** F
28:10 this is the burnt **o** for every sabbath, A
28:10 to the regular burnt **o** and its drink offering. A
28:10 to the regular burnt offering and its drink **o.** F
28:11 of your months you shall offer a burnt **o** to A
28:12 of an ephah of choice flour for a grain **o,** mixed B
28:12 and two-tenths of choice flour for a grain **o,** B
28:13 of choice flour mixed with oil as a grain **o** B
28:13 a burnt **o** of pleasing odor, A
28:13 an **o** by fire to the LORD. D
28:14 burnt **o** of every month throughout the months A
28:15 And there shall be one male goat for a sin **o** to C
28:15 offered in addition to the regular burnt **o** A
28:15 to the regular burnt offering and its drink **o.** F
28:16 of the first month there shall be a passover **o** to
28:19 You shall offer an **o** by fire, D
28:19 a burnt **o** to the LORD: A
28:20 Their grain **o** shall be of choice flour mixed B
28:22 also one male goat for a sin **o,** C
28:23 You shall offer these in addition to the burnt **o** A
28:23 which belongs to the regular burnt **o.** A
28:24 for seven days, the food of an **o** by fire, D
28:24 offered in addition to the regular burnt **o** A
28:24 to the regular burnt offering and its drink **o.** F
28:26 when you offer a grain **o** of new grain to B
28:27 You shall offer a burnt **o,** A
28:28 Their grain **o** shall be of choice flour mixed B
28:31 to the regular burnt **o** with its grain offering, A
28:31 to the regular burnt offering with its grain **o,** B
28:31 you shall offer them and their drink **o.** F
29:2 and you shall offer a burnt **o,** a pleasing odor to A
29:3 Their grain **o** shall be of choice flour mixed B
29:5 with one male goat for a sin **o,** C
29:6 the burnt **o** of the new moon and its grain A
29:6 of the new moon and its grain **o,** B
29:6 and the regular burnt **o** and its grain offering, A
29:6 and the regular burnt offering and its grain **o,** B
29:6 a pleasing odor, an **o** by fire to the LORD. D
29:8 You shall offer a burnt **o** to the LORD, A
29:9 Their grain **o** shall be of choice flour mixed B
29:11 with one male goat for a sin **o,** C
29:11 in addition to the sin **o** of atonement, C
29:11 and the regular burnt **o** and its grain offering, A
29:11 and the regular burnt offering and its grain **o,** B
29:13 You shall offer a burnt **o,** an offering by fire, A
29:13 You shall offer a burnt offering, an **o** by fire, D
29:14 Their grain **o** shall be of choice flour mixed B
29:16 also one male goat for a sin **o,** C
29:16 in addition to the regular burnt **o,** A
29:16 its grain **o** and its drink offering. B
29:16 its grain offering and its drink **o.** F
29:18 the grain **o** and the drink offerings for the bulls, B
29:19 also one male goat for a sin **o,** C
29:19 to the regular burnt **o** and its grain offering, A
29:19 to the regular burnt offering and its grain **o,** B
29:21 the grain **o** and the drink offerings for the bulls, B
29:22 also one male goat for a sin **o,** C
29:22 to the regular burnt **o** and its grain offering A
29:22 to the regular burnt offering and its grain **o** B
29:22 and its grain offering and its drink **o.** F
29:24 the grain **o** and the drink offerings for the bulls, B
29:25 also one male goat for a sin **o,** C
29:25 in addition to the regular burnt **o,** A
29:25 its grain **o** and its drink offering. B
29:25 its grain offering and its drink **o.** F
29:27 the grain **o** and the drink offerings for the bulls, B
29:28 also one male goat for a sin **o,** C
29:28 to the regular burnt **o** and its grain offering A
29:28 to the regular burnt offering and its grain **o** B
29:28 and its grain offering and its drink **o.** F
29:30 the grain **o** and the drink offerings for the bulls, B
29:31 also one male goat for a sin **o,** C
29:31 in addition to the regular burnt **o,** A
29:31 its grain **o,** and its drink offerings. B
29:33 the grain **o** and the drink offerings for the bulls, B
29:34 also one male goat for a sin **o,** C
29:34 besides the regular burnt **o,** its grain offering, A
29:34 besides the regular burnt offering, its grain **o,** B
29:34 its grain offering, and its drink **o.** F
29:36 You shall offer a burnt **o,** an offering by fire, A
29:36 You shall offer a burnt offering, an **o** by fire, D
29:37 the grain **o** and the drink offerings for the bull, B

Nu 29:38 also one male goat for a sin **o,** C
29:38 to the regular burnt **o** and its grain offering A
29:38 to the regular burnt offering and its grain **o** B
29:38 and its grain offering and its drink **o.** F
31:29 to Eleazar the priest as an **o** to the LORD.
31:41 Moses gave the tribute, the **o** for the LORD,
31:50 And we have brought the LORD's **o,** I
31:52 the gold of the **o** that they offered to the LORD,
Dt 13:16 as a whole burnt **o** to the LORD your God. A
16:10 contributing a freewill **o** in proportion to H
18:3 from those **o** a sacrifice, whether an ox or a sheep:
Jos 22:26 'Let us now build an altar, not for burnt **o,** A
22:29 the LORD by building an altar for burnt **o,** A
22:29 for burnt offering, grain **o,** or sacrifice, B
Jdg 6:26 take the second bull, and offer it as a burnt **o** A
11:31 to be offered up by me as a burnt **o."** A
13:16 but if you want to prepare a burnt **o,** A
13:19 So Manoah took the kid with the grain **o,** B
13:23 not have accepted a burnt **o** and a grain offering A
13:23 not have accepted a burnt offering and a grain **o** B
1Sa 2:29 the choicest parts of every **o** of my people Israel?'
3:14 not be expiated by sacrifice or **o** forever."
6:3 but by all means return him a guilt **o.** E
6:4 "What is the guilt **o** that we shall return to him?" E
6:8 which you are returning to him as a guilt **o.** E
6:14 and offered the cows as a burnt **o** to the LORD. A
6:17 the Philistines returned as a guilt **o** to the LORD: E
7:9 sucking lamb and offered it as a whole burnt **o** A
7:10 As Samuel was **o** up the burnt offering,
7:10 As Samuel was offering up the burnt **o,** A
13:9 So Saul said, "Bring the burnt **o** here to me, A
13:9 And he offered the burnt **o.** A
13:10 As soon as he had finished **o** the burnt offering,
13:10 As soon as he had finished offering the burnt **o,** A
13:12 so I forced myself, and offered the burnt **o."** A
26:19 up against me, may he accept an **o;**
2Sa 6:18 When David had finished **o** the burnt offerings
15:12 While Absalom was **o** the sacrifices,
24:22 here are the oxen for the burnt **o,** A
1Ki 8:54 Now when Solomon finished **o** all this prayer
9:25 **o** incense before the LORD.
18:29 on until the time of the **o** of the oblation,
18:33 and pour it on the burnt **o** and on the wood." A
18:36 At the time of the **o** of the oblation,
18:38 fire of the LORD fell and consumed the burnt **o,** A
2Ki 3:20 The next day, about the time of the morning **o,**
3:27 and offered him as a burnt **o** on the wall. A
5:17 for your servant will no longer offer burnt **o** A
10:25 soon as he had finished presenting the burnt **o,** A
16:13 and offered his burnt **o** and his grain offering, A
16:13 and offered his burnt offering and his grain **o,** B
16:13 and his grain offering, poured his drink **o,** F
16:15 "Upon the great altar offer the morning burnt **o,** A
16:15 evening grain **o,** and the king's burnt offering, B
16:15 and the king's burnt **o,** and his grain offering, A
16:15 and the king's burnt offering, and his grain **o,** B
16:15 with the burnt **o** of all the people of the land, A
16:15 their grain **o,** and their drink offering; B
16:15 their grain offering, and their drink **o;** F
16:15 then dash against it all the blood of the burnt **o,** A
23:10 or a daughter pass through fire as an **o** to Molech.
1Ch 6:49 his sons made offerings on the altar of burnt **o** A
16:2 When David had finished **o** the burnt offerings
16:29 bring an **o,** and come before him.
16:40 to the LORD on the altar of burnt **o** regularly, A
21:23 and the wheat for a grain **o.** B
21:26 with fire from heaven on the altar of burnt **o.** A
21:29 of burnt **o** were at that time in the high place A
22:1 of the LORD God and here the altar of burnt **o** A
23:29 the choice flour for the grain **o,** B
23:29 the wafers of unleavened bread, the baked **o,**
23:29 the baked offering, the **o** mixed with oil,
29:14 that we should be able to make this freewill **o?** H
29:17 who are present here, **o** freely and joyously to you.
2Ch 2:4 and dedicate it to him for **o** fragrant incense
2:4 and for the regular **o** of the rows of bread,
4:6 to rinse what was used for the burnt **o.** A
7:1 down from heaven and consumed the burnt **o** A
7:7 the burnt **o** and the grain offering and the fat A
7:7 the burnt offering and the grain **o** and the fat B
8:13 **o** according to the commandment of Moses for
26:16 and entered the temple of the LORD to make **o**
26:18 Uzziah, to make **o** to the LORD,
26:18 who are consecrated to make **o.**
26:19 Now he had a censer in his hand to make **o,**
29:18 the altar of burnt **o** and all its utensils, A
29:21 a sin **o** for the kingdom and for the sanctuary C
29:23 Then the male goats for the sin **o** were brought C
29:24 the priests slaughtered them and made a sin **o** C
29:24 the burnt **o** and the sin offering should be made A
29:24 the burnt offering and the sin **o** should be made C
29:27 Then Hezekiah commanded that the burnt **o** A
29:27 the burnt **o** began, the song to the LORD began A
29:28 all this continued until the burnt **o** was finished. A
29:29 When the **o** was finished, the king
29:32 all these were for a burnt **o** to the LORD. A
30:14 the altars for **o** incense they took away and threw
35:14 of Aaron were occupied in **o** the burnt offerings
Ezr 3:5 offerings of everyone who made a freewill **o** H
6:17 four hundred lambs, and as a sin **o** for all Israel, C
8:25 the **o** for the house of our God that the king,
8:28 silver and the gold are a freewill **o** to the LORD, H
8:35 and as a sin **o** twelve male goats; C
8:35 all this was a burnt **o** to the LORD. A
10:19 guilt **o** was a ram of the flock for their guilt. E
Ne 10:33 the regular grain **o,** the regular burnt offering, B
10:33 regular burnt **o,** the sabbaths, the new moons, A

Ne 10:34 the Levites, and the people, for the wood **o**,
13: 5 where they had previously put the grain **o**, B
13: 9 with the grain **o** and the frankincense. B
13:31 and I provided for the wood **o**,
Job 42: 8 and offer up for yourselves a burnt **o**; A
Ps 38: T *A Psalm of David, for the memorial* **o**.
40: 6 Sacrifice and **o** you do not desire,
40: 6 Burnt **o** and sin offering you have not required. A
40: 6 Burnt offering and sin **o** you have not required. C
51:16 if I were to give a burnt **o**, A
54: 6 With a freewill **o** I will sacrifice to you; H
66:15 I will make an **o** of bulls and goats.
70: T *To the leader. Of David, for the memorial* **o**.
96: 8 bring an **o**, and come into his courts.
Pr 14: 9 Fools mock at the guilt **o**, E
Isa 19:21 and will worship with sacrifice and burnt **o**, A
40:16 nor are its animals enough for a burnt **o**. A
53:10 When you make his life an **o** for sin,
57: 6 to them you have poured out a drink **o**, F
57: 6 you have brought a grain **o**. B
65: 3 sacrificing in gardens and **o** incense on bricks;
66: 3 whoever presents a grain **o**, B
66: 3 whoever makes a memorial **o** of frankincense,
66:20 from all the nations as an **o** to the LORD,
66:20 as the Israelites bring a grain **o** in a clean vessel B
Jer 14:12 although they offer burnt **o** and grain offering, A
14:12 although they offer burnt offering and grain **o**, B
Eze 16:21 and delivered them up as an **o** to them.
16:25 **o** yourself to every passer-by,
20:26 in their **o** up all their firstborn,
20:28 and presented the provocation of their **o**;
21:29 **O** false visions for you, divining lies for you,
40:38 where the burnt **o** was to be washed. A
40:39 on which the burnt **o** and the sin offering and A
40:39 on which the burnt offering and the sin **o** and C
40:39 and the sin offering and the guilt **o** were to E
40:42 also four tables of hewn stone for the burnt **o**, A
40:43 on the tables the flesh of the **o** was to be laid.
42:13 grain **o**, the sin offering, and the guilt offering, B
42:13 grain offering, the sin **o**, and the guilt offering, C
42:13 grain offering, the sin offering, and the guilt **o**, E
43:18 for **o** burnt offerings upon it and for dashing blood
43:19 says the Lord GOD, a bull for a sin **o**. C
43:21 You shall also take the bull of the sin **o**, C
43:22 a male goat without blemish for a sin **o**; C
43:24 and offer them up as a burnt **o** to the LORD. A
43:25 shall provide daily a goat for a sin **o**; C
44:11 they shall slaughter the burnt **o** and the sacrifice A
44:27 he shall offer his sin **o**, says the Lord GOD. C
44:29 They shall eat the grain **o**, the sin offering, B
44:29 They shall eat the grain offering, the sin **o**, C
44:29 the sin offering, and the guilt **o**; E
44:30 and every **o** of all kinds from all your offerings,
45:13 This is the **o** that you shall make:
45:15 This is the **o** for grain offerings, burnt offerings,
45:16 with the prince in Israel in making this **o**.
45:19 priest shall take some of the blood of the sin **o** C
45:22 the people of the land a young bull for a sin **o**. C
45:23 of the festival he shall provide as a burnt **o** to A
45:23 and a male goat daily for a sin **o**. C
45:24 He shall provide as a grain **o** an ephah B
46: 2 priests shall offer his burnt **o** and his offerings A
46: 4 The burnt **o** that the prince offers to the LORD A
46: 5 and the grain **o** with the ram shall be an ephah, B
46: 5 and the grain **o** with the lambs shall be as much B
46: 7 a grain **o** he shall provide an ephah with the bull B
46:11 festivals and the appointed seasons the grain **o** B
46:12 When the prince provides a freewill **o**, H
46:12 either a burnt **o** or offerings of well-being as A
46:12 of well-being as a freewill **o** to the LORD, H
46:12 and he shall offer his burnt **o** or his offerings A
46:13 without blemish, for a burnt **o** to the LORD A
46:14 a grain **o** with it morning by morning regularly, B
46:14 as a grain **o** to the LORD; B
46:15 Thus the lamb and the grain **o** and the oil shall B
46:15 morning by morning, as a regular burnt **o**. A
46:20 the place where the priests shall boil the guilt **o** E
46:20 the guilt offering and the sin **o**, C
46:20 and where they shall bake the grain **o**, B
Da 2:46 that a grain **o** and incense be offered to him. B
8:11 the regular burnt **o** away from him and A
8:12 over to it together with the regular burnt **o**; A
8:13 is this vision concerning the regular burnt **o**, A
9:27 of the week he shall make sacrifice and **o** cease;
11:31 They shall abolish the regular burnt **o** and set up A
12:11 the time that the regular burnt **o** is taken away A
Hos 11: 2 they kept sacrificing to the Baals, and **o** incense
Joel 1: 9 The grain **o** and the drink offering are cut off B
1: 9 The grain offering and the drink **o** are cut off F
1:13 Grain **o** and drink offering are withheld from B
1:13 Grain offering and drink **o** are withheld from F
2:14 a grain **o** and a drink offering for the LORD, B
2:14 a grain offering and a drink **o** for the LORD, F
Am 4: 5 bring a thank **o** of leavened bread,
Zep 3:10 my scattered ones, shall bring my **o**.
Mal 1: 7 By **o** polluted food on my altar.
1:10 and I will not accept an **o** from your hands.
1:11 to my name, and a pure **o**;
1:13 and this you bring as your **o**!
2:12 or to bring an **o** to the LORD of hosts.
2:13 and groaning because he no longer regards the **o**
3: 4 the **o** of Judah and Jerusalem will be pleasing to
Mt 5:23 So when you are **o** your gift at the altar,
Mk 7:11 from me is Corban' (that is, an **o** to God)—
Lk 1:10 Now at the time of the incense **o**,
5:14 make an **o** for your cleansing,
23:36 coming up and **o** him sour wine,
Jn 16: 2 that by doing so they are **o** worship to God.
Ac 14:18 the crowds from **o** sacrifice to them.
Ro 15:16 so that the **o** of the Gentiles may be acceptable,
Eph 5: 2 a fragrant **o** and sacrifice to God.
Php 2:17 a libation over the sacrifice and the **o** of your faith,
4:18 from Epaphroditus the gifts you sent, a fragrant **o**,
Heb 10:10 through the **o** of the body of Jesus Christ once
10:11 **o** again and again the same sacrifices
10:14 For by a single **o** he has perfected
10:18 there is no longer any **o** for sin.
Tob 4:11 is an excellent **o** in the presence of the Most High.
Jdt 16:16 For every sacrifice as a fragrant **o** is a small thing,
16:19 from his bedchamber she gave as a votive **o**.
Wis 3: 6 and like a sacrificial burnt **o** he accepted them. A
Sir 7: 9 and when I make an **o** to the Most High God,
7:31 the first fruits, the guilt **o**, E
34:21 one sacrifices ill-gotten goods, the **o** is blemished;
35: 2 the commandments makes an **o** of well-being. J
35: 4 and one who gives alms sacrifices a thank **o**.
35: 8 The **o** of the righteous enriches the altar,
38:11 and pour oil on your **o**, as much as you can afford.
47: 2 As the fat is set apart from the **o** of well-being, J
50:13 in their splendor held the Lord's **o** in their hands
50:14 and arranging the **o** to the Most High,
50:15 for the cup and poured a drink **o** of the blood of F
Bar 1:10 incense, and prepare a grain **o**, and offer them B
Aza 1:15 no burnt **o**, or sacrifice, or oblation, or incense, A
1:15 to make an **o** before you and to find mercy.
1Mc 1:54 a desolating sacrilege on the altar of burnt **o**. A
1:59 the altar that was on top of the altar of burnt **o**. A
4:44 to do about the altar of burnt **o**, A
4:53 on the new altar of burnt **o** that they had built. A
4:56 a sacrifice of well-being and a thanksgiving **o**.
7:33 to show him the burnt **o** that was being offered A
2Mc 1: 8 and we offered sacrifice and grain **o**, B
2:11 "They were consumed because the sin **o** had C
12:43 and sent it to Jerusalem to provide for a sin **o**. C
14:31 the great and holy temple while the priests were **o**
1Es 1:11 the **o** to the Lord as it is written in the book
1:14 because the priests were **o** the fat until nightfall;
8:66 and as a thank **o** twelve male goats—
2Es 10:45 in the world before any **o** was offered in it.
4Mc 3:16 he poured out the drink as an **o** to God.
18:11 and Isaac who was offered as a burnt **o**, A

OFFERINGS (339) [OFFER]

A. BURNT OFFERINGS (118)
B. OFFERINGS OF WELL-BEING (30)
C. DRINK OFFERINGS (27)
D. OFFERINGS BY FIRE (20)
E. GRAIN OFFERINGS (15)
F. FREEWILL OFFERINGS (14)
G. †LORD'S OFFERINGS (7)
H. SIN OFFERINGS (7)

Ge 8:20 and offered burnt **o** on the altar. A
Ex 10:25 let us have sacrifices and burnt **o** to sacrifice A
20:24 sacrifice on it your burnt **o** and your offerings A
20:24 your burnt offerings and your **o** of well-being, B
22:29 You shall not delay to make **o** from the fullness
24: 5 who offered burnt **o** and sacrificed oxen A
24: 5 and sacrificed oxen as **o** of well-being to B
25:29 flagons and bowls with which to pour drink **o**; C
29:28 from their sacrifice of **o** of well-being, B
32: 6 and offered burnt **o** and brought sacrifices A
36: 3 and they received from Moses all the freewill **o** F
36: 3 still kept bringing him freewill **o** every morning, F
37:16 bowls and flagons with which to pour drink **o**. C
Lev 2: 3 a most holy part of the **o** by fire to the LORD. D
2:10 a most holy part of the **o** by fire to the LORD. D
2:13 omit from your grain **o** the salt of the covenant E
2:13 with all your **o** you shall offer salt.
4:35 with the **o** by fire to the LORD. D
5:12 with the **o** by fire to the LORD; D
6:12 into smoke the fat pieces of the **o** of well-being. B
6:17 I have given it as their portion of my **o** by fire; D
6:18 from the LORD's **o** by fire; DG
7:35 to his sons from the **o** made by fire to the LORD,
7:38 the people of Israel to bring their **o** to the LORD,
8:31 with the bread that is in the basket of ordination **o**,
10:12 from the LORD's **o** by fire, DG
10:13 from the **o** by fire to the LORD; D
10:14 sacrifices of the **o** of well-being of the people B
10:15 together with the **o** by fire of the fat, D
14:32 who cannot afford the **o** for his cleansing.
21: 6 for they offer the LORD's **o** by fire, DG
21:21 shall come near to offer the LORD's **o** by fire; DG
22:22 or put any of them on the altar as **o** by fire D
23: 8 you shall present the LORD's **o** by fire; DG
23:18 along with their grain offering and their drink **o**, C
23:36 you shall present the LORD's **o** by fire; DG
23:36 convocation and present the LORD's **o** by fire; DG
23:37 for presenting to the LORD **o** by fire— D
23:37 burnt **o** and grain offerings, A
23:37 burnt offerings and grain **o**, E
23:37 sacrifices and drink **o**, each on its proper day— C
23:38 and apart from all your votive **o**,
23:38 and apart from all your freewill **o**, F
24: 9 most holy portions for him from the **o** by fire D
Nu 6:15 with their grain offering and their drink **o**. C
7: 2 who were over those who were enrolled, made **o**.
7: 3 They brought their **o** before the LORD,
7:10 The leaders also presented **o** for the dedication of
7:11 They shall present their **o**, one leader each day,
10:10 you shall blow the trumpets over your burnt **o** A
18: 8 I have given you charge of the **o** made to me,
Nu 18:11 the gifts of all the elevation **o** of the Israelites;
18:19 All the holy **o** that the Israelites present to
23: 3 "Stay here beside your burnt **o** while I go aside. A
23: 6 beside his burnt **o** with all the officials of Moab. A
23:15 "Stand here beside your burnt **o**, A
23:17 beside his burnt **o** with the officials of Moab. A
28: 2 My offering, the food for my **o** by fire, D
28:14 drink **o** shall be half a hin of wine for a bull, C
29: 6 and its grain offering, and their drink **o**, C
29:11 and its grain offering, and their drink **o**. C
29:18 the grain offering and the drink **o** for the bulls, C
29:19 and its grain offering, and their drink **o**. C
29:21 the grain offering and the drink **o** for the bulls, C
29:24 the grain offering and the drink **o** for the bulls, C
29:27 the grain offering and the drink **o** for the bulls, C
29:30 the grain offering and the drink **o** for the bulls, C
29:31 its grain offering, and its drink **o**. C
29:33 the grain offering and the drink **o** for the bulls, C
29:37 the grain offering and the drink **o** for the bull, C
29:39 to your votive **o** and your freewill offerings,
29:39 to your votive offerings and your freewill **o**, F
29:39 as your burnt **o**, your grain offerings, A
29:39 as your burnt offerings, your grain **o**, E
29:39 your drink **o**, and your offerings of well-being. C
29:39 your drink offerings, and your **o** of well-being. B
Dt 12: 6 bringing there your burnt **o** and your sacrifices, A
12: 6 your votive gifts, your freewill **o**, F
12:11 your burnt **o** and your sacrifices, A
12:13 not offer your burnt **o** at any place you happen A
12:14 there you shall offer your burnt **o** A
12:17 your freewill **o**, or your donations; F
12:27 You shall present your burnt **o**, A
27: 6 offer up burnt **o** on it to the LORD your God, A
33:10 and whole burnt **o** on your altar. A
Jos 8:31 and they offered on it burnt **o** to the LORD, A
8:31 and sacrificed **o** of well-being. B
13:14 the **o** by fire to the LORD God D
22:23 to offer burnt **o** or grain offerings or offerings A
22:23 to offer burnt offerings or grain **o** or offerings E
22:23 or grain offerings or **o** of well-being on it, B
22:27 of the LORD in his presence with our burnt **o** A
22:27 offerings and sacrifices and **o** of well-being; B
22:28 which our ancestors made, not for burnt **o**, A
Jdg 20:26 Then they offered burnt **o** and sacrifices A
21: 4 and offered burnt **o** and sacrifices of well-being. A
1Sa 2:17 they treated the **o** of the LORD with contempt.
2:28 the family of your ancestor all my **o** by fire D
2:29 at my sacrifices and my **o** that I commanded,
6:15 the people of Beth-shemesh offered burnt **o** A
10: 8 to you to present burnt **o** and offer sacrifices A
11:15 There they sacrificed **o** of well-being before B
13: 9 offering here to me, and the **o** of well-being." B
15:22 "Has the LORD as great delight in burnt **o** A
2Sa 6:17 and David offered burnt **o** and offerings A
6:17 offered burnt offerings and **o** of well-being B
6:18 When David had finished offering the burnt **o** A
6:18 the burnt offerings and the **o** of well-being, B
24:24 I will not offer burnt **o** to the LORD my God A
24:25 and offered burnt **o** and offerings of well-being. A
24:25 and offered burnt offerings and **o** of well-being. B
1Ki 3: 4 Solomon used to offer a thousand burnt **o** on A
3:15 He offered up burnt **o** and offerings of A
3:15 offered up burnt offerings and **o** of well-being, B
8:64 the burnt **o** and the grain offerings and A
8:64 the grain **o** and the fat pieces of the sacrifices E
8:64 to receive the burnt **o** and the grain offerings A
8:64 the grain **o** and the fat pieces of the sacrifices E
9:25 burnt **o** and sacrifices of well-being on the altar A
10: 5 and his burnt **o** that he offered at the house of A
2Ki 10:24 they proceeded to offer sacrifices and burnt **o**. A
12: 3 the people continued to sacrifice and make **o** on
12: 4 and the money from the voluntary **o** brought into
12:16 The money from the guilt **o** and the money from
12:16 and the money from the sin **o** was not brought H
14: 4 the people still sacrificed and made **o** on
15: 4 the people still sacrificed and made **o** on
15:35 the people still sacrificed and made **o** on
16: 4 He sacrificed and made **o** on the high places,
16:13 the blood of his **o** of well-being against the altar. B
17:11 there they made **o** on all the high places,
18: 4 until those days the people of Israel had made **o**
22:17 and have made **o** to other gods,
23: 5 to make **o** in the high places at the cities of Judah
23: 5 those also who made **o** to Baal, to the sun,
23: 8 the priests had made **o**, from Geba to Beer-sheba;
1Ch 6:49 and his sons made **o** on the altar of burnt offering
16: 1 and they offered burnt **o** and offerings A
16: 1 they offered burnt offerings and **o** of well-being B
16: 2 When David had finished offering the burnt **o** A
16: 2 and the **o** of well-being, he blessed the people B
16:40 to offer burnt **o** to the LORD on the altar A
21:23 see, I present the oxen for burnt **o**, A
21:24 nor offer burnt **o** that cost me nothing." A
21:26 presented burnt **o** and offerings of well-being. A
21:26 presented burnt offerings and **o** of well-being. B
23:13 that he and his sons forever should make **o**
23:31 and whenever burnt **o** are offered to the LORD A
29: 6 leaders of ancestral houses made their freewill **o**, F
29:21 the next day they offered sacrifices and burnt **o** A
2Ch 1: 6 and offered a thousand burnt **o** on it. A
2: 4 and for burnt **o** morning and evening, A
2: 6 except as a place to make **o** before him?
7: 7 for there he offered the burnt **o** and the fat of A
7: 7 and the fat of the **o** of well-being because B
8:12 Then Solomon offered up burnt **o** to the LORD A
9: 4 and his burnt **o** that he offered at the house of A
13:11 and every evening burnt **o** and fragrant incense, A

2Ch 23:18 to offer burnt **o** to the LORD, A
24:14 utensils for the service and for the burnt **o**, A
24:14 They offered burnt **o** in the house of A
25:14 and worshiped them, making **o** to them.
28: 3 and he made **o** in the valley of the son of Hinnom,
28: 4 He sacrificed and made **o** on the high places,
28:25 of Judah he made high places to make **o**
29: 7 and have not offered incense or made burnt **o** A
29:11 and to be his ministers and make **o** to him."
29:31 near, bring sacrifices and thank **o** to the house of
29:31 The assembly brought sacrifices and thank **o**;
29:31 all who were of a willing heart brought burnt **o**. A
29:32 The number of the burnt **o** that A
29:33 The consecrated **o** were six hundred bulls
29:34 and could not skin all the burnt **o**, so, A
29:35 the great number of burnt **o** there was the fat of A
29:35 there was the fat of the **o** of well-being, B
29:35 there were the drink **o** for the burnt offerings. C
29:35 there were the drink offerings for the burnt **o**. A
30:15 and brought burnt **o** into the house of the LORD. A
30:22 sacrificing **o** of well-being and giving thanks to B
30:24 a thousand bulls and seven thousand sheep for **o**,
31: 2 for burnt **o** and offerings of well-being, A
31: 2 for burnt offerings and **o** of well-being, B
31: 3 from his own possessions was for the burnt **o**: A
31: 3 the burnt **o** of morning and evening, A
31: 3 and the burnt **o** for the sabbaths, the new moons, A
31:14 was in charge of the freewill **o** to God, F
31:14 for the LORD and the most holy **o**.
32:12 and upon it you shall make your **o**'?
34:25 Because they have forsaken me and have made **o**
35: 7 as passover **o** for all that were present,
35: 8 the passover **o** two thousand six hundred lambs
35: 9 the Levites for the passover **o** five thousand lambs
35:12 the burnt **o** so that they might distribute them A
35:13 and they boiled the holy **o** in pots, in caldrons,
35:14 offering the burnt **o** and the fat parts until night; A
35:16 the passover and to offer burnt **o** on the altar of A
Ezr 1: 4 besides freewill **o** for the house of God F
2:68 heads of families made freewill **o** for the house F
3: 2 to offer burnt **o** on it, A
3: 3 and they offered burnt **o** upon it to the LORD, A
3: 4 offered the daily burnt **o** by number according A
3: 5 and after that the regular burnt **o**, A
3: 5 the **o** at the new moon and at all
3: 5 the **o** of everyone who made a freewill offering to
3: 6 the seventh month they began to offer burnt **o** A
6: 3 sacrifices are offered and burnt **o** are brought; A
6: 9 sheep for burnt **o** to the God of heaven, wheat, A
7:16 with the freewill **o** of the people and the priests, F
7:17 and their grain **o** and their drink offerings, E
7:17 and their grain offerings and their drink **o**, C
8:35 offered burnt **o** to the God of Israel, A
Ne 10:33 and the sin **o** to make atonement for Israel, H
Job 1: 5 in the morning and offer burnt **o** according to A
Ps 16: 4 their drink **o** of blood I will not pour out C
20: 3 May he remember all your **o**,
50: 8 your burnt **o** are continually before me. A
51:19 in burnt **o** and whole burnt offerings; A
51:19 in burnt offerings and whole burnt **o**; A
56:12 I will render thank **o** to you.
66:13 I will come into your house with burnt **o**; A
66:15 I will offer to you burnt **o** of fatlings, A
119:108 Accept my **o** of praise, O LORD,
Isa 1:11 I have had enough of burnt **o** of rams and the fat A
1:13 bringing **o** is futile; incense is an abomination
43:23 have not brought me your sheep for burnt **o**, A
43:23 I have not burdened you with **o**,
56: 7 burnt **o** and their sacrifices will be accepted A
Jer 1:16 they have made **o** to other gods,
6:20 Your burnt **o** are not acceptable, A
7: 9 commit adultery, swear falsely, make **o** to Baal,
7:18 and they pour out drink **o** to other gods, C
7:21 Add your burnt **o** to your sacrifices, A
7:22 to them or command them concerning burnt **o** A
11:12 and cry out to the gods to whom they make **o**,
11:13 up to shame, altars to make **o** to Baal.
11:17 provoking me to anger by making **o** to Baal.
17:26 bringing burnt **o** and sacrifices, A
17:26 and sacrifices, grain **o** and frankincense, E
17:26 and bringing thank **o** to the house of the LORD.
18:15 they burn **o** to a delusion;
19: 4 by making **o** in it to other gods whom neither they
19: 5 burn their children in the fire as burnt **o** to Baal, A
19:13 the houses upon whose roofs **o** have been made
32:29 the houses on whose roofs **o** have been made
33:11 as they bring thank **o** to the house of the LORD:
33:18 a man in my presence to offer burnt **o**, A
33:18 to offer burnt offerings, to make grain **o**, and E
41: 5 bringing grain **o** and incense to present at E
44: 3 in that they went to make **o** and serve other gods
44: 5 to turn from their wickedness and make no **o**
44: 8 making **o** to other gods in the land of Egypt
44:15 that their wives had been making **o** to other gods,
44:17 make **o** to the queen of heaven
44:18 from the time we stopped making **o** to the queen
44:19 "Indeed we will go on making **o** to the queen
44:21 "As for the **o** that you made in the towns of Judah
44:23 It is because you burned **o**,
44:25 to perform the vows that we have made, to make **o**
48:35 at a high place and make **o** to their gods.
Eze 20:28 and there they poured out their drink **o**. C
40:42 the burnt **o** and the sacrifices were slaughtered. A
42:13 the LORD shall eat the most holy **o**;
42:13 there they shall deposit the most holy **o**—
43:18 offering burnt **o** upon it and for dashing blood A
43:27 priests shall offer upon the altar your burnt **o** A
43:27 your burnt offerings and your **o** of well-being; B
44: 8 And you have not kept charge of my sacred **o**;
44:13 nor come near any of my sacred **o**,
44:30 and every offering of all kinds from all your **o**,
45:15 This is the offering for grain **o**, burnt offerings, E
45:15 This is the offering for grain offerings, burnt **o**, A
45:15 **o** of well-being, to make atonement for them, B
45:17 the burnt **o**, grain offerings, and drink offerings, A
45:17 grain **o**, and drink offerings, at the festivals, E
45:17 and drink **o**, at the festivals, the new moons, C
45:17 he shall provide the sin **o**, grain offerings, H
45:17 he shall provide the sin offerings, grain **o**, E
45:17 the burnt **o**, and the offerings of well-being, A
45:17 the burnt offerings, and the **o** of well-being, B
45:25 he shall make the same provision for sin **o**, H
45:25 burnt **o**, and grain offerings, and for the oil. A
45:25 burnt offerings, and grain **o**, and for the oil. E
46: 2 offer his burnt offering and his **o** of well-being, B
46:12 either a burnt offering or **o** of well-being as B
46:12 offer his burnt offering or his **o** of well-being B
Hos 4:13 and make **o** upon the hills, under oak, poplar,
6: 6 the knowledge of God rather than burnt **o**. A
9: 4 They shall not pour drink **o** of wine to the LORD, C
Am 4: 5 and proclaim freewill **o**, publish them; F
5:22 you offer me your burnt **o** and grain offerings, A
5:22 you offer me your burnt offerings and grain **o**, E
5:22 the **o** of well-being of your fatted animals I will B
5:25 to me sacrifices and **o** the forty years in
Mic 6: 6 Shall I come before him with burnt **o**, A
Hab 1:16 he sacrifices to his net and makes **o** to his seine;
Mal 2: 3 the dung of your **o**, and I will put you out
3: 3 until they present **o** to the LORD
3: 8 In your tithes and **o**!
Mk 12:33 much more important than all whole burnt **o** A
Heb 10: 5 he said, "Sacrifices and **o** you have not desired,
10: 6 in burnt **o** and sin offerings you have taken no A
10: 6 and sin **o** you have taken no pleasure. H
10: 8 in sacrifices and **o** and burnt offerings
10: 8 burnt **o** and sin offerings" (these are offered A
10: 8 sin **o**" (these are offered according to the law), H
Jdt 4:14 offered the daily burnt **o**, the votive offerings, A
4:14 the votive **o**, and freewill offerings of the people.
4:14 the votive offerings, and freewill **o** of the people. F
16:16 of all whole burnt **o** to you is a very little thing; A
16:18 offered their burnt **o**, their freewill offerings, A
16:18 offered their burnt offerings, their freewill **o**, F
Sir 14:11 and present worthy **o** to the Lord.
30:18 a mouth that is closed are like **o** of food placed
34:23 The Most High is not pleased with the **o** of
35: 1 The one who keeps the law makes many **o**;
Bar 1:10 burnt **o** and sin offerings and incense, A
1:10 burnt offerings and sin **o** and incense, H
Aza 1:17 though it were with burnt **o** of rams and bulls, A
1Mc 1:22 the cups for drink **o**, the bowls, C
1:45 forbid burnt **o** and sacrifices and drink offerings A
1:45 forbid burnt offerings and sacrifices and drink **o** C
4:56 and joyfully offered burnt **o**; A
5:54 and offered burnt **o**, because they had returned A
2Mc 2:10 came down and consumed the whole burnt **o**. A
2:13 and letters of kings about votive **o**.
5:16 the votive **o** that other kings had made to enhance
6: 5 with abominable **o** that were forbidden by
9:16 he would adorn with the finest **o**;
1Es 2: 7 the other things added as votive **o** for the temple
2: 9 of votive **o** from many whose hearts were stirred.
4:52 and an additional ten talents a year for burnt **o** A
4:52 with the commandment to make seventeen **o**;
5:49 to offer burnt **o** upon it, A
5:50 at the proper times and burnt **o** to the Lord A
5:52 the regular **o** and sacrifices on sabbaths and
3Mc 1: 9 and made thank **o** and did what was fitting for
3:17 with magnificent and most beautiful **o**,
2Es 10:46 Solomon built the city, and offered **o**;
13:13 and some were bringing others as **o**.

OFFERS (13) [OFFER]

Lev 6:26 The priest who **o** it as a sin offering shall eat of it;
7: 8 priest who **o** anyone's burnt offering shall keep
7: 9 shall belong to the priest who **o** it.
7:18 nor shall it be credited to the one who **o** it;
7:33 the one among the sons of Aaron who **o** the blood
17: 8 among them who **o** a burnt offering or sacrifice,
22:21 anyone **o** a sacrifice of well-being to the LORD,
Ezr 7:13 or Levites in my kingdom who freely **o** to go
Isa 66: 3 like one who **o** swine's blood;
Eze 46: 4 The burnt offering that the prince **o** to the LORD
Heb 9: 7 without taking the blood that he **o** for himself and
Sir 34:24 a son before his father's eyes is the person who **o**
35: 3 The one who returns a kindness **o** choice flour,

OFFICE (20) [OFFICER, OFFICERS, OFFICES]

Ge 40:13 up your head and restore you to your **o**;
41:13 I was restored to my **o**,
Dt 17: 9 with the levitical priests and the judge who is in **o**
19:17 priests and the judges who are in **o** in those days,
26: 3 You shall go to the priest who is in **o** at that time,
1Ch 9:22 and the seer Samuel established them in their **o**
Isa 22:19 I will thrust you from your **o**,
1Ti 3: 1 whoever aspires to the **o** of bishop desires
Heb 7: 5 the priestly **o** have a commandment in the law
7:20 for others who became priests took their **o** without
7:23 by death from continuing in **o**;
Sir 7: 4 Do not seek from the Lord high **o**,
46: 1 and was the successor of Moses in the prophetic **o**.
1Mc 11:63 intending to remove him from **o**.
2Mc 4:10 When the king assented and Jason came to **o**,
4:27 Although Menelaus continued to hold the **o**,
4:50 remained in **o**, growing in wickedness,
10:13 Unable to command the respect due his **o**,
13: 3 he thought that he would be established in **o**.
4Mc 4:17 that if the **o** were conferred on him he would pay

OFFICER (23) [OFFICE]

Ge 39: 1 an **o** of Pharaoh, the captain of the guard,
Jdg 9:28 the son of Jerubbaal and Zebul his **o** serve the men
1Ki 22: 9 Then the king of Israel summoned an **o** and said,
2Ki 25:19 the city he took an **o** who had been in command of
1Ch 9:11 son of Ahitub, the chief **o** of the house of God;
26:24 was chief **o** in charge of the treasuries.
27: 4 Mikloth was the chief **o** of his division.
27:16 Eliezer son of Zichri was chief **o**;
2Ch 18: 8 Then the king of Israel summoned an **o** and said,
24:11 the **o** of the chief priest would come and empty
26:11 by the secretary Jeiel and the **o** Maaseiah,
31:12 The chief **o** in charge of them was Conaniah
31:13 and of Azariah the chief **o** of the house of God.
Ne 11:11 son of Ahitub, **o** of the house of God,
Pr 6: 7 Without having any chief or **o** or ruler,
Jer 20: 1 who was chief **o** in the house of the LORD,
52:25 the city he took an **o** who had been in command of
Lk 12:58 and the judge hand you over to the **o**, and the **o** throw you in prison.
Jn 18:12 their **o**, and the Jewish police arrested Jesus
2Ti 2: 4 the soldier's aim is to please the enlisting **o**.
1Mc 2:25 the king's **o** who was forcing them to sacrifice,
1Es 4:49 that no **o** or satrap or governor

OFFICERS[‡] (86) [OFFICE]

Ge 40: 2 Pharaoh was angry with his two **o**,
40: 7 So he asked Pharaoh's **o**, who were with him
Ex 14: 7 the other chariots of Egypt with **o** over all of them.
15: 4 his picked **o** were sunk in the Red Sea.
18:21 set such men over them as **o** over thousands,
18:25 as **o** over thousands, hundreds, fifties, and tens.
Nu 11:16 to be the elders of the people and **o** over them;
31:14 Moses became angry with the **o** of the army,
31:48 the **o** who were over the thousands of the army,
Jos 1:10 Then Joshua commanded the **o** of the people,
3: 2 the end of three days the **o** went through the camp
8:33 with their elders and **o** and their judges,
23: 2 their elders and heads, their judges and **o**,
24: 1 the heads, the judges, and the **o** of Israel;
1Sa 8:15 and of your vineyards and give it to his **o**
2Sa 11: 1 David sent Joab with his **o** and all Israel with him;
19: 5 of all your **o** who have saved your life today,
19: 6 that commanders and **o** are nothing to you;
1Ki 9:23 the chief **o** who were over Solomon's work:
14:27 committed them to the hands of the **o** of the guard,
2Ki 6: 8 he took counsel with his **o**.
6:11 he called his **o** and said to them,
6:12 Then one of his **o** said, "No one, my lord king.
9:11 When Jehu came back to his master's **o**,
9:28 His **o** carried him in a chariot to Jerusalem,
10:25 Jehu said to the guards and to the **o**,
10:25 The guards and the **o** threw them out,
24:12 his servants, his **o**, and his palace officials.
1Ch 12:14 These Gadites were **o** of the army,
12:18 and made them **o** of his troops.
23: 4 six thousand shall be **o** and judges,
24: 5 for there were **o** of the sanctuary and **o** of God
24: 6 and the **o**, and Zadok the priest,
25: 1 and the **o** of the army also set apart for the service
26:26 and the **o** of the thousands and the hundreds,
26:29 to outside duties for Israel, as **o** and judges.
27: 1 and their **o** who served the king in all matters
28: 1 the **o** of the divisions that served the king,
28:21 also the **o** and all the people will be wholly
29: 6 and the **o** over the king's work.
2Ch 8: 9 they were soldiers, and his **o**,
8:10 These were the chief **o** of King Solomon,
12: 5 to the **o** of Judah, who had gathered at Jerusalem
12: 6 the **o** of Israel and the king humbled themselves
12:10 committed them to the hands of the **o** of the guard,
19:11 and the Levites will serve you as **o**.
24:11 Whenever the chest was brought to the king's **o** by
32: 3 with his **o** and his warriors to stop the flow of
32:21 and commanders and **o** in the camp of the king
35: 8 and Jehiel, the chief **o** of the house of God,
Ezr 7:28 and before all the king's mighty **o**.
Ne 2: 9 king had sent **o** of the army and cavalry with me.
Isa 31: 9 and his **o** desert the standard in panic,"
Jer 29:26 so that there may be **o** in the house of the LORD
39:13 and all the chief **o** of the king of Babylon sent
41: 1 of the royal family, one of the chief **o** of the king,
46:26 to King Nebuchadrezzar of Babylon and his **o**.
52:10 and also killed all the **o** of Judah at Riblah.
Eze 23:15 all of them looking like **o**—
23:23 **o** and warriors, all of them riding on horses.
Da 11: 5 of his **o** shall grow stronger than he and shall rule
Na 2: 5 He calls his **o**; they stumble
Mk 6:21 for his courtiers and **o** and for the leaders
Lk 22: 4 the chief priests and **o** of the temple police about
22:52 the **o** of the temple police,
Jdt 2:14 generals, and **o** of the Assyrian army.
5:22 Holofernes' **o** and all the inhabitants of
12:10 and did not invite any of his **o**.
14: 3 the camp and rouse the **o** of the Assyrian army.
14:12 and the captains and to all their other **o**.
AdE 2: 3 The king shall appoint **o** in all the provinces
2:18 and the **o** to celebrate his marriage to Esther;

1Mc 1: 6 So he summoned his most honored **o**,
1: 8 Then his **o** began to rule, each in his own place.
2:15 The king's **o** who were enforcing
2:17 Then the king's **o** spoke to Mattathias as follows:
2:31 And it was reported to the king's **o**,
5:40 Timothy said to the **o** of his forces,
5:42 he stationed the **o** of the army at the stream
10:37 Let their **o** and leaders be of their own number,
10:63 and he said to his **o**,
11:63 the **o** of Demetrius had come to Kadesh in Galilee
1Es 1: 8 Zechariah, and Jehiel, the chief **o** of the temple,
7: 2 assisting the elders of the Jews and the chief **o** of
3Mc 5:44 Then the Friends and **o** departed with great joy,

OFFICES (5) [OFFICE]

2Ch 8:14 for their **o** of praise and ministry alongside
31:16 for their service according to their **o**,
31:17 and upwards was according to their **o**,
35: 2 to their **o** and encouraged them in the service of
1Mc 13:15 in connection with the **o** he held,

OFFICIAL (14) [OFFICIALS, OFFICIALS', OFFICIATE]

1Ki 4:19 And there was one **o** in the land of Judah.
2Ki 8: 6 So the king appointed an **o** for her, saying,
Ne 2:10 and Tobiah the Ammonite **o** heard this,
2:19 the Horonite and Tobiah the Ammonite **o**,
Ecc 5: 8 for the high **o** is watched by a higher,
Da 2:15 the royal **o**, "Why is the decree of the king
11:20 in his place one who shall send an **o** for the glory
Mic 7: 3 the **o** and the judge ask for a bribe,
Jn 4:46 Now there was a royal **o** whose son lay ill
4:49 The **o** said to him, "Sir, come down
Ac 8:27 a court **o** of the Candace, queen of the Ethiopians,
18: 8 Crispus, the **o** of the synagogue,
18:17 of them seized Sosthenes, the **o** of the synagogue,
3Mc 6:30 the **o** in charge of the revenues and ordered him

OFFICIALS‡ (188) [OFFICIAL]

Ge 12:15 **o** of Pharaoh saw her, they praised her to Pharaoh.
37:36 one of Pharaoh's **o**, the captain of the guard.
Ex 5:21 into bad odor with Pharaoh and his **o**,
7:10 down his staff before Pharaoh and his **o**,
7:20 of his **o** he lifted up the staff and struck the water
8: 3 and into the houses of your **o** and of your people,
8: 4 up on you and on your people and on all your **o**.' "
8: 9 to pray for you and for your **o** and for your people,
8:11 and your houses and your **o** and your people;
8:21 your **o**, and your people, and into your houses;
8:29 from his **o**, and from his people;
8:31 from his **o**, and from his people;
9:14 and upon your **o**, and upon your people,
9:20 Those **o** of Pharaoh who feared the word of
9:30 But as for you and your **o**,
9:34 and hardened his heart, he and his **o**.
10: 1 I have hardened his heart and the heart of his **o**,
10: 6 the houses of all your **o** and of all the Egyptians—
10: 7 Pharaoh's **o** said to him,
11: 3 in the sight of Pharaoh's **o** and in the sight of
11: 8 Then all these **o** of yours shall come down to me,
12:30 he and all his **o** and all the Egyptians;
14: 5 the minds of Pharaoh and his **o** were changed
23: 8 You shall take no bribe, for a bribe blinds the **o**,
Nu 22: 8 so the **o** of Moab stayed with Balaam.
22:13 and said to the **o** of Balak, "Go to your own land,
22:14 So the **o** of Moab rose and went to Balak,
22:15 Once again Balak sent **o**, more numerous
22:21 saddled his donkey, and went with the **o** of Moab.
22:35 So Balaam went on with the **o** of Balak.
22:40 and sent them to Balaam and to the **o** who were
23: 6 beside his burnt offerings with all the **o** of Moab.
23:17 beside his burnt offerings with the **o** of Moab.
Dt 1:15 and **o**, throughout your tribes.
16:18 You shall appoint judges and **o**
20: 5 Then the **o** shall address the troops, saying,
20: 8 The **o** shall continue to address the troops, saying,
20: 9 When the **o** have finished addressing the troops,
29:10 the leaders of your tribes, your elders, and your **o**,
31:28 to me all the elders of your tribes and your **o**,
Jdg 8: 6 But the **o** of Succoth said,
8:14 and he listed for him the **o** and elders of Succoth,
2Sa 15:14 Then David said to all his **o** who were with him
15:15 The king's **o** said to the king,
15:18 All his **o** passed by him;
1Ki 1: 9 the king's sons, and all the royal **o** of Judah,
4: 2 and these were his high **o**:
4: 5 Azariah son of Nathan was over the **o**;
4: 7 Solomon had twelve **o** over all Israel,
4:27 Those **o** supplied provisions for King Solomon
9:22 they were the soldiers, they were his **o**,
10: 5 the food of his table, the seating of his **o**, and
2Ki 24:12 his servants, his officers, and his palace **o**.
24:14 He carried away all Jerusalem, all the **o**,
24:15 the king's mother, the king's wives, his **o**,
25:24 "Do not be afraid because of the Chaldean **o**;
1Ch 18:17 and David's sons were the chief **o** in the service of
19: 3 the **o** of the Ammonites said to Hanun,
28: 1 David assembled at Jerusalem all the **o** of Israel,
28: 1 the **o** of the tribes, the officers of the divisions
28: 1 together with the palace **o**, the mighty warriors,
2Ch 9: 4 the food of his table, the seating of his **o**, and
17: 7 In the third year of his reign he sent his **o**,
21: 4 and also some of the **o** of Israel.
22: 8 the **o** of Judah and the sons of Ahaziah's brothers,
24:17 of Jehoiada the **o** of Judah came and did obeisance
2Ch 24:23 and destroyed all the **o** of the people from
28:14 and the booty before the **o** and all the assembly.
28:21 the king and of the **o**, and gave tribute to the king
29:20 assembled the **o** of the city,
29:30 King Hezekiah and the **o** commanded the Levites
30: 2 For the king and his **o** and all the assembly
30: 6 and Judah with letters from the king and his **o**,
30:12 and the **o** commanded by the word of the LORD.
30:24 and the **o** gave the assembly a thousand bulls
31: 8 Hezekiah and the **o** came and saw the heaps,
32:31 in the matter of the envoys of the **o** of Babylon,
34:13 and some of the Levites were scribes, and **o**,
35: 8 His **o** contributed willingly to the people,
36:18 and the treasures of the king and of his **o**,
Ezr 4: 5 and they bribed **o** to frustrate their plan throughout
4: 9 the judges, the envoys, the **o**, the Persians,
8:20 whom David and his **o** had set apart to attend
9: 1 the **o** approached me and said,
9: 2 and in this faithlessness the **o** and leaders have led
10: 8 of the **o** and the elders all their property should
10:14 Let our **o** represent the whole assembly,
Ne 2:16 The **o** did not know where I had gone
2:16 the **o**, and the rest that were to do the work.
4:14 up and said to the nobles and the **o** and the rest of
4:19 And I said to the nobles, the **o**,
5: 7 I brought charges against the nobles and the **o**;
5:17 at my table one hundred fifty people, Jews and **o**,
7: 5 into my mind to assemble the nobles and the **o** and
9:32 upon our kings, our **o**, our priests, our prophets,
9:34 our **o**, our priests, and our ancestors have
9:38 the names of our **o**, our Levites,
12:32 after them went Hoshaiah and half the **o** of Judah,
12:40 and I and half of the **o** with me;
13:11 So I remonstrated with the **o** and said,
Est 1: 3 he gave a banquet for all his **o** and ministers.
1: 8 to all the **o** of his palace to do as each one desired.
1:11 in order to show the peoples and the **o** her beauty;
1:14 and Memucan, the seven **o** of Persia and Media,
1:16 in the presence of the king and the **o**,
1:16 also to all the **o** and all the peoples who are in all
1:18 the king's **o**, and there will be no end of contempt
1:21 This advice pleased the king and the **o**,
2:18 Then the king gave a great banquet to all his **o**
3: 1 and set his seat above all the **o** who were
3:12 and to the **o** of all the peoples, to every province
5:11 and how he had advanced him above the **o** and
6: 9 be handed over to one of the king's most noble **o**;
8: 9 and the **o** of the provinces from India to Ethiopia,
9: 3 All the **o** of the provinces,
9: 3 and the royal **o** were supporting the Jews,
Ps 105:22 to instruct his **o** at his pleasure,
Pr 25: 1 These are other proverbs of Solomon that the **o**
29:12 ruler listens to falsehood, all his **o** will be wicked.
Isa 30: 4 his **o** are at Zoan and his envoys reach Hanes,
Jer 2:26 their kings, their **o**, their priests, and their prophets,
4: 9 courage shall fail the king and the **o**;
8: 1 the bones of the kings of Judah, the bones of its **o**,
17:25 riding in chariots and on horses, they and their **o**,
24: 1 together with the **o** of Judah, the artisans,
24: 8 so will I treat King Zedekiah of Judah, his **o**,
25:18 its kings and **o**, to make them a desolation and
25:19 his servants, his **o**, and all his people;
26:10 When the **o** of Judah heard these things,
26:11 Then the priests and the prophets said to the **o** and
26:12 Jeremiah spoke to all the **o** and all the people,
26:16 Then the **o** and all the people said to the priests
26:21 with all his warriors and all the **o**,
29: 2 the court, the leaders of Judah and Jerusalem,
32:32 they, their kings and their **o**,
34:10 all the **o** and all the people who had entered into
34:19 the **o** of Judah, the **o** of Jerusalem, the eunuchs,
34:21 And as for King Zedekiah of Judah and his **o**,
35: 4 which was near the chamber of the **o**,
36:12 and all the **o** were sitting there:
36:12 Zedekiah son of Hananiah, and all the **o**.
36:14 Then all the **o** sent Jehudi son of Nethaniah son
36:19 Then the **o** said to Baruch, "Go and hide,
36:21 the king and all the **o** who stood beside the king.
37:14 and arrested Jeremiah and brought him to the **o**.
37:15 The **o** were enraged at Jeremiah,
38: 4 Then the **o** said to the king,
38:17 If you will only surrender to the **o** of the king
38:18 But if you do not surrender to the **o** of the king
38:22 the king of Judah being led out to the **o** of the king
38:25 If the **o** should hear that I have spoken with you,
38:27 the **o** did come to Jeremiah and questioned him;
39: 3 all the **o** of the king of Babylon came and sat in
39: 3 with all the rest of the **o** of the king of Babylon.
44:17 just as we and our ancestors, our kings and our **o**,
44:21 your kings and your **o**, and the people of the land,
49:38 and destroy their king and **o**, says the LORD.
50:35 and against her **o** and her sages!
51:57 I will make her **o** and her sages drunk,
Eze 11: 1 and Pelatiah son of Benaiah, **o** of the people.
17:12 to Jerusalem, took its king and its **o**,
22:27 Its **o** within it are like wolves tearing the prey,
Da 3: 2 the **o** of the provinces to assemble and come to
3: 3 the magistrates, and all the **o** of the provinces,
9: 8 falls on us, our kings, our **o**, and our ancestors,
Hos 7: 3 and the **o** by their treachery.
7: 5 On the day of our king the **o** became sick with
7:16 their **o** shall fall by the sword because of the rage
9:15 I will love them no more; all their **o** are rebels.
Am 1:15 he and his **o** together, says the LORD.
2: 3 and will kill all its **o** with him, says the LORD.
Zep 1: 8 of the LORD's sacrifice I will punish the **o** and
3: 3 The **o** within it are roaring lions;
Ac 13:15 the **o** of the synagogue sent them a message,
17: 8 the city **o** were disturbed when they heard this,
19:31 even some **o** of the province of Asia,
AdE 1:16 the king but also all the king's governors and **o**"
13: 1 from India to Ethiopia and to the **o** under them:
Sir 10: 2 As the people's judge is, so are his **o**;
1Mc 10:33 let all **o** cancel also the taxes on their livestock.
10:41 that the government **o** have not paid as they did in
10:42 of silver that my **o** have received every year from
12:45 and the remaining troops and all the **o**,
13:37 with you and to write to our **o** to grant you release
14:42 the sanctuary and appoint **o** over its tasks and over
1Es 8:67 and these **o** honored the people and the temple of
3Mc 5:39 But the **o** who were at table with him,

OFFICIALS' (1) [OFFICIAL]

Ex 8:24 into the house of Pharaoh and into his **o** houses;

OFFICIATE (1) [OFFICIAL]

Heb 13:10 from which those who **o** in the tent have no right

OFFSCOURING (KJV) See RUBBISH

OFFSETS (2) [OFF, SET]

1Ki 6: 6 for around the outside of the house he made **o** on
Eze 41: 6 There were **o** all around the wall of the temple

OFFSHOOTS (1) [OFF, SHOOT]

4Mc 1:28 so there are many **o** of these plants,

OFFSPRING (140) [OFFSPRINGS]

Ge 3:15 and between your **o** and hers;
12: 7 and said, "To your **o** I will give this land."
13:15 to you and to your **o** forever.
13:16 I will make your **o** like the dust of the earth;
13:16 your **o** also can be counted.
15: 3 And Abram said, "You have given me no **o**,
15:13 your **o** shall be aliens in a land that is not theirs,
16:10 "I will so greatly multiply your **o** that they cannot
17: 7 and your **o** after you throughout their generations,
17: 7 to be God to you and to your **o** after you.
17: 8 And I will give to you, and to your **o** after you,
17: 9 and your **o** after you throughout their generations.
17:10 between me and you and your **o** after you:
17:12 from any foreigner who is not of your **o**.
17:19 as an everlasting covenant for his **o** after him.
19:32 so that we may preserve **o** through our father."
19:34 so that we may preserve **o** through our father."
21:12 it is through Isaac that **o** shall be named for you.
21:13 a nation of him also, because he is your **o**."
21:23 that you will not deal falsely with me or with my **o**
22:17 and I will make your **o** as numerous as the stars
22:17 And your **o** shall possess the gate of their enemies,
22:18 and by your **o** shall all the nations of
24: 7 'To your **o** I will give this land,'
24:60 may your **o** gain possession of the gates
26: 4 I will make your **o** as numerous as the stars
26: 4 and will give to your **o** all these lands;
26: 4 for themselves through your **o**,
26:24 and will bless you and make your **o** numerous
28: 4 to you and to your **o** with you,
28:13 on which you lie I will give to you and to your **o**;
28:14 and your **o** shall be like the dust of the earth,
28:14 of the earth shall be blessed in you and in your **o**.
32:12 and make your **o** as the sand of the sea,
35:12 and I will give the land to your **o** after you."
38: 8 raise up **o** for your brother."
38: 9 But since Onan knew that the **o** would not be his,
38: 9 so that he would not give **o** to his brother.
46: 6 Jacob and all his **o** with him,
46: 7 all his **o** he brought with him into Egypt.
46: 8 Jacob and his **o**, who came to Egypt.
46:26 into Egypt, who were his own **o**, not including
48: 4 and will give this land to your **o** after you for
48: 6 the **o** born to you after them, they shall be yours.
48:19 and his **o** shall become a multitude of nations."
Lev 18:21 You shall not give any of your **o** to sacrifice them
20: 2 in Israel, who give any of their **o** to Molech shall
20: 3 because they have given of their **o** to Molech,
20: 4 when they give of their **o** to Molech,
21:15 that he may not profane his **o** among his kin;
21:17 of your **o** throughout their generations who has
22: 3 If anyone among all your **o**
22: 4 of Aaron's **o** who has a leprous disease or suffers
22:13 without **o**, and returns to her father's house,
Dt 1:28 We actually saw there the **o** of the Anakim!' "
2:33 along with his **o** and all his people.
9: 2 the **o** of the Anakim, whom you know.
28:59 the LORD will overwhelm both you and your **o**
Jos 24: 3 the land of Canaan and made his **o** many.
Jdg 8:30 Now Gideon had seventy sons, his own **o**,
2Sa 4: 8 the king this day on Saul and on his **o**."
7:12 I will raise up your **o** after you,
1Ki 1:48 of my **o** to sit on my throne and permitted me
1Ch 16:13 O **o** of his servant Israel,
17:11 I will raise up your **o** after you,
Job 5:25 and your **o** like the grass of the earth.
18:19 They have no **o** or descendant among their people,
21: 8 and their **o** before their eyes.
27:14 and their **o** have not enough to eat.
39: 3 when they crouch to give birth to their **o**,
Ps 21:10 You will destroy their **o** from the earth,
22:23 All you **o** of Jacob, glorify him;
22:23 stand in awe of him, all you **o** of Israel!

Ps 102:28 their **o** shall be established in your presence.
105: 6 O **o** of his servant Abraham,
Isa 1: 4 **o** who do evil, children who deal corruptly,
14:22 **o** and posterity, says the LORD.
22:24 the **o** and issue, every small vessel,
41: 8 Jacob, whom I have chosen, the **o** of Abraham,
43: 5 I will bring your **o** from the east,
44: 3 and my blessing on your **o**.
45:19 I did not say to the **o** of Jacob,
45:25 In the LORD all the **o** of Israel shall triumph
48:19 your **o** would have been like the sand,
53:10 he shall see his **o**, and shall prolong his days;
57: 3 you **o** of an adulterer and a whore.
57: 4 not children of transgression, the **o** of deceit—
61: 9 and their **o** among the peoples;
65:23 for they shall be **o** blessed by the LORD—
Jer 7:15 as I cast out all your kinsfolk, all the **o**
22:28 Why are he and his **o** hurled out and cast away in
22:30 of his **o** shall succeed in sitting on the throne
23: 8 the LORD lives who brought out and led the **o** of
30:10 and your **o** from the land of their captivity.
31:36 then also the **o** of Israel would cease to be a nation
31:37 be explored, then I will reject all the **o** of Israel
33:22 so I will increase the **o** of my servant David,
33:26 the **o** of Jacob and of my servant David and
33:26 his descendants as rulers over the **o** of Abraham,
36:31 And I will punish him and his **o** and his servants
46:27 and your **o** from the land of their captivity.
49:10 His **o** are destroyed, his kinsfolk
La 2:20 Should women eat their **o**,
Eze 17:13 He took one of the royal **o** and made a covenant
20: 5 I swore to the **o** of the house of Jacob—
Da 11: 6 and his **o** shall not endure.
Hos 9:16 I will kill the cherished **o** of their womb.
Mal 2: 3 I will rebuke your **o**, and spread dung
2:15 And what does the one God desire? Godly **o**.
Ac 17:28 'For we too are his **o**.'
17:29 Since we are God's **o**, we ought not to think that
Gal 3:16 the promises were made to Abraham and to his **o**;
3:16 but it says, "And to your **o**," that is, to one person,
3:19 until the **o** would come to whom
3:29 if you belong to Christ, then you are Abraham's **o**,
Wis 3:13 their **o** are accursed.
3:16 and the **o** of an unlawful union will perish.
Sir 10:19 Whose **o** are worthy of honor? Human **o**.
10:19 Whose **o** are worthy of honor? Those who fear
10:19 Whose **o** are unworthy of honor? Human **o**.
10:19 Whose **o** are unworthy of honor? Those who break
16: 1 and do not rejoice in ungodly **o**.
26:21 *So your o will prosper,*
41: 6 and on their **o** will be a perpetual disgrace.
44:13 Their **o** will continue forever,
44:21 that the nations would be blessed through his **o**;
44:21 and exalt his **o** like the stars,
Bar 4:32 wretched will be the city that received your **o**.
Sus 1:56 "You **o** of Canaan and not of Judah,
1Mc 1:38 she became strange to her **o**,
Man 1: 1 and Isaac and Jacob and of their righteous **o**;
2Es 2: 6 so that they may have no **o**.
12:32 who will arise from the **o** of David,
4Mc 14:14 have a sympathy and parental love for their **o**.
15: 4 a deeper sympathy toward their **o** than do
15:13 yearning of parents toward **o**,
16: 9 some unmarried, others married and without **o**.
18: 1 O Israelite children, **o** of the seed of Abraham,

OFFSPRINGS (1) [OFFSPRING]

Gal 3:16 it does not say, "And to **o**," as of many;

OFTEN[‡] (54) [OFTENTIMES]

1Sa 1: 7 as **o** as she went up to the house of the LORD,
18:30 and as **o** as they came out,
2Sa 8:10 Now Hadadezer had **o** been at war with Toi.
1Ki 14:28 **o** as the king went into the house of the LORD,
1Ch 18:10 Now Hadadezer had **o** been at war with Tou.
Job 21:17 "How **o** is the lamp of the wicked put out?
21:17 How **o** does calamity come upon them?
21:17 How **o** does God distribute pains in his anger?
21:18 How **o** are they like straw before the wind,
Ps 78:38 **o** he restrained his anger, and did not stir up all his
78:40 How **o** they rebelled against him in the wilderness
129: 1 "**O** have they attacked me
129: 2 "**o** have they attacked me from my youth,
Pr 29: 1 One who is **o** reproved, yet remains stubborn,
Isa 28:19 As **o** as it passes through, it will take you;
Jer 21: 2 a wonderful deed for us, as he has **o** done,
31:20 As **o** as I speak against him, I still remember him.
Mt 9:14 saying, "Why do we and the Pharisees fast **o**,
17:15 he **o** falls into the fire and **o** into the water.
18:21 against me, how **o** should I forgive?
23:37 How **o** have I desired to gather your children
Mk 5: 4 for he had **o** been restrained with shackles
9:22 It has **o** cast him into the fire and into the water,
Lk 13:34 How **o** have I desired to gather your children
Jn 18: 2 because Jesus **o** met there with his disciples.
Ac 24:26 and for that reason he used to send for him very **o**
26:11 By punishing them **o** in all the synagogues I tried
Ro 1:13 that I have **o** intended to come to you
15:22 This is the reason that I have so **o** been hindered
1Co 11:25 Do this, as **o** as you drink it,
11:26 For as **o** as you eat this bread and drink the cup,
2Co 7: 4 I **o** boast about you; I have great pride in you;
8:22 we are sending our brother whom we have **o** tested
11:23 with countless floggings, and **o** near death.
11:27 hungry and thirsty, **o** without food,
Php 3:18 I have **o** told you of them,
2Ti 1:16 because he **o** refreshed me and was not ashamed
Rev 11: 6 to strike the earth with every kind of plague, as **o**
Tob 1: 6 But I alone went **o** to Jerusalem for the festivals,
5: 6 I have **o** traveled to Media,
5:10 for I have **o** gone to Media
AdE 16: 5 And **o** many of those who are set in places
Sir 19:15 Question a friend, for **o** it is slander;
20:17 How many will ridicule him, and how **o**!
30: 1 He who loves his son will whip him **o**,
34:13 I have **o** been in danger of death,
1Mc 14:29 "Since wars **o** occurred in the country, Simon son
2Mc 9:25 whom I have **o** entrusted and commended to most
12:22 so that **o** they were injured by their own men
3Mc 6:26 toward us and **o** have accepted willingly the worst
2Es 4:26 and if you live long, you will **o** marvel,
5: 8 fire shall **o** break out, the wild animals shall roam
8:47 you have **o** compared yourself to the unrighteous.

OFTENTIMES (1) [OFTEN]

3Mc 2:12 **o** when our fathers were oppressed you helped

OG (20) [OG'S]

Nu 21:33 and King **O** of Bashan came out against them,
32:33 and the kingdom of King **O** of Bashan,
Dt 1: 4 who reigned in Heshbon, and King **O** of Bashan,
3: 1 King **O** of Bashan came out against us,
3: 3 over to us King **O** of Bashan and all his people.
3: 4 the kingdom of **O** in Bashan.
3:11 (Now only King **O** of Bashan was left of
4:47 and the land of King **O** of Bashan, the two kings of
29: 7 of Heshbon and King **O** of Bashan came out
31: 4 LORD will do to them as he did to Sihon and **O**,
Jos 2:10 to Sihon and **O**, whom you utterly destroyed.
9:10 and King **O** of Bashan who lived in Ashtaroth.
12: 4 and King **O** of Bashan, one of the last of
13:12 of **O** in Bashan, who reigned in Ashtaroth and
13:30 the whole kingdom of King **O** of Bashan,
13:31 the towns of the kingdom of **O** in Bashan;
1Ki 4:19 of King Sihon of the Amorites and of King **O**
Ne 9:22 of King Sihon of Heshbon and the land of King **O**
Ps 135:11 king of the Amorites, and **O**, king of Bashan,
136:20 and **O**, king of Bashan,

OG'S (2) [OG]

Dt 3:10 towns of **O** kingdom in Bashan.
3:13 the rest of Gilead and all of Bashan, **O** kingdom.

OH (25) [O] See Index of Articles Etc.

OHAD (2)

Ge 46:10 The children of Simeon: Jemuel, Jamin, **O**, Jachin,
Ex 6:15 The sons of Simeon: Jemuel, Jamin, **O**, Jachin,

OHEL (1)

1Ch 3:20 **O**, Berechiah, Hasadiah, and Jushab-hesed, five.

OHOLAH (5)

Eze 23: 4 **O** was the name of the elder and Oholibah
23: 4 As for their names, **O** is Samaria,
23: 5 **O** played the whore while she was mine;
23:36 Mortal, will you judge **O** and Oholibah?
23:44 Thus they went in to **O** and to Oholibah,

OHOLIAB (5)

Ex 31: 6 I have appointed with him **O** son of Ahisamach,
35:34 both him and **O** son of Ahisamach,
36: 1 Bezalel and **O** and every skillful one to whom
36: 2 then called Bezalel and **O** and every skillful one
38:23 and with him was **O** son of Ahisamach,

OHOLIBAH (6)

Eze 23: 4 the name of the elder and **O** the name of her sister.
23: 4 Oholah is Samaria, and **O** is Jerusalem.
23:11 Her sister **O** saw this, yet she was more corrupt
23:22 Therefore, O **O**, thus says the Lord GOD:
23:36 Mortal, will you judge Oholah and **O**?
23:44 Thus they went in to Oholah and to **O**,

OHOLIBAMAH (8)

Ge 36: 2 **O** daughter of Anah son of Zibeon the Hivite,
36: 5 and **O** bore Jeush, Jalam,
36:14 These were the sons of Esau's wife **O**,
36:18 These are the sons of Esau's wife **O**:
36:18 these are the clans born of Esau's wife **O**,
36:25 Dishon and **O** daughter of Anah.
36:41 **O**, Elah, Pinon,
1Ch 1:52 **O**, Elah, Pinon,

OIL[‡] (221) [OILS]

Ge 28:18 and set it up for a pillar and poured **o** on the top
35:14 a drink offering on it, and poured **o** on it.
Ex 25: 6 **o** for the lamps, spices for the anointing **o** and for
27:20 the Israelites to bring you pure **o** of beaten olives
29: 2 unleavened cakes mixed with **o**,
29: 2 and unleavened wafers spread with **o**.
29: 7 You shall take the anointing **o**,
29:21 and some of the anointing **o**,
29:23 one cake of bread made with **o**, and one wafer,
29:40 with one-fourth of a hin of beaten **o**,
30:24 and a hin of olive **o**;
30:25 a sacred anointing **o** blended as by the perfumer;
30:25 it shall be a holy anointing **o**.
Ex 30:31 "This shall be my holy anointing **o**
31:11 and the anointing **o** and the fragrant incense for
35: 8 **o** for the light, spices for the anointing **o** and for
35:14 and the **o** for the light;
35:15 and the anointing **o** and the fragrant incense,
35:28 spices and **o** for the light, and for the anointing **o**,
37:29 He made the holy anointing **o** also,
39:37 and the **o** for the light;
39:38 the anointing **o** and the fragrant incense,
40: 9 Then you shall take the anointing **o**,
Lev 2: 1 the worshiper shall pour **o** on it,
2: 2 taking from it a handful of the choice flour and **o**,
2: 4 unleavened cakes mixed with **o**,
2: 4 or unleavened wafers spread with **o**.
2: 5 it shall be of choice flour mixed with **o**,
2: 6 and pour **o** on it; it is a grain offering.
2: 7 it shall be made of choice flour in **o**.
2:15 You shall add **o** to it and lay frankincense on it;
2:16 of the coarse grain and **o** with all its frankincense;
5:11 you shall not put **o** on it or lay frankincense on it,
6:15 of the choice flour and **o** of the grain offering,
6:21 It shall be made with **o** on a griddle;
7:10 every other grain offering, mixed with **o** or dry,
7:12 the thank offering unleavened cakes mixed with **o**,
7:12 unleavened wafers spread with **o**,
7:12 and cakes of choice flour well soaked in **o**.
8: 2 the anointing **o**, the bull of sin offering,
8:10 the anointing **o** and anointed the tabernacle and all
8:12 the anointing **o** on Aaron's head and anointed him,
8:26 one cake of bread with **o**, and one wafer,
8:30 the anointing **o** and some of the blood that was on
9: 4 and a grain offering mixed with **o**.
10: 7 for the anointing **o** of the LORD is on you."
14:10 of choice flour mixed with **o**, and one log of **o**.
14:12 along with the log of **o**,
14:15 of **o** and pour it into the palm of his own left hand,
14:16 the **o** that is in his left hand and sprinkle some **o**
14:17 the **o** that remains in his hand the priest shall put
14:18 of the **o** that is in the priest's hand he shall put on
14:21 mixed with **o** for a grain offering and a log of **o**;
14:24 the lamb of the guilt offering and the log of **o**,
14:26 The priest shall pour some of the **o** into the palm
14:27 of the **o** that is in his left hand seven times before
14:28 the **o** that is in his hand on the lobe of the right ear
14:29 of the **o** that is in the priest's hand he shall put on
21:10 on whose head the anointing **o** has been poured
21:12 the consecration of the anointing **o** of his God is
23:13 an ephah of choice flour mixed with **o**, an offering
24: 2 Command the people of Israel to bring you pure **o**
Nu 4: 9 and all the vessels for **o** with which it is supplied;
4:16 of Aaron the priest shall have charge of the **o** for
4:16 the regular grain offering, and the anointing **o**,
5:15 He shall pour no **o** on it and put no frankincense
6:15 with **o** and unleavened wafers spread with **o**,
7:13 both of them full of choice flour mixed with **o** for
7:19 both of them full of choice flour mixed with **o** for
7:25 both of them full of choice flour mixed with **o** for
7:31 both of them full of choice flour mixed with **o** for
7:37 both of them full of choice flour mixed with **o** for
7:43 both of them full of choice flour mixed with **o** for
7:49 both of them full of choice flour mixed with **o** for
7:55 both of them full of choice flour mixed with **o** for
7:61 both of them full of choice flour mixed with **o** for
7:67 both of them full of choice flour mixed with **o** for
7:73 both of them full of choice flour mixed with **o** for
7:79 both of them full of choice flour mixed with **o** for
8: 8 of choice flour mixed with **o**,
11: 8 taste of it was like the taste of cakes baked with **o**.
15: 4 mixed with one-fourth of a hin of **o**.
15: 6 of choice flour mixed with one-third of a hin of **o**;
15: 9 mixed with half a hin of **o**,
18:12 the best of the **o** and all the best of the wine and of
28: 5 mixed with one-fourth of a hin of beaten **o**.
28: 9 mixed with **o**, and its drink offering—
28:12 mixed with **o**, for each bull;
28:12 mixed with **o**, for the one ram;
28:13 of choice flour mixed with **o** as a grain offering
28:20 be of choice flour mixed with **o**:
28:28 be of choice flour mixed with **o**:
29: 3 be of choice flour mixed with **o**,
29: 9 be of choice flour mixed with **o**,
29:14 be of choice flour mixed with **o**,
35:25 the high priest who was anointed with the holy **o**.
Dt 7:13 your grain and your wine and your **o**,
11:14 in your grain, your wine, and your **o**;
12:17 and your **o**, the firstlings of your herds
14:23 and your **o**, as well as the firstlings of your herd
18: 4 first fruits of your grain, your wine, and your **o**,
28:40 but you shall not anoint yourself with the **o**,
28:51 leaving you neither grain, wine, and **o**,
32:13 he nursed him with honey from the crags, with **o**
33:24 and may he dip his foot in **o**.
Jdg 9: 9 'Shall I stop producing my rich **o** by which gods
1Sa 10: 1 Samuel took a vial of **o** and poured it on his head,
16: 1 Fill your horn with **o** and set out;
16:13 Then Samuel took the horn of **o**,
2Sa 1:21 the shield of Saul, anointed with **o** no more.
14: 2 do not anoint yourself with **o**,
1Ki 1:39 the horn of **o** from the tent and anointed Solomon.
5:11 and twenty cors of fine **o**.
17:12 and a little **o** in a jug;
17:14 not be emptied and the jug of **o** will not fail until
17:16 neither did the jug of **o** fail,
2Ki 4: 2 in the house, except a jar of **o**."
4: 6 Then the **o** stopped flowing.
4: 7 and he said, "Go sell the **o** and pay your debts,
9: 1 take this flask of **o** in your hand,

2Ki 9: 3 Then take the flask of **o**, pour it on his head,
9: 6 the young man poured the **o** on his head,
18:32 a land of olive **o** and honey,
20:13 the gold, the spices, the precious **o**, his armory,
1Ch 9:29 the wine, the **o**, the incense, and the spices.
12:40 cakes of figs, clusters of raisins, wine, **o**, oxen,
23:29 the baked offering, the offering mixed with **o**,
27:28 Over the stores of **o** was Joash.
2Ch 2:10 and twenty thousand baths of **o**."
2:15 Now, as for the wheat, barley, **o**, and wine,
11:11 and stores of food, **o**, and wine.
31: 5 wine, **o**, honey, and of all the produce of the field;
32:28 also for the yield of grain, wine, and **o**;
Ezr 3: 7 and **o** to the Sidonians and the Tyrians
6: 9 wine, or **o**, as the priests in Jerusalem require—
7:22 one hundred baths of **o**, and unlimited salt.
Ne 5:11 and **o** that you have been exacting from them."
10:37 the fruit of every tree, the wine and the **o**,
10:39 and **o** to the storerooms where the vessels of
13: 5 the vessels, and the tithes of grain, wine, and **o**,
13:12 wine, and **o** into the storehouses.
Est 2:12 with **o** of myrrh and six months with perfumes
Job 24:11 between their terraces they press out **o**;
29: 6 and the rock poured out for me streams of **o**!
Ps 23: 5 you anoint my head with **o**; my cup overflows.
45: 7 with the **o** of gladness beyond your companions;
55:21 with words that were softer than **o**,
89:20 with my holy **o** I have anointed him;
92:10 you have poured over me fresh **o**.
104:15 **o** to make the face shine, and bread to strengthen
109:18 into his body like water, like **o** into his bones.
133: 2 It is like the precious **o** on the head,
141: 5 Never let the **o** of the wicked anoint my head,
Pr 5: 3 and her speech is smoother than **o**;
21:17 whoever loves wine and **o** will not be rich.
27:16 to restrain the wind or to grasp **o** in the right hand.
Ecc 9: 8 do not let **o** be lacking on your head.
Isa 1: 6 or bound up, or softened with **o**.
21: 5 Rise up, commanders, **o** the shield!
39: 2 the silver, the gold, the spices, the precious **o**,
57: 9 You journeyed to Molech with **o**,
61: 3 the **o** of gladness instead of mourning,
Jer 31:12 over the grain, the wine, and the **o**,
40:10 as for you, gather wine and summer fruits and **o**,
41: 8 barley, **o**, and honey hidden in the fields."
Eze 16: 9 the blood from you, and anointed you with **o**.
16:13 You had choice flour and honey and **o** for food.
16:18 and set my **o** and my incense before them.
16:19 I fed you with choice flour and **o** and honey—
23:41 on which you had placed my incense and my **o**.
27:17 millet, honey, **o**, and balm.
32:14 and cause their streams to run like **o**,
45:14 and as the fixed portion of **o**, one-tenth of a bath
45:24 and a hin of **o** to each ephah.
45:25 burnt offerings, and grain offerings, and for the **o**.
46: 5 together with a hin of **o** to each ephah.
46: 7 together with a hin of **o** to each ephah.
46:11 together with a hin of **o** to an ephah.
46:14 one-third of a hin of **o** to moisten the choice flour,
46:15 and the grain offering and the **o** shall be provided,
Hos 2: 5 my wool and my flax, my **o** and my drink."
2: 8 the **o**, and who lavished upon her silver and gold
2:22 the wine, and the **o**, and they shall answer Jezreel;
12: 1 they make a treaty with Assyria, and **o** is carried
Joel 1:10 grain is destroyed, the wine dries up, the **o** fails.
2:19 I am sending you grain, wine, and **o**,
2:24 the vats shall overflow with wine and **o**.
Mic 6: 7 with ten thousands of rivers of **o**?
6:15 but not anoint yourselves with **o**;
Hag 1:11 the new wine, the **o**, on what the soil produces,
2:12 or **o**, or any kind of food, does it become holy?
Zec 4:12 the **o** through the two golden pipes?"
Mt 6:17 you fast, put **o** on your head and wash your face,
25: 3 they took no **o** with them;
25: 4 but the wise took flasks of **o** with their lamps.
25: 8 foolish said to the wise, 'Give us some of your **o**,
Mk 6:13 with **o** many who were sick and cured them.
Lk 7:46 You did not anoint my head with **o**,
10:34 having poured **o** and wine on them.
16: 6 He answered, 'A hundred jugs of olive **o**.'
Heb 1: 9 with the **o** of gladness beyond your companions."
Jas 5:14 anointing them with **o** in the name of the Lord.
Rev 6: 6 but do not damage the olive **o** and the wine!"
18:13 spice, incense, myrrh, frankincense, wine, olive **o**,
Tob 1: 7 likewise the tenth of the grain, wine, olive **o**,
Jdt 10: 5 She gave her maid a skin of wine and a flask of **o**,
11:13 and **o**, which they had consecrated and set aside
AdE 2:12 while they are anointing themselves with **o**
Sir 38:11 and pour **o** on your offering,
39:26 the blood of the grape and **o** and clothing.
45:15 and anointed him with holy **o**;
Sus 1:17 "Bring me olive **o** and ointments,
1Es 6:30 and likewise wheat and salt and wine and **o**,
Pm 151: 4 and anointed me with his anointing **o**.

OILS (3) [OIL]

SS 1: 3 your anointing **o** are fragrant,
4:10 and the fragrance of your **o** than any spice!
Am 6: 6 and anoint themselves with the finest **o**,

OINTMENT (14) [OINTMENTS]

Job 41:31 it makes the sea like a pot of **o**.
Ecc 7: 1 A good name is better than precious **o**,
10: 1 Dead flies make the perfumer's **o** give off
Mt 26: 7 to him with an alabaster jar of very costly **o**,
26: 9 For this **o** could have been sold for a large sum,
26:12 By pouring this **o** on my body she has prepared me
Mk 14: 3 with an alabaster jar of very costly **o** of nard,
14: 3 and she broke open the jar and poured the **o**
14: 4 "Why was the **o** wasted in this way?
14: 5 For this **o** could have been sold
Lk 7:37 brought an alabaster jar of **o**.
7:38 and anointing them with the **o**.
7:46 but she has anointed my feet with **o**.
Jdt 10: 3 and anointed herself with precious **o**.

OINTMENTS (6) [OINTMENT]

Lk 23:56 Then they returned, and prepared spices and **o**.
Tob 2:10 with **o** the more my vision was obscured by
AdE 2: 3 let **o** and whatever else they need be given them.
2: 9 with **o** and her portion of food, as well
2:12 and six months with spices and **o** for women.
Sus 1:17 She said to her maids, "Bring me olive oil and **o**,

OLAM See Index to Footnotes

OLAMUS (1)

1Es 9:30 Of the descendants of Mani: **O**, Mamuchus,

OLD‡ (432) [OLDER, OLDEST, THREE-YEAR-OLD, YEAR-OLD]

A. OLD AGE (41)
B. FROM OF OLD (21)
C. OLD MAN (18)
D. DAYS OF OLD (17)
E. OLD MEN (9)

Ge 5:32 After Noah was five hundred years **o**,
6: 4 These were the heroes that were of **o**,
7: 6 Noah was six hundred years **o** when the flood
11:10 When Shem was one hundred years **o**,
12: 4 Abram was seventy-five years **o** when he departed
15: 9 He said to him, "Bring me a heifer three years **o**,
15: 9 a female goat three years **o**, a ram three years **o**,
15:15 you shall be buried in a good **o** age. A
16:16 Abram was eighty-six years **o**
17: 1 When Abram was ninety-nine years **o**,
17:12 be circumcised when he is eight days **o**,
17:17 be born to a man who is a hundred years **o**?
17:17 Can Sarah, who is ninety years **o**, bear a child?"
17:24 Abraham was ninety-nine years **o**
17:25 And his son Ishmael was thirteen years **o**
18:11 Abraham and Sarah were **o**, advanced in age;
18:12 "After I have grown **o**, and my husband is **o**,
18:13 'Shall I indeed bear a child, now that I am **o**?'
19: 4 both young and **o**, all the people to the last man,
19:31 the firstborn said to the younger, "Our father is **o**,
21: 2 and bore Abraham a son in his **o** age, A
21: 4 when he was eight days **o**,
21: 5 a hundred years **o** when his son Isaac was born
21: 7 Yet I have borne him a son in his **o** age." A
24: 1 Now Abraham was **o**, well advanced in years;
24:36 a son to my master when she was **o**;
25: 8 and died in a good **o** age, A
25: 8 an **o** man and full of years, C
25:20 Isaac was forty years **o** when he married Rebekah,
25:26 Isaac was sixty years **o** when she bore them.
26:34 When Esau was forty years **o**,
27: 1 When Isaac was **o** and his eyes were dim so
27: 2 "See, I am **o**; I do not know the day of my death.
35:29 and was gathered to his people, **o** and full of days;
37: 2 Joseph, being seventeen years **o**,
37: 3 because he was the son of his **o** age; A
41:46 Joseph was thirty years **o** when he entered
43:27 the **o** man of whom you spoke? C
44:20 we said to my lord, 'We have a father, an **o** man, C
44:20 and a young brother, the child of his **o** age. A
50:26 And Joseph died, being one hundred ten years **o**;
Ex 7: 7 Moses was eighty years **o** and Aaron eighty-three
10: 9 "We will go with our young and our **o**;
29:38 two lambs a year **o** regularly each day.
30:14 from twenty years **o** and upward,
38:26 from twenty years **o** and upward,
Lev 19:32 You shall rise before the aged, and defer to the **o**;
23:12 you shall offer a lamb a year **o**, without blemish,
23:18 the bread seven lambs a year **o** without blemish,
23:19 and two male lambs a year **o** as a sacrifice
25:22 you will be eating from the **o** crop;
25:22 when its produce comes in, you shall eat the **o**.
26:10 You shall eat **o** grain long stored,
26:10 and you shall have to clear out the **o** to make way
27: 7 And if the person is sixty years **o** or over,
Nu 1: 3 from twenty years **o** and upward,
1:18 to the number of names from twenty years **o**
1:20 every male from twenty years **o** and upward,
1:22 every male from twenty years **o** and upward,
1:24 from twenty years **o** and upward,
1:26 from twenty years **o** and upward,
1:28 from twenty years **o** and upward,
1:30 from twenty years **o** and upward,
1:32 from twenty years **o** and upward,
1:34 from twenty years **o** and upward,
1:36 from twenty years **o** and upward,
1:38 from twenty years **o** and upward,
1:40 from twenty years **o** and upward,
1:42 from twenty years **o** and upward,
1:45 from twenty years **o** and upward,
3:15 You shall enroll every male from a month **o**
3:22 the males from a month **o** and upward,
3:28 from a month **o** and upward,
Nu 3:34 the males from a month **o** and upward,
3:39 all the males from a month **o** and upward,
3:40 from a month **o** and upward,
3:43 the firstborn males from a month **o** and upward,
4: 3 from thirty years **o** up to fifty years **o**,
4:23 from thirty years **o** up to fifty years **o** you shall
4:30 from thirty years **o** up to fifty years **o** you shall
4:35 from thirty years **o** up to fifty years **o**,
4:39 from thirty years **o** up to fifty years **o**,
4:43 from thirty years **o** up to fifty years **o**,
4:47 from thirty years **o** up to fifty years **o**,
6:12 and bring a male lamb a year **o** as a guilt offering.
6:14 a year **o** without blemish as a burnt offering,
6:14 a year **o** without blemish as a sin offering,
7:15 one male lamb a year **o**, for a burnt offering;
7:17 five male goats, and five male lambs a year **o**.
7:21 one male lamb a year **o**, as a burnt offering;
7:23 five male goats, and five male lambs a year **o**.
7:27 one male lamb a year **o**, for a burnt offering;
7:29 five male goats, and five male lambs a year **o**.
7:33 one male lamb a year **o**, for a burnt offering;
7:35 five male goats, and five male lambs a year **o**.
7:39 one male lamb a year **o**, for a burnt offering;
7:41 five male goats, and five male lambs a year **o**.
7:45 one male lamb a year **o**, for a burnt offering;
7:47 five male goats, and five male lambs a year **o**.
7:51 one male lamb a year **o**, for a burnt offering;
7:53 five male goats, and five male lambs a year **o**.
7:57 one male lamb a year **o**, for a burnt offering;
7:59 five male goats, and five male lambs a year **o**.
7:63 one male lamb a year **o**, for a burnt offering;
7:65 five male goats, and five male lambs a year **o**.
7:69 one male lamb a year **o**, for a burnt offering;
7:71 five male goats, and five male lambs a year **o**.
7:75 one male lamb a year **o**, for a burnt offering;
7:77 five male goats, and five male lambs a year **o**.
7:81 one male lamb a year **o**, for a burnt offering;
7:83 five male goats, and five male lambs a year **o**.
7:87 twelve rams, twelve male lambs a year **o**,
7:88 the male lambs a year **o** sixty.
8:24 twenty-five years **o** and upward they shall begin to
14:29 from twenty years **o** and upward,
15:27 a female goat a year **o** for a sin offering.
26: 2 from twenty years **o** and upward,
26: 4 from twenty years **o** and upward,"
26:62 every male one month **o** and up;
28: 3 two male lambs a year **o** without blemish,
28: 9 two male lambs a year **o** without blemish,
28:11 seven male lambs a year **o** without blemish;
28:19 one ram, and seven male lambs a year **o**;
28:27 one ram, seven male lambs a year **o**.
29: 2 seven male lambs a year **o** without blemish.
29: 8 one ram, seven male lambs a year **o**.
29:13 two rams, fourteen male lambs a year **o**.
29:17 fourteen male lambs a year **o** without blemish,
29:20 fourteen male lambs a year **o** without blemish,
29:23 fourteen male lambs a year **o** without blemish,
29:26 fourteen male lambs a year **o** without blemish,
29:29 fourteen male lambs a year **o** without blemish,
29:32 fourteen male lambs a year **o** without blemish,
29:36 seven male lambs a year **o** without blemish,
32:11 from twenty years **o** and upward,
33:39 Aaron was one hundred twenty-three years **o**
Dt 28:50 a grim-faced nation showing no respect to the **o**
31: 2 "I am now one hundred twenty years **o**.
32: 7 the days of **o**, consider the years long past; D
32:25 nursing child and **o** gray head.
33:27 the ancient gods, shatters the forces of **o**;
34: 7 Moses was one hundred twenty years **o**
Jos 6:21 both men and women, young and **o**, oxen, sheep,
13: 1 Now Joshua was **o** and advanced in years;
13: 1 "You are **o** and advanced in years,
14: 7 I was forty years **o** when Moses the servant of
14:10 and here I am today, eighty-five years **o**.
23: 1 and Joshua was **o** and well advanced in years,
23: 2 "I am now **o** and well advanced in years;
24:29 died, being one hundred ten years **o**.
Jdg 6:25 the second bull seven years **o**,
8:32 Then Gideon son of Joash died at a good **o** age, A
19:16 an **o** man coming from his work in the field. C
19:17 When the **o** man looked up and saw the wayfarer C
19:20 The **o** man said, "Peace be to you. C
19:22 They said to the **o** man, the master of the house, C
Ru 1:12 go your way, for I am too **o** to have a husband.
4:15 a restorer of life and a nourisher of your **o** age; A
1Sa 2:22 Now Eli was very **o**.
2:31 so that no one in your family will live to **o** age. A
2:32 no one in your family shall ever live to **o** age. A
4:15 Eli was ninety-eight years **o** and his eyes were set,
4:18 for he was an **o** man, and heavy. C
5: 9 the inhabitants of the city, both young and **o**,
8: 1 When Samuel became **o**, he made his sons judges
8: 5 "You are **o** and your sons do not follow
12: 2 I am **o** and gray, but my sons are with you.
13: 1 Saul was . . . years **o** when he began to reign;
17:12 the man was already **o** and advanced in years.
28:14 She said, "An **o** man is coming up; C
2Sa 2:10 was forty years **o** when he began to reign
4: 4 He was five years **o** when the news about Saul
5: 4 David was thirty years **o** when he began to reign,
19:32 Barzillai was a very aged man, eighty years **o**.
19:35 Today I am eighty years **o**;
20:18 Then she said, "They used to say in the **o** days,
1Ki 1: 1 King David was **o** and advanced in years;
1:15 in his room. The king was very **o**;
11: 4 For when Solomon was **o**,
13:11 Now there lived an **o** prophet in Bethel.

1Ki 13:25 and told it in the town where the **o** prophet lived.
14:21 Rehoboam was forty-one years **o** when he began
15:23 But in his **o** age he was diseased in his feet. A
22:42 Jehoshaphat was thirty-five years **o**
2Ki 4:14 "Well, she has no son, and her husband is **o.**"
8:17 He was thirty-two years **o** when he became king,
8:26 Ahaziah was twenty-two years **o** when he began
11:21 Jehoash was seven years **o** when he began
14: 2 He was twenty-five years **o** when he began
14:21 of Judah took Azariah, who was sixteen years **o,**
15: 2 He was sixteen years **o** when he began to reign,
15:33 He was twenty-five years **o** when he began
16: 2 Ahaz was twenty years **o** when he began to reign;
18: 2 He was twenty-five years **o** when he began
19:25 from days of **o** what now I bring to pass, D
21: 1 Manasseh was twelve years **o** when he began
21:19 Amon was twenty-two years **o** when he began
22: 1 Josiah was eight years **o** when he began to reign;
23:31 Jehoahaz was twenty-three years **o** when he began
23:36 Jehoiakim was twenty-five years **o** when he began
24: 8 Jehoiachin was eighteen years **o** when he began
24:18 Zedekiah was twenty-one years **o** when he began
1Ch 2:21 whom he married when he was sixty years **o;**
23: 1 When David was **o** and full of days,
23: 3 The Levites, thirty years **o** and upward,
23:24 the names of the individuals from twenty years **o**
23:27 of the Levites from twenty years **o** and upward—
29:28 He died in a good **o** age, full of days, riches, A
2Ch 3: 3 the length, in cubits of the **o** standard,
12:13 Rehoboam was forty-one years **o** when he began
15:13 should be put to death, whether young or **o,**
20:31 He was thirty-five years **o** when he began to reign;
21: 5 Jehoram was thirty-two years **o** when he began
21:20 He was thirty-two years **o** when he began to reign;
22: 2 Ahaziah was forty-two years **o** when he began
24: 1 Joash was seven years **o** when he began to reign;
24:15 But Jehoiada grew **o** and full of days, and died;
24:15 he was one hundred thirty years **o** at his death.
25: 1 Amaziah was twenty-five years **o** when he began
25: 5 He mustered those twenty years **o** and upward,
26: 1 of Judah took Uzziah, who was sixteen years **o,**
26: 3 Uzziah was sixteen years **o** when he began
27: 1 Jotham was twenty-five years **o** when he began
27: 8 He was twenty-five years **o** when he began
28: 1 Ahaz was twenty years **o** when he began to reign;
29: 1 to reign when he was twenty-five years **o;**
31:15 **o** and young alike, by divisions,
31:16 males from three years **o** and upwards,
31:17 the Levites from twenty years **o** and upwards was
33: 1 Manasseh was twelve years **o** when he began
33:21 Amon was twenty-two years **o** when he began
34: 1 Josiah was eight years **o** when he began to reign;
36: 2 Jehoahaz was twenty-three years **o** when he began
36: 5 Jehoiakim was twenty-five years **o** when he began
36: 9 Jehoiachin was eight years **o** when he began
36:11 Zedekiah was twenty-one years **o** when he began
Ezr 3: 8 from twenty years **o** and upward,
3:12 **o** people who had seen the first house
Ne 3: 6 of Besodeiah repaired the **O** Gate;
12:39 by the **O** Gate, and by the Fish Gate and the Tower
Est 3:13 to kill, and to annihilate all Jews, young and **o,**
Job 5:26 You shall come to your grave in ripe **o** age, A
14: 8 Though its root grows **o** in the earth,
20: 4 Do you not know this from of **o,** B
21: 7 Why do the wicked live on, reach **o** age, A
22:15 to the **o** way that the wicked have trod?
29: 2 that I were as in the months of **o,**
32: 9 It is not the **o** that are wise,
42:17 And Job died, **o** and full of days.
Ps 25: 6 for they have been from of **o.** B
37:25 I have been young, and now am **o,**
44: 1 in their days, in the days of **o:** D
55:19 God, who is enthroned from of **o,** B
71: 9 Do not cast me off in the time of **o** age; A
71:18 So even to **o** age and gray hairs, O God, A
74:12 Yet God my King is from of **o,** B
77: 5 I consider the days of **o,** D
77:11 I will remember your wonders of **o.**
78: 2 I will utter dark sayings from of **o,** B
89:49 where is your steadfast love of **o,**
92:14 In **o** age they still produce fruit; A
93: 2 your throne is established from of **o;** B
119:52 When I think of your ordinances from of **o,** B
143: 5 I remember the days of **o,** D
148:12 and women alike, **o** and young together!
Pr 22: 6 Train children in the right way, and when **o,**
23:22 and do not despise your mother when she is **o.**
Ecc 4:13 a poor but wise youth than an **o** but foolish king,
SS 7:13 new as well as **o,** which I have laid up for you,
Isa 20: 4 both the young and the **o,** naked and barefoot,
22:11 between the two walls for the water of the **o** pool.
23: 7 from days of **o,** whose feet carried her D
25: 1 plans formed of **o,** faithful and sure.
37:26 from days of **o** what now I bring to pass, D
43:18 or consider the things of **o.**
44: 7 has announced from of **o** the things to come? B
44: 8 have I not told you from of **o** and declared it? B
45:21 Who declared it of **o?**
46: 4 even to your **o** age I am he, A
46: 9 remember the former things of **o;**
48: 8 from of **o** your ear has not been opened. B
51: 9 Awake, as in days of **o,** the generations of D
63: 9 and carried them all the days of **o.** D
63:11 Then they remembered the days of **o,** D
63:16 our Redeemer from of **o** is your name. B
65:20 or an **o** person who does not live out a lifetime;
Jer 6:11 the **o** folk and the very aged.
7: 7 that I gave of **o** to your ancestors forever and ever.
11:10 the iniquities of their ancestors of **o,** who refused
25: 5 you and your ancestors from of **o** and forever; B
30:20 Their children shall be as of **o,**
31:13 and the young men and the **o** shall be merry.
38:11 and took from there **o** rags and worn-out clothes,
46:26 be inhabited as in the days of **o,** D
51:22 with you I smash the **o** man and the boy; C
52: 1 Zedekiah was twenty-one years **o** when he began
La 1: 7 the precious things that were hers in days of **o.** D
2:21 The young and the **o** are lying on the ground in
5:14 The **o** men have left the city gate, E
5:21 renew our days as of **o—**
Eze 9: 6 Cut down **o** men, young men and young women, E
Da 5:31 being about sixty-two years **o.**
Joel 2: 2 their like has never been from of **o,** B
2:28 your **o** men shall dream dreams, E
Am 9:11 and rebuild it as in the days of **o;** D
Mic 5: 2 whose origin is from of **o,** from ancient days. B
6: 6 with burnt offerings, with calves a year **o?**
7:14 in Bashan and Gilead as in the days of **o.** D
7:20 to our ancestors from the days of **o.** D
Hab 1:12 Are you not from of **o,** O LORD my God, B
Zec 8: 4 **O** men and old women shall again sit in the E
8: 4 Old men and **o** women shall again sit in the streets
Mal 3: 4 be pleasing to the LORD as in the days of **o** and D
Mt 2:16 around Bethlehem who were two years **o** or under,
9:16 a piece of unshrunk cloth on an **o** cloak,
9:17 Neither is new wine put into **o** wineskins;
13:52 of his treasure what is new and what is **o.**"
Mk 2:21 a piece of unshrunk cloth on an **o** cloak;
2:21 the patch pulls away from it, the new from the **o,**
2:22 And no one puts new wine into **o** wineskins;
6:15 "It is a prophet, like one of the prophets of **o.**"
Lk 1:18 For I am an **o** man, C
1:36 your relative Elizabeth in her **o** age has A
1:70 the mouth of his holy prophets from of **o,** B
2:42 And when he was twelve years **o,**
3:23 about thirty years **o** when he began his work.
5:36 from a new garment and sews it on an **o** garment;
5:36 and the piece from the new will not match the **o.**
5:37 And no one puts new wine into **o** wineskins;
5:39 no one after drinking **o** wine desires new wine,
5:39 but says, 'The **o** is good.' "
8:42 about twelve years **o,** who was dying.
Jn 3: 4 "How can anyone be born after having grown **o?**
8:57 Jews said to him, "You are not yet fifty years **o,**
21:18 when you grow **o,** you will stretch out your hands,
Ac 2:17 and your **o** men shall dream dreams. E
4:22 had been performed was more than forty years **o.**
7:23 "When he was forty years **o,**
Ro 4:19 as dead (for he was about a hundred years **o**),
6: 6 We know that our **o** self was crucified with him so
7: 6 that we are slaves not under the **o** written code but
1Co 5: 7 the **o** yeast so that you may be a new batch,
5: 8 let us celebrate the festival, not with the **o** yeast,
2Co 3:14 when they hear the reading of the **o** covenant,
5:17 everything **o** has passed away;
Eph 4:22 your **o** self, corrupt and deluded by its lusts,
Col 3: 9 seeing that you have stripped off the **o** self
1Ti 4: 7 to do with profane myths and **o** wives' tales.
5: 9 on the list if she is not less than sixty years **o**
Phm 1: 9 and I, Paul, do this as an **o** man, C
Heb 8:13 and growing **o** will soon disappear.
11:11 even though he was too **o—**
1Jn 2: 7 but an **o** commandment that you have had from
2: 7 **o** commandment is the word that you have heard.
Tob 3:10 And I shall bring my father in his **o** age down A
4:12 Abraham, Isaac, and Jacob, our ancestors of **o,**
8: 7 and that we may grow **o** together."
14: 2 in peace when he was one hundred twelve years **o,**
14: 2 was sixty-two years **o** when he lost his eyesight,
14:13 with great respect in their **o** age, A
Jdt 16:23 and grew **o** in her husband's house,
Wis 3:17 and finally their **o** age will be without honor. A
4: 8 For **o** age is not honored for length of time, A
4: 9 and a blameless life is ripe **o** age. A
4:16 the prolonged **o** age of the unrighteous. A
8: 8 she knows the things of **o,**
Sir 2:10 Consider the generations of **o** and see:
3:12 My child, help your father in his **o** age, A
8: 6 Do not disdain one who is **o,**
8: 6 for some of us are also growing **o.**
9:10 Do not abandon **o** friends,
11:20 and grow **o** in your work.
14:17 All living beings become **o** like a garment,
14:17 for the decree from of **o** is, "You must die!" B
25: 2 and an **o** fool who commits adultery.
25: 3 how can you find anything in your **o** age? A
30:24 and anxiety brings on premature **o** age. A
42:18 he sees from of **o** the things that are to come. B
46: 9 which remained with him in his **o** age, A
50:23 as in the days of **o.** D
51: 8 O Lord, and your kindness from of **o,** B
Bar 3:10 that you are growing **o** in a foreign country,
3:26 giants were born there, who were famous of **o,**
Sus 1:52 "You **o** relic of wicked days,
1Mc 14: 9 **O** men sat in the streets; E
16: 3 But now I have grown **o,**
2Mc 5:13 Then there was massacre of young and **o,**
6:22 be treated kindly on account of his **o** friendship
6:23 his **o** age and the gray hairs that he had reached A
6:25 while I defile and disgrace my **o** age. A
6:27 I will show myself worthy of my **o** age A
1Es 1:34 who was twenty-three years **o,**
1:39 Jehoiakim was twenty-five years **o** when he began
1:43 when he was made king he was eighteen years **o,**
1Es 1:46 Zedekiah was twenty-one years **o,**
1:53 not spare young man or young woman, **o** man C
2:23 and kept setting up blockades in it from of **o.** B
2:26 that this city from of **o** has fought against kings, B
5:63 **o** men who had seen the former house, E
3Mc 1:23 and being barely restrained by the **o** men and E
3:27 whether **o** people or children or even infants,
4: 5 For a multitude of gray-headed **o** men, E
6: 1 who had attained a ripe **o** age and A
2Es 2:22 Protect the **o** and the young within your walls;
5:49 and a woman who has become **o** does
5:50 Or is she now approaching **o** age?" A
5:53 from those born during the time of **o** age, A
6:21 Children a year **o** shall speak with their voices,
9: 4 the Most High spoke from the days that were of **o,**
14:10 and the times begin to grow **o.**
14:17 the weaker the world becomes through **o** age, A
4Mc 5: 6 **o** man, I would advise you to save yourself C
5:12 on your **o** age by honoring my humane advice? A
5:31 not so **o** and cowardly as not to be young in reason
5:33 not so pity my **o** age as to break the ancestral A
5:36 not defile the honorable mouth of my **o** age, A
6: 2 First they stripped the **o** man, C
6: 6 yet while the **o** man's eyes were raised to heaven,
6:10 Like a noble athlete the **o** man, C
6:12 At that point, partly out of pity for his **o** age, A
6:18 to **o** age and having maintained in accordance A
7:13 Most amazing, indeed, though he was an **o** man, C
8: 5 as that of the **o** man who has just been tortured, C

OLDER‡ (15) [OLD]

1Ki 12: 6 the **o** men who had attended his father Solomon
12: 8 the advice that the **o** men gave him,
12:13 the advice that the **o** men had given him
2Ki 4:18 the child was **o,** he went out one day to his father
2Ch 10: 6 the **o** men who had attended his father Solomon
10: 8 he rejected the advice that the **o** men gave him,
10:13 King Rehoboam rejected the advice of the **o** men;
22: 1 the Arabs to the camp had killed all the **o** sons.
Job 15:10 the aged are on our side, those **o** than your father.
32: 4 because they were **o** than he.
1Ti 5: 1 Do not speak harshly to an **o** man,
5: 2 to **o** women as mothers, to younger women
Tit 2: 2 Tell the **o** men to be temperate, serious, prudent,
2: 3 tell the **o** women to be reverent in behavior,
Sir 32: 3 Speak, you who are **o,** for it is your right,

OLDEST (2) [OLD]

Ge 24: 2 Abraham said to his servant, the **o** of his house,
2Ki 3:21 from the youngest to the **o,**

OLDNESS (KJV) See OLD WRITTEN CODE

OLIVE (48) [OLIVES, OLIVET, OLIVEWOOD, OLIVEYARDS]

Ge 8:11 and there in its beak was a freshly plucked **o** leaf;
Ex 23:11 with your vineyard, and with your **o** orchard.
30:24 and a hin of **o** oil;
Dt 6:11 vineyards and **o** groves that you did not plant—
8: 8 a land of **o** trees and honey,
24:20 you beat your **o** trees, do not strip what is left;
28:40 You shall have **o** trees throughout all
Jdg 9: 8 So they said to the **o** tree, 'Reign over us.'
9: 9 The **o** tree answered them,
15: 5 as well as the vineyards and **o** groves.
1Sa 8:14 and **o** orchards and give them to his courtiers.
2Ki 5:26 **o** orchards and vineyards, sheep and oxen,
18:32 a land of **o** oil and honey,
1Ch 27:28 Over the **o** and sycamore trees in
Ne 5:11 their vineyards, their **o** orchards, and their houses,
8:15 "Go out to the hills and bring branches of **o,** wild **o,**
9:25 **o** orchards, and fruit trees in abundance;
Job 15:33 and cast off their blossoms, like the **o** tree.
Ps 52: 8 But I am like a green **o** tree in the house of God.
128: 3 be like **o** shoots around your table.
Isa 17: 6 as when an **o** tree is beaten—
24:13 as when an **o** tree is beaten,
41:19 the acacia, the myrtle, and the **o;**
Jer 11:16 The LORD once called you, "A green **o** tree,
Hos 14: 6 his beauty shall be like the **o** tree,
Am 4: 9 locust devoured your fig trees and your **o** trees;
Hab 3:17 produce of the **o** fails and the fields yield no food;
Hag 2:19 the pomegranate, and the **o** tree still yield nothing?
Zec 4: 3 And by it there are two **o** trees,
4:11 "What are these two **o** trees on the right and
4:12 "What are these two branches of the **o** trees,
Lk 16: 6 He answered, 'A hundred jugs of **o** oil.'
Ro 11:17 a wild **o** shoot, were grafted in their place to share
the rich root of the **o** tree,
11:24 from what is by nature a wild **o** tree and grafted,
contrary to nature, into a cultivated **o** tree,
11:24 be grafted back into their own **o** tree.
Rev 6: 6 but do not damage the **o** oil and the wine!"
11: 4 the two **o** trees and the two lampstands that stand
18:13 frankincense, wine, **o** oil, choice flour and wheat,
Tob 1: 7 likewise the tenth of the grain, wine, **o** oil,
Jdt 15:13 with her crowned themselves with **o** wreaths.
Sir 24:14 like a fair **o** tree in the field,
50:10 like an **o** tree laden with fruit,
Sus 1:17 "Bring me **o** oil and ointments,
2Mc 14: 4 of the customary **o** branches from the temple.
2Es 16:29 as in an **o** orchard three or four olives may be left

OLIVES (20) [OLIVE]

Ex 27:20 the Israelites to bring you pure oil of beaten **o** for
Lev 24: 2 to bring you pure oil of beaten **o** for the lamp,
Dt 28:40 for your **o** shall drop off.
2Sa 15:30 But David went up the ascent of the Mount of **O,**
Mic 6:15 You shall sow, but not reap; you shall tread **o,**
Zec 14: 4 On that day his feet shall stand on the Mount of **O,**
14: 4 and the Mount of **O** shall be split in two from east
Mt 21: 1 at the Mount of **O,** Jesus sent two disciples,
24: 3 When he was sitting on the Mount of **O,**
26:30 they went out to the Mount of **O.**
Mk 11: 1 at Bethphage and Bethany, near the Mount of **O,**
13: 3 When he was sitting on the Mount of **O** opposite
14:26 they went out to the Mount of **O.**
Lk 19:29 at the place called the Mount of **O,**
19:37 the path down from the Mount of **O,**
21:37 and spend the night on the Mount of **O,**
22:39 as was his custom, to the Mount of **O;**
Jn 8: 1 ⟦while Jesus went to the Mount of **O.**⟧
Jas 3:12 Can a fig tree, my brothers and sisters, yield **o,**
2Es 16:29 as in an olive orchard three or four **o** may be left

OLIVET (1) [OLIVE]

Ac 1:12 to Jerusalem from the mount called **O,**

OLIVET (KJV) See also OLIVES

OLIVEWOOD (4) [OLIVE, WOOD]

1Ki 6:23 In the inner sanctuary he made two cherubim of **o,**
6:31 to the inner sanctuary he made doors of **o;**
6:32 the two doors of **o** with carvings of cherubim,
6:33 for the entrance to the nave doorposts of **o,**

OLIVEYARD (KJV) See OLIVE ORCHARD

OLIVEYARDS (1) [OLIVE]

Jos 24:13 the fruit of vineyards and **o** that you did not plant.

OLYMPAS (1)

Ro 16:15 and **O,** and all the saints who are with them.

OLYMPIAN (1)

2Mc 6: 2 in Jerusalem and to call it the temple of **O** Zeus,

OMAR (3)

Ge 36:11 The sons of Eliphaz were Teman, **O,** Zepho,
36:15 the clans Teman, **O,** Zepho, Kenaz,
1Ch 1:36 The sons of Eliphaz: Teman, **O,** Zephi, Gatam,

OMEGA (3)

Rev 1: 8 "I am the Alpha and the **O,**" says the Lord God,
21: 6 I am the Alpha and the **O,**
22:13 I am the Alpha and the **O,** the first and the last,

OMEN (3) [OMENS]

1Ki 20:33 Now the men were watching for an **o;**
Zec 3: 8 For they are an **o** of things to come:
2Mc 5: 4 the apparition might prove to have been a good **o.**

OMENS (7) [OMEN]

Nu 24: 1 so he did not go, as at other times, to look for **o,**
Dt 13: 1 by dreams appear among you and promise you **o**
13: 2 the **o** or the portents declared by them take place,
Isa 44:25 who frustrates the **o** of liars, and makes fools
Mt 24:24 and produce great signs and **o,**
Mk 13:22 and produce signs and **o,** to lead astray,
Sir 34: 5 Divinations and **o** and dreams are unreal,

OMER (5) [OMERS]

Ex 16:16 **o** to a person according to the number of persons,
16:18 But when they measured it with an **o,**
16:32 an **o** of it be kept throughout your generations,
16:33 "Take a jar, and put an **o** of manna in it,
16:36 An **o** is a tenth of an ephah.

OMERS (1) [OMER]

Ex 16:22 they gathered twice as much food, two **o** apiece.

OMIT (1) [OMITTED, OMITTING]

Lev 2:13 You shall not **o** from your grain offerings the salt

OMITTED (2) [OMIT]

AdE 6:10 let nothing be **o** from what you have proposed."
1Es 8: 7 so that he **o** nothing from the law of the Lord or

OMITTING (1) [OMIT]

3Mc 4:13 not **o** any detail of their punishment.

OMNIPOTENCE See Index to Footnotes

OMNIPOTENT (KJV) See ALMIGHTY

OMRI (18)

1Ki 16:16 therefore all Israel made **O,** the commander of
16:17 So **O** went up from Gibbethon,
16:21 to make him king, and half followed **O.**
16:22 But the people who followed **O** overcame
16:22 so Tibni died, and **O** became king.
16:23 **O** began to reign over Israel;
16:25 **O** did what was evil in the sight of the LORD;
16:27 Now the rest of the acts of **O** that he did,
16:28 **O** slept with his ancestors,
16:29 Ahab son of **O** began to reign over Israel;
16:29 Ahab son of **O** reigned over Israel
16:30 Ahab son of **O** did evil in the sight of
2Ki 8:26 a granddaughter of King **O** of Israel.
1Ch 7: 8 Zemirah, Joash, Eliezer, Elioenai, **O,** Jeremoth,
9: 4 son of **O,** son of Imri, son of Bani,
27:18 for Issachar, **O** son of Michael;
2Ch 22: 2 name was Athaliah, a granddaughter of **O.**
Mic 6:16 the statutes of **O** and all the works of the house

ON (5 of 5394) [=HELIOPOLIS] See Index of Articles Etc. for an Exhaustive Listing (See Introduction, page xi)

Ge 41:45 daughter of Potiphera, priest of **O,** as his wife.
41:50 whom Asenath daughter of Potiphera, priest of **O,**
46:20 whom Asenath daughter of Potiphera, priest of **O,**
Nu 16: 1 and Abiram sons of Eliab, and **O** son of Peleth
Eze 30:17 The young men of **O** and of Pi-beseth shall fall

ONAM (4)

Ge 36:23 Alvan, Manahath, Ebal, Shepho, and **O.**
1Ch 1:40 Alian, Manahath, Ebal, Shephi, and **O.**
2:26 she was the mother of **O.**
2:28 The sons of **O:** Shammai and Jada.

ONAN (8)

Ge 38: 4 and bore a son whom she named **O.**
38: 8 to **O,** "Go in to your brother's wife and perform
38: 9 since **O** knew that the offspring would not be his,
46:12 The children of Judah: Er, **O,** Shelah, Perez,
46:12 Zerah (but Er and **O** died in the land of Canaan);
Nu 26:19 The sons of Judah: Er and **O;**
26:19 Er and **O** died in the land of Canaan.
1Ch 2: 3 The sons of Judah: Er, **O,** and Shelah;

ONCE‡ (179) [ONE]

Ge 18:32 not let the Lord be angry if I speak just **o** more.
25:29 **O** when Jacob was cooking a stew,
27:43 flee at **o** to my brother Laban in Haran,
28: 2 Go at **o** to Paddan-aram to the house of Bethuel,
31:10 of the flock I **o** had a dream in which I looked up
31:13 Now leave this land at **o** and return to the land
37: 5 **O** Joseph had a dream, and when he told it
41:10 **O** Pharaoh was angry with his servants,
Ex 9:34 he sinned **o** more and hardened his heart,
10:17 Do forgive my sin just this **o,**
30:10 **O** a year Aaron shall perform the rite of atonement
30:10 the atonement for it **o** a year with the blood of
32: 7 The LORD said to Moses, "Go down at **o!**
Lev 4:23 **o** the sin that he has committed is made known
7:35 **o** they have been brought forward to serve
16:34 the people of Israel **o** in the year for all their sins.
Nu 8:15 **o** you have cleansed them and presented them as
11:15 you are going to treat me, put me to death at **o—**
13:30 and said, "Let us go up at **o** and occupy it,
22:15 **O** again Balak sent officials,
Dt 4:10 how you **o** stood before the LORD your God
10:10 And **o** again the LORD listened to me.
28:62 **o** you were as numerous as the stars in heaven,
Jos 5:13 **O** when Joshua was by Jericho,
6: 3 all the warriors circling the city **o.**
6:11 of the LORD went around the city, circling it **o;**
6:14 the second day they marched around the city **o** and
8:19 took it, and at **o** set the city on fire.
Jdg 2:23 not driving them out at **o,**
6:39 please, make trial with the fleece just **o** more;
9: 8 trees **o** went out to anoint a king over themselves.
11:14 **O** again Jephthah sent messengers to the king of
14: 1 **O** Samson went down to Timnah,
16: 1 **O** Samson went to Gaza, where he saw a prostitute
16:28 remember me and strengthen me only this **o,**
20:28 "Shall we go out **o** more to battle
1Sa 23:22 Go and make sure **o** more;
2Sa 5:22 **O** again the Philistines came up,
19: 7 So go out at **o** and speak kindly to your servants;
20:13 **O** he was removed from the highway,
1Ki 1:13 Go in at **o** to King David, and say to him,
10:22 **O** every three years the fleet of ships
2Ki 4:26 run at **o** to meet her,
4:35 He got down, walked **o** to and fro in the room,
6: 8 **O** when the king of Aram was at war with Israel,
6:10 More than **o** or twice he warned such a place so
1Ch 14:13 **O** again the Philistines made a raid in the valley.
2Ch 2: 3 "**O** you dealt with my father David
9:21 **o** every three years the ships of Tarshish used
Ne 13:20 the night outside Jerusalem **o** or twice.
Job 1: 1 There was **o** a man in the land
9: 3 one could not answer him **o** in a thousand.
20:11 Their bodies, **o** full of youth,
33:21 and their bones, **o** invisible, now stick out.
40: 5 I have spoken **o,** and I will not answer;
Ps 62:11 **O** God has spoken; twice have I heard this:
71:21 will increase my honor, and comfort me **o** again.
76: 7 before you when **o** your anger is roused?
89:35 **O** and for all I have sworn by my holiness;
Pr 12:16 Fools show their anger at **o,**
Isa 4: 4 **o** the Lord has washed away the filth of
16: 8 whose clusters **o** made drunk the lords of
16: 8 their shoots **o** spread abroad and crossed over
Jer 2: 9 Therefore **o** more I accuse you, says the LORD,
11:16 The LORD **o** called you, "A green olive tree,
31:23 **O** more they shall use these words in the land
33:10 or animal, there shall **o** more be heard
La 1: 1 How lonely sits the city that **o** was full of people!
Eze 26:17 **o** mighty on the sea, you and your inhabitants,
47: 9 **o** these waters reach there.
Hos 9:13 **O** I saw Ephraim as a young palm planted in
Jnh 1: 2 "Go at **o** to Nineveh, that great city, and cry out
Hab 2:18 What use is an idol **o** its maker has shaped it—
Hag 2: 6 For thus says the LORD of hosts: **O** again,
Zec 11:15 Take **o** more the implements of
Mal 3:18 Then **o** more you shall see the difference between
Mt 21:19 And the fig tree withered at **o.**
21:20 saying, "How did the fig tree wither at **o?**"
22: 1 **O** more Jesus spoke to them in parables, saying:
25:16 the five talents went off at **o** and traded with them,
26:49 At **o** he came up to Jesus and said, "Greetings,
26:53 and he will at **o** send me more than twelve legions
27:48 At **o** one of them ran and got a sponge,
Mk 1:28 At **o** his fame began to spread throughout
1:30 and they told him about her at **o.**
1:43 After sternly warning him he sent him away at **o,**
2: 8 At **o** Jesus perceived in his spirit
4:29 the grain is ripe, at **o** he goes in with his sickle,
6:25 to give me at **o** the head of John the Baptist on
6:54 people at **o** recognized him,
14:40 And **o** more he came and found them sleeping,
14:45 So when he came, he went up to him at **o** and said,
Lk 1: 8 **O** when he was serving as priest before God
5: 1 **O** while Jesus was standing beside the lake
5:12 **O,** when he was in one of the cities,
8:55 Her spirit returned, and she got up at **o.**
9:18 **O** when Jesus was praying alone,
9:39 and all at **o** he shrieks.
13:25 When **o** the owner of the house has got up
14:21 'Go out at **o** into the streets and lanes of the town
17: 7 'Come here at **o** and take your place at the table'?
17:20 **O** Jesus was asked by the Pharisees when
22:32 and you, when **o** you have turned back,
Jn 5: 9 At **o** the man was made well,
8: 8 ⟦**o** again he bent down and wrote on the ground.⟧
13:32 in himself and will glorify him at **o.**
19:34 and at **o** blood and water came out.
Ac 23:30 I sent him to you at **o,**
Ro 6:10 The death he died, he died to sin, **o** for all;
6:17 having **o** been slaves of sin,
6:19 as you **o** presented your members as slaves
7: 9 I was **o** alive apart from the law,
11:30 Just as you were **o** disobedient to God but have
15:24 **o** I have enjoyed your company for a little while.
2Co 3:10 what **o** had glory has lost its glory because of
5:16 we **o** knew Christ from a human point of view,
11:25 **O** I received a stoning.
Gal 1:17 but I went away at **o** into Arabia,
1:23 now proclaiming the faith he **o** tried to destroy."
2:18 I build up again the very things that I **o** tore down,
3:15 **o** a person's will has been ratified,
5: 3 **O** again I testify to every man who lets himself
Eph 2: 2 in which you **o** lived, following the course
2: 3 All of us **o** lived among them in the passions
2:13 in Christ Jesus you who **o** were far off have been
5: 8 For **o** you were darkness,
Php 4:16 you sent me help for my needs more than **o.**
Col 1:21 you who were **o** estranged and hostile in mind,
3: 7 These are the ways you also **o** followed,
1Ti 3: 2 a bishop must be above reproach, married only **o,**
3:12 Let deacons be married only **o,**
5: 9 and has been married only **o;**
Tit 1: 6 married only **o,** whose children are believers,
3: 3 For we ourselves were **o** foolish, disobedient,
Heb 6: 4 to repentance those who have **o** been enlightened,
7:27 this he did **o** for all when he offered himself.
9: 7 and he but **o** a year,
9:12 he entered **o** for all into the Holy Place,
9:26 he has appeared **o** for all at the end of the age
9:27 And just as it is appointed for mortals to die **o,**
9:28 having been offered **o** to bear the sins of many,
10: 2 since the worshipers, cleansed **o** for all,
10:10 through the offering of the body of Jesus Christ **o**
12:26 now he has promised, "Yet **o** more I will shake
12:27 This phrase, "Yet **o** more,"
1Pe 2:10 **O** you were not a people,
2:10 **o** you had not received mercy,
3:18 For Christ also suffered for sins **o** for all,
Jude 1: 3 to contend for the faith that was **o** for all entrusted
1: 5 who **o** for all saved a people out of the land
Rev 4: 2 At **o** I was in the spirit,
19: 3 **O** more they said, "Hallelujah!
Tob 4:14 of those who work for you, but pay them at **o.**
8: 3 and at **o** bound him there hand and foot.
8:21 Take at **o** half of what I own and return in safety
Jdt 1:15 thus destroying him **o** and for all.
10:15 Go at **o** to his tent;
12:14 Whatever pleases him I will do at **o,**
AdE 8: 3 Then she spoke **o** again to the king and,
Wis 5: 4 "These are persons whom we **o** held in derision
5:12 the air, thus divided, comes together at **o,**
14:15 as a god what was **o** a dead human being,
18:17 Then at **o** apparitions in dreadful
Sus 1:15 **O,** while they were watching for an opportune day,
1Mc 3:15 **O** again a strong army of godless men went up
2Mc 3: 8 Heliodorus at **o** set out on his journey,
4:10 at **o** shifted his compatriots over to the Greek way
6:28 When he had said this, he went at **o** to the rack.
3Mc 1:11 and he only **o** a year—
5:25 the supreme God to help them again at **o.**

3Mc 5:38 the elephants now **o** more for the destruction of
6:41 at **o** and wrote the following letter for them to
2Es 5:22 and I began **o** more to speak words in the presence
6:43 your word went forth, and at **o** the work was done.
7:*49* and will admonish you **o** more.
7:*75* or whether we shall be tormented at **o**?"
16: 6 or quench a fire in the stubble **o** it has started
16:13 to the ends of the world will not miss **o**.
4Mc 12: 9 by the boy's declaration, they freed him at **o**.

ONE‡ (3714) [ANYONE, ANYONE'S, EVERYONE, EVERYONE'S, FIRST, ONCE, ONE'S, ONES, ONESELF]

A. ONE ANOTHER (207)
B. HOLY ONE (66)
C. ONE DAY (46)
D. EVERY ONE (39)
E. MIGHTY ONE (21)
F. LOVE ONE ANOTHER (15)
G. THE EVIL ONE (12)
H. ONE BODY (11)
I. ONE FLESH (8)
J. RIGHTEOUS ONE (8)

Ge 1: 9 under the sky be gathered together into **o** place,
2: 5 and there was no **o** to till the ground;
2:11 the **o** that flows around the whole land of Havilah,
2:13 the **o** that flows around the whole land of Cush.
2:21 then he took **o** of his ribs and closed up its place
2:23 this **o** shall be called Woman, for out of Man this **o** was taken."
2:24 and clings to his wife, and they become **o** flesh. I
3: 6 and that the tree was to be desired to make **o** wise,
3:22 "See, the man has become like **o** of us,
4:15 so that no **o** who came upon him would kill him.
4:19 the name of the **o** was Adah,
5: 3 When Adam had lived **o** hundred thirty years,
5: 6 When Seth had lived **o** hundred five years,
5:18 Jared had lived **o** hundred sixty-two years
5:25 Methuselah had lived **o** hundred eighty-seven
5:28 Lamech had lived **o** hundred eighty-two years,
5:29 the LORD has cursed this **o** shall bring us relief
6: 3 their days shall be **o** hundred twenty years."
7:24 on the earth for **o** hundred fifty days.
8: 3 of **o** hundred fifty days the waters had abated;
9: 5 each **o** for the blood of another,
10:25 the name of the **o** was Peleg,
11: 1 whole earth had **o** language and the same words.
11: 3 And they said to **o** another, "Come, A
11: 6 they are **o** people, and they have all **o** language;
11: 7 that they will not understand **o** another's speech."
11:10 When Shem was **o** hundred years old,
11:25 after the birth of Terah **o** hundred nineteen years,
12: 3 and the **o** who curses you I will curse;
13:16 so that if **o** can count the dust of the earth,
14:13 Then **o** who had escaped came and told Abram
14:20 And Abram gave him **o** tenth of everything.
15: 4 no **o** but your very own issue shall be your heir."
17:12 in your house and the **o** bought with your money
17:13 the slave born in your house and the **o** bought
18:10 Then **o** said, "I will surely return to you
19:20 near enough to flee to, and it is a little **o**.
19:20 is it not a little **o**?—and my life will be saved!"
21:15 she cast the child under **o** of the bushes.
22: 2 and offer him there as a burnt offering on **o** of
23: 1 Sarah lived **o** hundred twenty-seven years;
24:14 let her be the **o** whom you have appointed
25: 7 **o** hundred seventy-five years.
25:17 **o** hundred thirty-seven years;
25:23 the **o** shall be stronger than the other,
26:10 **O** of the people might easily have lain
26:21 and they quarreled over that **o** also;
27:38 Esau said to his father, "Have you only **o** blessing,
27:45 Why should I lose both of you in **o** day?" C
27:46 If Jacob marries **o** of the Hittite women such
27:46 **o** of the women of the land,
28: 1 "You shall not marry **o** of the Canaanite women.
28: 2 as wife from there **o** of the daughters of Laban,
28: 6 "You shall not marry **o** of the Canaanite women,"
28:11 Taking **o** of the stones of the place,
28:22 that you give me I will surely give **o** tenth to you."
29:27 Complete the week of this **o**,
30:33 Every **o** that is not speckled and spotted among D
30:35 every **o** that had white on it, D
31:49 when we are absent **o** from the other.
31:50 though no **o** else is with us,
32: 8 "If Esau comes to the **o** company and destroys it,
33:13 and if they are overdriven for **o** day, C
33:19 he bought for **o** hundred pieces of money the plot
34:14 to give our sister to **o** who is uncircumcised,
34:16 and we will live among you and become **o** people.
34:22 to live among us, to become **o** people:
35: 5 so that no **o** pursued them.
35:28 the days of Isaac were **o** hundred eighty years.
37:19 said to **o** another, "Here comes this dreamer. A
37:20 let us kill him and throw him into **o** of the pits;
37:36 **o** of Pharaoh's officials, the captain of the guard.
38:28 While she was in labor, **o** put out a hand;
38:28 saying, "This **o** came out first."
39:11 **O** day, however, when he went into the house C
39:11 and while no **o** else was in the house,
39:22 he was the **o** who did it.
40: 5 **O** night they both dreamed—
40: 8 and there is no **o** to interpret them."
41: 5 plump and good, were growing on **o** stalk.

Ge 41: 8 but there was no **o** who could interpret them
41:15 and there is no **o** who can interpret it.
41:21 when they had eaten them no **o** would have known
41:22 full and good, growing on **o** stalk,
41:24 there was no **o** who could explain it to me."
41:25 "Pharaoh's dreams are **o** and the same;
41:26 seven good ears are seven years; the dreams are **o**.
41:38 **o** in whom is the spirit of God?"
41:39 there is no **o** so discerning and wise as you.
41:44 and without your consent no **o** shall lift up hand
42: 1 "Why do you keep looking at **o** another? A
42:11 We are all sons of **o** man;
42:13 is now with our father, and **o** is no more."
42:16 Let **o** of you go and bring your brother,
42:19 let **o** of your brothers stay here
42:21 They said to **o** another, "Alas, A
42:27 When **o** of them opened his sack
42:28 and turned trembling to **o** another, A
42:32 **o** is no more, and the youngest is now
42:33 leave **o** of your brothers with me,
42:36 "I am the **o** you have bereaved of children:
43:33 the men looked at **o** another in amazement. A
44: 9 Should it be found with any **o** of your servants,
44:11 each **o** quickly lowered his sack to the ground,
44:13 Then each **o** loaded his donkey,
44:15 not know that **o** such as I can practice divination?"
44:16 then, my lord's slaves, both we and also the **o**
44:17 the **o** in whose possession the cup was found shall
44:28 **o** left me, and I said, Surely he has been torn
44:29 If you take this **o** also from me,
45: 1 So no **o** stayed with him
45:22 To each **o** of them he gave a set of garments;
47: 9 years of my earthly sojourn are **o** hundred thirty;
47:21 he made slaves of them from **o** end of Egypt to
47:28 were **o** hundred forty-seven years.
48:18 Since this **o** is the firstborn,
48:22 to you **o** portion more than to your brothers,
49:16 Dan shall judge his people as **o** of the tribes
49:24 by the hands of the Mighty **O** of Jacob, E
49:28 blessing each **o** of them with a suitable blessing.
50:22 and Joseph lived **o** hundred ten years.
50:26 And Joseph died, being **o** hundred ten years old;
Ex 1:15 **o** of whom was named Shiphrah and
2: 6 "This must be **o** of the Hebrews' children,"
2:11 **O** day, after Moses had grown up, C
2:11 an Egyptian beating a Hebrew, **o** of his kinsfolk.
2:12 and seeing no **o** he killed the Egyptian
2:13 and he said to the **o** who was in the wrong,
6:16 of Levi's life was **o** hundred thirty-seven years.
6:18 of Kohath's life was **o** hundred thirty-three years.
6:20 of Amram's life was **o** hundred thirty-seven years.
6:25 Aaron's son Eleazar married **o** of the daughters
7:12 Each **o** threw down his staff,
8:10 So that you may know that there is no **o** like
8:31 from his people; not **o** remained.
9: 6 but of the livestock of the Israelites not **o** died.
9: 7 not **o** of the livestock of the Israelites was dead.
9:14 that you may know that there is no **o** like me in all
10: 5 so that no **o** will be able to see the land.
10:23 People could not see **o** another, A
11: 1 "I will bring **o** more plague upon Pharaoh and
12: 4 it shall join its closest neighbor in obtaining **o**;
12:46 It shall be eaten in **o** house;
12:49 there shall be **o** law for the native and for
14:20 **o** did not come near the other all night.
14:28 into the sea; not **o** of them remained.
16:15 the Israelites saw it, they said to **o** another, A
16:19 "Let no **o** leave any of it over until morning."
17:12 Aaron and Hur held up his hands, **o** on **o** side,
18: 3 The name of the **o** was Gershom (for he said,
18:16 to me and I decide between **o** person and another,
19: 8 The people all answered as **o**:
21:18 and **o** strikes the other with a stone or fist so that
21:22 the **o** responsible shall be fined what
22: 6 **o** who started the fire shall make full restitution.
22: 9 clothing, or any other loss, of which **o** party says,
22: 9 the **o** whom God condemns shall pay double to
22:11 the two of them that the **o** has not laid hands on
23: 5 of **o** who hates you lying under its burden
23:15 No **o** shall appear before me empty-handed.
23:26 No **o** shall miscarry or be barren in your land;
23:29 not drive them out from before you in **o** year,
24: 3 and all the people answered with **o** voice,
25:12 two rings on the **o** side of it,
25:19 Make **o** cherub at the **o** end, and **o** cherub at the other; of **o** piece with the mercy seat
25:20 They shall face **o** to another;
25:23 **o** cubit wide, and a cubit and a half high.
25:31 and its petals shall be of **o** piece with it;
25:32 three branches of the lampstand out of **o** side of it
25:33 each with calyx and petals, on **o** branch,
25:35 of **o** piece with it under the first pair of branches,
25:35 of **o** piece with it under the next pair of branches,
25:35 of **o** piece with it under the last pair of branches—
25:36 and their branches shall be of **o** piece with it,
25:36 the whole of it **o** hammered piece of pure gold.
26: 3 Five curtains shall be joined to **o** another; A
26: 3 other five curtains shall be joined to **o** another. A
26: 5 You shall make fifty loops on the **o** curtain,
26: 5 the loops shall be opposite **o** another. A
26: 6 join the curtains to **o** another with the clasps, A
26: 6 so that the tabernacle may be **o** whole.
26:10 the edge of the curtain that is outermost in **o** set,
26:11 so that it may be **o** whole.
26:13 The cubit on the **o** side,
26:26 five for the frames of the **o** side of the tabernacle,
27: 2 its horns shall be of **o** piece with it,

Ex 27: 9 of fine twisted linen **o** hundred cubits long for
27:11 be hangings **o** hundred cubits long,
27:14 be fifteen cubits of hangings on the **o** side,
27:18 The length of the court shall be **o** hundred cubits,
28:10 six of their names on the **o** stone,
29: 1 Take **o** young bull and two rams without blemish,
29: 3 You shall put them in **o** basket and bring them in
29:15 Then you shall take **o** of the rams,
29:23 and **o** loaf of bread, **o** cake of bread made with oil, and **o** wafer,
29:33 but no **o** else shall eat of them,
29:39 **O** lamb you shall offer in the morning,
30: 2 It shall be **o** cubit long, and **o** cubit wide;
30: 2 its horns shall be of **o** piece with it.
30:13 This is what each **o** who is registered shall give:
30:14 Each **o** who is registered, from twenty years old
32:29 each **o** at the cost of a son or a brother,
32:35 they made the calf—the **o** that Aaron made.
33: 4 they mourned, and no **o** put on ornaments.
33:11 as **o** speaks to a friend.
33:20 for no **o** shall see me and live."
34: 3 No **o** shall come up with you,
34:20 No **o** shall appear before me empty-handed.
34:24 no **o** shall covet your land when you go up
36: 1 Bezalel and Oholiab and every skillful **o** to whom
36: 2 and Oholiab and every skillful **o** to whom
36:10 He joined five curtains to **o** another, A
36:10 the other five curtains he joined to **o** another. A
36:12 the **o** curtain, and he made fifty loops on the edge
36:12 the loops were opposite **o** another. A
36:13 and joined the curtains **o** to the other with clasps;
36:13 so the tabernacle was **o** whole.
36:17 on the edge of the outermost curtain of the **o** set,
36:18 the tent together so that it might be **o** whole.
36:31 five for the frames of the **o** side of the tabernacle,
37: 3 on its **o** side and two rings on its other side.
37: 8 **o** cherub at the **o** end, and **o** cherub at the other end; of **o** piece with the mercy seat
37: 9 They faced **o** another; A
37:10 **o** cubit wide, and a cubit and a half high.
37:17 its calyxes, and its petals were of **o** piece with it.
37:18 three branches of the lampstand out of **o** side of it
37:19 each with calyx and petals, on **o** branch,
37:21 of **o** piece with it under the first pair of branches,
37:21 of **o** piece with it under the next pair of branches,
37:21 of **o** piece with it under the last pair of branches.
37:22 Their calyxes and their branches were of **o** piece
37:22 the whole of it **o** hammered piece of pure gold.
37:25 **o** cubit long, and **o** cubit wide;
37:25 its horns were of **o** piece with it.
38: 2 its horns were of **o** piece with it,
38: 9 of fine twisted linen, **o** hundred cubits long;
38:11 side there were hangings **o** hundred cubits long;
38:14 hangings for **o** side of the gate were fifteen cubits,
38:25 who were counted was **o** hundred talents
38:25 **o** thousand seven hundred seventy-five shekels,
38:27 **o** hundred bases for the hundred talents,
Lev 3: 1 you shall offer **o** without blemish before
3: 6 male or female, you shall offer **o** without blemish.
4: 2 about things not to be done, and does any **o**
4:13 and they do any **o** of the things that by
4:22 doing unintentionally any **o** of all the things that
4:27 among you sins unintentionally in doing any **o** of
5: 1 though able to testify as **o** who has seen or learned
5: 3 by which **o** can become unclean—
5: 7 **o** for a sin offering and the other for
5: 8 who shall offer first the **o** for the sin offering,
6: 3 the various things that **o** may do and sin thereby—
6: 7 of the things that **o** may do and incur guilt thereby.
7:11 of the offering of well-being that **o** may offer to
7:14 From this you shall offer **o** cake
7:18 nor shall it be credited to the **o** who offers it;
7:18 and the **o** who eats of it shall incur guilt.
7:21 When any **o** of you touches any unclean thing—
7:25 If any **o** of you eats the fat from an animal
7:27 Any **o** of you who eats any blood shall be cut off
7:29 Any **o** of you who would offer to
7:33 the **o** among the sons of Aaron who offers
8:26 he took **o** cake of unleavened bread, **o** cake of bread with oil, and **o** wafer,
9:15 and presented it as a sin offering like the first **o**.
11:26 everyone who touches **o** of them shall be unclean.
11:28 the **o** who carries the carcass shall wash his clothes
11:31 whoever touches **o** of them
12: 8 **o** for a burnt offering and the other for
13: 2 to Aaron the priest or to **o** of his sons the priests.
13:23 if the spot remains in **o** place and does not spread,
13:28 the spot remains in **o** place and does not spread in
14: 4 be brought for the **o** who is to be cleansed,
14: 5 that **o** of the birds be slaughtered over fresh water
14: 7 the **o** who is to be cleansed of the leprous disease;
14: 8 The **o** who is to be cleansed shall wash his clothes,
14:10 and **o** ewe lamb in its first year without blemish,
14:10 an ephah of choice flour mixed with oil, and **o** log
14:12 The priest shall take **o** of the lambs,
14:14 on the lobe of the right ear of the **o** to be cleansed,
14:17 on the lobe of the right ear of the **o** to be cleansed,
14:18 the priest's hand he shall put on the head of the **o**
14:19 for the **o** to be cleansed from his uncleanness.
14:21 he shall take **o** male lamb for a guilt offering to
14:22 **o** for a sin offering and the other for
14:25 on the lobe of the right ear of the **o** to be cleansed,
14:28 on the lobe of the right ear of the **o** to be cleansed,
14:29 the priest's hand he shall put on the head of the **o**
14:31 **o** for a sin offering and the other for
14:31 the LORD on behalf of the **o** being cleansed.
14:32 the ritual for the **o** who has a leprous disease,

Lev 14:50 and shall slaughter o of the birds over fresh water
15: 4 the o with the discharge lies shall be unclean;
15: 6 All who sit on anything on which the o with
15: 7 the o with the discharge shall wash their clothes,
15: 8 If the o with the discharge spits
15: 9 the o with the discharge rides shall be unclean.
15:11 All those whom the o with the discharge touches
15:12 the o with the discharge touches shall be broken;
15:13 the o with a discharge is cleansed of his discharge,
15:15 o for a sin offering and the other for
15:30 The priest shall offer o for a sin offering and
16: 5 and o ram for a burnt offering.
16: 8 o lot for the LORD and the other lot for Azazel.
16:17 No o shall be in the tent of meeting from
16:26 The o who sets the goat free
16:28 The o who burns them shall wash his clothes
18: 5 by doing so o shall live: I am the LORD.
19:11 and you shall not lie to o another. A
21: 1 No o shall defile himself for a dead person
21:17 No o of your offspring throughout their generations
21:18 For no o who has a blemish shall draw near, o who is blind or lame, or o who has a mutilated face or
21:19 or o who has a broken foot or a broken hand,
22: 4 No o of Aaron's offspring who has
22:15 No o shall profane the sacred donations of
23:18 o young bull, and two rams;
23:19 You shall also offer o male goat for a sin offering,
23:30 a o I will destroy from the midst of the people.
24:16 O who blasphemes the name of the LORD shall
24:21 O who kills an animal shall make restitution for it;
24:21 o who kills a human being shall be put to death.
24:22 You shall have o law for the alien and for
25:10 you shall return, every o of you, D
25:10 of you, to your property and every o of you D
25:13 every o of you, to your property. D
25:14 you shall not cheat o another. A
25:17 You shall not cheat o another, A
25:26 If the person has no o to redeem it,
25:29 the right of redemption shall be o year.
25:46 no o shall rule over the other with harshness.
25:47 into difficulty with o of them and sell themselves
25:48 o of their brothers may redeem them,
26: 6 and no o shall make you afraid;
26:17 and you shall flee though no o pursues you.
26:36 and they shall flee as o flees from the sword,
26:36 and they shall fall though no o pursues.
26:37 They shall stumble over o another, A
26:37 as if to escape a sword, though no o pursues;
27: 6 If the age is from o month to five years,
27: 8 to what each o making a vow can afford.
27:10 and if o animal is substituted for another,
27:10 both that o and its substitute shall be holy.
27:15 o who consecrates the house wishes to redeem it,
27:19 o who consecrates the field wishes to redeem it,
27:24 In the year of jubilee the field shall return to the o
27:32 every tenth o that passes under
27:33 Let no o inquire whether it is good or bad,
27:33 if o makes substitution for it,
Nu 2: 9 is o hundred eighty-six thousand four hundred.
2:16 is o hundred fifty-one thousand four hundred fifty.
2:24 is o hundred eight thousand o hundred.
2:31 Dan is o hundred fifty-seven thousand six hundred.
3:50 o thousand three hundred sixty-five shekels,
5: 7 adding o fifth to it, and giving it to the o who was
6:11 and the priest shall offer o as a sin offering and
6:14 o male lamb a year old without blemish as
6:14 o ewe lamb a year old without blemish as
6:14 o ram without blemish as an offering
6:19 and o unleavened cake out of the basket,
6:19 and o unleavened wafer, and shall put them in
7: 3 and for each o an ox;
7:11 o leader each day, for the dedication of the altar.
7:12 The o who presented his offering
7:13 his offering was o silver plate weighing o hundred
7:13 o silver basin weighing seventy shekels,
7:14 o golden dish weighing ten shekels,
7:15 o young bull, o ram, o male lamb a year old,
7:16 o male goat for a sin offering;
7:19 his offering o silver plate weighing o hundred
7:19 o silver basin weighing seventy shekels,
7:20 o golden dish weighing ten shekels,
7:21 o young bull, o ram, o male lamb a year old,
7:22 o male goat as a sin offering;
7:25 his offering was o silver plate weighing o hundred
7:25 o silver basin weighing seventy shekels,
7:26 o golden dish weighing ten shekels,
7:27 o young bull, o ram, o male lamb a year old,
7:28 o male goat for a sin offering;
7:31 his offering was o silver plate weighing o hundred
7:31 o silver basin weighing seventy shekels,
7:32 o golden dish weighing ten shekels,
7:33 o young bull, o ram, o male lamb a year old,
7:34 o male goat for a sin offering;
7:37 his offering was o silver plate weighing o hundred
7:37 o silver basin weighing seventy shekels,
7:38 o golden dish weighing ten shekels,
7:39 o young bull, o ram, o male lamb a year old,
7:40 o male goat for a sin offering;
7:43 his offering was o silver plate weighing o hundred
7:43 o silver basin weighing seventy shekels,
7:44 o golden dish weighing ten shekels, full
7:45 o young bull, o ram, o male lamb a year old,
7:46 o male goat for a sin offering;
7:49 his offering was o silver plate weighing o hundred
7:49 o silver basin weighing seventy shekels,
7:50 o golden dish weighing ten shekels,
7:51 o young bull, o ram, o male lamb a year old,
Nu 7:52 o male goat for a sin offering;
7:55 his offering was o silver plate weighing o hundred
7:55 o silver basin weighing seventy shekels,
7:56 o golden dish weighing ten shekels,
7:57 o young bull, o ram, o male lamb a year old,
7:58 o male goat for a sin offering;
7:61 his offering was o silver plate weighing o hundred
7:61 o silver basin weighing seventy shekels,
7:62 o golden dish weighing ten shekels,
7:63 o young bull, o ram, o male lamb a year old,
7:64 o male goat for a sin offering;
7:67 his offering was o silver plate weighing o hundred
7:67 o silver basin weighing seventy shekels,
7:68 o golden dish weighing ten shekels,
7:69 o young bull, o ram, o male lamb a year old,
7:70 o male goat for a sin offering;
7:73 his offering was o silver plate weighing o hundred
7:73 o silver basin weighing seventy shekels,
7:74 o golden dish weighing ten shekels,
7:75 o young bull, o ram, o male lamb a year old,
7:76 o male goat for a sin offering;
7:79 his offering was o silver plate weighing o hundred
7:79 o silver basin weighing seventy shekels,
7:80 o golden dish weighing ten shekels,
7:81 o young bull, o ram, o male lamb a year old,
7:82 o male goat for a sin offering;
7:85 each silver plate weighing o hundred thirty shekels
7:86 of the dishes being o hundred twenty shekels;
8:12 and he shall offer the o for a sin offering and
9:13 such a o shall bear the consequences for the sin.
9:14 you shall have o statute for both the resident alien
10: 4 But if only o is blown, then the leaders,
11:19 You shall eat not only o day, or two days, C
11:26 Two men remained in the camp, o named Eldad,
11:28 the assistant of Moses, o of his chosen men, said,
12:12 Do not let her be like o stillborn,
13: 2 every o a leader among them." D
14: 4 So they said to o another, A
14:15 Now if you kill this people all at o time,
14:30 not o of you shall come into the land
15:12 so you shall do with each and every o. D
15:24 the whole congregation shall offer o young bull
15:24 and o male goat for a sin offering.
15:28 before the LORD for the o who commits an error,
16: 5 the o whom he will choose he will allow
16: 7 the LORD chooses shall be the holy o. B
16:15 I have not taken o donkey from them,
16:15 and I have not harmed any o of them."
16:17 and let each o of you take his censer,
16:17 and each o of you present his censer before
16:22 shall o person sin and you become angry with
17: 2 o for each ancestral house,
17: 3 be o staff for the head of each ancestral house.
17: 6 all their leaders gave him staffs, o for each leader,
18:16 reckoned from o month of age,
19: 8 The o who burns the heifer shall wash his clothes
19:10 The o who gathers the ashes of
19:16 in the open field touches o who has been killed by
19:21 The o who sprinkles the water
24: 4 the oracle of o who hears the words of God,
24:16 of o who hears the words of God, and knows
24:19 O out of Jacob shall rule,
25: 6 Just then o of the Israelites came and brought
26:51 six hundred and o thousand seven hundred thirty.
26:62 every male o month old and up;
26:64 Among these there was not o of those enrolled
26:65 Not o of them was left,
28: 4 O lamb you shall offer in the morning,
28: 8 a grain offering and a drink offering like the o in
28:11 two young bulls, o ram, seven male lambs
28:12 mixed with oil, for the o ram;
28:15 And there shall be o male goat for a sin offering to
28:19 o ram, and seven male lambs a year old;
28:22 also o male goat for a sin offering,
28:27 o ram, seven male lambs a year old.
28:28 of an ephah for each bull, two-tenths for o ram,
28:30 with o male goat, to make atonement for you.
29: 2 o young bull, o ram, seven male lambs
29: 3 three-tenths of o ephah for the bull,
29: 5 with o male goat for a sin offering,
29: 8 o young bull, one ram, seven male lambs
29: 8 o ram, seven male lambs a year old.
29: 9 of an ephah for the bull, two-tenths for the o ram,
29:11 with o male goat for a sin offering,
29:16 also o male goat for a sin offering,
29:19 also o male goat for a sin offering,
29:22 also o male goat for a sin offering,
29:25 also o male goat for a sin offering,
29:28 also o male goat for a sin offering,
29:31 also o male goat for a sin offering,
29:34 also o male goat for a sin offering,
29:36 o bull, o ram, seven male lambs a year old
29:38 also o male goat for a sin offering,
31:28 o item out of every five hundred, whether persons,
31:30 But from the Israelites' half you shall take o out
31:47 the Israelites' half Moses took o of every fifty,
31:49 and not o of us is missing.
33:39 Aaron was o hundred twenty-three years old
33:54 to a large o you shall give a large inheritance,
33:54 and to a small o you shall give a small inheritance;
34:18 You shall take o leader of every tribe to apportion
35:19 of blood is the o who shall put the murderer
35:21 the o who struck the blow shall be put to death;
35:30 but no o shall be put to death on the testimony of
35:32 Nor shall you accept ransom for o who has fled to
35:33 except by the blood of the o who shed it.
36: 7 of the Israelites shall be transferred from o tribe
Nu 36: 8 in any tribe of the Israelites shall marry o from
36: 9 No inheritance shall be transferred from o tribe
Dt 1:14 "The plan you have proposed is a good o."
1:16 and judge rightly between o person and another,
1:23 and I selected twelve of you, o from each tribe.
1:30 is the o who will fight for you,
1:31 just as o carries a child,
1:35 "Not o of these—not o of this evil generation—
1:38 for he is the o who will secure Israel's possession
4:32 ask from o end of heaven to the other:
4:42 homicide could flee to o of these cities and live:
7:24 no o will be able to stand against you,
8: 3 in order to make you understand that o does
9: 3 the LORD your God is the o who crosses over
11:25 No o will be able to stand against you;
12:14 that the LORD will choose in o of your tribes—
13: 7 from o end of the earth to the other,
13:12 If you hear it said about o of the towns that
15: 4 There will, however, be no o in need among you,
17: 2 in o of your towns that
17: 6 be put to death on the evidence of only o witness.
17: 8 to make between o kind of bloodshed and another,
17: 8 o kind of legal right and another,
17: 8 or o kind of assault and another—
17:15 O of your own community you may set as king
18:10 No o shall be found among you who makes a son
18:11 or o who casts spells, or who consults ghosts
19: 3 so that any homicide can flee to o of them.
19: 5 when o of them swings the ax to cut down a tree,
19: 5 the killer may flee to o of these cities and live.
19:11 and flees into o of these cities,
21: 3 o that has not pulled in the yoke;
21:15 o of them loved and the other disliked,
21:15 firstborn being the son of the o who is disliked,
21:17 the o who is disliked, giving him a double portion
22:19 they shall fine him o hundred shekels
22:27 but there was no o to rescue her.
23: 1 No o whose testicles are crushed
23:10 If o of you becomes unclean because of
23:16 in any place they choose in any o of your towns,
24: 5 He shall be free at home o year,
24: 6 No o shall take a mill or an upper millstone
24:14 or aliens who reside in your land in o
25: 1 declaring o to be in the right and the other to be
25: 2 If the o in the wrong deserves to be flogged,
25: 5 and o of them dies and has no son,
25:11 If men get into a fight with o another, A
25:11 and the wife of o intervenes to rescue her husband
28: 7 they shall come out against you o way,
28:25 you shall go out against them o way and flee
28:26 and there shall be no o to frighten them away.
28:64 from o end of the earth to the other;
31: 2 "I am now o hundred twenty years old.
31: 7 "Be strong and bold, for you are the o who will go
32:30 How could o have routed a thousand,
32:39 and no o can deliver from my hand.
33: 8 and your Urim to your loyal o,
33:16 and the favor of the o who dwells on Sinai.
34: 6 but no o knows his burial place to this day.
34: 7 Moses was o hundred twenty years old
Jos 1: 5 No o shall be able to stand against you all the days
3: 8 the o who shall command the priests who bear
3:12 now select twelve men from the tribes of Israel, o
4: 2 from the people, o from each tribe,
4: 4 whom he had appointed, o from each tribe.
4: 5 o for each of the tribes of the Israelites,
5:13 "Are you o of us, or o of our adversaries?"
6: 1 no o came out and no o went in.
7:14 that the LORD takes shall come near o by o.
7:15 And the o who is taken as having
7:18 And he brought near his household o by o,
7:20 I am the o who sinned against the LORD God
8:22 some on o side, and some on the other;
8:22 down until no o was left who survived or escaped.
9: 2 with o accord to fight Joshua and Israel.
10: 2 like o of the royal cities, and was larger than Ai,
10: 8 not o of them shall stand before you."
10:21 no o dared to speak against any of the Israelites.
10:28 in it; he left no o remaining.
10:30 he left no o remaining in it;
10:37 he left no o remaining, just as he had done
10:39 in it; he left no o remaining;
10:40 he left no o remaining, but utterly destroyed all
10:42 and their land at o time,
11: 8 until they had left no o remaining.
11:11 there was no o left who breathed,
12: 4 o of the last of the Rephaim,
12: 9 the king of Jericho o the king of Ai,
12: 9 which is next to Bethel o
12:10 the king of Jerusalem o the king of Hebron o
12:11 the king of Jarmuth o the king of Lachish o
12:12 the king of Eglon o the king of Gezer o
12:13 the king of Debir o the king of Geder o
12:14 the king of Hormah o the king of Arad o
12:15 the king of Libnah o the king of Adullam o
12:16 the king of Makkedah o the king of Bethel o
12:17 the king of Tappuah o the king of Hepher o
12:18 the king of Aphek o the king of Lasharon o
12:19 the king of Madon o the king of Hazor o
12:20 of Shimron-meron o the king of Achshaph o
12:21 the king of Taanach o the king of Megiddo o
12:22 king of Kedesh o the king of Jokneam in Carmel o
12:23 in Naphath-dor o the king of Goiim in Galilee, o
12:24 the king of Tirzah o thirty-one kings in all.
17:14 but o lot and o portion as an inheritance,
17:17 you shall not have o lot only,
20: 4 to o of these cities and shall stand at the entrance

Jos 20: 6 the death of the **o** who is high priest at the time:
21:10 **o** of the families of the Kohathites who belonged
21:27 **o** of the families of the Levites,
21:44 not **o** of all their enemies had withstood them,
21:45 Not **o** of all the good promises that
22: 7 Now to the **o** half of the tribe
22:14 **o** from each of the tribal families of Israel,
22:14 every **o** of them the head of a family among D
23: 9 no **o** has been able to withstand you to this day.
23:10 **O** of you puts to flight a thousand,
23:14 that not **o** thing has failed of all the good things
23:14 to pass for you, not **o** of them has failed.
24:29 died, being **o** hundred ten years old.
24:32 for **o** hundred pieces of money;
Jdg 2: 8 died at the age of **o** hundred ten years.
3:28 and allowed no **o** to cross over.
3:29 able-bodied men; no **o** escaped.
4:16 by the sword; no **o** was left.
5: 5 the **O** of Sinai, before the LORD,
6:16 you shall strike down the Midianites, every **o** D
6:29 So they said to **o** another, "Who has done this?" A
6:39 let me speak **o** more time;
7: 4 When I say, 'This **o** shall go with you,'
7: 4 and when I say, 'This **o** shall not go with you,'
7: 5 as a dog laps, you shall put to **o** side;
8:10 **o** hundred twenty thousand men bearing arms
8:14 **o** of the people of Succoth, and questioned him;
8:18 "As you are, so were they, every **o** of them; D
8:26 requested was **o** thousand seven hundred shekels
9: 2 or that **o** rule over you?'
9: 5 the sons of Jerubbaal, seventy men, on **o** stone;
9:18 and have killed his sons, seventy men on **o** stone,
9:37 and **o** company is coming from the direction
9:49 So every **o** of the troops cut down a bundle D
10:18 of the people of Gilead said to **o** another, A
11:27 the **o** who does me wrong by making war on me.
12: 5 Whenever **o** of the fugitives of Ephraim said,
14: 6 the lion apart barehanded as **o** might tear apart
16: 6 so that **o** could subdue you."
16:28 so that with this **o** act of revenge I may pay back
16:29 his right hand on the **o** and his left hand on
17: 5 and installed **o** of his sons, who became his priest.
17:11 the young man became to him like **o** of his sons.
18:19 for you to be priest to the house of **o** person,
19:13 "Come, let us try to reach **o** of these places,
19:15 but no **o** took them in to spend the night.
20: 1 and the congregation assembled in **o** body H
20: 8 All the people got up as **o**, saying,
20:11 of Israel gathered against the city, united as **o**.
20:16 every **o** could sling a stone at a hair, and not D
20:31 **o** of which goes up to Bethel and the other
20:35 destroyed twenty-five thousand **o** hundred men
21: 1 "No **o** of us shall give his daughter in marriage
21: 3 to pass that today there should be **o** tribe lacking
21: 5 saying, "That **o** shall be put to death."
21: 6 and said, "**O** tribe is cut off from Israel this day.
21: 8 that no **o** from Jabesh-gilead had come to
21: 9 not **o** of the inhabitants of Jabesh-gilead was there.
Ru 1: 4 the **o** was Orpah and the name of the other Ruth.
2: 8 do not go to glean in another field or leave this **o**,
2:13 even though I am not **o** of your servants."
2:20 also said to her, "The man is a relative of ours, **o**
3:14 got up before **o** person could recognize another;
4: 4 for there is no **o** prior to you to redeem it,
4: 7 the **o** took off a sandal and gave it to the other;
1Sa 1: 2 He had two wives; the name of the **o** was Hannah,
2: 2 "There is no Holy **O** like the LORD, B
2: 2 no **o** besides you; there is no Rock like our God.
2: 9 for not by might does **o** prevail.
2:15 and say to the **o** who was sacrificing, "Give meat
2:25 If **o** person sins against another,
2:31 so that no **o** in your family will live to old age.
2:32 and no **o** in your family shall ever live to old age.
2:33 The only **o** of you whom I shall not cut off
2:35 in and out before my anointed **o** forever.
2:36 Please put me in **o** of the priest's places,
6:12 in the direction of Beth-shemesh along **o** highway,
6:17 **o** for Ashdod, **o** for Gaza, **o** for Ashkelon, **o** for Gath, **o** for Ekron;
9: 3 "Take **o** of the boys with you;
9: 9 for the **o** who is now called
9:23 the **o** I asked you to put aside."
10: 3 at Bethel will meet you there, **o** carrying three kids,
10:11 the people said to **o** another, A
10:24 "Do you see the **o** whom the LORD has chosen?
10:24 There is no **o** like him among all the people."
10:27 No **o** was left of the Israelites across
11: 3 Then, if there is no **o** to save us,
11: 7 and they came out as **o**.
11:13 But Saul said, "No **o** shall be put to death this day,
13:17 **o** company turned toward Ophrah,
14: 1 **O** day Jonathan son of Saul said to C
14: 4 there was a rocky crag on **o** side and a rocky crag
14: 4 the name of the **o** was Bozez,
14: 5 **O** crag rose on the north in front of Michmash,
14:28 Then **o** of the soldiers said,
14:36 let us not leave **o** of them."
14:39 But there was no **o** among all
14:40 He said to all Israel, "You shall be on **o** side,
14:45 not **o** hair of his head shall fall to the ground;
16: 3 and you shall anoint for me the **o** whom I name
16: 8 He said, "Neither has the LORD chosen this **o**."
16: 9 he said, "Neither has the LORD chosen this **o**."
16:12 and anoint him; for this is the **o**."
16:18 **O** of the young men answered,
17: 3 Philistines stood on the mountain on the **o** side,
17:36 and this uncircumcised Philistine shall be like **o**
1Sa 18: 7 women sang to **o** another as they made merry, A
18:27 and killed **o** hundred of the Philistines;
20:15 the LORD were to cut off every **o** of the enemies D
21: 1 "Why are you alone, and no **o** with you?"
21: 2 'No **o** must know anything of the matter
21: 9 take it, for there is none here except that **o**."
21:11 Did they not sing to **o** another of him in dances, A
22: 7 give every **o** of you fields and vineyards, D
22: 8 No **o** discloses to me when my son makes a league
22:20 But **o** of the sons of Ahimelech son of Ahitub,
22:23 for the **o** who seeks my life seeks your life;
23:26 Saul went on **o** side of the mountain,
25:13 And every **o** of them strapped on his sword; D
25:14 But **o** of the young men told Abigail,
25:17 he is so ill-natured that no **o** can speak to him."
25:18 **o** hundred clusters of raisins,
25:22 so much as **o** male of all who belong to him."
25:34 not have been left to Nabal so much as **o** male."
26: 8 to the ground with **o** stroke of the spear;
26:12 No **o** saw it, or knew it, nor did anyone awake;
26:15 For **o** of the people came in to destroy your lord
26:20 like **o** who hunts a partridge in the mountains."
26:22 Let **o** of the young men come over and get it.
27: 1 "I shall now perish **o** day by the hand of Saul; C
27: 5 let a place be given me in **o** of the country towns,
27: 7 of the Philistines was **o** year and four months.
28: 8 and bring up for me the **o** whom I name to you."
29: 5 of whom they sing to **o** another in dances, A
30:17 of the next day. Not **o** of them escaped,
30:24 of the **o** who goes down into the battle shall be
30:24 as the share of the **o** who stays by the baggage;
2Sa 1:15 Then David called **o** of the young men and said,
2: 3 every **o** with his household; D
2:13 **O** group sat on **o** side of the pool,
2:21 and seize **o** of the young men, and take his spoil."
3:13 But **o** thing I require of you:
3:14 of **o** hundred foreskins of the Philistines."
3:29 of Joab never be without **o** who has a discharge,
3:34 as **o** falls before the wicked you have fallen."
3:39 The LORD pay back the **o** who does wickedly
4: 2 the name of the **o** was Baanah,
4:10 when the **o** who told me,
7: 5 Are you the **o** to build me a house to live in?
7:22 for there is no **o** like you,
8: 2 and **o** length for those who were to be spared.
8: 4 from him **o** thousand seven hundred horsemen,
9:11 like **o** of the king's sons.
10: 6 as well as the king of Maacah, **o** thousand men,
11: 2 It happened, late **o** afternoon,
11:25 for the sword devours now **o** and now another;
12: 1 the **o** rich and the other poor.
12: 3 the poor man had nothing but **o** little ewe lamb,
12: 4 and he was loath to take **o** of his own flock or herd
13:13 you, you would be as **o** of the scoundrels in Israel.
13:30 and not **o** of them was left.
14: 6 and they fought with **o** another in the field; A
14: 6 there was no **o** to part them,
14: 6 and **o** struck the other and killed him.
14: 7 Thus they would quench my **o** remaining ember,
14:11 not **o** hair of your son shall fall to the ground."
14:13 not bring his banished **o** home again.
14:19 **o** cannot turn right or left from anything
14:25 in all Israel there was no **o** to be praised so much
14:27 and **o** daughter whose name was Tamar;
15: 3 but there is no **o** deputed by the king to hear you."
16: 1 **o** hundred bunches of raisins, **o** hundred of summer fruits, and **o** skin of wine.
16:18 but the **o** whom the LORD and this people and all
16:23 that Ahithophel gave was as if **o** consulted
17: 3 You seek the life of only **o** man,
17: 9 Even now he has hidden himself in **o** of the pits,
17:22 by daybreak not **o** was left who had not crossed
18: 2 **o** third under the command of Joab, **o** third under
18: 2 and **o** third under the command of Ittai the Gittite.
18:27 of the first **o** is like the running of Ahimaaz son
19:14 the hearts of all the people of Judah as **o**,
20:11 And **o** of Joab's men took his stand by Amasa,
20:19 I am **o** of those who are peaceable and faithful
21:16 Ishbi-benob, **o** of the descendants of the giants,
21:18 who was **o** of the descendants of the giants.
22:42 They looked, but there was no **o** to save them;
23: 1 the favorite of the Strong **O** of Israel:
23: 3 **O** who rules over people justly,
23: 7 to touch them **o** uses an iron bar or the shaft of
23: 8 against eight hundred whom he killed at **o** time.
24:12 choose **o** of them, and I will do it to you."
24:13 to the **o** who sent me."
1Ki 1:48 who today has granted **o** of my offspring to sit
1:52 not **o** of his hairs shall fall to the ground;
2:16 And now I have **o** request to make of you;
2:20 she said, "I have **o** small request to make of you;
3:12 no **o** like you has been before you and no one
3:12 before you and no **o** like you shall arise after you.
3:17 The **o** woman said, "Please, my lord,
3:18 there was no **o** else with us in the house,
3:23 Then the king said, "The **o** says,
3:23 Your son is dead, and my son is the living **o**.' "
3:25 then give half to the **o**, and half to the other."
4: 7 each **o** had to make provision for **o** month in
4:19 And there was **o** official in the land of Judah.
4:22 Solomon's provision for **o** day was thirty cors C
4:23 **o** hundred sheep, besides deer, gazelles, roebucks,
4:27 each **o** in his month; they let nothing be lacking.
5: 6 that there is no **o** among us who knows how
6: 6 the middle **o** was six cubits wide,
6: 8 **o** went up by winding stairs to the middle story,
6:24 Five cubits was the length of **o** wing of the cherub,
1Ki 6:24 it was ten cubits from the tip of **o** wing to the tip
6:26 The height of **o** cherub was ten cubits,
6:27 a wing of **o** was touching the **o** wall,
6:34 the two leaves of the **o** door were folding,
6:36 with three courses of dressed stone to **o** course
7: 2 the Forest of the Lebanon **o** hundred cubits long,
7:12 to **o** layer of cedar beams all around;
7:15 Eighteen cubits was the height of the **o**,
7:16 the height of the **o** capital was five cubits,
7:17 seven for the **o** capital, and seven for
7:31 within the crown whose height was **o** cubit;
7:34 the supports were of **o** piece with the stands.
7:35 its stays and its borders were of **o** piece with it.
7:44 the **o** sea, and the twelve oxen underneath the sea.
8:46 for there is no **o** who does not sin—
8:56 not **o** word has failed of all his good promise,
8:63 and **o** hundred twenty thousand sheep.
9:14 to the king **o** hundred twenty talents of gold.
10:10 Then she gave the king **o** hundred twenty talents
10:14 in **o** year was six hundred sixty-six talents of gold,
10:20 **o** on each end of a step on the six steps.
10:25 Every **o** of them brought a present, D
10:29 and a horse for **o** hundred fifty;
11:13 I will give **o** tribe to your son,
11:32 **O** tribe will remain his, for the sake
11:36 Yet to his son I will give **o** tribe,
12:20 There was no **o** who followed the house of David,
12:21 **o** hundred eighty thousand chosen troops to fight
12:29 He set **o** in Bethel, and the other he put in Dan.
12:30 the **o** at Bethel and before the other as far as Dan.
13:11 **O** of his sons came and told him all that the man
13:27 for me." So they saddled **o**,
14:10 just as **o** burns up dung until it is all gone.
15:29 to the house of Jeroboam not **o** that breathed,
18: 6 Ahab went in **o** direction by himself,
18:23 let them choose **o** bull for themselves,
18:25 "Choose for yourselves **o** bull and prepare it first,
18:40 do not let **o** of them escape."
19: 2 if I do not make your life like the life of **o** of them
20:11 **O** who puts on armor should not brag like **o** who takes it off."
20:29 They encamped opposite **o** another seven days. A
20:29 Israelites killed **o** hundred thousand Aramean
20:29 thousand Aramean foot soldiers in **o** day. C
20:41 king of Israel recognized him as **o** of the prophets.
21:25 (Indeed, there was no **o** like Ahab,
22: 8 "There is still **o** other by whom we may inquire of
22:13 of the prophets with **o** accord are favorable to
22:13 let your word be like the word of **o** of them,
22:17 let each **o** go home in peace.' "
22:20 Then **o** said **o** thing, and another said another,
22:31 "Fight with no **o** small or great,
2Ki 2: 8 the water was parted to the **o** side and to the other,
2:14 the water was parted to the **o** side and to the other,
3: 4 to the king of Israel **o** hundred thousand lambs,
3: 4 and the wool of **o** hundred thousand rams.
3:11 **o** of the servants of the king of Israel answered,
3:23 must have fought together, and killed **o** another. A
4: 8 **O** day Elisha was passing through Shunem, C
4:11 **O** day when he came there, C
4:18 went out **o** day to his father among the reapers. C
4:22 "Send me **o** of the servants and **o** of the donkeys,
4:39 **O** of them went out into the field to gather herbs;
5: 2 on **o** of their raids had taken a young girl captive
5:18 may the LORD pardon your servant on **o** count:
5:18 the LORD pardon your servant on this **o** count."
6: 2 and let us collect logs there, **o** for each of us,
6: 3 **o** of them said, "Please come with your servants."
6: 5 **o** was felling a log, his ax head fell into the water;
6:12 Then **o** of his officers said, "No **o**, my lord king.
7: 3 who said to **o** another, "Why should we sit here A
7: 5 there was no **o** there at all.
7: 6 so that they said to **o** another, A
7: 9 Then they said to **o** another, A
7:10 but there was no **o** to be seen or heard there,
7:13 **O** of his servants said, "Let some men take five of
8:26 he reigned **o** year in Jerusalem.
9: 5 "For which **o** of us?"
9:10 and no **o** shall bury her."
9:15 then let no **o** slip out of the city to go and tell
9:37 so that no **o** can say, This is Jezebel.' "
10:21 so that there was no **o** left who did not come.
10:25 and kill them; let no **o** escape."
12: 9 the altar on the right side as **o** entered the house of
14: 8 "Come, let us look **o** another in the face." A
14:11 he and King Amaziah of Judah faced **o** another A
14:26 no **o** left, bond or free, and no **o** to help Israel.
15:13 he reigned **o** month in Samaria.
15:20 fifty shekels of silver from each **o**,
17:27 the king of Assyria commanded, "Send there **o** of
17:28 So **o** of the priests whom they had carried away
18: 5 that there was no **o** like him among all the kings
18:31 then every **o** of you will eat from your own vine D
19:22 Against the Holy **O** of Israel! B
19:35 down **o** hundred eighty-five thousand in the camp
21:13 I will wipe Jerusalem as **o** wipes a dish,
21:16 until he had filled Jerusalem from **o** end
23:10 so that no **o** would make a son or a daughter pass
23:18 He said, "Let him rest; let no **o** move his bones."
23:33 the land of **o** hundred talents of silver and a talent
24:14 no **o** remained, except the poorest people of
24:16 **o** thousand, all of them strong and fit for war.
25:16 As for the two pillars, the **o** sea, and the stands,
25:17 The height of the **o** pillar was eighteen cubits,
1Ch 1:10 he was the first to be a mighty **o** on the earth. E
1:19 the name of the **o** was Peleg (for in his days
5:21 and **o** hundred thousand captives.

1Ch 8:40 and grandchildren, **o** hundred fifty.
9:13 **o** thousand seven hundred sixty,
9:31 and Mattithiah, **o** of the Levites, the firstborn
11:11 against three hundred whom he killed at **o** time.
12:18 peace to you, and peace to the **o** who helps you!
12:18 For your God is the **o** who helps you."
12:25 mighty warriors, seven thousand **o** hundred.
12:37 **o** hundred twenty thousand armed with all
15: 2 that no **o** but the Levites were to carry the ark
15: 5 with **o** hundred twenty of his kindred;
15: 7 with **o** hundred thirty of his kindred;
15:10 with **o** hundred twelve of his kindred.
16:20 from **o** kingdom to another people,
16:21 he allowed no **o** to oppress them;
17:11 up your offspring after you, **o** of your own sons,
17:20 There is no **o** like you, O LORD,
17:21 **o** nation on the earth whom God went to redeem
18: 4 David took from him **o** thousand chariots,
18: 4 but left **o** hundred of them.
20: 4 who was **o** of the descendants of the giants;
21: 5 there were **o** million **o** hundred thousand men
21:10 choose **o** of them, so that I may do it to you.' "
21:12 to the **o** who sent me."
22:14 house of the LORD **o** hundred thousand talents of gold, **o** million talents of silver,
24: 6 **o** ancestral house being chosen for Eleazar and **o** chosen for Ithamar.
26:30 **o** thousand seven hundred men of ability,
27:18 Elihu, **o** of David's brothers;
29: 7 and **o** hundred thousand talents of iron.
2Ch 1:17 and a horse for **o** hundred fifty;
2:14 the son of **o** of the Danite women,
2:17 to be **o** hundred fifty-three thousand six hundred.
3: 4 and its height was **o** hundred twenty cubits.
3:11 **o** wing of the **o**, five cubits long,
3:12 of this cherub, **o** wing, five cubits long, touched
3:16 and he made **o** hundred pomegranates,
3:17 **o** on the right, the other on the left; the **o** on the right he called Jachin, and the **o** on the left, Boaz.
4: 8 And he made **o** hundred basins of gold.
4:15 the **o** sea, and the twelve oxen underneath it.
5:12 with **o** hundred twenty priests who were trumpeters
6: 5 and I chose no **o** as ruler over my people Israel;
6:36 for there is no **o** who does not sin—
6:42 O LORD God, do not reject your anointed **o.**
7: 5 and **o** hundred twenty thousand sheep.
9: 9 Then she gave the king **o** hundred twenty talents
9:13 in **o** year was six hundred sixty-six talents of gold,
9:19 **o** on each end of a step on the six steps.
9:24 Every **o** of them brought a present, D
11: 1 he assembled **o** hundred eighty thousand chosen
14:13 and the Ethiopians fell until no **o** remained alive;
17:18 with **o** hundred eighty thousand armed for war.
18: 7 "There is still **o** other by whom we may inquire of
18:12 of the prophets with **o** accord are favorable to
18:12 let your word be like the word of **o** of them,
18:16 let each **o** go home in peace.' "
18:19 Then **o** said **o** thing, and another said another,
18:30 "Fight with no **o** small or great,
20: 6 so that no **o** is able to withstand you.
20:23 they all helped to destroy **o** another. A
20:24 on the ground; no **o** had escaped.
22: 2 he reigned **o** year in Jerusalem.
22: 9 And the house of Ahaziah had no **o** able to rule
23: 4 This is what you are to do: **o** third of you,
23: 5 **o** third shall be at the king's house, and **o** third at the Gate of the Foundation;
23:19 of the LORD so that no **o** should enter who was
24:15 he was **o** hundred thirty years old at his death.
25: 6 He also hired **o** hundred thousand mighty warriors
25: 6 from Israel for **o** hundred talents of silver.
25:17 "Come, let us look **o** another in the face." A
25:21 he and King Amaziah of Judah faced **o** another A
26:11 **o** of the king's commanders.
27: 5 that year **o** hundred talents of silver,
28: 6 of Remaliah killed **o** hundred twenty thousand
28: 6 in Judah in **o** day, all of them valiant warriors, C
29:32 **o** hundred rams, and two hundred lambs;
30:12 on Judah to give them **o** heart to do what the king
32: 7 for there is **o** greater with us than with him.
32:12 saying, 'Before **o** altar you shall worship,
36: 3 a tribute of **o** hundred talents of silver and **o** talent
Ezr 1: 9 silver basins, **o** thousand;
1:10 other vessels, **o** thousand;
2: 3 two thousand **o** hundred seventy-two.
2: 7 Of Elam, **o** thousand two hundred fifty-four.
2:12 Of Azgad, **o** thousand two hundred twenty-two.
2:18 Of Jorah, **o** hundred twelve.
2:21 Of Bethlehem, **o** hundred twenty-three.
2:23 Of Anathoth, **o** hundred twenty-eight.
2:27 The people of Michmas, **o** hundred twenty-two.
2:30 Of Magbish, **o** hundred fifty-six.
2:31 **o** thousand two hundred fifty-four.
2:37 Of Immer, **o** thousand fifty-two.
2:38 Of Pashhur, **o** thousand two hundred forty-seven.
2:39 Of Harim, **o** thousand seventeen.
2:41 the descendants of Asaph, **o** hundred twenty-eight.
2:42 and of Shobai, in all **o** hundred thirty-nine.
2:61 and Barzillai (who had married **o** of the daughters
2:69 and **o** hundred priestly robes.
6: 4 with three courses of hewn stones and **o** course
6:17 of this house of God **o** hundred bulls,
7:22 up to **o** hundred talents of silver, **o** hundred cors of wheat, **o** hundred baths of wine, **o** hundred baths
8: 3 with whom were registered **o** hundred fifty males.
8:10 and with him **o** hundred sixty males.
8:12 and with him **o** hundred ten males.

Ezr 8:26 and **o** hundred silver vessels worth . . . talents, and **o** hundred talents of gold,
9:15 though no **o** can face you because of this."
10:13 Nor is this a task for **o** day or for two, C
Ne 1: 2 **o** of my brothers, Hanani, came with certain men
2:12 I told no **o** what my God had put into my heart
2:20 God of heaven is the **o** who will give us success,
3: 8 **o** of the goldsmiths, made repairs.
3: 8 Next to him Hananiah, **o** of the perfumers,
3:28 each **o** opposite his own house.
3:31 After him Malchijah, **o** of the goldsmiths,
4:17 a way that each labored on the work with **o** hand
4:19 we are separated far from **o** another on the wall. A
5:17 there were at my table **o** hundred fifty people,
5:18 that which was prepared for **o** day was one ox C
5:18 that which was prepared for one day was **o** ox
6: 2 and let us meet together in **o** of the villages in
6:10 **O** day when I went into the house of Shemaiah C
7: 8 two thousand **o** hundred seventy-two.
7:12 Of Elam, **o** thousand two hundred fifty-four.
7:24 Of Hariph, **o** hundred twelve.
7:26 and Netophah, **o** hundred eighty-eight.
7:27 Of Anathoth, **o** hundred twenty-eight.
7:31 Of Michmas, **o** hundred twenty-two.
7:32 Of Bethel and Ai, **o** hundred twenty-three.
7:34 **o** thousand two hundred fifty-four.
7:40 Of Immer, **o** thousand fifty-two.
7:41 Of Pashhur, **o** thousand two hundred forty-seven.
7:42 Of Harim, **o** thousand seventeen.
7:44 the descendants of Asaph, **o** hundred forty-eight.
7:45 of Hatita, of Shobai, **o** hundred thirty-eight.
7:63 of Barzillai (who had married **o** of the daughters
7:70 to the treasury **o** thousand darics of gold,
11: 1 the rest of the people cast lots to bring **o** out of ten
11:14 valiant warriors, **o** hundred twenty-eight;
11:19 were **o** hundred seventy-two.
12:31 **O** went to the right on the wall to the Dung Gate;
13:28 And **o** of the sons of Jehoiada,
Est 1: 1 over **o** hundred twenty-seven provinces from India
1: 4 **o** hundred eighty days in all.
1: 8 the officials of his palace to do as each **o** desired.
3:13 in **o** day, the thirteenth day of the twelfth month, C
4: 2 for no **o** might enter the king's gate clothed
4: 5 Esther called for Hathach, **o** of the king's eunuchs,
4:11 there is but **o** law—all alike are to be put to death.
5:12 "Even Queen Esther let no **o** but myself come
6: 9 Let the robes and the horse be handed over to **o** of
7: 9 **o** of the eunuchs in attendance on the king, said,
8: 9 **o** hundred twenty-seven provinces,
9: 2 and no **o** could withstand them,
9:19 on which they send gifts of food to **o** another. A
9:22 sending gifts of food to **o** another and presents A
9:30 to the **o** hundred twenty-seven provinces of
Job 1: 1 **o** who feared God and turned away from evil.
1: 4 to go and hold feasts in **o** another's houses in turn;
1: 6 **O** day the heavenly beings came C
1: 8 There is no **o** like him on the earth,
1:13 **O** day when his sons and daughters were eating C
2: 1 **O** day the heavenly beings came C
2: 3 There is no **o** like him on the earth,
2:13 and no **o** spoke a word to him,
3:20 "Why is light given to **o** in misery,
3:23 Why is light given to **o** who cannot see the way,
4: 2 "If **o** ventures a word with you,
5: 4 and there is no **o** to deliver them.
5:17 "How happy is the **o** whom God reproves;
6:10 for I have not denied the words of the Holy **O.** B
8:15 If **o** leans against its house, it will not stand;
8:15 if **o** lays hold of it, it will not endure.
9: 3 If **o** wished to contend with him,
9: 3 **o** could not answer him once in a thousand.
9:19 If it is a contest of strength, he is the strong **o!**
9:22 It is all **o;** therefore I say,
10: 7 and there is no **o** to deliver out of your hand?
11: 2 and should **o** full of talk be vindicated?
11: 3 and when you mock, shall no **o** shame you?
11:19 You will lie down, and no **o** will make you afraid;
12:14 If he tears down, no **o** can rebuild;
12:14 if he shuts someone in, no **o** can open up.
13: 9 as **o** person deceives another?
13:28 **O** wastes away like a rotten thing,
14: 3 Do you fix your eyes on such a **o?**
14: 4 bring a clean thing out of an unclean? No **o** can.
15:16 how much less **o** who is abominable and corrupt,
15:16 **o** who drinks iniquity like water!
15:28 in houses that no **o** should inhabit,
16:21 as **o** does for a neighbor.
17: 6 and I am **o** before whom people spit.
20:26 a fire fanned by no **o** will devour them;
21:23 **O** dies in full prosperity, being wholly at ease
25: 4 How can **o** born of woman be pure?
26: 2 "How you have helped **o** who has no power!
26: 3 How you have counseled **o** who has no wisdom,
29:25 like **o** who comforts mourners.
30:13 they promote my calamity; no **o** restrains them.
30:24 "Surely **o** does not turn against the needy,
31:15 And did not **o** fashion us in the womb?
31:35 that I had **o** to hear me!
32:12 but there was in fact no **o** that confuted Job,
32:12 no **o** among you that answered his words.
33:14 For God speaks in **o** way, and in two,
33:23 Then, if there should be for **o** of them an angel,
33:23 a mediator, **o** of a thousand,
33:23 **o** who declares a person upright,
34: 9 'It profits **o** nothing to take delight in God.'
34:17 Shall **o** who hates justice govern?
34:17 Will you condemn **o** who is righteous and mighty,

Job 35:10 But no **o** says, 'Where is God my Maker,
36: 4 **o** who is perfect in knowledge is with you.
37:16 of the **o** whose knowledge is perfect,
37:21 no **o** can look on the light when it is bright in
38:26 to bring rain on a land where no **o** lives,
40:24 Can **o** take it with hooks or pierce its nose with
41:10 No **o** is so fierce as to dare to stir it up.
41:16 **O** is so near to another that no air can come
41:17 They are joined **o** to another;
41:32 **o** would think the deep to be white-haired.
42:16 After this Job lived **o** hundred and forty years,
Ps 3: 3 my glory, and the **o** who lifts up my head.
7: 2 they will drag me away, with no **o** to rescue.
7:12 If **o** does not repent, God will whet his sword;
9:13 the **o** who lifts me up from the gates of death,
14: 1 there is no **o** who does good.
14: 3 there is no **o** who does good, no, not **o.**
16:10 or let your faithful **o** see the Pit.
18:41 but there was no **o** to save them;
22: 8 let him rescue the **o** in whom he delights!"
22:11 for trouble is near and there is no **o** to help.
27: 4 **O** thing I asked of the LORD,
31:12 I have passed out of mind like **o** who is dead;
31:23 but abundantly repays the **o** who acts haughtily.
34:20 not **o** of them will be broken.
35:14 I went about as **o** who laments for a mother,
38:14 Truly, I am like **o** who does not hear,
45: 3 Gird your sword on your thigh, O mighty **o,** E
49: 7 there is no price **o** can give to God for it.
49: 9 **o** should live on forever and never see the grave.
50: 1 The mighty **o,** God the LORD, speaks E
50:18 You make friends with a thief when you see **o,**
50:21 you thought that I was **o** just like yourself.
50:22 and there will be no **o** to deliver.
52: 1 O mighty **o,** of mischief done against the godly? E
52: 7 "See the **o** who would not take refuge in God,
53: 1 there is no **o** who does good.
53: 3 there is no **o** who does good, no, not **o.**
69:25 let no **o** live in their tents.
71:11 for there is no **o** to deliver."
71:22 will sing praises to you with the lyre, O Holy **O** B
73:20 They are like a dream when **o** awakes;
74: 9 and there is no **o** among us who knows how long.
75: 7 putting down **o** and lifting up another.
76:11 around him bring gifts to the **o** who is awesome,
78:41 and provoked the Holy **O** of Israel. B
79: 3 and there was no **o** to bury them.
80:17 But let your hand be upon the **o** at your right hand,
80:17 the **o** whom you made strong for yourself.
83: 5 They conspire with **o** accord;
87: 4 "This **o** was born there," they say.
87: 5 "This **o** and that **o** were born in it";
87: 6 the peoples, "This **o** was born there."
89: 3 "I have made a covenant with my chosen **o,**
89:18 our king to the Holy **O** of Israel. B
89:19 you spoke in a vision to your faithful **o,** and said:
89:19 "I have set the crown on **o** who is mighty,
89:19 I have exalted **o** chosen from the people.
101: 5 **O** who secretly slanders a neighbor I will destroy.
101: 7 No **o** who practices deceit shall remain
101: 7 no **o** who utters lies shall continue in my presence.
102: T *A prayer of **o** afflicted, when faint and pleading*
105:13 from **o** kingdom to another people,
105:14 he allowed no **o** to oppress them;
105:37 there was no **o** among their tribes who stumbled.
106:11 not **o** of them was left.
106:16 and of Aaron, the holy **o** of the LORD. B
106:23 had not Moses, his chosen **o,**
107:12 they fell down, with no **o** to help.
109:12 May there be no **o** to do him a kindness,
118:26 the **o** who comes in the name of the LORD.
119:160 of your word is truth; and every **o** D
119:162 I rejoice at your word like **o** who finds great spoil.
132: 2 the LORD and vowed to the Mighty **O** of Jacob, E
132: 5 a dwelling place for the Mighty **O** of Jacob." E
132:10 not turn away the face of your anointed **o.**
132:11 "**O** of the sons of your body I will set
132:17 I have prepared a lamp for my anointed **o.**
137: 3 saying, "Sing us **o** of the songs of Zion!"
141: 7 a rock that **o** breaks apart and shatters on the land,
142: 4 no **o** who takes notice of me; no **o** cares for me.
143: 2 for no **o** living is righteous before you.
144:10 the **o** who gives victory to kings,
145: 4 **O** generation shall laud your works to another,
Pr 1:14 we will all have **o** purse"—
1:24 have stretched out my hand and no **o** heeded,
3:12 for the LORD reproves the **o** he loves,
6:15 on such a **o** calamity will descend suddenly;
6:19 and **o** who sows discord in a family.
6:28 Or can **o** walk on hot coals without scorching
6:29 no **o** who touches her will go unpunished.
8: 9 They are all straight to **o** who understands
8:34 Happy is the **o** who listens to me,
9:10 and the knowledge of the Holy **O** is insight. B
10:10 but the **o** who rebukes boldly makes peace.
10:13 of **o** who has understanding wisdom is found,
10:13 but a rod is for the back of **o** who lacks sense.
10:17 but **o** who rejects a rebuke goes astray.
11:13 **o** who is trustworthy in spirit keeps a confidence.
11:25 and **o** who gives water will get water.
11:27 but evil comes to the **o** who searches for it.
12: 3 No **o** finds security by wickedness,
12: 8 **O** is commended for good sense,
12:14 the fruit of the mouth **o** is filled with good things,
12:23 **O** who is clever conceals knowledge,
13: 6 Righteousness guards **o** whose way is upright,
13:14 so that **o** may avoid the snares of death.

Pr 13:18 and disgrace are for the **o** who ignores instruction,
13:18 but **o** who heeds reproof is honored.
14: 2 but **o** who is devious in conduct despises him.
14: 6 but knowledge is easy for **o** who understands.
14:17 **O** who is quick-tempered acts foolishly,
14:25 but **o** who utters lies is a betrayer.
14:26 In the fear of the LORD **o** has strong confidence,
14:27 so that **o** may avoid the snares of death.
14:29 but **o** who has a hasty temper exalts folly.
14:33 at home in the mind of **o** who has understanding,
14:35 but his wrath falls on **o** who acts shamefully.
15: 5 but the **o** who heeds admonition is prudent.
15: 9 but he loves the **o** who pursues righteousness.
15:10 There is severe discipline for **o** who forsakes
15:10 but **o** who hates a rebuke will die.
15:14 of **o** who has understanding seeks knowledge,
15:21 Folly is a joy to **o** who has no sense,
16: 6 and by the fear of the LORD **o** avoids evil.
16:22 Wisdom is a fountain of life to **o** who has it,
16:30 **O** who winks the eyes plans perverse things;
16:30 **o** who compresses the lips brings evil to pass.
16:32 **O** who is slow to anger is better than the mighty,
16:32 **o** whose temper is controlled than **o** who captures
17: 2 and will share the inheritance as **o** of the family.
17: 9 **O** who forgives an affront fosters friendship,
17: 9 **o** who dwells on disputes will alienate a friend.
17:13 not depart from the house of **o** who returns evil
17:15 **O** who justifies the wicked and **o** who condemns
17:19 **O** who loves transgression loves strife;
17:19 **o** who builds a high threshold invites broken bones.
17:21 The **o** who begets a fool gets trouble;
17:27 **O** who spares words is knowledgeable;
17:27 **o** who is cool in spirit has understanding.
18: 1 The **o** who lives alone is self-indulgent,
18: 9 **O** who is slack in work is close kin to a vandal.
18:13 If **o** gives answer before hearing,
18:17 The **o** who first states a case seems right,
19: 1 the poor walking in integrity than **o** perverse
19: 2 and **o** who moves too hurriedly misses the way.
19:23 filled with it **o** rests secure and suffers no harm.
20: 6 but who can find **o** worthy of trust?
20:16 Take the garment of **o** who has given surety for
20:25 It is a snare for **o** to say rashly, "It is holy,"
21:12 Righteous **O** observes the house of the wicked; J
21:22 **O** wise person went up against a city of warriors
22:26 Do not be **o** of those who give pledges,
23:34 You will be like **o** who lies down in the midst of
23:34 like **o** who lies on the top of a mast.
24:26 **O** who gives an honest answer gives a kiss on
24:30 I passed by the field of **o** who was lazy,
25:14 Like clouds and wind without rain is **o** who boasts
25:18 a sharp arrow is **o** who bears false witness against
25:20 on a wound is **o** who sings songs to a heavy heart.
25:28 without walls, is **o** who lacks self-control.
26:10 an archer who wounds everybody is **o** who hires
26:17 a passing dog by the ears is **o** who meddles in
26:19 so is **o** who deceives a neighbor and says,
26:27 stone will come back on the **o** who starts it rolling.
27: 8 Like a bird that strays from its nest is **o** who strays
27:13 Take the garment of **o** who has given surety for
27:17 and **o** person sharpens the wits of another.
27:19 so **o** human heart reflects another.
28: 1 The wicked flee when no **o** pursues,
28: 8 **O** who augments wealth by exorbitant
28: 9 When **o** will not listen to the law,
28:13 No **o** who conceals transgressions will prosper, but
o who confesses and forsakes them will obtain
28:14 Happy is the **o** who is never without fear,
28:14 but **o** who is hard-hearted will fall into calamity.
28:16 but **o** who hates unjust gain will enjoy a long life.
28:17 a fugitive until death; let no **o** offer assistance.
28:18 **O** who walks in integrity will be safe,
28:19 **o** who follows worthless pursuits will have plenty
28:20 but **o** who is in a hurry to be rich will not go
28:23 will afterward find more favor than **o** who flatters
28:27 but **o** who turns a blind eye will get many a curse.
29: 1 **O** who is often reproved, yet remains stubborn,
29: 4 but **o** who makes heavy exactions ruins it.
29:22 **O** given to anger stirs up strife,
29:23 but **o** who is lowly in spirit will obtain honor.
29:24 **o** hears the victim's curse, but discloses nothing.
29:25 but **o** who trusts in the LORD is secure.
29:26 but it is from the LORD that **o** gets justice.
31: 6 Give strong drink to **o** who is perishing,
Ecc 1: 8 All things are wearisome; more than **o** can express;
2:12 for what can the **o** do who comes after the king?
2:21 because sometimes **o** who has toiled with wisdom
2:26 For to the **o** who pleases him God gives wisdom
2:26 only to give to **o** who pleases God.
3:19 as **o** dies, so dies the other.
3:20 All go to **o** place; all are from the
4: 1 with no **o** to comfort them!
4: 1 with no **o** to comfort them.
4: 3 but better than both is the **o** who has not yet been,
4: 4 and all skill in work come from **o** person's envy
4: 9 Two are better than **o**, because they have
4:10 For if they fall, **o** will lift up the other;
4:10 but woe to **o** who is alone and falls and does
4:11 but how can **o** keep warm alone?
4:12 And though **o** might prevail against another,
4:12 against another, two will withstand **o**.
4:14 **O** can indeed come out of prison to reign,
5:18 with which **o** toils under the sun the few days of
6: 6 do not all go to **o** place?
6:11 the more vanity, so how is **o** the better?
7:12 that wisdom gives life to the **o** who possesses it.
7:14 God has made the **o** as well as the other,
Ecc 7:18 It is good that you should take hold of the **o**,
7:18 for the **o** who fears God shall succeed with both.
7:20 Surely there is no **o** on earth so righteous as
7:26 **o** who pleases God escapes her,
7:27 adding **o** thing to another to find the sum,
7:28 **O** man among a thousand I found,
8: 8 No **o** has power over the wind to restrain the wind,
8: 9 while **o** person exercises authority over another to
8:17 no **o** can find out what is happening under the sun.
9: 1 whether it is love or hate **o** does not know.
9:12 For no **o** can anticipate the time of disaster.
9:15 Yet no **o** remembered that poor man.
9:18 but **o** bungler destroys much good.
10:10 If the iron is blunt, and **o** does not whet the edge,
10:10 but wisdom helps **o** to succeed.
10:14 No **o** knows what is to happen,
12: 4 and **o** rises up at the sound of a bird,
12: 5 **o** is afraid of heights, and terrors are in the road;
12:11 the collected sayings that are given by **o** shepherd.
SS 1: 7 for why should I be like **o** who is veiled beside
2:10 "Arise, my love, my fair **o**, and come away;
2:13 Arise, my love, my fair **o**, and come away.
4: 2 and not **o** among them is bereaved.
4: 9 with **o** jewel of your necklace.
5: 2 my sister, my love, my dove, my perfect **o**;
6: 6 and not **o** among them is bereaved.
6: 9 My dove, my perfect **o**, is the only **o**,
7: 6 How fair and pleasant you are, O loved **o**,
8: 1 I would kiss you, and no **o** would despise me.
8: 2 and into the chamber of the **o** who bore me.
8: 7 If **o** offered for love all the wealth of his house,
8:10 then I was in his eyes as **o** who brings peace.
8:11 each **o** was to bring for its fruit a thousand pieces
Isa 1: 4 who have despised the Holy **O** of Israel, B
1:24 the LORD of hosts, the Mighty **O** of Israel: E
1:31 with no **o** to quench them.
4: 1 Seven women shall take hold of **o** man in that day,
5: 8 until there is room for no **o** but you,
5:10 For ten acres of vineyard shall yield but **o** bath,
5:19 of the Holy **O** of Israel hasten to fulfillment, B
5:24 have despised the word of the Holy **O** of Israel. B
5:29 they carry it off, and no **o** can rescue.
5:30 And if **o** look to the land—
6: 3 And **o** called to another and said:
6: 6 Then **o** of the seraphs flew to me,
7:21 On that day **o** will keep alive a young cow
7:24 With bow and arrows **o** will go there,
8:14 a sanctuary, a stone **o** strikes against;
8:14 of Israel he will become a rock **o** stumbles over—
9:14 palm branch and reed in **o** day— C
9:19 for the fire; no **o** spared another.
10:14 and as **o** gathers eggs that have been forsaken,
10:15 Shall the ax vaunt itself over the **o** who wields it,
10:15 saw magnify itself against the **o** who handles it?
10:15 As if a rod should raise the **o** who lifts it up,
10:15 or as if a staff should lift the **o** who is not wood!
10:17 and his Holy **O** a flame; B
10:17 and devour his thorns and briers in **o** day. C
10:20 on the **o** who struck them,
10:20 but will lean on the LORD, the Holy **O** of Israel, B
12: 6 for great in your midst is the Holy **O** of Israel. B
13: 8 They will look aghast at **o** another; A
13:14 or like sheep with no **o** to gather them,
14: 8 no **o** comes to cut us down."
14:32 What will **o** answer the messengers of the nation?
17: 2 and no **o** will make them afraid.
17: 5 as when **o** gleans the ears of grain in the Valley
17: 7 and their eyes will look to the Holy **O** of Israel; B
19: 2 **o** against the other, neighbor against neighbor,
19:11 How can you say to Pharaoh, "I am **o** of the sages,
19:18 **O** of these will be called the City of the Sun.
21:10 O my threshed and winnowed **o**,
21:11 **O** is calling to me from Seir, "Sentinel,
22:22 he shall open, and no **o** shall shut;
22:22 he shall shut, and no **o** shall open.
23:15 for seventy years, the lifetime of **o** king.
24:10 every house is shut up so that no **o** can enter.
24:16 of glory to the Righteous **O**. J
26: 7 The way of the righteous is level; O Just **O**,
26:18 and no **o** is born to inhabit the world.
27: 3 I guard it night and day so that no **o** can harm it;
27:12 and you will be gathered **o** by **o**,
28: 2 See, the Lord has **o** who is mighty and strong;
28: 6 a spirit of justice to the **o** who sits in judgment,
28:16 "**O** who trusts will not panic."
28:28 but **o** does not thresh it forever;
28:28 **o** drives the cart wheel and horses over it,
29:16 or the thing formed say of the **o** who formed it,
29:19 people shall exult in the Holy **O** of Israel. B
29:21 without grounds deny justice to the **o** in the right.
29:23 they will sanctify the Holy **O** of Jacob, B
30:11 let us hear no more about the Holy **O** of Israel." B
30:12 Therefore thus says the Holy **O** of Israel: B
30:15 thus said the Lord GOD, the Holy **O** of Israel: B
30:17 A thousand shall flee at the threat of **o**,
30:29 as when **o** sets out to the sound of the flute to go
31: 1 but do not look to the Holy **O** of Israel or consult B
31: 3 the helper will stumble, and the **o** helped will fall,
33: 1 you treacherous **o**, with whom no **o** has dealt
treacherously!
33:18 "Where is the **o** who counted?
33:18 Where is the **o** who weighed the tribute?
33:18 Where is the **o** who counted the towers?"
34:10 no **o** shall pass through it forever and ever.
34:15 the buzzards shall gather, each **o** with its mate.
34:16 Not **o** of these shall be missing;
37:23 Against the Holy **O** of Israel! B
Isa 37:36 down **o** hundred eighty-five thousand in the camp
40:20 a gift **o** chooses mulberry wood—wood that will
40:25 or who is my equal? says the Holy **O**. B
40:26 mighty in power, not **o** is missing.
41: 6 Each **o** helps the other, saying to one another,
41: 6 Each one helps the other, saying to **o** another, A
41: 7 the **o** who smooths with the hammer encourages
the **o** who strikes
41:14 your Redeemer is the Holy **O** of Israel. B
41:16 in the Holy **O** of Israel you shall glory. B
41:20 the Holy **O** of Israel has created it. B
41:25 I stirred up **o** from the north, and he has come,
41:26 There was no **o** who declared it,
41:28 But when I look there is no **o**;
42:19 Who is blind like my dedicated **o**,
42:22 they have become a prey with no **o** to rescue,
42:22 a spoil with no **o** to say, "Restore!"
43: 3 I am the LORD your God, the Holy **O** of Israel, B
43:13 there is no **o** who can deliver from my hand;
43:14 your Redeemer, the Holy **O** of Israel: B
43:15 I am the LORD, your Holy **O**, B
44: 5 This **o** will say, "I am the LORD's,"
44: 8 There is no other rock; I know not **o**.
44:19 No **o** considers, nor is there knowledge
45: 6 that there is no **o** besides me;
45: 9 Does the clay say to the **o** who fashions it,
45:11 Thus says the LORD, the Holy **O** of Israel, B
45:21 there is no **o** besides me.
46: 7 If **o** cries out to it,
46: 9 I am God, and there is no **o** like me,
47: 3 I will take vengeance, and I will spare no **o**.
47: 4 is the Holy **O** of Israel. B
47: 8 "I am, and there is no **o** besides me;
47: 9 upon you in a moment, in **o** day: C
47:10 you said, "No **o** sees me."
47:10 "I am, and there is no **o** besides me."
47:15 there is no **o** to save you.
48:17 your Redeemer, the Holy **O** of Israel: B
49: 7 the Redeemer of Israel and his Holy **O**, B
49: 7 to **o** deeply despised, abhorred by the nations,
49: 7 the Holy **O** of Israel, who has chosen you." B
49:26 and your Redeemer, the Mighty **O** of Jacob. E
50: 2 Why was no **o** there when I came?
50: 2 Why did no **o** answer when I called?
51: 2 for he was but **o** when I called him,
51:18 There is no **o** to guide her among all
51:18 there is no **o** to take her by the hand among all
53: 3 as **o** from whom others hide their faces he was
53:11 The righteous **o**, my servant, J
54: 1 Sing, O barren **o** who did not bear;
54: 5 the Holy **O** of Israel is your Redeemer, B
54:11 O afflicted **o**, storm-tossed, and not comforted,
55: 5 the Holy **O** of Israel, for he has glorified you. B
56: 2 the **o** who holds it fast, who keeps the sabbath,
56:11 to their own gain, **o** and all.
57: 1 The righteous perish, and no **o** takes it to heart;
57: 1 devout are taken away, while no **o** understands.
57:15 the high and lofty **o** who inhabits eternity,
59: 4 No **o** brings suit justly, no **o** goes to law honestly;
59: 8 no **o** who walks in them knows peace.
59:16 He saw that there was no **o**,
59:16 and was appalled that there was no **o** to intervene;
60: 9 and for the Holy **O** of Israel, B
60:14 the Zion of the Holy **O** of Israel. B
60:15 with no **o** passing through,
60:16 and your Redeemer, the Mighty **O** of Jacob. E
60:22 and the smallest **o** a mighty nation;
63: 3 and from the peoples no **o** was with me;
63: 5 I stared, but there was no **o** to sustain me;
63:11 Where is the **o** who brought them up out of the sea
63:11 is the **o** who put within them his holy spirit,
64: 4 From ages past no **o** has heard,
64: 6 We have all become like **o** who is unclean,
64: 7 There is no **o** who calls on your name,
65:20 for **o** who dies at a hundred years will
65:20 and **o** who falls short of a hundred will
66: 2 But this is the **o** to whom I will look,
66: 3 Whoever slaughters an ox is like **o** who kills
66: 3 like **o** who breaks a dog's neck;
66: 3 like **o** who offers swine's blood,
66: 3 like **o** who blesses an idol.
66: 4 because, when I called, no **o** answered,
66: 8 Shall a land be born in **o** day? C
66: 8 Shall a nation be delivered in **o** moment?
66: 9 shall I, the **o** who delivers, shut the womb?
66:17 following the **o** in the center,
Jer 2: 6 in a land that no **o** passes through,
2: 6 that no one passes through, where no **o** lives?"
3: 6 Have you seen what she did, that faithless **o**,
3: 8 of that faithless **o**, Israel, I had sent her away with
3:14 **o** from a city and two from a family,
3:16 nor shall another **o** be made.
4: 4 and burn with no **o** to quench it,
4:25 I looked, and lo, there was no **o** at all,
4:29 all the towns are forsaken, and no **o** lives in them.
4:30 O desolate **o**, what do you mean that you dress
4:31 anguish as of **o** bringing forth her first child,
5: 1 and see if you can find **o** person who acts justly
7: 5 if you truly act justly **o** with another,
7:33 and no **o** will frighten them away.
8: 6 no **o** repents of wickedness, saying,
9: 5 and no **o** speaks the truth;
9:10 they are laid waste so that no **o** passes through,
9:12 so that no **o** passes through?
9:22 and no **o** shall gather them."
10: 7 the nations and in all their kingdoms there is no **o**
10:16 for he is the **o** who formed all things,

Jer 10:20 there is no o to spread my tent again,
12:11 but no o lays it to heart.
12:12 for the sword of the LORD devours from o end of the land to the other; no o shall be safe.
13:14 And I will dash them o against another,
13:19 of the Negeb are shut up with no o to open them;
14:16 There shall be no o to bury them—
16: 6 and no o shall lament for them;
16: 7 No o shall break bread for the mourner,
16:12 every o of you, following your stubborn evil D
18: 7 At o moment I may declare concerning a nation or
19:11 as o breaks a potter's vessel,
21:12 and burn, with no o to quench it,
22: 8 and all of them will say o to another,
22:28 a despised broken pot, a vessel no o wants?
23: 9 I have become like a drunkard, like o overcome
23:14 so that no o turns from wickedness;
23:27 by their dreams that they tell o another, A
23:28 the o who has my word speak my word faithfully.
23:30 who steal my words from o another. A
23:35 Thus shall you say to o another, A
24: 2 O basket had very good figs, like first-ripe figs,
25:26 far and near, o after another,
25:33 by the LORD on that day shall extend from o end
29:23 I am the o who knows and bears witness,
30:10 and no o shall make him afraid.
30:13 There is no o to uphold your cause,
30:17 "It is Zion; no o cares for her!"
30:21 Their prince shall be o of their own,
31:34 No longer shall they teach o another, A
32:39 I will give them o heart and o way,
33:13 under the hands of the o who counts them,
34: 9 so that no o should hold another Judean in slavery.
34:15 by proclaiming liberty to o another, and you A
35: 2 and bring them to the house of the LORD, into o
35: 7 nor shall you plant a vineyard, or even own o;
36:16 they turned to o another in alarm, A
36:19 and let no o know where you are."
36:30 He shall have no o to sit upon the throne of David,
40:15 and no o else will know.
41: 1 o of the chief officers of the king,
44:27 by the sword and by famine, until not o is left.
46:16 and o said to another, "Come,
46:18 o is coming like Tabor among the mountains,
46:27 and no o shall make him afraid.
48:10 Accursed is the o who is slack in doing the work
48:10 the o who keeps back the sword from bloodshed.
48:33 no o treads them with shouts of joy;
48:38 I have broken Moab like a vessel that no o wants,
49: 5 each headlong, with no o to gather the fugitives.
49:12 shall you be the o to go unpunished?
49:18 no o shall live there, nor shall anyone settle in it.
49:33 no o shall live there, nor shall anyone settle in it.
50: 3 and no o shall live in it;
50:29 Encamp all around her; let no o escape.
50:29 the LORD, the Holy O of Israel. B
50:31 I am against you, O arrogant o,
50:32 The arrogant o shall stumble and fall,
50:32 with no o to raise him up,
50:40 says the LORD, so no o shall live there,
51: 5 their land is full of guilt before the Holy O B
51:19 for he is the o who formed all things,
51:31 O runner runs to meet another,
51:31 and o messenger to meet another,
51:43 a land in which no o lives,
51:46 o year o rumor comes, the next year another,
52:20 As for the two pillars, the o sea,
52:21 the height of the o pillar was eighteen cubits,
52:22 the height of the o capital was five cubits;
52:23 the latticework numbered o hundred.
La 1: 2 among all her lovers she has no o to comfort her;
1: 4 for no o comes to the festivals;
1: 7 and there was no o to help her,
1:16 comforter is far from me, o to revive my courage;
1:17 but there is no o to comfort her;
1:21 with no o to comfort me.
2:22 the anger of the LORD no o escaped or survived;
3: 1 I am o who has seen affliction under the rod
3:26 that o should wait quietly for the salvation of
3:27 It is good for o to bear the yoke in youth,
4: 4 but no o gives them anything.
4:14 that no o was able to touch their garments.
4:20 the o of whom we said,
5: 8 there is no o to deliver us from their hand.
Eze 1: 9 their wings touched o another; A
1:15 o for each of the four of them.
1:23 wings were stretched out straight, o toward
3:13 the living creatures brushing against o another, A
4: 6 forty days I assign you, o day for each year. C
4: 8 from o side to the other until you have completed
4: 9 put them into o vessel, and make bread
4:17 they will look at o another in dismay, A
5: 2 O third of the hair you shall burn in the fire inside
5: 2 o third you shall take and strike with the sword all
5: 2 and o third you shall scatter to the wind,
5:12 O third of you shall die of pestilence or
5:12 o third shall fall by the sword around you;
5:12 and o third I will scatter to every wind
7:14 but no o goes to battle,
9: 6 but touch no o who has the mark.
10: 9 four wheels beside the cherubim, o beside each
10:14 Each o had four faces: the first face was
10:22 Each o moved straight ahead.
11:19 I will give them o heart, and put a new spirit
14:15 no o may pass through because of the animals;
15: 3 Does o take a peg from it on which
16:34 no o solicited you to play the whore;

Eze 17:13 He took o of the royal offspring and made
17:15 Can o escape who does such things?
17:22 a tender o from the topmost of its young twigs;
18: 9 acting faithfully—such a o is righteous;
19: 3 She raised up o of her cubs;
20: 7 every o of you, and do not defile yourselves D
20: 8 not o of them cast away
22: 5 you infamous o, full of tumult.
22:11 O commits abomination with his neighbor's wife;
22:20 As o gathers silver, bronze, iron, lead,
22:30 not destroy it; but I found no o.
23: 2 there were two women, the daughters of o mother;
23:44 they have gone in to her, as o goes in to a whore.
24: 5 Take the choicest o of the flock,
24:16 with o blow I am about to take away from you
24:23 in your iniquities and groan to o another. A
24:26 o who has escaped will come to you to report
24:27 be opened to the o who has escaped,
30:22 both the strong arm and the o that was broken;
30:24 with the groans of o mortally wounded.
32:10 each o of them, on the day of your downfall.
33: 2 of the land take o of their number as their sentinel;
33:24 "Abraham was only o man,
33:28 be so desolate that no o will pass through.
33:30 and at the doors of the houses, say to o another, A
33:32 o who has a beautiful voice and plays well on
34: 6 with no o to search or seek for them.
34:23 I will set up over them o shepherd,
34:28 and no o shall make them afraid.
37:17 and join them together into o stick,
37:17 so that they may become o in your hand.
37:19 the stick of Judah upon it, and make them o stick,
37:19 in order that they may be o in my hand.
37:22 I will make them o nation in the land,
37:22 and o king shall be king over them all.
37:24 and they shall all have o shepherd.
39: 7 that I am the LORD, the Holy O in Israel. B
39:26 when they live securely in their land with no o
40: 5 thickness of the wall, o reed; and the height, o reed.
40: 6 the threshold of the gate, o reed deep.
40: 7 each recess was o reed wide and o reed deep;
40: 7 of the gate at the inner end was o reed deep.
40: 8 the inner vestibule of the gateway, o cubit.
40:12 before the recesses, o cubit on either side;
40:13 the gate from the back of the o recess to the back
40:19 the outer front of the inner court, o hundred cubits.
40:23 he measured from gate to gate, o hundred cubits.
40:26 It had palm trees on its pilasters, o on either side.
40:27 to gate toward the south, o hundred cubits.
40:42 and o cubit and a half wide, and o cubit high,
40:43 There were pegs, o handbreadth long,
40:44 o at the side of the north gate facing south,
40:47 o hundred cubits deep, and o hundred cubits wide,
41: 6 o over another, thirty in each story.
41: 7 O ascended from the bottom story to the uppermost story by way of the middle o.
41:11 o door toward the north, and another door toward
41:13 he measured the temple, o hundred cubits deep;
41:13 the building with its walls, o hundred cubits deep;
41:14 of the temple and the yard, o hundred cubits.
41:15 with its galleries on either side, o hundred cubits.
41:19 toward the palm tree on the o side,
42: 2 that was on the north side was o hundred cubits,
42: 4 ten cubits wide and o hundred cubits deep,
42: 8 the temple were o hundred cubits long.
42: 9 that o entered from the east in order to enter them
43:13 of the altar by cubits (the cubit being o cubit and
43:13 its base shall be o cubit high, and o cubit wide,
43:13 with a rim of o span around its edge.
43:14 two cubits, with a width of o cubit;
43:14 four cubits, with a width of o cubit;
43:17 and its surrounding base, o cubit.
44: 2 it shall not be opened, and no o shall enter by it;
45: 7 corresponding in length to o of the tribal portions,
45:15 and o sheep from every flock of two hundred,
46:11 and with the lambs as much as o wishes to give,
46:17 But if he makes a gift out of his inheritance to o
47: 3 the man measured o thousand cubits,
47: 4 Again he measured o thousand,
47: 4 Again he measured o thousand,
47: 5 Again he measured o thousand,
47: 7 of the river a great many trees on the o side and on
48: 1 from the east side to the west, Dan, o portion.
48: 2 from the east side to the west, Asher, o portion.
48: 3 from the east side to the west, Naphtali, o portion.
48: 4 the east side to the west, Manasseh, o portion.
48: 5 from the east side to the west, Ephraim, o portion.
48: 6 from the east side to the west, Reuben, o portion.
48: 7 from the east side to the west, Judah, o portion.
48: 8 and in length equal to o of the tribal portions,
48:23 the east side to the west, Benjamin, o portion.
48:24 from the east side to the west, Simeon, o portion.
48:25 from the east side to the west, Issachar, o portion.
48:26 from the east side to the west, Zebulun, o portion.
48:27 from the east side to the west, Gad, o portion.
Da 1:19 no o was found to compare with Daniel,
2: 9 there is but o verdict for you.
2:10 "There is no o on earth who can reveal what
2:11 and no o can reveal it to the king except the gods,
2:43 so will they mix with o another in marriage, A
4:34 and praised and honored the o who lives forever.
4:35 There is no o who can stay his hand or say to him,
5:13 "So you are Daniel, o of the exiles of Judah,
6: 1 to set over the kingdom o hundred twenty satraps,
6:13 "Daniel, o of the exiles from Judah,
7: 3 up out of the sea, different from o another. A
7: 5 Another beast appeared, a second o,

Da 7: 5 It was raised up on o side,
7: 8 a little o coming up among them;
7: 9 and an Ancient O took his throne,
7:13 I saw o like a human being coming with
7:13 And he came to the Ancient O and was presented
7:14 and his kingship is o that shall never be destroyed.
7:16 I approached o of the attendants to ask him
7:22 until the Ancient O came;
7:24 This o shall be different from the former ones,
8: 1 Daniel, after the o that had appeared to me at first.
8: 3 horns were long, but o was longer than the other,
8: 3 and the longer o came up second.
8: 4 and no o could rescue from its power;
8: 7 upon it, and there was no o who could rescue
8: 9 Out of o of them came another horn, a little o,
8:13 Then I heard a holy o speaking, B
8:13 and another holy o said to the one that spoke, B
8:13 and another holy one said to the o that spoke,
9:26 anointed o shall be cut off and shall have nothing,
9:27 a strong covenant with many for o week,
10:13 So Michael, o of the chief princes,
10:16 Then o in human form touched my lips,
10:16 and said to the o who stood before me, "My lord,
10:18 Again o in human form touched me
10:21 There is no o with me who contends
11: 5 but o of his officers shall grow stronger than he
11: 6 and her child and the o who supported her.
11:16 and no o shall withstand him.
11:20 "Then shall arise in his place o who shall send
11:27 shall sit at o table and exchange lies.
11:37 or to the o beloved by women;
11:45 he shall come to his end, with no o to help him.
12: 5 o standing on this bank of the stream and o on
12: 6 O of them said to the man clothed in linen,
12: 7 the o who lives forever that it would be for a time,
12:11 there shall be o thousand two hundred ninety days.
Hos 1:11 and they shall appoint for themselves o head;
2:10 and no o shall rescue her out of my hand.
4: 4 Yet let no o contend, and let none accuse,
5:14 I will carry off, and no o shall rescue.
8: 1 O like a vulture is over the house of the LORD,
9:12 I will bereave them until no o is left.
11: 9 I am God and no mortal, the Holy O in your B
11:12 and is faithful to the Holy O. B
Joel 2: 8 They do not jostle o another, A
Am 1: 5 and the o who holds the scepter from Beth-eden;
1: 8 and the o who holds the scepter from Ashkelon;
4: 3 in the wall you shall leave, each o straight ahead;
4: 7 I would send rain on o city,
4: 7 o field would be rained upon,
4: 8 or three towns wandered to o town to drink water,
4:13 For lo, the o who forms the mountains,
5: 2 forsaken on her land, with no o to raise her up.
5: 6 and it will devour Bethel, with no o to quench it.
5: 8 The o who made the Pleiades and Orion,
5:10 They hate the o who reproves in the gate,
5:10 and they abhor the o who speaks the truth.
6: 9 If ten people remain in o house, they shall die.
6:10 And if a relative, o who burns the dead,
6:12 Does o plow the sea with oxen?
9: 1 not o of them shall flee away,
9: 1 not o of them shall escape.
9: 9 as o shakes with a sieve, but no pebble shall fall
9:13 the o who plows shall overtake the o who reaps,
9:13 and the treader of grapes the o who sows the seed;
Ob 1:11 you too were like o of them.
Jnh 1: 7 The sailors said to o another, "Come, A
Mic 2: 5 Therefore you will have no o to cast the line by lot
2: 6 "o should not preach of such things;
2: 7 not my words do good to o who walks uprightly?
2:11 such a o would be the preacher for this people!
2:13 The o who breaks out will go up before them;
4: 4 and no o shall make them afraid;
5: 2 who are o of the little clans of Judah,
5: 2 from you shall come forth for me o who is to rule
5: 5 and he shall be the o of peace.
5: 8 down and tears in pieces, with no o to deliver.
7: 1 For I have become like o who,
7: 2 and there is no o left who is upright;
7: 5 have no confidence in a loved o;
Na 1:11 From you o has gone out who plots evil against
1:15 the feet of o who brings good tidings,
2: 8 Halt!"—but no o turns back.
2:11 and the lion's cubs, with no o to disturb them?
3:17 no o knows where they have gone.
3:18 on the mountains with no o to gather them.
Hab 1:12 O LORD my God, my Holy O? B
3: 3 the Holy O from Mount Paran. B
Zep 2:15 that said to itself, "I am, and there is no o else"?
3: 6 I have laid waste their streets so that no o walks
3: 9 of the LORD and serve him with o accord.
3:13 and no o shall make them afraid.
Hag 1: 6 you clothe yourselves, but no o is warm;
2:12 If o carries consecrated meat in the fold
2:13 "If o who is unclean by contact with
2:16 When o came to a heap of twenty measures,
2:16 o came to the winevat to draw fifty measures,
2:22 every o by the sword of a comrade. D
Zec 2: 8 o who touches you touches the apple of my eye.
4: 1 and wakened me, as o is wakened from sleep.
4: 3 o on the right of the bowl and the other
5: 3 be cut off according to the writing on o side,
7: 9 show kindness and mercy to o another; A
7:10 not devise evil in your hearts against o another. A
7:14 so that no o went to and fro,
8:10 and I set them all against o other.
8:16 Speak the truth to o another, A

Zec 8:17 not devise evil in your hearts against **o** another, A
8:21 the inhabitants of **o** city shall go to another,
9:8 so that no **o** shall march to and fro;
11:6 I will cause them, every **o**, D
11:6 and I will deliver no **o** from their hand.
11:7 **o** I named Favor, the other I named Unity,
11:8 In **o** month I disposed of the three shepherds,
11:9 that are left devour the flesh of **o** another!" A
12:10 when they look on the **o** whom they have pierced,
12:10 as **o** mourns for an only child,
12:10 as **o** weeps over a firstborn.
13:4 every **o**, of their visions when they prophesy; D
13:9 refine them as **o** refines silver,
14:4 that **o** half of the Mount shall withdraw northward,
14:9 that day the LORD will be **o** and his name **o**.
14:13 the hand of the **o** will be raised against the hand of
Mal 2:10 Have we not all **o** father?
2:10 Has not **o** God created us?
2:10 Why then are we faithless to **o** another, A
2:15 Did not **o** God make her?
2:15 And what does the **o** God desire?
3:16 the LORD spoke with **o** another. A
3:18 between **o** who serves God and **o** who does not
Mt 3:3 This is the **o** of whom the prophet Isaiah spoke
3:3 "The voice of **o** crying out in the wilderness:
3:11 **o** who is more powerful than I is coming after me;
4:4 "It is written, '**O** does not live by bread alone,
5:15 No **o** after lighting a lamp puts it under
5:18 pass away, not **o** letter, not **o** stroke of a letter,
5:19 whoever breaks **o** of the least
5:29 it is better for you to lose **o** of your members than
5:30 it is better for you to lose **o** of your members than
5:36 for you cannot make **o** hair white or black.
5:37 anything more than this comes from the evil **o**. G
5:41 and if anyone forces you to go **o** mile,
6:13 but rescue us from the evil **o**. G
6:24 "No **o** can serve two masters;
6:24 a slave will either hate the **o** and love the other,
6:24 or be devoted to the **o** and despise the other.
6:29 in all his glory was not clothed like **o** of these.
7:21 the **o** who does the will of my Father in heaven.
7:29 for he taught them as **o** having authority,
8:9 and I say to **o**, 'Go,' and he goes, and to another,
8:10 in no **o** in Israel have I found such faith.
8:28 They were so fierce that no **o** could pass that way.
9:16 No **o** sews a piece of unshrunk cloth on
9:30 "See that no **o** knows of this."
9:33 the **o** who had been mute spoke;
10:4 and Judas Iscariot, the **o** who betrayed him.
10:22 But the **o** who endures to the end will be saved.
10:23 they persecute you in **o** town, flee to the next;
10:29 Yet not **o** of them will fall to the ground apart
10:40 welcomes me welcomes the **o** who sent me.
10:42 even a cup of cold water to **o** of these little ones in
11:3 "Are you the **o** who is to come,
11:10 This is the **o** about whom it is written, 'See,
11:11 of women no **o** has arisen greater than John
11:16 in the marketplaces and calling to **o** another, A
11:27 and no **o** knows the Son except the Father, and no
o knows the Father except
12:11 "Suppose **o** of you has only **o** sheep and it falls
12:22 that the **o** who had been mute could speak and see.
12:29 Or how can **o** enter a strong man's house
12:48 But to the **o** who had told him this, Jesus replied,
13:19 evil **o** comes and snatches away what is sown G
13:20 this is the **o** who hears the word
13:22 this is the **o** who hears the word,
13:23 the **o** who hears the word and understands it,
13:23 in **o** case a hundredfold, in another sixty,
13:37 **o** who sows the good seed is the Son of Man;
13:38 the weeds are the children of the evil **o**, G
13:46 on finding **o** pearl of great value,
15:14 And if **o** blind person guides another,
16:7 They said to **o** another, "It is A
16:14 and still others Jeremiah or **o** of the prophets."
17:4 **o** for you, **o** for Moses, and **o** for Elijah."
17:8 they saw no **o** except Jesus himself alone.
17:9 "Tell no **o** about the vision until after the Son
18:5 Whoever welcomes **o** such child
18:6 before **o** of these little ones who believe in me,
18:7 woe to the **o** by whom the stumbling block comes!
18:9 with **o** eye than to have two eyes and to be thrown
18:10 that you do not despise **o** of these little ones;
18:12 and **o** of them has gone astray,
18:12 and go in search of the **o** that went astray?
18:14 So it is not the will of your Father in heaven that **o**
18:15 member listens to you, you have regained that **o**.
18:16 take **o** or two others along with you,
18:17 the church, let such a **o** be to you as a Gentile and
18:24 **o** who owed him ten thousand talents was brought
18:28 came upon **o** of his fellow slaves who owed him
18:35 heavenly Father will also do to every **o** of you, D
19:4 "Have you not read that the **o** who made them at
19:5 and the two shall become **o** flesh'? I
19:6 So they are no longer two, but **o** flesh. I
19:6 what God has joined together, let no **o** separate."
19:17 There is only **o** who is good.
20:7 They said to him, 'Because no **o** has hired us.'
20:12 'These last worked only **o** hour,
20:13 But he replied to **o** of them, 'Friend,
20:21 will sit, **o** at your right hand and **o** at your left,
21:9 Blessed is the **o** who comes in the name of
21:24 Jesus said to them, "I will also ask you **o** question;
21:25 And they argued with **o** another, "If we say, A
21:35 But the tenants seized his slaves and beat **o**,
21:44 **o** who falls on this stone will be broken to pieces;
22:5 they made light of it and went away, **o** to his farm,

Mt 22:16 and show deference to no **o**;
22:35 and **o** of them, a lawyer, asked him a question
22:46 No **o** was able to give him an answer,
23:8 for you have **o** teacher, and you are all students.
23:9 And call no **o** your father on earth,
23:9 for you have **o** Father—the **o** in heaven.
23:10 for you have **o** instructor, the Messiah.
23:21 swears by it and by the **o** who dwells in it;
23:22 by the throne of God and by the **o** who is seated
23:39 the **o** who comes in the name of the Lord.' "
24:2 not **o** stone will be left here upon another;
24:4 "Beware that no **o** leads you astray.
24:10 they will betray **o** another and hate one another. A
24:10 they will betray one another and hate **o** another. A
24:13 But the **o** who endures to the end will be saved.
24:17 the **o** on the housetop must not go down
24:18 the **o** in the field must not turn back to get a coat.
24:22 if those days had not been cut short, no **o** would
24:31 from **o** end of heaven to the other.
24:36 "But about that day and hour no **o** knows,
24:40 **o** will be taken and **o** will be left.
24:41 **o** will be taken and **o** will be left.
24:47 he will put that **o** in charge of all his possessions.
25:15 to **o** he gave five talents,
25:15 to another **o**, to each according to his ability.
25:16 The **o** who had received the five talents went off
25:17 **o** who had the two talents made two more talents.
25:18 But the **o** who had received the **o** talent went off
25:20 **o** who had received the five talents came forward,
25:22 And the **o** with the two talents also came forward,
25:24 Then the **o** who had received the **o** talent
25:28 and give it to the **o** with the ten talents.
25:32 and he will separate people **o** from another as
25:40 to **o** of the least of these who are members
25:45 just as you did not do it to **o** of the least of these,
26:14 Then **o** of the twelve, who was called Judas
26:21 "Truly I tell you, **o** of you will betray me."
26:22 and began to say to him **o** after another,
26:23 "The **o** who has dipped his hand into the bowl
26:24 to that **o** by whom the Son of Man is betrayed!
26:24 It would have been better for that **o** not
26:40 "So, could you not stay awake with me **o** hour?
26:47 he was still speaking, Judas, **o** of the twelve,
26:48 saying, "The **o** I will kiss is the man; arrest him."
26:51 **o** of those with Jesus put his hand on his sword,
26:73 "Certainly you are also **o** of them,
27:9 the price of the **o** on whom a price had been set,
27:38 **o** on his right and **o** on his left.
27:48 At once **o** of them ran and got a sponge,
Mk 1:3 the voice of **o** crying out in the wilderness:
1:7 **o** who is more powerful than I is coming after me;
1:22 for he taught them as **o** having authority,
1:24 I know who you are, the Holy **O** of God." B
1:27 they kept on asking **o** another, "What is this? A
2:21 "No **o** sews a piece of unshrunk cloth on
2:22 And no **o** puts new wine into old wineskins;
2:22 but **o** puts new wine into fresh wineskins."
2:23 **O** sabbath he was going through the grainfields;
3:27 But no **o** can enter a strong man's house
4:41 with great awe and said to **o** another, A
5:3 and no **o** could restrain him any more,
5:4 and no **o** had the strength to subdue him.
5:22 Then **o** of the leaders of
5:37 He allowed no **o** to follow him except Peter,
5:43 that no **o** should know this,
6:15 "It is a prophet, like **o** of the prophets of old."
7:36 Then Jesus ordered them to tell no **o**;
8:4 "How can **o** feed these people with bread here in
8:14 and they had only **o** loaf with them in the boat.
8:16 They said to **o** another, "It is because we have A
8:28 and still others, **o** of the prophets."
9:3 such as no **o** on earth could bleach them.
9:5 **o** for you, **o** for Moses, and **o** for Elijah."
9:8 they saw no **o** with them any more, but only Jesus.
9:9 to tell no **o** about what they had seen,
9:23 All things can be done for the **o** who believes."
9:34 on the way they had argued with **o** another A
9:37 "Whoever welcomes **o** such child
9:37 not me but the **o** who sent me."
9:39 for no **o** who does a deed of power
9:42 before **o** of these little ones who believe in me,
9:47 with **o** eye than to have two eyes and to be thrown
9:50 and be at peace with **o** another." A
10:8 and the two shall become **o** flesh.' I
10:8 So they are no longer two, but **o** flesh. I
10:9 what God has joined together, let no **o** separate."
10:18 No **o** is good but God alone.
10:21 loved him and said, "You lack **o** thing;
10:26 and said to **o** another, "Then who can A
10:29 there is no **o** who has left house or brothers
10:37 **o** at your right hand and **o** at your left,
11:9 Blessed is the **o** who comes in the name of
11:14 "May no **o** ever eat fruit from you again."
11:29 Jesus said to them, "I will ask you **o** question;
11:31 They argued with **o** another, "If we say, A
12:4 this **o** they beat over the head and insulted.
12:5 Then he sent another, and that **o** they killed.
12:6 He had still **o** other, a beloved son.
12:7 those tenants said to **o** another, 'This is the heir; A
12:14 and show deference to no **o**;
12:16 And they brought **o**.
12:28 **O** of the scribes came near
12:28 near and heard them disputing with **o** another, A
12:29 the Lord our God, the Lord is **o**;
12:32 you have truly said that 'he is **o**,
12:34 After that no **o** dared to ask him any question.
13:1 **o** of his disciples said to him, "Look, Teacher,

Mk 13:2 Not **o** stone will be left here upon another;
13:5 "Beware that no **o** leads you astray.
13:13 But the **o** who endures to the end will be saved.
13:15 the **o** on the housetop must not go down or enter
13:16 the **o** in the field must not turn back to get a coat.
13:20 the Lord had not cut short those days, no **o** would
13:32 "But about that day or hour no **o** knows,
14:4 some were there who said to **o** another in anger, A
14:10 Then Judas Iscariot, who was **o** of the twelve,
14:18 "Truly I tell you, **o** of you will betray me,
14:18 **o** who is eating with me."
14:19 to be distressed and to say to him **o** after another,
14:20 He said to them, "It is **o** of the twelve,
14:20 **o** who is dipping bread into the bowl with me.
14:21 to that **o** by whom the Son of Man is betrayed!
14:21 It would have been better for that **o** not
14:37 Could you not keep awake **o** hour?
14:43 while he was still speaking, Judas, **o** of the twelve,
14:44 saying, "The **o** I will kiss is the man;
14:47 But **o** of those who stood near drew his sword
14:61 "Are you the Messiah, the Son of the Blessed **O**?"
14:66 **o** of the servant-girls of the high priest came by.
14:69 "This man is **o** of them."
14:70 "Certainly you are **o** of them;
15:27 **o** on his right and **o** on his left.
16:3 They had been saying to **o** another, A
16:16 ⟦The **o** who believes and is baptized will be saved⟧
16:16 ⟦the **o** who does not believe will be condemned.⟧
Lk 1:28 he came to her and said, "Greetings, favored **o**!
1:49 for the Mighty **O** has done great things for me, E
2:15 the shepherds said to **o** another, A
3:4 "The voice of **o** crying out in the wilderness:
3:16 but **o** who is more powerful than I is coming;
4:4 "It is written, '**O** does not live by bread alone.' "
4:34 I know who you are, the Holy **O** of God." B
4:36 and kept saying to **o** another, A
5:3 got into **o** of the boats, the **o** belonging to Simon,
5:12 Once, when he was in **o** of the cities,
5:14 And he ordered him to tell no **o**.
5:17 **O** day, while he was teaching, C
5:24 he said to the **o** who was paralyzed—
5:36 "No **o** tears a piece from a new garment
5:37 And no **o** puts new wine into old wineskins;
5:39 no **o** after drinking old wine desires new wine,
6:1 **O** sabbath while Jesus was going through
6:11 and discussed with **o** another what they might do A
6:48 That **o** is like a man building a house,
6:49 But the **o** who hears and does not act is like
7:8 and I say to **o**, 'Go,' and he goes, and to another,
7:19 "Are you the **o** who is to come,
7:20 'Are you the **o** who is to come,
7:27 This is the **o** about whom it is written, 'See,
7:28 of women no **o** is greater than John;
7:32 and calling to **o** another, 'We played the flute A
7:36 **O** of the Pharisees asked Jesus to eat with him,
7:41 **o** owed five hundred denarii, and the other fifty.
7:43 the **o** for whom he canceled the greater debt."
7:47 But the **o** to whom little is forgiven, loves little."
8:16 "No **o** after lighting a lamp hides it under a jar,
8:22 **O** day he got into a boat with his disciples, C
8:25 and said to **o** another, "Who then is this, A
8:36 how the **o** who had been possessed
8:43 on physicians, no **o** could cure her.
8:56 he ordered them to tell no **o** what had happened.
9:8 by others that **o** of the ancient prophets had arisen.
9:19 that **o** of the ancient prophets has arisen."
9:33 **o** for you, **o** for Moses, and **o** for Elijah"—
9:36 and in those days told no **o** any of
9:46 An argument arose among them as to which **o**
9:48 welcomes me welcomes the **o** who sent me;
9:62 "No **o** who puts a hand to the plow
10:4 and greet no **o** on the road.
10:16 whoever rejects me rejects the **o** who sent me."
10:22 and no **o** knows who the Son is except the Father,
10:37 He said, "The **o** who showed him mercy."
10:42 there is need of only **o** thing.
11:1 **o** of his disciples said to him, "Lord,
11:5 he said to them, "Suppose **o** of you has a friend,
11:14 the **o** who had been mute spoke,
11:22 But when **o** stronger than he attacks him
11:33 "No **o** after lighting a lamp puts it in a cellar,
11:40 the **o** who made the outside make the inside also?
11:45 **O** of the lawyers answered him, "Teacher,
12:1 so that they trampled on **o** another, A
12:6 Yet not **o** of them is forgotten in God's sight.
12:27 in all his glory was not clothed like **o** of these.
12:44 he will put that **o** in charge of all his possessions.
12:48 the **o** who did not know and did what deserved
12:48 and from the **o** to whom much has been entrusted,
12:52 From now on five in **o** household will be divided,
13:8 He replied, 'Sir, let it alone for **o** more year,
13:10 Now he was teaching in **o** of the synagogues on
13:22 through **o** town and village after another,
13:35 the **o** who comes in the name of the Lord.' "
14:1 On **o** occasion when Jesus was going to the house
14:5 "If **o** of you has a child or an ox that has fallen
14:12 He said also to the **o** who had invited him,
14:15 **O** of the dinner guests, on hearing this, said to him,
14:31 with ten thousand to oppose the **o** who comes
15:4 "Which **o** of you, having a hundred sheep
15:4 having a hundred sheep and losing **o** of them,
15:4 the ninety-nine in the wilderness and go after the **o**
15:7 in heaven over **o** sinner who repents than
15:8 if she loses **o** of them, does not light a lamp,
15:10 of the angels of God over **o** sinner who repents."
15:15 and hired himself out to **o** of the citizens of
15:16 and no **o** gave him anything.

Lk 15:19 treat me like **o** of your hired hands." '
15:22 bring out a robe—the best **o**—
15:26 He called **o** of the slaves
16: 5 So, summoning his master's debtors **o** by **o**,
16:13 a slave will either hate the **o** and love the other,
16:13 or be devoted to the **o** and despise the other.
16:17 for **o** stroke of a letter in the law to be dropped.
16:26 and no **o** can cross from there to us.'
17: 2 the sea than for you to cause **o** of these little ones
17:15 Then **o** of them, when he saw that he was healed,
17:22 "The days are coming when you will long to see **o**
17:24 and lights up the sky from **o** side to the other,
17:34 I tell you, on that night there will be two in **o** bed;
17:34 **o** will be taken and the other left.
17:35 **o** will be taken and the other left."
18:10 **o** a Pharisee and the other a tax collector.
18:19 No **o** is good but God alone.
18:22 he said to him, "There is still **o** thing lacking.
18:29 there is no **o** who has left house or wife
19: 7 "He has gone to be the guest of **o** who is a sinner."
19:24 from him and give it to the **o** who has ten pounds.'
19:44 not leave within you **o** stone upon another;
20: 1 **O** day, as he was teaching the people in the C
20: 5 They discussed it with **o** another, saying, A
20:11 that **o** also they beat and insulted
20:12 this **o** also they wounded and threw out.
20:21 and you show deference to no **o**,
21: 6 the days will come when not **o** stone will be left
22: 3 who was **o** of the twelve;
22:21 But see, the **o** who betrays me is with me,
22:22 but woe to that **o** by whom he is betrayed!"
22:23 Then they began to ask **o** another, A
22:23 which **o** of them it could be who would do this.
22:24 also arose among them as to which **o** of them was
22:26 and the leader like **o** who serves.
22:27 the **o** who is at the table or the **o** who serves?
22:27 Is it not the **o** at the table?
22:27 But I am among you as **o** who serves.
22:36 "But now, the **o** who has a purse must take it,
22:36 And the **o** who has no sword must sell his cloak
and buy **o**.
22:47 and the **o** called Judas, **o** of the twelve,
22:50 Then **o** of them struck the slave of the high priest
22:58 on seeing him, said, "You also are **o** of them."
23:14 as **o** who was perverting the people;
23:25 the **o** who had been put in prison for insurrection
23:33 **o** on his right and **o** on his left.
23:35 if he is the Messiah of God, his chosen **o**!"
23:39 **O** of the criminals who were hanged there
23:53 a rock-hewn tomb where no **o** had ever been laid.
24:18 Then **o** of them, whose name was Cleopas,
24:21 we had hoped that he was the **o** to redeem Israel.
Jn 1: 3 and without him not **o** thing came into being.
1:18 No **o** has ever seen God.
1:23 "I am the voice of **o** crying out in the wilderness,
1:26 Among you stands **o** whom you do not know,
1:27 the **o** who is coming after me;
1:33 **o** who sent me to baptize with water said to me,
1:33 the **o** who baptizes with the Holy Spirit.'
1:40 **O** of the two who heard John speak
2:25 and needed no **o** to testify about anyone;
3: 2 for no **o** can do these signs that you do apart from
3: 3 no **o** can see the kingdom of God
3: 4 Can **o** enter a second time into the mother's womb
3: 5 no **o** can enter the kingdom of God
3:13 No **o** has ascended into heaven except the **o** who
3:26 "Rabbi, the **o** who was with you across the Jordan,
3:27 "No **o** can receive anything except what has been
3:31 The **o** who comes from above is above all;
3:31 the **o** who is of the earth belongs to the earth
3:31 The **o** who comes from heaven is above all.
3:32 yet no **o** accepts his testimony.
4:18 and the **o** you have now is not your husband.
4:26 "I am he, the **o** who is speaking to you."
4:27 but no **o** said, "What do you want?"
4:33 So the disciples said to **o** another, A
4:33 "Surely no **o** has brought him something to eat?"
4:37 '**O** sows and another reaps.'
4:52 at **o** in the afternoon the fever left him."
5: 5 **O** man was there who had been ill
5: 7 I have no **o** to put me into the pool when
5:22 The Father judges no **o** but has given all judgment
5:44 when you accept glory from **o** another and do A
5:44 the glory that comes from the **o** who alone is God?
6: 8 **O** of his disciples, Andrew, Simon Peter's brother,
6:22 the sea saw that there had been only **o** boat there.
6:44 No **o** can come to me unless drawn by
6:46 the Father except the **o** who is from God;
6:50 so that **o** may eat of it and not die.
6:58 But the **o** who eats this bread will live forever."
6:64 and who was the **o** that would betray him.
6:65 that no **o** can come to me unless it is granted by
6:69 to believe and know that you are the Holy **O** B
6:70 Yet **o** of you is a devil."
6:71 though **o** of the twelve, was going to betray him.
7: 4 no **o** who wants to be widely known acts in secret.
7:13 Yet no **o** would speak openly about him for fear of
7:18 **o** who seeks the glory of him who sent him is true,
7:21 Jesus answered them, "I performed **o** work,
7:27 no **o** will know where he is from."
7:28 **o** who sent me is true, and you do not know him.
7:30 but no **o** laid hands on him,
7:35 The Jews said to **o** another, A
7:38 and let the **o** who believes in me drink.
7:44 but no **o** laid hands on him.
7:48 Has any **o** of the authorities or of
7:50 and who was **o** of them, asked,

Jn 8: 9 ⟦When they heard it, they went away, **o** by **o**,⟧
8:10 ⟦Has no **o** condemned you?"⟧
8:11 ⟦She said, "No **o**, sir."⟧
8:15 You judge by human standards; I judge no **o**.
8:20 the treasury of the temple, but no **o** arrested him,
8:26 but the **o** who sent me is true,
8:29 And the **o** who sent me is with me;
8:41 we have **o** father, God himself."
8:50 there is **o** who seeks it and he is the judge.
9: 4 night is coming when no **o** can work.
9:25 **O** thing I do know, that though I was blind,
9:31 to **o** who worships him and obeys his will.
9:37 and the **o** speaking with you is he."
10: 2 The **o** who enters by the gate is the shepherd of
10:16 So there will be **o** flock, **o** shepherd.
10:18 No **o** takes it from me,
10:21 "These are not the words of **o** who has a demon.
10:28 No **o** will snatch them out of my hand.
10:29 and no **o** can snatch it out of the Father's hand.
10:30 The Father and I are **o**."
10:36 the **o** whom the Father has sanctified and sent into
11: 2 the **o** who anointed the Lord with perfume
11:27 the Son of God, the **o** coming into the world."
11:49 But **o** of them, Caiaphas, who was high priest
11:50 to have **o** man die for the people than to have
11:52 but to gather into **o** the dispersed children of God.
11:56 and were asking **o** another as they stood A
12: 2 and Lazarus was **o** of those at the table with him.
12: 4 **o** of his disciples (the **o** who was about
12:13 the **o** who comes in the name of the Lord—
12:19 The Pharisees then said to **o** another, "You see, A
12:48 The **o** who rejects me and does
13:10 "**O** who has bathed does not need to wash,
13:14 you also ought to wash **o** another's feet.
13:16 are messengers greater than the **o** who sent them.
13:18 **o** who ate my bread has lifted his heel against me.'
13:20 whoever receives **o** whom I send receives me;
13:21 "Very truly, I tell you, **o** of you will betray me."
13:22 The disciples looked at **o** another, A
13:23 **O** of his disciples—the **o** whom Jesus loved—
13:26 "It is the **o** to whom I give this piece of bread
13:28 no **o** at the table knew why he said this to him.
13:34 a new commandment, that you love **o** another. AF
13:34 you also should love **o** another. AF
13:35 if you have love for **o** another." A
14: 6 No **o** comes to the Father except through me.
14:12 the **o** who believes in me will also do the works
15:12 that you love **o** another as I have loved you. AF
15:13 No **o** has greater love than this,
15:17 so that you may love **o** another. AF
15:24 among them the works that no **o** else did,
16:17 Then some of his disciples said to **o** another, A
16:22 and no **o** will take your joy from you.
16:32 each **o** to his home, and you will leave me alone.
17:11 so that they may be **o**, as we are **o**.
17:12 and not **o** of them was lost except the **o** destined
17:15 but I ask you to protect them from the evil **o**. G
17:21 that they may all be **o**.
17:22 so that they may be **o**, as we are **o**,
17:23 that they may become completely **o**,
18: 9 not lose a single **o** of those whom you gave me."
18:14 the **o** who had advised the Jews that it was better
to have **o** person die for the people.
18:17 "You are not also **o** of this man's disciples,
18:22 **o** of the police standing nearby struck Jesus on
18:25 "You are not also **o** of his disciples, are you?"
18:26 **O** of the slaves of the high priest,
19:11 the **o** who handed me over to you is guilty of
19:18 **o** on either side, with Jesus between them.
19:23 and divided them into four parts, **o** for each
19:23 woven in **o** piece from the top.
19:24 So they said to **o** another, "Let us not tear it, A
19:34 **o** of the soldiers pierced his side with a spear,
19:37 on the **o** whom they have pierced."
19:38 though a secret **o** because of his fear of the Jews,
19:41 a new tomb in which no **o** had ever been laid.
20: 2 the **o** whom Jesus loved, and said to them,
20:12 **o** at the head and the other at the feet.
20:24 the Twin), **o** of the twelve, was not with them
21:20 the **o** who had reclined next to Jesus at the supper
21:25 if every **o** of them were written down, D
Ac 1:15 about **o** hundred twenty persons) and said,
1:20 and let there be no **o** to live in it';
1:21 So **o** of the men who have accompanied us
1:22 **o** of these must become a witness with us
1:24 Show us which **o** of these two you have chosen
2: 1 they were all together in **o** place.
2: 6 because each **o** heard them speaking in
2:12 saying to **o** another, "What does this mean?" A
2:27 or let your Holy **O** experience corruption. B
2:30 to him that he would put **o** of his descendants
2:38 and be baptized every **o** of you in the name D
3: 1 **O** day Peter and John were going up to the C
3:10 and they recognized him as the **o** who used to sit
3:14 the Holy and Righteous **O** and asked to have J
4:12 There is salvation in no **o** else,
4:15 while they discussed the matter with **o** another. A
4:32 of those who believed were of **o** heart and soul,
4:32 and no **o** claimed private ownership
5:23 but when we opened them, we found no **o** inside."
7:24 When he saw **o** of them being wronged,
7:38 He is the **o** who was in the congregation in
7:52 the coming of the Righteous **O**, J
8: 6 with **o** accord listened eagerly to what was said
9: 7 because they heard the voice but saw no **o**.
10: 3 **O** afternoon at about three o'clock he had a vision
10:21 "I am the **o** you are looking for;

Ac 10:42 to testify that he is the **o** ordained by God as judge
11:19 and they spoke the word to no **o** except Jews.
11:28 **O** of them named Agabus stood up and predicted
13:25 No, but **o** is coming after me;
13:35 not let your Holy **O** experience corruption.' B
15: 7 be the **o** through whom the Gentiles would hear
15:38 with them **o** who had deserted them in Pamphylia
16:16 **O** day, as we were going to the place of prayer, C
17:26 From **o** ancestor he made all nations to inhabit
17:27 though indeed he is not far from each **o** of us.
18: 9 **O** night the Lord said to Paul in a vision,
18:10 and no **o** will lay a hand on you to harm you,
19: 4 the people to believe in the **o** who was to come
19:32 Meanwhile, some were shouting **o** thing,
19:38 let them bring charges there against **o** another. A
21: 6 and said farewell to **o** another. A
21: 7 the believers and stayed with them for **o** day. C
21: 8 **o** of the seven, and stayed with him.
21:19 he related **o** by **o** the things that God had done
21:34 Some in the crowd shouted **o** thing, some another;
22: 9 not hear the voice of the **o** who was speaking
22:14 to see the Righteous **O** and to hear his own voice; J
23:17 Paul called **o** of the centurions and said,
23:22 "Tell no **o** that you have informed me of this."
24:21 unless it was this **o** sentence that I called out
25:11 no **o** can turn me over to them.
26:31 said to **o** another, "This man is doing nothing A
28: 4 to **o** another, "This man must be a murderer; A
28:13 After **o** day there a south wind sprang up, C
28:25 they were leaving, Paul made **o** further statement:
Ro 1:17 "The **o** who is righteous will live by faith."
1:27 were consumed with passion for **o** another. A
2:28 For a person is not a Jew who is **o** outwardly,
2:29 Rather, a person is a Jew who is **o** inwardly,
3:10 "There is no **o** who is righteous, not even **o**; there
is no **o** who has understanding, there is no **o** who
seeks God.
3:12 no **o** who shows kindness there is not even **o**."
3:26 and that he justifies the **o** who has faith in Jesus.
3:30 since God is **o**; and he will justify the circumcised
4: 4 to **o** who works, wages are not reckoned as a gift
4: 5 to **o** who without works trusts him who justifies
4: 8 the **o** against whom the Lord will not reckon sin."
5:12 just as sin came into the world through **o** man,
5:14 who is a type of the **o** who was to come.
5:15 For if the many died through the **o** man's trespass,
5:15 of God and the free gift in the grace of the **o** man,
5:16 free gift is not like the effect of the **o** man's sin.
5:16 following **o** trespass brought condemnation,
5:17 If, because of the **o** man's trespass,
5:17 death exercised dominion through that **o**,
5:17 in life through the **o** man, Jesus Christ.
5:18 as **o** man's trespass led to condemnation for all,
5:18 so **o** man's act of righteousness leads
5:19 For just as by the **o** man's disobedience
5:19 so by the **o** man's obedience the many will
6:16 you are slaves of the **o** whom you obey,
8:20 but by the will of the **o** who subjected it,
9:10 when she had conceived children by **o** husband,
9:20 Will what is molded say to the **o** who molds it,
9:21 the same lump **o** object for special use and another
10:10 For **o** believes with the heart and so is justified,
10:10 and **o** confesses with the mouth and so is saved.
10:11 "No **o** who believes in him will be put to shame."
10:14 But how are they to call on **o** in whom they have
10:14 to believe in **o** of whom they have never heard?
12: 4 For as in **o** body we have many members, H
12: 5 who are many, are **o** body in Christ, H
12: 5 and individually we are members **o** of another.
12:10 love **o** another with mutual affection; AF
12:10 outdo **o** another in showing honor. A
12:16 Live in harmony with **o** another; A
13: 5 Therefore **o** must be subject,
13: 8 Owe no **o** anything, except to love one another;
13: 8 Owe no one anything, except to love **o** another; AF
13: 8 for the **o** who loves another has fulfilled the law.
14: 5 Some judge **o** day to be better than another, C
14:13 therefore no longer pass judgment on **o** another, A
14:15 Do not let what you eat cause the ruin of **o**
14:18 The **o** who thus serves Christ is acceptable to God
15: 5 to live in harmony with **o** another, A
15: 6 so that together you may with **o** voice glorify
15: 7 Welcome **o** another, therefore, A
15:12 the **o** who rises to rule the Gentiles;
15:14 and able to instruct **o** another. A
16:16 Greet **o** another with a holy kiss. A
1Co 1:15 no **o** can say that you were baptized in my name.
1:20 Where is the **o** who is wise?
1:29 so that no **o** might boast in the presence of God.
1:31 "Let the **o** who boasts, boast in the Lord."
2:11 also no **o** comprehends what is truly God's except
2:15 they are themselves subject to no **o** else's scrutiny.
3: 4 For when **o** says, "I belong to Paul," and another,
3: 7 So neither the **o** who plants nor the **o** who waters
3: 8 The **o** who plants and the **o** who waters have a
3:11 For no **o** can lay any foundation other than the **o**
3:21 So let no **o** boast about human leaders.
4: 5 each **o** will receive commendation from God.
4: 6 so that none of you will be puffed up in favor of **o**
5:11 Do not even eat with such a **o**.
6: 5 be that there is no **o** among you wise enough
6: 5 to decide between **o** believer and another,
6: 7 at all with **o** another is already a defeat for you. A
6:13 and God will destroy both **o** and the other.
6:16 to a prostitute becomes **o** body with her? H
6:16 For it is said, "The two shall be **o** flesh." I
6:17 But anyone united to the Lord becomes **o** spirit

1Co 7: 5 Do not deprive **o** another except perhaps A
7: 7 **o** having **o** kind and another a different kind.
7:25 as **o** who by the Lord's mercy is trustworthy.
8: 4 and that "there is no God but **o.**"
8: 6 yet for us there is **o** God,
8: 6 and for whom we exist, and **o** Lord, Jesus Christ,
8:13 so that I may not cause **o** of them to fall.
9:15 no **o** will deprive me of my ground for boasting!
9:20 as **o** under the law (though I myself am not under
9:21 To those outside the law I became as **o** outside
9:24 but only **o** receives the prize?
9:25 but we an imperishable **o.**
10:17 there is **o** bread, we who are many are one body,
10:17 there is one bread, we who are many are **o** body, H
10:17 for we all partake of the **o** bread.
10:28 out of consideration for the **o** who informed you,
11: 5 it is **o** and the same thing
11:21 and **o** goes hungry and another becomes drunk.
11:33 you come together to eat, wait for **o** another. A
12: 3 to understand that no **o** speaking by the Spirit
12: 3 and no **o** can say "Jesus is Lord" except by
12: 8 To **o** is given through the Spirit the utterance
12: 9 to another gifts of healing by the **o** Spirit,
12:11 All these are activated by **o** and the same Spirit,
12:11 to each **o** individually just as the Spirit chooses.
12:12 For just as the body is **o** and has many members,
12:12 though many, are **o** body, so it is with Christ. H
12:13 the **o** Spirit we were all baptized into one body—
12:13 one Spirit we were all baptized into **o** body— H
12:13 and we were all made to drink of **o** Spirit.
12:14 body does not consist of **o** member but of many.
12:18 each **o** of them, as he chose.
12:20 As it is, there are many members, yet **o** body. H
12:25 members may have the same care for **o** another. A
12:26 If **o** member suffers, all suffer together with it;
12:26 **o** member is honored, all rejoice together with it.
14: 5 **O** who prophesies is greater than **o** who speaks
14:13 **o** who speaks in a tongue should pray for
14:26 When you come together, each **o** has a hymn,
14:27 in turn; and let **o** interpret.
14:28 But if there is no **o** to interpret,
14:31 For you can all prophesy **o** by **o,**
15: 6 and sisters at **o** time, most of whom are still alive,
15: 8 Last of all, as to **o** untimely born,
15:27 that this does not include the **o** who put all things
15:28 the **o** who put all things in subjection under him,
15:39 but there is **o** flesh for human beings, I
15:40 but the glory of the heavenly is **o** thing,
15:41 There is **o** glory of the sun,
16:11 therefore let no **o** despise him.
16:20 Greet **o** another with a holy kiss. A
2Co 1:20 in him every **o** of God's promises is a "Yes." D
2: 2 to make me glad but the **o** whom I have pained?
2:16 to the **o** a fragrance from death to death,
3:16 but when **o** turns to the Lord, the veil is removed.
3:18 the same image from **o** degree of glory to another;
4: 2 the shameful things that **o** hides;
4:14 the **o** who raised the Lord Jesus will raise us also
5:14 because we are convinced that **o** has died for all;
5:16 we regard no **o** from a human point of view;
7: 2 we have wronged no **o,** we have corrupted no **o,**
we have taken advantage of no **o.**
7:12 it was not on account of the **o** who did the wrong,
nor on account of the **o** who was wronged,
8:12 the gift is acceptable according to what **o** has—
8:12 not according to what **o** does not have.
8:15 "The **o** who had much did not have too much, and
the **o** who had little did not have too little."
8:20 that no **o** should blame us about this generous gift
9: 6 the **o** who sows sparingly will also reap sparingly,
9: 6 **o** who sows bountifully will also reap bountifully.
10:12 But when they measure themselves by **o** another, A
10:12 and compare themselves with **o** another, A
10:17 "Let the **o** who boasts, boast in the Lord."
11: 2 for I promised you in marriage to **o** husband,
11: 4 the **o** we proclaimed, or if you receive a different
spirit from the **o** you received, or a different
gospel from the **o** you accepted,
11:16 I repeat, let no **o** think that I am a fool;
11:23 I am talking like a madman—I am a better **o:**
11:24 from the Jews the forty lashes minus **o.**
12: 5 On behalf of such a **o** I will boast,
12: 6 that no **o** may think better of me than what is seen
13:11 listen to my appeal, agree with **o** another, A
13:12 Greet **o** another with a holy kiss. A
Gal 1: 6 so quickly deserting the **o** who called you in
1: 8 contrary to what we proclaimed to you, let that **o**
1: 9 a gospel contrary to what you received, let that **o**
1:23 "The **o** who formerly was persecuting us is
2:10 They asked only **o** thing, that we remember
2:16 no **o** will be justified by the works of the law.
3:11 Now it is evident that no **o** is justified before God
3:11 for "The **o** who is righteous will live by faith."
3:15 no **o** adds to it or annuls it.
3:16 "And to your offspring," that is, to **o** person,
3:20 mediator involves more than **o** party; but God is **o.**
3:28 for all of you are **o** in Christ Jesus.
4:22 **o** by a slave woman and the other by
4:23 **O,** the child of the slave, was born according to
4:24 **O** woman, in fact, is Hagar, from Mount Sinai,
4:27 For it is written, "Rejoice, you childless **o,**
4:27 the children of the **o** who is married."
5: 8 not come from the **o** who calls you.
5:13 but through love become slaves to **o** another. A
5:15 If, however, you bite and devour **o** another, A
5:15 care that you are not consumed by **o** another. A
5:26 competing against **o** another, envying A
Gal 5:26 against one another, envying **o** another. A
6: 1 the Spirit should restore such a **o** in a spirit
6: 2 Bear **o** another's burdens,
6:17 From now on, let no **o** make trouble for me;
Eph 2: 9 not the result of works, so that no **o** may boast.
2:11 remember that at **o** time you Gentiles by birth,
2:14 into **o** and has broken down the dividing wall,
2:15 that he might create in himself **o** new humanity
2:16 might reconcile both groups to God in **o** body H
2:18 for through him both of us have access in **o** Spirit
4: 2 with patience, bearing with **o** another in love, A
4: 4 There is **o** body and one Spirit, H
4: 4 There is one body and **o** Spirit,
4: 4 as you were called to the **o** hope of your calling,
4: 5 **o** Lord, **o** faith, **o** baptism,
4: 6 **o** God and Father of all,
4:10 He who descended is the same **o** who ascended
4:25 for we are members of **o** another. A
4:32 and be kind to **o** another, A
4:32 tenderhearted, forgiving **o** another, A
5: 5 or **o** who is greedy (that is, an idolater),
5: 6 Let no **o** deceive you with empty words,
5:21 Be subject to **o** another out of reverence A
5:29 For no **o** ever hates his own body,
5:31 and the two will become **o** flesh." I
6:16 to quench all the flaming arrows of the evil **o.** G
Php 1: 4 with joy in every **o** of my prayers for all of you, D
1: 6 that the **o** who began a good work
1:27 I will know that you are standing firm in **o** spirit,
1:27 striving side by side with **o** mind for the faith of
2: 2 being in full accord and of **o** mind.
2:20 I have no **o** like him who will
2:27 so that I would not have **o** sorrow after another.
3: 9 but **o** that comes through faith in Christ,
3:13 but this **o** thing I do:
Col 2: 4 I am saying this so that no **o** may deceive you
2: 8 that no **o** takes you captive through philosophy
3: 9 Do not lie to **o** another, A
3:13 with **o** another and, if anyone has a complaint A
3:15 to which indeed you were called in the **o** body. H
3:16 teach and admonish **o** another in all wisdom; A
4: 9 the faithful and beloved brother, who is **o** of you.
4:12 Epaphras, who is **o** of you,
1Th 2:11 with each **o** of you like a father with his children,
3: 3 that no **o** would be shaken by these persecutions.
3:12 and abound in love for **o** another and for all, A
4: 4 that each **o** of you know how
4: 6 that no **o** wrong or exploit a brother or sister
4: 9 by God to love **o** another; AF
4:12 toward outsiders and be dependent on no **o.**
4:18 Therefore encourage **o** another with these words. A
5:11 encourage **o** another and build up each other, A
5:15 always seek to do good to **o** another and to all. A
5:24 **o** who calls you is faithful, and he will do this.
2Th 1: 3 of everyone of you for **o** another is increasing. A
2: 3 Let no **o** deceive you in any way;
2: 3 and the lawless **o** is revealed, the **o** destined for
destruction.
2: 7 only until the **o** who now restrains it is removed.
2: 8 And then the lawless **o** will be revealed,
2: 9 the lawless **o** is apparent in the working of Satan,
3: 3 and guard you from the evil **o.** G
1Ti 1: 8 that the law is good, if **o** uses it legitimately.
2: 5 there is **o** God; there is also **o** mediator between
3:15 how **o** ought to behave in the household of God,
4:12 Let no **o** despise your youth,
5:10 as **o** who has brought up children,
6:16 whom no **o** has ever seen or can see;
2Ti 1:12 for I know the **o** in whom I have put my trust,
2: 4 No **o** serving in the army gets entangled
2: 5 no **o** is crowned without competing according to
2:15 to present yourself to God as **o** approved by him,
4:16 At my first defense no **o** came to my support,
Tit 1:12 It was **o** of them, their very own prophet,
2:15 Let no **o** look down on you.
3: 2 to speak evil of no **o,**
3: 3 despicable, hating **o** another. A
Phm 1:22 **O** thing more—prepare a guest room
Heb 2:11 For the **o** who sanctifies
2:11 and those who are sanctified all have **o** Father.
2:14 that through death he might destroy the **o** who has
3: 2 was faithful to the **o** who appointed him,
3:13 But exhort **o** another every day, A
4: 4 For in **o** place it speaks about the seventh day
4:11 no **o** may fall through such disobedience as theirs.
4:13 but all are naked and laid bare to the eyes of the **o**
4:15 with our weaknesses, but we have **o** who
5: 4 And **o** does not presume to take this honor,
5: 5 but was appointed by the **o** who said to him,
5: 7 to the **o** who was able to save him from death,
6:11 And we want each **o** of you to show
6:13 because he had no **o** greater by whom to swear,
7: 8 In the **o** case, tithes are received
7: 8 by **o** of whom it is testified that he lives.
7: 9 **O** might even say that Levi himself,
7:11 rather than **o** according to the order of Aaron?
7:13 the **o** of whom these things are spoken belonged
7:13 from which no **o** has ever served at the altar.
7:16 **o** who has become a priest,
7:18 on the **o** hand, the abrogation of an earlier
7:21 but this **o** became a priest with an oath,
7:21 because of the **o** who said to him,
8: 1 a high priest, **o** who is seated at the right hand of
8: 5 that is a sketch and shadow of the heavenly **o;**
8: 7 to look for a second **o.**
8:11 shall not teach **o** another or say to each other, A
8:13 he has made the first **o** obsolete.
Heb 9: 2 For a tent was constructed, the first **o,**
9:16 death of the **o** who made it must be established.
9:17 not in force as long as the **o** who made it is alive.
9:24 a mere copy of the true **o,**
10:24 to provoke **o** another to love and good deeds, A
10:25 is the habit of some, but encouraging **o** another, A
10:30 For we know the **o** who said, "Vengeance is mine,
10:37 the **o** who is coming will come and will not delay;
10:38 but my righteous **o** will live by faith. J
11:12 from **o** person, and this **o** as good as dead,
11:16 they desire a better country, that is, a heavenly **o.**
12:14 the holiness without which no **o** will see the Lord.
12:15 See to it that no **o** fails to obtain the grace of God;
12:16 See to it that no **o** becomes like Esau,
12:25 See that you do not refuse the **o** who is speaking;
12:25 when they refused the **o** who warned them
12:25 if we reject the **o** who warns from heaven!
Jas 1: 6 for the **o** who doubts is like a wave of the sea,
1:12 a **o** has stood the test and will receive the crown
1:13 No **o,** when tempted, should say,
1:13 be tempted by evil and he himself tempts no **o.**
1:14 But **o** is tempted by one's own desire,
2: 3 if you take notice of the **o** wearing the fine clothes
2: 3 while to the **o** who is poor you say, "Stand there,"
2:10 but fails in **o** point has become accountable for all
2:11 the **o** who said, "You shall not commit adultery,"
2:16 and **o** of you says to them, "Go in peace;
2:19 You believe that God is **o;** you do well.
3: 8 but no **o** can tame the tongue—
4:11 Do not speak evil against **o** another, A
4:12 There is **o** lawgiver and judge who is able to save
5: 6 and murdered the righteous **o,** J
5: 9 Beloved, do not grumble against **o** another, A
5:16 Therefore confess your sins to **o** another, A
5:16 pray for **o** another, so that you may be healed. A
1Pe 1:17 the **o** who judges all people impartially according
1:22 love **o** another deeply from the heart. AF
2:23 he entrusted himself to the **o** who judges justly.
3: 8 unity of spirit, sympathy, love for **o** another, A
4: 8 Above all, maintain constant love for **o** another, A
4: 9 Be hospitable to **o** another without complaining. A
4:10 serve **o** another with whatever gift each A
4:11 Whoever speaks must do so as **o** speaking
5: 1 well as **o** who shares in the glory to be revealed,
5: 5 with humility in your dealings with **o** another, A
5:14 Greet **o** another with a kiss of love. A
2Pe 3: 8 But do not ignore this **o** fact, beloved,
3: 8 with the Lord **o** day is like a thousand years, C
3: 8 and a thousand years are like **o** day. C
1Jn 1: 7 we have fellowship with **o** another, A
2:13 because you have conquered the evil **o.** G
2:14 and you have overcome the evil **o.** G
2:20 But you have been anointed by the Holy **O,** B
2:22 Who is the liar but the **o** who denies that Jesus is
2:22 the **o** who denies the Father and the Son.
2:23 No **o** who denies the Son has the Father;
3: 6 No **o** who abides in him sins;
3: 6 no **o** who sins has either seen him or known him.
3: 7 Little children, let no **o** deceive you.
3:11 that we should love **o** another. AF
3:12 must not be like Cain who was from the evil **o** G
3:14 from death to life because we love **o** another. AF
3:16 we ought to lay down our lives for **o** another. A
3:23 of his Son Jesus Christ and love **o** another, AF
4: 4 the **o** who is in you is greater than the **o** who is
4: 7 Beloved, let us love **o** another, AF
4:11 we also ought to love **o** another. AF
4:12 No **o** has ever seen God;
4:12 if we love **o** another, God lives in us, AF
5: 5 the **o** who believes that Jesus is the Son of God?
5: 6 This is the **o** who came by water and blood,
5: 6 And the Spirit is the **o** that testifies,
5:16 you will ask, and God will give life to such a **o—**
5:18 but the **o** who was born of God protects them,
5:18 and the evil **o** does not touch them. G
5:19 whole world lies under the power of the evil **o.** G
2Jn 1: 5 but **o** we have had from the beginning,
1: 5 from the beginning, let us love **o** another. AF
Rev 1: 3 the **o** who reads aloud the words of the prophecy,
1:13 in the midst of the lampstands I saw **o** like the Son
1:18 and the living **o.** I was dead,
2:13 my faithful **o,** who was killed among you,
2:17 that no **o** knows except the **o** who receives it.
2:23 that I am the **o** who searches minds and hearts,
2:28 To the **o** who conquers I will also give
3: 7 These are the words of the holy **o,** the true one, B
3: 7 These are the words of the holy one, the true **o,**
3: 7 the key of David, who opens and no **o** will shut,
who shuts and no **o** opens:
3: 8 which no **o** is able to shut.
3:11 so that no **o** may seize your crown.
3:21 To the **o** who conquers I will give a place with me
4: 2 with **o** seated on the throne!
4: 3 the **o** seated there looks like jasper and carnelian,
4: 9 and thanks to the **o** who is seated on the throne,
4:10 the **o** who is seated on the throne and worship the
o who lives forever
5: 1 of the **o** seated on the throne a scroll written on the
5: 3 And no **o** in heaven or on earth or under
5: 4 because no **o** was found worthy to open the scroll
5: 5 Then **o** of the elders said to me, "Do not weep.
5: 7 from the right hand of the **o** who was seated on
5:13 "To the **o** seated on the throne and to the Lamb
6: 1 Then I saw the Lamb open **o** of the seven seals,
6: 1 and I heard **o** of the four living creatures call out,
6: 4 so that people would slaughter **o** another; A
6:16 of the **o** seated on the throne and from the wrath of

Rev 7: 4 **o** hundred forty-four thousand,
7: 9 there was a great multitude that no **o** could count,
7:13 Then **o** of the elders addressed me, saying,
7:14 I said to him, "Sir, you are the **o** that knows."
7:15 **o** who is seated on the throne will shelter them.
11: 3 for **o** thousand two hundred sixty days,
12: 6 for **o** thousand two hundred sixty days.
13: 3 **O** of its heads seemed to have received
13:17 no **o** can buy or sell who does not have the mark,
14: 1 with him were **o** hundred forty-four thousand
14: 3 No **o** could learn that song except the **o** hundred
forty-four thousand who have been redeemed
14:14 seated on the cloud was **o** like the Son of Man,
14:15 with a loud voice to the **o** who sat on the cloud,
14:16 the **o** who sat on the cloud swung his sickle over
15: 7 Then **o** of the four living creatures gave
15: 8 and no **o** could enter the temple until
16: 5 "You are just, O Holy **O**, who are and were, B
16:15 Blessed is the **o** who stays awake and is clothed,
17: 1 Then **o** of the seven angels who had
17:10 **o** is living, and the other has not yet come;
17:12 they are to receive authority as kings for **o** hour,
18:10 For in **o** hour your judgment has come."
18:11 since no **o** buys their cargo anymore,
18:17 For in **o** hour all this wealth has been laid waste!"
18:19 For in **o** hour she has been laid waste.
19:12 a name inscribed that no **o** knows but himself.
20:11 I saw a great white throne and the **o** who sat on it;
21: 5 And the **o** who was seated on the throne said,
21: 9 Then **o** of the seven angels who had
21:17 measured its wall, **o** hundred forty-four cubits
22: 7 the **o** who keeps the words of the prophecy
22: 8 I, John, am the **o** who heard and saw these things.
22:20 The **o** who testifies to these things says,
Tob 1:19 Then **o** of the Ninevites went and informed
2: 3 **o** of our own people has been murdered
2: 4 the square and laid it in **o** of the rooms until sunset
2:12 **O** day, the seventh of Dystrus, C
3: 7 was reproached by **o** of her father's maids.
3: 8 "You are the **o** who kills your husbands!
3: 8 and have not borne the name of a single **o** of them.
3:10 'You had only **o** beloved daughter
5: 3 we each took **o** part, and I put **o** with the money.
5: 9 a man who is **o** of our own Israelite kindred!"
5:13 the son of the great Hananiah, **o** of your relatives."
7:10 For no **o** except you, brother,
8:12 "Send **o** of the maids and have her go in to see
9: 4 if I delay even **o** day I will upset him very much. C
10: 2 and there is no **o** to give him the money?"
10: 6 with him is trustworthy and is **o** of our own kin.
10: 7 the road her son had taken, and would heed no **o**.
11:16 along in full vigor and with no **o** leading him,
12:15 **o** of the seven angels who stand ready and enter
14: 2 in peace when he was **o** hundred twelve years old,
14: 5 not like the first **o** until the period when the times
14:14 at the age of **o** hundred seventeen years.
Jdt 1: 3 At its gates he raised towers **o** hundred cubits high
1:11 but regarded him as only **o** man.
1:12 and all Judea, and every **o** in Egypt, D
1:16 and feasted for **o** hundred twenty days.
2: 3 They decided that every **o** who had D
2: 5 **o** hundred twenty thousand foot soldiers
2:15 **o** hundred twenty thousand of them,
5: 7 At **o** time they lived in Mesopotamia,
6: 3 we the king's servants will destroy them as **o** man.
6: 7 into the hill country and put you in **o** of the towns
7: 2 forces numbered **o** hundred seventy thousand
7: 4 they were greatly terrified and said to **o** another, A
7:13 to keep watch to see that no **o** gets out of the town.
7:25 For now we have no **o** to help us;
8: 8 No **o** spoke ill of her,
8:28 and there is no **o** who can deny your words.
10:13 and capture all the hill country without losing **o**
10:19 by her. They said to **o** another, A
10:19 It is not wise to leave **o** of their men alive,
11: 4 No **o** will hurt you.
11:18 and not **o** of them will be able to withstand you.
11:21 "No other woman from **o** end of the earth to
12:13 like **o** of the Assyrian women who serve in
12:20 much more than he had ever drunk in any **o** day C
13: 4 So everyone went out, and no **o**,
13:17 and said with **o** accord, "Blessed are you our God,
14: 6 and saw the head of Holofernes in the hand of **o** of
14:15 when no **o** answered, he opened it and went into
14:18 **O** Hebrew woman has brought disgrace on
15: 2 they did not wait for **o** another, A
15: 2 but with **o** impulse all rushed out and fled
15: 5 with **o** accord they fell upon the enemy,
15: 9 they all blessed her with **o** accord and said to her,
16: 6 For their mighty **o** did not fall by the hands of E
16:23 reaching the age of **o** hundred five.
16:25 No **o** ever again spread terror among the Israelites
AdE 1: 1 over **o** hundred twenty-seven provinces from India
1: 4 during the course of **o** hundred eighty days,
3: 7 taking the days and the months **o** by **o**,
3: 7 on **o** day to destroy the whole race of Mordecai. C
3:12 There were **o** hundred twenty-seven provinces
4: 2 because no **o** was allowed to enter
4:11 Only the **o** to whom the king stretches out
6: 9 both be given to **o** of the king's honored Friends,
7: 9 Then Bugathan, **o** of the eunuchs, said to the king,
8: 9 **o** hundred twenty-seven provinces,
9: 2 no **o** resisted, because they feared them.
9:19 and send presents of food to **o** another, A
9:19 also sending presents to **o** another. A
10:10 **o** for the people of God and **o** for all the nations,
11: 1 **o** of the residents of Jerusalem.

AdE 11: 4 was **o** of the captives whom King Nebuchadnezzar
13: 9 and there is no **o** who can oppose you
13:11 and there is no **o** who can resist you, the Lord.
15: 3 on **o** she leaned gently for support,
16: 1 **o** hundred twenty-seven provinces,
16:18 the **o** who did these things,
Wis 2: 1 and no **o** has been known to return from Hades.
2: 4 and no **o** will remember our works;
2: 5 because it is sealed up and no **o** turns back.
5: 3 They will speak to **o** another in repentance, A
5:12 so that no **o** knows its pathway.
6:14 **O** who rises early to seek her will have no
6:15 and **o** who is vigilant on her account will soon
6:19 and immortality brings **o** near to God;
7: 6 there is for all **o** entrance into life, and **o** way out.
7:27 Although she is but **o**, she can do all things,
8: 1 She reaches mightily from **o** end of the earth to
9: 6 even **o** who is perfect among human beings will
10:20 and praised with **o** accord your defending hand;
11:16 so that they might learn that **o** is punished by the
very things by which **o** sins.
12: 9 to destroy them at **o** blow by dread wild animals
12:27 the true God the **o** whom they had before refused
13: 1 to know the **o** who exists, nor did they recognize
13: 4 much more powerful is the **o** who formed them.
14: 1 **o** preparing to sail and about to voyage
14: 8 and so is the **o** who made it—
14:10 be punished together with the **o** who did it.
14:17 so that by their zeal they might flatter the absent **o**
14:20 the **o** whom shortly before they had honored as
14:24 but they either treacherously kill **o** another, A
14:24 or grieve **o** another by adultery, A
15:11 to know the **o** who formed them and inspired them
15:12 for they say **o** must get money however **o** can,
15:16 and **o** whose spirit is borrowed formed them;
15:19 in appearance that **o** would desire them,
16: 7 For the **o** who turned toward it was saved,
16:18 At **o** time the flame was restrained,
16:21 ministering to the desire of the **o** who took it,
16:28 that **o** must rise before the sun to give you thanks,
17:17 for with **o** chain of darkness they all were bound.
18: 5 and **o** child had been abandoned and rescued,
18: 9 and with **o** accord agreed to the divine law,
18:12 by the **o** form of death,
18:12 in **o** instant their most valued children had been
18:18 and **o** here and another there, hurled
18:23 dead had already fallen on **o** another in heaps, A
19: 8 by your hand passed through as **o** nation,
19:18 For the elements changed places with **o** another, A
Sir 1: 8 There is but **o** who is wise, greatly to be feared,
4: 2 Do not grieve the hungry, or anger **o** in need.
4: 5 and give no **o** reason to curse you;
4:14 Those who serve her minister to the Holy **O**; B
6: 6 but let your advisers be **o** in a thousand.
6:14 whoever finds **o** has found a treasure.
6:19 Come to her like **o** who plows and sows,
6:34 Attach yourself to such a **o**.
7: 8 not even for **o** will you go unpunished.
7:11 for there is **O** who humbles and exalts.
7:26 but do not trust yourself to **o** whom you detest.
8: 4 Do not make fun of **o** who is ill-bred,
8: 5 Do not reproach **o** who is turning away from sin;
8: 6 Do not disdain **o** who is old,
8:12 Do not lend to **o** who is stronger than you;
9:18 and the **o** who is reckless in speech is hated.
10:11 when **o** is dead he inherits maggots and vermin
10:13 and the **o** who clings to it pours out abominations.
10:23 not right to despise **o** who is intelligent but poor,
10:23 and it is not proper to honor **o** who is sinful.
10:24 of them is greater than the **o** who fears the Lord.
10:31 **O** who is honored in poverty,
10:31 And **o** dishonored in wealth,
11: 5 but **o** who was never thought of has worn a crown.
11:18 **O** becomes rich through diligence and self-denial,
11:27 An hour's misery makes **o** forget past delights,
11:28 Call no **o** happy before his death;
12: 3 to **o** who persists in evil or to **o** who does
12: 7 Give to the **o** who is good,
12: 9 One's enemies are friendly when **o** prospers,
12:11 Be to him like **o** who polishes a mirror,
12:14 So no **o** pities a person who associates with
13: 2 or associate with **o** mightier and richer than you.
14: 5 If **o** is mean to himself,
14: 6 No **o** is worse than **o** who is grudging to himself;
14:16 because in Hades **o** cannot look for luxury.
14:18 **o** dies and another is born.
14:19 and the **o** who made it will pass away with it.
15:17 and whichever **o** chooses will be given.
16: 3 for **o** can be better than a thousand,
16: 4 through **o** intelligent person a city can be filled
16:11 Even if there were only **o** stiff-necked person,
16:21 Like a tempest that no **o** can see,
16:23 the thoughts of **o** devoid of understanding;
16:28 They do not crowd **o** another, A
17:28 From the dead, as from **o** who does not exist,
18: 9 in their life is great if they reach **o** hundred years.
18:23 do not be like **o** who puts the Lord to the test.
18:27 **O** who is wise is cautious in everything;
18:27 sin is all around, **o** guards against wrongdoing.
18:28 and praises the **o** who finds her.
19: 1 The **o** who does this will not become rich;
19: 1 **o** who despises small things will fail little by little.
19: 4 **O** who trusts others too quickly has
19: 4 and **o** who sins does wrong to oneself.
19: 5 **O** who rejoices in wickedness will be condemned,
19: 6 but **o** who hates gossip has less evil.
19:27 and pretends not to hear, but when no **o** notices,

Sir 20: 3 **o** who admits his fault will be kept from failure.
20:15 such a **o** is hateful to God and humans.
20:21 **O** may be prevented from sinning by poverty;
20:22 **O** may lose his life through shame,
20:27 and **o** who is sensible pleases the great.
21: 8 like **o** who gathers stones for his burial mound.
21:12 The **o** who is not clever cannot be taught,
22: 1 and every **o** hisses at his disgrace. D
22: 4 but **o** who acts shamefully is a grief to her father.
22: 9 a fool is like **o** who glues potsherds together,
22:19 **O** who pricks the eye brings tears,
22:19 **o** who pricks the heart makes clear its feelings.
22:20 **O** who throws a stone at birds scares them away,
22:20 and **o** who reviles a friend destroys a friendship.
23: 7 the **o** who observes it will never be caught.
23: 9 nor habitually utter the name of the Holy **O**; B
23:11 The **o** who swears many oaths is full of iniquity,
23:16 **o** who commits fornication with his near
23:18 The **o** who sins against his marriage bed says
23:18 the walls hide me, and no **o** sees me.
24:28 nor will the last **o** fathom her.
25: 8 the **o** who does not plow with ox and ass together.
25: 8 Happy is the **o** who does not sin with the tongue,
25: 8 and the **o** who has not served an inferior.
25: 9 Happy is the **o** who finds a friend,
25: 9 and the **o** who speaks to attentive listeners.
25:10 How great is the **o** who finds wisdom!
25:10 But none is superior to the **o** who fears the Lord.
25:11 to whom can we compare the **o** who has it?
26:25 *but* **o** *who has a sense of shame will fear the Lord.*
28: 4 If **o** has no mercy toward another like himself,
28:19 Happy is the **o** who is protected from it,
28:26 and fall victim to **o** lying in wait.
29: 5 **O** kisses another's hands until he gets a loan,
29:14 the **o** who has lost all sense of shame will fail him.
30: 4 for he has left behind him **o** like himself,
30: 6 and **o** to repay the kindness of his friends.
30:19 So is the **o** punished by the Lord;
31: 5 **O** who loves gold will not be justified;
31: 5 **o** who pursues money will be led astray by it.
31:23 People bless the **o** who is liberal with food,
31:24 city complains of the **o** who is stingy with food,
31:27 What is life to **o** who is without wine?
32: 1 be among them as **o** of their number.
32: 8 be as **o** who knows and can still hold his tongue.
32:10 and approval goes before **o** who is modest.
32:14 The **o** who seeks God will accept his discipline,
32:15 The **o** who seeks the law will be filled with it,
32:24 The **o** who keeps the law preserves himself,
32:24 and the **o** who trusts the Lord will not suffer loss.
33: 1 No evil will befall the **o** who fears the Lord,
33: 1 in trials such a **o** will be rescued again and again.
33: 2 but the **o** who is hypocritical about it is like a boat
33: 3 a **o** the law is as dependable as a divine oracle.
33: 7 Why is **o** day more important than another, C
33:15 they come in pairs, **o** the opposite of the other.
33:31 If you have but **o** slave, treat him like yourself,
33:31 If you have but **o** slave, treat him like a brother,
34: 2 **o** who catches at a shadow and pursues the wind,
34: 9 An educated person knows many things, and **o**
34:21 If **o** sacrifices ill-gotten goods,
34:24 Like **o** who kills a son before his father's eyes is
34:28 When **o** builds and another tears down,
34:29 When **o** prays and another curses,
34:30 If **o** washes after touching a corpse,
34:31 So if **o** fasts for his sins,
35: 1 The **o** who keeps the law makes many offerings;
35: 2 **o** who heeds the commandments makes
35: 3 The **o** who returns a kindness offers choice flour,
35: 4 and **o** who gives alms sacrifices a thank offering.
35:13 For the Lord is the **o** who repays,
35:16 he will listen to the prayer of **o** who is wronged.
35:19 as she cries out against the **o** who causes them
35:20 The **o** whose service is pleasing to the Lord will
36:12 "There is no **o** but ourselves."
36:23 yet **o** food is better than another.
36:26 but **o** girl is preferable to another.
37:10 not consult the **o** who regards you with suspicion;
37:13 for no **o** is more faithful to you than it is.
37:26 **O** who is wise among his people will inherit honor,
37:28 and no **o** enjoys everything.
37:31 but the **o** who guards against it prolongs his life.
38:16 and as **o** in great pain begin the lament.
38:17 for **o** day, or two, to avoid criticism; C
38:24 the **o** who has little business can become wise.
38:25 How can **o** become wise who handles the plow,
38:34 the **o** who devotes himself to the study of the law
39:17 No **o** can say, 'What is this?'
39:21 No **o** can say, 'What is this?'
39:34 No **o** can say, "This is not as good as that,"
40: 3 From the **o** who sits on a splendid throne to the **o**
who grovels in dust
40: 4 from the **o** who wears purple and a crown
40: 4 to the **o** who is clothed in burlap,
40: 5 And when **o** rests upon his bed,
40: 6 by the visions of his mind like **o** who has escaped
40:19 but better than either is the **o** who finds wisdom.
40:19 Cattle and orchards make **o** prosperous;
40:25 Gold and silver make **o** stand firm,
40:29 When **o** looks to the table of another,
40:29 **O** loses self-respect with another person's food,
40:29 but **o** who is intelligent and well instructed guards
41: 1 how bitter is the thought of you to the **o** at peace
41: 2 how welcome is your sentence to the **o** who is needy
41: 2 to **o** who is contrary, and has lost all patience!
42:21 he is from all eternity **o** and the same.
42:21 and he needs no **o** to be his counselor.

Sir 42:24 All things come in pairs, **o** opposite the other,
43:10 On the orders of the Holy **O** they stand B
44:19 and no **o** has been found like him in glory.
46: 4 that the sun stood still and **o** day become as long C
46: 5 He called upon the Most High, the Mighty **O,** E
46: 6 for he was a devoted follower of the Mighty **O.** E
46:16 He called upon the Lord, the Mighty **O,** E
46:19 And no **o** accused him.
47: 8 In all that he did he gave thanks to the Holy **O,** B
47:22 the descendants of his chosen **o,**
47:23 and left behind him **o** of his sons,
48:20 The Holy **O** quickly heard them from heaven, B
50:19 before the Merciful **O,** until the order of worship
51: 7 and there was no **o** to help me;
51:12 *Give thanks to the mighty **o** of Jacob,* E
Bar 3:31 No **o** knows the way to her,
3:32 But the **o** who knows all things knows her,
3:32 The **o** who prepared the earth for all time filled it
3:33 the **o** who sends forth the light, and it goes;
4: 7 the **o** who made you by sacrificing to demons and
4:12 Let no **o** rejoice over me, a widow and bereaved
4:22 and joy has come to me from the Holy **O,** B
4:27 be remembered by the **o** who brought this
4:29 For the **o** who brought these calamities
4:30 for the **o** who named you will comfort you.
4:37 at the word of the Holy **O,** B
5: 5 from west and east at the word of the Holy **O,** B
LtJ 6:14 **O** of them holds a scepter, like a district judge,
6:34 Whether **o** does evil to them or good,
6:34 They cannot set up a king or depose **o.**
6:35 if **o** makes a vow to them and does not keep it,
6:37 they cannot rescue **o** who is in distress.
6:43 When **o** of them is led off by **o** of the passers-by
6:49 How then can **o** fail to see that these are not gods,
6:54 or deliver **o** who is wronged,
6:64 Therefore **o** must not think that they are gods,
Aza 1:12 of your servant Isaac and Israel your holy **o,** B
1:28 Then the three with **o** voice praised and glorified
Sus 1: 2 very beautiful woman and **o** who feared the Lord.
1:13 **O** day they said to each other, "Let us go home, C
1:16 No **o** was there except the two elders,
1:20 the garden doors are shut, and no **o** can see us.
1:25 And **o** of them ran and opened the garden doors.
1:52 he summoned **o** of them and said to him,
1:56 Then, putting him to **o** side,
1Mc 1:10 the **o** hundred thirty-seventh year of the kingdom
1:20 in the **o** hundred forty-third year,
1:41 to his whole kingdom that all should be **o** people,
1:54 in the **o** hundred forty-fifth year,
2:27 "Let every **o** who is zealous for the law D
2:70 in the **o** hundred forty-sixth year and was buried in
3:37 and left Antioch his capital in the **o** hundred
3:43 But they said to **o** another, A
3:45 not **o** of her children went in or out.
4: 1 and **o** thousand picked cavalry,
4: 5 the camp of Judas by night, he found no **o** there,
4:11 the Gentiles will know that there is **o** who redeems
4:38 or as on **o** of the mountains.
4:47 and built a new altar like the former **o.**
4:52 in the **o** hundred forty-eighth year,
5:42 "Permit no **o** to encamp, but make them all enter
5:48 No **o** will do you harm;
5:54 not **o** of them had fallen.
6:14 Then he called for Philip, **o** of his Friends,
6:16 in the **o** hundred forty-ninth year.
6:20 the citadel in the **o** hundred fiftieth year;
6:30 of his forces was **o** hundred thousand foot soldiers,
6:43 saw that **o** of the animals was equipped
7: 1 In the **o** hundred fifty-first year Demetrius son
7: 8 the king chose Bacchides, **o** of the king's Friends,
7:16 he seized sixty of them and killed them in **o** day, C
7:17 and there was no **o** to bury them."
7:26 the king sent Nicanor, **o** of his honored princes,
7:29 and they greeted **o** another peaceably; A
7:41 and struck down **o** hundred eighty-five thousand
7:46 not even **o** of them was left.
8: 6 against them with **o** hundred twenty elephants and
8:14 not **o** of them has put on a crown or worn purple
8:16 They trust **o** man each year to rule over them and
8:16 they all heed the **o** man,
9: 3 of the **o** hundred fifty-second year they encamped
9:29 of your brother Judas there has been no **o** like him
9:37 a daughter of **o** of the great nobles of Canaan,
9:49 about **o** thousand of Bacchides' men fell that day.
9:54 In the **o** hundred and fifty-third year,
9:58 and he will capture them all in **o** night."
10: 1 the **o** hundred sixtieth year Alexander Epiphanes,
10:21 the seventh month of the **o** hundred sixtieth year,
10:35 No **o** shall have authority to exact anything
10:38 so that they may be considered to be under **o** ruler
10:54 let us establish friendship with **o** another; A
10:56 so that we may see **o** another, A
10:57 to Ptolemais in the **o** hundred sixty-second year.
10:63 the city and proclaim that no **o** is to bring charges
10:63 and let no **o** annoy him for any reason."
10:67 In the **o** hundred sixty-fifth year Demetrius son
10:70 "You are the only **o** to rise up against us,
11: 6 they greeted **o** another and spent the night there. A
11:19 in the **o** hundred sixty-seventh year.
11:36 And not **o** of these grants shall be canceled
11:39 A certain Trypho had formerly been **o**
11:47 they killed on that day about **o** hundred thousand.
11:57 and set you over the four districts and make you **o**
11:70 not **o** of them was left except Mattathias son
12:47 while **o** thousand accompanied him.
12:50 they encouraged **o** another and kept marching A
13:16 Send now **o** hundred talents of silver and two

1Mc 13:28 also erected seven pyramids, opposite **o** another, A
13:41 In the **o** hundred seventieth year the yoke of
13:43 and battered and captured **o** tower.
13:51 in the **o** hundred seventy-first year,
14: 1 **o** hundred seventy-second year King Demetrius
14: 2 he sent **o** of his generals to take him alive.
14:13 No **o** was left in the land to fight them,
14:24 a large gold shield weighing **o** thousand minas,
14:27 in the **o** hundred seventy-second year,
14:39 made him **o** of his Friends,
15:10 **o** hundred seventy-fourth year Antiochus set out
15:13 with him were **o** hundred twenty thousand warriors
15:14 and permitted no **o** to leave or enter it.
15:18 a gold shield weighing **o** thousand minas.
15:28 He sent to him Athenobius, **o** of his Friends,
15:33 at **o** time had been unjustly taken by our enemies.
15:35 for them we will give you **o** hundred talents."
16:14 in the **o** hundred seventy-seventh year,
2Mc 1: 7 in the **o** hundred sixty-ninth year,
1: 9 in the **o** hundred eighty-eighth year.
2: 1 **O** finds in the records that
2:27 for **o** who prepares a banquet and seeks the benefit
2:29 while the **o** who undertakes its painting
2:31 the **o** who recasts the narrative should be allowed
3:31 to **o** who was lying quite at his last breath.
4: 3 a degree that even murders were committed by **o**
4: 9 to this he promised to pay **o** hundred fifty more
5:10 to lie unburied had no **o** to mourn for him;
6: 2 and to call the **o** in Gerizim the temple
6: 9 **O** could see, therefore, the misery that had come
6:18 Eleazar, **o** of the scribes in high position,
7: 2 **O** of them, acting as their spokesman, said,
7: 5 and their mother encouraged **o** another A
7:14 **"O** cannot but choose to die at the hands
8: 9 **o** of the king's chief Friends, and sent him,
8:19 when **o** hundred eighty-five thousand perished,
8:20 destroyed **o** hundred twenty thousand Galatians
8:32 and **o** who had greatly troubled the Jews.
8:33 who had fled into **o** little house;
9:10 Because of his intolerable stench no **o** was able
9:29 And Philip, **o** of his courtiers, took his body home;
10:11 appointed **o** Lysias to have charge of
10:28 the **o** having as pledge of success and victory
11:21 The **o** hundred forty-eighth year,
11:33 **o** hundred forty-eighth year, Xanthicus fifteenth."
11:36 you have considered them, send some **o** promptly
11:38 **o** hundred forty-eighth year, Xanthicus fifteenth."
12:18 in **o** place he had left a very strong garrison.
12:20 with him **o** hundred twenty thousand infantry
12:35 But a certain Dositheus, **o** of Bacenor's men,
12:35 when **o** of the Thracian cavalry bore down on him
12:40 of each **o** of the dead they found sacred tokens of
13: 1 the **o** hundred forty-ninth year word came to Judas
13: 2 a Greek force of **o** hundred ten thousand infantry,
14: 4 in about the **o** hundred fifty-first year,
14:20 and it had appeared that they were of **o** mind,
14:26 Alcimus noticed their goodwill for **o** another, A
14:36 O holy **O,** Lord of all holiness, B
14:37 A certain Razis, **o** of the elders of Jerusalem,
15:12 **o** who spoke fittingly and had been trained
15:22 and he killed fully **o** hundred eighty-five thousand
1Es 1:16 no **o** needed to interrupt his daily duties,
1:33 every **o** of the acts of Josiah, and his splendor, D
1:36 and fined the nation **o** hundred talents of silver and
o talent of gold.
2:13 **o** thousand gold cups, **o** thousand silver cups,
2:13 and **o** thousand other vessels.
3: 4 over the person of the king, said to **o** another, A
3: 5 "Let each of us state what **o** thing is strongest;
3: 5 and to the **o** whose statement seems wisest,
3: 9 and to the **o** whose statement the king and
4: 4 he tells them to make war on **o** another, A
4: 6 they compel **o** another to pay taxes to the king. A
4: 7 And yet he is only **o** man!
4:11 and no **o** may go away to attend to his own affairs,
4:33 the king and the nobles looked at **o** another; A
4:34 of the heavens and returns to its place in **o** day. C
4:35 Is not the **o** who does these things great?
5: 9 two thousand **o** hundred seventy-two.
5:12 **o** thousand two hundred fifty-four.
5:13 **o** thousand three hundred twenty-two.
5:16 The descendants of Annias, **o** hundred **o.**
5:16 The descendants of Arsiphurith, **o** hundred twelve.
5:17 of Bethlomon, **o** hundred twenty-three.
5:18 Those from Anathoth, **o** hundred fifty-eight.
5:21 Those from Macalon, **o** hundred twenty-two.
5:21 The descendants of Niphish, **o** hundred fifty-six.
5:24 descendants of Immer, **o** thousand and fifty-two.
5:25 **o** thousand two hundred forty-seven.
5:25 descendants of Charme, **o** thousand seventeen.
5:27 the descendants of Asaph, **o** hundred twenty-eight.
5:28 in all **o** hundred thirty-nine.
5:38 **o** of the daughters of Barzillai,
5:45 and **o** hundred priests' vestments.
5:63 came to the building of this **o** with outcries
6:25 of hewn stone and **o** course of new native timber;
7: 7 of the temple of the Lord **o** hundred bulls,
8:22 that no **o** has authority to impose any tax on them.
8:92 Shecaniah son of Jehiel, **o** of the men of Israel,
9:11 This is not a work we can do in **o** day or two, C
9:38 the whole multitude gathered with **o** accord in
3Mc 1:13 no **o** there had stopped him.
3: 1 that all should promptly be gathered into **o** place,
5:21 and joyfully with **o** accord gave their approval,
5:34 The king's Friends **o** by **o** sullenly slipped away
5:49 and falling into **o** another's arms—
5:50 they prostrated themselves with **o** accord on

3Mc 6:12 O Eternal **O,** who have all might and all power,
6:13 O honored **O,** who have power to save the nation
6:25 and foolishly gathered every **o** of them here? D
7: 8 with no **o** in any place doing them harm at all
7:16 joyfully and loudly giving thanks to the **o** God
7:21 at all to confiscation of their belongings by any **o.**
2Es 2:14 for I am the Living **O,** says the Lord.
2:26 Not **o** of the servants whom I have given you will
3: 7 And you laid upon him **o** commandment of yours;
3:11 But you left **o** of them, Noah with his household,
3:13 you chose for yourself **o** of them,
4: 4 If you can solve **o** of them for me,
4:11 And how can **o** who is already worn out by
5: 6 And **o** shall reign whom those who inhabit
5: 7 and **o** whom the many do
5: 9 and all friends shall conquer **o** another; A
5:11 **O** country shall ask its neighbor,
5:23 and from all its trees you have chosen **o** vine,
5:24 the world you have chosen for yourself **o** region,
5:24 of the world you have chosen for yourself **o** lily,
5:25 of the sea you have filled for yourself **o** river,
5:26 for yourself **o** dove, and from all the flocks
5:26 you have provided for yourself **o** sheep,
5:27 of peoples you have gotten for yourself **o** people;
5:28 why have you handed the **o** over to the many,
5:28 and dishonored the **o** root beyond the others,
5:28 and scattered your only **o** among the many?
5:40 "Just as you cannot do **o** of the things
5:43 at **o** time those who have been and those who are
5:44 at **o** time those who have been created in it."
5:45 that you will certainly give life at **o** time
5:45 If therefore all creatures will live at **o** time and
5:45 be able to support all of them present at **o** time."
5:46 'If you bear ten children, why **o** after another?'
5:46 Request it therefore to produce ten at **o** time."
6:32 the Mighty **O** has seen your uprightness and E
6:41 so that **o** part might move upward and
6:49 the **o** you called Behemoth and the name of
6:50 And you separated **o** from the other,
6:51 And you gave Behemoth **o** of the parts
7: 8 There is only **o** path lying between them, that is,
7: 8 so that only **o** person can walk on the path.
7:30 so that no **o** shall be left.
7:*50* the Most High has made not **o** world but two.
7:*79* If it is **o** of those who have shown scorn and have
7:*105* so no **o** shall ever pray for another on that day,
7:*109* [39] for the **o** who was dead, that he might live,
7:*115* [45] no **o** will then be able to have mercy
7:*138* [68] **o** ten-thousandth of humankind could have
8:35 For in truth there is no **o**
8:35 among those who have existed there is no **o** who
9:18 and no **o** opposed me then, for no **o** existed;
9:21 and saved for myself **o** grape out of a cluster,
9:21 and **o** plant out of a great forest.
9:45 and we gave great glory to the Mighty **O.** E
10: 8 you are sorrowing for **o** son, but we,
10:11 or you who are grieving for **o** alone?
10:24 that the Mighty **O** may be merciful to you again, E
10:59 So I slept that night and the following **o,**
11: 6 and no **o** spoke against it—
11:12 As I watched, **o** wing on the right side rose up,
11:17 you no **o** shall rule as long as you have ruled,
11:19 they wielded power **o** after another and
11:26 As I kept looking, **o** was set up,
11:29 **o** of the heads that were at rest (the **o** that was in
11:35 the head on the right side devour the **o** on the left.
11:39 'Are you not the **o** that remains of the four beasts
11:43 and your pride to the Mighty **O.** E
12:14 And twelve kings shall reign in it, **o** after another.
12:15 for a longer time than any other **o** of the twelve.
12:26 **o** of the kings shall die in his bed, but in agonies.
12:28 sword of **o** shall devour him who was with him;
12:47 Mighty **O** has not forgotten you in your struggle. E
12:49 Now go to your homes, every **o** of you, D
13:23 The **o** who brings the peril at
13:31 They shall plan to make war against **o** another, A
13:33 the warfare that they have against **o** another; A
13:52 as no **o** can explore or know what is in the depths
13:52 so no **o** on earth can see my Son or those who are
14:15 lay to **o** side the thoughts that are most grievous
14:21 so no **o** knows the things which have been done
14:36 But let no **o** come to me now,
14:36 and let no **o** seek me for forty days."
15:16 growing strong against **o** another, A
15:33 in ambush shall attack them and destroy **o**
15:35 against **o** another and shall pour out A
15:48 You have imitated that hateful **o** in all her deeds
16: 6 Can **o** drive off a hungry lion in the forest,
16: 7 Can **o** turn back an arrow shot by a strong archer?
16:23 and there shall be no **o** to console them;
16:24 No **o** shall be left to cultivate the earth or
16:41 Let the **o** who sells be like **o** who will flee;
16:41 let the **o** who buys be like **o** who will lose;
16:42 let the **o** who does business be like **o** who will
16:42 the **o** who builds a house be like **o** who will
16:43 let the **o** who sows be like **o** who will not reap;
16:43 so also the **o** who prunes the vines,
16:43 like **o** who will not gather the grapes;
16:50 the **o** who searches out every sin on earth.
16:71 They shall be like maniacs, sparing no **o,**
16:77 so that no **o** can pass through.
4Mc 1: 4 that it masters the emotions that hinder **o**
1: 6 but so that **o** may not give way to them.
1:33 I for **o** think so.
2: 6 with the emotions that hinder **o** from justice.
2: 8 as soon as **o** adopts a way of life in accordance
2: 8 **o** is forced to act contrary to natural ways and

4Mc 2: 9 If **o** is greedy, **o** is ruled by the law through reason so that **o** neither gleans the harvest
2:11 so that **o** rebukes her when she breaks the law.
2:12 so that **o** punishes them for misdeeds.
2:13 so that **o** rebukes friends when they act wickedly.
2:14 but **o** preserves the property of enemies
2:23 and **o** who lives subject to this will rule a kingdom
2:24 How is it then, **o** might say,
3: 2 No **o** of us can eradicate that kind of desire,
3: 3 No **o** of us can eradicate anger from the mind,
3: 4 No **o** of us can eradicate malice,
5: 4 When many persons had been rounded up, **o** man,
5:37 **o** who does not fear your violence even to death.
6: 8 **O** of the cruel guards rushed at him and began
8: 5 favorable feelings I admire each and every **o** D
8: 9 you will compel me to destroy each and every **o** D
8:29 all with **o** voice together, as from **o** mind, said:
9:15 or as **o** who acts impiously,
13: 5 How then can **o** fail to confess the sovereignty
13: 8 of religion and encouraged **o** another, A
13:11 While **o** said, "Courage, brother," another said,
13:13 and all of them together looking at **o** another, A
13:23 brothers were the more sympathetic to **o** another. A
13:24 they loved **o** another all the more. A
13:25 strengthened their goodwill toward **o** another, A
14:12 up under the rackings of each **o** of her children.
15:14 who saw them tortured and burned **o** by **o**,
15:19 the eyes of each **o** in his tortures gazing boldly at
15:26 **o** bearing death and the other deliverance
17: 1 into the flames so that no **o** might touch her body.

ONE'S‡ (62) [ONE]

Ge 42:35 there in each **o** sack was his bag of money.
43:21 and there was each **o** money in the top of his sack,
Lev 13:18 on the skin of **o** body a boil that has healed,
20:19 for that is to lay bare **o** own flesh;
1Sa 17:32 "Let no **o** heart fail because of him;
2Ch 21:20 He departed with no **o** regret.
Ps 49: 7 Truly, no ransom avails for **o** life,
127: 4 in the hand of a warrior are the sons of **o** youth.
Pr 6:27 in the bosom without burning **o** clothes?
14:26 and **o** children will have a refuge.
16: 2 All **o** ways may be pure in **o** own eyes,
18:12 Before destruction **o** heart is haughty,
18:20 From the fruit of the mouth **o** stomach is satisfied;
18:24 but a true friend sticks closer than **o** nearest kin.
19: 3 **O** own folly leads to ruin,
26: 6 like cutting off **o** foot and drinking down violence,
28: 6 and walk in integrity than to be crooked in **o** ways
28: 9 even **o** prayers are an abomination.
29: 3 with prostitutes is to squander **o** substance.
29:24 To be a partner of a thief is to hate **o** own life;
Ecc 8: 1 Wisdom makes **o** face shine,
8: 1 and the hardness of **o** countenance is changed.
8:16 how **o** eyes see sleep neither day nor night,
Jer 13:11 For as the loincloth clings to **o** loins,
La 3:29 to put **o** mouth to the dust (there may yet be hope),
3:30 to give **o** cheek to the smiter,
3:36 **o** case is subverted—does the Lord not see it?
Hag 2:12 in the fold of **o** garment,
Mal 2:16 and covering **o** garment with violence,
Mt 10:36 **o** foes will be members of **o** own household.
Mk 12:33 and 'to love **o** neighbor as oneself,'—
Lk 12:15 for **o** life does not consist in the abundance
Jn 15:13 to lay down **o** life for **o** friends.
Ac 20:33 I coveted no **o** silver or gold or clothing.
Ro 2: 6 For he will repay according to each **o** deeds:
Jas 1:14 But one is tempted by **o** own desire,
2Pe 1:20 of scripture is a matter of **o** own interpretation,
Wis 6:15 To fix **o** thought on her is perfect understanding,
Sir 1:22 for anger tips the scale to **o** ruin.
3:11 The glory of **o** father is **o** own glory,
8: 7 Do not rejoice over any **o** death;
11:27 and at the close of **o** life **o** deeds are revealed.
12: 9 **O** enemies are friendly when one prospers,
12: 9 but in adversity even **o** friend disappears.
16:12 he judges a person according to **o** deeds.
16:14 everyone receives in accordance with **o** deeds.
17:22 **O** almsgiving is like a signet ring with the Lord,
27:14 Their cursing and swearing make **o** hair stand
30:22 and rejoicing lengthens **o** life span.
31: 1 Wakefulness over wealth wastes away **o** flesh,
38:18 and a sorrowful heart saps **o** strength.
40:19 and the building of a city establish **o** name,
40:29 **o** way of life cannot be considered a life.
2Mc 5: 6 at the cost of **o** kindred is the greatest misfortune,
15:39 and delicious and enhances **o** enjoyment,
3Mc 4:16 even to communicate or to come to **o** help,
4Mc 2:11 It is superior to love for **o** wife,

ONE-FIFTH (10) [FIVE]

Ge 41:34 and take **o** of the produce of the land of Egypt
47:24 And at the harvests you shall give **o** to Pharaoh,
Lev 5:16 and shall add **o** to it and give it to the priest.
6: 5 the principal amount and shall add **o** to it.
22:14 he shall add **o** of its value to it,
27:13 **o** must be added to the assessment.
27:15 **o** shall be added to its assessed value,
27:19 then **o** shall be added to its assessed value,
27:27 be ransomed at its assessment, with **o** added;
27:31 they must add **o** to them.

ONE-FOURTH (9) [FOUR]

Ex 29:40 of choice flour mixed with **o** of a hin of beaten oil,
29:40 and **o** of a hin of wine for a drink offering.
Lev 23:13 drink offering with it shall be of wine, **o** of a hin.
Nu 15: 4 mixed with **o** of a hin of oil.
15: 5 you shall offer **o** of a hin of wine as
28: 5 mixed with **o** of a hin of beaten oil.
28: 7 Its drink offering shall be **o** of a hin for each lamb;
28:14 and **o** of a hin for a lamb.
2Ki 6:25 and **o** of a kab of dove's dung for five shekels

ONE-HALF (2) [HALF]

Jos 14: 2 for the nine and **o** tribes.
14: 3 an inheritance to the two and **o** tribes beyond

ONE-SIXTH (4) [SIX]

Eze 4:11 And you shall drink water by measure, **o** of a hin;
45:13 **o** of an ephah from each homer of wheat,
45:13 and **o** of an ephah from each homer of barley,
46:14 **o** of an ephah, and one-third of a hin of oil

ONE-TENTH (19) [TEN]

Ex 29:40 and with the first lamb **o** of a measure
Lev 5:11 for the sin that you have committed **o** of an ephah
6:20 **o** of an ephah of choice flour as a regular offering,
14:21 and **o** of an ephah of choice flour mixed with oil
Nu 5:15 **o** of an ephah of barley flour.
15: 4 **o** of an ephah of choice flour,
28: 5 **o** of an ephah of choice flour for a grain offering,
28:13 and **o** of choice flour mixed with oil as
28:21 **o** shall you offer for each of the seven lambs;
28:29 **o** for each of the seven lambs;
29: 4 and **o** for each of the seven lambs;
29:10 **o** for each of the seven lambs;
29:15 and **o** for each of the fourteen lambs;
1Sa 8:15 He will take **o** of your grain and of your vineyards
8:17 He will take **o** of your flocks,
Eze 45:11 the bath containing **o** of a homer, and the ephah **o** of a homer;
45:14 **o** of a bath from each cor (the cor, like the homer,
Heb 7: 2 to him Abraham apportioned "**o** of everything."

ONE-THIRD (8) [THREE]

Nu 15: 6 of an ephah of choice flour mixed with **o** of a hin
15: 7 a drink offering you shall offer **o** of a hin of wine,
28:14 **o** of a hin for a ram,
1Sa 13:21 and **o** of a shekel for sharpening the axes and
2Ki 11: 5 **o** of you, those who go off duty on the sabbath
Ne 10:32 the obligation to charge ourselves yearly **o** of
Eze 46:14 and **o** of a hin of oil to moisten the choice flour,
Zec 13: 8 and **o** shall be left alive.

ONES‡ (158) [ONE]

A. HOLY ONES (28)

Ge 34:29 All their wealth, all their little **o** and their wives,
41:19 Never had I seen such ugly **o** in all the land
43: 8 you and we and also our little **o**.
45:19 of Egypt for your little **o** and for your wives,
46: 5 their little **o**, and their wives,
47:24 and as food for your little **o**.
50:21 I myself will provide for you and your little **o**."
Ex 10: 8 But which **o** are to go?"
10:10 if ever I let your little **o** go with you!
34: 1 "Cut two tablets of stone like the former **o**,
34: 4 Moses cut two tablets of stone like the former **o**;
Nu 1:16 These were the **o** chosen from the congregation,
14: 3 Our wives and our little **o** will become booty;
14:31 your little **o**, who you said would become booty,
16:27 their children, and their little **o**.
19:19 The clean person shall sprinkle the unclean **o** on
31: 9 the women of Midian and their little **o** captive;
31:17 Now therefore, kill every male among the little **o**,
32:16 and towns for our little **o**,
32:17 Meanwhile our little **o** will stay in
32:24 Build towns for your little **o**,
32:26 Our little **o**, our wives, our flocks,
34:29 the **o** whom the LORD commanded to apportion
Dt 1:39 And as for your little **o**,
10: 1 "Carve out two tablets of stone like the former **o**,
10: 3 cut two tablets of stone like the former **o**,
14:12 But these are the **o** that you shall not eat:
32:17 to new **o** recently arrived,
33: 2 With him were myriads of holy **o**; A
33: 3 all his holy **o** were in your charge; A
Jos 1:14 your little **o**, and your livestock shall remain in
8:35 and the women, and the little **o**,
Jdg 11: 7 not the very **o** who rejected me and drove me out
11:24 And should we not be the **o** to possess everything
18:21 So they resumed their journey, putting the little **o**,
21:10 including the women and the little **o**.
1Sa 2: 9 "He will guard the feet of his faithful **o**,
2Sa 7: 9 like the name of the great **o** of the earth.
15:22 with all his men and all the little **o** who were
16:21 the **o** he has left to look after the house;
2Ki 8:12 dash in pieces their little **o**,
1Ch 16:13 children of Jacob, his chosen **o**.
16:22 "Do not touch my anointed **o**;
17: 8 like the name of the great **o** of the earth.
2Ch 20:13 with their little **o**, their wives, and their children.
Ne 4: 2 of rubbish—and burned **o** at that?"
Job 5: 1 To which of the holy **o** will you turn? A
15:15 God puts no trust even in his holy **o**, A
21:11 They send out their little **o** like a flock,
38:41 when its young **o** cry to God,
39: 4 Their young **o** become strong,
39:30 Its young **o** suck up blood;
Ps 16: 3 As for the holy **o** in the land, they are the noble, A
17:14 may they leave something over to their little **o**.
30: 4 Sing praises to the LORD, O you his faithful **o**,
34: 9 O fear the LORD, you his holy **o**, A
37:28 he will not forsake his faithful **o**.
50: 5 "Gather to me my faithful **o**,
89: 5 your faithfulness in the assembly of the holy **o**. A
89: 7 a God feared in the council of the holy **o**, A
103:20 you mighty **o** who do his bidding,
105: 6 children of Jacob, his chosen **o**.
105:15 saying, "Do not touch my anointed **o**; do my prophets no harm."
105:43 his chosen **o** with singing.
106: 5 that I may see the prosperity of your chosen **o**,
116:15 of the LORD is the death of his faithful **o**.
119:21 You rebuke the insolent, accursed **o**,
137: 9 be who take your little **o** and dash them against
149: 9 This is glory for all his faithful **o**.
Pr 1:22 O simple **o**, will you love being simple?
2: 8 justice and preserving the way of his faithful **o**.
7: 7 and I saw among the simple **o**,
8: 5 O simple **o**, learn prudence;
24: 5 Wise warriors are mightier than strong **o**,
30: 3 nor have I knowledge of the holy **o**. A
Ecc 5: 8 and there are yet higher **o** over them.
Isa 13: 3 I myself have commanded my consecrated **o**,
13: 3 my proudly exulting **o**, to execute my anger.
32:10 a year you will shudder, you complacent **o**;
32:11 shudder, you complacent **o**;
49:13 and will have compassion on his suffering **o**.
Jer 10: 7 among all the wise **o** of the nations and
48: 4 "Moab is destroyed!" her little **o** cry out.
49:20 the little **o** of the flock shall be dragged away;
50:45 the little **o** of the flock shall be dragged away;
Eze 21:29 place you over the necks of the vile, wicked **o**—
32:12 to fall by the swords of mighty **o**,
33: 8 If I say to the wicked, "O wicked **o**,
42: 6 the ground more than the lower and the middle **o**.
Da 4:17 the decision is given by order of the holy **o**, A
7:18 But the holy **o** of the Most High shall receive A
7:21 with the holy **o** and was prevailing over them, A
7:22 then judgment was given for the holy **o** of A
7:22 the holy **o** gained possession of the kingdom. A
7:24 This one shall be different from the former **o**,
7:25 shall wear out the holy **o** of the Most High, A
7:27 to the people of the holy **o** of the Most High; A
8:24 the powerful and the people of the holy **o**. A
Hos 13:16 their little **o** shall be dashed in pieces,
Zep 3:10 my scattered **o**, shall bring my offering.
3:11 from your midst your proudly exultant **o**,
Zec 4:14 the two anointed **o** who stand by the Lord of
6: 6 the white **o** go toward the west country,
6: 6 and the dappled **o** go toward the south country."
11:16 but devours the flesh of the fat **o**,
13: 7 I will turn my hand against the little **o**.
14: 5 and all the holy **o** with him. A
Mt 10:42 of cold water to one of these little **o** in the name
18: 6 before one of these little **o** who believe in me,
18:10 that you do not despise one of these little **o**;
18:14 in heaven that one of these little **o** should be lost.
19:18 He said to him, "Which **o**?"
20:25 and their great **o** are tyrants over them.
Mk 4:15 the **o** on the path where the word is sown:
4:16 And these are the **o** sown on rocky ground:
4:18 these are the **o** who hear the word,
4:20 And these are the **o** sown on the good soil:
9:42 before one of these little **o** who believe in me,
10:42 and their great **o** are tyrants over them.
Lk 8:12 The **o** on the path are those who have heard;
8:13 The **o** on the rock are those who,
8:14 these are the **o** who hear;
8:15 as for that in the good soil, these are the **o** who,
12:18 I will pull down my barns and build larger **o**,
17: 2 the sea than for you to cause one of these little **o**
18: 7 to his chosen **o** who cry to him day and night?
Jn 6:64 from the first who were the **o** that did not believe,
Ac 7:53 the **o** that received the law as ordained by angels,
1Co 14:36 Or are you the only **o** it has reached?)
2Co 12:11 the **o** commending me, for I am not at all inferior
Col 3:12 As God's chosen **o**, holy and beloved,
4:11 These are the only **o** of the circumcision
2Pe 2:10 they are not afraid to slander the glorious **o**,
Jude 1: 8 reject authority, and slander the glorious **o**.
1:14 Lord is coming with ten thousands of his holy **o**, A
Tob 8:15 let all your chosen **o** bless you.
Jdt 7:27 not witness our little **o** dying before our eyes,
Wis 3: 9 because grace and mercy are upon his holy **o**, A
4:15 and that he watches over his holy **o**. A
18: 1 But for your holy **o** there was very great light. A
18: 2 and were thankful that your holy **o**, A
18: 5 your holy **o**, and one child had been abandoned A
Sir 9:10 for new **o** cannot equal them.
42:17 The Lord has not empowered even his holy **o** A
45: 2 He made him equal in glory to the holy **o**, A
51:12 *praise for all his loyal **o**.*
1Mc 7:17 "The flesh of your faithful **o**
1Es 8:39 Of the descendants of Adonikam, the last **o**,
3Mc 2: 2 holy among the holy **o**, the only ruler, almighty, A
2:21 the first Father of all, holy among the holy **o**, A
2Es 7:18 while hoping for easier **o**;
7:18 and will never see the easier **o**."
8:57 they have even trampled on his righteous **o**,
10:22 our little **o** have been cast out,
11:18 and held the rule as the earlier **o** had done,
16:74 Listen, my elect **o**, says the Lord;
4Mc 14:15 the **o** that are tame protect their young by building
17:22 the blood of those devout **o** and their death as

ONESELF (9) [ONE]

Pr 19: 8 To get wisdom is to love **o;**
22:16 Oppressing the poor in order to enrich **o,**
Isa 28:20 For the bed is too short to stretch **o** on it,
28:20 and the covering too narrow to wrap **o** in it.
47:14 No coal for warming **o** is this, no fire to sit before!
58: 5 Is such the fast that I choose, a day to humble **o?**
Mk 12:33 and 'to love one's neighbor as **o,'—**
Jas 1:27 and to keep **o** unstained by the world.
Sir 19: 4 and one who sins does wrong to **o.**

ONESIMUS (2)

Col 4: 9 he is coming with **O,** the faithful and beloved
Phm 1:10 I am appealing to you for my child, **O,**

ONESIPHORUS (2)

2Ti 1:16 May the Lord grant mercy to the household of **O,**
4:19 Greet Prisca and Aquila, and the household of **O.**

ONIAS (24) [ONIAS'S]

Sir 50: 1 Simon son of **O,** who in his life repaired the house,
1Mc 12: 7 in time past a letter was sent to the high priest **O**
12: 8 **O** welcomed the envoy with honor,
12:19 This is a copy of the letter that they sent to **O:**
12:20 to the high priest **O,** greetings.
2Mc 3: 1 of the high priest **O** and his hatred of wickedness,
3: 5 Since he could not prevail over **O,**
3:31 of Heliodorus's friends quickly begged **O** to call
3:33 "Be very grateful to the high priest **O,**
3:35 and having bidden **O** farewell,
4: 1 the money against his own country, slandered **O,**
4: 4 **O** recognized that the rivalry was serious and
4: 7 of **O** obtained the high priesthood by corruption,
4:33 When **O** became fully aware of these acts,
4:34 taking Andronicus aside, urged him to kill **O.**
4:34 Andronicus came to **O,** and resorting to treachery,
4:36 with regard to the unreasonable murder of **O,**
4:38 where he had committed the outrage against **O,**
15:12 **O,** who had been high priest,
15:14 And **O** spoke, saying, "This is a man who loves
4Mc 4: 1 a political opponent of the noble and good man, **O,**
4: 1 of slander he was unable to injure **O** in the eyes of
4:13 Moved by these words, the high priest **O,**
4:16 who removed **O** from the priesthood

ONIAS'S (1) [ONIAS]

4Mc 4:16 from the priesthood and appointed **O** brother Jason

ONIONS (1)

Nu 11: 5 the cucumbers, the melons, the leeks, the **o,**

ONLY‡ (516)

A. ONLY SON (12)
B. ONLY CHILD (5)

Ge 6: 5 the thoughts of their hearts was **o** evil continually.
7:23 **O** Noah was left, and those that were with him in
9: 4 **O,** you shall not eat flesh with its life, that is,
11: 6 and this is **o** the beginning of what they will do;
19: 8 **o** do nothing to these men,
22: 2 He said, "Take your son, your **o** son Isaac, A
22:12 you have not withheld your son, your **o** son, A
22:16 and have not withheld your son, your **o** son, A
23:13 "If you **o** will listen to me!
24: 8 **o** you must not take my son back there."
24:42 you will **o** make successful the way I am going!
27:13 **o** obey my word, and go, get them for me."
27:38 Esau said to his father, "Have you **o** one blessing,
32:10 for with **o** my staff I crossed this Jordan;
34:12 **o** give me the girl to be my wife."
34:15 **O** on this condition will we consent to you:
34:22 **O** on this condition will they agree to live
34:23 **O** let us agree with them,
38:17 And she said, **"O** if you give me a pledge,
41:40 **o** with regard to the throne will I
44: 4 they had gone **o** a short distance from the city,
44:17 **O** the one in whose possession
44:26 **O** if our youngest brother goes with us,
47:22 **O** the land of the priests he did not buy;
50: 8 **O** their children, their flocks,
Ex 8: 9 and your houses and be left **o** in the Nile."
8:11 they shall be left **o** in the Nile."
8:29 **o** do not let Pharaoh again deal falsely by
9:26 **O** in the land of Goshen, where the Israelites were,
10:24 **O** your flocks and your herds shall remain behind.
12:16 **o** what everyone must eat,
14:14 and you have **o** to keep still."
16: 3 "If **o** we had died by the hand of the LORD in
20:20 for God has come **o** to test you and to put the fear
20:24 You need make for me **o** an altar of earth
22:15 if it was hired, **o** the hiring fee is due.
22:27 for it may be your neighbor's **o** clothing to use
32:32 But now, if you will **o** forgive their sin—
Lev 13: 6 shall pronounce him clean; it is **o** an eruption;
21:13 He shall marry **o** a woman who is a virgin.
25:12 you shall eat **o** what the field itself produces.
25:15 you shall pay **o** for the number of years since
25:15 the seller shall charge you **o** for
Nu 1:49 **O** the tribe of Levi you shall not enroll,
10: 4 But if **o** one is blown, then the leaders,
11: 4 and said, "If **o** we had meat to eat!
11:18 saying, 'If **o** we had meat to eat!
11:19 You shall eat not **o** one day, or two days,
Nu 12: 2 "Has the LORD spoken **o** through Moses?
14: 9 **O,** do not rebel against the LORD;
20:19 It is **o** a small matter;
22:20 but do **o** what I tell you to do."
22:35 but speak **o** what I tell you to speak."
23:13 you shall see **o** part of them,
36: 6 **o** it must be into a clan of their father's tribe
Dt 2:27 I will travel **o** along the road;
2:28 **O** allow me to pass through on foot—
2:35 **O** the livestock we kept as spoil for ourselves,
3:11 (Now **o** King Og of Bashan was left of
3:19 **O** your wives, your children, and your livestock—
3:24 "O Lord GOD, you have **o** begun
4:12 but saw no form; there was **o** a voice.
4:27 **o** a few of you will be left among the nations
5:29 If **o** they had such a mind as this,
10:12 **O** to fear the LORD your God,
11:13 If you will **o** heed his every commandment
12:14 But **o** at the place that the LORD will choose
12:23 **O** be sure that you do not eat the blood;
15: 5 if **o** you will obey the LORD your God
16: 6 **o** there shall you offer the passover sacrifice,
16:20 Justice, and **o** justice, you shall pursue,
17: 6 be put to death on the evidence of **o** one witness.
19:15 **O** on the evidence of two or three witnesses shall
20:20 You may destroy **o** the trees that you know do
22: 7 Let the mother go, taking **o** the young for yourself,
22:25 then **o** the man who lay with her shall die.
24:16 **o** for their own crimes may persons be put
25:15 You shall have **o** a full and honest weight;
25:15 you shall have **o** a full and honest measure,
28: 1 If you will **o** obey the LORD your God,
28:13 you shall be **o** at the top, and not at the bottom—
28:24 and **o** dust shall come down upon you from
28:67 the morning you shall say, "If **o** it were evening!"
28:67 evening you shall say, "If **o** it were morning!"—
29:14 not **o** with you who stand here with us today
Jos 1: 7 **O** be strong and very courageous,
1:17 **O** may the LORD your God be with you,
1:18 **O** be strong and courageous."
2: 3 they have come **o** to search out the whole land."
6:15 It was **o** on that day that they marched around
6:17 **O** Rahab the prostitute and all who are with her
6:24 **o** the silver and gold, and the vessels of bronze
8: 2 **o** its spoil and its livestock you may take as booty
8:27 **O** the livestock and the spoil of
11:22 some remained **o** in Gaza, in Gath, and in Ashdod.
13: 6 **o** allot the land to Israel for an inheritance,
14: 4 to the Levites in the land, but **o** towns to live in,
17: 3 of Manasseh had no sons, but **o** daughters;
17:17 you shall not have one lot **o,**
22:19 **o** do not rebel against the LORD,
Jdg 3: 2 (it was **o** that successive generations
6:39 let it be dry **o** on the fleece,
6:40 It was dry on the fleece **o,**
7: 2 Israel would **o** take the credit away from me,
9:29 If **o** this people were under my command!
11:34 She was his **o** child; B
15:13 we will **o** bind you and give you into their hands;
16: 3 But Samson lay **o** until midnight.
16:28 remember me and strengthen me **o** this once,
19:20 **o** do not spend the night in the square."
1Sa 1:11 if **o** you will look on the misery of your servant,
1:13 **o** her lips moved, but her voice was not heard;
1:23 **o—**may the LORD establish his word."
2:15 not accept boiled meat from you, but **o** raw."
2:33 The **o** one of you whom I shall not cut off
5: 4 **o** the trunk of Dagon was left to him.
7: 3 Direct your heart to the LORD, and serve him **o,**
7: 4 and they served the LORD **o.**
8: 9 Now then, listen to their voice; **o—**you shall
9:21 Saul answered, "I am **o** a Benjaminite,
12:24 **O** fear the LORD, and serve him faithfully
17:29 It was **o** a question."
17:42 he disdained him, for he was **o** a youth,
18:17 **o** be valiant for me and fight
20:39 **o** Jonathan and David knew the arrangement.
21: 4 "I have no ordinary bread at hand, **o** holy bread—
2Sa 15: 4 "If **o** I were judge in the land!
15:20 You came **o** yesterday,
17: 2 I will strike down **o** the king,
17: 3 You seek the life of **o** one man,
23:10 people came back to him—but **o** to strip the dead.
1Ki 2:22 not **o** for him but also for the priest Abiathar and
3: 3 **o,** he sacrificed and offered incense at
3: 7 although I am **o** a little child;
3:18 **o** the two of us were in the house.
8:25 if **o** your children look to their way,
8:39 for **o** you know what is in every human heart—
14: 8 doing **o** that which was right in my sight,
17:12 I have nothing baked, **o** a handful of meal in a jar,
18:22 Then Elijah said to the people, "I, even I **o,**
22: 8 anything favorable about me, but **o** disaster."
22:18 anything favorable about me, but **o** disaster?"
22:31 but **o** with the king of Israel."
2Ki 3:10 three kings, **o** to be handed over to Moab."
3:13 three kings, **o** to be handed over to Moab."
3:18 This is **o** a trifle in the sight of the LORD,
3:25 **O** at Kir-hareseth did the stone walls remain,
5: 3 "If **o** my lord were with the prophet who is
10:23 but **o** worshipers of Baal."
13:19 now you will strike down Aram **o** three times."
21: 8 if **o** they will be careful to do according to all
1Ch 2:34 Now Sheshan had no sons, **o** daughters;
22:12 **O,** may the LORD grant you discretion
23:22 Eleazar died having no sons, but **o** daughters;
2Ch 6:16 if **o** your children keep to their way,
2Ch 6:30 for **o** you know the human heart.
18: 7 anything favorable about me, but **o** disaster."
18:17 anything favorable about me, but **o** disaster?"
18:30 but **o** with the king of Israel."
27: 2 **o** he did not invade the temple of the LORD.
30:11 **O** a few from Asher, Manasseh,
33: 8 if **o** they will be careful to do all
33:17 but **o** to the LORD their God.
Ezr 10:15 **O** Jonathan son of Asahel and Jahzeiah son
Ne 2: 2 This can **o** be sadness of the heart."
2:12 The **o** animal I took was the animal I rode.
Est 1:16 "Not **o** has Queen Vashti done wrong to the king,
4:11 **O** if the king holds out the golden scepter
Job 1:12 **o** do not stretch out your hand against him!"
2: 6 in your power; **o** spare his life."
13: 5 If you would **o** keep silent,
13:20 **O** grant two things to me, then I will
14:22 They feel **o** the pain of their own bodies,
14:22 and mourn **o** for themselves."
23:17 If **o** I could vanish in darkness,
40:19 **o** its Maker can approach it with the sword.
Ps 9:20 let the nations know that they are **o** human.
37: 8 Do not fret—it leads **o** to evil.
38:16 For I pray, **"O** do not let them rejoice over me,
62: 4 Their **o** plan is to bring down a person
76:10 Human wrath serves **o** to praise you,
90:10 even then their span is **o** toil and trouble;
91: 8 You will **o** look with your eyes and see
Pr 6:26 for a prostitute's fee is **o** a loaf of bread,
6:30 not despised who steal **o** to satisfy their appetite
9: 8 A scoffer who is rebuked will **o** hate you;
11:23 The desire of the righteous ends **o** in good;
11:24 others withhold what is due, and **o** suffer want.
12:19 but a lying tongue lasts **o** a moment.
14:23 but mere talk leads **o** to poverty.
17:11 Evil people seek **o** rebellion,
18: 2 but **o** in expressing personal opinion.
19:19 you effect a rescue, you will **o** have to do it again.
20:25 and begin to reflect **o** after making a vow.
21: 5 but everyone who is hasty comes **o** to want.
22:16 and giving to the rich, will lead **o** to loss.
23: 9 who will **o** despise the wisdom of your words.
25:16 If you have found honey, eat **o** enough for you,
26:19 a neighbor and says, "I am **o** joking!"
Ecc 2:12 **O** what has already been done.
2:26 **o** to give to one who pleases God.
SS 6: 9 My dove, my perfect one, is the **o** one,
Isa 2:22 who have **o** breath in their nostrils,
5:30 to the land—**o** darkness and distress;
8:22 but will see **o** distress and darkness,
10:22 **o** a remnant of them will return.
26:18 we writhed, but we gave birth **o** to wind.
45:24 **O** in the LORD, it shall be said of me,
58: 4 you fast **o** to quarrel and to fight and to strike with
Jer 1: 6 for I am **o** a boy."
1: 7 LORD said to me, "Do not say, 'I am **o** a boy';
3:10 but **o** in pretense, says the LORD.
3:13 **O** acknowledge your guilt,
5: 4 I said, "These are **o** the poor, they have no sense;
6:26 make mourning as for an **o** child, B
7:10 **o** to go on doing all these abominations?
7:23 and walk **o** in the way that I command you,
9:25 to all those who are circumcised **o** in the foreskin:
22:17 your eyes and heart are **o** on your dishonest gain,
26:15 **O** know for certain that if you put me to death,
28:13 You have broken wooden bars **o** to forge iron bars
29:10 **O** when Babylon's seventy years are completed
33:21 **o** then could my covenant with my servant David
33:25 **O** if I had not established my covenant with day
34: 7 the **o** fortified cities of Judah that remained.
37:10 and there remained of them **o** wounded men
38: 6 Now there was no water in the cistern, but **o** mud,
38:17 If you will **o** surrender to the officials of the king
42: 2 For there are **o** a few of us left out of many,
42:10 If you will **o** remain in this land,
49: 9 even they would pillage **o** what they wanted.
51:58 and the nations weary themselves **o** for fire.
Eze 14:14 they would save **o** their own lives
14:20 they would save **o** their own lives
16:47 You not **o** followed their ways,
18: 4 it is **o** the person who sins that shall die.
33:24 "Abraham was **o** one man,
43: 8 with **o** a wall between me and them,
44: 3 **O** the prince, because he is a prince,
44:20 they shall **o** trim the hair of their heads.
44:22 but **o** a virgin of the stock of the house of Israel,
46:17 **o** his sons may keep a gift from his inheritance.
Da 11:24 against strongholds, but **o** for a time.
Hos 9: 4 for their bread shall be for their hunger **o;**
Am 3: 2 You **o** have I known of all the families of
8:10 I will make it like the mourning for an **o** son, A
Ob 1: 5 would they not steal **o** what they wanted?
Hab 2:13 not from the LORD of hosts that peoples labor **o**
2:18 though the product is **o** an idol that cannot speak!
Zec 1:15 for while I was **o** a little angry,
7: 6 do you not eat and drink **o** for yourselves?
12:10 as one mourns for an **o** child, B
Mal 3:15 evildoers not **o** prosper, but when they put God to
Mt 4:10 'Worship the Lord your God, and serve **o** him.' "
5:47 And if you greet **o** your brothers and sisters,
7:21 but **o** the one who does the will of my Father
8: 8 **o** speak the word, and my servant will be healed.
9:21 "If I **o** touch his cloak, I will be made well."
12: 4 not lawful for him or his companions to eat, but **o**
12:11 "Suppose one of you has **o** one sheep and it falls
12:24 Pharisees heard it, they said, "It is **o** by Beelzebul,
13:21 but endures **o** for a while,

Mt 15:24 "I was sent **o** to the lost sheep of the house
19:11 but **o** those to whom it is given.
19:17 There is **o** one who is good.
20:12 'These last worked **o** one hour,
21:21 **o** will you do what has been done to the fig tree,
24:36 nor the Son, but **o** the Father.
Mk 4:17 But they have no root, and endure **o** for a while;
5:36 of the synagogue, "Do not fear, **o** believe."
8:14 and they had **o** one loaf with them in the boat.
9:8 they saw no one with them any more, but **o** Jesus.
9:29 "This kind can come out **o** through prayer."
13:32 nor the Son, but **o** the Father.
Lk 4:8 'Worship the Lord your God, and serve **o** him.' "
7:7 **o** speak the word, and let my servant be healed.
7:12 was his mother's **o** son, and she was a widow; A
8:13 they believe **o** for a while and in a time
8:42 for he had an **o** daughter,
8:50 **O** believe, and she will be saved."
9:18 with **o** the disciples near him, he asked them,
9:38 to look at my son; he is my **o** child. B
10:42 there is need of **o** one thing.
13:23 "Lord, will **o** a few be saved?"
17:10 we have done **o** what we ought to have done!' "
19:42 had **o** recognized on this day the things that make
24:18 the **o** stranger in Jerusalem who does not know
Jn 1:14 the glory as of a father's **o** son, A
1:18 It is God the **o** Son, who is close to A
3:16 God so loved the world that he gave his **o** Son, A
3:18 not believed in the name of the **o** Son of God. A
5:18 because he was not **o** breaking the sabbath,
5:19 but **o** what he sees the Father doing;
6:22 the sea saw that there had been **o** one boat there.
10:10 The thief comes **o** to steal and kill and destroy.
10:33 because you, though **o** a human being,
11:52 and not for the nation **o**,
12:9 not **o** because of Jesus but also to see Lazarus,
13:9 not my feet **o** but also my hands and my head!"
13:33 Little children, I am with you **o** a little longer.
17:3 that they may know you, the **o** true God,
17:20 "I ask not **o** on behalf of these,
21:8 **o** about a hundred yards off.
Ac 2:15 for it is **o** nine o'clock in the morning.
5:2 brought **o** a part and laid it at the apostles' feet.
8:16 they had **o** been baptized in the name of
10:26 "Stand up; I am **o** a mortal."
15:20 to them to abstain **o** from things polluted by idols
18:25 though he knew **o** the baptism of John.
19:26 You also see and hear that not **o** in Ephesus but
19:27 And there is danger not **o** that this trade
20:24 if **o** I may finish my course and the ministry
21:13 not **o** to be bound but even to die in Jerusalem for
26:10 I not **o** locked up many of the saints in prison,
26:29 to God that not **o** you but also all who are listening
27:10 not **o** of the cargo and the ship,
27:22 for there will be no loss of life among you, but **o**
Ro 1:32 yet they not **o** do them but
3:29 Or is God the God of Jews **o**?
4:9 then, pronounced **o** on the circumcised,
4:12 of the circumcised who are not **o** circumcised
4:16 not **o** to the adherents of the law but also
5:3 And not **o** that, but we also boast in our sufferings,
7:1 on a person **o** during that person's lifetime?
8:23 and not **o** the creation, but we ourselves, who have
9:24 not from the Jews **o** but also from the Gentiles?
9:27 **o** a remnant of them will be saved;
11:20 but you stand **o** through faith.
13:5 **o** because of wrath but also because of conscience.
14:2 while the weak eat **o** vegetables.
16:4 to whom not **o** I give thanks,
16:27 to the **o** wise God, through Jesus Christ, to whom be
1Co 3:7 but **o** God who gives the growth.
3:15 the builder will be saved, but **o** as through fire.
7:39 to marry anyone she wishes, **o** in the Lord.
9:6 Or is it **o** Barnabas and I who have no right
9:24 but **o** one receives the prize?
11:19 for **o** so will it become clear who
11:28 and **o** then eat of the bread and drink of the cup.
13:9 we know **o** in part, and we prophesy **o** in part;
13:12 Now I know **o** in part;
14:27 let there be **o** two or at most three,
14:36 Or are you the **o** ones it has reached?)
15:19 If for this life **o** we have hoped in Christ,
2Co 3:14 since **o** in Christ is it set aside.
6:12 in our affections, but **o** in yours.
7:7 and not **o** by his coming,
7:8 with that letter, though **o** briefly).
8:10 for you who began last year not **o** to do something
8:17 For he not **o** accepted our appeal,
8:19 and not **o** that, but he has also been appointed by
8:21 to do what is right not **o** in the Lord's sight but
9:12 for the rendering of this ministry not **o** supplies
13:8 For we cannot do anything against the truth, but **o**
Gal 1:23 they **o** heard it said, "The one who formerly was
2:2 before them (though **o** in a private meeting with
2:10 They asked **o** one thing, that we remember
3:2 The **o** thing I want to learn from you is this:
4:18 and not **o** when I am present with you.
5:6 **o** thing that counts is faith working through love.
5:13 **o** do not use your freedom as an opportunity
6:12 **o** that they may not be persecuted for the cross
Eph 1:21 not **o** in this age but also in the age to come.
4:29 but **o** what is useful for building up,
6:6 not **o** while being watched,
Php 1:27 **O**, live your life in a manner worthy of the gospel
1:29 the privilege not **o** of believing in Christ,
2:12 not **o** in my presence, but much more now
2:27 and not **o** on him but on me also,
Php 3:16 **O** let us hold fast to what we have attained.
Col 2:17 These are **o** a shadow of what is to come,
3:22 not **o** while being watched and in order
4:11 These are the **o** ones of the circumcision
1Th 1:5 in word **o**, but also in power and in the Holy Spirit
1:8 of the Lord has sounded forth from you not **o**
2:8 not **o** the gospel of God but also our own selves,
2Th 2:7 **o** until the one who now restrains it is removed.
1Ti 1:17 the **o** God, be honor and glory forever and ever.
3:2 a bishop must be above reproach, married **o** once,
3:12 Let deacons be married **o** once,
5:9 and has been married **o** once;
5:23 No longer drink **o** water, but take a little wine for
6:15 he who is the blessed and **o** Sovereign,
2Ti 2:14 but **o** ruins those who are listening.
2:20 not **o** of gold and silver but also of wood and clay,
4:8 and not **o** to me but also to all who have longed
4:11 **O** Luke is with me.
Tit 1:6 married **o** once, whose children are believers,
Heb 3:14 if **o** we hold our first confidence firm to the end.
5:4 but takes it **o** when called by God,
9:7 but **o** the high priest goes into the second,
9:10 deal **o** with food and drink and various baptisms,
9:17 For a will takes effect **o** at death,
10:1 the law has **o** a shadow of the good things to come
11:17 the promises was ready to offer up his **o** son, A
12:26 "Yet once more I will shake not **o** the earth but
1Pe 2:18 not **o** those who are kind and gentle but
2Pe 2:22 and, "The sow is washed **o** to wallow in the mud."
1Jn 2:2 for ours **o** but also for the sins of the whole world.
4:9 God sent his **o** Son into the world so A
5:6 with the water **o** but with the water and the blood.
2Jn 1:1 and not **o** I but also all who know the truth,
Jude 1:4 into licentiousness and deny our **o** Master
1:25 to the **o** God our Savior,
Rev 2:25 **o** hold fast to what you have until I come.
9:4 but **o** those people who do not have the seal
17:10 when he comes, he must remain **o** a little while.
21:27 but **o** those who are written in the Lamb's book
Tob 3:10 'You had **o** one beloved daughter
3:15 I am my father's **o** child; he has no other child B
6:12 and no daughter except Sarah **o**,
6:15 So now, since I am the **o** son my father has, A
8:17 because you had compassion on two **o** children.
Jdt 1:11 but regarded him as **o** one man.
2:4 the chief general of his army, second **o** to himself,
4:3 For they had **o** recently returned from exile,
4:7 wide enough for **o** two at a time to pass.
8:34 **O**, do not try to find out what I am doing;
11:7 Not **o** do human beings serve him because of you,
11:23 You are not **o** beautiful in appearance,
12:10 a banquet for his personal attendants **o**,
14:2 against the Assyrian outpost; **o** do not go down.
AdE 1:16 not **o** the king but also all the king's governors
4:11 **O** the one to whom the king stretches out
14:3 "O my Lord, you **o** are our king;
15:10 for our law applies **o** to our subjects.
16:3 and not **o** seek to injure our subjects,
16:4 They not **o** take away thankfulness from others,
16:24 be made not **o** impassable for human beings,
Wis 10:8 not **o** were hindered from recognizing the good,
11:19 not **o** could the harm they did destroy people,
13:16 for it is **o** an image and has need of help.
19:15 not **o** so—but, while punishment of some
Sir Pr:1 not **o** themselves understand them,
Pr:2 Not **o** this book, but even the Law itself,
13:24 poverty is evil **o** in the opinion of the ungodly.
16:11 Even if there were **o** one stiff-necked person,
20:13 wise make themselves beloved by **o** few words,
32:7 but no more than twice, and **o** if asked.
37:1 but some friends are friends **o** in name.
38:24 the one who has little business can become wise.
41:9 you will beget them **o** for groaning.
45:13 but **o** his sons and his descendants in perpetuity.
45:25 that the king's heritage passes **o** from son to son,
LtJ 6:47 They have left **o** lies and reproach
Sus 1:15 she went in as before with **o** two maids,
Bel 1:7 for this thing is **o** clay inside and bronze outside,
1Mc 6:54 **O** a few men were left in the sanctuary;
9:55 But he **o** began to tear it down,
9:65 and he went with **o** a few men.
10:14 **O** in Beth-zur did some remain who had forsaken
10:70 "You are the **o** one to rise up against us,
11:42 **o** will I do these things for you and your nation,
15:10 so that there were **o** a few with Trypho.
15:33 but **o** the inheritance of our ancestors,
2Mc 1:20 that they had not found fire but **o** a thick liquid,
2:29 and decoration has to consider **o** what is suitable
4:35 For this reason not **o** Jews,
5:7 in the end he got **o** disgrace from his conspiracy,
6:31 **o** to the young but to the great body of his nation.
7:24 Antiochus not **o** appealed to him in words,
9:8 Thus he who **o** a little while before had thought
10:28 and victory not **o** their valor but also their reliance
11:9 to assail not **o** humans but the wildest animals
1Es 2:19 they will not **o** refuse to pay tribute but will
4:7 And yet he is **o** one man!
3Mc 1:11 **o** the high priest who was pre-eminent over all—
1:11 and he **o** once a year—
1:29 that not **o** the people but also the walls and
2:2 holy among the holy ones, the **o** ruler, almighty,
3:1 not **o** was he enraged against those Jews who lived
3:19 they become the **o** people
3:23 not **o** spurn the priceless citizenship,
5:50 Not **o** this, but when they considered the help
2Es 4:9 But now I have asked you **o** about fire and wind
4:21 the earth can understand **o** what is on the earth,
2Es 5:28 and scattered your **o** one among the many?
5:47 "Of course it cannot, but **o** each in its own time."
6:58 whom you have called your firstborn, **o** begotten,
7:8 There is **o** one path lying between them, that is,
7:8 so that **o** one person can walk on the path.
7:*34* **O** judgment shall remain, truth shall stand,
7:*42* but **o** the splendor of the glory of the Most High,
7:*54* And he said to me, "Not **o** that,
7:*140* [70] left **o** very few of the innumerable multitude."
8:1 but the world to come for the sake of **o** a few.
8:2 but **o** a little dust from which gold comes,
8:3 but **o** a few shall be saved."
8:5 for you have been given **o** a short time to live.
8:62 but **o** to you and a few like you."
9:24 and eat **o** of the flowers of the field,
9:24 and drink no wine, but eat **o** flowers,
10:34 I said, "Speak, my lord; **o** do not forsake me,
12:51 and I ate **o** of the flowers of the field,
13:10 but I saw **o** how he sent forth
13:11 the innumerable multitude but **o** the dust of ashes
16:47 do so **o** to have it plundered;
4Mc 2:4 Not **o** is reason proved to rule over
4:20 so that not **o** was a gymnasium constructed at
5:24 proper reverence we worship the **o** living God.
5:27 It would be tyrannical for you to compel us not **o**
6:35 not **o** that reason has mastered agonies,
7:6 which had room **o** for reverence and purity,
7:23 For **o** the wise and courageous are masters
8:5 Not **o** do I advise you not to display
8:15 not **o** were they not afraid,
9:10 the tyrant was not **o** indignant,
14:1 so that they not **o** despised their agonies,
14:9 they not **o** saw what was happening,
14:9 not **o** heard the direct word of threat,
15:9 Not **o** so, but also because of the nobility
16:2 not **o** that men have ruled over the emotions,
17:20 are honored, not **o** with this honor,
18:2 not **o** of sufferings from within,
18:3 for the sake of religion were not **o** admired

ONO (6)

1Ch 8:12 and Shemed, who built **O** and Lod with its towns,
Ezr 2:33 Of Lod, Hadid, and **O**, seven hundred twenty-five.
Ne 6:2 in one of the villages in the plain of **O**."
7:37 Of Lod, Hadid, and **O**, seven hundred twenty-one.
11:35 Lod, and **O**, the valley of artisans.
1Es 5:22 The descendants of the other Calamolalus and **O**,

ONRUSH (1) [RUSH]

2Es 13:9 When he saw the **o** of the approaching multitude,

ONRUSHING (3) [RUSH]

Jdg 5:21 torrent Kishon swept them away, the **o** torrent,
2Es 13:11 fell on the **o** multitude that was prepared to fight,
13:28 the **o** multitude that came to conquer him, this is

ONSLAUGHT (1)

2Mc 6:3 Harsh and utterly grievous was the **o** of evil.

ONTO (5)

Ge 49:4 because you went up **o** your father's bed;
49:4 you went up **o** my couch!
Nu 22:23 to turn it back **o** the road.
Ne 12:31 Then I brought the leaders of Judah up **o** the wall,
Eze 41:11 The side chambers opened **o** the area left free,

ONWARD (6)

Ex 33:6 of their ornaments, from Mount Horeb **o**.
2Ch 32:23 in the sight of all nations from that time **o**.
Ne 11:31 The people of Benjamin also lived from Geba **o**,
Isa 9:7 and with righteousness from this time **o**
Eze 43:27 from the eighth day **o** the priests shall offer upon
Sus 1:64 And from that day **o** Daniel had a great reputation

ONWARD (KJV) See also SET OUT

ONYCHA (2)

Ex 30:34 Take sweet spices, stacte, and **o**, and galbanum,
Sir 24:15 like galbanum, **o**, and stacte,

ONYX (12)

Ge 2:12 bdellium and **o** stone are there.
Ex 25:7 **o** stones and gems to be set in the ephod and for
28:9 You shall take two **o** stones,
28:20 and the fourth row a beryl, an **o**, and a jasper;
35:9 and **o** stones and gems to be set in the ephod and
35:27 the leaders brought **o** stones and gems to be set in
39:6 The **o** stones were prepared,
39:13 a beryl, an **o**, and a jasper;
1Ch 29:2 besides great quantities of **o** and stones for setting,
Job 28:16 in the gold of Ophir, in precious **o** or sapphire.
Eze 28:13 chrysolite, and moonstone, beryl, **o**, and jasper,
Rev 21:20 the fifth **o**, the sixth carnelian,

OPEN‡ (224) [OPENED, OPENING, OPENINGS, OPENLY, OPENS]

Ge 34:10 and the land shall be **o** to you;
Ex 9:19 and everything that you have in the **o** field brought
9:19 the **o** field and is not brought under shelter will die
9:21 and livestock in the **o** field.
9:25 in the **o** field throughout all the land of Egypt,
13:2 the first to **o** the womb among the Israelites,

Ex 21:33 If someone leaves a pit **o**,
Lev 1:17 He shall tear it **o** by its wings without severing it.
14: 7 and he shall let the living bird go into the **o** field.
14:53 the living bird go out of the city into the **o** field;
17: 5 that they offer in the **o** field,
25:31 around them shall be classed as **o** country;
25:34 But the **o** land around their cities may not be sold;
Nu 3:12 the firstborn that **o** the womb among the Israelites.
8:16 in place of all that **o** the womb,
19:15 And every **o** vessel with no cover fastened
19:16 in the **o** field touches one who has been killed by
Dt 15: 8 You should rather **o** your hand,
15:11 **"O** your hand to the poor and needy neighbor
21: 1 a body is found lying in **o** country,
22:25 man meets the engaged woman in the **o** country,
22:27 Since he found her in the **o** country,
28:12 The LORD will **o** for you his rich storehouse,
Jos 8:17 they left the city **o**, and pursued Israel.
8:24 in the **o** wilderness where they pursued them,
10:22 Then Joshua said, **"O** the mouth of the cave,
Jdg 3:25 he still did not **o** the doors of the roof chamber,
15:19 So God split **o** the hollow place that is at Lehi,
19:15 He went in and sat down in the **o** square of
19:17 and saw the wayfarer in the **o** square of the city,
20:31 as well as in the **o** country,
1Sa 30:11 In the **o** country they found an Egyptian,
2Sa 10: 8 were by themselves in the **o** country.
11:11 the servants of my lord are camping in the **o** field;
1Ki 6:18 the house had carvings of gourds and **o** flowers;
6:29 and **o** flowers, in the inner and outer rooms.
6:32 palm trees, and **o** flowers;
6:35 He carved cherubim, palm trees, and **o** flowers,
8:29 that your eyes may be **o** night and day
8:52 Let your eyes be **o** to the plea of your servant,
11:29 The two of them were alone in the **o** country
14:11 and anyone who dies in the **o** country,
21:24 in the **o** country the birds of the air shall eat."
2Ki 6:17 "O LORD, please **o** his eyes that he may see."
6:20 **o** the eyes of these men so that they may see."
7:12 the camp to hide themselves in the **o** country,
9: 3 Then **o** the door and flee; do not linger."
13:17 Then he said, **"O** the window eastward";
15:16 because they did not **o** it to him, he sacked it.
15:16 He ripped **o** all the pregnant women in it.
19:16 **o** your eyes, O LORD, and see;
1Ch 19: 9 by themselves in the **o** country.
2Ch 6:20 be **o** day and night toward this house,
6:40 let your eyes be **o** and your ears attentive to prayer
7:15 Now my eyes will be **o** and my ears attentive to
Ezr 10: 9 All the people sat in the **o** square before the house
10:13 we cannot stand in the **o**.
Ne 1: 6 and your eyes **o** to hear the prayer of your servant
4:13 behind the wall, in **o** places, I stationed the people
6: 5 to me with an **o** letter in his hand.
Est 4: 6 the **o** square of the city in front of the king's gate,
6: 9 the **o** square of the city, proclaiming before him:
6:11 and led him riding through the **o** square of
9:19 the Jews of the villages, who live in the **o** towns,
Job 11: 5 oh, that God would speak, and **o** his lips to you,
12:14 if he shuts someone in, no one can **o** up.
16:13 He slashes **o** my kidneys, and shows no mercy;
26: 8 and the cloud is not torn **o** by them.
27:19 they **o** their eyes, and it is gone.
28: 4 They **o** shafts in a valley away
32:20 I must **o** my lips and answer.
33: 2 I **o** my mouth; the tongue in my mouth speaks.
39: 4 they grow up in the **o**;
41:14 Who can **o** the doors of its face?
Ps 5: 9 their throats are **o** graves;
22:13 they **o** wide their mouths at me,
34:15 and his ears are **o** to their cry.
35:21 They **o** wide their mouths against me;
39: 9 I am silent; I do not **o** my mouth,
40: 6 but you have given me an **o** ear.
51:15 **o** my lips, and my mouth will declare your praise.
60: 2 to quake; you have torn it **o**;
78: 2 I will **o** my mouth in a parable;
78:15 He split rocks **o** in the wilderness,
81:10 **O** your mouth wide and I will fill it.
104:28 you **o** your hand, they are filled with good things.
118:19 **O** to me the gates of righteousness,
119:18 **O** my eyes, so that I may behold wondrous things
119:131 With **o** mouth I pant, because I long
145:16 You **o** your hand, satisfying the desire
Pr 3:20 by his knowledge the deeps broke **o**,
13: 3 those who **o** wide their lips come to ruin.
15:11 Sheol and Abaddon lie **o** before the LORD,
20:13 **o** your eyes, and you will have plenty of bread.
24: 7 in the gate they do not **o** their mouths.
27: 5 Better is **o** rebuke than hidden love.
SS 5: 2 **"O** to me, my sister, my love, my dove,
5: 5 I arose to **o** to my beloved,
Isa 9:12 and they devoured Israel with **o** mouth.
22:22 he shall **o**, and no one shall shut; he shall shut, and no one shall **o**.
26: 2 **O** the gates, so that the righteous nation
28:24 Do they continually **o** and harrow their ground?
37:17 **o** your eyes, O LORD, and see;
41:18 I will **o** rivers on the bare heights,
42: 7 to **o** the eyes that are blind,
42:20 his ears are **o**, but he does not hear.
45: 1 to **o** doors before him—and the gates shall not be
45: 8 let the earth **o**, that salvation may spring up,
48:21 he split **o** the rock and the water gushed out.
53: 7 and he was afflicted, yet he did not **o** his mouth;
53: 7 so he did not **o** his mouth.
57: 4 Against whom do you **o** your mouth wide

Isa 60:11 Your gates shall always be **o**;
64: 1 that you would tear **o** the heavens and come down,
66: 9 Shall I **o** the womb and not deliver?
Jer 5:16 Their quiver is like an **o** tomb;
9:22 like dung upon the **o** field,
13:19 of the Negeb are shut up with no one to **o** them;
17: 3 on the mountains in the **o** country.
32:11 the terms and conditions, and the **o** copy;
32:14 both this sealed deed of purchase and this **o** deed,
32:19 whose eyes are **o** to all the ways of mortals,
40: 7 When all the leaders of the forces in the **o** country
40:13 of the forces in the **o** country came to Gedaliah
50:26 from every quarter; **o** her granaries;
La 2:16 All your enemies **o** their mouths against you;
Eze 2: 8 **o** your mouth and eat what I give you.
3:27 But when I speak with you, I will **o** your mouth,
16: 5 but you were thrown out in the **o** field,
16:63 never **o** your mouth again because of your shame,
25: 9 therefore I will lay **o** the flank of Moab from
26: 2 it has swung **o** to me;
29: 5 you shall fall in the **o** field,
29:21 and I will **o** your lips among them.
32: 4 on the **o** field I will fling you,
33:27 in the **o** field I will give to the wild animals to
37:12 I am going to **o** your graves,
37:13 the LORD, when I **o** your graves, and bring you
39: 5 You shall fall in the **o** field;
42:14 before they go near to the area **o** to the people."
45: 2 with fifty cubits for an **o** space around it.
48:15 for dwellings and for **o** country.
48:17 The city shall have **o** land:
Da 6:10 which had windows in its upper room **o**
9: 7 O Lord, but **o** shame, as at this day, falls on us,
9: 8 **O** shame, O LORD, falls on us, our kings,
9:18 **O** your eyes and look at our desolation and the city
Hos 13: 8 and will tear **o** the covering of their heart;
13:16 and their pregnant women ripped **o**.
Am 1:13 because they have ripped **o** pregnant women
Mic 1: 4 under him and the valleys will burst **o**,
1: 6 I will make Samaria a heap in the **o** country,
4:10 from the city and camp in the **o** country;
Na 3:13 The gates of your land are wide **o** to your foes;
Hab 2: 5 They **o** their throats wide as Sheol;
Zec 11: 1 **O** your doors, O Lebanon,
Mal 3:10 see if I will not **o** the windows of heaven for you
Mt 13:35 "I will **o** my mouth to speak in parables;
17:27 and when you **o** its mouth, you will find a coin;
25:11 saying, 'Lord, lord, **o** to us.'
Mk 14: 3 and she broke **o** the jar and poured the ointment
Lk 12:36 so that they may **o** the door for him as soon
13:25 'Lord, **o** to us,' then in reply he will say to you,
Jn 9:26 How did he **o** your eyes?"
10:21 Can a demon **o** the eyes of the blind?"
Ac 1:18 and falling headlong, he burst **o** in the middle
8:32 so he does not **o** his mouth.
9: 8 and though his eyes were **o**, he could see nothing;
16:27 jailer woke up and saw the prison doors wide **o**,
19:38 the courts are **o**, and there are proconsuls;
26:18 to **o** their eyes so that they may turn from darkness
2Co 4: 2 but by the **o** statement of
6:11 our heart is wide **o** to you.
6:13 to children—**o** wide your hearts also.
Col 4: 3 as well that God will **o** to us a door for the word,
Heb 4: 1 while the promise of entering his rest is still **o**,
4: 6 Since therefore it remains **o** for some to enter it,
1Pe 3:12 and his ears are **o** to their prayer.
Rev 3: 8 Look, I have set before you an **o** door,
3:20 if you hear my voice and **o** the door,
4: 1 this I looked, and there in heaven a door stood **o**!
5: 2 to **o** the scroll and break its seals?"
5: 3 on earth or under the earth was able to **o** the scroll
5: 4 because no one was found worthy to **o** the scroll
5: 5 so that he can **o** the scroll and its seven seals."
5: 9 and to **o** its seals, for you were slaughtered and
6: 1 Then I saw the Lamb **o** one of the seven seals,
10: 2 He held a little scroll **o** in his hand.
10: 8 that is **o** in the hand of the angel who is standing
Tob 6: 5 "Cut **o** the fish and take out its gall, heart,
6: 6 So after cutting **o** the fish
Jdt 10: 9 they ordered the young men to **o** the gate for her,
13:11 to the sentries at the gates, **"O, o** the gate!
AdE 6: 9 and let it be proclaimed through the **o** square of
6:11 and made him ride through the **o** square of
13: 2 to make my kingdom peaceable and **o** to travel
14:10 to **o** the mouths of the nations for the praise
Sir 15: 5 and will **o** his mouth in the midst of the assembly.
22:22 If you **o** your mouth against your friend,
26:12 of every tent peg and **o** her quiver to the arrow.
29:24 as a guest you should not **o** your mouth;
Bar 1:15 but there is **o** shame on us today,
2: 6 but there is **o** shame on us
2:17 **o** your eyes, O Lord, and see, for the dead who are
Aza 1:10 And now we cannot **o** our mouths;
Bel 1:27 The dragon ate them, and burst **o**.
1Mc 5:48 But they refused to **o** to him.
2Mc 1: 4 May he **o** your heart to his law
6:18 forced to **o** his mouth to eat swine's flesh.
10:36 Others broke **o** the gates and let in the rest of
15:19 being anxious over the encounter in the **o** country.
1Es 4:19 and gape at her, and with **o** mouths stare at her,
9: 6 the multitude sat in the **o** square before the temple,
9:11 and we are not able to stand in the **o** air.
9:38 in the **o** square before the east gate of the temple;
9:41 He read aloud in the **o** square before the gate of
2Es 5:37 **o** for me the closed chambers, and bring out
9:11 an opportunity of repentance was still **o** to them,
14:38 **o** your mouth and drink what I give you to drink."

2Es 15:57 in the **o** country shall fall by the sword.
4Mc 4:11 down half dead in the temple area that was **o**
15: 2 Two courses were **o** to this mother,

OPENED[‡] (140) [OPEN]

Ge 3: 5 that when you eat of it your eyes will be **o**,
3: 7 Then the eyes of both were **o**,
4:11 from the ground, which has **o** its mouth
7:11 and the windows of the heavens were **o**.
8: 6 At the end of forty days Noah **o** the window of
21:19 Then God **o** her eyes and she saw a well of water.
29:31 he **o** her womb; but Rachel was barren.
30:22 and God heeded her and **o** her womb.
41:56 Joseph **o** all the storehouses,
42:27 of them **o** his sack to give his donkey fodder at
43:21 we came to the lodging place we **o** our sacks,
44:11 to the ground, and each **o** his sack.
Ex 2: 6 When she **o** it, she saw the child.
Nu 16:32 The earth **o** its mouth and swallowed them up,
22:28 Then the LORD **o** the mouth of the donkey,
22:31 Then the LORD **o** the eyes of Balaam,
26:10 and the earth **o** its mouth and swallowed them up
Dt 11: 6 how in the midst of all Israel the earth **o** its mouth
Jdg 3:25 they took the key and **o** them.
4:19 So she **o** a skin of milk and gave him a drink
11:35 For I have **o** my mouth to the LORD,
11:36 if you have **o** your mouth to the LORD,
19:27 **o** the doors of the house,
1Sa 3:15 then he **o** the doors of the house of the LORD.
2Sa 22:33 with strength has **o** wide my path.
2Ki 4:35 and the child **o** his eyes.
6:17 the LORD **o** the eyes of the servant, and he saw;
6:20 The LORD **o** their eyes, and they saw
9:10 Then he **o** the door and fled.
13:17 he said, "Open the window eastward"; and he **o** it.
2Ch 29: 3 he **o** the doors of the house of the LORD
Ne 7: 3 of Jerusalem are not to be **o** until the sun is hot;
8: 5 And Ezra **o** the book in the sight of all the people,
8: 5 and when he **o** it, all the people stood up.
13:19 be shut and gave orders that they should not be **o**
Job 3: 1 After this Job **o** his mouth and cursed the day
29:23 they **o** their mouths as for the spring rain.
31:32 I have **o** my doors to the traveler—
Ps 78:23 and **o** the doors of heaven;
105:41 He **o** the rock, and water gushed out;
106:17 The earth **o** and swallowed up Dathan,
109: 2 For wicked and deceitful mouths are **o** against me,
SS 5: 6 I **o** to my beloved, but my beloved had turned
7:12 whether the grape blossoms have **o** and
Isa 5:14 and **o** its mouth beyond measure;
10:14 there was none that moved a wing, or **o** its mouth,
24:18 For the windows of heaven are **o**,
35: 5 Then the eyes of the blind shall be **o**,
48: 8 from of old your ear has not been **o**.
50: 5 The Lord GOD has **o** my ear,
Jer 50:25 The LORD has **o** his armory,
La 3:46 All our enemies have **o** their mouths against us;
Eze 1: 1 the heavens were **o**, and I saw visions of God.
3: 2 So I **o** my mouth, and he gave me the scroll to eat.
24:27 On that day your mouth shall be **o** to
33:22 but he had **o** my mouth by the time
33:22 so my mouth was **o**, and I was no longer unable
41:11 The side chambers **o** onto the area left free,
44: 2 it shall not be **o**, and no one shall enter by it;
46: 1 but on the sabbath day it shall be **o** and on the day
46: 1 and on the day of the new moon it shall be **o**.
46:12 the gate facing east shall be **o** for him;
Da 7:10 The court sat in judgment, and the books were **o**.
10:16 and I **o** my mouth to speak,
Na 2: 6 The river gates are **o**, the palace trembles.
Zec 13: 1 a fountain shall be **o** for the house of David and
Mt 3:16 the heavens were **o** to him and he saw the Spirit
7: 7 knock, and the door will be **o** for you.
7: 8 and for everyone who knocks, the door will be **o**.
9:30 And their eyes were **o**.
20:33 They said to him, "Lord, let our eyes be **o**."
27:52 The tombs also were **o**, and many bodies of
Mk 7:34 "Ephphatha," that is, "Be **o**."
7:35 And immediately his ears were **o**,
Lk 1:64 Immediately his mouth was **o**
3:21 and was praying, the heaven was **o**,
11: 9 knock, and the door will be **o** for you.
11:10 and for everyone who knocks, the door will be **o**.
24:31 Then their eyes were **o**, and they recognized him;
24:45 Then he **o** their minds to understand the scriptures,
Jn 1:51 you will see heaven **o** and the angels
9:10 "Then how were your eyes **o**?"
9:14 when Jesus made the mud and **o** his eyes.
9:17 It was your eyes he **o**."
9:21 nor do we know who **o** his eyes.
9:30 and yet he **o** my eyes.
9:32 the world began has it been heard that anyone **o**
11:37 "Could not he who **o** the eyes of
Ac 5:19 the night an angel of the Lord **o** the prison doors,
5:23 but when we **o** them, we found no one inside."
7:56 "I see the heavens **o** and the Son of Man standing
9:40 Then she **o** her eyes, and seeing Peter, she sat up.
10:11 He saw the heaven **o** and something like
12:10 It **o** for them of its own accord,
12:16 they **o** the gate, they saw him and were amazed.
14:27 and how he had **o** a door of faith for the Gentiles.
16:14 The Lord **o** her heart to listen eagerly
16:26 and immediately all the doors were **o**
Ro 3:13 "Their throats are **o** graves;
1Co 16: 9 for a wide door for effective work has **o** to me,
2Co 2:12 a door was **o** for me in the Lord;

Heb 10:20 by the new and living way that he **o** for us through
Rev 6: 3 When he **o** the second seal,
6: 5 When he **o** the third seal,
6: 7 When he **o** the fourth seal,
6: 9 When he **o** the fifth seal, I saw under the altar
6:12 When he **o** the sixth seal, I looked,
8: 1 When the Lamb **o** the seventh seal,
9: 2 he **o** the shaft of the bottomless pit,
11:19 Then God's temple in heaven was **o,**
12:16 it **o** its mouth and swallowed the river that
13: 6 It **o** its mouth to utter blasphemies against God,
15: 5 the temple of the tent of witness in heaven was **o,**
19:11 Then I saw heaven **o,** and there was a white horse!
20:12 standing before the throne, and books were **o.**
20:12 Also another book was **o,** the book of life.
Tob 8:13 So they sent the maid, lit a lamp, and **o** the door;
11: 7 "I knowthat his eyes will be **o.**
Jdt 10: 9 be **o** for me so that I may go out and accomplish
13:13 They **o** the gate and welcomed them.
14:15 he **o** it and went into the bedchamber
Wis 10:21 for wisdom **o** the mouths of those who were mute,
Sir 43:14 Therefore the storehouses are **o,**
51:25 I **o** my mouth and said,
Sus 1:25 And one of them ran and **o** the garden doors.
1:39 and he **o** the doors and got away.
Bel 1:18 As soon as the doors were **o,**
1Mc 3:28 He **o** his coffers and gave a year's pay
3:48 And they **o** the book of the law to inquire
10:76 people of the city became afraid and **o** the gates,
11: 2 and the people of the towns **o** their gates to him
14: 5 and **o** a way to the isles of the sea.
2Mc 14:44 a space **o** and he fell in the middle of
1Es 9:46 When he **o** the law, they all stood erect.
3Mc 6:18 and true God revealed his holy face and **o**
2Es 6:20 books shall be **o** before the face of the firmament,
8:52 because it is for you that paradise is **o,**
9:28 Then my mouth was **o,** and I began to speak
14:39 I **o** my mouth, and a full cup was offered to me;
14:41 and my mouth was **o** and was no longer closed.

OPENING‡ (18) [OPEN]
Ex 28:32 It shall have an **o** for the head in the middle of it,
28:32 with a woven binding around the **o,** like the **o** in a coat of mail,
39:23 and the **o** of the robe in the middle of it was like the **o** in a coat of mail, with a binding around the **o,**
1Ki 7:31 Its **o** was within the crown whose height was one
7:31 its **o** was round, as a pedestal is made;
7:31 At its **o** there were carvings;
1Ch 9:27 and they had charge of **o** it every morning.
SS 5: 4 My beloved thrust his hand into the **o,**
Eze 40:11 he measured the width of the **o** of the gateway,
Mt 2:11 Then, **o** their treasure chests,
Lk 24:32 while he was **o** the scriptures to us?"
Ac 9:25 and let him down through an **o** in the wall,
12:14 she was so overjoyed that, instead of **o** the gate,
Jas 3:11 from the same **o** both fresh and brackish water?
2Mc 1:16 **O** a secret door in the ceiling,

OPENINGS (1) [OPEN]
Ps 74:15 You cut **o** for springs and torrents;

OPENLY‡ (10) [OPEN]
Eze 23:18 on her whorings so **o** and flaunted her nakedness,
Mk 1:45 so that Jesus could no longer go into a town **o,**
8:32 He said all this quite **o.**
Jn 7:13 Yet no one would speak **o** about him for fear of
7:26 And here he is, speaking **o,**
11:54 Jesus therefore no longer walked about **o** among
18:20 Jesus answered, "I have spoken **o** to the world;
2Co 8:24 Therefore **o** before the churches,
Sir 51:13 I sought wisdom **o** in my prayer.
2Es 14: 6 'These words you shall publish **o,**

OPENS‡ (20) [OPEN]
Ex 13:12 you shall set apart to the LORD all that first **o**
13:15 to the LORD every male that first **o** the womb,
34:19 All that first **o** the womb is mine,
Nu 16:30 and the ground **o** its mouth and swallows them up,
Job 33:16 then he **o** their ears, and terrifies them
35:16 Job **o** his mouth in empty talk,
36:10 He **o** their ears to instruction,
36:15 and **o** their ear by adversity.
Ps 146: 8 the LORD **o** the eyes of the blind.
Pr 18:16 A gift **o** doors; it gives access to the great.
31:20 She **o** her hand to the poor,
31:26 She **o** her mouth with wisdom,
Jn 10: 3 The gatekeeper **o** the gate for him,
Rev 3: 7 the key of David, who **o** and no one will shut, who shuts and no one **o:**
Sir 20:15 he **o** his mouth like a town crier.
24: 2 In the assembly of the Most High she **o** her mouth,
26:12 As a thirsty traveler **o** his mouth and drinks
27:25 and a treacherous blow **o** up many wounds.
39: 5 he **o** his mouth in prayer and asks pardon for his

OPERATION (KJV) See POWER, WORK

OPERATIONS (1)
1Es 6:10 These **o** are going on rapidly,

OPHEL (5)
2Ch 27: 3 and did extensive building on the wall of **O.**
2Ch 33:14 he carried it around **O,** and raised it to
Ne 3:26 the temple servants living on **O** made repairs up to
3:27 the great projecting tower as far as the wall of **O.**
11:21 But the temple servants lived on **O;**

OPHIR (15)
Ge 10:29 **O,** Havilah, and Jobab; all these were the
1Ki 9:28 They went to **O,** and imported
10:11 the fleet of Hiram, which carried gold from **O,**
10:11 brought from **O** a great quantity of almug wood
22:48 of the Tarshish type to go to **O** for gold;
1Ch 1:23 **O,** Havilah, and Jobab; all these were the
29: 4 of **O,** and seven thousand talents of refined silver,
2Ch 8:18 to **O,** together with the servants of Solomon,
9:10 from **O** brought algum wood and precious stones.
Job 22:24 and gold of **O** like the stones of the torrent-bed,
28:16 It cannot be valued in the gold of **O,**
Ps 45: 9 at your right hand stands the queen in gold of **O.**
Isa 13:12 and humans than the gold of **O.**
Tob 13:16 be paved with ruby and with stones of **O.**
Sir 7:18 or a real brother for the gold of **O.**

OPHNI (1)
Jos 18:24 **O,** and Geba—twelve towns with their

OPHRAH (8)
Jos 18:23 Avvim, Parah, **O,**
Jdg 6:11 of the LORD came and sat under the oak at **O,**
6:24 To this day it still stands at **O,**
8:27 an ephod of it and put it in his town, in **O;**
8:32 and was buried in the tomb of his father Joash at **O**
9: 5 He went to his father's house at **O,**
1Sa 13:17 one company turned toward **O,**
1Ch 4:14 Meonothai became the father of **O;**

OPINION (10) [OPINIONS]
Job 32: 6 I was timid and afraid to declare my **o** to you.
32:10 I say, 'Listen to me; let me also declare my **o.**'
32:17 I also will declare my **o.**
Pr 18: 2 but only in expressing personal **o.**
1Co 7:25 but I give my **o** as one who by
Sir 3:24 and wrong **o** has impaired their judgment.
13:24 poverty is evil only in the **o** of the ungodly.
2Mc 6:29 he had uttered were in their **o** sheer madness.
4Mc 5:10 by holding a vain **o** concerning the truth,
8:19 up this vain **o** and this arrogance that threatens

OPINIONS (3) [OPINION]
1Ki 18:21 long will you go limping with two different **o?**
Ro 14: 1 but not for the purpose of quarreling over **o.**
2Pe 2: 1 who will secretly bring in destructive **o.**

OPPONENT (6) [OPPONENT'S, OPPONENTS]
Dt 25:11 of his **o** by reaching out and seizing his genitals,
2Sa 2:16 Each grasped his **o** by the head,
Job 27: 7 and may my **o** be like the unrighteous.
Lk 18: 3 'Grant me justice against my **o.**'
Tit 2: 8 then any **o** will be put to shame,
4Mc 4: 1 a political **o** of the noble and good man, Onias,

OPPONENT'S (2) [OPPONENT]
2Sa 2:16 and thrust his sword in his **o** side;
Job 6:23 Or, 'Save me from an **o** hand'?

OPPONENTS (7) [OPPONENT]
Lk 13:17 When he said this, all his **o** were put to shame;
21:15 of your **o** will be able to withstand or contradict.
Php 1:28 and are in no way intimidated by your **o.**
2Ti 2:25 correcting **o** with gentleness.
AdE 8:11 to act as they wished against their **o** and enemies
Sir 46: 6 and on the slope he destroyed his **o,**
2Mc 8:35 the help of the Lord by **o** whom he regarded as of

OPPORTUNE‡ (3) [OPPORTUNITY]
Lk 4:13 he departed from him until an **o** time.
Sir 4:20 Watch for the **o** time, and beware of evil,
Sus 1:15 Once, while they were watching for an **o** day,

OPPORTUNITIES (1) [OPPORTUNITY]
2Mc 9:25 the neighbors of my kingdom keep watching for **o**

OPPORTUNITY‡ (39) [OPPORTUNE, OPPORTUNITIES]
Ge 43:18 so that he may have an **o** to fall upon us,
Mt 26:16 And from that moment he began to look for an **o**
Mk 6:21 But an **o** came when Herod on his birthday gave
14:11 So he began to look for an **o** to betray him.
Lk 21:13 This will give you an **o** to testify.
22: 6 and began to look for an **o** to betray him to them
Jn 7: 1 in Judea because the Jews were looking for an **o**
7:19 Why are you looking for an **o** to kill me?"
8:37 yet you look for an **o** to kill me,
Ac 24:25 when I have an **o,** I will send for you."
25:16 and had been given an **o** to make a defense against
Ro 7: 8 But sin, seizing an **o** in the commandment,
7:11 For sin, seizing an **o** in the commandment,
1Co 16:12 He will come when he has the **o.**
2Co 5:12 but giving you an **o** to boast about us,
11:12 to deny an **o** to those who want an **o** to be
Gal 5:13 not use your freedom as an **o** for self-indulgence,
Gal 6:10 So then, whenever we have an **o,**
Php 4:10 but had no **o** to show it.
Heb 11:15 they would have had **o** to return.
Jdt 12:16 an **o** to seduce her from the day he first saw her.
Wis 12:10 by little you gave them an **o** to repent,
12:20 and **o** to give up their wickedness,
Sir Pr: 3 I found **o** for no little instruction.
12:16 an **o** he will never have enough of your blood.
19:28 he will nevertheless do evil when he finds the **o.**
38:24 wisdom of the scribe depends on the **o** of leisure;
1Mc 11:42 on you and your nation, if I find an **o.**
12:25 for he gave them no **o** to invade his own country.
15:34 Now that we have the **o,**
2Mc 4:32 Menelaus, thinking he had obtained a suitable **o,**
14: 5 But he found an **o** that furthered his mad purpose
14:29 for an **o** to accomplish this by a stratagem.
2Es 5:50 "Since you have now given me the **o,**
8:56 For when they had **o** to choose,
9:11 and did not understand but despised it while an **o**
4Mc 1:12 I shall shortly have an **o** to speak of this;
11:12 through these noble sufferings you give us an **o**

OPPOSE (11) [OPPOSED, OPPOSES, OPPOSING, OPPOSITE, OPPOSITION]
Nu 22:34 that you were standing in the road to **o** me.
Lk 14:31 with ten thousand to **o** the one who comes
2Co 10: 2 to **o** those who think we are acting according
1Th 2:15 they displease God and **o** everyone
2Ti 3: 8 of corrupt mind and counterfeit faith, also **o**
AdE 13: 9 in your power and there is no one who can **o** you
1Mc 14: 7 and there was none to **o** him.
14:44 of these decisions or to **o** what he says,
2Mc 14:29 Since it was not possible to **o** the king,
1Es 1:27 Stand aside, and do not **o** the Lord."
2Es 15: 3 be troubled by the unbelief of those who **o** you.

OPPOSED (20) [OPPOSE]
Ezr 10:15 of Asahel and Jahzeiah son of Tikvah **o** this,
Da 10:13 of the kingdom of Persia **o** me twenty-one days.
Lk 2:34 and to be a sign that will be **o**
Ac 13: 8 (for that is the translation of his name) **o** them
18: 6 When they **o** and reviled him,
Gal 2:11 when Cephas came to Antioch, I **o** him to his face,
3:21 Is the law then **o** to the promises of God?
5:17 For what the flesh desires is **o** to the Spirit,
5:17 and what the Spirit desires is **o** to the flesh;
5:17 for these are **o** to each other,
2Ti 3: 8 As Jannes and Jambres **o** Moses, so these people,
4:15 for he strongly **o** our message.
Sir 46: 7 they **o** the congregation, restrained the people
1Mc 8:11 as ever **o** them, they destroyed and enslaved;
3Mc 3: 7 but were hostile and greatly **o** to his government.
6:19 They **o** the forces of the enemy and filled them
2Es 5:29 And those who **o** your promises have trampled
9:18 and no one **o** me then, for no one existed;
4Mc 1: 6 but those that are **o** to justice, courage,
8:15 they also **o** the tyrant with their own philosophy,

OPPOSES (4) [OPPOSE]
2Th 2: 4 He **o** and exalts himself above every so-called god
Jas 4: 6 "God **o** the proud, but gives grace to the humble."
1Pe 5: 5 "God **o** the proud, but gives grace to the humble."
Wis 2:12 because he is inconvenient to us and **o** our actions;

OPPOSING (5) [OPPOSE]
1Sa 15: 2 the Amalekites for what they did in **o** the Israelites
2Ch 35:21 Cease **o** God, who is with me,
Ac 7:51 you are forever **o** the Holy Spirit,
2Es 11: 3 I saw that out of its wings there grew **o** wings;
4Mc 3:16 Therefore, **o** reason to desire,

OPPOSITE‡ (91) [OPPOSE]
Ge 21:16 she went and sat down **o** him a good way off,
21:16 as she sat **o** him, she lifted up her voice and wept.
25:18 which is **o** Egypt in the direction of Assyria;
Ex 14: 2 you shall camp **o** it, by the sea.
26: 5 the loops shall be **o** one another.
26:35 the lampstand on the south side of the tabernacle **o**
30: 4 on two **o** sides of it you shall make them,
36:12 the loops were **o** one another.
37:27 on two **o** sides of it,
40:24 **o** the table on the south side of the tabernacle,
Nu 26: 3 in the plains of Moab by the Jordan **o** Jericho,
26:63 in the plains of Moab by the Jordan **o** Jericho.
Dt 1: 1 in the wilderness, on the plain **o** Suph,
3:29 So we remained in the valley **o** Beth-peor.
4:46 beyond the Jordan in the valley **o** Beth-peor,
11:30 **o** Gilgal, beside the oak of Moreh.
34: 1 to the top of Pisgah, which is **o** Jericho,
34: 6 **o** Beth-peor, but no one knows his burial place
Jos 3:16 Then the people crossed over **o** Jericho.
8:33 stood on **o** sides of the ark in front of
15: 7 which is **o** the ascent of Adummim,
18:14 **o** Beth-horon, and it ends at Kiriath-baal (that is,
18:17 which is **o** the ascent of Adummim;
19:46 Me-jarkon, and Rakkon at the border **o** Joppa.
Jdg 19:10 and arrived **o** Jebus (that is, Jerusalem).
1Sa 26: 1 on the hill of Hachilah, which is **o** Jeshimon."
26: 3 which is **o** Jeshimon beside the road.
2Sa 5:23 and come upon them **o** the balsam trees.
16:13 along on the hillside **o** him and cursed as he went,
1Ki 7: 5 **o,** facing each other in the three rows.
20:27 of Israel encamped **o** them like two little flocks
20:29 They encamped **o** one another seven days.

1Ki 21:10 seat two scoundrels **o** him,
21:13 The two scoundrels came in and sat **o** him;
2Ki 3:22 Moabites saw the water **o** them as red as blood.
3:26 **o** the king of Edom; but they could not.
1Ch 8:32 Now these also lived **o** their kindred in Jerusalem,
9:38 and these also lived **o** their kindred in Jerusalem,
14:14 go around and come on them **o** the balsam trees.
2Ch 7:6 **O** them the priests sounded trumpets;
Ne 3:10 of Harumaph made repairs **o** his house;
3:16 repaired from a point **o** the graves of David,
3:19 repaired another section **o** the ascent to the armory
3:23 and Hasshub made repairs **o** their house.
3:25 Palal son of Uzai repaired **o** the Angle and
3:26 up to a point **o** the Water Gate on the east and
3:27 After him the Tekoites repaired another section **o**
3:28 each one **o** his own house.
3:29 of Immer made repairs **o** his own house.
3:30 of Berechiah made repairs **o** his living quarters.
3:31 and of the merchants, **o** the Muster Gate,
12:9 and Unno their associates stood **o** them in
12:24 of David the man of God, section **o** to section.
Est 5:1 and stood in the inner court of the king's palace, **o**
5:1 on his royal throne inside the palace **o** the entrance
Eze 40:23 **O** the gate on the north, as on the east,
42:1 and he brought me to the chambers that were **o**
42:1 the temple yard and **o** the building on the north.
42:7 toward the outer court, **o** the chambers,
42:8 those **o** the temple were one hundred cubits long.
42:10 **o** the vacant area and opposite the building,
42:10 opposite the vacant area and **o** the building,
42:13 "The north chambers and the south chambers **o**
47:20 be the boundary to a point **o** Lebo-hamath.
Mt 27:61 and the other Mary were there, sitting **o** the tomb.
Mk 12:41 He sat down **o** the treasury,
13:3 When he was sitting on the Mount of Olives **o**
Lk 8:26 the country of the Gerasenes, which is **o** Galilee.
Ac 16:7 When they had come **o** Mysia,
20:15 and on the following day we arrived **o** Chios.
Tob 11:1 they came near to Kaserin, which is **o** Nineveh,
Jdt 2:21 and camped **o** Bectileth near the mountain that is
4:6 which faces Esdraelon **o** the plain near Dothan,
7:18 up and encamped in the hill country **o** Dothan;
Sir 33:14 Good is the **o** of evil, and life the **o** of death;
33:14 so the sinner is the **o** of the godly.
33:15 they come in pairs, one the **o** of the other.
42:24 All things come in pairs, one **o** the other,
1Mc 3:32 they encamped **o** them and prepared for battle
3:46 **o** Jerusalem, because Israel formerly had a place
5:37 and encamped **o** Raphon, on the other side of
6:32 **o** the camp of the king.
10:48 and encamped **o** Demetrius.
13:20 and his army kept marching along **o** him
13:28 He also erected seven pyramids, **o** one another,
2Mc 15:33 and would hang up these rewards of his folly **o**
3Mc 5:16 for the banquet to recline **o** him.
2Es 7:*36* and **o** it shall be the place of rest;
7:*36* and **o** it the paradise of delight.
14:1 suddenly a voice came out of a bush **o** me

OPPOSITION‡ (5) [OPPOSE]

Ac 4:14 they had nothing to say in **o**.
Ro 16:17 in **o** to the teaching that you have learned;
1Th 2:2 to you the gospel of God in spite of great **o**.
AdE 13:5 and it alone, stands constantly in **o** to every nation,
1Mc 11:38 before him and that there was no **o** to him,

OPPRESS (27) [OPPRESSED, OPPRESSES, OPPRESSING, OPPRESSION, OPPRESSIONS, OPPRESSIVE, OPPRESSIVELY, OPPRESSOR, OPPRESSORS]

Ex 1:11 over them to **o** them with forced labor.
3:9 I have also seen how the Egyptians **o** them.
22:21 You shall not wrong or **o** a resident alien,
23:9 You shall not **o** a resident alien;
Lev 19:33 you shall not **o** the alien
Dt 23:16 wherever they please; you shall not **o** them.
1Ch 16:21 he allowed no one to **o** them;
Job 10:3 Does it seem good to you to **o**,
Ps 56:1 all day long foes **o** me;
105:14 he allowed no one to **o** them;
119:122 do not let the godless **o** me.
Pr 14:31 Those who **o** the poor insult their Maker,
Isa 58:3 on your fast day, and **o** all your workers.
Jer 7:6 if you do not **o** the alien,
30:20 and I will punish all who **o** them.
Eze 18:7 does not **o** anyone, but restores to
45:8 And my princes shall no longer **o** my people;
Hos 12:7 in whose hands are false balances, he loves to **o**.
Am 4:1 who **o** the poor, who crush the needy,
6:14 and they shall **o** you from Lebo-hamath to
Mic 2:2 they **o** householder and house,
Zec 7:10 not **o** the widow, the orphan, the alien, or the poor;
Mal 3:5 against those who **o** the hired workers
Jas 2:6 Is it not the rich who **o** you?
Wis 2:10 Let us **o** the righteous poor man;
2Mc 1:28 Punish those who **o** and are insolent with pride.
5:22 He left governors to **o** the people:

OPPRESSED‡ (53) [OPPRESS]

Ge 15:13 and they shall be **o** for four hundred years;
Ex 1:12 But the more they were **o**,
Nu 20:15 and the Egyptians **o** us and our ancestors;
Jdg 2:18 because of those who persecuted and **o** them.
4:3 and had **o** the Israelites cruelly twenty years.
6:9 and from the hand of all who **o** you,
10:8 and they crushed and **o** the Israelites that year.
10:8 For eighteen years they **o** all the Israelites
10:12 and the Amalekites, and the Maonites, **o** you;
12:2 in conflict with the Ammonites who **o** us severely.
1Sa 12:3 Or whom have I defrauded? Whom have I **o**?
12:4 not defrauded us or **o** us or taken anything from
12:8 Jacob went into Egypt and the Egyptians **o** them,
2Ki 13:4 how the king of Aram **o** them.
13:22 Now King Hazael of Aram **o** Israel all the days
2Ch 28:20 and **o** him instead of strengthening him.
Ps 9:9 The LORD is a stronghold for the **o**,
10:12 up your hand; do not forget the **o**.
10:18 to do justice for the orphan and the **o**,
69:32 Let the **o** see it and be glad;
76:9 to save all the **o** of the earth.
103:6 and justice for all who are **o**.
106:42 Their enemies **o** them, and they were brought
146:7 who executes justice for the **o**;
Ecc 4:1 the tears of the **o**—with no one to comfort them!
Isa 1:17 seek justice, rescue the **o**, defend the orphan,
3:5 be **o**, everyone by another and everyone by
14:2 and rule over those who **o** them.
23:12 O **o** virgin daughter Sidon;
38:14 O Lord, I am **o**; be my security!
51:14 The **o** shall speedily be released;
52:4 the Assyrian, too, has **o** them without cause.
53:7 He was **o**, and he was afflicted,
58:6 to let the **o** go free, and to break every yoke?
60:14 of those who **o** you shall come bending low
61:1 he has sent me to bring good news to the **o**,
Jer 50:33 The people of Israel are **o**,
Eze 22:29 they have **o** the poor and needy,
Da 4:27 and your iniquities with mercy to the **o**,
Hos 5:11 Ephraim is **o**, crushed in judgment,
Lk 4:18 sight to the blind, to let the **o** go free,
Ac 7:24 the **o** man and avenged him by striking down
10:38 about doing good and healing all who were **o** by
Jdt 9:11 But you are the God of the lowly, helper of the **o**,
16:7 to exalt the **o** in Israel.
16:11 Then my **o** people shouted;
Wis 5:1 in the presence of those who have **o** them
15:14 are all the enemies who **o** your people.
Sir 4:9 Rescue the **o** from the oppressor;
1Mc 10:46 in Israel and how much he had **o** them.
2Mc 8:2 the Lord to look upon the people who were **o**
3Mc 2:12 when our fathers were **o** you helped them
2Es 11:42 you have **o** the meek and injured the peaceable;

OPPRESSES (4) [OPPRESS]

Nu 10:9 in your land against the adversary who **o** you,
Ps 42:9 about mournfully because the enemy **o** me?"
Pr 28:3 A ruler who **o** the poor is a beating rain
Eze 18:12 **o** the poor and needy, commits robbery, does

OPPRESSING (5) [OPPRESS]

1Sa 10:18 the hand of all the kingdoms that were **o** you.'
10:27 had been grievously **o** the Gadites and
Ps 37:35 I have seen the wicked **o**,
Pr 22:16 **O** the poor in order to enrich oneself,
Zep 3:1 Ah, soiled, defiled, **o** city!

OPPRESSION (24) [OPPRESS]

Dt 26:7 and saw our affliction, our toil, and our **o**.
2Ki 13:4 for he saw the **o** of Israel,
Ps 10:7 with cursing and deceit and **o**;
43:2 about mournfully because of the **o** of the enemy?
44:24 Why do you forget our affliction and **o**?
55:11 **o** and fraud do not depart from its marketplace.
72:14 From **o** and violence he redeems their life;
73:8 with malice; loftily they threaten **o**.
107:39 they are diminished and brought low through **o**,
119:134 Redeem me from human **o**,
Ecc 5:8 in a province the **o** of the poor and the violation
7:7 Surely **o** makes the wise foolish,
Isa 30:12 and put your trust in **o** and deceit,
33:15 who despise the gain of **o**,
54:14 you shall be far from **o**, for you shall not fear;
59:13 talking **o** and revolt, conceiving lying words
Jer 6:6 there is nothing but **o** within her.
9:6 **O** upon **o**, deceit upon deceit!
22:17 and for practicing **o** and violence.
Eze 45:9 Put away violence and **o**, and do what is just
AdE 16:20 against those who attack them at the time of **o**.
2Es 11:32 and with much **o** dominated its inhabitants;
11:40 and over all the earth with grievous **o**;

OPPRESSIONS (3) [OPPRESS]

Job 35:9 "Because of the multitude of **o** people cry out;
Ecc 4:1 Again I saw all the **o** that are practiced under
Am 3:9 and what **o** are in its midst."

OPPRESSIVE (2) [OPPRESS]

Isa 10:1 who make iniquitous decrees, who write **o** statutes,
3Mc 6:5 in his countless forces, **o** king of the Assyrians,

OPPRESSIVELY (1) [OPPRESS]

2Es 12:24 and its inhabitants more **o** than all who were

OPPRESSOR (12) [OPPRESS]

Ps 72:4 give deliverance to the needy, and crush the **o**.
Pr 28:16 A ruler who lacks understanding is a cruel **o**;
29:13 The poor and the **o** have this in common:
Isa 9:4 the rod of their **o**, you have broken as on the day
14:4 How the **o** has ceased! How his insolence has
16:4 When the **o** is no more, and destruction has ceased,
51:13 because of the fury of the **o**,
51:13 But where is the fury of the **o**?
Jer 21:12 the hand of the **o** anyone who has been robbed,
22:3 the hand of the **o** anyone who has been robbed.
Zec 9:8 no **o** shall again overrun them,
Sir 4:9 Rescue the oppressed from the **o**;

OPPRESSORS (11) [OPPRESS]

Job 6:23 Or, 'Ransom me from the hand of **o**'?
27:13 and the heritage that **o** receive from the Almighty:
Ps 119:121 do not leave me to my **o**.
Ecc 4:1 On the side of their **o** there was power—
Isa 3:12 children are their **o**, and women rule over them.
19:20 when they cry to the LORD because of **o**,
49:26 I will make your **o** eat their own flesh,
Zep 3:19 I will deal with all your **o** at that time.
Wis 10:11 When his **o** were covetous,
10:15 wisdom delivered from a nation of **o**.
16:4 that upon those **o** inescapable want should come,

OR (2379) See Index of Articles Etc.

ORACLE (39) [ORACLE-PRIESTS, ORACLES]

Nu 23:7 Then Balaam uttered his **o**, saying:
23:18 Then Balaam uttered his **o**, saying:
24:3 and he uttered his **o**, saying:
24:3 "The **o** of Balaam son of Beor,
24:3 the **o** of the man whose eye is clear,
24:4 the **o** of one who hears the words of God,
24:15 So he uttered his **o**, saying:
24:15 "The **o** of Balaam son of Beor,
24:15 the **o** of the man whose eye is clear,
24:16 the **o** of one who hears the words of God,
24:20 he looked on Amalek, and uttered his **o**, saying:
24:21 he looked on the Kenite, and uttered his **o**, saying:
24:23 Again he uttered his **o**, saying:
2Sa 16:23 that Ahithophel gave was as if one consulted the **o**
23:1 The **o** of David, son of Jesse, the **o** of the man
2Ki 9:25 how the LORD uttered this **o** against him:
Pr 30:1 The words of Agur son of Jakeh. An **o**.
31:1 An **o** that his mother taught him:
Isa 13:1 The **o** concerning Babylon that Isaiah son
14:28 In the year that King Ahaz died this **o** came:
15:1 An **o** concerning Moab.
17:1 An **o** concerning Damascus.
19:1 An **o** concerning Egypt. See,
21:1 The **o** concerning the wilderness of the sea.
21:11 The **o** concerning Dumah.
21:13 The **o** concerning the desert plain.
22:1 The **o** concerning the valley of vision.
23:1 The **o** concerning Tyre. Wail,
30:6 An **o** concerning the animals of the Negeb.
Eze 12:10 This **o** concerns the prince in Jerusalem and all
Na 1:1 An **o** concerning Nineveh.
Hab 1:1 The **o** that the prophet Habakkuk saw.
Zec 9:1 An **O**. The word of the LORD is against the
12:1 An **O**. The word of the LORD concerning Israel:
Mal 1:1 An **o**. The word of the LORD to Israel
Sir 33:3 such a one the law is as dependable as a divine **o**.
45:10 with the **o** of judgment, Urim and Thummim;
2Mc 2:4 the prophet, having received an **o**, ordered that

ORACLE-PRIESTS (1) [ORACLE, PRIEST]

Hos 11:6 sword rages in their cities, it consumes their **o**,

ORACLES (10) [ORACLE]

Dt 18:11 or who seeks **o** from the dead.
2Ch 24:27 and of the many **o** against him,
La 2:14 have seen **o** for you that are false and misleading.
Hos 4:12 and their divining rod gives them **o**.
Mic 3:11 its prophets give **o** for money;
Ac 7:38 and he received living **o** to give to us.
Ro 3:2 the first place the Jews were entrusted with the **o**
Heb 5:12 to teach you again the basic elements of the **o**
Wis 16:11 To remind them of your **o** they were bitten,
Sir 44:3 those who spoke in prophetic **o**;

ORCHARD (4) [ORCHARDS]

Ex 23:11 with your vineyard, and with your olive **o**.
SS 4:13 an **o** of pomegranates with all choicest fruits,
6:11 I went down to the nut **o**,
2Es 16:29 as in an olive **o** three or four olives may be left

ORCHARDS (5) [ORCHARD]

1Sa 8:14 the best of your fields and vineyards and olive **o**
2Ki 5:26 olive **o** and vineyards, sheep and oxen,
Ne 5:11 their vineyards, their olive **o**, and their houses,
9:25 vineyards, olive **o**, and fruit trees in abundance;
Sir 40:19 Cattle and **o** make one prosperous;

ORDAIN‡ (8) [FOREORDAINED, ORDAINED, ORDINANCE, ORDINANCES, ORDINATION]

Ex 28:41 shall anoint them and **o** them and consecrate them,
29:9 You shall then **o** Aaron and his sons.
29:33 to **o** and consecrate them,
29:35 through seven days you shall **o** them.

Lev 8:33 For it will take seven days to o you;
1Ki 1:36 the God of my lord the king, so o.
Isa 26:12 O LORD, you will o peace for us, for indeed,
1Ti 5:22 Do not o anyone hastily, and do not participate in

ORDAINED‡ (21) [ORDAIN]

Ex 29:29 they shall be anointed in them and o in them.
32:29 "Today you have o yourselves for the service of
Nu 3: 3 whom he o to minister as priests.
28: 6 o at Mount Sinai for a pleasing odor,
2Sa 17:14 For the LORD had o to defeat the good counsel
2Ki 23: 5 the kings of Judah had o to make offerings in
2Ch 2: 4 of the LORD our God, as o forever for Israel.
22: 7 But it was o by God that the downfall
Ps 133: 3 there the LORD o his blessing, life forevermore.
La 2:17 as he o long ago, he has demolished without pity;
3:37 if the Lord has not o it?
Ac 7:53 the ones that received the law as o by angels,
10:42 and to testify that he is the one o by God as judge
Gal 3:19 and it was o through angels by a mediator.
Heb 9:20 the blood of the covenant that God has o for you."
AdE 14: 9 to abolish what your mouth has o,
Sir 45:15 Moses o him, and anointed him with holy oil;
2Mc 8:36 because they followed the laws o by him.
1Es 1:32 it was o that this should always be done
3Mc 6:36 And when they had o a public rite for these things
2Es 7:17 you have o in your law that

ORDEAL (4)

2Co 8: 2 for during a severe o of affliction,
1Pe 4:12 not be surprised at the fiery o that is taking place
Rev 7:14 "These are they who have come out of the great o;
4Mc 13: 9 in Assyria who despised the same o of

ORDER‡ (267) [ORDERED, ORDERING, ORDERLY, ORDERS, WELL-ORDERED]

Ge 21:30 in o that you may be a witness for me
22: 9 an altar there and laid the wood in o.
25:13 named in the o of their birth:
32: 5 in o that I may find favor in your sight.' "
41:40 and all my people shall o themselves
42:16 in o that your words may be tested,
46:34 in o that you may settle in the land of Goshen,
50:20 in o to preserve a numerous people,
Ex 10: 1 of his officials, in o that I may show these signs
11: 9 in o that my wonders may be multiplied in
16:32 of it be kept throughout your generations, in o
19: 9 in o that the people may hear when I speak
28:10 in the o of their birth.
28:38 in o that they may find favor before the LORD.
30:30 in o that they may serve me as priests.
31:13 given in o that you may know that I, the LORD,
40:23 and set the bread in o on it before the LORD;
Lev 17: 5 This is in o that the people
24: 8 in o before the LORD regularly as a commitment
25:21 I will o my blessing for you in the sixth year,
Nu 4:19 with them in o that they may live and not die
8:19 in o that there may be no plague among
10:28 This was the o of march of the Israelites,
16: 9 to allow you to approach him in o to perform
18: 2 in o that they may be joined to you,
18: 4 They are attached to you in o to perform the duties
25: 4 in o that the fierce anger of the LORD may turn
Dt 2:30 and made his heart defiant in o to hand him over
6:23 He brought us out from there in o to bring us in,
8: 2 in o to humble you, testing you to know what was
8: 3 in o to make you understand that one does not live
9: 5 in o to fulfill the promise that the LORD made
17:16 the people to Egypt in o to acquire more horses,
20:19 making war against it in o to take it,
22: 7 in o that it may go well with you
29: 9 in o that you may succeed in everything
29:13 in o that he may establish you today as his people,
30: 6 in o that you may live.
31:19 in o that this song may be a witness for me against
Jos 11:20 in o that they might be utterly destroyed,
Jdg 2:22 In o to test Israel, whether or
6:26 on the top of the stronghold here, in proper o;
6:36 "In o to see whether you will deliver Israel
16: 5 so that we may bind him in o to subdue him;
21:17 in o that a tribe may not be blotted out from Israel.
Ru 4:10 in o that the name of the dead may not be cut off
1Sa 4: 9 in o not to become slaves to the Hebrews
2Sa 2:26 before you o your people to turn from the pursuit
3:21 in o that they may make a covenant with you,
14:20 In o to change the course
17:23 He set his house in o, and hanged himself;
24:21 "To buy the threshing floor from you in o to build
1Ki 5:17 costly stones in o to lay the foundation of
6: 6 the wall in o that the supporting beams should not
6:22 in o that the whole house might be perfect;
18:33 Next he put the wood in o, cut the bull in pieces,
2Ki 1:11 this is the king's o: Come down quickly!"
10:19 But Jehu was acting with cunning in o to destroy
20: 1 Set your house in o, for you shall die;
23: 4 the priests of the second o,
23:35 in o to meet Pharaoh's demand for money.
1Ch 6:32 and they performed their service in due o.
12:38 All these, warriors arrayed in battle o,
15:18 and with them their kindred of the second o,
25: 6 and Heman were under the o of the king.
2Ch 6: 6 but I have chosen Jerusalem in o
6:33 in o that all the peoples of
23:18 according to the o of David.
25:20 it was God's doing, in o to hand them over,
2Ch 32:18 in o that they might take the city.
32:31 in o to test him and to know all that was
35:20 After all this, when Josiah had set the temple in o,
35:22 but disguised himself in o to fight with him.
Ezr 1: 1 in o that the word of the LORD by the mouth
4:21 issue an o that these people be made to cease,
9: 8 in o that he may brighten our eyes and grant us
10: 8 by o of the officials and
Ne 5: 3 our houses in o to get grain during the famine."
6:13 and so they could give me a bad name, in o
8:13 the scribe Ezra in o to study the words of the law.
9:26 who had warned them in o to turn them back
9:29 And you warned them in o to turn them back
Est 1:11 in o to show the peoples and
1:19 it pleases the king, let a royal o go out from him,
2: 8 when the king's o and his edict were proclaimed,
3: 4 in o to see whether Mordecai's words would avail;
3:15 The couriers went quickly by o of the king,
8: 5 let an o be written to revoke the letters devised
Job 33: 5 set your words in o before me; take your stand.
Ps 59: T *Saul ordered his house be watched in o to kill him.*
110: 4 "You are a priest forever according to the o of
119:101 in o to keep your word.
Pr 15:24 in o to avoid Sheol below.
19:27 in o that you may hear instruction.
22:16 Oppressing the poor in o to enrich oneself,
28: 2 but with an intelligent ruler there is lasting o.
Isa 28:13 in o that they may go, and fall backward,
38: 1 Set your house in o, for you shall die;
Jer 13:11 in o that they might be for me a people, a name,
31:35 who gives the sun for light by day and the fixed o
31:36 this fixed o were ever to cease from my presence,
32:14 in o that they may last for a long time.
42: 6 in o that it may go well with us when we obey
43: 3 in o that they may kill us or take us into exile
44:29 in o that you may know that my words
47: 7 when the LORD has given it an o?
Eze 3:18 in o to save their life,
14: 5 in o that I may take hold of the hearts of the house
16:54 in o that you may bear your disgrace and
16:63 in o that you may remember and be confounded,
17:15 in o that they might give him horses and
17:23 in o that it may produce boughs and bear fruit,
20:26 in o that I might horrify them,
22:20 to blow the fire upon them in o to melt them;
23:25 in o that they may deal with you in fury.
31:14 in o that no trees by the waters may grow
37:19 in o that they may be one in my hand.
39:12 in o to cleanse the land.
40: 4 for you were brought here in o that I might show it
42: 9 that one entered from the east in o to enter them
44:30 in o that a blessing may rest on your house.
46:20 in o not to bring them out into the outer court and
Da 2:30 but in o that the interpretation may be known to
4: 6 in o that they might tell me the interpretation of
4:17 the decision is given by o of the holy ones,
4:17 in o that all who live may know that
11:14 up in o to fulfill the vision,
11:17 In o to destroy the kingdom,
Am 1:13 in Gilead in o to enlarge their territory.
9:12 in o that they may possess the remnant of Edom
Hab 2:15 in o to gaze on their nakedness!"
Zec 7:11 and stopped their ears in o not to hear.
7:12 They made their hearts adamant in o not to hear
13: 4 they will not put on a hairy mantle in o to deceive,
Mt 6: 1 of practicing your piety before others in o to
12:44 it comes, it finds it empty, swept, and put in o.
19:13 Then little children were being brought to him in o
26:58 and going inside, he sat with the guards in o to see
27: 1 of the people conferred together against Jesus in o
Mk 4:12 in o that 'they may indeed look, but not perceive,
7: 9 of rejecting the commandment of God in o
10:13 People were bringing little children to him in o
14:10 to the chief priests in o to betray him to them.
Lk 1: 5 who belonged to the priestly o of Abijah.
8:31 They begged him not to o them to go back into
11:25 When it comes, it finds it swept and put in o.
19:39 "Teacher, o your disciples to stop."
20:10 the tenants in o that they might give him his share
20:20 in o to trap him by what he said,
Jn 3:17 in o that the world might be saved through him.
7:23 If a man receives circumcision on the sabbath in o
10:17 because I lay down my life in o to take it up again.
19:28 he said (in o to fulfill the scripture), "I am thirsty."
Ac 5:15 in o that Peter's shadow might fall on some
6: 2 that we should neglect the word of God in o
16:18 "I o you in the name of Jesus Christ to come out
20:30 in o to entice the disciples to follow them.
22: 5 and I went there in o to bind those who were there
23: 3 yet in violation of the law you o me to be struck?"
25:23 Then Festus gave the o and Paul was brought in.
Ro 1:13 in o that I may reap some harvest among you
4:16 in o that the promise may rest on grace and
6: 1 in sin in o that grace may abound?
7: 4 from the dead in o that we may bear fruit for God.
7:13 in o that sin might be shown to be sin,
8:29 in o that he might be the firstborn within
9:23 so in o to make known the riches of his glory for
11:14 in o to make my own people jealous,
11:31 so they have now been disobedient in o that,
15: 8 the circumcised on behalf of the truth of God in o
15: 9 and in o that the Gentiles might glorify God
1Co 1:31 in o that, as it is written, "Let
7:35 but to promote good o and unhindered devotion to
9:20 To the Jews I became as a Jew, in o to win Jews.
14:19 in o to instruct others also,
14:40 but all things should be done decently and in o.
1Co 15:23 But each in his own o:
2Co 7:12 in o that your zeal for us might be made known
8:14 in o that there may be a fair balance.
9: 3 the brothers in o that our boasting about you may
11: 8 by accepting support from them in o to serve you.
11:12 in o to deny an opportunity to those who want
11:32 the city of Damascus in o to seize me,
13:11 Put things in o, listen to my appeal,
Gal 2: 2 in o to make sure that I was not running,
3:14 in o that in Christ Jesus the blessing
4: 5 in o to redeem those who were under the law,
Eph 5:26 in o to make her holy by cleansing her with
6: 6 and in o to please them, but as slaves of Christ,
Php 2:28 in o that you may rejoice at seeing him again,
3: 8 in o that I may gain Christ
Col 3:22 only while being watched and in o to please them,
2Th 3: 9 but in o to give you an example to imitate.
Tit 1: 5 that you should put in o what remained to be done,
3:14 to good works in o to meet urgent needs,
Phm 1:14 in o that your good deed might be voluntary and
Heb 5: 6 according to the o of Melchizedek."
5:10 a high priest according to the o of Melchizedek.
6:20 priest forever according to the o of Melchizedek.
7:11 priest arising according to the o of Melchizedek,
7:11 rather than one according to the o of Aaron?
7:17 according to the o of Melchizedek."
10: 9 He abolishes the first in o to establish the second.
11:35 in o to obtain a better resurrection.
12:10 in o that we may share his holiness.
12:20 (For they could not endure the o that was given,
13:12 also suffered outside the city gate in o to sanctify
Jas 4: 3 in o to spend what you get on your pleasures.
1Pe 2: 9 in o that you may proclaim the mighty acts
3:18 in o to bring you to God.
Rev 16:12 in o to prepare the way for the kings from the east.
20: 8 Gog and Magog, in o to gather them for battle;
Jdt 3:10 and remained for a whole month in o to collect all
8:27 the Lord scourges those who are close to him in o
10: 9 "O the gate of the town to be opened for me so
11:11 in o that my lord may not be defeated
11:14 in o to bring back permission from the council of
AdE 1:11 the queen to him in o to proclaim her as queen and
1:15 be done to Queen Vashti for not obeying the o that
8: 5 let an o be sent rescinding the letters
13: 2 in o to make my kingdom peaceable and open
16:16 and for our ancestors in the most excellent o.
Wis 16: 3 in o that those people,
16:23 in o that the righteous might be fed,
19: 4 in o that they might fill up the punishment
Sir 16:27 he arranged his works in an eternal o,
33:28 Put him to work, in o that he may not be idle,
38: 5 with a tree in o that its power might be known?
42:21 He has set in o the splendors of his wisdom;
50:19 until the o of worship of the Lord was ended,
LtJ 6:18 in o that they may not be plundered by robbers.
1Mc 1:16 in o that he might reign over both kingdoms.
4:35 to Antioch and enlisted mercenaries in o
6:40 and they advanced steadily and in good o.
12:36 in o to isolate it so
14:29 in o that their sanctuary and the law might
2Mc 1:18 in o that you also may celebrate the festival
6:11 in o to observe the seventh day secretly,
6:15 in o that he may not take vengeance
7:22 nor I who set in o the elements within each of you.
11:10 They advanced in battle o,
1Es 1: 5 in o in the temple according to the groupings of
1:10 stood in proper o according to kindred
2:21 in o that, if it seems good to you,
6: 4 "By whose o are you building this house
6:12 In o that we might inform you in writing who
6:31 in o that libations may be made to
8:12 in o to look into matters in Judea and Jerusalem,
Man 1: 2 you who made heaven and earth with all their o;
3Mc 1:10 he marveled at the good o of the temple,
2:30 In o that he might not appear to be an enemy
3:26 be established for ourselves in good o and in
5:19 he had carried out completely the o given him,
2Es 6:35 in o to complete the three weeks
7:*44* This is my judgment and its prescribed o;
7:*88* "Now this is the o of those who have kept
7:*92* The first o, because they have striven
7:*93* The second o, because they see the perplexity
7:*94* The third o, they see the witness
7:*95* The fourth o, they understand the rest that they
7:*96* The fifth o, they rejoice that they have
7:*97* The sixth o, when it is shown them
7:*98* The seventh o, which is greater than all
7:*99* This is the o of the souls of the righteous,
11:20 that followed also rose up on the right side, in o
14:13 set your house in o, and reprove your people;
14:46 in o to give them to the wise among your people.

ORDERED (127) [ORDER]

Ex 15:22 Then Moses o Israel to set out from the Red Sea,
Lev 10: 5 by their tunics out of the camp, as Moses had o.
10: 7 And they did as Moses had o.
Nu 16:47 So Aaron took it as Moses had o,
Dt 1:19 Then, just as the LORD our God had o us,
Jos 4:12 before the Israelites, as Moses had o them.
8: 8 doing as the LORD has o;
Ru 2: 9 I have o the young men not to bother you.
2Sa 1:18 (He o that The Song of the Bow be taught to
18: 5 The king o Joab and Abishai and Ittai, saying,
23: 5 o in all things and secure.
1Ki 22:26 The king of Israel then o, "Take Micaiah,
2Ch 18:25 The king of Israel then o, "Take Micaiah,

2Ch 27: 6 because he **o** his ways before the LORD his God.
Ezr 6: 13 with all diligence what King Darius had **o.**
Est 4: 5 and **o** him to go to Mordecai
4: 17 and did everything as Esther had **o** him.
Ps 59: T *Saul **o** his house be watched in order to kill him.*
Pr 20: 24 All our steps are **o** by the LORD;
Jer 36: 5 And Jeremiah **o** Baruch, saying,
36: 8 of Neriah did all that the prophet Jeremiah **o** him
Da 2: 23 for you have revealed to us what the king **o."**
3: 19 **o** the furnace heated up seven times more than
3: 20 and **o** some of the strongest guards in his army
Mt 9: 30 Then Jesus sternly **o** them,
12: 16 and he **o** them not to make him known.
14: 19 Then he **o** the crowds to sit down on the grass.
16: 20 Then he sternly **o** the disciples not to tell anyone
17: 9 Jesus **o** them, "Tell no one about the vision until
18: 25 as he could not pay, his lord **o** him to be sold,
20: 31 The crowd sternly **o** them to be quiet;
27: 58 then Pilate **o** it to be given to him.
Mk 3: 12 But he sternly **o** them not to make him known.
5: 43 He strictly **o** them that no one should know this,
6: 8 He **o** them to take nothing for their journey except
6: 39 Then he **o** them to get all the people to sit down
7: 36 Then Jesus **o** them to tell no one;
7: 36 but the more he **o** them,
8: 6 Then he **o** the crowd to sit down on the ground;
8: 7 he **o** that these too should be distributed.
8: 30 he sternly **o** them not to tell anyone about him.
9: 9 he **o** them to tell no one about what they had seen,
10: 48 Many sternly **o** him to be quiet,
Lk 5: 14 And he **o** him to tell no one.
8: 56 but he **o** them to tell no one what had happened.
9: 21 He sternly **o** and commanded them not
14: 22 the slave said, 'Sir, what you **o** has been done,
17: 10 when you have done all that you were **o** to do, say,
18: 15 disciples saw it, they sternly **o** them not to do it.
18: 39 Those who were in front sternly **o** him to be quiet;
18: 40 Jesus stood still and **o** the man to be brought
19: 15 having received royal power, he **o** these slaves,
Ac 1: 4 he **o** them not to leave Jerusalem,
4: 15 So they **o** them to leave the council
4: 18 and **o** them not to speak or teach at all in the name
5: 34 and **o** the men to be put outside for a short time.
5: 40 they **o** them not to speak in the name of Jesus,
10: 48 So he **o** them to be baptized in the name
12: 19 he examined the guards and **o** them to be put
15: 5 "It is necessary for them to be circumcised and **o**
16: 22 of their clothing and **o** them to be beaten
16: 23 into prison and **o** the jailer to keep them securely.
18: 2 because Claudius had **o** all Jews to leave Rome.
21: 33 and **o** him to be bound with two chains;
21: 34 he **o** him to be brought into the barracks.
22: 24 and **o** him to be examined by flogging,
22: 30 and **o** the chief priests and the entire council
23: 2 the high priest Ananias **o** those standing near him
23: 10 **o** the soldiers to go down, take him by force,
23: 35 Then he **o** that he be kept under guard
24: 23 Then he **o** the centurion to keep him in custody,
25: 6 on the tribunal and **o** Paul to be brought.
25: 17 on the next day took my seat on the tribunal and **o**
25: 21 I **o** him to be held until I could send him to
27: 43 He **o** those who could swim
Tob 8: 18 Then he **o** his servants to fill in the grave
8: 19 and brought two steers and four rams and **o** them
Jdt 2: 13 but carry them out exactly as I have **o** you;
2: 15 by divisions as his lord had **o** him to do,
4: 8 as they had been **o** by the high priest Joakim and
6: 10 Then Holofernes **o** his slaves,
7: 1 The next day Holofernes **o** his whole army,
10: 9 So they **o** the young men to open the gate for her,
12: 1 and **o** them to set a table for her with some
AdE 2: 23 Then the king **o** a memorandum to be deposited in
3: 14 all the nations were **o** to be prepared for that day.
4: 5 and **o** him to get accurate information for her
8: 11 He **o** the Jews in every city
12: 5 And the king **o** Mordecai to serve in the court,
Sir 10: 1 and the rule of an intelligent person is well **o.**
Bar 5: 7 For God has **o** that every high mountain and
LtJ 6: 63 and woods does what it is **o**
Sus 1: 32 the scoundrels **o** her to be unveiled,
1: 56 he **o** them to bring the other.
Bel 1: 14 Then Daniel **o** his servants to bring ashes,
1Mc 3: 28 and **o** them to be ready for any need.
4: 27 nor had they turned out as the king had **o.**
5: 49 Then Judas **o** proclamation to be made to the army
15: 41 as the king had **o** him.
2Mc 1: 20 he **o** them to dip it out and bring it.
1: 21 Nehemiah **o** the priests to sprinkle the liquid on
1: 31 Nehemiah **o** that the liquid that was left should
2: 1 prophet Jeremiah **o** those who were being deported
2: 4 **o** that the tent and the ark should follow with him,
5: 25 he **o** his troops to parade under arms.
7: 5 the king **o** them to take him to the fire,
9: 4 so he **o** his charioteer to drive without stopping
11: 20 I have **o** these men and my representatives
13: 4 for all the trouble, he **o** them to take him to Beroea
13: 10 he **o** the people to call upon the Lord day
13: 12 Judas exhorted them and **o** them to stand ready.
14: 41 they **o** that fire be brought and the doors burned.
15: 4 who **o** us to observe the seventh day,"
15: 30 **o** them to cut off Nicanor's head and arm
1Es 2: 26 So I **o** search to be made,
4: 57 everything that Cyrus had **o** to be done,
6: 24 he **o** the building of the house of the Lord
8: 46 and **o** them to tell Iddo and his kindred and
3Mc 3: 1 and he **o** that all should promptly be gathered
4: 13 **o** in his rage that these people be dealt with
4: 14 but to be tortured with the outrages that he had **o,**
5: 2 and **o** him on the following day to drug all
5: 16 and **o** those present for the banquet
6: 30 in charge of the revenues and **o** him to provide to
7: 8 We also have **o** all people to return
4Mc 5: 2 **o** the guards to seize each and every Hebrew and
8: 12 he **o** the instruments of torture to

ORDERING (6) [ORDER]

Mt 15: 35 Then **o** the crowd to sit down on the ground,
Ac 7: 44 **o** him to make it according to
23: 22 So the tribune dismissed the young man, **o** him,
23: 30 **o** his accusers also to state
Jdt 4: 7 **o** them to seize the mountain passes,
3Mc 5: 40 **o** now for a third time that they be destroyed,

ORDERLY (2) [ORDER]

Lk 1: 1 an **o** account of the events that have been fulfilled
1: 3 to write an **o** account for you,

ORDERS (59) [ORDER]

Ge 12: 20 And Pharaoh gave his men **o** concerning him;
42: 25 Joseph then gave **o** to fill their bags with grain,
Ex 6: 13 and gave them **o** regarding the Israelites
Nu 32: 27 to do battle for the LORD, just as my lord **o."**
Jos 1: 18 against your **o** and disobeys your words,
2: 3 Then the king of Jericho sent **o** to Rahab,
2Sa 14: 8 and I will give **o** concerning you."
18: 5 And all the people heard when the king gave **o**
1Ch 22: 2 David gave **o** to gather together
Ne 13: 9 Then I gave **o** and they cleansed the chambers,
13: 19 be shut and gave **o** that they should not be opened
Est 1: 8 for the king had given **o** to all the officials
3: 13 giving **o** to destroy, to kill,
6: 1 and he gave **o** to bring the book of records,
8: 5 which he wrote giving **o** to destroy
9: 25 he gave **o** in writing that the wicked plot
9: 31 and giving **o** that these days of Purim should
Jer 37: 21 So King Zedekiah gave **o,**
Mt 8: 18 he gave **o** to go over to the other side.
Mk 6: 27 a soldier of the guard with **o** to bring John's head.
Jn 11: 57 the Pharisees had given **o** that anyone who knew
Ac 5: 28 "We gave you strict **o** not to teach in this name,
Tob 6: 16 "Do you not remember your father's **o**
Jdt 2: 6 because they disobeyed my **o.**
7: 16 and he gave **o** to do as they had said.
12: 6 "Let my lord now give **o** to allow your servant
AdE 6: 1 so he gave **o** to his secretary to bring the book
Wis 8: 1 and she **o** all things well.
Sir 43: 5 at his **o** it hurries on its course.
43: 10 On the **o** of the Holy One they stand
1Mc 3: 34 and gave him **o** about all that he wanted done.
5: 58 So they issued **o** to the men of the forces that were
6: 57 So he quickly gave **o** to withdraw,
6: 62 he broke the oath he had sworn and gave **o** to tear
9: 54 Alcimus gave **o** to tear down the wall of
9: 63 and sent **o** to the men of Judea.
10: 62 The king gave **o** to take off Jonathan's garments
11: 23 he gave **o** to continue the siege.
14: 48 And they gave **o** to inscribe this decree
2Mc 3: 13 Heliodorus, because of the **o** he had from the king,
4: 25 After receiving the king's **o** he returned,
7: 3 and gave **o** to have pans and caldrons heated.
9: 7 and giving **o** to drive even faster.
12: 5 he gave **o** to his men
14: 13 with **o** to kill Judas and scatter his troops,
15: 10 he had aroused their courage, he issued his **o,**
1Es 2: 28 now issued **o** to prevent these people
7: 1 following the **o** of King Darius,
8: 10 I have given **o** that those of the Jewish nation and
8: 67 They delivered the king's **o** to the royal stewards
3Mc 1: 1 he gave **o** to all his forces,
3: 25 Therefore we have given **o** that,
5: 3 he had given these **o** he returned to his feasting,
5: 4 proceeded faithfully to carry out the **o.**
5: 37 must I give you **o** about these things?
2Es 7: *91* for they shall have rest in seven **o.**
4Mc 8: 3 the tyrant had given these **o,** seven brothers—
8: 6 as I am able to punish those who disobey my **o,**
10: 17 and utterly abominable Antiochus gave **o**

ORDINANCE (29) [ORDAIN]

Ex 12: 14 generations you shall observe it as a perpetual **o.**
12: 17 throughout your generations as a perpetual **o.**
12: 24 You shall observe this rite as a perpetual **o** for you
12: 43 This is the **o** for the passover:
13: 10 You shall keep this **o** at its proper time from year
15: 25 a statute and an **o** and there he put them to the test.
27: 21 It shall be a perpetual **o** to be observed
28: 43 be a perpetual **o** for him and for his descendants
29: 9 and the priesthood shall be theirs by a perpetual **o.**
29: 28 These things shall be a perpetual **o** for Aaron
30: 21 it shall be a perpetual **o** for them,
Nu 15: 16 with you shall have the same law and the same **o.**
15: 24 and its drink offering, according to the **o,**
27: 11 It shall be for the Israelites a statute and **o,**
29: 6 according to the **o** for them, a pleasing odor,
35: 29 These things shall be a statute and **o** for you
1Sa 30: 25 that day forward he made it a statute and an **o**
2Ch 8: 14 According to the **o** of his father David,
35: 13 the passover lamb with fire according to the **o;**
Ezr 3: 4 by number according to the **o,**
Ne 8: 18 a solemn assembly, according to the **o.**
Ps 81: 4 it is a statute for Israel, an **o** of the God of Jacob.
Isa 58: 2 and did not forsake the **o** of their God;
Jer 8: 7 but my people do not know the **o** of the LORD.
Eze 46: 14 this is the **o** for all time.
Da 6: 7 that the king should establish an **o** and enforce
6: 15 that no interdict or **o** that the king establishes can
Tob 1: 8 according to the **o** decreed concerning it in the law
2Es 8: 22 whose command is strong and whose **o** is terrible,

ORDINANCES (109) [ORDAIN]

Ex 21: 1 These are the **o** that you shall set before them:
24: 3 the words of the LORD and all the **o;**
Lev 18: 4 My **o** you shall observe
18: 5 You shall keep my statutes and my **o;**
18: 26 and my **o** and commit none of these abominations,
19: 37 You shall keep all my statutes and all my **o,**
20: 22 You shall keep all my statutes and all my **o,**
25: 18 and faithfully keep my **o,**
26: 15 if you spurn my statutes, and abhor my **o,** so
26: 43 because they dared to spurn my **o,**
26: 46 and **o** and laws that the LORD established
Nu 35: 24 in accordance with these **o;**
36: 13 the **o** that the LORD commanded through Moses
Dt 4: 1 to the statutes and **o** that I am teaching you
4: 5 now teach you statutes and **o** for you to observe in
4: 8 and **o** as just as this entire law that I am setting
4: 14 and **o** for you to observe in the land that you are
4: 45 These are the decrees and the statutes and **o**
5: 1 statutes and **o** that I am addressing to you today;
5: 31 the statutes and the **o,** that you shall teach them,
6: 1 this is the commandment—the statutes and the **o—**
6: 20 of the decrees and the statutes and the **o** that
7: 11 and the **o—**that I am commanding you today.
7: 12 If you heed these **o,** by diligently observing them,
8: 11 by failing to keep his commandments, his **o,**
11: 1 his decrees, his **o,** and his commandments always.
11: 32 you must diligently observe all the statutes and **o**
12: 1 the statutes and **o** that you must diligently observe
26: 16 to observe these statutes and **o;**
26: 17 to keep his statutes, his commandments, and his **o,**
30: 16 and observing his commandments, decrees, and **o,**
33: 10 They teach Jacob your **o,** and Israel your law;
33: 21 the justice of the LORD, and his **o** for Israel.
Jos 24: 25 and made statutes and **o** for them at Shechem.
2Sa 22: 23 For all his **o** were before me,
1Ki 2: 3 his commandments, his **o,** and his testimonies,
6: 12 if you will walk in my statutes, obey my **o,**
8: 58 and his **o,** which he commanded our ancestors.
9: 4 and keeping my statutes and my **o,**
11: 33 in my sight and keeping my statutes and my **o,**
2Ki 17: 34 and they do not follow the statutes or the **o** or
17: 37 and the **o** and the law and the commandment
1Ch 22: 13 if you are careful to observe the statutes and the **o**
28: 7 in keeping my commandments and my **o,**
2Ch 7: 17 and keeping my statutes and my **o,**
19: 10 statutes or **o,** then you shall instruct them,
33: 8 the statutes, and the **o** given through Moses."
Ezr 7: 10 and to teach the statutes and **o** in Israel.
Ne 1: 7 the **o** that you commanded your servant Moses.
9: 13 and gave them right **o** and true laws,
9: 29 but sinned against your **o,**
10: 29 of the LORD our Lord and his **o** and his statutes.
Job 38: 33 Do you know the **o** of the heavens?
Ps 18: 22 For all his **o** were before me,
19: 9 **o** of the LORD are true and righteous altogether.
89: 30 and do not walk according to my **o,**
119: 7 when I learn your righteous **o.**
119: 13 With my lips I declare all the **o** of your mouth.
119: 20 My soul is consumed with longing for your **o**
119: 30 I set your **o** before me.
119: 39 the disgrace that I dread, for your **o** are good.
119: 43 for my hope is in your **o.**
119: 52 When I think of your **o** from of old,
119: 62 because of your righteous **o.**
119: 102 I do not turn away from your **o,**
119: 106 to observe your righteous **o.**
119: 108 O LORD, and teach me your **o.**
119: 160 and every one of your righteous **o** endures forever.
119: 164 a day I praise you for your righteous **o.**
119: 175 and let your **o** help me.
147: 19 his statutes and **o** to Israel
147: 20 they do not know his **o.**
Jer 33: 25 with day and night and the **o** of heaven and earth,
Eze 5: 6 But she has rebelled against my **o** and my statutes,
5: 6 rejecting my **o** and not following my statutes.
5: 7 and have not followed my statutes or kept my **o,**
5: 7 but have acted according to the **o** of the nations
11: 12 and whose **o** you have not kept,
11: 12 to the **o** of the nations that are around you."
11: 20 that they may follow my statutes and keep my **o**
18: 9 and is careful to observe my **o,** acting faithfully—
18: 17 observes my **o,** and follows my statutes;
20: 11 I gave them my statutes and showed them my **o,**
20: 13 not observe my statutes but rejected my **o,**
20: 16 because they rejected my **o** and did
20: 18 the statutes of your parents, nor observe their **o,**
20: 19 and be careful to observe my **o,**
20: 21 and were not careful to observe my **o,**
20: 24 because they had not executed my **o,**
20: 25 that were not good and **o** by which they could
23: 24 and they shall judge you according to their **o.**
36: 27 and be careful to observe my **o.**
37: 24 They shall follow my **o** and be careful
43: 11 all its **o** and its entire plan and all its laws;
43: 11 and follow the entire plan and all its **o.**
43: 18 These are the **o** for the altar:
44: 5 the **o** of the temple of the LORD and all its laws;
Da 9: 5 turning aside from your commandments and **o.**

Mal 4: 4 the statutes and **o** that I commanded him at Horeb
Eph 2:15 the law with its commandments and **o**,
AdE 13: 4 of every nation and continually disregard the **o**
Sir 4:17 and she will test them with her **o**.
Bar 2:12 O Lord our God, against all your **o**.
1Mc 1:13 who authorized them to observe the **o** of
1:49 they would forget the law and change all the **o**.
2:21 Far be it from us to desert the law and the **o**.
2:40 with the Gentiles for our lives and for our **o**,
1Es 8: 7 but taught all Israel all the **o** and judgments.
4Mc 15:10 they obeyed her even to death in keeping the **o**.

ORDINARY (13)

Ex 30:32 It shall not be used in any **o** anointing of the body,
Lev 4:27 of the **o** people among you sins unintentionally
1Sa 21: 4 priest answered David, "I have no **o** bread at hand,
Eze 48:15 shall be for **o** use for the city,
Ac 4:13 and realized that they were uneducated and **o** men,
Ro 9:21 for special use and another for **o** use?
1Co 6: 3 to say nothing of **o** matters?
6: 4 If you have **o** cases, then, do you appoint
2Co 1:17 according to **o** human standards,
2Ti 2:20 some for special use, some for **o**.
AdE 4: 8 he said, "the days when you were an **o** person,
Sir 33: 9 and some he made **o** days.
3Mc 3: 7 So they attached no **o** reproach to them.

ORDINATION (11) [ORDAIN]

Ex 29:22 and the right thigh (for it is a ram of **o**),
29:26 You shall take the breast of the ram of Aaron's **o**
29:27 as an elevation offering from the ram of **o**,
29:31 You shall take the ram of **o**,
29:34 If any of the flesh for the **o**, or of the bread,
Lev 7:37 the offering of **o**, and the sacrifice of well-being,
8:22 he brought forward the second ram, the ram of **o**.
8:28 This was an **o** offering for a pleasing odor,
8:29 it was Moses' portion of the ram of **o**,
8:31 with the bread that is in the basket of **o** offerings,
8:33 until the day when your period of **o** is completed.

ORE (2)

Job 28: 2 and copper is smelted from **o**.
28: 3 and search out to the farthest bound the **o** in gloom

OREB (7)

Jdg 7:25 the two captains of Midian, **O** and Zeeb;
7:25 they killed **O** at the rock of **O**,
7:25 They brought the heads of **O** and Zeeb to Gideon
8: 3 your hands the captains of Midian, **O** and Zeeb;
Ps 83:11 Make their nobles like **O** and Zeeb,
Isa 10:26 as when he struck Midian at the rock of **O**;

OREN (1)

1Ch 2:25 Ram his firstborn, Bunah, **O**, Ozem, and Ahijah.

ORGAN (1) [ORGANS]

4Mc 10:18 But he said, "Even if you remove my **o** of speech,

ORGAN (KJV) See also PIPE

ORGANIZED (8) [ORGANIZING]

1Ch 23: 6 And David **o** them in divisions corresponding to
24: 3 David **o** them according to the appointed duties
24: 4 they **o** them under sixteen heads
24: 5 They **o** them by lot, all alike,
2Ch 23:18 to the levitical priests whom David had **o** to be
Jdt 2:16 and he **o** them as a great army is marshaled for
1Mc 2:44 They **o** an army, and struck down sinners
2Mc 8: 5 As soon as Maccabeus got his army **o**,

ORGANIZING (1) [ORGANIZED]

3Mc 4:16 **o** feasts in honor of all his idols,

ORGANS (1) [ORGAN]

Ex 12: 9 with its head, legs, and inner **o**.

ORGIES (2)

Jer 3:23 the hills are a delusion, the **o** on the mountains.
Hos 4:18 their drinking is ended, they indulge in sexual **o**;

ORIGIN (19) [ORIGINAL, ORIGINALLY, ORIGINATE]

Isa 23: 7 Is this your exultant city whose **o** is from days
Eze 16: 3 Your **o** and your birth were in the land of
21:30 in the land of your **o**, I will judge you.
29:14 to the land of Pathros, the land of their **o**;
Mic 5: 2 whose **o** is from of old, from ancient days.
Mt 21:25 or was it of human **o**?"
21:26 we say, 'Of human **o**,' we are afraid of the crowd;
Mk 7:26 the woman was a Gentile, of Syrophoenician **o**.
11:30 or was it of human **o**?
11:32 But shall we say, 'Of human **o**'?"—
Lk 20: 4 or was it of human **o**?"
20: 6 we say, 'Of human **o**,' all the people will stone us;
Ac 5:38 if this plan or this undertaking is of human **o**,
15:23 the elders, to the believers of Gentile **o** in Antioch
Gal 1:11 that was proclaimed by me is not of human **o**;
Rev 3:14 of the Amen, the faithful and true witness, the **o**
Wis 12:10 though you were not unaware that their **o** was evil
2Mc 7:23 the beginning of humankind and devised the **o**
2Es 15:31 And then the dragons, remembering their **o**,

ORIGINAL (6) [ORIGIN]

Lev 27:15 and it shall revert to the **o** owner.
27:19 and it shall revert to the **o** owner;
Nu 35:25 the slayer back to the **o** city of refuge.
35:26 at any time go outside the bounds of the **o** city
Sir Pr: 2 of the books differ not a little when read in the **o**.
2Mc 2:30 the duty of the **o** historian to occupy the ground,

ORIGINALLY (1) [ORIGIN]

Sir Pr: 2 For what was **o** expressed in Hebrew does

ORIGINATE (1) [ORIGIN]

1Co 14:36 Or did the word of God **o** with you?

ORION (3)

Job 9: 9 and **O**, the Pleiades and the chambers of the south;
38:31 or loose the cords of **O**?
Am 5: 8 The one who made the Pleiades and **O**,

ORNAMENT‡ (7) [ORNAMENTS]

Lev 8: 9 and on the turban, in front, he set the golden **o**,
Pr 25:12 Like a gold ring or an **o** of gold is a wise rebuke to
Isa 49:18 you shall put all of them on like an **o**,
Eze 7:20 From their beautiful **o**, in which they took pride,
Tit 2:10 that in everything they may be an **o** to the doctrine
Sir 6:30 Her yoke is a golden **o**,
21:21 the sensible person education is like a golden **o**,

ORNAMENTS‡ (13) [ORNAMENT]

Ge 24:53 to her brother and to her mother costly **o**.
Ex 33: 4 they mourned, and no one put on **o**.
33: 5 So now take off your **o**,
33: 6 the Israelites stripped themselves of their **o**,
2Sa 1:24 in luxury, who put **o** of gold on your apparel.
SS 1:10 Your cheeks are comely with **o**,
1:11 We will make you **o** of gold, studded with silver.
Jer 2:32 Can a girl forget her **o**, or a bride her attire?
4:30 that you deck yourself with **o** of gold,
Eze 16:11 I adorned you with **o**: I put bracelets on your
23:40 painted your eyes, and decked yourself with **o**;
1Pe 3: 3 and by wearing gold **o** or fine clothing;
LtJ 6: 9 as they might for a girl who loves **o**.

ORNAN (12) [=ARAUNAH]

1Ch 21:15 then standing by the threshing floor of **O**
21:18 an altar to the LORD on the threshing floor of **O**
21:20 **O** turned and saw the angel;
21:20 **O** continued to thresh wheat.
21:21 David came to **O**, **O** looked and saw David;
21:22 to **O**, "Give me the site of the threshing floor
21:23 Then **O** said to David, "Take it;
21:24 But King David said to **O**, "No;
21:25 So David paid **O** six hundred shekels of gold
21:28 at the threshing floor of **O** the Jebusite,
2Ch 3: 1 on the threshing floor of **O** the Jebusite.

ORPAH (2)

Ru 1: 4 of the one was **O** and the name of the other Ruth.
1:14 **O** kissed her mother-in-law, but Ruth clung to her.

ORPHAN (33) [ORPHANED, ORPHANS]

Ex 22:22 You shall not abuse any widow or **o**.
Dt 10:18 who executes justice for the **o** and the widow,
24:17 not deprive a resident alien or an **o** of justice;
24:19 it shall be left for the alien, the **o**, and the widow,
24:20 it shall be for the alien, the **o**, and the widow.
24:21 it shall be for the alien, the **o**, and the widow.
27:19 "Cursed be anyone who deprives the alien, the **o**,
Job 6:27 You would even cast lots over the **o**,
24: 3 They drive away the donkey of the **o**;
24: 9 "There are those who snatch the **o** child from
29:12 and the **o** who had no helper.
31:17 and the **o** has not eaten from it—
31:18 for from my youth I reared the **o** like a father,
31:21 the **o**, because I saw I had supporters at the gate;
Ps 10:14 you have been the helper of the **o**.
10:18 to do justice for the **o** and the oppressed,
82: 3 Give justice to the weak and the **o**;
94: 6 the widow and the stranger, they murder the **o**,
146: 9 he upholds the **o** and the widow,
Isa 1:17 defend the **o**, plead for the widow.
1:23 They do not defend the **o**,
Jer 5:28 they do not judge with justice the cause of the **o**,
7: 6 the **o**, and the widow, or shed innocent blood
22: 3 And do no wrong or violence to the alien, the **o**,
Eze 22: 7 the **o** and the widow are wronged in you.
Hos 14: 3 In you the **o** finds mercy."
Zec 7:10 the **o**, the alien, or the poor;
Mal 3: 5 in their wages, the widow and the **o**,
Tob 1: 8 for my father had died and left me an **o**.
Sir 35:17 He will not ignore the supplication of the **o**,
LtJ 6:38 on a widow or do good to an **o**.
1Es 3:19 It makes equal the mind of the king and the **o**,
2Es 2:20 give to the needy, defend the **o**, clothe the naked,

ORPHANED (2) [ORPHAN]

Ps 109:12 nor anyone to pity his **o** children.
Jn 14:18 "I will not leave you **o**; I am coming to you.

ORPHANS (21) [ORPHAN]

Ex 22:24 wives shall become widows and your children **o**.
Dt 14:29 the **o**, and the widows in your towns,
16:11 the **o**, and the widows who are among you—
16:14 the **o**, and the widows resident in your towns.
26:12 giving it to the Levites, the aliens, the **o**,
26:13 the resident aliens, the **o**, and the widows,
Job 22: 9 and the arms of the **o** you have crushed.
Ps 68: 5 Father of **o** and protector of widows is God
109: 9 May his children be **o**, and his wife a widow.
Pr 23:10 or encroach on the fields of **o**,
Isa 9:17 or compassion on their **o** and widows;
10: 2 and that you may make the **o** your prey!
Jer 49:11 Leave your **o**, I will keep them alive;
La 5: 3 We have become **o**, fatherless;
1Th 2:17 we were made **o** by being separated from you—
Jas 1:27 to care for **o** and widows in their distress,
Tob 1: 8 A third tenth I would give to the **o** and widows
Sir 4:10 to **o**, and be like a husband to their mother;
2Mc 3:10 some deposits belonging to widows and **o**,
8:28 and to the widows and **o**,
8:30 giving to those who had been tortured and to the **o**

ORTHOSIA (1)

1Mc 15:37 Trypho embarked on a ship and escaped to **O**.

OSEE (KJV) See HOSEA

OSHEA (KJV) See JOSHUA

OSNAPPAR (1)

Ezr 4:10 the nations whom the great and noble **O** deported

OSPREY (2)

Lev 11:13 the eagle, the vulture, the **o**,
Dt 14:12 the eagle, the vulture, the **o**,

OSSIFRAGE (KJV) See VULTURE

OSTENSIBLY (1)

2Mc 3: 8 **o** to make a tour of inspection of the cities

OSTRICH (2) [OSTRICH'S, OSTRICHES]

Lev 11:16 the **o**, the nighthawk, the sea gull, the hawk
Dt 14:15 the **o**, the nighthawk, the sea gull, the hawk,

OSTRICH'S (1) [OSTRICH]

Job 39:13 "The **o** wings flap wildly,

OSTRICHES (7) [OSTRICH]

Job 30:29 I am a brother of jackals, and a companion of **o**.
Isa 13:21 there **o** will live, and there goat-demons will dance.
34:13 It shall be the haunt of jackals, an abode for **o**.
43:20 wild animals will honor me, the jackals and the **o**;
Jer 50:39 with hyenas in Babylon, and **o** shall inhabit her;
La 4: 3 like the **o** in the wilderness.
Mic 1: 8 like the jackals, and mourning like the **o**.

OTHER‡ (606) [OTHER'S, OTHERS, OTHERWISE]

A. OTHER GODS (65)
B. OTHER SIDE (48)
C. NO OTHER (34)
D. EACH OTHER (33)
E. ANY OTHER (23)
F. OTHER NATIONS (11)
G. OTHER PEOPLE (9)

Ge 3: 1 serpent was more crafty than any **o** wild animal E
4:19 and the name of the **o** Zillah.
5: 4 and he had **o** sons and daughters.
5: 7 and had **o** sons and daughters.
5:10 and had **o** sons and daughters.
5:13 and had **o** sons and daughters.
5:16 and had **o** sons and daughters.
5:19 and had **o** sons and daughters.
5:22 and had **o** sons and daughters.
5:26 and had **o** sons and daughters.
5:30 and had **o** sons and daughters.
11:11 and had **o** sons and daughters.
11:13 and had **o** sons and daughters.
11:15 and had **o** sons and daughters.
11:17 and had **o** sons and daughters.
11:19 and had **o** sons and daughters.
11:21 and had **o** sons and daughters.
11:23 and had **o** sons and daughters.
11:25 and had **o** sons and daughters.
13:11 thus they separated from each **o**. D
15:10 laying each half over against the **o**;
25:23 the one shall be stronger than the **o**,
28:17 This is none **o** than the house of God,
29:19 to you than that I should give her to any **o** man; E
29:27 and we will give you the **o** also in return
31:49 when we are absent one from the **o**.
34:27 And the **o** sons of Jacob came upon the slain,
37: 3 Now Israel loved Joseph more than any **o** E
41: 3 Then seven **o** cows, ugly and thin,
41: 3 and stood by the **o** cows on the bank of the Nile.
41:19 Then seven **o** cows came up after them, poor,
42: 5 of Israel were among the **o** people who came G
43:14 he may send back your **o** brother and Benjamin.
47:21 of them from one end of Egypt to the **o**.
Ex 1:15 one of whom was named Shiphrah and the **o** Puah,

Ex 14: 7 the **o** chariots of Egypt with officers over all
14:20 one did not come near the **o** all night.
16: 5 it will be twice as much as they gather on **o** days."
17:12 one on one side, and the **o** on the other side;
17:12 one on one side, and the other on the **o** side; B
18: 4 and the name of the **o**,
20: 3 you shall have no **o** gods before me. AC
21:18 the **o** with a stone or fist so that the injured party,
22: 9 clothing, or any **o** loss, of which one party says, E
22: 9 whom God condemns shall pay double to the **o**.
22:10 ox, sheep, or any **o** animal for safekeeping, E
22:11 not laid hands on the property of the **o**;
22:20 to any god, **o** than the LORD alone, shall
23:13 Do not invoke the names of **o** gods; A
25:12 and two rings on the **o** side. B
25:19 and one cherub at the **o**;
25:32 of the lampstand out of the **o** side of it; B
25:33 each with calyx and petals, on the **o** branch—
26: 3 the **o** five curtains shall be joined to one another.
26:13 cubit on the one side, and the cubit on the **o** side, B
26:27 for the frames of the **o** side of the tabernacle, B
27:15 be fifteen cubits of hangings on the **o** side, B
28:10 and the names of the remaining six on the **o** stone,
29:19 You shall take the **o** ram;
29:39 and the **o** lamb you shall offer in the evening;
29:41 And the **o** lamb you shall offer in the evening,
30:32 and you shall make no **o** like it in composition; C
34:14 (for you shall worship no **o** god, C
36:10 and the **o** five curtains he joined to one another.
36:13 and joined the curtains one to the **o** with clasps;
36:17 fifty loops on the edge of the **o** connecting curtain.
36:32 for the frames of the **o** side of the tabernacle, B
37: 3 on its one side and two rings on its **o** side. B
37: 8 and one cherub at the **o** end;
37:18 of the lampstand out of the **o** side of it; B
37:19 each with calyx and petals, on the **o** branch—
38:15 And so for the **o** side; B
Lev 5: 7 for a sin offering and the **o** for a burnt offering.
6:11 and put on **o** garments, and carry the ashes out to
7:10 But every **o** grain offering, mixed with oil or dry,
7:19 for **o** flesh, all who are clean may eat such flesh.
11:10 in the waters and among all the **o** living creatures
11:23 But all **o** winged insects
12: 8 for a burnt offering and the **o** for a sin offering;
14:22 for a sin offering and the **o** for a burnt offering.
14:31 a sin offering and the **o** for a burnt offering,
14:42 They shall take **o** stones and put them in the place
14:42 and take **o** plaster and plaster the house.
15:15 for a sin offering and the **o** for a burnt offering;
15:30 for a sin offering and the **o** for a burnt offering;
16: 8 one lot for the LORD and the **o** lot for Azazel.
20:26 and I have separated you from the **o** peoples to
25:46 no one shall rule over the **o** with harshness.
Nu 1:49 not take a census of them with the **o** Israelites.
1:52 The **o** Israelites shall camp
2:33 Levites were not enrolled among the **o** Israelites.
4: 2 of the Kohathites separate from the **o** Levites,
5:20 some man **o** than your husband has had intercourse
6: 3 they shall drink no wine vinegar or **o** vinegar,
6:11 the priest shall offer one as a sin offering and the **o**
8:12 for a sin offering and the **o** for a burnt offering to
8:14 the Levites from among the **o** Israelites,
11:26 one named Eldad, and the **o** named Medad,
11:31 on this side and a day's journey on the **o** side, B
21:13 and camped on the **o** side of the Arnon, B
24: 1 so he did not go, as at **o** times, to look for omens,
28: 4 and the **o** lamb you shall offer at twilight
28: 8 The **o** lamb you shall offer at twilight with
32:19 them on the **o** side of the Jordan and beyond, B
Dt 4: 7 For what **o** great nation has a god so near to it as
4: 8 And what **o** great nation has statutes
4:28 There you will serve **o** gods made A
4:32 ask from one end of heaven to the **o**:
4:35 there is no **o** besides him. C
4:39 on the earth beneath; there is no **o**. C
5: 7 you shall have no **o** gods before me. AC
6:14 Do not follow **o** gods, any of the gods of A
7: 4 from following me, to serve **o** gods. A
7: 7 you were more numerous than any **o** people EG
8:19 the LORD your God and follow **o** gods to serve A
11:16 serving **o** gods and worshiping them, A
11:28 to follow **o** gods that you have not known. A
12:27 the blood of your **o** sacrifices shall be poured out
13: 2 "Let us follow **o** gods" (whom you have A
13: 6 saying, "Let us go worship **o** gods," A
13: 7 from one end of the earth to the **o**,
13:13 saying, "Let us go and worship **o** gods," A
17: 3 going to serve **o** gods and worshiping them— A
17:20 neither exalting himself above **o** members of
18: 2 among the **o** members of the community;
18:20 any prophet who speaks in the name of **o** gods, A
19: 5 the handle and strikes the **o** person who then dies;
19:19 as the false witness had meant to do to the **o**.
21:15 one of them loved and the **o** disliked,
24:14 whether **o** Israelites or aliens who reside
25: 1 declaring one to be in the right and the **o** to be in
28:14 following **o** gods to serve them. A
28:36 you shall serve **o** gods, of wood and stone. A
28:61 Every **o** malady and affliction,
28:64 from one end of the earth to the **o**;
28:64 and there you shall serve **o** gods, A
29:26 turned and served **o** gods, worshiping them, A
30:13 "Who will cross to the **o** side of the sea for us, B
30:17 but are led astray to bow down to **o** gods A
31:18 all the evil they have done by turning to **o** gods. A
31:20 they will turn to **o** gods and serve them, A
Jos 8:22 some on one side, and some on the **o**;
Jos 13: 8 With the **o** half-tribe of Manasseh the Reubenites
17: 5 which is on the **o** side of the Jordan, B
19:12 in the **o** direction eastward toward the sunrise to
22: 4 the LORD gave you on the **o** side of the Jordan. B
22: 7 but to the **o** half Joshua had given a possession
22:19 by building yourselves an altar **o** than the altar of
22:29 **o** than the altar of the LORD our God that stands
23:16 and go and serve **o** gods and bow down to them, A
24: 2 lived beyond the Euphrates and served **o** gods. A
24: 8 who lived on the **o** side of the Jordan; B
24:16 the LORD to serve **o** gods; A
Jdg 2:12 they followed **o** gods, from among the gods of A
2:17 lusted after **o** gods and bowed down to them. A
2:19 following **o** gods, worshiping them and bowing A
4:11 the Kenite had separated from the **o** Kenites,
7: 5 you shall put to the **o** side." B
7:14 "This is no **o** than the sword of Gideon son C
10:13 you have abandoned me and worshiped **o** gods; A
11:18 and camped on the **o** side of the Arnon. B
13:10 "The man who came to me the **o** day has appeared
16:20 he thought, "I will go out as at **o** times,
16:29 on the one and his left hand on the **o**.
20:31 of which goes up to Bethel and the **o** to Gibeah,
Ru 1: 4 of the one was Orpah and the name of the **o** Ruth.
4: 7 the one took off a sandal and gave it to the **o**;
1Sa 1: 2 and the name of the **o** Peninnah.
8: 5 then, a king to govern us, like **o** nations." F
8: 8 forsaking me and serving **o** gods, A
8:20 so that we also may be like **o** nations, F
14: 1 over to the Philistine garrison on the **o** side." B
14: 4 on one side and a rocky crag on the **o**;
14: 4 and the name of the **o** Seneh.
14: 5 and the **o** on the south in front of Geba.
14:20 and every sword was against the **o**,
14:40 I and my son Jonathan will be on the **o** side." B
17: 3 and Israel stood on the mountain on the **o** side, B
19:21 When Saul was told, he sent **o** messengers,
20:25 The king sat upon his seat, as at **o** times,
20:41 He bowed three times, and they kissed each **o**, D
20:41 they kissed each other, and wept with each **o**; D
23:26 and his men on the **o** side of the mountain. B
26:13 Then David went over to the **o** side, B
26:19 saying, 'Go, serve **o** gods.' A
28: 8 So Saul disguised himself and put on **o** clothes
30:20 which were driven ahead of the **o** cattle;
31: 7 When the men of Israel who were on the **o** side B
2Sa 2:13 while the **o** sat on the other side of the pool.
2:13 while the other sat on the **o** side of the pool. B
4: 2 and the name of the **o** Rechab.
12: 1 the one rich and the **o** poor.
13:16 in sending me away is greater than the **o**
14: 6 and one struck the **o** and killed him.
17: 9 in one of the pits, or in some **o** place.
18:13 On the **o** hand, if I had dealt treacherously
1Ki 3:13 no **o** king shall compare with you. C
3:22 But the **o** woman said, "No, the living son is mine,
3:23 while the **o** says, 'Not so!
3:25 then give half to the one, and half to the **o**."
3:26 The **o** said, "It shall be neither mine nor yours;
4:12 as far as the **o** side of Jokmeam; B
6:24 five cubits the length of the **o** wing of the cherub;
6:24 from the tip of one wing to the tip of the **o**.
6:25 The **o** cherub also measured ten cubits;
6:26 and so was that of the **o** cherub.
6:27 wing of the **o** cherub was touching the **o** wall;
6:27 their **o** wings toward the center of
6:34 and the two leaves of the **o** door were folding.
7: 4 facing each **o** in the three rows. D
7: 5 opposite, facing each **o** in the three rows. D
7: 8 in the **o** court back of the hall,
7:16 and the height of the **o** capital was five cubits.
7:17 and seven for the **o** capital.
7:18 he did the same with the **o** capital.
7:20 and so with the **o** capital.
8:60 that the LORD is God; there is no **o**. C
9: 6 but go and serve **o** gods and worship them, A
9: 9 and embraced **o** gods, worshiping them A
11: 4 his wives turned away his heart after **o** gods; A
11:10 that he should not follow **o** gods; A
12:29 He set one in Bethel, and the **o** he put in Dan.
12:30 the one at Bethel and before the **o** as far as Dan.
13:18 the **o** said to him, "I also am a prophet as you are,
14: 9 and have gone and made for yourself **o** gods, A
18:23 I will prepare the **o** bull and lay it on the wood,
22: 7 "Is there no **o** prophet of the LORD here C
22: 8 "There is still one **o** by whom we may inquire of
2Ki 2: 8 the water was parted to the one side and to the **o**,
2:14 the water was parted to the one side and to the **o**,
12: 7 the priest Jehoiada with the **o** priests and said
17: 7 They had worshiped **o** gods A
17:35 "You shall not worship **o** gods or bow A
17:37 You shall not worship **o** gods; A
17:38 You shall not worship **o** gods, A
22:17 and have made offerings to **o** gods, A
25:28 above the **o** seats of the kings who were with him
1Ch 2:52 Shobal father of Kiriath-jearim had **o** sons:
9:33 in the chambers of the temple free from **o** service,
23:17 Eliezer had no **o** sons, but the sons C
2Ch 2: 5 for our God is greater than **o** gods. A
3:11 touched the wall of the house, and its **o** wing,
3:11 five cubits long, touched the wing of the **o** cherub;
3:12 touched the wall of the house, and the **o** wing,
3:17 one on the right, the **o** on the left;
5:13 and cymbals and **o** musical instruments,
7:19 and go and serve **o** gods and worship them, A
7:22 and they adopted **o** gods, and worshiped them A
11:21 of Absalom more than all his **o** wives
2Ch 12: 8 and serving the kingdoms of **o** lands."
13: 9 for yourselves like the peoples of **o** lands?
18: 6 "Is there no **o** prophet of the LORD here C
18: 7 "There is still one **o** by whom we may inquire of
23: 6 for they are holy, but all the **o** people shall G
28:25 to make offerings to **o** gods, A
29:34 so, until **o** priests had sanctified themselves,
32:13 to all the peoples of **o** lands?
32:17 the nations in **o** lands did not rescue their people
34:12 **O** Levites, all skillful with instruments of music,
34:25 and have made offerings to **o** gods, A
Ezr 1:10 **o** silver bowls, four hundred ten;
1:10 four hundred ten; **o** vessels, one thousand;
2:31 the **o** Elam, one thousand two hundred fifty-four.
7:24 or **o** servants of this house of God.
Ne 4:17 on the work with one hand and with the **o** held
5: 8 Jewish kindred who had been sold to **o** nations; F
7:33 Of the **o** Nebo, fifty-two.
7:34 The descendants of the **o** Elam,
8:15 and **o** leafy trees to make booths, as it is written."
11: 1 while nine-tenths remained in the **o** towns.
12:38 The **o** company of those who gave thanks went to
Est 2:17 the king loved Esther more than all the **o** women;
3: 8 from those of every **o** people, G
4:13 you will escape any more than all the **o** Jews.
9:16 Now the **o** Jews who were in the king's provinces
Job 8:12 they wither before any **o** plant. E
31:10 and let **o** men kneel over her.
35: 8 and your righteousness, **o** human beings.
41:17 they clasp each **o** and cannot be separated. D
Ps 12: 2 They utter lies to each **o**; D
73: 5 they are not plagued like **o** people. G
73:25 there is nothing on earth that I desire **o** than you.
85:10 righteousness and peace will kiss each **o**. D
147:20 He has not dealt thus with any **o** nation; E
Pr 18:17 until the **o** comes and cross-examines.
25: 1 These are **o** proverbs of Solomon that the officials
Ecc 3:19 as one dies, so dies the **o**.
4:10 For if they fall, one will lift up the **o**;
7:14 God has made the one as well as the **o**,
7:18 without letting go of the **o**;
Isa 3: 7 But the **o** will cry out on that day, saying,
19: 2 one against the **o**, neighbor against neighbor,
26:13 **o** lords besides you have ruled over us,
34:14 goat-demons shall call to each **o**; D
41: 6 Each one helps the **o**, saying to one another,
42: 8 my glory I give to no **o**, nor my praise to idols. C
44: 8 There is no **o** rock; I know not one. C
45: 5 I am the LORD, and there is no **o**; C
45: 6 I am the LORD, and there is no **o**. C
45:14 "God is with you alone, and there is no **o**; C
45:18 I am the LORD, and there is no **o**. C
45:21 There is no **o** god besides me, C
45:22 For I am God, and there is no **o**. C
46: 9 for I am God, and there is no **o**; C
Jer 1:16 they have made offerings to **o** gods, A
7: 6 if you do not go after **o** gods to your own hurt, A
7: 9 and go after **o** gods that you have not known, A
7:18 and they pour out drink offerings to **o** gods, A
11:10 they have gone after **o** gods to serve them; A
12:12 from one end of the land to the **o**;
13:10 after **o** gods to serve them and worship them, A
16:11 after **o** gods and have served and worshiped A
16:13 and there you shall serve **o** gods day and night, A
19: 4 to **o** gods whom neither they nor their ancestors A
19:13 and libations have been poured out to **o** gods. A
22: 9 and worshiped **o** gods and served them." A
24: 2 but the **o** basket had very bad figs,
25: 6 not go after **o** gods to serve and worship them, A
25:33 from one end of the earth to the **o**.
31:34 or say to each **o**, "Know the LORD," D
32:29 and libations have been poured out to **o** gods, A
35:15 and do not go after **o** gods to serve them, A
40:11 the Ammonites and in Edom and in **o** lands heard
43: 2 and all the **o** insolent men said to Jeremiah,
44: 3 they went to make offerings and serve **o** gods A
44: 5 and make no offerings to **o** gods. A
44: 8 making offerings to **o** gods in the land of Egypt A
44:15 to **o** gods, and all the women who stood by, A
52:32 above the seats of the **o** kings who were with him
Eze 4: 8 from one side to the **o** until you have completed
15: 2 does the wood of the vine surpass all **o** wood—
16:34 So you were different from **o** women
25: 8 The house of Judah is like all the **o** nations, F
30: 7 be desolated among **o** desolated countries,
40:13 the back of the one recess to the back of the **o**,
40:40 and on the **o** side of the vestibule of B
40:44 the **o** at the side of the east gate facing north.
41:19 toward the palm tree on the **o** side. B
42:14 on **o** garments before they go near to the area open
44:19 and they shall put on **o** garments,
47: 7 a great many trees on the one side and on the **o**.
Da 1: 7 The palace master gave them **o** names:
1:10 in poorer condition than the **o** young men
2:30 that I have more than any **o** living being, E
3:21 their trousers, their hats, and their **o** garments,
3:29 for there is no **o** god who is able to deliver C
6: 3 above all the **o** presidents and satraps because
7:20 and concerning the **o** horn,
7:23 that shall be different from all the **o** kingdoms;
8: 3 horns were long, but one was longer than the **o**,
11:37 he shall pay no respect to any **o** god, E
12: 5 on this bank of the stream and one on the **o**.
Hos 3: 1 they turn to **o** gods and love raisin cakes." A
9: 1 Do not exult as **o** nations do; F
Joel 2:27 the LORD, am your God and there is no **o**. C
Mic 7: 2 and they hunt each **o** with nets. D

Zec 3:10 you shall invite each o to come under your vine D
4: 3 one on the right of the bowl and the o on its left."
5: 3 be cut off according to the writing on the o side. B
8:10 and I set them all against one o.
11: 7 one I named Favor, the o I named Unity,
14: 4 withdraw northward, and the o half southward.
14:13 of the one will be raised against the hand of the o;
Mt 4:21 As he went from there, he saw two o brothers,
5:39 on the right cheek, turn the o also;
6:24 for a slave will either hate the one and love the o,
6:24 or be devoted to the one and despise the o.
8:18 he gave orders to go over to the o side. B
8:28 When he came to the o side, B
12:13 and it was restored, as sound as the o.
12:45 along seven o spirits more evil than itself,
13: 5 O seeds fell on rocky ground,
13: 7 O seeds fell among thorns,
13: 8 O seeds fell on good soil and brought forth grain,
14:22 into the boat and go on ahead to the o side, B
16: 5 When the disciples reached the o side, B
21:36 Again he sent o slaves, more than the first;
21:41 to o tenants who will give him the produce at
22: 4 Again he sent o slaves, saying,
24:31 from one end of heaven to the o.
24:45 to give the o slaves their allowance of food at
25:11 Later the o bridesmaids came also, saying, 'Lord,
27:61 Mary Magdalene and the o Mary were there,
28: 1 Mary Magdalene and the o Mary went to see
Mk 4: 5 O seed fell on rocky ground,
4: 7 O seed fell among thorns, and the thorns grew up
4: 8 O seed fell into good soil and brought forth grain,
4:19 desire for o things come in and choke the word,
4:35 he said to them, "Let us go across to the o side." B
4:36 O boats were with him.
5: 1 They came to the o side of the sea, B
5:21 Jesus had crossed again in the boat to the o side, B
6:45 into the boat and go on ahead to the o side, B
7: 4 there are also many o traditions that they observe,
8:13 he went across to the o side. B
12: 6 He had still one o, a beloved son.
12:31 There is no o commandment greater than these." C
12:32 and besides him there is no o'; C
15:41 and there were many o women who had come up
Lk 3:18 So, with many o exhortations,
4:43 of the kingdom of God to the o cities also;
5: 7 So they signaled their partners in the o boat
6:29 anyone strikes you on the cheek, offer the o also;
7:41 one owed five hundred denarii, and the o fifty.
8:22 "Let us go across to the o side of the lake." B
10:31 when he saw him, he passed by on the o side. B
10:32 passed by on the o side. B
11:26 and brings seven o spirits more evil than itself,
12:45 and if he begins to beat the o slaves,
13: 2 they were worse sinners than all o Galileans?
14:32 If he cannot, then, while the o is still far away,
16:13 for a slave will either hate the one and love the o,
16:13 or be devoted to the one and despise the o.
17:17 But the o nine, where are they?
17:24 and lights up the sky from one side to the o,
17:34 one will be taken and the o left.
17:35 one will be taken and the o left."
18:10 one a Pharisee and the o a tax collector.
18:11 'God, I thank you that I am not like o people: G
18:14 down to his home justified rather than the o;
19:20 the o came, saying, 'Lord, here is your pound.
22:65 They kept heaping many o insults on him.
23:12 and Pilate became friends with each o; D
23:40 But the o rebuked him, saying,
24:10 o women with them who told this to the apostles.
24:14 and talking with each o about all these things D
24:17 "What are you discussing with each o D
24:32 said to each o, "Were not our hearts burning D
Jn 6: 1 Jesus went to the o side of the Sea of Galilee, B
6:22 that had stayed on the o side of the sea saw B
6:25 When they found him on the o side of the sea, B
10:16 I have o sheep that do not belong to this fold.
18:16 So the o disciple, who was known to
19:32 of the first and of the o who had been crucified
20: 2 and went to Simon Peter and the o disciple,
20: 3 the o disciple set out and went toward the tomb.
20: 4 o disciple outran Peter and reached the tomb first.
20: 8 Then the o disciple, who reached the tomb first,
20:12 one at the head and the o at the feet.
20:25 the o disciples told him, "We have seen the Lord."
20:30 Now Jesus did many o signs in the presence
21: 8 But the o disciples came in the boat,
21:25 But there are also many o things that Jesus did;
Ac 2: 4 the Holy Spirit and began to speak in o languages,
2:37 to the heart and said to Peter and to the o apostles,
2:40 with many o arguments and exhorted them,
4:12 for there is no o name under heaven given C
7:26 why do you wrong each o?' D
9:39 weeping and showing tunics and o clothing
12:12 the mother of John whose o name was Mark,
12:25 whose o name was Mark.
15:17 so that all o peoples may seek the Lord—
27: 1 they transferred Paul and some o prisoners to
28:25 So they disagreed with each o; D
Ro 13: 9 and any o commandment, E
1Co 3:11 For no one can lay any foundation o than the one
6:13 and God will destroy both one and the o.
9: 5 as do the o apostles and the brothers of the Lord
10:24 Do not seek your own advantage, but that of the o.
11:34 the o things I will give instructions when I come.
14: 2 in a tongue do not speak to o people but to God; G
14: 3 On the o hand, those who prophesy speak
14: 3 those who prophesy speak to o people G

1Co 14:17 but the o person is not built up.
15:37 perhaps of wheat or of some o grain.
16:12 to visit you with the o brothers,
2Co 1:13 we write you nothing o than what you can read
2:16 to the o a fragrance from life to life.
11: 8 I robbed o churches by accepting support
11:28 And, besides o things, I am under daily pressure
12:13 How have you been worse off than the o churches,
Gal 1:19 but I did not see any o apostle except James E
2:13 And the o Jews joined him in this hypocrisy,
4:22 one by a slave woman and the o by a free woman.
4:23 the o, the child of the free woman,
4:26 the o woman corresponds to the Jerusalem above;
5:17 for these are opposed to each o, D
Col 3:13 a complaint against another, forgive each o; D
1Th 5:11 encourage one another and build up each o, D
Heb 7: 8 in the o, by one of whom it is testified
7:19 on the o hand, the introduction of a better hope,
7:27 Unlike the o high priests, he has no need
8:11 they shall not teach one another or say to each o, D
Jas 5:12 either by heaven or by earth or by any o oath, E
2Pe 3:16 as they do the o scriptures.
Rev 2:24 to you I say, I do not lay on you any o burden; E
8:13 of the o trumpets that the three angels are about
17:10 one is living, and the o has not yet come;
Tob 3:15 he has no o child to be his heir; C
3:15 or o kindred for whom I should keep myself
6:12 have before all o men a hereditary claim on her.
6:13 he knows that you, rather than any o man, E
6:15 and they have no o son to bury them." C
7:10 at liberty to give her to any o man than yourself, E
7:15 "Sister, get the o room ready, and take her there."
8:21 the o half will be yours when my wife and I die.
Jdt 8:20 But we know no o god but him, C
9:14 there is no o who protects the people of Israel C
10: 4 bracelets, rings, earrings, and all her o jewelry.
10:21 emeralds and o precious stones.
11:21 "No o woman from one end of the earth to C
11:21 of the earth to the o looks so beautiful or speaks
13: 3 as she did on the o days;
13:18 the Most High God above all o women on earth;
14:12 and the captains and to all their o officers.
AdE 1: 3 for his Friends and o persons of various nations,
1: 6 on pillars of marble and o stones.
1:18 so now the o ladies who are wives of the Persian
2:17 and she found favor beyond all the o virgins,
3: 8 a certain nation scattered among the o nations F
3: 8 from those of every o nation,
9:16 Now the o Jews in the kingdom gathered
15: 4 while the o followed, carrying her train.
Wis 8: 1 from one end of the earth to the o,
Sir Pr: 1 and the Prophets and the o books of our ancestors,
1: 4 Wisdom was created before all o things,
21: 8 Whoever builds his house with o people's money
29: 6 the borrower has robbed the o of his money,
33:15 they come in pairs, one the opposite of the o.
36: 6 Give new signs, and work o wonders;
36:28 her husband is more fortunate than o men.
42:24 All things come in pairs, one opposite the o,
42:25 Each supplements the virtues of the o.
49:16 but above every o created living being was Adam.
Bar 1:22 of our own wicked hearts by serving o gods A
3:35 This is our God; no o can be compared to him. C
Aza 1:14 O Lord, have become fewer than any o nation, E
Sus 1:10 but they did not tell each o of their distress, D
1:13 One day they said to each o, "Let us go home, D
1:13 So they both left and parted from each o. D
1:14 and when each pressed the o for the reason,
1:51 "Separate them far from each o, D
1:52 When they were separated from each o, D
1:54 did you see them being intimate with each o?" D
1:56 he ordered them to bring the o.
1:58 did you catch them being intimate with each o?" D
Bel 1:41 God of Daniel, and there is no o besides you!" C
1Mc 1:47 to sacrifice swine and o unclean animals,
5:14 the letter was still being read, o messengers,
5:27 some have been shut up in the o towns of Gilead;
5:36 Maked, and Bosor, and the o towns of Gilead.
5:37 on the o side of the stream. B
5:41 shows fear and camps on the o side of the river, B
6:20 and he built siege towers and o engines of war.
6:29 from o kingdoms and from islands of the seas.
9:48 into the Jordan and swam across to the o side, B
10:38 be under one ruler and obey no o authority than C
10:71 and let us match strength with each o there, D
11: 9 "Come, let us make a covenant with each o, D
11:24 and gold and clothing and numerous o gifts.
11:27 and in as many o honors as he had formerly had,
11:35 the o payments henceforth due to us of the tithes,
12: 2 to the same effect to the Spartans and to o places.
12:11 both at our festivals and on o appropriate days,
12:14 We were unwilling to annoy you and our o allies
12:45 the o strongholds and the remaining troops and all
13:39 and whatever o tax has been collected
15: 5 and a release from all the o payments
16:19 He sent o troops to Gazara to do away with John;
16:20 and he sent o troops to take possession
2Mc 2: 3 And with o similar words he exhorted them that
4:32 o vessels, as it happened, he had sold to Tyre and
4:35 but many also of o nations, F
5:16 that o kings had made to enhance the glory
6:14 the case of the o nations the Lord waits patiently F
10:28 while the o made rage their leader in the fight.
11: 3 as he did on the sacred places of the o nations, F
11:27 to the senate of the Jews and to the o Jews,
12:11 and to help his people in all o ways.
13: 6 of sacrilege or notorious for o crimes.

2Mc 15: 2 and hallowed above o days,"
1Es 1:24 the Lord beyond any o people or kingdom, EG
1:26 "What have we to do with each o, D
2: 7 besides the o things added as votive offerings for
2:13 and one thousand o vessels.
2:16 living in Samaria and o places,
2:17 and the o members of their council, and the judges
2:22 troubling both kings and o cities,
4:18 and silver or any o beautiful thing, E
4:19 to gold or silver or any o beautiful thing. E
5:22 The descendants of the o Calamolalus and Ono,
5:50 some joined them from the o peoples of the land.
6: 4 and this roof and finishing all the o things?
8:22 that no tribute or any o tax is to be laid on any E
8:24 whether by death or some o punishment,
3Mc 1:13 he inquired why, when he entered every o temple,
3: 6 of o races paid no heed to their good service
3:21 Among o things, we made known
5:49 to lamentation and groans they kissed each o, D
2Es 1:24 to o nations and will give them my name, F
6:41 and the o part remain beneath.
6:49 and the name of the o Leviathan.
6:50 And you separated one from the o,
6:56 the o nations that have descended from Adam, F
7:62 of the dust like the o created things?
11: 4 the middle head was larger than the o heads,
11:29 it was greater than the o two heads.
12:15 for a longer time than any o one of the twelve. E
13:56 that after three more days I will tell you o things,
4Mc 2: 9 In all o matters we can recognize that reason rules
8:16 Let us consider, on the o hand,
15: 6 more than any o mother, loved her children. E
15:20 of children burned upon the flesh of o children,
15:20 and corpses fallen on o corpses,
15:26 one bearing death and the o deliverance

OTHER'S (5) [OTHER]

Ex 18: 7 each asked after the o welfare,
Ecc 8: 9 over another to the o hurt.
Ro 1:12 be mutually encouraged by each o faith,
1Co 10:29 I mean the o conscience,
Sir 12:14 with a sinner and becomes involved in the o sins.

OTHERS‡ (240) [OTHER]

Ex 24: 2 but the o shall not come near,
Nu 22:19 You remain here, as the o did,
31: 8 in addition to o who were slain by them;
Jos 8:22 And the o came out from the city against them;
Jdg 7: 7 Let all the o go to their homes."
1Ch 9:29 O of them were appointed over the furniture,
9:30 O, of the sons of the priests,
Ne 5: 5 and our fields and vineyards now belong to o."
7: 3 and o before their own houses."
Job 8:19 and out of the earth still o will spring.
11: 3 Should your babble put o to silence,
22:29 When o are humiliated, you say it is pride;
31:33 if I have concealed my transgressions as o do,
33:27 That person sings to o and says, 'I sinned,
34:24 and sets o in their place.
34:26 He strikes them for their wickedness while o look
35: 8 Your wickedness affects o like you,
Ps 17: 4 As for what o do, by the word
22: 6 scorned by o, and despised by the people.
49:10 and leave their wealth to o.
73: 5 They are not in trouble as o are;
Pr 5: 9 or you will give your honor to o,
11:24 o withhold what is due, and only suffer want.
13: 7 o pretend to be poor, yet have great wealth.
24:29 "I will do to o as they have done to me;
29:25 The fear of o lays a snare,
Ecc 7:22 that many times you have yourself cursed o.
Isa 51: 7 do not fear the reproach of o,
53: 3 He was despised and rejected by o;
53: 3 from whom o hide their faces he was despised,
56: 8 I will gather o to them besides those alread
Jer 5:26 they take over the goods of o.
6:12 Their houses shall be turned over to o,
8:10 to o and their fields to conquerors,
Eze 1:21 When they moved, the o moved;
1:21 when they stopped, the o stopped;
9: 5 To the o he said in my hearing,
10:11 the o followed without veering as they moved.
10:17 When they stopped, the o stopped,
10:17 and when they rose up, the o rose up with them;
40:24 they had the same dimensions as the o.
40:25 like the windows of the o;
40:28 it was of the same dimensions as the o.
40:29 and its vestibule were of the same size as the o;
40:32 it was of the same size as the o.
40:33 of the same dimensions as the o;
40:35 it had the same dimensions as the o.
40:36 and its vestibule were of the same size as the o;
Da 7:20 and that seemed greater than the o.
8:22 in place of which four o arose,
11: 4 be uprooted and go to o besides these.
12: 5 Then I, Daniel, looked, and two o appeared,
Mt 5:16 In the same way, let your light shine before o,
5:19 and teaches o to do the same,
5:47 what more are you doing than o?
6: 1 "Beware of practicing your piety before o in order
6: 2 so that they may be praised by o.
6: 5 so that they may be seen by o.
6:14 For if you forgive o their trespasses,
6:15 but if you do not forgive o,
6:16 for they disfigure their faces so as to show o
6:18 so that your fasting may be seen not by o but

Mt 7:12 "In everything do to o as you would have them do
10:32 therefore who acknowledges me before o, I
10:33 but whoever denies me before o,
15:30 the maimed, the blind, the mute, and many o.
16:14 "Some say John the Baptist, but o Elijah, and still o Jeremiah or one of the prophets."
17:25 From their children or from o?"
17:26 When Peter said, "From o," Jesus said to him,
18:16 take one or two o along with you,
19:12 eunuchs who have been made eunuchs by o,
20:3 he saw o standing idle in the marketplace;
20:6 and found o standing around;
21:8 and o cut branches from the trees and spread them
23:4 hard to bear, and lay them on the shoulders of o;
23:5 They do all their deeds to be seen by o;
23:13 and when o are going in, you stop them.
23:23 to have practiced without neglecting the o.
23:28 So you also on the outside look righteous to o,
27:42 "He saved o; he cannot save himself.
27:49 But the o said, "Wait, let us see whether Elijah
Mk 4:18 And o are those sown among the thorns:
6:15 But o said, "It is Elijah."
6:15 And o said, "It is a prophet,
8:28 And they answered him, "John the Baptist; and o,
8:28 and still o, one of the prophets."
11:8 and o spread leafy branches that they had cut in
12:5 And so it was with many o;
12:5 some they beat, and o they killed.
12:9 and destroy the tenants and give the vineyard to o.
15:31 "He saved o; he cannot save himself.
Lk 5:29 a large crowd of tax collectors and o sitting at
6:31 Do to o as you would have them do to you.
8:3 and Susanna, and many o,
8:10 but to o I speak in parables,
9:8 by o that one of the ancient prophets had arisen.
9:19 They answered, "John the Baptist; but o, Elijah; and still o, that one of the ancient prophets
10:1 the Lord appointed seventy o and sent them on
11:16 O, to test him, kept demanding from him a sign
11:42 to have practiced, without neglecting the o.
12:8 everyone who acknowledges me before o,
12:9 before o will be denied before the angels of God.
13:4 the o living in Jerusalem?
16:15 those who justify yourselves in the sight of o;
18:9 that they were righteous and regarded o
20:16 and give the vineyard to o."
23:32 Two o also, who were criminals,
23:35 the leaders scoffed at him, saying, "He saved o;
Jn 4:38 O have labored, and you have entered
7:12 o were saying, "No, he is deceiving the crowd."
7:41 O said, "This is the Messiah."
9:9 O were saying, "No, but it is someone like him."
9:16 But o said, "How can a man who is
10:21 O were saying, "These are not the words
12:29 O said, "An angel has spoken to him."
18:34 or did o tell you about me?"
19:18 There they crucified him, and with him two o,
21:2 the sons of Zebedee, and two o of his disciples.
Ac 2:13 But o sneered and said, "They are filled
6:9 and o of those from Cilicia and Asia,
7:6 be resident aliens in a country belonging to o,
8:7 many o who were paralyzed or lame were cured.
13:16 "You Israelites, and o who fear God, listen.
13:26 of Abraham's family, and o who fear God, to us
15:2 and Barnabas and some of the o were appointed
15:35 with many o, they taught and proclaimed the word
17:9 and after they had taken bail from Jason and the o,
17:18 O said, "He seems to be a proclaimer
17:32 but o said, "We will hear you again about this."
17:34 and a woman named Damaris, and o with them.
23:6 that some were Sadducees and o were Pharisees,
27:44 some on planks and o on pieces of the ship.
28:24 while o refused to believe.
Ro 1:32 but even applaud o who practice them.
2:1 whoever you are, when you judge o;
2:21 then, that teach o, will you not teach yourself?
2:29 a person receives praise not from o but from God.
14:5 while o judge all days to be alike.
14:20 it is wrong for you to make o fall by what you eat;
1Co 8:10 For if o see you, who possess knowledge,
9:2 If I am not an apostle to o, at least I am to you;
9:12 If o share this rightful claim on you,
9:27 so that after proclaiming to o I myself should not
14:19 in order to instruct o also,
14:29 and let the o weigh what is said.
2Co 5:11 the fear of the Lord, we try to persuade o;
8:8 of your love against the earnestness of o.
8:13 I do not mean that there should be relief for o
8:21 in the Lord's sight but also in the sight of o.
9:13 of your sharing with them and with all o,
10:15 that is, in the labors of o;
13:2 the o, and I warn them now while absent, as I did
Php 1:15 from envy and rivalry, but o from goodwill.
1:17 the o proclaim Christ out of selfish ambition,
2:3 but in humility regard o as better than yourselves.
2:4 but to the interests of o.
1Th 2:6 whether from you or from o,
4:13 you may not grieve as o do who have no hope.
5:6 So then let us not fall asleep as o do,
1Ti 5:22 and do not participate in the sins of o;
5:24 while the sins of o follow them there.
2Ti 2:2 to faithful people who will be able to teach o
3:13 deceiving o and being deceived.
Heb 7:20 for o who became priests took their office without
11:35 O were tortured, refusing to accept release,
11:36 O suffered mocking and flogging,
2Pe 2:5 a herald of righteousness, with seven o,
Jude 1:23 save o by snatching them out of the fire;
1:23 and have mercy on still o with fear,
Tob 3:17 before all o who had desired to marry her.
AdE 16:4 They not only take away thankfulness from o, but,
Wis 2:15 because his manner of life is unlike that of o,
3:4 For though in the sight of o they were punished,
15:13 For these persons, more than all o,
15:18 which are worse than all o when judged
16:4 while to these o it was merely shown
19:14 O had refused to receive strangers when they came
Sir Pr:1 to us through the Law and the Prophets and the o
1:29 Do not be a hypocrite before o,
11:6 and the honored have been handed over to o.
11:12 There are o who are slow and need help,
11:19 how long it will be until he leaves them to o
14:4 What he denies himself he collects for o;
14:4 and o will live in luxury on his goods.
14:18 a spreading tree that sheds some and puts forth o,
19:4 One who trusts o too quickly has a shallow mind,
20:5 while o are detested for being talkative.
20:6 o keep silent because they know when to speak.
27:14 and their quarrels make o stop their ears.
29:22 crude roof than sumptuous food in the house of o.
44:8 so that o declare their praise.
44:9 But of o there is no memory;
48:16 but o sinned more and more.
49:5 They gave their power to o,
Bar 2:3 of their sons and o the flesh of their daughters.
3:19 and o have arisen in their place.
LtJ 6:26 they are carried on the shoulders of o,
1Mc 6:43 It was taller than all the o,
8:5 and the o who rose up against them.
10:72 Ask and learn who I am and who the o are
2Mc 2:27 a banquet and seeks the benefit of o.
3:19 while o peered out of the windows.
4:41 and o took handfuls of the ashes that were lying
5:23 over his compatriots worse than the o did.
5:27 But Judas Maccabeus, with about nine o,
6:11 O who had assembled in the caves nearby,
7:39 and handled him worse than the o,
8:14 O sold all their remaining property,
8:33 and some o, who had fled into one little house;
9:6 the bowels of o with many and strange inflictions.
9:28 such as he had inflicted on o,
10:36 O who came up in the same way wheeled around
10:36 O broke open the gates and let in the rest of
11:7 and he urged the o to risk their lives with him
1Es 2:25 the o associated with them and living in Samaria
8:10 and of the priests and Levites and o in our realm,
3Mc 1:23 to the same posture of supplication as the o.
3:2 a report that they hindered o from the observance
4:9 o had their feet secured by unbreakable fetters,
4:13 with in precisely the same fashion as the o,
5:49 and children, mothers and daughters, and o
2Es 2:11 and will give to these o the everlasting habitations,
2:27 o shall weep and be sorrowful,
2:43 taller than any of the o,
5:28 and dishonored the one root beyond the o,
7:*85* how the habitations of the o are guarded by angels
7:*110* [40] and many o prayed for many?
10:10 all have been born of her, and o will come;
11:21 and o of them rose up, but did not hold the rule.
12:7 before you beyond many o,
13:13 and some were bringing o as offerings.
15:59 Unhappy above all o, you shall come
16:65 to shame when your sins come out before o,
4Mc 1:32 Some desires are mental, o are physical,
2:18 to correct some, and to render o powerless.
8:2 then in violent rage he commanded that o of
14:16 and the o, by building in precipitous chasms and
16:9 some unmarried, o married and without offspring.

OTHERWISE‡ (45) [OTHER]

Ge 11:4 o we shall be scattered abroad upon the face of
38:23 o we will be laughed at;
Ex 19:21 o many of them will perish.
19:24 o he will break out against them."
Lev 18:28 o the land will vomit you out for defiling it,
25:36 Do not take interest in advance or o make a profit
Nu 4:20 for a moment; o they will die.
18:3 o both they and you will die.
Dt 1:42 o you will be defeated by your enemies.' "
7:22 o the wild animals would become too numerous
9:28 o the land from which you have brought us might
22:8 o you might have bloodguilt on your house,
24:15 o they might cry to the LORD against you,
Ru 2:22 o you might be bothered in another field."
2Sa 17:16 o the king and all the people who are
1Ki 1:21 O it will come to pass,
19:7 o the journey will be too much for you."
2Ch 30:18 yet they ate the passover o than as prescribed.
Pr 25:17 o the neighbor will become weary of you
Jer 30:21 for who would o dare to approach me?
Eze 18:30 o iniquity will be your ruin.
Mt 9:17 Neither is new wine put into old wineskins; o,
27:64 o his disciples may go and steal him away,
Mk 2:21 o, the patch pulls away from it,
2:22 And no one puts new wine into old wineskins; o,
Lk 5:36 o the new will be torn,
5:37 o the new wine will burst the skins and will
14:29 O, when he has laid a foundation and is not able
Ro 11:6 o grace would no longer be grace.
11:22 o you also will be cut off.
1Co 7:14 O, your children would be unclean, but as it is,
14:16 O, if you say a blessing with the spirit,
15:29 O, what will those people do who receive baptism
2Co 9:4 o, if some Macedonians come with me and find
Gal 5:10 about you in the Lord that you will not think o.
1Ti 6:3 Whoever teaches o and does not agree with
Heb 10:2 O, would they not have ceased being offered,
Tob 4:19 if he chooses o, he casts down to deepest Hades.
Sir 23:3 O my mistakes may be multiplied,
Bel 1:12 o Daniel will, who is telling lies about us."
1Mc 15:31 O we will come and make war on you."
3Mc 2:17 o the transgressors will boast in their wrath
4Mc 1:33 O, how is it that when we are attracted
2:7 O how could it be that someone who is habitually
4:13 although o he had scruples about doing so,

OTHNI (1)

1Ch 26:7 The sons of Shemaiah: O, Rephael, Obed,

OTHNIEL (7)

Jos 15:17 O son of Kenaz, the brother of Caleb, took it;
Jdg 1:13 O son of Kenaz, Caleb's younger brother, took it;
3:9 O son of Kenaz, Caleb's younger brother.
3:11 Then O son of Kenaz died.
1Ch 4:13 The sons of Kenaz: O and Seraiah;
4:13 and the sons of O: Hathath and Meonothai.
27:15 of O; in his division were twenty-four thousand.

OTHONIAH (1)

1Es 9:28 Eliadas, Eliashib, O, Jeremoth,

OUCHES (KJV) See FILIGREE, SETTINGS

OUGHT‡ (54)

Ge 20:9 You have done things to me that o not to
34:7 for such a thing o not to be done.
Lev 4:13 by the LORD's commandments o not to be done
4:22 by commandments of the LORD his God o not to
4:27 by the LORD's commandments o not to be done
5:17 by the LORD's commandments o not to be done,
1Ki 2:9 you will know what you o to do to him,
1Ch 12:32 to know what Israel o to do, two hundred chiefs,
Jer 38:4 "This man o to be put to death,
Mt 23:23 It is these you o to have practiced
25:27 Then you o to have invested my money with
Mk 13:14 up where it o not to be (let the reader understand),
Lk 11:42 it is these you o to have practiced,
12:12 at that very hour what you o to say."
13:14 "There are six days on which work o to be done;
13:16 And o not this woman, a daughter
17:10 we have done only what we o to have done!' "
Jn 13:14 you also o to wash one another's feet.
19:7 that law he o to die because he has claimed to be
Ac 17:29 we o not to think that the deity is like gold,
19:36 you o to be quiet and do nothing rash.
24:19 they o to be here before you to make
25:24 shouting that he o not to live any longer.
26:9 I myself was convinced that I o to do many things
Ro 8:26 for we do not know how to pray as we o,
12:3 not to think of yourself more highly than you o
15:1 We who are strong o to put up with the failings of
15:27 to share in their spiritual blessings, they o also to
1Co 11:7 For a man o not to have his head veiled,
11:10 For this reason a woman o to have a symbol
2Co 12:14 for children o not to lay up for their parents,
Eph 5:24 so also wives o to be, in everything,
Col 4:6 you may know how you o to answer everyone.
1Th 4:1 from us how you o to live and to please God (as,
2Th 3:7 For you yourselves know how you o to imitate us;
1Ti 3:15 how one o to behave in the household of God,
2Ti 2:6 It is the farmer who does the work who o to have
Heb 5:12 For though by this time you o to be teachers,
Jas 3:10 My brothers and sisters, this o not to be so.
4:15 Instead you o to say, "If the Lord wishes,
2Pe 3:11 of persons o you to be in leading lives of holiness
1Jn 2:6 "I abide in him," o to walk just as he walked.
3:16 and we o to lay down our lives for one another.
4:11 we also o to love one another.
3Jn 1:8 Therefore we o to support such people,
Wis 14:21 on objects of stone or wood the name that o not to
2Mc 6:20 as all o to go who have the courage
3Mc 1:12 he did not cease to maintain that he o to enter,
1:12 "Even if those men are deprived of this honor, I o
3:9 for such a great community o not be left to its fate
2Es 10:9 and she will tell you that it is she who o to mourn
10:11 Who then o to mourn the more,
4Mc 11:15 we o likewise to die for the same principles.
16:19 you o to endure any suffering for the sake of God.

OUR (1674) [WE] See Index of Articles Etc.

OURS (19) [WE] See Index of Articles Etc.

OURSELVES (76) [WE] See Index of Articles Etc.

OUT (3056) [OUTER, OUTERMOST, OUTFLANKED, OUTWARD, OUTWARDLY, WITHOUT] See Index of Articles Etc.

OUTBIDDING (1)

2Mc 4:24 o Jason by three hundred talents of silver.

OUTBREAK (1) [BREAK]
Dt 24: 8 Guard against an **o** of a leprous skin disease

OUTBURST (1) [BURST]
2Sa 6: 8 the LORD had burst forth with an **o** upon Uzzah;

OUTCAST (3) [CAST]
2Sa 14:14 to keep an **o** banished forever from his presence.
Jer 30:17 because they have called you an **o:**
Zep 3:19 And I will save the lame and gather the **o,**

OUTCASTS (6) [CAST]
Ne 1: 9 though your **o** are under the farthest skies,
Ps 147: 2 he gathers the **o** of Israel.
Isa 11:12 and will assemble the **o** of Israel,
16: 3 hide the **o,** do not betray the fugitive;
16: 4 let the **o** of Moab settle among you;
56: 8 who gathers the **o** of Israel,

OUTCOME (6) [COME]
Isa 41:22 and that we may know their **o;**
Da 12: 8 "My lord, what shall be the **o** of these things?"
Heb 13: 7 consider the **o** of their way of life,
1Pe 1: 9 for you are receiving the **o** of your faith,
Wis 8: 8 and wonders and of the **o** of seasons and times.
2Mc 3:40 This was the **o** of the episode of Heliodorus and

OUTCRIES (1) [CRY]
1Es 5:63 the building of this one with **o** and loud weeping,

OUTCRY (12) [CRY]
Ge 18:20 "How great is the **o** against Sodom and Gomorrah
18:21 according to the **o** that has come to me;
19:13 because the **o** against its people has become great
Nu 16:34 All Israel around them fled at their **o,**
1Sa 4:14 When Eli heard the sound of the **o,** he said,
9:16 because their **o** has come to me."
Ne 5: 1 Now there was a great **o** of the people and
5: 6 when I heard their **o** and these complaints.
Job 16:18 let my **o** find no resting place.
Isa 24:11 There is an **o** in the streets for lack of wine;
Ac 22:24 to find out the reason for this **o** against him.
AdE 11:10 and at their **o,** as though from a tiny spring,

OUTDO (2) [DO]
Isa 49:17 Your builders **o** your destroyers,
Ro 12:10 **o** one another in showing honor.

OUTER‡ (39) [OUT]
Ex 26:14 of tanned rams' skins and an **o** covering
36:19 of tanned rams' skins and an **o** covering
Nu 4:25 the **o** covering of fine leather that is on top of it,
34: 4 and its **o** limit shall be south of Kadesh-barnea;
34: 8 and the **o** limit of the boundary shall be at Zedad;
Jos 2:15 the **o** side of the city wall and she resided within
1Ki 6:29 and open flowers, in the inner and **o** rooms.
6:30 in the inner and **o** rooms.
2Ki 16:18 and the **o** entrance for the king he removed from
2Ch 33:14 an **o** wall for the city of David west of Gihon,
Est 6: 4 Now Haman had just entered the **o** court of
Job 41:13 Who can strip off its **o** garment?
Eze 10: 5 of the cherubim was heard as far as the **o** court,
40:17 Then he brought me into the **o** court;
40:19 of the lower gate to the **o** front of the inner court,
40:20 Then he measured the gate of the **o** court
40:31 Its vestibule faced the **o** court,
40:34 Its vestibule faced the **o** court,
40:37 Its vestibule faced the **o** court,
41: 9 of the **o** wall of the side chambers was five cubits;
41:15 the temple and the inner room and the **o** vestibule
42: 1 Then he led me out into the **o** court,
42: 3 facing the pavement that belonged to the **o** court,
42: 6 they had no pillars like the pillars of the **o** court;
42: 7 toward the **o** court, opposite the chambers,
42: 8 the chambers on the **o** court were fifty cubits long,
42: 9 the east in order to enter them from the **o** court.
42:14 into the **o** court without laying there the vestments
44: 1 he brought me back to the **o** gate of the sanctuary,
44:19 When they go out into the **o** court to the people,
46:20 in order not to bring them out into the **o** court and
46:21 Then he brought me out to the **o** court,
47: 2 the outside to the **o** gate that faces toward the east;
Mt 8:12 of the kingdom will be thrown into the **o** darkness,
22:13 and throw him into the **o** darkness,
25:30 throw him into the **o** darkness,
Jn 13: 4 up from the table, took off his **o** robe, and tied
Ac 12:13 When he knocked at the **o** gate,
2Co 4:16 Even though our **o** nature is wasting away,

OUTERMOST (7) [OUT]
Ex 26: 4 of blue on the edge of the **o** curtain in the first set;
26: 4 on the edge of the **o** curtain in the second set.
26:10 on the edge of the curtain that is **o** in one set,
26:10 and fifty loops on the edge of the curtain that is **o**
36:11 He made loops of blue on the edge of the **o** curtain
36:11 on the edge of the **o** curtain of the second set;
36:17 He made fifty loops on the edge of the **o** curtain of

OUTFLANKED (2) [FLANK, OUT]
Jdt 15: 5 and in Galilee **o** them with great slaughter,
1Mc 7:46 and they **o** the enemy and drove them back

OUTFLOW (1) [FLOW]
Ex 22:29 from the fullness of your harvest and from the **o**

OUTGOINGS (KJV) See BORDERS, BOUNDARY, ENDED, ENDS, GATEWAYS

OUTLANDISH (KJV) See FOREIGN

OUTLAW (1) [OUTLAWS]
Pr 24:15 in wait like an **o** against the home of the righteous;

OUTLAWS (3) [OUTLAW]
Jdg 11: 3 **O** collected around Jephthah and went raiding
Sir 16: 4 but through a clan of **o** it becomes desolate.
1Mc 14:14 and did away with all the renegades and **o.**

OUTLAY (1)
2Ki 12:12 as well as for any **o** for repairs of the house.

OUTLET (2)
2Ch 32:30 This same Hezekiah closed the upper **o** of
Sir 25:25 Allow no **o** to water, and no boldness of speech to

OUTLINES (1)
2Mc 2:28 while devoting our effort to arriving at the **o** of

OUTLIVE (1) [LIVE]
Sir 41:12 since it will **o** you longer than a thousand hoards

OUTLIVED (2) [LIVE]
Jos 24:31 of the elders who **o** Joshua and had known all
Jdg 2: 7 and all the days of the elders who **o** Joshua,

OUTLYING (1)
Nu 11: 1 and consumed some **o** parts of the camp.

OUTMOST (KJV) See END, ENDS, OUTERMOST, TOP

OUTPOST (1) [OUTPOSTS]
Jdt 14: 2 down to the plain against the Assyrian **o;**

OUTPOSTS (2) [OUTPOST]
Jdg 7:11 with his servant Purah to the **o** of the armed men
1Mc 12:27 and he stationed **o** around the camp.

OUTPOURED (1) [POUR]
Ps 79:10 of the **o** blood of your servants be known among

OUTRAGE (6) [OUTRAGED, OUTRAGEOUS, OUTRAGEOUSLY, OUTRAGES]
Ge 34: 7 because he had committed an **o** in Israel by lying
Jdg 20: 6 for they have committed a vile **o** in Israel.
Jer 29:23 because they have perpetrated **o** in Israel
Wis 4:18 and an **o** among the dead forever;
2Mc 4:38 to that very place where he had committed the **o**
8:17 the lawless **o** that the Gentiles had committed

OUTRAGED (1) [OUTRAGE]
Heb 10:29 and **o** the Spirit of grace?

OUTRAGEOUS (4) [OUTRAGE]
Jos 7:15 and for having done an **o** thing in Israel.' "
Sir 10: 7 and injustice is **o** to both.
3Mc 6:26 with **o** treatment those who from
4Mc 4: 7 indignantly protested his words, considering it **o**

OUTRAGEOUSLY (1) [OUTRAGE]
3Mc 6: 9 who are being **o** treated by the abominable

OUTRAGES (2) [OUTRAGE]
2Mc 14:42 into the hands of sinners and suffer **o** unworthy
3Mc 4:14 but to be tortured with the **o** that he had ordered,

OUTRAN (2) [RUN]
2Sa 18:23 Then Ahimaaz ran by the way of the Plain, and **o**
Jn 20: 4 other disciple **o** Peter and reached the tomb first.

OUTSIDE (154) [OUTSIDER, OUTSIDERS]
Ge 9:22 and told his two brothers **o.**
15: 5 He brought him **o** and said,
19:16 and they brought him out and left him **o** the city.
19:17 When they had brought them **o,** they said,
24:11 He made the camels kneel down **o** the city by
24:31 Why do you stand **o** when I have prepared
39:12 he left his garment in her hand, and fled and ran **o.**
39:13 in her hand and had fled **o,**
39:15 he left his garment beside me, and fled **o."**
39:18 he left his garment beside me, and fled **o."**
Ex 12:22 None of you shall go **o** the door of your house
12:46 you shall not take any of the animal **o** the house,
21:19 but recovers and walks around **o** with the help of
25:11 inside and **o** you shall overlay it,
26:35 You shall set the table **o** the curtain,
27:21 **o** the curtain that is before the covenant,
29:14 and its dung, you shall burn with fire **o** the camp;
33: 7 Now Moses used to take the tent and pitch it **o**
33: 7 to the tent of meeting, which was **o** the camp.
37: 2 He overlaid it with pure gold inside and **o,**
40:22 on the north side of the tabernacle, **o** the curtain,
Lev 4:12 he shall carry out to a clean place **o** the camp,
4:21 He shall carry the bull **o** the camp,
6:11 carry the ashes out to a clean place **o** the camp.
8:17 he burned with fire **o** the camp,
8:33 not go **o** the entrance of the tent of meeting
9:11 flesh and the skin he burned with fire **o** the camp.
10: 4 the front of the sanctuary to a place **o** the camp."
10: 7 not go **o** the entrance of the tent of meeting,
13:46 his dwelling shall be **o** the camp.
13:55 the leprous spot is on the inside or on the **o.**
14: 8 but shall live **o** his tent seven days.
14:38 the priest shall go **o** to the door of the house
14:40 be taken out and thrown into an unclean place **o**
14:41 be dumped in an unclean place **o** the city.
14:45 and taken **o** the city to an unclean place.
16:27 shall be taken **o** the camp;
17: 3 or slaughters it **o** the camp,
21:12 He shall not go **o** the sanctuary and thus profane
24: 3 **o** the curtain of the covenant,
24:14 Take the blasphemer **o** the camp;
24:23 and they took the blasphemer **o** the camp,
Nu 5: 3 both male and female, putting them **o** the camp;
5: 4 The Israelites did so, putting them **o** the camp;
15:35 all the congregation shall stone him **o** the camp."
15:36 The whole congregation brought him **o** the camp
19: 3 and it shall be taken **o** the camp and slaughtered
19: 9 and deposit them **o** the camp in a clean place;
31:13 the congregation went to meet them **o** the camp.
31:19 Camp **o** the camp seven days;
35: 5 You shall measure, **o** the town,
35:26 But if the slayer shall at any time go **o** the bounds
35:27 and is found by the avenger of blood **o** the bounds
Dt 23:10 then he shall go **o** the camp;
23:12 You shall have a designated area **o** the camp
23:13 when you relieve yourself **o,**
24:11 You shall wait **o,** while the person
25: 5 of the deceased shall not be married **o** the family
Jos 6:23 and set them **o** the camp of Israel.
7: 5 chasing them from **o** the gate as far as Shebarim
Jdg 12: 9 He gave his thirty daughters in marriage **o** his clan
12: 9 in thirty young women from **o** for his sons.
1Ki 6: 6 for around the **o** of the house he made offsets on
7: 9 and from **o** to the great court.
8: 8 but they could not be seen from **o;**
21:13 they took him **o** the city, and stoned him to death.
2Ki 4: 3 "Go **o,** borrow vessels from all your neighbors,
7: 3 Now there were four leprous men **o** the city gate,
10:24 Now Jehu had stationed eighty men **o,** saying,
23: 4 he burned them **o** Jerusalem in the fields of
23: 6 **o** Jerusalem, to the Wadi Kidron,
1Ch 26:29 Chenaniah and his sons were appointed to **o** duties
2Ch 5: 9 but they could not be seen from **o;**
24: 8 and set it **o** the gate of the house of the LORD.
32: 3 to stop the flow of the springs that were **o** the city;
32: 5 and **o** it he built another wall;
Ne 11:16 who were over the **o** work of the house of God;
13:20 of merchandise spent the night **o** Jerusalem once
Pr 22:13 The lazy person says, "There is a lion **o!**
24:27 Prepare your work **o,** get everything ready for you
SS 8: 1 If I met you **o,** I would kiss you,
Jer 21: 4 the Chaldeans who are besieging you **o** the walls;
Eze 7:15 The sword is **o,** pestilence and famine are inside;
40: 5 a wall all around the **o** of the temple area.
40:40 On the **o** of the vestibule at the entrance of
40:41 and four tables on the **o** of the side of the gate,
40:44 the **o** of the inner gateway there were chambers
41:17 even to the inner room, and on the **o.**
41:25 a canopy of wood in front of the vestibule **o.**
42: 7 There was a wall **o** parallel to the chambers,
43:21 in the appointed place belonging to the temple, **o**
46: 2 by the vestibule of the gate from **o,**
47: 2 around on the **o** to the outer gate that faces toward
Hos 7: 1 the thief breaks in, and the bandits raid **o.**
Mt 9:25 But when the crowd had been put **o,**
12:46 his mother and his brothers were standing **o,**
12:47 your mother and your brothers are standing **o,**
23:25 For you clean the **o** of the cup and of the plate,
23:26 so that the **o** also may become clean.
23:27 which on the **o** look beautiful,
23:28 So you also on the **o** look righteous to others,
26:69 Now Peter was sitting **o** in the courtyard.
Mk 3:31 and standing **o,** they sent to him and called him.
3:32 "Your mother and your brothers and sisters are **o,**
4:11 but for those **o,** everything comes in parables;
5:40 Then he put them all **o,**
7:15 there is nothing **o** a person that by going
7:18 into a person from **o** cannot defile,
11: 4 and found a colt tied near a door, **o** in the street.
Lk 1:10 the whole assembly of the people was praying **o.**
8:20 "Your mother and your brothers are standing **o,**
11:39 "Now you Pharisees clean the **o** of the cup and of
11:40 not the one who made the **o** make the inside also?
11:53 When he went **o,** the scribes and
13:25 and you begin to stand **o** and to knock at the door,
13:33 for a prophet to be killed **o** of Jerusalem.'
Jn 18:16 but Peter was standing **o** at the gate.
19:13 he brought Jesus **o** and sat on the judge's bench at
20:11 But Mary stood weeping **o** the tomb.
Ac 2:23 you crucified and killed by the hands of those **o**
5:34 and ordered the men to be put **o** for a short time.
9:40 Peter put all of them **o,**

Ac 12:10 and they went **o** and walked along a lane,
14:13 priest of Zeus, whose temple was just **o** the city,
16:13 the sabbath day we went **o** the gate by the river,
16:30 Then he brought them **o** and said, "Sirs,
21: 5 with wives and children, escorted us **o** the city.
1Co 5:12 For what have I to do with judging those **o**?
5:13 God will judge those **o**.
6:18 Every sin that a person commits is **o** the body;
9:21 To those **o** the law I became as one **o** the law
9:21 under Christ's law) so that I might win those **o**
Heb 2: 8 God left nothing **o** their control.
13:11 the high priest as a sacrifice for sin are burned **o**
13:12 also suffered **o** the city gate in order to sanctify
13:13 to him **o** the camp and bear the abuse he endured.
Rev 11: 2 but do not measure the court **o** the temple;
14:20 And the wine press was trodden **o** the city,
22:15 **O** are the dogs and sorcerers and fornicators
Jdt 6: 1 When the disturbance made by the people **o**
10:18 They came and gathered around her as she stood **o**
13: 1 Bagoas closed the tent from **o** and shut out
13: 3 to stand **o** the bedchamber and to wait for her
AdE 9:19 the country **o** Susa keep the fourteenth of Adar as
Sir 21:22 but an experienced person waits respectfully **o**.
21:23 but a cultivated person remains **o**.
Bel 1: 7 for this thing is only clay inside and bronze **o**,
1:11 priests of Bel said, "See, we are now going **o**;
1Mc 7:47 and displayed them just **o** Jerusalem.
15:30 the places that you have conquered **o** the borders
2Mc 1:16 and threw them to the people **o**.
Pm 151: T *as his own composition (though it is **o** the number)*
4Mc 18: 7 a pure virgin and did not go **o** my father's house;

OUTSIDER (10) [OUTSIDE]

Nu 1:51 And any **o** who comes near shall be put to death.
3:10 and any **o** who comes near shall be put to death.
3:38 and any **o** who came near was to be put to death.
16:40 a reminder to the Israelites that no **o**, who is not of
18: 4 the service of the tent; no **o** shall approach you.
18: 7 any **o** who approaches shall be put to death.
1Co 14:16 of an **o** say the "Amen" to your thanksgiving,
14:16 since the **o** does not know what you are saying?
14:24 an unbeliever or **o** who enters is reproved by all
Sir 45:13 No **o** ever put them on,

OUTSIDERS (6) [OUTSIDE]

1Co 14:23 and **o** or unbelievers enter,
Col 4: 5 Conduct yourselves wisely toward **o**,
1Th 4:12 so that you may behave properly toward **o** and
1Ti 3: 7 Moreover, he must be well thought of by **o**,
Sir Pr: 1 through the spoken and written word to help the **o**.
45:18 **O** conspired against him, and envied him in

OUTSKIRTS (6)

Jos 18:15 southern side begins at the **o** of Kiriath-jearim;
Jdg 7:17 when I come to the **o** of the camp, do as I do.
7:19 and the hundred who were with him came to the **o**
1Sa 9:27 As they were going down to the **o** of the town,
14: 2 the **o** of Gibeah under the pomegranate tree that is
Job 26:14 These are indeed but the **o** of his ways;

OUTSPOKEN (1) [SPEAK]

3Mc 4: 1 in their minds was now made evident and **o**.

OUTSPREAD (1) [SPREAD]

Isa 8: 8 and its **o** wings will fill the breadth of your land,

OUTSTRETCHED (22) [STRETCH]

Ex 6: 6 with an **o** arm and with mighty acts of judgment.
Dt 4:34 by war, by a mighty hand and an **o** arm,
5:15 from there with a mighty hand and an **o** arm;
7:19 the mighty hand and the **o** arm by which
9:29 by your great power and by your **o** arm."
11: 2 his mighty hand and his **o** arm,
26: 8 an **o** arm, with a terrifying display of power,
1Ki 8:42 your mighty hand, and your **o** arm—
8:54 where he had knelt with hands **o** toward heaven;
2Ki 17:36 of Egypt with great power and with an **o** arm;
2Ch 6:32 and your mighty hand, and your **o** arm,
Ps 136:12 an **o** arm, for his steadfast love endures forever;
Isa 3:16 of Zion are haughty and walk with **o** necks,
Jer 21: 5 I myself will fight against you with **o** hand
27: 5 by my great power and my **o** arm have made
32:17 the earth by your great power and by your **o** arm!
32:21 with a strong hand and **o** arm,
Eze 20:33 surely with a mighty hand and an **o** arm,
20:34 with a mighty hand and an **o** arm,
Tob 3:11 with hands **o** toward the window,
Bar 2:11 and wonders and with great power and **o** arm,
2Mc 15:12 was praying with **o** hands for the whole body of

OUTWARD (4) [OUT]

Nu 35: 4 of the town **o** a thousand cubits all around.
1Sa 16: 7 they look on the **o** appearance,
2Co 5:12 to answer those who boast in **o** appearance and not
2Ti 3: 5 to the **o** form of godliness but denying its power.

OUTWARDLY (2) [OUT]

Ro 2:28 For a person is not a Jew who is one **o**,
1Pe 3: 3 Do not adorn yourselves **o** by braiding your hair,

OUTWEIGH (1) [WEIGH]

Sir 8: 2 in case their resources **o** yours;

OUTWEIGHS (1) [WEIGH]

Ecc 10: 1 so a little folly **o** wisdom and honor.

OUTWENT (KJV) See AHEAD

OUTWIT (1) [OUTWITTED]

Ps 89:22 The enemy shall not **o** him,

OUTWITTED (2) [OUTWIT]

2Co 2:11 And we do this so that we may not be **o** by Satan;
2Mc 14:31 that he had been cleverly **o** by the man,

OVEN (11) [OVENS]

Lev 2: 4 When you present a grain offering baked in the **o**,
7: 9 And every grain offering baked in the **o**,
11:35 whether an **o** or stove, it shall be broken in pieces;
26:26 ten women shall bake your bread in a single **o**,
La 5:10 Our skin is black as an **o** from the scorching heat
Hos 7: 4 They are all adulterers; they are like a heated **o**,
7: 6 For they are kindled like an **o**,
7: 7 All of them are hot as an **o**,
Mal 4: 1 See, the day is coming, burning like an **o**,
Mt 6:30 into the **o**, will he not much more clothe you—
Lk 12:28 into the **o**, how much more will he clothe you—

OVENS (3) [OVEN]

Ex 8: 3 and into your **o** and your kneading bowls.
Ne 3:11 and the Tower of the **O**.
12:38 above the Tower of the **O**, to the Broad Wall,

OVER‡ (1380)

Ge 1: 2 a wind from God swept **o** the face of the waters.
1:18 to rule **o** the day and **o** the night,
1:26 and let them have dominion **o** the fish of the sea, and **o** the birds of the air, and **o** the cattle, and **o** all the wild animals of the earth, and **o** every creeping
1:28 and have dominion **o** the fish of the sea and **o** the birds of the air and **o** every living thing
3:16 be for your husband, and he shall rule **o** you."
8: 1 And God made a wind blow **o** the earth,
9:14 When I bring clouds **o** the earth and
11: 8 So the LORD scattered them abroad from there **o**
11: 9 the LORD scattered them abroad **o** the face of all
15:10 laying each half **o** against the other;
22: 5 the boy and I will go **o** there;
24:65 "Who is the man **o** there,
26:21 and they quarreled **o** that one also;
26:22 and they did not quarrel **o** it;
27:29 Be lord **o** your brothers, and may your mother's
36:31 before any king reigned **o** the Israelites.
37: 8 "Are you indeed to reign **o** us?
37: 8 Are you indeed to have dominion **o** us?"
38:12 when Judah's time of mourning was **o**,
38:16 He went **o** to her at the road side, and said,
39: 5 that he made him overseer in his house and **o** all
41:33 and set him **o** the land of Egypt.
41:34 Let Pharaoh proceed to appoint overseers **o**
41:40 You shall be **o** my house,
41:41 "See, I have set you **o** all the land of Egypt."
41:43 Thus he set him **o** all the land of Egypt.
41:45 Thus Joseph gained authority **o** the land of Egypt.
41:56 And since the famine had spread **o** all the land,
42: 6 Now Joseph was governor **o** the land;
45: 8 to Pharaoh, and lord of all his house and ruler **o** all
45:26 He is even ruler **o** all the land of Egypt."
49:22 his branches run **o** the wall.
50: 1 on his father's face and wept **o** him
Ex 1: 8 Now a new king arose **o** Egypt,
1:11 Therefore they set taskmasters **o** them
2:14 "Who made you a ruler and judge **o** us?
5:14 whom Pharaoh's taskmasters had set **o** them,
7:19 and stretch out your hand **o** the waters of Egypt—
7:19 **o** its rivers, its canals, and its ponds,
8: 5 'Stretch out your hand with your staff **o** the rivers,
8: 6 So Aaron stretched out his hand **o** the waters
9: 9 It shall become fine dust all **o** the land of Egypt,
10:12 "Stretch out your hand **o** the land of Egypt,
10:13 Moses stretched out his staff **o** the land of Egypt,
10:21 so that there may be darkness **o** the land of Egypt,
12: 8 they shall eat it roasted **o** the fire
12: 9 but roasted **o** the fire, with its head, legs,
12:13 when I see the blood, I will pass **o** you,
12:23 and on the two doorposts, the LORD will pass **o**
12:27 he passed **o** the houses of the Israelites in Egypt,
14: 4 so that I will gain glory for myself **o** Pharaoh
14: 7 and all the other chariots of Egypt with officers **o**
14:16 and stretch out your hand **o** the sea and divide it,
14:17 and so I will gain glory for myself **o** Pharaoh
14:18 when I have gained glory for myself **o** Pharaoh,
14:21 Then Moses stretched out his hand **o** the sea.
14:26 "Stretch out your hand **o** the sea,
14:27 So Moses stretched out his hand **o** the sea,
16:18 those who gathered much had nothing **o**,
16:19 "Let no one leave any of it **o** until morning."
16:23 that is left **o** put aside to be kept until morning.' "
18:21 set such men **o** them as officers **o** thousands,
18:25 from all Israel and appointed them as heads **o**
18:25 as officers **o** thousands, hundreds, fifties, and tens.
22: 5 someone causes a field or vineyard to be grazed **o**,
23:31 for I will hand **o** to you the inhabitants of the land,
26: 7 also make curtains of goats' hair for a tent **o**
26: 9 the sixth curtain you shall double **o** at the front of
26:12 shall hang **o** the back of the tabernacle.
Ex 26:13 shall hang **o** the sides of the tabernacle,
30: 6 in front of the mercy seat that is **o** the covenant,
36:14 He also made curtains of goats' hair for a tent **o**
40:19 the tent **o** the tabernacle, and put the covering of the tent **o** it;
Lev 14: 5 be slaughtered **o** fresh water in an earthen vessel.
14: 6 of the bird that was slaughtered **o** the fresh water.
14:50 and shall slaughter one of the birds **o** fresh water
16:10 before the LORD to make atonement **o** it,
16:21 and confess **o** it all the iniquities of the people
19: 6 and anything left **o** until the third day shall
25:43 You shall not rule **o** them with harshness,
25:46 no one shall rule **o** the other with harshness.
25:53 however, rule with harshness **o** them in your sight.
26:17 your foes shall rule **o** you,
26:37 They shall stumble **o** one another,
27: 7 And if the person is sixty years old or **o**,
Nu 1:50 the Levites **o** the tabernacle of the covenant, and **o** all its equipment, and **o** all that belongs to it;
3:32 of Aaron the priest was to be chief **o** the leaders of
3:46 **o** and above the number of the Levites,
3:49 the redemption money from those who were **o** and
4: 6 and spread **o** that a cloth all of blue,
4: 7 **O** the table of the bread of
4: 8 then they shall spread **o** them a crimson cloth,
4:11 **O** the golden altar they shall spread a blue cloth,
4:13 and spread a purple cloth **o** it;
7: 2 who were **o** those who were enrolled,
9:15 and from evening until morning it was **o**
9:17 Whenever the cloud lifted from **o** the tent,
9:18 As long as the cloud rested **o** the tabernacle,
9:19 the cloud continued **o** the tabernacle many days,
9:20 Sometimes the cloud would remain a few days **o**
9:22 that the cloud continued **o** the tabernacle,
10:10 **o** your burnt offerings and **o** your sacrifices
10:11 cloud lifted from **o** the tabernacle of the covenant.
10:14 and **o** the whole company was Nahshon son
10:15 **O** the company of the tribe of Issachar
10:16 and **o** the company of the tribe of Zebulun
10:18 **o** the whole company was Elizur son of Shedeur.
10:19 **O** the company of the tribe of Simeon
10:20 and **o** the company of the tribe of Gad
10:22 and **o** the whole company was Elishama son
10:23 **O** the company of the tribe of Manasseh
10:24 and **o** the company of the tribe of Benjamin
10:25 and **o** the whole company was Ahiezer son
10:26 **O** the company of the tribe of Asher
10:27 and **o** the company of the tribe of Naphtali
10:34 the LORD being **o** them by day when they set out
11:16 to be the elders of the people and officers **o** them;
12:10 When the cloud went away from **o** the tent,
14:14 and your cloud stands **o** them and you go in front
16:13 that you must also lord it **o** us?
16:33 the earth closed **o** them, and they perished from
21: 3 and handed **o** the Canaanites;
22: 5 they have spread **o** the face of the earth,
22:11 'A people has come out of Egypt and has spread **o**
23:15 while I meet the LORD **o** there.
27:16 appoint someone **o** the congregation
31:48 the officers who were **o** the thousands of the army,
32: 7 of the Israelites from going **o** into the land that
32:27 but your servants will cross **o**,
32:29 will cross **o** the Jordan with you and the land shall
32:30 but if they will not cross **o** with you armed,
32:32 We will cross **o** armed before the LORD into
33:51 you cross **o** the Jordan into the land of Canaan,
Dt 1:15 and installed them as leaders **o** you,
1:27 to hand us **o** to the Amorites to destroy us.
2:13 "Now then, proceed to cross **o** the Wadi Zered."
2:13 So we crossed **o** the Wadi Zered.
2:24 I have handed **o** to you King Sihon the Amorite
2:30 and made his heart defiant in order to hand him **o**
2:31 I have begun to give Sihon and his land **o** to you.
2:33 the LORD our God gave him **o** to us;
3: 2 "Do not fear him, for I have handed him **o** to you,
3: 3 the LORD our God also handed **o** to us King Og
3:18 all your troops shall cross **o** armed as the vanguard
3:25 Let me cross **o** to see the good land beyond
3:27 Look well, for you shall not cross **o** this Jordan.
3:28 because it is he who shall cross **o** at the head
4:22 to die in this land without crossing **o** the Jordan,
4:22 but you are going to cross **o** to take possession of
7: 2 when the LORD your God gives them **o** to you
7:16 the peoples that the LORD your God is giving **o**
7:23 But the LORD your God will give them **o** to you,
7:24 He will hand their kings **o** to you
9: 3 that the LORD your God is the one who crosses **o**
11: 4 the Red Sea flow **o** them as they pursued you,
11: 8 in and occupy the land that you are crossing **o**
11:11 the land that you are crossing **o** to occupy is a land
12:10 When you cross **o** the Jordan and live in the land
15: 6 you will rule **o** many nations,
15: 6 but they will not rule **o** you.
17:14 and you say, "I will set a king **o** me,
17:15 you may indeed set **o** you a king whom
17:15 of your own community you may set as king **o**
17:15 you are not permitted to put a foreigner **o** you,
17:20 and his descendants may reign long **o** his kingdom
19:12 to have the culprit taken from there and handed **o**
21: 6 the body shall wash their hands **o**
21:10 and the LORD your God hands them **o** to you
23:14 to save you and to hand **o** your enemies to you,
27: 2 the day that you cross **o** the Jordan into the land
27: 3 the words of this law when you have crossed **o**,
27: 4 So when you have crossed **o** the Jordan,
27:12 When you have crossed **o** the Jordan,
28:23 The sky **o** your head shall be bronze,

Dt 28:36 and the king whom you set **o** you,
28:42 the fruit of your ground the cicada shall take **o**.
31: 2 'You shall not cross **o** this Jordan.'
31: 3 LORD your God himself will cross **o** before you.
31: 3 Joshua also will cross **o** before you,
31: 5 The LORD will give them **o** to you
31:13 that you are crossing **o** the Jordan to possess."
32:11 an eagle stirs up its nest, and hovers **o** its young;
32:47 that you are crossing **o** the Jordan to possess."
34: 4 but you shall not cross **o** there."
Jos 1:11 for in three days you are to cross **o** the Jordan,
1:14 But all the warriors among you shall cross **o**
2:23 They crossed **o**, came to Joshua son of Nun,
3: 1 They camped there before crossing **o**.
3:14 When the people set out from their tents to cross **o**
3:16 Then the people crossed **o** opposite Jericho.
3:17 While all Israel were crossing **o** on dry ground,
3:17 the entire nation finished crossing **o** the Jordan.
4: 1 entire nation had finished crossing **o** the Jordan,
4: 3 the priests' feet stood, carry them **o** with you,
4: 7 When it crossed **o** the Jordan,
4: 8 carried them **o** with them to the place
4:10 The people crossed **o** in haste.
4:11 As soon as all the people had finished crossing **o**,
4:11 and the priests, crossed **o** in front of the people.
4:12 of Manasseh crossed **o** armed before the Israelites,
4:13 for war crossed **o** before the LORD to the plains
4:22 'Israel crossed **o** the Jordan here on dry ground.'
4:23 of the Jordan for you until you crossed **o**,
4:23 which he dried up for us until we crossed **o**,
5: 1 for the Israelites until they had crossed **o**,
6: 2 "See, I have handed Jericho **o** to you,
7: 7 to hand us **o** to the Amorites so as to destroy us?
7:26 and raised **o** him a great heap of stones
8: 1 I have handed **o** to you the king of Ai
8:29 and raised **o** it a great heap of stones,
10: 8 for I have handed them **o** to you;
10:12 On the day when the LORD gave the Amorites **o**
11: 6 for tomorrow at this time I will hand **o** all of them,
11: 8 And the LORD handed them **o** to Israel,
12: 5 and ruled **o** Mount Hermon and Salecah
12: 5 and **o** half of Gilead to the boundary
15: 8 up to the top of the mountain that lies **o** against
22:19 cross **o** into the LORD's land where
24: 8 they fought with you, and I handed them **o** to you,
24:11 When you went **o** the Jordan and came to Jericho,
24:11 and I handed them **o** to you.
Jdg 2:14 he gave them **o** to plunderers who plundered them,
2:23 and had not handed them **o** to Joshua.
3:10 and his hand prevailed **o** Cushan-rishathaim.
3:22 and the fat closed **o** the blade,
3:28 and allowed no one to cross **o**.
6: 2 The hand of Midian prevailed **o** Israel;
8: 4 Then Gideon came to the Jordan and crossed **o**,
8:22 Then the Israelites said to Gideon, "Rule **o** us,
8:23 said to them, "I will not rule **o** you, and my son
will not rule **o** you; the LORD will rule **o** you."
9: 2 all seventy of the sons of Jerubbaal rule **o** you, or
that one rule **o** you?'
9: 8 trees once went out to anoint a king **o** themselves.
9: 8 So they said to the olive tree, 'Reign **o** us.'
9: 9 and go to sway **o** the trees?'
9:10 'You come and reign **o** us.'
9:11 and go to sway **o** the trees?'
9:12 trees said to the vine, 'You come and reign **o** us.'
9:13 and go to sway **o** the trees?'
9:14 'You come and reign **o** us.'
9:15 'If in good faith you are anointing me king **o** you,
9:18 king **o** the lords of Shechem,
9:22 Abimelech ruled **o** Israel three years.
9:49 and they set the stronghold on fire **o** them,
10:18 He shall be head **o** all the inhabitants of Gilead."
11: 8 and fight with the Ammonites, and become head **o**
11: 8 **o** all the inhabitants of Gilead."
11: 9 and the LORD gives them **o** to me,
11:11 people made him head and commander **o** them;
11:32 So Jephthah crossed **o** to the Ammonites to fight
12: 1 "Why did you cross **o** to fight against
12: 1 We will burn your house down **o** you!"
12: 3 and crossed **o** against the Ammonites,
12: 5 of the fugitives of Ephraim said, "Let me go **o**,"
14: 4 At that time the Philistines had dominion **o** Israel.
15:11 "Do you not know that the Philistines are rulers **o**
18: 3 so they went **o** and asked him,
18:19 Put your hand **o** your mouth, and come with us,
20:13 Now then, hand **o** those scoundrels in Gibeah,
Ru 2:14 and she had some left **o**.
2:18 Then she took out and gave her what was left **o**
3: 8 At midnight the man was startled, and turned **o**,
3: 9 spread your cloak **o** your servant,
4: 1 So Boaz said, "Come **o**, friend; sit down here."
4: 1 And he went **o** and sat down.
1Sa 4:18 Eli fell **o** backward from his seat by the side of
8: 1 he made his sons judges **o** Israel.
8: 7 but they have rejected me from being king **o** them.
8: 9 the ways of the king who shall reign **o** them."
8:11 be the ways of the king who will reign **o** you:
8:19 but we are determined to have a king **o** us,
8:22 "Listen to their voice and set a king **o** them."
9:16 and you shall anoint him to be ruler **o**
9:17 He it is who shall rule **o** my people."
10: 1 LORD has anointed you ruler **o** his people Israel.
10: 1 You shall reign **o** the people of the LORD
10: 1 the LORD has anointed you ruler **o** his heritage:
10:11 "What has come **o** the son of Kish?
10:19 but set a king **o** us.'
11:12 "Who is it that said, 'Shall Saul reign **o** us?'

1Sa 12: 1 and have set a king **o** you.
12:12 you said to me, 'No, but a king shall reign **o** us,'
12:13 see, the LORD has set a king **o** you.
12:14 and the king who reigns **o** you will follow
13: 1 and he reigned . . . and two years **o** Israel.
13:13 LORD would have established your kingdom **o**
13:14 and the LORD has appointed him to be ruler **o**
14: 1 let us go **o** to the Philistine garrison on
14: 4 to go **o** to the Philistine garrison, there was
14: 6 let us go **o** to the garrison of these uncircumcised;
14: 8 "Now we will cross **o** to those men
14:23 battle spread out **o** the hill country of Ephraim.
14:47 When Saul had taken the kingship **o** Israel,
15: 1 "The LORD sent me to anoint you king **o**
15:17 The LORD anointed you king **o** Israel.
15:26 the LORD has rejected you from being king **o**
15:35 but Samuel grieved **o** Saul.
15:35 that he had made Saul king **o** Israel.
16: 1 "How long will you grieve **o** Saul?
16: 1 I have rejected him from being king **o** Israel.
17:39 David strapped Saul's sword **o** the armor,
17:50 So David prevailed **o** the Philistine with a sling
17:51 Then David ran and stood **o** the Philistine;
18: 5 as a result, Saul set him **o** the army.
19:11 to David's house to keep watch **o** him,
22: 2 and he became captain **o** them.
23:17 you shall be king **o** Israel,
25:30 and has appointed you prince **o** Israel,
26:13 Then David went **o** to the other side,
26:15 Why then have you not kept watch **o** your lord
26:16 because you have not kept watch **o** your lord,
26:22 Let one of the young men come **o** and get it.
27: 2 So David set out and went **o**,
30:15 or hand me **o** to my master,
30:16 they were spread out all **o** the ground,
30:23 he has preserved us and handed **o** to us
2Sa 1: 9 He said to me, 'Come, stand **o** me and kill me;
1:10 So I stood **o** him, and killed him,
1:17 David intoned this lamentation **o** Saul
1:24 O daughters of Israel, weep **o** Saul,
2: 4 and there they anointed David king **o** the house
2: 7 the house of Judah has anointed me king **o** them."
2: 8 and brought him **o** to Mahanaim.
2: 9 He made him king **o** Gilead, the Ashurites,
2: 9 Jezreel, Ephraim, Benjamin, and **o** all Israel.
2:10 was forty years old when he began to reign **o**
2:11 in Hebron **o** the house of Judah was seven years
3:10 set up the throne of David **o** Israel and **o** Judah,
3:12 and I will give you my support to bring all Israel **o**
3:17 past you have been seeking David as king **o** you.
3:21 that you may reign **o** all that your heart desires."
3:31 and put on sackcloth, and mourn **o** Abner."
3:34 And all the people wept **o** him again.
5: 2 For some time, while Saul was king **o** us,
5: 2 you who shall be ruler **o** Israel."
5: 3 and they anointed David king **o** Israel.
5: 5 At Hebron he reigned **o** Judah seven years
5: 5 and at Jerusalem he reigned **o** all Israel and Judah
5:12 that the LORD had established him king **o** Israel,
5:17 that David had been anointed king **o** Israel, all
6:21 to appoint me as prince **o** Israel,
7: 8 the sheep to be prince **o** my people Israel;
7:11 that I appointed judges **o** my people Israel;
7:26 'The LORD of hosts is God **o** Israel';
8:15 So David reigned **o** all Israel;
8:16 Joab son of Zeruiah was **o** the army;
8:18 Benaiah son of Jehoiada was **o** the Cherethites and
11:23 "The men gained an advantage **o** us,
11:27 When the mourning was **o**,
12: 7 I anointed you king **o** Israel,
13:39 for he was now consoled **o** the death of Amnon.
16: 9 Let me go **o** and take off his head."
17:16 but by all means cross **o**;
17:19 stretched it **o** the well's mouth,
17:20 "They have crossed **o** the brook of water."
17:25 Now Absalom had set Amasa **o** the army in
18: 1 and set **o** them commanders of thousands
18: 8 The battle spread **o** the face of all the country;
18:17 and raised **o** him a very great heap of stones.
18:33 and went up to the chamber **o** the gate, and wept;
19:10 But Absalom, whom we anointed **o** us,
19:15 to meet the king and to bring him **o** the Jordan.
19:18 to bring **o** the king's household,
19:22 do I not know that I am this day king **o** Israel?"
19:31 to escort him **o** the Jordan.
19:33 The king said to Barzillai, "Come **o** with me,
19:36 Your servant will go a little way **o** the Jordan with
19:37 let him go **o** with my lord the king;
19:38 king answered, "Chimham shall go **o** with me,
19:39 Then all the people crossed **o** the Jordan, and the
king crossed **o**;
19:41 brought the king and his household **o** the Jordan,
19:42 Why then are you angry **o** this matter?
20: 8 Now Joab was wearing a soldier's garment and **o**
20:12 and threw a garment **o** him.
20:21 "His head shall be thrown **o** the wall to you."
21: 6 let seven of his sons be handed **o** to us,
21: 6 The king said, "I will hand them **o**."
22:30 and by my God I can leap **o** a wall.
23: 3 One who rules **o** people justly,
1Ki 1:34 and the prophet Nathan anoint him king **o** Israel;
1:35 appointed him to be ruler **o** Israel and **o** Judah."
2:11 time that David reigned **o** Israel was forty years;
2:35 The king put Benaiah son of Jehoiada **o** the army
4: 1 King Solomon was king **o** all Israel,
4: 5 Azariah son of Nathan was **o** the officials;
4: 7 Solomon had twelve officials **o** all Israel,

1Ki 4:21 Solomon was sovereign **o** all the kingdoms from
4:24 For he had dominion **o** all the region west of
4:24 **o** all the kings west of the Euphrates;
5: 7 to David a wise son to be **o** this great people."
5:16 thousand three hundred supervisors who were **o**
6: 1 in the fourth year of Solomon's reign **o** Israel,
8: 7 the cherubim spread out their wings **o** the place of
8:16 but I chose David to be **o** my people Israel.'
9: 5 I will establish your royal throne **o** Israel forever,
9:23 the chief officers who were **o** Solomon's work:
11:25 he despised Israel and reigned **o** Aram.
11:28 young man was industrious he gave him charge **o**
11:37 and you shall reign **o** all that your soul desires;
11:37 you shall be king **o** Israel.
11:42 The time that Solomon reigned in Jerusalem **o**
12:17 But Rehoboam reigned **o** the Israelites who
12:18 who was taskmaster **o** the forced labor,
12:20 to the assembly and made him king **o** all Israel.
13:30 they mourned **o** him, saying, "Alas, my brother!"
14: 2 who said of me that I should be king **o** this people.
14: 7 made you leader **o** my people Israel,
14:14 LORD will raise up for himself a king **o** Israel,
15: 1 Abijam began to reign **o** Judah.
15: 9 Asa began to reign **o** Judah;
15:25 Nadab son of Jeroboam began to reign **o** Israel in
15:25 he reigned **o** Israel two years.
15:33 Baasha son of Ahijah began to reign **o** all Israel
16: 2 the dust and made you leader **o** my people Israel,
16: 8 of Baasha began to reign **o** Israel in Tirzah;
16:16 king **o** Israel that day in the camp.
16:18 the king's house **o** himself with fire, and died—
16:23 Omri began to reign **o** Israel;
16:29 Ahab son of Omri began to reign **o** Israel;
16:29 Ahab son of Omri reigned **o** Israel
18: 9 that you would hand your servant **o** to Ahab,
18:28 and lances until the blood gushed out **o** them.
19:15 you shall anoint Hazael as king **o** Aram.
19:16 of Nimshi as king **o** Israel;
19:19 Elijah passed by him and threw his mantle **o** him.
20:38 disguising himself with a bandage **o** his eyes.
21:27 he tore his clothes and put sackcloth **o**
22:41 Jehoshaphat son of Asa began to reign **o** Judah in
22:51 to reign **o** Israel in Samaria in the seventeenth year
22:51 he reigned two years **o** Israel.
2Ki 2:14 to the one side and to the other, and Elisha went **o**.
3: 1 Jehoram son of Ahab became king **o** Israel
3:10 three kings, only to be handed **o** to Moab."
3:13 three kings, only to be handed **o** to Moab."
3:18 for he will also hand Moab **o** to you.
4:34 and while he lay bent **o** him,
4:35 then got up again and bent **o** him;
5:11 and would wave his hand **o** the spot,
8:13 that you are to be king **o** Aram."
8:15 in water and spread it **o** the king's face,
8:21 Then Joram crossed **o** to Zair with all his chariots.
9: 3 I anoint you king **o** Israel.'
9: 6 you king **o** the people of the LORD, **o** Israel.
9:12 I anoint you king **o** Israel.' "
9:29 Ahaziah began to reign **o** Judah.
10:36 The time that Jehu reigned **o** Israel
11: 3 while Athaliah reigned **o** the land.
11:15 the captains who were set **o** the army,
11:18 priest posted guards **o** the house of the LORD.
12: 7 from your donors but hand it **o** for the repair of
13: 1 Jehoahaz son of Jehu began to reign **o** Israel
13:10 Jehoash son of Jehoahaz began to reign **o** Israel
13:17 the arrow of victory **o** Aram!
15: 8 Zechariah son of Jeroboam reigned **o** Israel
15:17 Menahem son of Gadi began to reign **o** Israel;
15:23 Pekahiah son of Menahem began to reign **o** Israel
15:27 of Remaliah began to reign **o** Israel in Samaria;
17: 1 Hoshea son of Elah began to reign in Samaria **o**
21:13 I will stretch **o** Jerusalem the measuring line
24: 7 the king of Babylon had taken **o** all that belonged
25:22 as governor **o** the people who remained in the land
1Ch 1:43 of Edom before any king reigned **o** the Israelites:
9:20 And Phinehas son of Eleazar was chief **o** them
9:29 Others of them were appointed **o** the furniture, and
o all the holy utensils, also **o** the choice flour,
10:14 and turned the kingdom **o** to David son of Jesse.
11: 2 you who shall be ruler **o** my people Israel."
11: 3 And they anointed David king **o** Israel,
12: 4 among the Thirty and a leader **o** the Thirty;
12: 8 From the Gadites there went **o** to David at
12:23 to David in Hebron to turn the kingdom of Saul **o**
12:38 to Hebron with full intent to make David king **o**
14: 2 the LORD had established him as king **o** Israel,
14: 8 that David had been anointed king **o** all Israel, all
17: 7 to be ruler **o** my people Israel;
17:10 that I appointed judges **o** my people Israel;
18:14 So David reigned **o** all Israel;
18:15 Joab son of Zeruiah was **o** the army;
18:17 Benaiah son of Jehoiada was **o** the Cherethites and
21:16 and in his hand a drawn sword stretched out **o**
22:12 when he gives you charge **o** Israel you may keep
23: 1 he made his son Solomon king **o** Israel.
27:16 **O** the tribes of Israel, for the Reubenites,
27:25 **O** the king's treasuries was Azmaveth son
27:25 **O** the treasuries in the country, in the cities,
27:26 **O** those who did the work of the field,
27:27 **O** the vineyards was Shimei the Ramathite.
27:27 **O** the produce of the vineyards for
27:28 **O** the olive and sycamore trees in
27:28 **O** the stores of oil was Joash.
27:29 **O** the herds that pastured in Sharon was Shitrai
27:29 **O** the herds in the valleys was Shaphat son
27:30 **O** the camels was Obil the Ishmaelite.

1Ch 27:30 **O** the donkeys was Jehdeiah the Meronothite.
27:30 **O** the flocks was Jaziz the Hagrite.
28: 4 from all my ancestral house to be king **o** Israel
28: 4 in making me king **o** all Israel.
28: 5 the throne of the kingdom of the LORD **o** Israel.
29: 6 and the officers **o** the king's work.
29:12 and honor come from you, and you rule **o** all.
29:26 Thus David son of Jesse reigned **o** all Israel.
29:27 period that he reigned **o** Israel was forty years;
2Ch 1: 9 for you have made me king **o** a people
1:11 for yourself that you may rule my people **o**
1:13 And he reigned **o** Israel.
2:11 LORD loves his people he has made you king **o**
5: 8 the cherubim spread out their wings **o** the place of
6: 5 and I chose no one as ruler **o** my people Israel;
6: 6 I have chosen David to be **o** my people Israel.'
7:18 'You shall never lack a successor to rule **o** Israel.'
8:10 who exercised authority **o** the people.
9: 8 he has made you king **o** them,
9:26 He ruled **o** all the kings from the Euphrates to
9:30 in Jerusalem **o** all Israel forty years.
10:17 But Rehoboam reigned **o** the people
10:18 who was taskmaster **o** the forced labor,
13: 1 Abijah began to reign **o** Judah.
13: 5 the kingship **o** Israel forever to David and his sons
15:15 All Judah rejoiced **o** the oath;
19:11 Amariah the chief priest is **o** you in all matters of
20: 6 Do you not rule **o** all the kingdoms of the nations?
20:27 for the LORD had enabled them to rejoice **o**
20:31 So Jehoshaphat reigned **o** Judah.
21: 9 Then Jehoram crossed **o** with his commanders
22:12 while Athaliah reigned **o** the land.
23:14 the captains who were set **o** the army, saying
25:20 it was God's doing, in order to hand them **o,**
31:10 so that we have this great supply left **o.**"
32: 6 He appointed combat commanders **o** the people,
32:11 handing you **o** to die by famine and by thirst,
34: 4 he made dust of them and scattered it **o** the graves
34:12 **O** them were appointed the Levites Jahath
34:13 were **o** the burden bearers
36: 4 of Egypt made his brother Eliakim king **o** Judah
36:10 and made his brother Zedekiah king **o** Judah
Ezr 4:20 Jerusalem has had mighty kings who ruled **o**
5: 1 in the name of the God of Israel who was **o** them.
8:30 So the priests and the Levites took **o** the silver,
9: 7 and our priests have been handed **o** to the kings of
10: 6 he was mourning **o** the faithlessness of the exiles.
Ne 4: 4 and give them **o** as plunder in a land of captivity.
4:14 After I looked these things **o,**
5: 7 After thinking it **o,** I brought charges against
5:15 Even their servants lorded it **o** the people.
7: 2 I gave my brother Hanani charge **o** Jerusalem,
9:28 so that they had dominion **o** them;
9:30 you handed them **o** to the peoples of the lands.
9:37 to the kings whom you have set **o** us because
9:37 power also **o** our bodies and **o** our livestock
11:16 who were **o** the outside work of the house of God;
11:21 and Ziha and Gishpa were **o** the temple servants.
12:24 with their associates **o** against them,
12:44 On that day men were appointed **o** the chambers
12:44 for Judah rejoiced **o** the priests and
13: 4 who was appointed **o** the chambers of the house
13:13 And I appointed as treasurers **o** the storehouses
13:19 And I set some of my servants **o** the gates,
13:26 and God made him king **o** all Israel;
Est 1: 1 the same Ahasuerus who ruled **o**
3:12 and to the governors **o** all the provinces and to
6: 9 Let the robes and the horse be handed **o** to one of
8: 2 So Esther set Mordecai **o** the house of Haman.
9: 1 the enemies of the Jews hoped to gain power **o**
9: 1 when the Jews would gain power **o** their foes,
Job 6: 5 Does the wild ass bray **o** its grass,
6: 5 or the ox low **o** its fodder?
6:27 You would even cast lots **o** the orphan,
6:27 and bargain **o** your friend.
7:12 or the Dragon, that you set a guard **o** me?
8:16 and their shoots spread **o** the garden.
14:16 you would not keep watch **o** my sin;
14:17 and you would cover **o** my iniquity.
21:32 a watch is kept **o** their tomb.
26: 7 He stretches out Zaphon **o** the void,
26: 9 and spreads **o** it his cloud.
28: 8 the lion has not passed **o** it.
29: 2 as in the days when God watched **o** me;
29: 3 when his lamp shone **o** my head,
31:10 and let other men kneel **o** her.
34:13 Who gave him charge **o** the earth and who laid
39:11 and will you hand **o** your labor to it?
41: 6 Will traders bargain **o** it?
41:34 it is king **o** all that are proud."
Ps 1: 6 the LORD watches **o** the way of the righteous,
5:11 Spread your protection **o** them,
7: 7 and **o** it take your seat on high.
8: 6 You have given them dominion **o** the works
13: 2 How long shall my enemy be exalted **o** me?
17:14 may they leave something **o** to their little ones.
18:29 and by my God I can leap **o** a wall.
19:13 do not let them have dominion **o** me.
20: 5 May we shout for joy **o** your victory,
22:17 They stare and gloat **o** me;
22:28 and he rules **o** the nations.
25: 2 do not let my enemies exult **o** me.
29: 3 The voice of the LORD is **o** the waters;
29: 3 the LORD, **o** mighty waters.
29:10 The LORD sits enthroned **o** the flood;
30: 1 and did not let my foes rejoice **o** me.
35:19 Do not let my treacherous enemies rejoice **o** me,
Ps 35:24 and do not let them rejoice **o** me.
37: 7 do not fret **o** those who prosper in their way,
37: 7 **o** those who carry out evil devices.
38: 4 For my iniquities have gone **o** my head;
38:16 For I pray, "Only do not let them rejoice **o** me,
41:11 because my enemy has not triumphed **o** me.
42: 7 all your waves and your billows have gone **o** me.
47: 2 is awesome, a great king **o** all the earth.
47: 8 God is king **o** the nations;
57: 5 Let your glory be **o** all the earth.
57:11 Let your glory be **o** all the earth.
59:13 be known to the ends of the earth that God rules **o**
60: 8 **o** Philistia I shout in triumph."
61: 7 appoint steadfast love and faithfulness to watch **o**
63:10 they shall be given **o** to the power of the sword,
66:12 you let people ride **o** our heads;
68:34 Ascribe power to God, whose majesty is **o** Israel;
69: 2 and the flood sweeps **o** me.
69:15 Do not let the flood sweep **o** me,
69:15 or the Pit close its mouth **o** me.
73: 9 and their tongues range **o** the earth.
78:48 He gave **o** their cattle to the hail,
78:50 but gave their lives **o** to the plague.
81: 5 when he went out **o** the land of Egypt.
81:12 So I gave them **o** to their stubborn hearts,
83:18 are the Most High **o** all the earth.
88:16 Your wrath has swept **o** me;
92:10 you have poured **o** me fresh oil.
97: 9 For you, O LORD, are most high **o** all the earth;
99: 2 he is exalted **o** all the peoples.
103:16 for the wind passes **o** it,
103:19 and his kingdom rules **o** all.
106:27 scattering them **o** the lands.
106:41 so that those who hated them ruled **o** them.
108: 5 and let your glory be **o** all the earth.
108: 9 **o** Philistia I shout in triumph."
110: 6 he will shatter heads **o** the wide earth.
118:18 but he did not give me **o** to death.
119:133 and never let iniquity have dominion **o** me.
124: 4 the torrent would have gone **o** us;
124: 5 then **o** us would have gone the raging waters.
133: 2 running down **o** the collar of his robes.
136: 8 the sun to rule **o** the day,
136: 9 the moon and stars to rule **o** the night,
141: 3 Set a guard **o** my mouth, O LORD;
141: 3 keep watch **o** the door of my lips.
141: 6 When they are given **o** to those
145: 9 and his compassion is **o** all that he has made.
145:20 The LORD watches **o** all who love him,
146: 9 The LORD watches **o** the strangers;
Pr 2:11 prudence will watch **o** you;
4:19 they do not know what they stumble **o.**
6:22 when you lie down, they will watch **o** you;
17: 2 A slave who deals wisely will rule **o**
19:10 much less for a slave to rule **o** princes.
20:26 and drives the wheel **o** them.
21:23 To watch **o** mouth and tongue is to keep out
22: 7 The rich rules **o** the poor,
22:12 The eyes of the LORD keep watch **o** knowledge,
23:30 Those who linger late **o** wine,
24:12 not he who keeps watch **o** your soul know it?
28:15 a charging bear is a wicked ruler **o** a poor people.
Ecc 1:12 I, the Teacher, when king **o** Israel in Jerusalem,
1:16 surpassing all who were **o** Jerusalem before me;
3:19 and humans have no advantage **o** the animals;
5: 8 and there are yet higher ones **o** them.
5:20 they will scarcely brood **o** the days of their lives,
6: 6 though he should live a thousand years twice **o,**
6: 8 For what advantage have the wise **o** fools?
8: 8 No one has power **o** the wind to restrain the wind,
8: 8 or power **o** the day of death;
8: 9 while one person exercises authority **o** another to
SS 2: 8 leaping upon the mountains, bounding **o** the hills.
2:11 for now the winter is past, the rain is **o** and gone.
7: 9 that goes down smoothly, gliding **o** lips and teeth.
7:13 and **o** our doors are all choice fruits,
Isa 3: 4 and babes shall rule **o** them.
3:12 children are their oppressors, and women rule **o**
4: 5 Then the LORD will create **o** the whole site of
Mount Zion and **o** its places
4: 5 Indeed **o** all the glory there will be a canopy.
5:30 They will roar **o** it on that day,
8: 8 and, pouring **o,** it will reach up to the neck;
8:14 of Israel he will become a rock one stumbles **o**—
10:15 Shall the ax vaunt itself **o** the one who wields it,
10:26 his staff will be **o** the sea,
10:29 they have crossed **o** the pass, at Geba they lodge
11: 8 The nursing child shall play **o** the hole of the asp,
11:15 and will wave his hand **o** the River
14: 2 and rule **o** those who oppressed them.
14: 8 The cypresses exult **o** you, the cedars of Lebanon,
14:16 at you, and ponder **o** you:
14:26 the hand that is stretched out **o** all the nations.
15: 2 **o** Nebo and **o** Medeba Moab wails.
15: 7 up they carry away **o** the Wadi of the Willows.
16: 8 their shoots once spread abroad and crossed **o**
16: 9 for the shout **o** your fruit harvest
18: 5 when the blossom is **o** and the flower becomes
19: 4 a fierce king will rule **o** them, says the Sovereign,
23: 2 your messengers crossed **o** the sea
23: 5 they will be in anguish **o** the report about Tyre.
23: 6 Cross **o** to Tarshish—wail,
23:10 Cross **o** to your own land, O ships of Tarshish;
23:11 He has stretched out his hand **o** the sea,
23:12 cross **o** to Cyprus—even there you will have no
24:14 from the west **o** the majesty of the LORD.
25: 7 cast **o** all peoples, the sheet that is spread **o** all
Isa 26:13 other lords besides you have ruled **o** us,
28:27 nor is a cart wheel rolled **o** cummin;
28:28 one drives the cart wheel and horses **o** it,
31: 4 As a lion or a young lion growls **o** its prey, and—
34: 2 has given them **o** for slaughter.
34:11 He shall stretch the line of confusion **o** it,
34:11 and the plummet of chaos **o** its nobles.
34:13 Thorns shall grow **o** its strongholds,
44:12 The ironsmith fashions it and works it **o** the coals,
44:16 **o** this half he roasts meat, eats it and is satisfied.
45:14 tall of stature, shall come **o** to you and be yours,
45:14 they shall come **o** in chains and bow down to you.
51:10 of the sea a way for the redeemed to cross **o?**
54: 9 that the waters of Noah would never again go **o**
60: 2 and his glory will appear **o** you.
62: 5 and as the bridegroom rejoices **o** the bride,
62: 5 so shall your God rejoice **o** you.
62:10 clear it of stones, lift up an ensign **o** the peoples.
66:10 rejoice with her in joy, all you who mourn **o** her—
Jer 1:10 today I appoint you **o** nations and **o** kingdoms,
1:12 for I am watching **o** my word to perform it."
5:22 though they roar, they cannot pass **o** it.
5:26 they take **o** the goods of others.
6: 9 pass your hand again **o** its branches.
6:12 Their houses shall be turned **o** to others,
9:18 let them quickly raise a dirge **o** us,
13:21 as head **o** you those whom you have trained to
13:26 I myself will lift up your skirts **o** your face,
15: 3 I will appoint **o** them four kinds of destroyers,
15:20 but they shall not prevail **o** you,
18:21 Therefore give their children **o** to famine;
23: 4 up shepherds **o** them who will shepherd them,
26:24 not given **o** into the hands of the people to be put
30:15 Why do you cry out **o** your hurt?
31:12 be radiant **o** the goodness of the LORD,
31:12 **o** the grain, the wine, and the oil,
31:12 and **o** the young of the flock and the herd;
31:28 as I have watched **o** them to pluck up and break
31:28 so I will watch **o** them to build and to plant,
33:26 and not choose any of his descendants as rulers **o**
34: 3 but shall surely be captured and handed **o** to him;
34:20 shall be handed **o** to their enemies and
34:21 I will hand them **o** to their enemies and
37:17 "You shall be handed **o** to the king of Babylon."
38: 3 This city shall surely be handed **o** to the army of
38:16 or hand you **o** to these men who seek your life."
38:18 then this city shall be handed **o** to the Chaldeans,
38:19 be handed **o** to them and they would abuse me."
39:17 not be handed **o** to those whom you dread.
40:10 and live in the towns that you have taken **o.**"
40:11 of Ahikam son of Shaphan as governor **o** them,
41:10 and set out to cross **o** to the Ammonites.
41:18 whom the king of Babylon had made governor **o**
43: 3 to hand us **o** to the Chaldeans,
43:10 and he will spread his royal canopy **o** them.
44:27 I am going to watch **o** them for harm and not
46:24 she shall be handed **o** to a people from the north.
46:26 I will hand them **o** to those who seek their life,
48:17 Mourn **o** him, all you his neighbors,
48:32 Your branches crossed **o** the sea,
49:19 and I will appoint **o** it whomever I choose.
50:38 For it is a land of images, and they go mad **o** idols.
50:44 and I will appoint **o** her whomever I choose.
51:14 and they shall raise a shout of victory **o** you.
51:42 The sea has risen **o** Babylon;
51:48 shall shout for joy **o** Babylon;
La 1: 7 the foe looked on mocking **o** her downfall.
1:10 Enemies have stretched out their hands **o**
1:14 the Lord handed me **o** to those whom I cannot
2:17 he has made the enemy rejoice **o** you,
3:54 water closed **o** my head; I said, "I am lost."
5: 2 Our inheritance has been turned **o** to strangers,
5: 8 Slaves rule **o** us; there is no one to deliver
5:18 which lies desolate; jackals prowl **o** it.
Eze 1:22 **O** the heads of the living creatures there was
1:25 And there came a voice from above the dome **o**
1:26 above the dome **o** their heads there was something
5: 1 use it as a barber's razor and run it **o** your head
7:16 all of them moaning **o** their iniquity.
7:21 I will hand it **o** to strangers as booty,
9: 4 on the foreheads of those who sigh and groan **o** all
10: 1 and above the dome that was **o** the heads of
10: 2 and scatter them **o** the city."
11: 9 of it and give you **o** to the hands of foreigners,
12:13 I will spread my net **o** him,
16: 8 I spread the edge of my cloak **o** you,
17:20 I will spread my net **o** him,
19: 8 they spread their net **o** him;
20:33 and with wrath poured out, I will be king **o** you.
21:29 they place you **o** the necks of the vile,
25: 3 **o** my sanctuary when it was profaned,
25: 3 **o** the land of Israel when it was made desolate,
25: 3 and **o** the house of Judah when it went into exile;
25: 4 therefore I am handing you **o** to the people of
25: 7 and will hand you **o** as plunder to the nations.
26:17 And they shall raise a lamentation **o** you,
26:19 when I bring up the deep **o** you,
27: 2 Now you, mortal, raise a lamentation **o** Tyre,
27:30 and wail aloud **o** you,
27:31 and they weep **o** you in bitterness of soul,
27:32 a lamentation for you, and lament **o** you:
28:12 raise a lamentation **o** the king of Tyre,
29:15 that they will never again rule **o** the nations.
31:14 For all of them are handed **o** to death,
31:15 the day it went down to Sheol I closed the deep **o**
32: 2 raise a lamentation **o** Pharaoh king of Egypt,
32: 3 of many peoples I will throw my net **o** you;

Eze 32:16 **O** Egypt and all its hordes they shall chant it,
32:18 wail **o** the hordes of Egypt, and send them down,
32:20 Egypt has been handed **o** to the sword;
34: 6 they wandered **o** all the mountains and
34: 6 my sheep were scattered **o** all the face of the earth,
34:23 I will set up **o** them one shepherd,
35: 5 and gave **o** the people of Israel to the power of
35:15 As you rejoiced **o** the inheritance of the house
37:22 and one king shall be king **o** them all.
37:24 My servant David shall be king **o** them;
41: 6 side chambers were in three stories, one **o** another,
43:27 When these days are **o**, then from
Da 1:11 the palace master had appointed **o** Daniel,
2:38 and whom he has established as ruler **o** them all—
2:39 which shall rule **o** the whole earth.
2:48 and made him ruler **o** the whole province of Babylon and chief prefect **o** all the wise men
2:49 and Abednego **o** the affairs of the province
3:12 There are certain Jews whom you have appointed **o**
3:27 that the fire had not had any power **o** the bodies
4:16 And let seven times pass **o** him.
4:17 that the Most High is sovereign **o** the kingdom
4:17 and sets **o** it the lowliest of human beings.'
4:23 until seven times pass **o** him'—
4:25 and seven times shall pass **o** you,
4:25 that the Most High has sovereignty **o** the kingdom
4:32 and seven times shall pass **o** you,
4:32 that the Most High has sovereignty **o** the kingdom
4:34 When that period was **o**, I, Nebuchadnezzar,
4:36 I was re-established **o** my kingdom,
5:21 the Most High God has sovereignty **o** the kingdom
5:21 and sets **o** it whomever he will.
6: 1 to set **o** the kingdom one hundred twenty satraps,
6: 2 and **o** them three presidents, including Daniel;
6: 3 king planned to appoint him **o** the whole kingdom.
7:11 and its body destroyed and given **o** to be burned
7:21 with the holy ones and was prevailing **o** them,
8:12 the host was given **o** to it together with
8:13 and the giving **o** of the sanctuary and host to
9: 1 who became king **o** the realm of the Chaldeans—
9:14 So the LORD kept watch **o** this calamity
11:39 and shall appoint them as rulers **o** many,
Hos 7:12 As they go, I will cast my net **o** them;
8: 1 One like a vulture is **o** the house of the LORD,
9: 8 The prophet is a sentinel for my God **o** Ephraim,
10: 5 and its idolatrous priests shall wail **o** it,
10: 5 **o** its glory that has departed from it.
11: 8 How can I hand you **o**, O Israel?
Joel 1: 5 **o** the sweet wine, for it is cut off from your mouth.
1:11 wail, you vinedressers, **o** the wheat and the barley;
Am 1: 6 into exile entire communities, to hand them **o**
1: 9 they delivered entire communities **o** to Edom,
5: 1 Hear this word that I take up **o** you in lamentation,
5: 5 do not enter into Gilgal or cross **o** to Beer-sheba;
6: 2 Cross **o** to Calneh, and see;
6: 6 but are not grieved **o** the ruin of Joseph!
8: 5 will the new moon be **o** so that we may sell grain;
Ob 1:12 But you should not have gloated **o** your brother on
1:12 not have rejoiced **o** the people of Judah on the day
1:13 not have joined in the gloating **o** Judah's disaster
1:14 you should not have handed **o** his survivors on
Jnh 2: 3 all your waves and your billows passed **o** me.
2: 5 The waters closed in **o** me;
4: 6 made it come up **o** Jonah, to give shade **o** his head,
Mic 3: 6 and the day shall be black **o** them;
4: 7 the LORD will reign **o** them in Mount Zion now
5: 9 Your hand shall be lifted up **o** your adversaries,
6:14 and what you save, I will hand **o** to the sword.
7: 8 Do not rejoice **o** me, O my enemy;
7:18 pardoning iniquity and passing **o** the transgression
Na 3: 3 they stumble **o** the bodies!
3: 5 and will lift up your skirts **o** your face;
3:19 the news about you clap their hands **o** you.
Zep 1: 9 that day I will punish all who leap **o** the threshold,
3:17 he will rejoice **o** you with gladness,
3:17 he will exult **o** you with loud singing
Zec 1:16 measuring line shall be stretched out **o** Jerusalem.
5: 3 "This is the curse that goes out **o** the face of
9:14 Then the LORD will appear **o** them,
12: 7 the inhabitants of Jerusalem may not be exalted **o**
12:10 weep bitterly **o** him, as one weeps **o** a firstborn.
14: 9 And the LORD will become king **o** all the earth;
Mt 2: 9 until it stopped **o** the place where the child was.
2:22 when he heard that Archelaus was ruling **o** Judea
5:25 or your accuser may hand you **o** to the judge,
8:18 he gave orders to go **o** to the other side.
10: 1 and gave them authority **o** unclean spirits,
10:17 for they will hand you **o** to councils and flog you
10:19 When they hand you **o**, do not worry about
11:27 All things have been handed **o** to me
14:20 they took up what was left **o** of the broken pieces,
14:34 When they had crossed **o**,
15:37 and they took up the broken pieces left **o**,
18:13 he rejoices **o** it more than **o** the ninety-nine
18:34 And in anger his lord handed him **o** to be tortured
20:18 of Man will be handed **o** to the chief priests
20:19 then they will hand him **o** to the Gentiles to
20:25 "You know that the rulers of the Gentiles lord it **o**
20:25 and their great ones are tyrants **o** them.
24: 9 "Then they will hand you **o** to be tortured
25:20 saying, 'Master, you handed **o** to me five talents;
25:22 saying, 'Master, you handed **o** to me two talents;
26: 2 the Son of Man will be handed **o** to be crucified."
26:36 "Sit here while I go **o** there and pray."
27: 2 and handed him **o** to Pilate the governor.
27:18 of jealousy that they had handed him **o**.
27:26 flogging Jesus, he handed him **o** to be crucified.
Mt 27:36 then they sat down there and kept watch **o** him.
27:37 **O** his head they put the charge against him,
27:45 darkness came **o** the whole land until three in
27:54 who were keeping watch **o** Jesus,
Mk 6: 7 and gave them authority **o** the unclean spirits.
6:53 When they had crossed **o**,
8: 8 and they took up the broken pieces left **o**,
10:33 of Man will be handed **o** to the chief priests and
10:33 then they will hand him **o** to the Gentiles;
10:42 as their rulers lord it **o** them,
10:42 and their great ones are tyrants **o** them.
12: 4 this one they beat **o** the head and insulted.
13: 9 for they will hand you **o** to councils;
13:11 When they bring you to trial and hand you **o**,
14:65 The guards also took him **o** and beat him.
15: 1 led him away, and handed him **o** to Pilate.
15:10 that the chief priests had handed him **o**.
15:15 flogging Jesus, he handed him **o** to be crucified.
15:33 darkness came **o** the whole land until three in
16: 1 When the sabbath was **o**, Mary Magdalene,
Lk 1:33 He will reign **o** the house of Jacob forever,
1:65 Fear came **o** all their neighbors,
2: 8 keeping watch **o** their flock by night.
4: 2 and when they were **o**, he was famished.
4: 6 for it has been given **o** to me,
4:25 and there was a severe famine **o** all the land;
4:39 Then he stood **o** her and rebuked the fever,
6:38 pressed down, shaken together, running **o**,
9: 1 and gave them power and authority **o** all demons
9:17 What was left **o** was gathered up,
10:19 and **o** all the power of the enemy;
10:22 All things have been handed **o** to me
11:44 and people walk **o** them without realizing it."
12:14 who set me to be a judge or arbitrator **o** you?"
12:58 and the judge hand you **o** to the officer,
13:11 She was bent **o** and was quite unable to stand
13:12 When Jesus saw her, he called her **o** and said,
15: 7 joy in heaven **o** one sinner who repents than **o**
15:10 there is joy in the presence of the angels of God **o**
18:32 For he will be handed **o** to the Gentiles;
19:14 saying, 'We do not want this man to rule **o** us.'
19:19 He said to him, 'And you, rule **o** five cities.'
19:27 of mine who did not want me to be king **o** them—
19:41 As he came near and saw the city, he wept **o** it,
20:20 to hand him **o** to the jurisdiction and authority of
21:12 they will hand you **o** to synagogues and prisons,
22:25 "The kings of the Gentiles lord it **o** them;
22:25 those in authority **o** them are called benefactors.
23:25 and he handed Jesus **o** as they wished.
23:38 There was also an inscription **o** him,
23:44 and darkness came **o** the whole land until three in
24: 7 that the Son of Man must be handed **o** to sinners,
24:20 how our chief priests and leaders handed him **o** to
24:29 it is almost evening and the day is now nearly **o**."
Jn 4:43 When the two days were **o**,
6:12 "Gather up the fragments left **o**,
14:30 He has no power **o** me;
17: 2 since you have given him authority **o** all people,
18:30 we would not have handed him **o** to you."
18:35 and the chief priests have handed you **o** to me.
18:36 be fighting to keep me from being handed **o** to
19:11 "You would have no power **o** me
19:11 the one who handed me **o** to you is guilty of
19:16 Then he handed him **o** to them to be crucified.
20:11 As she wept, she bent **o** to look into the tomb;
Ac 2:23 handed **o** to you according to the definite plan
3:13 whom you handed **o** and rejected in the presence
7:10 who appointed him ruler **o** Egypt and **o** all his
7:18 not known Joseph ruled **o** Egypt.
7:27 saying, 'Who made you a ruler and a judge **o** us?
7:42 from them and handed them **o** to worship the host
8: 2 and made loud lamentation **o** him.
8:29 "Go **o** to this chariot and join it."
11:19 the persecution that took place **o** Stephen traveled
11:28 by the Spirit that there would be a severe famine **o**
12: 4 and handed him **o** to four squads of soldiers
12: 6 of the door were keeping watch **o** the prison.
12:18 among the soldiers **o** what had become of Peter.
12:20 and after winning **o** Blastus,
13:11 Immediately mist and darkness came **o** him,
14:19 from Antioch and Iconium and won **o** the crowds.
15:17 all the Gentiles **o** whom my name has been called.
16: 9 "Come **o** to Macedonia and help us."
16:10 we immediately tried to cross **o** to Macedonia,
18:27 And when he wished to cross **o** to Achaia,
19:13 of the Lord Jesus **o** those who had evil spirits,
20:10 and bending **o** him took him in his arms, and said,
20:28 Keep watch **o** yourselves and **o** all the flock,
21:11 the man who owns this belt and will hand him **o** to
24:10 that for many years you have been a judge **o**
25:11 no one can turn me **o** to them.
25:16 that it was not the custom of the Romans to hand **o**
28:17 yet I was arrested in Jerusalem and handed **o** to
Ro 3:25 because in his divine forbearance he had passed **o**
4:25 who was handed **o** to death for our trespasses
5:14 even **o** those whose sins were not like
6: 9 death no longer has dominion **o** him.
6:14 For sin will have no dominion **o** you,
9: 5 who is **o** all, God blessed forever.
9:21 Has the potter no right **o** the clay,
9:32 They have stumbled **o** the stumbling stone,
11:18 do not boast **o** the branches.
14: 1 but not for the purpose of quarreling **o** opinions.
16:19 so that I rejoice **o** you,
1Co 5: 5 to hand this man **o** to Satan for the destruction of
7: 4 the wife does not have authority **o** her own body,
7: 4 likewise the husband does not have authority **o** his
1Co 13: 3 and if I hand **o** my body so that I may boast,
15:24 when he hands **o** the kingdom to God the Father,
2Co 1:24 I do not mean to imply that we lord it **o** your faith;
3:13 a veil **o** his face to keep the people of Israel
3:15 a veil lies **o** their minds;
12:21 to mourn **o** many who previously sinned and have
Eph 1:22 under his feet and has made him the head **o**
3:13 I pray therefore that you may not lose heart **o**
Php 2:17 But even if I am being poured out as a libation **o**
Col 2:15 a public example of them, triumphing **o** them in it.
1Ti 1:20 whom I have turned **o** to Satan,
2:12 I permit no woman to teach or to have authority **o**
2Ti 2: 7 Think **o** what I say, for the Lord will give you
2:14 before God that they are to avoid wrangling **o**
Heb 3: 6 however, was faithful **o** God's house as a son,
6: 8 its end is to be burned **o**.
10:21 since we have a great priest **o** the house of God,
11:21 "bowing in worship **o** the top of his staff."
13:17 for they are keeping watch **o** your souls
Jas 2: 7 the excellent name that was invoked **o** you?
2:13 mercy triumphs **o** judgment.
5:14 for the elders of the church and have them pray **o**
1Pe 3: 1 be won **o** without a word by their wives' conduct,
5: 3 Do not lord it **o** those in your charge,
Rev 2:26 I will give authority **o** the nations;
6: 8 they were given authority **o** a fourth of the earth,
9:11 as king **o** them the angel of the bottomless pit;
10: 1 wrapped in a cloud, with a rainbow **o** his head;
11: 2 for it is given **o** to the nations, and they will trample **o** the holy city
11: 6 and they have authority **o** the waters to turn them
11:10 and the inhabitants of the earth will gloat **o** them
13: 7 It was given authority **o** every tribe and people
14:16 the one who sat on the cloud swung his sickle **o**
14:18 the angel who has authority **o** fire,
14:19 So the angel swung his sickle **o** the earth
16: 9 who had authority **o** these plagues,
17:18 The woman you saw is the great city that rules **o**
18: 9 will weep and wail **o** her when they see the smoke
18:20 Rejoice **o** her, O heaven, you saints and apostles
20: 3 and locked and sealed it **o** him,
20: 6 **O** these the second death has no power,
20: 9 up **o** the breadth of the earth and surrounded
Tob 1:21 the son of my brother Hanael **o** all the accounts
1:21 and he had authority **o** the entire administration.
2:14 I became flushed with anger against her **o** this.
3: 4 So you gave us **o** to plunder, exile, and death,
3:10 But she thought it **o** and said,
4:14 "Do not keep **o** until the next day the wages
10:13 praising the Lord of heaven and earth, King **o** all,
13:13 then, and rejoice **o** the children of the righteous,
14: 7 and it will be given **o** to them.
14:15 before he died he rejoiced **o** Nineveh,
Jdt 1: 1 who ruled **o** the Assyrians in the great city
1: 1 In those days Arphaxad ruled **o** the Medes
2: 7 to whom I will hand them **o** to be plundered.
2:11 but hand them **o** to slaughter and plunder
5: 3 Who rules **o** them as king and leads their army?
5:10 a famine spread **o** the land of Canaan they went
5:15 and crossing **o** the Jordan they took possession
6:10 and take him away to Bethulia and hand him **o** to
7: 3 and they spread out in breadth **o** Dothan as far
7: 7 he seized them and set guards of soldiers **o** them,
8:16 or like a mere mortal, to be won **o** by pleading.
8:19 That was why our ancestors were handed **o** to
10:12 about to be handed **o** to you to be devoured.
10:15 some of us will escort you and hand you **o** to him.
11: 3 from them and have come **o** to us.
11:15 on that very day they will be handed **o** to you to
14: 2 set a captain **o** them, as if you were going down to
14: 3 Then panic will come **o** them,
AdE 1: 1 the same Artaxerxes who ruled **o** one hundred
3: 1 advancing him and granting him precedence **o** all
8: 2 and Esther set Mordecai **o** everything
9:14 and handed **o** to the Jews of the city the bodies
13: 9 "O Lord, Lord, you rule as King **o** all things,
14: 6 and you have handed us **o** to our enemies
14:19 O God, whose might is **o** all,
16:18 for God, who rules **o** all things,
16:21 For God, who rules **o** all things,
Wis 3: 8 They will govern nations and rule **o** peoples,
3: 8 and the Lord will reign **o** them forever.
3: 9 and he watches **o** his elect.
4:15 and that he watches **o** his holy ones.
6: 2 Give ear, you that rule **o** multitudes,
6:21 O monarchs **o** the peoples, honor wisdom,
9: 2 to have dominion **o** the creatures you have made,
9: 7 be king of your people and to be judge **o** your sons
10:14 of a kingdom and authority **o** his masters.
10:18 She brought them **o** the Red Sea,
12:16 and your sovereignty **o** all causes you to spare all.
14: 1 about to voyage **o** raging waves calls upon a piece
14:26 confusion **o** what is good,
16:13 For you have power **o** life and death;
17:21 while **o** those people alone heavy night was spread,
19:19 and creatures that swim moved **o** to the land.
Sir 1:29 and keep watch **o** your lips.
3: 2 and he confirms a mother's right **o** her children.
4:19 and hand them **o** to their ruin.
5: 3 Do not say, "Who can have power **o** me?"
5:12 but if not, put your hand **o** your mouth.
6:11 and lord it **o** your servants;
8: 7 Do not rejoice **o** any one's death;
10: 4 **o** it he will raise up the right leader for the time.
11: 6 and the honored have been handed **o** to others.
17: 2 granted them authority **o** everything on the earth.
17: 4 and gave them dominion **o** beasts and birds.

Sir 20:12 but pay for it seven times **o**.
22:27 Who will set a guard **o** my mouth,
23: 2 Who will set whips **o** my thoughts,
23: 2 and the discipline of wisdom **o** my mind,
23: 3 and my enemy may rejoice **o** me.
23: 6 and do not give me **o** to shameless passion.
24: 6 **O** waves of the sea, **o** all the earth,
24: 6 and **o** every people and nation I have held sway.
24:26 It runs **o**, like the Euphrates, with understanding,
26:10 Keep strict watch **o** a headstrong daughter, or else,
26:28 and because of a third anger comes **o** me:
28:22 It has no power **o** the godly;
30:21 Do not give yourself **o** to sorrow,
31: 1 Wakefulness **o** wealth wastes away one's flesh,
33:20 to brother or friend, do not give power **o** yourself,
38: 8 and from him health spreads **o** all the earth.
38:19 When a person is taken away, sorrow is **o**;
38:29 he is always deeply concerned **o** his products,
42: 9 and worry **o** her robs him of sleep;
42:11 Keep strict watch **o** a headstrong daughter,
43:19 He pours frost **o** the earth like salt,
46:13 he established the kingdom and anointed rulers **o**
46:14 and the Lord watched **o** Jacob.
48:15 and were scattered **o** all the earth.
50:20 Then Simon came down and raised his hands **o**
Bar 2:34 Isaac, and Jacob, and they will rule **o** it;
3:16 and those who lorded it **o** the animals on earth;
3:30 Who has gone **o** the sea, and found her,
4: 6 but you were handed **o** to your enemies
4:12 Let no one rejoice **o** me, a widow and bereaved
LtJ 6: 7 and he is watching **o** your lives.
6:27 and if it is tipped **o**, it cannot straighten itself.
6:53 up a king **o** a country or give rain to people.
6:62 When God commands the clouds to go **o**
Aza 1: 9 You have handed us **o** to our enemies,
1:22 glorious **o** the whole world."
Bel 1: 5 and earth and has dominion **o** all living creatures."
1:22 king put them to death, and gave Bel **o** to Daniel,
1:29 Going to the king, they said, "Hand Daniel **o** to us,
1:30 under compulsion he handed Daniel **o** to them.
1:36 of the wind he set him down in Babylon, right **o**
1Mc 1: 4 He gathered a very strong army and ruled **o**
1:16 in order that he might reign **o** both kingdoms.
1:51 He appointed inspectors **o** all the people
2: 7 to live there when it was given **o** to the enemy,
2: 7 the sanctuary given **o** to aliens?
3:34 And he turned **o** to Lysias half of his forces and
5: 6 Then he crossed **o** to attack the Ammonites,
5:40 "If he crosses **o** to us first,
5:41 we will cross **o** to him and defeat him."
5:43 Then he crossed **o** against them first,
5:51 Then he passed through the town **o** the bodies of
6: 2 Macedonian king who first reigned **o** the Greeks.
6:14 and made him ruler **o** all his kingdom.
8:16 They trust one man each year to rule **o** them and
9:24 and the country went **o** to their side.
11: 9 and you shall reign **o** your father's kingdom.
11:40 insistently urged him to hand Antiochus **o** to him,
11:57 the high priesthood and set you **o** the four districts
11:66 and set a garrison **o** it.
12:34 for he had heard that they were ready to hand **o**
12:45 I will hand it **o** to you as well as
13:27 And Simon built a monument **o** the tomb
14: 7 he ruled **o** Gazara and Beth-zur and the citadel,
14:17 he was ruling **o** the country and the towns in it,
14:42 be governor **o** them and that he should take charge
of the sanctuary and appoint officials **o** its tasks
and **o** the country and the weapons
15:21 hand them **o** to the high priest Simon,
15:30 hand **o** the cities that you have seized and
16: 6 to cross the stream, so he crossed **o** first;
16: 6 when his troops saw him, they crossed **o** after him.
16:11 of Abubus had been appointed governor **o**
16:18 asking him to send troops to aid him and to turn **o**
2Mc 1:22 and when the sun, which had been clouded **o**,
3: 5 Since he could not prevail **o** Onias,
3:17 terror and bodily trembling had come **o** the man,
3:27 to the ground and deep darkness came **o** him,
3:39 For he who has his dwelling in heaven watches **o**
4:10 at once shifted his compatriots **o** to the Greek way
4:45 to Ptolemy son of Dorymenes to win **o** the king.
5: 2 that, for almost forty days, there appeared **o** all
5: 6 of victory **o** enemies and not **o** compatriots.
5:23 and besides these Menelaus, who lorded it **o**
6: 9 not choose to change **o** to Greek customs.
6:24 that Eleazar in his ninetieth year had gone **o** to
7: 6 "The Lord God is watching **o** us and
8:11 and promising to hand **o** ninety slaves for a talent,
9:16 the holy vessels he would give back, many times **o**;
10: 4 by him with forbearance and not be handed **o**
10:13 and had gone **o** to Antiochus Epiphanes.
11:13 he pondered **o** the defeat that had befallen him,
12:16 appeared to be running **o** with blood.
12:22 and fear came **o** the enemy at the manifestation
13:25 people of Ptolemais were indignant **o** the treaty;
14:31 and commanded them to hand the man **o**.
14:33 "If you do not hand Judas **o** to me as a prisoner,
15: 6 to erect a public monument of victory **o** Judas
15:19 being anxious **o** the encounter in the open country.
15:28 the action was **o** and they were returning with joy,
1Es 1: 9 and Joram, captains **o** thousands, gave the Levites
2:14 All the vessels were handed **o**, gold and silver,
3: 4 who kept guard **o** the person of the king,
4: 2 who rule **o** land and sea and all that is in them?
4:14 then, that rules them, or has the mastery **o** them?
4:15 to the king and to every people that rules **o** sea
4:22 you must realize that women rule **o** you!
1Es 5: 4 according to their ancestral houses in the tribes, **o**
6: 5 for the providence of the Lord was **o** the captives;
6:15 he gave them **o** into the hands
6:17 in the first year that Cyrus reigned **o** the country
8:72 as I mourned **o** this iniquity,
8:77 and our kings and our priests were given **o** to
9: 2 for he was mourning **o** the great iniquities of
9:13 until we are freed from the wrath of the Lord **o**
3Mc 1: 2 and crossed **o** by night to the tent of Ptolemy,
1:11 only the high priest who was pre-eminent **o** all—
2: 7 the Ruler **o** the whole creation.
5:17 to give themselves **o** to revelry and to make
5:28 This was the act of God who rules **o** all things,
5:51 the Ruler **o** every power to manifest himself and
6: 8 watched **o** and restored unharmed to all his family.
6:12 watch **o** us now and have mercy on us who by
7: 9 we always shall have not a mortal but the Ruler **o**
2Es 2:32 my springs run **o**, and my grace will not fail."
3:27 So you handed **o** your city to your enemies.
3:28 Is that why it has gained dominion **o** Zion?
4:23 why Israel has been given **o** to the Gentiles
4:23 why the people whom you loved has been given **o**
4:25 what will he do for his name that is invoked **o** us?
5:28 why have you handed the one **o** to the many,
5:33 "Are you greatly disturbed in mind **o** Israel?
6:54 and **o** these you placed Adam, as ruler **o** all the
6:57 domineer **o** us and devour us.
7:*60* for I will rejoice **o** the few who shall be saved,
7:*61* not grieve **o** the great number of those who perish;
7:*86* how some of them will cross **o** into torments.
7:*131* [61] as joy **o** those to whom salvation is assured."
8:39 but I will rejoice **o** the creation of the righteous,
8:39 **o** their pilgrimage also, and their salvation,
9:45 I rejoiced greatly **o** him, I and my husband
10: 9 to mourn **o** so many who have come into being
10:23 and given **o** into the hands of those that hate us.
10:39 for your people and mourned greatly **o** Zion.
11: 2 I saw it spread its wings **o** the whole earth,
11: 5 it reigned **o** the earth and **o** those who inhabit it.
11:12 and it reigned **o** all the earth.
11:32 it had greater power **o** the world than all the wings
11:34 like manner ruled **o** the earth and its inhabitants.
11:40 you have held sway **o** the world with great terror,
11:40 and **o** all the earth with grievous oppression;
12: 2 that had gone **o** to it rose up and set themselves up
12:29 As for your seeing two little wings passing **o** to
13:30 of mind shall come **o** those who inhabit the earth.
13:44 the channels of the river until they had crossed **o**.
13:47 so that they may be able to cross **o**.
14:34 will rule **o** your minds and discipline your hearts,
15:26 he will hand them **o** to death and slaughter.
15:29 their hissing shall spread **o** the earth,
15:39 the winds from the east shall prevail **o** the cloud
15:56 and will hand you **o** to adversities.
16:14 and shall not return until they come **o** the earth.
16:52 and righteousness will reign **o** us.
16:58 and by his word he has suspended the earth **o**
16:68 of a great multitude is kindled **o** you;
16:76 or your iniquities prevail **o** you.
4Mc 1: 1 whether devout reason is sovereign **o**
1: 3 it is evident that reason rules **o** those emotions
1: 5 not sovereign **o** forgetfulness and ignorance?"
1: 7 and various examples that reason is dominant **o**
1:11 the cause of the downfall of tyranny **o** their nation.
1:13 is whether reason is sovereign **o** the emotions.
1:14 and whether reason rules **o** all these.
1:19 Rational judgment is supreme **o** all of these,
1:19 since by means of it reason rules **o** the emotions.
1:30 but **o** the emotions it is sovereign.
1:30 that rational judgment is sovereign **o** the emotions
1:31 Self-control, then, is dominance **o** the desires.
1:32 and reason obviously rules **o** both.
1:33 Is it not because reason is able to rule **o** appetites?
2: 4 rule **o** the frenzied urge of sexual desire, but also **o**
2:10 For the law prevails even **o** affection for parents,
2:12 It takes precedence **o** love for children,
2:13 It is sovereign **o** the relationship of friends,
2:14 through the law, can prevail even **o** enmity.
2:16 for it is sovereign **o** even this.
2:22 the mind among the senses as a sacred governor **o**
3: 1 reason rules not **o** its own emotions, but **o** those
3:12 taking a pitcher climbed **o** the enemy's ramparts.
5:13 if there is some power watching **o** this religion
6:10 while being beaten, was victorious **o** his torturers;
6:31 then, devout reason is sovereign **o** the emotions.
6:32 For if the emotions had prevailed **o** reason,
7: 1 of our father Eleazar steered the ship of religion **o**
7:10 O supreme king **o** the passions, Eleazar!
8: 1 have prevailed **o** the most painful instruments
8:28 of the emotions and sovereign **o** agonies,
11:27 the tyrant but those of the divine law that are set **o**
13: 1 that devout reason is sovereign **o** the emotions.
13: 3 they prevailed **o** their emotions.
13: 4 The supremacy of the mind **o** these cannot
13: 5 of right reason **o** emotion in those who were
13: 6 For just as towers jutting out **o** harbors hold back
14:11 that reason had full command **o** these men
15: 1 O reason of the children, tyrant **o** the emotions!
16: 1 that devout reason is sovereign **o** the emotions.
16: 2 not only that men have ruled **o** the emotions,
16: 5 she would have mourned **o** them
17:20 that because of them our enemies did not rule **o**
18: 3 Therefore those who gave **o** their bodies

OVERBEARING (1)

Sir 33:30 Do not be **o** toward anyone, and do nothing unjust.

OVERBOARD (3)

Ac 27:18 on the next day they began to throw the cargo **o**,
27:19 their own hands they threw the ship's tackle **o**.
27:43 He ordered those who could swim to jump **o** first

OVERCAME (3) [OVERCOME]

1Ki 16:22 But the people who followed Omri **o**
4Mc 2: 2 because by mental effort he **o** sexual desire.
9: 6 which our aged instructor also **o**.

OVERCHARGE (KJV) See EXAGGERATE

OVERCOME (28) [OVERCAME]

Ge 43:30 because he was **o** with affection for his brother,
Nu 13:30 for we are well able to **o** it."
22: 3 Moab was **o** with fear of the people of Israel.
Isa 28: 1 of those bloated with rich food, of those **o**
Jer 23: 9 I have become like a drunkard, like one **o** by wine,
38:22 trusted friends have seduced you and have **o** you;
Da 8:27 So I, Daniel, was **o** and lay sick for some days;
Mt 17: 6 they fell to the ground and were **o** by fear.
Mk 5:42 At this they were **o** with amazement.
9:15 they were immediately **o** with awe,
Jn 1: 5 and the darkness did not **o** it.
Ac 20: 9 **O** by sleep, he fell to the ground three floors below
Ro 12:21 Do not be **o** by evil, but **o** evil with good.
1Jn 2:14 and you have **o** the evil one.
Jdt 8: 3 he was **o** by the burning heat,
15: 2 **O** with fear and trembling,
Wis 2: 4 that is chased by the rays of the sun and **o**
Sir 23: 6 Let neither gluttony nor lust **o** me,
3Mc 5:12 the Lord he was **o** by so pleasant and deep a sleep
5:27 he had been completely **o** by incomprehension—
6:34 groaned as they themselves were **o** by disgrace,
2Es 3:21 with an evil heart, transgressed and was **o**, as were
6:28 and corruption shall be **o**, and the truth,
7:92 to **o** the evil thought that was formed with them,
4Mc 3: 4 at our side so that we are not **o** by malice.
4:13 that Apollonius had been **o** by human treachery
7:22 not be able to **o** the emotions through godliness?

OVERCONFIDENT (1)

Sir 32:21 Do not be **o** on a smooth road,

OVERDRIVE (KJV) See OVERDRIVEN

OVERDRIVEN (1)

Ge 33:13 if they are **o** for one day, all the flocks will die.

OVEREATING (1) [EAT]

Sir 37:30 for **o** brings sickness, and gluttony leads

OVERFLOW (9) [OVERFLOWED, OVERFLOWING, OVERFLOWINGS, OVERFLOWS]

Ps 65:11 your wagon tracks **o** with richness.
65:12 The pastures of the wilderness **o**,
73: 7 their hearts **o** with follies.
Isa 8: 7 above all its channels and **o** all its banks;
Jer 47: 2 they shall **o** the land and all that fills it,
Joel 2:24 the vats shall **o** with wine and oil.
3:13 The vats **o**, for their wickedness is great.
Zec 1:17 My cities shall again **o** with prosperity;
Php 1: 9 that your love may **o** more and more

OVERFLOWED (5) [OVERFLOW]

Jos 4:18 to their place and **o** all its banks,
Ps 78:20 the rock so that water gushed out and torrents **o**,
2Co 8: 2 and their extreme poverty have **o** in a wealth
1Ti 1:14 and the grace of our Lord **o** for me with the faith
Sir 47:14 You **o** like the Nile with understanding.

OVERFLOWING (8) [OVERFLOW]

1Ch 12:15 when it was **o** all its banks,
Isa 10:22 Destruction is decreed, **o** with righteousness.
28: 2 like a storm of mighty, **o** waters;
30:28 his breath is like an **o** stream that reaches up to
54: 8 In **o** wrath for a moment I hid my face from you,
66:12 and the wealth of the nations like an **o** stream;
Jer 47: 2 of the north and shall become an **o** torrent;
Mal 3:10 for you and pour down for you an **o** blessing.

OVERFLOWINGS (1) [OVERFLOW]

Job 40:11 Pour out the **o** of your anger,

OVERFLOWS (5) [OVERFLOW]

Jos 3:15 Now the Jordan **o** all its banks throughout the time
Ps 23: 5 you anoint my head with oil; my cup **o**.
45: 1 My heart **o** with a goodly theme;
2Co 9:12 not only supplies the needs of the saints but also **o**
Sir 24:25 It **o**, like the Pishon, with wisdom,

OVERGROWN (3) [GROW]

Pr 15:19 The way of the lazy is **o** with thorns,
24:31 it was all **o** with thorns;
Isa 5: 6 and it shall be **o** with briers and thorns;

OVERHEAD (1)

Isa 31: 5 Like birds hovering **o**, so the LORD

OVERHEARD (3) [HEAR]

Jer 38:27 for the conversation had not been **o.**
Tob 7:10 But Raguel **o** it and said to the lad, "Eat and drink,
AdE 12: 2 He **o** their conversation and inquired

OVERHEARING (1) [HEAR]

Mk 5:36 But **o** what they said, Jesus said to the leader of

OVERHEATED (1) [HEAT]

Da 3:22 command was urgent and the furnace was so **o,**

OVERJOYED (5) [JOY]

Ac 12:14 On recognizing Peter's voice, she was so **o** that,
2Co 7: 4 I am **o** in all our affliction.
2Jn 1: 4 I was **o** to find some of your children walking in
3Jn 1: 3 I was **o** when some of the friends arrived
3Mc 7:20 they departed unharmed, free, and **o,**

OVERLAID (39) [OVERLAY]

Ex 26:32 You shall hang it on four pillars of acacia **o**
36:34 And he **o** the frames with gold,
36:34 and **o** the bars with gold.
36:36 For it he made four pillars of acacia, and **o** them
36:38 He **o** their capitals and their bases with gold,
37: 2 He **o** it with pure gold inside and outside,
37: 4 of acacia wood, and **o** them with gold,
37:11 He **o** it with pure gold,
37:15 of acacia wood to carry the table, and **o** them
37:26 He **o** it with pure gold, its top,
37:28 the poles of acacia wood, and **o** them with gold.
38: 2 its horns were of one piece with it, and he **o** it
38: 6 the poles of acacia wood, and **o** them with bronze.
38:28 and **o** their capitals and made bands for them.
1Ki 6:20 he **o** it with pure gold.
6:20 He also **o** the altar with cedar.
6:21 Solomon **o** the inside of the house with pure gold,
6:21 in front of the inner sanctuary, and **o** it with gold.
6:22 Next he **o** the whole house with gold,
6:22 that belonged to the inner sanctuary he **o** with gold.
6:28 He also **o** the cherubim with gold.
6:30 The floor of the house he **o** with gold,
6:32 he **o** them with gold, and spread gold on
10:18 and **o** it with the finest gold.
2Ki 18:16 of Judah had **o** and gave it to the king of Assyria.
2Ch 3: 4 He **o** it on the inside with pure gold.
3: 8 he **o** it with six hundred talents of fine gold.
3: 9 He **o** the upper chambers with gold.
3:10 two carved cherubim and **o** them with gold.
4: 9 he **o** their doors with bronze.
9:17 and **o** it with pure gold.
Heb 9: 4 the ark of the covenant **o** on all sides with gold,
LtJ 6: 8 and they themselves are **o** with gold and silver;
6:39 of wood and **o** with gold and silver are like stones
6:50 they are made of wood and **o** with gold and silver,
6:55 in a temple of wooden gods **o** with gold or silver,
6:57 of wood and **o** with silver and gold are unable
6:70 so are their gods of wood, **o** with gold and silver.
6:71 their gods of wood, **o** with gold and silver,

OVERLAY (12) [OVERLAID, OVERLAYING, OVERLAYS]

Ex 25:11 You shall **o** it with pure gold, inside and outside you shall **o** it,
25:13 of acacia wood, and **o** them with gold.
25:24 You shall **o** it with pure gold,
25:28 the poles of acacia wood, and **o** them with gold,
26:29 You shall **o** the frames with gold,
26:29 and you shall **o** the bars with gold.
26:37 for the screen five pillars of acacia, and **o** them
27: 2 and you shall **o** it with bronze.
27: 6 poles of acacia wood, and **o** them with bronze;
30: 3 You shall **o** it with pure gold, its top,
30: 5 the poles of acacia wood, and **o** them with gold.

OVERLAYING (4) [OVERLAY]

Ex 38:17 the **o** of their capitals was also of silver,
38:19 and the **o** of their capitals and their bands of silver.
1Ki 6:35 **o** them with gold evenly applied upon
1Ch 29: 4 for **o** the walls of the house,

OVERLAYS (1) [OVERLAY]

Isa 40:19 workman casts it, and a goldsmith **o** it with gold,

OVERLIVED (KJV) See OUTLIVED

OVERLOOK (7) [OVERLOOKED, OVERLOOKING, OVERLOOKS]

Pr 19:11 and it is their glory to **o** an offense.
Heb 6:10 not **o** your work and the love that you showed
Wis 11:23 for you can do all things, and you **o** people's sins,
Sir 23: 2 not to spare me in my errors, and not **o** my sins?
28: 7 the covenant of the Most High, and **o** faults.
32:18 sensible person will not **o** a thoughtful suggestion;
3Mc 1:27 in the present trouble and not to **o** this unlawful

OVERLOOKED (2) [OVERLOOK]

Ac 17:30 While God has **o** the times of human ignorance,
4Mc 13: 4 supremacy of the mind over these cannot be **o,**

OVERLOOKING (1) [OVERLOOK]

SS 7: 4 like a tower of Lebanon, **o** Damascus.

OVERLOOKS (4) [OVERLOOK]

Nu 21:20 of Moab by the top of Pisgah that **o** the wasteland.
23:28 So Balak took Balaam to the top of Peor, which **o**
Jos 18:16 that **o** the valley of the son of Hinnom, which is at
Sir 42:11 no spot that **o** the approaches to the house.

OVERMUCH (KJV) See EXCESSIVE

OVERNIGHT (1) [NIGHT]

Tob 14:10 do not stay **o** within the confines of the city.

OVERPASS (KJV) See NO LIMITS

OVERPAST (KJV) See PASS BY, PAST

OVERPLUS (KJV) See DIFFERENCES

OVERPOWER (1) [POWER]

Jdg 16: 5 and how we may **o** him, so that we may bind him

OVERPOWERED (4) [POWER]

Jer 20: 7 you have **o** me, and you have prevailed.
Da 6:24 the den the lions **o** them and broke all their bones
Ac 19:16 so **o** them that they fled out of the house naked
2Pe 2:20 they are again entangled in them and **o,**

OVERPOWERING (3) [POWER]

3Mc 5: 1 was filled with **o** anger and wrath;
5:30 But at these words he was filled with an **o** wrath,
2Es 10:28 it was he who brought me into this **o** bewilderment;

OVERPOWERS (1) [POWER]

Lk 11:22 when one stronger than he attacks him and **o** him,

OVERRUN (1)

Zec 9: 8 no oppressor shall again **o** them,

OVERSEE (1) [OVERSEEING, OVERSEER, OVERSEERS, OVERSEES, OVERSIGHT]

2Ch 2: 2 with three thousand six hundred to **o** them.

OVERSEEING (2) [OVERSEE]

Jdt 8: 3 For as he stood **o** those who were binding sheaves
Wis 7:23 sure, free from anxiety, all-powerful, **o** all,

OVERSEER‡ (7) [OVERSEE]

Ge 39: 4 he made him **o** of his house and put him in charge
39: 5 From the time that he made him **o** in his house and
Ne 11: 9 Joel son of Zichri was their **o;**
11:14 their **o** was Zabdiel son of Haggedolim.
11:22 The **o** of the Levites in Jerusalem was Uzzi son
Isa 60:17 I will appoint Peace as your **o** and Righteousness
Ac 1:20 and 'Let another take his position of **o.'**

OVERSEERS‡ (5) [OVERSEE]

Ge 41:34 Let Pharaoh proceed to appoint **o** over the land,
2Ch 2:18 and three thousand six hundred as **o** to make
31:13 and Benaiah were **o** assisting Conaniah
34:17 and have delivered it into the hand of the **o** and
Ac 20:28 of which the Holy Spirit has made you **o,**

OVERSEES (1) [OVERSEE]

3Mc 2:21 Thereupon God, who **o** all things,

OVERSHADOW (1) [OVERSHADOWED, OVERSHADOWING]

Lk 1:35 and the power of the Most High will **o** you;

OVERSHADOWED (3) [OVERSHADOW]

Mt 17: 5 suddenly a bright cloud **o** them,
Mk 9: 7 a cloud **o** them, and from the cloud there came
Lk 9:34 he was saying this, a cloud came and **o** them;

OVERSHADOWING (4) [OVERSHADOW]

Ex 25:20 **o** the mercy seat with their wings.
37: 9 **o** the mercy seat with their wings.
Heb 9: 5 the cherubim of glory **o** the mercy seat.
Wis 19: 7 The cloud was seen **o** the camp,

OVERSIGHT‡ (15) [OVERSEE]

Ge 43:12 of your sacks; perhaps it was an **o.**
Nu 3:32 and to have **o** of those who had charge of
4:16 the **o** of all the tabernacle and all that is in it,
4:28 be under the **o** of Ithamar son of Aaron the priest.
2Ki 12:11 into the hands of the workers who had the **o** of
22: 5 into the hand of the workers who have the **o** of
22: 9 the hand of the workers who have **o** of the house
1Ch 26:30 the **o** of Israel west of the Jordan for all the work
26:32 heads of families, to have the **o** of the Reubenites,
2Ch 34:10 They delivered it to the workers who had the **o** of
34:12 of the sons of the Kohathites, to have **o.**
Ezr 3: 8 the **o** of the work on the house of the LORD.

Eze 44:11 having **o** at the gates of the temple,
1Pe 5: 2 the **o,** not under compulsion but willingly,
Jdt 5:20 if there is any **o** in this people and they sin

OVERSPREAD (KJV) See PEOPLED

OVERSTEPPING (1) [STEP]

2Co 10:14 we were not **o** our limits when we reached you;

OVERSTUFFED (1)

Sir 31:21 If you are **o** with food, get up to vomit,

OVERTAKE (33) [OVERTAKEN, OVERTAKES, OVERTAKING, OVERTOOK]

Ge 19:19 for fear the disaster will **o** me and I die.
44: 4 and when you **o** them, say to them,
Ex 15: 9 The enemy said, 'I will pursue, I will **o,**
Lev 26: 5 Your threshing shall **o** the vintage,
26: 5 and the vintage shall **o** the sowing;
Dt 19: 6 in hot anger might pursue and **o** and put the killer
28: 2 all these blessings shall come upon you and **o** you,
28:15 all these curses shall come upon you and **o** you:
Jos 2: 5 Pursue them quickly, for you can **o** them."
1Sa 30: 8 "Shall I pursue this band? Shall I **o** them?"
30: 8 for you shall surely **o** and shall surely rescue."
2Sa 15:14 Hurry, or he will soon **o** us,
Job 27:20 Terrors **o** them like a flood;
Ps 7: 5 then let the enemy pursue and **o** me,
69:24 and let your burning anger **o** them.
Jer 42:16 then the sword that you fear shall **o** you there,
Hos 2: 7 She shall pursue her lovers, but not **o** them;
10: 9 Shall not war **o** them in Gibeah?
Am 9:10 who say, "Evil shall not **o** or meet us."
9:13 the one who plows shall **o** the one who reaps,
Mic 2: 6 of such things; disgrace will not **o** us."
Zec 1: 6 did they not **o** your ancestors?
Jn 12:35 so that the darkness may not **o** you.
Tob 12: 7 Do good and evil will not **o** you.
14: 4 that all these things will take place and **o** Assyria
Wis 14:30 But just penalties will **o** them on two counts:
Sir 7: 1 Do no evil, and evil will never **o** you.
11:10 If you pursue, you will not **o,**
31:22 and no sickness will **o** you.
1Mc 12:30 Jonathan pursued them, but he did not **o** them,
2Mc 8:11 from the Almighty that was about to **o** him.
3Mc 2:10 and tribulation should **o** us,
2:20 Speedily let your mercies **o** us,

OVERTAKEN (11) [OVERTAKE]

2Sa 16: 8 disaster has **o** you; for you are a man of blood."
Ps 40:12 my iniquities have **o** me, until I cannot see;
La 1: 3 her pursuers have all **o** her in the midst
1Co 10:13 No testing has **o** you that is not common
1Th 2:16 but God's wrath has **o** them at last.
Jdt 11:11 for a sin has **o** them by which they are about
Sir 23: 8 Sinners are **o** through their lips;
Bar 4:25 Your enemy has **o** you, but you will soon see
3Mc 2:13 subjected to our enemies, and **o** by helplessness.
2:23 seeing the severe punishment that had **o** him,
2Es 10:48 and that misfortune had **o** her,

OVERTAKES (3) [OVERTAKE]

1Ch 21:12 while the sword of your enemies **o** you;
Jer 4:20 Disaster **o** disaster, the whole land is laid waste.
Sir 36:31 but lodges wherever night **o** him?

OVERTAKING (1) [OVERTAKE]

Dt 28:45 pursuing and **o** you until you are destroyed,

OVERTHREW (13) [OVERTHROW]

Ge 19:25 and he **o** those cities, and all the Plain, and all
19:29 when he **o** the cities in which Lot had settled.
Ex 15: 7 of your majesty you **o** your adversaries;
1Ch 20: 1 Joab attacked Rabbah, and **o** it.
Ps 136:15 but **o** Pharaoh and his army in the Red Sea,
Isa 13:19 be like Sodom and Gomorrah when God **o** them.
14:17 who made the world like a desert and **o** its cities,
Jer 20:16 be like the cities that the LORD **o** without pity;
50:40 God **o** Sodom and Gomorrah and their neighbors,
Da 8:11 the regular burnt offering away from him and **o**
Am 4:11 I **o** some of you, as when God **o** Sodom and
2Mc 12:15 without battering-rams or engines of war **o** Jericho

OVERTHROW (21) [OVERTHREW, OVERTHROWING, OVERTHROWN, OVERTHROWS]

Ge 19:21 and will not **o** the city of which you have spoken.
19:29 and sent Lot out of the midst of the **o,**
2Sa 10: 3 to spy it out, and to **o** it?"
11:25 press your attack on the city, and **o** it.'
1Ch 19: 3 to you to search and to **o** and to spy out the land?"
2Ch 25: 8 for God has power to help or to **o."**
Ezr 6:12 God who has established his name there **o** any king
Ps 17:13 Rise up, O LORD, confront them, **o** them!
Jer 1:10 to pluck up and to pull down, to destroy and to **o,**
31:28 to **o,** destroy, and bring evil,
Da 11:12 and he shall **o** tens of thousands,
Hag 2:22 and to **o** the throne of kingdoms;
2:22 and **o** the chariots and their riders;
Ac 5:39 you will not be able to **o** them—
Ro 3:31 Do we then **o** the law by this faith?

Tob 13:12 all who **o** your towers and set your homes on fire.
Sir 1:30 The Lord will reveal your secrets and **o** you before
12:12 or he may **o** you and take your place.
2Mc 8:17 and besides, the **o** of their ancestral way of life.
2Es 16:46 **o** their houses, and take their children captive;
4Mc 3:18 it can **o** bodily agonies even

OVERTHROWING (1) [OVERTHROW]

Jdt 1:13 **o** the whole army of Arphaxad and all his cavalry

OVERTHROWN (13) [OVERTHROW]

Pr 11:11 but it is **o** by the mouth of the wicked.
12: 7 The wicked are **o** and are no more,
14:32 The wicked are **o** by their evildoing,
24:16 but the wicked are **o** by calamity.
Isa 1: 7 it is desolate, as **o** by foreigners.
Jer 6:15 at the time that I punish them, they shall be **o**,
8:12 at the time when I punish them, they shall be **o**,
31:40 It shall never again be uprooted or **o**.
49:18 Sodom and Gomorrah and their neighbors were **o**,
La 4: 6 which was **o** in a moment,
Jnh 3: 4 "Forty days more, and Nineveh shall be **o**!"
Sir 27: 3 his house will be quickly **o**.
2Es 1:10 For their sake I have **o** many kings;

OVERTHROWS (4) [OVERTHROW]

Job 12:19 He leads priests away stripped, and **o** the mighty.
Pr 13: 6 one whose way is upright, but sin **o** the wicked.
22:12 but he **o** the words of the faithless.
Sir 10:14 The Lord **o** the thrones of rulers,

OVERTOOK (15) [OVERTAKE]

Ge 31:25 Laban **o** Jacob. Now Jacob had pitched his tent
44: 6 When he **o** them, he repeated these words to them.
Ex 14: 9 they **o** them camped by the sea, by Pi-hahiroth,
Jdg 18:22 near Micah's house were called out, and they **o**
20:42 but the battle **o** them, and those who came out of
1Sa 31: 2 The Philistines **o** Saul and his sons;
2Ki 25: 5 and **o** him in the plains of Jericho;
1Ch 10: 2 The Philistines **o** Saul and his sons;
Job 31:29 or exulted when evil **o** them—
Ps 18:37 I pursued my enemies and **o** them;
Jer 39: 5 and **o** Zedekiah in the plains of Jericho;
52: 8 and **o** Zedekiah in the plains of Jericho;
Tob 6: 2 first night **o** them they camped by the Tigris river.
1Mc 2:32 Many pursued them, and **o** them;
2Mc 4:16 For this reason heavy disaster **o** them,

OVERTURN (2) [OVERTURNED, OVERTURNS]

Job 28: 9 and **o** mountains by the roots.
Wis 5:23 and evildoing will **o** the thrones of rulers.

OVERTURNED (5) [OVERTURN]

2Ki 3:25 The cities they **o**, and on every good piece
Mt 21:12 and he **o** the tables of the money changers and
Mk 11:15 and he **o** the tables of the money changers and
Jn 2:15 the coins of the money changers and **o** their tables.
Sir 28:14 and **o** the houses of the great.

OVERTURNS (2) [OVERTURN]

Job 9: 5 when he **o** them in his anger;
34:25 Thus, knowing their works, he **o** them in the night,

OVERWHELM‡ (11) [OVERWHELMED, OVERWHELMING, OVERWHELMS]

Dt 28:59 the LORD will **o** both you and your offspring
Job 12:15 if he sends them out, they **o** the land.
Ps 65: 3 When deeds of iniquity **o** us,
88: 7 and you **o** me with all your waves.
140: 9 let the mischief of their lips **o** them!
SS 6: 5 Turn away your eyes from me, for they **o** me!
Isa 28:17 and waters will **o** the shelter.
43: 2 and through the rivers, they shall not **o** you;
Hab 2:17 For the violence done to Lebanon will **o** you;
Jdt 6: 4 We will **o** them; their mountains will be drunk
Wis 5:22 and rivers will relentlessly **o** them;

OVERWHELMED (17) [OVERWHELM]

1Sa 4:19 for her labor pains **o** her.
Job 41: 9 were not even the gods **o** at the sight of it?
Ps 78:53 but the sea **o** their enemies.
90: 7 by your wrath we are **o**.
Mt 2:10 that the star had stopped, they were **o** with joy.
Lk 1:12 he was terrified; and fear **o** him.
2Co 2: 7 so that he may not be **o** by excessive sorrow.
2Ti 3: 6 **o** by their sins and swayed by all kinds of desires,
Wis 17:15 for sudden and unexpected fear **o** them.
Sir 46: 6 He **o** that nation in battle,
Sus 1:10 Both were **o** with passion for her,
1Mc 10:82 they were **o** by him and fled,
3Mc 2: 7 you **o** him in the depths of the sea,
2Es 16:77 choked by their sins and **o** by their iniquities!
16:77 choked with underbrush and its path **o** with thorns,
4Mc 7: 2 the tyrant and **o** by the mighty waves of tortures,
15:32 **o** from every side by the flood of your emotions

OVERWHELMING (3) [OVERWHELM]

Pr 27: 4 Wrath is cruel, anger is **o**,
Isa 28:15 **o** scourge passes through it will not come to us;
28:18 the **o** scourge passes through you will be beaten

OVERWHELMS (2) [OVERWHELM]

Job 22:10 snares are around you, and sudden terror **o** you,
Ps 55: 5 and trembling come upon me, and horror **o** me.

OWE (8) [OWED, OWES, OWING]

Mt 18:28 he said, 'Pay what you **o**.'
Lk 16: 5 'How much do you **o** my master?'
16: 7 he asked another, 'And how much do you **o**?'
Ro 13: 8 **O** no one anything, except to love one another;
15:27 and indeed they **o** it to them;
1Mc 10:43 because they **o** money to the king or are in debt,
13:39 and cancel the crown tax that you **o**;
15: 8 Every debt you **o** to the royal treasury

OWED (4) [OWE]

Mt 18:24 one who **o** him ten thousand talents was brought
18:28 of his fellow slaves who **o** him a hundred denarii;
Lk 7:41 one **o** five hundred denarii, and the other fifty.
1Mc 13:15 "It is for the money that your brother Jonathan **o**

OWES (2) [OWE]

Dt 15: 3 of your community **o** you.
Phm 1:18 or **o** you anything, charge that to my account.

OWING (1) [OWE]

Phm 1:19 I say nothing about your **o** me even your own self.

OWL (13)

Lev 11:17 the little **o**, the cormorant, the great **o**,
11:18 the water hen, the desert **o**, the carrion vulture,
Dt 14:16 the little **o** and the great **o**, the water hen
14:17 and the desert **o**, the carrion vulture and
Ps 102: 6 I am like an **o** of the wilderness,
102: 6 like a little **o** of the waste places.
Isa 34:11 the **o** and the raven shall live in it.
34:15 There shall the **o** nest and lay and hatch and brood
Zep 2:14 the desert **o** and the screech **o** shall lodge on its
capitals; the **o** shall hoot at the window,

OWN‡ (798) [LANDOWNER, OWNED, OWNER, OWNER'S, OWNERS, OWNERSHIP, OWNS, SLAVEOWNER]

Ge 9: 5 your **o** lifeblood I will surely require a reckoning:
9: 6 for in his **o** image God made humankind.
10: 5 with their **o** language, by their families,
15: 4 no one but your very **o** issue shall be your heir."
30:25 that I may go to my **o** home and country.
30:30 when shall I provide for my **o** household also?"
30:40 and he put his **o** droves apart,
37:27 for he is our brother, our **o** flesh."
38:23 Judah replied, "Let her keep the things as her **o**,
40: 5 his **o** dream, and each dream with its **o** meaning.
41:11 he and I, each having a dream with its **o** meaning.
45:12 of my brother Benjamin see that it is my **o** mouth
46: 4 and Joseph's **o** hand shall close your eyes."
46:26 who were his **o** offspring,
47:24 and four-fifths shall be your **o**,
Ex 5:16 You are unjust to your **o** people."
15:17 on the mountain of your **o** possession,
16:16 all providing for those in their **o** tents.' "
18:27 and he went off to his **o** country.
32:13 how you swore to them by your **o** self,
Lev 7:30 Your **o** hands shall bring the LORD's offering
14:15 of oil and pour it into the palm of his **o** left hand,
14:26 of the oil into the palm of his **o** left hand,
18:10 for their nakedness is your **o** nakedness.
20:19 for that is to lay bare one's **o** flesh;
21:14 He shall marry a virgin of his **o** kin,
25:41 they shall go back to their **o** family and return
25:49 of their **o** flesh may redeem them;
Nu 3:13 I consecrated for my **o** all the firstborn in Israel,
5:10 The sacred donations of all are their **o**;
5:18 In his **o** hand the priest shall have the water
10:30 I will go back to my **o** land and to my kindred."
15:39 follow the lust of your **o** heart and your **o** eyes.
16:28 it has not been of my **o** accord:
18:23 they shall bear responsibility for their **o** offenses,
22:13 to the officials of Balak, "Go to your **o** land,
24:13 to do either good or bad of my **o** will;
27: 3 but died for his **o** sin; and he had no sons.
36: 9 of the Israelites shall retain its **o** inheritance.' "
Dt 2:15 Indeed, the LORD's **o** hand was against them,
3:21 "Your **o** eyes have seen everything that
4:20 to become a people of his very **o** possession,
4:32 ask now about former ages, long before your **o**,
4:37 He brought you out of Egypt with his **o** presence,
4:40 for your **o** well-being and that of your descendants
7:10 who repays in their **o** person those who reject him.
7:10 but repays in their **o** person those who reject him.
8:17 of my **o** hand have gotten me this wealth."
9:26 the people who are your very **o** possession,
9:29 For they are the people of your very **o** possession,
10:13 commanding you today, for your **o** well-being.
10:21 and awesome things that your **o** eyes have seen.
11: 7 for it is your **o** eyes
12: 8 all of us according to our **o** desires,
13: 6 or your **o** son or daughter,
13: 9 your **o** hand shall be first against them
17:15 One of your **o** community you may set as king
17:15 who is not of your **o** community.
18:15 a prophet like me from among your **o** people;
18:18 a prophet like you from among their **o** people;
20: 1 an army larger than your **o**,
Dt 20: 8 the heart of his comrades to melt like his **o**."
22: 2 you shall bring it to your **o** house,
23:23 to the LORD your God with your **o** mouth.
24:16 for their **o** crimes may persons be put to death.
28:53 the flesh of your **o** sons and daughters whom
28:54 among you will begrudge food to his **o** brother,
28:56 to her **o** son, and to her **o** daughter,
29:19 we go our **o** stubborn ways" (thus bringing disaster
32: 9 the LORD's **o** portion was his people,
33: 2 at his right, a host of his **o**.
Jos 1:15 to your **o** land and take possession of it,
2:19 they shall be responsible for their **o** death,
7:11 and they have put them among their **o** belongings.
22: 9 their **o** land of which they had taken possession
24:30 in his **o** inheritance at Timnath-serah,
Jdg 2: 6 the Israelites all went to their **o** inheritances
3: 6 and their **o** daughters they gave to their sons;
7: 2 saying, 'My **o** hand has delivered me.'
7: 8 he sent all the rest of Israel back to their **o** tents,
8:29 Jerubbaal son of Joash went to live in his **o** house.
8:30 Now Gideon had seventy sons, his **o** offspring,
17: 6 all the people did what was right in their **o** eyes.
18:31 So they maintained as their **o** Micah's idol
21:24 and they went out from there to their **o** territories.
21:25 all the people did what was right in their **o** eyes.
Ru 4: 6 for myself without damaging my **o** inheritance.
1Sa 5:11 and let it return to its **o** place,
6: 9 And watch; if it goes up on the way to its **o** land,
13:14 the LORD has sought out a man after his **o** heart;
14:46 and the Philistines went to their **o** place.
15:17 "Though you are little in your **o** eyes,
18: 1 and Jonathan loved him as his **o** soul.
18: 3 because he loved him as his **o** soul.
20:17 for he loved him as he loved his **o** life.
20:30 the son of Jesse to your **o** shame,
25:26 and from taking vengeance with your **o** hand,
25:33 and from avenging myself by my **o** hand!
25:39 the evildoing of Nabal upon his **o** head."
28: 3 for him and buried him in Ramah, his **o** city.
31: 4 So Saul took his **o** sword and fell upon it.
2Sa 1:16 for your **o** mouth has testified against you, saying,
4:11 a righteous man on his bed in his **o** house!
6:22 and I will be abased in my **o** eyes;
7:10 so that they may live in their **o** place,
7:21 of your promise, and according to your **o** heart,
12: 4 and he was loath to take one of his **o** flock or herd
12:11 up trouble against you from within your **o** house;
12:20 he then went to his **o** house;
14:24 The king said, "Let him go to his **o** house;
14:24 So Absalom went to his **o** house,
16:11 "My **o** son seeks my life;
17:23 and went off home to his **o** city.
18:18 he called the pillar by his **o** name.
19:37 so that I may die in my **o** town,
19:39 and he returned to his **o** home.
23:21 and killed him with his **o** spear.
1Ki 1: 8 David's **o** warriors did not side with Adonijah.
1:12 so that you may save your **o** life and the life
1:33 and have my son Solomon ride on my **o** mule,
1:49 up trembling and went their **o** ways.
2:32 on his **o** head, because, without the knowledge
2:34 he was buried at his **o** house near the wilderness.
2:37 your blood shall be on your **o** head."
2:44 "You know in your **o** heart all the evil that you did
2:44 LORD will bring back your evil on your **o** head.
3: 1 until he had finished building his **o** house and
7: 1 Solomon was building his **o** house thirteen years,
7: 8 His **o** house where he would reside,
8:32 by bringing their conduct on their **o** head,
8:38 of their **o** hearts so that they stretch out their hands
9:15 to build the house of the LORD and his **o** house,
9:24 of David to her **o** house that Solomon had built
10: 6 that I heard in my **o** land of your accomplishments
10: 7 the reports until I came and my **o** eyes had seen it.
10:13 Then she returned to her **o** land, with her servants.
11:21 "Let me depart, that I may go to my **o** country."
11:22 that you now seek to go to your **o** country?"
12:16 Look now to your **o** house, O David."
13:30 He laid the body in his **o** grave;
15:15 of his father and his **o** votive gifts—
17:19 and laid him on his **o** bed
2Ki 2:12 he grasped his **o** clothes and tore them
3:27 from him and returned to their **o** land.
4:13 She answered, "I live among my **o** people."
7: 2 But he said, "You shall see it with your **o** eyes,
7:19 "You shall see it with your **o** eyes,
8:20 and set up a king of their **o**.
12:18 had dedicated, as well as his **o** votive gifts,
14: 6 but all shall be put to death for their **o** sins."
17:23 So Israel was exiled from their **o** land to Assyria
17:29 But every nation still made gods of its **o**
17:33 the LORD but also served their **o** gods,
18:27 to eat their **o** dung and to drink their **o** urine?"
18:31 will eat from your **o** vine and your **o** fig tree, and
drink water from your **o** cistern,
18:32 and take you away to a land like your **o** land,
19: 7 that he shall hear a rumor and return to his **o** land;
19: 7 to fall by the sword in his **o** land.' "
19:34 my **o** sake and for the sake of my servant David."
20: 6 for my **o** sake and for my servant David's sake."
20:18 Some of your **o** sons who are born to you shall
23:30 and buried him in his **o** tomb.
1Ch 10: 4 So Saul took his **o** sword and fell on it.
11:23 and killed him with his **o** spear.
12:28 from his **o** ancestral house.
17: 9 so that they may live in their **o** place,
17:11 up your offspring after you, one of your **o** sons,

1Ch 17:19 O LORD, and according to your **o** heart,
29: 3 I have a treasure of my **o** of gold and silver,
29:14 and of your **o** have we given you.
29:16 from your hand and is all your **o**.
2Ch 6:23 by bringing their conduct on their **o** head,
6:29 all knowing their **o** suffering and their **o** sorrows
7:11 and in his **o** house he successfully accomplished.
8: 1 the house of the LORD and his **o** house,
9: 5 that I heard in my **o** land of your accomplishments
9: 6 the reports until I came and my **o** eyes saw it.
9:12 Then she returned to her **o** land, with her servants.
10:16 Look now to your **o** house, O David."
11:15 and had appointed his **o** priests for the high places,
15:18 of his father and his **o** votive gifts—
21: 8 the rule of Judah and set up a king of their **o**.
25: 4 but all shall be put to death for their **o** sins."
25:15 not deliver their **o** people from your hand?"
29: 8 and of hissing, as you see with your **o** eyes.
31: 3 from his **o** possessions was for the burnt offerings:
32:21 So he returned in disgrace to his **o** land.
32:21 some of his **o** sons struck him down there with
Ezr 2: 1 to Jerusalem and Judah, all to their **o** towns.
Ne 3:23 of Ananiah made repairs beside his **o** house.
3:28 each one opposite his **o** house.
3:29 of Immer made repairs opposite his **o** house.
4: 4 turn their taunt back on their **o** heads,
5: 7 "You are all taking interest from your **o** people."
5: 8 but now you are selling your **o** kin,
6: 8 you are inventing them out of your **o** mind"
6:16 and fell greatly in their **o** esteem;
7: 3 and others before their **o** houses."
9:35 Even in their **o** kingdom,
Est 1:22 to every province in its **o** script and to every
people in its **o** language,
1:22 that every man should be master in his **o** house.
2: 7 Mordecai adopted her as his **o** daughter.
2:15 who had adopted her as his **o** daughter,
3:12 to every province in its **o** script and every people
in its **o** language;
7: 8 the queen in my presence, in my **o** house?"
8: 9 to every province in its **o** script and to every
people in its **o** language,
9:25 against the Jews should come upon his **o** head,
Job 5:13 He takes the wise in their **o** craftiness;
9:20 I am innocent, my **o** mouth would condemn me;
9:31 and my **o** clothes will abhor me.
14:22 They feel only the pain of their **o** bodies,
15: 6 Your **o** mouth condemns you, and not I;
15: 6 your **o** lips testify against you.
18: 7 and their **o** schemes throw them down.
18: 8 For they are thrust into a net by their **o** feet,
19:17 I am loathsome to my **o** family.
20: 7 they will perish forever like their **o** dung;
21:16 Is not their prosperity indeed their **o** achievement?
21:20 Let their **o** eyes see their destruction,
24: 6 a field not their **o** and they glean in the vineyard of
32: 1 because he was righteous in his **o** eyes.
37:24 not regard any who are wise in their **o** conceit."
39:16 as if they were not its **o**;
40:14 to you that your **o** right hand can give you victory.
Ps 5:10 let them fall by their **o** counsels;
7:16 Their mischief returns upon their **o** heads,
7:16 and on their **o** heads their violence descends.
9:15 the net that they hid has their **o** foot been caught.
9:16 the wicked are snared in the work of their **o** hands.
12: 4 our lips are our **o**—who is our master?"
36: 2 For they flatter themselves in their **o** eyes
37:15 their sword shall enter their **o** heart,
44: 2 you with your **o** hand drove out the nations,
44: 3 for not by their **o** sword did they win the land,
44: 3 nor did their **o** arm give them victory;
49:11 though they named lands their **o**.
50:20 you slander your **o** mother's child.
69:33 and does not despise his **o** that are in bonds.
81:12 to follow their **o** counsels.
83:12 the pastures of God for our **o** possession."
109:29 may they be wrapped in their **o** shame as in
125: 5 to their **o** crooked ways the LORD will lead away
135: 4 Israel as his **o** possession.
141:10 Let the wicked fall into their **o** nets,
Pr 1:18 and set an ambush—for their **o** lives!
1:31 of their way and be sated with their **o** devices.
3: 5 and do not rely on your **o** insight.
3: 7 Do not be wise in your **o** eyes;
5:15 Drink water from your **o** cistern,
5:15 flowing water from your **o** well.
11: 5 but the wicked fall by their **o** wickedness.
12:15 Fools think their **o** way is right,
14: 1 but the foolish tears it down with her **o** hands.
14:10 The heart knows its **o** bitterness,
16: 2 All one's ways may be pure in one's **o** eyes,
19: 3 One's **o** folly leads to ruin,
20:24 how then can we understand our **o** ways?
26: 5 or they will be wise in their **o** eyes.
26:12 Do you see persons wise in their **o** eyes?
27: 2 Let another praise you, and not your **o** mouth—
27: 2 a stranger, and not your **o** lips.
28:10 into evil ways will fall into pits of their **o** making,
28:26 Those who trust in their **o** wits are fools;
29:24 To be a partner of a thief is to hate one's **o** life;
30:12 There are those who are pure in their **o** eyes
Ecc 4: 5 Fools fold their hands and consume their **o** flesh.
SS 1: 6 but my **o** vineyard I have not kept!
8:12 My vineyard, my very **o**, is for myself;
Isa 2: 8 to what their **o** fingers have made.
4: 1 "We will eat our **o** bread and wear our **o** clothes;
5:21 wise in your **o** eyes, and shrewd in your **o** sight!
Isa 9:20 they devoured the flesh of their **o** kindred;
13:14 all will turn to their **o** people,
13:14 and all will flee to their **o** lands.
14: 1 and will set them in their **o** land;
14:18 of the nations lie in glory, each in his **o** tomb;
17: 8 not look to what their **o** fingers have made,
23:10 Cross over to your **o** land, O ships of Tarshish;
36:12 to eat their **o** dung and drink their **o** urine?"
36:16 will eat from your **o** vine and your **o** fig tree and
drink water from your **o** cistern,
36:17 and take you away to a land like your **o** land,
37: 7 and return to his **o** land;
37: 7 to fall by the sword in his **o** land.' "
37:35 my **o** sake and for the sake of my servant David."
39: 7 Some of your **o** sons who are born to you shall
43:25 for my **o** sake, and I will
47:15 they all wander about in their **o** paths;
48:11 For my **o** sake, for my **o** sake, I do it,
48:17 who teaches you for your **o** good,
49:26 I will make your oppressors eat their **o** flesh,
49:26 and they shall be drunk with their **o** blood as
53: 6 we have all turned to our **o** way,
56:11 they have all turned to their **o** way, to their **o** gain,
57:17 but they kept turning back to their **o** ways.
58: 3 Look, you serve your **o** interest on your fast day,
58: 7 and not to hide yourself from your **o** kin?
58:13 from pursuing your **o** interests on my holy day;
58:13 not going your **o** ways, serving your **o** interests, or
pursuing your **o** affairs;
59:16 so his **o** arm brought him victory,
63: 5 so my **o** arm brought me victory,
65: 2 following their **o** devices;
66: 3 These have chosen their **o** ways,
66: 5 Your **o** people who hate you and reject you
Jer 1:16 and worshiped the works of their **o** hands.
2:30 Your **o** sword devoured your prophets like
3:15 I will give you shepherds after my **o** heart,
3:17 shall no longer stubbornly follow their **o** evil will.
7: 6 if you do not go after other gods to your **o** hurt,
7:19 Is it not themselves, to their **o** hurt?
7:24 they walked in their **o** counsels,
8: 6 All of them turn to their **o** course,
9:14 but have stubbornly followed their **o** hearts
12: 6 For even your kinsfolk and your **o** family,
13:10 who stubbornly follow their **o** will and have gone
14:14 and the deceit of their **o** minds.
16:15 to their **o** land that I gave to their ancestors.
17: 4 By your **o** act you shall lose the heritage
18:12 We will follow our **o** plans,
23: 8 Then they shall live in their **o** land.
23:16 They speak visions of their **o** minds,
23:17 all who stubbornly follow their **o** stubborn hearts,
23:26 and who prophesy the deceit of their **o** heart?
23:31 says the LORD, who use their **o** tongues and say,
23:36 for the burden is everyone's **o** word,
25: 7 with the work of your hands to your **o** harm.
26:11 as you have heard with your **o** ears."
27: 7 until the time of his **o** land comes;
27:11 I will leave on its **o** land, says the LORD,
29:25 In your **o** name you sent a letter to all
30:21 Their prince shall be one of their **o**,
31:17 your children shall come back to their **o** country.
31:30 But all shall die for their **o** sins;
32:39 for their **o** good and the good of their children
35: 7 nor shall you plant a vineyard, or even **o** one;
37: 7 is going to return to its **o** land, to Egypt.
39:14 So he stayed with his **o** people.
44: 9 your **o** crimes and those of your wives,
46:16 let us go back to our **o** people and to the land
50:16 of them shall return to their **o** people,
50:16 and all of them shall flee to their **o** land.
51: 9 and let each of us go to our **o** country;
La 4:10 compassionate women have boiled their **o** children;
Eze 6: 9 Then they will be loathsome in their **o** sight for
7:27 according to their **o** judgments I will judge them.
11:15 your kinsfolk, your **o** kin, your fellow exiles,
11:21 I will bring their deeds upon their **o** heads,
12: 7 through the wall with my **o** hands;
13: 2 to those who prophesy out of their **o** imagination:
13: 3 the senseless prophets who follow their **o** spirit,
13:17 who prophesy out of their **o** imagination;
13:18 and maintain your **o** lives?
14:14 they would save only their **o** lives
14:20 they would save only their **o** lives
16:53 I will restore your **o** fortunes along with theirs,
18:20 the righteousness of the righteous shall be his **o**,
18:20 and the wickedness of the wicked shall be his **o**.
27:15 many coastlands were your **o** special markets;
28:25 of the nations, then they shall settle on their **o** soil
29: 3 saying, "My Nile is my **o**; I made it for myself."
33: 4 their blood shall be upon their **o** heads.
33:17 when it is their **o** way that is not just.
34:13 and will bring them into their **o** land;
36:17 when the house of Israel lived on their **o** soil,
36:24 and bring you into your **o** land.
37:14 and I will place you on your **o** soil;
37:21 and bring them to their **o** land.
39:28 and then gathered them into their **o** land.
46:18 of his **o** holding, so that none of my people shall
Da 1:10 the other young men of your **o** age,
3:28 and worship any god except their **o** God.
6:17 with his **o** signet and with the signet of his lords,
8:25 and in his **o** mind he shall be great.
9:17 and for your **o** sake, Lord,
9:19 For your **o** sake, O my God,
11: 5 and shall rule a realm greater than his **o** realm.
11: 9 but will return to his **o** land.
Da 11:14 among your **o** people shall lift themselves up
11:19 toward the fortresses of his **o** land,
11:28 He shall work his will, and return to his **o** land.
Hos 8: 4 and gold they made idols for their **o** destruction.
Joel 2: 7 Each keeps to its **o** course,
2: 8 each keeps to its **o** track;
3: 4 upon your **o** heads swiftly and speedily.
3: 6 removing them far from their **o** border.
3: 7 and I will turn your deeds back upon your **o** heads.
Am 6:13 by our **o** strength taken Karnaim for ourselves?"
Ob 1:15 your deeds shall return on your **o** head.
Jnh 4: 2 while I was still in my **o** country?
Mic 4: 4 under their **o** vines and under their **o** fig trees,
7: 6 your enemies are members of your **o** household.
Hab 1: 6 of the earth to seize dwellings not their **o**.
1:11 their **o** might is their god!
2: 5 and collect all peoples as their **o**.
2: 6 "Alas for you who heap up what is not your **o**!"
2: 7 Will not your **o** creditors suddenly rise,
3: 2 our **o** time revive it; in our **o** time make it known;
3:14 with his **o** arrows the head of his warriors,
Hag 1: 9 while all of you hurry off to your **o** houses.
Zec 2: 9 and they shall become plunder for their **o** slaves.
9: 8 for now I have seen with my **o** eyes.
11: 5 and their **o** shepherds have no pity on them.
Mal 1: 5 Your **o** eyes shall see this, and you shall say,
Mt 2:12 they left for their **o** country by another road.
6:34 for tomorrow will bring worries of its **o**.
7: 3 but do not notice the log in your **o** eye?
7: 4 while the log is in your **o** eye?
7: 5 You hypocrite, first take the log out of your **o** eye,
8:22 "Follow me, and let the dead bury their **o** dead."
9: 1 a boat he crossed the sea and came to his **o** town.
10:36 one's foes will be members of one's **o** household.
12:27 by whom do your **o** exorcists cast them out?
13:57 not without honor except in their **o** country and in
their **o** house."
25:27 on my return I would have received what was my **o**
27:31 they stripped him of the robe and put his **o** clothes
27:60 and laid it in his **o** new tomb,
Mk 6: 4 and among their **o** kin, and in their **o** house."
10:21 sell what you **o**, and give the money to the poor,
15:20 of the purple cloak and put his **o** clothes on him.
Lk 2: 3 All went to their **o** towns to be registered.
2:35 and a sword will pierce your **o** soul too."
2:39 to their **o** town of Nazareth.
6:41 but do not notice the log in your **o** eye?
6:42 you yourself do not see the log in your **o** eye?
6:42 You hypocrite, first take the log out of your **o** eye,
6:44 for each tree is known by its **o** fruit.
9:60 Jesus said to him, "Let the dead bury their **o** dead;
10:34 Then he put him on his **o** animal,
16: 8 with their **o** generation than are the children
16:12 who will give you what is your **o**?
18:22 that you **o** and distribute the money to the poor,
19:22 He said to him, 'I will judge you by your **o** words,
22:32 but I have prayed for you that your **o** faith may
22:71 We have heard it ourselves from his **o** lips!"
Jn 1:11 He came to what was his **o**, and his **o** people did
not accept him.
4:44 in the prophet's **o** country).
5:18 but was also calling God his **o** Father,
5:19 I tell you, the Son can do nothing on his **o**,
5:30 "I can do nothing on my **o**.
5:30 not my **o** will but the will of him who sent me.
5:43 another comes in his **o** name, you will accept him.
6:38 not to do my **o** will,
7:17 from God or whether I am speaking on my **o**.
7:18 Those who speak on their **o** seek their **o** glory;
7:28 I have not come on my **o**.
8:13 "You are testifying on your **o** behalf;
8:14 Jesus answered, "Even if I testify on my **o** behalf,
8:18 I testify on my **o** behalf,
8:28 and that I do nothing on my **o**,
8:42 I did not come on my **o**, but he sent me.
8:44 When he lies, he speaks according to his **o** nature,
8:50 Yet I do not seek my **o** glory;
10: 3 He calls his **o** sheep by name and leads them out.
10: 4 When he has brought out all his **o**,
10:12 who is not the shepherd and does not **o** the sheep,
10:14 I know my **o** and my **o** know me,
10:18 but I lay it down of my **o** accord.
11:51 He did not say this on his **o**,
12:49 for I have not spoken on my **o**,
13: 1 Having loved his **o** who were in the world,
14:10 words that I say to you I do not speak on my **o**;
15:19 the world would love you as its **o**.
16:13 for he will not speak on his **o**,
17: 5 glorify me in your **o** presence with the glory
18:34 Jesus answered, "Do you ask this on your **o**,
18:35 **o** nation and the chief priests have handed you
19:27 that hour the disciple took her into his **o** home.
21:18 you used to fasten your **o** belt and
Ac 1: 7 that the Father has set by his **o** authority.
1:25 to go to his **o** place."
2: 8 each of us, in our **o** native language?
2:11 in our **o** languages we hear them speaking
3:12 by our **o** power or piety we had made him walk?
3:22 up for you from your **o** people a prophet like me.
5: 4 it remained unsold, did it not remain your **o**?
7:21 and brought him up as her **o** son.
7:37 for you from your **o** people as he raised me up.'
12:10 It opened for them of its **o** accord,
13:36 of God in his **o** generation, died, was laid
14:16 the nations to follow their **o** ways;
17:28 as even some of your **o** poets have said,
18: 6 "Your blood be on your **o** heads!

Ac 18:15 and names and your **o** law, see to it yourselves;
20:28 that he obtained with the blood of his **o** Son.
20:30 from your **o** group will come distorting the truth
20:34 that I worked with my **o** hands to support myself
21:11 bound his **o** feet and hands with it, and said,
22:14 to see the Righteous One and to hear his **o** voice;
25:19 of disagreement with him about their **o** religion
26:4 from the beginning among my **o** people and
27:19 and on the third day with their **o** hands they threw
28:30 He lived there two whole years at his **o** expense
Ro 1:27 in their **o** persons the due penalty for their error.
2:15 to which their **o** conscience also bears witness;
4:19 in faith when he considered his **o** body,
7:15 I do not understand my **o** actions.
8:3 by sending his **o** Son in the likeness
8:20 not of its **o** will but by the will of
8:32 He who did not withhold his **o** Son,
9:3 from Christ for the sake of my **o** people,
10:3 and seeking to establish their **o**,
11:14 in order to make my **o** people jealous,
11:24 be grafted back into their **o** olive tree.
14:4 It is before their **o** lord that they stand or fall.
14:5 Let all be fully convinced in their **o** minds.
14:22 have as your **o** conviction before God.
16:18 not serve our Lord Christ, but their **o** appetites,
1Co 1:26 Consider your **o** call, brothers and sisters:
4:12 and we grow weary from the work of our **o** hands.
6:19 and that you are not your **o**?
7:2 have his **o** wife and each woman her **o** husband.
7:4 the wife does not have authority over her **o** body,
7:4 husband does not have authority over his **o** body,
7:35 I say this for your **o** benefit,
7:37 being under no necessity but having his **o** desire
7:37 and has determined in his **o** mind to keep her
9:17 For if I do this of my **o** will, I have a reward;
9:17 of my **o** will, I am entrusted with a commission.
10:24 Do not seek your **o** advantage,
10:29 the other's conscience, not your **o**.
10:33 not seeking my **o** advantage, but that of many,
11:21 each of you goes ahead with your **o** supper,
13:5 It does not insist on its **o** way;
15:23 But each in his **o** order:
15:38 and to each kind of seed its **o** body.
16:21 I, Paul, write this greeting with my **o** hand.
2Co 7:13 In addition to our **o** consolation,
8:17 he is going to you of his **o** accord.
11:26 danger from my **o** people, danger from Gentiles,
12:5 but on my **o** behalf I will not boast,
Gal 6:4 All must test their **o** work;
6:5 For all must carry their **o** loads.
6:8 If you sow to your **o** flesh,
6:11 when I am writing in my **o** hand!
Eph 1:14 toward redemption as God's **o** people,
2:8 and this is not your **o** doing;
4:28 and work honestly with their **o** hands,
5:28 as they do their **o** bodies.
5:29 For no one ever hates his **o** body,
Php 2:4 Let each of you look not to your **o** interests,
2:12 work out your **o** salvation with fear and trembling;
2:21 All of them are seeking their **o** interests,
3:9 a righteousness of my **o** that comes from the law,
3:12 but I press on to make it my **o**,
3:12 because Christ Jesus has made me his **o**.
3:13 I do not consider that I have made it my **o**;
Col 4:18 I, Paul, write this greeting with my **o** hand.
1Th 2:7 like a nurse tenderly caring for her **o** children.
2:8 not only the gospel of God but also our **o** selves,
2:12 who calls you into his **o** kingdom and glory.
2:14 from your **o** compatriots as they did from
4:4 how to control your **o** body in holiness and honor,
4:11 to live quietly, to mind your **o** affairs, and to work
2Th 3:12 to do their work quietly and to earn their **o** living.
3:17 I, Paul, write this greeting with my **o** hand.
1Ti 3:4 He must manage his **o** household well,
3:5 not know how to manage his **o** household,
5:4 to their **o** family and make some repayment
2Ti 1:9 to our works but according to his **o** purpose
4:3 for themselves teachers to suit their **o** desires,
Tit 1:12 It was one of them, their very **o** prophet, who said,
2:14 a people of his **o** who are zealous for good deeds.
Phm 1:12 I am sending him, that is, my **o** heart, back to you.
1:19 I, Paul, am writing this with my **o** hand:
1:19 about your owing me even your **o** self.
Heb 5:3 of this he must offer sacrifice for his **o** sins as well
6:6 since on their **o** they are crucifying again the Son
7:27 for his **o** sins, and then for those of the people;
9:12 of goats and calves, but with his **o** blood,
9:25 after year with blood that is not his **o**;
13:12 in order to sanctify the people by his **o** blood.
Jas 1:14 But one is tempted by one's **o** desire,
1:18 In fulfillment of his **o** purpose he gave us birth by
1Pe 2:9 a royal priesthood, a holy nation, God's **o** people,
2Pe 1:3 the knowledge of him who called us by his **o** glory
1:20 of scripture is a matter of one's **o** interpretation,
2:16 but was rebuked for his **o** transgression;
2:22 "The dog turns back to its **o** vomit," and,
3:3 scoffing and indulging their **o** lusts
3:16 and unstable twist to their **o** destruction,
3:17 the error of the lawless and lose your **o** stability.
1Jn 3:12 his **o** deeds were evil and his brother's righteous.
Jude 1:6 And the angels who did not keep their **o** position,
1:13 casting up the foam of their **o** shame;
1:16 they indulge their **o** lusts;
1:16 flattering people to their **o** advantage.
1:18 indulging their **o** ungodly lusts."
Rev 3:12 from my God out of heaven, and my **o** new name.
Tob 1:4 When I was in my **o** country, in the land of Israel,
Tob 1:9 a member of our **o** family,
2:3 of our **o** people has been murdered and thrown
5:9 a man who is one of our **o** Israelite kindred!"
8:21 Take at once half of what I **o** and return in safety
10:6 with him is trustworthy and is one of our **o** kin.
10:7 to let me go so that I may return to my **o** father.
12:10 and do wrong are their **o** worst enemies.
12:18 I was not acting on my **o** will,
Jdt 2:2 with his **o** lips, all the wickedness of the region.
2:12 I have spoken I will accomplish by my **o** hand.
6:21 Uzziah took him from the assembly to his **o** house
12:1 to set a table for her with some of his **o** delicacies,
12:1 and with some of his **o** wine to drink.
13:20 because you risked your **o** life
15:10 You have done all this with your **o** hand;
16:21 this they all returned home to their **o** inheritances.
16:24 and to her **o** nearest kindred.
AdE 1:22 to every province in its **o** language,
2:7 he brought her up to womanhood as his **o**.
3:12 governors were addressed each in his **o** language.
7:8 even assault my wife in my **o** house?"
8:9 to each province in its **o** language.
8:11 the Jews in every city to observe their **o** laws,
9:31 established this decision on their **o** responsibility,
9:31 pledging their **o** well-being to the plan.
16:3 to scheme against their **o** benefactors.
16:19 and permit the Jews to live under their **o** laws.
Wis 2:23 and made us in the image of his **o** eternity,
11:13 when they heard that through their **o** punishments
12:23 you tormented through their **o** abominations.
17:11 condemned by its **o** testimony;
19:17 to find the way through their **o** doors.
Sir 3:5 in their **o** children, and when they pray they will
3:11 The glory of one's father is one's **o** glory,
4:22 Do not show partiality, to your **o** harm,
9:1 or you will teach her an evil lesson to your **o** hurt.
11:34 and will make you a stranger to your **o** family.
12:12 or else he may try to take your **o** seat,
13:5 If you **o** something, he will live with you;
13:13 for you are walking about with your **o** downfall.
13:16 All living beings associate with their **o** kind,
14:5 He will not enjoy his **o** riches.
15:14 he left them in the power of their **o** free choice.
15:15 and to act faithfully is a matter of your **o** choice.
17:3 He endowed them with strength like his **o**,
17:3 and made them in his **o** image.
17:17 but Israel is the Lord's **o** portion.
22:4 A sensible daughter obtains a husband of her **o**,
26:20 *and sow it with your **o** seed, trusting in your fine*
27:9 Birds roost with their **o** kind,
27:23 and with your **o** words he will trip you up.
27:25 a stone straight up throws it on his **o** head,
28:4 can he then seek pardon for his **o** sins?
29:22 under their **o** crude roof than sumptuous food in
31:15 Judge your neighbor's feelings by your **o**,
31:30 the anger of a fool to his **o** hurt,
37:7 but some give counsel in their **o** interest.
37:13 And heed the counsel of your **o** heart,
37:14 our **o** mind sometimes keeps us better informed
37:22 If a person is wise to his **o** advantage,
37:23 A wise person instructs his **o** people,
38:20 drive it away, and remember your **o** end.
38:31 and all are skillful in their **o** work.
39:6 of wisdom of his **o** and give thanks to the Lord
39:21 for everything has been created for its **o** purpose.
47:7 he crushed their power to our **o** day.
47:22 and to David a root from his **o** family.
51:27 See with your **o** eyes that I have labored but little
51:30 and in his **o** time God will give you your reward.
Bar 1:22 of us followed the intent of our **o** wicked hearts
2:14 and for your **o** sake deliver us,
4:33 so she will be grieved at her **o** desolation.
LtJ 6:54 They cannot judge their **o** cause
Aza 1:7 done what you have commanded us for our **o** good.
Sus 1:61 of their **o** mouths Daniel had convicted them
Bel 1:4 But Daniel worshiped his **o** God.
1:39 immediately returned Habakkuk to his **o** place.
1Mc 1:8 his officers began to rule, each in his **o** place.
1:24 Taking them all, he went into his **o** land.
6:54 the rest scattered to their **o** homes
9:9 Let us rather save our **o** lives now,
9:69 Then he decided to go back to his **o** land.
9:72 then he turned and went back to his **o** land,
10:13 and went back to their **o** lands.
10:32 so that he may station in it men of his **o** choice
10:37 Let their officers and leaders be of their **o** number,
10:37 and let them live by their **o** laws,
10:72 to flight in their **o** land.
11:1 by trickery and add it to his **o** kingdom.
11:38 all of them to their **o** homes,
12:25 gave them no opportunity to invade his **o** country.
13:24 Then Trypho turned and went back to his **o** land.
14:12 All the people sat under their **o** vines and fig trees,
14:32 He spent great sums of his **o** money;
15:6 to mint your **o** coinage as money for your country,
2Mc 3:3 from his **o** revenues all the expenses connected
3:30 Lord who had acted marvelously for his **o** place.
3:36 which he had seen with his **o** eyes.
4:1 about the money against his **o** country,
4:21 and he took measures for his **o** security.
4:26 after supplanting his **o** brother was supplanted
4:29 Menelaus left his **o** brother Lysimachus as deputy
5:9 from their **o** country into exile died in exile,
6:16 he does not forsake his **o** people.
6:19 went up to the rack of his **o** accord,
6:21 to bring meat of his **o** providing,
7:18 we are suffering these things on our **o** account,
2Mc 7:18 because of our sins against our **o** God.
7:32 For we are suffering because of our **o** sins.
7:33 he will again be reconciled with his **o** servants.
8:15 if not for their **o** sake,
8:30 and also to the aged, shares equal to their **o**.
8:35 in the destruction of his **o** army!
9:12 And when he could not endure his **o** stench,
9:16 sacrifices he would provide from his **o** revenues;
10:7 to the purifying of his **o** holy place.
10:30 shielding him with their **o** armor and weapons,
11:23 be undisturbed in caring for their **o** affairs.
11:24 but prefer their **o** way of living and ask that their **o** customs be allowed them.
11:26 on happily in the conduct of their **o** affairs."
11:29 to return home and look after your **o** affairs.
11:31 for the Jews to enjoy their **o** food and laws,
12:22 so that often they were injured by their **o** men and pierced by the points of their **o** swords.
12:42 with their **o** eyes what had happened as the result
14:15 to him who established his **o** people forever and always upholds his **o** heritage
14:41 Being surrounded, Razis fell upon his **o** sword,
15:34 "Blessed is he who has kept his **o** place undefiled!"
1Es 3:8 Then each wrote his **o** statement,
4:11 and no one may go away to attend to his **o** affairs,
4:20 A man leaves his **o** father, who brought him up,
4:20 and his **o** country, and clings to his wife.
4:30 from the king's head and put it on her **o**,
4:46 to the King of heaven with your **o** lips."
5:8 and the rest of Judea, each to his **o** town.
5:47 and the Israelites were all in their **o** homes,
6:18 the house in Jerusalem and stored in his **o** temple,
Pm 151:T *psalm is ascribed to David as his **o** composition*
151:7 But I drew his **o** sword;
3Mc 1:11 members of their **o** nation were allowed to enter,
3:19 in defiance of kings and their **o** benefactors,
5:21 and all went to their **o** homes.
5:34 the assembled people to their **o** occupations.
5:47 with invulnerable heart and with his **o** eyes,
7:8 to return to their **o** homes,
7:10 of the king that at their **o** hands those of
7:18 until all of them arrived at their **o** houses.
7:20 by land and sea and river to their **o** homes.
2Es 3:8 And every nation walked after its **o** will;
4:20 but why have you not judged so in your **o** case?
5:30 they should be punished at your **o** hands."
5:47 "Of course it cannot, but only each in its **o** time."
7:*71* But now, understand from your **o** words—
7:*105* for then all shall bear their **o** righteousness
7:*134* [64] since they are his **o** creatures;
8:5 not of your **o** will did you come into the world,
8:33 in consequence of their **o** deeds.
8:44 by your hands and are called your **o** image
8:45 for you have mercy on your **o** creation."
8:51 But think of your **o** case,
11:8 let each sleep in its **o** place, and watch in its turn;
13:33 all the nations shall leave their **o** lands and
13:40 that were taken away from their **o** land into exile
13:42 that they had not kept in their **o** land.
13:54 because you have forsaken your **o** ways
15:35 a heavy tempest on the earth, and their **o** tempest;
15:58 **o** flesh in hunger for bread and drink their **o** blood
16:65 and your **o** iniquities shall stand as your accusers
4Mc 1:6 For reason does not rule its **o** emotions,
3:1 that reason rules not over its **o** emotions,
5:10 you continue to despise me to your **o** hurt.
5:33 as to break the ancestral law by my **o** act.
7:8 with their **o** blood and noble sweat in sufferings
8:15 also opposed the tyrant with their **o** philosophy,
10:8 he saw his **o** flesh torn all around and drops
11:3 I have come of my **o** accord,
14:17 warning them with their **o** calls.
15:25 of her **o** soul she saw mighty advocates—
17:15 and gave the crown to its **o** athletes.
17:23 as an example for their **o** endurance,

OWNED (4) [OWN]

Nu 32:1 and the Gadites **o** a very great number of cattle.
Jer 39:10 of Judah some of the poor people who **o** nothing,
Ac 4:32 but everything they **o** was held in common.
4:34 as **o** lands or houses sold them and brought

OWNER (46) [OWN]

Ge 38:25 "It was the **o** of these who made me pregnant."
Ex 21:20 a rod and the slave dies immediately, the **o** shall
21:26 the **o** shall let the slave go, a free person,
21:27 the **o** knocks out a tooth of a male or female slave,
21:28 but the **o** of the ox shall not be liable.
21:29 and its **o** has been warned but has not restrained it,
21:29 and its **o** also shall be put to death.
21:30 If a ransom is imposed on the **o**,
21:30 then the **o** shall pay whatever is imposed for
21:31 **o** shall be dealt with according to this same rule.
21:32 the **o** shall pay to the slaveowner thirty shekels
21:34 the **o** of the pit shall make restitution,
21:34 giving money to its **o**, but keeping
21:36 and its **o** has not restrained it,
21:36 the **o** shall restore ox for ox,
22:8 the **o** of the house shall be brought before God,
22:8 not the **o** had laid hands on the neighbor's goods.
22:11 the **o** shall accept the oath,
22:12 if it was stolen, restitution shall be made to its **o**.
22:14 and it is injured or dies, the **o** not being present,
22:15 If the **o** was present, there shall be no restitution;
Lev 6:5 to its **o** when you realize your guilt.
14:35 the **o** of the house shall come and tell the priest,

Lev 25:50 the **o** shall be rated as the time of a hired laborer.
27:15 and it shall revert to the original **o.**
27:19 and it shall revert to the original **o;**
Dt 22: 1 you shall take them back to their **o.**
22: 2 If the **o** does not reside near you or you do not know who the **o** is,
22: 2 and it shall remain with you until the **o** claims it;
1Ki 16:24 after the name of Shemer, the **o** of the hill.
Ecc 5:11 and what gain has their **o** but to see them
Isa 1: 3 ox knows its **o,** and the donkey its master's crib;
Mt 20: 8 the **o** of the vineyard said to his manager,
21:40 Now when the **o** of the vineyard comes,
24:43 if the **o** of the house had known in what part of
Mk 12: 9 What then will the **o** of the vineyard do?
14:14 say to the **o** of the house, 'The Teacher asks,
Lk 12:39 if the **o** of the house had known at what hour
13:25 When once the **o** of the house has got up and shut
14:21 **o** of the house became angry and said to his slave,
20:13 Then the **o** of the vineyard said, 'What shall I do?
20:15 What then will the **o** of the vineyard do to them?
22:11 and say to the **o** of the house,
Ac 27:11 and to the **o** of the ship than to what Paul said.
2Ti 2:21 dedicated and useful to the **o** of the house,

OWNER'S (3) [OWN]

Ex 21:21 for the slave is the **o** property.
22: 5 be made from the best in the **o** field or vineyard.
LtJ 6:59 or a household utensil that serves its **o** need,

OWNERS‡ (11) [OWN]

Dt 23:15 Slaves who have escaped to you from their **o** shall
Job 31:39 and caused the death of its **o;**
Ecc 5:13 riches were kept by their **o** to their hurt,
Lk 19:33 As they were untying the colt, its **o** asked them,
Ac 16:16 of divination and brought her **o** a great deal
16:19 But when her **o** saw that their hope
Gal 4: 1 though they are the **o** of all the property;
Tob 2:12 to the **o** and they would pay wages to her.
2:12 a piece she had woven and sent it to the **o,**
2:13 Return it to the **o;**
2:14 and told her to return it to the **o.**

OWNERSHIP (2) [OWN]

Ex 22: 9 In any case of disputed **o** involving ox, donkey,
Ac 4:32 and no one claimed private **o** of any possessions,

OWNS (3) [OWN]

Ge 23: 9 which he **o;** it is at the end of his field.
Lev 27:28 a person **o** that has been devoted to destruction for
Ac 21:11 the man who **o** this belt and will hand him over to

OX‡ (77) [OXEN, OXGOAD]

Ex 20:17 or male or female slave, or **o,** or donkey,
21:28 When an **o** gores a man or a woman to death,
21:28 **o** shall be stoned, and its flesh shall not be eaten;
21:28 but the owner of the **o** shall not be liable.
21:29 If the **o** has been accustomed to gore in the past,
21:29 or a woman, the **o** shall be stoned, and its owner
21:32 If the **o** gores a male or female slave,
21:32 and the **o** shall be stoned.
21:33 and an **o** or a donkey falls into it,
21:35 If someone's **o** hurts the **o** of another,
21:35 they shall sell the live **o** and divide the price of it;
21:36 if it was known that the **o** was accustomed to gore
21:36 the owner shall restore **o** for **o,**
22: 1 When someone steals an **o** or a sheep,
22: 1 the thief shall pay five oxen for an **o,**
22: 4 When the animal, whether **o** or donkey or sheep,
22: 9 In any case of disputed ownership involving **o,**
22:10 When someone delivers to another a donkey, **o,**
23: 4 upon your enemy's **o** or donkey going astray,
23:12 so that your **o** and your donkey may have relief,
Lev 4:10 as these are removed from the **o** of the sacrifice
7:23 You shall eat no fat of **o** or sheep or goat.
9: 4 and an **o** and a ram for an offering of well-being
9:18 the **o** and the ram as a sacrifice of well-being for
9:19 and the fat of the **o** and of the ram—
17: 3 If anyone of the house of Israel slaughters an **o** or
22:23 An **o** or a lamb that has a limb too long
22:27 When an **o** or a sheep or a goat is born,
27:26 whether **o** or sheep, it is the LORD's.
Nu 7: 3 and for each one an **o;**
15:11 Thus it shall be done for each **o** or ram,
22: 4 as an **o** licks up the grass of the field."
23:22 is like the horns of a wild **o** for them.
24: 8 is like the horns of a wild **o** for him;
Dt 5:14 or your **o** or your donkey,
5:21 or field, or male or female slave, or **o,** or donkey,
14: 4 These are the animals you may eat: the **o,**
15:19 not do work with your firstling **o** nor shear
17: 1 to the LORD your God an **o** or a sheep that has
18: 3 whether an **o** or a sheep:
22: 1 You shall not watch your neighbor's **o**
22: 4 not see your neighbor's donkey or **o** fallen on
22:10 not plow with an **o** and a donkey yoked together.
25: 4 You shall not muzzle an **o** while it is treading out
28:31 Your **o** shall be butchered before your eyes,
33:17 His horns are the horns of a wild **o;**
Jdg 6: 4 and no sheep or **o** or donkey.
1Sa 12: 3 Whose **o** have I taken?
15: 3 **o** and sheep, camel and donkey.' "
2Sa 6:13 he sacrificed an **o** and a fatling.
Ne 5:18 that which was prepared for one day was one **o**
Job 6: 5 or the **o** low over its fodder?
24: 3 they take the widow's **o** for a pledge.
39: 9 "Is the wild **o** willing to serve you?
40:15 it eats grass like an **o.**
Ps 29: 6 and Sirion like a young wild **o.**
69:31 the LORD more than an **o** or a bull with horns
92:10 you have exalted my horn like that of the wild **o;**
106:20 of God for the image of an **o** that eats grass.
Pr 7:22 and goes like an **o** to the slaughter,
14: 4 abundant crops come by the strength of the **o.**
15:17 where love is than a fatted **o** and hatred with it.
Isa 1: 3 The **o** knows its owner,
11: 7 and the lion shall eat straw like the **o.**
32:20 who let the **o** and the donkey range freely.
65:25 the lion shall eat straw like the **o;**
66: 3 Whoever slaughters an **o** is like one who kills
Eze 1:10 the face of an **o** on the left side,
Lk 13:15 Does not each of you on the sabbath untie his **o**
14: 5 "If one of you has a child or an **o** that has fallen
1Co 9: 9 "You shall not muzzle an **o** while it is treading out
1Ti 5:18 "You shall not muzzle an **o** while it is treading out
Rev 4: 7 the second living creature like an **o,**
Jdt 8: 1 the daughter of Merari son of **O** son of Joseph son
Sir 25: 8 one who does not plow with **o** and ass together.

OXEN (93) [OX]

Ge 12:16 and he had sheep, **o,** male donkeys,
20:14 Then Abimelech took sheep and **o,**
21:27 So Abraham took sheep and **o** and gave them
32: 5 I have **o,** donkeys, flocks, male and female slaves;
49: 6 and at their whim they hamstrung **o.**
Ex 20:24 of well-being, your sheep and your **o;**
22: 1 the thief shall pay five **o** for an ox,
22:30 the same with your **o** and with your sheep:
24: 5 and sacrificed **o** as offerings of well-being to
Nu 7: 3 six covered wagons and twelve **o,**
7: 6 So Moses took the wagons and the **o,**
7: 7 and four **o** he gave to the Gershonites,
7: 8 four wagons and eight **o** he gave to the Merarites,
7:17 two **o,** five rams, five male goats,
7:23 two **o,** five rams, five male goats,
7:29 two **o,** five rams, five male goats,
7:35 two **o,** five rams, five male goats,
7:41 two **o,** five rams, five male goats,
7:47 two **o,** five rams, five male goats,
7:53 two **o,** five rams, five male goats,
7:59 two **o,** five rams, five male goats,
7:65 two **o,** five rams, five male goats,
7:71 two **o,** five rams, five male goats,
7:77 two **o,** five rams, five male goats,
7:83 two **o,** five rams, five male goats,
22:40 Balak sacrificed **o** and sheep,
31:28 whether persons, **o,** donkeys, sheep, or goats.
31:30 whether persons, **o,** donkeys, sheep, or goats—
31:33 seventy-two thousand **o,**
31:38 The **o** were thirty-six thousand,
31:44 thirty-six thousand **o,**
Dt 14:26 **o,** sheep, wine, strong drink,
Jos 6:21 both men and women, young and old, **o,** sheep,
7:24 with his sons and daughters, with his **o,** donkeys,
1Sa 11: 5 Saul was coming from the field behind the **o;**
11: 7 He took a yoke of **o,**
11: 7 so shall it be done to his **o!"**
14:32 and took sheep and **o** and calves,
14:34 'Let all bring their **o** or their sheep,
14:34 of the troops brought their **o** with them that night,
22:19 men and women, children and infants, **o,** donkeys,
27: 9 the **o,** the donkeys, the camels, and the clothing,
2Sa 6: 6 of God and took hold of it, for the **o** shook it.
24:22 here are the **o** for the burnt offering,
24:22 and the threshing sledges and the yokes of the **o**
24:24 So David bought the threshing floor and the **o**
1Ki 1: 9 Adonijah sacrificed sheep, **o,**
1:19 He has sacrificed **o,** fatted cattle,
1:25 For today he has gone down and has sacrificed **o,**
4:23 ten fat **o,** and twenty pasture-fed cattle,
7:25 It stood on twelve **o,** three facing north,
7:29 that were set in the frames were lions, **o,**
7:29 both above and below the lions and **o,**
7:44 the one sea, and the twelve **o** underneath the sea.
8: 5 and **o** that they could not be counted or numbered.
8:63 to the LORD twenty-two thousand **o**
19:19 There were twelve yoke of **o** ahead of him,
19:20 He left the **o,** ran after Elijah, and said,
19:21 took the yoke of **o,** and slaughtered them;
19:21 using the equipment from the **o,**
2Ki 5:26 olive orchards and vineyards, sheep and **o,**
16:17 he removed the sea from the bronze **o** that were
1Ch 12:40 on donkeys, camels, mules, and **o—**
12:40 wine, oil, **o,** and sheep, for there was joy in Israel.
13: 9 to hold the ark, for the **o** shook it.
21:23 see, I present the **o** for burnt offerings,
2Ch 4: 4 It stood on twelve **o,** three facing north,
4:15 the one sea, and the twelve **o** underneath it.
5: 6 and **o** that they could not be numbered or counted.
7: 5 as a sacrifice twenty-two thousand **o**
15:11 seven hundred **o** and seven thousand sheep.
18: 2 Ahab slaughtered an abundance of sheep and **o**
Job 1: 3 three thousand camels, five hundred yoke of **o,**
1:14 "The **o** were plowing and
42:12 a thousand yoke of **o,** and a thousand donkeys.
Ps 8: 7 all sheep and **o,** and also the beasts of the field,
22:21 the horns of the wild **o** you have rescued me.
Pr 14: 4 Where there are no **o,** there is no grain;
Isa 22:13 killing **o** and slaughtering sheep,
30:24 **o** and donkeys that till the ground will eat silage,
34: 7 Wild **o** shall fall with them,
Da 4:25 You shall be made to eat grass like **o,**
4:32 You shall be made to eat grass like **o,**
4:33 ate grass like **o,** and his body was bathed with
5:21 he was fed grass like **o,**
Am 6:12 Does one plow the sea with **o?**
Mt 22: 4 my **o** and my fat calves have been slaughtered,
Lk 14:19 Another said, 'I have bought five yoke of **o,**
Ac 14:13 brought **o** and garlands to the gates;
1Co 9: 9 Is it for **o** that God is concerned?
Tob 10:10 male and female slaves, **o** and sheep,
Jdt 2:17 and innumerable sheep and **o** and goats for food;
Sir 38:25 who drives **o** and is occupied with their work,

OXGOAD (1) [OX]

Jdg 3:31 of the Philistines with an **o.**

OZEM (2)

1Ch 2:15 **O** the sixth, David the seventh;
2:25 Ram his firstborn, Bunah, Oren, **O,** and Ahijah.

OZIAS (KJV) See UZZIAH

OZIEL (1)

Jdt 8: 1 of Merari son of Ox son of Joseph son of **O** son

OZNI (1) [OZNITES]

Nu 26:16 of **O,** the clan of the Oznites;

OZNITES (1) [OZNI]

Nu 26:16 of Ozni, the clan of the **O;**

P

PAARAI (1)

2Sa 23:35 Hezro of Carmel; **P** the Arbite;

PACE (3) [PACES]

Ge 33:14 according to the **p** of the cattle that are before me
33:14 and according to the **p** of the children,
3Mc 4: 5 forced to march at a swift **p** by the violence

PACES (1) [PACE]

2Sa 6:13 the ark of the LORD had gone six **p,**

PACHON (1)

3Mc 6:38 from the twenty-fifth of **P** to the fourth of Epeiph,

PACK (1)

Jer 46:19 **P** your bags for exile, sheltered daughter Egypt!

PACT (1)

La 5: 6 We have made a **p** with Egypt and Assyria,

PADAN (KJV) See PADDAN

PADANARAM (KJV) See PADDAN-ARAM

PADDAN (1) [PADDAN-ARAM]

Ge 48: 7 For when I came from **P,** Rachel, alas,

PADDAN-ARAM (10) [ARAM, PADDAN]

Ge 25:20 daughter of Bethuel the Aramean of **P,**
28: 2 Go at once to **P** to the house of Bethuel,
28: 5 Thus Isaac sent Jacob away; and he went to **P,**
28: 6 and sent him away to **P** to take a wife from there,
28: 7 and his mother and gone to **P.**
31:18 in his possession that he had acquired in **P,**
33:18 in the land of Canaan, on his way from **P;**
35: 9 to Jacob again when he came from **P,**
35:26 the sons of Jacob who were born to him in **P.**
46:15 whom she bore to Jacob in **P,**

PADON (3)

Ezr 2:44 Keros, Siaha, **P,**
Ne 7:47 of Keros, of Sia, of **P,**
1Es 5:29 the descendants of **P,** the descendants of Lebanah,

PAGANS (4)

1Co 5: 1 and of a kind that is not found even among **p;**
10:20 No, I imply that what **p** sacrifice,
12: 2 You know that when you were **p,**
4Mc 18: 5 to compel the Israelites to become **p** and

PAGIEL (5)

Nu 1:13 From Asher, **P** son of Ochran,
2:27 leader of the Asherites shall be **P** son of Ochran,
7:72 On the eleventh day **P** son of Ochran,
7:77 This was the offering of **P** son of Ochran.

Nu 10:26 Over the company of the tribe of Asher was **P** son

PAHATH-MOAB (8)

Ezr 2: 6 Of **P**, namely the descendants of Jeshua and Joab,
8: 4 the descendants of **P**, Eliehoenai son of Zerahiah,
10:30 Of the descendants of **P**: Adna,
Ne 3:11 of **P** repaired another section and the Tower of
7:11 Of **P**, namely the descendants of Jeshua and Joab,
10:14 The leaders of the people: Parosh, **P**, Elam, Zattu,
1Es 5:11 The descendants of **P**, of the descendants
8:31 the descendants of **P**, Eliehoenai son of Zerahiah,

PAI (1)

1Ch 1:50 the name of his city was **P**,

PAID (43) [PAY]

Ge 39:23 The chief jailer **p** no heed to anything that was
Lev 27:23 and the assessment shall be **p** as of that day,
Jdg 1: 7 as I have done, so God has **p** me back."
2Ki 12:11 then they **p** it out to the carpenters and
17: 3 Hoshea became his vassal, and **p** him tribute.
1Ch 21:25 So David **p** Ornan six hundred shekels of gold
2Ch 26: 8 The Ammonites **p** tribute to Uzziah,
27: 5 The Ammonites **p** him the same amount in
Ezr 4:20 to whom tribute, custom, and toll were **p**.
6: 4 let the cost be **p** from the royal treasury.
6: 8 the cost is to be **p** to these people,
Job 15:32 It will be **p** in full before their time,
21:19 Let it be **p** back to them, so that they may know it.
33:27 and it was not **p** back to me.
Pr 7:14 and today I have **p** my vows;
Isa 40: 2 that she has served her term, that her penalty is **p**,
48:18 O that you had **p** attention to my commandments!
Jnh 1: 3 so he **p** his fare and went on board,
Mt 2:11 and they knelt down and **p** him homage.
5:26 you will never get out until you have **p**
26:15 They **p** him thirty pieces of silver.
Lk 10: 7 for the laborer deserves to be **p**.
12:59 you will never get out until you have **p**
Ac 18:17 But Gallio **p** no attention to any of these things.
27:11 But the centurion **p** more attention to the pilot and
Php 4:18 I have been **p** in full and have more than enough;
Col 3:25 be **p** back for whatever wrong has been done,
1Ti 5:18 and, "The laborer deserves to be **p**."
Heb 7: 9 who receives tithes, **p** tithes through Abraham,
Tob 2:12 they **p** her full wages and also gave her
Sir 20:10 and the gift to be **p** back double.
1Mc 7:11 But they **p** no attention to their words,
8: 4 the rest **p** them tribute every year.
10:41 the government officials have not **p** as they did in
10:44 the sanctuary be **p** from the revenues of the king.
10:45 also be **p** from the revenues of the king."
10:61 but the king **p** no attention to them.
10:64 When his accusers saw the honor that was **p** him,
11:60 the people of the city met him and **p** him honor.
14:32 the soldiers of his nation and **p** them wages.
14:39 of his Friends, and **p** him high honors.
1Es 6:25 the cost to be **p** from the treasury of King Cyrus;
3Mc 3: 6 of other races **p** no heed to their good service

PAIN‡ (61) [PAINED, PAINFUL, PAINLESS, PAINS]

Ge 3:16 in **p** you shall bring forth children,
34:25 On the third day, when they were still in **p**,
Nu 5:24 the curse shall enter her and cause bitter **p**.
5:27 the curse shall enter into her and cause bitter **p**,
18:32 not profane the holy gifts of the Israelites, on **p**
1Ch 4: 9 saying, "Because I bore him in **p**."
Job 6:10 I would even exult in unrelenting **p**;
14:22 They feel only the **p** of their own bodies,
15:20 The wicked writhe in **p** all their days,
16: 5 and the solace of my lips would assuage your **p**.
16: 6 "If I speak, my **p** is not assuaged, and if I forbear,
30:17 and the **p** that gnaws me takes no rest.
33:19 They are also chastened with **p** upon their beds,
Ps 13: 2 How long must I bear **p** in my soul,
38:17 For I am ready to fall, and my **p** is ever with me.
69:29 But I am lowly and in **p**;
73: 4 they have no **p**; their bodies are sound and sleek.
Ecc 2:23 For all their days are full of **p**,
11:10 and put away **p** from your body;
Isa 14: 3 When the LORD has given you rest from your **p**
17:11 in a day of grief and incurable **p**.
53:10 it was the will of the LORD to crush him with **p**.
65:14 but you shall cry out for **p** of heart,
66: 7 before her **p** came upon her she delivered a son.
Jer 4:19 my anguish! I writhe in **p**!
6:24 **p** as of a woman in labor.
15:18 Why is my **p** unceasing, my wound incurable,
22:23 **p** as of a woman in labor!
30:15 over your hurt? Your **p** is incurable.
45: 3 The LORD has added sorrow to my **p**;
50:43 **p** like that of a woman in labor.
Jn 16:20 you will have **p**, but your **p** will turn into joy.
16:21 When a woman is in labor, she has **p**,
16:22 So you have **p** now; but I will see you again,
2Co 2: 2 For if I cause you **p**,
2: 3 as I did, so that when I came, I might not suffer **p**
2: 4 of heart and with many tears, not to cause you **p**,
2: 5 But if anyone has caused **p**,
Gal 4:19 in the **p** of childbirth until Christ is formed in you,
1Pe 2:19 you endure **p** while suffering unjustly.
Rev 21: 4 mourning and crying and **p** will be no more,
Jdt 16:17 they shall weep in **p** forever.
Wis 8:16 and life with her has no **p**, but gladness and joy.
Sir 27:29 and **p** will consume them before their death.
38: 7 By them the physician heals and takes away **p**;
38:16 and as one in great **p** begin the lament.
Aza 1:27 not touch them at all and caused them no **p**
2Mc 3:17 to those who looked at him the **p** lodged
9: 5 a **p** in his bowels, for which there was no relief,
9: 9 and while he was still living in anguish and **p**,
9:11 for he was tortured with **p** every moment.
2Es 10:12 which I brought forth in **p** and bore in sorrow;
4Mc 1: 4 namely anger, fear, and **p**.
1:20 of the emotions are pleasure and **p**;
1:21 of both pleasure and **p** have many consequences.
1:23 Fear precedes **p** and sorrow comes after.
1:24 is an emotion embracing pleasure and **p**.
1:28 Just as pleasure and **p** are two plants growing from
9:31 I lighten my **p** by the joys that come from virtue,
16:23 who have religious knowledge not to withstand **p**."

PAINED (1) [PAIN]

2Co 2: 2 to make me glad but the one whom I have **p**?

PAINFUL (6) [PAIN]

2Co 2: 1 up my mind not to make you another **p** visit.
Heb 12:11 discipline always seems **p** rather than pleasant at
Rev 16: 2 a foul and **p** sore came on those who had the mark
Sir 13:26 but to devise proverbs requires **p** thinking.
4Mc 8: 1 have prevailed over the most **p** instruments
14:10 What could be more excruciatingly **p** than this?

PAINLESS (1) [PAIN]

4Mc 11:26 Your fire is cold to us, and the catapults **p**,

PAINS‡ (16) [PAIN]

1Sa 4:19 for her labor **p** overwhelmed her.
1Ch 22:14 With great **p** I have provided for the house of
Job 21:17 How often does God distribute **p** in his anger?
Ps 48: 6 **p** as of a woman in labor,
Da 10:16 because of the vision such **p** have come upon me
Mt 4:24 with various diseases and **p**,
Ro 8:22 the whole creation has been groaning in labor **p**
1Th 5: 3 as labor **p** come upon a pregnant woman,
1Ti 6:10 the faith and pierced themselves with many **p**.
Rev 16:11 and cursed the God of heaven because of their **p**
2Es 16:38 has great **p** around her womb for two
16:39 and **p** will seize it on every side.
4Mc 6: 9 the **p** and scorned the punishment and endured
13: 4 for the brothers mastered both emotions and **p**.
15: 7 and because of the many **p** she suffered with each
15:16 tried now by more bitter **p** than even

PAINT (4) [PAINTED, PAINTERS, PAINTING]

Jer 4:30 that you enlarge your eyes with **p**?
Wis 13:14 a coat of red **p** and coloring its surface red
13:14 and covering every blemish in it with **p**;
4Mc 17: 7 to **p** the history of your religion as an artist might,

PAINTED (2) [PAINT]

2Ki 9:30 she **p** her eyes, and adorned her head,
Eze 23:40 For them you bathed yourself, **p** your eyes,

PAINTERS (1) [PAINT]

Wis 15: 4 nor the fruitless toil of **p**,

PAINTING (3) [PAINT]

Jer 22:14 paneling it with cedar, and **p** it with vermilion.
Sir 38:27 they set their heart on **p** a lifelike image,
2Mc 2:29 the one who undertakes its **p** and decoration has

PAIR (14) [PAIRS]

Ge 7: 2 and a **p** of the animals that are not clean,
Ex 25:35 the first **p** of branches, a calyx of one piece with it under the next **p** of branches, and a calyx of one piece with it under the last **p** of branches—
37:21 the first **p** of branches, a calyx of one piece with it under the next **p** of branches, and a calyx of one piece with it under the last **p** of branches.
Jdg 15: 4 and put a torch between each **p** of tails.
Isa 6: 6 that had been taken from the altar with a **p**
Am 2: 6 and the needy for a **p** of sandals—
8: 6 buying the poor for silver and the needy for a **p**
Lk 2:24 "a **p** of turtledoves or two young pigeons."
Rev 6: 5 Its rider held a **p** of scales in his hand,
Sir 46:19 "No property, not so much as a **p** of shoes,

PAIRS (7) [PAIR]

Ge 7: 2 Take with you seven **p** of all clean animals,
7: 3 and seven **p** of the birds of the air also,
Isa 21: 7 When he sees riders, horsemen in **p**,
21: 9 Look, there they come, riders, horsemen in **p**!"
Lk 10: 1 and sent them on ahead of him in **p** to every town
Sir 33:15 they come in **p**, one the opposite of the other.
42:24 All things come in **p**, one opposite the other,

PALACE‡ (72) [PALACES, PALATIAL]

Ex 8: 3 they shall come up into your **p**,
1Ki 4: 6 Ahishar was in charge of the **p**;
16: 9 who was in charge of the **p** at Tirzah,
18: 3 who was in charge of the **p**.
21: 1 beside the **p** of King Ahab of Samaria.
2Ki 10: 5 the steward of the **p**, and the governor of the city,
11: 6 at the gate behind the guards), shall guard the **p**;
15: 5 Jotham the king's son was in charge of the **p**,
15:25 in the citadel of the **p** along with Argob and Arieh;
16:18 on the sabbath that had been built inside the **p**,
18:18 who was in charge of the **p**,
18:37 who was in charge of the **p**,
19: 2 And he sent Eliakim, who was in charge of the **p**,
20:18 be eunuchs in the **p** of the king of Babylon."
24:12 his servants, his officers, and his **p** officials.
1Ch 28: 1 together with the **p** officials, the mighty warriors,
2Ch 2: 1 and a royal **p** for himself.
2:12 and a royal **p** for himself.
26:21 His son Jotham was in charge of the **p** of the king,
28: 7 Azrikam the commander of the **p**,
36: 7 of the LORD to Babylon and put them in his **p**
Ezr 4:14 Now because we share the salt of the **p** and it is
Est 1: 5 in the court of the garden of the king's **p**.
1: 8 the officials of his **p** to do as each one desired.
1: 9 for the women in the **p** of King Ahasuerus.
2: 8 also was taken into the king's **p** and put in custody
2: 9 and with seven chosen maids from the king's **p**,
2:13 to take with her from the harem to the king's **p**.
2:16 to King Ahasuerus in his royal **p** in
4:13 in the king's **p** you will escape any more than all
5: 1 and stood in the inner court of the king's **p**,
5: 1 inside the **p** opposite the entrance to the **p**.
6: 4 the outer court of the king's **p** to speak to the king
7: 7 from the feast in wrath and went into the **p** garden,
7: 8 When the king returned from the **p** garden to
Ps 45:15 and gladness they are led along as they enter the **p**
144:12 cut for the building of a **p**.
Isa 25: 2 the **p** of aliens is a city no more,
32:14 the **p** will be forsaken, the populous city deserted;
36: 3 who was in charge of the **p**,
36:22 who was in charge of the **p**,
37: 2 And he sent Eliakim, who was in charge of the **p**,
39: 7 be eunuchs in the **p** of the king of Babylon."
Jer 32: 2 of the guard that was in the **p** of the king of Judah,
43: 9 at the entrance to Pharaoh's **p** in Tahpanhes.
Da 1: 3 Then the king commanded his **p** master Ashpenaz
1: 4 and competent to serve in the king's **p**;
1: 7 The **p** master gave them other names:
1: 8 the **p** master to allow him not to defile himself.
1: 9 and compassion from the **p** master.
1:10 The **p** master said to Daniel,
1:11 the guard whom the **p** master had appointed
1:18 the **p** master brought them into the presence
4: 4 at ease in my home and prospering in my **p**.
4:29 on the roof of the royal **p** of Babylon,
5: 5 on the plaster of the wall of the royal **p**,
6:18 the king went to his **p** and spent the night fasting;
Na 2: 6 The river gates are opened, the **p** trembles.
Mt 26: 3 of the people gathered in the **p** of the high priest,
Mk 15:16 soldiers led him into the courtyard of the **p** (that is,
Jdt 2: 1 there was talk in the **p** of Nebuchadnezzar,
2:18 a huge amount of gold and silver from the royal **p**.
11:23 the **p** of King Nebuchadnezzar and be renowned
12:13 of the Assyrian women who serve in the **p**
AdE 1: 5 for six days in the courtyard of the royal **p**,
1: 9 the women in the **p** where King Artaxerxes was.
2: 9 as well as seven maids chosen from the **p**;
2:13 and goes with him from the harem to the king's **p**.
LtJ 6:59 better also a wooden pillar in a **p**,
1Mc 7: 2 As he was entering the royal **p** of his ancestors,
11:46 But the king fled into the **p**.

PALACES‡ (14) [PALACE]

2Ch 36:19 burned all its **p** with fire,
Ps 45: 8 From ivory **p** stringed instruments make you glad;
Pr 30:28 yet it is found in kings' **p**.
Isa 13:22 and jackals in the pleasant **p**;
23:13 they tore down her **p**, they made her a ruin.
Jer 6: 5 "Up, and let us attack by night, and destroy her **p**!"
9:21 into our windows, it has entered our **p**, to cut off
17:27 it shall devour the **p** of Jerusalem and shall not
La 2: 5 He has destroyed all its **p**,
2: 7 into the hand of the enemy the walls of her **p**;
Hos 8:14 Israel has forgotten his Maker, and built **p**;
Mt 11: 8 Look, those who wear soft robes are in royal **p**.
Lk 7:25 on fine clothing and live in luxury are in royal **p**.
1Mc 2:10 not inherited her **p** and has not seized her spoils?

PALAL (1)

Ne 3:25 **P** son of Uzai repaired opposite the Angle and

PALANQUIN (1)

SS 3: 9 King Solomon made himself a **p** from the wood

PALATE‡ (3)

Job 12:11 Does not the ear test words as the **p** tastes food?
34: 3 for the ear tests words as the **p** tastes food.
Sir 36:24 As the **p** tastes the kinds of game,

PALATIAL (1) [PALACE]

Da 11:45 He shall pitch his **p** tents between the sea and

PALE (12)

Isa 19: 9 and the carders and those at the loom will grow **p**.
29:22 no longer shall his face grow **p**.
Jer 30: 6 Why has every face turned **p**?
Da 5: 6 Then the king's face turned **p**,
5: 9 became greatly terrified and his face turned **p**,
5:10 let your thoughts terrify you or your face grow **p**.
7:28 greatly terrified me, and my face turned **p**;
10: 8 and my complexion grew deathly **p**,

Joel 2: 6 them peoples are in anguish, all faces grow **p**.
Na 2:10 all loins quake, all faces grow **p!**
Rev 6: 8 I looked and there was a **p** green horse!
AdE 15: 7 The queen faltered, and turned **p** and faint,

PALESTINA, PALESTINE (KJV) See PHILISTIA

PALL (1)
Wis 11:18 or belch forth a thick **p** of smoke,

PALLU (5) [PALLUITES]
Ge 46: 9 Hanoch, **P**, Hezron, and Carmi.
Ex 6:14 Hanoch, **P**, Hezron, and Carmi;
Nu 26: 5 of **P**, the clan of the Palluites;
26: 8 And the descendants of **P**: Eliab.
1Ch 5: 3 Hanoch, **P**, Hezron, and Carmi.

PALLUITES (1) [PALLU]
Nu 26: 5 of Pallu, the clan of the **P**;

PALM (43) [PALMS]
Ex 15:27 of water and seventy **p** trees;
Lev 14:15 of oil and pour it into the **p** of his own left hand,
14:26 The priest shall pour some of the oil into the **p**
23:40 branches of **p** trees, boughs of leafy trees,
Nu 24: 6 Like **p** groves that stretch far away,
33: 9 of water and seventy **p** trees,
Dt 34: 3 that is, the valley of Jericho, the city of **p** trees—
Jdg 4: 5 the **p** of Deborah between Ramah and Bethel in
1Ki 6:29 **p** trees, and open flowers,
6:32 **p** trees, and open flowers;
6:32 spread gold on the cherubim and on the **p** trees.
6:35 He carved cherubim, **p** trees, and open flowers,
7:36 lions, and **p** trees, where each had space,
2Ch 28:15 to their kindred at Jericho, the city of **p** trees.
Ne 8:15 myrtle, **p**, and other leafy trees to make booths,
Ps 92:12 The righteous flourish like the **p** tree,
SS 7: 7 You are stately as a **p** tree,
7: 8 I say I will climb the **p** tree and lay hold
Isa 9:14 **p** branch and reed in one day—
19:15 Neither head nor tail, **p** branch or reed,
Eze 40:16 and on the pilasters were **p** trees.
40:22 and its **p** trees were of the same size as those of
40:26 It had **p** trees on its pilasters, one on either side.
40:31 and **p** trees were on its pilasters,
40:34 and it had **p** trees on its pilasters, on either side;
40:37 and it had **p** trees on its pilasters, on either side;
41:18 It was formed of cherubim and **p** trees,
41:18 a **p** tree between cherub and cherub.
41:19 a human face turned toward the **p** tree on
41:19 the face of a young lion turned toward the **p** tree
41:20 cherubim and **p** trees were carved on the wall.
41:25 the nave were carved cherubim and **p** trees, such
41:26 And there were recessed windows and **p** trees on
Hos 9:13 Once I saw Ephraim as a young **p** planted in
Joel 1:12 Pomegranate, **p**, and apple—
Jn 12:13 So they took branches of **p** trees and went out
Rev 7: 9 robed in white, with **p** branches in their hands.
Sir 24:14 I grew tall like a **p** tree in En-gedi,
50:12 on Lebanon surrounded by the trunks of **p** trees.
1Mc 13:37 We have received the gold crown and the **p** branch
13:51 the Jews entered it with praise and **p** branches,
2Mc 10: 7 and beautiful branches and also fronds of **p**,
14: 4 presenting to him a crown of gold and a **p**,

PALMERWORM (KJV) See [SWARMING] LOCUST

PALMS (12) [PALM]
Ex 29:24 these on the **p** of Aaron and on the **p** of his sons,
Lev 8:27 these on the **p** of Aaron and on the **p** of his sons,
Nu 6:19 and shall put them in the **p** of the nazirites,
Jdg 1:16 up with the people of Judah from the city of **p** into
3:13 and they took possession of the city of **p**.
2Ki 9:35 the skull and the feet and the **p** of her hands.
2Ch 3: 5 and made **p** and chains on it.
Isa 49:16 See, I have inscribed you on the **p** of my hands;
2Es 2:45 Now they are being crowned, and receive **p**."
2:46 on them and putting **p** in their hands?"

PALSY (KJV) See PARALYTIC, PARALYZED

PALTI (2)
Nu 13: 9 from the tribe of Benjamin, **P** son of Raphu;
1Sa 25:44 to **P** son of Laish, who was from Gallim.

PALTIEL (2)
Nu 34:26 Of the tribe of the Issacharites a leader, **P** son
2Sa 3:15 and took her from her husband **P** the son of Laish.

PALTITE (1)
2Sa 23:26 Helez the **P**; Ira son of Ikkesh of Tekoa;

PALTRY (1)
Wis 10: 4 steering the righteous man by a **p** piece of wood.

PAMPER (1) [PAMPERED]
Sir 30: 9 **P** a child, and he will terrorize you;

PAMPERED (3) [PAMPER]
Pr 29:21 A slave **p** from childhood will come to a bad end.
Mic 1:16 and cut off your hair for your **p** children;
Bar 4:26 My **p** children have traveled rough roads;

PAMPHYLIA (6)
Ac 2:10 and **P**, Egypt and the parts of Libya belonging
13:13 from Paphos and came to Perga in **P**.
14:24 Then they passed through Pisidia and came to **P**.
15:38 to take with them one who had deserted them in **P**
27: 5 across the sea that is off Cilicia and **P**,
1Mc 15:23 and to **P**, and to Lycia, and to Halicarnassus,

PAN (6) [FIREPANS, PANS]
Lev 2: 7 If your offering is grain prepared in a **p**,
7: 9 and all that is prepared in a **p** or on a griddle,
1Sa 2:14 and he would thrust it into the **p**, or kettle,
2Sa 13: 9 Then she took the **p** and set them out before him,
2Mc 7: 5 still breathing, and to fry him in a **p**.
7: 5 The smoke from the **p** spread widely,

PANELED (3) [PANELING, PANELS]
Eze 41:16 were **p**, and, all around, all three had windows
41:16 the threshold the temple was **p** with wood all
Hag 1: 4 a time for you yourselves to live in your **p** houses,

PANELING (1) [PANELED]
Jer 22:14 and who cuts out windows for it, **p** it with cedar,

PANELS (4) [PANELED]
1Ki 7:24 Under its brim were **p** all around it,
7:24 there were two rows of **p**, cast when it was cast.
2Ch 4: 3 Under it were **p** all around, each of ten cubits,
4: 3 there were two rows of **p**, cast when it was cast.

PANGS (22)
Ge 3:16 "I will greatly increase your **p** in childbearing;
Ex 15:14 **p** seized the inhabitants of Philistia.
1Sa 25:31 of grief, or **p** of conscience, for having shed blood
Ps 116: 3 the **p** of Sheol laid hold on me;
Isa 13: 8 **P** and agony will seize them;
21: 3 **p** have seized me, like the **p** of a woman in labor;
26:17 and cries out in her **p** when she is near her time,
Jer 13:21 Will not **p** take hold of you,
22:23 how you will groan when **p** come upon you,
Hos 13:13 The **p** of childbirth come for him,
Mic 4: 9 that **p** have seized you like a woman in labor?
Mt 24: 8 all this is but the beginning of the birth **p**.
Mk 13: 8 This is but the beginning of the birth **p**.
Gal 4:27 you who endure no birth **p**;
Rev 12: 2 She was pregnant and was crying out in birth **p**,
Sir 7:27 and do not forget the birth **p** of your mother.
19:11 the fool suffers birth **p** like a woman in labor with
2Es 4:42 in labor makes haste to escape the **p** of birth,
4Mc 15: 4 because of their birth **p** have a deeper sympathy
15:16 even the birth **p** you suffered for them!
16: 8 In vain, my sons, I endured many birth **p** for you,

PANIC (26) [PANIC-STRICKEN]
Ex 14:24 and threw the Egyptian army into **p**.
Dt 7:23 and throw them into great **p**,
20: 3 Do not lose heart, or be afraid, or **p**,
28:20 The LORD will send upon you disaster, **p**,
Jos 10:10 And the LORD threw them into a **p** before Israel,
Jdg 4:15 and all his chariots and all his army into a **p**
8:12 and threw all the army into a **p**.
1Sa 5: 9 against the city, causing a very great **p**;
5:11 there was a deathly **p** throughout the whole city.
14:15 There was a **p** in the camp, in the field,
14:15 and it became a very great **p**.
2Sa 17: 2 and throw him into a **p**;
Ps 48: 5 they were in **p**, they took to flight;
Pr 1:26 I will mock when **p** strikes you,
1:27 when **p** strikes you like a storm,
3:25 Do not be afraid of sudden **p**,
Isa 28:16 "One who trusts will not **p**."
31: 9 and his officers desert the standard in **p**,"
Jer 30: 5 We have heard a cry of **p**, of terror, and no peace.
49:24 she turned to flee, and **p** seized her;
51:32 and the soldiers are in **p**.
La 3:47 **p** and pitfall have come upon us,
Zec 12: 4 says the LORD, I will strike every horse with **p**,
14:13 On that day a great **p** from the LORD shall fall
Jdt 14: 3 Then **p** will come over them,
Sir 21: 4 **P** and insolence will waste away riches;

PANIC-STRICKEN (1) [PANIC]
3Mc 2:23 **p** in their exceedingly great fear.

PANNAG (KJV) See MILLET

PANS (2) [PAN]
2Ch 35:13 the holy offerings in pots, in caldrons, and in **p**,
2Mc 7: 3 and gave orders to have **p** and caldrons heated.

PANT (4)
Job 5: 5 and the thirsty **p** after their wealth.
Ps 119:131 With open mouth I **p**, because I long
Isa 42:14 like a woman in labor, I will gasp and **p**.
Jer 14: 6 they **p** for air like jackals;

PANTED, PANTETH (KJV) See LONGS, PANT, REELS, THROBS

PAPER (3)
2Jn 1:12 I would rather not use **p** and ink;
3Mc 4:20 and proved that both the **p** and the pens they used
2Es 15: 2 and cause them to be written on **p**;

PAPHOS (2)
Ac 13: 6 through the whole island as far as **P**,
13:13 Then Paul and his companions set sail from **P**

PAPYRUS (3)
Ex 2: 3 a **p** basket for him, and plastered it with bitumen
Job 8:11 "Can **p** grow where there is no marsh?
Isa 18: 2 sending ambassadors by the Nile in vessels of **p**

PARABLE‡ (31) [PARABLES]
Ps 78: 2 I will open my mouth in a **p**;
Mt 13:18 "Hear then the **p** of the sower.
13:24 He put before them another **p**:
13:31 He put before them another **p**:
13:33 He told them another **p**: "The kingdom of heaven
13:34 without a **p** he told them nothing.
13:36 "Explain to us the **p** of the weeds of the field."
15:15 But Peter said to him, "Explain this **p** to us."
21:33 "Listen to another **p**. There was a landowner who
Mk 4:13 he said to them, "Do you not understand this **p**?
4:30 or what **p** will we use for it?
7:17 his disciples asked him about the **p**.
12:12 they realized that he had told this **p** against them,
Lk 5:36 He also told them a **p**:
6:39 He also told them a **p**:
8: 4 from town after town came to him, he said in a **p**:
8: 9 Then his disciples asked him what this **p** meant.
8:11 "Now the **p** is this: The seed is the word of God.
12:16 Then he told them a **p**:
12:41 are you telling this **p** for us or for everyone?"
13: 6 Then he told this **p**: "A man had a fig tree planted
14: 7 the places of honor, he told them a **p**.
15: 3 So he told them this **p**:
18: 1 a **p** about their need to pray always and not
18: 9 also told this **p** to some who trusted in themselves
19:11 they were listening to this, he went on to tell a **p**,
20: 9 He began to tell the people this **p**:
20:19 and chief priests realized that he had told this **p**
21:29 Then he told them a **p**:
2Es 4:47 and I will show you the interpretation of a **p**."
8: 2 But I tell you a **p**, Ezra.

PARABLES‡ (20) [PARABLE]
Mt 13: 3 he told them many things in **p**, saying: "Listen!
13:10 "Why do you speak to them in **p**?"
13:13 to them in **p** is that 'seeing they do not perceive,
13:34 Jesus told the crowds all these things in **p**;
13:35 "I will open my mouth to speak in **p**;
13:53 Jesus had finished these **p**, he left that place.
21:45 the chief priests and the Pharisees heard his **p**,
22: 1 Once more Jesus spoke to them in **p**, saying:
Mk 3:23 he called them to him, and spoke to them in **p**,
4: 2 He began to teach them many things in **p**,
4:10 along with the twelve asked him about the **p**.
4:11 but for those outside, everything comes in **p**;
4:13 Then how will you understand all the **p**?
4:33 With many such **p** he spoke the word to them,
4:34 he did not speak to them except in **p**,
12: 1 Then he began to speak to them in **p**.
Lk 8:10 but to others I speak in **p**,
Sir 39: 2 of the famous and penetrates the subtleties of **p**;
39: 3 and is at home with the obscurities of **p**.
47:17 Your songs, proverbs, and **p**,

PARADE (2) [PARADED]
Sir 42:12 Do not let her **p** her beauty before any man,
2Mc 5:25 he ordered his troops to **p** under arms.

PARADED (1) [PARADE]
2Mc 6:10 They publicly **p** them around the city,

PARADISE (8)
Lk 23:43 "Truly I tell you, today you will be with me in **P**."
2Co 12: 4 was caught up into **P** and heard things that are not
Rev 2: 7 to eat from the tree of life that is in the **p** of God.
2Es 4: 7 or which are the entrances of **p**?'
6: 2 and before the foundations of **p** were laid,
7:*36* and opposite it the **p** of delight.
7:*123* [53] Or that a **p** shall be revealed,
8:52 because it is for you that **p** is opened,

PARADOXICAL (1)
4Mc 2:14 Do not consider it **p** when reason, through the law,

PARAH‡ (1)
Jos 18:23 Avvim, **P**, Ophrah,

PARALLEL (2)
Eze 42: 7 There was a wall outside **p** to the chambers,
48:21 to the west border, **p** to the tribal portions,

PARALYTIC (6) [PARALYZED]
Mt 9: 2 When Jesus saw their faith, he said to the **p**,
9: 6 he then said to the **p**—"Stand up, take your bed
Mk 2: 4 they let down the mat on which the **p** lay.
2: 5 When Jesus saw their faith, he said to the **p**, "Son,
2: 9 Which is easier, to say to the **p**,
2:10 on earth to forgive sins"—he said to the **p**—

PARALYTICS (1) [PARALYZED]
Mt 4:24 demoniacs, epileptics, and **p**, and he cured them.

PARALYZED (13) [PARALYTIC, PARALYTICS]
Mt 8: 6 my servant is lying at home **p**, in terrible distress."
9: 2 then some people were carrying a **p** man lying on
Mk 2: 3 Then some people came, bringing to him a **p** man,
Lk 5:18 carrying a **p** man on a bed.
5:24 he said to the one who was **p**—
Jn 5: 3 In these lay many invalids—blind, lame, and **p**.
Ac 8: 7 and many others who were **p** or lame were cured.
9:33 for eight years, for he was **p**.
Wis 17:15 and now were **p** by their souls' surrender;
17:19 a hollow of the mountains, it **p** them with terror.
1Mc 9:55 his mouth was stopped and he was **p**,
3Mc 2:22 besides being **p** in his limbs,
4Mc 11:24 We six boys have **p** your tyranny.

PARAMOURS (1)
Eze 23:20 and lusted after her **p** there,

PARAN (11) [EL-PARAN]
Ge 21:21 He lived in the wilderness of **P**;
Nu 10:12 and the cloud settled down in the wilderness of **P**.
12:16 and camped in the wilderness of **P**.
13: 3 So Moses sent them from the wilderness of **P**,
13:26 of the Israelites in the wilderness of **P**, at Kadesh;
Dt 1: 1 between **P** and Tophel, Laban, Hazeroth,
33: 2 he shone forth from Mount **P**.
1Sa 25: 1 up and went down to the wilderness of **P**.
1Ki 11:18 They set out from Midian and came to **P**;
11:18 they took people with them from **P** and came
Hab 3: 3 the Holy One from Mount **P**.

PARAPET (2)
Dt 22: 8 you shall make a **p** for your roof;
Jdt 14: 1 Take this head and hang it upon the **p**

PARAS (1)
Eze 27:10 **P** and Lud and Put were in your army,

PARAZ See Index to Footnotes

PARBAR (KJV) See COLONNADE; See also Index to Footnotes

PARCEL (1) [PARCELED, PARCELS]
Ru 4: 3 is selling the **p** of land that belonged

PARCELED (1) [PARCEL]
Am 7:17 and your land shall be **p** out by line;

PARCELS (1) [PARCEL]
Mic 2: 4 Among our captors he **p** out our fields."

PARCHED‡ (20) [PARCHES]
Lev 2:14 from fresh ears, **p** with fire.
23:14 You shall eat no bread or **p** grain or fresh ears
Jos 5:11 unleavened cakes and **p** grain.
Ru 2:14 and he heaped up for her some **p** grain.
1Sa 17:17 "Take for your brothers an ephah of this **p** grain
25:18 five sheep ready dressed, five measures of **p** grain,
2Sa 17:28 and earthen vessels, wheat, barley, meal, **p** grain,
Ps 68: 6 but the rebellious live in a **p** land.
69: 3 I am weary with my crying; my throat is **p**.
107:35 a **p** land into springs of water.
143: 6 my soul thirsts for you like a **p** land.
Isa 5:13 and their multitude is **p** with thirst.
19: 5 and the river will be **p** and dry;
41:17 and there is none, and their tongue is **p** with thirst,
58:11 and satisfy your needs in **p** places,
Jer 17: 6 They shall live in the **p** places of the wilderness,
48:18 Come down from glory, and sit on the **p** ground,
Hos 2: 3 and turn her into a **p** land, and kill her with thirst.
13:15 and his fountain shall dry up, his spring shall be **p**.
Joel 2:20 and drive it into a **p** and desolate land,

PARCHES (1) [PARCHED]
Sir 43: 3 At noon it **p** the land,

PARCHMENTS (1)
2Ti 4:13 also the books, and above all the **p**.

PARDON (20) [PARDONED, PARDONING]
Ex 23:21 for he will not **p** your transgression;
34: 9 **p** our iniquity and our sin,
Dt 29:20 the LORD will be unwilling to **p** them,
1Sa 15:25 Now therefore, I pray, **p** my sin,
2Ki 5:18 But may the LORD **p** your servant on one count:
5:18 may the LORD **p** your servant on this one count."
24: 4 and the LORD was not willing to **p**.
2Ch 30:18 for them, saying, "The good LORD **p** all
Job 7:21 Why do you not **p** my transgression
Ps 25:11 For your name's sake, O LORD, **p** my guilt,
Isa 55: 7 and to our God, for he will abundantly **p**.
Jer 5: 1 so that I may **p** Jerusalem.
5: 7 How can I **p** you?
50:20 for I will **p** the remnant that I have spared.
Wis 18: 2 and they begged their **p** for having been
Sir 28: 4 can he then seek **p** for his own sins?
39: 5 he opens his mouth in prayer and asks **p**
1Mc 13:39 We **p** any errors and offenses committed
3Mc 6:27 begging **p** for your former actions!
2Es 7:*139* [69] if he did not **p** those who were created by his

PARDONED (4) [PARDON]
Nu 14:19 just as you have **p** this people,
Ps 85: 2 of your people; you **p** all their sin.
Wis 6: 6 For the lowliest may be **p** in mercy,
Sir 28: 2 and then your sins will be **p** when you pray.

PARDONING (1) [PARDON]
Mic 7:18 **p** iniquity and passing over the transgression of

PARE (1)
Dt 21:12 she shall shave her head, **p** her nails,

PARENT (10) [GRANDPARENTS, PARENT'S, PARENTAL, PARENTS, PARENTS-IN-LAW]
Dt 8: 5 then in your heart that as a **p** disciplines a child so
Pr 17:21 the **p** of a fool has no joy.
27:10 not forsake your friend or the friend of your **p**;
29: 3 A child who loves wisdom makes a **p** glad,
Eze 18: 4 life of the **p** as well as the life of the child is mine:
18:20 A child shall not suffer for the iniquity of a **p**,
18:20 nor a **p** suffer for the iniquity of a child;
Heb 12: 7 what child is there whom a **p** does not discipline?
1Jn 5: 1 and everyone who loves the **p** loves the child.
Wis 11:10 For you tested them as a **p** does in warning,

PARENT'S (1) [PARENT]
Pr 15: 5 A fool despises a **p** instruction,

PARENTAL (5) [PARENT]
4Mc 14:14 have a sympathy and **p** love for their offspring.
15:13 O sacred nature and affection of **p** love,
15:23 to disregard, for the time, her **p** love.
15:25 family, **p** love, and the rackings of her children—
16: 3 as was her innate **p** love,

PARENTS‡ (74) [PARENT]
Ex 10: 6 something that neither your **p**
20: 5 punishing children for the iniquity of **p**,
34: 7 but visiting the iniquity of the **p** upon the children
Nu 14:18 the iniquity of the **p** upon the children to the third
Dt 5: 9 punishing children for the iniquity of **p**,
24:16 **P** shall not be put to death for their children, nor shall children be put to death for their **p**;
Jos 4:21 "When your children ask their **p** in time to come,
2Ki 14: 6 "The **p** shall not be put to death for the children, or the children be put to death for the **p**;
2Ch 25: 4 "The **p** shall not be put to death for the children, or the children be put to death for the **p**;
Pr 17: 6 and the glory of children is their **p**.
19:14 House and wealth are inherited from **p**,
28: 7 but companions of gluttons shame their **p**.
Ecc 5:14 though they are **p** of children,
Jer 6:21 **p** and children together, neighbor and friend shall
13:14 **p** and children together, says the LORD.
31:29 "The **p** have eaten sour grapes,
32:18 of **p** into the laps of their children after them,
47: 3 **p** do not turn back for children,
Eze 5:10 Surely, **p** shall eat their children in your midst, and children shall eat their **p**;
18: 2 'The **p** have eaten sour grapes,
20:18 Do not follow the statutes of your **p**,
Mal 3:17 as **p** spare their children who serve them.
4: 6 He will turn the hearts of **p** to their children and the hearts of children to their **p**,
Mt 10:21 and children will rise against **p** and have them put
Mk 13:12 and children will rise against **p** and have them put
Lk 1:17 to turn the hearts of **p** to their children,
2:27 and when the **p** brought in the child Jesus,
2:41 Now every year his **p** went to Jerusalem for
2:43 but his **p** did not know it.
2:48 When his **p** saw him they were astonished;
8:56 Her **p** were astounded;
18:29 or wife or brothers or **p** or children,
21:16 You will be betrayed even by **p** and brothers,
Jn 9: 2 this man or his **p**, that he was born blind?"
9: 3 "Neither this man nor his **p** sinned;
9:18 and had received his sight until they called the **p**
9:20 His **p** answered, "We know that this is our son,
9:22 His **p** said this because they were afraid of
9:23 Therefore his **p** said, "He is of age; ask him."
Ro 1:30 boastful, inventors of evil, rebellious toward **p**,
2Co 12:14 not to lay up for their **p**, but **p** for their children.
Eph 6: 1 Children, obey your **p** in the Lord, for this is right.
Col 3:20 Children, obey your **p** in everything,
1Ti 5: 4 and make some repayment to their **p**;
2Ti 3: 2 abusive, disobedient to their **p**, ungrateful, unholy,
Heb 11:23 by his **p** for three months after his birth,
12: 9 Moreover, we had human **p** to discipline us,
Tob 8: 4 the **p** had gone out and shut the door of the room,
10:12 as much your **p** as those who gave you birth.
AdE 2: 7 When her **p** died, he brought her up
Wis 4: 6 of evil against their **p** when God examines them.
12: 6 these **p** who murder helpless lives,
Sir 3: 7 they will serve their **p** as their masters.
7:28 Remember that it was of your **p** you were born;
8: 9 for they themselves learned from their **p**;
48:10 to turn the hearts of **p** to their children,
Sus 1: 3 Her **p** were righteous,
1:30 And she came with her **p**, her children,
1Mc 10: 9 and he returned them to their **p**.
2Mc 12:24 because he held the **p** of most of them,
3Mc 5:31 "If your **p** or children were present,
5:49 **p** and children, mothers and daughters,
6:14 of infants and their **p** entreat you with tears.
2Es 1: 6 that the sins of their **p** have increased in them,
7:*103* fathers for sons or sons for **p**,
4Mc 2:10 For the law prevails even over affection for **p**,
15: 4 the emotions of **p** who love their children?
15:13 yearning of **p** toward offspring,

PARENTS-IN-LAW (1) [PARENT]
Tob 14:13 He treated his **p** with great respect in their old age,

PARKS (1)
Ecc 2: 5 I made myself gardens and **p**,

PARMASHTA (1)
Est 9: 9 **P**, Arisai, Aridai, Vaizatha,

PARMENAS (1)
Ac 6: 5 Timon, **P**, and Nicolaus, a proselyte of Antioch.

PARNACH (1)
Nu 34:25 of the Zebulunites a leader, Eli-zaphan son of **P**.

PAROSH (9)
Ezr 2: 3 of **P**, two thousand one hundred seventy-two.
8: 3 Of **P**, Zechariah, with whom were registered
10:25 And of Israel: of the descendants of **P**:
Ne 3:25 After him Pedaiah son of **P**
7: 8 of **P**, two thousand one hundred seventy-two.
10:14 The leaders of the people: **P**, Pahath-moab, Elam,
1Es 5: 9 and their leaders: the descendants of **P**,
8:30 Of the descendants of **P**, Zechariah,
9:26 Of Israel: of the descendants of **P**:

PARSHANDATHA (1)
Est 9: 7 They killed **P**, Dalphon, Aspatha,

PARSIN‡ (1) [PERES]
Da 5:25 that was inscribed: MENE, MENE, TEKEL, and **P**.

PART‡ (102) [APART, PARTED, PARTIAL, PARTING, PARTLY, PARTS]
Ge 4: 4 Abel for his **p** brought of the firstlings of his flock,
6:17 For my **p**, I am going to bring a flood of waters on
27:16 on his hands and on the smooth **p** of his neck.
47: 6 settle your father and your brothers in the best **p** of
47:11 in the best **p** of the land, in the land of Rameses,
50:11 a grievous mourning on the **p** of the Egyptians."
Ex 16:20 some left **p** of it until morning,
26:12 The **p** that remains of the curtains of the tent,
28:27 in front to the lower **p** of the two shoulder-pieces
30:34 sweet spices with pure frankincense (an equal **p**
30:36 and put **p** of it before the covenant in the tent
39:20 in front to the lower **p** of the two shoulder-pieces
Lev 2: 3 most holy **p** of the offerings by fire to the LORD.
2:10 it is a most holy **p** of the offerings by fire to
6:27 you shall wash the bespattered **p** in a holy place.
10:18 not brought into the inner **p** of the sanctuary.
11:25 and whoever carries any **p** of the carcass of any
11:35 on which any **p** of their carcass falls shall
11:37 If any **p** of their carcass falls
11:38 on the seed and any **p** of their carcass falls on it,
27:22 which is not a **p** of the inherited landholding,
Nu 18:29 the best of all of them is the **p** to be consecrated.
22:41 from there he could see **p** of the people of Israel.
23:13 you shall see only **p** of them,
Jos 9: 4 they on their **p** acted with cunning:
19: 9 The inheritance of the tribe of Simeon formed **p** of
Jdg 2: 2 For your **p**, do not make a covenant with
Ru 2: 3 she came to the **p** of the field belonging to Boaz,
1Sa 23:20 and our **p** will be to surrender him into
30:26 he sent **p** of the spoil to his friends,
2Sa 3:37 that the king had no **p** in the killing of Abner son
14: 6 there was no one to **p** them,
1Ki 6:19 in the innermost **p** of the house,
6:27 the cherubim in the innermost **p** of the house;
7:50 the sockets for the doors of the innermost **p** of
2Ki 18:23 if you are able on your **p** to set riders on them.
2Ch 29:16 The priests went into the inner **p** of the house of
Ezr 4: 3 "You shall have no **p** with us in building a house
Ne 9: 3 of the LORD their God for a fourth **p** of the day,
Pr 20:27 searching every inmost **p**.
Isa 6:13 Even if a tenth **p** remain in it,
36: 8 if you are able on your **p** to set riders on them.
44:15 **P** of it he takes and warms himself;
Jer 1:18 I for my **p** have made you today a fortified city,

Eze 41:11 the **p** that was left free was five cubits all around.
Da 2:42 As the toes of the feet were **p** iron and **p** clay,
11:41 and the main **p** of the Ammonites shall escape
Am 3:12 with the corner of a couch and **p** of a bed.
Mt 23:30 we would not have taken **p** with them in shedding
24:43 if the owner of the house had known in what **p** of
Lk 10:42 Mary has chosen the better **p,**
11:36 with no **p** of it in darkness,
Jn 2:24 Jesus on his **p** would not entrust himself to them,
Ac 5: 2 brought only a **p** and laid it at the apostles' feet.
5: 3 the Holy Spirit and to keep back **p** of the proceeds
6: 4 for our **p,** will devote ourselves to prayer and
8:21 You have no **p** or share in this,
Ro 9:14 Is there injustice on God's **p?**
11:16 If the **p** of the dough offered as first fruits is holy,
11:25 a hardening has come upon **p** of Israel,
1Co 12:15 that would not make it any less a **p** of the body.
12:16 that would not make it any less a **p** of the body.
13: 9 we know only in **p,** and we prophesy only in **p;**
13:12 Now I know only in **p;**
2Co 1:14 as you have already understood us in **p—**
8: 2 in a wealth of generosity on their **p.**
Eph 4:16 as each **p** is working properly,
5:11 Take no **p** in the unfruitful works of darkness,
Rev 2: 9 the **p** of those who say that they are Jews and are
18: 4 my people, so that you do not take **p** in her sins,
Tob 5: 3 we each took one **p,** and I put one with the money.
AdE 14: 2 every **p** that she loved to adorn she covered
16: 5 of authority have been made in **p** responsible for
Wis 14:11 because, though **p** of what God created,
Sus 1:46 "I want no **p** in shedding this woman's blood!"
1Mc 6:40 Now a **p** of the king's army was spread out on
10:33 from the land of Judah into any **p** of my kingdom,
12:23 we on our **p** write to you that your livestock
12:37 **p** of the wall on the valley to the east had fallen,
2Mc 4:14 they hurried to take **p** in the unlawful proceedings
7:26 After much urging on his **p,**
14:22 to prevent sudden treachery on the **p** of the enemy;
3Mc 7: 6 always taking their **p** as a father does
2Es 4:45 or whether for us the greater **p** has gone by.
4:52 I can tell you in **p;**
5:34 and to search out some **p** of his judgment."
6:12 of which you showed me a **p** on a previous night."
6:41 so that one **p** might move upward and the other **p**
remain beneath.
6:42 to be gathered together in a seventh **p** of the earth;
6:47 "On the fifth day you commanded the seventh **p,**
6:50 from the other, for the seventh **p** where
6:52 to Leviathan you gave the seventh **p,** the watery **p;**
7: 5 how can they come to the broad **p** unless they pass
7: 5 unless they pass through the narrow **p?**
14:12 as well as half of the tenth **p;**
14:12 two of its parts remain, besides half of the tenth **p.**
15:38 and from the north, and another **p** from the west.
15:60 and shall destroy a **p** of your land and abolish

PARTAKE (10) [PARTOOK]

Ezr 2:63 the governor told them that they were not to **p** of
Ne 7:65 the governor told them that they were not to **p** of
1Co 10:17 for we all **p** of the one bread.
10:21 You cannot **p** of the table of the Lord and the table
10:30 If I **p** with thankfulness, why should I
Jdt 12: 2 But Judith said, "I cannot **p** of them,
Wis 16: 3 after suffering want a short time, might **p**
2Mc 6: 7 under bitter constraint, to **p** of the sacrifices;
6: 8 the same policy toward the Jews and make them **p**
7: 1 to **p** of unlawful swine's flesh.

PARTED (7) [PART]

2Ki 2: 8 the water was **p** to the one side and to the other,
2:14 the water was **p** to the one side and to the other,
Ac 15:39 so sharp that they **p** company;
21: 1 When we had **p** from them and set sail,
Tob 10:13 Tobias **p** from Raguel with happiness and joy,
Sus 1:13 So they both left and **p** from each other.
1Mc 6:45 and they **p** before him on both sides.

PARTHIANS (1)

Ac 2: 9 **P,** Medes, Elamites, and residents

PARTIAL (7) [PART]

Ex 23: 3 nor shall you be **p** to the poor in a lawsuit.
Lev 19:15 you shall not be **p** to the poor or defer to the great:
Dt 1:17 You must not be **p** in judging:
10:17 who is not **p** and takes no bribe,
Pr 18: 5 It is not right to be **p** to the guilty,
1Co 13:10 the **p** will come to an end.
Sir 7: 6 you may be **p** to the powerful,

PARTIALITY (25)

Dt 16:19 not distort justice; you must not show **p;**
2Ch 19: 7 or **p,** or taking of bribes."
Job 13: 8 Will you show **p** toward him,
13:10 He will surely rebuke you if in secret you show **p.**
32:21 I will not show **p** to any person or use flattery
34:19 who shows no **p** to nobles,
Ps 82: 2 "How long will you judge unjustly and show **p** to
Pr 24:23 **P** in judging is not good.
28:21 To show **p** is not good—
Mal 2: 9 as you have not kept my ways but have shown **p**
Mt 22:16 for you do not regard people with **p.**
Mk 12:14 for you do not regard people with **p,**
Ac 10:34 "I truly understand that God shows no **p,**
Ro 2:11 For God shows no **p.**
Gal 2: 6 makes no difference to me; God shows no **p)—**
Eph 6: 9 and with him there is no **p.**
Col 3:25 whatever wrong has been done, and there is no **p.**
1Ti 5:21 doing nothing on the basis of **p.**
Jas 2: 9 if you show **p,** you commit sin and are convicted
3:17 without a trace of **p** or hypocrisy.
Sir 4:22 Do not show **p,** to your own harm, or deference,
4:27 or show **p** to a ruler.
35:15 the Lord is the judge, and with him there is no **p.**
35:16 He will not show **p** to the poor;
1Es 4:39 With it there is no **p** or preference,

PARTICIPANTS (2) [PARTICIPATE]

2Pe 1: 4 and may become **p** of the divine nature.
3Mc 3:21 and to make them **p** in our regular religious rites.

PARTICIPATE (2) [PARTICIPANTS, PARTICIPATED]

1Ti 5:22 and do not **p** in the sins of others;
2Jn 1:11 for to welcome is to **p** in the evil deeds of such

PARTICIPATED (1) [PARTICIPATE]

2Mc 5:20 the nation and afterward **p** in its benefits;

PARTICULAR (4)

Nu 4:19 and his sons shall go in and assign each to a **p** task
1Co 7: 7 But each has a **p** gift from God,
Sir 42:23 each creature is preserved to meet a **p** need.
1Mc 1:42 and that all should give up their **p** customs.

PARTIES (4) [PARTY]

Ex 22: 9 the case of both **p** shall come before God;
Dt 19:17 **p** to the dispute shall appear before the LORD,
Eze 18: 8 executes true justice between contending **p,**
1Mc 8:30 both **p** shall determine to add or delete anything,

PARTING (3) [PART]

Jos 22: 9 **p** from the Israelites at Shiloh,
Eze 21:21 For the king of Babylon stands at the **p** of the way,
Mic 1:14 you shall give **p** gifts to Moresheth-gath;

PARTLY (9) [PART]

Da 2:33 its legs of iron, its feet **p** of iron and **p** of clay.
2:41 the feet and toes **p** of potter's clay and **p** of iron,
2:42 so the kingdom shall be **p** strong and **p** brittle.
4Mc 6:12 At that point, **p** out of pity for his old age,
6:13 **p** out of sympathy from their acquaintance with
him, **p** out of admiration for his endurance,

PARTNER (11) [PARTNERS, PARTNERSHIP]

Ge 2:18 I will make him a helper as his **p."**
2:20 for the man there was not found a helper as his **p.**
Pr 2:17 the **p** of her youth and forgets her sacred covenant;
28:24 "That is no crime," is **p** to a thug.
29:24 To be a **p** of a thief is to hate one's own life;
1Co 7:15 But if the unbelieving **p** separates, let it be so;
2Co 8:23 Titus, he is my **p** and co-worker in your service;
Phm 1:17 So if you consider me your **p,**
AdE 16:13 and of Esther, the blameless **p** of our kingdom,
Sir 41:18 of unjust dealing, before your **p** or your friend;
42: 3 a **p** or with traveling companions, and of dividing

PARTNERS‡ (7) [PARTNER]

Lk 5: 7 So they signaled their **p** in the other boat to come
5:10 sons of Zebedee, who were **p** with Simon.
1Co 10:18 are not those who eat the sacrifices **p** in the altar?
10:20 I do not want you to be **p** with demons.
Heb 3: 1 brothers and sisters, holy **p** in a heavenly calling,
3:14 For we have become **p** of Christ,
10:33 and sometimes being **p** with those so treated.

PARTNERSHIP (1) [PARTNER]

2Co 6:14 For what **p** is there between righteousness

PARTOOK (1) [PARTAKE]

Jos 9:14 So the leaders **p** of their provisions,

PARTRIDGE (3)

1Sa 26:20 like one who hunts a **p** in the mountains."
Jer 17:11 Like the **p** hatching what it did not lay,
Sir 11:30 Like a decoy **p** in a cage,

PARTS (56) [PART]

Ex 29:17 Then you shall cut the ram into its **p,**
29:17 and put them with its **p** and its head,
Lev 1: 6 burnt offering shall be flayed and cut up into its **p.**
1: 8 Aaron's sons the priests shall arrange the **p,**
1:12 It shall be cut up into its **p,**
8:20 The ram was cut into its **p,**
8:20 and Moses turned into smoke the head and the **p**
Nu 11: 1 and consumed some outlying **p** of the camp.
31:27 Divide the booty into two **p,**
Jdg 19: 1 in the remote **p** of the hill country of Ephraim,
19:18 to the remote **p** of the hill country of Ephraim,
Ru 1:17 and more as well, if even death **p** me from you!"
1Sa 2:29 by fattening yourselves on the choicest **p**
24: 3 and his men were sitting in the innermost **p** of
1Ki 6:38 the house was finished in all its **p,**
16:21 Then the people of Israel were divided into two **p;**
2Ki 10:32 In those days the LORD began to trim off **p**
2Ch 7: 7 and the grain offering and the fat **p.**
35:14 the burnt offerings and the fat **p** until night;
Ne 4:13 So in the lowest **p** of the space behind the wall,
Job 30:27 My inward **p** are in turmoil, and are never still;
38:36 Who has put wisdom in the inward **p,**
Ps 139:13 For it was you who formed my inward **p;**
Pr 18: 8 they go down into the inner **p** of the body.
20:30 beatings make clean the innermost **p.**
26:22 they go down into the inner **p** of the body.
Isa 3:17 and the LORD will lay bare their secret **p.**
Jer 6:22 a great nation is stirring from the farthest **p** of
25:32 and a great tempest is stirring from the farthest **p**
31: 8 and gather them from the farthest **p** of the earth,
34:18 when they cut it in two and passed between its **p:**
34:19 the people of the land who passed between the **p**
50:41 and many kings are stirring from the farthest **p** of
Eze 32:23 Their graves are set in the uttermost **p** of the Pit.
34:13 and in all the inhabited **p** of the land.
38: 6 Beth-togarmah from the remotest **p** of the north
38:15 and come from your place out of the remotest **p** of
39: 2 and bring you up from the remotest **p** of the north,
Da 11:24 Without warning he shall come into the richest **p**
Am 6:10 and shall say to someone in the innermost **p** of
Jn 19:23 they took his clothes and divided them into four **p,**
Ac 2:10 Egypt and the **p** of Libya belonging to Cyrene,
Eph 4: 9 but that he had also descended into the lower **p** of
Rev 16:19 The great city was split into three **p,**
Tob 8: 3 the demon that he fled to the remotest **p** of Egypt.
13:11 from far away, the inhabitants of the remotest **p** of
1Mc 7:24 Judas went out into all the surrounding **p** of Judea,
9:23 the renegades emerged in all **p** of Israel;
9:62 he rebuilt the **p** of it that had been demolished,
2Mc 8:21 then he divided his army into four **p.**
2Es 6:42 six **p** you dried up and kept so that some
6:51 of the **p** that had been dried up on the third day,
14:11 the age is divided into twelve **p,** and nine of its **p**
14:12 two of its **p** remain, besides half of the tenth part.
4Mc 14:13 toward an emotion felt in her inmost **p.**

PARTY (12) [PARTIES]

Ex 21:18 the other with a stone or fist so that the injured **p,**
22: 9 clothing, or any other loss, of which one **p** says,
Nu 5: 8 If the injured **p** has no next of kin
5: 8 with which atonement is made for the guilty **p.**
1Sa 30:15 "Will you take me down to this raiding **p?"**
30:23 over to us the raiding **p** that attacked us.
Da 11:23 and become strong with a small **p.**
Gal 3:20 Now a mediator involves more than one **p;**
AdE 1: 5 the end of the festivity the king gave a drinking **p**
1: 9 Queen Vashti gave a drinking **p** for the women in
3Mc 5:18 After the **p** had been going on for some time,
5:36 reconvened the **p** in the same manner and urged

PARUAH (1)

1Ki 4:17 Jehoshaphat son of **P,** in Issachar;

PARVAIM (1)

2Ch 3: 6 The gold was gold from **P.**

PAS-DAMMIM (1)

1Ch 11:13 at **P** when the Philistines were gathered there

PASACH (1)

1Ch 7:33 The sons of Japhlet: **P,** Bimhal, and Ashvath.

PASCHAL (1) [PASSOVER]

1Co 5: 7 For our **p** lamb, Christ, has been sacrificed.

PASEAH (4)

1Ch 4:12 Eshton became the father of Beth-rapha, **P,**
Ezr 2:49 Uzza, **P,** Besai,
Ne 3: 6 of **P** and Meshullam son of Besodeiah repaired
7:51 of Gazzam, of Uzza, of **P,**

PASHHUR (16)

1Ch 9:12 son of **P,** son of Malchijah,
Ezr 2:38 Of **P,** one thousand two hundred forty-seven.
10:22 Of the descendants of **P:** Elioenai,
Ne 7:41 Of **P,** one thousand two hundred forty-seven.
10: 3 **P,** Amariah, Malchijah,
11:12 of Zechariah son of **P** son of Malchijah,
Jer 20: 1 Now the priest **P** son of Immer,
20: 2 Then **P** struck the prophet Jeremiah,
20: 3 The next morning when **P** released Jeremiah from
20: 3 The LORD has named you not **P**
20: 6 And you, **P,** and all who live in your house,
21: 1 when King Zedekiah sent to him **P** son
38: 1 Shephatiah son of Mattan, Gedaliah son of **P,**
38: 1 and **P** son of Malchiah heard the words
1Es 5:25 of **P,** one thousand two hundred forty-seven.
9:22 Of the descendants of **P:** Elioenai,

PASS‡ (189) [PASSAGE, PASSAGES, PASSAGEWAY, PASSAGEWAYS, PASSED, PASSER-BY, PASSERS-BY, PASSES, PASSING, PAST]

Ge 18: 3 if I find favor with you, do not **p** by your servant.
18: 5 and after that you may **p** on—
30:32 let me **p** through all your flock today, removing
31:52 that I will not **p** beyond this heap to you,

Ge 31:52 and you will not **p** beyond this heap and this pillar
32:16 and said to his servants, "**P** on ahead of me,
33:14 Let my lord **p** on ahead of his servant,
Ex 12:12 For I will **p** through the land of Egypt that night,
12:13 when I see the blood, I will **p** over you,
12:23 For the LORD will **p** through to strike down
12:23 and on the two doorposts, the LORD will **p** over
26:28 shall **p** through from end to end.
33:19 "I will make all my goodness **p** before you,
36:33 He made the middle bar to **p** through from end
Lev 25:30 a house that is in a walled city shall **p** in perpetuity
Nu 20:17 Now let us **p** through your land.
20:17 We will not **p** through field or vineyard,
20:18 But Edom said to him, "You shall not **p** through,
20:19 just let us **p** through on foot."
20:20 But he said, "You shall not **p** through."
21:22 "Let me **p** through your land;
21:23 not allow Israel to **p** through his territory.
27: 7 among their father's brothers and **p** the inheritance
27: 8 then you shall **p** his inheritance on to his daughter.
Dt 2: 4 about to **p** through the territory of your kindred,
2:27 "If you let me **p** through your land,
2:28 Only allow me to **p** through on foot—
2:30 of Heshbon was not willing to let us **p** through,
18:10 among you who makes a son or daughter **p**
Jos 1:11 "**P** through the camp, and command the people:
3: 6 and **p** on in front of the people."
3:11 the earth is going to **p** before you into the Jordan.
4: 5 "**P** on before the ark of the LORD your God into
6: 7 have the armed men **p** on before the ark of
21:45 of Israel had failed; all came to **p.**
23:14 all have come to **p** for you,
Jdg 11:17 saying, 'Let us **p** through your land';
11:19 'Let us **p** through your land to our country.'
11:20 Sihon did not trust Israel to **p** through his territory;
21: 3 to **p** that today there should be one tribe lacking
1Sa 13:23 the Philistines had gone out to the **p** of Michmash.
14: 4 In the **p,** by which Jonathan tried to go over to
16: 8 and made him **p** before Samuel.
16: 9 Then Jesse made Shammah **p** by.
16:10 Jesse made seven of his sons **p** before Samuel,
1Ki 1:21 Otherwise it will come to **p,**
13:32 in the cities of Samaria, shall surely come to **p.**"
18: 6 So they divided the land between them to **p**
19:11 for the LORD is about to **p** by."
22:24 the spirit of the LORD **p** from me to speak
2Ki 6: 9 "Take care not to **p** this place,
16: 3 He even made his son **p** through fire,
17:17 They made their sons and their daughters **p**
19:25 I planned from days of old what now I bring to **p,**
21: 6 He made his son **p** through fire,
23:10 a daughter **p** through fire as an offering to Molech.
2Ch 18:23 the spirit of the LORD **p** from me to speak
28: 3 and made his sons **p** through fire,
33: 6 He made his son **p** through fire in the valley of
Ne 4:22 and his servant **p** the night inside Jerusalem,
Job 6:15 like a torrent-bed, like freshets that **p** away,
14: 5 you have appointed the bounds that they cannot **p,**
14:20 against them, and they **p** away;
19: 8 He has walled up my way so that I cannot **p,**
34:20 at midnight the people are shaken and **p** away,
Ps 51: 4 and blameless when you **p** judgment.
57: 1 until the destroying storms **p** by.
78:13 He divided the sea and let them **p** through it,
80:12 so that all who **p** along the way pluck its fruit?
89:41 All who **p** by plunder him;
90: 9 For all our days **p** away under your wrath;
102: 3 For my days **p** away like smoke,
102:26 You change them like clothing, and they **p** away;
104: 9 You set a boundary that they may not **p,**
105:19 until what he had said came to **p,**
129: 8 while those who **p** by do not say,
136:14 and made Israel **p** through the midst of it,
Pr 4:15 turn away from it and **p** on.
9:15 calling to those who **p** by,
16:30 one who compresses the lips brings evil to **p.**
Ecc 6:12 which they **p** like a shadow?
Isa 2:18 The idols shall utterly **p** away.
7: 7 It shall not stand, and it shall not come to **p.**
8:21 They will **p** through the land,
10:29 they have crossed over the **p,** at Geba they lodge
14:24 and as I have planned, so shall it come to **p:**
28:19 for morning by morning it will **p** through,
31: 9 His rock shall **p** away in terror,
33:21 with oars can go, nor stately ship can **p.**
34:10 no one shall **p** through it forever and ever.
37:26 I planned from days of old what now I bring to **p,**
42: 9 See, the former things have come to **p,**
43: 2 you **p** through the waters, I will be with you;
46:11 I have spoken, and I will bring it to **p;**
47: 2 uncover your legs, **p** through the rivers.
48: 3 then suddenly I did them and they came to **p.**
48: 5 before they came to **p** I announced them to you,
Jer 5:22 a perpetual barrier that it cannot **p;**
5:22 though they roar, they cannot **p** over it.
6: 9 **p** your hand again over its branches.
18:16 All who **p** by it are horrified
22: 8 And many nations will **p** by this city,
33:13 flocks shall again **p** under the hands of
La 1:12 Is it nothing to you, all you who **p** by?
2:15 All who **p** along the way clap their hands at you;
3:44 with a cloud so that no prayer can **p** through.
4:21 but to you also the cup shall **p;**
Eze 5:14 in the sight of all that **p** by.
5:17 pestilence and bloodshed shall **p** through you;
9: 5 "**P** through the city after him, and kill;
14:15 and no one may **p** through because of the animals;
14:17 'Let a sword **p** through the land,'
20:31 and make your children **p** through the fire,
20:37 I will make you **p** under the staff,
29:11 No human foot shall **p** through it,
29:11 and no animal foot shall **p** through it;
33:28 be so desolate that no one will **p** through.
39:14 They will set apart men to **p** through
39:15 As the searchers **p** through the land,
Da 4:16 And let seven times **p** over him.
4:23 until seven times **p** over him'—
4:25 and seven times shall **p** over you,
4:32 and seven times shall **p** over you,
7:14 an everlasting dominion that shall not **p** away,
11:10 which shall advance like a flood and **p** through,
11:40 He shall advance against countries and **p** through
Joel 1:13 Come, **p** the night in sackcloth,
3:17 and strangers shall never again **p** through it.
Am 5:17 for I will **p** through the midst of you,
6: 7 and the revelry of the loungers shall **p** away.
7: 8 I will never again **p** them by;
8: 2 I will never again **p** them by.
Mic 1:11 **P** on your way, inhabitants of Shaphir,
2: 8 from the peaceful, from those who **p** by trustingly
2:13 they will break through and **p** the gate,
2:13 Their king will **p** on before them,
Na 1:12 they will be cut off and **p** away.
Hag 2:15 consider what will come to **p** from this day on.
Zec 10:11 They shall **p** through the sea of distress,
Mt 5:18 For truly I tell you, until heaven and earth **p** away,
5:18 will **p** from the law until all is accomplished.
8:28 They were so fierce that no one could **p** that way.
24:34 not **p** away until all these things have taken place.
24:35 Heaven and earth will **p** away, but my words will not **p** away.
26:39 if it is possible, let this cup **p** from me;
26:42 "My Father, if this cannot **p** unless I drink it,
Mk 6:48 He intended to **p** them by.
11:23 but believe that what you say will come to **p,**
13:30 not **p** away until all these things have taken place.
13:31 Heaven and earth will **p** away, but my words will not **p** away.
14:35 if it were possible, the hour might **p** from him.
Lk 16:17 But it is easier for heaven and earth to **p** away,
16:26 so that those who might want to **p** from here
19: 4 because he was going to **p** that way.
21:32 not **p** away until all things have taken place.
21:33 Heaven and earth will **p** away, but my words will not **p** away.
Ro 14: 3 and those who abstain must not **p** judgment
14: 4 Who are you to **p** judgment on servants
14:10 Why do you **p** judgment on your brother or sister?
14:13 therefore no longer **p** judgment on one another,
1Co 16: 5 for I intend to **p** through Macedonia—
2Pe 3:10 then the heavens will **p** away with a loud noise,
Jdt 4: 7 wide enough for only two at a time to **p.**
5:21 then let my lord **p** them by;
7:31 But if these days **p** by, and no help comes for us,
Wis 1: 8 and justice, when it punishes, will not **p** them by.
2: 4 our life will **p** away like the traces of a cloud,
2: 7 and let no flower of spring **p** us by.
6:22 and I will not **p** by the truth;
Sir 13: 7 he will **p** you by and shake his head at you.
14:14 do not let your share of desired good **p** by you.
14:19 and the one who made it will **p** away with it.
1Mc 5:48 "Let us **p** through your land to get to our land.
5:48 we will simply **p** by on foot."
2Es 4:24 We **p** from the world like locusts,
4:29 where the evil has been sown does not **p** away,
6:20 seal is placed upon the age that is about to **p** away,
7: 5 how can they come to the broad part unless they **p**
7:14 Therefore unless the living **p** through the difficult
7:26 signs that I have foretold to you will come to **p,**
7:*33* and compassion shall **p** away,
9:23 "Now, if you will let seven days more **p**—
13:20 than to **p** from the world like a cloud,
13:58 and whatever things come to **p** in their seasons.
15:60 As they **p** by they shall crush the hateful city,
16:77 so that no one can **p** through.

PASSAGE‡ (10) [PASS]

Nu 20:21 to give Israel **p** through their territory;
Ne 2: 7 that they may grant me **p** until I arrive in Judah;
Eze 42: 4 In front of the chambers was a **p** on the inner side,
42: 9 the foot of these chambers ran a **p** that one entered
42:10 width of the **p** is fixed by the wall of the court.
42:11 with a **p** in front of them;
42:12 the entrance at the head of the corresponding **p,**
Jn 19:37 And again another **p** of scripture says,
Ac 8:32 the **p** of the scripture that he was reading was this:
Wis 5:11 no evidence of its **p** is found;

PASSAGES (1) [PASS]

2Es 13:43 in by the narrow **p** of the Euphrates river.

PASSAGEWAY (1) [PASS]

Eze 41: 7 The **p** of the side chambers widened from story

PASSAGEWAYS (1) [PASS]

LtJ 6:42 women, with cords around them, sit along the **p,**

PASSED‡ (140) [PASS]

Ge 12: 6 Abram **p** through the land to the place
15:17 and a flaming torch **p** between these pieces.
23:17 that were in the field, throughout its whole area, **p**
23:20 in it **p** from the Hittites into Abraham's possession
32:21 So the present **p** on ahead of him;
32:31 The sun rose upon him as he **p** Penuel,
37:28 When some Midianite traders **p** by,
Ex 7:25 Seven days **p** after the LORD had struck the Nile.
12:27 for he **p** over the houses of the Israelites in Egypt,
15:16 as a stone until your people, O LORD, **p** by,
15:16 until the people whom you acquired **p** by.
29:29 The sacred vestments of Aaron shall be **p** on
33:22 I will cover you with my hand until I have **p** by;
34: 6 The LORD **p** before him, and proclaimed,
Nu 20:17 to the left until we have **p** through your territory."
21:22 we will go by the King's Highway until we have **p**
31:23 shall be **p** through fire, and it shall be clean.
31:23 shall be **p** through the water.
33: 8 **p** through the sea into the wilderness,
Dt 2: 8 So we **p** by our kin,
29:16 the midst of the nations through which you **p.**
Jos 3: 4 for you have not **p** this way before.
6:13 of rams' horns before the ark of the LORD **p** on,
9:16 But when three days had **p** after they had made
10:29 Then Joshua **p** on from Makkedah,
10:31 Next Joshua **p** on from Libnah,
10:34 From Lachish Joshua **p** on with all Israel to Eglon;
24:17 and among all the peoples through whom we **p;**
Jdg 3:26 and **p** beyond the sculptured stones,
9:25 They robbed all who **p** by them along that way;
11:29 and he **p** through Gilead and Manasseh.
11:29 He **p** on to Mizpah of Gilead,
11:29 from Mizpah of Gilead he **p** on to the Ammonites.
18:13 From there they **p** on to the hill country
19:14 So they **p** on and went their way;
1Sa 7: 2 a long time **p,** some twenty years,
9: 4 He **p** through the hill country of Ephraim **p** through
9: 4 And they **p** through the land of Shaalim,
9: 4 Then he **p** through the land of Benjamin,
9:27 and when he has **p** on,
14:23 The battle **p** beyond Beth-aven,
15:12 and on returning he **p** on down to Gilgal."
2Sa 2:15 they came forward and were counted as they **p** by,
13: 1 Some time **p.** David's son Absalom had
15:18 All his officials **p** by him;
15:18 from Gath, **p** on before the king.
15:23 whole country wept aloud as all the people **p** by;
15:24 until the people had all **p** out of the city.
16: 1 When David had **p** a little beyond the summit,
20:14 Sheba **p** through all the tribes of Israel to Abel
1Ki 13:25 People **p** by and saw the body thrown in the road,
18:29 As midday **p,** they raved on until the time of
19:19 Elijah **p** by him and threw his mantle over him.
20:39 As the king **p** by, he cried to the king and said,
2Ki 4: 8 So whenever he **p** that way,
14: 9 a wild animal of Lebanon **p** by and trampled down
25: 6 to the king of Babylon at Riblah, who **p** sentence
2Ch 25:18 a wild animal of Lebanon **p** by and trampled down
Ne 9:11 so that they **p** through the sea on dry land,
Job 11:16 you will remember it as waters that have **p** away.
15:19 and no stranger **p** among them.
28: 8 the lion has not **p** over it.
30:15 and my prosperity has **p** away like a cloud.
37:21 when the wind has **p** and cleared them.
Ps 31:12 I have **p** out of mind like one who is dead;
37:36 Again I **p** by, and they were no more;
66: 6 they **p** through the river on foot.
148: 6 he fixed their bounds, which cannot be **p.**
Pr 24:30 I **p** by the field of one who was lazy,
SS 3: 4 Scarcely had I **p** them,
Isa 10:28 he has **p** through Migron, at Michmash he stores
Jer 8:13 and what I gave them has **p** away from them.
34:18 when they cut it in two and **p** between its parts:
34:19 the people of the land who **p** between the parts of
39: 5 and he **p** sentence on him.
52: 9 and he **p** sentence on him.
Eze 16: 6 I **p** by you, and saw you flailing about
16: 8 I **p** by you again and looked on you;
36:34 that it was in the sight of all who **p** by.
Jnh 2: 3 all your waves and your billows **p** over me.
Mt 15:29 he **p** along the Sea of Galilee,
27:39 Those who **p** by derided him, shaking their heads
Mk 1:16 As Jesus **p** along the Sea of Galilee,
9:30 They went on from there and **p** through Galilee.
11:20 In the morning as they **p** by,
15:29 Those who **p** by derided him,
Lk 2:21 After eight days had **p,** it was time to circumcise
4:30 But he **p** through the midst of them and went
10:31 and when he saw him, he **p** by on the other side.
10:32 **p** by on the other side.
Jn 5:24 but has **p** from death to life.
Ac 7:30 "Now when forty years had **p,**
9:23 After some time had **p,** the Jews plotted
12:10 After they had **p** the first and the second guard,
14:24 they **p** through Pisidia and came to Pamphylia.
15: 3 and as they **p** through both Phoenicia and Samaria,
17: 1 After Paul and Silas had **p** through Amphipolis
19: 1 Paul **p** through the interior regions and came
24:27 After two years had **p,** Felix was succeeded
25:13 After several days had **p,** King Agrippa
Ro 3:25 because in his divine forbearance he had **p** over
1Co 10: 1 and all **p** through the sea,
2Co 5:17 everything old has **p** away;
Heb 4:14 a great high priest who has **p** through the heavens,
11:29 By faith the people **p** through the Red Sea as
2Pe 2:21 the holy commandment that was **p** on to them.
1Jn 3:14 We know that we have **p** from death to life
Rev 9:12 The first woe has **p.**
11:14 The second woe has **p.**
21: 1 for the first heaven and the first earth had **p** away,

Rev 21: 4 for the first things have **p** away."
Tob 1:21 But not forty days **p** before two
5: 3 now twenty years have **p** since I left this money
10: 1 when the days had **p** and his son did not appear,
Jdt 2:24 and **p** through Mesopotamia and destroyed all
10:10 down the mountain and **p** through the valley,
13:10 They **p** through the camp,
Wis 5:10 and when it has **p** no trace can be found,
10: 8 For because they **p** wisdom by,
19: 8 where those protected by your hand **p** through
1Mc 5:51 he **p** through the town over the bodies of the dead.
5:66 the land of the Philistines, and **p** through Marisa.
11:62 And he **p** through the country as far as Damascus.
12:10 for considerable time has **p**
2Mc 1:20 But after many years had **p**, when it pleased God,
1:22 When this had been done and some time had **p**,
3Mc 6:35 arranged the aforementioned choral group and **p**
2Es 3:19 Your glory **p** through the four gates of fire
3:23 So the times **p** and the years were completed,
4:45 whether more time is to come than has **p**,
4:48 and lo, a flaming furnace **p** by before me,
4:49 And after this a cloud full of water **p** before me
4:49 and when the violent rainstorm had **p**,
4:50 so the quantity that **p** was far greater;
5:11 or anyone who does right, **p** through you?'
7:*113* [43] in which corruption has **p** away,
8:31 For we and our ancestors have **p** our lives in ways
8:54 sorrows have **p** away, and in the end the treasure
14:11 and nine of its parts have already **p**,

PASSER-BY (3) [PASS]

Eze 16:15 and lavished your whorings on any **p**.
16:25 offering yourself to every **p**,
Mk 15:21 They compelled a **p**, who was coming in from

PASSERS-BY (1) [PASS]

LtJ 6:43 of them is led off by one of the **p** and is taken

PASSES‡ (43) [PASS]

Ex 33:22 and while my glory **p** by I will put you in a cleft of
Lev 27:32 every tenth one that **p** under the shepherd's staff,
Jos 15: 3 the ascent of Akrabbim, **p** along to Zin, and goes
15: 4 **p** along to Azmon, goes out by the Wadi of Egypt,
15: 6 and **p** along north of Beth-arabah;
15: 7 the boundary **p** along to the waters of En-shemesh,
15:10 **p** along to the northern slope of Mount Jearim
15:10 down to Beth-shemesh, and **p** along by Timnah;
15:11 and **p** along to Mount Baalah,
16: 2 it **p** along to Ataroth, the territory of the Archites;
16: 6 and **p** along beyond it on the east to Janoah,
18:13 the boundary **p** along southward in the direction
18:19 then the boundary **p** on to the north of the slope
19:13 from there it **p** along on the east toward
2Ki 4: 9 I am sure that this man who regularly **p** our way is
Job 9:11 Look, he **p** by me, and I do not see him;
11:10 If he **p** through, and imprisons,
Ps 8: 8 whatever **p** along the paths of the seas.
78:39 a wind that **p** and does not come again.
103:16 for the wind **p** over it,
Pr 10:25 When the tempest **p**, the wicked are no more,
Isa 28:15 when the overwhelming scourge **p** through it will
28:18 the overwhelming scourge **p** through you will
28:19 As often as it **p** through, it will take you;
41: 3 He pursues them and **p** on safely,
Jer 2: 6 in a land that no one **p** through,
9:10 they are laid waste so that no one **p** through,
9:12 so that no one **p** through?
19: 8 everyone who **p** by it will be horrified
49:17 everyone who **p** by it will be horrified
50:13 everyone who **p** by Babylon shall be appalled
51:43 and through which no mortal **p**.
Zep 2:15 Everyone who **p** by it hisses and shakes the fist.
Jdt 4: 7 ordering them to seize the mountain **p**, since
5: 1 the mountain **p** and fortified all the high hilltops
6: 7 and put you in one of the towns beside the **p**.
7: 1 the **p** up into the hill country and make war on
14:11 and they went out in companies to the mountain **p**.
Wis 5: 9 and like a rumor that **p** by;
5:14 and it **p** like the remembrance of a guest who stays
7:27 in every generation she **p** into holy souls
Sir 10: 8 Sovereignty **p** from nation to nation on account
45:25 that the king's heritage **p** only from son to son,

PASSING‡ (35) [PASS]

Jos 18:18 and **p** on to the north of the slope
Jdg 19:18 "We are **p** from Bethlehem in Judah to
Ru 4: 1 of whom Boaz had spoken, came **p** by.
1Sa 29: 2 the lords of the Philistines were **p** on by hundreds
29: 2 and his men were **p** on in the rear with Achish,
2Sa 1:26 to me was wonderful, **p** the love of women.
1Ki 9: 8 everyone **p** by it will be astonished, and will hiss;
2Ki 4: 8 One day Elisha was **p** through Shunem,
2Ch 7:21 now exalted, everyone **p** by will be astonished,
Ps 39:12 I am your **p** guest, an alien, like all my forebears.
144: 4 their days are like a **p** shadow.
Pr 7: 8 **p** along the street near her corner,
26:10 is one who hires a **p** fool or drunkard.
26:17 a **p** dog by the ears is one who meddles in
Isa 60:15 and hated, with no one **p** through,
Eze 26:18 the coastlands by the sea are dismayed at your **p**.
Mic 7:18 pardoning iniquity and **p** over the transgression of
Mt 20:30 When they heard that Jesus was **p** by,
Lk 18:37 They told him, "Jesus of Nazareth is **p** by."
19: 1 He entered Jericho and was **p** through it.
Ac 8:40 and as he was **p** through the region,
Ac 16: 8 so, **p** by Mysia, they went down to Troas.
Ro 2: 1 in **p** judgment on another you condemn yourself,
1Co 7:31 For the present form of this world is **p** away.
16: 5 I will visit you after **p** through Macedonia—
16: 7 I do not want to see you now just in **p**,
Tit 3: 3 **p** our days in malice and envy, despicable,
1Jn 2: 8 because the darkness is **p** away and
2:17 And the world and its desire are **p** away,
Wis 2: 5 For our allotted time is the **p** of a shadow,
14: 5 even to the smallest piece of wood, and **p** through
17: 9 by the **p** of wild animals and the hissing of snakes
2Es 5:55 that already is aging and **p** the strength of youth."
7: 9 unless by **p** through the appointed danger?"
12:29 As for your seeing two little wings **p** over to

PASSION (16) [PASSIONS]

Dt 29:20 LORD's anger and **p** will smoke against them.
Pr 14:30 but **p** makes the bones rot.
SS 8: 6 for love is strong as death, **p** fierce as the grave.
Zep 1:18 the fire of his **p** the whole earth shall be consumed;
3: 8 in the fire of my **p** all the earth shall be consumed.
Ro 1:27 were consumed with **p** for one another.
1Co 7: 9 For it is better to marry than to be aflame with **p**.
Col 3: 5 fornication, impurity, **p**, evil desire,
1Th 4: 5 not with lustful **p**, like the Gentiles who do
Jdt 12:16 with her and his **p** was aroused,
Sir 6: 2 Do not fall into the grip of **p**,
6: 4 Evil **p** destroys those who have it,
9: 8 and by it **p** is kindled like a fire.
23: 6 and do not give me over to shameless **p**.
23:16 Hot **p** that blazes like a fire will not be quenched
Sus 1:10 Both were overwhelmed with **p** for her,

PASSIONS (13) [PASSION]

Ro 1:26 For this reason God gave them up to degrading **p**.
6:12 to make you obey their **p**.
7: 5 While we were living in the flesh, our sinful **p**,
1Co 7:36 if his **p** are strong, and so it has to be,
Gal 5:24 to Christ Jesus have crucified the flesh with its **p**
Eph 2: 3 of us once lived among them in the **p** of our flesh,
2Ti 2:22 Shun youthful **p** and pursue righteousness, faith,
Tit 2:12 training us to renounce impiety and worldly **p**,
3: 3 led astray, slaves to various **p** and pleasures,
1Pe 4: 3 living in licentiousness, **p**, drunkenness, revels,
4Mc 2: 3 by his reason he nullified the frenzy of the **p**.
7:10 O supreme king over the **p**, Eleazar!
7:18 these alone are able to control the **p** of the flesh,

PASSOVER (93) [PASCHAL]

Ex 12:11 It is the **p** of the LORD.
12:21 for your families, and slaughter the **p** lamb.
12:27 you shall say, 'It is the **p** sacrifice to the LORD,
12:43 This is the ordinance for the **p**:
12:48 with you wants to celebrate the **p** to the LORD,
34:25 and the sacrifice of the festival of the **p** shall not
Lev 23: 5 there shall be a **p** offering to the LORD,
Nu 9: 2 Let the Israelites keep the **p** at its appointed time.
9: 4 the Israelites that they should keep the **p**.
9: 5 They kept the **p** in the first month,
9: 6 so that they could not keep the **p** on that day.
9:10 shall still keep the **p** to the LORD.
9:12 to all the statute for the **p** they shall keep it.
9:13 and yet refrains from keeping the **p**,
9:14 to keep the **p** to the LORD shall do so according
9:14 the statute of the **p** and according to its regulation;
28:16 of the first month there shall be a **p** offering to
33: 3 the day after the **p** the Israelites went out boldly in
Dt 16: 1 Observe the month of Abib by keeping the **p** for
16: 2 the **p** sacrifice for the LORD your God,
16: 5 to offer the **p** sacrifice within any of your towns
16: 6 only there shall you offer the **p** sacrifice,
Jos 5:10 the **p** in the evening on the fourteenth day of
5:11 On the day after the **p**, on that very day,
2Ki 23:21 "Keep the **p** to the LORD your God as prescribed
23:22 No such **p** had been kept since the days of
23:23 the eighteenth year of King Josiah this **p** was kept
2Ch 30: 1 to keep the **p** to the LORD the God of Israel.
30: 2 in Jerusalem had taken counsel to keep the **p** in
30: 5 and keep the **p** to the LORD the God of Israel,
30:15 They slaughtered the **p** lamb on the fourteenth day
30:17 therefore the Levites had to slaughter the **p** lamb
30:18 yet they ate the **p** otherwise than as prescribed.
35: 1 Josiah kept a **p** to the LORD in Jerusalem;
35: 1 they slaughtered the **p** lamb on the fourteenth day
35: 6 Slaughter the **p** lamb, sanctify yourselves,
35: 7 as **p** offerings for all that were present,
35: 8 the **p** offerings two thousand six hundred lambs
35: 9 the Levites for the **p** offerings five thousand lambs
35:11 They slaughtered the **p** lamb,
35:13 the **p** lamb with fire according to the ordinance;
35:16 the **p** and to offer burnt offerings on the altar of
35:17 of Israel who were present kept the **p** at that time,
35:18 No **p** like it had been kept in Israel since the days
35:18 of Israel had kept such a **p** as was kept by Josiah,
35:19 of the reign of Josiah this **p** was kept.
Ezr 6:19 of the first month the returned exiles kept the **p**.
6:20 they killed the **p** lamb for all the returned exiles,
Eze 45:21 you shall celebrate the festival of the **p**,
Mt 26: 2 "You know that after two days the **P** is coming,
26:17 to make the preparations for you to eat the **P**?"
26:18 the **P** at your house with my disciples.' "
26:19 and they prepared the **P** meal.
Mk 14: 1 It was two days before the **P** and the festival
14:12 when the **P** lamb is sacrificed,
14:12 and make the preparations for you to eat the **P**?"
Mk 14:14 Where is my guest room where I may eat the **P**
14:16 and they prepared the **P** meal.
Lk 2:41 to Jerusalem for the festival of the **P**.
22: 1 which is called the **P**, was near.
22: 7 on which the **P** lamb had to be sacrificed.
22: 8 and prepare the **P** meal for us that we may eat it."
22:11 where I may eat the **P** with my disciples?" '
22:13 and they prepared the **P** meal.
22:15 "I have eagerly desired to eat this **P** with you
Jn 2:13 The **P** of the Jews was near,
2:23 When he was in Jerusalem during the **P** festival,
6: 4 Now the **P**, the festival of the Jews, was near.
11:55 Now the **P** of the Jews was near,
11:55 to Jerusalem before the **P** to purify themselves.
12: 1 Six days before the **P** Jesus came to Bethany,
13: 1 Now before the festival of the **P**,
18:28 and to be able to eat the **P**.
18:39 a custom that I release someone for you at the **P**.
19:14 Now it was the day of Preparation for the **P**;
Ac 12: 4 to bring him out to the people after the **P**.
Heb 11:28 By faith he kept the **P** and the sprinkling of blood,
1Es 1: 1 Josiah kept the **p** to his Lord in Jerusalem;
1: 1 he killed the **p** lamb on the fourteenth day of
1: 6 and kill the **p** lamb and prepare the sacrifices
1: 6 and keep the **p** according to the commandment of
1: 8 for the **p** two thousand six hundred sheep
1: 9 gave the Levites for the **p** five thousand sheep
1:12 They roasted the **p** lamb with fire, as required;
1:13 Afterward they prepared the **p** for themselves and
1:16 their kindred the Levites prepared the **p** for them.
1:17 were accomplished that day: the **p** was kept
1:19 of Israel who were present at that time kept the **p**
1:20 No **p** like it had been kept in Israel since the times
1:21 of Israel had kept such a **p** as was kept by Josiah
1:22 of the reign of Josiah this **p** was kept.
7:10 the **p** on the fourteenth day of the first month,
7:12 the **p** lamb for all the returned captives and

PAST‡ (34) [PASS]

Ge 50: 4 When the days of weeping for him were **p**,
Ex 4:10 in the **p** nor even now that you have spoken
21:29 If the ox has been accustomed to gore in the **p**,
21:36 that the ox was accustomed to gore in the **p**,
Dt 32: 7 consider the years long **p**;
2Sa 3:17 "For some time **p** you have been seeking David
15:34 as I have been your father's servant in time **p**,
Ne 2:13 by night by the Valley Gate **p** the Dragon's Spring
Job 4:15 A spirit glided **p** my face;
14:13 that you would conceal me until your wrath is **p**,
17:11 My days are **p**, my plans are broken off,
Ps 71:15 though their number is **p** my knowledge.
90: 4 in your sight are like yesterday when it is **p**,
Ecc 3:11 he has put a sense of **p** and future into their minds,
SS 2:11 for now the winter is **p**, the rain is over and gone.
Isa 16:13 that the LORD spoke concerning Moab in the **p**.
26:20 for a little while until the wrath is **p**.
64: 4 From ages **p** no one has heard,
Jer 8:20 "The harvest is **p**, the summer is ended,
Eze 46:21 and led me **p** the four corners of the court;
Ac 14:16 In **p** generations he allowed all the nations
15:21 For in every city, for generations **p**,
20:16 For Paul had decided to sail **p** Ephesus,
27: 8 Sailing **p** it with difficulty,
27:13 so they weighed anchor and began to sail **p** Crete,
2Pe 1: 9 and is forgetful of the cleansing of **p** sins.
3: 2 the words spoken in the **p** by the holy prophets,
Sir 11:27 An hour's misery makes one forget **p** delights,
21: 1 but ask forgiveness for your **p** sins.
Sus 1:52 which you have committed in the **p**,
1Mc 12: 7 in time **p** a letter was sent to the high priest Onias
3Mc 2: 4 You destroyed those who in the **p**
2Es 4: 5 or call back for me the day that is **p**."
12:40 that the seven days were **p** and I had not returned

PASTOR (KJV) See SHEPHERD

PASTORS (1)

Eph 4:11 some evangelists, some **p** and teachers,

PASTURE‡ (153) [PASTURE-FED, PASTURED, PASTURES, PASTURING]

Ge 29: 7 Water the sheep, and go, **p** them."
37:12 Now his brothers went to **p** their father's flock
47: 4 for there is no **p** for your servants' flocks because
Nu 35: 2 to the Levites **p** lands surrounding the towns.
35: 3 and their **p** lands shall be for their cattle,
35: 4 The **p** lands of the towns,
35: 5 this shall belong to them as **p** land for their towns.
35: 7 Levites shall total forty-eight, with their **p** lands.
Jos 14: 4 with their **p** lands for their flocks and herds.
21: 2 along with their **p** lands for our livestock."
21: 3 to the Levites the following towns and **p** lands out
21: 8 These towns and their **p** lands the Israelites gave
21:11 along with the **p** lands around it.
21:13 with its **p** lands, Libnah with its **p** lands,
21:14 Jattir with its **p** lands, Eshtemoa with its **p** lands,
21:15 Holon with its **p** lands, Debir with its **p** lands,
21:16 Ain with its **p** lands, Juttah with its **p** lands, and
Beth-shemesh with its **p** lands—
21:17 Gibeon with its **p** lands, Geba with its **p** lands,
21:18 Anathoth with its **p** lands, and Almon with its **p**
21:19 were thirteen in all, with their **p** lands.
21:21 with its **p** lands in the hill country of Ephraim,
Gezer with its **p** lands,

Jos 21:22 with its **p** lands, and Beth-horon with its **p** lands
21:23 Elteke with its **p** lands, Gibbethon with its **p** lands,
21:24 Aijalon with its **p** lands, Gath-rimmon with its **p**
21:25 with its **p** lands, and Gath-rimmon with its **p** lands
21:26 the Kohathites were ten in all, with their **p** lands.
21:27 Golan in Bashan with its **p** lands, the city of refuge
21:27 and Beeshterah with its **p** lands
21:28 Kishion with its **p** lands, Daberath with its **p** lands,
21:29 Jarmuth with its **p** lands, En-gannim with its **p**
21:30 Mishal with its **p** lands, Abdon with its **p** lands,
21:31 Helkath with its **p** lands, and Rehob with its **p**
21:32 Kedesh in Galilee with its **p** lands,
21:32 with its **p** lands, and Kartan with its **p** lands
21:33 in all thirteen, with their **p** lands.
21:34 Jokneam with its **p** lands, Kartah with its **p** lands,
21:35 Dimnah with its **p** lands, Nahalal with its **p** lands
21:36 Bezer with its **p** lands, Jahzah with its **p** lands,
21:37 with its **p** lands, and Mephaath with its **p** lands
21:38 Ramoth in Gilead with its **p** lands, the city of
21:38 Mahanaim with its **p** lands,
21:39 Heshbon with its **p** lands, Jazer with its **p** lands
21:41 in all forty-eight towns with their **p** lands.
21:42 Each of these towns had its **p** lands around it;
2Sa 7: 8 I took you from the **p**, from following the sheep to
1Ch 4:39 to seek **p** for their flocks,
4:40 good **p**, and the land was very broad, quiet,
4:41 because there was **p** there for their flocks.
5:16 and in all the **p** lands of Sharon to their limits.
6:55 in the land of Judah and its surrounding **p** lands,
6:57 Libnah with its **p** lands, Jattir, Eshtemoa with its **p**
6:58 Hilen with its **p** lands, Debir with its **p** lands,
6:59 with its **p** lands, and Beth-shemesh with its **p** lands.
6:60 Geba with its **p** lands, Alemeth with its **p** lands, and Anathoth with its **p** lands.
6:64 the Levites the towns with their **p** lands.
6:67 Shechem with its **p** lands in the hill country of Ephraim, Gezer with its **p** lands,
6:68 Jokmeam with its **p** lands, Beth-horon with its **p**
6:69 Aijalon with its **p** lands, Gath-rimmon with its **p**
6:70 with its **p** lands, and Bileam with its **p** lands,
6:71 with its **p** lands and Ashtaroth with its **p** lands;
6:72 Kedesh with its **p** lands, Daberath with its **p** lands,
6:73 Ramoth with its **p** lands, and Anem with its **p**
6:74 Mashal with its **p** lands, Abdon with its **p** lands,
6:75 Hukok with its **p** lands, and Rehob with its **p** lands;
6:76 Kedesh in Galilee with its **p** lands, Hammon with its **p** lands, and Kiriathaim with its **p** lands.
6:77 Rimmono with its **p** lands, Tabor with its **p** lands,
6:78 the steppe with its **p** lands, Jahzah with its **p** lands,
6:79 with its **p** lands, and Mephaath with its **p** lands;
6:80 Gilead with its **p** lands, Mahanaim with its **p** lands,
6:81 Heshbon with its **p** lands, and Jazer with its **p**
13: 2 and Levites in the cities that have **p** lands,
17: 7 I took you from the **p**, from following the sheep,
Job 24: 2 they seize flocks and **p** them.
39: 8 It ranges the mountains as its **p**,
Ps 74: 1 against the sheep of your **p**?
79:13 Then we your people, the flock of your **p**,
95: 7 For he is our God, and we are the people of his **p**,
100: 3 we are his people, and the sheep of his **p**.
SS 1: 7 you whom my soul loves, where you **p** your flock,
1: 8 and **p** your kids beside the shepherds' tents.
6: 2 to the beds of spices, to **p** his flock in the gardens,
Isa 5:17 Then the lambs shall graze as in their **p**,
32:14 the joy of wild asses, a **p** for flocks;
49: 9 on all the bare heights shall be their **p**;
65:10 Sharon shall become a **p** for flocks,
Jer 6: 2 I have likened daughter Zion to the loveliest **p**.
6: 3 they shall **p**, all in their places.
23: 1 and scatter the sheep of my **p**!
25:36 For the LORD is despoiling their **p**,
33:12 and in all its towns there shall again be **p**
49:19 a perennial **p**, I will suddenly chase Edom away
50: 7 the LORD, the true **p**, the LORD, the hope
50:19 I will restore Israel to its **p**,
50:44 the thickets of the Jordan against a perennial **p**,
La 1: 6 Her princes have become like stags that find no **p**;
Eze 25: 5 I will make Rabbah a **p** for camels and Ammon
34:14 I will feed them with good **p**,
34:14 the mountain heights of Israel shall be their **p**;
34:14 in good grazing land, and they shall feed on rich **p**
34:18 Is it not enough for you to feed on the good **p**,
34:18 down with your feet the rest of your **p**?
34:31 the sheep of my **p** and I am your God,
36: 5 took my land as their possession, because of its **p**,
Hos 4:16 now feed them like a lamb in a broad **p**?
Joel 1:18 of cattle wander about because there is no **p**
Mic 2:12 like a flock in its **p**; it will resound with people.
Zep 2: 7 of Judah, on which they shall **p**, and in the houses
3:13 Then they will **p** and lie down,
Jn 10: 9 and will come in and go out and find **p**.
2Es 9:19 with an unfailing table and an inexhaustible **p**,

PASTURE-FED (1) [FEED, PASTURE]

1Ki 4:23 and twenty **p** cattle, one hundred sheep,

PASTURED (2) [PASTURE]

Ge 36:24 as he **p** the donkeys of his father Zibeon.
1Ch 27:29 Over the herds that **p** in Sharon was Shitrai

PASTURES (16) [PASTURE]

Ps 23: 2 He makes me lie down in green **p**;
37:20 enemies of the LORD are like the glory of the **p**;
65:12 The **p** of the wilderness overflow,
83:12 "Let us take the **p** of God for our own possession."
SS 2:16 he **p** his flock among the lilies.
6: 3 he **p** his flock among the lilies.
Isa 7:19 and on all the thornbushes, and on all the **p**.
30:23 On that day your cattle will graze in broad **p**;
Jer 9:10 and a lamentation for the **p** of the wilderness,
23:10 and the **p** of the wilderness are dried up.
Eze 45:15 from every flock of two hundred, from the **p**
Joel 1:19 For fire has devoured the **p** of the wilderness,
1:20 and fire has devoured the **p** of the wilderness.
2:22 for the **p** of the wilderness are green;
Am 1: 2 the **p** of the shepherds wither,
Zep 2: 6 And you, O seacoast, shall be **p**,

PASTURING (3) [PASTURE]

Ge 30:36 while Jacob was **p** the rest of Laban's flock.
37:13 "Are not your brothers **p** the flock at Shechem?
37:16 "tell me, please, where they are **p** the flock."

PATARA (1)

Ac 21: 1 and the next day to Rhodes, and from there to **P**.

PATCH (2) [PATCHED]

Mt 9:16 for the **p** pulls away from the cloak,
Mk 2:21 otherwise, the **p** pulls away from it,

PATCHED (1) [PATCH]

Jos 9: 5 **p** sandals on their feet, and worn-out clothes;

PATH (59) [BYPATHS, PATHLESS, PATHS, PATHWAY, PATHWAYS]

Ge 49:17 a viper along the **p**, that bites the horse's heels so
Nu 22:24 Then the angel of the LORD stood in a narrow **p**
Dt 5:33 You must follow exactly the **p** that
2Sa 22:33 with strength has opened wide my **p**.
Job 18:10 a trap for them in the **p**.
28: 7 "That **p** no bird of prey knows,
30:13 They break up my **p**, they promote my calamity;
Ps 1: 1 or take the **p** that sinners tread,
16:11 You show me the **p** of life.
27:11 and lead me on a level **p** because of my enemies.
57: 6 They dug a pit in my **p**,
77:19 Your way was through the sea, your **p**,
78:50 He made a **p** for his anger;
85:13 and will make a **p** for his steps.
110: 7 He will drink from the stream by the **p**;
119:35 Lead me in the **p** of your commandments,
119:105 a lamp to my feet and a light to my **p**.
139: 3 You search out my **p** and my lying down,
142: 3 In the **p** where I walk they have hidden a trap for
143:10 Let your good spirit lead me on a level **p**.
Pr 2: 9 and justice and equity, every good **p**;
4:14 Do not enter the **p** of the wicked,
4:18 But the **p** of the righteous is like the light of dawn,
4:26 Keep straight the **p** of your feet,
5: 5 her steps follow the **p** to Sheol.
5: 6 She does not keep straight to the **p** of life;
10:17 Whoever heeds instruction is on the **p** to life,
12:28 In the **p** of righteousness there is life,
12:28 in walking its **p** there is no death.
15:19 but the **p** of the upright is a level highway.
15:24 For the wise the **p** of life leads upward,
Isa 26: 7 you make smooth the **p** of the righteous.
26: 8 In the **p** of your judgments, O LORD,
30:11 the way, turn aside from the **p**, let us hear no more
40:14 and who taught him the **p** of justice?
41: 3 scarcely touching the **p** with his feet.
43:16 a **p** in the mighty waters,
Jer 31: 9 in a straight **p** in which they shall not stumble;
Eze 39:11 it shall block the **p** of the travelers,
Mt 13: 4 And as he sowed, some seeds fell on the **p**,
13:19 this is what was sown on the **p**.
Mk 4: 4 And as he sowed, some seed fell on the **p**,
4:15 the ones on the **p** where the word is sown:
Lk 8: 5 he sowed, some fell on the **p** and was trampled on,
8:12 The ones on the **p** are those who have heard;
19:37 now approaching the **p** down from the Mount
Jdt 13:20 walking in the straight **p** before our God."
15: 2 and fled by every **p** across the plain and through
Wis 14: 3 because you have given it a **p** in the sea,
Sir 2:12 and to the sinner who walks a double **p**!
5: 9 Do not winnow in every wind, or follow every **p**.
32:20 Do not go on a **p** full of hazards,
50:29 for the fear of the Lord is their **p**.
51:15 my foot walked on the straight **p**;
Bar 3:31 or is concerned about the **p** to her.
2Es 7: 8 There is only one **p** lying between them, that is,
7: 8 so that only one person can walk on the **p**.
14:22 so that people may be able to find the **p**,
16:77 with underbrush and its **p** overwhelmed

PATHLESS (1) [PATH]

Job 12:24 and makes them wander in a **p** waste.

PATHROS (5)

Isa 11:11 from Assyria, from Egypt, from **P**, from Ethiopia,
Jer 44: 1 at Tahpanhes, at Memphis, and in the land of **P**,
44:15 all the people who lived in **P** in the land of Egypt,
Eze 29:14 and bring them back to the land of **P**,
30:14 I will make **P** a desolation,

PATHRUSIM (2)

Ge 10:14 **P**, Casluhim, and Caphtorim, from which
1Ch 1:12 **P**, Casluhim, and Caphtorim, from whom

PATHS‡ (56) [PATH]

Job 8:13 Such are the **p** of all who forget God;
13:27 in the stocks, and watch all my **p**;
19: 8 and he has set darkness upon my **p**.
24:13 and do not stay in its **p**.
33:11 in the stocks, and watches all my **p**.'
38:20 to its territory and that you may discern the **p**
Ps 8: 8 whatever passes along the **p** of the seas.
17: 5 My steps have held fast to your **p**;
23: 3 He leads me in right **p** for his name's sake.
25: 4 O LORD; teach me your **p**.
25:10 All the **p** of the LORD are steadfast love
Pr 1:15 keep your foot from their **p**;
2: 8 guarding the **p** of justice and preserving the way
2:13 who forsake the **p** of uprightness to walk in
2:15 those whose **p** are crooked,
2:18 and her **p** to the shades;
2:19 nor do they regain the **p** of life.
2:20 and keep to the **p** of the just.
3: 6 and he will make straight your **p**.
3:17 and all her **p** are peace.
4:11 I have led you in the **p** of uprightness.
5:21 and he examines all their **p**.
7:25 do not stray into her **p**.
8:20 in the way of righteousness, along the **p** of justice,
Isa 2: 3 and that we may walk in his **p**."
3:12 and confuse the course of your **p**.
42:16 by **p** they have not known I will guide them.
45:13 and I will make all his **p** straight;
47:15 they all wander about in their own **p**;
59: 8 and there is no justice in their **p**.
Jer 6:16 and look, and ask for the ancient **p**,
23:12 be to them like slippery **p** in the darkness,
La 3: 9 he has made my **p** crooked.
Hos 2: 6 so that she cannot find her **p**.
Joel 2: 7 they do not swerve from their **p**.
Mic 4: 2 and that we may walk in his **p**."
Mt 3: 3 the way of the Lord, make his **p** straight.' "
Mk 1: 3 the way of the Lord, make his **p** straight,' "
Lk 3: 4 'Prepare the way of the Lord, make his **p** straight.
Ac 13:10 will you not stop making crooked the straight **p** of
Ro 3:16 ruin and misery are in their **p**,
Heb 12:13 and make straight **p** for your feet,
Tob 4:19 and that all your **p** and plans may prosper.
Wis 5: 7 We took our fill of the **p** of lawlessness
6:16 and she graciously appears to them in their **p**,
9:18 And thus the **p** of those on earth were set right,
10:10 she guided him on straight **p**;
12:24 For they went far astray on the **p** of error,
Sir 4:17 For at first she will walk with them on tortuous **p**;
14:22 and lying in wait on her **p**;
32:22 and give good heed to your **p**.
Bar 3:20 nor understood her **p**, nor laid hold of her.
3:23 or given thought to her **p**.
4:13 or tread the **p** his righteousness showed them.
2Es 7:*48* the **p** of perdition and removed us far from life—
16:32 and its roads and all its **p** shall bring forth thorns,

PATHWAY (1) [PATH]

Wis 5:12 so that no one knows its **p**.

PATHWAYS (1) [PATH]

Hab 3: 6 along his ancient **p** the everlasting hills sank low.

PATIENCE‡ (26) [PATIENT]

Pr 25:15 With **p** a ruler may be persuaded,
Mic 2: 7 Is the LORD's **p** exhausted?
Mt 18:26 'Have **p** with me, and I will pay you everything.'
18:29 'Have **p** with me, and I will pay you.'
Ro 2: 4 the riches of his kindness and forbearance and **p**?
8:25 we wait for it with **p**.
9:22 with much **p** the objects of wrath that are made
2Co 6: 6 **p**, kindness, holiness of spirit, genuine love,
12:12 among you with utmost **p**,
Gal 5:22 joy, peace, **p**, kindness, generosity, faithfulness,
Eph 4: 2 with **p**, bearing with one another in love,
Col 1:11 may you be prepared to endure everything with **p**,
3:12 kindness, humility, meekness, and **p**.
1Ti 1:16 Jesus Christ might display the utmost **p**,
2Ti 3:10 my conduct, my aim in life, my faith, my **p**,
4: 2 and encourage, with the utmost **p** in teaching.
Heb 6:12 through faith and **p** inherit the promises.
Jas 5:10 As an example of suffering and **p**, beloved,
2Pe 3:15 and regard the **p** of our Lord as salvation.
Sir 16:13 and the **p** of the godly will not be frustrated.
41: 2 to one who is contrary, and has lost all **p**!
Bar 4:25 endure with **p** the wrath that has come upon you
Aza 1:19 with us in your **p** and in your abundant mercy.
1Mc 8: 4 of the whole region by their planning and **p**,
2Es 7:*33* and **p** shall be withdrawn.
7:*134* [64] he shows **p** toward those who have sinned,

PATIENT (25) [PATIENCE, PATIENTLY]

Ne 9:30 Many years you were **p** with them,
Job 6:11 And what is my end, that I should be **p**?
Ecc 7: 8 the **p** in spirit are better than the proud in spirit.
Lk 8:15 and bear fruit with **p** endurance.
Ro 12:12 Rejoice in hope, be **p** in suffering,
1Co 13: 4 Love is **p**; love is kind; love is
1Th 5:14 help the weak, be **p** with all of them.
2Ti 2:24 but kindly to everyone, an apt teacher, **p**,
Jas 5: 7 Be **p**, therefore, beloved, until the coming of the
5: 7 being **p** with it until it receives the early and
5: 8 You also must be **p**.

2Pe 3: 9 as some think of slowness, but is **p** with you,
Rev 1: 9 and the kingdom and the **p** endurance,
2: 2 your toil and your **p** endurance.
2:19 your love, faith, service, and **p** endurance.
3:10 Because you have kept my word of **p** endurance,
Wis 15: 1 But you, our God, are kind and true, **p,**
Sir 1:23 Those who are **p** stay calm until the right moment,
2: 4 and in times of humiliation be **p.**
3:13 even if his mind fails, be **p** with him;
18:11 the Lord is **p** with them and pours out his mercy
29: 8 be **p** with someone in humble circumstances,
35:22 a warrior will not be **p** until he crushes the loins of
2Es 7:*74* the Most High has been **p** with those who inhabit
7:*134* [64] and **p,** because he shows patience

PATIENTLY (10) [PATIENT]

Ps 37: 7 Be still before the LORD, and wait **p** for him;
40: 1 I waited **p** for the LORD;
Ac 26: 3 therefore I beg of you to listen to me **p.**
Ro 2: 7 to those who by **p** doing good seek for glory
2Co 1: 6 when you **p** endure the same sufferings that we are
Heb 6:15 And thus Abraham, having **p** endured,
1Pe 3:20 when God waited **p** in the days of Noah,
Rev 2: 3 also know that you are enduring **p** and bearing up
2Mc 6:14 the other nations the Lord waits **p** to punish them
4Mc 14: 9 but also bore the sufferings **p,**

PATMOS (1)

Rev 1: 9 on the island called **P** because of the word of God

PATRIARCH (1) [PATRIARCHS]

Heb 7: 4 Abraham the **p** gave him a tenth of the spoils.

PATRIARCHS (7) [PATRIARCH]

Jn 7:22 of course, not from Moses, but from the **p),**
Ac 7: 8 and Jacob of the twelve **p.**
7: 9 "The **p,** jealous of Joseph, sold him into Egypt;
Ro 9: 5 to them belong the **p,** and from them,
15: 8 that he might confirm the promises given to the **p,**
4Mc 7:19 like our **p** Abraham and Isaac and Jacob,
16:25 as do Abraham and Isaac and Jacob and all the **p.**

PATROBAS (1)

Ro 16:14 Greet Asyncritus, Phlegon, Hermes, **P,** Hermas,

PATROCLUS (1)

2Mc 8: 9 Ptolemy promptly appointed Nicanor son of **P,**

PATROL (4) [PATROLLED]

Zec 1:10 "They are those whom the LORD has sent to **p**
6: 7 they were impatient to get off and **p** the earth.
6: 7 And he said, "Go, **p** the earth."
Jdt 10:11 on through the valley, an Assyrian **p** met her

PATROLLED (2) [PATROL]

Zec 1:11 "We have **p** the earth, and lo,
6: 7 So they **p** the earth.

PATTERN (10)

Ex 25: 9 that I show you concerning the **p** of the tabernacle
25:40 that you make them according to the **p** for them,
Nu 8: 4 to the **p** that the LORD had shown Moses,
2Ki 16:10 and its **p,** exact in all its details.
Eze 41:17 in the inner room and the nave there was a **p.**
43:10 and let them measure the **p;**
Ac 7:44 to make it according to the **p** he had seen.
Heb 8: 5 "See that you make everything according to the **p**
Sir 38:28 and his eyes are on the **p** of the object.
4Mc 6:19 and ourselves become a **p** of impiety to the young

PAU (1)

Ge 36:39 the name of his city being **P;**

PAUL (169) [PAUL'S, =SAUL]

Ac 13: 9 But Saul, also known as **P,**
13:13 Then **P** and his companions set sail from Paphos
13:16 So **P** stood up and with a gesture began to speak:
13:42 As **P** and Barnabas were going out,
13:43 and devout converts to Judaism followed **P**
13:45 they contradicted what was spoken by **P.**
13:46 Then both **P** and Barnabas spoke out boldly,
13:50 stirred up persecution against **P** and Barnabas,
14: 1 where **P** and Barnabas went into
14: 9 He listened to **P** as he was speaking.
14: 9 And **P,** looking at him intently and seeing
14:11 When the crowds saw what **P** had done,
14:12 and **P** they called Hermes,
14:14 When the apostles Barnabas and **P** heard of it,
14:19 they stoned **P** and dragged him out of the city,
15: 2 And after **P** and Barnabas had no small dissension
15: 2 **P** and Barnabas and some of the others
15:12 and listened to Barnabas and **P** as they told of all
15:22 and to send them to Antioch with **P** and Barnabas.
15:25 along with our beloved Barnabas and **P,**
15:35 But **P** and Barnabas remained in Antioch,
15:36 After some days **P** said to Barnabas, "Come,
15:38 But **P** decided not to take with them
15:40 But **P** chose Silas and set out,
16: 1 **P** went on also to Derbe and to Lystra,
16: 3 **P** wanted Timothy to accompany him;
16: 9 During the night **P** had a vision:
16:14 to listen eagerly to what was said by **P.**
Ac 16:17 While she followed **P** and us, she would cry out,
16:18 But **P,** very much annoyed,
16:19 they seized **P** and Silas and dragged them into
16:25 About midnight **P** and Silas were praying
16:28 But **P** shouted in a loud voice,
16:29 he fell down trembling before **P** and Silas.
16:36 And the jailer reported the message to **P,** saying,
16:37 But **P** replied, "They have beaten us in public,
17: 1 After **P** and Silas had passed through Amphipolis
17: 2 And **P** went in, as was his custom,
17: 4 of them were persuaded and joined **P** and Silas,
17: 5 for **P** and Silas to bring them out to the assembly,
17:10 That very night the believers sent **P** and Silas off
17:13 that the word of God had been proclaimed by **P**
17:14 believers immediately sent **P** away to the coast,
17:15 Those who conducted **P** brought him as far
17:16 While **P** was waiting for them in Athens,
17:22 Then **P** stood in front of the Areopagus and said,
17:33 At that point **P** left them.
18: 1 After this **P** left Athens and went to Corinth.
18: 2 to leave Rome. **P** went to see them,
18: 5 **P** was occupied with proclaiming the word,
18: 8 of the Corinthians who heard **P** became believers
18: 9 One night the Lord said to **P** in a vision,
18:12 a united attack on **P** and brought him before
18:14 Just as **P** was about to speak,
18:18 **P** said farewell to the believers and sailed
19: 1 **P** passed through the interior regions and came
19: 4 **P** said, "John baptized with the baptism
19: 6 When **P** had laid his hands on them,
19:11 God did extraordinary miracles through **P,**
19:13 "I adjure you by the Jesus whom **P** proclaims."
19:15 "Jesus I know, and **P** I know; but who are you?"
19:21 **P** resolved in the Spirit to go through Macedonia
19:26 in almost the whole of Asia this **P** has persuaded
19:30 **P** wished to go into the crowd,
20: 1 the uproar had ceased, **P** sent for the disciples;
20: 7 **P** was holding a discussion with them;
20: 9 into a deep sleep while **P** talked still longer.
20:10 But **P** went down, and bending over him took him
20:11 Then **P** went upstairs,
20:13 intending to take **P** on board there;
20:16 For **P** had decided to sail past Ephesus,
20:37 they embraced **P** and kissed him,
21: 4 the Spirit they told **P** not to go on to Jerusalem.
21:13 Then **P** answered, "What are you doing,
21:18 The next day **P** went with us to visit James;
21:26 Then **P** took the men, and the next day,
21:29 and they supposed that **P** had brought him into
21:30 They seized **P** and dragged him out of the temple,
21:32 and the soldiers, they stopped beating **P.**
21:35 When **P** came to the steps,
21:37 as **P** was about to be brought into the barracks,
21:39 **P** replied, "I am a Jew, from Tarsus in Cilicia,
21:40 **P** stood on the steps and motioned to the people
22:25 **P** said to the centurion who was standing by,
22:27 The tribune came and asked **P,** "Tell me,
22:28 **P** said, "But I was born a citizen."
22:29 for he realized that **P** was a Roman citizen and
22:30 to find out what **P** was being accused of by
22:30 He brought **P** down and had him stand
23: 1 **P** was looking intently at the council he said,
23: 3 At this **P** said to him, "God will strike you,
23: 5 And **P** said, "I did not realize, brothers,
23: 6 When **P** noticed that some were Sadducees
23:10 fearing that they would tear **P** to pieces,
23:12 to eat nor drink until they had killed **P.**
23:14 by an oath to taste no food until we have killed **P.**
23:16 and gained entrance to the barracks and told **P.**
23:17 **P** called one of the centurions and said,
23:18 "The prisoner **P** called me and asked me
23:20 "The Jews have agreed to ask you to bring **P**
23:24 Also provide mounts for **P** to ride,
23:31 took **P** and brought him during the night
23:33 they presented **P** also before him.
24: 1 they reported their case against **P** to the governor.
24: 2 When **P** had been summoned,
24:10 the governor motioned to him to speak, **P** replied:
24:24 for **P** and heard him speak concerning faith
24:26 that money would be given him by **P,**
24:27 to grant the Jews a favor, Felix left **P** in prison.
25: 2 of the Jews gave him a report against **P.**
25: 3 as a favor to them against **P,**
25: 4 Festus replied that **P** was being kept at Caesarea,
25: 6 on the tribunal and ordered **P** to be brought.
25: 8 **P** said in his defense, "I have
25: 9 Festus, wishing to do the Jews a favor, asked **P,**
25:10 **P** said, "I am appealing to the emperor's tribunal;
25:19 who had died, but whom **P** asserted to be alive.
25:21 But when **P** had appealed to be kept in custody
25:23 Then Festus gave the order and **P** was brought in.
26: 1 Agrippa said to **P,** "You have permission to speak
26: 1 Then **P** stretched out his hand and began
26:24 Festus exclaimed, "You are out of your mind, **P!**
26:25 But **P** said, "I am not out of my mind,
26:28 to **P,** "Are you so quickly persuading me
26:29 **P** replied, "Whether quickly or not,
27: 1 they transferred **P** and some other prisoners to
27: 3 and Julius treated **P** kindly,
27: 9 the Fast had already gone by, **P** advised them,
27:11 and to the owner of the ship than to what **P** said.
27:21 **P** then stood up among them and said, "Men,
27:24 and he said, 'Do not be afraid, **P;**
27:31 **P** said to the centurion and the soldiers,
27:33 **P** urged all of them to take some food, saying,
27:43 but the centurion, wishing to save **P,** kept them
28: 3 **P** had gathered a bundle of brushwood
Ac 28: 8 **P** visited him and cured him by praying
28:15 On seeing them, **P** thanked God and took courage.
28:16 **P** was allowed to live by himself,
28:25 they were leaving, **P** made one further statement:
Ro 1: 1 **P,** a servant of Jesus Christ, called to be an apostle,
1Co 1: 1 **P,** called to be an apostle of Christ Jesus by
1:12 "I belong to **P,**" or "I belong to Apollos,"
1:13 Was **P** crucified for you?
1:13 Or were you baptized in the name of **P?**
3: 4 For when one says, "I belong to **P,**" and another,
3: 5 then is Apollos? What is **P?**
3:22 whether **P** or Apollos or Cephas or the world
16:21 I, **P,** write this greeting with my own hand.
2Co 1: 1 **P,** an apostle of Christ Jesus by the will of God,
10: 1 **P,** appeal to you by the meekness and gentleness
Gal 1: 1 **P** an apostle—sent neither by human
5: 2 **P,** am telling you that if you let yourselves
Eph 1: 1 **P,** an apostle of Christ Jesus by the will of God,
3: 1 that I **P** am a prisoner for Christ Jesus for the sake
Php 1: 1 **P** and Timothy, servants of Christ Jesus,
Col 1: 1 **P,** an apostle of Christ Jesus by the will of God,
1:23 I, **P,** became a servant of this gospel.
4:18 I, **P,** write this greeting with my own hand.
1Th 1: 1 **P,** Silvanus, and Timothy,
2:18 certainly I, **P,** wanted to again and again—
2Th 1: 1 **P,** Silvanus, and Timothy,
3:17 I, **P,** write this greeting with my own hand.
1Ti 1: 1 **P,** an apostle of Christ Jesus by the command
2Ti 1: 1 **P,** an apostle of Christ Jesus by the will of God,
Tit 1: 1 **P,** a servant of God and an apostle of Jesus Christ,
Phm 1: 1 **P,** a prisoner of Christ Jesus,
1: 9 and I, **P,** do this as an old man,
1:19 I, **P,** am writing this with my own hand:
2Pe 3:15 also our beloved brother **P** wrote to you according

PAUL'S (4) [PAUL]

Ac 19:29 Macedonians who were **P** travel companions.
21:11 He came to us and took **P** belt,
23:16 Now the son of **P** sister heard about the ambush;
25:14 Festus laid **P** case before the king, saying,

PAULUS (1)

Ac 13: 7 He was with the proconsul, Sergius **P,**

PAUPER (1)

Sir 25: 2 a **p** who boasts, a rich person who lies,

PAUSE (1)

2Es 2:24 **P** and be quiet, my people,

PAVED (2) [PAVEMENT]

Tob 13:16 of Jerusalem will be **p** with ruby and with stones
Sir 21:10 The way of sinners is **p** with smooth stones,

PAVEMENT (11) [PAVED]

Ex 24:10 Under his feet there was something like a **p**
2Ch 7: 3 they bowed down on the **p** with their faces to
Est 1: 6 of gold and silver on a mosaic **p** of porphyry,
Jer 43: 9 and bury them in the clay **p** that is at the entrance
Eze 40:17 there were chambers there, and a **p,**
40:17 thirty chambers fronted on the **p.**
40:18 The **p** ran along the side of the gates,
40:18 of the gates; this was the lower **p.**
42: 3 and facing the **p** that belonged to the outer court,
Jn 19:13 the judge's bench at a place called The Stone **P,**
Sir 20:18 A slip on the **p** is better than a slip of the tongue;

PAVILION (3)

Job 36:29 the thunderings of his **p?**
Isa 4: 6 It will serve as a **p,** a shade by day from the heat,
2Mc 13:15 he attacked the king's **p** at night and killed

PAW (2) [PAWS]

1Sa 17:37 who saved me from the **p** of the lion and from the **p** of the bear,

PAWN (1)

Ex 22:26 If you take your neighbor's cloak in **p,**

PAWS (2) [PAW]

Lev 11:27 that walk on their **p,** among the animals that walk
Job 39:21 It **p** violently, exults mightily;

PAY (125) [PAID, PAYING, PAYMENT, PAYMENTS, PAYS, REPAID, REPAY, REPAYING, REPAYMENT, REPAYS]

Ex 5: 9 at it and **p** no attention to deceptive words."
21:19 except to **p** for the loss of time,
21:30 then the owner shall **p** whatever is imposed for
21:32 the owner shall **p** to the slaveowner thirty shekels
22: 1 the thief shall **p** five oxen for an ox,
22: 4 in the thief's possession, the thief shall **p** double.
22: 7 then the thief, if caught, shall **p** double.
22: 9 the one whom God condemns shall **p** double to
22:17 he shall **p** an amount equal to the bride-price
Lev 6: 5 You shall **p** it to its owner
25:15 you shall **p** only for the number of years since
25:51 they shall **p** for their redemption in proportion to
Nu 16:15 "**P** no attention to their offering.
20:19 we and our livestock, then we will **p** for it.
Dt 1:45 neither heed your voice nor **p** you any attention.

Dt 9:27 **p** no attention to the stubbornness of this people,
24:15 You shall **p** them their wages daily before sunset,
Jdg 6:10 not **p** reverence to the gods of the Amorites,
16:28 so that with this one act of revenge I may **p** back
1Sa 1:21 the LORD the yearly sacrifice, and to **p** his vow.
2Sa 3:39 The LORD **p** back the one who does wickedly
15:7 and **p** the vow that I have made to the LORD.
1Ki 20:39 or else you shall **p** a talent of silver.'
2Ki 4:7 and he said, "Go sell the oil and **p** your debts,
12:15 into whose hand they delivered the money to **p** out
Ezr 4:13 they will not **p** tribute, custom, or toll,
Ne 5:4 to borrow money on our fields and vineyards to **p**
Est 3:9 and I will **p** ten thousand talents of silver into
4:7 to **p** into the king's treasuries for the destruction of
Job 20:2 **"P** attention! My thoughts urge me to answer,
22:27 and he will hear you, and you will **p** your vows.
33:31 **P** heed, Job, listen to me;
34:33 Will he then **p** back to suit you,
Ps 22:25 my vows I will **p** before those who fear him.
31:6 You hate those who **p** regard to worthless idols,
37:21 The wicked borrow, and do not **p** back,
50:14 and **p** your vows to the Most High.
61:8 as I **p** my vows day after day.
66:13 I will **p** you my vows,
116:14 I will **p** my vows to the LORD in the presence
116:18 I will **p** my vows to the LORD in the presence
137:8 be who **p** you back what you have done to us!
Pr 6:31 Yet if they are caught, they will **p** sevenfold;
19:19 A violent tempered person will **p** the penalty;
22:27 If you have nothing with which to **p**,
24:29 I will **p** them back for what they have done."
Isa 28:23 **P** attention, and hear my speech.
49:1 Listen to me, O coastlands, **p** attention,
66:15 to **p** back his anger in fury,
Jer 7:26 or **p** attention, but they stiffened their necks.
La 3:64 **P** them back for their deeds, O LORD,
5:4 We must **p** for the water we drink;
Eze 29:18 from Tyre to **p** for the labor that he had expended
Da 3:12 These **p** no heed to you, O King.
10:11 **p** attention to the words that I am going to speak
11:30 and **p** heed to those who forsake
11:37 He shall **p** no respect to the gods of his ancestors,
11:37 he shall **p** no respect to any other god,
Hos 2:12 "These are my **p**, which my lovers have given me."
9:1 a prostitute's **p** on all threshing floors.
12:14 down on him and **p** him back for his insults.
Jnh 2:9 what I have vowed I will **p**.
Mt 2:2 and have come to **p** him homage."
2:8 so that I may also go and **p** him homage."
17:24 "Does your teacher not **p** the temple tax?"
18:25 as he could not **p**, his lord ordered him to be sold,
18:26 and I will **p** you everything.'
18:28 he said, **'P** what you owe.'
18:29 'Have patience with me, and I will **p** you.'
18:30 and threw him into prison until he would **p**
18:34 to be tortured until he would **p** his entire debt.
20:4 and I will **p** you whatever is right.'
20:8 'Call the laborers and give them their **p**,
22:17 Is it lawful to **p** taxes to the emperor, or not?"
Mk 4:24 he said to them, **"P** attention to what you hear;
12:14 Is it lawful to **p** taxes to the emperor, or not?
12:15 Should we **p** them, or should we not?"
Lk 7:42 When they could not **p**, he canceled the debts for
8:18 Then **p** attention to how you listen;
19:8 I will **p** back four times as much."
20:22 Is it lawful for us to **p** taxes to the emperor,
23:2 forbidding us to **p** taxes to the emperor,
Ac 21:24 and **p** for the shaving of their heads.
Ro 13:6 For the same reason you also **p** taxes,
13:7 **P** to all what is due them—
Gal 5:10 But whoever it is that is confusing you will **p**
1Ti 4:16 **P** close attention to yourself and to your teaching;
2Ti 4:14 the Lord will **p** him back for his deeds.
Heb 2:1 Therefore we must **p** greater attention
Rev 6:6 "A quart of wheat for a day's **p**,
6:6 and three quarts of barley for a day's **p**,
Tob 2:12 to the owners and they would **p** wages to her.
4:14 the wages of those who work for you, but **p** them
5:3 and we will **p** him wages until you return.
5:7 and I will **p** you your wages."
5:10 I will **p** your wages, brother."
5:15 he added, "I will **p** you a drachma a day as wages,
12:2 He replied, "Father, how much shall I **p** him?
Jdt 7:15 Thus you will **p** them back with evil,
8:21 and he will make us **p** for its desecration
AdE 3:9 and I will **p** ten thousand talents of silver into
4:7 to **p** ten thousand talents into the royal treasury
Sir 6:33 and if you **p** attention you will become wise.
8:13 but if you give surety, be prepared to **p**.
16:24 and **p** close attention to my words.
20:12 but **p** for it seven times over.
28:16 Those who **p** heed to slander will not find rest,
29:6 If he can **p**, his creditor will hardly get back half,
29:6 If he cannot **p**, the borrower has robbed the other
33:19 and you leaders of the congregation, **p** heed!
34:6 by intervention from the Most High, **p** no attention
36:25 but a person with experience will **p** him back.
37:11 **p** no attention to any advice they give.
1Mc 2:68 **P** back the Gentiles in full,
3:28 He opened his coffers and gave a year's **p**
8:2 and forced them to **p** tribute,
8:7 and those who would reign after him should **p**
15:31 or else **p** me five hundred talents of silver for
2Mc 4:9 to this he promised to **p** one hundred fifty more
4:27 he did not **p** regularly any of the money promised
1Es 2:19 they will not only refuse to **p** tribute but will
4:6 they compel one another to **p** taxes to the king.
2Es 5:32 **p** attention to me, and I will tell you more."
4Mc 1:1 to advise you to **p** earnest attention to philosophy.
4:17 if the office were conferred on him he would **p**

PAYING (14) [PAY]

Ge 42:21 we are **p** the penalty for what we did
Ex 21:22 **p** as much as the judges determine.
Dt 26:12 When you have finished **p** all the tithe
Joel 3:4 Are you **p** me back for something?
3:4 If you are **p** me back,
2Th 3:8 and we did not eat anyone's bread without **p** for it;
1Ti 4:1 by **p** attention to deceitful spirits and teachings
Tit 1:14 not **p** attention to Jewish myths or
1Pe 3:7 **p** honor to the woman as the weaker sex,
Tob 12:1 see to **p** the wages of the man who went with you,
AdE 9:3 and the royal secretaries were **p** honor to the Jews,
Wis 13:1 nor did they recognize the artisan while **p** heed
Sir 18:22 Let nothing hinder you from **p** a vow promptly,
3Mc 2:32 and by **p** money in exchange

PAYMENT (19) [PAY]

Ex 21:11 she shall go out without debt, without **p** of money.
Lev 22:18 whether in **p** of a vow or as a freewill offering
25:52 according to the years involved they shall make **p**
Nu 18:31 it is your **p** for your service in the tent of meeting.
Dt 23:18 into the house of the LORD your God in **p**
Job 31:39 without **p**, and caused the death of its owners;
Isa 65:7 on the hills, I will measure into their laps full **p**
Eze 16:31 you were not like a whore, because you scorned **p**.
16:34 you gave **p**, while no **p** was given to you;
27:15 they brought you in **p** ivory tusks and ebony.
29:20 the land of Egypt as his **p** for which he labored,
Mt 10:8 You received without **p**; give without **p**.
18:25 and children and all his possessions, and **p** to
Tob 4:14 If you serve God you will receive **p**.
1Mc 10:29 "I now free you and exempt all the Jews from **p**
10:33 into any part of my kingdom, I set free without **p**;
2Mc 4:28 the captain of the citadel kept requesting **p**—

PAYMENTS (3) [PAY]

Eze 16:41 and you shall also make no more **p**.
1Mc 11:35 And the other **p** henceforth due to us of the tithes,
15:5 the other **p** from which they have released you.

PAYS‡ (5) [PAY]

Ge 50:15 and **p** us back in full for all the wrong that we did
Job 24:12 yet God **p** no attention to their prayer.
Da 6:13 **p** no attention to you, O king,
1Co 9:7 Who at any time **p** the expenses
Sir 29:5 and **p** back with empty promises,

PEACE‡ (323) [PEACEABLE, PEACEABLY, PEACEFUL, PEACEFULLY, PEACEMAKERS]

Ge 15:15 for yourself, you shall go to your ancestors in **p**;
26:29 but good and have sent you away in **p**.
26:31 and they departed from him in **p**.
28:21 so that I come again to my father's house in **p**,
34:5 so Jacob held his **p** until they came.
44:17 but as for you, go up in **p** to your father."
Ex 4:18 And Jethro said to Moses, "Go in **p**."
18:23 and all these people will go to their home in **p**."
Lev 26:6 And I will grant **p** in the land,
Nu 6:26 up his countenance upon you, and give you **p**.
25:12 say, 'I hereby grant him my covenant of **p**.
Dt 2:26 of Heshbon with the following terms of **p**:
20:10 to a town to fight against it, offer it terms of **p**.
20:11 If it accepts your terms of **p** and surrenders to you,
Jos 9:15 And Joshua made **p** with them,
10:1 the inhabitants of Gibeon had made **p** with Israel
10:4 it has made **p** with Joshua and with the Israelites."
11:19 that made **p** with the Israelites, except the Hivites,
Jdg 4:17 for there was **p** between King Jabin of Hazor and
6:23 But the LORD said to him, **"P** be to you;
6:24 and called it, The LORD is **p**.
18:6 The priest replied, "Go in **p**.
19:20 The old man said, **"P** be to you;
21:13 and proclaimed **p** to them.
1Sa 1:17 Then Eli answered, "Go in **p**;
7:14 There was **p** also between Israel and the Amorites.
10:27 But he held his **p**.
20:42 Then Jonathan said to David, "Go in **p**,
25:6 **'P** be to you, and **p** be to your house, and **p** be to all that you have.
25:35 he said to her, "Go up to your house in **p**;
2Sa 3:21 David dismissed Abner, and he went away in **p**.
3:22 and he had gone away in **p**.
3:23 and he has gone away in **p**."
10:19 that they had been defeated by Israel, they made **p**
15:9 The king said to him, "Go in **p**."
15:27 "Look, go back to the city in **p**, you and Abiathar,
17:3 and all the people will be at **p**."
1Ki 2:5 in time of **p** for blood that had been shed in war,
2:6 but do not let his gray head go down to Sheol in **p**.
2:33 there shall be **p** from the LORD forevermore."
4:24 and he had **p** on all sides.
5:12 There was **p** between Hiram and Solomon;
20:18 He said, "If they have come out for **p**,
22:17 let each one go home in **p**.' "
22:27 of bread and water until I come in **p**.' "
22:28 Micaiah said, "If you return in **p**,
22:44 Jehoshaphat also made **p** with the king of Israel.
2Ki 5:19 He said to him, "Go in **p**."
9:17 and let him say, 'Is it **p**?' "
9:18 he said, "Thus says the king, 'Is it **p**?' "
9:18 Jehu responded, "What have you to do with **p**?
9:19 "Thus says the king, 'Is it **p**?' "
9:19 Jehu answered, "What have you to do with **p**?
9:22 When Joram saw Jehu, he said, "Is it **p**, Jehu?"
9:22 He answered, "What **p** can there be,
9:31 As Jehu entered the gate, she said, "Is it **p**, Zimri,
18:31 'Make your **p** with me and come out to me;
20:19 if there will be **p** and security in my days?"
22:20 and you shall be gathered to your grave in **p**;
1Ch 12:18 **P**, **p** to you, and **p** to the one who helps you!
19:19 that they had been defeated by Israel, they made **p**
22:9 he shall be a man of **p**.
22:9 I will give him **p** from all his enemies on every
22:9 and I will give **p** and quiet to Israel in his days.
22:18 Has he not given you **p** on every side?
2Ch 14:6 for the LORD gave him **p**.
14:7 and he has given us **p** on every side."
18:16 let each one go home in **p**.' "
18:26 of bread and water until I return in **p**.' "
18:27 Micaiah said, "If you return in **p**,
34:28 and you shall be gathered to your grave in **p**;
Ezr 5:7 "To Darius the king, all **p**!
7:12 of the law of the God of heaven: **P**.
9:12 and never seek their **p** or prosperity,
Est 7:4 men and women, I would have held my **p**;
9:30 Letters were sent wishing **p** and security to all
Job 5:23 and the wild animals shall be at **p** with you.
12:6 The tents of robbers are at **p**,
21:13 and in **p** they go down to Sheol.
22:21 "Agree with God, and be at **p**;
25:2 he makes **p** in his high heaven.
Ps 4:8 I will both lie down and sleep in **p**;
28:3 who speak **p** with their neighbors,
29:11 May the LORD bless his people with **p**!
34:14 Depart from evil, and do good; seek **p**,
35:20 For they do not speak **p**,
39:2 I was silent and still; I held my **p** to no avail;
39:12 do not hold your **p** at my tears.
72:7 In his days may righteousness flourish and **p**
83:1 do not hold your **p** or be still, O God!
85:8 for he will speak **p** to his people, to his faithful,
85:10 righteousness and **p** will kiss each other.
119:165 Great **p** have those who love your law;
120:6 have I had my dwelling among those who hate **p**.
120:7 I am for **p**; but when I speak, they are for war.
122:6 Pray for the **p** of Jerusalem:
122:7 **P** be within your walls, and security
122:8 the sake of my relatives and friends I will say, **"P**
125:5 with evildoers. **P** be upon Israel!
128:6 see your children's children. **P** be upon Israel!
147:14 He grants **p** within your borders;
Pr 3:17 and all her paths are **p**.
10:10 but the one who rebukes boldly makes **p**.
12:20 but those who counsel **p** have joy.
16:7 he causes even their enemies to be at **p** with them.
Ecc 3:8 a time for war, and a time for **p**.
SS 8:10 then I was in his eyes as one who brings **p**.
Isa 9:6 Mighty God, Everlasting Father, Prince of **P**.
9:7 and there shall be endless **p** for the throne
26:3 Those of steadfast mind you keep in **p**—in **p** because they trust in you.
26:12 O LORD, you will ordain **p** for us, for indeed,
27:5 let it make **p** with me, let it make **p** with me.
32:17 The effect of righteousness will be **p**,
33:7 the envoys of **p** weep bitterly.
36:16 'Make your **p** with me and come out to me;
39:8 "There will be **p** and security in my days."
42:14 For a long time I have held my **p**,
48:22 "There is no **p**," says the LORD, "for the wicked."
52:7 the feet of the messenger who announces **p**,
54:10 and my covenant of **p** shall not be removed,
55:12 For you shall go out in joy, and be led back in **p**;
57:2 and they enter into **p**; those who walk uprightly will rest on their
57:19 **P**, **p**, to the far and the near, says the LORD;
57:21 There is no **p**, says my God, for the wicked.
59:8 The way of **p** they do not know,
59:8 no one who walks in them knows **p**.
60:17 I will appoint **P** as your overseer
Jer 6:14 saying, **"P, p,"** when there is no **p**.
8:11 saying, **"P, p,"** when there is no **p**.
8:15 We look for **p**, but find no good,
14:13 but I will give you true **p** in this place.' "
14:19 We look for **p**, but find no good;
16:5 for I have taken away my **p** from this people,
28:9 As for the prophet who prophesies **p**,
30:5 We have heard a cry of panic, of terror, and no **p**.
34:5 you shall die in **p**. And
La 3:17 my soul is bereft of **p**;
Eze 7:25 When anguish comes, they will seek **p**,
13:10 misled my people, saying, **"P,"** when there is no **p**;
13:16 concerning Jerusalem and saw visions of **p** for it,
13:16 when there was no **p**, says the Lord GOD.
34:25 a covenant of **p** and banish wild animals from
37:26 I will make a covenant of **p** with them;
Da 11:17 and he shall bring terms of **p** and perform them.
Mic 3:5 who cry **"P"** when they have something to eat,
5:5 and he shall be the one of **p**.
Na 1:15 of one who brings good tidings, who proclaims **p**!
Zec 1:11 and lo, the whole earth remains at **p**."
8:12 For there shall be a sowing of **p**;
8:16 that are true and make for **p**,
8:19 therefore love truth and **p**.
9:10 and he shall command **p** to the nations;
Mt 10:13 If the house is worthy, let your **p** come upon it;
10:13 but if it is not worthy, let your **p** return to you.

Mt 10:34 not think that I have come to bring **p** to the earth;
10:34 I have not come to bring **p**, but a sword.
Mk 4:39 up and rebuked the wind, and said to the sea, **"P!**
5:34 go in **p**, and be healed of your disease."
9:50 and be at **p** with one another."
Lk 1:79 to guide our feet into the way of **p."**
2:14 and on earth **p** among those whom he favors!"
2:29 now you are dismissing your servant in **p**,
7:50 "Your faith has saved you; go in **p."**
8:48 your faith has made you well; go in **p."**
10: 5 first say, **'P** to this house!'
10: 6 And if anyone is there who shares in **p**,
10: 6 your **p** will rest on that person;
12:51 Do you think that I have come to bring **p** to
14:32 he sends a delegation and asks for the terms of **p.**
19:38 **P** in heaven, and glory in the highest heaven!"
19:42 on this day the things that make for **p!**
24:36 among them and said to them, **"P** be with you."
Jn 14:27 **P** I leave with you; my **p** I give to you.
16:33 so that in me you may have **p.**
20:19 and stood among them and said, **"P** be with you."
20:21 Jesus said to them again, **"P** be with you.
20:26 and stood among them and said, **"P** be with you."
Ac 9:31 Galilee, and Samaria had **p** and was built up.
10:36 preaching **p** by Jesus Christ—he is Lord of all.
15:33 in **p** by the believers to those who had sent them.
16:36 therefore come out now and go in **p."**
24: 2 because of you we have long enjoyed **p,**
Ro 1: 7 Grace to you and **p** from God our Father and
2:10 and honor and **p** for everyone who does good,
3:17 and the way of **p** they have not known."
5: 1 since we are justified by faith, we have **p**
8: 6 but to set the mind on the Spirit is life and **p.**
14:17 not food and drink but righteousness and **p** and joy
14:19 Let us then pursue what makes for **p** and
15:13 May the God of hope fill you with all joy and **p**
15:33 The God of **p** be with all of you. Amen.
16:20 God of **p** will shortly crush Satan under your feet.
1Co 1: 3 Grace to you and **p** from God our Father and
7:15 It is to **p** that God has called you.
14:33 for God is a God not of disorder but of **p.**
16:11 Send him on his way in **p**,
2Co 1: 2 Grace to you and **p** from God our Father and
13:11 agree with one another, live in **p**; and the God of love and **p** will be with you.
Gal 1: 3 Grace to you and **p** from God our Father and
5:22 By contrast, the fruit of the Spirit is love, joy, **p,**
6:16 **p** be upon them, and mercy,
Eph 1: 2 Grace to you and **p** from God our Father and
2:14 For he is our **p**; in his flesh he has made both
2:15 new humanity in place of the two, thus making **p,**
2:17 and proclaimed **p** to you who were far off
2:17 and **p** to those who were near;
4: 3 to maintain the unity of the Spirit in the bond of **p.**
6:15 to proclaim the gospel of **p.**
6:23 **P** be to the whole community, and love with faith,
Php 1: 2 Grace to you and **p** from God our Father and
4: 7 the **p** of God, which surpasses all understanding,
4: 9 and the God of **p** will be with you.
Col 1: 2 Grace to you and **p** from God our Father.
1:20 by making **p** through the blood of his cross.
3:15 And let the **p** of Christ rule in your hearts,
1Th 1: 1 and the Lord Jesus Christ: Grace to you and **p.**
5: 3 When they say, "There is **p** and security,"
5:13 Be at **p** among yourselves.
5:23 May the God of **p** himself sanctify you entirely;
2Th 1: 2 Grace to you and **p** from God our Father and
3:16 the Lord of **p** himself give you **p** at all times
1Ti 1: 2 **p** from God the Father and Christ Jesus our Lord.
2Ti 1: 2 **p** from God the Father and Christ Jesus our Lord.
2:22 and **p**, along with those who call on the Lord from
Tit 1: 4 Grace and **p** from God the Father
Phm 1: 3 Grace to you and **p** from God our Father and
Heb 7: 2 next he is also king of Salem, that is, "king of **p."**
11:31 because she had received the spies in **p.**
12:14 Pursue **p** with everyone, and the holiness
13:20 Now may the God of **p,**
Jas 2:16 and one of you says to them, "Go in **p;**
3:18 And a harvest of righteousness is sown in **p** for those who make **p.**
1Pe 1: 2 May grace and **p** be yours in abundance.
3:11 let them seek **p** and pursue it.
5:14 **P** to all of you who are in Christ.
2Pe 1: 2 and **p** be yours in abundance in the knowledge
3:14 strive to be found by him at **p,**
2Jn 1: 3 and **p** will be with us from God the Father and
3Jn 1:15 **P** to you. The friends send you their greetings.
Jude 1: 2 May mercy, **p,** and love be yours in abundance.
Rev 1: 4 Grace to you and **p** from him who is and who was
6: 4 its rider was permitted to take **p** from the earth,
Tob 7:11 both this night and grant you mercy and **p."**
7:12 of heaven prosper your journey with his **p."**
10:12 Go in **p**, daughter, and may I hear a good report
10:12 Go in **p**, my child.
12:17 he said to them, "Do not be afraid; **p** be with you.
14: 2 in **p** when he was one hundred twelve years old,
Jdt 3: 1 They therefore sent messengers to him to sue for **p**
7:24 a great injury in not making **p** with the Assyrians.
8:35 Uzziah and the rulers said to her, "Go in **p,**
AdE 13: 2 to restore the **p** desired by all people.
Wis 3: 3 be their destruction; but they are at **p.**
14:22 they call such great evils **p.**
Sir 1:18 making **p** and perfect health to flourish.
13:18 What **p** is there between a hyena and a dog?
13:18 And what **p** between the rich and the poor?
26: 2 and he will complete his years in **p.**
28: 9 and sows discord among those who are at **p.**
Sir 28:13 for they destroy the **p** of many.
28:16 nor will they settle down in **p.**
41: 1 how bitter is the thought of you to the one at **p**
41:14 My children, be true to your training and be at **p;**
44:14 Their bodies are buried in **p,**
47:13 Solomon reigned in an age of **p,**
50:23 and may there be **p** in our days in Israel,
Bar 3:13 you would be living in **p** forever.
3:14 and life, where there is light for the eyes, and **p.**
4:20 I have taken off the robe of **p** and put on sackcloth
5: 4 "Righteous **P,** Godly Glory."
LtJ 6: 3 after that I will bring you away from there in **p.**
1Mc 6:49 He made **p** with the people of Beth-zur,
6:58 and make **p** with them and with all their nation.
6:60 and he sent to the Jews an offer of **p,**
7:13 among the Israelites to seek **p** from them,
7:28 with a few men to see you face to face in **p."**
8:20 to you to establish alliance and **p** with you,
8:22 with them there as a memorial of **p** and alliance:
9:70 to him to make **p** with him and obtain release of
10: 4 to make **p** with him before he makes **p** with
10:66 Jonathan returned to Jerusalem in **p** and gladness.
11:50 "Grant us **p,** and make the Jews stop fighting
11:51 And they threw down their arms and made **p.**
11:62 and he made **p** with them,
11:66 Then they asked him to grant them terms of **p,**
13:37 a general **p** with you and to write to our officials
13:40 and let there be **p** between us."
13:45 asking Simon to make **p** with them;
13:50 Then they cried to Simon to make **p** with them,
14: 8 They tilled their land in **p;**
14:11 He established **p** in the land,
2Mc 1: 1 in Egypt, Greetings and true **p.**
1: 4 and his commandments, and may he bring **p.**
3: 1 in unbroken **p** and the laws were strictly observed
12: 2 would not let them live quietly and in **p.**
12:12 agreed to make **p** with them;
14:10 it is impossible for the government to find **p."**
1Es 8:85 do not seek ever to have **p** with them,
3Mc 2:20 and broken in spirit, and give us **p."**
6:27 Send them back to their homes in **p,**
7:19 in **p** with appropriate thanksgiving,
2Es 13:47 you saw the multitude gathered together in **p.**
16:21 that people will imagine that **p** is assured for them,
4Mc 3:20 when our ancestors were enjoying profound **p**
8:26 when we can live in **p** if we obey the king?"
18: 4 Because of them the nation gained **p,**

PEACEABLE (16) [PEACE]

2Sa 20:19 I am one of those who are **p** and faithful in Israel;
Ps 37:37 for there is posterity for the **p.**
1Ti 2: 2 that we may lead a quiet and **p** life in all godliness
Jas 3:17 But the wisdom from above is first pure, then **p,**
AdE 13: 2 in order to make my kingdom **p** and open to travel
16: 8 to render our kingdom quiet and **p** for all,
1Mc 1:30 Deceitfully he spoke **p** words to them,
7:10 and his brothers with **p** but treacherous words.
7:15 Alcimus spoke **p** words to them
7:27 to Judas and his brothers this **p** message,
10: 3 Demetrius sent Jonathan a letter in **p** words
10:47 he had been the first to speak **p** words to them,
11: 2 He set out for Syria with **p** words,
2Es 11:42 you have oppressed the meek and injured the **p;**
13:12 and call to himself another multitude that was **p.**
13:39 to himself another multitude that was **p,**

PEACEABLY (14) [PEACE]

Ge 37: 4 they hated him, and could not speak **p** to him.
Jdg 11:13 now therefore restore it **p."**
1Sa 16: 4 and said, "Do you come **p?"**
16: 5 He said, **"P;** I have come to sacrifice
29: 7 So go back now; and go **p;**
1Ki 2:13 She asked, "Do you come **p?"**He said, **"P."**
Ro 12:18 so far as it depends on you, live **p** with all.
Jdt 7:15 because they rebelled and did not receive you **p."**
1Mc 5:25 who met them **p** and told them all
7:29 he came to Judas, and they greeted one another **p;**
7:33 of the elders of the people came out to greet him **p**
2Mc 5:25 he pretended to be **p** disposed and waited until
12: 4 they wished to live **p** and suspected nothing,

PEACEFUL (10) [PEACE]

1Ch 4:40 and the land was very broad, quiet, and **p;**
Isa 32:18 My people will abide in a **p** habitation,
Jer 25:37 and the **p** folds are devastated,
Mic 2: 8 you strip the robe from the **p,**
Zec 6:13 with **p** understanding between the two of them.
Heb 12:11 but later it yields the **p** fruit of righteousness
Sir 47:16 and you were loved for your **p** reign.
2Mc 4: 6 not again reach a **p** settlement,
10:12 and attempted to maintain **p** relations with them.
3Mc 6:32 they formed choruses as a sign of **p** joy.

PEACEFULLY (2) [PEACE]

Dt 20:12 If it does not submit to you **p,**
Sir 44: 6 with resources, living **p** in their homes—

PEACEMAKERS (1) [PEACE]

Mt 5: 9 "Blessed are the **p,** for they will be called children

PEACOCKS (2)

1Ki 10:22 to come bringing gold, silver, ivory, apes, and **p.**
2Ch 9:21 to come bringing gold, silver, ivory, apes, and **p.**

PEACOCKS (KJV) See also OSTRICH

PEAK (2) [MANY-PEAKED]

SS 4: 8 Depart from the **p** of Amana, from the **p** of Senir and Hermon,

PEALS (4) [THUNDERPEALS]

Rev 4: 5 and rumblings and **p** of thunder,
8: 5 and there were **p** of thunder, rumblings,
11:19 **p** of thunder, an earthquake, and heavy hail.
16:18 rumblings, **p** of thunder, and a violent earthquake,

PEARL (2) [MOTHER-OF-PEARL, PEARLS]

Mt 13:46 on finding one **p** of great value,
Rev 21:21 each of the gates is a single **p,**

PEARLS (8) [PEARL]

Job 28:18 the price of wisdom is above **p.**
Mt 7: 6 and do not throw your **p** before swine,
13:45 of heaven is like a merchant in search of fine **p;**
1Ti 2: 9 not with their hair braided, or with gold, **p,**
Rev 17: 4 and adorned with gold and jewels and **p,**
18:12 jewels and **p,** fine linen, purple, silk and scarlet,
18:16 adorned with gold, with jewels, and with **p!**
21:21 And the twelve gates are twelve **p,**

PEASANTRY (2)

Jdg 5: 7 The **p** prospered in Israel,
5:11 the triumphs of his **p** in Israel.

PEBBLE (3)

2Sa 17:13 until not even a **p** is to be found there."
Am 9: 9 but no **p** shall fall to the ground.
1Mc 10:73 where there is no stone or **p,** or place to flee."

PEBBLES See Index to Footnotes

PECKED (1)

Pr 30:17 a father and scorns to obey a mother will be **p** out

PEDAHEL (1)

Nu 34:28 of the Naphtalites a leader, **P** son of Ammihud.

PEDAHZUR (5)

Nu 1:10 from Manasseh, Gamaliel son of **P.**
2:20 of Manasseh shall be Gamaliel son of **P,**
7:54 On the eighth day Gamaliel son of **P,**
7:59 This was the offering of Gamaliel son of **P.**
10:23 of the tribe of Manasseh was Gamaliel son of **P,**

PEDAIAH (9)

2Ki 23:36 His mother's name was Zebidah daughter of **P**
1Ch 3:18 **P,** Shenazzar, Jekamiah, Hoshama, and Nedabiah;
3:19 The sons of **P:** Zerubbabel
27:20 for the half-tribe of Manasseh, Joel son of **P;**
Ne 3:25 After him **P** son of Parosh
8: 4 and **P,** Mishael, Malchijah, Hashum,
11: 7 Sallu son of Meshullam son of Joed son of **P** son
13:13 the scribe Zadok, and **P** of the Levites,
1Es 9:44 and on his left **P,** Mishael,

PEDDLERS (1)

2Co 2:17 For we are not **p** of God's word like so many;

PEDESTAL (1)

1Ki 7:31 its opening was round, as a **p** is made;

PEDIMENT (1)

2Ki 16:17 and put it on a **p** of stone.

PEEL (1) [PEELED]

Tob 11: 8 the white films shrink and **p** off from his eyes,

PEELED (3) [PEEL]

Ge 30:37 and **p** white streaks in them,
30:38 He set the rods that he had **p** in front of the flocks
Tob 11:13 with both his hands he **p** off the white films from

PEERED (2) [PEERS]

Jdg 5:28 "Out of the window she **p,**
2Mc 3:19 while others **p** out of the windows.

PEERS (2) [PEERED]

Sir 14:23 who **p** through her windows and listens
21:23 A boor **p** into the house from the door,

PEG (10) [PEGS]

Jdg 4:21 But Jael wife of Heber took a tent **p,**
4:21 went softly to him and drove the **p** into his temple,
4:22 with the tent **p** in his temple.
5:26 She put her hand to the tent **p** and her right hand
Isa 22:23 I will fasten him like a **p** in a secure place,
22:25 the **p** that was fastened in
Eze 15: 3 a **p** from it on which to hang any object?
Zec 10: 4 out of them the tent **p,** out of them the battle bow,
Sir 14:24 near her house and fastens his tent **p** to her walls;
26:12 of every tent **p** and open her quiver to the arrow.

PEGS (17) [PEG]
Ex 26:17 be two **p** in each frame to fit the frames together;
26:19 two bases under the first frame for its two **p,** and two bases under the next frame for its two **p;**
27:19 and all its **p** and all the **p** of the court,
35:18 the **p** of the tabernacle and the **p** of the court,
36:22 Each frame had two **p** for fitting together;
36:24 two bases under the first frame for its two **p,** and two bases under the next frame for its two **p.**
38:20 All the **p** for the tabernacle and for the court all
38:31 all the **p** of the tabernacle, and all the **p** around the
39:40 for the gate of the court, its cords, and its **p;**
Nu 3:37 with their bases and **p** and cords.
4:32 **p,** and cords, with all their equipment
Eze 40:43 There were **p,** one handbreadth long,

PEKAH (11)
2Ki 15:25 **P** son of Remaliah, his captain,
15:27 **P** son of Remaliah began to reign over Israel
15:29 In the days of King **P** of Israel,
15:30 against **P** son of Remaliah, attacked him,
15:31 Now the rest of the acts of **P,** and all that he did,
15:32 In the second year of King **P** son of Remaliah
15:37 of Aram and **P** son of Remaliah against Judah.
16:1 In the seventeenth year of **P** son of Remaliah,
16:5 and King **P** son of Remaliah of Israel came up
2Ch 28:6 **P** son of Remaliah killed one hundred twenty
Isa 7:1 King Rezin of Aram and King **P** son of Remaliah

PEKAHIAH (3)
2Ki 15:22 and his son **P** succeeded him.
15:23 **P** son of Menahem began to reign over Israel
15:26 Now the rest of the deeds of **P,** and all that he did,

PEKOD (2)
Jer 50:21 and attack the inhabitants of **P** and utterly destroy
Eze 23:23 the Chaldeans, **P** and Shoa and Koa, and all

PELAIAH (4)
1Ch 3:24 Hodaviah, Eliashib, **P,** Akkub, Johanan, Delaiah,
Ne 8:7 Kelita, Azariah, Jozabad, Hanan, **P,** the Levites,
10:10 Shebaniah, Hodiah, Kelita, **P,** Hanan,
1Es 9:48 Hanan, **P,** the Levites, taught the law of the Lord,

PELALIAH (1)
Ne 11:12 and Adaiah son of Jeroham son of **P** son

PELATIAH (5)
1Ch 3:21 **P** and Jeshaiah, his son Rephaiah, his son Arnan,
4:42 went to Mount Seir, having as their leaders **P,**
Ne 10:22 **P,** Hanan, Anaiah,
Eze 11:1 and **P** son of Benaiah, officials of the people.
11:13 while I was prophesying, **P** son of Benaiah died.

PELEG (8)
Ge 10:25 the name of the one was **P,**
11:16 he became the father of **P;**
11:17 after the birth of **P** four hundred thirty years,
11:18 When **P** had lived thirty years,
11:19 and **P** lived after the birth
1Ch 1:19 the name of the one was **P** (for in his days
1:25 Eber, **P,** Reu;
Lk 3:35 son of Reu, son of **P,** son of Eber, son of Shelah,

PELET (2)
1Ch 2:47 Regem, Jotham, Geshan, **P,** Ephah, and Shaaph.
12:3 also Jeziel and **P** sons of Azmaveth;

PELETH (2) [PELETHITES]
Nu 16:1 and Abiram sons of Eliab, and On son of **P**—
1Ch 2:33 The sons of Jonathan: **P** and Zaza.

PELETHITES (7) [PELETH]
2Sa 8:18 of Jehoiada was over the Cherethites and the **P;**
15:18 and all the Cherethites, and all the **P,**
20:7 along with the Cherethites, the **P,**
20:23 in command of the Cherethites and the **P;**
1Ki 1:38 and the Cherethites and the **P,**
1:44 and the Cherethites and the **P;**
1Ch 18:17 of Jehoiada was over the Cherethites and the **P;**

PELICAN (KJV) See DESERT OWL, OWL; See also Index to Footnotes

PELONITE (3)
1Ch 11:27 Shammoth of Harod, Helez the **P,**
11:36 Hepher the Mecherathite, Ahijah the **P,**
27:10 Seventh, for the seventh month, was Helez the **P,**

PELUSIUM (2)
Eze 30:15 I will pour my wrath upon **P,**
30:16 I will set fire to Egypt; **P** shall be in great agony;

PEN (5) [PENS]
Job 19:24 with an iron **p** and with lead they were engraved
Ps 45:1 my tongue is like the **p** of a ready scribe.
Jer 8:8 the false **p** of the scribes has made it into a lie?
17:1 The sin of Judah is written with an iron **p;**
3Jn 1:13 but I would rather not write with **p** and ink;

PENALTIES (4) [PENALTY]
Wis 14:30 But just **p** will overtake them on two counts:
Sir 9:5 or you may stumble and incur **p** for her.
3Mc 7:3 and to punish them with barbarous **p** as traitors;
2Es 9:6 and the end in **p** and in signs.

PENALTY (20) [PENALTIES]
Ge 42:21 the **p** for what we did to our brother;
Lev 5:6 as your **p** for the sin that you have committed,
5:7 as your **p** for the sin that you have committed,
Nu 35:31 of a murderer who is subject to the death **p;**
Dt 17:7 against the person to execute the death **p,**
Pr 19:19 A violent tempered person will pay the **p;**
Isa 40:2 that she has served her term, that her **p** is paid,
Eze 16:58 the **p** of your lewdness and your abominations,
23:49 and you shall bear the **p** for your sinful idolatry;
Ac 28:18 there was no reason for the death **p** in my case.
Ro 1:27 in their own persons the due **p** for their error.
Gal 5:10 whoever it is that is confusing you will pay the **p.**
Heb 2:2 or disobedience received a just **p,**
2Pe 2:13 suffering the **p** for doing wrong.
Tob 3:5 now your many judgments are true in exacting **p**
6:13 the **p** of death according to the decree of the book
Wis 14:31 but the just **p** for those who sin,
18:11 slave was punished with the same **p** as the master,
2Mc 4:48 and the holy vessels quickly suffered the unjust **p.**
2Es 6:19 and when I require from the doers of iniquity the **p**

PENCE (KJV) See DENARII

PENDANTS (5)
Ex 35:22 and earrings and signet rings and **p,**
Nu 31:50 signet rings, earrings, and **p,**
Jdg 8:26 the **p** and the purple garments worn by the kings
Pr 1:9 a fair garland for your head, and **p** for your neck.
Isa 3:19 the **p,** the bracelets, and the scarfs;

PENETRATE (1) [PENETRATES, PENETRATING]
Job 41:13 Who can **p** its double coat of mail?

PENETRATES (2) [PENETRATE]
Wis 7:24 of her pureness she pervades and **p** all things.
Sir 39:2 of the famous and **p** the subtleties of parables;

PENETRATING (1) [PENETRATE]
Wis 7:23 and **p** through all spirits that are intelligent, pure,

PENIEL (1) [=PENUEL]
Ge 32:30 So Jacob called the place **P,** saying,

PENINNAH (3)
1Sa 1:2 and the name of the other **P.**
1:2 **P** had children, but Hannah had no children.
1:4 to his wife **P** and to all her sons and daughters;

PENIS (1)
Dt 23:1 whose testicles are crushed or whose **p** is cut off

PENITENT (2)
2Ki 22:19 because your heart was **p,**
2Ch 34:27 because your heart was **p**

PENKNIFE (1) [KNIFE]
Jer 36:23 a **p** and throw them into the fire in the brazier,

PENNIES (1) [PENNY]
Lk 12:6 Are not five sparrows sold for two **p?**

PENNY (4) [PENNIES]
Mt 5:26 until you have paid the last **p.**
10:29 Are not two sparrows sold for a **p?**
Mk 12:42 in two small copper coins, which are worth a **p**
Lk 12:59 until you have paid the very last **p.**"

PENNYWORTH (KJV) See DENARII, SIX MONTHS' WAGES

PENS (1) [PEN]
3Mc 4:20 and proved that both the paper and the **p** they used

PENT-UP (1)
Isa 59:19 a **p** stream that the wind of the LORD drives on.

PENTAPOLIS See Index to Footnotes

PENTECOST (5)
Ac 2:1 When the day of **P** had come,
20:16 if possible, on the day of **P.**
1Co 16:8 But I will stay in Ephesus until **P,**
Tob 2:1 At our festival of **P,** which is the sacred festival
2Mc 12:32 After the festival called **P,**

PENUEL (8) [=PENIEL]
Ge 32:31 The sun rose upon him as he passed **P,**
Jdg 8:8 From there he went up to **P,**
8:8 and the people of **P** answered him as the people
Jdg 8:9 So he said to the people of **P,**
8:17 He also broke down the tower of **P,**
1Ki 12:25 he went out from there and built **P.**
1Ch 4:4 and **P** was the father of Gedor,
8:25 Iphdeiah, and **P** were the sons of Shashak.

PEOPLE‡ (2840) [PEOPLE'S, PEOPLED, PEOPLES, TOWNSPEOPLE]
A. ALL ... PEOPLE (384)
B. PEOPLE OF ISRAEL (209)
C. PEOPLE ISRAEL (85)
D. PEOPLE OF JUDAH (72)
E. PEOPLE OF THE LAND (52)
F. ELDERS OF THE/MY PEOPLE (14)
G. PEOPLE OF THE EAST (11)
H. PEOPLE OF THE †LORD (10)
I. OTHER PEOPLE (9)
J. PEOPLE OF THE CITY (9)
K. HOLY PEOPLE (8)

Ge 4:26 At that time **p** began to invoke the name of
6:1 **p** began to multiply on the face of the ground,
6:7 **p** together with animals and creeping things
11:6 And the LORD said, "Look, they are one **p,**
13:13 Now the **p** of Sodom were wicked,
14:16 and the women and the **p.**
17:14 of his foreskin shall be cut off from his **p;**
19:4 all the **p** to the last man, surrounded the house; A
19:13 against its **p** has become great before the LORD,
20:4 he said, "Lord, will you destroy an innocent **p?**
23:7 and bowed to the Hittites, the **p** of the land. E
23:11 in the presence of my **p** I give it to you;
23:12 Abraham bowed down before the **p** of the land. E
23:13 to Ephron in the hearing of the **p** of the land, E
25:8 and was gathered to his **p.**
25:17 and was gathered to his **p.)**
25:18 he settled down alongside of all his **p.** A
26:10 of the **p** might easily have lain with your wife,
26:11 So Abimelech warned all the **p,** saying, A
29:1 and came to the land of the **p** of the east. G
29:22 Laban gathered together all the **p** of the place, A
32:7 and he divided the **p** that were with him,
33:15 "Let me leave with you some of the **p** who are
34:16 and we will live among you and become one **p.**
34:21 "These **p** are friendly with us;
34:22 to live among us, to become one **p:**
35:6 he and all the **p** who were with him, A
35:29 he died and was gathered to his **p,**
41:40 all my **p** shall order themselves as you A
41:55 the **p** cried to Pharaoh for bread.
42:5 of Israel were among the other **p** who came I
42:6 it was he who sold to all the **p** of the land. AE
47:21 As for the **p,** he made slaves of them from one end
47:23 Then Joseph said to the **p,**
48:19 he also shall become a **p,**
49:16 Dan shall judge his **p** as one of the tribes of Israel.
49:29 "I am about to be gathered to my **p.**
49:33 breathed his last, and was gathered to his **p.**
50:20 in order to preserve a numerous **p,**
Ex 1:5 The total number of **p** born to Jacob was seventy.
1:9 to his **p,** "Look, the Israelite **p** are more numerous
1:20 and the **p** multiplied and became very strong.
1:22 Then Pharaoh commanded all his **p,** A
2:11 he went out to his **p** and saw their forced labor.
3:7 "I have observed the misery of my **p** who are
3:10 come, I will send you to Pharaoh to bring my **p,**
3:12 when you have brought the **p** out of Egypt,
3:21 I will bring this **p** into such favor with
4:16 He indeed shall speak for you to the **p;**
4:21 so that he will not let the **p** go.
4:30 and performed the signs in the sight of the **p.**
4:31 The **p** believed; and when they heard
5:1 the LORD, the God of Israel, 'Let my **p** go,
5:4 why are you taking the **p** away from their work?
5:5 they are more numerous than the **p** of the land E
5:6 commanded the taskmasters of the **p,** as well
5:7 "You shall no longer give the **p** straw
5:10 and the supervisors of the **p** went out and said to
5:10 of the people went out and said to the **p,**
5:12 So the **p** scattered throughout the land of Egypt,
5:16 You are unjust to your own **p.**"
5:22 "O LORD, why have you mistreated this **p?**
5:23 to speak in your name, he has mistreated this **p,**
5:23 you have done nothing at all to deliver your **p.**"
6:7 I will take you as my **p,** and I will be your God.
7:4 I will lay my hand upon Egypt and bring my **p**
7:14 he refuses to let the **p** go.
7:16 sent me to you to say, "Let my **p** go,
8:1 Let my **p** go, so that they may worship me.
8:3 into the houses of your officials and of your **p,**
8:4 The frogs shall come up on you and on your **p** and
8:8 to take away the frogs from me and my **p,**
8:8 and I will let the **p** go to sacrifice to the LORD."
8:9 for you and for your officials and for your **p,**
8:11 and your houses and your officials and your **p;**
8:20 Let my **p** go, so that they may worship me.
8:21 For if you will not let my **p** go,
8:21 your officials, and your **p,** and into your houses;
8:22 where my **p** live, so that no swarms of flies shall
8:23 make a distinction between my **p** and your **p.**
8:29 from his officials, and from his **p;**
8:29 by not letting the **p** go to sacrifice to the LORD."
8:31 and from his **p;** not one remained.
8:32 and would not let the **p** go.
9:1 Let my **p** go, so that they may worship me.
9:7 and he would not let the **p** go.

Ex 9:13 Let my **p** go, so that they may worship me.
9:14 and upon your officials, and upon your **p**,
9:15 and struck you and your **p** with pestilence,
9:17 You are still exalting yourself against my **p**,
9:27 and I and my **p** are in the wrong.
10: 3 Let my **p** go, so that they may worship me.
10: 4 For if you refuse to let my **p** go,
10: 7 Let the **p** go, so that they may worship
10:23 **P** could not see one another,
11: 2 Tell the **p** that every man is to ask his neighbor
11: 3 The LORD gave the **p** favor in the sight of
11: 3 of Pharaoh's officials and in the sight of the **p**.
11: 7 not at **p**, not at animals—
11: 8 'Leave us, you and all the **p** who follow you.' A
11:10 he did not let the **p** of Israel go out of his land. B
12: 4 in proportion to the number of **p** who eat of it.
12:27 And the **p** bowed down and worshiped.
12:31 go away from my **p**, both you and the Israelites!
12:33 the **p** to hasten their departure from the land,
12:34 So the **p** took their dough before it was leavened,
12:36 and the LORD had given the **p** favor in the sight
13: 3 Moses said to the **p**, "Remember this day
13:17 When Pharaoh let the **p** go,
13:17 for God thought, "If the **p** face war,
13:18 the **p** by the roundabout way of the wilderness
13:22 of fire by night left its place in front of the **p**.
14: 5 the king of Egypt was told that the **p** had fled,
14: 5 and his officials were changed toward the **p**,
14:13 But Moses said to the **p**, "Do not be afraid,
14:31 So the **p** feared the LORD and believed in
15:13 the **p** whom you redeemed;
15:16 they became still as a stone until your **p**,
15:16 until the **p** whom you acquired passed by.
15:24 And the **p** complained against Moses, saying,
16: 4 and each day the **p** shall go out and gather enough
16:27 the seventh day some of the **p** went out to gather,
16:30 So the **p** rested on the seventh day.
17: 1 but there was no water for the **p** to drink.
17: 2 The **p** quarreled with Moses, and said,
17: 3 But the **p** thirsted there for water;
17: 3 and the **p** complained against Moses and said,
17: 4 "What shall I do with this **p**?
17: 5 The LORD said to Moses, "Go on ahead of the **p**,
17: 6 so that the **p** may drink."
17:13 Joshua defeated Amalek and his **p** with the sword.
18: 1 God had done for Moses and for his **p** Israel, C
18:11 because he delivered the **p** from the Egyptians,
18:13 The next day Moses sat as judge for the **p**,
18:13 **p** stood around him from morning until evening.
18:14 that he was doing for the **p**,
18:14 "What is this that you are doing for the **p**?
18:14 while all the **p** stand around you from morning A
18:15 "Because the **p** come to me to inquire of God.
18:18 both you and these **p** with you.
18:19 You should represent the **p** before God,
18:21 all the **p**, men who fear God, are trustworthy, A
18:22 Let them sit as judges for the **p** at all times;
18:23 and all these **p** will go to their home in peace." A
18:25 and appointed them as heads over the **p**,
18:26 And they judged the **p** at all times;
19: 7 So Moses came, summoned the elders of the **p**, F
19: 8 The **p** all answered as one:
19: 8 Moses reported the words of the **p** to the LORD.
19: 9 that the **p** may hear when I speak with you and
19: 9 Moses had told the words of the **p** to the LORD,
19:10 to the **p** and consecrate them today and tomorrow.
19:11 down upon Mount Sinai in the sight of all the **p**. A
19:12 You shall set limits for the **p** all around, saying,
19:14 So Moses went down from the mountain to the **p**.
19:14 He consecrated the **p**,
19:15 And he said to the **p**, "Prepare for the third day;
19:16 a blast of a trumpet so loud that all the **p** who A
19:17 Moses brought the **p** out of the camp to meet God.
19:21 and warn the **p** not to break through to the LORD
19:23 **p** are not permitted to come up to Mount Sinai;
19:24 or the **p** break through to come up to the LORD;
19:25 So Moses went down to the **p** and told them.
20:18 all the **p** witnessed the thunder and lightning, A
20:20 Moses said to the **p**, "Do not be afraid;
20:21 Then the **p** stood at a distance,
21: 8 he shall have no right to sell her to a foreign **p**,
21:22 When **p** who are fighting injure a pregnant woman
22:25 If you lend money to my **p**,
22:28 or curse a leader of your **p**.
22:31 You shall be **p** consecrated to me;
23:11 so that the poor of your **p** may eat;
23:27 and will throw into confusion all the **p** A
24: 2 and the **p** shall not come up with him."
24: 3 and told the **p** all the words of the LORD and
24: 3 and all the **p** answered with one voice, and said, A
24: 5 He sent young men of the **p** of Israel, B
24: 7 and read it in the hearing of the **p**;
24: 8 Moses took the blood and dashed it on the **p**,
24:11 his hand on the chief men of the **p** of Israel; B
24:17 the mountain in the sight of the **p** of Israel. B
30:33 an unqualified person shall be cut off from the **p**."
30:38 to use as perfume shall be cut off from the **p**.
31:14 on it shall be cut off from among the **p**.
31:17 a sign forever between me and the **p** of Israel B
32: 1 When the **p** saw that Moses delayed to come down
32: 1 the **p** gathered around Aaron, and said to him,
32: 3 all the **p** took off the gold rings from their ears, A
32: 6 **p** sat down to eat and drink, and rose up to revel.
32: 7 Your **p**, whom you brought up out of the land
32: 9 The LORD said to Moses, "I have seen this **p**,
32:11 why does your wrath burn hot against your **p**,
32:12 and do not bring disaster on your **p**.

Ex 32:14 the disaster that he planned to bring on his **p**.
32:17 Joshua heard the noise of the **p** as they shouted,
32:21 "What did this **p** do to you that you have brought
32:22 you know the **p**, that they are bent on evil.
32:25 When Moses saw that the **p** were running wild
32:28 and about three thousand of the **p** fell on that day.
32:30 On the next day Moses said to the **p**,
32:31 "Alas, this **p** has sinned a great sin;
32:34 lead the **p** to the place about which I have spoken
32:35 Then the LORD sent a plague on the **p**,
33: 1 you and the **p** whom you have brought up out of
33: 3 for you are a stiff-necked **p**."
33: 4 When the **p** heard these harsh words,
33: 5 "Say to the Israelites, 'You are a stiff-necked **p**;
33: 8 all the **p** would rise and stand, each of them, A
33:10 When all the **p** saw the pillar of cloud standing A
33:10 all the **p** would rise and bow down, all of them, A
33:12 "See, you have said to me, 'Bring up this **p**';
33:13 Consider too that this nation is your **p**."
33:16 I and your **p**, unless you go with us?
33:16 In this way, we shall be distinct, I and your **p**,
33:16 from every **p** on the face of the earth."
34: 9 Although this is a stiff-necked **p**,
34:10 Before all your **p** I will perform marvels, A
34:10 all the **p** among whom you live shall see A
36: 5 "The **p** are bringing much more than enough
36: 6 So the **p** were restrained from bringing;
Lev 1: 2 Speak to the **p** of Israel and say to them: B
4: 2 Speak to the **p** of Israel, saying: B
4: 3 thus bringing guilt on the **p**,
4:27 of the ordinary **p** among you sins unintentionally
5: 4 whatever **p** utter in an oath, and are unaware of it,
7:23 Speak to the **p** of Israel, saying: B
7:29 Speak to the **p** of Israel, saying: B
7:34 the thigh that is offered, from the **p** of Israel, B
7:34 as a perpetual due from the **p** of Israel. B
7:36 from the **p** of Israel throughout their generations. B
7:38 the **p** of Israel to bring their offerings to B
9: 3 And say to the **p** of Israel, B
9: 7 and make atonement for yourself and for the **p**;
9: 7 and sacrifice the offering of the **p**,
9:15 the goat of the sin offering that was for the **p**,
9:18 and the ram as a sacrifice of well-being for the **p**.
9:22 Aaron lifted his hands toward the **p**
9:23 and then came out and blessed the **p**;
9:23 and the glory of the LORD appeared to all the **p**. A
9:24 and when all the **p** saw it, A
10: 3 and before all the **p** I will be glorified.' " A
10:11 you are to teach the **p** of Israel all the statutes B
10:14 of the offerings of well-being of the **p** of Israel. B
11: 2 Speak to the **p** of Israel, saying: B
12: 2 Speak to the **p** of Israel, saying: B
15: 2 Speak to the **p** of Israel and say to them: B
15:31 the **p** of Israel separate from their uncleanness, B
16: 5 the **p** of Israel two male goats for a sin offering, B
16:15 the sin offering that is for the **p** and bring its blood
16:16 because of the uncleannesses of the **p** of Israel, B
16:19 from the uncleannesses of the **p** of Israel. B
16:21 over it all the iniquities of the **p** of Israel, B
16:24 and the burnt offering of the **p**,
16:24 making atonement for himself and for the **p**.
16:33 for the priests and for all the **p** of the assembly. A
16:34 the **p** of Israel once in the year for all their sins. B
17: 2 to Aaron and his sons and to all the **p** of Israel AB
17: 4 and he shall be cut off from the **p**.
17: 5 that the **p** of Israel may bring their sacrifices B
17: 9 shall be cut off from the **p**.
17:10 and will cut that person off from the **p**.
17:12 Therefore I have said to the **p** of Israel: B
17:13 And anyone of the **p** of Israel, B
17:14 therefore I have said to the **p** of Israel: B
18: 2 Speak to the **p** of Israel and say to them: B
18:29 these abominations shall be cut off from their **p**.
19: 2 to all the congregation of the **p** of Israel and say B
19: 8 and any such person shall be cut off from the **p**.
19:16 around as a slanderer among your **p**, and you shall
19:18 of your **p**, but you shall love your neighbor
20: 2 Say further to the **p** of Israel: B
20: 2 Any of the **p** of Israel, or of the aliens who B
20: 2 the **p** of the land shall stone them to death. E
20: 3 and will cut them off from the **p**,
20: 4 **p** of the land should ever close their eyes to E
20: 5 and will cut them off from among their **p**,
20: 6 and will cut them off from the **p**.
20:17 and they shall be cut off in the sight of their **p**;
20:18 both of them shall be cut off from their **p**.
21: 4 as a husband among his **p** and so profane himself.
21:24 Aaron and to his sons and to all the **p** of Israel. AB
22: 2 with the sacred donations of the **p** of Israel, B
22: 3 which the **p** of Israel dedicate to the LORD, B
22:15 profane the sacred donations of the **p** of Israel, B
22:18 to Aaron and his sons and all the **p** of Israel AB
22:32 that I may be sanctified among the **p** of Israel: B
23: 2 Speak to the **p** of Israel and say to them: B
23:10 Speak to the **p** of Israel and say to them: B
23:24 Speak to the **p** of Israel, saying: B
23:29 during that entire day shall be cut off from the **p**.
23:30 such a one I will destroy from the midst of the **p**.
23:34 Speak to the **p** of Israel, saying: B
23:43 may know that I made the **p** of Israel live in B
23:44 to the **p** of Israel the appointed festivals of B
24: 2 Command the **p** of Israel to bring you pure oil B
24: 8 regularly as a commitment of the **p** of Israel, B
24:10 an Egyptian came out among the **p** of Israel; B
24:15 And speak to the **p** of Israel, saying: B
24:23 Moses spoke thus to the **p** of Israel; B
24:23 The **p** of Israel did as the LORD had B

Lev 25: 2 Speak to the **p** of Israel and say to them: B
25:33 are their possession among the **p** of Israel. B
25:55 For to me the **p** of Israel are servants; B
26:12 and will be your God, and you shall be my **p**.
26:46 the **p** of Israel on Mount Sinai through Moses. B
27: 2 Speak to the **p** of Israel and say to them: B
27:34 that the LORD gave to Moses for the **p** of Israel B
Nu 2: 3 The leader of the **p** of Judah shall be Nahshon D
2:18 of the **p** of Ephraim shall be Elishama son
2:20 of the **p** of Manasseh shall be Gamaliel son
5:21 an execration and an oath among your **p**,
5:27 woman shall become an execration among her **p**.
9: 6 Now there were certain **p** who were unclean
9:13 the **p** for not presenting the LORD's offering
11: 1 the **p** complained in the hearing of the LORD
11: 2 But the **p** cried out to Moses;
11: 8 The **p** went around and gathered it,
11:10 the **p** weeping throughout their families,
11:11 that you lay the burden of all this **p** on me? A
11:12 Did I conceive all this **p**? A
11:13 Where am I to get meat to give to all this **p**? A
11:14 I am not able to carry all this **p** alone, A
11:16 to be the elders of the **p** and officers over them; F
11:17 the burden of the **p** along with you so that you
11:18 And say to the **p**: Consecrate yourselves
11:21 **p** I am with number six hundred thousand on foot;
11:24 So Moses went out and told the **p** the words of
11:24 and he gathered seventy elders of the **p**, F
11:29 Would that all the LORD's **p** were prophets,
11:32 So the **p** worked all that day and night and all
11:33 the anger of the LORD was kindled against the **p**,
11:33 the LORD struck the **p** with a very great plague.
11:34 there they buried the **p** who had the craving.
11:35 From Kibroth-hattaavah the **p** journeyed
12:15 and the **p** did not set out on the march
12:16 After that the **p** set out from Hazeroth,
13:18 whether the **p** who live in it are strong or weak,
13:28 Yet the **p** who live in the land are strong,
13:30 But Caleb quieted the **p** before Moses, and said,
13:31 "We are not able to go up against this **p**,
13:32 and all the **p** that we saw in it are of great size. A
14: 1 and the **p** wept that night.
14: 9 and do not fear the **p** of the land, E
14:11 "How long will this **p** despise me?
14:13 for in your might you brought up this **p** from
14:14 O LORD, are in the midst of this **p**;
14:15 Now if you kill this **p** all at one time,
14:16 to bring this **p** into the land he swore to give them
14:19 the iniquity of this **p** according to the greatness
14:19 just as you have pardoned this **p**,
14:22 of the **p** who have seen my glory and the signs
14:39 to all the Israelites, the **p** mourned greatly.
15:26 because the whole **p** was involved in the error.
15:30 and shall be cut off from among the **p**.
16:29 If these **p** die a natural death,
16:41 saying, "You have killed the **p** of the LORD." H
16:47 where the plague had already begun among the **p**.
16:47 and made atonement for the **p**.
20: 1 and the **p** stayed in Kadesh.
20: 3 The **p** quarreled with Moses and said,
20:13 where the **p** of Israel quarreled with the LORD, B
20:24 "Let Aaron be gathered to his **p**.
20:26 But Aaron shall be gathered to his **p**,
21: 2 "If you will indeed give this **p** into our hands,
21: 4 but the **p** became impatient on the way.
21: 5 The **p** spoke against God and against Moses,
21: 6 the LORD sent poisonous serpents among the **p**,
21: 6 and they bit the **p**, so that many Israelites died.
21: 7 The **p** came to Moses and said,
21: 7 So Moses prayed for the **p**.
21:16 the LORD said to Moses, "Gather the **p** together,
21:18 that the nobles of the **p** dug, with the scepter,
21:23 Sihon gathered all his **p** together, A
21:29 You are undone, O **p** of Chemosh!
21:33 he and all his **p**, to battle at Edrei. A
21:34 I have given him into your hand, with all his **p**, A
21:35 So they killed him, his sons, and all his **p**, A
22: 3 Moab was in great dread of the **p**,
22: 3 Moab was overcome with fear of the **p** of Israel. B
22: 5 saying, "A **p** has come out of Egypt;
22: 6 Come now, curse this **p** for me,
22:11 'A **p** has come out of Egypt and has spread over
22:12 you shall not curse the **p**, for they are blessed."
22:17 come, curse this **p** for me.' "
22:41 from there he could see part of the **p** of Israel. B
23: 9 Here is a **p** living alone, and not reckoning itself
23:24 Look, a **p** rising up like a lioness,
24:14 So now, I am going to my **p**;
24:14 what this **p** will do to your **p** in days to come."
25: 1 the **p** began to have sexual relations with
25: 2 These invited the **p** to the sacrifices of their gods,
25: 2 and the **p** ate and bowed down to their gods.
25: 4 "Take all the chiefs of the **p**,
25: 5 of your **p** who have yoked themselves to the Baal
25: 8 the plague was stopped among the **p** of Israel. B
26: 4 "Take a census of the **p**,
27:13 you also shall be gathered to your **p**,
31: 2 afterward you shall be gathered to your **p**."
31: 3 So Moses said to the **p**,
31:11 but they took all the spoil and all the booty, both **p**
32:11 'Surely none of the **p** who came up out of Egypt,
32:15 and you will destroy all this **p**." A
33:14 where there was no water for the **p** to drink.
Dt 1:28 'The **p** are stronger and taller than we;
2: 4 and charge the **p** as follows:
2:10 a large and numerous **p**, as tall as the Anakim—
2:16 as all the warriors had died off from among the **p**,

Dt 2:21 a strong and numerous **p**,
2:32 he and all his **p** for battle at Jahaz, A
2:33 along with his offspring and all his **p**. A
3: 1 he and all his **p**, for battle at Edrei. A
3: 2 along with his **p** and his land.
3: 3 over to us King Og of Bashan and all his **p**. A
3:28 of this **p** and who shall secure their possession of
4: 6 this great nation is a wise and discerning **p**!"
4:10 the **p** for me, and I will let them hear my words,
4:20 to become a **p** of his very own possession,
4:33 Has any **p** ever heard the voice of a god speaking
5:28 "I have heard the words of this **p**,
7: 6 For you are a **p** holy to the LORD your God;
7: 6 of all the peoples on earth to be his **p**,
7: 7 you were more numerous than any other **p** I
9: 2 a strong and tall **p**, the offspring of the Anakim,
9: 6 for you are a stubborn **p**.
9:12 for your **p** whom you have brought
9:13 that this **p** is indeed a stubborn people.
9:13 that this people is indeed a stubborn **p**.
9:26 the **p** who are your very own possession,
9:27 pay no attention to the stubbornness of this **p**,
9:29 For they are the **p** of your very own possession,
10:11 "Get up, go on your journey at the head of the **p**,
13: 9 and afterwards the hand of all the **p**. A
14: 2 For you are a **p** holy to the LORD your God;
14: 2 of all the peoples on earth to be his **p**,
14:21 For you are a **p** holy to the LORD your God.
16:18 and they shall render just decisions for the **p**.
17: 7 and afterward the hands of all the **p**. A
17:13 All the **p** will hear and be afraid, A
17:16 the **p** to Egypt in order to acquire more horses,
18: 3 This shall be the priests' due from the **p**,
18:15 a prophet like me from among your own **p**;
18:18 a prophet like you from among their own **p**;
20:11 all the **p** in it shall serve you at forced labor. A
21: 8 Absolve, O LORD, your **p** Israel, C
21: 8 in the midst of your **p** Israel." C
26:15 and bless your **p** Israel and the ground C
26:18 to be his treasured **p**, as he promised you,
26:19 for you to be a **p** holy to the LORD your God,
27: 1 the elders of Israel charged all the **p** as follows: A
27: 9 very day you have become the **p** of the LORD H
27:11 The same day Moses charged the **p** as follows:
27:12 on Mount Gerizim for the blessing of the **p**:
27:15 All the **p** shall respond, saying, "Amen!" A
27:16 All the **p** shall say, "Amen!" A
27:17 All the **p** shall say, "Amen!" A
27:18 All the **p** shall say, "Amen!" A
27:19 All the **p** shall say, "Amen!" A
27:20 All the **p** shall say, "Amen!" A
27:21 All the **p** shall say, "Amen!" A
27:22 All the **p** shall say, "Amen!" A
27:23 All the **p** shall say, "Amen!" A
27:24 All the **p** shall say, "Amen!" A
27:25 All the **p** shall say, "Amen!" A
27:26 All the **p** shall say, "Amen!" A
28: 9 The LORD will establish you as his holy **p**, K
28:29 at noon as blind **p** grope in darkness,
28:32 and daughters shall be given to another **p**,
28:33 A **p** whom you do not know shall eat up the fruit
29:13 in order that he may establish you today as his **p**,
31: 7 with this **p** into the land that the LORD has sworn
31:12 Assemble the **p**—men, women,
31:16 Then this **p** will begin to prostitute themselves to
32: 6 O foolish and senseless **p**?
32: 9 the LORD's own portion was his **p**,
32:21 So I will make them jealous with what is no **p**,
32:36 Indeed the LORD will vindicate his **p**,
32:43 Praise, O heavens, his **p**, worship him,
32:43 and cleanse the land for his **p**.
32:44 the words of this song in the hearing of the **p**,
33: 5 when the leaders of the **p** assembled—
33: 7 give heed to Judah, and bring him to his **p**;
33:21 he came at the head of the **p**,
33:29 Who is like you, a **p** saved by the LORD,
Jos 1: 2 proceed to cross the Jordan, you and all this **p**, A
1: 6 for you shall put this **p** in possession of the land
1:10 Then Joshua commanded the officers of the **p**,
1:11 through the camp, and command the **p**:
3: 3 and commanded the **p**, "When you see the ark of
3: 5 Then Joshua said to the **p**, "Sanctify yourselves;
3: 6 and pass on in front of the **p**."
3: 6 the ark of the covenant and went in front of the **p**.
3:14 **p** set out from their tents to cross over the Jordan,
3:14 the ark of the covenant were in front of the **p**.
3:16 Then the **p** crossed over opposite Jericho.
4: 2 "Select twelve men from the **p**,
4:10 that the LORD commanded Joshua to tell the **p**,
4:10 The **p** crossed over in haste.
4:11 As soon as all the **p** had finished crossing over, A
4:11 and the priests, crossed over in front of the **p**.
4:19 The **p** came up out of the Jordan on the tenth day
5: 4 all the males of the **p** who came out of Egypt,
5: 5 all the **p** who came out had been circumcised, A
5: 5 yet all the **p** born on the journey through A
6: 5 then all the **p** shall shout with a great shout; A
6: 5 and all the **p** shall charge straight ahead." A
6: 7 To the **p** he said, "Go forward and march around
6: 8 As Joshua had commanded the **p**,
6:10 To the **p** Joshua gave this command:
6:16 Joshua said to the **p**, "Shout!
6:20 So the **p** shouted, and the trumpets were blown.
6:20 As soon as the **p** heard the sound of the trumpets,
6:20 so the **p** charged straight ahead into the city
7: 3 "Not all the **p** need go up; A
7: 3 do not make the whole **p** toil up there."

Jos 7: 4 So about three thousand of the **p** went up there;
7: 5 The hearts of the **p** melted and turned to water.
7: 7 Why have you brought this **p** across the Jordan
7:13 Proceed to sanctify the **p**, and say,
8: 1 over to you the king of Ai with his **p**,
8: 5 I and all the **p** who are with me will approach A
8:10 the morning Joshua rose early and mustered the **p**,
8:10 with the elders of Israel, before the **p** to Ai.
8:14 When the king of Ai saw this, he and all his **p**, A
8:16 So all the **p** who were in the city were called A
8:20 for the **p** who fled to the wilderness turned back
8:25 was twelve thousand—all the **p** of Ai. A
8:33 that they should bless the **p** of Israel. B
10:21 all the **p** returned safe to Joshua in the camp A
10:33 and Joshua struck him and his **p**,
11:14 but all the **p** they struck down with the edge A
13:31 to the **p** of Machir son of Manasseh according
14: 4 For the **p** of Joseph were two tribes,
14: 6 Then the **p** of Judah came to Joshua at Gilgal; D
14: 8 up with me made the heart of the **p** melt;
15: 1 The lot for the tribe of the **p** of Judah according D
15:12 This is the boundary surrounding the **p** of Judah D
15:13 of Jephunneh a portion among the **p** of Judah, D
15:20 of the **p** of Judah according to their families. D
15:21 the tribe of the **p** of Judah in the extreme South, D
15:63 the **p** of Judah could not drive out the Jebusites, D
15:63 Jebusites live with the **p** of Judah in Jerusalem D
17:14 since we are a numerous **p**,
17:15 Joshua said to them, "If you are a numerous **p**,
17:17 "You are indeed a numerous **p**,
22:12 And when the **p** of Israel heard of it, B
24: 2 And Joshua said to all the **p**, A
24:16 Then the **p** answered, "Far be it from us
24:19 But Joshua said to the **p**,
24:21 **p** said to Joshua, "No, we will serve the LORD!"
24:22 Then Joshua said to the **p**,
24:24 The **p** said to Joshua, "The LORD our God we will
24:25 So Joshua made a covenant with the **p** that day,
24:27 Joshua said to all the **p**, "See, A
24:28 So Joshua sent the **p** away to their inheritances.
Jdg 1: 8 **p** of Judah fought against Jerusalem and took it. D
1: 9 Afterward the **p** of Judah went down to fight D
1:16 up with the **p** of Judah from the city of palms D
2: 4 the **p** lifted up their voices and wept.
2: 6 When Joshua dismissed the **p**,
2: 7 **p** worshiped the LORD all the days of Joshua,
2:20 "Because this **p** have transgressed my covenant
3:18 he sent the **p** who carried the tribute on their way.
5: 2 when the **p** offer themselves willingly—
5: 9 who offered themselves willingly among the **p**.
5:11 down to the gates marched the **p** of the LORD. H
5:13 the **p** of the LORD marched down for him H
5:18 Zebulun is a **p** that scorned death;
6: 3 the **p** of the east would come up against them. G
6:33 and the Amalekites and the **p** of the east G
7:12 and the Amalekites and all the **p** of the east AG
8: 5 So he said to the **p** of Succoth,
8: 8 the **p** of Penuel answered him as the **p** of Succoth
8: 9 So he said to the **p** of Penuel,
8:10 who were left of all the army of the **p** of the east; G
8:14 one of the **p** of Succoth, and questioned him;
8:14 and elders of Succoth, seventy-seven **p**.
8:15 Then he came to the **p** of Succoth, and said,
8:16 and with them he trampled the **p** of Succoth.
9:29 If only this **p** were under my command!
9:36 **p** are coming down from the mountain tops!"
9:36 shadows on the mountains look like **p** to you."
9:37 "Look, **p** are coming down from Tabbur-erez,
9:42 the following day the **p** went out into the fields.
9:43 he looked and saw the **p** coming out of the city,
9:45 he took the city, and killed the **p** that were in it;
9:49 all the **p** of the Tower of Shechem also died, A
9:54 so **p** will not say about me,
9:57 and God also made all the wickedness of the **p**
10:18 The commanders of the **p** of Gilead said
11:11 the **p** made him head and commander over them;
11:20 so Sihon gathered all his **p** together, A
11:21 gave Sihon and all his **p** into the hand of Israel, A
11:23 the Amorites for the benefit of his **p** Israel. C
11:33 Ammonites were subdued before the **p** of Israel. B
12: 2 "My **p** and I were engaged in conflict with
14: 3 a woman among your kin, or among all our **p**, A
14:11 the **p** saw him, they brought thirty companions to
14:16 You have asked a riddle of my **p**,
14:17 Then she explained the riddle to her **p**.
16:24 When the **p** saw him, they praised their god;
16:30 house fell on the lords and all the **p** who were A
17: 6 all the **p** did what was right in their own eyes. A
18: 7 the **p** who were there living securely,
18:10 you go, you will come to an unsuspecting **p**.
18:20 and the idol, and went along with the **p**.
18:27 came to Laish, to a **p** quiet and unsuspecting,
19:12 who do not belong to the **p** of Israel; B
19:16 (The **p** of the place were Benjaminites.)
20: 2 The chiefs of all the **p**, of all the tribes of Israel, A
20: 2 presented themselves in the assembly of the **p**
20: 3 that the **p** of Israel had gone up to Mizpah.) B
20: 8 All the **p** got up as one, saying, A
20:48 the city, the **p**, the animals, and all that remained.
21: 2 And the **p** came to Bethel,
21: 4 On the next day, the **p** got up early,
21: 9 For when the roll was called among the **p**,
21:15 The **p** had compassion on Benjamin because
21:25 all the **p** did what was right in their own eyes. A
Ru 1: 6 of Moab that the LORD had considered his **p**
1:10 "No, we will return with you to your **p**."
1:15 your sister-in-law has gone back to her **p** and

Ru 1:16 your **p** shall be my **p**, and your God my God.
2:11 and your native land and came to a **p** that you did
3:11 for all the assembly of my **p** know that you are
4: 4 and in the presence of the elders of my **p**. F
4: 9 Then Boaz said to the elders and all the **p**, A
4:11 Then all the **p** who were at the gate, A
1Sa 2:13 or for the duties of the priests to the **p**.
2:23 For I hear of your evil dealings from all these **p**. A
2:24 that I hear the **p** of the LORD spreading abroad. H
2:26 and in favor with the LORD and with the **p**.
2:28 offerings by fire from the **p** of Israel. B
2:29 of every offering of my **p** Israel?' C
4: 4 So the **p** sent to Shiloh,
5: 3 When the **p** of Ashdod rose early the next day,
5: 6 of the LORD was heavy upon the **p** of Ashdod,
5:10 the **p** of Ekron cried out,
5:10 the ark of the God of Israel to kill us and our **p**?"
5:11 that it may not kill us and our **p**."
6: 6 did they not let the **p** go, and they departed?
6:13 Now the **p** of Beth-shemesh
6:15 the **p** of Beth-shemesh offered burnt offerings
6:19 the **p** of Beth-shemesh when they greeted the ark
6:19 The **p** mourned because the LORD had made
6:19 a great slaughter among the **p**.
6:20 Then the **p** of Beth-shemesh said,
7: 1 the **p** of Kiriath-jearim came and took up the ark
7: 6 And Samuel judged the **p** of Israel at Mizpah. B
7: 7 that the **p** of Israel had gathered at Mizpah, B
7: 7 when the **p** of Israel heard of it they were afraid B
7: 8 The **p** of Israel said to Samuel, B
8: 7 "Listen to the voice of the **p** in all that they say
8:10 of the LORD to the **p** who were asking him for
8:19 But the **p** refused to listen to the voice of Samuel;
8:21 When Samuel had heard all the words of the **p**,
8:22 Samuel then said to the **p** of Israel, B
9: 2 among the **p** of Israel more handsome than he; B
9:12 because the **p** have a sacrifice today at the shrine.
9:13 For the **p** will not eat until he comes,
9:16 you shall anoint him to be ruler over my **p** Israel. C
9:16 He shall save my **p** from the hand of the Philistines
9:16 for I have seen the suffering of my **p**,
9:17 He it is who shall rule over my **p**."
10: 1 LORD has anointed you ruler over his **p** Israel. C
10: 1 the **p** of the LORD and you will save them from H
10:11 the **p** said to one another,
10:17 Samuel summoned the **p** to the LORD at Mizpah
10:23 When he took his stand among the **p**,
10:24 Samuel said to all the **p**, A
10:24 There is no one like him among all the **p**." A
10:24 And all the **p** shouted, "Long live the king!" A
10:25 the **p** the rights and duties of the kingship;
10:25 Then Samuel sent all the **p** back to their homes. A
11: 4 they reported the matter in the hearing of the **p**;
11: 4 and all the **p** wept aloud. A
11: 5 and Saul said, "What is the matter with the **p**,
11: 7 Then the dread of the LORD fell upon the **p**,
11:11 The next day Saul put the **p** in three companies.
11:12 The **p** said to Samuel, "Who is it that said,
11:14 Samuel said to the **p**, "Come,
11:15 So all the **p** went to Gilgal, A
12: 6 Samuel said to the **p**, "The LORD is witness,
12:18 all the **p** greatly feared the LORD and Samuel. A
12:19 All the **p** said to Samuel, "Pray to the LORD A
12:20 And Samuel said to the **p**, "Do not be afraid;
12:22 For the LORD will not cast away his **p**,
12:22 because it has pleased the LORD to make you a **p**
13: 2 the rest of the **p** he sent home to their tents.
13: 4 the **p** were called out to join Saul at Gilgal.
13: 6 the **p** hid themselves in caves and in holes and
13: 7 and all the **p** followed him trembling. A
13: 8 and the **p** began to slip away from Saul.
13:11 I saw that the **p** were slipping away from me,
13:14 LORD has appointed him to be ruler over his **p**,
13:15 The rest of the **p** followed Saul to join the army;
13:15 Saul counted the **p** who were present with him,
13:16 the **p** who were present with them stayed in Geba
13:22 to be found in the possession of any of the **p**
14: 3 Now the **p** did not know that Jonathan had gone.
14:15 in the field, and among all the **p**; A
14:20 Then Saul and all the **p** who were with him A
14:38 Saul said, "Come here, all you leaders of the **p**;
14:39 among all the **p** who answered him. A
14:40 The **p** said to Saul, "Do what seems good to you."
14:41 if this guilt is in your **p** Israel, give Thummim." C
14:41 by the lot, but the **p** were cleared.
14:45 Then the **p** said to Saul, "Shall Jonathan die,
14:45 So the **p** ransomed Jonathan, and he did not die.
15: 1 to anoint you king over his **p** Israel; C
15: 4 So Saul summoned the **p**,
15: 6 to all the **p** of Israel when they came up out AB
15: 8 but utterly destroyed all the **p** with the edge of A
15: 9 Saul and the **p** spared Agag,
15:15 the **p** spared the best of the sheep and the cattle,
15:21 But from the spoil the **p** took sheep and cattle,
15:24 because I feared the **p** and obeyed their voice.
15:30 yet honor me now before the elders of my **p** and F
17:27 The **p** answered him in the same way,
17:30 and the **p** answered him again as before.
18: 5 And all the **p**, even the servants of Saul, A
23: 8 Saul summoned all the **p** to war, A
26:15 one of the **p** came in to destroy your lord the king.
27:12 made himself utterly abhorrent to his **p** Israel; C
30: 4 and the **p** who were with him raised their voices
30: 6 for the **p** spoke of stoning him,
30: 6 all the **p** were bitter in spirit for their sons A
30:20 **p** said, "This is David's spoil."
30:21 to meet David and to meet the **p** who were

1Sa 30:21 When David drew near to the **p** he saluted them.
31: 9 to the houses of their idols and to the **p.**
2Sa 1:18 Song of the Bow be taught to the **p** of Judah; D
2: 4 Then the **p** of Judah came, D
2: 4 "It was the **p** of Jabesh-gilead who buried Saul,"
2: 5 David sent messengers to the **p** of Jabesh-gilead,
2:26 be before you order your **p** to turn from the pursuit
2:27 **p** would have continued to pursue their kinsmen,
2:28 Joab sounded the trumpet and all the **p** stopped; A
2:30 and when he had gathered all the **p** together, A
3:18 my servant David I will save my **p** Israel C
3:31 David said to Joab and to all the **p** who were A
3:32 wept at the grave of Abner, and all the **p** wept. A
3:34 And all the **p** wept over him again. A
3:35 Then all the **p** came to persuade David to eat A
3:36 All the **p** took notice of it, and it pleased them; A
3:36 just as everything the king did pleased all the **p.** A
3:37 So all the **p** and all Israel understood that day A
4: 3 the **p** of Beeroth had fled to Gittaim and are there
5: 2 It is you who shall be shepherd of my **p** Israel, C
5:12 for the sake of his **p** Israel. C
6: 2 and all the **p** with him set out and went from A
6:18 he blessed the **p** in the name of the LORD
6:19 and distributed food among all the **p,** A
6:19 Then all the **p** went back to their homes. A
6:21 the **p** of the LORD, that I have danced before H
7: 6 house since the day I brought up the **p** of Israel B
7: 7 I have moved about among all the **p** of Israel, AB
7: 7 whom I commanded to shepherd my **p** Israel, C
7: 8 the sheep to be prince over my **p** Israel; C
7:10 a place for my **p** Israel and will plant them, C
7:11 time that I appointed judges over my **p** Israel; C
7:19 May this be instruction for the **p,** O Lord GOD!
7:23 Who is like your **p,** like Israel?
7:23 on earth whose God went to redeem it as a **p,**
7:23 by driving out before his **p** nations and their gods?
7:24 And you established your **p** Israel for yourself C
7:24 for yourself to be your **p** forever;
8:15 administered justice and equity to all his **p.** A
10:12 and let us be courageous for the sake of our **p,**
10:13 and the **p** who were with him moved forward
11: 7 David asked how Joab and the **p** fared,
11:17 some of the servants of David among the **p** fell.
12:28 Now, then, gather the rest of the **p** together,
12:29 So David gathered all the **p** together and went A
12:31 He brought out the **p** who were in it,
12:31 Then David and all the **p** returned to Jerusalem. A
13:34 he saw many **p** coming from the Horonaim road
14:13 then have you planned such a thing against the **p**
14:15 the king because the **p** have made me afraid;
15: 5 Whenever **p** came near to do obeisance to him,
15: 6 so Absalom stole the hearts of the **p** of Israel. B
15:12 and the **p** with Absalom kept increasing.
15:17 The king left, followed by all the **p;** A
15:23 whole country wept aloud as all the **p** passed by; A
15:23 and all the **p** moved on toward the wilderness. A
15:24 until the **p** had all passed out of the city.
15:30 all the **p** who were with him covered their heads A
16: 6 all the **p** and all the warriors were on his right A
16:14 and all the **p** who were with him arrived weary A
16:18 but the one whom the LORD and this **p** and all
17: 2 and all the **p** who are with him will flee. A
17: 3 all the **p** back to you as a bride comes home A
17: 3 and all the **p** will be at peace." A
17:16 all the **p** who are with him will be swallowed A
17:22 So David and all the **p** who were with him set A
17:29 for David and the **p** with him to eat;
18: 5 And all the **p** heard when the king gave orders A
19: 9 All the **p** were disputing throughout all the A
19:14 Amasa swayed the hearts of all the **p** of Judah AD
19:16 down with the **p** of Judah to meet King David; D
19:17 with him were a thousand **p** from Benjamin.
19:39 Then all the **p** crossed over the Jordan, A
19:40 all the **p** of Judah, and also half the people AD
19:40 and also half the **p** of Israel, B
19:41 Then all the **p** of Israel came to the king, AB
19:41 our kindred the **p** of Judah stolen you away, D
19:42 All the **p** of Judah answered the people of AD
19:42 the people of Judah answered the **p** of Israel, B
19:43 the **p** of Israel answered the people of Judah, B
19:43 the people of Israel answered the **p** of Judah, D
19:43 But the words of the **p** of Judah were fiercer D
19:43 were fiercer than the words of the **p** of Israel. B
20: 2 So all the **p** of Israel withdrew from David AB
20: 2 the **p** of Judah followed their king steadfastly D
20:12 and the man saw that all the **p** were stopping. A
20:13 all the **p** went on after Joab to pursue Sheba A
20:22 the woman went to all the **p** with her wise plan. A
21: 2 (Now the Gibeonites were not of the **p** of Israel, B
21: 2 the **p** of Israel had sworn to spare them, B
21: 2 to wipe them out in his zeal for the **p** of Israel B
21:12 of his son Jonathan from the **p** of Jabesh-gilead,
22:28 You deliver a humble **p,** but your eyes are upon
22:44 **p** whom I had not known served me.
23: 3 One who rules over **p** justly,
23:10 **p** came back to him—but only to strip the dead.
24: 1 saying, "Go, count the **p** of Israel and Judah." B
24: 2 and take a census of the **p,**
24: 3 the LORD your God increase the number of the **p**
24: 4 the king to take a census of the **p** of Israel. B
24:10 to the heart because he had numbered the **p.**
24:15 and seventy thousand of the **p** died,
24:16 among the **p,** "It is enough;
24:17 David saw the angel who was destroying the **p,**
24:21 so that the plague may be averted from the **p.**"
1Ki 1:39 Then they blew the trumpet, and all the **p** said, A
1:40 And all the **p** went up following him, A
1Ki 3: 2 The **p** were sacrificing at the high places,
3: 8 midst of the **p** whom you have chosen, a great **p,**
3: 9 therefore an understanding mind to govern your **p,**
3: 9 for who can govern this your great **p?"**
4:30 the wisdom of all the **p** of the east, AG
4:34 **P** came from all the nations to hear the wisdom
5: 7 to David a wise son to be over this great **p."**
5:16 having charge of the **p** who did the work.
6:13 and will not forsake my **p** Israel." C
8: 2 All the **p** of Israel assembled to King Solomon AB
8:16 the day that I brought my **p** Israel out of Egypt, C
8:16 but I chose David to be over my **p** Israel.' C
8:30 your **p** Israel when they pray toward this place; C
8:33 "When your **p** Israel, having sinned against you, C
8:34 forgive the sin of your **p** Israel, C
8:36 forgive the sin of your servants, your **p** Israel, C
8:36 which you have given to your **p** as an inheritance.
8:38 all your **p** Israel, all knowing the afflictions AC
8:41 who is not of your **p** Israel, C
8:43 as do your **p** Israel, and so that they may know C
8:44 "If your **p** go out to battle against their enemy,
8:50 and forgive your **p** who have sinned against you,
8:51 (for they are your **p** and heritage,
8:52 and to the plea of your **p** Israel, C
8:56 who has given rest to his **p** Israel according to C
8:59 the cause of his **p** Israel, as each day requires; C
8:63 and all the **p** of Israel dedicated the house AB
8:65 **p** from Lebo-hamath to the Wadi of Egypt—
8:66 On the eighth day he sent the **p** away;
8:66 to his servant David and to his **p** Israel. C
9:20 All the **p** who were left of the Amorites, A
9:20 who were not of the **p** of Israel— B
9:23 who had charge of the **p** who carried on the work.
11:18 they took **p** with them from Paran and came
12: 5 So the **p** went away.
12: 6 saying, "How do you advise me to answer this **p?"**
12: 7 be a servant to this **p** today and serve them,
12: 9 that we answer this **p** who have said to me,
12:10 "Thus you should say to this **p** who spoke to you,
12:12 and all the **p** came to Rehoboam the third day, A
12:13 The king answered the **p** harshly.
12:15 So the king did not listen to the **p,**
12:16 the **p** answered the king, "What share do we have
12:23 and to the rest of the **p,**
12:24 up or fight against your kindred the **p** of Israel. B
12:27 If this **p** continues to go up to offer sacrifices in
12:27 the heart of this **p** will turn again to their master,
12:28 He said to the **p,** "You have gone up
12:30 the **p** went to worship before the one at Bethel and
12:31 and appointed priests from among all the **p,** A
12:33 he appointed a festival for the **p** of Israel, B
13:25 **P** passed by and saw the body thrown in the road,
13:33 for the high places again from among all the **p;** A
14: 2 who said of me that I should be king over this **p.**
14: 7 Because I exalted you from among the **p,**
14: 7 made you leader over my **p** Israel, C
14:24 that the LORD drove out before the **p** of Israel. B
16: 2 and made you leader over my **p** Israel, C
16: 2 and have caused my **p** Israel to sin, C
16:21 Then the **p** of Israel were divided into two parts; B
16:21 half of the **p** followed Tibni son of Ginath,
16:22 But the **p** who followed Omri overcame
16:22 the **p** who followed Tibni son of Ginath;
18:21 Elijah then came near to all the **p,** and said, A
18:21 The **p** did not answer him a word.
18:22 Then Elijah said to the **p,** "I, even I only,
18:24 All the **p** answered, "Well spoken!" A
18:30 Elijah said to all the **p,** "Come closer to me"; A
18:30 and all the **p** came closer to him. A
18:37 answer me, so that this **p** may know that you,
18:39 When all the **p** saw it, they fell on their faces A
19:21 he boiled their flesh, and gave it to the **p,**
20: 8 Then all the elders and all the **p** said to him, A
20:10 a handful for each of the **p** who follow me."
20:15 after them he mustered all the **p** of Israel, AB
20:27 the **p** of Israel encamped opposite them B
20:42 and your **p** for his **p.'** "
21:13 in the presence of the **p,** saying,
22: 4 my **p** are your **p,** my horses are your horses."
22:43 and the **p** still sacrificed and offered incense on
2Ki 2:19 Now the **p** of the city said to Elisha, J
3: 7 I am with you, my **p** are your **p,**
4:13 She answered, "I live among my own **p."**
4:41 and said, "Serve the **p** and let them eat."
4:42 Elisha said, "Give it to the **p** and let them eat."
4:43 "How can I set this before a hundred **p?"**
4:43 So he repeated, "Give it to the **p** and let them eat,
6:18 and said, "Strike this **p,** please, with blindness."
6:30 the city wall, the **p** could see that he had sackcloth
7:16 Then the **p** went out, and plundered the camp of
7:17 the **p** trampled him to death in the gate,
7:20 the **p** trampled him to death in the gate.
8:12 I know the evil that you will do to the **p** of Israel; B
9: 6 I anoint you king over the **p** of the LORD, H
10: 9 he stood and said to all the **p,** "You are innocent. A
10:18 Then Jehu assembled all the **p** and said to them, A
11:13 Athaliah heard the noise of the guard and of the **p,**
11:13 she went into the house of the LORD to the **p;**
11:14 all the **p** of the land rejoicing and AE
11:17 and **p,** that they should be the LORD's **p;**
11:17 also between the king and the **p.**
11:18 all the **p** of the land went to the house of Baal, AE
11:19 Carites, the guards, and all the **p** of the land; AE
11:20 So all the **p** of the land rejoiced; AE
12: 3 the **p** continued to sacrifice and make offerings on
12: 8 from the **p** nor repair the house.
13: 5 the **p** of Israel lived in their homes as formerly. B
2Ki 14: 4 the **p** still sacrificed and made offerings on
14:21 All the **p** of Judah took Azariah, AD
15: 4 the **p** still sacrificed and made offerings on
15: 5 governing the **p** of the land. E
15:29 and he carried the **p** captive to Assyria.
15:35 the **p** still sacrificed and made offerings on
16: 3 the LORD drove out before the **p** of Israel. B
16: 9 carrying its **p** captive to Kir; then he killed Rezin.
16:15 with the burnt offering of all the **p** of the land, AE
17: 7 This occurred because the **p** of Israel had sinned B
17: 8 the LORD drove out before the **p** of Israel, B
17: 9 The **p** of Israel secretly did things that were B
17:22 The **p** of Israel continued in all the sins B
17:24 The king of Assyria brought **p** from Babylon,
17:24 the cities of Samaria in place of the **p** of Israel; B
17:29 of the high places that the **p** of Samaria had made,
17:30 the **p** of Babylon made Succoth-benoth, the people
17:30 the **p** of Cuth made Nergal,
17:30 the **p** of Hamath made Ashima;
17:32 from among themselves all sorts of **p** as priests A
18: 4 those days the **p** of Israel had made offerings B
18:26 within the hearing of the **p** who are on the wall."
18:27 and not to the **p** sitting on the wall,
18:36 the **p** were silent and answered him not a word,
19:12 Rezeph, and the **p** of Eden who were in Telassar?
20: 5 and say to Hezekiah prince of my **p,**
21: 2 that the LORD drove out before the **p** of Israel. B
21: 9 that the LORD destroyed before the **p** of Israel. B
21:24 But the **p** of the land killed all those who had E
21:24 the **p** of the land made his son Josiah king in E
22: 4 of the threshold have collected from the **p;**
22:13 inquire of the LORD for me, for the **p,**
23: 2 and with him went all the **p** of Judah, AD
23: 2 the prophets, and all the **p,** both small and great; A
23: 3 All the **p** joined in the covenant. A
23: 6 the dust of it upon the graves of the common **p.**
23:17 The **p** of the city told him, J
23:21 The king commanded all the **p,** A
23:30 The **p** of the land took Jehoahaz son of Josiah, E
23:35 the silver and the gold from the **p** of the land, E
24:14 one remained, except the poorest **p** of the land. E
25: 3 there was no food for the **p** of the land. E
25:11 into exile the rest of the **p** who were left in the city
25:12 the guard left some of the poorest **p** of the land E
25:19 of the army who mustered the **p** of the land; E
25:19 sixty men of the **p** of the land who were found E
25:22 of Shaphan as governor over the **p** who remained
25:26 Then all the **p,** high and low and the captains of A
1Ch 6:64 So the **p** of Israel gave the Levites the towns B
7:21 Now the **p** of Gath, who were born in the land,
9: 3 And some of the **p** of Judah, Benjamin, D
10: 9 to carry the good news to their idols and to the **p.**
11: 2 It is you who shall be shepherd of my **p** Israel, C
11: 2 you who shall be ruler over my **p** Israel." C
11:13 Now the **p** had fled from the Philistines,
12:22 Indeed from day to day **p** kept coming to David
12:24 The **p** of Judah bearing shield D
13: 4 for the thing pleased all the **p.** A
14: 2 for the sake of his **p** Israel. C
16: 2 he blessed the **p** in the name of the LORD;
16:20 from one kingdom to another **p,**
16:36 Then all the **p** said "Amen!" A
16:43 Then all the **p** departed to their homes, A
17: 6 whom I commanded to shepherd my **p,** saying,
17: 7 to be ruler over my **p** Israel; C
17: 9 I will appoint a place for my **p** Israel, C
17:10 the time that I appointed judges over my **p** Israel; C
17:21 Who is like your **p** Israel, C
17:21 the earth whom God went to redeem to be his **p,**
17:21 before your **p** whom you redeemed from Egypt?
17:22 made your **p** Israel to be your people forever; C
17:22 made your people Israel to be your **p** forever;
18:14 he administered justice and equity to all his **p.** A
19:13 and let us be courageous for our **p** and for
20: 3 He brought out the **p** who were in it,
20: 3 Then David and all the **p** returned to Jerusalem. A
21: 1 and incited David to count the **p** of Israel. B
21: 3 "May the LORD increase the number of his **p**
21: 5 Joab gave the total count of the **p** to David.
21:17 not I who gave the command to count the **p?**
21:17 but do not let your **p** be plagued!"
21:22 so that the plague may be averted from the **p."**
22:18 the land is subdued before the LORD and his **p.**
23:25 the God of Israel, has given rest to his **p;**
27: 1 This is the list of the **p** of Israel, B
28: 2 "Hear me, my brothers and my **p.**
28:21 and all the **p** will be wholly at your command." A
29: 9 the **p** rejoiced because these had given willingly,
29:14 "But who am I, and what is my **p,**
29:17 and now I have seen your **p,** who are present here,
29:18 and thoughts in the hearts of your **p,**
2Ch 1: 9 for you have made me king over a **p** as numerous
1:10 to go out and come in before this **p,**
1:10 for who can rule this great **p** of yours?"
1:11 for yourself that you may rule my **p**
2:11 the LORD loves his **p** he has made you king
2:18 as overseers to make the **p** work.
5: 2 leaders of the ancestral houses of the **p** of Israel, B
5:10 a covenant with the **p** of Israel after they came B
6: 5 'Since the day that I brought my **p** out of the land
6: 5 and I chose no one as ruler over my **p** Israel; C
6: 6 and I have chosen David to be over my **p** Israel.' C
6:11 of the LORD that he made with the **p** of Israel." B
6:21 the plea of your servant and of your **p** Israel, C
6:24 "When your **p** Israel, having sinned against you, C
6:25 and forgive the sin of your **p** Israel, C
6:27 forgive the sin of your servants, your **p** Israel, C

2Ch 6:27 which you have given to your **p** as an inheritance.
6:29 from any individual or from all your **p** Israel, AC
6:32 who are not of your **p** Israel, C
6:33 as do your **p** Israel, and that they may know C
6:34 "If your **p** go out to battle against their enemies,
6:39 and forgive your **p** who have sinned against you.
7: 3 all the **p** of Israel saw the fire come down AB
7: 4 Then the king and all the **p** offered sacrifice A
7: 5 king and all the **p** dedicated the house of God. A
7:10 of the seventh month he sent the **p** away
7:10 to David and to Solomon and to his **p** Israel. C
7:13 or send pestilence among my **p**,
7:14 if my **p** who are called by my name humble
8: 2 and settled the **p** of Israel in them. B
8: 7 All the **p** who were left of the Hittites, A
8: 8 whom the **p** of Israel had not destroyed— B
8: 9 But of the **p** of Israel Solomon made no slaves B
8:10 who exercised authority over the **p**.
9: 7 Happy are your **p**! Happy are these your servants,
10: 5 So the **p** went away.
10: 6 saying, "How do you advise me to answer this **p**?"
10: 7 "If you will be kind to this **p** and please them,
10: 9 that we answer this **p** who have said to me,
10:10 "Thus should you speak to the **p** who said to you,
10:12 and all the **p** came to Rehoboam the third day, A
10:15 So the king did not listen to the **p**,
10:16 the **p** answered the king, "What share do we have
10:17 over the **p** of Israel who were living in the cities B
10:18 the **p** of Israel stoned him to death. B
13:15 Then the **p** of Judah raised the battle shout. D
13:15 And when the **p** of Judah shouted, D
13:18 and the **p** of Judah prevailed, D
14:13 **p** of Judah carried away a great quantity of D
16:10 And Asa inflicted cruelties on some of the **p** at
17: 9 the cities of Judah and taught among the **p**.
18: 2 of sheep and oxen for him and for the **p** who were
18: 3 "I am with you, my **p** are your **p**.
19: 4 then he went out again among the **p**,
20: 7 the inhabitants of this land before your **p** Israel, C
20:10 See now, the **p** of Ammon, Moab, and Mount Seir,
20:21 When he had taken counsel with the **p**,
20:25 and his **p** came to take the booty from them,
20:27 Then all the **p** of Judah and Jerusalem, AD
20:33 the **p** had not yet set their hearts upon the God
21:14 the LORD will bring a great plague on your **p**,
21:19 His **p** made no fire in his honor,
23: 5 and all the **p** shall be in the courts of the house A
23: 6 but all the other **p** shall observe the instructions AI
23:10 and he set all the **p** as a guard for the king, A
23:12 the **p** running and praising the king, she went into
23:12 she went into the house of the LORD to the **p**;
23:13 and all the **p** of the land rejoicing and AE
23:16 a covenant between himself and all the **p** and A
23:16 and the king that they should be the LORD's **p**.
23:17 Then all the **p** went to the house of Baal, A
23:20 the nobles, the governors of the **p**,
23:20 and all the **p** of the land, AE
23:21 So all the **p** of the land rejoiced, AE
24:10 and all the **p** rejoiced and brought their tax and A
24:20 he stood above the **p** and said to them,
24:23 and destroyed all the officials of the **p** from
25: 5 Amaziah assembled the **p** of Judah, D
25:11 Amaziah took courage, and led out his **p**;
25:12 **p** of Judah captured another ten thousand alive, D
25:13 they killed three thousand **p** in them,
25:14 he brought the gods of the **p** of Seir,
25:15 a people's gods who could not deliver their own **p**
26: 1 Then all the **p** of Judah took Uzziah, AD
26:21 governing the **p** of the land. E
27: 2 But the **p** still followed corrupt practices.
28: 3 the LORD drove out before the **p** of Israel. B
28: 5 a great number of his **p** and brought them
28: 8 The **p** of Israel took captive two hundred B
28:10 Now you intend to subjugate the **p** of Judah D
29:36 all the **p** rejoiced because of what God had done A
29:36 because of what God had done for the **p**;
30: 3 nor had the **p** assembled in Jerusalem).
30: 5 that the **p** should come and keep the passover to
30: 6 saying, "O **p** of Israel, return to the LORD, B
30:13 Many **p** came together in Jerusalem to keep
30:18 For a multitude of the **p**,
30:20 The LORD heard Hezekiah, and healed the **p**.
30:21 The **p** of Israel who were present B
30:22 So the **p** ate the food of the festival for seven days,
30:27 priests and the Levites stood up and blessed the **p**,
31: 1 Then all the **p** of Israel returned to their cities, AB
31: 4 He commanded the **p** who lived in Jerusalem
31: 5 the **p** of Israel gave in abundance the first fruits B
31: 6 The **p** of Israel and Judah who lived in the cities B
31: 8 they blessed the LORD and his **p** Israel. C
31:10 for the LORD has blessed his **p**,
31:19 the **p** designated by name were
32: 4 A great many **p** were gathered,
32: 6 He appointed combat commanders over the **p**,
32: 8 The **p** were encouraged by the words
32: 9 to all the **p** of Judah that were in Jerusalem, AD
32:14 to save his **p** from my hand,
32:15 to save his **p** from my hand or from the hand
32:17 of the nations in other lands did not rescue their **p**
32:17 of Hezekiah will not rescue his **p** from my hand."
32:18 a loud voice in the language of Judah to the **p**
33: 2 the LORD drove out before the **p** of Israel. B
33: 9 the LORD had destroyed before the **p** of Israel. B
33:10 The LORD spoke to Manasseh and to his **p**,
33:17 The **p**, however, still sacrificed at the high places,
33:25 But the **p** of the land killed all those who had E
33:25 and the **p** of the land made his son Josiah king E

2Ch 34:12 The **p** did the work faithfully.
34:30 with all the **p** of Judah, the inhabitants of AD
34:30 all the **p** both great and small; A
34:33 the territory that belonged to the **p** of Israel, B
35: 3 Now serve the LORD your God and his **p** Israel. C
35: 5 of the ancestral houses of your kindred the **p**,
35: 7 Then Josiah contributed to the **p**,
35: 8 His officials contributed willingly to the **p**,
35:12 to the groupings of the ancestral houses of the **p**,
35:13 in pans, and carried them quickly to all the **p**. A
35:17 The **p** of Israel who were present kept B
36: 1 The **p** of the land took Jehoahaz son of Josiah E
36:14 and the **p** also were exceedingly unfaithful,
36:15 because he had compassion on his **p** and
36:16 until the wrath of the LORD against his **p** became
36:23 Whoever is among you of all his **p**, A
Ezr 1: 3 Any of those among you who are of his **p**—
1: 4 be assisted by the **p** of their place with silver
2: 1 Now these were the **p** of the province who came
2: 2 The number of the Israelite **p**:
2:22 The **p** of Netophah, fifty-six.
2:27 The **p** of Michmas, one hundred twenty-two.
2:70 some of the **p** lived in Jerusalem and its vicinity;
3: 1 the **p** gathered together in Jerusalem.
3: 8 together with the rest of their **p**,
3:11 And all the **p** responded with a great shout A
3:12 old **p** who had seen the first house
3:13 so that the **p** could not distinguish the sound of
3:13 for the **p** shouted so loudly that
4: 4 **p** of the land discouraged the people of Judah, E
4: 4 people of the land discouraged the **p** of Judah, D
4: 9 the **p** of Erech, the Babylonians, the **p** of Susa,
4:11 the **p** of the province Beyond the River,
4:21 issue an order that these **p** be made to cease,
5:12 who destroyed this house and carried away the **p**
6: 8 the cost is to be paid to these **p**,
6:12 or **p** that shall put forth a hand to alter this,
6:16 The **p** of Israel, the priests and the Levites, B
6:21 It was eaten by the **p** of Israel who had returned B
7: 7 Some of the **p** of Israel, and some of the priests B
7:13 I decree that any of the **p** of Israel or their B
7:16 with the freewill offerings of the **p** and the priests,
7:25 all the **p** in the province Beyond the River A
8:15 As I reviewed the **p** and the priests,
8:36 and they supported the **p** and the house of God.
9: 1 "The **p** of Israel, the priests, B
10: 1 to him out of Israel; the **p** also wept bitterly.
10: 9 all the **p** of Judah and Benjamin assembled AD
10: 9 All the **p** sat in the open square before the house A
10:13 But the **p** are many, and it is a time of heavy rain;
Ne 1: 6 day and night for your servants, the **p** of Israel, B
1: 6 confessing the sins of the **p** of Israel, B
1:10 They are your servants and your **p**,
2:10 to seek the welfare of the **p** of Israel. B
4: 6 for the **p** had a mind to work.
4:13 I stationed the **p** according to their families,
4:14 to the nobles and the officials and the rest of the **p**,
4:19 the officials, and the rest of the **p**,
4:22 I also said to the **p** at that time,
5: 1 the **p** and of their wives against their Jewish kin.
5: 7 "You are all taking interest from your own **p**."
5:13 And the **p** did as they had promised.
5:15 before me laid heavy burdens on the **p**,
5:15 Even their servants lorded it over the **p**.
5:17 there were at my table one hundred fifty **p**,
5:18 because of the heavy burden of labor on the **p**.
5:19 O my God, all that I have done for this **p**.
7: 4 **p** within it were few and no houses had been built.
7: 5 the officials and the **p** to be enrolled by genealogy.
7: 6 These are the **p** of the province who came up out
7: 7 The number of the Israelite **p**:
7:26 The **p** of Bethlehem and Netophah,
7:72 of the **p** gave was twenty thousand darics of gold,
7:73 the singers, some of the **p**, the temple servants,
7:73 the **p** of Israel being settled in their towns— B
8: 1 all the **p** gathered together into the square A
8: 3 the ears of all the **p** were attentive to the book A
8: 5 Ezra opened the book in the sight of all the **p**, A
8: 5 for he was standing above all the **p**; A
8: 5 and when he opened it, all the **p** stood up. A
8: 6 the great God, and all the **p** answered, "Amen, A
8: 7 the Levites, helped the **p** to understand the law,
8: 7 while the **p** remained in their places.
8: 8 so that the **p** understood the reading.
8: 9 Levites who taught the **p** said to all the people,
8: 9 Levites who taught the people said to all the **p**, A
8: 9 For all the **p** wept when they heard the words A
8:11 So the Levites stilled all the **p**, saying, A
8:12 And all the **p** went their way to eat and drink A
8:13 the heads of ancestral houses of all the **p**, A
8:14 that the **p** of Israel should live in booths during B
8:16 So the **p** went out and brought them,
8:17 to that day the **p** of Israel had not done so. B
9: 1 twenty-fourth day of this month the **p** of Israel B
9:10 Pharaoh and all his servants and all the **p** of his A
9:32 our prophets, our ancestors, and all your **p**, A
10:14 The leaders of the **p**: Parosh,
10:28 The rest of the **p**, the priests, the Levites,
10:34 the Levites, and the **p**, for the wood offering,
10:39 For the **p** of Israel and the sons of Levi shall B
11: 1 Now the leaders of the **p** lived in Jerusalem;
11: 1 of the **p** cast lots to bring one out of ten to live in
11: 2 And the **p** blessed all those who willingly offered
11:24 at the king's hand in all matters concerning the **p**.
11:25 some of the **p** of Judah lived in Kiriath-arba D
11:31 The **p** of Benjamin also lived from Geba onward,
12:30 and they purified the **p** and the gates and the wall.

Ne 12:38 and I followed them with half of the **p** on the wall,
13: 1 from the book of Moses in the hearing of the **p**;
13: 3 When the **p** heard the law,
13:15 in Judah **p** treading wine presses on the sabbath,
13:16 and sold them on the sabbath to the **p** of Judah, D
Est 1: 5 the king gave for all the **p** present in the citadel A
1:22 to every province in its own script and to every **p**
2:10 Esther did not reveal her **p** or kindred,
2:20 Now Esther had not revealed her kindred or her **p**,
3: 6 So, having been told who Mordecai's **p** were,
3: 6 the **p** of Mordecai, throughout the whole kingdom
3: 8 "There is a certain **p** scattered and separated
3: 8 from those of every other **p**, I
3:11 "The money is given to you, and the **p** as well,
3:12 in its own script and every **p** in its own language;
4: 8 to him and entreat him for her **p**.
4:11 the **p** of the king's provinces know that if any man
6:13 of the Jewish **p**, you will not prevail against him,
7: 3 and the lives of my **p**—that is my request.
7: 4 For we have been sold, I and my **p**,
8: 6 to see the calamity that is coming on my **p**?
8: 9 to every province in its own script and to every **p**
8:11 to annihilate any armed force of any **p** or province
9: 6 the Jews killed and destroyed five hundred **p**.
9:12 of Susa the Jews have killed five hundred **p** and
10: 3 for he sought the good of his **p** and interceded for
Job 1: 3 man was the greatest of all the **p** of the east. AG
1:19 and it fell on the young **p**, and they are dead;
2: 4 All that **p** have they will give to save their lives.
12: 2 "No doubt you are the **p**,
17: 6 and I am one before whom **p** spit.
18:19 or descendant among their **p**,
28: 4 they sway suspended, remote from **p**.
30: 5 **p** shout after them as after a thief.
33:14 and in two, though **p** do not perceive it.
34:20 at midnight the **p** are shaken and pass away,
34:30 or those who ensnare the **p**.
35: 9 of the multitude of oppressions **p** cry out;
36:25 All **p** have looked on it; A
Ps 3: 6 of ten thousands of **p** who have set themselves
3: 8 may your blessing be on your **p**!
4: 2 How long, you **p**, shall my honor suffer shame?
14: 4 the evildoers who eat up my **p** as they eat bread,
14: 7 When the LORD restores the fortunes of his **p**,
18:27 For you deliver a humble **p**,
18:43 **p** whom I had not known served me.
22: 6 scorned by others, and despised by the **p**.
22:31 and proclaim his deliverance to a **p** yet unborn,
28: 8 The LORD is the strength of his **p**;
28: 9 O save your **p**, and bless your heritage;
29:11 May the LORD give strength to his **p**!
29:11 May the LORD bless his **p** with peace!
33:12 the **p** whom he has chosen as his heritage.
36: 7 All **p** may take refuge in the shadow A
42: 3 while **p** say to me continually,
43: 1 and defend my cause against an ungodly **p**;
44:12 You have sold your **p** for a trifle,
45:10 forget your **p** and your father's house,
45:12 the **p** of Tyre will seek your favor with gifts, the richest of the **p**
47: 9 gather as the **p** of the God of Abraham.
50: 4 that he may judge his **p**:
50: 7 O my **p**, and I will speak, O Israel,
53: 4 who eat up my **p** as they eat bread,
53: 6 When God restores the fortunes of his **p**,
56: 1 O God, for **p** trample on me;
58: 1 Do you judge **p** fairly?
58:11 **P** will say, "Surely there is a reward for
59:11 Do not kill them, or my **p** may forget;
60: 3 You have made your **p** suffer hard things;
62: 8 Trust in him at all times, O **p**;
65: 9 you provide the **p** with grain,
66:12 you let **p** ride over our heads;
68: 7 O God, when you went out before your **p**,
68:18 in your train and receiving gifts from **p**,
68:35 he gives power and strength to his **p**.
72: 2 May he judge your **p** with righteousness,
72: 3 May the mountains yield prosperity for the **p**,
72: 4 May he defend the cause of the poor of the **p**,
72:16 and may **p** blossom in the cities like the grass of
73: 3 they are not plagued like other **p**. I
73:10 **p** turn and praise them, and find no fault in them.
74:18 and an impious **p** reviles your name.
75: 1 **P** tell of your wondrous deeds.
77:15 With your strong arm you redeemed your **p**,
77:20 You led your **p** like a flock by the hand of Moses
78: 1 O my **p**, to my teaching;
78:20 can he also give bread, or provide meat for his **p**?"
78:52 Then he led out his **p** like sheep,
78:62 He gave his **p** to the sword,
78:71 to be the shepherd of his **p** Jacob,
79:13 Then we your **p**, the flock of your pasture,
81: 8 O my **p**, while I admonish you;
81:11 "But my **p** did not listen to my voice;
81:13 O that my **p** would listen to me,
83: 3 They lay crafty plans against your **p**;
85: 2 You forgave the iniquity of your **p**;
85: 6 so that your **p** may rejoice in you?
85: 8 for he will speak peace to his **p**, to his faithful,
89:15 Happy are the **p** who know the festal shout,
89:19 I have exalted one chosen from the **p**.
94: 5 They crush your **p**, O LORD,
94: 8 Understand, O dullest of the **p**;
94:14 For the LORD will not forsake his **p**;
95: 7 For he is our God, and we are the **p** of his pasture,
95:10 "They are a **p** whose hearts go astray,
100: 3 we are his **p**, and the sheep of his pasture.

Ps 102:18 so that a **p** yet unborn may praise the LORD:
103: 7 his acts to the **p** of Israel. B
104:14 and plants for **p** to use,
104:23 **P** go out to their work and to their labor until
105:13 from one kingdom to another **p**,
105:24 And the LORD made his **p** very fruitful,
105:25 whose hearts he then turned to hate his **p**,
105:43 So he brought his **p** out with joy,
106: 4 O LORD, when you show favor to your **p**;
106:40 the anger of the LORD was kindled against his **p**,
106:48 And let all the **p** say, "Amen." A
107:32 Let them extol him in the congregation of the **p**,
110: 3 Your **p** will offer themselves willingly on
111: 6 He has shown his **p** the power of his works,
111: 9 He sent redemption to his **p**;
113: 8 with the princes of his **p**.
114: 1 the house of Jacob from a **p** of strange language,
116:14 vows to the LORD in the presence of all his **p**. A
116:18 vows to the LORD in the presence of all his **p**, A
119: 9 How can young **p** keep their way pure?
125: 2 so the LORD surrounds his **p**,
135:12 a heritage to his **p** Israel. C
135:14 For the LORD will vindicate his **p**,
136:16 who led his **p** through the wilderness,
144:15 Happy are the **p** to whom such blessings fall;
144:15 happy are the **p** whose God is the LORD.
145:12 to make known to all **p** your mighty deeds, A
148:14 He has raised up a horn for his **p**,
148:14 for the **p** of Israel who are close to him. B
149: 4 For the LORD takes pleasure in his **p**;
Pr 3: 4 and good repute in the sight of God and of **p**.
8: 4 "To you, O **p**, I call, and my cry is to all that live.
11:26 The **p** curse those who hold back grain,
14:28 The glory of a king is a multitude of **p**;
14:28 without **p** a prince is ruined.
14:34 but sin is a reproach to any **p**.
16: 7 When the ways of **p** please the LORD,
17:11 Evil **p** seek only rebellion,
22:29 they will not serve common **p**.
28:12 but when the wicked prevail, **p** go into hiding.
28:15 or a charging bear is a wicked ruler over a poor **p**.
28:28 When the wicked prevail, **p** go into hiding;
29: 2 When the righteous are in authority, the **p** rejoice;
29: 2 but when the wicked rule, the **p** groan.
29:18 there is no prophecy, the **p** cast off restraint,
30:25 a **p** without strength, yet they provide their food in
30:26 a **p** without power, yet they make their homes in
30:31 the he-goat, and a king striding before his **p**.
Ecc 1: 3 What do **p** gain from all the toil at which they toil
1:11 The **p** of long ago are not remembered,
1:11 of **p** yet to come by those who come after them.
4:16 there was no end to all those **p** whom he led. A
7:15 there are righteous **p** who perish
7:15 and there are wicked **p** who prolong their life
7:21 Do not give heed to everything that **p** say,
8:14 that there are righteous **p** who are treated
8:14 and there are wicked **p** who are treated according
8:15 for there is nothing better for **p** under the sun than
9:14 There was a little city with few **p** in it.
12: 9 the Teacher also taught the **p** knowledge,
Isa 1: 3 but Israel does not know, my **p** do not understand.
1: 4 Ah, sinful nation, **p** laden with iniquity,
1:10 to the teaching of our God, you **p** of Gomorrah!
2: 6 For you have forsaken the ways of your **p**,
2: 9 so **p** are humbled, and everyone is brought low—
2:11 The haughty eyes of **p** shall be brought low,
2:17 The haughtiness of **p** shall be humbled,
2:20 On that day **p** will throw away to the moles and to
3: 5 The **p** will be oppressed, everyone by another
3: 7 you shall not make me leader of the **p**."
3:12 My **p**—children are their oppressors,
3:12 O my **p**, your leaders mislead you,
3:14 into judgment with the elders and princes of his **p**:
3:15 What do you mean by crushing my **p**,
5: 3 now, inhabitants of Jerusalem and **p** of Judah, D
5: 7 and the **p** of Judah are his pleasant planting; D
5:13 Therefore my **p** go into exile without knowledge;
5:15 **P** are bowed down, everyone is brought low,
5:25 the anger of the LORD was kindled against his **p**,
5:26 and whistle for a **p** at the ends of the earth;
6: 5 and I live among a **p** of unclean lips;
6: 9 And he said, "Go and say to this **p**:
6:10 Make the mind of this **p** dull, and stop their ears,
6:11 houses without **p**, and the land is utterly desolate;
7: 2 the heart of his **p** shook as the trees of the forest
7: 8 Ephraim will be shattered, no longer a **p**.)
7:17 The LORD will bring on you and on your **p** and
8: 6 Because this **p** has refused the waters of Shiloah
8:11 and warned me not to walk in the way of this **p**,
8:12 not call conspiracy all that this **p** calls conspiracy,
8:19 Now if **p** say to you, "Consult the ghosts and
8:19 should not a **p** consult their gods,
9: 2 **p** who walked in darkness have seen a great light;
9: 3 as **p** exult when dividing plunder.
9: 9 and all the **p** knew it— A
9:13 The **p** did not turn to him who struck them,
9:16 for those who led this **p** led them astray,
9:17 on their young **p**, or compassion on their orphans
9:19 and the **p** became like fuel for the fire;
10: 2 the needy from justice and to rob the poor of my **p**
10: 6 and against the **p** of my wrath I command him,
10:22 your **p** Israel were like the sand of the sea, C
10:24 O my **p**, who live in Zion,
11:11 to recover the remnant that is left of his **p**,
11:14 together they shall plunder the **p** of the east. G
11:16 from Assyria for the remnant that is left of his **p**,
13:14 all will turn to their own **p**,
Isa 14:20 destroyed your land, you have killed your **p**.
14:32 the needy among his **p** will find refuge in her."
17: 7 On that day **p** will regard their Maker,
18: 2 to a **p** feared near and far,
18: 7 to the LORD of hosts from a **p** tall and smooth,
18: 7 from a **p** feared near and far,
19:25 saying, "Blessed be Egypt my **p**,
22: 4 to comfort me for the destruction of my beloved **p**.
23:13 This is the **p**; it was not Assyria.
24: 2 And it shall be, as with the **p**, so with the priest;
24: 6 of the earth dwindled, and few **p** are left.
25: 8 the disgrace of his **p** he will take away from all
26:11 Let them see your zeal for your **p**,
26:20 Come, my **p**, enter your chambers,
27:11 For this is a **p** without understanding;
27:12 you will be gathered one by one, O **p** of Israel. B
28: 5 and a diadem of beauty, to the remnant of his **p**;
28:11 and with alien tongue he will speak to this **p**,
28:14 you scoffers who rule this **p** in Jerusalem.
29:13 Because these **p** draw near with their mouths
29:14 so I will again do amazing things with this **p**,
29:19 neediest **p** shall exult in the Holy One of Israel.
30: 5 to shame through a **p** that cannot profit them,
30: 6 to a **p** that cannot profit them.
30: 9 For they are a rebellious **p**, faithless children,
30:19 Truly, O **p** in Zion, inhabitants of Jerusalem,
30:26 when the LORD binds up the injuries of his **p**,
31: 6 you have deeply betrayed, O **p** of Israel. B
32:13 the soil of my **p** growing up in thorns and briers;
32:18 My **p** will abide in a peaceful habitation,
33:19 No longer will you see the insolent **p**,
33:19 the **p** of an obscure speech
33:24 the **p** who live there will be forgiven their iniquity.
34: 5 upon the **p** I have doomed to judgment.
35: 8 but it shall be for God's **p**;
36:11 within the hearing of the **p** who are on the wall."
36:12 and not to the **p** sitting on the wall,
37:12 Rezeph, and the **p** of Eden who were in Telassar?
38:16 O Lord, by these things **p** live,
40: 1 Comfort, O comfort my **p**, says your God.
40: 5 and all **p** shall see it together, A
40: 6 All **p** are grass, their constancy is like the flower A
40: 7 blows upon it; surely the **p** are grass.
42: 5 to the **p** upon it and spirit to those who walk in it:
42: 6 I have given you as a covenant to the **p**,
42:22 But this is a **p** robbed and plundered,
43: 4 I give **p** in return for you, nations in exchange for
43: 8 Bring forth the **p** who are blind, yet have eyes,
43:20 rivers in the desert, to give drink to my chosen **p**,
43:21 the **p** whom I formed for myself so
47: 6 I was angry with my **p**, I profaned my heritage;
49: 8 and given you as a covenant to the **p**, to establish
49:13 For the LORD has comforted his **p**,
51: 4 Listen to me, my **p**, and give heed to me,
51: 7 you **p** who have my teaching in your hearts;
51:16 and saying to Zion, "You are my **p**."
51:22 your God who pleads the cause of his **p**:
52: 4 my **p** went down into Egypt to reside there
52: 5 seeing that my **p** are taken away without cause?
52: 6 Therefore my **p** shall know my name;
52: 9 for the LORD has comforted his **p**,
53: 8 stricken for the transgression of my **p**.
56: 3 "The LORD will surely separate me from his **p**";
58: 1 Announce to my **p** their rebellion,
60:21 Your **p** shall all be righteous;
61: 9 that they are a **p** whom the LORD has blessed.
62:10 go through the gates, prepare the way for the **p**;
62:12 They shall be called, "The Holy **P**, K
63: 8 For he said, "Surely they are my **p**,
63:14 led your **p**, to make for yourself a glorious name.
63:18 Your holy **p** took possession for a little while; K
64: 9 Now consider, we are all your **p**. A
65: 2 I held out my hands all day long to a rebellious **p**,
65: 3 a **p** who provoke me to my face continually,
65:10 for my **p** who have sought me.
65:18 to create Jerusalem as a joy, and its **p** as a delight.
65:19 I will rejoice in Jerusalem, and delight in my **p**;
65:22 like the days of a tree shall the days of my **p** be,
66: 5 Your own **p** who hate you and reject you
66:24 at the dead bodies of the **p** who have rebelled
Jer 1:18 its princes, its priests, and the **p** of the land. E
2:11 But my **p** have changed their glory for something
2:13 for my **p** have committed two evils:
2:16 the **p** of Memphis and Tahpanhes have broken
2:31 Why then do my **p** say, "We are free,
2:32 my **p** have forgotten me, days without number.
4: 3 For thus says the LORD to the **p** of Judah and D
4: 4 O **p** of Judah and inhabitants of Jerusalem, D
4:10 utterly you have deceived this **p** and Jerusalem,
4:11 that time it will be said to this **p** and to Jerusalem:
4:11 of the bare heights in the desert toward my poor **p**,
4:22 "For my **p** are foolish, they do not know me;
5:14 and this **p** wood, and the fire shall devour them.
5:19 And when your **p** say, "Why has
5:21 O foolish and senseless **p**, who have eyes,
5:23 But this **p** has a stubborn and rebellious heart;
5:26 For scoundrels are found among my **p**;
5:31 my **p** love to have it so, but what will you do when
6:14 They have treated the wound of my **p** carelessly,
6:19 I am going to bring disaster on this **p**,
6:21 See, I am laying before this **p** stumbling blocks
6:22 See, a **p** is coming from the land of the north,
6:26 O my poor **p**, put on sackcloth, and roll in ashes;
6:27 I have made you a tester and a refiner among my **p**
7: 2 Hear the word of the LORD, all you **p** of Judah, AD
7:12 to it for the wickedness of my **p** Israel. C
7:16 As for you, do not pray for this **p**,
Jer 7:23 and I will be your God, and you shall be my **p**;
7:30 For the **p** of Judah have done evil in my sight, D
7:33 The corpses of this **p** will be food for the birds of
8: 4 When **p** fall, do they not get up again?
8: 5 Why then has this **p** turned away
8: 7 but my **p** do not know the ordinance of the LORD.
8:11 They have treated the wound of my **p** carelessly,
8:19 cry of my poor **p** from far and wide in the land:
8:21 For the hurt of my poor **p** I am hurt, I mourn,
8:22 the health of my poor **p** not been restored?
9: 1 and night for the slain of my poor **p**!
9: 2 that I might leave my **p** and go away from them!
9: 7 for what else can I do with my sinful **p**?
9:15 I am feeding this **p** with wormwood,
10: 4 **p** deck it with silver and gold;
11: 2 the **p** of Judah and the inhabitants of Jerusalem. D
11: 4 So shall you be my **p**, and I will be your God,
11: 9 the **p** of Judah and the inhabitants of Jerusalem. D
11:14 As for you, do not pray for this **p**,
11:21 concerning the **p** of Anathoth, who seek your life,
11:23 For I will bring disaster upon the **p** of Anathoth,
12: 4 and because **p** said, "He is blind to our ways."
12:14 the heritage that I have given my **p** Israel C
12:16 if they will diligently learn the ways of my **p**,
12:16 as they taught my **p** to swear by Baal,
12:16 then they shall be built up in the midst of my **p**.
13:10 This evil **p**, who refuse to hear my words,
13:11 in order that they might be for me a **p**, a name,
14:10 Thus says the LORD concerning this **p**:
14:11 Do not pray for the welfare of this **p**.
14:16 the **p** to whom they prophesy shall be thrown out
14:17 for the virgin daughter—my **p**—
15: 1 yet my heart would not turn toward this **p**.
15: 7 I have bereaved them, I have destroyed my **p**;
15:20 I will make you to this **p** a fortified wall of bronze;
16: 5 for I have taken away my peace from this **p**,
16:10 And when you tell this **p** all these words,
16:14 "As the LORD lives who brought the **p** of Israel B
16:15 "As the LORD lives who brought the **p** of Israel B
17:25 the **p** of Judah and the inhabitants of Jerusalem; D
17:26 And **p** shall come from the towns of Judah and
18:11 the **p** of Judah and the inhabitants of Jerusalem: D
18:15 But my **p** have forgotten me,
19: 1 elders of the **p** and some of the senior priests, F
19: 4 Because the **p** have forsaken me,
19:11 So will I break this **p** and this city,
19:14 of the LORD's house and said to all the **p**: A
21: 7 and his servants, and the **p** in this city—
21: 8 And to this **p** you shall say:
22: 2 and your **p** who enter these gates.
22: 4 they, and their servants, and their **p**.
23: 2 concerning the shepherds who shepherd my **p**:
23: 7 "As the LORD lives who brought the **p** of Israel B
23:13 by Baal and led my **p** Israel astray. C
23:22 they would have proclaimed my words to my **p**,
23:27 to make my **p** forget my name by their dreams
23:32 and who lead my **p** astray by their lies
23:32 so they do not profit this **p** at all, says the LORD.
23:33 When this **p**, or a prophet, or a priest asks you,
23:34 And as for the prophet, priest, or the **p** who say,
24: 7 and they shall be my **p** and I will be their God,
25: 1 to Jeremiah concerning all the **p** of Judah, AD
25: 2 to all the **p** of Judah and all the inhabitants AD
25:19 his servants, his officials, and all his **p**; A
25:20 all the mixed **p**; all the kings of the land A
26: 7 all the **p** heard Jeremiah speaking these words A
26: 8 to speak to all the **p**, A
26: 8 priests and the prophets and all the **p** laid hold A
26: 9 And all the **p** gathered around Jeremiah A
26:11 the prophets said to the officials and to all the **p**, A
26:12 Jeremiah spoke to all the officials and all the **p**, A
26:16 Then the officials and all the **p** said to the priests A
26:17 arose and said to all the assembled **p**, A
26:18 said to all the **p** of Judah: AD
26:23 into the burial place of the common **p**.
26:24 that he was not given over into the hands of the **p**
27: 5 with the **p** and animals that are on the earth,
27:12 and serve him and his **p**, and live.
27:13 Why should you and your **p** die by the sword,
27:16 Then I spoke to the priests and to all this **p**, A
28: 1 in the presence of the priests and all the **p**, A
28: 5 of the priests and all the **p** who were standing in A
28: 7 in your hearing and in the hearing of all the **p**. A
28:11 And Hananiah spoke in the presence of all the **p**, A
28:15 and you made this **p** trust in a lie.
29: 1 and to the priests, the prophets, and all the **p**, A
29:16 and concerning all the **p** who live in this city, A
29:25 a letter to all the **p** who are in Jerusalem, A
29:32 living among this **p** to see the good that I am
going to do to my **p**,
30: 3 when I will restore the fortunes of my **p**,
30:22 And you shall be my **p**, and I will be your God.
31: 1 and they shall be my **p**.
31: 2 The **p** who survived the sword found grace in
31: 7 "Save, O LORD, your **p**, the remnant of Israel."
31:14 and my **p** shall be satisfied with my bounty,
31:33 and I will be their God, and they shall be my **p**.
32:21 brought your **p** Israel out of the land of Egypt C
32:30 For the **p** of Israel and the people B
32:30 of Israel and the **p** of Judah have done nothing D
32:30 the **p** of Israel have done nothing but provoke B
32:32 evil of the **p** of Israel and the people of Judah B
32:32 evil of the people of Israel and the **p** of Judah D
32:38 They shall be my **p**, and I will be their God.
32:42 upon this **p**, so I will bring upon them all
33:24 Have you not observed how these **p** say,
33:24 and how they hold my **p** in such contempt

Jer 34: 8 all the **p** in Jerusalem to make a proclamation A
34:10 all the officials and all the **p** who had entered A
34:19 and all the **p** of the land who passed between AE
35:13 the **p** of Judah and the inhabitants of Jerusalem, D
35:16 but this **p** has not obeyed me.
36: 6 of the **p** in the LORD's house you shall read
36: 6 also in the hearing of all the **p** of Judah AD
36: 7 that the LORD has pronounced against this **p."**
36: 9 all the **p** in Jerusalem and all the people who A
36: 9 all the people in Jerusalem and all the **p** who A
36:10 Then, in the hearing of all the **p,** A
36:13 Baruch read the scroll in the hearing of the **p.**
36:14 the scroll that you read in the hearing of the **p,**
36:31 of Jerusalem, and on the **p** of Judah, D
37: 2 nor his servants nor the **p** of the land listened to E
37: 4 Jeremiah was still going in and out among the **p,**
37:12 to receive his share of property among the **p** there.
37:18 to you or your servants or this **p,**
38: 1 the words that Jeremiah was saying to all the **p,** A
38: 4 and all the **p,** by speaking such words to them. A
38: 4 For this man is not seeking the welfare of this **p,**
39: 8 the king's house and the houses of the **p,**
39: 9 to Babylon the rest of the **p** who were left in
39: 9 to him, and the **p** who remained.
39:10 of Judah some of the poor **p** who owned nothing,
39:14 So he stayed with his own **p.**
40: 5 and stay with him among the **p;**
40: 6 and stayed with him among the **p** who were left in
41:10 the rest of the **p** who were in Mizpah,
41:10 the king's daughters and all the **p** who were left A
41:13 all the **p** who were with Ishmael saw Johanan A
41:14 all the **p** whom Ishmael had carried away A
41:16 took all the rest of the **p** whom Ishmael
42: 1 and all the **p** from the least to the greatest, A
42: 8 and all the **p** from the least to the greatest, A
42:17 All the **p** who have determined to go to Egypt A
43: 1 all the **p** all these words of the LORD their God, A
43: 4 and all the **p** did not obey the voice of the LORD, A
44:15 all the **p** who lived in Pathros in the land of A
44:20 Jeremiah said to all the **p,** men and women, A
44:20 all the **p** who were giving him this answer: A
44:21 and the **p** of the land, E
44:24 Jeremiah said to all the **p** and all the women, A
44:26 pronounced on the lips of any of the **p** of Judah D
44:27 all the **p** of Judah who are in the land AD
46:16 let us go back to our own **p** and to the land
46:24 she shall be handed over to a **p** from the north.
47: 2 **P** shall cry out, and all the inhabitants of the land
48:31 for the **p** of Kir-heres I mourn.
48:36 my heart moans like a flute for the **p** of Kir-heres;
48:42 Moab shall be destroyed as a **p,**
48:45 the scalp of the **p** of tumult.
48:46 The **p** of Chemosh have perished,
49: 1 and his **p** settled in its towns?
49:28 Destroy the **p** of the east! G
50: 4 says the LORD, the **p** of Israel shall come, B
50: 4 they and the **p** of Judah together; D
50: 6 My **p** have been lost sheep;
50:16 of them shall return to their own **p,**
50:33 The **p** of Israel are oppressed, B
50:33 and so too are the **p** of Judah; D
50:41 Look, a **p** is coming from the north;
51:45 Come out of her, my **p!**
52: 6 that there was no food for the **p** of the land. E
52:15 poorest of the **p** and the rest of the **p** who were left
52:16 the guard left some of the poorest **p** of the land E
52:25 of the army who mustered the **p** of the land; E
52:25 sixty men of the **p** of the land who were found E
52:28 the number of the **p** whom Nebuchadrezzar took
La 1: 1 How lonely sits the city that once was full of **p!**
1: 7 When her **p** fell into the hand of the foe,
1:11 All her **p** groan as they search for bread; A
2:11 on the ground because of the destruction of my **p,**
3:14 I have become the laughingstock of all my **p,** A
3:48 of tears because of the destruction of my **p.**
4: 3 but my **p** has become cruel,
4: 6 the chastisement of my **p** has been greater than
4:10 they became their food in the destruction of my **p.**
4:15 **p** shouted at them: "Away!
Eze 2: 3 Mortal, I am sending you to the **p** of Israel, B
3: 5 a **p** of obscure speech and difficult language,
3:11 to your **p,** and speak to them.
3:25 so that you cannot go out among the **p;**
4:13 "Thus shall the **p** of Israel eat their bread, B
6: 5 corpses of the **p** of Israel in front of their idols; B
7:27 and the hands of the **p** of the land shall tremble. E
11: 1 and Pelatiah son of Benaiah, officials of the **p.**
11:20 Then they shall be my **p,** and I will be their God.
12:19 to the **p** of the land, Thus says the Lord GOD E
13: 9 they shall not be in the council of my **p,**
13:10 Because, in truth, because they have misled my **p,**
13:10 and because, when the **p** build a wall,
13:17 set your face against the daughters of your **p,**
13:18 Will you hunt down lives among my **p,**
13:19 among my **p** for handfuls of barley and for pieces
13:19 by your lies to my **p,** who listen to lies.
13:21 and save my **p** from your hands;
13:23 I will save my **p** from your hand.
14: 8 and cut them off from the midst of my **p;**
14: 9 will destroy him from the midst of my **p** Israel. C
14:11 Then they shall be my **p,** and I will be their God,
18:18 and did what is not good among his **p,**
19: 6 to catch prey; he devoured **p.**
21:12 Cry and wail, O mortal, for it is against my **p;**
21:12 they are thrown to the sword, together with my **p.**
22:29 The **p** of the land have practiced extortion E
24:18 So I spoke to the **p** in the morning,

Eze 24:19 Then the **p** said to me,
25: 4 I am handing you over to the **p** of the east G
25:10 with Ammon to the **p** of the east as a possession. G
25:14 upon Edom by the hand of my **p** Israel; C
26:11 He shall put your **p** to the sword,
26:20 to the **p** of long ago,
30: 5 and the **p** of the allied land shall fall with them by
30:11 He and his **p** with him, the most terrible of
33: 2 speak to your **p** and say to them,
33: 2 and the **p** of the land take one of their number E
33: 3 the land and blows the trumpet and warns the **p;**
33: 6 so that the **p** are not warned,
33:12 And you, mortal, say to your **p,**
33:17 Yet your **p** say, "The way of the Lord is not just,"
33:30 your **p** who talk together about you by the walls,
33:31 to you as **p** come, and they sit before you as my **p,**
34:30 and that they, the house of Israel, are my **p,**
35: 5 over the **p** of Israel to the power of the sword B
36: 3 an object of gossip and slander among the **p;**
36: 8 and yield your fruit to my **p** Israel; C
36:12 I will lead **p** upon you—
36:12 I will lead people upon you—my **p** Israel— C
36:13 Because they say to you, "You devour **p,**
36:14 therefore you shall no longer devour **p**
36:20 "These are the **p** of the LORD, H
36:28 and you shall be my **p,** and I will be your God.
36:38 shall the ruined towns be filled with flocks of **p.**
37:12 and bring you up from your graves, O my **p;**
37:13 and bring you up from your graves, O my **p.**
37:18 And when your **p** say to you,
37:21 I will take the **p** of Israel from the nations B
37:23 they shall be my **p,** and I will be their GOD.
37:27 and I will be their God, and they shall be my **p.**
38: 8 a land where **p** were gathered from many nations
38: 8 its **p** were brought out from the nations and
38:11 I will fall upon the quiet **p** who live in safety,
38:12 and the **p** who were gathered from the nations,
38:14 that day when my **p** Israel are living securely, C
38:16 you will come up against my **p** Israel, C
39: 7 name I will make known among my **p** Israel; C
39:13 All the **p** of the land shall bury them; AE
42:14 before they go near to the area open to the **p."**
43: 7 I will reside among the **p** of Israel forever. B
44: 9 all the foreigners who are among the **p** of Israel, B
44:11 the burnt offering and the sacrifice for the **p,**
44:15 my sanctuary when the **p** of Israel went astray B
44:19 When they go out into the outer court to the **p,**
44:19 that they may not communicate holiness to the **p**
44:23 They shall teach my **p** the difference between
45: 8 And my princes shall no longer oppress my **p;**
45: 9 Cease your evictions of my **p,**
45:16 All the **p** of the land shall join with the prince AE
45:22 himself and all the **p** of the land a young bull AE
46: 3 The **p** of the land shall bow down at the entrance E
46: 9 When the **p** of the land come before the LORD E
46:18 of the inheritance of the **p,** thrusting them out
46:18 of my **p** shall be dispossessed of their holding.
46:20 and so communicate holiness to the **p."**
46:24 at the temple shall boil the sacrifices of the **p."**
47:10 **P** will stand fishing beside the sea from En-gedi
48:11 not go astray when the **p** of Israel went astray, B
Da 2:44 nor shall this kingdom be left to another **p.**
3:29 Therefore I make a decree: Any **p,** nation,
6:26 that in all my royal dominion **p** should tremble
7:27 under the whole heaven shall be given to the **p** of
8:24 He shall destroy the powerful and the **p** of
9: 6 and our ancestors, and to all the **p** of the land. AE
9: 7 the **p** of Judah, the inhabitants of Jerusalem, D
9:15 who brought your **p** out of the land of Egypt with
9:16 Jerusalem and your **p** have become a disgrace
9:19 because your city and your **p** bear your name!"
9:20 confessing my sin and the sin of my **p** Israel, C
9:24 "Seventy weeks are decreed for your **p**
10: 7 the **p** who were with me did not see the vision,
10:14 to help you understand what is to happen to your **p**
11:14 among your own **p** shall lift themselves up
11:32 the **p** who are loyal to their God shall stand firm
11:33 The wise among the **p** shall give understanding
12: 1 the great prince, the protector of your **p,**
12: 1 But at that time your **p** shall be delivered,
12: 7 the shattering of the power of the holy **p** comes K
Hos 1: 9 for you are not my **p** and I am not your God."
1:10 number of the **p** of Israel shall be like the sand B
1:10 "You are not my **p,"** it shall be said to them,
1:11 The **p** of Judah and the people of Israel shall D
1:11 and the **p** of Israel shall be gathered together, B
2:23 and I will say to Lo-ammi, "You are my **p"**;
3: 1 just as the LORD loves the **p** of Israel, B
4: 1 Hear the word of the LORD, O **p** of Israel; B
4: 6 My **p** are destroyed for lack of knowledge;
4: 8 They feed on the sin of my **p;**
4: 9 And it shall be like **p,** like priest;
4:12 My **p** consult a piece of wood,
4:14 thus a **p** without understanding comes to ruin.
6:11 When I would restore the fortunes of my **p,**
10: 5 Its **p** shall mourn for it, and its idolatrous priests
10:10 I will come against the wayward **p** to punish them;
10:14 the tumult of war shall rise against your **p,**
11: 7 My **p** are bent on turning away from me.
13: 2 **P** are kissing calves!
Joel 1:12 surely, joy withers away among the **p.**
2:16 gather the **p.** Sanctify the congregation;
2:17 Let them say, "Spare your **p,** O LORD,
2:18 and had pity on his **p.**
2:19 In response to his **p** the LORD said:
2:26 And my **p** shall never again be put to shame.
2:27 And my **p** shall never again be put to shame.

Joel 3: 2 on account of my **p** and my heritage Israel,
3: 3 and cast lots for my **p,**
3: 6 You have sold the **p** of Judah and Jerusalem to D
3: 8 the hand of the **p** of Judah, and they will sell D
3:16 But the LORD is a refuge for his **p,**
3:16 a stronghold for the **p** of Israel. B
3:19 because of the violence done to the **p** of Judah, D
Am 1: 5 and the **p** of Aram shall go into exile to Kir,
2:11 Is it not indeed so, O **p** of Israel? B
3: 1 O **p** of Israel, against the whole family B
3: 6 and the **p** are not afraid?
3:12 so shall the **p** of Israel who live in Samaria B
4: 5 for so you love to do, O **p** of Israel! B
6: 9 If ten **p** remain in one house, they shall die.
7: 8 a plumb line in the midst of my **p** Israel; C
7:15 'Go, prophesy to my **p** Israel.' C
8: 2 "The end has come upon my **p** Israel; C
9: 1 and shatter them on the heads of all the **p;** A
9: 7 not like the Ethiopians to me, O **p** of Israel? B
9:10 All the sinners of my **p** shall die by the sword,
9:14 I will restore the fortunes of my **p** Israel, C
Ob 1:12 should not have rejoiced over the **p** of Judah D
1:13 You should not have entered the gate of my **p** on
Jnh 1: 8 And of what **p** are you?"
3: 5 And the **p** of Nineveh believed God;
Mic 1: 9 it has reached to the gate of my **p,** to Jerusalem.
2: 2 they oppress householder and house, **p**
2: 4 the LORD alters the inheritance of my **p;**
2: 8 But you rise up against my **p** as an enemy;
2: 9 of my **p** you drive out from their pleasant houses;
2:11 such a one would be the preacher for this **p!**
2:12 in its pasture; it will resound with **p.**
3: 2 who tear the skin off my **p,**
3: 3 who eat the flesh of my **p,**
3: 5 concerning the prophets who lead my **p** astray,
5: 3 rest of his kindred shall return to the **p** of Israel. B
5: 7 not depend upon **p** or wait for any mortal.
6: 2 for the LORD has a controversy with his **p,**
6: 3 "O my **p,** what have I done to you?
6: 5 O my **p,** remember now what King Balak
6:16 so you shall bear the scorn of my **p.**
7:14 Shepherd your **p** with your staff,
Na 3:18 Your **p** are scattered on the mountains with no one
Hab 1:14 You have made **p** like the fish of the sea,
2: 6 Shall not everyone taunt such **p** and,
3:13 You came forth to save your **p,**
3:16 of calamity to come upon the **p** who attack us.
Zep 1:12 and I will punish the **p** who rest complacently
1:17 upon **p** that they shall walk like the blind;
2: 4 Ashdod's **p** shall be driven out at noon,
2: 8 how they have taunted my **p** and made boasts
2: 9 The remnant of my **p** shall plunder them,
2:10 and boasted against the **p** of the LORD of hosts. H
3: 6 their cities have been made desolate, without **p,**
3:12 For I will leave in the midst of you a **p** humble
Hag 1: 2 These **p** say the time has not yet come to rebuild
1:12 the high priest, with all the remnant of the **p,**
1:12 and the **p** feared the LORD.
1:13 spoke to the **p** with the LORD's message, saying,
1:14 and the spirit of all the remnant of the **p;**
2: 2 the high priest, and to the remnant of the **p,**
2: 4 take courage, all you **p** of the land, AE
2:14 Haggai then said, So is it with this **p,**
Zec 1:21 against the land of Judah to scatter its **p."**
2: 4 because of the multitude of **p** and animals in it.
2:11 and shall be my **p;** and I will dwell in your midst.
2:13 Be silent, all **p,** before the LORD; A
7: 2 Now the **p** of Bethel had sent Sharezer
7: 5 Say to all the **p** of the land and the priests: AE
8: 6 to the remnant of this **p** in these days,
8: 7 I will save my **p** from the east country and from
8: 8 They shall be my **p** and I will be their God,
8:10 For before those days there were no wages for **p**
8:11 now I will not deal with the remnant of this **p** as in
8:12 the remnant of this **p** to possess all these things.
9: 6 a mongrel **p** shall settle in Ashdod,
9:16 for they are the flock of his **p;**
10: 2 Therefore the **p** wander like sheep;
10: 7 Then the **p** of Ephraim shall become like warriors,
13: 9 I will say, "They are my **p"**;
14: 2 the rest of the **p** shall not be cut off from the city
Mal 1: 4 the **p** with whom the LORD is angry forever.
2: 7 and **p** should seek instruction from his mouth,
2: 9 I make you despised and abased before all the **p,** A
Mt 1:21 for he will save his **p** from their sins."
2: 4 the chief priests and scribes of the **p,**
2: 6 a ruler who is to shepherd my **p** Israel.' " C
3: 5 the **p** of Jerusalem and all Judea were going out
4:16 the **p** who sat in darkness have seen a great light,
4:19 "Follow me, and I will make you fish for **p."**
4:23 and every sickness among the **p.**
5:11 when **p** revile you and persecute you
9: 2 then some **p** were carrying a paralyzed man lying
12:31 **p** will be forgiven for every sin and blasphemy,
12:41 The **p** of Nineveh will rise up at the judgment
13:17 and righteous **p** longed to see what you see,
13:54 and began to teach the **p** in their synagogue,
14:35 After the **p** of that place recognized him,
15: 8 'This **p** honors me with their lips,
16:13 "Who do **p** say that the Son of Man is?"
21:23 the chief priests and the elders of the **p** came F
21:43 from you and given to a **p** that produces the fruits
22:16 for you do not regard **p** with partiality.
23: 7 and to have **p** call them rabbi.
23:13 For you lock **p** out of the kingdom of heaven.
25:32 and he will separate **p** one from another as
26: 3 the chief priests and the elders of the **p** gathered F

Mt 26: 5 or there may be a riot among the **p.**"
26:47 from the chief priests and the elders of the **p.** F
27: 1 elders of the **p** conferred together against Jesus F
27: 9 on whom some of the **p** of Israel had set a price, B
27:25 Then the **p** as a whole answered,
27:64 and tell the **p,** 'He has been raised from the dead,'
Mk 1: 5 And **p** from the whole Judean countryside and all
1: 5 all the **p** of Jerusalem were going out to him, A
1:17 "Follow me and I will make you fish for **p.**"
1:45 and **p** came to him from every quarter.
2: 3 Then some **p** came, bringing to him
2:18 and **p** came and said to him,
3:21 for **p** were saying, "He has gone out of his mind."
3:28 **p** will be forgiven for their sins
5:14 Then **p** came to see what it was that had happened.
5:35 some **p** came from the leader's house to say,
5:38 **p** weeping and wailing loudly.
6: 5 except that he laid his hands on a few sick **p**
6:39 he ordered them to get all the **p** to sit down A
6:41 and gave them to his disciples to set before the **p;**
6:54 they got out of the boat, **p** at once recognized him,
7: 6 as it is written, 'This **p** honors me with their lips,
8: 4 "How can one feed these **p** with bread here in
8: 9 Now there were about four thousand **p.**
8:22 Some **p** brought a blind man to him
8:24 And the man looked up and said, "I can see **p,**
8:27 "Who do **p** say that I am?"
10:13 **P** were bringing little children to him in order
11: 8 Many **p** spread their cloaks on the road,
12:14 for you do not regard **p** with partiality,
12:41 Many rich **p** put in large sums.
14: 2 or there may be a riot among the **p.**"
Lk 1:10 the whole assembly of the **p** was praying outside.
1:16 many of the **p** of Israel to the Lord their God. B
1:17 to make ready a **p** prepared for the Lord."
1:21 Meanwhile the **p** were waiting for Zechariah,
1:25 the disgrace I have endured among my **p.**"
1:68 for he has looked favorably on his **p**
1:77 to give knowledge of salvation to his **p** by
2:10 good news of great joy for all the **p:** A
2:32 to the Gentiles and for glory to your **p** Israel." C
3:15 As the **p** were filled with expectation,
3:18 he proclaimed the good news to the **p.**
3:21 Now when all the **p** were baptized, A
5:10 from now on you will be catching **p.**"
6:17 of his disciples and a great multitude of **p**
6:22 "Blessed are you when **p** hate you,
7: 1 all his sayings in the hearing of the **p,**
7: 5 loves our **p,** and it is he who built our synagogue
7:16 and "God has looked favorably on his **p!**"
7:21 Jesus had just then cured many **p** of diseases,
7:29 (And all the **p** who heard this, A
7:31 then will I compare the **p** of this generation,
8: 4 and **p** from town after town came to him, he said
8:35 Then **p** came out to see what had happened,
8:37 Then all the **p** of the surrounding country of A
8:47 presence of all the **p** why she had touched him, A
9:13 we are to go and buy food for all these **p.**" A
10: 8 and its **p** welcome you, eat what is set before you;
11:30 just as Jonah became a sign to the **p** of Nineveh,
11:31 with the **p** of this generation and condemn them,
11:32 The **p** of Nineveh will rise up at the judgment
11:44 and **p** walk over them without realizing it."
11:46 For you load **p** with burdens hard to bear,
13:29 Then **p** will come from east and west,
14: 3 "Is it lawful to cure **p** on the sabbath, or not?"
14:23 and compel **p** to come in,
16: 4 **p** may welcome me into their homes.'
18: 2 who neither feared God nor had respect for **p.**
18:11 'God, I thank you that I am not like other **p:** I
18:15 **P** were bringing even infants to him
18:43 and all the **p,** when they saw it, praised God. A
19:36 **p** kept spreading their cloaks on the road.
19:47 leaders of the **p** kept looking for a way to kill him;
19:48 all the **p** were spellbound by what they heard. A
20: 1 as he was teaching the **p** in the temple and telling
20: 6 say, 'Of human origin,' all the **p** will stone us; A
20: 9 He began to tell the **p** this parable:
20:19 on him at that very hour, but they feared the **p.**
20:26 the presence of the **p** to trap him by what he said;
20:45 the hearing of all the **p** he said to the disciples, A
21: 1 and saw rich **p** putting their gifts into the treasury;
21:23 on the earth and wrath against this **p;**
21:26 **P** will faint from fear and foreboding
21:38 And all the **p** would get up early in the morning A
22: 2 for they were afraid of the **p.**
22:66 day came, the assembly of the elders of the **p,** F
23: 5 up the **p** by teaching throughout all Judea,
23:13 the chief priests, the leaders, and the **p,**
23:14 as one who was perverting the **p;**
23:27 A great number of the **p** followed him,
23:35 And the **p** stood by, watching;
24:19 in deed and word before God and all the **p,** A
Jn 1: 4 was life, and the life was the light of all **p.** A
1:11 and his own **p** did not accept him.
2:14 In the temple he found **p** selling cattle, sheep,
2:24 entrust himself to them, because he knew all **p** A
3:19 and **p** loved darkness rather than light
3:23 and **p** kept coming and were being baptized
4:20 but you say that the place where **p** must worship is
4:28 She said to the **p,**
6: 5 "Where are we to buy bread for these **p** to eat?"
6: 9 But what are they among so many **p?**"
6:10 Jesus said, "Make the **p** sit down."
6:14 When the **p** saw the sign that he had done,
7:25 Now some of the **p** of Jerusalem were saying,
7:51 not judge **p** without first giving them a hearing

Jn 8: 2 ⟦All the **p** came to him and he sat down and⟧ A
11:50 for the **p** than to have the whole nation destroyed."
12:32 from the earth, I will draw all **p** to myself." A
17: 2 since you have given him authority over all **p,** A
18:14 that it was better to have one person die for the **p.**
Ac 2:47 God and having the goodwill of all the **p.** A
3: 2 **P** would lay him daily at the gate of
3: 9 All the **p** saw him walking and praising God, A
3:11 all the **p** ran together to them in A
3:12 When Peter saw it, he addressed the **p,**
3:22 up for you from your own **p** a prophet like me.
3:23 to that prophet will be utterly rooted out of the **p.**'
4: 1 While Peter and John were speaking to the **p,**
4: 2 because they were teaching the **p** and proclaiming
4: 8 said to them, "Rulers of the **p** and elders,
4:10 and to all the **p** of Israel, AB
4:17 But to keep it from spreading further among the **p,**
4:21 finding no way to punish them because of the **p,**
5:12 and wonders were done among the **p** through
5:13 but the **p** held them in high esteem.
5:16 A great number of **p** would also gather from
5:20 and tell the **p** the whole message about this life."
5:25 in the temple and teaching the **p!**"
5:26 for they were afraid of being stoned by the **p.**
5:34 a teacher of the law, respected by all the **p,** A
5:37 at the time of the census and got **p** to follow him;
6: 8 did great wonders and signs among the **p.**
6:12 They stirred up the **p** as well as the elders and
7:17 our **p** in Egypt increased and multiplied
7:34 surely seen the mistreatment of my **p** who are
7:37 for you from your own **p** as he raised me up.'
7:51 "You stiff-necked **p,** uncircumcised in heart
8: 9 in the city and amazed the **p** of Samaria,
9:15 Gentiles and kings and before the **p** of Israel; B
10: 2 to the **p** and prayed constantly to God.
10:36 You know the message he sent to the **p** of Israel, B
10:41 to all the **p** but to us who were chosen by God A
10:42 He commanded us to preach to the **p** and to
10:47 the water for baptizing these **p** who have received
11:24 And a great many **p** were brought to the Lord.
11:26 with the church and taught a great many **p,**
12: 4 to bring him out to the **p** after the Passover.
12:11 and from all that the Jewish **p** were expecting."
12:20 Herod was angry with the **p** of Tyre and Sidon.
12:22 The **p** kept shouting, "The voice of a god,
13:15 if you have any word of exhortation for the **p,**
13:17 The God of this **p** Israel chose our ancestors C
13:17 and made the **p** great during their stay in the land
13:24 a baptism of repentance to all the **p** of Israel. AB
13:31 and they are now his witnesses to the **p.**
13:42 the **p** urged them to speak about these things again
15:14 to take from among them a **p** for his name.
17: 6 "These **p** who have been turning the world upside
17: 8 The **p** and the city officials were disturbed
17:30 now he commands all **p** everywhere to repent, A
18:10 for there are many in this city who are my **p.**"
18:13 "This man is persuading **p** to worship God in ways
19: 4 the **p** to believe in the one who was to come
19:26 of **p** by saying that gods made with hands are
19:29 and **p** rushed together to the theater,
19:33 and tried to make a defense before the **p.**
21:12 the **p** there urged him not to go up to Jerusalem.
21:28 against our **p,** our law, and this place;
21:30 all the city was aroused, and the **p** rushed together.
21:39 I beg you, let me speak to the **p.**"
21:40 on the steps and motioned to the **p** for silence;
23: 5 'You shall not speak evil of a leader of your **p.**' "
24: 2 and reforms have been made for this **p** because
24:16 have a clear conscience toward God and all **p.** A
26: 4 the beginning among my own **p** and in Jerusalem.
26:17 I will rescue you from your **p** and from
26:23 he would proclaim light both to our **p** and to
28: 9 of the **p** on the island who had diseases also came
28:17 against our **p** or the customs of our ancestors,
28:26 'Go to this **p** and say,
Ro 3: 8 And why not say (as some **p** slander us by saying
9: 3 and cut off from Christ for the sake of my own **p,**
9:25 "Those who were not my **p** I will call 'my **p,**'
9:26 not my **p,**' there they shall be called children of
9:33 in Zion a stone that will make **p** stumble,
10:21 to a disobedient and contrary **p.**"
11: 1 I ask, then, has God rejected his **p?**
11: 2 God has not rejected his **p** whom he foreknew.
11:14 in order to make my own **p** jealous,
15:10 "Rejoice, O Gentiles, with his **p**";
16:18 For such **p** do not serve our Lord Christ,
1Co 1:11 by Chloe's **p** that there are quarrels among you,
3: 1 I could not speak to you as spiritual **p,**
3: 1 but rather as **p** of the flesh, as infants in Christ.
4:19 and I will find out not the talk of these arrogant **p**
9:22 I have become all things to all **p,** A
10: 7 as it is written, "The **p** sat down to eat and drink,
10:15 I speak as to sensible **p;**
10:18 Consider the **p** of Israel; are B
14: 2 in a tongue do not speak to other **p** but to God; I
14: 3 prophesy speak to other **p** for their upbuilding I
14:21 "By **p** of strange tongues and by the lips of
14:21 I will speak to this **p;** yet even then they will not
15:19 we are of all **p** most to be pitied. A
15:29 what will those **p** do who receive baptism
15:29 why are **p** baptized on their behalf?
15:34 for some **p** have no knowledge of God.
16:16 to put yourselves at the service of such **p,**
2Co 3: 7 in glory so that the **p** of Israel could not gaze B
3:13 over his face to keep the **p** of Israel from gazing B
4:15 so that grace, as it extends to more and more **p,**
6:16 and I will be their God, and they shall be my **p.**

2Co 9: 2 of my boasting about you to the **p** of Macedonia,
10:11 Let such **p** understand that what we say by letter
11:26 danger from my own **p,** danger from Gentiles,
Gal 1:10 Or am I trying to please **p?**
1:10 If I were still pleasing **p,**
1:14 I advanced in Judaism beyond many among my **p**
2:12 for until certain **p** came from James,
Eph 1:14 toward redemption as God's own **p,**
4: 8 he gave gifts to his **p.**"
5:12 even to mention what such **p** do secretly;
5:15 not as unwise **p** but as wise,
Php 2:29 then in the Lord with all joy, and honor such **p,**
3: 5 a member of the **p** of Israel, B
1Th 1: 9 the **p** of those regions report about us what kind
2Th 3: 2 that we may be rescued from wicked and evil **p;**
1Ti 1: 3 in Ephesus so that you may instruct certain **p** not
1: 6 Some **p** have deviated from these and turned
4:10 the living God, who is the Savior of all **p,** A
5:24 of some **p** are conspicuous and precede them
6: 9 and harmful desires that plunge **p** into ruin
2Ti 2: 2 to faithful **p** who will be able to teach others
2:16 for it will lead **p** into more and more impiety,
3: 2 For **p** will be lovers of themselves,
3: 8 Jannes and Jambres opposed Moses, so these **p,**
3:13 But wicked **p** and impostors will go from bad
4: 3 For the time is coming when **p** will not put up
Tit 1:10 There are also many rebellious **p,**
2:14 a **p** of his own who are zealous for good deeds.
3:14 And let **p** learn to devote themselves
Heb 2:17 a sacrifice of atonement for the sins of the **p.**
4: 9 then, a sabbath rest still remains for the **p** of God;
5: 3 for his own sins as well as for those of the **p.**
7: 5 in the law to collect tithes from the **p,**
7:11 for the **p** received the law under this priesthood—
7:27 first for his own sins, and then for those of the **p;**
8:10 and I will be their God, and they shall be my **p.**
9: 7 for the sins committed unintentionally by the **p.**
9:19 all the **p** by Moses in accordance with the law, A
9:19 and sprinkled both the scroll itself and all the **p,** A
10:30 And again, "The Lord will judge his **p.**"
11:14 for **p** who speak in this way make it clear
11:25 the **p** of God than to enjoy the fleeting pleasures
11:29 By faith the **p** passed through the Red Sea as
13:12 in order to sanctify the **p** by his own blood.
Jas 5: 1 now, you rich **p,** weep and wail for the miseries
1Pe 1:17 the one who judges all **p** impartially according A
2: 9 a royal priesthood, a holy nation, God's own **p,**
2:10 not a **p,** but now you are God's **p;**
2:16 As servants of God, live as free **p,**
2Pe 2: 1 But false prophets also arose among the **p,**
2:12 These **p,** however, are like irrational animals,
2:18 of the flesh they entice **p** who have just escaped
2:19 for **p** are slaves to whatever masters them.
1Jn 2:13 I am writing to you, young **p,**
2:14 I write to you, young **p,** because you are strong
3Jn 1: 8 Therefore we ought to support such **p,**
Jude 1: 4 **p** who long ago were designated
1: 5 who once for all saved a **p** out of the land
1:10 these **p** slander whatever they do not understand,
1:16 flattering **p** to their own advantage.
1:19 It is these worldly **p,** devoid of the Spirit,
Rev 2:14 to put a stumbling block before the **p** of Israel, B
5: 9 from every tribe and language and **p** and nation;
6: 4 so that **p** would slaughter one another;
7: 4 sealed out of every tribe of the **p** of Israel: B
9: 4 but only those **p** who do not have the seal of God
9: 6 in those days **p** will seek death but will not find it;
9:10 and in their tails is their power to harm **p**
11:13 seven thousand **p** were killed in the earthquake,
13: 7 over every tribe and **p** and language and nation,
14: 6 to every nation and tribe and language and **p.**
16:10 **p** gnawed their tongues in agony,
16:18 as had not occurred since **p** were upon the earth,
16:21 dropped from heaven on **p,**
18: 4 "Come out of her, my **p,** so that you do not take
21:26 **P** will bring into it the glory and the honor of
Tob 1: 3 of charity for my kindred and my **p** who had gone
1:10 everyone of my kindred and my **p** ate the food of
1:17 if I saw the dead body of any of my **p** thrown out
2: 2 of our **p** among the exiles in Nineveh,
2: 3 to look for some poor person of our **p.**
2: 3 of our own **p** has been murdered and thrown into
4:13 the sons and daughters of your **p,**
5:10 I hear **p** but I cannot see them."
5:14 Your kindred are good **p;**
6:14 I have heard **p** saying that it was a demon
11:16 When the **p** of Nineveh saw him coming,
12: 6 With fitting honor declare to all **p** the deeds A
13: 8 Let all **p** speak of his majesty, A
13:14 Happy also are all **p** who grieve with you A
14:10 while the **p** are without shame.
14:15 Tobias praised God for all he had done to the **p**
Jdt 1: 6 all the **p** of the hill country and all those who A
1:12 and the **p** of Ammon, and all Judea,
2:28 and dread of him fell upon all the **p** who lived A
3: 7 These **p** and all in the countryside welcomed him
4: 3 all the **p** of Judea had just now gathered A
4: 6 wrote to the **p** of Bethulia and Betomesthaim,
4: 8 and the senate of the whole **p** of Israel, B
4:13 for the **p** fasted many days throughout Judea and
4:14 and freewill offerings of the **p.**
5: 1 that the **p** of Israel had prepared for war B
5: 3 what **p** is this that lives in the hill country?
5: 5 and I will tell you the truth about this **p** that lives
5: 6 These **p** are descended from the Chaldeans.
5:14 They drove out all the **p** of the desert, A
5:20 if there is any oversight in this **p** and they sin

Jdt 5:22 all the **p** standing around the tent began to A
5:23 a **p** with no strength or power for making war.
6: 1 When the disturbance made by the **p** outside
6: 2 tell us not to make war against the **p** of Israel B
6:16 They set Achior in the midst of all their **p,** A
6:18 the **p** fell down and worshiped God, and cried out:
6:19 and have pity on our **p** in their humiliation,
7:10 This **p,** the Israelites, do not rely on their spears
7:13 where all the **p** of Bethulia get their water. A
7:13 we and our **p** will go up to the tops of the nearby
7:23 Then all the **p,** the young men, the women, A
7:32 Then he dismissed the **p** to their various posts,
8: 9 the harsh words spoken by the **p** against the ruler,
8:11 "Listen to me, rulers of the **p** of Bethulia!
8:11 What you have said to the **p** today is not right;
8:18 has there been any tribe or family or **p** or town
8:29 all the **p** have recognized your understanding, A
8:30 the **p** were so thirsty that they compelled us to do
9:14 there is no other who protects the **p** of Israel B
10: 8 that the **p** of Israel may glory and Jerusalem B
10:12 They asked her, "To what **p** do you belong,
10:19 "Who can despise these **p,**
11: 2 if your **p** who live in the hill country had
11: 9 for the **p** of Bethulia spared him
11:13 for any of the **p** even to touch with their hands.
11:14 even the **p** in Jerusalem have been doing this,
11:16 the whole world wherever **p** shall hear about them.
11:22 "God has done well to send you ahead of the **p,**
12: 3 For none of your **p** are here with us."
12: 8 of Israel to direct her way for the triumph of his **p.**
13:12 When the **p** of her town heard her voice,
13:17 All the **p** were greatly astonished. A
13:17 this day humiliated the enemies of your **p."**
13:20 And all the **p** said, "Amen. A
14: 6 of one of the men in the assembly of the **p,**
14: 8 So Judith told him in the presence of the **p** all
14: 9 the **p** raised a great shout and made a joyful noise
14:17 he rushed out to the **p** and shouted,
15: 6 of the **p** of Bethulia fell upon the Assyrian camp
15:10 And all the **p** said, "Amen." A
15:11 All the **p** plundered the camp for thirty days. A
15:13 She went before all the **p** in the dance, A
15:14 and all the **p** loudly sang this song of praise. A
16: 2 he sets up his camp among his **p;**
16:11 Then my oppressed **p** shouted;
16:11 my weak **p** cried out, and the enemy trembled;
16:17 Woe to the nations that rise up against my **p!**
16:18 As soon as the **p** were purified,
16:19 which the **p** had given her;
16:20 the **p** continued feasting in Jerusalem before
16:22 and was gathered to his **p.**
AdE 1: 5 for the **p** of various nations who lived in the city.
1:11 to all the governors and the **p** of various nations,
2:10 Now Esther had not disclosed her **p** or country,
3:13 the Jewish **p** on a given day of the twelfth month,
4: 8 the king and plead for his favor in behalf of the **p.**
6:13 "If Mordecai is of the Jewish **p,**
7: 3 and my **p** at my request.
7: 4 For we have been sold, I and my **p,**
8: 6 How can I look on the ruin of my **p?**
8:15 The **p** in Susa rejoiced on seeing him.
9: 6 in the city of Susa the Jews killed five hundred **p,**
9:12 the Jews have destroyed five hundred **p.**
9:15 on the fourteenth and killed three hundred **p,**
10: 9 The Lord has saved his **p;**
10:10 one for the **p** of God and one for all the nations,
10:12 And God remembered his **p**
10:13 to generation forever among his **p** Israel." C
12: 6 and his **p** because of the two eunuchs of the king.
13: 2 to restore the peace desired by all **p.** A
13: 4 in the world there is scattered a certain hostile **p,**
13: 5 We understand that this **p,** and it alone,
13:15 God of Abraham, spare your **p;**
16: 2 "Many **p,** the more they are honored with
16:21 for his chosen **p** instead of a day of destruction
Wis 1: 3 For perverse thoughts separate **p** from God,
4: 2 When it is present, **p** imitate it,
6:24 and a sensible king is the stability of any **p.**
8:15 among the **p** I shall show myself capable,
9: 7 be king of your **p** and to be judge over your sons
9:12 and I shall judge your **p** justly,
9:18 and **p** were taught what pleases you,
10:15 A holy **p** and blameless race wisdom delivered K
10:17 She gave to holy **p** the reward of their labors; K
11:19 not only could the harm they did destroy **p,**
11:20 **p** could fall at a single breath when pursued
12:13 any god besides you, whose care is for all **p,** A
12:17 when **p** doubt the completeness of your power,
12:19 Through such works you have taught your **p** that
13: 1 all **p** who were ignorant of God were foolish A
13: 3 in the beauty of these things **p** assumed them to
13: 4 And if **p** were amazed at their power and working,
13: 6 Yet these **p** are little to be blamed,
14: 5 therefore **p** trust their lives even to
14:17 **p** could not honor monarchs in their presence,
14:21 a hidden trap for humankind, because **p,**
14:31 it is not the power of the things by which **p** swear,
15:14 are all the enemies who oppressed your **p.**
15:17 **P** are mortal, and what they make
16: 1 Therefore those **p** were deservedly punished
16: 2 to your **p,** and you prepared quails to eat,
16: 3 that those **p,** when they desired food, might lose
16: 3 while your **p,** after suffering want a short time,
16: 5 the terrible rage of wild animals came upon your **p**
16:12 but it was your word, O Lord, that heals all **p.** A
16:20 of these things you gave your **p** food of angels,
17: 2 For when lawless **p** supposed that they held

Wis 17:21 while over those **p** alone heavy night was spread,
18: 7 of their enemies were expected by your **p.**
18: 9 the holy children of good **p** offered sacrifices,
18:13 they acknowledged your **p** to be God's child.
19: 2 though they themselves had permitted your **p**
19: 5 your **p** might experience an incredible journey,
19:22 O Lord, you have exalted and glorified your **p,**
Sir 7: 7 and do not disgrace yourself among the **p.**
9:15 Let your conversation be with intelligent **p,**
10: 1 A wise magistrate educates his **p,**
10: 3 An undisciplined king ruins his **p,**
13:16 and **p** stick close to those like themselves.
14: 8 he turns away and disregards **p.**
16: 4 one intelligent person a city can be filled with **p,**
16:17 Among so many **p** I am unknown,
19:25 and there are **p** who abuse favors to gain a verdict.
20: 5 Some **p** keep silent and are thought to be wise,
20: 6 Some **p** keep silent because they have nothing
24: 1 and tells of her glory in the midst of her **p.**
24: 6 and over every **p** and nation I have held sway.
24:12 I took root in an honored **p,**
25: 2 I hate three kinds of **p,** and I loathe their manner
27: 7 for this is the way **p** are tested.
27:12 Among stupid **p** limit your time,
27:12 but among thoughtful **p** linger on.
31: 9 For he has done wonders among his **p.**
31:23 **P** bless the one who is liberal with food,
31:27 It has been created to make **p** happy.
33:19 Hear me, you who are great among the **p,**
35:25 of his **p** and makes them rejoice in his mercy.
36:10 and let **p** recount your mighty deeds.
36:11 and may those who harm your **p** meet destruction.
36:17 O Lord, on the **p** called by your name, on Israel,
36:22 according to your goodwill toward your **p,**
37:19 Some **p** may be clever enough to teach many,
37:23 A wise person instructs his own **p,**
37:26 One who is wise among his **p** will inherit honor,
38:32 they are not sought out for the council of the **p,**
41:18 before the congregation and the **p;**
42:11 a byword in the city and the assembly of the **p,**
44: 4 the **p** by their counsels and by their knowledge of
44:22 The blessing of all **p** and the covenant A
45: 1 and was beloved by God and **p,**
45: 3 He gave him commandments for his **p,**
45: 7 and gave him the priesthood of the **p.**
45: 9 in the temple as a reminder to his **p;**
45:15 and serve as priest and bless his **p** in his name.
45:16 to make atonement for the **p.**
45:22 But in the land of the **p** he has no inheritance,
45:22 and he has no portion among the **p;**
45:23 and standing firm, when the **p** turned away,
45:24 he should be leader of the sanctuary and of his **p,**
45:26 the Lord grant you wisdom of mind to judge his **p**
46: 7 they opposed the congregation, restrained the **p**
46: 8 to lead the **p** into their inheritance,
46:13 the kingdom and anointed rulers over his **p.**
46:20 to blot out the wickedness of the **p.**
47: 5 and to exalt the power of his **p.**
47:23 Rehoboam, whose policy drove the **p** to revolt.
48:15 Despite all this the **p** did not repent,
48:15 The **p** were left very few in number,
49: 2 He did what was right by reforming the **p,**
49:10 the **p** of Jacob and delivered them
50: 1 and the pride of his **p** was the high priest,
50: 4 He considered how to save his **p** from ruin,
50: 5 How glorious he was, surrounded by the **p,**
50:17 all the **p** together quickly fell to the ground A
50:19 the **p** of the Lord Most High offered their prayers
50:25 and the third is not even a **p:**
50:26 and the foolish **p** that live in Shechem.
51:12 *He has raised up a horn for his p,*
51:12 *For the children of Israel the p close to him.*
Bar 1: 3 and to all the **p** who came to hear the book, A
1: 4 to the elders, and to all the **p,** small and great, A
1: 7 and to all the **p** who were present with him A
1: 9 prisoners and the nobles and the **p** of the land, E
1:15 the **p** of Judah, on the inhabitants of Jerusalem, D
2: 1 our kings and our rulers and the **p** of Israel B
2:11 who brought your **p** out of the land of Egypt with
2:28 write your law in the presence of the **p** of Israel B
2:30 for they are a stiff-necked **p.**
2:35 with them to be their God and they shall be my **p;**
2:35 and I will never again remove my **p** Israel from C
3: 4 hear now the prayer of the **p** of Israel, B
3:17 which **p** trust, and there is no end to their getting;
4: 3 or your advantages to an alien **p.**
4: 5 my **p,** who perpetuate Israel's name!
LtJ 6: 4 which **p** carry on their shoulders,
6: 9 **P** take gold and make crowns for the heads
6:53 up a king over a country or give rain to **p.**
Aza 1:60 "Bless the Lord, all **p** on earth; A
Sus 1: 5 That year two elders from the **p** were appointed
1: 5 who were supposed to govern the **p."**
1: 7 When the **p** left at noon,
1:26 **p** in the house heard the shouting in the garden,
1:28 the **p** gathered at the house of her husband Joakim,
1:28 In the presence of the **p** they said,
1:34 up before the **p** and laid their hands on her head.
1:41 Because they were elders of the **p** and judges, F
1:47 All the **p** turned to him and asked, A
1:50 So all the **p** hurried back. A
1:64 a great reputation among the **p.**
1Mc 1:13 and some of the **p** eagerly went to the king,
1:30 and destroyed many **p** of Israel. B
1:34 They stationed there a sinful **p,**
1:41 to his whole kingdom that all should be one **p,**
1:51 all the **p** and commanded the towns of Judah A

1Mc 1:52 Many of the **p,** everyone who forsook the law,
2: 7 Why was I born to see this, the ruin of my **p,**
2:18 as all the Gentiles and the **p** of Judah and D
2:67 and avenge the wrong done to your **p.**
3: 3 He extended the glory of his **p.**
3: 5 he burned those who troubled his **p.**
3:42 to do to the **p** to cause their final destruction.
3:43 restore the ruins of our **p,** and fight for our **p** and
3:55 After this Judas appointed leaders of the **p,**
4:17 the **p,** "Do not be greedy for plunder, for there is
4:31 Hem in this army by the hand of your **p** Israel, C
4:55 All the **p** fell on their faces and worshiped A
4:58 There was very great joy among the **p,**
4:61 the **p** might have a stronghold that faced Idumea.
5: 2 So they began to kill and destroy among the **p.**
5: 4 a trap and a snare to the **p** and ambushed them on
5: 6 where he found a strong band and many **p,**
5:15 that the **p** of Ptolemais and Tyre and Sidon,
5:16 When Judas and the **p** heard these messages,
5:18 son of Zechariah, and Azariah, a leader of the **p,**
5:19 "Take charge of this **p,** but do not engage in battle
5:27 and destroy all these **p** in a single day." A
5:47 But the **p** of the town shut them out and blocked
5:53 and encouraging the **p** all the way until he came to
5:60 as two thousand of the **p** of Israel fell that day. B
5:61 Thus the **p** suffered a great rout because,
5:64 **P** gathered to them and praised them.
6:19 and assembled all the **p** to besiege them. A
6:24 of our **p** besieged the citadel and became hostile
6:44 So he gave his life to save his **p** and to win
6:49 He made peace with the **p** of Beth-zur,
6:58 Now then let us come to terms with these **p,**
7: 6 to the king this accusation against the **p:**
7:18 Then the fear and dread of them fell on all the **p,** A
7:19 of the **p,** and killed them and threw them into
7:22 and all who were troubling their **p** joined him.
7:26 and he commanded him to destroy the **p.**
7:33 elders of the **p** came out to greet him peaceably F
7:37 be for your **p** a house of prayer and supplication.
7:46 **P** came out of all the surrounding villages
7:48 The **p** rejoiced greatly and celebrated that day as
8:15 senators constantly deliberate concerning the **p,**
8:20 and his brothers and the **p** of the Jews have sent us
8:29 the Romans make a treaty with the Jewish **p.**
9: 2 and they took it and killed many **p.**
9:66 down Odomera and his kindred and the **p**
9:73 in Michmash and began to judge the **p;**
10: 7 read the letter in the hearing of all the **p** and A
10:46 When Jonathan and the **p** heard these words,
10:72 **P** will tell you that you cannot stand before us,
10:75 but the **p** of the city closed its gates, J
10:76 **p** of the city became afraid and opened the gates, J
10:86 and the **p** of the city came out to meet him J
11: 2 and the **p** of the towns opened their gates to him
11:14 because the **p** of that region were in revolt.
11:45 Then the **p** of the city assembled within the city, J
11:46 **p** of the city seized the main streets of the city J
11:49 When the **p** of the city saw that the Jews J
11:51 of the king and of all the **p** in his kingdom, A
11:60 the **p** of the city met him and paid him honor. J
11:61 but the **p** of Gaza shut him out.
11:62 Then the **p** of Gaza pleaded with Jonathan,
12: 4 Romans gave them letters to the **p** in every place,
12: 6 rest of the Jewish **p** to their brothers the Spartans,
12:35 the elders of the **p** and planned with them F
12:44 have you put all these **p** to so much trouble A
12:48 **p** of Ptolemais closed the gates and seized him,
13: 2 and he saw that the **p** were trembling with fear.
13: 2 and gathering the **p** together
13: 7 the **p** was rekindled when they heard these words,
13:17 he would not arouse great hostility among the **p,**
13:42 **p** began to write in their documents and contracts,
14:12 All the **p** sat under their own vines and fig trees, A
14:14 He gave help to all the humble among his **p;**
14:20 and the priests and the rest of the Jewish **p,**
14:21 to our **p** have told us about your glory and honor,
14:23 It has pleased our **p** to receive these men
14:23 the **p** of the Spartans may have a record of them.
14:25 When the **p** heard these things they said,
14:28 of the priests and the **p** and the rulers of the nation
14:30 and was gathered to his **p.**
14:35 "The **p** saw Simon's faithfulness and the glory
14:35 He sought in every way to exalt his **p.**
14:44 of the **p** or priests shall be permitted to nullify any
14:46 All the **p** agreed to grant Simon the right to act A
15:17 by the high priest Simon and by the Jewish **p**
15:35 they were causing great damage among the **p** and
15:39 and to make war on the **p;**
15:40 the **p** and invade Judea and take the **p** captive
2Mc 1:10 The **p** of Jerusalem and of Judea and the senate
1:16 and threw them to the **p** outside.
1:26 this sacrifice on behalf of all your **p** Israel AC
1:27 Gather together our scattered **p,**
1:29 Plant your **p** in your holy place,
1:36 but by most **p** it is called naphtha.
2: 7 until God gathers his **p** together again
2:15 send **p** to get them for you.
2:17 It is God who has saved all his **p,** A
3:12 be done to those **p** who had trusted in the holiness
3:18 **P** also hurried out of their houses in crowds
3:34 report to all **p** the majestic power of God." A
4: 5 both public and private, of all the **p.** A
4: 9 to enroll the **p** of Jerusalem as citizens of Antioch.
4:30 that the **p** of Tarsus and of Mallus revolted
5:22 He left governors to oppress the **p:**
5:26 and killed great numbers of **p.**
6: 2 as did the **p** who lived in that place.

2Mc 6: 6 **P** could neither keep the sabbath,
6: 8 of the **p** of Ptolemais a decree was issued to
6:12 not to destroy but to discipline our **p.**
6:16 he does not forsake his own **p.**
7: 6 that bore witness against the **p** to their faces,
7:16 But do not think that God has forsaken our **p.**
8: 2 the Lord to look upon the **p** who were oppressed
8:36 of the **p** of Jerusalem proclaimed that the Jews had
9: 2 Therefore the **p** rushed to the rescue with arms,
9:24 the **p** throughout the realm would not be troubled,
10:21 he gathered the leaders of the **p,**
11: 6 they and all the **p,** with lamentations and tears, A
11:16 "Lysias to the **p** of the Jews, greetings.
11:34 envoys of the Romans, to the **p** of the Jews,
12: 3 And the **p** of Joppa did so ungodly a deed as this:
12: 4 the **p** of Joppa took them out to sea
12: 8 the **p** in Jamnia meant in the same way to wipe out
12:11 promising to give him livestock and to help his **p**
12:26 and slaughtered twenty-five thousand **p.**
12:27 where Lysias lived with multitudes of **p**
12:30 that the **p** of Scythopolis had shown them
12:42 the **p** to keep themselves free from sin,
13:10 he ordered the **p** to call upon the Lord day
13:11 to let the **p** who had just begun to revive fall into
13:22 The king negotiated a second time with the **p**
13:25 The **p** of Ptolemais were indignant over the treaty;
14:15 to him who established his own **p** forever
14:20 and the leader had informed the **p,**
14:23 but dismissed the flocks of **p** that had gathered.
15:14 the family of Israel and prays much for the **p** and
15:24 against your holy **p** be struck down." K
15:30 in body and soul the defender of his **p,**
1Es 1: 4 the Lord your God and serve his **p** Israel; C
1: 5 minister before your kindred the **p** of Israel, B
1: 7 To the **p** who were present Josiah gave
1: 7 to the **p** and the priests and Levites.
1:11 before the **p,** to make the offering to the Lord
1:13 and carried them to all the **p.** A
1:19 the **p** of Israel who were present at that time B
1:21 the priests and Levites and the **p** of Judah and D
1:24 toward the Lord beyond any other **p** or kingdom, I
1:49 of the **p** and of the priests committed many acts
1:52 until in his anger against his **p** because
2: 5 If any of you, therefore, are of his **p,**
2: 6 by the **p** of your place with gold and silver,
2:27 that the **p** in it were given to rebellion and war,
2:28 to prevent these **p** from building the city and
3:22 When **p** drink they forget to be friendly
3:24 since it forces **p** to do these things?"
4:10 All his **p** and his armies obey him. A
4:15 Women gave birth to the king and to every **p**
4:41 he stopped speaking, all the **p** shouted and said, A
5:46 some of the **p** settled in Jerusalem and its vicinity;
5:62 And all the **p** sounded trumpets and shouted A
5:65 so that the **p** could not hear the trumpets because
of the weeping of the **p.**
6:16 and carried the **p** away captive to Babylon.
7: 6 And the **p** of Israel, the priests, the Levites, B
7:10 The **p** of Israel who came from exile kept B
7:13 The **p** of Israel who had returned from exile ate B
8: 5 the **p** of Israel and some of the priests and B
8:67 and these officials honored the **p** and the temple
8:69 "The **p** of Israel and the rulers and the priests B
8:70 of these **p,** and the holy race has been mixed with
9:37 when the **p** of Israel were in their settlements, B
9:53 The Levites commanded all the **p,** saying, A
Pm 151: 7 and took away disgrace from the **p** of Israel. B
3Mc 1:27 they turned, together with our **p,**
1:29 for it seemed that not only the **p** but also the walls
2: 5 and sulfur the **p** of Sodom who acted arrogantly,
2: 6 Pharaoh who had enslaved your holy **p** Israel. CK
2:16 graciously bestowed your glory on your **p** Israel, C
3: 5 of life with the good deeds of upright **p,**
3: 7 alleging that these **p** were loyal neither to the king
3: 8 an unexpected tumult around these **p** and
3:16 went up to honor the temple of those wicked **p,**
3:19 toward us, they become the only **p**
3:24 not have these impious **p** behind our backs
3:27 whether old **p** or children or even infants,
4: 4 at the most miserable expulsion of these **p.**
4:11 When these **p** had been brought to
4:13 in his rage that these **p** be dealt with in precisely
4:15 of these **p** was therefore conducted
5: 5 the hands of the wretched **p** and arranged
5:34 the assembled **p** to their own occupations.
5:41 it is crowded with masses of **p,**
5:46 of **p** crowding their way into the hippodrome—
5:47 and pitiful destruction of the aforementioned **p.**
6: 3 a **p** of your consecrated portion who are perishing
6:11 at the destruction of your beloved **p,**
7: 4 of the ill-will that these **p** had toward all nations.
7: 6 toward all **p** we barely spared their lives. A
7: 8 We also have ordered all **p** to return A
2Es 1: 5 declare to my **p** their evil deeds,
1: 8 not obeyed my law—they are a rebellious **p.**
1:29 you should be my **p** and I should be your God,
1:35 I will give your houses to a **p** that will come,
1:37 to witness the gratitude of the **p** that is to come,
1:38 with pride and see the **p** coming from the east;
2: 1 I brought this **p** out of bondage,
2:10 "Tell my **p** that I will give them the kingdom
2:24 Pause and be quiet, my **p,**
2:40 close the list of your **p** who are clothed in white,
2:41 implore the Lord's authority that your **p,**
2:48 tell my **p** how great and how many are
3:22 in the hearts of the **p** along with the evil root;
3:30 and have destroyed your **p,**

2Es 4:23 why the **p** whom you loved has been given over
5: 3 and **p** shall see it desolate.
5:12 At that time **p** shall hope but not obtain;
5:16 Now on the second night Phaltiel, a chief of the **p,**
5:27 of peoples you have gotten for yourself one **p;**
5:27 and to this **p,** whom you have loved,
5:30 If you really hate your **p,**
5:35 of Jacob and the exhaustion of the **p** of Israel?" B
5:40 the goal of the love that I have promised to my **p."**
6:54 the **p** whom you have chosen.
6:58 we your **p,** whom you have called your firstborn,
7:*106* [36] that first Abraham prayed for the **p** of Sodom,
7:*110* [40] Hezekiah for the **p** in the days of Sennacherib,
7:*129* [59] to the **p,** saying, 'Choose life for yourself,
8:15 but I will speak about your **p,**
8:26 O do not look on the sins of your **p,**
8:44 But **p,** who have been formed by your hands
8:45 spare your **p** and have mercy on your inheritance,
8:62 I have not shown this to all **p,** A
10:39 and that you have sorrowed continually for your **p**
12:34 But in mercy he will set free the remnant of my **p,**
12:38 you shall teach them to the wise among your **p,**
12:40 all the **p** heard that the seven days were past A
12:50 So the **p** went into the city, as I told them to do.
13: 5 of **p** were gathered together from the four winds
13:13 Then many **p** came to him,
13:31 **p** against **p,** and kingdom against kingdom.
13:36 Zion shall come and be made manifest to all **p,** A
13:48 But those who are left of your **p,**
13:49 he will defend the **p** who remain.
14: 3 and spoke to Moses when my **p** were in bondage
14: 4 and I sent him and led my **p** out of Egypt;
14:13 set your house in order, and reprove your **p;**
14:20 and I will reprove the **p** who are now living;
14:22 so that **p** may be able to find the path,
14:23 He answered me and said, "Go and gather the **p,**
14:27 and I gathered all the **p** together, and said, A
14:33 you are here, and your **p** are farther in the interior.
14:46 in order to give them to the wise among your **p.**
15: 1 of my **p** the words of the prophecy that I will put
15:10 my **p** are being led like a flock to the slaughter;
15:16 For there shall be unrest among **p;**
15:18 the houses shall be destroyed, and **p** shall
15:19 **P** shall have no pity for their neighbors,
15:53 if you had not killed my chosen **p** continually,
15:56 As you will do to my chosen **p,** says the Lord,
15:57 be wiped out, and all your **p** who are in A
16:21 that **p** will imagine that peace is assured for them,
16:40 Hear my words, O my **p;**
16:54 The Lord certainly knows everything that **p** do;
4Mc 1:11 All **p,** even their torturers, marveled A
4: 7 The **p** indignantly protested his words,
4:12 the blessedness of the holy place before all **p.** A
4:22 that a rumor of his death had spread and that the **p**
4:26 I say, his decrees were despised by the **p,**
5:15 he began to address the **p** as follows:
6:28 to your **p,** and let our punishment suffice
7:11 ran through the multitude of the **p** and conquered
16:23 for **p** who have religious knowledge not
17: 8 on their tomb these words as a reminder to the **p**

PEOPLE'S[‡] (17) [PEOPLE]

Lev 9:15 Next he presented the **p** offering.
2Ch 25:15 a **p** gods who could not deliver their own people
Ezr 3:13 the joyful shout from the sound of the **p** weeping,
Ps 80: 4 how long will you be angry with your **p** prayers?
Isa 57:14 remove every obstruction from my **p** way."
Jer 17:19 Go and stand in the **P** Gate,
Mt 13:15 For this **p** heart has grown dull,
Ac 28:27 For this **p** heart has grown dull,
Eph 4:14 about by every wind of doctrine, by **p** trickery,
Wis 11:23 for you can do all things, and you overlook **p** sins,
18: 3 of fire as a guide for your **p** unknown journey,
Sir 9:17 so a **p** leader is proved wise by his words.
10: 2 As the **p** judge is, so are his officials;
21: 8 with other **p** money is like one who gathers stones
44: 4 and by their knowledge of the **p** lore;
47: 4 and take away the **p** disgrace,
4Mc 4:24 in any way to put an end to the **p** observance of

PEOPLED (2) [PEOPLE]

Ge 9:19 and from these the whole earth was **p.**
Jer 50:39 she shall never again be **p,** or inhabited

PEOPLES[‡] (257) [PEOPLE]

A. ALL ... PEOPLES (61)
B. PEOPLES OF THE LAND (15)
C. PEOPLES OF THE EARTH (9)

Ge 10: 5 From these the coastland **p** spread.
17:16 kings of **p** shall come from her."
25:23 and two **p** born of you shall be divided;
27:29 Let **p** serve you, and nations bow down to you.
28: 3 that you may become a company of **p.**
48: 4 I will make of you a company of **p,**
49:10 and the obedience of the **p** is his.
Ex 15:14 The **p** heard, they trembled;
19: 5 be my treasured possession out of all the **p.** A
Lev 20:24 I have separated you from the **p.**
20:26 I have separated you from the other **p** to be mine.
Dt 2:25 the dread and fear of you upon the **p** everywhere
4: 6 and discernment to the **p,**
4:19 to all the **p** everywhere under heaven. A
4:27 The LORD will scatter you among the **p;**
6:14 any of the gods of the **p** who are all around you,

Dt 7: 6 you out of all the **p** on earth to be his people, A
7: 7 for you were the fewest of all **p.** A
7:14 You shall be the most blessed of **p,**
7:16 all the **p** that the LORD your God is giving A
7:19 LORD your God will do the same to all the **p** A
10:15 their descendants after them, out of all the **p,** A
13: 7 any of the gods of the **p** that are around you,
14: 2 the LORD has chosen out of all the **p** on earth to A
20:16 of these **p** that the LORD your God is giving you
28:10 All the **p** of the earth shall see that you are AC
28:37 among all the **p** where the LORD will lead you. A
28:64 The LORD will scatter you among all **p,** A
30: 3 gathering you again from all the **p** among whom A
32: 8 the boundaries of the **p** according to the number
33: 3 Indeed, O favorite among **p,**
33:17 with them he gores the **p,**
33:19 They call **p** to the mountain;
Jos 4:24 all the **p** of the earth may know that the hand AC
24:17 and among all the **p** through whom we passed; A
24:18 and the LORD drove out before us all the **p,** A
Jdg 2:12 the **p** who were all around them, and bowed down
2Sa 22:44 You delivered me from strife with the **p;**
22:48 and brought down **p** under me,
1Ki 8:43 all the **p** of the earth may know your name AC
8:53 them from among all the **p** of the earth, AC
8:60 so that all the **p** of the earth may know that AC
9: 7 a proverb and a taunt among all **p.** A
22:28 And he said, "Hear, you **p,** all of you!"
1Ch 5:25 themselves to the gods of the **p** of the land, B
16: 8 make known his deeds among the **p.**
16:24 his marvelous works among all the **p.** A
16:26 For all the gods of the **p** are idols,
16:28 Ascribe to the LORD, O families of the **p,**
2Ch 6:33 all the **p** of the earth may know your name AC
7:20 make it a proverb and a byword among all **p.** A
13: 9 and made priests for yourselves like the **p**
18:27 And he said, "Hear, you **p,** all of you!"
32:13 and my ancestors have done to all the **p** A
32:19 as if he were like the gods of the **p** of the earth, C
Ezr 3: 3 because they were in dread of the neighboring **p,**
9: 1 not separated themselves from the **p** of the lands
9: 2 Thus the holy seed has mixed itself with the **p** of
9:11 a land unclean with the pollutions of the **p** of
9:14 with the **p** who practice these abominations?
10: 2 married foreign women from the **p** of the land, B
10:11 separate yourselves from the **p** of the land and B
Ne 1: 8 I will scatter you among the **p;**
9:22 And you gave them kingdoms and **p,**
9:24 with their kings and the **p** of the land, B
9:30 you handed them over to the **p** of the lands.
10:28 and all who have separated themselves from the **p**
10:30 will not give our daughters to the **p** of the land B
10:31 the **p** of the land bring in merchandise or any B
13:24 but spoke the language of various **p.**
Est 1:11 in order to show the **p** and the officials her beauty;
1:16 to all the officials and all the **p** who are in all A
3: 8 among the **p** in all the provinces of your kingdom;
3:12 to the officials of all the **p,** to every province A
3:14 calling on all the **p** to be ready for that day. A
8:13 decree in every province and published to all **p,** A
8:17 many of the **p** of the country professed to be Jews,
9: 2 because the fear of them had fallen upon all **p.** A
Job 17: 6 "He has made me a byword of the **p,**
36:20 when **p** are cut off in their place.
36:31 For by these he governs **p;**
Ps 2: 1 and the **p** plot in vain?
7: 7 Let the assembly of the **p** be gathered around you,
7: 8 The LORD judges the **p;**
9: 8 he judges the **p** with equity.
9:11 Declare his deeds among the **p.**
18:43 You delivered me from strife with the **p;**
18:47 the God who gave me vengeance and subdued **p**
33:10 he frustrates the plans of the **p.**
44: 2 you afflicted the **p,** but them you set free;
44:14 a laughingstock among the **p.**
45: 5 of the king's enemies; the **p** fall under you.
45:17 therefore the **p** will praise you forever and ever.
47: 1 Clap your hands, all you **p;** shout to God A
47: 3 He subdued **p** under us, and nations
47: 9 the **p** gather as the people of the God of Abraham.
49: 1 Hear this, all you **p;** give ear, A
56: 7 in wrath cast down the **p,** O God!
57: 9 I will give thanks to you, O Lord, among the **p;**
65: 7 the roaring of their waves, the tumult of the **p.**
66: 8 O **p,** let the sound of his praise be heard,
67: 3 Let the **p** praise you, O God;
67: 3 let all the **p** praise you. A
67: 4 the **p** with equity and guide the nations upon earth.
67: 5 Let the **p** praise you, O God;
67: 5 let all the **p** praise you. A
68:30 the herd of bulls with the calves of the **p.**
68:30 scatter the **p** who delight in war.
77:14 you have displayed your might among the **p.**
87: 6 The LORD records, as he registers the **p,**
89:50 how I bear in my bosom the insults of the **p,**
96: 3 his marvelous works among all the **p.** A
96: 5 For all the gods of the **p** are idols,
96: 7 Ascribe to the LORD, O families of the **p,**
96:10 He will judge the **p** with equity."
96:13 and the **p** with his truth.
97: 6 and all the **p** behold his glory. A
98: 9 with righteousness, and the **p** with equity.
99: 1 The LORD is king; let the **p** tremble!
99: 2 he is exalted over all the **p.** A
102:22 when **p** gather together, and kingdoms, to worship
105: 1 make known his deeds among the **p.**
105:20 the ruler of the **p** set him free.

Ps 105:44 and they took possession of the wealth of the **p**,
106:34 They did not destroy the **p**,
108: 3 I will give thanks to you, O LORD, among the **p**,
117: 1 Extol him, all you **p**! A
144: 2 who subdues the **p** under me.
148:11 Kings of the earth and all **p**, A
149: 7 on the nations and punishment on the **p**,
Pr 24:24 will be cursed by **p**, abhorred by nations;
Isa 2: 3 Many **p** shall come and say, "Come,
2: 4 and shall arbitrate for many **p**;
3:13 he stands to judge the **p**.
8: 9 Band together, you **p**, and be dismayed;
10:13 I have removed the boundaries of **p**,
10:14 like a nest, the wealth of the **p**;
11:10 the root of Jesse shall stand as a signal to the **p**;
14: 6 struck down the **p** in wrath with unceasing blows,
17:12 Ah, the thunder of many **p**,
25: 3 Therefore strong **p** will glorify you;
25: 6 of hosts will make for all **p** a feast of rich food, A
25: 7 the shroud that is cast over all **p**, A
30:28 the jaws of the **p** a bridle that leads them astray.
33: 3 At the sound of tumult, **p** fled;
33:12 And the **p** will be as if burned to lime,
34: 1 Draw near, O nations, to hear; O **p**, give heed!
41: 1 let the **p** renew their strength;
43: 9 the nations gather together, and let the **p** assemble.
49: 1 O coastlands, pay attention, you **p** from far away!
49:22 and raise my signal to the **p**;
51: 4 and my justice for a light to the **p**.
51: 5 and my arms will rule the **p**;
55: 4 See, I made him a witness to the **p**,
55: 4 a leader and commander for the **p**.
56: 7 house shall be called a house of prayer for all **p**. A
60: 2 and thick darkness the **p**;
61: 9 and their offspring among the **p**;
62:10 clear it of stones, lift up an ensign over the **p**.
63: 3 and from the **p** no one was with me;
63: 6 I trampled down **p** in my anger,
Jer 10: 3 For the customs of the **p** are false:
10:25 and on the **p** that do not call on your name;
25:24 of Arabia and all the kings of the mixed **p** that
34: 1 and all the **p** under his dominion were fighting A
51:58 The **p** exhaust themselves for nothing,
La 1:18 but hear, all you **p**, and behold my suffering; A
3:45 You have made us filth and rubbish among the **p**.
Eze 3: 6 not to many **p** of obscure speech
11:17 I will gather you from the **p**,
20:34 I will bring you out from the **p** and gather you out
20:35 and I will bring you into the wilderness of the **p**,
20:41 when I bring you out from the **p**,
23:24 with chariots and wagons and a host of **p**;
25: 7 from the **p** and will make you perish out of
26: 2 "Aha, broken is the gateway of the **p**;
27: 3 merchant of the **p** on many coastlands,
27:33 from the seas, you satisfied many **p**;
27:36 The merchants among the **p** hiss at you;
28:19 All who know you among the **p** are appalled
28:25 When I gather the house of Israel from the **p**
29:13 from the **p** among whom they were scattered;
31:12 all the **p** of the earth went away from its shade AC
32: 3 In an assembly of many **p** I will throw my net
32: 9 I will trouble the hearts of many **p**,
32:10 I will make many **p** appalled at you;
34:13 I will bring them out from the **p** and gather them
36:15 no longer shall you bear the disgrace of the **p**;
38: 6 with all its troops—many **p** are with you.
38: 9 you and all your troops, and many **p** with you.
38:15 you and many **p** with you,
38:22 and his troops and the many **p** that are with him.
39: 4 and all your troops and the **p** that are with you;
39:27 when I have brought them back from the **p**
Da 3: 4 "You are commanded, O **p**, nations,
3: 7 as soon as all the **p** heard the sound of the horn, A
3: 7 drum, and entire musical ensemble, all the **p**, A
4: 1 King Nebuchadnezzar to all **p**, nations, A
5:19 because of the greatness that he gave him, all **p**, A
6:25 to all **p** and nations of every language A
7:14 and glory and kingship, that all **p**, nations, A
Hos 7: 8 Ephraim mixes himself with the **p**;
Joel 2: 6 Before them **p** are in anguish, all faces grow pale.
2:17 Why should it be said among the **p**,
Mic 1: 2 you **p**, all of you; listen, O earth,
4: 1 raised up above the hills. **P** shall stream to it,
4: 3 He shall judge between many **p**,
4: 5 For all the **p** walk, each in the name of its god, A
4:13 you shall beat in pieces many **p**,
5: 7 the remnant of Jacob, surrounded by many **p**,
5: 8 the remnant of Jacob, surrounded by many **p**,
Na 3: 4 and **p** through her sorcery,
Hab 2: 5 and collect all **p** as their own. A
2: 8 all that survive of the **p** shall plunder you—
2:10 for your house by cutting off many **p**;
2:13 Is it not from the LORD of hosts that **p** labor only
Zep 3: 9 At that time I will change the speech of the **p** to
3:20 and praised among all the **p** of the earth, AC
Zec 8:20 **P** shall yet come, the inhabitants of many cities;
8:22 Many **p** and strong nations shall come to seek
11:10 the covenant that I had made with all the **p**. A
12: 2 a cup of reeling for all the surrounding **p**; A
12: 3 a heavy stone for all the **p**; A
12: 4 when I strike every horse of the **p** with blindness.
12: 6 to the right and to the left all the surrounding **p**, A
14:12 the LORD will strike all the **p** that wage war A
Lk 2:31 you have prepared in the presence of all **p**, A
Ac 4:25 and the **p** imagine vain things?
4:27 with the Gentiles and the **p** of Israel,
15:17 so that all other **p** may seek the Lord— A

Ro 15:11 all you Gentiles, and let all the **p** praise him"; A
Rev 7: 9 from all tribes and **p** and languages,
10:11 "You must prophesy again about many **p**
11: 9 and a half days members of the **p** and tribes
17:15 are **p** and multitudes and nations and languages.
21: 3 be his **p**, and God himself will be with them;
Wis 3: 8 They will govern nations and rule over **p**,
4:15 Yet the **p** saw and did not understand,
6:21 O monarchs over the **p**, honor wisdom,
8:14 I shall govern **p**, and nations will be subject to me;
Bar 2: 4 and a desolation among all the surrounding **p**,
1Mc 2:66 the army for you and fight the battle against the **p**.
1Es 5:50 some joined them from the other **p** of the land. B
5:50 for all the **p** of the land were hostile to them AB
5:72 **p** of the land pressed hard upon those in Judea, B
7:13 the abominations of the **p** of the land and sought B
8:69 away from themselves the alien **p** of the land B
8:70 has been mixed with the alien **p** of the land; B
8:87 with the uncleanness of the **p** of the land. B
8:92 married foreign women from the **p** of the land; B
9: 9 the **p** of the land and from your foreign wives." B
2Es 1:11 and scattered in the east the **p** of two provinces,
3: 7 **p** and clans without number.
3:12 they produced children and **p** and many nations,
5: 5 the **p** shall be troubled, and the stars shall fall.
5:27 and from all the multitude of **p** you have gotten
9: 3 tumult of **p**, intrigues of nations,

PEOR (10) [BAAL-PEOR, BETH-PEOR]

Nu 23:28 So Balak took Balaam to the top of **P**,
25: 3 Thus Israel yoked itself to the Baal of **P**,
25: 5 who have yoked themselves to the Baal of **P**."
25:18 with which they deceived you in the affair of **P**,
25:18 on the day of the plague that resulted from **P**."
31:16 against the LORD in the affair of **P**,
Dt 4: 3 the LORD did with regard to the Baal of **P**—
4: 3 among you everyone who followed the Baal of **P**,
Jos 22:17 not had enough of the sin at **P** from which even
Ps 106:28 Then they attached themselves to the Baal of **P**,

PERATH See Index to Footnotes

PERAZIM (1) [BAAL-PERAZIM]

Isa 28:21 For the LORD will rise up as on Mount **P**,

PERCEIVE (22) [PERCEIVED, PERCEIVES, PERCEIVING, PERCEPTION, PERCEPTIVE]

2Sa 19: 6 for I **p** that if Absalom were alive and all
Job 9:11 he moves on, but I do not **p** him.
23: 8 or backward, I cannot **p** him;
33:14 and in two, though people do not **p** it.
Ps 94: 7 the God of Jacob does not **p**."
Pr 24:12 does not he who weighs the heart **p** it?
Isa 43:19 now it springs forth, do you not **p** it?
Mt 13:13 to them in parables is that 'seeing they do not **p**,
13:14 and you will indeed look, but never **p**.
16: 9 Do you still not **p**?
16:11 How could you fail to **p** that I was not speaking
Mk 4:12 but not **p**, and may indeed listen,
8:17 Do you still not **p** or understand?
Lk 8:10 'looking they may not **p**, and listening they may
9:45 so that they could not **p** it.
Ac 28:26 and you will indeed look, but never **p**.
Eph 3: 4 which will enable you to **p** my understanding of
Phm 1: 6 your faith may become effective when you **p** all
Tob 5: 4 but he did not **p** that he was an angel of God.
Wis 13: 4 let them **p** from them how much more powerful is
LtJ 6:41 they themselves cannot **p** this and abandon them,
2Mc 5:17 and did not **p** that the Lord was angered for a little

PERCEIVED (22) [PERCEIVE]

Jdg 6:22 Gideon **p** that it was the angel of the LORD;
1Sa 3: 8 Then Eli **p** that the LORD was calling the boy.
2Sa 5:12 then **p** that the LORD had established him king
12:19 he **p** that the child was dead;
14: 1 of Zeruiah **p** that the king's mind was
1Ki 3:28 they **p** that the wisdom of God was in him,
1Ch 14: 2 David then **p** that the LORD had established him
Ne 6:12 Then I **p** and saw that God had not sent him at all,
6:16 for they **p** that this work had been accomplished
Ps 73:17 went into the sanctuary of God; then I **p** their end.
Ecc 1:17 I **p** that this also is but a chasing after wind.
2:14 Yet I **p** that the same fate befalls all of them.
Isa 64: 4 From ages past no one has heard, no ear has **p**,
Da 9: 2 I, Daniel, **p** in the books the number of years that,
Mk 2: 8 At once Jesus **p** in his spirit
Lk 5:22 When Jesus **p** their questionings,
20:23 But he **p** their craftiness and said to them,
Wis 8:21 But I **p** that I would not possess wisdom
11:13 they **p** it was the Lord's doing.
Sir 6:22 she is not readily **p** by many.
1Mc 1: 5 After this he fell sick and **p** that he was dying.
4:21 When they **p** this, they were greatly frightened,

PERCEIVES (2) [PERCEIVE]

Ps 138: 6 but the haughty he **p** from far away.
Pr 31:18 She **p** that her merchandise is profitable.

PERCEIVING (2) [PERCEIVE]

Mt 9: 4 But Jesus, **p** their thoughts, said,
3Mc 4: 4 **p** the common object of pity before their eyes,

PERCEPTION (1) [PERCEIVE]

Wis 13: 5 comes a corresponding **p** of their Creator.

PERCEPTIVE (1) [PERCEIVE]

Pr 16:21 The wise of heart is called **p**,

PERCHES (1)

LtJ 6:71 a thornbush in a garden on which every bird **p**;

PERDITION (4)

2Sa 22: 5 the torrents of **p** assailed me;
Ps 18: 4 the torrents of **p** assailed me;
2Es 7:*48* the paths of **p** and removed us far from life—
10:10 and, lo, almost all go to **p**,

PERENNIAL (2)

Jer 49:19 from the thickets of the Jordan against a **p** pasture,
50:44 from the thickets of the Jordan against a **p** pasture,

PERES (1) [PARSIN]

Da 5:28 **P**, your kingdom is divided and given to

PERESH (1)

1Ch 7:16 of Machir bore a son, and she named him **P**;

PEREZ (18) [PEREZITES]

Ge 38:29 Therefore he was named **P**.
46:12 The children of Judah: Er, Onan, Shelah, **P**,
46:12 and the children of **P** were Hezron and Hamul.
Nu 26:20 of **P**, the clan of the Perezites;
26:21 The descendants of **P** were:
Ru 4:12 may your house be like the house of **P**,
4:18 descendants of **P**: **P** became the father of Hezron,
1Ch 2: 4 His daughter-in-law Tamar also bore him **P**
2: 5 The sons of **P**: Hezron and Hamul.
4: 1 **P**, Hezron, Carmi, Hur, and Shobal.
9: 4 son of Bani, from the sons of **P** son of Judah.
27: 3 He was a descendant of **P**,
Ne 11: 4 of Mahalalel, of the descendants of **P**;
11: 6 All the descendants of **P** who lived
Mt 1: 3 and Judah the father of **P** and Zerah by Tamar, and **P** the father of Hezron,
Lk 3:33 son of Hezron, son of **P**, son of Judah,

PEREZ-UZZAH (2) [UZZAH]

2Sa 6: 8 so that place is called **P**, to this day.
1Ch 13:11 so that place is called **P** to this day.

PEREZITES (1) [PEREZ]

Nu 26:20 of Perez, the clan of the **P**;

PERFECT‡ (48) [PERFECTED, PERFECTER, PERFECTION, PERFECTLY]

Lev 22:21 to be acceptable it must be **p**;
Dt 32: 4 The Rock, his work is **p**, and all his ways are just.
2Sa 22:31 This God—his way is **p**;
1Ki 6:22 in order that the whole house might be **p**;
Job 36: 4 one who is **p** in knowledge is with you.
37:16 of the one whose knowledge is **p**,
Ps 18:30 This God—his way is **p**;
19: 7 The law of the LORD is **p**, reviving the soul;
139:22 I hate them with **p** hatred;
SS 5: 2 my sister, my love, my dove, my **p** one;
6: 9 My dove, my **p** one, is the only one,
Eze 16:14 for it was **p** because of my splendor
27: 3 O Tyre, you have said, "I am **p** in beauty."
27: 4 your builders made **p** your beauty.
27:11 around your walls; they made **p** your beauty.
28:12 of perfection, full of wisdom and **p** in beauty.
Mt 5:48 Be **p**, therefore, as your heavenly Father is **p**.
19:21 Jesus said to him, "If you wish to be **p**, go,
Ac 3:16 that is through Jesus has given him this **p** health in
Ro 12: 2 what is good and acceptable and **p**.
2Co 7: 1 making holiness **p** in the fear of God.
12: 9 for power is made **p** in weakness."
13: 9 This is what we pray for, that you may become **p**.
Col 3:14 which binds everything together in **p** harmony.
Tit 2:10 but to show complete and **p** fidelity,
Heb 2:10 the pioneer of their salvation **p** through sufferings.
5: 9 and having been made **p**, he became the source
7:19 (for the law made nothing **p**);
7:28 appoints a Son who has been made **p** forever.
9: 9 that cannot **p** the conscience of the worshiper,
9:11 the greater and **p** tent (not made with hands,
10: 1 year after year, make **p** those who approach.
11:40 that they would not, apart from us, be made **p**.
12:23 and to the spirits of the righteous made **p**,
Jas 1:17 Every generous act of giving, with every **p** gift,
1:25 But those who look into the **p** law,
3: 2 Anyone who makes no mistakes in speaking is **p**,
1Jn 4:18 There is no fear in love, but **p** love casts out fear;
Rev 3: 2 not found your works **p** in the sight of my God.
AdE 15: 5 She was radiant with **p** beauty,
Wis 6:15 To fix one's thought on her is **p** understanding,
9: 6 for even one who is **p** among human beings will
Sir 1:18 making peace and **p** health to flourish.
31:10 Who has been tested by it and been found **p**?
44:17 Noah was found **p** and righteous;
45: 8 He clothed him in **p** splendor,
50:11 and clothed himself in **p** splendor,

PERFECTED (8) [PERFECT]
Heb 10:14 For by a single offering he has **p** for all time
1Jn 4:12 God lives in us, and his love is **p** in us.
4:17 Love has been **p** among us in this:
Wis 4:13 Being **p** in a short time, they fulfilled long years;
4:16 and youth that is quickly **p** will condemn
2Es 8:52 goodness is established and wisdom **p** beforehand.
9:22 because with much labor I have **p** them.
4Mc 7:15 whom the faithful seal of death has **p!**

PERFECTER (1) [PERFECT]
Heb 12:2 looking to Jesus the pioneer and **p** of our faith,

PERFECTION (8) [PERFECT]
Ps 50:2 Out of Zion, the **p** of beauty, God shines forth.
119:96 I have seen a limit to all **p**,
La 2:15 "Is this the city that was called the **p** of beauty,
Eze 28:12 You were the signet of **p**, full of wisdom and
Heb 6:1 Therefore let us go on toward **p**,
7:11 Now if **p** had been attainable through
1Jn 2:5 truly in this person the love of God has reached **p**.
4:18 and whoever fears has not reached **p** in love.

PERFECTLY (2) [PERFECT]
3Mc 7:22 So the supreme God **p** performed great deeds
2Es 7:*89* so that they might keep the law of the Lawgiver **p**.

PERFIDY (1)
2Mc 15:10 at the same time pointing out the **p** of the Gentiles

PERFORM (47) [PERFORMED, PERFORMING, PERFORMS]
Ge 38:8 "Go in to your brother's wife and **p** the duty of
Ex 3:20 and strike Egypt with all my wonders that I will **p**
4:17 with which you shall **p** the signs."
4:21 see that you **p** before Pharaoh all the wonders
7:9 '**P** a wonder,' then you shall say to Aaron,
30:10 Once a year Aaron shall **p** the rite of atonement
30:10 Throughout your generations he shall **p**
34:10 Before all your people I will **p** marvels,
Nu 1:53 the Levites shall **p** the guard duty of the tabernacle
3:7 They shall **p** duties for him and for
8:26 but they shall **p** no service.
16:9 to **p** the duties of the LORD's tabernacle,
18:3 They shall **p** duties for you and for the whole tent.
18:4 They are attached to you in order to **p** the duties of
18:5 You yourselves shall **p** the duties of the sanctuary
18:6 to **p** the service of the tent of meeting.
18:7 with you shall diligently **p** your priestly duties
18:21 a possession in return for the service that they **p**,
18:23 Levites shall **p** the service of the tent of meeting,
Dt 3:24 in heaven or on earth can **p** deeds and mighty acts
23:23 Whatever your lips utter you must diligently **p**,
25:7 not **p** the duty of a husband's brother to me."
34:11 that the LORD sent him to **p** in the land of Egypt,
Jos 22:27 that we do **p** the service of the LORD
2Sa 14:15 be that the king will **p** the request of his servant.
2Ki 23:3 to **p** the words of this covenant that were written
2Ch 34:31 to **p** the words of the covenant that were written
Ne 5:13 and from property who does not **p** this promise.
Ps 56:12 My vows to you I must **p**, O God;
76:11 Make vows to the LORD your God, and **p** them;
119:112 I incline my heart to **p** your statutes forever,
Isa 19:21 they will make vows to the LORD and **p** them.
48:14 he shall **p** his purpose on Babylon,
Jer 1:12 for I am watching over my word to **p** it."
11:5 I may **p** the oath that I swore to your ancestors,
21:2 perhaps the LORD will **p** a wonderful deed
44:25 in words, saying, 'We are determined to **p**
Da 11:17 and he shall bring terms of peace and **p** them.
Mic 2:1 When the morning dawns, they **p** it,
Lk 23:8 about him and was hoping to see him **p** some sign.
Jn 6:28 "What must we do to **p** the works of God?"
9:16 "How can a man who is a sinner **p** such signs?"
Rev 13:14 and by the signs that it is allowed to **p** on behalf of
AdE 8:14 with all speed to **p** what the king had commanded;
Sir 3:17 My child, **p** your tasks with humility;
1Es 8:16 **p** it in accordance with the will of your God;
2Es 12:25 up his wickedness and **p** his last actions.

PERFORMED‡ (38) [PERFORM]
Ex 4:30 and **p** the signs in the sight of the people.
11:10 and Aaron **p** all these wonders before Pharaoh;
34:10 as have not been **p** in all the earth or in any nation;
36:4 each from the task being **p**,
Dt 34:12 the terrifying displays of power that Moses **p** in
Jdg 16:25 So they called Samson out of the prison, and he **p**
16:27 who looked on while Samson **p**.
1Sa 12:7 to you all the saving deeds of the LORD that he **p**
1Ch 6:32 and they **p** their service in due order.
Ne 9:10 You **p** signs and wonders against Pharaoh
9:17 and were not mindful of the wonders that you **p**
12:45 They **p** the service of their God and the service
Est 1:15 to be done to Queen Vashti because she has not **p**
Ps 44:1 what deeds you **p** in their days, in the days of old:
65:1 and to you shall vows be **p**,
105:27 They **p** his signs among them,
111:8 to be **p** with faithfulness and uprightness.
Isa 41:4 Who has **p** and done this,
Mt 26:10 She has **p** a good service for me.
Mk 14:6 She has **p** a good service for me.
Jn 7:21 Jesus answered them, "I **p** one work,
10:41 and they were saying, "John **p** no sign,
12:18 also because they heard that he had **p** this sign that
12:37 he had **p** so many signs in their presence,
Ac 4:22 healing had been **p** was more than forty years old.
4:30 and signs and wonders are **p** through the name
7:36 having **p** wonders and signs in Egypt,
2Co 12:12 The signs of a true apostle were **p** among you
Rev 19:20 with it the false prophet who had **p** in its presence
Tob 1:3 I **p** many acts of charity for my kindred
1:16 the days of Shalmaneser I **p** many acts of charity
Jdt 15:12 and some of them **p** a dance in her honor.
Sir 45:3 By his words he **p** swift miracles;
45:19 he **p** wonders against them to consume them
48:12 He **p** twice as many signs,
3Mc 7:22 So the supreme God perfectly **p** great deeds
2Es 7:24 and have not **p** his works.
13:44 For at that time the Most High **p** signs for them,

PERFORMING (6) [PERFORM]
Dt 25:5 and **p** the duty of a husband's brother to her,
1Ch 29:19 your decrees, and your statutes, **p** all of them,
Lk 13:32 I am casting out demons and **p** cures today
Jn 6:30 What work are you **p?**
11:47 This man is **p** many signs.
Rev 16:14 These are demonic spirits, **p** signs,

PERFORMS (1) [PERFORM]
Rev 13:13 It **p** great signs, even making fire come down

PERFUME (12) [MYRRH-PERFUMED, PERFUMED, PERFUMER, PERFUMER'S, PERFUMERS, PERFUMES]
Ex 30:38 like it to use as **p** shall be cut off from the people.
Pr 27:9 **P** and incense make the heart glad,
SS 1:3 your name is **p** poured out;
Isa 3:20 the sashes, the **p** boxes, and the amulets;
3:24 Instead of **p** there will be a stench;
Jn 11:2 the Lord with **p** and wiped his feet with her hair;
12:3 Mary took a pound of costly **p** made of pure nard,
12:3 The house was filled with the fragrance of the **p**.
12:5 "Why was this **p** not sold for three hundred denarii
Jdt 16:7 She anointed her face with **p**;
Sir 24:15 Like cassia and camel's thorn I gave forth **p**,
2Es 2:12 The tree of life shall give them fragrant **p**,

PERFUMED (2) [PERFUME]
Pr 7:17 I have **p** my bed with myrrh, aloes, and cinnamon.
SS 3:6 **p** with myrrh and frankincense,

PERFUMER (4) [PERFUME]
Ex 30:25 a sacred anointing oil blended as by the **p**;
30:35 as by the **p**, seasoned with salt, pure and holy;
37:29 and the pure fragrant incense, blended as by the **p**.
Sir 49:1 prepared by the skill of the **p**;

PERFUMER'S (2) [PERFUME]
2Ch 16:14 with various kinds of spices prepared by the **p** art;
Ecc 10:1 Dead flies make the **p** ointment give off

PERFUMERS (2) [PERFUME]
1Sa 8:13 He will take your daughters to be **p** and cooks
Ne 3:8 Next to him Hananiah, one of the **p**, made repairs;

PERFUMES (4) [PERFUME]
Est 2:12 and six months with **p** and cosmetics for women.
Isa 57:9 to Molech with oil, and multiplied your **p**;
AdE 14:2 and instead of costly **p** she covered her head
Wis 2:7 Let us take our fill of costly wine and **p**,

PERGA (3)
Ac 13:13 from Paphos and came to **P** in Pamphylia.
13:14 but they went on from **P** and came to Antioch
14:25 When they had spoken the word in **P**,

PERGAMOS (KJV) See PERGAMUM

PERGAMUM (2)
Rev 1:11 to **P**, to Thyatira, to Sardis, to Philadelphia,
2:12 "And to the angel of the church in **P** write:

PERHAPS (49)
Ge 24:5 "**P** the woman may not be willing to follow me
24:39 '**P** the woman will not follow me.'
27:12 **P** my father will feel me,
32:20 I shall see his face; **p** he will accept me."
43:12 in the top of your sacks; **p** it was an oversight.
Ex 32:30 **p** I can make atonement for your sin."
Nu 22:6 **p** I shall be able to defeat them and drive them
22:11 **p** I shall be able to fight against them
23:3 **P** the LORD will come to meet me.
23:27 **p** it will please God that you may curse them
Jos 9:7 But the Israelites said to the Hivites, "**P** you live
1Sa 6:5 **p** he will lighten his hand on you and your gods
9:6 **p** he will tell us about the journey
1Ki 18:5 **p** we may find grass to keep the horses
18:27 or **p** he is asleep and must be awakened."
20:31 **p** he will spare your life."
Est 4:14 **P** you have come to royal dignity for just such
Ps 90:10 The days of our life are seventy years, or **p** eighty,
Isa 47:12 **p** you may be able to succeed,
47:12 be able to succeed, **p** you may inspire terror.
Jer 20:10 "**P** he can be enticed, and we can prevail against
21:2 **p** the LORD will perform a wonderful deed
51:8 Bring balm for her wound; **p** she may be healed.
Eze 12:3 **P** they will understand, though they are
Jnh 1:6 **P** the god will spare us a thought so that we do
Zep 2:3 **p** you may be hidden on the day of
Mk 11:13 he went to see whether **p** he would find anything
Lk 20:13 will send my beloved son; **p** they will respect him.'
Ac 17:27 so that they would search for God and **p** grope
Ro 2:15 their conflicting thoughts will accuse or **p** excuse
5:7 though **p** for a good person someone might
11:21 **p** he will not spare you.
1Co 7:5 Do not deprive one another except **p** by agreement
15:37 but a bare seed, **p** of wheat or of some other grain.
16:6 **p** I will stay with you or even spend the winter,
2Co 12:20 I fear that there may **p** be quarreling, jealousy,
2Ti 2:25 God may **p** grant that they will repent and come
Phm 1:15 **P** this is the reason he was separated from you for
Tob 13:6 **p** he may look with favor upon you
Wis 13:6 for **p** they go astray while seeking God
14:19 For he, **p** wishing to please his ruler,
Sir 19:13 Question a friend; **p** he did not do it;
19:14 Question a neighbor; **p** he did not say it;
2Es 4:8 **p** you would have said to me,
4:39 It is **p** on account of us that the time
7:*69* **p** it would have been better for us."
4Mc 1:5 Some might **p** ask, "If reason rules the emotions,
7:17 Some **p** might say, "Not all have full command
16:5 she would have mourned over them and **p** spoken

PERIDA (1)
Ne 7:57 of Sotai, of Sophereth, of **P**,

PERIL (7)
La 5:9 We get our bread at the **p** of our lives,
Ro 8:35 or persecution, or famine, or nakedness, or **p**,
2Co 1:10 from so deadly a **p** will continue to rescue us;
2Es 9:20 in **p** because of the devices of those who had come
13:20 to come into these things, though incurring **p**, than
13:23 the **p** at that time will protect those who fall
13:23 at that time will protect those who fall into **p**,

PERIMETER (1)
3Mc 4:11 with a monstrous **p** wall in front of the city,

PERIOD (19) [PERIODS]
Lev 8:33 the day when your **p** of ordination is completed.
15:33 for her who is in the infirmity of her **p**,
25:8 **p** of seven weeks of years gives forty-nine years.
Dt 34:8 then the **p** of mourning for Moses was ended.
2Sa 11:4 (Now she was purifying herself after her **p**.)
1Ch 29:27 The **p** that he reigned over Israel was forty years;
Est 2:12 this was the regular **p** of their cosmetic treatment,
Eze 18:6 or approach a woman during her menstrual **p**,
36:17 the uncleanness of a woman in her menstrual **p**.
Da 4:34 When that **p** was over, I, Nebuchadnezzar,
8:19 tell you what will take place later in the **p** of wrath;
11:36 He shall prosper until the **p** of wrath is completed,
Tob 14:5 but not like the first one until the **p** when the times
AdE 2:12 Now the **p** after which a girl was to go to
Wis 7:2 within the **p** of ten months,
2Mc 4:23 After a **p** of three years Jason sent Menelaus,
2Es 5:4 into confusion after the third **p**;
10:47 that was the **p** of residence in Jerusalem.
4Mc 13:20 of time and was shaped during the same **p** of time;

PERIODS (3) [PERIOD]
Eze 22:10 in you they violate women in their menstrual **p**.
Ac 1:7 or **p** that the Father has set by his own authority.
LtJ 6:29 to them may even be touched by women in their **p**

PERISH (138) [PERISHABLE, PERISHED, PERISHES, PERISHING]
Ge 41:36 so that the land may not **p** through the famine."
Ex 19:21 otherwise many of them will **p**.
Lev 26:38 You shall **p** among the nations,
Nu 17:13 Are we all to **p?"**
24:20 but its end is to **p** forever."
24:24 and he also shall **p** forever."
Dt 4:26 against you today that you will soon utterly **p** from
8:19 I solemnly warn you today that you shall surely **p**.
8:20 before you, so shall you **p**, because you would
11:17 then you will **p** quickly off the good land that
28:20 until you are destroyed and **p** quickly,
28:22 they shall pursue you until you **p**.
28:51 until it has made you **p**.
30:18 I declare to you today that you shall **p**;
Jos 22:20 And he did not **p** alone for his iniquity!' "
23:13 on your sides, and thorns in your eyes, until you **p**
23:16 and you shall **p** quickly from the good land
Jdg 5:31 "So **p** all your enemies, O LORD!
1Sa 26:10 or he will go down into battle and **p**.
27:1 "I shall now **p** one day by the hand of Saul;
2Ki 9:8 For the whole house of Ahab shall **p**;
Est 4:14 but you and your father's family will **p**.
4:16 though it is against the law; and if I **p**, I **p**."
Job 3:3 "Let the day **p** in which I was born,
4:9 By the breath of God they **p**,
4:20 they **p** forever without any regarding it.
6:18 they go up into the waste, and **p**.
8:13 the hope of the godless shall **p**.
20:7 they will **p** forever like their own dung;
31:19 if I have seen anyone **p** for lack of clothing,

Job 34:15 all flesh would **p** together,
36:12 But if they do not listen, they shall **p** by the sword,
Ps 1: 6 but the way of the wicked will **p.**
2:12 or he will be angry, and you will **p** in the way;
9:18 nor the hope of the poor **p** forever.
10:16 the nations shall **p** from his land.
37:20 the wicked **p,** and the enemies of the LORD are
41: 5 in malice when I will die, and my name **p.**
49:10 fool and dolt **p** together and leave their wealth
49:12 they are like the animals that **p.**
49:20 they are like the animals that **p.**
68: 2 let the wicked **p** before God.
73:27 Indeed, those who are far from you will **p;**
80:16 may they **p** at the rebuke of your countenance.
83:17 and dismayed forever; let them **p** in disgrace.
92: 9 O LORD, for your enemies shall **p;**
102:26 They will **p,** but you endure;
146: 4 on that very day their plans **p.**
Pr 11:10 and when the wicked **p,** there is jubilation.
19: 9 not go unpunished, and the liar will **p.**
21:28 A false witness will **p,** but
28:28 but when they **p,** the righteous increase.
Ecc 7:15 are righteous people who **p** in their righteousness,
Isa 22:25 and the load that was on it will **p,**
29:14 The wisdom of their wise shall **p,**
31: 3 and they will all **p** together.
41:11 against you shall be as nothing and shall **p.**
57: 1 The righteous **p,** and no one takes it to heart;
60:12 and kingdom that will not serve you shall **p;**
Jer 6:21 neighbor and friend shall **p.**
8:14 **p** there; for the LORD our God has doomed us to **p,**
10:11 not make the heavens and the earth shall **p** from
10:15 at the time of their punishment they shall **p.**
16: 4 They shall **p** by the sword and by famine,
18:18 for instruction shall not **p** from the priest,
27:10 I will drive you out, and you will **p.**
27:15 the result that I will drive you out and you will **p,**
40:15 and the remnant of Judah would **p?"**
44:12 and they shall **p,** everyone;
44:12 by the sword and by famine they shall **p;**
44:27 of Judah who are in the land of Egypt shall **p** by
48: 8 the valley shall **p,** and the plain shall be destroyed,
51: 6 Do not **p** because of her guilt,
51:18 at the time of their punishment they shall **p.**
La 4: 5 Those who feasted on delicacies **p** in the streets;
Eze 7:26 instruction shall **p** from the priest,
13:14 when it falls, you shall **p** within it;
25: 7 from the peoples and will make you **p** out of
32:12 and all its hordes shall **p.**
Da 2:18 the rest of the wise men of Babylon might not **p.**
Hos 10: 7 Samaria's king shall **p** like a chip on the face of
Am 1: 8 and the remnant of the Philistines shall **p,**
2:14 Flight shall **p** from the swift,
3:15 and the houses of ivory shall **p,**
Jnh 1: 6 the god will spare a thought so that we do not **p."**
1:14 do not let us **p** on account of this man's life.
3: 9 from his fierce anger, so that we do not **p."**
Zec 9: 5 The king shall **p** from Gaza;
13: 8 says the LORD, two-thirds shall be cut off and **p,**
Mt 26:52 for all who take the sword will **p** by the sword.
Lk 13: 3 but unless you repent, you will all **p** as they did.
13: 5 unless you repent, you will all **p** just as they did."
21:18 But not a hair of your head will **p.**
Jn 3:16 so that everyone who believes in him may not **p**
10:28 I give them eternal life, and they will never **p.**
Ac 8:20 Peter said to him, "May your silver **p** with you,
13:41 and **p,** for in your days I am doing a work, a work
Ro 2:12 from the law will also **p** apart from the law,
1Co 2: 6 or of the rulers of this age, who are doomed to **p.**
Col 2:22 All these regulations refer to things that **p**
Heb 1:11 they will **p,** but you remain;
11:31 not **p** with those who were disobedient,
2Pe 3: 9 but is patient with you, not wanting any to **p,**
Jude 1:11 and **p** in Korah's rebellion.
Jdt 6: 4 will survive our attack; they will utterly **p.**
6: 8 You will not die until you **p** along with them.
AdE 4:14 but you and your father's family will **p.**
11: 9 that threatened them, and were ready to **p.**
Wis 3:16 and the offspring of an unlawful union will **p.**
4:19 and the memory of them will **p.**
18:19 not **p** without knowing why they suffered.
Sir 3:26 and whoever loves danger will **p** in it.
5: 7 and at the time of punishment you will **p.**
8:15 and through their folly you will **p** with them.
41: 6 The inheritance of the children of sinners will **p,**
47:22 or cause any of his works to **p;**
2Mc 7:20 she saw her seven sons **p** within a single day,
1Es 4:37 in them and in their unrighteousness they will **p.**
2Es 2:26 one of the servants whom I have given you will **p,**
7:15 why are you disturbed, seeing that you are to **p?**
7:17 but that the ungodly shall **p.**
7:20 Let many **p** who are now living,
7:31 and that which is corruptible shall **p.**
7:*61* not grieve over the great number of those who **p;**
7:*64* because we **p** and we know it.
8:55 about the great number of those who **p.**
9:15 there are more who **p** than those who will
9:22 So let the multitude **p** that has been born in vain,
9:32 yet the fruit of the law did not **p—**
9:36 we who have received the law and sinned will **p,**
9:37 however, does not **p** but survives in its glory."
12:21 two of them shall **p** when the middle
15:58 in the mountains and highlands shall **p** of hunger,
16:18 the beginning of famine, when many shall **p;**
16:22 of those who live on the earth shall **p** by famine;
16:34 and their husbands shall **p** of famine.

PERISHABLE (11) [PERISH]

1Co 9:25 they do it to receive a **p** wreath,
15:42 What is sown is **p,** what is raised is imperishable.
15:50 nor does the **p** inherit the imperishable.
15:53 For this **p** body must put on imperishability,
15:54 When this **p** body puts on imperishability,
1Pe 1: 7 being more precious than gold that, though **p,**
1:18 not with **p** things like silver or gold,
1:23 not of **p** but of imperishable seed,
Wis 9:15 for a **p** body weighs down the soul,
14: 8 and the **p** thing because it was named a god.
19:21 the flesh of **p** creatures that walked among them,

PERISHED (48) [PERISH]

Nu 16:33 and they **p** from the midst of the assembly.
21:30 So their posterity **p** from Heshbon to Dibon,
Dt 2:14 until the entire generation of warriors had **p** from
2:15 to root them out from the camp, until all had **p.**
Jos 5: 6 **p,** not having listened to the voice of the LORD.
2Sa 1:27 the mighty have fallen, and the weapons of war **p!**
21: 9 The seven of them **p** together.
2Ki 7:13 the whole multitude of Israel that have **p** already;
Job 4: 7 "Think now, who that was innocent ever **p?**
Ps 9: 3 they stumbled and **p** before you.
9: 6 the very memory of them has **p.**
119:92 I would have **p** in my misery.
Ecc 9: 6 and their hate and their envy have already **p;**
Jer 7:28 truth has **p;** it is cut off from their lips.
44:18 we have lacked everything and have **p** by
48:36 for the riches they gained have **p.**
48:46 The people of Chemosh have **p,**
49: 7 Has counsel **p** from the prudent?
La 1:19 and elders **p** in the city while seeking food
Jnh 4:10 it came into being in a night and **p** in a night.
Mic 4: 9 Has your counselor **p,** that pangs have seized you
Zep 1:11 for all the traders have **p;**
Mal 3: 6 therefore you, O children of Jacob, have not **p.**
Mt 8:32 the steep bank into the sea and **p** in the water.
Lk 11:51 who **p** between the altar and the sanctuary.
Ac 5:37 and got people to follow him; he also **p,**
1Co 15:18 Then those also who have died in Christ have **p.**
2Pe 3: 6 of that time was deluged with water and **p.**
Tob 10: 4 "My child has **p** and is no longer among
10: 7 Stop trying to deceive me! My child has **p."**
Jdt 16:12 they **p** before the army of my Lord.
AdE 9: 2 On that same day the enemies of the Jews **p;**
Wis 10: 3 he **p** because in rage he killed his brother.
17:10 they **p** in trembling fear, refusing to look even at
Sir 34: 7 and those who put their hope in them have **p.**
44: 9 they have **p** as though they had never existed;
Bar 2:25 They **p** in great misery, by famine and sword
3:28 so they **p** because they had no wisdom,
3:28 they **p** through their folly.
1Mc 2:63 and their plans will have **p.**
12:50 that Jonathan had been seized and had **p** along
13: 4 By reason of this all my brothers have **p** for
13:18 the money and the sons, that Jonathan **p."**
13:49 and many of them **p** from famine.
16:21 at Gazara that his father and brothers had **p,**
2Mc 8:19 when one hundred eighty-five thousand **p,**
1Es 4:27 Many have **p,** or stumbled,
2Es 9:33 Yet those who received it **p,**

PERISHES (6) [PERISH]

Job 4:11 The strong lion **p** for lack of prey,
18:17 Their memory **p** from the earth,
Pr 11: 7 When the wicked die, their hope **p,**
Jn 6:27 Do not work for the food that **p,**
Jas 1:11 its flower falls, and its beauty **p.**
2Es 8:43 or if it has been ruined by too much rain, it **p.**

PERISHING (17) [PERISH]

Nu 17:12 The Israelites said to Moses, "We are **p;**
Pr 31: 6 Give strong drink to one who is **p,**
Hos 4: 3 even the fish of the sea are **p.**
Zec 11:16 in the land a shepherd who does not care for the **p,**
Mt 8:25 "Lord, save us! We are **p!"**
Mk 4:38 "Teacher, do you not care that we are **p!"**
Lk 8:24 shouting, "Master, Master, we are **p!"**
1Co 1:18 about the cross is foolishness to those who are **p,**
2Co 2:15 and among those who are **p;**
4: 3 it is veiled to those who are **p.**
2Th 2:10 of wicked deception for those who are **p,**
Wis 10: 6 a righteous man when the ungodly were **p;**
14: 6 in the beginning, when arrogant giants were **p,**
Bar 3: 3 you are enthroned forever, and we are **p** forever.
1Mc 3: 9 he gathered in those who were **p.**
6:13 **p** of bitter disappointment in a strange land."
3Mc 6: 3 a people of your consecrated portion who are **p**

PERIZZITE (1) [PERIZZITES]

Ne 9: 8 the Hittite, the Amorite, the **P,** the Jebusite,

PERIZZITES (25) [PERIZZITE]

Ge 13: 7 At that time the Canaanites and the **P** lived in
15:20 the Hittites, the **P,** the Rephaim,
34:30 the Canaanites and the **P;**
Ex 3: 8 the Hittites, the Amorites, the **P,** the Hivites,
3:17 the Hittites, the Amorites, the **P,** the Hivites,
23:23 the Hittites, the **P,** the Canaanites, the Hivites,
33: 2 the Hittites, the **P,** the Hivites, and the Jebusites.
34:11 the Hittites, the **P,** the Hivites, and the Jebusites.
Dt 7: 1 the Amorites, the Canaanites, the **P,** the Hivites,
20:17 the Canaanites and the **P,**
Jos 3:10 Hivites, **P,** Girgashites, Amorites, and Jebusites:
9: 1 the Hittites, the Amorites, the Canaanites, the **P,**
11: 3 the **P,** and the Jebusites in the hill country,
12: 8 Amorites, Canaanites, **P,** Hivites, and Jebusites):
17:15 for yourselves in the land of the **P** and
24:11 and also the Amorites, the **P,** the Canaanites,
Jdg 1: 4 up and the LORD gave the Canaanites and the **P**
1: 5 and defeated the Canaanites and the **P.**
3: 5 the Hittites, the Amorites, the **P,** the Hivites,
1Ki 9:20 the Hittites, the **P,** the Hivites, and the Jebusites,
2Ch 8: 7 the **P,** the Hivites, and the Jebusites,
Ezr 9: 1 the Hittites, the **P,** the Jebusites, the Ammonites,
Jdt 5:16 They drove out before them the Canaanites, the **P,**
1Es 8:69 the **P,** the Jebusites, the Moabites, the Egyptians,
2Es 1:21 I drove out the Canaanites, the **P,**

PERJURERS (1) [PERJURY]

1Ti 1:10 fornicators, sodomites, slave traders, liars, **p,**

PERJURY (2) [PERJURERS]

Wis 14:25 corruption, faithlessness, tumult, **p,**
14:28 or live unrighteously, or readily commit **p;**

PERMANENT (6) [PERMANENTLY]

Nu 15:14 or who takes up **p** residence among you,
Jn 8:35 slave does not have a **p** place in the household;
2Co 3:11 much more has the **p** come in glory!
AdE 12: 4 The king made a **p** record of these things,
1Mc 13:29 of armor for a **p** memorial,
2Es 3:22 Thus the disease became **p;**

PERMANENTLY (1) [PERMANENT]

Heb 7:24 but he holds his priesthood **p,**

PERMISSION‡ (16) [PERMIT]

Mk 5:13 So he gave them **p.**
Lk 8:32 So he gave them **p.**
Jn 19:38 take away the body of Jesus. Pilate gave him **p;**
Ac 21:40 When he had given him **p,**
26: 1 "You have **p** to speak for yourself."
Rev 2: 7 I will give **p** to eat from the tree of life that is in
Jdt 11:14 to bring back **p** from the council of the elders.
Sir 15:20 and he has not given anyone **p** to sin.
Bel 1:26 But give me **p,** O king, and I will kill the dragon
1:26 The king said, "I give you **p."**
1Mc 9:35 for **p** to store with them the great amount
14:44 an assembly in the country without his **p,**
2Mc 4: 9 to pay one hundred fifty more if **p** were given
11:30 will have our pledge of friendship and full **p**
1Es 4:62 because he had given them release and **p**
4Mc 5:15 When he had received **p** to speak,

PERMIT‡ (16) [PERMISSION, PERMITS, PERMITTED]

Ge 31: 7 but God did not **p** him to harm me.
31:28 And why did you not **p** me to kiss my sons
Ex 22:18 You shall not **p** a female sorcerer to live.
Nu 35: 6 where you shall **p** a slayer to flee,
Dt 18:14 the LORD your God does not **p** you to do so.
1Sa 24: 7 and did not **p** them to attack Saul.
Ps 55:22 he will never **p** the righteous to be moved.
Hos 5: 4 Their deeds do not **p** them to return to their God.
Mk 1:34 and he would not **p** the demons to speak,
7:12 then you no longer **p** doing anything for a father
1Ti 2:12 I **p** no woman to teach or to have authority over
AdE 16:19 and **p** the Jews to live under their own laws.
1Mc 5:42 **"P** no one to encamp, but make them all enter
12:40 He feared that Jonathan might not **p** him to do so,
15: 6 I **p** you to mint your own coinage as money
1Es 6:27 to keep away from the place, and to **p** Zerubbabel,

PERMITS (2) [PERMIT]

1Co 16: 7 to spend some time with you, if the Lord **p.**
Heb 6: 3 And we will do this, if God **p.**

PERMITTED (20) [PERMIT]

Ex 19:23 "The people are not **p** to come up to Mount Sinai;
Dt 16: 5 not **p** to offer the passover sacrifice within any
17:15 you are not **p** to put a foreigner over you,
21:16 not **p** to treat the son of the loved as the firstborn
22:19 he shall not be **p** to divorce her as long as he lives.
22:29 not be **p** to divorce her as long as he lives.
24: 4 is not **p** to take her again to be his wife
1Ki 1:48 of my offspring to sit on my throne and **p** me
Ezr 1: 3 are now **p** to go up to Jerusalem in Judah,
Jn 18:31 "We are not **p** to put anyone to death."
1Co 14:34 For they are not **p** to speak,
2Co 12: 4 that no mortal is **p** to repeat.
Rev 6: 4 its rider was **p** to take peace from the earth,
AdE 9:14 So he **p** this to be done,
Wis 19: 2 though they themselves had **p** your people
1Mc 14:44 of the people or priests shall be **p** to nullify any
15:14 and **p** no one to leave or enter it.
3Mc 1:11 When they said that this was not **p,**
2Es 5:13 These are the signs that I am **p** to tell you,
4Mc 5:26 He has **p** us to eat what will be most suitable

PERPETRATED (2) [PERPETRATOR]

Jer 29:23 because they have **p** outrage in Israel
2Mc 3:32 the notion that some foul play had been **p** by

PERPETRATOR (2) [PERPETRATED]
Ezr 6:11 a beam shall be pulled out of the house of the **p**,
1Es 6:32 a beam should be taken out of the house of the **p**,

PERPETUAL (42) [PERPETUALLY, PERPETUATE, PERPETUATED, PERPETUITY]
Ge 17: 8 for a **p** holding; and I will be their God."
48: 4 to your offspring after you for a **p** holding.'
Ex 12:14 generations you shall observe it as a **p** ordinance.
12:17 throughout your generations as a **p** ordinance.
12:24 You shall observe this rite as a **p** ordinance
27:21 It shall be a **p** ordinance to be observed
28:43 be a **p** ordinance for him and for his descendants
29: 9 the priesthood shall be theirs by a **p** ordinance.
29:28 These things shall be a **p** ordinance for Aaron
30:21 it shall be a **p** ordinance for them,
31:16 throughout their generations, as a **p** covenant.
40:15 a **p** priesthood throughout all generations to come.
Lev 3:17 It shall be a **p** statute throughout your generations,
6:13 A **p** fire shall be kept burning on the altar;
6:18 as their **p** due throughout your generations,
6:22 a **p** due—to be turned entirely into smoke.
7:34 as a **p** due from the people of Israel.
7:36 as a **p** due from the people of Israel
24: 9 from the offerings by fire to the LORD, a **p** due.
Nu 10: 8 this shall be a **p** institution for you
15:15 a **p** statute throughout your generations;
18:11 together with your sons and daughters, as a **p** due,
18:19 together with your sons and daughters, as a **p** due;
18:23 it shall be a **p** statute throughout your generations.
19:10 This shall be a **p** statute for the Israelites and for
19:21 It shall be a **p** statute for them.
25:13 after him a covenant of **p** priesthood,
Dt 13:16 It shall remain a **p** ruin, never to be rebuilt.
Ps 74: 3 Direct your steps to the **p** ruins;
Jer 5:22 a **p** barrier that it cannot pass;
8: 5 then has this people turned away in **p** backsliding?
23:40 upon you everlasting disgrace and **p** shame,
49:13 and all her towns shall be **p** wastes.
51:26 but you shall be a **p** waste, says the LORD.
51:39 sleep a **p** sleep and never wake, says the LORD.
51:57 they shall sleep a **p** sleep and never wake,
Eze 35: 9 I will make you a **p** desolation,
Jdt 13:20 May God grant this to be a **p** honor to you,
AdE 16:13 our savior and **p** benefactor, and of Esther,
Sir 41: 6 and on their offspring will be a **p** disgrace.
1Es 6:24 where they sacrifice with **p** fire;
2Es 2:35 because **p** light will shine on you forevermore.

PERPETUALLY (1) [PERPETUAL]
Am 1:11 he maintained his anger **p**, and kept his wrath

PERPETUATE (2) [PERPETUAL]
Dt 25: 7 to **p** his brother's name in Israel;
Bar 4: 5 Take courage, my people, who **p** Israel's name!

PERPETUATED (2) [PERPETUAL]
Ge 48:16 and in them let my name be **p**,
Na 1:14 "Your name shall be **p** no longer;

PERPETUITY (4) [PERPETUAL]
Lev 25:23 land shall not be sold in **p**, for the land is mine;
25:30 in **p** to the purchaser, throughout the generations;
Nu 18: 8 and your sons as a priestly portion due you in **p**.
Sir 45:13 but only his sons and his descendants in **p**.

PERPLEXED (13) [PERPLEXITY]
Da 5: 9 and his face turned pale, and his lords were **p**.
Mk 6:20 When he heard him, he was greatly **p**;
10:24 And the disciples were **p** at these words.
Lk 1:29 But she was much **p** by his words
9: 7 about all that had taken place, and he was **p**,
24: 4 While they were **p** about this,
Ac 2:12 All were amazed and **p**, saying to one another,
5:24 the chief priests heard these words, they were **p**
2Co 4: 8 but not crushed; **p**, but not driven to despair;
Gal 4:20 change my tone, for I am **p** about you.
Sir 18: 7 and when they stop, they are still **p**.
1Mc 3:31 He was greatly **p** in mind;
4:27 When he heard it, he was **p** and discouraged,

PERPLEXITIES (1) [PERPLEXITY]
Sir 40: 2 **P** and fear of heart are theirs,

PERPLEXITY (2) [PERPLEXED, PERPLEXITIES]
2Es 7:*93* the **p** in which the souls of the ungodly wander
12: 3 Then I woke up in great **p** of mind and great fear,

PERSECUTE‡ (16) [PERSECUTED, PERSECUTING, PERSECUTION, PERSECUTIONS, PERSECUTOR, PERSECUTORS]
Job 19:28 If you say, 'How we will **p** him!'
30:21 with the might of your hand you **p** me.
Ps 10: 2 In arrogance the wicked **p** the poor—
69:26 For they **p** those whom you have struck down,
119:84 When will you judge those who **p** me?
119:150 Those who **p** me with evil purpose draw near;
Ps 119:161 Princes **p** me without cause,
Mt 5:11 and **p** you and utter all kinds of evil
5:44 Love your enemies and pray for those who **p** you,
10:23 When they **p** you in one town, flee to the next;
Lk 11:49 some of whom they will kill and **p**,'
21:12 all this occurs, they will arrest you and **p** you;
Jn 15:20 If they persecuted me, they will **p** you;
Ac 7:52 Which of the prophets did your ancestors not **p**?
9: 4 "Saul, Saul, why do you **p** me?"
Ro 12:14 Bless those who **p** you; bless

PERSECUTED‡ (14) [PERSECUTE]
Jdg 2:18 to pity by their groaning because of those who **p**
Ps 119:86 I am **p** without cause; help me!
Mt 5:10 "Blessed are those who are **p** for righteousness'
5:12 for in the same way they **p** the prophets who were
Jn 15:20 If they **p** me, they will persecute you;
Ac 22: 4 I **p** this Way up to the point of death by binding
1Co 4:12 When reviled, we bless; when **p**, we endure;
15: 9 because I **p** the church of God.
2Co 4: 9 **p**, but not forsaken; struck down,
Gal 4:29 to the flesh **p** the child who was born according to
5:11 why am I still being **p** if I am still preaching
6:12 only that they may not be **p** for the cross of Christ.
2Ti 3:12 to live a godly life in Christ Jesus will be **p**.
Heb 11:37 about in skins of sheep and goats, destitute, **p**,

PERSECUTING (8) [PERSECUTE]
Jn 5:16 Therefore the Jews started **p** Jesus,
Ac 9: 5 The reply came, "I am Jesus, whom you are **p**.
22: 7 'Saul, Saul, why are you **p** me?'
22: 8 'I am Jesus of Nazareth whom you are **p**.'
26:14 'Saul, Saul, why are you **p** me?
26:15 The Lord answered, 'I am Jesus whom you are **p**.
Gal 1:13 I was violently **p** the church of God
1:23 "The one who formerly was **p** us is

PERSECUTION (13) [PERSECUTE]
Isa 14: 6 that ruled the nations in anger with unrelenting **p**.
Mt 13:21 when trouble or **p** arises on account of the word,
Mk 4:17 when trouble or **p** arises on account of the word,
Jn 16:33 In the world you face **p**.
Ac 8: 1 a severe **p** began against the church in Jerusalem,
11:19 the **p** that took place over Stephen traveled as far
13:50 and stirred up **p** against Paul and Barnabas,
Ro 8:35 Will hardship, or distress, or **p**, or famine,
1Th 1: 6 of **p** you received the word with joy inspired by
3: 4 we told you beforehand that we were to suffer **p**;
3: 7 and **p** we have been encouraged about you
Heb 10:33 sometimes being publicly exposed to abuse and **p**,
Rev 1: 9 the **p** and the kingdom and the patient endurance,

PERSECUTIONS (8) [PERSECUTE]
Mk 10:30 mothers and children, and fields with **p**—
Ac 14:22 through many **p** that we must enter the kingdom
20:23 in every city that imprisonment and **p** are waiting
2Co 12:10 hardships, **p**, and calamities for the sake of Christ;
1Th 3: 3 so that no one would be shaken by these **p**.
2Th 1: 4 for your steadfastness and faith during all your **p**
2Ti 3:11 my **p** and suffering the things that happened to me
3:11 What **p** I endured! Yet the Lord rescued me

PERSECUTOR (3) [PERSECUTE]
Php 3: 6 as to zeal, a **p** of the church;
1Ti 1:13 a **p**, and a man of violence.
AdE 8: 1 to Esther all the property of the **p** Haman.

PERSECUTORS (7) [PERSECUTE]
Ps 31:15 deliver me from the hand of my enemies and **p**.
49: 5 when the iniquity of my **p** surrounds me,
119:157 Many are my **p** and my adversaries,
142: 6 Save me from my **p**, for they are too strong for me.
Jer 15:15 and bring down retribution for me on my **p**.
17:18 Let my **p** be shamed, but do not let me be shamed;
20:11 my **p** will stumble, and they will not prevail.

PERSEPOLIS (1)
2Mc 9: 2 the city called **P** and attempted to rob the temples

PERSEUS (1)
1Mc 8: 5 and King **P** of the Macedonians,

PERSEVERANCE (1) [PERSEVERE]
Heb 12: 1 and let us run with **p** the race that is set before us,

PERSEVERE (5) [PERSEVERANCE, PERSEVERED]
Da 12:12 Happy are those who **p** and attain
Ro 12:12 be patient in suffering, **p** in prayer.
Eph 6:18 that end keep alert and always **p** in supplication
Jas 1:25 and **p**, being not hearers who forget
3Mc 3:11 that he would **p** constantly in his same purpose,

PERSEVERED (2) [PERSEVERE]
Heb 11:27 for he **p** as though he saw him who is invisible.
Sir 2:10 Or has anyone **p** in the fear of the Lord

PERSIA‡ (42) [PERSIAN, PERSIANS]
2Ch 36:20 until the establishment of the kingdom of **P**,
36:22 In the first year of King Cyrus of **P**,
36:22 up the spirit of King Cyrus of **P** so that he sent
2Ch 36:23 "Thus says King Cyrus of **P**:
Ezr 1: 1 In the first year of King Cyrus of **P**,
1: 1 up the spirit of King Cyrus of **P** so that he sent
1: 2 "Thus says King Cyrus of **P**:
1: 8 King Cyrus of **P** had them released into
3: 7 to the grant that they had from King Cyrus of **P**.
4: 3 as King Cyrus of **P** has commanded us."
4: 5 throughout the reign of King Cyrus of **P** and until the reign of King Darius of **P**.
4: 7 of their associates wrote to King Artaxerxes of **P**;
4:24 the second year of the reign of King Darius of **P**.
6:14 Darius, and King Artaxerxes of **P**;
7: 1 After this, in the reign of King Artaxerxes of **P**,
9: 9 to us his steadfast love before the kings of **P**,
Est 1: 3 of **P** and Media and the nobles and governors of
1:14 and Memucan, the seven officials of **P** and Media,
1:18 the noble ladies of **P** and Media who have heard
10: 2 in the annals of the kings of Media and **P**?
Eze 38: 5 **P**, Ethiopia, and Put are with them,
Da 8:20 these are the kings of Media and **P**.
10: 1 of King Cyrus of **P** a word was revealed
10:13 of the kingdom of **P** opposed me twenty-one days.
10:13 with the prince of the kingdom of **P**,
10:20 Now I must return to fight against the prince of **P**,
11: 2 Three more kings shall arise in **P**.
Jdt 1: 7 to all who lived in **P** and to all who lived in
1Mc 3:31 to **P** and collect the revenues from those regions
6: 1 when he heard that Elymais in **P** was a city famed
6: 5 Then someone came to him in **P** and reported that
6:56 from **P** and Media with the forces that had gone
14: 2 When King Arsaces of **P** and Media heard
2Mc 1:13 When the leader reached **P** with a force
1:19 when our ancestors were being led captive to **P**,
1:20 having been commissioned by the king of **P**,
9: 1 in disorder from the region of **P**.
9:21 On my way back from the region of **P** I suffered
1Es 3: 1 and all the nobles of Media and **P**,
3: 9 of **P** judge to be wisest the victory shall be given
3:14 and summoned all the nobles of **P** and Media and

PERSIAN (5) [PERSIA]
Ne 12:22 also the priests until the reign of Darius the **P**.
Da 6:28 the reign of Darius and the reign of Cyrus the **P**.
AdE 1:18 so now the other ladies who are wives of the **P**
16:10 a Macedonian (really an alien to the **P** blood,
Bel 1: 1 Cyrus the **P** succeeded to his kingdom.

PERSIANS (30) [PERSIA]
Ezr 4: 9 the **P**, the people of Erech, the Babylonians,
Est 1:19 be written among the laws of the **P** and the Medes
Da 5:28 and given to the Medes and **P**."
6: 8 according to the law of the Medes and the **P**,
6:12 according to the law of the Medes and **P**,
6:15 of the Medes and **P** that no interdict or ordinance
Jdt 16:10 The **P** trembled at her boldness,
AdE 1: 3 the **P** and Median nobles,
1:14 the **P** and Medes who were closest to the king—
1:19 the Medes and **P** so that it may not be altered,
10: 2 in the annals of the kings of the **P** and the Medes.
16:14 and would transfer the kingdom of the **P** to
16:23 for you and the loyal **P**,
1Mc 1: 1 had defeated King Darius of the **P** and the Medes,
2Mc 1:33 and it was reported to the king of the **P** that,
1Es 1:57 to him and to his sons until the **P** began to reign,
2: 1 In the first year of Cyrus as king of the **P**,
2: 2 up the spirit of King Cyrus of the **P**, and he made
2: 3 "Thus says Cyrus king of the **P**:
2:11 When King Cyrus of the **P** brought these out,
2:16 In the time of King Artaxerxes of the **P**, Bishlam,
2:30 of the reign of King Darius of the **P**.
5: 6 before King Darius of the **P**,
5:55 that they had in writing from King Cyrus of the **P**.
5:71 as Cyrus, the king of the **P**, has commanded us."
7: 4 and Darius and Artaxerxes, kings of the **P**,
8: 1 these things, when Artaxerxes, the king of the **P**,
8:80 he brought us into favor with the kings of the **P**,
2Es 1: 3 in the reign of Artaxerxes, king of the **P**.
4Mc 18: 5 he left Jerusalem and marched against the **P**.

PERSIS (1)
Ro 16:12 Greet the beloved **P**, who has worked hard in

PERSIST (4) [PERSISTENCE, PERSISTENT, PERSISTENTLY, PERSISTS]
Job 2: 9 "Do you still **p** in your integrity?
Ro 11:23 even those of Israel, if they do not **p** in unbelief,
1Ti 5:20 As for those who **p** in sin,
Heb 10:26 For if we willfully **p** in sin after having received

PERSISTED See Index to Footnotes

PERSISTENCE (1) [PERSIST]
Lk 11: 8 at least because of his **p** he will get up

PERSISTENT (1) [PERSIST]
2Ti 4: 2 be **p** whether the time is favorable or unfavorable;

PERSISTENTLY (11) [PERSIST]
2Ch 36:15 sent **p** to them by his messengers,
Jer 7:13 and when I spoke to you **p**, you did not listen,
7:25 I have **p** sent all my servants the prophets to them,

Jer 11: 7 warning them **p,** even to this day, saying,
25: 3 and I have spoken **p** to you,
25: 4 LORD **p** sent you all his servants the prophets,
29:19 when I **p** sent to you my servants the prophets,
32:33 though I have taught them **p,**
35:14 But I myself have spoken to you **p,**
35:15 sending them **p,** saying, 'Turn now everyone
44: 4 Yet I **p** sent to you all my servants the prophets,

PERSISTS (3) [PERSIST]

Dt 25: 8 If he **p,** saying, "I have no desire to marry her,"
Job 2: 3 He still **p** in his integrity,
Sir 12: 3 to one who **p** in evil or to one who does

PERSON‡ (334) [PERSON'S, PERSONAL, PERSONS]

Ex 12:48 But no uncircumcised **p** shall eat of it;
16:16 omer to a **p** according to the number of persons,
18:16 to me and I decide between one **p** and another,
21: 2 but in the seventh he shall go out a free **p,**
21: 5 I will not go out a free **p,"**
21:12 Whoever strikes a **p** mortally shall be put to death.
21:16 Whoever kidnaps a **p,** whether that **p** has been sold
21:26 the owner shall let the slave go, a free **p,**
21:27 a free **p,** to compensate for the tooth.
22:27 in what else shall that **p** sleep?
30:33 or whoever puts any of it on an unqualified **p** shall
Lev 13: 2 When a **p** has on the skin of his body a swelling or
13: 4 priest shall confine the diseased **p** for seven days.
13: 9 When a **p** contracts a leprous disease,
13:12 so that it covers all the skin of the diseased **p**
13:17 the priest shall pronounce the diseased **p** clean.
13:31 the **p** with the itching disease for seven days.
13:33 The priest shall confine the **p** with the itch
13:45 The **p** who has the leprous disease shall wear torn
14: 2 This shall be the ritual for the leprous **p** at the time
14: 3 If the disease is healed in the leprous **p,**
14:11 priest who cleanses shall set the **p** to be cleansed,
17:10 I will set my face against that **p** who eats blood,
17:10 and will cut that **p** off from the people.
17:12 No **p** among you shall eat blood,
19: 8 and any such **p** shall be cut off from the people.
21: 1 No one shall defile himself for a dead **p**
22: 3 that **p** shall be cut off from my presence:
22: 6 the **p** who touches any such shall be unclean
22:10 No lay **p** shall eat of the sacred donations.
22:11 priest acquires anyone by purchase, the **p** may eat
22:13 No lay **p** shall eat of it.
25:26 If the **p** has no one to redeem it,
25:27 and the difference shall be refunded to the **p**
27: 2 When a **p** makes an explicit vow to the LORD
27: 4 the **p** is a female, the equivalent is thirty shekels.
27: 7 And if the **p** is sixty years old or over,
27:14 If a **p** consecrates a house to the LORD,
27:16 If a **p** consecrates to the LORD any inherited
27:17 the **p** consecrates the field as of the year of jubilee,
27:28 that a **p** owns that has been devoted to destruction
Nu 5: 6 breaking faith with the LORD, that **p** incurs guilt
5: 7 The **p** shall make full restitution for the wrong,
15:28 to make atonement for the **p,**
15:31 such a **p** shall be utterly cut off and bear the guilt.
16:22 shall one **p** sin and you become angry with
19:18 then a clean **p** shall take hyssop,
19:19 The clean **p** shall sprinkle the unclean ones on
19:22 Whatever the unclean **p** touches shall be unclean,
21: 9 **p** would look at the serpent of bronze and live.
31:19 of you has killed any **p** or touched a corpse,
33:54 the inheritance shall belong to the **p** on whom
35:11 slayer who kills a **p** without intent may flee there.
35:15 who kills a **p** without intent may flee there.
35:21 shall be put to death; that **p** is a murderer;
Dt 1:16 and judge rightly between one **p** and another,
4:42 someone who unintentionally kills another **p,**
5:24 to someone and the **p** may still live.
7:10 who repays in their own **p** those who reject him.
7:10 but repays in their own **p** those who reject him.
15:12 in the seventh year you shall set that **p** free.
15:13 when you send a male slave out from you a free **p,**
17: 6 a **p** must not be put to death on the evidence
17: 7 the witnesses shall be the first raised against the **p**
17:12 or the judge, that **p** shall die.
19: 4 someone who has killed another **p** unintentionally
19: 5 the handle and strikes the other **p** who then dies;
19:10 so that the blood of an innocent **p** may not be shed
19:11 in wait and attacks and takes the life of that **p,**
19:15 A single witness shall not suffice to convict a **p**
21: 1 and it is not known who struck the **p** down,
24:11 the **p** to whom you are making the loan brings
24:12 If the **p** is poor, you shall not sleep in
25: 2 the judge shall make that **p** lie down and be beaten
27:18 be anyone who misleads a blind **p** on the road."
Jos 10:28 he utterly destroyed every **p** in it;
10:30 with the edge of the sword, and every **p** in it;
10:32 and every **p** in it, as he had done to Libnah.
10:35 and every **p** in it he utterly destroyed that day,
10:37 and its king and its towns, and every **p** in it;
10:37 and utterly destroyed it with every **p** in it.
10:39 and utterly destroyed every **p** in it;
20: 3 kills a **p** without intent or by mistake may flee
20: 9 who killed a **p** without intent could flee there,
Jdg 18:19 for you to be priest to the house of one **p,**
Ru 3:14 but got up before one **p** could recognize another;
1Sa 2:25 If one **p** sins against another,
10: 6 along with them and be turned into a different **p.**
19: 5 an innocent **p** by killing David without cause?"

2Sa 15: 2 the **p** said, "Your servant is of such and such
17:11 and that you go to battle in **p.**
2Ki 8: 5 the king how Elisha had restored a dead **p** to life,
12: 4 the money for which each **p** is assessed—
1Ch 16: 3 and he distributed to every **p** in Israel—
Ne 9:29 by the observance of which a **p** shall live.
Est 4:11 the golden scepter to someone, may that **p** live.
Job 8:20 "See, God will not reject a blameless **p,**
11:12 But a stupid **p** will get understanding,
13: 9 can you deceive him, as one **p** deceives another?
17:10 and I shall not find a sensible **p** among you.
23: 7 There an upright **p** could reason with him,
31:19 or a poor **p** without covering,
32:21 I will not show partiality to any **p** or use flattery
33:23 one of a thousand, one who declares a **p** upright,
33:24 to that **p,** and says, 'Deliver him from going down
33:27 That **p** sings to others and says, 'I sinned,
Ps 37:16 a little that the righteous **p** has than the abundance
62: 3 How long will you assail a **p,**
62: 4 Their only plan is to bring down a **p**
71:11 "Pursue and seize that **p** whom God has forsaken,
Pr 10:23 wise conduct is pleasure to a **p** of understanding.
11:12 but an intelligent **p** remains silent.
11:25 A generous **p** will be enriched,
14:12 There is a way that seems right to a **p,**
15:21 but a **p** of understanding walks straight ahead.
16:28 A perverse **p** spreads strife,
17:10 A rebuke strikes deeper into a discerning **p** than
17:24 The discerning **p** looks to wisdom,
19:15 an idle **p** will suffer hunger.
19:19 A violent tempered **p** will pay the penalty;
19:22 What is desirable in a **p** is loyalty,
19:24 The lazy **p** buries a hand in the dish,
20: 4 The lazy **p** does not plow in season;
21:22 One wise **p** went up against a city of warriors
21:24 The proud, haughty **p,** named "Scoffer,"
21:25 The craving of the lazy **p** is fatal,
22:13 The lazy **p** says, "There is a lion outside!
24:30 by the vineyard of a stupid **p;**
25:19 a bad tooth or a lame foot is trust in a faithless **p**
26: 7 The legs of a disabled **p** hang limp;
26:13 The lazy **p** says, "There is a lion in the road!
26:14 a door turns on its hinges, so does a lazy **p** in bed.
26:15 The lazy **p** buries a hand in the dish,
26:16 The lazy **p** is wiser in self-esteem
26:21 so is a quarrelsome **p** for kindling strife.
27:17 and one **p** sharpens the wits of another.
27:21 so a **p** is tested by being praised.
28:11 but an intelligent poor **p** sees through the pose.
28:21 yet for a piece of bread a **p** may do wrong.
28:23 rebukes a **p** will afterward find more favor
28:25 The greedy **p** stirs up strife,
Ecc 8: 9 while one **p** exercises authority over another to
Isa 29: 8 as when a hungry **p** dreams of eating and wakes
29: 8 a thirsty **p** dreams of drinking and wakes up faint,
29:21 those who cause a **p** to lose a lawsuit,
65:20 or an old **p** who does not live out a lifetime;
Jer 5: 1 and see if you can find one **p** who acts justly
Eze 18: 4 it is only the **p** who sins that shall die.
18:20 The **p** who sins shall die.
44:25 not defile themselves by going near to a dead **p;**
Da 11:21 a contemptible **p** on whom royal majesty had
Mt 10:41 and whoever welcomes a righteous **p** in the name
of a righteous **p** will receive the reward
12:35 good **p** brings good things out of a good treasure,
12:35 the evil **p** brings evil things out of an evil treasure.
12:43 "When the unclean spirit has gone out of a **p,**
12:45 and the last state of that **p** is worse than the first.
13:21 yet such a **p** has no root,
13:21 that **p** immediately falls away.
15: 5 then that **p** need not honor the father.
15:11 it is not what goes into the mouth that defiles a **p,**
15:14 And if one blind **p** guides another,
15:20 These are what defile a **p,**
19:23 it will be hard for a rich **p** to enter the kingdom
Mk 7:15 there is nothing outside a **p** that by going
7:18 Do you not see that whatever goes into a **p**
7:20 he said, "It is what comes out of a **p** that defiles.
7:23 evil things come from within, and they defile a **p.**"
Lk 6:39 "Can a blind **p** guide a blind **p**?
6:45 The good **p** out of the good treasure of the heart
6:45 and the evil **p** out of evil treasure produces evil;
10: 6 your peace will rest on that **p;**
11:24 "When the unclean spirit has gone out of a **p,**
11:26 and the last state of that **p** is worse than the first."
14: 9 and say to you, 'Give this **p** your place,'
17: 4 if the same **p** sins against you seven times a day,
Jn 6:44 and I will raise that **p** up on the last day.
9:32 that anyone opened the eyes of a **p** born blind.
18:14 that it was better to have one **p** die for the people.
Ac 4:34 There was not a needy **p** among them,
Ro 2:28 For a **p** is not a Jew who is one outwardly,
2:29 Rather, a **p** is a Jew who is one inwardly,
2:29 a **p** receives praise not from others but from God.
3:28 For we hold that a **p** is justified by faith apart
5: 7 Indeed, rarely will anyone die for a righteous **p**—
5: 7 for a good **p** someone might actually dare to die.
7: 1 on a **p** only during that person's lifetime?
10: 5 "the **p** who does these things will live by them."
13: 1 Let every **p** be subject to the governing authorities;
1Co 3:17 destroys God's temple, God will destroy that **p.**
5:13 "Drive out the wicked **p** from among you."
6:18 Every sin that a **p** commits is outside the body;
7:22 in the Lord as a slave is a freed **p** belonging to
14:17 but the other **p** is not built up.
14:25 **p** will bow down before God and worship him,
14:30 let the first **p** be silent.

2Co 2: 6 by the majority is enough for such a **p;**
12: 2 a **p** in Christ who fourteen years ago was caught
12: 3 And I know that such a **p**—
Gal 2:16 that a **p** is justified not by the works of the law but
3:16 it says, "And to your offspring," that is, to one **p,**
Eph 5: 5 Be sure of this, that no fornicator or impure **p,**
1Th 2:17 from you—in **p,** not in heart—
Tit 3:11 you know that such a **p** is perverted and sinful,
Heb 11:12 Therefore from one **p,** and this one as good as dead
12:16 like Esau, an immoral and godless **p,**
Jas 2: 2 if a **p** with gold rings and in fine clothes comes
2: 2 and if a poor **p** in dirty clothes also comes in,
2:20 Do you want to be shown, you senseless **p,**
2:24 a **p** is justified by works and not by faith alone.
1Pe 1:11 inquiring about the **p** or time that the Spirit
1Jn 2: 4 is a liar, and in such a **p** the truth does not exist;
2: 5 in this **p** the love of God has reached perfection.
2:10 and in such a **p** there is no cause for stumbling.
2Jn 1: 7 any such **p** is the deceiver and the antichrist!
1:11 to participate in the evil deeds of such a **p.**
Rev 13:18 for it is the number of a **p.**
22:18 if anyone adds to them, God will add to that **p**
Tob 2: 2 and bring whatever poor **p** you may find
2: 3 So Tobias went to look for some poor **p**
4:18 Seek advice from every wise **p** and do
6: 8 and never remain with that **p** any longer.
AdE 2:13 she is handed to the **p** appointed,
4: 8 he said, "the days when you were an ordinary **p,**
4:11 there is no escape for that **p.**
6: 6 "What shall I do for the **p** whom I wish to honor?"
6: 7 "For a **p** whom the king wishes to honor,
6: 9 the **p** whom the king loves and mount him on
7: 5 "Who is the **p** that would dare to do this thing?"
16:11 down to by all as the **p** second to the royal throne.
Wis 7:28 for God loves nothing so much as the **p** who lives
14: 4 so that even a **p** who lacks skill may put to sea.
16:14 A **p** in wickedness kills another,
16:29 hope of an ungrateful **p** will melt like wintry frost,
Sir 6:36 If you see an intelligent **p,** rise early to visit him;
7:11 Do not ridicule a **p** who is embittered in spirit,
10: 1 and the rule of an intelligent **p** is well ordered.
10:25 and an intelligent **p** will not complain.
11:28 by how he ends, a **p** becomes known.
12:14 So no one pities a **p** who associates with a sinner
13: 1 and whoever associates with a proud **p** becomes
13: 3 A rich **p** does wrong, and even adds insults;
13: 3 a poor **p** suffers wrong, and must add apologies.
13: 4 rich **p** will exploit you if you can be of use to him,
13: 9 When an influential **p** invites you, be reserved,
13:15 and every **p** the neighbor.
13:21 When the rich **p** totters, he is supported by friends,
13:22 If the rich **p** slips, many come to the rescue;
13:22 If the humble **p** slips, they even criticize him;
13:23 The rich **p** speaks and all are silent;
13:23 poor **p** speaks and they say, "Who is this fellow?"
14: 3 Riches are inappropriate for a small-minded **p;**
14: 8 The miser is an evil **p;**
14: 9 eye of the greedy **p** is not satisfied with his share;
14:20 Happy is the **p** who meditates on wisdom
15:17 Before each **p** are life and death,
16: 4 one intelligent **p** a city can be filled with people,
16:11 Even if there were only one stiff-necked **p,**
16:12 he judges a **p** according to one's deeds.
16:23 a senseless and misguided **p** thinks foolishly.
18:17 Both are to be found in a gracious **p.**
18:28 Every intelligent **p** knows wisdom,
19: 3 and the reckless **p** will be snatched away.
19:16 A **p** may make a slip without intending it.
19:29 A **p** is known by his appearance,
19:29 and a sensible **p** is known when first met,
20: 1 there is the **p** who is wise enough to keep silent.
20: 4 a girl is the **p** who does right under compulsion.
20: 9 There may be good fortune for a **p** in adversity,
20:19 A coarse **p** is like an inappropriate story,
20:24 A lie is an ugly blot on a **p;**
20:27 The wise **p** advances himself by his words,
21: 7 when they slip, the sensible **p** knows it.
21:15 When an intelligent **p** hears a wise saying,
21:17 utterance of a sensible **p** is sought in the assembly,
21:19 To a senseless **p** education is fetters on his feet,
21:21 the sensible **p** education is like a golden ornament,
21:22 but an experienced **p** waits respectfully outside.
21:23 but a cultivated **p** remains outside.
21:24 It is ill-mannered for a **p** to listen at a door;
21:27 ungodly **p** curses an adversary, he curses himself.
22:13 with a senseless **p** or visit an unintelligent **p.**
22:15 a piece of iron are easier to bear than a stupid **p.**
23:10 so also the **p** who always swears and utters
25: 2 a pauper who boasts, a rich **p** who lies,
26:27 *and every **p** like this lives in the anarchy of war.*
27: 3 If a **p** is not steadfast in the fear of the Lord,
27: 5 so the test of a **p** is in his conversation.
27:18 For as a **p** destroys his enemy,
27:27 If a **p** does evil, it will roll back upon him,
29:14 A good **p** will be surety for his neighbor,
29:17 and the ungrateful **p** abandons his rescuer.
29:28 for a sensible **p** to bear scolding about lodging and
31: 3 The rich **p** toils to amass a fortune,
31: 4 The poor **p** toils to make a meager living,
31: 8 Blessed is the rich **p** who is found blameless,
31:16 before you like a well brought-up **p,**
31:19 How ample a little is for a well-disciplined **p!**
32:18 A sensible **p** will not overlook
32:18 insolent and proud **p** will not be deterred by fear.
33: 3 The sensible **p** will trust in the law;
34: 9 An educated **p** knows many things,
34:10 An inexperienced **p** knows few things,

Sir 34:24 a son before his father's eyes is the **p** who offers
36:25 but a **p** with experience will pay him back.
37:12 with a godly **p** whom you know to be a keeper of
37:22 If a **p** is wise to his own advantage,
37:23 A wise **p** instructs his own people,
37:24 A wise **p** will have praise heaped upon him,
38:19 When a **p** is taken away, sorrow is over;
40:14 As a generous **p** has cause to rejoice,
40:27 and covers a **p** better than any glory.
Bar 2:18 but the **p** who is deeply grieved,
LtJ 6:73 such a **p** will be far above reproach.
Sus 1:53 'You shall not put an innocent and righteous **p**
1Mc 2: 8 Her temple has become like a **p** without honor;
2Mc 3:37 of **p** would be suitable to send on another mission
1Es 3: 4 who kept guard over the **p** of the king,
3Mc 5:14 the **p** who was in charge of the invitations,
2Es 6:10 The beginning of a **p** is the hand,
6:10 and the end of a **p** is the heel;
7: 8 so that only one **p** can walk on the path.
7:*59* for the **p** who has what is hard
7:*59* the **p** who has what is plentiful.
7:*78* from the Most High that a **p** shall die,
15:17 For a **p** will desire to go into a city,
15:46 in the splendor of Babylon and the glory of her **p**—
16:27 a **p** will long to see another human being,
16:61 and gave each **p** breath and life and understanding
4Mc 1:24 as a **p** will see by reflecting on this experience,
7:21 What **p** who lives as a philosopher by

PERSON'S (19) [PERSON]

Ge 9: 6 by a human shall that **p** blood be shed;
1Ki 18:44 a little cloud no bigger than a **p** hand is rising out
Pr 13: 8 Wealth is a ransom for a **p** life,
29:23 A **p** pride will bring humiliation,
30: 4 What is the **p** name? And what is the name of the **p** child?
Ecc 4: 4 and all skill in work come from one **p** envy
Ro 7: 1 on a person only during that **p** lifetime?
Gal 3:15 once a **p** will has been ratified,
Rev 22:19 that **p** share in the tree of life and in the holy city,
Tob 6: 9 anoint a **p** eyes where white films have appeared
Sir 17:22 he will keep a **p** kindness like the apple of his eye.
19:12 Like an arrow stuck in a **p** thigh,
19:30 A **p** attire and hearty laughter,
27: 4 so do a **p** faults when he speaks.
27: 6 so a **p** speech discloses the cultivation of his mind.
28:10 in proportion to a **p** strength will be his anger,
37:25 The days of a **p** life are numbered,
40:29 One loses self-respect with another **p** food,

PERSONAL (4) [PERSON]

Pr 18: 2 but only in expressing **p** opinion.
Jdt 12:10 a banquet for his **p** attendants only,
12:11 the eunuch who had charge of his **p** affairs,
14:13 to the steward in charge of all his **p** affairs,

PERSONS‡ (73) [PERSON]

Ge 12: 5 and the **p** whom they had acquired in Haran;
14:21 the king of Sodom said to Abram, "Give me the **p**,
46:18 and these she bore to Jacob—sixteen **p**).
46:22 who were born to Jacob—fourteen **p** in all).
46:25 and these she bore to Jacob—seven **p** in all).
46:26 the **p** belonging to Jacob who came into Egypt,
46:26 the wives of his sons, were sixty-six **p** in all.
46:27 all the **p** of the house of Jacob who came
Ex 16:16 an omer to a person according to the number of **p**,
Lev 15: 8 one with the discharge spits on **p** who are clean,
17:15 All **p**, citizens or aliens, who eat what dies
27:31 If **p** wish to redeem any of their tithes,
Nu 19:13 such **p** shall be cut off from Israel.
19:18 on all the furnishings, on the **p** who were there,
19:20 those **p** shall be cut off from the assembly,
31:28 one item out of every five hundred, whether **p**,
31:30 whether **p**, oxen, donkeys, sheep, or goats—
31:35 and thirty-two thousand **p** in all,
31:40 The **p** were sixteen thousand,
31:40 of which the LORD's tribute was thirty-two **p**.
31:46 and sixteen thousand **p**.
31:47 both of **p** and of animals, and gave them to
Dt 10:22 Your ancestors went down to Egypt seventy **p**;
13: 8 you must not yield to or heed any such **p**.
15:18 when you send them out from you free **p**, because
24:16 only for their own crimes may **p** be put to death.
25: 1 Suppose two **p** have a dispute and enter
2Ki 10: 6 Now the king's sons, seventy **p**,
10: 7 the king's sons and killed them, seventy **p**;
12: 4 the money from the assessment of **p**—
1Ch 21:14 and seventy thousand **p** fell in Israel.
Est 9:15 the month of Adar and they killed three hundred **p**
Pr 13: 2 the fruit of their words good **p** eat good things,
26:12 Do you see **p** wise in their own eyes?
Jer 52:29 from Jerusalem eight hundred thirty-two **p**;
52:30 of the Judeans seven hundred forty-five **p**;
52:30 all the **p** were four thousand six hundred.
Eze 3:18 those wicked **p** shall die for their iniquity;
13:18 and make veils for the heads of **p** of every height,
13:19 putting to death **p** who should not die and keeping alive **p** who should not live,
Jnh 4:11 a hundred and twenty thousand **p** who do
Zep 3: 4 Its prophets are reckless, faithless **p**;
Lk 15: 7 ninety-nine righteous **p** who need no repentance.
Ac 1:15 the crowd numbered about one hundred twenty **p**)
2:41 and that day about three thousand **p** were added.
15:24 that certain **p** who have gone out from us,
17:17 in the synagogue with the Jews and the devout **p**,
Ac 27:37 (We were in all two hundred seventy-six **p** in
Ro 1:27 in their own **p** the due penalty for their error.
1Co 5: 9 not to associate with sexually immoral **p**—
16:18 So give recognition to such **p**.
2Co 2:17 but in Christ we speak as **p** of sincerity,
2:17 as **p** sent from God and standing in his presence.
1Th 1: 5 just as you know what kind of **p** we proved to be
2Th 3:12 Now such **p** we command and exhort in
1Ti 1:19 certain **p** have suffered shipwreck in the faith;
1Pe 3:20 that is, eight **p**, were saved through water.
2Pe 3:11 of **p** ought you to be in leading lives of holiness
Rev 3: 4 Yet you have still a few **p** in Sardis who have
AdE 1: 3 for his Friends and other **p** of various nations,
16: 6 when these **p** by the false trickery
Wis 5: 4 "These are **p** whom we once held in derision
15:13 For these **p**, more than all others,
Sir 31:18 If you are seated among many **p**,
1Mc 2:38 to the number of a thousand **p**.
5:13 and have destroyed about a thousand **p** there."
2Mc 1:35 with those **p** whom the king favored he exchanged
1Es 8:22 or gatekeepers or temple servants or **p** employed
2Es 16:47 their houses and possessions, and their **p**,
4Mc 3:21 that time certain **p** attempted a revolution against
5: 4 When many **p** had been rounded up, one man,
7:20 therefore arises when some **p** appear to

PERSUADE‡ (9) [PERSUADED, PERSUADES, PERSUADING, PERSUASION, PERSUASIVELY, PERSUASIVENESS]

2Sa 3:35 to **p** David to eat something while it was still day;
2Co 5:11 knowing the fear of the Lord, we try to **p** others;
Jdt 12:11 "Go and **p** the Hebrew woman who is in your care
2Mc 7:26 she undertook to **p** her son.
11:14 promising that he would **p** the king,
4Mc 8:12 so as to **p** them out of fear to eat the defiling food.
11:25 not been able to **p** us to change our mind or
12: 2 to come nearer and tried to **p** him,
12: 6 and to influence her to **p** the surviving son to obey

PERSUADED (14) [PERSUADE]

Pr 25:15 With patience a ruler may be **p**,
Mt 27:20 the chief priests and the elders **p** the crowds to ask
Ac 17: 4 Some of them were **p** and joined Paul and Silas,
19:26 the whole of Asia this Paul has **p** and drawn away
21:14 Since he would not be **p**,
23:21 But do not be **p** by them,
Ro 14:14 and am **p** in the Lord Jesus that nothing is unclean
2Mc 4:34 he **p** him, though still suspicious,
11:14 and **p** them to settle everything on just terms,
3Mc 1:11 the king was by no means **p**.
7: 3 **p** us to gather together the Jews of the kingdom in
2Es 10:20 not do that, but let yourself be **p**—
4Mc 5:16 who have been **p** to govern our lives by
16:24 of the seven encouraged and **p** each of her sons

PERSUADES (1) [PERSUADE]

Pr 7:21 With much seductive speech she **p** him;

PERSUADING (2) [PERSUADE]

Ac 18:13 "This man is **p** people to worship God in ways
26:28 "Are you so quickly **p** me to become a Christian?"

PERSUASION (3) [PERSUADE]

Gal 5: 8 Such **p** does not come from the one who calls you.
AdE 16: 5 by the **p** of friends who have been entrusted with
4Mc 12: 5 but if you yield to **p** you will be my friend and

PERSUASIVELY (1) [PERSUADE]

Ac 19: 8 and argued **p** about the kingdom of God.

PERSUASIVENESS‡ (2) [PERSUADE]

Pr 16:21 and pleasant speech increases **p**.
16:23 their speech judicious, and adds **p** to their lips.

PERTAIN (2) [PERTAINING, PERTAINS]

Tob 7:11 nor drink anything until you settle the things that **p**
2Es 7:*70* and the things that **p** to the judgment.

PERTAINING (7) [PERTAIN]

Lev 11:46 This is the law **p** to land animal and bird
Nu 3:26 all the service **p** to these.
3:31 all the service **p** to these.
3:36 all the service **p** to these;
1Ch 26:32 of the Manassites for everything **p** to God and for
Heb 5: 1 among mortals is put in charge of things **p** to God
Sir Pr: 1 to write something **p** to instruction and wisdom,

PERTAINS (1) [PERTAIN]

Hos 5: 1 O house of the king! For the judgment **p** to you;

PERTURBED (1)

2Ki 6:11 of the king of Aram was greatly **p** because of this;

PERUDA (2)

Ezr 2:55 of Solomon's servants: Sotai, Hassophereth, **P**,
1Es 5:33 descendants of Assaphioth, the descendants of **P**,

PERVADES (1)

Wis 7:24 of her pureness she **p** and penetrates all things.

PERVERSE (29) [PERVERSELY, PERVERSENESS, PERVERSION, PERVERSITY, PERVERT, PERVERTED, PERVERTING, PERVERTS]

Nu 22:32 because your way is **p** before me.
Dt 32: 5 a **p** and crooked generation.
32:20 for they are a **p** generation,
Jdg 19:22 the men of the city, a **p** lot, surrounded the house,
1Sa 20:30 He said to him, "You son of a **p**,
2Sa 22:27 and with the crooked you show yourself **p**.
Job 9:20 though I am blameless, he would prove me **p**.
Ps 14: 3 They have all gone astray, they are all alike **p**;
18:26 and with the crooked you show yourself **p**.
53: 3 They have all fallen away, they are all alike **p**;
Pr 3:32 for the **p** are an abomination to the LORD,
10: 9 but whoever follows **p** ways will be found out.
10:31 but the **p** tongue will be cut off.
10:32 but the mouth of the wicked what is **p**.
12: 8 but a **p** mind is despised.
14:14 The **p** get what their ways deserve, and the good,
16:28 A **p** person spreads strife,
16:30 One who winks the eyes plans **p** things;
17:20 and the **p** of tongue fall into calamity.
19: 1 in integrity than one **p** of speech who is a fool.
22: 5 Thorns and snares are in the way of the **p**;
23:33 and your mind utter **p** things.
Jer 17: 9 The heart is devious above all else; it is **p**—
Mt 17:17 Jesus answered, "You faithless and **p** generation,
Lk 9:41 Jesus answered, "You faithless and **p** generation,
Php 2:15 in the midst of a crooked and **p** generation,
Wis 1: 3 For **p** thoughts separate people from God,
Sir 36:25 A **p** mind will cause grief,
2Es 7:*124* [54] because we have lived in **p** ways?

PERVERSELY (4) [PERVERSE]

Ex 32: 7 up out of the land of Egypt, have acted **p**;
Pr 2:12 from the way of evil, from those who speak **p**,
Isa 26:10 the land of uprightness they deal **p** and do not see
AdE 13: 5 **p** following a strange manner of life and laws,

PERVERSENESS (3) [PERVERSE]

Ps 101: 4 **P** of heart shall be far from me;
Pr 2:14 who rejoice in doing evil and delight in the **p**
15: 4 but **p** in it breaks the spirit.

PERVERSION (5) [PERVERSE]

Lev 18:23 to have sexual relations with it: it is **p**.
20:12 they have committed **p**, their blood is upon them.
2Ch 19: 7 there is no **p** of justice with the LORD our God,
Isa 53: 8 By a **p** of justice he was taken away.
Wis 14:26 forgetfulness of favors, defiling of souls, sexual **p**,

PERVERSITY (2) [PERVERSE]

Eze 9: 9 the land is full of bloodshed and the city full of **p**;
Jdt 6: 5 you have said these words in a moment of **p**;

PERVERT (13) [PERVERSE]

Ex 23: 2 not side with the majority so as to **p** justice;
23: 6 not **p** the justice due to your poor in their lawsuits.
Job 8: 3 Does God **p** justice? Or does the Almighty **p** the right?
34:12 and the Almighty will not **p** justice.
Pr 17:23 The wicked accept a concealed bribe to **p** the ways
31: 5 and will **p** the rights of all the afflicted.
Jer 23:36 and so you **p** the words of the living God,
Mic 3: 9 who abhor justice and **p** all equity,
7: 3 dictate what they desire; thus they **p** justice.
Gal 1: 7 and want to **p** the gospel of Christ.
Jude 1: 4 who **p** the grace of our God into licentiousness
4Mc 15:11 the various tortures strong enough to **p** her reason.

PERVERTED (10) [PERVERSE]

1Sa 8: 3 they took bribes and **p** justice.
Job 33:27 'I sinned, and **p** what was right,
Pr 6:14 with **p** mind devising evil,
8:13 and the way of evil and **p** speech I hate.
Jer 3:21 because they have **p** their way,
La 3:35 when human rights are **p** in the presence of the
Hab 1: 4 therefore judgment comes forth **p**.
Tit 3:11 since you know that such a person is **p** and sinful,
Sir 8: 2 and has **p** the minds of kings.
Sus 1:56 beauty has beguiled you and lust has **p** your heart.

PERVERTING (2) [PERVERSE]

Lk 23: 2 saying, "We found this man **p** our nation,
23:14 "You brought me this man as one who was **p**

PERVERTS (1) [PERVERSE]

Wis 4:12 and roving desire **p** the innocent mind.

PESTERED (1)

Jdg 16:16 and **p** him, he was tired to death.

PESTILENCE (59) [PESTILENT]

Ex 5: 3 or he will fall upon us with **p** or sword."
9: 3 with a deadly **p** your livestock in the field:
9:15 and struck you and your people with **p**,
23:28 And I will send the **p** in front of you,
Lev 26:25 if you withdraw within your cities, I will send **p**
Nu 14:12 I will strike them with **p** and disinherit them,

Dt 7:20 the LORD your God will send the **p** against them,
28:21 the **p** cling to you until it has consumed you off
32:24 burning consumption, bitter **p.**
2Sa 24:13 Or shall there be three days' **p** in your land?
24:15 the LORD sent a **p** on Israel from that morning
1Ch 21:12 or three days of the sword of the LORD, **p** on
21:14 So the LORD sent a **p** on Israel;
2Ch 7:13 or send **p** among my people,
20: 9 or **p,** or famine, we will stand before this house,
Job 27:15 Those who survive them the **p** buries,
Ps 91: 3 the snare of the fowler and from the deadly **p;**
91: 6 or the **p** that stalks in darkness,
Jer 14:12 by famine, and by **p** I consume them.
15: 2 Those destined for **p,** to **p,**
18:21 May their men meet death by **p,**
21: 6 they shall die of a great **p.**
21: 7 those who survive the **p,** sword, and famine—
21: 9 by the sword, by famine, and by **p;**
24:10 And I will send sword, famine, and **p** upon them,
27: 8 with famine, and with **p,** says the LORD,
27:13 by famine, and by **p,** as the LORD has spoken
28: 8 and **p** against many countries and great kingdoms.
29:17 and **p,** and I will make them like rotten figs
29:18 and with **p,** and will make them a horror to all
32:24 and the city, faced with sword, famine, and **p,**
32:36 of Babylon by the sword, by famine, and by **p":**
34:17 a release to the sword, to **p,** and to famine.
38: 2 by the sword, by famine, and by **p;**
42:17 by the sword, by famine, and by **p;**
42:22 and by **p** in the place where you desire to go
43:11 giving those who are destined for **p,** to **p,**
44:13 with the sword, with famine, and with **p,**
Eze 5:12 of you shall die of **p** or be consumed by famine
5:17 **p** and bloodshed shall pass through you;
6:11 they shall fall by the sword, by famine, and by **p.**
6:12 Those far off shall die of **p;**
7:15 The sword is outside, **p** and famine are inside;
7:15 famine and **p** devour them.
12:16 from famine and **p,** so that they may tell
14:19 Or if I send a **p** into that land,
14:21 and **p,** to cut off humans and animals from it!
28:23 I will send **p** into it, and bloodshed into its streets;
33:27 in strongholds and in caves shall die by **p.**
38:22 With **p** and bloodshed I will enter into judgment
Am 4:10 I sent among you a **p** after the manner of Egypt;
Hab 3: 5 him went **p,** and plague followed close behind.
Rev 6: 8 and **p,** and by the wild animals of the earth.
18: 8 **p** and mourning and famine—
Sir 39:29 Fire and hail and famine and **p,**
Bar 2:25 by famine and sword and **p.**
2Es 15:49 widowhood, poverty, famine, sword, and **p,**

PESTILENCES See Index to Footnotes

PESTILENT (2) [PESTILENCE]
Ac 24: 5 We have, in fact, found this man a **p** fellow,
AdE 16: 7 wickedly accomplished through the **p** behavior

PESTLE (1)
Pr 27:22 in a mortar with a **p** along with crushed grain,

PETALS (8)
Ex 25:31 its calyxes, and its **p** shall be of one piece with it;
25:33 each with calyx and **p,** on one branch,
25:33 each with calyx and **p,** on the other branch—
25:34 each with its calyxes and **p.**
37:17 its calyxes, and its **p** were of one piece with it.
37:19 each with calyx and **p,** on one branch,
37:19 each with calyx and **p,** on the other branch—
37:20 each with its calyxes and **p.**

PETER (157) [=CEPHAS, PETER'S, =SIMON]
Mt 4:18 Simon, who is called **P,** and Andrew his brother,
10: 2 first, Simon, also known as **P,**
14:28 **P** answered him, "Lord, if it is you,
14:29 So **P** got out of the boat,
15:15 But **P** said to him, "Explain this parable to us."
16:16 Simon **P** answered, "You are the Messiah,
16:18 And I tell you, you are **P,**
16:22 And **P** took him aside and began to rebuke him,
16:23 he turned and said to **P,** "Get behind me, Satan!
17: 1 with him **P** and James and his brother John
17: 4 **P** said to Jesus, "Lord, it is good for us to be here;
17:24 collectors of the temple tax came to **P** and said,
17:26 When **P** said, "From others," Jesus said to him,
18:21 Then **P** came and said to him, "Lord,
19:27 Then **P** said in reply, "Look,
26:33 **P** said to him, "Though all become deserters
26:35 **P** said to him, "Even though I must die with you,
26:37 He took with him **P** and the two sons of Zebedee,
26:40 and he said to **P,** "So, could you not stay awake
26:58 But **P** was following him at a distance,
26:69 Now **P** was sitting outside in the courtyard.
26:73 little while the bystanders came up and said to **P,**
26:75 Then **P** remembered what Jesus had said:
Mk 3:16 Simon (to whom he gave the name **P);**
5:37 He allowed no one to follow him except **P,**
8:29 **P** answered him, "You are the Messiah."
8:32 And **P** took him aside and began to rebuke him.
8:33 he rebuked **P** and said, "Get behind me, Satan!
9: 2 Jesus took with him **P** and James and John,
9: 5 Then **P** said to Jesus, "Rabbi,
10:28 **P** began to say to him, "Look,
11:21 **P** remembered and said to him, "Rabbi, look!
13: 3 **P,** James, John, and Andrew asked him privately,
14:29 **P** said to him, "Even though all become deserters,
14:33 He took with him **P** and James and John,
14:37 and he said to **P,** "Simon, are you asleep?
14:54 **P** had followed him at a distance,
14:66 While **P** was below in the courtyard,
14:67 When she saw **P** warming himself,
14:70 after a little while the bystanders again said to **P,**
14:72 Then **P** remembered that Jesus had said to him,
16: 7 and **P** that he is going ahead of you to Galilee;
16: S ⟦they told briefly to those around **P.**⟧
Lk 5: 8 But when Simon **P** saw it,
6:14 whom he named **P,** and his brother Andrew,
8:45 When all denied it, **P** said, "Master,
8:51 except **P,** John, and James,
9:20 **P** answered, "The Messiah of God."
9:28 after these sayings Jesus took with him **P**
9:32 Now **P** and his companions were weighed down
9:33 Just as they were leaving him, **P** said to Jesus,
12:41 **P** said, "Lord, are you telling this parable for us or
18:28 Then **P** said, "Look, we have left our homes
22: 8 So Jesus sent **P** and John, saying,
22:34 "I tell you, **P,** the cock will not crow this day,
22:54 But **P** was following at a distance.
22:55 of the courtyard and sat down together, **P** sat
22:58 But **P** said, "Man, I am not!"
22:60 But **P** said, "Man, I do
22:61 The Lord turned and looked at **P.**
22:61 Then **P** remembered the word of the Lord,
24:12 But **P** got up and ran to the tomb;
Jn 1:42 to be called Cephas" (which is translated **P).**
1:44 the city of Andrew and **P.**
6:68 Simon **P** answered him, "Lord,
13: 6 He came to Simon **P,** who said to him, "Lord,
13: 8 **P** said to him, "You will never wash my feet."
13: 9 Simon **P** said to him, "Lord,
13:24 Simon **P** therefore motioned to him to ask Jesus
13:36 Simon **P** said to him, "Lord,
13:37 **P** said to him, "Lord, why can I
18:10 Then Simon **P,** who had a sword, drew it,
18:11 Jesus said to **P,** "Put your sword back
18:15 Simon **P** and another disciple followed Jesus.
18:16 but **P** was standing outside at the gate.
18:16 the gate, and brought **P** in.
18:17 The woman said to **P,** "You are not also one
18:18 **P** also was standing with them
18:25 Now Simon **P** was standing and warming himself.
18:26 a relative of the man whose ear **P** had cut off,
18:27 Again **P** denied it, and at that moment
20: 2 and went to Simon **P** and the other disciple,
20: 3 Then **P** and the other disciple set out and went
20: 4 other disciple outran **P** and reached the tomb first.
20: 6 Then Simon **P** came, following him,
21: 2 Gathered there together were Simon **P,**
21: 3 Simon **P** said to them, "I am going fishing."
21: 7 That disciple whom Jesus loved said to **P,**
21: 7 When Simon **P** heard that it was the Lord,
21:11 Simon **P** went aboard and hauled the net ashore,
21:15 Jesus said to Simon **P,** "Simon son of John,
21:17 **P** felt hurt because he said to him the third time,
21:20 **P** turned and saw the disciple whom Jesus loved
21:21 When **P** saw him, he said to Jesus, "Lord,
Ac 1:13 **P,** and John, and James, and Andrew,
1:15 In those days **P** stood up among
2:14 But **P,** standing with the eleven,
2:37 to the heart and said to **P** and to the other apostles,
2:38 **P** said to them, "Repent, and be baptized
3: 1 One day **P** and John were going up to the temple
3: 3 he saw **P** and John about to go into the temple,
3: 4 **P** looked intently at him, as did John, and said,
3: 6 But **P** said, "I have no silver or gold,
3:11 While he clung to **P** and John,
3:12 When **P** saw it, he addressed the people,
4: 1 While **P** and John were speaking to the people,
4: 8 Then **P,** filled with the Holy Spirit, said to them,
4:13 Now when they saw the boldness of **P** and John
4:19 But **P** and John answered them,
5: 3 **P** asked, "why has Satan filled your heart to lie to
5: 8 **P** said to her, "Tell me whether you
5: 9 Then **P** said to her, "How is it
5:29 But **P** and the apostles answered,
8:14 they sent **P** and John to them.
8:17 Then **P** and John laid their hands on them,
8:20 But **P** said to him, "May your silver perish
8:25 Now after **P** and John had testified and spoken
9:32 as **P** went here and there among all the believers,
9:34 **P** said to him, "Aeneas, Jesus Christ heals you;
9:38 the disciples, who heard that **P** was there,
9:39 So **P** got up and went with them;
9:40 **P** put all of them outside,
9:40 she opened her eyes, and seeing **P,** she sat up.
10: 5 to Joppa for a certain Simon who is called **P;**
10: 9 **P** went up on the roof to pray.
10:13 he heard a voice saying, "Get up, **P;** kill and eat."
10:14 But **P** said, "By no means, Lord;
10:17 while **P** was greatly puzzled about what to make
10:18 who was called **P,** was staying there.
10:19 While **P** was still thinking about the vision,
10:21 So **P** went down to the men and said,
10:23 So **P** invited them in and gave them lodging.
10:26 But **P** made him get up, saying, "Stand up;
10:32 to Joppa and ask for Simon, who is called **P;**
10:34 Then **P** began to speak to them:
10:44 While **P** was still speaking,
10:45 with **P** were astounded that the gift of the Holy
10:46 in tongues and extolling God. Then **P** said,
Ac 11: 2 So when **P** went up to Jerusalem,
11: 4 Then **P** began to explain it to them, step by step,
11: 7 I also heard a voice saying to me, 'Get up, **P;**
11:13 'Send to Joppa and bring Simon, who is called **P;**
12: 3 he proceeded to arrest **P** also.
12: 5 While **P** was kept in prison, the church prayed
12: 6 **P,** bound with two chains, was sleeping
12: 7 He tapped **P** on the side and woke him, saying,
12: 9 **P** went out and followed him;
12:11 Then **P** came to himself and said,
12:14 in and announced that **P** was standing at the gate.
12:16 Meanwhile **P** continued knocking;
12:18 among the soldiers over what had become of **P.**
12:19 Then **P** went down from Judea to Caesarea
15: 7 **P** stood up and said to them, "My brothers,
Gal 2: 7 just as **P** had been entrusted with the gospel for
2: 8 (for he who worked through **P** making him
1Pe 1: 1 **P,** an apostle of Jesus Christ,
2Pe 1: 1 Simeon **P,** a servant and apostle of Jesus Christ,

PETER'S (6) [PETER]
Mt 8:14 When Jesus entered **P** house,
Jn 1:40 and followed him was Andrew, Simon **P** brother.
6: 8 One of his disciples, Andrew, Simon **P** brother,
Ac 5:15 in order that **P** shadow might fall on some of them
10:25 On **P** arrival Cornelius met him,
12:14 On recognizing **P** voice, she was so overjoyed

PETHAHIAH (5)
1Ch 24:16 the nineteenth to **P,** the twentieth to Jehezkel,
Ezr 10:23 Jozabad, Shimei, Kelaiah (that is, Kelita), **P,**
Ne 9: 5 Sherebiah, Hodiah, Shebaniah, and **P,** said,
11:24 And **P** son of Meshezabel,
1Es 9:23 who was Kelita, and **P** and Judah and Jonah.

PETHOR (2)
Nu 22: 5 He sent messengers to Balaam son of Beor at **P,**
Dt 23: 4 from **P** of Mesopotamia, to curse you.

PETHUEL (1)
Joel 1: 1 word of the LORD that came to Joel son of **P:**

PETITION‡ (17) [PETITIONED, PETITIONS]
1Sa 1:17 God of Israel grant the **p** you have made to him."
1:27 LORD has granted me the **p** that I made to him.
25:35 and I have granted your **p."**
Est 5: 6 the king said to Esther, "What is your **p?**
5: 7 Then Esther said, "This is my **p** and request:
5: 8 the king to grant my **p** and fulfill my request,
7: 2 the king again said to Esther, "What is your **p,**
7: 3 let my life be given me—that is my **p—**
9:12 Now what is your **p?**
AdE 5: 7 She said, "My **p** and request is:
7: 2 What is your **p** and what is your request?
7: 3 let my life be granted me at my **p,**
Sir 39: 5 and to **p** the Most High;
2Mc 13:12 in the same **p** and had implored the merciful Lord
3Mc 2:10 to our **p** when we come to this place and pray.
6:40 on which also they made the **p** for their dismissal.
2Es 8:24 and give ear to the **p** of your creature;

PETITIONED (3) [PETITION]
Ezr 8:23 So we fasted and **p** our God for this,
Ac 25:24 about whom the whole Jewish community **p** me,
3Mc 6:37 Then they **p** the king, asking for dismissal

PETITIONS (1) [PETITION]
Ps 20: 5 May the LORD fulfill all your **p.**

PETRA, PETROS See Index to Footnotes

PETTY (1)
4Mc 5:19 Therefore do not suppose that it would be a **p** sin

PEULLETHAI (1)
1Ch 26: 5 **P** the eighth; for God blessed him.

PHALANX (3) [PHALANXES]
1Mc 6:45 He courageously ran into the midst of the **p**
9:12 the **p** advanced to the sound of the trumpets;
10:82 the **p** in battle (for the cavalry was exhausted);

PHALANXES (2) [PHALANX]
1Mc 6:35 They distributed the animals among the **p;**
6:38 while being themselves protected by the **p.**

PHALARIS (2)
3Mc 5:20 possessed by a savagery worse than that of **P,**
5:42 a **P** in everything and filled with madness,

PHALEC (KJV) See PELEG

PHALLU (KJV) See PALLU

PHALLUS See Index to Footnotes

PHALTI, PHALTIEL (KJV) See PALTI, PALTIEL

PHALTIEL (1)

2Es 5:16 Now on the second night **P,** a chief of the people,

PHANTOMS (2)

Ps 73:20 on awaking you despise their **p.**
Wis 17: 4 and dismal **p** with gloomy faces appeared.

PHANUEL (1)

Lk 2:36 There was also a prophet, Anna the daughter of **P,**

PHARADATHA (1)

AdE 9: 8 **P,** Barea, Sarbacha,

PHARAKIM (1)

1Es 5:31 the descendants of **P,** the descendants of Bazluth,

PHARAOH‡ (236) [PHARAOH'S]

Ge 12:15 the officials of **P** saw her, they praised her to **P.**
12:17 But the LORD afflicted **P** and his house
12:18 So **P** called Abram, and said,
12:20 And **P** gave his men orders concerning him;
39: 1 an officer of **P,** the captain of the guard,
40: 2 **P** was angry with his two officers,
40:13 within three days **P** will lift up your head
40:14 the kindness to make mention of me to **P,**
40:17 for **P,** but the birds were eating it out of the basket
40:19 within three days **P** will lift up your head—
41: 1 **P** dreamed that he was standing by the Nile,
41: 4 the seven sleek and fat cows. And **P** awoke.
41: 7 **P** awoke, and it was a dream.
41: 8 and all its wise men. **P** told them his dreams,
41: 8 there was no one who could interpret them to **P.**
41: 9 Then the chief cupbearer said to **P,**
41:10 Once **P** was angry with his servants,
41:14 Then **P** sent for Joseph,
41:14 and changed his clothes, he came in before **P.**
41:15 And **P** said to Joseph, "I have had a dream,
41:16 Joseph answered **P,** "It is not I; God will give **P** a favorable answer."
41:17 Then **P** said to Joseph, "In my dream
41:25 Then Joseph said to **P,** "Pharaoh's dreams are one
41:25 God has revealed to **P** what he is about to do.
41:28 as I told **P;** God has shown to **P** what he is about
41:33 let **P** select a man who is discerning and wise,
41:34 Let **P** proceed to appoint overseers over the land,
41:35 and lay up grain under the authority of **P** for food
41:37 The proposal pleased **P** and all his servants.
41:38 **P** said to his servants, "Can we find anyone else
41:39 So **P** said to Joseph,
41:41 And **P** said to Joseph, "See,
41:42 **P** put it on Joseph's hand;
41:44 Moreover **P** said to Joseph, "I am **P,**
41:45 **P** gave Joseph the name Zaphenath-paneah;
41:46 when he entered the service of **P** king of Egypt.
41:46 And Joseph went out from the presence of **P,**
41:55 the people cried to **P** for bread.
41:55 **P** said to all the Egyptians, "Go to Joseph;
42:15 Here is how you shall be tested: as **P** lives,
42:16 or else, as **P** lives, surely you are spies."
44:18 for you are like **P** himself.
45: 2 and the household of **P** heard it.
45: 8 he has made me a father to **P,**
45:16 **P** and his servants were pleased.
45:17 **P** said to Joseph, "Say to your brothers, 'Do this:
45:21 according to the instruction of **P,**
46: 5 in the wagons that **P** had sent to carry him.
46:31 "I will go up and tell **P,** and will say to him,
46:33 **P** calls you, and says, 'What is your occupation?'
47: 1 So Joseph went and told **P,**
47: 2 he took five men and presented them to **P.**
47: 3 **P** said to his brothers, "What is your occupation?"
47: 3 And they said to **P,** "Your servants are shepherds,
47: 4 They said to **P,** "We have come to reside as aliens
47: 5 Then **P** said to Joseph, "Your father and your
47: 7 and presented him before **P,** and Jacob blessed **P.**
47: 8 **P** said to Jacob, "How many are the years
47: 9 Jacob said to **P,** "The years
47:10 Then Jacob blessed **P,** and went out from
47:10 and went out from the presence of **P.**
47:11 in the land of Rameses, as **P** had instructed.
47:19 We with our land will become slaves to **P;**
47:20 So Joseph bought all the land of Egypt for **P.**
47:22 for the priests had a fixed allowance from **P,**
47:22 and lived on the allowance that **P** gave them;
47:23 I have this day bought you and your land for **P,**
47:24 And at the harvests you shall give one-fifth to **P,**
47:25 may it please my lord, we will be slaves to **P."**
47:26 that **P** should have the fifth.
50: 4 Joseph addressed the household of **P,**
50: 4 please speak to **P** as follows:
50: 6 **P** answered, "Go up, and bury your father,
50: 7 With him went up all the servants of **P,**
Ex 1:11 Pithom and Rameses, for **P.**
1:19 to **P,** "Because the Hebrew women are not like
1:22 Then **P** commanded all his people,
2: 5 daughter of **P** came down to bathe at the river,
2:15 When **P** heard of it, he sought to kill Moses.
2:15 But Moses fled from **P.**
3:10 So come, I will send you to **P** to bring my people,
3:11 "Who am I that I should go to **P,**
4:21 see that you perform before **P** all the wonders
4:22 Then you shall say to **P,** 'Thus says the LORD:
5: 1 Afterward Moses and Aaron went to **P** and said,
5: 2 But **P** said, "Who is the LORD,
Ex 5: 5 **P** continued, "Now they are more numerous than
5: 6 That same day **P** commanded the taskmasters of
5:10 "Thus says **P,** 'I will not give you straw.
5:15 the Israelite supervisors came to **P** and cried,
5:20 As they left **P,** they came upon Moses
5:21 You have brought us into bad odor with **P**
5:23 Since I first came to **P** to speak in your name,
6: 1 "Now you shall see what I will do to **P:**
6:11 and tell **P** king of Egypt to let the Israelites go out
6:12 then shall **P** listen to me, poor speaker that I am?"
6:13 the Israelites and **P** king of Egypt,
6:27 It was they who spoke to **P** king of Egypt to bring
6:29 tell **P** king of Egypt all that I am speaking
6:30 why would **P** listen to me?"
7: 1 "See, I have made you like God to **P,**
7: 2 and your brother Aaron shall tell **P** to let
7: 4 When **P** does not listen to you,
7: 7 and Aaron eighty-three when they spoke to **P.**
7: 9 "When **P** says to you, 'Perform a wonder,'
7: 9 'Take your staff and throw it down before **P,**
7:10 to **P** and did as the LORD had commanded;
7:10 down his staff before **P** and his officials,
7:11 **P** summoned the wise men and the sorcerers;
7:15 Go to **P** in the morning, as he is going out to
7:20 In the sight of **P** and of his officials he lifted up
7:23 **P** turned and went into his house,
8: 1 LORD said to Moses, "Go to **P** and say to him,
8: 8 Then **P** called Moses and Aaron, and said,
8: 9 to **P,** "Kindly tell me when I am to pray for you
8:12 Then Moses and Aaron went out from **P;**
8:12 concerning the frogs that he had brought upon **P.**
8:15 But when **P** saw that there was a respite,
8:19 magicians said to **P,** "This is the finger of God!"
8:20 and present yourself before **P,** as he goes out to
8:24 into the house of **P** and into his officials' houses;
8:25 Then **P** summoned Moses and Aaron, and said,
8:28 So **P** said, "I will let you go to sacrifice to
8:29 the swarms of flies may depart tomorrow from **P,**
8:29 only do not let **P** again deal falsely by not letting
8:30 Moses went out from **P** and prayed to the LORD.
8:31 he removed the swarms of flies from **P,**
8:32 But **P** hardened his heart this time also,
9: 1 Then the LORD said to Moses, "Go to **P,**
9: 7 **P** inquired and found that not one of the livestock
9: 7 But the heart of **P** was hardened,
9: 8 and let Moses throw it in the air in the sight of **P.**
9:10 they took soot from the kiln, and stood before **P,**
9:12 But the LORD hardened the heart of **P,**
9:13 before **P,** and say to him, 'Thus says the LORD,
9:20 Those officials of **P** who feared the word of
9:27 Then **P** summoned Moses and Aaron,
9:33 So Moses left **P,** went out of the city,
9:34 But when **P** saw that the rain and the hail and
9:35 So the heart of **P** was hardened,
10: 1 Then the LORD said to Moses, "Go to **P;**
10: 3 So Moses and Aaron went to **P,** and said to him,
10: 6 Then he turned and went out from **P.**
10: 8 So Moses and Aaron were brought back to **P,**
10:16 **P** hurriedly summoned Moses and Aaron
10:18 So he went out from **P** and prayed to the LORD.
10:24 Then **P** summoned Moses, and said, "Go,
10:28 Then **P** said to him, "Get away from me!
11: 1 "I will bring one more plague upon **P** and
11: 5 from the firstborn of **P** who sits on his throne to
11: 8 And in hot anger he left **P.**
11: 9 LORD said to Moses, **"P** will not listen to you,
11:10 and Aaron performed all these wonders before **P;**
12:29 from the firstborn of **P** who sat on his throne to
12:30 **P** arose in the night, he and all his officials and all
13:15 When **P** stubbornly refused to let us go,
13:17 When **P** let the people go,
14: 3 **P** will say of the Israelites,
14: 4 so that I will gain glory for myself over **P**
14: 5 the minds of **P** and his officials were changed
14: 8 of **P** king of Egypt and he pursued the Israelites,
14:10 As **P** drew near, the Israelites looked back,
14:17 and so I will gain glory for myself over **P**
14:18 when I have gained glory for myself over **P,**
14:28 the entire army of **P** that had followed them into
15:19 of **P** with his chariots and his chariot drivers went
18: 4 and delivered me from the sword of **P").**
18: 8 the LORD had done to **P** and to the Egyptians
18:10 from the Egyptians and from **P.**
Dt 6:22 against **P** and all his household.
7: 8 from the hand of **P** king of Egypt.
7:18 the LORD your God did to **P** and to all Egypt,
11: 3 his signs and his deeds that he did in Egypt to **P,**
29: 2 to **P** and to all his servants and to all his land,
34:11 against **P** and all his servants and his entire land,
1Sa 2:27 in Egypt when they were slaves to the house of **P.**
6: 6 as the Egyptians and **P** hardened their hearts?
1Ki 3: 1 Solomon made a marriage alliance with **P** king
9:16 (**P** king of Egypt had gone up and captured Gezer
11: 1 along with the daughter of **P:**
11:18 to **P** king of Egypt, who gave him a house,
11:19 Hadad found great favor in the sight of **P,**
11:20 in Pharaoh's house among the children of **P.**
11:21 Hadad said to **P,** "Let me depart,
11:22 But **P** said to him, "What do you lack with me
2Ki 17: 7 of Egypt from under the hand of **P** king of Egypt.
18:21 Such is **P** king of Egypt to all who rely on him.
23:29 In his days **P** Neco king of Egypt went up to
23:29 when **P** Neco met him at Megiddo, he killed him.
23:33 **P** Neco confined him at Riblah in the land
23:34 **P** Neco made Eliakim son of Josiah king in place
23:35 Jehoiakim gave the silver and the gold to **P,**
23:35 to give it to **P** Neco.
1Ch 4:17 These are the sons of Bithiah, daughter of **P,**
Ne 9:10 and wonders against **P** and all his servants and all
Ps 135: 9 O Egypt, against **P** and all his servants.
136:15 but overthrew **P** and his army in the Red Sea,
Isa 19:11 the wise counselors of **P** give stupid counsel.
19:11 How can you say to **P,** "I am one of the sages,
30: 2 to take refuge in the protection of **P,**
30: 3 the protection of **P** shall become your shame,
36: 6 Such is **P** king of Egypt to all who rely on him.
Jer 25:19 **P** king of Egypt, his servants, his officials,
37: 5 Meanwhile, the army of **P** had come out of Egypt;
44:30 I am going to give **P** Hophra, king of Egypt,
46: 2 Concerning Egypt, about the army of **P** Neco,
46:17 Give **P,** king of Egypt, the name "Braggart who
46:25 **P,** and Egypt and her gods and her kings, upon **P**
47: 1 the Philistines, before **P** attacked Gaza:
Eze 17:17 **P** with his mighty army and great company will
29: 2 set your face against **P** king of Egypt,
29: 3 I am against you, **P** king of Egypt,
30:21 I have broken the arm of **P** king of Egypt;
30:22 I am against **P** king of Egypt,
30:24 but I will break the arms of **P,**
30:25 but the arms of **P** shall fall.
31: 2 say to **P** king of Egypt and to his hordes:
31:18 This is **P** and all his horde, says the Lord GOD.
32: 2 raise a lamentation over **P** king of Egypt,
32:31 When **P** sees them, he will be consoled
32:31 **P** and all his army, killed by the sword,
32:32 **P** and all his multitude, says the Lord GOD.
Ac 7:10 and to show wisdom when he stood before **P,**
7:13 and Joseph's family became known to **P.**
Ro 9:17 For the scripture says to **P,**
1Mc 4: 9 when **P** with his forces pursued them.
1Es 1:25 After all these acts of Josiah, it happened that **P,**
3Mc 2: 6 **P** who had enslaved your holy people Israel.
6: 4 **P** with his abundance of chariots,
2Es 1:10 down **P** with his servants and all his army.

PHARAOH'S (49) [PHARAOH]

Ge 12:15 And the woman was taken into **P** house.
37:36 one of **P** officials, the captain of the guard.
40: 7 So he asked **P** officers, who were with him
40:11 **P** cup was in my hand;
40:11 and I took the grapes and pressed them into **P** cup,
40:11 and placed the cup in **P** hand."
40:13 and you shall place **P** cup in his hand,
40:20 On the third day, which was **P** birthday,
40:21 and he placed the cup in **P** hand;
41:25 **"P** dreams are one and the same;
41:32 of **P** dream means that the thing is fixed by God,
45:16 When the report was heard in **P** house,
47:14 and Joseph brought the money into **P** house.
47:20 upon them; and the land became **P.**
47:26 The land of the priests alone did not become **P.**
Ex 2: 7 Then his sister said to **P** daughter,
2: 8 **P** daughter said to her, "Yes."
2: 9 **P** daughter said to her, "Take this child
2:10 the child grew up, she brought him to **P** daughter,
5:14 whom **P** taskmasters had set over them,
7: 3 But I will harden **P** heart,
7:13 Still **P** heart was hardened,
7:14 the LORD said to Moses, **"P** heart is hardened;
7:22 so **P** heart remained hardened,
8:19 But **P** heart was hardened,
10: 7 **P** officials said to him,
10:11 And they were driven out from **P** presence.
10:20 But the LORD hardened **P** heart,
10:27 But the LORD hardened **P** heart,
11: 3 in the sight of **P** officials and in the sight of
11:10 but the LORD hardened **P** heart,
14: 4 I will harden **P** heart, and he will pursue them,
14: 9 Egyptians pursued them, all **P** horses and chariots,
14:23 and went into the sea after them, all of **P** horses,
15: 4 **"P** chariots and his army he cast into the sea;
Dt 6:21 "We were **P** slaves in Egypt,
1Ki 3: 1 he took **P** daughter and brought her into the city
7: 8 also made a house like this hall for **P** daughter,
9:24 But **P** daughter went up from the city of David
11:20 whom Tahpenes weaned in **P** house;
11:20 Genubath was in **P** house among the children
2Ki 23:35 but he taxed the land in order to meet **P** demand
2Ch 8:11 Solomon brought **P** daughter from the city
SS 1: 9 my love, to a mare among **P** chariots.
Jer 37: 7 who sent you to me to inquire of me, **P** army,
37:11 from Jerusalem at the approach of **P** army,
43: 9 that is at the entrance to **P** palace in Tahpanhes.
Ac 7:21 **P** daughter adopted him and brought him up
Heb 11:24 refused to be called a son of **P** daughter,

PHARAOH-NECHO (KJV) See PHARAOH NECO

PHARATHON (1)

1Mc 9:50 and Beth-horon, and Bethel, and Timnath, and **P,**

PHARES (1)

1Es 5: 5 of the house of David, of the lineage of **P,**

PHARES, PHAREZ (KJV) See also PEREZ

PHARISEE (11) [PHARISEE'S, PHARISEES, PHARISEES']

Mt 23:26 You blind **P!** First clean the inside of the cup,

Lk 7:39 Now when the **P** who had invited him saw it,
11:37 a **P** invited him to dine with him;
11:38 The **P** was amazed to see that he did not first wash
18:10 one a **P** and the other a tax collector.
18:11 The **P**, standing by himself, was praying thus,
Jn 3: 1 Now there was a **P** named Nicodemus,
Ac 5:34 But a **P** in the council named Gamaliel,
23: 6 he called out in the council, "Brothers, I am a **P**,
26: 5 the strictest sect of our religion and lived as a **P**.
Php 3: 5 as to the law, a **P**;

PHARISEE'S (2) [PHARISEE]

Lk 7:36 and he went into the **P** house and took his place at
7:37 having learned that he was eating in the **P** house,

PHARISEES‡ (84) [PHARISEE]

Mt 3: 7 But when he saw many **P** and Sadducees coming
5:20 that of the scribes and **P**,
9:11 When the **P** saw this, they said to his disciples,
9:14 saying, "Why do we and the **P** fast often,
9:34 But the **P** said, "By the ruler of the demons
12: 2 When the **P** saw it, they said to him, "Look,
12:14 But the **P** went out and conspired against him,
12:24 But when the **P** heard it, they said,
12:38 Then some of the scribes and **P** said to him,
15: 1 Then **P** and scribes came to Jesus from Jerusalem
15:12 "Do you know that the **P** took offense
16: 1 The **P** and Sadducees came,
16: 6 and beware of the yeast of the **P** and Sadducees."
16:11 Beware of the yeast of the **P** and Sadducees!"
16:12 but of the teaching of the **P** and Sadducees.
19: 3 Some **P** came to him, and to test him they asked,
21:45 the chief priests and the **P** heard his parables,
22:15 **P** went and plotted to entrap him in what he said.
22:34 the **P** heard that he had silenced the Sadducees,
22:41 Now while the **P** were gathered together,
23: 2 "The scribes and the **P** sit on Moses' seat;
23:13 "But woe to you, scribes and **P**, hypocrites!
23:15 Woe to you, scribes and **P**, hypocrites!
23:23 "Woe to you, scribes and **P**, hypocrites!
23:25 "Woe to you, scribes and **P**, hypocrites!
23:27 "Woe to you, scribes and **P**, hypocrites!
23:29 "Woe to you, scribes and **P**, hypocrites!
27:62 the chief priests and the **P** gathered before Pilate
Mk 2:16 When the scribes of the **P** saw that he was eating
2:18 Now John's disciples and the **P** were fasting;
2:18 and the disciples of the **P** fast,
2:24 The **P** said to him, "Look,
3: 6 The **P** went out and immediately conspired with
7: 1 the **P** and some of the scribes who had come
7: 3 (For the **P**, and all the Jews,
7: 5 So the **P** and the scribes asked him,
8:11 The **P** came and began to argue with him,
8:15 of the yeast of the **P** and the yeast of Herod."
10: 2 Some **P** came, and to test him they asked,
12:13 to him some **P** and some Herodians to trap him
Lk 5:17 **P** and teachers of the law were sitting near
5:21 Then the scribes and the **P** began to question,
5:30 The **P** and their scribes were complaining
5:33 "John's disciples, like the disciples of the **P**,
6: 2 But some of the **P** said, "Why are you doing
6: 7 the **P** watched him to see whether he would cure
7:30 the **P** and the lawyers rejected God's purpose
7:36 One of the **P** asked Jesus to eat with him,
11:39 you **P** clean the outside of the cup and of the dish,
11:42 "But woe to you **P**! For you tithe mint and rue
11:43 Woe to you **P**! For you love to have the seat
11:53 and the **P** began to be very hostile toward him and
12: 1 "Beware of the yeast of the **P**, that is,
13:31 At that very hour some **P** came and said to him,
14: 1 to the house of a leader of the **P** to eat a meal on
14: 3 And Jesus asked the lawyers and **P**,
15: 2 the **P** and the scribes were grumbling and saying,
16:14 The **P**, who were lovers of money, heard all this,
17:20 Once Jesus was asked by the **P** when the kingdom
19:39 Some of the **P** in the crowd said to him, "Teacher,
Jn 1:24 Now they had been sent from the **P**.
4: 1 Now when Jesus learned that the **P** had heard,
7:32 The **P** heard the crowd muttering such things
7:32 and the chief priests and **P** sent temple police
7:45 went back to the chief priests and **P**,
7:47 Then the **P** replied, "Surely you have
7:48 Has any one of the authorities or of the **P** believed
8: 3 ⟦the **P** brought a woman who had been caught⟧
8:13 Then the **P** said to him, "You are testifying
9:13 to the **P** the man who had formerly been blind.
9:15 Then the **P** also began to ask him
9:16 Some of the **P** said, "This man is not from God,
9:40 of the **P** near him heard this and said to him,
11:46 to the **P** and told them what he had done.
11:47 So the chief priests and the **P** called a meeting of
11:57 and the **P** had given orders that anyone who knew
12:19 The **P** then said to one another, "You see,
12:42 But because of the **P** they did not confess it,
18: 3 with police from the chief priests and the **P**,
Ac 15: 5 to the sect of the **P** stood up and said,
23: 6 that some were Sadducees and others were **P**,
23: 6 "Brothers, I am a Pharisee, a son of **P**.
23: 7 dissension began between the **P** and the Sadducees
23: 8 but the **P** acknowledge all three.)

PHARISEES' (1) [PHARISEE]

Ac 23: 9 and certain scribes of the **P** group stood up

PHARMACIST (1)

Sir 38: 8 the **p** makes a mixture from them.

PHAROSH (KJV) See PAROSH

PHARPAR (1)

2Ki 5:12 Are not Abana and **P**, the rivers of Damascus,

PHARSANNESTAIN (1)

AdE 9: 7 including **P**, Delphon, Phasga,

PHARZITES (KJV) See PEREZITES

PHASEAH (KJV) See PASEAH

PHASELIS (1)

1Mc 15:23 and to Rhodes, and to **P**, and to Cos, and to Side,

PHASGA (1)

AdE 9: 7 including Pharsannestain, Delphon, **P**,

PHASIRON (1)

1Mc 9:66 and his kindred and the people of **P** in their tents.

PHEBE (KJV) See PHOEBE

PHENICE (KJV) See PHOENIX, PHOENICIA

PHENICIA (KJV) See PHOENICIA

PHICHOL (KJV) See PHICOL

PHICOL (3)

Ge 21:22 with **P** the commander of his army,
21:32 Abimelech, with **P** the commander of his army,
26:26 with Ahuzzath his adviser and **P** the commander

PHILADELPHIA (2)

Rev 1:11 to Thyatira, to Sardis, to **P**, and to Laodicea."
3: 7 "And to the angel of the church in **P** write:

PHILEMON (1)

Phm 1: 1 To **P** our dear friend and co-worker,

PHILETUS (1)

2Ti 2:17 Among them are Hymenaeus and **P**,

PHILIP‡ (44) [PHILIP'S]

Mt 10: 3 **P** and Bartholomew; Thomas
Mk 3:18 and **P**, and Bartholomew, and Matthew,
Lk 3: 1 and his brother **P** ruler of the region of Ituraea
6:14 and James, and John, and **P**, and Bartholomew,
Jn 1:43 He found **P** and said to him, "Follow me."
1:44 Now **P** was from Bethsaida,
1:45 **P** found Nathanael and said to him,
1:46 **P** said to him, "Come and see."
1:48 "I saw you under the fig tree before **P** called you."
6: 5 to **P**, "Where are we to buy bread for these people
6: 7 **P** answered him, "Six months' wages would not
12:21 to **P**, who was from Bethsaida in Galilee, and said
12:22 **P** went and told Andrew; then Andrew and **P** went
14: 8 **P** said to him, "Lord, show us the Father,
14: 9 "Have I been with you all this time, **P**,
Ac 1:13 and John, and James, and Andrew, **P** and Thomas,
6: 5 together with **P**, Prochorus, Nicanor, Timon,
8: 5 **P** went down to the city of Samaria
8: 6 to what was said by **P**,
8:12 But when they believed **P**,
8:13 with **P** and was amazed when he saw the signs
8:26 Then an angel of the Lord said to **P**,
8:29 Then the Spirit said to **P**,
8:30 So **P** ran up to it and heard him reading
8:31 And he invited **P** to get in and sit beside him.
8:34 The eunuch asked **P**, "About whom,
8:35 Then **P** began to speak, and starting
8:38 **P** and the eunuch, went down into the water, and **P** baptized him.
8:39 the Spirit of the Lord snatched **P** away;
8:40 But **P** found himself at Azotus,
21: 8 and we went into the house of **P** the evangelist,
1Mc 1: 1 After Alexander son of **P**, the Macedonian,
6: 2 and weapons left there by Alexander son of **P**,
6:14 Then he called for **P**, one of his Friends,
6:55 Then Lysias heard that **P**,
6:63 He found **P** in control of the city,
8: 5 They had crushed in battle and conquered **P**,
2Mc 5:22 at Jerusalem, **P**, by birth a Phrygian and
6:11 were betrayed to **P** and were all burned together,
8: 8 When **P** saw that the man was gaining ground
9:29 And **P**, one of his courtiers, took his body home;
13:23 he got word that **P**, who had been left in charge of

PHILIP'S (2) [PHILIP]

Mt 14: 3 on account of Herodias, his brother **P** wife,
Mk 6:17 on account of Herodias, his brother **P** wife,

PHILIPPI (6) [PHILIPPIANS]

Mt 16:13 when Jesus came into the district of Caesarea **P**,
Mk 8:27 with his disciples to the villages of Caesarea **P**;
Ac 16:12 and from there to **P**, which is a leading city of
20: 6 from **P** after the days of Unleavened Bread,
Php 1: 1 To all the saints in Christ Jesus who are in **P**,
1Th 2: 2 and been shamefully mistreated at **P**,

PHILIPPIANS (1) [PHILIPPI]

Php 4:15 You **P** indeed know that in the early days of

PHILISTIA (8) [PHILISTINE, PHILISTINES]

Ex 15:14 pangs seized the inhabitants of **P**.
Ps 60: 8 over **P** I shout in triumph."
83: 7 **P** with the inhabitants of Tyre;
87: 4 **P** too, and Tyre, with Ethiopia—
108: 9 over **P** I shout in triumph."
Isa 14:31 melt in fear, O **P**, all of you!
Joel 3: 4 O Tyre and Sidon, and all the regions of **P**?
Zec 9: 6 and I will make an end of the pride of **P**.

PHILISTIM (KJV) See PHILISTINES

PHILISTINE (41) [PHILISTIA]

Jdg 14: 1 and at Timnah he saw a **P** woman.
14: 2 "I saw a **P** woman at Timnah;
1Sa 10: 5 at the place where the **P** garrison is;
14: 1 let us go over to the **P** garrison on the other side."
14: 4 the **P** garrison, there was a rocky crag on one side
17: 8 Am I not a **P**, and are you not servants of Saul?
17:10 And the **P** said, "Today I defy the ranks of Israel!
17:11 Saul and all Israel heard these words of the **P**,
17:16 forty days the **P** came forward and took his stand,
17:23 he talked with them, the champion, the **P** of Gath,
17:26 "What shall be done for the man who kills this **P**,
17:26 For who is this uncircumcised **P**
17:32 your servant will go and fight with this **P**."
17:33 not able to go against this **P** to fight with him;
17:36 this uncircumcised **P** shall be like one of them,
17:37 will save me from the hand of this **P**."
17:40 and he drew near to the **P**.
17:41 The **P** came on and drew near to David,
17:42 When the **P** looked and saw David,
17:43 The **P** said to David, "Am I a dog,
17:43 And the **P** cursed David by his gods.
17:44 The **P** said to David, "Come to me,
17:45 to the **P**, "You come to me with sword and spear
17:46 the **P** army this very day to the birds of the air and
17:48 When the **P** drew nearer to meet David,
17:48 toward the battle line to meet the **P**.
17:49 slung it, and struck the **P** on his forehead;
17:50 over the **P** with a sling and a stone, striking down the **P** and killing him;
17:51 Then David ran and stood over the **P**;
17:54 the head of the **P** and brought it to Jerusalem;
17:55 When Saul saw David go out against the **P**,
17:57 On David's return from killing the **P**,
17:57 with the head of the **P** in his hand.
18: 6 when David returned from killing the **P**,
19: 5 in his hand when he attacked the **P**,
21: 9 The priest said, "The sword of Goliath the **P**,
22:10 and gave him the sword of Goliath the **P**."
2Sa 21:17 and attacked the **P** and killed him.
1Ch 14:16 and they struck down the **P** army from Gibeon
Pm 151: 6 I went out to meet the **P**,

PHILISTINES‡ (262) [PHILISTIA]

Ge 10:14 and Caphtorim, from which the **P** come.
21:32 left and returned to the land of the **P**.
21:34 as an alien many days in the land of the **P**.
26: 1 Isaac went to Gerar, to King Abimelech of the **P**.
26: 8 King Abimelech of the **P** looked out of a window
26:14 and a great household, so that the **P** envied him.
26:15 the **P** had stopped up and filled with earth all
26:18 for the **P** had stopped them up after the death
Ex 13:17 of the land of the **P**, although that was nearer;
23:31 the **P**, and from the wilderness to the Euphrates;
Jos 13: 2 all the regions of the **P**,
13: 3 there are five rulers of the **P**, those of Gaza,
Jdg 3: 3 the five lords of the **P**,
3:31 who killed six hundred of the **P** with an oxgoad.
10: 6 the gods of the Ammonites, and the gods of the **P**.
10: 7 and he sold them into the hand of the **P** and into
10:11 from the Ammonites and from the **P**?
13: 1 into the hand of the **P** forty years.
13: 5 to deliver Israel from the hand of the **P**."
14: 3 to take a wife from the uncircumcised **P**?"
14: 4 for he was seeking a pretext to act against the **P**.
14: 4 At that time the **P** had dominion over Israel.
15: 3 "This time, when I do mischief to the **P**,
15: 5 the foxes go into the standing grain of the **P**,
15: 6 Then the **P** asked, "Who has done this?"
15: 6 So the **P** came up, and burned her and her father.
15: 9 Then the **P** came up and encamped in Judah,
15:11 "Do you not know that the **P** are rulers over us?
15:12 so that we may give you into the hands of the **P**."
15:14 the **P** came shouting to meet him;
15:20 he judged Israel in the days of the **P** twenty years.
16: 5 The lords of the **P** came to her and said to her,
16: 8 the **P** brought her seven fresh bowstrings that had
16: 9 she said to him, "The **P** are upon you, Samson!"
16:12 and said to him, "The **P** are upon you, Samson!"
16:14 she said to him, "The **P** are upon you, Samson!"
16:18 she sent and called the lords of the **P**, saying,

Jdg 16:18 Then the lords of the **P** came up to her,
16:20 Then she said, "The **P** are upon you, Samson!"
16:21 So the **P** seized him and gouged out his eyes.
16:23 of the **P** gathered to offer a great sacrifice
16:27 all the lords of the **P** were there,
16:28 with this one act of revenge I may pay back the **P**
16:30 Then Samson said, "Let me die with the **P**."
1Sa 4: 1 the **P** mustered for war against Israel,
4: 1 and the **P** encamped at Aphek.
4: 2 The **P** drew up in line against Israel,
4: 2 Israel was defeated by the **P**,
4: 3 the LORD put us to rout today before the **P**?
4: 6 When the **P** heard the noise of the shouting,
4: 7 the **P** were afraid; for they said,
4: 9 Take courage, and be men, O **P**,
4:10 So the **P** fought; Israel was defeated,
4:17 messenger replied, "Israel has fled before the **P**,
5: 1 When the **P** captured the ark of God,
5: 2 then the **P** took the ark of God and brought it into
5: 8 and gathered together all the lords of the **P**,
5:11 and gathered together all the lords of the **P**,
6: 1 in the country of the **P** seven months.
6: 2 **P** called for the priests and the diviners and said,
6: 4 according to the number of the lords of the **P**;
6:12 to the left, and the lords of the **P** went after them
6:16 When the five lords of the **P** saw it,
6:17 the **P** returned as a guilt offering to the LORD:
6:18 the number of all the cities of the **P** belonging to
6:21 "The **P** have returned the ark of the LORD.
7: 3 and he will deliver you out of the hand of the **P**."
7: 7 the **P** heard that the people of Israel had gathered
7: 7 the lords of the **P** went up against Israel.
7: 7 of Israel heard of it they were afraid of the **P**.
7: 8 pray that he may save us from the hand of the **P**."
7:10 the **P** drew near to attack Israel;
7:10 against the **P** and threw them into confusion;
7:11 of Israel went out of Mizpah and pursued the **P**,
7:13 So the **P** were subdued and did not again enter
7:13 the hand of the LORD was against the **P** all
7:14 that the **P** had taken from Israel were restored
7:14 recovered their territory from the hand of the **P**.
9:16 He shall save my people from the hand of the **P**;
12: 9 and into the hand of the **P**,
13: 3 Jonathan defeated the garrison of the **P** that was
13: 3 and the **P** heard of it.
13: 4 that Saul had defeated the garrison of the **P**,
13: 4 and also that Israel had become odious to the **P**,
13: 5 The **P** mustered to fight with Israel,
13:11 and that the **P** were mustering at Michmash,
13:12 'Now the **P** will come down upon me at Gilgal,
13:16 but the **P** encamped at Michmash.
13:17 And raiders came out of the camp of the **P**
13:19 the **P** said, "The Hebrews must not make swords
13:20 the **P** to sharpen their plowshare, mattocks, axes,
13:23 Now a garrison of the **P** had gone out to the pass
14:11 to the garrison of the **P**;
14:11 and the **P** said, "Look, Hebrews are coming out of
14:13 The **P** fell before Jonathan, and his armor-bearer,
14:19 the tumult in the camp of the **P** increased more
14:21 the Hebrews who previously had been with the **P**
14:22 of Ephraim heard that the **P** were fleeing,
14:30 the slaughter among the **P** has not been great."
14:31 down the **P** that day from Michmash to Aijalon,
14:36 down after the **P** by night and despoil them until
14:37 "Shall I go down after the **P**?
14:46 Then Saul withdrew from pursuing the **P**;
14:46 and the **P** went to their own place.
14:47 against the kings of Zobah, and against the **P**;
14:52 There was hard fighting against the **P** all the days
17: 1 Now the **P** gathered their armies for battle;
17: 2 and formed ranks against the **P**.
17: 3 The **P** stood on the mountain on the one side,
17: 4 the camp of the **P** a champion named Goliath,
17:19 were in the valley of Elah, fighting with the **P**.
17:21 Israel and the **P** drew up for battle,
17:23 came up out of the ranks of the **P**,
17:51 the **P** saw that their champion was dead, they fled.
17:52 and Judah rose up with a shout and pursued the **P**
17:52 that the wounded **P** fell on the way from Shaaraim
17:53 The Israelites came back from chasing the **P**,
18:17 let the **P** deal with him."
18:21 a snare for him and that the hand of the **P** may be
18:25 a hundred foreskins of the **P**,
18:25 to make David fall by the hand of the **P**.
18:27 and killed one hundred of the **P**;
18:30 Then the commanders of the **P** came out to battle;
19: 8 and David went out to fight the **P**.
23: 1 "The **P** are fighting against Keilah,
23: 2 "Shall I go and attack these **P**?"
23: 2 "Go and attack the **P** and save Keilah."
23: 3 if we go to Keilah against the armies of the **P**?"
23: 4 for I will give the **P** into your hand."
23: 5 fought with the **P**, brought away their livestock,
23:27 for the **P** have made a raid on the land."
23:28 stopped pursuing David, and went against the **P**;
24: 1 When Saul returned from following the **P**,
27: 1 for me than to escape to the land of the **P**;
27: 7 of the **P** was one year and four months.
27:11 the time he lived in the country of the **P**.
28: 1 In those days the **P** gathered their forces for war,
28: 4 **P** assembled, and came and encamped at Shunem.
28: 5 When Saul saw the army of the **P**, he was afraid,
28:15 for the **P** are warring against me,
28:19 along with you into the hands of the **P**;
28:19 the army of Israel into the hands of the **P**."
29: 1 Now the **P** gathered all their forces at Aphek,
29: 2 As the lords of the **P** were passing on by hundreds
1Sa 29: 3 the commanders of the **P** said,
29: 3 Achish said to the commanders of the **P**,
29: 4 the commanders of the **P** were angry with him;
29: 4 and the commanders of the **P** said to him,
29: 7 do nothing to displease the lords of the **P**."
29: 9 nevertheless, the commanders of the **P** have said,
29:11 to return to the land of the **P**.
29:11 But the **P** went up to Jezreel.
30:16 from the land of the **P** and from the land of Judah.
31: 1 Now the **P** fought against Israel;
31: 1 and the men of Israel fled before the **P**,
31: 2 The **P** overtook Saul and his sons;
31: 2 **P** killed Jonathan and Abinadab and Malchishua,
31: 7 and the **P** came and occupied them.
31: 8 The next day, when the **P** came to strip the dead,
31: 9 and sent messengers throughout the land of the **P**
31:11 of Jabesh-gilead heard what the **P** had done
2Sa 1:20 or the daughters of the **P** will rejoice,
3:14 at the price of one hundred foreskins of the **P**."
3:18 my people Israel from the hand of the **P**,
5:17 the **P** heard that David had been anointed king
5:17 all the **P** went up in search of David;
5:18 Now the **P** had come and spread out in the valley
5:19 "Shall I go up against the **P**?
5:19 for I will certainly give the **P** into your hand."
5:21 The **P** abandoned their idols there,
5:22 Once again the **P** came up,
5:24 before you to strike down the army of the **P**."
5:25 and he struck down the **P** from Geba all the way
8: 1 David attacked the **P** and subdued them;
8: 1 took Metheg-ammah out of the hand of the **P**.
8:12 Moab, the Ammonites, the **P**, Amalek,
19: 9 and saved us from the hand of the **P**;
21:12 where the **P** had hung them up,
21:12 on the day the **P** killed Saul on Gilboa.
21:15 The **P** went to war again with Israel,
21:15 They fought against the **P**,
21:18 After this a battle took place with the **P**, at Gob;
21:19 Then there was another battle with the **P** at Gob;
23: 9 when they defied the **P** who were gathered there
23:10 He struck down the **P** until his arm grew weary,
23:11 The **P** gathered together at Lehi,
23:11 and the army fled from the **P**.
23:12 defended it, and killed the **P**;
23:13 while a band of **P** was encamped in the valley
23:14 and the garrison of the **P** was then at Bethlehem.
23:16 three warriors broke through the camp of the **P**,
1Ki 4:21 to the land of the **P**, even to the border of Egypt;
15:27 which belonged to the **P**;
16:15 which belonged to the **P**.
2Ki 8: 2 and settled in the land of the **P** seven years.
8: 3 when the woman returned from the land of the **P**,
18: 8 He attacked the **P** as far as Gaza and its territory,
1Ch 1:12 and Caphtorim, from whom the **P** come.
10: 1 Now the **P** fought against Israel;
10: 1 and the men of Israel fled before the **P**,
10: 2 The **P** overtook Saul and his sons;
10: 2 **P** killed Jonathan and Abinadab and Malchishua,
10: 7 and the **P** came and occupied them.
10: 8 The next day when the **P** came to strip the dead,
10: 9 and sent messengers throughout the land of the **P**
10:11 that the **P** had done to Saul,
11:13 at Pas-dammim when the **P** were gathered there
11:13 Now the people had fled from the **P**,
11:14 defended it, and killed the **P**;
11:15 while the army of **P** was encamped in the valley
11:16 and the garrison of the **P** was then at Bethlehem.
11:18 Then the Three broke through the camp of the **P**,
12:19 to David when he came with the **P** for the battle
12:19 rulers of the **P** took counsel and sent him away,
14: 8 the **P** heard that David had been anointed king
14: 8 all the **P** went up in search of David;
14: 9 Now the **P** had come and made a raid in the valley
14:10 "Shall I go up against the **P**?
14:13 Once again the **P** made a raid in the valley.
14:15 before you to strike down the army of the **P**."
18: 1 David attacked the **P** and subdued them;
18: 1 he took Gath and its villages from the **P**.
18:11 Moab, the Ammonites, the **P**, and Amalek.
20: 4 After this, war broke out with the **P** at Gezer;
20: 4 of the giants; and the **P** were subdued.
20: 5 Again there was war with the **P**;
2Ch 9:26 the kings from the Euphrates to the land of the **P**,
17:11 Some of the **P** brought Jehoshaphat presents,
21:16 the anger of the **P** and of the Arabs who are near
26: 6 He went out and made war against the **P**,
26: 6 of Ashdod and elsewhere among the **P**.
26: 7 God helped him against the **P**,
28:18 And the **P** had made raids on the cities in
Ps 56: T *A Miktam, when the* **P** *seized him in Gath.*
Isa 2: 6 from the east and of soothsayers like the **P**,
9:12 the Arameans on the east and the **P** on the west,
11:14 But they shall swoop down on the backs of the **P**
14:29 all you **P**, that the rod that struck you is broken,
Jer 25:20 all the kings of the land of the **P**—
47: 1 concerning the **P**, before Pharaoh attacked Gaza:
47: 4 of the day that is coming to destroy all the **P**,
47: 4 For the LORD is destroying the **P**,
Eze 16:27 the will of your enemies, the daughters of the **P**,
16:57 and to the daughters of the **P**,
25:15 Because with unending hostilities the **P** acted
25:16 I will stretch out my hand against the **P**,
Am 1: 8 and the remnant of the **P** shall perish,
6: 2 then go down to Gath of the **P**.
9: 7 the **P** from Caphtor and the Arameans from Kir?
Ob 1:19 and those of the Shephelah the land of the **P**;
Zep 2: 5 O Canaan, land of the **P**;
Sir 46:18 of the enemy and all the rulers of the **P**.
47: 7 and annihilated his adversaries the **P**;
50:26 in Seir, and the **P**, and the foolish people that live
1Mc 3:24 and the rest fled into the land of the **P**.
3:41 from Syria and the land of the **P** joined with them.
4:22 they all fled into the land of the **P**.
4:30 the camp of the **P** into the hands of Jonathan son
5:66 Then he marched off to go into the land of the **P**,
5:68 Judas turned aside to Azotus in the land of the **P**;
2Es 1:21 the Perizzites, and the **P** before you.
4Mc 3: 7 David had been attacking the **P** all day long,

PHILOLOGUS (1)

Ro 16:15 Greet **P**, Julia, Nereus and his sister,

PHILOMETOR (4)

2Mc 4:21 to Egypt for the coronation of **P** as king,
4:21 that **P** had become hostile to his government,
9:29 he withdrew to Ptolemy **P** in Egypt.
10:13 which **P** had entrusted to him,

PHILOPATOR (3)

3Mc 1: 1 When **P** learned from those who returned that
3:12 "King Ptolemy **P** to his generals and soldiers
7: 1 "King Ptolemy **P** to the generals in Egypt and all

PHILOSOPHER (3) [PHILOSOPHY]

4Mc 5: 7 not seem to me that you are a **p** when you observe
7: 7 in harmony with the law and **p** of divine life!
7:21 What person who lives as a **p** by the whole rule

PHILOSOPHERS (1) [PHILOSOPHY]

Ac 17:18 some Epicurean and Stoic **p** debated with him.

PHILOSOPHICAL (2) [PHILOSOPHY]

4Mc 1: 1 The subject that I am about to discuss is most **p**,
5:35 I will not put you to shame, **p** reason,

PHILOSOPHIZE (1) [PHILOSOPHY]

4Mc 5:11 **p** according to the truth of what is beneficial,

PHILOSOPHY (9) [PHILOSOPHER, PHILOSOPHERS, PHILOSOPHICAL, PHILOSOPHIZE]

Col 2: 8 See to it that no one takes you captive through **p**
4Mc 1: 1 for me to advise you to pay earnest attention to **p**.
5: 4 to many in the tyrant's court because of his **p**.
5:11 Will you not awaken from your foolish **p**,
5:22 at our **p** as though living by it were irrational,
7: 9 deeds you made your words of divine **p** credible.
7:21 as a philosopher by the whole rule of **p**,
8: 1 a **p** in accordance with devout reason,
8:15 but they also opposed the tyrant with their own **p**,

PHINEAS (2) [=PHINEHAS]

1Es 8: 2 of Uzzi son of Bukki son of Abishua son of **P** son
8:29 Of the descendants of **P**, Gershom.

PHINEHAS (33) [=PHINEAS]

Ex 6:25 of the daughters of Putiel, and she bore him **P**.
Nu 25: 7 When **P** son of Eleazar, son of Aaron the priest,
25:11 "**P** son of Eleazar, son of Aaron
31: 6 along with **P** son of Eleazar the priest,
Jos 22:13 Then the Israelites sent the priest **P** son of Eleazar
22:30 the priest **P** and the chiefs of the congregation,
22:31 The priest **P** son of Eleazar said to the Reubenites
22:32 the priest **P** son of Eleazar and the chiefs returned
24:33 they buried him at Gibeah, the town of his son **P**,
Jdg 20:28 and **P** son of Eleazar, son of Aaron, ministered
1Sa 1: 3 Hophni and **P**, were priests of the LORD.
2:34 The fate of your two sons, Hophni and **P**,
4: 4 The two sons of Eli, Hophni and **P**,
4:11 and the two sons of Eli, Hophni and **P**, died.
4:17 your two sons also, Hophni and **P**, are dead,
4:19 Now his daughter-in-law, the wife of **P**,
14: 3 Ichabod's brother, son of **P** son of Eli,
1Ch 6: 4 Eleazar became the father of **P**, **P** of Abishua,
6:50 Eleazar his son, **P** his son, Abishua his son,
9:20 And **P** son of Eleazar was chief over them
Ezr 7: 5 son of **P**, son of Eleazar, son of
8: 2 Of the descendants of **P**, Gershom.
8:33 and with him was Eleazar son of **P**,
Ps 106:30 Then **P** stood up and interceded,
Sir 45:23 **P** son of Eleazar ranks third in glory
1Mc 2:26 just as **P** did against Zimri son of Salu.
2:54 **P** our ancestor, because he was deeply zealous,
1Es 5: 5 the descendants of **P** son of Aaron;
8:63 with him was Eleazar son of **P**,
2Es 1: 2 of **P** son of Eli son of Amariah son of Azariah son
1: 2 of Uzzi son of Borith son of Abishua son of **P** son
4Mc 18:12 He told you of the zeal of **P**,

PHINOE (1)

1Es 5:31 the descendants of **P**, the descendants of Hasrah,

PHLEGON (1)

Ro 16:14 Greet Asyncritus, **P**, Hermes, Patrobas, Hermas,

PHOEBE (1)

Ro 16: 1 I commend to you our sister **P**,

PHOENICIA (27) [SYROPHOENICIAN]

Ob 1:20 of the Israelites who are in Halah shall possess **P**
Ac 11:19 that took place over Stephen traveled as far as **P**,
15: 3 and as they passed through both **P** and Samaria,
21: 2 When we found a ship bound for **P**,
2Mc 3: 5 at that time was governor of Coelesyria and **P**,
3: 8 of inspection of the cities of Coelesyria and **P**,
4: 4 and governor of Coelesyria and **P**,
4:22 Then he marched his army into **P**.
8: 8 the governor of Coelesyria and **P**,
10:11 and to be chief governor of Coelesyria and **P**.
1Es 2:17 and the judges in Coelesyria and **P**:
2:24 will no longer have access to Coelesyria and **P**."
2:25 with them and living in Samaria and Syria and **P**,
2:27 and exacted tribute from Coelesyria and **P**.
4:48 the governors in Coelesyria and **P** and to those
6: 3 the governor of Syria and **P** and Sathrabuzanes
6: 7 the governor of Syria and **P**, and Sathrabuzanes,
6: 7 their associates the local rulers in Syria and **P**,
6:27 the governor of Syria and **P**,
6:27 as local rulers in Syria and **P**,
6:29 and that out of the tribute of Coelesyria and **P**
7: 1 Then Sisinnes the governor of Coelesyria and **P**,
8:19 and **P** that whatever Ezra the priest and reader of
8:23 throughout all Syria and **P**;
8:67 and to the governors of Coelesyria and **P**;
3Mc 3:15 not rule the nations inhabiting Coelesyria and **P**
4Mc 4: 2 So he came to Apollonius, governor of Syria, **P**,

PHOENIX (2)

Job 29:18 and I shall multiply my days like the **p**;
Ac 27:12 on the chance that somehow they could reach **P**,

PHOGOR (1)

Tob 1: 2 above Asher toward the west, and north of **P**.

PHRASE (1) [PHRASES]

Heb 12:27 This **p**, "Yet once more," indicates the removal

PHRASES (2) [PHRASE]

Mt 6: 7 do not heap up empty **p** as the Gentiles do;
Sir Pr: 2 to have rendered some **p** imperfectly.

PHRYGIA (3) [PHRYGIAN]

Ac 2:10 **P** and Pamphylia, Egypt and the parts
16: 6 They went through the region of **P** and Galatia,
18:23 to place through the region of Galatia and **P**,

PHRYGIAN (1) [PHRYGIA]

2Mc 5:22 by birth a **P** and in character more barbarous than

PHURAH (KJV) See PURAH

PHUT (KJV) See PUT

PHYGELUS (1)

2Ti 1:15 away from me, including **P** and Hermogenes.

PHYLACTERIES (1)

Mt 23: 5 for they make their **p** broad and their fringes long.

PHYSICAL (10) [PHYSICALLY]

Da 1: 4 young men without **p** defect and handsome,
Ro 2:28 nor is true circumcision something external and **p**.
1Co 15:44 It is sown a **p** body, it is raised a spiritual body.
15:44 If there is a **p** body, there is also a spiritual body.
15:46 But it is not the spiritual that is first, but the **p**,
Gal 4:13 of a **p** infirmity that I first announced the gospel
Eph 2:11 a **p** circumcision made in the flesh
1Ti 4: 8 while **p** training is of some value,
Heb 7:16 through a legal requirement concerning **p** descent,
4Mc 1:32 Some desires are mental, others are **p**,

PHYSICALLY (1) [PHYSICAL]

Ro 2:27 Then those who are **p** uncircumcised but keep

PHYSICIAN (9) [PHYSICIANS]

Jer 8:22 Is there no **p** there?
Mt 9:12 he said, "Those who are well have no need of a **p**,
Mk 2:17 "Those who are well have no need of a **p**,
Lk 5:31 "Those who are well have no need of a **p**,
Col 4:14 Luke, the beloved **p**, and Demas greet you.
Sir 10:10 A long illness baffles the **p**;
38: 7 By them the **p** heals and takes away pain;
38:12 give the **p** his place, for the Lord created him;
38:15 will be defiant toward the **p**.

PHYSICIANS‡ (10) [PHYSICIAN]

Ge 50: 2 the **p** in his service to embalm his father.
50: 2 So the **p** embalmed Israel;
2Ch 16:12 not seek the LORD, but sought help from **p**.
Job 13: 4 all of you are worthless **p**.
Mk 5:26 She had endured much under many **p**,
Lk 8:43 and though she had spent all she had on **p**,
Tob 2:10 I went to **p** to be healed,
Sir 38: 1 Honor **p** for their services,
38: 3 The skill of **p** makes them distinguished,
38:13 a time when recovery lies in the hands of **p**,

PI-BESETH (1)

Eze 30:17 young men of On and of **P** shall fall by the sword;

PI-HAHIROTH (4)

Ex 14: 2 in front of **P**, between Migdol and the sea, in front
14: 9 they overtook them camped by the sea, by **P**,
Nu 33: 7 They set out from Etham, and turned back to **P**,
33: 8 They set out from **P**, passed through the sea into

PICK (10) [GRAPE-PICKER, GRAPE-PICKERS, PICKED, PICKS]

Jdg 1: 7 with their thumbs and big toes cut off used to **p**
2Ki 5: 7 and see how he is trying to **p** a quarrel with me."
6: 7 He said, "**P** it up."
Job 30: 4 they **p** mallow and the leaves of bushes,
Jer 43:12 and he shall **p** clean the land of Egypt,
Eze 17:21 All the **p** of his troops shall fall by the sword,
Jnh 1:12 "**P** me up and throw me into the sea;
Mk 16:18 ⟦they will **p** up snakes in their hands,⟧
Sir 8:16 Do not **p** a fight with the quick-tempered,
LtJ 6:27 they themselves must **p** it up.

PICKED (31) [PICK]

Ge 42:24 And he **p** out Simeon and had him bound
Ex 14: 7 he took six hundred **p** chariots and all
15: 4 his **p** officers were sunk in the Red Sea.
Jdg 20:16 seven hundred **p** men who were left-handed;
20:34 against Gibeah ten thousand **p** men out
Ru 2:18 She **p** it up and came into the town,
2Sa 4: 4 His nurse **p** him up and fled;
10: 9 he chose some of the **p** men of Israel,
23: 6 for they cannot be **p** up with the hand;
2Ki 2:13 He **p** up the mantle of Elijah that had fallen
1Ch 19:10 of the **p** men of Israel and arrayed them against
2Ch 13: 3 four hundred thousand **p** men;
13: 3 with eight hundred thousand **p** mighty warriors.
13:17 five hundred thousand **p** men of Israel fell slain.
25: 5 that they were three hundred thousand **p** troops fit
Da 11:15 not even his **p** troops, for there shall be no strength
Jnh 1:15 So they **p** Jonah up and threw him into the sea;
Lk 6:44 nor are grapes **p** from a bramble bush.
Jn 8:59 So they **p** up stones to throw at him,
Ac 20: 9 he fell to the ground three floors below and was **p**
Jdt 2:15 He mustered the **p** troops by divisions
2:19 with their chariots and cavalry and **p** foot soldiers.
3: 6 in the fortified towns and took **p** men from them
1Mc 4: 1 and one thousand **p** cavalry,
4:28 next year he mustered sixty thousand **p** infantry
6:35 and five hundred **p** horsemen were assigned
9: 5 and with him were three thousand **p** men.
12:41 to meet him with forty thousand **p** warriors,
15:26 Simon sent to Antiochus two thousand **p** troops,
2Mc 4:41 some **p** up stones, some blocks of wood,
13:15 and with a **p** force of the bravest young men,

PICKS (4) [PICK]

2Sa 12:31 to work with saws and iron **p** and iron axes,
1Ch 20: 3 set them to work with saws and iron **p** and axes.
Jer 43:12 as a shepherd **p** his cloak clean of vermin;
Sir 22: 2 anyone that **p** it up will shake it off his hand.

PICTURE (2)

Eze 23:15 **p** of Babylonians whose native land was Chaldea.
2Es 5:37 or show me the **p** of a voice;

PIECE‡ (55) [APIECE, BREASTPIECE, PIECEMEAL, PIECES, SHOULDER-PIECES]

Ge 23:15 a **p** of land worth four hundred shekels of silver—
Ex 15:25 and the LORD showed him a **p** of wood;
25:19 of one **p** with the mercy seat you shall make
25:31 its calyxes, and its petals shall be of one **p** with it;
25:35 of one **p** with it under the first pair of branches,
25:35 of one **p** with it under the next pair of branches,
25:35 of one **p** with it under the last pair of branches—
25:36 Their calyxes and their branches shall be of one **p**
25:36 the whole of it one hammered **p** of pure gold.
27: 2 its horns shall be of one **p** with it,
30: 2 its horns shall be of one **p** with it.
37: 8 of one **p** with the mercy seat he made
37:17 its calyxes, and its petals were of one **p** with it.
37:21 of one **p** with it under the first pair of branches,
37:21 of one **p** with it under the next pair of branches,
37:21 of one **p** with it under the last pair of branches.
37:22 Their calyxes and their branches were of one **p**
37:22 the whole of it one hammered **p** of pure gold.
37:25 its horns were of one **p** with it.
38: 2 its horns were of one **p** with it,
Lev 9:13 they brought him the burnt offering **p** by **p**,
25:25 of your kin falls into difficulty and sells a **p**
1Sa 2:36 to implore him for a **p** of silver or a loaf of bread,
30:12 they also gave him a **p** of fig cake and two clusters
1Ki 7:34 the supports were of one **p** with the stands.
7:35 its stays and its borders were of one **p** with it.
2Ki 3:19 every good **p** of land you shall ruin with stones."
3:25 on every good **p** of land everyone threw a stone,
Job 33: 6 I too was formed from a **p** of clay.
42:11 of them gave him a **p** of money and a gold ring.
Pr 28:21 yet for a **p** of bread a person may do wrong.
Eze 24: 6 Empty it **p** by **p**, making no choice at all.
Hos 4:12 My people consult a **p** of wood,
Am 3:12 the mouth of the lion two legs, or a **p** of an ear,
Mt 9:16 a **p** of unshrunk cloth on an old cloak,
Mk 2:21 "No one sews a **p** of unshrunk cloth on
Lk 5:36 "No one tears a **p** from a new garment and sews it
5:36 and the **p** from the new will not match the old.
14:18 The first said to him, 'I have bought a **p** of land,
19:20 I wrapped it up in a **p** of cloth,
24:42 They gave him a **p** of broiled fish,
Jn 13:26 "It is the one to whom I give this **p** of bread
13:26 So when he had dipped the **p** of bread,
13:27 he received the **p** of bread, Satan entered into him.
13:30 receiving the **p** of bread, he immediately went out.
19:23 tunic was seamless, woven in one **p** from the top.
Ac 5: 1 with the consent of his wife Sapphira, sold a **p**
Tob 2:12 when she cut off a **p** she had woven and sent it to
Wis 10: 4 steering the righteous man by a paltry **p** of wood.
13:13 But a cast-off **p** from among them,
14: 1 about to voyage over raging waves calls upon a **p**
14: 5 even to the smallest **p** of wood,
Sir 22:15 a **p** of iron are easier to bear than a stupid person.

PIECEMEAL (1) [PIECE]

2Mc 15:33 and said that he would feed it **p** to the birds

PIECES (109) [PIECE]

Ge 15:17 and a flaming torch passed between these **p**.
20:16 I have given your brother a thousand **p** of silver;
33:19 he bought for one hundred **p** of money the plot
37:28 sold him to the Ishmaelites for twenty **p** of silver.
37:33 Joseph is without doubt torn to **p**."
44:28 and I said, Surely he has been torn to **p**;
45:22 but to Benjamin he gave three hundred **p** of silver
Ex 23:24 and break their pillars in **p**.
Lev 2: 6 break it in **p**, and pour oil on it;
6:12 into smoke the fat **p** of the offerings of well-being.
6:21 as a grain offering of baked **p**,
11:35 whether an oven or stove, it shall be broken in **p**;
Jos 24:32 for one hundred **p** of money;
Jdg 5:30 for Sisera, spoil of dyed stuffs embroidered, two **p**
9: 4 They gave him seventy **p** of silver out of
16: 5 we will each give you eleven hundred **p** of silver."
17: 2 "The eleven hundred **p** of silver that were taken
17: 3 Then he returned the eleven hundred **p** of silver
17: 4 his mother took two hundred **p** of silver,
17:10 and I will give you ten **p** of silver a year,
19:29 grasping his concubine he cut her into twelve **p**,
20: 6 Then I took my concubine and cut her into **p**,
1Sa 11: 7 and cut them in **p** and sent them throughout all
15:33 And Samuel hewed Agag in **p** before the LORD
2Sa 18:11 I would have been glad to give you ten **p** of silver
18:12 a thousand **p** of silver, I would not raise my hand
1Ki 8:64 the grain offerings and the fat **p** of the sacrifices
8:64 the grain offerings and the fat **p** of the sacrifices
11:30 garment he was wearing and tore it into twelve **p**.
11:31 to Jeroboam: Take for yourself ten **p**;
18:23 cut it in **p**, and lay it on the wood,
18:33 Next he put the wood in order, cut the bull in **p**,
19:11 in **p** before the LORD, but the LORD was not in
2Ki 2:12 and tore them in two **p**.
8:12 with the sword, dash in **p** their little ones,
11:18 his altars and his images they broke in **p**,
18: 4 in **p** the bronze serpent that Moses had made,
23:12 he pulled down from there and broke in **p**,
23:14 He broke the pillars in **p**,
24:13 he cut in **p** all the vessels of gold in the temple of
25:13 the Chaldeans broke in **p**,
2Ch 15: 6 in **p**, nation against nation and city against city,
23:17 his altars and his images they broke in **p**,
25:12 so that all of them were dashed to **p**.
28:24 and cut in **p** the utensils of the house of God.
Job 16:12 he seized me by the neck and dashed me to **p**;
19: 2 and break me in **p** with words?
Ps 2: 9 and dash them in **p** like a potter's vessel."
119:72 to me than thousands of gold and silver **p**.
SS 8:11 each one was to bring for its fruit a thousand **p**
Isa 13:16 Their infants will be dashed to **p** before their eyes;
27: 9 of the altars like chalkstones crushed to **p**,
45: 2 in **p** the doors of bronze and cut through the bars
51: 9 Was it not you who cut Rahab in **p**,
Jer 5: 6 everyone who goes out of them shall be torn in **p**—
23:29 and like a hammer that breaks a rock in **p**?
48:12 and empty his vessels, and break his jars in **p**.
52:17 the Chaldeans broke in **p**,
La 3:11 he led me off my way and tore me to **p**;
Eze 13:19 among my people for handfuls of barley and for **p**
16:40 and they shall stone you and cut you to **p**
24: 4 put in it the **p**, all the good **p**, the thigh and
24: 5 boil its **p**, seethe also its bones in it.
Da 2:34 on its feet of iron and clay and broke them in **p**.
2:35 were all broken in **p** and became like the chaff of
6:24 and broke all their bones in **p**.
7: 7 breaking in **p**, and stamping what was left
7:19 and which devoured and broke in **p**,
7:23 and trample it down, and break it to **p**.
Hos 8: 6 The calf of Samaria shall be broken to **p**.
10:14 the day of battle when mothers were dashed in **p**
13:16 their little ones shall be dashed in **p**,
Am 6:11 and the little house to **p**.
Mic 1: 7 All her images shall be beaten to **p**,
3: 3 break their bones in **p**, and chop them up like meat
4:13 you shall beat in **p** many peoples,
5: 8 treads down and tears in **p**, with no one to deliver.
Na 1: 6 and by him the rocks are broken in **p**.
3:10 even her infants were dashed in **p** at the head
Mt 14:20 they took up what was left over of the broken **p**,
15:37 and they took up the broken **p** left over,
21:44 one who falls on this stone will be broken to **p**;

Mt 24:51 He will cut him in **p** and put him with
26:15 They paid him thirty **p** of silver.
27: 3 he repented and brought back the thirty **p** of silver
27: 5 Throwing down the **p** of silver in the temple,
27: 6 But the chief priests, taking the **p** of silver, said,
27: 9 "And they took the thirty **p** of silver,
Mk 5: 4 and the shackles he broke in **p**;
6:43 up twelve baskets full of broken **p** and of the fish.
8: 8 and they took up the broken **p** left over,
8:19 many baskets full of broken **p** did you collect?"
8:20 many baskets full of broken **p** did you collect?"
Lk 9:17 twelve baskets of broken **p**.
12:46 and will cut him in **p**,
20:18 on that stone will be broken to **p**;
Ac 23:10 the tribune, fearing that they would tear Paul to **p**,
27:44 some on planks and others on **p** of the ship.
Jdt 5:22 and Moab insisted that he should be cut to **p**.
Wis 13:12 burn the cast-off **p** of his work to prepare his food,
Sir 43:15 and the hailstones are broken in **p**.
1Mc 1:56 The books of the law that they found they tore to **p**
2Mc 1:13 they were cut to **p** in the temple of Nanea by
10:30 they were thrown into disorder and cut to **p**.
3Mc 6: 5 broke in **p**, showing your power to many nations.
2Es 1:32 and killed them and torn their bodies in **p**;
4Mc 6: 6 and his sides were being cut to **p**.
9:20 and **p** of flesh were falling off the axles of

PIERCE (8) [PIERCED, PIERCES, PIERCING]

Ex 21: 6 and his master shall **p** his ear with an awl;
2Ki 18:21 which will **p** the hand of anyone who leans on it.
Job 40:24 Can one take it with hooks or **p** its nose with
41: 2 or **p** its jaw with a hook?
Isa 36: 6 which will **p** the hand of anyone who leans on it.
Zec 13: 3 and their mothers who bore them shall **p** them
Lk 2:35 and a sword will **p** your own soul too."
Jdt 6: 6 and the spear of my servants shall **p** your sides,

PIERCED[‡] (20) [PIERCE]

Nu 25: 8 and **p** the two of them,
Jdg 5:26 she shattered and **p** his temple.
2Ki 9:24 so that the arrow **p** his heart;
Job 26:13 his hand **p** the fleeing serpent.
Ps 109:22 I am poor and needy, and my heart is **p** within me.
Isa 14:19 clothed with the dead, those **p** by the sword,
51: 9 not you who cut Rahab in pieces, who **p**
La 4: 9 Happier were those **p** by the sword than those **p** by hunger,
Hab 3:14 You **p** with his own arrows the head
Zec 12:10 when they look on the one whom they have **p**,
Jn 19:34 Instead, one of the soldiers **p** his side with a spear,
19:37 "They will look on the one whom they have **p**."
1Ti 6:10 from the faith and **p** themselves with many pains.
Rev 1: 7 every eye will see him, even those who **p** him;
Jdt 16:12 of slave-girls **p** them through and wounded them
Wis 5:11 and **p** by the force of its rushing flight, is traversed
2Mc 12:22 and **p** by the points of their own swords.
4Mc 11:19 **p** his ribs so that his entrails were burned through.
18:21 **p** the pupils of their eyes and cut out their tongues,

PIERCES (2) [PIERCE]

Pr 7:23 until an arrow **p** its entrails.
Sir 35:21 The prayer of the humble **p** the clouds,

PIERCING (2) [PIERCE]

Eze 28:24 a pricking brier or a **p** thorn
Heb 4:12 **p** until it divides soul from spirit,

PIETY (14) [PIOUS, PIOUSLY]

Job 22: 4 Is it for your **p** that he reproves you,
Mt 6: 1 of practicing your **p** before others in order to
Ac 3:12 by our own power or **p** we had made him walk?
Col 2:23 of wisdom in promoting self-imposed **p**,
2Mc 3: 1 the laws were strictly observed because of the **p** of
6:11 their **p** kept them from defending themselves,
4Mc 5:18 be right for us to invalidate our reputation for **p**.
5:24 and it teaches us **p**, so that
5:31 as not to be young in reason on behalf of **p**.
6: 2 with the gracefulness of his **p**.
7:16 of **p** an aged man despised tortures even to death,
13:10 not be cowardly in the demonstration of our **p**."
17: 5 lighting the way of your star-like seven sons to **p**,
18: 1 obey this law and exercise **p** in every way,

PIG (2) [PIG'S, PIGS]

Lev 11: 7 The **p**, for even though it has divided hoofs
Dt 14: 8 And the **p**, because it divides the hoof but does

PIG'S (1) [PIG]

Pr 11:22 Like a gold ring in a **p** snout is a beautiful woman

PIGEON (2) [PIGEONS]

Ge 15: 9 a ram three years old, a turtledove, and a young **p**."
Lev 12: 6 and a **p** or a turtledove for a sin offering.

PIGEONS (10) [PIGEON]

Lev 1:14 shall choose your offering from turtledoves or **p**.
5: 7 or two **p**, one for a sin offering and the other for
5:11 But if you cannot afford two turtledoves or two **p**,
12: 8 she shall take two turtledoves or two **p**,
14:22 also two turtledoves or two **p**,
14:30 of the turtledoves or **p** such as he can afford,
Lev 15:14 or two **p** and come before the LORD to
15:29 or two **p** and bring them to the priest to
Nu 6:10 or two young **p** to the priest at the entrance of
Lk 2:24 "a pair of turtledoves or two young **p**."

PIGS (3) [PIG]

Isa 66:17 eating the flesh of **p**, vermin, and rodents,
Lk 15:15 who sent him to his fields to feed the **p**.
15:16 with the pods that the **p** were eating;

PILASTER (1) [PILASTERS]

Eze 40:14 the gate next to the **p** on every side of the court.

PILASTERS[‡] (18) [PILASTER]

Eze 40: 9 eight cubits; and its **p**, two cubits;
40:10 and the **p** on either side were of the same size.
40:16 The recesses and their **p** had windows,
40:16 and on the **p** were palm trees.
40:21 and its **p** and its vestibule were of the same size
40:24 and he measured its **p** and its vestibule;
40:26 It had palm trees on its **p**, one on either side.
40:29 its **p**, and its vestibule were of the same size as
40:31 and palm trees were on its **p**,
40:33 its **p**, and its vestibule were of
40:34 and it had palm trees on its **p**, on either side;
40:36 its **p**, and its vestibule were of the same size as
40:37 and it had palm trees on its **p**, on either side;
40:48 and measured the **p** of the vestibule, five cubits on
40:49 and there were pillars beside the **p** on either side.
41: 1 he brought me to the nave, and measured the **p**;
41: 1 on each side six cubits was the width of the **p**.
41: 3 and measured the **p** of the entrance, two cubits;

PILATE (56) [PILATE'S]

Mt 27: 2 and handed him over to **P** the governor.
27:13 Then **P** said to him, "Do you not hear
27:17 So after they had gathered, **P** said to them,
27:22 **P** said to them, "Then what should I do
27:24 So when **P** saw that he could do nothing,
27:58 He went to **P** and asked for the body of Jesus;
27:58 then **P** ordered it to be given to him.
27:62 chief priests and the Pharisees gathered before **P**
27:65 **P** said to them, "You have a guard of soldiers;
Mk 15: 1 led him away, and handed him over to **P**.
15: 2 **P** asked him, "Are you the King of the Jews?"
15: 4 **P** asked him again, "Have you no answer?
15: 5 Jesus made no further reply, so that **P** was amazed.
15: 8 the crowd came and began to ask **P** to do for them
15:12 **P** spoke to them again,
15:14 **P** asked them, "Why, what evil has he done?"
15:15 So **P**, wishing to satisfy the crowd,
15:43 went boldly to **P** and asked for the body of Jesus.
15:44 Then **P** wondered if he were already dead;
Lk 3: 1 when Pontius **P** was governor of Judea,
13: 1 about the Galileans whose blood **P** had mingled
23: 1 as a body and brought Jesus before **P**.
23: 3 **P** asked him, "Are you the king of the Jews?"
23: 4 Then **P** said to the chief priests and the crowds,
23: 6 When **P** heard this, he asked whether the man was
23:11 an elegant robe on him, and sent him back to **P**.
23:12 That same day Herod and **P** became friends
23:13 **P** then called together the chief priests,
23:20 **P**, wanting to release Jesus,
23:24 So **P** gave his verdict that their demand should
23:52 This man went to **P** and asked for the body
Jn 18:29 So **P** went out to them and said,
18:31 **P** said to them, "Take him yourselves
18:33 Then **P** entered the headquarters again,
18:35 **P** replied, "I am not a Jew, am I?
18:37 **P** asked him, "So you are a king?"
18:38 **P** asked him, "What is truth?"
19: 1 Then **P** took Jesus and had him flogged.
19: 4 **P** went out again and said to them, "Look,
19: 5 **P** said to them, "Here is the man!"
19: 6 **P** said to them, "Take him yourselves
19: 8 when **P** heard this, he was more afraid than ever.
19:10 **P** therefore said to him, "Do you refuse to speak
19:12 From then on **P** tried to release him,
19:13 When **P** heard these words,
19:15 **P** asked them, "Shall I crucify your King?"
19:19 **P** also had an inscription written and put on
19:21 Then the chief priests of the Jews said to **P**,
19:22 **P** answered, "What I have written I have written."
19:31 So they asked **P** to have the legs of
19:38 asked **P** to let him take away the body of Jesus. **P** gave him permission;
Ac 3:13 over and rejected in the presence of **P**,
4:27 For in this city, in fact, both Herod and Pontius **P**,
13:28 they asked **P** to have him killed.
1Ti 6:13 who in his testimony before Pontius **P** made

PILATE'S (1) [PILATE]

Jn 18:28 they took Jesus from Caiaphas to **P** headquarters.

PILDASH (1)

Ge 22:22 Chesed, Hazo, **P**, Jidlaph, and Bethuel."

PILE (8) [PILED, PILES]

2Ch 31: 7 In the third month they began to **p** up the heaps,
Job 27:16 and **p** up clothing like clay—
27:17 they may **p** it up, but the just will wear it,
Jer 50:26 **p** her up like heaps of grain,
Eze 24: 5 the choicest one of the flock, **p** the logs under it;
Eze 24: 9 I will even make the **p** great.
Zec 12: 6 a blazing pot on a **p** of wood, like a flaming torch
Lk 14:35 It is fit neither for the soil nor for the manure **p**;

PILED (3) [PILE]

Ex 15: 8 At the blast of your nostrils the waters **p** up,
Jdt 15:11 and hitched up her carts and **p** the things on them.
1Mc 11: 4 for they had **p** them in heaps along his route.

PILEHA (KJV) See PILHA

PILES (1) [PILE]

Na 3: 3 **p** of dead, heaps of corpses, dead bodies without

PILFER (1)

Tit 2:10 not to **p**, but to show complete and perfect fidelity,

PILGRIMAGE (1)

2Es 8:39 over their **p** also, and their salvation,

PILGRIMS (KJV) See ALIENS, STRANGERS

PILHA (1)

Ne 10:24 Hallohesh, **P**, Shobek,

PILLAGE (2) [PILLAGED]

Jer 49: 9 even they would **p** only what they wanted.
Jdt 8:19 handed over to the sword and to **p**,

PILLAGED (1) [PILLAGE]

Ob 1: 6 How Esau has been **p**, his treasures searched out!

PILLAR[‡] (60) [PILLARS]

A. PILLAR OF CLOUD (13)
B. PILLAR OF FIRE (8)

Ge 19:26 looked back, and she became a **p** of salt.
28:18 and set it up for a **p** and poured oil on the top of it.
28:22 which I have set up for a **p**, shall be God's house;
31:13 where you anointed a **p** and made a vow to me.
31:45 So Jacob took a stone, and set it up as a **p**.
31:49 and the **p** Mizpah, for he said, "The LORD watch
31:51 Laban said to Jacob, "See this heap and see the **p**,
31:52 This heap is a witness, and the **p** is a witness,
31:52 and you will not pass beyond this heap and this **p**
35:14 Jacob set up a **p** in the place where he had spoken with him, a **p** of stone;
35:20 set up a **p** at her grave; it is the **p** of Rachel's tomb,
Ex 13:21 The LORD went in front of them in a **p** of cloud A
13:21 and in a **p** of fire by night, to give them light, B
13:22 Neither the **p** of cloud by day nor the pillar A
13:22 pillar of cloud by day nor the **p** of fire by night B
14:19 and the **p** of cloud moved from in front of them A
14:24 the LORD in the **p** of fire and cloud looked down B
33: 9 the **p** of cloud would descend and stand at A
33:10 When all the people saw the **p** of cloud standing A
Nu 12: 5 Then the LORD came down in a **p** of cloud, A
14:14 you go in front of them, in a **p** of cloud by day A
14:14 pillar of cloud by day and in a **p** of fire by night. B
Dt 16:22 nor shall you set up a stone **p**—
31:15 the LORD appeared at the tent in a **p** of cloud; A
31:15 the **p** of cloud stood at the entrance to the tent. A
Jdg 9: 6 by the oak of the **p** at Shechem.
2Sa 18:18 in his lifetime had taken and set up for himself a **p**
18:18 he called the **p** by his own name.
1Ki 7:15 the second **p** was the same.
7:21 he set up the **p** on the south and called it Jachin;
7:21 and he set up the **p** on the north and called it Boaz.
2Ki 3: 2 he removed the **p** of Baal that his father had made.
10:26 They brought out the **p** that was in the temple
10:27 Then they demolished the **p** of Baal,
11:14 there was the king standing by the **p**,
23: 3 by the **p** and made a covenant before the LORD,
25:17 The height of the one **p** was eighteen cubits,
25:17 The second **p** had the same, with the latticework.
2Ch 23:13 the king standing by his **p** at the entrance,
Ne 9:12 you led them by day with a **p** of cloud, A
9:12 and by night with a **p** of fire, B
9:19 the **p** of cloud that led them in the way did A
9:19 nor the **p** of fire by night that gave them light B
Ps 99: 7 He spoke to them in the **p** of cloud; A
Isa 19:19 and a **p** to the LORD at its border.
Jer 1:18 an iron **p**, and a bronze wall,
52:21 pillars, the height of the one **p** was eighteen cubits,
52:22 the second **p** had the same, with pomegranates.
Hos 3: 4 without sacrifice or **p**, without ephod or teraphim.
1Ti 3:15 the **p** and bulwark of the truth.
Rev 3:12 I will make you a **p** in the temple of my God;
Wis 10: 7 not ripen, and a **p** of salt standing as a monument
18: 3 Therefore you provided a flaming **p** of fire as B
Sir 24: 4 and my throne was in a **p** of cloud. A
36:29 a helper fit for him and a **p** of support.
LtJ 6:59 better also a wooden **p** in a palace,
3Mc 7:20 after inscribing them as holy on a **p** and dedicating
2Es 1:14 I provided light for you from a **p** of fire, B

PILLARS[‡] (101) [PILLAR]

Ex 23:24 and break their **p** in pieces.
24: 4 the mountain, and set up twelve **p**, corresponding
26:32 You shall hang it on four **p** of acacia overlaid

Ex 26:37 You shall make for the screen five **p** of acacia,
27:10 its twenty **p** and their twenty bases shall be
27:10 hooks of the **p** and their bands shall be of silver.
27:11 their **p** twenty and their bases twenty, of bronze,
27:11 hooks of the **p** and their bands shall be of silver.
27:12 with ten **p** and ten bases.
27:14 with three **p** and three bases.
27:15 with three **p** and three bases.
27:16 it shall have four **p** and with them four bases.
27:17 the **p** around the court shall be banded with silver;
34:13 You shall tear down their altars, break their **p**,
35:11 its clasps and its frames, its bars, its **p**,
35:17 its **p** and its bases, and the screen for the gate of
36:36 For it he made four **p** of acacia,
36:38 and its five **p** with their hooks.
38:10 its twenty **p** and their twenty bases were
38:10 the hooks of the **p** and their bands were of silver.
38:11 its twenty **p** and their twenty bases were
38:11 the hooks of the **p** and their bands were of silver.
38:12 with ten **p** and ten bases;
38:12 the hooks of the **p** and their bands were of silver.
38:14 with three **p** and three bases.
38:15 with three **p** and three bases.
38:17 The bases for the **p** were of bronze,
38:17 the hooks of the **p** and their bands were of silver;
38:17 and all the **p** of the court were banded with silver.
38:19 There were four **p**; their four bases were of bronze,
38:28 the **p**, and overlaid their capitals and made bands
39:33 its hooks, its frames, its bars, its **p**, and its bases;
39:40 its **p**, and its bases, and the screen for the gate of
40:18 and put in its poles, and raised up its **p**;
Lev 26: 1 and erect no carved images or **p**, and you shall
Nu 3:36 the **p**, the bases, and all their accessories—
3:37 also the **p** of the court all around,
4:31 the frames of the tabernacle, with its bars, **p**,
4:32 the **p** of the court all around with their bases, pegs,
Dt 7: 5 break down their altars, smash their **p**,
12: 3 Break down their altars, smash their **p**,
Jdg 16:25 They made him stand between the **p**;
16:26 "Let me feel the **p** on which the house rests,
16:29 And Samson grasped the two middle **p** on which
1Sa 2: 8 For the **p** of the earth are the LORD's,
1Ki 7: 2 built on four rows of cedar **p**,
7: 2 with cedar beams on the **p**.
7: 3 fifteen in each row, which were on the **p**.
7: 6 Hall of **P** fifty cubits long and thirty cubits wide.
7: 6 There was a porch in front with **p**,
7:15 He cast two **p** of bronze.
7:16 to set on the tops of the **p**;
7:17 of chain work for the capitals on the tops of the **p**;
7:19 the tops of the **p** in the vestibule were of lily-work,
7:20 the two **p** and also above the rounded projection
7:21 He set up the **p** at the vestibule of the temple;
7:22 On the tops of the **p** was lily-work.
7:22 Thus the work of the **p** was finished.
7:41 the two **p**, the two bowls of the capitals that were on the tops of the **p**, the two latticeworks
7:41 of the capitals that were on the tops of the **p**;
7:42 the two bowls of the capitals that were on the **p**;
14:23 For they also built for themselves high places, **p**,
2Ki 17:10 they set up for themselves **p** and sacred poles
18: 4 He removed the high places, broke down the **p**,
23:14 He broke the **p** in pieces,
25:13 bronze **p** that were in the house of the LORD,
25:16 As for the two **p**, the one sea, and the stands,
1Ch 18: 8 the bronze sea and the **p** and the vessels of bronze.
2Ch 3:15 of the house he made two **p** thirty-five cubits high,
3:16 and put them on the tops of the **p**;
3:17 He set up the **p** in front of the temple,
4:12 the two **p**, the bowls, and the two capitals on the top of the **p**;
4:12 of the capitals that were on the top of the **p**;
4:13 the two bowls of the capitals that were on the **p**.
14: 3 broke down the **p**, hewed down the sacred poles,
31: 1 to the cities of Judah and broke down the **p**,
Est 1: 6 and purple to silver rings and marble **p**.
Job 9: 6 the earth out of its place, and its **p** tremble;
26:11 The **p** of heaven tremble, and are astounded
Ps 75: 3 it is I who keep its **p** steady.
144:12 our daughters like corner **p**,
Pr 9: 1 she has hewn her seven **p**.
Jer 27:19 thus says the LORD of hosts concerning the **p**,
52:17 **p** of bronze that were in the house of the LORD,
52:20 As for the two **p**, the one sea,
52:21 As for the **p**, the height of one pillar
Eze 26:11 and your strong **p** shall fall to the ground.
40:49 there were **p** beside the pilasters on either side.
42: 6 they had no **p** like the the **p** of the outer court;
Hos 10: 1 as his country improved, he improved his **p**.
10: 2 down their altars, and destroy their **p**.
Mic 5:13 and your **p** from among you, and you shall bow
Gal 2: 9 who were acknowledged **p**,
Rev 10: 1 and his legs like **p** of fire.
AdE 1: 6 and silver blocks on **p** of marble and other stones.
Sir 26:18 Like golden **p** on silver bases,
1Mc 14:27 on bronze tablets and put it on **p** on Mount Zion.
4Mc 17: 3 Nobly set like a roof on the **p** of your sons,

PILLED (KJV) See PEELED

PILLOW (1)
1Es 3: 8 and they sealed them and put them under the **p**

PILOT (3) [PILOTS]
Ac 27:11 But the centurion paid more attention to the **p** and
Jas 3: 4 small rudder wherever the will of the **p** directs.
4Mc 7: 1 For like a most skillful **p**, the reason of our father

PILOTS (4) [PILOT]
Eze 27: 8 of Zemer were within you, they were your **p**.
27:27 your merchandise, your mariners and your **p**,
27:28 of the cry of your **p** the countryside shakes,
27:29 mariners and all the **p** of the sea stand on the shore

PILTAI (1)
Ne 12:17 of Abijah, Zichri; of Miniamin, of Moadiah, **P**;

PIM See Index to Footnotes

PIN (6)
Jdg 16:13 with the web and make it tight with the **p**,
16:14 and made them tight with the **p**.
16:14 he awoke from his sleep, and pulled away the **p**,
1Sa 18:11 for he thought, "I will **p** David to the wall."
19:10 Saul sought to **p** David to the wall with the spear;
26: 8 now therefore let me **p** him to the ground

PINE (7) [PINED]
Lev 26:16 that waste the eyes and cause life to **p** away.
SS 1:17 the beams of our house are cedar, our rafters are **p**.
Isa 24:16 But I say, I **p** away, I **p** away.
41:19 the plane and the **p** together,
60:13 and the **p**, to beautify the place of my sanctuary;
Eze 24:23 you shall not mourn or weep, but you shall **p** away

PINED (1) [PINE]
Wis 1:16 they **p** away and made a covenant with him,

PINES (1)
Eze 27: 6 they made your deck of **p** from the coasts

PINIONS (6)
Dt 32:11 takes them up, and bears them aloft on its **p**,
Job 39:13 though its **p** lack plumage.
Ps 68:13 a dove covered with silver, its **p** with green gold.
91: 4 he will cover you with his **p**, and
Eze 17: 3 A great eagle, with great wings and long **p**,
Wis 5:11 the light air, lashed by the beat of its **p** and pierced

PINNACLE (2) [PINNACLES]
Mt 4: 5 to the holy city and placed him on the **p** of
Lk 4: 9 and placed him on the **p** of the temple,

PINNACLES (1) [PINNACLE]
Isa 54:12 I will make your **p** of rubies, your gates of jewels,

PINON (2)
Ge 36:41 Oholibamah, Elah, **P**,
1Ch 1:52 Oholibamah, Elah, **P**,

PINS (KJV) See HANDBAGS, PEGS

PIONEER (2)
Heb 2:10 the **p** of their salvation perfect through sufferings.
12: 2 looking to Jesus the **p** and perfecter of our faith,

PIOUS (5) [PIETY]
Sir 11:22 The blessing of the Lord is the reward of the **p**,
26:23 *a **p** wife is given to the man who fears the Lord.*
2Mc 1:19 the **p** priests of that time took some of the fire of
12:45 it was a holy and **p** thought.
4Mc 10:15 and by the everlasting life of the **p**,

PIOUSLY (1) [PIETY]
4Mc 9: 6 the Hebrews because of their religion lived **p**

PIPE (8) [PIPES, PIPING]
Ge 4:21 the ancestor of all those who play the lyre and **p**.
Job 21:12 and rejoice to the sound of the **p**.
30:31 and my **p** to the voice of those who weep.
Ps 150: 4 praise him with strings and **p**!
Da 3: 5 horn, **p**, lyre, trigon, harp, drum,
3: 7 horn, **p**, lyre, trigon, harp, drum,
3:10 horn, **p**, lyre, trigon, harp, drum,
3:15 horn, **p**, lyre, trigon, harp, drum,

PIPES (2) [PIPE]
1Ki 1:40 playing on **p** and rejoicing with great joy,
Zec 4:12 which pour out the oil through the two golden **p**?"

PIPING (1) [PIPE]
Jdg 5:16 to hear the **p** for the flocks?

PIRAM (1)
Jos 10: 3 to King **P** of Jarmuth, to King Japhia of Lachish,

PIRATHON (4) [PIRATHONITE]
Jdg 12:15 and was buried at **P** in the land of Ephraim,
2Sa 23:30 Benaiah of **P**; Hiddai of the torrents of Gaash;
1Ch 11:31 of Gibeah of the Benjaminites, Benaiah of **P**,
27:14 for the eleventh month, was Benaiah of **P**,

PIRATHONITE (2) [PIRATHON]
Jdg 12:13 After him Abdon son of Hillel the **P** judged Israel.
12:15 Then Abdon son of Hillel the **P** died,

PISGAH (8)
Nu 21:20 the region of Moab by the top of **P** that overlooks
23:14 to the field of Zophim, to the top of **P**.
Dt 3:17 with the lower slopes of **P** on the east.
3:27 to the top of **P** and look around you to the west,
4:49 as the Sea of the Arabah, under the slopes of **P**.
34: 1 to the top of **P**, which is opposite Jericho,
Jos 12: 3 southward to the foot of the slopes of **P**;
13:20 and the slopes of **P**, and Beth-jeshimoth,

PISHON (2)
Ge 2:11 The name of the first is **P**;
Sir 24:25 It overflows, like the **P**, with wisdom,

PISIDIA (2)
Ac 13:14 on from Perga and came to Antioch in **P**.
14:24 they passed through **P** and came to Pamphylia.

PISON (KJV) See PISHON

PISPA (1)
1Ch 7:38 The sons of Jether: Jephunneh, **P**, and Ara.

PISS (KJV) See URINE

PISSETH (KJV) See MALE

PISTACHIO (1)
Ge 43:11 a little balm and a little honey, gum, resin, **p** nuts,

PIT‡ (89) [DUNG-PIT, PITFALL, PITFALLS, PITS]
Ge 37:22 throw him into this **p** here in the wilderness,
37:24 and they took him and threw him into a **p**.
37:24 The **p** was empty; there was no water in it.
37:28 they drew Joseph up, lifting him out of the **p**,
37:29 to the **p** and saw that Joseph was not in the **p**,
Ex 21:33 If someone leaves a **p** open, or digs a **p** and does
21:34 the owner of the **p** shall make restitution,
2Sa 18:17 threw him into a great **p** in the forest,
23:20 also went down and killed a lion in a **p** on a day
2Ki 10:14 and slaughtered them at the **p** of Beth-eked,
1Ch 11:22 also went down and killed a lion in a **p** on a day
Job 17:14 if I say to the **P**, 'You are my father,'
33:18 to spare their souls from the **P**,
33:22 Their souls draw near the **P**,
33:24 'Deliver him from going down into the **P**;
33:28 from going down to the **P**,
33:30 to bring back their souls from the **P**,
Ps 7:15 They make a **p**, digging it out,
9:15 The nations have sunk in the **p** that they made;
16:10 or let your faithful one see the **P**.
28: 1 I shall be like those who go down to the **P**.
30: 3 to life from among those gone down to the **P**.
30: 9 if I go down to the **P**?
35: 7 without cause they dug a **p** for my life.
40: 2 He drew me up from the desolate **p**,
55:23 O God, will cast them down into the lowest **p**;
57: 6 They dug a **p** in my path,
69:15 or the **P** close its mouth over me.
88: 4 I am counted among those who go down to the **P**;
88: 6 You have put me in the depths of the **P**,
94:13 until a **p** is dug for the wicked.
103: 4 who redeems your life from the **P**,
143: 7 or I shall be like those who go down to the **P**.
Pr 1:12 like those who go down to the **P**.
22:14 The mouth of a loose woman is a deep **p**;
23:27 For a prostitute is a deep **p**;
26:27 Whoever digs a **p** will fall into it,
28:18 whoever follows crooked ways will fall into the **P**.
Ecc 10: 8 Whoever digs a **p** will fall into it;
Isa 14:15 to the depths of the **P**.
14:19 who go down to the stones of the **P**,
24:17 Terror, and the **p**, and the snare are upon you,
24:18 at the sound of the terror shall fall into the **p**;
24:18 and whoever climbs out of the **p** shall be caught in
24:22 be gathered together like prisoners in a **p**;
38:17 but you have held back my life from the **p**
38:18 down to the **P** cannot hope for your faithfulness.
51:14 they shall not die and go down to the **P**,
Jer 18:20 Yet they have dug a **p** for my life.
18:22 For they have dug a **p** to catch me,
48:43 Terror, **p**, and trap are before you,
48:44 from the terror shall fall into the **p**,
48:44 and everyone who climbs out of the **p** shall
La 3:53 they flung me alive into a **p** and hurled stones
3:55 O LORD, from the depths of the **p**;
Eze 19: 4 he was caught in their **p**;
19: 8 he was caught in their **p**.
26:20 down with those who descend into the **P**,
26:20 with those who go down to the **P**,
28: 8 They shall thrust you down to the **P**,
31:14 with those who go down to the **P**.
31:16 down to Sheol with those who go down to the **P**;
32:18 with those who go down to the **P**.
32:23 in the uttermost parts of the **P**.
32:24 with those who go down to the **P**.
32:25 with those who go down to the **P**;

Eze 32:29 with those who go down to the **P.**
32:30 with those who go down to the **P.**
Hos 5: 2 and a **p** dug deep in Shittim;
Jnh 2: 6 yet you brought up my life from the **P,**
Zec 9:11 I will set your prisoners free from the waterless **p.**
Mt 12:11 of you has only one sheep and it falls into a **p** on
15:14 both will fall into a **p."**
Mk 12: 1 dug a **p** for the wine press, and built a watchtower;
Lk 6:39 Will not both fall into a **p?**
Rev 9: 1 the key to the shaft of the bottomless **p;**
9: 2 he opened the shaft of the bottomless **p,**
9:11 as king over them the angel of the bottomless **p;**
11: 7 up from the bottomless **p** will make war on them
17: 8 about to ascend from the bottomless **p** and go
20: 1 holding in his hand the key to the bottomless **p**
20: 3 and threw him into the **p,**
Sir 12:16 but in his heart he plans to throw you into a **p;**
21:10 but at its end is the **p** of Hades.
27:26 Whoever digs a **p** will fall into it,
1Mc 7:19 and killed them and threw them into a great **p.**
2Es 7:*36* The **p** of torment shall appear,

PITCH (13) [PITCHED, PITCHER, PITCHERS, PITCHES]

Ge 6:14 and cover it inside and out with **p.**
Ex 2: 3 and plastered it with bitumen and **p;**
33: 7 Now Moses used to take the tent and **p** it outside
Isa 13:20 Arabs will not **p** their tents there,
34: 9 And the streams of Edom shall be turned into **p,**
34: 9 her land shall become burning **p.**
Jer 6: 3 They shall **p** their tents around her;
Eze 25: 4 among you and **p** their tents in your midst;
Da 11:45 He shall **p** his palatial tents between the sea and
Sir 13: 1 Whoever touches **p** gets dirty,
Aza 1:23 in kept stoking the furnace with naphtha, **p,** tow,
Bel 1:27 Then Daniel took **p,** fat, and hair,
2Es 2: 9 whose land lies in lumps of **p** and heaps of ashes.

PITCHED (13) [PITCH]

Ge 12: 8 and **p** his tent, with Bethel on the west and Ai on
26:25 on the name of the LORD, and **p** his tent there.
31:25 Now Jacob had **p** his tent in the hill country,
33:19 the plot of land on which he had **p** his tent.
35:21 and **p** his tent beyond the tower of Eder.
Nu 1:51 the tabernacle is to be **p,** the Levites shall set it up.
2Sa 6:17 inside the tent that David had **p** for it;
16:22 So they **p** a tent for Absalom upon the roof;
1Ch 15: 1 and he prepared a place for the ark of God and **p**
16: 1 and set it inside the tent that David had **p** for it;
2Ch 1: 4 for he had **p** a tent for it in Jerusalem.)
Wis 11: 2 and **p** their tents in untrodden places.
2Mc 13:14 and commonwealth, he **p** his camp near Modein.

PITCHER (2) [PITCH]

Ecc 12: 6 and the **p** is broken at the fountain,
4Mc 3:12 and taking a **p** climbed over the enemy's ramparts.

PITCHERS (1) [PITCH]

Jer 35: 5 Then I set before the Rechabites **p** full of wine,

PITCHES (1) [PITCH]

Sir 14:25 who **p** his tent near her, and so occupies

PITEOUS (1) [PITY]

Wis 18:10 of their enemies echoed back, and their **p** lament

PITEOUSLY (1) [PITY]

4Mc 15:18 nor when the second in torments looked at you **p**

PITFALL (2) [PIT]

Job 18: 8 and they walk into a **p.**
La 3:47 panic and **p** have come upon us,

PITFALLS (2) [PIT]

Ps 119:85 arrogant have dug **p** for me; they flout your law.
Sir 39:24 but full of **p** for the wicked.

PITHOM (1)

Ex 1:11 They built supply cities, **P** and Rameses,

PITHON (2)

1Ch 8:35 The sons of Micah: **P,** Melech, Tarea, and Ahaz.
9:41 The sons of Micah: **P,** Melech, Tahrea, and Ahaz;

PITIABLE (3) [PITY]

Rev 3:17 You do not realize that you are wretched, **p,** poor,
2Mc 3:21 There was something **p** in the prostration of
9:28 came to the end of his life by a most **p** fate,

PITIED‡ (4) [PITY]

Ps 106:46 to be **p** by all who held them captive.
Eze 16: 5 No eye **p** you, to do any of these things
1Co 15:19 we are of all people most to be **p.**
2Es 1:19 I **p** your groanings and gave you manna for food;

PITIES (2) [PITY]

Sir 12:13 Who **p** a snake charmer when he is bitten,
12:14 So no one **p** a person who associates with a sinner

PITIFUL (2) [PITY]

3Mc 5:24 city had been assembled for this most **p** spectacle
5:47 and **p** destruction of the aforementioned people.

PITILESS (2) [PITY]

Wis 19: 1 the ungodly were assailed to the end by **p** anger,
3Mc 5:10 the **p** elephants until they had been filled with

PITS‡ (9) [PIT]

Ge 14:10 Now the Valley of Siddim was full of bitumen **p;**
37:20 let us kill him and throw him into one of the **p;**
2Sa 17: 9 Even now he has hidden himself in one of the **p,**
Ps 140:10 Let them be flung into **p,** no more to rise!
Pr 28:10 into evil ways will fall into **p** of their own making,
Jer 2: 6 in a land of deserts and **p,**
La 4:20 the breath of our life, was taken in their **p—**
Zep 2: 9 a land possessed by nettles and salt **p,**
1Mc 11:35 and the salt **p** and the crown taxes due to us—

PITY (64) [PITEOUS, PITEOUSLY, PITIABLE, PITIED, PITIES, PITIFUL, PITILESS]

Ex 2: 6 He was crying, and she took **p** on him,
Dt 7:16 over to you, showing them no **p;**
13: 8 Show them no **p** or compassion and do
19:13 Show no **p;** you shall purge the guilt of innocent
19:21 Show no **p:** life for life, eye for eye,
25:12 you shall cut off her hand; show no **p.**
Jdg 2:18 be moved to **p** by their groaning because
2Sa 12: 6 and because he had no **p."**
Job 19:21 Have **p** on me, have **p** on me, O you my friends,
27:22 It hurls at them without **p;**
Ps 17:10 They close their hearts to **p;**
69:20 I looked for **p,** but there was none;
72:13 He has **p** on the weak and the needy,
102:14 and have **p** on its dust.
109:12 nor anyone to **p** his orphaned children.
Isa 9:17 not have **p** on their young people, or compassion
13:18 their eyes will not **p** children.
49:10 for he who has **p** on them will lead them,
63: 9 in his love and in his **p** he redeemed them;
Jer 13:14 I will not **p** or spare or have compassion
15: 5 Who will have **p** on you, O Jerusalem,
20:16 the cities that the LORD overthrew without **p;**
21: 7 he shall not **p** them, or spare them,
La 2:17 he has demolished without **p;**
3:43 with anger and pursued us, killing without **p;**
Eze 5:11 my eye will not spare, and I will have no **p.**
7: 4 My eye will not spare you, I will have no **p.**
7: 9 My eye will not spare; I will have no **p.**
8:18 my eye will not spare, nor will I have **p;**
9: 5 your eye shall not spare, and you shall show no **p.**
9:10 for me, my eye will not spare, nor will I have **p,**
Hos 1: 6 for I will no longer have **p** on the house of Israel
1: 7 But I will have **p** on the house of Judah,
2: 4 Upon her children also I will have no **p,**
2:23 And I will have **p** on Lo-ruhamah,
Joel 2:18 and had **p** on his people.
Am 1:11 with the sword and cast off all **p;**
Zec 11: 5 and their own shepherds have no **p** on them.
11: 6 For I will no longer have **p** on the inhabitants of
Mt 18:27 And out of **p** for him,
Mk 1:41 Moved with **p,** Jesus stretched out his hand
9:22 have **p** on us and help us."
Lk 10:33 and when he saw him, he was moved with **p.**
Jdt 6:19 and have **p** on our people in their humiliation,
AdE 13: 6 the swords of their enemies, without **p** or restraint,
Sir 16: 9 He showed no **p** on the doomed nation,
36:18 Have **p** on the city of your sanctuary,
Bar 4:15 which had no respect for the aged and no **p** for
LtJ 6:38 They cannot take **p** on a widow or do good to
2Mc 4:37 Antiochus was grieved at heart and filled with **p,**
7:27 "My son, have **p** on me.
8: 2 to have **p** on the temple that had been profaned by
3Mc 4: 4 the common object of **p** before their eyes,
6:22 the king's anger was turned to **p** and tears because
2Es 8:32 For if you have desired to have **p** on us,
15:19 People shall have no **p** for their neighbors,
4Mc 5:33 not so **p** my old age as to break the ancestral law
6:12 At that point, partly out of **p** for his old age,
8:10 Therefore take **p** on yourselves.
8:20 Let us take **p** on our youth and have compassion
9: 3 for us do not **p** us more than we **p** ourselves.
9: 4 For we consider this **p** of yours,

PIVOTS (1)

Isa 6: 4 The **p** on the thresholds shook at the voices

PLACE‡ (940) [PLACED, PLACES, PLACING, REPLACED]

A. HOLY PLACE (78)
B. HIGH PLACE (16)
C. MOST HOLY PLACE (13)

Ge 1: 9 under the sky be gathered together into one **p,**
2:21 then he took one of his ribs and closed up its **p**
8: 9 but the dove found no **p** to set its foot,
12: 6 Abram passed through the land to the **p**
13: 3 to the **p** where his tent had been at the beginning,
13: 4 to the **p** where he had made an altar at the first;
13:14 and look from the **p** where you are,
18:24 will you then sweep away the **p** and not forgive it
18:26 I will forgive the whole **p** for their sake."
18:33 and Abraham returned to his **p.**
19:12 bring them out of the **p.**
19:13 For we are about to destroy this **p,**
19:14 to marry his daughters, "Up, get out of this **p;**
19:27 in the morning to the **p** where he had stood before
20:11 There is no fear of God at all in this **p,**
20:13 at every **p** to which we come, say of me,
21:31 Therefore that **p** was called Beer-sheba;
22: 3 the burnt offering, and set out and went to the **p** in
22: 4 up and saw the **p** far away.
22: 9 When they came to the **p** that God had shown him,
22:14 Abraham called that **p** "The LORD will provide";
23: 4 give me property among you for a burying **p,**
23: 9 in your presence as a possession for a burying **p."**
23:20 into Abraham's possession as a burying **p.**
24:25 of straw and fodder and a **p** to spend the night."
24:31 when I have prepared the house and a **p** for
26: 7 When the men of the **p** asked him about his wife,
26: 7 of the **p** might kill me for the sake of Rebekah,
28:11 to a certain **p** and stayed there for the night,
28:11 Taking one of the stones of the **p,**
28:11 he put it under his head and lay down in that **p.**
28:16 "Surely the LORD is in this **p—**
28:17 he was afraid, and said, "How awesome is this **p!**
28:19 He called that **p** Bethel;
29: 3 the stone back in its **p** on the mouth of the well.
29:22 So Laban gathered together all the people of the **p,**
30: 2 "Am I in the **p** of God,
32: 2 So he called that **p** Mahanaim.
32:30 So Jacob called the **p** Peniel, saying,
33:17 therefore the **p** is called Succoth.
35: 7 there he built an altar and called the **p** El-bethel,
35:13 from him at the **p** where he had spoken with him.
35:14 up a pillar in the **p** where he had spoken with him,
35:15 the **p** where God had spoken with him Bethel.
39:20 the **p** where the king's prisoners were confined;
40:13 and you shall **p** Pharaoh's cup in his hand,
40:14 and so get me out of this **p.**
42:15 as Pharaoh lives, you shall not leave this **p**
42:27 to give his donkey fodder at the lodging **p,**
43:21 we came to the lodging **p** we opened our sacks,
44:33 as a slave to my lord in **p** of the boy;
47:30 of Egypt and bury me in their burial **p."**
49:15 he saw that a resting **p** was good,
50:11 Therefore the **p** was named Abel-mizraim;
50:19 Am I in the **p** of God?
Ex 3: 5 the **p** on which you are standing is holy ground."
4:24 On the way, at a **p** where they spent the night,
9:19 in the open field brought to a secure **p;**
9:20 and livestock off to a secure **p.**
13:22 nor the pillar of fire by night left its **p** in front of
14:19 from in front of them and took its **p** behind them.
15:17 the **p,** O LORD, that you made your abode,
16:29 do not leave your **p** on the seventh day."
16:33 and **p** it before the LORD,
17: 7 He called the **p** Massah and Meribah,
20:24 in every **p** where I cause my name to
21:13 for you a **p** to which the killer may flee.
23:20 to guard you on the way and to bring you to the **p**
26:33 curtain shall separate for you the holy **p** from A
26:34 on the ark of the covenant in the most holy **p.** AC
28:29 on his heart when he goes into the holy **p,** A
28:35 when he goes into the holy **p** before the LORD, A
28:43 come near the altar to minister in the holy **p;** A
29:24 and you shall **p** all these on the palms of Aaron
29:30 in his **p** shall wear them seven days,
29:30 the tent of meeting to minister in the holy **p.** A
29:31 and boil its flesh in a holy **p;** A
30: 6 You shall **p** it in front of the curtain that is above
31:11 and the fragrant incense for the holy **p.** A
32:34 lead the people to the **p** about which I have spoken
33: 1 The LORD said to Moses, "Go, leave this **p,**
33:21 a **p** by me where you shall stand on the rock;
35:19 for ministering in the holy **p,** A
39: 1 for ministering in the holy **p;** A
39:41 for ministering in the holy **p,** A
40: 7 and **p** the basin between the tent of meeting and
40:28 in **p** the screen for the entrance of the tabernacle.
Lev 1:16 and throw it at the east side of the altar, in the **p**
4:12 he shall carry out to a clean **p** outside the camp,
4:29 and the sin offering shall be slaughtered at the **p** of
6:10 and **p** them beside the altar.
6:11 carry the ashes out to a clean **p** outside the camp.
6:16 it shall be eaten as unleavened cakes in a holy **p;** A
6:26 it shall be eaten in a holy **p,** A
6:27 you shall wash the bespattered part in a holy **p.** A
6:30 the tent of meeting for atonement in the holy **p;** A
7: 6 it shall be eaten in a holy **p;** it is most holy. A
10: 4 the front of the sanctuary to a **p** outside the camp."
10:13 shall eat it in a holy **p,** because it is your due A
10:14 and daughters as well may eat in any clean **p;**
13:19 the **p** of the boil there appears a white swelling or
13:23 if the spot remains in one **p** and does not spread,
13:28 if the spot remains in one **p** and does not spread in
14:13 the lamb in the **p** where the sin offering and
14:13 the burnt offering are slaughtered in the holy **p;** A
14:40 be taken out and thrown into an unclean **p** outside
14:41 be dumped in an unclean **p** outside the city.
14:42 They shall take other stones and put them in the **p**
14:45 and taken outside the city to an unclean **p.**
16: 3 Thus shall Aaron come into the holy **p:** A
16:20 When he has finished atoning for the holy **p** A
16:23 that he put on when he went into the holy **p,** A
16:24 He shall bathe his body in water in a holy **p,** A
16:27 in the holy **p,** shall be taken outside the camp; A
16:32 as priest in his father's **p** shall make atonement,
24: 6 You shall **p** them in two rows, six in a row,

Lev 24: 9 who shall eat them in a holy **p,** A
26: 1 and you shall not **p** figured stones in your land,
26:11 I will **p** my dwelling in your midst,
Nu 4: 6 and shall put its poles in **p.**
4: 8 and shall put its poles in **p.**
4:11 and shall put its poles in **p;**
4:14 and shall put its poles in **p.**
5:18 **p** in her hands the grain offering of remembrance,
8:16 in **p** of all that open the womb,
8:18 in **p** of all the firstborn among the Israelites.
9:17 and in the **p** where the cloud settled down,
10:29 for the **p** of which the LORD said, 'I will give it
10:33 to seek out a resting **p** for them,
11: 3 So that **p** was called Taberah,
11:16 and have them take their **p** there with you.
11:34 So that **p** was called Kibroth-hattaavah,
13:24 That **p** was called the Wadi Eshcol,
14:40 up to the **p** that the LORD has promised,
17: 4 **P** them in the tent of meeting before the covenant,
18:31 You may eat it in any **p,** you and your households;
19: 9 and deposit them outside the camp in a clean **p;**
20: 5 to bring us to this wretched **p?**
20: 5 It is no **p** for grain, or figs, or vines,
21: 3 so the **p** was called Hormah.
22:26 and stood in a narrow **p,**
23:13 to another **p** from which you may see them;
23:27 "Come now, I will take you to another **p;**
24:21 "Enduring is your dwelling **p,**
24:25 Then Balaam got up and went back to his **p,**
32: 1 and the land of Gilead was a good **p** for cattle,
32:14 a brood of sinners, have risen in **p** of your fathers,
32:17 until we have brought them to their **p.**
Dt 1:31 the way that you traveled until you reached this **p.**
1:33 who goes before you on the way to seek out a **p**
2:12 destroying them and settling in their **p,**
2:21 they could dispossess them and settle in their **p.**
2:22 and settle in their **p** even to this day.
2:23 destroyed them and settled in their **p.**)
9: 7 of the land of Egypt until you came to this **p.**
11: 5 until you came to this **p;**
11:24 Every **p** on which you set foot shall be yours;
12: 5 the **p** that the LORD your God will choose out
12:11 to the **p** that the LORD your God will choose as
12:13 not offer your burnt offerings at any **p** you happen
12:14 But only at the **p** that the LORD will choose
12:18 the presence of the LORD your God at the **p** that
12:21 If the **p** where the LORD your God will choose
12:26 to the **p** that the LORD will choose.
13: 2 the omens or the portents declared by them take **p,**
14:23 in the **p** that he will choose as a dwelling
14:24 the **p** where the LORD your God will choose
14:25 go to the **p** that the LORD your God will choose;
15:20 of the LORD your God year by year at the **p** that
16: 2 at the **p** that the LORD will choose as a dwelling
16: 6 But at the **p** that the LORD your God will choose
16: 7 at the **p** that the LORD your God will choose;
16:11 at the **p** that the LORD your God will choose as
16:15 the festival for the LORD your God at the **p** that
16:16 the LORD your God at the **p** that he will choose:
17: 8 up to the **p** that the LORD your God will choose,
17:10 the decision that they announce to you from the **p**
18: 6 and comes to the **p** that the LORD will choose
18:22 of the LORD but the thing does not take **p**
21:19 to the elders of his town at the gate of that **p.**
23:16 in any **p** they choose in any one of your towns,
26: 2 and you shall put it in a basket and go to the **p** that
26: 9 and he brought us into this **p** and gave us this land,
28:65 no resting **p** for the sole of your foot.
29: 7 When you came to this **p,**
31:11 the LORD your God at the **p** that he will choose,
33:10 they **p** incense before you,
34: 6 but no one knows his burial **p** to this day.
Jos 1: 3 Every **p** that the sole of your foot will tread
1:13 LORD your God is providing you a **p** of rest,
3: 3 then you shall set out from your **p.**
4: 3 from the **p** where the priests' feet stood,
4: 3 down in the **p** where you camp tonight.' "
4: 8 over with them to the **p** where they camped,
4: 9 the **p** where the feet of the priests bearing the ark
4:18 the waters of the Jordan returned to their **p**
5: 7 it was their children, whom he raised up in their **p,**
5: 9 And so that **p** is called Gilgal to this day.
5:15 for the **p** where you stand is holy."
7:26 that **p** to this day is called the Valley of Achor.
8: 9 and they went to the **p** of ambush,
8:14 in the morning to the meeting **p** facing the Arabah
8:19 the troops in ambush rose quickly out of their **p**
9:27 in the **p** that he should choose.
20: 4 fugitive shall be taken into the city, and given a **p,**
Jdg 2: 5 So they named that **p** Bochim,
7:21 Every man stood in his **p** all around the camp,
11:23 Do you intend to take their **p?**
15:17 and that **p** was called Ramath-lehi.
15:19 So God split open the hollow **p** that is at Lehi,
17: 8 to live wherever he could find a **p.**
17: 9 and I am going to live wherever I can find a **p."**
18: 3 What are you doing in this **p?**
18:10 a **p** where there is no lack of anything on earth."
18:12 On this account that **p** is called Mahaneh-dan
19:16 (The people of the **p** were Benjaminites.)
20:22 and again formed the battle line in the same **p**
20:33 in ambush rushed out of their **p** west of Geba.
20:43 from Nohah and trod them down as far as a **p** east
21:19 yearly festival of the LORD is taking **p** at Shiloh,
Ru 1: 7 she set out from the **p** where she had been living,
3: 4 When he lies down, observe the **p** where he lies;
4:10 and from the gate of his native **p;**
1Sa 3: 9 So Samuel went and lay down in his **p.**
5: 3 So they took Dagon and put him back in his **p.**
5:11 and let it return to its own **p,**
6: 2 Tell us what we should send with it to its **p."**
6: 8 Take the ark of the LORD and **p** it on the cart,
9:22 a **p** at the head of those who had been invited,
10: 5 at the **p** where the Philistine garrison is;
10:12 man of the **p** answered, "And who is their father?"
12: 8 and settled them in this **p.**
14: 9 then we will stand still in our **p,**
14:46 and the Philistines went to their own **p.**
19: 2 stay in a secret **p** and hide yourself.
20:18 you will be missed, because your **p** will be empty.
20:19 go to the **p** where you hid yourself earlier,
20:25 but David's **p** was empty.
20:27 the day after the new moon, David's **p** was empty.
20:37 to the **p** where Jonathan's arrow had fallen,
21: 2 with the young men for such and such a **p.**
23:28 therefore that **p** was called the Rock of Escape.
26: 5 and came to the **p** where Saul had encamped;
26: 5 and David saw the **p** where Saul lay,
26:25 So David went his way, and Saul returned to his **p.**
27: 5 let a **p** be given me in one of the country towns,
29: 4 that he may return to the **p** that you have assigned
29:10 and go to the **p** that I appointed for you.
2Sa 2:16 Therefore that **p** was called Helkath-hazzurim,
2:23 to the **p** where Asahel had fallen and died,
5:20 Therefore that **p** is called Baal-perazim.
6: 8 so that **p** is called Perez-uzzah, to this day.
6:17 in its **p,** inside the tent that David had pitched
6:21 in **p** of your father and all his household,
7:10 a **p** for my people Israel and will plant them,
7:10 so that they may live in their own **p,**
11:16 the **p** where he knew there were valiant warriors.
15:25 and let me see both it and the **p** where it stays.
16: 8 in whose **p** you have reigned;
17: 9 in one of the pits, or in some other **p.**
17:12 in whatever **p** he may be found, and we shall light
17:25 over the army in the **p** of Joab.
19:13 not the commander of my army from now on, in **p**
19:18 while the crossing was taking **p,**
21: 5 we should have no **p** in all the territory of Israel—
21:18 this a battle took **p** with the Philistines, at Gob;
22:20 He brought me out into a broad **p;**
1Ki 1:30 and he shall sit on my throne in my **p,'**
1:35 he shall be king in my **p;**
2:35 of Jehoiada over the army in his **p,**
2:35 the king put the priest Zadok in the **p** of Abiathar.
2:36 and do not go out from there to any **p** whatever.
2:42 on the day you go out and go to any **p** whatever,
3: 4 for that was the principal high **p;** B
3: 7 in **p** of my father David, although I am only
4:28 also brought to the required **p** barley and straw for
5: 1 that they had anointed him king in **p** of his father;
5: 5 whom I will set on your throne in your **p,**
5: 9 into rafts to go by sea to the **p** you indicate.
6:16 as an inner sanctuary, as the most holy **p.** AC
7:50 innermost part of the house, the most holy **p,** AC
8: 6 the ark of the covenant of the LORD to its **p,**
8: 6 of the house, in the most holy **p,** underneath AC
8: 7 For the cherubim spread out their wings over the **p**
8: 8 ends of the poles were seen from the holy **p** in A
8:10 And when the priests came out of the holy **p,** A
8:13 a **p** for you to dwell in forever."
8:20 for I have risen in the **p** of my father David;
8:21 There I have provided a **p** for the ark,
8:29 the **p** of which you said, 'My name shall be there,'
8:29 the prayer that your servant prays toward this **p.**
8:30 when they pray toward this **p;**
8:30 O hear in heaven your dwelling **p;**
8:35 and then they pray toward this **p,**
8:39 then hear in heaven your dwelling **p,** forgive, act,
8:43 then hear in heaven your dwelling **p,**
8:49 then hear in heaven your dwelling **p** their prayer
11: 7 a high **p** for Chemosh the abomination of Moab, B
13: 8 nor will I eat food or drink water in this **p.**
13:16 will I eat food or drink water with you in this **p,**
13:22 and drunk water in the **p** of which he said to you,
19: 9 At that **p** he came to a cave,
19:16 of Shaphat of Abel-meholah as prophet in your **p.**
20:24 and put commanders in **p** of them;
21: 1 Later the following events took **p:**
21:19 the **p** where dogs licked up the blood of Naboth,
2Ki 6: 1 the **p** where we live under your charge is too small
6: 2 and build a **p** there for us to live."
6: 6 When he showed him the **p,** he cut off a stick,
6: 8 He said, "At such and such a **p** shall be my camp."
6: 9 "Take care not to pass this **p,**
6:10 The king of Israel sent word to the **p** of which
6:10 More than once or twice he warned such a **p** so
15:10 and reigned in **p** of him.
15:14 he reigned in **p** of him.
15:25 he killed him, and reigned in **p** of him.
15:30 he reigned in **p** of him,
16:14 from the **p** between his altar and the house of
17:24 in the cities of Samaria in **p** of the people of Israel;
18:25 that I have come up against this **p** to destroy it?
21:24 of the land made his son Josiah king in **p** of him.
22:16 I will indeed bring disaster on this **p** and
22:17 therefore my wrath will be kindled against this **p,**
22:19 when you heard how I spoke against this **p,**
22:20 not see all the disaster that I will bring on this **p."**
23:15 the high **p** erected by Jeroboam son of Nebat, B
23:15 he pulled down that altar along with the high **p.** B
23:15 He burned the high **p,** crushing it to dust; B
23:30 and made him king in **p** of his father.
23:34 of Josiah king in **p** of his father Josiah,
2Ki 24:17 king in his **p,** and changed his name to Zedekiah.
1Ch 4:41 in their **p,** because there was pasture there
6:49 doing all the work of the most holy **p,** AC
13:11 so that **p** is called Perez-uzzah to this day.
14:11 Therefore that **p** is called Baal-perazim.
15: 1 and he prepared a **p** for the ark of God and pitched
15: 3 to bring up the ark of the LORD to its **p,**
15:12 to the **p** that I have prepared for it.
16:27 strength and joy are in his **p.**
16:39 the tabernacle of the LORD in the high **p** that B
17: 9 I will appoint a **p** for my people Israel,
17: 9 so that they may live in their own **p,**
21:29 of burnt offering were at that time in the high **p** B
2Ch 1: 3 went to the high **p** that was at Gibeon; B
1: 4 the ark of God up from Kiriath-jearim to the **p**
1:13 So Solomon came from the high **p** at Gibeon, B
2: 6 except as a **p** to make offerings before him?
3: 1 at the **p** that David had designated,
3: 8 He made the most holy **p;** AC
3:10 the most holy **p** he made two carved cherubim AC
4:22 the inner doors to the most holy **p** and the AC
5: 7 the ark of the covenant of the LORD to its **p,**
5: 7 of the house, in the most holy **p,** underneath AC
5: 8 the cherubim spread out their wings over the **p**
5: 9 ends of the poles were seen from the holy **p** in A
5:11 when the priests came out of the holy **p** (for all A
6: 2 a **p** for you to reside in forever."
6:20 the **p** where you promised to set your name,
6:20 the prayer that your servant prays toward this **p.**
6:21 when they pray toward this **p;**
6:21 may you hear from heaven your dwelling **p;**
6:26 and then they pray toward this **p,**
6:30 from heaven, your dwelling **p,** forgive, and render
6:33 may you hear from heaven your dwelling **p,**
6:39 from heaven your dwelling **p** their prayer
6:40 and your ears attentive to prayer from this **p.**
6:41 rise up, O LORD God, and go to your resting **p,**
7:12 "I have heard your prayer, and have chosen this **p**
7:15 to the prayer that is made in this **p.**
12:10 but King Rehoboam made in **p** of them shields
20:26 that **p** has been called the Valley of Beracah
24:11 the chest and take it and return it to its **p.**
29: 5 and carry out the filth from the holy **p.** A
29: 7 made burnt offerings in the holy **p** to the God A
34:24 I will indeed bring disaster upon this **p** and
34:25 my wrath will be poured out on this **p** and will not
34:27 when you heard his words against this **p**
34:28 not see all the disaster that I will bring on this **p**
34:31 in his **p** and made a covenant before the LORD,
35: 5 in the holy **p** according to the groupings of A
35:10 the priests stood in their **p,**
35:15 in their **p** according to the command of David,
36:15 on his people and on his dwelling **p;**
Ezr 1: 4 in whatever **p** they reside,
1: 4 be assisted by the people of their **p** with silver
6: 3 of God at Jerusalem, let the house be rebuilt, the **p**
6: 5 to the temple in Jerusalem, each to its **p;**
8:17 the leader at the **p** called Casiphia,
9: 8 and given us a stake in his holy **p,** A
Ne 1: 9 and bring them to the **p** at which I have chosen
2: 3 when the city, the **p** of my ancestors' graves,
2:14 but there was no **p** for the animal I was riding
9: 3 They stood up in their **p** and read from the book of
13: 6 While this was taking **p** I was not in Jerusalem,
Est 2: 9 and advanced her and her maids to the best **p** in
Job 6:17 when it is hot, they vanish from their **p.**
8: 6 for you and restore to you your rightful **p.**
8:18 If they are destroyed from their **p,**
9: 6 the earth out of its **p,** and its pillars tremble;
14:18 and the rock is removed from its **p;**
16: 4 I also could talk as you do, if you were in my **p;**
16:18 let my outcry find no resting **p.**
18: 4 or the rock be removed out of its **p?**
18:21 such is the **p** of those who do not know God."
20: 9 nor will their **p** behold them any longer.
27:21 it sweeps them out of their **p.**
27:23 and hisses at them from its **p.**
28: 1 and a **p** for gold to be refined.
28: 6 Its stones are the **p** of sapphires,
28:12 And where is the **p** of understanding?
28:20 And where is the **p** of understanding?
28:23 the way to it, and he knows its **p.**
34:24 and sets others in their **p.**
36:16 He also allured you out of distress into a broad **p**
36:20 when peoples are cut off in their **p.**
37: 1 and leaps out of its **p.**
38:12 and caused the dawn to know its **p,**
38:19 and where is the **p** of darkness,
38:24 the way to the **p** where the light is distributed,
39: 6 the salt land for its dwelling **p?**
Ps 12: 5 "I will **p** them in the safety for which they long."
18:19 He brought me out into a broad **p;**
18:36 You gave me a wide **p** for my steps under me,
24: 3 And who shall stand in his holy **p?** A
26: 8 and the **p** where your glory abides.
31: 8 you have set my feet in a broad **p.**
32: 7 You are a hiding **p** for me;
37:10 though you look diligently for their **p,**
45:16 In the **p** of ancestors you, O king, shall have sons;
66:12 yet you have brought us out to a spacious **p.**
68:17 the Lord came from Sinai into the holy **p.** A
74: 4 Your foes have roared within your holy **p;** A
74: 7 they desecrated the dwelling **p** of your name,
76: 2 in Salem, his dwelling **p** in Zion.
81: 7 I answered you in the secret **p** of thunder;
82: 1 God has taken his **p** in the divine council;
84: 1 How lovely is your dwelling **p,**

Ps 84: 6 the valley of Baca they make it a p of springs;
90: 1 you have been our dwelling p in all generations.
91: 9 the Most High your dwelling p,
103:16 and it is gone, and its p knows it no more.
104: 8 ran down to the valleys to the p that you appointed
118: 5 the LORD answered me and set me in a broad p.
119:114 You are my hiding p and my shield;
132: 5 until I find a p for the LORD,
132: 5 a dwelling p for the Mighty One of Jacob."
132: 7 "Let us go to his dwelling p;
132: 8 Rise up, O LORD, and go to your resting p,
132:14 "This is my resting p forever;
134: 2 Lift up your hands to the holy p, A
Pr 4: 9 She will p on your head a fair garland;
15: 3 The eyes of the LORD are in every p,
24:15 do no violence to the p where the righteous live;
25: 6 the king's presence or stand in the p of the great;
Ecc 1: 5 and hurries to the p where it rises.
1: 7 to the p where the streams flow,
3:16 I saw under the sun that in the p of justice,
3:16 and in the p of righteousness,
3:20 All go to one p; all are from the
6: 6 do not all go to one p?
8:10 they used to go in and out of the holy p, A
8:14 There is a vanity that takes p on earth,
10: 6 and the rich sit in a low p.
11: 3 in the p where the tree falls, there it will lie.
Isa 7:23 On that day every p where there used to be
7:25 but they will become a p where cattle are let loose
9:10 but we will put cedars in their p."
13:13 and the earth will be shaken out of its p,
14: 2 nations will take them and bring them to their p,
16:12 when he wearies himself upon the high p, B
18: 7 the p of the name of the LORD of hosts.
22:22 I will p on his shoulder the key of the house
22:23 I will fasten him like a peg in a secure p,
22:25 peg that was fastened in a secure p will give way;
25: 5 of aliens like heat in a dry p, you subdued the heat
25:10 in their p as straw is trodden down in a dung-pit.
26:21 from his p to punish the inhabitants of the earth
28: 8 covered with filthy vomit; no p is clean.
28:25 and plant wheat in rows and barley in its proper p,
30:28 of destruction, and to p on the jaws of the peoples
30:33 For his burning p has long been prepared;
32: 2 Each will be like a hiding p from the wind,
32: 2 like streams of water in a dry p,
33:21 But there the LORD in majesty will be for us a p
33:23 it cannot hold the mast firm in its p,
34:14 there too Lilith shall repose, and find a p to rest.
46: 7 they carry it, they set it in its p, and it stands there;
46: 7 it cannot move from its p.
49:20 "The p is too crowded for me;
57:15 I dwell in the high and holy p, A
60:13 and the pine, to beautify the p of my sanctuary;
65:10 and the Valley of Achor a p for herds to lie down,
66: 1 and what is my resting p?
Jer 4: 7 he has gone out from his p to make your land
7: 3 and let me dwell with you in this p.
7: 6 and the widow, or shed innocent blood in this p,
7: 7 then I will dwell with you in this p,
7:12 Go now to my p that was in Shiloh,
7:14 to the p that I gave to you and to your ancestors,
7:20 on this p, on human beings and animals,
7:31 And they go on building the high p of Topheth, B
9: 2 O that I had in the desert a traveler's lodging p,
13: 7 the loincloth from the p where I had hidden it.
14:13 but I will give you true peace in this p.' "
16: 2 nor shall you have sons or daughters in this p.
16: 3 the sons and daughters who are born in this p, and
16: 9 I am going to banish from this p,
19: 3 I am going to bring such disaster upon this p that
19: 4 and have profaned this p by making offerings in it
19: 4 and because they have filled this p with the blood
19: 6 when this p shall no more be called Topheth,
19: 7 And in this p I will make void the plans of Judah
19:12 Thus will I do to this p, says the LORD,
19:13 of Judah shall be defiled like the p of Topheth—
22: 3 and the widow, or shed innocent blood in this p.
22:11 and who went away from this p:
22:12 but in the p where they have carried him captive
24: 5 from Judah, whom I have sent away from this p to
26:23 and threw his dead body into the burial p of
27:22 I will bring them up and restore them to this p.
28: 3 to this p all the vessels of the LORD's house,
28: 3 of Babylon took away from this p and carried
28: 4 to this p King Jeconiah son of Jehoiakim of Judah,
28: 6 that you have prophesied, and bring back to this p
28:13 to forge iron bars in p of them!
29:10 to you my promise and bring you back to this p.
29:14 to the p from which I sent you into exile.
32:37 I will bring them back to this p,
33:10 Thus says the LORD: In this p of which you say,
33:12 In this p that is waste,
40: 2 "The LORD your God threatened this p
42:18 You shall see this p no more.
42:22 and by pestilence in the p where you desire to go
44:29 that I am going to punish you in this p,
45: 5 as a prize of war in every p to which you may go."
48:35 at a high p and make offerings to their gods. B
51:62 to destroy this p so that neither human beings
La 1: 3 now among the nations, and finds no resting p;
Eze 3:12 and as the glory of the LORD rose from its p,
4: 3 an iron plate and p it as an iron wall between you
4: 4 p the punishment of the house of Israel upon it;
7:22 so that they may profane my treasured p;
12: 3 from your p to another p in their sight.
14: 4 and p their iniquity as a stumbling block

Eze 16:24 and made yourself a lofty p in every square;
16:25 at the head of every street you built your lofty p
16:31 and making your lofty p in every square!
17:16 the p where the king resides who made him king,
20:29 What is the high p to which you go? B
21:29 they p you over the necks of the vile,
21:30 In the p where you were created,
26: 5 in the midst of the sea, a p for spreading nets.
26:14 you shall be a p for spreading nets.
26:20 be inhabited or have a p in the land of the living.
31: 4 making its rivers flow around the p it was planted,
37:14 and I will p you on your own soil;
37:27 My dwelling p shall be with them;
38:15 and come from your p out of the remotest parts of
39:11 that day I will give to Gog a p for burial in Israel,
41: 4 And he said to me, This is the most holy p. AC
41:21 In front of the holy p was something resembling A
41:23 The nave and the holy p had each a double door. A
42:13 and the guilt offering, for the p is holy.
42:14 When the priests enter the holy p, A
43: 7 Mortal, this is the p of my throne and the p for
43:21 and it shall be burnt in the appointed p belonging
44:27 On the day that he goes into the holy p, A
44:27 into the inner court, to minister in the holy p, A
45: 3 which shall be the sanctuary, the most holy p. AC
45: 4 be both a p for their houses and a holy place for
45: 4 be both a place for their houses and a holy p for A
46:19 and there I saw a p at the extreme western end
46:20 the p where the priests shall boil the guilt offering
47:10 it will be a p for the spreading of nets;
48:12 a most holy p, adjoining the territory of AC
Da 7: 9 thrones were set in p, and an Ancient One took
8: 8 the great horn was broken, and in its p there came
8:11 from him and overthrew the p of his sanctuary.
8:19 and I will tell you what will take p later in
8:22 in p of which four others arose,
9:24 and to anoint a most holy p. AC
9:27 in their p shall be an abomination that desolates,
11: 7 a branch from her roots shall rise up in his p.
11:20 "Then shall arise in his p one who shall send
11:21 In his p shall arise a contemptible person
Hos 1:10 and in the p where it was said to them,
5:15 to my p until they acknowledge their guilt
Am 2:13 So, I will press you down in your p,
8: 3 dead bodies shall be many, cast out in every p.
Mic 1: 3 For lo, the LORD is coming out of his p,
1: 4 like waters poured down a steep p.
1: 5 And what is the high p of Judah? B
1: 6 a p for planting vineyards.
2:10 Arise and go; for this is no p to rest,
Hab 3:11 the moon stood still in its exalted p,
Zep 1: 4 from this p every remnant of Baal and the name of
2:11 and to him shall bow down, each in its p,
Hag 2: 9 and in this p I will give prosperity,
Zec 6:12 for he shall branch out in his p,
12: 6 while Jerusalem shall again be inhabited in its p,
14:10 the Gate of Benjamin to the p of the former gate,
Mal 1:11 and in every p incense is offered to my name,
Mt 1:18 the birth of Jesus the Messiah took p in this way.
1:22 All this took p to fulfill what had been spoken by
2: 9 until it stopped over the p where the child was.
2:22 that Archelaus was ruling over Judea in p
12: 9 He left that p and entered their synagogue;
12:43 through waterless regions looking for a resting p,
13:53 Jesus had finished these parables, he left that p.
14:13 he withdrew from there in a boat to a deserted p
14:15 "This is a deserted p, and the hour is now late;
14:35 After the people of that p recognized him,
15:21 Jesus left that p and went away to the district
15:29 After Jesus had left that p,
18:31 and reported to their lord all that had taken p.
21: 4 This took p to fulfill what had been spoken
23: 6 They love to have the p of honor at banquets and
24: 6 for this must take p, but the end is not yet.
24:15 the desolating sacrilege standing in the holy p, A
24:34 not pass away until all these things have taken p.
26:20 it was evening, he took his p with the twelve;
26:36 Jesus went with them to a p called Gethsemane;
26:52 "Put your sword back into its p;
26:56 But all this has taken p,
27: 7 to buy the potter's field as a p to bury foreigners.
27:33 to a p called Golgotha (which means P of a Skull),
27:54 saw the earthquake and what took p,
28: 6 Come, see the p where he lay.
Mk 1:35 he got up and went out to a deserted p,
6: 1 He left that p and came to his hometown,
6:10 stay there until you leave the p.
6:11 If any p will not welcome you and they refuse
6:31 to a deserted p all by yourselves and rest a while."
6:32 And they went away in the boat to a deserted p
6:35 a deserted p, and the hour is now very late;
10: 1 that p and went to the region of Judea and beyond
13: 7 this must take p, but the end is still to come.
13:29 So also, when you see these things taking p,
13:30 not pass away until all these things have taken p.
14:32 They went to a p called Gethsemane;
15:22 p called Golgotha (which means the p of a skull).
16: 6 Look, there is the p they laid him.
Lk 2: 7 because there was no p for them in the inn.
2:15 to Bethlehem and see this thing that has taken p,
4:17 the scroll and found the p where it was written:
4:37 And a report about him began to reach every p in
4:42 and went into a deserted p.
6:17 He came down with them and stood on a level p,
7:36 the Pharisee's house and took his p at the table.
9: 7 Herod the ruler heard about all that had taken p,
9:12 for we are here in a deserted p."

Lk 10: 1 to every town and p where he himself intended
10:32 when he came to the p and saw him,
11: 1 He was praying in a certain p,
11:24 through waterless regions looking for a resting p,
11:37 so he went in and took his p at the table.
12:17 for I have no p to store my crops?'
14: 8 do not sit down at the p of honor,
14: 9 'Give this person your p,'
14: 9 in disgrace you would start to take the lowest p.
14:10 you are invited, go and sit down at the lowest p,
15:14 a severe famine took p throughout that country,
16:28 they will not also come into this p of torment.'
17: 7 'Come here at once and take your p at the table'?
19: 5 When Jesus came to the p,
19:29 at the p called the Mount of Olives,
20:35 but those who are considered worthy of a p in
21: 7 what will be the sign that this is about to take p?"
21: 9 for these things must take p first,
21:28 Now when these things begin to take p,
21:31 So also, when you see these things taking p,
21:32 not pass away until all things have taken p.
21:36 to escape all these things that will take p,
22:14 When the hour came, he took his p at the table,
22:40 When he reached the p, he said to them,
23: 5 from Galilee where he began even to this p."
23:19 in prison for an insurrection that had taken p in
23:33 When they came to the p that is called The Skull,
23:47 When the centurion saw what had taken p,
23:48 for this spectacle saw what had taken p,
24:18 the things that have taken p there in these days?"
24:21 it is now the third day since these things took p.
Jn 1:28 This took p in Bethany across the Jordan
4:20 the p where people must worship is in Jerusalem."
4:43 he went from that p to Galilee
6:10 Now there was a great deal of grass in the p;
6:23 Then some boats from Tiberias came near the p
8:35 permanent p in the household; the son has a p there
8:37 because there is no p in you for my word.
10:22 the festival of the Dedication took p in Jerusalem.
10:40 to the p where John had been baptizing earlier,
11: 6 he stayed two days longer in the p where he was.
11:30 but was still at the p where Martha had met him.
11:48 Romans will come and destroy both our holy p A
14: 2 would I have told you that I go to prepare a p
14: 3 And if I go and prepare a p for you,
14: 4 you know the way to the p where I am going."
18: 1 the Kidron valley to a p where there was a garden,
18: 2 Now Judas, who betrayed him, also knew the p,
19:13 and sat on the judge's bench at a p called
19:17 he went out to what is called The P of the Skull,
19:20 the p where Jesus was crucified was near the city;
19:41 a garden in the p where he was crucified,
20: 7 the linen wrappings but rolled up in a p by itself.
Ac 1:25 to take the p in this ministry and apostleship
1:25 from which Judas turned aside to go to his own p."
2: 1 they were all together in one p.
4:28 and your plan had predestined to take p.
4:31 When they had prayed, the p
6:13 against this holy p and the law; A
6:14 of Nazareth will destroy this p and will change
7: 7 that they shall come out and worship me in this p.'
7:33 for the p where you are standing is holy ground.
7:46 and asked that he might find a dwelling p for
7:49 says the Lord, or what is the p of my rest?
8: 4 those who were scattered went from p to p,
8:13 the signs and great miracles that took p.
11:19 the persecution that took p over Stephen traveled
11:28 and this took p during the reign of Claudius.
12:17 Then he left and went to another p.
16:13 where we supposed there was a p of prayer;
16:16 One day, as we were going to the p of prayer,
18:23 from p to p through the region of Galatia and
21:28 against our people, our law, and this p;
21:28 into the temple and has defiled this holy p." A
26:18 that they may receive forgiveness of sins and a p
26:22 the prophets and Moses said would take p:
27: 8 we came to a p called Fair Havens,
28: 7 that p were lands belonging to the leading man of
Ro 3: 2 the first p the Jews were entrusted with the oracles
9:26 "And in the very p where it was said to them,
11:17 in their p to share the rich root of the olive tree,
15:23 now, with no further p for me in these regions,
1Co 1: 2 with all those who in every p call on the name
2Co 2:14 and through us spreads in every p the fragrance
Eph 2:15 in himself one new humanity in p of the two,
2:22 also are built together spiritually into a dwelling p
5: 4 Entirely out of p is obscene, silly, and vulgar talk;
Col 1:18 that he might come to have first p in everything.
1Th 1: 8 in every p your faith in God has become known,
1Ti 2: 8 I desire, then, that in every p the men should pray,
2Ti 2:18 that the resurrection has already taken p.
Phm 1:13 in your p during my imprisonment for the gospel;
Heb 4: 4 For in one p it speaks about the seventh day
4: 5 And again in this p it says,
5: 6 as he says also in another p,
7: 2 in the first p, means "king of righteousness";
9: 2 this is called the Holy P. A
9:12 he entered once for all into the Holy P, A
9:25 the high priest enters the Holy P year after year A
11: 8 when he was called to set out for a p that he was
1Pe 4:12 not be surprised at the fiery ordeal that is taking p
2Pe 1:19 to this as to a lamp shining in a dark p,
Rev 1: 1 to show his servants what must soon take p;
1:19 what is, and what is to take p after this.
2: 5 to you and remove your lampstand from its p,
3:21 To the one who conquers I will give a p with me
4: 1 and I will show you what must take p after this."

Rev 6:14 and island was removed from its **p.**
12: 6 where she has a **p** prepared by God,
12: 8 and there was no longer any **p** for them in heaven.
12:14 to her **p** where she is nourished for a time,
16:16 at the **p** that in Hebrew is called Harmagedon.
18: 2 It has become a dwelling **p** of demons,
20:11 and no **p** was found for them.
21: 8 their **p** will be in the lake that burns with fire
22: 6 to show his servants what must soon take **p."**
Tob 1:15 and his son Sennacherib reigned in his **p,**
2: 3 and thrown into the market **p,**
4:17 **P** your bread on the grave of the righteous,
7:16 Lord of heaven grant you joy in **p** of your sorrow.
14: 4 that all these things will take **p**
Jdt 5: 9 Then their God commanded them to leave the **p**
6:17 He answered and told them what had taken **p** at
8:12 and to set yourselves up in the **p** of God
15: 4 to tell what had taken **p** and to urge all to rush out
AdE 1:11 to him in order to proclaim her as queen and to **p**
13: 3 and has attained the second **p** in the kingdom—
16:19 post a copy of this letter publicly in every **p,**
Wis 3:14 and a **p** of great delight in the temple of the Lord.
19:18 be clearly inferred from the sight of what took **p.**
Sir 4:13 and the Lord blesses the **p** she enters.
10:14 and enthrones the lowly in their **p.**
10:15 and plants the humble in their **p.**
12:12 or he may overthrow you and take your **p.**
14:25 and so occupies an excellent lodging **p;**
17:27 in Hades in **p** of the living who give thanks?
22:18 Fences set on a high **p** will not stand firm B
24: 7 Among all these I sought a resting **p;**
24: 8 and my Creator chose the **p** for my tent.
24:11 Thus in the beloved city he gave me a resting **p,**
32: 2 take your **p,** so that you may be merry along
33:12 and turned them out of their **p.**
33:21 do not let anyone take your **p.**
36:18 Jerusalem, the **p** of your dwelling.
38:12 give the physician his **p,** for the Lord created him;
41:19 in the **p** where you live.
Bar 2:24 be brought out of their resting **p;**
3:15 Who has found her **p?**
3:19 and others have arisen in their **p.**
Aza 1:15 no **p** to make an offering before you and
Bel 1:23 Now in that **p** there was a great dragon,
1:39 God immediately returned Habakkuk to his own **p.**
1Mc 1: 8 Then his officers began to rule, each in his own **p.**
1:53 into hiding in every **p** of refuge they had.
2:12 And see, our holy **p,** our beauty, A
3: 1 was called Maccabeus, took command in his **p.**
3:35 he was to banish the memory of them from the **p,**
3:45 it was a lodging **p** for the Gentiles.
3:46 Israel formerly had a **p** of prayer in Mizpah.
4:43 and removed the defiled stones to an unclean **p.**
4:46 the stones in a convenient **p** on the temple hill
5:29 He left the **p** at night,
6:57 the **p** against which we are fighting is strong,
6:62 and saw what a strong fortress the **p** was,
8: 4 even though the **p** was far distant from them.
9:30 therefore we have chosen you today to take his **p**
9:31 at that time in **p** of his brother Judas.
9:45 there is no **p** to turn.
10:14 for it served as a **p** of refuge.
10:73 where there is no stone or pebble, or **p** to flee."
11:37 up in a conspicuous **p** on the holy mountain.' "
11:40 to become king in **p** of his father.
12: 4 to the people in every **p,**
13: 8 in **p** of Judas and your brother Jonathan.
13:14 Trypho learned that Simon had risen up in **p**
13:20 along opposite him to every **p** he went.
13:32 and became king in his **p,** putting on the crown
14:48 to put them up in a conspicuous **p** in the precincts
16: 3 Take my **p** and my brother's,
2Mc 1:14 Antiochus came to the **p** together with his Friends,
1:19 that the **p** was unknown to anyone.
1:29 Plant your people in your holy **p,** A
1:33 the **p** where the exiled priests had hidden the fire,
1:34 and enclosed the **p** and made it sacred.
2: 7 "The **p** shall remain unknown
2: 8 that the **p** should be specially consecrated."
2:18 from everywhere under heaven into his holy **p,** A
2:18 from great evils and has purified the **p.**
3: 2 the kings themselves honored the **p** and glorified
3:12 of the **p** and in the sanctity and inviolability of
3:18 holy **p** was about to be brought into dishonor. A
3:30 the Lord who had acted marvelously for his own **p.**
3:38 there is certainly some power of God about the **p.**
3:39 in heaven watches over that **p** himself
4:33 to a **p** of sanctuary at Daphne near Antioch.
4:34 to come out from the **p** of sanctuary;
4:38 to that very **p** where he had committed the outrage
5:10 he had no funeral of any sort and no **p** in the tomb
5:16 to enhance the glory and honor of the **p.**
5:17 the reason he was disregarding the holy **p.** A
5:19 not choose the nation for the sake of the holy **p,** A
5:19 but the **p** for the sake of the nation.
5:20 the **p** itself shared in the misfortunes that befell
6: 2 as did the people who lived in that **p.**
8:17 the Gentiles had committed against the holy **p,** A
8:20 against the Galatians that took **p** in Babylonia,
9:17 and would visit every inhabited **p** to proclaim
10: 5 the purification of the sanctuary took **p,** that is,
10: 7 to the purifying of his own holy **p.** A
10:10 we will tell what took **p** under Antiochus Eupator,
10:34 The men within, relying on the strength of the **p,**
11: 5 a fortified **p** about five stadia from Jerusalem,
12:18 though in one **p** he had left a very strong garrison.
12:21 and also the baggage to a **p** called Carnaim;
2Mc 12:21 that **p** was hard to besiege and difficult of access
13: 4 to death by the method that is customary in that **p.**
13:23 sanctuary and showed generosity to the holy **p.** A
14:21 seats of honor were set in **p;**
15:34 "Blessed is he who has kept his own **p** undefiled!"
1Es 1:10 This is what took **p.**
1:15 were in their **p** according to the arrangement made
1:43 His son Jehoiachin became king in his **p;**
1:50 he would have spared them and his dwelling **p.**
2: 6 by the people of your **p** with gold and silver,
4:34 of the heavens and returns to its **p** in one day.
5:50 And they erected the altar in its **p,**
6:27 to keep away from the **p,**
8:45 who was the leading man at the **p** of the treasury,
8:46 and the treasurers at that **p** to send us men to serve
8:78 to leave to us a root and a name in your holy **p,** A
9:13 with the elders and judges of each **p,**
9:45 for he had the **p** of honor in the presence of all.
3Mc 1: 9 and did what was fitting for the holy **p.** A
1: 9 the **p** and being impressed by its excellence
1:23 created a considerable disturbance in the holy **p;** A
1:29 to the profanation of the **p.**
2: 9 chose this city and sanctified this **p** for your name,
2:10 to our petition when we come to this **p** and pray.
2:14 profane man undertakes to violate the holy **p** A
2:16 on your people Israel, you sanctified this **p.**
3: 1 that all should promptly be gathered into one **p,**
3:14 When our expedition took **p** in Asia,
3:29 Every **p** detected sheltering a Jew is to
4: 1 In every **p,** then, where this decree arrived,
4: 3 What district or city, or what habitable **p** at all,
4: 7 along as far as the **p** of embarkation.
4:11 to the **p** called Schedia,
4:18 in their homes, and some at the **p;**
6:30 in that same **p** in which they had expected
6:31 and full of joy they apportioned to celebrants the **p**
7: 8 with no one in any **p** doing them harm at all
7:17 because of a characteristic of the **p,**
7:20 as holy on a pillar and dedicating a **p** of prayer at
2Es 2:23 and I will give you the first **p** in my resurrection.
4:19 and the locale of the sea a **p** to carry its waves."
4:29 and if the **p** where the evil has been sown does
6: 1 before the portals of the world were in **p,**
6:14 if the **p** where you are standing is greatly shaken
6:29 by little the **p** where I was standing began to rock
7: 4 but it has an entrance set in a narrow **p,**
7: 7 entrance to it is narrow and set in a precipitous **p,**
7:*36* and opposite it shall be the **p** of rest;
7:*104* to be ill or sleep or eat or be healed in his **p,**
10:27 and a **p** of huge foundations showed itself.
10:54 of human construction could endure in a **p** where
11: 8 let each sleep in its own **p,** and watch in its turn;
11:13 so that even its **p** was no longer visible.
11:24 but four remained in their **p.**
12:37 put it in a hidden **p;**
12:41 that you have forsaken us and sit in this **p?**
12:42 and like a lamp in a dark **p,**
12:48 but I have come to this **p** to pray on account of
13: 7 And I tried to see the region or **p** from which
13:31 **p** against **p,** people against people,
13:32 When these things take **p** and the signs occur
14:16 now seen happen shall take **p** hereafter.
15:40 and shall pour out upon every high and lofty **p**
4Mc 4: 9 to shield the holy **p** that was being treated A
4:12 the blessedness of the holy **p** before all people. A
5: 1 in state with his counselors on a certain high **p,** B
15:20 when you saw the **p** filled with many spectators of

PLACED (69) [PLACE]

Ge 3:24 the east of the garden of Eden he **p** the cherubim,
40:11 and **p** the cup in Pharaoh's hand."
40:21 and he **p** the cup in Pharaoh's hand;
50:26 he was embalmed and **p** in a coffin in Egypt.
Ex 2: 3 the child in it and **p** it among the reeds on the bank
16:34 so Aaron **p** it before the covenant, for safekeeping.
Lev 8: 8 He **p** the breastpiece on him,
8:26 and **p** them on the fat and on the right thigh.
8:27 He **p** all these on the palms of Aaron and on
14:28 where the blood of the guilt offering was **p.**
Nu 11:24 and **p** them all around the tent.
17: 7 So Moses **p** the staffs before the LORD in
1Sa 5: 2 into the house of Dagon and **p** it beside Dagon.
2Sa 12:30 and it was **p** on David's head.
1Ki 2:24 who has established me and **p** me on the throne
8: 9 the two tablets of stone that Moses had **p** there
12: 4 of your father and his heavy yoke that he **p** on us,
12:32 And he **p** in Bethel the priests of the high places
2Ki 17: 6 He **p** them in Halah, on the Habor,
17:24 and **p** them in the cities of Samaria in place of
17:26 and **p** in the cities of Samaria do not know the law
1Ch 20: 2 and it was **p** on David's head.
2Ch 4: 8 He also made ten tables and **p** them in the temple,
10: 4 of your father and his heavy yoke that he **p** on us,
17: 2 He **p** forces in all the fortified cities of Judah,
17:19 besides those whom the king had **p** in
Ezr 1: 7 from Jerusalem and **p** in the house of his gods.
Job 20: 4 ever since mortals were **p** on earth,
Jer 5:22 I **p** the sand as a boundary for the sea,
24: 1 The LORD showed me two baskets of figs **p**
Eze 3:25 As for you, mortal, cords shall be **p** on you,
11: 7 The slain whom you have **p** within it are the meat,
14: 3 **p** their iniquity as a stumbling block before them;
17: 5 to take a seed from the land, **p** it in fertile soil;
21:11 the sword is polished, to be **p** in the slayer's hand.
23:41 on which you had **p** my incense and my oil.
24: 7 she **p** it on a bare rock;
Eze 24: 8 I have **p** the blood she shed on a bare rock,
28:14 With an anointed cherub as guardian I **p** you;
32:25 they are **p** among the slain.
43: 8 When they **p** their threshold by my threshold
Da 1: 2 and **p** the vessels in the treasury of his gods.
Hag 2:15 stone was **p** upon a stone in the LORD's temple,
Mt 4: 5 Then the devil took him to the holy city and **p** him
Lk 4: 9 and **p** him on the pinnacle of the temple,
Jn 3:35 The Father loves the Son and has **p** all things
Jas 3: 6 The tongue is **p** among our members as a world
Rev 1:17 But he **p** his right hand on me, saying,
11: 9 at their dead bodies and refuse to let them be **p** in
Tob 2: 2 for me and an abundance of food **p** before me,
Jdt 6:14 and brought him into Bethulia and **p** him before
13:10 who **p** it in her food bag.
AdE 1: 6 Gold and silver couches were **p** on a mosaic floor
Sir 15:16 He has **p** before you fire and water;
30:18 a mouth that is closed are like offerings of food **p**
47: 9 He **p** singers before the altar,
LtJ 6:27 Gifts are **p** before them just as before the dead.
1Mc 4:51 They **p** the bread on the table and hung up
7:20 He **p** Alcimus in charge of the country and left
9:51 And he **p** garrisons in them to harass Israel.
14:33 and he **p** there a garrison of Jews.
16: 7 Then he divided the army and **p** the cavalry in
1Es 1: 2 having **p** the priests according to their divisions,
6:26 to be **p** where they had been."
2Es 2:43 and on the head of each of them he **p** a crown,
6:20 seal is **p** upon the age that is about to pass away,
6:54 over these you **p** Adam, as ruler over all the works
4Mc 8:13 When the guards had **p** before them wheels
9:12 they **p** him upon the wheel.

PLACES‡ (186) [PLACE]

A. HIGH PLACES (68)

Ge 23: 6 Bury your dead in the choicest of our burial **p;**
30:38 the watering **p,** where the flocks came to drink.
Lev 26:30 I will destroy your high **p** and cut A
Nu 33: 2 these are their stages according to their starting **p.**
33:52 and demolish all their high **p.** A
Dt 12: 2 You must demolish completely all the **p** where
12: 3 and thus blot out their name from their **p.**
Jos 5: 8 in their **p** in the camp until they were healed.
Jdg 5:11 To the sound of musicians at the watering **p,**
6: 2 the Israelites provided for themselves hiding **p** in
19:13 "Come, let us try to reach one of these **p,**
1Sa 2:36 Please put me in one of the priest's **p,**
7:16 and he judged Israel in all these **p.**
23:23 around and learn all the hiding **p** where he lurks,
30:31 all the **p** where David and his men had roamed.
2Sa 1:19 O Israel, lies slain upon your high **p!** A
1:25 Jonathan lies slain upon your high **p.** A
1Ki 3: 2 The people were sacrificing at the high **p,** A
3: 3 he sacrificed and offered incense at the high **p.** A
12:31 He also made houses on high **p,** A
12:32 he placed in Bethel the priests of the high **p** A
13: 2 priests of the high **p** who offer incense on you, A
13:32 and against all the houses of the high **p** that are A
13:33 for the high **p** again from among all the people; A
13:33 to be priests he consecrated for the high **p.** A
14:23 they also built for themselves high **p,** pillars, A
15:14 But the high **p** were not taken away. A
22:43 yet the high **p** were not taken away. A
22:43 and offered incense on the high **p.** A
2Ki 12: 3 Nevertheless the high **p** were not taken away; A
12: 3 to sacrifice and make offerings on the high **p.** A
14: 4 But the high **p** were not removed; A
14: 4 and made offerings on the high **p.** A
15: 4 Nevertheless the high **p** were not taken away; A
15: 4 and made offerings on the high **p.** A
15:35 Nevertheless the high **p** were not removed; A
15:35 and made offerings on the high **p.** A
16: 4 He sacrificed and made offerings on the high **p,** A
17: 9 built for themselves high **p** at all their towns, A
17:11 there they made offerings on all the high **p,** A
17:29 the high **p** that the people of Samaria had made, A
17:32 of people as priests of the high **p,** A
17:32 for them in the shrines of the high **p.** A
18: 4 He removed the high **p,** broke down the pillars, A
18:22 is it not he whose high **p** A
21: 3 high **p** that his father Hezekiah had destroyed; A
23: 5 to make offerings in the high **p** at the cities A
23: 8 the high **p** where the priests had made offerings, A
23: 8 he broke down the high **p** of the gates that were A
23: 9 The priests of the high **p,** however, A
23:13 The king defiled the high **p** that were east A
23:19 of the high **p** that were in the towns of Samaria, A
23:20 the priests of the high **p** who were there, A
1Ch 6:54 These are their dwelling **p** according
2Ch 8:11 for the **p** to which the ark of the LORD
11:15 had appointed his own priests for the high **p,** A
14: 3 He took away the foreign altars and the high **p,** A
14: 5 of Judah the high **p** and the incense altars. A
15:17 But the high **p** were not taken out of Israel. A
17: 6 the high **p** and the sacred poles from Judah. A
20:33 Yet the high **p** were not removed; A
21:11 he made high **p** in the hill country of Judah, A
28: 4 He sacrificed and made offerings on the high **p,** A
28:25 of Judah he made high **p** to make offerings A
31: 1 the high **p** and the altars throughout all Judah A
32:12 this same Hezekiah who took away his high **p** A
33: 3 the high **p** that his father Hezekiah had pulled A
33:17 people, however, still sacrificed at the high **p,** A
33:19 the sites on which he built high **p** and set up A
34: 3 to purge Judah and Jerusalem of the high **p,** A

Ne 4:12 "From all the **p** where they live they will come up
4:13 of the space behind the wall, in open **p**, I stationed
8: 7 while the people remained in their **p**.
12:27 the Levites in all their **p**,
Job 7:10 nor do their **p** know them any more.
Ps 10: 8 in hiding **p** they murder the innocent.
16: 6 boundary lines have fallen for me in pleasant **p**;
49:11 their dwelling **p** to all generations,
73:18 Truly you set them in slippery **p**;
74: 8 they burned all the meeting **p** of God in the land.
74:20 for the dark **p** of the land are full of the haunts
78:58 they provoked him to anger with their high **p**; A
102: 6 like a little owl of the waste **p**.
103:22 all his works, in all **p** of his dominion.
Pr 9: 3 she calls from the highest **p** in the town,
9:14 on a seat at the high **p** of the town, A
Ecc 10: 6 folly is set in many high **p**, A
Isa 4: 5 Mount Zion and over its **p** of assembly a cloud
15: 2 to the high **p** to weep; A
17: 2 they will be **p** for flocks, which will lie down,
17: 9 the deserted **p** of the Hivites and the Amorites,
19: 7 There will be bare **p** by the Nile,
32:18 in secure dwellings, and in quiet resting **p**.
36: 7 is it not he whose high **p** A
40: 4 and the rough **p** a plain.
42:16 the rough **p** into level ground.
45: 3 of darkness and riches hidden in secret **p**,
49:19 and your desolate **p** and your devastated land—
51: 3 he will comfort all her waste **p**,
58:11 and satisfy your needs in parched **p**,
64:11 and all our pleasant **p** have become ruins.
65: 4 and spend the night in secret **p**;
Jer 6: 3 they shall pasture, all in their **p**.
8: 3 that remains of this evil family in all the **p**
17: 6 They shall live in the parched **p** of the wilderness,
17:26 the towns of Judah and the **p** around Jerusalem,
19: 5 high **p** of Baal to burn their children in the fire A
21:13 or who can enter our **p** of refuge?"
23:24 in secret **p** so that I cannot see them?
24: 9 and a curse in all the **p** where I shall drive them.
29:14 the nations and all the **p** where I have driven you,
32:35 They built the high **p** of Baal in the valley of A
32:44 in the **p** around Jerusalem,
33:13 the **p** around Jerusalem, and in the towns of Judah,
40:12 the **p** to which they had been scattered and came
49:10 I have uncovered his hiding **p**,
49:30 Flee, wander far away, hide in deep **p**,
51:51 for aliens have come into the holy **p** of
Eze 6: 3 and I will destroy your high **p**. A
6: 6 towns shall be waste and your high **p** ruined, A
7:24 and their holy **p** shall be profaned.
16:39 down your platform and break down your lofty **p**;
33:24 of these waste **p** in the land of Israel keep saying,
33:27 surely those who are in the waste **p** shall fall by
34:12 the **p** to which they have been scattered on a day
36:10 towns shall be inhabited and the waste **p** rebuilt;
36:33 and the waste **p** shall be rebuilt.
36:36 the LORD, have rebuilt the ruined **p**,
38:12 to assail the waste **p** that are now inhabited,
Hos 10: 8 The high **p** of Aven, the sin of Israel, A
Joel 3: 7 to leave the **p** to which you have sold them,
Am 4: 6 and lack of bread in all your **p**,
7: 9 the high **p** of Isaac shall be made desolate, A
Mic 1: 3 and will come down and tread upon the high **p** A
Mt 24: 7 be famines and earthquakes in various **p**:
Mk 12:39 and to have the best seats in the synagogues and **p**
13: 8 there will be earthquakes in various **p**;
14:18 And when they had taken their **p** and were eating,
Lk 5:16 But he would withdraw to deserted **p** and pray.
14: 7 he noticed how the guests chose the **p** of honor,
20:46 and to have the best seats in the synagogues and **p**
21:11 and in various **p** famines and plagues;
Jn 14: 2 In my Father's house there are many dwelling **p**.
Ac 16: 3 because of the Jews who were in those **p**,
17:26 and the boundaries of the **p** where they would live,
Eph 1: 3 with every spiritual blessing in the heavenly **p**,
1:20 and seated him at his right hand in the heavenly **p**,
2: 6 with him and seated us with him in the heavenly **p**
3:10 to the rulers and authorities in the heavenly **p**.
6:12 the spiritual forces of evil in the heavenly **p**.
Jdt 5:19 from the **p** where they were scattered,
AdE 16: 5 And often many of those who are set in **p**
Wis 6: 5 severe judgment falls on those in high **p**. A
11: 2 and pitched their tents in untrodden **p**.
19:18 For the elements changed **p** with one another,
19:22 not neglected to help them at all times and in all **p**.
Sir 14:26 who **p** his children under her shelter, and lodges
43:10 of the Holy One they stand in their appointed **p**;
1Mc 2:31 down to the hiding **p** in the wilderness.
2:36 or hurl a stone at them or block up their hiding **p**,
2:41 not all die as our kindred died in their hiding **p**."
10:13 all of them left their **p** and went back
10:40 of the king's revenues from appropriate **p**.
11:69 in ambush emerged from their **p** and joined battle.
12: 2 to the same effect to the Spartans and to other **p**.
15:29 and you have taken possession of many **p**
15:30 the **p** that you have conquered outside the borders
2Mc 8:31 and carefully stored all of them in strategic **p**;
10:17 they gained possession of the **p**,
10:19 for **p** where he was more urgently needed.
11: 3 as he did on the sacred **p** of the other nations,
12: 2 But some of the governors in various **p**,
14:22 at key **p** to prevent sudden treachery on the part of
1Es 2:16 living in Samaria and other **p**,
2:18 repairing its market **p** and walls and laying
5:48 took their **p** and prepared the altar of the God
3Mc 5:44 the **p** in the city most favorable for keeping guard.
2Es 2:16 And I will raise up the dead from their **p**,
2:31 I will bring them out of the hiding **p** of the earth,
4:42 so also do these **p** hasten to give back those things
5: 8 There shall be chaos also in many **p**,
6:22 Sown **p** shall suddenly appear unsown,
16:26 For in all **p** there shall be great solitude;
16:56 At his word the stars were fixed in their **p**,
16:62 and searches out hidden things in hidden **p**.
16:70 For in many **p** and in neighboring cities there shall

PLACING‡ (3) [PLACE]

Eze 14: 7 and **p** their iniquity as a stumbling block
Ac 15:10 therefore why are you putting God to the test by **p**
2Es 2:46 "Who is that young man who is **p** crowns on them

PLAGUE‡ (45) [PLAGUED, PLAGUES]

Ex 8: 2 I will **p** your whole country with frogs.
11: 1 "I will bring one more **p** upon Pharaoh and
12:13 over you, and no **p** shall destroy you when I strike
30:12 no **p** may come upon them for being registered.
32:35 Then the LORD sent a **p** on the people,
Lev 26:21 I will continue to **p** you sevenfold for your sins.
Nu 8:19 be no **p** among the Israelites for coming too close
11:33 the LORD struck the people with a very great **p**.
14:37 an unfavorable report about the land died by a **p**
16:46 from the LORD; the **p** has begun."
16:47 where the **p** had already begun among the people.
16:48 and the living; and the **p** was stopped.
16:49 by the **p** were fourteen thousand seven hundred,
16:50 When the **p** was stopped, Aaron returned to Moses
25: 8 So the **p** was stopped among the people of Israel.
25: 9 that died by the **p** were twenty-four thousand.
25:18 she was killed on the day of the **p** that resulted
26: 1 the **p** the LORD said to Moses and to Eleazar son
31:16 **p** came among the congregation of the LORD.
Jos 22:17 and for which a **p** came upon the congregation of
1Sa 4: 8 with every sort of **p** in the wilderness.
6: 4 same **p** was upon all of you and upon your lords.
2Sa 24:21 so that the **p** may be averted from the people."
24:25 and the **p** was averted from Israel.
1Ki 8:37 "If there is famine in the land, if there is **p**, blight,
8:37 whatever **p**, whatever sickness there is;
1Ch 21:22 so that the **p** may be averted from the people."
2Ch 6:28 "If there is famine in the land, if there is **p**, blight,
21:14 the LORD will bring a great **p** on your people,
Ps 78:50 but gave their lives over to the **p**.
106:29 and a **p** broke out among them.
106:30 up and interceded, and the **p** was stopped.
Hab 3: 5 him went pestilence, and **p** followed close behind.
Zec 14:12 be the **p** with which the LORD will strike all
14:15 And a **p** like this **p** shall fall on the horses,
14:18 on them shall come the **p** that the LORD inflicts
Rev 11: 6 and to strike the earth with every kind of **p**,
16:21 for the **p** of the hail, so fearful was that **p**.
Wis 18:20 and a **p** came upon the multitude in the desert,
Sir 40: 9 calamities and famine and ruin and **p**.
2Es 7:*108* [38] and David for the **p**, and Solomon for those at
15:12 because of the **p** of chastisement and castigation
16:19 and **p**, tribulation and anguish are sent as scourges

PLAGUED (4) [PLAGUE]

Jos 24: 5 and I **p** Egypt with what I did in its midst;
1Ch 21:17 but do not let your people be **p**!"
Ps 73: 5 they are not **p** like other people.
73:14 For all day long I have been **p**,

PLAGUES (18) [PLAGUE]

Ge 12:17 and his house with great **p** because of Sarai,
Ex 9:14 this time I will send all my **p** upon you yourself,
Hos 13:14 O Death, where are your **p**?
Lk 7:21 of diseases, **p**, and evil spirits, and had given sight
21:11 and in various places famines and **p**;
Rev 9:18 By these three **p** a third of humankind was killed,
9:20 who were not killed by these **p**,
15: 1 seven angels with seven **p**, which are the last,
15: 6 the seven angels with the seven **p**,
15: 8 until the seven **p** of the seven angels were ended.
16: 9 who had authority over these **p**,
18: 4 and so that you do not share in her **p**;
18: 8 therefore her **p** will come in a single day—
21: 9 the seven bowls full of the seven last **p** came
22:18 God will add to that person the **p** described
Jdt 5:12 the whole land of Egypt with incurable **p**.
2Mc 7:37 and **p** to make you confess that he alone is God,
2Es 15:11 and will strike Egypt with **p**, as before,

PLAIN‡ (73) [PLAINLY, PLAINS]

Ge 11: 2 upon a **p** in the land of Shinar and settled there.
13:10 the **p** of the Jordan was well watered everywhere
13:11 So Lot chose for himself all the **p** of the Jordan,
13:12 of the **P** and moved his tent as far as Sodom.
19:17 do not look back or stop anywhere in the **P**;
19:25 and all the **P**, and all the inhabitants of the cities,
19:28 the **P** and saw the smoke of the land going up like
19:29 when God destroyed the cities of the **P**,
Dt 1: 1 in the wilderness, on the **p** opposite Suph,
34: 3 the Negeb, and the **P**—
Jos 17:16 the Canaanites who live in the **p** have chariots
Jdg 1:19 but could not drive out the inhabitants of the **p**,
1:34 they did not allow them to come down to the **p**.
2Sa 18:23 Then Ahimaaz ran by the way of the **P**,
1Ki 7:46 In the **p** of the Jordan the king cast them,
20:23 but let us fight against them in the **p**,
20:25 then we will fight against them in the **p**,
2Ch 4:17 In the **p** of the Jordan the king cast them,
26:10 both in the Shephelah and in the **p**,
35:22 but joined battle in the **p** of Megiddo.
Ne 6: 2 in one of the villages in the **p** of Ono."
Isa 21:13 The oracle concerning the desert **p**.
21:13 In the scrub of the desert **p** you will lodge,
40: 4 and the rough places a **p**.
52: 8 in **p** sight they see the return of the LORD to Zion.
Jer 21:13 O inhabitant of the valley, O rock of the **p**,
48: 8 valley shall perish, and the **p** shall be destroyed,
Da 3: 1 up on the **p** of Dura in the province of Babylon.
Hab 2: 2 make it **p** on tablets, so that a runner may read it.
Zec 4: 7 Before Zerubbabel you shall become a **p**;
12:11 as the mourning for Hadad-rimmon in the **p**
14:10 The whole land shall be turned into a **p** from Geba
Ro 1:19 For what can be known about God is **p** to them,
1Co 15:27 it is **p** that this does not include
2Ti 3: 9 their folly will become **p** to everyone.
1Jn 2:19 But by going out they made it **p** that none
Tob 5: 6 while Ecbatana is in the middle of the **p**."
Jdt 1: 5 against King Arphaxad in the great **p** that is on
1: 6 and, on the **p**, Arioch, king of the Elymeans.
1: 8 and Upper Galilee and the great **p** of Esdraelon,
2:21 for three days from Nineveh to the **p** of Bectileth,
2:27 Then he went down into the **p** of Damascus during
4: 6 which faces Esdraelon opposite the **p** near Dothan,
6:11 and led him out of the camp into the **p**,
6:11 the **p** they went up into the hill country and came
7:18 The rest of the Assyrian army encamped in the **p**,
14: 2 over them, as if you were going down to the **p**
15: 2 and fled by every path across the **p** and through
15: 7 in the hill country and in the **p** got a great amount
Wis 19: 7 and a grassy **p** out of the raging waves,
Sir 26:20 *Seek a fertile field within the whole p,*
1Mc 3:24 down the descent of Beth-horon to the **p**;
3:40 they arrived they encamped near Emmaus in the **p**.
4: 6 At daybreak Judas appeared in the **p**
4:14 The Gentiles were crushed, and fled into the **p**,
4:21 the army of Judas drawn up in the **p** for battle,
5:52 Then they crossed the Jordan into the large **p**
6:40 and some troops were on the **p**,
10:71 come down to the **p** to meet us,
10:73 and such an army in the **p**,
10:77 At the same time he advanced into the **p**,
10:83 and the cavalry was dispersed in the **p**.
11:67 in the morning they marched to the **p** of Hazor,
11:68 there in the **p** the army of the foreigners met him;
12:49 and the Great **P** to destroy all Jonathan's soldiers.
13:13 Simon encamped in Adida, facing the **p**.
16: 5 and marched into the **p**, where a large force
16:11 had been appointed governor over the **p** of Jericho;
1Es 1:29 He joined battle with him in the **p** of Megiddo,
2Es 4:13 "I went into a forest of trees of the **p**,
4:15 the **p** so that there also we may gain more territory
7: 6 There is a city built and set on a **p**,
4Mc 18: 8 No seducer corrupted me on a desert **p**,

PLAINLY (9) [PLAIN]

Ge 26:28 "We see **p** that the LORD has been with you;
Ex 10:10 **P**, you have some evil purpose in mind.
Ecc 12:10 and he wrote words of truth **p**.
Mk 7:35 his tongue was released, and he spoke **p**.
Jn 10:24 If you are the Messiah, tell us **p**."
11:14 Then Jesus told them **p**, "Lazarus is dead.
16:25 but will tell you **p** of the Father.
16:29 His disciples said, "Yes, now you are speaking **p**,
2Mc 3:17 which **p** showed to those who looked at him

PLAINS (21) [PLAIN]

Nu 22: 1 in the **p** of Moab across the Jordan from Jericho.
26: 3 in the **p** of Moab by the Jordan opposite Jericho,
26:63 in the **p** of Moab by the Jordan opposite Jericho.
31:12 at the camp on the **p** of Moab by the Jordan
33:48 the mountains of Abarim and camped in the **p**
33:49 as far as Abel-shittim in the **p** of Moab.
33:50 In the **p** of Moab by the Jordan at Jericho,
35: 1 In the **p** of Moab by the Jordan at Jericho,
36:13 through Moses to the Israelites in the **p** of Moab
Dt 34: 1 up from the **p** of Moab to Mount Nebo, to the top
34: 8 for Moses in the **p** of Moab thirty days;
Jos 4:13 for war crossed over before the LORD to the **p**
5:10 on the fourteenth day of the month in the **p**
13:32 the inheritances that Moses distributed in the **p**
2Ki 25: 5 and overtook him in the **p** of Jericho;
Jer 39: 5 and overtook Zedekiah in the **p** of Jericho;
52: 8 and overtook Zedekiah in the **p** of Jericho;
Tob 5:10 to Media and have crossed all its **p**,
Jdt 5: 1 the high hilltops and set up barricades in the **p**.
1Mc 4:15 and to the **p** of Idumea, and to Azotus and Jamnia;
14: 8 and the trees of the **p** their fruit.

PLAINTIVE (1)

Jer 3:21 the **p** weeping of Israel's children,

PLAITING (KJV) See BRAIDING

PLAN‡ (63) [PLANNED, PLANNING, PLANS]

Ex 26:30 the **p** for it that you were shown on the mountain.
Dt 1:14 "The **p** you have proposed is a good one."
1:23 The **p** seemed good to me,
2Sa 20:22 the woman went to all the people with her wise **p**.
1Ch 28: 9 and understands every **p** and thought.
28:11 Then David gave his son Solomon the **p** of
28:12 and the **p** of all that he had in mind:

1Ch 28:18 also his **p** for the golden chariot of the cherubim
28:19 the **p** of all the works."
2Ch 30: 4 **p** seemed right to the king and all the assembly.
Ezr 4: 5 and they bribed officials to frustrate their **p**
Ps 21:11 If they **p** evil against you, if they devise mischief,
62: 4 Their only **p** is to bring down a person
140: 2 who **p** evil things in their minds and stir
Pr 3:29 Do not **p** harm against your
12:20 Deceit is in the mind of those who **p** evil,
14:22 Do they not err that **p** evil?
14:22 Those who **p** good find loyalty and faithfulness.
Isa 5:19 let the **p** of the Holy One of Israel hasten
14:26 the **p** that is planned concerning the whole earth;
19:17 to whom it is mentioned will fear because of the **p**
29:15 You who hide a **p** too deep for the LORD,
30: 1 says the LORD, who carry out a **p**, but not mine;
32: 8 But those who are noble **p** noble things,
Jer 18:11 a potter shaping evil against you and devising a **p**
23:27 They **p** to make my people forget my name
49:20 the **p** that the LORD has made against Edom and
49:30 a **p** against you and formed a purpose against you.
50:45 the **p** that the LORD has made against Babylon,
Eze 43:11 make known to them the **p** of the temple,
43:11 all its ordinances and its entire **p** and all its laws;
43:11 so that they may observe and follow the entire **p**
Mic 4:12 they do not understand his **p**,
Mt 28:12 they devised a **p** to give a large sum of money to
Lk 23:51 had not agreed to their **p** and action.
Ac 2:23 handed over to you according to the definite **p**
4:28 and your **p** had predestined to take place.
5:38 if this **p** or this undertaking is of human origin,
27:42 The soldiers' **p** was to kill the prisoners,
27:43 kept them from carrying out their **p**.
Eph 1:10 as a **p** for the fullness of time,
3: 9 and to make everyone see what is the **p** of
Jdt 2: 2 and all his nobles and set before them his secret **p**
2: 4 When he had completed his **p**, Nebuchadnezzar,
9: 9 a widow, the strong hand to do what I **p**.
AdE 9:31 pledging their own well-being to the **p**.
14:11 but turn their **p** against them,
Sir 43:23 By his **p** he stilled the deep and planted islands
1Mc 6: 3 but he could not because his **p** had become known
7:31 Nicanor learned that his **p** had been disclosed,
9:60 because their **p** became known.
9:68 for his **p** and his expedition had been in vain.
3Mc 1:25 to change his arrogant mind from the **p**
1:26 to bring the aforesaid **p** to a conclusion.
3:14 it was brought to conclusion, according to **p**,
5:12 and was completely frustrated in his inflexible **p**.
2Es 4:13 a forest of trees of the plain, and they made a **p**
4:15 In like manner the waves of the sea also made a **p**
4:16 But the **p** of the forest was in vain,
4:17 likewise also the **p** of the waves of the sea was
4:19 I answered and said, "Each made a foolish **p**,
13:31 They shall **p** to make war against one another,
13:41 But they formed this **p** for themselves,

PLANE (5)

Ge 30:37 Jacob took fresh rods of poplar and almond and **p**,
Isa 41:19 the **p** and the pine together,
60:13 the cypress, the **p**, and the pine,
Eze 31: 8 the **p** trees were as nothing compared
Sir 24:14 and like a **p** tree beside water I grew tall.

PLANES (1)

Isa 44:13 fashions it with **p**, and marks it with a compass;

PLANKS (3)

1Ki 6: 9 he roofed the house with beams and **p** of cedar.
Eze 27: 5 They made all your **p** of fir trees from Senir;
Ac 27:44 some on **p** and others on pieces of the ship.

PLANNED (40) [PLAN]

Ex 32:14 about the disaster that he **p** to bring on his people.
1Sa 18:25 Now Saul **p** to make David fall by the hand of
2Sa 14:13 then have you **p** such a thing against the people
21: 5 "The man who consumed us and **p** to destroy us,
2Ki 19:25 I **p** from days of old what now I bring to pass,
1Ch 22: 7 I had **p** to build a house to the name of
28: 2 I had **p** to build a house of rest for the ark of
2Ch 7:11 all that Solomon had **p** to do in the house of
32: 3 he **p** with his officers and his warriors to stop
Ps 140: 4 from the violent who have **p** my downfall.
Isa 14:24 and as I have **p**, so shall it come to pass:
14:26 the plan that is **p** concerning the whole earth;
14:27 the LORD of hosts has **p**, and who will annul it?
19:12 and make known what the LORD of hosts has **p**
22:11 or have regard for him who **p** it long ago.
23: 8 Who has **p** this against Tyre,
23: 9 The LORD of hosts has **p** it—
37:26 I **p** from days of old what now I bring to pass,
46:11 I have **p**, and I will do it.
Jer 48: 2 In Heshbon they **p** evil against her:
51:12 for the LORD has both **p** and done what he spoke
Da 6: 3 king **p** to appoint him over the whole kingdom.
Zec 1: 6 just as he **p** to do."
Mt 1:19 and unwilling to expose her to public disgrace, **p**
Jn 11:53 So from that day on they **p** to put him to death.
12:10 the chief priests **p** to put Lazarus to death as well,
Ac 27:39 on which they **p** to run the ship ashore,
Jdt 9:13 and bruise on those who have **p** cruel things
11:12 they have **p** to kill their livestock
AdE 8: 3 to avert all the evil that Haman had **p** against
Wis 14: 2 For it was desire for gain that **p** that vessel,
14:14 and therefore their speedy end has been **p**.

Sus 1:61 as they had wickedly **p** to do to their neighbor.
1Mc 5: 9 the Israelites who lived in their territory, and **p**
6: 8 things had not turned out for him as he had **p**.
8: 9 The Greeks **p** to come and destroy them,
12:35 of the people and **p** with them to build strongholds
2Mc 9:15 but had **p** to throw out with their children for
2Es 6: 6 then I **p** these things, and they were made
11:25 that these little wings **p** to set themselves up

PLANNING (9) [PLAN]

Ge 27:42 "Your brother Esau is consoling himself by **p**
1Sa 19:11 **p** to kill him in the morning.
Isa 19:17 because of the plan that the LORD of hosts is **p**
Jer 9: 8 but inwardly are **p** to lay an ambush.
Ac 25: 3 in fact, **p** an ambush to kill him along the way.
1Mc 8: 4 of the whole region by their **p** and patience,
2Es 11:28 the two that remained were **p** between themselves
11:29 and while they were **p**, one of the heads that were
11:31 and devoured the two little wings that were **p**

PLANS (36) [PLAN]

2Sa 14:14 he will devise **p** so as not to keep
Job 17:11 My days are past, my **p** are broken off,
21:16 The **p** of the wicked are repugnant to me.
22:18 but the **p** of the wicked are repugnant to me.
Ps 14: 6 You would confound the **p** of the poor,
20: 4 grant you your heart's desire, and fulfill all your **p**.
33:10 he frustrates the **p** of the peoples.
83: 3 They lay crafty **p** against your people;
146: 4 on that very day their **p** perish.
Pr 6:18 a heart that devises wicked **p**,
15:22 Without counsel, **p** go wrong,
15:26 Evil **p** are an abomination to the LORD,
16: 1 The **p** of the mind belong to mortals,
16: 3 and your **p** will be established.
16: 9 The human mind **p** the way,
16:30 One who winks the eyes **p** perverse things;
19:21 The human mind may devise many **p**,
20:18 **P** are established by taking advice;
21: 5 The **p** of the diligent lead surely to abundance,
24: 8 Whoever **p** to do evil will be called
Isa 19: 3 and I will confound their **p**;
25: 1 you have done wonderful things, **p** formed of old,
Jer 18:12 We will follow our own **p**,
19: 7 And in this place I will make void the **p** of Judah
29:11 I know the **p** I have for you, **p** for your welfare
Da 11:24 He shall devise **p** against strongholds,
2Co 1:17 Do I make my **p** according
Tob 4:19 and that all your paths and **p** may prosper.
Jdt 10: 8 of our ancestors grant you favor and fulfill your **p**,
Wis 6: 3 search out your works and inquire into your **p**.
Sir 12:16 but in his heart he **p** to throw you into a pit;
1Mc 2:63 and their **p** will have perished.
16:13 made treacherous **p** against Simon and his sons,
2Mc 15: 1 he made **p** to attack them with complete safety on
3Mc 1:22 of his **p** or the fulfillment of his intended purpose.

PLANT‡ (56) [IMPLANTED, PLANTED, PLANTERS, PLANTING, PLANTS, REPLANTED, TRANSPLANTED]

Ge 1:29 I have given you every **p** yielding seed that is
1:30 I have given every green **p** for food."
2: 5 when no **p** of the field was yet in the earth
9:20 a man of the soil, was the first to **p** a vineyard.
Ex 10:12 that the locusts may come upon it and eat every **p**
10:15 nothing green was left, no tree, no **p** in the field,
Lev 19:23 into the land and **p** all kinds of trees for food,
Dt 6:11 vineyards and olive groves that you did not **p**—
16:21 You shall not **p** any tree as a sacred pole beside
28:30 You shall **p** a vineyard, but not enjoy its fruit.
28:39 You shall **p** vineyards and dress them,
Jos 24:13 of vineyards and oliveyards that you did not **p**.
2Sa 7:10 a place for my people Israel and will **p** them,
2Ki 19:29 then in the third year sow, reap, **p** vineyards,
1Ch 17: 9 and will **p** them, so that they may live
Job 8:12 they wither before any other **p**.
14: 9 and put forth branches like a young **p**.
Ps 107:37 and **p** vineyards, and get a fruitful yield.
Ecc 3: 2 time to **p**, and a time to pluck up what is planted;
Isa 17:10 though you **p** pleasant plants and set out slips of
17:11 the day that you **p** them, and make them blossom
28:25 and **p** wheat in rows and barley in its proper place,
37:30 then in the third year sow, reap, **p** vineyards,
53: 2 For he grew up before him like a young **p**,
65:21 they shall **p** vineyards and eat their fruit.
65:22 they shall not **p** and another eat;
Jer 1:10 to destroy and to overthrow, to build and to **p**."
12: 2 You **p** them, and they take root;
18: 9 a nation or a kingdom that I will build and **p** it,
24: 6 I will **p** them, and not pluck them up.
29: 5 **p** gardens and eat what they produce.
29:28 and **p** gardens and eat what they produce."
31: 5 Again you shall **p** vineyards on the mountains
31: 5 the planters shall **p**, and shall enjoy the fruit.
31:28 so I will watch over them to build and to **p**,
32:41 and I will **p** them in this land in faithfulness,
35: 7 nor shall you **p** a vineyard, or even own one;
42:10 I will **p** you, and not pluck you up;
Eze 4: 2 and **p** battering rams against it all around.
16: 7 and grow up like a **p** of the field."
17: 5 A **p** by abundant waters, he set it like a willow
17:22 I myself will **p** it on a high and lofty mountain.
17:23 On the mountain height of Israel I will **p** it,
28:26 and shall build houses and **p** vineyards.

Am 9:14 they shall **p** vineyards and drink their wine,
9:15 I will **p** them upon their land,
Zep 1:13 though they **p** vineyards, they shall not drink wine
Mt 15:13 "Every **p** that my heavenly Father has
Sir 3:28 for an evil **p** has taken root in him.
49: 7 and likewise to build and to **p**.
2Mc 1:29 **P** your people in your holy place,
1Es 4: 9 if he tells them to **p**, they **p**.
4:16 and women brought up the very men who **p**
2Es 9:21 and one **p** out of a great forest.
9:22 but let my grape and my **p** be saved,

PLANTED (41) [PLANT]

Ge 2: 8 the LORD God **p** a garden in Eden, in the east;
21:33 Abraham **p** a tamarisk tree in Beer-sheba,
Ex 15:17 You brought them in and **p** them on the mountain
Nu 24: 6 like aloes that the LORD has **p**,
Dt 20: 6 Has anyone **p** a vineyard but not
29:23 nothing **p**, nothing sprouting,
Ps 1: 3 They are like trees **p** by streams of water,
44: 2 the nations, but them you **p**;
80: 8 you drove out the nations and **p** it.
80:15 the stock that your right hand **p**.
92:13 They are **p** in the house of the LORD;
94: 9 He who **p** the ear, does he not hear?
104:16 the cedars of Lebanon that he **p**.
Ecc 2: 4 I built houses and **p** vineyards for myself;
2: 5 and **p** in them all kinds of fruit trees.
3: 2 a time to plant, and a time to pluck up what is **p**;
Isa 5: 2 and **p** it with choice vines;
40:24 Scarcely are they **p**, scarcely sown,
60:21 They are the shoot that I **p**, the work of my hands,
Jer 2:21 I **p** you as a choice vine, from the purest stock.
11:17 The LORD of hosts, who **p** you,
17: 8 They shall be like a tree **p** by water,
45: 4 pluck up what I have **p**—that is, the whole land.
Eze 17: 7 From the bed where it was **p**
31: 4 making its rivers flow around the place it was **p**,
Hos 9:13 Once I saw Ephraim as a young palm **p** in
Am 5:11 you have **p** pleasant vineyards,
Mt 15:13 that my heavenly Father has not **p** will
21:33 There was a landowner who **p** a vineyard,
Mk 12: 1 "A man **p** a vineyard, put a fence around it,
Lk 13: 6 "A man had a fig tree **p** in his vineyard;
17: 6 'Be uprooted and **p** in the sea,'
20: 9 "A man **p** a vineyard, and leased it to tenants,
1Co 3: 6 I **p**, Apollos watered, but God gave the growth.
Sir 43:23 By his plan he stilled the deep and **p** islands in it.
2Es 3: 4 not speak at the beginning when you **p** the earth—
3: 6 into the garden that your right hand had **p** before
6:42 be **p** and cultivated and be of service before you.
8:41 and not all that were **p** will take root;
8:52 the tree of life is **p**, the age to come is prepared,
4Mc 2:21 he **p** in them emotions and inclinations,

PLANTERS (1) [PLANT]

Jer 31: 5 the **p** shall plant, and shall enjoy the fruit.

PLANTING‡ (5) [PLANT]

Isa 5: 7 and the people of Judah are his pleasant **p**;
61: 3 the **p** of the LORD, to display his glory.
Mic 1: 6 in the open country, a place for **p** vineyards.
Lk 17:28 buying and selling, **p** and building,
1Mc 3:56 or were about to be married, or were **p** a vineyard,

PLANTS (28) [PLANT]

Ge 1:11 **p** yielding seed, and fruit trees of every kind
1:12 **p** yielding seed of every kind,
3:18 and you shall eat the **p** of the field.
9: 3 and just as I gave you the green **p**,
Ex 9:22 on humans and animals and all the **p** of the field in
9:25 the hail also struck down all the **p** of the field,
10:15 and they ate all the **p** in the land and all the fruit of
2Ki 19:26 they have become like **p** of the field and
Job 12: 8 ask the **p** of the earth, and they will teach you;
40:21 Under the lotus **p** it lies,
Ps 104:14 and **p** for people to use,
144:12 May our sons in their youth be like **p** full grown,
Pr 31:16 with the fruit of her hands she **p** a vineyard.
Isa 17:10 though you plant pleasant **p** and set out slips of
37:27 they have become like **p** of the field and
44:14 He **p** a cedar and the rain nourishes it.
Mt 13:26 So when the **p** came up and bore grain,
1Co 3: 7 the one who **p** nor the one who waters is anything,
3: 8 The one who **p** and the one who waters have
9: 7 Who **p** a vineyard and does not eat any of its fruit?
Wis 7:20 the varieties of **p** and the virtues of roots;
10: 7 **p** bearing fruit that does not ripen,
Sir 10:15 and **p** the humble in their place.
2Es 8:41 the ground and **p** a multitude of seedlings,
9:26 there I sat among the flowers and ate of the **p** of
12:51 and my food was of **p** during those days.
4Mc 1:28 Just as pleasure and pain are two **p** growing from
1:28 so there are many offshoots of these **p**,

PLASTER (8) [PLASTERED]

Lev 14:41 and the **p** that is scraped off shall be dumped in
14:42 and take other **p** and **p** the house.
14:45 its stones and timber and all the **p** of the house,
Dt 27: 2 up large stones and cover them with **p**.
27: 4 on Mount Ebal, and you shall cover them with **p**.
Da 5: 5 and began writing on the **p** of the wall of
Hab 2:11 and the **p** will respond from the woodwork.

PLASTERED (3) [PLASTER]
Ex 2: 3 and **p** it with bitumen and pitch;
Lev 14:43 the stones and scraped the house and **p** it,
14:48 after the house was **p**, the priest shall pronounce

PLATE‡ (17) [BREASTPLATE, BREASTPLATES, PLATED, PLATES]
Nu 7:13 his offering was one silver **p** weighing one hundred
7:19 his offering one silver **p** weighing one hundred
7:25 his offering was one silver **p** weighing one hundred
7:31 his offering was one silver **p** weighing one hundred
7:37 his offering was one silver **p** weighing one hundred
7:43 his offering was one silver **p** weighing one hundred
7:49 his offering was one silver **p** weighing one hundred
7:55 his offering was one silver **p** weighing one hundred
7:61 his offering was one silver **p** weighing one hundred
7:67 his offering was one silver **p** weighing one hundred
7:73 his offering was one silver **p** weighing one hundred
7:79 his offering was one silver **p** weighing one hundred
7:85 each silver **p** weighing one hundred thirty shekels
Eze 4: 3 an iron **p** and place it as an iron wall between you
Mt 23:25 For you clean the outside of the cup and of the **p**,
1Mc 11:58 He also sent him gold **p** and a table service,
15:32 and the sideboard with its gold and silver **p**,

PLATED (1) [PLATE]
Hab 2:19 See, it is gold and silver **p**,

PLATES (5) [PLATE]
Ex 25:29 You shall make its **p** and dishes for incense,
37:16 its **p** and dishes for incense,
Nu 4: 7 and put on it the **p**, the dishes for incense,
7:84 twelve silver **p**, twelve silver basins,
16:38 Make them into hammered **p** as a covering for

PLATFORM (9)
2Ch 6:13 Solomon had made a bronze **p** five cubits long,
Ne 8: 4 a wooden **p** that had been made for the purpose;
Eze 16:24 you built yourself a **p** and made yourself
16:31 building your **p** at the head of every street,
16:39 down your **p** and break down your lofty places;
41: 8 also that the temple had a raised **p** all around;
Ac 12:21 took his seat on the **p**,
2Mc 13:26 Lysias took the public **p**, made
1Es 9:42 and reader of the law stood on the wooden **p**

PLATTED (KJV) See TWISTING, WOVE

PLATTER (4)
Mt 14: 8 Give me the head of John the Baptist here on a **p**."
14:11 The head was brought on a **p** and given to the girl,
Mk 6:25 at once the head of John the Baptist on a **p**."
6:28 brought his head on a **p**,

PLAUSIBLE (2)
1Co 2: 4 and my proclamation were not with **p** words
Col 2: 4 so that no one may deceive you with **p** arguments.

PLAY‡ (27) [PLAYED, PLAYERS, PLAYING, PLAYS]
Ge 4:21 the ancestor of all those who **p** the lyre and pipe.
19: 9 and he would **p** the judge!
1Sa 16:16 the evil spirit from God is upon you, he will **p** it,
16:17 "Provide for me someone who can **p** well,
21:15 that you have brought this fellow to **p** the madman
1Ch 15:16 as the singers to **p** on musical instruments,
15:20 Benaiah were to **p** harps according to Alamoth;
Job 40:20 for it where all the wild animals **p**.
41: 5 Will you **p** with it as with a bird,
Ps 33: 3 **p** skillfully on the strings, with loud shouts.
144: 9 upon a ten-stringed harp I will **p** to you,
Pr 18:24 Some friends **p** at friendship but
Isa 11: 8 The nursing child shall **p** over the hole of the asp,
Eze 16:34 no one solicited you to **p** the whore;
Hos 3: 3 you shall not **p** the whore,
4:10 they shall **p** the whore, but not multiply;
4:13 Therefore your daughters **p** the whore,
4:14 when they **p** the whore, nor your daughters-in-law
4:15 Though you **p** the whore, O Israel,
1Co 10: 7 down to eat and drink, and they rose up to **p**."
Sir 29:25 you will **p** the host and provide drink
30: 9 **p** with him, and he will grieve you.
34:16 or **p** the coward, for he is their hope.
1Mc 3:45 the flute and the harp ceased to **p**.
2Mc 3:32 that some foul **p** had been perpetrated by the Jews
4Mc 5:34 I will not **p** false to you, O law that trained me,
10:14 "You do not have a fire hot enough to make me **p**

PLAYED (25) [PLAY]
Ge 38:24 "Your daughter-in-law Tamar has **p** the whore;
1Sa 16:23 David took the lyre and **p** it with his hand,
Jer 2:20 and under every green tree you sprawled and **p**
3: 1 You have **p** the whore with many lovers;
3: 6 and under every green tree, and **p** the whore there?
3: 8 but she too went and **p** the whore.
Eze 16:15 and **p** the whore because of your fame,
16:16 and on them **p** the whore;
16:17 and with them **p** the whore;
16:26 You **p** the whore with the Egyptians,
16:28 You **p** the whore with the Assyrians,
16:28 you **p** the whore with them,
Eze 23: 3 they **p** the whore in Egypt;
23: 3 they **p** the whore in their youth;
23: 5 Oholah **p** the whore while she was mine;
23:19 when she **p** the whore in the land of Egypt
23:30 because you **p** the whore with the nations,
Hos 2: 5 For their mother has **p** the whore;
4:12 and they have **p** the whore, forsaking their God.
5: 3 for now, O Ephraim, you have **p** the whore;
9: 1 you have **p** the whore, departing from your God.
Mt 11:17 'We **p** the flute for you, and you did not dance;
Lk 7:32 'We **p** the flute for you, and you did not dance;
1Co 14: 7 how will anyone know what is being **p**?
Sir 47: 3 He **p** with lions as though they were young goats,

PLAYERS (1) [PLAY]
Mt 9:23 the flute **p** and the crowd making a commotion,

PLAYING (12) [PLAY]
Ge 21: 9 whom she had borne to Abraham, **p** with her son
1Sa 10: 5 tambourine, flute, and lyre **p** in front of them;
16:16 to look for someone who is skillful in **p** the lyre;
16:18 in **p**, a man of valor, a warrior, prudent in speech,
18:10 while David was **p** the lyre, as he did day by day.
19: 9 while David was **p** music.
1Ki 1:40 **p** on pipes and rejoicing with great joy,
2Ki 3:15 And then, while the musician was **p**,
Ps 68:25 between them girls **p** tambourines:
Eze 16:41 I will stop you from **p** the whore,
Zec 8: 5 of the city shall be full of boys and girls **p**
Rev 14: 2 the voice I heard was like the sound of harpists **p**

PLAYS‡ (3) [PLAY]
Jer 29:26 of the LORD to control any madman who **p**
29:27 not rebuked Jeremiah of Anathoth who **p**
Eze 33:32 a beautiful voice and **p** well on an instrument;

PLEA (21) [PLEAS]
1Ki 8:28 Regard your servant's prayer and his **p**,
8:30 the **p** of your servant and of your people Israel
8:38 whatever **p** there is from any individual or
8:45 then hear in heaven their prayer and their **p**,
8:49 your dwelling place their prayer and their **p**,
8:52 the **p** of your servant, and to the **p** of your people
8:54 and this **p** to the LORD, he arose from facing
9: 3 "I have heard your prayer and your **p**,
2Ch 6:19 Regard your servant's prayer and his **p**,
6:21 the **p** of your servant and of your people Israel,
6:29 whatever **p** from any individual or
6:35 then hear from heaven their prayer and their **p**,
33:13 and God received his entreaty, heard his **p**,
Isa 32: 7 even when the **p** of the needy is right.
Jer 36: 7 be that their **p** will come before the LORD,
37:20 be good enough to listen to my **p**,
38:26 'I was presenting my **p** to the king not
42: 2 "Be good enough to listen to our **p**,
42: 9 to whom you sent me to present your **p**
La 3:56 you heard my **p**, "Do not close your ear to my cry

PLEAD (20) [PLEADED, PLEADING, PLEADINGS, PLEADS]
1Sa 24:15 May he see to it, and **p** my cause,
1Ki 8:33 pray and **p** with you in this house,
8:47 and **p** with you in the land of their captors, saying,
2Ch 6:24 pray and **p** with you in this house,
6:37 and **p** with you in the land of their captivity,
Job 13: 8 will you **p** the case for God?
19:16 I must myself **p** with him.
Ps 5: 3 in the morning I **p** my case to you, and watch.
74:22 Rise up, O God, **p** your cause;
119:154 **P** my cause and redeem me;
Pr 6: 3 go, hurry, and **p** with your neighbor.
23:11 he will **p** their cause against you.
Isa 1:17 defend the orphan, **p** for the widow.
Jer 50:34 He will surely **p** their cause,
Hos 2: 2 **P** with your mother, **p**—
Mic 6: 1 Rise, **p** your case before the mountains,
Lk 15:28 His father came out and began to **p** with him.
AdE 4: 8 to go in to the king and **p** for his favor in behalf of
Wis 12:12 Or who will come before you to **p** as an advocate

PLEADED (7) [PLEAD]
Ge 42:21 we saw his anguish when he **p** with us,
2Sa 12:16 David therefore **p** with God for the child;
1Ki 8:59 with which I **p** before the LORD,
Mt 18:29 Then his fellow slave fell down and **p** with him,
18:32 I forgave you all that debt because you **p** with me.
1Mc 11:62 Then the people of Gaza **p** with Jonathan,
2Mc 4:47 if they had **p** even before Scythians.

PLEADING (7) [PLEAD]
Est 8: 3 and **p** with him to avert the evil design of Haman
Ps 102: T *when faint and **p** before the LORD.*
Jer 31:18 Indeed I heard Ephraim **p**:
Ac 16: 9 a man of Macedonia **p** with him and saying,
1Th 2:12 urging and encouraging you and **p** that you lead
Jdt 8:16 or like a mere mortal, to be won over by **p**.
AdE 7: 8 on the couch, **p** with the queen.

PLEADINGS (2) [PLEAD]
Job 13: 6 and listen to the **p** of my lips.
Ps 28: 6 for he has heard the sound of my **p**.

PLEADS (3) [PLEAD]
Pr 22:23 for the LORD **p** their cause and despoils
Isa 51:22 your God who **p** the cause of his people:
Ro 11: 2 how he **p** with God against Israel?

PLEAS (2) [PLEA]
2Ch 6:39 and their **p**, maintain their cause
Isa 59: 4 they rely on empty **p**, they speak lies,

PLEASANT‡ (34) [PLEASANTNESS]
Ge 2: 9 the LORD God made to grow every tree that is **p**
49:15 and that the land was **p**;
2Sa 19:35 can I discern what is **p** and what is not?
Ps 16: 6 The boundary lines have fallen for me in **p** places;
55:14 with whom I kept **p** company;
106:24 Then they despised the **p** land,
133: 1 and **p** it is when kindred live together in unity!
141: 6 then they shall learn that my words were **p**.
Pr 2:10 and knowledge will be **p** to your soul;
9:17 and bread eaten in secret is **p**."
16:21 and **p** speech increases persuasiveness.
16:24 **P** words are like a honeycomb,
22:18 for it will be **p** if you keep them within you,
23: 8 and you will waste your **p** words.
24: 4 the rooms are filled with all precious and **p** riches.
Ecc 11: 7 and it is **p** for the eyes to see the sun.
SS 7: 6 How fair and **p** you are, O loved one,
Isa 5: 7 and the people of Judah are his **p** planting;
13:22 and jackals in the **p** palaces;
17:10 you plant **p** plants and set out slips of an alien god,
27: 2 On that day: A **p** vineyard, sing about it!
32:12 Beat your breasts for the **p** fields,
64:11 and all our **p** places have become ruins.
Jer 3:19 and give you a **p** land, the most beautiful heritage
12:10 they have made my **p** portion
31:26 and my sleep was **p** to me.
Am 5:11 you have planted **p** vineyards,
Mic 2: 9 of my people you drive out from their **p** houses;
Zec 7:14 and a **p** land was made desolate.
Heb 12:11 discipline always seems painful rather than **p** at
Sir 6: 5 **P** speech multiplies friends,
40:21 but a **p** voice is better than either.
3Mc 5:12 by the action of the Lord he was overcome by so **p**
4Mc 8:23 Why do we banish ourselves from this most **p** life

PLEASANTNESS (2) [PLEASANT]
Job 36:11 in prosperity, and their years in **p**.
Pr 3:17 Her ways are ways of **p**,

PLEASE (124) [PLEASED, PLEASES, PLEASING, PLEASURE, PLEASURES]
Ge 16: 6 do to her as you **p**."
19: 2 "**P**, my lords, turn aside to your servant's house
19: 8 and do to them as you **p**;
24:12 **p** grant me success today and show steadfast love
24:14 '**P** offer your jar that I may drink,'
24:17 "**P** let me sip a little water from your jar."
24:43 "**P** give me a little water from your jar to drink,"
24:45 I said to her, '**P** let me drink.'
28: 8 the Canaanite women did not **p** his father Isaac,
30:14 "**P** give me some of your son's mandrakes."
32:11 Deliver me, **p**, from the hand of my brother,
32:29 Then Jacob asked him, "**P** tell me your name."
33:10 Jacob said, "No, **p**; if I find favor with you,
33:11 **P** accept my gift that is brought to you,
34: 8 **p** give her to him in marriage.
37:16 "tell me, **p**, where they are pasturing the flock."
38:25 And she said, "Take note, **p**, whose these are,
40: 8 **P** tell them to me."
40:14 **p** do me the kindness to make mention of me
44:18 let your servant **p** speak a word in my lord's ears,
44:33 **p** let your servant remain as a slave to my lord
47:25 may it **p** my lord, we will be slaves to Pharaoh."
48: 9 And he said, "Bring them to me, **p**,
50: 4 **p** speak to Pharaoh as follows:
50:17 Now therefore **p** forgive the crime of the servants
Ex 4:13 But he said, "O my Lord, **p** send someone else."
4:18 "**P** let me go back to my kindred in Egypt
21: 8 If she does not **p** her master,
Nu 12:13 Moses cried to the LORD, "O God, **p** heal her."
23:27 perhaps it will **p** God that you may curse them
Dt 23:16 wherever they **p**; you shall not oppress them.
24: 1 but she does not **p** him because he finds something
Jdg 4:19 he said to her, "**P** give me a little water to drink;
6:39 **p**, make trial with the fleece just once more;
8: 5 "**P** give some loaves of bread to my followers,
16: 6 "**P** tell me what makes your strength so great,
16:10 **p** tell me how you could be bound."
Ru 2: 7 '**P**, let me glean and gather among the sheaves
1Sa 2:36 **P** put me in one of the priest's places,
9:18 "Tell me, **p**, where is the house of the seer?"
22: 3 "**P** let my father and mother come to you,
25: 8 **P** give whatever you have at hand to your servants
25:24 **p** let your servant speak in your ears,
25:28 **P** forgive the trespass of your servant;
2Sa 7:29 now therefore may it **p** you to bless the house
13: 6 the king, "**P** let my sister Tamar come and make
13:24 the king and his servants **p** go with your servant?"
13:26 "If not, **p** let my brother Amnon go with us."
14:11 "**P**, may the king keep the LORD your God
14:12 "**P** let your servant speak a word to my lord
15: 7 "**P** let me go to Hebron and pay the vow
19:37 **P** let your servant return, so that I may die
1Ki 2:17 He said, "**P** ask King Solomon—

1Ki 3:17 The one woman said, **"P,** my lord,
3:26 **"P,** my lord, give her the living boy;
9:12 that Solomon had given him, they did not **p** him.
20:32 "Your servant Ben-hadad says, **'P** let me live.' "
2Ki 1:13 and entreated him, "O man of God, **p** let my life,
2: 9 **"P** let me inherit a double share of your spirit."
2:16 **p** let them go and seek your master;
5:15 **p** accept a present from your servant."
5:17 **p** let two mule-loads of earth be given
5:22 **p** give them a talent of silver and two changes
5:23 Naaman said, **"P** accept two talents."
6: 3 one of them said, **"P** come with your servants."
6:17 "O LORD, **p** open his eyes that he may see."
6:18 and said, "Strike this people, **p,** with blindness."
18:26 **"P** speak to your servants in
1Ch 17:27 may it **p** you to bless the house of your servant,
2Ch 10: 7 "If you will be kind to this people and **p** them,
Est 8: 8 You may write as you **p** with regard to the Jews,
Job 6: 9 that it would **p** God to crush me,
Ps 69:31 This will **p** the LORD more than an ox or a bull
Pr 16: 7 When the ways of people **p** the LORD,
Isa 36:11 **"P** speak to your servants in Aramaic,
56: 4 the things that **p** me and hold fast my covenant,
66: 4 and chose what did not **p** me.
Jer 21: 2 **"P** inquire of the LORD on our behalf,
27: 5 and I give it to whomever I **p.**
37: 3 **"P** pray for us to the LORD our God."
37:20 Now **p** hear me, my lord king:
40:15 **"P** let me go and kill Ishmael son of Nethaniah,
Da 1:12 **"P** test your servants for ten days.
Hos 9: 4 and their sacrifices shall not **p** him.
Jnh 1:14 Then they cried out to the LORD, **"P,** O LORD,
4: 3 And now, O LORD, **p** take my life from me,
Lk 4: 6 and I give it to anyone I **p.**
14:18 and see it; **p** accept my regrets.'
14:19 to try them out; **p** accept my regrets.'
Ac 9:38 **"P** come to us without delay."
Ro 8: 8 and those who are in the flesh cannot **p** God.
15: 1 the failings of the weak, and not to **p** ourselves.
15: 2 of us must **p** our neighbor for the good purpose
15: 3 For Christ did not **p** himself;
1Co 7:32 about the affairs of the Lord, how to **p** the Lord;
7:33 about the affairs of the world, how to **p** his wife,
7:34 the affairs of the world, how to **p** her husband.
10:33 just as I try to **p** everyone in everything I do,
2Co 5: 9 we make it our aim to **p** him.
Gal 1:10 Or am I trying to **p** people?
Eph 6: 6 and in order to **p** them, but as slaves of Christ,
Col 3:22 only while being watched and in order to **p** them,
1Th 2: 4 even so we speak, not to **p** mortals, but to **p** God
who tests our hearts.
4: 1 from us how you ought to live and to **p** God (as,
2Ti 2: 4 the soldier's aim is to **p** the enlisting officer.
Heb 11: 6 And without faith it is impossible to **p** God,
Jas 2: 3 and say, "Have a seat here, **p,"**
Jdt 3: 3 do with them as you **p.**
5: 5 "May my lord **p** listen to a report from the mouth
9:12 **P, p,** God of my father,
Wis 14:19 For he, perhaps wishing to **p** his ruler,
Sir 2:16 Those who fear the Lord seek to **p** him,
8:15 for they will act as they **p,**
20:28 and those who **p** the great atone for injustice.
1Mc 12:18 And now **p** send us a reply to this."
12:22 **p** write us concerning your welfare;
2Mc 2:16 Will you therefore **p** keep the days?
2:25 we have aimed to **p** those who wish to read,
7:16 though you also are mortal, you do what you **p.**
14: 9 may it **p** you to take thought for our country
2Es 15:47 for prostitution to **p** and glory in your lovers,
4Mc 8:26 and such a fatal stubbornness **p** us,

PLEASED[‡] (79) [PLEASE]

Ge 34:18 Their words **p** Hamor and Hamor's son Shechem.
41:37 The proposal **p** Pharaoh and all his servants.
45:16 Pharaoh and his servants were **p.**
Nu 14: 8 If the LORD is **p** with us,
24: 1 Balaam saw that it **p** the LORD to bless Israel,
Jos 22:33 The report **p** the Israelites;
Jdg 14: 7 and talked with the woman, and she **p** Samson.
1Sa 12:22 because it has **p** the LORD to make you a people
18:20 Saul was told, and the thing **p** him.
18:26 David was well **p** to be the king's son-in-law.
2Sa 3:36 All the people took notice of it, and it **p** them;
3:36 just as everything the king did **p** all the people.
17: 4 The advice **p** Absalom and all the elders of Israel.
19: 6 of us were dead today, then you would be **p.**
1Ki 3:10 It **p** the Lord that Solomon had asked this.
1Ch 13: 4 for the thing **p** all the people.
Ne 2: 6 So it **p** the king to send me, and I set him a date.
9:24 to do with them as they **p.**
Est 1:21 This advice **p** the king and the officials,
2: 4 This **p** the king, and he did so.
2: 9 The girl **p** him and won his favor,
5:14 This advice **p** Haman, and he had
9: 5 and did as they **p** to those who hated them.
Job 6:28 be **p** to look at me; for I will not lie to your face.
Ps 40:13 Be **p,** O LORD, to deliver me;
41:11 By this I know that you are **p** with me;
49:13 the end of those who are **p** with their lot.
51:16 to give a burnt offering, you would not be **p.**
70: 1 Be **p,** O God, to deliver me.
Isa 42:21 The LORD was **p,** for the sake
Da 4: 2 that the Most High God has worked for me I am **p**
6: 1 It **p** Darius to set over the kingdom
8: 4 it did as it **p** and became strong.
Jnh 1:14 for you, O LORD, have done as it **p** you."
Mic 6: 7 Will the LORD be **p** with thousands of rams,
Mal 1: 8 will he be **p** with you or show you favor?
Mt 3:17 the Beloved, with whom I am well **p."**
12:18 my beloved, with whom my soul is well **p.**
14: 6 before the company, and she **p** Herod
17: 5 with him I am well **p;** listen to him!"
17:12 but they did to him whatever they **p.**
Mk 1:11 with you I am well **p."**
6:22 she **p** Herod and his guests;
9:13 and they did to him whatever they **p,**
14:11 When they heard it, they were greatly **p,**
Lk 3:22 with you I am well **p."**
22: 5 They were greatly **p** and agreed
Ac 6: 5 What they said **p** the whole community,
12: 3 After he saw that it **p** the Jews,
Ro 15:26 and Achaia have been **p** to share their resources
15:27 They were **p** to do this, and indeed they owe it
1Co 10: 5 Nevertheless, God was not **p** with most of them,
Gal 1:15 and called me through his grace, was **p**
Col 1:19 For in him all the fullness of God was **p** to dwell,
1:20 him God was **p** to reconcile to himself all things,
Heb 11: 5 before he was taken away that "he had **p** God."
2Pe 1:17 my Beloved, with whom I am well **p."**
Jdt 7:16 These words **p** Holofernes and all his attendants,
11:20 Her words **p** Holofernes and all his servants.
12:20 Holofernes was greatly **p** with her,
15:10 and God is well **p** with it.
AdE 1:21 This speech **p** the king and the governors,
2: 4 This **p** the king, and he did so.
2: 9 The girl **p** him and won his favor,
5:14 This advice **p** Haman,
Wis 4:10 There were some who **p** God and were loved
Sir 34:23 The Most High is not **p** with the offerings of
44:16 Enoch **p** the Lord and was taken up,
45:19 The Lord saw it and was not **p,**
1Mc 1:12 This proposal **p** them,
6:60 The speech **p** the king and the commanders,
8:21 The proposal **p** them,
11:49 the Jews had gained control of the city as they **p,**
14:23 It has **p** our people to receive these men
2Mc 1:20 But after many years had passed, when it **p** God,
14:35 you were **p** that there should be a temple
Pm 151: 5 but the Lord was not **p** with them.
4Mc 8: 4 about their mother as though a chorus, he was **p**
12: 9 Extremely **p** by the boy's declaration,

PLEASES[‡] (38) [PLEASE]

Ge 20:15 before you; settle where it **p** you."
Jdg 14: 3 "Get her for me, because she **p** me."
1Ki 20: 6 and lay hands on whatever **p** them,
Ne 2: 5 Then I said to the king, "If it **p** the king,
2: 7 Then I said to the king, "If it **p** the king,
Est 1:19 If it **p** the king, let a royal order go out from him,
2: 4 And let the girl who **p** the king be queen instead
3: 9 If it **p** the king, let a decree be issued
5: 4 Then Esther said, "If it **p** the king,
5: 8 and if it **p** the king to grant my petition
7: 3 and if it **p** the king, let my life be given me—
8: 5 She said, "If it **p** the king,
9:13 Esther said, "If it **p** the king,
Ps 115: 3 Our God is in the heavens; he does whatever he **p.**
135: 6 Whatever the LORD **p** he does,
Ecc 2:26 For to the one who **p** him God gives wisdom
2:26 only to give to one who **p** God.
7:26 one who **p** God escapes her,
8: 3 for he does whatever he **p.**
Da 11: 3 with great dominion and take action as he **p.**
11:16 against him shall take the actions he **p,**
11:36 "The king shall act as he **p.**
1Jn 3:22 we obey his commandments and do what **p** him.
Tob 4: 3 Do whatever **p** her, and do not grieve her
Jdt 8:15 he has power to protect us within any time he **p,**
8:17 and he will hear our voice, if it **p** him.
12:14 Whatever **p** him I will do at once,
AdE 1:19 If therefore it **p** the king, let him issue
2: 4 the woman who **p** the king shall be queen instead
3: 9 If it **p** the king, let it be decreed that they are to
5: 4 If it **p** the king, let him and Haman come to
8: 5 Esther said, "If it **p** you, and if I have found favor,
Wis 9:18 and people were taught what **p** you,
Sir 7:26 Do you have a wife who **p** you?
9:12 Do not delight in what **p** the ungodly;
20:27 and one who is sensible **p** the great.
33:13 to be molded as he **p,**
2Es 12:39 so that you may be shown whatever it **p**

PLEASING[‡] (73) [PLEASE]

Ge 8:21 And when the LORD smelled the **p** odor,
Ex 29:18 it is a **p** odor, an offering by fire to the LORD.
29:25 of the burnt offering of **p** odor before the LORD;
29:41 for a **p** odor, an offering by fire to the LORD.
Lev 1: 9 an offering by fire of **p** odor to the LORD.
1:13 an offering by fire of **p** odor to the LORD.
1:17 an offering by fire of **p** odor to the LORD.
2: 2 an offering by fire of **p** odor to the LORD.
2: 9 an offering by fire of **p** odor to the LORD.
2:12 they shall not be offered on the altar for a **p** odor.
3: 5 as an offering by fire of **p** odor to the LORD.
3:16 on the altar as a food offering by fire for a **p** odor.
4:31 into smoke on the altar for a **p** odor to the LORD.
6:15 into smoke on the altar as a **p** odor to the LORD.
6:21 and you shall present it as a **p** odor to the LORD.
8:21 it was a burnt offering for a **p** odor,
8:28 This was an ordination offering for a **p** odor,
17: 6 turn the fat into smoke as a **p** odor to the LORD,
23:13 an offering by fire of **p** odor to the LORD;
Lev 23:18 an offering by fire of **p** odor to the LORD.
26:31 and I will not smell your **p** odors.
Nu 15: 3 to make a **p** odor for the LORD,
15: 7 a **p** odor to the LORD.
15:10 as an offering by fire, a **p** odor to the LORD.
15:13 a **p** odor to the LORD.
15:14 a **p** odor to the LORD, shall do as you do.
15:24 a **p** odor to the LORD,
18:17 as an offering by fire for a **p** odor to the LORD;
28: 2 the food for my offerings by fire, my **p** odor,
28: 6 ordained at Mount Sinai for a **p** odor,
28: 8 you shall offer it as an offering by fire, a **p** odor to
28:13 a burnt offering of **p** odor,
28:24 a **p** odor to the LORD;
28:27 a **p** odor to the LORD:
29: 2 a **p** odor to the LORD:
29: 6 according to the ordinance for them, a **p** odor,
29: 8 a burnt offering to the LORD, a **p** odor:
29:13 an offering by fire, a **p** odor to the LORD:
29:36 an offering by fire, a **p** odor to the LORD:
1Ki 14:13 in him there is found something **p** to the LORD,
Ezr 6:10 they may offer **p** sacrifices to the God of heaven,
Ps 104:34 May my meditation be **p** to him,
Ecc 12:10 The Teacher sought to find **p** words,
Jer 6:20 nor are your sacrifices **p** to me.
Eze 6:13 wherever they offered **p** odor to all their idols.
16:19 you set it before them as a **p** odor;
20:28 there they sent up their **p** odors,
20:41 As a **p** odor I will accept you,
Mal 3: 4 of Judah and Jerusalem will be **p** to the LORD as
Jn 8:29 for I always do what is **p** to him."
Gal 1:10 If I were still **p** people,
Eph 5:10 Try to find out what is **p** to the Lord.
Php 4: 8 whatever is just, whatever is pure, whatever is **p,**
4:18 a sacrifice acceptable and **p** to God.
Col 1:10 that you may lead lives worthy of the Lord, fully **p**
1Ti 5: 4 for this is **p** in God's sight.
Heb 13:16 for such sacrifices are **p** to God.
13:21 working among us that which is **p** in his sight,
Tob 3:15 But if it is not **p** to you, O Lord, to take my life,
14:8,9 serve God faithfully and do what is **p** in his sight.
Wis 4:14 for their souls were **p** to the Lord,
9: 9 she understands what is **p** in your sight
9:10 and that I may learn what is **p** to you.
13:11 then with **p** workmanship make a useful vessel
Sir 35: 5 To keep from wickedness is **p** to the Lord,
35: 8 and its **p** odor rises before the Most High.
35:20 The one whose service is **p** to the Lord will
45:16 incense and a **p** odor as a memorial portion,
48:22 For Hezekiah did what was **p** to the Lord,
50:15 a **p** odor to the Most High, the king of all.
Bar 4: 4 O Israel, for we know what is **p** to God.
1Mc 14: 4 his rule was **p** to them, as was the honor shown
1Es 1:12 in bronze pots and caldrons, with a **p** odor,

PLEASURE[‡] (58) [PLEASE]

Ge 18:12 and my husband is old, shall I have **p?"**
2Sa 15:26 But if he says, 'I take no **p** in you,' here I am,
19:18 over the king's household, and to do his **p.**
1Ch 29:17 and take **p** in uprightness;
Ezr 5:17 Let the king send us his **p** in this matter."
Ne 9:37 over our bodies and over our livestock at their **p,**
Job 22: 3 Is it any **p** to the Almighty if you are righteous,
Ps 51:18 Do good to Zion in your good **p;**
62: 4 They take **p** in falsehood;
105:22 to instruct his officials at his **p,**
147:10 nor his **p** in the speed of a runner;
147:11 but the LORD takes **p** in those who fear him,
149: 4 For the LORD takes **p** in his people;
Pr 10:23 wise conduct is **p** to a person of understanding.
18: 2 A fool takes no **p** in understanding,
21:17 Whoever loves **p** will suffer want;
Ecc 2: 1 I will make a test of **p;** enjoy yourself."
2: 2 I said of laughter, "It is mad," and of **p,** "What use
2:10 I kept my heart from no **p,** for my heart found **p** in
all my toil,
3:13 that all should eat and drink and take **p**
4: 8 they ask, "and depriving myself of **p?"**
5: 4 for he has no **p** in fools.
12: 1 "I have no **p** in them";
Jer 6:10 they take no **p** in it.
Eze 16:37 with whom you took **p,** all those you loved
18:23 Have I any **p** in the death of the wicked,
18:32 For I have no **p** in the death of anyone,
33:11 I have no **p** in the death of the wicked,
Hag 1: 8 so that I may take **p** in it and be honored,
Mal 1:10 I have no **p** in you, says the LORD of hosts,
Lk 12:32 for it is your Father's good **p** to give you
Eph 1: 5 according to the good **p** of his will,
1: 9 according to his good **p** that he set forth in Christ,
Php 2:13 both to will and to work for his good **p.**
2Th 2:12 that all who have not believed the truth but took **p**
1Ti 5: 6 but the widow who lives for **p** is dead even
2Ti 3: 4 lovers of **p** rather than lovers of God,
Heb 10: 6 and sin offerings you have taken no **p.**
10: 8 "You have neither desired nor taken **p** in sacrifices
10:38 My soul takes no **p** in anyone who shrinks back."
Jas 5: 5 You have lived on the earth in luxury and in **p;**
2Pe 2:13 They count it a **p** to revel in the daytime.
AdE 1: 8 to comply with his **p** and with that of the guests.
5:13 But these things give me no **p** as long
Wis 7: 2 from the seed of a man and the **p** of marriage.
16:20 providing every **p** and suited to every taste.
Sir 9:10 when it has aged, you can drink it with **p.**
18:31 If you allow your soul to take **p** in base desire,
25: 1 I take **p** in three things, and they are beautiful in

4Mc 1:20 of the emotions are p and pain;
1:21 of both p and pain have many consequences.
1:22 Thus desire precedes p and delight follows it.
1:24 is an emotion embracing p and pain.
1:25 In p there exists even a malevolent tendency,
1:28 Just as p and pain are two plants growing from
1:33 to forbidden foods we abstain from the p to be had
8:18 why do we take p in vain resolves and venture

PLEASURES‡ (8) [PLEASE]

Ps 16:11 in your right hand are p forevermore.
Isa 47:8 Now therefore hear this, you lover of p,
Lk 8:14 they are choked by the cares and riches and p
Tit 3:3 led astray, slaves to various passions and p,
Heb 11:25 with the people of God than to enjoy the fleeting p
Jas 4:3 in order to spend what you get on your p.
4Mc 5:23 so that we master all p and desires,
6:35 that it masters p and in no respect yields to them.

PLEDGE‡ (38) [PLEDGED, PLEDGES, PLEDGING]

Ge 38:17 And she said, "Only if you give me a p,
38:18 He said, "What p shall I give you?"
38:20 to recover the p from the woman,
Lev 6:2 a neighbor in a matter of a deposit or a p,
Nu 30:2 or swears an oath to bind himself by a p,
30:3 or binds herself by a p,
30:4 or her p by which she has bound herself,
30:4 any p by which she has bound herself shall stand.
30:5 and no p by which she has bound herself,
30:10 or bound herself by a p with an oath,
30:11 and any p by which she bound herself shall stand.
30:12 or concerning her p of herself, shall not stand.
Dt 24:6 a mill or an upper millstone in p,
24:6 for that would be taking a life in p.
24:10 you shall not go into the house to take the p.
24:11 to whom you are making the loan brings the p out
24:12 not sleep in the garment given you as the p.
24:13 You shall give the p back by sunset,
24:17 you shall not take a widow's garment in p.
2Ch 34:32 in Jerusalem and in Benjamin p themselves to it.
Ne 5:3 "We are having to p our fields, our vineyards,
Job 17:3 "Lay down a p for me with yourself;
24:3 they take the widow's ox for a p.
24:9 and take as a p the infant of the poor.
Pr 6:1 if you have given your p to your neighbor,
17:18 It is senseless to give a p,
20:16 seize the p given as surety for foreigners.
27:13 seize the p given as surety for foreigners.
Eze 18:7 but restores to the debtor his p,
18:12 commits robbery, does not restore the p,
18:16 exacts no p, commits no robbery,
33:15 the p, give back what they have taken by robbery,
Am 2:8 down beside every altar on garments taken in p;
Hab 2:6 will you load yourselves with goods taken in p?
Eph 1:14 this is the p of our inheritance toward redemption
1Ti 5:12 for having violated their first p.
2Mc 10:28 as p of success and victory not only their valor but
11:30 by the thirtieth of Xanthicus will have our p

PLEDGED (5) [PLEDGE]

1Ch 29:24 p their allegiance to King Solomon.
Ezr 10:19 They p themselves to send away their wives,
Eze 16:8 I p myself to you and entered into a covenant
1Mc 8:1 that they p friendship to those who came to them,
1Es 9:20 They p themselves to put away their wives,

PLEDGES (10) [PLEDGE]

Nu 30:7 her p by which she has bound herself shall stand.
30:14 then he validates all her vows, or all her p,
Job 22:6 For you have exacted p from your family
Pr 22:26 Do not be one of those who give p,
2Mc 4:34 offered him sworn p and gave him his right hand;
11:26 to them and give them p of friendship,
12:11 to grant them p of friendship,
12:12 after receiving his p they went back to their tents.
13:22 gave p, received theirs, withdrew,
14:19 and Mattathias to give and receive p of friendship.

PLEDGING (2) [PLEDGE]

AdE 9:31 p their own well-being to the plan.
3Mc 3:10 of them aside privately and were p to protect them

PLEIADES (3)

Job 9:9 the P and the chambers of the south;
38:31 "Can you bind the chains of the P,
Am 5:8 The one who made the P and Orion,

PLENTEOUS (3) [PLENTY]

Ge 41:34 of the land of Egypt during the seven p years.
41:47 the seven p years the earth produced abundantly.
Isa 30:23 which will be rich and p.

PLENTIFUL (8) [PLENTY]

2Ch 1:15 and he made cedar as p as the sycamore of
9:27 and cedar as p as the sycamore of the Shephelah.
Jer 2:7 into a p land to eat its fruits and its good things.
Mt 9:37 Then he said to his disciples, "The harvest is p,
Lk 10:2 He said to them, "The harvest is p,
2Es 7:58 "O sovereign Lord, what is p is of less worth,
7:59 the person who has what is p.
4Mc 3:10 and though springs were p there,

PLENTY (21) [PLENTEOUS, PLENTIFUL]

Ge 24:25 "We have p of straw and fodder and a place
27:28 and p of grain and wine.
41:29 of great p throughout all the land of Egypt.
41:30 and all the p will be forgotten in the land of Egypt;
41:31 The p will no longer be known in the land because
41:48 when there was p in the land of Egypt, and stored
41:53 of p that prevailed in the land of Egypt came to
2Ch 31:10 we have had enough to eat and have p to spare;
Pr 3:10 then your barns will be filled with p,
12:11 Those who till their land will have p of food,
20:13 open your eyes, and you will have p of bread.
28:19 Anyone who tills the land will have p of bread,
28:19 one who follows worthless pursuits will have p
Jer 44:17 We used to have p of food, and prospered,
Joel 2:26 You shall eat in p and be satisfied,
Php 4:12 and I know what it is to have p.
4:12 of having p and of being in need.
Sir 10:27 Better is the worker who has goods in p than
18:25 In the time of p think of the time of hunger;
3Mc 5:2 with large handfuls of frankincense and p
2Es 8:52 p is provided, a city is built, rest is appointed,

PLIABLE (1)

Sir 38:30 the clay with his arm and makes it p with his feet;

PLOT (34) [PLOTS, PLOTTED, PLOTTER, PLOTTING]

Ge 33:19 he bought for one hundred pieces of money the p
2Sa 23:11 where there was a p of ground full of lentils;
23:12 But he took his stand in the middle of the p,
2Ki 9:25 and throw him on the p of ground belonging
9:26 I swear I will repay you on this very p of ground.'
9:26 lift him out and throw him on the p of ground,
1Ch 11:13 There was a p of ground full of barley.
11:14 and David took their stand in the middle of the p,
Ne 4:15 our enemies heard that their p was known to us,
Est 8:3 the Agagite and the p that he had devised against
9:25 in writing that the wicked p that he had devised
Ps 2:1 and the peoples p in vain?
31:13 as they p to take my life.
36:4 They p mischief while on their beds;
37:12 The wicked p against the righteous,
59:5 spare none of those who treacherously p evil.
64:6 We have thought out a cunningly conceived p."
140:8 do not further their evil p.
Isa 32:6 For fools speak folly, and their minds p iniquity:
Eze 45:2 a square p of five hundred
Hos 7:15 yet they p evil against me.
Na 1:9 Why do you p against the LORD?
Jn 4:5 near the p of ground that Jacob had given
Ac 9:24 but their p became known to Saul.
20:3 about to set sail for Syria when a p was made
23:30 When I was informed that there would be a p
AdE 2:22 who in turn revealed the p to the king.
9:25 but the wicked p he had devised against
16:23 be a reminder of destruction for those who p
Sus 1:28 of their wicked p to have Susanna put to death.
1Mc 3:52 you know what they p against us.
3Mc 1:2 determined to carry out the p he had devised,
1:6 Now that he had foiled the p,
5:8 with vengeance the evil p against them and in

PLOTS (11) [PLOT]

Ps 31:20 of your presence you hide them from human p;
64:2 Hide me from the secret p of the wicked,
Jer 18:18 "Come, let us make p against Jeremiah—
La 3:60 have seen all their malice, all their p against me.
3:61 O LORD, all their p against me.
Da 11:25 for p shall be devised against him
Na 1:11 From you one has gone out who p evil against
Ac 20:19 enduring the trials that came to me through the p
Sir 27:22 Whoever winks the eye p mischief,
1Es 5:73 and by p and demagoguery
2Es 15:3 Do not fear the p against you,

PLOTTED (10) [PLOT]

Ne 4:8 and all p together to come and fight
Est 3:6 Haman p to destroy all the Jews,
8:7 because he p to lay hands on the Jews.
9:24 had p against the Jews to destroy them,
Isa 7:5 has p evil against you, saying,
Mt 22:15 Then the Pharisees went and p to entrap him
Ac 9:23 some time had passed, the Jews p to kill him,
AdE 2:21 and they p to kill King Artaxerxes.
3:6 p to destroy all the Jews under Artaxerxes' rule.
1Mc 9:58 Then all the lawless p and said, "See!

PLOTTER (3) [PLOT]

2Mc 3:38 or p against your government, send him there,
4:2 as a p against the government the man who was
4:50 having become the chief p against his compatriots.

PLOTTING‡ (5) [PLOT]

1Sa 23:9 David learned that Saul was p evil against him,
Ps 52:2 you are p destruction. Your tongue is like a
119:23 Even though princes sit p against me,
Jer 18:23 Yet you, O LORD, know all their p to kill me.
3Mc 1:21 because of what the king was profanely p.

PLOUGH (KJV) See PLOW

PLOW‡ (12) [PLOWED, PLOWERS, PLOWING, PLOWS, PLOWSHARE, PLOWSHARES]

Dt 22:10 not p with an ox and a donkey yoked together.
1Sa 8:12 and some to p his ground and to reap his harvest,
Job 4:8 those who p iniquity and sow trouble reap
Pr 20:4 The lazy person does not p in season;
Isa 28:24 Do those who p for sowing p continually?
Hos 10:11 Judah must p; Jacob must harrow for himself.
Am 6:12 Does one p the sea with oxen?
Lk 9:62 to the p and looks back is fit for the kingdom
1Co 9:10 for whoever plows should p in hope
Sir 25:8 the one who does not p with ox and ass together.
38:25 How can one become wise who handles the p,

PLOWED (8) [PLOW]

Dt 21:4 which is neither p nor sown,
Jdg 14:18 he said to them, "If you had not p with my heifer,
Ps 129:3 The plowers p on my back;
Ecc 5:9 an advantage for a land: a king for a p field.
Jer 26:18 Zion shall be p as a field; Jerusalem shall become
Hos 10:13 You have p wickedness, you have reaped injustice,
Mic 3:12 because of you Zion shall be p as a field;
2Es 16:32 and its fields shall be p up,

PLOWERS (1) [PLOW]

Ps 129:3 The p plowed on my back;

PLOWING (6) [PLOW]

Ge 45:6 in which there will be neither p nor harvest.
Ex 34:21 even in p time and in harvest time you shall rest.
1Ki 19:19 and found Elisha son of Shaphat, who was p.
Job 1:14 "The oxen were p and the donkeys were feeding
Lk 17:7 to your slave who has just come in from p
Sir 38:26 He sets his heart on p furrows,

PLOWS (3) [PLOW]

Am 9:13 the one who p shall overtake the one who reaps,
1Co 9:10 for whoever p should plow in hope
Sir 6:19 Come to her like one who p and sows,

PLOWSHARE‡ (1) [PLOW]

1Sa 13:20 the Philistines to sharpen their p, mattocks, axes,

PLOWSHARES (4) [PLOW]

1Sa 13:21 The charge was two-thirds of a shekel for the p
Isa 2:4 they shall beat their swords into p,
Joel 3:10 Beat your p into swords, and your pruning hooks
Mic 4:3 they shall beat their swords into p,

PLUCK (16) [PLUCKED, PLUCKS]

Dt 23:25 you may p the ears with your hand,
2Ch 7:20 then I will p you up from the land
Ps 25:15 for he will p my feet out of the net.
80:12 so that all who pass along the way p its fruit?
Ecc 3:2 a time to plant, and a time to p up what is planted;
Jer 1:10 to p up and to pull down,
12:14 I am about to p them up from their land,
12:14 I will p up the house of Judah from among them.
18:7 that I will p up and break down and destroy it,
24:6 I will plant them, and not p them up.
31:28 as I have watched over them to p up and break
42:10 I will plant you, and not p you up;
45:4 and p up what I have planted—
Mt 12:1 and they began to p heads of grain and to eat.
Mk 2:23 his disciples began to p heads of grain.
Sir 49:7 to p up and ruin and destroy,

PLUCKED‡ (12) [PLUCK]

Ge 8:11 and there in its beak was a freshly p olive leaf;
Dt 28:63 be p off the land that you are entering to possess.
Job 4:21 Their tent-cord is p up within them,
Isa 38:12 My dwelling is p up and removed from me like
Jer 12:15 And after I have p them up,
Eze 19:12 But it was p up in fury, cast down to the ground;
Da 7:4 Then, as I watched, its wings were p off,
7:8 three of the earlier horns were p up by the roots.
Am 9:15 and they shall never again be p up out of the land
Zec 3:2 Is not this man a brand p from the fire?"
Lk 6:1 his disciples p some heads of grain,
Sir 40:16 The reeds by any water or river bank are p up

PLUCKS (1) [PLUCK]

Sir 10:15 The Lord p up the roots of the nations,

PLUMAGE (3) [PLUMES]

Job 39:13 wings flap wildly, though its pinions lack p.
Eze 17:3 rich in p of many colors, came to the Lebanon.
17:7 with great wings and much p.

PLUMB‡ (5)

Am 7:7 a wall built with a p line, with a p line in his hand.
7:8 And I said, "A p line."
7:8 a p line in the midst of my people Israel;
Jdt 8:14 You cannot p the depths of the human heart

PLUMES (1) [PLUMAGE]

Job 39:18 When it spreads its p aloft,

PLUMMET (4)

2Ki 21:13 and the **p** for the house of Ahab;
Isa 28:17 will make justice the line, and righteousness the **p;**
34:11 and the **p** of chaos over its nobles.
Zec 4:10 and shall see the **p** in the hand of Zerubbabel.

PLUMP (2)

Ge 41: 5 seven ears of grain, **p** and good,
41: 7 thin ears swallowed up the seven **p** and full ears.

PLUNDER (66) [PLUNDERED, PLUNDERERS, PLUNDERING, PLUNDERS]

Ex 3:22 and so you shall **p** the Egyptians."
Nu 31:53 (The troops had all taken **p** for themselves.)
Dt 2:35 as well as the **p** of the towns that we had captured.
3: 7 the **p** of the towns we kept as spoil for ourselves.
Jdg 5: 7 peasantry prospered in Israel, they grew fat on **p,**
2Ch 14:14 for there was much **p** in them.
Ne 4: 4 and give them over as **p** in a land of captivity.
Est 3:13 which is the month of Adar, and to **p** their goods.
8:11 and women, and to **p** their goods
9:10 but they did not touch the **p.**
9:15 but they did not touch the **p.**
9:16 but they laid no hands on the **p.**
Ps 89:41 All who pass by **p** him;
109:11 may strangers **p** the fruits of his toil.
Isa 9: 3 as people exult when dividing **p.**
10: 6 to take spoil and seize **p,** and to tread them down
11:14 together they shall **p** the people of the east.
17:14 and the lot of those who **p** us.
Jer 2:14 Why then has he become **p?**
15:13 Your wealth and your treasures I will give as **p,**
20: 5 who shall **p** them, and seize them,
30:16 those who **p** you shall be plundered,
50:10 all who **p** her shall be sated, says the LORD.
Eze 7:21 to the wicked of the earth as **p;**
23:46 and make them an object of terror and of **p.**
25: 7 and will hand you over as **p** to the nations.
26: 5 It shall become **p** for the nations,
26:12 They will **p** your riches
29:19 he shall carry off its wealth and despoil it and **p** it;
34:28 They shall no more be **p** for the nations,
36: 4 a source of **p** and an object of derision to the rest
36: 5 because of its pasture, to **p** it.
38:12 to seize spoil and carry off **p;**
38:13 Have you assembled your horde to carry off **p,**
39:10 and **p** those who plundered them,
Da 11:24 lavishing **p,** spoil, and wealth on them.
11:33 and suffer captivity and **p.**
Na 2: 9 "**P** the silver, **p** the gold!
3: 1 full of booty—no end to the **p!**
Hab 2: 8 all that survive of the peoples shall **p** you—
Zep 2: 9 The remnant of my people shall **p** them,
Zec 2: 9 and they shall become **p** for their own slaves.
14: 1 **p** taken from you will be divided in your midst.
Mt 12:29 a strong man's house and **p** his property,
Mk 3:27 and **p** his property without first tying up
Lk 11:22 in which he trusted and divides his **p.**
Tob 3: 4 So you gave us over to **p,** exile, and death,
Jdt 2:11 to slaughter and **p** throughout your whole region.
AdE 3:13 which is Adar, and to **p** their goods.
9:10 and they indulged themselves in **p.**
9:15 and killed three hundred people, but took no **p.**
9:16 but did not engage in **p.**
Sir 16:13 The sinner will not escape with **p,**
48:15 until they were carried off as **p** from their land,
1Mc 4:17 not be greedy for **p,** for there is a battle before us;
4:18 and afterward seize the **p** boldly."
4:23 Then Judas returned to **p** the camp,
6: 3 So he came and tried to take the city and **p** it,
7:47 Then the Jews seized the spoils and the **p;**
13:34 for all that Trypho did was to **p.**
2Mc 8:30 and they divided a very large amount of **p,**
2Es 15:19 and **p** their goods, because of hunger for bread and
15:63 **p** your wealth, and mar the glory
16:46 and **p** their goods, overthrow their houses,
16:72 For they shall destroy and **p** their goods,

PLUNDERED (50) [PLUNDER]

Ge 34:27 the other sons of Jacob came upon the slain, and **p**
Ex 12:36 And so they **p** the Egyptians.
Jdg 2:14 and he gave them over to plunderers who **p** them,
2:16 of the power of those who **p** them.
1Sa 14:48 of the hands of those who **p** them.
17:53 the Philistines, and they **p** their camp.
2Ki 7:16 people went out, and **p** the camp of the Arameans.
2Ch 14:14 on them. They **p** all the cities;
28:21 For Ahaz **p** the house of the LORD and
Ps 7: 4 if I have repaid my ally with harm or **p** my foe
Isa 10:13 and have **p** their treasures;
13:16 their houses will be **p,** and their wives ravished.
42:22 But this is a people robbed and **p,**
Jer 30:16 those who plunder you shall be **p,**
50:10 Chaldea shall be **p;** all who plunder her shall be
50:37 against all her treasures, that they may be **p!**
Eze 39:10 and plunder those who **p** them,
Am 3:11 and your strongholds shall be **p.**
Hab 2: 8 Because you have **p** many nations,
Zep 1:13 Their wealth shall be **p,**
Zec 2: 8 his glory sent me) regarding the nations that **p** you:
Mt 12:29 Then indeed the house can be **p.**
Mk 3:27 then indeed the house can be **p.**
Jdt 1:14 **p** its markets, and turned its glory into disgrace.
Jdt 2: 7 to whom I will hand them over to be **p.**
2:23 and **p** all the Rassisites and the Ishmaelites on
2:26 and burned their tents and **p** their sheepfolds.
4: 1 and how he had **p** and destroyed all their temples,
8:21 be captured and our sanctuary will be **p;**
15: 6 of Bethulia fell upon the Assyrian camp and **p** it,
15:11 All the people **p** the camp for thirty days.
AdE 7: 4 to be destroyed, **p,** and made slaves—
Wis 10:20 Therefore the righteous **p** the ungodly;
Sir 36:30 Where there is no fence, the property will be **p;**
LtJ 6:18 in order that they may not be **p** by robbers.
1Mc 1: 3 to the ends of the earth, and **p** many nations.
1:19 and he **p** the land of Egypt.
1:31 He **p** the city, burned it with fire,
5:35 and he killed every male in it, **p** it,
5:51 and razed and **p** the town.
5:68 he **p** the towns and returned to the land of Judah.
8:10 they **p** them, conquered the land,
10:84 and the surrounding towns and **p** them;
11:61 and burned its suburbs with fire and **p** them.
12:31 and he crushed them and **p** them.
2Mc 9:16 which he had formerly **p,**
3Mc 5:41 and also in constant danger of being **p."**
2Es 10:22 the ark of our covenant has been **p,**
16:47 do so only to have it **p;**
4Mc 4:23 after he had **p** them he issued a decree that if any

PLUNDERERS (4) [PLUNDER]

Jdg 2:14 and he gave them over to **p** who plundered them,
2Ki 17:20 and gave them into the hand of **p,**
Jer 50:11 you rejoice, though you exult, O **p** of my heritage,
Ob 1: 5 if **p** by night—how you have been destroyed!—

PLUNDERING (5) [PLUNDER]

Ezr 9: 7 to the sword, to captivity, to **p,** and to utter shame,
Isa 33:23 even the lame will fall to **p.**
Heb 10:34 you cheerfully accepted the **p** of your possessions,
1Es 8:77 to the sword and exile and **p,**
2Es 16:71 but **p** and destroying those who continue to fear

PLUNDERS (1) [PLUNDER]

1Es 4:24 and when he steals and robs and **p,**

PLUNGE (2) [PLUNGED, PLUNGING]

Job 9:31 yet you will **p** me into filth,
1Ti 6: 9 and harmful desires that **p** people into ruin

PLUNGED (3) [PLUNGE]

Rev 16:10 and its kingdom was **p** into darkness;
Sir 9: 9 and in blood you may be **p** into destruction.
1Mc 6:11 And into what a great flood I now am **p!**

PLUNGING (1) [PLUNGE]

Jer 8: 6 like a horse **p** headlong into battle.

PLY (1)

Jer 14:18 both prophet and priest **p** their trade throughout

POCHERETH-HAZZEBAIM (3)

Ezr 2:57 Shephatiah, Hattil, **P,** and Ami.
Ne 7:59 of Shephatiah, of Hattil, of **P,** of Amon.
1Es 5:34 the descendants of **P,** the descendants of Sarothie,

PODS (1)

Lk 15:16 He would gladly have filled himself with the **p**

POETS (1)

Ac 17:28 as even some of your own **p** have said,

POINT (38) [MID-POINT, POINTED, POINTING, POINTS]

Ge 31:32 **p** out what I have that is yours, and take it."
Nu 22:36 at the farthest **p** of the boundary.
2Ki 20: 1 and was at the **p** of death.
2Ch 32:24 and was at the **p** of death.
Ne 3:16 repaired from a **p** opposite the graves of David,
3:26 up to a **p** opposite the Water Gate on the east and
Job 20:25 and the glittering **p** comes out of their gall;
Pr 5:14 I am at the **p** of utter ruin in the public assembly."
Isa 38: 1 and was at the **p** of death.
Jer 17: 1 with a diamond **p** it is engraved on the tablet
Eze 21:15 At all their gates I have set the **p** of the sword.
47:20 be the boundary to a **p** opposite Lebo-hamath.
Mt 18:15 and point out the fault when the two of you are alone.
24: 1 his disciples came to **p** out to him the buildings of
Mk 5:23 "My little daughter is at the **p** of death.
14:59 But even on this **p** their testimony did not agree.
Jn 4:47 for he was at the **p** of death.
Ac 17:33 At that **p** Paul left them.
22: 4 to the **p** of death by binding both men and women
22:22 Up to this **p** they listened to him,
1Co 8:10 be encouraged to the **p** of eating food sacrificed
2Co 5:16 we regard no one from a human **p** of view;
5:16 we once knew Christ from a human **p** of view,
7:11 At every **p** you have proved yourselves guiltless in
9: 6 The **p** is this: the one who sows sparingly will
Gal 3:17 My **p** is this: the law, which came four hundred
4: 1 My **p** is this: heirs, as long as they are minors,
Php 2: 8 and became obedient to the **p** of death—
2Ti 2: 9 even to the **p** of being chained like a criminal.
Heb 8: 1 Now the main **p** in what we are saying is this:
Heb 12: 4 not yet resisted to the **p** of shedding your blood.
Jas 2:10 but fails in one **p** has become accountable for all
Rev 3: 2 strengthen what remains and is on the **p** of death,
2Mc 2:32 At this **p** therefore let us begin our narrative,
7:27 and have reared you and brought you up to this **p**
13:10 to help those who were on the **p** of being deprived
15:38 If it is well told and to the **p,**
4Mc 6:12 At that **p,** partly out of pity for his old age,

POINTED (5) [POINT]

AdE 13: 4 **p** out to us that among all the nations in
Sir 43:19 and icicles form like **p** thorns.
3Mc 5:15 he **p** out that the hour of the banquet
5:19 with the corroboration of his Friends, **p** out that
5:29 Then Hermon and all the king's Friends **p** out that

POINTING (4) [POINT]

Pr 6:13 winking the eyes, shuffling the feet, **p** the fingers,
Isa 58: 9 the **p** of the finger, the speaking of evil,
Mt 12:49 And **p** to his disciples, he said,
2Mc 15:10 at the same time **p** out the perfidy of the Gentiles

POINTS (4) [POINT]

Nu 33: 2 Moses wrote down their starting **p,** stage by stage,
Ac 25:19 Instead they had certain **p** of disagreement
Ro 15:15 on some **p** I have written to you rather boldly
2Mc 12:22 and pierced by the **p** of their own swords.

POISON‡ (9) [POISONED, POISONOUS]

Dt 32:32 their grapes are grapes of **p,**
32:33 their wine is the **p** of serpents,
Job 6: 4 in me; my spirit drinks their **p;**
20:16 They will suck the **p** of asps;
Ps 69:21 They gave me **p** for food,
Am 6:12 But you have turned justice into **p** and the fruit
Jas 3: 8 a restless evil, full of deadly **p.**
Wis 1:14 and there is no destructive **p** in them,
2Mc 10:13 he took **p** and ended his life.

POISONED (3) [POISON]

Jer 8:14 and has given us **p** water to drink,
23:15 and give them **p** water to drink;
Ac 14: 2 stirred up the Gentiles and **p** their minds against

POISONOUS (6) [POISON]

Nu 21: 6 the LORD sent **p** serpents among the people,
21: 8 the LORD said to Moses, "Make a **p** serpent,
Dt 8:15 an arid wasteland with **p** snakes and scorpions.
29:18 among you a root sprouting **p** and bitter growth.
Jer 9:15 and giving them **p** water to drink.
Hos 10: 4 so litigation springs up like **p** weeds in the furrows

POLE (15) [POLES]

Ge 40:19 and hang you on a **p;**
Nu 13:23 and they carried it on a **p** between two of them.
21: 8 "Make a poisonous serpent, and set it on a **p;**
21: 9 a serpent of bronze, and put it upon a **p;**
Dt 16:21 You shall not plant any tree as a sacred **p** beside
Jdg 6:25 and cut down the sacred **p** that is beside it;
6:26 the wood of the sacred **p** that you shall cut down."
6:28 and the sacred **p** beside it was cut down,
6:30 down the altar of Baal and cut down the sacred **p**
1Ki 16:33 Ahab also made a sacred **p.**
2Ki 13: 6 the sacred **p** also remained in Samaria.
17:16 a sacred **p,** worshiped all the host of heaven,
18: 4 broke down the pillars, and cut down the sacred **p.**
21: 3 he erected altars for Baal, made a sacred **p,**
23:15 he also burned the sacred **p.**

POLES (60) [POLE]

Ex 25:13 You shall make **p** of acacia wood,
25:14 And you shall put the **p** into the rings on the sides
25:15 The **p** shall remain in the rings of the ark;
25:27 the **p** used for carrying the table shall be close to
25:28 You shall make the **p** of acacia wood,
27: 6 You shall make **p** for the altar,
27: 6 **p** of acacia wood, and overlay them with bronze;
27: 7 the **p** shall be put through the rings,
27: 7 so that the **p** shall be on the two sides of the altar
30: 4 and they shall hold the **p** with which to carry it.
30: 5 You shall make the **p** of acacia wood,
34:13 and cut down their sacred **p**
35:12 the ark with its **p,** the mercy seat, and the curtain
35:13 with its **p** and all its utensils, and the bread of
35:15 with its **p,** and the anointing oil and
35:16 its **p,** and all its utensils, the basin with its stand;
37: 4 He made **p** of acacia wood,
37: 5 and put the **p** into the rings on the sides of the ark,
37:14 the **p** used for carrying the table were close to
37:15 He made the **p** of acacia wood to carry the table,
37:27 to hold the **p** with which to carry it.
37:28 And he made the **p** of acacia wood,
38: 5 of the bronze grating to hold the **p;**
38: 6 he made the **p** of acacia wood,
38: 7 And he put the **p** through the rings on the sides of
39:35 ark of the covenant with its **p** and the mercy seat;
39:39 and its grating of bronze, its **p,** and all its utensils;
40:18 and put in its **p,** and raised up its pillars;
40:20 and put the **p** on the ark,
Nu 4: 6 and shall put its **p** in place.
4: 8 and shall put its **p** in place.
4:11 and shall put its **p** in place;
4:14 and shall put its **p** in place.

Dt 7: 5 smash their pillars, hew down their sacred **p**,
12: 3 smash their pillars, burn their sacred **p** with fire,
1Ki 8: 7 cherubim made a covering above the ark and its **p**.
8: 8 The **p** were so long that the ends of the **p** were seen
14:15 because they have made their sacred **p**,
14:23 and sacred **p** on every high hill and
2Ki 17:10 they set up for themselves pillars and sacred **p**
23:14 in pieces, cut down the sacred **p**, and covered
1Ch 15:15 the ark of God on their shoulders with the **p**,
2Ch 5: 8 cherubim made a covering above the ark and its **p**.
5: 9 The **p** were so long that the ends of the **p** were seen
14: 3 broke down the pillars, hewed down the sacred **p**,
17: 6 the high places and the sacred **p** from Judah.
19: 3 for you destroyed the sacred **p** out of the land,
24:18 and served the sacred **p** and the idols.
31: 1 hewed down the sacred **p**,
33: 3 made sacred **p**, worshiped all the host of heaven,
33:19 and set up the sacred **p** and the images,
34: 3 the sacred **p**, and the carved and the cast images.
34: 4 the sacred **p** and the carved and the cast images;
34: 7 beat the sacred **p** and the images into powder,
Isa 17: 8 either the sacred **p** or the altars of incense.
27: 9 no sacred **p** or incense altars will remain standing.
Jer 17: 2 and their sacred **p**, beside every green tree,
Mic 5:14 and I will uproot your sacred **p** from among you

POLICE (14)

Lk 22: 4 the chief priests and officers of the temple **p** about
22:52 the officers of the temple **p**,
Jn 7:32 and the chief priests and Pharisees sent temple **p**
7:45 Then the temple **p** went back to the chief priests
7:46 **p** answered, "Never has anyone spoken like this!"
18: 3 of soldiers together with **p** from the chief priests
18:12 and the Jewish **p** arrested Jesus and bound him.
18:18 the **p** had made a charcoal fire because it was cold,
18:22 of the **p** standing nearby struck Jesus on the face,
19: 6 When the chief priests and the **p** saw him,
Ac 5:22 But when the temple **p** went there,
5:26 captain went with the temple **p** and brought them,
16:35 When morning came, the magistrates sent the **p**,
16:38 The **p** reported these words to the magistrates,

POLICY (5)

Sir 47:23 Rehoboam, whose **p** drove the people to revolt.
2Mc 6: 8 that they should adopt the same **p** toward the Jews
9:27 that he will follow my **p** and will treat you
11:26 so that they may know our **p** and be of good cheer
3Mc 3:23 they secretly suspect that we may soon alter our **p**.

POLISHED (8) [POLISHES]

Ezr 8:27 two vessels of fine **p** bronze as precious as gold.
Isa 49: 2 he made me a **p** arrow, in his quiver he hid me
Eze 21: 9 A sword, a sword is sharpened, it is also **p**;
21:11 sword is given to be **p**, to be grasped in the hand;
21:11 It is sharpened, the sword is **p**,
21:15 It is made for flashing, it is **p** for slaughter.
21:28 Drawn for slaughter **P** to consume,
1Mc 13:27 with **p** stone at the front and back.

POLISHES (1) [POLISHED]

Sir 12:11 Be to him like one who **p** a mirror,

POLITARCHS See Index to Footnotes

POLITELY (1)

Sir 4: 8 a hearing to the poor, and return their greeting **p**.

POLITICAL (1)

4Mc 4: 1 a **p** opponent of the noble and good man, Onias,

POLL (1)

3Mc 2:28 be subjected to a registration involving **p** tax and

POLLUTE (4) [POLLUTED, POLLUTES, POLLUTION, POLLUTIONS]

Nu 35:33 You shall not **p** the land in which you live;
Jdt 9: 8 for they intend to defile your sanctuary, and to **p**
2Mc 6: 2 also to **p** the temple in Jerusalem and to call it
2Es 15:25 Do not **p** my sanctuary.

POLLUTED (20) [POLLUTE]

2Ch 36:14 and they **p** the house of the LORD
Ps 106:38 and the land was **p** with blood.
Pr 25:26 or a **p** fountain are the righteous who give way
Isa 24: 5 The earth lies **p** under its inhabitants;
Jer 3: 1 Would not such a land be greatly **p**?
3: 2 You have **p** the land with your whoring and
3: 9 she took her whoredom so lightly, she **p** the land,
16:18 because they have **p** my land with the carcasses
Eze 20:43 and all the deeds by which you have **p** yourselves;
23:30 and **p** yourself with their idols.
Mal 1: 7 By offering **p** food on my altar.
1: 7 And you say, "How have we **p** it?"
1:12 when you say that the Lord's table is **p**,
Ac 15:20 to them to abstain only from things **p** by idols and
Rev 21: 8 But as for the cowardly, the faithless, the **p**,
Jdt 9: 2 and **p** her womb to disgrace her;
2Mc 5:16 He took the holy vessels with his **p** hands,
1Es 1:49 and **p** the temple of the Lord in Jerusalem—
8:83 to take possession of is a land **p** with the pollution
2Es 10:22 our holy things have been **p**,

POLLUTES (1) [POLLUTE]

Nu 35:33 for blood **p** the land, and no expiation can be made

POLLUTION (3) [POLLUTE]

Jdt 9: 4 with zeal for you and abhorred the **p** of their blood
2Mc 6:19 with honor rather than life with **p**,
1Es 8:83 a land polluted with the **p** of the aliens of the land,

POLLUTIONS (4) [POLLUTE]

Ezr 6:21 and separated themselves from the **p** of the nations
9:11 a land unclean with the **p** of the peoples of
1Mc 13:50 from there and cleansed the citadel from its **p**.
1Es 8:69 the alien peoples of the land and their **p**,

POMEGRANATE (8) [POMEGRANATES]

Ex 28:34 and a **p** alternating all around the lower hem of
39:26 a bell and a **p**, a bell and a **p** all around
1Sa 14: 2 in the outskirts of Gibeah under the **p** tree that is
SS 4: 3 like halves of a **p** behind your veil.
6: 7 like halves of a **p** behind your veil.
Joel 1:12 **P**, palm, and apple—all the trees of the field are
Hag 2:19 Do the vine, the fig tree, the **p**,

POMEGRANATES (25) [POMEGRANATE]

Ex 28:33 On its lower hem you shall make **p** of blue,
39:24 On the lower hem of the robe they made **p** of blue,
39:25 and put the bells between the **p** on the lower hem
39:25 of the robe all around, between the **p**;
Nu 13:23 They also brought some **p** and figs.
20: 5 It is no place for grain, or figs, or vines, or **p**;
Dt 8: 8 of vines and fig trees and **p**,
1Ki 7:18 to cover the capitals that were above the **p**;
7:20 there were two hundred **p** in rows all around;
7:42 the four hundred **p** for the two latticeworks,
7:42 two rows of **p** for each latticework,
2Ki 25:17 latticework and **p**, all of bronze,
2Ch 3:16 and he made one hundred **p**,
4:13 the four hundred **p** for the two latticeworks,
4:13 two rows of **p** for each latticework,
SS 4:13 an orchard of **p** with all choicest fruits,
6:11 whether the **p** were in bloom.
7:12 the grape blossoms have opened and the **p** are
8: 2 to drink, the juice of my **p**.
Jer 52:22 latticework and **p**, all of bronze,
52:22 And the second pillar had the same, with **p**.
52:23 There were ninety-six **p** on the sides;
52:23 the **p** encircling the latticework numbered
Tob 1: 7 likewise the tenth of the grain, wine, olive oil, **p**,
Sir 45: 9 And he encircled him with **p**,

POMP (9)

Est 1: 4 the splendor and **p** of his majesty for many days,
Ps 49:12 Mortals cannot abide in their **p**;
49:20 Mortals cannot abide in their **p**;
Isa 14:11 Your **p** is brought down to Sheol,
Ac 25:23 and Bernice came with great **p**,
1Mc 10:58 celebrated her wedding at Ptolemais with great **p**,
10:60 with **p** to Ptolemais and met the two kings;
10:86 of the city came out to meet him with great **p**.
11: 6 Jonathan met the king at Joppa with **p**,

PONDER (5) [PONDERED, PONDERS]

Ps 4: 4 **p** it on your beds, and be silent.
48: 9 We **p** your steadfast love,
64: 9 about, and **p** what he has done.
Isa 14:16 who see you will stare at you, and **p** over you:
Sir 21:17 and they **p** his words in their minds.

PONDERED (5) [PONDER]

Lk 1:29 and **p** what sort of greeting this might be.
1:66 All who heard them **p** them and said,
2:19 But Mary treasured all these words and **p** them
Wis 8:17 and **p** in my heart that in kinship
2Mc 11:13 he **p** over the defeat that had befallen him,

PONDERS (2) [PONDER]

Pr 15:28 The mind of the righteous **p** how to answer,
Sir 14:21 in his heart on her ways and **p** her secrets,

PONDS (1)

Ex 7:19 over its rivers, its canals, and its **p**,

PONTIUS (3)

Lk 3: 1 when **P** Pilate was governor of Judea,
Ac 4:27 For in this city, in fact, both Herod and **P** Pilate,
1Ti 6:13 who in his testimony before **P** Pilate made

PONTUS (3)

Ac 2: 9 Judea and Cappadocia, **P** and Asia,
18: 2 a native of **P**, who had recently come from Italy
1Pe 1: 1 To the exiles of the Dispersion in **P**, Galatia,

POOL‡ (24) [POOLS]

2Sa 2:13 went out and met them at the **p** of Gibeon.
2:13 One group sat on one side of the **p**, while the other sat on the other side of the **p**.
4:12 and hung their bodies beside the **p** at Hebron.
1Ki 22:38 They washed the chariot by the **p** of Samaria;
2Ki 18:17 and stood by the conduit of the upper **p**,
20:20 the **p** and the conduit and brought water into
Ne 2:14 on to the Fountain Gate and to the King's **P**;
Ne 3:15 the wall of the **P** of Shelah of the king's garden,
3:16 far as the artificial **p** and the house of the warriors.
Ps 114: 8 who turns the rock into a **p** of water,
Isa 7: 3 The upper **p** on the highway to the Fuller's Field,
22: 9 and you collected the waters of the lower **p**.
22:11 between the two walls for the water of the old **p**.
35: 7 a **p**, and the thirsty ground springs of water;
36: 2 the upper **p** on the highway to the Fuller's Field.
41:18 I will make the wilderness a **p** of water,
Jer 41:12 They came upon him at the great **p** that is
Na 2: 8 Nineveh is like a **p** whose waters run away.
Jn 5: 2 Now in Jerusalem by the Sheep Gate there is a **p**,
5: 7 to put me into the **p** when the water is stirred up;
9: 7 wash in the **p** of Siloam" (which means Sent).
Sir 43:20 it settles on every **p** of water,
1Mc 9:33 and camped by the water of the **p** of Asphar.

POOLS (10) [POOL]

Ex 7:19 its canals, and its ponds, and all its **p** of water—
8: 5 the canals, and the **p**, and make frogs come up on
2Ki 3:16 'I will make this wadi full of **p**.'
Ps 84: 6 the early rain also covers it with **p**.
107:35 He turns a desert into **p** of water,
Ecc 2: 6 I made myself **p** from which to water the forest
SS 7: 4 Your eyes are **p** in Heshbon,
Isa 14:23 and **p** of water, and I will sweep it with the broom
42:15 I will turn the rivers into islands, and dry up the **p**.
2Es 16:60 and **p** on the tops of the mountains,

POOR‡ (204) [IMPOVERISH, IMPOVERISHED, POORER, POOREST, POORLY, POVERTY]

Ge 41:19 Then seven other cows came up after them, **p**,
Ex 6:12 shall Pharaoh listen to me, **p** speaker that I am?"
6:30 "Since I am a **p** speaker,
22:25 the **p** among you, you shall not deal with them as
23: 3 nor shall you be partial to the **p** in a lawsuit.
23: 6 You shall not pervert the justice due to your **p**
23:11 so that the **p** of your people may eat;
30:15 and the **p** shall not give less, than the half shekel,
Lev 14:21 But if he is **p** and cannot afford so much,
19:10 you shall leave them for the **p** and the alien:
19:15 not be partial to the **p** or defer to the great:
23:22 you shall leave them for the **p** and for the alien:
Nu 13:20 and whether the land is rich or **p**,
Dt 15:11 "Open your hand to the **p** and needy neighbor
24:12 If the person is **p**, you shall not sleep in
24:14 not withhold the wages of **p** and needy laborers,
24:15 they are **p** and their livelihood depends on them;
Ru 3:10 you have not gone after young men, whether **p**
1Sa 2: 7 The LORD makes **p** and makes rich;
2: 8 He raises up the **p** from the dust;
18:23 seeing that I am a **p** man and of no repute?"
2Sa 12: 1 the one rich and the other **p**.
12: 3 but the **p** man had nothing but one little ewe lamb,
12: 4 but he took the **p** man's lamb,
Est 9:22 of food to one another and presents to the **p**.
Job 5:16 So the **p** have hope, and injustice shuts its mouth.
20:10 Their children will seek the favor of the **p**,
20:19 For they have crushed and abandoned the **p**,
24: 4 the **p** of the earth all hide themselves.
24: 9 and take as a pledge the infant of the **p**.
24:14 The murderer rises at dusk to kill the **p** and needy,
29:12 because I delivered the **p** who cried,
30:25 Was not my soul grieved for the **p**?
31:16 "If I have withheld anything that the **p** desired,
31:19 or a **p** person without covering,
34:19 nor regards the rich more than the **p**,
34:28 that they caused the cry of the **p** to come to him,
Ps 9:18 nor the hope of the **p** perish forever.
10: 2 In arrogance the wicked persecute the **p**—
10: 9 they lurk that they may seize the **p**;
10: 9 they seize the **p** and drag them off in their net.
12: 5 "Because the **p** are despoiled,
14: 6 You would confound the plans of the **p**,
22:26 The **p** shall eat and be satisfied;
34: 6 This **p** soul cried, and was heard by the LORD,
37:14 the **p** and needy, to kill those who walk uprightly;
40:17 As for me, I am **p** and needy,
41: 1 Happy are those who consider the **p**;
49: 2 both low and high, rich and **p** together.
70: 5 But I am **p** and needy; hasten to me, O God!
72: 2 with righteousness, and your **p** with justice.
72: 4 May he defend the cause of the **p** of the people,
72:12 the **p** and those who have no helper.
74:19 do not forget the life of your **p** forever.
74:21 let the **p** and needy praise your name.
86: 1 O LORD, and answer me, for I am **p** and needy.
109:16 the **p** and needy and the brokenhearted
109:22 For I am **p** and needy,
112: 9 they have given to the **p**;
113: 7 He raises the **p** from the dust,
132:15 I will satisfy its **p** with bread.
140:12 and executes justice for the **p**.
Pr 10:15 the poverty of the **p** is their ruin.
13: 7 others pretend to be **p**, yet have great wealth.
13: 8 but the **p** get no threats.
13:23 The field of the **p** may yield much food,
14:20 The **p** are disliked even by their neighbors,
14:21 but happy are those who are kind to the **p**.
14:31 Those who oppress the **p** insult their Maker,
15:15 All the days of the **p** are hard,
16:19 It is better to be of a lowly spirit among the **p** than
17: 5 Those who mock the **p** insult their Maker;
18:23 The **p** use entreaties, but the rich answer roughly.

Pr 19: 1 Better the **p** walking in integrity than one perverse
19: 4 but the **p** are left friendless.
19: 7 If the **p** are hated even by their kin,
19:17 Whoever is kind to the **p** lends to the LORD,
19:22 and it is better to be **p** than a liar.
21:13 If you close your ear to the cry of the **p,**
22: 2 The rich and the **p** have this in common:
22: 7 The rich rules over the **p,**
22: 9 for they share their bread with the **p.**
22:16 Oppressing the **p** in order to enrich oneself,
22:22 Do not rob the **p** because they are **p,**
28: 3 A ruler who oppresses the **p** is a beating rain
28: 6 to be **p** and walk in integrity than to be crooked
28: 8 for another who is kind to the **p.**
28:11 but an intelligent **p** person sees through the pose.
28:15 a charging bear is a wicked ruler over a **p** people.
28:27 Whoever gives to the **p** will lack nothing,
29: 7 The righteous know the rights of the **p;**
29:13 The **p** and the oppressor have this in common:
29:14 If a king judges the **p** with equity,
30: 9 or I shall be **p,** and steal, and profane the name of
30:14 to devour the **p** from off the earth,
31: 9 defend the rights of the **p** and needy.
31:20 She opens her hand to the **p,**
Ecc 4:13 a **p** but wise youth than an old but foolish king,
4:14 even though born **p** in the kingdom.
5: 8 the oppression of the **p** and the violation of justice
6: 8 the **p** have who know how to conduct themselves
9:15 Now there was found in it a **p** wise man,
9:15 Yet no one remembered that **p** man.
9:16 yet the **p** man's wisdom is despised,
Isa 3:14 the spoil of the **p** is in your houses.
3:15 by grinding the face of the **p?**
10: 2 and to rob the **p** of my people of their right,
11: 4 the **p,** and decide with equity for the meek of
14:30 The firstborn of the **p** will graze,
25: 4 For you have been a refuge to the **p,**
26: 6 The foot tramples it, the feet of the **p,**
32: 7 they devise wicked devices to ruin the **p**
41:17 When the **p** and needy seek water,
58: 7 and bring the homeless **p** into your house;
Jer 2:34 the lifeblood of the innocent **p,**
4:11 the bare heights in the desert toward my **p** people,
5: 4 I said, "These are only the **p,** they have no sense;
6:26 O my **p** people, put on sackcloth, and roll in ashes;
8:19 cry of my **p** people from far and wide in the land:
8:21 For the hurt of my **p** people I am hurt, I mourn,
8:22 the health of my **p** people not been restored?
9: 1 and night for the slain of my **p** people!
22:16 He judged the cause of the **p** and needy;
39:10 of the **p** people who owned nothing,
Eze 16:49 but did not aid the **p** and needy.
18:12 oppresses the **p** and needy,
22:29 they have oppressed the **p** and needy,
Am 2: 7 they who trample the head of the **p** into the dust of
4: 1 who oppress the **p,** who crush the needy,
5:11 Therefore because you trample on the **p** and take
8: 4 and bring to ruin the **p** of the land,
8: 6 the **p** for silver and the needy for a pair of sandals,
Hab 3:14 as if ready to devour the **p** who were in hiding.
Zec 7:10 the orphan, the alien, or the **p;**
Mt 5: 3 "Blessed are the **p** in spirit,
11: 5 and the **p** have good news brought to them.
19:21 and give the money to the **p,**
26: 9 and the money given to the **p."**
26:11 For you always have the **p** with you,
Mk 10:21 sell what you own, and give the money to the **p,**
12:42 **p** widow came and put in two small copper coins,
12:43 to them, "Truly I tell you, this **p** widow has put
14: 5 and the money given to the **p."**
14: 7 For you always have the **p** with you,
Lk 4:18 he has anointed me to bring good news to the **p.**
6:20 "Blessed are you who are **p,**
7:22 the **p** have good news brought to them.
14:13 But when you give a banquet, invite the **p,**
14:21 and lanes of the town and bring in the **p,**
16:20 And at his gate lay a **p** man named Lazarus,
16:22 The **p** man died and was carried away by
18:22 that you own and distribute the money to the **p,**
19: 8 half of my possessions, Lord, I will give to the **p;**
21: 2 also saw a **p** widow put in two small copper coins.
21: 3 this **p** widow has put in more than all of them;
Jn 12: 5 and the money given to the **p?"**
12: 6 (He said this not because he cared about the **p,**
12: 8 You always have the **p** with you,
13:29 or, that he should give something to the **p.**
Ro 15:26 to share their resources with the **p** among
2Co 6:10 as **p,** yet making many rich;
8: 9 yet for your sakes he became **p,**
9: 9 "He scatters abroad, he gives to the **p;**
Gal 2:10 the **p,** which was actually what I was eager
Jas 2: 2 and if a **p** person in dirty clothes also comes in,
2: 3 while to the one who is **p** you say, "Stand there,"
2: 5 the **p** in the world to be rich in faith and to be heirs
2: 6 But you have dishonored the **p.**
Rev 3:17 pitiable, **p,** blind, and naked.
13:16 it causes all, both small and great, both rich and **p,**
Tob 2: 2 and bring whatever **p** person you may find
2: 3 So Tobias went to look for some **p** person
4: 7 Do not turn your face away from anyone who is **p,**
4:21 my son, because we have become **p.**
AdE 1:20 to their husbands, rich and **p** alike."
9:22 of food to their friends and to the **p.**
Wis 2:10 Let us oppress the righteous **p** man;
Sir 4: 1 My child, do not cheat the **p** of their living,
4: 4 or turn your face away from the **p.**
4: 8 Give a hearing to the **p,**
Sir 7:32 Stretch out your hand to the **p,**
10:22 The rich, and the eminent, and the **p**—
10:23 not right to despise one who is intelligent but **p,**
10:30 The **p** are honored for their knowledge,
11:21 the sight of the Lord to make the **p** rich suddenly,
13: 3 a **p** person suffers wrong, and must add apologies.
13:18 And what peace between the rich and the **p?**
13:19 likewise the **p** are feeding grounds for the rich.
13:20 likewise the **p** are an abomination to the rich.
13:23 The **p** person speaks and they say,
21: 5 The prayer of the **p** goes from their lips to the ears
26: 4 Whether rich or **p,** his heart is content,
29: 9 Help the **p** for the commandment's sake,
29:22 Better is the life of the **p** under their own crude
30:14 Better off **p,** healthy, and fit than rich and afflicted
31: 4 The **p** person toils to make a meager living,
34:24 a sacrifice from the property of the **p.**
34:25 The bread of the needy is the life of the **p;**
35:16 He will not show partiality to the **p;**
38:19 but the life of the **p** weighs down the heart.
LtJ 6:28 but give none to the **p** or helpless.
1Es 3:19 of the slave and the free, of the **p** and the rich.
3Mc 5:37 "How many times, you **p** wretch,

POORER (1) [POOR]

Da 1:10 in **p** condition than the other young men

POOREST (5) [POOR]

2Ki 24:14 no one remained, except the **p** people of the land.
25:12 the captain of the guard left some of the **p** people
Jer 40: 7 the **p** of the land who had not been taken into exile
52:15 into exile some of the **p** of the people and the rest
52:16 the captain of the guard left some of the **p** people

POORLY (2) [POOR]

1Co 4:11 we are **p** clothed and beaten and homeless,
2Mc 15:38 if it is **p** done and mediocre,

POPLAR (2)

Ge 30:37 Jacob took fresh rods of **p** and almond and plane,
Hos 4:13 and make offerings upon the hills, under oak, **p,**

POPLARS See Index to Footnotes

POPULACE (2) [POPULATION]

2Mc 3:21 in the prostration of the whole **p** and the anxiety of
4:39 the **p** gathered against Lysimachus,

POPULAR (1)

Est 10: 3 among the Jews and **p** with his many kindred,

POPULATION (4) [POPULACE, POPULOUS]

2Ki 25:11 all the rest of the **p.**
Eze 36:10 and I will multiply your **p,** the whole house
36:37 to increase their **p** like a flock.
Bar 4:34 I will take away her pride in her great **p,**

POPULOUS (2) [POPULATION]

Dt 26: 5 and there he became a great nation, mighty and **p.**
Isa 32:14 the palace will be forsaken, the **p** city deserted;

POPULOUS (KJV) See also THEBES

PORATHA (1)

Est 9: 8 **P,** Adalia, Aridatha,

PORCH (3)

1Ki 7: 6 There was a **p** in front with pillars,
Eze 8:16 between the **p** and the altar,
Mt 26:71 When he went out to the **p,**

PORCIUS (1)

Ac 24:27 Felix was succeeded by **P** Festus;

PORK (3)

4Mc 5: 2 and to compel them to eat **p** and food sacrificed
5: 6 I would advise you to save yourself by eating **p,**
6:15 save yourself by pretending to eat **p."**

PORPHYRY (1)

Est 1: 6 of gold and silver on a mosaic pavement of **p,**

PORTAL (1) [PORTALS]

2Ki 16:18 The covered **p** for use on the sabbath

PORTALS (2) [PORTAL]

Pr 8: 3 at the entrance of the **p** she cries out:
2Es 6: 1 before the **p** of the world were in place,

PORTENT (7) [PORTENTS]

Dt 28:46 and your descendants as a sign and a **p** forever.
Ps 71: 7 I have been like a **p** to many,
Isa 20: 3 for three years as a sign and a **p** against Egypt
Rev 12: 1 A great **p** appeared in heaven:
12: 3 Then another **p** appeared in heaven:
15: 1 I saw another **p** in heaven, great and amazing:
3Mc 1:14 that it was wrong to take that as a **p.**

PORTENTS (6) [PORTENT]

Dt 13: 1 among you and promise you omens or **p,**
13: 2 the omens or the **p** declared by them take place,
Isa 8:18 the LORD has given me are signs and **p** in Israel
Joel 2:30 I will show **p** in the heavens and on the earth,
Lk 21:11 and there will be dreadful **p** and great signs
Ac 2:19 And I will show **p** in the heaven above and signs

PORTICO (4) [PORTICOES]

Jn 10:23 and Jesus was walking in the temple, in the **p**
Ac 3:11 to them in the **p** called Solomon's **P,**
5:12 And they were all together in Solomon's **P.**

PORTICOES (1) [PORTICO]

Jn 5: 2 called in Hebrew Beth-zatha, which has five **p.**

PORTION‡ (120) [APPORTION, APPORTIONED, PORTIONED, PORTIONS]

Ge 31:14 "Is there any **p** or inheritance left to us
43:34 but Benjamin's **p** was five times as much as any
48:22 now give to you one **p** more than to your brothers,
48:22 the **p** that I took from the hand of the Amorites
Ex 29:26 and it shall be your **p.**
Lev 2: 2 the priest shall turn this token **p** into smoke on
2: 9 from the grain offering its token **p** and turn this
2:16 the priest shall turn a token **p** of it into smoke—
5:12 of it as its memorial **p,** and turn this into smoke on
6:15 and they shall turn its memorial **p** into smoke on
6:17 I have given it as their **p** of my offerings by fire;
7:33 of well-being shall have the right thigh for a **p.**
7:35 This is the **p** allotted to Aaron and to his sons from
8:29 it was Moses' **p** of the ram of ordination,
Nu 5:26 of the grain offering, as its memorial **p,** and turn it
6:20 they are a holy **p** for the priest,
18: 8 to you and your sons as a priestly **p** due you
18:24 to the Levites as their **p** the tithe of the Israelites,
18:26 that I have given you from them for your **p,**
31:36 the **p** of those who had gone out to war,
36: 3 so it will be taken away from the allotted **p**
Dt 3:13 all that **p** of Bashan used to be called a land
18: 1 the sacrifices that are the LORD's **p**
21:17 giving him a double **p** of all that he has;
26:13 "I have removed the sacred **p** from the house,
32: 9 the LORD's own **p** was his people,
Jos 14: 4 and no **p** was given to the Levites in the land,
15:13 to Caleb son of Jephunneh a **p** among the people
17:14 "Why have you given me but one lot and one **p** as
18: 7 The Levites have no **p** among you,
18:10 the land to the Israelites, to each a **p.**
19: 9 the **p** of the tribe of Judah was too large for them,
22:25 you have no **p** in the LORD.'
22:27 "You have no **p** in the LORD."'
24:32 in the **p** of ground that Jacob had bought from
1Sa 1: 5 but to Hannah he gave a double **p,**
9:23 Samuel said to the cook, "Bring the **p** I gave you,
2Sa 6:19 to each a cake of bread, a **p** of meat,
20: 1 "We have no **p** in David,
2Ki 25:30 a **p** every day, as long as he lived.
1Ch 16: 3 to each a loaf of bread, a **p** of meat,
16:18 the land of Canaan as your **p** for an inheritance."
2Ch 31: 4 in Jerusalem to give the **p** due to the priests and
Est 2: 9 with her cosmetic treatments and her **p** of food,
Job 20:29 This is the **p** of the wicked from God,
24:18 their **p** in the land is cursed;
27:13 "This is the **p** of the wicked with God,
31: 2 What would be my **p** from God above,
Ps 11: 6 a scorching wind shall be the **p** of their cup.
16: 5 The LORD is my chosen **p** and my cup;
17:14 from mortals whose **p** in life is in this world.
60: 6 and **p** out the Vale of Succoth.
73:26 God is the strength of my heart and my **p** forever.
105:11 the land of Canaan as your **p** for an inheritance."
108: 7 and **p** out the Vale of Succoth.
119:57 LORD is my **p;** I promise to keep your words.
142: 5 my **p** in the land of the living."
Ecc 9: 9 because that is your **p** in life and in your toil
Isa 53:12 Therefore I will allot him a **p** with the great,
57: 6 Among the smooth stones of the valley is your **p;**
61: 7 therefore they shall possess a double **p;**
Jer 10:16 Not like these is the LORD, the **p** of Jacob,
12:10 they have trampled down my **p,**
12:10 they have made my pleasant **p** a desolate
13:25 This is your lot, the **p** I have measured out to you,
51:19 Not like these is the LORD, the **p** of Jacob,
La 3:24 "The LORD is my **p,"** says my soul,
Eze 45: 1 you shall set aside for the LORD a **p** of the land
45: 4 It shall be a holy **p** of the land;
45: 6 the **p** set apart as the holy district you shall assign
45:14 and as the fixed **p** of oil, one-tenth of a bath
48: 1 from the east side to the west, Dan, one **p.**
48: 2 from the east side to the west, Asher, one **p.**
48: 3 from the east side to the west, Naphtali, one **p.**
48: 4 from the east side to the west, Manasseh, one **p.**
48: 5 from the east side to the west, Ephraim, one **p.**
48: 6 from the east side to the west, Reuben, one **p.**
48: 7 from the east side to the west, Judah, one **p.**
48: 8 shall be the **p** that you shall set apart,
48: 9 The **p** that you shall set apart for the LORD shall
48:10 These shall be the allotments of the holy **p:**
48:12 as a special **p** from the holy **p** of the land,
48:14 they shall not transfer this choice **p** of the land,
48:18 the holy **p** shall be ten thousand cubits to the east,
48:18 and it shall be alongside the holy **p.**

Eze 48:20 The whole **p** that you shall set apart shall
48:20 the holy **p** together with the property of the city.
48:21 on both sides of the holy **p** and of the property of
48:21 from the twenty-five thousand cubits of the holy **p**
48:21 The holy **p** with the sanctuary of the temple in
48:22 The **p** of the prince shall lie between the territory
48:23 from the east side to the west, Benjamin, one **p.**
48:24 from the east side to the west, Simeon, one **p.**
48:25 from the east side to the west, Issachar, one **p.**
48:26 from the east side to the west, Zebulun, one **p.**
48:27 from the east side to the west, Gad, one **p.**
Da 1: 5 a daily **p** of the royal rations of food and wine.
Hab 1:16 for by them his **p** is lavish, and his food is rich.
Zec 2:12 The LORD will inherit Judah as his **p** in
AdE 2: 9 and her **p** of food, as well as seven maids chosen
13:16 Do not neglect your **p,** which you redeemed
Wis 2: 9 because this is our **p,** and this our lot.
Sir 7:31 and give him his **p,** as you have been commanded:
17:17 but Israel is the Lord's own **p.**
24:12 in the **p** of the Lord, his heritage.
26:23 *A godless wife is given as a p to a lawless man,*
38:11 and a memorial **p** of choice flour,
41:21 of taking away someone's **p** or gift,
45:16 incense and a pleasing odor as a memorial **p,**
45:22 and he has no **p** among the people;
45:22 for the Lord himself is his **p** and inheritance.
2Mc 1:26 of all your people Israel and preserve your **p**
1Es 6:29 of the tribute of Coelesyria and Phoenicia a **p**
3Mc 5:11 But the Lord sent upon the king a **p** of sleep,
5:17 and to make the present **p** of the banquet joyful
6: 3 a people of your consecrated **p** who are perishing
2Es 7:10 He said to me, "So also is Israel's **p.**
15:30 with their tusks they shall devastate a **p** of the land
15:60 a part of your land and abolish a **p** of your glory,

PORTIONED (1) [PORTION]

Isa 34:17 his hand has **p** it out to them with the line;

PORTIONS (23) [PORTION]

Ge 4: 4 of the firstlings of his flock, their fat **p.**
43:34 **P** were taken to them from Joseph's table,
Lev 24: 9 for they are most holy **p** for him from
Dt 18: 8 They shall have equal **p** to eat,
Jos 17: 5 Thus there fell to Manasseh ten **p,**
18: 5 They shall divide it into seven **p,**
1Sa 1: 4 he would give **p** to his wife Peninnah and
2Ch 31:15 to distribute the **p** to their kindred,
31:19 to distribute **p** to every male among the priests and
Ne 8:10 and drink sweet wine and send **p** of them to those
8:12 and to send **p** and to make great rejoicing,
12:44 into them the **p** required by the law for the priests
12:47 in the days of Nehemiah all Israel gave the daily **p**
13:10 the **p** of the Levites had not been given to them;
Eze 45: 7 corresponding in length to one of the tribal **p,**
47:13 Joseph shall have two **p.**
48: 8 and in length equal to one of the tribal **p,**
48:21 to the west border, parallel to the tribal **p,**
48:29 and these are their **p,** says the Lord GOD.
Sir 44:23 divided his **p,** and distributed them among twelve
50:12 he received the **p** from the hands of the priests,
1Es 9:51 and send **p** to those who have none;
9:54 and to give **p** to those who had none,

PORTRAY (1) [PORTRAYED]

Eze 4: 1 On it **p** a city, Jerusalem;

PORTRAYED (2) [PORTRAY]

Eze 8:10 there, **p** on the wall all around,
23:14 images of the Chaldeans **p** in vermilion,

PORTS (1)

Ac 27: 2 of Adramyttium that was about to set sail to the **p**

POSE (1)

Pr 28:11 but an intelligent poor person sees through the **p.**

POSIDONIUS (1)

2Mc 14:19 Therefore he sent **P,** Theodotus,

POSITION (17) [POSITIONS]

Nu 2:17 they shall set out just as they camp, each in **p,**
Jdg 4: 6 commands you, 'Go, take **p** at Mount Tabor,
2Ch 20:17 This battle is not for you to fight; take your **p,**
35: 5 Take **p** in the holy place according to
Est 1:19 and let the king give her royal **p**
Ps 109: 8 May his days be few; may another seize his **p.**
Da 11:16 He shall take a **p** in the beautiful land,
Lk 16: 3 now that my master is taking the **p** away from me?
Ac 1:20 and 'Let another take his **p** of overseer.'
1Co 14:16 how can anyone in the **p** of an outsider say
Jude 1: 6 And the angels who did not keep their own **p,**
AdE 14:16 that I abhor the sign of my proud **p,**
1Mc 1:34 These strengthened their **p;**
6:36 These took their **p** beforehand wherever
10:54 to you and to her in keeping with your **p.**"
2Mc 3:11 a man of very prominent **p,**
6:18 Eleazar, one of the scribes in high **p,**

POSITIONS (8) [POSITION]

1Ki 20:12 he said to his men, "Take your **p!**"
20:12 And they took their **p** against the city.
Jer 50:14 Take up your **p** around Babylon,
1Ti 2: 2 for kings and all who are in high **p,**
1Mc 10:37 of them be put in **p** of trust in the kingdom.
2Mc 8: 6 He captured strategic **p** and put to flight not a few
13:18 tried strategy in attacking their **p.**
4Mc 8: 7 and you will have **p** of authority

POSSESS‡ (78) [POSSESSED, POSSESSES, POSSESSING, POSSESSION, POSSESSIONS, POSSESSORS]

Ge 15: 7 to give you this land to **p.**"
15: 8 how am I to know that I shall **p** it?"
22:17 your offspring shall **p** the gate of their enemies,
47: 1 with their flocks and herds and all that they **p,**
Ex 23:30 until you have increased and **p** the land.
Lev 20:24 and I will give it to you to **p,**
Nu 14:24 and his descendants shall **p** it.
27: 7 you shall indeed let them **p** an inheritance
27:11 the nearest kinsman of his clan, and he shall **p** it.
33:53 for I have given you the land to **p.**
35: 2 from the inheritance that they **p,**
36: 8 to **p** their ancestral inheritance.
Dt 5:31 in the land that I am giving them to **p.**"
5:33 you may live long in the land that you are to **p.**
19: 2 that the LORD your God is giving you to **p.**
19:14 that the LORD your God is giving you to **p.**
21: 1 that the LORD your God is giving you to **p,**
23:20 in the land that you are about to enter and **p.**
25:19 to **p,** you shall blot out the remembrance
26: 1 an inheritance to **p,** and you **p** it, and settle in it,
28:21 the land that you are entering to **p.**
28:63 be plucked off the land that you are entering to **p.**
30: 5 that your ancestors possessed, and you will **p** it;
30:16 in the land that you are entering to **p.**
30:18 that you are crossing the Jordan to enter and **p.**
31:13 land that you are crossing over the Jordan to **p.**"
32:47 land that you are crossing over the Jordan to **p.**"
33:23 full of the blessing of the LORD, **p** the west
Jos 1:11 that the LORD your God gives you to **p.**' "
17:18 you shall clear it and **p** it to its farthest borders;
23: 5 and you shall **p** their land,
24: 4 I gave Esau the hill country of Seir to **p,**
Jdg 11:24 not **p** what your god Chemosh gives you to **p?**
11:24 And should we not be the ones to **p** everything
18: 9 Do not be slow to go, but enter in and **p** the land.
1Sa 10: 6 Then the spirit of the LORD will **p** you,
1Ch 28: 8 that you may **p** this good land,
Ezr 7:25 Ezra, according to the God-given wisdom you **p,**
9:11 that you are entering to **p** is a land unclean with
Ne 9:15 to go in to **p** the land that you swore to give them.
9:23 that you had told their ancestors to enter and **p.**
Job 22: 8 The powerful **p** the land, and the favored live in it.
Ps 25:13 and their children shall **p** the land.
69:35 and his servants shall live there and **p** it;
Isa 14: 2 and the house of Israel will **p** the nations as male
14:21 Let them never rise to **p** the earth or cover the face
34:11 But the hawk and the hedgehog shall **p** it;
34:17 shall **p** it forever, from generation to generation
54: 3 and your descendants will **p** the nations
57:13 But whoever takes refuge in me shall **p** the land
60:21 they shall **p** the land forever.
61: 7 therefore they shall **p** a double portion;
Eze 33:24 the land is surely given us to **p.**"
33:25 shall you then **p** the land?
33:26 shall you then **p** the land?
36:12 and they shall **p** you, and you shall
Da 7:18 of the Most High shall receive the kingdom and **p**
Hos 9: 6 Nettles shall **p** their precious things of silver;
Am 2:10 to **p** the land of the Amorite.
9:12 in order that they may **p** the remnant of Edom
Ob 1:19 Those of the Negeb shall **p** Mount Esau,
1:19 they shall **p** the land of Ephraim and the land
1:19 and Benjamin shall **p** Gilead.
1:20 the Israelites who are in Halah shall **p** Phoenicia
1:20 in Sepharad shall **p** the towns of the Negeb.
Zep 2: 9 and the survivors of my nation shall **p** them.
Zec 8:12 the remnant of this people to **p** all these things.
Ro 2:14 When Gentiles, who do not **p** the law,
1Co 8: 1 we know that "all of us **p** knowledge."
8:10 For if others see you, who **p** knowledge,
12:30 Do all **p** gifts of healing?
Jdt 9:13 and against the house your children **p.**
Wis 8:21 that I would not **p** wisdom unless God gave her
Sir 25: 4 and for the aged to **p** good counsel!
LtJ 6: 5 or of letting fear for these gods **p** you
2Es 6:59 why do we not **p** our world as an inheritance?

POSSESSED (20) [POSSESS]

Ex 35:23 And everyone who **p** blue or purple
35:24 and everyone who **p** acacia wood of any use in
Dt 30: 5 that your ancestors **p,** and you will possess it;
Jos 13: 1 and very much of the land still remains to be **p.**
1Sa 10:10 and the spirit of God **p** him,
Ne 9:24 So the descendants went in and **p** the land,
Zep 2: 9 a land **p** by nettles and salt pits,
Mt 8:16 to him many who were **p** with demons;
Mk 1:32 to him all who were sick or **p** with demons.
5:18 the man who had been **p** by demons begged him
Lk 8:36 how the one who had been **p**
Ac 8: 7 came out of many who were **p;**
Heb 10:34 knowing that you yourselves **p** something better
Jdt 8:10 who was in charge of all she **p,**
Wis 11:12 for a twofold grief **p** them,
1Mc 5:23 with their wives and children, and all they **p,**
2Mc 2: 9 that being **p** of wisdom Solomon offered sacrifice
1Es 8: 7 For Ezra **p** great knowledge,
3Mc 5:20 **p** by a savagery worse than that of Phalaris,
7:21 They also **p** greater prestige among their enemies,

POSSESSES (3) [POSSESS]

Nu 36: 8 Every daughter who **p** an inheritance in any tribe
Ecc 7:12 that wisdom gives life to the one who **p** it.
Bar 3:24 how vast the territory that he **p!**

POSSESSING (4) [POSSESS]

Jdg 18: 7 lacking nothing on earth, and **p** wealth.
2Co 6:10 as having nothing, and yet **p** everything.
1Mc 1:57 Anyone found **p** the book of the covenant,
2Mc 4:25 **p** no qualification for the high priesthood,

POSSESSION‡ (149) [POSSESS]

Ge 23: 9 to me in your presence as a **p** for a burying place."
23:18 to Abraham as a **p** in the presence of the Hittites,
23:20 in it passed from the Hittites into Abraham's **p** as
24:60 may your offspring gain **p** of the gates
28: 4 so that you may take **p** of the land where you
31:18 in his **p** that he had acquired in Paddan-aram,
44:16 also the one in whose **p** the cup has been found."
44:17 Only the one in whose **p** the cup was found shall
Ex 6: 8 I will give it to you for a **p.**
13: 7 no leavened bread shall be seen in your **p,**
15:17 and planted them on the mountain of your own **p,**
19: 5 you shall be my treasured **p** out of all the peoples.
21:16 that person has been sold or is still held in **p,**
22: 4 is found alive in the thief's **p,**
Lev 14:34 which I give you for a **p,**
14:34 a leprous disease in a house in the land of your **p,**
25:33 the Levites are their **p** among the people of Israel.
25:34 for that is their **p** for all time.
25:46 You may keep them as a **p** for your children
Nu 18:20 I am your share and your **p** among the Israelites.
18:21 for a **p** in return for the service that they perform,
21:24 took **p** of his land from the Arnon to the Jabbok,
21:35 and they took **p** of his land.
24:18 Edom will become a **p,** Seir a **p** of its enemies,
27: 4 Give to us a **p** among our father's brothers."
32: 5 let this land be given to your servants for a **p;**
32:22 and this land shall be your **p** before the LORD.
32:29 you shall give them the land of Gilead for a **p;**
32:32 but the **p** of our inheritance shall remain with us
33:53 You shall take **p** of the land and settle in it,
35: 8 as for the towns that you shall give from the **p** of
Dt 1: 8 go in and take **p** of the land that I swore
1:21 go up, take **p,** as the LORD,
1:38 for he is the one who will secure Israel's **p** of it.
1:39 to them I will give it, and they shall take **p** of it.
2: 5 since I have given Mount Seir to Esau as a **p.**
2: 9 for I will not give you any of its land as a **p,**
2: 9 I have given Ar as a **p** to the descendants of Lot."
2:12 in the land that the LORD gave them as a **p.**)
2:19 not give the land of the Ammonites to you as a **p,**
2:24 Begin to take **p** by engaging him in battle.
2:31 Begin now to take **p** of his land."
3:12 As for the land that we took **p** of at that time,
3:28 of this people and who shall secure their **p** of
4:20 to become a people of his very own **p,**
4:21 that the LORD your God is giving for your **p.**
4:22 but you are going to cross over to take **p** of
4:38 giving you their land for a **p,** as it is still today.
7: 6 on earth to be his people, his treasured **p.**
9:26 not destroy the people who are your very own **p,**
9:29 For they are the people of your very own **p,**
12: 9 and the **p** that the LORD your God is giving you.
14: 2 on earth to be his people, his treasured **p.**
15: 4 that the LORD your God is giving you as a **p**
17:14 and have taken **p** of it and settled in it,
19: 3 that the LORD your God gives you as a **p,**
21:23 that the LORD your God is giving you for **p.**
24: 4 that the LORD your God is giving you as a **p.**
31: 7 and you will put them in **p** of it.
32:49 which I am giving to the Israelites for a **p;**
33: 4 as a **p** for the assembly of Jacob.
Jos 1: 6 in **p** of the land that I swore to their ancestors
1:11 over the Jordan, to go in to take **p** of the land that
1:15 and they too take **p** of the land that
1:15 you shall return to your own land and take **p** of it,
12: 6 the servant of the LORD gave their land for a **p**
12: 7 of Israel as a **p** according to their allotments,
17:12 the Manassites could not take **p** of those towns;
18: 3 be slack about going in and taking **p** of the land
19:47 they took **p** of it and settled in it, calling Leshem,
21:43 and having taken **p** of it, they settled there.
22: 4 and go to your tents in the land where your **p** lies,
22: 7 of the tribe of Manasseh Moses had given a **p**
22: 7 a **p** beside their fellow Israelites in the land west
22: 9 of which they had taken **p** by command of
22:19 and take for yourselves a **p** among us;
24: 8 and you took **p** of their land,
Jdg 1:19 and he took **p** of the hill country,
2: 6 to their own inheritances to take **p** of the land.
3:13 and they took **p** of the city of palms.
6:34 But the spirit of the LORD took **p** of Gideon;
8: 6 in your **p** the hands of Zebah and Zalmunna,
8:15 in your **p** the hands of Zebah and Zalmunna,
17: 2 that silver is in my **p;**
1Sa 13:22 to be found in the **p** of any of the people with Saul
1Ki 21:15 take **p** of the vineyard of Naboth the Jezreelite,
21:16 to the vineyard of Naboth the Jezreelite, to take **p**
21:18 where he has gone to take **p.**
21:19 Have you killed, and also taken **p?**"

2Ki 17:24 they took **p** of Samaria, and settled in its cities.
2Ch 20:11 they reward us by coming to drive us out of your **p**
24:20 Then the spirit of God took **p** of Zechariah son of
Ezr 4:16 then have no **p** in the province Beyond the River."
Ne 9:22 so they took **p** of the land of King Sihon
9:25 and took **p** of houses filled with all sorts of goods,
Ps 2:8 and the ends of the earth your **p**.
78:55 for a **p** and settled the tribes of Israel in their tents.
83:12 "Let us take the pastures of God for our own **p**."
105:44 and they took **p** of the wealth of the peoples,
135:4 for himself, Israel as his own **p**.
Isa 14:23 And I will make it a **p** of the hedgehog,
63:18 Your holy people took **p** for a little while;
Jer 30:3 that I gave to their ancestors and they shall take **p**
32:8 for the right of **p** and redemption is yours;
32:23 and they entered and took **p** of it.
Eze 7:24 the worst of the nations to take **p** of their houses.
11:15 to us this land is given for a **p**."
25:4 over to the people of the east for a **p**.
25:10 with Ammon to the people of the east as a **p**.
33:24 yet he got **p** of the land;
35:10 and we will take **p** of them,"—
36:2 and, "The ancient heights have become our **p**,"
36:3 so that you became the **p** of the rest of the nations,
36:5 took my land as their **p**, because of its pasture,
Da 7:22 and the time arrived when the holy ones gained **p**
Hos 1:11 and they shall take **p** of the land,
Ob 1:17 and the house of Jacob shall take **p**
Mic 7:18 over the transgression of the remnant of your **p**?
Zep 2:7 The seacoast shall become the **p** of the remnant of
Zec 13:5 for the land has been my **p** since my youth."
Mal 3:17 my special **p** on the day when I act,
Ac 7:5 to him as his **p** and to his descendants after him,
Jdt 1:14 Thus he took **p** of his towns and came
5:15 over the Jordan they took **p** of all the hill country.
7:12 let your servants take **p** of the spring of water
15:7 when they returned from the slaughter, took **p**
Wis 8:5 If riches are a desirable **p** in life,
Sir 19:3 Decay and worms will take **p** of him,
24:20 and the **p** of me sweeter than the honeycomb.
36:29 He who acquires a wife gets his best **p**,
51:21 therefore I have gained a prize **p**.
1Mc 10:76 and Jonathan gained **p** of Joppa.
10:89 also gave him Ekron and all its environs as his **p**.
11:1 and he tried to get **p** of Alexander's kingdom
11:34 We have confirmed as their **p** both the territory
11:66 He removed them from there, took **p** of the town,
13:38 let the strongholds that you have built be your **p**.
15:29 you have taken **p** of many places in my kingdom.
16:20 and he sent other troops to take **p** of Jerusalem and
2Mc 2:14 and they are in our **p**.
2:22 and regained **p** of the temple famous throughout
8:30 and got **p** of some exceedingly high strongholds,
10:17 they gained **p** of the places,
13:13 before the king's army could enter Judea and get **p**
14:2 and had taken **p** of the country,
15:37 and from that time the city has been in the **p** of
1Es 8:83 that you are entering to take **p** of is a land polluted
2Es 14:31 land was given to you for a **p** in the land of Zion;

POSSESSIONS (53) [POSSESS]

Ge 12:5 and all the **p** that they had gathered,
13:6 for their **p** were so great that they could
15:14 and afterward they shall come out with great **p**.
26:14 He had **p** of flocks and herds,
36:7 their **p** were too great for them to live together;
45:20 Give no thought to your **p**,
47:27 and they gained **p** in it,
Nu 32:30 they shall have **p** among you in the land
Dt 18:8 they have income from the sale of family **p**.
21:16 then on the day when he wills his **p** to his sons,
1Ch 7:28 Their **p** and settlements were Bethel and its towns,
9:2 in their **p** in their towns were Israelites,
2Ch 1:11 and you have not asked for **p**, wealth, honor,
1:12 I will also give you riches, **p**, and honor,
21:3 of silver, gold, and valuable **p**,
21:14 your children, your wives, and all your **p**,
21:17 the **p** they found that belonged to the king's house,
31:3 The contribution of the king from his own **p** was
32:29 for God had given him very great **p**.
35:7 these were from the king's **p**.
Ezr 8:21 our children, and all our **p**.
Job 1:10 and his **p** have increased in the land.
20:28 The **p** of their house will be carried away,
Ps 105:21 and ruler of all his **p**,
Ecc 2:7 I also had great **p** of herds and flocks,
5:19 and **p** and whom he enables to enjoy them,
6:2 **p**, and honor, so that they lack nothing of all
Zec 9:4 the Lord will strip it of its **p** and hurl its wealth
Mt 18:25 together with his wife and children and all his **p**,
19:21 go, sell your **p**, and give the money to the poor,
19:22 he went away grieving, for he had many **p**.
24:47 he will put that one in charge of all his **p**.
Mk 10:22 and went away grieving, for he had many **p**.
Lk 12:15 one's life does not consist in the abundance of **p**."
12:33 Sell your **p**, and give alms.
12:44 he will put that one in charge of all his **p**.
14:33 if you do not give up all your **p**.
19:8 "Look, half of my **p**, Lord, I will give to the poor;
Ac 2:45 they would sell their **p** and goods and distribute
4:32 and no one claimed private ownership of any **p**,
1Co 7:30 and those who buy as though they had no **p**,
13:3 If I give away all my **p**,
Heb 10:34 you cheerfully accepted the plundering of your **p**,
Tob 4:7 from your **p**, and do not let your eye begrudge
4:8 If you have many **p**, make your gift from them
Tob 6:12 Also it is right for you to inherit her father's **p**.
12:2 to give him half of the **p** brought back with me.
Jdt 16:19 also dedicated to God all the **p** of Holofernes,
Wis 13:17 he prays about **p** and his marriage and children,
Sir 25:21 and do not desire a woman for her **p**.
41:1 the thought of you to the one at peace among **p**,
1Es 1:7 these were given from the king's **p**,
2Es 16:47 more they adorn their cities, their houses and **p**,

POSSESSORS (1) [POSSESS]

Pr 1:19 it takes away the life of its **p**.

POSSIBLE (28) [POSSIBLY]

1Ch 17:25 your servant has found it **p** to pray before you.
Mt 19:26 but for God all things are **p**."
24:24 to lead astray, if **p**, even the elect.
26:39 "My Father, if it is **p**, let this cup pass from me;
Mk 10:27 for God all things are **p**."
13:22 to lead astray, if **p**, the elect.
14:35 if it were **p**, the hour might pass from him.
14:36 He said, "Abba, Father, for you all things are **p**;
Lk 18:27 "What is impossible for mortals is **p** for God."
Ac 8:22 if **p**, the intent of your heart may be forgiven you.
17:15 to have Silas and Timothy join him as soon as **p**,
20:16 he was eager to be in Jerusalem, if **p**,
Ro 12:18 If it is **p**, so far as it depends on you,
Gal 4:15 For I testify that, had it been **p**,
Tob 8:10 "It is **p** that he will die and we will become
10:2 "Is it **p** that he has been detained?
Sir 18:6 It is not **p** to diminish or increase them,
18:6 nor is it **p** to fathom the wonders of the Lord.
22:22 do not worry, for reconciliation is **p**.
1Mc 11:22 for a conference at Ptolemais as quickly as **p**.
2Mc 3:6 but that it was **p** for them to fall under the control
11:18 and he has agreed to what was **p**.
13:26 made the best **p** defense, convinced them,
14:29 Since it was not **p** to oppose the king,
3Mc 1:8 the more eager to visit them as soon as **p**.
2Es 4:44 "If I have found favor in your sight, and if it is **p**,
10:55 as far as it is **p** for your eyes to see it,
4Mc 17:7 If it were **p** for us to paint the history

POSSIBLY (1) [POSSIBLE]

Jer 25:29 and how can you **p** avoid punishment?

POST (9) [BED-POST, DOORPOST, DOORPOSTS, GUIDEPOSTS, POSTED, POSTS, SIGNPOST, WATCHPOST]

1Ki 20:24 Also do this: remove the kings, each from his **p**,
Ecc 10:4 of the ruler rises against you, do not leave your **p**,
Isa 21:6 "Go, **p** a lookout, let him announce what he sees.
21:8 and at my **p** I am stationed throughout the night.
22:19 and you will be pulled down from your **p**.
Jer 51:12 **p** sentinels; prepare the ambushes;
Eze 46:2 and shall take his stand by the **p** of the gate.
AdE 16:19 **p** a copy of this letter publicly in every place,
4Mc 9:23 "Do not leave your **p** in my struggle

POSTED (9) [POST]

2Ki 11:18 The priest **p** guards over the house of the LORD.
Ne 4:16 the leaders **p** themselves behind the whole house
Isa 62:6 Upon your walls, O Jerusalem, I have **p** sentinels;
AdE 3:14 Copies of the document were **p** in every province,
4:3 the king's proclamation had been **p** there was
4:8 also gave him a copy of what had been **p** in Susa
8:13 "Let copies of the decree be **p** conspicuously in all
2Mc 14:22 Judas **p** armed men in readiness at key places
3Mc 5:44 and they confidently **p** the armed forces at

POSTERITY (11)

Ge 21:23 with me or with my offspring or with my **p**,
Nu 21:30 So their **p** perished from Heshbon to Dibon,
Ps 22:30 **P** will serve him; future generations will be told
37:37 for there is **p** for the peaceable.
37:38 the **p** of the wicked shall be cut off.
109:13 May his **p** be cut off;
Isa 14:22 offspring and **p**, says the LORD.
Da 11:4 but not to his **p**, nor according to the dominion
Ac 13:23 Of this man's **p** God has brought to Israel
Tob 4:12 and their **p** will inherit the land.
2Es 3:19 and your commandment to the **p** of Israel.

POSTPONE (2)

Dt 23:21 to the LORD your God, do not **p** fulfilling it;
Sir 5:7 and do not **p** it from day to day;

POSTS (9) [POST]

Jdg 16:3 of the doors of the city gate and the two **p**,
2Ch 7:6 The priests stood at their **p**;
30:16 They took their accustomed **p** according to the law
Ne 7:3 of Jerusalem, some at their watch **p**, and others
SS 3:10 He made its **p** of silver, its back of gold,
Eze 45:19 and the **p** of the gate of the inner court.
Jdt 7:32 Then he dismissed the people to their various **p**,
8:36 So they returned from the tent and went to their **p**.
13:9 the bed and pulled down the canopy from the **p**.

POSTURE (1)

3Mc 1:23 they resorted to the same **p** of supplication as

POT (23) [FLESHPOTS, POTS, POTSHERD, POTSHERDS, POTTER, POTTER'S, POTTERS]

Ge 15:17 a smoking fire **p** and a flaming torch passed
Jdg 6:19 and the broth he put in a **p**,
1Sa 2:14 or kettle, or caldron, or **p**;
2Ki 4:38 he said to his servant, "Put the large **p** on,
4:39 and came and cut them up into the **p** of stew,
4:40 "O man of God, there is death in the **p**!"
4:41 He threw it into the **p**, and said,
4:41 And there was nothing harmful in the **p**.
Job 41:20 as from a boiling **p** and burning rushes.
41:31 It makes the deep boil like a **p**;
41:31 it makes the sea like a **p** of ointment.
Ecc 7:6 For like the crackling of thorns under a **p**,
Jer 1:13 And I said, "I see a boiling **p**,
22:28 Is this man Coniah a despised broken **p**,
Eze 11:3 this city is the **p**, and we are the meat.'
11:7 within it are the meat, and this city is the **p**;
11:11 This city shall not be your **p**,
24:3 Set on the **p**, set it on, pour in water also;
24:6 Woe to the bloody city, the **p** whose rust is in it,
Zec 12:6 a blazing **p** on a pile of wood, like a flaming torch
14:21 and every cooking **p** in Jerusalem and Judah shall
Sir 13:2 How can the clay **p** associate with the iron kettle?
13:2 The **p** will strike against it and be smashed.

POTENTATE (KJV) See SOVEREIGN

POTIPHAR (2)

Ge 37:36 the Midianites had sold him in Egypt to **P**,
39:1 Now Joseph was taken down to Egypt, and **P**,

POTIPHERA (3)

Ge 41:45 and he gave him Asenath daughter of **P**,
41:50 whom Asenath daughter of **P**, priest of On,
46:20 whom Asenath daughter of **P**, priest of On,

POTS (17) [POT]

Ex 27:3 You shall make **p** for it to receive its ashes,
38:3 He made all the utensils of the altar, the **p**,
Nu 11:8 then boiled it in **p** and made cakes of it;
1Ki 7:40 Hiram also made the **p**, the shovels,
7:45 The **p**, the shovels, and the basins,
2Ki 25:14 They took away the **p**, the shovels, the snuffers,
2Ch 4:11 Huram made the **p**, the shovels, and the basins.
4:16 The **p**, the shovels, the forks,
35:13 and they boiled the holy offerings in **p**,
Ps 58:9 Sooner than your **p** can feel the heat of thorns,
Jer 52:18 They took away the **p**, the shovels, the snuffers,
52:19 the firepans, the basins, the **p**, the lampstands,
La 4:2 how they are reckoned as earthen **p**,
Zec 14:20 the cooking **p** in the house of the LORD shall be
Mk 7:4 the washing of cups, **p**, and bronze kettles.)
Rev 2:27 as when clay **p** are shattered—
1Es 1:12 they boiled the sacrifices in bronze **p** and caldrons,

POTSHERD (3) [POT, SHERD]

Job 2:8 Job took a **p** with which to scrape himself,
Ps 22:15 dried up like a **p**, and my tongue sticks to my jaws;
Jer 19:2 of the son of Hinnom at the entry of the **P** Gate,

POTSHERDS‡ (2) [POT, SHERD]

Job 41:30 Its underparts are like sharp **p**;
Sir 22:9 a fool is like one who glues **p** together,

POTTAGE (KJV) See LENTIL STEW, RED STUFF, STEW

POTTER‡ (10) [POT]

Isa 29:16 Shall the **p** be regarded as the clay?
41:25 on rulers as on mortar, as the **p** treads clay.
45:9 earthen vessels with the **p**!
64:8 we are the clay, and you are our **p**;
Jer 18:6 O house of Israel, just as this **p** has done?
18:11 a **p** shaping evil against you and devising a plan
Ro 9:21 Has the **p** no right over the clay,
Wis 15:7 A **p** kneads the soft earth
Sir 33:13 Like clay in the hand of the **p**,
38:29 the **p** sitting at his work and turning the wheel

POTTER'S (13) [POT]

Ps 2:9 and dash them in pieces like a **p** vessel."
Isa 30:14 that of a **p** vessel that is smashed so ruthlessly that
Jer 18:2 go down to the **p** house,
18:3 So I went down to the **p** house,
18:4 of clay was spoiled in the **p** hand,
18:6 Just like the clay in the **p** hand,
19:1 Go and buy a **p** earthenware jug.
19:11 and this city, as one breaks a **p** vessel,
La 4:2 as earthen pots, the work of a **p** hands!
Da 2:41 and toes partly of **p** clay and partly of iron, it shall
Mt 27:7 to buy the **p** field as a place to bury foreigners.
27:10 and they gave them for the **p** field,
Sir 27:5 The kiln tests the **p** vessels;

POTTERS‡ (1) [POT]

1Ch 4:23 the **p** and inhabitants of Netaim and Gederah;

POUCH (1)

1Sa 17:40 and put them in his shepherd's bag, in the **p;**

POULTICE (1)

Wis 16:12 For neither herb nor **p** cured them,

POUND‡ (5) [POUNDED, POUNDING, POUNDS]

Lk 19:16 'Lord, your **p** has made ten more pounds.'
19:18 saying, 'Lord, your **p** has made five pounds.'
19:20 the other came, saying, 'Lord, here is your **p.**
19:24 'Take the **p** from him and give it to
Jn 12: 3 a **p** of costly perfume made of pure nard,

POUNDED (1) [POUND]

Ac 27:18 We were being **p** by the storm so violently that on

POUNDING (1) [POUND]

Jdg 19:22 surrounded the house, and started **p** on the door.

POUNDS (7) [POUND]

Lk 19:13 and gave them ten **p,** and said to them,
19:16 'Lord, your pound has made ten more **p.'**
19:18 saying, 'Lord, your pound has made five **p.'**
19:24 from him and give it to the one who has ten **p.'**
19:25 (And they said to him, 'Lord, he has ten **p!'**)
Jn 19:39 weighing about a hundred **p.**
Rev 16:21 each weighing about a hundred **p,**

POUR (84) [OUTPOURED, POURED, POURING, POURS]

Ex 4: 9 you shall take some water from the Nile and **p** it
25:29 and bowls with which to **p** drink offerings;
29: 7 and **p** it on his head and anoint him.
29:12 of the blood you shall **p** out at the base of the altar.
30: 9 and you shall not **p** a drink offering on it.
37:16 and flagons with which to **p** drink offerings.
Lev 2: 1 the worshiper shall **p** oil on it,
2: 6 and **p** oil on it; it is a grain offering.
4: 7 and the rest of the blood of the bull he shall **p** out
4:18 and the rest of the blood he shall **p** out at the base
4:25 and **p** out the rest of its blood at the base of
4:30 and he shall **p** out the rest of its blood at the base
4:34 **p** out the rest of its blood at the base of the altar.
14:15 The priest shall take some of the log of oil and **p** it
14:26 The priest shall **p** some of the oil into the palm
17:13 that may be eaten shall **p** out its blood and cover it
Nu 5:15 He shall **p** no oil on it and put no frankincense
28: 7 in the sanctuary you shall **p** out a drink offering
Dt 12:16 you shall **p** it out on the ground like water.
12:24 you shall **p** it out on the ground like water.
15:23 you shall **p** it out on the ground like water.
Jdg 6:20 and put them on this rock, and **p** out the broth."
1Ki 18:33 and **p** it on the burnt offering and on the wood."
2Ki 3:11 who used to **p** water on the hands of Elijah,
9: 3 Then take the flask of oil, **p** it on his head,
Job 10:10 not **p** me out like milk and curdle me like cheese?
36:28 which the skies **p** down and drop
40:11 **P** out the overflowings of your anger,
Ps 16: 4 their drink offerings of blood I will not **p** out
42: 4 These things I remember, as I **p** out my soul:
62: 8 **p** out your heart before him;
69:24 **P** out your indignation upon them,
75: 8 he will **p** a draught from it,
79: 6 **P** out your anger on the nations that do
94: 4 They **p** out their arrogant words;
119:171 My lips will **p** forth praise,
142: 2 I **p** out my complaint before him;
Pr 1:23 I will **p** out my thoughts to you;
15: 2 but the mouths of fools **p** out folly.
Isa 1:24 Ah, I will **p** out my wrath on my enemies,
44: 3 For I will **p** water on the thirsty land,
44: 3 I will **p** my spirit upon your descendants,
Jer 6:11 **P** it out on the children in the street,
7:18 and they **p** out drink offerings to other gods,
10:25 **P** out your wrath on the nations that do
14:16 For I will **p** out their wickedness upon them.
44:17 to the queen of heaven and **p** out libations to her,
44:25 the queen of heaven and to **p** out libations to her.'
La 2:19 **P** out your heart like water before the presence of
Eze 7: 8 Soon now I will **p** out my wrath upon you;
9: 8 as you **p** out your wrath upon Jerusalem?"
14:19 and **p** out my wrath upon it with blood,
20: 8 Then I thought I would **p** out my wrath upon them
20:13 Then I thought I would **p** out my wrath upon them
20:21 Then I thought I would **p** out my wrath upon them
21:31 I will **p** out my indignation upon you,
24: 3 Set on the pot, set it on, **p** in water also;
24: 7 she did not **p** it out on the ground,
30:15 I will **p** my wrath upon Pelusium,
38:22 and I will **p** down torrential rains and hailstones,
39:29 when I **p** out my spirit upon the house of Israel,
Hos 5:10 on them I will **p** out my wrath like water.
9: 4 not **p** drink offerings of wine to the LORD,
Joel 2:28 Then afterward I will **p** out my spirit on all flesh;
2:29 in those days, I will **p** out my spirit.
Mic 1: 6 I will **p** down her stones into the valley,
Zep 3: 8 to **p** out upon them my indignation,
Zec 4:12 which **p** out the oil through the two golden pipes?"
12:10 And I will **p** out a spirit of compassion
Mal 3:10 not open the windows of heaven for you and **p**
Ac 2:17 that I will **p** out my Spirit upon all flesh,
2:18 in those days I will **p** out my Spirit;
Jas 3:11 a spring **p** forth from the same opening both fresh
Rev 16: 1 "Go and **p** out on the earth the seven bowls of
Sir 18:29 become wise themselves, and **p** forth apt proverbs.
24:33 I will again **p** out teaching like prophecy,
32: 4 Where there is entertainment, do not **p** out talk;
36: 8 Rouse your anger and **p** out your wrath;
38:11 and **p** oil on your offering,
39: 6 he will **p** forth words of wisdom of his own
39:28 the day of reckoning they will **p** out their strength
2Es 15:35 and shall **p** out a heavy tempest on the earth,
15:40 and shall **p** out upon every high and lofty place
15:44 they shall **p** out on it the tempest and all its fury;

POURED‡ (103) [POUR]

Ge 28:18 and set it up for a pillar and **p** oil on the top of it.
35:14 and he **p** out a drink offering on it, and **p** oil
Ex 9:33 and the rain no longer **p** down on the earth.
Lev 8:12 He **p** some of the anointing oil on Aaron's head
8:15 then he **p** out the blood at the base of the altar.
9: 9 rest of the blood he **p** out at the base of the altar.
21:10 on whose head the anointing oil has been **p**
Dt 12:27 be **p** out beside the altar of the LORD your God,
Jdg 5: 4 the earth trembled, and the heavens **p,**
5: 4 the clouds indeed **p** water.
1Sa 7: 6 and drew water and **p** it out before the LORD.
10: 1 Samuel took a vial of oil and **p** it on his head,
2Sa 20:10 the belly so that his entrails **p** out on the ground,
23:16 he **p** it out to the LORD,
1Ki 13: 3 and the ashes that are on it shall be **p** out.' "
13: 5 and the ashes **p** out from the altar,
2Ki 9: 6 the young man **p** the oil on his head,
16:13 and his grain offering, **p** his drink offering,
1Ch 11:18 he **p** it out to the LORD,
2Ch 12: 7 not be **p** out on Jerusalem by the hand of Shishak.
34:21 wrath of the LORD that is **p** out on us is great,
34:25 my wrath will be **p** out on this place and will not
Job 3:24 and my groanings are **p** out like water.
29: 6 and the rock **p** out for me streams of oil!
30:16 "And now my soul is **p** out within me;
Ps 22:14 I am **p** out like water, and all my bones are out
45: 2 grace is **p** upon your lips;
68: 8 the heavens **p** down rain at the presence of God,
77:17 The clouds **p** out water; the skies thundered;
79: 3 They have **p** out their blood like water all
92:10 you have **p** over me fresh oil.
106:38 they **p** out innocent blood, the blood of their sons
SS 1: 3 your name is perfume **p** out;
Isa 19:14 The LORD has **p** into them a spirit of confusion;
26:16 they **p** out a prayer when your chastening was
29:10 LORD has **p** out upon you a spirit of deep sleep;
32:15 until a spirit from on high is **p** out on us,
42:25 So he **p** upon him the heat of his anger and
53:12 because he **p** out himself to death,
57: 6 to them you have **p** out a drink offering,
63: 6 and I **p** out their lifeblood on the earth."
Jer 7:20 and my wrath shall be **p** out on this place,
19:13 and libations have been **p** out to other gods.
32:29 and libations have been **p** out to other gods,
42:18 Just as my anger and my wrath were **p** out on
42:18 of Jerusalem, so my wrath will be **p** out on you
44: 6 So my wrath and my anger were **p** out and kindled
44:19 with her image, and **p** out libations to her
La 2: 4 he has **p** out his fury like fire.
2:11 my bile is **p** out on the ground because of
2:12 as their life is **p** out on their mothers' bosom.
4:11 he **p** out his hot anger,
Eze 16:36 Because your lust was **p** out
20:28 and there they **p** out their drink offerings.
20:33 and with wrath **p** out, I will be king over you.
20:34 and an outstretched arm, and with wrath **p** out;
22:22 that I the LORD have **p** out my wrath upon you.
22:31 Therefore I have **p** out my indignation upon them;
23: 8 and fondled her virgin bosom and **p** out their lust
36:18 So I **p** out my wrath upon them for the blood
Da 9:11 the servant of God, have been **p** out upon us,
9:27 until the decreed end is **p** out upon the desolator."
Joel 2:23 he has **p** down for you abundant rain,
Mic 1: 4 like waters **p** down a steep place.
Na 1: 6 His wrath is **p** out like fire,
Zep 1:17 their blood shall be **p** out like dust,
Mt 26: 7 and she **p** it on his head as he sat at the table.
26:28 which is **p** out for many for the forgiveness
Mk 14: 3 and she broke open the jar and **p** the ointment
14:24 which is **p** out for many.
Lk 10:34 having **p** oil and wine on them.
22:20 "This cup that is **p** out for you is the new covenant
Jn 2:15 He also **p** out the coins of the money changers
13: 5 Then he **p** water into a basin and began to wash
Ac 2:33 he has **p** out this that you both see and hear.
10:45 that the gift of the Holy Spirit had been **p** out even
Ro 5: 5 because God's love has been **p** into our hearts
Php 2:17 if I am being **p** out as a libation over the sacrifice
2Ti 4: 6 As for me, I am already being **p** out as a libation,
Tit 3: 6 This Spirit he **p** out on us richly
Rev 12:15 the serpent **p** water like a river after the woman,
12:16 the river that the dragon had **p** from his mouth.
14:10 **p** unmixed into the cup of his anger,
16: 2 the first angel went and **p** his bowl on the earth,
16: 3 The second angel **p** his bowl into the sea,
16: 4 The third angel **p** his bowl into the rivers and
16: 8 The fourth angel **p** his bowl on the sun,
16:10 fifth angel **p** his bowl on the throne of the beast,
16:12 The sixth angel **p** his bowl on
16:17 The seventh angel **p** his bowl into the air,
Sir 1: 9 he **p** her out upon all his works,
30:18 Good things **p** out upon a mouth that is closed
50:15 for the cup and **p** a drink offering of the blood of
50:15 he **p** it out at the foot of the altar,
50:27 whose mind **p** forth wisdom.
Aza 1:24 flames **p** out above the furnace forty-nine cubits,
1Mc 7:17 of your faithful ones and their blood they **p** out all
2Mc 1:31 the liquid that was left should be **p** on large stones.
2Es 4:49 a cloud full of water passed before me and **p** down
14:40 I had drunk it, my heart **p** forth understanding,
4Mc 3:16 he **p** out the drink as an offering to God.
6:25 and **p** stinking liquids into his nostrils.

POURING (8) [POUR]

1Sa 1:15 but I have been **p** out my soul before the LORD.
2Ki 4: 4 and start **p** into all these vessels;
4: 5 they kept bringing vessels to her, and she kept **p.**
Isa 8: 8 and, **p** over, it will reach up to the neck;
Jer 44:18 to the queen of heaven and **p** out libations to her,
44:19 to the queen of heaven and **p** out libations to her;
Hab 2:15 **p** out your wrath until they are drunk,
Mt 26:12 By **p** this ointment on my

POURS (15) [POUR]

Job 12:21 He **p** contempt on princes,
16:13 he **p** out my gall on the ground.
16:20 My friends scorn me; my eye **p** out tears to God,
Ps 19: 2 Day to day **p** forth speech,
107:40 he **p** contempt on princes and makes them wander
Pr 15:28 but the mouth of the wicked **p** out evil.
Am 5: 8 and **p** them out on the surface of the earth,
9: 6 and **p** them out upon the surface of the earth—
Rev 11: 5 fire **p** from their mouth and consumes their foes;
Sir 10:13 and the one who clings to it **p** out abominations.
16:11 but he also **p** out wrath.
18:11 the Lord is patient with them and **p** out his mercy
24:27 It **p** forth instruction like the Nile,
35:17 or the widow when she **p** out her complaint.
43:19 He **p** frost over the earth like salt,

POURTRAY[ED] (KJV) See PORTRAY[ED]

POVERTY‡ (28) [POOR]

Ge 45:11 and all that you have, will not come to **p.'**
Pr 6:11 and **p** will come upon you like a robber,
10: 4 A slack hand causes **p,** but the hand of
10:15 the **p** of the poor is their ruin.
13:18 **P** and disgrace are for the one who ignores
14:23 but mere talk leads only to **p.**
20:13 Do not love sleep, or else you will come to **p;**
23:21 for the drunkard and the glutton will come to **p,**
24:34 and **p** will come upon you like a robber,
28:19 follows worthless pursuits will have plenty of **p.**
30: 8 give me neither **p** nor riches;
31: 7 let them drink and forget their **p,**
Mk 12:44 but she out of her **p** has put in everything she had,
Lk 21: 4 she out of her **p** has put in all she had to live on."
2Co 8: 2 and their extreme **p** have overflowed in a wealth
8: 9 so that by his **p** you might become rich.
Rev 2: 9 "I know your affliction and your **p,**
Tob 4:13 And in idleness there is loss and dire **p,**
Sir 10:31 who is honored in **p,** how much more in wealth!
10:31 one dishonored in wealth, how much more in **p!**
11:12 who lack strength and abound in **p;**
11:14 Good things and bad, life and death, **p** and wealth,
13:24 **p** is evil only in the opinion of the ungodly.
18:25 in days of wealth think of **p** and need.
20:21 One may be prevented from sinning by **p;**
22:23 Gain the trust of your neighbor in his **p,**
26:28 a warrior in want through **p,**
2Es 15:49 widowhood, **p,** famine, sword, and pestilence,

POWDER (4) [POWDERS]

Ex 30:36 of it into **p,** and put part of it before the covenant
32:20 ground it to **p,** scattered it on the water,
Dt 28:24 LORD will change the rain of your land into **p,**
2Ch 34: 7 beat the sacred poles and the images into **p,**

POWDERS (1) [POWDER]

SS 3: 6 with all the fragrant **p** of the merchant?

POWER‡ (380) [ALL-POWERFUL, EMPOWERED, OVERPOWER, OVERPOWERED, OVERPOWERING, OVERPOWERS, POWERFUL, POWERFULLY, POWERLESS, POWERS]

A. POWER OF *GOD (23)
B. GREAT POWER (20)
C. DEEDS OF POWER (12)

Ge 16: 6 "Your slave-girl is in your **p;**
31:29 It is in my **p** to do you harm;
49: 3 excelling in rank and excelling in **p.**
Ex 4:21 the wonders that I have put in your **p;**
9:16 to show you my **p,** and to make my name resound
15: 6 Your right hand, O LORD, glorious in **p—**
32:11 of Egypt with great **p** and with a mighty hand? B
Lev 26:37 you shall have no **p** to stand against your enemies.
Nu 11:23 "Is the LORD's **p** limited?
14:17 let the **p** of the LORD be great in the way
22:38 but do I have **p** to say just anything?
Dt 4:34 and by terrifying displays of **p,**
4:37 of Egypt with his own presence, by his great **p,** B
8:17 not say to yourself, "My **p** and the might

Dt 8:18 for it is he who gives you **p** to get wealth,
9:29 by your great **p** and by your outstretched arm." B
26: 8 with a terrifying display of **p**,
32:36 when he sees that their **p** is gone,
34:12 the terrifying displays of **p** that Moses performed
Jos 8:20 They had no **p** to flee this way or that,
17:17 a numerous people, and have great **p**; B
Jdg 2:14 and he sold them into the **p** of their enemies all
2:16 of the **p** of those who plundered them.
1Sa 2:10 and exalt the **p** of his anointed."
4: 3 among us and save us from the **p** of our enemies."
4: 8 from the **p** of these mighty gods?
11: 6 upon Saul in **p** when he heard these words,
2Sa 18:19 that the LORD has delivered him from the **p**
18:31 delivering you from the **p** of all who rose up
1Ki 15:23 Now the rest of all the acts of Asa, all his **p**,
16: 5 rest of the acts of Baasha, what he did, and his **p**,
16:27 and the **p** that he showed,
22:45 and his **p** that he showed, and how he waged war,
2Ki 3:15 the **p** of the LORD came on him.
10:34 all that he did, and all his **p**,
14: 5 As soon as the royal **p** was firmly
15:19 he might help him confirm his hold on the royal **p**.
17:36 with great **p** and with an outstretched arm; B
18:20 Do you think that mere words are strategy and **p**
20:20 The rest of the deeds of Hezekiah, all his **p**,
1Ch 29:11 Yours, O LORD, are the greatness, the **p**,
29:12 In your hand are **p** and might;
2Ch 13:20 Jeroboam did not recover his **p** in the days
20: 6 In your hand are **p** and might,
25: 3 As soon as the royal **p** was firmly
25: 8 for God has **p** to help or to overthrow."
26:13 who could make war with mighty **p**,
Ezr 4:23 in Jerusalem and by force and **p** made them cease.
8:22 but his **p** and his wrath are
Ne 1:10 by your great **p** and your strong hand. B
9:37 they have **p** also over our bodies and
Est 9: 1 when the enemies of the Jews hoped to gain **p**
9: 1 a day when the Jews would gain **p** over their foes,
10: 2 All the acts of his **p** and might,
Job 1:12 "Very well, all that he has is in your **p**;
2: 6 LORD said to Satan, "Very well, he is in your **p**;
5:20 and in war from the **p** of the sword.
8: 4 he delivered them into the **p** of their transgression.
21: 7 reach old age, and grow mighty in **p**?
23: 6 with me in the greatness of his **p**?
24:22 Yet God prolongs the life of the mighty by his **p**;
26: 2 "How you have helped one who has no **p**!
26:12 By his **p** he stilled the Sea;
26:14 But the thunder of his **p** who can understand?"
27:22 they flee from its **p** in headlong flight.
36:22 See, God is exalted in his **p**;
37:23 he is great in **p** and justice,
40:16 and its **p** in the muscles of its belly.
Ps 21:13 We will sing and praise your **p**.
22:20 my life from the **p** of the dog!
37:33 The LORD will not abandon them to their **p**,
49:15 But God will ransom my soul from the **p** of Sheol,
59:11 make them totter by your **p**, and bring them down,
62:11 twice have I heard this: that **p** belongs to God,
63: 2 beholding your **p** and glory.
63:10 they shall be given over to the **p** of the sword,
66: 3 of your great **p**, your enemies cringe before you. B
67: 2 your saving **p** among all nations.
68:34 Ascribe **p** to God, whose majesty is over Israel;
68:34 and whose **p** is in the skies.
68:35 he gives **p** and strength to his people.
71:18 the generations to come. Your **p**
78:22 and did not trust his saving **p**.
78:26 and by his **p** he led out the south wind;
78:42 They did not keep in mind his **p**,
78:61 and delivered his **p** to captivity,
79:11 according to your great **p** preserve those B
89:48 Who can escape the **p** of Sheol?
90:11 Who considers the **p** of your anger?
90:16 and your glorious **p** to their children.
106: 8 so that he might make known his mighty **p**.
106:42 they were brought into subjection under their **p**.
111: 6 He has shown his people the **p** of his works,
130: 7 and with him is great **p** to redeem. B
145:11 of the glory of your kingdom, and tell of your **p**,
147: 5 Great is our Lord, and abundant in **p**;
Pr 3:27 when it is in your **p** to do it.
6: 3 for you have come into your neighbor's **p**:
18:21 Death and life are in the **p** of the tongue,
30:26 without **p**, yet they make their homes in the rocks;
Ecc 4: 1 On the side of their oppressors there was **p**—
8: 8 No one has **p** over the wind to restrain the wind,
8: 8 or **p** over the day of death;
Isa 10:33 will lop the boughs with terrifying **p**;
36: 5 Do you think that mere words are strategy and **p**
40:26 because he is great in strength, mighty in **p**,
40:29 He gives **p** to the faint,
47: 9 in spite of your many sorceries and the great **p** B
47:14 they cannot deliver themselves from the **p** of
50: 2 Or have I no **p** to deliver?
Jer 10:12 It is he who made the earth by his **p**,
16:21 this time I am going to teach them my **p**
18:21 hurl them out to the **p** of the sword,
27: 5 by my great **p** and my outstretched arm have B
32:17 by your great **p** and by your outstretched arm! B
47: 5 O remnant of their **p**! How long will you gash
51:15 It is he who made the earth by his **p**,
Eze 22: 6 everyone according to his **p**,
24:21 I will profane my sanctuary, the pride of your **p**,
35: 5 to the **p** of the sword at the time of their calamity,
Da 1: 2 Lord let King Jehoiakim of Judah fall into his **p**,

Da 2:20 for wisdom and **p** are his.
2:23 for you have given me wisdom and **p**,
2:37 the **p**, the might, and the glory,
3:27 that the fire had not had any **p** over the bodies
4:30 by my mighty **p** and for my glorious majesty?"
5:23 but the God in whose **p** is your very breath,
6:27 for he has saved Daniel from the **p** of the lions."
7:25 and they shall be given into his **p** for a time,
8: 4 and no one could rescue from its **p**;
8: 7 The ram did not have **p** to withstand it;
8: 7 no one who could rescue the ram from its **p**.
8: 8 but at the height of its **p**,
8:22 from his nation, but not with his **p**.
8:24 He shall grow strong in **p**,
11: 4 And while still rising in **p**,
11: 6 But she shall not retain her **p**,
11:16 and all of it shall be in his **p**.
11:25 He shall stir up his **p** and determination against
11:41 of the Ammonites shall escape from his **p**.
12: 7 the shattering of the **p** of the holy people comes to
Hos 10:13 in your **p** and in the multitude of your warriors,
13:14 Shall I ransom them from the **p** of Sheol?
Mic 2: 1 they perform it, because it is in their **p**.
3: 8 But as for me, I am filled with **p**,
Na 1: 3 The LORD is slow to anger but great in **p**,
Hab 3: 4 from his hand, where his **p** lay hidden.
Zec 4: 6 Not by might, nor by **p**, but by my spirit,
Mt 7:22 and do many deeds of **p** in your name?' C
11:20 in which most of his deeds of **p** had been done, C
11:21 deeds of **p** done in you had been done in Tyre C
11:23 deeds of **p** done in you had been done in Sodom, C
13:54 this man get this wisdom and these deeds of **p**? C
13:58 And he did not do many deeds of **p** there, C
22:29 know neither the scriptures nor the **p** of God. A
24:30 on the clouds of heaven' with **p** and great glory.
26:64 of Man seated at the right hand of **P** and coming
Mk 5:30 Immediately aware that **p** had gone forth
6: 2 What deeds of **p** are being done by his hands! C
6: 5 And he could do no deed of **p** there,
9: 1 that the kingdom of God has come with **p**."
9:39 for no one who does a deed of **p** in my name will
12:24 know neither the scriptures nor the **p** of God? A
13:26 Son of Man coming in clouds' with great **p** B
14:62 the Son of Man seated at the right hand of the **P**,'
Lk 1:17 the spirit and **p** of Elijah he will go before him,
1:35 and the **p** of the Most High will overshadow you;
4:14 Then Jesus, filled with the **p** of the Spirit,
4:36 and **p** he commands the unclean spirits,
5:17 and the **p** of the Lord was with him to heal.
6:19 for **p** came out from him and healed all of them.
8:46 for I noticed that **p** had gone out from me."
9: 1 the twelve together and gave them **p** and authority
10:13 deeds of **p** done in you had been done in Tyre C
10:19 and over all the **p** of the enemy;
19:12 to a distant country to get royal **p** for himself and
19:15 When he returned, having received royal **p**,
19:37 for all the deeds of **p** that they had seen, C
21:27 of Man coming in a cloud' with **p** and great glory.
22:53 But this is your hour, and the **p** of darkness!"
22:69 seated at the right hand of the **p** of God." A
24:49 in the city until you have been clothed with **p** from
Jn 1:12 he gave **p** to become children of God,
10:18 I have **p** to lay it down, and I have **p** to take it up
14:30 He has no **p** over me;
19:10 Do you not know that I have **p** to release you, and
p to crucify you?"
19:11 "You would have no **p** over me
Ac 1: 8 But you will receive **p** when
2:11 we hear them speaking about God's deeds of **p**." C
2:22 a man attested to you by God with deeds of **p**, C
2:24 it was impossible for him to be held in its **p**.
3:12 by our own **p** or piety we had made him walk?
4: 7 "By what **p** or by what name did you do this?"
4:33 With great **p** the apostles gave their testimony B
6: 8 Stephen, full of grace and **p**,
8:10 "This man is the **p** of God that is called Great." A
8:19 "Give me also this **p** so that anyone
10:38 of Nazareth with the Holy Spirit and with **p**;
26:18 from darkness to light and from the **p** of Satan
Ro 1: 4 of God with **p** according to the spirit of holiness
1:16 it is the **p** of God for salvation A
1:20 Ever since the creation of the world his eternal **p**
3: 9 both Jews and Greeks, are under the **p** of sin,
9:17 up for the very purpose of showing my **p** in you,
9:22 to show his wrath and to make known his **p**,
11:23 for God has the **p** to graft them in again.
15:13 so that you may abound in hope by the **p** of
15:19 by the **p** of signs and wonders,
15:19 by the **p** of the Spirit of God,
1Co 1:17 the cross of Christ might not be emptied of its **p**.
1:18 but to us who are being saved it is the **p** of God. A
1:24 Christ the **p** of God and the wisdom of God. A
2: 4 but with a demonstration of the Spirit and of **p**,
2: 5 not on human wisdom but on the **p** of God. A
4:19 not the talk of these arrogant people but their **p**.
4:20 the kingdom of God depends not on talk but on **p**.
5: 4 my spirit is present with the **p** of our Lord Jesus,
6:14 the Lord and will also raise us by his **p**.
12:28 then deeds of **p**, then gifts of healing, C
14:13 one who speaks in a tongue should pray for the **p**
15:24 and every authority and **p**.
15:43 It is sown in weakness, it is raised in **p**.
15:56 sting of death is sin, and the **p** of sin is the law.
2Co 4: 7 that this extraordinary **p** belongs to God and does
6: 7 truthful speech, and the **p** of God; A
10: 4 but they have divine **p** to destroy strongholds.
12: 9 for **p** is made perfect in weakness."

2Co 12: 9 so that the **p** of Christ may dwell in me.
13: 4 but lives by the **p** of God. A
13: 4 we will live with him by the **p** of God. A
Gal 3:22 the scripture has imprisoned all things under the **p**
Eph 1:19 and what is the immeasurable greatness of his **p**
1:19 according to the working of his great **p**. B
1:20 God put this **p** to work in Christ
1:21 above all rule and authority and **p** and dominion,
2: 2 following the ruler of the **p** of the air,
3: 7 that was given me by the working of his **p**.
3:16 in your inner being with **p** through his Spirit,
3:18 I pray that you may have the **p** to comprehend,
3:20 Now to him who by the **p** at work within us is able
6:10 be strong in the Lord and in the strength of his **p**.
Php 3:10 I want to know Christ and the **p** of his resurrection
3:21 by the **p** that also enables him
Col 1:11 the strength that comes from his glorious **p**,
1:13 from the **p** of darkness and transferred us into
2:12 raised with him through faith in the **p** of God, A
1Th 1: 5 but also in **p** and in the Holy Spirit and
2Th 1:11 by his **p** every good resolve and work of faith,
2: 9 who uses all **p**, signs, lying wonders,
2Ti 1: 7 a spirit of **p** and of love and of self-discipline.
1: 8 relying on the **p** of God, A
3: 5 to the outward form of godliness but denying its **p**.
Heb 2:14 the one who has the **p** of death,
7:16 but through the **p** of an indestructible life.
11:11 By faith he received **p** of procreation,
Jas 1:21 with meekness the implanted word that has the **p**
1Pe 1: 5 by the **p** of God through faith for a salvation A
4:11 To him belong the glory and the **p** forever
5:11 To him be the **p** forever and ever. Amen.
2Pe 1: 3 His divine **p** has given us everything needed
1:16 to you the **p** and coming of our Lord Jesus Christ,
2:11 though greater in might and **p**,
1Jn 5:19 the whole world lies under the **p** of the evil one.
Jude 1:25 be glory, majesty, **p**, and authority,
Rev 3: 8 I know that you have but little **p**,
4:11 to receive glory and honor and **p**,
5:12 to receive **p** and wealth and wisdom and might
7: 2 to the four angels who had been given **p**
7:12 and honor and **p** and might be to our God forever
9:10 and in their tails is their **p** to harm people
9:19 **p** of the horses is in their mouths and in their tails;
11:17 you have taken your great **p** and begun to reign. B
12:10 "Now have come the salvation and the **p** and
13: 2 And the dragon gave it his **p** and his throne
15: 8 with smoke from the glory of God and from his **p**,
17:13 These are united in yielding their **p** and authority
18: 3 of the earth have grown rich from the **p**
19: 1 Salvation and glory and **p** to our God,
20: 6 Over these the second death has no **p**,
Tob 13: 6 and show his **p** and majesty to a nation of sinners:
Jdt 2:12 For as I live, and by the **p** of my kingdom,
5: 3 and in what does their **p** and strength consist?
5:23 a people with no strength or **p** for making war.
8:15 he has **p** to protect us within any time he pleases,
9: 8 and bring down their **p** in your anger;
9:14 the God of all **p** and might,
11: 7 and by the **p** of him who has sent you
11: 7 the birds of the air will live, because of your **p**,
13:11 still showing his **p** in Israel and his strength
13:19 the hearts of those who remember the **p** of God. A
AdE 10: 2 And as for his **p** and bravery,
13: 9 in your **p** and there is no one who can oppose you
Wis 1: 3 and when his **p** is tested, it exposes the foolish;
7:25 For she is a breath of the **p** of God, A
11:20 by justice and scattered by the breath of your **p**.
11:21 For it is always in your **p** to show great strength,
12:15 to your **p** to condemn anyone who does
12:17 when people doubt the completeness of your **p**,
12:18 for you have **p** to act whenever you choose.
13: 4 if people were amazed at their **p** and working,
13: 9 the **p** to know so much that they could investigate
14:31 it is not the **p** of the things by which people swear,
15: 2 For even if we sin we are yours, knowing your **p**;
15: 3 and to know your **p** is the root of immortality.
16:13 For you have **p** over life and death;
16:23 be fed, even forgot its native **p**.
17: 2 that they held the holy nation in their **p**,
17: 5 And no **p** of fire was able to give light,
19:20 Fire even in water retained its normal **p**,
Sir 3:21 nor investigate what is beyond your **p**.
5: 3 Do not say, "Who can have **p** over me?"
9:13 Keep far from those who have **p** to kill,
15:14 and he left them in the **p** of their own free choice.
15:18 he is mighty in **p** and sees everything;
18: 4 To none has he given **p** to proclaim his works;
18: 5 Who can measure his majestic **p**?
28:22 It has no **p** over the godly;
28:23 Those who forsake the Lord will fall into its **p**;
31:10 the **p** to transgress and did not transgress,
33:20 to brother or friend, do not give **p** over yourself,
38: 5 with a tree in order that its **p** might be known?
39:18 and none can limit his saving **p**.
43:29 the Lord and very great, and marvelous is his **p**.
46: 5 with hailstones of mighty **p**.
47: 5 and to exalt the **p** of his people.
47: 7 he crushed their **p** to our own day.
47:11 Lord took away his sins, and exalted his **p** forever;
49: 5 They gave their **p** to others,
Bar 2:11 and with signs and wonders and with great **p** B
3: 5 but in this crisis remember your **p** and your name.
4:21 and he will deliver you from the **p** and hand of
LtJ 6:54 or deliver one who is wronged, for they have no **p**;
6:63 not to be compared with them in appearance or **p**.
Aza 1:21 let them be disgraced and deprived of all **p**,

Aza 1:66 and saved us from the **p** of death, and delivered us
1Mc 6:11 For I was kind and beloved in my **p.'**
10:71 for I have with me the **p** of the cities.
2Mc 3:24 were astounded by the **p** of God, A
3:28 They recognized clearly the sovereign **p** of God. A
3:34 report to all people the majestic **p** of God." A
3:38 there is certainly some **p** of God about the place. A
4:50 But Menelaus, because of the greed of those in **p,**
7:17 and see how his mighty **p** will torture you
9:8 making the **p** of God manifest to all. A
9:17 to proclaim the **p** of God. A
11:4 He took no account whatever of the **p** of God, A
12:28 upon the Sovereign who with **p** shatters the might
1Es 4:28 "Is not the king great in his **p?**
4:40 and the kingship and the **p** and the majesty of all
8:52 **p** of our Lord will be with those who seek him,
Man 1:4 and tremble before your **p,**
3Mc 1:27 to call upon him who has all **p** to defend them in
2:2 puffed up in his audacity and **p.**
2:6 You made known your mighty **p**
3:15 and Phoenicia by the **p** of the spear,
3:18 but they were spared the exercise of our **p** because
5:7 upon the Almighty Lord and Ruler of all **p,**
5:51 over every **p** to manifest himself and be merciful
6:2 "King of great **p,** Almighty God Most High, B
6:5 broke in pieces, showing your **p** to many nations.
6:12 you, O Eternal One, who have all might and all **p,**
6:13 who have **p** to save the nation of Jacob.
7:9 not a mortal but the Ruler over every **p,**
2Es 2:29 My **p** will protect you, so that your children may
4:22 why have I been endowed with the **p**
5:18 like a shepherd who leaves the flock in the **p**
11:19 they wielded **p** one after another and
11:32 it had greater **p** over the world than all the wings
12:18 it shall not fall then, but shall regain its former **p.**
15:30 with great **p** they shall come and engage them B
15:31 if they combine in great **p** and turn to pursue B
15:32 be disorganized and silenced by their **p,**
16:12 at the presence of the Lord and the glory of his **p.**
4Mc 1:30 over the emotions by virtue of the restraining **p**
2:15 lust for **p,** vainglory, boasting, arrogance,
5:13 if there is some **p** watching over this religion
6:33 we properly attribute to it the **p** to govern.
14:10 For the **p** of fire is intense and swift,

POWERFUL (37) [POWER]

Ge 26:16 you have become too **p** for us."
Ex 1:9 Israelite people are more numerous and more **p**
Est 9:4 For Mordecai was **p** in the king's house,
9:4 as the man Mordecai grew more and more **p.**
10:3 and he was **p** among the Jews and popular
Job 22:8 The **p** possess the land, and the favored live in it.
Ps 29:4 The voice of the LORD is **p;**
Pr 18:18 to disputes and decides between **p** contenders.
Ecc 8:4 For the word of the king is **p,**
Eze 26:7 chariots, cavalry, and a great and **p** army.
Da 2:10 In fact no king, however great and **p,**
8:24 shall destroy the **p** and the people of the holy ones.
Joel 1:6 a nation has invaded my land, **p** and innumerable;
2:2 upon the mountains a great and **p** army comes;
2:5 like a **p** army drawn up for battle.
Mic 7:3 and the **p** dictate what they desire;
Mt 3:11 but one who is more **p** than I is coming after me;
Mk 1:7 "The one who is more **p** than I is coming after me;
Lk 1:52 He has brought down the **p** from their thrones,
3:16 but one who is more **p** than I is coming;
Ac 7:22 the Egyptians and was **p** in his words and deeds.
9:22 Saul became increasingly more **p** and confounded
1Co 1:26 not many were **p,** not many were of noble birth.
2Co 13:3 not weak in dealing with you, but is **p** in you.
2Th 2:11 For this reason God sends them a **p** delusion,
Heb 1:3 and he sustains all things by his **p** word.
Jas 5:16 The prayer of the righteous is **p** and effective.
Rev 6:15 and the generals and the rich and the **p,**
Jdt 9:11 nor your might on the **p.**
Wis 10:12 that godliness is more **p** than anything else.
13:4 let them perceive from them how much more **p** is
Sir 7:6 you may be partial to the **p,**
8:1 Do not contend with the **p,**
4Mc 5:16 there is no compulsion more **p** than our obedience
7:10 O aged man, more **p** than tortures;
9:17 your wheel is not so **p** as to strangle my reason.
16:14 in word and deed you have proved more **p** than

POWERFULLY (2) [POWER]

Ac 18:28 for he **p** refuted the Jews in public,
Col 1:29 and struggle with all the energy that he **p** inspires

POWERLESS (13) [POWER]

Dt 28:32 for them all day but be **p** to do anything.
2Sa 3:39 Today I am **p,** even though anointed king;
2Ch 20:12 For we are **p** against this great multitude
Ne 5:5 we are **p,** and our fields and vineyards now belong
Isa 40:29 He gives power to the faint, and strengthens the **p.**
Jer 38:5 for the king is **p** against you."
Da 8:4 All beasts were **p** to withstand it,
Wis 17:14 which was really **p** and which came upon them
17:14 upon them from the recesses of **p** Hades,
2Es 10:22 and our strong men made **p.**
4Mc 2:1 for the enjoyment of beauty are rendered **p?**
2:18 to correct some, and to render others **p.**
11:26 and the catapults painless, and your violence **p.**

POWERS (16) [POWER]

Mt 14:2 and for this reason these **p** are at work in him."
24:29 and the **p** of heaven will be shaken.
Mk 6:14 and for this reason these **p** are at work in him."
13:25 and the **p** in the heavens will be shaken.
Lk 21:26 for the **p** of the heavens will be shaken.
Ro 8:38 nor things present, nor things to come, nor **p,**
1Co 13:2 And if I have prophetic **p,**
14:37 or to have spiritual **p,** must acknowledge
Eph 6:12 against the cosmic **p** of this present darkness,
Col 1:16 whether thrones or dominions or rulers or **p—**
Heb 6:5 of the word of God and the **p** of the age to come,
1Pe 3:22 authorities, and **p** made subject to him.
Wis 7:20 the **p** of spirits and the thoughts of human beings,
Aza 1:39 Bless the Lord, all you **p** of the Lord;
2Es 6:3 and before the **p** of movements were established,
16:18 beginning of wars, when the **p** shall be terrified;

PRACTICE (28) [PRACTICED, PRACTICES, PRACTICING]

Ge 44:15 not know that one such as I can **p** divination?"
Lev 19:26 You shall not **p** augury or witchcraft.
23:29 For anyone who does not **p** self-denial during
1Sa 27:11 Such was his **p** all the time he lived in the country
2Ki 17:34 to **p** their former customs.
17:40 but they continued to **p** their former custom.
Ezr 9:14 with the peoples who **p** these abominations?
Ps 111:10 all those who **p** it have a good understanding.
Ecc 8:8 nor does wickedness deliver those who **p** it.
Isa 32:6 **p** ungodliness, to utter error concerning the LORD,
Eze 13:23 shall no longer see false visions or **p** divination;
Am 8:5 and **p** deceit with false balances,
Zec 7:3 "Should I mourn and **p** abstinence in
Mt 23:3 for they do not **p** what they teach.
Ro 1:32 that those who **p** such things deserve to die—
1:32 but even applaud others who **p** them.
2Co 4:2 we refuse to **p** cunning or to falsify God's word;
Eph 4:19 greedy to **p** every kind of impurity.
1Ti 4:15 Put these things into **p,** devote yourself to them,
Heb 5:14 for those whose faculties have been trained by **p**
Rev 2:14 eat food sacrificed to idols and **p** fornication.
2:20 to **p** fornication and to eat food sacrificed to idols.
Tob 4:6 To all those who **p** righteousness
4:11 Indeed, almsgiving, for all who **p** it,
Sir 27:9 so honesty comes home to those who **p** it.
50:29 For if they put them into **p,**
4Mc 9:2 unless we should **p** ready obedience to the law and
12:11 and torture on the wheel those who **p** religion?

PRACTICED (18) [PRACTICE]

Jos 13:22 the sword Balaam son of Beor, who **p** divination.
2Ki 21:6 he **p** soothsaying and augury,
2Ch 33:6 **p** soothsaying and augury and sorcery,
Ecc 4:1 Again I saw all the oppressions that are **p** under
Isa 58:2 if they were a nation that **p** righteousness and did
Eze 18:18 As for his father, because he **p** extortion,
22:29 the land have **p** extortion and committed robbery;
23:8 She did not give up her whorings that she had **p**
39:26 and all the treachery they have **p** against me,
Mt 23:23 It is these you ought to have **p** without neglecting
Lk 11:42 it is these you ought to have **p,**
Ac 8:9 certain man named Simon had previously **p** magic
19:19 of those who **p** magic collected their books
2Co 12:21 and licentiousness that they have **p.**
Tob 14:10 and that much deceit is **p** within it,
Jdt 9:3 which was ashamed of the deceit they had **p,**
Wis 19:13 for they **p** a more bitter hatred of strangers.
2Es 7:*125* [55] of those who **p** self-control shall shine more

PRACTICES (20) [PRACTICE]

Ex 23:24 or worship them, or follow their **p,**
Lev 18:24 for by all these **p** the nations I am casting out
20:23 not follow the **p** of the nation that I am driving out
Dt 18:9 you must not learn to imitate the abhorrent **p**
18:10 or who **p** divination, or is a soothsayer,
18:12 it is because of such abhorrent **p** that
Jdg 2:19 not drop any of their **p** or their stubborn ways.
2Ki 16:3 to the abominable **p** of the nations whom
21:2 following the abominable **p** of the nations that
2Ch 27:2 But the people still followed corrupt **p.**
28:3 to the abominable **p** of the nations whom
33:2 to the abominable **p** of the nations whom
Est 9:32 command of Queen Esther fixed these **p** of Purim,
Ps 101:7 No one who **p** deceit shall remain in my house;
Ac 19:18 became believers confessed and disclosed their **p.**
Col 3:9 that you have stripped off the old self with its **p**
Rev 21:27 nor anyone who **p** abomination or falsehood,
22:15 and everyone who loves and **p** falsehood.
Wis 12:4 you hated for their detestable **p,**
2Es 15:8 neither will I tolerate their wicked **p.**

PRACTICING (3) [PRACTICE]

Jer 22:17 and for **p** oppression and violence.
Mt 6:1 "Beware of **p** your piety before others in order to
1Co 7:9 if they are not **p** self-control, they should marry.

PRAETORIUM See Index to Footnotes

PRAISE‡ (300) [PRAISED, PRAISES, PRAISEWORTHY, PRAISING]

A. PRAISE THE †LORD (42)
B. SING PRAISE (41)

Ge 29:35 and said, "This time I will **p** the LORD"; A
49:8 Judah, your brothers shall **p** you;
Ex 15:2 this is my God, and I will **p** him, my father's God,
Dt 10:21 He is your **p;** he is your God,
26:19 in **p** and in fame and in honor;
32:43 **P,** O heavens, his people, worship him,
1Ch 16:4 to thank, and to **p** the LORD, the God of Israel. A
16:35 to your holy name, and glory in your **p.**
23:5 with the instruments that I have made for **p."**
25:3 with the lyre in thanksgiving and **p** to the LORD.
29:13 we give thanks to you and **p** your glorious name.
2Ch 5:13 in unison in **p** and thanksgiving to the LORD,
5:13 in **p** to the LORD, "For he is good,
8:14 of **p** and ministry alongside the priests as the duty
20:19 stood up to **p** the LORD, the God of Israel, A
20:21 to sing to the LORD and **p** him in holy splendor,
20:22 As they began to sing and **p,**
31:2 the camp of the LORD and to give thanks and **p.**
Ezr 3:10 in their vestments were stationed to **p** the LORD A
Ne 9:5 which is exalted above all blessing and **p."**
12:24 with their associates over against them, to **p** and
12:46 there were songs of **p** and thanksgiving to God.
Ps 6:5 in Sheol who can give you **p?**
7:17 and sing **p** to the name of the LORD, B
9:2 I will sing **p** to your name, O Most High. B
21:13 We will sing and **p** your power.
22:22 in the midst of the congregation I will **p** you:
22:23 You who fear the LORD, **p** him!
22:25 From you comes my **p** in the great congregation;
22:26 those who seek him shall **p** the LORD. A
30:9 the dust **p** you? Will it tell of your faithfulness?
30:12 so that my soul may **p** you and not be silent.
33:1 O you righteous. **P** befits the upright.
33:2 **P** the LORD with the lyre; A
34:1 his **p** shall continually be in my mouth.
35:18 in the mighty throng I will **p** you.
35:28 of your righteousness and of your **p** all day long.
40:3 a song of **p** to our God.
42:5 Hope in God; for I shall again **p** him,
42:11 for I shall again **p** him, my help and my God.
43:4 and I will **p** you with the harp, O God, my God.
43:5 for I shall again **p** him, my help and my God.
45:17 therefore the peoples will **p** you forever and ever.
48:10 Your name, O God, like your **p,**
51:15 open my lips, and my mouth will declare your **p.**
56:4 In God, whose word I **p,** in God I trust;
56:10 In God, whose word I **p,** in the LORD,
56:10 in the LORD, whose word I **p,**
63:3 steadfast love is better than life, my lips will **p** you.
65:1 **P** is due to you, O God, in Zion;
66:2 sing the glory of his name; give to him glorious **p.**
66:8 O peoples, let the sound of his **p** be heard,
67:3 the peoples **p** you, O God; let all the peoples **p** you.
67:5 the peoples **p** you, O God; let all the peoples **p** you.
69:30 I will **p** the name of God with a song;
69:34 Let heaven and earth **p** him,
71:6 My **p** is continually of you.
71:8 My mouth is filled with your **p,**
71:14 and will **p** you yet more and more.
71:16 I will **p** your righteousness, yours alone.
71:22 also **p** you with the harp for your faithfulness,
73:10 people turn and **p** them, and find no fault in them.
74:21 let the poor and needy **p** your name.
76:10 Human wrath serves only to **p** you,
79:13 to generation we will recount your **p.**
84:4 in your house, ever singing your **p.**
88:10 Do the shades rise up to **p** you?
89:5 Let the heavens **p** your wonders,
89:12 Tabor and Hermon joyously **p** your name.
95:2 let us make a joyful noise to him with songs of **p!**
99:3 Let them **p** your great and awesome name.
100:4 with thanksgiving, and his courts with **p.**
102:18 so that a people yet unborn may **p** the LORD: A
102:21 may be declared in Zion, and his **p** in Jerusalem,
104:33 I will sing **p** to my God while I have being. B
104:35 Bless the LORD, O my soul. **P** the LORD! A
105:45 and observe his laws. **P** the LORD! A
106:1 **P** the LORD! O give thanks to the LORD, A
106:2 mighty doings of the LORD, or declare all his **p?**
106:12 Then they believed his words; they sang his **p.**
106:47 to your holy name and glory in your **p.**
106:48 And let all the people say, "Amen." **P** the LORD! A
107:32 and **p** him in the assembly of the elders.
109:1 Do not be silent, O God of my **p.**
109:30 I will **p** him in the midst of the throng.
111:1 **P** the LORD! I will give thanks to the LORD A
111:10 His **p** endures forever.
112:1 **P** the LORD! Happy are those who fear the LORD, A
113:1 **P** the LORD! Praise, O servants of the LORD; A
113:1 **P,** O servants of the LORD;
113:1 **p** the name of the LORD.
113:9 joyous mother of children. **P** the LORD! A
115:17 The dead do not **p** the LORD, A
115:18 from this time on and forevermore. **P** the LORD! A
116:19 O Jerusalem. **P** the LORD! A
117:1 **P** the LORD, all you nations! A
117:2 of the LORD endures forever. **P** the LORD! A
119:7 I will **p** you with an upright heart,
119:62 At midnight I rise to **p** you,
119:108 Accept my offerings of **p,** O LORD,
119:164 a day I **p** you for your righteous ordinances.
119:171 My lips will pour forth **p,**
119:175 Let me live that I may **p** you,
135:1 **P** the LORD! Praise the name of the LORD; A
135:1 **P** the name of the LORD; give **p,**
135:3 **P** the LORD, for the LORD is good; A
135:21 who resides in Jerusalem. **P** the LORD! A
138:1 before the gods I sing your **p;**
138:4 All the kings of the earth shall **p** you, O LORD,

Ps 139:14 I **p** you, for I am fearfully and wonderfully made.
145: T ***P.*** *Of David.*
145: 2 and **p** your name forever and ever.
145:21 My mouth will speak the **p** of the LORD,
146: 1 **P** the LORD! Praise the LORD, O my soul! A
146: 1 Praise the LORD! **P** the LORD, O my soul! A
146: 2 I will **p** the LORD as long as I live; A
146:10 for all generations. **P** the LORD! A
147: 1 **P** the LORD! How good it is to sing A
147: 1 for he is gracious, and a song of **p** is fitting.
147:12 **P** the LORD, O Jerusalem! A
147:12 **P** your God, O Zion!
147:20 not know his ordinances. **P** the LORD! A
148: 1 **P** the LORD! Praise the LORD from the heavens; A
148: 1 **P** the LORD from the heavens; A
148: 1 from the heavens; **p** him in the heights!
148: 2 **P** him, all his angels; **p** him, all his host!
148: 3 **P** him, sun and moon; **p** him, all you shining stars!
148: 4 **P** him, you highest heavens,
148: 5 Let them **p** the name of the LORD,
148: 7 **P** the LORD from the earth, A
148:13 Let them **p** the name of the LORD,
148:14 **p** for all his faithful, for the people of Israel
148:14 of Israel who are close to him. **P** the LORD! A
149: 1 **P** the LORD! Sing to the LORD a new song, A
149: 1 his **p** in the assembly of the faithful.
149: 3 Let them **p** his name with dancing,
149: 9 for all his faithful ones. **P** the LORD! A
150: 1 **P** the LORD! Praise God in his sanctuary; A
150: 1 **P** God in his sanctuary;
150: 1 **p** him in his mighty firmament!
150: 2 **P** him for his mighty deeds;
150: 2 **p** him according to his surpassing greatness!
150: 3 **P** him with trumpet sound;
150: 3 **p** him with lute and harp!
150: 4 **P** him with tambourine and dance;
150: 4 **p** him with strings and pipe!
150: 5 **P** him with clanging cymbals;
150: 5 **p** him with loud clashing cymbals!
150: 6 Let everything that breathes **p** the LORD! A
150: 6 that breathes praise the LORD! **P** the LORD! A
Pr 27: 2 Let another **p** you, and not your own mouth—
28: 4 Those who forsake the law **p** the wicked,
31:31 and let her works **p** her in the city gates.
Isa 24:16 From the ends of the earth we hear songs of **p**,
25: 1 I will exalt you, I will **p** your name;
38:18 For Sheol cannot thank you, death cannot **p** you;
42: 8 my glory I give to no other, nor my **p** to idols.
42:10 his **p** from the end of the earth!
42:12 and declare his **p** in the coastlands.
43:21 for myself so that they might declare my **p**.
48: 9 for the sake of my **p** I restrain it for you,
60: 6 and shall proclaim the **p** of the LORD.
60:18 shall call your walls Salvation, and your gates **P**.
61: 3 the mantle of **p** instead of a faint spirit.
61:11 so the Lord GOD will cause righteousness and **p**
62: 9 those who garner it shall eat it and **p** the LORD, A
Jer 13:11 a name, a **p**, and a glory.
17:14 and I shall be saved; for you are my **p**.
20:13 Sing to the LORD; **p** the LORD! A
31: 7 proclaim, give **p**, and say, "Save, O LORD,
33: 9 a **p** and a glory before all the nations of
Da 2:23 O God of my ancestors, I give thanks and **p**,
4:37 **p** and extol and honor the King of heaven,
6:10 a day to pray to his God and **p** him,
Joel 2:26 and **p** the name of the LORD your God,
Hab 3: 3 and the earth was full of his **p**.
Zep 3:19 and I will change their shame into **p** and renown
Mt 21:16 of infants and nursing babies you have prepared **p**
Lk 2:38 and began to **p** God and to speak about the child
17:18 to return and give **p** to God except this foreigner?"
19:37 of the disciples began to **p** God joyfully with
Ro 2:29 a person receives **p** not from others but from God.
14:11 and every tongue shall give **p** to God."
15:11 "**P** the Lord, all you Gentiles, and let all the peoples **p** him";
1Co 14:15 I will sing **p** with the spirit, B
14:15 but I will sing **p** with the mind also. B
Eph 1: 6 the **p** of his glorious grace that he freely bestowed
1:12 might live for the **p** of his glory.
1:14 to the **p** of his glory.
Php 1:11 through Jesus Christ for the glory and **p** of God.
4: 8 and if there is anything worthy of **p**,
1Th 2: 6 nor did we seek **p** from mortals,
Heb 2:12 in the midst of the congregation I will **p** you."
13:15 let us continually offer a sacrifice of **p** to God,
Jas 5:13 They should sing songs of **p**.
1Pe 1: 7 may be found to result in **p** and glory and honor
2:14 and to **p** those who do right.
Rev 19: 5 "**P** our God, all you his servants,
Tob 3:11 let all your works **p** you forever.
12: 6 Bless and sing **p** to his name. B
13:11 Generation after generation will give joyful **p**
13:13 for they will be gathered together and will **p**
14: 1 So ended Tobit's words of **p**.
14: 7 and in righteousness they will **p** the eternal God.
Jdt 13:14 with a loud voice, "**P** God, O **p** him! **P** God,
13:19 Your **p** will never depart from the hearts
15:14 and all the people loudly sang this song of **p**.
AdE 2:23 in the royal library in **p** of the goodwill shown
13:17 we may live and sing **p** to your name, O Lord; B
13:17 do not destroy the lips of those who **p** you."
14: 9 of those who **p** you and to quench your altar and
14:10 the mouths of the nations for the **p** of vain idols,
Wis 15:19 but they have escaped both the **p** of God
Sir Pr: 1 and for these we should **p** Israel for instruction
11: 2 Do not **p** individuals for their good looks,
Sir 15: 9 **P** is unseemly on the lips of a sinner,
15:10 For in wisdom must **p** be uttered,
17:10 And they will **p** his holy name,
24: 1 THE **P** OF WISDOM Wisdom praises herself,
27: 7 Do not **p** anyone before he speaks,
31: 9 Who is he, that we may **p** him?
37: 7 All counselors **p** the counsel they give,
37:24 A wise person will have **p** heaped upon him,
39: 9 Many will **p** his understanding;
39:10 and the congregation will proclaim his **p**.
39:14 Scatter the fragrance, and sing a hymn of **p**;
39:15 with **p**, with songs on your lips, and with harps;
39:35 So now sing **p** with all your heart and voice, B
43:11 Look at the rainbow, and **p** him who made it;
43:28 Where can we find the strength to **p** him?
43:30 for you cannot **p** him enough.
44: 8 so that others declare their **p**.
44:15 and the congregation proclaims their **p**.
47: 8 he sang **p** with all his heart,
51: 1 O Lord and King, and **p** you, O God my Savior.
51:11 I will **p** your name continually,
51:12 For this reason I thank you and **p** you,
51:12 *a horn for his people, **p** for all his loyal ones.*
51:12 *Israel, the people close to him. **P** the LORD!* A
51:22 and I will **p** him with it.
51:29 and may you never be ashamed to **p** him.
Bar 2:32 they will **p** me in the land of their exile,
3: 6 and it is you, O Lord, whom we will **p**.
3: 7 and we will **p** you in our exile,
Aza 1: 3 O Lord, God of our ancestors, and worthy of **p**;
1:35 sing **p** to him and highly exalt him forever. B
1:36 sing **p** to him and highly exalt him forever. B
1:37 sing **p** to him and highly exalt him forever. B
1:38 sing **p** to him and highly exalt him forever. B
1:39 sing **p** to him and highly exalt him forever. B
1:40 sing **p** to him and highly exalt him forever. B
1:41 sing **p** to him and highly exalt him forever. B
1:42 sing **p** to him and highly exalt him forever. B
1:43 sing **p** to him and highly exalt him forever. B
1:44 sing **p** to him and highly exalt him forever. B
1:45 sing **p** to him and highly exalt him forever. B
1:46 sing **p** to him and highly exalt him forever. B
1:47 sing **p** to him and highly exalt him forever. B
1:48 sing **p** to him and highly exalt him forever. B
1:49 sing **p** to him and highly exalt him forever. B
1:50 sing **p** to him and highly exalt him forever. B
1:51 sing **p** to him and highly exalt him forever. B
1:52 sing **p** to him and highly exalt him forever. B
1:53 sing **p** to him and highly exalt him forever. B
1:54 sing **p** to him and highly exalt him forever. B
1:55 sing **p** to him and highly exalt him forever. B
1:56 sing **p** to him and highly exalt him forever. B
1:57 sing **p** to him and highly exalt him forever. B
1:58 sing **p** to him and highly exalt him forever. B
1:59 sing **p** to him and highly exalt him forever. B
1:60 sing **p** to him and highly exalt him forever. B
1:61 sing **p** to him and highly exalt him forever. B
1:62 sing **p** to him and highly exalt him forever. B
1:63 sing **p** to him and highly exalt him forever. B
1:64 sing **p** to him and highly exalt him forever. B
1:65 sing **p** to him and highly exalt him forever. B
1:66 sing **p** to him and highly exalt him forever. B
1:68 sing **p** to him and give thanks to him, B
1Mc 4:33 let all who know your name **p** you with hymns."
13:47 and then entered it with hymns and **p**.
13:51 the Jews entered it with **p** and palm branches,
2Mc 8:27 giving great **p** and thanks to the Lord,
Man 1:15 I will **p** you continually all the days of my life.
1:15 For all the host of heaven sings your **p**,
3Mc 6:11 the vain-minded **p** their vanities at the destruction
7:16 in words of **p** and all kinds of melodious songs.
2Es 2:47 to **p** those who had stood valiantly for the name of
13:57 giving great glory and **p** to the Most High for
4Mc 1: 2 in addition it includes the **p** of the highest virtue—
1:10 On this anniversary it is fitting for me to **p**
4:12 that if he were spared he would **p** the blessedness
13:17 and all the fathers will **p** us."

PRAISED‡ (62) [PRAISE]

Ge 12:15 When the officials of Pharaoh saw her, they **p** her
Jdg 16:24 When the people saw him, they **p** their god;
2Sa 14:25 Now in all Israel there was no one to be **p** so much
22: 4 I call upon the LORD, who is worthy to be **p**,
1Ch 16:25 For great is the LORD, and greatly to be **p**;
16:36 Then all the people said "Amen!" and **p** the LORD.
2Ch 30:21 Levites and the priests **p** the LORD day by day,
Ezr 3:11 with a great shout when they **p** the LORD,
Ne 5:13 all the assembly said, "Amen," and **p** the LORD.
Ps 18: 3 I call upon the LORD, who is worthy to be **p**,
48: 1 Great is the LORD and greatly to be **p** in the city
49:18 —for you are **p** when you do well for yourself—
96: 4 For great is the LORD, and greatly to be **p**;
113: 3 to its setting the name of the LORD is to be **p**.
145: 3 Great is the LORD, and greatly to be **p**;
Pr 27:21 so a person is tested by being **p**.
31:30 but a woman who fears the LORD is to be **p**.
Ecc 8:10 in and out of the holy place, and were **p** in the city
SS 6: 9 the queens and concubines also, and they **p** her.
Isa 64:11 where our ancestors **p** you,
Da 4:34 and **p** and honored the one who lives forever.
5: 4 They drank the wine and **p** the gods of gold
5:23 You have **p** the gods of silver and gold, of bronze,
Zep 3:20 for I will make you renowned and **p** among all
Mt 6: 2 so that they may be **p** by others.
15:31 And they **p** the God of Israel.
Lk 2:28 Simeon took him in his arms and **p** God, saying,
Lk 4:15 He began to teach in their synagogues and was **p**
18:43 and all the people, when they saw it, **p** God.
23:47 the centurion saw what had taken place, he **p** God
Ac 4:21 for all of them **p** God for what had happened.
11:18 And they **p** God, saying, "Then God has given
13:48 they were glad and **p** the word of the Lord;
19:17 and the name of the Lord Jesus was **p**.
21:20 When they heard it, they **p** God.
Tob 14:15 Tobias **p** God for all he had done to the people
Jdt 6:20 Then they reassured Achior, and **p** him highly.
Wis 10:20 and **p** with one accord your defending hand;
Sir 9:17 A work is **p** for the skill of the artisan;
47: 6 and **p** him for the blessings bestowed by the Lord,
47:10 while they **p** God's holy name,
50:18 Then the singers **p** him with their voices in sweet
Aza 1:28 with one voice **p** and glorified and blessed God in
1:29 and to be **p** and highly exalted forever;
1:30 and to be highly **p** and highly exalted forever.
1:32 and to be **p** and highly exalted forever.
Sus 1:63 and his wife **p** God for their daughter Susanna,
1Mc 5:64 People gathered to them and **p** them.
2Mc 3:30 they **p** the Lord who had acted marvelously
11: 9 And together they all **p** the merciful God,
1Es 4:58 and **p** the King of heaven, saying,
4:62 And they **p** the God of their ancestors,
3Mc 2: 8 they had seen works of your hands, they **p** you,
5:13 the appointed hour, **p** their holy God
5:35 **p** the manifest Lord God, King of kings,
6:29 **p** their holy God and Savior,
2Es 10:16 and will be **p** among women.
4Mc 2: 2 certainly, that the temperate Joseph is **p**,
4: 4 he **p** Simon for his service to the king and went up
7: 9 and you did not abandon the holiness that you **p**,
13: 3 Instead, by reason, which is **p** before God,
18:13 He **p** Daniel in the den of the lions

PRAISES‡ (51) [PRAISE]

2Sa 22:50 among the nations, and sing **p** to your name.
1Ch 16: 7 on that day David first appointed the singing of **p**
16: 9 Sing to him, sing **p** to him,
23: 5 and four thousand shall offer **p** to the LORD with
2Ch 7: 6 whenever David offered **p** by their ministry.
29:30 the Levites to sing **p** to the LORD with the words
29:30 They sang **p** with gladness,
Ps 9:11 Sing **p** to the LORD, who dwells in Zion.
9:14 so that I may recount all your **p**,
18:49 among the nations, and sing **p** to your name.
22: 3 Yet you are holy, enthroned on the **p** of Israel.
30: 4 Sing **p** to the LORD, O you his faithful ones,
47: 6 Sing **p** to God, sing **p**;
47: 6 sing **p** to our King, sing **p**.
47: 7 of all the earth; sing **p** with a psalm.
57: 9 I will sing **p** to you among the nations.
59:17 O my strength, I will sing **p** to you, for you,
61: 8 So I will always sing **p** to your name,
63: 5 and my mouth **p** you with joyful lips
66: 4 they sing **p** to you, sing **p** to your name."
68: 4 Sing to God, sing **p** to his name;
68:32 of the earth; sing **p** to the Lord,
71:22 I will sing **p** to you with the lyre,
71:23 My lips will shout for joy when I sing **p** to you;
75: 9 I will sing **p** to the God of Jacob.
92: 1 to sing **p** to your name, O Most High;
98: 4 break forth into joyous song and sing **p**.
98: 5 Sing **p** to the LORD with the lyre,
105: 2 Sing to him, sing **p** to him;
108: 3 and I will sing **p** to you among the nations.
146: 2 I will sing **p** to my God all my life long.
147: 1 How good it is to sing **p** to our God;
149: 6 Let the high **p** of God be in their throats
Pr 31:28 her husband too, and he **p** her:
Isa 12: 5 Sing **p** to the LORD, for he has done gloriously;
Ro 15: 9 and sing **p** to your name";
Tob 12:18 Bless him each and every day; sing his **p**.
12:22 They kept blessing God and singing his **p**,
Wis 18: 9 already they were singing the **p** of the ancestors.
Sir 17:27 Who will sing **p** to the Most High in Hades
17:28 those who are alive and well sing the Lord's **p**.
18:28 and **p** the one who finds her.
21:15 he **p** it and adds to it;
24: 1 Wisdom **p** herself, and tells of her glory
44: 1 Let us now sing the **p** of famous men,
51:12 *Give thanks to the God of **p**,*
1Mc 4:24 On their return they sang hymns and **p**
3Mc 2:20 and put **p** in the mouth of those who are downcast

PRAISEWORTHY (3) [PRAISE]

Isa 63: 7 the **p** acts of the LORD,
Sir 37:22 the fruits of his good sense will be **p**.
2Es 8:48 in this respect you will be **p** before the Most High,

PRAISING (21) [PRAISE]

1Ch 23:30 every morning, thanking and **p** the LORD,
2Ch 23:12 the people running and **p** the king, she went into
Ezr 3:11 **p** and giving thanks to the LORD,
Ps 71:16 I will come **p** the mighty deeds of the Lord GOD,
Lk 1:64 and he began to speak, **p** God.
2:13 the angel a multitude of the heavenly host, **p** God
2:20 glorifying and **p** God for all they had heard
13:13 she stood up straight and began **p** God.
17:15 turned back, **p** God with a loud voice.
Ac 2:47 **p** God and having the goodwill of all the people.
3: 8 walking and leaping and **p** God.
3: 9 All the people saw him walking and **p** God,
Tob 10:13 **p** the Lord of heaven and earth, King over all,

Tob 11:15 So Tobit went in rejoicing and **p** God at the top
11:16 Then Tobit, rejoicing and **p** God,
Wis 19: 9 and leaped like lambs, **p** you, O Lord,
1Es 5:60 **p** the Lord and blessing him,
5:62 **p** the Lord for the erection of the house of the Lord
3Mc 4:16 **p** speechless things that are not able even
6:32 **p** God, their Savior and worker of wonders.
2Es 2:42 and they all were **p** the Lord with songs.

PRANCE (1)

Na 2: 3 when he musters them; the chargers **p.**

PRAY‡ (155) [PRAYED, PRAYER, PRAYERS, PRAYING, PRAYS]

Ge 20: 7 and he will **p** for you and you shall live.
Ex 8: 8 "**P** to the LORD to take away the frogs from me
8: 9 when I am to **p** for you and for your officials and
8:28 do not go very far away. **P** for me."
8:29 I will **p** to the LORD that the swarms
9:28 **P** to the LORD! Enough of God's thunder and hail!
10:17 and **p** to the LORD your God that at the least
33:18 Moses said, "Show me your glory, I **p.**"
34: 9 O Lord, I **p,** let the Lord go with us.
Nu 21: 7 **p** to the LORD to take away the serpents
Jdg 13: 8 and said, "O, LORD, I **p,**
1Sa 7: 5 and I will **p** to the LORD for you."
7: 8 and **p** that he may save us from the hand of
12:19 "**P** to the LORD your God for your servants,
12:23 against the LORD by ceasing to **p** for you;
15:25 Now therefore, I **p,** pardon my sin,
2Sa 7:27 to **p** this prayer to you.
15:31 And David said, "O LORD, I **p** you,
24:10 But now, O LORD, I **p** you,
24:17 I **p,** be against me and against my father's house."
1Ki 1:48 and went on to **p** thus,
8:30 and of your people Israel when they **p**
8:33 **p** and plead with you in this house,
8:35 and then they **p** toward this place,
8:44 and they **p** to the LORD toward the city
8:48 and **p** to you toward their land,
13: 6 the favor of the LORD your God, and **p** for me,
2Ki 19:19 So now, O LORD our God, save us, I **p** you,
1Ch 17:25 your servant has found it possible to **p** before you.
21: 8 now, I **p** you, take away the guilt of your servant;
21:17 Let your hand, I **p,** O LORD my God,
2Ch 6:21 when they **p** toward this place;
6:24 **p** and plead with you in this house,
6:26 and then they **p** toward this place,
6:32 when they come and **p** toward this house,
6:34 and they **p** to you toward this city
6:38 and **p** toward their land, which you gave
7:14 **p,** seek my face, and turn from their wicked ways,
Ezr 6:10 and **p** for the life of the king and his children.
Ne 1: 6 now **p** before you day and night for your servants,
Job 6:29 Turn, I **p,** let no wrong be done.
21:15 And what profit do we get if we **p** to him?'
22:27 You will **p** to him, and he will hear you,
42: 8 and my servant Job shall **p** for you,
Ps 5: 2 my King and my God, for to you I **p.**
38:16 For I **p,** "Only do not let them rejoice over me,
116: 4 "O LORD, I **p,** save my life!"
122: 6 **P** for the peace of Jerusalem:
Isa 16:12 when he comes to his sanctuary to **p,**
Jer 7:16 As for you, do not **p** for this people,
11:14 As for you, do not **p** for this people,
14:11 Do not **p** for the welfare of this people.
29: 7 and **p** to the LORD on its behalf,
29:12 when you call upon me and come and **p** to me,
37: 3 "Please **p** for us to the LORD our God."
42: 2 and **p** to the LORD your God for us—
42: 4 to **p** to the LORD your God as you request,
42:20 saying, '**P** for us to the LORD our God,
Da 6:10 to get down on his knees three times a day to **p**
9:16 we **p,** turn away from your city Jerusalem,
Jnh 1:14 "Please, O LORD, we **p,**
Mt 5:44 and **p** for those who persecute you,
6: 5 whenever you **p,** do not be like the hypocrites;
6: 5 for they love to stand and **p** in the synagogues and
6: 6 But whenever you **p,** go into your room and shut the door and **p** to your Father who is in secret;
6: 9 "**P** then in this way: Our Father in heaven,
14:23 he went up the mountain by himself to **p.**
19:13 that he might lay his hands on them and **p.**
24:20 **P** that your flight may not be in winter or on
26:36 "Sit here while I go over there and **p.**"
26:41 and **p** that you may not come into the time of trial;
Mk 6:46 he went up on the mountain to **p.**
13:18 **P** that it may not be in winter.
14:32 and he said to his disciples, "Sit here while I **p.**"
14:38 and **p** that you may not come into the time of trial;
Lk 5:16 But he would withdraw to deserted places and **p.**
5:33 frequently fast and **p,** but your disciples eat
6:12 those days he went out to the mountain to **p;**
6:28 **p** for those who abuse you.
9:28 and went up on the mountain to **p.**
11: 1 "Lord, teach us to **p,** as John taught his disciples."
11: 2 He said to them, "When you **p,** say:
18: 1 about their need to **p** always and not to lose heart.
18:10 "Two men went up to the temple to **p,**
22:40 "**P** that you may not come into the time of trial."
22:46 Get up and **p** that you may not come into the time
Ac 8:22 and **p** to the Lord that, if possible,
8:24 Simon answered, "**P** for me to the Lord,
10: 9 Peter went up on the roof to **p.**
26:29 I **p** to God that not only you but
Ro 8:26 for we do not know how to **p** as we ought,
1Co 11:13 for a woman to **p** to God with her head unveiled?
14:13 in a tongue should **p** for the power to interpret.
14:14 For if I **p** in a tongue, my spirit prays but my mind
14:15 I will **p** with the spirit, but I will **p** with the mind
2Co 9:14 while they long for you and **p** for you because of
13: 7 But we **p** to God that you may
13: 9 This is what we **p** for,
Eph 1:17 I **p** that the God of our Lord Jesus Christ,
3:13 I **p** therefore that you may not lose heart
3:16 I **p** that, according to the riches of his glory,
3:18 I **p** that you may have the power to comprehend,
6:18 **P** in the Spirit at all times in every prayer
6:19 **P** also for me, so that when I speak,
6:20 **P** that I may declare it boldly, as I must speak.
Col 4: 3 the same time **p** for us as well that God will open
1Th 3:10 Night and day we **p** most earnestly
5:17 **p** without ceasing,
5:25 Beloved, **p** for us.
2Th 1:11 To this end we always **p** for you,
3: 1 Finally, brothers and sisters, **p** for us,
1Ti 2: 8 then, that in every place the men should **p,**
Phm 1: 6 I **p** that the sharing of your faith may become
Heb 13:18 **P** for us; we are sure that we have a clear
Jas 5:13 Are any among you suffering? They should **p.**
5:14 for the elders of the church and have them **p**
5:16 and **p** for one another, so that you may be healed.
1Jn 5:16 I do not say that you should **p** about that.
3Jn 1: 2 I **p** that all may go well with you and that you may
Jude 1:20 on your most holy faith; **p** in the Holy Spirit;
Tob 3: 1 and with groaning began to **p:**
3:10 but to **p** the Lord that I may die and not listen
6:18 both of you must first stand up and **p,**
8: 4 and let us **p** and implore our Lord
8: 5 and they began to **p** and implore that they might
Jdt 8:31 Now since you are a God-fearing woman, **p** for us,
11:17 into the valley and **p** to God.
12: 6 to allow your servant to go out and **p.**"
Wis 16:28 and must **p** to you at the dawning of the light;
Sir 3: 5 and when they **p** they will be heard.
7:10 Do not grow weary when you **p;**
7:14 and do not repeat yourself when you **p.**
17:25 **p** in his presence and lessen your offense.
28: 2 and then your sins will be pardoned when you **p.**
37:15 But above all **p** to the Most High
38: 9 when you are ill, do not delay, but **p** to the Lord,
38:14 for they too **p** to the Lord
Bar 1:11 **p** for the life of King Nebuchadnezzar of Babylon,
1:13 **P** also for us to the Lord our God,
LtJ 6:40 they bring Bel and **p** that the mute may speak,
1Mc 3:44 and to **p** and ask for mercy and compassion.
2Mc 12:44 it would have been superfluous and foolish to **p**
1Es 4:46 I **p** therefore that you fulfill
3Mc 2:10 to our petition when we come to this place and **p.**
2Es 2:13 **p** that your days may be few,
5:13 and if you **p** again, and weep as you do now,
6:31 you will **p** again and fast again for seven days,
7:*105* so no one shall ever **p** for another on that day,
8: 6 grant to your servant that we may **p** before you,
8:17 I will **p** before you for myself and for them,
9:25 and **p** to the Most High continually.
12:48 but I have come to this place to **p** on account of
4Mc 4:11 the Hebrews to **p** for him and propitiate the wrath

PRAYED (83) [PRAY]

Ge 20:17 Then Abraham **p** to God;
25:21 Isaac **p** to the LORD for his wife,
Ex 8:30 So Moses went out from Pharaoh and **p** to
10:18 So he went out from Pharaoh and **p** to the LORD.
Nu 11: 2 and Moses **p** to the LORD, and the fire abated.
21: 7 So Moses **p** for the people.
Dt 9:26 I **p** to the LORD and said,
1Sa 1:10 She was deeply distressed and **p** to the LORD,
1:27 For this child I **p;** and the LORD has granted me
2: 1 Hannah **p** and said, "My heart exults in
8: 6 Samuel **p** to the LORD,
2Ki 4:33 the door on the two of them, and **p** to the LORD.
6:17 Then Elisha **p:** "O LORD,
6:18 Elisha **p** to the LORD, and said,
19:15 And Hezekiah **p** before the LORD, and said:
20: 2 Then Hezekiah turned his face to the wall and **p** to
2Ch 30:18 But Hezekiah **p** for them, saying,
32:20 the prophet Isaiah son of Amoz **p** because of this
32:24 He **p** to the LORD, and he answered him
33:13 He **p** to him, and God received his entreaty,
Ezr 10: 1 While Ezra **p** and made confession,
Ne 2: 4 So I **p** to the God of heaven.
4: 9 So we **p** to our God,
Job 42:10 the fortunes of Job when he had **p** for his friends;
Ps 35:13 I **p** with head bowed on my bosom,
Isa 37:15 And Hezekiah **p** to the LORD, saying:
37:21 Because you have **p** to me
38: 2 Then Hezekiah turned his face to the wall, and **p**
Jer 32:16 I **p** to the LORD, saying:
Da 9: 4 I **p** to the LORD my God and made confession,
Jnh 2: 1 Then Jonah **p** to the LORD his God from
4: 2 He **p** to the LORD and said, "O LORD!
Mt 26:39 he threw himself on the ground and **p,**
26:42 Again he went away for the second time and **p,**
26:44 he went away and **p** for the third time,
Mk 1:35 and went out to a deserted place, and there he **p.**
14:35 he threw himself on the ground and **p** that,
14:39 again he went away and **p,** saying the same words.
Lk 22:32 I have **p** for you that your own faith may not fail;
22:41 about a stone's throw, knelt down, and **p,**
22:44 ⟦In his anguish he **p** more earnestly,⟧
Ac 1:24 Then they **p** and said, "Lord, you know everyone's
4:31 When they had **p,** the place in which they were
6: 6 who **p** and laid their hands on them.
7:59 While they were stoning Stephen, he **p,**
8:15 down and **p** for them that they might receive
9:40 and then he knelt down and **p,**
10: 2 to the people and **p** constantly to God.
12: 5 the church **p** fervently to God for him.
20:36 he knelt down with them all and **p.**
21: 5 There we knelt down on the beach and **p**
27:29 they let down four anchors from the stern and **p**
Jas 5:17 and he **p** fervently that it might not rain,
5:18 Then he **p** again, and the heaven gave rain and
Tob 3:11 she **p** and said, "Blessed are you, merciful God!
12:12 So now when you and Sarah **p,**
Jdt 12: 8 she **p** the Lord God of Israel to direct her way for
AdE 13: 8 Then Mordecai **p** to the Lord,
14: 3 She **p** to the Lord God of Israel, and said:
Wis 7: 7 Therefore I **p,** and understanding was given me;
Bar 1: 5 Then they wept, and fasted, and **p** before the Lord;
Aza 1: 2 Then Azariah stood still in the fire and **p** aloud:
1Mc 4:30 When he saw that their army was strong, he **p,**
7:40 with three thousand men. Then Judas **p** and said,
11:71 put dust on his head, and **p.**
2Mc 1: 8 We **p** to the Lord and were heard,
2:10 Just as Moses **p** to the Lord,
2:10 and consumed the sacrifices, so also Solomon **p,**
5: 4 Therefore everyone **p** that the apparition
11: 6 **p** the Lord to send a good angel to save Israel.
14:15 they sprinkled dust on their heads and **p**
1Es 8:53 And again we **p** to our Lord about these things,
3Mc 2: 1 and extending his hands with calm dignity, **p**
6: 1 to stop calling upon the holy God, and he **p**
2Es 4:51 Then I **p** and said, "Do you think that I shall live
7:*46* But what of those for whom I **p?**
7:*106* [36] "How then do we find that first Abraham **p** for
7:*110* [40] and many others **p** for many?
7:*111* [41] the righteous have **p** for the ungodly,
7:*112* [42] those who were strong **p** for the weak.
9:44 during those thirty years I **p** to the Most High,
13:13 I woke up in great terror, and **p** to the Most High,
4Mc 4:13 **p** for him so that King Seleucus would not

PRAYER‡ (148) [PRAY]

Ge 25:21 and the LORD granted his **p,**
2Sa 7:27 to pray this **p** to you.
1Ki 8:28 Regard your servant's **p** and his plea,
8:28 heeding the cry and the **p** that your servant prays
8:29 that you may heed the **p** that your servant prays
8:38 whatever **p,** whatever plea there is
8:45 then hear in heaven their **p** and their plea,
8:49 then hear in heaven your dwelling place their **p**
8:54 Now when Solomon finished offering all this **p**
9: 3 "I have heard your **p** and your plea,
2Ki 19: 4 lift up your **p** for the remnant that is left."
19:20 I have heard your **p** to me about King Sennacherib
20: 5 I have heard your **p,** I have seen your tears;
2Ch 6:19 Regard your servant's **p** and his plea,
6:19 heeding the cry and the **p** that your servant prays
6:20 and may you heed the **p** that your servant prays
6:29 whatever **p,** whatever plea from any individual or
6:35 then hear from heaven their **p** and their plea,
6:39 then hear from heaven your dwelling place their **p**
6:40 let your eyes be open and your ears attentive to **p**
7: 1 When Solomon had ended his **p,**
7:12 "I have heard your **p,** and have chosen this place
7:15 be open and my ears attentive to the **p** that is made
30:27 their **p** came to his holy dwelling in heaven.
33:18 the rest of the acts of Manasseh, his **p** to his God,
33:19 His **p,** and how God received his entreaty,
Ne 1: 6 and your eyes open to hear the **p** of your servant
1:11 let your ear be attentive to the **p** of your servant,
1:11 and to the **p** of your servants who delight
11:17 who was the leader to begin the thanksgiving in **p,**
Job 16:17 in my hands, and my **p** is pure.
24:12 yet God pays no attention to their **p.**
42: 8 for you, for I will accept his **p** not to deal with you
42: 9 and the LORD accepted Job's **p.**
Ps 4: 1 Be gracious to me, and hear my **p.**
6: 9 the LORD accepts my **p.**
17: T *A P of David.*
17: 1 give ear to my **p** from lips free of deceit.
32: 6 Therefore let all who are faithful offer **p** to you;
39:12 "Hear my **p,** O LORD, and give ear to my cry;
42: 8 a **p** to the God of my life.
54: 2 Hear my **p,** O God; give ear to the
55: 1 Give ear to my **p,** O God;
61: 1 Hear my cry, O God; listen to my **p.**
65: 2 O you who answer **p!** To you all flesh shall come.
66:19 he has given heed to the words of my **p.**
66:20 not rejected my **p** or removed his steadfast love
69:13 But as for me, my **p** is to you, O LORD.
72:15 May **p** be made for him continually,
84: 8 O LORD God of hosts, hear my **p;**
86: T *A P of David.*
86: 6 Give ear, O LORD, to my **p;**
88: 2 let my **p** come before you;
88:13 in the morning my **p** comes before you.
90: T *A P of Moses, the man of God.*
102: T *A p of one afflicted, when faint and pleading*
102: 1 Hear my **p,** O LORD; let my cry come to you.
102:17 He will regard the **p** of the destitute,
102:17 and will not despise their **p.**
109: 4 even while I make **p** for them.
109: 7 let his **p** be counted as sin.
141: 2 Let my **p** be counted as incense before you,

Ps 141: 5 for my **p** is continually against their wicked deeds.
142: T *A Maskil of David. When he was in the cave. A **P**.*
143: 1 Hear my **p**, O LORD; give ear to my
Pr 15: 8 but the **p** of the upright is his delight.
15:29 but he hears the **p** of the righteous.
Isa 26:16 they poured out a **p** when your chastening was
37: 4 lift up your **p** for the remnant that is left."
38: 5 I have heard your **p**, I have seen your tears;
56: 7 and make them joyful in my house of **p**;
56: 7 for my house shall be called a house of **p**
Jer 7:16 do not raise a cry or **p** on their behalf,
11:14 or lift up a cry or **p** on their behalf,
La 3: 8 though I call and cry for help, he shuts out my **p**;
3:44 with a cloud so that no **p** can pass through.
Da 9: 3 by **p** and supplication with fasting and sackcloth
9:17 to the **p** of your servant and to his supplication,
9:21 while I was speaking in **p**,
Jnh 2: 7 and my **p** came to you, into your holy temple.
Hab 3: 1 A **p** of the prophet Habakkuk according
Mt 21:13 'My house shall be called a house of **p**';
21:22 Whatever you ask for in **p** with faith,
Mk 9:29 "This kind can come out only through **p**."
11:17 'My house shall be called a house of **p** for all
11:24 So I tell you, whatever you ask for in **p**,
Lk 1:13 Zechariah, for your **p** has been heard.
2:37 but worshiped there with fasting and **p** night
6:12 and he spent the night in **p** to God.
19:46 "It is written, 'My house shall be a house of **p**';
22:45 When he got up from **p**,
Ac 1:14 to **p**, together with certain women, including Mary
3: 1 up to the temple at the hour of **p**,
6: 4 will devote ourselves to **p** and to serving
10:31 'Cornelius, your **p** has been heard
14:23 with **p** and fasting they entrusted them to the Lord
16:13 where we supposed there was a place of **p**;
16:16 One day, as we were going to the place of **p**,
Ro 10: 1 and **p** to God for them is that they may be saved.
12:12 be patient in suffering, persevere in **p**.
15:30 to join me in earnest **p** to God on my behalf,
1Co 7: 5 to devote yourselves to **p**,
Eph 6:18 the Spirit at all times in every **p** and supplication.
Php 1: 9 And this is my **p**, that your love may overflow
4: 6 but in everything by **p** and supplication
Col 4: 2 Devote yourselves to **p**, keeping alert in it
1Ti 4: 5 for it is sanctified by God's word and by **p**.
Jas 5:15 The **p** of faith will save the sick,
5:16 The **p** of the righteous is powerful and effective.
1Pe 3:12 and his ears are open to their **p**.
Tob 12: 8 **P** with fasting is good, but better than
12:12 it was I who brought and read the record of your **p**
Jdt 9:12 King of all your creation, hear my **p**!
13:10 as they were accustomed to do for **p**.
AdE 13:17 Hear my **p**, and have mercy
15: 1 On the third day, when she ended her **p**,
Wis 18:21 **p** and propitiation by incense;
Sir 4: 6 their Creator will hear their **p**.
21: 5 The **p** of the poor goes from their lips to the ears
34:31 who will listen to his **p**?
35:16 but he will listen to the **p** of one who is wronged.
35:20 and his **p** will reach to the clouds.
35:21 The **p** of the humble pierces the clouds,
36:22 Hear, O Lord, the **p** of your servants,
39: 5 opens his mouth in **p** and asks pardon for his sins.
39: 6 of his own and give thanks to the Lord in **p**.
51: 1 **P** OF JESUS SON OF SIRACH I give you thanks,
51: 9 And I sent up my **p** from the earth,
51:11 sing hymns of thanksgiving." My **p** was heard,
51:13 I sought wisdom openly in my **p**.
Bar 2:14 Hear, O Lord, our **p** and our supplication,
2:19 or our kings that we bring before you our **p**
3: 4 hear now the **p** of the people of Israel,
1Mc 3:46 Israel formerly had a place of **p** in Mizpah.
5:33 who sounded their trumpets and cried aloud in **p**.
7:37 be for your people a house of **p** and supplication.
2Mc 1:23 the priests offered **p**—the priests and everyone.
1:24 The **p** was to this effect:
10:27 from their **p** they took up their arms and advanced
15:24 With these words he ended his **p**.
3Mc 1:24 as before, was engaged in **p**,
6:16 Just as Eleazar was ending his **p**,
7:20 on a pillar and dedicating a place of **p** at the site of
2Es 8:19 The beginning of the words of Ezra's **p**,
10:24 O Lord, the **p** of your servant,
10:28 my end has become corruption, and my **p**
12: 7 and if my **p** has indeed come up before your face,
13:14 and have deemed me worthy to have my **p** heard

PRAYERS‡ (37) [PRAY]

Ps 72:20 The **p** of David son of Jesse are ended.
80: 4 long will you be angry with your people's **p**?
Pr 28: 9 even one's **p** are an abomination.
Isa 1:15 even though you make many **p**, I will not listen;
Da 6:13 but he is saying his **p** three times a day."
Mk 12:40 and for the sake of appearance say long **p**.
Lk 20:47 and for the sake of appearance say long **p**.
Ac 2:42 to the breaking of bread and the **p**.
10: 4 "Your **p** and your alms have ascended as
Ro 1: 9 without ceasing I remember you always in my **p**,
2Co 1:11 as you also join in helping us by your **p**,
1:11 for the blessing granted us through the **p** of many.
Eph 1:16 to give thanks for you as I remember you in my **p**.
Php 1: 4 constantly praying with joy in every one of my **p**
1:19 for I know that through your **p** and the help of
Col 1: 3 In our **p** for you we always thank God,
4:12 He is always wrestling in his **p** on your behalf,
1Th 1: 2 to God for all of you and mention you in our **p**,
1Ti 2: 1 First of all, then, I urge that supplications, **p**,
5: 5 on God and continues in supplications and **p** night
2Ti 1: 3 I remember you constantly in my **p** night and day.
Phm 1: 4 When I remember you in my **p**,
1:22 I am hoping through your **p** to be restored to you.
Heb 5: 7 Jesus offered up **p** and supplications,
1Pe 3: 7 so that nothing may hinder your **p**.
4: 7 and discipline yourselves for the sake of your **p**.
Rev 5: 8 which are the **p** of the saints.
8: 3 of incense to offer with the **p** of all the saints on
8: 4 the smoke of the incense, with the **p** of the saints,
Tob 3:16 the **p** of both of them were heard in
Jdt 4:13 The Lord heard their **p** and had regard
13: 3 for she said she would be going out for her **p**.
Sir 50:19 the people of the Lord Most High offered their **p**
1Mc 12:11 at the sacrifices that we offer and in our **p**,
2Mc 1: 5 May he hear your **p** and be reconciled to you,
15:26 the enemy in battle with invocations to God and **p**.
1Es 6:31 and **p** be offered for their lives."

PRAYING (33) [PRAY]

1Sa 1:12 As she continued **p** before the LORD,
1:13 Hannah was **p** silently; only her lips moved,
1:26 in your presence, **p** to the LORD.
Ne 1: 4 fasting and **p** before the God of heaven.
Isa 45:20 and keep on **p** to a god that cannot save.
Da 6:11 The conspirators came and found Daniel **p**
9:20 and was **p** and confessing my sin and the sin
Mt 6: 7 "When you are **p**, do not heap up empty phrases
Mk 11:25 "Whenever you stand **p**, forgive,
Lk 1:10 the whole assembly of the people was **p** outside.
3:21 and when Jesus also had been baptized and was **p**,
9:18 Once when Jesus was **p** alone,
9:29 And while he was **p**, the appearance
11: 1 He was **p** in a certain place,
18:11 The Pharisee, standing by himself, was **p** thus,
21:36 **p** that you may have the strength
Ac 9:11 At this moment he is **p**,
10:30 I was **p** in my house when suddenly a man
11: 5 "I was in the city of Joppa **p**,
12:12 where many had gathered and were **p**.
13: 3 after fasting and **p** they laid their hands on them
16:25 and Silas were **p** and singing hymns to God,
22:17 to Jerusalem and while I was **p** in the temple,
28: 8 and cured him by **p** and putting his hands on him.
Php 1: 4 constantly **p** with joy in every one of my prayers
Col 1: 9 not ceased **p** for you and asking that you may
Jdt 4:12 **p** fervently to the God of Israel not
2Mc 1: 6 We are now **p** for you here.
12:42 **p** that the sin that had been committed might
15:12 was **p** with outstretched hands for the whole body
15:27 with their hands and **p** to God in their hearts,
1Es 8:91 While Ezra was **p** and making his confession,
3Mc 5: 7 of all power, their merciful God and Father, **p**

PRAYS (16) [PRAY]

1Ki 8:28 heeding the cry and the prayer that your servant **p**
8:29 that you may heed the prayer that your servant **p**
8:42 when a foreigner comes and **p** toward this house,
2Ch 6:19 heeding the cry and the prayer that your servant **p**
6:20 and may you heed the prayer that your servant **p**
Job 33:26 Then he **p** to God, and is accepted by him,
Isa 44:17 he **p** to it and says, "Save me,
Da 6: 7 that whoever **p** to anyone, divine or human,
6:12 that anyone who **p** to anyone, divine or human,
1Co 11: 4 Any man who **p** or prophesies with something
11: 5 but any woman who **p** or prophesies
14:14 my spirit **p** but my mind is unproductive.
Wis 13:17 When he **p** about possessions and his marriage
13:18 for life he **p** to a thing that is dead;
Sir 34:29 When one **p** and another curses,
2Mc 15:14 the family of Israel and **p** much for the people and

PRE-EMINENCE (1) [PRE-EMINENT]

Eze 7:11 not their wealth; no **p** among them.

PRE-EMINENT (1) [PRE-EMINENCE]

3Mc 1:11 but only the high priest who was **p** over all—

PREACH (10) [PREACHER, PREACHING]

Eze 20:46 set your face toward the south, **p** against the south,
21: 2 toward Jerusalem and **p** against the sanctuaries;
Am 7:16 and do not **p** against the house of Isaac.'
Mic 2: 6 "Do not **p**"—thus they **p**—"one should not **p** of
2:11 saying, "I will **p** to you of wine and strong drink,"
Ac 10:42 He commanded us to **p** to the people and to testify
Ro 2:21 While you **p** against stealing, do you steal?
Tit 1: 9 that he may be able both to **p** with sound doctrine

PREACHER‡ (1) [PREACH]

Mic 2:11 such a one would be the **p** for this people!

PREACHING (3) [PREACH]

Ac 10:36 **p** peace by Jesus Christ—he is Lord of all.
Gal 5:11 being persecuted if I am still **p** circumcision?
1Ti 5:17 especially those who labor in **p** and teaching;

PRECAUTIONS (2)

2Mc 1:19 they took such **p** that the place was unknown
3Mc 3:24 we have taken **p** so that, if a sudden disorder

PRECEDE (4) [PRECEDED, PRECEDENCE, PRECEDES, PRECEDING]

1Th 4:15 will by no means **p** those who have died.
1Ti 5:24 of some people are conspicuous and **p** them
Sir 22:24 The vapor and smoke of the furnace **p** the fire; so insults **p** bloodshed.

PRECEDED (3) [PRECEDE]

Jer 28: 8 The prophets who **p** you and me
34: 5 the earlier kings who **p** you,
Da 7: 7 It was different from all the beasts that **p** it,

PRECEDENCE (2) [PRECEDE]

AdE 3: 1 and granting him **p** over all the king's Friends.
4Mc 2:12 It takes **p** over love for children,

PRECEDES (3) [PRECEDE]

Sir 37:16 and counsel **p** every undertaking.
4Mc 1:22 Thus desire **p** pleasure and delight follows it.
1:23 Fear **p** pain and sorrow comes after.

PRECEDING (2) [PRECEDE]

AdE 11: 1 and his son Ptolemy brought to Egypt the **p** Letter
1Mc 3:30 that he used to give more lavishly than **p** kings.

PRECEPT (8) [PRECEPTS]

Isa 28:10 For it is **p** upon **p**, **p** upon **p**, line upon line,
28:13 "**P** upon **p**, **p** upon **p**, line upon line,

PRECEPTS (29) [PRECEPT]

Ps 19: 8 the **p** of the LORD are right, rejoicing the heart;
111: 7 and just; all his **p** are trustworthy.
119: 4 You have commanded your **p** to
119:15 I will meditate on your **p**,
119:27 Make me understand the way of your **p**,
119:40 See, I have longed for your **p**;
119:45 I shall walk at liberty, for I have sought your **p**.
119:56 for I have kept your **p**.
119:63 of those who keep your **p**.
119:69 but with my whole heart I keep your **p**.
119:78 as for me, I will meditate on your **p**.
119:87 but I have not forsaken your **p**.
119:93 I will never forget your **p**,
119:94 I am yours; save me, for I have sought your **p**.
119:100 the aged, for I keep your **p**.
119:104 Through your **p** I get understanding;
119:110 but I do not stray from your **p**.
119:128 Truly I direct my steps by all your **p**;
119:134 that I may keep your **p**.
119:141 yet I do not forget your **p**.
119:159 Consider how I love your **p**;
119:168 I keep your **p** and decrees,
119:173 for I have chosen your **p**.
Pr 4: 2 for I give you good **p**: do not forsake my teaching.
Jer 35:18 of your ancestor Jonadab, and kept all his **p**,
Mt 15: 9 teaching human **p** as doctrines.' "
Mk 7: 7 teaching human **p** as doctrines.'
Sir 18:14 and who are eager for his **p**.
2Es 16:76 You who keep my commandments and **p**,

PRECINCT (1) [PRECINCTS]

2Mc 1:15 with a few men inside the wall of the sacred **p**,

PRECINCTS‡ (8) [PRECINCT]

2Ki 23:11 the eunuch Nathan-melech, which was in the **p**;
1Mc 1:47 to build altars and sacred **p** and shrines for idols,
5:43 and fled into the sacred **p** at Carnaim.
5:44 But he took the town and burned the sacred **p**
10:43 in Jerusalem, or in any of its **p**,
14:48 to put them up in a conspicuous place in the **p** of
2Mc 6: 4 with women within the sacred **p**,
10: 2 and also destroyed the sacred **p**.

PRECIOUS‡ (74)

1Sa 26:21 because my life was **p** in your sight today;
26:24 As your life was **p** today in my sight, so may my life be **p** in the sight of the LORD,
2Sa 12:30 and in it was a **p** stone;
1Ki 10: 2 and very much gold, and **p** stones;
10:10 a great quantity of spices, and **p** stones;
10:11 a great quantity of almug wood and **p** stones.
2Ki 1:13 of these fifty servants of yours, be **p** in your sight.
1:14 but now let my life be **p** in your sight."
20:13 the gold, the spices, the **p** oil, his armory,
1Ch 20: 2 and in it was a **p** stone;
29: 2 antimony, colored stones, all sorts of **p** stones,
29: 8 Whoever had **p** stones gave them to the treasury of
2Ch 3: 6 He adorned the house with settings of **p** stones.
9: 1 and very much gold and **p** stones.
9: 9 a very great quantity of spices, and **p** stones:
9:10 from Ophir brought algum wood and **p** stones.
20:25 goods, clothing, and **p** things,
32:23 in Jerusalem and **p** things to King Hezekiah
32:27 for gold, for **p** stones, for spices, for shields,
36:10 with the **p** vessels of the house of the LORD,
36:19 and destroyed all its **p** vessels.
Ezr 8:27 two vessels of fine polished bronze as **p** as gold.
Job 22:25 and if the Almighty is your gold and your **p** silver,
28:10 and their eyes see every **p** thing.
28:16 in the gold of Ophir, in **p** onyx or sapphire.
Ps 36: 7 How **p** is your steadfast love, O God!
72:14 and **p** is their blood in his sight.

Ps 116:15 **P** in the sight of the LORD is the death
133: 2 It is like the **p** oil on the head,
Pr 3:15 She is more **p** than jewels,
12:27 but the diligent obtain **p** wealth.
20:15 but the lips informed by knowledge are a **p** jewel.
21:20 **P** treasure remains in the house of the wise,
24: 4 the rooms are filled with all **p** and pleasant riches.
31:10 She is far more **p** than jewels.
Ecc 7: 1 A good name is better than **p** ointment,
Isa 28:16 a tested stone, a **p** cornerstone, a sure foundation:
39: 2 the gold, the spices, the **p** oil, his whole armory,
43: 4 Because you are **p** in my sight, and honored,
54:12 your gates of jewels, and all your wall of **p** stones.
Jer 15:19 If you utter what is **p**, and not what is worthless,
La 1: 7 all the **p** things that were hers in days of old.
1:10 stretched out their hands over all her **p** things;
4: 2 The **p** children of Zion, worth their weight
Eze 22:25 they have taken treasure and **p** things;
27:22 and all **p** stones, and gold.
28:13 every **p** stone was your covering, carnelian,
Da 11: 8 with their idols and with their **p** vessels of silver
11:38 with **p** stones and costly gifts.
Hos 9: 6 Nettles shall possess their **p** things of silver;
13:15 It shall strip his treasury of every **p** thing.
Na 2: 9 An abundance of every **p** thing!"
1Co 3:12 silver, **p** stones, wood, hay, straw—
Jas 5: 7 The farmer waits for the **p** crop from the earth,
1Pe 1: 7 your faith—being more **p** than gold that,
1:19 but with the **p** blood of Christ,
2: 4 though rejected by mortals yet chosen and **p**
2: 6 a cornerstone chosen and **p;**
2: 7 To you then who believe, he is **p;**
3: 4 which is very **p** in God's sight.
2Pe 1: 1 a faith as **p** as ours through the righteousness
1: 4 his **p** and very great promises,
Tob 13:16 and all your walls with **p** stones.
Jdt 10: 3 and anointed herself with **p** ointment.
10:21 emeralds and other **p** stones.
AdE 15: 6 all covered with gold and **p** stones.
Wis 12: 7 so that the land most **p** of all to you might receive
Sir 26:14 and nothing is so **p** as her self-discipline.
45:11 with **p** stones engraved like seals,
50: 9 with all kinds of **p** stones;
2Es 7:*52* "If you have just a few **p** stones,
7:*57* Judge therefore which things are **p** and desirable,
7:*58* for what is more rare is more **p.**"

PRECIPITOUS (2) [PRECIPITOUSLY]

2Es 7: 7 the entrance to it is narrow and set in a **p** place,
4Mc 14:16 by building in **p** chasms and in holes and tops

PRECIPITOUSLY (1) [PRECIPITOUS]

2Mc 13: 5 around it that on all sides inclines **p** into the ashes.

PRECISELY (2)

Sir 16:25 I will impart discipline **p**
3Mc 4:13 be dealt with in **p** the same fashion as the others,

PREDECESSORS (5)

2Ki 19:12 the nations that my **p** destroyed, Gozan, Haran,
Isa 37:12 the nations that my **p** destroyed, Gozan, Haran,
Da 11:24 and do what none of his **p** had ever done,
1Mc 11:26 the king treated him as his **p** had treated him;
11:38 the troops who had served under his **p** hated him.

PREDESTINATE, PREDESTINATED (KJV) See DESTINED, PREDESTINED

PREDESTINED (3)

Ac 4:28 to do whatever your hand and your plan had **p**
Ro 8:29 also **p** to be conformed to the image of his Son,
8:30 And those whom he **p** he also called;

PREDICT (1) [PREDICTED, PREDICTION, PREDICTIONS]

Isa 47:13 and at each new moon **p** what shall befall you.

PREDICTED (8) [PREDICT]

2Ki 23:16 of the man of God who had **p** these things.
23:17 from Judah and **p** these things that you have done
Ac 3:24 and those after him, also **p** these days.
11:28 One of them named Agabus stood up and **p** by
Ro 9:29 And as Isaiah **p**, "If the Lord of hosts had
2Es 8:59 For just as the things that I have **p** await you,
9: 1 you see that some of the **p** signs have occurred,
9: 8 will survive the dangers that have been **p**,

PREDICTION (1) [PREDICT]

Isa 44:26 and fulfills the **p** of his messengers;

PREDICTIONS (1) [PREDICT]

Jude 1:17 the **p** of the apostles of our Lord Jesus Christ;

PREFACE (1)

2Mc 2:32 be foolish to lengthen the **p** while cutting short

PREFECT (1) [PREFECTS]

Da 2:48 over the whole province of Babylon and chief **p**

PREFECTS (5) [PREFECT]

Da 3: 2 King Nebuchadnezzar sent for the satraps, the **p**,
3: 3 So the satraps, the **p**, and the governors,
3:27 And the satraps, the **p**, the governors,
6: 7 the kingdom, the **p** and the satraps, the counselors
1Es 3:14 and the satraps and generals and governors and **p**,

PREFER (6) [PREFERABLE, PREFERENCE, PREFERRED, PREFERRING, PREFERS]

1Ki 21: 6 if you **p**, I will give you another vineyard for it';
1Co 4:21 What would you **p?** Am I to come
Php 1:22 and I do not know which I **p.**
2Mc 11:24 but **p** their own way of living and ask
1Es 4:19 and all **p** her to gold or silver
3Mc 2:30 of them **p** to join those who have been initiated

PREFERABLE (3) [PREFER]

Sir 20:25 A thief is **p** to a habitual liar,
28:21 its death is an evil death, and Hades is **p** to it.
36:26 but one girl is **p** to another.

PREFERENCE (2) [PREFER]

Dt 21:16 the son of the loved as the firstborn in **p** to the son
1Es 4:39 With it there is no partiality or **p**,

PREFERRED (4) [PREFER]

Jer 8: 3 be **p** to life by all the remnant that remains
Phm 1:14 but I **p** to do nothing without your consent,
Wis 7: 8 I **p** her to scepters and thrones,
3Mc 1:29 at that time **p** death to the profanation of the place.

PREFERRING (1) [PREFER]

2Mc 14:42 **p** to die nobly rather than to fall into the hands

PREFERS (2) [PREFER]

Wis 17:13 **p** ignorance of what causes the torment.
4Mc 1:15 Now reason is the mind that with sound logic **p**

PREFIGURED (1)

1Pe 3:21 And baptism, which this **p**, now saves you—

PREGNANCIES (2) [PREGNANT]

4Mc 15: 6 In seven **p** she had implanted in herself tender
16: 7 O seven childbirths all in vain, seven profitless **p**,

PREGNANCY (1) [PREGNANT]

Hos 9:11 no birth, no **p**, no conception!

PREGNANT (20) [PREGNANCIES, PREGNANCY]

Ge 19:36 the daughters of Lot became **p** by their father.
38:24 moreover she is **p** as a result of whoredom."
38:25 "It was the owner of these who made me **p.**"
Ex 21:22 When people who are fighting injure a **p** woman
1Sa 4:19 his daughter-in-law, the wife of Phinehas, was **p**,
2Sa 11: 5 and she sent and told David, "I am **p.**"
2Ki 8:12 and rip up their **p** women."
15:16 He ripped open all the **p** women in it.
Ps 7:14 and are **p** with mischief, and bring forth lies.
Hos 13:16 and their **p** women ripped open.
Am 1:13 because they have ripped open **p** women in Gilead
Mt 24:19 Woe to those who are **p** and
Mk 13:17 Woe to those who are **p** and
Lk 21:23 Woe to those who are **p** and
1Th 5: 3 as labor pains come upon a **p** woman,
Rev 12: 2 She was **p** and was crying out in birth pangs,
Sir 42:10 be seduced and become **p** in her father's house;
2Es 4:40 "Go and ask a **p** woman whether,
6:21 and **p** women shall give birth
16:38 as a **p** woman, in the ninth month when the time

PREJUDICE (1)

1Ti 5:21 I warn you to keep these instructions without **p**,

PREMATURE (2)

Sir 30:24 and anxiety brings on **p** old age.
2Es 6:21 and pregnant women shall give birth to **p** children

PREMEDITATED (1)

Ex 21:13 If it was not **p**, but came about by an act of God,

PREPARATION (8) [PREPARE]

1Ch 22: 5 I will therefore make **p** for it."
Mt 27:62 The next day, that is, after the day of **P**,
Mk 15:42 evening had come, and since it was the day of **P**,
Lk 23:54 It was the day of **P**,
Jn 19:14 Now it was the day of **P** for the Passover;
19:31 Since it was the day of **P**,
19:42 And so, because it was the Jewish day of **P**,
Jdt 4: 5 the villages on them and stored up food in **p**

PREPARATIONS (14) [PREPARE]

1Ch 28: 2 and I made **p** for building.
2Ch 35: 4 Make **p** by your ancestral houses
35: 6 and on behalf of your kindred make **p**,
35:14 Afterward they made **p** for themselves and for
35:14 Levites made **p** for themselves and for the priests,
2Ch 35:15 for their kindred the Levites made **p** for them.
Mt 26:17 "Where do you want us to make the **p** for you
Mk 14:12 to go and make the **p** for you to eat the Passover?"
14:15 Make **p** for us there."
Lk 22: 9 "Where do you want us to make **p** for it?"
22:12 Make **p** for us there."
Heb 9: 6 Such **p** having been made,
Tob 8:19 So they began to make **p.**
3Mc 5:10 in the morning to report to the king about these **p.**

PREPARE‡ (78) [PREPARATION, PREPARATIONS, PREPARED, PREPARES, PREPARING]

Ge 18: 7 and gave it to the servant, who hastened to **p** it.
27: 4 Then **p** for me savory food, such as I like,
27: 7 and **p** for me savory food to eat,
27: 9 I may **p** from them savory food for your father,
Ex 16: 5 On the sixth day, when they **p** what they bring in,
19:11 and **p** for the third day,
19:15 And he said to the people, **"P** for the third day;
Lev 6:22 Aaron's descendants as a successor, shall **p** it;
Nu 23: 1 and **p** seven bulls and seven rams for me."
23:29 and **p** seven bulls and seven rams for me."
Jos 1:11 and command the people: **'P** your provisions;
Jdg 13:15 "Allow us to detain you, and **p** a kid for you."
13:16 but if you want to **p** a burnt offering,
2Sa 12: 4 to take one of his own flock or herd to **p** for
13: 5 and **p** the food in my sight,
13: 7 to your brother Amnon's house, and **p** food
1Ki 17:12 I may go home and **p** it for myself and my son,
18:23 I will **p** the other bull and lay it on the wood,
18:25 "Choose for yourselves one bull and **p** it first,
1Ch 9:32 to **p** them for each sabbath.
22: 2 to **p** dressed stones for building the house of God.
2Ch 2: 9 to **p** timber for me in abundance,
31:11 to **p** store-chambers in the house of the LORD;
Est 5: 8 to the banquet that I will **p** for them,
Ps 23: 5 You **p** a table before me in the presence
Pr 24:27 **P** your work outside, get everything ready for you
Isa 14:21 **P** slaughter for his sons because of the guilt
21: 5 They **p** the table, they spread the rugs, they eat,
40: 3 "In the wilderness **p** the way of the LORD,
57:14 It shall be said, "Build up, build up, **p** the way,
62:10 go through the gates, **p** the way for the people;
Jer 6: 4 **"P** war against her; up, and let us attack at noon!"
22: 7 I will **p** destroyers against you,
46: 3 **P** buckler and shield, and advance for battle!
51:12 post sentinels; **p** the ambushes;
51:27 **p** the nations for war against her,
51:28 **P** the nations for war against her,
Eze 4:15 on which you may **p** your bread."
12: 3 mortal, **p** for yourself an exile's baggage,
35: 6 I will **p** you for blood, and blood shall pursue you;
Joel 3: 9 **P** war, stir up the warriors.
Am 4:12 I will do this to you, **p** to meet your God, O Israel!
Mal 3: 1 I am sending my messenger to **p** the way
Mt 3: 3 **'P** the way of the Lord, make his paths straight.' "
11:10 who will **p** your way before you.'
Mk 1: 2 ahead of you, who will **p** your way;
1: 3 **'P** the way of the Lord, make his paths straight,' "
Lk 1:76 for you will go before the Lord to **p** his ways,
3: 4 **'P** the way of the Lord, make his paths straight.
7:27 who will **p** your way before you.'
12:47 but did not **p** himself or do what was wanted,
17: 8 **'P** supper for me, put on your apron and serve me
21:14 your minds not to **p** your defense in advance;
22: 8 and **p** the Passover meal for us that we may eat it."
Jn 14: 2 would I have told you that I go to **p** a place
14: 3 And if I go and **p** a place for you,
Phm 1:22 One thing more—**p** a guest room for me,
1Pe 1:13 Therefore **p** your minds for action;
Rev 16:12 in order to **p** the way for the kings from the east.
Tob 5:17 **p** supplies for the journey and set out
11: 3 and **p** the house while they are still on the way."
Jdt 2: 7 Tell them to **p** earth and water,
AdE 5: 4 to the dinner that I shall **p** today."
5: 8 and Haman come to the dinner that I shall **p** them,
Wis 13:12 burn the cast-off pieces of his work to **p** his food,
Sir 2: 1 when you come to serve the Lord, **p** yourself
2:17 Those who fear the Lord **p** their hearts,
18:23 Before making a vow, **p** yourself;
26:28 the Lord will **p** him for the sword!
29:26 **p** the table; let me eat what you have there."
33: 4 **P** what to say, and then you will be listened to;
Bar 1:10 and incense, and **p** a grain offering, and offer them
Bel 1:11 O king, set out the food and **p** the wine,
1Es 1: 4 **p** yourselves by your families and kindred,
1: 6 and kill the passover lamb and **p** the sacrifices
3Mc 5:20 without delay **p** the elephants in the same way for
2Es 14:24 But **p** for yourself many writing tablets,
16:40 Hear my words, O my people; **p** for battle,

PREPARED‡ (119) [PREPARE]

Ge 18: 8 he took curds and milk and the calf that he had **p**,
24:31 Why do you stand outside when I have **p**
27:14 his mother **p** savory food, such as his father loved.
27:17 and the bread that she had **p**, to her son Jacob.
27:31 He also **p** savory food, and brought it to his father.
Ex 12:16 that alone may be **p** by you.
12:39 nor had they **p** any provisions for themselves.
13:18 The Israelites went up out of the land of Egypt **p**
23:20 and to bring you to the place that I have **p.**
39: 6 The onyx stones were **p**, enclosed in settings
Lev 2: 5 If your offering is grain **p** on a griddle,
2: 7 If your offering is grain **p** in a pan,

Lev 2: 8 the grain offering that is **p** in any of these ways;
7: 9 and all that is **p** in a pan or on a griddle,
Jos 9: 4 they went and **p** provisions,
Jdg 6:19 So Gideon went into his house and **p** a kid,
19: 5 up early in the morning, and he **p** to go;
2Sa 12: 4 and **p** that for the guest who had come to him."
1Ki 1: 5 he **p** for himself chariots and horsemen,
5:18 the Gebalites did the stonecutting and **p** the timber
6:19 The inner sanctuary he **p** in the innermost part of
18:26 So they took the bull that was given them, **p** it,
2Ki 6:23 So he **p** for them a great feast;
7:12 "I will tell you what the Arameans have **p**
1Ch 9:30 **p** the mixing of the spices,
15: 1 and he **p** a place for the ark of God and pitched
15: 3 which he had **p** for it.
15:12 the God of Israel, to the place that I have **p** for it.
2Ch 1: 4 from Kiriath-jearim to the place that David had **p**
16:14 that had been filled with various kinds of spices **p**
31:11 in the house of the LORD; and they **p** them.
35:10 When the service had been **p** for,
35:16 So all the service of the LORD was **p** that day,
Ne 5:18 Now that which was **p** for one day was one ox
5:18 also fowls were **p** for me,
8:10 for whom nothing is **p**, for this day is holy
13: 5 **p** for Tobiah a large room
Est 5: 4 and Haman come today to a banquet that I have **p**
5: 5 and Haman came to the banquet that Esther had **p.**
5:12 with the king to the banquet that she **p.**
6: 4 on the gallows that he had **p** for him.
6:14 to the banquet that Esther had **p.**
7: 9 the very gallows that Haman has **p** for Mordecai,
7:10 on the gallows that he had **p** for Mordecai.
Job 13:18 I have indeed **p** my case;
15:24 they prevail against them, like a king **p** for battle.
Ps 7:13 he has **p** his deadly weapons,
65: 9 the people with grain, for so you have **p** it.
132:17 I have **p** a lamp for my anointed one.
Isa 30:33 For his burning place has long been **p;**
Eze 28:13 On the day that you were created they were **p.**
Jnh 4: 8 When the sun rose, God **p** a sultry east wind,
Zep 1: 7 the LORD has **p** a sacrifice,
Zec 5:11 when this is **p**, they will set the basket down there
Mt 20:23 for those for whom it has been **p** by my Father."
21:16 of infants and nursing babies you have **p** praise
22: 4 Look, I have **p** my dinner,
25:34 inherit the kingdom **p** for you from the foundation
25:41 depart from me into the eternal fire **p** for the devil
26:12 on my body she has **p** me for burial.
26:19 and they **p** the Passover meal.
Mk 10:40 but it is for those for whom it has been **p."**
14:16 and they **p** the Passover meal.
Lk 1:17 to make ready a people **p** for the Lord."
2:31 which you have **p** in the presence of all peoples,
12:20 And the things you have **p**, whose will they be?'
22:13 and they **p** the Passover meal.
23:56 Then they returned, and **p** spices and ointments.
24: 1 taking the spices that they had **p.**
Ac 10:10 and while it was being **p**, he fell into a trance.
Ro 9:23 which he has **p** beforehand for glory—
1Co 2: 9 what God has **p** for those who love him"—
2Co 3: 3 **p** by us, written not with ink but with the Spirit of
5: 5 He who has **p** us for this very thing is God,
Eph 2:10 which God **p** beforehand to be our way of life.
Col 1:11 may you be **p** to endure everything with patience,
Heb 10: 5 but a body you have **p** for me;
11: 3 By faith we understand that the worlds were **p** by
11:16 indeed, he has **p** a city for them.
Rev 12: 6 where she has a place **p** by God,
21: 2 **p** as a bride adorned for her husband.
Tob 2: 1 a good dinner was **p** for me and I reclined to eat.
Jdt 5: 1 the people of Israel had **p** for war and had closed
9: 6 For all your ways are **p** in advance,
12:19 Then she took what her maid had **p** and ate
AdE 3:14 all the nations were ordered to be **p** for that day.
5:14 and so the gallows was **p.**
6: 4 on the gallows that he had **p.**
6:14 to the banquet that Esther had **p.**
7: 9 "Look, Haman has even **p** a gallows for Mordecai,
7:10 So Haman was hanged on the gallows he had **p**
11: 7 At their roaring every nation **p** for war,
Wis 9: 8 of the holy tent that you **p** from the beginning.
16: 2 and you **p** quails to eat, a delicacy to satisfy
Sir 8:13 but if you give surety, be **p** to pay.
45:20 and **p** bread of first fruits in abundance;
49: 1 of Josiah is like blended incense **p** by the skill of
Bar 3:32 The one who **p** the earth for all time filled it
1Mc 2:32 and **p** for battle against them on the sabbath day.
12:28 and his troops were **p** for battle, they were afraid
15: 7 the weapons that you have **p** and the strongholds
1Es 1:13 Afterward they **p** the passover for themselves and
1:14 so the Levites **p** it for themselves and
1:16 their kindred the Levites **p** the passover for them.
5:48 took their places and **p** the altar of the God
9:42 on the wooden platform that had been **p;**
3Mc 1:19 for marriage abandoned the bridal chambers **p**
5: 8 from the fate now **p** for them.
5:31 I would have **p** them to be a rich feast for
6:31 that had been **p** for their destruction and burial.
2Es 2:11 which I had **p** for Israel.
2:13 kingdom is already **p** for you; be on the watch!
2:18 to their counsel I have consecrated and **p**
7:*70* he first **p** the judgment and the things that pertain
8:52 the tree of life is planted, the age to come is **p,**
8:59 so the thirst and torment that are **p** await them.
8:60 and have been ungrateful to him who **p** life
13:11 fell on the onrushing multitude that was **p** to fight,
13:36 **p** and built, as you saw the mountain carved out

PREPARES (4) [PREPARE]

Job 15:35 and bring forth evil and their heart **p** deceit."
Ps 147: 8 **p** rain for the earth, makes grass grow on the hills.
Pr 6: 8 it **p** its food in summer,
2Mc 2:27 as it is not easy for one who **p** a banquet and seeks

PREPARING (10) [PREPARE]

Ne 13: 7 **p** a room for him in the courts of the house
Eze 39:17 from all around to the sacrificial feast that I am **p**
39:19 at the sacrificial feast that I am **p** for you.
2Co 4:17 For this slight momentary affliction is **p** us for
Jude 1: 3 while eagerly **p** to write to you about
AdE 12: 2 that they were **p** to lay hands on King Artaxerxes;
Wis 14: 1 one **p** to sail and about to voyage
1Mc 5:11 They are **p** to come and capture the stronghold
7:29 but the enemy were **p** to kidnap Judas.
2Es 9:18 in this age when I was **p** for those who now exist,

PRESBYTER See Index to Footnotes

PRESBYTERY (KJV) See ELDERS; See also Index to Footnotes

PRESCRIBED (25)

Nu 29:18 as **p** in accordance with their number;
29:21 as **p** in accordance with their number;
29:24 as **p** in accordance with their number;
29:27 as **p** in accordance with their number;
29:30 as **p** in accordance with their number;
29:33 as **p** in accordance with their number;
29:37 as **p** in accordance with their number;
2Ki 23:21 "Keep the passover to the LORD your God as **p**
2Ch 4: 7 He made ten golden lampstands as **p,**
4:20 to burn before the inner sanctuary, as **p;**
30: 5 for they had not kept it in great numbers as **p.**
30:18 yet they ate the passover otherwise than as **p.**
Ezr 3: 2 as **p** in the law of Moses the man of God.
3: 4 And they kept the festival of booths, as **p,**
Job 36:23 Who has **p** for him his way, or who can say,
38:10 and **p** bounds for it, and set bars and doors,
Lk 3:13 "Collect no more than the amount **p** for you."
Ro 3:20 be justified in his sight" by deeds **p** by the law,
3:28 a person is justified by faith apart from works **p** by
Tob 1: 6 as it is **p** for all Israel by an everlasting decree.
Jdt 5:18 they departed from the way he had **p** for them,
1Es 6:34 that it be done with all diligence as here **p."**
8:21 Let all things **p** in the law of God
2Es 6:35 to complete the three weeks that had been **p**
7:*44* This is my judgment and its **p** order;

PRESENCE (260) [PRESENT]

Ge 3: 8 the man and his wife hid themselves from the **p** of
4:16 Then Cain went away from the **p** of the LORD,
23: 9 For the full price let him give it to me in your **p** as
23:11 in the **p** of my people I give it to you;
23:18 to Abraham as a possession in the **p** of the Hittites,
23:18 in the **p** of all who went in at the gate of his city.
27:30 when Jacob had scarcely gone out from the **p**
31:32 In the **p** of our kinsfolk,
41:46 And Joseph went out from the **p** of Pharaoh,
45: 3 so dismayed were they at his **p.**
47:10 and went out from the **p** of Pharaoh.
Ex 6:30 But Moses said in the LORD's **p,**
10:11 And they were driven out from Pharaoh's **p.**
18:12 to eat bread with Moses' father-in-law in the **p**
25:30 the bread of the **P** on the table before me always.
33:14 He said, "My **p** will go with you,
33:15 And he said to him, "If your **p** will not go,
35:13 and the bread of the **P;**
35:20 of the Israelites withdrew from the **p** of Moses.
39:36 and the bread of the **P;**
Lev 10: 2 from the **p** of the LORD and consumed them,
22: 3 that person shall be cut off from my **p:**
Nu 4: 7 the **P** they shall spread a blue cloth, and put on it
19: 3 the camp and slaughtered in his **p.**
36: 1 came forward and spoke in the **p** of Moses and
Dt 1:27 He brought you out of Egypt with his own **p,**
12: 7 And you shall eat there in the **p** of
12:18 in the **p** of the LORD your God at the place that
12:18 rejoicing in the **p** of the LORD your God
14:23 In the **p** of the LORD your God,
14:26 And you shall eat there in the **p** of
15:20 in the **p** of the LORD your God year by year at
17:18 a copy of this law written for him in the **p** of
25: 2 in his **p** with the number of lashes proportionate to
25: 9 then his brother's wife shall go up to him in the **p**
Jos 8:32 And there, in the **p** of the Israelites,
22:27 of the LORD in his **p** with our burnt offerings
Jdg 3:19 and all his attendants went out from his **p.**
Ru 4: 4 Buy it in the **p** of those sitting here,
4: 4 and in the **p** of the elders of my people.
1Sa 1:22 that he may appear in the **p** of the LORD,
1:26 I am the woman who was standing here in your **p,**
2:11 in the **p** of the priest Eli.
2:21 the boy Samuel grew up in the **p** of the LORD.
16:13 and anointed him in the **p** of his brothers;
16:18 prudent in speech, and a man of good **p;**
18:13 So Saul removed him from his **p,**
19: 7 and he was in his **p** as before.
21: 6 the **P**, which is removed from before the LORD,
21:13 he pretended to be mad when in their **p.**
21:15 to play the madman in my **p?**
26:20 away from the **p** of the LORD;
2Sa 3:13 in my **p** unless you bring Saul's daughter Michal
3:26 When Joab came out from David's **p,**
11:13 to eat and drink in his **p** and made him drunk;
13:17 "Put this woman out of my **p,**
14:14 not to keep an outcast banished forever from his **p.**
14:24 he is not to come into my **p."**
14:24 and did not come into the king's **p.**
14:28 without coming into the king's **p.**
14:32 Now let me go into the king's **p;**
24: 4 of the army went out from the **p** of the king to take
1Ki 1:28 So she came into the king's **p,**
7:48 the golden table for the bread of the **P,**
8:22 the altar of the LORD in the **p** of all the assembly
10:24 The whole earth sought the **p** of Solomon
21:13 in the **p** of the people, saying,
2Ki 5:27 So he left his **p** leprous, as white as snow.
6:32 So he dispatched a man from his **p.**
13:23 nor has he banished them from his **p** until now.
17:20 until he had banished them from his **p.**
24:20 the LORD that he expelled them from his **p.**
25:29 of his life he dined regularly in the king's **p.**
1Ch 16:11 and his strength, seek his **p** continually.
17:24 of your servant David will be established in your **p.**
24: 6 a Levite, recorded them in the **p** of the king,
24:31 the descendants of Aaron, in the **p** of King David,
29:10 Then David blessed the LORD in the **p** of all
2Ch 4:19 the golden altar, the tables for the bread of the **P,**
6:12 of the LORD in the **p** of the whole assembly
6:13 on his knees in the **p** of the whole assembly
9:23 All the kings of the earth sought the **p** of Solomon
26:19 in the **p** of the priests in the house of the LORD,
29:11 for the LORD has chosen you to stand in his **p**
34: 4 In his **p** they pulled down the altars of the Baals;
Ne 2: 1 Now, I had never been sad in his **p** before.
4: 2 the **p** of his associates and of the army of Samaria,
6:19 Also they spoke of his good deeds in my **p,**
8: 3 in the **p** of the men and the women
Est 1:16 Then Memucan said in the **p** of the king and
2:23 It was recorded in the book of the annals in the **p**
7: 8 "Will he even assault the queen in my **p,**
8:15 Then Mordecai went out from the **p** of the king,
Job 1:12 So Satan went out from the **p** of the LORD.
2: 7 So Satan went out from the **p** of the LORD,
21: 8 Their children are established in their **p,**
23:15 Therefore I am terrified at his **p;**
30:11 they have cast off restraint in my **p.**
33:26 he comes into his **p** with joy,
Ps 16:11 In your **p** there is fullness of joy;
21: 6 you make him glad with the joy of your **p.**
23: 5 a table before me in the **p** of my enemies;
31:20 of your **p** you hide them from human plots;
39: 1 on my mouth as long as the wicked are in my **p."**
41:12 and set me in your **p** forever.
51:11 Do not cast me away from your **p,**
52: 9 In the **p** of the faithful I will proclaim your name,
68: 8 the heavens poured down rain at the **p** of God,
68: 8 at the **p** of God, the God of Israel.
88: 1 when, at night, I cry out in your **p,**
95: 2 Let us come into his **p** with thanksgiving;
98: 9 at the **p** of the LORD,
100: 2 come into his **p** with singing.
101: 7 no one who utters lies shall continue in my **p.**
102:28 their offspring shall be established in your **p.**
105: 4 and his strength; seek his **p** continually.
114: 7 Tremble, O earth, at the **p** of the LORD,
114: 7 at the **p** of the God of Jacob,
116:14 I will pay my vows to the LORD in the **p**
116:18 I will pay my vows to the LORD in the **p**
139: 7 Or where can I flee from your **p?**
140:13 the upright shall live in your **p.**
Pr 14: 7 Leave the **p** of a fool,
25: 5 take away the wicked from the **p** of the king,
25: 6 not put yourself forward in the king's **p** or stand in
25: 7 than to be put lower in the **p** of a noble.
Ecc 8: 3 Do not be terrified; go from his **p,**
Isa 1: 7 in your very **p** aliens devour your land;
3: 8 against the LORD, defying his glorious **p.**
19: 1 the idols of Egypt will tremble at his **p,**
23:18 and fine clothing for those who live in the **p** of
63: 9 It was no messenger or angel but his **p**
64: 1 so that the mountains would quake at your **p—**
64: 2 so that the nations might tremble at your **p!**
64: 3 you came down, the mountains quaked at your **p.**
Jer 3:17 to the **p** of the LORD in Jerusalem,
4: 1 if you remove your abominations from my **p,**
16:17 they are not hidden from my **p,**
23:39 surely lift you up and cast you away from my **p,**
28: 1 in the **p** of the priests and all the people, saying,
28: 5 the prophet Hananiah in the **p** of the priests and all
28:11 And Hananiah spoke in the **p** of all the people,
31:36 If this fixed order were ever to cease from my **p,**
32:12 in the **p** of my cousin Hanamel,
32:12 in the **p** of the witnesses who signed the deed
32:12 and in the **p** of all the Judeans who were sitting in
32:13 In their **p** I charged Baruch, saying,
33:18 the levitical priests shall never lack a man in my **p**
39:16 they shall be accomplished in your **p** on that day.
52: 3 the LORD that he expelled them from his **p.**
La 2:19 Pour out your heart like water before the **p** of
3:35 when human rights are perverted in the **p** of
Eze 28: 9 "I am a god," in the **p** of those who kill you,
38:20 at my **p**, and the mountains shall be thrown down,
Da 1:18 the palace master brought them into the **p**
5: 1 and he was drinking wine in the **p** of the thousand.
5:17 Then Daniel answered in the **p** of the king,
5:24 "So from his **p** the hand was sent
7:10 A stream of fire issued and flowed out from his **p.**

Jnh 1: 3 But Jonah set out to flee to Tarshish from the **p** of
1: 3 away from the **p** of the LORD.
1:10 For the men knew that he was fleeing from the **p**
Mal 2: 3 and I will put you out of my **p.**
Mt 12: 4 the house of God and ate the bread of the **P,**
Mk 2:26 and ate the bread of the **P,**
Lk 1:19 I stand in the **p** of God,
2:31 which you have prepared in the **p** of all peoples,
6: 4 of God and took and ate the bread of the **P,**
8:47 and falling down before him, she declared in the **p**
14:10 then you will be honored in the **p** of all who sit at
15:10 there is joy in the **p** of the angels of God
19:27 bring them here and slaughter them in my **p.**' "
20:26 in the **p** of the people to trap him by what he said;
23:14 and here I have examined him in your **p** and have
24:43 and he took it and ate in their **p.**
Jn 3: 2 that you do apart from the **p** of God."
8:38 I declare what I have seen in the Father's **p;**
12:37 he had performed so many signs in their **p,**
17: 5 Father, glorify me in your own **p** with the glory
that I had in your **p** before the world existed.
20:30 Now Jesus did many other signs in the **p**
Ac 2:28 you will make me full of gladness with your **p.'**
3:13 whom you handed over and rejected in the **p**
3:16 in the **p** of all of you.
3:20 so that times of refreshing may come from the **p**
10:33 So now all of us are here in the **p** of God to listen
27:35 and giving thanks to God in the **p** of all,
Ro 4:17 in the **p** of the God in whom he believed,
1Co 1:29 so that no one might boast in the **p** of God.
2Co 2:10 has been for your sake in the **p** of Christ.
2:17 as persons sent from God and standing in his **p.**
4:14 and will bring us with you into his **p.**
10:10 but his bodily **p** is weak,
Php 2:12 not only in my **p,** but much more now
2Th 1: 9 the **p** of the Lord and from the glory of his might,
1Ti 5:20 rebuke them in the **p** of all,
5:21 In the **p** of God and of Christ Jesus and of
6:12 for which you made the good confession in the **p**
6:13 In the **p** of God, who gives life to all things,
2Ti 4: 1 In the **p** of God and of Christ Jesus,
Heb 9: 2 the table, and the bread of the **P;**
9:24 now to appear in the **p** of God on our behalf.
Jude 1:24 and to make you stand without blemish in the **p**
Rev 14:10 in the **p** of the holy angels and in the **p** of the Lamb
19:20 the false prophet who had performed in its **p**
20:11 the earth and the heaven fled from his **p,**
Tob 3:16 both of them were heard in the glorious **p** of God.
4:11 is an excellent offering in the **p** of the Most High.
6: 8 in the **p** of a man or woman afflicted by a demon
12: 6 and acknowledge him in the **p** of all the living for
13: 4 Exalt him in the **p** of every living being,
Jdt 2: 5 Leave my **p** and take with you men confident
2:14 So Holofernes left the **p** of his lord,
5: 8 their ancestors drove them out from the **p**
6: 1 to Achior in the **p** of all the foreign contingents:
6:17 that he had said in the **p** of the Assyrian leaders,
8:15 or even to destroy us in the **p** of our enemies.
10:23 When Judith came into the **p** of Holofernes
11: 5 and let your servant speak in your **p.**
11:13 and set aside for the priests who minister in the **p**
12:13 So Bagoas left the **p** of Holofernes,
12:13 to come to my lord to be honored in his **p,**
13: 1 and shut out the attendants from his master's **p.**
14: 8 So Judith told him in the **p** of the people all
AdE 1:19 that the queen may no longer come into his **p;**
7: 6 Haman was terrified in the **p** of the king
Wis 5: 1 in the **p** of those who have oppressed them
8:10 the multitudes and honor in the **p** of the elders,
14:17 When people could not honor monarchs in their **p,**
Sir 8:18 In the **p** of strangers do nothing that is to
17:25 pray in his **p** and lessen your offense.
23:14 or you may forget yourself in their **p,**
24: 2 and in the **p** of his hosts she tells of her glory:
27:23 In your **p** his mouth is all sweetness,
38: 3 and in the **p** of the great they are admired.
45: 3 the Lord glorified him in the **p** of kings.
Bar 2:28 to write your law in the **p** of the people of Israel,
Aza 1:18 we fear you and seek your **p.**
Sus 1:28 In the **p** of the people they said,
Bel 1:14 the whole temple in the **p** of the king alone.
1Mc 1:22 He took also the table for the bread of the **P,**
11:26 he exalted him in the **p** of all his Friends.
2Mc 6:18 a man now advanced in age and of noble **p,**
10: 3 and lighted lamps and set out the bread of the **P.**
14:24 And he kept Judas always in his **p;**
1Es 3:15 and the writing was read in their **p.**
8:90 for we can no longer stand in your **p** because
9:41 in the **p** of both men and women;
9:45 for he had the place of honor in the **p** of all.
3Mc 3:17 They accepted our **p** by word,
2Es 1:30 I will cast you out from my **p.**
3: 5 and he was made alive in your **p.**
5:22 and I began once more to speak words in the **p** of
6:36 and I began to speak in the **p** of the Most High.
7:*87* the glory of the Most High in whose **p** they sinned
7:*87* in whose **p** they are to be judged in the last times.
14:19 I answered and said, "Let me speak in your **p,**
16:11 and who will not be utterly shattered at his **p?**
16:12 and the fish with them shall be troubled at the **p** of

PRESENT‡ (183) [PRESENCE, PRESENTED, PRESENTING, PRESENTS]

Ge 32:13 and from what he had with him he took a **p**
32:18 they are a **p** sent to my lord Esau;
32:20 "I may appease him with the **p** that goes ahead
32:21 So the **p** passed on ahead of him;
33:10 then accept my **p** from my hand;
34:12 Put the marriage **p** and gift as high as you like,
43:11 and carry them down as a **p** to the man—
43:15 So the men took the **p,**
43:25 they made the **p** ready for Joseph's coming
43:26 they brought him the **p** that they had carried into
Ex 8:20 and **p** yourself before Pharaoh, as he goes out to
9:13 in the morning and **p** yourself before Pharaoh,
22:14 and it is injured or dies, the owner not being **p,**
22:15 If the owner was **p,** there shall be no restitution;
34: 2 the morning to Mount Sinai and **p** yourself there
Lev 2: 4 When you **p** a grain offering baked in the oven,
3: 7 If you **p** a sheep as your offering,
3: 9 You shall **p** its fat from the sacrifice of well-being,
3:14 You shall **p** as your offering from it,
6:21 you shall **p** it as a pleasing odor to the LORD.
16: 9 Aaron shall **p** the goat on which the lot fell for
16:11 Aaron shall **p** the bull as a sin offering for himself,
16:20 he shall **p** the live goat.
17: 4 to **p** it as an offering to the LORD before
22:23 that has a limb too long or too short you may **p** for
23: 8 For seven days you shall **p** the LORD's offerings
23:16 then you shall **p** an offering of new grain to
23:18 You shall **p** with the bread seven lambs a year old
23:25 and you shall **p** the LORD's offering by fire.
23:27 and **p** the LORD's offering by fire;
23:36 Seven days you shall **p** the LORD's offerings
23:36 a holy convocation and **p** the LORD's offerings
Nu 6:16 The priest shall **p** them before the LORD
7:11 They shall **p** their offerings, one leader each day,
8:11 and Aaron shall **p** the Levites before the LORD
8:13 and you shall **p** them as an elevation offering to
15: 4 to the LORD shall **p** also a grain offering,
15: 9 then you shall **p** with the bull a grain offering,
15:10 you shall **p** as a drink offering half a hin of wine,
15:19 you shall **p** a donation to the LORD.
15:20 From your first batch of dough you shall **p** a loaf
15:20 you shall **p** it just as you **p** a donation from
15:27 An individual who sins unintentionally shall **p**
16:16 be **p** tomorrow before the LORD,
16:17 each one of you **p** his censer before the LORD,
18:19 the Israelites **p** to the LORD I have given to you,
Dt 6:15 who is **p** with you, is a jealous God.
7:21 who is **p** with you, is a great and awesome God.
12:27 You shall **p** your burnt offerings,
31:14 and **p** yourselves in the tent of meeting,
Jos 15:19 She said to him, "Give me a **p;**
Jdg 1:15 She said to him, "Give me a **p;**
6:18 and bring out my **p,** and set it before you."
1Sa 9: 7 and there is no **p** to bring to the man of God.
10: 8 then I will come down to you to **p** burnt offerings
10:19 Now therefore **p** yourselves before the LORD
10:27 They despised him and brought him no **p.**
13:15 Saul counted the people who were **p** with him,
13:16 the people who were **p** with them stayed in Geba
18:25 'The king desires no marriage **p** except
25:27 And now let this **p** that your servant has brought
30:25 it continues to the **p** day.
30:26 "Here is a **p** for you from the spoil of the enemies
2Sa 11: 8 and there followed him a **p** from the king.
1Ki 10:25 Every one of them brought a **p,**
15:19 I am sending you a **p** of silver and gold;
18: 1 **p** yourself to Ahab; I will send rain on the earth."
18: 2 So Elijah went to **p** himself to Ahab.
2Ki 5:15 please accept a **p** from your servant."
8: 8 a **p** with you and go to meet the man of God.
8: 9 So Hazael went to meet him, taking a **p** with him,
16: 8 and sent a **p** to the king of Assyria.
20:12 of Babylon sent envoys with letters and a **p**
1Ch 21:23 see, I **p** the oxen for burnt offerings,
29:17 and now I have seen your people, who are **p** here,
2Ch 5:11 the priests who were **p** had sanctified themselves,
9:24 Every one of them brought a **p,**
28:13 the LORD in addition to our **p** sins and guilt.
29:29 the king and all who were **p** with him bowed
30:21 The people of Israel who were **p** at Jerusalem kept
31: 1 all Israel who were **p** went out to the cities
34:32 Then he made all who were **p** in Jerusalem and
35: 7 as passover offerings for all that were **p,**
35:17 The people of Israel who were **p** kept the passover
35:18 by all Judah and Israel who were **p,**
Ezr 8:25 his lords, and all Israel there **p** had offered;
Est 1: 3 the nobles and governors of the provinces were **p,**
1: 5 the king gave for all the people **p** in the citadel
Job 1: 6 the heavenly beings came to **p** themselves before
2: 1 the heavenly beings came to **p** themselves before
2: 1 and Satan also came among them to **p** himself
Ps 46: 1 a very **p** help in trouble.
Isa 39: 1 of Babylon sent envoys with letters and a **p**
45:21 Declare and **p** your case; let them take counsel
Jer 40: 5 the guard gave him an allowance of food and a **p,**
41: 5 and incense to **p** at the temple of the LORD.
42: 9 to whom you sent me to **p** your plea before him:
Eze 43:24 You shall **p** them before the LORD,
Da 3:16 we have no need to **p** a defense to you
9:18 not **p** our supplication before you on the ground
Hos 13:13 the proper time he does not **p** himself at the mouth
Zec 8: 9 from the mouths of the prophets who were **p** when
14:18 family of Egypt do not go up and **p** themselves,
Mal 3: 3 until they **p** offerings to the LORD
Lk 2:22 they brought him up to Jerusalem to **p** him to
12:56 why do you not know how to interpret the **p** time?
13: 1 At that very time there were some **p** who told him
22: 6 to betray him to them when no crowd was **p.**
Ac 5:38 So in the **p** case, I tell you,
21:18 and all the elders were **p.**
24:25 and said, "Go away for the **p;**
25:24 Festus said, "King Agrippa and all here **p** with us,
Ro 3:26 to prove at the **p** time that he himself is righteous
6:13 No longer **p** your members to sin as instruments of
wickedness, but **p** yourselves to God
6:13 and **p** your members to God as instruments
6:16 if you **p** yourselves to anyone as obedient slaves,
6:19 so now **p** your members as slaves to righteousness
8:18 I consider that the sufferings of this **p** time are
8:38 nor things **p,** nor things to come, nor powers,
11: 5 So too at the **p** time there is a remnant,
12: 1 to **p** your bodies as a living sacrifice,
15:25 At **p,** however, I am going to Jerusalem in
1Co 3:22 or Cephas or the world or life or death or the **p** or
4:11 To the **p** hour we are hungry and thirsty,
5: 3 For though absent in body, I am **p** in spirit;
5: 3 and as if **p** I have already pronounced judgment
5: 4 my spirit is **p** with the power of our Lord Jesus,
7:21 make use of your **p** condition now more than ever.
7:31 For the **p** form of this world is passing away.
2Co 8:14 your **p** abundance and their need,
10: 2 when I am **p** I need not show boldness by daring
10:11 we will also do when **p.**
11: 2 to **p** you as a chaste virgin to Christ.
13: 2 as I did when **p** on my second visit,
Gal 1: 4 for our sins to set us free from the **p** evil age,
4:18 and not only when I am **p** with you.
4:20 I wish I were **p** with you now
4:25 in Arabia and corresponds to the **p** Jerusalem,
Eph 5:27 as to **p** the church to himself in splendor,
6:12 against the cosmic powers of this **p** darkness,
Col 1:22 as to **p** you holy and blameless and irreproachable
1:28 so that we may **p** everyone mature in Christ.
1Ti 4: 8 holding promise for both the **p** life and the life
6:17 As for those who in the **p** age are rich,
2Ti 2:15 Do your best to **p** yourself to God as one approved
4:10 with this **p** world, has deserted me and gone
Tit 2:12 in the **p** age to live lives that are self-controlled,
Heb 9: 9 This is a symbol of the **p** time,
2Pe 3: 7 the **p** heavens and earth have been reserved
Tob 11:18 Ahikar and his nephew Nadab were also **p**
Jdt 8:18 "For never in our generation, nor in these **p** days,
AdE 13: 6 of the twelfth month, Adar, of this **p** year,
Wis 4: 2 When it is **p,** people imitate it,
9: 9 she who knows your works and was **p**
11:11 Whether absent or **p,** they were equally distressed,
14:17 the absent one as though **p.**
Sir 14:11 and **p** worthy offerings to the Lord.
Bar 1: 7 the people who were **p** with him in Jerusalem.
2Mc 4:18 at Tyre and the king was **p,**
4:30 because their cities had been given as a **p**
6:26 for the **p** I would avoid the punishment of mortals,
7: 9 you dismiss us from this **p** life,
9:26 to you and to maintain your **p** goodwill,
1Es 1: 7 who were **p** Josiah gave thirty thousand lambs
1:19 of Israel who were **p** at that time kept the passover
3Mc 1:16 to aid in the **p** situation and to avert the violence
1:27 in the **p** trouble and not to overlook this unlawful
3:11 Then the king, boastful of his **p** good fortune,
5:16 and ordered those **p** for the banquet
5:17 and to make the **p** portion of the banquet joyful
5:18 to remain alive through the **p** day.
5:21 all those **p** readily and joyfully
5:31 "If your parents or children were **p,**
2Es 5:45 it might even now be able to support all of them **p**
6: 5 and before the **p** years were reckoned and before
7:16 rather than what is now **p?"**
7:*112* [42] "This **p** world is not the end;
8: 2 so is the course of the **p** world.
8:46 "Things that are **p** are for those who live now,
4Mc 3:19 The **p** occasion now invites us to
12:18 on you he will take vengeance both in this **p** life

PRESENTATION See Index to Footnotes

PRESENTED‡ (40) [PRESENT]

Ge 46:29 He **p** himself to him, fell on his neck,
47: 2 among his brothers he took five men and **p** them
47: 7 and **p** him before Pharaoh,
Lev 2: 8 it is **p** to the priest, he shall take it to the altar.
9: 9 The sons of Aaron **p** the blood to him,
9:15 Next he **p** the people's offering.
9:15 and **p** it as a sin offering like the first one.
9:16 He **p** the burnt offering, and sacrificed it according
9:17 He **p** the grain offering, and, taking a handful of it,
16:10 be **p** alive before the LORD to make atonement
27:11 the animal shall be **p** before the priest.
Nu 7: 3 they **p** them before the tabernacle.
7:10 The leaders also **p** offerings for the dedication of
7:10 the leaders **p** their offering before the altar.
7:12 The one who **p** his offering
7:18 the leader of Issachar, **p** an offering;
7:19 he **p** for his offering one silver plate weighing one
8:15 once you have cleansed them and **p** them as
8:21 then Aaron **p** them as an elevation offering before
16:38 for they **p** them before the LORD
16:39 the priest took the bronze censers that had been **p**
Dt 31:14 So Moses and Joshua went and **p** themselves in
Jos 24: 1 and they **p** themselves before God.
Jdg 3:17 Then he **p** the tribute to King Eglon of Moab.
6:19 brought them to him under the oak and **p** them.
20: 2 **p** themselves in the assembly of the people
1Sa 1: 9 Hannah rose and **p** herself before the LORD.
6:15 and **p** sacrifices on that day to the LORD.
1Ch 21:26 and **p** burnt offerings and offerings of well-being.
2Ch 11:13 the Levites who were in all Israel **p** themselves

Eze 20:28 there they offered their sacrifices and **p**
Da 7:13 he came to the Ancient One and was **p** before him.
Ac 1: 3 After his suffering he **p** himself alive to them
23:33 they **p** Paul also before him.
Ro 6:19 as you once **p** your members as slaves to impurity
Jdt 9: 6 the things you decided on **p** themselves and said,
2Mc 1:21 When the materials for the sacrifices were **p**,
4:24 But he, when **p** to the king,
4:44 three men sent by the senate **p** the case
3Mc 5:10 **p** himself at the courtyard early in the morning

PRESENTING (12) [PRESENT]

Lev 23:37 for **p** to the LORD offerings by fire—
Nu 9: 7 from **p** the LORD's offering at its appointed time
9:13 not **p** the LORD's offering at its appointed time;
15:13 in **p** an offering by fire,
Jdg 3:18 When Ehud had finished **p** the tribute,
2Ki 10:25 As soon as he had finished **p** the burnt offering,
Jer 38:26 'I was **p** my plea to the king not to send me back
Da 9:20 and **p** my supplication before the LORD my God
Zec 6: 5 **p** themselves before the LORD of all the earth.
Mal 1: 8 Try **p** that to your governor;
Ac 17:19 we know what this new teaching is that you are **p**?
2Mc 14: 4 **p** to him a crown of gold and a palm,

PRESENTS (13) [PRESENT]

Lev 2: 1 When anyone **p** a grain offering to the LORD,
22:18 or of the aliens residing in Israel **p** an offering,
Nu 15: 4 then whoever **p** such an offering to the LORD
2Ch 17:11 Some of the Philistines brought Jehoshaphat **p**,
Est 9:22 days for sending gifts of food to one another and **p**
Isa 16:12 When Moab **p** himself, when he wearies himself
66: 3 whoever **p** a grain offering,
Rev 11:10 over them and celebrate and exchange **p**,
AdE 9:19 and send **p** of food to one another,
9:19 also sending **p** to one another.
9:22 a time for feasting and gladness and for sending **p**
Sir 23:22 a woman who leaves her husband and **p** him with
2Mc 3: 2 and glorified the temple with the finest **p**,

PRESERVE (22) [PRESERVED, PRESERVES, PRESERVING]

Ge 19:32 so that we may **p** offspring through our father."
19:34 so that we may **p** offspring through our father."
45: 5 for God sent me before you to **p** life.
45: 7 God sent me before you to **p** for you a remnant
50:20 in order to **p** a numerous people,
Ps 25:21 May integrity and uprightness **p** me,
32: 7 for me; you **p** me from trouble;
64: 1 **p** my life from the dread enemy.
79:11 according to your great power **p** those doomed
86: 2 **P** my life, for I am devoted to you;
119:149 O LORD, in your justice **p** my life.
119:159 **p** my life according to your steadfast love.
138: 7 you **p** me against the wrath of my enemies;
143:11 For your name's sake, O LORD, **p** my life.
Pr 6:24 to **p** you from the wife of another,
13: 3 Those who guard their mouths **p** their lives;
14: 3 but the lips of the wise **p** them.
16:17 those who guard their way **p** their lives.
20:28 Loyalty and faithfulness **p** the king,
LtJ 6:28 Likewise their wives **p** some of the meat with salt,
2Mc 1:26 of all your people Israel and **p** your portion
4Mc 15:27 She did not approve the deliverance that would **p**

PRESERVED (12) [PRESERVE]

Ge 32:30 and yet my life is **p**."
1Sa 30:23 he has **p** us and handed over to us the raiding party
Job 10:12 and your care has **p** my spirit.
Mt 9:17 into fresh wineskins, and so both are **p**."
Wis 10: 5 recognized the righteous man and **p** him blameless
11:25 not called forth by you have been **p**?
Sir 42:23 each creature is **p** to meet a particular need.
1Mc 14:29 that their sanctuary and the law might be **p**;
2Mc 8:27 who had **p** them for that day and allotted it to them
2Es 7:67 that we shall be **p** alive but cruelly tormented?
8: 8 what you have created is **p** amid fire and water,
4Mc 17:22 divine Providence **p** Israel

PRESERVES (5) [PRESERVE]

Ps 31:23 The LORD **p** the faithful,
Sir 32:24 The one who keeps the law **p** himself,
39: 2 he **p** the sayings of the famous and penetrates
4Mc 2:14 but one **p** the property of enemies from marauders
15: 3 the religion that **p** them for eternal life according

PRESERVING (3) [PRESERVE]

Pr 2: 8 of justice and **p** the way of his faithful ones.
Sir 38:14 for the sake of **p** life.
4Mc 15: 2 and that of **p** her seven sons for a time,

PRESIDE See Index to Footnotes

PRESIDENTS (5)

Da 6: 2 and over them three **p**, including Daniel;
6: 3 above all the other **p** and satraps because
6: 4 So the **p** and the satraps tried to find grounds
6: 6 the **p** and satraps conspired and came to the king
6: 7 All the **p** of the kingdom,

PRESS (30) [HARD-PRESSED, PRESSED, PRESSES, PRESSING, PRESSURE]

Nu 18:27 the threshing floor and the fullness of the wine **p**.
18:30 and as produce of the wine **p**.
Dt 15:14 your threshing floor, and your wine **p**,
16:13 from your threshing floor and your wine **p**.
Jdg 6:11 in the wine **p**, to hide it from
7:25 and Zeeb they killed at the wine **p** of Zeeb,
Ru 1:16 "Do not **p** me to leave you or to turn back
2Sa 11:25 **p** your attack on the city, and overthrow it.'
2Ki 6:27 From the threshing floor or from the wine **p**?"
Job 24:11 between their terraces they **p** out oil;
41: 1 or **p** down its tongue with a cord?
Isa 63: 2 your garments like theirs who tread the wine **p**?"
63: 3 "I have trodden the wine **p** alone,
La 1:15 as in a wine **p** the virgin daughter Judah.
Eze 4: 3 be in a state of siege, and **p** the siege against it.
Hos 6: 3 Let us know, let us **p** on to know the LORD;
Joel 3:13 Go in, tread, for the wine **p** is full.
Am 2:13 So, I will **p** you down in your place,
Mt 21:33 dug a wine **p** in it, and built a watchtower.
Mk 12: 1 dug a pit for the wine **p**, and built a watchtower;
Lk 8:45 the crowds surround you and **p** in on you."
Php 3:12 but I **p** on to make it my own,
3:14 I **p** on toward the goal for the prize of
Rev 14:19 and he threw it into the great wine **p** of the wrath
14:20 And the wine **p** was trodden outside the city,
14:20 and blood flowed from the wine **p**,
19:15 he will tread the wine **p** of the fury of the wrath
Sir 33:17 and like a grape-picker I filled my wine **p**.
1Mc 6:57 and the affairs of the kingdom **p** urgently on us.
2Es 7:*98* for they **p** forward to see the face of him

PRESSED (26) [PRESS]

Ge 19: 9 Then they **p** hard against the man Lot,
40:11 I took the grapes and **p** them into Pharaoh's cup,
49:23 they shot at him and **p** him hard.
Jdg 1:34 Amorites **p** the Danites back into the hill country;
1Sa 13: 6 in distress (for the troops were hard **p**),
31: 3 The battle **p** hard upon Saul;
2Sa 13:25 He **p** him, but he would not go
13:27 But Absalom **p** him until he let Amnon and all
1Ch 10: 3 The battle **p** hard on Saul;
Zec 5: 8 and **p** the leaden weight down on its mouth.
Mk 3:10 that all who had diseases **p** upon him to touch him.
5:24 And a large crowd followed him and **p** in on him.
Lk 6:38 A good measure, **p** down, shaken together,
8:42 As he went, the crowds **p** in on him.
Php 1:23 I am hard **p** between the two:
Sir 46: 5 when enemies **p** him on every side,
46:16 when his enemies **p** him on every side,
Sus 1:14 and when each **p** the other for the reason,
1Mc 2:30 because troubles **p** heavily upon them.
9:68 They **p** him very hard, for his plan
10:50 He **p** the battle strongly until the sun set,
15:14 he **p** the town hard from land and sea,
2Mc 8:20 yet when the Macedonians were hard **p**,
11: 5 about five stadia from Jerusalem, and **p** it hard.
12:23 Judas **p** the pursuit with the utmost vigor,
1Es 5:72 the peoples of the land **p** hard upon those in Judea,

PRESSES (7) [PRESS]

Ex 22:29 of your harvest and from the outflow of your **p**.
Ne 13:15 in Judah people treading wine **p** on the sabbath,
Job 24:11 they tread the wine **p**, but suffer thirst.
Isa 16:10 no treader treads out wine in the **p**;
Jer 48:33 I have stopped the wine from the wine **p**;
Am 2:13 just as a cart **p** down when it is full of sheaves.
Zec 14:10 from the Tower of Hananel to the king's wine **p**.

PRESSING (8) [PRESS]

Pr 30:33 For as **p** milk produces curds, and **p** the nose
produces blood, so **p** anger produces strife.
Hab 1: 9 They all come for violence, with faces **p** forward;
Mk 5:31 "You see the crowd **p** in on you;
Lk 5: 1 crowd was **p** in on him to hear the word of God,
Bel 1:30 The king saw that they were **p** him hard,
1Es 5:58 **p** forward the work on the house of God with

PRESSURE (3) [PRESS]

Job 33: 7 my **p** will not be heavy on you.
2Co 8:13 that there should be relief for others and **p** on you,
11:28 I am under daily **p** because of my anxiety for all

PRESTIGE (2)

2Mc 4:15 the highest value upon Greek forms of **p**.
3Mc 7:21 also possessed greater **p** among their enemies,

PRESUME (4) [PRESUMED, PRESUMES, PRESUMPTION, PRESUMPTUOUSLY]

Mt 3: 9 Do not **p** to say to yourselves,
Lk 7: 7 therefore I did not **p** to come to you.
Heb 5: 4 And one does not **p** to take this honor,
Tob 6:18 I **p** that you will have children by her,

PRESUMED (2) [PRESUME]

Nu 14:44 they **p** to go up to the heights of the hill country,
Est 7: 5 and where is he, who has **p** to do this?"

PRESUMES (2) [PRESUME]

Dt 17:12 for anyone who **p** to disobey the priest appointed
18:20 or who **p** to speak in my name a word that I have

PRESUMPTION (2) [PRESUME]

1Sa 17:28 I know your **p** and the evil of your heart;
AdE 13: 2 of the whole world (not elated with **p** of authority

PRESUMPTUOUSLY (5) [PRESUME]

Dt 1:43 against the command of the LORD and **p** went up
17:13 and will not act **p** again.
18:22 The prophet has spoken it **p**;
Ne 9:16 and our ancestors acted **p** and stiffened their necks
9:29 Yet they acted **p** and did

PRETEND (6) [PRETENDED, PRETENDING, PRETENDS, PRETENSE]

2Sa 13: 5 "Lie down on your bed, and **p** to be ill;
14: 2 He said to her, "**P** to be a mourner;
1Ki 14: 6 why do you **p** to be another?
Pr 13: 7 Some **p** to be rich, yet have nothing;
13: 7 others **p** to be poor, yet have great wealth.
2Mc 6:21 and to **p** that he was eating the flesh of

PRETENDED (5) [PRETEND]

1Sa 21:13 he **p** to be mad when in their presence.
2Sa 13: 6 So Amnon lay down, and **p** to be ill;
1Ki 14: 5 When she came, she **p** to be another woman.
Lk 20:20 So they watched him and sent spies who **p** to
2Mc 5:25 he **p** to be peaceably disposed and waited until

PRETENDING (2) [PRETEND]

Sir 12:17 **p** to help, he will trip you up.
4Mc 6:15 save yourself by **p** to eat pork."

PRETENDS (2) [PRETEND]

Sir 19:27 He hides his face and **p** not to hear,
20: 8 and whoever **p** to authority is hated.

PRETENSE (4) [PRETEND]

Jos 8:15 and all Israel made a **p** of being beaten
Jer 3:10 but only in **p**, says the LORD.
2Mc 6:24 "Such **p** is not worthy of our time of life," he said,
6:25 and through my **p**, for the sake of living

PRETEXT (7)

Jdg 14: 4 he was seeking a **p** to act against the Philistines.
Ac 23:15 on the **p** that you want to make
27:30 on the **p** of putting out anchors from the bow,
1Th 2: 5 we never came with words of flattery or with a **p**
1Pe 2:16 yet do not use your freedom as a **p** for evil.
2Mc 1:14 On the **p** of intending to marry her,
3Mc 3: 2 a **p** being given by a report

PRETTIER (1) [PRETTY]

Jdg 15: 2 Is not her younger sister **p** than she?

PRETTY (1) [PRETTIER]

Jdt 12:13 "Let this **p** girl not hesitate to come to my lord to

PREVAIL‡ (31) [PREVAILED, PREVAILING, PREVAILS]

Ge 32:25 When the man saw that he did not **p** against Jacob,
1Sa 2: 9 for not by might does one **p**.
17: 9 but if I **p** against him and kill him,
2Ch 14:11 let no mortal **p** against you."
Est 6:13 you will not **p** against him,
Job 14:20 You **p** forever against them, and they pass away;
15:24 they **p** against them, like a king prepared
Ps 9:19 O LORD! Do not let mortals **p**;
12: 4 "With our tongues we will **p**;
Pr 28:12 but when the wicked **p**, people go into hiding.
28:28 When the wicked **p**, people go into hiding;
30: 1 I am weary, O God. How can I **p**?
Ecc 4:12 And though one might **p** against another,
Isa 16:12 to his sanctuary to pray, he will not **p**.
Jer 1:19 but they shall not **p** against you, for I am with you,
5:22 though the waves toss, they cannot **p**,
15:20 but they shall not **p** over you,
20:10 and we can **p** against him,
20:11 my persecutors will stumble, and they will not **p**.
Da 11: 7 and he shall take action against them and **p**.
11:12 of thousands, but he shall not **p**.
Mt 16:18 and the gates of Hades will not **p** against it.
Ro 3: 4 "So that you may be justified in your words, and **p**
Jdt 11:10 nor can the sword **p** against them,
Wis 7:30 but against wisdom evil does not **p**.
Sir 49: 3 in lawless times he made godliness **p**.
2Mc 3: 5 Since he could not **p** over Onias,
2Es 7:*60* it is they who have made my glory to **p** now,
15:39 from the east shall **p** over the cloud that was raised
16:76 or your iniquities **p** over you.
4Mc 2:14 through the law, can **p** even over enmity.

PREVAILED (25) [PREVAIL]

Ge 30: 8 I have wrestled with my sister, and have **p**";
32:28 with God and with humans, and have **p**."
41:53 of plenty that **p** in the land of Egypt came to
Ex 17:11 Whenever Moses held up his hand, Israel **p**;
17:11 and whenever he lowered his hand, Amalek **p**.
Jdg 3:10 and his hand **p** over Cushan-rishathaim.
6: 2 The hand of Midian **p** over Israel;
1Sa 17:50 So David **p** over the Philistine with a sling and
2Sa 24: 4 But the king's word **p** against Joab and

1Ch 21: 4 But the king's word **p** against Joab.
2Ch 13:18 and the people of Judah **p**,
27: 5 He fought with the king of the Ammonites and **p**
Ps 13: 4 and my enemy will say, "I have **p**";
129: 2 yet they have not **p** against me.
Jer 20: 7 you have overpowered me, and you have **p**.
La 1:16 my children are desolate, for the enemy has **p**.
Hos 12: 4 He strove with the angel and **p**,
Ob 1: 7 your confederates have **p** against you;
Lk 23:23 be crucified; and their voices **p**.
Ac 16:15 And she **p** upon us.
19:20 So the word of the Lord grew mightily and **p**.
1Es 9: 6 shivering because of the bad weather that **p**.
4Mc 6:32 For if the emotions had **p** over reason,
8: 1 have **p** over the most painful instruments
13: 3 they **p** over their emotions.

PREVAILING (2) [PREVAIL]

2Ch 1:16 from Kue at the **p** price.
Da 7:21 this horn made war with the holy ones and was **p**

PREVAILS (3) [PREVAIL]

Hab 1: 4 So the law becomes slack and justice never **p**.
1Es 4:38 and lives and **p** forever and ever.
4Mc 2:10 For the law **p** even over affection for parents,

PREVENT (12) [PREVENTED, PREVENTING, PREVENTS]

1Ki 15:17 to **p** anyone from going out or coming in
2Ch 16: 1 to **p** anyone from going out or coming into
Ne 5: 9 to **p** the taunts of the nations our enemies?
13:19 to **p** any burden from being brought in on
Lk 4:42 they wanted to **p** him from leaving them.
Ac 8:36 What is to **p** me from being baptized?"
24:23 but to let him have some liberty and not to **p** any
Gal 5:17 to **p** you from doing what you want.
1Mc 6:27 unless you quickly **p** them,
2Mc 14:22 in readiness at key places to **p** sudden treachery on
1Es 2:28 now issued orders to **p** these people from building
4Mc 4: 7 and did all that they could to **p** it.

PREVENTED‡ (11) [PREVENT]

Ge 16: 2 that the LORD has **p** me from bearing children;
2Ch 11:14 and his sons had **p** them from serving as priests of
Jer 36: 5 "I am **p** from entering the house of the LORD;
Mt 3:14 John would have **p** him, saying,
Ro 1:13 to come to you (but thus far have been **p**),
Gal 5: 7 who **p** you from obeying the truth?
Heb 7:23 they were **p** by death from continuing in office;
Sir 20:21 One may be **p** from sinning by poverty;
1Mc 13:49 Those who were in the citadel at Jerusalem were **p**
1Es 5:73 by plots and demagoguery and uprisings they **p**
6: 6 they were not **p** from building until word could

PREVENTING (1) [PREVENT]

1Mc 7:24 on those who had deserted and **p** those in the city

PREVENTS (2) [PREVENT]

3Jn 1:10 even **p** those who want to do so and expels them
Sir 31: 2 Wakeful anxiety **p** slumber,

PREVIOUS (2) [PREVIOUSLY]

2Es 5:31 to me on a **p** night was sent to me.
6:12 of which you showed me a part on a **p** night."

PREVIOUSLY (24) [PREVIOUS]

Ex 5: 8 the same quantity of bricks as they have made **p**;
Jdg 20:32 "They are being routed before us, as **p**."
1Sa 14:21 the Hebrews who **p** had been with the Philistines
1Ch 9:18 stationed **p** in the king's gate on the east side.
Ne 13: 5 for Tobiah a large room where they had **p** put
Da 6:10 just as he had done **p**.
Ac 8: 9 a certain man named Simon had **p** practiced magic
21:29 For they had **p** seen Trophimus the Ephesian
Ro 3:25 he had passed over the sins **p** committed;
2Co 12:21 that I may have to mourn over many who **p** sinned
13: 2 I warned those who sinned **p** and all the others,
Gal 3:17 does not annul a covenant **p** ratified by God,
Wis 18: 2 though **p** wronged, were doing them no injury;
1Mc 1: 1 (He had **p** become king of Greece.)
9:72 the captives whom he had taken **p** from the land
2Mc 4: 1 The **p** mentioned Simon, who had informed about
4:23 the brother of the **p** mentioned Simon,
3Mc 1: 2 the Ptolemaic arms that had been **p** issued to him,
2:25 abetted by the **p** mentioned drinking companions
4:17 But after the **p** mentioned interval of time
5:28 a forgetfulness of the things he had **p** devised.
6:34 Those who had **p** believed that the Jews would
2Es 7:99 and the **p** mentioned are the ways of torment
4Mc 17:22 that **p** had been mistreated.

PREY‡ (46) [PREYS]

Ge 15:11 And when birds of **p** came down on the carcasses,
34:29 they captured and made their **p**.
49: 9 from the **p**, my son, you have gone up.
49:27 in the morning devouring the **p**,
Nu 23:24 down until it has eaten the **p** and drunk the blood
Dt 31:17 from them; they will become easy **p**,
2Ki 21:14 a **p** and a spoil to all their enemies,
Job 4:11 The strong lion perishes for lack of **p**,
9:26 like an eagle swooping on the **p**.
28: 7 "That path no bird of **p** knows,
29:17 and made them drop their **p** from their teeth.
38:39 "Can you hunt the **p** for the lion,
38:41 Who provides for the raven its **p**,
39:29 From there it spies the **p**;
Ps 57: 4 down among lions that greedily devour human **p**;
63:10 they shall be **p** for jackals.
104:21 The young lions roar for their **p**,
124: 6 who has not given us as **p** to their teeth.
Isa 5:29 they growl and seize their **p**, they carry it off,
10: 2 and that you may make the orphans your **p**!
18: 6 the birds of **p** of the mountains and to the animals
18: 6 And the birds of **p** will summer on them,
31: 4 As a lion or a young lion growls over its **p**, and—
33:23 Then **p** and spoil in abundance will be divided;
42:22 they have become a **p** with no one to rescue,
46:11 calling a bird of **p** from the east,
49:24 Can the **p** be taken from the mighty,
49:25 and the **p** of the tyrant be rescued;
Jer 12: 9 Are the birds of **p** all around her?
30:16 and all who **p** on you I will make a **p**.
Eze 13:21 they shall no longer be **p** in your hands;
19: 3 and he learned to catch **p**; he devoured humans.
19: 6 and he learned to catch **p**; he devoured people.
22:25 within it are like a roaring lion tearing the **p**;
22:27 Its officials within it are like wolves tearing the **p**,
34: 8 because my sheep have become a **p**,
39: 4 to birds of **p** of every kind and to the wild animals
Am 3: 4 Does a lion roar in the forest, when it has no **p**?
Na 2:12 for his whelps and strangled **p** for his lionesses;
2:12 he has filled his caves with **p** and his dens
2:13 I will cut off your **p** from the earth,
Ac 11: 6 beasts of **p**, reptiles, and birds of the air.
Sir 13:19 Wild asses in the wilderness are the **p** of lions;
27:10 A lion lies in wait for **p**; so does sin for evildoers.
1Mc 3: 4 like a lion's cub roaring for **p**.

PREYS (1) [PREY]

2Co 11:20 or **p** upon you, or takes advantage of you,

PRICE‡ (38) [BRIDE-PRICE, PRICELESS]

Ge 23: 9 the full **p** let him give it to me in your presence as
23:13 I will give the **p** of the field;
Ex 21:35 they shall sell the live ox and divide the **p** of it;
Lev 25:16 If the years are more, you shall increase the **p**,
25:16 you shall diminish the **p**;
25:50 the **p** of the sale shall be applied to the number
25:51 in proportion to the purchase **p**;
27:18 the **p** for it according to the years that remain until
Nu 3:46 As the **p** of redemption of the two hundred
18:16 Their redemption **p**, reckoned from one month
2Sa 3:14 the **p** of one hundred foreskins of the Philistines."
24:24 "No, but I will buy them from you for a **p**;
1Ki 10:28 the king's traders received them from Kue at a **p**.
1Ch 21:22 give it to me at its full **p**—
21:24 I will buy them for the full **p**.
2Ch 1:16 from Kue at the prevailing **p**.
Job 28:15 and silver cannot be weighed out as its **p**.
28:18 the **p** of wisdom is above pearls.
Ps 44:12 demanding no high **p** for them.
49: 7 there is no **p** one can give to God for it.
Pr 17:16 Why should fools have a **p** in hand
27:26 and the goats the **p** of a field;
Isa 45:13 not for **p** or reward, says the LORD of hosts.
55: 1 buy wine and milk without money and without **p**.
Jer 15:13 without **p**, for all your sins,
17: 3 and all your treasures I will give for spoil as the **p**
Da 11:39 and shall distribute the land for a **p**.
Mic 3:11 its priests teach for a **p**, its prophets give oracles
Zec 11:13 this lordly **p** at which I was valued by them.
Mt 27: 9 the **p** of the one on whom a **p** had been set, on whom some of the people of Israel had set a **p**,
Ac 5: 8 the land for such and such a **p**."
5: 8 And she said, "Yes, that was the **p**."
1Co 6:20 For you were bought with a **p**;
7:23 You were bought with a **p**;
Sir 6:15 Faithful friends are beyond **p**;
3Mc 2:31 with an obvious abhorrence of the **p** to be exacted

PRICELESS (2) [PRICE]

Wis 7: 9 Neither did I liken to her any **p** gem,
3Mc 3:23 they not only spurn the **p** citizenship,

PRICKED (1) [PRICKING, PRICKS]

Ps 73:21 my soul was embittered, when I was **p** in heart,

PRICKING (1) [PRICKED]

Eze 28:24 The house of Israel shall no longer find a **p** brier

PRICKS (2) [PRICKED]

Sir 22:19 One who **p** the eye brings tears,
22:19 and one who **p** the heart makes clear its feelings.

PRICKS (KJV) See also BARBS, GOADS

PRIDE‡ (74) [PRIDING, PROUD, PROUDLY]

2Ch 32:26 Hezekiah humbled himself for the **p** of his heart,
Job 22:29 When others are humiliated, you say it is **p**;
33:17 from their deeds, and keep them from **p**,
35:12 because of the **p** of evildoers.
Ps 10: 4 In the **p** of their countenance the wicked say,
20: 7 Some take **p** in chariots, and some in horses,
20: 7 but our **p** is in the name of the LORD our God.
31:18 that speak insolently against the righteous with **p**
47: 4 the **p** of Jacob whom he loves.
59:12 let them be trapped in their **p**.
73: 6 Therefore **p** is their necklace;
Pr 8:13 **P** and arrogance and the way of evil
11: 2 When **p** comes, then comes disgrace;
16:18 **P** goes before destruction,
21:24 named "Scoffer," acts with arrogant **p**.
29:23 A person's **p** will bring humiliation,
Isa 2:11 and the **p** of everyone shall be humbled;
2:17 and the **p** of everyone shall be brought low;
4: 2 and the fruit of the land shall be the **p** and glory of
9: 9 but in **p** and arrogance of heart they said:
10:12 of the king of Assyria and his haughty **p**.
13:11 I will put an end to the **p** of the arrogant,
13:19 the splendor and **p** of the Chaldeans,
16: 6 We have heard of the **p** of Moab—how proud he is!—of his arrogance, his **p**, and his insolence;
23: 9 to defile the **p** of all glory,
25:11 their **p** will be laid low despite the struggle
Jer 13: 9 the **p** of Judah and the great **p** of Jerusalem.
13:17 my soul will weep in secret for your **p**;
48:29 We have heard of the **p** of Moab—he is very proud—of his loftiness, his **p**, and his arrogance,
49:16 and the **p** of your heart have deceived you,
51:41 Sheshach is taken, the **p** of the whole earth seized!
La 2: 4 in whom we took **p** in the tent of daughter Zion;
Eze 7:10 The rod has blossomed, **p** has budded.
7:20 their beautiful ornament, in which they took **p**,
16:49 she and her daughters had **p**, excess of food,
16:56 a byword in your mouth in the day of your **p**,
24:21 I will profane my sanctuary, the **p** of your power,
32:12 They shall bring to ruin the **p** of Egypt,
Da 4:37 and he is able to bring low those who walk in **p**.
Hos 5: 5 Israel's **p** testifies against him;
7:10 Israel's **p** testifies against him;
Am 6: 8 I abhor the **p** of Jacob and hate his strongholds;
8: 7 The LORD has sworn by the **p** of Jacob:
Zep 2:10 This shall be their lot in return for their **p**,
Zec 9: 6 and I will make an end of the **p** of Philistia.
10:11 The **p** of Assyria shall be laid low,
Mk 7:22 deceit, licentiousness, envy, slander, **p**, folly.
2Co 7: 4 I often boast about you; I have great **p** in you;
Gal 6: 4 will become a cause for **p**.
Heb 3: 6 the confidence and the **p** that belong to hope.
1Jn 2:16 the desire of the eyes, the **p** in riches—
Tob 4:13 For in **p** there is ruin and great confusion.
Jdt 9: 9 Look at their **p**, and send your wrath
15: 9 you are the great **p** of our nation!
AdE 13:12 that it was not in insolence or **p** or for any love
13:14 and I will not do these things in **p**.
Sir 10:12 The beginning of human **p** is to forsake the Lord;
10:13 For the beginning of **p** is sin,
10:18 **P** was not created for human beings,
26:26 *but if she dishonors him in her **p** she will be known*
43: 1 **p** of the higher realms is the clear vault of the sky,
44: 7 and were the **p** of their times.
50: 1 and the **p** of his people was the high priest,
Bar 4:34 I will take away her **p** in her great population,
1Mc 8:14 on a crown or worn purple as a mark of **p**,
2Mc 1:28 Punish those who oppress and are insolent with **p**.
2Es 1:38 with **p** and see the people coming from the east;
8:50 because they have walked in great **p**.
11:43 and your **p** to the Mighty One.
15:18 Because of their **p** the cities shall be in confusion,
4Mc 8:24 against compulsion or take hollow **p** in being put

PRIDING (1) [PRIDE]

Jdt 9: 7 **p** themselves in their horses and riders,

PRIEST (576) [HIGH-PRIESTLY, ORACLE-PRIESTS, PRIEST'S, PRIESTHOOD, PRIESTLY, PRIESTS, PRIESTS']

A. HIGH PRIEST (126)
B. ELEAZAR THE PRIEST (19)
C. AARON THE PRIEST (17)
D. PRIEST JEHOIADA (16)
E. PRIEST ZADOK (11)
F. CHIEF PRIEST (10)
G. PRIEST HILKIAH (10)
H. EZRA THE PRIEST (8)

Ge 14:18 he was **p** of God Most High.
41:45 gave him Asenath daughter of Potiphera, **p** of On,
41:50 whom Asenath daughter of Potiphera, **p** of On,
46:20 whom Asenath daughter of Potiphera, **p** of On,
Ex 2:16 The **p** of Midian had seven daughters.
3: 1 of his father-in-law Jethro, the **p** of Midian;
18: 1 Jethro, the **p** of Midian, Moses' father-in-law,
29:30 The son who is **p** in his place
31:10 for the **p** Aaron and the vestments of his sons,
35:19 the holy vestments for the **p** Aaron,
38:21 under the direction of Ithamar son of the **p** Aaron.
39:41 the sacred vestments for the **p** Aaron,
40:13 so that he may serve me as **p**.
Lev 1: 7 The sons of the **p** Aaron shall put fire on the altar
1: 9 the **p** shall turn the whole into smoke on the altar
1:12 and the **p** shall arrange them on the wood that is
1:13 the **p** shall offer the whole and turn it into smoke
1:15 **p** shall bring it to the altar and wring off its head,
1:17 Then the **p** shall turn it into smoke on the altar,
2: 2 the **p** shall turn this token portion into smoke on
2: 8 it is presented to the **p**, he shall take it to the altar.
2: 9 The **p** shall remove from the grain offering its
2:16 the **p** shall turn a token portion of it into smoke—

Lev 3:11 Then the **p** shall turn these into smoke on the altar
3:16 Then the **p** shall turn these into smoke on the altar
4: 3 If it is the anointed **p** who sins,
4: 5 The anointed **p** shall take some of the blood of
4: 6 The **p** shall dip his finger in the blood
4: 7 The **p** shall put some of the blood on the horns of
4:10 The **p** shall turn them into smoke upon the altar
4:16 The anointed **p** shall bring some of the blood of
4:17 and the **p** shall dip his finger in the blood
4:20 The **p** shall make atonement for them,
4:25 The **p** shall take some of the blood of
4:26 Thus the **p** shall make atonement on his behalf
4:30 The **p** shall take some of its blood with his finger
4:31 and the **p** shall turn it into smoke on the altar for
4:31 Thus the **p** shall make atonement on your behalf,
4:34 The **p** shall take some of the blood of
4:35 and the **p** shall turn it into smoke on the altar,
4:35 Thus the **p** shall make atonement on your behalf
5: 6 and the **p** shall make atonement on your behalf
5: 8 You shall bring them to the **p,**
5:10 Thus the **p** shall make atonement on your behalf
5:12 You shall bring it to the **p,**
5:12 and the **p** shall scoop up a handful of it
5:13 Thus the **p** shall make atonement on your behalf
5:13 Like the grain offering, the rest shall be for the **p.**
5:16 and shall add one-fifth to it and give it to the **p.**
5:16 The **p** shall make atonement on your behalf with
5:18 to the **p** a ram without blemish from the flock,
5:18 and the **p** shall make atonement on your behalf for
6: 6 And you shall bring to the **p,**
6: 7 The **p** shall make atonement on your behalf before
6:10 The **p** shall put on his linen vestments after putting
6:12 Every morning the **p** shall add wood to it,
6:22 the **p,** anointed from among Aaron's descendants
6:23 Every grain offering of a **p** shall
6:26 The **p** who offers it as a sin offering shall eat of it;
7: 5 The **p** shall turn them into smoke on the altar as
7: 7 the **p** who makes atonement with it shall have it.
7: 8 **p** who offers anyone's burnt offering shall keep
7: 9 shall belong to the **p** who offers it.
7:14 it shall belong to the **p** who dashes the blood of
7:31 The **p** shall turn the fat into smoke on the altar,
7:32 of well-being you shall give to the **p** as
7:34 have given them to Aaron the **p** and to his sons, C
12: 6 the **p** at the entrance of the tent of meeting a lamb
12: 8 and the **p** shall make atonement on her behalf,
13: 2 to Aaron the **p** or to one of his sons the priests. C
13: 3 The **p** shall examine the disease on the skin
13: 3 **p** has examined him he shall pronounce him
13: 4 **p** shall confine the diseased person for seven days.
13: 5 The **p** shall examine him on the seventh day,
13: 5 then the **p** shall confine him seven days more.
13: 6 The **p** shall examine him again on the seventh day,
13: 6 the **p** shall pronounce him clean;
13: 7 in the skin after he has shown himself to the **p**
13: 7 he shall appear again before the **p.**
13: 8 The **p** shall make an examination,
13: 8 the **p** shall pronounce him unclean;
13: 9 he shall be brought to the **p.**
13:10 The **p** shall make an examination,
13:11 The **p** shall pronounce him unclean;
13:12 so far as the **p** can see,
13:13 then the **p** shall make an examination,
13:15 the **p** shall examine the raw flesh
13:16 he shall come to the **p;**
13:17 the **p** shall examine him,
13:17 the **p** shall pronounce the diseased person clean.
13:19 it shall be shown to the **p.**
13:20 The **p** shall make an examination,
13:20 the **p** shall pronounce him unclean;
13:21 if the **p** examines it and the hair on it is not white,
13:21 the **p** shall confine him seven days.
13:22 the **p** shall pronounce him unclean; it is diseased.
13:23 the **p** shall pronounce him clean.
13:25 the **p** shall examine it.
13:25 and the **p** shall pronounce him unclean.
13:26 **p** examines it and the hair in the spot is not white,
13:26 the **p** shall confine him seven days,
13:27 The **p** shall examine him the seventh day;
13:27 the **p** shall pronounce him unclean.
13:28 and the **p** shall pronounce him clean;
13:30 the **p** shall examine the disease.
13:30 the **p** shall pronounce him unclean;
13:31 If the **p** examines the itching disease,
13:31 the **p** shall confine the person with
13:32 On the seventh day the **p** shall examine the itch;
13:33 The **p** shall confine the person with the itch
13:34 On the seventh day the **p** shall examine the itch;
13:34 the **p** shall pronounce him clean.
13:36 the **p** shall examine him.
13:36 the **p** need not seek for the yellow hair;
13:37 and the **p** shall pronounce him clean.
13:39 the **p** shall make an examination, and if the spots
13:43 The **p** shall examine him;
13:44 The **p** shall pronounce him unclean;
13:49 it is a leprous disease and shall be shown to the **p.**
13:50 The **p** shall examine the disease,
13:53 If the **p** makes an examination,
13:54 the **p** shall command them to wash the article
13:55 The **p** shall examine the diseased article
13:56 If the **p** makes an examination,
14: 2 He shall be brought to the **p;**
14: 3 the **p** shall go out of the camp,
14: 3 and the **p** shall make an examination.
14: 4 the **p** shall command that two living clean birds
14: 5 The **p** shall command that one of the birds
14:11 **p** who cleanses shall set the person to be cleansed,

Lev 14:12 The **p** shall take one of the lambs,
14:13 like the sin offering, belongs to the **p:**
14:14 The **p** shall take some of the blood of
14:15 The **p** shall take some of the log of oil and pour it
14:17 that remains in his hand the **p** shall put on the lobe
14:18 the **p** shall make atonement on his behalf before
14:19 the **p** shall offer the sin offering,
14:20 and the **p** shall offer the burnt offering and
14:20 Thus the **p** shall make atonement on his behalf
14:23 to the **p,** to the entrance of the tent of meeting,
14:24 and the **p** shall take the lamb of the guilt offering
14:24 and the **p** shall raise them as an elevation offering
14:25 The **p** shall slaughter the lamb of the guilt offering
14:26 The **p** shall pour some of the oil into the palm
14:28 The **p** shall put some of the oil that is in his hand
14:31 and the **p** shall make atonement before the LORD
14:35 the owner of the house shall come and tell the **p,**
14:36 The **p** shall command that they empty the house
14:36 the **p** goes to examine the disease, or all that is in
14:36 afterward the **p** shall go in to inspect the house.
14:38 the **p** shall go outside to the door of the house
14:39 The **p** shall come again on the seventh day
14:40 the **p** shall command that the stones in which
14:44 the **p** shall go and make inspection;
14:48 If the **p** comes and makes an inspection,
14:48 the **p** shall pronounce the house clean;
15:14 of the tent of meeting and give them to the **p.**
15:15 The **p** shall offer them, one for a sin offering and
15:15 the **p** shall make atonement on his behalf before
15:29 and bring them to the **p** to the entrance of the tent
15:30 The **p** shall offer one for a sin offering and
15:30 the **p** shall make atonement on her behalf before
16:32 The **p** who is anointed and consecrated as **p**
17: 5 to the **p** at the entrance of the tent of meeting,
17: 6 The **p** shall dash the blood against the altar of
19:22 the **p** shall make atonement for him with the ram
21: 9 of a **p** profanes herself through prostitution,
21:10 The **p** who is exalted above his fellows,
21:21 of Aaron the **p** who has a blemish shall come C
22:10 No bound or hired servant of the **p** shall eat of
22:11 but if a **p** acquires anyone by purchase,
22:14 and give the sacred donation to the **p.**
23:10 the sheaf of the first fruits of your harvest to the **p.**
23:11 on the day after the sabbath the **p** shall raise it.
23:20 The **p** shall raise them with the bread of
23:20 they shall be holy to the LORD for the **p.**
27: 8 before the **p** and the **p** shall assess them;
27: 8 the **p** shall assess them according
27:11 the animal shall be presented before the **p.**
27:12 The **p** shall assess it: whether good
27:12 according to the assessment of the **p,** so it shall be.
27:14 a house to the LORD, the **p** shall assess it:
27:14 whether good or bad, as the **p** assesses it,
27:18 the **p** shall compute the price for it according to
27:23 the **p** shall compute for it
Nu 3: 6 and set them before Aaron the **p,** C
3:32 of Aaron the **p** was to be chief over the leaders C
4:16 Eleazar son of Aaron the **p** shall have charge of C
4:28 the oversight of Ithamar son of Aaron the **p.** C
4:33 under the hand of Ithamar son of Aaron the **p.** C
5: 8 for wrong shall go to the LORD for the **p,**
5: 9 every gift that they bring to the **p** shall be his.
5:10 whatever anyone gives to the **p** shall be his.
5:15 then the man shall bring his wife to the **p.**
5:16 Then the **p** shall bring her near,
5:17 the **p** shall take holy water in an earthen vessel,
5:18 The **p** shall set the woman before the LORD,
5:18 the **p** shall have the water of bitterness that brings
5:19 Then the **p** shall make her take an oath, saying,
5:21 the **p** make the woman take the oath of the curse
5:23 Then the **p** shall put these curses in writing,
5:25 The **p** shall take the grain offering of jealousy out
5:26 and the **p** shall take a handful of the grain offering,
5:30 and the **p** shall apply this entire law to her.
6:10 or two young pigeons to the **p** at the entrance of
6:11 the **p** shall offer one as a sin offering and the other
6:16 The **p** shall present them before the LORD
6:17 **p** also shall make the accompanying grain offering
6:19 The **p** shall take the shoulder of the ram,
6:20 the **p** shall elevate them as an elevation offering
6:20 they are a holy portion for the **p,**
7: 8 the direction of Ithamar son of Aaron the **p.** C
15:25 The **p** shall make atonement for all
15:28 the **p** shall make atonement before the LORD for
16:37 Aaron the **p** to take the censers out of the blaze; C
16:39 So Eleazar the **p** took the bronze censers B
18:28 the LORD's offering to the **p** Aaron.
19: 3 You shall give it to the **p** Eleazar,
19: 4 The **p** Eleazar shall take some of its blood
19: 6 The **p** shall take cedarwood, hyssop,
19: 7 the **p** shall wash his clothes and bathe his body
19: 7 but the **p** shall remain unclean until evening.
25: 7 Phinehas son of Eleazar, son of Aaron the **p,** C
25:11 of Aaron the **p,** has turned back my wrath from C
26: 1 to Moses and to Eleazar son of Aaron the **p,** C
26: 3 and Eleazar the **p** spoke with them in the plains B
26:63 by Moses and Eleazar the **p,** B
26:64 of those enrolled by Moses and Aaron the **p,** C
27: 2 They stood before Moses, Eleazar the **p,** B
27:19 before Eleazar the **p** and all the congregation, B
27:21 But he shall stand before Eleazar the **p,** B
27:22 before Eleazar the **p** and the whole congregation; B
31: 6 along with Phinehas son of Eleazar the **p,** B
31:12 booty and the spoil to Moses, to Eleazar the **p,** B
31:13 Eleazar the **p,** and all the leaders of the B
31:21 Eleazar the **p** said to the troops who had gone B
31:26 Eleazar the **p** and the heads of the ancestral B

Nu 31:29 it from their half and give it to Eleazar the **p** B
31:31 Eleazar the **p** did as the LORD had commanded B
31:41 the offering for the LORD, to Eleazar the **p,** B
31:51 and Eleazar the **p** received the gold from them, B
31:54 So Moses and Eleazar the **p** received the gold B
32: 2 to Moses, to Eleazar the **p,** and to the leaders of B
32:28 concerning them to Eleazar the **p,** B
33:38 Aaron the **p** went up Mount Hor at the C
34:17 the **p** Eleazar and Joshua son of Nun.
35:25 the high **p** who was anointed with the holy oil. A
35:28 the city of refuge until the death of the high **p;** A
35:28 death of the high **p** the slayer may return home. A
35:32 to live in the land before the death of the high **p.** A
Dt 10: 6 his son Eleazar succeeded him as **p.**
17:12 to disobey the **p** appointed to minister there to
18: 3 they shall give to the **p** the shoulder,
20: 2 the **p** shall come forward and speak to the troops,
26: 3 You shall go to the **p** who is in office at that time,
26: 4 the **p** takes the basket from your hand and sets it
Jos 14: 1 which the **p** Eleazar, and Joshua son of Nun,
17: 4 before the **p** Eleazar and Joshua son of Nun and
19:51 the **p** Eleazar and Joshua son of Nun and the heads
20: 6 the death of the one who is high **p** at the time: A
21: 1 to the **p** Eleazar and to Joshua son of Nun and to
21: 4 descendants of Aaron the **p** received by lot C
21:13 descendants of Aaron the **p** they gave Hebron, C
22:13 the Israelites sent the **p** Phinehas son of Eleazar to
22:30 the **p** Phinehas and the chiefs of the congregation,
22:31 The **p** Phinehas son of Eleazar said to
22:32 Then the **p** Phinehas son of Eleazar and
Jdg 17: 5 and installed one of his sons, who became his **p.**
17:10 "Stay with me, and be to me a father and a **p,**
17:12 and the young man became his **p,**
17:13 because the Levite has become my **p."**
18: 4 and he hired me, and I have become his **p."**
18: 6 The **p** replied, "Go in peace.
18:17 The **p** was standing by the entrance of the gate
18:18 the ephod, and the teraphim, the **p** said to them,
18:19 and come with us, and be to us a father and a **p.**
18:19 for you to be **p** to the house of one person,
18:19 or to be **p** to a tribe and clan in Israel?"
18:20 Then the **p** accepted the offer.
18:24 and the **p,** and go away, and what have I left?
18:27 and the **p** who belonged to him, came to Laish,
1Sa 1: 9 the **p** was sitting on the seat beside the doorpost of
2:11 in the presence of the **p** Eli.
2:14 the fork brought up the **p** would take for himself.
2:15 "Give meat for the **p** to roast;
2:28 to be my **p,** to go up to my altar, to offer incense,
2:35 I will raise up for myself a faithful **p,**
14: 3 the **p** of the LORD in Shiloh, carrying an ephod.
14:19 While Saul was talking to the **p,**
14:19 and Saul said to the **p,** "Withdraw your hand."
14:36 But the **p** said, "Let us draw near to God here."
21: 1 David came to Nob to the **p** Ahimelech.
21: 2 David said to the **p** Ahimelech,
21: 4 The **p** answered David, "I have no ordinary bread
21: 5 the **p,** "Indeed women have been kept from us
21: 6 So the **p** gave him the holy bread;
21: 9 The **p** said, "The sword of Goliath the Philistine,
22:11 The king sent for the **p** Ahimelech son of Ahitub
23: 9 he said to the **p** Abiathar, "Bring the ephod here."
30: 7 David said to the **p** Abiathar son of Ahimelech,
2Sa 15:27 The king also said to the **p** Zadok, "Look, E
20:26 and Ira the Jairite was also David's **p.**
1Ki 1: 7 with Joab son of Zeruiah and with the **p** Abiathar,
1: 8 But the **p** Zadok, and Benaiah son of Jehoiada, E
1:19 **p** Abiathar, and Joab the commander of the army;
1:25 the army, and the **p** Abiathar, who are now eating
1:26 and the **p** Zadok, and Benaiah son of Jehoiada, E
1:32 King David said, "Summon to me the **p** Zadok, E
1:34 There let the **p** Zadok and E
1:38 So the **p** Zadok, the prophet Nathan, E
1:39 the **p** Zadok took the horn of oil from the tent E
1:42 Jonathan son of the **p** Abiathar arrived.
1:44 the **p** Zadok, the prophet Nathan, and Benaiah E
1:45 the **p** Zadok and the prophet Nathan have E
2:22 for the **p** Abiathar and for Joab son of Zeruiah!"
2:26 The king said to the **p** Abiathar, "Go to Anathoth,
2:27 So Solomon banished Abiathar from being **p** to
2:35 king put the **p** Zadok in the place of Abiathar. E
4: 2 Azariah son of Zadok was the **p;**
4: 5 Zabud son of Nathan was **p** and king's friend;
2Ki 11: 9 according to all that the **p** Jehoiada commanded; D
11: 9 and came to the **p** Jehoiada. D
11:10 The **p** delivered to the captains the spears
11:15 Then the **p** Jehoiada commanded D
11:15 For the **p** said, "Let her not be killed in the house
11:18 and they killed Mattan, the **p** of Baal,
11:18 The **p** posted guards over the house of the LORD.
12: 2 because the **p** Jehoiada instructed him. D
12: 7 King Jehoash summoned the **p** Jehoiada D
12: 9 Then the **p** Jehoiada took a chest, D
12:10 the king's secretary and the high **p** went up, A
16:10 King Ahaz sent to the **p** Uriah a model of the altar,
16:11 The **p** Uriah built the altar;
16:11 just so did the **p** Uriah build it,
16:15 King Ahaz commanded the **p** Uriah, saying,
16:16 The **p** Uriah did everything
22: 4 "Go up to the high **p** Hilkiah, and have him AG
22: 8 high **p** Hilkiah said to Shaphan the secretary, AG
22:10 "The **p** Hilkiah has given me a book." G
22:12 Then the king commanded the **p** Hilkiah, G
22:14 So the **p** Hilkiah, Ahikam, Achbor, Shaphan, G
23: 4 The king commanded the high **p** Hilkiah, AG
23:24 book that the **p** Hilkiah had found in the house G
25:18 captain of the guard took the chief **p** Seraiah, F

2Ki 25:18 the second **p** Zephaniah, and the three guardians
1Ch 6:10 Johanan of Azariah (it was he who served as **p**
16:39 he left the **p** Zadok and his kindred the priests E
24: 6 and Zadok the **p**, and Ahimelech son of Abiathar,
27: 5 was Benaiah son of the **p** Jehoiada, as chief; D
29:22 as the LORD's prince, and Zadok as **p**.
2Ch 13: 9 or seven rams becomes a **p** of what are no gods.
15: 3 and without a teaching **p**, and without law;
19:11 Amariah the chief **p** is over you in all matters of F
22:11 of King Jehoram and wife of the **p** Jehoiada— D
23: 8 according to all that the **p** Jehoiada commanded; D
23: 8 for the **p** Jehoiada did not dismiss the divisions. D
23: 9 **p** Jehoiada delivered to the captains the spears D
23:14 Then the **p** Jehoiada brought out D
23:14 the **p** said, "Do not put her to death in the house
23:17 and they killed Mattan, the **p** of Baal,
24: 2 of the LORD all the days of the **p** Jehoiada. D
24:11 officer of the chief **p** would come and empty F
24:20 of Zechariah son of the **p** Jehoiada; D
24:25 of the blood of the son of the **p** Jehoiada, D
26:17 But the **p** Azariah went in after him,
26:20 When the chief **p** Azariah, and all the priests, F
31:10 The chief **p** Azariah, who was of the house F
34: 9 They came to the high **p** Hilkiah and delivered AG
34:14 the **p** Hilkiah found the book of the law of G
34:18 "The **p** Hilkiah has given me a book." G
Ezr 2:63 until there should be a **p** to consult Urim
7: 5 son of Eleazar, son of the chief **p** Aaron— F
7:11 the letter that King Artaxerxes gave to the **p** Ezra,
7:12 king of kings, to the **p** Ezra,
7:21 Whatever the **p** Ezra, the scribe of the law of
8:33 into the hands of the **p** Meremoth son of Uriah,
10:10 Then Ezra the **p** stood up and said to them, H
10:16 Ezra the **p** selected men, heads of families, H
Ne 3: 1 Then the high **p** Eliashib set to work A
3:20 to the door of the house of the high **p** Eliashib. A
7:65 until a **p** with Urim and Thummim should come.
8: 2 the **p** Ezra brought the law before the assembly,
8: 9 was the governor, and Ezra the **p** and scribe, H
10:38 And the **p**, the descendant of Aaron,
12:26 of the governor Nehemiah and of the **p** Ezra,
13: 4 Now before this, the **p** Eliashib,
13:13 the storehouses the **p** Shelemiah, the scribe Zadok,
13:28 son of the high **p** Eliashib, A
Ps 110: 4 "You are a **p** forever according to the order
Isa 8: 2 the **p** Uriah and Zechariah son of Jeberechiah.
24: 2 And it shall be, as with the people, so with the **p**;
28: 7 the **p** and the prophet reel with strong drink,
Jer 6:13 and from prophet to **p**, everyone deals falsely.
8:10 from prophet to **p** everyone deals falsely.
14:18 prophet and **p** ply their trade throughout the land,
18:18 for instruction shall not perish from the **p**,
20: 1 Now the **p** Pashhur son of Immer,
21: 1 of Malchiah and the **p** Zephaniah son of Maaseiah,
23:11 Both prophet and **p** are ungodly;
23:33 When this people, or a prophet, or a **p** asks you,
23:34 And as for the prophet, **p**, or the people who say,
29:25 and to the **p** Zephaniah son of Maaseiah,
29:26 The LORD himself has made you **p** instead of
29:26 of the **p** Jehoiada, so that there may be officers D
29:29 The **p** Zephaniah read this letter in the hearing of
37: 3 and the **p** Zephaniah son of Maaseiah to
52:24 captain of the guard took the chief **p** Seraiah, F
52:24 the second **p** Zephaniah, and the three guardians
La 2: 6 in his fierce indignation has spurned king and **p**.
2:20 Should **p** and prophet be killed in the sanctuary of
Eze 1: 3 the word of the LORD came to the **p** Ezekiel son
7:26 instruction shall perish from the **p**,
44:13 They shall not come near to me, to serve me as **p**,
44:21 No **p** shall drink wine when he enters
44:22 or a widow who is the widow of a **p**.
45:19 The **p** shall take some of the blood of
Hos 4: 4 for with you is my contention, O **p**.
4: 6 I reject you from being a **p** to me.
4: 9 And it shall be like people, like **p**;
Am 7:10 Then Amaziah, the **p** of Bethel,
Hag 1: 1 and to Joshua son of Jehozadak, the high **p**: A
1:12 the high **p**, with all the remnant of the people, A
1:14 the high **p**, and the spirit of all the remnant of A
2: 2 the high **p**, and to the remnant of the people, A
2: 4 O Joshua, son of Jehozadak, the high **p**; A
Zec 3: 1 Then he showed me the high **p** Joshua standing A
3: 8 Now listen, Joshua, high **p**, A
6:11 the head of the high **p** Joshua son of Jehozadak; A
6:13 There shall be a **p** by his throne,
Mal 2: 7 For the lips of a **p** should guard knowledge,
Mt 8: 4 but go, show yourself to the **p**,
26: 3 the people gathered in the palace of the high **p**, A
26:51 drew it, and struck the slave of the high **p**, A
26:57 Caiaphas the high **p**, in whose house the scribes A
26:58 as far as the courtyard of the high **p**; A
26:62 high **p** stood up and said, "Have you no answer? A
26:63 Then the high **p** said to him, A
26:65 Then the high **p** tore his clothes and said, A
Mk 1:44 but go, show yourself to the **p**,
2:26 when Abiathar was high **p**, A
14:47 and struck the slave of the high **p**, A
14:53 They took Jesus to the high **p**; A
14:54 right into the courtyard of the high **p**; A
14:60 high **p** stood up before them and asked Jesus, A
14:61 Again the high **p** asked him, A
14:63 Then the high **p** tore his clothes and said, A
14:66 one of the servant-girls of the high **p** came by. A
Lk 1: 5 there was a **p** named Zechariah,
1: 8 as **p** before God and his section was on duty,
5:14 "Go," he said, "and show yourself to the **p**, and,
10:31 Now by chance a **p** was going down that road;
Lk 22:50 Then one of them struck the slave of the high **p** A
Jn 11:49 of them, Caiaphas, who was high **p** that year, A
11:51 but being high **p** that year he prophesied A
18:13 father-in-law of Caiaphas, the high **p** that year. A
18:15 Since that disciple was known to the high **p**, A
18:15 with Jesus into the courtyard of the high **p**, A
18:16 other disciple, who was known to the high **p**, A
18:19 the high **p** questioned Jesus about his disciples A
18:22 saying, "Is that how you answer the high **p**?" A
18:24 Annas sent him bound to Caiaphas the high **p**. A
18:26 One of the slaves of the high **p**, A
Ac 4: 6 the high **p**, Caiaphas, John, and Alexander, A
5:17 Then the high **p** took action; A
5:21 When the high **p** and those with him arrived, A
5:27 The high **p** questioned them, A
7: 1 the high **p** asked him, "Are these things so?" A
9: 1 the disciples of the Lord, went to the high **p** A
14:13 The **p** of Zeus, whose temple was just outside
19:14 a Jewish high **p** named Sceva were doing this. A
22: 5 as the high **p** and the whole council A
23: 2 the high **p** Ananias ordered those standing A
23: 4 "Do you dare to insult God's high **p**?" A
23: 5 "I did not realize, brothers, that he was high **p**; A
24: 1 high **p** Ananias came down with some elders A
Heb 2:17 that he might be a merciful and faithful high **p** A
3: 1 the apostle and high **p** of our confession, A
4:14 we have a great high **p** who has passed through A
4:15 not have a high **p** who is unable to sympathize A
5: 1 Every high **p** chosen from among mortals is put A
5: 5 a high **p**, but was appointed by the one who said A
5: 6 a **p** forever, according to the order of Melchizedek.
5:10 been designated by God a high **p** according A
6:20 having become a high **p** forever according to A
7: 1 **p** of the Most High God, met Abraham
7: 3 the Son of God, he remains a **p** forever.
7:11 of another **p** arising according to the order
7:15 It is even more obvious when another **p** arises,
7:16 one who has become a **p**,
7:17 a **p** forever, according to the order of Melchizedek.
7:21 but this one became a **p** with an oath,
7:21 not change his mind, 'You are a **p** forever' "—
7:26 it was fitting that we should have such a high **p**, A
8: 1 we have such a high **p**, one who is seated at A
8: 3 For every high **p** is appointed to offer gifts A
8: 3 for this **p** also to have something to offer.
8: 4 if he were on earth, he would not be a **p** at all,
9: 7 but only the high **p** goes into the second, A
9:11 when Christ came as a high **p** of the good things A
9:25 as the high **p** enters the Holy Place year after A
10:11 And every **p** stands day after day at his service,
10:21 since we have a great **p** over the house of God,
13:11 by the high **p** as a sacrifice for sin are burned A
Jdt 4: 6 The high **p**, Joakim, who was in Jerusalem at A
4: 8 as they had been ordered by the high **p** Joakim A
4:14 The high **p** Joakim and all the priests who stood A
15: 8 Then the high **p** Joakim and the elders of A
AdE 11: 1 Dositheus, who said that he was a **p** and a Levite,
Sir 7:31 Fear the Lord and honor the **p**,
45:15 and serve as **p** and bless his people in his name.
50: 1 and the pride of his people was the high **p**, A
Bar 1: 7 to the high **p** Jehoiakim son of Hilkiah son A
1Mc 2: 1 a **p** of the family of Joarib,
7: 5 by Alcimus, who wanted to be high **p**. A
7: 9 the ungodly Alcimus, whom he made high **p**; A
7:14 A **p** of the line of Aaron has come with the army,
10:20 so we have appointed you today to be the high **p** A
10:32 the citadel in Jerusalem and give it to the high **p**, A
10:38 and obey no other authority than the high **p**. A
10:69 the following message to the high **p** Jonathan: A
12: 3 "The high **p** Jonathan and A
12: 6 "The high **p** Jonathan, the senate of the nation, A
12: 7 in time past a letter was sent to the high **p** Onias A
12:20 to the high **p** Onias, greetings. A
13:36 the high **p** and friend of kings, A
13:42 the great high **p** and commander and leader of A
14:17 that his brother Simon had become high **p** A
14:20 the city of the Spartans to the high **p** Simon A
14:23 a copy of this to the high **p** Simon.' " A
14:27 is the third year of the great high **p** Simon, A
14:29 Simon son of Mattathias, a **p** of the sons of Joarib,
14:30 Jonathan rallied the nation, became their high **p**, A
14:35 and they made him their leader and high **p**, A
14:41 be their leader and high **p** forever, A
14:47 So Simon accepted and agreed to be high **p**, A
15: 1 the **p** and ethnarch of the Jews, A
15: 2 Simon the high **p** and ethnarch and to the nation A
15:17 They had been sent by the high **p** Simon and by A
15:21 hand them over to the high **p** Simon, A
15:24 a copy of these things to the high **p** Simon. A
16:12 for he was son-in-law of the high **p**. A
16:24 the time that he became high **p** after his father. A
2Mc 3: 1 the high **p** Onias and his hatred of wickedness, A
3: 4 with the high **p** about the administration of A
3: 9 and had been kindly welcomed by the high **p** A
3:10 The high **p** explained A
3:16 the appearance of the high **p** was to be wounded A
3:21 the anxiety of the high **p** in his great anguish. A
3:32 So the high **p**, fearing that the king might get A
3:33 While the high **p** was making an atonement, A
3:33 "Be very grateful to the high **p** Onias, A
4:13 who was ungodly and no true high **p**, A
14: 3 who had formerly been high **p** A
14:13 to install Alcimus as high **p** of the great temple. A
15:12 Onias, who had been high **p**, A
1Es 5:40 until a high **p** should appear wearing Urim A
8: 2 Phineas son of Eleazar son of Aaron the high **p**. A
8: 8 to Ezra the **p** and reader of the law of the Lord: H
1Es 8: 9 to Ezra the **p** and reader of the law of the Lord, H
8:19 Phoenicia that whatever Ezra the **p** and reader H
8:62 in the house of our Lord to the **p** Meremoth son
9:16 Ezra the **p** chose for himself the leading men H
9:39 the chief **p** and reader to bring the law of Moses F
9:40 So Ezra the chief **p** brought the law, F
9:42 Ezra the **p** and reader of the law stood on H
9:49 Attharates said to Ezra the chief **p** and reader, F
3Mc 1:11 only the high **p** who was pre-eminent over all— A
2: 1 Then the high **p** Simon, facing the sanctuary, A
2Es 1:13 I gave you Moses as leader and Aaron as **p**;
4Mc 4:13 Moved by these words, the high **p** Onias, A
4:16 and appointed Onias's brother Jason as high **p**. A
4:18 appointed him high **p** and ruler of the nation. A
7: 6 O **p**, worthy of the priesthood,
17: 9 "Here lie buried an aged **p** and an aged woman

PRIEST'S (10) [PRIEST]

Lev 14:18 in the **p** hand he shall put on the head of the one to
14:29 in the **p** hand he shall put on the head of the one to
22:12 If a **p** daughter marries a layman,
22:13 but if a **p** daughter is widowed or divorced,
27:21 as a devoted field; it becomes the **p** holding.
1Sa 2:13 the **p** servant would come,
2:15 the **p** servant would come and say to the one
2:36 and shall say, Please put me in one of the **p** places,
Lk 22:54 bringing him into the high **p** house.
Jn 18:10 who had a sword, drew it, struck the high **p** slave,

PRIESTHOOD (41) [PRIEST]

Ex 28: 3 to consecrate him for my **p**.
29: 9 and the **p** shall be theirs by a perpetual ordinance.
40:15 a perpetual **p** throughout all generations to come.
Nu 3:10 it is they who shall attend to the **p**,
16:10 yet you seek the **p** as well!
18: 1 for offenses connected with the **p**.
18: 7 I give your **p** as a gift;
25:13 after him a covenant of perpetual **p**,
Jos 18: 7 for the **p** of the LORD is their heritage;
Ezr 2:62 and so they were excluded from the **p** as unclean;
Ne 7:64 so they were excluded from the **p** as unclean;
13:29 O my God, because they have defiled the **p**,
Lk 1: 9 according to the custom of the **p**,
3: 2 during the high **p** of Annas and Caiaphas,
Heb 7:11 had been attainable through the levitical **p**—
7:11 for the people received the law under this **p**—
7:12 For when there is a change in the **p**,
7:24 but he holds his **p** permanently,
1Pe 2: 5 be a holy **p**, to offer spiritual sacrifices acceptable
2: 9 But you are a chosen race, a royal **p**,
Sir 45: 7 and gave him the **p** of the people.
45:24 the dignity of the **p** forever.
1Mc 2:54 received the covenant of everlasting **p**.
3:49 They also brought the vestments of the **p** and
7:21 Alcimus struggled to maintain his high **p**,
11:27 in the high **p** and in as many other honors
11:57 in the high **p** and set you over the four districts
14:38 King Demetrius confirmed him in the high **p**,
16:24 are written in the annals of his high **p**,
2Mc 2:17 and the kingship and the **p** and the consecration,
4: 7 Jason the brother of Onias obtained the high **p**
4:24 and secured the high **p** for himself,
4:25 possessing no qualification for the high **p**,
4:29 as deputy in the high **p**,
11: 3 and to put up the high **p** for sale every year.
14: 7 laid aside my ancestral glory—I mean the high **p**—
1Es 5:38 Of the priests the following had assumed the **p**
4Mc 4: 1 Onias, who then held the high **p** for life.
4:16 from the **p** and appointed Onias's brother Jason
5:35 honored **p** and knowledge of the law.
7: 6 O priest, worthy of the **p**,

PRIESTLY‡ (11) [PRIEST]

Ex 19: 6 be for me a **p** kingdom and a holy nation.
Nu 18: 7 with you shall diligently perform your **p** duties
18: 8 and your sons as a **p** portion due you in perpetuity.
Ezr 2:69 of silver, and one hundred **p** robes.
Ne 7:70 fifty basins, and five hundred thirty **p** robes.
7:72 of silver, and sixty-seven **p** robes.
Lk 1: 5 who belonged to the **p** order of Abijah.
Ro 15:16 the Gentiles in the **p** service of the gospel of God,
Heb 7: 5 the **p** office have a commandment in the law
2Mc 3:15 before the altar in their **p** vestments and called
4Mc 5: 4 He was a man of **p** family, learned in the law,

PRIESTS‡ (510) [PRIEST]

A. CHIEF PRIESTS (65)
B. PRIESTS AND [THE] LEVITES (55)
C. LEVITICAL PRIESTS (13)

Ge 47:22 Only the land of the **p** he did not buy;
47:22 for the **p** had a fixed allowance from Pharaoh,
47:26 The land of the **p** alone did not become Pharaoh's.
Ex 19:22 Even the **p** who approach
19:24 either the **p** or the people break through to come
28: 1 from among the Israelites, to serve me as **p**—
28: 4 and his sons to serve me as **p**,
28:41 so that they may serve me as **p**.
29: 1 so that they may serve me as **p**.
29:44 and his sons I will consecrate, to serve me as **p**.
30:30 in order that they may serve me as **p**.
31:10 the vestments of his sons, for their service as **p**,
35:19 the vestments of his sons, for their service as **p**.
39:41 and the vestments of his sons to serve as **p**.
40:15 that they may serve me as **p**:

Lev 1: 5 and Aaron's sons the **p** shall offer the blood,
1: 8 Aaron's sons the **p** shall arrange the parts,
1:11 the **p** shall dash its blood against all sides of
2: 2 and bring it to Aaron's sons the **p.**
3: 2 the **p** shall dash the blood against all sides of
6:29 Every male among the **p** shall eat of it;
7: 6 Every male among the **p** shall eat of it;
7:35 to serve the LORD as **p;**
13: 2 to Aaron the priest or to one of his sons the **p.**
16:33 and he shall make atonement for the **p** and for all
21: 1 The LORD said to Moses: Speak to the **p,**
Nu 3: 3 the names of the sons of Aaron, the anointed **p,**
3: 3 whom he ordained to minister as **p.**
3: 4 Eleazar and Ithamar served as **p** in the lifetime
3:31 vessels of the sanctuary with which the **p** minister,
10: 8 The sons of Aaron, the **p,** shall blow the trumpets;
Dt 17: 9 the levitical **p** and the judge who is in office C
17:18 for him in the presence of the levitical **p.** C
18: 1 The levitical **p,** the whole tribe of Levi, C
19:17 **p** and the judges who are in office in those days,
21: 5 Then the **p,** the sons of Levi, shall come forward,
24: 8 observe whatever the levitical **p** instruct you, C
27: 9 Moses and the levitical **p** spoke to all Israel, C
31: 9 Moses wrote down this law, and gave it to the **p,**
Jos 3: 3 by the levitical **p,** then you shall set out C
3: 6 To the **p** Joshua said, "Take up the ark of
3: 8 the one who shall command the **p** who bear
3:13 of the **p** who bear the ark of the LORD, the Lord
3:14 the **p** bearing the ark of the covenant were in front
3:15 of the **p** bearing the ark were dipped in the edge of
3:17 the **p** who bore the ark of the covenant of
4: 9 the place where the feet of the **p** bearing the ark of
4:10 The **p** who bore the ark remained standing in
4:11 and the **p,** crossed over in front of the people.
4:16 the **p** who bear the ark of the covenant,
4:17 Joshua therefore commanded the **p,**
4:18 When the **p** bearing the ark of the covenant of
6: 4 with seven **p** bearing seven trumpets
6: 4 the **p** blowing the trumpets.
6: 6 So Joshua son of Nun summoned the **p** and said
6: 6 and have seven **p** carry seven trumpets
6: 8 the seven **p** carrying the seven trumpets
6: 9 And the armed men went before the **p** who blew
6:12 and the **p** took up the ark of the LORD.
6:13 The seven **p** carrying the seven trumpets
6:16 when the **p** had blown the trumpets,
8:33 levitical **p** who carried the ark of the covenant C
21:19 the **p**—were thirteen in all, with their pasture
Jdg 18:30 and his sons were **p** to the tribe of the Danites
1Sa 1: 3 Hophni and Phinehas, were **p** of the LORD.
2:13 or for the duties of the **p** to the people.
5: 5 This is why the **p** of Dagon and all who enter
6: 2 the Philistines called for the **p** and the diviners
22:11 the **p** who were at Nob;
22:17 "Turn and kill the **p** of the LORD,
22:17 the king would not raise their hand to attack the **p**
22:18 "You, Doeg, turn and attack the **p.**"
22:18 Doeg the Edomite turned and attacked the **p;**
22:19 Nob, the city of the **p,** he put to the sword;
22:21 Abiathar told David that Saul had killed the **p** of
2Sa 8:17 of Ahitub and Ahimelech son of Abiathar were **p;**
8:18 and the Pelethites; and David's sons were **p.**
15:35 The **p** Zadok and Abiathar will be with you there.
15:35 tell it to the **p** Zadok and Abiathar.
17:15 Then Hushai said to the **p** Zadok and Abiathar,
19:11 King David sent this message to the **p** Zadok
20:25 Sheva was secretary; Zadok and Abiathar were **p;**
1Ki 4: 4 Zadok and Abiathar were **p;**
8: 3 and the **p** carried the ark.
8: 4 the **p** and the Levites brought them up. B
8: 6 Then the **p** brought the ark of the covenant of
8:10 And when the **p** came out of the holy place,
8:11 **p** could not stand to minister because of the cloud;
12:31 and appointed **p** from among all the people,
12:32 And he placed in Bethel the **p** of the high places
13: 2 the **p** of the high places who offer incense on you,
13:33 but made **p** for the high places again from
13:33 any who wanted to be **p** he consecrated for
2Ki 10:11 close friends, and **p,** until he left him no survivor.
10:19 all his worshipers, and all his **p;**
12: 4 the **p,** "All the money offered as sacred donations
12: 5 let the **p** receive from each of the donors;
12: 6 of King Jehoash the **p** had made no repairs on
12: 7 the priest Jehoiada with the other **p** and said
12: 8 So the **p** agreed that they would neither accept
12: 9 the **p** who guarded the threshold put in it all
12:16 of the LORD; it belonged to the **p.**
17:27 "Send there one of the **p** whom you carried away
17:28 So one of the **p** whom they had carried away
17:32 from among themselves all sorts of people as **p** of
19: 2 and Shebna the secretary, and the senior **p,**
23: 2 the **p,** the prophets, and all the people,
23: 4 the **p** of the second order,
23: 5 He deposed the idolatrous **p** whom the kings
23: 8 He brought all the **p** out of the towns of Judah,
23: 8 the high places where the **p** had made offerings,
23: 9 The **p** of the high places, however,
23:20 the **p** of the high places who were there,
1Ch 9: 2 **p,** Levites, and temple servants.
9:10 Of the **p:** Jedaiah, Jehoiarib, Jachin,
9:30 Others, of the sons of the **p,**
13: 2 including the **p** and Levites in the cities B
15:11 David summoned the **p** Zadok and Abiathar,
15:14 So the **p** and the Levites sanctified themselves B
15:24 Amasai, Zechariah, Benaiah, and Eliezer, the **p,**
16: 6 and the **p** Benaiah and Jahaziel were
16:39 And he left the priest Zadok and his kindred the **p**
1Ch 18:16 of Ahitub and Ahimelech son of Abiathar were **p;**
23: 2 the leaders of Israel and the **p** and the Levites. B
24: 2 so Eleazar and Ithamar became the **p.**
24: 6 of ancestral houses of the **p** and of the Levites; B
24:31 of ancestral houses of the **p** and of the Levites, B
28:13 the divisions of the **p** and of the Levites, and all B
28:21 Here are the divisions of the **p** and the Levites B
2Ch 4: 6 The sea was for the **p** to wash in.
4: 9 He made the court of the **p,** and the great court,
5: 5 the **p** and the Levites brought them up. B
5: 7 Then the **p** brought the ark of the covenant of
5:11 when the **p** came out of the holy place (for all
5:11 the **p** who were present had sanctified themselves,
5:12 with one hundred twenty **p** who were trumpeters).
5:14 **p** could not stand to minister because of the cloud;
6:41 Let your **p,** O LORD God,
7: 2 The **p** could not enter the house of the LORD,
7: 6 The **p** stood at their posts;
7: 6 Opposite them the **p** sounded trumpets;
8:14 the divisions of the **p** for their service,
8:14 of praise and ministry alongside the **p** as the duty
8:15 the **p** and Levites regarding anything at all, B
11:13 The **p** and the Levites who were B
11:14 his sons had prevented them from serving as **p**
11:15 and had appointed his own **p** for the high places,
13: 9 Have you not driven out the **p** of the LORD,
13: 9 and made **p** for yourselves like the peoples
13:10 have **p** ministering to the LORD who are
13:12 and his **p** have their battle trumpets to sound
13:14 and the **p** blew the trumpets.
17: 8 with these Levites, the **p** Elishama and Jehoram.
19: 8 and **p** and heads of families of Israel,
23: 4 one third of you, **p** and Levites, B
23: 6 the LORD except the **p** and ministering Levites;
23:18 to the levitical **p** whom David had organized C
24: 5 the **p** and the Levites and said to them, "Go out B
26:17 with eighty **p** of the LORD who were men
26:18 but for the **p** the descendants of Aaron,
26:19 the **p** a leprous disease broke out on his forehead,
26:19 the presence of the **p** in the house of the LORD,
26:20 When the chief priest Azariah, and all the **p,**
29: 4 in the **p** and the Levites and assembled them in B
29:16 The **p** went into the inner part of the house of
29:21 the **p** the descendants of Aaron to offer them on
29:22 and the **p** received the blood and dashed it against
29:24 the **p** slaughtered them and made a sin offering
29:26 and the **p** with the trumpets.
29:34 But the **p** were too few and could not skin all
29:34 so, until other **p** had sanctified themselves,
29:34 for the Levites were more conscientious than the **p**
30: 3 not keep it at its proper time because the **p** had
30:15 The **p** and the Levites were ashamed, B
30:16 the **p** dashed the blood that they received from
30:21 Levites and the **p** praised the LORD day by day,
30:24 The **p** sanctified themselves in great numbers.
30:25 whole assembly of Judah, the **p** and the Levites, B
30:27 **p** and the Levites stood up and blessed the B
31: 2 the divisions of the **p** and of the Levites, B
31: 2 according to his service, the **p** and the Levites, B
31: 4 to give the portion due to the **p** and the Levites, B
31: 9 Hezekiah questioned the **p** and the Levites B
31:15 in the cities of the **p,**
31:17 of the **p** was according to their ancestral houses;
31:18 The **p** were enrolled with all their little children,
31:19 And for the descendants of Aaron, the **p,**
31:19 to every male among the **p** and to everyone among
34: 5 He also burned the bones of the **p** on their altars,
34:30 inhabitants of Jerusalem, the **p** and the Levites, B
35: 2 the **p** to their offices and encouraged them in
35: 8 to the **p,** and to the Levites. B
35: 8 of the house of God, gave to the **p** for
35:10 the **p** stood in their place,
35:11 **p** dashed the blood that they received from them,
35:14 and for the **p,** because the **p** the descendants of
35:14 for themselves and for the **p,**
35:18 as was kept by Josiah, by the **p** and the Levites, B
36:14 All the leading **p** and the people
Ezr 1: 5 and the **p** and the Levites— B
2:36 The **p:** the descendants of Jedaiah,
2:61 Also, of the descendants of the **p:**
2:70 The **p,** the Levites, and some of the people lived
3: 2 Then Jeshua son of Jozadak, with his fellow **p,**
3: 8 the **p** and the Levites and all who had come B
3:10 the **p** in their vestments were stationed to praise
3:12 many of the **p** and Levites and heads of families, B
6: 9 salt, wine, or oil, as the **p** in Jerusalem require—
6:16 The people of Israel, the **p** and the Levites, B
6:18 Then they set the **p** in their divisions and
6:20 the **p** and the Levites had purified themselves; B
6:20 for their fellow **p,** and for themselves.
7: 7 and some of the **p** and Levites, B
7:13 I decree that any of the people of Israel or their **p**
7:16 with the freewill offerings of the people and the **p,**
7:24 or toll on any of the **p,** the Levites, the singers,
8:15 As I reviewed the people and the **p,**
8:24 Then I set apart twelve of the leading **p:**
8:29 before the chief **p** and the Levites and the AB
8:30 So the **p** and the Levites took over the silver, B
9: 1 "The people of Israel, the **p,** and the Levites B
9: 7 and our **p** have been handed over to the kings of
10: 5 Then Ezra stood up and made the leading **p,**
10:18 of the **p** who had married foreign women,
Ne 2:16 I had not yet told the Jews, the **p,** the nobles,
3: 1 with his fellow **p** and rebuilt the Sheep Gate.
3:22 After him the **p,** the men of the surrounding area,
3:28 Above the Horse Gate the **p** made repairs,
5:12 And I called the **p,** and made them take an oath
Ne 7:39 The **p:** the descendants of Jedaiah,
7:63 of the **p:** the descendants of Hobaiah,
7:73 So the **p,** the Levites, the gatekeepers, the singers,
8:13 with the **p** and the Levites, came together B
9:32 upon our kings, our officials, our **p,** our prophets,
9:34 our **p,** and our ancestors have not kept your law
9:38 the names of our officials, our Levites, and our **p.**
10: 8 Maaziah, Bilgai, Shemaiah; these are the **p.**
10:28 The rest of the people, the **p,** the Levites,
10:34 We have also cast lots among the **p,** the Levites,
10:36 to the **p** who minister in the house of our God,
10:37 to the **p,** to the chambers of the house of our God;
10:39 and where the **p** that minister,
11: 3 Israel, the **p,** the Levites, the temple servants,
11:10 Of the **p:** Jedaiah son of Joiarib, Jachin,
11:20 the rest of Israel, and of the **p** and the Levites, B
12: 1 These are the **p** and the Levites who came up B
12: 7 the **p** and of their associates in the days of Jeshua.
12:12 In the days of Joiakim the **p,**
12:22 also the **p** until the reign of Darius the Persian.
12:30 And the **p** and the Levites purified themselves; B
12:35 and some of the young **p** with trumpets:
12:41 and the **p** Eliakim, Maaseiah,
12:44 the **p** and for the Levites from the fields B
12:44 over the **p** and the Levites who ministered. B
13: 5 and gatekeepers, and the contributions for the **p.**
13:29 the covenant of the **p** and the Levites. B
13:30 I established the duties of the **p** and Levites, B
Job 12:19 He leads **p** away stripped,
Ps 78:64 Their **p** fell by the sword,
99: 6 Moses and Aaron were among his **p,**
132: 9 Let your **p** be clothed with righteousness,
132:16 Its **p** I will clothe with salvation,
Isa 37: 2 and Shebna the secretary, and the senior **p,**
61: 6 but you shall be called **p** of the LORD, you shall
66:21 will also take some of them as **p** and as Levites, B
Jer 1: 1 of the **p** who were in Anathoth in the land
1:18 against the kings of Judah, its princes, its **p,**
2: 8 The **p** did not say, "Where is the LORD?"
2:26 they, their kings, their officials, their **p,**
4: 9 **p** shall be appalled and the prophets astounded.
5:31 and the **p** rule as the prophets direct;
8: 1 the bones of the **p,** the bones of the prophets,
13:13 the kings who sit on David's throne, the **p,**
19: 1 the elders of the people and some of the senior **p,**
26: 7 The **p** and the prophets and all
26: 8 the **p** and the prophets and all the people laid hold
26:11 Then the **p** and the prophets said to the officials
26:16 Then the officials and all the people said to the **p**
27:16 Then I spoke to the **p** and to all this people,
28: 1 in the presence of the **p** and all the people, saying,
28: 5 of the **p** and all the people who were standing in
29: 1 and to the **p,** the prophets, and all the people,
29:25 of Maaseiah, and to all the **p,**
31:14 I will give the **p** their fill of fatness,
32:32 their **p** and their prophets,
33:18 and the levitical **p** shall never lack a man C
34:19 the officials of Jerusalem, the eunuchs, the **p,**
48: 7 with his **p** and his attendants.
49: 3 with his **p** and his attendants.
La 1: 4 all her gates are desolate, her **p** groan;
1:19 my **p** and elders perished in the city
4:13 the sins of her prophets and the iniquities of her **p,**
4:16 no honor was shown to the **p,**
Eze 22:26 Its **p** have done violence to my teaching
40:45 that faces south is for the **p** who have charge of
40:46 that faces north is for the **p** who have charge of
42:13 where the **p** who approach the LORD shall eat
42:14 When the **p** enter the holy place,
43:19 you shall give to the levitical **p** of the family C
43:24 the **p** shall throw salt on them and offer them up as
43:27 from the eighth day onward the **p** shall offer upon
44:15 But the levitical **p,** the descendants of Zadok, C
44:30 from all your offerings, shall belong to the **p;**
44:30 you shall also give to the **p** the first of your dough,
44:31 The **p** shall not eat of anything,
45: 4 the **p,** who minister in the sanctuary and approach
46: 2 The **p** shall offer his burnt offering
46:19 to the north row of the holy chambers for the **p;**
46:20 the place where the **p** shall boil the guilt offering
48:10 **p** shall have an allotment measuring twenty-five
48:11 This shall be for the consecrated **p,**
48:13 Alongside the territory of the **p,**
Hos 5: 1 Hear this, O **p!** Give heed,
6: 9 so the **p** are banded together;
10: 5 and its idolatrous **p** shall wail over it,
Joel 1: 9 The **p** mourn, the ministers of the LORD.
1:13 Put on sackcloth and lament, you **p;**
2:17 Between the vestibule and the altar let the **p,**
Mic 3:11 its **p** teach for a price, its prophets give oracles
Zep 1: 4 of Baal and the name of the idolatrous **p;**
3: 4 its **p** have profaned what is sacred,
Hag 2:11 Ask the **p** for a ruling:
2:12 does it become holy? The **p** answered,
2:13 The **p** answered, "Yes, it becomes unclean."
Zec 7: 3 to ask the **p** of the house of the LORD of hosts
7: 5 Say to all the people of the land and the **p:**
Mal 1: 6 says the LORD of hosts to you, O **p,**
2: 1 And now, O **p,** this command is for you.
Mt 2: 4 and calling together all the chief **p** and scribes A
12: 4 or his companions to eat, but only for the **p.**
12: 5 the sabbath the **p** in the temple break the sabbath
16:21 the hands of the elders and chief **p** and scribes, A
20:18 Son of Man will be handed over to the chief **p** A
21:15 chief **p** and the scribes saw the amazing things A
21:23 the chief **p** and the elders of the people came A
21:45 the chief **p** and the Pharisees heard his parables, A

Mt 26: 3 chief **p** and the elders of the people gathered A
26:14 was called Judas Iscariot, went to the chief **p** A
26:47 from the chief **p** and the elders of the people. A
26:59 the chief **p** and the whole council were looking A
27: 1 all the chief **p** and the elders of A
27: 3 the thirty pieces of silver to the chief **p** and A
27: 6 But the chief **p**, taking the pieces of silver, said, A
27:12 when he was accused by the chief **p** and elders, A
27:20 the chief **p** and the elders persuaded the crowds A
27:41 In the same way the chief **p** also, A
27:62 chief **p** and the Pharisees gathered before Pilate A
28:11 told the chief **p** everything that had happened. A
28:12 After the **p** had assembled with the elders,
Mk 2:26 which it is not lawful for any but the **p** to eat,
8:31 the chief **p**, and the scribes, and be killed, A
10:33 Son of Man will be handed over to the chief **p** A
11:18 And when the chief **p** and the scribes heard it, A
11:27 As he was walking in the temple, the chief **p**, A
14: 1 chief **p** and the scribes were looking for a way A
14:10 to the chief **p** in order to betray him to them. A
14:43 from the chief **p**, the scribes, and the elders. A
14:53 and all the chief **p**, the elders, A
14:55 the chief **p** and the whole council were looking A
15: 1 the chief **p** held a consultation with the elders A
15: 3 Then the chief **p** accused him of many things. A
15:10 jealousy that the chief **p** had handed him over. A
15:11 But the chief **p** stirred up the crowd A
15:31 In the same way the chief **p**, A
Lk 6: 4 which it is not lawful for any but the **p** to eat,
9:22 be rejected by the elders, chief **p**, and scribes, A
17:14 "Go and show yourselves to the **p**."
19:47 The chief **p**, the scribes, and the leaders of A
20: 1 the chief **p** and the scribes came with the elders A
20:19 and chief **p** realized that he had told this parable A
22: 2 chief **p** and the scribes were looking for a way A
22: 4 chief **p** and officers of the temple police about A
22:52 Then Jesus said to the chief **p**, A
22:66 both chief **p** and scribes, gathered together, A
23: 4 Then Pilate said to the chief **p** and the crowds, A
23:10 The chief **p** and the scribes stood by, A
23:13 Pilate then called together the chief **p**, A
24:20 how our chief **p** and leaders handed him over A
Jn 1:19 given by John when the Jews sent **p** and Levites B
7:32 and the chief **p** and Pharisees sent temple police A
7:45 Then the temple police went back to the chief **p** A
11:47 the chief **p** and the Pharisees called a meeting A
11:57 the chief **p** and the Pharisees had given orders A
12:10 chief **p** planned to put Lazarus to death as well, A
18: 3 of soldiers together with police from the chief **p** A
18:35 Your own nation and the chief **p** have handed A
19: 6 When the chief **p** and the police saw him, A
19:15 The chief **p** answered, "We have no king but A
19:21 Then the chief **p** of the Jews said to Pilate, A
Ac 4: 1 Peter and John were speaking to the people, the **p**,
4:23 to their friends and reported what the chief **p** A
5:24 of the temple and the chief **p** heard these words, A
6: 7 a great many of the **p** became obedient to the faith.
9:14 the chief **p** to bind all who invoke your name." A
9:21 of bringing them bound before the chief **p**?" A
22:30 and ordered the chief **p** and the entire council A
23:14 They went to the chief **p** and elders and said, A
25: 2 the chief **p** and the leaders of the Jews gave him A
25:15 chief **p** and the elders of the Jews informed me A
26:10 with authority received from the chief **p**, A
26:12 the authority and commission of the chief **p**, A
Heb 7:14 with that tribe Moses said nothing about **p**.
7:20 for others who became **p** took their office without
7:23 Furthermore, the former **p** were many in number,
7:27 Unlike the other high **p**, he has no need
7:28 the law appoints as high **p** those who are subject
8: 4 there are **p** who offer gifts according to the law.
9: 6 the **p** go continually into the first tent
Rev 1: 6 **p** serving his God and Father,
5:10 to be a kingdom and **p** serving our God,
20: 6 but they will be **p** of God and of Christ,
Tob 1: 7 I would give these to the **p**, the sons of Aaron,
Jdt 4:14 the **p** who stood before the Lord and ministered to
11:13 for the **p** who minister in the presence of our God
Sir 7:29 With all your soul fear the Lord, and revere his **p**.
50:12 he received the portions from the hands of the **p**,
51:12 *who has chosen the sons of Zadok to be p,*
Bar 1: 7 of Hilkiah son of Shallum, and to the **p**, and to all
1:16 our rulers, our **p**, our prophets, and our ancestors,
LtJ 6:10 the **p** secretly take gold and silver from their gods
6:18 so the **p** make their temples secure with doors
6:28 The **p** sell the sacrifices that are offered
6:31 in their temples the **p** sit with their clothes torn,
6:33 The **p** take some of the clothing of their gods
6:48 the **p** consult together as to where they can hide
6:55 their **p** will flee and escape,
Aza 1:62 Bless the Lord, you **p** of the Lord;
Bel 1: 8 Then the king was angry and called the **p** of Bel
1:10 Now there were seventy **p** of Bel,
1:11 **p** of Bel said, "See, we are now going outside;
1:15 During the night the **p** came as usual,
1:21 and he arrested the **p** and their wives and children.
1:28 and killed the dragon, and slaughtered the **p**."
1Mc 1:46 to defile the sanctuary and the **p**,
3:51 and your **p** mourn in humiliation.
4:38 They saw also the chambers of the **p** in ruins.
4:42 He chose blameless **p** devoted to the law,
4:57 they restored the gates and the chambers for the **p**,
5:67 On that day some **p**, who wished to do
7:33 the **p** from the sanctuary and some of the elders of
7:36 At this the **p** went in and stood before the altar and
10:42 because it belongs to the **p** who minister there.
11:23 of the elders of Israel and some of the **p**,
1Mc 12: 6 the senate of the nation, the **p**,
14:20 the high priest Simon and to the elders and the **p**
14:28 of the **p** and the people and the rulers of the nation
14:41 and their **p** have resolved that Simon should
14:44 of the people or **p** shall be permitted to nullify any
14:47 to be commander and ethnarch of the Jews and **p**,
2Mc 1:10 who is of the family of the anointed **p**,
1:13 of Nanea by a deception employed by the **p** of
1:15 When the **p** of the temple of Nanea had set out
1:19 the pious **p** of that time took some of the fire of
1:20 the descendants of the **p** who had hidden the fire
1:21 Nehemiah ordered the **p** to sprinkle the liquid on
1:23 the **p** offered prayer—the **p** and everyone.
1:30 Then the **p** sang the hymns.
1:33 in the place where the exiled **p** had hidden the fire,
3:15 The **p** prostrated themselves before the altar
4:14 that the **p** were no longer intent upon their service
14:31 while the **p** were offering the customary sacrifices,
14:34 the **p** stretched out their hands toward heaven
15:31 and stationed the **p** before the altar,
1Es 1: 2 having placed the **p** according to their divisions,
1: 7 to the people and the **p** and Levites. B
1: 8 the chief officers of the temple, gave to the **p** for
1:10 The **p** and the Levites, having the unleavened B
1:13 for themselves and for their kindred the **p**,
1:14 because the **p** were offering the fat until nightfall;
1:14 for themselves and for their kindred the **p**,
1:21 the **p** and Levites and the people of Judah and B
1:49 of the people and of the **p** committed many acts
2: 8 and the **p** and the Levites, B
4:53 they and their children and all the **p** who came.
5: 5 the **p**, the descendants of Phinehas son of Aaron;
5:24 The **p**: the descendants of Jedaiah
5:38 Of the **p** the following had assumed the priesthood
5:39 they were excluded from serving as **p**.
5:46 The **p**, the Levites, and some of the people settled
5:48 Then Jeshua son of Jozadak, with his fellow **p**,
5:56 and the levitical **p** and all who had come back C
5:59 And the **p** stood arrayed in their vestments,
5:63 of the levitical **p** and heads of ancestral houses, C
6:30 for daily use as the **p** in Jerusalem may indicate,
7: 6 And the people of Israel, the **p**, the Levites,
7: 9 and the **p** and the Levites stood arrayed B
7:10 the **p** and the Levites were purified together. B
7:12 the returned captives and for their kindred the **p**
8: 5 people of Israel and some of the **p** and Levites B
8:10 and of the **p** and Levites and others in our realm, B
8:22 the **p** or Levites or temple singers or gatekeepers
8:42 of the descendants of the **p** or of the Levites,
8:46 at that place to send us men to serve as **p** in
8:54 Then I set apart twelve of the leaders of the **p**,
8:59 to the leaders of the **p** and the Levites, B
8:60 So the **p** and the Levites who took the silver B
8:69 Israel and the rulers and the **p** and the Levites B
8:77 and our kings and our **p** were given over to
8:96 leaders of the **p** and Levites of all Israel swear B
9:18 Of the **p**, those who were brought in and found
9:37 The **p** and the Levites and the Israelites settled B
9:40 men and women, and all the **p** to hear the law,
3Mc 1:11 not even all of the **p**, but only
1:16 the **p** in all their vestments prostrated themselves
6: 1 famous among the **p** of the country,
7:13 their **p** and the whole multitude shouted
2Es 10:22 our **p** have been burned to death,
4Mc 4: 9 While the **p** together with women

PRIESTS' (5) [PRIEST]

Dt 18: 3 This shall be the **p** due from the people,
Jos 4: 3 from the place where the **p** feet stood,
4:18 and the soles of the **p** feet touched dry ground,
1Es 4:54 also concerning their support and the **p** vestments
5:45 and one hundred **p** vestments.

PRIME (3)

Job 29: 4 in my **p**, when the friendship of God was
3Mc 4: 8 Their husbands, in the **p** of youth,
4Mc 2: 3 when he was young and in his **p** for intercourse,

PRIMEVAL (2)

Eze 26:20 among **p** ruins, with those who go down to the Pit,
2Es 7:30 Then the world shall be turned back to **p** silence

PRINCE[‡] (65) [PRINCES, PRINCESS, PRINCESSES]

Ge 23: 6 you are a mighty **p** among us.
34: 2 Shechem son of Hamor the Hivite, **p** of the region,
Dt 33:16 on the brow of the **p** among his brothers.
1Sa 25:30 and has appointed you **p** over Israel,
2Sa 3:38 a **p** and a great man has fallen this day in Israel?
6:21 to appoint me as **p** over Israel,
7: 8 from the pasture, from following the sheep to be **p**
2Ki 20: 5 and say to Hezekiah **p** of my people,
1Ch 2:10 **p** of the sons of Judah.
29:22 they anointed him as the LORD's **p**,
2Ch 11:22 of Maacah as chief **p** among his brothers,
Ezr 1: 8 who counted them out to Sheshbazzar the **p**
Job 21:28 For you say, 'Where is the house of the **p**?
31:37 like a **p** I would approach him.
Ps 82: 7 you shall die like mortals, and fall like any **p**."
Pr 14:28 without people a **p** is ruined.
SS 6:12 my fancy set me in a chariot beside my **p**.
Isa 9: 6 Mighty God, Everlasting Father, **P** of Peace.
Jer 30:21 Their **p** shall be one of their own,
Eze 7:27 the **p** shall be wrapped in despair,
Eze 12:10 This oracle concerns the **p** in Jerusalem and all
12:12 the **p** who is among them shall lift his baggage
21:25 As for you, vile, wicked **p** of Israel,
28: 2 say to the **p** of Tyre, Thus says the Lord GOD:
30:13 there shall no longer be a **p** in the land of Egypt;
31:11 I gave it into the hand of the **p** of the nations;
34:24 and my servant David shall be **p** among them;
37:25 and my servant David shall be their **p** forever.
38: 2 the chief **p** of Meshech and Tubal.
38: 3 O Gog, chief **p** of Meshech and Tubal;
39: 1 O Gog, chief **p** of Meshech and Tubal!
44: 3 Only the **p**, because he is a **p**, may sit in it
45: 7 And to the **p** shall belong the land on both sides of
45:16 All the people of the land shall join with the **p**
45:17 But this shall be the obligation of the **p** regarding
45:22 On that day the **p** shall provide for himself and all
46: 2 The **p** shall enter by the vestibule of the gate
46: 4 the **p** offers to the LORD on the sabbath day shall
46: 8 the **p** enters, he shall come in by the vestibule of
46:10 they come in, the **p** shall come in with them;
46:12 When the **p** provides a freewill offering,
46:16 If the **p** makes a gift to any of his sons out
46:17 then it shall revert to the **p**;
46:18 The **p** shall not take any of the inheritance of
48:21 of the property of the city shall belong to the **p**.
48:21 it shall belong to the **p**.
48:22 be in the middle of that which belongs to the **p**.
48:22 The portion of the **p** shall lie between the territory
Da 8:11 Even against the **p** of the host it acted arrogantly;
8:25 and shall even rise up against the **P** of princes.
9:25 of an anointed **p**, there shall be seven weeks;
9:26 of the **p** who is to come shall destroy the city and
10:13 But the **p** of the kingdom of Persia opposed me
10:13 and I left him there with the **p** of the kingdom
10:20 Now I must return to fight against the **p** of Persia,
10:20 the **p** of Greece will come.
10:21 against these princes except Michael, your **p**.
11:22 and the **p** of the covenant as well.
12: 1 "At that time Michael, the great **p**,
Hos 3: 4 or **p**, without sacrifice or pillar, without ephod
Jdt 9:10 the slave with the **p** and the **p** with his servant;
Sir 10:24 The **p** and the judge and the ruler are honored,
41:17 and of a lie, before a **p** or a ruler;

PRINCES[‡] (77) [PRINCE]

Ge 17:20 he shall be the father of twelve **p**,
25:16 twelve **p** according to their tribes.
Jos 13:21 as **p** of Sihon, who lived in the land.
Jdg 5: 3 "Hear, O kings; give ear, O **p**;
1Sa 2: 8 to make them sit with **p** and inherit a seat of honor.
2Sa 10: 3 the **p** of the Ammonites said to their lord Hanun,
2Ki 10:13 the royal **p** and the sons of the queen mother."
1Ch 7:40 select mighty warriors, chief of the **p**.
Job 3:15 or with **p** who have gold,
12:21 He pours contempt on **p**, and looses the belt of
29:10 the voices of **p** were hushed,
34:18 and to **p**, 'You wicked men!';
Ps 45:16 you will make them **p** in all the earth.
47: 9 The **p** of the peoples gather as the people of
68:27 the **p** of Judah in a body, the **p** of Zebulun, the **p** of Naphtali.
76:12 who cuts off the spirit of **p**,
83:11 all their **p** like Zebah and Zalmunna,
107:40 on **p** and makes them wander in trackless wastes;
113: 8 to make them sit with **p**, with the **p** of his people.
118: 9 in the LORD than to put confidence in **p**.
119:23 Even though **p** sit plotting against me,
119:161 **P** persecute me without cause,
146: 3 Do not put your trust in **p**, in mortals,
148:11 **p** and all rulers of the earth!
Pr 19:10 much less for a slave to rule over **p**.
Ecc 10: 7 and **p** walking on foot like slaves.
10:16 and your **p** feast in the morning!
10:17 and your **p** feast at the proper time—
Isa 1:23 Your **p** are rebels and companions of thieves.
3: 4 And I will make boys their **p**,
3:14 into judgment with the elders and **p** of his people:
19:11 The **p** of Zoan are utterly foolish;
19:13 The **p** of Zoan have become fools,
19:13 and the **p** of Memphis are deluded;
23: 8 the bestower of crowns, whose merchants were **p**,
32: 1 and **p** will rule with justice.
34:12 and all its **p** shall be nothing.
40:23 who brings **p** to naught, and makes the rulers of
43:28 Therefore I profaned the **p** of the sanctuary,
49: 7 **p**, and they shall prostrate themselves,
Jer 1:18 against the kings of Judah, its **p**, its priests,
La 1: 6 Her **p** have become like stags that find no pasture;
2: 9 her king and **p** are among the nations;
4: 7 Her **p** were purer than snow, whiter than milk;
5:12 **P** are hung up by their hands;
Eze 19: 1 for you, raise up a lamentation for the **p** of Israel,
21:12 it is against all Israel's **p**;
22: 6 The **p** of Israel in you,
22:25 Its **p** within it are like a roaring lion tearing
26:16 the **p** of the sea shall step down from their thrones;
27:21 and all the **p** of Kedar were your favored dealers
32:29 Edom is there, its kings and all its **p**,
32:30 The **p** of the north are there, all of them,
39:18 and drink the blood of the **p** of the earth—
45: 8 And my **p** shall no longer oppress my people;
45: 9 Thus says the Lord GOD: Enough, O **p** of Israel!
Da 8:25 and shall even rise up against the Prince of **p**.
9: 6 who spoke in your name to our kings, our **p**,
10:13 So Michael, one of the chief **p**, came to help me,
10:21 against these **p** except Michael,

Hos 5:10 The **p** of Judah have become
8: 4 they set up **p**, but without my knowledge.
8:10 under the burden of kings and **p**.
Jdt 5: 2 In great anger he called together all the **p** of Moab
9: 3 and you struck down slaves along with **p**, and **p** on their thrones.
AdE 9: 3 The chief provincial governors, the **p**,
Sir 8: 8 you will learn discipline and how to serve **p**.
Bar 1: 4 and to the nobles and the **p**,
1: 9 and the **p** and the prisoners and the nobles and
1Mc 1: 4 nations, and **p**, and they became tributary to him.
7:26 Then the king sent Nicanor, one of his honored **p**,
2Mc 9:25 how the **p** along the borders and the neighbors
2Es 9: 3 wavering of leaders, confusion of **p**,

PRINCESS (2) [PRINCE]
Ps 45:13 The **p** is decked in her chamber
La 1: 1 She that was a **p** among the provinces has become

PRINCESSES (2) [PRINCE]
1Ki 11: 3 Among his wives were seven hundred **p**
Jer 43: 6 the women, the children, the **p**,

PRINCIPAL (4)
Lev 6: 5 the **p** amount and shall add one-fifth to it.
1Ki 3: 4 for that was the **p** high place;
2Mc 10:10 and will give a brief summary of the **p** calamities
1Es 1:32 and the **p** men, with the women,

PRINCIPLE (1) [PRINCIPLES]
4Mc 1:12 my custom is, I shall begin by stating my main **p**,

PRINCIPLES (3) [PRINCIPLE]
4Mc 5:38 but you shall not dominate my religious **p**,
11:15 we ought likewise to die for the same **p**.
18: 6 The mother of seven sons expressed also these **p**

PRIOR (2)
Ru 4: 4 for there is no one **p** to you to redeem it,
Wis 19:13 upon the sinners without **p** signs in the violence

PRISCA (3) [=PRISCILLA]
Ro 16: 3 Greet **P** and Aquila, who work with me
1Co 16:19 Aquila and **P**, together with the church
2Ti 4:19 Greet **P** and Aquila, and the household

PRISCILLA (3) [=PRISCA]
Ac 18: 2 who had recently come from Italy with his wife **P**,
18:18 accompanied by **P** and Aquila.
18:26 but when **P** and Aquila heard him,

PRISON (75) [IMPRISONED, IMPRISONMENT, IMPRISONMENTS, IMPRISONS, PRISONER, PRISONERS, PRISONS]
Ge 39:20 Joseph's master took him and put him into the **p**,
39:20 prisoners were confined; he remained there in **p**.
39:22 the prisoners who were in the **p**,
40: 3 in the **p** where Joseph was confined.
40: 5 who were confined in the **p**—
42:16 while the rest of you remain in **p**,
42:17 And he put them all together in **p** for three days.
Jdg 16:21 and he ground at the mill in the **p**.
16:25 So they called Samson out of the **p**,
1Ki 22:27 in **p**, and feed him on reduced rations of bread
2Ki 25:27 released King Jehoiachin of Judah from **p**;
25:29 So Jehoiachin put aside his **p** clothes.
2Ch 16:10 in **p**, for he was in a rage with him because of this.
18:26 in **p**, and feed him on reduced rations of bread
Ps 142: 7 Bring me out of **p**, so that I may give thanks
Ecc 4:14 One can indeed come out of **p** to reign,
Isa 24:22 they will be shut up in a **p**,
42: 7 from the **p** those who sit in darkness.
Jer 37: 4 for he had not yet been put in **p**.
37:15 for it had been made a **p**.
37:18 that you have put me in **p**?
52:11 and put him in **p** until the day of his death.
52:31 of Judah and brought him out of **p**;
52:33 So Jehoiachin put aside his **p** clothes,
Mt 5:25 and you will be thrown into **p**.
11: 2 John heard in **p** what the Messiah was doing,
14: 3 and put him in **p** on account of Herodias,
14:10 he sent and had John beheaded in the **p**.
18:30 and threw him into **p** until he would pay the debt.
25:36 I was in **p** and you visited me.'
25:39 that we saw you sick or in **p** and visited you?'
25:43 sick and in **p** and you did not visit me.'
25:44 or thirsty or a stranger or naked or sick or in **p**,
Mk 6:17 and put him in **p** on account of Herodias,
6:27 He went and beheaded him in the **p**,
15: 7 in **p** with the rebels who had committed murder
Lk 3:20 added to them all by shutting up John in **p**.
12:58 and the officer throw you in **p**.
22:33 I am ready to go with you to **p** and to death!"
23:19 a man who had been put in **p** for an insurrection
23:25 the one who had been put in **p** for insurrection
Jn 3:24 —John, of course, had not yet been thrown into **p**.
Ac 5:18 arrested the apostles and put them in the public **p**.
5:19 the night an angel of the Lord opened the **p** doors,
5:21 and sent to the **p** to have them brought.
5:22 they did not find them in the **p**;
5:23 the **p** securely locked and the guards standing at
5:25 in **p** are standing in the temple and teaching
8: 3 both men and women, he committed them to **p**.
12: 4 in **p** and handed him over to four squads
12: 5 While Peter was kept in **p**,
12: 6 of the door were keeping watch over the **p**.
12:17 how the Lord had brought him out of the **p**.
16:23 they threw them into **p** and ordered the jailer
16:26 violent that the foundations of the **p** were shaken;
16:27 the jailer woke up and saw the **p** doors wide open,
16:37 and have thrown us into **p**;
16:40 After leaving the **p** they went to Lydia's home;
22: 4 both men and women and putting them in **p**,
24:27 to grant the Jews a favor, Felix left Paul in **p**.
25:14 "There is a man here who was left in **p** by Felix.
26:10 I not only locked up many of the saints in **p**,
Ro 16: 7 my relatives who were in **p** with me;
Col 4: 3 declare the mystery of Christ, for which I am in **p**,
Heb 10:34 For you had compassion for those who were in **p**,
13: 3 Remember those who are in **p**,
13: 3 as though you were in **p** with them;
1Pe 3:19 and made a proclamation to the spirits in **p**,
Rev 2:10 about to throw some of you into **p** so that you may
20: 7 Satan will be released from his **p**
Wis 10:14 and when he was in **p** she did not leave him,
17:16 and thus was kept shut up in a **p** not made of iron;
2Mc 13:21 he was sought for, caught, and put in **p**.
1Es 1:38 Jehoiakim put the nobles in **p**,
4Mc 18:11 as a burnt offering, and about Joseph in **p**.

PRISONER (16) [PRISON]
Ex 12:29 on his throne to the firstborn of the **p** who was in
2Ki 24:12 The king of Babylon took him **p** in the eighth year
Mt 27:15 the governor was accustomed to release a **p** for
27:16 At that time they had a notorious **p**,
Mk 15: 6 Now at the festival he used to release a **p** for them,
Ac 23:18 "The **p** Paul called me and asked me
25:27 to me unreasonable to send a **p** without indicating
Eph 3: 1 a **p** for Christ Jesus for the sake of you Gentiles—
4: 1 I therefore, the **p** in the Lord,
Col 4:10 Aristarchus my fellow **p** greets you,
2Ti 1: 8 of the testimony about our Lord or of me his **p**,
Phm 1: 1 Paul, a **p** of Christ Jesus, and Timothy our brother,
1: 9 and now also as a **p** of Christ Jesus.
1:23 Epaphras, my fellow **p** in Christ Jesus,
2Mc 14:27 to send Maccabeus to Antioch as a **p**
14:33 "If you do not hand Judas over to me as a **p**,

PRISONERS (25) [PRISON]
Ge 39:20 the place where the king's **p** were confined;
39:22 to Joseph's care all the **p** who were in the prison,
Job 3:18 There the **p** are at ease together;
Ps 68: 6 he leads out the **p** to prosperity,
79:11 Let the groans of the **p** come before you;
102:20 the **p**, to set free those who were doomed to die;
107:10 **p** in misery and in irons,
146: 7 The LORD sets the **p** free;
Isa 10: 4 not to crouch among the **p** or fall among the slain?
14:17 who would not let his **p** go home?"
24:22 They will be gathered together like **p** in a pit;
42: 7 to bring out the **p** from the dungeon,
49: 9 saying to the **p**, "Come out," to those who are
61: 1 to the captives, and release to the **p**;
La 3:34 When all the **p** of the land are crushed under foot,
Zec 9:11 I will set your **p** free from the waterless pit.
9:12 Return to your stronghold, O **p** of hope;
Ac 4: 7 When they had made the **p** stand in their midst,
16:25 and the **p** were listening to them.
16:27 since he supposed that the **p** had escaped.
27: 1 they transferred Paul and some other **p** to
27:42 The soldiers' plan was to kill the **p**,
Tob 14:15 and he saw its **p** being led into Media,
Wis 17: 2 they themselves lay as captives of darkness and **p**
Bar 1: 9 from Jerusalem Jeconiah and the princes and the **p**

PRISONS (2) [PRISON]
Isa 42:22 all of them are trapped in holes and hidden in **p**;
Lk 21:12 they will hand you over to synagogues and **p**,

PRIVACY (1) [PRIVATE]
Sir 29:21 bread, and clothing, and also a house to assure **p**.

PRIVATE (11) [PRIVACY, PRIVATELY]
Ge 43:30 So he went into a **p** room and wept there.
1Sa 18:22 "Speak to David in **p** and say, 'See,
18:23 Saul's servants reported these words to David in **p**.
Mk 4:34 but he explained everything in **p** to his disciples.
7:33 He took him aside in **p**, away from the crowd,
Ac 4:32 no one claimed **p** ownership of any possessions,
Gal 2: 2 in a **p** meeting with the acknowledged leaders)
2Mc 4: 5 both public and **p**, of all the people.
9:26 to remember the public and **p** services rendered
4Mc 4: 3 in **p** funds, which are not the property of
4: 6 with the king's authority to seize the **p** funds in

PRIVATELY (13) [PRIVATE]
2Sa 3:27 in the gateway to speak with him **p**,
Mt 17:19 Then the disciples came to Jesus **p** and said,
24: 3 the disciples came to him **p**, saying, "Tell us,
Mk 9:28 his disciples asked him **p**,
13: 3 Peter, James, John, and Andrew asked him **p**,
Lk 9:10 He took them with him and withdrew **p** to
10:23 Then turning to the disciples, Jesus said to them **p**,
Jn 11:28 and told her **p**, "The Teacher is here and is calling
Ac 23:19 tribune took him by the hand, drew him aside **p**,
Tob 12: 6 Raphael called the two of them **p** and said to them,
2Mc 6:21 **p** urged him to bring meat of his own providing,
13:13 After consulting **p** with the elders,
3Mc 3:10 of them aside **p** and were pledging to protect them

PRIVILEGE (2)
2Co 8: 4 for the **p** of sharing in this ministry to the saints—
Php 1:29 For he has graciously granted you the **p** not only

PRIZE (12) [PRIZED, PRIZES]
Pr 4: 8 **P** her highly, and she will exalt you;
Jer 21: 9 and shall have their lives as a **p** of war.
38: 2 they shall have their lives as a **p** of war, and live.
39:18 but you shall have your life as a **p** of war,
45: 5 a **p** of war in every place to which you may go."
1Co 9:24 but only one receives the **p**?
Php 3:14 the **p** of the heavenly call of God in Christ Jesus.
Wis 2:22 nor discerned the **p** for blameless souls;
Sir 51:21 therefore I have gained a **p** possession.
4Mc 9: 8 shall have the **p** of virtue and shall be with God,
15:29 who carried away the **p** of the contest
17:12 The **p** was immortality in endless life.

PRIZED (4) [PRIZE]
Jer 20: 5 all its gains, all its **p** belongings,
Lk 16:15 for what is **p** by human beings is an abomination
Sir 45:12 a distinction to be **p**, the work of an expert,
2Mc 4:15 the honors **p** by their ancestors and putting

PRIZES (1) [PRIZE]
Wis 4: 2 victor in the contest for **p** that are undefiled.

PROBABLY (2)
Tob 10: 6 **P** something unexpected has happened there.
2Es 7:*140* [70] there would **p** be left only very few of

PROBE (1)
Job 28:11 The sources of the rivers they **p**;

PROBLEMS (3)
Da 5:12 and solve **p** were found in this Daniel,
5:16 that you can give interpretations and solve **p**.
2Es 4: 3 and to put before you three **p**.

PROCEDURE (2) [PROCEED]
1Ch 24:19 the **p** established for them by their ancestor Aaron,
Est 1:13 the king's **p** toward all who were versed in law

PROCEED (10) [PROCEDURE, PROCEEDED, PROCEEDINGS, PROCEEDS, PROCESSION, PROCESSIONS]
Ge 41:34 Let Pharaoh **p** to appoint overseers over the land,
Dt 2:13 "Now then, **p** to cross over the Wadi Zered."
2:24 "**P** on your journey and cross the Wadi Arnon.
Jos 1: 2 Now **p** to cross the Jordan, you and all this people,
7:13 **P** to sanctify the people, and say,
Job 40: 5 twice, but will **p** no further."
Jer 9: 3 for they **p** from evil to evil,
Hab 1: 7 their justice and dignity **p** from themselves.
Ro 14:23 for whatever does not **p** from faith is sin.
1Mc 15: 4 to make a landing in the country so that I may **p**

PROCEEDED (12) [PROCEED]
Jdg 8:21 So Gideon **p** to kill Zebah and Zalmunna;
18:17 the land **p** to enter and take the idol of cast metal,
20:18 The Israelites **p** to go up to Bethel,
2Ki 10:24 Then they **p** to offer sacrifices and burnt offerings.
Ecc 10: 5 as great an error as if it **p** from the ruler:
Ac 12: 3 he **p** to arrest Peter also.
21: 5 we left and **p** on our journey;
Jdt 12:15 So she **p** to dress herself in all her woman's finery.
2Mc 4:21 upon arriving at Joppa he **p** to Jerusalem.
3Mc 5: 4 **p** faithfully to carry out the orders.
2Es 14:37 as he commanded me, and we **p** to the field,
4Mc 4: 5 he **p** quickly to our country accompanied by

PROCEEDINGS (2) [PROCEED]
2Mc 4:14 in the unlawful **p** in the wrestling arena after
1Es 2:29 that such wicked **p** go no further to the annoyance

PROCEEDS (9) [PROCEED]
Nu 30: 2 according to all that **p** out of his mouth.
30:12 whatever **p** out of her lips concerning her vows,
Pr 12:12 The wicked covet the **p** of wickedness,
Mt 15:18 But what comes out of the mouth **p** from the heart,
Ac 2:45 and goods and distribute the **p** to all,
4:34 or houses sold them and brought the **p**
5: 2 he kept back some of the **p**,
5: 3 to the Holy Spirit and to keep back part of the **p** of
5: 4 after it was sold, were not the **p** at your disposal?

PROCESS (1)
1Es 6:20 Although it has been in **p** of construction from

PROCESSION (7) [PROCEED]
Ne 12:31 that gave thanks and went in **p**.
Ps 42: 4 and led them in **p** to the house of God,

Ps 118:27 Bind the festal **p** with branches,
Isa 60:11 with their kings led in **p.**
2Co 2:14 who in Christ always leads us in triumphal **p,**
1Mc 9:39 a tumultuous **p** with a great amount of baggage;
2Mc 6: 7 of ivy and to walk in the **p** in honor of Dionysus.

PROCESSIONS (2) [PROCEED]

Ps 68:24 Your solemn **p** are seen, O God,
68:24 the **p** of my God, my King, into the sanctuary—

PROCHORUS (1)

Ac 6: 5 **P,** Nicanor, Timon, Parmenas, and Nicolaus,

PROCLAIM (105) [PROCLAIMED, PROCLAIMER, PROCLAIMING, PROCLAIMS, PROCLAMATION]

Ex 33:19 and will **p** before you the name, 'The LORD';
Lev 23: 2 the LORD that you shall **p** as holy convocations,
25:10 the fiftieth year and you shall **p** liberty throughout
Dt 32: 3 For I will **p** the name of the LORD;
Jdg 7: 3 Now therefore **p** this in the hearing of the troops,
2Sa 1:20 **p** it not in the streets of Ashkelon;
1Ki 21: 9 She wrote in the letters, **"P** a fast,
Ne 6: 7 You have also set up prophets to **p** in Jerusalem
8:15 that they should publish and **p** in all their towns
Ps 22:31 and **p** his deliverance to a people yet unborn,
40: 5 Were I to **p** and tell of them,
52: 9 In the presence of the faithful I will **p** your name,
71:17 and I still **p** your wondrous deeds.
71:18 until I **p** your might to all the generations to come.
89: 1 with my mouth I will **p** your faithfulness
97: 6 The heavens **p** his righteousness;
Pr 20: 6 Many **p** themselves loyal,
Isa 3: 9 they **p** their sin like Sodom, they do not hide it.
12: 4 **p** that his name is exalted.
44: 7 Let them **p** it, let them declare and set it forth
48:20 **p** it, send it forth to the end of the earth;
60: 6 and shall **p** the praise of the LORD.
61: 1 to **p** liberty to the captives,
61: 2 to **p** the year of the LORD's favor, and the day
Jer 2: 2 Go and **p** in the hearing of Jerusalem, Thus says
3:12 Go, and **p** these words toward the north, and say:
4: 5 Declare in Judah, and **p** in Jerusalem, and say:
4:16 **P** against Jerusalem, "Besiegers come from
5:20 Declare this in the house of Jacob, **p** it in Judah:
7: 2 and **p** there this word, and say,
11: 6 **P** all these words in the cities of Judah,
19: 2 and **p** there the words that I tell you.
23:18 Who has given heed to his word so as to **p** it?
31: 7 **p,** give praise, and say, "Save, O LORD,
46:14 in Egypt, and **p** in Migdol;
46:14 **p** in Memphis and Tahpanhes;
50: 2 among the nations and **p,** set up a banner and **p,**
Joel 3: 9 **P** this among the nations:
Am 3: 9 **P** to the strongholds in Ashdod,
4: 5 and **p** freewill offerings, publish them;
Jnh 3: 2 and **p** to it the message that I tell you."
Zec 1:14 with me said to me, **P** this message:
1:17 **P** further: Thus says the LORD of hosts:
Mt 4:17 From that time Jesus began to **p,** "Repent,
10: 7 As you go, **p** the good news,
10:27 what you hear whispered, **p** from the housetops.
11: 1 he went on from there to teach and **p** his message
12:18 and he will **p** justice to the Gentiles.
13:35 I will **p** what has been hidden from the foundation
Mk 1:38 so that I may **p** the message there also;
1:45 But he went out and began to **p** it freely,
3:14 and to be sent out to **p** the message,
5:20 to **p** in the Decapolis how much Jesus had done
16:15 ⟦"Go into all the world and **p** the good news to⟧
Lk 4:18 to **p** release to the captives and recovery of sight
4:19 to **p** the year of the Lord's favor."
4:43 "I must **p** the good news of the kingdom of God to
9: 2 and he sent them out to **p** the kingdom of God and
9:60 but as for you, go and **p** the kingdom of God."
Jn 4:25 "When he comes, he will **p** all things to us."
Ac 5:42 at home they did not cease to teach and **p** Jesus as
9:20 and immediately he began to **p** Jesus in
15:21 Moses has had those who **p** him,
16:10 that God had called us to **p** the good news to them.
16:17 who **p** to you a way of salvation."
17:23 therefore you worship as unknown, this I **p** to you.
26:23 he would **p** light both to our people and to
Ro 1:15 —hence my eagerness to **p** the gospel to you
10: 8 the word of faith that we **p**);
10:14 how are they to hear without someone to **p** him?
10:15 And how are they to **p** him unless they are sent?
15:20 Thus I make it my ambition to **p** the good news,
1Co 1:17 For Christ did not send me to baptize but to **p**
1:23 but we **p** Christ crucified,
9:14 that those who **p** the gospel should get their living
9:16 If I **p** the gospel, this gives me no ground for
9:16 and woe to me if I do not **p** the gospel!
11:26 you **p** the Lord's death until he comes.
15:11 so we **p** and so you have come to believe.
2Co 2:12 I came to Troas to **p** the good news of Christ,
4: 5 we do not **p** ourselves; we **p** Jesus Christ as Lord
10:16 that we may **p** the good news in lands beyond you,
Gal 1: 8 or an angel from heaven should **p** to you a gospel
1:16 so that I might **p** him among the Gentiles,
2: 2 with the acknowledged leaders) the gospel that I **p**
Eph 6:15 on whatever will make you ready to **p** the gospel
Php 1:15 Some **p** Christ from envy and rivalry,
1:16 These **p** Christ out of love,
Php 1:17 the others **p** Christ out of selfish ambition,
Col 1:28 It is he whom we **p,** warning everyone and
2Ti 4: 2 **p** the message; be persistent
Heb 2:12 "I will **p** your name to my brothers and sisters,
1Pe 2: 9 in order that you may **p** the mighty acts
1Jn 1: 5 This is the message we have heard from him and **p**
Rev 14: 6 with an eternal gospel to **p** to those who live on
AdE 1:11 in order to **p** her as queen and to place the diadem
Sir 17: 9 to **p** the grandeur of his works.
18: 4 To none has he given power to **p** his works;
31:11 and the assembly will **p** his acts of charity.
39:10 and the congregation will **p** his praise.
1Mc 10:63 "Go out with him into the middle of the city and **p**
2Mc 9:17 a Jew and would visit every inhabited place to **p**
2Es 2:32 until I come, and **p** mercy to them;

PROCLAIMED (78) [PROCLAIM]

Ex 34: 5 and **p** the name, "The LORD."
34: 6 The LORD passed before him, and **p,**
36: 6 and word was **p** throughout the camp:
Dt 15: 2 because the LORD's remission has been **p.**
Jdg 21:13 at the rock of Rimmon, and **p** peace to them.
1Ki 13: 2 and **p** against the altar by the word of the LORD,
13:21 and he **p** to the man of God who came from Judah,
13:32 the saying that he **p** by the word of the LORD
21:12 they **p** a fast and seated Naboth at the head of
2Ki 7:11 Then the gatekeepers called out and **p** it to
9:13 and they blew the trumpet, and **p,** "Jehu is king."
10:20 a solemn assembly for Baal." So they **p** it.
11:12 they **p** him king, and anointed him;
23:16 to the word of the LORD that the man of God **p,**
2Ch 20: 3 and **p** a fast throughout all Judah.
23:11 they **p** him king, and Jehoiada
Ezr 8:21 Then I **p** a fast there, at the river Ahava,
Est 1:20 by the king is **p** throughout all his kingdom,
2: 8 So when the king's order and his edict were **p,**
Ps 145: 6 The might of your awesome deeds shall be **p,**
Isa 41:26 There was no one who declared it, none who **p,**
43:12 I declared and saved and **p,**
61: 7 and dishonor was **p** as their lot,
62:11 The LORD has **p** to the end of the earth:
Jer 23:22 then they would have **p** my words to my people,
36: 9 of Judah to Jerusalem **p** a fast before the LORD.
La 1:15 he **p** a time against me to crush my young men;
Da 3: 4 the herald **p** aloud, "You are commanded,
Jnh 3: 5 they **p** a fast, and everyone, great and small,
Zec 1: 4 to whom the former prophets **p,**
7: 7 Were not these the words that the LORD **p** by
Mt 24:14 of the kingdom will be **p** throughout the world,
26:13 wherever this good news is **p** in the whole world,
Mk 1: 7 He **p,** "The one who is more powerful than I
6:12 So they went out and **p** that all should repent.
7:36 the more zealously they **p** it.
13:10 And the good news must first be **p** to all nations.
14: 9 wherever the good news is **p** in the whole world,
16:20 ⟦they went out and **p** the good news everywhere,⟧
Lk 3:18 he **p** the good news to the people.
12: 3 behind closed doors will be **p** from the housetops.
16:16 then the good news of the kingdom of God is **p,**
24:47 that repentance and forgiveness of sins is to be **p**
Ac 8: 5 to the city of Samaria and **p** the Messiah to them.
8:35 he **p** to him the good news about Jesus.
8:40 he **p** the good news to all the towns until he came
13: 5 they **p** the word of God in the synagogues of
13:24 before his coming John had already **p** a baptism
13:38 through this man forgiveness of sins is **p** to you;
14:21 After they had **p** the good news to that city
15:35 they taught and **p** the word of the Lord.
15:36 the believers in every city where we **p** the word of
17:13 that the word of God had been **p** by Paul in Beroea
Ro 1: 8 because your faith is **p** throughout the world.
9:17 so that my name may be **p** in all the earth."
15:19 around as Illyricum I have fully **p** the good news
1Co 15: 1 of the good news that I **p** to you,
15: 2 if you hold firmly to the message that I **p** to you—
15:12 Now if Christ is **p** as raised from the dead,
2Co 1:19 Son of God, Jesus Christ, whom we **p** among you,
11: 4 and proclaims another Jesus than the one we **p,**
11: 7 I **p** God's good news to you free of charge?
Gal 1: 8 to you a gospel contrary to what we **p** to you,
1:11 gospel that was **p** by me is not of human origin;
Eph 2:17 So he came and **p** peace to you who were far off
Php 1:18 Just this, that Christ is **p** in every way,
Col 1:23 which has been **p** to every creature under heaven.
1Th 2: 9 that we might not burden any of you while we **p**
1Ti 3:16 **p** among Gentiles, believed in throughout the
2Ti 4:17 through me the message might be fully **p** and all
1Pe 4: 6 For this is the reason the gospel was **p** even to
AdE 1:20 Let whatever law the king enacts be **p**
2: 8 So, when the decree of the king was **p,**
6: 9 and let it be **p** through the open square of the city,
1Mc 14:28 the following was **p** to us:
2Mc 8:36 by the capture of the people of Jerusalem **p** that
1Es 8:50 There I **p** a fast for the young men
4Mc 17:23 **p** them to his soldiers as an example

PROCLAIMER (1) [PROCLAIM]

Ac 17:18 "He seems to be a **p** of foreign divinities."

PROCLAIMING‡ (33) [PROCLAIM]

Est 6: 9 through the open square of the city, **p** before him:
6:11 the open square of the city, **p,** "Thus shall it
Jer 34:15 and did what was right in my sight by **p** liberty
Mt 3: 1 the Baptist appeared in the wilderness of Judea, **p,**
4:23 teaching in their synagogues and **p** the good news
Mt 9:35 and **p** the good news of the kingdom,
Mk 1: 4 **p** a baptism of repentance for the forgiveness
1:14 Jesus came to Galilee, **p** the good news of God,
1:39 **p** the message in their synagogues
Lk 3: 3 **p** a baptism of repentance for the forgiveness
4:44 So he continued **p** the message in the synagogues
8: 1 **p** and bringing the good news of the kingdom
8:39 **p** throughout the city how much Jesus had done
Ac 4: 2 because they were teaching the people and **p** that
8: 4 from place to place, **p** the word.
8:12 who was **p** the good news about the kingdom
8:25 **p** the good news to many villages of
11:20 spoke to the Hellenists also, **p** the Lord Jesus.
14: 7 and there they continued **p** the good news.
17: 3 "This is the Messiah, Jesus whom I am **p** to you."
18: 5 Paul was occupied with **p** the word,
20:20 **p** the message to you and teaching you publicly
20:25 among whom I have gone about **p** the kingdom,
28:31 **p** the kingdom of God and teaching about
1Co 2: 1 I did not come **p** the mystery of God to you
9:27 **p** to others I myself should not be disqualified.
2Co 8:18 among all the churches for his **p** the good news;
Gal 1:23 now **p** the faith he once tried to destroy."
1Th 3: 2 our brother and co-worker for God in **p** the gospel
Rev 5: 2 and I saw a mighty angel **p** with a loud voice,
12:10 Then I heard a loud voice in heaven, **p,**
AdE 6:11 through the open square of the city, **p,**
Sir 47: 8 the Most High, **p** his glory;

PROCLAIMS (9) [PROCLAIM]

Ps 19: 1 and the firmament **p** his handiwork.
Jer 4:15 from Dan and **p** disaster from Mount Ephraim.
Na 1:15 of one who brings good tidings, who **p** peace!
Ac 19:13 saying, "I adjure you by the Jesus whom Paul **p."**
2Co 11: 4 and **p** another Jesus than the one we proclaimed,
Gal 1: 9 if anyone **p** to you a gospel contrary
Sir 25: 7 and a tenth my tongue **p:**
43: 2 **p** as it rises what a marvelous instrument it is,
44:15 and the congregation **p** their praise.

PROCLAMATION (27) [PROCLAIM]

Ex 32: 5 and Aaron made **p** and said,
Lev 23:21 On that same day you shall make **p;**
1Ki 15:22 King Asa made a **p** to all Judah, none was exempt:
2Ch 24: 9 A **p** was made throughout Judah and Jerusalem
30: 5 So they decreed to make a **p** throughout all Israel,
Ezr 10: 7 They made a **p** throughout Judah and Jerusalem
Est 3:14 to be issued as a decree in every province by **p,**
Jer 34: 8 the people in Jerusalem to make a **p** of liberty
Da 5:29 and a **p** was made concerning him
Jnh 3: 7 Then he had a **p** made in Nineveh:
Mt 12:41 because they repented at the **p** of Jonah, and see,
Mk 16: S ⟦sacred and imperishable **p** of eternal salvation.⟧
Lk 11:32 because they repented at the **p** of Jonah, and see,
Ro 16:25 according to my gospel and the **p** of Jesus Christ,
1Co 1:21 God decided, through the foolishness of our **p,**
2: 4 and my **p** were not with plausible words
9:18 that in my **p** I may make the gospel free of charge,
15:14 then our **p** has been in vain
2Th 2:14 For this purpose he called you through our **p** of
Tit 1: 3 through the **p** with which I have been entrusted by
1Pe 3:19 also he went and made a **p** to the spirits in prison,
AdE 4: 3 the king's **p** had been posted there was a loud cry
8:17 wherever the **p** was made,
1Mc 5:49 Then Judas ordered **p** to be made to the army
10:64 the honor that was paid him, in accord with the **p,**
1Es 2: 2 and he made a **p** throughout all his kingdom and
9: 3 a **p** was made throughout Judea and Jerusalem

PROCONSUL (4) [PROCONSULS]

Ac 13: 7 He was with the **p,** Sergius Paulus,
13: 8 and tried to turn the **p** away from the faith.
13:12 When the **p** saw what had happened, he believed,
18:12 But when Gallio was **p** of Achaia,

PROCONSULS (1) [PROCONSUL]

Ac 19:38 the courts are open, and there are **p;**

PROCREATION (1)

Heb 11:11 By faith he received power of **p,**

PRODUCE (55) [PRODUCED, PRODUCES, PRODUCING, PRODUCT, PRODUCTION, PRODUCTS]

Ge 41:34 and take one-fifth of the **p** of the land of Egypt
Ex 8:18 The magicians tried to **p** gnats by their secret arts,
Lev 23:39 when you have gathered in the **p** of the land,
25:22 until the ninth year, when its **p** comes in,
26: 4 and the land shall yield its **p,**
26:20 your land shall not yield its **p,**
Nu 18:12 the choice **p** that they give to the LORD,
18:30 then the rest shall be reckoned to the Levites as **p**
18:30 and as **p** of the wine press.
Dt 1:25 and gathered some of the land's **p,**
14:28 the full tithe of your **p** for that year, and store it
16:13 in the **p** from your threshing floor
16:15 the LORD your God will bless you in all your **p**
20:20 the trees that you know do not **p** food;
26:12 of your **p** in the third year (which is the year of
32:13 and fed him with **p** of the field;
33:15 with the finest **p** of the ancient mountains,
Jos 5:11 on that very day, they ate the **p** of the land,
5:12 The manna ceased on the day they ate the **p** of

Jdg 6:4 against them and destroy the **p** of the land,
Ru 4:11 May you **p** children in Ephrathah and bestow
2Sa 9:10 and shall bring in the **p**, so
1Ch 27:27 Over the **p** of the vineyards for
2Ch 31:5 wine, oil, honey, and of all the **p** of the field;
Ps 92:14 In old age they still **p** fruit;
144:13 May our barns be filled, with **p** of every kind;
Pr 3:9 and with the first fruits of all your **p**;
Isa 30:23 and grain, the **p** of the ground,
Jer 29:5 plant gardens and eat what they **p**.
29:28 and plant gardens and eat what they **p**."
La 4:9 deprived of the **p** of the field.
Eze 17:8 that it might **p** branches and bear fruit and become
17:23 in order that it may **p** boughs and bear fruit,
36:30 the fruit of the tree and the **p** of the field abundant,
48:18 Its **p** shall be food for the workers of the city.
Hab 3:17 the **p** of the olive fails and the fields yield no food;
Hag 1:10 and the earth has withheld its **p**.
Zec 8:12 the ground shall give its **p**,
Mal 3:11 so that it will not destroy the **p** of your soil;
Mt 21:34 he sent his slaves to the tenants to collect his **p**.
21:41 to other tenants who will give him the **p** at
24:24 and false prophets will appear and **p** great signs
Mk 12:2 the tenants to collect from them his share of the **p**
13:22 and false prophets will appear and **p** signs
Lk 20:10 in order that they might give him his share of the **p**
1Co 14:7 with lifeless instruments that **p** sound,
2Co 9:11 which will **p** thanksgiving to God through us;
Jas 1:20 for your anger does not **p** God's righteousness.
Sir 1:17 and their storehouses with her **p**.
6:19 and soon you will eat of her **p**.
2Es 3:20 so that your law might **p** fruit in them.
4:30 and will **p** until the time of threshing comes!
5:46 Request it therefore to **p** ten at one time."
7:*55* Say to her, 'You **p** gold and silver and bronze,
16:46 in captivity and famine they will **p** their children.

PRODUCED (18) [PRODUCE]
Ge 4:1 "I have **p** a man with the help of the LORD."
30:39 and so the flocks **p** young that were striped,
41:47 the seven plenteous years the earth **p** abundantly.
Nu 6:4 as nazirites they shall eat nothing that is **p** by
17:8 It put forth buds, **p** blossoms,
Lk 8:8 and when it grew, it **p** a hundredfold."
12:16 "The land of a rich man **p** abundantly.
Ro 7:8 **p** in me all kinds of covetousness.
2Co 7:11 see what earnestness this godly grief has **p** in you,
Php 1:11 having **p** the harvest of righteousness that comes
Tob 2:10 into my eyes and **p** white films.
2Es 3:12 they **p** children and peoples and many nations,
4:30 and how much ungodliness it has **p** until now—
4:31 of ungodliness a grain of evil seed has **p**.
6:48 The dumb and lifeless water **p** living creatures,
7:*116* [46] if the earth had not **p** Adam, or else, when it
had **p** him, had restrained him from sinning.
8:6 of our understanding so that fruit may be **p**,

PRODUCES (21) [PRODUCE]
Lev 25:12 you shall eat only what the field itself **p**.
Pr 25:23 The north wind **p** rain, and a backbiting tongue,
30:33 For as pressing milk **p** curds, and pressing the
nose **p** blood, so pressing anger **p** strife.
Isa 54:16 and **p** a weapon fit for its purpose;
Hag 1:11 on what the soil **p**, on human beings and animals,
Mt 21:43 from you and given to a people that **p** the fruits of
Mk 4:28 The earth **p** of itself, first the stalk, then the head,
Lk 6:45 of the good treasure of the heart **p** good,
6:45 and the evil person out of evil treasure **p** evil;
Ro 5:3 knowing that suffering **p** endurance,
5:4 and endurance **p** character,
5:4 produces character, and character **p** hope,
2Co 7:10 For godly grief **p** a repentance that leads
7:10 but worldly grief **p** death.
Heb 6:7 **p** a crop useful to those for whom it is cultivated,
6:8 But if it **p** thorns and thistles,
Jas 1:3 that the testing of your faith **p** endurance;
Sir 11:3 but what it **p** is the best of sweet things.
38:29 and he **p** them in quantity.

PRODUCING (5) [PRODUCE]
Jdg 9:9 'Shall I stop **p** my rich oil by which gods
9:11 'Shall I stop **p** my sweetness
9:13 'Shall I stop **p** my wine that cheers gods
Rev 22:2 of fruit, **p** its fruit each month;
Wis 19:10 instead of **p** animals the earth brought forth gnats,

PRODUCT (3) [PRODUCE]
Jer 10:9 they are all the **p** of skilled workers.
Hab 2:18 though the **p** is only an idol that cannot speak!
2Es 9:17 and as is the work, so is the **p**;

PRODUCTION‡ (1) [PRODUCE]
Wis 16:26 that it is not the **p** of crops that feeds humankind

PRODUCTS (3) [PRODUCE]
Lev 2:12 to the LORD as an offering of choice **p**,
Hag 2:17 the **p** of your toil with blight and mildew and hail;
Sir 38:29 he is always deeply concerned over his **p**,

PROFANATION (3) [PROFANE]
Jdt 4:3 and the temple had been consecrated after their **p**.
3Mc 1:29 at that time preferred death to the **p** of the place.
2:17 or call us to account for this **p**,

PROFANE‡ (43) [PROFANATION, PROFANED, PROFANELY, PROFANERS, PROFANES, PROFANING]
Ex 20:25 for if you use a chisel upon it you **p** it.
Lev 18:21 and so **p** the name of your God: I am the LORD.
19:29 not **p** your daughter by making her a prostitute,
21:4 as a husband among his people and so **p** himself.
21:6 and not **p** the name of their God;
21:12 the sanctuary and thus **p** the sanctuary of his God;
21:15 that he may not **p** his offspring among his kin;
21:23 that he may not **p** my sanctuaries;
22:2 so that they may not **p** my holy name;
22:15 No one shall **p** the sacred donations of the people
22:32 You shall not **p** my holy name,
Nu 18:32 But you shall not **p** the holy gifts of the Israelites,
Pr 30:9 and steal, and **p** the name of my God.
Isa 56:6 and do not **p** it, and hold fast my covenant—
Eze 7:21 as plunder; they shall **p** it.
7:22 so that they may **p** my treasured place;
7:22 the violent shall enter it, they shall **p** it.
20:39 but my holy name you shall no more **p**
23:39 the same day they came into my sanctuary to **p** it.
24:21 I will **p** my sanctuary, the pride of your power,
28:16 I cast you as a **p** thing from the mountain of God,
Da 11:31 by him shall occupy and **p** the temple and fortress.
Mal 1:12 But you **p** it when you say that
Ac 10:14 I have never eaten anything that is **p** or unclean."
10:15 "What God has made clean, you must not call **p**."
10:28 that I should not call anyone **p** or unclean.
11:8 nothing **p** or unclean has ever entered my mouth.'
11:9 'What God has made clean, you must not call **p**.'
24:6 He even tried to **p** the temple,
1Ti 1:9 for the godless and sinful, for the unholy and **p**,
4:7 to do with **p** myths and old wives' tales.
6:20 Avoid the **p** chatter and contradictions
2Ti 2:16 Avoid **p** chatter, for it will lead people into more
1Mc 1:45 to **p** sabbaths and festivals,
1:48 by everything unclean and **p**,
1:63 to be defiled by food or to **p** the holy covenant;
2:34 nor will we do what the king commands and so **p**
2Mc 5:16 and swept away with **p** hands the votive offerings
15:32 the vile Nicanor's head and that **p** man's arm,
3Mc 2:2 from an impious and **p** man,
2:14 and **p** man undertakes to violate the holy place
4:16 a mind alienated from truth and with a **p** mouth,
4Mc 12:11 "You **p** tyrant, most impious of all the wicked,

PROFANED (45) [PROFANE]
Lev 19:8 because they have **p** what is holy to the LORD;
22:9 and die in the sanctuary for having **p** it:
Isa 43:28 Therefore I **p** the princes of the sanctuary,
47:6 I was angry with my people, I **p** my heritage;
48:11 I do it, for why should my name be **p**?
Jer 19:4 and have **p** this place by making offerings in it
34:16 then you turned around and **p** my name when each
Eze 7:24 and their holy places shall be **p**.
13:19 You have **p** me among my people for handfuls
20:9 that it should not be **p** in the sight of the nations
20:13 and my sabbaths they greatly **p**.
20:14 that it should not be **p** in the sight of the nations,
20:16 not observe my statutes, and **p** my sabbaths;
20:21 everyone shall live; they **p** my sabbaths.
20:22 that it should not be **p** in the sight of the nations,
20:24 but had rejected my statutes and **p** my sabbaths,
22:8 have despised my holy things, and **p** my sabbaths.
22:16 I shall be **p** through you in the sight of the nations;
22:26 to my teaching and have **p** my holy things;
22:26 so that I am **p** among them.
23:38 on the same day and **p** my sabbaths.
25:3 over my sanctuary when it was **p**,
28:18 of your trade, you **p** your sanctuaries.
36:20 they **p** my holy name, in that it was said of them,
36:21 which the house of Israel had **p** among the nations
36:22 for the sake of my holy name, which you have **p**
36:23 which has been **p** among the nations,
36:23 and which you have **p** among them;
39:7 and I will not let my holy name be **p** any more;
Am 2:7 so that my holy name is **p**;
Mic 4:11 "Let her be **p**, and let our eyes gaze upon Zion."
Zep 3:4 its priests have **p** what is sacred,
Mal 2:11 for Judah has **p** the sanctuary of the LORD,
Heb 10:29 **p** the blood of the covenant
Jdt 4:12 to be **p** and desecrated to the malicious joy of
1Mc 1:43 they sacrificed to idols and **p** the sabbath.
2:12 the Gentiles have **p** them.
3:51 Your sanctuary is trampled down and **p**,
4:38 There they saw the sanctuary desolate, the altar **p**,
4:44 the altar of burnt offering, which had been **p**.
4:54 and on the very day that the Gentiles had **p** it,
2Mc 8:2 and to have pity on the temple that had been **p** by
10:5 the same day on which the sanctuary had been **p**
2Es 10:22 name by which we are called has been almost **p**;
4Mc 7:6 nor **p** your stomach, which had room only

PROFANELY (1) [PROFANE]
3Mc 1:21 because of what the king was **p** plotting.

PROFANERS (1) [PROFANE]
3Mc 7:15 since they had destroyed the **p**.

PROFANES (3) [PROFANE]
Ex 31:14 everyone who **p** it shall be put to death;
Lev 21:9 daughter of a priest **p** herself through prostitution,
Lev 21:9 she **p** her father; she shall be burned to death.

PROFANEST See Index to Footnotes

PROFANING (7) [PROFANE]
Lev 19:12 **p** the name of your God: I am the LORD.
20:3 defiling my sanctuary and **p** my holy name.
Ne 13:17 that you are doing, **p** the sabbath day?
13:18 you bring more wrath on Israel by **p** the sabbath."
Isa 56:2 not **p** it, and refrains from doing any evil.
Eze 44:7 **p** my temple when you offer to me my food,
Mal 2:10 **p** the covenant of our ancestors?

PROFESS (2) [PROFESSED, PROFESSES, PROFESSING]
1Ti 2:10 as is proper for women who **p** reverence for God.
Tit 1:16 They **p** to know God, but they deny him

PROFESSED (1) [PROFESS]
Est 8:17 many of the peoples of the country **p** to be Jews,

PROFESSES (1) [PROFESS]
Wis 2:13 He **p** to have knowledge of God,

PROFESSING (1) [PROFESS]
1Ti 6:21 by **p** it some have missed the mark as regards

PROFICIENCY (1) [PROFICIENT]
Sir Pr:1 and had acquired considerable **p** in them,

PROFICIENT (1) [PROFICIENCY]
2Ti 3:17 so that everyone who belongs to God may be **p**,

PROFIT (35) [PROFITABLE, PROFITED, PROFITLESS, PROFITS]
Ge 37:26 "What **p** is it if we kill our brother
Lev 19:16 and you shall not **p** by the blood of your neighbor:
25:36 not take interest in advance or otherwise make a **p**
25:37 or provide them food at a **p**.
1Sa 12:21 not turn aside after useless things that cannot **p**
Job 20:18 the **p** of their trading they will get no enjoyment.
21:15 And what **p** do we get if we pray to him?'
Ps 30:9 "What **p** is there in my death,
Pr 10:2 Treasures gained by wickedness do not **p**,
11:4 Riches do not **p** in the day of wrath,
14:23 In all toil there is **p**,
Isa 30:5 to shame through a people that cannot **p** them,
30:5 that brings neither help nor **p**,
30:6 to a people that cannot **p** them.
44:9 and the things they delight in do not **p**;
Jer 2:8 and went after things that do not **p**.
2:11 for something that does not **p**.
12:13 they have tired themselves out but **p** nothing.
16:19 worthless things in which there is no **p**.
23:32 they do not **p** this people at all, says the LORD.
Hos 7:16 They turn to that which does not **p**;
Mal 3:14 What do we **p** by keeping his command or
Mt 16:26 For what will it **p** them if they gain
Mk 8:36 For what will it **p** them to gain the whole world
Lk 9:25 What does it **p** them if they gain the whole world,
Php 4:17 but I seek the **p** that accumulates to your account.
Wis 6:25 be instructed by my words, and you will **p**.
15:12 and life a festival held for **p**,
Sir 20:14 A fool's gift will **p** you nothing,
29:11 and it will **p** you more than gold.
30:2 He who disciplines his son will **p** by him,
42:5 of **p** from dealing with merchants,
2Mc 2:25 to memorize, and to **p** all readers.
2Es 7:*67* What does it **p** us that we shall be preserved alive
16:42 be like one who will not make a **p**;

PROFITABLE (4) [PROFIT]
Pr 31:18 She perceives that her merchandise is **p**.
Tit 3:8 these things are excellent and **p** to everyone
Wis 8:7 nothing in life is more **p** for mortals than these.
Sir 7:22 Look after them; if they are **p** to you, keep them.

PROFITED (1) [PROFIT]
Wis 5:8 What has our arrogance **p** us?

PROFITLESS (1) [PROFIT]
4Mc 16:7 in vain, seven **p** pregnancies, fruitless nurturings

PROFITS (3) [PROFIT]
Job 34:9 'It **p** one nothing to take delight in God.'
Isa 23:18 her **p** will not be stored or hoarded,
Sir 20:10 There is the gift that **p** you nothing,

PROFLIGATES (1)
2Ti 3:3 implacable, slanderers, **p**, brutes, haters of good,

PROFOUND (3) [PROFOUNDLY]
2Es 7:*85* of the others are guarded by angels in **p** quiet.
7:*95* and guarded by angels in **p** quiet,
4Mc 3:20 a time when our ancestors were enjoying **p** peace

PROFOUNDLY (1) [PROFOUND]
2Es 10:50 that you are sincerely grieved and **p** distressed

PROFUSE (1)

Pr 27: 6 but **p** are the kisses of an enemy.

PROGENITORS See Index to Footnotes

PROGRESS (5) [PROGRESSED]

Php 1:25 and continue with all of you for your **p** and joy
1Ti 4:15 so that all may see your **p**.
2Ti 3: 9 But they will not make much **p**, because,
Sir Pr: 1 even greater **p** in living according to the law.
51:17 I made **p** in her; to him who gives wisdom

PROGRESSED (1) [PROGRESS]

2Mc 4: 3 When his hatred **p** to such a degree that

PROJECTING (4) [PROJECTION]

Ne 3:25 the Angle and the tower **p** from the upper house of
3:26 the Water Gate on the east and the **p** tower.
3:27 the great **p** tower as far as the wall of Ophel.
Eze 43:15 and from the altar hearth **p** upward, four horns.

PROJECTION (1) [PROJECTING]

1Ki 7:20 on the two pillars and also above the rounded **p**

PROLIFIC (2)

Ex 1: 7 But the Israelites were fruitful and **p**;
Wis 4: 3 But the **p** brood of the ungodly will be of no use,

PROLONG (6) [PROLONGED, PROLONGS]

Ps 61: 6 **P** the life of the king;
85: 5 Will you **p** your anger to all generations?
Ecc 7:15 and there are wicked people who **p** their life
8:12 sinners do evil a hundred times and **p** their lives,
8:13 neither will they **p** their days like a shadow,
Isa 53:10 he shall see his offspring, and shall **p** his days;

PROLONGED (7) [PROLONG]

Isa 13:22 its time is close at hand, and its days will not be **p**.
Eze 12:22 which says, "The days are **p**,
Da 4:27 so that your prosperity may be **p**."
7:12 but their lives were **p** for a season and a time.
Wis 4:16 the **p** old age of the unrighteous.
Sir 13:11 for he will test you by **p** talk,
48:23 and he **p** the life of the king.

PROLONGS (3) [PROLONG]

Job 24:22 Yet God **p** the life of the mighty by his power;
Pr 10:27 The fear of the LORD **p** life,
Sir 37:31 but the one who guards against it **p** his life.

PROMINENCE (1) [PROMINENT]

Ps 62: 4 Their only plan is to bring down a person of **p**.

PROMINENT (6) [PROMINENCE]

Ru 2: 1 a **p** rich man, of the family of Elimelech,
1Ch 5: 2 though Judah became **p** among his brothers and
Da 8: 8 and in its place there came up four **p** horns toward
Ac 25:23 the military tribunes and the **p** men of the city.
Ro 16: 7 they are **p** among the apostles,
2Mc 3:11 a man of very **p** position,

PROMISE (78) [PROMISED, PROMISES, PROMISING]

Ge 47:29 under my thigh and **p** to deal loyally and truly
Dt 9: 5 in order to fulfill the **p** that the LORD made
13: 1 by dreams appear among you and **p** you omens
2Sa 7:21 Because of your **p**, and according
22:31 the **p** of the LORD proves true;
1Ki 6:12 then I will establish my **p** with you,
8:20 Now the LORD has upheld the **p** that he made;
8:56 not one word has failed of all his good **p**,
2Ki 15:12 This was the **p** of the LORD that he gave to Jehu,
1Ch 16:16 that he made with Abraham, his sworn **p** to Isaac,
25: 5 according to the **p** of God to exalt him;
2Ch 1: 9 let your **p** to my father David now be fulfilled,
6:10 Now the LORD has fulfilled his **p** that he made;
Ne 5:13 and from property who does not perform this **p**.
9: 8 you have fulfilled your **p**, for you are righteous.
Ps 18:30 the **p** of the LORD proves true;
105: 9 that he made with Abraham, his sworn **p** to Isaac,
105:42 For he remembered his holy **p**, and Abraham,
106:24 having no faith in his **p**.
119:38 Confirm to your servant your **p**,
119:41 O LORD, your salvation according to your **p**.
119:50 that your **p** gives me life.
119:57 The LORD is my portion; I **p** to keep your words.
119:58 be gracious to me according to your **p**.
119:76 according to your **p** to your servant.
119:82 My eyes fail with watching for your **p**;
119:116 Uphold me according to your **p**, that I may live,
119:123 and for the fulfillment of your righteous **p**.
119:133 Keep my steps steady according to your **p**,
119:140 Your **p** is well tried, and your servant loves it.
119:148 that I may meditate on your **p**.
119:154 give me life according to your **p**.
119:170 deliver me according to your **p**.
119:172 My tongue will sing of your **p**,
Jer 29:10 and I will fulfill to you my **p** and bring you back
32:42 upon them all the good fortune that I now **p** them.
Jer 33:14 the **p** I made to the house of Israel and the house
Hag 2: 5 to the **p** that I made you when you came out
Lk 1:55 according to the **p** he made to our ancestors,
Ac 1: 4 but to wait there for the **p** of the Father.
2:33 and having received from the Father the **p** of
2:39 For the **p** is for you, for your children,
7:17 near for the fulfillment of the **p** that God had made
26: 6 of my hope in the **p** made by God to our ancestors,
26: 7 a **p** that our twelve tribes hope to attain,
Ro 4:13 the **p** that he would inherit the world did not come
4:14 faith is null and the **p** is void.
4:16 that the **p** may rest on grace and be guaranteed
4:20 No distrust made him waver concerning the **p**
9: 8 the children of the **p** are counted as descendants.
9: 9 For this is what the **p** said,
Gal 3:14 we might receive the **p** of the Spirit through faith.
3:17 by God, so as to nullify the **p**.
3:18 it no longer comes from the **p**;
3:18 but God granted it to Abraham through the **p**.
3:19 to whom the **p** had been made;
3:29 are Abraham's offspring, heirs according to the **p**.
4:23 of the free woman, was born through the **p**.
4:28 you, my friends, are children of the **p**, like Isaac.
Eph 2:12 and strangers to the covenants of **p**,
3: 6 sharers in the **p** in Christ Jesus through the gospel.
6: 2 this is the first commandment with a **p**:
1Ti 4: 8 holding **p** for both the present life and the life
2Ti 1: 1 for the sake of the **p** of life that is in Christ Jesus,
Heb 4: 1 while the **p** of entering his rest is still open,
6:13 When God made a **p** to Abraham,
6:15 having patiently endured, obtained the **p**.
6:17 the **p** the unchangeable character of his purpose,
11: 9 who were heirs with him of the same **p**.
2Pe 2:19 They **p** them freedom,
3: 4 "Where is the **p** of his coming?
3: 9 The Lord is not slow about his **p**,
3:13 But, in accordance with his **p**,
Tob 6:13 or **p** her to another man without incurring
Sir 29: 3 Keep your **p** and be honest with him,
1Mc 10:24 of encouragement and **p** them honor and gifts,
2Mc 12:25 with many words he had confirmed his solemn **p**
4Mc 15: 3 for eternal life according to God's **p**.

PROMISED (129) [PROMISE]

Ge 18:19 about for Abraham what he has **p** him."
21: 1 and the LORD did for Sarah as he had **p**.
28:15 until I have done what I have **p** you."
Ex 12:25 as he has **p**, you shall keep this observance.
32:13 that I have **p** I will give to your descendants,
Nu 10:29 for the LORD has **p** good to Israel."
11:12 to the land that you **p** on oath to their ancestors?
14:17 be great in the way that you **p** when you spoke,
14:40 We will go up to the place that the LORD has **p**,
23:19 Has he **p**, and will he not do it?
32:24 but do what you have **p**."
Dt 1:11 and bless you, as he has **p** you!
1:21 has **p** you; do not fear or be dismayed."
6: 3 the God of your ancestors, has **p** you.
6:19 from before you, as the LORD has **p**.
6:23 the land that he **p** on oath to our ancestors.
8: 1 in and occupy the land that the LORD **p** on oath
9: 3 as the LORD has **p** you.
9:28 not able to bring them into the land that he **p** them,
10: 9 as the LORD your God **p** him.)
11:25 on all the land on which you set foot, as he **p** you.
12:20 as he has **p** you, and you say,
15: 6 LORD your God has blessed you, as he **p** you,
18: 2 the LORD is their inheritance, as he **p** them.
19: 8 the land that he **p** your ancestors to give you,
26:18 to be his treasured people, as he **p** you,
26:19 be a people holy to the LORD your God, as he **p**.
27: 3 as the LORD, the God of your ancestors, **p** you.
28:68 by a route that I **p** you would never see again;
29:13 as he **p** you and as he swore to your ancestors,
31: 3 also will cross over before you, as the LORD **p**.
31:20 which I **p** on oath to their ancestors,
31:21 into the land that I **p** them on oath."
31:23 the Israelites into the land that I **p** them;
Jos 1: 3 upon I have given to you, as I **p** to Moses.
22: 4 to your kindred, as he **p** them;
23: 5 as the LORD your God **p** you.
23:10 LORD your God who fights for you, as he **p** you.
23:14 of all the good things that the LORD your God **p**
23:15 as all the good things that the LORD your God **p**
Jdg 2: 1 into the land that I had **p** to your ancestors.
1Sa 2:30 'I **p** that your family and the family
2Sa 3:18 for the LORD has **p** David:
7:25 confirm it forever; do as you have **p**.
7:28 and you have **p** this good thing to your servant;
1Ki 2:24 and who has made me a house as he **p**,
5:12 the LORD gave Solomon wisdom, as he **p** him.
8:15 who with his hand has fulfilled what he **p**
8:20 I sit on the throne of Israel, as the LORD **p**,
8:24 you **p** with your mouth and have this day fulfilled
8:25 servant my father David that which you **p** him,
8:26 which you **p** to your servant my father David.
8:53 to be your heritage, just as you **p** through Moses,
8:56 to his people Israel according to all that he **p**;
9: 5 as I **p** your father David, saying,
2Ki 8:19 since he had **p** to give a lamp to him and
20: 9 that the LORD will do the thing that he has **p**:
1Ch 17:23 let it be established forever, and do as you have **p**.
17:26 and you have **p** this good thing to your servant;
27:23 for the LORD had **p** to make Israel as numerous
2Ch 6: 4 who with his hand has fulfilled what he **p**
6:10 and sit on the throne of Israel, as the LORD **p**,
2Ch 6:15 my father David, what you **p** to him.
6:15 you **p** with your mouth and this day have fulfilled
6:16 my father David, that which you **p** him, saying,
6:17 which you **p** to your servant David.
6:20 the place where you **p** to set your name,
21: 7 and since he had **p** to give a lamp to him and
23: 3 as the LORD **p** concerning the sons of David.
Ne 5:12 and made them take an oath to do as they had **p**.
5:13 And the people did as they had **p**.
Est 4: 7 that Haman had **p** to pay into the king's treasuries
Ps 60: 6 God has **p** in his sanctuary:
66:14 that my lips uttered and my mouth **p** when I was
108: 7 God has **p** in his sanctuary:
Isa 38: 7 that the LORD will do this thing that he has **p**:
Mt 14: 7 so much that he **p** on oath
Mk 14:11 and **p** to give him money.
Lk 1:72 Thus he has shown the mercy **p** to our ancestors,
24:49 see, I am sending upon you what my Father **p**;
Ac 7: 5 but **p** to give it to him as his possession and
13:23 to Israel a Savior, Jesus, as he **p**;
13:32 And we bring you the good news that what God **p**
Ro 1: 2 which he **p** beforehand through his prophets in
4:21 that God was able to do what he had **p**.
7:10 and the very commandment that **p** life proved to
2Co 9: 5 in advance for this bountiful gift that you have **p**,
11: 2 for I **p** you in marriage to one husband,
Gal 3:22 so that what was **p** through faith in Jesus Christ
Eph 1:13 were marked with the seal of the **p** Holy Spirit;
Col 1:23 without shifting from the hope **p** by the gospel
Tit 1: 2 who never lies, **p** before the ages began—
Heb 9:15 may receive the **p** eternal inheritance,
10:23 for he who has **p** is faithful.
10:36 you may receive what was **p**.
11: 9 for a time in the land he had been **p**,
11:11 because he considered him faithful who had **p**.
11:39 did not receive what was **p**,
12:26 but now he has **p**, "Yet once more I will shake
Jas 1:12 of life that the Lord has **p** to those who love him.
2: 5 the kingdom that he has **p** to those who love him?
1Jn 2:25 And this is what he has **p** us, eternal life.
Jdt 8: 9 how he **p** them under oath to surrender the town to
8:30 to do for them what we have **p**,
8:33 after which you have **p** to surrender the town
AdE 4: 7 how Haman had **p** to pay ten thousand talents into
14: 5 and that you did for them all that you **p**.
Wis 17: 8 For those who **p** to drive off the fears
Aza 1:13 to whom you **p** to multiply their descendants like
1Mc 11:28 and **p** him three hundred talents.
11:53 But he broke his word about all that he had **p**;
2Mc 1:29 Plant your people in your holy place, as Moses **p**."
2:18 as he **p** through the law.
4: 9 to this he **p** to pay one hundred fifty more
4:27 not pay regularly any of the money **p** to the king.
4:45 **p** a substantial bribe to Ptolemy son of Dorymenes
7:24 but **p** with oaths that he would make him rich
1Es 1: 7 as he **p**, to the people and the priests and Levites.
Man 1: 6 immeasurable and unsearchable is your **p** mercy,
1: 7 to your great goodness you have **p** repentance
3Mc 2:10 you **p** that if we should have reverses
2Es 3:15 an everlasting covenant with him, and **p** him
4:27 not be able to bring the things that have been **p** to
5:40 or the goal of the love that I have **p** to my people."
7:*60* So also will be the judgment that I have **p**;
7:*66* of any torment or salvation **p** to them after death.
7:*119* [49] if an immortal time has been **p** to us,
7:*120* [50] that an everlasting hope has been **p** to us,
4Mc 15: 2 for a time, as the tyrant had **p**.

PROMISES (23) [PROMISE]

Jos 21:45 the good **p** that the LORD had made to the house
Ps 12: 6 The **p** of the LORD are **p** that are pure,
77: 8 Are his **p** at an end for all time?
Ac 13:34 'I will give you the holy **p** made to David.'
Ro 9: 4 the giving of the law, the worship, and the **p**;
15: 8 of God in order that he might confirm the **p** given
2Co 1:20 For in him every one of God's **p** is a "Yes."
7: 1 Since we have these **p**, beloved,
Gal 3:16 the **p** were made to Abraham and to his offspring;
3:21 Is the law then opposed to the **p** of God?
Heb 6:12 through faith and patience inherit the **p**.
7: 6 and blessed him who had received the **p**.
8: 6 which has been enacted through better **p**.
11:13 in faith without having received the **p**,
11:17 He who had received the **p** was ready to offer
11:33 obtained **p**, shut the mouths of lions,
2Pe 1: 4 his precious and very great **p**,
Wis 12:21 and covenants full of good **p**!
Sir 20:23 Another out of shame makes **p** to a friend,
29: 5 and pays back with empty **p**,
1Mc 10:15 of all the **p** that Demetrius had sent to Jonathan,
2Es 5:29 And those who opposed your **p** have trampled

PROMISING (8) [PROMISE]

2Ki 19:10 by **p** that Jerusalem will not be given into the hand
Isa 37:10 by **p** that Jerusalem will not be given into the hand
Jdt 8:11 and pronounced this oath between God and you, **p**
2Mc 4: 8 **p** the king at an interview three hundred sixty
8:11 inviting them to buy Jewish slaves and **p** to hand
11:14 **p** that he would persuade the king,
12:11 **p** to give him livestock and to help his people
3Mc 1: 4 **p** to give them each two minas of gold if they won

PROMOTE (5) [PROMOTED, PROMOTES, PROMOTING, PROMOTIONS]

Dt 23: 6 You shall never **p** their welfare or their prosperity

Job 30:13 They break up my path, they **p** my calamity;
1Co 7:35 but to **p** good order and unhindered devotion to
1Ti 1: 4 that **p** speculations rather than the divine training
2Mc 11:19 in the future to help **p** your welfare.

PROMOTED (4) [PROMOTE]

Est 3: 1 After these things King Ahasuerus **p** Haman son
Da 2:48 the king **p** Daniel, gave him many great gifts,
3:30 Then the king **p** Shadrach, Meshach,
AdE 3: 1 After these events King Artaxerxes **p** Haman son

PROMOTES (1) [PROMOTE]

Eph 4:16 **p** the body's growth in building itself up in love.

PROMOTING (1) [PROMOTE]

Col 2:23 an appearance of wisdom in **p** self-imposed piety,

PROMOTIONS (1) [PROMOTE]

Est 5:11 all the **p** with which the king had honored him,

PROMPT (1) [PROMPTED]

Ex 25: 2 from all whose hearts **p** them

PROMPTED (1) [PROMPT]

Mt 14: 8 **P** by her mother, she said,

PROMPTLY‡ (6)

1Ki 11:40 but Jeroboam **p** fled to Egypt,
Tob 10:10 So Raguel **p** gave Tobias his wife Sarah,
Sir 18:22 Let nothing hinder you from paying a vow **p**,
2Mc 8: 9 Ptolemy **p** appointed Nicanor son of Patroclus,
11:36 as you have considered them, send some one **p** so
3Mc 3: 1 and he ordered that all should **p** be gathered

PRONOUNCE (27) [PRONOUNCED, PRONOUNCING]

Lev 13: 3 he shall **p** him ceremonially unclean.
13: 6 the priest shall **p** him clean;
13: 8 the priest shall **p** him unclean;
13:11 The priest shall **p** him unclean;
13:13 he shall **p** him clean of the disease;
13:15 the raw flesh and **p** him unclean.
13:17 the priest shall **p** the diseased person clean.
13:20 the priest shall **p** him unclean;
13:22 the priest shall **p** him unclean; it is diseased.
13:23 the priest shall **p** him clean.
13:25 and the priest shall **p** him unclean.
13:27 the priest shall **p** him unclean.
13:28 and the priest shall **p** him clean;
13:30 the priest shall **p** him unclean;
13:34 the priest shall **p** him clean.
13:37 and the priest shall **p** him clean.
13:44 The priest shall **p** him unclean;
14: 7 then he shall **p** him clean,
14:48 the priest shall **p** the house clean;
Dt 21: 5 to minister to him and to **p** blessings in the name
Jdg 12: 6 "Sibboleth," for he could not **p** it right.
1Ki 7: 7 of the Throne where he was to **p** judgment,
1Ch 23:13 to him and **p** blessings in his name forever;
Ps 72:17 in him; may they **p** him happy.
1Co 4: 5 Therefore do not **p** judgment before the time,
Wis 9: 3 and **p** judgment in uprightness of soul,
Sir 50:20 to **p** the blessing of the Lord with his lips,

PRONOUNCED (15) [PRONOUNCE]

Lev 13:35 if the itch spreads in the skin after he was **p** clean,
Jos 6:26 Joshua then **p** this oath, saying,
Ne 6:12 but he had **p** the prophecy against me
Jer 11:17 who planted you, has **p** evil against you,
16:10 the LORD **p** all this great evil against us?
19:15 and upon all its towns all the disaster that I have **p**
26:13 about the disaster that he has **p** against you.
26:19 about the disaster that he had **p** against them?
35:17 of Jerusalem every disaster that I have **p**
36: 7 that the LORD has **p** against this people."
44:26 be **p** on the lips of any of the people of Judah in all
Ro 4: 9 then, **p** only on the circumcised,
1Co 5: 3 and as if present I have already **p** judgment
2Pe 2: 3 Their condemnation, **p** against them long ago,
Jdt 8:11 you have even sworn and **p** this oath between God

PRONOUNCING (1) [PRONOUNCE]

Sus 1:53 **p** unjust judgments, condemning the innocent

PROOF (3) [PROVE]

Ps 95: 9 put me to the **p**, though they had seen my work.
2Co 8:24 the **p** of your love and of our reason for boasting
13: 3 since you desire **p** that Christ is speaking in me.

PROOFS (2) [PROVE]

Isa 41:21 bring your **p**, says the King of Jacob.
Ac 1: 3 himself alive to them by many convincing **p**,

PROPER‡ (32) [PROPERLY]

Ex 13:10 You shall keep this ordinance at its **p** time
Lev 23:37 sacrifices and drink offerings, each on its **p** day—
Jdg 6:26 on the top of the stronghold here, in **p** order;
1Ch 15:13 because we did not give it **p** care."
2Ch 24:13 of God to its **p** condition and strengthened it.
30: 3 (for they could not keep it at its **p** time because
Ecc 10:17 and your princes feast at the **p** time—
Isa 28:25 and plant wheat in rows and barley in its **p** place,
Hos 13:13 for at the **p** time he does not present himself at
Mt 3:15 for it is **p** for us in this way
24:45 of food at the **p** time?
Lk 12:42 to give them their allowance of food at the **p** time?
1Co 11:13 is it **p** for a woman to pray to God
Eph 5: 3 be mentioned among you, as is **p** among saints.
1Ti 2:10 as is **p** for women who profess reverence for God.
Jude 1: 6 but left their **p** dwelling, he has kept
Tob 4: 3 "My son, when I die, give me a **p** burial.
Sir 4:23 Do not refrain from speaking at the **p** moment,
10:23 and it is not **p** to honor one who is sinful.
20:20 for he does not tell it at the **p** time.
31:28 the **p** time and in moderation is rejoicing of heart
42: 1 Then you will show **p** shame,
1Mc 12:11 as it is right and **p** to remember brothers.
2Mc 6:21 **p** for him to use, and to pretend that he was eating
8:33 so these received the **p** reward for their impiety.
1Es 1:10 stood in **p** order according to kindred
5:50 and they offered sacrifices at the **p** times
5:51 and offered the **p** sacrifices every day,
3Mc 1:19 and, neglecting **p** modesty,
3:20 to their folly and did as was **p**,
4Mc 5:24 with **p** reverence we worship the only living God.
17: 8 be **p** to inscribe on their tomb these words as

PROPERLY (4) [PROPER]

1Co 7:36 that he is not behaving **p** toward his fiancée,
Eph 4:16 as each part is working **p**,
1Th 4:12 so that you may behave **p** toward outsiders and
4Mc 6:33 we **p** attribute to it the power to govern.

PROPERTIES (1) [PROPERTY]

2Ch 31: 1 to their cities, all to their individual **p**.

PROPERTY (63) [PROPERTIES]

Ge 23: 4 give me **p** among you for a burying place,
31:16 All the **p** that God has taken away
31:18 all the **p** that he had gained,
34:10 live and trade in it, and get **p** in it."
34:23 Will not their livestock, their **p**,
36: 6 all the **p** he had acquired in the land of Canaan;
Ex 21:21 for the slave is the owner's **p**.
22:11 of them that the one has not laid hands on the **p** of
Lev 25:10 to your **p** and every one of you to your family.
25:13 every one of you, to your **p**.
25:25 into difficulty and sells a piece of **p**,
25:27 and the **p** shall be returned.
25:28 and the **p** shall be returned.
25:33 Such **p** as may be redeemed from the Levites—
25:41 to their own family and return to their ancestral **p**.
25:45 and they may be your **p**.
25:46 for them to inherit as **p**.
Dt 3:20 of you may return to the **p** that I have given
19:14 on the **p** that will be allotted to you in the land that
1Sa 25: 2 a man in Maon, whose **p** was in Carmel.
2Ki 9:21 they met him at the **p** of Naboth the Jezreelite.
1Ch 27:31 All these were stewards of King David's **p**.
28: 1 of all the **p** and cattle of the king and his sons,
Ezr 10: 8 of the officials and the elders all their **p** should
Ne 5:13 and from **p** who does not perform this promise.
11: 3 but in the towns of Judah all lived on their **p**
Jer 37:12 to receive his share of **p** among the people there.
Eze 45: 8 It is to be his **p** in Israel.
48:20 the holy portion together with the **p** of the city.
48:21 and of the **p** of the city shall belong to the prince.
48:22 and the **p** of the Levites and of the city,
Mt 12:29 a strong man's house and plunder his **p**,
25:14 summoned his slaves and entrusted his **p** to them;
Mk 3:27 and plunder his **p** without first tying up
Lk 11:21 fully armed, guards his castle, his **p** is safe.
15:12 give me the share of the **p** that will belong to me.'
15:12 So he divided his **p** between them.
15:13 and there he squandered his **p** in dissolute living.
15:30 who has devoured your **p** with prostitutes,
16: 1 to him that this man was squandering his **p**
Ac 5: 1 of his wife Sapphira, sold a piece of **p**;
Gal 4: 1 though they are the owners of all the **p**;
Tob 1:20 Then all my **p** was confiscated;
10:10 as well as half of all his **p**:
14:13 both the **p** of Raguel and that of his father Tobit.
Jdt 16:24 Before she died she distributed her **p**
AdE 8: 1 to Esther all the **p** of the persecutor Haman.
8: 7 "Now that I have granted all of Haman's **p** to you
Sir 28:24 As you fence in your **p** with thorns,
29:16 A sinner wastes the **p** of his guarantor,
33:20 and do not give your **p** to another,
34:24 the person who offers a sacrifice from the **p** of
36:30 Where there is no fence, the **p** will be plundered;
46:19 "No **p**, not so much as a pair of shoes,
1Mc 10:43 let them be released and receive back all their **p**
12:23 to you that your livestock and your **p** belong to us,
15:33 nor seized foreign **p**, but only the inheritance
2Mc 8:14 Others sold all their remaining **p**,
1Es 6:32 and all **p** forfeited to the king.
3Mc 3:28 the **p** of those who incur the punishment,
7:22 Besides, they all recovered all of their **p**,
4Mc 2:14 the **p** of enemies from marauders and helps raise
4: 3 the **p** of the temple but belong to King Seleucus."

PROPHECIES‡ (6) [PROPHESY]

1Co 13: 8 But as for **p**, they will come to an end;
1Ti 1:18 in accordance with the **p** made earlier about you,
Tob 14: 4 not a single word of the **p** will fail.
Sir Pr: 2 Not only this book, but even the Law itself, the **P**,
36:20 and fulfill the **p** spoken in your name.
39: 1 of all the ancients, and is concerned with **p**;

PROPHECY (24) [PROPHESY]

2Ch 9:29 and in the **p** of Ahijah the Shilonite,
15: 8 the **p** of Azariah son of Oded, he took courage,
Ne 6:12 but he had pronounced the **p** against me
Pr 29:18 Where there is no **p**, the people cast off restraint,
Mt 13:14 With them indeed is fulfilled the **p** of Isaiah
Lk 1:67 with the Holy Spirit and spoke this **p**:
Ac 21: 9 four unmarried daughters who had the gift of **p**.
Ro 12: 6 the grace to us: **p**, in proportion to faith;
1Co 12:10 to another **p**, to another the discernment of spirits,
14: 6 in some revelation or knowledge or **p** or teaching?
14:22 while **p** is not for unbelievers but for believers.
1Ti 4:14 which was given to you through **p** with the laying
2Pe 1:20 that no **p** of scripture is a matter
1:21 because no **p** ever came by human will,
Rev 1: 3 the words of the **p**, and blessed are those who hear
19:10 For the testimony of Jesus is the spirit of **p**."
22: 7 Blessed is the one who keeps the words of the **p**
22:10 "Do not seal up the words of the **p** of this book,
22:18 I warn everyone who hears the words of the **p**
22:19 from the words of the book of this **p**,
Tob 2: 6 Then I remembered the **p** of Amos,
Sir 24:33 I will again pour out teaching like **p**,
46:20 and lifted up his voice from the ground in **p**,
2Es 15: 1 Speak in the ears of my people the words of the **p**

PROPHESIED (37) [PROPHESY]

Nu 11:25 and when the spirit rested upon them, they **p**.
11:26 and so they **p** in the camp.
1Sa 10:11 When all who knew him before saw how he **p**
1Ch 25: 2 who **p** under the direction of the king.
25: 3 under the direction of their father Jeduthun, who **p**
2Ch 20:37 of Dodavahu of Mareshah **p** against Jehoshaphat,
Ezr 5: 1 **p** to the Jews who were in Judah and Jerusalem,
Jer 2: 8 the prophets **p** by Baal, and went after things
20: 6 to whom you have **p** falsely.
23:13 they **p** by Baal and led my people Israel astray.
23:21 I did not speak to them, yet they **p**.
25:13 which Jeremiah **p** against all the nations.
26: 9 Why have you **p** in the name of the LORD,
26:11 of death because he has **p** against this city,
26:18 who **p** during the days of King Hezekiah of Judah,
26:20 He **p** against this city and against this land
28: 6 may the LORD fulfill the words that you have **p**,
28: 8 and me from ancient times **p** war,
29:31 Because Shemaiah has **p** to you,
37:19 Where are your prophets who **p** to you, saying,
Eze 13:16 the prophets of Israel who **p** concerning Jerusalem
37: 7 So I **p** as I had been commanded; and as I **p**,
37:10 I **p** as he commanded me,
38:17 in those days **p** for years that I would bring you
Mt 11:13 For all the prophets and the law **p** until John came;
15: 7 Isaiah **p** rightly about you when he said:
Mk 7: 6 "Isaiah **p** rightly about you hypocrites,
Jn 11:51 but being high priest that year he **p** that Jesus was
Ac 19: 6 and they spoke in tongues and **p**—
1Pe 1:10 the prophets who **p** of the grace that was to
Jude 1:14 in the seventh generation from Adam, **p**, saying,
Sir 46:20 he **p** and made known to the king his death,
48:13 and when he was dead, his body **p**.
1Es 6: 1 and Zechariah son of Iddo **p** to the Jews who were
6: 1 they **p** to them in the name of the Lord God
7: 3 while the prophets Haggai and Zechariah **p**;

PROPHESIES (7) [PROPHESY]

1Ki 22: 8 for he never **p** anything favorable about me,
2Ch 18: 7 for he never **p** anything favorable about me,
Jer 28: 9 As for the prophet who **p** peace,
Eze 12:27 for many years ahead; he **p** for distant times."
1Co 11: 4 Any man who prays or **p** with something on his
11: 5 or **p** with her head unveiled disgraces her head—
14: 5 One who **p** is greater than one who speaks

PROPHESY (76) [PROPHECIES, PROPHECY, PROPHESIED, PROPHESIES, PROPHESYING, PROPHET, PROPHET'S, PROPHETESS, PROPHETIC, PROPHETICALLY, PROPHETS]

1Ki 22:18 not tell you that he would not **p** anything favorable
1Ch 25: 1 and of Jeduthun, who should **p** with lyres, harps,
2Ch 18:17 not tell you that he would not **p** anything favorable
Isa 30:10 and to the prophets, "Do not **p** to us what is right;
30:10 speak to us smooth things, **p** illusions,
Jer 5:31 the prophets **p** falsely, and the priests rule as
11:21 "You shall not **p** in the name of the LORD,
14:15 the prophets who **p** in my name though I did
14:16 to whom they **p** shall be thrown out into the streets
19:14 where the LORD had sent him to **p**,
23:16 Do not listen to the words of the prophets who **p**
23:25 the prophets have said who **p** lies in my name,
23:26 who **p** lies, and who **p** the deceit of their own
23:32 See, I am against those who **p** lying dreams,
25:30 therefore, shall **p** against them all these words,
26:12 the LORD who sent me to **p** against this house
32: 3 Zedekiah had said, "Why do you **p** and say:
Eze 4: 7 and with your arm bared you shall **p** against it.
6: 2 the mountains of Israel, and **p** against them,
11: 4 Therefore **p** against them; **p**, O mortal."

Eze 13: 2 **p** against the prophets of Israel
13: 2 say to those who **p** out of their own imagination:
13:17 who **p** out of their own imagination; **p** against them
20:46 and **p** against the forest land in the Negeb;
21: 2 **p** against the land of Israel
21: 9 **p** and say: Thus says the Lord;
21:14 And you, mortal, **p**; Strike hand to hand.
21:28 As for you, mortal, **p**, and say,
25: 2 toward the Ammonites and **p** against them.
28:21 set your face toward Sidon, and **p** against it,
29: 2 and **p** against him and against all Egypt;
30: 2 **p**, and say, Thus says the Lord GOD:
34: 2 **p** against the shepherds of Israel: **p**, and say to
35: 2 set your face against Mount Seir, and **p** against it,
36: 1 you, mortal, **p** to the mountains of Israel, and say:
36: 3 therefore **p**, and say: Thus says the Lord GOD:
36: 6 Therefore **p** concerning the land of Israel,
37: 4 he said to me, **"P** to these bones, and say to them:
37: 9 Then he said to me, **"P** to the breath, **p**,
37:12 **p**, and say to them, Thus says the Lord GOD:
38: 2 prince of Meshech and Tubal. **P** against him
38:14 Therefore, mortal, **p**, and say to Gog:
39: 1 And you, mortal, **p** against Gog, and say:
Joel 2:28 your sons and your daughters shall **p**,
Am 2:12 the prophets, saying, "You shall not **p."**
3: 8 The Lord GOD has spoken; who can but **p?**
7:12 earn your bread there, and **p** there;
7:13 but never again **p** at Bethel,
7:15 'Go, **p** to my people Israel.'
7:16 You say, 'Do not **p** against Israel,
Zec 13: 3 shall pierce them through when they **p.**
13: 4 every one, of their visions when they **p;**
Mt 7:22 'Lord, Lord, did we not **p** in your name,
26:68 **"P** to us, you Messiah! Who is it that struck you?"
Mk 14:65 and to strike him, saying to him, **"P!"**
Lk 22:64 also blindfolded him and kept asking him, **"P!**
Ac 2:17 and your sons and your daughters shall **p**,
2:18 I will pour out my Spirit; and they shall **p.**
1Co 13: 9 For we know only in part, and we **p** only in part;
14: 1 and especially that you may **p.**
14: 3 those who **p** speak to other people
14: 4 but those who **p** build up the church.
14: 5 of you to speak in tongues, but even more to **p.**
14:24 But if all **p**, an unbeliever or outsider who enters
14:31 For you can all **p** one by one,
14:39 So, my friends, be eager to **p**,
Rev 10:11 "You must **p** again about many peoples
11: 3 And I will grant my two witnesses authority to **p**
Jdt 6: 2 to **p** among us as you have done today and tell us
Wis 14:28 their worshipers either rave in exultation, or **p** lies,
Sir 47: 1 him Nathan rose up to **p** in the days of David.

PROPHESYING (21) [PROPHESY]

Nu 11:27 "Eldad and Medad are **p** in the camp."
1Ki 22:10 and all the prophets were **p** before them.
22:12 All the prophets were **p** the same and saying,
2Ch 18: 9 and all the prophets were **p** before them.
18:11 All the prophets were **p** the same and saying,
Ezr 6:14 the **p** of the prophet Haggai and Zechariah son
Jer 14:14 The prophets are **p** lies in my name;
14:14 They are **p** to you a lying vision,
20: 1 heard Jeremiah **p** these things.
26:20 There was another man **p** in the name of
27:10 For they are **p** a lie to you,
27:14 for they are **p** a lie to you.
27:15 but they are **p** falsely in my name,
27:15 you and the prophets who are **p** to you.
27:16 not listen to the words of your prophets who are **p**
27:16 for they are **p** a lie to you.
29: 9 for it is a lie that they are **p** to you in my name;
29:21 who are **p** a lie to you in my name:
Eze 11:13 Now, while I was **p**, Pelatiah son of Benaiah died.
13: 2 prophesy against the prophets of Israel who are **p;**
Rev 11: 6 so that no rain may fall during the days of their **p**,

PROPHET‡ (254) [PROPHESY]

A. FALSE PROPHET (4)

Ge 20: 7 Now then, return the man's wife; for he is a **p**,
Ex 7: 1 and your brother Aaron shall be your **p.**
15:20 Then the **p** Miriam, Aaron's sister,
Dt 18:15 for you a **p** like me from among your own people;
18:15 you shall heed such a **p.**
18:18 a **p** like you from among their own people;
18:18 I will put my words in the mouth of the **p**,
18:19 the words that the **p** shall speak in my name,
18:20 But any **p** who speaks in the name of other gods,
18:20 not commanded the **p** to speak—that **p** shall die."
18:22 If a **p** speaks in the name of the LORD but
18:22 The **p** has spoken it presumptuously;
34:10 since has there arisen a **p** in Israel like Moses,
Jdg 6: 8 the LORD sent a **p** to the Israelites;
1Sa 3:20 that Samuel was a trustworthy **p** of the LORD.
9: 9 the one who is now called a **p** was formerly called
22: 5 Then the **p** Gad said to David,
2Sa 7: 2 the king said to the **p** Nathan,
12:25 and sent a message by the **p** Nathan;
24:11 the word of the LORD came to the **p** Gad,
1Ki 1: 8 and Benaiah son of Jehoiada, and the **p** Nathan,
1:10 not invite the **p** Nathan or Benaiah or the warriors
1:22 with the king, the **p** Nathan came in.
1:23 The king was told, "Here is the **p** Nathan."
1:32 "Summon to me the priest Zadok, the **p** Nathan,
1:34 the priest Zadok and the **p** Nathan anoint him king
1:38 So the priest Zadok, the **p** Nathan,
1:44 the **p** Nathan, and Benaiah son of Jehoiada,
1Ki 1:45 the **p** Nathan have anointed him king at Gihon;
11:29 the **p** Ahijah the Shilonite found him on the road.
13:11 Now there lived an old **p** in Bethel.
13:18 the other said to him, "I also am a **p** as you are,
13:20 to the **p** who had brought him back;
13:23 to the **p** who had brought him back.
13:25 and told it in the town where the old **p** lived.
13:26 When the **p** who had brought him back from
13:29 The **p** took up the body of the man of God,
14: 2 for the **p** Ahijah is there,
14:18 which he spoke by his servant the **p** Ahijah.
16: 7 of the LORD came by the **p** Jehu son of Hanani
16:12 which he spoke against Baasha by the **p** Jehu—
18:22 "I, even I only, am left a **p** of the LORD;
18:36 the **p** Elijah came near and said, "O LORD,
19:16 of Shaphat of Abel-meholah as **p** in your place.
20:13 certain **p** came up to King Ahab of Israel and said,
20:22 **p** approached the king of Israel and said to him,
20:38 Then the **p** departed, and waited for the king along
22: 7 "Is there no other **p** of the LORD here
2Ki 3:11 "Is there no **p** of the LORD here,
5: 3 only my lord were with the **p** who is in Samaria!
5: 8 that he may learn that there is a **p** in Israel."
5:13 **p** had commanded you to do something difficult,
6:12 It is Elisha, the **p** in Israel,
9: 1 the **p** Elisha called a member of the company
9: 4 young man, the young **p**, went to Ramoth-gilead.
14:25 the **p**, who was from Gath-hepher.
17:13 the LORD warned Israel and Judah by every **p**
19: 2 to the **p** Isaiah son of Amoz.
20: 1 The **p** Isaiah son of Amoz came to him,
20:11 The **p** Isaiah cried to the LORD;
20:14 Then the **p** Isaiah came to King Hezekiah,
23:18 with the bones of the **p** who came out of Samaria.
1Ch 17: 1 David said to the **p** Nathan,
29:29 and in the records of the **p** Nathan,
2Ch 9:29 are they not written in the history of the **p** Nathan,
12: 5 Then the **p** Shemaiah came to Rehoboam and to
12:15 not written in the records of the **p** Shemaiah and
13:22 are written in the story of the **p** Iddo.
18: 6 "Is there no other **p** of the LORD here
21:12 A letter came to him from the **p** Elijah, saying:
25:15 with Amaziah and sent to him a **p**,
25:16 So the **p** stopped, but said,
26:22 from first to last, the **p** Isaiah son of Amoz wrote.
28: 9 But a **p** of the LORD was there,
29:25 and of Gad the king's seer and of the **p** Nathan,
32:20 the **p** Isaiah son of Amoz prayed because of this
32:32 the vision of the **p** Isaiah son of Amoz in the Book
34:22 the king had sent went to the **p** Huldah,
35:18 in Israel since the days of the **p** Samuel;
36:12 before the **p** Jeremiah who spoke from the mouth
Ezr 6:14 of the **p** Haggai and Zechariah son of Iddo.
Ps 51: T *A Psalm of David, when the* **p** *Nathan came to him,*
74: 9 there is no longer any **p**,
Isa 3: 2 judge and **p**, diviner and elder,
28: 7 the priest and the **p** reel with strong drink,
37: 2 to the **p** Isaiah son of Amoz.
38: 1 The **p** Isaiah son of Amoz came to him,
39: 3 **p** Isaiah came to King Hezekiah and said to him,
Jer 1: 5 I appointed you a **p** to the nations."
6:13 and from **p** to priest, everyone deals falsely.
8:10 from **p** to priest everyone deals falsely.
14:18 **p** and priest ply their trade throughout the land,
18:18 from the wise, nor the word from the **p.**
20: 2 Then Pashhur struck the **p** Jeremiah,
23:11 Both **p** and priest are ungodly;
23:28 Let the **p** who has a dream tell the dream,
23:33 When this people, or a **p**, or a priest asks you,
23:34 And as for the **p**, priest, or the people who say,
23:37 Thus you shall ask the **p**,
25: 2 the **p** Jeremiah spoke to all the people of Judah
28: 1 the **p** Hananiah son of Azzur, from Gibeon,
28: 5 the **p** Jeremiah spoke to the **p** Hananiah in
28: 6 and the **p** Jeremiah said, "Amen!
28: 9 As for the **p** who prophesies peace, when the word of that **p** comes true, then it will be known that the LORD has truly sent the **p."**
28:10 Then the **p** Hananiah took the yoke from the neck of the **p** Jeremiah,
28:11 At this, the **p** Jeremiah went his way.
28:12 the **p** Hananiah had broken the yoke from the neck of the **p** Jeremiah, the word of the LORD came
28:15 And the **p** Jeremiah said to the **p** Hananiah,
28:17 in the seventh month, the **p** Hananiah died.
29: 1 the letter that the **p** Jeremiah sent from Jerusalem
29:26 to control any madman who plays the **p**,
29:27 not rebuked Jeremiah of Anathoth who plays the **p**
29:29 in the hearing of the **p** Jeremiah.
32: 2 and the **p** Jeremiah was confined in the court of
34: 6 Then the **p** Jeremiah spoke all these words
36: 8 of Neriah did all that the **p** Jeremiah ordered him
36:26 to arrest the secretary Baruch and the **p** Jeremiah.
37: 2 the LORD that he spoke through the **p** Jeremiah.
37: 3 of Maaseiah to the **p** Jeremiah saying,
37: 6 the word of the LORD came to the **p** Jeremiah:
37:13 of Hananiah arrested the **p** Jeremiah saying,
38: 9 to the **p** Jeremiah by throwing him into the cistern
38:10 the **p** Jeremiah up from the cistern before he dies."
38:14 for the **p** Jeremiah and received him at
42: 2 the **p** Jeremiah and said, "Be good enough
42: 4 The **p** Jeremiah said to them, "Very well:
43: 6 also the **p** Jeremiah and Baruch son of Neriah.
45: 1 that the **p** Jeremiah spoke to Baruch son of Neriah,
46: 1 of the LORD that came to the **p** Jeremiah
46:13 The word that the LORD spoke to the **p** Jeremiah
47: 1 to the **p** Jeremiah concerning the Philistines,
Jer 49:34 that came to the **p** Jeremiah concerning Elam,
50: 1 the land of the Chaldeans, by the **p** Jeremiah:
51:59 that the **p** Jeremiah commanded Seraiah son
La 2:20 Should priest and **p** be killed in the sanctuary of
Eze 2: 5 they shall know that there has been a **p**
7:26 they shall keep seeking a vision from the **p;**
14: 4 before them, and yet come to the **p—**
14: 7 and yet come to a **p** to inquire of me by him,
14: 9 If a **p** is deceived and speaks a word, I, the LORD, have deceived that **p**,
14:10 the inquirer and the punishment of the **p** shall be
33:33 they shall know that a **p** has been among them.
Da 9: 2 to the word of the LORD to the **p** Jeremiah,
9:24 to seal both vision and **p**,
Hos 4: 5 the **p** also shall stumble with you by night,
9: 7 "The **p** is a fool, the man of the spirit is mad!"
9: 8 The **p** is a sentinel for my God over Ephraim,
12:13 By a **p** the LORD brought Israel up from Egypt,
12:13 and by a **p** he was guarded.
Am 7:14 Then Amos answered Amaziah, "I am no **p**,
Hab 1: 1 The oracle that the **p** Habakkuk saw.
3: 1 of the **p** Habakkuk according to Shigionoth.
Hag 1: 1 by the **p** Haggai to Zerubbabel son of Shealtiel,
1: 3 word of the LORD came by the **p** Haggai, saying:
1:12 and the words of the **p** Haggai,
2: 1 the word of the LORD came by the **p** Haggai,
2:10 the word of the LORD came by the **p** Haggai,
Zec 1: 1 to the **p** Zechariah son of Berechiah son of Iddo,
1: 7 to the **p** Zechariah son of Berechiah son of Iddo;
13: 5 "I am no **p**, I am a tiller of the soil;
Mal 4: 5 the **p** Elijah before the great and terrible day of
Mt 1:22 by the Lord through the **p:**
2: 5 for so it has been written by the **p:**
2:15 spoken by the Lord through the **p**,
2:17 what had been spoken through the **p** Jeremiah:
3: 3 the one of whom the **p** Isaiah spoke when he said,
4:14 through the **p** Isaiah might be fulfilled:
8:17 through the **p** Isaiah, "He took our infirmities
10:41 welcomes a **p** in the name of a **p** will receive
11: 9 then did you go out to see? A **p?**
11: 9 Yes, I tell you, and more than a **p.**
12:17 fulfill what had been spoken through the **p** Isaiah:
12:39 be given to it except the sign of the **p** Jonah.
13:35 to fulfill what had been spoken through the **p:**
14: 5 because they regarded him as a **p.**
21: 4 to fulfill what had been spoken through the **p**,
21:11 "This is the **p** Jesus from Nazareth in Galilee."
21:26 for all regard John as a **p."**
21:46 because they regarded him as a **p.**
24:15 of by the **p** Daniel (let the reader understand),
27: 9 the **p** Jeremiah, "And they took the thirty pieces
Mk 1: 2 As it is written in the **p** Isaiah, "See,
6:15 And others said, "It is a **p**,
11:32 for all regarded John as truly a **p.**
Lk 1:76 you, child, will be called the **p** of the Most High;
2:36 There was also a **p**, Anna the daughter of Phanuel,
3: 4 the book of the words of the **p** Isaiah, "The voice
4:17 and the scroll of the **p** Isaiah was given to him.
4:24 no **p** is accepted in the prophet's hometown.
4:27 in Israel in the time of the **p** Elisha,
7:16 saying, "A great **p** has risen among us!"
7:26 then did you go out to see? A **p?**
7:26 Yes, I tell you, and more than a **p.**
7:39 he said to himself, "If this man were a **p**,
13:33 because it is impossible for a **p** to be killed outside
20: 6 for they are convinced that John was a **p."**
24:19 who was a **p** mighty in deed and word before God
Jn 1:21 "I am not." "Are you the **p?"**
1:23 the way of the Lord,' " as the **p** Isaiah said.
1:25 the Messiah, nor Elijah, nor the **p?"**
4:19 woman said to him, "Sir, I see that you are a **p.**
4:44 a **p** has no honor in the prophet's own country).
6:14 "This is indeed the **p** who is to come into
7:40 some in the crowd said, "This is really the **p."**
7:52 Search and you will see that no **p** is to arise
9:17 He said, "He is a **p."**
12:38 to fulfill the word spoken by the **p** Isaiah:
Ac 2:16 No, this is what was spoken through the **p** Joel:
2:30 Since he was a **p**, he knew that God had sworn
3:22 up for you from your own people a **p** like me.
3:23 be that everyone who does not listen to that **p** will
7:37 up a **p** for you from your own people
7:48 with human hands; as the **p** says,
8:28 seated in his chariot, he was reading the **p** Isaiah.
8:30 up to it and heard him reading the **p** Isaiah.
8:34 "About whom, may I ask you, does the **p** say this,
13: 6 they met a certain magician, a Jewish false **p**, A
13:20 until the time of the **p** Samuel.
21:10 a **p** named Agabus came down from Judea.
28:25 in saying to your ancestors through the **p** Isaiah,
1Co 14:37 Anyone who claims to be a **p**,
Tit 1:12 It was one of them, their very own **p**, who said,
Rev 2:20 a **p** and is teaching and beguiling my servants
16:13 and from the mouth of the false **p.** A
19:20 the false **p** who had performed in its presence A
20:10 where the beast and the false **p** were, A
Wis 11: 1 by the hand of a holy **p.**
Sir 46:13 Samuel was beloved by his Lord; a **p** of the Lord,
46:15 By his faithfulness he was proved to be a **p**,
48: 1 Then Elijah arose, a **p** like fire,
48:22 as he was commanded by the **p** Isaiah,
49: 7 who even in the womb had been consecrated a **p**,
Aza 1:15 In our day we have no ruler, or **p**, or leader,
Bel 1:33 Now the **p** Habakkuk was in Judea;
1Mc 4:46 until a **p** should come to tell what to do with them.
14:41 until a trustworthy **p** should arise,
2Mc 2: 1 **p** Jeremiah ordered those who were being deported

2Mc 2: 2 and that the **p,** after giving them
2: 4 It was also in the same document that the **p,**
15:14 and the holy city—Jeremiah, the **p** of God."
1Es 1:20 in Israel since the times of the **p** Samuel;
1:28 and did not heed the words of the **p** Jeremiah from
1:32 The **p** Jeremiah lamented for Josiah,
1:47 by the **p** Jeremiah from the mouth of the Lord.
2Es 1: 1 of the **p** Ezra son of Seraiah son of Azariah son

PROPHET'S (5) [PROPHESY]

Am 7:14 "I am no prophet, nor a **p** son;
Mt 10:41 in the name of a prophet will receive a **p** reward;
Lk 4:24 no prophet is accepted in the **p** hometown.
Jn 4:44 that a prophet has no honor in the **p** own country).
2Pe 2:16 with a human voice and restrained the **p** madness.

PROPHETESS (4) [PROPHESY]

Jdg 4: 4 At that time Deborah, a **p,** wife of Lappidoth,
2Ki 22:14 the **p** Huldah the wife of Shallum son of Tikvah,
Ne 6:14 and also the **p** Noadiah and the rest of
Isa 8: 3 I went to the **p,** and she conceived and bore a son.

PROPHETIC (11) [PROPHESY]

1Sa 10: 5 they will be in a **p** frenzy.
10: 6 and you will be in a **p** frenzy along with them and
10:10 and he fell into a **p** frenzy along with them.
10:13 When his **p** frenzy had ended, he went home.
19:20 and they also fell into a **p** frenzy.
19:23 As he was going, he fell into a **p** frenzy,
Ro 16:26 the **p** writings is made known to all the Gentiles,
1Co 13: 2 And if I have **p** powers,
2Pe 1:19 So we have the **p** message more fully confirmed.
Sir 44: 3 those who spoke in **p** oracles;
46: 1 and was the successor of Moses in the **p** office.

PROPHETICALLY (1) [PROPHESY]

Rev 11: 8 of the great city that is **p** called Sodom and Egypt,

PROPHETS‡ (272) [PROPHESY]

A. SERVANTS THE PROPHETS (23)
B. COMPANY OF PROPHETS (11)
C. FALSE PROPHETS (7)

Nu 11:29 Would that all the LORD's people were **p,**
12: 6 When there are **p** among you,
Dt 13: 1 If **p** or those who divine by dreams appear
13: 3 not heed the words of those **p** or those who divine
13: 5 But those **p** or those who divine by dreams shall
1Sa 10: 5 the town, you will meet a band of **p** coming down
10:10 a band of **p** met him;
10:11 before saw how he prophesied with the **p,**
10:11 Is Saul also among the **p?"**
10:12 it became a proverb, "Is Saul also among the **p?"**
19:20 When they saw the company of the **p** in a frenzy,
19:24 Therefore it is said, "Is Saul also among the **p?"**
28: 6 not by dreams, or by Urim, or by **p.**
28:15 either by **p** or by dreams;
1Ki 18: 4 when Jezebel was killing off the **p** of the LORD,
18: 4 Obadiah took a hundred **p,** hid them fifty to a cave,
18:13 when Jezebel killed the **p** of the LORD,
18:13 I hid a hundred of the LORD's **p** fifty to a cave,
18:19 with the four hundred fifty **p** of Baal and
18:19 of Baal and the four hundred **p** of Asherah,
18:20 and assembled the **p** at Mount Carmel.
18:22 but Baal's **p** number four hundred fifty.
18:25 Then Elijah said to the **p** of Baal,
18:40 Elijah said to them, "Seize the **p** of Baal;
19: 1 and how he had killed all the **p** with the sword.
19:10 and killed your **p** with the sword.
19:14 and killed your **p** with the sword.
20:35 a certain member of a company of **p** said B
20:41 The king of Israel recognized him as one of the **p.**
22: 6 Then the king of Israel gathered the **p** together,
22:10 and all the **p** were prophesying before them.
22:12 All the **p** were prophesying the same and saying,
22:13 of the **p** with one accord are favorable to the king;
22:22 and be a lying spirit in the mouth of all his **p.'**
22:23 a lying spirit in the mouth of all these your **p;**
2Ki 2: 3 The company of **p** who were in Bethel came out B
2: 5 company of **p** who were at Jericho drew near B
2: 7 Fifty men of the company of **p** also went, B
2:15 the company of **p** who were at Jericho saw him B
3:13 Go to your father's **p** or to your mother's."
4: 1 a member of the company of **p** cried to Elisha, B
4:38 As the company of **p** was sitting before him, B
4:38 and make some stew for the company of **p."** B
5:22 'Two members of a company of **p** have just B
6: 1 Now the company of **p** said to Elisha, B
9: 1 a member of the company of **p** and said to him, B
9: 7 on Jezebel the blood of my servants the **p,** A
10:19 Now therefore summon to me all the **p** of Baal,
17:13 and that I sent to you by my servants the **p."** A
17:23 as he had foretold through all his servants the **p.** A
21:10 The LORD said by his servants the **p,** A
23: 2 the inhabitants of Jerusalem, the priests, the **p,**
24: 2 of the LORD that he spoke by his servants the **p.** A
1Ch 16:22 not touch my anointed ones; do my **p** no harm."
2Ch 18: 5 Then the king of Israel gathered the **p** together,
18: 9 and all the **p** were prophesying before them.
18:11 All the **p** were prophesying the same and saying,
18:12 of the **p** with one accord are favorable to the king;
18:21 and be a lying spirit in the mouth of all his **p.'**
18:22 a lying spirit in the mouth of these your **p;**
20:20 be established; believe his **p."**
2Ch 24:19 Yet he sent **p** among them to bring them back to
29:25 from the LORD through his **p.**
36:16 despising his words, and scoffing at his **p,**
Ezr 5: 1 Now the **p,** Haggai and Zechariah son of Iddo,
5: 2 and with them were the **p** of God, helping them.
9:11 which you commanded by your servants the **p,** A
Ne 6: 7 You have also set up **p** to proclaim in Jerusalem
6:14 the rest of the **p** who wanted to make me afraid.
9:26 behind their backs and killed your **p,**
9:30 and warned them by your spirit through your **p;**
9:32 upon our kings, our officials, our priests, our **p,**
Ps 105:15 not touch my anointed ones; do my **p** no harm."
Isa 9:15 and **p** who teach lies are the tail;
29:10 he has closed your eyes, you **p,**
30:10 and to the **p,** "Do not prophesy to us what is right;
Jer 2: 8 the **p** prophesied by Baal,
2:26 their officials, their priests, and their **p,**
2:30 Your own sword devoured your **p** like
4: 9 the priests shall be appalled and the **p** astounded.
5:13 The **p** are nothing but wind,
5:31 the **p** prophesy falsely, and the priests rule as the **p** direct;
7:25 I have persistently sent all my servants the **p** A
8: 1 the bones of the priests, the bones of the **p,**
13:13 kings who sit on David's throne, the priests, the **p,**
14:13 Here are the **p** saying to them,
14:14 The **p** are prophesying lies in my name;
14:15 the **p** who prophesy in my name though I did
14:15 By sword and famine those **p** shall be consumed.
23: 9 Concerning the **p:** My heart is crushed within me,
23:13 In the **p** of Samaria I saw a disgusting thing:
23:14 But in the **p** of Jerusalem I have seen
23:15 thus says the LORD of hosts concerning the **p:**
23:15 from the **p** of Jerusalem ungodliness has spread
23:16 Do not listen to the words of the **p** who prophesy
23:21 I did not send the **p,** yet they ran;
23:25 the **p** have said who prophesy lies in my name,
23:26 Will the hearts of the **p** ever turn back—
23:30 See, therefore, I am against the **p,**
23:31 See, I am against the **p,** says the LORD,
25: 4 LORD persistently sent you all his servants the **p,** A
26: 5 the words of my servants the **p** whom I send A
26: 7 The priests and the **p** and all
26: 8 the priests and the **p** and all the people laid hold
26:11 and the **p** said to the officials and to all the people,
26:16 and all the people said to the priests and the **p,**
27: 9 You, therefore, must not listen to your **p,**
27:14 not listen to the words of the **p** who are telling you
27:15 you and the **p** who are prophesying to you.
27:16 the words of your **p** who are prophesying to you,
27:18 If indeed they are **p,** and if the word of
28: 8 The **p** who preceded you and me
29: 1 and to the priests, the **p,** and all the people,
29: 8 Do not let the **p** and the diviners who are
29:15 LORD has raised up **p** for us in Babylon,"—
29:19 I persistently sent to you my servants the **p,** A
32:32 and their officials, their priests and their **p,**
35:15 I have sent to you all my servants the **p,** A
37:19 Where are your **p** who prophesied to you, saying,
44: 4 I persistently sent to you all my servants the **p,** A
La 2: 9 and her **p** obtain no vision from the LORD.
2:14 Your **p** have seen for you false
4:13 the sins of her **p** and the iniquities of her priests,
Eze 13: 2 against the **p** of Israel who are prophesying;
13: 3 for the senseless **p** who follow their own spirit,
13: 4 Your **p** have been like jackals among ruins,
13: 9 be against the **p** who see false visions
13:10 these **p** smear whitewash on it.
13:16 the **p** of Israel who prophesied concerning
22:28 Its **p** have smeared whitewash on their behalf,
38:17 in former days by my servants the **p** of Israel, A
Da 9: 6 We have not listened to your servants the **p,** A
9:10 which he set before us by his servants the **p.** A
Hos 6: 5 Therefore I have hewn them by the **p,**
12:10 I spoke to the **p;** it was I who multiplied visions,
12:10 and through the **p** I will bring destruction.
Am 2:11 of your children to be **p** and some of your youths
2:12 and commanded the **p,** saying,
3: 7 without revealing his secret to his servants the **p.** A
Mic 3: 5 concerning the **p** who lead my people astray,
3: 6 The sun shall go down upon the **p,**
3:11 its **p** give oracles for money;
Zep 3: 4 Its **p** are reckless, faithless persons;
Zec 1: 4 to whom the former **p** proclaimed,
1: 5 And the **p,** do they live forever?
1: 6 which I commanded my servants the **p,** A
7: 3 of the house of the LORD of hosts and the **p,**
7: 7 that the LORD proclaimed by the former **p,**
7:12 by his spirit through the former **p.**
8: 9 from the mouths of the **p** who were present when
13: 2 and also I will remove from the land the **p** and
13: 3 And if any **p** appear again,
13: 4 On that day the **p** will be ashamed, every one,
Mt 2:23 so that what had been spoken through the **p** might
5:12 in the same way they persecuted the **p** who were
5:17 that I have come to abolish the law or the **p;**
7:12 for this is the law and the **p.**
7:15 of false **p,** who come to you in sheep's clothing C
11:13 all the **p** and the law prophesied until John came;
13:17 many **p** and righteous people longed
13:57 **"P** are not without honor except
16:14 and still others Jeremiah or one of the **p."**
22:40 two commandments hang all the law and the **p."**
23:29 of the **p** and decorate the graves of the righteous,
23:30 with them in shedding the blood of the **p.'**
23:31 of those who murdered the **p.**
23:34 Therefore I send you **p,** sages, and scribes,
Mt 23:37 that kills the **p** and stones those who are sent to it!
24:11 many false **p** will arise and lead many astray. C
24:24 and false **p** will appear and produce great signs C
26:56 so that the scriptures of the **p** may be fulfilled."
Mk 6: 4 Jesus said to them, **"P** are not without honor,
6:15 "It is a prophet, like one of the **p** of old."
8:28 and still others, one of the **p."**
13:22 and false **p** will appear and produce signs C
Lk 1:70 as he spoke through the mouth of his holy **p** from
6:23 for that is what their ancestors did to the **p.**
6:26 for that is what their ancestors did to the false **p.** C
9: 8 and by others that one of the ancient **p** had arisen.
9:19 still others, that one of the ancient **p** has arisen."
10:24 that many **p** and kings desired to see what you see,
11:47 the tombs of the **p** whom your ancestors killed.
11:49 'I will send them **p** and apostles,
11:50 of all the **p** shed since the foundation of the world,
13:28 and Isaac and Jacob and all the **p** in the kingdom
13:34 that kills the **p** and stones those who are sent to it!
16:16 "The law and the **p** were in effect until John came;
16:29 Abraham replied, 'They have Moses and the **p;**
16:31 'If they do not listen to Moses and the **p,**
18:31 that is written about the Son of Man by the **p** will
24:25 of heart to believe all that the **p** have declared!
24:27 Then beginning with Moses and all the **p,**
24:44 the **p,** and the psalms must be fulfilled."
Jn 1:45 in the law and also the **p** wrote,
6:45 It is written in the **p,** 'And they shall all be taught
8:52 Abraham died, and so did the **p;**
8:53 our father Abraham who died? The **p** also died.
Ac 3:18 fulfilled what he had foretold through all the **p,**
3:21 that God announced long ago through his holy **p.**
3:24 And all the **p,** as many as have spoken,
3:25 the descendants of the **p** and of the covenant
7:42 as it is written in the book of the **p:**
7:52 Which of the **p** did your ancestors not persecute?
10:43 the **p** testify about him that everyone who believes
11:27 that time **p** came down from Jerusalem to Antioch.
13: 1 the church at Antioch there were **p** and teachers:
13:15 After the reading of the law and the **p,**
13:27 the words of the **p** that are read every sabbath,
13:40 that what the **p** said does not happen to you:
15:15 This agrees with the words of the **p,**
15:32 Judas and Silas, who were themselves **p,**
24:14 down according to the law or written in the **p.**
26:22 but what the **p** and Moses said would take place:
26:27 King Agrippa, do you believe the **p?**
28:23 both from the law of Moses and from the **p.**
Ro 1: 2 which he promised beforehand through his **p** in
3:21 and is attested by the law and the **p,**
11: 3 "Lord, they have killed your **p,**
1Co 12:28 the church first apostles, second **p,** third teachers;
12:29 Are all apostles? Are all **p?**
14:29 Let two or three **p** speak,
14:32 And the spirits of **p** are subject to the **p,**
Eph 2:20 built upon the foundation of the apostles and **p,**
3: 5 now been revealed to his holy apostles and **p** by
4:11 some **p,** some evangelists,
1Th 2:15 both the Lord Jesus and the **p,** and drove us out;
5:20 Do not despise the words of **p,**
Heb 1: 1 in many and various ways by the **p,**
11:32 Jephthah, of David and Samuel and the **p**—
Jas 5:10 take the **p** who spoke in the name of the Lord.
1Pe 1:10 the **p** who prophesied of the grace that was to
2Pe 2: 1 But false **p** also arose among the people, C
3: 2 the words spoken in the past by the holy **p,**
1Jn 4: 1 for many false **p** have gone out into the world. C
Rev 10: 7 as he announced to his servants the **p."** A
11:10 because these two **p** had been a torment to
11:18 the **p** and saints and all who fear your name,
16: 6 because they shed the blood of saints and **p,**
18:20 O heaven, you saints and apostles and **p!**
18:24 And in you was found the blood of **p** and of saints,
22: 6 for the Lord, the God of the spirits of the **p,**
22: 9 with you and your comrades the **p,**
Tob 4:12 for we are the descendants of the **p.**
14: 4 everything that was spoken by the **p** of Israel,
14: 5 just as the **p** of Israel have said concerning it.
Wis 7:27 and makes them friends of God, and **p;**
Sir Pr: 1 to us through the Law and the **P** and the others
Pr: 1 and the **P** and the other books of our ancestors,
36:21 Reward those who wait for you and let your **p**
48: 8 to inflict retribution, and **p** to succeed you.
49:10 the bones of the Twelve **P** send forth new life
Bar 1:16 our rulers, our priests, our **p,** and our ancestors,
1:21 in all the words of the **p** whom he sent to us,
2:20 as you declared by your servants the **p,** saying: A
2:24 which you spoke by your servants the **p,** A
1Mc 9:27 such as had not been since the time that **p** ceased
9:54 He tore down the work of the **p!**
2Mc 2:13 and collected the books about the kings and **p,**
15: 9 Encouraging them from the law and the **p,**
1Es 1:51 the Lord spoke, they scoffed at his **p,**
6: 1 the **p** Haggai and Zechariah son of Iddo
6: 2 the help of the **p** of the Lord who were with them.
7: 3 while the **p** Haggai and Zechariah prophesied;
8:82 which you gave by your servants the **p,** saying, A
2Es 1:32 I sent you my servants the **p,** A
1:36 have seen no **p,** yet will recall their former state.
2: 1 through my servants the **p;** A
7:*130* [60] they did not believe him or the **p** after him,
12:42 For of all the **p** you alone are left to us,
4Mc 18:10 he taught you the law and the **p.**

PROPITIATE (1) [PROPITIATION]

4Mc 4:11 the Hebrews to pray for him and **p** the wrath of

PROPITIATION (1) [PROPITIATE]

Wis 18:21 the shield of his ministry, prayer and **p** by incense;

PROPITIATION (KJV) See also ATONEMENT, ATONING SACRIFICE

PROPORTION (10) [PROPORTIONATE]

Ex 12: 4 be divided in **p** to the number of people who eat
Lev 25:51 for their redemption in **p** to the purchase price;
Nu 35: 8 each, in **p** to the inheritance that it obtains,
Dt 16:10 contributing a freewill offering in **p** to the blessing
Ro 12: 6 to us: prophecy, in **p** to faith;
Tob 4: 8 make your gift from them in **p**;
Sir 28:10 In **p** to the fuel, so will the fire burn,
28:10 and in **p** to the obstinacy, so will strife increase;
28:10 in **p** to a person's strength will be his anger,
28:10 and in **p** to his wealth he will increase his wrath.

PROPORTIONATE (2) [PROPORTION]

Lev 27:23 the priest shall compute for it the **p** assessment up
Dt 25: 2 in his presence with the number of lashes **p** to

PROPOSAL (4) [PROPOSE]

Ge 41:37 The **p** pleased Pharaoh and all his servants.
Da 1:14 he agreed to this **p** and tested them for ten days.
1Mc 1:12 This **p** pleased them,
8:21 The **p** pleased them,

PROPOSALS (1) [PROPOSE]

2Mc 11:36 so that we may make **p** appropriate for you.

PROPOSE (3) [PROPOSAL, PROPOSALS, PROPOSED]

Ge 11: 6 that they **p** to do will now be impossible for them.
2Ch 28:13 for you **p** to bring on us guilt against the LORD
Ac 5:35 consider carefully what you **p** to do to these men.

PROPOSED (7) [PROPOSE]

Dt 1:14 "The plan you have **p** is a good one."
Est 1:21 and the king did as Memucan **p**;
Ac 1:23 So they **p** two, Joseph called Barsabbas,
AdE 6:10 And let nothing be omitted from what you have **p.**"
3Mc 2:27 He **p** to inflict public disgrace on
3:17 when we **p** to enter their inner temple and honor it
2Es 7:23 and **p** to themselves wicked frauds;

PROPOUND (1)

Eze 17: 2 **p** a riddle, and speak an allegory to the house

PROPPED (2)

1Ki 22:35 king was **p** up in his chariot facing the Arameans,
2Ch 18:34 the king of Israel **p** himself up in his chariot facing

PROSELYTE (1) [PROSELYTES]

Ac 6: 5 Timon, Parmenas, and Nicolaus, a **p** of Antioch.

PROSELYTE (KJV) See also CONVERT

PROSELYTES (1) [PROSELYTE]

Ac 2:10 and visitors from Rome, both Jews and **p,**

PROSPECT (1)

Heb 10:27 but a fearful **p** of judgment,

PROSPER (43) [PROSPERED, PROSPERING, PROSPERITY, PROSPEROUS, PROSPERS]

Ge 39: 3 the LORD caused all that he did to **p** in his hands.
39:23 and whatever he did, the LORD made it **p.**
Lev 25:47 If resident aliens among you **p,**
25:49 or if they **p** they may redeem themselves.
Jdg 17:13 "Now I know that the LORD will **p** me,
2Sa 23: 5 Will he not cause to **p** all my help and my desire?
1Ki 2: 3 so that you may **p** in all that you do
1Ch 22:13 Then you will **p** if you are careful to observe
2Ch 24:20 of the LORD, so that you cannot **p?**
26: 5 long as he sought the LORD, God made him **p.**
Ps 1: 3 In all that they do, they **p.**
10: 5 Their ways **p** at all times;
37: 7 do not fret over those who **p** in their way,
90:17 and **p** for us the work of our hands—O **p** the work
122: 6 "May they **p** who love you.
Pr 16:20 Those who are attentive to a matter will **p,**
17: 8 wherever they turn they **p.**
17:20 The crooked of mind do not **p,**
19: 8 to keep understanding is to **p.**
28:13 No one who conceals transgressions will **p,**
Ecc 11: 6 for you do not know which will **p,** this or that,
Isa 48:15 I have brought him, and he will **p** in his way.
52:13 my servant shall **p;** he shall be exalted
53:10 through him the will of the LORD shall **p.**
54:17 No weapon that is fashioned against you shall **p,**
Jer 2:37 and you will not **p** through them.
5:28 with justice the cause of the orphan, to make it **p,**
12: 1 Why does the way of the guilty **p?**
La 1: 5 Her foes have become the masters, her enemies **p,**
Eze 17: 9 Say: Thus says the Lord GOD: Will it **p?**
Da 8:25 By his cunning he shall make deceit **p**
11:36 He shall **p** until the period of wrath is completed,
Mal 3:15 evildoers not only **p,** but when they put God to
Tob 4: 6 for those who act in accordance with truth will **p**
4:19 and that all your paths and plans may **p.**
7:11 and **p** you both this night and grant you mercy
7:12 the God of heaven **p** your journey with his peace."
10:11 The Lord of heaven **p** you and your wife Sarah,
10:12 May we all **p** together all the days of our lives."
Sir 15:10 and the Lord will make it **p.**
26:21 *So your offspring will p,*
2Es 5:12 they shall labor, but their ways shall not **p.**

PROSPERED (21) [PROSPER]

Ge 26:13 he **p** more and more until he became very wealthy.
Jdg 5: 7 The peasantry **p** in Israel, they grew fat
2Ki 18: 7 LORD was with him; wherever he went, he **p.**
1Ch 29:23 he **p,** and all Israel obeyed him.
2Ch 14: 7 So they built and **p.**
31:21 he did with all his heart; and he **p.**
32:30 Hezekiah **p** in all his works.
Ezr 6:14 So the elders of the Jews built and **p,**
Jer 10:21 they have not **p,** and all their flock is scattered.
44:17 We used to have plenty of food, and **p,**
Da 6:28 So this Daniel **p** during the reign of Darius and
Rev 3:17 you say, 'I am rich, I have **p,** and I need nothing.'
Jdt 5:17 long as they did not sin against their God they **p,**
Wis 10:10 she **p** him in his labors,
11: 1 Wisdom **p** their works by the hand of
1Mc 2:47 and the work **p** in their hands.
3: 6 and deliverance **p** by his hand.
4:55 and blessed Heaven, who had **p** them.
14:36 In his days things **p** in his hands,
16: 2 until this day, and things have **p** in our hands so
1Es 7: 3 The holy work **p,** while the prophets Haggai

PROSPERING (6) [PROSPER]

Dt 30: 9 For the LORD will again take delight in **p** you, just as he delighted in **p** your ancestors,
Da 4: 4 was living at ease in my home and **p** in my palace.
8:12 and kept **p** in what it did.
1Es 6:10 the work is **p** in their hands and being completed
4Mc 3:20 because of their observance of the law and were **p,**

PROSPERITY‡ (47) [PROSPER]

Dt 23: 6 You shall never promote their welfare or their **p**
28:11 The LORD will make you abound in **p,**
30:15 See, I have set before you today life and **p,**
1Sa 2:32 with greedy eye on all the **p** that shall be bestowed
1Ki 10: 7 and **p** far surpass the report that I had heard.
Ezr 9:12 and never seek their peace or **p,**
Job 15:21 in **p** the destroyer will come upon them.
20:21 therefore their **p** will not endure.
21:13 They spend their days in **p,**
21:16 Is not their **p** indeed their own achievement?
21:23 One dies in full **p,** being wholly at ease
30:15 and my **p** has passed away like a cloud.
36:11 and serve him, they complete their days in **p,**
Ps 25:13 in **p,** and their children shall possess
30: 6 for me, I said in my **p,** "I shall never be moved."
37:11 and delight themselves in abundant **p.**
68: 6 he leads out the prisoners to **p,**
72: 3 May the mountains yield **p** for the people,
73: 3 I saw the **p** of the wicked.
106: 5 that I may see the **p** of your chosen ones,
128: 5 May you see the **p** of Jerusalem all the days
Pr 8:18 and honor are with me, enduring wealth and **p.**
13:21 but **p** rewards the righteous.
Ecc 7:14 In the day of **p** be joyful,
Isa 48:18 Then your **p** would have been like a river,
54:13 and great shall be the **p** of your children.
66:12 I will extend **p** to her like a river,
Jer 22:21 I spoke to you in your **p,** but you said,
33: 6 and reveal to them abundance of **p** and security.
33: 9 because of all the good and all the **p** I provide
Da 4: 1 May you have abundant **p!**
4:27 so that your **p** may be prolonged."
6:25 "May you have abundant **p!**
Hag 2: 9 and in this place I will give **p,**
Zec 1:17 My cities shall again overflow with **p;**
7: 7 when Jerusalem was inhabited and in **p,**
Tob 13:14 and happy are those who rejoice in your **p.**
14: 2 and after regaining it he lived in **p,**
AdE 16: 3 but in their inability to stand **p,**
Sir 11:25 In the day of **p,** adversity is forgotten,
11:25 and in the day of adversity, **p** is not remembered.
12: 8 A friend is not known in **p,**
22:23 so that you may rejoice with him in his **p.**
31:11 His **p** will be established,
45:26 so that their **p** may not vanish,
2Mc 9:19 and good wishes for their health and **p.**
14:14 of the Jews would mean **p** for themselves.

PROSPEROUS‡ (14) [PROSPER]

Dt 28:63 as the LORD took delight in making you **p**
30: 5 he will make you more **p** and numerous
30: 9 the LORD your God will make you abundantly **p**
Jos 1: 8 For then you shall make your way **p,**
Eze 16:49 and **p** ease, but did not aid the poor and needy.
Jdt 5: 9 and grew very **p** in gold and silver
Wis 13:18 for a **p** journey, a thing that cannot take a step;
Sir 2: 3 so that your last days may be **p.**
6:11 When you are **p,** they become your second self,
29:18 Being surety has ruined many who were **p,**
40:19 Cattle and orchards make one **p;**
41: 1 who has nothing to worry about and is **p**
1Es 8: 6 by the **p** journey that the Lord gave them.
8:50 a **p** journey for ourselves and for our children and

PROSPERS (3) [PROSPER]

Lev 25:26 but then **p** and finds sufficient means to do so,
Ezr 5: 8 this work is being done diligently and **p**
Sir 12: 9 One's enemies are friendly when one **p,**

PROSTITUTE (38) [PROSTITUTE'S, PROSTITUTED, PROSTITUTES, PROSTITUTING, PROSTITUTION, PROSTITUTIONS]

Ge 38:15 When Judah saw her, he thought her to be a **p,**
38:21 the temple **p** who was at Enaim by the wayside?"
38:21 But they said, "No **p** has been here."
38:22 the townspeople said, 'No **p** has been here.' "
Ex 34:15 when they **p** themselves to their gods and sacrifice
34:16 and their daughters who **p** themselves to their gods
34:16 also **p** themselves to their gods.
Lev 17: 7 goat-demons, to whom they **p** themselves.
19:29 Do not profane your daughter by making her a **p,**
21: 7 not marry a **p** or a woman who has been defiled;
21:14 or a woman who has been defiled, a **p,**
Dt 23:17 of the daughters of Israel shall be a temple **p;**
23:17 none of the sons of Israel shall be a temple **p.**
23:18 You shall not bring the fee of a **p** or the wages of a male **p** into the house of the LORD your God
31:16 to **p** themselves to the foreign gods in their midst,
Jos 2: 1 entered the house of a **p** whose name was Rahab,
6:17 Only Rahab the **p** and all who are with her
6:25 the **p,** with her family and all who belonged
Jdg 11: 1 Now Jephthah the Gileadite, the son of a **p,**
16: 1 where he saw a **p** and went in to her.
Pr 7:10 a woman comes toward him, decked out like a **p,**
23:27 a **p** is a deep pit; an adulteress is a narrow well.
Isa 23:15 it will happen to Tyre as in the song about the **p:**
23:16 go about the city, you forgotten **p!**
23:17 and will **p** herself with all the kingdoms of
Am 7:17 'Your wife shall become a **p** in the city,
Mic 1: 7 for as the wages of a **p** she gathered them,
1: 7 and as the wages of a **p** they shall again be used.
Na 3: 4 Because of the countless debaucheries of the **p,**
1Co 6:15 of Christ and make them members of a **p?**
6:16 that whoever is united to a **p** becomes one body
Heb 11:31 By faith Rahab the **p** did not perish
Jas 2:25 was not Rahab the **p** also justified by works
Sir 26:22 *A p is regarded as spittle,*
41:20 before those who greet you; of looking at a **p,**
2Es 15:55 The reward of a **p** is in your lap;
16:49 as a respectable and virtuous woman abhors a **p,**

PROSTITUTE'S (3) [PROSTITUTE]

Jos 6:22 "Go into the **p** house, and bring the woman out
Pr 6:26 for a **p** fee is only a loaf of bread,
Hos 9: 1 You have loved a **p** pay on all threshing floors.

PROSTITUTED‡ (6) [PROSTITUTE]

Lev 19:29 that the land not become **p** and full of depravity.
Jdg 8:27 and all Israel **p** themselves to it there,
8:33 the Israelites relapsed and **p** themselves with
1Ch 5:25 and **p** themselves to the gods of the peoples of
Ps 106:39 and **p** themselves in their doings.
Eze 16:25 and **p** your beauty, offering yourself

PROSTITUTES‡ (18) [PROSTITUTE]

1Ki 3:16 two women who were **p** came to the king
14:24 there were also male temple **p** in the land.
15:12 He put away the male temple **p** out of the land,
22:38 and the **p** washed themselves in it,
22:46 of the male temple **p** who were still in the land in
2Ki 23: 7 down the houses of the male temple **p** that were in
Pr 29: 3 with **p** is to squander one's substance.
Jer 5: 7 and trooped to the houses of **p.**
Hos 4:14 and sacrifice with temple **p;**
Joel 3: 3 and traded boys for **p,** and sold girls for wine,
Mt 21:31 the **p** are going into the kingdom of God ahead
21:32 but the tax collectors and the **p** believed him;
Lk 15:30 who has devoured your property with **p,**
1Co 6: 9 Fornicators, idolaters, adulterers, male **p,**
Sir 9: 6 Do not give yourself to **p,**
19: 2 and the man who consorts with **p** is reckless.
LtJ 6:11 or even give some of it to the **p** on the terrace.
2Mc 6: 4 with **p** and had intercourse with women within

PROSTITUTING (3) [PROSTITUTE]

Lev 20: 5 all who follow them in **p** themselves to Molech.
20: 6 If any turn to mediums and wizards, **p** themselves
Dt 22:21 in Israel by **p** herself in her father's house.

PROSTITUTION (2) [PROSTITUTE]

Lev 21: 9 daughter of a priest profanes herself through **p,**
2Es 15:47 you have decked out your daughters for **p**

PROSTITUTIONS (1) [PROSTITUTE]

Jer 13:27 your shameless **p** on the hills of the countryside.

PROSTRATE (13) [PROSTRATED, PROSTRATING, PROSTRATION]

Dt 9:18 Then I lay **p** before the LORD as before,
9:25 the forty days and forty nights that I lay **p** before
Ru 2:10 Then she fell **p,** with her face to the ground,

Ps 36:12 There the evildoers lie **p;**
38: 6 I am utterly bowed down and **p;**
Isa 49: 7 princes, and they shall **p** themselves,
Eze 9: 8 I fell **p** on my face and cried out,
Da 8:17 and when he came, I became frightened and fell **p.**
Jdt 3: 2 the Great King, lie **p** before you.
10: 2 she rose from where she lay **p.**
2Mc 3:29 While he lay **p,** speechless because of
10: 4 they fell **p** and implored the Lord
13:12 and lying **p** for three days without ceasing,

PROSTRATED (13) [PROSTRATE]
1Sa 20:41 beside the stone heap and **p** himself with his face
2Sa 14:22 Joab **p** himself with his face to the ground
14:33 So he came to the king and **p** himself with his face
18:28 He **p** himself before the king with his face to
24:20 and **p** himself before the king with his face to
1Ch 29:20 and **p** themselves before the LORD and the king.
Lk 17:16 He **p** himself at Jesus' feet and thanked him.
Jdt 4:11 and children living at Jerusalem **p** themselves
9: 1 Then Judith **p** herself, put ashes on her head,
10:23 She **p** herself and did obeisance to him,
2Mc 3:15 The priests **p** themselves before the altar
3Mc 1:16 in all their vestments **p** themselves and entreated
5:50 they **p** themselves with one accord on the ground,

PROSTRATING (1) [PROSTRATE]
Eze 8:16 **p** themselves to the sun toward the east.

PROSTRATION (1) [PROSTRATE]
2Mc 3:21 in the **p** of the whole populace and the anxiety of

PROTECT (25) [PROTECTED, PROTECTING, PROTECTION, PROTECTOR, PROTECTS]
2Sa 18:12 For my sake **p** the young man Absalom!
Ezr 8:22 and cavalry to **p** us against the enemy on our way,
Ps 12: 7 You, O LORD, will **p** us;
16: 1 **P** me, O God, for in you I take refuge.
20: 1 The name of the God of Jacob **p** you!
59: 1 **p** me from those who rise up against me.
69:29 let your salvation, O God, **p** me.
83: 3 they consult together against those you **p.**
91:14 I will **p** those who know my name.
140: 1 **p** me from those who are violent,
140: 4 **p** me from the violent who have planned my
Isa 31: 5 so the LORD of hosts will **p** Jerusalem;
31: 5 he will **p** and deliver it, he will spare and rescue it.
Zec 9:15 The LORD of hosts will **p** them,
Lk 4:10 concerning you, to **p** you,'
Jn 17:11 **p** them in your name that you have given me,
17:15 but I ask you to **p** them from the evil one.
Jdt 8:15 he has power to **p** us within any time he pleases,
3Mc 3:10 to **p** them and to exert more earnest efforts
2Es 2:21 do not ridicule the lame, **p** the maimed,
2:22 **P** the old and the young within your walls;
2:29 My power will **p** you, so that your children may
13:23 at that time will **p** those who fall into peril,
4Mc 9:15 but because I **p** the divine law."
14:15 the ones that are tame **p** their young by building

PROTECTED‡ (16) [PROTECT]
Jos 24:17 He **p** us along all the way that we went,
1Sa 25:21 that I **p** all that this fellow has in the wilderness,
Job 11:18 you will be **p** and take your rest in safety.
Mk 6:20 a righteous and holy man, and he **p** him.
Jn 17:12 I **p** them in your name that you have given me.
1Pe 1: 5 who are being **p** by the power of God
Jdt 13:16 the Lord lives, who has **p** me in the way I went,
Wis 2:20 for, according to what he says, he will be **p."**
10: 1 Wisdom **p** the first-formed father of the world,
10:12 She **p** him from his enemies,
17: 4 inner chamber that held them **p** them from fear,
19: 8 where those **p** by your hand passed through
Sir 28:19 Happy is the one who is **p** from it,
1Mc 6:38 to harass the enemy while being themselves **p** by
2Mc 13:17 because the Lord's help **p** him.
2Es 3:30 have destroyed your people, and **p** your enemies,

PROTECTING (1) [PROTECT]
1Mc 3: 3 and waged battles, **p** the camp by his sword.

PROTECTION‡ (17) [PROTECT]
Nu 14: 9 their **p** is removed from them,
Dt 32:38 Let them rise up and help you, let them be your **p!**
Ne 4: 9 and set a guard as a **p** against them day and night.
Ps 5:11 Spread your **p** over them, so that those who love
Ecc 7:12 the **p** of wisdom is like the **p** of money,
Isa 27: 5 Or else let it cling to me for **p,**
30: 2 to take refuge in the **p** of Pharaoh,
30: 3 the **p** of Pharaoh shall become your shame,
AdE 4:14 and **p** will come to the Jews from another quarter,
Bar 1:12 we shall live under the **p** of King Nebuchadnezzar
1:12 and under the **p** of his son Belshazzar,
1Mc 11:16 So Alexander fled into Arabia to find **p** there,
2Mc 3:40 of the episode of Heliodorus and the **p** of
5: 9 the Lacedaemonians in hope of finding **p** because
3Mc 5:42 of mind that had come about within him for the **p**
2Es 1:15 I gave you camps for your **p,**

PROTECTOR (7) [PROTECT]
Ps 68: 5 and **p** of widows is God in his holy habitation.
Da 12: 1 the great prince, the **p** of your people, shall arise.
Jdt 9:11 **p** of the forsaken, savior of those without hope.
Sir 51: 2 for you have been my **p** and helper
1Mc 14:47 and to be **p** of them all.
2Mc 4: 2 the **p** of his compatriots, and a zealot for the laws.
3Mc 6: 9 you who hate insolence, all-merciful and **p** of all,

PROTECTS (6) [PROTECT]
Ps 41: 2 The LORD **p** them and keeps them alive;
116: 6 The LORD **p** the simple;
Na 1: 7 he **p** those who take refuge in him,
1Jn 5:18 but the one who was born of God **p** them,
Jdt 9:14 that there is no other who **p** the people of Israel
LtJ 6:59 better even the door of a house that **p** its contents,

PROTEST (3) [PROTESTED]
Lk 10:11 we wipe off in **p** against you.
Ac 13:51 So they shook the dust off their feet in **p**
18: 6 in **p** he shook the dust from his clothes and said

PROTESTED (1) [PROTEST]
4Mc 4: 7 The people indignantly **p** his words,

PROUD‡ (51) [PRIDE]
Lev 26:19 I will break your **p** glory,
2Ch 26:16 But when he had become strong he grew **p,**
32:25 to the benefit done to him, for his heart was **p.**
Job 28: 8 The **p** wild animals have not trodden it;
38:11 and here shall your **p** waves be stopped'?
40:11 and look on all who are **p,** and abase them.
40:12 Look on all who are **p,** and bring them low;
41:34 it is king over all that are **p."**
Ps 40: 4 who do not turn to the **p,** to those who go astray
94: 2 give to the **p** what they deserve!
123: 4 of the contempt of the **p.**
Pr 15:25 The LORD tears down the house of the **p,**
16:19 among the poor than to divide the spoil with the **p.**
21: 4 Haughty eyes and a **p** heart—
21:24 The **p,** haughty person, named "Scoffer,"
Ecc 7: 8 the patient in spirit are better than the **p** in spirit.
Isa 2:12 the LORD of hosts has a day against all that is **p**
16: 6 of the pride of Moab—how **p** he is!—
28: 1 Ah, the **p** garland of the drunkards of Ephraim,
28: 3 under foot will be the **p** garland of the drunkards
Jer 48:29 of the pride of Moab—he is very **p—**
Eze 28: 2 your heart is **p** and you have said, "I am a god;
28: 5 and your heart has become **p** in your wealth.
28:17 Your heart was **p** because of your beauty;
30: 6 and its **p** might shall come down;
30:18 and its **p** might shall come to an end;
31:10 and its heart was **p** of its height,
33:28 and its **p** might shall come to an end;
Hos 13: 6 they were satisfied, and their heart was **p;**
Ob 1: 3 Your **p** heart has deceived you,
Hab 2: 4 Look at the **p!** Their spirit is
Zec 10: 3 and will make them like his **p** war horse.
Lk 1:51 he has scattered the **p** in the thoughts
Ro 11:20 So do not become **p,** but stand in awe.
2Co 10: 5 and every **p** obstacle raised up against
Jas 4: 6 God opposes the **p,** but gives grace to the humble.
1Pe 5: 5 God opposes the **p,** but gives grace to the humble.
AdE 13:12 and refused to bow down to this **p** Haman;
14:16 that I abhor the sign of my **p** position,
16: 2 the more **p** do they become,
Sir 3:28 When calamity befalls the **p,** there is no healing,
10: 9 How can dust and ashes be **p?**
11:30 so is the mind of the **p,**
13: 1 and whoever associates with a **p** person becomes
13:20 Humility is an abomination to the **p;**
21: 4 thus the house of the **p** will be laid waste.
27:15 The strife of the **p** leads to bloodshed,
27:28 Mockery and abuse issue from the **p,**
32:12 but do not sin through **p** speech.
32:18 insolent and **p** person will not be deterred by fear.
51:10 when there is no help against the **p.**

PROUDLY (4) [PRIDE]
1Sa 2: 3 Talk no more so very **p,** let not arrogance come
Isa 13: 3 have summoned my warriors, my **p** exulting ones,
Da 5:20 up and his spirit was hardened so that he acted **p,**
Zep 3:11 from your midst your **p** exultant ones,

PROVE (22) [PROOF, PROOFS, PROVED, PROVES, PROVING]
Dt 18:22 but the thing does not take place or **p** true,
Ezr 2:59 they could not **p** their families or their descent,
Ne 7:61 not **p** their ancestral houses or their descent,
Job 9:20 though I am blameless, he would **p** me perverse.
24:25 If it is not so, who will **p** me a liar,
Ps 26: 2 **P** me, O LORD, and try me;
Jer 17:11 and at their end they will **p** to be fools.
Jn 16: 8 he will **p** the world wrong about sin
Ac 24:13 Neither can they **p** to you the charge that they
25: 7 against him, which they could not **p.**
Ro 3:26 to **p** at the present time that he himself is righteous
2Co 9: 3 in order that our boasting about you may not **p**
1Ti 3:10 then, if they **p** themselves blameless,
Heb 6:18 in which it is impossible that God would **p** false,
Wis 12:13 to whom you should **p** that you have
Sir 31:25 Do not try to **p** your strength by wine-drinking,
Bel 1: 9 But if you **p** that Bel is eating them,
2Mc 5: 4 the apparition might **p** to have been a good omen.
7:29 but **p** worthy of your brothers.
1Es 5:37 though they could not **p** by their ancestral houses
4Mc 1: 7 I could **p** to you from many and various examples
2: 6 I could **p** to you all the more that reason is able

PROVED‡ (17) [PROVE]
Dt 17: 4 and the charge is **p** true that such
Isa 43:26 set forth your case, so that you may be **p** right.
Ro 3: 4 Although everyone is a liar, let God be **p** true,
7:10 and the very commandment that promised life **p** to
2Co 7:11 At every point you have **p** yourselves guiltless in
7:14 so our boasting to Titus has **p** true as well.
1Th 1: 5 just as you know what kind of persons we **p** to be
Sir 9:17 so a people's leader is **p** wise by his words.
44:20 and when he was tested he **p** faithful.
46: 7 And in the days of Moses he **p** his loyalty,
46:15 By his faithfulness he was **p** to be a prophet,
1Mc 6:54 for the famine **p** too much for them.
3Mc 4:20 and **p** that both the paper and the pens they used
4Mc 2: 4 Not only is reason **p** to rule over the frenzied urge
6:35 I have **p** not only that reason has mastered agonies,
14: 4 the seven youths **p** coward or shrank from death,
16:14 in word and deed you have **p** more powerful than

PROVENDER (KJV) See FED, FODDER, SILAGE

PROVERB (19) [PROVERBIAL, PROVERBS]
Dt 28:37 You shall become an object of horror, a **p,**
1Sa 10:12 it became a **p,** "Is Saul also among the prophets?"
24:13 As the ancient **p** says, 'Out of
1Ki 9: 7 and Israel will become a **p** and a taunt
2Ch 7:20 will make it a **p** and a byword among all peoples.
Ps 49: 4 I will incline my ear to a **p;**
Pr 1: 6 to understand a **p** and a figure,
26: 7 so does a **p** in the mouth of a fool.
26: 9 by the hand of a drunkard is a **p** in the mouth of
Eze 12:22 what is this **p** of yours about the land of Israel,
12:23 I will put an end to this **p,**
12:23 and they shall use it no more as a **p** in Israel."
16:44 everyone who uses proverbs will use this **p**
18: 2 What do you mean by repeating this **p** concerning
18: 3 this **p** shall no more be used by you in Israel.
Lk 4:23 "Doubtless you will quote to me this **p,** 'Doctor,
2Pe 2:22 It has happened to them according to the true **p,**
Sir 20:20 A **p** from a fool's lips will be rejected,
4Mc 18:16 He recounted to you Solomon's **p,**

PROVERBIAL (1) [PROVERB]
Sir 20:27 P SAYINGS The wise person advances himself by

PROVERBS (14) [PROVERB]
1Ki 4:32 He composed three thousand **p,**
Job 13:12 Your maxims are **p** of ashes,
Pr 1: 1 The **p** of Solomon son of David, king of Israel:
10: 1 The **p** of Solomon. A wise child makes a glad
25: 1 These are other **p** of Solomon that the officials
Ecc 12: 9 weighing and studying and arranging many **p.**
Eze 16:44 everyone who uses **p** will use this proverb
Sir 3:29 The mind of the intelligent appreciates **p,**
6:35 and let no wise **p** escape you.
13:26 but to devise **p** requires painful thinking.
18:29 become wise themselves, and pour forth apt **p.**
39: 3 the hidden meanings of **p** and is at home with
47:15 and you filled it with **p** having deep meaning.
47:17 Your songs, **p,** and parables,

PROVES (7) [PROVE]
2Sa 22:31 the promise of the LORD **p** true;
1Ki 1:52 Solomon responded, "If he **p** to be a worthy man,
Ps 18:30 the promise of the LORD **p** true;
Pr 30: 5 Every word of God **p** true;
Ro 5: 8 But God **p** his love for us in that
Wis 2:11 for what is weak **p** itself to be useless.
Sir 39:34 for everything **p** good in its appointed time.

PROVIDE (46) [PROVIDED, PROVIDENCE, PROVIDES, PROVIDING, PROVISION, PROVISIONED, PROVISIONS]
Ge 22: 8 "God himself will **p** the lamb for a burnt offering,
22:14 Abraham called that place "The LORD will **p"**;
30:30 now when shall I **p** for my own household also?"
45:11 I will **p** for you there—
49:20 and he shall **p** royal delicacies.
50:21 I myself will **p** for you and your little ones."
Lev 25:24 you shall **p** for the redemption of the land.
25:37 or **p** them food at a profit.
Nu 20: 8 thus you shall **p** drink for the congregation
Dt 15:14 **P** liberally out of your flock, your threshing floor,
Jos 18: 4 **P** three men from each tribe,
1Sa 16:17 **"P** for me someone who can play well,
2Sa 19:33 and I will **p** for you in Jerusalem at my side."
1Ki 20:10 if the dust of Samaria will **p** a handful for each of
2Ch 2:10 I will **p** for your servants,
Ezr 7:20 you may **p** out of the king's treasury.
Ps 65: 9 you **p** the people with grain,
78:20 can he also give bread, or **p** meat for his people?"
Pr 27:26 the lambs will **p** your clothing, and the goats
30:25 yet they **p** their food in the summer;
Isa 40:16 Lebanon would not **p** fuel enough,

Isa 61: 3 to **p** for those who mourn in Zion—
Jer 33: 9 because of all the good and all the prosperity I **p**
Eze 34:29 I will **p** for them a splendid vegetation so
43:25 For seven days you shall **p** daily a goat for
45:17 he shall **p** the sin offerings, grain offerings,
45:22 the prince shall **p** for himself and all the people of
45:23 during the seven days of the festival he shall **p** as
45:24 He shall **p** as a grain offering an ephah
46: 7 a grain offering he shall **p** an ephah with the bull
46:13 He shall **p** a lamb, a yearling, without blemish,
46:13 morning by morning he shall **p** it.
46:14 And he shall **p** a grain offering with it morning
Lk 10: 7 eating and drinking whatever they **p,**
Ac 23:24 Also **p** mounts for Paul to ride,
1Co 10:13 but with the testing he will also **p** the way out so
2Co 9: 8 And God is able to **p** you with every blessing
1Ti 5: 8 And whoever does not **p** for relatives,
Sir 29:25 the host and **p** drink without being thanked,
47:13 so that he might build a house in his name and **p**
1Mc 12: 4 asking them to **p** for the envoys safe conduct to
2Mc 9:16 the expenses incurred for the sacrifices he would **p**
12:43 and sent it to Jerusalem to **p** for a sin offering.
1Es 8:18 you may **p** out of the royal treasury.
3Mc 6:30 in charge of the revenues and ordered him to **p** to
4Mc 3: 2 but reason can **p** a way for us not to be enslaved

PROVIDED (56) [PROVIDE]

Ge 22:14 "On the mount of the LORD it shall be **p."**
47:12 And Joseph **p** his father, his brothers,
Ex 8:28 **p** you do not go very far away.
Dt 19: 9 **p** you diligently observe this entire commandment
Jdg 6: 2 the Israelites **p** for themselves hiding places in
1Sa 16: 1 for I have **p** for myself a king among his sons."
21: 4 **p** that the young men have kept themselves
2Sa 19:32 He had **p** the king with food while he stayed
20: 3 and **p** for them, but did not go in to them.
1Ki 3:15 and **p** a feast for all his servants.
4: 7 who **p** food for the king and his household;
8:21 There I have **p** a place for the ark,
18: 4 and **p** them with bread and water.)
18:13 and **p** them with bread and water?
1Ch 12:39 for their kindred had **p** for them.
22: 3 also **p** great stores of iron for nails for the doors of
22: 5 So David **p** materials in great quantity
22:14 With great pains I have **p** for the house of
22:14 timber and stone too I have **p.**
29: 2 So I have **p** for the house of my God,
29: 3 in addition to all that I have **p** for the holy house,
29:16 all this abundance that we have **p** for building you
2Ch 2: 7 whom my father David **p.**
26:14 Uzziah **p** for all the army the shields, spears,
28:15 **p** them with food and drink, and anointed them;
32:29 He likewise **p** cities for himself,
Ne 13:31 and I **p** for the wood offering,
Est 2: 9 and he quickly **p** her with her cosmetic treatments
Ps 68:10 in your goodness, O God, you **p** for the needy.
Eze 43:25 without blemish, shall be **p.**
46:15 and the grain offering and the oil shall be **p,**
Da 4:12 its fruit abundant, and it **p** food for all.
4:21 and which **p** food for all, under which animals of
Jnh 1:17 the LORD **p** a large fish to swallow up Jonah;
Mt 27:55 they had followed Jesus from Galilee and had **p**
Mk 15:41 to follow him and **p** for him when he was
Lk 8: 3 who **p** for them out of their resources.
Ro 11:22 **p** you continue in his kindness;
Col 1:23 **p** that you continue securely established
1Ti 2:15 **p** they continue in faith and love and holiness,
4: 4 **p** it is received with thanksgiving;
Heb 11:40 since God had **p** something better so
2Pe 1:11 and Savior Jesus Christ will be richly **p** for you.
AdE 2: 9 and he quickly **p** her with ointments
Wis 18: 3 Therefore you **p** a flaming pillar of fire as a guide
Bel 1: 3 and every day they **p** for it twelve bushels
1Mc 14:34 and **p** in those towns whatever was necessary
2Mc 4:49 **p** magnificently for their funeral.
12: 3 that they had **p,** as though there were no ill will to
1Es 4:55 that the support for the Levites should be **p** until
4:56 and wages should be **p** for all who guarded
3Mc 6:40 they feasted, being **p** with everything by the king,
7:18 for the king had generously **p** all things to them
2Es 1:14 I **p** light for you from a pillar of fire,
5:26 the flocks that have been made you have **p**
8:52 plenty is **p,** a city is built, rest is appointed,

PROVIDENCE (8) [PROVIDE]

Wis 14: 3 but it is your **p,** O Father, that steers its course,
17: 2 shut in under their roofs, exiles from eternal **p.**
1Es 6: 5 for the **p** of the Lord was over the captives;
3Mc 4:21 an act of the invincible **p** of him who was aiding
5:30 the **p** of God his whole mind had been deranged
4Mc 9:24 the just **P** of our ancestors may become merciful
13:19 and all-wise **P** has bequeathed through the fathers
17:22 as an atoning sacrifice, divine **P** preserved Israel

PROVIDES‡ (6) [PROVIDE]

Job 38:41 Who **p** for the raven its prey,
Ps 111: 5 He **p** food for those who fear him;
Pr 31:15 while it is still night and **p** food for her household
Eze 46:12 When the prince **p** a freewill offering,
1Ti 6:17 but rather on God who richly **p** us with everything
2Es 8: 2 it will tell you that it **p** a large amount of clay

PROVIDING (7) [PROVIDE]

Ex 16:16 all **p** for those in their own tents.' "
Dt 10:18 **p** them food and clothing.
Jos 1:13 'The LORD your God is **p** you a place of rest,
1Ki 5: 9 And you shall meet my needs by **p** food
Ezr 7:20 which you are responsible for **p,**
Wis 16:20 **p** every pleasure and suited to every taste.
2Mc 6:21 privately urged him to bring meat of his own **p,**

PROVINCE (53) [PROVINCES, PROVINCIAL]

Ezr 2: 1 Now these were the people of the **p** who came
4:10 and in the rest of the **p** Beyond the River wrote—
4:11 the people of the **p** Beyond the River,
4:16 you will then have no possession in the **p** Beyond
4:17 in Samaria and in the rest of the **p** Beyond
4:20 over the whole **p** Beyond the River,
5: 3 At the same time Tattenai the governor of the **p**
5: 6 of the **p** Beyond the River and Shethar-bozenai
5: 6 and his associates the envoys who were in the **p**
5: 8 May it be known to the king that we went to the **p**
6: 2 it was in Ecbatana, the capital in the **p** of Media,
6: 6 you, Tattenai, governor of the **p** Beyond the River,
6: 6 the envoys in the **p** Beyond the River, keep away;
6: 8 the tribute of the **p** Beyond the River.
6:13 Tattenai, the governor of the **p** Beyond the River,
7:16 that you shall find in the whole **p** of Babylonia,
7:21 to all the treasurers in the **p** Beyond the River:
7:25 and judges who may judge all the people in the **p**
8:36 to the king's satraps and to the governors of the **p**
Ne 1: 3 in the **p** who escaped captivity are in great trouble
2: 7 let letters be given me to the governors of the **p**
2: 9 I came to the governors of the **p** Beyond the River,
3: 7 the jurisdiction of the governor of the **p** Beyond
7: 6 These are the people of the **p** who came up out of
11: 3 the leaders of the **p** who lived in Jerusalem;
Est 1:22 to every **p** in its own script and to every people
3:12 to every **p** in its own script and every people
3:14 be issued as a decree in every **p** by proclamation,
4: 3 In every **p,** wherever the king's command
8: 9 to every **p** in its own script and to every people
8:11 to annihilate any armed force of any people or **p**
8:13 as a decree in every **p** and published to all peoples,
8:17 In every **p** and in every city,
9:28 in every family, **p,** and city;
Ecc 5: 8 in a **p** the oppression of the poor and the violation
Da 2:48 the whole **p** of Babylon and chief prefect over all
2:49 Abednego over the affairs of the **p** of Babylon.
3: 1 up on the plain of Dura in the **p** of Babylon.
3:12 over the affairs of the **p** of Babylon:
3:30 Meshach, and Abednego in the **p** of Babylon.
8: 2 in the **p** of Elam, and I was by the river Ulai.
11:24 into the richest parts of the **p** and do what none
Ac 19:31 even some officials of the **p** of Asia,
23:34 he asked what **p** he belonged to,
25: 1 Three days after Festus had arrived in the **p,**
AdE 1:22 to every **p** in its own language,
3:12 the governors in every **p** from India to Ethiopia.
3:14 Copies of the document were posted in every **p,**
4: 3 And in every **p** where the king's proclamation
8: 9 to each **p** in its own language.
8:17 and **p** wherever the decree was published;
1Mc 7: 8 governor of the **p** Beyond the River;
10:65 and made him general and governor of the **p.**

PROVINCES‡ (41) [PROVINCE]

Ezr 4:15 that this is a rebellious city, hurtful to kings and **p,**
Est 1: 1 over one hundred twenty-seven **p** from India
1: 3 the nobles and governors of the **p** were present,
1:16 and all the peoples who are in all the **p**
1:22 he sent letters to all the royal **p,**
2: 3 the king appoint commissioners in all the **p**
2:18 He also granted a holiday to the **p,**
3: 8 among the peoples in all the **p** of your kingdom;
3:12 to the governors over all the **p** and to the officials
3:13 Letters were sent by couriers to all the king's **p,**
4:11 the king's **p** know that if any man or woman goes
8: 5 to destroy the Jews who are in all the **p** of
8: 9 and the officials of the **p** from India to Ethiopia,
one hundred twenty-seven **p,**
8:12 throughout all the **p** of King Ahasuerus,
9: 2 throughout all the **p** of King Ahasuerus
9: 3 All the officials of the **p,**
9: 4 and his fame spread throughout all the **p** as
9:12 What have they done in the rest of the king's **p?**
9:16 in the king's **p** also gathered to defend their lives,
9:20 the Jews who were in all the **p** of King Ahasuerus,
9:30 to the one hundred twenty-seven **p** of the kingdom
Ecc 2: 8 and gold and the treasure of kings and of the **p;**
La 1: 1 She that was a princess among the **p** has become
Eze 19: 8 The nations set upon him from the **p** all around;
Da 3: 2 of the **p** to assemble and come to the dedication of
3: 3 the magistrates, and all the officials of the **p,**
AdE 1: 1 over one hundred twenty-seven **p** from India
1: 3 and the governors of the **p.**
2: 3 The king shall appoint officers in all the **p**
3:12 There were one hundred twenty-seven **p** in all,
8: 9 and governors of the **p** from Media to Ethiopia,
one hundred twenty-seven **p,**
13: 1 the hundred twenty-seven **p** from India to Ethiopia
16: 1 to the governors of the **p** from India to Ethiopia,
one hundred twenty-seven **p,**
1Mc 3:37 the Euphrates river and went through the upper **p.**
6: 1 through the upper **p** when he heard that Elymais
8: 7 and surrender some of their best **p,**
2Mc 9:25 to most of you when I hurried off to the upper **p;**
2Es 1:11 and scattered in the east the peoples of two **p,**

PROVINCIAL (1) [PROVINCE]

AdE 9: 3 The chief **p** governors, the princes,

PROVING (2) [PROVE]

Ac 9:22 in Damascus by **p** that Jesus was the Messiah.
17: 3 and **p** that it was necessary for the Messiah

PROVISION (7) [PROVIDE]

Ge 45:23 bread, and **p** for his father on the journey.
1Ki 4: 7 each one had to make **p** for one month in the year.
4:22 Solomon's **p** for one day was thirty cors
1Ch 29:19 he may build the temple for which I have made **p."**
Ne 11:23 and a settled **p** for the singers,
Eze 45:25 he shall make the same **p** for sin offerings,
Ro 13:14 and make no **p** for the flesh, to gratify its desires.

PROVISIONED (1) [PROVIDE]

1Ki 20:27 After the Israelites had been mustered and **p,**

PROVISIONS‡ (24) [PROVIDE]

Ge 14:11 and all their **p,** and went their way;
42:25 and to give them **p** for their journey.
45:21 and he gave them **p** for the journey.
Ex 12:39 nor had they prepared any **p** for themselves.
Dt 23:19 interest on **p,** interest on anything that is lent.
Jos 1:11 and command the people: 'Prepare your **p;**
9: 4 they went and prepared **p,**
9: 5 and all their **p** were dry and moldy.
9:11 'Take **p** in your hand for the journey;
9:14 So the leaders partook of their **p,**
Jdg 20:10 to bring **p** for the troops,
1Sa 17:20 left the sheep with a keeper, took the **p,**
22:10 of the LORD for him, gave him **p,** and gave him
1Ki 4:27 Those officials supplied **p** for King Solomon and
1Ch 12:40 abundant **p** of meal, cakes of figs,
2Ch 11:23 he gave them abundant **p,**
Ps 132:15 I will abundantly bless its **p;**
Lk 9:12 and countryside, to lodge and get **p;**
Ac 28:10 they put on board all the **p** we needed.
Bel 1: 8 "If you do not tell me who is eating these **p,**
1:13 to go in regularly and consume the **p.**
1Mc 6:49 the town because they had no **p** there to withstand
2Mc 12:14 the strength of the walls and on their supply of **p,**
2Es 16:21 **p** will be so cheap upon earth

PROVOCATION‡ (4) [PROVOKE]

Dt 32:27 but I feared **p** by the enemy,
Job 17: 2 and my eye dwells on their **p.**
Pr 27: 3 but a fool's **p** is heavier than both.
Eze 20:28 and presented the **p** of their offering;

PROVOCATIONS (1) [PROVOKE]

2Ki 23:26 the **p** with which Manasseh had provoked him.

PROVOKE (22) [PROVOCATION, PROVOCATIONS, PROVOKED, PROVOKES, PROVOKING]

Dt 32:21 **p** them with a foolish nation.
1Sa 1: 6 Her rival used to **p** her severely, to irritate her,
1: 7 up to the house of the LORD, she used to **p** her.
1Ki 16:33 Ahab did more to **p** the anger of the LORD,
2Ki 14:10 for why should you **p** trouble so that you fall,
2Ch 25:19 why should you **p** trouble so that you fall,
Job 12: 6 and those who **p** God are secure,
Isa 65: 3 a people who **p** me to my face continually,
Jer 7:18 to other gods, to **p** me to anger.
7:19 Is it I whom they **p?**
25: 6 do not **p** me to anger with the work of your hands.
32:29 to other gods, to **p** me to anger.
32:30 of Israel have done nothing but **p** me to anger by
32:32 and the people of Judah that they did to **p** me
44: 8 Why do you **p** me to anger with the works
Eze 8:17 and **p** my anger still further?
16:26 multiplying your whoring, to **p** me to anger.
Eph 6: 4 And, fathers, do not **p** your children to anger,
Col 3:21 Fathers, do not **p** your children,
Heb 10:24 And let us consider how to **p** one another to love
Jdt 11:11 by which they are about to **p** their God to anger
1Mc 15:40 So Cendebeus came to Jamnia and began to **p**

PROVOKED (25) [PROVOKE]

Dt 9: 7 and do not forget how you **p** the LORD your God
9: 8 Even at Horeb you **p** the LORD to wrath,
9:22 you **p** the LORD to wrath.
32:16 with abhorrent things they **p** him.
32:21 with what is no god, **p** me with their idols.
Jdg 2:12 and they **p** the LORD to anger.
1Ki 14:22 they **p** him to jealousy with their sins
15:30 because of the anger to which he **p** the LORD,
21:22 because you have **p** me to anger
22:53 he **p** the LORD, the God of Israel, to anger,
2Ki 21:15 in my sight and have **p** me to anger,
22:17 so that they have **p** me to anger with all the work
23:26 the provocations with which Manasseh had **p** him.
2Ch 34:25 so that they have **p** me to anger with all the works
Ps 78:41 and **p** the Holy One of Israel.
78:58 For they **p** him to anger with their high places;
106:29 they **p** the LORD to anger with their deeds,
Jer 7:29 and forsaken the generation that **p** his wrath.
8:19 ("Why have they **p** me to anger with their images,
25: 7 and so you have **p** me to anger with the work
Zec 8:14 when your ancestors **p** me to wrath,

Bar 4: 7 For you **p** the one who made you by sacrificing
2Mc 14:27 **p** by the false accusations of that depraved man,
1Es 6:15 and **p** him, he gave them over into the hands
Man 1:10 for I have **p** your wrath and have done what is evil

PROVOKES (3) [PROVOKE]

Job 16: 3 Or what **p** you that you keep on talking?
Pr 20: 2 anyone who **p** him to anger forfeits life itself.
Eze 8: 3 of the image of jealousy, which **p** to jealousy.

PROVOKING (18) [PROVOKE]

Dt 4:25 in the sight of the LORD your God, and **p** him
9:18 **p** the LORD by doing what was evil in his sight.
31:29 **p** him to anger through the work of your hands."
1Ki 14: 9 and cast images, **p** me to anger,
14:15 because they have made their sacred poles, **p**
16: 2 **p** me to anger with their sins,
16: 7 **p** him to anger with the work of his hands,
16:13 **p** the LORD God of Israel to anger
16:26 **p** the LORD, the God of Israel,
2Ki 17:11 They did wicked things, **p** the LORD to anger;
17:17 to do evil in the sight of the LORD, **p** him
21: 6 in the sight of the LORD, **p** him to anger.
23:19 of Samaria, which kings of Israel had made, **p**
2Ch 28:25 **p** to anger the LORD, the God of his ancestors.
33: 6 in the sight of the LORD, **p** him to anger.
Jer 11:17 **p** me to anger by making offerings to Baal.
44: 3 **p** me to anger, in that they went to make offerings
1Co 10:22 Or are we **p** the Lord to jealousy?

PROWL (2) [PROWLED, PROWLING, PROWLS]

Ps 12: 8 On every side the wicked **p**,
La 5:18 which lies desolate; jackals **p** over it.

PROWLED (1) [PROWL]

Eze 19: 6 He **p** among the lions; he became a young lion,

PROWLING (2) [PROWL]

Ps 59: 6 howling like dogs and **p** about the city.
59:14 howling like dogs and **p** about the city.

PROWLS (1) [PROWL]

1Pe 5: 8 a roaring lion your adversary the devil **p** around,

PRUDENCE (10) [PRUDENT]

Pr 1: 4 knowledge and **p** to the young—
2:11 **p** will watch over you;
3:21 keep sound wisdom and **p**,
5: 2 so that you may hold on to **p**,
8: 5 learn **p**; acquire intelligence, you who lack it.
8:12 live with **p**, and I attain knowledge and discretion.
19:25 Strike a scoffer, and the simple will learn **p**;
Da 2:14 Daniel responded with **p** and discretion to Arioch,
Wis 8: 7 for she teaches self-control and **p**,
Sir 19:22 nor is there **p** in the counsel of sinners.

PRUDENT (15) [PRUDENCE]

1Sa 16:18 **p** in speech, and a man of good presence;
1Ch 26:14 a **p** counselor, and his lot came out for the north.
Pr 10: 5 A child who gathers in summer is **p**,
10:19 but the **p** are restrained in speech.
12:16 but the **p** ignore an insult.
15: 5 but the one who heeds admonition is **p**.
19:14 but a **p** wife is from the LORD.
Jer 49: 7 Has counsel perished from the **p**?
Am 5:13 Therefore the **p** will keep silent in such a time;
Lk 12:42 and **p** manager whom his master will put in charge
Tit 1: 8 a lover of goodness, **p**, upright, devout,
2: 2 Tell the older men to be temperate, serious, **p**,
Sir 1: 4 and **p** understanding from eternity.
21:25 but the words of the **p** are weighed in the balance.
4Mc 7:17 because not all have **p** reason."

PRUNE (2) [PRUNED, PRUNES, PRUNING]

Lev 25: 3 and six years you shall **p** your vineyard,
25: 4 you shall not sow your field or **p** your vineyard.

PRUNED (1) [PRUNE]

Isa 5: 6 I will make it a waste; it shall not be **p** or hoed,

PRUNES (3) [PRUNE]

Jn 15: 2 that bears fruit he **p** to make it bear more fruit.
2Es 16:43 so also the one who **p** the vines,
4Mc 1:29 weeds and **p** and ties up and waters

PRUNING (4) [PRUNE]

Isa 2: 4 and their spears into **p** hooks;
18: 5 he will cut off the shoots with **p** hooks,
Joel 3:10 and your **p** hooks into spears;
Mic 4: 3 and their spears into **p** hooks;

PRUNINGHOOKS (KJV) See PRUNING HOOKS

PRYING (1)

4Mc 10: 5 dismembering him by **p** his limbs

PSALM (63) [PSALMIST, PSALMS]

Ps 3: T *A **P** of David, when he fled from his son Absalom.*
4: T *with stringed instruments. A **P** of David.*
5: T *To the leader: for the flutes. A **P** of David.*
6: T *according to The Sheminith. A **P** of David.*
8: T *according to The Gittith. A **P** of David.*
9: T *according to Muth-labben. A **P** of David.*
12: T *according to The Sheminith. A **P** of David.*
13: T *To the leader. A **P** of David.*
15: T *A **P** of David.*
18: T *A **P** of David the servant of the LORD,*
19: T *To the leader. A **P** of David.*
20: T *To the leader. A **P** of David.*
21: T *To the leader. A **P** of David.*
22: T *according to The Deer of the Dawn. A **P** of David.*
23: T *A **P** of David.*
24: T *Of David. A **P**.*
29: T *A **P** of David.*
30: T *A **P**. A Song at the dedication of the temple.*
31: T *To the leader. A **P** of David.*
38: T *A **P** of David, for the memorial offering.*
39: T *To the leader: to Jeduthun. A **P** of David.*
40: T *To the leader. Of David. A **P**.*
41: T *To the leader. A **P** of David.*
47: T *To the leader. Of the Korahites. A **P**.*
47: 7 king of all the earth; sing praises with a **p**.
48: T *A Song. A **P** of the Korahites.*
49: T *To the leader. Of the Korahites. A **P**.*
50: T *A **P** of Asaph.*
51: T *To the leader. A **P** of David, when the prophet*
62: T *according to Jeduthun. A **P** of David.*
63: T *A **P** of David, when he was in the Wilderness of*
64: T *To the leader. A **P** of David.*
65: T *To the leader. A **P** of David.*
66: T *To the leader. A Song. A **P**.*
67: T *with stringed instruments. A **P**. A Song.*
68: T *To the leader. Of David. A **P**. A Song.*
73: T *A **P** of Asaph.*
75: T *To the leader: Do Not Destroy. A **P** of Asaph.*
76: T *with stringed instruments. A **P** of Asaph. A Song.*
77: T *according to Jeduthun. Of Asaph. A **P**.*
79: T *A **P** of Asaph.*
80: T *on Lilies, a Covenant. Of Asaph. A **P**.*
82: T *A **P** of Asaph.*
83: T *A Song. A **P** of Asaph.*
84: T *according to The Gittith. Of the Korahites. A **P**.*
85: T *To the leader. Of the Korahites. A **P**.*
87: T *Of the Korahites. A **P**. A Song.*
88: T *A Song. A **P** of the Koroahites. To the leader:*
92: T *A **P**. A Song for the Sabbath Day.*
98: T *A **P**.*
100: T *A **P** of thanksgiving.*
101: T *Of David. A **P**.*
108: T *A Song. A **P** of David.*
109: T *To the leader. Of David. A **P**.*
110: T *Of David. A **P**.*
139: T *To the leader. Of David. A **P**.*
140: T *To the leader. A **P** of David.*
141: T *A **P** of David.*
143: T *A **P** of David.*
Ac 13:33 it is written in the second **p**, 'You are my Son;
13:35 Therefore he has also said in another **p**,
Jdt 16: 1 Raise to him a new **p**; exalt him, and call upon his
Pm 151: T *This **p** is ascribed to David as his own composition*

PSALMIST (1) [PSALM]

4Mc 18:15 He sang to you songs of the **p** David, who said,

PSALMS (6) [PSALM]

Lk 20:42 For David himself says in the book of **P**,
24:44 the prophets, and the **p** must be fulfilled."
Ac 1:20 "For it is written in the book of **P**,
Eph 5:19 as you sing **p** and hymns and spiritual songs
Col 3:16 and with gratitude in your hearts sing **p**, hymns,
3Mc 6:35 the accompaniment of joyous thanksgiving and **p**.

PTOLEMAIC (1) [PTOLEMY]

3Mc 1: 2 the **P** arms that had been previously issued to him,

PTOLEMAIS (22)

Ac 21: 7 the voyage from Tyre, we arrived at **P**;
1Mc 5:15 they said that the people of **P** and Tyre and Sidon,
5:22 He pursued them to the gate of **P**;
5:55 and their brother Simon was in Galilee before **P**,
10: 1 son of Antiochus, landed and occupied **P**.
10:39 **P** and the land adjoining it I have given as a gift
10:56 I will do for you as you wrote, but meet me at **P**,
10:57 came to **P** in the one hundred sixty-second year.
10:58 and celebrated her wedding at **P** with great pomp,
10:60 he went with pomp to **P** and met the two kings;
11:22 as soon as he heard it he set out and came to **P**;
11:22 but to meet him for a conference at **P** as quickly
11:24 for he went to the king at **P**,
12:45 and come with me to **P**.
12:48 But when Jonathan entered **P**,
12:48 the people of **P** closed the gates and seized him,
13:12 Then Trypho left **P** with a large army to invade
2Mc 6: 8 of the people of **P** a decree was issued to
13:24 left Hegemonides as governor from **P** to Gerar,
13:25 and went to **P**. The people of **P** were indignant
3Mc 7:17 When they had arrived at **P**,

PTOLEMIES See Index to Footnotes

PTOLEMY‡ (33) [MACRON, PTOLEMAIC]

AdE 11: 1 In the fourth year of the reign of **P** and Cleopatra,
11: 1 and his son **P** brought to Egypt the preceding
11: 1 and had been translated by Lysimachus son of **P**,
1Mc 1:18 He engaged King **P** of Egypt in battle,
1:18 and **P** turned and fled before him,
3:38 Lysias chose **P** son of Dorymenes,
10:51 to **P** king of Egypt with the following message:
10:55 **P** the king replied and said,
10:57 So **P** set out from Egypt,
10:58 **P** gave him his daughter Cleopatra in marriage,
11: 3 But when **P** entered the towns he stationed forces
11: 8 So King **P** gained control of the coastal cities
11:13 **P** entered Antioch and put on the crown of Asia.
11:15 **P** marched out and met him with a strong force,
11:16 and King **P** was triumphant.
11:17 the head of Alexander and sent it to **P**.
11:18 But King **P** died three days later,
15:16 consul of the Romans, to King **P**, greetings.
16:11 Now **P** son of Abubus had been appointed
16:16 **P** and his men rose up, took their weapons,
16:18 Then **P** wrote a report about these things
2Mc 1:10 teacher of King **P**, and to the Jews in Egypt,
4:45 a substantial bribe to **P** son of Dorymenes to win
4:46 Therefore **P**, taking the king aside into
8: 8 to **P**, the governor of Coelesyria and Phoenicia,
8: 9 **P** promptly appointed Nicanor son of Patroclus,
9:29 he withdrew to **P** Philometor in Egypt.
10:12 **P**, who was called Macron,
3Mc 1: 2 and crossed over by night to the tent of **P**,
1: 6 **P** decided to visit the neighboring cities
3:12 "King **P** Philopator to his generals and soldiers
7: 1 "King **P** Philopator to the generals in Egypt
4Mc 4:22 For when he was warring against **P** in Egypt,

PUA (KJV) See PUVAH

PUAH (3) [=PUVAH]

Ex 1:15 of whom was named Shiphrah and the other **P**,
Jdg 10: 1 After Abimelech, Tola son of **P** son of Dodo,
1Ch 7: 1 Tola, **P**, Jashub, and Shimron, four.

PUBLIC (41) [PUBLICLY]

Lev 5: 1 that you have heard a **p** adjuration to testify and—
Dt 13:16 All of its spoil you shall gather into its **p** square;
2Sa 21:12 who had stolen them from the **p** square
2Ki 15:10 and struck him down in **p** and killed him,
Pr 5:14 I am at the point of utter ruin in the **p** assembly."
Isa 59:14 for truth stumbles in the **p** square,
Da 2: 5 king answered the Chaldeans, "This is a **p** decree:
Mt 1:19 and unwilling to expose her to **p** disgrace,
Ac 5:18 arrested the apostles and put them in the **p** prison.
12:21 and delivered a **p** address to them.
16:37 But Paul replied, "They have beaten us in **p**,
18:28 for he powerfully refuted the Jews in **p**,
21:26 making **p** the completion of the days
Col 2:15 the rulers and authorities and made a **p** example
1Ti 4:13 give attention to the **p** reading of scripture,
AdE 14:16 upon my head on days when I appear in **p**.
16: 5 with the administration of **p** affairs,
Sir 7: 7 Commit no offense against the **p**,
38:33 nor do they attain eminence in the **p** assembly.
42:11 and put you to shame in **p** gatherings.
1Mc 14:22 We have recorded what they said in our **p** decrees,
14:23 and to put a copy of their words in the **p** archives,
2Mc 4: 5 both **p** and private, of all the people.
4: 6 the king's attention **p** affairs could not again reach
7:24 for his Friend and entrust him with **p** affairs.
9:26 to remember the **p** and private services rendered
10: 2 down the altars that had been built in the **p** square
10: 8 They decreed by **p** edict, ratified by vote,
12: 4 and this was done by **p** vote of the city.
13:26 Lysias took the **p** platform,
15: 6 to erect a **p** monument of victory over Judas
15:36 by **p** vote never to let this day go unobserved,
3Mc 2:27 to inflict **p** disgrace on the Jewish community,
4: 1 a feast at **p** expense was arranged for the Gentiles
4: 7 in **p** view they were violently dragged along as far
6:36 a **p** rite for these things in their whole community
7:14 And so on their way they punished and put to a **p**
2Es 14:26 you have finished, some things you shall make **p**,
14:45 "Make **p** the twenty-four books
16:64 and will make a **p** spectacle of all of you.
4Mc 3:21 against the **p** harmony and caused many

PUBLICAN (KJV) See TAX COLLECTOR

PUBLICLY (10) [PUBLIC]

Lk 1:80 in the wilderness until the day he appeared **p**
Jn 7:10 then he also went, not **p** but as it were in secret.
Ac 19:19 magic collected their books and burned them **p**;
20:20 and teaching you **p** and from house to house,
Gal 3: 1 before your eyes that Jesus Christ was **p** exhibited
Heb 10:33 sometimes being **p** exposed to abuse
AdE 16:19 post a copy of this letter **p** in every place,
2Mc 4:33 he **p** exposed them, having first withdrawn to
6:10 They **p** paraded them around the city,
2Es 2:36 I **p** call on my savior to witness.

PUBLISH (4) [PUBLISHED]

Ne 8:15 that they should **p** and proclaim in all their towns
Am 4: 5 **p** them; for so you love to do, O people of Israel!
Sir Pr: 3 and **p** the book for those living abroad who wished

2Es 14: 6 'These words you shall **p** openly,

PUBLISHED (3) [PUBLISH]

Est 8:13 as a decree in every province and **p** to all peoples,
AdE 8:14 and the decree was **p** also in Susa.
8:17 and province wherever the decree was **p;**

PUBLIUS (2)

Ac 28: 7 to the leading man of the island, named **P,**
28: 8 It so happened that the father of **P** lay sick in bed

PUDENS (1)

2Ti 4:21 as do **P** and Linus and Claudia and all the brothers

PUFFED (5) [PUFFS]

1Co 4: 6 so that none of you will be **p** up in favor of one
Col 2:18 **p** up without cause by a human way of thinking,
1Ti 3: 6 or he may be **p** up with conceit and fall into
2Mc 7:34 not be elated in vain and **p** up by uncertain hopes,
3Mc 2: 2 **p** up in his audacity and power.

PUFFS (1) [PUFFED]

1Co 8: 1 Knowledge **p** up, but love builds up.

PUHITES (KJV) See PUTHITES

PUL‡ (3) [=TIGLATH-PILESER]

2Ki 15:19 King **P** of Assyria came against the land;
15:19 Menahem gave **P** a thousand talents of silver,
1Ch 5:26 So the God of Israel stirred up the spirit of King **P**

PULL (13) [PULLED, PULLS]

Dt 25: 9 **p** his sandal off his foot, spit in his face,
Jdg 6:25 and **p** down the altar of Baal that belongs
Ru 2:16 also **p** out some handfuls for her from the bundles,
Jer 1:10 to pluck up and to **p** down,
12: 3 **P** them out like sheep for the slaughter,
38:10 and **p** the prophet Jeremiah up from the cistern
42:10 then I will build you up and not **p** you down;
Eze 17: 9 Will he not **p** up its roots,
17: 9 or mighty army will be needed to **p** it from its
Lk 12:18 I will **p** down my barns and build larger ones,
14: 5 not immediately **p** it out on a sabbath day?"
Tob 13:12 cursed are all who conquer you and **p** down your
2Es 1: 8 **p** out the hair of your head and hurl all evils

PULLED (25) [PULL]

Dt 21: 3 one that has not **p** in the yoke;
25:10 as "the house of him whose sandal was **p** off."
Jdg 6:30 for he has **p** down the altar of Baal and cut down
6:31 because his altar has been **p** down."
6:32 because he **p** down his altar.
16: 3 **p** them up, bar and all, put them on his shoulders,
16:14 But he awoke from his sleep, and **p** away the pin,
2Ki 23:12 he **p** down from there and broke in pieces,
23:15 he **p** down that altar along with the high place.
2Ch 31: 1 and **p** down the high places and the altars
33: 3 the high places that his father Hezekiah had **p**
34: 4 In his presence they **p** down the altars of
Ezr 6:11 be **p** out of the house of the perpetrator,
9: 3 and **p** hair from my head and beard,
Ne 13:25 and beat some of them and **p** out their hair;
Isa 22:19 and you will be **p** down from your post.
33:20 whose stakes will never be **p** up,
50: 6 and my cheeks to those who **p** out the beard;
Jer 38:13 up by the ropes and **p** him out of the cistern.
Ac 11:10 then everything was **p** up again to heaven.
Jdt 13: 9 Next she rolled his body off the bed and **p** down
13:15 Then she **p** the head out of the bag and showed it
Bel 1:42 Then he **p** Daniel out, and threw into
1Es 6:16 and they **p** down the house,
8:71 and **p** out hair from my head and beard,

PULLS (2) [PULL]

Mt 9:16 for the patch **p** away from the cloak,
Mk 2:21 otherwise, the patch **p** away from it,

PULSE (KJV) See VEGETABLES

PULVERIZE (1)

Isa 28:28 the cart wheel and horses over it, but does not **p** it.

PUNISH‡ (81) [PUNISHABLE, PUNISHED, PUNISHES, PUNISHING, PUNISHMENT, PUNISHMENTS]

Ex 32:34 I will **p** them for their sin."
Lev 26:18 I will continue to **p** you sevenfold for your sins.
26:28 I in turn will **p** you myself sevenfold for your sins.
Nu 12:11 do not **p** us for a sin that we have
Dt 22:18 elders of that town shall take the man and **p** him;
1Sa 3:13 that I am about to **p** his house forever,
15: 2 'I will **p** the Amalekites for what they did
2Sa 7:14 I will **p** him with a rod such as mortals use,
13:21 but he would not **p** his son Amnon,
1Ki 8:35 and turn from their sin, because you **p** them,
11:39 For this reason I will **p** the descendants of David,
2Ch 6:26 and turn from their sin, because you **p** them,
Job 35:15 And now, because his anger does not **p,**
Ps 59: 5 Awake to **p** all the nations;
89:32 then I will **p** their transgression with the rod
Isa 10:12 he will **p** the arrogant boasting of the king
13:11 I will **p** the world for its evil,
24:21 On that day the LORD will **p** the host of heaven
26:21 to **p** the inhabitants of the earth for their iniquity;
27: 1 and great and strong sword will **p** Leviathan
64:12 Will you keep silent, and **p** us so severely?
Jer 2:19 Your wickedness will **p** you,
5: 9 Shall I not **p** them for these things?
5:29 Shall I not **p** them for these things?
6:15 at the time that I **p** them, they shall be overthrown,
8:12 at the time when I **p** them,
9: 9 Shall I not **p** them for these things?
11:22 I am going to **p** them;
14:10 he will remember their iniquity and **p** their sins.
21:14 I will **p** you according to the fruit of your doings,
23:34 I will **p** them and their households.
25:12 I will **p** the king of Babylon and that nation,
27: 8 then I will **p** that nation with the sword,
29:32 to **p** Shemaiah of Nehelam and his descendants;
30:20 and I will **p** all who oppress them.
36:31 And I will **p** him and his offspring
44:13 I will **p** those who live in the land of Egypt,
44:29 that I am going to **p** you in this place,
49: 8 the time when I **p** him.
50:18 I am going to **p** the king of Babylon and his land,
50:31 for your day has come, the time when I will **p** you.
51:44 I will **p** Bel in Babylon,
51:47 the days are coming when I will **p** the images
51:52 says the LORD, when I will **p** her idols,
La 4:22 but your iniquity, O daughter Edom, he will **p,**
Eze 7: 3 I will **p** you for all your abominations.
7: 4 I will **p** you for your ways,
7: 8 and **p** you for all your abominations.
7: 9 I will **p** you according to your ways,
Hos 1: 4 for in a little while I will **p** the house of Jehu for
2:13 I will **p** her for the festival days of the Baals,
4: 9 I will **p** them for their ways,
4:14 not **p** your daughters when they play the whore,
5: 2 but I will **p** all of them.
8:13 he will remember their iniquity, and **p** their sins;
9: 9 will remember their iniquity, he will **p** their sins.
10:10 I will come against the wayward people to **p** them;
12: 2 and will **p** Jacob according to his ways,
Am 3: 2 therefore I will **p** you for all your iniquities.
3:14 On the day I **p** Israel for its transgressions,
3:14 I will **p** the altars of Bethel,
Zep 1: 8 of the LORD's sacrifice I will **p** the officials and
1: 9 that day I will **p** all who leap over the threshold,
1:12 and I will **p** the people who rest complacently
Zec 10: 3 and I will **p** the leaders;
Ac 4:21 finding no way to **p** them because of the people,
1Co 9:27 but I **p** my body and enslave it,
2Co 10: 6 We are ready to **p** every disobedience
1Pe 2:14 as sent by him to **p** those who do wrong and
Tob 3: 3 Do not **p** me for my sins and for my unwitting
Wis 11:15 a multitude of irrational creatures to **p** them,
16:24 exerts itself to **p** the unrighteous,
Sir 5: 3 for the Lord will surely **p** you.
1Mc 7: 7 and let him **p** them and all who help them."
15:21 so that he may **p** them according to their law."
2Mc 1:28 **P** those who oppress and are insolent with pride.
6:13 but to **p** them immediately.
6:14 to **p** them until they have reached the full measure
3Mc 2:17 Do not **p** us for the defilement committed
7: 3 and to **p** them with barbarous penalties as traitors;
4Mc 8: 6 as I am able to **p** those who disobey my orders,

PUNISHABLE (2) [PUNISH]

Dt 21:22 When someone is convicted of a crime **p** by death
22:26 the young woman has not committed an offense **p**

PUNISHED‡ (44) [PUNISH]

Ex 21:20 the slave dies immediately, the owner shall be **p.**
Lev 18:25 and I **p** it for its iniquity,
2Ki 17:20 he **p** them and gave them into the hand
Ezr 9:13 have **p** us less than our iniquities deserved
Job 31:28 also would be an iniquity to be **p** by the judges,
Ps 73:14 I have been plagued, and am **p** every morning.
118:18 The LORD has **p** me severely,
Pr 21:11 When a scoffer is **p,** the simple become wiser;
Isa 24:22 and after many days they will be **p.**
26:14 because you have **p** and destroyed them,
Jer 6: 6 This is the city that must be **p;**
44:13 as I have **p** Jerusalem, with the sword,
50:18 as I **p** the king of Assyria.
Hos 10:10 be gathered against them when they are **p**
2Co 6: 9 as **p,** and yet not killed;
Heb 12: 5 or lose heart when you are **p** by him;
Jdt 11:10 Indeed our nation cannot be **p,**
Wis 3: 4 For though in the sight of others they were **p,**
3:10 the ungodly will be **p** as their reasoning deserves,
11: 5 the very things by which their enemies were **p,**
11: 8 at that time how you **p** their enemies.
11:16 that one is **p** by the very things by which one sins.
12:14 about those whom you have **p.**
12:15 to condemn anyone who does not deserve to be **p.**
12:20 For if you **p** with such great care and indulgence
12:27 being **p** by means of them,
14:10 for what was done will be **p** together with
16: 1 Therefore those people were deservedly **p**
16: 9 because they deserved to be **p** by such things.
18: 8 by which you **p** our enemies you called us
18:11 slave was **p** with the same penalty as the master,
Sir 23:21 This man will be **p** in the streets of the city,
30:19 So is the one **p** by the Lord;
Bar 3: 8 and **p** for all the iniquities of our ancestors,
2Mc 4:16 completely became their enemies and **p** them.
7: 7 "Will you eat rather than have your body **p** limb
1Es 8:24 or the law of the kingdom shall be strictly **p,**
3Mc 2:24 a while he recovered, and though he had been **p,**
3:26 For when all of these have been **p,**
7:14 And so on their way they **p** and put to a public
2Es 5:30 they should be **p** at your own hands."
9:13 to be curious about how the ungodly will be **p;**
4Mc 17:21 the tyrant was **p,** and the homeland purified—
18: 5 The tyrant Antiochus was both **p** on earth

PUNISHES (4) [PUNISH]

Jdt 7:28 who **p** us for our sins and the sins of our ancestors;
Wis 1: 8 and justice, when it **p,** will not pass them by.
Sir 39:30 and the sword that **p** the ungodly with destruction.
4Mc 2:12 so that one **p** them for misdeeds.

PUNISHING (5) [PUNISH]

Ex 20: 5 **p** children for the iniquity of parents,
Dt 5: 9 **p** children for the iniquity of parents,
Joel 2:13 in steadfast love, and relents from **p.**
Jnh 4: 2 and ready to relent from **p.**
Ac 26:11 By **p** them often in all the synagogues I tried

PUNISHMENT‡ (98) [PUNISH]

Ge 4:13 "My **p** is greater than I can bear!
19:15 or else you will be consumed in the **p** of the city."
Ex 21:21 if the slave survives a day or two, there is no **p;**
32:34 day comes for **p,** I will punish them for their sin."
Lev 5: 1 does not speak up, you are subject to **p.**
5:17 you have incurred guilt, and are subject to **p.**
19: 8 All who eat it shall be subject to **p,**
20:17 he shall be subject to **p.**
20:19 they shall be subject to **p.**
20:20 they shall be subject to **p;** they shall die childless.
1Sa 28:10 no **p** shall come upon you for this thing."
Job 19:29 for wrath brings the **p** of the sword,
34:31 "For has anyone said to God, 'I have endured **p;**
Ps 39:11 "You chastise mortals in **p** for sin,
91: 8 You will only look with your eyes and see the **p** of
149: 7 to execute vengeance on the nations and **p** on
Pr 16:22 but folly is the **p** of fools.
Isa 10: 3 What will you do on the day of **p,**
30:32 the staff of **p** that the LORD lays upon him will
53: 5 upon him was the **p** that made us whole,
Jer 10:15 at the time of their **p** they shall perish.
10:19 But I said, "Truly this is my **p,** and I must bear it."
11:23 upon the people of Anathoth, the year of their **p.**
23:12 upon them in the year of their **p,**
25:29 and how can you possibly avoid **p?**
30:14 for I have dealt you the blow of an enemy, the **p** of
46:21 upon them, the time of their **p.**
46:25 See, I am bringing **p** upon Amon of Thebes,
48:44 upon Moab in the year of their **p,**
50:27 their day has come, the time of their **p!**
51:18 at the time of their **p** they shall perish.
La 3:39 about the **p** of their sins?
4: 6 of my people has been greater than the **p**
4:22 The **p** of your iniquity, O daughter Zion,
Eze 4: 4 and place the **p** of the house of Israel upon it;
4: 4 you shall bear their **p** for the number of the days
4: 5 equal to the number of the years of their **p;**
4: 5 and so you shall bear the **p** of the house of Israel.
4: 6 and bear the **p** of the house of Judah;
4:17 and waste away under their **p.**
14:10 And they shall bear their **p—**the **p** of the inquirer and the **p** of the prophet shall be the same—
21:25 you whose day has come, the time of final **p,**
21:29 those whose day has come, the time of final **p.**
35: 5 at the time of their final **p;**
44:10 when Israel went astray, shall bear their **p.**
44:12 says the Lord GOD, that they shall bear their **p.**
Hos 5: 9 a desolation in the day of **p;**
9: 7 The days of **p** have come,
Am 1: 3 and for four, I will not revoke the **p;**
1: 6 and for four, I will not revoke the **p;**
1: 9 and for four, I will not revoke the **p;**
1:11 and for four, I will not revoke the **p;**
1:13 and for four, I will not revoke the **p;**
2: 1 and for four, I will not revoke the **p;**
2: 4 and for four, I will not revoke the **p;**
2: 6 and for four, I will not revoke the **p;**
Mic 7: 4 The day of their sentinels, of their **p,** has come;
Hab 1:12 and you, O Rock, have established them for **p.**
Zec 14:19 Such shall be the **p** of Egypt and the **p** of all the
Mt 25:46 And these will go away into eternal **p,**
Ac 22: 5 and to bring them back to Jerusalem for **p.**
2Co 2: 6 This **p** by the majority is enough for such
7:11 what alarm, what longing, what zeal, what **p!**
2Th 1: 9 These will suffer the **p** of eternal destruction,
Heb 10:29 How much worse **p** do you think will be deserved
2Pe 2: 9 the unrighteous under **p** until the day of judgment
1Jn 4:18 for fear has to do with **p,**
Jude 1: 7 as an example by undergoing a **p** of eternal fire.
Jdt 2:10 you shall hold them for me until the day of their **p.**
AdE 16:18 over all things, has speedily inflicted on him the **p**
Wis 16: 2 of this **p** you showed kindness to your people,
18: 5 you in **p** took away a multitude of their children;
19: 4 up the **p** that their torments still lacked,
19:15 while **p** of some sort will come upon the former
Sir 5: 7 and at the time of **p** you will perish.
7:17 for the **p** of the ungodly is fire and worms.
8: 5 remember that we all deserve **p.**
12: 6 the Most High also hates sinners and will inflict **p**
14: 6 this is the **p** for his meanness.

Sir 23:24 and her **p** will extend to her children.
1Mc 14:45 or rejects any of them shall be liable to **p.**”
2Mc 4:38 The Lord thus repaid him with the **p** he deserved.
6:26 if for the present I would avoid the **p** of mortals,
7:36 will receive just **p** for your arrogance.
1Es 8:24 whether by death or some other **p,**
3Mc 2:23 seeing the severe **p** that had overtaken him,
3:28 the property of those who incur the **p,**
4:13 not omitting any detail of their **p.**
7:10 the law of God should receive the **p** they deserved.
2Es 7:21 and what they should observe to avoid **p.**
7:*93* of the ungodly wander and the **p** that awaits them.
7:*117* [47] that they live in sorrow now and expect **p**
4Mc 6:9 and scorned the **p** and endured the tortures.
6:28 and let our **p** suffice for them.
11:3 so that by murdering me you will incur **p** from

PUNISHMENTS (10) [PUNISH]
Lev 26:23 in spite of these **p** you have not turned back to me,
Eze 5:15 on you in anger and fury, and with furious **p**—
25:17 execute great vengeance on them with wrathful **p.**
Wis 11:13 For when they heard that through their own **p**
19:13 The **p** did not come upon the sinners
2Mc 6:12 but to recognize that these **p** were designed not
3Mc 2:6 by inflicting many and varied **p** on
4:4 that at the sight of their unusual **p,**
4Mc 4:24 that all his threats and **p** were being disregarded
8:9 of you with dreadful **p** through tortures.

PUNITES (1) [PUVAH]
Nu 26:23 of Puvah, the clan of the **P;**

PUNON (2)
Nu 33:42 They set out from Zalmonah and camped at **P.**
33:43 They set out from **P** and camped at Oboth.

PUNY (1)
2Es 11:3 but they became little, **p** wings.

PUPIL (1) [PUPILS]
1Ch 25:8 small and great, teacher and **p** alike.

PUPILS (1) [PUPIL]
4Mc 18:21 the **p** of their eyes and cut out their tongues,

PUR (3) [PURIM]
Est 3:7 the twelfth year of King Ahasuerus, they cast **P**—
9:24 against the Jews to destroy them, and had cast **P**—
9:26 these days are called Purim, from the word **P.**

PURAH (2)
Jdg 7:10 go down to the camp with your servant **P;**
7:11 down with his servant **P** to the outposts of

PURCHASE (9) [PURCHASED, PURCHASER]
Lev 22:11 a priest acquires anyone by **p,** the person may eat
25:51 for their redemption in proportion to the **p** price;
Dt 2:6 You shall **p** food from them for money,
Jer 32:7 for the right of redemption by **p** is yours.”
32:11 Then I took the sealed deed of **p,**
32:12 of **p** to Baruch son of Neriah son of Mahseiah,
32:12 of the witnesses who signed the deed of **p,**
32:14 both this sealed deed of **p** and this open deed,
32:16 I had given the deed of **p** to Baruch son of Neriah,

PURCHASED (5) [PURCHASE]
Ge 25:10 the field that Abraham **p** from the Hittites.
49:32 and the cave that is in it were **p** from the Hittites.”
Ex 12:44 but any slave who has been **p** may eat of it
Lev 27:22 to the LORD a field that has been **p,**
Jdt 4:10 and hired laborer and **p** slave—

PURCHASER (3) [PURCHASE]
Lev 25:28 what was sold shall remain with the **p** until
25:30 in perpetuity to the **p,** throughout the generations;
25:50 They shall compute with the **p** the total from

PURE‡ (108) [PURENESS, PURER, PUREST, PURIFICATION, PURIFIED, PURIFIER, PURIFY, PURIFYING, PURITY]
A. PURE GOLD (44)

Ex 25:11 You shall overlay it with **p** gold, A
25:17 Then you shall make a mercy seat of **p** gold; A
25:24 You shall overlay it with **p** gold, A
25:29 you shall make them of **p** gold. A
25:31 You shall make a lampstand of **p** gold. A
25:36 the whole of it one hammered piece of **p** gold. A
25:38 Its snuffers and trays shall be of **p** gold. A
25:39 shall be made from a talent of **p** gold. A
27:20 the Israelites to bring you **p** oil of beaten olives
28:14 and two chains of **p** gold, twisted like cords; A
28:22 for the breastpiece chains of **p** gold, twisted A
28:36 You shall make a rosette of **p** gold, A
30:3 You shall overlay it with **p** gold, its top, A
30:34 and galbanum, sweet spices with **p** frankincense
30:35 seasoned with salt, **p** and holy;
31:8 and the **p** lampstand with all its utensils,
37:2 He overlaid it with **p** gold inside and outside, A
Ex 37:6 He made a mercy seat of **p** gold; A
37:11 He overlaid it with **p** gold, A
37:16 And he made the vessels of **p** gold that were to A
37:17 He also made the lampstand of **p** gold. A
37:22 the whole of it one hammered piece of **p** gold. A
37:23 and its snuffers and its trays of **p** gold. A
37:24 made it and all its utensils of a talent of **p** gold. A
37:26 He overlaid it with **p** gold, its top, A
37:29 and the **p** fragrant incense,
39:15 They made on the breastpiece chains of **p** gold, A
39:25 They also made bells of **p** gold, A
39:30 the rosette of the holy diadem of **p** gold, A
39:37 the **p** lampstand with its lamps set on it
Lev 24:2 Command the people of Israel to bring you **p** oil
24:4 up the lamps on the lampstand of **p** gold before A
24:6 six in a row, on the table of **p** gold. A
24:7 You shall put **p** frankincense with each row,
2Sa 22:27 with the **p** you show yourself **p,**
1Ki 6:20 he overlaid it with **p** gold. A
6:21 the inside of the house with **p** gold, A
7:49 the lampstands of **p** gold, five on the south side A
7:50 dishes for incense, and firepans, of **p** gold; A
10:21 of the Forest of Lebanon were of **p** gold; A
1Ch 28:17 and **p** gold for the forks, the basins, and the A
2Ch 3:4 He overlaid it on the inside with **p** gold. A
4:20 lampstands and their lamps of **p** gold to burn A
4:22 basins, ladles, and firepans, of **p** gold. A
9:17 and overlaid it with **p** gold. A
9:20 of the Forest of Lebanon were of **p** gold; A
13:11 set out the rows of bread on the table of **p** gold, A
Job 4:17 Can human beings be **p** before their Maker?
8:6 if you are **p** and upright,
11:4 For you say, ‘My conduct is **p,**
16:17 in my hands, and my prayer is **p.**
25:4 How can one born of woman be **p?**
25:5 even the moon is not bright and the stars are not **p**
28:19 nor can it be valued in **p** gold. A
33:9 I am **p,** and there is no iniquity in me.
Ps 12:6 promises of the LORD are promises that are **p,**
18:26 with the **p** you show yourself **p;**
19:9 the fear of the LORD is **p,** enduring forever;
24:4 Those who have clean hands and **p** hearts,
73:1 to those who are **p** in heart.
119:9 How can young people keep their way **p?**
Pr 15:26 to the LORD, but gracious words are **p.**
16:2 All one’s ways may be **p** in one’s own eyes,
20:9 I am **p** from my sin”?
20:11 by whether what they do is **p** and right.
21:8 but the conduct of the **p** is right.
22:11 a **p** heart and are gracious in speech will have
30:12 There are those who are **p** in their own eyes
La 4:1 gold has grown dim, how the **p** gold is changed! A
Da 7:9 and the hair of his head like **p** wool;
Hab 1:13 Your eyes are too **p** to behold evil,
Zep 3:9 the speech of the peoples to a **p** speech,
Mal 1:11 to my name, and a **p** offering;
Mt 5:8 “Blessed are the **p** in heart, for they will see God.
Jn 12:3 a pound of costly perfume made of **p** nard,
2Co 11:3 be led astray from a sincere and **p** devotion
Php 1:10 in the day of Christ you may be **p** and blameless,
4:8 whatever is **p,** whatever is pleasing,
1Th 2:10 You are witnesses, and God also, how **p,** upright,
1Ti 1:5 that comes from a **p** heart,
5:22 of others; keep yourself **p.**
2Ti 2:22 with those who call on the Lord from a **p** heart.
Tit 1:15 To the **p** all things are **p,** but to the corrupt and unbelieving nothing is **p.**
Heb 10:22 and our bodies washed with **p** water.
Jas 1:27 Religion that is **p** and undefiled before God,
3:17 But the wisdom from above is first **p,**
1Pe 2:2 Like newborn infants, long for the **p,**
1Jn 3:3 in him purify themselves, just as he is **p.**
Rev 15:6 with the seven plagues, robed in **p** bright linen,
19:8 to be clothed with fine linen, bright and **p**”—
19:14 armies of heaven, wearing fine linen, white and **p,**
21:18 wall is built of jasper, while the city is **p** gold, A
21:21 and the street of the city is **p** gold, A
Tob 8:15 “Blessed are you, O God, with every **p** blessing;
13:16 and their battlements with **p** gold. A
Wis 7:23 through all spirits that are intelligent, **p,**
7:25 and a **p** emanation of the glory of the Almighty;
8:18 **p** delight, and in the labors of her hands,
14:24 either their lives or their marriages **p,**
Bar 3:30 and found her, and will buy her for **p** gold? A
2Es 7:*122* [52] a **p** life, but we have walked in
4Mc 5:37 My ancestors will receive me as **p,**
18:7 “I was a **p** virgin and did
18:23 and have received **p** and immortal souls from God,

PURENESS (1) [PURE]
Wis 7:24 of her **p** she pervades and penetrates all things.

PURER (1) [PURE]
La 4:7 Her princes were **p** than snow, whiter than milk;

PUREST (2) [PURE]
2Ch 4:21 the flowers, the lamps, and the tongs, of **p** gold;
Jer 2:21 I planted you as a choice vine, from the **p** stock.

PURGE (16) [PURGED, PURGES]
Dt 13:5 So you shall **p** the evil from your midst.
17:7 So you shall **p** the evil from your midst.
17:12 So you shall **p** the evil from Israel.
19:13 you shall **p** the guilt of innocent blood from Israel,
19:19 So you shall **p** the evil from your midst.
Dt 21:9 So you shall **p** the guilt of innocent blood
21:21 So you shall **p** the evil from your midst;
22:21 So you shall **p** the evil from your midst.
22:22 So you shall **p** the evil from Israel.
22:24 So you shall **p** the evil from your midst.
24:7 So you shall **p** the evil from your midst.
Jdg 20:13 and **p** the evil from Israel.”
2Ch 34:3 to **p** Judah and Jerusalem of the high places,
Ps 51:7 **P** me with hyssop, and I shall be clean;
Eze 20:38 I will **p** out the rebels among you,
22:15 and I will **p** your filthiness out of you.

PURGED (2) [PURGE]
2Ch 34:5 on their altars, and **p** Judah and Jerusalem.
34:8 when he had **p** the land and the house,

PURGES (1) [PURGE]
Tob 12:9 from death and **p** away every sin.

PURGETH (KJV) See PRUNES

PURIFICATION (22) [PURE]
Lev 12:4 Her time of blood **p** shall be thirty-three days;
12:4 until the days of her **p** are completed.
12:5 her time of blood **p** shall be sixty-six days.
12:6 When the days of her **p** are completed,
Nu 8:7 sprinkle the water of **p** on them,
19:9 It is a **p** offering.
19:17 of the burnt **p** offering, and running water shall
31:23 it shall also be purified with the water for **p;**
Ne 12:45 the service of their God and the service of **p,**
Lk 2:22 the time came for their **p** according to the law
Jn 2:6 for the Jewish rites of **p,**
3:25 about **p** arose between John’s disciples and a Jew.
Ac 21:24 Join these men, go through the rite of **p** with them,
21:26 of the days of **p** when the sacrifice would be made
24:18 completing the rite of **p,** without any crowd
Heb 1:3 When he had made **p** for sins,
2Mc 1:18 of Chislev we shall celebrate the **p** of the temple,
1:36 called this “nephthar,” which means **p,**
2:16 we are about to celebrate the **p,** we write to you.
2:19 and the **p** of the great temple,
10:5 the **p** of the sanctuary took place, that is,
4Mc 6:29 Make my blood their **p,** and take my life

PURIFIED (26) [PURE]
Nu 8:21 The Levites **p** themselves from sin
31:23 it shall also be **p** with the water for purification;
Ezr 6:20 both the priests and the Levites had **p** themselves;
Ne 12:30 And the priests and the Levites **p** themselves;
12:30 and they **p** the people and the gates and the wall.
Ps 12:6 in a furnace on the ground, **p** seven times.
Eze 43:22 the altar shall be **p,** as it was **p** with the bull.
Da 11:35 so that they may be refined, **p,** and cleansed,
12:10 Many shall be **p,** cleansed, and refined,
Ac 21:26 and the next day, having **p** himself,
Heb 9:13 so that their flesh is **p,**
9:22 under the law almost everything is **p** with blood,
9:23 of the heavenly things to be **p** with these rites,
1Pe 1:22 that you have **p** your souls by your obedience to
Jdt 12:9 Then she returned **p** and stayed in the tent
16:18 As soon as the people were **p,**
2Mc 2:18 for he has rescued us from great evils and has **p**
10:3 They **p** the sanctuary, and made another altar
12:38 they **p** themselves according to the custom,
14:36 that has been so recently **p.**”
1Es 7:10 after the priests and the Levites were **p** together.
7:11 Not all of the returned captives were **p,**
7:11 but the Levites were all **p** together,
4Mc 1:11 and thus their native land was **p** through them.
17:21 the tyrant was punished, and the homeland **p**—

PURIFIER (1) [PURE]
Mal 3:3 he will sit as a refiner and **p** of silver,

PURIFY‡ (18) [PURE]
Ge 35:2 and **p** yourselves, and change your clothes;
Nu 19:12 They shall **p** themselves with the water on
19:12 if they do not **p** themselves on the third day and on
19:13 and do not **p** themselves, defile the tabernacle of
19:20 Any who are unclean but do not **p** themselves,
31:19 **p** yourselves and your captives on the third and on
31:20 You shall **p** every garment, every article of skin,
Ne 13:22 that they should **p** themselves and come and guard
Isa 52:11 go out from the midst of it, **p** yourselves,
66:17 Those who sanctify and **p** themselves to go into
Eze 43:20 thus you shall **p** it and make atonement for it.
45:18 a young bull without blemish, and **p** the sanctuary.
Mal 3:3 and he will **p** the descendants of Levi
Jn 11:55 to Jerusalem before the Passover to **p** themselves.
Tit 2:14 that he might redeem us from all iniquity and **p**
Heb 9:14 **p** our conscience from dead works to worship
Jas 4:8 and **p** your hearts, you double-minded.
1Jn 3:3 And all who have this hope in him **p** themselves,

PURIFYING (5) [PURE]
Lev 8:15 on each of the horns of the altar, **p** the altar;
Nu 19:19 thus **p** them on the seventh day.
2Sa 11:4 (Now she was **p** herself after her period.)
Eze 43:23 When you have finished **p** it,
2Mc 10:7 to him who had given success to the **p**

PURIM (10) [PUR]

Est 9:26 these days are called **P,** from the word Pur.
9:28 of **P** should never fall into disuse among the Jews,
9:29 confirming this second letter about **P.**
9:31 and giving orders that these days of **P** should
9:32 of Queen Esther fixed these practices of **P,**
AdE 9:26 Therefore these days were called **"P,"**
9:27 These days of **P** should be a memorial and kept
9:28 These days of **P** were to be observed for all time,
9:29 and gave full authority to the letter about **P.**
11: 1 to Egypt the preceding Letter about **P,**

PURITY (9) [PURE]

2Co 6: 6 by **p,** knowledge, patience, kindness, holiness
1Ti 4:12 in speech and conduct, in love, in faith, in **p.**
5: 2 as sisters—with absolute **p.**
1Pe 3: 2 when they see the **p** and reverence of your lives.
Sir 51:20 I directed my soul to her, and in **p** I found her.
1Mc 14:36 doing great damage to its **p.**
2Es 6:32 the **p** that you have maintained from your youth.
4Mc 7: 6 which had room only for reverence and **p,**
18: 8 the deceitful serpent, defile the **p** of my virginity.

PURLOINING (KJV) See PILFER

PURPLE (71)

Ex 25: 4 **p,** and crimson yarns and fine linen, goats' hair,
26: 1 and blue, **p,** and crimson yarns;
26:31 You shall make a curtain of blue, **p,**
26:36 **p,** and crimson yarns, and of fine twisted linen,
27:16 **p,** and crimson yarns, and of fine twisted linen,
28: 5 blue, **p,** and crimson yarns, and fine linen.
28: 6 They shall make the ephod of gold, of blue, **p,**
28: 8 **p,** and crimson yarns, and of fine twisted linen.
28:15 of gold, of blue and **p** and crimson yarns,
28:33 **p,** and crimson yarns, all around the lower hem,
35: 6 **p,** and crimson yarns, and fine linen;
35:23 or **p** or crimson yarn or fine linen or goats' hair
35:25 in blue and **p** and crimson yarns and fine linen;
35:35 **p,** and crimson yarns, and in fine linen,
36: 8 they were made of fine twisted linen, and blue, **p,**
36:35 He made the curtain of blue, **p,** and crimson yarns,
36:37 **p,** and crimson yarns, and fine twisted linen,
38:18 **p,** and crimson yarns and fine twisted linen.
38:23 engraver, designer, and embroiderer in blue, **p,**
39: 1 Of the blue, **p,** and crimson yarns they made finely
39: 2 He made the ephod of gold, of blue, **p,**
39: 3 to work into the blue, **p,** and crimson yarns and
39: 5 **p,** and crimson yarns, and of fine twisted linen;
39: 8 **p,** and crimson yarns, and of fine twisted linen.
39:24 **p,** and crimson yarns, and of fine twisted linen.
39:29 and of blue, **p,** and crimson yarns,
Nu 4:13 and spread a **p** cloth over it;
Jdg 8:26 the pendants and the **p** garments worn by the kings
2Ch 2: 7 and iron, and in **p,** crimson, and blue fabrics,
2:14 and in **p,** blue, and crimson fabrics and fine linen,
3:14 of blue and **p** and crimson fabrics and fine linen,
Est 1: 6 with cords of fine linen and **p** to silver rings
8:15 and a mantle of fine linen and **p,**
Pr 31:22 her clothing is fine linen and **p.**
SS 3:10 its seat of **p;** its interior was inlaid with love.
7: 5 and your flowing locks are like **p;**
Jer 10: 9 their clothing is blue and **p;**
La 4: 5 those who were brought up in **p** cling to ash heaps.
Eze 27: 7 and **p** from the coasts of Elishah was your awning.
27:16 they exchanged for your wares turquoise, **p,**
Da 5: 7 and tell me its interpretation shall be clothed in **p,**
5:16 you shall be clothed in **p,**
5:29 and Daniel was clothed in **p,**
Mk 15:17 And they clothed him in a **p** cloak;
15:20 of the **p** cloak and put his own clothes on him.
Lk 16:19 a rich man who was dressed in **p** and fine linen
Jn 19: 2 and they dressed him in a **p** robe.
19: 5 wearing the crown of thorns and the **p** robe.
Ac 16:14 from the city of Thyatira and a dealer in **p** cloth.
Rev 17: 4 The woman was clothed in **p** and scarlet,
18:12 jewels and pearls, fine linen, **p,** silk and scarlet,
18:16 in **p** and scarlet, adorned with gold, with jewels,
Jdt 10:21 on his bed under a canopy that was woven with **p**
AdE 1: 6 of **p** linen attached to gold and silver blocks
8:15 and wearing a gold crown and a turban of **p** linen.
Sir 6:30 and her bonds a **p** cord.
40: 4 from the one who wears **p** and a crown to
45:10 and violet and **p,** the work of an embroiderer;
LtJ 6:12 When they have been dressed in **p** robes,
6:72 the **p** and linen that rot upon them you will know
1Mc 4:23 and cloth dyed blue and sea **p,** and great riches.
8:14 not one of them has put on a crown or worn **p** as
10:20 He also sent him a **p** robe and a golden crown.
10:62 and to clothe him in **p,**
10:64 and saw him clothed in **p,** they all fled.
11:58 to drink from gold cups and dress in **p** and wear
14:43 and that he should be clothed in **p** and wear gold.
14:44 or to be clothed in **p** or put on a gold buckle.
2Mc 4:38 he immediately stripped off the **p** robe
4:38 from Andronicus, tore off his **p** robe, and led him
1Es 3: 6 in **p,** and drink from gold cups, and sleep on

PURPOSE‡ (69) [PURPOSED, PURPOSES]

Ex 10:10 Plainly, you have some evil **p** in mind.
Lev 5: 4 a rash oath for a bad or a good **p,**
11:32 any article that is used for any **p;**
26:20 Your strength shall be spent to no **p:**
1Ch 12:33 to help David with singleness of **p.**
Ne 6:13 He was hired for this **p,**
8: 4 a wooden platform that had been made for the **p;**
Job 10:13 I know that this was your **p.**
42: 2 and that no **p** of yours can be thwarted.
Ps 57: 2 to God who fulfills his **p** for me.
64: 5 They hold fast to their evil **p;**
119:150 Those who persecute me with evil **p** draw near;
138: 8 The LORD will fulfill his **p** for me;
Pr 16: 4 The LORD has made everything for its **p,**
19:21 it is the **p** of the LORD that will be established.
Isa 44:28 and he shall carry out all my **p";**
46:10 "My **p** shall stand, and I will fulfill my intention,"
46:11 the man for my **p** from a far country.
48:14 he shall perform his **p** on Babylon,
54:16 and produces a weapon fit for its **p;**
55:11 but it shall accomplish that which I **p,**
Jer 49:30 a plan against you and formed a **p** against you.
51:11 because his **p** concerning Babylon is to destroy it,
Lk 4:43 for I was sent for this **p."**
7:30 and the lawyers rejected God's **p** for themselves.)
Ac 9:21 not come here for the **p** of bringing them bound
13:36 he had served the **p** of God in his own generation,
20:27 not shrink from declaring to you the whole **p**
26:16 for I have appeared to you for this **p,**
27:13 they thought they could achieve their **p;**
Ro 4:11 The **p** was to make him the ancestor
8:28 who are called according to his **p.**
9:11 or bad (so that God's **p** of election might continue,
9:17 up for the very **p** of showing my power in you,
14: 1 but not for the **p** of quarreling over opinions.
15: 2 of us must please our neighbor for the good **p**
1Co 1:10 you be united in the same mind and the same **p.**
3: 8 and the one who waters have a common **p,**
Gal 4:17 They make much of you, but for no good **p;**
4:18 to be made much of for a good **p** at all times,
Eph 1:11 to the **p** of him who accomplishes all things
3:11 This was in accordance with the eternal **p**
6:22 I am sending him to you for this very **p,**
Col 4: 8 I have sent him to you for this very **p,**
2Th 2:14 For this **p** he called you through our proclamation
2Ti 1: 9 to our works but according to his own **p** and grace.
Heb 6:17 the promise the unchangeable character of his **p,**
Jas 1:18 of his own **p** he gave us birth by the word of truth,
5:11 and you have seen the **p** of the Lord,
1Jn 3: 8 The Son of God was revealed for this **p,**
Rev 17:17 into their hearts to carry out his **p** by agreeing
Jdt 11:11 not be defeated and his **p** frustrated,
AdE 10:10 For this **p** he made two lots,
Wis 6: 4 or walk according to the **p** of God,
Sir 39:18 When he commands, his every **p** is fulfilled,
39:21 for everything has been created for its own **p.**
2Mc 3: 8 but in fact to carry out the king's **p.**
4:19 but to expend it for another **p.**
14: 5 that furthered his mad **p** when he was invited
1Es 5:47 a single **p** in the square before the first gate toward
5:58 the work on the house of God with a single **p.**
3Mc 1:22 of his plans or the fulfillment of his intended **p.**
2:26 intently observing the king's **p,**
3:11 that he would persevere constantly in his same **p,**
5:12 in his lawless **p** and was completely frustrated
5:29 "O king, according to your eager **p."**
2Es 8:14 to what **p** was it made?
4Mc 1: 6 and it is not for the **p** of destroying them,
4: 1 he fled the country with the **p** of betraying it.

PURPOSED (5) [PURPOSE]

Jer 4:28 for I have spoken, I have **p;**
La 2:17 The LORD has done what he **p,**
Zec 8:14 Just as I **p** to bring disaster upon you,
8:15 so again I have **p** in these days to do good
Wis 4:17 and will not understand what the Lord **p** for them,

PURPOSES (11) [PURPOSE]

1Ch 29:18 keep forever such **p** and thoughts in the hearts
Ps 106:43 but they were rebellious in their **p,**
Pr 20: 5 The **p** in the human mind are like deep water,
Jer 49:20 against Edom and the **p** that he has formed against
50:45 and the **p** that he has formed against the land of
51:29 for the LORD's **p** against Babylon stand,
1Co 4: 5 now hidden in darkness and will disclose the **p** of
Jdt 8:16 Do not try to bind the **p** of the Lord our God;
11: 6 and my lord will not fail to achieve his **p.**
AdE 12: 2 into their **p,** and learned that they were preparing
Wis 2:22 the secret **p** of God, nor hoped for the wages

PURSE (8) [PURSES]

Pr 1:14 we will all have one **p"**—
Isa 46: 6 Those who lavish gold from the **p,**
Lk 10: 4 Carry no **p,** no bag, no sandals;
22:35 "When I sent you out without a **p,** bag, or sandals,
22:36 "But now, the one who has a **p** must take it,
Jn 12: 6 the common **p** and used to steal what was put
13:29 because Judas had the common **p,**
Sir 18:33 when you have nothing in your **p.**

PURSES (1) [PURSE]

Lk 12:33 Make **p** for yourselves that do not wear out,

PURSUE (47) [PURSUED, PURSUER, PURSUERS, PURSUES, PURSUING, PURSUIT, PURSUITS]

Ex 14: 4 I will harden Pharaoh's heart, and he will **p** them,
15: 9 The enemy said, 'I will **p,** I will overtake,
Dt 16:20 Justice, and only justice, you shall **p,**
19: 6 of blood in hot anger might **p** and overtake
28:22 they shall **p** you until you perish.
Jos 2: 5 **P** them quickly, for you can overtake them."
8:16 in the city were called together to **p** them,
10:19 **p** your enemies, and attack them from the rear.
1Sa 24:14 of Israel come out? Whom do you **p?**
25:29 up to **p** you and to seek your life, the life
26:18 And he added, "Why does my lord **p** his servant?
30: 8 of the LORD, "Shall I **p** this band?
30: 8 He answered him, **"P;** for you shall surely
2Sa 2:27 people would have continued to **p** their kinsmen,
17: 1 and I will set out and **p** David tonight.
20: 6 take your lord's servants and **p** him,
20: 7 they went out from Jerusalem to **p** Sheba son
20:13 all the people went on after Joab to **p** Sheba son
24:13 before your foes while they **p** you?
Job 13:25 a windblown leaf and **p** dry chaff?
19:22 Why do you, like God, **p** me,
Ps 7: 5 then let the enemy **p** and overtake me,
34:14 and do good; seek peace, and **p** it.
71:11 **"P** and seize that person whom God has forsaken,
83:15 so **p** them with your tempest and terrify them
Isa 51: 1 Listen to me, you that **p** righteousness,
Jer 29:18 I will **p** them with the sword, with famine,
48: 2 to silence; the sword shall **p** you.
La 3:66 **P** them in anger and destroy them from under
Eze 35: 6 for blood, and blood shall **p** you;
35: 6 not hate bloodshed, bloodshed shall **p** you.
Hos 2: 7 She shall **p** her lovers, but not overtake them;
8: 3 Israel has spurned the good; the enemy shall **p** him.
Na 1: 8 and will **p** his enemies into darkness.
Mt 23:34 and some you will flog in your synagogues and **p**
Ro 14:19 Let us then **p** what makes for peace and
1Co 14: 1 **P** love and strive for the spiritual gifts,
1Ti 6:11 **p** righteousness, godliness, faith, love, endurance,
2Ti 2:22 Shun youthful passions and **p** righteousness, faith,
Heb 12:14 **P** peace with everyone, and the holiness
1Pe 3:11 let them seek peace and **p** it.
Jdt 14: 4 the borders of Israel will **p** them and cut them
Wis 19: 2 they would change their minds and **p** them.
Sir 11:10 If you **p,** you will not overtake,
27: 8 If you **p** justice, you will attain it and wear it like
2Es 15:31 if they combine in great power and turn to **p** them,
4Mc 18:22 For these crimes divine justice pursued and will **p**

PURSUED‡ (67) [PURSUE]

Ge 14:15 and routed them and **p** them to Hobah,
31:23 with him and **p** him for seven days until he caught
31:36 What is my sin, that you have hotly **p** me?
35: 5 so that no one **p** them.
Ex 14: 8 of Pharaoh king of Egypt and he **p** the Israelites,
14: 9 The Egyptians **p** them, all Pharaoh's horses
14:23 The Egyptians **p,** and went into the sea after them,
Dt 11: 4 the Red Sea flow over them as they **p** you,
Jos 2: 7 So the men **p** them on the way to the Jordan as far
8:16 and as they **p** Joshua they were drawn away from
8:17 they left the city open, and **p** Israel.
8:24 of Ai in the open wilderness where they **p** them,
24: 6 and the Egyptians **p** your ancestors with chariots
Jdg 1: 6 Adoni-bezek fled; but they **p** him, and caught him,
4:16 while Barak **p** the chariots and the army
7:23 and they **p** after the Midianites.
7:25 the wine press of Zeeb, as they **p** the Midianites.
8:12 and he **p** them and took the two kings of Midian,
20:43 they **p** them from Nohah and trod them down
20:45 and they were **p** as far as Gidom,
1Sa 7:11 of Israel went out of Mizpah and **p** the Philistines,
17:52 up with a shout and **p** the Philistines as far as Gath
23:25 he **p** David into the wilderness of Maon.
2Sa 2:19 Asahel **p** Abner, turning neither to the right nor to
2:24 But Joab and Abishai **p** Abner.
2:28 they no longer **p** Israel or engaged
20:10 Then Joab and his brother Abishai **p** Sheba son
22:38 I **p** my enemies and destroyed them,
1Ki 20:20 the Arameans fled and Israel **p** them,
2Ki 9:27 Jehu **p** him, saying, "Shoot him also!"
25: 5 But the army of the Chaldeans **p** the king,
2Ch 13:19 Abijah **p** Jeroboam, and took cities from him:
14:13 Asa and the army with him **p** them as far as Gerar,
Job 30:15 my honor is **p** as by the wind,
Ps 18:37 I **p** my enemies and overtook them;
109:16 but **p** the poor and needy and the brokenhearted
143: 3 For the enemy has **p** me,
Jer 39: 5 But the army of the Chaldeans **p** them,
52: 8 But the army of the Chaldeans **p** the king,
La 3:43 You have wrapped yourself with anger and **p** us,
Am 1:11 because he **p** his brother with the sword
Ac 26:11 I **p** them even to foreign cities.
Jude 1: 7 in sexual immorality and **p** unnatural lust,
Rev 12:13 he **p** the woman who had given birth to the male
Wis 11:20 a single breath when **p** by justice and scattered by
16:16 **p** by unusual rains and hail and relentless storms,
16:18 that they were being **p** by the judgment of God;
19: 3 and **p** as fugitives those whom they had begged
1Mc 2:32 Many **p** them, and overtook them;
3: 5 He searched out and **p** those who broke the law;
3:24 They **p** them down the descent of Beth-horon to
4: 9 when Pharaoh with his forces **p** them.
4:15 They **p** them to Gazara, and to the plains
5:22 He **p** them to the gate of Ptolemais;
5:60 and were **p** to the borders of Judea;
7:45 The Jews **p** them a day's journey,
9:15 and he **p** them as far as Mount Azotus.
10:49 and Alexander **p** him and defeated them.
10:78 Jonathan **p** him to Azotus,
12:30 Then Jonathan **p** them, but he did not overtake

1Mc 15:11 Antiochus **p** him, and Trypho came in his flight
15:39 on the people; but the king **p** Trypho.
16: 9 but John **p** them until Cendebeus reached Kedron,
2Mc 2:21 in number they seized the whole land and **p**
5: 8 **p** by everyone, hated as a rebel against the laws,
3Mc 2: 7 he **p** them with chariots and a mass of troops,
4Mc 18:22 For these crimes divine justice **p** and will pursue

PURSUER‡ (1) [PURSUE]

La 1: 6 they fled without strength before the **p.**

PURSUERS (15) [PURSUE]

Jos 2: 7 As soon as the **p** had gone out, the gate was shut.
2:16 so that the **p** may not come upon you.
2:16 Hide yourselves there three days, until the **p** have
2:22 and stayed there three days, until the **p** returned.
2:22 The **p** had searched all along the way
8:20 to the wilderness turned back against the **p.**
Ne 9:11 but you threw their **p** into the depths,
Ps 7: 1 save me from all my **p,** and deliver me,
35: 3 Draw the spear and javelin against my **p;**
Isa 30:16 therefore your **p** shall be swift!
La 1: 3 her **p** have all overtaken her in the midst
4:19 Our **p** were swifter than the eagles in the heavens;
Jdt 16: 2 he delivered me from the hands of my **p.**
1Mc 7:46 and drove them back to their **p,** so that they all fell
12:51 their **p** saw that they would fight for their lives,

PURSUES (13) [PURSUE]

Lev 26:17 and you shall flee though no one **p** you.
26:36 and they shall fall though no one **p.**
26:37 as if to escape a sword, though no one **p;**
Pr 11:19 but whoever **p** evil will die.
13:21 Misfortune **p** sinners, but prosperity rewards
15: 9 but he loves the one who **p** righteousness.
21:21 Whoever **p** righteousness and kindness
28: 1 The wicked flee when no one **p,**
Isa 41: 3 He **p** them and passes on safely,
Hos 12: 1 and **p** the east wind all day long;
Wis 14:31 that always **p** the transgression of the unrighteous.
Sir 31: 5 one who **p** money will be led astray by it.
34: 2 As one who catches at a shadow and **p** the wind,

PURSUING‡ (15) [PURSUE]

Nu 14:45 **p** them as far as Hormah.
Dt 28:45 **p** and overtaking you until you are destroyed,
Jdg 8: 5 and I am **p** Zebah and Zalmunna,
1Sa 14:46 Then Saul withdrew from **p** the Philistines;
23:28 So Saul stopped **p** David, and went against
2Sa 18:16 and the troops came back from **p** Israel,
1Ki 22:33 they turned back from **p** him.
2Ch 18:32 they turned back from **p** him.
Ps 35: 6 with the angel of the LORD **p** them.
Isa 58:13 from **p** your own interests on my holy day;
58:13 serving your own interests, or **p** your own affairs;
Sir 5: 2 Do not follow your inclination and strength in **p**
14:22 **p** her like a hunter, and lying in wait on her paths;
1Mc 4:16 Judas and his force turned back from **p** them,
2Mc 8:25 After **p** them for some distance,

PURSUIT (12) [PURSUE]

Ge 14:14 and went in **p** as far as Dan.
Jos 20: 5 And if the avenger of blood is in **p,**
Jdg 4:22 Then, as Barak came in **p** of Sisera,
1Sa 30:10 But David went on with the **p,**
2Sa 2:26 before you order your people to turn from the **p**
2:30 Joab returned from the **p** of Abner;
Isa 5:11 you who rise early in the morning in **p**
Lk 17:23 Do not go, do not set off in **p.**
Sir 29:19 his **p** of gain involves him in lawsuits.
1Mc 11:73 they returned to him and joined him in the **p** as far
2Mc 8:26 and for that reason they did not continue their **p.**
12:23 Judas pressed the **p** with the utmost vigor,

PURSUITS (2) [PURSUE]

Pr 12:11 but those who follow worthless **p** have no sense.
28:19 but one who follows worthless **p** will have plenty

PUSH (7) [PUSHED, PUSHES, PUSHING]

Jos 23: 5 LORD your God will **p** them back before you,
2Ki 4:27 Gehazi approached to **p** her away.
Ps 44: 5 Through you we **p** down our foes;
Am 2: 7 and **p** the afflicted out of the way;
5:12 and **p** aside the needy in the gate.
Sir 13:23 And should he stumble, they even **p** him down.
2Mc 13: 6 There they all **p** to destruction anyone guilty

PUSHED (6) [PUSH]

Ps 118:13 I was **p** hard, so that I was falling,
Eze 34:21 Because you **p** with flank and shoulder,
Ac 7:27 who was wronging his neighbor **p** Moses aside,
7:39 instead, they **p** him aside,
19:33 whom the Jews had **p** forward.
Sir 13:21 he is **p** away even by friends.

PUSHES (2) [PUSH]

Nu 35:20 Likewise, if someone **p** another from hatred,
35:22 if someone **p** another suddenly without enmity,

PUSHING (1) [PUSH]

2Mc 8: 8 that he was **p** ahead with more frequent successes,

PUT‡ (1105) [PUTS, PUTTING]

Ge 1:11 Then God said, "Let the earth **p** forth vegetation:
2: 8 and there he **p** the man whom he had formed.
2:15 the man and **p** him in the garden of Eden to till it
3:15 I will **p** enmity between you and the woman,
4:15 And the LORD **p** a mark on Cain,
6:16 and **p** the door of the ark in its side;
8: 9 So he **p** out his hand and took it and brought it
10: 6 Cush, Egypt, **P,** and Canaan.
24: 2 "**P** your hand under my thigh
24: 9 So the servant **p** his hand under the thigh
24:47 So I **p** the ring on her nose,
26:11 "Whoever touches this man or his wife shall be **p**
27:15 and **p** them on her younger son Jacob;
27:16 and she **p** the skins of the kids on his hands and on
28:11 he **p** it under his head and lay down in that place.
28:18 the stone that he had **p** under his head and set it up
29: 3 and **p** the stone back in its place on the mouth of
30:35 and **p** them in charge of his sons;
30:40 and he **p** his own droves apart,
30:40 and did not **p** them with Laban's flock.
31:34 the household gods and **p** them in the camel's
32:16 and **p** a space between drove and drove."
32:25 and Jacob's hip was **p** out of joint as he wrestled
33: 2 He **p** the maids with their children in front,
34:12 **P** the marriage present and gift as high as you
35: 2 "**P** away the foreign gods that are among you,
37:34 and **p** sackcloth on his loins,
38: 7 and the LORD **p** him to death.
38:10 and he **p** him to death also.
38:14 she **p** off her widow's garments,
38:14 **p** on a veil, wrapped herself up,
38:19 and taking off her veil she **p** on the garments
38:28 While she was in labor, one **p** out a hand;
39: 4 of his house and **p** him in charge of all that he had.
39: 8 and he has **p** everything that he has in my hand.
39:20 And Joseph's master took him and **p** him into
40: 3 and he **p** them in custody in the house of
40:15 that they should have **p** me into the dungeon."
41:10 and **p** me and the chief baker in custody in
41:42 Pharaoh **p** it on Joseph's hand;
41:42 and **p** a gold chain around his neck.
42:17 he **p** them all together in prison for three days.
42:28 "My money has been **p** back;
42:37 **P** him in my hands, and I will bring him back
43:22 We do not know who **p** our money in our sacks."
43:23 of your father must have **p** treasure in your sacks
44: 1 and **p** each man's money in the top of his sack.
44: 2 **P** my cup, the silver cup, in the top of the sack of
47: 6 **p** them in charge of my livestock."
47:29 **p** your hand under my thigh and promise
48:18 **p** your right hand on his head."
48:20 So he **p** Ephraim ahead of Manasseh.
Ex 2: 3 she **p** the child in it and placed it among the reeds
3:22 and you shall **p** them on your sons and
4: 6 "**P** your hand inside your cloak."
4: 6 He **p** his hand into his cloak;
4: 7 God said, "**P** your hand back into your cloak"—
4: 7 so he **p** his hand back into his cloak,
4:15 You shall speak to him and **p** the words
4:20 **p** them on a donkey and went back to the land
4:21 before Pharaoh all the wonders that I have **p**
5:21 and have **p** a sword in their hand to kill us."
12: 7 of the blood and **p** it on the two doorposts and
15:25 a statute and an ordinance and there he **p** them to
16:23 that is left over **p** aside to be kept until morning.' "
16:24 So they **p** it aside until morning,
16:33 "Take a jar, and **p** an omer of manna in it,
17:12 so they took a stone and **p** it under him,
19:12 Any who touch the mountain shall be **p** to death.
20:20 and to **p** the fear of him upon you so that you do
21:12 Whoever strikes a person mortally shall be **p**
21:15 Whoever strikes father or mother shall be **p**
21:16 or is still held in possession, shall be **p** to death.
21:17 Whoever curses father or mother shall be **p**
21:29 and its owner also shall be **p** to death.
22:19 Whoever lies with an animal shall be **p** to death.
24: 6 Moses took half of the blood and **p** it in basins,
25:12 You shall cast four rings of gold for it and **p** them
25:14 And you shall **p** the poles into the rings on
25:16 You shall **p** into the ark the covenant
25:21 You shall **p** the mercy seat on the top of the ark;
25:21 and in the ark you shall **p** the covenant
26:11 and **p** the clasps into the loops,
26:34 You shall **p** the mercy seat on the ark of
26:35 and you shall **p** the table on the north side.
27: 7 the poles shall be **p** through the rings,
28:23 and **p** the two rings on the two edges of
28:24 You shall **p** the two cords of gold in the two rings
28:26 and **p** them at the two ends of the breastpiece,
28:30 the breastpiece of judgment you shall **p** the Urim
28:41 You shall **p** them on your brother Aaron,
29: 3 You shall **p** them in one basket and bring them in
29: 5 **p** on Aaron the tunic and the robe of the ephod,
29: 6 and **p** the holy diadem on the turban.
29: 8 you shall bring his sons, and **p** tunics on them,
29:12 and **p** it on the horns of the altar with your finger,
29:17 and **p** them with its parts and its head,
29:20 and **p** it on the lobe of Aaron's right ear and on
30:18 You shall **p** it between the tent of meeting and
30:18 and you shall **p** water in it;
30:36 and **p** part of it before the covenant in the tent
31:14 everyone who profanes it shall be **p** to death;
31:15 on the sabbath day shall be **p** to death.
32:27 the God of Israel, '**P** your sword on your side,
33: 4 they mourned, and no one **p** on ornaments.
Ex 33:22 while my glory passes by I will **p** you in a cleft of
34:33 he **p** a veil on his face;
34:35 and Moses would **p** the veil on his face again,
35: 2 whoever does any work on it shall be **p** to death.
37: 5 **p** the poles into the rings on the sides of the ark,
38: 7 And he **p** the poles through the rings on the sides
39:16 and **p** the two rings on the two edges of
39:17 and they **p** the two cords of gold in the two rings
39:19 and **p** them at the two ends of the breastpiece,
39:25 and **p** the bells between the pomegranates on
40: 3 You shall **p** in it the ark of the covenant,
40: 5 You shall **p** the golden altar for incense before
40: 7 the tent of meeting and the altar, and **p** water in it.
40:13 and **p** on Aaron the sacred vestments,
40:14 You shall bring his sons also and **p** tunics
40:18 and **p** in its poles, and raised up its pillars;
40:19 and **p** the covering of the tent over it;
40:20 He took the covenant and **p** it into the ark,
40:20 and **p** the poles on the ark,
40:22 He **p** the table in the tent of meeting,
40:24 He **p** the lampstand in the tent of meeting,
40:26 He **p** the golden altar in the tent of meeting before
40:28 He also **p** in place the screen for the entrance of
40:30 and **p** water in it for washing,
40:33 and **p** up the screen at the gate of the court.
Lev 1: 7 The sons of the priest Aaron shall **p** fire on
2: 1 on it, and **p** frankincense on it,
4: 7 The priest shall **p** some of the blood on the horns
4:18 He shall **p** some of the blood on the horns of
4:25 and **p** it on the horns of the altar of burnt offering,
4:30 of its blood with his finger and **p** it on the horns of
4:34 and **p** it on the horns of the altar of burnt offering,
5:11 you shall not **p** oil on it or lay frankincense on it,
6:10 The priest shall **p** on his linen vestments
6:11 Then he shall take off his vestments and **p**
7:24 or was torn by wild animals may be **p** to any use,
8: 7 He **p** the tunic on him, fastened the sash around
8: 7 and **p** the ephod on him.
8: 7 He then **p** the decorated band of the ephod
8: 8 the breastpiece he **p** the Urim and the Thummim.
8:15 and with his finger **p** some on each of the horns of
8:23 Moses took some of its blood and **p** it on the lobe
8:24 Moses **p** some of the blood on the lobes
9: 9 and he dipped his finger in the blood and **p** it on
10: 1 **p** fire in it, and laid incense on it;
11:38 but if water is **p** on the seed and any part
13:50 and **p** the diseased article aside for seven days.
13:54 and he shall **p** it aside seven days more.
14:14 the blood of the guilt offering and **p** it on the lobe
14:17 of the oil that remains in his hand the priest shall **p**
14:18 the priest's hand he shall **p** on the head of the one
14:25 and **p** it on the lobe of the right ear of the one to
14:28 The priest shall **p** some of the oil that is
14:29 the priest's hand he shall **p** on the head of the one
14:34 and I **p** a leprous disease in a house in the land
14:42 They shall take other stones and **p** them in
16: 4 He shall **p** on the holy linen tunic,
16: 4 in water, and then **p** them on.
16:13 and **p** the incense on the fire before the LORD,
16:18 and **p** it on each of the horns of the altar.
16:23 the linen vestments that he **p** on when he went into
16:24 in water in a holy place, and **p** on his vestments;
19:14 the deaf or **p** a stumbling block before the blind;
19:19 nor shall you **p** on a garment made
19:20 They shall not be **p** to death,
20: 2 of their offspring to Molech shall be **p** to death;
20: 4 and do not **p** them to death,
20: 9 All who curse father or mother shall be **p** to death;
20:10 the adulterer and the adulteress shall be **p** to death.
20:11 both of them shall be **p** to death;
20:12 both of them shall be **p** to death;
20:13 they shall be **p** to death; their blood is upon them.
20:15 he shall be **p** to death;
20:16 they shall be **p** to death, their blood is upon them.
20:27 a woman who is a medium or a wizard shall be **p**
22:22 or **p** any of them on the altar as offerings by fire to
24: 7 You shall **p** pure frankincense with each row,
24:12 and they **p** him in custody,
24:16 who blasphemes the name of the LORD shall be **p**
to death;
24:16 they blaspheme the Name, shall be **p** to death.
24:17 who kills a human being shall be **p** to death.
24:21 one who kills a human being shall be **p** to death.
26:36 the sound of a driven leaf shall **p** them to flight,
27:29 they shall be **p** to death.
Nu 1:51 any outsider who comes near shall be **p** to death.
3:10 any outsider who comes near shall be **p** to death.
3:38 any outsider who came near was to be **p** to death.
4: 6 then they shall **p** on it a covering of fine leather,
4: 6 and shall **p** its poles in place.
4: 7 and **p** on it the plates, the dishes for incense,
4: 8 and shall **p** its poles in place.
4:10 and they shall **p** it with all its utensils in
4:10 and **p** it on the carrying frame.
4:11 and shall **p** its poles in place;
4:12 and **p** them in a blue cloth,
4:12 and **p** them on the carrying frame.
4:14 and they shall **p** on it all the utensils of the altar,
4:14 and shall **p** its poles in place.
5: 2 to **p** out of the camp everyone who is leprous,
5: 3 you shall **p** out both male and female,
5:15 He shall pour no oil on it and **p** no frankincense
5:17 the floor of the tabernacle and **p** it into the water.
5:23 Then the priest shall **p** these curses in writing,
6:18 the consecrated head and **p** it on the fire under
6:19 and shall **p** them in the palms of the nazirites,
6:27 So they shall **p** my name on the Israelites,

Nu 11:15 **p** me to death at once—
11:17 of the spirit that is on you and **p** it on them;
11:25 that was on him and **p** it on the seventy elders;
11:29 and that the LORD would **p** his spirit on them!"
15:34 They **p** him in custody, because it was
15:35 "The man shall be **p** to death;
15:38 throughout their generations and to **p** a blue cord
16: 7 and tomorrow **p** fire in them, and lay incense
16:14 Would you **p** out the eyes of these men?
16:17 and **p** incense on it, and each one
16:18 they **p** fire in the censers and laid incense on them,
16:46 **p** fire on it from the altar and lay incense on it,
16:47 He **p** on the incense, and made atonement for
17: 5 thus I will **p** a stop to the complaints of
17: 8 It **p** forth buds, produced blossoms,
17:10 "**P** back the staff of Aaron before the covenant,
18: 7 any outsider who approaches shall be **p** to death.
20:26 and **p** them on his son Eleazar.
20:28 and **p** them on his son Eleazar;
21: 9 and **p** it upon a pole;
21:24 Israel **p** him to the sword,
23: 5 The LORD **p** a word in Balaam's mouth,
23:16 The LORD met Balaam, **p** a word into his mouth,
35:16 the murderer shall be **p** to death.
35:17 the murderer shall be **p** to death.
35:18 the murderer shall be **p** to death.
35:19 is the one who shall **p** the murderer to death;
35:21 the one who struck the blow shall be **p** to death;
35:21 the avenger of blood shall **p** the murderer to death,
35:30 the murderer shall be **p** to death on the evidence
35:30 be **p** to death on the testimony of a single witness.
35:31 a murderer must be **p** to death.
Dt 2:25 This day I will begin to **p** the dread and fear
6:16 Do not **p** the LORD your God to the test,
10: 2 and you shall **p** them in the ark."
10: 5 and **p** the tablets in the ark that I had made;
11:18 You shall **p** these words of mine in your heart
11:25 the LORD your God will **p** the fear and dread
12: 5 as his habitation to **p** his name there.
12:21 to **p** his name is too far from you,
13: 5 or those who divine by dreams shall be **p** to death
13:15 you shall **p** the inhabitants of that town to
16: 9 the seven weeks from the time the sickle is first **p**
17: 6 be **p** to death on the evidence of only one witness.
17:15 you are not permitted to **p** a foreigner over you,
18:18 I will **p** my words in the mouth of the prophet,
19: 6 in hot anger might pursue and overtake and **p**
19:12 and handed over to the avenger of blood to be **p**
20:13 you shall **p** all its males to the sword.
22: 5 nor shall a man **p** on a woman's garment;
23:24 but you shall not **p** any in a container.
23:25 not **p** a sickle to your neighbor's standing grain.
24:16 Parents shall not be **p** to death for their children,
nor shall children be **p** to death for their parents;
24:16 for their own crimes may persons be **p** to death.
26: 2 and you shall **p** it in a basket and go to the place
28:48 He will **p** an iron yoke on your neck
30: 7 The LORD your God will **p** all these curses
31: 7 and you will **p** them in possession of it.
31:19 **p** it in their mouths, in order that this song may be
31:26 "Take this book of the law and **p** it beside the ark
32:30 and two **p** a myriad to flight,
Jos 1: 6 for you shall **p** this people in possession of
1:18 whatever you command, shall be **p** to death.
6:24 and iron, they **p** into the treasury of the house of
7: 6 and they **p** dust on their heads.
7:11 they have **p** them among their own belongings.
10:24 **p** your feet on the necks of these kings."
10:24 they came near and **p** their feet on their necks.
10:26 Afterward Joshua struck them down and **p** them
11:11 And they **p** to the sword all who were in it,
11:17 struck them down, and **p** them to death.
13:22 Along with the rest of those they **p** to death,
13:22 Israelites also **p** to the sword Balaam son of Beor,
17:13 they **p** the Canaanites to forced labor,
24: 7 he **p** darkness between you and the Egyptians,
24:14 **p** away the gods that your ancestors served
24:23 **p** away the foreign gods that are among you,
Jdg 1: 8 They **p** it to the sword and set the city on fire.
1:25 and they **p** the city to the sword,
1:28 they **p** the Canaanites to forced labor,
5:26 She **p** her hand to the tent peg and her right hand
6: 3 For whenever the Israelites **p** in seed,
6:19 meat he **p** in a basket, and the broth he **p** in a pot,
6:20 and **p** them on this rock, and pour out the broth."
6:31 Whoever contends for him shall be **p** to death
7: 5 as a dog laps, you shall **p** to one side;
7: 5 you shall **p** to the other side."
7:16 and **p** trumpets into the hands of all of them,
8:27 Gideon made an ephod of it and **p** it in his town,
9:26 the lords of Shechem **p** confidence in him.
9:49 a bundle and following Abimelech **p** it against
10:16 So they **p** away the foreign gods from among them
14:12 "Let me now **p** a riddle to you.
15: 4 and **p** a torch between each pair of tails.
16: 3 bar and all, **p** them on his shoulders,
18:19 **P** your hand over your mouth, and come with us,
18:27 **p** them to the sword, and burned down the city.
19:25 man seized his concubine, and **p** her out to them.
19:28 Then he **p** her on the donkey;
20:13 so that we may **p** them to death,
20:37 Then they **p** the whole city to the sword.
20:48 and **p** them to the sword—
21: 5 saying, "That one shall be **p** to death."
21:10 **p** the inhabitants of Jabesh-gilead to the sword,
Ru 3: 3 and **p** on your best clothes and go down to
3:15 and **p** it on her back; then he went into the city.

1Sa 1:14 of yourself? **P** away your wine."
2:36 Please **p** me in one of the priest's places,
4: 3 "Why has the LORD **p** us to rout today before
5: 3 So they took Dagon and **p** him back in his place.
6: 8 and **p** in a box at its side the figures of gold,
6:11 They **p** the ark of the LORD on the cart,
7: 3 then **p** away the foreign gods and the Astartes
7: 4 So Israel **p** away the Baals and the Astartes,
8:16 and **p** them to his work.
9:23 the one I asked you to **p** aside."
11: 2 and thus **p** disgrace upon all Israel."
11:11 next day Saul **p** the people in three companies.
11:12 Give them to us so that we may **p** them to death."
11:13 Saul said, "No one shall be **p** to death this day,
14:26 but they did not **p** their hands to their mouths,
14:27 and **p** his hand to his mouth;
17:38 he **p** a bronze helmet on his head and clothed him
17:40 and **p** them in his shepherd's bag, in the pouch;
17:49 David **p** his hand in his bag, took out a stone,
17:54 but he **p** his armor in his tent.
19: 6 "As the LORD lives, he shall not be **p** to death."
19:13 she **p** a net of goats' hair on its head,
20:32 "Why should he be **p** to death?
20:33 that it was the decision of his father to **p** David
22:19 Nob, the city of the priests, he **p** to the sword;
22:19 oxen, donkeys, and sheep, he **p** to the sword.
24:18 in that you did not kill me when the LORD **p** me
28: 8 So Saul disguised himself and **p** on other clothes
28:25 She **p** them before Saul and his servants,
31:10 They **p** his armor in the temple of Astarte;
2Sa 1:24 who **p** ornaments of gold on your apparel.
3:31 and **p** on sackcloth, and mourn over Abner."
7:15 whom I **p** away from before you.
8: 2 of cord for those who were to be **p** to death,
8: 6 Then David **p** garrisons among the Arameans
8:14 He **p** garrisons in Edom; throughout all Edom he **p**
garrisons,
10:10 the rest of his men he **p** in the charge
12:13 "Now the LORD has **p** away your sin;
13:17 "**P** this woman out of my presence,
13:18 his servant **p** her out, and bolted the door after her.
13:19 But Tamar **p** ashes on her head,
13:19 she **p** her hand on her head, and went away,
14: 2 **p** on mourning garments, do not anoint yourself
14: 3 And Joab **p** the words into her mouth.
14:19 it was he who **p** all these words into the mouth
15: 5 he would **p** out his hand and take hold of them,
19:21 "Shall not Shimei be **p** to death for this,
19:22 Shall anyone be **p** to death in Israel this day?
20: 3 and **p** them in a house under guard,
21: 1 because he **p** the Gibeonites to death."
21: 4 neither is it for us to **p** anyone to death in Israel."
21: 9 They were **p** to death in the first days of harvest,
23:23 And David **p** him in charge of his bodyguard.
1Ki 2: 8 'I will not **p** you to death with the sword.'
2:24 today Adonijah shall be **p** to death."
2:26 But I will not at this time **p** you to death,
2:35 The king **p** Benaiah son of Jehoiada over the army
2:35 king **p** the priest Zadok in the place of Abiathar.
5: 3 the LORD **p** them under the soles of his feet.
6:27 He **p** the cherubim in the innermost part of
9: 3 and **p** my name there forever;
10:17 and the king **p** them in the House of the Forest
10:24 which God had **p** into his mind.
11:36 the city where I have chosen to **p** my name.
12: 9 'Lighten the yoke that your father **p** on us'?"
12:29 He set one in Bethel, and the other he **p** in Dan.
14:21 of all the tribes of Israel, to **p** his name there.
15:12 He **p** away the male temple prostitutes out of
18:23 and lay it on the wood, but **p** no fire to it;
18:23 the other bull and lay it on the wood, but **p** no fire
18:25 call on the name of your god, but **p** no fire to it."
18:33 Next he **p** the wood in order, cut the bull in pieces,
18:42 upon the earth and **p** his face between his knees.
20:24 and **p** commanders in place of them;
20:31 let us **p** sackcloth around our waists and ropes
20:32 **p** ropes on their heads, went to the king of Israel,
21:27 and **p** sackcloth over his bare flesh;
22:23 the LORD has **p** a lying spirit in the mouth
22:27 **P** this fellow in prison, and feed him
2Ki 2:20 He said, "Bring me a new bowl, and **p** salt in it."
3:21 all who were able to **p** on armor,
4:10 and **p** there for him a bed, a table, a chair,
4:38 he said to his servant, "**P** the large pot on,
10: 7 they **p** their heads in baskets and sent them to him
10:25 So they **p** them to the sword.
11: 2 she **p** him and his nurse in a bedroom.
11: 4 and **p** them under oath in the house of the LORD;
11:12 he brought out the king's son, **p** the crown on him,
11:16 and there she was **p** to death.
12: 9 the priests who guarded the threshold **p** in it all
14: 6 not **p** to death the children of the murderers;
14: 6 parents shall not be **p** to death for the children, or
the children be **p** to death for the parents; but all
shall be **p** to death for their own sins."
16:14 and **p** it on the north side of his altar.
16:17 and **p** it on a pediment of stone.
17:29 and **p** them in the shrines of the high places that
19: 7 I myself will **p** a spirit in him,
19:28 I will **p** my hook in your nose and my bit
21: 4 "In Jerusalem I will **p** my name."
21: 7 I will **p** my name forever;
23:24 Moreover Josiah **p** away the mediums, wizards,
25: 7 then **p** out the eyes of Zedekiah;
25:21 of Babylon struck them down and **p** them to death
25:29 So Jehoiachin **p** aside his prison clothes.
1Ch 1: 8 Cush, Egypt, **P**, and Canaan.

1Ch 2: 3 and he **p** him to death.
6:31 the men whom David **p** in charge of the service
8:13 who **p** to flight the inhabitants of Gath);
10:10 They **p** his armor in the temple of their gods,
10:14 Therefore the LORD **p** him to death and turned
11:25 And David **p** him in charge of his bodyguard.
12:15 and **p** to flight all those in the valleys,
13: 9 Uzzah **p** out his hand to hold the ark,
13:10 he struck him down because he **p** out his hand to
18: 6 Then David **p** garrisons in Aram of Damascus;
18:13 He **p** garrisons in Edom;
19:11 the rest of his troops he **p** in the charge
21:27 and he **p** his sword back into its sheath.
2Ch 3:16 He made encircling chains and **p** them on the tops
3:16 and **p** them on the chains.
5:10 the ark except the two tablets that Moses **p** there
9:16 and the king **p** them in the House of the Forest
9:23 which God had **p** into his mind.
10: 9 'Lighten the yoke that your father **p** on us'?"
11:11 and **p** commanders in them, and stores of food,
11:12 He also **p** large shields and spears in all the cities,
12:13 of all the tribes of Israel to **p** his name there.
15: 8 and **p** away the abominable idols from all the land
15:13 should be **p** to death, whether young or old,
16:10 and **p** him in the stocks, in prison,
18:22 the LORD has **p** a lying spirit in the mouth
18:26 **P** this fellow in prison, and feed him
21: 4 he **p** all his brothers to the sword,
22: 9 in Samaria and was brought to Jehu, and **p**
22:11 she **p** him and his nurse in a bedroom.
23:11 he brought out the king's son, **p** the crown on him,
23:14 anyone who follows her is to be **p** to the sword."
23:14 not **p** her to death in the house of the LORD."
23:15 and there they **p** her to death.
25: 4 But he did not **p** their children to death,
25: 4 parents shall not be **p** to death for the children, or
the children be **p** to death for the parents; but all
shall be **p** to death for their own sins."
25:16 Why should you be **p** to death?"
29: 7 They also shut the doors of the vestibule and **p** out
33: 7 I will **p** my name forever;
33:14 He also **p** commanders of the army in all
35: 3 "**P** the holy ark in the house that Solomon son
36: 7 of the LORD to Babylon and **p** them in his palace
Ezr 5:15 go and **p** them in the temple in Jerusalem,
6: 5 you shall **p** them in the house of God."
6:12 or people that shall **p** forth a hand to alter this,
7:27 who **p** such a thing as this into the heart of
Ne 2:12 I told no one what my God had **p** into my heart
3: 5 not **p** their shoulders to the work of their Lord.
7: 5 Then my God **p** it into my mind to assemble
13: 5 where they had previously **p** the grain offering,
Est 2: 8 Esther also was taken into the king's palace and **p**
3: 9 so that they may **p** it into the king's treasuries."
4: 1 and **p** on sackcloth and ashes, and went through
4:11 all alike are to be **p** to death.
5: 1 the third day Esther **p** on her royal robes and stood
Job 1:10 Have you not **p** a fence around him and his house
9:27 I will **p** off my sad countenance and be
11: 3 Should your babble **p** others to silence,
11:14 If iniquity is in your hand, **p** it far away,
13:14 and **p** my life in my hand.
13:27 You **p** my feet in the stocks,
14: 9 the scent of water it will bud and **p** forth branches
18: 5 "Surely the light of the wicked is **p** out,
18: 6 and the lamp above them is **p** out.
19: 6 know then that God has **p** me in the wrong,
19:13 "He has **p** my family far from me,
21:17 "How often is the lamp of the wicked **p** out?
27: 5 until I die I will not **p** away my integrity from me.
28: 3 Miners **p** an end to darkness,
28: 9 "They **p** their hand to the flinty rock,
29:14 I **p** on righteousness, and it clothed me;
32:22 or my Maker would soon **p** an end to me!
38:27 and to make the ground **p** forth grass?
38:36 Who has **p** wisdom in the inward parts,
40: 8 Will you even **p** me in the wrong?
41: 2 Can you **p** a rope in its nose,
41: 5 or will you **p** it on leash for your girls?
Ps 4: 5 and **p** your trust in the LORD.
4: 7 You have **p** gladness in my heart more than
6:10 and in a moment be **p** to shame.
8: 6 you have **p** all things under their feet,
9:10 those who know your name **p** their trust in you,
9:20 **P** them in fear, O LORD;
18:22 and his statutes I did not **p** away from me.
21:12 For you will **p** them to flight;
22: 5 in you they trusted, and were not **p** to shame.
25: 2 do not let me be **p** to shame;
25: 3 Do not let those who wait for you be **p** to shame;
25:20 do not let me be **p** to shame,
31: 1 do not let me ever be **p** to shame;
31:17 Do not let me be **p** to shame, O LORD,
31:17 let the wicked be **p** to shame;
33: 7 he **p** the deeps in storehouses.
35: 4 Let them be **p** to shame and dishonor who seek
35:26 Let all those who rejoice at my calamity be **p**
37:19 they are not **p** to shame in evil times,
40: 3 He **p** a new song in my mouth,
40: 3 and **p** their trust in the LORD.
40:14 be **p** to shame and confusion who seek
44: 7 and have **p** to confusion those who hate us.
51:10 O God, and **p** a new and right spirit within me.
53: 5 they will be **p** to shame,
54: 5 In your faithfulness, **p** an end to them.
56: 3 when I am afraid, I **p** my trust in you.
56: 8 **p** my tears in your bottle.

Ps 57: 3 he will **p** to shame those who trample on me.
62:10 **P** no confidence in extortion,
69: 6 Do not let those who hope in you be **p** to shame
70: 2 be **p** to shame and confusion who seek my life.
71: 1 let me never be **p** to shame.
71:13 Let my accusers be **p** to shame and consumed;
71:24 for those who tried to do me harm have been **p**
73:27 you **p** an end to those who are false to you.
74:21 Do not let the downtrodden be **p** to shame;
78:66 He **p** his adversaries to rout;
78:66 he **p** them to everlasting disgrace.
83:17 Let them be **p** to shame and dismayed forever;
85: 4 and **p** away your indignation toward us.
86:17 those who hate me may see it and be **p** to shame,
88: 6 You have **p** me in the depths of the Pit,
95: 9 and **p** me to the proof,
97: 7 All worshipers of images are **p** to shame,
105:18 his neck was **p** in a collar of iron;
106:14 and **p** God to the test in the desert;
109:28 Let my assailants be **p** to shame;
118: 8 to take refuge in the LORD than to **p** confidence
118: 9 to take refuge in the LORD than to **p** confidence
119: 6 Then I shall not be **p** to shame,
119:29 **P** false ways far from me;
119:31 let me not be **p** to shame.
119:46 and shall not be **p** to shame;
119:78 Let the arrogant be **p** to shame,
119:80 so that I may not be **p** to shame.
119:116 and let me not be **p** to shame in my hope.
119:147 I **p** my hope in your words.
127: 5 be **p** to shame when he speaks with his enemies in
129: 5 May all who hate Zion be **p** to shame
143: 8 for in you I **p** my trust.
146: 3 Do not **p** your trust in princes, in mortals,
Pr 4:24 **P** away from you crooked speech,
4:24 and **p** devious talk far from you.
12:24 while the lazy will be **p** to forced labor.
21:29 The wicked **p** on a bold face,
23: 2 **p** a knife to your throat if you have a big appetite.
25: 6 Do not **p** yourself forward in the king's presence
25: 7 than to be **p** lower in the presence of a noble.
30:32 **p** your hand on your mouth.
Ecc 3:11 moreover he has **p** a sense of past and future
11:10 and **p** away pain from your body;
SS 5: 3 I had **p** off my garment; how could I **p** it on again?
Isa 5:20 who **p** darkness for light and light for darkness,
5:20 who **p** bitter for sweet and sweet for bitter!
7:12 and I will not **p** the LORD to the test.
9:10 but we will **p** cedars in their place."
11: 8 weaned child shall **p** its hand on the adder's den.
11:14 They shall **p** forth their hand against Edom
13:11 I will **p** an end to the pride of the arrogant,
27: 6 Israel shall blossom and **p** forth shoots,
30:12 and **p** your trust in oppression and deceit,
31: 8 and his young men shall be **p** to forced labor.
32:11 and **p** sackcloth on your loins.
37: 7 I myself will **p** a spirit in him,
37:29 I will **p** my hook in your nose and my bit
41:19 I will **p** in the wilderness the cedar, the acacia,
42: 1 I have **p** my spirit upon him;
42:17 be turned back and utterly **p** to shame—
44: 9 And so they will be **p** to shame.
44:11 Look, all its devotees shall be **p** to shame;
44:11 they shall be terrified, they shall all be **p** to shame.
45:16 All of them are **p** to shame and confounded,
45:17 not be **p** to shame or confounded to all eternity.
46:13 I will **p** salvation in Zion, for Israel my glory.
49:18 you shall **p** all of them on like an ornament,
49:21 I was bereaved and barren, exiled and **p** away—
49:23 those who wait for me shall not be **p** to shame.
50: 1 bill of divorce with which I **p** her away?
50: 1 for your transgressions your mother was **p** away.
50: 7 and I know that I shall not be **p** to shame;
51: 9 Awake, awake, **p** on strength,
51:16 I have **p** my words in your mouth,
51:23 And I will **p** it into the hand of your tormentors,
52: 1 Awake, awake, **p** on your strength, O Zion!
52: 1 **P** on your beautiful garments, O Jerusalem,
59:17 He **p** on righteousness like a breastplate,
59:17 he **p** on garments of vengeance for clothing,
59:21 and my words that I have **p** in your mouth,
63:11 is the one who **p** within them his holy spirit,
65:13 but you shall be **p** to shame;
65:15 and the Lord GOD will **p** you to death;
66: 5 but it is they who shall be **p** to shame.
66:19 to Tarshish, **P**, and Lud—
Jer 1: 9 the LORD **p** out his hand and touched my mouth;
1: 9 "Now I have **p** my words in your mouth.
2:36 You shall be **p** to shame by Egypt as you were **p**
4: 8 Because of this **p** on sackcloth, lament and wail:
6:26 O my poor people, **p** on sackcloth,
8: 9 The wise shall be **p** to shame,
9: 4 and **p** no trust in any of your kin;
10:14 goldsmiths are all **p** to shame by their idols;
12: 1 but let me **p** my case to you.
13: 1 and **p** it on your loins, but do not dip it in water."
13: 2 and **p** it on my loins.
17:13 All who forsake you shall be **p** to shame;
20: 2 and **p** him in the stocks that were in
25:31 and the guilty he will **p** to the sword,
26:15 Only know for certain that if you **p** me to death,
26:19 of Judah and all Judah actually **p** him to death?
26:21 heard his words, the king sought to **p** him to death;
26:24 not given over into the hands of the people to be **p**
27: 2 and **p** them on your neck.
27: 8 **p** its neck under the yoke of the king of Babylon,
28:14 I have **p** an iron yoke on the neck

Jer 29:26 to **p** him in the stocks and the collar.
31:33 I will **p** my law within them,
32:14 and **p** them in an earthenware jar,
32:40 and I will **p** the fear of me in their hearts,
37: 4 for he had not yet been **p** in prison.
37:16 Thus Jeremiah was **p** in the cistern house,
37:18 that you have **p** me in prison?
38: 4 "This man ought to be **p** to death,
38: 7 heard that they had **p** Jeremiah into the cistern.
38:12 "Just **p** the rags and clothes between your armpits
38:15 "If I tell you, you will **p** me to death, will you not?
38:16 I will not **p** you to death or hand you over
38:25 or we will **p** you to death.
39: 7 He **p** out the eyes of Zedekiah,
46: 4 whet your lances, **p** on your coats of mail!
46: 9 Ethiopia and **P** who carry the shield, the Ludim,
46:24 Daughter Egypt shall be **p** to shame;
47: 6 **P** yourself into your scabbard, rest and be still!
48: 1 Kiriathaim is **p** to shame, it is taken;
48: 1 the fortress is **p** to shame and broken down;
48:20 Moab is **p** to shame, for it is broken down;
49: 3 **P** on sackcloth, lament, and slash yourselves with
50: 2 Babylon is taken, Bel is **p** to shame,
50: 2 Her images are **p** to shame,
51:17 goldsmiths are all **p** to shame by their idols;
51:47 her whole land shall be **p** to shame,
51:51 We are **p** to shame, for we have heard insults;
52:11 He **p** out the eyes of Zedekiah,
52:11 and **p** him in prison until the day of his death.
52:27 **p** them to death at Riblah in the land of Hamath.
52:33 So Jehoiachin **p** aside his prison clothes,
La 2:10 they have thrown dust on their heads and **p**
3: 7 he has **p** heavy chains on me;
3:29 to **p** one's mouth to the dust (there may yet
Eze 4: 2 and **p** siegeworks against it, and build a siege wall
4: 9 **p** them into one vessel, and make bread
7:18 They shall **p** on sackcloth,
7:24 I will **p** an end to the arrogance of the strong,
9: 4 and **p** a mark on the foreheads of those who sigh
10: 7 and **p** it into the hands of the man clothed in linen,
11:19 and **p** a new spirit within them;
12:23 I will **p** an end to this proverb,
15: 4 It is **p** in the fire for fuel;
16:11 I **p** bracelets on your arms, a chain on your neck,
17: 6 it brought forth branches, **p** forth foliage.
19: 9 With hooks they **p** him in a cage,
22:20 and I will **p** you in and melt you.
23:27 So I will **p** an end to your lewdness
23:42 and they **p** bracelets on the arms of the women,
23:48 Thus will I **p** an end to lewdness in the land,
24: 4 **p** in it the pieces, all the good pieces, the thigh and
24:17 and **p** your sandals on your feet;
26: 8 Your daughter-towns in the country he shall **p** to
26:11 He shall **p** your people to the sword,
27:10 Paras and Lud and **P** were in your army,
27:31 and **p** on sackcloth, and they weep over you
29: 4 I will **p** hooks in your jaws,
30: 5 Ethiopia, and **P**, and Lud, and all Arabia,
30:10 I will **p** an end to the hordes of Egypt,
30:13 I will destroy the idols and **p** an end to the images
30:13 so I will **p** fear in the land of Egypt.
30:24 and **p** my sword in his hand;
30:25 when I **p** my sword into the hand of the king
32: 8 and **p** darkness on your land, says the Lord GOD.
34:10 and **p** a stop to their feeding the sheep;
36:26 and a new spirit I will **p** within you;
36:27 I will **p** my spirit within you,
37: 6 and cover you with skin, and **p** breath in you,
37:14 I will **p** my spirit within you, and you shall live,
37:19 and I will **p** the stick of Judah upon it,
38: 4 I will turn you around and **p** hooks into your jaws,
38: 5 Persia, Ethiopia, and **P** are with them,
42:14 they shall **p** on other garments before they go near
43: 9 Now let them **p** away their idolatry and
43:20 and **p** it on the four horns of the altar,
44:19 and they shall **p** on other garments,
45: 9 **P** away violence and oppression,
45:19 of the sin offering and **p** it on the doorposts of
Da 5:29 a chain of gold was **p** around his neck,
7:11 And as I watched, the beast was **p** to death,
7:24 and shall **p** down three kings.
9:24 to finish the transgression, to **p** an end to sin,
11:18 But a commander shall **p** an end to his insolence;
Hos 1: 4 of Jezreel, and I will **p** an end to the kingdom of
2: 2 that she **p** away her whoring from her face,
2:11 I will **p** an end to all her mirth, her festivals,
10: 6 Ephraim shall be **p** to shame,
Joel 1:13 **P** on sackcloth and lament, you priests;
2:26 And my people shall never again be **p** to shame.
2:27 And my people shall never again be **p** to shame.
3:13 **P** in the sickle, for the harvest is ripe.
Am 6: 3 O you that **p** far away the evil day,
Jnh 3: 5 and everyone, great and small, **p** on sackcloth.
Mic 3: 5 against those who **p** nothing into their mouths.
3: 7 and the diviners **p** to shame;
6:14 you shall **p** away, but not save, and what you save,
7: 5 **P** no trust in a friend, have no confidence in
Na 3: 9 **P** and the Libyans were her helpers.
Zep 3:11 that day you shall not be **p** to shame because of all
Hag 1: 6 and you that earn wages earn wages to **p** them into
Zec 3: 5 I said, "Let them **p** a clean turban on his head."
3: 5 So they **p** a clean turban on his head
10: 5 and they shall **p** to shame the riders on horses.
13: 4 not **p** on a hairy mantle in order to deceive,
13: 9 And I will **p** this third into the fire,
Mal 2: 3 and I will **p** you out of my presence.
3:10 and thus **p** me to the test,

Mal 3:15 but when they **p** God to the test they escape."
Mt 4: 7 'Do not **p** the Lord your God to the test.' "
6:17 you fast, **p** oil on your head and wash your face,
9:17 Neither is new wine **p** into old wineskins;
9:17 but new wine is **p** into fresh wineskins,
9:25 But when the crowd had been **p** outside,
10:21 against parents and have them **p** to death;
12:18 I will **p** my Spirit upon him,
12:44 it comes, it finds it empty, swept, and **p** in order.
13:24 He **p** before them another parable:
13:31 He **p** before them another parable:
13:48 and **p** the good into baskets but threw out the bad.
14: 3 and **p** him in prison on account of Herodias,
14: 5 Though Herod wanted to **p** him to death,
15:30 They **p** them at his feet, and he cured them,
17:17 How much longer must I **p** up with you?
18: 2 He called a child, whom he **p** among them,
18: 6 "If any of you **p** a stumbling block before one
21: 7 and **p** their cloaks on them, and he sat on them.
21:33 **p** a fence around it, dug a wine press in it,
21:41 "He will **p** those wretches to a miserable death,
22:44 until I **p** your enemies under your feet" '?
24: 9 over to be tortured and will **p** you to death,
24:45 whom his master has **p** in charge of his household,
24:47 he will **p** that one in charge of all his possessions.
24:51 He will cut him in pieces and **p** him with
25:21 I will **p** you in charge of many things;
25:23 I will **p** you in charge of many things;
25:33 and he will **p** the sheep at his right hand and
26:51 one of those with Jesus **p** his hand on his sword,
26:52 "**P** your sword back into its place;
26:59 against Jesus so that they might **p** him to death,
26:63 "I **p** you under oath before the living God,
27: 6 said, "It is not lawful to **p** them into the treasury,
27:28 They stripped him and **p** a scarlet robe on him,
27:29 some thorns into a crown, they **p** it on his head.
27:29 They **p** a reed in his right hand and knelt
27:31 of the robe and **p** his own clothes on him.
27:37 Over his head they **p** the charge against him,
27:48 **p** it on a stick, and gave it to him to drink.
Mk 4:21 a lamp brought in to be **p** under the bushel basket,
5:40 Then he **p** them all outside,
6: 9 but to wear sandals and not to **p** on two tunics.
6:17 and **p** him in prison on account of Herodias,
7:33 and **p** his fingers into his ears,
8:23 and when he had **p** saliva on his eyes
9:19 How much longer must I **p** up with you?
9:36 Then he took a little child and **p** it among them;
9:42 "If any of you **p** a stumbling block before one
12: 1 "A man planted a vineyard, **p** a fence around it,
12:36 until I **p** your enemies under your feet." '
12:41 Many rich people **p** in large sums.
12:42 and **p** in two small copper coins,
12:43 to them, "Truly I tell you, this poor widow has **p**
12:44 she out of her poverty has **p** in everything she had,
13:12 against parents and have them **p** to death;
14:55 for testimony against Jesus to **p** him to death;
15:17 after twisting some thorns into a crown, they **p** it
15:20 of the purple cloak and **p** his own clothes on him.
15:36 **p** it on a stick, and gave it to him to drink, saying,
Lk 4:12 'Do not **p** the Lord your God to the test.' "
5: 3 and asked him to **p** out a little way from the shore.
5: 4 "**P** out into the deep water and let down your nets
5:38 But new wine must be **p** into fresh wineskins.
6:38 running over, will be **p** into your lap;
7:25 those who **p** on fine clothing and live in luxury are
8:22 of the lake." So they **p** out,
9:47 took a little child and **p** it by his side,
10:34 Then he **p** him on his own animal,
11:25 When it comes, it finds it swept and **p** in order.
12:42 and prudent manager whom his master will **p**
12:44 he will **p** that one in charge of all his possessions.
12:46 and **p** him with the unfaithful.
13: 8 until I dig around it and **p** manure on it.
13:17 he said this, all his opponents were **p** to shame;
15:20 he ran and **p** his arms around him and kissed him.
15:22 the best one—and **p** it on him;
15:22 **p** a ring on his finger and sandals on his feet.
17: 8 **p** on your apron and serve me while I eat
19:23 Why then did you not **p** my money into the bank?
21: 2 a poor widow **p** in two small copper coins.
21: 3 this poor widow has **p** in more than all of them;
21: 4 of her poverty has **p** in all she had to live on."
21:16 and they will **p** some of you to death.
22: 2 and the scribes were looking for a way to **p** Jesus
23:11 then he **p** an elegant robe on him,
23:19 (This was a man who had been **p** in prison for
23:25 the one who had been **p** in prison for insurrection
23:32 were led away to be **p** to death with him.
Jn 5: 7 to **p** me into the pool when the water is stirred up;
9:15 He said to them, "He **p** mud on my eyes.
9:22 be the Messiah would be **p** out of the synagogue.
11:53 from that day on they planned to **p** him to death.
12: 6 the common purse and used to steal what was **p**
12:10 chief priests planned to **p** Lazarus to death as well,
12:42 for fear that they would be **p** out of the synagogue;
13: 2 The devil had already **p** it into the heart
13:12 After he had washed their feet, had **p** on his robe,
16: 2 They will **p** you out of the synagogues.
18:11 "**P** your sword back into its sheath.
18:31 "We are not permitted to **p** anyone to death."
19: 2 And the soldiers wove a crown of thorns and **p** it
19:19 also had an inscription written and **p** on the cross.
19:29 So they **p** a sponge full of the wine on a branch
20:25 and **p** my finger in the mark of the nails
20:27 "**P** your finger here and see my hands.
20:27 Reach out your hand and **p** it in my side.

Jn 21: 7 he **p** on some clothes, for he was naked,
Ac 2:30 to him that he would **p** one of his descendants
4: 3 So they arrested them and **p** them in custody until
5: 9 that you have agreed together to **p** the Spirit of
5:18 the apostles and **p** them in the public prison.
5:25 the men whom you **p** in prison are standing in
5:34 stood up and ordered the men to be **p** outside for
9:40 Peter **p** all of them outside,
10:39 They **p** him to death by hanging him on a tree;
12: 4 he **p** him in prison and handed him over
12: 8 "Fasten your belt and **p** on your sandals."
12:19 he examined the guards and ordered them to be **p**
12:21 On an appointed day Herod **p** on his royal robes,
13:18 For about forty years he **p** up with them in
16:24 he **p** them in the innermost cell
27: 2 we **p** to sea, accompanied by Aristarchus,
27: 3 The next day we **p** in at Sidon;
27: 6 an Alexandrian ship bound for Italy and **p** us
28:10 they **p** on board all the provisions we needed.
28:12 We **p** in at Syracuse and stayed there
Ro 3:25 whom God **p** forward as a sacrifice of atonement
8:13 by the Spirit you **p** to death the deeds of the body,
9:33 whoever believes in him will not be **p** to shame."
10:11 "No one who believes in him will be **p** to shame."
13:12 the works of darkness and **p** on the armor of light;
13:14 Instead, **p** on the Lord Jesus Christ,
14:13 but resolve instead never to **p** a stumbling block
15: 1 We who are strong ought to **p** up with the failings
1Co 7:35 not to **p** any restraint upon you,
9:12 but we endure anything rather than **p** an obstacle
10: 9 We must not **p** Christ to the test,
13:11 I became an adult, I **p** an end to childish ways.
15:25 For he must reign until he has **p** all his enemies
15:27 "God has **p** all things in subjection under his feet."
15:27 But when it says, "All things are **p** in subjection,"
15:27 that this does not include the one who **p** all things
15:28 the one who **p** all things in subjection under him,
15:53 this perishable body must **p** on imperishability,
15:53 and this mortal body must **p** on immortality.
16: 2 to **p** aside and save whatever extra you earn,
16:16 to **p** yourselves at the service of such people,
2Co 3:13 who **p** a veil over his face to keep the people
8:16 But thanks be to God who **p** in the heart of Titus
11:19 you gladly **p** up with fools, being wise yourselves!
11:20 For you **p** up with it when someone makes slaves
13:11 **P** things in order, listen to my appeal,
Gal 4:14 though my condition **p** you to the test,
Eph 1:20 God **p** this power to work in Christ
1:22 And he has **p** all things under his feet
4:22 You were taught to **p** away your former way
4:31 **P** away from you all bitterness and wrath
6:11 **P** on the whole armor of God,
6:14 and **p** on the breastplate of righteousness.
6:15 for your feet **p** on whatever will make you ready
Php 1:16 knowing that I have been **p** here for the defense of
1:20 and hope that I will not be **p** to shame in any way,
Col 3: 5 **P** to death, therefore, whatever in you is earthly:
3:23 Whatever your task, **p** yourselves into it,
1Th 5: 8 and **p** on the breastplate of faith and love,
1Ti 4: 6 If you **p** these instructions before the brothers
4:15 **P** these things into practice,
5: 9 Let a widow be **p** on the list if she is
5:11 But refuse to **p** younger widows on the list;
2Ti 1:12 for I know the one in whom I have **p** my trust,
4: 3 For the time is coming when people will not **p** up
Tit 1: 5 you should **p** in order what remained to be done,
2: 8 then any opponent will be **p** to shame,
Heb 2:13 And again, "I will **p** my trust in him."
3: 9 where your ancestors **p** me to the test,
5: 1 Every high priest chosen from among mortals is **p**
8:10 I will **p** my laws in their minds,
10:16 I will **p** my laws in their hearts,
11:17 By faith Abraham, when **p** to the test,
11:34 became mighty in war, **p** foreign armies to flight.
12:13 so that what is lame may not be **p** out of joint,
Jas 3: 3 If we **p** bits into the mouths of horses
1Pe 2: 6 whoever believes in him will not be **p** to shame."
3:16 for your good conduct in Christ may be **p**
3:18 He was **p** to death in the flesh,
1Jn 2:28 and not be **p** to shame before him at his coming.
3Jn 1: 9 but Diotrephes, who likes to **p** himself first,
Rev 2:14 to **p** a stumbling block before the people of Israel,
17:17 For God has **p** it into their hearts
Tob 1:18 I also buried any whom King Sennacherib **p**
1:18 For in his anger he **p** to death many Israelites;
1:19 about me and that I was being searched for to be **p**
2: 8 He has already been hunted down to be **p** to death
5: 3 and I **p** one with the money.
6:17 and **p** them on the embers of the incense.
8: 2 where he had them and **p** them on the embers of
Jdt 2:23 He ravaged **P** and Lud, and plundered all
2:27 and ravaged their lands and **p** all their young men
4:10 they all **p** sackcloth around their waists.
4:11 before the temple and **p** ashes on their heads
6: 7 into the hill country and **p** you in one of the towns
8: 5 She **p** sackcloth around her waist and dressed
8:12 Who are you to **p** God to the test today,
9: 1 Judith prostrated herself, **p** ashes on her head,
9: 2 and exposed her thighs to **p** her to shame,
10: 3 She combed her hair, **p** on a tiara,
10: 4 She **p** sandals on her feet, and **p** on her anklets,
16: 7 For she **p** away her widow's clothing to exalt
16: 8 with a tiara and **p** on a linen gown to beguile him.
AdE 2:17 so he **p** on her the queen's diadem.
4: 1 **p** on sackcloth, and sprinkled himself with ashes;
4: 3 and they **p** on sackcloth and ashes.
4: 4 and sent some clothes to Mordecai to **p** on instead
AdE 6:11 he **p** the robe on Mordecai and made him ride
14: 2 and **p** on the garments of distress and mourning,
14:13 **P** eloquent speech in my mouth before the lion,
16:17 not to **p** in execution the letters sent by Haman son
Wis 1: 2 he is found by those who do not **p** him to the test,
4: 4 For even if they **p** forth boughs for a while,
5:18 he will **p** on righteousness as a breastplate,
8:12 they will **p** their hands on their mouths.
10: 5 when the nations in wicked agreement had been **p**
12: 2 be freed from wickedness and **p** their trust in you,
14: 4 so that even a person who lacks skill may **p** to sea.
18:21 he withstood the anger and **p** an end to
Sir 5:12 but if not, **p** your hand over your mouth.
6:24 **P** your feet into her fetters,
6:31 and **p** her on like a splendid crown.
12:12 Do not **p** him next to you,
15: 4 and he will rely on her and not be **p** to shame.
17: 4 He **p** the fear of them in all living beings,
17: 8 He **p** the fear of him into their hearts to show them
24:22 Whoever obeys me will not be **p** to shame,
28:12 if you spit on it, it will be **p** out;
28:23 it will burn among them and will not be **p** out.
33:28 **P** him to work, in order that he may not be idle,
34: 7 and those who **p** their hope in them have perished.
36: 2 and **p** all the nations in fear of you.
39:14 and **p** forth blossoms like a lily.
40:15 The children of the ungodly **p** out few branches;
42: 7 and when you give or receive, **p** it all in writing.
42:11 and **p** you to shame in public gatherings.
44: 5 composed musical tunes, or **p** verses in writing;
45: 7 and **p** a glorious robe on him.
45:13 No outsider ever **p** them on,
50:11 When he **p** on his glorious robe
50:29 For if they **p** them into practice,
51:26 **P** your neck under her yoke,
Bar 3: 7 For you have **p** the fear of you in our hearts so
3: 7 for we have **p** away from our hearts all
4:20 of peace and **p** on sackcloth for my supplication;
4:22 I have **p** my hope in the Everlasting to save you,
5: 1 and **p** on forever the beauty of the glory from God.
5: 2 **P** on the robe of the righteousness that comes
5: 2 **p** on your head the diadem of the glory of
LtJ 6:26 And those who serve them are **p** to shame
6:39 and those who serve them will be **p** to shame.
Aza 1:19 Do not **p** us to shame,
1:21 Let all who do harm to your servants be **p**
Sus 1:28 of their wicked plot to have Susanna **p** to death.
1:53 'You shall not **p** an innocent and righteous person
1:62 in accordance with the law of Moses, they **p** them
Bel 1:22 Therefore the king **p** them to death,
1Mc 1: 2 and **p** to death the kings of the earth.
1: 9 They all **p** on crowns after his death,
1:60 According to the decree, they **p** to death
2:14 **p** on sackcloth, and mourned greatly.
2:61 of those who **p** their trust in him will lack strength.
3: 3 Like a giant he **p** on his breastplate;
3:47 **p** on sackcloth and sprinkled ashes on their heads,
4:20 They saw that their army had been **p** to flight,
6:24 moreover, they have **p** to death as many of us
8:14 not one of them has **p** on a crown or worn purple
9:25 Bacchides chose the godless and **p** them in charge
9:52 and in them he **p** troops and stores of food.
9:53 of the land as hostages and **p** them under guard in
10:21 So Jonathan **p** on the sacred vestments in
10:37 of them be **p** in positions of trust in the kingdom.
10:72 for your ancestors were twice **p** to flight
10:77 a large troop of cavalry and **p** confidence in it.
11:13 Then Ptolemy entered Antioch and **p** on the crown
11:13 Thus he **p** two crowns on his head,
11:15 and met him with a strong force, and **p** him
11:23 and some of the priests, and **p** himself in danger,
11:37 to Jonathan and **p** up in a conspicuous place on
11:54 to reign and **p** on the crown.
11:71 Jonathan tore his clothes, **p** dust on his head,
12:39 to become king in Asia and **p** on the crown,
12:44 "Why have you **p** all these people to
13:29 and on the columns he **p** suits of armor for
14: 3 and took him to Arsaces, who **p** him under guard.
14: 9 and the youths **p** on splendid military attire.
14:23 to **p** a copy of their words in the public archives,
14:27 So they made a record on bronze tablets and **p** it
14:36 so that the Gentiles were **p** out of the country,
14:44 or to be clothed in purple or to **p** on a gold buckle.
14:48 to **p** them up in a conspicuous place in
16: 8 and Cendebeus and his army were **p** to flight;
2Mc 3:27 his men took him up, **p** him on a stretcher,
4:34 he immediately **p** him out of the way.
4:42 and killed some, and **p** all the rest to flight;
5:26 He **p** to the sword all those who came out
7:10 he quickly **p** out his tongue
8: 6 He captured strategic positions and **p** to flight not
9: 2 that Antiochus was **p** to flight by the inhabitants
9: 4 the injury done by those who had **p** him to flight;
11: 3 to **p** up the high priesthood for sale every year.
12:37 when they were not expecting it, and **p** them
13: 4 to **p** him to death by the method that is customary
13:21 he was sought for, caught, and **p** in prison.
1Es 1: 3 to the Lord and **p** the holy ark of the Lord in
1:38 Jehoiakim **p** the nobles in prison,
2: 2 throughout all his kingdom and also **p** it
3: 8 and they sealed them and **p** them under the pillow
4:30 and take the crown from the king's head and **p** it
6:19 and **p** them in the temple at Jerusalem,
8:25 who **p** this into the heart of the king,
8:69 and the Levites have not **p** away from themselves
8:93 that we will **p** away all our foreign wives,
9:20 They pledged themselves to **p** away their wives,
1Es 9:36 and they **p** them away together with their children.
3Mc 2: 7 through safely those who had **p** their confidence
2:20 and **p** praises in the mouth
2:28 to this are to be taken by force and **p** to death;
3: 1 and **p** to death by the most cruel means.
5:40 how long will you **p** us to the test,
7: 5 without any inquiry or examination to **p** them
7:14 so on their way they punished and **p** to a public
7:15 In that day they **p** to death
2Es 2:45 "These are they who have **p** off mortal clothing
and have **p** on the immortal,
4: 3 and to **p** before you three problems.
8:13 You **p** it to death as your creation,
8:30 but love those who have always **p** their trust
9:34 or what was launched or what was **p**
10: 2 So all of us **p** out our lamps,
10:22 the light of our lampstand has been **p** out,
12:37 that you have seen in a book, **p** it in a hidden place;
14:14 and **p** away from you mortal thoughts;
14:25 which shall not be **p** out until what you are about
15: 1 of the prophecy that I will **p** in your mouth,
16:15 not be **p** out until it consumes the foundations of
16:60 he has **p** springs of water in the desert,
16:61 He formed human beings and **p** a heart in
16:65 You shall be **p** to shame when your sins come out
4Mc 4:24 in any way to **p** an end to the people's observance
5:35 I will not **p** you to shame, philosophical reason,
8:24 or take hollow pride in being **p** to the rack.
8:25 even the law itself would arbitrarily **p** us to death
9: 7 Therefore, tyrant, **p** us to the test;
13:16 Therefore let us **p** on the full armor of self-control,
13:18 "Do not **p** us to shame, brother,
17: 1 about to be seized and **p** to death she threw herself
18:21 and **p** them to death with various tortures.

PUTEOLI (1)

Ac 28:13 and on the second day we came to **P.**

PUTHITES (1)

1Ch 2:53 the Ithrites, the **P**, the Shumathites,

PUTIEL (1)

Ex 6:25 Eleazar married one of the daughters of **P**,

PUTS‡ (34) [PUT]

Ex 30:33 Whoever compounds any like it or whoever **p** any
Nu 22:38 word God **p** in my mouth, that is what I must say."
23:12 "Must I not take care to say what the LORD **p** into
Dt 24: 1 **p** it in her hand, and sends her out of his house;
24: 3 writes her a bill of divorce, **p** it in her hand,
Jos 23:10 One of you **p** to flight a thousand,
1Ki 20:11 One who **p** on armor should not brag
Job 4:18 Even in his servants he **p** no trust,
15:15 God **p** no trust even in his holy ones,
33:11 he **p** my feet in the stocks,
Pr 18:18 Casting the lot **p** an end to disputes and decides
25: 8 when your neighbor **p** you to shame?
31:19 She **p** her hands to the distaff,
SS 2:13 The fig tree **p** forth its figs,
Mt 5:15 after lighting a lamp **p** it under the bushel basket,
24:32 and **p** forth its leaves, you know
Mk 2:22 And no one **p** new wine into old wineskins;
2:22 but one **p** new wine into fresh wineskins."
4:32 and **p** forth large branches,
13:28 and **p** forth its leaves, you know
13:34 when he leaves home and **p** his slaves in charge,
Lk 5:37 And no one **p** new wine into old wineskins;
8:16 or **p** it under a bed, but **p** it on a lampstand,
9:62 "No one who **p** a hand to the plow
11:33 "No one after lighting a lamp **p** it in a cellar,
1Co 15:54 When this perishable body **p** on imperishability,
and this mortal body **p** on immortality,
2Co 11:20 or **p** on airs, or gives you a slap in the face.
Heb 6:16 oath given as confirmation **p** an end to all dispute.
Sir 14:18 and **p** forth others, so are the generations of flesh
18:23 do not be like one who **p** the Lord to the test.
26:13 and her skill **p** flesh on his bones.
43:20 and the water **p** it on like a breastplate.

PUTTING‡ (45) [PUT]

Ge 21:14 and gave it to Hagar, **p** it on her shoulder,
Lev 6:10 The priest shall put on his linen vestments after **p**
16:21 all their sins, **p** them on the head of the goat,
Nu 5: 3 both male and female, **p** them outside the camp;
5: 4 The Israelites did so, **p** them outside the camp;
Dt 13:15 even **p** its livestock to the sword.
Jos 19:47 and after capturing it and **p** it to the sword,
Jdg 7: 5 **p** their hands to their mouths,
18:21 So they resumed their journey, **p** the little ones,
1Ki 2: 5 **p** the blood of war on the belt around his waist,
2Ki 4:34 **p** his mouth upon his mouth,
Ps 75: 7 **p** down one and lifting up another.
Isa 22:12 to baldness and **p** on sackcloth;
Eze 4: 8 I am **p** cords on you so that you cannot turn
8:17 See, they are **p** the branch to their nose!
13:19 **p** to death persons who should not die
17:13 **p** him under oath (he had taken away
Mt 22:18 "Why are you **p** me to the test, you hypocrites?
Mk 12:15 he said to them, "Why are you **p** me to the test?
12:41 and watched the crowd **p** money into the treasury.
Lk 21: 1 He looked up and saw rich people **p** their gifts into
Ac 15:10 therefore why are you **p** God to the test by placing
22: 4 by binding both men and women and **p** them
27: 4 **P** out to sea from there,

Ac 27:12 the majority was in favor of **p** to sea from there,
27:30 on the pretext of **p** out anchors from the bow,
28: 3 a bundle of brushwood and was **p** it on the fire,
28: 8 and cured him by praying and **p** his hands on him.
1Co 15:30 why are we **p** ourselves in danger every hour?
2Co 1:22 by **p** his seal on us and giving us his Spirit
6: 3 We are **p** no obstacle in anyone's way,
Eph 2:16 thus **p** to death that hostility through it.
4:25 So then, **p** away falsehood,
Col 2:11 by **p** off the body of the flesh in the circumcision
Jdt 8:13 You are **p** the Lord Almighty to the test,
8:25 who is **p** us to the test as he did our ancestors.
Sus 1:56 Then, **p** him to one side, he ordered them to bring
1Mc 13:32 **p** on the crown of Asia;
2Mc 4:15 and **p** the highest value upon Greek forms
7:40 **p** his whole trust in the Lord.
8:22 **p** fifteen hundred men under each.
12:23 **p** the sinners to the sword,
3Mc 6:32 **P** an end to all mourning and wailing,
2Es 2:46 on them and **p** palms in their hands?"
4Mc 9: 2 we are obviously **p** our forebears to shame

PUVAH (2) [=PUAH, PUNITES]
Ge 46:13 Tola, **P**, Jashub, and Shimron.
Nu 26:23 of **P**, the clan of the Punites;

PUZZLED (1)
Ac 10:17 while Peter was greatly **p** about what to make of

PYGARG (KJV) See IBEX

PYRAMIDS (2)
1Mc 13:28 He also erected seven **p**, opposite one another,
13:29 For the **p** he devised an elaborate setting,

PYRE (1)
Isa 30:33 its **p** made deep and wide,

PYRRHUS (1)
Ac 20: 4 He was accompanied by Sopater son of **P**

Q

QAYITS, QESITAH, QETS, QIQAYON, QOHELETH See Index to Footnotes

QUADRENNIAL (1)
2Mc 4:18 When the **q** games were being held at Tyre and

QUAILS (7)
Ex 16:13 In the evening **q** came up and covered the camp;
Nu 11:31 and it brought **q** from the sea and let them fall
11:32 and night and all the next day, gathering the **q**;
Ps 105:40 They asked, and he brought **q**,
Wis 16: 2 and you prepared **q** to eat,
19:12 for, to give them relief, **q** came up from the sea.
2Es 1:15 The **q** were a sign to you;

QUAKE (10) [EARTHQUAKE, EARTHQUAKES, QUAKED, QUAKES, QUAKING]
Ps 60: 2 You have caused the land to **q**;
99: 1 upon the cherubim; let the earth **q**!
Isa 64: 1 so that the mountains would **q** at your presence—
Eze 31:16 I made the nations **q** at the sound of its fall,
38:20 the face of the earth, shall **q** at my presence,
Na 1: 5 The mountains **q** before him, and the hills melt;
2:10 all loins **q**, all faces grow pale!
Sir 16:19 the earth quiver and **q** when he looks upon them.
1Es 4:36 All God's works **q** and tremble,
2Es 16:12 The earth and its foundations **q**,

QUAKED (8) [QUAKE]
Jdg 5: 5 The mountains **q** before the LORD,
1Sa 14:15 the earth **q**; and it became a very great panic.
2Sa 22: 8 the foundations of the heavens trembled and **q**,
1Ki 1:40 so that the earth **q** at their noise.
Ps 18: 7 foundations also of the mountains trembled and **q**,
68: 8 the earth **q**, the heavens poured down rain at
Isa 5:25 the mountains **q**, and their corpses were like refuse
64: 3 you came down, the mountains **q** at your presence.

QUAKES (3) [QUAKE]
Jer 8:16 of the neighing of their stallions the whole land **q**.
10:10 At his wrath the earth **q**, and the nations cannot
Joel 2:10 The earth **q** before them, the heavens tremble.

QUAKING (2) [QUAKE]
Jer 4:24 I looked on the mountains, and lo, they were **q**,
Eze 12:18 with **q**, and drink your water with trembling and

QUALIFICATION (1) [QUALIFY]
2Mc 4:25 possessing no **q** for the high priesthood,

QUALIFIED (9) [QUALIFY]
Nu 4:35 everyone who **q** for work relating to the tent
4:39 everyone who **q** for work relating to the tent
4:43 everyone who **q** for work relating to the tent
4:47 everyone who **q** to do the work of service and
2Ki 10: 3 select the son of your master who is the best **q**,
1Ch 9:13 **q** for the work of the service of the house of God.
26: 8 were able men **q** for the service;
Lk 6:40 everyone who is fully **q** will be like the teacher.
1Mc 13:40 any of you are **q** to be enrolled in our bodyguard,

QUALIFIES (1) [QUALIFY]
Nu 4:30 everyone who **q** to do the work of the tent

QUALIFY (2) [QUALIFICATION, QUALIFIED, QUALIFIES]
Nu 4: 3 all who **q** to do work relating to the tent
4:23 all who **q** to do work in the tent of meeting.

QUALITY (1)
2Es 16:73 Then the tested **q** of my elect shall be manifest,

QUALM (1)
Sir 13: 5 he will drain your resources without a **q**.

QUANTITIES (4) [QUANTITY]
1Ch 22: 3 as well as bronze in **q** beyond weighing,
22: 4 the Sidonians and Tyrians brought great **q** of cedar
29: 2 besides great **q** of onyx and stones for setting,
2Ch 4:18 Solomon made all these things in great **q**,

QUANTITY (18) [QUANTITIES]
Ex 5: 8 the same **q** of bricks as they have made previously;
5:14 the required **q** of bricks yesterday and today,
Lev 19:35 not cheat in measuring length, weight, or **q**.
Dt 17:17 also silver and gold he must not acquire in great **q**
Jos 22: 8 bronze, and iron, and with a great **q** of clothing;
1Ki 10:10 a great **q** of spices, and precious stones;
10:10 in such **q** as that which the queen of Sheba gave
10:11 a great **q** of almug wood and precious stones.
1Ch 18: 8 cities of Hadadezer, David took a vast **q** of bronze;
22: 5 So David provided materials in great **q**
23:29 and all measures of **q** or size.
2Ch 9: 9 a very great **q** of spices, and precious stones:
14:13 people of Judah carried away a great **q** of booty.
Rev 8: 3 a great **q** of incense to offer with the prayers of all
Jdt 12:20 and drank a great **q** of wine,
15: 7 since there was a vast **q** of it.
Sir 38:29 and he produces them in **q**.
2Es 4:50 so the **q** that passed was far greater;

QUARREL‡ (14) [QUARRELED, QUARRELING, QUARRELS, QUARRELSOME]
Ge 26:22 and they did not **q** over it;
45:24 "Do not **q** along the way."
Ex 17: 2 Moses said to them, "Why do you **q** with me?
21:18 When individuals **q** and one strikes the other with
2Ki 5: 7 and see how he is trying to pick a **q** with me."
Pr 3:30 Do not **q** with anyone without cause,
17:14 so stop before the **q** breaks out.
20: 3 but every fool is quick to **q**.
26:17 by the ears is one who meddles in the **q** of another.
Isa 58: 4 to **q** and to fight and to strike with a wicked fist.
Sir 6: 9 and tell of the **q** to your disgrace.
8: 2 Do not **q** with the rich,
28:11 A hasty **q** kindles a fire,
31:26 so wine tests hearts when the insolent **q**.
27:14 and their **q** make others stop their ears.
31:29 to bitterness of spirit, to **q** and stumbling.

QUARRELED (7) [QUARREL]
Ge 26:20 the herders of Gerar **q** with Isaac's herders,
26:21 and they **q** over that one also;
Ex 17: 2 The people **q** with Moses, and said,
17: 7 because the Israelites **q** and tested the LORD,
Nu 20: 3 The people **q** with Moses and said,
20:13 where the people of Israel **q** with the LORD,
27:14 in the wilderness of Zin when the congregation **q**

QUARRELING (10) [QUARREL]
Pr 18:19 such **q** is like the bars of a castle.
19:13 and a wife's **q** is a continual dripping of rain.
22:10 and strife goes out; **q** and abuse will cease.
26:20 and where there is no whisperer, **q** ceases.
Ac 7:26 of them as they were **q** and tried to reconcile them,
Ro 13:13 not in debauchery and licentiousness, not in **q**
14: 1 but not for the purpose of **q** over opinions.
1Co 3: 3 For as long as there is jealousy and **q** among you,
2Co 12:20 I fear that there may perhaps be **q**, jealousy, anger,
Tit 3: 2 to speak evil of no one, to avoid **q**, to be gentle,

QUARRELS (6) [QUARREL]
1Co 1:11 by Chloe's people that there are **q** among you,
Gal 5:20 enmities, strife, jealousy, anger, **q**, dissensions,
2Ti 2:23 you know that they breed **q**.
Tit 3: 9 genealogies, dissensions, and **q** about the law,

QUARRELSOME (3) [QUARREL]
Pr 26:21 so is a **q** person for kindling strife.
1Ti 3: 3 not **q**, and not a lover of money.
2Ti 2:24 And the Lord's servant must not be **q** but kindly

QUARRIED (4) [QUARRY]
1Ki 5:17 At the king's command, they **q** out great,
2Ki 12:12 as to buy timber and **q** stone for making repairs on
22: 6 to buy timber and **q** stone to repair the house.
2Ch 34:11 to the carpenters and the builders to buy **q** stone,

QUARRIES (1) [QUARRY]
Ecc 10: 9 Whoever **q** stones will be hurt by them;

QUARRY (2) [QUARRIED, QUARRIES]
1Ki 6: 7 The house was built with stone finished at the **q**,
Isa 51: 1 and to the **q** from which you were dug.

QUART (1) [QUARTS]
Rev 6: 6 "A **q** of wheat for a day's pay,

QUARTER (10) [HEADQUARTERS, QUARTERS]
1Sa 9: 8 "Here, I have with me a **q** shekel of silver;
2Ki 22:14 she resided in Jerusalem in the Second **Q**,
2Ch 34:22 in Jerusalem in the Second **Q**) and spoke to her to
Est 4:14 for the Jews from another **q**,
Jer 50:26 Come against her from every **q**;
Eze 37:21 and will gather them from every **q**,
Zep 1:10 a wail from the Second **Q**,
Mk 1:45 and people came to him from every **q**.
AdE 4:14 to the Jews from another **q**,
2Mc 12:16 so that the adjoining lake, a **q** of a mile wide,

QUARTERMASTER (1)
Jer 51:59 fourth year of his reign. Seraiah was the **q**.

QUARTERS (3) [QUARTER]
1Sa 1:18 Then the woman went to her **q**,
Ne 3:30 of Berechiah made repairs opposite his living **q**.
Jer 49:36 upon Elam the four winds from the four **q**

QUARTS (1) [QUART]
Rev 6: 6 and three **q** of barley for a day's pay,

QUARTUS (1)
Ro 16:23 Erastus, the city treasurer, and our brother **Q**,

QUATERNIONS (KJV) See SQUADS

QUEEN (77) [QUEEN'S, QUEENLY, QUEENS]
1Ki 10: 1 the **q** of Sheba heard of the fame of Solomon,
10: 4 When the **q** of Sheba had observed all the wisdom
10:10 in such quantity as that which the **q** of Sheba gave
10:13 to the **q** of Sheba every desire that she expressed,
11:19 for a wife, the sister of **Q** Tahpenes.
15:13 from being **q** mother, because she had made
2Ki 10:13 the royal princes and the sons of the **q** mother."
2Ch 9: 1 the **q** of Sheba heard of the fame of Solomon,
9: 3 **q** of Sheba had observed the wisdom of Solomon,
9: 9 as those that the **q** of Sheba gave to King Solomon.
9:12 the **q** of Sheba every desire that she expressed,
15:16 from being **q** mother because she had made
Ne 2: 6 king said to me (the **q** also was sitting beside him),
Est 1: 9 **Q** Vashti gave a banquet for the women in
1:11 to bring **Q** Vashti before the king, wearing
1:12 But **Q** Vashti refused to come at
1:15 what is to be done to **Q** Vashti because she has
1:16 "Not only has **Q** Vashti done wrong to the king,
1:17 of the **q** will be made known to all women,
1:17 'King Ahasuerus commanded **Q** Vashti to
2: 4 And let the girl who pleases the king be **q** instead
2:17 on her head and made her **q** instead of Vashti.
2:22 and he told it to **Q** Esther,
4: 4 the **q** was deeply distressed;
5: 2 as the king saw **Q** Esther standing in the court,
5: 3 The king said to her, "What is it, **Q** Esther?
5:12 "Even **Q** Esther let no one but myself come with
7: 1 king and Haman went in to feast with **Q** Esther.
7: 2 "What is your petition, **Q** Esther?
7: 3 Then **Q** Esther answered,
7: 5 Then King Ahasuerus said to **Q** Esther,
7: 6 Haman was terrified before the king and the **q**.
7: 7 but Haman stayed to beg his life from **Q** Esther,
7: 8 "Will he even assault the **q** in my presence,
8: 1 to **Q** Esther the house of Haman, the enemy of
8: 7 Then King Ahasuerus said to **Q** Esther and to
9:12 The king said to **Q** Esther,
9:29 **Q** Esther daughter of Abihail,
9:31 Mordecai and **Q** Esther enjoined on the Jews,
9:32 The command of **Q** Esther fixed these practices
Ps 45: 9 at your right hand stands the **q** in gold of Ophir.
Jer 7:18 to make cakes for the **q** of heaven;
13:18 Say to the king and the **q** mother;
29: 2 This was after King Jeconiah, and the **q** mother,
44:17 to the **q** of heaven and pour out libations to her,

Jer 44:18 to the **q** of heaven and pouring out libations to her,
44:19 to the **q** of heaven and pouring out libations to her;
44:25 to the **q** of heaven and to pour out libations to her.'
Eze 16:13 You grew exceedingly beautiful, fit to be a **q**.
Da 5:10 The **q**, when she heard the discussion of the king
5:10 The **q** said, "O king, live forever!
Mt 12:42 The **q** of the South will rise up at the judgment
Lk 11:31 The **q** of the South will rise at the judgment with
Ac 8:27 a court official of the Candace, **q** of the Ethiopians,
Rev 18:7 Since in her heart she says, 'I rule as a **q**;
AdE 1:9 **Q** Vashti gave a drinking party for the women in
1:11 the **q** to him in order to proclaim her as **q** and
1:12 But **Q** Vashti refused to obey him and would
1:15 be done to **Q** Vashti for not obeying the order that
1:16 "**Q** Vashti has insulted not only the king but
1:17 the **q** had said and how she had defied the king).
1:19 that the **q** may no longer come into his presence;
2:4 the woman who pleases the king shall be **q** instead
4:14 not for such a time as this that you were made **q**?"
5:6 the king said to Esther, "What is it, **Q** Esther?
5:12 "The **q** did not invite anyone to the dinner with
7:1 the king and Haman went in to drink with the **q**.
7:2 the king said, "What is it, **Q** Esther?
7:6 in the presence of the king and **q**.
7:7 and Haman began to beg for his life from the **q**,
7:8 on the couch, pleading with the **q**.
9:29 Then **Q** Esther daughter of Aminadab along
9:31 and **Q** Esther established this decision
10:6 whom the king married and made **q**.
14:1 Then **Q** Esther, seized with deadly anxiety,
15:7 The **q** faltered, and turned pale and faint,

QUEEN'S (3) [QUEEN]

Est 1:18 of the **q** behavior will rebel against
AdE 2:17 so he put on her the **q** diadem.
4:4 When the **q** maids and eunuchs came and told her,

QUEENLY (1) [QUEEN]

SS 7:1 graceful are your feet in sandals, O **q** maiden!

QUEENS (3) [QUEEN]

SS 6:8 There are sixty **q** and eighty concubines,
6:9 the **q** and concubines also, and they praised her.
Isa 49:23 and their **q** your nursing mothers.

QUENCH (17) [FIRE-QUENCHING, QUENCHED, QUENCHES]

2Sa 14:7 Thus they would **q** my one remaining ember,
21:17 so that you do not **q** the lamp of Israel."
Ps 104:11 the wild asses **q** their thirst.
SS 8:7 Many waters cannot **q** love, neither can floods
Isa 1:31 with no one to **q** them.
42:3 and a dimly burning wick he will not **q**;
Jer 4:4 and burn with no one to **q** it,
21:12 with no one to **q** it, because of your evil doings.
Am 5:6 and it will devour Bethel, with no one to **q** it.
Mt 12:20 not break a bruised reed or **q** a smoldering wick
Eph 6:16 be able to **q** all the flaming arrows of the evil one.
1Th 5:19 Do not **q** the Spirit.
AdE 14:9 and to **q** your altar and the glory of your house,
2Es 16:4 and who is there to **q** it?
16:6 **q** a fire in the stubble once it has started to burn?
16:9 and who is there to **q** it?
4Mc 3:17 the emotions and **q** the flames of frenzied desires;

QUENCHED (17) [QUENCH]

2Ki 22:17 and it will not be **q**.
2Ch 34:25 be poured out on this place and will not be **q**.
Isa 34:10 Night and day it shall not be **q**;
43:17 they are extinguished, **q** like a wick:
66:24 their worm shall not die, their fire shall not be **q**,
Jer 7:20 it will burn and not be **q**.
17:27 the palaces of Jerusalem and shall not be **q**.
Eze 20:47 the blazing flame shall not be **q**,
20:48 that I the LORD have kindled it; it shall not be **q**.
Mk 9:48 their worm never dies, and the fire is never **q**.
Heb 11:34 **q** raging fire, escaped the edge of the sword,
Sir 23:16 Hot passion that blazes like a fire will not be **q**
3Mc 6:34 their fire-breathing boldness was ignominiously **q**.
2Es 6:27 For evil shall be blotted out, and deceit shall be **q**;
4Mc 9:20 heap of coals was being **q** by the drippings of gore,
16:4 But the mother **q** so many and such great emotions
18:20 of the Greeks **q** fire with fire in his cruel caldrons,

QUENCHES (1) [QUENCH]

Wis 16:17 in water, which **q** all things,

QUERY (1)

4Mc 18:17 He confirmed the **q** of Ezekiel,

QUESTION‡ (29) [QUESTIONED, QUESTIONING, QUESTIONINGS, QUESTIONS]

Jdg 5:29 indeed, she answers the **q** herself:
1Sa 17:29 "What have I done now? It was only a **q**."
2Sa 14:32 that I may send you to the king with the **q**,
Job 38:3 Gird up your loins like a man, I will **q** you,
40:7 I will **q** you, and you declare to me.
42:4 I will **q** you, and you declare to me.'
Isa 45:11 Will you **q** me about my children,
Mt 21:24 Jesus said to them, "I will also ask you one **q**;
22:23 and they asked him a **q**, saying,
22:35 a lawyer, asked him a **q** to test him.
22:41 gathered together, Jesus asked them this **q**:
Mk 11:29 Jesus said to them, "I will ask you one **q**;
12:18 came to him and asked him a **q**, saying,
12:34 After that no one dared to ask him any **q**.
Lk 5:21 Then the scribes and the Pharisees began to **q**,
20:3 He answered them, "I will also ask you a **q**,
20:28 and asked him a **q**, "Teacher, Moses wrote for us
20:40 For they no longer dared to ask him another **q**.
22:68 and if I **q** you, you will not answer.
Jn 16:30 and do not need to have anyone **q** you;
Ac 15:2 to Jerusalem to discuss this **q** with the apostles and
1Co 10:25 without raising any **q** on the ground of conscience,
10:27 without raising any **q** on the ground of conscience.
2Co 8:13 but it is a **q** of a fair balance between
Sir 19:13 **Q** a friend; perhaps he did not do it;
19:14 **Q** a neighbor; perhaps he did not say it;
19:15 **Q** a friend, for often it is slander;
19:17 **Q** your neighbor before you threaten him;
1Mc 9:10 and leave no cause to **q** our honor."

QUESTIONED (15) [QUESTION]

Ge 43:7 "The man **q** us carefully about ourselves
Jdg 8:14 one of the people of Succoth, and **q** him;
2Ki 8:6 When the king **q** the woman, she told him.
2Ch 31:9 Hezekiah **q** the priests and the Levites about
Jer 36:17 Then they **q** Baruch, "Tell us now,
37:17 The king **q** him secretly in his house, and said,
38:27 All the officials did come to Jeremiah and **q** him;
Lk 23:9 He **q** him at some length,
Jn 18:19 Then the high priest **q** Jesus about his disciples and
Ac 4:9 if we are **q** today because of a good deed done
5:27 before the council. The high priest **q** them,
Tob 6:7 Then the young man **q** the angel and said to him,
7:3 Then Edna **q** them, saying, "Where are you from,
Jdt 6:16 and Uzziah **q** him about what had happened.
1Es 6:12 we **q** them and asked them for a list of the names

QUESTIONING (5) [QUESTION]

Jer 38:27 So they stopped **q** him, for the conversation had
Mk 2:6 of the scribes were sitting there, **q** in their hearts,
9:10 **q** what this rising from the dead could mean.
Lk 3:15 and all were **q** in their hearts concerning John,
Jn 8:7 ⟦When they kept on **q** him,⟧

QUESTIONINGS (1) [QUESTION]

Lk 5:22 When Jesus perceived their **q**, he answered them,

QUESTIONS (16) [QUESTION]

Ge 43:7 What we told him was in answer to these **q**.
1Ki 10:1 she came to test him with hard **q**.
10:3 Solomon answered all her **q**;
2Ch 9:1 she came to Jerusalem to test him with hard **q**,
9:2 Solomon answered all her **q**;
Mt 22:46 that day did anyone dare to ask him any more **q**.
Mk 2:8 in his spirit that they were discussing these **q**
2:8 "Why do you raise such **q** in your hearts?
Lk 2:46 listening to them and asking them **q**.
5:22 "Why do you raise such **q** in your hearts?
Ac 18:15 of **q** about words and names and your own law,
23:29 that he was accused concerning **q** of their law,
25:20 Since I was at a loss how to investigate these **q**,
Sir 39:17 at the appointed time all such **q** will be answered.
41:4 there are no **q** asked in Hades.
2Es 8:55 not ask any more **q** about the great number

QUIBBLING (1)

1Es 6:30 regularly every year, without **q**, for daily use

QUICK (15) [QUICK-MELTING, QUICK-TEMPERED, QUICKLY]

Ex 32:8 they have been **q** to turn aside from the way
Lev 13:10 and there is **q** raw flesh in the swelling,
Dt 7:22 you will not be able to make a **q** end of them,
9:12 They have been **q** to turn from the way
9:16 you had been **q** to turn from the way that
1Sa 20:38 Jonathan called after the boy, "Hurry, be **q**,
22:14 and is **q** to do your bidding,
Job 5:13 and the schemes of the wily are brought to a **q** end.
Pr 20:3 but every fool is **q** to quarrel.
Ecc 5:2 nor let your heart be **q** to utter a word before God,
7:9 Do not be **q** to anger,
Jas 1:19 let everyone be **q** to listen, slow to speak,
Wis 18:21 a blameless man was **q** to act as their champion;
Sir 5:11 Be **q** to hear, but deliberate in answering.
2Es 6:34 Do not be **q** to think vain thoughts concerning

QUICK (KJV) See also ACTIVE, ALIVE, LIVING, RAW

QUICK-MELTING (1) [MELT, QUICK]

Wis 19:21 the crystalline, **q** kind of heavenly food.

QUICK-TEMPERED (3) [QUICK, TEMPER]

Pr 14:17 One who is **q** acts foolishly,
Tit 1:7 not be arrogant or **q** or addicted to wine or violent
Sir 8:16 Do not pick a fight with the **q**,

QUICKEN (KJV) See GIVE LIFE, LIFE, PRESERVE LIFE, REVIVE, SPARE LIFE

QUICKLY (105) [QUICK]

Ge 18:6 "Make ready **q** three measures of choice flour,
24:18 and **q** lowered her jar upon her hand and gave him
24:20 So she **q** emptied her jar into the trough
24:46 She **q** let down her jar from her shoulder, and said,
24:64 she slipped **q** from the camel,
27:20 "How is it that you have found it so **q**, my son?"
44:11 Then each one **q** lowered his sack to the ground,
Ex 34:8 And Moses **q** bowed his head toward the earth,
Nu 16:46 and carry it **q** to the congregation
Dt 7:4 and he would destroy you **q**.
9:3 so that you may dispossess and destroy them **q**,
9:12 LORD said to me, "Get up, go down **q** from here,
11:17 then you will perish **q** off the good land that
28:20 until you are destroyed and perish **q**,
Jos 2:5 Pursue them **q**, for you can overtake them."
8:19 the troops in ambush rose **q** out of their place
10:6 come up to us **q**, and save us, and help us;
23:16 and you shall perish **q** from the good land
Jdg 9:48 "What you have seen me do, do **q**,
13:10 So the woman ran **q** and told her husband,
20:37 The troops in ambush rushed **q** upon Gibeah.
1Sa 4:14 Then the man came **q** and told Eli.
17:17 and carry them **q** to the camp to your brothers;
17:48 David ran **q** toward the battle line to meet
28:24 She **q** slaughtered it, and she took flour,
2Sa 17:16 Therefore send **q** and tell David,
17:18 so both of them went away **q**,
17:21 They said to David, "Go and cross the water **q**;
1Ki 20:33 they **q** took it up from him and said, "Yes,
20:41 Then he **q** took the bandage away from his eyes.
22:9 "Bring **q** Micaiah son of Imlah."
2Ki 1:11 this is the king's order: Come down **q**!"
4:22 so that I may **q** go to the man of God
2Ch 18:8 "Bring **q** Micaiah son of Imlah."
24:5 and see that you act **q**."
24:5 But the Levites did not act **q**.
35:13 and in pans, and carried them **q** to all the people.
Est 2:9 and won his favor, and he **q** provided her
3:15 The couriers went **q** by order of the king,
5:5 Then the king said, "Bring Haman **q**,
6:10 Then the king said to Haman, "**Q**,
Ps 2:12 for his wrath is **q** kindled.
22:19 O my help, come **q** to my aid!
81:14 Then I would **q** subdue their enemies,
141:1 upon you, O LORD; come **q** to me;
143:7 Answer me **q**, O LORD; my spirit fails.
Pr 20:21 An estate **q** acquired in the beginning will not
Ecc 4:12 A threefold cord is not **q** broken.
Isa 58:8 and your healing shall spring up **q**;
60:22 in its time I will accomplish it **q**.
Jer 9:18 let them **q** raise a dirge over us,
Da 2:25 Then Arioch **q** brought Daniel before the king
3:24 Nebuchadnezzar was astonished and rose up **q**.
Joel 3:11 Come **q**, all you nations all around,
Mt 5:25 Come to terms **q** with your accuser while you are
13:5 and they sprang up **q**, since they had no depth
28:7 Then go **q** and tell his disciples,
28:8 So they left the tomb **q** with fear and great joy,
Mk 4:5 and it sprang up **q**, since it had no depth of soil.
Lk 15:22 father said to his slaves, '**Q**, bring out a robe—
16:6 He said to him, 'Take your bill, sit down **q**,
18:8 I tell you, he will **q** grant justice to them.
Jn 11:29 when she heard it, she got up **q** and went to him.
11:31 consoling her, saw Mary get up **q** and go out.
13:27 "Do **q** what you are going to do."
Ac 12:7 on the side and woke him, saying, "Get up **q**."
22:18 'Hurry and get out of Jerusalem **q**,
26:28 so **q** persuading me to become a Christian?"
26:29 Paul replied, "Whether **q** or not,
Ro 9:28 the Lord will execute his sentence on the earth **q**
Gal 1:6 that you are so **q** deserting the one who called you
2Th 2:2 not to be **q** shaken in mind or alarmed,
Jdt 13:1 When evening came, his slaves **q** withdrew.
AdE 2:9 and he **q** provided her with ointments
5:5 Then the king said, "Bring Haman **q**,
Wis 4:14 he took them **q** from the midst of wickedness.
4:16 and youth that is **q** perfected will condemn
16:11 and then were **q** delivered,
Sir 11:22 and **q** God causes his blessing to flourish.
19:4 One who trusts others too **q** has a shallow mind,
27:3 his house will be **q** overthrown.
32:11 go home **q** and do not linger.
43:22 A mist **q** heals all things;
48:20 The Holy One **q** heard them from heaven,
50:17 Then all the people together **q** fell to the ground
1Mc 2:35 Then the enemy **q** attacked them.
2:40 they will **q** destroy us from the earth."
5:28 and his army **q** turned back by the wilderness road
6:27 unless you **q** prevent them,
6:57 So he **q** gave orders to withdraw,
11:22 but to meet him for a conference at Ptolemais as **q**
2Mc 3:31 of Heliodorus's friends **q** begged Onias to call
4:48 and the holy vessels **q** suffered the unjust penalty.
6:23 to the holy God-given law, he declared himself **q**,
7:10 he **q** put out his tongue and courageously
14:11 **q** inflamed Demetrius still more.
14:44 But as they **q** drew back,
1Es 2:30 the scribe Shimshai and their associates went **q**
3Mc 2:23 that he would lose his life, **q** dragged him out,
5:43 to him would **q** render it forever empty
6:9 reveal yourself **q** to those of the nation of Israel—
2Es 8:14 If then you will suddenly and **q** destroy what with
11:27 and this disappeared more **q** than the first.
4Mc 4:5 he proceeded **q** to our country accompanied by
14:10 and it consumed their bodies **q**.

QUIET (55) [QUIETED, QUIETLY, QUIETNESS]

Ge 25:27 a man of the field, while Jacob was a **q** man,
Jdg 16: 2 They kept **q** all night, thinking,
18: 7 **q** and unsuspecting, lacking nothing on earth,
18:19 They said to him, "Keep **q**!
18:27 came to Laish, to a people **q** and unsuspecting,
2Sa 13:20 Be **q** for now, my sister;
2Ki 11:20 the city was **q** after Athaliah had been killed with
1Ch 4:40 good pasture, and the land was very broad, **q**,
22: 9 and I will give peace and **q** to Israel in his days.
2Ch 20:30 And the realm of Jehoshaphat was **q**,
23:21 the city was **q** after Athaliah had been killed with
Ne 8:11 So the Levites stilled all the people, saying, "Be **q**,
Job 3:13 Now I would be lying down and **q**;
3:26 I am not at ease, nor am I **q**;
20:20 "They knew no **q** in their bellies;
34:29 When he is **q**, who can condemn?
Ps 35:20 against those who are **q** in the land.
107:30 Then they were glad because they had **q**,
Pr 17: 1 a dry morsel with **q** than a house full of feasting
Ecc 4: 6 a handful with **q** than two handfuls with toil,
9:17 The **q** words of the wise are more to
Isa 7: 4 Take heed, be **q**, do not fear,
14: 7 The whole earth is at rest and **q**;
32:18 in secure dwellings, and in **q** resting places.
33:20 Your eyes will see Jerusalem, a **q** habitation,
Jer 30:10 Jacob shall return and have **q** and ease,
46:27 Jacob shall return and have **q** and ease,
47: 6 How long until you are **q**?
47: 7 How can it be **q**, when the LORD has given it
49:23 they are troubled like the sea that cannot be **q**.
Eze 38:11 I will fall upon the **q** people who live in safety,
Jnh 1:11 that the sea may **q** down for us?"
1:12 then the sea will **q** down for you;
Mt 20:31 The crowd sternly ordered them to be **q**;
Mk 10:48 Many sternly ordered him to be **q**,
Lk 18:39 in front sternly ordered him to be **q**;
Ac 19:36 you ought to be **q** and do nothing rash.
22: 2 they became even more **q**.
1Ti 2: 2 a **q** and peaceable life in all godliness and dignity.
1Pe 3: 4 with the lasting beauty of a gentle and **q** spirit,
Tob 10: 6 Tobit kept saying to her, "Be **q** and stop worrying,
10: 7 She answered him, "Be **q** yourself!
AdE 4:14 For if you keep **q** at such a time as this,
16: 8 to render our kingdom **q** and peaceable for all,
Sir 25:20 such is a garrulous wife to a **q** husband.
1Mc 1: 3 When the earth became **q** before him,
9:58 and his men are living in **q** and confidence.
11:38 When King Demetrius saw that the land was **q**
11:52 and the land was **q** before him.
2Mc 14: 4 During that day he kept **q**.
2Es 2:24 Pause and be **q**, my people,
7:*85* of the others are guarded by angels in profound **q**.
7:*95* and guarded by angels in profound **q**,
10: 2 I remained **q** until the evening of the second day.
10: 3 encouraging me to be **q**, I got up in the night and

QUIETED (3) [QUIET]

Nu 13:30 But Caleb **q** the people before Moses, and said,
Ps 131: 2 But I have calmed and **q** my soul,
Ac 19:35 But when the town clerk had **q** the crowd, he said,

QUIETLY (9) [QUIET]

Pr 29:11 but the wise **q** holds it back.
Isa 18: 4 I will **q** look from my dwelling like clear heat
La 3:26 It is good that one should wait **q** for the salvation
Hab 3:16 I wait **q** for the day of calamity to come upon
Mt 1:19 to public disgrace, planned to dismiss her **q**.
1Th 4:11 to aspire to live **q**, to mind your own affairs,
2Th 3:12 to do their work **q** and to earn their own living.
Sir 21:20 when he laughs, but the wise smile **q**.
2Mc 12: 2 would not let them live **q** and in peace.

QUIETNESS (2) [QUIET]

Isa 30:15 in **q** and in trust shall be your strength.
32:17 and the result of righteousness, **q** and trust forever.

QUINTUS (1)

2Mc 11:34 "**Q** Memmius and Titus Manius,

QUIRINIUS (1)

Lk 2: 2 and was taken while **Q** was governor of Syria.

QUIT (1)

Isa 33: 8 highways are deserted, travelers have **q** the road.

QUITE (8)

Mk 8:32 He said all this **q** openly.
12:27 but of the living; you are **q** wrong."
Lk 13:11 She was bent over and was **q** unable to stand
1Co 4: 8 **Q** apart from us you have become kings!
AdE 16:10 and **q** devoid of our kindliness),
2Mc 3:31 the Most High to grant life to one who was lying **q**
3Mc 5:12 by so pleasant and deep a sleep that he **q** failed
4Mc 3: 8 evening fell, he came, sweating and **q** exhausted,

QUIVER (11) [QUIVERS]

Ge 27: 3 then, take your weapons, your **q** and your bow,
Job 39:23 Upon it rattle the **q**, the flashing spear,
Ps 127: 5 Happy is the man who has his **q** full of them.
Isa 15: 4 therefore the loins of Moab **q**; his soul trembles.
Isa 22: 6 Elam bore the **q** with chariots and cavalry,
49: 2 in his **q** he hid me away.
Jer 5:16 Their **q** is like an open tomb;
La 3:13 He shot into my vitals the arrows of his **q**;
Hab 3:16 my lips **q** at the sound.
Sir 16:19 of the earth **q** and quake when he looks upon them.
26:12 of every tent peg and open her **q** to the arrow.

QUIVERING See Index to Footnotes

QUIVERS (2) [QUIVER]

Jer 51:11 Sharpen the arrows! Fill the **q**!
Eze 27:11 They hung their **q** all around your walls;

QUOTE (1) [QUOTED]

Lk 4:23 "Doubtless you will **q** to me this proverb, 'Doctor,

QUOTED (1) [QUOTE]

Heb 4: 7 through David much later, in the words already **q**,

---

R

RAAMA (1) [=RAAMAH]

1Ch 1: 9 Seba, Havilah, Sabta, **R**, and Sabteca.

RAAMAH (4) [=RAAMA]

Ge 10: 7 Seba, Havilah, Sabtah, **R**, and Sabteca.
10: 7 The descendants of **R**: Sheba and Dedan.
1Ch 1: 9 The descendants of **R**: Sheba and Dedan.
Eze 27:22 The merchants of Sheba and **R** traded with you;

RAAMIAH (1)

Ne 7: 7 Nehemiah, Azariah, **R**, Nahamani, Mordecai,

RAAMSES (1) [=RAMESES]

Jdt 1: 9 Tahpanhes and **R** and the whole land of Goshen,

RAAMSES (KJV) See RAMESES

RABBAH (15)

Dt 3:11 can still be seen in **R** of the Ammonites.
Jos 13:25 to Aroer, which is east of **R**,
15:60 Kiriath-baal (that is, Kiriath-jearim), and **R**:
2Sa 11: 1 they ravaged the Ammonites, and besieged **R**.
12:26 Now Joab fought against **R** of the Ammonites,
12:27 and said, "I have fought against **R**;
12:29 the people together and went to **R**,
17:27 Shobi son of Nahash from **R** of the Ammonites,
1Ch 20: 1 and came and besieged **R**.
20: 1 Joab attacked **R**, and overthrew it.
Jer 49: 2 when I will sound the battle alarm against **R** of
49: 3 Cry out, O daughters of **R**!
Eze 21:20 for the sword to come to **R** of the Ammonites or
25: 5 I will make **R** a pasture for camels and Ammon
Am 1:14 So I will kindle a fire against the wall of **R**,

RABBATH (KJV) See RABBAH

RABBI (15) [RABBOUNI]

Mt 23: 7 and to have people call them **r**.
23: 8 But you are not to be called **r**,
26:25 Judas, who betrayed him, said, "Surely not I, **R**?"
26:49 up to Jesus and said, "Greetings, **R**!"
Mk 9: 5 Peter said to Jesus, "**R**, it is good for us to be here,
11:21 Then Peter remembered and said to him, "**R**, look!
14:45 he came, he went up to him at once and said, "**R**!"
Jn 1:38 "**R**" (which translated means Teacher),
1:49 Nathanael replied, "**R**, you are the Son of God!
3: 2 He came to Jesus by night and said to him, "**R**,
3:26 They came to John and said to him, "**R**,
4:31 Meanwhile the disciples were urging him, "**R**,
6:25 they said to him, "**R**, when did you come here?"
9: 2 His disciples asked him, "**R**, who sinned,
11: 8 The disciples said to him, "**R**,

RABBITH (1)

Jos 19:20 **R**, Kishion, Ebez,

RABBLE (3)

Nu 11: 4 The **r** among them had a strong craving;
Job 30:12 On my right hand the **r** rise up;
Eze 23:42 of the **r** brought in drunken from the wilderness;

RABBOUNI‡ (1) [RABBI]

Jn 20:16 She turned and said to him in Hebrew, "**R**!"

RABMAG (2)

Jer 39: 3 Sarsechim the Rabsaris, Nergal-sharezer the **R**,
39:13 Nebushazban the Rabsaris, Nergal-sharezer the **R**,

RABSARIS (3)

2Ki 18:17 The king of Assyria sent the Tartan, the **R**,
Jer 39: 3 Nergal-sharezer, Samgar-nebo, Sarsechim the **R**,
39:13 Nebushazban the **R**, Nergal-sharezer the Rabmag,

RABSHAKEH (16)

2Ki 18:17 and the **R** with a great army from Lachish
18:19 The **R** said to them, "Say to Hezekiah:
18:26 and Shebnah, and Joah said to the **R**,
18:27 But the **R** said to them,
18:28 Then the **R** stood and called out in a loud voice in
18:37 and told him the words of the **R**.
19: 4 the LORD your God heard all the words of the **R**,
19: 8 The **R** returned, and found the king
Isa 36: 2 The king of Assyria sent the **R** from Lachish
36: 4 The **R** said to them, "Say to Hezekiah:
36:11 Then Eliakim, Shebna, and Joah said to the **R**,
36:12 But the **R** said, "Has my master sent me
36:13 Then the **R** stood and called out in a loud voice in
36:22 and told him the words of the **R**.
37: 4 the LORD your God heard the words of the **R**,
37: 8 The **R** returned, and found the king

RACA See Index to Footnotes

RACAL (1)

1Sa 30:29 in **R**, in the towns of the Jerahmeelites,

RACE‡ (24) [RACED, RACES]

Job 15: 7 "Are you the firstborn of the human **r**?
Pr 8:31 and delighting in the human **r**.
Ecc 9:11 the sun the **r** is not to the swift, nor the battle to
Na 2: 4 The chariots **r** madly through the streets,
Ac 7:19 with our **r** and forced our ancestors
1Co 9:24 not know that in a **r** the runners all compete,
2Ti 4: 7 I have fought the good fight, I have finished the **r**,
Heb 12: 1 and let us run with perseverance the **r** that is set
1Pe 2: 9 But you are a chosen **r**, a royal priesthood,
Tob 8: 6 From the two of them the human **r** has sprung.
Jdt 5:10 a multitude that their **r** could not be counted.
6: 5 until I take revenge on this **r** that came out
AdE 3: 7 on one day to destroy the whole **r** of Mordecai.
Wis 10:15 A holy people and blameless **r** wisdom delivered
12:11 For they were an accursed **r** from the beginning,
Sir 44:17 in the time of wrath he kept the **r** alive;
2Mc 7:28 in the same way the human **r** came into being.
8: 9 to wipe out the whole **r** of Judea.
12:31 and exhorted them to be well disposed to their **r** in
1Es 8:70 the holy **r** has been mixed with the alien peoples
3Mc 4:14 The entire **r** was to be registered individually,
2Es 7:*65* Let the human **r** lament, but let the wild animals
8:34 or what is a corruptible **r**,
4Mc 17:14 the world and the human **r** were the spectators.

RACED (1) [RACE]

Jer 12: 5 If you have **r** with foot-runners

RACES (1) [RACE]

3Mc 3: 6 of other **r** paid no heed to their good service

RACHAB (KJV) See RAHAB

RACHAL (KJV) See RACAL

RACHEL (42) [RACHEL'S]

Ge 29: 6 "Yes," they replied, "and here is his daughter **R**,
29: 9 **R** came with her father's sheep; for she kept them.
29:10 Now when Jacob saw **R**, the daughter
29:11 Then Jacob kissed **R**, and wept aloud.
29:12 Jacob told **R** that he was her father's kinsman,
29:16 and the name of the younger was **R**.
29:17 and **R** was graceful and beautiful.
29:18 Jacob loved **R**; so he said,
29:18 for your younger daughter **R**."
29:20 So Jacob served seven years for **R**,
29:25 Did I not serve with you for **R**?
29:28 then Laban gave him his daughter **R** as a wife.
29:29 (Laban gave his maid Bilhah to his daughter **R** to
29:30 So Jacob went in to **R** also,
29:30 and he loved **R** more than Leah.
29:31 he opened her womb; but **R** was barren.
30: 1 When **R** saw that she bore Jacob no children,
30: 2 Jacob became very angry with **R** and said,
30: 6 Then **R** said, "God has judged me,
30: 8 Then **R** said, "With mighty wrestlings
30:14 Then **R** said to Leah, "Please give me some
30:15 **R** said, "Then he may lie with you tonight
30:22 Then God remembered **R**, and God heeded her
30:25 When **R** had borne Joseph, Jacob said to Laban,
31: 4 So Jacob sent and called **R** and Leah into the field
31:14 Then **R** and Leah answered him,
31:19 and **R** stole her father's household gods.
31:32 Jacob did not know that **R** had stolen the gods.
31:34 Now **R** had taken the household gods and put them
33: 1 the children among Leah and **R** and the two maids.
33: 2 and **R** and Joseph last of all.
33: 7 and finally Joseph and **R** drew near,
35:16 **R** was in childbirth, and she had hard labor.
35:19 So **R** died, and she was buried on the way
35:24 The sons of **R**: Joseph and Benjamin.
46:19 children of Jacob's wife **R**: Joseph and Benjamin.
46:22 the children of **R**, who were born to Jacob—

Ge 46:25 whom Laban gave to his daughter **R,**
48: 7 For when I came from Paddan, **R,** alas,
Ru 4:11 the woman who is coming into your house like **R**
Jer 31:15 **R** is weeping for her children;
Mt 2:18 **R** weeping for her children;

RACHEL'S (5) [RACHEL]

Ge 30: 7 **R** maid Bilhah conceived again and bore Jacob
31:33 And he went out of Leah's tent, and entered **R.**
35:20 it is the pillar of **R** tomb, which is there to this day.
35:25 The sons of Bilhah, **R** maid: Dan and Naphtali.
1Sa 10: 2 from me today you will meet two men by **R** tomb

RACK (6) [RACKINGS, RACKS]

2Mc 6:19 went up to the **r** of his own accord,
6:28 When he had said this, he went at once to the **r.**
4Mc 7:14 he rendered the many-headed **r** ineffective.
8:11 nothing remains for you but to die on the **r?"**
8:13 **r** and hooks and catapults and caldrons,
8:24 or take hollow pride in being put to the **r.**

RACKINGS (4) [RACK]

4Mc 9:22 by fire into immortality, he nobly endured the **r.**
14:12 of the seven young men bore up under the **r**
15:24 of seven children and the ingenious and various **r,**
15:25 family, parental love, and the **r** of her children—

RACKS (3) [RACK]

Job 30:17 The night **r** my bones, and the pain
Sir 33:27 and for a wicked slave there are **r** and tortures.
4Mc 7: 4 his sacred life was consumed by tortures and **r,**

RADDAI (1)

1Ch 2:14 Nethanel the fourth, **R** the fifth,

RADIANCE (2) [RADIANT]

Rev 21:11 the glory of God and a **r** like a very rare jewel,
Wis 7:10 because her **r** never ceases.

RADIANT (7) [RADIANCE]

Ps 34: 5 and be **r;** so your faces shall never be ashamed.
SS 5:10 My beloved is all **r** and ruddy,
Isa 26:19 For your dew is a **r** dew, and the earth will give
60: 5 Then you shall see and be **r;**
Jer 31:12 they shall be **r** over the goodness of the LORD,
AdE 15: 5 She was **r** with perfect beauty,
Wis 6:12 Wisdom is **r** and unfading,

RAFT (2) [RAFTS]

Wis 14: 5 through the billows on a **r** they come safely
14: 6 the hope of the world took refuge on a **r,**

RAFTERS (4)

1Ki 6:15 from the floor of the house to the **r** of the ceiling,
6:16 with boards of cedar from the floor to the **r,**
7: 3 It was roofed with cedar on the forty-five **r,**
SS 1:17 the beams of our house are cedar, our **r** are pine.

RAFTS (3) [RAFT]

1Ki 5: 9 into **r** to go by sea to the place you indicate.
2Ch 2:16 and bring it to you as **r** by sea to Joppa;
1Es 5:55 from Lebanon and convey them in **r** to the harbor

RAG (1) [RAGS]

AdE 14:16 I abhor it like a filthy **r,**

RAGAU (2)

Jdt 1: 5 in the great plain that is on the borders of **R.**
1:15 He captured Arphaxad in the mountains of **R**

RAGAU (KJV) See also REU

RAGE (28) [ENRAGED, RAGED, RAGES, RAGING]

2Ki 5:12 He turned and went away in a **r.**
2Ch 16:10 for he was in a **r** with him because of this.
28: 9 but you have killed them in a **r** that has reached up
Job 39:24 With fierceness and **r** it swallows the ground;
Ps 78:21 when the LORD heard, he was full of **r;**
Isa 28:21 he will **r** as in the valley of Gibeon;
Da 2:12 a violent **r** and commanded that all the wise men
3:13 in furious **r** commanded that Shadrach, Meshach,
3:19 Then Nebuchadnezzar was so filled with **r**
11:11 Moved with **r,** the king of the south shall go out
Hos 7:16 by the sword because of the **r** of their tongue.
Hab 3: 8 or your **r** against the sea,
Lk 4:28 all in the synagogue were filled with **r.**
Ac 4:25 'Why did the Gentiles **r,** and the peoples imagine
Wis 5:22 the water of the sea will **r** against them,
10: 3 he perished because in **r** he killed his brother.
11:18 or newly-created unknown beasts full of **r,** or such
16: 5 For when the terrible **r** of wild animals came
2Mc 4:25 of a cruel tyrant and the **r** of a savage wild beast.
7: 3 The king fell into a **r,**
7:39 The king fell into a **r,**
9: 4 with **r,** he conceived the idea of turning upon
9: 7 breathing fire in his **r** against the Jews,
10:28 while the other made **r** their leader in the fight.
3Mc 4:13 in his **r** that these people be dealt with in precisely
5:47 he had filled his impious mind with a deep **r,**
4Mc 8: 2 then in violent **r** he commanded that others of
18:20 and in his burning **r** brought those seven sons of

RAGED (5) [RAGE]

2Ki 19:28 Because you have **r** against me
Isa 37:29 Because you have **r** against me
Ac 27:20 for many days, and no small tempest **r,** all hope
Rev 11:18 The nations **r,** but your wrath has come,
1Mc 9:13 and the battle **r** from morning until evening.

RAGES‡ (11) [RAGE]

Pr 19: 3 yet the heart **r** against the LORD.
Hos 11: 6 The sword **r** in their cities,
Na 1: 2 on his adversaries and **r** against his enemies.
Tob 4: 1 that he had left in trust with Gabael at **R** in Media,
4:20 in trust with Gabael son of Gabrias, at **R** in Media.
5: 6 with our kinsman Gabael who lives in **R** of Media.
5: 6 It is a journey of two days from Ecbatana to **R;**
6:13 we return from **R** we will celebrate her marriage.
6:13 from **R** we will take her and bring her back with us
9: 2 and two camels with you and travel to **R.**
9: 5 with the four servants and two camels went to **R**

RAGING (16) [RAGE]

2Ki 19:27 and coming in, and your **r** against me.
Ps 55: 8 a shelter for myself from the **r** wind and tempest."
89: 9 You rule the **r** of the sea;
124: 5 then over us would have gone the **r** waters.
SS 8: 6 Its flashes are flashes of fire, a **r** flame.
Isa 37:28 down, your going out and coming in, and your **r**
Da 3:22 the **r** flames killed the men who lifted Shadrach,
Jnh 1:15 and the sea ceased from its **r.**
Lk 8:24 up and rebuked the wind and the **r** waves;
Heb 11:34 quenched **r** fire, escaped the edge of the sword,
Wis 14: 1 about to voyage over **r** waves calls upon a piece
14:25 and all is a **r** riot of blood and murder,
19: 7 and a grassy plain out of the **r** waves,
2Mc 5:11 So, **r** inwardly, he left Egypt and took the city
2Es 15:30 Also the Carmonians, **r** in wrath,
4Mc 16: 3 the **r** fiery furnace of Mishael so intensely hot,

RAGS (4) [RAG]

Pr 23:21 and drowsiness will clothe them with **r.**
Isa 30:22 You will scatter them like filthy **r;**
Jer 38:11 and took from there old **r** and worn-out clothes,
38:12 "Just put the **r** and clothes between your armpits

RAGUEL‡ (24) [RAGUEL'S]

Tob 3: 7 it also happened that Sarah, the daughter of **R,**
3:17 and Sarah, daughter of **R,**
3:17 daughter of **R** came down from her upper room.
6:11 "We must stay this night in the home of **R.**
6:13 For I know that **R** can by no means keep her
7: 1 take me straight to our brother **R."**
7: 6 At that **R** jumped up and kissed him and wept.
7: 9 Then **R** slaughtered a ram from the flock
7: 9 ask **R** to give me my kinswoman Sarah."
7:10 But **R** overheard it and said to the lad,
7:11 So **R** said, "I will do so.
7:12 Then **R** summoned his daughter Sarah.
7:15 **R** called his wife Edna and said to her, "Sister,
8: 9 But **R** arose and called his servants to him,
8:11 **R** went into his house and called his wife,
8:15 So they blessed the God of heaven, and **R** said,
9: 3 You are witness to the oath **R** has sworn,
10: 7 that **R** had sworn to observe for his daughter,
10: 8 **R** said to Tobias, "Stay, my child, stay with me;
10:10 So **R** promptly gave Tobias his wife Sarah,
10:13 Tobias parted from **R** with happiness and joy,
10:13 Finally, he blessed **R** and his wife Edna, and said,
14:12 and settled in Ecbatana with **R** his father-in-law.
14:13 both the property of **R** and that of his father Tobit.

RAGUEL (KJV) See also REUEL

RAGUEL'S (3) [RAGUEL]

Tob 7: 1 So he took him to **R** house,
9: 6 into **R** house they found Tobias reclining at table.
11:15 that he had married **R** daughter Sarah,

RAHAB (14)

Jos 2: 1 the house of a prostitute whose name was **R,**
2: 3 Then the king of Jericho sent orders to **R,**
6:17 Only **R** the prostitute and all who are with her
6:23 in and brought **R** out,
6:25 But **R** the prostitute, with her family
Job 9:13 the helpers of **R** bowed beneath him.
26:12 by his understanding he struck down **R.**
Ps 87: 4 Among those who know me I mention **R**
89:10 You crushed **R** like a carcass;
Isa 30: 7 therefore I have called her, **"R** who sits still."
51: 9 Was it not you who cut **R** in pieces,
Mt 1: 5 and Salmon the father of Boaz by **R,**
Heb 11:31 By faith **R** the prostitute did not perish
Jas 2:25 was not **R** the prostitute also justified by works

RAHAM (1)

1Ch 2:44 Shema became father of **R,** father of Jorkeam;

RAHEL (KJV) See RACHEL

RAID (12) [RAIDED, RAIDERS, RAIDING, RAIDS]

Ge 49:19 but he shall **r** at their heels.
Jdg 15: 9 and made a **r** on Lehi.
1Sa 23:27 for the Philistines have made a **r** on the land."
27:10 "Against whom have you made a **r** today?"
30: 1 the Amalekites had made a **r** on the Negeb and
30:14 We had made a **r** on the Negeb of the Cherethites
2Sa 3:22 the servants of David arrived with Joab from a **r,**
1Ch 7:21 because they came down to **r** their cattle.
14: 9 Now the Philistines had come and made a **r** in
14:13 Once again the Philistines made a **r** in the valley.
Job 1:17 made a **r** on the camels and carried them off,
Hos 7: 1 the thief breaks in, and the bandits **r** outside.

RAIDED (1) [RAID]

Ge 49:19 Gad shall be **r** by raiders,

RAIDERS (4) [RAID]

Ge 49:19 Gad shall be raided by **r,**
1Sa 13:17 And **r** came out of the camp of the Philistines
14:15 the garrison and even the **r** trembled;
1Ch 12:21 They helped David against the band of **r,**

RAIDING (5) [RAID]

Jdg 11: 3 Outlaws collected around Jephthah and went **r**
1Sa 30:15 "Will you take me down to this **r** party?"
30:23 and handed over to us the **r** party that attacked us.
2Sa 4: 2 Saul's son had two captains of **r** bands;
2Ki 6:23 Arameans no longer came **r** into the land of Israel.

RAIDS (4) [RAID]

1Sa 27: 8 up and made **r** on the Geshurites, the Girzites,
2Ki 5: 2 on one of their **r** had taken a young girl captive
2Ch 28:18 And the Philistines had made **r** on the cities in
1Mc 15:41 so that they might go out and make **r** along

RAIL (1) [RAILING]

Nu 16:11 What is Aaron that you **r** against him?"

RAILING (1) [RAIL]

2Mc 12:14 **r** at them and even blaspheming and saying unholy

RAIMENT (KJV) See CLOAK, CLOTH, CLOTHED, CLOTHES, CLOTHING, COATS, GARB, GARMENT[S], ROBES

RAIN (116) [RAINBOW, RAINDROPS, RAINED, RAINS, RAINSTORM, RAINY]

Ge 2: 5 LORD God had not caused it to **r** upon the earth,
7: 4 For in seven days I will send **r** on the earth
7:12 The **r** fell on the earth forty days and forty nights.
8: 2 the **r** from the heavens was restrained,
Ex 9:33 and the **r** no longer poured down on the earth.
9:34 that the **r** and the hail and the thunder had ceased,
16: 4 "I am going to **r** bread from heaven for you,
Dt 11:11 watered by **r** from the sky,
11:14 he will give the **r** for your land in its season, the early **r** and the later **r,**
11:17 there will be no **r** and the land will yield no fruit;
28:12 to give the **r** of your land in its season and
28:24 The LORD will change the **r** of your land
32: 2 May my teaching drop like the **r,**
32: 2 like gentle **r** on grass, like showers on new growth.
1Sa 12:17 that he may send thunder and **r;**
12:18 and the LORD sent thunder and **r** that day;
2Sa 1:21 let there be no dew or **r** upon you,
21:10 from the beginning of harvest until **r** fell on them
23: 4 gleaming from the **r** on the grassy land.
1Ki 8:35 up and there is no **r** because they have sinned
8:36 and grant **r** on your land,
17: 1 there shall be neither dew nor **r** these years,
17: 7 wadi dried up, because there was no **r** in the land.
17:14 not fail until the day that the LORD sends **r** on
18: 1 I will send **r** on the earth."
18:41 for there is a sound of rushing **r."**
18:44 and go down before the **r** stops you.' "
18:45 and wind; there was a heavy **r.**
2Ki 3:17 'You shall see neither wind nor **r,**
2Ch 6:26 up and there is no **r** because they have sinned
6:27 and send down **r** upon your land,
7:13 When I shut up the heavens so that there is no **r,**
Ezr 10: 9 because of this matter and because of the heavy **r.**
10:13 the people are many, and it is a time of heavy **r;**
Job 5:10 He gives **r** on the earth and sends waters on
20:23 and **r** it upon them as their food.
24: 8 They are wet with the **r** of the mountains,
28:26 a decree for the **r,** and a way for the thunderbolt;
29:23 They waited for me as for the **r;**
29:23 they opened their mouths as for the spring **r.**
36:27 he distills his mist in **r,**
37: 6 and the shower of **r,** his heavy shower of **r,**
38:25 "Who has cut a channel for the torrents of **r,**
38:26 to bring **r** on a land where no one lives,
38:28 "Has the **r** a father, or who has begotten the drops
Ps 11: 6 On the wicked he will **r** coals of fire and sulfur;
68: 8 heavens poured down **r** at the presence of God,
68: 9 **R** in abundance, O God, you showered abroad;
72: 6 May he be like **r** that falls on the mown grass,
84: 6 the early **r** also covers it with pools.
105:32 He gave them hail for **r,**

Ps 135: 7 he makes lightnings for the **r** and brings out
147: 8 the heavens with clouds, prepares **r** for the earth,
Pr 16:15 his favor is like the clouds that bring the spring **r**.
19:13 a wife's quarreling is a continual dripping of **r**.
25:14 Like clouds and wind without **r** is one who boasts
25:23 The north wind produces **r**,
26: 1 Like snow in summer or **r** in harvest,
28: 3 A ruler who oppresses the poor is a beating **r**
Ecc 11: 3 When clouds are full, they empty **r** on the earth;
12: 2 and the clouds return with the **r**;
SS 2:11 for now the winter is past, the **r** is over and gone.
Isa 4: 6 and a refuge and a shelter from the storm and **r**.
5: 6 I will also command the clouds that they **r** no **r**
30:23 He will give **r** for the seed with which you sow
44:14 He plants a cedar and the **r** nourishes it.
45: 8 and let the skies **r** down righteousness;
55:10 as the **r** and the snow come down from heaven,
Jer 3: 3 and the spring **r** has not come;
5:24 the **r** in its season, the autumn **r** and the spring **r**,
10:13 He makes lightnings for the **r**,
14: 4 Because there has been no **r** on the land
14:22 Can any idols of the nations bring **r**?
51:16 He makes lightnings for the **r**,
Eze 13:11 There will be a deluge of **r**,
13:13 and in my anger there shall be a deluge of **r**,
Hos 10:12 that he may come and **r** righteousness upon you.
Joel 2:23 the early **r** for your vindication, he has poured
down for you abundant **r**, the early and the later **r**,
Am 4: 7 the **r** from you when there were still three months
4: 7 I would send **r** on one city, and send no **r** on
4: 7 and the field on which it did not **r** withered;
Zec 10: 1 Ask **r** from the LORD in the season of the spring **r**,
10: 1 who gives showers of **r** to you,
14:17 the LORD of hosts, there will be no **r** upon them.
Mt 5:45 sends **r** on the righteous and on the unrighteous.
7:25 The **r** fell, the floods came,
7:27 The **r** fell, and the floods came,
Lk 12:54 you immediately say, 'It is going to **r**';
Ac 28: 2 Since it had begun to **r** and was cold,
Heb 6: 7 that drinks up the **r** falling on it repeatedly,
Jas 5:17 and he prayed fervently that it might not **r**, and for
three years and six months it did not **r** on
5:18 the heaven gave **r** and the earth yielded its harvest.
Rev 11: 6 no **r** may fall during the days of their prophesying,
Jdt 8:31 so that the Lord may send us **r** to fill our cisterns.
Wis 16:22 in the hail and flashed in the showers of **r**;
Sir 1: 2 The sand of the sea, the drops of **r**,
35:26 as welcome in time of distress as clouds of **r**
LtJ 6:53 up a king over a country or give **r** to people.
Aza 1:42 "Bless the Lord, all **r** and dew;
2Es 4:49 before me and poured down a heavy and violent **r**,
4:50 for just as the **r** is more than the drops,
7:*41* or hail or **r** or dew,
7:*109* [39] and Elijah for those who received the **r**,
8:43 because it has not received your **r** in due season,
8:43 or if it has been ruined by too much **r**, it perishes.

RAINBOW (4) [RAIN]

Rev 4: 3 around the throne is a **r** that looks like an emerald.
10: 1 wrapped in a cloud, with a **r** over his head;
Sir 43:11 Look at the **r**, and praise him who made it;
50: 7 like the **r** gleaming in splendid clouds;

RAINDROPS (1) [RAIN]

2Es 5:36 and gather for me the scattered **r**,

RAINED (8) [RAIN]

Ge 19:24 the LORD **r** on Sodom and Gomorrah sulfur
Ex 9:23 And the LORD **r** hail on the land of Egypt;
Ps 78:24 he **r** down on them manna to eat,
78:27 he **r** flesh upon them like dust, winged birds like
Eze 22:24 not **r** upon in the day of indignation.
Am 4: 7 one field would be **r** upon,
Lk 17:29 it **r** fire and sulfur from heaven and destroyed all
Sir 1:19 She **r** down knowledge and discerning

RAINS (6) [RAIN]

Lev 26: 4 I will give you your **r** in their season,
Eze 38:22 and I will pour down torrential **r** and hailstones,
Hos 6: 3 like the spring **r** that water the earth."
Ac 14:17 giving you **r** from heaven and fruitful seasons,
Jas 5: 7 with it until it receives the early and the late **r**.
Wis 16:16 by unusual **r** and hail and relentless storms,

RAINSTORM (3) [RAIN, STORM]

Isa 25: 4 a shelter from the **r** and a shade from the heat.
25: 4 When the blast of the ruthless was like a winter **r**,
2Es 4:49 and when the violent **r** had passed,

RAINY (2) [RAIN]

Pr 27:15 on a **r** day and a contentious wife are alike;
Eze 1:28 Like the bow in a cloud on a **r** day,

RAISE (106) [RISE]

Ge 13:14 "**R** your eyes now, and look from the place
38: 8 **r** up offspring for your brother."
39:15 and when he heard me **r** my voice and cry out,
Ex 29:24 **r** them as an elevation offering before the LORD.
29:26 the breast of the ram of Aaron's ordination and **r** it
Lev 10:15 to **r** for an elevation offering before the LORD;
14:12 **r** them as an elevation offering before the LORD.
14:24 and the priest shall **r** them as an elevation offering
23:11 He shall **r** the sheaf before the LORD,
Lev 23:11 on the day after the sabbath the priest shall **r** it.
23:12 On the day when you **r** the sheaf,
23:20 The priest shall **r** them with the bread of
Dt 18:15 The LORD your God will **r** up for you a prophet
18:18 I will **r** up for them a prophet like you from
1Sa 2:35 I will **r** up for myself a faithful priest,
18:17 For Saul thought, "I will not **r** a hand against him;
22:17 But the servants of the king would not **r** their hand
24: 6 the LORD's anointed, to **r** my hand against him;
24:10 I said, 'I will not **r** my hand against my lord;
26: 9 who can **r** his hand against the LORD's anointed,
26:11 The LORD forbid that I should **r** my hand against
26:23 into my hand today, but I would not **r** my hand
2Sa 7:12 I will **r** up your offspring after you,
12:11 I will **r** up trouble against you from
18:12 I would not **r** my hand against the king's son;
1Ki 14:14 LORD will **r** up for himself a king over Israel,
1Ch 15:16 to **r** loud sounds of joy.
17:11 I will **r** up your offspring after you,
Ps 41:10 you, O LORD, be gracious to me, and **r** me up,
81: 2 **R** a song, sound the tambourine,
Pr 2: 3 and **r** your voice for understanding;
8: 1 and does not understanding **r** her voice?
Isa 5:26 He will **r** a signal for a nation far away,
10:15 As if a rod should **r** the one who lifts it up,
11:12 He will **r** a signal for the nations,
13: 2 On a bare hill **r** a signal, cry aloud to them;
14:13 I will **r** my throne above the stars of God;
15: 5 the road to Horonaim they **r** a cry of destruction;
29: 3 I will besiege you with towers and **r** siegeworks
44:26 "They shall be rebuilt, and I will **r** up their ruins";
49: 6 that you should be my servant to **r** up the tribes
49:22 and **r** my signal to the peoples;
58:12 you shall **r** up the foundations
61: 4 they shall **r** up the former devastations;
Jer 4: 6 **R** a standard toward Zion, flee for safety,
6: 1 and **r** a signal on Beth-haccherem;
7:16 do not **r** a cry or prayer on their behalf,
7:29 **r** a lamentation on the bare heights,
9:18 let them quickly **r** a dirge over us,
23: 4 I will **r** up shepherds over them
23: 5 when I will **r** up for David a righteous Branch,
30: 9 whom I will **r** up for them.
31: 7 and **r** shouts for the chief of the nations;
50:15 **R** a shout against her from all sides,
50:32 with no one to **r** him up,
51:12 **R** a standard against the walls of Babylon;
51:14 and they shall **r** a shout of victory over you.
51:27 **R** a standard in the land, blow the trumpet among
Eze 19: 1 you, **r** up a lamentation for the princes of Israel,
26: 8 and **r** a roof of shields against you.
26:17 And they shall **r** a lamentation over you,
27: 2 Now you, mortal, **r** a lamentation over Tyre,
27:32 In their wailing they **r** a lamentation for you,
28:12 **r** a lamentation over the king of Tyre,
32: 2 **r** a lamentation over Pharaoh king of Egypt,
Da 11:13 For the king of the north shall again **r** a multitude,
Hos 6: 2 on the third day he will **r** us up,
11: 7 but he does not **r** them up at all.
Am 5: 2 forsaken on her land, with no one to **r** her up.
9:11 On that day I will **r** up the booth of David
9:11 and repair its breaches, and **r** up its ruins,
Mic 5: 5 we will **r** against them seven shepherds
Zec 2: 9 See now, I am going to **r** my hand against them,
Mt 3: 9 for I tell you, God is able from these stones to **r**
10: 8 Cure the sick, **r** the dead, cleanse the lepers,
22:24 and **r** up children for his brother.'
Mk 2: 8 "Why do you **r** such questions in your hearts?
12:19 the man shall marry the widow and **r** up children
Lk 3: 8 for I tell you, God is able from these stones to **r**
5:22 "Why do you **r** such questions in your hearts?
20:28 the man shall marry the widow and **r** up children
21:28 stand up and **r** your heads,
Jn 2:19 and in three days I will **r** it up."
2:20 and will you **r** it up in three days?"
6:39 but **r** it up on the last day.
6:40 and I will **r** them up on the last day."
6:44 and I will **r** that person up on the last day.
6:54 and I will **r** them up on the last day;
Ac 3:22 'The Lord your God will **r** up for you
7:37 'God will **r** up a prophet for you
1Co 6:14 And God raised the Lord and will also **r** us
15:15 whom he did not **r** if it is true that the dead are
2Co 4:14 the one who raised the Lord Jesus will **r** us also
Heb 11:19 the fact that God is able even to **r** someone from
Jas 5:15 and the Lord will **r** them up;
Tob 3:12 I turn my face to you, and **r** my eyes toward you.
Jdt 16: 1 **R** to him a new psalm; exalt him, and call upon his
Sir 10: 4 over it he will **r** up the right leader for the time.
1Mc 3:31 and collect the revenues from those regions and **r**
12:39 and to **r** his hand against King Antiochus.
12:42 he was afraid to **r** his hand against him.
2Mc 7: 9 the universe will **r** us up to an everlasting renewal
7:34 you **r** your hand against the children of heaven.
2Es 2:16 And I will **r** up the dead from their places,
12:23 the Most High will **r** up three kings,
4Mc 2:14 from marauders and helps **r** up what has fallen.

RAISED‡ (163) [RISE]

Ge 39:18 but as soon as I **r** my voice and cried out,
Ex 29:27 the breast that was **r** as an elevation offering and
29:27 as an elevation offering and the thigh that was **r** as
40:18 and put in its poles, and **r** up its pillars;
Lev 7:30 so that the breast may be **r** as an elevation offering
8:27 **r** them as an elevation offering before the LORD.
8:29 the breast and **r** it as an elevation offering before
Lev 9:21 the right thigh Aaron **r** as an elevation offering
10:14 the breast that is elevated and the thigh that is **r**,
10:15 The thigh that is **r** and the breast
Nu 14: 1 Then all the congregation **r** a loud cry,
Dt 17: 7 the witnesses shall be the first **r** against the person
Jos 5: 7 it was their children, whom he **r** up in their place,
6:20 they **r** a great shout, and the wall fell down flat;
7:26 and **r** over him a great heap of stones that remains
8:29 and **r** over it a great heap of stones,
Jdg 2:16 Then the LORD **r** up judges,
2:18 Whenever the LORD **r** up judges for them,
3: 9 the LORD **r** up a deliverer for the Israelites,
3:15 the LORD **r** up for them a deliverer,
1Sa 30: 4 and the people who were with him **r** their voices
2Sa 13:36 and **r** their voices and wept;
18:17 and **r** over him a very great heap of stones.
18:28 who has delivered up the men who **r** their hand
1Ki 11:14 the LORD **r** up an adversary against Solomon,
11:23 God **r** up another adversary against Solomon,
2Ki 19:22 Against whom have you **r** your voice
2Ch 5:13 and when the song was **r**,
13:15 Then the people of Judah **r** the battle shout.
32: 5 **r** towers on it, and outside it he built another wall;
33:14 and **r** it to a very great height.
Job 2:12 and they **r** their voices and wept aloud;
31:21 if I have **r** my hand against the orphan,
Ps 83: 2 those who hate you have **r** their heads.
106:26 Therefore he **r** his hand and swore to them
107:25 For he commanded and **r** the stormy wind,
131: 1 my eyes are not **r** too high;
148:14 He has **r** up a horn for his people,
Isa 2: 2 and shall be **r** above the hills;
9:11 So the LORD **r** adversaries against them,
16:10 the vineyards no songs are sung, no shouts are **r**;
18: 3 when a signal is **r** on the mountains, look!
37:23 Against whom have you **r** your voice
49:11 and my highways shall be **r** up.
Jer 6:17 Also I **r** up sentinels for you:
29:15 LORD has **r** up prophets for us in Babylon,"—
La 2: 7 a clamor was **r** in the house of the LORD as on
Eze 19: 3 She **r** up one of her cubs;
41: 8 also that the temple had a **r** platform all around;
Da 7: 5 It was **r** up on one side,
12: 7 **r** his right hand and his left hand toward heaven.
Am 2:11 And I **r** up some of your children to be prophets
Mic 4: 1 and shall be **r** up above the hills.
Hab 3:10 The sun **r** high its hands;
Zec 1:21 so that no head could be **r**;
14:13 and the hand of the one will be **r** against the hand
Mt 11: 5 the deaf hear, the dead are **r**,
14: 2 he has been **r** from the dead,
16:21 and be killed, and on the third day be **r**.
17: 9 after the Son of Man has been **r** from the dead."
17:23 and on the third day he will be **r**."
20:19 and on the third day he will be **r**."
26:32 after I am **r** up, I will go ahead of you to Galilee."
27:52 of the saints who had fallen asleep were **r**.
27:64 and tell the people, 'He has been **r** from the dead,'
28: 6 He is not here; for he has been **r**, as he said.
28: 7 'He has been **r** from the dead,
Mk 6:14 "John the baptizer has been **r** from the dead;
6:16 he said, "John, whom I beheaded, has been **r**."
12:26 And as for the dead being **r**,
14:28 after I am **r** up, I will go before you to Galilee."
16: 6 He has been **r**; he is not here.
Lk 1:69 He has **r** up a mighty savior for us in the house
7:22 the deaf hear, the dead are **r**,
9: 7 because it was said by some that John had been **r**
9:22 and be killed, and on the third day be **r**."
11:27 a woman in the crowd **r** her voice and said to him,
20:37 the fact that the dead are **r** Moses himself showed,
Jn 2:22 After he was **r** from the dead,
12: 1 whom he had **r** from the dead.
12: 9 whom he had **r** from the dead.
12:17 when he called Lazarus out of the tomb and **r** him
21:14 that Jesus appeared to the disciples after he was **r**
Ac 2:14 **r** his voice and addressed them,
2:24 But God **r** him up, having freed him from death,
2:32 This Jesus God **r** up, and of that all
3: 7 And he took him by the right hand and **r** him up;
3:15 whom God **r** from the dead.
3:26 When God **r** up his servant, he sent him first to you
4:10 whom you crucified, whom God **r** from the dead.
4:24 they **r** their voices together to God and said,
5:30 The God of our ancestors **r** up Jesus,
7:37 for you from your own people as he **r** me up.'
10:40 but God **r** him on the third day and allowed him
13:30 But God **r** him from the dead;
13:37 but he whom God **r** up experienced no corruption.
Ro 4:24 to us who believe in him who **r** Jesus our Lord
4:25 for our trespasses and was **r** for our justification.
6: 4 just as Christ was **r** from the dead by the glory of
6: 9 We know that Christ, being **r** from the dead,
7: 4 to him who has been **r** from the dead in order
8:11 the Spirit of him who **r** Jesus from the dead dwells
8:11 he who **r** Christ from the dead will give life
8:34 It is Christ Jesus, who died, yes, who was **r**,
9:17 "I have **r** you up for the very purpose
10: 9 and believe in your heart that God **r** him from
1Co 6:14 And God **r** the Lord and will also raise us
15: 4 that he was **r** on the third day in accordance with
15:12 Now if Christ is proclaimed as **r** from the dead,
15:13 then Christ has not been **r**;
15:14 and if Christ has not been **r**,
15:15 because we testified of God that he **r** Christ—
15:15 not raise if it is true that the dead are not **r**.
15:16 if the dead are not **r**, then Christ has not been **r**.

1Co 15:17 If Christ has not been **r**, your faith is futile
15:20 But in fact Christ has been **r** from the dead,
15:29 If the dead are not **r** at all,
15:32 If the dead are not **r**, "Let us eat and drink,
15:35 But someone will ask, "How are the dead **r**?
15:42 is sown is perishable, what is **r** is imperishable.
15:43 It is sown in dishonor, it is **r** in glory.
15:43 It is sown in weakness, it is **r** in power.
15:44 It is sown a physical body, it is **r** a spiritual body.
15:52 and the dead will be **r** imperishable,
2Co 4:14 that the one who **r** the Lord Jesus will raise us also
5:15 but for him who died and was **r** for them.
10: 5 and every proud obstacle **r** up against
Gal 1: 1 who **r** him from the dead—
Eph 1:20 to work in Christ when he **r** him from the dead
2: 6 and **r** us up with him and seated us with him in
Col 2:12 also **r** with him through faith in the power of God,
2:12 who **r** him from the dead.
3: 1 So if you have been **r** with Christ,
1Th 1:10 whom he **r** from the dead—
2Ti 2: 8 Remember Jesus Christ, **r** from the dead,
Jas 1: 9 Let the believer who is lowly boast in being **r** up,
1Pe 1:21 who **r** him from the dead and gave him glory,
Rev 10: 5 on the sea and the land **r** his right hand to heaven
Jdt 1: 3 At its gates he **r** towers one hundred cubits high
10:23 but his slaves **r** her up.
14: 7 they **r** him up he threw himself at Judith's feet,
14: 9 the people **r** a great shout and made a joyful noise
AdE 15:11 Then he **r** the golden scepter and touched her neck
Sir 20:11 and there are some who have **r** their heads
48: 5 You **r** a corpse from death and from Hades,
49:12 the house and **r** a temple holy to the Lord,
49:13 he **r** our fallen walls, and set up gates and bars,
50:20 down and **r** his hands over the whole congregation
51:12 *He has r up a horn for his people,*
Bar 2: 5 They were brought down and not **r** up,
LtJ 6:18 of the dust **r** by the feet of those who enter.
Sus 1:60 whole assembly **r** a great shout and blessed God,
2Mc 7:14 and to cherish the hope God gives of being **r** again
12:37 the language of their ancestors he **r** the battle cry,
1Es 8:81 and **r** Zion from desolation,
3Mc 5:48 the Jews saw the dust **r** by the elephants going out
6:17 the Jews observed this they **r** great cries to heaven
2Es 3:23 and you **r** up for yourself a servant, named David.
7:37 to the nations that have been **r** from the dead,
11:18 Then the third wing **r** itself up,
15:39 the cloud that was **r** in wrath, and shall dispel it;
4Mc 6: 6 yet while the old man's eyes were **r** to heaven,

RAISES (15) [RISE]

1Sa 2: 6 he brings down to Sheol and **r** up.
2: 8 He **r** up the poor from the dust;
Job 41:25 When it **r** itself up the gods are afraid;
Ps 107:41 but he **r** up the needy out of distress,
113: 7 He **r** the poor from the dust,
145:14 and **r** up all who are bowed down.
Pr 1:20 in the squares she **r** her voice.
Isa 14: 9 it **r** from their thrones all who were kings of the
19:16 the hand that the LORD of hosts **r** against them.
Jn 5:21 just as the Father **r** the dead and gives them life,
Ac 26: 8 by any of you that God **r** the dead?
2Co 1: 9 not on ourselves but on God who **r** the dead.
Sir 11:13 **r** up their heads to the amazement of the many.
21:20 A fool **r** his voice when he laughs,
28:17 The blow of a whip **r** a welt,

RAISIN (2) [RAISINS]

Isa 16: 7 utterly stricken, for the **r** cakes of Kir-hareseth.
Hos 3: 1 though they turn to other gods and love **r** cakes."

RAISING (9) [RISE]

Eze 21:22 to call out for slaughter, for **r** the battle cry,
Am 6:14 Indeed, I am **r** up against you a nation,
Zec 11:16 now **r** up in the land a shepherd who does not care
Ac 13:33 for us, their children, by **r** Jesus;
13:34 As to his **r** him from the dead,
17:31 of this he has given assurance to all by **r** him from
1Co 10:25 in the meat market without **r** any question on
10:27 before you without **r** any question on the ground
3Mc 4: 6 all together **r** a lament instead of a wedding song,

RAISINS (7) [RAISIN]

1Sa 25:18 one hundred clusters of **r**,
30:12 a piece of fig cake and two clusters of **r**.
2Sa 6:19 a portion of meat, and a cake of **r**.
16: 1 one hundred bunches of **r**,
1Ch 12:40 cakes of figs, clusters of **r**, wine, oil, oxen,
16: 3 a portion of meat, and a cake of **r**.
SS 2: 5 Sustain me with **r**, refresh me with apples;

RAKKATH (1)

Jos 19:35 The fortified towns are Ziddim, Zer, Hammath, **R**,

RAKKON (1)

Jos 19:46 Me-jarkon, and **R** at the border opposite Joppa.

RALLIED (6) [RALLY]

1Sa 14:20 Then Saul and all the people who were with him **r**
2Sa 2:25 The Benjaminites **r** around Abner and formed
Jdt 1: 6 There **r** to him all the people of the hill country
1Mc 11:47 and they all **r** around him and then spread out
14:30 Jonathan **r** the nation, became their high priest,
15:10 All the troops **r** to him,

RALLY (4) [RALLIED, RALLYING]

2Sa 3:21 "Let me go and **r** all Israel to my lord the king,
Ne 4:20 **R** to us wherever you hear the sound of
Ps 60: 4 to **r** to it out of bowshot.
1Mc 2:67 You shall **r** around you all who observe the law,

RALLYING (1) [RALLY]

1Mc 5:53 Judas kept **r** the laggards and encouraging

RAM (97) [RAM'S, RAMS, RAMS']

Ge 15: 9 a female goat three years old, a **r** three years old,
22:13 And Abraham looked up and saw a **r**,
22:13 Abraham went and took the **r** and offered it up as
Ex 29:15 lay their hands on the head of the **r**,
29:16 and you shall slaughter the **r**,
29:17 Then you shall cut the **r** into its parts,
29:18 and turn the whole **r** into smoke on the altar;
29:19 You shall take the other **r**;
29:19 lay their hands on the head of the **r**,
29:20 and you shall slaughter the **r**,
29:22 You shall also take the fat of the **r**, the fat tail,
29:22 and the right thigh (for it is a **r** of ordination),
29:26 of the **r** of Aaron's ordination and raise it as
29:27 that was raised as an elevation offering from the **r**
29:31 You shall take the **r** of ordination,
29:32 and Aaron and his sons shall eat the flesh of the **r**
Lev 5:15 a **r** without blemish from the flock,
5:16 on your behalf with the **r** of the guilt offering,
5:18 to the priest a **r** without blemish from the flock,
6: 6 a **r** without blemish from the flock,
8:18 Then he brought forward the **r** of burnt offering.
8:18 and his sons laid their hands on the head of the **r**,
8:20 The **r** was cut into its parts,
8:21 Moses turned into smoke the whole **r** on the altar;
8:22 Then he brought forward the second **r**, the **r** of
8:22 and his sons laid their hands on the head of the **r**,
8:29 it was Moses' portion of the **r** of ordination,
9: 2 "Take a bull calf for a sin offering and a **r** for
9: 4 a **r** for an offering of well-being to sacrifice before
9:18 the **r** as a sacrifice of well-being for the people.
9:19 and the fat of the ox and of the **r**—
16: 3 with a young bull for a sin offering and a **r** for
16: 5 and one **r** for a burnt offering.
19:21 of the tent of meeting, a **r** as guilt offering.
19:22 the priest shall make atonement for him with the **r**
Nu 5: 8 the **r** of atonement with which atonement is made
6:14 one **r** without blemish as an offering
6:17 and shall offer the **r** as a sacrifice of well-being to
6:19 The priest shall take the shoulder of the **r**,
7:15 one **r**, one male lamb a year old,
7:21 one **r**, one male lamb a year old,
7:27 one **r**, one male lamb a year old,
7:33 one **r**, one male lamb a year old,
7:39 one **r**, one male lamb a year old,
7:45 one **r**, one male lamb a year old,
7:51 one **r**, one male lamb a year old,
7:57 one **r**, one male lamb a year old,
7:63 one **r**, one male lamb a year old,
7:69 one **r**, one male lamb a year old,
7:75 one **r**, one male lamb a year old,
7:81 one **r**, one male lamb a year old,
15: 6 For a **r**, you shall offer a grain offering,
15:11 Thus it shall be done for each ox or **r**,
23: 2 and Balaam offered a bull and a **r** on each altar.
23: 4 and have offered a bull and a **r** on each altar."
23:14 and offered a bull and a **r** on each altar.
23:30 and offered a bull and a **r** on each altar.
28:11 two young bulls, one **r**, seven male lambs
28:12 mixed with oil, for the one **r**;
28:14 one-third of a hin for a **r**,
28:19 one **r**, and seven male lambs a year old;
28:20 for a bull, and two-tenths for a **r**;
28:27 one **r**, seven male lambs a year old.
28:28 of an ephah for each bull, two-tenths for one **r**,
29: 2 one young bull, one **r**, seven male lambs
29: 3 of one ephah for the bull, two-tenths for the **r**,
29: 8 one **r**, seven male lambs a year old.
29: 9 of an ephah for the bull, two-tenths for the one **r**,
29:36 one bull, one **r**, seven male lambs a year old
29:37 for the **r**, and for the lambs,
Ru 4:19 Hezron of **R**, **R** of Amminadab,
1Ch 2: 9 Jerahmeel, **R**, and Chelubai.
2:10 **R** became the father of Amminadab,
2:25 **R** his firstborn, Bunah, Oren, Ozem, and Ahijah.
2:27 The sons of **R**, the firstborn of Jerahmeel:
Ezr 10:19 and their guilt offering was a **r** of the flock
Job 32: 2 of the family of **R**, became angry.
Eze 43:23 you shall offer a bull without blemish and a **r** from
43:25 also a bull and a **r** from the flock,
45:24 for each bull, an ephah for each **r**, and a hin of oil
46: 4 without blemish and a **r** without blemish;
46: 5 and the grain offering with the **r** shall be an ephah,
46: 6 six lambs and a **r**, which shall be without blemish;
46: 7 an ephah with the bull and an ephah with the **r**,
46:11 and with a **r** an ephah,
Da 8: 3 I looked up and saw a **r** standing beside the river.
8: 4 I saw the **r** charging westward and northward
8: 6 the **r** with the two horns that I had seen standing
8: 7 I saw it approaching the **r**.
8: 7 It was enraged against it and struck the **r**,
8: 7 The **r** did not have power to withstand it;
8: 7 it threw the **r** down to the ground and trampled
8: 7 and there was no one who could rescue the **r**
8:20 As for the **r** that you saw with the two horns,
Tob 7: 9 a **r** from the flock and received them very warmly.

RAM'S (1) [RAM]

Jos 6: 5 When they make a long blast with the **r** horn,

RAMAH (37) [RAMATHAIM, RAMATHITE]

Jos 18:25 Gibeon, **R**, Beeroth,
19: 8 towns as far as Baalath-beer, **R** of the Negeb.
19:29 to **R**, reaching to the fortified city of Tyre;
19:36 Adamah, **R**, Hazor,
Jdg 4: 5 under the palm of Deborah between **R** and Bethel
19:13 and spend the night at Gibeah or at **R**."
1Sa 1:19 then they went back to their house at **R**.
2:11 Then Elkanah went home to **R**,
7:17 he would come back to **R**, for his home was there;
8: 4 and came to Samuel at **R**,
15:34 Then Samuel went to **R**;
16:13 Samuel then set out and went to **R**.
19:18 he came to Samuel at **R**,
19:19 Saul was told, "David is at Naioth in **R**."
19:22 Then he himself went to **R**.
19:22 And someone said, "They are at Naioth in **R**."
19:23 He went there, toward Naioth in **R**;
19:23 until he came to Naioth in **R**.
20: 1 David fled from Naioth in **R**.
25: 1 They buried him at his home in **R**.
28: 3 for him and buried him in **R**,
1Ki 15:17 up against Judah, and built **R**, to prevent anyone
15:21 he stopped building **R** and lived in Tirzah.
15:22 they carried away the stones of **R** and its timber,
2Ki 8:29 that the Arameans had inflicted on him at **R**,
2Ch 16: 1 up against Judah, and built **R**, to prevent anyone
16: 5 When Baasha heard of it, he stopped building **R**,
16: 6 they carried away the stones of **R** and its timber,
22: 6 in Jezreel of the wounds that he had received at **R**,
Ezr 2:26 Of **R** and Geba, six hundred twenty-one.
Ne 7:30 Of **R** and Geba, six hundred twenty-one.
11:33 Hazor, **R**, Gittaim,
Isa 10:29 **R** trembles, Gibeah of Saul has fled.
Jer 31:15 A voice is heard in **R**, lamentation and bitter
40: 1 the captain of the guard had let him go from **R**,
Hos 5: 8 Blow the horn in Gibeah, the trumpet in **R**.
Mt 2:18 "A voice was heard in **R**, wailing and loud

RAMATH-LEHI (1) [LEHI]

Jdg 15:17 and that place was called **R**.

RAMATH-MIZPEH (1)

Jos 13:26 and from Heshbon to **R** and Betonim,

RAMATHAIM (1) [RAMAH]

1Sa 1: 1 There was a certain man of **R**, a Zuphite from

RAMATHAIM-ZOPHIM (KJV)

RAMATHAIM, ZUPHITE; See also Index to Footnotes

RAMATHITE (1) [RAMAH]

1Ch 27:27 Over the vineyards was Shimei the **R**.

RAMESES (5) [=RAAMSES]

Ge 47:11 in the best part of the land, in the land of **R**,
Ex 1:11 They built supply cities, Pithom and **R**,
12:37 The Israelites journeyed from **R** to Succoth,
Nu 33: 3 They set out from **R** in the first month,
33: 5 Israelites set out from **R**, and camped at Succoth.

RAMIAH (2)

Ezr 10:25 And of Israel: of the descendants of Parosh: **R**,
1Es 9:26 Of Israel: of the descendants of Parosh: **R**, Izziah,

RAMOTH (6) [RAMOTH-GILEAD]

Dt 4:43 **R** in Gilead belonging to the Gadites,
Jos 20: 8 from the tribe of Reuben, and **R** in Gilead,
21:38 **R** in Gilead with its pasture lands,
1Sa 30:27 in **R** of the Negeb, in Jattir,
1Ch 6:73 **R** with its pasture lands, and Anem
6:80 **R** in Gilead with its pasture lands,

RAMOTH-GILEAD (20) [GILEAD, RAMOTH]

1Ki 4:13 in **R** (he had the villages of Jair son of Manasseh,
22: 3 "Do you know that **R** belongs to us,
22: 4 "Will you go with me to battle at **R**?"
22: 6 "Shall I go to battle against **R**, or shall I refrain?"
22:12 "Go up to **R** and triumph;
22:15 shall we go to **R** to battle, or shall we refrain?"
22:20 so that he may go up and fall at **R**?'
22:29 and King Jehoshaphat of Judah went up to **R**.
2Ki 8:28 to wage war against King Hazael of Aram at **R**,
9: 1 take this flask of oil in your hand, and go to **R**.
9: 4 So the young man, the young prophet, went to **R**.
9:14 Joram with all Israel had been on guard at **R**
2Ch 18: 2 and induced him to go up against **R**.
18: 3 "Will you go with me to **R**?"
18: 5 and said to them, "Shall we go to battle against **R**,
18:11 "Go up to **R** and triumph;
18:14 shall we go to **R** to battle, or shall I refrain?"
18:19 so that he may go up and fall at **R**?'
18:28 and King Jehoshaphat of Judah went up to **R**.
22: 5 to make war against King Hazael of Aram at **R**.

RAMP‡ (6) [RAMPS]

2Sa 20:15 they threw up a siege **r** against the city,
2Ki 19:32 or cast up a siege **r** against it.
Isa 37:33 or cast up a siege **r** against it.
Jer 6: 6 cast up a siege **r** against Jerusalem.
Eze 4: 2 and cast up a **r** against it;
26: 8 cast up a **r** against you,

RAMPART (5) [RAMPARTS]

2Sa 20:15 against the city, and it stood against the **r**.
La 2: 8 he caused **r** and wall to lament;
Na 3: 8 with water around her, her **r** a sea, water her wall?
Hab 2: 1 and station myself on the **r**;
Zec 9: 3 Tyre has built itself a **r**,

RAMPARTS (4) [RAMPART]

Ps 48:13 consider well its **r**; go through its citadels,
Na 2: 1 Guard the **r**; watch the road; gird your lions;
Lk 19:43 when your enemies will set up **r** around you
4Mc 3:12 and taking a pitcher climbed over the enemy's **r**.

RAMPS (4) [RAMP]

Jer 32:24 the siege **r** have been cast up against the city
33: 4 a defense against the siege **r** and before the sword:
Eze 17:17 when **r** are cast up and siege walls built
21:22 to set battering rams against the gates, to cast up **r**,

RAMS‡ (75) [RAM]

Ge 31:38 and I have not eaten the **r** of your flocks.
32:14 two hundred ewes and twenty **r**,
Ex 29: 1 Take one young bull and two **r** without blemish,
29: 3 and bring the bull and the two **r**.
29:15 Then you shall take one of the **r**,
Lev 8: 2 the two **r**, and the basket of unleavened bread;
23:18 one young bull, and two **r**;
Nu 7:17 two oxen, five **r**, five male goats,
7:23 two oxen, five **r**, five male goats,
7:29 two oxen, five **r**, five male goats,
7:35 two oxen, five **r**, five male goats,
7:41 two oxen, five **r**, five male goats,
7:47 two oxen, five **r**, five male goats,
7:53 two oxen, five **r**, five male goats,
7:59 two oxen, five **r**, five male goats,
7:65 two oxen, five **r**, five male goats,
7:71 two oxen, five **r**, five male goats,
7:77 two oxen, five **r**, five male goats,
7:83 two oxen, five **r**, five male goats,
7:87 twelve **r**, twelve male lambs a year old,
7:88 the **r** sixty, the male goats sixty,
23: 1 and prepare seven bulls and seven **r** for me."
23:29 and prepare seven bulls and seven **r** for me."
29:13 thirteen young bulls, two **r**,
29:14 two-tenths for each of the two **r**,
29:17 On the second day: twelve young bulls, two **r**,
29:18 for the **r**, and for the lambs,
29:20 On the third day: eleven bulls, two **r**,
29:21 for the **r**, and for the lambs,
29:23 On the fourth day: ten bulls, two **r**,
29:24 for the **r**, and for the lambs,
29:26 On the fifth day: nine bulls, two **r**,
29:27 for the **r**, and for the lambs,
29:29 On the sixth day: eight bulls, two **r**,
29:30 for the **r**, and for the lambs,
29:32 On the seventh day: seven bulls, two **r**,
29:33 for the **r**, and for the lambs,
Dt 32:14 and milk from the flock, with fat of lambs and **r**;
1Sa 15:22 and to heed than the fat of **r**.
2Ki 3: 4 and the wool of one hundred thousand **r**.
1Ch 15:26 they sacrificed seven bulls and seven **r**.
29:21 a thousand **r**, and a thousand lambs,
2Ch 13: 9 consecrated with a young bull or seven **r**
17:11 also brought him seven thousand seven hundred **r**
29:21 They brought seven bulls, seven **r**, seven lambs,
29:22 the **r** and their blood was dashed against the altar;
29:32 one hundred **r**, and two hundred lambs;
Ezr 6: 9 Whatever is needed—young bulls, **r**,
6:17 two hundred **r**, four hundred lambs,
7:17 then, you shall with all diligence buy bulls, **r**,
8:35 twelve bulls for all Israel, ninety-six **r**,
Job 42: 8 Now therefore take seven bulls and seven **r**,
Ps 66:15 with the smoke of the sacrifice of **r**;
114: 4 The mountains skipped like **r**, the hills like lambs.
114: 6 O mountains, that you skip like **r**?
Isa 1:11 of burnt offerings of **r** and the fat of fed beasts;
34: 6 with the fat of the kidneys of **r**.
60: 7 the **r** of Nebaioth shall minister to you;
Jer 51:40 down like lambs to the slaughter, like **r** and goats.
Eze 4: 2 and plant battering **r** against it all around.
21:22 to set battering **r**, to call out for slaughter,
21:22 to set battering **r** against the gates,
26: 9 of his battering **r** against your walls and break
27:21 **r**, and goats; in these they did business with you.
34:17 I shall judge between sheep and sheep, between **r**
39:18 of **r**, of lambs, and of goats, of bulls,
45:23 to the LORD seven young bulls and seven **r**
Mic 6: 7 Will the LORD be pleased with thousands of **r**,
Tob 8:19 and four **r** and ordered them to be slaughtered.
Aza 1:17 though it were with burnt offerings of **r** and bulls,
1Es 6:29 for bulls and **r** and lambs,
7: 7 two hundred **r**, four hundred lambs,
8:14 and silver for bulls and **r** and lambs and what goes
8:65 twelve bulls for all Israel, ninety-six **r**,
9:20 and to offer **r** in expiation of their error.

RAMS' (10) [RAM]

Ex 25: 5 tanned **r** skins, fine leather, acacia wood,
26:14 for the tent a covering of tanned **r** skins and
35: 7 tanned **r** skins, and fine leather; acacia wood,
35:23 or goats' hair or tanned **r** skins or fine leather,
36:19 for the tent a covering of tanned **r** skins and
39:34 of tanned **r** skins and the covering of fine leather,
Jos 6: 4 trumpets of **r** horns before the ark.
6: 6 trumpets of **r** horns in front of the ark of the
6: 8 trumpets of **r** horns before the LORD
6:13 the seven trumpets of **r** horns before the ark of

RAN (75) [RUN]

Ge 16: 6 and she **r** away from her.
18: 2 he **r** from the tent entrance to meet them,
18: 7 Abraham **r** to the herd, and took a calf,
24:17 Then the servant **r** to meet her and said,
24:20 into the trough and **r** again to the well to draw,
24:28 Then the girl **r** and told her mother's household
24:29 and Laban **r** out to the man, to the spring.
29:12 and she **r** and told her father.
29:13 about his sister's son Jacob, he **r** to meet him;
33: 4 But Esau **r** to meet him, and embraced him,
39:12 in her hand, and fled and **r** outside.
Nu 11:27 And a young man **r** and told Moses,
16:47 and **r** into the middle of the assembly,
Jos 7:22 So Joshua sent messengers, and they **r** to the tent;
15: 2 And their south boundary **r** from the end of
19:33 And its boundary **r** from Heleph,
Jdg 1:36 of the Amorites **r** from the ascent of Akrabbim,
7:21 and all the men in camp **r**; they cried out and fled.
9:21 Then Jotham **r** away and fled, going to Beer,
13:10 So the woman **r** quickly and told her husband,
1Sa 3: 5 **r** to Eli, and said, "Here I am, for you called me."
4:12 A man of Benjamin **r** from the battle line,
10:23 Then they **r** and brought him from there.
17:22 **r** to the ranks, and went and greeted his brothers.
17:48 David **r** quickly toward the battle line to meet
17:51 Then David **r** and stood over the Philistine;
20:36 As the boy **r**, he shot an arrow beyond him.
2Sa 18:21 The Cushite bowed before Joab, and **r**.
18:23 Then Ahimaaz **r** by the way of the Plain,
1Ki 2:39 of three years that two of Shimei's slaves **r** away
18:35 so that the water **r** all around the altar,
18:46 up his loins and **r** in front of Ahab to the entrance
19:20 He left the oxen, **r** after Elijah, and said,
Ps 104: 8 **r** down to the valleys to the place
Jer 23:21 I did not send the prophets, yet they **r**;
Eze 40:18 The pavement **r** along the side of the gates,
42: 9 of these chambers **r** a passage that one entered
Da 8: 6 and it **r** at it with savage force.
Mt 8:33 The swineherds **r** off, and on going into the town,
27:48 At once one of them **r** and got a sponge,
28: 8 and **r** to tell his disciples.
Mk 5: 6 he **r** and bowed down before him;
5:14 The swineherds **r** off and told it in the city and in
9:15 and they **r** forward to greet him.
10:17 a man **r** up and knelt before him, and asked him,
14:52 but he left the linen cloth and **r** off naked.
15:36 And someone **r**, filled a sponge with sour wine,
Lk 8:34 they **r** off and told it in the city and in the country.
15:20 he **r** and put his arms around him and kissed him.
19: 4 So he **r** ahead and climbed a sycamore tree
24:12 But Peter got up and **r** to the tomb;
Jn 20: 2 So she **r** and went to Simon Peter and
Ac 3:11 all the people **r** together to them in
8:30 So Philip **r** up to it and heard him reading
12:14 she **r** in and announced that Peter was standing at
21:32 Immediately he took soldiers and centurions and **r**
27:41 But striking a reef, they **r** the ship aground;
Tob 1:19 I was afraid and **r** away.
2: 8 to be put to death for doing this, and he **r** away;
11: 9 Then Anna **r** up to her son and threw her arms
Jdt 6:12 they seized their weapons and **r** out of the town to
6:16 all their young men and women **r** to the assembly.
13:13 They all **r** together, both small and great,
Sus 1:19 the two elders got up and **r** to her.
1:25 And one of them **r** and opened the garden doors.
1:38 and when we saw this wickedness we **r** to them.
1Mc 2:24 he **r** and killed him on the altar.
6:45 He courageously **r** into the midst of the phalanx
16:21 But someone **r** ahead and reported to John
2Mc 3:19 young women who were kept indoors **r** together
8:13 and distrustful of God's justice **r** off and got away.
11:22 The king's letter **r** thus: "King Antiochus to his
14:43 He courageously **r** up on the wall,
14:45 and his wounds were severe he **r** through
4Mc 7:11 **r** through the multitude of the people

RANG (1) [RING]

Wis 17: 4 but terrifying sounds **r** out around them,

RANGE (5) [RANGED, RANGES]

Nu 27:12 "Go up this mountain of the Abarim **r**,
2Ch 16: 9 eyes of the LORD **r** throughout the entire earth,
Ps 73: 9 and their tongues **r** over the earth.
Isa 32:20 who let the ox and the donkey **r** freely.
Zec 4:10 which **r** through the whole earth."

RANGED (1) [RANGE]

Wis 19: 9 For they **r** like horses, and leaped like lambs,

RANGES (1) [RANGE]

Job 39: 8 It **r** the mountains as its pasture,

RANGING (KJV) See CHARGING

RANK (10) [RANKS]

Ge 49: 3 excelling in **r** and excelling in power.
1Ch 17:17 You regard me as someone of high **r**,
Est 10: 3 the Jew was next in **r** to King Ahasuerus,
Pr 30:27 yet all of them march in **r**;
Da 5: 7 and **r** third in the kingdom."
5:16 and **r** third in the kingdom."
5:29 that he should **r** third in the kingdom.
Jas 1:21 of all sordidness and **r** growth of wickedness,
AdE 1:19 but let the king give her royal **r** to a woman better
2Mc 4:31 leaving Andronicus, a man of high **r**,

RANKS (16) [RANK]

1Sa 17: 2 and formed **r** against the Philistines.
17: 8 He stood and shouted to the **r** of Israel,
17:10 the Philistine said, "Today I defy the **r** of Israel!
17:22 ran to the **r**, and went and greeted his brothers.
17:23 came up out of the **r** of the Philistines,
2Ki 11: 8 and whoever approaches the **r** is to be killed.
11:15 "Bring her out between the **r**,
2Ch 23:14 saying to them, "Bring her out between the **r**;
Isa 14:31 and there is no straggler in its **r**.
Jn 1:15 'He who comes after me **r** ahead of me
1:30 'After me comes a man who **r** ahead of me
Ac 10: 7 of his slaves and a devout soldier from the **r**
Jdt 1: 4 in force and his infantry to form their **r**.
Sir 7:16 Do not enroll in the **r** of sinners;
45:23 of Eleazar **r** third in glory for being zealous in
2Mc 13:21 But Rhodocus, a man from the **r** of the Jews,

RANSOM (20) [RANSOMED]

Ex 21:30 If a **r** is imposed on the owner,
30:12 of them shall give a **r** for their lives to the LORD,
30:16 to the Israelites of the **r** given for your lives.
Nu 35:31 shall accept no **r** for the life of a murderer
35:32 Nor shall you accept **r** for one who has fled to
Job 6:23 Or, '**R** me from the hand of oppressors'?
33:24 from going down into the Pit; I have found a **r**;
36:18 and do not let the greatness of the **r** turn you aside.
Ps 49: 7 Truly, no **r** avails for one's life,
49: 8 For the **r** of life is costly, and can never suffice
49:15 But God will **r** my soul from the power of Sheol,
Pr 13: 8 Wealth is a **r** for a person's life,
21:18 The wicked is a **r** for the righteous,
Isa 43: 3 I give Egypt as your **r**, Ethiopia and Seba in
Hos 13:14 Shall I **r** them from the power of Sheol?
Mt 20:28 and to give his life a **r** for many."
Mk 10:45 and to give his life a **r** for many."
1Ti 2: 6 who gave himself a **r** for all—this was attested at
Tob 5:19 but let it be a **r** for our child.
4Mc 17:21 as it were, a **r** for the sin of our nation.

RANSOMED (10) [RANSOM]

Lev 19:20 for another man but not **r** or given her freedom,
27:27 it shall be **r** at its assessment,
27:29 who have been devoted to destruction can be **r**;
1Sa 6: 3 Then you will be healed and will be **r**;
14:45 So the people **r** Jonathan, and he did not die.
Isa 35:10 And the **r** of the LORD shall return,
51:11 So the **r** of the LORD shall return,
Jer 31:11 For the LORD has **r** Jacob,
1Pe 1:18 that you were **r** from the futile ways inherited
Rev 5: 9 for you were slaughtered and by your blood you **r**

RANTING (1)

Pr 29: 9 there is **r** and ridicule without relief.

RAPED (6)

Jdg 19:25 They wantonly **r** her, and abused her all through
20: 5 and they **r** my concubine until she died.
2Sa 13:22 because he had **r** his sister Tamar.
13:32 from the day Amnon **r** his sister Tamar.
La 5:11 Women are **r** in Zion, virgins in the towns
Zec 14: 2 be taken and the houses looted and the women **r**;

RAPHA (1) [BETH-RAPHA]

1Ch 8: 2 Nohah the fourth, and **R** the fifth.

RAPHAEL‡ (20)

Tob 1: 1 of Hananiel son of Aduel son of Gabael son of **R**
3:17 So **R** was sent to heal both of them:
5: 4 and found the angel **R** standing in front of him;
5:16 **R** answered, "I will go with him; so do not fear.
6:11 **R** said to the young man,
6:11 Then **R** said to him, "We must stay this night in
6:14 Then Tobias said in answer to **R**,
6:16 But **R** said to him, "Do you
6:18 When Tobias heard the words of **R** and learned
7: 9 Tobias said to **R**, "Brother Azariah,
8: 2 Then Tobias remembered the words of **R**,
8: 3 of Egypt. But **R** followed him,
9: 1 Then Tobias called **R** and said to him,
9: 5 So **R** with the four servants and two camels went
9: 5 **R** gave him the bond and informed him
11: 1 which is opposite Nineveh, **R** said,
11: 4 As they went on together **R** said to him,
11: 7 **R** said to Tobias, before he had approached
12: 6 Then **R** called the two of them privately and said
12:15 I am **R**, one of the seven angels who stand ready

RAPHAH (1)
1Ch 8:37 **R** was his son, Eleasah his son, Azel his son.

RAPHAIN (1)
Jdt 8: 1 of Gideon son of **R** son of Ahitub son of Elijah son

RAPHIA (1)
3Mc 1: 1 and marched out to the region near **R**,

RAPHON (1)
1Mc 5:37 and encamped opposite **R**,

RAPHU (1)
Nu 13: 9 from the tribe of Benjamin, Palti son of **R**;

RAPIDLY (4)
2Th 3: 1 so that the word of the Lord may spread **r** and
1Es 6:10 These operations are going on **r**,
3Mc 5:43 against Judea and **r** level it to the ground with fire
2Es 14:24 these five, who are trained to write **r**;

RARE (5) [RARELY]
1Sa 3: 1 The word of the LORD was **r** in those days;
Isa 13:12 I will make mortals more **r** than fine gold,
Rev 21:11 of God and a radiance like a very **r** jewel,
2Es 7:*57* those that are abundant or those that are **r**?"
7:*58* for what is more **r** is more precious."

RARELY (1) [RARE]
Ro 5: 7 Indeed, **r** will anyone die for a righteous person—

RASE (KJV) See RAZE

RASH (10) [RASHLY]
Lev 5: 4 Or when any of you utter aloud a **r** oath for a bad
13:39 it is a **r** that has broken out on the skin;
1Sa 14:24 Now Saul committed a very **r** act on that day.
Job 6: 3 therefore my words have been **r**.
Ps 106:33 and he spoke words that were **r**.
Pr 12:18 **R** words are like sword thrusts,
Ecc 5: 2 Never be **r** with your mouth,
Isa 32: 4 The minds of the **r** will have good judgment,
Ac 19:36 you ought to be quiet and do nothing **r**.
2Mc 5:18 from his **r** act as soon as he came forward,

RASHLY (1) [RASH]
Pr 20:25 It is a snare for one to say **r**, "It is holy,"

RASSISITES (1)
Jdt 2:23 and plundered all the **R** and the Ishmaelites on

RATED (1)
Lev 25:50 the owner shall be **r** as the time of a hired laborer.

RATHAMIN (1)
1Mc 11:34 the three districts of Aphairema and Lydda and **R**;

RATHER (84)
Nu 1:50 **R** you shall appoint the Levites over the tabernacle
Dt 9: 4 it is **r** because of the wickedness of these nations
15: 8 You should **r** open your hand,
32:47 for you, but **r** your very life;
2Ki 20:10 **r** let the shadow retreat ten intervals."
2Ch 25: 8 **R**, go by yourself and act;
Job 7:15 and death **r** than this body.
32: 2 at Job because he justified himself **r** than God;
Ps 84:10 I would **r** be a doorkeeper in the house
Pr 8:10 and knowledge **r** than choice gold;
16:16 To get understanding is to be chosen **r** than silver.
22: 1 A good name is to be chosen **r** than great riches,
Ecc 6: 5 yet it finds rest **r** than he.
Isa 59: 2 **R**, your iniquities have been barriers between you
Jer 7:24 and looked backward **r** than forward.
22:10 weep **r** for him who goes away,
Eze 18:23 **r** that they should turn from their ways and live?
Da 3:28 yielded up their bodies **r** than serve and worship
Hos 6: 6 the knowledge of God **r** than burnt offerings.
Mt 10: 6 but go **r** to the lost sheep of the house of Israel.
10:28 **r** fear him who can destroy both soul and body
27:24 but **r** that a riot was beginning,
Mk 5:26 and she was no better, but **r** grew worse.
Lk 11:28 "Blessed **r** are those who hear the word of God
12:51 No, I tell you, but **r** division!
17: 8 Would you not **r** say to him,
18:14 this man went down to his home justified **r** than
22:26 **r** the greatest among you must become like
Jn 3:19 and people loved darkness **r** than light
11: 4 **r** it is for God's glory,
Ac 4:19 to listen to you **r** than to God, you must judge;
5:29 "We must obey God **r** than any human authority.
17:20 It sounds **r** strange to us,
24:22 Felix, who was **r** well informed about the Way,
Ro 1:12 or **r** so that we may be mutually encouraged
1:25 a lie and worshiped and served the creature **r** than
2:29 **R**, a person is a Jew who is one inwardly,
15:15 on some points I have written to you **r** boldly
1Co 3: 1 but **r** as people of the flesh, as infants in Christ.
5: 2 Should you not **r** have mourned,
6: 7 Why not **r** be wronged?
6: 7 Why not **r** be defrauded?
1Co 9:12 but we endure anything **r** than put an obstacle in
9:15 Indeed, I would **r** die than that—
14:19 church I would **r** speak five words with my mind,
14:20 **r**, be infants in evil, but in thinking be adults.
2Co 1:24 **r**, we are workers with you for your joy,
5: 8 and we would **r** be away from the body and
Gal 4: 9 or **r** to be known by God,
6: 4 then that work, **r** than their neighbor's work,
Eph 4:28 **r** let them labor and work honestly
1Ti 1: 4 that promote speculations **r** than
6: 2 **r** they must serve them all the more,
6:17 but **r** on God who richly provides us
2Ti 1: 7 but **r** a spirit of power and of love and
3: 4 lovers of pleasure **r** than lovers of God,
Phm 1: 9 yet I would **r** appeal to you on the basis of love—
Heb 7:11 **r** than one according to the order of Aaron?
11:25 choosing **r** to share ill-treatment with the people
12:11 discipline always seems painful **r** than pleasant at
12:13 that what is lame may not be put out of joint, but **r**
1Pe 3: 4 **r**, let your adornment be the inner self with
2Jn 1:12 I would **r** not use paper and ink;
3Jn 1:13 but I would **r** not write with pen and ink;
Tob 6:13 Indeed he knows that you, **r** than any other man,
Jdt 11: 4 **R**, all will treat you well, as they do the servants
Wis 7:10 and I chose to have her **r** than light,
8:20 or **r**, being good, I entered an undefiled body.
Sir 25:16 I would **r** live with a lion and a dragon than live
Sus 1:23 **r** than sin in the sight of the Lord."
1Mc 1:63 They chose to die **r** than to be defiled by food or
9: 9 Let us **r** save our own lives now,
2Mc 6:19 welcoming death with honor **r** than life
7: 2 to die **r** than transgress the laws of our ancestors."
7: 7 "Will you eat **r** than have your body punished limb
14:42 preferring to die nobly **r** than to fall into the hands
3Mc 1: 4 matters were turning out **r** in favor of Antiochus,
6:31 those disgracefully treated and near to death, or **r**,
7: 5 as slaves, or **r** as traitors, and, girding themselves
2Es 7:16 **r** than what is now present?"
7:20 **r** than that the law of God that is set before them
7:*135* [65] because he would **r** give than take away;
4Mc 9: 1 die **r** than transgress our ancestral commandments;
16:24 to die **r** than violate God's commandment.

RATIFIED (3) [RATIFY]
Gal 3:15 once a person's will has been **r**,
3:17 does not annul a covenant previously **r** by God,
2Mc 10: 8 They decreed by public edict, **r** by vote,

RATIFY (1) [RATIFIED]
Da 11: 6 the south shall come to the king of the north to **r**

RATIONAL‡ (4)
4Mc 1: 2 I mean, of course, **r** judgment.
1:18 Now the kinds of wisdom are **r** judgment, justice,
1:19 **R** judgment is supreme over all of these,
1:30 that **r** judgment is sovereign over the emotions

RATIONED (1) [RATIONS]
Jdt 7:21 for their drinking water was **r**.

RATIONS (10) [RATIONED]
1Ki 22:27 and feed him on reduced **r** of bread and water
2Ch 18:26 and feed him on reduced **r** of bread and water
Eze 16:27 against you, reduced your **r**, and gave you up to
Da 1: 5 a daily portion of the royal **r** of food and wine.
1: 8 that he would not defile himself with the royal **r**
1:13 of the young men who eat the royal **r**,
1:15 the young men who had been eating the royal **r**.
1:16 the guard continued to withdraw their royal **r** and
11:26 by those who eat of the royal **r**.
Jdt 2:18 also ample **r** for everyone,

RATTLE (2) [RATTLING]
Job 39:23 Upon it **r** the quiver, the flashing spear,
41:29 it laughs at the **r** of javelins.

RATTLING (1) [RATTLE]
Eze 37: 7 as I prophesied, suddenly there was a noise, a **r**,

RAUCOUS (1)
Eze 23:42 The sound of a **r** multitude was around her,

RAVAGE (3) [RAVAGED, RAVAGER, RAVAGERS, RAVAGES, RAVAGING]
1Sa 6: 5 that **r** the land, and give glory to the God of Israel;
Jer 43:11 He shall come and **r** the land of Egypt,
Eze 14:15 If I send wild animals through the land to **r** it,

RAVAGED (10) [RAVAGE]
2Sa 11: 1 they **r** the Ammonites, and besieged Rabbah.
1Ch 20: 1 **r** the country of the Ammonites,
Isa 3:26 **r**, she shall sit upon the ground.
Eze 19: 7 he **r** their strongholds, and laid waste their towns;
34:22 and they shall no longer be **r**;
Na 2: 2 ravagers have **r** them and ruined their branches.)
Jdt 2:23 He **r** Put and Lud, and plundered all the Rassisites
2:27 and herds and sacked their towns and **r** their lands
4Mc 17:24 and he **r** and conquered all his enemies.
18: 4 of the law in the homeland they **r** the enemy.

RAVAGER (2) [RAVAGE]
Jdg 16:24 the **r** of our country, who has killed many of us."
Isa 54:16 I have also created the **r** to destroy.

RAVAGERS (1) [RAVAGE]
Na 2: 2 **r** have ravaged them and ruined their branches.)

RAVAGES (2) [RAVAGE]
Ps 35:17 Rescue me from their **r**, my life from the lions!
80:13 The boar from the forest **r** it,

RAVAGING (1) [RAVAGE]
Ac 8: 3 But Saul was **r** the church by entering house

RAVE (1) [RAVED]
Wis 14:28 For their worshipers either **r** in exultation,

RAVED (2) [RAVE]
1Sa 18:10 and he **r** within his house,
1Ki 18:29 they **r** on until the time of the offering of

RAVEN (7) [RAVENS]
Ge 8: 7 and sent out the **r**; and it went to and
Lev 11:15 every **r** of any kind;
Dt 14:14 every **r** of any kind;
Job 38:41 Who provides for the **r** its prey,
SS 5:11 his locks are wavy, black as a **r**.
Isa 34:11 the owl and the **r** shall live in it.
Zep 2:14 the **r** croak on the threshold;

RAVENING (2) [RAVENOUS]
Ps 22:13 like a **r** and roaring lion.
Jer 2:30 own sword devoured your prophets like a **r** lion.

RAVENOUS (4) [RAVENING]
Ge 49:27 a **r** wolf, in the morning devouring the prey,
Pr 27: 7 but to a **r** appetite even the bitter is sweet.
Isa 35: 9 nor shall any **r** beast come up on it;
Mt 7:15 in sheep's clothing but inwardly are **r** wolves.

RAVENS (5) [RAVEN]
1Ki 17: 4 and I have commanded the **r** to feed you there."
17: 6 The **r** brought him bread and meat in the morning,
Ps 147: 9 and to the young **r** when they cry.
Pr 30:17 scorns to obey a mother will be pecked out by the **r**
Lk 12:24 Consider the **r**: they neither sow nor reap,

RAVIN (KJV) See RAVENOUS, TORN FLESH

RAVINE (1) [RAVINES]
Jos 8:11 with a **r** between them and Ai.

RAVINES (3) [RAVINE]
Isa 7:19 And they will all come and settle in the steep **r**,
Eze 6: 3 to the **r** and the valleys:
Jdt 2: 8 Their wounded shall fill their **r** and gullies,

RAVISH (1) [RAVISHED]
Jdg 19:24 **R** them and do whatever you want to them;

RAVISHED (7) [RAVISH]
Ne 5: 5 and some of our daughters have been **r**;
SS 4: 9 You have **r** my heart, my sister, my bride,
4: 9 you have **r** my heart with a glance of your eyes,
Isa 13:16 their houses will be plundered, and their wives **r**.
Jdt 12:16 Holofernes' heart was **r** with her
16: 9 Her sandal **r** his eyes, her beauty captivated his
2Es 10:22 and our wives have been **r**;

RAW (8)
Ex 12: 9 Do not eat any of it **r** or boiled in water,
Lev 13:10 and there is quick **r** flesh in the swelling,
13:14 if **r** flesh ever appears on him, he shall be unclean;
13:15 the **r** flesh and pronounce him unclean.
13:15 **R** flesh is unclean, for it is a leprous disease.
13:16 But if the **r** flesh again turns white,
13:24 the body has a burn on the skin and the **r** flesh of
1Sa 2:15 not accept boiled meat from you, but only **r**."

RAY (2) [RAYS]
Wis 16:27 when simply warmed by a fleeting **r** of the sun,
2Es 6:40 Then you commanded a **r** of light to

RAYS (5) [RAY]
Hab 3: 4 **r** came forth from his hand,
Lk 11:36 of light as when a lamp gives you light with its **r**."
Wis 2: 4 and be scattered like mist that is chased by the **r** of
Sir 43: 4 and its bright **r** blind the eyes.
3Mc 5:26 The **r** of the sun were not yet shed abroad,

RAZED (3)
Jdg 9:45 and he **r** the city and sowed it with salt.
Jdt 5:18 The temple of their God was **r** to the ground,
1Mc 5:51 and **r** and plundered the town.

RAZIS (2)
2Mc 14:37 A certain **R,** one of the elders of Jerusalem,
14:41 Being surrounded, **R** fell upon his own sword,

RAZOR (8)
Nu 6: 5 All the days of their nazirite vow no **r** shall come
8: 7 have them shave their whole body with a **r**
Jdg 13: 5 No **r** is to come on his head,
16:17 "A **r** has never come upon my head;
1Sa 1:11 and no **r** shall touch his head."
Ps 52: 2 Your tongue is like a sharp **r,**
Isa 7:20 that day the Lord will shave with a **r** hired beyond
Eze 5: 1 use it as a barber's **r** and run it over your head

RE-ESTABLISHED (3) [ESTABLISH]
Da 4:26 your kingdom shall be **r** for you from the time
4:36 I was **r** over my kingdom,
2Mc 2:22 and **r** the laws that were about to be abolished,

REACH‡ (33) [REACHED, REACHES, REACHING]
Ge 3:22 he might **r** out his hand and take also from the tree
Ex 4: 4 Then the LORD said to Moses, **"R** out your hand,
28:42 they shall **r** from the hips to the thighs;
Nu 34:11 and **r** the eastern slope of the sea of Chinnereth;
35: 4 shall **r** from the wall of the town outward
Dt 1: 2 eleven days to **r** Kadesh-barnea from Horeb.)
Jdg 19:13 "Come, let us try to **r** one of these places,
Job 21: 7 Why do the wicked live on, **r** old age,
Ps 32: 6 the rush of mighty waters shall not **r** them.
71:19 O God, **r** the high heavens.
Isa 8: 8 and, pouring over, it will **r** up to the neck;
30: 4 his officials are at Zoan and his envoys **r** Hanes,
49: 6 that my salvation may **r** to the end of the earth."
59: 9 and righteousness does not **r** us;
Eze 31:14 and that no trees that drink water may **r** up to them
47: 9 very many fish, once these waters **r** there.
Hab 2: 9 setting your nest on high to be safe from the **r**
Zec 14: 5 the valley between the mountains shall **r** to Azal;
Lk 4:37 And a report about him began to **r** every place in
8:19 but they could not **r** him because of the crowd.
Jn 20:27 **R** out your hand and put it in my side.
Ac 27:12 on the chance that somehow they could **r** Phoenix,
2Co 10:13 to **r** out even as far as you.
Heb 4: 1 that none of you should seem to have failed to **r** it.
Jdt 7:10 for it is not easy to **r** the tops of their mountains.
Sir 14:13 and **r** out and give to them as much as you can.
18: 9 in their life is great if they **r** one hundred years.
31:14 Do not **r** out your hand for everything you see,
35:20 and his prayer will **r** to the clouds.
1Mc 6:45 into the midst of the phalanx to **r** it;
2Mc 4: 6 not again **r** a peaceful settlement,
2Es 7: 5 If there are those who wish to **r** the sea,
15:44 then the dust and smoke shall **r** the sky,

REACHED (80) [REACH]
Ge 19:10 the men inside **r** out their hands and brought Lot
22:10 Then Abraham **r** out his hand and took the knife
42: 5 for the famine had **r** the land of Canaan.
Ex 4: 4 so he **r** out his hand and grasped it,
Dt 1:19 until we **r** Kadesh-barnea.
1:20 "You have **r** the hill country of the Amorites,
1:24 when they **r** the Valley of Eshcol they spied it out
1:31 all the way that you traveled until you **r** this place.
Jos 9:17 Israelites set out and **r** their cities on the third day.
15: 1 of Judah according to their families **r** southward to
17: 7 of Manasseh **r** from Asher to Michmethath,
17:10 on the north Asher is **r,** and on the east Issachar.
19:10 The boundary of its inheritance **r** as far as Sarid;
Jdg 3:21 Then Ehud **r** with his left hand,
6:21 the angel of the LORD **r** out the tip of the staff
15:15 a donkey, **r** down and took it, and with it he killed
19: 3 When he **r** her father's house,
2Sa 6: 6 Uzzah **r** out his hand to the ark of God
6: 7 because he **r** out his hand to the ark;
22:17 He **r** from on high, he took me,
2Ki 6: 7 So he **r** out his hand and took it.
9:18 sentinel reported, saying, "The messenger **r** them,
9:20 Again the sentinel reported, "He **r** them,
10: 7 When the letter **r** them, they took the king's sons
2Ch 28: 9 but you have killed them in a rage that has **r** up
Ezr 5: 5 and they did not stop them until a report **r** Darius
Ps 18: 6 and my cry to him **r** his ears.
18:16 He **r** down from on high, he took me;
107: 7 until they **r** an inhabited town.
Isa 10:10 As my hand has **r** to the kingdoms of
16: 8 **r** to Jazer and strayed to the desert;
24:11 all joy has **r** its eventide;
Jer 4:18 It has **r** your very heart."
37:13 When he **r** the Benjamin Gate,
41: 7 When they **r** the middle of the city,
48:32 over the sea, **r** as far as Jazer;
51: 9 for her judgment has **r** up to heaven
Da 4:11 The tree grew great and strong, its top **r** to heaven,
4:20 that its top **r** to heaven and was visible to the end
6:24 Before they **r** the bottom of the den
8:23 when the transgressions have **r** their full measure,
Jnh 3: 6 When the news **r** the king of Nineveh,
Mic 1: 9 it has **r** to the gate of my people, to Jerusalem.
Mt 14:31 Jesus immediately **r** out his hand and caught him,
16: 5 When the disciples **r** the other side,
17:24 When they **r** Capernaum, the collectors of
21: 1 near Jerusalem and had **r** Bethphage,
Lk 4:42 and when they **r** him, they wanted to prevent him
22:40 When he **r** the place, he said to them,
Jn 6:21 the boat **r** the land toward which they were going.
20: 4 the other disciple outran Peter and **r** the tomb first.
20: 8 Then the other disciple, who **r** the tomb first,
Ac 15:19 Therefore I have **r** the decision that we should
16: 4 for observance the decisions that had been **r** by
18:19 When they **r** Ephesus, he left them there,
28: 1 After we had **r** safety, we then learned that
1Co 14:36 Or are you the only ones it has **r?)**
2Co 10:14 not overstepping our limits when we **r** you;
Php 3:12 that I have already obtained this or have already **r**
Jas 5: 4 the harvesters have **r** the ears of the Lord of hosts.
1Jn 2: 5 in this person the love of God has **r** perfection.
4:18 and whoever fears has not **r** perfection in love.
Wis 19: 3 they **r** another foolish decision,
Sir 47:16 Your fame **r** to far-off islands,
1Mc 3:26 His fame **r** the king, and the Gentiles talked of
12:52 So they all **r** the land of Judah safely,
13:47 So Simon **r** an agreement with them
13:53 Simon saw that his son John had **r** manhood,
16: 9 but John pursued them until Cendebeus **r** Kedron,
2Mc 1:13 When the leader **r** Persia with a force
5:11 When news of what had happened **r** the king,
6:14 to punish them until they have **r** the full measure
6:15 on us afterward when our sins have **r** their height.
6:23 that he had **r** with distinction and his excellent life
8:35 across the country until he **r** Antioch,
12: 1 When this agreement had been **r,**
12:35 so Gorgias escaped and **r** Marisa.
1Es 6:20 it has not yet **r** completion.'
2Es 11:44 they have ended, and his ages have **r** completion.
15: 6 and their harmful doings have **r** their limit.

REACHES (15) [REACH]
2Ki 5: 6 which read, "When this letter **r** you,
Job 20: 6 and their head **r** to the clouds,
41:26 Though the sword **r** it, it does not avail,
Ps 48:10 O God, like your praise, **r** to the ends of the earth.
108: 4 and your faithfulness **r** to the clouds.
Pr 31:20 and **r** out her hands to the needy.
Isa 15: 8 the wailing **r** to Eglaim, the wailing **r** to Beer-elim.
30:28 like an overflowing stream that **r** up to the neck—
Da 4:22 Your greatness has increased and **r** to heaven,
Jdt 7:14 before the sword **r** them they will be strewn about
11:15 When the response **r** them and they act upon it,
Wis 8: 1 She **r** mightily from one end of the earth to
Sir 35:21 and it will not rest until it **r** its goal;
40: 7 At the moment he **r** safety he wakes up,

REACHETH (KJV) See EXTENDS, REACHED, REACHES, SPREAD, TOUCHES, TOUCHING

REACHING (5) [REACH]
Ge 28:12 ladder set up on the earth, the top of it **r** to heaven;
Dt 25:11 of his opponent by **r** out and seizing his genitals,
Jos 19:29 **r** to the fortified city of Tyre;
2Ch 33:14 in the valley, **r** the entrance at the Fish Gate;
Jdt 16:23 **r** the age of one hundred five.

READ‡ (97) [READER, READERS, READING, READS]
Ex 24: 7 and **r** it in the hearing of the people;
Dt 17:19 with him and he shall **r** in it all the days of his life,
31:11 you shall **r** this law before all Israel
Jos 8:34 And afterward he **r** all the words of the law,
8:35 of all that Moses commanded that Joshua did not **r**
2Ki 5: 6 He brought the letter to the king of Israel, which **r,**
5: 7 When the king of Israel **r** the letter,
19:14 the letter from the hand of the messengers and **r** it;
22: 8 When Hilkiah gave the book to Shaphan, he **r** it.
22:10 Shaphan then **r** it aloud to the king.
22:16 the words of the book that the king of Judah has **r.**
23: 2 he **r** in their hearing all the words of the book of
2Ch 34:18 Shaphan then **r** it aloud to the king.
34:24 the curses that are written in the book that was **r**
34:30 he **r** in their hearing all the words of the book of
Ezr 4:18 that you sent to us has been **r** in translation
4:23 when the copy of King Artaxerxes' letter was **r**
Ne 8: 3 He **r** from it facing the square before
8: 8 So they **r** from the book, from the law of God,
8:18 he **r** from the book of the law of God.
9: 3 up in their place and **r** from the book of the law of
13: 1 On that day they **r** from the book of Moses in
Est 6: 1 the annals, and they were **r** to the king.
Isa 29:11 If it is given to those who can **r,**
29:11 **"R** this," they say, "We cannot, for it is sealed."
29:12 And if it is given to those who cannot **r,** saying,
29:12 saying, **"R** this," they say, "We cannot **r."**
34:16 Seek and **r** from the book of the LORD:
37:14 the letter from the hand of the messengers and **r** it;
Jer 29:29 The priest Zephaniah **r** this letter in the hearing of
36: 6 of the people in the LORD's house you shall **r**
36: 6 You shall **r** them also in the hearing of all
36:10 Baruch **r** the words of Jeremiah from the scroll,
36:13 Baruch **r** the scroll in the hearing of the people.
36:14 the scroll that you **r** in the hearing of the people,
36:15 And they said to him, "Sit down and **r** it to us."
36:15 So Baruch **r** it to them.
36:21 and Jehudi **r** it to the king and all
36:23 As Jehudi **r** three or four columns,
51:61 see that you **r** all these words,
Da 5: 7 wise men of Babylon, "Whoever can **r** this writing
5: 8 not **r** the writing or tell the king the interpretation.
5:15 have been brought in before me to **r** this writing
5:16 to **r** the writing and tell me its interpretation,
5:17 Nevertheless I will **r** the writing to the king
Hab 2: 2 make it plain on tablets, so that a runner may **r** it.
Mt 12: 3 "Have you not **r** what David did when he
12: 5 not **r** in the law that on the sabbath the priests in
19: 4 "Have you not **r** that the one who made them at
21:16 Jesus said to them, "Yes; have you never **r,**
21:42 "Have you never **r** in the scriptures:
22:31 have you not **r** what was said to you by God,
27:37 which **r,** "This is Jesus, the King of the Jews."
Mk 2:25 "Have you never **r** what David did when he
12:10 Have you not **r** this scripture:
12:26 have you not **r** in the book of Moses,
15:26 The inscription of the charge against him **r,**
Lk 4:16 as was his custom. He stood up to **r,**
6: 3 "Have you not **r** what David did when he
10:26 What do you **r** there?"
Jn 19:19 It **r,** "Jesus of Nazareth, the King of the Jews."
19:20 Many of the Jews **r** this inscription,
Ac 13:27 the words of the prophets that are **r** every sabbath,
15:21 for he has been **r** aloud every sabbath in
15:31 its members **r** it, they rejoiced at the exhortation.
2Co 1:13 we write you nothing other than what you can **r**
3: 2 written on our hearts, to be known and **r** by all;
3:15 Indeed, to this very day whenever Moses is **r,**
Col 4:16 And when this letter has been **r** among you,
4:16 have it **r** also in the church of the Laodiceans;
4:16 and see that you **r** also the letter from Laodicea.
1Th 5:27 by the Lord that this letter be **r** to all of them.
Tob 12:12 and **r** the record of your prayer before the glory of
AdE 6: 1 to bring the book of daily records, and to **r** to him.
Sir Pr: 1 those who **r** the scriptures must not only
Pr: 2 You are invited therefore to **r** it with goodwill
Pr: 2 the books differ not a little when **r** in the original.
Bar 1: 3 Baruch **r** the words of this book to Jeconiah son
1:14 And you shall **r** aloud this scroll
1Mc 5:14 While the letter was still being **r,**
10: 7 and **r** the letter in the hearing of all the people and
14:19 these were **r** before the assembly in Jerusalem.
2Mc 2:25 we have aimed to please those who wish to **r,**
6:12 Now I urge those who **r** this book not to
8:23 to **r** aloud from the holy book, and gave
11:34 The Romans also sent them a letter, which **r** thus:
15:39 the story delights the ears of those who **r** the work.
1Es 2:26 "I have **r** the letter that you sent me.
2:30 when the letter from King Artaxerxes was **r,**
3:13 the writing and gave it to him, and he **r** it.
3:15 and the writing was **r** in their presence.
9:41 He **r** aloud in the open square before the gate of
9:48 at the same time explaining what was **r.**
3Mc 1:12 Even after the law had been **r** to him,
2Es 14:45 and let the worthy and the unworthy **r** them;
4Mc 18:11 He **r** to you about Abel slain by Cain,

READER (8) [READ]
Mt 24:15 by the prophet Daniel (let the **r** understand),
Mk 13:14 the **r** understand), then those in Judea must flee to
1Es 8: 8 to Ezra the priest and **r** of the law of the Lord:
8: 9 to Ezra the priest and **r** of the law of the Lord,
8:19 and Phoenicia that whatever Ezra the priest and **r**
9:39 the chief priest and **r** to bring the law of Moses
9:42 and **r** of the law stood on the wooden platform
9:49 Then Attharates said to Ezra the chief priest and **r,**

READERS (1) [READ]
2Mc 2:25 to memorize, and to profit all **r.**

READILY (6) [READY]
Isa 32: 4 tongues of stammerers will speak **r** and distinctly.
2Co 11: 4 you submit to it **r** enough.
Wis 14:28 or live unrighteously, or **r** commit perjury;
Sir 6:22 she is not **r** perceived by many.
3Mc 2:31 the religion of their city, **r** gave themselves up
5:21 all those present **r** and joyfully

READINESS (1) [READY]
2Mc 14:22 in **r** at key places to prevent sudden treachery on

READING (13) [READ]
Ne 8: 8 so that the people understood the **r.**
Jer 36: 8 about **r** from the scroll the words of the LORD in
51:63 When you finish **r** this scroll, tie a stone to it,
Ac 8:28 seated in his chariot, he was **r** the prophet Isaiah.
8:30 up to it and heard him **r** the prophet Isaiah.
8:30 He asked, "Do you understand what you are **r?"**
8:32 the passage of the scripture that he was **r** was this:
13:15 After the **r** of the law and the prophets,
23:34 On **r** the letter, he asked what province he
2Co 3:14 when they hear the **r** of the old covenant,
Eph 3: 4 a **r** of which will enable you
1Ti 4:13 give attention to the public **r** of scripture,
Sir Pr: 1 who had devoted himself especially to the **r** of

READS (1) [READ]
Rev 1: 3 the one who **r** aloud the words of the prophecy,

READY‡ (121) [READILY, READINESS]
Ge 18: 6 "Make **r** quickly three measures of choice flour,
43:16 and slaughter an animal and make **r,**
43:25 they made the present **r** for Joseph's coming
46:29 Joseph made **r** his chariot and went up
Ex 14: 6 So he had his chariot made **r,**

Ex 17: 4 They are almost **r** to stone me."
34: 2 Be **r** in the morning, and come up in the morning
Dt 1:41 We are **r** to go up and fight,
9: 8 the LORD was so angry with you that he was **r**
9:20 so angry with Aaron that he was **r** to destroy him,
1Sa 6: 7 get **r** a new cart and two milch cows
25:18 two skins of wine, five sheep **r** dressed,
2Sa 3:19 and the whole house of Benjamin were **r** to do.
15:15 "Your servants are **r** to do whatever our lord
2Ki 9:21 Joram said, "Get **r**." And they got his chariot **r**.
10: 6 and if you are **r** to obey me,
1Ch 5:18 in war, forty-four thousand seven hundred sixty, **r**
7:11 thousand two hundred, **r** for service in war.
12:36 forty thousand seasoned troops **r** for battle.
2Ch 29:19 we have made **r** and sanctified;
Ezr 1: 5 got **r** to go up and rebuild the house of the LORD
Ne 9:17 But you are a God **r** to forgive,
Est 3:14 calling on all the peoples to be **r** for that day.
8:13 be **r** on that day to take revenge on their enemies.
Job 12: 5 but it is **r** for those whose feet are unstable.
15:23 They know that a day of darkness is **r** at hand;
17: 1 my days are extinct, the grave is **r** for me.
18:12 and calamity is **r** for their stumbling.
32:19 like new wineskins, it is **r** to burst.
Ps 38:17 For I am **r** to fall, and my pain is ever with me.
45: 1 my tongue is like the pen of a **r** scribe.
59: 4 for no fault of mine, they run and make **r**.
119:173 Let your hand be **r** to help me,
Pr 19:29 Condemnation is **r** for scoffers,
21:31 The horse is made **r** for the day of battle,
22:18 if all of them are **r** on your lips.
24:27 get everything **r** for you in the field;
SS 2: 7 do not stir up or awaken love until it is **r**!
3: 5 do not stir up or awaken love until it is **r**!
8: 4 do not stir up or awaken love until it is **r**!
Isa 30:33 truly it is made **r** for the king,
65: 1 I was **r** to be sought out by those who did not ask,
Jer 46:14 Say, "Take your stations and be **r**,
Eze 7:14 the horn and made everything **r**;
38: 7 Be **r** and keep **r**, you and all the companies
Da 3:15 if you are **r** when you hear the sound of the horn,
Jnh 4: 2 and **r** to relent from punishing.
Hab 3:14 as if **r** to devour the poor who were in hiding.
Mt 22: 4 calves have been slaughtered, and everything is **r**;
22: 8 Then he said to his slaves, 'The wedding is **r**,
24:44 Therefore you also must be **r**,
25:10 and those who were **r** went with him into
Mk 3: 9 to have a boat **r** for him because of the crowd,
14:15 a large room upstairs, furnished and **r**.
Lk 1:17 to make **r** a people prepared for the Lord."
9:52 a village of the Samaritans to make **r** for him;
12:40 You also must be **r**, for the Son of Man is coming
14:17 'Come; for everything is **r** now.'
22:33 I am **r** to go with you to prison and to death!"
Ac 21:13 For I am **r** not only to be bound but even to die
21:15 After these days we got **r** and started to go up
23:15 we are **r** to do away with him before he arrives."
23:21 They are **r** now and are waiting for your consent."
23:23 "Get **r** to leave by nine o'clock tonight
1Co 3: 2 not solid food, for you were not **r** for solid food.
3: 2 Even now you are still not **r**,
14: 8 who will get **r** for battle?
2Co 1:17 **r** to say "Yes, yes" and "No, no" at the same time?
9: 2 saying that Achaia has been **r** since last year;
9: 3 so that you may be **r**, as I said you would be;
9: 4 come with me and find that you are not **r**,
9: 5 so that it may be **r** as a voluntary gift and not as
10: 6 We are **r** to punish every disobedience
12:14 Here I am, **r** to come to you this third time.
Eph 6:15 for your feet put on whatever will make you **r**
1Ti 6:18 to be rich in good works, generous, and **r** to share,
2Ti 2:21 to the owner of the house, **r** for every good work.
Tit 3: 1 to be obedient, to be **r** for every good work,
Heb 11:17 He who had received the promises was **r** to offer
1Pe 1: 5 the power of God through faith for a salvation **r** to
3:15 Always be **r** to make your defense
4: 5 to give an accounting to him who stands **r** to judge
Rev 8: 6 the seven trumpets made **r** to blow them.
9:15 who had been held **r** for the hour, the day,
19: 7 and his bride has made herself **r**;
Tob 7:15 "Sister, get the other room **r**, and take her there."
11: 4 on together Raphael said to him, "Have the gall **r**."
11: 9 that I have seen you, my child, I am **r** to die."
12:15 of the seven angels who stand **r** and enter before
AdE 8:13 be **r** on that day to fight against their enemies."
11: 6 two great dragons came forward, both **r** to fight,
11: 9 that threatened them, and were **r** to perish.
Wis 16:20 supplied them from heaven with bread **r** to eat,
Sir 6:35 Be **r** to listen to every godly discourse,
39:31 always **r** for his service on earth;
Bar 2: 9 And the Lord has kept the calamities **r**,
1Mc 3:28 and ordered them to be **r** for any need.
3:44 So the congregation assembled to be **r** for battle,
3:58 Be **r** early in the morning to fight
4:35 and how **r** they were either to live or to die nobly,
5:27 the enemy are getting **r** to attack
5:39 **r** to come and fight against you."
6:33 and his troops made **r** for battle
12:27 to keep their arms at hand so as to be **r** all night
12:34 for he had heard that they were **r** to hand over
12:50 and kept marching in close formation, **r** for battle.
13:22 So Trypho got all his cavalry **r** to go,
13:37 and we are **r** to make a general peace with you and
2Mc 7: 2 For we are **r** to die rather than transgress the laws
8:21 with courage and made them **r** to die for their laws
11: 9 **r** to assail not only humans but the wildest animals
13:12 Judas exhorted them and ordered them to stand **r**.
3Mc 5:26 that what the king desired was **r** for action.
5:29 that the animals and the armed forces were **r**,
2Es 2:35 Be **r** for the rewards of the kingdom,
4Mc 5:32 Therefore get your torture wheels **r** and fan
9: 1 "Why do you delay, O tyrant? For we are **r**
9: 2 to shame unless we should practice **r** obedience to
15: 9 of the nobility of her sons and their **r** obedience to

REAFFIRM (1) [AFFIRM]

2Co 2: 8 So I urge you to **r** your love for him.

REAIAH (4)

1Ch 4: 2 **R** son of Shobal became the father of Jahath,
5: 5 Micah his son, **R** his son, Baal his son,
Ezr 2:47 Giddel, Gahar, **R**,
Ne 7:50 of **R**, of Rezin, of Nekoda,

REAL (7) [REALITIES, REALLY]

Pr 11:18 The wicked earn no **r** gain,
Ac 12: 9 with the angel's help was **r**;
Ro 2:29 and **r** circumcision is a matter of the heart—
1Ti 5: 5 The **r** widow, left alone, has set her hope on God
5:16 so that it can assist those who are **r** widows.
Sir 7:18 or a **r** brother for the gold of Ophir.
2Mc 4: 1 and had been the **r** cause of the misfortune.

REALITIES (1) [REAL]

Heb 10: 1 things to come and not the true form of these **r**,

REALIZE (15) [REALIZED, REALIZING]

Lev 5: 5 When you **r** your guilt in any of these,
6: 4 when you have sinned and **r** your guilt,
6: 5 to its owner when you **r** your guilt.
Jdg 20:34 the Benjaminites did not **r** that disaster was close
Jn 8:28 then you will **r** that I am he,
Ac 12: 9 he did not **r** that what was happening with
23: 5 And Paul said, "I did not **r**, brothers,
Ro 2: 4 not **r** that God's kindness is meant to lead you
2Co 13: 5 Do you not **r** that Jesus Christ is in you?—
Heb 6:11 as to **r** the full assurance of hope to the very end,
Rev 3:17 You do not **r** that you are wretched, pitiable, poor,
Sir 12:12 and at last you will **r** the truth of my words,
23:19 to human eyes and he does not **r** that the eyes of
1Es 4:22 Therefore you must **r** that women rule over you!
3Mc 7: 6 Since we have come to **r** that the God of heaven

REALIZED (22) [REALIZE]

Jdg 13:21 Manoah **r** that it was the angel of the LORD.
16:18 Delilah **r** that he had told her his whole secret,
1Sa 18:28 But when Saul **r** that the LORD was with David,
Pr 13:19 A desire **r** is sweet to the soul,
Mt 21:45 they **r** that he was speaking about them.
27:18 For he **r** that it was out of jealousy
Mk 12:12 they **r** that he had told this parable against them,
15:10 For he **r** that it was out of jealousy that
Lk 1:22 they **r** that he had seen a vision in the sanctuary.
20:19 and chief priests **r** that he had told this parable
Jn 4:53 The father **r** that this was the hour when Jesus
6:15 When Jesus **r** that they were about to come
Ac 4:13 of Peter and John and **r** that they were uneducated
12:12 As soon as he **r** this, he went to the house of Mary,
22:29 the tribune also was afraid, for he **r** that Paul was
Tob 1:19 But when I **r** that the king knew about me and
1Mc 5:34 the army of Timothy **r** that it was Maccabeus,
6: 9 and he **r** that he was dying.
7:25 and **r** that he could not withstand them,
12:50 But they **r** that Jonathan had been seized
2Mc 11:13 and **r** that the Hebrews were invincible because
14: 3 **r** that there was no way for him to be safe or

REALIZING (4) [REALIZE]

Ge 50:15 **R** that their father was dead,
Lk 11:44 and people walk over them without **r** it."
2Mc 5: 6 not **r** that success at the cost of one's kindred is
12:12 **r** that they might indeed be useful in many ways,

REALLY (25) [REAL]

Ge 16:13 "Have I **r** seen God and remained alive
27:21 to know whether you are **r** my son Esau or not."
27:24 He said, "Are you **r** my son Esau?"
Jdg 14:16 you do not **r** love me.
2Sa 10: 3 to their lord Hanun, "Do you **r** think
Jn 7:26 Can it be that the authorities **r** know that this is
7:40 some in the crowd said, "This is **r** the prophet."
1Co 5: 7 be a new batch, as you **r** are unleavened.
8: 4 we know that "no idol in the world **r** exists,"
11:20 it is not **r** to eat the Lord's supper.
14:25 declaring, "God is **r** among you."
Gal 3: 4 if it **r** was for nothing.
1Th 2:13 not as a human word but as what it **r** is,
1Ti 5: 3 Honor widows who are **r** widows.
5:16 believing woman has relatives who are **r** widows,
6:19 so that they may take hold of the life that **r** is life.
Jas 2: 1 do you with your acts of favoritism **r** believe
2: 8 if you **r** fulfill the royal law according to
Tob 12:19 I **r** did not eat or drink anything—
Jdt 6: 9 If you **r** hope in your heart that they will not
AdE 16:10 a Macedonian (**r** an alien to the Persian blood,
Wis 17:14 which was **r** powerless and which came
Sus 1:54 Now then, if you **r** saw this woman, tell me this:
2Mc 3: 9 and he inquired whether this **r** was the situation.
2Es 5:30 If you **r** hate your people,

REALM (10) [REALMS]

2Ki 20:13 or in all his **r** that Hezekiah did not show them.
2Ch 20:30 And the **r** of Jehoshaphat was quiet,
Ezr 7:23 or wrath will come upon the **r** of the king
Isa 39: 2 or in all his **r** that Hezekiah did not show them.
Da 9: 1 who became king over the **r** of the Chaldeans—
11: 5 and shall rule a **r** greater than his own **r**.
11: 9 latter shall invade the **r** of the king of the south,
2Mc 9:24 the people throughout the **r** would not be troubled,
1Es 8:10 and of the priests and Levites and others in our **r**,

REALMS (1) [REALM]

Sir 43: 1 pride of the higher **r** is the clear vault of the sky,

REAP (38) [REAPED, REAPER, REAPERS, REAPING, REAPS]

Lev 19: 9 When you **r** the harvest of your land, you shall not **r** to the very edges of your field,
23:10 the land that I am giving you and you **r** its harvest,
23:22 When you **r** the harvest of your land, you shall not **r** to the very edges of your field,
25: 5 You shall not **r** the aftergrowth of your harvest
25:11 you shall not sow, or **r** the aftergrowth,
Dt 24:19 When you **r** your harvest in your field and forget
1Sa 8:12 and some to plow his ground and to **r** his harvest,
2Ki 19:29 then in the third year sow, **r**, plant vineyards,
Job 4: 8 those who plow iniquity and sow trouble **r**
13:26 and make me **r** the iniquities of my youth.
24: 6 They **r** in a field not their own and they glean in
Ps 126: 5 May those who sow in tears **r** with shouts of joy.
Pr 22: 8 Whoever sows injustice will **r** calamity,
Ecc 11: 4 and whoever regards the clouds will not **r**.
Isa 37:30 then in the third year sow, **r**, plant vineyards,
Hos 8: 7 they sow the wind, and they shall **r** the whirlwind.
10:12 for yourselves righteousness; **r** steadfast love;
Mic 6:15 You shall sow, but not **r**;
Mt 6:26 they neither sow nor **r** nor gather into barns,
25:26 You knew, did you, that I **r** where I did not sow,
Lk 12:24 Consider the ravens: they neither sow nor **r**,
19:21 and **r** what you did not sow.'
Jn 4:38 I sent you to **r** that for which you did not labor.
Ro 1:13 that I may **r** some harvest among you as I have
1Co 9:11 is it too much if we **r** your material benefits?
2Co 9: 6 the one who sows sparingly will also **r** sparingly,
9: 6 one who sows bountifully will also **r** bountifully.
Gal 6: 7 God is not mocked, for you **r** whatever you sow.
6: 8 you will **r** corruption from the flesh;
6: 8 you will **r** eternal life from the Spirit.
6: 9 for we will **r** at harvest time, if we do not give up.
Rev 14:15 on the cloud, "Use your sickle and **r**, for the hour
14:15 for the hour to **r** has come,
Sir 7: 3 and you will not **r** a sevenfold crop.
1Es 4: 6 whenever they sow and **r**,
2Es 16:43 let the one who sows be like one who will not **r**;

REAPED (6) [REAP]

Ge 26:12 and in the same year **r** a hundredfold.
Ru 2: 9 Keep your eyes on the field that is being **r**,
Jer 12:13 They have sown wheat and have **r** thorns,
Hos 10:13 you have **r** injustice, you have eaten the fruit
Rev 14:16 over the earth, and the earth was **r**.
2Es 4:29 If therefore that which has been sown is not **r**,

REAPER (3) [REAP]

Jer 9:22 like sheaves behind the **r**,
Jn 4:36 The **r** is already receiving wages
4:36 so that sower and **r** may rejoice together.

REAPERS (12) [REAP]

Ru 2: 3 She came and gleaned in the field behind the **r**.
2: 4 He said to the **r**, "The LORD be with you."
2: 5 to his servant who was in charge of the **r**,
2: 6 The servant who was in charge of the **r** answered,
2: 7 and gather among the sheaves behind the **r**.'
2:14 So she sat beside the **r**,
2Ki 4:18 he went out one day to his father among the **r**.
Ps 129: 7 with which **r** do not fill their hands or binders
Isa 17: 5 And it shall be as when **r** gather standing grain
Mt 13:30 and at harvest time I will tell the **r**,
13:39 harvest is the end of the age, and the **r** are angels.
Bel 1:33 and was going into the field to take it to the **r**.

REAPING (3) [REAP]

1Sa 6:13 of Beth-shemesh were **r** their wheat harvest in
Mt 25:24 **r** where you did not sow, and gathering
Lk 19:22 taking what I did not deposit and **r** what I did

REAPPEARED (1) [APPEAR]

1Mc 9:23 in all parts of Israel; all the wrongdoers **r**.

REAPPOINTED (1) [APPOINT]

Tob 1:22 Sennacherib of Assyria; so Esar-haddon **r** him.

REAPS (2) [REAP]

Am 9:13 the one who plows shall overtake the one who **r**,
Jn 4:37 'One sows and another **r**.'

REAR (22) [REARED, REARING]

Ex 26:22 for the **r** of the tabernacle westward you shall make
26:23 for corners of the tabernacle in the **r**;
26:27 of the side of the tabernacle at the **r** westward.

Ex 36:27 **r** of the tabernacle westward he made six frames.
36:28 for corners of the tabernacle in the **r.**
36:32 for the frames of the tabernacle at the **r** westward.
Nu 10:25 acting as the **r** guard of all the camps, set out,
Jos 6: 9 the **r** guard came after the ark,
6:13 and the **r** guard came after the ark of the LORD,
8:13 that was north of the city and its **r** guard west of
10:19 pursue your enemies, and attack them from the **r.**
1Sa 29: 2 and his men were passing on in the **r** with Achish,
2Sa 5:23 around to their **r,** and come upon them opposite
10: 9 the **r,** he chose some of the picked men of Israel,
1Ki 6:16 of the **r** of the house with boards of cedar from
1Ch 19:10 in the **r,** he chose some of the picked men of Israel
Isa 52:12 and the God of Israel will be your **r** guard.
58: 8 the glory of the LORD shall be your **r** guard.
Joel 2:20 and its **r** into the western sea;
Zec 10: 9 and they shall **r** their children and return.
1Mc 4:15 and all those in the **r** fell by the sword.
9:47 but he eluded him and went to the **r.**

REARED (8) [REAR]

Job 31:18 for from my youth I **r** the orphan like a father,
Isa 1: 2 I **r** children and brought them up,
23: 4 nor given birth, I have neither **r** young men
49:21 and put away—so who has **r** these?
La 2:22 those whom I bore and **r** my enemy has destroyed.
Tob 14:10 my son, what Nadab did to Ahikar who had **r** him.
Bar 4: 8 and you grieved Jerusalem, who **r** you.
2Mc 7:27 and have **r** you and brought you up to this point

REARING (1) [REAR]

Eze 19: 2 She lay down among young lions, **r** her cubs.

REASON‡ (168) [REASONABLY, REASONED, REASONING, REASONINGS, REASONS]

Nu 6:11 because they incurred guilt by **r** of the corpse.
18:32 You shall incur no guilt by **r** of it,
Dt 15:15 for this **r** I lay this command upon you today.
Jos 5: 4 This is the **r** why Joshua circumcised them:
1Sa 20:29 For this **r** he has not come to the king's table."
1Ki 11:27 following was the **r** he rebelled against the king.
11:39 For this **r** I will punish the descendants of David,
Job 2: 3 to destroy him for no **r."**
22: 6 from your family for no **r,**
23: 7 There an upright person could **r** with him,
Eze 41: 7 For this **r** the structure became wider from story
42: 6 for this **r** the upper chambers were set back from
Da 4:34 lifted my eyes to heaven, and my **r** returned to me.
4:36 At that time my **r** returned to me;
Mt 13:13 The **r** I speak to them in parables is
14: 2 and for this **r** these powers are at work in him."
18:23 "For this **r** the kingdom of heaven may
19: 5 'For this **r** a man shall leave his father and mother
27: 8 For this **r** that field has been called the Field
Mk 6:14 and for this **r** these powers are at work in him."
10: 7 'For this **r** a man shall leave his father and mother
12:24 "Is not this the **r** you are wrong,
Jn 1:31 but I came baptizing with water for this **r,**
3:29 For this **r** my joy has been fulfilled.
5:18 For this **r** the Jews were seeking all the more
6:65 "For this **r** I have told you that no one can come
8:47 The **r** you do not hear them is that you are not
10:17 For this **r** the Father loves me,
12:27 No, it is for this **r** that I have come to this hour.
13:11 for this **r** he said, "Not all of you are clean."
16:15 For this **r** I said that he will take what is mine
Ac 10:21 what is the **r** for your coming?"
22:24 to find out the **r** for this outcry against him.
24:26 and for that **r** he used to send for him very often
26:21 For this **r** the Jews seized me in the temple
28:18 there was no **r** for the death penalty in my case.
28:20 For this **r** therefore I have asked to see you
Ro 1:26 this **r** God gave them up to degrading passions.
4:16 For this **r** it depends on faith,
8: 7 For this **r** the mind that is set on the flesh is hostile
13: 6 For the same **r** you also pay taxes,
14:22 Blessed are those who have no **r** to condemn
15:17 then, I have **r** to boast of my work for God.
15:22 This is the **r** that I have so often been hindered
1Co 4:17 For this **r** I sent you Timothy,
11:10 For this **r** a woman ought to have a symbol
11:30 For this **r** many of you are weak and ill,
2Co 1:20 this **r** it is through him that we say the "Amen,"
2: 9 I wrote for this **r:** to test you and to know
8:24 of your love and of our **r** for boasting about you.
Gal 3: 9 For this **r,** those who believe are blessed
Eph 1:15 and your love toward all the saints, and for this **r**
3: 1 the **r** that I Paul am a prisoner for Christ Jesus for
3:14 For this **r** I bow my knees before the Father,
5:31 "For this **r** a man will leave his father and mother
Php 3: 4 I, too, have **r** for confidence in the flesh.
3: 4 If anyone else has **r** to be confident in the flesh,
Col 1: 9 For this **r,** since the day we heard it,
1Th 3: 5 For this **r,** when I could bear it no longer,
3: 7 For this **r,** brothers and sisters,
2Th 2:11 For this **r** God sends them a powerful delusion,
1Ti 1:16 But for that very **r** I received mercy, so that in me,
2Ti 1: 6 For this **r** I remind you to rekindle the gift of God
1:12 and for this **r** I suffer as I do.
Tit 1: 5 I left you behind in Crete for this **r,**
1:13 For this **r** rebuke them sharply,
Phm 1: 8 For this **r,** though I am bold enough in Christ
1:15 Perhaps this is the **r** he was separated from you for
Heb 2:11 For this **r** Jesus is not ashamed to call them
9:15 For this **r** he is the mediator of a new covenant,
1Pe 4: 6 For this is the **r** the gospel was proclaimed even to
2Pe 1: 5 For this very **r,** you must make every effort
1Jn 3: 1 The **r** the world does not know us is that it did
Rev 7:15 For this **r** they are before the throne of God,
Wis 2: 2 **r** is a spark kindled by the beating of our hearts;
12:25 Therefore, as though to children who cannot **r,**
17:12 but a giving up of the helps that come from **r;**
Sir 4: 5 and give no one **r** to curse you;
31:13 Therefore it sheds tears for any **r.**
51:12 For this **r** I thank you and praise you,
Sus 1:14 and when each pressed the other for the **r,**
1Mc 6:12 to destroy the inhabitants of Judah without good **r.**
6:24 For this **r** the sons of our people besieged
10:63 and let no one annoy him for any **r."**
13: 4 By **r** of this all my brothers have perished for
2Mc 4:16 For this **r** heavy disaster overtook them,
4:35 For this **r** not only Jews,
5:17 this was the **r** he was disregarding the holy place.
8:26 and for that **r** they did not continue their pursuit.
12:40 to all that this was the **r** these men had fallen.
3Mc 3: 4 For this **r** they appeared hateful to some;
2Es 5: 9 then shall **r** hide itself, and wisdom shall withdraw
7:25 the **r,** Ezra, that empty things are for the empty,
7:*50* For this **r** the Most High has made not one world
7:*72* For this **r,** therefore, those who live on earth shall
10:45 the **r** is that there were three thousand years in
13:19 for those also who are left, and for that very **r!**
4Mc 1: 1 whether devout **r** is sovereign over the emotions.
1: 3 it is evident that **r** rules over those emotions
1: 5 Some might perhaps ask, "If **r** rules the emotions,
1: 6 For **r** does not rule its own emotions,
1: 7 and various examples that **r** is dominant over
1: 9 demonstrated that **r** controls the emotions.
1:13 is whether **r** is sovereign over the emotions.
1:14 We shall decide just what **r** is
1:14 and whether **r** rules over all these.
1:15 Now **r** is the mind that with sound logic prefers
1:19 since by means of it **r** rules over the emotions.
1:29 the master cultivator, **r,** weeds and prunes and ties
1:30 For **r** is the guide of the virtues,
1:32 and **r** obviously rules over both.
1:33 Is it not because **r** is able to rule over appetites?
1:34 we abstain because of domination by **r.**
1:35 and all the impulses of the body are bridled by **r.**
2: 2 It is for this **r,** certainly,
2: 3 by his **r** he nullified the frenzy of the passions.
2: 4 Not only is **r** proved to rule over the frenzied urge
2: 6 to you all the more that **r** is able to control desires.
2: 7 unless **r** is clearly lord of the emotions?
2: 9 through **r** so that one neither gleans the harvest
2: 9 In all other matters we can recognize that **r** rules
2:14 Do not consider it paradoxical when **r,**
2:15 that **r** rules even the more violent emotions:
2:17 but controlled his anger by **r.**
2:20 For if **r** could not control anger,
2:24 one might say, that if **r** is master of the emotions,
3: 1 it is evident that **r** rules not over its own emotions,
3: 2 but **r** can provide a way for us not to be enslaved
3: 3 but **r** can help to deal with anger.
3: 4 but **r** can fight at our side so that we are
3: 5 For **r** does not uproot the emotions
3:16 Therefore, opposing **r** to desire,
3:18 and by nobility of **r** spurn all domination by
3:19 to a narrative demonstration of temperate **r.**
5:31 not so old and cowardly as not to be young in **r**
5:35 I will not put you to shame, philosophical **r,**
6: 7 he kept his **r** upright and unswerving.
6:30 in the tortures of death he resisted, by virtue of **r,**
6:31 then, devout **r** is sovereign over the emotions.
6:32 For if the emotions had prevailed over **r,**
6:33 But now that **r** has conquered the emotions,
6:34 of **r** when it masters even external agonies.
6:35 not only that **r** has mastered agonies,
7: 1 the **r** of our father Eleazar steered the ship
7: 4 the besiegers with the shield of his devout **r.**
7:12 remained unmoved in his **r.**
7:14 in spirit through **r;** and by **r** like that of Isaac he rendered the many-headed rack ineffective.
7:16 most certainly devout **r** is governor of
7:17 because not all have prudent **r."**
7:20 because of the weakness of their **r.**
8: 1 a philosophy in accordance with devout **r,**
9:17 your wheel is not so powerful as to strangle my **r.**
10:19 in spite of this you will not make our **r** speechless.
11:27 therefore, unconquered, we hold fast to **r."**
13: 1 everyone must concede that devout **r** is sovereign
13: 3 Instead, by **r,** which is praised before God,
13: 5 to confess the sovereignty of right **r** over emotion
13: 7 so the seven-towered right **r** of the youths,
13:16 on the full armor of self-control, which is divine **r.**
14: 2 O **r,** more royal than kings and freer than the free!
14:11 not consider it amazing that **r** had full command
15: 1 O **r** of the children, tyrant over the emotions!
15:11 the various tortures strong enough to pervert her **r.**
15:23 But devout **r,** giving her heart a man's courage in
16: 1 it must be admitted that devout **r** is sovereign over
16: 4 so many and such great emotions by devout **r.**
18: 2 knowing that devout **r** is master of all emotions,

REASONABLE See Index to Footnotes

REASONABLY (1) [REASON]

AdE 13: 2 with presumption of authority but always acting **r**

REASONED (3) [REASON]

1Co 13:11 I thought like a child, I **r** like a child,
Wis 2: 1 For they **r** unsoundly, saying to themselves,
2:21 Thus they **r,** but they were led astray,

REASONING‡ (5) [REASON]

Job 13: 6 Hear now my **r,** and listen to the pleadings
Wis 3:10 the ungodly will be punished as their **r** deserves,
9:14 For the **r** of mortals is worthless,
2Mc 7:21 she reinforced her woman's **r** with
4Mc 8:15 and by their right **r** nullified his tyranny.

REASONINGS (1) [REASON]

4Mc 5:11 from your foolish philosophy, dispel your futile **r,**

REASONS (1) [REASON]

Sir 14:20 who meditates on wisdom and **r** intelligently,

REASSURE (1) [ASSURANCE]

1Jn 3:19 that we are from the truth and will **r** our hearts

REASSURED (2) [ASSURANCE]

Ge 50:21 In this way he **r** them, speaking kindly to them.
Jdt 6:20 Then they **r** Achior, and praised him highly.

REBA (2)

Nu 31: 8 Evi, Rekem, Zur, Hur, and **R,**
Jos 13:21 Evi and Rekem and Zur and Hur and **R,**

REBECCA (1) [=REBEKAH]

Ro 9:10 to **R** when she had conceived children

REBEKAH (28) [=REBECCA, REBEKAH'S]

Ge 22:23 Bethuel became the father of **R.**
24:15 Before he had finished speaking, there was **R,**
24:29 **R** had a brother whose name was Laban;
24:30 and when he heard the words of his sister **R,**
24:45 there was **R** coming out with her water jar
24:51 Look, **R** is before you, take her and go,
24:53 and garments, and gave them to **R;**
24:58 And they called **R,** and said to her,
24:59 So they sent away their sister **R** and her nurse
24:60 And they blessed **R** and said to her, "May you,
24:61 Then **R** and her maids rose up,
24:61 thus the servant took **R,** and went his way.
24:64 And **R** looked up, and when she saw Isaac,
24:67 He took **R,** and she became his wife;
25:20 and Isaac was forty years old when he married **R,**
25:21 and his wife **R** conceived.
25:28 he was fond of game; but **R** loved Jacob.
26: 7 of the place might kill me for the sake of **R,**
26: 8 of a window and saw him fondling his wife **R.**
26:35 and they made life bitter for Isaac and **R.**
27: 5 **R** was listening when Isaac spoke to his son Esau.
27: 6 **R** said to her son Jacob,
27:11 But Jacob said to his mother **R,** "Look,
27:15 **R** took the best garments of her elder son Esau,
27:42 the words of her elder son Esau were told to **R;**
27:46 Then **R** said to Isaac, "I am weary of my life
28: 5 the brother of **R,** Jacob's and Esau's mother.
49:31 there Isaac and his wife **R** were buried;

REBEKAH'S (2) [REBEKAH]

Ge 29:12 her father's kinsman, and that he was **R** son;
35: 8 And Deborah, **R** nurse, died,

REBEL‡ (18) [REBELLED, REBELLING, REBELLION, REBELLIOUS, REBELS]

Ex 23:21 do not **r** against him, for he will
Nu 14: 9 Only, do not **r** against the LORD;
Jos 22:18 If you **r** against the LORD today,
22:19 only do not **r** against the LORD, or **r** against us
22:29 be it from us that we should **r** against the LORD,
1Sa 12:14 and serve him and heed his voice and not **r** against
12:15 but **r** against the commandment of the LORD,
Ne 6: 6 that you and the Jews intend to **r;**
Est 1:18 of the queen's behavior will **r** against
Job 24:13 "There are those who **r** against the light,
Ps 68:18 even from those who **r** against
Isa 1: 5 Why do you continue to **r?**
1:20 but if you refuse and **r,** you shall be devoured by
48: 8 and that from birth you were called a **r.**
Hos 7:14 and wine; they **r** against me.
Sir 47:21 and a **r** kingdom arose out of Ephraim.
2Mc 5: 8 pursued by everyone, hated as a **r** against the laws,

REBELLED (51) [REBEL]

Ge 14: 4 but in the thirteenth year they **r.**
Nu 16:41 the Israelites **r** against Moses and against Aaron,
20:24 because you **r** against my command at the waters
26: 9 who **r** against Moses and Aaron in the company
26: 9 when they **r** against the LORD,
27:14 because you **r** against my word in the wilderness
Dt 1:26 You **r** against the command of the LORD
1:43 You **r** against the command of the LORD
9:23 you **r** against the command of the LORD
1Ki 11:26 a widow, **r** against the king.
11:27 following was the reason he **r** against the king.
2Ki 1: 1 After the death of Ahab, Moab **r** against Israel.
3: 5 the king of Moab **r** against the king of Israel.
3: 7 "The king of Moab has **r** against me;

2Ki 18: 7 He **r** against the king of Assyria and would
18:20 that you have **r** against me?
24: 1 then he turned and **r** against him.
24:20 Zedekiah **r** against the king of Babylon.
2Ch 13: 6 rose up and **r** against his lord;
36:13 He also **r** against King Nebuchadnezzar,
Ne 9:26 "Nevertheless they were disobedient and **r**
Ps 5:10 for they have **r** against you.
78:40 How often they **r** against him in the wilderness
78:56 they tested the Most High God, and **r** against him.
105:28 and made the land dark; they **r** against his words.
106: 7 but **r** against the Most High at the Red Sea.
107:11 for they had **r** against the words of God,
Isa 1: 2 but they have **r** against me.
36: 5 that you have **r** against me?
63:10 But they **r** and grieved his holy spirit;
66:24 dead bodies of the people who have **r** against me;
Jer 2:29 You have all **r** against me, says the LORD.
3:13 that you have **r** against the LORD your God,
4:17 because she has **r** against me, says the LORD.
52: 3 Zedekiah **r** against the king of Babylon.
La 1:18 for I have **r** against his word;
3:42 We have transgressed and **r**,
Eze 2: 3 to a nation of rebels who have **r** against me;
5: 6 she has **r** against my ordinances and my statutes,
17:15 But he **r** against him by sending ambassadors
20: 8 But they **r** against me and would not listen to me;
20:13 the house of Israel **r** against me in the wilderness;
20:21 But the children **r** against me;
Da 9: 5 and **r**, turning aside from your commandments
9: 9 for we have **r** against him,
Hos 7:13 Destruction to them, for they have **r** against me!
13:16 because she has **r** against her God;
Zep 3:11 of all the deeds by which you have **r** against me;
Jdt 7:15 they **r** and did not receive you peaceably."
Wis 3:10 those who disregarded the righteous and **r** against
1Es 1:48 he broke his oath and **r**;

REBELLING (2) [REBEL]

Ne 2:19 Are you **r** against the king?"
Ps 78:17 **r** against the Most High in the desert.

REBELLION‡ (17) [REBEL]

Jos 22:16 by building yourselves an altar today in **r** against
22:22 it was in **r** or in breach of faith toward the LORD,
1Sa 15:23 For **r** is no less a sin than divination,
1Ki 12:19 So Israel has been in **r** against the house of David
2Ch 10:19 So Israel has been in **r** against the house of David
Ezr 4:19 and that **r** and sedition have been made in it.
Job 34:37 For he adds **r** to his sin;
Pr 17:11 Evil people seek only **r**, but
Isa 58: 1 Announce to my people their **r**,
Jer 28:16 because you have spoken **r** against the LORD."
29:32 for he has spoken **r** against the LORD.
33: 8 and I will forgive all the guilt of their sin and **r**
2Th 2: 3 that day will not come unless the **r** comes first and
Heb 3: 8 do not harden your hearts as in the **r**,
3:15 do not harden your hearts as in the **r**."
Jude 1:11 for the sake of gain, and perish in Korah's **r**.
1Es 2:27 that the people in it were given to **r** and war,

REBELLIOUS‡ (43) [REBEL]

A. REBELLIOUS HOUSE (15)

Dt 9: 7 you have been **r** against the LORD from
9:24 You have been **r** against the LORD as long
21:18 and **r** son who will not obey his father and mother,
21:20 "This son of ours is stubborn and **r**.
31:27 For I know well how **r** and stubborn you are.
31:27 If you already have been so **r** toward the LORD
1Sa 20:30 He said to him, "You son of a perverse, **r** woman!
Ezr 4:12 They are rebuilding that **r** and wicked city;
4:15 You will discover in the annals that this is a **r** city,
Ps 66: 7 let the **r** not exalt themselves.
68: 6 but the **r** live in a parched land.
78: 8 a stubborn and **r** generation,
106:43 but they were **r** in their purposes,
Isa 30: 1 Oh, **r** children, says the LORD,
30: 9 For they are a **r** people, faithless children,
50: 5 Lord GOD has opened my ear, and I was not **r**,
65: 2 I held out my hands all day long to a **r** people,
Jer 5:23 But this people has a stubborn and **r** heart;
6:28 They are all stubbornly **r**,
La 1:20 because I have been very **r**.
Eze 2: 5 or refuse to hear (for they are a **r** house), A
2: 6 dismayed at their looks, for they are a **r** house. A
2: 7 for they are a **r** house. A
2: 8 do not be **r** like that rebellious house;
2: 8 do not be rebellious like that **r** house; A
3: 9 dismayed at their looks, for they are a **r** house. A
3:26 for they are a **r** house. A
3:27 for they are a **r** house. A
12: 2 you are living in the midst of a **r** house, A
12: 3 for they are a **r** house. A
12: 3 though they are a **r** house. A
12: 9 the **r** house, said to you, "What are you doing?" A
12:25 but in your days, O **r** house, I will speak A
17:12 Say now to the **r** house: Do you not know A
24: 3 utter an allegory to the **r** house and say to them, A
44: 6 Say to the **r** house, to the house of Israel, A
Ro 1:30 boastful, inventors of evil, **r** toward parents,
Tit 1: 6 not accused of debauchery and not **r**.
1:10 There are also many **r** people,
Heb 3:16 Now who were they who heard and yet were **r**?
1Es 2:18 and are building that **r** and wicked city,
1Es 2:22 and will learn that this city was **r**,
2Es 1: 8 not obeyed my law—they are a **r** people.

REBELS‡ (12) [REBEL]

Nu 17:10 to be kept as a warning to **r**,
20:10 and he said to them, "Listen, you **r**,
Jos 1:18 Whoever **r** against your orders
Pr 28: 2 When a land **r** it has many rulers;
Isa 1:23 Your princes are **r** and companions of thieves.
1:28 But **r** and sinners shall be destroyed together,
Eze 2: 3 to a nation of **r** who have rebelled against me;
20:38 I will purge out the **r** among you,
Hos 9:15 I will love them no more; all their officials are **r**.
Mk 15: 7 in prison with the **r** who had committed murder
Aza 1: 9 lawless and hateful **r**, and to an unjust king,
1Es 2:23 the Jews were **r** and kept setting up blockades in it

REBIRTH (2) [BEAR]

Tit 3: 5 the water of **r** and renewal by the Holy Spirit.
4Mc 16:13 and giving **r** for immortality to the whole number

REBUFFED (1)

Sir 13:10 Do not be forward, or you may be **r**;

REBUILD (22) [BUILD]

Ezr 1: 3 and **r** the house of the LORD, the God of Israel—
1: 5 got ready to go up and **r** the house of the LORD
5: 2 of Shealtiel and Jeshua son of Jozadak set out to **r**
6: 7 of the Jews and the elders of the Jews **r** this house
Ne 2: 5 so that I may **r** it."
2:17 Come, let us **r** the wall of Jerusalem,
Job 3:14 with kings and counselors of the earth who **r** ruins
12:14 If he tears down, no one can **r**;
Ps 51:18 in your good pleasure; **r** the walls of Jerusalem,
69:35 For God will save Zion and **r** the cities of Judah;
Jer 33: 7 and **r** them as they were at first.
Da 9:25 the word went out to restore and **r** Jerusalem until
Am 9:11 and raise up its ruins, and **r** it as in the days of old;
9:14 and they shall **r** the ruined cities and inhabit them;
Hag 1: 2 These people say the time has not yet come to **r**
Mal 1: 4 "We are shattered but we will **r** the ruins,"
Ac 15:16 and I will **r** the dwelling of David,
15:16 from its ruins I will **r** it, and I will set it up,
Tob 14: 5 and they will **r** the temple of God,
14: 5 from their exile and will **r** Jerusalem in splendor;
1Mc 10:10 in Jerusalem and began to **r** and restore the city.
12:37 So they gathered together to **r** the city;

REBUILDING (9) [BUILD]

2Ch 24:27 and of the **r** of the house of God are written in
Ezr 4:12 They are **r** that rebellious and wicked city;
5:11 we are **r** the house that was built many years ago,
5:17 by King Cyrus for the **r** of this house of God
6: 8 for these elders of the Jews for the **r** of this house
Zec 8: 9 the foundation was laid for the **r** of the temple,
1Mc 10:44 of **r** and restoring the structures of the sanctuary
10:45 of **r** the walls of Jerusalem and fortifying it all
10:45 and the cost of **r** the walls in Judea,

REBUILT (43) [BUILD]

Nu 32:34 And the Gadites **r** Dibon, Ataroth, Aroer,
32:37 And the Reubenites **r** Heshbon, Elealeh,
32:38 and they gave names to the towns that they **r**.
Dt 13:16 It shall remain a perpetual ruin, never to be **r**.
Jos 19:50 he **r** the town, and settled in it.
Jdg 18:28 They **r** the city, and lived in it.
21:23 and **r** the towns, and lived in them.
1Ki 9:17 so Solomon **r** Gezer), Lower Beth-horon,
2Ki 14:22 He **r** Elath and restored it to Judah,
21: 3 For he **r** the high places
2Ch 8: 2 Solomon **r** the cities that Huram had given to him,
26: 2 He **r** Eloth and restored it to Judah,
33: 3 For he **r** the high places
Ezr 4:13 if this city is **r** and the walls finished,
4:16 if this city is **r** and its walls finished,
4:21 and that this city not be **r**, until I make a decree.
5:13 made a decree that this house of God should be **r**.
5:15 and let the house of God be **r** on its site."
6: 3 the house of God at Jerusalem, let the house be **r**,
Ne 3: 1 with his fellow priests and **r** the Sheep Gate.
3:13 they **r** it and set up its doors, its bolts, and its bars,
3:14 he **r** it and set up its doors, its bolts, and its bars.
3:15 he **r** it and covered it and set up its doors, its bolts,
4: 6 So we **r** the wall, and all
Isa 25: 2 of aliens is a city no more, it will never be **r**.
44:26 "They shall be **r**, and I will raise up their ruins";
44:28 and who says of Jerusalem, "It shall be **r**,"
58:12 Your ancient ruins shall be **r**;
Jer 30:18 the city shall be **r** upon its mound,
31:38 be **r** for the LORD from the tower of Hananel to
Eze 26:14 You shall never again be **r**,
36:10 towns shall be inhabited and the waste places **r**;
36:33 and the waste places shall be **r**.
36:36 the LORD, have **r** the ruined places,
Tob 13:10 so that his tent may be **r** in you in joy.
14: 5 and in it the temple of God will be **r**,
Sir 49:13 and set up gates and bars, and **r** our ruined houses.
51:12 *Give thanks to him who **r** his city*
1Mc 4:48 also **r** the sanctuary and the interior of the temple,
5: 1 the altar had been **r** and the sanctuary dedicated
9:62 he **r** the parts of it that had been demolished,
1Es 6:17 King Cyrus wrote that this house should be **r**.
6:19 that this temple of the Lord should be **r** on its site.

REBUKE (49) [REBUKED, REBUKES]

Ru 2:16 and leave them for her to glean, and do not **r** her."
2Sa 22:16 at the **r** of the LORD, at the blast of the breath of
2Ki 19: 3 This day is a day of distress, of **r**, and of disgrace;
19: 4 and will **r** the words that the LORD your God
Job 13:10 surely **r** you if in secret you show partiality.
26:11 and are astounded at his **r**.
Ps 6: 1 do not **r** me in your anger,
18:15 at your **r**, O LORD, at the blast of the breath of
38: 1 do not **r** me in your anger,
50: 8 Not for your sacrifices do I **r** you;
50:21 But now I **r** you, and lay the charge before you.
68:30 **R** the wild animals that live among the reeds,
76: 6 At your **r**, O God of Jacob,
80:16 may they perish at the **r** of your countenance.
104: 7 At your **r** they flee;
119:21 You **r** the insolent, accursed ones,
Pr 10:17 but one who rejects a **r** goes astray.
13: 1 but a scoffer does not listen to **r**.
15:10 but one who hates a **r** will die.
17:10 A **r** strikes deeper into a discerning person than
24:25 but those who **r** the wicked will have delight,
25:12 Like a gold ring or an ornament of gold is a wise **r**
27: 5 Better is open **r** than hidden love.
30: 6 Do not add to his words, or else he will **r** you,
Ecc 7: 5 It is better to hear the **r** of the wise than to hear
Isa 17:13 but he will **r** them, and they will flee far away,
37: 3 This day is a day of distress, of **r**, and of disgrace;
37: 4 and will **r** the words that the LORD your God
50: 2 my **r** I dry up the sea, I make the rivers a desert;
51:20 of the wrath of the LORD, the **r** of your God.
54: 9 not be angry with you and will not **r** you.
66:15 and his **r** in flames of fire.
Zec 3: 2 the LORD said to Satan, "The LORD **r** you,
3: 2 The LORD who has chosen Jerusalem **r** you!
Mal 2: 3 I will **r** your offspring, and spread dung
3:11 I will **r** the locust for you,
Mt 16:22 And Peter took him aside and began to **r** him,
Mk 8:32 And Peter took him aside and began to **r** him.
Lk 17: 3 If another disciple sins, you must **r** the offender,
1Ti 5:20 **r** them in the presence of all,
2Ti 4: 2 convince, **r**, and encourage, with the utmost
Tit 1:13 For this reason **r** them sharply,
Jude 1: 9 but said, "The Lord **r** you!"
Wis 11: 7 in **r** for the decree to kill the infants,
12:17 you **r** any insolence among those who know it.
Sir 20: 1 There is a **r** that is untimely,
20: 2 How much better it is to **r** than to fume!
48: 7 You heard **r** at Sinai and judgments of vengeance
2Mc 7:33 to **r** and discipline us, he will again be reconciled

REBUKED (28) [REBUKE]

Ge 31:42 and the labor of my hands, and **r** you last night."
37:10 his father **r** him, and said to him,
1Ch 16:21 he **r** kings on their account,
Ps 9: 5 You have **r** the nations, you have destroyed
105:14 he **r** kings on their account,
106: 9 He **r** the Red Sea, and it became dry;
Pr 9: 8 A scoffer who is **r** will only hate you;
9: 8 the wise, when **r**, will love you.
12: 1 but those who hate to be **r** are stupid.
15:12 Scoffers do not like to be **r**;
Jer 29:27 not **r** Jeremiah of Anathoth who plays the prophet
Mt 8:26 Then he got up and **r** the winds and the sea;
17:18 And Jesus **r** the demon, and it came out of him,
Mk 1:25 But Jesus **r** him, saying, "Be silent,
4:39 He woke up and **r** the wind, and said to the sea,
8:33 he **r** Peter and said, "Get behind me, Satan!
9:25 he **r** the unclean spirit, saying to it,
Lk 3:19 who had been **r** by him because of Herodias,
4:35 But Jesus **r** him, saying, "Be silent,
4:39 he stood over her and **r** the fever, and it left her.
4:41 But he **r** them and would not allow them to speak,
8:24 he woke up and **r** the wind and the raging waves;
9:42 But Jesus **r** the unclean spirit, healed the boy,
9:55 But he turned and **r** them.
23:40 But the other **r** him, saying, "Do you not fear God,
2Pe 2:16 but was **r** for his own transgression;
Wis 17: 7 and their boasted wisdom was scornfully **r**.
2Mc 2: 7 Jeremiah learned of it, he **r** them and declared:

REBUKES (9) [REBUKE]

Pr 9: 7 whoever **r** the wicked gets hurt.
10:10 but the one who **r** boldly makes peace.
28:23 Whoever **r** a person will afterward find more favor
Na 1: 4 He **r** the sea and makes it dry,
Wis 12:26 not heeded the warning of mild **r** will experience
Sir 18:13 He **r** and trains and teaches them,
43:17 The voice of his thunder **r** the earth;
4Mc 2:11 so that one **r** her when she breaks the law.
2:13 so that one **r** friends when they act wickedly.

RECAH (1)

1Ch 4:12 These are the men of **R.**

RECALL (5) [RECALLED, RECALLING]

Isa 46: 8 Remember this and consider, **r** it to mind,
Eze 29:16 they will **r** their iniquity, when they turned
Heb 10:32 But **r** those earlier days when,
2Pe 1:15 be able at any time to **r** these things.
2Es 1:36 yet will **r** their former state.

RECALLED (1) [RECALL]

Wis 19:10 For they still **r** the events of their sojourn,

RECALLING (1) [RECALL]
2Ti 1: 4 **R** your tears, I long to see you so that I may

RECANT (1)
1Sa 15:29 the Glory of Israel will not **r** or change his mind;

RECASTS (1)
2Mc 2:31 but the one who **r** the narrative should be allowed

RECEDE (1) [RECEDED]
2Es 4:14 that it may **r** before us and so that we may make

RECEDED (1) [RECEDE]
Ge 8: 3 and the waters gradually **r** from the earth.

RECEIPT OF CUSTOM (KJV) See TAX BOOTH

RECEIVE‡ (146) [RECEIVED, RECEIVES, RECEIVING, RECEPTIVE]
Ge 4:11 to **r** your brother's blood from your hand.
Ex 25: 2 to give you shall **r** the offering for me.
25: 3 This is the offering that you shall **r** from them:
27: 3 You shall make pots for it to **r** its ashes,
Nu 18:26 When you **r** from the Israelites the tithe
18:28 to the LORD from all the tithes that you **r** from
Dt 9: 9 I went up the mountain to **r** the stone tablets,
Jos 11:20 and might **r** no mercy, but be exterminated,
1Ki 8:64 to **r** the burnt offerings and the grain offerings and
2Ki 12: 5 let the priests **r** from each of the donors;
Ne 10:38 be with the Levites when the Levites **r** the tithes;
Job 2:10 Shall we **r** the good at the hand of God,
2:10 the good at the hand of God, and not **r** the bad?"
3:12 Why were there knees to **r** me,
22:22 **R** instruction from his mouth,
27:13 the heritage that oppressors **r** from the Almighty:
35: 7 or what does he **r** from your hand?
Ps 24: 5 They will **r** blessing from the LORD,
49:15 from the power of Sheol, for he will **r** me.
69:19 the insults I **r**, and my shame and dishonor;
73:24 and afterward you will **r** me with honor.
Jer 9:20 and let your ears **r** the word of his mouth;
17:23 and would not hear or **r** instruction.
37:12 to **r** his share of property among the people there.
Eze 3:10 that I shall speak to you **r** in your heart and hear
Da 1: 9 to **r** favor and compassion from the palace master.
2: 6 you shall **r** from me gifts and rewards
7:18 of the Most High shall **r** the kingdom and possess
11:34 When they fall victim, they shall **r** a little help,
Mt 5: 7 "Blessed are the merciful, for they will **r** mercy.
10:41 in the name of a prophet will **r** a prophet's reward;
10:41 in the name of a righteous person will **r** the reward
11: 5 the blind **r** their sight, the lame walk,
19:29 will **r** a hundredfold, and will inherit eternal life.
20:10 the first came, they thought they would **r** more;
21:22 for in prayer with faith, you will **r**."
Mk 4:16 they hear the word, they immediately **r** it with joy.
10:15 whoever does not **r** the kingdom of God as
10:30 who will not **r** a hundredfold now in this age—
12:40 They will **r** the greater condemnation."
Lk 6:34 If you lend to those from whom you hope to **r**,
6:34 Even sinners lend to sinners, to **r** as much again.
7:22 the blind **r** their sight, the lame walk,
8:13 when they hear the word, **r** it with joy.
9:53 but they did not **r** him,
12:47 not prepare himself or do what was wanted, will **r**
12:48 not know and did what deserved a beating will **r**
18:17 whoever does not **r** the kingdom of God as
18:42 Jesus said to him, "**R** your sight;
20:47 They will **r** the greater condemnation."
Jn 3:11 yet you do not **r** our testimony.
3:27 No one can **r** anything except what has been given
7:39 which believers in him were to **r**;
12:48 and does not **r** my word has a judge;
14:17 whom the world cannot **r**,
16:24 Ask and you will **r**, so that your joy may
20:22 on them and said to them, "**R** the Holy Spirit.
Ac 1: 8 But you will **r** power when the Holy Spirit
2:38 and you will **r** the gift of the Holy Spirit.
3: 5 expecting to **r** something from them.
7:59 he prayed, "Lord Jesus, **r** my spirit."
8:15 down and prayed for them that they might **r**
8:19 on whom I lay my hands may **r** the Holy Spirit."
19: 2 "Did you **r** the Holy Spirit when you became
20:35 'It is more blessed to give than to **r**.' "
26:18 so that they may **r** forgiveness of sins and a place
Ro 5:17 much more surely will those who **r** the abundance
8:15 For you did not **r** a spirit of slavery to fall back
11:31 they too may now **r** mercy.
11:35 who has given a gift to him, to **r** a gift in return?"
13: 3 Then do what is good, and you will **r** its approval;
1Co 2:14 Those who are unspiritual do not **r** the gifts
3: 8 each will **r** wages according to the labor of each.
3:14 the builder will **r** a reward.
4: 5 Then each one will **r** commendation from God.
4: 7 What do you have that you did not **r**?
9:25 they do it to **r** a perishable wreath,
15:29 what will those people do who **r** baptism on behalf
2Co 5:10 so that each may **r** recompense
11: 4 you **r** a different spirit from the one you received,
Gal 1:12 for I did not **r** it from a human source,
3: 2 Did you **r** the Spirit by doing the works of the law
3:14 we might **r** the promise of the Spirit through faith.
Gal 4: 5 so that we might **r** adoption as children.
Eph 6: 8 we will **r** the same again from the Lord,
Col 3:24 the Lord you will **r** the inheritance as your reward;
Heb 4:16 that we may **r** mercy and find grace to help in time
7: 5 descendants of Levi who **r** the priestly office have
9:15 so that those who are called may **r** the promised
10:36 you may **r** what was promised.
11: 8 for a place that he was to **r** as an inheritance;
11:19 and figuratively speaking, he did **r** him back.
11:39 did not **r** what was promised,
Jas 1:7,8 must not expect to **r** anything from the Lord.
1:12 a one has stood the test and will **r** the crown of life
4: 3 You ask and do not **r**, because you ask wrongly,
1Jn 3:22 and we **r** from him whatever we ask,
5: 9 If we **r** human testimony, the testimony
2Jn 1: 8 but may **r** a full reward.
1:10 Do not **r** into the house
Rev 4:11 to **r** glory and honor and power,
5:12 to **r** power and wealth and wisdom and might
14: 9 and **r** a mark on their foreheads or on their hands,
17:12 but they are to **r** authority as kings for one hour,
Tob 4:14 If you serve God you will **r** payment.
12: 4 my child, to **r** half of all that he brought back."
Jdt 7:15 they rebelled and did not **r** you peaceably."
Wis 3: 5 they will **r** great good, because God tested them
5:16 Therefore they will **r** a glorious crown and
12: 7 so that the land most precious of all to you might **r**
17:21 image of the darkness that was destined to **r** them;
19:14 Others had refused to **r** strangers when they came
Sir 4:31 not let your hand be stretched out to **r** and closed
11:34 **R** strangers into your home and they will stir
12: 5 then you will **r** twice as much evil for all
24: 8 and in Israel **r** your inheritance.'
32: 2 so that you may be merry along with them and **r**
42: 7 and when you give or **r**, put it all in writing.
50:21 to **r** the blessing from the Most High.
51:26 and let your souls **r** instruction;
1Mc 2:51 you will **r** great honor and an everlasting name.
10:30 and the half of the fruit of the trees that I should **r**,
10:43 let them be released and **r** back all their property
14:23 to **r** these men with honor and to put a copy
15:27 But he refused to **r** them,
2Mc 7:36 will **r** just punishment for your arrogance.
14:19 and Mattathias to give and **r** pledges of friendship.
3Mc 3:28 Any who are willing to give information will **r**
7:10 against the holy God and the law of God should **r**
2Es 2:13 Go and you will **r**; pray that your days may be few,
2:36 **r** the joy of your glory;
2:37 **R** what the Lord has entrusted to you and
2:45 Now they are being crowned, and **r** palms."
7: 9 the heir **r** the inheritance unless by passing
7:14 they can never **r** those things
7:*96* the spacious liberty that they are to **r** and enjoy
7:*98* in life and from whom they are to **r** their reward
7:*128* [58] if they are victorious they shall **r** what I have
8:33 shall **r** their reward in consequence
8:49 You will **r** the greatest glory,
10:16 you will **r** your son back in due time,
15: 9 and will **r** to myself all the innocent blood from
15:51 so that you cannot **r** your mighty lovers.
15:55 therefore you shall **r** your recompense.
16:36 **r** it and do not disbelieve what the Lord says.
4Mc 5:37 My ancestors will **r** me as pure,

RECEIVED‡ (176) [RECEIVE]
Ge 33:10 since you have **r** me with such favor.
43:23 treasure in your sacks for you; I **r** your money."
Ex 36: 3 and they **r** from Moses all the freewill offerings
Nu 23:20 See, I **r** a command to bless;
31:51 and Eleazar the priest **r** the gold from them,
31:54 So Moses and Eleazar the priest **r** the gold from
Dt 16:10 in proportion to the blessing that you have **r** from
Jos 13: 8 the Reubenites and the Gadites **r** their inheritance,
14: 1 These are the inheritances that the Israelites **r** in
16: 4 and Ephraim—**r** their inheritance.
17: 6 of Manasseh **r** an inheritance along with his sons
18: 7 the half-tribe of Manasseh have **r** their inheritance
21: 4 the priest **r** by lot thirteen towns from the tribes
21: 5 the Kohathites **r** by lot ten towns from the families
21: 6 The Gershonites **r** by lot thirteen towns from
21: 7 according to their families **r** twelve towns from
1Sa 25:35 David **r** from her hand what she had brought him;
1Ki 7:13 King Solomon invited and **r** Hiram from Tyre.
10:28 and the king's traders **r** them from Kue at a price.
2Ki 19:14 Hezekiah **r** the letter from the hand of the
1Ch 5:20 and when they **r** help against them,
12:18 Then David **r** them, and made them officers
2Ch 1:16 the king's traders **r** them from Kue at
22: 6 to be healed in Jezreel of the wounds that he had **r**
29:22 priests **r** the blood and dashed it against the altar;
30:16 the priests dashed the blood that they **r** from
33:13 He prayed to him, and God **r** his entreaty,
33:19 His prayer, and how God **r** his entreaty,
35:11 the priests dashed the blood that they **r** from them,
Job 4:12 my ear **r** the whisper of it.
Pr 24:32 I saw and considered it; I looked and **r** instruction.
Isa 37:14 Hezekiah **r** the letter from the hand of
40: 2 that she has **r** from the LORD's hand double
Jer 37:17 Then King Zedekiah sent for him, and **r** him.
38:14 and **r** him at the third entrance of the temple of
Da 5:31 And Darius the Mede **r** the kingdom,
10: 1 having **r** understanding in the vision.
Zec 13: 6 the answer will be "The wounds I **r** in the house
Mt 6: 2 Truly I tell you, they have **r** their reward.
6: 5 Truly I tell you, they have **r** their reward.
6:16 Truly I tell you, they have **r** their reward.
Mt 10: 8 You **r** without payment; give without payment.
20: 9 each of them **r** the usual daily wage.
20:10 but each of them also **r** the usual daily wage.
20:11 And when they **r** it, they grumbled against
25:16 The one who had **r** the five talents went off
25:18 the one who had **r** the one talent went off and dug
25:20 the one who had **r** the five talents came forward,
25:24 one who had **r** the one talent also came forward,
25:27 on my return I would have **r** what was my own
Mk 11:24 believe that you have **r** it, and it will be yours.
Lk 6:24 for you have **r** your consolation.
16:25 that during your lifetime you **r** your good things,
19:15 When he returned, having **r** royal power,
Jn 1:12 But to all who **r** him, who believed in his name,
1:16 From his fullness we have all **r**, grace upon grace.
9:11 Then I went and washed and **r** my sight."
9:15 also began to ask him how he had **r** his sight.
9:18 and had **r** his sight until they called the parents of the man who had **r** his sight
10:18 I have **r** this command from my Father."
13:27 he **r** the piece of bread, Satan entered into him.
17: 8 and they have **r** them and know in truth
19:30 Jesus had **r** the wine, he said, "It is finished."
Ac 2:33 and having **r** from the Father the promise of
7:38 and he **r** living oracles to give to us.
7:53 the ones that **r** the law as ordained by angels,
8:17 and they **r** the Holy Spirit.
10:47 the water for baptizing these people who have **r**
20:24 and the ministry that I **r** from the Lord Jesus,
22: 5 also **r** letters to the brothers in Damascus,
26:10 with authority **r** from the chief priests,
28: 7 who **r** us and entertained us hospitably
28:21 "We have **r** no letters from Judea about you,
Ro 1: 5 through whom we have **r** grace and apostleship
1:27 Men committed shameless acts with men and **r**
4:11 He **r** the sign of circumcision as a seal of
5:11 through whom we have now **r** reconciliation.
8:15 but you have **r** a spirit of adoption.
11:30 now **r** mercy because of their disobedience,
1Co 2:12 Now we have **r** not the spirit of the world,
4: 7 you **r** it, why do you boast as if it were not a gift?
11:23 I **r** from the Lord what I also handed on to you,
15: 1 which you in turn **r**, in which also you stand,
15: 3 to you as of first importance what I in turn had **r**:
2Co 1: 9 we felt that we had **r** the sentence of death so
11: 4 if you receive a different spirit from the one you **r**,
11:24 Five times I have **r** from the Jews the forty lashes
11:25 Once I **r** a stoning.
Gal 1: 9 to you a gospel contrary to what you **r**,
1:12 but I **r** it through a revelation of Jesus Christ.
6: 1 you who have **r** the Spirit should restore such
Php 4: 9 the things that you have learned and **r** and heard
4:18 that I have **r** from Epaphroditus the gifts you sent,
Col 2: 6 As you therefore have **r** Christ Jesus the Lord,
4:10 concerning whom you have **r** instructions—
4:17 "See that you complete the task that you have **r** in
1Th 1: 6 of persecution you **r** the word with joy inspired by
2:13 you **r** the word of God that you heard from us,
2Th 3: 6 not according to the tradition that they **r** from us.
1Ti 1:13 But I **r** mercy because I had acted ignorantly
1:16 But for that very reason I **r** mercy, so that in me,
4: 3 to be **r** with thanksgiving by those who believe
4: 4 provided it is **r** with thanksgiving;
Phm 1: 7 I have indeed **r** much joy and encouragement
Heb 2: 2 and every transgression or disobedience **r**
4: 6 and those who formerly **r** the good news failed
7: 6 Abraham and blessed him who had **r** the promises.
7: 8 tithes are **r** by those who are mortal;
7:11 for the people **r** the law under this priesthood—
10:26 in sin after having **r** the knowledge of the truth,
11: 2 Indeed, by faith our ancestors **r** approval.
11: 4 Through this he **r** approval as righteous,
11:11 By faith he **r** power of procreation,
11:13 these died in faith without having **r** the promises,
11:17 He who had **r** the promises was ready to offer
11:31 because she had **r** the spies in peace.
11:35 Women **r** their dead by resurrection.
1Pe 2:10 you had not **r** mercy, but now you have **r** mercy.
4:10 with whatever gift each of you has **r**.
2Pe 1: 1 To those who have **r** a faith as precious as ours
1:17 For he **r** honor and glory from God the Father
1Jn 2:27 the anointing that you **r** from him abides in you,
Rev 2:28 even as I also **r** authority from my Father.
3: 3 Remember then what you **r** and heard;
13: 3 One of its heads seemed to have **r** a death-blow,
17:12 that you saw are ten kings who have not yet **r**
19:20 by which he deceived those who had **r** the mark of
20: 4 not **r** its mark on their foreheads or their hands.
Tob 7: 9 a ram from the flock and **r** them very warmly.
14:11 and he **r** an honorable funeral.
Jdt 12:15 before Holofernes the lambskins she had **r**
Wis 7:15 and to have thoughts worthy of what I have **r**;
11: 5 they themselves **r** benefit in their need.
11:13 the righteous had **r** benefit,
16: 6 and **r** a symbol of deliverance to remind them
19:15 the former for having **r** strangers with hostility,
19:16 having first **r** them with festal celebrations,
Sir 50:12 he **r** the portions from the hands of the priests,
51:16 I inclined my ear a little and **r** her,
Bar 4:32 wretched will be the city that **r** your offspring.
Sus 1:55 for the angel of God has **r** the sentence from God
1Mc 2:54 **r** the covenant of everlasting priesthood.
2:56 **r** an inheritance in the land.
10:42 of silver that my officials have **r** every year from
11:34 that the king formerly **r** from them each year,
12: 8 with honor, and **r** the letter, which contained
12:43 So he **r** him with honor and commended him

1Mc 13:37 We have r the gold crown and the palm branch
14:40 Romans had r the envoys of Simon with honor.
16:15 The son of Abubus r them treacherously in
2Mc 2: 4 that the prophet, having r an oracle, ordered that
8:33 so these r the proper reward for their impiety.
10:15 they r those who were banished from Jerusalem,
13:22 r theirs, withdrew, attacked Judas and his men,
13:24 He r Maccabeus, left Hegemonides as governor
3Mc 5:35 since this also was his aid that they had r.
5:50 but when they considered the help that they had r
7:16 to God even to death and had r the full enjoyment
2Es 2:33 r a command from the Lord on Mount Horeb
2:39 the shadow of this age have r glorious garments
7:*72* and though they r the commandments,
7:*72* they dealt unfaithfully with what they r.
7:*109* [39] and Elijah for those who r the rain,
8:43 because it has not r your rain in due season,
9:10 though they r my benefits,
9:32 But though our ancestors r the law,
9:33 Yet those who r it perished,
9:34 when the ground has r seed, or the sea a ship,
9:36 For we who have r the law and sinned will perish,
9:36 as well as our hearts that r it;
14:30 and r the law of life,
4Mc 5:15 When he had r permission to speak,
12:11 since you have r good things and
18:23 and have r pure and immortal souls from God,

RECEIVES (19) [RECEIVE]

Eze 16:32 who r strangers instead of her husband!
Mt 7: 8 For everyone who asks r,
13:20 the one who hears the word and immediately r it
Lk 11:10 For everyone who asks r,
Jn 7:23 a man r circumcision on the sabbath in order that
13:20 whoever r one whom I send r me; and whoever r
me r him who sent me."
Ac 10:43 that everyone who believes in him r forgiveness
Ro 2:29 a person r praise not from others but from God.
1Co 9:24 but only one r the prize?
Heb 6: 7 a crop useful to those for whom it is cultivated, r
7: 9 who r tithes, paid tithes through Abraham,
Jas 5: 7 with it until it r the early and the late rains.
Rev 2:17 that no one knows except the one who r it.
14:11 and its image and for anyone who r the mark
Sir 16:14 everyone r in accordance with one's deeds.
2Es 7:*91* with great joy the glory of him who r them,

RECEIVING‡ (17) [RECEIVE]

Ps 68:18 leading captives in your train and r gifts
Jn 4:36 The reaper is already r wages
13:30 r the piece of bread, he immediately went out.
Ac 17:15 and after r instructions to have Silas
Php 4:15 with me in the matter of giving and r,
Heb 12:28 since we are r a kingdom that cannot be shaken,
1Pe 1: 9 for you are r the outcome of your faith,
Sir 41:19 of surliness in r or giving,
1Mc 8:26 shall keep their obligations without r any return.
2Mc 4:25 After r the king's orders he returned,
10:20 and on r seventy thousand drachmas let some
12:12 after r his pledges they went back to their tents.
3Mc 5:26 and while the king was r his Friends,
5:27 on r the report and being struck by
7:10 On r this letter the Jews did not immediately hurry
2Es 8:39 and their salvation, and their r their reward.
4Mc 4: 5 On r authority to deal with this matter,

RECENT (1) [RECENTLY]

1Ti 3: 6 He must not be a r convert,

RECENTLY‡ (10) [RECENT]

Dt 32:17 to new ones r arrived, whom your ancestors had
Jer 34:15 You yourselves r repented and did what was right
Zec 8: 9 you that have r been hearing these words from
Ac 18: 2 who had r come from Italy with his wife Priscilla,
21:38 not the Egyptian who r stirred up a revolt and led
Jdt 4: 3 For they had only r returned from exile,
4: 5 since their fields had r been harvested.
2Mc 14:36 that has been so r purified."
3Mc 1:19 Those women who had r been arrayed
2Es 5:52 'Why are those whom you have borne r not

RECEPTIVE (1) [RECEIVE]

Ac 17:11 These Jews were more r than those in Thessalonica

RECESS (2) [RECESSED, RECESSES]

Eze 40: 7 and each r was one reed wide and one reed deep;
40:13 from the back of the one r to the back of the other,

RECESSED (3) [RECESS]

1Ki 6: 4 For the house he made windows with r frames.
Eze 41:16 all around, all three had windows with r frames.
41:26 And there were r windows and palm trees on

RECESSES (14) [RECESS]

2Ki 19:23 to the far r of Lebanon;
Job 38:16 or walked in the r of the deep?
Isa 37:24 to the far r of Lebanon;
Eze 40: 7 r, and each recess was one reed wide
40: 7 and the space between the r, five cubits;
40:10 There were three r on either side of the east gate;
40:12 There was a barrier before the r,
40:12 and the r were six cubits on either side.
40:16 The r and their pilasters had windows,
Eze 40:21 Its r, three on either side, and its pilasters
40:29 Its r, its pilasters, and its vestibule were of
40:33 Its r, its pilasters, and its vestibule were of
40:36 Its r, its pilasters, and its vestibule were of
Wis 17:14 upon them from the r of powerless Hades,

RECHAB (13) [RECHABITES]

2Sa 4: 2 and the name of the other R.
4: 5 the sons of Rimmon the Beerothite, R and Baanah,
4: 6 then R and his brother Baanah escaped.
4: 9 David answered R and his brother Baanah,
2Ki 10:15 he met Jehonadab son of R coming to meet him;
10:23 the temple of Baal with Jehonadab son of R;
1Ch 2:55 father of the house of R.
Ne 3:14 Malchijah son of R, ruler of the district
Jer 35: 6 for our ancestor Jonadab son of R commanded us,
35: 8 the charge of our ancestor Jonadab son of R in all
35:14 son of R gave to his descendants to drink no wine;
35:16 of Jonadab son of R have carried out the command
35:19 of R shall not lack a descendant to stand before me

RECHABITES (4) [RECHAB]

Jer 35: 2 of the R, and speak with them, and bring them to
35: 3 and all his sons, and the whole house of the R.
35: 5 I set before the R pitchers full of wine, and cups;
35:18 But to the house of the R Jeremiah said:

RECHAH (KJV) See RECAH

RECITE (4) [RECITED, RECITING]

Ex 17:14 as a reminder in a book and r it in the hearing
Dt 6: 7 R them to your children and talk about them
31:28 so that I may r these words in their hearing
Ps 50:16 "What right have you to r my statutes,

RECITED (2) [RECITE]

Dt 31:30 Then Moses r the words of this song,
32:44 and r all the words of this song in the hearing of

RECITING (1) [RECITE]

Dt 32:45 Moses had finished r all these words to all Israel,

RECKLESS (8) [RECKLESSNESS]

Jdg 9: 4 which Abimelech hired worthless and r fellows,
Zep 3: 4 Its prophets are r, faithless persons;
2Ti 3: 4 r, swollen with conceit, lovers
Sir 4:29 Do not be r in your speech,
8:15 Do not go traveling with the r,
9:18 and the one who is r in speech is hated.
19: 2 and the man who consorts with prostitutes is r.
19: 3 and the r person will be snatched away.

RECKLESSNESS (1) [RECKLESS]

Jer 23:32 by their lies and their r, when I did not send them

RECKON (1) [RECKONED, RECKONING, RECKONS]

Ro 4: 8 the one against whom the Lord will not r sin."

RECKONED‡ (29) [RECKON]

Ge 15: 6 and the LORD r it to him as righteousness.
Nu 3:50 r by the shekel of the sanctuary;
18:16 Their redemption price, r from one month of age,
18:27 It shall be r to you as your gift,
18:30 then the rest shall be r to the Levites as produce of
Dt 2:11 Like the Anakim, they are usually r as Rephaim,
2:20 (It also is usually r as a land of Rephaim.
Jos 13: 3 to the boundary of Ekron, it is r as Canaanite;
1Ch 5: 7 when the genealogy of their generations was r:
23:14 his sons were to be r among the tribe of Levi.
Ps 106:31 And that has been r to him as righteousness
La 4: 2 how they are r as earthen pots,
Ro 4: 3 and it was r to him as righteousness."
4: 4 wages are not r as a gift but as something due.
4: 5 such faith is r as righteousness.
4: 9 "Faith was r to Abraham as righteousness."
4:10 How then was it r to him?
4:11 and who thus have righteousness r to them,
4:22 his faith "was r to him as righteousness."
4:23 Now the words, "it was r to him,"
4:24 It will be r to us who believe
5:13 but sin is not r when there is no law.
Gal 3: 6 and it was r to him as righteousness,"
Jas 2:23 and it was r to him as righteousness,"
Wis 4:20 They will come with dread when their sins are r
1Mc 2:52 and it was r to him as righteousness?
11:27 and caused him to be r among his chief Friends.
2Mc 3: 6 so that the amount of the funds could not be r,
2Es 6: 5 and before the present years were r and before

RECKONING (8) [RECKON]

Ge 9: 5 For your own lifeblood I will surely require a r:
9: 5 I will require a r for human life.
42:22 So now there comes a r for his blood."
Nu 3:47 r by the shekel of the sanctuary,
23: 9 and not r itself among the nations!
Mt 18:24 When he began the r, one who owed him ten
Sir 2:14 What will you do when the Lord's r comes?
39:28 on the day of r they will pour out their strength

RECKONS (1) [RECKON]

Ro 4: 6 to whom God r righteousness apart from works:

RECLINE (1) [RECLINED, RECLINES, RECLINING]

3Mc 5:16 for the banquet to r opposite him.

RECLINED‡ (3) [RECLINE]

Jn 21:20 the one who had r next to Jesus at the supper
Tob 2: 1 a good dinner was prepared for me and I r to eat.
7: 9 and washed themselves and had r to dine,

RECLINES (1) [RECLINE]

1Es 4:10 Furthermore, he r, he eats and drinks and sleeps,

RECLINING‡ (5) [RECLINE]

Est 7: 8 on the couch where Esther was r;
Jn 13:23 the one whom Jesus loved—was r next to him;
13:25 r next to Jesus, he asked him, "Lord, who is it?"
Tob 9: 6 into Raguel's house they found Tobias r at table.
Jdt 12:15 from Bagoas for her daily use in r.

RECOGNITION (1) [RECOGNIZE]

1Co 16:18 So give r to such persons.

RECOGNIZE‡ (19) [RECOGNITION, RECOGNIZED, RECOGNIZES, RECOGNIZING]

Ge 27:23 He did not r him, because his hands were hairy
42: 8 Joseph had recognized his brothers, they did not r
Dt 18:21 can we r a word that the LORD has not spoken?"
Ru 3:14 but got up before one person could r another;
Job 2:12 they saw him from a distance, they did not r him,
Mt 17:12 Elijah has already come, and they did not r him,
Mk 10:42 that among the Gentiles those whom they r
Lk 19:44 because you did not r the time of your visitation
Ac 13:27 not r him or understand the words of the prophets
27:39 In the morning they did not r the land,
1Co 14:38 Anyone who does not r this is not to
Tob 5: 2 What evidence am I to give him so that he will r
Jdt 14: 5 and r the man who despised the house of Israel
Wis 13: 1 the one who exists, nor did they r the artisan
Sir 23:27 Those who survive her will r that there is
2Mc 6:12 but to r that these punishments were designed not
7:28 and r that God did not make them out of things
2Es 2:16 because I r my name in them.
4Mc 2: 9 In all other matters we can r that reason rules

RECOGNIZED (26) [RECOGNIZE]

Ge 37:33 He r it, and said, "It is my son's robe!
42: 7 When Joseph saw his brothers, he r them,
42: 8 Although Joseph had r his brothers,
Jdg 18: 3 they r the voice of the young Levite;
1Sa 26:17 Saul r David's voice, and said, "Is this your voice,
1Ki 18: 7 Obadiah r him, fell on his face, and said,
20:41 The king of Israel r him as one of the prophets.
La 4: 8 they are not r in the streets.
Mt 14:35 After the people of that place r him,
Mk 6:33 Now many saw them going and r them,
6:54 they got out of the boat, people at once r him,
Lk 19:42 had only r on this day the things that make
24:31 Then their eyes were opened, and they r him;
Ac 3:10 and they r him as the one who used to sit and ask
4:13 they were amazed and r them as companions
19:34 But when they r that he was a Jew,
1Co 14:38 Anyone who does not recognize this is not to be r.
2Co 11:12 to be r as our equals in what they boast about.
Gal 2: 9 r the grace that had been given to me,
Jdt 8:29 the people have r your understanding,
Wis 10: 5 r the righteous man and preserved him blameless
12:27 and r as the true God the one whom they had
2Mc 3:28 They r clearly the sovereign power of God.
4: 4 Onias r that the rivalry was serious and
15:28 they r Nicanor, lying dead, in full armor.
4Mc 3:20 the temple service and r their commonwealth—

RECOGNIZES (1) [RECOGNIZE]

Sir 18:12 He sees and r that their end is miserable;

RECOGNIZING (3) [RECOGNIZE]

Lk 24:16 but their eyes were kept from r him.
Ac 12:14 On r Peter's voice, she was so overjoyed that,
Wis 10: 8 they not only were hindered from r the good,

RECOILS (1)

Hos 11: 8 My heart r within me; my compassion grows

RECOMMENDATION (1) [RECOMMENDED]

2Co 3: 1 as some do, letters of r to you or from you, do we?

RECOMMENDED (1) [RECOMMENDATION]

AdE 1:21 and the king did as Muchaeus had r.

RECOMPENSE‡ (15) [RECOMPENSED]

Dt 32:35 Vengeance is mine, and r,
2Sa 19:36 Why should the king r me with such a reward?

Job 15:31 for emptiness will be their **r**.
Isa 35: 4 He will come with vengeance, with terrible **r**.
40:10 his reward is with him, and his **r** before him.
61: 8 I will faithfully give them their **r**,
62:11 his reward is with him, and his **r** before him."
Jer 18:20 Is evil a **r** for good?
51:56 for the LORD is a God of **r**, he will repay in full.
Hos 9: 7 the days of **r** have come;
2Co 5:10 so that each may receive **r** for what has been done
Sir 17:23 and he will bring their **r** on their heads.
20:14 for he looks for **r** sevenfold.
2Es *7:35* **R** shall follow, and the reward shall be manifested;
15:55 therefore you shall receive your **r**.

RECOMPENSED (4) [RECOMPENSE]

2Sa 22:21 according to the cleanness of my hands he **r** me.
22:25 LORD has **r** me according to my righteousness,
Ps 18:20 according to the cleanness of my hands he **r** me.
18:24 LORD has **r** me according to my righteousness,

RECONCILE (4) [RECONCILED, RECONCILIATION, RECONCILING]

1Sa 29: 4 For how could this fellow **r** himself to his lord?
Ac 7:26 as they were quarreling and tried to **r** them,
Eph 2:16 and might **r** both groups to God in one body
Col 1:20 him God was pleased to **r** to himself all things,

RECONCILED (13) [RECONCILE]

Mt 5:24 first be **r** to your brother or sister,
Ro 5:10 we were **r** to God through the death of his Son,
5:10 having been **r**, will we be saved by his life.
1Co 7:11 her remain unmarried or else be **r** to her husband),
2Co 5:18 who **r** us to himself through Christ,
5:20 we entreat you on behalf of Christ, be **r** to God.
Col 1:22 he has now **r** in his fleshly body through death,
2Mc 1: 5 May he hear your prayers and be **r** to you,
5:20 in all its glory when the great Lord became **r**.
7:33 he will again be **r** with his own servants.
8:29 the merciful Lord to be wholly **r** with his servants.
1Es 4:31 he flatters her, so that she may be **r** to him.
3Mc 5:13 and again implored him who is easily **r** to show

RECONCILIATION (7) [RECONCILE]

Ac 12:20 the king's chamberlain, they asked for a **r**,
Ro 5:11 through whom we have now received **r**.
11:15 For if their rejection is the **r** of the world,
2Co 5:18 and has given us the ministry of **r**;
5:19 and entrusting the message of **r** to us.
Sir 22:22 do not worry, for **r** is possible.
27:21 and there is **r** after abuse,

RECONCILING (1) [RECONCILE]

2Co 5:19 in Christ God was **r** the world to himself,

RECONNOITERED (1)

Jdt 7: 7 He **r** the approaches to their town,

RECONVENED (1) [CONVENE]

3Mc 5:36 **r** the party in the same manner and urged

RECORD (9) [RECORDED, RECORDER, RECORDS]

1Ch 4:33 And they kept a genealogical **r**.
Ezr 6: 2 on which this was written: "A **r**.
Ps 56: 8 Are they not in your **r**?
Jer 22:30 **R** this man as childless, a man who shall not
Col 2:14 the **r** that stood against us with its legal demands.
Tob 12:12 it was I who brought and read the **r** of your prayer
AdE 12: 4 The king made a permanent **r** of these things,
1Mc 14:23 the people of the Spartans may have a **r** of them.
14:27 So they made a **r** on bronze tablets and put it

RECORDED (25) [RECORD]

Ge 48: 6 be **r** under the names of their brothers with regard
Dt 28:61 even though not **r** in the book of this law,
2Sa 24: 9 to the king the number of those who had been **r**:
1Ch 24: 6 a Levite, **r** them in the presence of the king,
2Ch 12:15 Shemaiah and of the seer Iddo, **r** by genealogy?
20:34 which are **r** in the Book of the Kings of Israel.
35:25 they are **r** in the Laments.
Ezr 8:34 and the weight of everything was **r**.
Ne 12:22 there were **r** the heads of ancestral houses;
12:23 were **r** in the Book of the Annals until the days
Est 2:23 It was **r** in the book of the annals in the presence
9:20 Mordecai **r** these things, and sent letters to all
9:32 and it was **r** in writing.
Ps 102:18 Let this be **r** for a generation to come,
Isa 4: 3 everyone who has been **r** for life in Jerusalem,
Jer 17:13 those who turn away from you shall be **r** in
Rev 20:12 according to their works, as **r** in the books.
AdE 9:20 Mordecai **r** these things in a book,
10: 2 they were **r** in the annals of the kings of
1Mc 9:22 have not been **r**, but they were very many.
14:22 We have **r** what they said in our public decrees,
1Es 1:24 the events of his reign have been **r**—
1:33 are **r** in the book of the kings of Israel and Judah.
6:23 a scroll was found in which this was **r**:
8:64 the weight of everything was **r** at that very time.

RECORDER (11) [RECORD]

2Sa 8:16 Jehoshaphat son of Ahilud was **r**;
20:24 Jehoshaphat son of Ahilud was the **r**;
1Ki 4: 3 Jehoshaphat son of Ahilud was **r**;
2Ki 18:18 and Joah son of Asaph, the **r**.
18:37 and Joah son of Asaph, the **r**,
1Ch 18:15 Jehoshaphat son of Ahilud was **r**;
2Ch 34: 8 the **r**, to repair the house of the LORD his God.
Isa 36: 3 and Joah son of Asaph, the **r**.
36:22 the **r**, came to Hezekiah with their clothes torn,
1Es 2:17 the **r** Rehum and the scribe Shimshai and
2:25 Then the king, in reply to the **r** Rehum,

RECORDS (16) [RECORD]

Ex 38:21 These are the **r** of the tabernacle,
1Ch 4:22 but returned to Lehem (now the **r** are ancient).
29:29 are written in the **r** of the seer Samuel,
29:29 and in the **r** of the prophet Nathan,
29:29 and in the **r** of the seer Gad,
2Ch 12:15 not written in the **r** of the prophet Shemaiah and
33:19 these are written in the **r** of the seers.
Ezr 2:62 the genealogical **r**, but they were not found there,
Est 6: 1 and he gave orders to bring the book of **r**,
Ps 87: 6 The LORD **r**, as he registers the peoples,
AdE 6: 1 to his secretary to bring the book of daily **r**,
16: 7 so much from the more ancient **r** that we hand on,
2Mc 2: 1 One finds in the **r** that the prophet Jeremiah
2:13 The same things are reported in the **r** and in
4:23 the money to the king and to complete the **r**
1Es 2:21 search may be made in the **r** of your ancestors.

RECOUNT‡ (8) [RECOUNTED]

Ps 9:14 so that I may **r** all your praises,
79:13 to generation we will **r** your praise.
118:17 but I shall live, and **r** the deeds of the LORD.
Isa 63: 7 I will **r** the gracious deeds of the LORD,
Da 4: 2 for me I am pleased to **r**.
Sir 18: 5 And who can fully **r** his mercies?
36:10 and let people **r** your mighty deeds.
42:17 even his holy ones to **r** all his marvelous works,

RECOUNTED (4) [RECOUNT]

Jdg 6:13 that our ancestors **r** to us,
Est 5:11 and Haman **r** to them the splendor of his riches,
Jdt 2: 2 and set before them his secret plan and **r** fully,
4Mc 18:16 He **r** to you Solomon's proverb,

RECOVER (17) [RECOVERED, RECOVERING, RECOVERS, RECOVERY]

Ge 38:20 to **r** the pledge from the woman,
Lev 25:28 But if there is not sufficient means to **r** it,
Jdg 11:26 why did you not **r** them within that time?
2Ki 1: 2 whether I shall **r** from this injury."
8: 8 whether I shall **r** from this illness."
8: 9 saying, 'Shall I **r** from this illness?' "
8:10 "Go, say to him, 'You shall certainly **r**';
8:14 "He told me that you would certainly **r**."
20: 1 for you shall die; you shall not **r**."
20: 7 and apply it to the boil, so that he may **r**."
2Ch 13:20 Jeroboam did not **r** his power in the days
Isa 11:11 yet a second time to **r** the remnant that is left
38: 1 for you shall die; you shall not **r**."
38:21 and apply it to the boil, so that he may **r**."
Mk 16:18 ⟦lay their hands on the sick, and they will **r**."⟧
Jn 4:52 So he asked them the hour when he began to **r**,
1Es 3:23 And when they **r** from the wine,

RECOVERED‡ (12) [RECOVER]

1Sa 7:14 and Israel **r** their territory from the hand of
30:18 David **r** all that the Amalekites had taken;
30:22 not give them any of the spoil that we have **r**,
2Ki 13:25 Three times Joash defeated him and **r** the towns
14:28 and how he **r** for Israel Damascus and Hamath,
16: 6 At that time the king of Edom **r** Elath for Edom,
Isa 38: 9 after he had been sick and had **r** from his sickness:
39: 1 for he heard that he had been sick and had **r**.
2Mc 10: 1 Lord leading them on, **r** the temple and the city;
3Mc 2:24 a while he **r**, and though he had been punished, he
7:22 Besides, they all **r** all of their property,
2Es 5:22 Then my soul **r** the spirit of understanding,

RECOVERING (1) [RECOVER]

2Mc 9:22 for I have good hope of **r** from my illness,

RECOVERS (1) [RECOVER]

Ex 21:19 but **r** and walks around outside with the help of

RECOVERY (6) [RECOVER]

Ex 21:19 and to arrange for full **r**.
Jer 33: 6 I am going to bring it **r** and healing;
Lk 4:18 to proclaim release to the captives and **r** of sight to
Sir 38:13 There may come a time when **r** lies in the hands
2Mc 3:29 and deprived of any hope of **r**,
3:32 offered sacrifice for the man's **r**.

RECRUIT (2) [RECRUITED]

1Mc 10: 6 So Demetrius gave him authority to **r** troops,
10: 8 that the king had given him authority to **r** troops.

RECRUITED (3) [RECRUIT]

1Mc 10:21 and he **r** troops and equipped them with arms
11:38 the foreign troops that he had **r** from the islands of
15: 3 and have **r** a host of mercenary troops

RED‡ (48) [REDDISH, REDDISH-WHITE, REDNESS]

A. RED SEA (30)

Ge 25:25 first came out **r**, all his body like a hairy mantle;
25:30 "Let me eat some of that **r** stuff,
Ex 10:19 the locusts and drove them into the **R** Sea; A
13:18 of the wilderness toward the **R** Sea. A
15: 4 his picked officers were sunk in the **R** Sea. A
15:22 Moses ordered Israel to set out from the **R** Sea, A
23:31 I will set your borders from the **R** Sea to the sea A
Nu 14:25 for the wilderness by the way to the **R** Sea." A
19: 2 Tell the Israelites to bring you a **r** heifer
21: 4 by the way to the **R** Sea, to go around the land A
33:10 set out from Elim and camped by the **R** Sea. A
33:11 the **R** Sea and camped in the wilderness of Sin. A
Dt 1:40 in the direction of the **R** Sea." A
2: 1 in the direction of the **R** Sea, A
11: 4 the **R** Sea flow over them as they pursued you, A
Jos 2:10 **R** Sea before you when you came out of Egypt, A
4:23 as the LORD your God did to the **R** Sea, A
24: 6 with chariots and horsemen to the **R** Sea. A
Jdg 11:16 wilderness to the **R** Sea and came to Kadesh. A
1Ki 9:26 which is near Eloth on the shore of the **R** Sea, A
2Ki 3:22 the Moabites saw the water opposite them as **r**
Ne 9: 9 in Egypt and heard their cry at the **R** Sea. A
Job 16:16 My face is **r** with weeping,
Ps 106: 7 but rebelled against the Most High at the **R** Sea. A
106: 9 He rebuked the **R** Sea, and it became dry; A
106:22 and awesome deeds by the **R** Sea. A
136:13 who divided the **R** Sea in two, A
136:15 overthrew Pharaoh and his army in the **R** Sea, A
Pr 23:31 Do not look at wine when it is **r**,
Isa 1:18 though they are **r** like crimson,
63: 2 "Why are your robes **r**, and your garments
Jer 49:21 sound of their cry shall be heard at the **R** Sea. A
Na 2: 3 The shields of his warriors are **r**;
Zec 1: 8 In the night I saw a man riding on a **r** horse!
1: 8 and behind him were **r**, sorrel, and white horses.
6: 2 The first chariot had **r** horses,
Mt 16: 2 you say, 'It will be fair weather, for the sky is **r**.'
16: 3 for the sky is **r** and threatening.'
Ac 7:36 the **R** Sea, and in the wilderness for forty years. A
Heb 11:29 By faith the people passed through the **R** Sea as A
Rev 6: 4 And out came another horse, bright **r**;
12: 3 a great **r** dragon, with seven heads and ten horns,
Jdt 5:13 Then God dried up the **R** Sea before them, A
Wis 10:18 She brought them over the **R** Sea, A
13:14 a coat of **r** paint and coloring its surface **r**
19: 7 an unhindered way out of the **R** Sea, A
1Mc 4: 9 how our ancestors were saved at the **R** Sea, A

REDDISH (2) [RED]

Lev 13:49 if the disease shows greenish or **r** in the garment,
14:37 in the walls of the house with greenish or **r** spots,

REDDISH-WHITE (4) [RED, WHITE]

Lev 13:19 the boil there appears a white swelling or a **r** spot,
13:24 and the raw flesh of the burn becomes a spot, **r**
13:42 or the bald forehead a **r** diseased spot,
13:43 if the diseased swelling is **r** on his bald head or

REDEEM‡ (46) [REDEEMABLE, REDEEMED, REDEEMER, REDEEMING, REDEEMS, REDEMPTION]

Ex 6: 6 I will **r** you with an outstretched arm and
13:13 every firstborn donkey you shall **r** with a sheep;
13:13 if you do not **r** it, you must break its neck.
13:13 among your children you shall **r**.
13:15 but every firstborn of my sons I **r**.'
34:20 The firstborn of a donkey you shall **r** with a lamb,
34:20 or if you will not **r** it you shall break its neck.
34:20 All the firstborn of your sons you shall **r**.
Lev 25:25 of kin shall come and **r** what the relative has sold.
25:26 If the person has no one to **r** it,
25:48 one of their brothers may **r** them,
25:49 or their uncle or their uncle's son may **r** them,
25:49 of their own flesh may **r** them;
25:49 or if they prosper they may **r** themselves.
27:15 the one who consecrates the house wishes to **r** it,
27:19 if the one who consecrates the field wishes to **r** it,
27:31 If persons wish to **r** any of their tithes,
Nu 18:15 but the firstborn of human beings you shall **r**,
18:15 and the firstborn of unclean animals you shall **r**.
18:17 or the firstborn of a goat, you shall not **r**;
Ru 4: 4 If you will **r** it, **r** it; but if you will not,
4: 4 for there is no one prior to you to **r** it,
4: 4 So he said, "I will **r** it."
4: 6 "I cannot **r** it for myself without damaging my own
4: 6 my right of redemption yourself, for I cannot **r** it."
2Sa 7:23 on earth whose God went to **r** it as a people,
1Ch 17:21 on the earth whom God went to **r** to be his people,
Job 5:20 In famine he will **r** you from death,
Ps 25:22 **R** Israel, O God, out of all its troubles.
26:11 **r** me, and be gracious to me.
44:26 **R** us for the sake of your steadfast love.
55:18 He will **r** me unharmed from the battle
69:18 **r** me, set me free because of my enemies.
119:134 **R** me from human oppression,
119:154 Plead my cause and **r** me;
130: 7 and with him is great power to **r**.
130: 8 It is he who will **r** Israel from all its iniquities.
Isa 50: 2 Is my hand shortened, that it cannot **r**?
Jer 15:21 and **r** you from the grasp of the ruthless.

Hos 7:13 I would **r** them, but they speak lies against me.
13:14 Shall I **r** them from Death?
Mic 4:10 there the LORD will **r** you from the hands
Lk 24:21 But we had hoped that he was the one to **r** Israel.
Gal 4: 5 in order to **r** those who were under the law,
Tit 2:14 He it is who gave himself for us that he might **r** us

REDEEMABLE (1) [REDEEM]

Lev 27:20 sold to someone else, it shall no longer be **r.**

REDEEMED‡ (52) [REDEEM]

Ge 48:16 angel who has **r** me from all harm, bless the boys;
Ex 15:13 steadfast love you led the people whom you **r;**
21: 8 then he shall let her be **r;**
Lev 25:29 it may be **r** until a year has elapsed since its sale;
25:30 If it is not **r** before a full year has elapsed,
25:31 they may be **r,** and they shall be released in
25:33 Such property as may be **r** from the Levites—
25:54 And if they have not been **r** in any of these ways,
27:13 But if it is to be **r,** one-fifth must be added
27:20 but if the field is not **r,** or if it has been sold
27:27 if it is not **r,** it shall be sold at its assessment.
27:28 or inherited landholding, may be sold or **r;**
27:33 it and the substitute shall be holy and cannot be **r.**
Nu 3:48 by which the excess number of them is **r.**
3:49 from those who were over and above those **r** by
Dt 7: 8 and **r** you from the house of slavery,
9:26 whom you **r** in your greatness,
13: 5 of Egypt and **r** you from the house of slavery—
15:15 and the LORD your God **r** you;
21: 8 O LORD, your people Israel, whom you **r;**
24:18 a slave in Egypt and the LORD your God **r** you
2Sa 4: 9 who has **r** my life out of every adversity,
1Ch 17:21 before your people whom you **r** from Egypt?
Ne 1:10 whom you **r** by your great power
Job 33:28 He has **r** my soul from going down to the Pit,
Ps 31: 5 you have **r** me, O LORD, faithful God.
74: 2 which you **r** to be the tribe of your heritage.
77:15 With your strong arm you **r** your people,
78:42 or the day when he **r** them from the foe;
107: 2 Let the **r** of the LORD say so, those he **r** from
Isa 1:27 Zion shall be **r** by justice,
29:22 Therefore thus says the LORD, who **r** Abraham,
35: 9 but the **r** shall walk there.
43: 1 Do not fear, for I have **r** you;
44:22 return to me, for I have **r** you.
44:23 LORD has **r** Jacob, and will be glorified in Israel.
48:20 say, "The LORD has **r** his servant Jacob!"
51:10 the depths of the sea a way for the **r** to cross over?
52: 3 and you shall be **r** without money.
52: 9 has comforted his people, he has **r** Jerusalem.
62:12 "The Holy People, The **R** of the LORD";
63: 9 in his love and in his pity he **r** them;
Jer 31:11 and has **r** him from hands too strong for him.
La 3:58 O Lord, you have **r** my life.
Mic 6: 4 and **r** you from the house of slavery;
Zec 10: 8 for I have **r** them, and they shall be as numerous
Lk 1:68 he has looked favorably on his people and **r** them.
Gal 3:13 Christ **r** us from the curse of the law by becoming
Rev 14: 3 one hundred forty-four thousand who have been **r**
14: 4 They have been **r** from humankind as first fruits
AdE 13:16 which you **r** for yourself out of the land of Egypt.

REDEEMER (19) [REDEEM]

Job 19:25 For I know that my **R** lives,
Ps 19:14 O LORD, my rock and my **r.**
78:35 the Most High God their **r.**
Pr 23:11 for their **r** is strong; he will plead their cause
Isa 41:14 your **R** is the Holy One of Israel.
43:14 Thus says the LORD, your **R,**
44: 6 the King of Israel, and his **R,** the LORD of hosts:
44:24 Thus says the LORD, your **R,**
47: 4 Our **R**—the LORD of hosts
48:17 Thus says the LORD, your **R,**
49: 7 the **R** of Israel and his Holy One,
49:26 and your **R,** the Mighty One of Jacob.
54: 5 the Holy One of Israel is your **R,**
54: 8 on you, says the LORD, your **R.**
59:20 And he will come to Zion as **R,**
60:16 the LORD, am your Savior and your **R,**
63:16 our **R** from of old is your name.
Jer 50:34 Their **R** is strong; the LORD of hosts is his name.
Sir 51:12 *Give thanks to the r of Israel,*

REDEEMING (2) [REDEEM]

Ru 4: 7 the custom in former times in Israel concerning **r**
Isa 63: 4 and the year for my **r** work had come.

REDEEMS (5) [REDEEM]

Ps 34:22 The LORD **r** the life of his servants;
72:14 From oppression and violence he **r** their life;
103: 4 who **r** your life from the Pit,
Heb 9:15 because a death has occurred that **r** them from
1Mc 4:11 the Gentiles will know that there is one who **r**

REDEMPTION‡ (25) [REDEEM]

Ex 21:30 the owner shall pay whatever is imposed for the **r**
Lev 25:24 you shall provide for the **r** of the land.
25:29 the right of **r** shall be one year.
25:32 the right of **r** of the houses in the cities belonging
25:48 have sold themselves they shall have the right of **r;**
25:51 for their **r** in proportion to the purchase price;
25:52 they shall make payment for their **r.**
Nu 3:46 As the price of **r** of the two hundred seventy-three
3:49 So Moses took the **r** money from those who were
3:51 Moses gave the **r** money to Aaron and his sons,
18:16 Their **r** price, reckoned from one month of age,
Ru 4: 6 Take my right of **r** yourself,
Ps 111: 9 He sent **r** to his people;
Jer 32: 7 for the right of **r** by purchase is yours."
32: 8 for the right of possession and **r** is yours;
Lk 2:38 about the child to all who were looking for the **r**
21:28 because your **r** is drawing near."
Ro 3:24 through the **r** that is in Christ Jesus,
8:23 while we wait for adoption, the **r** of our bodies.
1Co 1:30 and righteousness and sanctification and **r,**
Eph 1: 7 In him we have **r** through his blood,
1:14 of our inheritance toward **r** as God's own people,
4:30 with a seal for the day of **r.**
Col 1:14 in whom we have **r,** the forgiveness of sins.
Heb 9:12 but with his own blood, thus obtaining eternal **r.**

REDNESS (1) [RED]

Pr 23:29 has wounds without cause? Who has **r** of eyes?

REDOUND (KJV) See INCREASE

REDRESS (1)

Eze 22:29 and have extorted from the alien without **r.**

REDUCE (3) [REDUCED, REDUCES, REDUCING]

Dt 28:55 the enemy siege will **r** you in all your towns.
28:57 the enemy siege will **r** you in your towns.
1Co 1:28 things that are not, to **r** to nothing things that are,

REDUCED (8) [REDUCE]

Lev 6:10 the ashes to which the fire has **r** the burnt offering
27:18 and the assessment shall be **r.**
Dt 9:21 grinding it thoroughly, until it was **r** to dust;
1Ki 22:27 Put this fellow in prison, and feed him on **r** rations
2Ch 18:26 Put this fellow in prison, and feed him on **r** rations
Ezr 4:13 custom, or toll, and the royal revenue will be **r.**
Eze 16:27 against you, **r** your rations, and gave you up to
3Mc 2:29 they shall also be **r** to their former limited status."

REDUCES (1) [REDUCE]

Dt 28:53 straits to which the enemy siege **r** you,

REDUCING (1) [REDUCE]

Sir 31:30 **r** his strength and adding wounds.

REED (31) [REEDS]

Ge 41: 2 and they grazed in the **r** grass.
41:18 came up out of the Nile and fed in the **r** grass.
1Ki 14:15 as a **r** is shaken in the water;
2Ki 18:21 relying now on Egypt, that broken **r** of a staff,
Job 9:26 They go by like skiffs of **r,**
Isa 9:14 palm branch and **r** in one day—
19:15 Neither head nor tail, palm branch or **r,**
36: 6 you are relying on Egypt, that broken **r** of a staff,
42: 3 a bruised **r** he will not break,
Eze 29: 6 that I am the LORD because you were a staff of **r**
40: 3 with a linen cord and a measuring **r** in his hand;
40: 5 The length of the measuring **r** in
40: 5 thickness of the wall, one **r;** and the height, one **r.**
40: 6 the threshold of the gate, one **r** deep.
40: 7 each recess was one **r** wide and one **r** deep;
40: 7 of the gate at the inner end was one **r** deep.
41: 8 of the side chambers measured a full **r**
42:16 He measured the east side with the measuring **r,**
42:16 five hundred cubits by the measuring **r.**
42:17 five hundred cubits by the measuring **r.**
42:18 five hundred cubits by the measuring **r.**
42:19 five hundred cubits by the measuring **r.**
Mt 11: 7 A **r** shaken by the wind?
12:20 not break a bruised **r** or quench a smoldering wick
27:29 They put a **r** in his right hand and knelt before him
27:30 and took the **r** and struck him on the head.
Mk 15:19 They struck his head with a **r,** spat upon him,
Lk 7:24 A **r** shaken by the wind?
3Mc 2:22 He shook him on this side and that as a **r** is shaken

REEDS‡ (8) [REED]

Ex 2: 3 she put the child in it and placed it among the **r** on
2: 5 She saw the basket among the **r** and sent her maid
Job 8:11 Can **r** flourish where there is no water?
40:21 in the covert of the **r** and in the marsh.
Ps 68:30 Rebuke the wild animals that live among the **r,**
Isa 19: 6 **r** and rushes will rot away.
35: 7 the grass shall become **r** and rushes.
Sir 40:16 The **r** by any water or river bank are plucked up

REEF (1)

Ac 27:41 But striking a **r,** they ran the ship aground;

REEFS See Index to Footnotes

REEL (3) [REELED, REELING, REELS]

Ps 60: 3 you have given us wine to drink that made us **r.**
Isa 28: 7 also **r** with wine and stagger with strong drink;
28: 7 the priest and the prophet **r** with strong drink,

REELAIAH (1) [=REELIAH]

Ezr 2: 2 Nehemiah, Seraiah, **R,** Mordecai, Bilshan, Mispar,

REELED (3) [REEL]

2Sa 22: 8 Then the earth **r** and rocked;
Ps 18: 7 Then the earth **r** and rocked;
107:27 they **r** and staggered like drunkards,

REELIAH (1) [=REELAIAH]

1Es 5: 8 Aspharasus, **R,** Rehum, and Baanah, their leaders.

REELING (1) [REEL]

Zec 12: 2 I am about to make Jerusalem a cup of **r** for all

REELS (1) [REEL]

Isa 21: 4 My mind **r,** horror has appalled me;

REFER (1) [REFERRED, REFERRING, REFERS]

Col 2:22 All these regulations **r** to things that perish

REFERRED (1) [REFER]

2Mc 11:36 But as to the matters that he decided are to be **r** to

REFERRING (2) [REFER]

Jn 11:13 but they thought that he was **r** merely to sleep.
Php 4:11 Not that I am **r** to being in need;

REFERS (2) [REFER]

Da 8:19 for it **r** to the appointed time of the end.
8:26 for it **r** to many days from now."

REFINE (3) [REFINED, REFINEMENT, REFINER, REFINER'S, REFINES, REFINING]

Jer 9: 7 I will now **r** and test them,
Zec 13: 9 **r** them as one refines silver,
Mal 3: 3 the descendants of Levi and **r** them like gold

REFINED (12) [REFINE]

Dt 28:54 Even the most **r** and gentle of men
28:56 She who is the most **r** and gentle among you,
28:56 so gentle and **r** that she does not venture to set
1Ch 28:18 the altar of incense made of **r** gold, and its weight;
29: 4 and seven thousand talents of **r** silver,
Job 28: 1 and a place for gold to be **r.**
Ps 12: 6 silver **r** in a furnace on the ground,
Isa 48:10 See, I have **r** you, but not like silver;
Da 11:35 Some of the wise shall fall, so that they may be **r,**
12:10 Many shall be purified, cleansed, and **r,**
Rev 1:15 **r** as in a furnace, and his voice was like the sound
3:18 from me gold **r** by fire so that you may be rich;

REFINEMENT (1) [REFINE]

Sus 1:31 a woman of great **r** and beautiful in appearance.

REFINER (2) [REFINE]

Jer 6:27 I have made you a tester and a **r** among my people
Mal 3: 3 he will sit as a **r** and purifier of silver,

REFINER'S (1) [REFINE]

Mal 3: 2 For he is like a **r** fire and like fullers' soap;

REFINES (1) [REFINE]

Zec 13: 9 refine them as one **r** silver,

REFINING (1) [REFINE]

Jer 6:29 in vain the **r** goes on, for the wicked are not

REFLECT (3) [REFLECTED, REFLECTING, REFLECTION, REFLECTIONS, REFLECTS]

Pr 20:25 and begin to **r** only after making a vow.
Sir 3:22 **R** upon what you have been commanded,
6:37 **R** on the statutes of the Lord,

REFLECTED (2) [REFLECT]

2Co 3:18 as though **r** in a mirror, are being transformed into
3Mc 4: 4 **r** on the uncertainty of life and shed tears at

REFLECTING (2) [REFLECT]

Da 9:13 turning from our iniquities and **r** on his fidelity.
4Mc 1:24 as a person will see by **r** on this experience,

REFLECTION (6) [REFLECT]

1Co 11: 7 image and **r** of God; but woman is the **r** of man.
Heb 1: 3 He is the **r** of God's glory and the exact imprint
Wis 7:26 For she is a **r** of eternal light,
Sir 22:16 so the mind firmly resolved after due **r** will not
34: 3 What is seen in dreams is but a **r,**

REFLECTIONS (1) [REFLECT]

2Es 10: 5 I broke off the **r** with which I was still engaged,

REFLECTS (3) [REFLECT]
Pr 27:19 as water **r** the face, so one human heart **r** another.
Sir 14:21 who **r** in his heart on her ways

REFORMING (1) [REFORMS]
Sir 49: 2 He did what was right by **r** the people,

REFORMS (1) [REFORMING]
Ac 24: 2 and **r** have been made for this people because

REFRAIN (17) [REFRAINED, REFRAINS]
Dt 23:22 But if you **r** from vowing, you will not incur guilt.
Ru 1:13 Would you then **r** from marrying?
1Ki 22: 6 to battle against Ramoth-gilead, or shall I **r?"**
22:15 to Ramoth-gilead to battle, or shall we **r?"**
2Ch 18: 5 to battle against Ramoth-gilead, or shall I **r?"**
18:14 to Ramoth-gilead to battle, or shall I **r?"**
Ps 37: 8 **R** from anger, and forsake wrath.
Pr 20: 3 It is honorable to **r** from strife,
Ecc 3: 5 time to embrace, and a time to **r** from embracing;
Isa 58:13 If you **r** from trampling the sabbath,
Eze 24:14 I will not **r**, I will not spare, I will not relent.
Da 11: 8 For some years he shall **r** from attacking the king
1Co 9: 6 Or is it only Barnabas and I who have no right to **r**
2Co 11: 9 and will continue to **r** from burdening you
12: 6 But I **r** from it, so that no one may think better
Sir 4:23 Do not **r** from speaking at the proper moment,
28: 8 **R** from strife, and your sins will be fewer;

REFRAINED (3) [REFRAIN]
Job 29: 9 the nobles **r** from talking, and laid their hands
Jer 41: 8 So he **r**, and did not kill them along
2Co 11: 9 So I **r** and will continue to refrain

REFRAINETH (KJV) See RESTRAINED

REFRAINS (3) [REFRAIN]
Nu 9:13 and yet **r** from keeping the passover,
Isa 56: 2 not profaning it, and **r** from doing any evil.
1Co 7:38 and he who **r** from marriage will do better.

REFRESH (5) [REFRESHED, REFRESHES, REFRESHING, REFRESHMENT]
Ge 18: 5 that you may **r** yourselves,
Pr 25:13 they **r** the spirit of their masters.
SS 2: 5 Sustain me with raisins, **r** me with apples;
Phm 1:20 **R** my heart in Christ.
2Pe 1:13 as long as I am in this body, to **r** your memory,

REFRESHED (8) [REFRESH]
Ex 23:12 and the resident alien may be **r.**
31:17 and on the seventh day he rested, and was **r."**
2Sa 16:14 at the Jordan; and there he **r** himself.
Ro 15:32 to you with joy and be **r** in your company.
1Co 16:18 for they **r** my spirit as well as yours.
2Ti 1:16 he often **r** me and was not ashamed of my chain;
Phm 1: 7 the hearts of the saints have been **r** through you,
2Es 11:46 freed from your violence, may be **r** and relieved,

REFRESHES (1) [REFRESH]
Pr 15:30 and good news **r** the body.

REFRESHING (1) [REFRESH]
Ac 3:20 so that times of **r** may come from the presence of

REFRESHMENT (3) [REFRESH]
Pr 3: 8 be a healing for your flesh and a **r** for your body.
Sir 43:22 the falling dew gives **r** from the heat.
2Mc 4:46 taking the king aside into a colonnade as if for **r,**

REFUGE‡ (106) [REFUGEES]
A. CITY OF REFUGE (10)
B. CITIES OF REFUGE (7)

Nu 35: 6 to the Levites shall include the six cities of **r,** B
35:11 you shall select cities to be cities of **r** for you, B
35:12 The cities shall be for you a **r** from the avenger,
35:13 cities that you designate shall be six cities of **r** B
35:14 in the land of Canaan, to be cities of **r.** B
35:15 These six cities shall serve as **r** for the Israelites,
35:25 the slayer back to the original city of **r.** A
35:26 the bounds of the original city of **r,** A
35:27 of blood outside the bounds of the city of **r,** A
35:28 in the city of **r** until the death of the high priest; A
35:32 for one who has fled to a city of **r,** A
Dt 32:37 are their gods, the rock in which they took **r,**
Jos 20: 2 'Appoint the cities of **r,** of which I spoke to you B
20: 3 they shall be for you a **r** from the avenger
21:13 the city of **r** for the slayer, with its pasture A
21:21 the city of **r** for the slayer, A
21:27 the city of **r** for the slayer, A
21:32 the city of **r** for the slayer, A
21:38 the city of **r** for the slayer, A
Jdg 9:15 then come and take **r** in my shade;
Ru 2:12 under whose wings you have come for **r!"**
2Sa 22: 3 my rock, in whom I take **r,**
22: 3 my stronghold and my **r,** my savior;
22:31 he is a shield for all who take **r** in him.
1Ch 6:57 To the sons of Aaron they gave the cities of **r:** B
6:67 They were given the cities of **r:** B
Ps 2:12 Happy are all who take **r** in him.
5:11 But let all who take **r** in you rejoice;
7: 1 O LORD my God, in you I take **r;**
11: 1 In the LORD I take **r;**
14: 6 but the LORD is their **r.**
16: 1 Protect me, O God, for in you I take **r.**
17: 7 of those who seek **r** from their adversaries
18: 2 my God, my rock in whom I take **r,** my shield,
18:30 he is a shield for all who take **r** in him.
25:20 do not let me be put to shame, for I take **r** in you.
28: 8 he is the saving **r** of his anointed.
31: 1 In you, O LORD, I seek **r;**
31: 2 Be a rock of **r** for me, a strong fortress to save me.
31: 4 of the net that is hidden for me, for you are my **r.**
31:19 and accomplished for those who take **r** in you,
34: 8 happy are those who take **r** in him.
34:22 of those who take **r** in him will be condemned.
36: 7 All people may take **r** in the shadow
37:39 he is their **r** in the time of trouble.
37:40 and saves them, because they take **r** in him.
43: 2 For you are the God in whom I take **r;**
46: 1 God is our **r** and strength,
46: 7 the God of Jacob is our **r.**
46:11 the God of Jacob is our **r.**
52: 7 "See the one who would not take **r** in God,
52: 7 in abundant riches, and sought **r** in wealth!"
57: 1 be merciful to me, for in you my soul takes **r;**
57: 1 in the shadow of your wings I will take **r,**
59:16 a fortress for me and a **r** in the day of my distress.
61: 3 for you are my **r,** a strong tower against
61: 4 find **r** under the shelter of your wings.
62: 7 my mighty rock, my **r** is in God.
62: 8 God is a **r** for us.
64:10 Let the righteous rejoice in the LORD and take **r**
71: 1 In you, O LORD, I take **r;**
71: 3 Be to me a rock of **r,** a strong fortress, to save me,
71: 7 but you are my strong **r.**
73:28 I have made the Lord GOD my **r,**
91: 2 "My **r** and my fortress; my God, in whom I trust."
91: 4 and under his wings you will find **r;**
91: 9 Because you have made the LORD your **r,**
94:22 and my God the rock of my **r.**
104:18 the rocks are a **r** for the coneys.
118: 8 to take **r** in the LORD than to put confidence
118: 9 to take **r** in the LORD than to put confidence
141: 8 in you I seek **r;** do not leave me defenseless.
142: 4 no **r** remains to me; no one cares for me.
142: 5 I cry to you, O LORD; I say, "You are my **r,**
143: 9 I have fled to you for **r.**
144: 2 my shield, in whom I take **r,**
Pr 14:26 and one's children will have a **r.**
14:32 but the righteous find a **r** in their integrity.
30: 5 he is a shield to those who take **r** in him.
Isa 4: 6 and a **r** and a shelter from the storm and rain.
14:32 the needy among his people will find **r** in her."
16: 4 be a **r** to them from the destroyer."
17:10 and have not remembered the Rock of your **r;**
25: 4 For you have been a **r** to the poor,
25: 4 a **r** to the needy in their distress,
28:15 for we have made lies our **r,**
28:17 hail will sweep away the **r** of lies,
30: 2 to take **r** in the protection of Pharaoh,
33:16 their **r** will be the fortresses of rocks;
57:13 But whoever takes **r** in me shall possess the land
Jer 16:19 my **r** in the day of trouble,
17:17 you are my **r** in the day of disaster;
21:13 or who can enter our places of **r?"**
Joel 3:16 But the LORD is a **r** for his people,
Na 1: 7 he protects those who take **r** in him,
3:11 you will seek a **r** from the enemy.
Zep 3:12 They shall seek **r** in the name of the LORD—
Heb 6:18 we who have taken **r** might
Wis 14: 6 the hope of the world took **r** on a raft,
1Mc 1:53 into hiding in every place of **r** they had.
10:14 for it served as a place of **r.**
10:43 And all who take **r** at the temple in Jerusalem,
10:84 temple of Dagon, and those who had taken **r** in it,
2Mc 5: 5 Menelaus took **r** in the citadel.
10:18 When at least nine thousand took **r**
12: 6 and massacred those who had taken **r** there

REFUGEES (1) [REFUGE]
Jer 50:28 and **r** from the land of Babylon are coming

REFUNDED (1)
Lev 25:27 be computed and the difference shall be **r** to

REFUSE (48) [REFUSED, REFUSES, REFUSING]
Ex 8: 2 If you **r** to let them go,
9: 2 For if you **r** to let them go and still hold them,
10: 3 long will you **r** to humble yourself before me?
10: 4 For if you **r** to let my people go,
16:28 "How long will you **r** to keep my commandments
Nu 14:11 And how long will they **r** to believe in me,
1Ki 2:16 I have one request to make of you; do not **r** me."
2:17 "Please ask King Solomon—he will not **r** you—
2:20 one small request to make of you; do not **r** me."
2:20 my mother; for I will not **r** you."
20: 7 and my gold; and I did not **r** him."
Ps 28: 1 my rock, do not **r** to hear me,
Pr 21: 7 because they **r** to do what is just.
21:25 for lazy hands **r** to labor.
Isa 1:20 but if you **r** and rebel, you shall be devoured by
5:25 and their corpses were like **r** in the streets.
7:15 by the time he knows how to **r** the evil and choose
7:16 the child knows how to **r** the evil and choose
Jer 3: 3 yet you have the forehead of a whore, you **r** to
9: 6 They **r** to know me, says the LORD.
13:10 This evil people, who **r** to hear my words,
25:28 they **r** to accept the cup from your hand to drink,
50:33 all their captors have held them fast and **r**
Eze 2: 5 or **r** to hear (for they are a rebellious house),
2: 7 whether they hear or **r** to hear;
3:11 whether they hear or **r** to hear.
3:27 and let those who **r** to hear, **r;**
Mt 5:42 do not **r** anyone who wants to borrow from you.
Mk 6:11 If any place will not welcome you and they **r**
6:26 he did not want to **r** her.
Jn 5:40 Yet you **r** to come to me to have life.
19:10 "Do you **r** to speak to me?
2Co 4: 2 we **r** to practice cunning or to falsify God's word;
1Ti 5:11 But **r** to put younger widows on the list;
Heb 12:25 See that you do not **r** the one who is speaking;
Rev 11: 9 at their dead bodies and **r** to let them be placed in
Tob 4: 5 and **r** to sin or to transgress his commandments.
Jdt 12:14 Judith replied, "Who am I to **r** my lord?
Sir 7:13 **R** to utter any lie, for it is a habit that results
27: 4 When a sieve is shaken, the **r** appears;
29: 7 Many **r** to lend, not because of meanness,
Sus 1:21 If you **r,** we will testify against you that
1Mc 2:40 and **r** to fight with the Gentiles for our lives and
2Mc 6:20 as all ought to go who have the courage to **r** things
1Es 2:19 not only **r** to pay tribute but will even resist kings.
4Mc 8: 2 but if any were to **r,**
11: 2 "I will not **r,** tyrant, to be tortured for the sake

REFUSED (46) [REFUSE]
Ge 37:35 but he **r** to be comforted, and said, "No,
39: 8 But he **r** and said to his master's wife, "Look,
48:19 his father **r,** and said, "I know, my son, I know;
Ex 4:23 But you **r** to let him go;
13:15 When Pharaoh stubbornly **r** to let us go,
Nu 20:21 Thus Edom **r** to give Israel passage
22:13 for the LORD has **r** to let me go with you."
Dt 23: 5 (Yet the LORD your God **r** to heed Balaam;
1Sa 8:19 But the people **r** to listen to the voice of Samuel;
28:23 He **r,** and said, "I will not eat."
2Sa 2:23 But he **r** to turn away.
13: 9 the pan and set them out before him, but he **r**
1Ki 20:35 But the man **r** to strike him.
21:15 which he **r** to give you for money;
2Ki 5:16 He urged him to accept, but he **r.**
Ne 9:17 they **r** to obey, and were not mindful of the
Est 1:12 Queen Vashti **r** to come at the king's command
Ps 78:10 but **r** to walk according to his law.
Pr 1:24 Because I have called and you **r,**
Isa 8: 6 Because this people has **r** the waters of Shiloah
30:15 in trust shall be your strength. But you **r**
Jer 5: 3 but they **r** to take correction.
5: 3 they have **r** to turn back.
8: 5 held fast to deceit, they have **r** to return.
11:10 who **r** to heed my words;
Hos 11: 5 because they have **r** to return to me.
Zec 7:11 But they **r** to listen, and turned
Mt 2:18 she **r** to be consoled, because they are no more."
18:30 But he **r;** then he went
Mk 5:19 But Jesus **r,** and said to him,
Lk 15:28 Then he became angry and **r** to go in.
18: 4 For a while he **r;** but later he said to himself,
Ac 19: 9 When some stubbornly **r** to believe and spoke evil
28:24 by what he had said, while others **r** to believe.
2Th 2:10 because they **r** to love the truth and so be saved.
Heb 11:24 **r** to be called a son of Pharaoh's daughter,
12:25 not escape when they **r** the one who warned them
Jdt 1:11 king of the Assyrians, and **r** to join him in the war;
5: 4 **r** to come out and meet me?"
AdE 1:12 But Queen Vashti **r** to obey him and would
13:12 and **r** to bow down to this proud Haman;
Wis 12:27 as the true God the one whom they had before **r**
19:14 Others had **r** to receive strangers when they came
1Mc 5:48 But they **r** to open to him.
15:27 But he **r** to receive them,
2Es 2:33 When I came to them they rejected me and i

REFUSES (13) [REFUSE]
Ex 7:14 he **r** to let the people go.
22:17 But if her father **r** to give her to him,
Nu 22:14 and said, "Balaam **r** to come with us."
Dt 25: 7 at the gate and say, "My husband's brother **r**
Job 6: 7 My appetite **r** to touch them;
Ps 77: 2 my soul **r** to be comforted.
Pr 6:35 and **r** a bribe no matter how great.
Jer 31:15 she **r** to be comforted for her children,
Mt 18:17 member **r** to listen to them, tell it to the church;
18:17 and if the offender **r** to listen even to the church,
1Jn 3:17 and sees a brother or sister in need and yet **r** help?
3Jn 1:10 he **r** to welcome the friends,
Rev 2:21 but she **r** to repent of her fornication.

REFUSING (10) [REFUSE]
Pr 11:15 but there is safety in **r** to do so.
Jer 15:18 my wound incurable, **r** to be healed?
16:12 following your stubborn evil will, **r** to listen
19:15 because they have stiffened their necks, **r** to hear
Da 9:11 and turned aside, **r** to obey your voice.
Lk 7:30 But by **r** to be baptized by him,
Heb 11:35 Others were tortured, **r** to accept release,
Tob 4:13 by **r** to take a wife for yourself from among them.

Wis 16:16 for the ungodly, **r** to know you, were flogged by
17:10 **r** to look even at the air,

REFUTE (1) [REFUTED]

Tit 1: 9 and to **r** those who contradict it.

REFUTED (1) [REFUTE]

Ac 18:28 for he powerfully **r** the Jews in public,

REGAIN (6) [REGAINED, REGAINING]

Pr 2:19 nor do they **r** the paths of life.
Ac 9:12 on him so that he might **r** his sight."
9:17 so that you may **r** your sight and be filled with
22:13 he said, 'Brother Saul, **r** your sight!'
Tob 11: 8 and your father will **r** his sight and see the light."
2Es 12:18 it shall not fall then, but shall **r** its former power.

REGAINED (7) [REGAIN]

Mt 18:15 If the member listens to you, you have **r** that one.
20:34 Immediately they **r** their sight and followed him.
Mk 10:52 Immediately he **r** his sight and followed him on
Lk 18:43 Immediately he **r** his sight and followed him,
Ac 9:19 and after taking some food, he **r** his strength.
22:13 In that very hour I **r** my sight and saw him.
2Mc 2:22 and **r** possession of the temple famous throughout

REGAINING (1) [REGAIN]

Tob 14: 2 and after **r** it he lived in prosperity,

REGARD (80) [REGARDED, REGARDING, REGARDS]

Ge 4: 4 And the LORD had **r** for Abel and his offering,
4: 5 but for Cain and his offering he had no **r**.
31: 2 And Jacob saw that Laban did not **r** him
31: 5 "I see that your father does not **r** me as favorably
41:40 with **r** to the throne will I be greater than you."
48: 6 of their brothers with **r** to their inheritance.
Ex 9:21 not **r** the word of the LORD left their slaves
Lev 11:11 and their carcasses you shall **r** as detestable.
11:13 These you shall **r** as detestable among the birds.
19:23 then you shall **r** their fruit as forbidden;
Nu 4:26 and they shall do all that needs to be done with **r**
Dt 4: 3 for yourselves what the LORD did with **r** to
15:17 You shall do the same with **r** to your female slave.
33: 9 of his father and mother, "I **r** them not";
Jos 7: 1 the Israelites broke faith in **r** to the devoted things:
1Sa 1:16 Do not **r** your servant as a worthless woman,
2:12 they had no **r** for the LORD
1Ki 8:28 **R** your servant's prayer and his plea,
2Ki 3:14 not that I have **r** for King Jehoshaphat of Judah,
1Ch 17:17 You **r** me as someone of high rank,
2Ch 5:11 without **r** to their divisions,
6:19 **R** your servant's prayer and his plea,
Est 8: 8 You may write as you please with **r** to the Jews,
Job 34:27 and had no **r** for any of his ways,
35:13 nor does the Almighty **r** it.
37:24 not **r** any who are wise in their own conceit."
Ps 20: 3 and **r** with favor your burnt sacrifices.
28: 5 Because they do not **r** the works of the LORD,
31: 6 You hate those who pay **r** to worthless idols,
74:20 Have **r** for your covenant,
80:14 and see; have **r** for this vine,
95:10 and they do not **r** my ways."
102:17 He will **r** the prayer of the destitute,
119:117 be safe and have **r** for your statutes continually.
144: 3 what are human beings that you **r** them,
Ecc 3:18 with **r** to human beings that God is testing them
Isa 5:12 but who do not **r** the deeds of the LORD,
8:13 But the LORD of hosts, him you shall **r** as holy;
13:17 who have no **r** for silver and do not delight
17: 7 On that day people will **r** their Maker,
17: 8 they will not have **r** for the altars,
22:11 or have **r** for him who planned it long ago.
Jer 24: 5 so I will **r** as good the exiles from Judah,
33:24 in such contempt that they no longer **r** them as
La 4:16 he will **r** them no more;
Mt 14: 9 yet out of **r** for his oaths and for the guests,
21:26 for all **r** John as a prophet."
22:16 for you do not **r** people with partiality.
Mk 6:26 yet out of **r** for his oaths and for the guests,
12:14 for you do not **r** people with partiality,
Ac 28:22 for with **r** to this sect we know
Ro 6:20 you were free in **r** to righteousness.
2Co 5:16 we **r** no one from a human point of view;
11:17 What I am saying in **r** to this boastful confidence,
Php 2: 3 but in humility **r** others as better than yourselves.
2: 6 did not **r** equality with God as something to
3: 7 these I have come to **r** as loss because of Christ.
3: 8 I **r** everything as loss because of the surpassing
3: 8 and I **r** them as rubbish,
2Th 3:15 Do not **r** them as enemies,
1Ti 6: 1 of slavery **r** their masters as worthy of all honor,
Heb 12: 5 do not **r** lightly the discipline of the Lord,
1Pe 1:12 in **r** to the things that have now been announced
2Pe 3:15 and **r** the patience of our Lord as salvation.
Jdt 4:13 The Lord heard their prayers and had **r**
Wis 2:10 let us not spare the widow or **r** the gray hairs of
Sir 29: 4 Many **r** a loan as a windfall,
29: 6 and will **r** that as a windfall.
41:12 Have **r** for your name,
Bar 4:13 They had no **r** for his statutes;
LtJ 6:25 They are bought without **r** to cost,
2Mc 3:32 by the Jews with **r** to Heliodorus,
4:34 then, with no **r** for justice,
4:36 the Jews in the city appealed to him with **r** to
6:11 in view of their **r** for that most holy day.
11:15 Maccabeus, having **r** for the common good,
11:35 With **r** to what Lysias the kinsman of
14: 8 second because I have **r** also for my compatriots.
3Mc 3:19 and are unwilling to **r** any action as sincere.
2Es 8:29 but **r** those who have gloriously taught your law.

REGARDED (21) [REGARD]

Ge 31:15 Are we not **r** by him as foreigners?
Ex 12:48 he shall be **r** as a native of the land.
30:37 it shall be **r** by you as holy to the LORD.
Ps 106:44 he **r** their distress when he heard their cry.
Isa 29:16 Shall the potter be **r** as the clay?
29:17 and the fruitful field be **r** as a forest?
Hos 8:12 they are **r** as a strange thing.
Mt 14: 5 because they **r** him as a prophet.
21:46 because they **r** him as a prophet.
Mk 11:32 for all **r** John as truly a prophet.
Lk 18: 9 that they were righteous and **r** others
22:24 among them as to which one of them was to be **r**
Ro 2:26 not their uncircumcision be **r** as circumcision?
Jdt 1:11 but **r** him as only one man.
Wis 9: 6 among human beings will be **r** as nothing without
14:20 now **r** as an object of worship
Sir 26:22 *A prostitute is **r** as spittle,*
26:25 *A headstrong wife is **r** as a dog,*
2Mc 7:12 for he **r** his sufferings as nothing.
8:35 the help of the Lord by opponents whom he **r** as of
4Mc 3:15 to his soul to drink what was **r** as equivalent

REGARDING‡ (14) [REGARD]

Ex 6:13 and gave them orders **r** the Israelites
Lev 6: 3 if you swear falsely **r** any of the various things
Dt 1:22 a report to us **r** the route by which we should go
2Ki 22:18 **R** the words that you have heard,
2Ch 7:21 And **r** this house, now exalted,
8:15 and Levites **r** anything at all, or **r** the treasuries.
34:26 **R** the words that you have heard,
Ezr 6: 8 a decree **r** what you shall do for these elders of
Job 4:20 they perish forever without any **r** it.
Eze 44:24 and my statutes **r** all my appointed festivals,
45:17 of the prince **r** the burnt offerings, grain offerings,
Zec 2: 8 the LORD of hosts (after his glory sent me) **r** the
2Es 4: 2 "Your understanding has utterly failed **r** this world,

REGARDS (8) [REGARD]

Job 34:19 nor **r** the rich more than the poor,
Ps 138: 6 For though the LORD is high, he **r** the lowly;
Ecc 11: 4 and whoever **r** the clouds will not reap.
Mal 2:13 with weeping and groaning because he no longer **r**
Ro 11:28 As **r** the gospel they are enemies of God
11:28 but as **r** election they are beloved,
1Ti 6:21 by professing it some have missed the mark as **r**
Sir 37:10 Do not consult the one who **r** you with suspicion;

REGEM (1)

1Ch 2:47 **R**, Jotham, Geshan, Pelet, Ephah, and Shaaph.

REGEM-MELECH (1)

Zec 7: 2 Now the people of Bethel had sent Sharezer and **R**

REGENERATION (KJV) See REBIRTH, RENEWAL

REGIMENTAL (5) [REGIMENTS]

Nu 1:52 in their respective **r** camps, by companies;
2: 3 the sunrise shall be of the **r** encampment of Judah
2:10 be the **r** encampment of Reuben by companies.
2:18 be the **r** encampment of Ephraim by companies.
2:25 the north side shall be the **r** encampment of Dan

REGIMENTS‡ (3) [REGIMENTAL]

Nu 2: 2 in their respective **r**, under ensigns
2:17 each in position, by their **r**.
2:34 They camped by **r**, and they set out the same way,

REGION (68) [REGIONS]

Ge 20: 1 From there Abraham journeyed toward the **r** of
34: 1 went out to visit the women of the **r**.
34: 2 Shechem son of Hamor the Hivite, prince of the **r**,
47:27 in the land of Egypt, in the **r** of Goshen;
Lev 16:22 on itself all their iniquities to a barren **r**;
Nu 21:20 the **r** of Moab by the top of Pisgah that overlooks
Dt 2:37 the whole upper **r** of the Wadi Jabbok as well as
3: 4 sixty towns, the whole **r** of Argob,
3:13 Og's kingdom. (The whole **r** of Argob:
3:14 Jair the Manassite acquired the whole **r** of Argob
Jos 13:11 and the **r** of the Geshurites and Maacathites,
22:10 When they came to the **r** near the Jordan that lies
22:11 in the **r** near the Jordan,
24:15 the **r** beyond the River or the gods of the Amorites
Jdg 5: 4 when you marched from the **r** of Edom,
1Ki 4:13 which are in Gilead, and he had the **r** of Argob,
4:24 the **r** west of the Euphrates from Tiphsah to Gaza,
1Ch 5:10 in their tents throughout all the **r** east of Gilead.
Ne 12:29 also from Beth-gilgal and from the **r** of Geba
Eze 34:26 I will make them and the **r** around my hill
47: 8 "This water flows toward the eastern **r** and goes
Mt 3: 5 and all the **r** along the Jordan,
4:16 in the **r** and shadow of death light has dawned."
14:35 throughout the **r** and brought all who were sick
15:22 Just then a Canaanite woman from that **r** came out
15:39 he got into the boat and went to the **r** of Magadan.
19: 1 he left Galilee and went to the **r** of Judea beyond
Mk 1:28 to spread throughout the surrounding **r** of Galilee.
3: 8 and the **r** around Tyre and Sidon.
6:55 and rushed about that whole **r** and began to bring
7:24 From there he set out and went away to the **r** of
7:31 Then he returned from the **r** of Tyre,
7:31 in the **r** of the Decapolis.
10: 1 and went to the **r** of Judea and beyond the Jordan.
Lk 2: 8 In that **r** there were shepherds living in the fields,
3: 1 and his brother Philip ruler of the **r** of Ituraea
3: 3 He went into all the **r** around the Jordan,
4:37 about him began to reach every place in the **r**.
17:11 through the **r** between Samaria and Galilee.
Jn 11:54 from there to a town called Ephraim in the **r** near
Ac 8:40 and as he was passing through the **r**,
13:49 the word of the Lord spread throughout the **r**.
13:50 and drove them out of their **r**.
16: 6 They went through the **r** of Phrygia and Galatia,
18:23 to place through the **r** of Galatia and Phrygia,
Jdt 1:11 But all who lived in the whole **r** disregarded
1:12 with this whole **r**, and swore by his throne
2: 1 about carrying out his revenge on the whole **r**,
2: 2 with his own lips, all the wickedness of the **r**.
2:11 to slaughter and plunder throughout your whole **r**.
Bar 2:23 to cease from the towns of Judah and from the **r**
1Mc 3:41 the traders of the **r** heard what was said to them,
8: 4 and how they had gained control of the whole **r**
11:14 because the people of that **r** were in revolt.
11:34 the latter, with all the **r** bordering them,
12:25 from Jerusalem and met them in the **r** of Hamath,
12:32 and marched through all that **r**.
2Mc 4:36 When the king returned from the **r** of Cilicia,
9: 1 Antiochus had retreated in disorder from the **r**
9:21 from the **r** of Persia I suffered an annoying illness,
10:14 When Gorgias became governor of the **r**,
12:18 They did not find Timothy in that **r**,
15: 1 that Judas and his troops were in the **r** of Samaria,
3Mc 1: 1 and marched out to the **r** near Raphia,
2Es 5:24 of the world you have chosen for yourself one **r**,
13: 7 And I tried to see the **r** or place from which
13:41 of the nations and go to a more distant **r**,
13:45 Through that **r** there was a long way to go,

REGIONS (16) [REGION]

Dt 1: 7 of the Amorites as well as into the neighboring **r**—
19: 3 the distances and divide into three **r** the land that
Jos 13: 2 all the **r** of the Philistines,
Ps 88: 6 in the **r** dark and deep.
Joel 3: 4 O Tyre and Sidon, and all the **r** of Philistia?
Mt 12:43 through waterless **r** looking for a resting place,
Lk 11:24 through waterless **r** looking for a resting place,
Ac 19: 1 Paul passed through the interior **r** and came
20: 2 When he had gone through those **r** and had given
Ro 15:23 But now, with no further place for me in these **r**,
2Co 11:10 of mine will not be silenced in the **r** of Achaia.
Gal 1:21 Then I went into the **r** of Syria and Cilicia,
1Th 1: 9 the people of those **r** report about us what kind
Tob 13: 2 down to Hades in the lowest **r** of the earth,
1Mc 3:31 the revenues from those **r** and raise a large fund.
3Mc 1: 1 that the **r** that he had controlled had been seized

REGISTER (4) [REGISTERED, REGISTERS, REGISTRATION]

Ex 30:12 When you take a census of the Israelites to **r** them,
Nu 3:10 you shall make a **r** of Aaron and his descendants;
Eze 13: 9 nor be enrolled in the **r** of the house of Israel,
1Es 5:39 a search was made in the **r** and the genealogy

REGISTERED (14) [REGISTER]

Ex 30:12 that no plague may come upon them for being **r**.
30:13 This is what each one who is **r** shall give:
30:14 Each one who is **r**, from twenty years old
Nu 1:18 They **r** themselves in their clans,
11:26 they were among those **r**,
1Ch 4:41 **r** by name, came in the days of King Hezekiah
Ezr 8: 3 with whom were **r** one hundred fifty males.
Lk 2: 1 that all the world should be **r**.
2: 3 All went to their own towns to be **r**.
2: 5 He went to be **r** with Mary,
1Es 5:38 the priesthood but were not found **r**:
3Mc 2:29 those who are **r** are also to be branded
4:14 The entire race was to be **r** individually,
6:34 for birds, and had joyfully **r** them, groaned

REGISTERS (1) [REGISTER]

Ps 87: 6 The LORD records, as he **r** the peoples,

REGISTRATION (8) [REGISTER]

Ex 30:12 at **r** all of them shall give a ransom for their lives
Ne 7:64 These sought their **r** among those enrolled in
Lk 2: 2 This was the first **r** and was taken
3Mc 2:28 to a **r** involving poll tax and to the status of slaves.
2:32 to save themselves from the **r**.
4:15 The **r** of these people was therefore conducted
6:38 So their **r** was carried out from the twenty-fifth
7:22 the **r**, so that those who held any of it restored it

REGRET (7) [REGRETS]

1Sa 15:11 "I **r** that I made Saul king,
2Ch 21:20 He departed with no one's **r**.

2Co 7: 8 I do not **r** it (though I did **r** it, for I see that
7:10 that leads to salvation and brings no **r,**
Sir 32:19 but when you have acted, do not **r** it.
1Mc 11:10 I now **r** that I gave him my daughter,

REGRETS (2) [REGRET]

Lk 14:18 and see it; please accept my **r.'**
14:19 to try them out; please accept my **r.'**

REGULAR (40) [REGULARLY]

Ex 29:42 be a **r** burnt offering throughout your generations
30: 8 a **r** incense offering before the LORD
Lev 6:20 of an ephah of choice flour as a **r** offering,
15:19 of blood that is her **r** discharge from her body,
Nu 4: 7 the **r** bread also shall be on it;
4:16 the **r** grain offering, and the anointing oil,
28: 3 a year old without blemish, daily, as a **r** offering.
28: 6 It is a **r** burnt offering,
28:10 to the **r** burnt offering and its drink offering.
28:15 to the **r** burnt offering and its drink offering.
28:23 which belongs to the **r** burnt offering.
28:24 to the **r** burnt offering and its drink offering.
28:31 to the **r** burnt offering with its grain offering,
29: 6 and the **r** burnt offering and its grain offering,
29:11 and the **r** burnt offering and its grain offering,
29:16 in addition to the **r** burnt offering,
29:19 to the **r** burnt offering and its grain offering,
29:22 to the **r** burnt offering and its grain offering
29:25 in addition to the **r** burnt offering,
29:28 to the **r** burnt offering and its grain offering
29:31 in addition to the **r** burnt offering,
29:34 besides the **r** burnt offering, its grain offering,
29:38 to the **r** burnt offering and its grain offering
2Ki 25:30 a **r** allowance was given him by the king,
2Ch 2: 4 and for the **r** offering of the rows of bread,
Ezr 3: 5 and after that the **r** burnt offerings,
Ne 10:33 the **r** grain offering, the **r** burnt offering,
Est 2:12 this was the **r** period of their cosmetic treatment,
Jer 52:34 a **r** daily allowance was given him by the king
Eze 46:15 morning by morning, as a **r** burnt offering.
Da 8:11 the **r** burnt offering away from him and overthrew
8:12 over to it together with the **r** burnt offering;
8:13 long is this vision concerning the **r** burnt offering,
11:31 They shall abolish the **r** burnt offering and set up
12:11 the time that the **r** burnt offering is taken away
Ac 19:39 it must be settled in the **r** assembly.
Jdt 7:11 my lord, do not fight against them in **r** formation,
1Es 5:52 the **r** offerings and sacrifices on sabbaths and
3Mc 3:21 to make them participants in our **r** religious rites.

REGULARLY (19) [REGULAR]

Ex 27:20 so that a lamp may be set up to burn **r.**
29:38 two lambs a year old **r** each day.
Lev 24: 2 that a light may be kept burning **r.**
24: 3 from evening to morning before the LORD **r;**
24: 4 the lampstand of pure gold before the LORD **r.**
24: 8 in order before the LORD **r** as a commitment of
2Ki 4: 9 that this man who **r** passes our way is a holy man
25:29 of his life he dined **r** in the king's presence.
1Ch 16: 6 and Jahaziel were to blow trumpets **r,**
16:37 the ark of the covenant of the LORD to minister **r**
16:40 to the LORD on the altar of burnt offering **r,**
23:31 the number required of them, **r** before the LORD.
2Ch 24:14 the house of the LORD **r** all the days of Jehoiada.
Jer 52:33 every day of his life he dined **r** at the king's table.
Eze 39:14 They will set apart men to pass through the land **r**
46:14 a grain offering with it morning by morning **r,**
Bel 1:13 through which they used to go in **r** and consume
2Mc 4:27 not pay **r** any of the money promised to the king.
1Es 6:30 **r** every year, without quibbling,

REGULATION (3) [REGULATIONS]

Lev 5:10 for a burnt offering according to the **r.**
9:16 and sacrificed it according to **r.**
Nu 9:14 the statute of the passover and according to its **r;**

REGULATIONS (9) [REGULATION]

Nu 9: 3 to all its statutes and all its **r** you shall keep it.
Est 2:12 being twelve months under the **r** for the women,
9:31 and for their descendants **r** concerning their fasts
Lk 1: 6 according to all the commandments and **r** of
Col 2:20 Why do you submit to **r,**
2:22 All these **r** refer to things that perish with use;
Heb 9: 1 Now even the first covenant had **r** for worship and
9:10 **r** for the body imposed until the time comes
13: 9 for the heart to be strengthened by grace, not by **r**

REHABIAH (5)

1Ch 23:17 The sons of Eliezer: **R** the chief;
23:17 but the sons of **R** were very numerous.
24:21 Of **R:** of the sons of **R,** Isshiah the chief.
26:25 from Eliezer were his son **R,** his son Jeshaiah,

REHEARSE (KJV) See RECITE, REPEAT

REHOB (10) [BETH-REHOB]

Nu 13:21 the land from the wilderness of Zin to **R,**
Jos 19:28 Ebron, **R,** Hammon, Kanah, as far as Great Sidon;
19:30 and **R**—twenty-two towns with their villages.
21:31 and **R** with its pasture lands—four towns.
Jdg 1:31 or of Achzib, or of Helbah, or of Aphik, or of **R;**
2Sa 8: 3 David also struck down King Hadadezer son of **R**
8:12 the spoil of King Hadadezer son of **R** of Zobah.
10: 8 but the Arameans of Zobah and of **R,**
1Ch 6:75 and **R** with its pasture lands;
Ne 10:11 Mica, **R,** Hashabiah,

REHOBOAM (53)

1Ki 11:43 and his son **R** succeeded him.
12: 1 **R** went to Shechem, for all Israel had come
12: 3 and all the assembly of Israel came and said to **R,**
12: 6 Then King **R** took counsel with
12:12 and all the people came to **R** the third day,
12:17 But **R** reigned over the Israelites who were living
12:18 When King **R** sent Adoram,
12:18 King **R** then hurriedly mounted his chariot to flee
12:21 When **R** came to Jerusalem,
12:21 to restore the kingdom to **R** son of Solomon.
12:23 Say to King **R** of Judah,
12:27 to their master, King **R** of Judah;
12:27 they will kill me and return to King **R** of Judah."
14:21 Now **R** son of Solomon reigned in Judah.
14:21 **R** was forty-one years old when he began to reign,
14:25 In the fifth year of King **R,**
14:27 so King **R** made shields of bronze instead,
14:29 Now the rest of the acts of **R,** and all that he did,
14:30 between **R** and Jeroboam continually.
14:31 **R** slept with his ancestors and was buried
15: 6 between **R** and Jeroboam continued all the days
1Ch 3:10 The descendants of Solomon: **R,** Abijah his son,
2Ch 9:31 and his son **R** succeeded him.
10: 1 **R** went to Shechem, for all Israel had come
10: 3 and Jeroboam and all Israel came and said to **R,**
10: 6 Then King **R** took counsel with
10:12 and all the people came to **R** the third day,
10:13 King **R** rejected the advice of the older men;
10:17 But **R** reigned over the people
10:18 When King **R** sent Hadoram,
10:18 King **R** hurriedly mounted his chariot to flee
11: 1 When **R** came to Jerusalem,
11: 1 to restore the kingdom to **R.**
11: 3 Say to King **R** of Judah,
11: 5 **R** resided in Jerusalem, and he built cities
11:17 three years they made **R** son of Solomon secure,
11:18 **R** took as his wife Mahalath daughter
11:21 **R** loved Maacah daughter
11:22 **R** appointed Abijah son of Maacah as chief prince
12: 1 the rule of **R** was established and he grew strong,
12: 2 In the fifth year of King **R,**
12: 5 Then the prophet Shemaiah came to **R** and to
12:10 King **R** made in place of them shields of bronze,
12:13 So King **R** established himself in Jerusalem
12:13 **R** was forty-one years old when he began to reign;
12:15 Now the acts of **R,** from first to last,
12:15 There were continual wars between **R**
12:16 **R** slept with his ancestors and was buried in
13: 7 around him and defied **R** son of Solomon,
13: 7 when **R** was young and irresolute and could
Mt 1: 7 and Solomon the father of **R,** and **R** the father of
Sir 47:23 **R,** whose policy drove the people to revolt.

REHOBOTH (3)

Ge 26:22 so he called it **R,** saying,
36:37 and Shaul of **R** on the Euphrates succeeded him
1Ch 1:48 Shaul of **R** on the Euphrates succeeded him.

REHOBOTH-IR (1)

Ge 10:11 and built Nineveh, **R,** Calah,

REHUM (13)

Ezr 2: 2 Reelaiah, Mordecai, Bilshan, Mispar, Bigvai, **R,**
4: 8 **R** the royal deputy and Shimshai the scribe wrote
4: 9 (then **R** the royal deputy, Shimshai the scribe,
4:17 "To **R** the royal deputy and Shimshai the scribe
4:23 of King Artaxerxes' letter was read before **R** and
Ne 3:17 After him the Levites made repairs: **R** son of Bani;
10:25 **R,** Hashabnah, Maaseiah,
12: 3 Shecaniah, **R,** Meremoth,
1Es 2:16 Bishlam, Mithridates, Tabeel, **R,** Beltethmus,
2:17 the recorder **R** and the scribe Shimshai and
2:25 Then the king, in reply to the recorder **R,**
2:30 **R** and the scribe Shimshai
5: 8 Aspharasus, Reeliah, **R,** and Baanah, their leaders.

REI (1)

1Ki 1: 8 and the prophet Nathan, and Shimei, and **R,**

REIGN (191) [REIGNED, REIGNING, REIGNS]

Ge 37: 8 "Are you indeed to **r** over us?
Ex 15:18 The LORD will **r** forever and ever."
Dt 17:20 and his descendants may **r** long over his kingdom
Jdg 9: 8 So they said to the olive tree, **'R** over us.'
9:10 'You come and **r** over us.'
9:12 trees said to the vine, 'You come and **r** over us.'
9:14 'You come and **r** over us.'
1Sa 8: 9 and show them the ways of the king who shall **r**
8:11 "These will be the ways of the king who will **r**
10: 1 You shall **r** over the people of the LORD
11:12 "Who is it that said, 'Shall Saul **r** over us?'
12:12 you said to me, 'No, but a king shall **r** over us,'
13: 1 Saul was . . . years old when he began to **r;**
2Sa 2:10 was forty years old when he began to **r** over Israel,
3:21 that you may **r** over all that your heart desires."
5: 4 David was thirty years old when he began to **r,**
1Ki 2:15 and that all Israel expected me to **r;**
6: 1 in the fourth year of Solomon's **r** over Israel,
11:37 and you shall **r** over all that your soul desires;
14:21 to **r,** and he reigned seventeen years in Jerusalem,
15: 1 Abijam began to **r** over Judah.
15: 9 Asa began to **r** over Judah;
15:25 Nadab son of Jeroboam began to **r** over Israel in
15:33 Baasha son of Ahijah began to **r** over all Israel
16: 8 of Baasha began to **r** over Israel in Tirzah;
16:11 to **r,** as soon as he had seated himself
16:23 Omri began to **r** over Israel;
16:29 Ahab son of Omri began to **r** over Israel;
22:41 Jehoshaphat son of Asa began to **r** over Judah in
22:42 to **r,** and he reigned twenty-five years
22:51 to **r** over Israel in Samaria in the seventeenth year
2Ki 8:16 of King Jehoshaphat of Judah began to **r.**
8:25 Ahaziah son of King Jehoram of Judah began to **r.**
8:26 twenty-two years old when he began to **r;**
9:29 Ahaziah began to **r** over Judah.
11:21 Jehoash was seven years old when he began to **r.**
12: 1 In the seventh year of Jehu, Jehoash began to **r;**
13: 1 Jehoahaz son of Jehu began to **r** over Israel
13:10 Jehoash son of Jehoahaz began to **r** over Israel
14: 1 King Amaziah son of Joash of Judah, began to **r.**
14: 2 He was twenty-five years old when he began to **r,**
14:23 King Jeroboam son of Joash of Israel began to **r**
15: 1 of Amaziah of Judah began to **r.**
15: 2 He was sixteen years old when he began to **r,**
15:13 of Jabesh began to **r** in the thirty-ninth year
15:17 Menahem son of Gadi began to **r** over Israel;
15:23 Pekahiah son of Menahem began to **r** over Israel
15:27 of Remaliah began to **r** over Israel in Samaria;
15:32 King Jotham son of Uzziah of Judah began to **r.**
15:33 He was twenty-five years old when he began to **r**
16: 1 King Ahaz son of Jotham of Judah began to **r.**
16: 2 Ahaz was twenty years old when he began to **r;**
17: 1 Hoshea son of Elah began to **r** in Samaria
18: 1 Hezekiah son of King Ahaz of Judah began to **r.**
18: 2 He was twenty-five years old when he began to **r;**
21: 1 Manasseh was twelve years old when he began to **r**
21:19 was twenty-two years old when he began to **r;**
22: 1 Josiah was eight years old when he began to **r;**
23:31 was twenty-three years old when he began to **r;**
23:33 so that he might not **r** in Jerusalem,
23:36 was twenty-five years old when he began to **r;**
24: 8 was eighteen years old when he began to **r;**
24:12 in the eighth year of his **r.**
24:18 was twenty-one years old when he began to **r;**
25: 1 And in the ninth year of his **r,** in the tenth month,
25:27 in the year that he began to **r,**
1Ch 26:31 (In the fortieth year of David's **r** search was made,
2Ch 3: 2 of the second month of the fourth year of his **r.**
12:13 was forty-one years old when he began to **r;**
13: 1 Abijah began to **r** over Judah.
15:10 in the third month of the fifteenth year of the **r**
15:19 until the thirty-fifth year of the **r** of Asa.
16: 1 In the thirty-sixth year of the **r** of Asa,
16:12 In the thirty-ninth year of his **r** Asa was diseased
16:13 dying in the forty-first year of his **r.**
17: 7 In the third year of his **r** he sent his officials,
20:31 He was thirty-five years old when he began to **r;**
21: 5 was thirty-two years old when he began to **r;**
21:20 He was thirty-two years old when he began to **r;**
22: 2 was forty-two years old when he began to **r;**
23: 3 Let him **r,** as the LORD promised concerning
24: 1 Joash was seven years old when he began to **r;**
25: 1 to **r,** and he reigned twenty-nine years
26: 3 Uzziah was sixteen years old when he began to **r,**
27: 1 was twenty-five years old when he began to **r;**
27: 8 He was twenty-five years old when he began to **r;**
28: 1 Ahaz was twenty years old when he began to **r;**
29: 1 to **r** when he was twenty-five years old;
29: 3 In the first year of his **r,** in the first month,
29:19 the utensils that King Ahaz repudiated during his **r**
33: 1 Manasseh was twelve years old when he began to **r**
33:21 was twenty-two years old when he began to **r;**
34: 1 Josiah was eight years old when he began to **r;**
34: 3 For in the eighth year of his **r,**
34: 8 In the eighteenth year of his **r,**
35:19 of the **r** of Josiah this passover was kept.
36: 2 was twenty-three years old when he began to **r;**
36: 5 was twenty-five years old when he began to **r;**
36: 9 Jehoiachin was eight years old when he began to **r;**
36:11 was twenty-one years old when he began to **r;**
Ezr 4: 5 throughout the **r** of King Cyrus of Persia and until
4: 5 of Persia and until the **r** of King Darius of Persia.
4: 6 In the **r** of Ahasuerus, in his accession year,
4:24 the second year of the **r** of King Darius of Persia.
5:13 King Cyrus of Babylon, in the first year of his **r,**
6: 3 In the first year of his **r,**
6:15 in the sixth year of the **r** of King Darius.
7: 1 After this, in the **r** of King Artaxerxes of Persia,
8: 1 in the **r** of King Artaxerxes:
Ne 12:22 also the priests until the **r** of Darius the Persian.
Est 1: 3 in the third year of his **r,**
2:16 in the seventh year of his **r,**
Job 34:30 so that the godless should not **r,**
Ps 146:10 The LORD will **r** forever, your God, O Zion,
Pr 8:15 By me kings **r,** and rulers decree what is just;
Ecc 4:14 One can indeed come out of prison to **r,**
Isa 24:23 for the LORD of hosts will **r** on Mount Zion and
32: 1 See, a king will **r** in righteousness,
Jer 1: 2 in the thirteenth year of his **r.**
23: 5 and he shall **r** as king and deal wisely,
26: 1 of the **r** of King Jehoiakim son of Josiah of Judah,
27: 1 of the **r** of King Zedekiah son of Josiah of Judah,
28: 1 the beginning of the **r** of King Zedekiah of Judah,
33:21 so that he would not have a son to **r** on his throne,

Jer 49:34 the beginning of the **r** of King Zedekiah of Judah.
51:59 in the fourth year of his **r**.
52: 1 was twenty-one years old when he began to **r**;
52: 4 And in the ninth year of his **r**, in the tenth month,
52:31 in the year he began to **r**,
La 5:19 But you, O LORD, **r** forever;
Da 1: 1 the third year of the **r** of King Jehoiakim of Judah,
2: 1 In the second year of Nebuchadnezzar's **r**,
6:28 the **r** of Darius and the **r** of Cyrus the Persian.
8: 1 the **r** of King Belshazzar a vision appeared to me,
9: 2 in the first year of his **r**,
Am 6: 3 and bring near a **r** of violence?
Mic 4: 7 the LORD will **r** over them in Mount Zion now
Lk 1:33 He will **r** over the house of Jacob forever,
3: 1 In the fifteenth year of the **r** of Emperor Tiberius,
Ac 11:28 and this took place during the **r** of Claudius.
1Co 15:25 For he must **r** until he has put all his enemies
2Ti 2:12 we will also **r** with him;
Rev 5:10 and they will **r** on earth."
11:15 and he will **r** forever and ever."
11:17 you have taken your great power and begun to **r**.
20: 6 and they will **r** with him a thousand years.
22: 5 and they will **r** forever and ever.
Tob 2: 1 Then during the **r** of Esar-haddon I returned home,
Jdt 1: 1 the twelfth year of the **r** of Nebuchadnezzar,
AdE 1: 3 in the third year of his **r**,
2:16 which is Adar, in the seventh year of his **r**,
11: 1 the fourth year of the **r** of Ptolemy and Cleopatra,
11: 2 the second year of the **r** of Artaxerxes the Great,
Wis 3: 8 and the Lord will **r** over them forever.
6:21 honor wisdom, so that you may **r** forever.
Sir Pr: 3 of the **r** of Euergetes and stayed for some time,
47:16 and you were loved for your peaceful **r**.
1Mc 1:10 to **r** in the one hundred thirty-seventh year of
1:16 in order that he might **r** over both kingdoms.
6:17 he set up Antiochus the king's son to **r**.
7: 1 to a town by the sea, and there began to **r**.
8: 7 and those who would **r** after him should pay
10: 1 They welcomed him, and there he began to **r**.
11: 9 and you shall **r** over your father's kingdom.
11:54 with him the young boy Antiochus who began to **r**
2Mc 1: 7 the **r** of Demetrius, in the one hundred sixty-ninth
1Es 1:22 of the **r** of Josiah this passover was kept.
1:24 the events of his **r** have been recorded—
1:39 when he began to **r** in Judea and Jerusalem;
1:57 and to his sons until the Persians began to **r**,
2:30 in Jerusalem stopped until the second year of the **r**
5: 6 in the second year of his **r**, in the month of Nisan,
5:73 from building for two years, until the **r** of Darius.
6: 1 Now in the second year of the **r** of Darius,
6:24 of the **r** of King Cyrus, he ordered the building of
8: 6 of the **r** of Artaxerxes, in the fifth month (this was
8:28 in the **r** of King Artaxerxes:
2Es 1: 3 in the country of the Medes in the **r** of Artaxerxes,
5: 6 And one shall **r** whom those who inhabit
11:13 And after a time its **r** came to an end,
11:13 and it continued to **r** a long time.
11:28 between themselves to **r** together;
11:31 the two little wings that were planning to **r**.
11:39 that remains of the four beasts that I had made to **r**
12: 2 over to it rose up and set themselves up to **r**,
12: 2 and their **r** was brief and full of tumult.
12:14 And twelve kings shall **r** in it, one after another.
12:15 But the second that is to **r** shall hold sway for
12:30 this was the **r** which was brief and full of tumult,
16:52 and righteousness will **r** over us.

REIGNED (118) [REIGN]

Ge 36:31 These are the kings who **r** in the land of Edom,
36:31 before any king **r** over the Israelites.
36:32 Bela son of Beor **r** in Edom,
Dt 1: 4 who **r** in Heshbon, and King Og of Bashan,
1: 4 who **r** in Ashtaroth and in Edrei.
3: 2 as you did to King Sihon of the Amorites, who **r**
4:46 of King Sihon of the Amorites, who **r** at Heshbon,
Jos 13:10 who **r** in Heshbon, as far as the boundary of
13:12 who **r** in Ashtaroth and in Edrei (he alone was left
13:21 of King Sihon of the Amorites, who **r** in Heshbon,
Jdg 4: 2 the hand of King Jabin of Canaan, who **r** in Hazor;
1Sa 13: 1 and he **r** . . . and two years over Israel.
2Sa 2:10 to reign over Israel, and he **r** two years.
5: 4 when he began to reign, and he **r** forty years.
5: 5 At Hebron he **r** over Judah seven years and six
5: 5 and at Jerusalem he **r** over all Israel
8:15 So David **r** over all Israel;
16: 8 in whose place you have **r**;
1Ki 2:11 The time that David **r** over Israel was forty years;
he **r** seven years in Hebron,
11:25 he despised Israel and **r** over Aram.
11:42 The time that Solomon **r** in Jerusalem
12:17 But Rehoboam **r** over the Israelites who were
14:19 how he warred and how he **r**,
14:20 The time that Jeroboam **r** was twenty-two years;
14:21 Now Rehoboam son of Solomon **r** in Judah.
14:21 and he **r** seventeen years in Jerusalem,
15: 2 He **r** for three years in Jerusalem.
15:10 he **r** forty-one years in Jerusalem.
15:25 he **r** over Israel two years.
15:33 at Tirzah; he **r** twenty-four years.
16: 8 over Israel in Tirzah; he **r** two years.
16:15 Zimri **r** seven days in Tirzah.
16:23 he **r** for twelve years, six of them in Tirzah.
16:29 of Omri **r** over Israel in Samaria twenty-two years.
22:42 and he **r** twenty-five years in Jerusalem.
22:51 he **r** two years over Israel.
2Ki 3: 1 in Samaria; he **r** twelve years.
8:17 and he **r** eight years in Jerusalem.
8:26 he **r** one year in Jerusalem.
10:36 The time that Jehu **r** over Israel
11: 3 while Athaliah **r** over the land.
12: 1 he **r** forty years in Jerusalem.
13: 1 in Samaria; he **r** seventeen years.
13:10 in Samaria; he **r** sixteen years.
14: 2 and he **r** twenty-nine years in Jerusalem.
14:23 in Samaria; he **r** forty-one years.
15: 2 and he **r** fifty-two years in Jerusalem.
15: 8 of Jeroboam **r** over Israel in Samaria six months.
15:10 and **r** in place of him.
15:13 he **r** one month in Samaria.
15:14 he **r** in place of him.
15:17 he **r** ten years in Samaria.
15:23 in Samaria; he **r** two years.
15:25 he killed him, and **r** in place of him.
15:27 in Samaria; he **r** twenty years.
15:30 he **r** in place of him,
15:33 when he began to reign and **r** sixteen years
16: 2 he **r** sixteen years in Jerusalem.
17: 1 over Israel; he **r** nine years.
18: 2 he **r** twenty-nine years in Jerusalem.
21: 1 he **r** fifty-five years in Jerusalem.
21:19 he **r** two years in Jerusalem.
22: 1 he **r** thirty-one years in Jerusalem.
23:31 he **r** three months in Jerusalem.
23:36 he **r** eleven years in Jerusalem.
24: 8 he **r** three months in Jerusalem.
24:18 he **r** eleven years in Jerusalem.
1Ch 1:43 These are the kings who **r** in the land of Edom
1:43 of Edom before any king **r** over the Israelites:
3: 4 where he **r** for seven years and six months.
3: 4 And he **r** thirty-three years in Jerusalem.
18:14 So David **r** over all Israel;
29:26 Thus David son of Jesse **r** over all Israel.
29:27 The period that he **r** over Israel was forty years;
29:27 he **r** seven years in Hebron,
2Ch 1:13 And he **r** over Israel.
9:30 Solomon **r** in Jerusalem over all Israel forty years.
10:17 But Rehoboam **r** over the people
12:13 Rehoboam established himself in Jerusalem and **r**.
12:13 he **r** seventeen years in Jerusalem,
13: 2 He **r** for three years in Jerusalem.
20:31 So Jehoshaphat **r** over Judah.
20:31 he **r** twenty-five years in Jerusalem.
21: 5 he **r** eight years in Jerusalem.
21:20 he **r** eight years in Jerusalem.
22: 1 So Ahaziah son of Jehoram **r** as king of Judah.
22: 2 he **r** one year in Jerusalem.
22:12 while Athaliah **r** over the land.
24: 1 he **r** forty years in Jerusalem;
25: 1 and he **r** twenty-nine years in Jerusalem.
26: 3 and he **r** fifty-two years in Jerusalem.
27: 1 he **r** sixteen years in Jerusalem.
27: 8 he **r** sixteen years in Jerusalem.
28: 1 he **r** sixteen years in Jerusalem.
29: 1 he **r** twenty-nine years in Jerusalem.
33: 1 he **r** fifty-five years in Jerusalem.
33:21 he **r** two years in Jerusalem.
34: 1 he **r** thirty-one years in Jerusalem.
36: 2 he **r** three months in Jerusalem.
36: 5 he **r** eleven years in Jerusalem.
36: 9 he **r** three months and ten days in Jerusalem.
36:11 he **r** eleven years in Jerusalem.
Jer 52: 1 he **r** eleven years in Jerusalem.
Ac 13:21 of the tribe of Benjamin, who **r** for forty years.
Rev 20: 4 to life and **r** with Christ a thousand years.
Tob 1:15 and his son Sennacherib **r** in his place,
1:21 and his son Esar-haddon **r** after him.
Sir 47:13 Solomon **r** in an age of peace,
1Mc 1: 7 And after Alexander had **r** twelve years, he died.
6: 2 the Macedonian king who first **r** over the Greeks.
1Es 1:35 He **r** three months in Judah and Jerusalem.
1:44 and he **r** three months and ten days in Jerusalem.
1:46 twenty-one years old, and he **r** eleven years.
6:17 But in the first year that Cyrus **r** over the country
2Es 11: 5 it **r** over the earth and over those who inhabit it.
11:12 and it **r** over all the earth.
11:13 Then the next wing rose up and **r**,

REIGNING (3) [REIGN]

1Es 1:35 king of Egypt deposed him from **r** in Jerusalem,
8: 1 when Artaxerxes, the king of the Persians, was **r**,
2Es 11:14 While it was **r** its end came also,

REIGNS (3) [REIGN]

1Sa 12:14 both you and the king who **r** over you will follow
Isa 52: 7 who says to Zion, "Your God **r**."
Rev 19: 6 For the Lord our God the Almighty **r**.

REIN (1) [REINED]

Ps 50:19 "You give your mouth free **r** for evil,

REINED (1) [REIN]

2Ki 9:23 Then Joram **r** about and fled, saying to Ahaziah,

REINFORCED (2) [REINFORCEMENTS]

1Mc 2:43 to escape their troubles joined them and **r** them.
2Mc 7:21 she **r** her woman's reasoning with

REINFORCEMENTS (1) [REINFORCED]

AdE 16:20 And give them **r**, so that on the thirteenth day of

REINS See Index to Footnotes

REJECT (26) [REJECTED, REJECTING, REJECTION, REJECTS]

Ex 20: 5 and the fourth generation of those who **r** me,
Dt 5: 9 the third and fourth generation of those who **r** me,
7:10 who repays in their own person those who **r** him.
7:10 but repays in their own person those who **r** him.
2Ki 23:27 and I will **r** this city that I have chosen, Jerusalem,
2Ch 6:42 O LORD God, do not **r** your anointed one.
Job 8:20 "See, God will not **r** a blameless person,
34:33 then pay back to suit you, because you **r** it?
Ps 36: 4 not good; they do not **r** evil.
Pr 1: 8 and do not **r** your mother's teaching;
Isa 30:12 Because you **r** this word, and put your trust in
66: 5 and **r** you for my name's sake have said, "Let
Jer 31:37 be explored, then I will **r** all the offspring of Israel
33:26 would I **r** the offspring of Jacob and
La 3:31 For the Lord will not **r** forever.
Hos 4: 6 I **r** you from being a priest to me.
9:17 they have not listened to him, my God will **r** them;
Ac 13:46 Since you **r** it and judge yourselves to
Tit 1:14 or to commandments of those who **r** the truth.
Heb 12:25 on earth, how much less will we escape if we **r**
Jude 1: 8 **r** authority, and slander the glorious ones.
Wis 9: 4 and do not **r** me from among your servants.
Sir 4: 4 Do not **r** a suppliant in distress,
6:23 and accept my judgment; do not **r** my counsel.
41: 4 why then should you **r** the will of the Most High?
4Mc 5:35 philosophical reason, nor will I **r** you,

REJECTED (74) [REJECT]

Nu 11:20 you have **r** the LORD who is among you,
Jdg 11: 7 not the very ones who **r** me and drove me out
15: 2 Her father said, "I was sure that you had **r** her;
1Sa 8: 7 for they have not **r** you,
8: 7 but they have **r** me from being king over them.
10:19 But today you have **r** your God,
15:23 Because you have **r** the word of the LORD,
15:23 he has also **r** you from being king."
15:26 for you have **r** the word of the LORD,
15:26 LORD has **r** you from being king over Israel."
16: 1 I have **r** him from being king over Israel.
16: 7 on the height of his stature, because I have **r** him;
2Ki 17:16 They **r** all the commandments of the LORD
17:20 The LORD **r** all the descendants of Israel;
2Ch 10: 8 But he **r** the advice that the older men gave him,
10:13 King Rehoboam **r** the advice of the older men;
Job 31:13 "If I have **r** the cause of my male or female slaves,
Ps 44: 9 Yet you have **r** us and abased us,
53: 5 they will be put to shame, for God has **r** them.
60: 1 you have **r** us, broken our defenses;
60:10 Have you not **r** us, O God?
66:20 not **r** my prayer or removed his steadfast love
78:59 he was full of wrath, and he utterly **r** Israel.
78:67 He **r** the tent of Joseph, he did not choose the tribe
89:38 But now you have spurned and **r** him;
108:11 Have you not **r** us, O God?
118:22 the builders **r** has become the chief cornerstone.
Isa 5:24 they have **r** the instruction of the LORD of hosts,
53: 3 He was despised and **r** by others;
Jer 2:37 for the LORD has **r** those in whom you trust,
6:19 and as for my teaching, they have **r** it.
6:30 are called "**r** silver," for the LORD has **r** them.
7:29 for the LORD has **r** and forsaken the generation
8: 9 since they have **r** the word of the LORD,
14:19 Have you completely **r** Judah?
15: 6 You have **r** me, says the LORD,
33:24 that the LORD chose have been **r** by him,"
La 1:15 LORD has **r** all my warriors in the midst of me;
5:22 unless you have utterly **r** us,
Eze 20:13 not observe my statutes but **r** my ordinances,
20:16 because they **r** my ordinances and did
20:24 but had **r** my statutes and profaned my sabbaths,
Hos 4: 6 because you have **r** knowledge,
8: 5 Your calf is **r**, O Samaria.
Am 2: 4 because they have **r** the law of the LORD,
Zec 10: 6 and they shall be as though I had not **r** them;
Mt 21:42 that the builders **r** has become the cornerstone;
Mk 8:31 and be **r** by the elders, the chief priests,
12:10 that the builders **r** has become the cornerstone;
Lk 7:30 and the lawyers **r** God's purpose for themselves.)
9:22 and be **r** by the elders, chief priests, and scribes,
17:25 But first he must endure much suffering and be **r**
20:17 that the builders **r** has become the cornerstone'?
Ac 3:13 whom you handed over and **r** in the presence
3:14 But you **r** the Holy and Righteous One and asked
4:11 This Jesus is 'the stone that was **r** by you,
7:35 "It was this Moses whom they **r** when they said,
Ro 11: 1 I ask, then, has God **r** his people?
11: 2 God has not **r** his people whom he foreknew.
1Ti 4: 4 to be **r**, provided it is received with thanksgiving;
Heb 12:17 when he wanted to inherit the blessing, he was **r**,
1Pe 2: 4 though **r** by mortals yet chosen and precious
2: 7 that the builders **r** has become the very head of
Wis 11:14 For though they had mockingly **r** him who long
Sir 20:20 A proverb from a fool's lips will be **r**,
1Mc 2:31 the city of David, that those who had **r**
2Mc 1:27 look on those who are **r** and despised,
Man 1:10 so that I am **r** because of my sins,
2Es 1:31 for I have **r** your festal days, and new moons,
2:33 When I came to them they **r** me and refused
3: 8 in your sight and **r** your commands,
3:16 You set apart Jacob for yourself, but Esau you **r**;
9: 9 and those who have **r** them

REJECTING (4) [REJECT]

Eze 5: 6 **r** my ordinances and not following my statutes.
Mk 7: 9 a fine way of **r** the commandment of God in order
1Ti 1:19 By **r** conscience, certain persons have suffered
Sir 41:21 and of **r** the appeal of a relative;

REJECTION‡ (1) [REJECT]

Ro 11:15 For if their **r** is the reconciliation of the world,

REJECTS (9) [REJECT]

Pr 10:17 but one who **r** a rebuke goes astray.
Lk 10:16 whoever **r** you **r** me, and whoever **r** me **r** the one who sent me."
Jn 12:48 The one who **r** me and does not receive my word
1Th 4: 8 Therefore whoever **r** this **r** not human authority
1Mc 14:45 Whoever acts contrary to these decisions or **r** any

REJOICE‡ (175) [REJOICED, REJOICES, REJOICING]

Lev 23:40 and you shall **r** before the LORD your God
Dt 12:12 And you shall **r** before the LORD your God,
16:11 **R** before the LORD your God—
16:14 **R** during your festival, you and your sons
33:18 **R,** Zebulun, in your going out;
Jdg 9:19 **r** in Abimelech, and let him also rejoice in you;
9:19 and let him also **r** in you;
16:23 a great sacrifice to their god Dagon, and to **r;**
1Sa 2: 1 because I **r** in my victory.
6:19 The descendants of Jeconiah did not **r** with
2Sa 1:20 or the daughters of the Philistines will **r,**
1Ch 16:10 let the hearts of those who seek the LORD **r.**
16:31 Let the heavens be glad, and let the earth **r,**
2Ch 6:41 and let your faithful **r** in your goodness.
20:27 LORD had enabled them to **r** over their enemies.
Ne 12:43 for God had made them **r** with great joy;
Job 3: 6 let it not **r** among the days of the year;
3:22 who **r** exceedingly, and are glad when they find
21:12 and **r** to the sound of the pipe.
Ps 5:11 But let all who take refuge in you **r;**
9:14 the gates of daughter Zion, **r** in your deliverance.
13: 4 my foes will **r** because I am shaken.
13: 5 my heart shall **r** in your salvation.
14: 7 Jacob will **r;** Israel will be glad.
30: 1 and did not let my foes **r** over me.
31: 7 I will exult and **r** in your steadfast love,
32:11 Be glad in the LORD and **r,** O righteous,
33: 1 **R** in the LORD, O you righteous.
35: 9 Then my soul shall **r** in the LORD,
35:19 Do not let my treacherous enemies **r** over me,
35:24 and do not let them **r** over me.
35:26 Let all those who **r** at my calamity be put to shame
38:16 For I pray, "Only do not let them **r** over me,
40:16 But may all who seek you **r** and be glad in you;
48:11 the towns of Judah **r** because of your judgments.
51: 8 let the bones that you have crushed **r.**
53: 6 Jacob will **r;** Israel will be glad.
58:10 righteous will **r** when they see vengeance done;
63:11 But the king shall **r** in God;
64:10 Let the righteous **r** in the LORD and take refuge
70: 4 Let all who seek you **r** and be glad in you.
75: 9 But I will **r** forever; I will sing praises to the
85: 6 so that your people may **r** in you?
89:42 you have made all his enemies **r.**
90:14 so that we may **r** and be glad all our days.
96:11 Let the heavens be glad, and let the earth **r;**
97: 1 Let the earth **r;** let the many coastlands be glad!
97: 8 Zion hears and is glad, and the towns of Judah **r,**
97:12 **R** in the LORD, O you righteous,
104:31 may the LORD **r** in his works—
104:34 for I **r** in the LORD.
105: 3 let the hearts of those who seek the LORD **r.**
106: 5 that I may **r** in the gladness of your nation,
118:24 let us **r** and be glad in it.
119:74 Those who fear you shall see me and **r,**
119:162 I **r** at your word like one who finds great spoil.
149: 2 let the children of Zion **r** in their King.
Pr 2:14 who **r** in doing evil and delight in the perverseness
5:18 and **r** in the wife of your youth,
23:16 My soul will **r** when your lips speak what is right.
23:24 The father of the righteous will greatly **r;**
23:25 let her who bore you **r.**
24:17 Do not **r** when your enemies fall,
29: 2 When the righteous are in authority, the people **r;**
29: 6 but the righteous sing and **r.**
Ecc 4:16 Yet those who come later will not **r** in him.
11: 8 those who live many years should **r** in them all;
11: 9 **R,** young man, while you are young,
SS 1: 4 We will exult and **r** in you;
Isa 9: 3 they **r** before you as with joy at the harvest,
14:29 Do not **r,** all you Philistines, that the rod
25: 9 let us be glad and **r** in his salvation.
35: 1 the desert shall **r** and blossom;
35: 2 and **r** with joy and singing.
41:16 Then you shall **r** in the LORD;
60: 5 your heart shall thrill and **r,**
61:10 I will greatly **r** in the LORD,
62: 5 so shall your God **r** over you.
65:13 my servants shall **r,** but you shall be put to shame;
65:18 But be glad and **r** forever in what I am creating;
65:19 I will **r** in Jerusalem, and delight in my people;
66:10 **R** with Jerusalem, and be glad for her,
66:10 **r** with her in joy, all you who mourn over her—
66:14 You shall see, and your heart shall **r;**
Jer 15:17 in the company of merrymakers, nor did I **r;**
Jer 31:13 Then shall the young women **r** in the dance,
32:41 I will **r** in doing good to them,
50:11 Though you **r,** though you exult,
La 2:17 he has made the enemy **r** over you,
4:21 **R** and be glad, O daughter Edom,
Eze 7:12 let not the buyer **r,** nor the seller mourn,
Hos 9: 1 Do not **r,** O Israel!
Joel 2:21 Do not fear, O soil; be glad and **r,**
2:23 be glad and **r** in the LORD your God;
Am 6:13 you who **r** in Lo-debar, who say, "Have we not
Mic 7: 8 Do not **r** over me, O my enemy;
Hab 3:18 yet I will **r** in the LORD;
Zep 3:14 **R** and exult with all your heart,
3:17 he will **r** over you with gladness,
Zec 2:10 Sing and **r,** O daughter Zion!
4:10 the day of small things shall **r,**
9: 9 **R** greatly, O daughter Zion!
10: 7 Their children shall see it and **r,**
Mt 5:12 **R** and be glad, for your reward is great in heaven,
Lk 1:14 and many will **r** at his birth,
6:23 **R** in that day and leap for joy,
10:20 Nevertheless, do not **r** at this,
10:20 but **r** that your names are written in heaven."
15: 6 saying to them, '**R** with me,
15: 9 '**R** with me, for I have found the coin
15:32 But we had to celebrate and **r,**
Jn 4:36 so that sower and reaper may **r** together.
5:35 and you were willing to **r** for a while in his light.
14:28 you would **r** that I am going to the Father,
16:20 you will weep and mourn, but the world will **r;**
16:22 but I will see you again, and your hearts will **r,**
Ro 12:12 **R** in hope, be patient in suffering,
12:15 **R** with those who **r,** weep with those who weep.
15:10 "**R,** O Gentiles, with his people";
16:19 so that I **r** over you,
1Co 7:30 and those who **r** as though they were not rejoicing,
12:26 if one member is honored, all **r** together with it.
13: 6 it does not **r** in wrongdoing,
16:17 I **r** at the coming of Stephanas and Fortunatus
2Co 2: 3 from those who should have made me **r;**
7: 9 Now I **r,** not because you were grieved,
7:16 I **r,** because I have complete confidence in you.
13: 9 For we **r** when we are weak and you are strong.
Gal 4:27 For it is written, "**R,** you childless one,
Php 1:18 and in that I **r.** Yes, and I will continue to **r,**
2:17 I am glad and **r** with all of you—
2:18 and in the same way you also must be glad and **r**
2:28 in order that you may **r** at seeing him again,
3: 1 Finally, my brothers and sisters, **r** in the Lord.
4: 4 **R** in the Lord always; again I will say, **R.**
4:10 I **r** in the Lord greatly that now
Col 2: 5 and I **r** to see your morale and the firmness
1Th 5:16 **R** always,
1Pe 1: 6 In this you **r,** even if now for a little
1: 8 not see him now, you believe in him and **r** with
4:13 **r** insofar as you are sharing Christ's sufferings,
Rev 12:12 **R** then, you heavens and those who dwell in them!
18:20 **R** over her, O heaven, you saints and apostles
19: 7 Let us **r** and exult and give him the glory,
Tob 13:13 Go, then, and **r** over the children of the righteous,
13:14 and happy are those who **r** in your prosperity.
13:14 for they will **r** with you and witness all your glory
14: 7 Those who sincerely love God will **r,**
Wis 18: 6 that they might **r** in sure knowledge of the oaths
Sir 8: 7 Do not **r** over any one's death;
16: 1 and do not **r** in ungodly offspring.
16: 2 If they multiply, do not **r** in them,
22:23 so that you may **r** with him in his prosperity.
23: 3 and my enemy may **r** over me.
25: 7 a man who can **r** in his children;
27:29 Those who **r** in the fall of the godly will be caught
30: 1 so that he may **r** at the way he turns out.
35:25 of his people and makes them **r** in his mercy.
37: 4 Some companions **r** in the happiness of a friend,
40:14 As a generous person has cause to **r,**
51:29 May your soul **r** in God's mercy,
Bar 4:12 Let no one **r** over me, a widow and bereaved
1Mc 12:12 And we **r** in your glory.
2Es 1:37 whose children **r** with gladness;
2:27 but you shall **r** and have abundance.
2:30 "**R,** O mother, with your children,
7:28 and those who remain shall **r** four hundred years.
7:*60* for I will **r** over the few who shall be saved,
7:*65* but let the cattle and the flocks **r.**
7:*96* The fifth order, they **r** that they have
7:*98* because they shall **r** with boldness,
8:39 but I will **r** over the creation of the righteous,

REJOICED‡ (47) [REJOICE]

Ex 18: 9 Jethro **r** for all the good that the LORD had done
1Sa 11: 9 and told the inhabitants of Jabesh, they **r.**
11:15 and there Saul and all the Israelites **r** greatly.
19: 5 You saw it, and **r;** then why will you sin
1Ki 5: 7 Hiram heard the words of Solomon, he **r** greatly,
2Ki 11:20 So all the people of the land **r;**
1Ch 29: 9 the people **r** because these had given willingly,
29: 9 King David also **r** greatly.
2Ch 15:15 All Judah **r** over the oath;
23:21 So all the people of the land **r,**
24:10 the people **r** and brought their tax and dropped it
29:36 and all the people **r** because of what God had done
30:25 and the resident aliens who lived in Judah, **r.**
Ne 12:43 They offered great sacrifices that day and **r,**
12:43 the women and children also **r.**
12:44 for Judah **r** over the priests and
Est 8:15 while the city of Susa shouted and **r.**
Job 31:25 if I have **r** because my wealth was great,
31:29 "If I have **r** at the ruin of those who hated me,
Ps 66: 6 on foot. There we **r** in him,
126: 3 LORD has done great things for us, and we **r.**
Eze 25: 6 and stamped your feet and **r** with all the malice
35:15 you **r** over the inheritance of the house of Israel,
Ob 1:12 you should not have **r** over the people of Judah on
Lk 1:58 to her, and they **r** with her.
10:21 that same hour Jesus **r** in the Holy Spirit and said,
Jn 8:56 Your ancestor Abraham **r**
20:20 Then the disciples **r** when they saw the Lord.
Ac 2:26 therefore my heart was glad, and my tongue **r;**
5:41 they **r** that they were considered worthy
11:23 When he came and saw the grace of God, he **r,**
15:31 its members read it, they **r** at the exhortation.
16:34 and his entire household **r** that he had become
2Co 7: 7 your zeal for me, so that I **r** still more.
7:13 we **r** still more at the joy of Titus,
Tob 14:15 before he died he **r** over Nineveh,
AdE 8:15 The people in Susa **r** on seeing him.
Wis 7:12 I **r** in them all, because wisdom leads them;
Bar 4:31 be those who mistreated you and who **r**
4:33 as she **r** at your fall and was glad for your ruin,
1Mc 7:48 The people **r** greatly and celebrated that day as
10:26 we have heard of it and **r.**
11:44 the king **r** at their arrival.
14:11 and Israel **r** with great joy.
14:21 and we **r** at their coming.
2Es 9:45 I **r** greatly over him, I and my husband
4Mc 4:22 and that the people of Jerusalem had **r** greatly.

REJOICES (16) [REJOICE]

Ps 16: 9 Therefore my heart is glad, and my soul **r;**
21: 1 In your strength the king **r,**
Pr 11:10 When it goes well with the righteous, the city **r;**
13: 9 The light of the righteous **r,**
15:30 The light of the eyes **r** the heart,
Isa 62: 5 and as the bridegroom **r** over the bride,
Eze 35:14 As the whole earth **r,** I will make you desolate.
Hab 1:15 in his seine; so he **r** and exults.
Mt 18:13 he **r** over it more than over the ninety-nine
Lk 1:47 and my spirit **r** in God my Savior,
15: 5 he has found it, he lays it on his shoulders and **r.**
Jn 3:29 **r** greatly at the bridegroom's voice.
1Co 13: 6 not rejoice in wrongdoing, but **r** in the truth.
Tob 13: 7 and my soul **r** in the King of heaven.
Sir 19: 5 One who **r** in wickedness will be condemned,
2Es 7:*59* the person who has what is hard to get **r** more than

REJOICING (43) [REJOICE]

Lev 19:24 the fourth year all their fruit shall be set apart for **r**
Nu 10:10 on your days of **r,** at your appointed festivals,
Dt 12: 7 **r** in all the undertakings in which
12:18 **r** in the presence of the LORD your God
14:26 you and your household **r** together.
27: 7 and eat them there, **r** before the LORD your God.
1Sa 6:13 they went with **r** to meet it.
2Sa 6:12 of Obed-edom to the city of David with **r;**
1Ki 1:40 playing on pipes and **r** with great joy,
1:45 and they have gone up from there **r,**
2Ki 11:14 all the people of the land **r** and blowing trumpets.
1Ch 15:25 the LORD from the house of Obed-edom with **r.**
2Ch 23:13 all the people of the land **r** and blowing trumpets,
23:18 law of Moses, with **r** and with singing,
Ne 8:12 and to send portions and to make great **r,**
8:17 And there was very great **r.**
12:27 to Jerusalem to celebrate the dedication with **r,**
Ps 19: 8 the precepts of the LORD are right, **r** the heart;
Pr 8:30 and I was daily his delight, **r** before him always,
8:31 **r** in his inhabited world and delighting in
Lk 13:17 the entire crowd was **r** at all the wonderful things
Ac 8:39 eunuch saw him no more, and went on his way **r.**
1Co 7:30 and those who rejoice as though they were not **r,**
2Co 6:10 as sorrowful, yet always **r;**
Col 1:24 I am now **r** in my sufferings for your sake,
Jude 1:24 in the presence of his glory with **r,**
Tob 11:15 So Tobit went in **r** and praising God at the top
11:16 Then Tobit, **r** and praising God,
11:17 that day there was **r** among all the Jews who were
Jdt 8: 6 the festivals and days of **r** of the house of Israel.
Sir 1:11 and gladness and a crown of **r.**
15: 6 He will find gladness and a crown of **r,**
30:22 and **r** lengthens one's life span.
31:28 at the proper time and in moderation is **r** of heart
Bar 4:37 at the word of the Holy One, **r** in the glory of God.
5: 5 **r** that God has remembered them.
1Mc 5:23 and led them to Judea with great **r.**
13:52 every year they should celebrate this day with **r.**
2Mc 10: 6 They celebrated it for eight days with **r,**
1Es 4:63 they feasted, with music and **r,** for seven days.
7:14 the festival of unleavened bread seven days, **r**
9:54 to those who had none, and to make great **r;**
2Es 10:22 and our **r** has been ended;

REKEM (6)

Nu 31: 8 They killed the kings of Midian: Evi, **R,** Zur, Hur,
Jos 13:21 Evi and **R** and Zur and Hur and Reba,
18:27 **R,** Irpeel, Taralah,
1Ch 2:43 sons of Hebron: Korah, Tappuah, **R,** and Shema.
2:44 and **R** became the father of Shammai.
7:16 and his sons were Ulam and **R.**

REKINDLE (1) [KINDLE]

2Ti 1: 6 For this reason I remind you to **r** the gift of God

REKINDLED (2) [KINDLE]
Isa 57:10 found your desire r, and so you did not weaken.
1Mc 13: 7 of the people was r when they heard these words,

RELAPSE (1) [RELAPSED]
Jdg 2:19 But whenever the judge died, they would r

RELAPSED (1) [RELAPSE]
Jdg 8:33 the Israelites r and prostituted themselves with

RELATED (10) [RELATION]
Nu 4:32 with all their equipment and all their r service;
Dt 24: 5 with the army or be charged with any r duty.
Ru 3:12 there is another kinsman more closely r than I.
1Sa 19: 7 So Jonathan called David and r all these things
Ne 13: 4 and who was r to Tobiah,
Ac 14:27 the church together and r all that God had done
15:14 Simeon has r how God first looked favorably on
21:19 he r one by one the things that God had done
Tob 6:18 r through his father's lineage,
AdE 8: 1 for Esther had told the king that he was r to her.

RELATING (9) [RELATION]
Nu 4: 3 all who qualify to do work r to the tent
4: 4 of the Kohathites r to the tent of meeting concerns
4:28 the service of the clans of the Gershonites r to
4:33 the whole of their service r to the tent of meeting,
4:35 everyone who qualified for work r to the tent
4:39 everyone who qualified for work r to the tent
4:43 everyone who qualified for work r to the tent
4:47 of service and the work of bearing burdens r to
2Mc 15:11 and he cheered them all by r a dream,

RELATION (1) [RELATED, RELATING, RELATIONS, RELATIONSHIP, RELATIVE, RELATIVES]
Ro 2:17 and rely on the law and boast of your r to God

RELATIONS (9) [RELATION]
Lev 18:20 not have sexual r with your kinsman's wife,
18:23 You shall not have sexual r with any animal
18:23 to an animal to have sexual r with it:
19:20 a man has sexual r with a woman who is a slave,
20:15 If a man has sexual r with an animal,
20:16 a woman approaches any animal and has sexual r
Nu 25: 1 the people began to have sexual r with the women
Mt 1:25 but had no marital r with her until she had borne
2Mc 10:12 and attempted to maintain peaceful r with them.

RELATIONSHIP (1) [RELATION]
4Mc 2:13 It is sovereign over the r of friends,

RELATIVE (13) [RELATION]
Lev 25:25 of kin shall come and redeem what the r has sold.
Ru 2:20 Naomi also said to her, "The man is a r of ours,
Isa 3: 6 Someone will even seize a r,
Am 6:10 And if a r, one who burns the dead,
6:10 Then the r shall say, "Hush!
Lk 1:36 your r Elizabeth in her old age has also conceived
Jn 18:26 a r of the man whose ear Peter had cut off, asked,
Ro 16:11 Greet my r Herodion. Greet those in the
Tob 1:22 He was my nephew and so a close r.
3:15 and he has no close r or other kindred
6:11 He is your r, and he has a daughter named Sarah.
7:10 because you are my nearest r.
Sir 41:21 and of rejecting the appeal of a r;

RELATIVES (24) [RELATION]
Lev 21: 1 for a dead person among his r,
2Ki 10:13 Jehu met r of King Ahaziah of Judah and said,
Job 19:14 My r and my close friends have failed me;
Ps 122: 8 For the sake of my r and friends I will say,
Isa 22:16 Who are your r here, that you have cut out
Lk 1:58 Her neighbors and r heard that
1:61 They said to her, "None of your r has this name."
2:44 Then they started to look for him among their r
14:12 not invite your friends or your brothers or your r
21:16 even by parents and brothers, by r and friends;
Ac 7: 3 'Leave your country and your r and go to the land
7:14 and invited his father Jacob and all his r to come
7:23 it came into his heart to visit his r, the Israelites.
10:24 and had called together his r and close friends.
Ro 16: 7 my r who were in prison with me;
16:21 so do Lucius and Jason and Sosipater, my r.
1Ti 5: 8 And whoever does not provide for r,
5:16 any believing woman has r who are really widows,
Tob 5:13 the son of the great Hananiah, one of your r."
Sus 1:30 her children, and all her r.
1:63 and so did her husband Joakim and all her r,
2Mc 15:18 and also for brothers and sisters and r,
3Mc 5:49 embracing r and falling into one another's arms—
2Es 7:*103* brothers for brothers, r for their kindred,

RELAX (2) [RELAXES]
Lk 12:19 for many years; r, eat, drink, be merry.'
Sir 43:10 they never r in their watches.

RELAXES (1) [RELAX]
Wis 16:24 in kindness r on behalf of those who trust in you.

RELEASE‡ (41) [RELEASED]
Ge 42:34 Then I will r your brother to you,
Job 14:14 of my service I would wait until my r should come.
Isa 61: 1 to proclaim liberty to the captives, and r to
Jer 34:17 not obeyed me by granting a r to your neighbors
34:17 I am going to grant a r to you, says the LORD—
34:17 a r to the sword, to pestilence, and to famine.
Mt 27:15 at the festival the governor was accustomed to r
27:17 "Whom do you want me to r for you,
27:21 "Which of the two do you want me to r for you?"
Mk 15: 6 at the festival he used to r a prisoner for them,
15: 9 "Do you want me to r for you the King of
15:11 to have him r Barabbas for them instead.
Lk 4:18 to proclaim r to the captives and recovery of sight
23:16 I will therefore have him flogged and r him."
23:18 with this fellow! R Barabbas for us!"
23:20 Pilate, wanting to r Jesus, addressed them again;
23:22 I will therefore have him flogged and then r him."
Jn 18:39 But you have a custom that I r someone for you at
18:39 Do you want me to r for you the King of the Jews?
19:10 Do you not know that I have power to r you,
19:12 From then on Pilate tried to r him,
19:12 but the Jews cried out, "If you r this man,
Ac 3:13 though he had decided to r him.
28:18 the Romans wanted to r me,
Heb 11:35 Others were tortured, refusing to accept r,
Rev 9:14 "R the four angels who are bound at
Tob 3: 6 r me to go to the eternal home, and do not,
1Mc 9:70 to him to make peace with him and obtain r of
10:30 I r them from this day and henceforth.
10:32 I r also my control of the citadel in Jerusalem
10:34 and r for all the Jews who are in my kingdom.
11:34 in Jerusalem we have granted r from
11:35 from all these we shall grant them r.
13:16 not revolt against us, and we will r him."
13:19 but Trypho broke his word and did not r Jonathan.
13:37 to write to our officials to grant you r from tribute.
15: 5 and a r from all the other payments
1Es 4: 7 if he tells them to r, they r;
4:62 because he had given them r and permission
3Mc 6:28 R the children of the almighty and living God

RELEASED (34) [RELEASE]
Lev 25:28 in the jubilee it shall be r,
25:30 it shall not be r in the jubilee.
25:31 and they shall be r in the jubilee.
25:33 shall be r in the jubilee;
27:21 But when the field is r in the jubilee,
Jos 2:17 be r from this oath that you have made us swear
2:20 be r from this oath that you made us swear
2Ki 25:27 r King Jehoiachin of Judah from prison;
Ezr 1: 8 of Persia had them r into the charge of Mithredath
Ps 105:20 The king sent and r him;
Isa 51:14 The oppressed shall speedily be r;
Jer 20: 3 The next morning when Pashhur r Jeremiah from
40: 4 I have just r you today from the fetters
Mt 18:27 lord of that slave r him and forgave him the debt.
27:26 So he r Barabbas for them;
Mk 7:35 his tongue was r, and he spoke plainly.
15:15 wishing to satisfy the crowd, r Barabbas for them;
Lk 23:25 He r the man they asked for,
Ac 4:23 After they were r, they went to their friends
22:30 the next day he r him and ordered the chief priests
Rev 9:15 So the four angels were r,
20: 7 Satan will be r from his prison
Tob 3: 6 be taken from me, so that I may be r from the face
3: 6 Command, O Lord, that I be r from this distress;
3:13 Command that I be r from the earth and not listen
Sir 18:22 and do not wait until death to be r from it.
1Mc 10: 6 that the hostages in the citadel should be r to him.
10: 9 But those in the citadel r the hostages to Jonathan,
10:43 let them be r and receive back all their property
13:16 so that when r he will not revolt against us,
15: 5 the other payments from which they have r you.
3Mc 6:29 and the Jews, immediately r,
4Mc 9:16 to eat so that you may be r from the tortures,"
11:13 inquired whether he was willing to eat and be r,

RELENT (6) [RELENTED, RELENTING, RELENTLESS, RELENTLESSLY, RELENTS]
Eze 24:14 I will not refrain, I will not spare, I will not r.
Joel 2:14 Who knows whether he will not turn and r,
Jnh 3: 9 God may r and change his mind;
4: 2 and ready to r from punishing.
Zec 8:14 and I did not r, says the LORD of hosts,
Man 1: 7 and very merciful, and you r at human suffering.

RELENTED (5) [RELENT]
2Sa 24:16 the LORD r concerning the evil,
1Ch 21:15 LORD took note and r concerning the calamity;
Jer 4:28 I have not r nor will I turn back.
Am 7: 3 The LORD r concerning this;
7: 6 The LORD r concerning this;

RELENTING (1) [RELENT]
Jer 15: 6 and destroyed you—I am weary of r.

RELENTLESS (1) [RELENT]
Wis 16:16 pursued by unusual rains and hail and r storms,

RELENTLESSLY (3) [RELENT]
Wis 5:22 and rivers will r overwhelm them;
2Mc 5: 6 But Jason kept r slaughtering his compatriots,
5:12 to cut down r everyone they met and

RELENTS (1) [RELENT]
Joel 2:13 to anger, and abounding in steadfast love, and r

RELIABLE (1) [RELY]
Isa 8: 2 and have it attested for me by r witnesses,

RELIANCE (2) [RELY]
Eze 29:16 The Egyptians shall never again be the r of
2Mc 10:28 and victory not only their valor but also their r on

RELIC (1)
Sus 1:52 "You old r of wicked days,

RELIED (3) [RELY]
2Ch 13:18 because they r on the LORD,
16: 7 "Because you r on the king of Aram,
16: 8 Yet because you r on the LORD,

RELIEF (20) [RELIEVE]
Ge 5:29 the LORD has cursed this one shall bring us r
Ex 23:12 so that your ox and your donkey may have r,
Est 4:14 r and deliverance will rise for the Jews
9:16 and gained r from their enemies,
9:22 on which the Jews gained r from their enemies,
Job 32:20 I must speak, so that I may find r;
Pr 29: 9 there is ranting and ridicule without r.
Jer 17: 6 and shall not see when r comes.
La 3:56 to my cry for help, but give me r!"
Ac 11:29 each would send r to the believers living in Judea;
2Co 8:13 I do not mean that there should be r for others
2Th 1: 7 and to give r to the afflicted as well as to us,
AdE 9:16 and got r from their enemies.
9:22 on these days the Jews got r from their enemies.
Wis 19:12 for, to give them r, quails came up from the sea.
Sir 18:16 Does not the dew give r from the scorching heat?
31:21 get up to vomit, and you will have r.
1Mc 13:34 to King Demetrius with a request to grant r to
2Mc 9: 5 for which there was no r, and
Man 1:10 because of my sins, and I have no r;

RELIES (1) [RELY]
Isa 50:10 in the name of the LORD and r upon his God?

RELIEVE (3) [RELIEF, RELIEVED, RELIEVING]
Dt 23:13 when you r yourself outside,
1Sa 24: 3 and Saul went in to r himself.
Ps 25:17 R the troubles of my heart,

RELIEVED (4) [RELIEVE]
1Sa 16:23 and Saul would be r and feel better,
Ps 81: 6 "I r your shoulder of the burden;
2Es 7:*138* [68] be r of them, not one ten-thousandth
11:46 freed from your violence, may be refreshed and r,

RELIEVING (1) [RELIEVE]
Jdg 3:24 "He must be r himself in the cool chamber."

RELIGION (45) [RELIGION'S, RELIGIOUS]
Ac 25:19 of disagreement with him about their own r and
26: 5 the strictest sect of our r and lived as a Pharisee.
1Ti 3:16 Without any doubt, the mystery of our r is great:
Jas 1:26 but deceive their hearts, their r is worthless.
1:27 R that is pure and undefiled before God,
1Mc 1:43 Many even from Israel gladly adopted his r;
2:19 of them abandoning the r of their ancestors,
2:22 by turning aside from our r to the right hand or to
2Mc 6:24 in his ninetieth year had gone over to an alien r,
3Mc 1: 3 by birth who later changed his r and apostatized
2:31 to be exacted for maintaining the r of their city,
2:32 a courageous spirit and did not abandon their r;
4Mc 5: 7 a philosopher when you observe the r of the Jews.
5:13 there is some power watching over this r of yours,
6:22 O children of Abraham, die nobly for your r!
7: 1 of our father Eleazar steered the ship of r over
7: 3 the rudder of r until he sailed into the haven
7:18 But as many as attend to r with a whole heart,
9: 6 of the Hebrews because of their r lived piously
9: 7 and if you take our lives because of our r,
9:24 Fight the sacred and noble battle for r.
9:29 "How sweet is any kind of death for the r
9:30 by our endurance for the sake of r?
11:20 to an arena of sufferings for r,
12:11 and torture on the wheel those who practice r?
13: 7 by fortifying the harbor of r,
13: 8 a holy chorus of r and encouraged one another,
13:12 to being slain for the sake of r."
13:26 with the aid of their r.
13:27 those who were left endured for the sake of r,
14: 3 of the seven brothers on behalf of r!
14: 7 of creation move in choral dance around r,
15: 1 r, more desirable to the mother than her children!
15: 2 Two courses were open to this mother, that of r,
15: 3 She loved r more, the r that preserves them
15:14 because of r did not change her attitude.
15:29 vindicator of the law and champion of r,
15:32 and withstood the wintry storms that assail r.
16:13 and urged them on to death for the sake of r.

4Mc 16:14 O mother, soldier of God in the cause of **r**,
16:17 aged man endures such agonies for the sake of **r**,
17: 7 to paint the history of your **r** as an artist might,
17: 7 to death for the sake of **r**?
18: 3 the sake of **r** were not only admired by mortals,

RELIGION'S (1) [RELIGION]

4Mc 15:12 the mother urged on to death for **r** sake.

RELIGIOUS (7) [RELIGION]

Ac 17:22 I see how extremely **r** you are in every way.
1Ti 5: 4 they should first learn their **r** duty
Jas 1:26 If any think they are **r**,
3Mc 3:21 to make them participants in our regular **r** rites.
4Mc 5:38 but you shall not dominate my **r** principles,
11:21 For **r** knowledge, O tyrant, is invincible.
16:23 for people who have **r** knowledge not

RELUCTANTLY (1)

2Co 9: 7 made up your mind, not **r** or under compulsion,

RELY (28) [RELIABLE, RELIANCE, RELIED, RELIES, RELYING]

2Ki 18:20 On whom do you now **r**,
18:21 Such is Pharaoh king of Egypt to all who **r**
18:22 if you say to me, 'We **r** on the LORD our God,'
18:24 you **r** on Egypt for chariots and for horsemen?
18:30 Do not let Hezekiah make you **r** on the LORD
19:10 Do not let your God on whom you **r** deceive you
2Ch 14:11 Help us, O LORD our God, for we **r** on you,
16: 7 and did not **r** on the LORD your God,
Pr 3: 5 and do not **r** on your own insight.
Isa 30:12 and put your trust in oppression and deceit, and **r**
31: 1 down to Egypt for help and who **r** on horses,
36: 5 On whom do you now **r**,
36: 6 Such is Pharaoh king of Egypt to all who **r**
36: 7 if you say to me, 'We **r** on the LORD our God,'
36: 9 you **r** on Egypt for chariots and for horsemen?
36:15 Do not let Hezekiah make you **r** on the LORD
37:10 Do not let your God on whom you **r** deceive you
59: 4 they **r** on empty pleas, they speak lies,
Ro 2:17 and **r** on the law and boast of your relation to God
2Co 1: 9 of death so that we would **r** not on ourselves but
Gal 3:10 For all who **r** on the works of the law are under
Jdt 7:10 do not **r** on their spears but on the height of
Sir 5: 1 Do not **r** on your wealth, or say, "I have enough."
15: 4 and he will **r** on her and not be put to shame.
16: 3 not trust in their survival, or **r** on their numbers;
35:15 and do not **r** on a dishonest sacrifice;
38:31 All these **r** on their hands,
1Mc 8:12 but with their friends and those who **r**

RELYING (6) [RELY]

2Ki 18:21 See, you are **r** now on Egypt,
2Ch 32:10 On what are you **r**, that you undergo the siege
Isa 36: 6 you are **r** on Egypt, that broken reed of a staff,
2Ti 1: 8 **r** on the power of God,
2Mc 10:34 The men within, **r** on the strength of the place,
12:14 **r** on the strength of the walls and on their supply

REMAIN‡ (151) [REMAINDER, REMAINED, REMAINING, REMAINS]

Ge 24:55 "Let the girl **r** with us a while, at least ten days;
38:11 "**R** a widow in your father's house
42:16 while the rest of you **r** in prison,
44:33 please let your servant **r** as a slave to my lord
Ex 10:24 Only your flocks and your herds shall **r** behind.
12:10 You shall let none of it **r** until the morning;
22:30 seven days it shall **r** with its mother;
23:18 or let the fat of my festival **r** until the morning.
25:15 The poles shall **r** in the rings of the ark;
Lev 6: 9 The burnt offering itself shall **r** on the hearth upon
8:35 You shall **r** at the entrance of the tent
11:11 and detestable they shall **r**.
11:35 they are unclean, and shall **r** unclean for you.
13:46 He shall **r** unclean as long as he has the disease;
22:27 it shall **r** seven days with its mother,
25:28 what was sold shall **r** with the purchaser until
25:40 They shall **r** with you as hired or bound laborers.
25:51 If many years **r**, they shall pay
25:52 and if few years **r** until the jubilee year,
27:18 the price for it according to the years that **r** until
Nu 9:18 the cloud rested over the tabernacle, they would **r**
9:20 the cloud would **r** a few days over the tabernacle,
9:20 to the command of the LORD they would **r**
9:21 the cloud would **r** from evening until morning;
9:22 Israelites would **r** in camp and would not set out;
19: 7 but the priest shall **r** unclean until evening.
19: 8 he shall **r** unclean until evening.
19:13 they **r** unclean; their uncleanness is still on them.
22:19 You **r** here, as the others did,
32:26 and all our livestock shall **r** there in the towns
32:32 the possession of our inheritance shall **r** with us
33:55 then those whom you let **r** shall be as barbs
35:28 For the slayer must **r** in the city of refuge until
Dt 4:40 so that you may long **r** in the land that
13:16 It shall **r** a perpetual ruin, never to be rebuilt.
16: 4 the evening of the first day shall **r** until morning.
17:19 It shall **r** with him and he shall read in it all
18:13 You must **r** completely loyal to
20:16 you must not let anything that breathes **r** alive.
21: 8 do not let the guilt of innocent blood **r** in the midst
21:13 and shall **r** in your house a full month,
Dt 21:23 his corpse must not **r** all night upon the tree;
22: 2 and it shall **r** with you until the owner claims it;
22:19 She shall **r** his wife;
28:41 but they shall not **r** yours,
31:26 let it **r** there as a witness against you.
Jos 1:14 and your livestock shall **r** in the land
10:27 the mouth of the cave, which **r** to this very day.
20: 4 and given a place, and shall **r** with them.
20: 6 The slayer shall **r** in that city until there is a trial
23: 4 an inheritance for your tribes those nations that **r**,
Ru 3:13 **R** this night, and in the morning,
1Sa 1:22 in the presence of the LORD, and **r** there forever;
5: 7 "The ark of the God of Israel must not **r** with us;
16:22 saying, "Let David **r** in my service,
20:19 and **r** beside the stone there.
22: 5 "Do not **r** in the stronghold;
2Sa 10: 5 "**R** at Jericho until your beards have grown,
11:11 "The ark and Israel and Judah **r** in booths;
11:12 Then David said to Uriah, "**R** here today also,
16:18 his I will be, and with him I will **r**.
1Ki 11:32 One tribe will **r** his, for the sake
2Ki 3:25 Only at Kir-hareseth did the stone walls **r**,
1Ch 13: 2 let us send abroad to our kindred who **r** in all
19: 5 "**R** at Jericho until your beards have grown,
Job 37: 8 the animals go into their lairs and **r** in their dens.
Ps 89:21 my hand shall always **r** with him;
101: 7 No one who practices deceit shall **r** in my house;
Pr 2:21 and the innocent will **r** in it;
10:30 but the wicked will not **r** in the land.
Isa 6:13 Even if a tenth part **r** in it, it will be burned again,
27: 9 no sacred poles or incense altars will **r** standing.
66:22 which I will make, shall **r** before me,
66:22 so shall your descendants and your name **r**.
Jer 24: 8 the remnant of Jerusalem who **r** in this land,
25: 5 and you will **r** upon the land that
32: 5 and there he shall **r** until I attend to him,
40: 5 If you **r**, then return to Gedaliah son
42:10 If you will only **r** in this land, then I will build you
51:30 they **r** in their strongholds;
Eze 7:11 None of them shall **r**, not their abundance,
7:13 to what has been sold as long as they **r** alive.
9: 8 will you destroy all who **r** of Israel
21:26 things shall not **r** as they are.
22:14 or can your hands **r** strong in the days
39:14 the land regularly and bury any invaders who **r** on
44: 2 The LORD said to me: This gate shall **r** shut;
44: 2 therefore it shall **r** shut.
46: 1 of the inner court that faces east shall **r** closed on
Da 12: 9 the words are to **r** secret and sealed until the time
Hos 3: 3 I said to her, "You must **r** as mine for many days;
3: 4 For the Israelites shall **r** many days without king
9: 3 They shall not **r** in the land of the LORD;
Am 6: 9 If ten people **r** in one house, they shall die.
Zec 14:10 But Jerusalem shall **r** aloft on its site from
Mt 2:13 and flee to Egypt, and **r** there until I tell you;
26:38 **r** here, and stay awake with me."
Mk 14:34 "I am deeply grieved, even to death; **r** here,
Lk 8:47 When the woman saw that she could not **r** hidden,
10: 7 **R** in the same house, eating
Jn 1:33 'He on whom you see the Spirit descend and **r** is
12:46 so that everyone who believes in me should not **r**
21:22 "If it is my will that he **r** until I come,
21:23 but, "If it is my will that he **r** until I come,
Ac 3:21 who must **r** in heaven until the time
5: 4 While it remained unsold, did it not **r** your own?
11:23 and he exhorted them all to **r** faithful to the Lord
1Co 7: 8 that it is well for them to **r** unmarried as I am.
7:11 let her **r** unmarried or else be reconciled to her
7:20 of you **r** in the condition in which you were called.
7:24 brothers and sisters, there **r** with God.
7:26 it is well for you to **r** as you are.
Gal 2: 5 the truth of the gospel might always **r** with you.
4: 2 but they **r** under guardians and trustees until
Php 1:24 but to **r** in the flesh is more necessary for you.
1:25 I know that I will **r** and continue with all of you
1Ti 1: 3 as I did when I was on my way to Macedonia, to **r**
5:25 and even when they are not, they cannot **r** hidden.
Heb 1:11 they will perish, but you **r**;
12:27 so that what cannot be shaken may **r**.
Rev 17:10 and when he comes, he must **r** only a little while.
Tob 6: 8 and every affliction will flee away and never **r**
14:8,9 So now, my son, leave Nineveh; do not **r** here.
Jdt 7:12 **R** in your camp, and keep all the men
11:17 So, my lord, I will **r** with you;
AdE 13: 7 and **r** so may in a single day go down in violence
Sir 4:16 If they **r** faithful, they will inherit her;
6:20 to the undisciplined; fools cannot **r** with her.
20: 7 The wise **r** silent until the right moment,
42:23 All these things live and **r** forever;
44:11 their wealth will **r** with their descendants,
Bar 2:21 you will **r** in the land that I gave to your ancestors.
LtJ 6: 3 when you have come to Babylon you will **r** there
1Mc 8:22 to Jerusalem to **r** with them there as a memorial
10:14 in Beth-zur did some **r** who had forsaken the law
13:38 All the grants that we have made to you **r** valid,
15: 7 that you have built and now hold shall **r** yours.
2Mc 2: 7 "The place shall **r** unknown
15:19 And those who had to **r** in the city were
3Mc 5:18 to know why the Jews had been allowed to **r** alive
2Es 4:35 saying, 'How long are we to **r** here?
6:41 and the other part **r** beneath.
7:28 and those who **r** shall rejoice four hundred years.
7:*34* Only judgment shall **r**, truth shall stand,
7:*112* [42] the full glory does not **r** in it;
9:35 but the things that held them **r**;
10:51 to **r** in the field where no house had been built,
10:58 But tomorrow night you shall **r** here,
2Es 13:49 he will defend the people who **r**.
14:12 so two of its parts **r**, besides half of the tenth part.
15:27 and you shall **r** in them;

REMAINDER (4) [REMAIN]

Ex 29:34 then you shall burn the **r** with fire;
Jos 21:40 that is, the **r** of the families of the Levites,
Eze 48:15 The **r**, five thousand cubits in width
48:18 The **r** of the length alongside the holy portion

REMAINED (113) [REMAIN]

Ge 16:13 for she said, "Have I really seen God and **r** alive
18:22 while Abraham **r** standing before the LORD.
39:20 prisoners were confined; he **r** there in prison.
49:24 Yet his bow **r** taut, and his arms were made agile
50:22 Joseph **r** in Egypt, he and his father's household;
Ex 7:22 so Pharaoh's heart **r** hardened,
8:31 from his people; not one **r**.
14:28 into the sea; not one of them **r**.
Nu 11:26 Two men **r** in the camp, one named Eldad,
14:38 of Nun and Caleb son of Jephunneh alone **r** alive,
36:12 and their inheritance **r** in the tribe
Dt 3:29 So we **r** in the valley opposite Beth-peor.
5:26 speaking out of fire, as we have, and **r** alive?
9: 9 I **r** on the mountain forty days and forty nights;
Jos 4:10 the ark **r** standing in the middle of the Jordan,
5: 8 they **r** in their places in the camp
11:22 some **r** only in Gaza, in Gath, and in Ashdod.
18: 2 There **r** among the Israelites seven tribes whose
Jdg 7: 3 twenty-two thousand returned, and ten thousand **r**.
9:21 where he **r** for fear of his brother Abimelech.
11:17 So Israel **r** at Kadesh.
19: 4 made him stay, and he **r** with him three days;
20:47 and **r** at the rock of Rimmon for four months.
20:48 the city, the people, the animals, and all that **r**.
Ru 1: 2 They went into the country of Moab and **r** there.
1Sa 1:23 So the woman **r** and nursed her son,
2:11 while the boy **r** to minister to the LORD,
23:14 David **r** in the strongholds in the wilderness,
23:18 David **r** at Horesh, and Jonathan went home.
25:13 while two hundred **r** with the baggage.
26: 3 But David **r** in the wilderness.
2Sa 1: 1 David **r** two days in Ziklag.
6:11 of the LORD **r** in the house of Obed-edom
11: 1 But David **r** at Jerusalem.
11:12 So Uriah **r** in Jerusalem that day.
13:20 So Tamar **r**, a desolate woman,
15:29 the ark of God back to Jerusalem, and they **r** there.
1Ki 11:16 (for Joab and all Israel **r** there six months,
11:40 and **r** in Egypt until the death of Solomon.
2Ki 2:18 When they came back to him (he had **r** at Jericho),
11: 3 he **r** with her six years,
13: 6 the sacred pole also **r** in Samaria.
24:14 no one **r**, except the poorest people of the land.
25:22 of Shaphan as governor over the people who **r** in
1Ch 13:14 of God **r** with the household of Obed-edom
20: 1 But David **r** at Jerusalem.
2Ch 14:13 and the Ethiopians fell until no one **r** alive;
22:12 he **r** with them six years,
Ezr 8:32 We came to Jerusalem and **r** there three days.
Ne 8: 7 while the people **r** in their places.
11: 1 while nine-tenths **r** in the other towns.
Ecc 2: 9 also my wisdom **r** with me.
Jer 34: 7 these were the only fortified cities of Judah that **r**.
37:10 there **r** of them only wounded men in their tents,
37:16 in the cells, and **r** there many days.
37:21 So Jeremiah **r** in the court of the guard.
38:13 And Jeremiah **r** in the court of the guard.
38:28 And Jeremiah **r** in the court of the guard until
39: 9 to him, and the people who **r**.
48:11 his flavor has **r** and his aroma is unspoiled.
Eze 17: 6 Its branches turned toward him, its roots **r**
Da 2:49 But Daniel **r** at the king's court.
Mt 2:15 and **r** there until the death of Herod.
11:23 it would have **r** until this day.
Lk 1:22 He kept motioning to them and **r** unable to speak.
1:24 and for five months she **r** in seclusion.
1:56 And Mary **r** with her about three months and
Jn 1:32 from heaven like a dove, and it **r** on him
1:39 and they **r** with him that day.
2:12 and they **r** there a few days.
7: 9 After saying this, he **r** in Galilee.
10:40 John had been baptizing earlier, and he **r** there.
11:54 and he **r** there with the disciples.
Ac 5: 4 While it **r** unsold, did it not remain your own?
14: 3 So they **r** for a long time,
15:35 But Paul and Barnabas **r** in Antioch, and there,
16:12 We **r** in this city for some days.
17:14 but Silas and Timothy **r** behind.
21:14 we **r** silent except to say,
27:41 the bow stuck and **r** immovable,
2Ti 4:20 Erastus **r** in Corinth; Trophimus I left ill in
Tit 1: 5 so that you should put in order what **r** to be done,
1Jn 2:19 they would have **r** with us.
Tob 2:10 For four years I **r** unable to see.
Jdt 3:10 and **r** for a whole month in order to collect all
7: 5 they **r** on guard all that night.
8: 4 Judith **r** as a widow for three years
12: 7 She **r** in the camp three days.
15: 7 took possession of what **r**.
16:20 in Jerusalem before the sanctuary, and Judith **r**
16:21 Judith went to Bethulia, and **r** on her estate.
Sir 16:11 it would be a wonder if he **r** unpunished.
46: 9 which **r** with him in his old age,
1Mc 10:47 and they **r** his allies all his days.
13:11 he drove out its occupants and **r** there.

2Mc 4:50 because of the greed of those in power, **r** in office,
3Mc 1:17 those who **r** behind in the city were agitated
2:33 They **r** resolutely hopeful of obtaining help,
2Es 3:22 but what was good departed, and the evil **r.**
4:48 by I looked, and lo, the smoke **r.**
4:49 drops still **r** in the cloud.
4:50 passed was far greater; but drops and smoke **r.**"
10: 2 I **r** quiet until the evening of the second day.
11:23 and nothing **r** on the eagle's body except
11:24 that two little wings separated from the six and **r**
11:24 but four **r** in their place.
11:28 the two that **r** were planning between themselves
11:34 the two heads **r,** which also in like manner ruled
12:27 as for the two who **r,** the sword shall devour them.
14:37 and we proceeded to the field, and **r** there.
4Mc 6: 2 he **r** adorned with the gracefulness of his piety.
7:12 though being consumed by the fire, **r** unmoved
18: 9 In the time of my maturity I **r** with my husband,

REMAINING‡ (30) [REMAIN]

Ex 28:10 and the names of the **r** six on the other stone,
Lev 10:12 Moses spoke to Aaron and to his **r** sons,
10:16 with Eleazar and Ithamar, Aaron's **r** sons,
25:15 seller shall charge you only for the **r** crop years.
Nu 31:32 The booty **r** from the spoil that the troops
Dt 28:54 and to the last of his **r** children,
32:36 that their power is gone, neither bond nor free **r.**
Jos 10:28 destroyed every person in it; he left no one **r.**
10:30 every person in it; he left no one **r** in it;
10:37 he left no one **r,** just as he had done to Eglon,
10:39 destroyed every person in it; he left no one **r.**
10:40 he left no one **r,** but utterly destroyed all
11: 8 until they had left no one **r.**
Jdg 20:48 Also the **r** towns they set on fire.
2Sa 9: 3 "Is there anyone **r** of the house of Saul
14: 7 Thus they would quench my one **r** ember,
2Ki 7:13 "Let some men take five of the **r** horses,
Isa 21:17 and the **r** bows of Kedar's warriors will be few;
Jer 29: 1 from Jerusalem to the **r** elders among the exiles,
38:22 of all the women **r** in the house of the king
Ac 27:33 that you have been in suspense and **r**
Jdt 14:10 and joined the house of Israel, **r** so to this day.
Wis 7:27 and while **r** in herself, she renews all things;
1Mc 3:37 the **r** half of his forces and left Antioch his capital
8:11 The **r** kingdoms and islands,
12:45 as well as the other strongholds and the **r** troops
2Mc 8:14 Others sold all their **r** property,
3Mc 3:26 we are sure that for the **r** time the government will
4: 8 spent the **r** days of their marriage festival
2Es 12: 2 and saw that the **r** head had disappeared.

REMAINS‡ (56) [REMAIN]

Ex 12:10 anything that **r** until the morning you shall burn.
22:13 restitution shall not be made for the mangled **r.**
26:12 The part that **r** of the curtains of the tent,
26:12 the half curtain that **r,** shall hang over the back of
26:13 of what **r** in the length of the curtains of the tent,
29:34 or of the bread, **r** until the morning,
Lev 8:32 and what **r** of the flesh and
13:23 But if the spot **r** in one place and does not spread,
13:28 But if the spot **r** in one place and does not spread
14:17 that **r** in his hand the priest shall put on the lobe of
16:16 and so he shall do for the tent of meeting, which **r**
Dt 28:55 because nothing else **r** to him,
Jos 7:26 over him a great heap of stones that **r** to this day.
13: 1 and very much of the land still **r** to be possessed.
13: 2 This is the land that still **r:**
1Sa 16:11 And he said, "There **r** yet the youngest,
2Sa 9: 3 Ziba said to the king, "There **r** a son of Jonathan;
16: 3 Ziba said to the king, "He **r** in Jerusalem;
Ne 9:10 a name for yourself, which **r** to this day.
Job 18:15 In their tents nothing **r;** sulfur is scattered upon
19: 4 if it is true that I have erred, my error **r** with me.
Ps 142: 4 no refuge **r** to me; no one cares for me.
Pr 11:12 but an intelligent person **r** silent.
21:20 Precious treasure **r** in the house of the wise,
29: 1 One who is often reproved, yet **r** stubborn,
Ecc 1: 4 and a generation comes, but the earth **r** forever.
Isa 4: 3 Whoever is left in Zion and **r** in Jerusalem will
6:13 an oak whose stump **r** standing when it is felled."
Jer 8: 3 to life by all the remnant that **r** of this evil family
47: 4 to cut off from Tyre and Sidon every helper that **r.**
Eze 19:14 so that there **r** in it no strong stem,
48:21 What **r** on both sides of the holy portion and of
Da 10:17 For I am shaking, no strength **r** in me,
11:27 for there **r** an end at the time appointed.
Zec 1:11 and lo, the whole earth **r** at peace."
Jn 9:41 But now that you say, 'We see,' your sin **r.**
12:24 it **r** just a single grain; but if it dies, it bears much
12:34 from the law that the Messiah **r** forever.
1Co 7:40 But in my judgment she is more blessed if she **r**
2Ti 2:13 he **r** faithful—for he cannot deny himself.
Heb 4: 6 Since therefore it **r** open for some to enter it,
4: 9 then, a sabbath rest still **r** for the people of God;
7: 3 but resembling the Son of God, he **r** a priest
10:26 there no longer **r** a sacrifice for sins,
Rev 3: 2 and strengthen what **r** and is on the point of death,
Wis 10: 7 Evidence of their wickedness still **r:**
19:18 while each note **r** the same.
Sir 1: 1 and with him it **r** forever.
11:17 The Lord's gift **r** with the devout,
21:23 but a cultivated person **r** outside.
23:11 If he swears in error, his sin **r** on him,
1Mc 13:30 in Modein; it **r** to this day.
2Es 6:25 be that whoever **r** after all that I have foretold
7:*123* [53] whose fruit **r** unspoiled and

2Es 11:39 that **r** of the four beasts that I had made to reign
4Mc 8:11 nothing **r** for you but to die on the rack?"

REMALIAH (13)

2Ki 15:25 Pekah son of **R,** his captain,
15:27 of **R** began to reign over Israel in Samaria;
15:30 a conspiracy against Pekah son of **R,** attacked him,
15:32 the second year of King Pekah son of **R** of Israel,
15:37 to send King Rezin of Aram and Pekah son of **R**
16: 1 In the seventeenth year of Pekah son of **R,**
16: 5 of **R** of Israel came up to wage war on Jerusalem;
2Ch 28: 6 of **R** killed one hundred twenty thousand in Judah
Isa 7: 1 of Aram and King Pekah son of **R** of Israel went
7: 4 of Rezin and Aram and the son of **R.**
7: 5 Because Aram—with Ephraim and the son of **R—**
7: 9 and the head of Samaria is the son of **R.**
8: 6 and melt in fear before Rezin and the son of **R;**

REMARKABLY (1)

2Mc 3:26 Two young men also appeared to him, **r** strong,

REMEDY (3)

2Ch 36:16 so great that there was no **r.**
Wis 2: 1 and there is no **r** when a life comes to its end,
11: 4 and from hard stone a **r** for their thirst.

REMEMBER (212) [REMEMBERED, REMEMBERING, REMEMBERS, REMEMBRANCE]

Ge 9:15 I will **r** my covenant that is between me and you
9:16 and **r** the everlasting covenant between God
31:50 **r** that God is witness between you and me."
40:14 But **r** me when it is well with you;
40:23 chief cupbearer did not **r** Joseph, but forgot him.
41: 9 to Pharaoh, "I **r** my faults today.
Ex 13: 3 "**R** this day on which you came out of Egypt,
20: 8 **R** the sabbath day, and keep it holy.
32:13 **R** Abraham, Isaac, and Israel, your servants,
Lev 26:42 then will I **r** my covenant with Jacob; I will **r** also
my covenant with Isaac and also my covenant
with Abraham, and I will **r** the land.
26:45 but I will **r** in their favor the covenant
Nu 11: 5 We **r** the fish we used to eat in Egypt for nothing,
15:39 you will **r** all the commandments of the LORD
15:40 So you shall **r** and do all my commandments,
Dt 5:15 **R** that you were a slave in the land of Egypt,
7:18 Just **r** what the LORD your God did to Pharaoh
8: 2 **R** the long way that the LORD your God has led
8:18 But **r** the LORD your God,
9: 7 **R** and do not forget how you provoked
9:27 **R** your servants, Abraham, Isaac, and Jacob;
11: 2 **R** today that it was not your children (who have
15:15 **R** that you were a slave in the land of Egypt,
16: 3 so that all the days of your life you may **r** the day
16:12 **R** that you were a slave in Egypt,
24: 9 **R** what the LORD your God did to Miriam
24:18 **R** that you were a slave in Egypt and
24:22 **R** that you were a slave in the land of Egypt;
25:17 **R** what Amalek did to you on your journey out
32: 7 **R** the days of old, consider the years long past;
Jos 1:13 "**R** the word that Moses the servant of
Jdg 8:34 The Israelites did not **r** the LORD their God,
9: 2 **R** also that I am your bone and your flesh."
16:28 **r** me and strengthen me only this once, O God,
1Sa 1:11 and **r** me, and not forget your servant,
25:31 with my lord, then **r** your servant."
2Sa 19:19 "May my lord not hold me guilty or **r**
2Ki 9:25 for **r,** when you and I rode side by side
20: 3 "**R** now, O LORD, I implore you,
1Ch 16:12 **R** the wonderful works he has done, his miracles,
16:15 **R** his covenant forever, the word
2Ch 6:42 **R** your steadfast love for your servant David."
24:22 King Joash did not **r** the kindness that Jehoiada,
Ne 1: 8 **R** the word that you commanded your servant
4:14 **R** the LORD, who is great and awesome,
5:19 **R** for my good, O my God,
6:14 **R** Tobiah and Sanballat, O my God,
13:14 **R** me, O my God, concerning this,
13:22 **R** this also in my favor, O my God,
13:29 **R** them, O my God, because they have defiled
13:31 **R** me, O my God, for good.
Job 7: 7 "**R** that my life is a breath;
10: 9 **R** that you fashioned me like clay;
11:16 you will **r** it as waters that have passed away.
14:13 that you would appoint me a set time, and **r** me!
36:24 "**R** to extol his work, of which mortals have sung.
Ps 20: 3 May he **r** all your offerings,
22:27 of the earth shall **r** and turn to the LORD;
25: 7 not **r** the sins of my youth or my transgressions;
25: 7 according to your steadfast love **r** me,
42: 4 These things I **r,** as I pour out my soul:
42: 6 I **r** you from the land of Jordan and of Hermon,
74: 2 **R** your congregation, which you acquired long ago,
74: 2 **R** Mount Zion, where you came to dwell.
74:18 **R** this, O LORD, how the enemy scoffs,
74:22 **r** how the impious scoff at you all day long.
77: 5 and **r** the years of long ago.
77:11 I will **r** your wonders of old.
79: 8 Do not **r** against us the iniquities of our ancestors;
88: 5 like those whom you **r** no more,
89:47 **R** how short my time is—
89:50 **R,** O Lord, how your servant is taunted;
103:18 to those who keep his covenant and **r**
105: 5 **R** the wonderful works he has done, his miracles,

Ps 106: 4 **R** me, O LORD, when you show favor
106: 7 not **r** the abundance of your steadfast love,
109:16 For he did not **r** to show kindness,
119:49 **R** your word to your servant,
119:55 I **r** your name in the night, O LORD,
132: 1 **r** in David's favor all the hardships he endured;
137: 6 if I do not **r** you, if I do not set Jerusalem above
137: 7 **R,** O LORD, against the Edomites the day
143: 5 I **r** the days of old, I think about all your deeds,
Pr 31: 7 and **r** their misery no more.
Ecc 11: 8 let them **r** that the days of darkness will be many.
12: 1 **R** your creator in the days of your youth,
Isa 38: 3 "**R** now, O LORD, I implore you,
43:18 Do not **r** the former things,
43:25 and I will not **r** your sins.
44:21 **R** these things, O Jacob, and Israel,
46: 8 **R** this and consider, recall it to mind,
46: 9 **r** the former things of old;
47: 7 you did not lay these things to heart or **r** their end.
54: 4 disgrace of your widowhood you will **r** no more.
57:11 and did not **r** me or give me a thought?
64: 5 those who **r** you in your ways.
64: 9 O LORD, and do not **r** iniquity forever.
Jer 2: 2 I **r** the devotion of your youth,
14:10 now he will **r** their iniquity and punish their sins.
14:21 **r** and do not break your covenant with us.
15:15 O LORD, you know; **r** me and visit me,
17: 2 their children **r** their altars and their sacred poles,
18:20 **R** how I stood before you to speak good for them,
31:20 As often as I speak against him, I still **r** him.
31:34 and **r** their sin no more.
44:21 did not the LORD **r** them?
51:50 **R** the LORD in a distant land,
La 5: 1 **R,** O LORD, what has befallen us;
Eze 6: 9 of you who escape shall **r** me among the nations
16:22 and your whorings you did not **r** the days
16:60 yet I will **r** my covenant with you in the days
16:61 Then you will **r** your ways,
16:63 in order that you may **r** and be confounded,
20:43 There you shall **r** your ways and all the deeds
23:27 you shall not long for them, or **r** Egypt any more.
36:31 Then you shall **r** your evil ways,
Hos 7: 2 they do not consider that I **r** all their wickedness.
8:13 Now he will **r** their iniquity, and punish their sins;
9: 9 he will **r** their iniquity, he will punish their sins.
Am 1: 9 and did not **r** the covenant of kinship.
Mic 6: 5 **r** now what King Balak of Moab devised,
Hab 3: 2 in wrath may you **r** mercy.
Zec 10: 9 yet in far countries they shall **r** me,
Mal 4: 4 **R** the teaching of my servant Moses,
Mt 5:23 if you **r** that your brother or sister has something
16: 9 Do you not **r** the five loaves for the five thousand,
27:63 we **r** what that impostor said
28:20 **r,** I am with you always, to the end of the age."
Mk 8:18 And do you not **r?**
Lk 16:25 But Abraham said, 'Child, **r** that during your
17:32 **R** Lot's wife.
23:42 "Jesus, **r** me when you come into your kingdom."
24: 6 **R** how he told you, while he was still in Galilee,
Jn 15:20 **R** the word that I said to you,
16: 4 when their hour comes you may **r** that I told you
Ro 1: 9 that without ceasing I **r** you always in my prayers,
11:18 **r** that it is not you that support the root,
1Co 11: 2 I commend you because you **r** me in everything
Gal 2:10 They asked only one thing, that we **r** the poor,
Eph 1:16 to give thanks for you as I **r** you in my prayers.
2:11 So then, **r** that at one time you Gentiles by birth,
2:12 **r** that you were at that time without Christ,
Php 1: 3 I thank my God every time I **r** you,
Col 4:18 greeting with my own hand. **R** my chains.
1Th 2: 9 You **r** our labor and toil, brothers and sisters;
3: 6 that you always **r** us kindly and long to see us—
2Th 2: 5 not **r** that I told you these things when I was still
2Ti 1: 3 I **r** you constantly in my prayers night and day.
2: 8 **R** Jesus Christ, raised from the dead,
Phm 1: 4 When I **r** you in my prayers,
Heb 8:12 and I will **r** their sins no more."
10:17 also adds, "I will **r** their sins
13: 3 **R** those who are in prison,
13: 7 **R** your leaders, those who spoke the word of God
2Pe 3: 2 that you should **r** the words spoken in the past by
Jude 1:17 must **r** the predictions of the apostles
Rev 2: 5 **R** then from what you have fallen;
3: 3 **R** then what you received and heard;
Tob 3: 3 now, O Lord, **r** me and look favorably upon me.
4: 4 **R** her, my son, because she faced many dangers
4:12 **R,** my son, that Noah, Abraham, Isaac, and Jacob,
4:19 So now, my child, **r** these commandments,
6:16 "Do you not **r** your father's orders
Jdt 8:26 **R** what he did with Abraham,
13:19 from the hearts of those who **r** the power of God.
AdE 4: 8 "**R,**" he said, "the days when you were
10: 5 I **r** the dream that I had concerning these matters,
14:12 **R,** O Lord; make yourself known in this
Wis 2: 4 and no one will **r** our works;
Sir 7:16 **r** that retribution does not delay.
7:28 **R** that it was of your parents you were born;
7:36 In all you do, **r** the end of your life,
8: 5 **r** that we all deserve punishment.
8: 7 **r** that we must all die.
9:12 **r** that they will not be held guiltless all their lives.
14:12 **R** that death does not tarry,
23:14 **R** your father and mother when you sit among
23:18 The Most High will not **r** sins."
28: 6 **R** the end of your life, and set enmity aside;
28: 6 **r** corruption and death, and be true to
28: 7 **R** the commandments, and do not be angry

Sir 28: 7 **r** the covenant of the Most High,
31:13 **R** that a greedy eye is a bad thing.
36:10 Hasten the day, and **r** the appointed time,
38:20 drive it away, and **r** your own end.
38:22 **R** his fate, for yours is like it;
41: 3 **r** those who went before you
Bar 2:32 in the land of their exile, and will **r** my name
2:33 for they will **r** the ways of their ancestors,
3: 5 Do not **r** the iniquities of our ancestors,
3: 5 but in this crisis **r** your power and your name.
4:14 **r** the capture of my sons and daughters,
1Mc 2:51 **"R** the deeds of the ancestors,
4: 9 **R** how our ancestors were saved at the Red Sea,
4:10 to see whether he will favor us and **r** his covenant
6:12 But now I **r** the wrong I did in Jerusalem.
7:38 **r** their blasphemies, and let them live no longer."
10: 5 for he will **r** all the wrongs that we did to him and
12:11 We therefore **r** you constantly on every occasion,
12:11 as it is right and proper to **r** brothers.
2Mc 1: 2 and may he **r** his covenant with Abraham
8: 4 to **r** also the lawless destruction of
9:21 I **r** with affection your esteem and goodwill.
9:26 to **r** the public and private services rendered
1Es 3:23 they do not **r** what they have done.
4:43 **"R** the vow that you made on the day
2Es 2: 8 **r** what I did to Sodom and Gomorrah,
2:31 **R** your children that sleep,
8:28 but **r** those who have willingly acknowledged
4Mc 13:12 and another reminded them, **"R** whence you came,
16:18 **R** that it is through God that you have had a share

REMEMBERED (68) [REMEMBER]

Ge 8: 1 But God **r** Noah and all the wild animals and all
19:29 God **r** Abraham, and sent Lot out of the midst of
30:22 Then God **r** Rachel, and God heeded her
42: 9 also **r** the dreams that he had dreamed about them.
Ex 2:24 and God **r** his covenant with Abraham, Isaac,
6: 5 and I have **r** my covenant.
20:24 where I cause my name to be **r** I will come to you
Nu 10: 9 so that you may be **r** before the LORD your God
1Sa 1:19 knew his wife Hannah, and the LORD **r** her.
Est 2: 1 he **r** Vashti and what she had done
9:28 be **r** and kept throughout every generation,
Job 24:20 no longer **r;** so wickedness is broken like a tree.
Ps 78:35 They **r** that God was their rock,
78:39 He **r** that they were but flesh,
83: 4 let the name of Israel be **r** no more."
98: 3 He has **r** his steadfast love and faithfulness to
105:42 he **r** his holy promise, and Abraham, his servant.
106:45 For their sake he **r** his covenant,
109:14 the iniquity of his father be **r** before the LORD,
112: 6 will never be moved; they will be **r** forever.
136:23 It is he who **r** us in our low estate,
137: 1 down and there we wept when we **r** Zion.
Ecc 1:11 The people of long ago are not **r,**
9:15 Yet no one **r** that poor man.
Isa 17:10 and have not **r** the Rock of your refuge;
23:16 sing many songs, that you may be **r.**
63:11 Then they **r** the days of old, of Moses his servant.
65:17 the former things shall not be **r** or come to mind.
Jer 3:16 It shall not come to mind, or be **r,** or missed;
11:19 so that his name will no longer be **r!"**
La 2: 1 he has not **r** his footstool in the day of his anger.
Eze 3:20 that they have done shall not be **r;**
16:43 Because you have not **r** the days of your youth,
18:22 that they have committed shall be **r** against them;
18:24 the righteous deeds that they have done shall be **r;**
21:32 shall be **r** no more, for I the LORD have spoken.
25:10 Thus Ammon shall be **r** no more among
33:13 none of their righteous deeds shall be **r;**
33:16 that they have committed shall be **r** against them;
Jnh 2: 7 As my life was ebbing away, I **r** the LORD;
Zec 13: 2 so that they shall be **r** no more;
Mt 26:75 Then Peter **r** what Jesus had said:
Mk 11:21 Then Peter **r** and said to him, "Rabbi, look!
14:72 Then Peter **r** that Jesus had said to him,
Lk 1:72 and has **r** his holy covenant,
22:61 Then Peter **r** the word of the Lord,
24: 8 Then they **r** his words,
Jn 2:17 His disciples **r** that it was written,
2:22 his disciples **r** that he had said this;
12:16 then they **r** that these things had been written
Ac 10:31 and your alms have been **r** before God.
11:16 And I **r** the word of the Lord, how he had said,
Rev 16:19 God **r** great Babylon and gave her the wine-cup of
18: 5 and God has **r** her iniquities.
Tob 2: 6 Then I **r** the prophecy of Amos,
4: 1 That same day Tobit **r** the money that he had left
8: 2 Then Tobias **r** the words of Raphael,
AdE 2: 1 about Vashti or **r** what he had said and
10:12 God **r** his people and vindicated his inheritance.
Sir 3:15 the day of your distress it will be **r** in your favor;
11:25 and in the day of adversity, prosperity is not **r.**
51: 8 Then I **r** your mercy, O Lord,
Bar 4:27 for you will be **r** by the one who brought this
5: 5 rejoicing that God has **r** them.
Bel 1:38 Daniel said, "You have **r** me, O God,
1Mc 5: 4 He also **r** the wickedness of the sons of Baean,
10:46 because they **r** the great wrongs
4Mc 15:28 of God-fearing Abraham she **r** his fortitude.

REMEMBERING (8) [REMEMBER]

Eze 23:19 **r** the days of her youth, when she played the whore
Ac 20:31 **r** that for three years I did not cease night or day
20:35 **r** the words of the Lord Jesus, for he himself said,
1Th 1: 3 **r** before our God and Father your work of faith
Sus 1: 9 to Heaven or **r** their duty to administer justice.
1Mc 9:38 **R** how their brother John had been killed,
2Mc 10: 6 of the festival of booths, **r** how not long before,
2Es 15:31 dragons, **r** their origin, shall become still stronger;

REMEMBERS (4) [REMEMBER]

Ps 103:14 he **r** that we are dust.
La 1: 7 Jerusalem **r,** in the days of her affliction
Jn 16:21 she no longer **r** the anguish because of the joy
2Co 7:15 as he **r** the obedience of all of you,

REMEMBRANCE (31) [REMEMBER]

Ex 12:14 This day shall be a day of **r** for you.
17:14 I will utterly blot out the **r** of Amalek from
28:12 as stones of **r** for the sons of Israel;
28:12 before the LORD on his two shoulders for **r.**
28:29 for a continual **r** before the LORD.
39: 7 to be stones of **r** for the sons of Israel;
Nu 5:15 a grain offering of **r,** bringing iniquity to **r.**
5:18 and place in her hands the grain offering of **r,**
Dt 25:19 you shall blot out the **r** of Amalek from
2Sa 18:18 for he said, "I have no son to keep my name in **r";**
1Ki 17:18 You have come to me to bring my sin to **r,**
Ps 6: 5 For in death there is no **r** of you;
34:16 to cut off the **r** of them from the earth.
Ecc 1:11 be any **r** of people yet to come by those who come
2:16 For there is no enduring **r** of the wise or of fools,
Eze 21:23 but he brings their guilt to **r,**
21:24 Because you have brought your guilt to **r,**
21:24 you have come to **r,** you shall be taken in hand.
Mal 3:16 of **r** was written before him of those who revered
Mt 26:13 what she has done will be told in **r** of her."
Mk 14: 9 what she has done will be told in **r** of her."
Lk 1:54 He has helped his servant Israel, in **r** of his mercy,
22:19 Do this in **r** of me."
1Co 11:24 Do this in **r** of me."
11:25 Do this, as often as you drink it, in **r** of me."
AdE 13: 8 calling to **r** all the works of the Lord.
Wis 5:14 it passes like the **r** of a guest who stays but a day.
8:13 leave an everlasting **r** to those who come after me.
Sir 38:23 When the dead is at rest, let his **r** rest too,
2Es 12:47 for the Most High has you in **r,**

REMETH (1)

Jos 19:21 **R,** En-gannim, En-haddah, Beth-pazzez;

REMIND (12) [REMINDED, REMINDER, REMINDING]

Isa 62: 6 You who **r** the LORD, take no rest,
Jn 14:26 and **r** you of all that I have said to you.
1Co 4:17 to **r** you of my ways in Christ Jesus,
15: 1 Now I would **r** you, brothers and sisters,
2Co 10: 7 **r** yourself of this, that just as you belong to Christ,
2Ti 1: 6 For this reason I **r** you to rekindle the gift of God
2:14 **R** them of this, and warn them before God
Tit 3: 1 **R** them to be subject to rulers and authorities,
Jude 1: 5 Now I desire to **r** you,
Wis 12: 2 and you **r** and warn them of the things
16: 6 of deliverance to **r** them of your law's command.
16:11 To **r** them of your oracles they were bitten,

REMINDED (3) [REMIND]

2Ti 1: 5 I am **r** of your sincere faith,
4Mc 13:12 and another **r** them, "Remember whence you came,
18:14 He **r** you of the scripture of Isaiah, which says,

REMINDER (13) [REMIND]

Ex 13: 9 and as a **r** on your forehead, so that the teaching of
17:14 a **r** in a book and recite it in the hearing of Joshua:
30:16 before the LORD it will be a **r** to the Israelites of
Nu 10:10 as a **r** on your behalf before the LORD your God:
16:40 a **r** to the Israelites that no outsider, who is not of
Ro 15:15 to you rather boldly by way of **r,**
Heb 10: 3 But in these sacrifices there is a **r** of sin year
AdE 16:23 that it may be a **r** of destruction for those who plot
Wis 10: 8 but also left for humankind a **r** of their folly,
Sir 45: 9 to make their ringing heard in the temple as a **r**
50:16 a mighty fanfare as a **r** before the Most High.
2Mc 6:17 Let what we have said serve as a **r;**
4Mc 17: 8 to inscribe on their tomb these words as a **r** to

REMINDING (3) [REMIND]

2Pe 1:12 I intend to keep on **r** you of these things,
3: 1 to arouse your sincere intention by **r** you
2Mc 15: 9 and **r** them also of the struggles they had won,

REMISS (2)

Lev 5:16 for the holy thing in which you were **r,**
Sir 4:29 or sluggish and **r** in your deeds.

REMISSION (6) [REMIT]

Dt 15: 1 Every seventh year you shall grant a **r** of debts.
15: 2 And this is the manner of the **r:**
15: 2 because the LORD's **r** has been proclaimed.
15: 9 thinking, "The seventh year, the year of **r,**
31:10 "Every seventh year, in the scheduled year of **r,**
AdE 2:18 and he granted a **r** of taxes to those who were

REMISSION (KJV) See also FORGIVEN, FORGIVENESS, PASSED OVER

REMISSIONS (1) [REMIT]

1Mc 15: 5 now therefore I confirm to you all the tax **r** that

REMIT (2) [REMISSION, REMISSIONS]

Dt 15: 2 every creditor shall **r** the claim that is held against
15: 3 but you must **r** your claim on whatever

REMMON, REMMON-METHOAR (KJV)

See RIMMON

REMNANT‡ (82)

Ge 45: 7 God sent me before you to preserve for you a **r**
Ex 10: 5 They shall devour the last **r** left you after the hail,
Dt 3:11 (Now only King Og of Bashan was left of the **r** of
Jdg 5:13 Then down marched the **r** of the noble;
2Sa 14: 7 to my husband neither name nor **r** on the face of
21: 2 but of the **r** of the Amorites;
1Ki 22:46 The **r** of the male temple prostitutes who were still
2Ki 19: 4 therefore lift up your prayer for the **r** that is left."
19:30 The surviving **r** of the house
19:31 for from Jerusalem a **r** shall go out,
21:14 I will cast off the **r** of my heritage,
1Ch 4:43 the **r** of the Amalekites that had escaped,
2Ch 30: 6 to the **r** of you who have escaped from the hand of
34: 9 the **r** of Israel and from all Judah and Benjamin
Ezr 9: 8 who has left us a **r,** and given us a stake
9:13 and have given us such a **r** as this,
9:14 not be angry with us until you destroy us without **r**
9:15 but we have escaped as a **r,** as is now the case.
Isa 10:19 The **r** of the trees of his forest will be so few that
10:20 On that day the **r** of Israel and the survivors of
10:21 A **r** will return, the **r** of Jacob,
10:22 only a **r** of them will return.
11:11 yet a second time to recover the **r** that is left
11:16 a highway from Assyria for the **r** that is left
14:22 and will cut off from Babylon name and **r,**
14:30 of famine, and your **r** I will kill.
15: 9 those of Moab who escape, for the **r** of the land.
17: 3 the **r** of Aram will be like the glory of the children
28: 5 and a diadem of beauty, to the **r** of his people;
37: 4 therefore lift up your prayer for the **r** that is left."
37:31 The surviving **r** of the house of Judah
37:32 for from Jerusalem a **r** shall go out,
46: 3 O house of Jacob, all the **r** of the house of Israel,
Jer 6: 9 Glean thoroughly as a vine the **r** of Israel;
8: 3 to life by all the **r** that remains of this evil family
11:23 and not even a **r** shall be left of them.
23: 3 Then I myself will gather the **r** of my flock out
24: 8 the **r** of Jerusalem who remain in this land,
25:20 Ashkelon, Gaza, Ekron, and the **r** of Ashdod;
31: 7 "Save, O LORD, your people, the **r** of Israel."
40:11 that the king of Babylon had left a **r** in Judah
40:15 and the **r** of Judah would perish?"
42: 2 to the LORD your God for us—for all this **r.**
42:15 then hear the word of the LORD, O **r** of Judah.
42:17 they shall have no **r** or survivor from the disaster
42:19 The LORD has said to you, O **r** of Judah,
43: 5 the forces took all the **r** of Judah who had returned
44: 7 leaving yourselves without a **r?**
44:12 the **r** of Judah who are determined to come to
44:14 the **r** of Judah who have come to settle in the land
44:28 and all the **r** of Judah,
47: 4 the **r** of the coastland of Caphtor.
47: 5 O **r** of their power! How long will you gash
50:20 for I will pardon the **r** that I have spared.
Eze 11:13 will you make a full end of the **r** of Israel?"
Am 1: 8 and the **r** of the Philistines shall perish,
5:15 will be gracious to the **r** of Joseph.
9:12 the **r** of Edom and all the nations who are called
Mic 4: 7 The lame I will make the **r,**
5: 7 Then the **r** of Jacob, surrounded by many peoples,
5: 8 And among the nations the **r** of Jacob,
7:18 over the transgression of the **r** of your possession?
Zep 1: 4 and I will cut off from this place every **r** of Baal
2: 7 The seacoast shall become the possession of the **r**
2: 9 The **r** of my people shall plunder them,
3:13 the **r** of Israel; they shall do no wrong
Hag 1:12 the high priest, with all the **r** of the people,
1:14 and the spirit of all the **r** of the people;
2: 2 the high priest, and to the **r** of the people, and say,
Zec 8: 6 though it seems impossible to the **r** of this people
8:11 But now I will not deal with the **r** of this people as
8:12 the **r** of this people to possess all these things.
9: 7 it too shall be a **r** for our God;
Ro 9:27 only a **r** of them will be saved;
11: 5 So too at the present time there is a **r,**
Tob 13:16 be if a **r** of my descendants should survive
Wis 16: 3 might lose the least **r** of appetite because of
Sir 44:17 a **r** was left on the earth when the flood came.
47:22 So he gave a **r** to Jacob, and to David a root from
1Mc 3:35 the strength of Israel and the **r** of Jerusalem;
2Es 12:34 But in mercy he will set free the **r** of my people,

REMONSTRATED (3)

Ne 13:11 So I **r** with the officials and said,
13:17 I **r** with the nobles of Judah and said to them,
3Mc 5:39 wondering at his instability of mind, **r** as follows:

REMORSE (2)

Sir 14: 1 and need not suffer **r** for sin.
20:21 so when he rests he feels no **r.**

REMOTE‡ (3) [REMOTEST]
Jdg 19: 1 in the **r** parts of the hill country of Ephraim,
19:18 to the **r** parts of the hill country of Ephraim,
Job 28: 4 they sway suspended, **r** from people.

REMOTEST (6) [REMOTE]
Isa 37:24 I came to its **r** height, its densest forest.
Eze 38: 6 from the **r** parts of the north with all its troops—
38:15 from your place out of the **r** parts of the north, you
39: 2 and bring you up from the **r** parts of the north,
Tob 8: 3 so repelled the demon that he fled to the **r** parts
13:11 to you from far away, the inhabitants of the **r** parts

REMOVAL (4) [REMOVE]
Isa 27: 9 and this will be the full fruit of the **r** of his sin:
Heb 12:27 indicates the **r** of what is shaken—
1Pe 3:21 not as a **r** of dirt from the body,
2Mc 3: 7 and sent him with commands to effect the **r** of

REMOVE (67) [REMOVAL, REMOVED, REMOVES, REMOVING]
Ge 48:17 to **r** it from Ephraim's head to Manasseh's head.
Ex 3: 5 **R** the sandals from your feet,
10:17 that at the least he **r** this deadly thing from me."
12:15 the first day you shall **r** leaven from your houses,
Lev 1:16 He shall **r** its crop with its contents and throw it at
2: 9 The priest shall **r** from the grain offering its token
3: 4 which he shall **r** with the kidneys.
3:10 which you shall **r** with the kidneys.
3:15 which you shall **r** with the kidneys.
4: 8 He shall **r** all the fat from the bull of sin offering:
4: 9 which he shall **r** with the kidneys,
4:19 He shall **r** all its fat and turn it into smoke on
4:31 He shall **r** all its fat,
4:35 You shall **r** all its fat,
10:17 that you may **r** the guilt of the congregation,
26: 6 I will **r** dangerous animals from the land,
Jos 5:15 "**R** the sandals from your feet,
Jdg 9:29 Then I would **r** Abimelech;
1Ki 20:24 Also do this: **r** the kings, each from his post,
2Ki 23:27 LORD said, "I will **r** Judah also out of my sight,
24: 3 to **r** them out of his sight,
2Ch 33: 8 I will never again **r** the feet of Israel from the land
Job 22:23 if you **r** unrighteousness from your tents,
24: 2 The wicked **r** landmarks; they seize flocks
Ps 39:10 **R** your stroke from me; I am worn down by
89:33 but I will not **r** from him my steadfast love,
Pr 22:28 Do not **r** the ancient landmark
23:10 Do not **r** an ancient landmark or encroach on
30: 8 **R** far from me falsehood and lying;
Isa 1:16 **r** the evil of your doings from before my eyes;
1:25 as with lye and **r** all your alloy.
5: 5 I will **r** its hedge, and it shall be devoured;
47: 2 Take the millstones and grind meal, **r** your veil,
57:14 **r** every obstruction from my people's way."
58: 9 If you **r** the yoke from among you,
Jer 4: 1 if you **r** your abominations from my presence,
4: 4 **r** the foreskin of your hearts,
32:31 so that I will **r** it from my sight
Eze 11:18 they will **r** from it all its detestable things
11:19 I will **r** the heart of stone from their flesh
21:26 **R** the turban, take off the crown;
26:16 shall **r** their robes and strip off their embroidered
36:26 and I will **r** from your body the heart of stone
44:19 they shall **r** the vestments
Hos 2:17 I will **r** the names of the Baals from her mouth,
5:10 of Judah have become like those who **r**
Joel 2:20 I will **r** the northern army far from you,
Mic 1:11 Beth-ezel is wailing and shall **r** its support
2: 3 an evil from which you cannot **r** your necks;
Zep 3:11 I will **r** from your midst your proudly exultant
3:18 I will **r** disaster from you,
Zec 3: 9 and I will **r** the guilt of this land in a single day.
13: 2 and also I will **r** from the land the prophets and
Mk 14:36 for you all things are possible; **r** this cup from me;
Lk 22:42 if you are willing, **r** this cup from me;
Ac 7:43 so I will **r** you beyond Babylon.'
1Co 7:18 Let him not seek to **r** the marks of circumcision.
13: 2 and if I have all faith, so as to **r** mountains,
Heb 9:26 for all at the end of the age to **r** sin by the sacrifice
Rev 2: 5 to you and **r** your lampstand from its place,
Tob 1:18 but I would secretly **r** the bodies and bury them.
Sir 23: 5 and **r** evil desire from me.
30:23 and **r** sorrow far from you,
Bar 2:35 and I will never again **r** my people Israel from
1Mc 11:41 to King Demetrius the request that he **r** the troops
11:63 intending to **r** him from office.
4Mc 10:18 But he said, "Even if you **r** my organ of speech,

REMOVED‡ (80) [REMOVE]
Ge 8:13 and Noah **r** the covering of the ark, and looked,
30:35 that day Laban **r** the male goats that were striped
48:12 Then Joseph **r** them from his father's knees,
Ex 8: 9 be **r** from you and your houses and be left only in
8:31 he **r** the swarms of flies from Pharaoh,
Lev 3: 9 which shall be **r** close to the backbone,
4:10 just as these are **r** from the ox of the sacrifice
4:31 as the fat is **r** from the offering of well-being,
4:35 of the sheep is **r** from the sacrifice of well-being,
7: 4 which shall be **r** with the kidneys.
Nu 14: 9 their protection is **r** from them,
Dt 26:13 "I have **r** the sacred portion from the house,
26:14 I have not **r** any of it while I was unclean;
1Sa 17:39 I am not used to them." So David **r** them.
1Sa 18:13 So Saul **r** him from his presence,
21: 6 which is **r** from before the LORD,
2Sa 20:13 Once he was **r** from the highway,
1Ki 15:12 and **r** all the idols that his ancestors had made.
15:13 He also **r** his mother Maacah
2Ki 3: 2 for he **r** the pillar of Baal that his father had made.
14: 4 But the high places were not **r;**
15:35 Nevertheless the high places were not **r;**
16:14 that was before the LORD he **r** from the front of
16:17 and **r** the laver from them; he **r** the sea from
16:18 the outer entrance for the king he **r** from the house
17:18 with Israel and **r** them out of his sight;
17:23 until the LORD **r** Israel out of his sight,
18: 4 He **r** the high places, broke down the pillars,
18:22 and altars Hezekiah has **r,**
23:11 He **r** the horses that the kings
23:19 Josiah **r** all the shrines of the high places that were
23:27 also out of my sight, as I have **r** Israel;
2Ch 14: 5 also **r** from all the cities of Judah the high places
15:16 King Asa even **r** his mother Maacah
17: 6 and furthermore he **r** the high places and
20:33 Yet the high places were not **r;**
30:14 to work and **r** the altars that were in Jerusalem,
Job 14:18 and the rock is **r** from its place;
18: 4 or the rock be **r** out of its place?
Ps 66:20 not rejected my prayer or **r** his steadfast love
89:44 You have **r** the scepter from his hand,
Pr 10:30 The righteous will never be **r,**
Isa 10:13 I have **r** the boundaries of peoples,
10:27 that day his burden will be **r** from your shoulder,
14:25 his yoke shall be **r** from them,
27: 8 with his fierce blast he **r** them in the day of
36: 7 and altars Hezekiah has **r,**
38:12 My dwelling is plucked up and **r** from me like
54:10 For the mountains may depart and the hills be **r,**
54:10 and my covenant of peace shall not be **r,**
Jer 6:29 the refining goes on, for the wicked are not **r.**
27:10 the result that you will be **r** far from your land;
Eze 11:16 Though I **r** them far away among the nations,
16:50 therefore I **r** them when I saw it.
Jnh 3: 6 **r** his robe, covered himself with sackcloth,
Mk 2: 4 they **r** the roof above him;
Jn 19:31 of the crucified men broken and the bodies **r.**
19:38 so he came and **r** his body.
20: 1 to the tomb and saw that the stone had been **r** from
Ac 13:22 When he had **r** him, he made David their king.
1Co 5: 2 that he who has done this would have been **r** from
2Co 3:16 but when one turns to the Lord, the veil is **r.**
Gal 5:11 In that case the offense of the cross has been **r.**
2Th 2: 7 but only until the one who now restrains it is **r.**
Rev 6:14 every mountain and island was **r** from its place.
Tob 2: 4 and **r** the body from the square and laid it in one
Jdt 10: 3 She **r** the sackcloth she had been wearing,
1Mc 1:15 and **r** the marks of circumcision,
4:43 and **r** the defiled stones to an unclean place.
4:58 and the disgrace brought by the Gentiles was **r.**
11:66 He **r** them from there, took possession of
13:41 the yoke of the Gentiles was **r** from Israel,
13:48 He **r** all uncleanness from it,
13:51 a great enemy had been crushed and **r** from Israel.
14: 7 and he **r** its uncleanness from it;
1Es 1:45 A year later Nebuchadnezzar sent and **r** him
2Es 7:*48* the paths of perdition and **r** us far from life—
16:52 a very short time iniquity will be **r** from the earth,
4Mc 4:16 who **r** Onias from the priesthood

REMOVES (5) [REMOVE]
Job 9: 5 he who **r** mountains, and they do not know it,
Ps 103:12 so far he **r** our transgressions from us.
Mic 2: 4 inheritance of my people; how he **r** it from me!
Jn 15: 2 He **r** every branch in me that bears no fruit.
Sir 10:17 He **r** some of them and destroys them,

REMOVING (6) [REMOVE]
Ge 30:32 **r** from it every speckled and spotted sheep
41:42 **R** his signet ring from his hand,
Joel 3: 6 **r** them far from their own border.
Tob 3:17 Tobit, by **r** the white films from his eyes,
Sir 49: 2 and **r** the wicked abominations.
3Mc 5:50 **r** the babies from their breasts,

REMPHAN (KJV) See REPHAN

RENAMED (2) [NAME]
Nu 32:41 captured their villages, and **r** them Havvoth-jair.
32:42 and **r** it Nobah after himself.

REND (1)
Joel 2:13 **r** your hearts and not your clothing.

RENDER‡ (19) [RENDERED, RENDERING, RENDERS]
Lev 19:15 You shall not **r** an unjust judgment;
Nu 18: 9 of theirs that they **r** to me as a most holy thing,
Dt 16:18 and they shall **r** just decisions for the people.
1Ki 8:39 forgive, act, and **r** to all whose hearts you know—
1Ch 16:41 of those chosen and expressly named to **r** thanks
2Ch 6:30 forgive, and **r** to all whose heart you know,
Ps 28: 4 of their hands; **r** them their due reward.
38:20 Those who **r** me evil for good are my adversaries
56:12 I will **r** thank offerings to you.
72:10 the kings of Tarshish and of the isles **r** him tribute,
Isa 59:18 to the coastlands he will **r** requital.
Zec 7: 9 **R** true judgments, show kindness and mercy
8:16 the truth to one another, **r** in your gates judgments
Eph 6: 7 **R** service with enthusiasm,
Heb 4:13 of the one to whom we must **r** an account.
Rev 18: 6 **R** to her as she herself has rendered,
AdE 16: 8 the future we will take care to **r** our kingdom quiet
3Mc 5:43 to him would quickly **r** it forever empty
4Mc 2:18 to correct some, and to **r** others powerless.

RENDERED (8) [RENDER]
1Ki 3:28 of the judgment that the king had **r;**
Da 4:17 The sentence is **r** by decree of the watchers,
2Ti 1:18 And you know very well how much service he **r**
Rev 18: 6 Render to her as she herself has **r,**
Sir Pr: 2 we may seem to have **r** some phrases imperfectly.
2Mc 9:26 to remember the public and private services **r**
4Mc 2: 1 for the enjoyment of beauty are **r** powerless?
7:14 of Isaac he **r** the many-headed rack ineffective.

RENDERING (2) [RENDER]
2Co 9:12 the **r** of this ministry not only supplies the needs
Sir 42: 2 and of **r** judgment to acquit the ungodly;

RENDERS (1) [RENDER]
Zep 3: 5 Every morning he **r** his judgment,

RENEGADE (1) [RENEGADES]
1Mc 7: 5 Then there came to him all the **r** and godless men

RENEGADES (9) [RENEGADE]
1Mc 1:11 In those days certain **r** came out from Israel
1:34 a sinful people, men who were **r.**
2:44 down sinners in their anger and **r** in their wrath;
9:23 death of Judas, the **r** emerged in all parts of Israel;
9:69 at the **r** who had counseled him to come into
10:61 A group of malcontents from Israel, **r,**
11:21 But certain **r** who hated their nation went to
11:25 certain **r** of his nation kept making complaints
14:14 and did away with all the **r** and outlaws.

RENEW (16) [RENEWAL, RENEWED, RENEWING, RENEWS]
1Sa 11:14 let us go to Gilgal and there **r** the kingship."
Job 10:17 You **r** your witnesses against me,
Ps 104:30 and you **r** the face of the ground.
Isa 40:31 for the LORD shall **r** their strength,
41: 1 let the peoples **r** their strength;
La 5:21 **r** our days as of old—
Zep 3:17 he will **r** you in his love;
1Mc 12: 1 to confirm and **r** the friendship with them.
12: 3 to **r** the former friendship and alliance with them."
12:10 we have undertaken to send to **r** our family ties
12:16 to **r** our former friendship and alliance with them.
14:18 they wrote to him on bronze tablets to **r** with him
14:22 have come to us to **r** their friendship with us.
15:17 as our friends and allies to **r** our ancient friendship
2Es 7:*75* in rest until those times come when you will **r**
12:23 and they shall **r** many things in it,

RENEWAL (5) [RENEW]
Mt 19:28 "Truly I tell you, at the **r** of all things,
Col 3:11 In that **r** there is no longer Greek and Jew,
Tit 3: 5 the water of rebirth and **r** by the Holy Spirit.
1Mc 12:17 from us concerning the **r** of our family ties.
2Mc 7: 9 of the universe will raise us up to an everlasting **r**

RENEWED (6) [RENEW]
Ps 90: 5 like grass that is **r** in the morning;
90: 6 in the morning it flourishes and is **r;**
103: 5 as you live so that your youth is **r** like the eagle's.
2Co 4:16 our inner nature is being **r** day by day.
Eph 4:23 and to be **r** in the spirit of your minds,
Col 3:10 which is being **r** in knowledge according to

RENEWING (1) [RENEW]
Ro 12: 2 but be transformed by the **r** of your minds,

RENEWS‡ (2) [RENEW]
Wis 7:27 and while remaining in herself, she **r** all things;
Sir 43: 8 The new moon, as its name suggests, **r** itself;

RENOUNCE (11) [RENOUNCED]
Ps 10: 3 those greedy for gain curse and **r** the LORD.
10:13 Why do the wicked **r** God, and say in their hearts,
1Ti 4: 1 that in later times some will **r** the faith
Tit 2:12 training us to **r** impiety and worldly passions,
2Es 14:13 And now **r** the life that is corruptible,
4Mc 4:26 the nation to eat defiling foods and to **r** Judaism.
5:34 O law that trained me, nor will I **r** you,
8: 7 of authority in my government if you will **r**
9:23 in my struggle or **r** our courageous family ties.
10: 3 I do not **r** the noble kinship that binds me
10:15 I will not **r** our noble family ties.

RENOUNCED (2) [RENOUNCE]
Ps 89:39 You have **r** the covenant with your servant;
2Co 4: 2 We have **r** the shameful things that one hides;

RENOWN (9) [RENOWNED]
Ge 6: 4 the heroes that were of old, warriors of **r.**

Ps 111: 4 He has gained **r** by his wonderful deeds;
135:13 Your name, O LORD, endures forever, your **r**,
Isa 26: 8 your name and your **r** are the soul's desire.
Jer 48: 2 the **r** of Moab is no more.
Hab 3: 2 O LORD, I have heard of your **r**,
Zep 3:19 and I will change their shame into praise and **r**
Wis 8:18 understanding, and **r** in sharing her words,
1Mc 14:10 until his **r** spread to the ends of the earth.

RENOWNED‡ (12) [RENOWN]

Ru 4:14 and may his name be **r** in Israel!
2Sa 23:19 He was the most **r** of the Thirty,
23:23 He was **r** among the Thirty,
1Ch 11:21 He was the most **r** of the Thirty,
11:25 He was **r** among the Thirty,
Isa 62: 7 until he establishes Jerusalem and makes it **r**
Eze 26:17 How you have vanished from the seas, O city **r**,
Da 9:15 with a mighty hand and made your name **r** even
Zep 3:20 for I will make you **r** and praised among all
Jdt 11:23 in the palace of King Nebuchadnezzar and be **r**
Wis 3:15 For the fruit of good labors is **r**,
1Mc 3: 9 He was **r** to the ends of the earth;

REPAID (11) [PAY]

Jdg 9:56 Thus God **r** Abimelech for the crime he committed
1Sa 24:17 for you have **r** me good, whereas I have **r** you evil.
Ps 7: 4 if I have **r** my ally with harm or plundered my foe
Pr 11:31 If the righteous are **r** on earth,
19:17 and will be **r** in full.
Lk 14:12 invite you in return, and you would be **r**.
14:14 you will be **r** at the resurrection of the righteous."
Tob 14:10 God **r** him to his face for this shameful treatment.
Sir 12: 2 Do good to the devout, and you will be **r**—
2Mc 4:38 Lord thus **r** him with the punishment he deserved.

REPAIR (13) [REPAIRED, REPAIRER, REPAIRING, REPAIRS]

2Ki 12: 5 and let them **r** the house wherever any need
12: 7 from your donors but hand it over for the **r** of
12: 8 from the people nor **r** the house.
22: 6 to buy timber and quarried stone to **r** the house.
2Ch 24: 5 and gather money from all Israel to **r** the house
24:12 and also workers in iron and bronze to **r** the house
34: 8 the recorder, to **r** the house of the LORD his God.
Ezr 9: 9 to set up the house of our God, to **r** its ruins,
Ps 60: 2 **r** the cracks in it, for it is tottering.
Pr 6:15 in a moment, damage beyond **r**.
Isa 61: 4 they shall **r** the ruined cities,
Eze 22:30 among them who would **r** the wall and stand in
Am 9:11 and **r** its breaches, and raise up its ruins,

REPAIRED (21) [REPAIR]

1Ki 18:30 First he **r** the altar of the LORD
1Ch 11: 8 and Joab **r** the rest of the city.
2Ch 15: 8 He **r** the altar of the LORD that was in front of
29: 3 the doors of the house of the LORD and **r** them.
Ne 3: 6 and Meshullam son of Besodeiah **r** the Old Gate;
3:11 of Pahath-moab **r** another section and the Tower
3:13 and the inhabitants of Zanoah **r** the Valley Gate;
3:13 and its bars, and **r** a thousand cubits of the wall,
3:14 the district of Beth-haccherem, **r** the Dung Gate;
3:15 of Col-hozeh, ruler of the district of Mizpah, **r**
3:16 **r** from a point opposite the graves of David,
3:19 **r** another section opposite the ascent to the armory
3:20 After him Baruch son of Zabbai **r** another section
3:21 of Uriah son of Hakkoz **r** another section from
3:24 him Binnui son of Henadad **r** another section,
3:25 Palal son of Uzai **r** opposite the Angle and
3:27 After him the Tekoites **r** another section opposite
3:30 and Hanun sixth son of Zalaph **r** another section.
Eze 13: 5 or **r** a wall for the house of Israel,
Sir 50: 1 Simon son of Onias, who in his life **r** the house,
1Mc 12:37 and he **r** the section called Chaphenatha.

REPAIRER (1) [REPAIR]

Isa 58:12 you shall be called the **r** of the breach,

REPAIRING (8) [REPAIR]

2Ki 12: 7 "Why are you not **r** the house?
12:14 the workers who were **r** the house of the LORD
22: 5 who are at the house of the LORD, **r** the house,
2Ch 24:13 and the **r** went forward at their hands,
34:10 the house of the LORD gave it for **r** and restoring
Ezr 4:12 they are finishing the walls and **r** the foundations.
Ne 4: 7 the **r** of the walls of Jerusalem was going forward
1Es 2:18 **r** its market places and walls and laying

REPAIRS (28) [REPAIR]

2Ki 12: 5 the house wherever any need of **r** is discovered."
12: 6 of King Jehoash the priests had made no **r** on
12:12 to buy timber and quarried stone for making **r** on
12:12 as well as for any outlay for **r** of the house.
Ne 3: 4 son of Uriah son of Hakkoz made **r**.
3: 4 son of Berechiah son of Meshezabel made **r**.
3: 4 Next to them Zadok son of Baana made **r**.
3: 5 Next to them the Tekoites made **r**;
3: 7 to them **r** were made by Melatiah the Gibeonite
3: 8 one of the goldsmiths, made **r**.
3: 8 one of the perfumers, made **r**;
3: 9 ruler of half the district of Jerusalem, made **r**.
3:10 son of Harumaph made **r** opposite his house;
3:10 next to him Hattush son of Hashabneiah made **r**.
3:12 ruler of half the district of Jerusalem, made **r**,
Ne 3:17 After him the Levites made **r**:
3:17 the district of Keilah, made **r** for his district.
3:18 After him their kin made **r**:
3:22 the men of the surrounding area, made **r**.
3:23 and Hasshub made **r** opposite their house.
3:23 son of Ananiah made **r** beside his own house.
3:26 and the temple servants living on Ophel made **r** up
3:28 Above the Horse Gate the priests made **r**,
3:29 son of Immer made **r** opposite his own house.
3:29 the keeper of the East Gate, made **r**.
3:30 of Berechiah made **r** opposite his living quarters.
3:31 made **r** as far as the house of the temple servants
3:32 the goldsmiths and the merchants made **r**.

REPAY‡ (60) [PAY]

Lev 6: 5 you shall **r** the principal amount
Dt 32: 6 Do you thus **r** the LORD,
32:41 and will **r** those who hate me.
32:43 he will **r** those who hate him,
Jdg 20:10 who are going to **r** Gibeah of Benjamin for all
1Sa 2:20 the LORD **r** you with children by this woman for
2Sa 16:12 the LORD will **r** me with good for this cursing
2Ki 9:26 I swear I will **r** you on this very plot of ground.'
Job 34:11 For according to their deeds he will **r** them,
Ps 28: 4 **R** them according to their work,
28: 4 **r** them according to the work of their hands;
35:12 They **r** me evil for good; my soul is forlorn.
41:10 and raise me up, that I may **r** them.
54: 5 He will **r** my enemies for their evil.
56: 7 so **r** them for their crime;
62:12 For you **r** to all according to their work.
94:23 He will **r** them for their iniquity
103:10 nor **r** us according to our iniquities.
Pr 20:22 Do not say, "I will **r** evil";
24:12 And will he not **r** all according to their deeds?
Isa 57:18 I will lead them and **r** them with comfort,
59:18 According to their deeds, so will he **r**;
65: 6 but I will **r**; I will indeed **r** into their laps
Jer 16:18 And I will doubly **r** their iniquity and their sin,
25:14 and I will **r** them according to their deeds and
32:18 but **r** the guilt of parents into the laps
50:29 **R** her according to her deeds;
51:24 I will **r** Babylon and all the inhabitants of Chaldea
51:56 LORD is a God of recompense, he will **r** in full.
Eze 23:49 They shall **r** you for your lewdness,
Hos 4: 9 and **r** them for their deeds.
12: 2 and **r** him according to his deeds.
Joel 2:25 I will **r** you for the years that
Mt 16:27 then he will **r** everyone for what has been done.
Lk 10:35 I will **r** you whatever more you spend.'
14:14 you will be blessed, because they cannot **r** you,
Ro 2: 6 For he will **r** according to each one's deeds:
12:17 Do not **r** anyone evil for evil,
12:19 for it is written, "Vengeance is mine, I will **r**,
2Th 1: 6 of God to **r** with affliction those who afflict you,
Phm 1:19 with my own hand: I will **r** it.
Heb 10:30 "Vengeance is mine, I will **r**."
1Pe 3: 9 Do not **r** evil for evil or abuse for abuse; but, on the contrary, **r** with a blessing.
Rev 18: 6 and **r** her double for her deeds;
22:12 to **r** according to everyone's work.
Sir 3:31 Those who **r** favors give thought to the future;
7:28 how can you **r** what they have given to you?
17:23 Afterward he will rise up and **r** them,
29: 2 **r** your neighbor when a loan falls due.
29: 6 he will **r** him with curses and reproaches,
29: 6 and instead of glory will **r** him with dishonor.
30: 6 and one to **r** the kindness of his friends.
35:13 and he will **r** you sevenfold.
LtJ 6:34 they will not be able to **r** it.
1Mc 10:27 we will **r** you with good for what you do for us.
11:53 he became estranged from Jonathan and did not **r**
2Es 15:20 to turn and **r** what they have given them.
15:21 so I will do, and will **r** into their bosom.

REPAYING (2) [PAY]

2Ch 6:23 **r** the guilty by bringing their conduct
Jer 51: 6 he is **r** her what is due.

REPAYMENT (2) [PAY]

1Ti 5: 4 to their own family and make some **r**
Sir 29: 5 but at the time for **r** he delays,

REPAYS (9) [PAY]

Dt 7:10 who **r** in their own person those who reject him.
7:10 but **r** in their own person those who reject him.
Job 21:31 and who **r** them for what they have done?
33:26 and God **r** him for his righteousness.
Ps 31:23 but abundantly **r** the one who acts haughtily.
1Th 5:15 See that none of you **r** evil for evil,
Sir 35:13 For the Lord is the one who **r**,
35:23 and **r** vengeance on the nations;
35:24 until he **r** mortals according to their deeds,

REPEAT (8) [REPEATED, REPEATEDLY, REPEATING]

Jdg 5:11 there they **r** the triumphs of the LORD,
Job 10:16 you **r** your exploits against me.
2Co 11:16 I **r**, let no one think that I am a fool;
12: 4 that no mortal is permitted to **r**.
Gal 1: 9 As we have said before, so now I **r**,
Sir 7:14 and do not **r** yourself when you pray.
19: 7 Never **r** a conversation, and you will lose nothing
19:14 or if he said it, so that he may not **r** it.

REPEATED (4) [REPEAT]

Ge 44: 6 When he overtook them, he **r** these words to them.
1Sa 8:21 he **r** them in the ears of the LORD.
17:31 they **r** them before Saul; and he sent for him.
2Ki 4:43 So he **r**, "Give it to the people and let them eat,

REPEATEDLY (5) [REPEAT]

2Ki 13: 3 that he gave them **r** into the hand of King Hazael
Ecc 7:28 which my mind has sought **r**,
Mk 5:23 and begged him **r**, "My little daughter is at
Heb 6: 7 Ground that drinks up the rain falling on it **r**,
4Mc 10: 1 and many **r** urged him to save himself by tasting

REPEATING (2) [REPEAT]

Eze 18: 2 What do you mean by **r** this proverb concerning
Sir 42: 1 Be ashamed of **r** what you hear,

REPEL (1) [REPELLED, REPELS]

Wis 5:17 and will arm all creation to **r** his enemies;

REPELLED (1) [REPEL]

Tob 8: 3 The odor of the fish so **r** the demon that he fled to

REPELS (2) [REPEL]

4Mc 2:16 For the temperate mind **r** all these malicious emotions, just as it **r** anger—

REPENT (45) [REPENTANCE, REPENTED, REPENTS]

1Ki 8:47 and **r**, and plead with you in the land
8:48 if they **r** with all their heart and soul in the land
2Ch 6:37 and **r**, and plead with you in the land
6:38 if they **r** with all their heart and soul in the land
Job 42: 6 and **r** in dust and ashes."
Ps 7:12 If one does not **r**, God will whet his sword;
Isa 1:27 and those in her who **r**, by righteousness.
Jer 9: 5 they commit iniquity and are too weary to **r**.
Eze 14: 6 **R** and turn away from your idols;
18:30 **R** and turn from all your transgressions;
Mt 3: 2 "**R**, for the kingdom of heaven has come near."
4:17 From that time Jesus began to proclaim, "**R**,
11:20 of power had been done, because they did not **r**.
Mk 1:15 **r**, and believe in the good news."
6:12 So they went out and proclaimed that all should **r**.
Lk 13: 3 but unless you **r**, you will all perish as they did.
13: 5 unless you **r**, you will all perish just as they did."
16:30 someone goes to them from the dead, they will **r**.'
17: 4 and turns back to you seven times and says, 'I **r**,'
Ac 2:38 "**R**, and be baptized every one of you in the name
3:19 **R** therefore, and turn to God so that your sins may
8:22 **R** therefore of this wickedness of yours,
17:30 now he commands all people everywhere to **r**,
26:20 that they should **r** and turn to God
2Ti 2:25 God may perhaps grant that they will **r** and come
Heb 12:17 he was rejected, for he found no chance to **r**,
Rev 2: 5 **r**, and do the works you did at first.
2: 5 from its place, unless you **r**.
2:16 **R** then. If not, I will come to you
2:21 I gave her time to **r**,
2:21 but she refuses to **r** of her fornication.
2:22 unless they **r** of her doings;
3: 3 then what you received and heard; obey it, and **r**.
3:19 Be earnest, therefore, and **r**.
9:20 did not **r** of the works of their hands or give
9:21 not **r** of their murders or their sorceries
16: 9 and they did not **r** and give him glory.
16:11 and they did not **r** of their deeds.
Wis 11:23 and you overlook people's sins, so that they may **r**.
12:10 by little you gave them an opportunity to **r**,
Sir 17:24 Yet to those who **r** he grants a return,
18:21 and when you have sinned, **r**.
21: 6 but those who fear the Lord **r** in their heart.
48:15 Despite all this the people did not **r**,
Man 1:13 For you, O Lord, are the God of those who **r**,

REPENTANCE‡ (31) [REPENT]

Mt 3: 8 Bear fruit worthy of **r**.
3:11 "I baptize you with water for **r**,
Mk 1: 4 proclaiming a baptism of **r** for the forgiveness
Lk 3: 3 proclaiming a baptism of **r** for the forgiveness
3: 8 Bear fruits worthy of **r**.
5:32 to call not the righteous but sinners to **r**."
15: 7 over ninety-nine righteous persons who need no **r**.
17: 3 you must rebuke the offender, and if there is **r**,
24:47 that **r** and forgiveness of sins is to be proclaimed
Ac 5:31 as Leader and Savior that he might give **r** to Israel
11:18 "Then God has given even to the Gentiles the **r**
13:24 a baptism of **r** to all the people of Israel.
19: 4 Paul said, "John baptized with the baptism of **r**,
20:21 as I testified to both Jews and Greeks about **r**
26:20 and turn to God and do deeds consistent with **r**.
Ro 2: 4 that God's kindness is meant to lead you to **r**?
2Co 7: 9 but because your grief led to **r**;
7:10 For godly grief produces a **r** that leads to salvation
Heb 6: 1 **r** from dead works and faith toward God,
6: 4 to **r** those who have once been enlightened,
2Pe 3: 9 not wanting any to perish, but all to come to **r**.
Wis 5: 3 They will speak to one another in **r**,
12:19 because you give **r** for sins.
Sir 44:16 an example of **r** to all generations.
Man 1: 7 to your great goodness you have promised **r**
1: 7 of your mercies you have appointed **r** for sinners,

Man 1: 8 have not appointed **r** for the righteous,
1: 8 but you have appointed **r** for me, who am a sinner.
2Es 7:*82* because they cannot now make a good **r** so
7:*133* [63] gracious to those who turn in **r** to his law;
9:11 while an opportunity of **r** was still open to them,

REPENTED (11) [REPENT]

Ps 78:34 they **r** and sought God earnestly.
Jer 31:19 For after I had turned away I **r;**
34:15 You yourselves recently **r** and did what was right
Zec 1: 6 So they **r** and said, "The LORD of hosts has dealt
Mt 11:21 they would have **r** long ago in sackcloth
12:41 because they **r** at the proclamation of Jonah,
27: 3 he **r** and brought back the thirty pieces of silver to
Lk 10:13 they would have **r** long ago,
11:32 because they **r** at the proclamation of Jonah,
2Co 12:21 over many who previously sinned and have not **r**
3Mc 2:24 though he had been punished, he by no means **r,**

REPENTS (3) [REPENT]

Jer 8: 6 no one **r** of wickedness, saying, "What have I
Lk 15: 7 be more joy in heaven over one sinner who **r** than
15:10 of the angels of God over one sinner who **r."**

REPHAEL (1)

1Ch 26: 7 The sons of Shemaiah: Othni, **R,** Obed,

REPHAH (1)

1Ch 7:25 **R** was his son, Resheph his son, Telah his son,

REPHAIAH (5)

1Ch 3:21 Pelatiah and Jeshaiah, his son **R,** his son Arnan,
4:42 having as their leaders Pelatiah, Neariah, **R,**
7: 2 The sons of Tola: Uzzi, **R,** Jeriel, Jahmai, Ibsam,
9:43 and **R** was his son, Eleasah his son, Azel his son.
Ne 3: 9 Next to them **R** son of Hur,

REPHAIM (18) [=ZAMZUMMIM, EMIM]

Ge 14: 5 and subdued the **R** in Ashteroth-karnaim,
15:20 the Hittites, the Perizzites, the **R,**
Dt 2:11 Like the Anakim, they are usually reckoned as **R,**
2:20 (It also is usually reckoned as a land of **R. R**
formerly inhabited it,
3:11 Og of Bashan was left of the remnant of the **R.**
3:13 of Bashan used to be called a land of **R;**
Jos 12: 4 Og of Bashan, one of the last of the **R,**
13:12 alone was left of the survivors of the **R);**
15: 8 on the west, at the northern end of the valley of **R;**
17:15 in the land of the Perizzites and the **R,**
18:16 which is at the north end of the valley of **R;**
2Sa 5:18 and spread out in the valley of **R.**
5:22 and were spread out in the valley of **R.**
23:13 of Philistines was encamped in the valley of **R.**
1Ch 11:15 of Philistines was encamped in the valley of **R.**
14: 9 and made a raid in the valley of **R.**
Isa 17: 5 one gleans the ears of grain in the Valley of **R.**

REPHAN (1)

Ac 7:43 and the star of your god **R,**

REPHIDIM (5)

Ex 17: 1 They camped at **R,** but there was no water for
17: 8 Then Amalek came and fought with Israel at **R.**
19: 2 They had journeyed from **R,**
Nu 33:14 They set out from Alush and camped at **R,**
33:15 They set out from **R** and camped in the wilderness

REPLACED (3) [PLACE]

Ge 43:18 **r** in our sacks the first time,
1Sa 21: 6 to be **r** by hot bread on the day it is taken away.
Ecc 4:15 follow that youth who **r** the king;

REPLANTED (1) [PLANT]

Eze 36:36 and **r** that which was desolate;

REPLENISH (1) [REPLENISHED]

Jer 31:25 and all who are faint I will **r.**

REPLENISH (KJV) See also FILL

REPLENISHED‡ (1) [REPLENISH]

Eze 26: 2 I shall be **r,** now that it is wasted."

REPLIED‡ (118) [REPLY]

Ge 19: 9 But they **r,** "Stand back!"
29: 6 "Yes," they **r,** "and here is his daughter Rachel,
38:18 She **r,** "Your signet and your cord,
38:23 Judah **r,** "Let her keep the things as her own,
43: 7 They **r,** "The man questioned us carefully
43:23 He **r,** "Rest assured, do not be afraid;
Nu 22:18 But Balaam **r** to the servants of Balak,
Dt 18:17 Then the LORD **r** to me:
Jos 5:14 He **r,** "Neither; but as commander of the
Jdg 8: 7 Gideon **r,** "Well then,
8:19 And he **r,** "They were my brothers,
15:11 He **r,** "As they did to me, so I have done to them."
17: 9 He **r,** "I am a Levite of Bethlehem in Judah,
18: 6 The priest **r,** "Go in peace.
18:24 He **r,** "You take my gods that I made,
Ru 3:18 She **r,** "Wait, my daughter,
1Sa 4:17 The messenger **r,** "Israel has fled before
5: 8 The inhabitants of Gath **r,**
9: 7 Then Saul **r** to the boy, "But if we go,
10:14 And he **r,** "To seek the donkeys;
13:11 Saul **r,** "When I saw that the people
15:16 LORD said to me last night." He **r,** "Speak."
20:11 Jonathan **r** to David, "Come,
26:14 Abner **r,** "Who are you that calls to the king?"
26:22 David **r,** "Here is the spear, O king!
29: 9 Achish **r** to David, "I know that you are
1Ki 2:31 The king **r** to him, "Do as he has said,
22: 4 Jehoshaphat **r** to the king of Israel,
22:22 He **r,** 'I will go out and be a lying spirit in
22:25 Micaiah **r,** "You will find out on that day
2Ki 4:16 She **r,** "No, my lord, O man of God;
5:22 He **r,** "Yes, but my master has sent me to say,
6:16 He **r,** "Do not be afraid, for there are more
2Ch 18:21 He **r,** 'I will go out and be a lying spirit in
18:24 Micaiah **r,** "You will find out on that day
Ne 1: 3 They **r,** "The survivors there in
2:20 Then I **r** to them, "The God of heaven is
Da 3:25 He **r,** "But I see four men unbound,
Jnh 1: 9 "I am a Hebrew," he **r.**
Zec 1:13 the LORD **r** with gracious and comforting words
Mt 12:48 But to the one who had told him this, Jesus **r,**
13:29 But he **r,** 'No; for in gathering
14:17 They **r,** "We have nothing here but five loaves
17:11 He **r,** "Elijah is indeed coming
20:13 But he **r** to one of them, 'Friend,
25: 9 But the wise **r,** 'No!
25:12 But he **r,** 'Truly I tell you, I do not know you.'
25:26 But his master **r,** 'You wicked and lazy slave!
26:25 He **r,** "You have said so."
Mk 3:33 And he **r,** "Who are my mother and my brothers?"
5: 9 He **r,** "My name is Legion; for we are many."
6:24 She **r,** "The head of John the baptizer."
8: 4 His disciples **r,** "How can one feed these people
10:39 They **r,** "We are able."
Lk 1:19 The angel **r,** "I am Gabriel.
7:40 "Teacher," he **r,** "Speak."
8:50 When Jesus heard this, he **r,** "Do not fear.
10:30 Jesus **r,** "A man was going down from Jerusalem
13: 8 He **r,** 'Sir, let it alone for one more year,
15:27 He **r,** 'Your brother has come,
16: 7 He **r,** 'A hundred containers of wheat.'
16:29 Abraham **r,** 'They have Moses and the prophets;
17: 6 The Lord **r,** "If you had faith the size of
18:21 He **r,** "I have kept all these since my youth."
18:27 He **r,** "What is impossible for mortals is possible
22:38 He **r,** "It is enough."
22:67 He **r,** "If I tell you, you will not believe;
23:43 He **r,** "Truly I tell you, today you will be with me
24:19 They **r,** "The things about Jesus of Nazareth,
Jn 1:49 Nathanael **r,** "Rabbi, you are the Son of God!
7:47 Then the Pharisees **r,** "Surely you have
7:52 They **r,** "Surely you are not also from Galilee,
10:32 Jesus **r,** "I have shown you many good works
18: 5 Jesus **r,** "I am he."
18:31 The Jews **r,** "We are not permitted to put anyone
18:35 Pilate **r,** "I am not a Jew, am I?
Ac 1: 7 He **r,** "It is not for you to know the times
7: 2 Stephen **r:** "Brothers and fathers, listen to me.
8:31 He **r,** "How can I, unless someone guides me?"
10:30 Cornelius **r,** "Four days ago at this very hour,
11: 8 But I **r,** 'By no means, Lord;
15:13 After they finished speaking, James **r,**
16:37 But Paul **r,** "They have beaten us in public,
19: 2 They **r,** "No, we have not even heard that there is
21:37 The tribune **r,** "Do you know Greek?
21:39 Paul **r,** "I am a Jew, from Tarsus in Cilicia,
24:10 the governor motioned to him to speak, Paul **r:**
25: 4 Festus **r** that Paul was being kept at Caesarea,
25:12 Festus, after he had conferred with his council, **r,**
26:29 Paul **r,** "Whether quickly or not,
28:21 They **r,** "We have received no letters from Judea
Tob 2: 3 And I **r,** "Here I am, my child."
2:14 Then she **r** to me, "Where are your acts of charity?
5: 5 "From your kindred, the Israelites," he **r,**
5: 6 "Yes," he **r,** "I have been there many times;
5: 8 He **r,** "All right, I will wait;
5: 9 He **r,** "Call the man in, my son,
5:10 He **r,** "Joyous greetings to you!"
5:12 He **r,** "Why do you need to know my tribe?"
5:13 He **r,** "I am Azariah, the son of
6: 8 He **r,** "As for the fish's heart and liver,
7: 1 They greeted him first, and he **r,**
7: 4 And they **r,** "Yes, we know him."
7: 5 They **r,** "He is alive and in good health."
12: 2 He **r,** "Father, how much shall I pay him?
Jdt 10:12 She **r,** "I am a daughter of the Hebrews,
12: 4 Judith **r,** "As surely as you live, my lord,
12:14 Judith **r,** "Who am I to refuse my lord?
1Mc 3:18 Judas **r,** "It is easy for many to be hemmed in
10:55 Ptolemy the king **r** and said,
2Mc 3:37 to send on another mission to Jerusalem, he **r,**
7: 8 He **r** in the language of his ancestors and said
15: 5 he **r,** "But I am a sovereign also, on earth,
2Es 4: 3 And he **r** to me, "I have been sent
5:44 He **r** to me and said, "The creation cannot move
5:51 He **r** to me, "Ask a woman who bears children,
7:62 I **r** and said, "O earth, what have you brought forth,
4Mc 9:17 he **r,** "You abominable lackeys, your wheel is not

REPLY (19) [REPLIED]

Ezr 5: 5 and then answer was returned by letter in **r** to it.
5:11 This was their **r** to us:
Est 4:13 Mordecai told them to **r** to Esther,
4:15 Then Esther said in **r** to Mordecai,
Job 13:22 or let me speak, and you **r** to me.
Mt 19:27 Then Peter said in **r,** "Look,
Mk 15: 5 But Jesus made no further **r,**
Lk 3:11 In **r** he said to them,
13:25 'Lord, open to us,' then in **r** he will say to you,
14: 6 And they could not **r** to this.
Jn 18:40 They shouted in **r,** "Not this man, but Barabbas!"
Ac 9: 5 **r** came, "I am Jesus, whom you are persecuting.
19:15 But the evil spirit said to them in **r,** "Jesus I know,
Ro 11: 4 But what is the divine **r** to him?
1Mc 8:22 of the letter that they wrote in **r,** on bronze tablets,
12:18 And now please send us a **r** to this."
13:35 King Demetrius sent him a favorable **r**
15:33 Simon said to him in **r:**
1Es 2:25 Then the king, in **r** to the recorder Rehum,

REPORT (54) [REPORTED, REPORTING, REPORTS]

Ge 37: 2 and Joseph brought a bad **r** of them to their father.
45:16 When the **r** was heard in Pharaoh's house,
Ex 23: 1 You shall not spread a false **r.**
Nu 13:32 So they brought to the Israelites an unfavorable **r**
14:36 against him by bringing a bad **r** about the land—
14:37 an unfavorable **r** about the land died by a plague
Dt 1:22 for us and bring back a **r** to us regarding the route
1:25 They brought back a **r** to us, and said,
2:25 when they hear **r** of you,
Jos 9: 9 for we have heard a **r** of him,
14: 7 and I brought him an honest **r.**
22:33 The **r** pleased the Israelites;
Jdg 18: 8 they said to them, "What do you **r?"**
1Sa 2:24 it is not a good **r** that I hear the people of
29:10 As for the evil **r,** do not take it to heart,
2Sa 13:30 the **r** came to David that Absalom had killed all
15:36 by them you shall **r** to me everything you hear."
1Ki 10: 6 "The **r** was true that I heard in my own land
10: 7 and prosperity far surpass the **r** that I had heard.
1Ch 21: 2 from Beer-sheba to Dan, and bring me a **r,**
2Ch 9: 5 "The **r** was true that I heard in my own land
9: 6 you far surpass the **r** that I had heard.
Ezr 5: 5 a **r** reached Darius and then answer was returned
5: 7 they sent him a **r,** in which was written as follows:
Ne 6: 6 according to this **r** you wish to become their king.
Isa 23: 5 When the **r** comes to Egypt,
23: 5 they will be in anguish over the **r** about Tyre.
Jer 36:16 "We certainly must **r** all these words to the king."
Eze 24:26 one who has escaped will come to you to **r** to you
Hos 7:12 I will discipline them according to the **r** made
Ob 1: 1 We have heard a **r** from the LORD,
Mt 9:26 And the **r** of this spread throughout that district.
Lk 4:14 and a **r** about him spread through all
4:37 And a **r** about him began to reach every place in
Ac 23:17 for he has something to **r** to him."
23:19 and asked, "What is it that you have to **r** to me?"
25: 2 the leaders of the Jews gave him a **r** against Paul.
1Th 1: 9 the people of those regions **r** about us what kind
Tob 10:12 may I hear a good **r** about you as long as I live."
Jdt 5: 5 "May my lord please listen to a **r** from the mouth
10:13 to give him a true **r;**
Wis 1: 9 and a **r** of their words will come to the Lord,
Sir 19: 8 With friend or foe do not **r** it,
1Mc 5:14 came from Galilee and made a similar **r;**
12:23 We therefore command that our envoys **r**
16:18 a **r** about these things and sent it to the king,
2Mc 3:34 **r** to all people the majestic power of God."
4:39 and when **r** of them had spread abroad,
1Es 6: 6 be sent to Darius concerning them and a **r** made.
3Mc 3: 2 a **r** that they hindered others from the observance
5:10 the courtyard early in the morning to **r** to the king
5:27 the **r** and being struck by the unusual invitation
4Mc 4: 3 because I am loyal to the king's government, to **r**
4:14 went away to **r** to the king what had happened

REPORTED (61) [REPORT]

Ex 19: 8 Moses **r** the words of the people to the LORD.
Dt 17: 4 and if it is **r** to you or you hear of it,
Jdg 9:25 and it was **r** to Abimelech.
1Sa 8:10 So Samuel **r** all the words of the LORD to
11: 4 they **r** the matter in the hearing of the people;
14:33 Then it was **r** to Saul, "Look,
18:23 Saul's servants **r** these words to David in private.
2Sa 1:13 David said to the young man who had **r** to him,
11: 3 It was **r,** "This is Bathsheba daughter of Eliam,
24: 9 Joab **r** to the king the number
1Ki 20:17 Ben-hadad had sent out scouts, and they **r** to him,
2Ki 9:18 The sentinel **r,** saying, "The messenger reached
9:20 Again the sentinel **r,** "He reached them,
22: 9 and **r** to the king, "Your servants have emptied out
2Ch 34:16 and further **r** to the king,
Ne 6: 1 Now when it was **r** to Sanballat and Tobiah and
6: 6 In it was written, "It is **r** among the nations—
6: 7 it will be **r** to the king according to these words.
6:19 and **r** my words to him.
Est 9:11 of those killed in the citadel of Susa was **r** to
Jer 36:20 and they **r** all the words to the king.
Mt 18:31 and **r** to their lord all that had taken place.
Mk 2: 1 it was **r** that he was at home.
5:16 to the demoniac and to the swine **r** it.
Lk 7:18 The disciples of John **r** all these things to him.
14:21 So the slave returned and **r** this to his master.
Ac 4:23 and **r** what the chief priests and the elders had said
5:22 in the prison; so they returned and **r,**
15: 3 they **r** the conversion of the Gentiles,

Ac 15: 4 and they **r** all that God had done with them.
16:36 And the jailer **r** the message to Paul, saying,
16:38 The police **r** these words to the magistrates,
24: 1 and they **r** their case against Paul to the governor.
28:21 and none of the brothers coming here has **r**
1Co 1:11 For it has been **r** to me by Chloe's people
5: 1 It is actually **r** that there is sexual immorality
Tob 11:15 **r** to his father that his journey had been
Jdt 5: 1 It was **r** to Holofernes, the general of
10:18 for her arrival was **r** from tent to tent.
11: 8 and it is **r** throughout the whole world
AdE 1:17 (for he had **r** to them what the queen had said and
9:11 the number of those killed in Susa was **r** to
1Mc 2:31 And it was **r** to the king's officers,
4:26 Those of the foreigners who escaped went and **r**
5:38 and they **r** to him, "All the Gentiles
6: 5 in Persia and **r** that the armies that had gone into
9:37 After these things it was **r** to Jonathan
11:21 the king and **r** to him that Jonathan was besieging
11:40 He also **r** to Imalkue what Demetrius had done
12:26 and **r** to him that the enemy were being drawn up
15:32 When he **r** to him the king's message,
15:36 in wrath to the king and **r** to him these words,
16: 1 John went up from Gazara and **r**
16:21 But someone ran ahead and **r** to John at Gazara
2Mc 1:20 And when they **r** to us that they had not found fire
1:33 and it was **r** to the king of the Persians that,
2:13 The same things are **r** in the records and in
3: 6 and **r** to him that the treasury
3: 7 to effect the removal of the **r** wealth.
1Es 1:42 But the things that are **r** about Jehoiakim,
8:49 the list of all their names was **r**.

REPORTING (3) [REPORT]
Dt 1:28 Our kindred have made our hearts melt by **r**,
2Sa 1: 5 David asked the young man who was **r** to him,
1: 6 The young man **r** to him said,

REPORTS (6) [REPORT]
1Ki 10: 7 the **r** until I came and my own eyes had seen it.
2Ch 9: 6 the **r** until I came and my own eyes saw it.
Da 11:44 But **r** from the east and the north shall alarm him,
Mt 14: 1 At that time Herod the ruler heard **r** about Jesus;
1Mc 3:27 When King Antiochus heard these **r**,
3Mc 2:26 that he framed evil **r** in the various localities;

REPOSE (2)
Isa 28:12 and this is **r**"; yet they would not hear.
34:14 there too Lilith shall **r**, and find a place to rest.

REPRESENT (4) [REPRESENTATIVES, REPRESENTED, REPRESENTING]
Ex 18:19 You should **r** the people before God,
Ezr 10:14 Let our officials **r** the whole assembly,
Jer 40:10 to **r** you before the Chaldeans who come to us;
AdE 16:23 that both now and hereafter it may **r** deliverance

REPRESENTATIVES (2) [REPRESENT]
Ac 15:25 we have decided unanimously to choose **r**
2Mc 11:20 I have ordered these men and my **r** to confer

REPRESENTED (1) [REPRESENT]
1Es 1:15 Zechariah, and Eddinus, who **r** the king.

REPRESENTING (1) [REPRESENT]
Nu 1:44 twelve men, each **r** his ancestral house.

REPROACH‡ (32) [REPROACHED, REPROACHES, REPROACHFUL, REPROACHING]
Ge 30:23 and said, "God has taken away my **r**";
Ru 2:15 among the standing sheaves, and do not **r** her.
1Sa 17:26 and takes away the **r** from Israel?
Job 19: 3 These ten times you have cast **r** upon me;
27: 6 my heart does not **r** me for any of my days
Ps 15: 3 nor take up a **r** against their neighbors;
69: 7 It is for your sake that I have borne **r**,
Pr 14:34 but sin is a **r** to any people.
19:26 are children who cause shame and bring **r**.
Isa 51: 7 do not fear the **r** of others,
Jer 20: 8 For the word of the LORD has become for me a **r**
Eze 21:28 and concerning their **r**; say: A sword, a sword!
Zep 3:18 so that you will not bear **r** for it.
Mt 11:20 Then he began to **r** the cities in which most
1Ti 3: 2 Now a bishop must be above **r**,
5: 7 so that they may be above **r**.
Tob 3: 4 and an object of **r** among all the nations
3:10 "Never shall they **r** my father, saying to him,
Wis 5: 4 in derision and made a byword of **r**—
Sir 6: 1 for a bad name incurs shame and **r**;
8: 5 Do not **r** one who is turning away from sin;
18:15 My child, do not mix **r** with your good deeds,
29:23 and you will hear no **r** for being a guest.
31:31 speak no word of **r** to him,
LtJ 6:47 and **r** for those who come after.
6:72 and be a **r** in the land.
6:73 such a person will be far above **r**.
Aza 1:10 have become a shame and a **r**.
1Mc 1:39 her sabbaths into a **r**, her honor into contempt.
3Mc 3: 7 So they attached no ordinary **r** to them.
2Es 10:28 end has become corruption, and my prayer a **r**."
13:38 and will **r** them to their face

REPROACHED (3) [REPROACH]
Tob 3: 7 was **r** by one of her father's maids.
Bar 3: 8 be **r** and cursed and punished for all the iniquities
4Mc 12: 2 the tyrant had been vehemently **r** by the brothers,

REPROACHES (5) [REPROACH]
Pr 27:11 so that I may answer whoever **r** me.
Tob 3:10 that I may die and not listen to these **r** anymore."
3:13 from the earth and not listen to such **r** any more.
Wis 2:12 he **r** us for sins against the law,
Sir 29: 6 he will repay him with curses and **r**,

REPROACHFUL (1) [REPROACH]
2Mc 7:24 and he was suspicious of her **r** tone.

REPROACHING (1) [REPROACH]
3Mc 7: 8 in any place doing them harm at all or **r** them for

REPROBATE, REPROBATES (KJV) See COUNTERFEIT, DEBASED, FAIL, FAILED, REJECTED, UNFIT

REPROOF (12) [REPROVE]
Job 6:25 But your **r**, what does it reprove?
Pr 1:23 Give heed to my **r**; I will pour out my thoughts to
1:25 and would have none of my **r**,
1:30 none of my counsel, and despised all my **r**,
3:11 the LORD's discipline or be weary of his **r**,
5:12 how I hated discipline, and my heart despised **r**!
13:18 but one who heeds **r** is honored.
29:15 The rod and **r** give wisdom,
2Ti 3:16 for teaching, for **r**, for correction, and for training
Wis 2:14 He became to us a **r** of our thoughts;
Sir 21: 6 Those who hate **r** walk in the sinner's steps,
32:17 The sinner will shun **r**, and will find a decision

REPROOF, REPROVE (KJV) See also ACCUSE, ADMONITION, CONVICT, CONVINCE, CORRECT, DECIDE, EXPOSE, PROVE, REBUKE, REBUKED

REPROOFS‡ (2) [REPROVE]
Pr 6:23 and the **r** of discipline are the way of life,
Sir 20:29 like a muzzle on the mouth they stop **r**.

REPROVE (11) [REPROOF, REPROOFS, REPROVED, REPROVES, REPROVING]
Lev 19:17 you shall **r** your neighbor,
Job 6:25 But your reproof, what does it **r**?
6:26 Do you think that you can **r** words,
Pr 19:25 **r** the intelligent, and they will gain knowledge.
Eze 3:26 that you shall be speechless and unable to **r** them;
Tit 2:15 exhort and **r** with all authority.
Rev 3:19 I **r** and discipline those whom I love.
Sir 31:31 Do not **r** your neighbor at a banquet of wine,
2Es 13:37 will **r** the assembled nations
14:13 set your house in order, and **r** your people;
14:20 and I will **r** the people who are now living;

REPROVED‡ (4) [REPROVE]
Pr 29: 1 One who is often **r**, yet remains stubborn,
1Co 14:24 an unbeliever or outsider who enters is **r** by all
2Es 8:12 and **r** it in your wisdom.
12:33 and when he has **r** them,

REPROVES (4) [REPROVE]
Job 5:17 "How happy is the one whom God **r**;
22: 4 Is it for your piety that he **r** you,
Pr 3:12 for the LORD **r** the one he loves,
Am 5:10 They hate the one who **r** in the gate,

REPROVING (1) [REPROVE]
2Es 12:31 and roaring and speaking to the eagle and **r** him

REPTILE (1) [REPTILES]
Jas 3: 7 and bird, of **r** and sea creature, can be tamed

REPTILES (4) [REPTILE]
1Ki 4:33 he would speak of animals, and birds, and **r**,
Ac 10:12 of four-footed creatures and **r** and birds of the air.
11: 6 beasts of prey, **r**, and birds of the air.
Ro 1:23 or birds or four-footed animals or **r**.

REPUDIATED (1)
2Ch 29:19 All the utensils that King Ahaz **r** during his reign

REPUGNANT (2)
Job 21:16 The plans of the wicked are **r** to me.
22:18 but the plans of the wicked are **r** to me.

REPULSE (2) [REPULSED, REPULSIVE]
2Ki 18:24 then can you **r** a single captain among the least
Isa 36: 9 then can you **r** a single captain among the least

REPULSED (1) [REPULSE]
1Mc 14:26 they have fought and **r** Israel's enemies

REPULSIVE (1) [REPULSE]
Job 19:17 My breath is **r** to my wife;

REPUTABLE (2) [REPUTE]
Dt 1:13 discerning, and **r** to be your leaders."
1:15 the leaders of your tribes, wise and **r** individuals,

REPUTATION (5) [REPUTE]
Sir 11:33 and they may ruin your **r** forever.
Sus 1:64 from that day onward Daniel had a great **r** among
3Mc 2:31 to enhance their **r** by their future association with
4Mc 5:18 even so would it be right for us to invalidate our **r**
6:18 in accordance with law the **r** of such a life,

REPUTE (6) [REPUTABLE, REPUTATION, REPUTED]
1Sa 18:23 seeing that I am a poor man and of no **r**?"
Pr 3: 4 So you will find favor and good **r** in the sight
25:10 and your ill **r** will have no end.
2Co 6: 8 in honor and dishonor, in ill **r** and good **r**.
3Mc 3: 5 they were established in good **r** with everyone.

REPUTED (1) [REPUTE]
2Es 6:57 these nations, which are **r** to be as nothing,

REQUEST (32) [REQUESTED, REQUESTING, REQUESTS]
Jdg 8: 8 and made the same **r** of them;
8:24 Gideon said to them, "Let me make a **r** of you;
2Sa 14:15 be that the king will perform the **r** of his servant.
14:22 in that the king has granted the **r** of his servant."
1Ki 2:16 I have one **r** to make of you; do not refuse me."
2:20 Then she said, "I have one small **r** to make of you;
2:20 the king said to her, "Make your **r**, my mother;
Ne 2: 4 Then the king said to me, "What do you **r**?"
Est 5: 3 Queen Esther? What is your **r**?
5: 6 And what is your **r**?
5: 7 Then Esther said, "This is my petition and **r**:
5: 8 the king to grant my petition and fulfill my **r**,
7: 2 And what is your **r**?
7: 3 and the lives of my people—that is my **r**.
9:12 And what further is your **r**?
Job 6: 8 "O that I might have my **r**,
Ps 21: 2 and have not withheld the **r** of his lips.
Jer 42: 4 to the LORD your God as you **r**, and whatever
Da 2:49 Daniel made a **r** of the king,
Ac 9:38 sent two men to him with the **r**,
AdE 5: 3 "What do you wish, Esther? What is your **r**?
5: 7 She said, "My petition and **r** is:
7: 2 What is your petition and what is your **r**?
7: 3 and my people at my **r**.
8: 7 against the Jews, what else do you **r**?
1Mc 11:41 to King Demetrius the **r** that he remove the troops
13:34 to King Demetrius with a **r** to grant relief to
13:35 a favorable reply to this **r**,
2Mc 11:15 For the king granted every **r** in behalf of
1Es 4:46 O lord the king, this is what I ask and **r** of you,
3Mc 6:41 The king granted their **r** at once and wrote
2Es 5:46 **R** it therefore to produce ten at one time."

REQUESTED (8) [REQUEST]
Ex 8:13 And the LORD did as Moses **r**:
Dt 18:16 This is what you **r** of the LORD your God
Jdg 8:26 that he **r** was one thousand seven hundred shekels
Da 2:16 and **r** that the king give him time and he would tell
Mk 6:25 Immediately she rushed back to the king and **r**,
Ac 25: 3 and **r**, as a favor to them against Paul,
Jdt 10: 9 the young men to open the gate for her, as she **r**.
3Mc 7:10 but they **r** of the king that at their own hands those

REQUESTING (1) [REQUEST]
2Mc 4:28 the captain of the citadel kept **r** payment—

REQUESTS‡ (3) [REQUEST]
Php 4: 6 and supplication with thanksgiving let your **r**
1Jn 5:15 we know that we have obtained the **r** made of him.
1Es 8: 4 for he found favor before the king in all his **r**.

REQUIRE (22) [REQUIRED, REQUIREMENT, REQUIREMENTS, REQUIRES, REQUIRING]
Ge 9: 5 For your own lifeblood I will surely **r** a reckoning:
9: 5 from every animal I will **r** it and
9: 5 I will **r** a reckoning for human life.
Ex 5: 8 But you shall **r** of them the same quantity
Dt 10:12 what does the LORD your God **r** of you?
23:21 for the LORD your God will surely **r** it of you,
2Sa 3:13 But one thing I **r** of you:
4:11 And now shall I not **r** his blood at your hand,
1Ki 18:10 he would **r** an oath of the kingdom or nation,
1Ch 21: 3 Why then should my lord **r** this?
Ezr 6: 9 salt, wine, or oil, as the priests in Jerusalem **r**—
Eze 3:18 but their blood I will **r** at your hand.
3:20 but their blood I will **r** at your hand.
20:40 and there I will **r** your contributions and
33: 6 but their blood I will **r** at the sentinel's hand.
33: 8 but their blood I will **r** at your hand.
Mic 6: 8 what does the LORD **r** of you but to do justice,
Ro 16: 2 and help her in whatever she may **r** from you,
LtJ 6:35 to them and does not keep it, they will not **r** it.

2Es 1:32 I will **r** their blood of you, says the Lord.
2:26 for I will **r** them from among your number.
6:19 and when I **r** from the doers of iniquity the penalty

REQUIRED (26) [REQUIRE]
Ge 31:39 of my hand you **r** it.
50: 3 for that is the time **r** for embalming.
Ex 5:14 the **r** quantity of bricks yesterday and today,
13:19 the bones of Joseph who had **r** a solemn oath of
Nu 4:32 by name the objects that they are **r** to carry.
5:15 And he shall bring the offering **r** for her,
1Sa 21: 8 because the king's business **r** haste."
1Ki 4:28 They also brought to the **r** place barley and straw
1Ch 9:28 for they were **r** to count them
16:37 to minister regularly before the ark as each day **r**,
23:31 according to the number **r** of them,
2Ch 6:22 against another and is **r** to take an oath and comes
8:13 as the duty of each day **r**, offering according to
8:14 as the duty of each day **r**, and the gatekeepers
24: 6 "Why have you not **r** the Levites to bring in
31:16 the house of the LORD as the duty of each day **r**,
Ezr 3: 4 according to the ordinance, as **r** for each day,
7:20 And whatever else is **r** for the house of your God,
Ne 11:23 for the singers, as was **r** every day.
12:44 into them the portions **r** by the law for the priests
Ps 40: 6 Burnt offering and sin offering you have not **r**.
Lk 2:39 When they had finished everything **r** by the law of
12:48 to whom much has been given, much will be **r**;
1Co 4: 2 it is **r** of stewards that they be found trustworthy.
AdE 9: 4 The king's decree **r** that Mordecai's name be held
1Es 1:12 They roasted the passover lamb with fire, as **r**;

REQUIREMENT (2) [REQUIRE]
Ro 8: 4 that the just **r** of the law might be fulfilled in us,
Heb 7:16 not through a legal **r** concerning physical descent,

REQUIREMENTS (3) [REQUIRE]
Lev 27:16 be in accordance with its seed **r**:
Zec 3: 7 If you will walk in my ways and keep my **r**,
Ro 2:26 if those who are uncircumcised keep the **r** of

REQUIRES (5) [REQUIRE]
1Ki 8:59 and the cause of his people Israel, as each day **r**;
Ezr 7:21 **r** of you, let it be done with all diligence,
Ro 2:14 do instinctively what the law **r**, these,
2:15 that what the law **r** is written on their hearts,
Sir 13:26 but to devise proverbs **r** painful thinking.

REQUIRING (1) [REQUIRE]
Lev 22:16 causing them to bear guilt **r** a guilt offering,

REQUITAL (2)
Isa 59:18 wrath to his adversaries, **r** to his enemies;
59:18 to the coastlands he will render **r**.

REQUITE, REQUITED, REQUITING
(KJV) See PAID BACK, PAY BACK, REPAY, REPAYING, REPAYMENT, RETURNED, REWARD, TAKE INTO

REREWARD (KJV) See REAR, REAR GUARD

RESAIAH (1)
1Es 5: 8 **R**, Eneneus, Mordecai, Beelsarus, Aspharasus,

RESCINDING (1)
AdE 8: 5 let an order be sent **r** the letters that Haman wrote

RESCUE‡ (61) [RESCUED, RESCUER, RESCUES, RESCUING]
Ge 37:22 that he might **r** him out of their hand
Nu 35:25 and the congregation shall **r** the slayer from
Dt 22:27 but there was no one to **r** her.
25:11 the wife of one intervenes to **r** her husband from
1Sa 12:10 but now **r** us out of the hand of our enemies,
26:24 and may he **r** me from all tribulation."
30: 8 for you shall surely overtake and shall surely **r**."
2Ki 16: 7 and **r** me from the hand of the king of Aram and
1Ch 16:35 and gather and **r** us from among the nations,
2Ch 32:17 of the nations in other lands did not **r** their people
32:17 of Hezekiah will not **r** his people from my hand."
Ps 7: 2 they will drag me away, with no one to **r**.
22: 8 let him **r** the one in whom he delights!"
31: 2 Incline your ear to me; **r** me speedily.
35:17 **R** me from their ravages, my life from the lions!
69:14 **r** me from sinking in the mire;
71: 2 In your righteousness deliver me and **r** me;
71: 4 **R** me, O my God, from the hand of the wicked,
82: 4 **R** the weak and the needy;
91:15 I will **r** them and honor them.
119:153 Look on my misery and **r** me,
144: 7 set me free and **r** me from the mighty waters,
144:11 **R** me from the cruel sword,
Pr 19:19 if you effect a **r**, you will only have to do it again.
Isa 1:17 seek justice, **r** the oppressed, defend the orphan,
5:29 they carry it off, and no one can **r**.
31: 5 he will protect and deliver it, he will spare and **r** it.
42:22 they have become a prey with no one to **r**,
Jer 42:11 to save you and to **r** you from his hand.
Eze 34:10 I will **r** my sheep from their mouths,
34:12 I will **r** them from all the places
Da 6:14 the sun went down he made every effort to **r** him.
8: 4 and no one could **r** from its power;
8: 7 upon it, and there was no one who could **r** the ram
Hos 2:10 and no one shall **r** her out of my hand.
5:14 I will carry off, and no one shall **r**.
Mic 5: 6 they shall **r** us from the Assyrians if they come
Mt 6:13 but **r** us from the evil one.
Ac 7:34 and I have come down to **r** them.
26:17 I will **r** you from your people and from
Ro 7:24 Who will **r** me from this body of death?
2Co 1:10 from so deadly a peril will continue to **r** us;
1:10 that he will **r** us again,
2Ti 4:18 The Lord will **r** me from every evil attack
2Pe 2: 9 then the Lord knows how to **r** the godly from trial,
Sir 4: 9 **R** the oppressed from the oppressor;
13:22 If the rich person slips, many come to the **r**;
29:12 and it will **r** you from every disaster;
51: 8 for you **r** those who wait for you and save them
51: 9 and begged for **r** from death.
LtJ 6:36 They cannot save anyone from death or **r** the weak
6:37 they cannot **r** one who is in distress.
1Mc 5:12 Now then, come and **r** us from their hands,
5:17 "Choose your men and go and **r** your kindred
2Mc 1:25 You **r** Israel from every evil;
8:14 the Lord to **r** those who had been sold by
9: 2 Therefore the people rushed to the **r** with arms,
3Mc 5: 8 in a glorious manifestation **r** them from the fate
6:10 **r** us from the hand of the enemy, and destroy us,
6:30 deciding that they should celebrate their **r**
6:33 for the unexpected **r** that he had experienced.

RESCUED‡ (46) [RESCUE]
Jos 24:10 so I **r** you out of his hand.
Jdg 8:34 who had **r** them from the hand of all their enemies
9:17 and **r** you from the hand of Midian;
1Sa 10:18 and I **r** you from the hand of the Egyptians and
12:11 and **r** you out of the hand of your enemies
14:48 and **r** Israel out of the hands
23: 5 Thus David **r** the inhabitants of Keilah.
30:18 and David **r** his two wives.
2Sa 12: 7 and I **r** you from the hand of Saul;
Ne 9:28 many times you **r** them according to your mercies.
Job 21:30 and are **r** in the day of wrath?
Ps 22:21 From the horns of the wild oxen you have **r** me.
60: 5 so that those whom you love may be **r**.
71:23 my soul also, which you have **r**.
81: 7 In distress you called, and I **r** you;
108: 6 so that those whom you love may be **r**.
136:24 and **r** us from our foes,
Isa 49:24 or the captives of a tyrant be **r**?
49:25 and the prey of the tyrant be **r**;
Jer 30: 7 yet he shall be **r** from it.
Am 3:12 shall the people of Israel who live in Samaria be **r**,
Mic 4:10 There you shall be **r**, there the LORD will redeem
Lk 1:74 being **r** from the hands of our enemies,
Ac 7:10 and **r** him from all his afflictions,
12:11 and **r** me from the hands of Herod and from all
23:27 I came with the guard and **r** him.
Ro 15:31 that I may be **r** from the unbelievers in Judea,
2Co 1:10 He who **r** us from so deadly a peril will continue
Col 1:13 He has **r** us from the power of darkness
2Th 3: 2 that we may be **r** from wicked and evil people;
2Ti 3:11 Yet the Lord **r** me from all of them.
4:17 So I was **r** from the lion's mouth.
2Pe 2: 7 and if he **r** Lot, a righteous man greatly distressed
AdE 10: 9 the Lord has **r** us from all these evils;
Wis 10: 6 Wisdom **r** a righteous man when the ungodly
10: 9 Wisdom **r** from troubles those who served her.
18: 5 and one child had been abandoned and **r**,
Sir 33: 1 but in trials such a one will be **r** again and again.
51:12 from destruction and **r** me in time of trouble.
Aza 1:66 For he has **r** us from Hades and saved us from
1Mc 2:48 They **r** the law out of the hands of the Gentiles
2Mc 2:18 for he has **r** us from great evils and has purified
3Mc 2:12 and **r** them from great evils,
6: 6 you **r** unharmed, even to a hair,
6:11 saying, 'Not even their god has **r** them.'
6:39 and **r** them all together and unharmed.

RESCUER (1) [RESCUE]
Sir 29:17 and the ungrateful person abandons his **r**.

RESCUES (10) [RESCUE]
Ps 34:17 and **r** them from all their troubles.
34:19 but the LORD **r** them from them all.
37:40 The LORD helps them and **r** them;
37:40 he **r** them from the wicked, and saves them,
97:10 he **r** them from the hand of the wicked.
144:10 to kings, who **r** his servant David.
Da 6:27 and **r**, he works signs and wonders in heaven and
Am 3:12 shepherd **r** from the mouth of the lion two legs,
1Th 1:10 Jesus, who **r** us from the wrath that is coming.
Sir 40:24 but almsgiving **r** better than either.

RESCUING (3) [RESCUE]
1Sa 17:35 **r** the lamb from its mouth;
Pr 24:11 if you hold back from **r** those taken away to death,
Ac 7:25 that God through him was **r** them,

RESEMBLED (1) [RESEMBLES, RESEMBLING, SEMBLANCE]
Jdg 8:18 they **r** the sons of a king."

RESEMBLES (2) [RESEMBLED]
Lev 13:43 which **r** a leprous disease in the skin of the body,
Tob 7: 2 "How much the young man **r** my kinsman Tobit!"

RESEMBLING (5) [RESEMBLED]
Eze 10: 1 above them something like a sapphire, in form **r**
41:21 In front of the holy place was something **r**
Ro 1:23 for images **r** a mortal human being or birds
Heb 7: 3 but **r** the Son of God, he remains a priest forever.
7:15 when another priest arises, **r** Melchizedek,

RESEN (1)
Ge 10:12 **R** between Nineveh and Calah;

RESENTFUL (3) [RESENTMENT]
1Ki 20:43 king of Israel set out toward home, **r** and sullen,
21: 4 Ahab went home **r** and sullen because
1Co 13: 5 it is not irritable or **r**;

RESENTMENT (1) [RESENTFUL]
Ecc 5:17 in much vexation and sickness and **r**.

RESERVE (2) [RESERVED]
Ge 41:36 a **r** for the land against the seven years of famine
Eze 38: 7 and hold yourselves in **r** for them.

RESERVED (14) [RESERVE]
Ge 27:36 Then he said, "Have you not **r** a blessing for me?"
Nu 18: 9 be yours from the most holy things, **r** from
Dt 33:21 for there a commander's allotment was **r**;
2Ch 31:14 to apportion the contribution **r** for the LORD and
Job 38:23 which I have **r** for the time of trouble,
2Ti 4: 8 on there is **r** for me the crown of righteousness,
2Pe 2:17 for them the deepest darkness has been **r**.
3: 7 the present heavens and earth have been **r** for fire,
Jude 1:13 for whom the deepest darkness has been **r** forever.
Sir 13: 9 When an influential person invites you, be **r**,
2Es 7:14 that have been **r** for them.
7:*121* [51] and healthful habitations have been **r** for us,
11: 9 but let the heads be **r** for the last."
13:18 because they understand the things that are **r** for

RESERVOIR (2) [RESERVOIRS]
Isa 22:11 You made a **r** between the two walls for the water
Sir 50: 3 a **r** like the sea in circumference.

RESERVOIRS (1) [RESERVOIR]
Sir 39:17 and the **r** of water at the word of his mouth.

RESHEPH‡ (1)
1Ch 7:25 Rephah was his son, **R** his son, Telah his son,

RESIDE (29) [RESIDED, RESIDENCE, RESIDENT, RESIDENTS, RESIDES, RESIDING]
Ge 12:10 Abram went down to Egypt to **r** there as an alien,
26: 3 **R** in this land as an alien, and I will be with you,
47: 4 "We have come to **r** as aliens in the land;
Lev 17: 8 or of the aliens who **r** among them who offers
17:10 or of the aliens who **r** among them eats any blood,
17:13 or of the aliens who **r** among them,
20: 2 or of the aliens who **r** in Israel,
Dt 12:12 and the Levites who **r** in your towns
22: 2 If the owner does not **r** near you or you do
23:16 They shall **r** with you, in your midst,
24:14 or aliens who **r** in your land in one of your towns.
25: 5 When brothers **r** together,
26:11 with the Levites and the aliens who **r** among you,
1Ki 7: 8 His own house where he would **r**,
2Ch 6: 1 LORD has said that he would **r** in thick darkness.
6: 2 a place for you to **r** in forever."
6:18 "But will God indeed **r** with mortals on earth?
Ezr 1: 4 in whatever place they **r**, be assisted by the people
Job 11:14 and do not let wickedness **r** in your tents.
Ps 68:16 where the LORD will **r** forever?
132:14 here I will **r**, for I have desired it.
Isa 52: 4 my people went down into Egypt to **r** there
Jer 35: 7 you may live many days in the land where you **r**.'
Eze 14: 7 or of the aliens who **r** in Israel,
20:38 I will bring them out of the land where they **r**
43: 7 where I will **r** among the people of Israel forever.
43: 9 and I will **r** among them forever.
47:22 for yourselves and for the aliens who **r** among you
47:23 In whatever tribe aliens **r**,

RESIDED (14) [RESIDE]
Ge 21:23 and with the land where you have **r** as an alien."
21:34 And Abraham **r** as an alien many days in the land
35:27 where Abraham and Isaac had **r** as aliens.
Ex 6: 4 the land in which they **r** as aliens.
Jos 2:15 on the outer side of the city wall and she **r** within
8:35 and the aliens who **r** among them.
Jdg 9:41 So Abimelech **r** at Arumah;
1Ki 12:25 in the hill country of Ephraim, and **r** there;
15:18 who **r** in Damascus, saying,
2Ki 22:14 she **r** in Jerusalem in the Second Quarter,
1Ch 11: 7 David **r** in the stronghold;
2Ch 11: 5 Rehoboam **r** in Jerusalem,
16: 2 who **r** in Damascus, saying,
19: 4 Jehoshaphat **r** at Jerusalem;

RESIDENCE (4) [RESIDE]
Nu 15:14 or who takes up permanent **r** among you,
Jdt 5:15 and took up **r** in the land of the Amorites,
1Mc 10:10 up **r** in Jerusalem and began to rebuild and restore
2Es 10:47 that was the period of **r** in Jerusalem.

RESIDENT (25) [RESIDE]
Ex 20:10 your livestock, or the alien **r** in your towns.
22:21 You shall not wrong or oppress a **r** alien,
23: 9 You shall not oppress a **r** alien;
23:12 and your homeborn slave and the **r** alien may
Lev 25:35 they shall live with you as though **r** aliens.
25:47 If **r** aliens among you prosper,
Nu 9:14 you shall have one statute for both the **r** alien and
15:15 and the **r** alien a single statute, a perpetual statute
35:15 for the **r** or transient alien among them,
Dt 1:16 whether citizen or **r** alien.
5:14 or the **r** alien in your towns,
12:18 and the Levites **r** in your towns,
14:27 As for the Levites **r** in your towns,
14:29 as well as the **r** aliens, the orphans,
16:11 the Levites **r** in your towns,
16:14 the orphans, and the widows **r** in your towns.
24:17 not deprive a **r** alien or an orphan of justice;
26:13 and I have given it to the Levites, the **r** aliens,
2Sa 1:13 He answered, "I am the son of a **r** alien,
4: 3 to Gittaim and are there as **r** aliens to this day).
2Ch 30:25 the **r** aliens who came out of the land of Israel,
30:25 and the **r** aliens who lived in Judah, rejoiced.
Ac 7: 6 be **r** aliens in a country belonging to others,
7:29 Moses fled and became a **r** alien in the land
Jdt 4:10 and their children and their cattle and every **r** alien

RESIDENTS (10) [RESIDE]
Ac 1:19 This became known to all the **r** of Jerusalem,
2: 9 and **r** of Mesopotamia, Judea and Cappadocia,
9:35 the **r** of Lydda and Sharon saw him and turned to
13:27 Because the **r** of Jerusalem and their leaders did
14: 4 But the **r** of the city were divided;
19:10 so that all the **r** of Asia, both Jews and Greeks,
19:17 When this became known to all **r** of Ephesus,
AdE 11: 1 one of the **r** of Jerusalem.
1Mc 1:38 Because of them the **r** of Jerusalem fled;
3:34 As for the **r** of Judea and Jerusalem,

RESIDES (12) [RESIDE]
Ex 12:48 If an alien who **r** with you wants to celebrate
12:49 for the native and for the alien who **r** among you.
Lev 16:29 neither the citizen nor the alien who **r** among you.
17:12 nor shall any alien who **r** among you eat blood.
18:26 either the citizen or the alien who **r** among you
19:33 When an alien **r** with you in your land,
19:34 The alien who **r** with you shall be to you as
Nu 15:16 the alien who **r** with you shall have the same law
1Ch 23:25 and he **r** in Jerusalem forever.
Ps 135:21 be the LORD from Zion, he who **r** in Jerusalem.
Eze 17:16 in the place where the king **r** who made him king,
Jdt 9: 8 the tabernacle where your glorious name **r**,

RESIDING (23) [RESIDE]
Ge 20: 1 While **r** in Gerar as an alien,
23: 4 "I am a stranger and an alien **r** among you;
Ex 2:22 he said, "I have been an alien **r** in a foreign land."
Lev 22:18 or of the aliens **r** in Israel presents an offering,
25:45 the aliens **r** with you, and from their families
Nu 9:14 Any alien **r** among you who wishes to keep
15:26 as well as the aliens **r** among them,
15:29 among the Israelites and the alien **r** among them—
19:10 for the Israelites and for the alien **r** among them.
Dt 14:21 you may give it to aliens **r** in your towns for them
18: 6 from wherever he has been **r** in Israel,
23: 7 because you were an alien **r** in their land.
28:43 Aliens **r** among you shall ascend above you higher
31:12 as well as the aliens **r** in your towns—
Jos 20: 9 and for the aliens **r** among them,
Jdg 17: 7 He was a Levite **r** there.
19: 1 **r** in the remote parts of the hill country
19:16 and he was **r** in Gibeah.
1Ch 22: 2 to gather together the aliens who were **r** in
2Ch 2:17 of all the aliens who were **r** in the land of Israel,
15: 9 and Simeon who were **r** as aliens with them,
Eze 22: 7 the alien **r** within you suffers extortion;
3Mc 4:18 some still **r** in their homes, and some at the place;

RESIDUE (KJV) See LEFT, OTHER, REMAIN, REMAINDER, REMAINING, REMAINS, REMNANT, REST, SOME, SURVIVORS

RESIN (3)
Ge 37:25 and **r**, on their way to carry it down to Egypt.
43:11 a little balm and a little honey, gum, **r**,
Nu 11: 7 and its color was like the color of gum **r**.

RESIST (14) [RESISTANCE, RESISTED, RESISTING, RESISTS]
Da 11:15 for there shall be no strength to **r**.
Mt 5:39 But I say to you, Do not **r** an evildoer.
Ro 9:19 For who can **r** his will?"
13: 2 and those who **r** will incur judgment.
Jas 4: 7 **R** the devil, and he will flee from you.
Jas 5: 6 the righteous one, who does not **r** you.
1Pe 5: 9 **R** him, steadfast in your faith,
Jdt 2:11 But to those who **r** show no mercy,
6: 3 They cannot **r** the might of our cavalry.
16:14 there is none that can **r** your voice.
AdE 13:11 and there is no one who can **r** you, the Lord.
Wis 12:12 Or will **r** your judgment?
1Mc 5:40 we will not be able to **r** him,
1Es 2:19 to pay tribute but will even **r** kings.

RESISTANCE (1) [RESIST]
LtJ 6:56 Besides, they can offer no **r** to king or enemy.

RESISTED (6) [RESIST]
Job 9: 4 and mighty in strength—who has **r** him,
Heb 12: 4 In your struggle against sin you have not yet **r** to
Jdt 2:25 and killed everyone who **r** him.
AdE 9: 2 no one **r**, because they feared them.
1Mc 14:29 exposed themselves to danger and **r** the enemies
4Mc 6:30 even in the tortures of death he **r**,

RESISTING (1) [RESIST]
AdE 3: 4 Then they informed Haman that Mordecai was **r**

RESISTS (2) [RESIST]
Ro 13: 2 whoever **r** authority **r** what God has appointed,

RESOLUTE (1) [RESOLVE]
1Ch 28: 7 if he continues **r** in keeping my commandments

RESOLUTELY (2) [RESOLVE]
2Ch 32: 5 Hezekiah set to work **r** and built up the entire wall
3Mc 2:33 They remained **r** hopeful of obtaining help,

RESOLVE (5) [RESOLUTE, RESOLUTELY, RESOLVED, RESOLVES]
Ro 14:13 but **r** instead never to put a stumbling block
1Co 7:37 But if someone stands firm in his **r**,
2Th 1:11 by his power every good **r** and work of faith,
Sir 22:18 with a fool's **r** will not stand firm against any fear.
2Mc 6:23 But making a high **r**, worthy of his years and

RESOLVED (10) [RESOLVE]
Da 1: 8 But Daniel **r** that he would not defile himself with
Mt 1:20 But just when he had **r** to do this,
Ac 19:21 Paul **r** in the Spirit to go through Macedonia
Wis 18: 5 they had **r** to kill the infants of your holy ones,
Sir 22:16 so the mind firmly **r** after due reflection will not
51:18 For I **r** to live according to wisdom,
1Mc 1:62 and were **r** in their hearts not to eat unclean food.
6:19 Judas therefore **r** to destroy them,
14:35 and the glory that he had **r** to win for his nation,
14:41 and their priests have **r** that Simon should

RESOLVES (2) [RESOLVE]
Jn 7:17 Anyone who **r** to do the will of God
4Mc 8:18 why do we take pleasure in vain **r** and venture

RESORT (1) [RESORTED, RESORTING, RESORTS]
Sir 10: 6 and do not **r** to acts of insolence.

RESORTED (2) [RESORT]
2Ch 25:15 "Why have you **r** to a people's gods who could
3Mc 1:23 they **r** to the same posture of supplication as

RESORTING (1) [RESORT]
2Mc 4:34 Andronicus came to Onias, and **r** to treachery,

RESORTS (1) [RESORT]
Am 6: 1 to whom the house of Israel **r**!

RESOUND (3) [RESOUNDED, RESOUNDING, RESOUNDS]
Ex 9:16 and to make my name **r** through all the earth.
Jer 25:31 The clamor will **r** to the ends of the earth,
Mic 2:12 in its pasture; it will **r** with people.

RESOUNDED (3) [RESOUND]
1Sa 4: 5 all Israel gave a mighty shout, so that the earth **r**.
Sir 47:10 and the sanctuary **r** from early morning.
3Mc 6:17 even the nearby valleys **r** with them and brought

RESOUNDING (1) [RESOUND]
2Es 6:13 "Rise to your feet and you will hear a full, **r** voice.

RESOUNDS (1) [RESOUND]
Jer 51:55 the sound of their clamor **r**;

RESOURCE (1) [RESOURCES]
Job 6:13 and any **r** is driven from me.

RESOURCES‡ (6) [RESOURCE]
Ezr 2:69 According to their **r** they gave to
Lk 8: 3 who provided for them out of their **r**.
Ro 15:26 and Achaia have been pleased to share their **r** with
Sir 8: 2 in case their **r** outweigh yours;
Sir 13: 5 he will drain your **r** without a qualm.
44: 6 rich men endowed with **r**, living peacefully

RESPECT‡ (42) [RESPECTABLE, RESPECTED, RESPECTFUL, RESPECTFULLY, RESPECTING, RESPECTIVE, RESPECTS, SELF-RESPECT]
Dt 28:50 a grim-faced nation showing no **r** to the old
Pr 13:13 those who **r** the commandment will be rewarded.
La 5:12 no **r** is shown to the elders.
Da 11:37 He shall pay no **r** to the gods of his ancestors,
11:37 he shall pay no **r** to any other god,
Mal 1: 6 And if I am a master, where is the **r** due me?
Mt 21:37 saying, 'They will **r** my son.'
23: 7 and to be greeted with **r** in the marketplaces,
Mk 12: 6 saying, 'They will **r** my son.'
12:38 and to be greeted with **r** in the marketplaces,
Lk 11:43 in the synagogues and to be greeted with **r** in
18: 2 a judge who neither feared God nor had **r**
18: 4 I have no fear of God and no **r** for anyone,
20:13 send my beloved son; perhaps they will **r** him.'
20:46 and love to be greeted with **r** in the marketplaces,
Ro 13: 7 to whom revenue is due, **r** to whom **r** is due,
1Co 9:19 For though I am free with **r** to all,
12:23 less respectable members are treated with greater **r**
Eph 5:33 and a wife should **r** her husband.
1Th 5:12 to **r** those who labor among you,
Tit 2: 9 and to give satisfaction in every **r**;
Heb 2:17 to become like his brothers and sisters in every **r**,
4:15 but we have one who in every **r** has been tested
Tob 14:13 He treated his parents-in-law with great **r**
AdE 1:22 so that in every house **r** would be shown
8: 9 that he commanded with **r** to the Jews was given
Sir 3: 4 and those who **r** their mother are
3: 6 Those who **r** their father will have long life,
3:11 it is a disgrace for children not to **r** their mother.
20:22 or lose it because of human **r**.
41:16 Therefore show **r** for my words;
Bar 4:15 which had no **r** for the aged and no pity for
2Mc 10:13 Unable to command the **r** due his office,
15: 2 but show **r** for the day
3Mc 3: 4 they kept their separateness with **r** to foods.
2Es 8:48 But even in this **r** you will be praiseworthy before
15:16 they shall in their might have no **r** for their king or
4Mc 5: 7 for I **r** your age and your gray hairs.
5:17 that we should not transgress it in any **r**.
6:35 it masters pleasures and in no **r** yields to them.
8: 5 and greatly **r** the beauty and the number

RESPECTABLE (4) [RESPECT]
1Co 12:23 less **r** members are treated with greater respect;
12:24 whereas our more **r** members do not need this.
1Ti 3: 2 temperate, sensible, **r**, hospitable, an apt teacher,
2Es 16:49 Just as a **r** and virtuous woman abhors a prostitute,

RESPECTED (5) [RESPECT]
Mk 15:43 Joseph of Arimathea, a **r** member of the council,
Ac 5:34 a teacher of the law, **r** by all the people,
Heb 11: 7 **r** the warning and built an ark
12: 9 human parents to discipline us, and we **r** them.
Tob 14:14 He died highly **r** at the age of one hundred

RESPECTER (KJV) See PARTIALITY

RESPECTFUL (1) [RESPECT]
1Ti 3: 4 keeping his children submissive and **r** in every way

RESPECTFULLY (1) [RESPECT]
Sir 21:22 but an experienced person waits **r** outside.

RESPECTING (1) [RESPECT]
4Mc 3:12 two staunch young soldiers, **r** the king's desire,

RESPECTIVE (3) [RESPECT]
Nu 1:52 in their **r** regimental camps, by companies;
2: 2 The Israelites shall camp each in their **r** regiments,
Sir 46:11 The judges also, with their **r** names,

RESPECTS (1) [RESPECT]
Tit 2: 7 Show yourself in all **r** a model of good works,

RESPITE (6)
Ex 8:15 But when Pharaoh saw that there was a **r**,
1Sa 11: 3 of Jabesh said to him, "Give us seven days' **r**
Ps 94:13 giving them **r** from days of trouble,
La 2:18 Give yourself no rest, your eyes no **r**!
3:49 My eyes will flow without ceasing, without **r**,
2Es 10:24 and the Most High may give you rest, a **r**

RESPLENDENT (1)
2Mc 10:29 to the enemy from heaven five **r** men on horses

RESPOND (7) [RESPONDED, RESPONDS, RESPONSE, RESPONSIVELY]
Dt 27:15 All the people shall **r**, saying, "Amen!"
2Sa 24:23 "May the LORD your God **r** favorably to you."
2Ch 32:25 not **r** according to the benefit done to him,

Job 40: 2 Anyone who argues with God must **r**."
Hos 2:15 There she shall **r** as in the days of her youth,
Hab 2:11 and the plaster will **r** from the woodwork.
Rev 16: 7 And I heard the altar **r**, "Yes, O Lord God,

RESPONDED‡ (12) [RESPOND]

Jdg 6:15 He **r**, "But sir, how can I deliver Israel?
1Ki 1:52 So Solomon **r**, "If he proves to be a worthy man,
3:27 the king **r**: "Give the first woman the living boy;
20:34 king of Israel **r**, "I will let you go on those terms."
2Ki 2:10 He **r**, "You have asked a hard thing;
2:16 He **r**, "No, do not send them."
9:18 Jehu **r**, "What have you to do with peace?
Ezr 3:11 the people **r** with a great shout when they praised
Isa 21: 9 Then he **r**, "Fallen, fallen is Babylon;
Da 2:14 Daniel **r** with prudence and discretion to Arioch,
6:13 Then they **r** to the king, "Daniel,
2Mc 1:23 Jonathan led, and the rest **r**, as did Nehemiah.

RESPONDS (1) [RESPOND]

Sir 35:21 it will not desist until the Most High **r**

RESPONSE (6) [RESPOND]

Dt 26: 5 you shall make this **r** before
1Ki 18:29 but there was no voice, no answer, and no **r**.
Joel 2:19 In **r** to his people the LORD said:
Gal 2: 2 I went up in **r** to a revelation.
Jdt 11:15 When the **r** reaches them and they act upon it,
4Mc 6: 1 When Eleazar in this manner had made eloquent **r**

RESPONSIBILITIES (1) [RESPONSIBLE]

Nu 4:28 and their **r** are to be under the oversight

RESPONSIBILITY (10) [RESPONSIBLE]

Nu 3:25 The **r** of the sons of Gershon in the tent
3:31 Their **r** was to be the ark, the table, the lampstand,
3:36 The **r** assigned to the sons of Merari was to be
18: 1 with you shall bear **r** for offenses connected with
18: 1 while you and your sons alone shall bear **r**
18:23 and they shall bear **r** for their own offenses;
Jos 2:19 we shall bear the **r** for their death.
AdE 9:31 on their own **r**, pledging their own well-being to
2Mc 2:28 leaving the **r** for exact details to the compiler,
4:28 for the collection of the revenue was his **r**—

RESPONSIBLE (6) [RESPONSIBILITIES, RESPONSIBILITY]

Ex 21:22 the one **r** shall be fined what
Jos 2:19 they shall be **r** for their own death,
1Sa 22:22 I am **r** for the lives of all your father's house.
Ezr 7:20 which you are **r** for providing,
Ac 20:26 to you this day that I am not **r** for the blood of any
AdE 16: 5 in places of authority have been made in part **r** for

RESPONSIVELY (1) [RESPOND]

Ezr 3:11 and they sang **r**, praising and giving thanks to

REST‡ (364) [RESTED, RESTING, RESTS]

Ge 8: 4 the ark came to **r** on the mountains of Ararat.
9: 2 The fear and dread of you shall **r** on every animal
14:10 and the **r** fled to the hill country.
18: 4 and **r** yourselves under the tree.
30:36 while Jacob was pasturing the **r** of Laban's flock.
42:16 while the **r** of you remain in prison,
42:19 The **r** of you shall go and carry grain for
43:23 He replied, "**R** assured, do not be afraid;
44: 9 the **r** of us will become my lord's slaves."
44:10 but the **r** of you shall go free."
Ex 4: 7 it was restored like the **r** of his body—
16:23 'Tomorrow is a day of solemn **r**,
23:11 the seventh year you shall let it **r** and lie fallow,
23:12 but on the seventh day you shall **r**,
26:32 which have hooks of gold and **r** on four bases
29:12 the **r** of the blood you shall pour out at the base of
29:20 and dash the **r** of the blood against all sides of
31:15 but the seventh day is a sabbath of solemn **r**,
33:14 and I will give you **r**."
34:21 but on the seventh day you shall **r**;
34:21 in plowing time and in harvest time you shall **r**.
35: 2 a holy sabbath of solemn **r** to the LORD;
Lev 4: 7 and the **r** of the blood of the bull he shall pour out
4:12 all the **r** of the bull—
4:18 and the **r** of the blood he shall pour out at the base
4:25 and pour out the **r** of its blood at the base of
4:30 and he shall pour out the **r** of its blood at the base
4:34 pour out the **r** of its blood at the base of the altar.
5: 9 the **r** of the blood shall be drained out at the base
5:13 the **r** shall be for the priest.
8:24 the **r** of the blood against all sides of the altar.
9: 9 and the **r** of the blood he poured out at the base of
14:18 The **r** of the oil that is in
14:29 The **r** of the oil that is in
16:31 It is a sabbath of complete **r** to you,
23: 3 but the seventh day is a sabbath of complete **r**,
23:24 you shall observe a day of complete **r**,
23:32 It shall be to you a sabbath of complete **r**,
23:39 a complete **r** on the first day, and a complete **r** on the eighth day.
25: 4 a sabbath of complete **r** for the land, a sabbath for
25: 5 it shall be a year of complete **r** for the land.
26:34 then the land shall **r**, and enjoy its sabbath years.
26:35 it shall have the **r** it did not have on your sabbaths
Nu 10:36 And whenever it came to **r**, he would say,
18:30 the **r** shall be reckoned to the Levites as produce
Dt 3:13 the half-tribe of Manasseh the **r** of Gilead and all
3:20 When the LORD gives **r** to your kindred,
5:14 your male and female slave may **r** as well as you.
12: 9 not yet come into the **r** and the possession that
12:10 when he gives you **r** from your enemies all around
19:20 The **r** shall hear and be afraid,
25:19 when the LORD your God has given you **r**
Jos 1:13 LORD your God is providing you a place of **r**,
1:15 until the LORD gives **r** to your kindred as well as
3:13 **r** in the waters of the Jordan,
11:23 And the land had **r** from war.
13:22 Along with the **r** of those they put to death,
13:27 the **r** of the kingdom of King Sihon of Heshbon,
14:15 And the land had **r** from war.
17: 2 And allotments were made to the **r** of the tribe
17: 6 of Gilead was allotted to the **r** of the Manassites.
21: 5 The **r** of the Kohathites received by lot ten towns
21:20 As to the **r** of the Kohathites belonging to
21:26 of the families of the **r** of the Kohathites were ten
21:34 To the **r** of the Levites—
21:44 And the LORD gave them **r** on every side just
22: 4 the LORD your God has given **r** to your kindred,
23: 1 when the LORD had given **r** to Israel
Jdg 3:11 So the land had **r** forty years.
3:30 And the land had **r** eighty years.
5:31 And the land had **r** forty years.
7: 6 all the **r** of the troops knelt down to drink water.
7: 8 he sent all the **r** of Israel back to their own tents,
8:28 the land had **r** forty years in the days of Gideon.
Ru 3:18 for the man will not **r**, but will settle the matter
1Sa 13: 2 the **r** of the people he sent home to their tents.
13:15 **r** of the people followed Saul to join the army;
15:15 but the **r** we have utterly destroyed."
2Sa 4: 5 while he was taking his noonday **r**.
7: 1 the LORD had given him **r** from all his enemies
7:11 and I will give you **r** from all your enemies.
10:10 the **r** of his men he put in the charge
12:28 Now, then, gather the **r** of the people together,
14:17 'The word of my lord the king will set me at **r**';
1Ki 5: 4 the LORD my God has given me **r** on every side;
8:56 who has given **r** to his people Israel according
11:41 Now the **r** of the acts of Solomon,
12:23 and to the **r** of the people,
14:19 Now the **r** of the acts of Jeroboam,
14:29 Now the **r** of the acts of Rehoboam,
15: 7 The **r** of the acts of Abijam, and all that he did,
15:23 Now the **r** of all the acts of Asa, all his power,
15:31 Now the **r** of the acts of Nadab, and all that he did,
16: 5 Now the **r** of the acts of Baasha, what he did,
16:14 Now the **r** of the acts of Elah, and all that he did,
16:20 Now the **r** of the acts of Zimri,
16:27 Now the **r** of the acts of Omri that he did,
20:30 The **r** fled into the city of Aphek;
22:39 Now the **r** of the acts of Ahab, and all that he did,
22:45 Now the **r** of the acts of Jehoshaphat,
2Ki 1:18 Now the **r** of the acts of Ahaziah that he did,
4: 7 and you and your children can live on the **r**."
8:23 Now the **r** of the acts of Joram, and all that he did,
10:34 Now the **r** of the acts of Jehu, all that he did,
12:19 Now the **r** of the acts of Joash, and all that he did,
13: 8 the **r** of the acts of Jehoahaz and all that he did,
13:12 Now the **r** of the acts of Joash, and all that he did,
14:15 Now the **r** of the acts that Jehoash did, his might,
14:18 Now the **r** of the deeds of Amaziah,
14:28 Now the **r** of the acts of Jeroboam,
15: 6 Now the **r** of the acts of Azariah,
15:11 Now the **r** of the deeds of Zechariah are written in
15:15 Now the **r** of the deeds of Shallum,
15:21 Now the **r** of the deeds of Menahem,
15:26 Now the **r** of the deeds of Pekahiah,
15:31 Now the **r** of the acts of Pekah, and all that he did,
15:36 Now the **r** of the acts of Jotham,
16:19 Now the **r** of the acts of Ahaz that he did,
20:20 The **r** of the deeds of Hezekiah, all his power,
21:17 Now the **r** of the acts of Manasseh, all that he did,
21:25 Now the **r** of the acts of Amon that he did,
23:18 He said, "Let him **r**; let no one move his bones."
23:28 Now the **r** of the acts of Josiah, and all that he did,
24: 5 Now the **r** of the deeds of Jehoiakim,
25:11 the captain of the guard carried into exile the **r** of
25:11 all the **r** of the population.
1Ch 6:31 after the ark came to **r** there.
6:61 To the **r** of the Kohathites were given by lot out of
6:70 for the **r** of the families of the Kohathites.
6:77 the **r** of the Merarites out of the tribe of Zebulun:
11: 8 and Joab repaired the **r** of the city.
12:38 likewise all the **r** of Israel were of a single mind
16:41 and the **r** of those chosen and expressly named
19:11 the **r** of his troops he put in the charge
23:25 the God of Israel, has given **r** to his people;
24:20 And of the **r** of the sons of Levi:
28: 2 to build a house of **r** for the ark of the covenant of
2Ch 9:29 Now the **r** of the acts of Solomon,
13:22 The **r** of the acts of Abijah,
14: 1 In his days the land had **r** for ten years.
14: 5 And the kingdom had **r** under him.
14: 6 in Judah while the land had **r**.
15:15 and the LORD gave them **r** all around.
20:30 for his God gave him **r** all around.
20:34 Now the **r** of the acts of Jehoshaphat,
24:14 the **r** of the money to the king and Jehoiada,
25:26 Now the **r** of the deeds of Amaziah,
26:22 Now the **r** of the acts of Uzziah, from first to last,
27: 7 Now the **r** of the acts of Jotham,
28:26 Now the **r** of his acts and all his ways,
32:22 he gave them **r** on every side.
2Ch 32:32 Now the **r** of the acts of Hezekiah,
33:18 Now the **r** of the acts of Manasseh,
35:26 the **r** of the acts of Josiah and his faithful deeds
36: 8 Now the **r** of the acts of Jehoiakim,
Ezr 3: 8 together with the **r** of their people,
4: 3 **r** of the heads of families in Israel said to them,
4: 7 the **r** of their associates wrote to King Artaxerxes
4: 9 Shimshai the scribe, and the **r** of their associates,
4:10 and the **r** of the nations whom the great
4:10 in the **r** of the province Beyond the River wrote—
4:17 the **r** of their associates who live in Samaria and in the **r** of the province
6:16 and the **r** of the returned exiles,
7:18 and your colleagues to do with the **r** of the silver
Ne 2:16 the officials, and the **r** that were to do the work.
4:14 the nobles and the officials and the **r** of the people,
4:19 the officials, and the **r** of the people,
6: 1 and Tobiah and to Geshem the Arab and to the **r**
6:14 and also the prophetess Noadiah and the **r** of
7:72 what the **r** of the people gave was twenty thousand
9:28 after they had **r**, they again did evil before you,
10:28 The **r** of the people, the priests, the Levites,
11: 1 the **r** of the people cast lots to bring one out of ten
11:20 And the **r** of Israel, and of the priests and
Est 9:12 in the **r** of the king's provinces?
Job 3:13 then I would be at **r**
3:17 and there the weary are at **r**.
3:26 I am not at ease, nor am I quiet; I have no **r**;
11:18 you will be protected and take your **r** in safety.
30:17 and the pain that gnaws me takes no **r**.
Ps 22: 2 and by night, but find no **r**.
55: 6 I would fly away and be at **r**;
95:11 in my anger I swore, "They shall not enter my **r**."
116: 7 Return, O my soul, to your **r**,
125: 3 of wickedness shall not **r** on the land allotted to
127: 2 It is in vain that you rise up early and go late to **r**,
Pr 6:10 a little slumber, a little folding of the hands to **r**,
21:16 the way of understanding will **r** in the assembly of
24:33 a little slumber, a little folding of the hands to **r**,
29:17 and they will give you **r**;
Ecc 2:23 even at night their minds do not **r**.
6: 5 yet it finds **r** rather than he.
Isa 11: 2 The spirit of the LORD shall **r** on him,
14: 3 When the LORD has given you **r** from your pain
14: 7 The whole earth is at **r** and quiet;
23:12 even there you will have no **r**.
25:10 the hand of the LORD will **r** on this mountain.
28:12 "This is **r**; give **r** to the weary;
30:15 In returning and **r** you shall be saved;
34:14 there too Lilith shall repose, and find a place to **r**.
38:10 I am consigned to the gates of Sheol for the **r**
44:17 The **r** of it he makes into a god, his idol,
44:19 Now shall I make the **r** of it an abomination?
57: 2 those who walk uprightly will **r** on their couches.
60:13 and I will glorify where my feet **r**.
62: 1 and for Jerusalem's sake I will not **r**,
62: 6 You who remind the LORD, take no **r**,
62: 7 and give him no **r** until he establishes Jerusalem
63:14 the spirit of the LORD gave them **r**.
Jer 6:16 and walk in it, and find **r** for your souls.
15: 9 And the **r** of them I will give to the sword
27:19 and the **r** of the vessels that are left in this city,
31: 2 in the wilderness; when Israel sought for **r**,
39: 3 the Rabmag, with all the **r** of the officials of
39: 9 the captain of the guard exiled to Babylon the **r** of
41:10 the **r** of the people who were in Mizpah,
41:16 the leaders of the forces with him took all the **r** of
45: 3 I am weary with my groaning, and I find no **r**."
47: 6 Put yourself into your scabbard, **r** and be still!
50:34 that he may give **r** to the earth,
52:15 of the people and the **r** of the people who were left
52:15 together with the **r** of the artisans.
La 2:18 Give yourself no **r**, your eyes no respite!
5: 5 we are weary, we are given no **r**.
Eze 25:16 and destroy the **r** of the seacoast.
32:19 Be laid to **r** with the uncircumcised!"
32:32 he shall be laid to **r** among the uncircumcised,
34:18 but you must tread down with your feet the **r**
34:18 must you foul the **r** with your feet?
36: 3 you became the possession of the **r** of the nations,
36: 4 of plunder and an object of derision to the **r** of
36: 5 I am speaking in my hot jealousy against the **r** of
44:30 in order that a blessing may **r** on your house.
48:23 As for the **r** of the tribes:
Da 2:18 the **r** of the wise men of Babylon might not perish.
7:12 As for the **r** of the beasts,
7:19 which was different from all the **r**,
12:13 But you, go your way, and **r**;
Mic 2:10 Arise and go; for this is no place to **r**,
5: 3 **r** of his kindred shall return to the people of Israel.
Zep 1:12 and I will punish the people who **r** complacently
Zec 6: 8 toward the north country have set my spirit at **r** in
9: 1 the land of Hadrach and will **r** upon Damascus.
14: 2 **r** of the people shall not be cut off from the city.
Mt 11:28 and I will give you **r**.
11:29 and you will find **r** for your souls.
22: 6 while the **r** seized his slaves,
26:45 "Are you still sleeping and taking your **r**?
Mk 6:31 a deserted place all by yourselves and **r** a while."
14:41 "Are you still sleeping and taking your **r**?
16:13 ⟦And they went back and told the **r**,⟧
Lk 10: 6 your peace will **r** on that person;
12:26 why do you worry about the **r**?
24: 9 they told all this to the eleven and to all the **r**.
Ac 5:13 None of the **r** dared to join them,
7:49 says the Lord, or what is the place of my **r**?
27:44 and the **r** to follow, some on planks and others

Ac 28: 9 the **r** of the people on the island who had diseases
Ro 1:13 among you as I have among the **r** of the Gentiles.
4:16 that the promise may **r** on grace and be guaranteed
11: 7 The elect obtained it, but the **r** were hardened,
1Co 2: 5 that your faith might **r** not on human wisdom but
7:12 To the **r** I say—I and not the Lord—
2Co 2:13 not **r** because I did not find my brother Titus there.
7: 5 we came into Macedonia, our bodies had no **r**,
7:13 because his mind has been set at **r** by all of you.
Gal 3:12 But the law does not **r** on faith;
Php 4: 3 with Clement and the **r** of my co-workers,
1Ti 5:20 so that the **r** also may stand in fear.
Heb 3:11 in my anger I swore, 'They will not enter my **r**.' "
3:18 that they would not enter his **r**,
4: 1 while the promise of entering his **r** is still open,
4: 3 For we who have believed enter that **r**,
4: 3 'They shall not enter my **r**,' "
4: 5 "They shall not enter my **r**."
4: 8 For if Joshua had given them **r**,
4: 9 a sabbath **r** still remains for the people of God;
4:10 for those who enter God's **r** also cease from their
4:11 Let us therefore make every effort to enter that **r**,
1Pe 4: 2 so as to live for the **r** of your earthly life no longer
Rev 2:24 But to the **r** of you in Thyatira,
6:11 They were each given a white robe and told to **r**
9:20 The **r** of humankind, who were not killed
11:13 and the **r** were terrified and gave glory to the God
12:17 and went off to make war on the **r** of her children,
14:11 There is no **r** day or night for those who worship
14:13 says the Spirit, "they will **r** from their labors,
19:21 And the **r** were killed by the sword of the rider on
20: 5 (The **r** of the dead did not come to life until
Tob 1: 7 and the **r** of the fruits to the sons
Jdt 7:18 The **r** of the Assyrian army encamped in the plain,
15: 6 The **r** of the people of Bethulia fell upon
16:21 For the **r** of her life she was honored throughout
AdE 9:17 and made that same day a day of **r**,
9:18 also on the fourteenth, but did not **r**.
12: 1 Now Mordecai took his **r** in the courtyard
Wis 4: 7 the righteous, though they die early, will be at **r**.
8:16 When I enter my house, I shall find **r** with her;
Sir Pr: 2 and the **r** of the books differ not a little when read
5: 6 and his anger will **r** on sinners.
6:28 For at last you will find the **r** she gives,
11:19 "I have found **r**, and now I shall feast
22:11 Weep less bitterly for the dead, for he is at **r**;
22:13 Avoid him and you will find **r**,
28:16 Those who pay heed to slander will not find **r**,
33:26 Set your slave to work, and you will find **r**;
35:21 and it will not **r** until it reaches its goal;
38:23 When the dead is at **r**, let his remembrance **r** too,
39:11 and if he goes to **r**, it is enough for him.
40: 6 He gets little or no **r**;
44:23 he made to **r** on the head of Jacob;
Sus 1:50 And the **r** of the elders said to him, "Come,
Bel 1: 1 King Astyages was laid to **r** with his ancestors,
1Mc 3:11 Many were wounded and fell, and the **r** fled.
3:12 and used it in battle the **r** of his life.
3:24 and the **r** fled into the land of the Philistines.
5:18 a leader of the people, with the **r** of the forces,
6:38 The **r** of the cavalry were stationed on either side,
6:54 the **r** scattered to their own homes,
7:32 and the **r** fled into the city of David.
7:42 let the **r** learn that Nicanor has spoken wickedly
7:50 So the land of Judah had **r** for a few days.
8: 4 the **r** paid them tribute every year.
9:18 Judas also fell, and the **r** fled.
9:22 Now the **r** of the acts of Judas,
9:40 and the **r** fled to the mountain;
9:57 and the land of Judah had **r** for two years.
12: 6 and the **r** of the Jewish people to their brothers
14: 4 The land had **r** all the days of Simon.
14:20 and the priests and the **r** of the Jewish people,
16: 8 many of them fell wounded and the **r** fled into
16:23 The **r** of the acts of John and his wars and
2Mc 1:23 Jonathan led, and the **r** responded,
4:42 and killed some, and put all the **r** to flight;
7: 4 the **r** of the brothers and the mother looked on.
8:28 the **r** among themselves and their children.
8:31 the **r** of the spoils they carried to Jerusalem.
10:36 Others broke open the gates and let in the **r** of
11:11 and forced all the **r** to flee.
14:11 When he had said this, the **r** of the king's Friends,
15: 1 with complete safety on the day of **r**.
1Es 2:16 the scribe Shimshai, and the **r** of their associates,
5: 8 and who returned to Jerusalem and the **r** of Judea,
7: 6 and the **r** of those who returned
2Es 2:24 my people, because your **r** will come.
2:34 he will give you everlasting **r**,
7:*32* and the dust those who **r** there in silence;
7:*36* and opposite it shall be the place of **r**;
7:*38* here are delight and **r**, and there are fire
7:*75* in **r** until those times come when you will renew
7:*91* for they shall have **r** in seven orders.
7:*95* they understand the **r** that they now enjoy,
8:52 plenty is provided, a city is built, **r** is appointed,
10:24 and the Most High may give you **r**,
11: 4 But its heads were at **r**;
11: 4 but it too was at **r** with them.
11:23 the three heads that were at **r** and six little wings.
11:29 one of the heads that were at **r** (the one that was in
12:22 "As for your seeing three heads at **r**,
4Mc 3: 9 Now all the **r** were at supper,

RESTED (21) [REST]

Ge 2: 2 and he **r** on the seventh day from all the work
2: 3 on it God **r** from all the work that he had done
Ex 16:30 So the people **r** on the seventh day.
20:11 and all that is in them, but **r** the seventh day;
31:17 and on the seventh day he **r**, and was refreshed."
Nu 9:18 As long as the cloud **r** over the tabernacle,
11:25 and when the spirit **r** upon them, they prophesied.
11:26 and the spirit **r** on them;
Jdg 1:35 the hand of the house of Joseph **r** heavily on them,
16:29 the two middle pillars on which the house **r**,
Est 9:17 on the fourteenth day they **r** and made that a day
9:18 and **r** on the fifteenth day,
Eze 9: 3 up from the cherub on which it **r** to the threshold
Am 5:19 went into the house and **r** a hand against the wall,
Lk 2:25 and the Holy Spirit **r** on him.
23:56 the sabbath they **r** according to the commandment.
Ac 2: 3 and a tongue **r** on each of them.
Heb 4: 4 God **r** on the seventh day from all his works."
Jdt 1:16 and there he and his forces **r** and feasted
AdE 9:17 the fourteenth day they **r** and made that same day
Sir 47:23 Solomon **r** with his ancestors,

RESTING‡ (20) [REST]

Ge 49:15 a **r** place was good, and that the land was pleasant;
Nu 9:22 **r** upon it, the Israelites would remain in camp
10:33 to seek out a **r** place for them,
Dt 28:65 no **r** place for the sole of your foot.
Ru 2: 7 without **r** even for a moment."
2Ch 6:41 rise up, O LORD God, and go to your **r** place,
Job 16:18 let my outcry find no **r** place.
Ps 132: 8 Rise up, O LORD, and go to your **r** place,
132:14 "This is my **r** place forever;
Isa 32:18 in secure dwellings, and in quiet **r** places.
66: 1 for me, and what is my **r** place?
Jer 33:12 be pasture for shepherds **r** their flocks.
La 1: 3 now among the nations, and finds no **r** place;
Mt 12:43 through waterless regions looking for a **r** place,
Lk 11:24 through waterless regions looking for a **r** place,
1Pe 4:14 which is the Spirit of God, is **r** on you.
Jdt 10:21 Holofernes was **r** on his bed under a canopy
Sir 24: 7 Among all these I sought a **r** place;
24:11 Thus in the beloved city he gave me a **r** place,
Bar 2:24 be brought out of their **r** place;

RESTITUTION (15)

Ex 21:34 the owner of the pit shall make **r**,
22: 1 The thief shall make **r**, but if unable to do so,
22: 5 **r** shall be made from the best in the owner's field
22: 6 the one who started the fire shall make full **r**.
22:11 the owner shall accept the oath, and no **r** shall
22:12 But if it was stolen, **r** shall be made to its owner.
22:13 **r** shall not be made for the mangled remains.
22:14 the owner not being present, full **r** shall be made.
22:15 If the owner was present, there shall be no **r**;
Lev 5:16 And you shall make **r** for the holy thing
24:18 Anyone who kills an animal shall make **r** for it,
24:21 One who kills an animal shall make **r** for it;
Nu 5: 7 The person shall make full **r** for the wrong,
5: 8 no next of kin to whom **r** may be made
5: 8 the **r** for wrong shall go to the LORD for the priest,

RESTIVE (1)

Jer 2:23 a **r** young camel interlacing her tracks,

RESTLESS (1)

Jas 3: 8 a **r** evil, full of deadly poison.

RESTORATION (2) [RESTORE]

Ac 3:21 of universal **r** that God announced long ago
1Mc 14:34 in those towns whatever was necessary for their **r**.

RESTORE‡ (78) [RESTORATION, RESTORED, RESTORER, RESTORES, RESTORING]

Ge 20: 7 But if you do not **r** her
37:22 of their hand and **r** him to his father.
40:13 up your head and **r** you to your office;
Ex 21:36 the owner shall **r** ox for ox,
22:26 you shall **r** it before the sun goes down;
Lev 6: 4 and would **r** what you took by robbery or by fraud
Dt 30: 3 then the LORD your God will **r** your fortunes
Jdg 11:13 now therefore **r** it peaceably."
1Sa 12: 3 Testify against me and I will **r** it to you."
2Sa 8: 3 he went to **r** his monument at the river Euphrates.
9: 7 I will **r** to you all the land
12: 6 he shall **r** the lamb fourfold,
1Ki 12:21 to **r** the kingdom to Rehoboam son of Solomon.
20:34 "I will **r** the towns that my father took
2Ki 8: 6 saying, "**R** all that was hers,
2Ch 11: 1 to **r** the kingdom to Rehoboam.
24: 4 Some time afterward Joash decided to **r** the house
24:12 and carpenters to **r** the house of the LORD,
Ne 4: 2 are these feeble Jews doing? Will they **r** things?
5:11 **R** to them, this very day, their fields,
5:12 "We will **r** everything and demand nothing more
Job 8: 6 surely then he will rouse himself for you and **r**
Ps 51:12 **R** to me the joy of your salvation,
60: 1 you have been angry; now **r** us!
69: 4 What I did not steal must I now **r**?
80: 3 **R** us, O God; let your face shine,
80: 7 **R** us, O God of hosts;
80:19 **R** us, O LORD God of hosts;
85: 4 **R** us again, O God of our salvation,
126: 4 **R** our fortunes, O LORD,
Isa 1:26 And I will **r** your judges as at the first,
38:16 Oh, **r** me to health and make me live!
42:22 a spoil with no one to say, "**R!**"
49: 6 the tribes of Jacob and to **r** the survivors of Israel;
Jer 27:22 Then I will bring them up and **r** them to this place.
29:14 and I will **r** your fortunes and gather you from all
30: 3 when I will **r** the fortunes of my people,
30:17 For I will **r** health to you,
30:18 I am going to **r** the fortunes of the tents of Jacob,
31:23 of Judah and in its towns when I **r** their fortunes:
32:44 for I will **r** their fortunes, says the LORD.
33: 7 I will **r** the fortunes of Judah and the fortunes
33:11 For I will **r** the fortunes of the land as at first,
33:26 For I will **r** their fortunes,
42:12 and he will have mercy on you and **r** you
48:47 Yet I will **r** the fortunes of Moab in the latter days,
49: 6 afterward I will **r** the fortunes of the Ammonites,
49:39 But in the latter days I will **r** the fortunes of Elam,
50:19 I will **r** Israel to its pasture,
La 2:14 not exposed your iniquity to **r** your fortunes,
5:21 **R** us to yourself, O LORD,
Eze 16:53 I will **r** their fortunes, the fortunes of Sodom
16:53 and I will **r** your own fortunes along with theirs,
18:12 does not **r** the pledge, lifts up his eyes to the idols,
29:14 and I will **r** the fortunes of Egypt,
33:15 if the wicked **r** the pledge,
39:25 Now I will **r** the fortunes of Jacob,
Da 9:25 the word went out to **r** and rebuild Jerusalem until
Hos 6:11 When I would **r** the fortunes of my people,
Joel 3: 1 when I **r** the fortunes of Judah and Jerusalem,
Am 9:14 I will **r** the fortunes of my people Israel,
Zep 2: 7 be mindful of them and **r** their fortunes.
3:20 when I **r** your fortunes before your eyes,
Zec 9:12 today I declare that I will **r** to you double.
Mt 17:11 "Elijah is indeed coming and will **r** all things;
Mk 9:12 "Elijah is indeed coming first to **r** all things.
Ac 1: 6 the time when you will **r** the kingdom to Israel?"
Gal 6: 1 you who have received the Spirit should **r** such
1Th 3:10 to face and **r** whatever is lacking in your faith.
Heb 6: 4 For it is impossible to **r** again
1Pe 5:10 will himself **r**, support, strengthen,
AdE 13: 2 to **r** the peace desired by all people.
Sir 48:10 and to **r** the tribes of Jacob.
LtJ 6:37 They cannot **r** sight to the blind;
1Mc 3:43 "Let us **r** the ruins of our people,
10:10 in Jerusalem and began to rebuild and **r** the city.
15: 3 the kingdom so that I may **r** it as it formerly was,
2Mc 12:25 to **r** them unharmed, they let him go, for the sake

RESTORED (52) [RESTORE]

Ge 20:14 and **r** his wife Sarah to him.
40:21 He **r** the chief cupbearer to his cupbearing,
41:13 I was **r** to my office, and the baker was hanged."
Ex 4: 7 it was **r** like the rest of his body—
Dt 28:31 and shall not be **r** to you.
1Sa 7:14 from Israel were **r** to Israel, from Ekron to Gath;
1Ki 13: 6 and pray for me, so that my hand may be **r** to me."
13: 6 and the king's hand was **r** to him,
2Ki 5:10 and your flesh shall be **r** and you shall be clean."
5:14 his flesh was **r** like the flesh of a young boy,
8: 1 to the woman whose son he had **r** to life, "Get up
8: 5 the king how Elisha had **r** a dead person to life,
8: 5 the woman whose son he had **r** to life appealed to
8: 5 and here is her son whom Elisha **r** to life."
14:22 He rebuilt Elath and **r** it to Judah,
14:25 He **r** the border of Israel from Lebo-hamath as far
2Ch 24:13 and they **r** the house of God to its proper condition
26: 2 He rebuilt Eloth and **r** it to Judah,
29:35 Thus the service of the house of the LORD was **r**.
33:13 and **r** him again to Jerusalem and to his kingdom.
33:16 He also **r** the altar of the LORD and offered
Ezr 6: 5 be **r** and brought back to the temple in Jerusalem,
Ne 3: 8 and they **r** Jerusalem as far as the Broad Wall.
Job 22:23 If you return to the Almighty, you will be **r**,
42:10 And the LORD **r** the fortunes of Job
Ps 30: 3 **r** me to life from among those gone down to
68: 9 you **r** your heritage when it languished;
85: 1 you **r** the fortunes of Jacob.
126: 1 When the LORD **r** the fortunes of Zion,
Jer 8:22 then has the health of my poor people not been **r**?
La 5:21 O LORD, that we may be **r**;
Eze 38: 8 in the latter years you shall go against a land **r**
Da 4:36 and my majesty and splendor were **r** to me for
8:14 then the sanctuary shall be **r** to its rightful state."
Mt 5:13 if salt has lost its taste, how can its saltiness be **r**?
12:13 He stretched it out, and it was **r**,
Mk 3: 5 He stretched it out, and his hand was **r**.
8:25 and he looked intently and his sight was **r**,
Lk 6:10 He did so, and his hand was **r**.
14:34 if salt has lost its taste, how can its saltiness be **r**?
Ac 9:18 like scales fell from his eyes, and his sight was **r**.
Phm 1:22 I am hoping through your prayers to be **r** to you.
Heb 13:19 so that I may be **r** to you very soon.
Tob 2: 1 my wife Anna and my son Tobias were **r** to me.
11:17 to him and had **r** his sight.
1Mc 4:57 they **r** the gates and the chambers for the priests,
9:72 He **r** to him the captives whom he had taken
2Mc 5:20 of the Almighty was **r** again in all its glory when
11:25 our decision is that their temple be **r** to them and
1Es 6:26 should be **r** to the house in Jerusalem,
3Mc 6: 8 watched over and **r** unharmed to all his family.
7:22 so that those who held any of it **r** it to them

RESTORER (2) [RESTORE]

Ru 4:15 to you a **r** of life and a nourisher of your old age;
Isa 58:12 the **r** of streets to live in.

RESTORES (4) [RESTORE]
Ps 14: 7 When the LORD **r** the fortunes of his people,
23: 3 he **r** my soul. He leads me in right paths
53: 6 When God **r** the fortunes of his people,
Eze 18: 7 but **r** to the debtor his pledge,

RESTORING (3) [RESTORE]
2Ch 34:10 the house of the LORD gave it for repairing and **r**
Na 2: 2 (For the LORD is **r** the majesty of Jacob,
1Mc 10:44 of rebuilding and **r** the structures of the sanctuary

RESTRAIN (13) [RESTRAINED, RESTRAINING, RESTRAINS, RESTRAINT]
1Sa 3:13 and he did not **r** them.
Job 7:11 "Therefore I will not **r** my mouth;
37: 4 not **r** the lightnings when his voice is heard.
Pr 27:16 to **r** her is to **r** the wind or to grasp oil in
Ecc 8: 8 No one has power over the wind to **r** the wind,
Isa 48: 9 for the sake of my praise I **r** it for you,
64:12 After all this, will you **r** yourself, O LORD?
Jer 2:24 Who can **r** her lust?
Mk 3:21 When his family heard it, they went out to **r** him,
5: 3 no one could **r** him any more, even with a chain;
AdE 16:12 But, unable to **r** his arrogance,
Sir 18:30 not follow your base desires, but **r** your appetites.

RESTRAINED (23) [RESTRAIN]
Ge 8: 2 the rain from the heavens was **r**,
Ex 21:29 and its owner has been warned but has not **r** it,
21:36 and its owner has not **r** it,
36: 6 So the people were **r** from bringing;
1Sa 25:26 since the LORD has **r** you from bloodguilt and
25:34 who has **r** me from hurting you,
2Sa 18:16 from pursuing Israel, for Joab **r** the troops.
Est 5:10 nevertheless Haman **r** himself and went home.
Ps 40: 9 see, I have not **r** my lips, as you know, O LORD.
78:38 he **r** his anger, and did not stir up all his wrath.
Pr 10:19 but the prudent are **r** in speech.
Isa 42:14 I have kept still and **r** myself;
Jer 14:10 to wander, they have not **r** their feet;
Eze 31:15 I **r** its rivers, and its mighty waters were checked.
Mk 5: 4 for he had often been **r** with shackles and chains,
Ac 14:18 they scarcely **r** the crowds from offering sacrifice
2Pe 2:16 with a human voice and **r** the prophet's madness.
Wis 16:18 At one time the flame was **r**,
Sir 46: 7 they opposed the congregation, **r** the people
Bel 1:19 But Daniel laughed and **r** the king from going in.
3Mc 1:23 and being barely **r** by the old men and the elders,
2Es 7:*116* [46] or else, when it had produced him, had **r** him
4Mc 1:35 For the emotions of the appetites are **r**,

RESTRAINING (2) [RESTRAIN]
2Th 2: 6 And you know what is now **r** him,
4Mc 1:30 over the emotions by virtue of the **r** power

RESTRAINS (2) [RESTRAIN]
Job 30:13 they promote my calamity; no one **r** them.
2Th 2: 7 but only until the one who now **r** it is removed.

RESTRAINT‡ (9) [RESTRAIN]
2Ch 28:19 without **r** in Judah and had been faithless to
Est 1: 8 Drinking was by flagons, without **r**;
Job 30:11 they have cast off **r** in my presence.
Pr 6:34 and he shows no **r** when he takes revenge.
14:16 but the fool throws off **r** and is careless.
29:18 Where there is no prophecy, the people cast off **r**,
1Co 7:35 not to put any **r** upon you,
AdE 13: 6 by the swords of their enemies, without pity or **r**,
Sir 37:29 and do not eat without **r**;

RESTRICTION (1)
2Co 6:12 There is no **r** in our affections, but only in yours.

RESTRICTED See Index to Footnotes

RESTS‡ (17) [REST]
Dt 33:12 The beloved of the LORD **r** in safety—
33:12 the beloved **r** between his shoulders.
Jdg 16:26 "Let me feel the pillars on which the house **r**,
1Ki 10:19 arm **r** and two lions standing beside the arm **r**,
2Ki 2:15 they declared, "The spirit of Elijah **r** on Elisha."
2Ch 9:18 arm **r** and two lions standing beside the arm **r**,
Ps 16: 9 and my soul rejoices; my body also **r** secure.
62: 7 On God **r** my deliverance and my honor;
Pr 19:23 filled with it one **r** secure and suffers no harm.
Isa 9: 6 authority **r** upon his shoulders;
Jdt 8:24 and the altar—**r** upon us.
Sir 20:21 so when he **r** he feels no remorse.
31: 3 and when he **r** he fills himself with his dainties.
31: 4 and if ever he **r** he becomes needy.
40: 5 And when one **r** upon his bed,

RESULT (18) [RESULTED, RESULTS]
Ge 38:24 moreover she is pregnant as a **r** of whoredom."
1Sa 18: 5 as a **r**, Saul set him over the army.
Isa 32:17 and the **r** of righteousness,
Jer 27:10 the **r** that you will be removed far from your land;
27:15 the **r** that I will drive you out and you will perish,
Ro 5:20 with the **r** that the trespass multiplied;
Eph 2: 9 not the **r** of works, so that no one may boast.
1Pe 1: 7 may be found to **r** in praise and glory and honor
Wis 1:11 because no secret word is without **r**,
Sir 20: 9 and a windfall may **r** in a loss.
38:18 For grief may **r** in death,
2Mc 4:42 As a **r**, they wounded many of them,
7:12 As a **r** the king himself and those
9: 2 with the **r** that Antiochus was put to flight by
10:13 As a **r** he was accused before Eupator by
12:42 with their own eyes what had happened as the **r** of
3Mc 5:41 **r** the city is in a tumult because of its expectation;
4Mc 12: 3 "You see the **r** of your brothers' stupidity,

RESULTED (3) [RESULT]
Nu 25:18 she was killed on the day of the plague that **r**
3Mc 1: 4 a bitter fight **r**, and matters were turning out rather
1:28 of the crowds **r** in an immense uproar;

RESULTS (1) [RESULT]
Sir 7:13 for it is a habit that **r** in no good.

RESUME (1) [RESUMED]
Dt 1: 7 **R** your journey, and go into the hill country of

RESUMED (2) [RESUME]
Jdg 18:21 So they **r** their journey, putting the little ones,
4Mc 8:13 and wedges and bellows, the tyrant **r** speaking:

RESURRECTION (45)
Mt 22:23 Sadducees came to him, saying there is no **r**;
22:28 In the **r**, then, whose wife of the seven
22:30 the **r** they neither marry nor are given in marriage,
22:31 And as for the **r** of the dead,
27:53 After his **r** they came out of the tombs and entered
Mk 12:18 Some Sadducees, who say there is no **r**,
12:23 In the **r** whose wife will she be?
Lk 14:14 for you will be repaid at the **r** of the righteous."
20:27 Some Sadducees, those who say there is no **r**,
20:33 In the **r**, therefore, whose wife will
20:35 in the **r** from the dead neither marry nor are given
20:36 and are children of God, being children of the **r**.
Jn 5:29 those who have done good, to the **r** of life,
5:29 of life, and those who have done evil, to the **r**
11:24 that he will rise again in the **r** on the last day."
11:25 Jesus said to her, "I am the **r** and the life.
Ac 1:22 of these must become a witness with us to his **r**."
2:31 David spoke of the **r** of the Messiah, saying,
4: 2 and proclaiming that in Jesus there is the **r** of
4:33 the apostles gave their testimony to the **r** of
17:18 the good news about Jesus and the **r**.)
17:32 they heard of the **r** of the dead, some scoffed;
23: 6 on trial concerning the hope of the **r** of the dead."
23: 8 (The Sadducees say that there is no **r**, or angel,
24:15 be a **r** of both the righteous and the unrighteous.
24:21 'It is about the **r** of the dead that I am on trial
Ro 1: 4 with power according to the spirit of holiness by **r**
6: 5 we will certainly be united with him in a **r** like his.
1Co 15:12 can some of you say there is no **r** of the dead?
15:13 If there is no **r** of the dead,
15:21 the **r** of the dead has also come through
15:42 So it is with the **r** of the dead.
Php 3:10 the power of his **r** and the sharing of his sufferings
3:11 if somehow I may attain the **r** from the dead.
2Ti 2:18 by claiming that the **r** has already taken place.
Heb 6: 2 **r** of the dead, and eternal judgment.
11:35 Women received their dead by **r**.
11:35 in order to obtain a better **r**.
1Pe 1: 3 a living hope through the **r** of Jesus Christ from
3:21 through the **r** of Jesus Christ,
Rev 20: 5 This is the first **r**.
20: 6 Blessed and holy are those who share in the first **r**.
2Mc 7:14 But for you there will be no **r** to life!"
12:43 and honorably, taking account of the **r**.
2Es 2:23 and I will give you the first place in my **r**.

RETAIN (7) [RETAINED, RETAINING]
Nu 36: 7 for all Israelites shall **r** the inheritance
36: 9 of the Israelites shall **r** its own inheritance.' "
Da 10:16 upon me that I **r** no strength.
11: 6 But she shall not **r** her power,
Am 2:14 and the strong shall not **r** their strength,
Mic 7:18 He does not **r** his anger forever,
Jn 20:23 if you **r** the sins of any, they are retained."

RETAINED (5) [RETAIN]
Jdg 7: 8 the rest of Israel back to their own tents, but **r**
Da 10: 8 complexion grew deathly pale, and I **r** no strength.
Jn 20:23 if you retain the sins of any, they are **r**."
Wis 19:20 Fire even in water **r** its normal power,
2Es 14:40 for my spirit **r** its memory,

RETAINING (1) [RETAIN]
Sir 50: 2 the high **r** walls for the temple enclosure.

RETALIATING (1)
1Ki 2: 5 **r** in time of peace for blood that had been shed

RETINUE (4)
1Ki 10: 2 She came to Jerusalem with a very great **r**,
2Ch 9: 1 having a very great **r** and camels bearing spices
2Mc 3:28 with a great **r** and all his bodyguard but was
4Mc 6:13 some of the king's **r** came to him and said,

RETIRE (2)
Nu 8:25 the age of fifty years they shall **r** from the duty of
Tob 8: 1 finished eating and drinking they wanted to **r**;

RETORT (1) [RETORTED]
Ps 38:14 and in whose mouth is no **r**.

RETORTED (1) [RETORT]
Tob 5:10 But Tobit **r**, "What joy is left for me any more?

RETREAT (6) [RETREATED]
Jdg 20:32 "Let us **r** and draw them away from the city
2Ki 19:23 I entered its farthest **r**, its densest forest.
20: 9 advanced ten intervals; shall it **r** ten intervals?"
20:10 rather let the shadow **r** ten intervals."
Ps 56: 9 Then my enemies will **r** in the day when I call.
2Mc 9: 2 to flight by the inhabitants and beat a shameful **r**.

RETREATED (1) [RETREAT]
2Mc 9: 1 Antiochus had **r** in disorder from the region

RETRIBUTION (11)
Isa 66: 6 The voice of the LORD, dealing **r** to his enemies!
Jer 5: 9 and shall I not bring **r** on a nation such as this?
5:29 and shall I not bring **r** on a nation such as this?
9: 9 and shall I not bring **r** on a nation such as this?
11:20 let me see your **r** upon them,
15:15 and bring down **r** for me on my persecutors.
20:12 let me see your **r** upon them,
46:10 a day of **r**, to gain vindication from his foes.
Ro 11: 9 a stumbling block and a **r** for them;
Sir 7:16 remember that **r** does not delay.
48: 8 You anointed kings to inflict **r**,

RETURN‡ (275) [RETURNED, RETURNING, RETURNS]
Ge 3:19 you **r** to the ground, for out of it you were taken;
3:19 you are dust, and to dust you shall **r**."
8:12 and it did not **r** to him any more.
14:17 After his **r** from the defeat of Chedorlaomer and
16: 9 "**R** to your mistress, and submit to her."
18:10 one said, "I will surely **r** to you in due season,
18:14 At the set time I will **r** to you, in due season,
20: 7 Now then, **r** the man's wife;
29:27 also in **r** for serving me another seven years."
31: 3 "**R** to the land of your ancestors and
31:13 Now leave this land at once and **r** to the land
32: 9 '**R** to your country and to your kindred,
42:25 to **r** every man's money to his sack,
50: 5 that I may bury my father; then I will **r**."
Ex 13:17 they may change their minds and **r** to Egypt."
33:11 Then he would **r** to the camp;
Lev 24:19 maims another shall suffer the same injury in **r**:
25:10 It shall be a jubilee for you: you shall **r**,
25:13 In this year of jubilee you shall **r**,
25:41 they shall go back to their own family and **r**
27:24 In the year of jubilee the field shall **r** to the one
Nu 10:36 And whenever it came to rest, he would say, "**R**,
18:21 a possession in **r** for the service that they perform,
22:34 if it is displeasing to you, I will **r** home."
23: 5 "**R** to Balak, and this is what you must say."
23:16 put a word into his mouth, and said, "**R** to Balak,
32:18 We will not **r** to our homes until all
32:22 then after that you may **r** and be free of obligation
35:28 the death of the high priest the slayer may **r** home.
35:32 the fugitive to **r** to live in the land before the death
Dt 3:20 of you may **r** to the property that I have given
4:30 you will **r** to the LORD your God and heed him.
5:30 Go say to them, '**R** to your tents.'
17:16 or **r** the people to Egypt in order
17:16 "You must never **r** that way again."
22: 2 until the owner claims it; then you shall **r** it.
30: 2 and **r** to the LORD your God,
Jos 1:15 Then you shall **r** to your own land
20: 6 then the slayer may **r** home,
Jdg 6:18 And he said, "I will stay until you **r**."
7: 3 and trembling, let him **r** home.' "
8:35 in **r** for all the good that he had done to Israel.
11:31 when I **r** victorious from the Ammonites,
17: 2 but now I will **r** it to you."
20: 8 nor will any of us **r** to our houses.
Ru 1: 6 to **r** with her daughters-in-law from the country
1:10 "No, we will **r** with you to your people."
1:15 **r** after your sister-in-law."
1Sa 2:20 and then they would **r** to their home.
5:11 and let it **r** to its own place,
6: 3 but by all means **r** him a guilt offering.
6: 4 "What is the guilt offering that we shall **r** to him?"
8:22 to the people of Israel, "Each of you **r** home."
15:25 therefore, I pray, pardon my sin, and **r** with me,
15:26 Samuel said to Saul, "I will not **r** with you;
15:30 the elders of my people and before Israel, and **r**
17:57 On David's **r** from killing the Philistine,
18: 2 Saul took him that day and would not let him **r**
29: 4 that he may **r** to the place that you have assigned
29:11 to **r** to the land of the Philistines.
2Sa 1:22 nor the sword of Saul **r** empty.
10: 5 until your beards have grown, and then **r**."
12:23 I shall go to him, but he will not **r** to me."
15:34 But if you **r** to the city and say to Absalom,
19:14 "**R**, both you and all your servants."
19:37 Please let your servant **r**, so that I may die
24:13 and decide what answer I shall **r** to

1Ki 12:27 they will kill me and **r** to King Rehoboam
13: 9 or drink water, or **r** by the way that you came."
13:10 did not **r** by the way that he had come to Bethel.
13:16 he said, "I cannot **r** with you, or go in with you;
13:17 or **r** by the way that you came."
19:15 **r** on your way to the wilderness of Damascus;
22:26 and **r** him to Amon the governor of the city and
22:28 Micaiah said, "If you **r** in peace,
2Ki 19: 7 that he shall hear a rumor and **r** to his own land;
19:33 By the way that he came, by the same he shall **r;**
1Ch 19: 5 until your beards have grown, and then **r."**
21:12 Now decide what answer I shall **r** to
2Ch 11: 4 Let everyone **r** home, for this thing is from me."
18:25 and **r** him to Amon the governor of the city and
18:26 on reduced rations of bread and water until I **r**
18:27 Micaiah said, "If you **r** in peace,
24:11 the chest and take it and **r** it to its place.
30: 6 **r** to the LORD, the God of Abraham, Isaac,
30: 9 For as you **r** to the LORD,
30: 9 with their captors, and **r** to this land.
30: 9 not turn away his face from you, if you **r** to him."
Ne 1: 9 but if you **r** to me and keep my commandments
2: 6 be gone, and when will you **r?"**
9:17 but they stiffened their necks and determined to **r**
Job 1:21 and naked shall I **r** there;
7:10 they **r** no more to their houses,
10:21 before I go, never to **r,** to the land of gloom
16:22 I shall go the way from which I shall not **r.**
22:23 If you **r** to the Almighty, you will be restored,
33:25 let him **r** to the days of his youthful vigor.'
34:15 and all mortals **r** to dust.
36:10 and commands that they **r** from iniquity.
39: 4 they go forth, and do not **r** to them.
39:12 Do you have faith in it that it will **r,**
Ps 51:13 and sinners will **r** to you.
60: T *Joab on his r killed twelve thousand Edomites*
79:12 **R** sevenfold into the bosom of our neighbors
94:15 for justice will **r** to the righteous,
104:29 they die and **r** to their dust.
109: 4 In **r** for my love they accuse me,
116: 7 **R,** O my soul, to your rest,
116:12 What shall I **r** to the LORD for all his bounty
146: 4 When their breath departs, they **r** to the earth;
Ecc 12: 2 and the stars are darkened and the clouds **r** with
SS 6:13 **R, r,** O Shulammite! **R, r,** that we may look upon
Isa 10:21 A remnant will **r,** the remnant of Jacob,
10:22 only a remnant of them will **r.**
19:22 they will **r** to the LORD,
23:17 and she will **r** to her trade,
35:10 And the ransomed of the LORD shall **r,**
37: 7 and **r** to his own land;
37:34 By the way that he came, by the same he shall **r;**
43: 4 and I love you, I give people in **r** for you,
44:22 **r** to me, for I have redeemed you.
45:23 in righteousness a word that shall not **r:**
51:11 So the ransomed of the LORD shall **r,**
52: 8 in plain sight they see the **r** of the LORD to Zion.
55: 7 let them **r** to the LORD,
55:10 do not **r** there until they have watered the earth,
55:11 it shall not **r** to me empty,
Jer 3: 1 and becomes another man's wife, will he **r** to her?
3: 1 and would you **r** to me?
3: 7 "After she has done all this she will **r** to me";
3: 7 but she did not **r,** and her false sister Judah saw it.
3:10 for all this her false sister Judah did not **r** to me
3:12 **R,** faithless Israel, says the LORD.
3:14 **R,** O faithless children, says the LORD,
3:22 **R,** O faithless children, I will heal your
4: 1 If you **r,** O Israel, says the LORD, if you **r** to me,
8: 5 to deceit, they have refused to **r.**
14: 3 they **r** with their vessels empty.
22:10 for he shall **r** no more to see his native land.
22:11 He shall **r** here no more,
22:27 they shall not **r** to the land to which they long to **r.**
24: 7 for they shall **r** to me with their whole heart.
30:10 Jacob shall **r** and have quiet and ease,
31: 8 a great company, they shall **r** here.
31:21 **R,** O virgin Israel, **r** to these your cities.
37: 7 is going to **r** to its own land, to Egypt.
37: 8 the Chaldeans shall **r** and fight against this city;
40: 5 then **r** to Gedaliah son of Ahikam son of Shaphan,
44:14 in the land of Egypt shall escape or survive or **r** to
44:28 And those who escape the sword shall **r** from
46:27 Jacob shall **r** and have quiet and ease,
50: 9 of a skilled warrior who does not **r** empty-handed.
50:16 because of the destroying sword all of them shall **r**
La 3:40 and examine our ways, and **r** to the LORD.
Eze 7:13 the sellers shall not **r** to what has been sold as long
16:55 and her daughters shall **r** to their former state,
16:55 and her daughters shall **r** to their former state,
16:55 and your daughters shall **r** to your former state.
17:19 surely **r** upon his head my oath that he despised,
21:30 **R** it to its sheath!
46: 9 not **r** by way of the gate by which they entered,
Da 10:20 Now I must **r** to fight against the prince of Persia,
11: 9 but will **r** to his own land.
11:28 He shall **r** to his land with great wealth,
11:28 He shall work his will, and **r** to his own land.
11:29 "At the time appointed he shall **r** and come into
Hos 2: 7 she shall say, "I will go and **r** to my first husband,
3: 5 Afterward the Israelites shall **r** and seek
5: 4 Their deeds do not permit them to **r** to their God.
5:15 I will **r** again to my place
6: 1 let us **r** to the LORD;
7:10 yet they do not **r** to the LORD their God,
8:13 and punish their sins; they shall **r** to Egypt.
9: 3 but Ephraim shall **r** to Egypt,
Hos 11: 5 They shall **r** to the land of Egypt,
11: 5 because they have refused to **r** to me.
11:11 and I will **r** them to their homes, says the LORD.
12: 6 But as for you, **r** to your God,
14: 1 **R,** O Israel, to the LORD your God,
14: 2 Take words with you and **r** to the LORD;
Joel 2:12 now, says the LORD, **r** to me with all your heart,
2:13 **R** to the LORD, your God,
Am 4: 6 yet you did not **r** to me, says the LORD.
4: 8 yet you did not **r** to me, says the LORD.
4: 9 yet you did not **r** to me, says the LORD.
4:10 yet you did not **r** to me, says the LORD.
4:11 yet you did not **r** to me, says the LORD.
Ob 1:15 your deeds shall **r** on your own head.
Mic 5: 3 rest of his kindred shall **r** to the people of Israel.
Zep 2:10 This shall be their lot in **r** for their pride,
Hag 2:17 yet you did not **r** to me, says the LORD.
Zec 1: 3 **R** to me, says the LORD of hosts, and I will **r** to you
1: 4 **R** from your evil ways and from your evil deeds."
8: 3 Thus says the LORD: I will **r** to Zion,
9:12 **R** to your stronghold, O prisoners of hope;
10: 9 and they shall rear their children and **r.**
Mal 3: 7 **R** to me, and I will **r** to you,
3: 7 But you say, "How shall we **r?"**
Mt 2:12 having been warned in a dream not to **r** to Herod,
10:13 but if it is not worthy, let your peace **r** to you.
12:44 it says, 'I will **r** to my house from which I came.'
16:26 Or what will they give in **r** for their life?
25:27 on my **r** I would have received what was my own
Mk 8:37 Indeed, what can they give in **r** for their life?
Lk 2:43 When the festival was ended and they started to **r,**
6:35 do good, and lend, expecting nothing in **r.**
8:39 **"R** to your home, and declare
9:10 On their **r** the apostles told Jesus all they had done.
10: 6 but if not, it will **r** to you.
11:24 it says, 'I will **r** to my house from which I came.'
12:36 be like those who are waiting for their master to **r**
14:12 in case they may invite you in **r,**
17:18 to **r** and give praise to God except this foreigner?"
19:12 to get royal power for himself and then **r.**
Ac 13:34 no more to **r** to corruption,
15:16 'After this I will **r,** and I will rebuild the dwelling
15:36 let us **r** and visit the believers in every city
18:21 he said, "I will **r** to you, if God wills."
20: 3 and so he decided to **r** through Macedonia.
Ro 9: 9 "About this time I will **r** and Sarah shall have
11:35 who has given a gift to him, to receive a gift in **r?"**
2Co 6:13 In **r**—I speak as to children—
1Th 3: 9 How can we thank God enough for you in **r** for all
Heb 11:15 they would have had opportunity to **r.**
1Pe 2:23 When he was abused, he did not **r** abuse;
Tob 2:13 is it? **R** it to the owners;
2:14 and told her to **r** it to the owners.
5: 3 and we will pay him wages until you **r.**
5:16 in good health and **r** to you in good health,
5:17 in heaven bring you safely there and **r** you
5:21 our child will leave in good health and **r** to us
6:13 we **r** from Rages we will celebrate her marriage.
6:13 And when we **r** from Rages we will take her
8:21 Take at once half of what I own and **r** in safety
10: 7 to let me go so that I may **r** to my own father.
14: 5 After this they all will **r** from their exile
Jdt 6: 6 Then at my **r** the sword of my army and the spear
Wis 2: 1 and no one has been known to **r** from Hades.
2: 5 and there is no **r** from our death,
11:15 In **r** for their foolish and wicked thoughts,
15: 8 the time comes to **r** the souls that were borrowed.
Sir 4: 8 and **r** their greeting politely.
16:30 and into it they must **r.**
17: 1 and makes them **r** to it again.
17:24 Yet to those who repent he grants a **r,**
17:26 **R** to the Most High and turn away from iniquity,
17:29 and his forgiveness for those who **r** to him!
40: 1 until the day they **r** to the mother of all the living.
Bar 1: 8 to **r** them to the land of Judah—
4:28 **r** with tenfold zeal to seek him.
Sus 1:49 **R** to court, for these men have given false evidence
Bel 1:12 When you **r** in the morning,
1Mc 4:24 On their **r** they sang hymns and praises
5:19 not engage in battle with the Gentiles until we **r."**
6: 4 in great disappointment left there to **r** to Babylon.
7:35 then if I **r** safely I will burn up this house."
8:26 keep their obligations without receiving any **r.**
2Mc 8:25 they were obliged to **r** because the hour was late.
11:29 Menelaus has informed us that you wish to **r** home
3Mc 5:36 in the same manner and urged the guests to **r**
7: 8 We also have ordered all people to **r**
2Es 7:*78* the body to **r** again to him who gave it,
10: 4 now I intend not to **r** to the town, but to stay here;
15:60 when they **r** from devastated Babylon.
16:14 and shall not **r** until they come over the earth.
16:16 as an arrow shot by a mighty archer does not **r,**
16:16 calamities that are sent upon the earth shall not **r.**

RETURNED[‡] (233) [RETURN]

Ge 8: 9 and it **r** to him to the ark,
18:33 and Abraham **r** to his place.
21:32 left and **r** to the land of the Philistines.
22:19 So Abraham **r** to his young men,
31:55 then he departed and **r** home.
32: 6 The messengers **r** to Jacob, saying,
33:16 So Esau **r** that day on his way to Seir.
37:29 When Reuben **r** to the pit and saw that Joseph was
37:30 He **r** to his brothers, and said, "The boy is gone;
38:22 So he **r** to Judah, and said, "I have not found her;
42:24 then he **r** and spoke to them.
Ge 43:10 we had not delayed, we would now have **r** twice."
43:12 the money that was **r** in the top of your sacks;
44: 4 say to them, 'Why have you **r** evil for good?
44:13 each one loaded his donkey, and they **r** to the city.
50:14 Joseph **r** to Egypt with his brothers
Ex 2:18 When they **r** to their father Reuel, he said,
14:27 and at dawn the sea **r** to its normal depth.
14:28 The waters **r** and covered the chariots and
32:31 So Moses **r** to the LORD and said, "Alas,
34:31 and all the leaders of the congregation **r** to him,
Lev 25:27 and the property shall be **r.**
25:28 and the property shall be **r.**
Nu 11:30 And Moses and the elders of Israel **r** to the camp.
13:25 At the end of forty days they **r** from spying out
14:36 who **r** and made all the congregation complain
16:50 Aaron **r** to Moses at the entrance of the tent
23: 6 So he **r** to Balak, who was standing
Dt 1:45 When you **r** and wept before the LORD,
Jos 2:16 until the pursuers have **r;**
2:22 and stayed there three days, until the pursuers **r.**
4:18 the waters of the Jordan **r** to their place
6:14 around the city once and then **r** to the camp.
7: 3 Then they **r** to Joshua and said to him,
8:24 of the sword, all Israel **r** to Ai, and attacked it with
10:15 Then Joshua **r,** and all Israel with him,
10:21 all the people **r** safe to Joshua in the camp
10:43 Then Joshua **r,** and all Israel with him,
22: 9 and the half-tribe of Manasseh **r** home,
22:32 the priest Phinehas son of Eleazar and the chiefs **r**
Jdg 7: 3 Gideon sifted them out; twenty-two thousand **r,**
7:15 and he **r** to the camp of Israel, and said, "Get up;
8:13 of Joash **r** from the battle by the ascent of Heres,
11:39 At the end of two months, she **r** to her father,
14: 8 After a while he **r** to marry her,
15:19 When he drank, his spirit **r,** and he revived.
17: 3 Then he **r** the eleven hundred pieces of silver
17: 4 So when he **r** the money to his mother,
21:14 Benjamin **r** at that time;
21:23 Then they went and **r** to their territory,
Ru 1:22 So Naomi **r** together with Ruth the Moabite,
1Sa 6:16 they **r** that day to Ekron.
6:17 the Philistines **r** as a guilt offering to the LORD:
6:21 "The Philistines have **r** the ark of the LORD.
18: 6 when David **r** from killing the Philistine,
24: 1 When Saul **r** from following the Philistines,
25:21 but he has **r** me evil for good.
25:39 the LORD has **r** the evildoing of Nabal
26:25 So David went his way, and Saul **r** to his place.
2Sa 1: 1 when David had **r** from defeating the Amalekites,
2:30 Joab **r** from the pursuit of Abner;
3:27 When Abner **r** to Hebron,
6:20 David **r** to bless his household.
8:13 When he **r,** he killed eighteen thousand Edomites
10:14 Then Joab **r** from fighting against the Ammonites,
11: 4 Then she **r** to her house.
12:31 Then David and all the people **r** to Jerusalem.
17:20 and could not find them, they **r** to Jerusalem.
19:39 and he **r** to his own home.
20:22 while Joab **r** to Jerusalem to the king.
1Ki 2:41 from Jerusalem to Gath and **r,**
10:13 Then she **r** to her own land, with her servants.
12: 2 then Jeroboam **r** from Egypt.
12:20 When all Israel heard that Jeroboam had **r,**
19:21 He **r** from following him, took the yoke of oxen,
2Ki 1: 5 The messengers **r** to the king, who said to them,
1: 5 who said to them, "Why have you **r?"**
2:25 on to Mount Carmel, and then **r** to Samaria.
3:27 they withdrew from him and **r** to their own land.
4:38 Elisha **r** to Gilgal, there was a famine in the land.
5:15 he **r** to the man of God, he and all his company;
7:15 So the messengers **r,** and told the king.
8: 3 the woman **r** from the land of the Philistines,
8:29 King Joram **r** to be healed in Jezreel of
9:15 but King Joram had **r** to be healed in Jezreel of
14:14 as hostages; then he **r** to Samaria.
19: 8 The Rabshakeh **r,** and found the king
23:20 Then he **r** to Jerusalem.
1Ch 4:22 but **r** to Lehem (now the records are ancient).
20: 3 Then David and all the people **r** to Jerusalem.
2Ch 9:12 Then she **r** to her own land, with her servants.
10: 2 then Jeroboam **r** from Egypt.
14:15 Then they **r** to Jerusalem.
19: 1 King Jehoshaphat of Judah **r** in safety to his house
20:27 and Jerusalem, with Jehoshaphat at their head, **r**
22: 6 and he **r** to be healed in Jezreel of the wounds
25:10 and **r** home in fierce anger.
25:24 also hostages; then he **r** to Samaria.
28:15 Then they **r** to Samaria.
31: 1 Then all the people of Israel **r** to their cities,
32:21 So he **r** in disgrace to his own land.
34: 7 Then he **r** to Jerusalem.
Ezr 2: 1 they **r** to Jerusalem and Judah,
4: 1 and Benjamin heard that the **r** exiles were building
5: 5 a report reached Darius and then answer was **r**
6:16 and the rest of the **r** exiles,
6:19 of the first month the **r** exiles kept the passover.
6:20 they killed the passover lamb for all the **r** exiles,
6:21 It was eaten by the people of Israel who had **r**
8:35 the **r** exiles, offered burnt offerings to the God
9: 4 because of the faithlessness of the **r** exiles,
10: 7 throughout Judah and Jerusalem to all the **r** exiles
10:16 Then the **r** exiles did so.
Ne 2:15 and entered by the Valley Gate, and so **r.**
4:15 and that God had frustrated it, we all **r** to the wall,
7: 6 they **r** to Jerusalem and Judah, each to his town.
8:17 of those who had **r** from the captivity made booths
13: 7 and **r** to Jerusalem. I then discovered the wrong

Est 6:12 Then Mordecai **r** to the king's gate,
7: 8 king **r** from the palace garden to the banquet hall,
Isa 37: 8 The Rabshakeh **r,** and found the king
Jer 40:12 then all the Judeans **r** from all the places
43: 5 the forces took all the remnant of Judah who had **r**
Eze 16:43 therefore, I have **r** your deeds upon your head,
22:31 I have **r** their conduct upon their heads,
Da 4:34 lifted my eyes to heaven, and my reason **r** to me.
4:36 At that time my reason **r** to me;
Zec 1:16 I have **r** to Jerusalem with compassion;
Mt 21:18 In the morning, when he **r** to the city,
Mk 2: 1 When he **r** to Capernaum after some days,
7:31 Then he **r** from the region of Tyre,
Lk 1:56 about three months and then **r** to her home.
2:20 The shepherds **r,** glorifying and praising God
2:39 they **r** to Galilee, to their own town of Nazareth.
2:45 they **r** to Jerusalem to search for him.
4: 1 **r** from the Jordan and was led by the Spirit in
4:14 filled with the power of the Spirit, **r** to Galilee,
7:10 When those who had been sent **r** to the house,
8:37 So he got into the boat and **r.**
8:40 Now when Jesus **r,** the crowd welcomed him,
8:55 Her spirit **r,** and she got up at once.
10:17 The seventy **r** with joy, saying, "Lord,
14:21 So the slave **r** and reported this to his master.
19:15 When he **r,** having received royal power,
19:23 when I **r,** I could have collected it with interest.'
23:48 they **r** home, beating their breasts.
23:56 Then they **r,** and prepared spices and ointments.
24:33 That same hour they got up and **r** to Jerusalem;
24:52 and **r** to Jerusalem with great joy;
Jn 13:12 had put on his robe, and had **r** to the table,
20:10 Then the disciples **r** to their homes.
Ac 1:12 they **r** to Jerusalem from the mount called Olivet,
5:22 in the prison; so they **r** and reported,
8:25 they **r** to Jerusalem, proclaiming the good news
12:25 and Saul **r** to Jerusalem and brought
13:13 John, however, left them and **r** to Jerusalem;
14:21 they **r** to Lystra, then on to Iconium and Antioch.
21: 6 Then we went on board the ship, and they **r** home.
22:17 "After I had **r** to Jerusalem and
23:32 while they **r** to the barracks.
Gal 1:17 and afterwards I **r** to Damascus.
1Pe 2:25 but now you have **r** to the shepherd and guardian
Tob 1:22 Ahikar interceded for me, and I **r** to Nineveh.
2: 1 Then during the reign of Esar-haddon I **r** home,
2: 3 When he had **r** he said, "Father!"
2: 5 I **r,** I washed myself and ate my food in sorrow.
2:13 When she **r** to me, the goat began to bleat.
3:17 At the same time that Tobit **r** from the courtyard
14:12 and his wife and children **r** to Media and settled
Jdt 1:16 Then he **r** to Nineveh,
4: 3 For they had only recently **r** from exile,
5:19 But now they have **r** to their God,
6:13 and left him lying at the foot of the hill, and **r**
7: 7 and set guards of soldiers over them, and then **r**
8:36 So they **r** from the tent and went to their posts.
12: 9 Then she **r** purified and stayed in the tent
13:13 for it seemed unbelievable that she had **r.**
15: 7 And the Israelites, when they **r** from the slaughter,
16:21 this they all **r** home to their own inheritances.
AdE 6:12 Then Mordecai **r** to the courtyard,
7: 8 When the king **r** from the garden,
Bel 1:39 of God immediately **r** Habakkuk to his own place.
1Mc 1:20 Antiochus **r** in the one hundred forty-third year.
2:63 because they will have **r** to the dust,
3:33 also to take care of his son Antiochus until he **r.**
4:23 Then Judas **r** to plunder the camp,
5: 8 and its villages; then he **r** to Judea.
5:54 because they had **r** in safety;
5:68 he plundered the towns and **r** to the land of Judah.
6:56 had **r** from Persia and Media with the forces
6:63 Then he set off in haste and **r** to Antioch.
7:25 he **r** to the king and brought malicious charges
9:42 they **r** to the marshes of the Jordan.
9:50 Then Bacchides **r** to Jerusalem
9:57 When Bacchides saw that Alcimus was dead, he **r**
10: 9 and he **r** them to their parents.
10:52 "Since I have **r** to my kingdom
10:55 "Happy was the day on which you **r** to the land
10:66 Jonathan **r** to Jerusalem in peace and gladness.
10:68 he was greatly distressed and **r** to Antioch.
10:87 then **r** to Jerusalem with a large amount of booty.
11: 7 the river called Eleutherus; then he **r** to Jerusalem.
11:51 they **r** to Jerusalem with a large amount of spoil.
11:54 After this Trypho **r,** and with him
11:73 they **r** to him and joined him in the pursuit as far
11:74 And Jonathan **r** to Jerusalem.
12:24 that the commanders of Demetrius had **r,**
12:26 and they **r** and reported to him that
12:35 When Jonathan **r** he convened the elders of
12:46 and they **r** to the land of Judah.
15:36 but **r** in wrath to the king and reported
16:10 He then **r** to Judea safely.
16:17 an act of great treachery and **r** evil for good.
2Mc 2:17 and has **r** the inheritance to all,
4:25 After receiving the king's orders he **r,**
4:36 When the king **r** from the region of Cilicia,
12: 1 When this agreement had been reached, Lysias **r**
1Es 5: 8 and who **r** to Jerusalem and the rest of Judea,
5:67 that those who had **r** from exile were building
6:28 to help those who have **r** from the exile of Judea,
7: 6 rest of those who **r** from exile who joined them,
7:11 Not all of the **r** captives were purified,
7:12 the **r** captives and for their kindred the priests and
7:13 The people of Israel who had **r** from exile ate it,
8:65 And those who had **r** from exile offered sacrifices
1Es 9: 3 throughout Judea and Jerusalem to all who had **r**
9: 4 from the multitude of those who had **r** from
9:15 And those who had **r** from exile acted
3Mc 1: 1 When Philopator learned from those who **r** that
5: 3 he had given these orders he **r** to his feasting,
5:16 The king, after considering this, **r** to his drinking,
6:30 Then the king, when he had **r** to the city,
2Es 12:40 that the seven days were past and I had not **r** to

RETURNING (11) [RETURN]

1Sa 6: 8 which you are **r** to him as a guilt offering.
7: 3 "If you are **r** to the LORD with all your heart,
15:12 and on **r** he passed on down to Gilgal."
Job 15:22 They despair of **r** from darkness,
Isa 30:15 In **r** and rest you shall be saved;
Lk 24: 9 and **r** from the tomb, they told all this to
Ac 8:28 and was **r** home; seated in his chariot,
Heb 7: 1 met Abraham as he was **r** from defeating the kings
Tob 10: 1 many days Tobias would need for going and for **r.**
2Mc 15:28 the action was over and they were **r** with joy,
1Es 2:15 by Sheshbazzar with the **r** exiles from Babylon

RETURNS (13) [RETURN]

Lev 22:13 without offspring, and **r** to her father's house,
Ps 7:16 Their mischief **r** upon their own heads,
Pr 17:13 not depart from the house of one who **r** evil
26:11 that **r** to its vomit is a fool who reverts to his folly.
Ecc 1: 6 and on its circuits the wind **r.**
12: 7 and the dust **r** to the earth as it was, and the breath
r to God who gave it.
Tob 5:21 Your eyes will see him on the day when he **r**
Sir 35: 3 The one who **r** a kindness offers choice flour,
40:11 All that is of earth **r** to earth, and what is from
above **r** above.
41:10 Whatever comes from earth **r** to earth;
1Es 4:34 for it makes the circuit of the heavens and **r**

REU (6)

Ge 11:18 he became the father of **R;**
11:19 after the birth of **R** two hundred nine years,
11:20 When **R** had lived thirty-two years,
11:21 and **R** lived after the birth of Serug
1Ch 1:25 Eber, Peleg, **R;**
Lk 3:35 son of **R,** son of Peleg, son of Eber, son of Shelah,

REUBEN (44) [REUBEN'S, REUBENITE, REUBENITES]

Ge 29:32 and bore a son, and she named him **R;**
30:14 of wheat harvest **R** went and found mandrakes in
35:22 **R** went and lay with Bilhah his father's concubine;
35:23 The sons of Leah: **R** (Jacob's firstborn), Simeon,
37:21 But when **R** heard it, he delivered him out
37:22 **R** said to them, "Shed no blood;
37:29 When **R** returned to the pit and saw
42:22 Then **R** answered them, "Did I not tell you not
42:37 Then **R** said to his father,
46: 8 and his offspring, who came to Egypt. **R,**
46: 9 and the children of **R:** Hanoch,
48: 5 Ephraim and Manasseh shall be mine, just as **R**
49: 3 **R,** you are my firstborn, my might and
Ex 1: 2 **R,** Simeon, Levi, and Judah,
6:14 the sons of **R,** the firstborn of Israel:
6:14 these are the families of **R.**
Nu 1: 5 From **R,** Elizur son of Shedeur.
1:20 The descendants of **R,** Israel's firstborn,
1:21 of **R** were forty-six thousand five hundred.
2:10 be the regimental encampment of **R** by companies.
2:16 The total enrollment of the camp of **R,**
10:18 Next the standard of the camp of **R** set out,
13: 4 From the tribe of **R,** Shammua son of Zaccur;
16: 1 of Peleth—descendants of **R—**
26: 5 **R,** the firstborn of Israel. The descendants of **R:**
Dt 11: 6 of Eliab son of **R,** how in the midst of all Israel
27:13 **R,** Gad, Asher, Zebulun, Dan, and Naphtali.
33: 6 May **R** live, and not die out,
Jos 18: 7 and Gad and **R** and the half-tribe
20: 8 from the tribe of **R,** and Ramoth in Gilead,
21: 7 from the tribe of **R,** the tribe of Gad, and the tribe
21:36 Out of the tribe of **R:**
Jdg 5:15 clans of **R** there were great searchings of heart.
5:16 clans of **R** there were great searchings of heart.
1Ch 2: 1 These are the sons of Israel: **R,** Simeon, Levi,
5: 1 The sons of **R** the firstborn of Israel.
5: 3 The sons of **R,** the firstborn of Israel:
6:63 allotted twelve towns out of the tribes of **R,** Gad,
6:78 on the east side of the Jordan, out of the tribe of **R:**
Eze 48: 6 from the east side to the west, **R,** one portion.
48: 7 Adjoining the territory of **R,**
48:31 the gate of **R,** the gate of Judah,
Rev 7: 5 from the tribe of **R** twelve thousand,

REUBEN'S (2) [REUBEN]

Jos 15: 6 boundary goes up to the Stone of Bohan, **R** son;
18:17 then it goes down to the Stone of Bohan, **R** son;

REUBENITE (1) [REUBEN]

1Ch 11:42 Adina son of Shiza the **R,**

REUBENITES (45) [REUBEN]

Nu 2:10 The leader of the **R** shall be Elizur son of Shedeur,
7:30 of Shedeur, the leader of the **R:**
26: 7 These are the clans of the **R;**
32: 1 the **R** and the Gadites owned a very great number
Nu 32: 2 the Gadites and the **R** came and spoke to Moses,
32: 6 But Moses said to the Gadites and to the **R,**
32:25 Then the Gadites and the **R** said to Moses,
32:29 Moses said to them, "If the Gadites and the **R,**
32:31 The Gadites and the **R** answered,
32:33 and to the **R** and to the half-tribe of Manasseh son
32:37 And the **R** rebuilt Heshbon, Elealeh, Kiriathaim,
34:14 for the tribe of the **R** by their ancestral houses and
Dt 3:12 to the **R** and Gadites the territory north of Aroer,
3:16 And to the **R** and the Gadites I gave the territory
4:43 the wilderness on the tableland belonging to the **R,**
29: 8 and gave it as an inheritance to the **R,**
Jos 1:12 To the **R,** the Gadites, and the half-tribe
4:12 The **R,** the Gadites, and the half-tribe
12: 6 for a possession to the **R** and the Gadites and
13: 8 the **R** and the Gadites received their inheritance,
13:15 Moses gave an inheritance to the tribe of the **R**
13:23 the border of the **R** was the Jordan and its banks.
13:23 This was the inheritance of the **R,**
22: 1 Then Joshua summoned the **R,** the Gadites,
22: 9 So the **R** and the Gadites and the half-tribe
22:10 the **R** and the Gadites and the half-tribe
22:11 The Israelites heard that the **R** and the Gadites and
22:13 the priest Phinehas son of Eleazar to the **R** and
22:15 They came to the **R,** the Gadites,
22:21 Then the **R,** the Gadites, and the half-tribe
22:25 the Jordan a boundary between us and you, you **R**
22:30 the **R** and the Gadites and the Manassites spoke,
22:31 The priest Phinehas son of Eleazar said to the **R**
22:32 from the **R** and the Gadites in the land of Gilead to
22:33 the land where the **R** and the Gadites were settled.
22:34 The **R** and the Gadites called the altar Witness;
1Sa 10:27 grievously oppressing the Gadites and the **R.**
2Ki 10:33 all the land of Gilead, the Gadites, the **R,**
1Ch 5: 6 he was a chieftain of the **R.**
5:18 The **R,** the Gadites, and the half-tribe
5:26 the **R,** the Gadites, and the half-tribe of Manasseh,
11:42 a leader of the **R,** and thirty with him,
12:37 the **R** and Gadites and the half-tribe of Manasseh
26:32 heads of families, to have the oversight of the **R,**
27:16 Over the tribes of Israel, for the **R,**

REUEL (11)

Ge 36: 4 Adah bore Eliphaz to Esau; Basemath bore **R;**
36:10 **R,** the son of Esau's wife Basemath.
36:13 These were the sons of **R:**
36:17 These are the sons of Esau's son **R:**
36:17 these are the clans of **R** in the land of Edom;
Ex 2:18 When they returned to their father **R,** he said,
Nu 2:14 leader of the Gadites shall be Eliasaph son of **R,**
10:29 Moses said to Hobab son of **R** the Midianite,
1Ch 1:35 sons of Esau: Eliphaz, **R,** Jeush, Jalam, and Korah.
1:37 sons of **R:** Nahath, Zerah, Shammah, and Mizzah.
9: 8 and Meshullam son of Shephatiah, son of **R,**

REUMAH (1)

Ge 22:24 Moreover, his concubine, whose name was **R,**

REVEAL‡ (23) [REVEALED, REVEALER, REVEALING, REVEALS, REVELATION, REVELATIONS]

Est 2:10 Esther did not **r** her people or kindred,
Job 20:27 The heavens will **r** their iniquity,
Jer 33: 6 I will heal them and **r** to them abundance
Da 2: 4 and we will **r** the interpretation."
2:10 on earth who can **r** what the king demands!
2:11 and no one can **r** it to the king except the gods,
2:47 for you have been able to **r** this mystery!"
Mt 11:27 and anyone to whom the Son chooses to **r** him.
Lk 10:22 and anyone to whom the Son chooses to **r** him."
Jn 14:21 and I will love them and **r** myself to them."
14:22 "Lord, how is it that you will **r** yourself to us,
Gal 1:16 to **r** his Son to me, so that I might proclaim him
Php 3:15 this too God will **r** to you.
Col 4: 4 so that I may **r** it clearly, as I should.
Tob 12: 7 but to acknowledge and **r** the works of God,
12:11 but to **r** with due honor the works of God.'
Sir 1:30 The Lord will **r** your secrets and overthrow you
4:18 and will **r** her secrets to them.
8:19 Do not **r** your thoughts to anyone,
19: 8 and unless it would be a sin for you, do not **r** it;
3Mc 2:19 and **r** your mercy at this hour.
6: 9 **r** yourself quickly to those of the nation
2Es 10:52 that the Most High would **r** these things to you.

REVEALED (84) [REVEAL]

Ge 35: 7 because it was there that God had **r** himself to him
41:25 God has **r** to Pharaoh what he is about to do.
Ex 5: 3 "The God of the Hebrews has **r** himself to us;
Dt 29:29 **r** things belong to us and to our children forever,
1Sa 2:27 'I **r** myself to the family of your ancestor in Egypt
3: 7 the word of the LORD had not yet been **r** to him.
3:21 for the LORD **r** himself to Samuel at Shiloh by
9:15 the LORD had **r** to Samuel:
1Ch 17:25 have **r** to your servant that you will build a house
Est 2:20 Now Esther had not **r** her kindred or her people,
Job 38:17 Have the gates of death been **r** to you,
Ps 98: 2 he has **r** his vindication in the sight of the nations.
Isa 22:14 The LORD of hosts has **r** himself in my ears:
40: 5 Then the glory of the LORD shall be **r,**
53: 1 And to whom has the arm of the LORD been **r?**
56: 1 salvation will come, and my deliverance be **r.**
Da 2:19 mystery was **r** to Daniel in a vision of the night,
2:23 and have now **r** to me what we asked of you,

Da 2:23 for you have **r** to us what the king ordered."
2:30 this mystery has not been **r** to me because
10:1 of King Cyrus of Persia a word was **r** to Daniel,
Hos 7:1 the corruption of Ephraim is **r**,
Mt 11:25 from the wise and the intelligent and have **r** them
16:17 For flesh and blood has not **r** this to you,
Lk 2:26 It had been **r** to him by the Holy Spirit
2:35 so that the inner thoughts of many will be **r**—
10:21 from the wise and the intelligent and have **r** them
17:30 be like that on the day that the Son of Man is **r**.
Jn 1:31 that he might be **r** to Israel."
2:11 and **r** his glory; and his disciples believed in him.
9:3 he was born blind so that God's works might be **r**
12:38 and to whom has the arm of the Lord been **r**?"
Ro 1:17 in it the righteousness of God is **r** through faith
1:18 of God is **r** from heaven against all ungodliness
2:5 when God's righteous judgment will be **r**.
8:18 not worth comparing with the glory about to be **r**
1Co 2:10 these things God has **r** to us through the Spirit;
3:13 because it will be **r** with fire,
Gal 3:23 and guarded under the law until faith would be **r**.
Eph 3:5 now been **r** to his holy apostles and prophets by
Col 1:26 and generations but has now been **r** to his saints.
3:4 When Christ who is your life is **r**,
3:4 then you also will be **r** with him in glory.
2Th 1:7 when the Lord Jesus is **r** from heaven
2:3 the rebellion comes first and the lawless one is **r**,
2:6 so that he may be **r** when his time comes.
2:8 And then the lawless one will be **r**,
1Ti 3:16 He was **r** in flesh, vindicated in spirit,
2Ti 1:10 but it has now been **r** through the appearing
Tit 1:3 in due time he **r** his word through
1Pe 1:5 of God through faith for a salvation ready to be **r**
1:7 and glory and honor when Jesus Christ is **r**.
1:12 It was **r** to them that they were serving
1:13 that Jesus Christ will bring you when he is **r**.
1:20 but was **r** at the end of the ages for your sake.
4:13 also be glad and shout for joy when his glory is **r**.
5:1 as well as one who shares in the glory to be **r**,
1Jn 1:2 this life was **r**, and we have seen it and testify
1:2 the eternal life that was with the Father and was **r**
2:28 that when he is **r** we may have confidence and not
3:2 what we will be has not yet been **r**.
3:2 What we do know is this: when he is **r**,
3:5 You know that he was **r** to take away sins,
3:8 The Son of God was **r** for this purpose,
3:10 and the children of the devil are **r** in this way:
4:9 God's love was **r** among us in this way:
Rev 15:4 for your judgments have been **r**."
AdE 2:22 who in turn **r** the plot to the king.
Sir 1:6 The root of wisdom—to whom has it been **r**?
11:27 and at the close of one's life one's deeds are **r**.
17:12 and **r** to them his decrees.
45:3 and **r** to him his glory.
48:25 He **r** what was to occur to the end of time,
3Mc 6:18 and true God **r** his holy face and opened
6:39 the Lord of all most gloriously **r** his mercy
2Es 3:14 and to him alone you **r** the end of the times,
6:28 which has been so long without fruit, shall be **r**."
7:28 the Messiah shall be **r** with those who are
7:*33* The Most High shall be **r** on the seat of judgment,
7:*123* [53] Or that a paradise shall be **r**,
10:38 for the Most High has **r** many secrets to you.
10:54 where the city of the Most High was to be **r**.
13:32 then my Son will be **r**,
14:3 "I **r** myself in a bush and spoke to Moses

REVEALER (2) [REVEAL]
Da 2:29 the **r** of mysteries disclosed to you what is to be,
2:47 of gods and Lord of kings and a **r** of mysteries,

REVEALING (4) [REVEAL]
Am 3:7 without **r** his secret to his servants the prophets.
Ro 8:19 For the creation waits with eager longing for the **r**
1Co 1:7 as you wait for the **r** of our Lord Jesus Christ.
LtJ 6:26 **r** to humankind their worthlessness.

REVEALS‡ (7) [REVEAL]
Pr 20:19 A gossip **r** secrets,
Da 2:22 He **r** deep and hidden things;
2:28 but there is a God in heaven who **r** mysteries,
Am 4:13 creates the wind, **r** his thoughts to mortals,
Sir 14:7 and in the end he **r** his meanness.
42:19 and he **r** the traces of hidden things.
2Mc 12:41 who **r** the things that are hidden;

REVEL (4) [REVELED, REVELERS, REVELING, REVELRY, REVELS]
Ex 32:6 people sat down to eat and drink, and rose up to **r**.
2Pe 2:13 They count it a pleasure to **r** in the daytime.
Sir 9:9 or **r** with her at wine;
18:32 Do not **r** in great luxury,

REVELATION (12) [REVEAL]
2Sa 7:27 have made this **r** to your servant, saying,
Mic 3:6 without vision, and darkness to you, without **r**.
Lk 2:32 a light for **r** to the Gentiles and for glory
Ro 16:25 to the **r** of the mystery that was kept secret
1Co 14:6 in some **r** or knowledge or prophecy or teaching?
14:26 each one has a hymn, a lesson, a **r**, a tongue,
14:30 If a **r** is made to someone else sitting nearby,
Gal 1:12 but I received it through a **r** of Jesus Christ.
2:2 I went up in response to a **r**.
Eph 1:17 of wisdom and **r** as you come to know him,
3:3 and how the mystery was made known to me by **r**,
Rev 1:1 The **r** of Jesus Christ, which God gave him

REVELATIONS (2) [REVEAL]
2Co 12:1 but I will go on to visions and **r** of the Lord.
12:7 considering the exceptional character of the **r**.

REVELED (1) [REVEL]
Ac 7:41 and **r** in the works of their hands.

REVELER See Index to Footnotes

REVELERS (1) [REVEL]
Ex 32:18 it is the sound of **r** that I hear."

REVELING (4) [REVEL]
Eze 7:7 of tumult, not of **r** on the mountains.
Ro 13:13 not in **r** and drunkenness, not in debauchery
2Pe 2:13 **r** in their dissipation while they feast with you.
2Mc 6:4 For the temple was filled with debauchery and **r**

REVELRY (4) [REVEL]
Am 6:7 and the **r** of the loungers shall pass away.
Wis 2:9 Let none of us fail to share in our **r**;
3Mc 4:8 of good cheer and youthful **r**,
5:17 over to **r** and to make the present portion of

REVELS (2) [REVEL]
1Pe 4:3 living in licentiousness, passions, drunkenness, **r**,
Wis 14:23 or hold frenzied **r** with strange customs,

REVENGE (10) [VENGEANCE]
Jdg 15:7 I swear I will not stop until I have taken **r** on you."
16:28 so that with this one act of **r** I may pay back
Est 8:13 and the Jews were to be ready on that day to take **r**
Pr 6:34 and he shows no restraint when he takes **r**.
Jer 20:10 and take our **r** on him."
Eze 25:15 and with malice of heart took **r** in destruction;
Jdt 1:12 by his throne and kingdom that he would take **r** on
2:1 about carrying out his **r** on the whole region,
6:5 not see my face again from this day until I take **r**
9:2 to take **r** on those strangers who had torn off

REVENGEFULLY (1) [VENGEANCE]
Eze 25:12 Because Edom acted **r** against the house of Judah

REVENUE (9) [REVENUES]
2Ki 8:6 together with all the **r** of the fields from the day
Ezr 4:13 custom, or toll, and the royal **r** will be reduced.
6:8 in full and without delay, from the royal **r**,
Pr 3:14 and her **r** better than gold.
Isa 23:3 your **r** was the grain of Shihor,
Ro 13:7 **r** to whom **r** is due, respect to whom respect is due,
2Mc 4:8 and from another source of **r** eighty talents.
4:28 for the collection of the **r** was his responsibility—

REVENUES (10) [REVENUE]
1Mc 3:29 and that the **r** from the country were small because
3:31 to go to Persia and collect the **r** from those regions
10:31 Jerusalem and its environs, its tithes and its **r**,
10:40 of the king's **r** from appropriate places.
10:44 the structures of the sanctuary be paid from the **r**
10:45 also be paid from the **r** of the king."
2Mc 3:3 from his own **r** all the expenses connected with
9:16 the sacrifices he would provide from his own **r**;
3Mc 3:16 when we had granted very great **r** to the temples
6:30 in charge of the **r** and ordered him to provide to

REVERE (12) [REVERED, REVERENCE, REVERENCED, REVERENT, REVERENTLY, REVERING]
Lev 19:3 You shall each **r** your mother and father,
Jos 24:14 "Now therefore **r** the LORD,
Ps 67:7 let all the ends of the earth **r** him.
86:11 give me an undivided heart to **r** your name.
119:48 I **r** your commandments, which I love,
Mal 4:2 But for you who **r** my name the sun
Tob 4:5 "**R** the Lord all your days, my son,
13:12 But blessed forever will be all who **r** you.
Sir 7:29 With all your soul fear the Lord, and **r** his priests.
Bel 1:5 "Because I do not **r** idols made with hands,
4Mc 8:14 whatever justice you **r** will be merciful to you
11:5 Is it because we **r** the Creator of all things and live

REVERED (11) [REVERE]
1Ki 18:3 (Now Obadiah **r** the LORD greatly;
18:12 I your servant have **r** the LORD from my youth.
1Ch 16:25 he is to be **r** above all gods.
Ps 96:4 he is to be **r** above all gods.
130:4 so that you may be **r**.
Mal 2:5 and he **r** me and stood in awe of my name.
3:16 those who **r** the LORD spoke with one another.
3:16 before him of those who **r** the LORD and thought
Bel 1:4 The king **r** it and went every day to worship it.
1:23 a great dragon, which the Babylonians **r**.
2Mc 6:28 to die a good death willingly and nobly for the **r**

REVERENCE (12) [REVERE]
Lev 19:30 You shall keep my sabbaths and **r** my sanctuary:
Lev 26:2 You shall keep my sabbaths and **r** my sanctuary:
Jdg 6:10 you shall not pay **r** to the gods of the Amorites,
Mal 2:5 this called for **r**, and he revered me and stood
Eph 5:21 Be subject to one another out of **r** for Christ.
1Ti 2:10 as is proper for women who profess **r** for God.
Heb 12:28 to God an acceptable worship with **r** and awe;
1Pe 3:2 when they see the purity and **r** of your lives.
3:16 yet do it with gentleness and **r**.
4Mc 5:24 that with proper **r** we worship the only living God.
7:6 which had room only for **r** and purity,
17:15 **R** for God was victor and gave the crown

REVERENCED (1) [REVERE]
Mal 1:14 and my name is **r** among the nations.

REVERENT (3) [REVERE]
Tit 2:3 Likewise, tell the older women to be **r** in behavior,
Heb 5:7 and he was heard because of his **r** submission.
1Pe 1:17 live in **r** fear during the time of your exile.

REVERENTLY (1) [REVERE]
4Mc 1:17 by which we learn divine matters **r**

REVERING (1) [REVERE]
Ne 1:11 of your servants who delight in **r** your name.

REVERSES (1)
3Mc 2:10 you promised that if we should have **r**

REVERT (4) [REVERTS]
Lev 27:15 and it shall **r** to the original owner.
27:19 and it shall **r** to the original owner;
1Ki 12:26 the kingdom may well **r** to the house of David.
Eze 46:17 then it shall **r** to the prince;

REVERTS (1) [REVERT]
Pr 26:11 that returns to its vomit is a fool who **r** to his folly.

REVIEWED (1)
Ezr 8:15 As I **r** the people and the priests,

REVILE (7) [REVILED, REVILER, REVILERS, REVILES, REVILING, REVILINGS]
Ex 22:28 You shall not **r** God, or curse a leader
Lev 19:14 You shall not **r** the deaf or put a stumbling block
Ps 74:10 Is the enemy to **r** your name forever?
Isa 51:7 and do not be dismayed when they **r** you.
Mt 5:11 when people **r** you and persecute you
Lk 6:22 and when they exclude you, **r** you,
1Ti 5:14 so as to give the adversary no occasion to **r** us.

REVILED (9) [REVILE]
2Ki 19:6 the servants of the king of Assyria have **r** me.
19:22 Whom have you mocked and **r**?
Isa 37:6 the servants of the king of Assyria have **r** me.
37:23 Whom have you mocked and **r**?
65:7 on the mountains and **r** me on the hills,
Jn 9:28 Then they **r** him, saying, "You are his disciple,
Ac 18:6 When they opposed and **r** him,
1Co 4:12 When **r**, we bless; when persecuted, we endure;
1Pe 4:14 If you are **r** for the name of Christ,

REVILER (2) [REVILE]
1Co 5:11 or is an idolater, **r**, drunkard, or robber.
Sir 23:8 by them the **r** and the arrogant are tripped up.

REVILERS (2) [REVILE]
Ps 44:16 at the words of the taunters and **r**,
1Co 6:10 the greedy, drunkards, **r**, robbers—

REVILES (2) [REVILE]
Ps 74:18 and an impious people **r** your name.
Sir 22:20 and one who **r** a friend destroys a friendship.

REVILING (2) [REVILE]
Isa 43:28 to utter destruction, and Israel to **r**.
Sir 22:22 But as for **r**, arrogance, disclosure of secrets,

REVILINGS (1) [REVILE]
Zep 2:8 the taunts of Moab and the **r** of the Ammonites,

REVIVE (13) [REVIVED, REVIVING]
Ne 4:2 Will they **r** the stones out of the heaps
Ps 69:32 you who seek God, let your hearts **r**.
71:20 and calamities will **r** me again;
85:6 Will you not **r** us again,
119:25 **r** me according to your word.
Isa 57:15 to **r** the spirit of the humble,
57:15 and to **r** the heart of the contrite.
La 1:11 for food to **r** their strength.
1:16 a comforter is far from me, one to **r** my courage;
1:19 in the city while seeking food to **r** their strength.
Hos 6:2 After two days he will **r** us;
Hab 3:2 our own time **r** it; in our own time make it known;
2Mc 13:11 to let the people who had just begun to **r** fall into

REVIVED (6) [REVIVE]

Ge 45:27 the spirit of their father Jacob r.
Jdg 15:19 When he drank, his spirit returned, and he r.
1Sa 30:12 When he had eaten, his spirit r;
1Ki 17:22 the life of the child came into him again, and he r.
Ro 7: 9 the law, but when the commandment came, sin r
Php 4:10 that now at last you have r your concern for me;

REVIVING (2) [REVIVE]

Ps 19: 7 The law of the LORD is perfect, r the soul;
4Mc 18: 4 and by r observance of the law in the homeland

REVOKE (10) [REVOKED, REVOKING]

Nu 23:20 he has blessed, and I cannot r it.
Est 8: 5 be written to r the letters devised by Haman son
Am 1: 3 and for four, I will not r the punishment;
1: 6 and for four, I will not r the punishment;
1: 9 and for four, I will not r the punishment;
1:11 and for four, I will not r the punishment;
1:13 and for four, I will not r the punishment;
2: 1 and for four, I will not r the punishment;
2: 4 and for four, I will not r the punishment;
2: 6 and for four, I will not r the punishment;

REVOKED (4) [REVOKE]

Est 8: 8 and sealed with the king's ring cannot be r."
Eze 7:13 vision concerns all their multitude; it shall not be r.
Da 6: 8 of the Medes and the Persians, which cannot be r."
6:12 of the Medes and Persians, which cannot be r."

REVOKING‡ (1) [REVOKE]

3Mc 5:40 and again r your decree in the matter?

REVOLT (8) [REVOLTED, REVOLUTION]

2Ki 8:22 So Edom has been in r against the rule of Judah
2Ch 21:10 So Edom has been in r against the rule of Judah
Isa 59:13 talking oppression and r, conceiving lying words
Ac 21:38 up a r and led the four thousand assassins out into
Sir 47:23 Rehoboam, whose policy drove the people to r.
1Mc 11:14 because the people of that region were in r.
13:16 so that when released he will not r against us,
2Mc 5:11 he took it to mean that Judea was in r.

REVOLTED (9) [REVOLT]

2Ki 8:20 In his days Edom r against the rule of Judah,
8:22 Libnah also r at the same time.
2Ch 21: 8 In his days Edom r against the rule of Judah
21:10 At that time Libnah also r against his rule,
Sir 16: 7 not forgive the ancient giants who r in their might.
1Mc 11:43 for all my troops have r."
2Mc 1: 7 in those years after Jason and his company r from
4:30 of Mallus r because their cities had been given as
13:23 in charge of the government, had r in Antioch;

REVOLUTION (1) [REVOLT]

4Mc 3:21 at that time certain persons attempted a r against

REVULSION (1)

2Mc 9: 9 of the stench the whole army felt r at his decay.

REWARD‡ (77) [REWARDED, REWARDING, REWARDS]

Ge 15: 1 your r shall be very great."
Nu 24:11 I said, 'I will r you richly,'
24:11 but the LORD has denied you any r."
Ru 2:12 May the LORD r you for your deeds, and may you have a full r from the LORD,
1Sa 24:19 So may the LORD r you with good
2Sa 2: 6 I too will r you because you have done this thing.
4:10 this was the r I gave him for his news.
18:22 my son, seeing that you have no r for the tidings?"
19:36 the king recompense me with such a r?
2Ch 20:11 they r us by coming to drive us out
Job 17: 5 Those who denounce friends for r—
Ps 19:11 in keeping them there is great r.
28: 4 of their hands; render them their due r.
58:11 "Surely there is a r for the righteous;
109: 5 they r me evil for good, and hatred for my love.
109:20 that be the r of my accusers from the LORD,
127: 3 the fruit of the womb a r.
Pr 11:17 Those who are kind r themselves,
11:18 but those who sow righteousness get a true r.
12:14 and manual labor has its r.
22: 4 The r for humility and fear of the LORD is riches
25:22 and the LORD will r you.
Ecc 2:10 and this was my r for all my toil.
4: 9 because they have a good r for their toil.
9: 5 they have no more r, and even the memory
Isa 40:10 his r is with him, and his recompense before him.
45:13 not for price or r, says the LORD of hosts.
49: 4 yet surely my cause is with the LORD, and my r
62:11 his r is with him, and his recompense before him."
Jer 31:16 for there is a r for your work, says the LORD:
Da 12:13 you shall rise for your r at the end of the days."
Mt 5:12 Rejoice and be glad, for your r is great in heaven,
5:46 you love those who love you, what r do you have?
6: 1 then you have no r from your Father in heaven.
6: 2 Truly I tell you, they have received their r.
6: 4 and your Father who sees in secret will r you.
6: 5 Truly I tell you, they have received their r.
6: 6 and your Father who sees in secret will r you.
6:16 Truly I tell you, they have received their r.
Mt 6:18 and your Father who sees in secret will r you.
10:41 the name of a prophet will receive a prophet's r;
10:41 the name of a righteous person will receive the r
10:42 truly I tell you, none of these will lose their r."
Mk 9:41 the name of Christ will by no means lose the r.
Lk 6:23 for surely your r is great in heaven;
6:35 Your r will be great, and you will be children of
Ac 1:18 (Now this man acquired a field with the r
1Co 3:14 the builder will receive a r.
9:17 For if I do this of my own will, I have a r;
9:18 What then is my r?
Col 3:24 you will receive the inheritance as your r;
Heb 10:35 that confidence of yours; it brings a great r.
11:26 for he was looking ahead to the r.
2Jn 1: 8 but may receive a full r.
Rev 22:12 "See, I am coming soon; my r is with me,
Jdt 13:20 and may he r you with blessings,
Wis 5:15 righteous live forever, and their r is with the Lord;
10:17 She gave to holy people the r of their labors;
Sir 2: 8 trust in him, and your r will not be lost.
11:18 and the r allotted to him is this:
11:22 The blessing of the Lord is the r of the pious,
11:26 for the Lord on the day of death to r individuals
36:21 R those who wait for you and let your prophets
51:22 The Lord gave me my tongue as a r,
51:30 and in his own time God will give you your r.
2Mc 8:33 so these received the proper r for their impiety.
12:45 But if he was looking to the splendid r that is laid
2Es 3:33 Yet their r has not appeared
4:35 And when will the harvest of our r come?
7:35 and the r shall be manifested;
7:83 the r laid up for those who have trusted
7:98 in life and from whom they are to receive their r
8:33 shall receive their r in consequence
8:39 and their salvation, and their receiving their r.
13:56 for there is a r laid up with the Most High.
15:55 The r of a prostitute is in your lap;

REWARDED (6) [REWARD]

2Sa 22:21 The LORD r me according to my righteousness;
2Ch 15: 7 for your work shall be r."
Ps 18:20 The LORD r me according to my righteousness;
Pr 13:13 but those who respect the commandment will be r.
AdE 12: 5 and r him for these things.
Sir 38: 2 and they are r by the king.

REWARDING (4) [REWARD]

1Ki 8:32 and vindicating the righteous by r them according
2Ch 6:23 by r them in accordance with their righteousness.
Jer 32:19 the ways of mortals, r all according to their ways
Rev 11:18 the time for judging the dead, for r your servants,

REWARDS (7) [REWARD]

1Sa 26:23 The LORD r everyone for his righteousness
Pr 13:21 but prosperity r the righteous.
Da 2: 6 you shall receive from me gifts and r
5:17 or give your r to someone else!
Heb 11: 6 that he exists and that he r those who seek him.
2Mc 15:33 and would hang up these r of his folly opposite
2Es 2:35 Be ready for the r of the kingdom,

REWORKED (1) [WORK]

Jer 18: 4 and he r it into another vessel,

REZEPH (2)

2Ki 19:12 R, and the people of Eden who were in Telassar?
Isa 37:12 R, and the people of Eden who were in Telassar?

REZIA (KJV) See RIZIA

REZIN‡ (9)

2Ki 15:37 In those days the LORD began to send King R
16: 5 Then King R of Aram and King Pekah son
16: 9 carrying its people captive to Kir; then he killed R.
Ezr 2:48 R, Nekoda, Gazzam,
Ne 7:50 of Reaiah, of R, of Nekoda,
Isa 7: 1 King R of Aram and King Pekah son of Remaliah
7: 4 because of the fierce anger of R and Aram and
7: 8 and the head of Damascus is R.
8: 6 and melt in fear before R and the son of Remaliah;

REZON (1)

1Ki 11:23 R son of Eliada, who had fled from his master,

RHEGIUM (1)

Ac 28:13 then we weighed anchor and came to R.

RHESA (1)

Lk 3:27 son of R, son of Zerubbabel, son of Shealtiel,

RHODA (1)

Ac 12:13 a maid named R came to answer.

RHODES (2) [RHODIANS]

Ac 21: 1 and the next day to R, and from there to Patara.
1Mc 15:23 and to R, and to Phaselis, and to Cos, and to Side,

RHODIANS (1) [RHODES]

Eze 27:15 The R traded with you; many coastlands were

RHODOCUS (1)

2Mc 13:21 But R, a man from the ranks of the Jews,

RHYTHM (2)

Wis 17:18 or the r of violently rushing water,
19:18 as on a harp the notes vary the nature of the r,

RIB (2) [RIBS]

Ge 2:22 And the r that the LORD God had taken from
4Mc 18: 7 but I guarded the r from which woman was made.

RIBAI (2)

2Sa 23:29 Ittai son of R of Gibeah of the Benjaminites;
1Ch 11:31 Ithai son of R of Gibeah of the Benjaminites,

RIBBAND (KJV) See CORD

RIBEBOTH-KODESH See Index to Footnotes

RIBLAH (12)

Nu 34:11 down from Shepham to R on the east side of Ain;
2Ki 23:33 Pharaoh Neco confined him at R in the land
25: 6 and brought him up to the king of Babylon at R,
25:20 and brought them to the king of Babylon at R.
25:21 and put them to death at R in the land of Hamath.
Jer 39: 5 at R, in the land of Hamath;
39: 6 of Babylon slaughtered the sons of Zedekiah at R
52: 9 to the king of Babylon at R in the land of Hamath,
52:10 and also killed all the officers of Judah at R.
52:26 and brought them to the king of Babylon at R.
52:27 and put them to death at R in the land of Hamath.
Eze 6:14 all their settlements, from the wilderness to R.

RIBS‡ (2) [RIB]

Ge 2:21 then he took one of his r and closed up its place
4Mc 11:19 that had been heated in the fire, and pierced his r

RICH‡ (143) [ENRICH, ENRICHED, ENRICHES, RICHER, RICHES, RICHEST, RICHLY, RICHNESS]

Ge 13: 2 Now Abram was very r in livestock, in silver,
14:23 so that you might not say, 'I have made Abram r.'
26:13 and the man became r; he prospered more
30:43 Thus the man grew exceedingly r,
49:20 Asher's food shall be r,
Ex 30:15 The r shall not give more,
Nu 13:20 and whether the land is r or poor,
Dt 28:12 The LORD will open for you his r storehouse,
33:14 and the r yield of the months;
Jdg 5:10 you who sit on r carpets and you who walk by
9: 9 'Shall I stop producing my r oil by which gods
Ru 2: 1 a prominent r man, of the family of Elimelech,
3:10 not gone after young men, whether poor or r.
1Sa 2: 7 The LORD makes poor and makes r;
25: 2 in Carmel. The man was very r;
2Sa 12: 1 the one r and the other poor.
12: 2 The r man had very many flocks and herds;
12: 4 Now there came a traveler to the r man,
1Ch 4:40 where they found r, good pasture,
Ne 9:25 And they captured fortress cities and a r land,
9:35 in the large and r land that you set before them,
9:37 Its r yield goes to the kings whom you have set
Job 15:29 not be r, and their wealth will not endure,
34:19 nor regards the r more than the poor,
Ps 21: 3 For you meet him with r blessings;
49: 2 both low and high, r and poor together.
49:16 Do not be afraid when some become r,
63: 5 My soul is satisfied as with a r feast,
Pr 10: 4 but the hand of the diligent makes r.
10:15 The wealth of the r is their fortress;
10:22 The blessing of the LORD makes r,
13: 7 Some pretend to be r, yet have nothing;
14:20 but the r have many friends.
18:11 The wealth of the r is their strong city;
18:23 The poor use entreaties, but the r answer roughly.
21:17 whoever loves wine and oil will not be r.
22: 2 The r and the poor have this in common:
22: 7 The r rules over the poor,
22:16 and giving to the r, will lead only to loss.
23: 4 Do not wear yourself out to get r;
28: 6 to be crooked in one's ways even though r.
28:11 The r is wise in self-esteem,
28:20 in a hurry to be r will not go unpunished.
28:22 a hurry to get r and does not know that loss is sure
Ecc 5:12 but the surfeit of the r will not let them sleep.
10: 6 and the r sit in a low place.
10:20 or curse the r, even in your bedroom;
Isa 3:24 and instead of a r robe, a binding of sackcloth;
25: 6 of hosts will make for all peoples a feast of r food,
25: 6 of r food filled with marrow,
28: 1 which is on the head of those bloated with r food,
28: 4 which is on the head of those bloated with r food,
30:23 which will be r and plenteous.
34: 7 and their soil made r with fat.
53: 9 with the wicked and his tomb with the r,
55: 2 and delight yourselves in r food.
Jer 5: 5 Let me go to the r and speak to them;
5:27 therefore they have become great and r,
51:13 You who live by mighty waters, r in treasures,
Eze 16:10 in fine linen and covered you with r fabric.

Eze 16:13 while your clothing was of fine linen, **r** fabric,
17: 3 **r** in plumage of many colors,
34:14 and they shall feed on **r** pasture on the mountains
Da 10: 3 I had eaten no **r** food,
Hos 12: 8 Ephraim has said, "Ah, I am **r**,
Joel 3: 5 and have carried my **r** treasures into your temples.
Hab 1:16 for by them his portion is lavish, and his food is **r**.
Zec 11: 5 "Blessed be the LORD, for I have become **r**";
Mt 19:23 it will be hard for a **r** person to enter the kingdom
19:24 eye of a needle than for someone who is **r** to enter
27:57 there came a **r** man from Arimathea,
Mk 10:25 eye of a needle than for someone who is **r** to enter
12:41 Many **r** people put in large sums.
Lk 1:53 and sent the **r** away empty.
6:24 "But woe to you who are **r**,
12:16 "The land of a **r** man produced abundantly.
12:21 for themselves but are not **r** toward God."
14:12 or your brothers or your relatives or **r** neighbors,
16: 1 "There was a **r** man who had a manager,
16:19 a **r** man who was dressed in purple and fine linen
16:21 with what fell from the **r** man's table;
16:22 The **r** man also died and was buried.
18:23 he heard this, he became sad; for he was very **r**.
18:25 of a needle than for someone who is **r** to enter
19: 2 he was a chief tax collector and was **r**.
21: 1 He looked up and saw **r** people putting their gifts
Ro 11:17 in their place to share the **r** root of the olive tree,
1Co 4: 8 Already you have become **r**!
2Co 6:10 as poor, yet making many **r**;
8: 9 of our Lord Jesus Christ, that though he was **r**, yet
8: 9 so that by his poverty you might become **r**.
Eph 2: 4 But God, who is **r** in mercy,
3:10 of God in its **r** variety might now be made known
1Ti 6: 9 But those who want to be **r** fall into temptation
6:10 to be **r** some have wandered away from the faith
6:17 As for those who in the present age are **r**,
6:18 They are to do good, to be **r** in good works,
Jas 1:10 and the **r** in being brought low,
1:10 the **r** will disappear like a flower in the field.
1:11 It is the same way with the **r**;
2: 5 Has not God chosen the poor in the world to be **r**
2: 6 Is it not the **r** who oppress you?
5: 1 Come now, you **r** people,
Rev 2: 9 and your poverty, even though you are **r**.
3:17 For you say, 'I am **r**, I have prospered,
3:18 by fire so that you may be **r**;
6:15 and the magnates and the generals and the **r** and
13:16 it causes all, both small and great, both **r** and poor,
18: 3 and the merchants of the earth have grown **r** from
18:19 all who had ships at sea grew **r** by her wealth!
AdE 1:20 to their husbands, **r** and poor alike."
Wis 10:11 she stood by him and made him **r**.
Sir 8: 2 Do not quarrel with the **r**,
10:22 The **r**, and the eminent, and the poor—
10:30 while the **r** are honored for their wealth.
11:18 One becomes **r** through diligence and self-denial,
11:21 the sight of the Lord to make the poor **r** suddenly,
13: 3 A **r** person does wrong, and even adds insults;
13: 4 A **r** person will exploit you if you can be of use
13:18 And what peace between the **r** and the poor?
13:19 likewise the poor are feeding grounds for the **r**.
13:20 likewise the poor are an abomination to the **r**.
13:21 When the **r** person totters,
13:22 If the **r** person slips, many come to the rescue;
13:23 The **r** person speaks and all are silent;
19: 1 The one who does this will not become **r**;
25: 2 a pauper who boasts, a **r** person who lies,
25: 6 **R** experience is the crown of the aged,
26: 4 Whether **r** or poor, his heart is content,
27: 1 and those who seek to get **r** will avert their eyes.
30:14 healthy, and fit than **r** and afflicted in body.
31: 3 The **r** person toils to amass a fortune,
31: 8 Blessed is the **r** person who is found blameless,
32: 6 of emerald in a **r** setting of gold is the melody
44: 6 **r** men endowed with resources, living peacefully
Sus 1: 4 Joakim was very **r**, and had a fine garden
1Mc 6: 2 Its temple was very **r**, containing golden shields,
2Mc 7:24 but promised with oaths that he would make him **r**
1Es 3: 5 King Darius will give **r** gifts and great honors
3:19 of the slave and the free, of the poor and the **r**.
3:21 It makes all hearts feel **r**,
3Mc 5:31 to be a **r** feast for the savage animals instead of
4Mc 4: 4 up to Seleucus to inform him of the **r** treasure.

RICHER (4) [RICH]

Pr 11:24 Some give freely, yet grow all the **r**;
Da 11: 2 The fourth shall be far **r** than all of them,
Wis 8: 5 in life, what is **r** than wisdom, the active cause
Sir 13: 2 or associate with one mightier and **r** than you.

RICHES‡ (69) [RICH]

1Ki 3:11 and have not asked for yourself long life or **r**,
3:13 both **r** and honor all your life;
10:23 the kings of the earth in **r** and in wisdom.
1Ch 29:12 **R** and honor come from you, and you rule over all.
29:28 He died in a good old age, full of days, **r**,
2Ch 1:12 I will also give you **r**, possessions, and honor,
9:22 the kings of the earth in **r** and in wisdom.
17: 5 and he had great **r** and honor.
18: 1 Now Jehoshaphat had great **r** and honor;
32:27 Hezekiah had very great **r** and honor;
Est 5:11 Haman recounted to them the splendor of his **r**,
Job 20:15 They swallow down **r** and vomit them up again;
Ps 49: 6 and boast of the abundance of their **r**?
52: 7 but trusted in abundant **r**,
62:10 if **r** increase, do not set your heart on them.
73:12 always at ease, they increase in **r**.
112: 3 Wealth and **r** are in their houses,
119:14 in the way of your decrees as much as in all **r**.
Pr 3:16 in her left hand are **r** and honor.
8:18 **R** and honor are with me,
11: 4 **R** do not profit in the day of wrath,
11:16 timid become destitute, but the aggressive gain **r**.
11:28 Those who trust in their **r** will wither,
22: 1 A good name is to be chosen rather than great **r**,
22: 4 for humility and fear of the LORD is **r** and honor
24: 4 with all precious and pleasant **r**.
27:24 for **r** do not last forever,
30: 8 give me neither poverty nor **r**;
Ecc 4: 8 and their eyes are never satisfied with **r**.
5:13 **r** were kept by their owners to their hurt,
5:14 and those **r** were lost in a bad venture;
9:11 nor **r** to the intelligent, nor favor to the skillful;
Isa 30: 6 they carry their **r** on the backs of donkeys,
45: 3 of darkness and **r** hidden in secret places,
61: 6 and in their **r** you shall glory.
Jer 48:36 for the **r** they gained have perished.
Eze 26:12 They will plunder your **r**
27:27 Your **r**, your wares, your merchandise,
Da 11: 2 and when he has become strong through his **r**,
11:43 and all the **r** of Egypt;
Lk 8:14 they are choked by the cares and **r** and pleasures
16:11 who will entrust to you the true **r**?
Ro 2: 4 Or do you despise the **r** of his kindness
9:23 to make known the **r** of his glory for the objects
11:12 Now if their stumbling means **r** for the world,
11:12 and if their defeat means **r** for Gentiles,
11:33 O the depth of the **r** and wisdom and knowledge
Eph 1: 7 according to the **r** of his grace
1:18 the **r** of his glorious inheritance among the saints,
2: 7 the immeasurable **r** of his grace in kindness
3: 8 the Gentiles the news of the boundless **r** of Christ,
3:16 I pray that, according to the **r** of his glory,
Php 4:19 of yours according to his **r** in glory in Christ Jesus.
Col 1:27 the Gentiles are the **r** of the glory of this mystery,
2: 2 the **r** of assured understanding and have
1Ti 6:17 or to set their hopes on the uncertainty of **r**,
Jas 5: 2 Your **r** have rotted, and your clothes are
1Jn 2:16 the desire of the eyes, the pride in **r**—
Jdt 15: 6 and plundered it, acquiring great **r**.
AdE 1: 4 to them the **r** of his kingdom and the splendor
5:11 And he told them about his **r** and the honor that
Wis 8: 5 If **r** are a desirable possession in life,
Sir 13:24 **R** are good if they are free from sin;
14: 3 **R** are inappropriate for a small-minded person;
14: 5 He will not enjoy his own **r**.
21: 4 Panic and insolence will waste away **r**;
30:15 and a robust body than countless **r**.
40:26 **R** and strength build up confidence,
1Mc 4:23 and cloth dyed blue and sea purple, and great **r**.

RICHEST (2) [RICH]

Ps 45:12 will seek your favor with gifts, the **r** of the people
Da 11:24 Without warning he shall come into the **r** parts of

RICHLY (7) [RICH]

Nu 24:11 I said, 'I will reward you **r**,'
Pr 13: 4 while the appetite of the diligent is **r** supplied.
Col 3:16 Let the word of Christ dwell in you **r**;
1Ti 6:17 on God who **r** provides us with everything
Tit 3: 6 on us **r** through Jesus Christ our Savior,
2Pe 1:11 and Savior Jesus Christ will be **r** provided for you.
Sir 45:12 a delight to the eyes, **r** adorned.

RICHNESS‡ (1) [RICH]

Ps 65:11 your wagon tracks overflow with **r**.

RID (4)

1Sa 6:20 To whom shall he go so that we may be **r**
Col 3: 8 But now you must get **r** of all such things—
Jas 1:21 Therefore **r** yourselves of all sordidness
1Pe 2: 1 **R** yourselves, therefore, of all malice,

RIDDEN (4) [RIDE]

Nu 22:30 which you have **r** all your life to this day?
Est 6: 8 and a horse that the king has **r**,
Mk 11: 2 a colt that has never been **r**;
Lk 19:30 a colt that has never been **r**.

RIDDLE‡ (10) [RIDDLES]

Jdg 14:12 Samson said to them, "Let me now put a **r** to you.
14:13 So they said to him, "Ask your **r**; let us hear it."
14:14 But for three days they could not explain the **r**.
14:15 "Coax your husband to explain the **r** to us,
14:16 You have asked a **r** of my people,
14:17 Then she explained the **r** to her people.
14:18 you would not have found out my **r**."
14:19 to those who had explained the **r**.
Ps 49: 4 I will solve my **r** to the music of the harp.
Eze 17: 2 propound a **r**, and speak an allegory to the house

RIDDLES (5) [RIDDLE]

Nu 12: 8 With him I speak face to face—clearly, not in **r**;
Pr 1: 6 the words of the wise and their **r**.
Da 5:12 and understanding to interpret dreams, explain **r**,
Hab 2: 6 with mocking **r**, say about them,
Wis 8: 8 of speech and the solutions of **r**;

RIDE (20) [RIDDEN, RIDER, RIDER'S, RIDERS, RIDES, RIDING, RODE]

Ge 41:43 He had him **r** in the chariot
Jdg 5:10 "Tell of it, you who **r** on white donkeys,
2Sa 16: 2 "The donkeys are for the king's household to **r**,
19:26 so that I may **r** on it and go with the king.'
1Ki 1:33 and have my son Solomon **r** on my own mule,
1:38 down and had Solomon **r** on King David's mule,
1:44 and they had him **r** on the king's mule;
2Ki 10:16 So he had him **r** in his chariot.
Job 30:22 You lift me up on the wind, you make me **r** on it,
Ps 45: 4 In your majesty **r** on victoriously for the cause
66:12 you let people **r** over our heads;
104: 3 you **r** on the wings of the wind,
Isa 30:16 and, "We will **r** upon swift steeds"—
58:14 I will make you **r** upon the heights of the earth;
Jer 6:23 they **r** on horses, equipped like a warrior for battle,
50:42 they **r** upon horses, set in array as a warrior
Hos 14: 3 we will not **r** upon horses;
Am 2:15 nor shall those who **r** horses save their lives;
Ac 23:24 Also provide mounts for Paul to **r**,
AdE 6:11 the robe on Mordecai and made him **r** through

RIDER (18) [RIDE]

Ge 49:17 bites the horse's heels so that its **r** falls backward.
Ex 15: 1 horse and **r** he has thrown into the sea.
15:21 horse and **r** he has thrown into the sea."
Job 39:18 it laughs at the horse and its **r**.
Ps 68:33 O **r** in the heavens, the ancient heavens;
76: 6 O God of Jacob, both **r** and horse lay stunned.
Jer 51:21 with you I smash the horse and its **r**;
Zec 12: 4 with panic, and its **r** with madness.
Rev 6: 2 and there was a white horse! Its **r** had a bow;
6: 4 its **r** was permitted to take peace from the earth,
6: 5 Its **r** held a pair of scales in his hand,
19:11 Its **r** is called Faithful and True,
19:19 against the **r** on the horse and against his army.
19:21 rest were killed by the sword of the **r** on the horse,
Sir 33: 6 like a stallion that neighs no matter who the **r** is.
2Mc 3:25 with a **r** of frightening mien;
3:25 Its **r** was seen to have armor and weapons of gold.
13:15 He stabbed the leading elephant and its **r**.

RIDER'S (1) [RIDE]

Rev 6: 8 Its **r** name was Death, and Hades followed

RIDERS (12) [RIDE]

2Ki 18:23 if you are able on your part to set **r** on them.
Isa 21: 7 When he sees **r**, horsemen in pairs, **r** on donkeys, **r** on camels,
21: 9 Look, there they come, **r**, horsemen in pairs!"
36: 8 if you are able on your part to set **r** on them.
Hag 2:22 and overthrow the chariots and their **r**; and the horses and their **r** shall fall,
Zec 10: 5 and they shall put to shame the **r** on horses.
Rev 9:17 the **r** wore breastplates the color of fire and
19:18 the flesh of horses and their **r**—
Jdt 9: 7 priding themselves in their horses and **r**,

RIDES (4) [RIDE]

Lev 15: 9 the one with the discharge **r** shall be unclean.
Dt 33:26 who **r** through the heavens to your help,
Ps 68: 4 lift up a song to him who **r** upon the clouds—
AdE 6: 8 and the horse on which the king **r**,

RIDGE (1) [RIDGES]

Jdt 3: 9 near Dothan, facing the great **r** of Judea;

RIDGES (1) [RIDGE]

Ps 65:10 You water its furrows abundantly, settling its **r**,

RIDICULE (11) [RIDICULED, RIDICULOUS]

Pr 29: 9 there is ranting and **r** without relief.
Jer 42:18 of execration and horror, of cursing and **r**.
44: 8 an object of cursing and **r** among all the nations of
44:12 of execration and horror, of cursing and **r**.
49:13 Bozrah shall become an object of horror and **r**,
Lk 14:29 all who see it will begin to **r** him,
Tob 8:10 that he will die and we will become an object of **r**
Sir 7:11 Do not **r** a person who is embittered in spirit,
20:17 How many will **r** him, and how often!
1Mc 10:70 I have fallen into **r** and disgrace because of you.
2Es 2:21 do not **r** the lame, protect the maimed,

RIDICULED (3) [RIDICULE]

Jdg 9:27 ate and drank, and **r** Abimelech.
Ne 2:19 they mocked and **r** us, saying,
Lk 16:14 heard all this, and they **r** him.

RIDICULOUS (4) [RIDICULE]

Wis 17: 8 of a sick soul were sick themselves with **r** fear.
4Mc 1: 5 Their attempt at argument is **r**!
3: 1 But this argument is entirely **r**;
6:34 It would be **r** to deny it.

RIDING (13) [RIDE]

Nu 22:22 Now he was **r** on the donkey,
2Sa 18: 9 Absalom was **r** on his mule,
Ne 2:14 but there was no place for the animal I was **r**
Est 6:11 and led him **r** through the open square of the city,
8:10 by mounted couriers **r** on fast steeds bred from

Isa 19: 1 LORD is **r** on a swift cloud and comes to Egypt;
Jer 17:25 **r** in chariots and on horses,
22: 4 **r** in chariots and on horses, they,
Eze 23:23 officers and warriors, all of them **r** on horses.
27:20 Dedan traded with you in saddlecloths for **r.**
38:15 all of them **r** on horses, a great horde,
Zec 1: 8 In the night I saw a man **r** on a red horse!
9: 9 humble and **r** on a donkey, on a colt,

RIE (KJV) See SPELT

RIFLED (KJV) See LOOTED

RIGGING (1)

Isa 33:23 Your **r** hangs loose; it cannot hold the mast firm in its

RIGHT‡ (510) [ARIGHT, BIRTHRIGHT, RIGHTFUL, RIGHTLY, RIGHTS]

A. RIGHT HAND (137)
B. DO WHAT IS ... RIGHT (19)
C. IN THE RIGHT (19)
D. NOT RIGHT (13)

Ge 13: 9 If you take the left hand, then I will go to the **r;**
13: 9 if you take the **r** hand, then I will go to the left." A
24:48 who had led me by the **r** way to obtain
24:49 I may turn either to the **r** hand or to the left." A
38:26 "She is more in the **r** than I, C
48:13 Ephraim in his **r** hand toward Israel's left, A
48:13 and Manasseh in his left hand toward Israel's **r,** A
48:14 But Israel stretched out his **r** hand and laid it on A
48:17 When Joseph saw that his father laid his **r** hand A
48:18 put your **r** hand on his head." A
Ex 8:26 But Moses said, "It would not be **r** to do so;
9:27 the LORD is in the **r,** I and my people are C
14:22 the waters forming a wall for them on their **r** and
14:29 the waters forming a wall for them on their **r** and
15: 6 Your **r** hand, O LORD, glorious in power— A
15: 6 your **r** hand, O LORD, shattered the enemy. A
15:12 You stretched out your **r** hand, A
15:26 and do what is **r** in his sight, B
21: 8 he shall have no **r** to sell her to a foreign people,
23: 7 and do not kill the innocent and those in the **r,** C
23: 8 and subverts the cause of those who are in the **r.** C
29:20 and put it on the lobe of Aaron's **r** ear and on the lobes of the **r** ears of his sons, and on the thumbs of their **r** hands, and on the big toes of their **r** feet,
29:22 and the **r** thigh (for it is a ram of ordination),
Lev 7:32 And the **r** thigh from your sacrifices
7:33 of the offering of well-being shall have the **r** thigh
8:23 of its blood and put it on the lobe of Aaron's **r** ear
8:23 on the thumb of his **r** hand and on the big toe A
8:23 of his right hand and on the big toe of his **r** foot.
8:24 on the lobes of their **r** ears and on the thumbs of their **r** hands and on the big toes of their **r** feet;
8:25 with their fat—and the **r** thigh.
8:26 and placed them on the fat and on the **r** thigh.
9:21 the **r** thigh Aaron raised as an elevation offering
14:14 the guilt offering and put it on the lobe of the **r** ear
14:14 and on the thumb of the **r** hand, A
14:14 and on the big toe of the **r** foot.
14:16 and dip his **r** finger in the oil that is
14:17 on the lobe of the **r** ear of the one to be cleansed,
14:17 and on the thumb of the **r** hand, A
14:17 and on the big toe of the **r** foot,
14:25 on the lobe of the **r** ear of the one to be cleansed,
14:25 and on the thumb of the **r** hand, A
14:25 and on the big toe of the **r** foot.
14:27 and shall sprinkle with his **r** finger some of the oil
14:28 the oil that is in his hand on the lobe of the **r** ear of
14:28 and on the thumb of the **r** hand, A
14:28 and the big toe of the **r** foot,
25:29 the **r** of redemption shall be one year.
25:32 the Levites shall forever have the **r** of redemption
25:48 themselves they shall have the **r** of redemption;
Nu 18:18 that is elevated and as the **r** thigh are yours.
20:17 to the **r** hand or to the left until we have passed A
22:26 where there was no way to turn either to the **r** or
22:29 I would kill you **r** now!"
27: 7 of Zelophehad are **r** in what they are saying;
36: 5 the tribe of Joseph are **r** in what they are saying.
Dt 1:39 who today do not yet know **r** from wrong,
2:27 I will turn aside neither to the **r** nor to the left.
5:28 they are **r** in all that they have spoken.
5:32 you shall not turn to the **r** or to the left.
6:18 Do what is **r** and good in the sight of the LORD, B
6:25 as he has commanded us, we will be in the **r."** C
12:25 you do what is **r** in the sight of the LORD. B
12:28 because you will be doing what is good and **r** in
13:18 doing what is **r** in the sight of
16:19 and subverts the cause of those who are in the **r.** C
17: 8 one kind of legal **r** and another,
17:11 either to the **r** or to the left.
17:20 either to the **r** or to the left,
18:17 "They are **r** in what they have said.
21: 9 you must do what is **r** in the sight of the LORD. B
21:17 the **r** of the firstborn is his.
25: 1 declaring one to be in the **r** and the other to be C
28:14 either to the **r** or to the left,
33: 2 at his **r,** a host of his own.
33:19 there they offer the **r** sacrifices;
Jos 1: 7 do not turn from it to the **r** hand or to the left, A
9:25 as it seems good and **r** in your sight to do to us."
Jos 23: 6 turning aside from it neither to the **r** nor to the left,
Jdg 3:16 and he fastened it on his **r** thigh under his clothes.
3:21 took the sword from his **r** thigh,
5:26 She put her hand to the tent peg and her **r** hand A
7:20 and in their **r** hands the trumpets to blow;
12: 6 "Sibboleth," for he could not pronounce it **r.**
16:29 his **r** hand on the one and his left hand on A
17: 6 all the people did what was **r** in their own eyes.
21:25 all the people did what was **r** in their own eyes.
Ru 4: 6 Take my **r** of redemption yourself,
1Sa 6:12 they turned neither to the **r** nor to the left,
10:27 He would gouge out the **r** eye of each of them
10:27 across the Jordan whose **r** eye Nahash,
11: 2 namely that I gouge out everyone's **r** eye,
12:23 and I will instruct you in the good and the **r** way.
29: 6 to me it seems **r** that you should march out and in
2Sa 2:19 to the **r** nor to the left as he followed him.
2:21 Abner said to him, "Turn to your **r** or to your left,
14:19 one cannot turn **r** or left from anything
15: 3 "See, your claims are good and **r;**
16: 6 and all the warriors were on his **r** and on his left.
19:28 What further **r** have I, then, to appeal to the king?"
20: 9 by the beard with his **r** hand to kiss him. A
1Ki 2:19 for the king's mother, and she sat on his **r.**
3:11 for yourself understanding to discern what is **r,**
11:33 doing what is **r** in my sight
11:38 and do what is **r** in my sight B
14: 8 doing only that which was **r** in my sight,
14:14 the house of Jeroboam today, even **r** now!
15: 5 David did what was **r** in the sight of the LORD,
15:11 Asa did what was **r** in the sight of the LORD,
22:19 the host of heaven standing beside him to the **r**
22:43 doing what was **r** in the sight of the LORD;
2Ki 4:23 She said, "It will be all **r."**
4:26 and say to her, Are you all **r?**
4:26 Is your husband all **r?**
4:26 Is the child all **r?"**
4:26 She answered, "It is all **r."**
5:21 to meet him and said, "Is everything all **r?"**
9:11 they said to him, "Is everything all **r?**
10: 5 make anyone king; do whatever you think **r."**
10:30 in carrying out what I consider **r,**
12: 2 Jehoash did what was **r** in the sight of the LORD
12: 9 the **r** side as one entered the house of the LORD;
14: 3 He did what was **r** in the sight of the LORD,
15: 3 He did what was **r** in the sight of the LORD,
15:34 He did what was **r** in the sight of the LORD,
16: 2 He did not do what was **r** in the sight of
17: 9 of Israel secretly did things that were not **r** D
18: 3 He did what was **r** in the sight of the LORD just
22: 2 He did what was **r** in the sight of the LORD,
22: 2 he did not turn aside to the **r** or to the left.
1Ch 6:39 who stood on his **r,** namely,
12: 2 sling stones with either the **r** hand or the left; A
2Ch 3:17 one on the **r,** the other on the left;
3:17 the one on the **r** he called Jachin,
4: 6 and set five on the **r** side, and five on the left.
4: 8 five on the **r** side and five on the left.
6:23 in the **r** by rewarding them in accordance C
12: 6 "The LORD is in the **r."** C
14: 2 Asa did what was good and **r** in the sight of
18:18 with all the host of heaven standing to the **r** and to
20:32 doing what was **r** in the sight of the LORD.
24: 2 Joash did what was **r** in the sight of the LORD all
25: 2 He did what was **r** in the sight of the LORD,
26: 4 He did what was **r** in the sight of the LORD,
27: 2 He did what was **r** in the sight of the LORD just
28: 1 not do what was **r** in the sight of the LORD, B
29: 2 He did what was **r** in the sight of the LORD,
30: 4 plan seemed **r** to the king and all the assembly.
31:20 he did what was good and **r** and faithful before
34: 2 He did what was **r** in the sight of the LORD,
34: 2 he did not turn aside to the **r** or to the left.
Ne 2:20 but you have no share or claim or historic **r**
4:23 each kept his weapon in his **r** hand. A
8: 4 Uriah, Hilkiah, and Maaseiah on his **r** hand; A
9:13 and gave them **r** ordinances and true laws,
12:31 One went to the **r** on the wall to the Dung Gate;
Est 8: 5 and if the thing seems **r** before the king,
Job 8: 3 Or does the Almighty pervert the **r?**
16:21 that he would maintain the **r** of a mortal with God,
23: 9 I turn to the **r,** but I cannot see him.
27: 2 who has taken away my **r,** and the Almighty,
27: 5 Far be it from me to say that you are **r;**
30:12 On my **r** hand the rabble rise up; A
32: 9 nor the aged that understand what is **r.**
33:12 "But in this you are not **r.** D
33:27 'I sinned, and perverted what was **r,**
34: 4 Let us choose what is **r;**
34: 5 'I am innocent, and God has taken away my **r;**
34: 6 in spite of being **r** I am counted a liar;
35: 2 You say, 'I am in the **r** before God.' C
36: 6 but gives the afflicted their **r.**
40:14 that your own **r** hand can give you victory. A
42: 7 for you have not spoken of me what is **r,**
42: 8 for you have not spoken of me what is **r,**
Ps 4: 1 when I call, O God of my **r!**
4: 5 Offer **r** sacrifices, and put your trust in
15: 2 Those who walk blamelessly, and do what is **r,** B
16: 8 he is at my **r** hand, I shall not be moved. A
16:11 in your **r** hand are pleasures forevermore. A
17: 2 let your eyes see the **r.**
17: 7 from their adversaries at your **r** hand. A
18:35 and your **r** hand has supported me; A
19: 8 precepts of the LORD are **r,** rejoicing the heart;
20: 6 with mighty victories by his **r** hand. A
21: 8 your **r** hand will find out those who hate you. A
Ps 23: 3 He leads me in **r** paths for his name's sake.
25: 9 He leads the humble in what is **r,**
26:10 and whose **r** hands are full of bribes.
44: 3 but your **r** hand, and your arm, A
45: 4 for the cause of truth and to defend the **r;**
45: 4 let your **r** hand teach you dread deeds. A
45: 9 at your **r** hand stands the queen in gold of Ophir. A
48:10 Your **r** hand is filled with victory. A
50:16 "What **r** have you to recite my statutes,
50:23 the **r** way I will show the salvation of God."
51:10 O God, and put a new and **r** spirit within me.
51:19 then you will delight in **r** sacrifices,
58: 1 Do you indeed decree what is **r,**
60: 5 Give victory with your **r** hand, A
63: 8 My soul clings to you; your **r** hand upholds me. A
73:23 I am continually with you; you hold my **r** hand. A
77:10 that the **r** hand of the Most High has changed." A
78:54 to the mountain that his **r** hand had won. A
80:15 the stock that your **r** hand planted. A
80:17 let your hand be upon the one at your **r** hand, A
82: 3 maintain the **r** of the lowly and the destitute.
89:13 strong is your hand, high your **r** hand. A
89:25 I will set his hand on the sea and his **r** hand on A
89:42 You have exalted the **r** hand of his foes; A
91: 7 ten thousand at your **r** hand, A
98: 1 **r** hand and his holy arm have gotten him A
108: 6 Give victory with your **r** hand, and answer me, A
109: 6 let an accuser stand on his **r.**
109:31 For he stands at the **r** hand of the needy, A
110: 1 The LORD says to my lord, "Sit at my **r** hand A
110: 5 The Lord is at your **r** hand; A
118:15 "The **r** hand of the LORD does valiantly; A
118:16 the **r** hand of the LORD is exalted; A
118:16 the **r** hand of the LORD does valiantly." A
119:75 I know, O LORD, that your judgments are **r,**
119:121 I have done what is just and **r;**
119:137 O LORD, and your judgments are **r.**
119:172 for all your commandments are **r.**
121: 5 the LORD is your shade at your **r** hand. A
137: 5 I forget you, O Jerusalem, let my **r** hand wither! A
138: 7 and your **r** hand delivers me. A
139:10 and your **r** hand shall hold me fast. A
142: 4 Look on my **r** hand and see— A
144: 8 and whose **r** hands are false.
144:11 and whose **r** hands are false.
Pr 3:16 Long life is in her **r** hand; A
4:27 Do not swerve to the **r** or to the left;
7:22 **R** away he follows her, and goes like an ox to
8: 6 and from my lips will come what is **r;**
8: 9 They are all straight to one who understands and **r**
12:15 Fools think their own way is **r,**
14:12 There is a way that seems **r** to a person,
16:13 and he loves those who speak what is **r.**
16:25 Sometimes there is a way that seems to be **r,**
17:26 To impose a fine on the innocent is not **r,** D
18: 5 It is not **r** to be partial to the guilty, D
18:17 The one who first states a case seems **r,**
20:11 by whether what they do is pure and **r.**
21: 2 All deeds are **r** in the sight of the doer,
21: 8 but the conduct of the pure is **r.**
22: 6 Train children in the **r** way, and when old, C
22:21 to show you what is **r** and true,
23:16 when your lips speak what is **r.**
27:16 restrain the wind or to grasp oil in the **r** hand. AC
Ecc 5: 8 the violation of justice and **r,** do not be amazed at
10: 2 The heart of the wise inclines to the **r,**
SS 2: 6 and that his **r** hand embraced me! A
8: 3 and that his **r** hand embraced me! A
Isa 9:20 They gorged on the **r,** but still were hungry,
10: 2 and to rob the poor of my people of their **r,**
16: 5 and is swift to do what is **r.** B
22:16 What **r** do you have here?
29:21 without grounds deny justice to the one in the **r.** C
30:10 to the prophets, "Do not prophesy to us what is **r;**
30:21 you turn to the **r** or when you turn to the left,
32: 7 even when the plea of the needy is **r.**
40:27 and my **r** is disregarded by my God"?
41:10 I will uphold you with my victorious **r** hand. A
41:13 For I, the LORD your God, hold your **r** hand; A
41:26 and beforehand, so that we might say, "He is **r"**?
43:26 set forth your case, so that you may be proved **r.**
44:20 "Is not this thing in my **r** hand a fraud?" A
45: 1 whose **r** hand I have grasped to subdue nations A
45:19 I the LORD speak the truth, I declare what is **r.**
48: 1 and invoke the God of Israel, but not in truth or **r.**
48:13 and my **r** hand spread out the heavens; A
54: 3 For you will spread out to the **r** and to the left,
56: 1 Maintain justice, and do what is **r,** B
62: 8 The LORD has sworn by his **r** hand and A
63:12 to march at the **r** hand of Moses, A
64: 5 You meet those who gladly do **r,**
Jer 11:15 What **r** has my beloved in my house,
12: 1 You will be in the **r,** O LORD, C
22:24 of Judah were the signet ring on my **r** hand, A
23:10 and their might is not **r.** D
26:14 Do with me as seems good and **r** to you.
32: 7 for the **r** of redemption by purchase is yours."
32: 8 for the **r** of possession and redemption is yours;
34:15 and did what was **r** in my sight
40: 4 go wherever you think it good and **r** to go.
40: 5 or go wherever you think it **r** to go."
La 1:18 The LORD is in the **r,** for I have rebelled C
2: 3 he has withdrawn his **r** hand from them A
2: 4 with his **r** hand set like a foe; A
Eze 1:10 the face of a lion on the **r** side,
4: 6 but on your **r** side, and bear the punishment of
16:52 they are more in the **r** than you. C

Eze 18: 5 a man is righteous and does what is lawful and **r**—
18:19 When the son has done what is lawful and **r**,
18:21 do what is lawful and **r**, they shall surely live; B
18:27 and do what is lawful and **r**, B
21:16 Attack to the **r**! Engage to the left!
21:22 Into his **r** hand comes the lot for Jerusalem, A
21:27 Until he comes whose **r** it is; to him I will give it.
33:14 from their sin and do what is lawful and **r**— B
33:16 they have done what is lawful and **r**,
33:19 and do what is lawful and **r**, they shall live by it. B
39: 3 will make your arrows drop out of your **r** hand. A
45: 9 and do what is just and **r**. B
Da 9:14 the LORD our God is **r** in all that he has done;
12: 7 his **r** hand and his left hand toward heaven. A
Hos 14: 9 For the ways of the LORD are **r**,
Am 3:10 They do not know how to do **r**, says the LORD,
Jnh 4: 4 And the LORD said, "Is it **r** for you to be angry?"
4: 9 "Is it **r** for you to be angry about the bush?"
4:11 not know their **r** hand from their left, A
Hab 2: 4 Their spirit is not **r** in them, D
2:16 The cup in the LORD's **r** hand will come around A
Zec 3: 1 and Satan standing at his **r** hand to accuse him. A
3: 7 of my courts, and I will give you the **r** of access
4: 3 one on the **r** of the bowl and the other on its left."
4:11 "What are these two olive trees on the **r** and
11:12 I then said to them, "If it seems **r** to you,
11:17 May the sword strike his arm and his **r** eye!
11:17 be completely withered, his **r** eye utterly blinded!
12: 6 to the **r** and to the left all the surrounding peoples,
Mt 5:29 If your **r** eye causes you to sin,
5:30 And if your **r** hand causes you to sin, A
5:39 But if anyone strikes you on the **r** cheek,
6: 3 your left hand know what your **r** hand is doing, A
20: 4 and I will pay you whatever is **r**.'
20:21 one at your **r** hand and one at your left, A
20:23 but to sit at my **r** hand and at my left, A
22:44 "Sit at my **r** hand, until I put your enemies A
25:33 the sheep at his **r** hand and the goats at the left. A
25:34 Then the king will say to those at his **r** hand, A
26:64 Son of Man seated at the **r** hand of Power A
27:29 put a reed in his **r** hand and knelt before him A
27:38 one on his **r** and one on his left.
Mk 5:15 clothed and in his **r** mind,
10:37 one at your **r** hand and one at your left, A
10:40 but to sit at my **r** hand or at my left is not mine A
12:32 Then the scribe said to him, "You are **r**, Teacher;
12:36 "Sit at my **r** hand, until I put your enemies A
14:54 **r** into the courtyard of the high priest;
14:62 Son of Man seated at the **r** hand of the Power,' A
15:27 one on his **r** and one on his left.
16: 5 dressed in a white robe, sitting on the **r** side;
16:19 ⟦into heaven and sat down at the **r** hand of God.⟧ A
Lk 1:11 standing at the **r** side of the altar of incense.
6: 6 a man there whose **r** hand was withered. A
8:35 clothed and in his **r** mind.
10:28 he said to him, "You have given the **r** answer;
12:57 why do you not judge for yourselves what is **r**?
20:21 we know that you are **r** in what you say and teach,
20:42 'The Lord said to my Lord, "Sit at my **r** hand, A
22:50 the slave of the high priest and cut off his **r** ear.
22:69 Son of Man will be seated at the **r** hand of the A
23:33 one on his **r** and one on his left.
Jn 4:17 Jesus said to her, "You are **r** in saying,
7:24 but judge with **r** judgment."
8:48 we not **r** in saying that you are a Samaritan and D
11:12 "Lord, if he has fallen asleep, he will be all **r**."
13:13 and you are **r**, for that is what I am.
18:10 struck the high priest's slave, and cut off his **r** ear.
21: 6 "Cast the net to the **r** side of the boat,
Ac 2:25 he is at my **r** hand so that I will not be shaken; A
2:33 Being therefore exalted at the **r** hand of God, A
2:34 'The Lord said to my Lord, "Sit at my **r** hand, A
3: 7 he took him by the **r** hand and raised him up; A
4:19 "Whether it is **r** in God's sight to listen
5:31 God exalted him at his **r** hand as Leader A
6: 2 is not **r** that we should neglect the word of God D
7:55 glory of God and Jesus standing at the **r** hand A
7:56 the Son of Man standing at the **r** hand of God!" A
8:21 for your heart is not **r** before God. D
10:35 and does what is **r** is acceptable to him.
28:25 "The Holy Spirit was **r** in saying to your ancestors
Ro 5: 6 at the **r** time Christ died for the ungodly.
7:18 I can will what is **r**, but I cannot do it.
8:34 who was raised, who is at the **r** hand of God, A
9:21 Has the potter no **r** over the clay,
1Co 9: 4 Do we not have the **r** to our food and drink?
9: 5 the **r** to be accompanied by a believing wife,
9: 6 and I who have no **r** to refrain from working for
9:12 Nevertheless, we have not made use of this **r**,
15:34 Come to a sober and **r** mind, and sin no more;
2Co 5:13 if we are in our **r** mind, it is for you.
6: 7 the weapons of righteousness for the **r** hand A
8:21 to do what is **r** not only in the Lord's sight but B
13: 7 but that you may do what is **r**, B
Gal 2: 9 to Barnabas and me the **r** hand of fellowship, A
6: 9 So let us not grow weary in doing what is **r**,
Eph 1:20 from the dead and seated him at his **r** hand in A
5: 9 the light is found in all that is good and **r** and true.
6: 1 obey your parents in the Lord, for this is **r**.
Php 1: 7 It is **r** for me to think this way about all of you,
Col 3: 1 where Christ is, seated at the **r** hand of God. A
2Th 1: 3 as is **r**, because your faith is growing abundantly,
3: 9 This was not because we do not have that **r**,
3:13 do not be weary in doing what is **r**.
1Ti 2: 3 This is **r** and is acceptable in the sight
2: 6 a ransom for all—this was attested at the **r** time.
6:15 which he will bring about at the **r** time—

Tit 1:11 by teaching for sordid gain what it is not **r** D
Heb 1: 3 sat down at the **r** hand of the Majesty on high, A
1:13 "Sit at my **r** hand until I make your enemies A
8: 1 a high priest, one who is seated at the **r** hand of A
9:10 until the time comes to set things **r**.
10:12 "he sat down at the **r** hand of God," A
12: 2 and has taken his seat at the **r** hand of the throne A
13:10 in the tent have no **r** to eat.
Jas 4:17 who knows the **r** thing to do and fails to do it,
1Pe 2:14 and to praise those who do **r**.
2:15 that by doing **r** you should silence the ignorance
2:20 But if you endure when you do **r** and suffer for it,
3:14 you do suffer for doing what is **r**, you are blessed.
3:22 who has gone into heaven and is at the **r** hand A
2Pe 1:13 I think it **r**, as long as I am in this body,
1Jn 2:29 that everyone who does **r** has been born of him.
3: 7 Everyone who does what is **r** is righteous,
3:10 all who do not do what is **r** are not from God, B
Rev 1:16 In his **r** hand he held seven stars, A
1:17 But he placed his **r** hand on me, saying, A
1:20 of the seven stars that you saw in my **r** hand, A
2: 1 the seven stars in his **r** hand, who walks among A
5: 1 Then I saw in the **r** hand of the one seated on AC
5: 7 He went and took the scroll from the **r** hand of A
10: 2 Setting his **r** foot on the sea and his left foot on
10: 5 and the land raised his **r** hand to heaven A
13:16 to be marked on the **r** hand or the forehead, A
22:11 and the righteous still do **r**,
22:14 the **r** to the tree of life and may enter the city by
Tob 2:13 for we have no **r** to eat anything stolen."
5: 8 He replied, "All **r**, I will wait;
6:12 it is **r** for you to inherit her father's possessions.
6:13 "You have every **r** to take her in marriage.
7:10 brother, has the **r** to marry my daughter Sarah.
10: 6 and stop worrying, my dear; he is all **r**.
13: 6 you sinners, and do what is **r** before him; B
14:8,9 commanded to do what is **r** and to give alms, B
Jdt 8:11 What you have said to the people today is not **r**; D
8:29 for your heart's disposition is **r**.
Wis 2:11 But let our might be our law of **r**,
5:16 because with his **r** hand he will cover them, A
9: 9 and what is **r** according to your commandments.
9:18 And thus the paths of those on earth were set **r**,
Sir 1:23 the **r** moment, and then cheerfulness comes back
1:24 They hold back their words until the **r** moment;
2: 2 Set your heart **r** and be steadfast,
3: 2 and he confirms a mother's **r** over her children.
10: 4 over it he will raise up the **r** leader for the time.
10:23 not **r** to despise one who is intelligent but poor, D
12:12 Do not let him sit at your **r** hand, A
20: 4 a girl is the person who does **r** under compulsion.
20: 7 The wise remain silent until the **r** moment,
20: 7 but a boasting fool misses the **r** moment.
21:19 and like manacles on his **r** hand. A
21:21 and like a bracelet on the **r** arm.
32: 3 Speak, you who are older, for it is your **r**,
36: 7 make your hand and **r** arm glorious.
47: 5 and he gave strength to his **r** arm to strike down
48:16 Some of them did what was **r**,
49: 2 He did what was **r** by reforming the people,
49:11 He was like a signet ring on the **r** hand, A
Bar 1:15 And you shall say: The Lord our God is in the **r**, C
2: 6 The Lord our God is in the **r**, C
LtJ 6:15 Another has a dagger in its **r** hand, and an ax, A
Aza 1: 4 all your works are true and your ways **r**,
Bel 1:36 of the wind he set him down in Babylon, **r** over
1Mc 2:22 turning aside from our religion to the **r** hand or A
5:46 they could not go around it to the **r** or to the left;
6:45 he killed men **r** and left,
7:47 the **r** hand that he had so arrogantly stretched A
9: 1 and with them the **r** wing of the army.
9:12 Bacchides was on the **r** wing.
9:14 and the strength of his army were on the **r**;
9:15 and they crushed the **r** wing,
9:16 on the left wing saw that the **r** wing was crushed,
11:58 the **r** to drink from gold cups and dress in purple
12:11 as it is **r** and proper to remember brothers.
14:46 All the people agreed to grant Simon the **r** to act
2Mc 4:12 in establishing a gymnasium **r** under the citadel,
4:34 and gave him his **r** hand; A
6:20 courage to refuse things that it is not **r** to taste, D
9:12 "It is **r** to be subject to God;
14:33 he stretched out his **r** hand toward the sanctuary, A
15:15 Jeremiah stretched out his **r** hand and gave A
1Es 4:29 she would sit at the king's **r** hand A
9:43 Uriah, Hezekiah, and Baalsamus on his **r**,
2Es 3: 6 the garden that your **r** hand had planted before A
4:47 And he said to me, "Stand at my **r** side,
5:11 or anyone who does **r**, passed through you?'
7: 7 there is fire on the **r** hand and deep water on A
7:10 I said, "That is **r**, lord."
9:38 I looked around, and on my **r** I saw a woman;
10:30 he grasped my **r** hand and strengthened me A
11:12 As I watched, one wing on the **r** side rose up,
11:20 the wings that followed also rose up on the **r** side,
11:24 under the head that was on the **r** side;
11:35 the head on the **r** side devour the one on the left.
12:29 over to the head which was on the **r** side,
15:22 My **r** hand will not spare the sinners, A
16:13 For his **r** hand that bends the bow is strong, A
4Mc 1: 1 So it is **r** for me to advise you
5:18 so would it be **r** for us to invalidate our reputation
6:34 It is **r** for us to acknowledge the dominance
8:15 and by their **r** reasoning nullified his tyranny.
13: 5 of **r** reason over emotion in those who were
13: 7 so the seven-towered **r** reason of the youths,
13:24 in the same virtues and brought up in **r** living,

RIGHTEOUS‡ (348) [RIGHTEOUSLY, RIGHTEOUSNESS, RIGHTEOUSNESS']

A. RIGHTEOUS MAN (14)
B. RIGHTEOUS DEEDS (11)
C. RIGHTEOUS ONE (8)

Ge 6: 9 Noah was a **r** man, blameless in his generation; A
7: 1 that you alone are **r** before me in this generation.
18:23 "Will you indeed sweep away the **r** with
18:24 Suppose there are fifty **r** within the city;
18:24 the place and not forgive it for the fifty **r** who are
18:25 to slay the **r** with the wicked,
18:25 so that the **r** fare as the wicked!
18:26 LORD said, "If I find at Sodom fifty **r** in the city,
18:28 Suppose five of the fifty **r** are lacking?
1Sa 24:17 He said to David, "You are more **r** than I;
2Sa 4:11 wicked men have killed a **r** man on his bed A
1Ki 2:32 the sword two men more **r** and better than himself,
8:32 and vindicating the **r** by rewarding them according
Ne 9: 8 and you have fulfilled your promise, for you are **r**.
Job 4:17 'Can mortals be **r** before God?
10:15 If I am **r**, I cannot lift up my head,
15:14 Or those born of woman, that they can be **r**?
17: 9 Yet the **r** hold to their way,
22: 3 Is it any pleasure to the Almighty if you are **r**,
22:19 The **r** see it and are glad;
25: 4 How then can a mortal be **r** before God?
32: 1 because he was **r** in his own eyes.
34:17 Will you condemn one who is **r** and mighty,
35: 7 If you are **r**, what do you give to him;
36: 7 He does not withdraw his eyes from the **r**,
Ps 1: 5 nor sinners in the congregation of the **r**;
1: 6 for the LORD watches over the way of the **r**,
5:12 For you bless the **r**, O LORD;
7: 9 but establish the **r**, you who test the minds and hearts, O **r** God.
7:11 God is a **r** judge, and a God who has indignation
9: 4 you have sat on the throne giving **r** judgment.
11: 3 the foundations are destroyed, what can the **r** do?"
11: 5 The LORD tests the **r** and the wicked,
11: 7 For the LORD is **r**; he loves righteous deeds;
11: 7 loves **r** deeds; the upright shall behold his face. B
14: 5 for God is with the company of the **r**.
19: 9 of the LORD are true and **r** altogether.
31:18 that speak insolently against the **r** with pride
32:11 Be glad in the LORD and rejoice, O **r**,
33: 1 Rejoice in the LORD, O you **r**.
34:15 The eyes of the LORD are on the **r**,
34:17 When the **r** cry for help, the LORD hears,
34:19 Many are the afflictions of the **r**,
34:21 and those who hate the **r** will be condemned.
37:12 The wicked plot against the **r**,
37:16 a little that the **r** person has than the abundance
37:17 but the LORD upholds the **r**.
37:21 but the **r** are generous and keep giving;
37:25 the **r** forsaken or their children begging bread.
37:28 The **r** shall be kept safe forever,
37:29 The **r** shall inherit the land, and live in it forever.
37:30 The mouths of the **r** utter wisdom,
37:32 The wicked watch for the **r**, and seek to kill them.
37:39 The salvation of the **r** is from the LORD;
52: 6 The **r** will see, and fear, and will laugh at
55:22 he will never permit the **r** to be moved.
58:10 The **r** will rejoice when they see vengeance done;
58:11 "Surely there is a reward for the **r**;
64:10 the **r** rejoice in the LORD and take refuge in him.
68: 3 But let the **r** be joyful;
69:28 let them not be enrolled among the **r**.
71:15 My mouth will tell of your **r** acts,
71:24 All day long my tongue will talk of your **r** help,
75:10 but the horns of the **r** shall be exalted.
92:12 The **r** flourish like the palm tree,
94:15 for justice will return to the **r**,
94:21 They band together against the life of the **r**,
97:11 Light dawns for the **r**, and joy for the upright
97:12 Rejoice in the LORD, O you **r**,
112: 4 they are gracious, merciful, and **r**.
112: 6 For the **r** will never be moved;
116: 5 Gracious is the LORD, and **r**;
118:15 of victory in the tents of the **r**:
118:20 the gate of the LORD; the **r** shall enter through it.
119: 7 when I learn your **r** ordinances.
119:62 because of your **r** ordinances.
119:106 to observe your **r** ordinances.
119:123 and for the fulfillment of your **r** promise.
119:137 You are **r**, O LORD,
119:144 Your decrees are **r** forever;
119:160 every one of your **r** ordinances endures forever.
119:164 a day I praise you for your **r** ordinances.
125: 3 not rest on the land allotted to the **r**,
125: 3 **r** might not stretch out their hands to do wrong.
129: 4 LORD is **r**; he has cut the cords of the wicked.
140:13 Surely the **r** shall give thanks to your name;
141: 5 Let the **r** strike me; let the faithful correct me.
142: 7 The **r** will surround me, for you will deal
143: 2 for no one living is **r** before you.
146: 8 those who are bowed down; the LORD loves the **r**.
Pr 3:33 but he blesses the abode of the **r**.
4:18 But the path of the **r** is like the light of dawn,
8: 8 All the words of my mouth are **r**;
9: 9 teach the **r** and they will gain in learning.
10: 3 The LORD does not let the **r** go hungry,
10: 6 Blessings are on the head of the **r**,
10: 7 The memory of the **r** is a blessing,
10:11 The mouth of the **r** is a fountain of life,
10:16 The wage of the **r** leads to life,

Pr 10:20 The tongue of the **r** is choice silver;
10:21 The lips of the **r** feed many,
10:24 but the desire of the **r** will be granted.
10:25 but the **r** are established forever.
10:28 The hope of the **r** ends in gladness,
10:30 The **r** will never be removed,
10:31 The mouth of the **r** brings forth wisdom,
10:32 The lips of the **r** know what is acceptable,
11: 8 The **r** are delivered from trouble,
11: 9 but by knowledge the **r** are delivered.
11:10 When it goes well with the **r**, the city rejoices;
11:21 but those who are **r** will escape.
11:23 The desire of the **r** ends only in good;
11:28 but the **r** will flourish like green leaves.
11:30 The fruit of the **r** is a tree of life,
11:31 If the **r** are repaid on earth,
12: 3 but the root of the **r** will never be moved.
12: 5 The thoughts of the **r** are just;
12: 7 but the house of the **r** will stand.
12:10 The **r** know the needs of their animals,
12:12 but the root of the **r** bears fruit.
12:13 but the **r** escape from trouble.
12:21 No harm happens to the **r**,
12:26 The **r** gives good advice to friends,
13: 5 The **r** hate falsehood, but the wicked act
13: 9 The light of the **r** rejoices,
13:21 but prosperity rewards the **r**.
13:22 but the sinner's wealth is laid up for the **r**.
13:25 The **r** have enough to satisfy their appetite,
14:19 the wicked at the gates of the **r**.
14:32 but the **r** find a refuge in their integrity.
15: 6 In the house of the **r** there is much treasure,
15:28 The mind of the **r** ponders how to answer,
15:29 but he hears the prayer of the **r**.
16:13 **R** lips are the delight of a king,
16:31 it is gained in a **r** life.
17:15 the **r** are both alike an abomination to the LORD.
18:10 the **r** run into it and are safe.
20: 7 The **r** walk in integrity—happy are the children
21:12 The **R** One observes the house of the wicked; C
21:15 When justice is done, it is a joy to the **r**,
21:18 The wicked is a ransom for the **r**,
21:26 but the **r** give and do not hold back.
23:24 The father of the **r** will greatly rejoice;
24:15 in wait like an outlaw against the home of the **r**;
24:15 do no violence to the place where the **r** live;
25:26 a polluted fountain are the **r** who give way before
28: 1 but the **r** are as bold as a lion.
28:12 When the **r** triumph, there is great glory,
28:28 but when they perish, the **r** increase.
29: 2 When the **r** are in authority, the people rejoice;
29: 6 but the **r** sing and rejoice.
29: 7 The **r** know the rights of the poor;
29:16 but the **r** will look upon their downfall.
29:27 The unjust are an abomination to the **r**,
Ecc 3:17 God will judge the **r** and the wicked,
7:15 there are **r** people who perish
7:16 Do not be too **r**, and do not act too wise;
7:20 Surely there is no one on earth so **r** as to do good
8:14 that there are **r** people who are treated according
8:14 according to the conduct of the **r**.
9: 1 the **r** and the wise and their deeds are in the hand
9: 2 to the **r** and the wicked, to the good and the evil,
Isa 24:16 songs of praise, of glory to the **R** One. C
26: 2 so that the **r** nation that keeps faith may enter in.
26: 7 The way of the **r** is level;
26: 7 O Just One, you make smooth the path of the **r**.
45:21 a **r** God and a Savior; there is no one besides me.
53:11 The **r** one, my servant, shall make many C
53:11 righteous one, my servant, shall make many **r**,
57: 1 The **r** perish, and no one takes it to heart;
57: 1 For the **r** are taken away from calamity,
58: 2 they ask of me **r** judgments,
60:21 Your people shall all be **r**;
64: 6 and all our **r** deeds are like a filthy cloth. B
Jer 20:12 O LORD of hosts, you test the **r**,
23: 5 when I will raise up for David a **r** Branch,
33:15 and at that time I will cause a **r** Branch to spring
La 4:13 who shed the blood of the **r** in the midst of her.
Eze 3:20 if the **r** turn from their righteousness
3:20 and their **r** deeds that they have done shall not B
3:21 If, however, you warn the **r** not to sin,
13:22 Because you have disheartened the **r** falsely,
16:51 and have made your sisters appear **r** by all
16:52 for you have made your sisters appear **r**.
18: 5 If a man is **r** and does what is lawful and right—
18: 9 acting faithfully—such a one is **r**;
18:20 the righteousness of the **r** shall be his own,
18:24 But when the **r** turn away from their righteousness
18:24 None of the **r** deeds that they have done shall B
18:26 When the **r** turn away from their righteousness
21: 3 and will cut off from you both **r** and wicked.
21: 4 Because I will cut off from you both **r** and wicked,
23:45 But **r** judges shall declare them guilty of adultery
33:12 of the **r** shall not save them when they transgress;
33:12 and the **r** shall not be able to live
33:13 Though I say to the **r** that they shall surely live,
33:13 none of their **r** deeds shall be remembered; B
33:18 When the **r** turn from their righteousness,
Da 9:16 O Lord, in view of all your **r** acts,
Am 2: 6 because they sell the **r** for silver,
5:12 you who afflict the **r**, who take a bribe,
Hab 1: 4 The wicked surround the **r**—
1:13 when the wicked swallow those more **r** than they?
2: 4 but the **r** live by their faith.
Zep 3: 5 The LORD within it is **r**; he does no wrong.
Mal 3:18 the difference between the **r** and the wicked,

Mt 1:19 being a **r** man and unwilling to expose her A
5:45 and sends rain on the **r** and on the unrighteous.
9:13 For I have come to call not the **r** but sinners."
10:41 and whoever welcomes a **r** person in the name of a **r** person will receive the reward of the **r**;
13:17 and **r** people longed to see what you see,
13:43 Then the **r** will shine like the sun in the kingdom
13:49 and separate the evil from the **r**
23:28 So you also on the outside look **r** to others,
23:29 of the prophets and decorate the graves of the **r**,
23:35 upon you may come all the **r** blood shed on earth,
23:35 the blood of **r** Abel to the blood of Zechariah son
25:37 Then the **r** will answer him, 'Lord,
25:46 but the **r** into eternal life."
Mk 2:17 I have come to call not the **r** but sinners."
6:20 knowing that he was a **r** and holy man,
Lk 1: 6 Both of them were **r** before God,
1:17 and the disobedient to the wisdom of the **r**,
2:25 this man was **r** and devout,
5:32 to call not the **r** but sinners to repentance."
14:14 for you will be repaid at the resurrection of the **r**."
15: 7 ninety-nine **r** persons who need no repentance.
18: 9 in themselves that they were **r** and regarded others
23:50 there was a good and **r** man named Joseph, A
Jn 17:25 "**R** Father, the world does not know you,
Ac 3:14 But you rejected the Holy and **R** One and asked C
7:52 the coming of the **R** One, C
22:14 to see the **R** One and to hear his own voice; C
24:15 be a resurrection of both the **r** and the unrighteous.
Ro 1:17 it is written, "The one who is **r** will live by faith."
2: 5 when God's **r** judgment will be revealed.
2:13 the hearers of the law who are **r** in God's sight,
3:10 "There is no one who is **r**, not even one;
3:26 to prove at the present time that he himself is **r**
5: 7 Indeed, rarely will anyone die for a **r** person—
5:19 the one man's obedience the many will be made **r**.
Gal 3:11 for "The one who is **r** will live by faith."
2Th 1: 5 This is evidence of the **r** judgment of God,
2Ti 4: 8 the **r** judge, will give me on that day,
Heb 1: 8 and the **r** scepter is the scepter of your kingdom.
10:38 but my **r** one will live by faith. C
11: 4 Through this he received approval as **r**,
12:23 and to the spirits of the **r** made perfect,
Jas 5: 6 You have condemned and murdered the **r** one, C
5:16 The prayer of the **r** is powerful and effective.
1Pe 3:12 For the eyes of the Lord are on the **r**,
3:18 For Christ also suffered for sins once for all, the **r**
4:18 And "If it is hard for the **r** to be saved,
2Pe 2: 7 a **r** man greatly distressed by the licentiousness A
2: 8 (for that **r** man, living among them day A
2: 8 was tormented in his **r** soul by their lawless deeds
1Jn 2: 1 an advocate with the Father, Jesus Christ the **r**;
2:29 If you know that he is **r**,
3: 7 who does what is right is **r**, just as he is **r**.
3:12 his own deeds were evil and his brother's **r**.
Rev 19: 8 for the fine linen is the **r** deeds of the saints. B
22:11 and the filthy still be filthy, and the **r** still do right,
Tob 2:14 Where are your **r** deeds? B
3: 2 "You are **r**, O Lord, and all your deeds are just;
4:17 Place your bread on the grave of the **r**,
13: 9 but will again have mercy on the children of the **r**.
13:13 Go, then, and rejoice over the children of the **r**,
AdE 11: 7 to fight against the **r** nation.
11: 9 And the whole **r** nation was troubled;
14: 7 You are **r**, O Lord!
16:15 but are governed by most **r** laws
Wis 2:10 Let us oppress the **r** poor man;
2:12 "Let us lie in wait for the **r** man, A
2:16 he calls the last end of the **r** happy,
2:18 for if the **r** man is God's child, A
3: 1 But the souls of the **r** are in the hand of God,
3:10 those who disregarded the **r** and rebelled against
4: 7 But the **r**, though they die early, will be at rest.
4:16 The **r** who have died will condemn
5: 1 Then the **r** will stand with great confidence in
5: 2 be amazed at the unexpected salvation of the **r**.
5:15 **r** live forever, and their reward is with the Lord;
10: 4 steering the **r** man by a paltry piece of wood. A
10: 5 the **r** man and preserved him blameless A
10: 6 a **r** man when the ungodly were perishing; A
10:10 When a **r** man fled from his brother's wrath, A
10:13 When a **r** man was sold, A
10:20 Therefore the **r** plundered the ungodly;
11:13 the **r** had received benefit,
11:14 when they felt thirst in a different way from the **r**.
12: 9 the ungodly into the hands of the **r** in battle,
12:15 You are **r** and you rule all things righteously,
12:19 that the **r** must be kind,
16:17 for the universe defends the **r**.
16:23 in order that the **r** might be fed,
18: 7 The deliverance of the **r** and the destruction
18:20 The experience of death touched also the **r**,
19:17 just as were those at the door of the **r** man— A
Sir 9:16 Let the **r** be your dinner companions,
32:16 and they will kindle **r** deeds like a light. B
35: 8 The offering of the **r** enriches the altar,
35: 9 The sacrifice of the **r** is acceptable,
35:22 and does justice for the **r**,
44:10 whose **r** deeds have not been forgotten; B
44:17 Noah was found perfect and **r**;
Bar 2:19 of any **r** deeds of our ancestors or our kings B
5: 4 God will give you evermore the name, "**R** Peace,
Aza 1:64 Bless the Lord, spirits and souls of the **r**;
Sus 1: 3 Her parents were **r**, and had trained their daughter
1:53 'You shall not put an innocent and **r** person
1Mc 2:24 He gave vent to **r** anger;
2Mc 12: 6 the **r** judge, attacked the murderers of his kindred.

2Mc 12:41 they all blessed the ways of the Lord, the **r** judge,
1Es 4:39 but it does what is **r** instead of anything
Man 1: 1 and Isaac and Jacob and of their **r** offspring;
1: 8 Therefore you, O Lord, God of the **r**,
1: 8 have not appointed repentance for the **r**,
3Mc 2:22 since he was smitten by a **r** judgment.
2Es 3:11 and all the **r** who have descended from him.
4:27 the things that have been promised to the **r**
4:35 of the **r** in their chambers ask about these matters,
4:39 that the time of threshing is delayed for the **r**—
7:17 in your law that the **r** shall inherit these things,
7:18 The **r**, therefore, can endure difficult circumstances
7:*35* **r** deeds shall awake, and unrighteous deeds B
7:*51* Inasmuch as you have said that the **r** are not many
7:*99* This is the order of the souls of the **r**,
7:*102* the day of judgment the **r** will be able to intercede
7:*111* [41] the **r** have prayed for the ungodly,
8:33 For the **r**, who have many works laid up with you,
8:39 but I will rejoice over the creation of the **r**,
8:49 have not considered yourself to be among the **r**.
8:57 Moreover, they have even trampled on his **r** ones,
9:13 but inquire how the **r** will be saved,
10:22 our **r** men have been carried off,
10:39 He has seen your **r** conduct,
12: 7 and if I have been accounted **r** before you
14:32 And since he is a **r** judge,
14:35 then the names of the **r** shall become manifest,
15: 8 Innocent and **r** blood cries out to me,
15: 8 and the souls of the **r** cry out continually.
4Mc 15:10 For they were **r** and self-controlled and brave
16:21 Daniel the **r** was thrown to the lions,
18:15 who said, 'Many are the afflictions of the **r**.'

RIGHTEOUSLY (4) [RIGHTEOUS]

Pr 31: 9 judge **r**, defend the rights of the poor and needy.
Isa 33:15 Those who walk **r** and speak uprightly,
Jer 11:20 But you, O LORD of hosts, who judge **r**,
Wis 12:15 You are righteous and you rule all things **r**,

RIGHTEOUSNESS‡ (262) [RIGHTEOUS]

Ge 15: 6 and the LORD reckoned it to him as **r**.
18:19 the way of the LORD by doing **r** and justice;
Dt 9: 4 because of my **r** that the LORD has brought me
9: 5 because of your **r** or the uprightness of your heart
9: 6 to occupy because of your **r**;
1Sa 26:23 The LORD rewards everyone for his **r**
2Sa 22:21 The LORD rewarded me according to my **r**;
22:25 LORD has recompensed me according to my **r**,
1Ki 3: 6 because he walked before you in faithfulness, in **r**,
8:32 by rewarding them according to their **r**.
10: 9 he has made you king to execute justice and **r**."
2Ch 6:23 by rewarding them in accordance with their **r**.
9: 8 that you may execute justice and **r**."
Job 27: 6 I hold fast my **r**, and will not let it go;
29:14 I put on **r**, and it clothed me;
33:26 and God repays him for his **r**.
35: 8 and your **r**, other human beings.
36: 3 and ascribe **r** to my Maker.
37:23 and abundant **r** he will not violate.
Ps 5: 8 O LORD, in your **r** because of my enemies;
7: 8 according to my **r** and according to the integrity
7:17 I will give to the LORD the thanks due to his **r**,
9: 8 He judges the world with **r**;
17:15 As for me, I shall behold your face in **r**;
18:20 The LORD rewarded me according to my **r**;
18:24 LORD has recompensed me according to my **r**,
31: 1 to shame; in your **r** deliver me.
33: 5 He loves **r** and justice; the earth is full of the
35:24 O LORD, my God, according to your **r**,
35:28 of your **r** and of your praise all day long.
36: 6 Your **r** is like the mighty mountains,
45: 7 you love **r** and hate wickedness.
50: 6 heavens declare his **r**, for God himself is judge.
71: 2 In your **r** deliver me and rescue me;
71:16 I will praise your **r**, yours alone.
71:19 and your **r**, O God, reach the high heavens.
72: 1 O God, and your **r** to a king's son.
72: 2 May he judge your people with **r**,
72: 3 for the people, and the hills, in **r**.
72: 7 In his days may **r** flourish and peace abound,
85:10 **r** and peace will kiss each other.
85:11 and **r** will look down from the sky.
85:13 **R** will go before him, and will make a path
89:14 **R** and justice are the foundation of your throne;
89:16 in your name all day long, and extol your **r**.
96:13 He will judge the world with **r**,
97: 2 **r** and justice are the foundation of his throne.
97: 6 The heavens proclaim his **r**;
98: 9 He will judge the world with **r**,
99: 4 you have executed justice and **r** in Jacob.
103:17 and his **r** to children's children,
106: 3 who do **r** at all times.
106:31 to him as **r** from generation to generation forever.
111: 3 and his **r** endures forever.
112: 3 and their **r** endures forever.
112: 9 to the poor; their **r** endures forever;
118:19 Open to me the gates of **r**,
119:40 in your **r** give me life.
119:138 You have appointed your decrees in **r** and
119:142 Your **r** is an everlasting **r**,
132: 9 Let your priests be clothed with **r**,
143: 1 in your faithfulness; answer me in your **r**.
143:11 In your **r** bring me out of trouble.
145: 7 and shall sing aloud of your **r**.
Pr 1: 3 for gaining instruction in wise dealing, **r**, justice,
2: 9 Then you will understand **r** and justice and equity,

Pr 8:20 I walk in the way of **r**, along the paths of justice,
10: 2 but **r** delivers from death.
11: 4 but **r** delivers from death.
11: 5 The **r** of the blameless keeps their ways straight,
11: 6 The **r** of the upright saves them,
11:18 but those who sow **r** get a true reward.
11:19 Whoever is steadfast in **r** will live,
12:28 In the path of **r** there is life,
13: 6 **R** guards one whose way is upright,
14:34 **R** exalts a nation, but sin is a reproach
15: 9 but he loves the one who pursues **r**.
16: 8 a little with **r** than large income with injustice.
16:12 for the throne is established by **r**.
20:28 and his throne is upheld by **r**.
21: 3 To do **r** and justice is more acceptable to
21:21 Whoever pursues **r** and kindness will find life
25: 5 and his throne will be established in **r**.
Ecc 3:16 wickedness was there, and in the place of **r**,
7:15 there are righteous people who perish in their **r**,
Isa 1:21 **r** lodged in her—but now murderers!
1:26 Afterward you shall be called the city of **r**,
1:27 and those in her who repent, by **r**.
5: 7 justice, but saw bloodshed; **r**, but heard a cry!
5:16 and the Holy God shows himself holy by **r**.
9: 7 with justice and with **r** from this time onward and
10:22 Destruction is decreed, overflowing with **r**.
11: 4 but with **r** he shall judge the poor, and decide
11: 5 **R** shall be the belt around his waist,
26: 9 the inhabitants of the world learn **r**.
26:10 favor is shown to the wicked, they do not learn **r**;
28:17 I will make justice the line, and **r** the plummet;
32: 1 See, a king will reign in **r**,
32:16 and **r** abide in the fruitful field.
32:17 The effect of **r** will be peace,
32:17 and the result of **r**, quietness and trust forever.
33: 5 he filled Zion with justice and **r**;
42: 6 in **r**, I have taken you by the hand and kept you;
42:21 The LORD was pleased, for the sake of his **r**,
45: 8 from above, and let the skies rain down **r**;
45: 8 and let it cause **r** to sprout up also;
45:13 I have aroused Cyrus in **r**,
45:23 from my mouth has gone forth in **r** a word
45:24 it shall be said of me, are **r** and strength;
51: 1 Listen to me, you that pursue **r**,
51: 7 Listen to me, you who know **r**,
54:14 In **r** you shall be established;
57:12 I will concede your **r** and your works,
58: 2 that practiced **r** and did not forsake the ordinance
59: 9 justice is far from us, and **r** does not reach us;
59:14 Justice is turned back, and **r** stands at a distance;
59:16 arm brought him victory, and his **r** upheld him.
59:17 He put on **r** like a breastplate,
60:17 I will appoint Peace as your overseer and **R**
61: 3 They will be called oaks of **r**,
61:10 he has covered me with the robe of **r**,
61:11 the Lord GOD will cause **r** and praise to spring
Jer 9:24 I act with steadfast love, justice, and **r** in the earth,
22: 3 Thus says the LORD: Act with justice and **r**,
22:15 and drink and do justice and **r**?
23: 5 and shall execute justice and **r** in the land.
23: 6 be called: "The LORD is our **r**."
31:23 LORD bless you, O abode of **r**, O holy hill!"
33:15 and he shall execute justice and **r** in the land.
33:16 be called: "The LORD is our **r**."
Eze 3:20 righteous turn from their **r** and commit iniquity,
14:14 they would save only their own lives by their **r**,
14:20 they would save only their own lives by their **r**.
18:20 the **r** of the righteous shall be his own,
18:22 for the **r** that they have done they shall live.
18:24 But when the righteous turn away from their **r**
18:26 from their **r** and commit iniquity, they shall die
33:12 The **r** of the righteous shall not save them
33:12 the righteous shall not be able to live by their **r**
33:13 yet if they trust in their **r** and commit iniquity,
33:18 When the righteous turn from their **r**,
Da 4:27 atone for your sins with **r**,
9: 7 "**R** is on your side, O Lord, but open shame,
9:18 before you on the ground of our **r**,
9:24 and to atone for iniquity, to bring in everlasting **r**,
12: 3 and those who lead many to **r**,
Hos 2:19 I will take you for my wife in **r** and in justice,
10:12 Sow for yourselves **r**; reap steadfast love;
10:12 that he may come and rain **r** upon you.
Am 5: 7 and bring **r** to the ground!
5:24 and **r** like an ever-flowing stream.
6:12 into poison and the fruit of **r** into wormwood—
Zep 2: 3 seek **r**, seek humility; perhaps you may be hidden
Zec 8: 8 and I will be their God, in faithfulness and in **r**.
Mal 3: 3 until they present offerings to the LORD in **r**.
4: 2 you who revere my name the sun of **r** shall rise,
Mt 3:15 for it is proper for us in this way to fulfill all **r**."
5: 6 "Blessed are those who hunger and thirst for **r**,
5:20 your **r** exceeds that of the scribes and Pharisees,
6:33 But strive first for the kingdom of God and his **r**,
21:32 For John came to you in the way of **r** and you did
Lk 1:75 in holiness and **r** before him all our days.
Jn 16: 8 the world wrong about sin and **r** and judgment:
16:10 about **r**, because I am going to the Father
Ac 13:10 you enemy of all **r**, full of all deceit and villainy,
17:31 a day on which he will have the world judged in **r**
Ro 1:17 the **r** of God is revealed through faith for faith;
3:21 apart from law, the **r** of God has been disclosed,
3:22 the **r** of God through faith in Jesus Christ
3:25 He did this to show his **r**,
4: 3 and it was reckoned to him as **r**."
4: 5 such faith is reckoned as **r**.
4: 6 to whom God reckons **r** apart from works:
Ro 4: 9 We say, "Faith was reckoned to Abraham as **r**."
4:11 of circumcision as a seal of the **r** that he had
4:11 and who thus have **r** reckoned to them,
4:13 through the law but through the **r** of faith.
4:22 Therefore his faith "was reckoned to him as **r**."
5:17 the free gift of **r** exercise dominion in life through
5:18 so one man's act of **r** leads to justification and life
6:13 present your members to God as instruments of **r**.
6:16 or of obedience, which leads to **r**?
6:18 set free from sin, have become slaves of **r**.
6:19 so now present your members as slaves to **r**
6:20 you were free in regard to **r**.
8:10 the Spirit is life because of **r**.
9:30 Gentiles, who did not strive for **r**, have attained it, that is, **r** through faith;
9:31 who did strive for the **r** that is based on the law,
10: 3 For, being ignorant of the **r** that comes from God,
10: 3 they have not submitted to God's **r**.
10: 4 so that there may be **r** for everyone who believes.
10: 5 Moses writes concerning the **r** that comes from
10: 6 But the **r** that comes from faith says,
14:17 the kingdom of God is not food and drink but **r**
1Co 1:30 and **r** and sanctification and redemption,
2Co 5:21 so that in him we might become the **r** of God.
6: 7 with the weapons of **r** for the right hand and for
6:14 For what partnership is there between **r**
9: 9 he gives to the poor; his **r** endures forever."
9:10 for sowing and increase the harvest of your **r**.
11:15 also disguise themselves as ministers of **r**.
Gal 3: 6 and it was reckoned to him as **r**,"
3:21 then **r** would indeed come through the law.
5: 5 Spirit, by faith, we eagerly wait for the hope of **r**.
Eph 4:24 created according to the likeness of God in true **r**
6:14 and put on the breastplate of **r**.
Php 1:11 of **r** that comes through Jesus Christ for the glory
3: 6 as to **r** under the law, blameless.
3: 9 having a **r** of my own that comes from the law,
3: 9 the **r** from God based on faith.
1Ti 6:11 pursue **r**, godliness, faith, love, endurance,
2Ti 2:22 Shun youthful passions and pursue **r**, faith, love,
3:16 for reproof, for correction, and for training in **r**,
4: 8 now on there is reserved for me the crown of **r**,
Tit 3: 5 not because of any works of **r** that we had done,
Heb 1: 9 You have loved **r** and hated wickedness;
5:13 being still an infant, is unskilled in the word of **r**.
7: 2 His name, in the first place, means "king of **r**";
11: 7 and became an heir to the **r** that is in accordance
12:11 of **r** to those who have been trained by it.
Jas 1:20 for your anger does not produce God's **r**.
2:23 and it was reckoned to him as **r**,"
3:18 of **r** is sown in peace for those who make peace.
1Pe 2:24 so that, free from sins, we might live for **r**;
2Pe 1: 1 through the **r** of our God and Savior Jesus Christ:
2: 5 even though he saved Noah, a herald of **r**,
2:21 for them never to have known the way of **r** than,
3:13 for new heavens and a new earth, where **r** is
Rev 19:11 and in **r** he judges and makes war.
Tob 1: 3 in the ways of truth and **r** all the days of my life.
4: 6 To all those who practice **r**
12: 8 but better than both is almsgiving with **r**.
12: 8 little with **r** is better than wealth with wrongdoing.
13: 6 Bless the Lord of **r**, and exalt the King of the ages.
14: 7 and in **r** they will praise the eternal God.
Wis 1: 1 Love **r**, you rulers of the earth,
1:15 For **r** is immortal.
5: 6 and the light of **r** did not shine on us,
5:18 on **r** as a breastplate, and wear impartial justice as
8: 7 And if anyone loves **r**, her labors are virtues;
9: 3 and rule the world in holiness and **r**,
12:16 For your strength is the source of **r**,
14: 7 For blessed is the wood by which **r** comes.
15: 3 For to know you is complete **r**,
Sir 7: 5 Do not assert your **r** before the Lord,
26:28 and a man who turns back from **r** to sin—
Bar 2:18 will declare your glory and **r**, O Lord.
4:13 or tread the paths his **r** showed them.
5: 2 Put on the robe of the **r** that comes from God;
5: 9 with the mercy and **r** that come from him.
1Mc 2:29 At that time many who were seeking **r**
2:52 and it was reckoned to him as **r**?
2Es 5:11 One country shall ask its neighbor, 'Has **r**,
7:*105* all shall bear their own **r** and unrighteousness."
7:*114* [44] and **r** has increased and truth has appeared.
8:12 You have nurtured it in your **r**,
8:32 who have no works of **r**,
8:36 O Lord, your **r** and goodness will be declared,
16:50 so **r** shall abhor iniquity,
16:52 and **r** will reign over us.

RIGHTEOUSNESS' (1) [RIGHTEOUS]

Mt 5:10 "Blessed are those who are persecuted for **r** sake,

RIGHTFUL‡ (4) [RIGHT]

Job 8: 6 for you and restore to you your **r** place.
Jer 30:18 and the citadel set on its **r** site.
Da 8:14 then the sanctuary shall be restored to its **r** state."
1Co 9:12 If others share this **r** claim on you,

RIGHTLY (14) [RIGHT]

Ge 27:36 Esau said, "Is he not **r** named Jacob?
Dt 1:16 and judge **r** between one person and another,
Job 11:13 "If you direct your heart **r**,
Pr 8:16 by me rulers rule, and nobles, all who govern **r**.
SS 1: 4 your love more than wine; **r** do they love you.
Mt 15: 7 Isaiah prophesied **r** about you when he said:
Mk 7: 6 "Isaiah prophesied **r** about you hypocrites,
Lk 7:43 And Jesus said to him, "You have judged **r**."
Jn 18:23 But if I have spoken **r**, why do you strike me?"
2Ti 2:15 **r** explaining the word of truth.
Wis 6: 4 as servants of his kingdom you did not rule **r**,
Sir 38:10 Give up your faults and direct your hands **r**,
2Es 4:20 He answered me and said, "You have judged **r**,
8:37 "Some things you have spoken **r**,

RIGHTS (18) [RIGHT]

Ex 21:10 clothing, or marital **r** of the first wife.
Dt 22:30 thereby violating his father's **r**.
27:20 because he has violated his father's **r**."
1Sa 10:25 the people the **r** and duties of the kingship;
Pr 29: 7 The righteous know the **r** of the poor;
31: 5 and will pervert the **r** of all the afflicted.
31: 8 for the **r** of all the destitute.
31: 9 defend the **r** of the poor and needy.
Isa 5:23 and deprive the innocent of their **r**!
Jer 5:28 and they do not defend the **r** of the needy.
La 3:35 when human **r** are perverted in the presence of
1Co 7: 3 husband should give to his wife her conjugal **r**,
9:15 But I have made no use of any of these **r**,
9:18 so as not to make full use of my **r** in the gospel.
Wis 19:16 those who had already shared the same **r**.
1Mc 8:32 we will defend their **r** and fight you on sea and
2Mc 13:23 yielded and swore to observe all their **r**,
2Es 2:20 "Guard the **r** of the widow,

RIGID (1)

Mk 9:18 and he foams and grinds his teeth and becomes **r**;

RIGOUR (KJV) See HARSHNESS, RUTHLESS

RIM (14) [RIMS]

Ex 25:25 You shall make around it a **r** a handbreadth wide,
25:25 and a molding of gold around the **r**.
25:27 for carrying the table shall be close to the **r**.
37:12 He made around it a **r** a handbreadth wide,
37:12 and made a molding of gold around the **r**.
37:14 for carrying the table were close to the **r**.
2Ch 4: 2 it was round, ten cubits from **r** to **r**,
4: 5 its **r** was made like the **r** of a cup,
Eze 43:13 with a **r** of one span around its edge.
43:17 with a **r** around it half a cubit wide,
43:20 and upon the **r** all around;
2Mc 13: 5 and it has a **r** running around it that

RIMMON (16) [EN-RIMMON, GATH-RIMMON, HADAD-RIMMON, RIMMON-PEREZ]

Jos 15:32 Shilhim, Ain, and **R**: in all,
19: 7 **R**, Ether, and Ashan—four towns with their
19:13 and going on to **R** it bends toward Neah;
Jdg 20:45 and fled toward the wilderness to the rock of **R**,
20:47 and fled toward the wilderness to the rock of **R**,
20:47 and remained at the rock of **R** for four months.
21:13 to the Benjaminites who were at the rock of **R**,
2Sa 4: 2 of **R** a Benjaminite from Beeroth—
4: 5 Now the sons of **R** the Beerothite,
4: 9 the sons of **R** the Beerothite, "As the LORD lives,
2Ki 5:18 when my master goes into the house of **R**
5:18 and I bow down in the house of **R**,
5:18 when I do bow down in the house of **R**,
1Ch 4:32 And their villages were Etam, Ain, **R**, Tochen,
Isa 10:27 He has gone up from **R**,
Zec 14:10 into a plain from Geba to **R** south of Jerusalem.

RIMMON-PEREZ (2) [RIMMON]

Nu 33:19 They set out from Rithmah and camped at **R**.
33:20 They set out from **R** and camped at Libnah.

RIMMONO (1)

1Ch 6:77 **R** with its pasture lands, Tabor with its pasture

RIMS (4) [RIM]

1Ki 7:33 their axles, their **r**, their spokes,
Eze 1:18 Their **r** were tall and awesome,
1:18 for the **r** of all four were full of eyes all around.
10:12 Their entire body, their **r**, their spokes,

RING (25) [EARRING, EARRINGS, NOSE-RING, RANG, RINGING, RINGLEADER, RINGS]

Ge 24:47 So I put the **r** on her nose,
41:42 Removing his signet **r** from his hand,
Ex 26:24 but joined at the top, at the first **r**;
36:29 but joined at the top, at the first **r**;
Est 3:10 So the king took his signet **r** from his hand
3:12 of King Ahasuerus and sealed with the king's **r**.
8: 2 Then the king took off his signet **r**,
8: 8 and seal it with the king's **r**;
8: 8 and sealed with the king's **r** cannot be revoked."
8:10 sealed them with the king's **r**,
Job 42:11 of them gave him a piece of money and a gold **r**.
Pr 11:22 Like a gold **r** in a pig's snout is a beautiful woman
25:12 a gold **r** or an ornament of gold is a wise rebuke to
Jer 22:24 of Judah were the signet **r** on my right hand,
Eze 16:12 a **r** on your nose, earrings in your ears,
Hos 2:13 to them and decked herself with her **r** and jewelry,

Hag 2:23 says the LORD, and make you like a signet **r**;
Lk 15:22 put a **r** on his finger and sandals on his feet.
AdE 3:10 the king took off his signet **r** and gave it to Haman
8:2 king took the **r** that had been taken from Haman,
8:8 and seal it with my **r**;
8:8 the king's command and sealed with my **r** cannot
8:10 with the king's authority and sealed with his **r**,
Sir 17:22 One's almsgiving is like a signet **r** with the Lord,
49:11 He was like a signet **r** on the right hand,

RINGING (1) [RING]
Sir 45:9 to make their **r** heard in the temple as a reminder

RINGLEADER (1) [LEAD, RING]
Ac 24:5 and a **r** of the sect of the Nazarenes.

RINGS (47) [RING]
Ge 35:4 and the **r** that were in their ears;
Ex 25:12 You shall cast four **r** of gold for it and put them
25:12 two **r** on the one side of it, and two **r** on the other
25:14 And you shall put the poles into the **r** on the sides
25:15 The poles shall remain in the **r** of the ark;
25:26 make for it four **r** of gold, and fasten the **r** to the
25:27 The **r** that hold the poles used for carrying
26:29 and shall make their **r** of gold to hold the bars;
27:4 and on the net you shall make four bronze **r**
27:7 the poles shall be put through the **r**,
28:23 you shall make for the breastpiece two **r** of gold,
28:23 put the two **r** on the two edges of the breastpiece.
28:24 of gold in the two **r** at the edges of the breastpiece;
28:26 You shall make two **r** of gold,
28:27 You shall make two **r** of gold,
28:28 The breastpiece shall be bound by its **r** to the **r** of
30:4 And you shall make two golden **r** for it;
32:2 the gold **r** that are on the ears of your wives,
32:3 all the people took off the gold **r** from their ears,
35:22 and earrings and signet **r** and pendants,
36:34 and made **r** of gold for them to hold the bars,
37:3 He cast for it four **r** of gold for its four feet, two **r** on its one side and two **r** on its other side.
37:5 and put the poles into the **r** on the sides of the ark,
37:13 He cast for it four **r** of gold, and fastened the **r** to
37:14 The **r** that held the poles used for carrying
37:27 and made two golden **r** for it under its molding,
38:5 He cast four **r** on the four corners of
38:7 And he put the poles through the **r** on the sides of
39:16 and two gold **r**, and put the two **r** on the two
39:17 of gold in the two **r** at the edges of the breastpiece.
39:19 Then they made two **r** of gold,
39:20 They made two **r** of gold,
39:21 They bound the breastpiece by its **r** to the **r** of
Nu 31:50 articles of gold, armlets and bracelets, signet **r**,
Est 1:6 with cords of fine linen and purple to silver **r**
Isa 3:21 the signet **r** and nose **r**;
Jas 2:2 if a person with gold **r** and in fine clothes comes
Jdt 10:4 bracelets, **r**, earrings, and all her other jewelry.

RINGSTRAKED (KJV) See MOTTLED, SPECKLED, SPOTTED, STRIPED

RINNAH (1)
1Ch 4:20 Amnon, **R**, Ben-hanan, and Tilon.

RINSE (1) [RINSED]
2Ch 4:6 to **r** what was used for the burnt offering.

RINSED (3) [RINSE]
Lev 6:28 that shall be scoured and **r** in water.
15:11 without his having **r** his hands
15:12 and every vessel of wood shall be **r** in water.

RIOT (4) [RIOTING, RIOTS]
Mt 26:5 or there may be a **r** among the people."
27:24 but rather that a **r** was beginning,
Mk 14:2 or there may be a **r** among the people."
Wis 14:25 and all is a raging **r** of blood and murder,

RIOTING (1) [RIOT]
Ac 19:40 we are in danger of being charged with **r** today,

RIOTS (1) [RIOT]
2Co 6:5 imprisonments, **r**, labors, sleepless nights, hunger;

RIP (1) [RIPPED]
2Ki 8:12 and **r** up their pregnant women."

RIPATH See Index to Footnotes

RIPE (11) [FIRST-RIPE, RIPEN, RIPENED, RIPENING]
Nu 13:20 Now it was the season of the first **r** grapes.
17:8 produced blossoms, and bore **r** almonds.
Job 5:26 You shall come to your grave in **r** old age,
Joel 3:13 Put in the sickle, for the harvest is **r**.
Mk 4:29 But when the grain is **r**,
Jn 4:35 and see how the fields are **r** for harvesting.
Rev 14:15 because the harvest of the earth is fully **r**."
14:18 of the vine of the earth, for its grapes are **r**."
Wis 4:5 and their fruit will be useless, not **r** enough to eat,
4:9 and a blameless life is **r** old age.
3Mc 6:1 who had attained a **r** old age and

RIPEN (2) [RIPE]
Wis 10:7 plants bearing fruit that does not **r**,
2Es 16:26 The grapes shall **r**, but who will tread them?

RIPENED (1) [RIPE]
Ge 40:10 its blossoms came out and the clusters **r**

RIPENING (2) [RIPE]
Isa 18:5 blossom is over and the flower becomes a **r** grape,
Sir 51:15 the first blossom to the **r** grape my heart delighted

RIPHATH (1)
Ge 10:3 Ashkenaz, **R**, and Togarmah.

RIPPED (3) [RIP]
2Ki 15:16 He **r** open all the pregnant women in it.
Hos 13:16 and their pregnant women **r** open.
Am 1:13 because they have **r** open pregnant women

RISE‡ (170) [ARISE, ARISEN, ARISES, ARISING, AROSE, RAISE, RAISED, RAISES, RAISING, RISEN, RISES, RISING, ROSE, SUNRISE]
Ge 2:6 but a stream would **r** from the earth, and water
13:17 **R** up, walk through the length and the breadth of
17:16 I will bless her, and she shall give **r** to nations;
19:2 then you can **r** early and go on your way."
31:35 not my lord be angry that I cannot **r** before you,
Ex 8:20 "**R** early in the morning and present yourself
9:13 "**R** up early in the morning and present yourself
12:31 and said, "**R** up, go away from my people,
33:8 all the people would **r** and stand, each of them,
33:10 all the people would **r** and bow down, all of them,
Lev 19:32 You shall **r** before the aged, and defer to the old;
Nu 23:18 "**R**, Balak, and hear; listen to me, O son of Zippor:
24:17 and a scepter shall **r** out of Israel;
Dt 6:7 when you lie down and when you **r**.
11:19 when you lie down and when you **r**.
28:7 The LORD will cause your enemies who **r**
29:22 next generation, your children who **r** up after you,
32:38 Let them **r** up and help you,
33:11 of those that hate him, so that they do not **r** again.
Jos 8:7 you shall **r** up from the ambush and seize the city;
Jdg 20:40 a column of smoke, began to **r** out of the city,
1Sa 16:12 The LORD said, "**R** and anoint him;
25:29 If anyone should **r** up to pursue you and
29:10 Now then **r** early in the morning,
2Sa 12:17 urging him to **r** from the ground;
15:2 Absalom used to **r** early and stand beside the road
18:32 and all who **r** up to do you harm,
22:39 I struck them down, so that they did not **r**;
2Ch 6:41 "Now **r** up, O LORD God,
Est 4:14 relief and deliverance will **r** for the Jews
Job 1:5 and he would **r** early in the morning
7:4 When I lie down I say, 'When shall I **r**?'
9:7 the sun, and it does not **r**;
14:12 so mortals lie down and do not **r** again;
19:18 when I **r**, they talk against me.
20:27 and the earth will **r** up against them.
24:22 they **r** up when they despair of life.
30:12 On my right hand the rabble **r** up;
Ps 3:7 **R** up, O LORD! Deliver me,
7:6 **R** up, O LORD, in your anger;
9:19 **R** up, O LORD! Do not let mortals prevail;
10:12 **R** up, O LORD; O God, lift up your
12:5 because the needy groan, I will now **r** up,"
17:13 **R** up, O LORD, confront them, overthrow them!
18:38 so that they were not able to **r**;
20:8 but we shall **r** and stand upright.
27:3 war **r** up against me, yet I will be confident.
35:2 and **r** up to help me!
35:11 Malicious witnesses **r** up;
36:12 they are thrust down, unable to **r**.
41:8 that I will not **r** again from where I lie.
44:26 **R** up, come to our help.
59:1 protect me from those who **r** up against me.
68:1 Let God **r** up, let his enemies be scattered;
74:22 **R** up, O God, plead your cause;
78:6 and **r** up and tell them to their children,
82:8 **R** up, O God, judge the earth;
86:14 O God, the insolent **r** up against me;
88:10 Do the shades **r** up to praise you?
89:9 when its waves **r**, you still them.
94:2 **R** up, O judge of the earth;
102:13 You will **r** up and have compassion on Zion,
112:4 They **r** in the darkness as a light for the upright;
119:62 At midnight I **r** to praise you,
119:147 I **r** before dawn and cry for help;
127:2 It is in vain that you **r** up early and go late to rest,
132:8 **R** up, O LORD, and go to your resting place,
135:7 He it is who makes the clouds **r** at the end of
139:2 You know when I sit down and when I **r** up;
139:21 And do I not loathe those who **r** up against you?
140:10 Let them be flung into pits, no more to **r**!
Pr 6:9 When will you **r** from your sleep?
24:16 for though they fall seven times, they will **r** again;
31:28 Her children **r** up and call her happy;
SS 3:2 "I will **r** now and go about the city,
Isa 5:11 you who **r** early in the morning in pursuit
8:7 it will **r** above all its channels
14:21 Let them never **r** to possess the earth or cover
14:22 I will **r** up against them, says the LORD of hosts,
21:5 **R** up, commanders, oil the shield!
23:12 **r**, cross over to Cyprus—
24:20 and it falls, and will not **r** again.
26:14 The dead do not live; shades do not **r**—
26:19 Your dead shall live, their corpses shall **r**.
28:21 For the LORD will **r** up as on Mount Perazim,
30:18 therefore he will **r** up to show mercy to you.
31:2 but will **r** against the house of the evildoers,
32:9 **R** up, you women who are at ease, hear my voice;
34:3 and the stench of their corpses shall **r**;
43:17 they lie down, they cannot **r**,
52:2 Shake yourself from the dust, **r** up,
58:10 then your light shall **r** in the darkness
Jer 10:13 he makes the mist **r** from the ends of the earth.
25:27 Drink, get drunk and vomit, fall and **r** no more,
37:10 they would **r** up and burn this city with fire.
46:8 It said, Let me **r**, let me cover the earth,
49:14 and come against her, and **r** up for battle!"
49:28 **R** up, advance against Kedar!
49:31 **R** up, advance against a nation at ease,
51:16 he makes the mist **r** from the ends of the earth.
51:64 'Thus shall Babylon sink, to **r** no more,
La 3:63 Whether they sit or **r**—see, I am the object of their
Eze 3:22 and he said to me, **R** up, go out into the valley,
10:16 and when the cherubim lifted up their wings to **r**
Da 8:25 and shall even **r** up against the Prince of princes.
11:7 a branch from her roots shall **r** up in his place.
11:14 "In those times many shall **r** against the king of
12:13 you shall **r** for your reward at the end of the days."
Hos 10:14 the tumult of war shall **r** against your people,
Joel 2:20 its stench and foul smell will **r** up.
Am 5:2 no more to **r**, is maiden Israel;
7:9 and I will **r** against the house of Jeroboam with
8:8 and all of it **r** like the Nile,
8:14 they shall fall, and never **r** again.
Ob 1:1 the nations: "**R** up! Let us **r** against it for battle!"
Mic 2:8 But you **r** up against my people as an enemy;
6:1 **R**, plead your case before the mountains,
7:8 when I fall, I shall **r**;
Na 1:9 He will make an end; no adversary will **r** up twice.
Hab 2:7 Will not your own creditors suddenly **r**,
Mal 4:2 the sun of righteousness shall **r**,
Mt 5:45 for he makes his sun **r** on the evil and on the good,
10:21 and children will **r** against parents
12:41 The people of Nineveh will **r** up at the judgment
12:42 The queen of the South will **r** up at the judgment
24:7 For nation will **r** against nation,
27:63 'After three days I will **r** again.'
Mk 4:27 and would sleep and **r** night and day,
8:31 and be killed, and after three days **r** again.
9:31 and three days after being killed, he will **r** again."
10:34 and after three days he will **r** again."
12:25 For when they **r** from the dead,
13:8 For nation will **r** against nation,
13:12 and children will **r** against parents
Lk 7:14 And he said, "Young man, I say to you, **r**!"
11:31 The queen of the South will **r** at the judgment with
11:32 The people of Nineveh will **r** up at the judgment
18:33 and on the third day he will **r** again."
21:10 he said to them, "Nation will **r** against nation,
24:7 and be crucified, and on the third day **r** again."
24:46 that the Messiah is to suffer and to **r** from the dead
Jn 11:23 Jesus said to her, "Your brother will **r** again."
11:24 "I know that he will **r** again in the resurrection on
14:31 **R**, let us be on our way.
20:9 that he must **r** from the dead.
Ac 17:3 for the Messiah to suffer and to **r** from the dead,
26:23 and that, by being the first to **r** from the dead,
Eph 5:14 **R** from the dead, and Christ will shine on you."
1Th 4:16 and the dead in Christ will **r** first.
Jdt 16:17 Woe to the nations that **r** up against my people!
Wis 5:6 and the sun did not **r** upon us.
5:23 a mighty wind will **r** against them,
16:28 that one must **r** before the sun to give you thanks,
Sir 6:36 you see an intelligent person, **r** early to visit him;
17:23 Afterward he will **r** up and repay them,
32:14 and those who **r** early to seek him will find favor.
39:5 to **r** early to seek the Lord who made him,
1Mc 10:70 "You are the only one to **r** up against us,
2Mc 12:44 that those who had fallen would **r** again,
1Es 8:95 **R** up and take action, for it is your task,
2Es 2:38 **R**, stand erect and see the number
5:18 **R** therefore and eat some bread,
6:13 "**R** to your feet and you will hear a full,
7:2 "**R**, Ezra, and listen to the words that I have come
11:7 Then I saw the eagle **r** upon its talons,
12:13 days are coming when a kingdom shall **r** on earth,
15:15 and nation shall **r** up to fight against nation,
15:40 shall **r** and destroy all the earth and its inhabitants,
15:50 like a flower when the heat shall **r** that is sent

RISEN‡ (24) [RISE]
Ge 19:23 sun had **r** on the earth when Lot came to Zoar.
Nu 32:14 a brood of sinners, have **r** in place of your fathers,
Jdg 9:18 but you have **r** up against my
1Sa 22:13 so that he has **r** against me, to lie in wait,
2Sa 14:7 Now the whole family has **r** against your servant.
1Ki 8:20 for I have **r** in the place of my father David;
Ezr 4:19 and discovered that this city has **r** against kings
9:6 for our iniquities have **r** higher than our heads,
Job 16:8 my leanness has **r** up against me,
Ps 27:12 for false witnesses have **r** against me,
54:3 For the insolent have **r** against me,
Isa 60:1 and the glory of the LORD has **r** upon you.
Jer 51:42 The sea has **r** over Babylon;

Eze 47: 5 a river that I could not cross, for the water had **r**;
Mk 3:26 if Satan has **r** up against himself and is divided,
9: 9 until after the Son of Man had **r** from the dead.
16: 2 when the sun had **r**, they went to the tomb.
16:14 ⟦not believed those who saw him after he had **r**.⟧
Lk 7:16 saying, "A great prophet has **r** among us!"
24: 5 He is not here, but has **r**.
24:34 They were saying, "The Lord has **r** indeed,
Jdt 13: 5 to destroy the enemies who have **r** up against us."
1Mc 13:14 Trypho learned that Simon had **r** up in place
1Es 8:75 For our sins have **r** higher than our heads,

RISES (31) [RISE]

Jos 11:17 from Mount Halak, which **r** toward Seir, as far
12: 7 that **r** toward Seir (and Joshua gave their land to
Jdg 5:31 But may your friends be like the sun as it **r**
9:33 Then early in the morning, as soon as the sun **r**,
2Sa 11:20 if the king's anger **r**, and if he says to you,
Job 24:14 The murderer **r** at dusk to kill the poor and needy,
31:14 what then shall I do when God **r** up?
Ps 94:16 Who **r** up for me against the wicked?
104:22 sun **r**, they withdraw and lie down in their dens.
Pr 31:15 She **r** while it is still night and provides food
Ecc 1: 5 The sun **r** and the sun goes down, and hurries to
the place where it **r**.
10: 4 If the anger of the ruler **r** against you,
12: 4 and one **r** up at the sound of a bird,
Isa 2:19 when he **r** to terrify the earth.
2:21 when he **r** to terrify the earth.
3:13 The LORD **r** to argue his case;
54:17 and you shall confute every tongue that **r**
Jer 46: 8 Egypt **r** like the Nile, like rivers
Am 9: 5 and all of it **r** like the Nile, and sinks again,
Mic 7: 6 the daughter **r** up against her mother,
Na 3:17 when the sun **r**, they fly away;
Lk 16:31 be convinced even if someone **r** from the dead.' "
Ro 15:12 the one who **r** to rule the Gentiles;
Jas 1:11 sun **r** with its scorching heat and withers the field;
2Pe 1:19 until the day dawns and the morning star **r**
Jdt 14: 2 As soon as day breaks and the sun **r** on the earth,
Wis 6:14 One who **r** early to seek her will have no difficulty,
Sir 31:20 on moderate eating; he **r** early,
35: 8 and its pleasing odor **r** before the Most High.
43: 2 proclaims as it **r** what a marvelous instrument it is,

RISING‡ (34) [RISE]

Nu 23:24 Look, a people **r** up like a lioness,
Jos 3:16 **r** up in a single heap far off at Adam,
8:20 the smoke of the city was **r** to the sky.
8:21 the city and that the smoke of the city was **r**,
2Sa 23: 4 like the sun **r** on a cloudless morning,
1Ki 18:44 a person's hand is **r** out of the sea."
2Ki 19:27 "But I know your **r** and your sitting,
Ps 3: 1 how many are my foes! Many are **r** against me;
19: 6 Its **r** is from the end of the heavens,
50: 1 and summons the earth from the **r** of the sun
113: 3 From the **r** of the sun to its setting the name of
Pr 27:14 **r** early in the morning, will be counted as cursing.
Isa 13:10 the sun will be dark at its **r**,
30:27 burning with his anger, and in thick **r** smoke;
37:28 I know your **r** up and your sitting down,
41:25 from the **r** of the sun he was summoned by name.
45: 6 from the **r** of the sun and from the west,
Jer 46: 7 Who is this, **r** like the Nile,
47: 2 See, waters are **r** out of the north and shall become
Da 11: 4 And while still **r** in power,
Hos 13:15 a blast from the LORD, **r** from the wilderness;
Mal 1:11 the **r** of the sun to its setting my name is great
Mt 2: 2 For we observed his star at its **r**,
2: 9 went the star that they had seen at its **r**,
Mk 9:10 questioning what this **r** from the dead could mean.
Lk 2:34 "This child is destined for the falling and the **r**
12:54 "When you see a cloud **r** in the west,
Rev 7: 2 I saw another angel ascending from the **r** of
13: 1 And I saw a beast **r** out of the sea having ten horns
Sir 26:16 Like the sun **r** in the heights of the Lord,
2Mc 10:27 And **r** from their prayer they took up their arms
3Mc 4:15 with bitter haste and zealous intensity from the **r**
2Es 11: 1 I saw **r** from the sea an eagle
15:20 says God, from the **r** sun and from the south,

RISK‡ (5) [RISKED, RISKING]

2Sa 17:17 for they could not **r** being seen entering the city.
23:17 of the men who went at the **r** of their lives?"
1Ki 2:23 for Adonijah has devised this scheme at the **r**
1Ch 11:19 For at the **r** of their lives they brought it."
2Mc 11: 7 and he urged the others to **r** their lives with him

RISKED (5) [RISK]

Jdg 9:17 and **r** his life, and rescued you from the hand
Ac 15:26 who have **r** their lives for the sake
Ro 16: 4 and who **r** their necks for my life,
Jdt 13:20 because you **r** your own life
2Mc 14:38 he had most zealously **r** body and life for Judaism.

RISKING (1) [RISK]

Php 2:30 **r** his life to make up for those services

RISSAH (2)

Nu 33:21 They set out from Libnah and camped at **R**.
33:22 They set out from **R** and camped at Kehelathah.

RITE (5) [RITES, RITUAL]

Ex 12:24 You shall observe this **r** as a perpetual ordinance
30:10 a year Aaron shall perform the **r** of atonement
Ac 21:24 go through the **r** of purification with them,
24:18 completing the **r** of purification,
3Mc 6:36 when they had ordained a public **r** for these things

RITES (6) [RITE]

Nu 3:38 having charge of the **r** within the sanctuary,
Jn 2: 6 for the Jewish **r** of purification,
Heb 9:23 of the heavenly things to be purified with these **r**,
Wis 12: 4 their works of sorcery and unholy **r**,
14:15 on to his dependents secret **r** and initiations.
3Mc 3:21 make them participants in our regular religious **r**.

RITHMAH (2)

Nu 33:18 They set out from Hazeroth and camped at **R**.
33:19 from **R** and camped at Rimmon-perez.

RITUAL (16) [RITE]

Lev 6: 9 This is the **r** of the burnt offering.
6:14 This is the **r** of the grain offering:
6:25 This is the **r** of the sin offering.
7: 1 This is the **r** of the guilt offering. It is most holy;
7: 7 there is the same **r** for them;
7:11 the **r** of the sacrifice of the offering of well-being
7:37 This is the **r** of the burnt offering,
13:59 the **r** for a leprous disease in a cloth of wool
14: 2 This shall be the **r** for the leprous person at
14:32 This is the **r** for the one who has a leprous disease,
14:54 This is the **r** for any leprous disease: for an itch,
14:57 This is the **r** for leprous diseases.
15:32 This is the **r** for those who have a discharge:
Jn 18:28 so as to avoid **r** defilement and to be able to eat
Heb 9: 6 into the first tent to carry out their **r** duties;
Sir 50:19 and they completed his **r**.

RIVAL (6) [RIVALRY]

Lev 18:18 you shall not take a woman as a **r** to her sister,
1Sa 1: 6 Her **r** used to provoke her severely, to irritate her,
Eze 31: 8 The cedars in the garden of God could not **r** it,
Sir 26: 6 and sorrow when a wife is jealous of a **r**,
37:11 a woman about her **r** or with a coward about war,
2Es 11:11 I counted its **r** wings, and there were eight

RIVALRY (3) [RIVAL]

Php 1:15 Some proclaim Christ from envy and **r**,
2Mc 4: 4 that the **r** was serious and that Apollonius son
4Mc 1:26 covetousness, thirst for honor, **r**, and malice;

RIVER‡ (144) [RIVERS]

Ge 2:10 A **r** flows out of Eden to water the garden,
2:13 The name of the second **r** is Gihon;
2:14 The name of the third **r** is Tigris,
2:14 And the fourth **r** is the Euphrates.
15:18 from the **r** of Egypt to the great **r**, the **r** Euphrates,
Ex 2: 3 and placed it among the reeds on the bank of the **r**.
2: 5 daughter of Pharaoh came down to bathe at the **r**,
2: 5 while her attendants walked beside the **r**.
7:15 stand by at the **r** bank to meet him,
7:18 The fish in the **r** shall die, the **r** itself shall stink,
7:20 and struck the water in the **r**, and all the water in
the **r** was turned into blood,
7:21 and the fish in the **r** died. The **r** stank so that
7:24 for they could not drink the water of the **r**.
8: 3 The **r** shall swarm with frogs;
Nu 24: 6 beside a **r**, like aloes that the LORD has planted,
Dt 1: 7 as far as the great **r**, the **r** Euphrates.
11:24 from the **R**, the **r** Euphrates, to the Western Sea.
Jos 1: 4 the Lebanon as far as the great **r**, the **r** Euphrates,
12: 2 the middle of the valley as far as the **r** Jabbok,
24: 3 the **R** and led him through all the land of Canaan
24:14 the gods that your ancestors served beyond the **R**
24:15 beyond the **R** or the gods of the Amorites
2Sa 8: 3 to restore his monument at the **r** Euphrates.
2Ki 17: 6 the **r** of Gozan, and in the cities of the Medes.
18:11 the **r** of Gozan, and in the cities of the Medes,
23:29 up to the king of Assyria to the **r** Euphrates.
24: 7 from the Wadi of Egypt to the **R** Euphrates.
1Ch 5:26 Habor, Hara, and the **r** Gozan, to this day.
18: 3 he went to set up a monument at the **r** Euphrates.
Ezr 4:10 in the rest of the province Beyond the **R** wrote—
4:11 the people of the province Beyond the **R**,
4:16 in the province Beyond the **R**."
4:17 and in the rest of the province Beyond the **R**,
4:20 over the whole province Beyond the **R**,
5: 3 of the province Beyond the **R** and Shethar-bozenai
5: 6 of the province Beyond the **R** and Shethar-bozenai
5: 6 in the province Beyond the **R** sent to King Darius;
6: 6 Tattenai, governor of the province Beyond the **R**,
6: 6 the envoys in the province Beyond the **R**,
6: 8 the tribute of the province Beyond the **R**.
6:13 the governor of the province Beyond the **R**,
7:21 to all the treasurers in the province Beyond the **R**:
7:25 in the province Beyond the **R** who know the laws
8:15 I gathered them by the **r** that runs to Ahava,
8:21 Then I proclaimed a fast there, at the **r** Ahava,
8:31 the **r** Ahava on the twelfth day of the first month,
8:36 to the governors of the province Beyond the **R**;
Ne 2: 7 to the governors of the province Beyond the **R**,
2: 9 to the governors of the province Beyond the **R**,
3: 7 of the governor of the province Beyond the **R**.
Job 14:11 and a **r** wastes away and dries up,
33:18 their lives from traversing the **R**.
40:23 Even if the **r** is turbulent, it is not frightened;
Ps 36: 8 you give them drink from the **r** of your delights.
46: 4 There is a **r** whose streams make glad the city
65: 9 the **r** of God is full of water;
66: 6 they passed through the **r** on foot.
72: 8 and from the **R** to the ends of the earth.
80:11 its branches to the sea, and its shoots to the **R**.
105:41 it flowed through the desert like a **r**.
Isa 7:20 with a razor hired beyond the **R**—
8: 7 up against it the mighty flood waters of the **R**,
11:15 over the **R** with his scorching wind;
19: 5 and the **r** will be parched and dry;
48:18 Then your prosperity would have been like a **r**,
66:12 I will extend prosperity to her like a **r**,
Jer 46: 2 which was by the **r** Euphrates at Carchemish
46: 6 in the north by the **r** Euphrates they have stumbled
46:10 in the land of the north by the **r** Euphrates.
Eze 1: 1 as I was among the exiles by the **r** Chebar,
1: 3 in the land of the Chaldeans by the **r** Chebar;
3:15 who lived by the **r** Chebar.
3:23 like the glory that I had seen by the **r** Chebar;
10:15 the living creatures that I saw by the **r** Chebar.
10:20 the God of Israel by the **r** Chebar;
10:22 whose appearance I had seen by the **r** Chebar.
43: 3 and like the vision that I had seen by the **r** Chebar;
47: 5 and it was a **r** that I could not cross,
47: 5 a **r** that could not be crossed.
47: 6 Then he led me back along the bank of the **r**.
47: 7 of the **r** a great many trees on the one side and on
47: 9 Wherever the **r** goes, every living creature
47: 9 and everything will live where the **r** goes.
47:12 On the banks, on both sides of the **r**,
Da 8: 2 in the province of Elam, and I was by the **r** Ulai.
8: 3 I looked up and saw a ram standing beside the **r**.
8: 6 that I had seen standing beside the **r**,
10: 4 I was standing on the bank of the great **r** (that is,
Mic 7:12 and from Egypt to the **R**, from sea to sea
Na 2: 6 The **r** gates are opened, the palace trembles.
Zec 9:10 and from the **R** to the ends of the earth.
Mt 3: 6 and they were baptized by him in the **r** Jordan,
Mk 1: 5 and were baptized by him in the **r** Jordan,
Lk 6:48 **r** burst against that house but could not shake it,
6:49 When the **r** burst against it, immediately it fell,
Ac 16:13 the sabbath day we went outside the gate by the **r**,
Rev 9:14 angels who are bound at the great **r** Euphrates."
12:15 the serpent poured water like a **r** after the woman,
12:16 the **r** that the dragon had poured from his mouth.
16:12 the great **r** Euphrates, and its water was dried up
22: 1 the angel showed me the **r** of the water of life,
22: 2 of the **r** is the tree of life with its twelve kinds
Tob 6: 2 overtook them they camped by the Tigris **r**.
6: 3 down to wash his feet in the Tigris **r**.
Jdt 1: 9 and Bethany and Chelous and Kadesh and the **r**
2: 8 and the swelling **r** shall be filled with their dead.
AdE 10: 6 There was the little spring that became a **r**,
10: 6 the **r** is Esther, whom the king married
11:10 as though from a tiny spring, there came a great **r**,
Wis 11: 6 Instead of the fountain of an ever-flowing **r**,
19:10 and instead of fish the **r** spewed out vast numbers
Sir 4:26 and do not try to stop the current of a **r**.
24:30 As for me, I was like a canal from a **r**,
24:31 And lo, my canal became a **r**, and my **r** a sea.
39:22 "His blessing covers the dry land like a **r**,
40:13 The wealth of the unjust will dry up like a **r**,
40:16 The reeds by any water or **r** bank are plucked up
Bar 1: 4 all who lived in Babylon by the **r** Sud.
1Mc 3:32 from the **r** Euphrates to the borders of Egypt.
3:37 He crossed the Euphrates **r** and went through
5:41 and camps on the other side of the **r**,
7: 8 governor of the province Beyond the **R**;
11: 7 with the king as far as the **r** called Eleutherus;
11:60 and traveled beyond the **r** and among the towns,
12:30 for they had crossed the Eleutherus **r**.
1Es 8:41 I assembled them at the **r** called Theras,
8:61 the **r** Theras on the twelfth day of the first month;
3Mc 7:20 of them been brought safely by land and sea and **r**
2Es 5:25 of the sea you have filled for yourself one **r**,
7: 4 so that it is like a **r**.
13:40 he took them across the **r**,
13:43 in by the narrow passages of the Euphrates **r**.
13:44 the channels of the **r** until they had crossed over.
13:47 Most High will stop the channels of the **r** again,
14:47 the fountain of wisdom, and the **r** of knowledge."

RIVERS‡ (42) [RIVER]

Ex 7:19 over its **r**, its canals, and its ponds,
8: 5 'Stretch out your hand with your staff over the **r**,
2Ki 5:12 Are not Abana and Pharpar, the **r** of Damascus,
Job 20:17 They will not look on the **r**,
28:11 The sources of the **r** they probe;
Ps 24: 2 and established it on the **r**.
78:16 and caused waters to flow down like **r**.
78:44 He turned their **r** to blood,
89:25 on the sea and his right hand on the **r**.
107:33 He turns **r** into a desert,
137: 1 By the **r** of Babylon—there we sat down and
Isa 18: 1 land of whirring wings beyond the **r** of Ethiopia,
18: 2 and conquering, whose land the **r** divide.
18: 7 whose land the **r** divide, to Mount Zion,
33:21 in majesty will be for us a place of broad **r**
41:18 I will open **r** on the bare heights,
42:15 I will turn the **r** into islands, and dry up the pools.
43: 2 and through the **r**, they shall not overwhelm you;
43:19 I will make a way in the wilderness and **r** in
43:20 for I give water in the wilderness, **r** in the desert,

Isa 44:27 I will dry up your r";
47: 2 uncover your legs, pass through the r.
50: 2 I make the r a desert;
Jer 46: 7 rising like the Nile, like r whose waters surge?
46: 8 like r whose waters surge.
La 3:48 with r of tears because of the destruction
Eze 31: 4 making its r flow around the place it was planted,
31:15 and covered it; I restrained its r,
Mic 6: 7 with ten thousands of r of oil?
Na 1: 4 and he dries up all the r;
Hab 3: 8 Was your wrath against the r, O LORD?
3: 8 Or your anger against the r,
3: 9 You split the earth with r.
Zep 3:10 From beyond the r of Ethiopia my suppliants,
Jn 7:38 the believer's heart shall flow r of living water.' "
2Co 11:26 in danger from r, danger from bandits,
Rev 8:10 and it fell on a third of the r and on the springs
16: 4 The third angel poured his bowl into the r and
Wis 5:22 and r will relentlessly overwhelm them;
Aza 1:55 Bless the Lord, seas and r;
1Es 4:23 and rob and steal and to sail the sea and r;
2Es 16:60 so as to send r from the heights to water the earth.

RIZIA (1)

1Ch 7:39 The sons of Ulla: Arah, Hanniel, and R.

RIZPAH (4)

2Sa 3: 7 a concubine whose name was R daughter of Aiah.
21: 8 The king took the two sons of R daughter of Aiah,
21:10 Then R the daughter of Aiah took sackcloth,
21:11 When David was told what R daughter of Aiah,

ROAD (78) [CROSSROADS, ROADS, ROADSIDE]

Ge 38:14 which is on the r to Timnah.
38:16 He went over to her at the r side, and said, "Come,
Nu 21:33 Then they turned and went up the r to Bashan;
22:22 and the angel of the LORD took his stand in the r
22:23 the LORD standing in the r, with a drawn sword
22:23 donkey turned off the r, and went into the field;
22:23 to turn it back onto the r.
22:31 he saw the angel of the LORD standing in the r,
22:34 for I did not know that you were standing in the r
Dt 2:27 I will travel only along the r;
3: 1 When we headed up the r to Bashan,
22: 4 or ox fallen on the r and ignore it;
27:18 be anyone who misleads a blind person on the r."
Jdg 4: 9 nevertheless, the r on which you are going will
1Sa 4:13 Eli was sitting upon his seat by the r watching,
24: 3 He came to the sheepfolds beside the r,
26: 3 which is opposite Jeshimon beside the r.
2Sa 13:34 he saw many people coming from the Horonaim r
15: 2 Absalom used to rise early and stand beside the r
16:13 So David and his men went on the r,
1Ki 11:29 prophet Ahijah the Shilonite found him on the r.
13:24 a lion met him on the r and killed him.
13:24 His body was thrown in the r,
13:25 by and saw the body thrown in the r,
13:28 and he went and found the body thrown in the r,
20:38 and waited for the king along the r,
1Ch 26:16 at the gate of Shallecheth on the ascending r.
26:18 the colonnade on the west there were four at the r
Job 24: 4 They thrust the needy off the r;
Ps 140: 5 along the r they have set snares for me.
Pr 7: 8 near her corner, taking the r to her house
26:13 The lazy person says, "There is a lion in the r!
Ecc 10: 3 Even when fools walk on the r, they lack sense,
12: 5 and terrors are in the r;
Isa 15: 5 the r to Horonaim they raise a cry of destruction;
33: 8 highways are deserted, travelers have quit the r.
42:16 I will lead the blind by a r they do not know,
49:11 And I will turn all my mountains into a r,
Jer 6:25 Do not go out into the field, or walk on the r;
31:21 Set up r markers for yourself,
31:21 the highway, the r by which you went.
48:19 Stand by the r and watch, you inhabitant of Aroer!
Eze 21:19 make it for a fork in the r leading to a city;
21:20 mark out the r for the sword to come to Rabbah of
48: 1 on the Hethlon r, from Lebo-hamath,
Hos 6: 9 they murder on the r to Shechem,
Na 2: 1 Guard the ramparts; watch the r;
Mt 2:12 they left for their own country by another r.
4:15 on the r by the sea, across the Jordan,
7:13 for the gate is wide and the r is easy that leads
7:14 gate is narrow and the r is hard that leads to life,
21: 8 A very large crowd spread their cloaks on the r,
21: 8 from the trees and spread them on the r.
21:19 And seeing a fig tree by the side of the r,
Mk 10:32 They were on the r, going up to Jerusalem,
11: 8 Many people spread their cloaks on the r,
Lk 9:57 As they were going along the r,
10: 4 and greet no one on the r.
10:31 Now by chance a priest was going down that r;
19:36 people kept spreading their cloaks on the r.
24:32 within us while he was talking to us on the r,
24:35 Then they told what had happened on the r,
Ac 8:26 up and go toward the south to the r that goes down
8:26 (This is a wilderness r.)
8:36 As they were going along the r,
9:27 and described for them how on the r he had seen
26:13 when at midday along the r,
Jas 2:25 the messengers and sent them out by another r?
2Pe 2:15 They have left the straight r and have gone astray,
2:15 following the r of Balaam son of Bosor,
Tob 10: 7 and watch the r her son had taken,
Tob 11: 5 Meanwhile Anna sat looking intently down the r
Sir 32:21 Do not be overconfident on a smooth r,
1Mc 5:28 by the wilderness r to Bozrah;
5:46 This was a large and very strong town on the r,
6:33 by a forced march along the r to Beth-zechariah,
9: 2 by the r that leads to Gilgal and encamped
2Es 1:13 for you where there was no r;

ROADS[‡] (18) [ROAD]

Lev 26:22 and your r shall be deserted.
Jdg 20:31 the troops, along the main r, one of which goes up
20:32 and draw them away from the city toward the r."
20:45 of them were cut down on the main r,
Job 21:29 Have you not asked those who travel the r,
30:12 they send me sprawling, and build r for my ruin.
Isa 59: 8 Their r they have made crooked;
Jer 18:15 they have stumbled in their ways, in the ancient r,
La 1: 4 r to Zion mourn, for no one comes to the festivals;
Eze 21:19 mark out two r for the sword of the king
21:21 at the fork in the two r, to use divination;
Lk 14:23 'Go out into the r and lanes,
Tob 5: 2 I do not know the r to Media, or how to get there."
5: 6 I am acquainted with it and know all the r.
5:10 "I can go with him and I know all the r,
5:10 I am familiar with its mountains and all of its r."
Bar 4:26 My pampered children have traveled rough r;
2Es 16:32 and its r and all its paths shall bring forth thorns,

ROADSIDE (4) [ROAD]

Ge 49:17 Dan shall be a snake by the r,
Mt 20:30 There were two blind men sitting by the r.
Mk 10:46 a blind beggar, was sitting by the r.
Lk 18:35 a blind man was sitting by the r begging.

ROAM (2) [ROAMED]

Ps 59:15 They r about for food, and growl if they do
2Es 5: 8 the wild animals shall r beyond their haunts,

ROAMED (1) [ROAM]

1Sa 30:31 all the places where David and his men had r.

ROAMS See Index to Footnotes

ROAR (24) [ROARED, ROARING, ROARS]

1Ch 16:32 Let the sea r, and all that fills it;
Job 4:10 The r of the lion, the voice of the fierce lion,
30:22 and you toss me about in the r of the storm.
Ps 46: 3 though its waters r and foam,
96:11 let the sea r, and all that fills it;
98: 7 Let the sea r, and all that fills it;
104:21 The young lions r for their prey,
Isa 5:29 like a lion, like young lions they r;
5:30 They will r over it on that day,
17:12 Ah, the r of nations, they r like the roaring of
17:13 The nations r like the roaring of many waters,
42:10 Let the sea r and all that fills it,
51:15 who stirs up the sea so that its waves r—
Jer 5:22 the waves toss, they cannot prevail, though they r,
11:16 with the r of a great tempest he will set fire to it,
25:30 The LORD will r from on high,
25:30 he will r mightily against his fold, and shout,
31:35 who stirs up the sea so that its waves r—
51:38 Like lions they shall r together;
51:55 Their waves r like mighty waters,
Da 10: 6 the sound of his words like the r of a multitude.
Am 3: 4 Does a lion r in the forest, when it has no prey?
Zec 11: 3 Listen, the r of the lions, for the thickets of the

ROARED (6) [ROAR]

Jdg 14: 5 suddenly a young lion r at him.
Ps 74: 4 Your foes have r within your holy place;
Jer 2:15 lions have r against him, they have r loudly.
Am 3: 8 The lion has r; who will not fear?
AdE 11: 6 both ready to fight, and they r terribly.

ROARING (23) [ROAR]

Ps 22:13 like a ravening and r lion.
65: 7 You silence the r of the seas, the r of their waves,
93: 3 the floods lift up their r.
Pr 28:15 Like a r lion or a charging bear is a wicked ruler
Isa 5:29 Their r is like a lion, like young lions they roar;
5:30 like the r of the sea.
17:12 they roar like the r of mighty waters!
17:13 The nations roar like the r of many waters,
30: 6 a land of trouble and distress, of lioness and r lion,
Jer 6:23 their sound is like the r sea;
50:42 The sound of them is like the r sea;
Eze 19: 7 and all in it, at the sound of his r.
22:25 Its princes within it are like a r lion tearing
Zep 3: 3 The officials within it are r lions;
Lk 21:25 the earth distress among nations confused by the r
1Pe 5: 8 a r lion your adversary the devil prowls around,
Rev 10: 3 a great shout, like a lion r.
AdE 11: 7 At their r every nation prepared for war,
Wis 17:19 or the sound of the most savage r beasts,
1Mc 3: 4 like a lion's cub r for prey.
2Es 11:37 to be a lion roused from the forest, r;
12:31 up out of the forest and r and speaking to the eagle

ROARS (5) [ROAR]

Job 37: 4 After it his voice r; he thunders with his
Hos 11:10 They shall go after the LORD, who r like a lion;
Hos 11:10 when he r, his children shall come trembling from
Joel 3:16 The LORD r from Zion, and utters his voice
Am 1: 2 The LORD r from Zion, and utters his voice

ROAST (2) [ROASTED, ROASTS]

1Sa 2:15 "Give meat for the priest to r;
Pr 12:27 The lazy do not r their game,

ROASTED (9) [ROAST]

Ex 12: 8 they shall eat it r over the fire
12: 9 but r over the fire, with its head, legs,
2Ch 35:13 They r the passover lamb with fire according to
Isa 44:19 I also baked bread on its coals, I r meat
Jer 29:22 whom the king of Babylon r in the fire,"
Tob 6: 6 then he r and ate some of the fish,
Jdt 10: 5 and filled a bag with r grain, dried fig cakes,
1Es 1:12 They r the passover lamb with fire, as required;
4Mc 11:18 and he was r from underneath.

ROASTS (1) [ROAST]

Isa 44:16 over this half he r meat, eats it and is satisfied.

ROB (8) [ROBBED, ROBBER, ROBBERS, ROBBERY, ROBBING, ROBS]

Pr 22:22 Do not r the poor because they are poor,
Isa 10: 2 and to r the poor of my people of their right,
Eze 5:17 and they will r you of your children;
Mal 3: 8 Will anyone r God? Yet you are robbing me!
Ro 2:22 You that abhor idols, do you r temples?
Sir 9:13 make no misstep, or they may r you of your life.
2Mc 9: 2 the city called Persepolis and attempted to r
1Es 4:23 and goes out to travel and r and steal and to sail

ROBBED (12) [ROB]

Dt 28:29 and you shall be continually abused and r,
Jdg 9:25 They r all who passed by them along that way;
2Sa 17: 8 like a bear r of her cubs in the field.
Pr 4:16 are r of sleep unless they have made someone
17:12 to meet a she-bear r of its cubs than to confront
Isa 42:22 But this is a people r and plundered,
Jer 21:12 the hand of the oppressor anyone who has been r,
22: 3 the hand of the oppressor anyone who has been r.
Eze 18:18 because he practiced extortion, r his brother,
Hos 13: 8 I will fall upon them like a bear r of her cubs,
2Co 11: 8 I r other churches by accepting support from them
Sir 29: 6 the borrower has r the other of his money,

ROBBER (6) [ROB]

Pr 6:11 and poverty will come upon you like a r,
23:28 She lies in wait like a r and increases the number
24:34 and poverty will come upon you like a r,
1Co 5:11 or is an idolater, reviler, drunkard, or r.
Sir 36:31 For who will trust a nimble r that skips from city
2Mc 4:42 temple r himself they killed close by the treasury.

ROBBERS (15) [ROB]

Job 12: 6 The tents of r are at peace,
Isa 42:24 up Jacob to the spoiler, and Israel to the r?
Jer 7:11 become a den of r in your sight?
Hos 6: 9 As r lie in wait for someone,
Mt 21:13 but you are making it a den of r."
Mk 11:17 But you have made it a den of r."
Lk 10:30 and fell into the hands of r, who stripped him,
10:36 to the man who fell into the hands of the r?"
19:46 but you have made it a den of r."
Ac 19:37 brought these men here who are neither temple r
1Co 5:10 or the greedy and r, or idolaters,
6:10 r—none of these will inherit the kingdom of God.
LtJ 6:15 and an ax, but cannot defend itself from war and r.
6:18 in order that they may not be plundered by r.
6:57 to save themselves from thieves or r.

ROBBERY (10) [ROB]

Lev 6: 2 or by r, or if you have defrauded a neighbor,
6: 4 by r or by fraud or the deposit that was committed
Ps 62:10 and set no vain hopes on r;
Isa 61: 8 the LORD love justice, I hate r and wrongdoing;
Eze 18: 7 commits no r, gives his bread to the hungry
18:12 commits r, does not restore the pledge,
18:16 exacts no pledge, commits no r,
22:29 the land have practiced extortion and committed r;
33:15 give back what they have taken by r,
Am 3:10 up violence and r in their strongholds.

ROBBING (4) [ROB]

1Sa 23: 1 and are r the threshing floors."
Mal 3: 8 Will anyone rob God? Yet you are r me!
3: 8 But you say, "How are we r you?"
3: 9 You are cursed with a curse, for you are r me—

ROBE (70) [ROBED, ROBES]

Ge 37: 3 and he had made him a long r with sleeves.
37:23 they stripped him of his r, the long r with sleeves
37:31 Then they took Joseph's r, slaughtered a goat, and dipped the r in the blood.
37:32 the long r with sleeves taken to their father,
37:32 see now whether it is your son's r or not."
37:33 He recognized it, and said, "It is my son's r!
49:11 he washes his garments in wine and his r in
Ex 28: 4 a breastpiece, an ephod, a r, a checkered tunic,
28:31 You shall make the r of the ephod all of blue.
28:34 around the lower hem of the r.

Ex 29: 5 and put on Aaron the tunic and the **r** of the ephod,
39:22 He also made the **r** of the ephod woven all
39:23 of the **r** in the middle of it was like the opening in
39:24 the lower hem of the **r** they made pomegranates
39:25 the pomegranates on the lower hem of the **r** all
39:26 around on the lower hem of the **r** for ministering;
Lev 8: 7 clothed him with the **r**, and put the ephod on him.
1Sa 2:19 for him a little **r** and take it to him each year,
15:27 Saul caught hold of the hem of his **r**, and it tore.
18: 4 Jonathan stripped himself of the **r**
28:14 he is wrapped in a **r**."
2Sa 13:18 (Now she was wearing a long **r** with sleeves;
13:19 and tore the long **r** that she was wearing;
1Ch 15:27 David was clothed with a **r** of fine linen,
Est 6: 9 let him **r** the man whom the king wishes to honor,
Job 1:20 Then Job arose, tore his **r**, shaved his head,
29:14 my justice was like a **r** and a turban.
Isa 3:24 and instead of a rich **r**, a binding of sackcloth;
6: 1 and the hem of his **r** filled the temple.
22:21 and will clothe him with your **r** and bind your sash
47: 2 strip off your **r**, uncover your legs,
61:10 he has covered me with the **r** of righteousness,
Eze 5: 3 and bind them in the skirts of your **r**.
Jnh 3: 6 removed his **r**, covered himself with sackcloth,
Mic 2: 8 you strip the **r** from the peaceful,
Mt 22:11 a man there who was not wearing a wedding **r**,
22:12 how did you get in here without a wedding **r**?'
27:28 They stripped him and put a scarlet **r** on him,
27:31 they stripped him of the **r** and put his own clothes
Mk 16: 5 dressed in a white **r**, sitting on the right side;
Lk 15:22 father said to his slaves, 'Quickly, bring out a **r**—
23:11 then he put an elegant **r** on him,
Jn 13: 4 up from the table, took off his outer **r**, and tied
13:12 After he had washed their feet, had put on his **r**,
19: 2 and they dressed him in a purple **r**.
19: 5 wearing the crown of thorns and the purple **r**.
Rev 1:13 a long **r** and with a golden sash across his chest.
6:11 They were each given a white **r** and told to rest
19:13 He is clothed in a **r** dipped in blood,
19:16 On his **r** and on his thigh he has a name inscribed,
AdE 6: 8 the king's servants bring out the fine linen **r** that
6: 9 and let him **r** the person whom the king loves
6:11 So Haman got the **r** and the horse;
6:11 the **r** on Mordecai and made him ride through
8:15 the royal **r** and wearing a gold crown and a turban
Wis 18:24 For on his long **r** the whole world was depicted,
Sir 6:29 and her collar a glorious **r**.
6:31 You will wear her like a glorious **r**,
27: 8 you will attain it and wear it like a glorious **r**.
45: 7 and put a glorious **r** on him.
45: 8 the linen undergarments, the long **r**,
50:11 When he put on his glorious **r** and clothed himself
Bar 4:20 I have taken off the **r** of peace and put
5: 2 the **r** of the righteousness that comes from God;
1Mc 6:15 He gave him the crown and his **r** and the signet,
10:20 He also sent him a purple **r** and a golden crown.
2Mc 4:38 he immediately stripped off the purple **r**
4:38 tore off his purple **r**, and led him around

ROBED (7) [ROBE]

Est 6:11 and the horse and **r** Mordecai and led him riding
Ps 93: 1 The LORD is king, he is **r** in majesty;
93: 1 the LORD is **r**, he is girded with strength.
Isa 63: 1 Who is this so splendidly **r**,
Rev 7: 9 **r** in white, with palm branches in their hands.
7:13 **r** in white, and where have they come from?"
15: 6 with the seven plagues, **r** in pure bright linen,

ROBES‡ (38) [ROBE]

1Ki 22:10 in their **r**, at the threshing floor at the entrance of
22:30 and go into battle, but you wear your **r**."
2Ch 18: 9 on their thrones, arrayed in their **r**;
18:29 and go into battle, but you wear your **r**."
Ezr 2:69 and one hundred priestly **r**.
Ne 7:70 fifty basins, and five hundred thirty priestly **r**.
7:72 and sixty-seven priestly **r**.
Est 5: 1 the third day Esther put on her royal **r** and stood in
6: 8 let royal **r** be brought, which the king has worn,
6: 9 Let the **r** and the horse be handed over to one of
6:10 take the **r** and the horse, as you have said,
6:11 the **r** and the horse and robed Mordecai
8:15 wearing royal **r** of blue and white,
Job 2:12 they tore their **r** and threw dust in the air
Ps 45: 8 your **r** are all fragrant with myrrh and aloes
45:13 in her chamber with gold-woven **r**;
45:14 in many-colored **r** she is led to the king;
133: 2 running down over the collar of his **r**.
Isa 3:22 festal **r**, the mantles, the cloaks, and the handbags;
45: 1 and strip kings of their **r**, to open doors
63: 2 "Why are your **r** red, and your garments
63: 3 on my garments, and stained all my **r**.
Eze 26:16 shall remove their **r** and strip off their embroidered
Mt 11: 8 Someone dressed in soft **r**?
11: 8 Look, those who wear soft **r** are in royal palaces.
Mk 12:38 who like to walk around in long **r**,
Lk 7:25 Someone dressed in soft **r**?
20:46 who like to walk around in long **r**,
Ac 1:10 suddenly two men in white **r** stood by them.
12:21 On an appointed day Herod put on his royal **r**,
Rev 3: 5 you will be clothed like them in white **r**,
3:18 and white **r** to clothe you and to keep the shame
4: 4 dressed in white **r**, with golden crowns
7:14 they have washed their **r** and made them white in
22:14 Blessed are those who wash their **r**,
LtJ 6:12 When they have been dressed in purple **r**,
6:20 from the earth devour them and their **r**.
6:58 of their gold and silver and of the **r** they wear,

ROBOAM (KJV) See REHOBOAM

ROBS (3) [ROB]

Pr 28:24 Anyone who **r** father or mother and says,
Sir 42: 9 and worry over her **r** him of sleep;
1Es 4:24 and when he steals and **r** and plunders,

ROBUST (1)

Sir 30:15 and a **r** body than countless riches.

ROCK‡ (129) [ROCK-HEWN, ROCKED, ROCKS, ROCKY]

Ge 49:24 by the name of the Shepherd, the **R** of Israel,
Ex 17: 6 be standing there in front of you on the **r** at Horeb.
17: 6 Strike the **r**, and water will come out of it,
33:21 a place by me where you shall stand on the **r**;
33:22 a cleft of the **r**, and I will cover you with my hand
Lev 11: 5 The **r** badger, for even though it chews the cud,
Nu 20: 8 command the **r** before their eyes to yield its water.
20: 8 Thus you shall bring water out of the **r** for them;
20:10 the assembly together before the **r**,
20:10 shall we bring water for you out of this **r**?"
20:11 up his hand and struck the **r** twice with his staff;
24:21 and your nest is set in the **r**;
Dt 8:15 He made water flow for you from flint **r**,
14: 7 the camel, the hare, and the **r** badger,
32: 4 **R**, his work is perfect, and all his ways are just.
32:13 with honey from the crags, with oil from flinty **r**;
32:15 and scoffed at the **R** of his salvation.
32:18 You were unmindful of the **R** that bore you;
32:30 unless their **R** had sold them,
32:31 Indeed their **r** is not like our **R**;
32:37 are their gods, the **r** in which they took refuge,
Jdg 6:20 and put them on this **r**, and pour out the broth."
6:21 and fire sprang up from the **r** and consumed
7:25 they killed Oreb at the **r** of Oreb,
13:19 and offered it on the **r** to the LORD,
15: 8 and he went down and stayed in the cleft of the **r**
15:11 of Judah went down to the cleft of the **r** of Etam,
15:13 and brought him up from the **r**.
20:45 toward the wilderness to the **r** of Rimmon,
20:47 toward the wilderness to the **r** of Rimmon,
20:47 and remained at the **r** of Rimmon for four months.
21:13 to the Benjaminites who were at the **r** of Rimmon,
1Sa 2: 2 there is no **R** like our God.
23:25 he went down to the **r** and stayed in the wilderness
23:28 therefore that place was called the **R** of Escape.
2Sa 21:10 and spread it on a **r** for herself,
22: 2 He said: The LORD is my **r**, my fortress,
22: 3 my **r**, in whom I take refuge,
22:32 And who is a **r**, except our God?
22:47 Blessed be my **r**, and exalted be my God,
22:47 and exalted be my God, the **r** of my salvation,
23: 3 the **R** of Israel has said to me:
1Ch 11:15 of the thirty chiefs went down to the **r** to David at
Ne 9:15 for them out of the **r**,
Job 14:18 and the **r** is removed from its place;
18: 4 or the **r** be removed out of its place?
19:24 and with lead they were engraved on a **r** forever!
24: 8 and cling to the **r** for want of shelter.
28: 9 "They put their hand to the flinty **r**,
29: 6 and the **r** poured out for me streams of oil!
39:28 It lives on the **r** and makes its home in the fastness
Ps 18: 2 The LORD is my **r**, my fortress,
18: 2 my God, my **r** in whom I take refuge, my shield,
18:31 And who is a **r** besides our God?—
18:46 Blessed be my **r**, and exalted be the God
19:14 O LORD, my **r** and my redeemer.
27: 5 he will set me high on a **r**.
28: 1 my **r**, do not refuse to hear me,
31: 2 Be a **r** of refuge for me, a strong fortress to save
31: 3 You are indeed my **r** and my fortress;
40: 2 and set my feet upon a **r**, making my steps secure.
42: 9 I say to God, my **r**, "Why have you forgotten me?
61: 2 Lead me to the **r** that is higher than I;
62: 2 He alone is my **r** and my salvation, my fortress;
62: 6 He alone is my **r** and my salvation, my fortress;
62: 7 my mighty **r**, my refuge is in God.
71: 3 Be to me a **r** of refuge, a strong fortress,
71: 3 to save me, for you are my **r** and my fortress.
78:16 He made streams come out of the **r**,
78:20 though he struck the **r** so that water gushed out
78:35 They remembered that God was their **r**,
81:16 and with honey from the **r** I would satisfy you."
89:26 my God, and the **R** of my salvation!'
92:15 he is my **r**, and there is no unrighteousness in him.
94:22 and my God the **r** of my refuge.
95: 1 let us make a joyful noise to the **r** of our salvation!
105:41 He opened the **r**, and water gushed out;
114: 8 who turns the **r** into a pool of water,
137: 9 and dash them against the **r**!
141: 7 a **r** that one breaks apart and shatters on the land,
144: 1 my **r**, who trains my hands for war,
144: 2 my **r** and my fortress, my stronghold
Pr 30:19 the way of a snake on a **r**,
SS 2:14 O my dove, in the clefts of the **r**,
Isa 2:10 into the **r**, and hide in the dust from the terror of
8:14 of Israel he will become a **r** one stumbles over—
10:26 as when he struck Midian at the **r** of Oreb;
17:10 and have not remembered the **R** of your refuge;
22:16 and carving a habitation for yourself in the **r**?
26: 4 in the LORD GOD you have an everlasting **r**.
30:29 to the mountain of the LORD, to the **R** of Israel.
31: 9 His **r** shall pass away in terror,
32: 2 like the shade of a great **r** in a weary land.
44: 8 There is no other **r**; I know not one.
48:21 he made water flow for them from the **r**;
48:21 he split open the **r** and the water gushed out.
51: 1 Look to the **r** from which you were hewn,
Jer 5: 3 They have made their faces harder than **r**;
13: 4 and hide it there in a cleft of the **r**."
21:13 O inhabitant of the valley, O **r** of the plain,
23:29 and like a hammer that breaks a **r** in pieces?
48:28 Leave the towns, and live on the **r**,
49:16 you who live in the clefts of the **r**,
Eze 24: 7 she placed it on a bare **r**;
24: 8 I have placed the blood she shed on a bare **r**,
26: 4 I will scrape its soil from it and make it a bare **r**.
26:14 I will make you a bare **r**;
Ob 1: 3 you that live in the clefts of the **r**,
Hab 1:12 you, O **R**, have established them for punishment.
Mt 7:24 be like a wise man who built his house on **r**.
7:25 because it had been founded on **r**.
16:18 you are Peter, and on this **r** I will build my church,
27:60 which he had hewn in the **r**.
Mk 15:46 laid it in a tomb that had been hewn out of the **r**.
Lk 6:48 who dug deeply and laid the foundation on **r**;
8: 6 Some fell on the **r**; and
8:13 The ones on the **r** are those who,
Ro 9:33 a **r** that will make them fall,
1Co 10: 4 they drank from the spiritual **r** that followed them,
10: 4 that followed them, and the **r** was Christ.
1Pe 2: 8 and a **r** that makes them fall."
Wis 11: 4 and water was given them out of flinty **r**,
Sir 40:15 they are unhealthy roots on sheer **r**.
48:17 he tunneled the **r** with iron tools,
51:12 *Give thanks to the r of Isaac,*
2Mc 14:45 and standing upon a steep **r**,
2Es 1:20 not split the **r** so that waters flowed in abundance?
6:29 by little the place where I was standing began to **r**

ROCK-HEWN (1) [HEW, ROCK]

Lk 23:53 in a **r** tomb where no one had ever been laid.

ROCKED (2) [ROCK]

2Sa 22: 8 Then the earth reeled and **r**;
Ps 18: 7 Then the earth reeled and **r**;

ROCKS (25) [ROCK]

1Sa 13: 6 and in holes and in **r** and in tombs and in cisterns.
24: 2 for David and his men in the direction of the **R** of
1Ki 19:11 and breaking **r** in pieces before the LORD,
Job 8:17 around the stoneheap; they live among the **r**.
28:10 They cut out channels in the **r**,
30: 6 in holes in the ground, and in the **r**.
Ps 78:15 He split **r** open in the wilderness,
104:18 the **r** are a refuge for the coneys.
Pr 30:26 yet they make their homes in the **r**;
Isa 2:19 the caves of the **r** and the holes of the ground,
2:21 the caverns of the **r** and the clefts in the crags,
7:19 and in the clefts of the **r**,
33:16 their refuge will be the fortresses of **r**;
57: 5 under the clefts of the **r**?
Jer 4:29 they enter thickets; they climb among **r**;
16:16 and out of the clefts of the **r**.
Am 6:12 Do horses run on **r**?
Na 1: 6 and by him the **r** are broken in pieces.
Mt 27:51 The earth shook, and the **r** were split.
Ac 27:29 Fearing that we might run on the **r**,
Rev 6:15 hid in the caves and among the **r** of the mountains,
6:16 the mountains and **r**, "Fall on us and hide us from
Jdt 16:15 before your glance the **r** shall melt like wax.
Wis 17:19 or the harsh crash of **r** hurled down,
2Es 16:28 in thick groves and clefts in the **r**.

ROCKY (7) [ROCK]

1Sa 14: 4 a **r** crag on one side and a **r** crag on the other,
Job 39:28 and makes its home in the fastness of the **r** crag.
Mt 13: 5 Other seeds fell on **r** ground,
13:20 As for what was sown on **r** ground,
Mk 4: 5 Other seed fell on **r** ground,
4:16 And these are the ones sown on **r** ground:

ROD (38) [RODS]

Ex 21:20 with a **r** and the slave dies immediately,
2Sa 7:14 I will punish him with a **r** such as mortals use,
Job 9:34 If he would take his **r** away from me,
21: 9 and no **r** of God is upon them.
Ps 2: 9 You shall break them with a **r** of iron,
23: 4 your **r** and your staff—they comfort me.
89:32 then I will punish their transgression with the **r**
Pr 10:13 but a **r** is for the back of one who lacks sense.
13:24 Those who spare the **r** hate their children,
14: 3 The talk of fools is a **r** for their backs,
22: 8 and the **r** of anger will fail.
22:15 but the **r** of discipline drives it far away.
23:13 if you beat them with a **r**, they will not die.
23:14 If you beat them with the **r**,
26: 3 and a **r** for the back of fools.
29:15 The **r** and reproof give wisdom,
Isa 9: 4 the **r** of their oppressor, you have broken as on
10: 5 Ah, Assyria, the **r** of my anger—
10:15 As if a **r** should raise the one who lifts it up,
10:24 the Assyrians when they beat you with a **r** and lift
11: 4 he shall strike the earth with the **r** of his mouth,
14:29 that the **r** that struck you is broken,

Isa 28:27 with a stick, and cummin with a **r**.
30:31 when he strikes with his **r**.
La 3: 1 I am one who has seen affliction under the **r**
Eze 7:10 The **r** has blossomed, pride has budded.
7:11 Violence has grown into a **r** of wickedness.
21:10 You have despised the **r**, and all discipline.
21:13 If you despise the **r**, will it not happen?
Hos 4:12 and their divining **r** gives them oracles.
Mic 5: 1 a **r** they strike the ruler of Israel upon the cheek.
Heb 9: 4 and Aaron's **r** that budded,
Rev 2:27 with an iron **r**, as when clay pots are shattered—
11: 1 Then I was given a measuring **r** like a staff,
12: 5 who is to rule all the nations with a **r** of iron.
19:15 and he will rule them with a **r** of iron;
21:15 The angel who talked to me had a measuring **r**
21:16 and he measured the city with his **r**,

RODANIM (2)

Ge 10: 4 Elishah, Tarshish, Kittim, and **R**.
1Ch 1: 7 Elishah, Tarshish, Kittim, and **R**.

RODE (11) [RIDE]

Jdg 10: 4 He had thirty sons who **r** on thirty donkeys;
12:14 who **r** on seventy donkeys;
1Sa 25:20 As she **r** on the donkey and came down
25:42 Abigail got up hurriedly and **r** away on a donkey;
2Sa 22:11 He **r** on a cherub, and flew;
1Ki 18:45 Ahab **r** off and went to Jezreel.
2Ki 9:25 and I **r** side by side behind his father Ahab how
Ne 2:12 The only animal I took was the animal I **r**.
Ps 18:10 He **r** on a cherub, and flew;
Lk 19:36 As he **r** along, people kept spreading their cloaks
2Mc 9: 4 But the judgment of heaven **r** with him!

RODENTS (1)

Isa 66:17 vermin, and **r**, shall come to an end together,

RODS‡ (8) [ROD]

Ge 30:37 Then Jacob took fresh **r** of poplar and almond
30:37 exposing the white of the **r**.
30:38 the **r** that he had peeled in front of the flocks in
30:39 the flocks bred in front of the **r**,
30:41 Jacob laid the **r** in the troughs before the eyes of
30:41 that they might breed among the **r**,
Ac 16:22 and ordered them to be beaten with **r**.
2Co 11:25 Three times I was beaten with **r**.

ROEBUCK (1) [ROEBUCKS]

Dt 14: 5 the **r**, the wild goat, the ibex, the antelope,

ROEBUCKS (1) [ROEBUCK]

1Ki 4:23 one hundred sheep, besides deer, gazelles, **r**,

ROES (KJV) See GAZELLE, GAZELLES

ROGELIM (2)

2Sa 17:27 and Barzillai the Gileadite from **R**,
19:31 Barzillai the Gileadite had come down from **R**;

ROGUES (1)

Lk 18:11 **r**, adulterers, or even like this tax collector.

ROHGAH (1)

1Ch 7:34 The sons of Shemer: Ahi, **R**, Hubbah, and Aram.

ROLE (1)

4Mc 6:17 that out of cowardice we feign a **r** unbecoming

ROLL (16) [ROLLED, ROLLING]

Ge 29: 3 the shepherds would **r** the stone from the mouth of
Jos 10:18 "**R** large stones against the mouth of the cave,
Jdg 21: 9 For when the **r** was called among the people,
1Sa 14:17 "Call the **r** and see who has gone from us."
14:17 When they had called the **r**,
14:33 **r** a large stone before me here."
Job 30:14 wide breach they come; amid the crash they **r** on.
Isa 34: 4 and the skies **r** up like a scroll.
Jer 6:26 put on sackcloth, and **r** in ashes;
25:34 Wail, you shepherds, and cry out; **r** in ashes,
51:25 and **r** you down from the crags,
Am 5:24 But let justice **r** down like waters,
Mic 1:10 in Beth-leaphrah **r** yourselves in the dust.
Mk 16: 3 "Who will **r** away the stone for us from
Heb 1:12 like a cloak you will **r** them up,
Sir 27:27 If a person does evil, it will **r** back upon him,

ROLLED (16) [ROLL]

Ge 29: 8 and the stone is **r** from the mouth of the well;
29:10 up and **r** the stone from the well's mouth,
Jos 5: 9 "Today I have **r** away from you the disgrace
2Ki 2: 8 Then Elijah took his mantle and **r** it up,
Isa 9: 5 the garments **r** in blood shall be burned as fuel for
28:27 nor is a cart wheel **r** over cummin;
38:12 like a weaver I have **r** up my life;
Mt 27:60 He then **r** a great stone to the door of the tomb
28: 2 came and **r** back the stone and sat on it.
Mk 9:20 and he fell on the ground and **r** about,
15:46 He then **r** a stone against the door of the tomb.
16: 4 which was very large, had already been **r** back.
Lk 4:20 And he **r** up the scroll,
24: 2 They found the stone **r** away from the tomb,
Jn 20: 7 the linen wrappings but **r** up in a place by itself.
Jdt 13: 9 Next she **r** his body off the bed and pulled down

ROLLING (2) [ROLL]

Pr 26:27 a stone will come back on the one who starts it **r**.
Rev 6:14 The sky vanished like a scroll **r** itself up,

ROMAMTI-EZER (2)

1Ch 25: 4 Eliathah, Giddalti, and **R**, Joshbekashah, Mallothi,
25:31 to **R**, his sons and his brothers, twelve.

ROMAN (8) [ROME]

Ac 16:12 of the district of Macedonia and a **R** colony.
16:37 uncondemned, men who are **R** citizens,
16:38 when they heard that they were **R** citizens;
22:25 for you to flog a **R** citizen who is uncondemned?"
22:26 This man is a **R** citizen."
22:27 "Tell me, are you a **R** citizen?"
22:29 for he realized that Paul was a **R** citizen and
23:27 but when I had learned that he was a **R** citizen,

ROMANS (20) [ROME]

Jn 11:48 the **R** will come and destroy both our holy place
Ac 16:21 not lawful for us as **R** to adopt or observe."
25:16 the custom of the **R** to hand over anyone before
28:17 in Jerusalem and handed over to the **R**.
28:18 the **R** wanted to release me,
1Mc 8: 1 Now Judas heard of the fame of the **R**,
8:10 and the **R** took captive their wives and children;
8:23 "May all go well with the **R** and with the nation of
8:27 the **R** shall willingly act as their allies,
8:29 Thus on these terms the **R** make a treaty with
12: 4 **R** gave them letters to the people in every place,
14:24 to confirm the alliance with the **R**.
14:40 that the Jews were addressed by the **R** as friends
14:40 **R** had received the envoys of Simon with honor.
15:16 consul of the **R**, to King Ptolemy, greetings.
2Mc 4:11 to establish friendship and alliance with the **R**;
8:10 to make up for the king the tribute due to the **R**,
8:36 to secure tribute for the **R** by the capture of
11:34 The **R** also sent them a letter, which read thus:
11:34 envoys of the **R**, to the people of the Jews,

ROME (22) [ROMAN, ROMANS]

Ac 2:10 and visitors from **R**, both Jews and proselytes,
18: 2 because Claudius had ordered all Jews to leave **R**.
19:21 "After I have gone there, I must also see **R**."
23:11 so you must bear witness also in **R**."
28:14 And so we came to **R**.
28:16 into **R**, Paul was allowed to live by himself,
Ro 1: 7 To all God's beloved in **R**, who are called to
1:15 to proclaim the gospel to you also who are in **R**.
2Ti 1:17 when he arrived in **R**, he eagerly searched for me
1Mc 1:10 he had been a hostage in **R**.
7: 1 of Seleucus set out from **R**,
8:17 sent them to **R** to establish friendship and alliance,
8:19 They went to **R**, a very long journey;
8:24 to **R** or to any of their allies in all their dominion,
8:26 arms, money, or ships, just as **R** has decided;
8:28 arms, money, or ships, just as **R** has decided;
12: 1 he chose men and sent them to **R** to confirm
12: 3 So they went to **R** and entered the senate chamber
12:16 to **R** to renew our former friendship and alliance
14:16 It was heard in **R**, and as far away as Sparta,
14:24 After this Simon sent Numenius to **R** with
15:15 Numenius and his companions arrived from **R**,

ROOF‡ (37) [ROOFED, ROOFS]

Ge 6:16 Make a **r** for the ark, and finish it to a cubit above;
19: 8 for they have come under the shelter of my **r**."
Dt 22: 8 you shall make a parapet for your **r**;
Jos 2: 6 brought them up to the **r** and hidden them with the
stalks of flax that she had laid out on the **r**.
2: 8 she came up to them on the **r**
Jdg 3:20 while he was sitting alone in his cool **r** chamber,
3:23 and closed the doors of the **r** chamber on him,
3:24 that the doors of the **r** chamber were locked,
3:25 he still did not open the doors of the **r** chamber,
9:51 and they went to the **r** of the tower.
16:27 the Philistines were there, and on the **r** there were
1Sa 9:25 a bed was spread for Saul on the **r**,
9:26 of dawn Samuel called to Saul upon the **r**,
2Sa 11: 2 and was walking about on the **r** of the king's
house, that he saw from the **r** a woman bathing;
16:22 So they pitched a tent for Absalom upon the **r**;
18:24 sentinel went up to the **r** of the gate by the wall,
2Ki 4:10 Let us make a small **r** chamber with walls,
23:12 The altars on the **r** of the upper chamber of Ahaz,
Job 29:10 and their tongues stuck to the **r** of their mouths.
Ps 137: 6 Let my tongue cling to the **r** of my mouth,
Ecc 10:18 Through sloth the **r** sinks in,
La 4: 4 of the infant sticks to the **r** of its mouth for thirst;
Eze 3:26 and I will make your tongue cling to the **r**
26: 8 and raise a **r** of shields against you.
Da 4:29 the end of twelve months he was walking on the **r**
Hab 3:13 laying it bare from foundation to **r**.
Mt 8: 8 I am not worthy to have you come under my **r**;
Mk 2: 4 they removed the **r** above him;
Lk 5:19 up on the **r** and let him down with his bed through
7: 6 I am not worthy to have you come under my **r**;
Ac 10: 9 Peter went up on the **r** to pray.
Jdt 8: 5 at home where she set up a tent for herself on the **r**
Sir 29:22 under their own crude **r** than sumptuous food in
1Es 6: 4 and this **r** and finishing all the other things?
4Mc 17: 3 Nobly set like a **r** on the pillars of your sons,

ROOFED (2) [ROOF]

1Ki 6: 9 he **r** the house with beams and planks of cedar.
7: 3 It was **r** with cedar on the forty-five rafters,

ROOFS (5) [ROOF]

Ne 8:16 each on the **r** of their houses,
Jer 19:13 upon whose **r** offerings have been made to
32:29 the houses on whose **r** offerings have been made
Zep 1: 5 those who bow down on the **r** to the host of
Wis 17: 2 and prisoners of long night, shut in under their **r**,

ROOM‡ (52) [BEDROOM, GUARDROOM, GUESTROOM, ROOMS, STOREROOMS]

Ge 24:23 Is there **r** in your father's house for us to spend
26:22 saying, "Now the LORD has made **r** for us,
43:30 So he went into a private **r** and wept there.
Jdg 15: 1 He said, "I want to go into my wife's **r**."
1Sa 3: 2 was lying down in his **r**;
1Ki 1:15 So Bathsheba went to the king in his **r**.
2Ki 4:35 He got down, walked once to and fro in the **r**,
1Ch 28:11 and of the **r** for the mercy seat;
Ne 3:31 and to the upper **r** of the corner.
3:32 the upper **r** of the corner and the Sheep Gate
13: 5 for Tobiah a large **r** where they had previously put
13: 7 preparing a **r** for him in the courts of the house
13: 8 the household furniture of Tobiah out of the **r**.
Ps 4: 1 You gave me **r** when I was in distress.
Isa 5: 8 until there is **r** for no one but you,
49:20 make **r** for me to settle."
Jer 7:32 they will bury in Topheth until there is no more **r**.
19:11 In Topheth they shall bury until there is no more **r**
Eze 8:12 each in his **r** of images?
41: 3 into the inner **r** and measured the pilasters of
41: 4 He measured the depth of the **r**, twenty cubits,
41:15 the temple and the inner **r** and the outer vestibule
41:17 even to the inner **r**, and on the outside.
41:17 And on all the walls all around in the inner **r** and
Da 6:10 which had windows in its upper **r** open
7: 8 to make **r** for it, three of
7:20 and to make **r** for which three of them fell out—
Joel 2:16 Let the bridegroom leave his **r**,
Zec 10:10 until there is no **r** for them.
Mt 6: 6 go into your **r** and shut the door and pray
Mk 2: 2 around that there was no longer **r** for them,
14:14 Where is my guest **r** where I may eat the Passover
14:15 He will show you a large **r** upstairs,
Lk 14:22 you ordered has been done, and there is still **r**.'
22:11 'The teacher asks you, "Where is the guest **r**,
22:12 He will show you a large **r** upstairs,
Ac 1:13 to the **r** upstairs where they were staying,
9:37 they had washed her, they laid her in a **r** upstairs.
9:39 when he arrived, they took him to the **r** upstairs.
20: 8 in the **r** upstairs where we were meeting.
Ro 12:19 but leave **r** for the wrath of God;
2Co 7: 2 Make **r** in your hearts for us;
Eph 4:27 and do not make **r** for the devil.
Phm 1:22 One thing more—prepare a guest **r** for me,
Tob 3:10 When she had gone up to her father's upper **r**,
3:17 of Raguel came down from her upper **r**.
7:15 "Sister, get the other **r** ready, and take her there."
7:16 and made the bed in the **r** as he had told her,
8: 4 parents had gone out and shut the door of the **r**,
Sir 16:14 He makes **r** for every act of mercy;
42:11 See that there is no lattice in her **r**,
4Mc 7: 6 which had **r** only for reverence and purity,

ROOMS (9) [ROOM]

Ge 6:14 make **r** in the ark, and cover it inside and out
1Ki 6:29 and open flowers, in the inner and outer **r**.
6:30 in the inner and outer **r**.
1Ch 28:11 its treasuries, its upper **r**, and its inner chambers,
Pr 24: 4 by knowledge the **r** are filled with all precious
Jer 22:13 and his upper **r** by injustice;
22:14 a spacious house with large upper **r**,"
Mt 24:26 He is in the inner **r**,' do not believe it.
Tob 2: 4 the body from the square and laid it in one of the **r**

ROOST (1)

Sir 27: 9 Birds **r** with their own kind,

ROOSTER (1)

Pr 30:31 the strutting **r**, the he-goat, and a king striding

ROOT‡ (61) [ROOTED, ROOTS]

Dt 2:15 to **r** them out from the camp,
29:18 be that there is among you a **r** sprouting poisonous
1Ki 14:15 he will **r** up Israel out of this good land
2Ki 19:30 the house of Judah shall again take **r** downward,
Job 5: 3 I have seen fools taking **r**,
14: 8 Though its **r** grows old in the earth,
15:29 nor will they strike **r** in the earth;
19:28 and, 'The **r** of the matter is found in him';
31:12 and it would burn to the **r** all my harvest.
Ps 80: 9 it took deep **r** and filled the land.
Pr 12: 3 but the **r** of the righteous will never be moved.
12:12 but the **r** of the righteous bears fruit.
Isa 5:24 so their **r** will become rotten,
11:10 the **r** of Jesse shall stand as a signal to the peoples;
14:29 from the **r** of the snake will come forth an adder,
14:30 but I will make your **r** die of famine,
27: 6 In days to come Jacob shall take **r**,

Isa 37:31 the house of Judah shall again take **r** downward,
40:24 scarcely has their stem taken **r** in the earth,
53: 2 and like a **r** out of dry ground;
Jer 12: 2 You plant them, and they take **r**;
Hos 9:16 Ephraim is stricken, their **r** is dried up,
14: 5 he shall strike **r** like the forests of Lebanon.
Mal 4: 1 so that it will leave them neither **r** nor branch.
Mt 3:10 Even now the ax is lying at the **r** of the trees;
13: 6 and since they had no **r**, they withered away.
13:21 yet such a person has no **r**,
Mk 4: 6 and since it had no **r**, it withered away.
4:17 But they have no **r**, and endure only for a while;
Lk 3: 9 Even now the ax is lying at the **r** of the trees;
8:13 with joy. But these have no **r**;
Ro 11:16 if the **r** is holy, then the branches also are holy.
11:17 in their place to share the rich **r** of the olive tree,
11:18 remember that it is not you that support the **r**, but
the **r** that supports you.
15:12 "The **r** of Jesse shall come,
1Ti 6:10 For the love of money is a **r** of all kinds of evil,
Heb 12:15 no **r** of bitterness springs up and causes trouble,
Rev 5: 5 See, the Lion of the tribe of Judah, the **R** of David,
22:16 I am the **r** and the descendant of David,
Wis 3:15 and the **r** of understanding does not fail.
4: 3 of their illegitimate seedlings will strike a deep **r**
15: 3 and to know your power is the **r** of immortality.
Sir 1: 6 The **r** of wisdom—to whom has it been revealed?
1:20 To fear the Lord is the **r** of wisdom,
3:28 for an evil plant has taken **r** in him.
7: 6 or you may be unable to **r** out injustice;
23:25 Her children will not take **r**,
24:12 I took **r** in an honored people,
37:17 The mind is the **r** of all conduct;
47:22 and to David a **r** from his own family.
1Mc 1:10 From them came forth a sinful **r**,
2Mc 12: 7 to come again and **r** out the whole community
1Es 8:78 to leave to us a **r** and a name in your holy place,
8:87 and gave us such a **r** as this;
8:88 to destroy us without leaving a **r** or seed or name?
8:89 for we are left as a **r** to this day.
2Es 3:22 in the hearts of the people along with the evil **r**;
5:28 and dishonored the one **r** beyond the others,
8:41 and not all that were planted will take **r**;
8:53 The **r** of evil is sealed up from you,

ROOTED (6) [ROOT]

Job 31: 8 and let what grows for me be **r** out.
Ps 9: 6 their cities you have **r** out;
Pr 2:22 and the treacherous will be **r** out of it.
Ac 3:23 to that prophet will be utterly **r** out of the people.'
Eph 3:17 as you are being **r** and grounded in love.
Col 2: 7 **r** and built up in him and established in the faith,

ROOTS (24) [ROOT]

Job 8:17 Their **r** twine around the stoneheap;
18:16 Their **r** dry up beneath,
28: 9 and overturn mountains by the **r**.
29:19 my **r** spread out to the waters,
30: 4 and to warm themselves the **r** of broom.
36:30 around him and covers the **r** of the sea.
Isa 11: 1 and a branch shall grow out of his **r**.
Jer 17: 8 sending out its **r** by the stream.
Eze 17: 6 its **r** remained where it stood.
17: 7 This vine stretched out its **r** toward him;
17: 9 Will he not pull up its **r**, cause its fruit to rot and
17: 9 or mighty army will be needed to pull it from its **r**.
31: 7 for its **r** went down to abundant water.
Da 4:15 But leave its stump and **r** in the ground,
4:23 but leave its stump and **r** in the ground,
4:26 As it was commanded to leave the stump and **r** of
7: 8 of the earlier horns were plucked up by the **r**.
11: 7 a branch from her **r** shall rise up in his place.
Am 2: 9 I destroyed his fruit above, and his **r** beneath.
Jnh 2: 6 at the **r** of the mountains.
Mk 11:20 they saw the fig tree withered away to its **r**.
Wis 7:20 the varieties of plants and the virtues of **r**;
Sir 10:15 The Lord plucks up the **r** of the nations,
40:15 they are unhealthy **r** on sheer rock.

ROPE (4) [ROPES]

Jos 2:15 she let them down by a **r** through the window,
Job 18:10 A **r** is hid for them in the ground,
41: 2 Can you put a **r** in its nose,
Isa 3:24 and instead of a sash, a **r**;

ROPES (18) [ROPE]

Jdg 15:13 So they bound him with two new **r**,
15:14 of the LORD rushed on him, and the **r** that were
16:11 they bind me with new **r** that have not been used,
16:12 So Delilah took new **r** and bound him with them,
16:12 But he snapped the **r** off his arms like a thread.
2Sa 17:13 then all Israel will bring **r** to that city,
1Ki 20:31 around our waists and **r** on our heads, and go out
20:32 put **r** on their heads, went to the king of Israel,
Job 39:10 Can you tie it in the furrow with **r**,
Isa 5:18 who drag sin along as with cart **r**,
33:20 and none of whose **r** will be broken.
Jer 38: 6 letting Jeremiah down by **r**.
38:11 which he let down to Jeremiah in the cistern by **r**.
38:12 and clothes between your armpits and the **r**."
38:13 up by the **r** and pulled him out of the cistern.
Ac 27:32 soldiers cut away the **r** of the boat and set it adrift.
27:40 At the same time they loosened the **r** that tied
3Mc 4: 8 their necks encircled with **r** instead of garlands,

ROSE‡ (135) [RISE, ROSE-BEARING, ROSEBUDS, ROSEBUSHES, ROSES]

Ge 4: 8 Cain **r** up against his brother Abel, and killed him.
7:17 and bore up the ark, and it **r** high above the earth.
19: 1 When Lot saw them, he **r** to meet them,
19:33 not know when she lay down or when she **r**.
19:35 and the younger **r**, and lay with him;
19:35 not know when she lay down or when she **r**.
20: 8 So Abimelech **r** early in the morning,
21:14 So Abraham **r** early in the morning,
22: 3 So Abraham **r** early in the morning,
23: 3 Abraham **r** up from beside his dead,
23: 7 Abraham **r** and bowed to the Hittites,
24:54 When they **r** in the morning, he said,
24:61 Then Rebekah and her maids **r** up,
25:34 and he ate and drank, and **r** and went his way.
26:31 In the morning they **r** early and exchanged oaths;
28:18 So Jacob **r** early in the morning,
31:55 Early in the morning Laban **r** up,
32:31 The sun **r** upon him as he passed Penuel,
37: 7 Suddenly my sheaf **r** and stood upright;
Ex 2:23 Out of the slavery their cry for help **r** up to God.
24: 4 He **r** early in the morning,
32: 6 They **r** early the next day,
32: 6 and the people sat down to eat and drink, and **r** up
34: 4 and he **r** early in the morning and went up
Nu 14:40 They **r** early in the morning and went up to
22:13 So Balaam **r** in the morning,
22:14 So the officials of Moab **r** and went to Balak,
Jos 3: 1 in the morning Joshua **r** and set out from Shittim
6:12 Then Joshua **r** early in the morning,
6:15 On the seventh day they **r** early, at dawn,
7:16 So Joshua **r** early in the morning,
8:10 In the morning Joshua **r** early and mustered
8:19 the troops in ambush **r** quickly out of their place
Jdg 3:20 So he **r** from his seat.
6:28 When the townspeople **r** early in the morning,
6:38 he **r** early next morning and squeezed the fleece,
7: 1 with him **r** early and encamped beside the spring
9:35 and the troops with him **r** from the ambush.
9:43 he **r** against them and killed them.
10: 1 in the hill country of Ephraim, **r** to deliver Israel.
16: 3 Then at midnight he **r** up,
20: 5 The lords of Gibeah **r** up against me,
1Sa 1: 9 Hannah **r** and presented herself before
1:19 They **r** early in the morning and worshiped before
5: 3 When the people of Ashdod **r** early the next day,
5: 4 But when they **r** early on the next morning,
14: 5 One crag **r** on the north in front of Michmash,
15:12 Samuel **r** early in the morning to meet Saul,
17:20 David **r** early in the morning,
17:52 of Israel and Judah **r** up with a shout and pursued
18:27 David **r** and went, along with his men,
20:34 Jonathan **r** from the table in fierce anger
20:41 David **r** from beside the stone heap
21:10 David **r** and fled that day from Saul;
24: 8 also **r** up and went out of the cave and called
25:41 She **r** and bowed down, with her face to
26: 2 Saul **r** and went down to the Wilderness of Ziph,
28:25 Then they **r** and went away that night.
2Sa 11: 2 when David **r** from his couch and was walking
12:20 Then David **r** from the ground, washed,
12:21 but when the child died, you **r** and ate food."
13:29 Then all the king's sons **r**,
13:31 king **r**, tore his garments, and lay on the ground;
14:31 Then Joab **r** and went to Absalom at his house,
18:31 delivering you from the power of all who **r** up
24:11 When David **r** in the morning,
1Ki 2:19 The king **r** to meet her, and bowed down to her;
3:21 When I **r** in the morning to nurse my son,
2Ki 3:22 When they **r** early in the morning,
3:24 the Israelites **r** up and attacked the Moabites,
4:30 So he **r** up and followed her.
6:15 When an attendant of the man of God **r** early in
1Ch 28: 2 Then King David **r** to his feet and said:
2Ch 13: 6 **r** up and rebelled against his lord;
20:20 They **r** early in the morning and went out into
29:20 Then King Hezekiah **r** early,
Est 5: 9 and observed that he neither **r** nor trembled
7: 7 The king **r** from the feast in wrath and went into
8: 5 and Esther **r** and stood before the king.
Job 29: 8 and the aged **r** up and stood;
Ps 76: 9 when God **r** up to establish judgment,
78:31 of God **r** against them and he killed the strongest
104: 8 They **r** up to the mountains,
SS 2: 1 I am a **r** of Sharon, a lily of the valleys.
Eze 1:19 living creatures **r** from the earth, the wheels **r**.
1:20 they went, and the wheels **r** along with them;
1:21 and when they **r** from the earth, the wheels **r** along
3:12 and as the glory of the LORD **r** from its place,
3:23 So I **r** up and went out into the valley;
10: 4 Then the glory of the LORD **r** up from the cherub
10:15 The cherubim **r** up. These were the living creatures
10:17 and when they **r** up, the others **r** up with them;
10:19 up their wings and **r** up from the earth in my sight
42: 3 the chambers **r** gallery by gallery in three stories.
Da 3:24 Then King Nebuchadnezzar was astonished and **r**
Jnh 3: 6 he **r** from his throne, removed his robe,
4: 8 When the sun **r**, God prepared a sultry east wind,
Mt 13: 6 But when the sun **r**, they were scorched;
Mk 4: 6 And when the sun **r**, it was scorched;
16: 9 ⟦Now after he **r** early on the first day of the week,⟧
Lk 23: 1 Then the assembly **r** as a body and brought Jesus
Ac 5:36 For some time ago Theudas **r** up,
5:37 After him Judas the Galilean **r** up at the time of
10:41 and who ate and drank with him after he **r** from
1Co 10: 7 "The people sat down to eat and drink, and they **r**
1Th 4:14 For since we believe that Jesus died and **r** again,
Rev 8: 4 **r** before God from the hand of the angel.
9: 2 and from the shaft **r** smoke like the smoke of
13:11 Then I saw another beast that **r** out of the earth;
Jdt 10: 2 she **r** from where she lay prostrate.
14:19 and their loud cries and shouts **r** up throughout
AdE 7: 7 king **r** from the banquet and went into the garden,
8: 4 and she **r** and stood before the king.
11:11 and the sun **r**, and the lowly were exalted
Sir 39:13 blossom like a **r** growing by a stream of water.
46: 1 to take vengeance on the enemies that **r**
47: 1 him Nathan **r** up to prophesy in the days of David.
47:12 a wise son **r** up who because of him lived
Bel 1:16 Early in the morning the king **r** and came,
1Mc 4:53 they **r** and offered sacrifice,
8: 5 and the others who **r** up against them.
14:32 then Simon **r** up and fought for his nation.
16:16 Ptolemy and his men **r** up, took their weapons,
2Mc 14:45 Still alive and aflame with anger, he **r**,
1Es 8:73 Then I **r** from my fast,
8:96 Then Ezra **r** up and made the leaders of the priests
2Es 11:12 As I watched, one wing on the right side **r** up,
11:13 Then the next wing **r** up and reigned,
11:20 the wings that followed also **r** up on the right side,
11:21 and others of them **r** up, but did not hold the rule.
12: 2 that had gone over to it **r** up and set themselves up
14: 2 I answered, "Here I am, Lord," and I **r** to my feet.

ROSE-BEARING (1) [BEAR, ROSE]

3Mc 7:17 called "**r**" because of a characteristic of the place,

ROSEBUDS (1) [BUD, ROSE]

Wis 2: 8 Let us crown ourselves with **r** before they wither.

ROSEBUSHES (1) [BUSH, ROSE]

Sir 24:14 like a palm tree in En-gedi, and like **r** in Jericho;

ROSES (3) [ROSE]

AdE 1: 6 with **r** arranged around them.
Sir 50: 8 like **r** in the days of first fruits, like lilies by
2Es 2:19 and seven mighty mountains on which **r**

ROSETTE (2)

Ex 28:36 You shall make a **r** of pure gold,
39:30 They made the **r** of the holy diadem of pure gold,

ROSH (1)

Ge 46:21 Bela, Becher, Ashbel, Gera, Naaman, Ehi, **R**,

ROT (10) [ROTTED, ROTTEN, ROTTENNESS]

Pr 10: 7 but the name of the wicked will **r**.
14:30 but passion makes the bones **r**.
Isa 19: 6 reeds and rushes will **r** away.
34: 4 All the host of heaven shall **r** away,
40:20 chooses mulberry wood—wood that will not **r**—
Eze 17: 9 cause its fruit to **r** and wither,
Zec 14:12 their flesh shall **r** while they are still on their feet;
their eyes shall **r** in their sockets, and their tongues
shall **r** in their mouths.
LtJ 6:72 that **r** upon them you will know that they are

ROTE (1)

Isa 29:13 of me is a human commandment learned by **r**;

ROTTED (2) [ROT]

Jas 5: 2 Your riches have **r**, and your clothes are
2Mc 9: 9 in anguish and pain, his flesh **r** away,

ROTTEN (4) [ROT]

Job 13:28 One wastes away like a **r** thing,
41:27 It counts iron as straw, and bronze as **r** wood.
Isa 5:24 so their root will become **r**,
Jer 29:17 like **r** figs that are so bad they cannot be eaten.

ROTTENNESS (3) [ROT]

Pr 12: 4 but she who brings shame is like **r** in his bones.
Hos 5:12 and like **r** to the house of Judah.
Hab 3:16 **R** enters into my bones, and my steps tremble

ROUGH (5) [ROUGHLY]

Isa 40: 4 and the **r** places a plain.
42:16 the **r** places into level ground.
Lk 3: 5 and the **r** ways made smooth;
Jn 6:18 sea became **r** because a strong wind was blowing.
Bar 4:26 My pampered children have traveled **r** roads;

ROUGHLY (1) [ROUGH]

Pr 18:23 The poor use entreaties, but the rich answer **r**.

ROUND (13) [ROUNDABOUT, ROUNDED, ROUNDS]

Lev 19:27 You shall not **r** off the hair on your temples or mar
1Ki 7:23 Then he made the molten sea; it was **r**,
7:31 its opening was **r**, as a pedestal is made;
7:31 its borders were four-sided, not **r**.
7:35 of the stand there was a **r** band half a cubit high;
2Ch 4: 2 Then he made the molten sea; it was **r**,

Job 37:12 They turn r and r by his guidance,
Ecc 1: 6 r and r goes the wind,
Isa 22:18 whirl you r and r, and throw you like a ball
29: 1 Add year to year; let the festivals run their r.

ROUNDABOUT (2) [ROUND]

Ex 13:18 the people by the r way of the wilderness toward
2Ki 3: 9 and when they had made a r march of seven days,

ROUNDED (6) [ROUND]

1Ki 7:20 on the two pillars and also above the r projection
10:19 The top of the throne was r in the back,
SS 5:14 His arms are r gold, set with jewels.
7: 1 Your r thighs are like jewels,
7: 2 a r bowl that never lacks mixed wine.
4Mc 5: 4 When many persons had been r up, one man,

ROUNDS (1) [ROUND]

SS 5: 7 Making their r in the city the sentinels found me;

ROUSE (17) [AROUSE, AROUSED, AROUSES, AROUSING, ROUSED, ROUSES, ROUSING]

Ge 49: 9 like a lioness—who dares r him up?
Nu 24: 9 like a lioness; who will r him up?
Job 3: 8 those who are skilled to r up Leviathan.
8: 6 surely then he will r himself for you and restore
Ps 44:23 R yourself! Why do you sleep,
59: 4 R yourself, come to my help and see!
Isa 51:17 R yourself, r yourself!
Eze 23:22 I will r against you your lovers
24: 8 To r my wrath, to take vengeance,
38:14 Israel are living securely, you will r yourself
Joel 3: 7 But now I will r them to leave the places
3:12 Let the nations r themselves,
Hab 2:19 to silent stone, "R yourself!"
Jdt 14: 3 the camp and r the officers of the Assyrian army.
Sir 36: 8 R your anger and pour out your wrath;
4Mc 8: 9 But if by disobedience you r my anger,

ROUSED (8) [ROUSE]

Job 14:12 they will not awake or be r out of their sleep.
Ps 76: 7 before you when once your anger is r?
Isa 41: 2 Who has r a victor from the east,
Da 10:10 hand touched me and r me to my hands and knees.
Zec 2:13 for he has r himself from his holy dwelling.
3Mc 5:15 And when he had with difficulty r him,
2Es 7:31 the world that is not yet awake shall be r,
11:37 I saw what seemed to be a lion r from the forest,

ROUSES (2) [ROUSE]

Isa 14: 9 it r the shades to greet you,
Sir 22: 9 or who r a sleeper from deep slumber.

ROUSING (3) [ROUSE]

Nu 23:24 and r itself like a lion!
Hab 1: 6 For I am r the Chaldeans,
2Es 12:31 for the lion whom you saw r up out of the forest

ROUT (6) [ROUTED]

1Sa 4: 3 "Why has the LORD put us to r today before
Ps 78:66 He put his adversaries to r;
144: 6 send out your arrows and r them.
1Mc 4:35 When Lysias saw the r of his troops and observed
5:61 Thus the people suffered a great r because,
2Mc 12:27 After the r and destruction of these,

ROUTE (7)

Dt 1:22 for us and bring back a report to us regarding the r
1:33 to show you the r you should take."
2: 8 leaving behind the r of the Arabah,
2: 8 When we had headed out along the r of
28:68 by a r that I promised you would never see again;
Jdg 8:11 So Gideon went up by the caravan r east of Nobah
1Mc 11: 4 for they had piled them in heaps along his r.

ROUTED (13) [ROUT]

Ge 14:15 and r them and pursued them to Hobah,
Dt 32:30 How could one have r a thousand,
Jdg 20:32 "They are being r before us, as previously."
1Sa 7:10 and they were r before Israel.
14:47 wherever he turned he r them.
2Sa 22:15 and scattered them—lightning, and r them.
2Ch 20:22 who had come against Judah, so that they were r.
Ps 18:14 he flashed forth lightnings, and r them.
1Mc 5:60 Then Joseph and Azariah were r,
6: 5 that had gone into the land of Judah had been r;
11:55 against Demetrius, and he fled and was r.
11:72 to the battle against the enemy and r them,
3Mc 1: 5 it came about that the enemy was r in the action,

ROVERS (KJV) See RAIDERS

ROVING (1)

Wis 4:12 and r desire perverts the innocent mind.

ROW (15) [ROWED, ROWERS, ROWS, VINE-ROWS]

Ex 28:17 A r of carnelian, chrysolite, and emerald shall be the first r;
28:18 second r a turquoise, a sapphire and a moonstone;
28:19 the third r a jacinth, an agate, and an amethyst;
28:20 and the fourth r a beryl, an onyx, and a jasper;
39:10 A r of carnelian, chrysolite, and emerald was the first r;
39:11 and the second r, a turquoise, a sapphire,
39:12 the third r, a jacinth, an agate, and an amethyst;
39:13 and the fourth r, a beryl, an onyx, and a jasper;
Lev 24: 6 You shall place them in two rows, six in a r,
24: 7 You shall put pure frankincense with each r,
1Ki 7: 3 fifteen in each r, which were on the pillars.
Eze 46:19 to the north r of the holy chambers for the priests;
46:23 around each of the four courts was a r of masonry,

ROWED (2) [ROW]

Jnh 1:13 the men r hard to bring the ship back to land,
Jn 6:19 When they had r about three or four miles,

ROWERS (2) [ROW]

Eze 27: 8 The inhabitants of Sidon and Arvad were your r;
27:26 Your r have brought you into the high seas.

ROWING (KJV) See AT THE OARS

ROWS (24) [ROW]

Ex 28:17 You shall set in it four r of stones.
39:10 They set in it four r of stones.
Lev 24: 6 You shall place them in two r, six in a row,
1Ki 7: 2 built on four r of cedar pillars,
7: 4 There were window frames in the three r,
7: 4 facing each other in the three r.
7: 5 opposite, facing each other in the three r.
7:18 the columns with two r around each latticework
7:20 were two hundred pomegranates in r all around;
7:24 there were two r of panels, cast when it was cast.
7:42 two r of pomegranates for each latticework,
1Ch 9:32 of the Kohathites had charge of the r of bread,
23:29 to assist also with the r of bread,
28:16 weight of gold for each table for the r of bread,
2Ch 2: 4 and for the regular offering of the r of bread,
4: 3 there were two r of panels, cast when it was cast.
4:13 two r of pomegranates for each latticework,
13:11 set out the r of bread on the table of pure gold,
29:18 and the table for the r of bread and all its utensils.
Ne 10:33 for the r of bread, the regular grain offering,
Job 41:15 Its back is made of shields in r,
Isa 28:25 and plant wheat in r and barley in its proper place,
Eze 46:23 at the bottom of the r all around.
Wis 18:24 of the ancestors were engraved on the four r

ROYAL (108)

Ge 49:20 and he shall provide r delicacies.
Jos 10: 2 like one of the r cities, and was larger than Ai,
1Sa 27: 5 for why should your servant live in the r city
2Sa 12:26 of the Ammonites, and took the r city.
1Ki 1: 9 the king's sons, and all the r officials of Judah,
1:46 Solomon now sits on the r throne.
9: 5 I will establish your r throne over Israel forever,
10:13 as what he gave her out of Solomon's r bounty.
11:14 he was of the r house in Edom.
2Ki 10:13 the r princes and the sons of the queen mother."
11: 1 she set about to destroy all the r family.
14: 5 As soon as the r power was firmly
15:19 he might help him confirm his hold on the r power.
25:25 of the r family, came with ten men;
1Ch 22:10 and I will establish his r throne in Israel forever.'
29:25 and bestowed upon him such r majesty as had
2Ch 2: 1 and a r palace for himself.
2:12 and a r palace for himself.
7:18 then I will establish your r throne,
22:10 to destroy all the r family of the house of Judah.
23:20 They set the king on the r throne.
25: 3 As soon as the r power was firmly
25:16 "Have we made you a r counselor?
Ezr 4: 8 Rehum the r deputy and Shimshai the scribe wrote
4: 9 (then Rehum the r deputy,
4:13 custom, or toll, and the r revenue will be reduced.
4:17 "To Rehum the r deputy and Shimshai the scribe
5:17 a search made in the r archives there in Babylon,
6: 4 let the cost be paid from the r treasury.
6: 8 in full and without delay, from the r revenue,
Est 1: 2 when King Ahasuerus sat on his r throne in
1: 7 the r wine was lavished according to the bounty of
1:11 wearing the r crown, in order to show the peoples
1:19 it pleases the king, let a r order go out from him,
1:19 and let the king give her r position to another
1:22 he sent letters to all the r provinces,
2:16 to King Ahasuerus in his r palace in
2:17 and devotion, so that he set the r crown
2:18 and gave gifts with r liberality.
4:14 Perhaps you have come to r dignity for just such
5: 1 the third day Esther put on her r robes and stood
5: 1 The king was sitting on his r throne inside
6: 8 let r robes be brought, which the king has worn,
6: 8 with a r crown on its head.
8:10 on fast steeds bred from the r herd.
8:14 So the couriers, mounted on their swift r steeds,
8:15 wearing r robes of blue and white,
9: 3 and the r officials were supporting the Jews,
Ps 45: 6 Your r scepter is a scepter of equity;
Isa 12: 6 Shout aloud and sing for joy, O r Zion,
62: 3 and a r diadem in the hand of your God.
Jer 41: 1 of Nethaniah son of Elishama, of the r family, one
43:10 and he will spread his r canopy over them.
Eze 17:13 of the r offspring and made a covenant with him,
Da 1: 3 of the Israelites of the r family and of the nobility,
1: 5 a daily portion of the r rations of food and wine.
1: 8 that he would not defile himself with the r rations
1:13 of the young men who eat the r rations,
1:15 the young men who had been eating the r rations.
1:16 to withdraw their r rations and the wine they were
2:15 the r official, "Why is the decree of the king
4:29 on the roof of the r palace of Babylon,
4:30 as a r capital by my mighty power and
5: 5 on the plaster of the wall of the r palace,
6:26 that in all my r dominion people should tremble
11:21 a contemptible person on whom r majesty had
11:26 by those who eat of the r rations.
Zec 6:13 he shall bear r honor, and shall sit and rule
Mt 11: 8 Look, those who wear soft robes are in r palaces.
Lk 7:25 on fine clothing and live in luxury are in r palaces.
19:12 to a distant country to get r power for himself and
19:15 When he returned, having received r power,
Jn 4:46 Now there was a r official whose son lay ill
Ac 12:21 On an appointed day Herod put on his r robes,
Jas 2: 8 if you really fulfill the r law according to
1Pe 2: 9 But you are a chosen race, a r priesthood,
Tob 1:20 not taken into the r treasury except my wife Anna
Jdt 2:18 huge amount of gold and silver from the r palace.
AdE 1: 5 for six days in the courtyard of the r palace,
1:19 it pleases the king, let him issue a r decree,
1:19 but let the king give her r rank to a woman better
2:23 in the r library in praise of the goodwill shown
4: 7 into the r treasury to bring about the destruction of
6: 2 the two r eunuchs who were on guard and sought
8:15 the r robe and wearing a gold crown and a turban
9: 3 the r secretaries were paying honor to the Jews,
15: 6 He was seated on his r throne,
16:11 to by all as the person second to the r throne.
Wis 14:21 in bondage to misfortune or to r authority,
18:15 from heaven, from the r throne, into the midst of
Bar 5: 6 carried in glory, as on a r throne.
1Mc 3:32 He left Lysias, a distinguished man of r lineage,
6:43 of the animals was equipped with r armor.
6:47 the Jews saw the r might and the fierce attack of
7: 2 As he was entering the r palace of his ancestors,
11:34 from the r taxes that the king formerly received
13:15 that your brother Jonathan owed the r treasury,
15: 8 to the r treasury and any such future debts shall
2Mc 4:11 the existing r concessions to the Jews, secured
1Es 1:54 the treasure chests of the Lord, and the r stores,
6:21 let search be made in the r archives of our lord
6:23 in the r archives that were deposited in Babylon.
8:18 you may provide out of the r treasury.
8:67 They delivered the king's orders to the r stewards
3Mc 3:28 also two thousand drachmas from the r treasury,
7:12 and without r authority or supervision,
4Mc 3: 8 sweating and quite exhausted, to the r tent,
14: 2 more r than kings and freer than the free!.

RUBBED (3)

Eze 16: 4 nor r with salt, nor wrapped in cloths.
29:18 and every shoulder was r bare;
Lk 6: 1 r them in their hands, and ate them.

RUBBISH (5)

Ne 4: 2 Will they revive the stones out of the heaps of r—
4:10 and there is too much r so that we are unable
La 3:45 You have made us filth and r among the peoples.
1Co 4:13 We have become like the r of the world,
Php 3: 8 and I regard them as r,

RUBBLE (1)

2Ki 23:12 and threw the r into the Wadi Kidron.

RUBIES (2) [RUBY]

Isa 54:12 I will make your pinnacles of r,
Eze 27:16 purple, embroidered work, fine linen, coral, and r.

RUBY (3) [RUBIES]

Tob 13:16 of Jerusalem will be paved with r and with stones
AdE 1: 7 and a miniature cup was displayed, made of r,
Sir 32: 5 A r seal in a setting of gold is a concert of music

RUDDER (2)

Jas 3: 4 yet they are guided by a very small r wherever
4Mc 7: 3 the r of religion until he sailed into the haven

RUDDY (4)

1Sa 16:12 Now he was r, and had beautiful eyes,
17:42 r and handsome in appearance.
SS 5:10 My beloved is all radiant and r,
La 4: 7 their bodies were more r than coral,

RUDE (2) [RUDELY]

1Co 13: 5 or r. It does not insist on its own way;
Sir 29:25 and besides this you will hear r words like these:

RUDELY (1) [RUDE]

2Mc 14:30 was meeting him more r than had been his custom,

RUDIMENTS (KJV) See ELEMENTAL SPIRITS; See also Index to Footnotes

RUE (1)
Lk 11:42 For you tithe the mint and **r** and herbs of all kinds,

RUFFIANS (3)
Ps 35:15 **r** whom I did not know tore at me without ceasing;
86:14 a band of **r** seeks my life,
Ac 17: 5 of some **r** in the marketplaces they formed a mob

RUFUS (2)
Mk 15:21 the father of Alexander and **R.**
Ro 16:13 Greet **R,** chosen in the Lord;

RUG (1) [RUGS]
Jdg 4:18 and she covered him with a **r.**

RUGS (1) [RUG]
Isa 21: 5 They prepare the table, they spread the **r,** they eat,

RUHAMAH (1) [LO-RUHAMAH]
Hos 2: 1 Say to your brother, Ammi, and to your sister, **R.**

RUIN‡ (72) [RUINED, RUINS]
Dt 13:16 It shall remain a perpetual **r,** never to be rebuilt.
28:63 the LORD will take delight in bringing you to **r**
2Sa 17:14 so that the LORD might bring **r** on Absalom.
2Ki 3:19 every good piece of land you shall **r** with stones."
2Ch 22: 4 of his father they were his counselors, to his **r.**
28:23 But they were the **r** of him, and of all Israel.
34:11 that the kings of Judah had let go to **r.**
Est 9: 2 to lay hands on those who had sought their **r;**
Job 30:12 they send me sprawling, and build roads for my **r.**
31:29 "If I have rejoiced at the **r** of those who hated me,
Ps 35: 8 Let **r** come on them unawares.
35: 8 let them fall in it—to their **r.**
38:12 those who seek to hurt me speak of **r,**
55:11 **r** is in its midst; oppression
64: 8 Because of their tongue he will bring them to **r;**
73:18 you make them fall to **r.**
146: 9 but the way of the wicked he brings to **r.**
Pr 5:14 I am at the point of utter **r** in the public assembly."
10: 8 but a babbling fool will come to **r.**
10:14 but the babbling of a fool brings **r** near.
10:15 the poverty of the poor is their **r.**
13: 3 those who open wide their lips come to **r.**
13:15 but the way of the faithless is their **r.**
18: 7 The mouths of fools are their **r,**
19: 3 One's own folly leads to **r,**
19:13 A stupid child is **r** to a father,
21:12 he casts the wicked down to **r.**
24:22 and who knows the **r** that both can bring?
26:28 and a flattering mouth works **r.**
SS 2:15 foxes, that **r** the vineyards—for our vineyards
Isa 23:13 they tore down her palaces, they made her a **r.**
25: 2 the city a heap, the fortified city a **r;**
32: 7 they devise wicked devices to **r** the poor
47:11 and **r** shall come on you suddenly,
Jer 13: 9 so I will **r** the pride of Judah and the great pride
25:11 This whole land shall become a **r** and a waste,
46:19 For Memphis shall become a waste, a **r,**
La 2:13 For vast as the sea is your **r;** who can heal you?
Eze 18:30 otherwise iniquity will be your **r.**
21:27 A **r,** a **r,** a **r**—I will make it!
27:27 sink into the heart of the seas on the day of your **r.**
32:12 They shall bring to **r** the pride of Egypt,
Da 11:44 with great fury to bring **r** and complete destruction
Hos 4:14 thus a people without understanding comes to **r.**
Am 6: 6 but are not grieved over the **r** of Joseph!
8: 4 and bring to **r** the poor of the land,
Ob 1:12 over the people of Judah on the day of their **r;**
Zep 1:15 a day of **r** and devastation,
Lk 6:49 and great was the **r** of that house."
Ro 3:16 **r** and misery are in their paths,
14:15 Do not let what you eat cause the **r** of one
1Ti 6: 9 and harmful desires that plunge people into **r**
Tob 4:13 For in pride there is **r** and great confusion.
Jdt 13:20 and you averted our **r,** walking in the straight path
AdE 8: 6 How can I look on the **r** of my people?
Sir 1:22 for anger tips the scale to one's **r.**
4:19 and hand them over to their **r.**
11:33 and they may **r** your reputation forever.
20:25 but the lot of both is **r.**
31: 6 Many have come to **r** because of gold,
40: 9 calamities and famine and **r** and plague.
49: 7 to pluck up and **r** and destroy,
50: 4 He considered how to save his people from **r,**
Bar 4:33 at your fall and was glad for your **r,**
1Mc 2: 7 see this, the **r** of my people, the **r** of the holy city,
2:49 it is a time of **r** and furious anger.
7: 7 the **r** that Judas has brought on us and on the land
2Es 2: 6 on them and bring their mother to **r,**
15:49 sword, and pestilence, bringing **r** to your houses,

RUINED (27) [RUIN]
Ex 8:24 in all of Egypt the land was **r** because of the flies.
9:31 (Now the flax and the barley were **r,**
9:32 But the wheat and the spelt were not **r,**
10: 7 do you not yet understand that Egypt is **r?"**
Pr 14:28 without people a prince is **r.**
Isa 61: 4 they shall repair the **r** cities,
Jer 4:13 woe to us, for we are **r!**
9:12 Why is the land **r** and laid waste like a wilderness,
9:19 from Zion: "How we are **r!**
13: 7 now the loincloth was **r;** it was good for nothing.
La 2: 9 he has **r** and broken her bars;
Eze 6: 6 your towns shall be waste and your high places **r,**
6: 6 so that your altars will be waste and **r,**
36:35 and **r** towns are now inhabited and fortified."
36:36 the LORD, have rebuilt the **r** places,
36:38 so shall the **r** towns be filled with flocks of people.
Joel 1:11 for the crops of the field are **r.**
1:17 the granaries are **r** because the grain has failed.
Am 9:14 they shall rebuild the **r** cities and inhabit them;
Mic 2: 4 and say, "We are utterly **r;**
Na 2: 2 ravagers have ravaged them and **r** their branches.)
Zec 11: 2 for the glorious trees are **r!**
Sir 8: 2 for gold has **r** many, and has perverted the minds
29:18 Being surety has **r** many who were prosperous,
49:13 and set up gates and bars, and rebuilt our **r** houses.
2Es 8:43 or if it has been **r** by too much rain, it perishes.
15:13 to grow and their trees shall be **r** by blight and hail

RUINS (50) [RUIN]
Jos 8:28 Joshua burned Ai, and made it forever a heap of **r,**
1Ki 9: 8 This house will become a heap of **r;**
2Ki 19:25 make fortified cities crash into heaps of **r,**
2Ch 34: 6 and as far as Naphtali, in their **r** all around,
Ezr 9: 9 to set up the house of our God, to repair its **r,**
Ne 2:17 how Jerusalem lies in **r** with its gates burned.
Job 3:14 of the earth who rebuild **r** for themselves,
15:28 houses destined to become heaps of **r;**
Ps 9: 6 The enemies have vanished in everlasting **r;**
74: 3 Direct your steps to the perpetual **r;**
79: 1 they have laid Jerusalem in **r.**
89:40 you have laid his strongholds in **r.**
109:10 may they be driven out of the **r** they inhabit.
Pr 29: 4 but one who makes heavy exactions **r** it.
Isa 3: 6 and this heap of **r** shall be under your rule."
5:17 fatlings and kids shall feed among the **r.**
17: 1 and will become a heap of **r.**
24:12 the gates are battered into **r.**
37:26 make fortified cities crash into heaps of **r,**
44:26 "They shall be rebuilt, and I will raise up their **r**";
52: 9 into singing, you **r** of Jerusalem;
58:12 Your ancient **r** shall be rebuilt;
61: 4 They shall build up the ancient **r,**
64:11 and all our pleasant places have become **r.**
Jer 2:15 his cities are in **r,** without inhabitant.
4: 7 your cities will be **r** without inhabitant.
4:26 and all its cities were laid in **r** before the LORD,
9:11 I will make Jerusalem a heap of **r,**
26:18 Jerusalem shall become a heap of **r,**
51:37 and Babylon shall become a heap of **r,**
La 2: 5 laid in **r** its strongholds, and multiplied
2: 8 The LORD determined to lay in **r** the wall
Eze 13: 4 Your prophets have been like jackals among **r,**
26:20 among primeval **r,** with those who go down to
35: 4 I lay your towns in **r;**
Da 2: 5 and your houses shall be laid in **r.**
3:29 and their houses laid in **r;**
Am 9:11 and repair its breaches, and raise up its **r,**
Mic 3:12 Jerusalem shall become a heap of **r,**
Zep 3: 6 I have cut off nations; their battlements are in **r;**
Hag 1: 4 while this house lies in **r?**
1: 9 Because my house lies in **r,**
Mal 1: 4 "We are shattered but we will rebuild the **r,**"
Ac 15:16 from its **r** I will rebuild it, and I will set it up,
1Co 15:33 "Bad company **r** good morals."
2Ti 2:14 but only **r** those who are listening.
Sir 10: 3 An undisciplined king **r** his people,
21:18 Like a house in **r** is wisdom to a fool,
1Mc 3:43 "Let us restore the **r** of our people,
4:38 They saw also the chambers of the priests in **r.**

RULE‡ (112) [RULED, RULER, RULER'S, RULERS, RULES, RULING]
Ge 1:16 to **r** the day and the lesser light to **r** the night—
1:18 to **r** over the day and over the night,
3:16 be for your husband, and he shall **r** over you."
Ex 21:31 owner shall be dealt with according to this same **r.**
Lev 25:43 You shall not **r** over them with harshness,
25:46 no one shall **r** over the other with harshness.
25:53 **r** with harshness over them in your sight.
26:17 your foes shall **r** over you,
Nu 24:19 One out of Jacob shall **r,**
Dt 15: 6 you will **r** over many nations,
15: 6 but they will not **r** over you.
Jdg 8:22 Then the Israelites said to Gideon, **"R** over us,
8:23 Gideon said to them, "I will not **r** over you, and
my son will not **r** over you; the LORD will **r** over
9: 2 all seventy of the sons of Jerubbaal **r** over you, or
that one **r** over you?'
13:12 what is to be the boy's **r** of life; what is he to do?"
1Sa 9:17 He it is who shall **r** over my people."
2Ki 8:20 In his days Edom revolted against the **r** of Judah,
8:22 So Edom has been in revolt against the **r** of Judah
1Ch 29:12 and honor come from you, and you **r** over all.
29:30 with accounts of all his **r** and his might and of
2Ch 1:10 for who can **r** this great people of yours?"
1:11 for yourself that you may **r** my people
7:18 'You shall never lack a successor to **r** over Israel.'
12: 1 When the **r** of Rehoboam was established
20: 6 Do you not **r** over all the kingdoms of the nations?
21: 8 In his days Edom revolted against the **r** of Judah
21:10 So Edom has been in revolt against the **r** of Judah
21:10 At that time Libnah also revolted against his **r,**
22: 9 And the house of Ahaziah had no one able to **r**
Job 38:33 Can you establish their **r** on the earth?
Ps 89: 9 You **r** the raging of the sea;
110: 2 **R** in the midst of your foes.
136: 8 the sun to **r** over the day,
136: 9 the moon and stars to **r** over the night,
Pr 8:16 by me rulers **r,** and nobles, all who govern rightly.
12:24 The hand of the diligent will **r,**
17: 2 A slave who deals wisely will **r** over
19:10 much less for a slave to **r** over princes.
29: 2 but when the wicked **r,** the people groan.
Isa 3: 4 and babes shall **r** over them.
3: 6 and this heap of ruins shall be under your **r."**
3:12 children are their oppressors, and women **r**
14: 2 and **r** over those who oppressed them.
19: 4 a fierce king will **r** over them, says the Sovereign,
28:14 you scoffers who **r** this people in Jerusalem.
32: 1 and princes will **r** with justice.
51: 5 my salvation has gone out and my arms will **r**
63:19 We have long been like those whom you do not **r,**
Jer 5:31 and the priests **r** as the prophets direct;
La 5: 8 Slaves **r** over us; there is no one to deliver
Eze 29:15 that they will never again **r** over the nations.
Da 2:39 which shall **r** over the whole earth.
8:23 At the end of their **r,**
11: 3 who shall **r** with great dominion and take action
11: 5 and shall **r** a realm greater than his own realm.
Ob 1:21 up to Mount Zion to **r** Mount Esau;
Mic 5: 2 from you shall come forth for me one who is to **r**
5: 6 They shall **r** the land of Assyria with the sword,
Zec 3: 7 then you shall **r** my house and have charge
6:13 and shall sit and **r** on his throne.
Lk 19:14 saying, 'We do not want this man to **r** over us.'
19:19 He said to him, 'And you, **r** over five cities.'
Ro 15:12 the one who rises to **r** the Gentiles;
1Co 7:17 This is my **r** in all the churches.
Gal 6:16 As for those who will follow this **r**—
Eph 1:21 above all **r** and authority and power and dominion,
Col 3:15 And let the peace of Christ **r** in your hearts,
1Ti 5:17 Let the elders who **r** well be considered worthy
Rev 2:27 to **r** them with an iron rod,
12: 5 who is to **r** all the nations with a rod of iron.
18: 7 Since in her heart she says, 'I **r** as a queen;
19:15 and he will **r** them with a rod of iron;
AdE 1: 8 The drinking was not according to a fixed **r;**
2:18 of taxes to those who were under his **r.**
3: 6 to destroy all the Jews under Artaxerxes' **r.**
13: 9 "O Lord, Lord, you **r** as King over all things,
Wis 3: 8 They will govern nations and **r** over peoples,
6: 2 Give ear, you that **r** over multitudes,
6: 4 as servants of his kingdom you did not **r** rightly,
9: 3 and **r** the world in holiness and righteousness,
10: 2 and gave him strength to **r** all things.
12:15 You are righteous and you **r** all things righteously,
13: 2 or the luminaries of heaven were the gods that **r**
Sir 10: 1 and the **r** of an intelligent person is well ordered.
Bar 2:34 Isaac, and Jacob, and they will **r** over it;
1Mc 1: 8 his officers began to **r,** each in his own place.
2:19 "Even if all the nations that live under the **r** of
8:16 They trust one man each year to **r** over them and
10:52 the throne of my ancestors, and established my **r**—
14: 4 his **r** was pleasing to them,
1Es 4: 2 who **r** over land and sea and all that is in them?
4:22 you must realize that women **r** over you!
3Mc 3:15 and we considered that we should not **r**
2Es 5:49 so I have made the same **r** for the world
9:34 Now this is the general **r** that,
11:17 After you no one shall **r** as long as you have ruled,
11:18 and held the **r** as the earlier ones had done,
11:20 also rose up on the right side, in order to **r.**
11:21 and others of them rose up, but did not hold the **r.**
11:25 to set themselves up and hold the **r.**
12:23 and they shall renew many things in it, and shall **r**
14:34 will **r** over your minds and discipline your hearts,
4Mc 1: 6 For reason does not **r** its own emotions,
1:33 Is it not because reason is able to **r** over appetites?
2: 4 to **r** over the frenzied urge of sexual desire,
2:23 and one who lives subject to this will **r** a kingdom
7:21 as a philosopher by the whole **r** of philosophy,
17:20 the fact that because of them our enemies did not **r**

RULED (20) [RULE]
Nu 21:34 as you did to King Sihon of the Amorites, who **r**
Jos 12: 2 of the Amorites who lived at Heshbon, and **r**
12: 5 and **r** over Mount Hermon and Salecah
Jdg 9:22 Abimelech **r** over Israel three years.
Ru 1: 1 In the days when the judges **r,**
2Ch 9:26 He **r** over all the kings from the Euphrates to
Ezr 4:20 Jerusalem has had mighty kings who **r** over
Est 1: 1 the same Ahasuerus who **r** over
Ps 106:41 so that those who hated them **r** over them.
Isa 14: 6 that **r** the nations in anger
26:13 other lords besides you have **r** over us,
Eze 34: 4 but with force and harshness you have **r** them.
Da 11: 4 nor according to the dominion with which he **r;**
Ac 7:18 until another king who had not known Joseph **r**
Jdt 1: 1 who **r** over the Assyrians in the great city
1: 1 In those days Arphaxad **r** over the Medes
AdE 1: 1 the same Artaxerxes who **r** over
Sir 44: 3 There were those who **r** in their kingdoms,
Bar 2: 1 against our judges who **r** Israel,
1Mc 1: 4 a very strong army and **r** over countries,
14: 7 he **r** over Gazara and Beth-zur and the citadel,
1Es 2:27 and cruel kings **r** in Jerusalem and exacted tribute
2Es 11:16 you who have **r** the earth all this time;
11:17 After you no one shall rule as long as you have **r,**
11:20 There were some of them that **r,**
11:34 in like manner **r** over the earth and its inhabitants.
4Mc 2: 9 one is **r** by the law through reason so

4Mc 16: 2 not only that men have r over the emotions,

RULER‡ (99) [RULE]

Ge 45: 8 to Pharaoh, and lord of all his house and r over all
45:26 He is even r over all the land of Egypt."
Ex 2:14 "Who made you a r and judge over us?
Lev 4:22 When a r sins, doing unintentionally any one
Jdg 9:30 When Zebul the r of the city heard the words
1Sa 9:16 you shall anoint him to be r over my people Israel.
10: 1 LORD has anointed you r over his people Israel.
10: 1 the sign to you that the LORD has anointed you r
13:14 LORD has appointed him to be r over his people,
2Sa 5: 2 you who shall be r over Israel."
1Ki 1:35 for I have appointed him to be r over Israel and
11:34 but will make him r all the days of his life,
1Ch 5: 2 among his brothers and a r came from him,
11: 2 you who shall be r over my people Israel."
17: 7 to be r over my people Israel;
2Ch 6: 5 and I chose no one as r over my people Israel;
Ne 3: 9 r of half the district of Jerusalem, made repairs.
3:12 r of half the district of Jerusalem, made repairs,
3:14 r of the district of Beth-haccherem,
3:15 r of the district of Mizpah,
3:16 r of half the district of Beth-zur,
3:17 r of half the district of Keilah,
3:18 son of Henadad, r of half the district of Keilah;
3:19 r of Mizpah, repaired another section opposite
Ps 105:20 the r of the peoples set him free.
105:21 and r of all his possessions,
Pr 6: 7 Without having any chief or officer or r,
17: 7 still less is false speech to a r.
23: 1 When you sit down to eat with a r,
25:15 With patience a r may be persuaded,
28: 2 but with an intelligent r there is lasting order.
28: 3 A r who oppresses the poor is a beating rain
28:15 a roaring lion or a charging bear is a wicked r over
28:16 A r who lacks understanding is a cruel oppressor;
29:12 If a r listens to falsehood,
29:26 Many seek the favor of a r,
Ecc 9:17 to be heeded than the shouting of a r among fools.
10: 4 If the anger of the r rises against you,
10: 5 as great an error as if it proceeded from the r:
Isa 16: 1 Send lambs to the r of the land, from Sela,
16: 5 r who seeks justice and is swift to do what is right.
33:22 For the LORD is our judge, the LORD is our r,
Jer 30:21 their r shall come from their midst;
51:46 of violence in the land and of r against r.
Da 2:38 and whom he has established as r over them all—
2:48 and made him r over the whole province
11:43 He shall become r of the treasures of gold and
Am 2: 3 I will cut off the r from its midst,
Mic 5: 1 a rod they strike the r of Israel upon the cheek.
Hab 1:14 like crawling things that have no r.
Mt 2: 6 a r who is to shepherd my people Israel.' "
9:34 "By the r of the demons he casts out the demons."
12:24 "It is only by Beelzebul, the r of the demons,
14: 1 At that time Herod the r heard reports about Jesus;
Mk 3:22 and by the r of the demons he casts out demons."
Lk 3: 1 and Herod was r of Galilee, and his brother Philip
r of the region of Ituraea and Trachonitis, and
Lysanias r of Abilene,
3:19 But Herod the r, who had been rebuked by him
9: 7 Herod the r heard about all that had taken place,
11:15 by Beelzebul, the r of the demons."
18:18 A certain r asked him, "Good Teacher,
Jn 12:31 now the r of this world will be driven out.
14:30 for the r of this world is coming.
16:11 because the r of this world has been condemned.
Ac 7:10 who appointed him r over Egypt and
7:27 saying, 'Who made you a r and a judge over us?
7:35 'Who made you a r and a judge?'
7:35 and whom God now sent as both r and liberator
13: 1 Manaen a member of the court of Herod the r,
1Co 15:24 after he has destroyed every r and every authority
Eph 2: 2 following the r of the power of the air,
Col 2:10 who is the head of every r and authority.
Rev 1: 5 and the r of the kings of the earth.
Jdt 8: 9 by the people against the r,
AdE 13: 2 "Having become r of many nations and master of
Wis 14:19 For he, perhaps wishing to please his r,
Sir 4:27 or show partiality to a r.
10: 2 as the r of the city is, so are all its inhabitants.
10:24 The prince and the judge and the r are honored,
17:17 He appointed a r for every nation,
41:17 and of a lie, before a prince or a r;
48:12 Never in his lifetime did he tremble before any r,
48:15 but with a r from the house of David.
Aza 1:15 In our day we have no r, or prophet, or leader,
1Mc 6:14 and made him r over all his kingdom.
9:30 to take his place as our r and leader,
10:38 to be under one r and obey no other authority than
2Mc 5: 8 Accused before Aretas the r of the Arabs,
3Mc 2: 2 holy among the holy ones, the only r, almighty,
2: 3 of all things and the governor of all, are a just R,
2: 7 the R over the whole creation.
5: 7 upon the Almighty Lord and R of all power,
5:51 the R over every power to manifest himself and
6: 4 the former r of this Egypt,
7: 9 we always shall have not a mortal but the R
2Es 6:54 as r over all the works that you had made;
4Mc 4:18 king appointed him high priest and r of the nation.

RULER'S (3) [RULE]

Ge 49:10 nor the r staff from between his feet,
Pr 23: 3 Do not desire the r delicacies,
Eze 19:11 Its strongest stem became a r scepter;

RULERS (76) [RULE]

Jos 13: 3 there are five r of the Philistines, those of Gaza,
Jdg 15:11 "Do you not know that the Philistines are r
2Ki 10: 1 to the r of Jezreel, to the elders,
1Ch 12:19 for the r of the Philistines took counsel
Ps 2: 2 and the r take counsel together,
2:10 O kings, be wise; be warned, O r of the earth.
94:20 Can wicked r be allied with you,
148:11 princes and all r of the earth!
Pr 8:15 By me kings reign, and r decree what is just;
8:16 by me r rule, and nobles, all who govern rightly.
28: 2 When a land rebels it has many r;
31: 4 or for r to desire strong drink;
Ecc 7:19 Wisdom gives strength to the wise more than ten r
Isa 1:10 Hear the word of the LORD, you r of Sodom!
14: 5 the staff of the wicked, the scepter of r,
22: 3 Your r have all fled together;
40:23 and makes the r of the earth as nothing.
41:25 He shall trample on r as on mortar,
49: 7 the slave of r, "Kings shall see and stand up,
52: 5 Their r howl, says the LORD, and continually,
Jer 2: 8 the r transgressed against me;
33:26 and not choose any of his descendants as r over
La 2: 2 to the ground in dishonor the kingdom and its r.
Da 9:12 which he spoke against us and against our r,
11:39 and shall appoint them as r over many,
Hos 7: 7 as an oven, and they devour their r.
13:10 Where in all your cities are your r,
13:10 of whom you said, "Give me a king and r"?
Mic 3: 1 you heads of Jacob and r of the house of Israel!
3: 9 you r of the house of Jacob and chiefs of
3:11 Its r give judgment for a bribe,
5: 5 them seven shepherds and eight installed as r.
Hab 1:10 At kings they scoff, and of r they make sport.
Mt 2: 6 are by no means least among the r of Judah;
20:25 "You know that the r of the Gentiles lord it
Mk 10:42 as their r lord it over them,
Lk 12:11 they bring you before the synagogues, the r,
Ac 3:17 that you acted in ignorance, as did also your r.
4: 5 The next day their r, elders,
4: 8 said to them, "R of the people and elders,
4:26 and the r have gathered together against the Lord
14: 5 with their r, to mistreat them and to stone them,
Ro 8:38 nor life, nor angels, nor r, nor things present,
13: 3 For r are not a terror to good conduct, but to bad.
1Co 2: 6 though it is not a wisdom of this age or of the r
2: 8 None of the r of this age understood this;
Eph 3:10 now be made known to the r and authorities in
6:12 but against the r, against the authorities,
Col 1:16 whether thrones or dominions or r or powers—
2:15 the r and authorities and made a public example
Tit 3: 1 Remind them to be subject to r and authorities,
Jdt 7:23 around Uzziah and the r of the town and cried out
8:11 "Listen to me, r of the people of Bethulia!
8:35 Uzziah and the r said to her, "Go in peace,
9: 3 So you gave up their r to be killed, and their bed,
Wis 1: 1 Love righteousness, you r of the earth,
5:23 and evildoing will overturn the thrones of r.
8:11 and in the sight of r I shall be admired.
Sir 10: 3 to live in through the understanding of its r.
10:14 The Lord overthrows the thrones of r,
11: 6 Many r have been utterly disgraced,
36:12 Crush the heads of hostile r who say,
38:33 and they are not found among the r.
39: 4 He serves among the great and appears before r;
46:13 the kingdom and anointed r over his people.
46:18 he subdued the leaders of the enemy and all the r
Bar 1:16 our r, our priests, our prophets, and our ancestors,
2: 1 and against our kings and our r and the people
3:16 Where are the r of the nations,
1Mc 1:26 r and elders groaned, young women
11:62 of their r as hostages and sent them to Jerusalem.
14:20 "The r and the city of the Spartans to
14:28 the people and the r of the nation and the elders of
1Es 6: 7 their associates the local r in Syria and Phoenicia,
6:27 and those who were appointed as local r in Syria
8:69 "The people of Israel and the r and the priests and

RULES‡ (26) [RULE]

2Sa 23: 3 One who r over people justly,
1Ki 21:18 to meet King Ahab of Israel, who r in Samaria;
2Ch 30:19 though not in accordance with the sanctuary's r
Ps 22:28 and he r over the nations.
59:13 to the ends of the earth that God r over Jacob.
66: 7 who r by his might forever,
103:19 and his kingdom r over all.
Pr 22: 7 The rich r over the poor,
Isa 40:10 and his arm r for him;
2Ti 2: 5 without competing according to the r.
Rev 17:18 The woman you saw is the great city that r over
Jdt 5: 3 Who r over them as king and leads their army?
AdE 16:18 for God, who r over all things,
16:21 For God, who r over all things,
Sir 37:18 and it is the tongue that continually r them.
1Es 4:14 Who is it, then, that r them,
4:15 to the king and to every people that r over sea
3Mc 5:28 This was the act of God who r over all things,
4Mc 1: 3 it is evident that reason r over those emotions
1: 5 "If reason r the emotions,
1:14 and whether reason r over all these.
1:19 since by means of it reason r over the emotions.
1:32 and reason obviously r over both.
2: 9 In all other matters we can recognize that reason r
2:15 that reason r even the more violent emotions:
3: 1 that reason r not over its own emotions,

RULING (11) [RULE]

Dt 17:11 for you or the r that they announce to you;
2Sa 23: 3 One who rules over people justly, r in the fear
Jer 22:30 on the throne of David, and r again in Judah.
Eze 19:14 in it no strong stem, no scepter for r.
Hag 2:11 Ask the priests for a r:
Mt 2:22 when he heard that Archelaus was r over Judea
AdE 1:13 therefore your r and judgment on this matter."
Wis 15: 1 patient, and r all things in mercy.
1Mc 14:17 that he was r over the country and the towns in it,
1Es 9: 4 in accordance with the decision of the r elders,
2Es 5: 3 land that you now see r shall be a trackless waste,

RUMAH (1)

2Ki 23:36 name was Zebidah daughter of Pedaiah of R.

RUMBLE (1) [RUMBLING, RUMBLINGS]

Na 3: 2 The crack of whip and r of wheel,

RUMBLING (5) [RUMBLE]

Job 37: 2 of his voice and the r that comes from his mouth.
Jer 47: 3 at the r of their wheels,
Eze 3:12 I heard behind me the sound of loud r;
3:13 that sounded like a loud r.
Joel 2: 5 As with the r of chariots,

RUMBLINGS (5) [RUMBLE]

Rev 4: 5 and r and peals of thunder,
8: 5 and there were peals of thunder, r,
11:19 and there were flashes of lightning, r,
16:18 And there came flashes of lightning, r,
2Es 6: 2 and before the r of thunder sounded,

RUMOR (11) [RUMORS]

2Ki 19: 7 so that he shall hear a r and return to his own land;
Job 28:22 'We have heard a r of it with our ears.'
Isa 37: 7 so that he shall hear a r,
Jer 51:46 one year one r comes, the next year another,
Eze 7:26 Disaster comes upon disaster, r follows r;
Jn 21:23 So the r spread in the community
Wis 5: 9 and like a r that passes by;
2Mc 5: 5 When a false r arose that Antiochus was dead,
3Mc 3: 2 a hostile r was circulated against the Jewish nation
4Mc 4:22 that a r of his death had spread and that the people

RUMORS (4) [RUMOR]

Jer 51:46 Do not be fainthearted or fearful at the r heard in
51:46 r of violence in the land and of ruler against ruler.
Mt 24: 6 And you will hear of wars and r of wars;
Mk 13: 7 you hear of wars and r of wars, do not be alarmed;

RUMP (KJV) See BROAD TAIL, FAT TAIL

RUN (61) [FOOT-RUNNERS, FORERUNNER, FORERUNNERS, OUTRAN, RAN, RUNAWAY, RUNNER, RUNNERS, RUNNING, RUNS]

Ge 49:22 his branches r over the wall.
Ex 32:25 (for Aaron had let them r wild,
1Sa 8:11 and to r before his chariots;
20: 6 'David earnestly asked leave of me to r
20:36 "R and find the arrows that I shoot."
21:13 and let his spittle r down his beard.
2Sa 15: 1 and fifty men to r ahead of him.
18:19 Then Ahimaaz son of Zadok said, "Let me r,
18:22 "Come what may, let me also r after the Cushite."
18:22 And Joab said, "Why will you r, my son,
18:23 "Come what may," he said, "I will r."
18:23 So he said to him, "R."
1Ki 1: 5 and fifty men to r before him.
2Ki 4:26 r at once to meet her, and say to her,
5:20 I will r after him and get something out of him."
Ne 6:11 But I said, "Should a man like me r away?
Job 1: 5 And when the feast days had r their course,
6:16 that r dark with ice, turbid with melting snow.
Ps 59: 4 for no fault of mine, they r and make ready.
119:32 I r the way of your commandments,
Pr 1:16 for their feet r to evil,
4:12 and if you r, you will not stumble.
6:18 feet that hurry to r to evil,
18:10 the righteous r into it and are safe.
Ecc 1: 7 All streams r to the sea, but the sea is not full;
Isa 29: 1 Add year to year; let the festivals r their round.
40:31 they shall r and not be weary,
55: 5 and nations that do not know you shall r to you,
59: 7 Their feet r to evil, and they rush
Jer 5: 1 R to and fro through the streets of Jerusalem,
9:18 so that our eyes may r down with tears,
13:17 my eyes will weep bitterly and r down with tears,
14:17 Let my eyes r down with tears night and day,
17:16 not r away from being a shepherd in your service,
18:14 Do the mountain waters r dry,
Eze 5: 1 use it as a barber's razor and r it over your head
24:16 nor shall your tears r down.
32:14 and cause their streams to r like oil,
47:17 the boundary shall r from the sea to Hazar-enon,
47:19 it shall r from Tamar as far as the waters
48:28 the boundary shall r from Tamar to the waters
Joel 2: 9 They leap upon the city, they r upon the walls;
Am 6:12 Do horses r on rocks?
8:12 they shall r to and fro,

Na 2: 8 Nineveh is like a pool whose waters **r** away.
Zec 2: 4 "**R,** say to that young man:
Jn 10: 5 but they will **r** from him because they do
Ac 27:17 then, fearing that they would **r** on the Syrtis,
27:26 But we will have to **r** aground on some island."
27:29 Fearing that we might **r** on the rocks,
27:39 on which they planned to **r** the ship ashore,
1Co 9:24 **R** in such a way that you may win it.
9:26 not **r** aimlessly, nor do I box as though beating
Gal 2: 2 to make sure that I was not running, or had not **r,**
Php 2:16 that I can boast on the day of Christ that I did not **r**
Heb 12: 1 and let us **r** with perseverance the race that is set
Tob 11: 3 Let us **r** ahead of your wife and prepare the house
Wis 3: 7 and will **r** like sparks through the stubble.
Sir 35:18 Do not the tears of the widow **r** down her cheek
3Mc 5:25 at their last gasp—since the time had **r** out—
2Es 2:32 my springs **r** over, and my grace will not fail."

RUNAWAY (1) [RUN]
2Mc 8:35 and made his way alone like a **r** slave across

RUNNER (4) [RUN]
Job 9:25 "My days are swifter than a **r;**
Ps 147:10 nor his pleasure in the speed of a **r;**
Jer 51:31 One **r** runs to meet another,
Hab 2: 2 make it plain on tablets, so that a **r** may read it.

RUNNERS (1) [RUN]
1Co 9:24 Do you not know that in a race the **r** all compete,

RUNNING (29) [RUN]
Ge 16: 8 She said, "I am **r** away from my mistress Sarai."
Ex 32:25 When Moses saw that the people were **r** wild
Nu 19:17 and **r** water shall be added in a vessel;
Dt 21: 4 the heifer down to a wadi with **r** water,
2Sa 18:24 and when he looked up, he saw a man **r** alone.
18:26 Then the sentinel saw another man **r;**
18:26 "See, another man **r** alone!"
18:27 the **r** of the first one is like the **r** of Ahimaaz
1Ki 6: 5 **r** around the walls of the house,
2Ki 5:21 When Naaman saw someone **r** after him,
2Ch 23:12 the people **r** and praising the king, she went into
Job 15:26 **r** stubbornly against him with a thick-bossed shield
Ps 133: 2 **r** down upon the beard, on the beard of Aaron,
133: 2 **r** down over the collar of his robes.
Isa 30:25 and every high hill there will be brooks **r**
Da 12: 4 Many shall be **r** back and forth,
Mk 9:25 When Jesus saw that a crowd came **r** together,
Lk 6:38 shaken together, **r** over, will be put into your lap;
Jn 20: 4 The two were **r** together,
Ac 27:16 By **r** under the lee of a small island called Cauda
Gal 2: 2 in order to make sure that I was not **r,**
5: 7 You were **r** well; who prevented you from obeying
Wis 17:19 or the unseen **r** of leaping animals,
1Mc 4: 5 because he said, "These men are **r** away from us."
2Mc 12:16 appeared to be **r** over with blood.
13: 5 and it has a rim **r** around it that
4Mc 12:10 **R** to the nearest of the braziers,
14: 5 as though **r** the course toward immortality,

RUNS‡ (14) [RUN]
Dt 9:21 of it into the stream that **r** down the mountain.
Jos 15: 5 And the boundary on the north side **r** from the bay
Ezr 8:15 I gathered them by the river that **r** to Ahava,
Job 38:38 the dust **r** into a mass and the clods cling together?
Ps 19: 5 and like a strong man **r** its course with joy.
58: 7 Let them vanish like water that **r** away;
147:15 to the earth; his word **r** swiftly.
Isa 1:23 Everyone loves a bribe and **r** after gifts.
Jer 51:31 One runner **r** to meet another,
Jn 10:12 and leaves the sheep and **r** away—
10:13 The hired hand **r** away because a hired hand does
Jdt 12: 3 Holofernes said to her, "If your supply **r** out,
Sir 24:26 It **r** over, like the Euphrates, with understanding,
33:32 If you ill-treat him, and he leaves you and **r** away,

RURAL (1)
Ne 10:37 Levites who collect the tithes in all our **r** towns.

RUSH (10) [ONRUSH, ONRUSHING, RUSHED, RUSHES, RUSHING]
Jdg 9:33 as soon as the sun rises, get up and **r** on the city;
Ps 32: 6 the **r** of mighty waters shall not reach them.
Isa 59: 7 and they **r** to shed innocent blood;
Da 11:40 of the north shall **r** upon him like a whirlwind,
Na 2: 4 they **r** to and fro through the squares;
Ac 2: 2 from heaven there came a sound like the **r** of
Tob 10: 7 She would **r** out every day and watch
Jdt 14: 3 They will **r** into the tent of Holofernes and will
15: 4 to tell what had taken place and to urge all to **r** out
3Mc 1:19 in a disorderly **r** flocked together in the city.

RUSHED (39) [RUSH]
Jos 8:19 of their place and **r** forward.
Jdg 5:15 into the valley they **r** out at his heels.
9:44 with him **r** forward and stood at the entrance of
9:44 the two companies **r** on all who were in the fields
14: 6 The spirit of the LORD **r** on him,
14:19 Then the spirit of the LORD **r** on him,
15:14 and the spirit of the LORD **r** on him,
20:33 while those Israelites who were in ambush **r** out
20:37 The troops in ambush **r** quickly upon Gibeah.
1Sa 18:10 The next day an evil spirit from God **r** upon Saul,
2Sa 19:17 **r** down to the Jordan ahead of the king,
Mt 8:32 the whole herd **r** down the steep bank into the sea
Mk 5:13 **r** down the steep bank into the sea,
6:25 Immediately she **r** back to the king and requested,
6:55 and **r** about that whole region and began to bring
Lk 8:33 and the herd **r** down the steep bank into the lake
Ac 7:57 and with a loud shout all **r** together against him.
14:14 they tore their clothes and **r** out into the crowd,
19:29 and people **r** together to the theater,
21:30 all the city was aroused, and the people **r** together.
27:14 called the northeaster, **r** down from Crete.
Jdt 14:17 he **r** out to the people and shouted,
15: 2 with one impulse all **r** out and fled by every path
15: 3 everyone that was a soldier, **r** out upon them.
AdE 4: 1 he **r** through the street of the city, shouting loudly:
Sus 1:26 they **r** in at the side door to see what had happened
1Mc 3:23 he **r** suddenly against Seron and his army,
9:40 Then they **r** on them from the ambush
16:16 **r** in against Simon in the banquet hall
2Mc 3:25 it **r** furiously at Heliodorus and struck at him
5:26 then **r** into the city with his armed warriors
9: 2 Therefore the people **r** to the rescue with arms,
10:16 **r** to the strongholds of the Idumeans.
11: 7 Then they eagerly **r** off together.
12:15 **r** furiously upon the walls.
12:22 In their flight they **r** headlong in every direction,
3Mc 1:18 in their chambers **r** out with their mothers,
5:47 **r** out in full force along with the animals,
4Mc 6: 8 of the cruel guards **r** at him and began to kick him

RUSHES (7) [BULRUSH, RUSH]
Job 16:14 he **r** at me like a warrior.
40:23 it is confident though Jordan **r** against its mouth.
41:20 as from a boiling pot and burning **r.**
Isa 19: 6 reeds and **r** will rot away.
35: 7 the grass shall become reeds and **r.**
Hos 13:15 Although he may flourish among **r,**
Sir 21:22 The foot of a fool **r** into a house,

RUSHING (9) [RUSH]
1Ki 18:41 for there is a sound of **r** rain."
Pr 7:23 He is like a bird **r** into a snare,
Na 1: 8 even in a **r** flood. He will make a full end of his
Ac 16:29 The jailer called for lights, and **r** in,
Rev 9: 9 like the noise of many chariots with horses **r**
Wis 5:11 and pierced by the force of its **r** flight, is traversed
17:18 or the rhythm of violently **r** water,
2Mc 9: 7 that he fell out of his chariot as it was **r** along,
14:43 and the crowd was now **r** in through the doors.

RUST (10) [RUSTED]
Eze 24: 6 Woe to the bloody city, the pot whose **r** is in it,
24: 6 whose **r** has not gone out of it!
24:11 its filth melt in it, its **r** be consumed.
24:12 its thick **r** does not depart.
24:12 To the fire with its **r!**
Mt 6:19 and **r** consume and where thieves break in
6:20 nor **r** consumes and where thieves do not break in
Jas 5: 3 and their **r** will be evidence against you,
Sir 29:10 and do not let it **r** under a stone and be lost.
LtJ 6:12 that cannot save themselves from **r** and corrosion.

RUSTED (1) [RUST]
Jas 5: 3 Your gold and silver have **r,**

RUTH (13)
Ru 1: 4 of the one was Orpah and the name of the other **R.**
1:14 Orpah kissed her mother-in-law, but **R** clung to her
1:16 But **R** said, "Do not press me to leave you or
1:22 So Naomi returned together with **R** the Moabite,
2: 2 And **R** the Moabite said to Naomi,
2: 8 Then Boaz said to **R,** "Now listen, my daughter,
2:21 Then **R** the Moabite said, "He even said to me,
2:22 Naomi said to **R,** her daughter-in-law, "It is better,
3: 9 And she answered, "I am **R,** your servant;
4: 5 you are also acquiring **R** the Moabite,
4:10 I have also acquired **R** the Moabite,
4:13 So Boaz took **R** and she became his wife.
Mt 1: 5 and Boaz the father of Obed by **R,**

RUTHLESS (11) [RUTHLESSLY]
Ex 1:13 The Egyptians became **r** in imposing tasks on
1:14 They were **r** in all the tasks that they imposed
Job 15:20 through all the years that are laid up for the **r.**
Ps 54: 3 insolent have risen against me, the **r** seek my life;
Isa 25: 3 cities of **r** nations will fear you.
25: 4 the blast of the **r** was like a winter rainstorm,
25: 5 the song of the **r** was stilled.
Jer 15:21 and redeem you from the grasp of the **r.**
Ro 1:31 foolish, faithless, heartless, **r.**
Bar 4:15 a nation **r** and of a strange language,
3Mc 4: 4 a harsh and **r** spirit were they being sent off,

RUTHLESSLY (1) [RUTHLESS]
Isa 30:14 so **r** that among its fragments not a sherd is found

S

SABACHTHANI (2)
Mt 27:46 with a loud voice, "Eli, Eli, lema **s?**"
Mk 15:34 with a loud voice, "Eloi, Eloi, lema **s?**"

SABANNUS See Index to Footnotes

SABAOTH (KJV) See OF HOSTS

SABBAIAS (1)
1Es 9:32 and Melchias and **S** and Simon Chosamaeus.

SABBATH (157) [SABBATHS, SABBATICAL]
Ex 16:23 'Tomorrow is a day of solemn rest, a holy **s** to
16:25 "Eat it today, for today is a **s** to the LORD;
16:26 but on the seventh day, which is a **s,**
16:29 The LORD has given you the **s,**
20: 8 Remember the **s** day, and keep it holy.
20:10 But the seventh day is a **s** to the LORD your God;
20:11 the LORD blessed the **s** day and consecrated it.
31:14 You shall keep the **s,** because it is holy for you;
31:15 but the seventh day is a **s** of solemn rest,
31:15 whoever does any work on the **s** day shall be put
31:16 Therefore the Israelites shall keep the **s,**
31:16 observing the **s** throughout their generations,
35: 2 but on the seventh day you shall have a holy **s**
35: 3 in all your dwellings on the **s** day.
Lev 16:31 It is a **s** of complete rest to you,
23: 3 but the seventh day is a **s** of complete rest,
23: 3 it is a **s** to the LORD throughout your settlements.
23:11 on the day after the **s** the priest shall raise it.
23:15 And from the day after the **s,**
23:16 You shall count until the day after the seventh **s,**
23:32 It shall be to you a **s** of complete rest,
23:32 from evening to evening you shall keep your **s.**
24: 8 Every **s** day Aaron shall set them in order before
25: 2 the land shall observe a **s** for the LORD.
25: 4 a **s** of complete rest for the land, a **s** for the LORD:
25: 6 You may eat what the land yields during its **s**—
26:34 Then the land shall enjoy its **s** years as long
26:34 then the land shall rest, and enjoy its **s** years.
26:43 enjoy its **s** years by lying desolate without them,
Nu 15:32 they found a man gathering sticks on the **s** day.
28: 9 On the **s** day: two male lambs a year old without
28:10 this is the burnt offering for every **s,**
Dt 5:12 Observe the **s** day and keep it holy,
5:14 But the seventh day is a **s** to the LORD your God;
5:15 LORD your God commanded you to keep the **s** day.
2Ki 4:23 It is neither new moon nor **s.**"
11: 5 of you, those who go off duty on the **s** and guard
11: 7 on duty in force on the **s** and guard the house of
11: 9 to go off duty on the **s,**
11: 9 with those who were to come on duty on the **s,**
16:18 on the **s** that had been built inside the palace,
1Ch 9:32 to prepare them for each **s.**
2Ch 23: 4 who come on duty on the **s,** shall be gatekeepers,
23: 8 who were to come on duty on the **s,**
23: 8 with those who were to go off duty on the **s;**
36:21 All the days that it lay desolate it kept **s,**
Ne 9:14 and you made known your holy **s** to them
10:31 or any grain on the **s** day to sell, we will not buy it
from them on the **s** or on a holy day;
13:15 in Judah people treading wine presses on the **s,**
13:15 which they brought into Jerusalem on the **s** day;
13:16 and sold them on the **s** to the people of Judah,
13:17 that you are doing, profaning the **s** day?
13:18 bring more wrath on Israel by profaning the **s.**"
13:19 to be dark at the gates of Jerusalem before the **s,**
13:19 that they should not be opened until after the **s.**
13:19 from being brought in on the **s** day.
13:21 From that time on they did not come on the **s.**
13:22 to keep the **s** day holy.
Ps 92: T *A Psalm. A Song for the **S** Day.*
Isa 1:13 New moon and **s** and calling of convocation—
56: 2 the one who holds it fast, who keeps the **s,**
56: 6 and to be his servants, all who keep the **s,**
58:13 If you refrain from trampling the **s,**
58:13 if you call the **s** a delight and the holy day of the
66:23 from **s** to **s,** all flesh shall come to worship
Jer 17:21 the **s** day or bring it in by the gates of Jerusalem.
17:22 not carry a burden out of your houses on the **s** day,
but keep the **s** day holy,
17:24 in no burden by the gates of this city on the **s** day,
17:24 but keep the **s** day holy and do no work on it,
17:27 if you do not listen to me, to keep the **s** day holy,
17:27 of Jerusalem on the **s** day, then I will kindle a fire
La 2: 6 the LORD has abolished in Zion festival and **s,**
Eze 46: 1 but on the **s** day it shall be opened and on the day
46: 4 the prince offers to the LORD on the **s** day shall
46:12 of well-being as he does on the **s** day.
Am 8: 5 and the **s,** so that we may offer wheat for sale?
Mt 12: 1 through the grainfields on the **s;**
12: 2 not lawful to do on the **s.**"
12: 5 that on the **s** the priests in the temple break the **s**

Mt 12: 8 For the Son of Man is lord of the s."
12:10 and they asked him, "Is it lawful to cure on the s?"
12:11 and it falls into a pit on the s;
12:12 So it is lawful to do good on the s."
24:20 that your flight may not be in winter or on a s.
28: 1 After the s, as the first day of
Mk 1:21 the s came, he entered the synagogue and taught.
2:23 One s he was going through the grainfields;
2:24 why are they doing what is not lawful on the s?"
2:27 he said to them, "The s was made for humankind, and not humankind for the s;
2:28 so the Son of Man is lord even of the s."
3: 2 to see whether he would cure him on the s,
3: 4 "Is it lawful to do good or to do harm on the s,
6: 2 On the s he began to teach in the synagogue,
15:42 that is, the day before the s,
16: 1 When the s was over, Mary Magdalene,
Lk 4:16 he went to the synagogue on the s day,
4:31 a city in Galilee, and was teaching them on the s.
6: 1 One s while Jesus was going through
6: 2 "Why are you doing what is not lawful on the s?"
6: 5 he said to them, "The Son of Man is lord of the s."
6: 6 On another s he entered the synagogue and taught,
6: 7 to see whether he would cure on the s,
6: 9 is it lawful to do good or to do harm on the s,
13:10 he was teaching in one of the synagogues on the s.
13:14 indignant because Jesus had cured on the s,
13:14 on those days and be cured, and not on the s day."
13:15 not each of you on the s untie his ox or his donkey
13:16 be set free from this bondage on the s day?"
14: 1 of a leader of the Pharisees to eat a meal on the s,
14: 3 "Is it lawful to cure people on the s, or not?"
14: 5 will you not immediately pull it out on a s day?"
23:54 the day of Preparation, and the s was beginning.
23:56 the s they rested according to the commandment.
Jn 5: 9 Now that day was a s.
5:10 to the man who had been cured, "It is the s;
5:16 because he was doing such things on the s.
5:18 because he was not only breaking the s,
7:22 and you circumcise a man on the s.
7:23 a man receives circumcision on the s in order that
7:23 because I healed a man's whole body on the s?
9:14 Now it was a s day when Jesus made the mud
9:16 for he does not observe the s."
19:31 not want the bodies left on the cross during the s,
19:31 because that s was a day of great solemnity.
Ac 1:12 which is near Jerusalem, a s day's journey away.
13:14 And on the s day they went into the synagogue
13:27 the words of the prophets that are read every s,
13:42 to speak about these things again the next s.
13:44 The next s almost the whole city gathered to hear
15:21 he has been read aloud every s in the synagogues."
16:13 On the s day we went outside the gate by the river,
17: 2 and on three s days argued with them from
18: 4 Every s he would argue in the synagogue
Heb 4: 9 then, a s rest still remains for the people of God;
Jdt 8: 6 except the day before the s and the s itself,
1Mc 1:43 they sacrificed to idols and profaned the s.
2:32 and prepared for battle against them on the s day.
2:34 the king commands and so profane the s day."
2:38 So they attacked them on the s, and they died,
2:41 to attack us on the s day;
9:34 Bacchides found this out on the s day,
9:43 with a large force on the s day to the banks of
2Mc 5:25 and waited until the holy s day;
6: 6 People could neither keep the s,
8:26 It was the day before the s,
8:27 of their spoils, they kept the s, giving great praise
8:28 After the s they gave some of the spoils
12:38 according to the custom, and kept the s there.
15: 3 had commanded the keeping of the s day.
1Es 1:58 it shall keep s all the time of its desolation until

SABBATHS‡ (33) [SABBATH]

Ex 31:13 "You shall keep my s, for this is a sign
Lev 19: 3 and you shall keep my s:
19:30 You shall keep my s and reverence my sanctuary:
23:38 apart from the s of the LORD,
26: 2 You shall keep my s and reverence my sanctuary:
26:35 not have on your s when you were living on it.
1Ch 23:31 on s, new moons, and appointed festivals,
2Ch 2: 4 on the s and the new moons and
8:13 to the commandment of Moses for the s,
31: 3 and the burnt offerings for the s, the new moons,
36:21 until the land had made up for its s.
Ne 10:33 the regular burnt offering, the s, the new moons,
Isa 56: 4 To the eunuchs who keep my s,
Eze 20:12 Moreover I gave them my s,
20:13 and my s they greatly profaned.
20:16 not observe my statutes, and profaned my s;
20:20 and hallow my s that they may be a sign
20:21 they profaned my s.
20:24 but had rejected my statutes and profaned my s,
22: 8 have despised my holy things, and profaned my s.
22:26 and they have disregarded my s,
23:38 on the same day and profaned my s.
44:24 and they shall keep my s holy.
45:17 at the festivals, the new moons, and the s,
46: 3 before the LORD on the s and on the new moons.
Hos 2:11 her s, and all her appointed festivals.
Col 2:16 or of observing festivals, new moons, or s.
Jdt 10: 2 and went down into the house where she lived on s
1Mc 1:39 her s into a reproach, her honor into contempt.
1:45 and drink offerings in the sanctuary, to profane s
10:34 and s and new moons and appointed days,
1Es 1:58 "Until the land has enjoyed its s,
5:52 and sacrifices on s and at new moons and at all

SABBATICAL (1) [SABBATH]

1Mc 6:49 since it was a s year for the land.

SABEANS (3)

Job 1:15 the S fell on them and carried them off, and killed
Isa 45:14 of Ethiopia, and the S, tall of stature, shall come
Joel 3: 8 and they will sell them to the S,

SABTA (1) [=SABTAH]

1Ch 1: 9 Seba, Havilah, S, Raama, and Sabteca.

SABTAH (1) [=SABTA]

Ge 10: 7 Seba, Havilah, S, Raamah, and Sabteca.

SABTECA (2)

Ge 10: 7 Seba, Havilah, Sabtah, Raamah, and S.
1Ch 1: 9 Seba, Havilah, Sabta, Raama, and S.

SACHAR (2)

1Ch 11:35 Ahiam son of S the Hararite, Eliphal son of Ur,
26: 4 Jehozabad the second, Joah the third, S the fourth,

SACHERDONOS See Index to Footnotes

SACHIA (1)

1Ch 8:10 S, and Mirmah. These were his sons,

SACK (12) [SACKCLOTH, SACKING, SACKS]

Ge 42:25 to return every man's money to his s,
42:27 of them opened his s to give his donkey fodder at
42:27 he saw his money at the top of the s.
42:28 here it is in my s!"
42:35 there in each one's s was his bag of money.
43:21 there was each one's money in the top of his s,
44: 1 and put each man's money in the top of his s.
44: 2 the silver cup, in the top of the s of the youngest,
44:11 each one quickly lowered his s to the ground,
44:11 to the ground, and each opened his s.
44:12 and the cup was found in Benjamin's s.
2Ki 4:42 of barley and fresh ears of grain in his s.

SACKBUT (KJV) See LYRE

SACKCLOTH (65) [CLOTH, SACK]

Ge 37:34 Jacob tore his garments, and put s on his loins,
2Sa 3:31 and put on s, and mourn over Abner."
21:10 Then Rizpah the daughter of Aiah took s,
1Ki 20:31 let us put s around our waists and ropes
20:32 So they tied s around their waists,
21:27 he tore his clothes and put s over his bare flesh;
21:27 he fasted, lay in the s, and went about dejectedly.
2Ki 6:30 on the city wall, the people could see that he had s
19: 1 he tore his clothes, covered himself with s,
19: 2 covered with s, to the prophet Isaiah son of Amoz.
1Ch 21:16 Then David and the elders, clothed in s,
Ne 9: 1 of Israel were assembled with fasting and in s,
Est 4: 1 Mordecai tore his clothes and put on s and ashes,
4: 2 no one might enter the king's gate clothed with s.
4: 3 and most of them lay in s and ashes.
4: 4 so that he might take off his s;
Job 16:15 I have sewed s upon my skin,
Ps 30:11 you have taken off my s and clothed me with joy,
35:13 But as for me, when they were sick, I wore s;
69:11 I made s my clothing, I became a byword to them.
Isa 3:24 and instead of a rich robe, a binding of s;
15: 3 in the streets they bind on s;
20: 2 and loose the s from your loins
22:12 to baldness and putting on s;
32:11 and make yourselves bare, and put s on your loins.
37: 1 he tore his clothes, covered himself with s,
37: 2 covered with s, to the prophet Isaiah son of Amoz.
50: 3 and make s their covering.
58: 5 and to lie in s and ashes?
Jer 4: 8 Because of this put on s, lament and wail:
6:26 O my poor people, put on s, and roll in ashes;
48:37 the hands there are gashes, and on the loins s.
49: 3 Put on s, lament, and slash yourselves with whips!
La 2:10 they have thrown dust on their heads and put on s;
Eze 7:18 They shall put on s, horror shall cover them.
27:31 on s, and they weep over you in bitterness of soul,
Da 9: 3 and supplication with fasting and s and ashes.
Joel 1: 8 a virgin dressed in s for the husband of her youth.
1:13 Put on s and lament, you priests;
1:13 Come, pass the night in s,
Am 8:10 I will bring s on all loins, and baldness on every
Jnh 3: 5 and everyone, great and small, put on s.
3: 6 removed his robe, covered himself with s,
3: 8 and animals shall be covered with s,
Mt 11:21 they would have repented long ago in s and ashes.
Lk 10:13 have repented long ago, sitting in s and ashes.
Rev 6:12 the sun became black as s,
11: 3 one thousand two hundred sixty days, wearing s."
Jdt 4:10 they all put s around their waists.
4:11 and put ashes on their heads and spread out their s
4:12 They even draped the altar with s and cried out
4:14 before the Lord and ministered to the Lord, with s
8: 5 She put s around her waist and dressed
9: 1 and uncovered the s she was wearing.
Jdt 10: 3 She removed the s she had been wearing,
AdE 4: 1 put on s, and sprinkled himself with ashes:
4: 2 to enter the courtyard clothed in s and ashes.
4: 3 and they put on s and ashes.
4: 4 to Mordecai to put on instead of s;
Bar 4:20 the robe of peace and put on s for my supplication;
1Mc 2:14 Mattathias and his sons tore their clothes, put on s,
3:47 put on s and sprinkled ashes on their heads,
2Mc 3:19 Women, girded with s under their breasts,
10:25 on their heads and girded their loins with s,
2Es 16: 2 Bind on s and cloth of goats' hair,

SACKED (3)

2Ki 15:16 At that time Menahem s Tiphsah,
15:16 because they did not open it to him, he s it.
Jdt 2:27 and s their towns and ravaged their lands

SACKING (1) [SACK]

Lev 11:32 whether an article of wood or cloth or skin or s,

SACKS (10) [SACK]

Ge 42:35 As they were emptying their s,
43:12 the money that was returned in the top of your s;
43:18 replaced in our s the first time,
43:21 we came to the lodging place we opened our s,
43:22 We do not know who put our money in our s."
43:23 of your father must have put treasure in your s
44: 1 "Fill the men's s with food,
44: 8 Look, the money that we found at the top of our s,
Jos 9: 4 and took worn-out s for their donkeys,
1Sa 9: 7 For the bread in our s is gone,

SACRED (107)

Ex 28: 2 You shall make s vestments for the glorious
28: 4 When they make these s vestments
28:38 that the Israelites consecrate as their s donations;
29:29 The s vestments of Aaron shall be passed on
30:25 a s anointing oil blended as by the perfumer;
34:13 and cut down their s poles
35:21 and for all its service, and for the s vestments.
39: 1 they made the s vestments for Aaron;
39:41 the s vestments for the priest Aaron,
40:13 and put on Aaron the s vestments,
Lev 10:17 not eat the sin offering in the s area?
22: 2 to deal carefully with the s donations of the people
22: 3 near the s donations, which the people
22: 4 or suffers a discharge may eat of the s donations
22: 6 of the s donations unless he has washed his body
22: 7 and afterward he may eat of the s donations,
22:10 No lay person shall eat of the s donations.
22:10 of the priest shall eat of the s donations;
22:12 she shall not eat of the offering of the s donations;
22:14 If a man eats of the s donation unintentionally,
22:14 and give the s donation to the priest.
22:15 No one shall profane the s donations of the people
22:16 by eating their s donations:
27:23 a s donation to the LORD.
Nu 5: 9 Among all the s donations of the Israelites,
5:10 The s donations of all are their own;
Dt 7: 5 smash their pillars, hew down their s poles,
12: 3 smash their pillars, burn their s poles with fire,
12:26 But the s donations that are due from you,
16:21 You shall not plant any tree as a s pole beside
26:13 "I have removed the s portion from the house,
Jos 6:19 and gold, and vessels of bronze and iron, are s to
Jdg 6:25 and cut down the s pole that is beside it;
6:26 the wood of the s pole that you shall cut down."
6:28 and the s pole beside it was cut down,
6:30 down the altar of Baal and cut down the s pole
1Sa 20: 8 into a s covenant with you.
1Ki 14:15 because they have made their s poles,
14:23 and s poles on every high hill and
16:33 Ahab also made a s pole.
2Ki 12: 4 the money offered as s donations that is brought
13: 6 the s pole also remained in Samaria.
17:10 they set up for themselves pillars and s poles
17:16 a s pole, worshiped all the host of heaven,
18: 4 broke down the pillars, and cut down the s pole.
21: 3 he erected altars for Baal, made a s pole,
23:14 in pieces, cut down the s poles, and covered
23:15 he also burned the s pole.
1Ch 16:42 and instruments for s song.
2Ch 14: 3 broke down the pillars, hewed down the s poles,
17: 6 the high places and the s poles from Judah.
19: 3 for you destroyed the s poles out of the land,
24:18 and served the s poles and the idols.
31: 1 down the s poles, and pulled down the high places
33: 3 made s poles, worshiped all the host of heaven,
33:19 and set up the s poles and the images,
34: 3 the s poles, and the carved and the cast images.
34: 4 the s poles and the carved and the cast images;
34: 7 beat the s poles and the images into powder,
Ezr 3: 5 at the new moon and at all the s festivals of
Ne 10:33 the appointed festivals, the s donations,
Pr 2:17 of her youth and forgets her s covenant;
Ecc 8: 2 Keep the king's command because of your s oath.
Isa 17: 8 either the s poles or the altars of incense.
27: 9 no s poles or incense altars will remain standing.
Jer 17: 2 and their s poles, beside every green tree,
31:40 shall be s to the LORD.
La 4: 1 The s stones lie scattered at the head of every
Eze 20:40 the choicest of your gifts, with all your s things.
43:21 to the temple, outside the s area.
44: 8 And you have not kept charge of my s offerings;
44:13 nor come near any of my s offerings,

Eze 44:13 the things that are most s;
Da 7:25 shall attempt to change the s seasons and the law;
Mic 5:14 and I will uproot your s poles from among you
Zep 3: 4 its priests have profaned what is s,
Zec 14:21 in Jerusalem and Judah shall be s to the LORD
Mt 23:17 gold or the sanctuary that has made the gold s?
23:19 the gift or the altar that makes the gift s?
Mk 16: S ⟦the s and imperishable proclamation of eternal⟧
2Ti 3:15 from childhood you have known the s writings
Tob 2: 1 which is the s festival of weeks,
Jdt 3: 8 and cut down their s groves;
4: 3 and the s vessels and the altar and
9:13 and against your s house, and against Mount Zion,
Sir 45:10 with the s vestment, of gold and violet and purple,
1Mc 1:47 to build altars and s precincts and shrines for idols,
5:43 and fled into the s precincts at Carnaim.
5:44 But he took the town and burned the s precincts
10:21 on the s vestments in the seventh month of
2Mc 1:15 with a few men inside the wall of the s precinct,
1:34 and enclosed the place and made it s.
6: 4 with women within the s precincts,
8:33 they burned those who had set fire to the s gates,
10: 2 and also destroyed the s precincts.
11: 3 as he did on the s places of the other nations,
12:40 of each one of the dead they found s tokens of
1Es 5:45 that they would give to the s treasury for the work
3Mc 1: 7 and by endowing their s enclosures with gifts,
4Mc 2:22 among the senses as a s governor over them all.
4: 7 to the s treasury should be deprived of them,
5:29 the s oaths of my ancestors concerning the keeping
7: 4 his s life was consumed by tortures and racks,
7: 6 you neither defiled your s teeth
9:24 Fight the s and noble battle for religion.
14: 3 O s and harmonious concord of the seven brothers
15:13 O s nature and affection of parental love,

SACRIFICE‡ (220) [SACRIFICED, SACRIFICES, SACRIFICIAL, SACRIFICING]

Ge 31:54 offered a s on the height and called his kinsfolk
Ex 3:18 so that we may s to the LORD our God.'
5: 3 a three days' journey into the wilderness to s to
5: 8 is why they cry, 'Let us go and offer s to our God.'
5:17 is why you say, 'Let us go and s to the LORD.'
8: 8 and I will let the people go to s to the LORD."
8:25 and said, "Go, s to your God within the land."
8:27 and s to the LORD our God as he commands us."
8:28 "I will let you go to s to the LORD your God in
8:29 by not letting the people go to s to the LORD."
10:25 also let us have sacrifices and burnt offerings to s
12:27 you shall say, 'It is the passover s to the LORD,
13:15 Therefore I s to the LORD every male
20:24 and s on it your burnt offerings and your offerings
23:18 the blood of my s with anything leavened,
29:28 be an offering by the Israelites from their s
34:15 to their gods and s to their gods,
34:15 and you will eat of the s.
34:25 You shall not offer the blood of my s with leaven,
34:25 the s of the festival of the passover shall not be left
Lev 3: 1 If the offering is a s of well-being,
3: 3 You shall offer from the s of well-being,
3: 6 a s of well-being to the LORD is from the flock,
3: 9 You shall present its fat from the s of well-being,
4:10 just as these are removed from the ox of the s
4:26 like the fat of the s of well-being.
4:35 of the sheep is removed from the s of well-being,
7:11 the ritual of the s of the offering of well-being
7:13 With your thanksgiving s of well-being
7:15 the flesh of your thanksgiving s of well-being shall
7:16 But if the s you offer is a votive offering or
7:16 it shall be eaten on the day that you offer your s,
7:17 but what is left of the flesh of the s shall be burned
7:18 If any of the flesh of your s of well-being is eaten
7:20 from the LORD's s of well-being while in a state
7:21 then eats flesh from the LORD's s of well-being,
7:29 of you who would offer to the LORD your s
7:29 to the LORD your offering from your s
7:37 the offering of ordination, and the s of well-being,
9: 4 and a ram for an offering of well-being to s before
9: 7 and s your sin offering and your burnt offering,
9: 7 and s the offering of the people,
9:18 and the ram as a s of well-being for the people.
17: 8 among them who offers a burnt offering or s,
17: 9 to s it to the LORD,
18:21 You shall not give any of your offspring to s them
19: 5 When you offer a s of well-being to the LORD,
22:21 anyone offers a s of well-being to the LORD,
22:29 you s a thanksgiving offering to the LORD,
22:29 you shall s it so that it may be acceptable
23:19 two male lambs a year old as a s of well-being.
Nu 6:17 as a s of well-being to the LORD, with the basket
6:18 and put it on the fire under the s of well-being.
7:17 and for the s of well-being,
7:23 and for the s of well-being,
7:29 and for the s of well-being,
7:35 and for the s of well-being,
7:41 and for the s of well-being,
7:47 and for the s of well-being,
7:53 and for the s of well-being,
7:59 and for the s of well-being,
7:65 and for the s of well-being,
7:71 and for the s of well-being,
7:77 and for the s of well-being,
7:83 and for the s of well-being,
7:88 for the s of well-being twenty-four bulls,
Nu 15: 3 whether a burnt offering or a s,
15: 5 as a drink offering with the burnt offering or the s,
15: 8 When you offer a bull as a burnt offering or a s,
Dt 15:21 you shall not s it to the LORD your God;
16: 2 the passover s for the LORD your God,
16: 5 to offer the passover s within any of your towns
16: 6 only there shall you offer the passover s,
17: 1 You must not s to the LORD your God an ox or
18: 3 from those offering a s, whether an ox or a sheep:
Jos 22:26 not for burnt offering, nor for s,
22:28 nor for s, but to be a witness between us and you.'
22:29 for burnt offering, grain offering, or s, other than
Jdg 16:23 a great s to their god Dagon, and to rejoice;
1Sa 1: 3 up year by year from his town to worship and to s
1:21 up to offer to the LORD the yearly s,
2:13 to the people. When anyone offered s,
2:19 she went up with her husband to offer the yearly s.
3:14 not be expiated by s or offering forever."
9:12 because the people have a s today at the shrine.
9:13 since he must bless the s;
15:15 to s to the LORD your God;
15:21 to s to the LORD your God in Gilgal."
15:22 Surely, to obey is better than s,
16: 2 and say, 'I have come to s to the LORD.'
16: 3 to the s, and I will show you what you shall do;
16: 5 I have come to s to the LORD;
16: 5 sanctify yourselves and come with me to the s."
16: 5 and his sons and invited them to the s.
20: 6 for there is a yearly s there for all the family.'
20:29 for our family is holding a s in the city,
1Ki 3: 4 The king went to Gibeon to s there,
8:62 offered s before the LORD.
13: 2 and he shall s on you the priests of
2Ki 5:17 or s to any god except the LORD.
10:19 for I have a great s to offer to Baal;
12: 3 the people continued to s and make offerings on
16:15 and all the blood of the s;
17:35 or bow yourselves to them or serve them or s
17:36 to him, and to him you shall s.
2Ch 7: 4 Then the king and all the people offered s before
7: 5 as a s twenty-two thousand oxen
7:12 have chosen this place for myself as a house of s.
11:16 the tribes of Israel to Jerusalem to s to the LORD,
28:23 I will s to them so that they may help me."
Ezr 9: 4 around me while I sat appalled until the evening s.
9: 5 At the evening s I got up from my fasting,
Ne 4: 2 Will they restore things? Will they s?
Ps 40: 6 S and offering you do not desire,
50: 5 who made a covenant with me by s!"
50:14 Offer to God a s of thanksgiving,
50:23 Those who bring thanksgiving as their s honor me;
51:16 For you have no delight in s;
51:17 The s acceptable to God is a broken spirit;
54: 6 With a freewill offering I will s to you;
66:15 with the smoke of the s of rams;
116:17 I will offer to you a thanksgiving s and call
141: 2 and the lifting up of my hands as an evening s.
Pr 15: 8 s of the wicked is an abomination to the LORD,
21: 3 and justice is more acceptable to the LORD than s.
21:27 The s of the wicked is an abomination;
Ecc 5: 1 near to listen is better than the s offered by fools;
9: 2 to those who s and those who do not s.
Isa 19:21 and will worship with s and burnt offering,
34: 6 For the LORD has a s in Bozrah,
57: 7 and there you went up to offer s.
Jer 46:10 a s in the land of the north by the river Euphrates.
48:35 those who offer s at a high place
Eze 44:11 they shall slaughter the burnt offering and the s for
Da 9:21 to me in swift flight at the time of the evening s.
9:27 of the week he shall make s and offering cease;
Hos 3: 4 without s or pillar, without ephod or teraphim.
4:13 They s on the tops of the mountains,
4:14 and s with temple prostitutes;
6: 6 For I desire steadfast love and not s,
12:11 In Gilgal they s bulls, so their altars shall be like
13: 2 "S to these," they say. People are kissing calves!
Jnh 1:16 they offered a s to the LORD and made vows.
2: 9 But I with the voice of thanksgiving will s to you;
Zep 1: 7 the LORD has prepared a s,
1: 8 of the LORD's s I will punish the officials and
Zec 14:21 so that all who s may come and use them to boil the flesh of the s.
Mal 1: 8 you offer blind animals in s, is that not wrong?
Mt 9:13 and learn what this means, 'I desire mercy, not s.'
12: 7 'I desire mercy and not s,'
Lk 2:24 and they offered a s according to what is stated in
Ac 7:41 they made a calf, offered a s to the idol,
14:13 he and the crowds wanted to offer s.
14:18 they scarcely restrained the crowds from offering s
21:26 the days of purification when the s would be made
Ro 3:25 whom God put forward as a s of atonement
12: 1 to present your bodies as a living s,
1Co 10:20 No, I imply that what pagans s,
10:20 they s to demons and not to God.
10:28 someone says to you, "This has been offered in s,"
Eph 5: 2 a fragrant offering and s to God.
Php 2:17 over the s and the offering of your faith, I am glad
4:18 a s acceptable and pleasing to God.
Heb 2:17 a s of atonement for the sins of the people.
5: 3 of this he must offer s for his own sins as well as
9:26 for all at the end of the age to remove sin by the s
10:12 Christ had offered for all time a single s for sins,
10:26 there no longer remains a s for sins,
11: 4 to God a more acceptable s than Cain's.
13:11 by the high priest as a s for sin are burned outside
13:15 let us continually offer a s of praise to God, that is,
1Jn 2: 2 and he is the atoning s for our sins,
1Jn 4:10 and sent his Son to be the atoning s for our sins.
Tob 1: 4 where all the tribes of Israel should offer s and
Jdt 16:16 For every s as a fragrant offering is a small thing,
Sir 7:31 the gift of the shoulders, the s of sanctification,
28: 5 who will make an atoning s for his sins?
30:19 Of what use to an idol is a s?
34:24 the person who offers a s from the property of
35: 9 The s of the righteous is acceptable,
35:15 and do not rely on a dishonest s;
38:11 Offer a sweet-smelling s, and a memorial portion
45:16 He chose him out of all the living to offer s to
46:16 and he offered in s a suckling lamb.
Aza 1:15 no burnt offering, or s, or oblation, or incense,
1:17 such may our s be in your sight today,
1Mc 1:47 to s swine and other unclean animals,
1:51 and commanded the towns of Judah to offer s,
1:59 the twenty-fifth day of the month they offered s on
2:15 to the town of Modein to make them offer s.
2:23 a Jew came forward in the sight of all to offer s on
2:25 the king's officer who was forcing them to s,
4:53 and offered s, as the law directs, on the new altar
4:56 a s of well-being and a thanksgiving offering.
11:34 To all those who offer s
2Mc 1: 8 and we offered s and grain offering,
1:23 And while the s was being consumed,
1:26 Accept this s on behalf of all your people Israel
1:31 After the materials of the s had been consumed,
1:33 his associates had burned the materials of the s,
2: 9 that being possessed of wisdom Solomon offered s
3:32 offered s for the man's recovery.
3:35 Then Heliodorus offered s to the Lord
4:19 to carry three hundred silver drachmas for the s
4:19 however, thought best not to use it for s,
4:20 So this money was intended by the sender for the s
6: 4 and besides brought in things for s that were unfit.
6:21 Those who were in charge of that unlawful s took
10: 3 and made another altar of s;
13:23 settled with them and offered s,
1Es 6:24 where they s with perpetual fire;
8:66 all as a s to the Lord.
8:72 and I sat grief-stricken until the evening s.
9: 4 be seized for s and the men themselves expelled
3Mc 1: 9 he offered s to the supreme God
2:28 of those who do not s shall enter their sanctuaries,
4Mc 16:20 to s his son Isaac, the ancestor of our nation;
17:22 and their death as an atoning s,

SACRIFICED (47) [SACRIFICE]

Ex 24: 5 and s oxen as offerings of well-being to
32: 8 and have worshiped it and s to it, and said,
Lev 9:16 and s it according to regulation.
Nu 22:40 Balak s oxen and sheep, and sent them to Balaam
Dt 32:17 They s to demons, not God,
Jos 8:31 and s offerings of well-being.
Jdg 2: 5 and there they s to the LORD.
1Sa 1: 4 On the day when Elkanah s,
11:15 There they s offerings of well-being before
2Sa 6:13 he s an ox and a fatling.
1Ki 1: 9 Adonijah s sheep, oxen, and fatted cattle by
1:19 He has s oxen, fatted cattle,
1:25 For today he has gone down and has s oxen,
3: 3 only, he s and offered incense at the high places.
11: 8 who offered incense and s to their gods.
22:43 and the people still s and offered incense on
2Ki 14: 4 the people still s and made offerings on
15: 4 the people still s and made offerings on
15:35 the people still s and made offerings on
16: 4 He s and made offerings on the high places,
17:32 who s for them in the shrines of the high places.
1Ch 15:26 they s seven bulls and seven rams.
2Ch 15:11 They s to the LORD on that day,
28: 4 He s and made offerings on the high places,
28:23 For he s to the gods of Damascus,
33:17 The people, however, still s at the high places,
33:22 Amon s to all the images that his father
34: 4 and scattered it over the graves of those who had s
Ps 106:37 They s their sons and their daughters to
106:38 whom they s to the idols of Canaan;
Eze 16:20 and these you s to them to be devoured
Mk 14:12 when the Passover lamb is s,
Lk 22: 7 on which the Passover lamb had to be s.
Ac 15:29 that you abstain from what has been s to idols and
21:25 from what has been s to idols and from blood and
1Co 5: 7 For our paschal lamb, Christ, has been s.
8: 1 Now concerning food s to idols:
8:10 be encouraged to the point of eating food s
9:13 and those who serve at the altar share in what is s
10:19 That food s to idols is anything,
Rev 2:14 the people of Israel, so that they would eat food s
2:20 to practice fornication and to eat food s to idols.
Tob 1: 5 and our ancestral house of Naphtali s to the calf
1Mc 1:43 they s to idols and profaned the sabbath.
1Es 7:12 and they s the passover lamb for all
2Es 16:68 of you away and force you to eat what was s
4Mc 5: 2 and to compel them to eat pork and food s to idols.

SACRIFICES‡ (130) [SACRIFICE]

Ge 46: 1 he offered s to the God of his father Isaac.
Ex 8:26 for the s that we offer to the LORD
8:26 in the sight of the Egyptians s that are offensive
10:25 also let us have s and burnt offerings to sacrifice to
18:12 brought a burnt offering and s to God;
22:20 Whoever s to any god, other than
32: 6 and offered burnt offerings and brought s
Lev 7:32 from your s of well-being you shall give to
7:34 from their s of well-being,

Lev 10:14 the s of the offerings of well-being of the people
17: 5 in order that the people of Israel may bring their s
17: 5 and offer them as s of well-being to the LORD.
17: 7 they may no longer offer their s for goat-demons,
23:37 s and drink offerings, each on its proper day—
Nu 10:10 over your burnt offerings and over your s
25: 2 These invited the people to the s of their gods,
Dt 12: 6 bringing there your burnt offerings and your s,
12:11 your burnt offerings and your s,
12:27 of your other s shall be poured out beside the altar
18: 1 They may eat the s that are the LORD's portion
27: 7 make s of well-being, and eat them there, rejoicing
32:38 who ate the fat of their s,
33:19 there they offer the right s;
Jos 22:27 in his presence with our burnt offerings and s
Jdg 20:26 Then they offered burnt offerings and s
21: 4 and offered burnt offerings and s of well-being.
1Sa 2:29 at my s and my offerings that I commanded,
6:15 and presented s on that day to the LORD.
10: 8 down to you to present burnt offerings and offer s
15:22 as great delight in burnt offerings and s,
2Sa 15:12 While Absalom was offering the s,
1Ki 8:63 Solomon offered as s of well-being to
8:64 and the grain offerings and the fat pieces of the s
8:64 and the grain offerings and the fat pieces of the s
9:25 up burnt offerings and s of well-being on the altar
12:27 to offer s in the house of the LORD at Jerusalem,
12:32 and he offered s on the altar;
2Ki 10:24 Then they proceeded to offer s and burnt offerings.
1Ch 21:28 of Ornan the Jebusite, he made his s there.
29:21 On the next day they offered s and burnt offerings
29:21 and s in abundance for all Israel;
2Ch 7: 1 and consumed the burnt offering and the s;
29:31 near, bring s and thank offerings to the house of
29:31 The assembly brought s and thank offerings;
33:16 the LORD and offered on it s of well-being and
Ezr 6: 3 the house be rebuilt, the place where s are offered
6:10 they may offer pleasing s to the God of heaven,
Ne 12:43 They offered great s that day and rejoiced,
Ps 4: 5 Offer right s, and put your trust in the LORD.
20: 3 and regard with favor your burnt s.
27: 6 and I will offer in his tent s with shouts of joy;
50: 8 Not for your s do I rebuke you;
51:19 then you will delight in right s, in burnt offerings
106:28 and ate s offered to the dead;
107:22 And let them offer thanksgiving s,
Pr 7:14 "I had to offer s, and today I have paid my vows;
Isa 1:11 What to me is the multitude of your s?
43:23 or honored me with your s.
43:24 or satisfied me with the fat of your s.
56: 7 their burnt offerings and their s will be accepted
66: 3 whoever s a lamb, like one who breaks
Jer 6:20 nor are your s pleasing to me.
7:21 Add your burnt offerings to your s,
7:22 concerning burnt offerings and s.
17:26 bringing burnt offerings and s,
33:18 to make grain offerings, and to make s for all time.
Eze 20:28 there they offered their s and presented
36:38 Like the flock for s, like the flock at Jerusalem
40:41 eight tables, on which the s were to be slaughtered.
40:42 the burnt offerings and the s were slaughtered.
46:24 at the temple shall boil the s of the people."
Hos 8:13 Though they offer choice s, though they eat flesh,
9: 4 and their s shall not please him.
9: 4 Such s shall be like mourners' bread;
Am 4: 4 bring your s every morning,
5:25 Did you bring to me s and offerings the forty years
Hab 1:16 he s to his net and makes offerings to his seine;
Mal 1:14 and yet s to the Lord what is blemished;
Mk 12:33 important than all whole burnt offerings and s."
Lk 13: 1 whose blood Pilate had mingled with their s.
Ac 7:42 to me slain victims and s forty years in
24:17 to bring alms to my nation and to offer s.
1Co 10:18 are not those who eat the s partners in the altar?
Heb 5: 1 to offer gifts and s for sins.
7:27 he has no need to offer s day after day,
8: 3 every high priest is appointed to offer gifts and s;
9: 9 and s are offered that cannot perfect
9:23 heavenly things themselves need better s than
10: 1 by the same s that are continually offered year
10: 3 in these s there is a reminder of sin year after year.
10: 5 he said, "S and offerings you have not desired,
10: 8 "You have neither desired nor taken pleasure in s
10:11 the same s that can never take away sins.
13:16 for such s are pleasing to God.
1Pe 2: 5 to offer spiritual s acceptable to God
Wis 18: 9 the holy children of good people offered s, and
Sir 34:21 If one s ill-gotten goods, the offering is blemished;
34:23 nor for a multitude of s does he forgive sins.
35: 4 and one who gives alms s a thank offering.
45:14 His s shall be wholly burned twice every day
45:21 for they eat the s of the Lord,
LtJ 6:28 The priests sell the s that are offered to these gods
6:29 S to them may even be touched by women
1Mc 1:45 to forbid burnt offerings and s and drink offerings
12:11 at the s that we offer and in our prayers,
2Mc 1:18 who built the temple and the altar, offered s.
1:21 When the materials for the s were presented,
2:10 fire came down from heaven and consumed the s,
3: 3 the expenses connected with the service of the s.
3: 6 that they did not belong to the account of the s,
4:14 Despising the sanctuary and neglecting the s,
6: 7 under bitter constraint, to partake of the s;
6: 8 toward the Jews and make them partake of the s,
7:42 about the eating of s and the extreme tortures.
9:16 for the s he would provide from his own revenues;
10: 3 then, striking fire out of flint, they offered s,
2Mc 14:31 while the priests were offering the customary s,
1Es 1: 6 and kill the passover lamb and prepare the s
1:12 and they boiled the s in bronze pots and caldrons,
1:17 with the s to the Lord were accomplished that day:
1:18 and the s were offered on the altar of the Lord,
5:50 and they offered s at the proper times
5:51 and offered the proper s every day,
5:52 and s on sabbaths and at new moons and at all
5:53 to God began to offer s to God,
6:29 for s to the Lord, for bulls and rams and lambs,
8:15 so as to offer s on the altar of their Lord that is
8:65 And those who had returned from exile offered s
3Mc 5:43 of those who offered s there.
2Es 1: 6 for they have forgotten me and have offered s

SACRIFICIAL (7) [SACRIFICE]

Jer 11:15 Can vows and s flesh avert your doom?
Eze 39:17 from all around to the s feast that I am preparing
39:17 a great s feast on the mountains of Israel,
39:19 at the s feast that I am preparing for you.
Wis 3: 6 and like a s burnt offering he accepted them.
12: 5 and their s feasting on human flesh and blood.
2Mc 6:21 the s meal that had been commanded by the king,

SACRIFICING (12) [SACRIFICE]

Lev 9:22 and he came down after s the sin offering,
1Sa 2:15 to the one who was s, "Give meat for the priest
1Ki 3: 2 The people were s at the high places, however,
8: 5 s so many sheep and oxen that they could not
12:32 he did in Bethel, s to the calves that he had made.
2Ch 5: 6 s so many sheep and oxen that they could not
30:22 s offerings of well-being and giving thanks to
Ezr 4: 2 and we have been s to him ever since the days
Isa 65: 3 s in gardens and offering incense on bricks;
Hos 11: 2 they kept s to the Baals, and offering incense to
Bar 4: 7 the one who made you by s to demons and not
1Es 5:69 as you do and we have been s to him ever since

SACRILEGE (6)

Mt 24:15 you see the desolating s standing in the holy place,
Mk 13:14 the desolating s set up where it ought not to be (let
1Mc 1:54 a desolating s on the altar of burnt offering.
2Mc 4:39 of s had been committed in the city by Lysimachus
13: 6 to destruction anyone guilty of s or notorious
1Es 1:49 of s and lawlessness beyond all the unclean deeds

SACRILEGE (KJV) See also ROB TEMPLES

SAD (13) [SADNESS]

1Sa 1: 8 Why is your heart s?
1:18 and her countenance was s no longer.
Ne 2: 1 Now, I had never been s in his presence before.
2: 2 So the king said to me, "Why is your face s,
2: 3 Why should my face not be s, when the city,
Job 9:27 I will put off my s countenance and be
Pr 14:13 Even in laughter the heart is s,
Lk 18:23 he heard this, he became s; for he was very rich.
24:17 They stood still, looking s.
2Es 5:16 And why is your face s?
7:*80* always grieving and s, in seven ways.
8:16 for whom I am s, and about the seed of Jacob,
13:17 For those who are not left will be s

SADDLE (5) [SADDLECLOTHS, SADDLED]

Ge 31:34 the household gods and put them in the camel's s,
Lev 15: 9 Any s on which the one with
2Sa 19:26 for your servant said to him, 'S a donkey for me,
1Ki 13:13 Then he said to his sons, "S a donkey for me."
13:27 Then he said to his sons, "S a donkey for me."

SADDLECLOTHS (1) [CLOTH, SADDLE]

Eze 27:20 Dedan traded with you in s for riding.

SADDLED (10) [SADDLE]

Ge 22: 3 Abraham rose early in the morning, s his donkey,
Nu 22:21 So Balaam got up in the morning, s his donkey,
Jdg 19:10 He had with him a couple of s donkeys,
2Sa 16: 1 with a couple of donkeys s,
17:23 he s his donkey and went off home to his own city.
1Ki 2:40 Shimei arose and s a donkey, and went to Achish
13:13 So they s a donkey for him, and he mounted it.
13:23 they s for him a donkey belonging to
13:27 "Saddle a donkey for me." So they s one,
2Ki 4:24 Then she s the donkey and said to her servant,

SADDUCEES (14)

Mt 3: 7 he saw many Pharisees and S coming for baptism,
16: 1 The Pharisees and S came,
16: 6 and beware of the yeast of the Pharisees and S."
16:11 Beware of the yeast of the Pharisees and S!"
16:12 but of the teaching of the Pharisees and S.
22:23 The same day some S came to him,
22:34 the Pharisees heard that he had silenced the S,
Mk 12:18 Some S, who say there is no resurrection,
Lk 20:27 Some S, those who say there is no resurrection,
Ac 4: 1 the captain of the temple, and the S came to them,
5:17 the sect of the S), being filled with jealousy,
23: 6 that some were S and others were Pharisees,
23: 7 dissension began between the Pharisees and the S,
23: 8 (The S say that there is no resurrection, or angel,

SADNESS (4) [SAD]

Ne 2: 2 This can only be s of the heart."
Ecc 7: 3 for by s of countenance the heart is made glad.
2Es 4:27 because this age is full of s and infirmities.
10:24 Therefore shake off your great s

SADOC (KJV) See ZADOK

SAFE (44) [SAFEGUARD, SAFEKEEPING, SAFELY, SAFER, SAFETY]

Dt 29:19 in their hearts, "We are s even
Jos 10:21 all the people returned s to Joshua in the camp
1Sa 20:21 it is s for you and there is no danger.
22:23 you will be s with me."
2Ch 15: 5 In those times it was not s for anyone to go
Ezr 8:21 to seek from him a s journey for ourselves,
Job 5:24 You shall know that your tent is s,
21: 9 Their houses are s from fear,
41:11 Who can confront it and be s?
Ps 18:32 with strength, and made my way s.
22: 9 you kept me s on my mother's breast.
31:20 you hold them s under your shelter
37:28 The righteous shall be kept s forever,
40:11 and your faithfulness keep me s forever.
119:117 be s and have regard for your statutes continually.
Pr 18:10 the righteous run into it and are s.
28:18 One who walks in integrity will be s,
Jer 7:10 which is called by my name, and say, "We are s!"
12: 5 And if in a s land you fall down,
12:12 to the other; no one shall be s.
Da 10:19 He said, "Do not fear, greatly beloved, you are s.
Hab 2: 9 setting your nest on high to be s from the reach
Lk 11:21 fully armed, guards his castle, his property is s.
15:27 because he has got him back s and sound.'
Jude 1: 1 who are beloved in God the Father and kept s
Tob 5:16 to you in good health, because the way is s."
5:17 Tobit then said to him, "Have a s journey."
8: 5 to pray and implore that they might be kept s.
8:17 Be merciful to them, O Master, and keep them s;
10:11 "Farewell, my child; have a s journey.
AdE 4:11 the king stretches out the golden scepter is s—
8: 6 can I be s if my ancestral nation is destroyed?"
Wis 4:17 and for what he kept them s.
10:12 and kept him s from those who lay in wait for him;
14: 3 and a s way through the waves,
1Mc 12: 4 asking them to provide for the envoys s conduct to
2Mc 3:15 that he should keep them s for those who had
3:22 that he would keep what had been entrusted s
14: 3 realized that there was no way for him to be s or
1Es 4:47 that they should give s conduct to him and
8:51 and an escort to keep us s from our adversaries;
2Es 1:13 made s highways for you where there was no road;
7:13 the entrances of the greater world are broad and s,
7:*121* [51] s and healthful habitations have been reserved

SAFEGUARD (1) [GUARD, SAFE]

Php 3: 1 not troublesome to me, and for you it is a s.

SAFEKEEPING (3) [KEEP, SAFE]

Ex 16:34 so Aaron placed it before the covenant, for s.
22: 7 to a neighbor money or goods for s,
22:10 ox, sheep, or any other animal for s,

SAFELY‡ (21) [SAFE]

Ge 33:18 Jacob came s to the city of Shechem,
1Sa 24:19 and sent the enemy s away?
2Sa 19:30 since my lord the king has arrived home s."
Pr 28:26 but those who walk in wisdom come through s.
Isa 41: 3 He pursues them and passes on s,
Jer 43:12 and he shall depart from there s.
Ac 23:24 and take him s to Felix the governor."
27:44 And so it was that all were brought s to land.
Tob 5:17 in heaven bring you s there and return you
7:12 Take her and bring her s to your father.
10:11 Then he saw them s off;
10:12 the Lord of heaven bring you back s,
10:12 Then she kissed them both and saw them s off.
12: 3 For he has led me back to you s,
Wis 14: 5 through the billows on a raft they come s to land.
Bar 5: 7 so that Israel may walk s in the glory of God.
1Mc 7:35 then if I return s I will burn up this house."
12:52 So they all reached the land of Judah s,
16:10 He then returned to Judea s.
3Mc 2: 7 through s those who had put their confidence
7:20 of them been brought s by land and sea and river

SAFER (1) [SAFE]

Tob 14: 4 it will be s in Media than in Assyria and Babylon.

SAFETY (50) [SAFE]

Dt 12:10 from your enemies all around so that you live in s,
33:12 The beloved of the LORD rests in s—
33:28 in s, untroubled is Jacob's abode in a land of grain
1Sa 12:11 on every side; and you lived in s.
20:13 and send you away, so that you may go in s.
2Sa 19:24 the king left until the day he came back in s.
1Ki 4:25 in s, from Dan even to Beer-sheba, all of them
2Ch 19: 1 of Judah returned in s to his house in Jerusalem.
Job 5: 4 Their children are far from s,
5:11 and those who mourn are lifted to s.
11:18 you will be protected and take your rest in s.
Ps 4: 8 for you alone, O LORD, make me lie down in s.

Ps 12: 5 "I will place them in the s for which they long."
78:53 He led them in s, so that they were not afraid;
Pr 11:14 but in an abundance of counselors there is s.
11:15 but there is s in refusing to do so.
Isa 10:31 the inhabitants of Gebim flee for s.
14:30 and the needy lie down in s;
Jer 4: 6 Raise a standard toward Zion, flee for s,
6: 1 Flee for s, O children of Benjamin,
23: 6 be saved and Israel will live in s.
32:37 and I will settle them in s.
33:16 be saved and Jerusalem will live in s.
Eze 28:26 They shall live in s in it,
28:26 They shall live in s, when I execute judgments
34:28 of the land devour them; they shall live in s,
38: 8 from the nations and now are living in s,
38:11 I will fall upon the quiet people who live in s,
Hos 2:18 and I will make you lie down in s.
Zec 8:10 nor was there any s from the foe
Ac 27:24 God has granted s to all those who are sailing
28: 1 After we had reached s, we then learned that
Tob 5:17 my son, accompany you both for your s."
6:18 of heaven that mercy and s may be granted to you.
8: 4 implore our Lord that he grant us mercy and s."
8:21 Take at once half of what I own and return in s
14: 7 they will go to Jerusalem and live in s forever in
Jdt 11: 3 In any event, you have come to s.
Sir 3: 1 act accordingly, that you may be kept in s.
40: 7 At the moment he reaches s he wakes up,
1Mc 2:44 the survivors fled to the Gentiles for s.
5:54 because they had returned in s;
6:53 those who had found s in Judea from
10:83 the temple of their idol, for s.
14:37 in it and fortified it for the s of the country and of
2Mc 12:24 With great guile he begged them to let him go in s,
15: 1 to attack them with complete s on the day of rest.
1Es 5: 2 to Jerusalem in s, with the music of drums
4Mc 9: 4 which insures our s through transgression of
15: 8 of the fear of God she disdained the temporary s

SAFFRON (1)

SS 4:14 nard and s, calamus and cinnamon, with all trees

SAGES (8)

Est 1:13 Then the king consulted the s who knew the laws
Job 15:18 what s have told, and their ancestors have
Isa 19:11 How can you say to Pharaoh, "I am one of the s,
19:12 Where now are your s?
Jer 50:35 and against her officials and her s!
51:57 I will make her officials and her s drunk,
Mt 23:34 Therefore I send you prophets, s, and scribes,
Sir 8: 8 Do not slight the discourse of the s,

SAID‡ (4322) [SAY]

Ge 1: 3 God s, "Let there be light"; and there was light.
1: 6 And God s, "Let there be a dome in the midst of
1: 9 And God s, "Let the waters under the sky
1:11 Then God s, "Let the earth put forth vegetation:
1:14 And God s, "Let there be lights in the dome of
1:20 And God s, "Let the waters bring forth swarms
1:24 And God s, "Let the earth bring forth living
1:26 Then God s, "Let us make humankind
1:28 God blessed them, and God s to them,
1:29 God s, "See, I have given you every plant yielding
2:18 Then the LORD God s, "It is not good that
2:23 Then the man s, "This at last is bone of my bones
3: 1 He s to the woman, "Did God say,
3: 2 The woman s to the serpent,
3: 3 but God s, 'You shall not eat of the fruit of
3: 4 But the serpent s to the woman, "You will not die;
3: 9 the LORD God called to the man, and s to him,
3:10 He s, "I heard the sound of you in the garden,
3:11 He s, "Who told you that you were naked?
3:12 The man s, "The woman whom you gave to be
3:13 Then the LORD God s to the woman,
3:13 The woman s, "The serpent tricked me, and I ate."
3:14 The LORD God s to the serpent,
3:16 To the woman he s, "I will greatly increase your
3:17 And to the man he s, "Because you have listened
3:22 Then the LORD God s, "See,
4: 6 The LORD s to Cain, "Why are you angry,
4: 8 Cain s to his brother Abel,
4: 9 LORD s to Cain, "Where is your brother Abel?"
4: 9 He s, "I do not know; am I my brother's keeper?"
4:10 And the LORD s, "What have you done?
4:13 Cain s to the LORD, "My punishment is greater
4:15 Then the LORD s to him, "Not so!
4:23 Lamech s to his wives: "Adah
4:25 and she bore a son and named him Seth, for she s,
6: 3 Then the LORD s, "My spirit shall not abide
6: 7 So the LORD s, "I will blot out from the earth
6:13 And God s to Noah, "I have determined to make
7: 1 Then the LORD s to Noah, "Go into the ark,
8:15 Then God s to Noah,
8:21 the LORD s in his heart, "I will never again curse
9: 1 God blessed Noah and his sons, and s to them,
9: 8 Then God s to Noah and to his sons with him,
9:12 God s, "This is the sign of the covenant
9:17 God s to Noah, "This is the sign of the covenant
9:25 he s, "Cursed be Canaan; lowest of slaves
9:26 also s, "Blessed by the LORD my God be Shem;
10: 9 therefore it is s, "Like Nimrod a mighty hunter
11: 3 And they s to one another, "Come,
11: 4 Then they s, "Come, let us build ourselves a city,
11: 6 And the LORD s, "Look, they are one people,
12: 1 Now the LORD s to Abram,

Ge 12: 7 Then the LORD appeared to Abram, and s,
12:11 he was about to enter Egypt, he s to his wife Sarai,
12:18 So Pharaoh called Abram, and s,
13: 8 Then Abram s to Lot, "Let there be no strife
13:14 The LORD s to Abram, after Lot had separated
14:19 He blessed him and s, "Blessed be Abram
14:21 Then the king of Sodom s to Abram,
14:22 But Abram s to the king of Sodom,
15: 2 But Abram s, "O Lord GOD,
15: 3 And Abram s, "You have given me no offspring,
15: 5 He brought him outside and s,
15: 5 Then he s to him, "So shall your descendants be."
15: 7 Then he s to him, "I am the LORD who brought you
15: 8 But he s, "O Lord GOD,
15: 9 He s to him, "Bring me a heifer three years old,
15:13 Then the LORD s to Abram,
16: 2 and Sarai s to Abram, "You see that
16: 5 Then Sarai s to Abram, "May the wrong done
16: 6 But Abram s to Sarai, "Your slave-girl is
16: 8 And he s, "Hagar, slave-girl of Sarai,
16: 8 She s, "I am running away
16: 9 The angel of the LORD s to her,
16:10 The angel of the LORD also s to her,
16:11 And the angel of the LORD s to her,
16:13 for she s, "Have I really seen God
17: 1 the LORD appeared to Abram, and s to him,
17: 3 Then Abram fell on his face; and God s to him,
17: 9 God s to Abraham, "As for you,
17:15 God s to Abraham, "As for Sarai your wife,
17:17 Then Abraham fell on his face and laughed, and s
17:18 And Abraham s to God, "O that Ishmael might
17:19 God s, "No, but your wife Sarah shall bear you
17:23 as God had s to him.
18: 3 He s, "My lord, if I find favor with you,
18: 5 So they s, "Do as you have s."
18: 6 Abraham hastened into the tent to Sarah, and s,
18: 9 They s to him, "Where is your wife Sarah?"
18: 9 And he s, "There, in the tent."
18:10 Then one s, "I will surely return to you
18:13 The LORD s to Abraham, "Why did Sarah laugh,
18:15 He s, "Oh yes, you did laugh."
18:17 The LORD s, "Shall I hide
18:20 Then the LORD s, "How great is the outcry
18:23 Then Abraham came near and s,
18:26 the LORD s, "If I find at Sodom fifty righteous in
18:28 And he s, "I will not destroy it
18:30 he s, "Oh do not let the Lord be angry if I speak.
18:31 He s, "Let me take it upon myself to speak to
18:32 Then he s, "Oh do not let the Lord be angry
19: 2 He s, "Please, my lords, turn aside
19: 2 They s, "No; we will spend the night
19: 7 and s, "I beg you, my brothers, do not act
19: 9 And they s, "This fellow came here as an alien,
19:12 the men s to Lot, "Have you anyone else here?
19:14 So Lot went out and s to his sons-in-law,
19:17 When they had brought them outside, they s,
19:18 And Lot s to them, "Oh, no, my lords;
19:21 He s to him, "Very well, I grant you this favor too,
19:31 And the firstborn s to the younger,
19:34 On the next day, the firstborn s to the younger,
20: 2 Abraham s of his wife Sarah,
20: 3 and s to him, "You are about to die because of
20: 4 he s, "Lord, will you destroy an innocent people?
20: 5 And she herself s, 'He is my brother.'
20: 6 Then God s to him in the dream, "Yes,
20: 9 Then Abimelech called Abraham, and s to him,
20:10 And Abimelech s to Abraham,
20:11 Abraham s, "I did it because I thought,
20:13 I s to her, 'This is the kindness you must do me:
20:15 Abimelech s, "My land is before you;
20:16 To Sarah he s, "Look, I have given your brother
21: 1 The LORD dealt with Sarah as he had s,
21: 6 Now Sarah s, "God has brought laughter for me;
21: 7 And she s, "Who would ever have said
21: 7 "Who would ever have s to Abraham
21:10 So she s to Abraham, "Cast out this slave woman
21:12 But God s to Abraham, "Do not be distressed
21:16 for she s, "Do not let me look on the death of
21:17 and s to her, "What troubles you, Hagar?
21:22 s to Abraham, "God is with you in all that you do;
21:24 And Abraham s, "I swear it."
21:26 Abimelech s, "I do not know who has done this;
21:29 And Abimelech s to Abraham,
21:30 He s, "These seven ewe lambs you shall accept
22: 1 He s to him, "Abraham!"
22: 1 And he s, "Here I am."
22: 2 He s, "Take your son, your only son Isaac,
22: 5 Then Abraham s to his young men,
22: 7 Isaac s to his father Abraham, "Father!"
22: 7 And he s, "Here I am, my son."
22: 7 He s, "The fire and the wood are here,
22: 8 Abraham s, "God himself will provide the lamb
22:11 and s, "Abraham, Abraham!"
22:11 And he s, "Here I am."
22:12 He s, "Do not lay your hand on the boy
22:14 as it is s to this day,
22:16 and s, "By myself I have sworn, says the LORD:
23: 3 up from beside his dead, and s to the Hittites,
23: 8 He s to them, "If you are willing
23:13 He s to Ephron in the hearing of the people of
24: 2 Abraham s to his servant, the oldest of his house,
24: 5 The servant s to him, "Perhaps the woman may
24: 6 Abraham s to him, "See to it that you do
24:12 And he s, "O LORD, God of my master
24:17 Then the servant ran to meet her and s,
24:18 she s, and quickly lowered her jar upon her hand
24:19 When she had finished giving him a drink, she s,

Ge 24:23 and s, "Tell me whose daughter you are.
24:24 She s to him, "I am the daughter of Bethuel son
24:27 and s, "Blessed be the LORD, the God
24:31 He s, "Come in, O blessed of the LORD.
24:33 he s, "I will not eat until I have told my errand."
24:33 He s, "Speak on."
24:34 So he s, "I am Abraham's servant.
24:39 I s to my master, 'Perhaps the woman will
24:40 But he s to me, 'The LORD, before whom I walk,
24:42 "I came today to the spring, and s, 'O LORD,
24:45 I s to her, 'Please let me drink.'
24:46 and s, 'Drink, and I will also water your camels.'
24:47 She s, 'The daughter of Bethuel, Nahor's son,
24:54 When they rose in the morning, he s,
24:55 Her brother and her mother s,
24:56 But he s to them, "Do not delay me,
24:57 They s, "We will call the girl, and ask her."
24:58 And they called Rebekah, and s to her,
24:58 "Will you go with this man?" She s, "I will."
24:60 And they blessed Rebekah and s to her, "May you,
24:65 and s to the servant, "Who is the man
24:65 The servant s, "It is my master."
25:22 and she s, "If it is to be this way, why do I live?"
25:23 And the LORD s to her, "Two nations are
25:30 Esau s to Jacob, "Let me eat some of that red stuff,
25:31 Jacob s, "First sell me your birthright."
25:32 Esau s, "I am about to die;
25:33 Jacob s, "Swear to me first."
26: 2 The LORD appeared to Isaac and s,
26: 7 men of the place asked him about his wife, he s,
26: 9 So Abimelech called for Isaac, and s,
26: 9 Isaac s to him, "Because I thought I might die
26:10 Abimelech s, "What is this you have done to us?
26:16 And Abimelech s to Isaac, "Go away from us;
26:24 that very night the LORD appeared to him and s,
26:27 Isaac s to them, "Why have you come to me,
26:28 They s, "We see plainly that the LORD has been
26:32 and s to him, "We have found water!"
27: 1 he called his elder son Esau and s to him,
27: 2 He s, "See, I am old;
27: 6 Rebekah s to her son Jacob,
27:11 But Jacob s to his mother Rebekah, "Look,
27:13 His mother s to him, "Let your curse be on me,
27:18 So he went in to his father, and s, "My father";
27:18 and he s, "Here I am; who are you, my son?"
27:19 Jacob s to his father, "I am Esau your firstborn.
27:20 But Isaac s to his son,
27:21 Then Isaac s to Jacob, "Come near,
27:22 who felt him and s, "The voice is Jacob's voice,
27:24 He s, "Are you really my son Esau?"
27:25 Then he s, "Bring it to me,
27:26 Then his father Isaac s to him,
27:27 and blessed him, and s, "Ah,
27:31 And he s to his father,
27:32 His father Isaac s to him, "Who are you?"
27:33 Then Isaac trembled violently, and s,
27:34 and s to his father, "Bless me, me also, father!"
27:35 But he s, "Your brother came deceitfully,
27:36 Esau s, "Is he not rightly named Jacob?
27:36 he s, "Have you not reserved a blessing for me?"
27:38 Esau s to his father, "Have you only one blessing,
27:41 and Esau s to himself, "The days of mourning
27:42 so she sent and called her younger son Jacob and s
27:46 Then Rebekah s to Isaac, "I am weary of my life
28:13 And the LORD stood beside him and s,
28:16 Then Jacob woke from his sleep and s,
28:17 he was afraid, and s, "How awesome is this place!
29: 4 Jacob s to them, "My brothers,
29: 4 They s, "We are from Haran."
29: 5 He s to them, "Do you know Laban son
29: 5 "Do you know Laban son of Nahor?" They s,
29: 6 He s to them, "Is it well with him?"
29: 7 He s, "Look, it is still broad daylight;
29: 8 But they s, "We cannot until all
29:14 and Laban s to him, "Surely you are my bone
29:15 Then Laban s to Jacob,
29:18 Jacob loved Rachel; so he s,
29:19 Laban s, "It is better that I give her to you than
29:21 Then Jacob s to Laban, "Give me my wife
29:25 it was Leah! And Jacob s to Laban,
29:26 Laban s, "This is not done in our country—
29:32 for she s, "Because the LORD has looked
29:33 She conceived again and bore a son, and s,
29:34 Again she conceived and bore a son, and s,
29:35 She conceived again and bore a son, and s,
30: 1 she s to Jacob, "Give me children, or I shall die!"
30: 2 Jacob became very angry with Rachel and s,
30: 3 Then she s, "Here is my maid Bilhah;
30: 6 Then Rachel s, "God has judged me,
30: 8 Then Rachel s, "With mighty wrestlings
30:11 And Leah s, "Good fortune!"
30:13 And Leah s, "Happy am I!
30:14 Then Rachel s to Leah, "Please give me some
30:15 But she s to her, "Is it a small matter
30:15 Rachel s, "Then he may lie with you tonight
30:16 Leah went out to meet him, and s,
30:18 Leah s, "God has given me my hire
30:20 Leah s, "God has endowed me with a good dowry;
30:23 She conceived and bore a son, and s,
30:25 When Rachel had borne Joseph, Jacob s to Laban,
30:27 But Laban s to him, "If you will allow me to say
30:29 Jacob s to him, "You yourself know
30:31 He s, "What shall I give you?"
30:31 Jacob s, "You shall not give me anything;
30:34 Laban s, "Good! Let it be as you have said."
30:34 Laban said, "Good! Let it be as you have s."
31: 3 Then the LORD s to Jacob,

Ge 31: 5 and s to them, "I see that your father does
31: 8 If he s, 'The speckled shall be your wages,'
31: 8 and if he s, 'The striped shall be your wages,'
31:11 Then the angel of God s to me in the dream,
31:11 'Jacob,' and I s, 'Here I am!'
31:12 And he s, 'Look up and see that all the goats
31:16 now then, do whatever God has s to you."
31:24 by night, and s to him, "Take heed that you say not
31:26 Laban s to Jacob, "What have you done?
31:35 And she s to her father,
31:36 Jacob s to Laban, "What is my offense?
31:43 Then Laban answered and s to Jacob,
31:46 And Jacob s to his kinsfolk, "Gather stones,"
31:48 Laban s, "This heap is a witness between you
31:49 for he s, "The LORD watch between you and me,
31:51 Then Laban s to Jacob, "See this heap and see
32: 2 and when Jacob saw them he s,
32: 9 And Jacob s, "O God of my father Abraham
32: 9 O LORD who s to me,
32:12 Yet you have s, 'I will surely do you good,
32:16 and s to his servants, "Pass on ahead of me,
32:26 Then he s, "Let me go, for the day is breaking."
32:26 But Jacob s, "I will not let you go,
32:27 So he s to him, "What is your name?"
32:27 "What is your name?" And he s, "Jacob."
32:28 the man s, "You shall no longer be called Jacob,
32:29 But he s, "Why is it that you ask my name?"
33: 5 he s, "Who are these with you?"
33: 5 "Who are these with you?" Jacob s,
33: 8 Esau s, "What do you mean by all this company
33: 9 But Esau s, "I have enough, my brother;
33:10 Jacob s, "No, please; if I find favor with you,
33:12 Then Esau s, "Let us journey on our way,
33:13 But Jacob s to him, "My lord knows that
33:15 So Esau s, "Let me leave with you some of
33:15 But he s, "Why should my lord be so kind to me?"
34:11 Shechem also s to her father and to her brothers,
34:14 They s to them, "We cannot do this thing,
34:30 Then Jacob s to Simeon and Levi,
34:31 they s, "Should our sister be treated like a whore?"
35: 1 God s to Jacob, "Arise, go up to Bethel,
35: 2 So Jacob s to his household and to all who were
35:10 God s to him, "Your name is Jacob;
35:11 God s to him, "I am God Almighty:
35:17 she was in her hard labor, the midwife s to her,
37: 6 He s to them, "Listen to this dream that I dreamed.
37: 8 His brothers s to him, "Are you indeed to reign
37:10 his father rebuked him, and s to him,
37:13 And Israel s to Joseph, "Are not your brothers
37:14 So he s to him, "Go now,
37:16 "I am seeking my brothers," he s;
37:17 The man s, "They have gone away,
37:19 They s to one another, "Here comes this dreamer.
37:22 Reuben s to them, "Shed no blood;
37:26 Then Judah s to his brothers,
37:30 He returned to his brothers, and s,
37:32 and they s, "This we have found;
37:33 He recognized it, and s, "It is my son's robe!
37:35 but he refused to be comforted, and s, "No,
38: 8 Then Judah s to Onan, "Go in to your brother's
38:11 Then Judah s to his daughter-in-law Tamar,
38:16 He went over to her at the road side, and s,
38:16 She s, "What will you give me,
38:17 And she s, "Only if you give me a pledge,
38:18 He s, "What pledge shall I give you?"
38:21 But they s, "No prostitute has been here."
38:22 he returned to Judah, and s, "I have not found her;
38:22 the townspeople s, 'No prostitute has been here.' "
38:24 Judah s, "Bring her out, and let her be burned."
38:25 And she s, "Take note, please, whose these are,
38:26 Then Judah acknowledged them and s,
38:29 and she s, "What a breach you have made
39: 7 his master's wife cast her eyes on Joseph and s,
39: 8 But he refused and s to his master's wife, "Look,
39:14 to the members of her household and s to them,
40: 8 They s to him, "We have had dreams,
40: 8 And Joseph s to them, "Do not interpretations
40: 9 the chief cupbearer told his dream to Joseph, and s
40:12 Then Joseph s to him, "This is its interpretation:
40:16 he s to Joseph, "I also had a dream:
41: 9 Then the chief cupbearer s to Pharaoh,
41:15 And Pharaoh s to Joseph, "I have had a dream,
41:15 I have heard it s of you that when you hear
41:17 Then Pharaoh s to Joseph, "In my dream
41:25 Then Joseph s to Pharaoh, "Pharaoh's dreams
41:38 Pharaoh s to his servants, "Can we find anyone
41:39 So Pharaoh s to Joseph, "Since God has shown
41:41 And Pharaoh s to Joseph, "See, I have set you
41:44 Moreover Pharaoh s to Joseph, "I am Pharaoh,
41:51 Joseph named the firstborn Manasseh, "For," he s,
41:54 of famine began to come, just as Joseph had s.
41:55 Pharaoh s to all the Egyptians, "Go to Joseph;
42: 1 that there was grain in Egypt, he s to his sons,
42: 2 I have heard," he s, "that there is grain in Egypt;
42: 7 "Where do you come from?" he s.
42: 7 They s, "From the land of Canaan, to buy food."
42: 9 He s to them, "You are spies;
42:10 They s to him, "No, my lord;
42:12 But he s to them, "No, you have come to see
42:13 They s, "We, your servants, are twelve brothers,
42:14 Joseph s to them, "It is just as I have said to you;
42:14 Joseph said to them, "It is just as I have s to you;
42:18 On the third day Joseph s to them,
42:21 They s to one another, "Alas,
42:28 He s to his brothers, "My money has been put
42:31 we s to him, 'We are honest men, we are not spies.
42:33 Then the man, the lord of the land, s to us,

Ge 42:36 And their father Jacob s to them,
42:37 Then Reuben s to his father,
42:38 But he s, "My son shall not go down with you,
43: 2 their father s to them, "Go again,
43: 3 But Judah s to him, "The man solemnly warned us,
43: 5 for the man s to us, 'You shall not see my face,
43: 6 Israel s, "Why did you treat me so badly as to tell
43: 8 Then Judah s to his father Israel,
43:11 Then their father Israel s to them, "If it must be so,
43:16 he s to the steward of his house,
43:17 The man did as Joseph s,
43:18 and they s, "It is because of the money,
43:20 They s, "Oh, my lord, we came down
43:27 He inquired about their welfare, and s,
43:28 They s, "Your servant our father is well;
43:29 and s, "Is this your youngest brother,
43:31 and controlling himself he s, "Serve the meal."
44: 4 Joseph s to his steward, "Go, follow after the men;
44: 7 They s to him, "Why does my lord speak such
44:10 He s, "Even so; in accordance
44:15 Joseph s to them, "What deed is this
44:16 And Judah s, "What can we say to my lord?
44:17 But he s, "Far be it from me that I should do so!
44:18 Then Judah stepped up to him and s, "O my lord,
44:20 And we s to my lord, 'We have a father,
44:21 Then you s to your servants,
44:22 We s to my lord, 'The boy cannot leave his father,
44:23 Then you s to your servants,
44:25 And when our father s, 'Go again,
44:26 we s, 'We cannot go down.
44:27 Then your servant my father s to us,
44:28 and I s, Surely he has been torn to pieces;
45: 3 Joseph s to his brothers, "I am Joseph.
45: 4 Joseph s to his brothers, "Come closer to me."
45: 4 He s, "I am your brother, Joseph,
45:17 Pharaoh s to Joseph, "Say to your brothers,
45:24 and as they were leaving he s to them,
45:27 the words of Joseph that he had s to them,
45:28 Israel s, "Enough! My son Joseph is still alive.
46: 2 God spoke to Israel in visions of the night, and s,
46: 2 And he s, "Here I am."
46: 3 Then he s, "I am God, the God of your father;
46:30 Israel s to Joseph, "I can die now,
46:31 Joseph s to his brothers and
47: 3 Pharaoh s to his brothers, "What is your
47: 3 "What is your occupation?" And they s to Pharaoh,
47: 4 They s to Pharaoh, "We have come to reside
47: 5 Then Pharaoh s to Joseph,
47: 8 Pharaoh s to Jacob, "How many are the years
47: 9 Jacob s to Pharaoh, "The years
47:15 all the Egyptians came to Joseph, and s,
47:18 they came to him the following year, and s to him,
47:23 Then Joseph s to the people,
47:25 They s, "You have saved our lives;
47:29 he called his son Joseph and s to him,
47:30 He answered, "I will do as you have s."
47:31 And he s, "Swear to me"; and he swore to him.
48: 3 And Jacob s to Joseph, "God Almighty appeared
48: 4 and s to me, 'I am going to make you fruitful
48: 8 Israel saw Joseph's sons, he s, "Who are these?"
48: 9 Joseph s to his father, "They are my sons,
48: 9 And he s, "Bring them to me, please,
48:11 Israel s to Joseph, "I did not expect
48:15 He blessed Joseph, and s, "The God
48:18 Joseph s to his father, "Not so, my father!
48:19 his father refused, and s, "I know, my son, I know;
48:21 Then Israel s to Joseph, "I am about to die,
49: 1 Then Jacob called his sons, and s:
49:28 and this is what their father s to them
50: 5 he s, 'I am about to die.
50:11 they s, "This is a grievous mourning on the part of
50:15 Joseph's brothers s, "What if Joseph still bears
50:18 and s, "We are here as your slaves."
50:19 But Joseph s to them, "Do not be afraid!
50:24 Then Joseph s to his brothers, "I am about to die;
Ex 1: 9 He s to his people, "Look,
1:15 The king of Egypt s to the Hebrew midwives,
1:18 of Egypt summoned the midwives and s to them,
1:19 The midwives s to Pharaoh,
2: 6 be one of the Hebrews' children," she s.
2: 7 Then his sister s to Pharaoh's daughter,
2: 8 Pharaoh's daughter s to her, "Yes."
2: 9 Pharaoh's daughter s to her, "Take this child
2:10 She named him Moses, "because," she s,
2:13 and he s to the one who was in the wrong,
2:18 When they returned to their father Reuel, he s,
2:19 They s, "An Egyptian helped us against
2:20 He s to his daughters, "Where is he?
2:22 for he s, "I have been an alien residing in
3: 3 Then Moses s, "I must turn aside and look
3: 4 And he s, "Here I am."
3: 5 Then he s, "Come no closer!
3: 6 He s further, "I am the God of your father,
3: 7 Then the LORD s, "I have observed the misery
3:11 But Moses s to God, "Who am I that I should go
3:12 He s, "I will be with you;
3:13 But Moses s to God, "If I come to the Israelites
3:14 God s to Moses, "I AM WHO I AM."
3:14 He s further, "Thus you shall say to the Israelites,
3:15 God also s to Moses, "Thus you shall say to
4: 2 The LORD s to him, "What is that in your hand?"
4: 2 "What is that in your hand?" He s,
4: 3 And he s, "Throw it on the ground."
4: 4 Then the LORD s to Moses, "Reach out your hand,
4: 6 Again, the LORD s to him, "Put your hand
4: 7 God s, "Put your hand back into your cloak"—
4:10 But Moses s to the LORD, "O my Lord,

Ex 4:11 LORD s to him, "Who gives speech to mortals?
4:13 But he s, "O my Lord, please send someone else."
4:14 the LORD was kindled against Moses and he s,
4:18 Moses went back to his father-in-law Jethro and s
4:18 And Jethro s to Moses, "Go in peace."
4:19 LORD s to Moses in Midian, "Go back to Egypt;
4:21 And the LORD s to Moses, "When you go back
4:23 I s to you, "Let my son go
4:25 and touched Moses' feet with it, and s,
4:26 It was then she s, "A bridegroom of blood
4:27 The LORD s to Aaron, "Go into the wilderness
5: 1 and Aaron went to Pharaoh and s,
5: 2 But Pharaoh s, "Who is the LORD,
5: 3 Then they s, "The God of the Hebrews
5: 4 But the king of Egypt s to them,
5:10 and the supervisors of the people went out and s to
5:17 He s, "You are lazy, lazy;
5:21 They s to them, "The LORD look upon you
5:22 Then Moses turned again to the LORD and s,
6: 1 Then the LORD s to Moses, "Now you shall see
6: 2 God also spoke to Moses and s to him:
6:26 and Moses to whom the LORD s,
6:29 he s to him, "I am the LORD;
6:30 But Moses s in the LORD's presence,
7: 1 The LORD s to Moses, "See,
7: 8 The LORD s to Moses and Aaron,
7:13 not listen to them, as the LORD had s.
7:14 LORD s to Moses, "Pharaoh's heart is hardened;
7:19 The LORD s to Moses, "Say to Aaron,
7:22 to them; as the LORD had s.
8: 1 Then the LORD s to Moses, "Go to Pharaoh
8: 5 And the LORD s to Moses, "Say to Aaron,
8: 8 Then Pharaoh called Moses and Aaron, and s,
8: 9 Moses s to Pharaoh, "Kindly tell me when I am
8:10 And he s, "Tomorrow." Moses s, "As you say!
8:15 just as the LORD had s.
8:16 Then the LORD s to Moses, "Say to Aaron,
8:19 And the magicians s to Pharaoh,
8:19 just as the LORD had s.
8:20 Then the LORD s to Moses,
8:25 Pharaoh summoned Moses and Aaron, and s,
8:26 But Moses s, "It would not be right to do so;
8:28 So Pharaoh s, "I will let you go to sacrifice to
8:29 Then Moses s, "As soon as I leave you,
9: 1 Then the LORD s to Moses, "Go to Pharaoh,
9: 8 Then the LORD s to Moses and Aaron,
9:13 Then the LORD s to Moses, "Rise up early
9:22 The LORD s to Moses, "Stretch out your hand
9:27 and s to them, "This time I have sinned;
9:29 Moses s to him, "As soon as I have gone out of
10: 1 Then the LORD s to Moses, "Go to Pharaoh;
10: 3 Moses and Aaron went to Pharaoh, and s to him,
10: 7 Pharaoh's officials s to him, "How long
10: 8 and Aaron were brought back to Pharaoh, and he s
10: 9 Moses s, "We will go with our young and our old;
10:10 He s to them, "The LORD indeed will be
10:12 Then the LORD s to Moses, "Stretch out your hand
10:16 and Aaron and s, "I have sinned against
10:21 Then the LORD s to Moses, "Stretch out your hand
10:24 Then Pharaoh summoned Moses, and s, "Go,
10:25 But Moses s, "You must also let us have sacrifices
10:28 Then Pharaoh s to him, "Get away from me!
10:29 Moses s, "Just as you say!
11: 1 The LORD s to Moses, "I will bring one more
11: 4 Moses s, "Thus says the LORD:
11: 9 The LORD s to Moses, "Pharaoh will not listen
12: 1 The LORD s to Moses and Aaron in the land
12:21 Moses called all the elders of Israel and s to them,
12:31 and s, "Rise up, go away from my people,
12:31 Go, worship the LORD, as you s.
12:32 Take your flocks and your herds, as you s,
12:33 for they s, "We shall all be dead."
12:43 The LORD s to Moses and Aaron:
13: 1 The LORD s to Moses:
13: 3 Moses s to the people, "Remember this day
14: 1 Then the LORD s to Moses:
14: 5 and they s, "What have we done,
14:11 They s to Moses, "Was it
14:13 But Moses s to the people, "Do not be afraid,
14:15 LORD s to Moses, "Why do you cry out to me?
14:25 The Egyptians s, "Let us flee from the Israelites,
14:26 Then the LORD s to Moses, "Stretch out your
15: 9 The enemy s, 'I will pursue, I will overtake,
15:26 He s, "If you will listen carefully to the voice of
16: 3 The Israelites s to them, "If only we had died by
16: 4 Then the LORD s to Moses,
16: 6 So Moses and Aaron s to all the Israelites,
16: 8 And Moses s, "When the LORD gives you meat
16: 9 Then Moses s to Aaron, "Say to
16:11 The LORD spoke to Moses and s,
16:15 When the Israelites saw it, they s to one another,
16:15 Moses s to them, "It is the bread that
16:19 And Moses s to them, "Let no one leave any of it
16:23 he s to them, "This is what
16:25 Moses s, "Eat it today, for today is a sabbath to
16:28 The LORD s to Moses,
16:32 Moses s, "This is what the LORD has commanded:
16:33 And Moses s to Aaron, "Take a jar,
17: 2 The people quarreled with Moses, and s,
17: 2 Moses s to them, "Why do you quarrel with me?
17: 3 and the people complained against Moses and s,
17: 5 The LORD s to Moses, "Go on ahead of
17: 9 Moses s to Joshua, "Choose some men for us
17:14 Then the LORD s to Moses,
17:16 He s, "A hand upon the banner of the LORD!
18: 3 The name of the one was Gershom (for he s,
18: 4 the name of the other, Eliezer (for he s, "The God

Ex 18:10 Jethro s, "Blessed be the LORD,
18:14 the people, he s, "What is this that you are doing
18:15 Moses s to his father-in-law,
18:17 Moses' father-in-law s to him,
18:24 to his father-in-law and did all that he had s.
19: 9 Then the LORD s to Moses,
19:10 the LORD s to Moses: "Go to the
19:15 And he s to the people, "Prepare for the third day;
19:21 Then the LORD s to Moses,
19:23 Moses s to the LORD, "The people are
19:24 The LORD s to him, "Go down,
20:19 s to Moses, "You speak to us, and we will listen;
20:20 Moses s to the people, "Do not be afraid;
20:22 The LORD s to Moses: Thus you shall say to the
23:13 Be attentive to all that I have s to you.
24: 1 Then he s to Moses, "Come up to the LORD,
24: 3 and all the people answered with one voice, and s,
24: 7 of the people; and they s, "All that
24: 8 and dashed it on the people, and s, "See the blood
24:12 The LORD s to Moses, "Come up to me on
24:14 To the elders he had s, "Wait here for us,
25: 1 The LORD s to Moses:
30:34 The LORD s to Moses: Take sweet spices,
31:12 The LORD s to Moses:
32: 1 the people gathered around Aaron, and s to him,
32: 2 Aaron s to them, "Take off the gold rings that are
32: 4 and they s, "These are your gods, O Israel,
32: 5 and Aaron made proclamation and s,
32: 7 The LORD s to Moses, "Go down at once!
32: 8 and have worshiped it and sacrificed to it, and s,
32: 9 The LORD s to Moses, "I have seen this people,
32:11 But Moses implored the LORD his God, and s,
32:17 as they shouted, he s to Moses, "There is a noise
32:18 But he s, "It is not the sound made by victors,
32:21 Moses s to Aaron, "What did this people do to you
32:22 And Aaron s, "Do not let the anger
32:23 They s to me, 'Make us gods,
32:24 So I s to them, 'Whoever has gold, take it off';
32:26 and s, "Who is on the LORD's side?
32:27 He s to them, "Thus says the LORD,
32:29 Moses s, "Today you have ordained yourselves for
32:30 On the next day Moses s to the people,
32:31 So Moses returned to the LORD and s, "Alas,
32:33 But the LORD s to Moses,
33: 1 The LORD s to Moses, "Go, leave this place,
33: 5 For the LORD had s to Moses,
33:12 Moses s to the LORD, "See, you have s to me,
33:12 Yet you have s, 'I know you by name,
33:14 He s, "My presence will go with you,
33:15 And he s to him, "If your presence will not go,
33:17 The LORD s to Moses, "I will do the very thing
33:18 Moses s, "Show me your glory, I pray."
33:19 And he s, "I will make all my goodness pass
33:20 But," he s, "you cannot see my face;
34: 1 The LORD s to Moses, "Cut two tablets of stone
34: 9 He s, "If now I have found favor in your sight,
34:10 He s: I hereby make a covenant.
34:27 The LORD s to Moses: Write these words;
35: 1 the congregation of the Israelites and s to them:
35: 4 Moses s to all the congregation of the Israelites:
35:30 Then Moses s to the Israelites:
36: 5 and s to Moses, "The people are bringing much
Lev 8: 5 Moses s to the congregation,
8:31 And Moses s to Aaron and his sons,
9: 2 He s to Aaron, "Take a bull calf for a sin offering
9: 6 And Moses s, "This is the thing that
9: 7 Then Moses s to Aaron, "Draw near to the altar
10: 3 Then Moses s to Aaron, "This is what
10: 3 "This is what the LORD meant when he s,
10: 4 sons of Uzziel the uncle of Aaron, and s to them,
10: 6 And Moses s to Aaron and to his sons Eleazar
10:16 Aaron's remaining sons, and s,
16: 2 The LORD s to Moses: Tell your brother Aaron
17:12 Therefore I have s to the people of Israel:
17:14 therefore I have s to the people of Israel:
20:24 But I have s to you: You shall inherit
21: 1 The LORD s to Moses: Speak to the priests,
24:13 The LORD s to Moses, saying:
Nu 1:48 The LORD had s to Moses:
3:40 Then the LORD s to Moses: Enroll all the
7: 4 Then the LORD s to Moses:
7:11 The LORD s to Moses: They shall present their
9: 7 and s to him, "Although we are unclean
10:29 Moses s to Hobab son of Reuel the Midianite,
10:29 for the place of which the LORD s, 'I will give it
10:30 But he s to him, "I will not go,
10:31 He s, "Do not leave us, for you know
11: 4 and the Israelites also wept again, and s,
11:11 So Moses s to the LORD, "Why have you
11:16 So the LORD s to Moses, "Gather for me
11:21 But Moses s, "The people I am with
11:23 The LORD s to Moses, "Is the LORD's power
11:28 the assistant of Moses, one of his chosen men, s,
11:29 Moses s to him, "Are you jealous for my sake?
12: 2 and they s, "Has the LORD spoken only
12: 4 Suddenly the LORD s to Moses, Aaron,
12: 6 And he s, "Hear my words:
12:11 Then Aaron s to Moses, "Oh, my lord,
12:14 But the LORD s to Moses, "If her father
13: 1 The LORD s to Moses,
13:17 and s to them, "Go up there into the Negeb,
13:30 But Caleb quieted the people before Moses, and s,
13:31 Then the men who had gone up with him s,
14: 2 the whole congregation s to them,
14: 4 So they s to one another, "Let us choose a captain,
14: 7 and s to all the congregation of the Israelites,
14:11 And the LORD s to Moses, "How long

Nu 14:13 But Moses s to the LORD, "Then the Egyptians
14:20 LORD s, "I do forgive, just as you have asked;
14:31 your little ones, who you s would become booty,
14:41 But Moses s, "Why do you continue to transgress
15:35 Then the LORD s to Moses, "The man shall be put
15:37 The LORD s to Moses:
16: 3 and s to them, "You have gone too far!
16: 5 Then he s to Korah and all his company,
16: 8 Then Moses s to Korah, "Hear now, you Levites!
16:12 but they s, "We will not come!
16:15 Moses was very angry and s to the LORD,
16:16 And Moses s to Korah, "As for you
16:22 They fell on their faces, and s, "O God,
16:26 He s to the congregation, "Turn away from
16:28 And Moses s, "This is how you shall know that
16:34 for they s, "The earth will swallow us too!"
16:40 just as the LORD had s to him through Moses.
16:46 Moses s to Aaron, "Take your censer,
17:10 And the LORD s to Moses, "Put back the staff
17:12 The Israelites s to Moses, "We are perishing;
18: 1 The LORD s to Aaron: You and your sons
18:20 Then the LORD s to Aaron: You shall have no
18:24 Therefore I have s of them that they shall have no
20: 3 The people quarreled with Moses and s,
20:10 and he s to them, "Listen, you rebels,
20:12 But the LORD s to Moses and Aaron,
20:18 But Edom s to him, "You shall not pass through,
20:19 Israelites s to him, "We will stay on the highway;
20:20 But he s, "You shall not pass through."
20:23 the LORD s to Moses and Aaron at Mount Hor,
21: 2 Then Israel made a vow to the LORD and s,
21: 7 The people came to Moses and s,
21: 8 And the LORD s to Moses, "Make a poisonous
21:14 Wherefore it is s in the Book of the Wars of
21:16 that is the well of which the LORD s to Moses,
21:34 the LORD s to Moses, "Do not be afraid of him;
22: 4 And Moab s to the elders of Midian,
22: 8 He s to them, "Stay here tonight,
22: 9 God came to Balaam and s, "Who are these men
22:10 Balaam s to God, "King Balak son of Zippor
22:12 God s to Balaam, "You shall not go with them;
22:13 and s to the officials of Balak,
22:14 officials of Moab rose and went to Balak, and s,
22:16 They came to Balaam and s to him,
22:20 That night God came to Balaam and s to him,
22:28 and it s to Balaam, "What have I done to you,
22:29 Balaam s to the donkey, "Because you have made
22:30 But the donkey s to Balaam, "Am I not your
22:30 And he s, "No."
22:32 The angel of the LORD s to him,
22:34 Then Balaam s to the angel of the LORD,
22:35 The angel of the LORD s to Balaam,
22:37 Balak s to Balaam, "Did I not send
22:38 Balaam s to Balak, "I have come to you now,
23: 1 Then Balaam s to Balak, "Build me seven altars
23: 2 Balak did as Balaam had s;
23: 3 Then Balaam s to Balak, "Stay here
23: 4 Then God met Balaam; and Balaam s to him,
23: 5 The LORD put a word in Balaam's mouth, and s,
23:11 Balak s to Balaam, "What have you done to me?
23:13 So Balak s to him, "Come with me
23:15 Balaam s to Balak, "Stand here
23:16 put a word into his mouth, and s,
23:17 Balak s to him, "What has the LORD s?"
23:23 now it shall be s of Jacob and Israel,
23:25 Then Balak s to Balaam, "Do not curse them at all,
23:27 So Balak s to Balaam, "Come now,
23:29 Balaam s to Balak, "Build me seven altars here,
23:30 So Balak did as Balaam had s,
24:10 Balak s to Balaam, "I summoned you
24:11 I s, 'I will reward you richly,'
24:12 And Balaam s to Balak, "Did I not tell
25: 4 The LORD s to Moses, "Take all the chiefs of
25: 5 And Moses s to the judges of Israel,
25:16 The LORD s to Moses,
26: 1 After the plague the LORD s to Moses and
26:65 For the LORD had s of them,
27: 2 at the entrance of the tent of meeting, and they s,
27:12 The LORD s to Moses, "Go up this mountain of
27:18 So the LORD s to Moses, "Take Joshua
30: 1 Moses s to the heads of the tribes of the Israelites:
30:11 and her husband heard it and s nothing to her,
30:14 he has validated them, because he s nothing to her
31: 3 So Moses s to the people, "Arm some of your
31:15 Moses s to them, "Have you allowed all
31:21 the priest s to the troops who had gone to battle:
31:49 and s to Moses, "Your servants have counted
32: 6 But Moses s to the Gadites and to the Reubenites,
32:16 Then they came up to him and s,
32:20 So Moses s to them, "If you do this—
32:25 Then the Gadites and the Reubenites s to Moses,
32:29 And Moses s to them, "If the Gadites and
36: 2 they s, "The LORD commanded my lord to give
Dt 1: 9 At that time I s to you, "I am unable
1:20 I s to you, "You have reached the hill country of
1:22 All of you came to me and s,
1:25 They brought back a report to us, and s,
1:27 you grumbled in your tents and s,
1:29 I s to you, "Have no dread or fear of them.
1:42 The LORD s to me, "Say to them,
2: 2 Then the LORD s to me:
2: 9 the LORD s to me: "Do not harass Moab
2:31 The LORD s to me, "See, I have begun
3: 2 The LORD s to me, "Do not fear him,
3:26 The LORD s to me, "Enough from you!
4:10 when the LORD s to me, "Assemble the people
5: 1 Moses convened all Israel, and s to them:

Dt 5: 5 not go up the mountain.) And he s:
5:24 and you s, "Look, the LORD our God has shown us
5:28 and the LORD s to me: "I have heard
9: 2 You have heard it s of them, "Who can stand
9:12 Then the LORD s to me, "Get up,
9:13 Furthermore the LORD s to me, "I have seen
9:26 I prayed to the LORD and s, "Lord GOD,
10: 1 At that time the LORD s to me,
10:11 The LORD s to me, "Get up,
13:12 If you hear it s about one of the towns that
17:16 since the LORD has s to you,
18:16 at Horeb on the day of the assembly when you s:
18:17 "They are right in what they have s.
29: 2 Moses summoned all Israel and s to them:
31: 2 he s to them: "I am now one hundred twenty
31: 7 Then Moses summoned Joshua and s to him in
31:14 The LORD s to Moses, "Your time to die is near;
31:16 The LORD s to Moses, "Soon you will lie down
31:23 LORD commissioned Joshua son of Nun and s,
32:20 He s: I will hide my face from them,
32:46 he s to them: "Take to heart
33: 2 He s: The LORD came from Sinai,
33: 7 And this he s of Judah: O LORD,
33: 8 And of Levi he s: Give to Levi
33: 9 who s of his father and mother,
33:12 Of Benjamin he s: The beloved of the LORD
33:13 And of Joseph he s: Blessed by the LORD
33:18 And of Zebulun he s: Rejoice,
33:20 of Gad he s: Blessed be the enlargement of Gad!
33:22 And of Dan he s: Dan is a lion's whelp
33:23 And of Naphtali he s: O Naphtali,
33:24 And of Asher he s: Most blessed of sons
33:27 he drove out the enemy before you, and s,
34: 4 The LORD s to him, "This is the land
Jos 1:12 and the half-tribe of Manasseh Joshua s,
2: 4 Then she s, "True, the men came to me,
2: 9 and s to the men: "I know
2:14 The men s to her, "Our life for yours!
2:16 She s to them, "Go toward the hill country,
2:17 The men s to her, "We will be released
2:21 She s, "According to your words, so be it."
2:24 They s to Joshua, "Truly the LORD has given all
3: 5 Then Joshua s to the people, "Sanctify yourselves;
3: 6 To the priests Joshua s, "Take up the ark of
3: 7 The LORD s to Joshua, "This day I will begin
3: 9 Joshua then s to the Israelites,
3:10 Joshua s, "By this you shall know that
4: 1 over the Jordan, the LORD s to Joshua:
4: 5 Joshua s to them, "Pass on before the ark of
4:15 The LORD s to Joshua,
5: 2 At that time the LORD s to Joshua,
5: 9 The LORD s to Joshua, "Today I have rolled away
5:13 Joshua went to him and s to him,
5:14 on his face to the earth and worshiped, and he s
5:15 commander of the army of the LORD s to Joshua,
6: 2 The LORD s to Joshua, "See,
6: 6 So Joshua son of Nun summoned the priests and s
6: 7 the people he s, "Go forward and march around
6:16 Joshua s to the people, "Shout!
6:22 Joshua s to the two men who had spied out
7: 2 and s to them, "Go up and spy out the land."
7: 3 Then they returned to Joshua and s to him,
7: 7 Joshua s, "Ah, Lord GOD!
7:10 The LORD s to Joshua, "Stand up!
7:19 Then Joshua s to Achan, "My son,
7:25 Joshua s, "Why did you bring trouble on us?
8: 1 LORD s to Joshua, "Do not fear or be dismayed;
8:18 Then the LORD s to Joshua,
9: 6 and s to him and to the Israelites,
9: 7 But the Israelites s to the Hivites,
9: 8 They s to Joshua, "We are your servants."
9: 8 And Joshua s to them, "Who are you?
9: 9 They s to him, "Your servants have come from
9:11 and all the inhabitants of our country s to us,
9:19 But all the leaders s to all the congregation,
9:21 The leaders s to them, "Let them live."
9:22 Joshua summoned them, and s to them,
10: 8 The LORD s to Joshua, "Do not fear them,
10:12 and he s in the sight of Israel, "Sun,
10:18 Joshua s, "Roll large stones against the mouth of
10:22 Then Joshua s, "Open the mouth of the cave,
10:24 and s to the chiefs of the warriors who had gone
10:25 Joshua s to them, "Do not be afraid or dismayed;
11: 6 And the LORD s to Joshua,
13: 1 and the LORD s to him,
13:14 of Israel are their inheritance, as he s to them.
13:33 of Israel is their inheritance, as he s to them.
14: 6 Caleb son of Jephunneh the Kenizzite s to him,
14: 6 You know what the LORD s to Moses the man
14:10 as you see, the LORD has kept me alive, as he s,
14:12 and I shall drive them out, as the LORD s."
15:16 And Caleb s, "Whoever attacks Kiriath-sepher
15:18 she dismounted from her donkey, Caleb s to her,
15:19 She s to him, "Give me a present;
17: 4 and s, "The LORD commanded Moses to give us
17:15 And Joshua s to them, "If you are
17:16 of Joseph s, "The hill country is not enough for us;
17:17 Then Joshua s to the house of Joseph,
18: 3 So Joshua s to the Israelites,
21: 2 they s to them at Shiloh in the land of Canaan,
22: 2 and s to them, "You have observed all that Moses
22: 8 he s to them, "Go back to your tents
22:15 in the land of Gilead, and they s to them,
22:21 the half-tribe of Manasseh s in answer to the heads
22:26 Therefore we s, 'Let us now build an altar,
22:28 be s to us or to our descendants in time to come,
22:31 of Eleazar s to the Reubenites and the Gadites and

Jos 22:34 "For," s they, "it is a witness between us that
23: 2 their judges and officers, and s to them,
24: 2 And Joshua s to all the people,
24:19 But Joshua s to the people,
24:21 And the people s to Joshua, "No,
24:22 Then Joshua s to the people,
24:22 And they s, "We are witnesses."
24:23 He s, "Then put away the foreign gods that are
24:24 The people s to Joshua, "The LORD our God we
24:27 Joshua s to all the people, "See,
Jdg 1: 2 The LORD s, "Judah shall go up.
1: 3 Judah s to his brother Simeon,
1: 7 Adoni-bezek s, "Seventy kings with their thumbs
1:12 Then Caleb s, "Whoever attacks Kiriath-sepher
1:14 she dismounted from her donkey, Caleb s to her,
1:15 She s to him, "Give me a present;
1:20 Hebron was given to Caleb, as Moses had s;
1:24 they s to him, "Show us the way into the city,
2: 1 and s, "I brought you up from Egypt,
2: 1 I s, 'I will never break my covenant with you.
2:20 of the LORD was kindled against Israel; and he s,
3:19 and s, "I have a secret message for you, O king."
3:19 So the king s, "Silence!"
3:20 and s, "I have a message from God for you."
3:28 He s to them, "Follow after me;
4: 6 and s to him, "The LORD, the God of Israel,
4: 8 Barak s to her, "If you will go with me, I will go;
4: 9 And she s, "I will surely go with you;
4:14 Then Deborah s to Barak, "Up!
4:18 Jael came out to meet Sisera, and s to him,
4:19 he s to her, "Please give me a little water to drink;
4:20 He s to her, "Stand at the entrance of the tent,
4:22 Jael went out to meet him, and s to him, "Come,
6: 8 and he s to them, "Thus says the LORD,
6:10 and I s to you, 'I am the LORD your God;
6:12 angel of the LORD appeared to him and s to him,
6:14 Then the LORD turned to him and s,
6:16 The LORD s to him, "But I will be with you,
6:17 Then he s to him, "If now I have found favor
6:18 And he s, "I will stay until you return."
6:20 The angel of God s to him,
6:22 and Gideon s, "Help me, Lord GOD!
6:23 But the LORD s to him, "Peace be to you;
6:25 That night the LORD s to him,
6:29 So they s to one another, "Who has done this?"
6:30 Then the townspeople s to Joash,
6:31 But Joash s to all who were arrayed against him,
6:36 Then Gideon s to God, "In order
6:36 deliver Israel by my hand, as you have s,
6:37 deliver Israel by my hand, as you have s."
6:39 Then Gideon s to God, "Do
7: 2 The LORD s to Gideon, "The troops
7: 4 Then the LORD s to Gideon,
7: 5 and the LORD s to Gideon,
7: 7 Then the LORD s to Gideon,
7: 9 That same night the LORD s to him, "Get up,
7:13 and he s, "I had a dream,
7:15 he returned to the camp of Israel, and s, "Get up;
7:17 he s to them, "Look at me, and do the same;
8: 1 Then the Ephraimites s to him,
8: 2 So he s to them, "What have I done now
8: 3 When he s this, their anger against him subsided.
8: 5 So he s to the people of Succoth,
8: 6 But the officials of Succoth s,
8: 9 So he s to the people of Penuel,
8:15 Then he came to the people of Succoth, and s,
8:18 Then he s to Zebah and Zalmunna,
8:20 So he s to Jether his firstborn, "Go kill them!"
8:21 Zebah and Zalmunna s, "You come and kill us;
8:22 Then the Israelites s to Gideon, "Rule over us,
8:23 Gideon s to them, "I will not rule over you,
8:24 Gideon s to them, "Let me make a request of you;
9: 1 to Shechem to his mother's kinsfolk and s to them
9: 3 for they s, "He is our brother."
9: 7 and cried aloud and s to them, "Listen to me,
9: 8 So they s to the olive tree, 'Reign over us.'
9:10 Then the trees s to the fig tree,
9:12 trees s to the vine, 'You come and reign over us.'
9:13 But the vine s to them,
9:14 So all the trees s to the bramble,
9:15 And the bramble s to the trees,
9:28 Gaal son of Ebed s, "Who is Abimelech,
9:36 And when Gaal saw them, he s to Zebul, "Look,
9:36 And Zebul s to him, "The shadows on
9:37 Gaal spoke again and s, "Look,
9:38 Then Zebul s to him, "Where is your boast now,
9:38 "Where is your boast now, you who s,
9:48 Then he s to the troops with him,
9:54 the young man who carried his armor and s to him,
10:11 And the LORD s to the Israelites,
10:15 The Israelites s to the LORD, "We have sinned;
10:18 The commanders of the people of Gilead s
11: 6 They s to Jephthah, "Come and
11: 7 But Jephthah s to the elders of Gilead,
11: 8 The elders of Gilead s to Jephthah, "Nevertheless,
11: 9 Jephthah s to the elders of Gilead,
11:10 And the elders of Gilead s to Jephthah,
11:12 to the king of the Ammonites and s,
11:15 and s to him: "Thus says Jephthah:
11:19 and Israel s to him, 'Let us pass through your land
11:30 And Jephthah made a vow to the LORD, and s,
11:35 When he saw her, he tore his clothes, and s, "Alas,
11:36 She s to him, "My father,
11:37 she s to her father, "Let this thing be done for me:
11:38 "Go," he s and sent her away for two months.
12: 1 and they crossed to Zaphon and s to Jephthah,
12: 2 Jephthah s to them, "My people
Jdg 12: 4 men of Gilead defeated Ephraim, because they s,
12: 5 Whenever one of the fugitives of Ephraim s,
12: 5 "Are you an Ephraimite?" When he s,
12: 6 they s to him, "Then say Shibboleth,"
12: 6 "Then say Shibboleth," and he s, "Sibboleth,"
13: 3 of the LORD appeared to the woman and s to her,
13: 7 but he s to me, 'You shall conceive and bear
13: 8 Then Manoah entreated the LORD, and s, "O,
13:11 and came to the man and s to him,
13:11 And he s, "I am."
13:12 Then Manoah s, "Now when your words come
13:13 The angel of the LORD s to Manoah,
13:13 "Let the woman give heed to all that I s to her.
13:15 Manoah s to the angel of the LORD,
13:16 The angel of the LORD s to Manoah,
13:17 Then Manoah s to the angel of the LORD,
13:18 But the angel of the LORD s to him,
13:22 And Manoah s to his wife, "We shall surely die,
13:23 But his wife s to him,
14: 3 But his father and mother s to him,
14: 3 But Samson s to his father, "Get her for me,
14:12 Samson s to them, "Let me now put a riddle
14:13 So they s to him, "Ask your riddle; let us hear it."
14:14 He s to them, "Out of the eater came something
14:15 On the fourth day they s to Samson's wife,
14:16 He s to her, "Look, I have not told my father
14:18 The men of the town s to him on the seventh day
14:18 And he s to them, "If you had not plowed
15: 1 He s, "I want to go into my wife's room."
15: 2 Her father s, "I was sure that you had rejected her;
15: 3 Samson s to them, "This time,
15: 6 And they s, "Samson, the son-in-law of
15: 7 Samson s to them, "If this is what you do,
15:10 The men of Judah s, "Why have you come up
15:10 They s, "We have come up to bind Samson,
15:11 of Etam, and they s to Samson, "Do you not know
15:12 They s to him, "We have come down to bind you,
15:13 They s to him, "No, we will only bind you
15:16 And Samson s, "With the jawbone of a donkey,
16: 5 lords of the Philistines came to her and s to her,
16: 6 So Delilah s to Samson, "Please tell me what
16: 7 Samson s to her, "If they bind me
16: 9 she s to him, "The Philistines are upon you,
16:10 Then Delilah s to Samson,
16:11 He s to her, "If they bind me with new ropes
16:12 and s to him, "The Philistines are upon you,
16:13 Then Delilah s to Samson,
16:13 He s to her, "If you weave the seven locks
16:14 Then she s to him, "The Philistines are upon you,
16:15 Then she s to him, "How can you say,
16:17 So he told her his whole secret, and s to her,
16:20 she s, "The Philistines are upon you, Samson!"
16:23 for they s, "Our god has given Samson our enemy
16:24 for they s, "Our god has given our enemy
16:25 And when their hearts were merry, they s,
16:26 and Samson s to the attendant who held him by
16:28 Then Samson called to the LORD and s,
16:30 Then Samson s, "Let me die with the Philistines."
17: 2 He s to his mother, "The eleven hundred pieces
17: 2 And his mother s, "May my son be blessed by
17: 3 and his mother s, "I consecrate the silver to
17: 9 Micah s to him, "From where do you come?"
17:10 Then Micah s to him, "Stay with me,
17:13 Then Micah s, "Now I know that
18: 2 and they s to them, "Go, explore the land."
18: 4 He s to them, "Micah did such and such for me,
18: 5 Then they s to him, "Inquire of God
18: 8 they s to them, "What do you report?"
18: 9 They s, "Come, let us go up against them;
18:14 s to their comrades, "Do you know that
18:18 the ephod, and the teraphim, the priest s to them,
18:19 They s to him, "Keep quiet!
18:23 who turned around and s to Micah,
18:25 And the Danites s to him,
19: 5 but the girl's father s to his son-in-law,
19: 6 and the girl's father s to the man,
19: 8 and the girl's father s, "Fortify yourself."
19: 9 his father-in-law, the girl's father, s to him, "Look,
19:11 and the servant s to his master, "Come now,
19:12 But his master s to him, "We will not turn aside
19:13 Then he s to his servant, "Come,
19:17 the wayfarer in the open square of the city, he s,
19:20 The old man s, "Peace be to you.
19:22 They s to the old man, the master of the house,
19:23 went out to them and s to them, "No, my brothers,
19:28 "Get up," he s to her, "we are going."
20: 3 And the Israelites s, "Tell us,
20:23 And the LORD s, "Go up against them."
20:32 But the Israelites s, "Let us retreat
21: 3 They s, "O LORD, the God of Israel,
21: 5 Then the Israelites s, "Which of all the tribes
21: 6 and s, "One tribe is cut off from Israel this day.
21: 8 Then they s, "Is there anyone from the tribes
21:16 So the elders of the congregation s,
21:17 And they s, "There must be heirs for the survivors
21:19 So they s, "Look, the yearly festival of
Ru 1: 8 But Naomi s to her two daughters-in-law,
1:10 They s to her, "No, we will return with you
1:11 But Naomi s, "Turn back, my daughters,
1:15 So she s, "See, your sister-in-law has gone back
1:16 But Ruth s, "Do not press me to leave you or
1:18 she s no more to her.
1:19 and the women s, "Is this Naomi?"
1:20 She s to them, "Call me no longer Naomi,
2: 2 And Ruth the Moabite s to Naomi,
2: 2 She s to her, "Go, my daughter."
2: 4 He s to the reapers, "The LORD be with you."
Ru 2: 5 Then Boaz s to his servant who was in charge of
2: 7 She s, 'Please, let me glean and gather among
2: 8 Then Boaz s to Ruth, "Now listen, my daughter,
2:10 with her face to the ground, and s to him,
2:13 Then she s, "May I continue to find favor
2:14 At mealtime Boaz s to her, "Come here,
2:19 Her mother-in-law s to her,
2:19 with whom she had worked, and s, "The name of
2:20 Then Naomi s to her daughter-in-law,
2:20 Naomi also s to her, "The man is a relative of ours,
2:21 Then Ruth the Moabite s, "He even s to me,
2:22 Naomi s to Ruth, her daughter-in-law, "It is better,
3: 1 Naomi her mother-in-law s to her, "My daughter,
3: 5 She s to her, "All that you tell me I will do."
3: 9 He s, "Who are you?"
3:10 He s, "May you be blessed by the LORD,
3:14 for he s, "It must not be known that
3:15 Then he s, "Bring the cloak you are wearing
3:16 She came to her mother-in-law, who s,
3:17 of barley, for he s, 'Do not go back
4: 1 So Boaz s, "Come over, friend; sit down here."
4: 2 Boaz took ten men of the elders of the city, and s,
4: 3 He then s to the next-of-kin, "Naomi,
4: 4 So he s, "I will redeem it."
4: 5 Then Boaz s, "The day you acquire the field from
4: 6 the next-of-kin s, "I cannot redeem it for myself
4: 8 So when the next-of-kin s to Boaz,
4: 9 Then Boaz s to the elders and all the people,
4:11 along with the elders, s, "We are witnesses.
4:14 Then the women s to Naomi,
1Sa 1: 8 Her husband Elkanah s to her, "Hannah,
1:14 So Eli s to her, "How long will you make
1:18 she s, "Let your servant find favor in your sight."
1:20 She named him Samuel, for she s,
1:22 Hannah did not go up, for she s to her husband,
1:23 Her husband Elkanah s to her,
1:26 And she s, "Oh, my lord!
2: 1 Hannah prayed and s, "My heart exults in
2:16 And if the man s to him,
2:23 He s to them, "Why do you do such things?
2:27 A man of God came to Eli and s to him,
2:27 to him, "Thus the LORD has s, 'I revealed myself
3: 4 and he s, "Here I am!"
3: 5 ran to Eli, and s, "Here I am, for you called me."
3: 5 But he s, "I did not call; lie down again."
3: 6 Samuel got up and went to Eli, and s, "Here I am,
3: 6 But he s, "I did not call, my son; lie down again."
3: 8 And he got up and went to Eli, and s, "Here I am,
3: 9 Therefore Eli s to Samuel, "Go, lie down;
3:10 Samuel s, "Speak, for your servant is listening."
3:11 Then the LORD s to Samuel, "See,
3:16 But Eli called Samuel and s, "Samuel, my son."
3:16 He s, "Here I am."
3:17 Eli s, "What was it that he told you?
3:18 Then he s, "It is the LORD;
4: 3 the troops came to the camp, the elders of Israel s,
4: 6 Philistines heard the noise of the shouting, they s,
4: 7 for they s, "Gods have come into the camp."
4: 7 They also s, "Woe to us!
4:14 When Eli heard the sound of the outcry, he s,
4:16 man s to Eli, "I have just come from the battle;
4:16 He s, "How did it go, my son?"
4:20 the women attending her s to her,
4:22 She s, "The glory has departed from Israel,
5: 7 they s, "The ark of the God of Israel must
5: 8 and s, "What shall we do with the ark of the God
5:11 and s, "Send away the ark of the God of Israel,
6: 2 for the priests and the diviners and s,
6: 3 They s, "If you send away the ark of the God
6: 4 And they s, "What is the guilt offering
6:20 Then the people of Beth-shemesh s,
7: 3 Then Samuel s to all the house of Israel,
7: 5 Then Samuel s, "Gather all Israel at Mizpah,
7: 6 They fasted that day, and s,
7: 8 The people of Israel s to Samuel,
7:12 for he s, "Thus far the LORD has helped us."
8: 5 and s to him, "You are old and your sons do
8: 6 But the thing displeased Samuel when they s,
8: 7 and the LORD s to Samuel, "Listen to the voice
8:11 He s, "These will be the ways of the king
8:19 to the voice of Samuel; they s,
8:22 The LORD s to Samuel, "Listen to their voice
8:22 Samuel then s to the people of Israel,
9: 3 So Kish s to his son Saul,
9: 5 Saul s to the boy who was with him,
9: 6 he s to him, "There is a man of God in this town;
9:10 Saul s to the boy, "Good; come, let us go."
9:11 and s to them, "Is the seer here?"
9:18 Saul approached Samuel inside the gate, and s,
9:23 And Samuel s to the cook,
9:24 Samuel s, "See, what was kept is set before you.
9:27 Samuel s to Saul, "Tell the boy to go on before us,
10: 1 he s, "The LORD has anointed you ruler
10:11 the people s to one another,
10:14 Saul's uncle s to him and to the boy,
10:15 Saul's uncle s, "Tell me what Samuel s to you."
10:16 Saul s to his uncle, "He told us that
10:18 and s to them, "Thus says the LORD, the God
10:19 and your distresses; and you have s,
10:22 the LORD s, "See, he has hidden himself among
10:24 Samuel s to all the people,
10:27 But some worthless fellows s,
11: 1 and all the men of Jabesh s to Nahash,
11: 2 But Nahash the Ammonite s to them,
11: 3 The elders of Jabesh s to him,
11: 5 and Saul s, "What is the matter with the people,
11: 9 They s to the messengers who had come,

1Sa 11:10 So the inhabitants of Jabesh s,
11:12 The people s to Samuel, "Who is it that s,
11:13 But Saul s, "No one shall be put to death this day,
11:14 Samuel s to the people, "Come,
12: 1 Samuel s to all Israel, "I have listened to you in all
12: 1 "I have listened to you in all that you have s to me,
12: 4 They s, "You have not defrauded us
12: 5 He s to them, "The LORD is witness against you,
12: 5 And they s, "He is witness."
12: 6 Samuel s to the people, "The LORD is witness,
12:10 Then they cried to the LORD, and s,
12:12 you s to me, 'No, but a king shall reign over us,'
12:19 All the people s to Samuel,
12:20 And Samuel s to the people, "Do not be afraid;
13: 9 So Saul s, "Bring the burnt offering here to me,
13:11 Samuel s, "What have you done?"
13:12 I s, 'Now the Philistines will come down upon me
13:13 Samuel s to Saul, "You have done foolishly;
13:19 for the Philistines s, "The Hebrews must
14: 1 of Saul s to the young man who carried his armor,
14: 6 Jonathan s to the young man who carried his armor
14: 7 His armor-bearer s to him,
14: 8 Then Jonathan s, "Now we will cross over
14:11 and the Philistines s, "Look,
14:12 Jonathan s to his armor-bearer,
14:17 Then Saul s to the troops that were with him,
14:18 Saul s to Ahijah, "Bring the ark of God here."
14:19 and Saul s to the priest, "Withdraw your hand."
14:28 Then one of the soldiers s,
14:29 Then Jonathan s, "My father has troubled the land;
14:33 And he s, "You have dealt treacherously;
14:34 Saul s, "Disperse yourselves among the troops,
14:36 Then Saul s, "Let us go down after the Philistines
14:36 They s, "Do whatever seems good to you."
14:36 But the priest s, "Let us draw near to God here."
14:38 Saul s, "Come here, all you leaders of the people;
14:40 He s to all Israel, "You shall be on one side,
14:40 people s to Saul, "Do what seems good to you."
14:41 Then Saul s, "O LORD God of Israel,
14:42 Then Saul s, "Cast the lot between me
14:43 Saul s to Jonathan, "Tell me what you have done."
14:44 Saul s, "God do so to me and more also;
14:45 Then the people s to Saul, "Shall Jonathan die,
15: 1 Samuel s to Saul, "The LORD sent me
15: 6 Saul s to the Kenites, "Go!
15:13 When Samuel came to Saul, Saul s to him,
15:14 But Samuel s, "What then is this bleating of sheep
15:15 Saul s, "They have brought them from
15:16 Then Samuel s to Saul, "Stop!
15:16 I will tell you what the LORD s to me last night."
15:17 Samuel s, "Though you are little
15:18 And the LORD sent you on a mission, and s, 'Go,
15:20 Saul s to Samuel, "I have obeyed the voice of
15:22 And Samuel s, "Has the LORD as great delight
15:24 Saul s to Samuel, "I have sinned;
15:26 Samuel s to Saul, "I will not return with you;
15:28 And Samuel s to him, "The LORD has torn
15:30 Then Saul s, "I have sinned;
15:32 Then Samuel s, "Bring Agag king of
15:32 Agag s, "Surely this is the bitterness of death."
15:33 But Samuel s, "As your sword has made women
16: 1 The LORD s to Samuel,
16: 2 Samuel s, "How can I go?
16: 2 And the LORD s, "Take a heifer with you,
16: 4 and s, "Do you come peaceably?"
16: 5 He s, "Peaceably; I have come to sacrifice
16: 7 But the LORD s to Samuel,
16: 8 He s, "Neither has the LORD chosen this one."
16: 9 he s, "Neither has the LORD chosen this one."
16:10 of his sons pass before Samuel, and Samuel s
16:11 Samuel s to Jesse, "Are all your sons here?"
16:11 And he s, "There remains yet the youngest,
16:11 And Samuel s to Jesse, "Send and bring him;
16:12 The LORD s, "Rise and anoint him;
16:15 And Saul's servants s to him, "See now,
16:17 So Saul s to his servants,
16:19 So Saul sent messengers to Jesse, and s,
17:10 the Philistine s, "Today I defy the ranks of Israel!
17:17 Jesse s to his son David, "Take for your brothers
17:25 The Israelites s, "Have you seen this man who has
17:26 David s to the men who stood by him,
17:28 He s, "Why have you come down?
17:29 David s, "What have I done now?
17:32 David s to Saul, "Let no one's heart fail because
17:33 Saul s to David, "You are not able to go
17:34 But David s to Saul, "Your servant used
17:37 David s, "The LORD, who saved me from
17:37 So Saul s to David, "Go, and may the LORD be
17:39 Then David s to Saul, "I cannot walk with these;
17:43 The Philistine s to David, "Am I a dog,
17:44 The Philistine s to David, "Come to me,
17:45 But David s to the Philistine,
17:55 he s to Abner, the commander of the army,
17:55 Abner s, "As your soul lives, O king,
17:56 The king s, "Inquire whose son the stripling is."
17:58 Saul s to him, "Whose son are you, young man?"
18: 8 He s, "They have ascribed to David ten thousands,
18:17 Then Saul s to David, "Here is my elder daughter
18:18 David s to Saul, "Who am I
18:21 Therefore Saul s to David a second time,
18:23 And David s, "Does it seem to you a little thing
18:24 servants of Saul told him, "This is what David s."
18:25 Then Saul s, "Thus shall you say to David,
19:14 When Saul sent messengers to take David, she s,
19:15 He s, "Bring him up to me in the bed,
19:17 Saul s to Michal, "Why have you deceived me
19:17 Michal answered Saul, "He s to me, 'Let me go;

1Sa 19:22 And someone s, "They are at Naioth in Ramah."
19:24 it is s, "Is Saul also among the prophets?"
20: 1 He came before Jonathan and s,
20: 2 He s to him, "Far from it!
20: 4 Then Jonathan s to David, "Whatever you say,
20: 5 David s to Jonathan, "Tomorrow is the new moon,
20: 9 Jonathan s, "Far be it from you!
20:10 Then David s to Jonathan,
20:12 Jonathan s to David, "By the LORD,
20:18 Jonathan s to him, "Tomorrow is the new moon;
20:27 And Saul s to his son Jonathan,
20:29 he s, 'Let me go; for our family is holding a
20:30 He s to him, "You son of a perverse,
20:36 He s to the boy, "Run and find the arrows
20:37 Jonathan called after the boy and s,
20:40 Jonathan gave his weapons to the boy and s
20:42 Then Jonathan s to David, "Go in peace,
21: 1 and s to him, "Why are you alone,
21: 2 David s to the priest Ahimelech,
21: 2 "The king has charged me with a matter, and s
21: 8 David s to Ahimelech, "Is there no spear
21: 9 The priest s, "The sword of Goliath the Philistine,
21: 9 David s, "There is none like it; give it to me."
21:11 The servants of Achish s to him,
21:14 Achish s to his servants, "Look,
22: 3 He s to the king of Moab,
22: 5 Then the prophet Gad s to David,
22: 7 Saul s to his servants who stood around him,
22:12 Saul s, "Listen now, son of Ahitub."
22:13 Saul s to him, "Why have you conspired
22:16 The king s, "You shall surely die, Ahimelech,
22:17 The king s to the guard who stood around him,
22:18 Then the king s to Doeg, "You, Doeg,
22:22 David s to Abiathar, "I knew on that day,
23: 2 The LORD s to David, "Go and attack
23: 3 But David's men s to him, "Look,
23: 7 And Saul s, "God has given him into my hand;
23: 9 he s to the priest Abiathar, "Bring the ephod here."
23:10 David s, "O LORD, the God of Israel,
23:11 The LORD s, "He will come down."
23:12 Then David s, "Will the men
23:12 The LORD s, "They will surrender you."
23:17 He s to him, "Do not be afraid;
23:19 some Ziphites went up to Saul at Gibeah and s,
23:21 Saul s, "May you be blessed by the LORD
24: 4 The men of David s to him,
24: 4 "Here is the day of which the LORD s to you,
24: 6 He s to his men, "The LORD forbid
24: 9 David s to Saul, "Why do you listen to the words
24:10 I s, 'I will not raise my hand against my lord;
24:16 Saul s, "Is this your voice, my son David?"
24:17 He s to David, "You are more righteous than I;
25: 5 and David s to the young men, "Go up to Carmel,
25: 9 they s all this to Nabal in the name of David;
25:13 David s to his men, "Every man strap
25:19 and s to her young men, "Go on ahead of me;
25:21 Now David had s, "Surely it was in vain
25:24 She fell at his feet and s, "Upon me alone,
25:32 David s to Abigail, "Blessed be the LORD,
25:35 he s to her, "Go up to your house in peace;
25:39 When David heard that Nabal was dead, he s,
25:40 they s to her, "David has sent us to you to take you
25:41 with her face to the ground, and s,
26: 6 Then David s to Ahimelech the Hittite,
26: 6 Abishai s, "I will go down with you."
26: 8 Abishai s to David, "God has given your enemy
26: 9 But David s to Abishai, "Do not destroy him;
26:10 David s, "As the LORD lives,
26:15 David s to Abner, "Are you not a man?
26:17 Saul recognized David's voice, and s,
26:17 David s, "It is my voice, my lord, O king."
26:21 Then Saul s, "I have done wrong;
26:25 Saul s to David, "Blessed be you, my son David!
27: 1 David s in his heart, "I shall now perish one day
27: 5 Then David s to Achish, "If I have found favor
28: 1 Achish s to David, "You know, of course,
28: 2 David s to Achish, "Very well,
28: 2 Achish s to David, "Very well,
28: 7 Then Saul s to his servants,
28: 7 His servants s to him, "There is a medium
28: 8 And he s, "Consult a spirit for me,
28: 9 The woman s to him,
28:11 the woman s, "Whom shall I bring up for you?"
28:12 woman s to Saul, "Why have you deceived me?
28:13 king s to her, "Have no fear; what do you see?"
28:13 The woman s to Saul, "I see a divine being coming
28:14 He s to her, "What is his appearance?"
28:14 She s, "An old man is coming up;
28:15 Then Samuel s to Saul, "Why have you disturbed
28:16 Samuel s, "Why then do you ask me,
28:21 she s to him, "Your servant has listened to you;
28:21 and have listened to what you have s to me.
28:23 He refused, and s, "I will not eat."
29: 3 the commanders of the Philistines s,
29: 3 Achish s to the commanders of the Philistines,
29: 4 and the commanders of the Philistines s to him,
29: 6 Then Achish called David and s to him,
29: 8 David s to Achish, "But what have I done?
29: 9 the commanders of the Philistines have s,
30: 7 David s to the priest Abiathar son of Ahimelech,
30:13 Then David s to him, "To whom do you belong?
30:13 He s, "I am a young man of Egypt,
30:15 David s to him, "Will you take me down
30:15 He s, "Swear to me by God that you will
30:20 people s, "This is David's spoil."
30:22 among the men who had gone with David s,
30:23 But David s, "You shall not do so, my brothers,

1Sa 31: 4 Then Saul s to his armor-bearer,
2Sa 1: 3 David s to him, "Where have you come from?"
1: 3 He s to him, "I have escaped from the camp
1: 4 David s to him, "How did things go?
1: 6 The young man reporting to him s,
1: 8 And he s to me, 'Who are you?'
1: 9 He s to me, 'Come, stand over me and kill me;
1:13 David s to the young man who had reported
1:14 David s to him, "Were you not afraid
1:15 Then David called one of the young men and s,
1:16 David s to him, "Your blood be on your head;
1:18 written in the Book of Jashar.) He s:
2: 1 The LORD s to him, "Go up."
2: 1 David s, "To which shall I go up?"
2: 1 "To which shall I go up?" He s,
2: 5 to the people of Jabesh-gilead, and s to them,
2:14 Abner s to Joab, "Let the young men come forward
2:14 Joab s, "Let them come forward."
2:20 Abner looked back and s, "Is it you, Asahel?"
2:21 Abner s to him, "Turn to your right or to your left,
2:22 Abner s again to Asahel, "Turn away
2:27 Joab s, "As God lives, if you had not spoken,
3: 7 And Ishbaal s to Abner, "Why have you gone in
3: 8 he s, "Am I a dog's head for Judah?
3:13 He s, "Good; I will make a covenant with you.
3:16 Then Abner s to him, "Go back home!"
3:21 Abner s to David, "Let me go and rally all Israel
3:24 Then Joab went to the king and s,
3:28 Afterward, when David heard of it, he s,
3:31 Then David s to Joab and to all
3:38 And the king s to his servants,
4: 8 and s to the king, "Here is the head of Ishbaal, son
5: 1 and s, "Look, we are your bone and flesh.
5: 2 and brought it in. The LORD s to you:
5: 6 who s to David, "You will not come in here,
5: 8 David had s on that day,
5: 8 Therefore it is s, "The blind and the lame shall
5:19 The LORD s to David, "Go up;
5:20 He s, "The LORD has burst forth
5:23 When David inquired of the LORD, he s,
6: 9 David was afraid of the LORD that day; he s,
6:20 of Saul came out to meet David, and s, "How
6:21 David s to Michal, "It was before the LORD,
7: 2 the king s to the prophet Nathan,
7: 3 Nathan s to the king, "Go,
7:18 and s, "Who am I, O Lord GOD,
9: 2 The king s to him, "Are you Ziba?"
9: 2 And he s, "At your service!"
9: 3 The king s, "Is there anyone remaining of
9: 3 Ziba s to the king, "There remains a son
9: 4 The king s to him, "Where is he?"
9: 4 Ziba s to the king, "He is in the house
9: 6 David s, "Mephibosheth!"
9: 7 David s to him, "Do not be afraid,
9: 8 He did obeisance and s, "What is your servant,
9: 9 king summoned Saul's servant Ziba, and s to him,
9:11 Then Ziba s to the king,
10: 2 David s, "I will deal loyally with Hanun son
10: 3 princes of the Ammonites s to their lord Hanun,
10: 5 The king s, "Remain at Jericho
10:11 He s, "If the Arameans are too strong for me,
11: 8 Then David s to Uriah, "Go down to your house,
11:10 not go down to his house," David s to Uriah,
11:11 Uriah s to David, "The ark and Israel
11:12 Then David s to Uriah, "Remain here today also,
11:23 The messenger s to David,
11:25 David s to the messenger,
12: 1 He came to him, and s to him,
12: 5 He s to Nathan, "As the LORD lives,
12: 7 Nathan s to David, "You are the man!
12:13 David s to Nathan, "I have sinned against
12:13 s to David, "Now the LORD has put away your sin;
12:18 for they s, "While the child was still alive,
12:19 and David s to his servants, "Is the child dead?"
12:19 They s, "He is dead."
12:21 Then his servants s to him,
12:22 He s, "While the child was still alive,
12:22 I fasted and wept; for I s,
12:27 Joab sent messengers to David, and s,
13: 4 He s to him, "O son of the king,
13: 4 Amnon s to him, "I love Tamar,
13: 5 Jonadab s to him, "Lie down on your bed,
13: 6 the king came to see him, Amnon s to the king,
13: 9 Amnon s, "Send out everyone from me."
13:10 Then Amnon s to Tamar, "Bring the food into
13:11 and s to her, "Come, lie with me, my sister."
13:15 Amnon s to her, "Get out!"
13:16 But she s to him, "No, my brother;
13:17 He called the young man who served him and s,
13:20 Her brother Absalom s to her,
13:24 Absalom came to the king, and s,
13:25 But the king s to Absalom, "No, my son,
13:26 Then Absalom s, "If not, please let my brother
13:26 The king s to him, "Why should he go with you?"
13:32 Jonadab, the son of David's brother Shimeah, s,
13:35 Jonadab s to the king, "See,
13:35 as your servant s, so it has come about."
14: 2 He s to her, "Pretend to be a mourner;
14: 4 on her face to the ground and did obeisance, and s,
14: 8 Then the king s to the woman, "Go to your house,
14: 9 The woman of Tekoa s to the king,
14:10 The king s, "If anyone says anything to you,
14:11 Then she s, "Please, may the king keep
14:11 He s, "As the LORD lives,
14:12 Then the woman s, "Please let your servant speak
14:12 to my lord the king." He s,
14:13 The woman s, "Why then have you planned such

2Sa 14:18 The woman **s**, "Let my lord the king speak."
14:19 king **s**, "Is the hand of Joab with you in all this?"
14:19 The woman answered and **s**,
14:19 or left from anything that my lord the king has **s**.
14:21 Then the king **s** to Joab, "Very well, I grant this;
14:22 and Joab **s**, "Today your servant knows
14:24 The king **s**, "Let him go to his own house;
14:30 Then he **s** to his servants, "Look,
14:31 and went to Absalom at his house, and **s** to him,
15: 2 the person **s**, "Your servant is of such and such
15: 4 Absalom **s** moreover, "If only I were judge in
15: 7 At the end of four years Absalom **s** to the king,
15: 9 The king **s** to him, "Go in peace."
15:14 Then David **s** to all his officials who were
15:15 The king's officials **s** to the king,
15:19 Then the king **s** to Ittai the Gittite,
15:22 David **s** to Ittai, "Go then, march on."
15:25 Then the king **s** to Zadok,
15:27 The king also **s** to the priest Zadok, "Look,
15:31 And David **s**, "O LORD, I pray you,
15:33 David **s** to him, "If you go on with me,
16: 2 king **s** to Ziba, "Why have you brought these?"
16: 3 The king **s**, "And where is your master's son?"
16: 3 Ziba **s** to the king, "He remains in Jerusalem;
16: 3 for he **s**, 'Today the house of Israel
16: 4 Then the king **s** to Ziba,
16: 4 now yours." Ziba **s**, "I do obeisance;
16: 9 Then Abishai son of Zeruiah **s** to the king,
16:10 But the king **s**, "What have I to do with you,
16:10 If he is cursing because the LORD has **s** to him,
16:11 David **s** to Abishai and to all his servants,
16:16 Hushai **s** to Absalom, "Long live the king!
16:17 Absalom **s** to Hushai, "Is this your loyalty
16:18 Hushai **s** to Absalom, "No;
16:20 Absalom **s** to Ahithophel, "Give us your counsel;
16:21 Ahithophel **s** to Absalom,
17: 1 Moreover Ahithophel **s** to Absalom,
17: 5 Then Absalom **s**, "Call Hushai the Archite also,
17: 6 Hushai came to Absalom, Absalom **s** to him,
17: 6 "This is what Ahithophel has **s**;
17: 7 Then Hushai **s** to Absalom,
17:14 Absalom and all the men of Israel **s**,
17:15 Then Hushai **s** to the priests Zadok and Abiathar,
17:20 they **s**, "Where are Ahimaaz and Jonathan?"
17:20 The woman **s** to them, "They have crossed over
17:21 They **s** to David, "Go and cross the water quickly;
17:29 for they **s**, "The troops are hungry and weary
18: 2 The king **s** to the men,
18: 3 But the men **s**, "You shall not go out.
18: 4 The king **s** to them, "Whatever seems best
18:11 Joab **s** to the man who told him, "What,
18:12 But the man **s** to Joab, "Even if I felt in my hand
18:14 Joab **s**, "I will not waste time like this with you."
18:18 for he **s**, "I have no son to keep my name
18:19 Then Ahimaaz son of Zadok **s**, "Let me run,
18:20 Joab **s** to him, "You are not to carry tidings today;
18:21 Then Joab **s** to a Cushite, "Go,
18:22 Then Ahimaaz son of Zadok **s** again to Joab,
18:22 And Joab **s**, "Why will you run, my son,
18:23 "Come what may," he **s**, "I will run."
18:23 So he **s** to him, "Run."
18:25 The king **s**, "If he is alone,
18:26 and the sentinel called to the gatekeeper and **s**,
18:26 The king **s**, "He also is bringing tidings."
18:27 The sentinel **s**, "I think the running of
18:27 The king **s**, "He is a good man,
18:28 and **s**, "Blessed be the LORD your God,
18:29 king **s**, "Is it well with the young man Absalom?"
18:30 The king **s**, "Turn aside, and stand here."
18:31 the Cushite **s**, "Good tidings for my lord the king!
18:32 The king **s** to the Cushite,
18:33 and as he went, he **s**, "O my son Absalom,
19: 5 Then Joab came into the house to the king, and **s**,
19:19 and **s** to the king, "May my lord not hold me guilty
19:22 But David **s**, "What have I to do with you,
19:23 The king **s** to Shimei, "You shall not die."
19:25 the king **s** to him, "Why did you not go with me,
19:26 for your servant **s** to him,
19:29 The king **s** to him, "Why speak any more
19:30 Mephibosheth **s** to the king, "Let him take it all,
19:33 The king **s** to Barzillai, "Come over with me,
19:34 But Barzillai **s** to the king,
19:41 the people of Israel came to the king, and **s** to him,
20: 4 Then the king **s** to Amasa,
20: 6 David **s** to Abishai, "Now Sheba son
20: 9 Joab **s** to Amasa, "Is it well with you,
20:11 one of Joab's men took his stand by Amasa, and **s**,
20:17 and the woman **s**, "Are you Joab?"
20:17 Then she **s** to him, "Listen to the words
20:18 Then she **s**, "They used to say in the old days,
20:21 The woman **s** to Joab, "His head shall be thrown
21: 1 The LORD **s**, "There is bloodguilt on Saul and
21: 3 David **s** to the Gibeonites,
21: 4 The Gibeonites **s** to him, "It is not a matter
21: 4 He **s**, "What do you say that I should do for you?"
21: 5 They **s** to the king, "The man who consumed us
21: 6 The king **s**, "I will hand them over."
21:16 with new weapons, **s** he would kill David.
22: 2 He **s**: The LORD is my rock,
23: 3 the Rock of Israel has **s** to me:
23:15 David **s** longingly, "O that someone would give
23:17 for he **s**, "The LORD forbid that I should do this.
24: 2 king **s** to Joab and the commanders of the army,
24: 3 But Joab **s** to the king,
24:10 David **s** to the LORD, "I have sinned greatly
24:14 Then David **s** to Gad, "I am in great distress;
24:16 and **s** to the angel who was bringing destruction
2Sa 24:17 he **s** to the LORD, "I alone have sinned,
24:18 That day Gad came to David and **s** to him,
24:21 Araunah **s**, "Why has my lord the king come
24:21 David **s**, "To buy the threshing floor from you
24:22 Then Araunah **s** to David,
24:23 And Araunah **s** to the king,
24:24 But the king **s** to Araunah, "No,
1Ki 1: 2 So his servants **s** to him, "Let a young virgin
1:11 Then Nathan **s** to Bathsheba, Solomon's mother,
1:16 and the king **s**, "What do you wish?"
1:17 She **s** to him, "My lord, you swore to your servant
1:24 Nathan **s**, "My lord the king, have you **s**,
1:31 and **s**, "May my lord King David live forever!"
1:32 King David **s**, "Summon to me the priest Zadok,
1:33 the king **s** to them, "Take with you the servants
1:39 Then they blew the trumpet, and all the people **s**,
1:41 When Joab heard the sound of the trumpet, he **s**,
1:42 Adonijah **s**, "Come in, for you are a worthy man
1:53 and Solomon **s** to him, "Go home."
2:13 He **s**, "Peaceably."
2:14 Then he **s**, "May I have a word with you?"
2:14 "May I have a word with you?" She **s**,
2:15 He **s**, "You know that the kingdom was mine,
2:16 She **s** to him, "Go on."
2:17 He **s**, "Please ask King Solomon—
2:18 Bathsheba **s**, "Very well; I will speak to the
2:20 she **s**, "I have one small request to make of you;
2:20 the king **s** to her, "Make your request, my mother;
2:21 She **s**, "Let Abishag the Shunammite be given
2:26 The king **s** to the priest Abiathar, "Go to Anathoth,
2:30 So Benaiah came to the tent of the LORD and **s**
2:30 But he **s**, "No, I will die here."
2:30 saying, "Thus **s** Joab, and thus he answered me."
2:31 The king replied to him, "Do as he has **s**,
2:36 the king sent and summoned Shimei, and **s** to him,
2:38 And Shimei **s** to the king, "The sentence is fair;
2:38 as my lord the king has **s**, so will your servant do."
2:42 the king sent and summoned Shimei, and **s** to him,
2:42 And you **s** to me, 'The sentence is fair; I accept.'
2:44 The king also **s** to Shimei,
3: 5 and God **s**, "Ask what I should give you."
3: 6 And Solomon **s**, "You have shown great
3:11 God **s** to him, "Because you have asked this,
3:17 The one woman **s**, "Please, my lord,
3:22 But the other woman **s**, "No,
3:22 The first **s**, "No, the dead son is yours,
3:23 Then the king **s**, "The one says,
3:24 So the king **s**, "Bring me a sword,"
3:25 The king **s**, "Divide the living boy in two;
3:26 the woman whose son was alive **s** to the king—
3:26 The other **s**, "It shall be neither mine nor yours;
5: 5 as the LORD **s** to my father David, 'Your son,
5: 7 and **s**, "Blessed be the LORD today,
8:12 Then Solomon **s**, "The LORD has said
8:12 "The LORD has **s** that he would dwell
8:15 He **s**, "Blessed be the LORD, the God of Israel,
8:18 But the LORD **s** to my father David,
8:23 He **s**, "O LORD, God of Israel,
8:29 the place of which you **s**,
9: 3 The LORD **s** to him, "I have heard your prayer
9:13 Therefore he **s**, "What kind of cities are these
10: 6 So she **s** to the king, "The report was true
11: 2 the nations concerning which the LORD had **s** to
11:11 Therefore the LORD **s** to Solomon,
11:21 Hadad **s** to Pharaoh, "Let me depart,
11:22 But Pharaoh **s** to him, "What do you lack with me
11:22 And he **s**, "No, do let me go."
11:31 He then **s** to Jeroboam: Take for yourself ten
12: 3 the assembly of Israel came and **s** to Rehoboam,
12: 5 He **s** to them, "Go away for three days,
12: 9 He **s** to them, "What do you advise
12: 9 that we answer this people who have **s** to me,
12:10 young men who had grown up with him **s** to him,
12:12 to Rehoboam the third day, as the king had **s**,
12:26 Then Jeroboam **s** to himself,
12:28 He **s** to the people, "You have gone up
13: 2 and **s**, "O altar, altar, thus says the LORD:
13: 6 The king **s** to the man of God,
13: 7 Then the king **s** to the man of God,
13: 8 But the man of God **s** to the king,
13:12 Their father **s** to them, "Which way did he go?"
13:13 Then he **s** to his sons, "Saddle a donkey for me."
13:14 He **s** to him, "Are you the man of God who came
13:15 Then he **s** to him, "Come home with me
13:16 he **s**, "I cannot return with you, or go in with you;
13:17 for it was **s** to me by the word of the LORD:
13:18 the other **s** to him, "I also am a prophet as you are,
13:22 and drunk water in the place of which he **s** to you,
13:26 he **s**, "It is the man of God who disobeyed
13:27 Then he **s** to his sons, "Saddle a donkey for me."
13:31 After he had buried him, he **s** to his sons,
14: 2 Jeroboam **s** to his wife, "Go, disguise yourself,
14: 2 who **s** of me that I should be king over this people.
14: 5 But the LORD **s** to Ahijah,
14: 6 as she came in at the door, he **s**, "Come in,
16:16 and the troops who were encamped heard it **s**,
17: 1 Elijah the Tishbite, of Tishbe in Gilead, **s** to Ahab,
17:10 he called to her and **s**,
17:11 she was going to bring it, he called to her and **s**,
17:12 But she **s**, "As the LORD your God lives,
17:13 Elijah **s** to her, "Do not be afraid;
17:13 go and do as you have **s**;
17:15 She went and did as Elijah **s**,
17:18 She then **s** to Elijah, "What have you against me,
17:19 But he **s** to her, "Give me your son."
17:23 then Elijah **s**, "See, your son is alive."
17:24 So the woman **s** to Elijah,
1Ki 18: 5 Then Ahab **s** to Obadiah, "Go through the land
18: 7 Obadiah recognized him, fell on his face, and **s**,
18: 9 And he **s**, "How have I sinned,
18:15 Elijah **s**, "As the LORD of hosts lives,
18:17 When Ahab saw Elijah, Ahab **s** to him, "Is it you,
18:21 Elijah then came near to all the people, and **s**,
18:22 Then Elijah **s** to the people, "I, even I only,
18:25 Then Elijah **s** to the prophets of Baal,
18:30 Elijah **s** to all the people, "Come closer to me";
18:33 He **s**, "Fill four jars with water and pour it on
18:34 Then he **s**, "Do it a second time";
18:34 Again he **s**, "Do it a third time";
18:36 the prophet Elijah came near and **s**, "O LORD,
18:39 all the people saw it, they fell on their faces and **s**,
18:40 Elijah **s** to them, "Seize the prophets of Baal;
18:41 Elijah **s** to Ahab, "Go up, eat and drink;
18:43 He **s** to his servant, "Go up now,
18:43 He went up and looked, and **s**, "There is nothing."
18:43 Then he **s**, "Go again seven times."
18:44 At the seventh time he **s**, "Look,
18:44 Then he **s**, "Go say to Ahab,
19: 5 Suddenly an angel touched him and **s** to him,
19: 7 touched him, and **s**, "Get up and eat,
19:11 He **s**, "Go out and stand on the mountain before
19:13 Then there came a voice to him that **s**,
19:15 Then the LORD **s** to him, "Go,
19:20 He left the oxen, ran after Elijah, and **s**,
19:20 Then Elijah **s** to him, "Go back again;
20: 2 into the city to King Ahab of Israel, and **s** to him:
20: 5 The messengers came again and **s**:
20: 7 of Israel called all the elders of the land, and **s**,
20: 8 Then all the elders and all the people **s** to him,
20: 9 So he **s** to the messengers of Ben-hadad,
20:10 Ben-hadad sent to him and **s**,
20:12 he **s** to his men, "Take your positions!"
20:13 prophet came up to King Ahab of Israel and **s**,
20:14 Ahab **s**, "By whom?" He **s**, "Thus says the LORD,
20:14 Then he **s**, "Who shall begin the battle?"
20:18 He **s**, "If they have come out for peace,
20:22 prophet approached the king of Israel and **s** to him,
20:23 The servants of the king of Aram **s** to him,
20:28 man of God approached and **s** to the king of Israel,
20:28 Because the Arameans have **s**,
20:31 His servants **s** to him, "Look,
20:32 and **s**, "Your servant Ben-hadad says,
20:32 And he **s**, "Is he still alive?
20:33 they quickly took it up from him and **s**, "Yes,
20:33 Then he **s**, "Go and bring him."
20:34 Ben-hadad **s** to him, "I will restore the towns
20:35 a certain member of a company of prophets **s**
20:36 Then he **s** to him, "Because you have not obeyed
20:37 Then he found another man and **s**, "Strike me!"
20:39 As the king passed by, he cried to the king and **s**,
20:39 a soldier turned and brought a man to me, and **s**,
20:40 The king of Israel **s** to him,
20:42 Then he **s** to him, "Thus says the LORD,
21: 2 And Ahab **s** to Naboth, "Give me your vineyard,
21: 3 But Naboth **s** to Ahab, "The LORD forbid
21: 4 Naboth the Jezreelite had **s** to him; for he had **s**,
21: 5 His wife Jezebel came to him and **s**,
21: 6 He **s** to her, "Because I spoke to Naboth
21: 6 I spoke to Naboth the Jezreelite and **s** to him,
21: 7 His wife Jezebel **s** to him,
21:15 Jezebel **s** to Ahab, "Go, take possession of
21:20 Ahab **s** to Elijah, "Have you found me,
21:23 Also concerning Jezebel the LORD **s**,
22: 3 The king of Israel **s** to his servants,
22: 4 He **s** to Jehoshaphat, "Will you go with me
22: 5 But Jehoshaphat also **s** to the king of Israel,
22: 6 about four hundred of them, and **s** to them,
22: 6 They **s**, "Go up;
22: 7 But Jehoshaphat **s**, "Is there no other prophet of
22: 8 The king of Israel **s** to Jehoshaphat,
22: 8 Jehoshaphat **s**, "Let the king not say such a thing."
22: 9 the king of Israel summoned an officer and **s**,
22:11 and he **s**, "Thus says the LORD:
22:13 to summon Micaiah **s** to him, "Look, the words of
22:14 But Micaiah **s**, "As the LORD lives,
22:15 When he had come to the king, the king **s** to him,
22:16 But the king **s** to him,
22:17 Then Micaiah **s**, "I saw all Israel scattered on
22:17 and the LORD **s**, 'These have no master;
22:18 The king of Israel **s** to Jehoshaphat,
22:19 Then Micaiah **s**, "Therefore hear the word of
22:20 And the LORD **s**, 'Who will entice Ahab,
22:20 Then one **s** one thing, and another **s** another,
22:22 Then the LORD **s**, 'You are to entice him,
22:24 slapped him on the cheek, and **s**,
22:28 Micaiah **s**, "If you return in peace,
22:28 And he **s**, "Hear, you peoples, all of you!"
22:30 The king of Israel **s** to Jehoshaphat,
22:32 captains of the chariots saw Jehoshaphat, they **s**,
22:34 so he **s** to the driver of his chariot, "Turn around,
22:49 Then Ahaziah son of Ahab **s** to Jehoshaphat,
2Ki 1: 3 the angel of the LORD **s** to Elijah the Tishbite,
1: 5 messengers returned to the king, who **s** to them,
1: 6 who **s** to us, 'Go back to the king who sent you,
1: 7 He **s** to them, "What sort of man was he who came
1: 8 He **s**, "It is Elijah the Tishbite."
1: 9 who was sitting on the top of a hill, and **s** to him,
1:11 He went up and **s** to him, "O man of God,
1:15 Then the angel of the LORD **s** to Elijah,
1:16 and **s** to him, "Thus says the LORD:
2: 2 Elijah **s** to Elisha, "Stay here;
2: 2 But Elisha **s**, "As the LORD lives,
2: 3 to Elisha, and **s** to him, "Do you know that today
2: 3 And he **s**, "Yes, I know; keep silent."

2Ki 2: 4 Elijah s to him, "Elisha, stay here;
2: 4 But he s, "As the LORD lives,
2: 5 to Elisha, and s to him, "Do you know that today
2: 6 Then Elijah s to him, "Stay here;
2: 6 But he s, "As the LORD lives,
2: 9 When they had crossed, Elijah s to Elisha,
2: 9 Elisha s, "Please let me inherit a double share
2:16 They s to him, "See now, we have fifty strong men
2:17 when they urged him until he was ashamed, he s,
2:18 he s to them, "Did I not say to you, Do not go?"
2:19 Now the people of the city s to Elisha,
2:20 He s, "Bring me a new bowl, and put salt in it."
2:21 and s, "Thus says the LORD,
3:10 Then the king of Israel s, "Alas!
3:11 But Jehoshaphat s, "Is there no prophet of
3:12 Jehoshaphat s, "The word of the LORD is
3:13 Elisha s to the king of Israel,
3:13 But the king of Israel s to him, "No;
3:14 Elisha s, "As the LORD of hosts lives,
3:16 And he s, "Thus says the LORD,
3:23 They s, "This is blood; the kings must have fought
4: 2 Elisha s to her, "What shall I do for you?
4: 3 He s, "Go outside, borrow vessels
4: 6 When the vessels were full, she s to her son,
4: 6 But he s to her, "There are no more."
4: 7 She came and told the man of God, and he s,
4: 9 She s to her husband, "Look,
4:12 He s to his servant Gehazi,
4:13 He s to him, "Say to her,
4:14 He s, "What then may be done for her?"
4:15 He s, "Call her." When he had called her,
4:16 He s, "At this season, in due time,
4:19 father s to his servant, "Carry him to his mother."
4:22 Then she called to her husband, and s,
4:23 He s, "Why go to him today?
4:23 She s, "It will be all right."
4:24 Then she saddled the donkey and s to her servant,
4:25 he s to Gehazi his servant, "Look,
4:27 But the man of God s, "Let her alone,
4:28 Then she s, "Did I ask my lord for a son?
4:29 He s to Gehazi, "Gird up your loins,
4:30 Then the mother of the child s,
4:36 Elisha summoned Gehazi and s,
4:36 When she came to him, he s, "Take your son."
4:38 he s to his servant, "Put the large pot on,
4:41 He s, "Then bring some flour."
4:41 He threw it into the pot, and s,
4:42 Elisha s, "Give it to the people and let them eat."
4:43 But his servant s, "How can I set this before
5: 3 She s to her mistress, "If only my lord were with
5: 4 the girl from the land of Israel had s.
5: 5 And the king of Aram s, "Go then,
5: 7 he tore his clothes and s, "Am I God,
5:13 But his servants approached and s to him, "Father,
5:13 How much more, when all he s to you was, 'Wash,
5:15 he came and stood before him and s,
5:16 But he s, "As the LORD lives, whom I serve,
5:17 Then Naaman s, "If not, please let two mule-loads
5:19 He s to him, "Go in peace."
5:21 down from the chariot to meet him and s,
5:23 Naaman s, "Please accept two talents."
5:25 Elisha s to him, "Where have you been, Gehazi?"
5:26 But he s to him, "Did I not go with you in spirit
6: 1 Now the company of prophets s to Elisha,
6: 3 one of them s, "Please come with your servants."
6: 6 Then the man of God s, "Where did it fall?"
6: 7 He s, "Pick it up."
6: 8 He s, "At such and such a place shall
6:11 he called his officers and s to them,
6:12 Then one of his officers s, "No one, my lord king.
6:13 He s, "Go and find where he is;
6:15 His servant s, "Alas, master!
6:18 and s, "Strike this people, please, with blindness."
6:19 Elisha s to them, "This is not the way,
6:20 As soon as they entered Samaria, Elisha s,
6:21 When the king of Israel saw them he s to Elisha,
6:27 He s, "No! Let the LORD help you.
6:28 She answered, "This woman s to me,
6:29 The next day I s to her,
6:31 and he s, "So may God do to me, and more,
6:32 the messenger arrived, Elisha s to the elders,
6:33 the king came down to him and s,
7: 1 But Elisha s, "Hear the word of the LORD;
7: 2 Then the captain on whose hand the king leaned s
7: 2 But he s, "You shall see it with your own eyes,
7: 3 who s to one another, "Why should we sit here
7: 6 so that they s to one another,
7: 9 Then they s to one another,
7:12 The king got up in the night, and s to his servants,
7:13 One of his servants s, "Let some men take five of
7:17 as the man of God had s when the king came down
7:18 For when the man of God had s to the king,
8: 1 Now Elisha had s to the woman whose son he had
8: 5 Gehazi s, "My lord king, here is the woman,
8: 8 the king s to Hazael, "Take a present with you
8: 9 When he entered and stood before him, he s,
8:10 Elisha s to him, "Go, say to him,
8:13 Hazael s, "What is your servant,
8:14 and went to his master Ben-hadad, who s to him,
9: 1 of the company of prophets and s to him, "Gird
9:11 they s to him, "Is everything all right?
9:12 They s, "Liar! Come on, tell us!"
9:12 So he s, "This is just what he s to me:
9:15 So Jehu s, "If this is your wish,
9:17 and s, "I see a company."
9:17 Joram s, "Take a horseman;
9:18 he s, "Thus says the king, 'Is it peace?' "

2Ki 9:19 who came to them and s, "Thus says the king,
9:21 Joram s, "Get ready."
9:22 When Joram saw Jehu, he s, "Is it peace, Jehu?"
9:25 Jehu s to his aide Bidkar, "Lift him out,
9:31 As Jehu entered the gate, she s, "Is it peace, Zimri,
9:32 He looked up to the window and s,
9:33 He s, "Throw her down."
9:34 he s, "See to that cursed woman and bury her;
9:36 When they came back and told him, he s,
10: 4 But they were utterly terrified and s, "Look,
10: 8 he s, "Lay them in two heaps
10: 9 he stood and s to all the people,
10:10 for the LORD has done what he s
10:13 of King Ahaziah of Judah and s,
10:14 He s, "Take them alive."
10:15 he greeted him, and s to him,
10:15 Jehu s, "If it is, give me your hand."
10:16 He s, "Come with me, and see my zeal for
10:18 Then Jehu assembled all the people and s to them,
10:22 He s to the keeper of the wardrobe,
10:23 he s to the worshipers of Baal,
10:25 Jehu s to the guards and to the officers,
10:30 The LORD s to Jehu,
11:15 For the priest s, "Let her not be killed in the house
12: 4 Jehoash s to the priests, "All the money offered
12: 7 the priest Jehoiada with the other priests and s
13:15 Elisha s to him, "Take a bow and arrows";
13:16 Then he s to the king of Israel, "Draw the bow";
13:17 Then he s, "Open the window eastward";
13:17 Elisha s, "Shoot"; and he shot.
13:17 Then he s, "The LORD's arrow of victory,
13:18 He s to the king of Israel,
13:19 Then the man of God was angry with him, and s,
14:27 But the LORD had not s that he would blot out
17:12 of which the LORD had s to them,
18:19 The Rabshakeh s to them, "Say to Hezekiah:
18:25 The LORD s to me, Go up against this land,
18:26 and Shebnah, and Joah s to the Rabshakeh,
18:27 But the Rabshakeh s to them,
19: 3 They s to him, "Thus says Hezekiah,
19: 6 Isaiah s to them, "Say to your master, 'Thus says
19:15 And Hezekiah prayed before the LORD, and s:
19:23 you have mocked the Lord, and you have s,
20: 1 and s to him, "Thus says the LORD:
20: 7 Then Isaiah s, "Bring a lump of figs.
20: 8 Hezekiah s to Isaiah, "What shall be the sign that
20: 9 Isaiah s, "This is the sign to you from the LORD,
20:14 and s to him, "What did these men say?
20:15 He s, "What have they seen in your house?"
20:16 Then Isaiah s to Hezekiah,
20:19 Then Hezekiah s to Isaiah,
21: 4 of which the LORD had s,
21: 7 in the house of which the LORD s to David and
21:10 The LORD s by his servants the prophets,
22: 8 The high priest Hilkiah s to Shaphan the secretary,
23:17 Then he s, "What is that monument that I see?"
23:18 He s, "Let him rest; let no one move his bones."
23:27 The LORD s, "I will remove Judah also out
23:27 Jerusalem, and the house of which I s,
1Ch 10: 4 Then Saul s to his armor-bearer,
11: 1 to David at Hebron and s,
11: 2 The LORD your God s to you:
11: 5 The inhabitants of Jebus s to David,
11: 6 David had s, "Whoever attacks
11:17 David s longingly, "O that someone would give
11:19 and s, "My God forbid
12:17 David went out to meet them and s to them,
12:18 chief of the Thirty, and he s, "We are yours,
13: 2 David s to the whole assembly of Israel,
13:12 David was afraid of God that day; he s,
14:10 The LORD s to him, "Go up,
14:11 David s, "God has burst out against my enemies
14:14 When David again inquired of God, God s to him,
15:12 He s to them, "You are the heads of families of
16:36 Then all the people s "Amen!"
17: 1 David s to the prophet Nathan,
17: 2 Nathan s to David, "Do all that you have in mind,
17:16 and s, "Who am I, O LORD God,
19: 2 David s, "I will deal loyally with Hanun son
19: 3 the officials of the Ammonites s to Hanun,
19: 5 The king s, "Remain at Jericho
19:12 He s, "If the Arameans are too strong for me,
21: 2 David s to Joab and the commanders of the army
21: 3 But Joab s, "May the LORD increase the number
21: 8 David s to God, "I have sinned greatly in
21:11 So Gad came to David and s to him,
21:13 Then David s to Gad, "I am in great distress;
21:15 he s to the destroying angel, "Enough!
21:17 And David s to God, "Was it not I who gave
21:22 David s to Ornan, "Give me the site of
21:23 Then Ornan s to David, "Take it;
21:24 But King David s to Ornan, "No;
22: 1 Then David s, "Here shall be the house of
22: 5 For David s, "My son Solomon is young
22: 7 David s to Solomon, "My son,
23: 4 "Twenty-four thousand of these," David s,
23:25 For David s, "The LORD, the God of Israel,
28: 2 Then King David rose to his feet and s:
28: 3 But God s to me, 'You shall not build a house
28: 6 He s to me, 'It is your son Solomon who shall
28:20 David s further to his son Solomon,
29: 1 King David s to the whole assembly,
29:10 David s: "Blessed are you, O LORD
29:20 Then David s to the whole assembly,
2Ch 1: 7 night God appeared to Solomon, and s to him,
1: 8 Solomon s to God, "You have shown great
2:12 Huram also s, "Blessed be the LORD God

2Ch 6: 1 Then Solomon s, "The LORD has s that he would
6: 4 And he s, "Blessed be the LORD,
6: 8 But the LORD s to my father David,
6:14 He s, "O LORD, God of Israel,
7:12 to Solomon in the night and s to him:
8:11 that he had built for her, for he s, "My wife shall
9: 5 So she s to the king, "The report was true
10: 3 Jeroboam and all Israel came and s to Rehoboam,
10: 5 He s to them, "Come to me again in three days."
10: 9 He s to them, "What do you advise
10: 9 that we answer this people who have s to me,
10:10 young men who had grown up with him s to him,
10:10 "Thus should you speak to the people who s
10:12 to Rehoboam the third day, as the king had s,
12: 5 and s to them, "Thus says the LORD:
12: 6 of Israel and the king humbled themselves and s,
13: 4 and s, "Listen to me, Jeroboam and all Israel!
14: 7 He s to Judah, "Let us build these cities,
15: 2 He went out to meet Asa and s to him, "Hear me,
16: 7 the seer Hanani came to King Asa of Judah, and s
18: 3 King Ahab of Israel s to King Jehoshaphat
18: 4 But Jehoshaphat also s to the king of Israel,
18: 5 four hundred of them, and s to them,
18: 5 They s, "Go up; for God will give it
18: 6 But Jehoshaphat s, "Is there no other prophet of
18: 7 The king of Israel s to Jehoshaphat,
18: 7 Jehoshaphat s, "Let the king not say such a thing."
18: 8 the king of Israel summoned an officer and s,
18:10 and he s, "Thus says the LORD:
18:12 to summon Micaiah s to him, "Look, the words of
18:13 But Micaiah s, "As the LORD lives,
18:14 When he had come to the king, the king s to him,
18:15 But the king s to him, "How many times
18:16 Then Micaiah s, "I saw all Israel scattered on
18:16 and the LORD s, 'These have no master;
18:17 The king of Israel s to Jehoshaphat,
18:18 Then Micaiah s, "Therefore hear the word of
18:19 And the LORD s, 'Who will entice King Ahab
18:19 Then one s one thing, and another s another,
18:21 Then the LORD s, 'You are to entice him,
18:23 slapped him on the cheek, and s,
18:27 Micaiah s, "If you return in peace,
18:27 And he s, "Hear, you peoples, all of you!"
18:29 The king of Israel s to Jehoshaphat,
18:31 captains of the chariots saw Jehoshaphat, they s,
18:33 so he s to the driver of his chariot, "Turn around,
19: 2 of Hanani the seer went out to meet him and s
19: 6 and s to the judges, "Consider what you are doing,
20: 6 and s, "O LORD, God of our ancestors, are you
20:15 He s, "Listen, all Judah and inhabitants
20:20 and as they went out, Jehoshaphat stood and s,
22: 9 They buried him, for they s,
23: 3 Jehoiada s to them, "Here is the king's son!
23:14 the priest s, "Do not put her to death in the house
24: 5 and the Levites and s to them, "Go out to the cities
24: 6 king summoned Jehoiada the chief, and s to him,
24:20 he stood above the people and s to them,
24:22 he s, "May the LORD see and avenge!"
25: 7 But a man of God came to him and s, "O king,
25: 9 Amaziah s to the man of God,
25:15 a prophet, who s to him, "Why have you resorted
25:16 But as he was speaking the king s to him,
25:16 So the prophet stopped, but s,
26:18 and s to him, "It is not for you, Uzziah,
26:23 for they s, "He is leprous."
28: 9 and s to them, "Because the LORD,
28:13 and s to them, "You shall not bring the captives
28:23 which had defeated him, and s,
29: 5 He s to them, "Listen to me, Levites!
29:18 Then they went inside to King Hezekiah and s,
29:31 Then Hezekiah s, "You have
32:16 His servants s still more against the Lord GOD
33: 4 of which the LORD had s,
33: 7 of which God s to David and to his son Solomon,
34:15 Hilkiah s to the secretary Shaphan,
35: 3 He s to the Levites who taught all Israel
35:23 and the king s to his servants, "Take me away,
Ezr 4: 2 and the heads of families and s to them,
4: 3 the rest of the heads of families in Israel s to them,
5:15 He s to him, "Take these vessels;
8:28 And I s to them, "You are holy to the LORD,
9: 1 the officials approached me and s,
9: 6 and s, "O my God, I am too ashamed
10: 5 all Israel swear that they would do as had been s.
10:10 Then Ezra the priest stood up and s to them,
10:12 we must do as you have s.
Ne 1: 5 I s, "O LORD God of heaven,
2: 2 So the king s to me, "Why is your face sad,
2: 3 I s to the king, "May the king live forever!
2: 4 Then the king s to me, "What do you request?"
2: 5 Then I s to the king, "If it pleases the king,
2: 6 The king s to me (the queen also was sitting
2: 7 Then I s to the king, "If it pleases the king,
2:17 Then I s to them, "You see the trouble we are in,
2:18 Then they s, "Let us start building!"
4: 2 He s in the presence of his associates and of
4: 3 Tobiah the Ammonite was beside him, and he s,
4:10 But Judah s, "The strength of the burden bearers
4:11 And our enemies s, "They will not know
4:12 they s to us ten times,
4:14 up and s to the nobles and the officials and the rest
4:19 And I s to the nobles, the officials,
4:22 I also s to the people at that time,
5: 2 For there were those who s,
5: 3 There were also those who s,
5: 4 And there were those who s,
5: 7 I s to them, "You are all taking interest

Ne 5: 8 and s to them, "As far as we
5: 9 So I s, "The thing that you are doing is not good.
5: 12 Then they s, "We will restore everything
5: 13 I also shook out the fold of my garment and s,
5: 13 And all the assembly s, "Amen,"
6: 10 he s, "Let us meet together in the house of God,
6: 11 But I s, "Should a man like me run away?
7: 3 And I s to them, "The gates of Jerusalem are not to
8: 9 Levites who taught the people s to all the people,
8: 10 Then he s to them, "Go your way,
9: 5 Sherebiah, Hodiah, Shebaniah, and Pethahiah, s,
9: 6 And Ezra s: "You are the LORD,
9: 18 an image of a calf for themselves and s,
13: 11 So I remonstrated with the officials and s,
13: 17 with the nobles of Judah and s to them,
13: 21 But I warned them and s to them,
Est 1: 16 Then Memucan s in the presence of the king and
2: 2 Then the king's servants who attended him s,
3: 3 the king's servants who were at the king's gate s
3: 8 Then Haman s to King Ahasuerus,
3: 11 The king s to Haman, "The money is given to you,
4: 9 and told Esther what Mordecai had s.
4: 12 When they told Mordecai what Esther had s,
4: 15 Then Esther s in reply to Mordecai,
5: 3 The king s to her, "What is it, Queen Esther?
5: 4 Then Esther s, "If it pleases the king,
5: 5 Then the king s, "Bring Haman quickly,
5: 6 they were drinking wine, the king s to Esther,
5: 7 Then Esther s, "This is my petition and request:
5: 8 and then I will do as the king has s."
5: 14 Then his wife Zeresh and all his friends s to him,
6: 3 Then the king s, "What honor
6: 3 The king's servants who attended him s,
6: 4 The king s, "Who is in the court?"
6: 5 The king s, "Let him come in."
6: 6 So Haman came in, and the king s to him,
6: 6 Haman s to himself, "Whom would the king wish
6: 7 So Haman s to the king,
6: 10 Then the king s to Haman, "Quickly,
6: 10 take the robes and the horse, as you have s,
6: 13 his advisers and his wife Zeresh s to him,
7: 2 the king again s to Esther, "What is your petition,
7: 5 Then King Ahasuerus s to Queen Esther,
7: 6 Esther s, "A foe and enemy, this wicked Haman!"
7: 8 and the king s, "Will he even assault the queen
7: 9 one of the eunuchs in attendance on the king, s,
7: 9 And the king s, "Hang him on that."
8: 5 She s, "If it pleases the king,
8: 7 Then King Ahasuerus s to Queen Esther and to
9: 12 The king s to Queen Esther,
9: 13 Esther s, "If it pleases the king,
Job 1: 5 for Job s, "It may be that my children have sinned,
1: 7 LORD s to Satan, "Where have you come from?"
1: 8 The LORD s to Satan, "Have you considered my
1: 12 The LORD s to Satan, "Very well,
1: 14 a messenger came to Job and s,
1: 16 While he was still speaking, another came and s,
1: 17 While he was still speaking, another came and s,
1: 18 While he was still speaking, another came and s,
1: 21 He s, "Naked I came from my mother's womb,
2: 2 LORD s to Satan, "Where have you come from?"
2: 3 The LORD s to Satan, "Have you considered my
2: 6 The LORD s to Satan, "Very well,
2: 9 Then his wife s to him, "Do you still persist
2: 10 But he s to her, "You speak as any foolish
3: 2 Job s:
3: 3 and the night that s, 'A man-child is conceived.'
6: 22 Have I s, 'Make me a gift'?
22: 17 They s to God, 'Leave us alone,'
27: 1 Job again took up his discourse and s:
28: 28 And he s to humankind, 'Truly,
29: 1 Job again took up his discourse and s:
31: 31 of my tent ever s, 'O that we might be sated
32: 7 I s, 'Let days speak, and many years teach
34: 1 Then Elihu continued and s:
34: 5 For Job has s, 'I am innocent,
34: 9 For he has s, 'It profits one nothing to take delight
34: 31 has anyone s to God, 'I have endured punishment;
35: 1 Elihu continued and s:
36: 1 Elihu continued and s:
38: 11 and s, 'Thus far shall you come, and no farther,
40: 1 And the LORD s to Job:
42: 7 the LORD s to Eliphaz the Temanite:
Ps 2: 7 He s to me, "You are my son;
18: T *and from the hand of Saul. He s:*
30: 6 I s in my prosperity, "I shall never be moved."
31: 22 I had s in my alarm,
32: 5 I s, "I will confess my transgressions to
39: 1 I s, "I will guard my ways that I may not sin
40: 7 Then I s, "Here I am;
41: 4 As for me, I s, "O LORD, be gracious to me;
52: T *came to Saul and s to him, "David has come*
68: 22 The Lord s, "I will bring them back from Bashan,
73: 15 If I had s, "I will talk on in this way,"
74: 8 They s to themselves, "We will utterly subdue
83: 12 who s, "Let us take the pastures of God
87: 5 And of Zion it shall be s,
89: 3 You s, "I have made a covenant
89: 19 you spoke in a vision to your faithful one, and s:
95: 10 For forty years I loathed that generation and s,
105: 19 until what he had s came to pass,
106: 23 Therefore he s he would destroy them—
116: 10 I kept my faith, even when I s,
116: 11 I s in my consternation, "Everyone is a liar."
122: 1 I was glad when they s to me,
126: 2 then it was s among the nations,
137: 7 how they s, "Tear it down!
Pr 4: 4 and s to me, "Let your heart hold fast my words;
Ecc 1: 10 Is there a thing of which it is s, "See, this is new"?
1: 16 I s to myself, "I have acquired great wisdom,
2: 1 I s to myself, "Come now,
2: 2 I s of laughter, "It is mad," and of pleasure,
2: 15 Then I s to myself, "What happens to
2: 15 And I s to myself that this also is vanity.
3: 17 I s in my heart, God will judge the righteous and
3: 18 I s in my heart with regard to human beings
7: 23 I s, "I will be wise," but it was far from me.
8: 14 I s that this also is vanity.
9: 16 So I s, "Wisdom is better than might;
Isa 3: 16 The LORD s: Because the daughters of Zion
6: 3 And one called to another and s:
6: 5 And I s: "Woe is me!
6: 7 The seraph touched my mouth with it and s:
6: 8 And I s, "Here am I; send me!"
6: 9 And he s, "Go and say to this people:
6: 11 Then I s, "How long, O Lord?" And he s:
7: 3 Then the LORD s to Isaiah, Go out to meet Ahaz,
7: 12 But Ahaz s, I will not ask,
7: 13 Then Isaiah s: "Hear then, O house of David!
8: 1 Then the LORD s to me,
8: 3 Then the LORD s to me,
9: 9 but in pride and arrogance of heart they s:
14: 13 You s in your heart, "I will ascend to heaven;
18: 4 For thus the LORD s to me:
20: 3 Then the LORD s, "Just
21: 6 For thus the Lord s to me:
21: 16 For thus the Lord s to me:
22: 4 Therefore I s: Look away from me,
23: 12 He s: You will exult no longer,
25: 9 It will be s on that day, Lo, this is our God;
28: 12 to whom he has s, "This is rest;
28: 15 Because you have s, "We have made a covenant
29: 13 The Lord s: Because these people draw near with
30: 15 For thus s the Lord GOD, the Holy One of Israel:
30: 16 and s, "No! We will flee upon horses"—
31: 4 For thus the LORD s to me,
32: 5 nor a villain s to be honorable.
36: 4 The Rabshakeh s to them, "Say to Hezekiah:
36: 10 The LORD s to me, Go up against this land,
36: 11 Eliakim, Shebna, and Joah s to the Rabshakeh,
36: 12 But the Rabshakeh s, "Has my master sent me
37: 3 They s to him, "Thus says Hezekiah,
37: 6 Isaiah s to them, "Say to your master, 'Thus says
37: 24 you have mocked the Lord, and you have s,
38: 1 and s to him, "Thus says the LORD:
38: 10 I s: In the noontide of my days
38: 11 I s, I shall not see the LORD in the land of
38: 21 Now Isaiah had s, "Let them take a lump of figs,
38: 22 also had s, "What is the sign that I shall go up to
39: 3 the prophet Isaiah came to King Hezekiah and s
39: 4 He s, "What have they seen in your house?"
39: 5 Then Isaiah s to Hezekiah,
39: 8 Then Hezekiah s to Isaiah,
40: 6 And I s, "What shall I cry?"
45: 24 Only in the LORD, it shall be s of me,
47: 7 You s, "I shall be mistress forever,"
47: 10 You felt secure in your wickedness; you s,
47: 10 and you s in your heart, "I am, and there is no one
49: 3 And he s to me, "You are my servant, Israel,
49: 4 But I s, "I have labored in vain,
49: 14 But Zion s, "The LORD has forsaken me,
51: 23 who have s to you, "Bow down,
57: 14 It shall be s, "Build up, build up, prepare the way,
63: 8 For he s, "Surely they are my people,
65: 1 I s, "Here I am, here I am,"
66: 5 and reject you for my name's sake have s, "Let
Jer 1: 6 Then I s, "Ah, Lord GOD!
1: 7 LORD s to me, "Do not say, 'I am only a boy';
1: 9 and the LORD s to me,
1: 11 And I s, "I see a branch of an almond tree."
1: 12 Then the LORD s to me, "You have seen well,
1: 13 And I s, "I see a boiling pot,
1: 14 Then the LORD s to me:
2: 20 and you s, "I will not serve!"
2: 25 But you s, "It is hopeless,
3: 6 The LORD s to me in the days of King Josiah:
3: 11 Then the LORD s to me:
4: 10 Then I s, "Ah, Lord GOD,
4: 11 At that time it will be s to this people and
5: 4 I s, "These are only the poor, they have no sense;
5: 12 and have s, "He will do nothing.
6: 16 But they s, "We will not walk in it."
6: 17 But they s, "We will not give heed."
10: 19 But I s, "Truly this is my punishment,
11: 6 And the LORD s to me:
11: 9 And the LORD s to me:
12: 4 and because people s, "He is blind to our ways."
13: 1 Thus s the LORD to me,
13: 6 And after many days the LORD s to me,
14: 11 The LORD s to me: Do
14: 13 Then I s: "Ah, Lord GOD!
14: 14 And the LORD s to me:
15: 1 Then the LORD s to me:
15: 11 The LORD s: Surely I have intervened in your
16: 14 says the LORD, when it shall no longer be s,
17: 19 Thus s the LORD to me:
18: 18 Then they s, "Come, let us make plots
19: 1 Thus s the LORD: Go
19: 14 he stood in the court of the LORD's house and s
20: 3 Jeremiah s to him, The LORD has named you
21: 3 Then Jeremiah s to them:
22: 21 I spoke to you in your prosperity, but you s,
23: 7 says the LORD, when it shall no longer be s,
23: 25 the prophets have s who prophesy lies
Jer 23: 38 Because you have s these words,
24: 3 the LORD s to me, "What do you see, Jeremiah?"
24: 3 I s, "Figs, the good figs very good,
25: 5 when they s, "Turn now, everyone of you,
25: 15 For thus the LORD, the God of Israel, s to me:
26: 11 the prophets s to the officials and to all the people,
26: 16 Then the officials and all the people s to the priests
26: 17 of the land arose and s to all the assembled people,
26: 18 s to all the people of Judah:
27: 2 Thus the LORD s to me:
28: 6 and the prophet Jeremiah s,
28: 15 the prophet Jeremiah s to the prophet Hananiah,
29: 3 to King Nebuchadnezzar of Babylon. It s:
29: 15 Because you have s, "The LORD has raised
32: 3 Zedekiah had s, "Why do you prophesy and say:
32: 6 Jeremiah s, The word of the LORD came to me:
32: 8 and s to me, "Buy my field that is at Anathoth in
32: 25 Yet you, O Lord GOD, have s to me,
35: 5 and I s to them, "Have some wine."
35: 11 we s, 'Come, and let us go to Jerusalem for fear of
35: 18 But to the house of the Rechabites Jeremiah s:
36: 15 And they s to him, "Sit down and read it to us."
36: 16 to one another in alarm, and s to Baruch,
36: 19 Then the officials s to Baruch, "Go and hide,
37: 14 And Jeremiah s, "That is a lie;
37: 17 king questioned him secretly in his house, and s,
37: 17 Jeremiah s, "There is!"
37: 17 Then he s, "You shall be handed over to the king
37: 18 Jeremiah also s to King Zedekiah,
38: 4 Then the officials s to the king,
38: 5 King Zedekiah s, "Here he is;
38: 12 Then Ebed-melech the Ethiopian s to Jeremiah,
38: 14 king s to Jeremiah, "I have something to ask you;
38: 15 Jeremiah s to Zedekiah, "If I tell you,
38: 17 Then Jeremiah s to Zedekiah,
38: 19 King Zedekiah s to Jeremiah,
38: 20 Jeremiah s, "That will not happen.
38: 24 Then Zedekiah s to Jeremiah,
38: 25 'Just tell us what you s to the king;
40: 2 captain of the guard took Jeremiah and s to him,
40: 3 and has done as he s,
40: 14 and s to him, "Are you at all aware
40: 16 But Gedaliah son of Ahikam s to Johanan son
41: 6 As he met them, he s to them,
41: 8 there were ten men among them who s to Ishmael,
42: 2 the prophet Jeremiah and s, "Be good enough
42: 4 The prophet Jeremiah s to them, "Very well:
42: 5 They in their turn s to Jeremiah,
42: 9 and s to them, "Thus says the LORD, the God
42: 19 The LORD has s to you, O remnant of Judah,
43: 2 and all the other insolent men s to Jeremiah,
44: 19 And the women s, "Indeed we will go
44: 20 Then Jeremiah s to all the people,
44: 24 Jeremiah s to all the people and all the women,
45: 3 You s, "Woe is me! The LORD has added sorrow
46: 8 It s, Let me rise, let me cover the earth,
46: 16 and one s to another, "Come,
46: 25 The LORD of hosts, the God of Israel, s:
50: 7 and their enemies have s, "We are not guilty,
51: 61 And Jeremiah s to Seraiah:
La 3: 54 water closed over my head; I s, "I am lost."
3: 57 You came near when I called on you; you s,
4: 15 it was s among the nations,
4: 20 the one of whom we s,
Eze 2: 1 He s to me: O mortal, stand up on
2: 3 He s to me, Mortal, I am sending you to the people
3: 1 He s to me, O mortal, eat what is offered to you;
3: 3 He s to me, Mortal, eat this scroll that I give you
3: 4 He s to me: Mortal, go to the
3: 10 He s to me: Mortal, all my words
3: 22 and he s to me, Rise up, go out into the valley,
3: 24 and he spoke with me and s to me:
4: 13 The LORD s, "Thus shall the people
4: 14 Then I s, "Ah Lord GOD!
4: 15 Then he s to me, "See, I will let you have cow's
4: 16 Then he s to me, Mortal, I am going to break
8: 5 Then God s to me, "O mortal,
8: 6 He s to me, "Mortal, do you see what they are
8: 8 Then he s to me, "Mortal, dig through the wall";
8: 9 He s to me, "Go in, and see the vile abominations
8: 12 Then he s to me, "Mortal,
8: 13 He s also to me, "You will see still greater
8: 15 Then he s to me, "Have you seen this, O mortal?
8: 17 Then he s to me, "Have you seen this, O mortal?
9: 4 and s to him, "Go through the city,
9: 5 To the others he s in my hearing,
9: 7 Then he s to them, "Defile the house,
9: 9 He s to me, "The guilt of the house of Israel
10: 2 He s to the man clothed in linen,
11: 2 He s to me, "Mortal, these are
11: 5 spirit of the LORD fell upon me, and he s to me,
11: 13 cried with a loud voice, and s, "Ah Lord GOD!
11: 15 of Jerusalem have s, "They have gone far from
12: 9 s to you, "What are you doing?"
13: 7 when you have s, "Says the LORD,"
13: 12 When the wall falls, will it not be s to you,
16: 6 As you lay in your blood, I s to you, "Live!
20: 7 And I s to them, Cast away
20: 18 I s to their children in the wilderness,
20: 29 (I s to them, What is the high place
20: 49 Then I s, "Ah Lord GOD!
23: 36 The LORD s to me: Mortal,
23: 43 Then I s, Ah, she is worn out with adulteries,
24: 19 Then the people s to me,
24: 20 Then I s to them: The word of the
25: 3 Thus says the Lord GOD, Because you s, "Aha!"
25: 8 Thus says the Lord GOD: Because Moab s,

Eze 26: 2 because Tyre s concerning Jerusalem, "Aha,
27: 3 O Tyre, you have s, "I am perfect in beauty."
28: 2 your heart is proud and you have s, "I am a god;
29: 9 Because you s, "The Nile is mine, and I made it,"
33:10 mortal, say to the house of Israel, Thus you have s:
33:21 from Jerusalem came to me and s,
35:10 Because you s, "These two nations
36: 2 Because the enemy s of you, "Aha!"
36:20 in that it was s of them,
37: 3 He s to me, "Mortal, can these bones live?"
37: 4 Then he s to me, "Prophesy to these bones,
37: 9 Then he s to me, "Prophesy to the breath,
37:11 Then he s to me, "Mortal,
40: 4 The man s to me, "Mortal,
40:45 He s to me, "This chamber that faces south is for
41: 4 And he s to me, This is the most holy place.
41:22 He s to me, "This is the table that stands before
42:13 Then he s to me, "The north chambers and
43: 7 He s to me: Mortal, this is the place of my
43:18 Then he s to me: Mortal, thus says the Lord GOD:
44: 2 The LORD s to me: This gate shall remain shut;
44: 5 The LORD s to me: Mortal,
46:20 He s to me, "This is the place where
46:24 Then he s to me, "These are the kitchens
47: 6 He s to me, "Mortal, have you seen this?"
47: 8 He s to me, "This water flows toward
Da 1:10 The palace master s to Daniel,
2: 3 he s to them, "I have had such a dream
2: 4 The Chaldeans s to the king (in Aramaic),
2:20 Daniel s: "Blessed be the name of God
2:24 and s to him, "Do not destroy the wise men
2:25 before the king and s to him:
2:26 king s to Daniel, whose name was Belteshazzar,
2:47 The king s to Daniel, "Truly,
3: 9 They s to King Nebuchadnezzar, "O king,
3:14 Nebuchadnezzar s to them, "Is it true, O Shadrach,
3:24 He s to his counselors, "Was it not three men
3:26 the door of the furnace of blazing fire and s,
3:28 Nebuchadnezzar s, "Blessed be the God
4:14 He cried aloud and s: 'Cut down the
4:19 The king s, "Belteshazzar,
4:30 and the king s, "Is this not magnificent Babylon,
5: 7 and the king s to the wise men of Babylon,
5:10 The queen s, "O king, live forever!
5:13 The king s to Daniel, "So you are Daniel,
6: 5 The men s, "We shall not find any ground
6: 6 and satraps conspired and came to the king and s
6:12 Then they approached the king and s concerning
6:15 the conspirators came to the king and s to him,
6:16 The king s to Daniel, "May your God,
6:21 Daniel then s to the king, "O king, live forever!
7:16 So he s that he would disclose to me
7:23 This is what he s: "As
8:13 and another holy one s to the one that spoke,
8:17 But he s to me, "Understand, O mortal,
8:19 He s, "Listen, and I will tell you what will take
9:22 He came and s to me, "Daniel,
10:11 He s to me, "Daniel, greatly beloved,
10:12 He s to me, "Do not fear, Daniel,
10:16 and s to the one who stood before me, "My lord,
10:19 He s, "Do not fear, greatly beloved, you are safe.
10:19 When he spoke to me, I was strengthened and s,
10:20 he s, "Do you know why I have come to you?
12: 6 One of them s to the man clothed in linen,
12: 8 I heard but could not understand; so I s, "My lord,
12: 9 He s, "Go your way, Daniel,
Hos 1: 2 the LORD s to Hosea, "Go,
1: 4 And the LORD s to him, "Name him Jezreel;
1: 6 Then the LORD s to him, "Name her Lo-ruhamah,
1: 9 Then the LORD s, "Name him Lo-ammi,
1:10 and in the place where it was s to them,
1:10 it shall be s to them, "Children of the living God."
2: 5 For she s, "I will go after my lovers;
2:12 of which she s, "These are my pay,
3: 1 The LORD s to me again, "Go,
3: 3 And I s to her, "You must remain as mine
12: 8 Ephraim has s, "Ah, I am rich,
13:10 of whom you s, "Give me a king and rulers"?
Joel 2:17 Why should it be s among the peoples,
2:19 In response to his people the LORD s:
2:32 be those who escape, as the LORD has s,
Am 1: 2 And he s: The LORD roars from Zion,
5:14 will be with you, just as you have s.
7: 2 they had finished eating the grass of the land, I s,
7: 3 "It shall not be," s the LORD.
7: 5 Then I s, "O Lord GOD, cease, I beg you!
7: 6 "This also shall not be," s the Lord GOD.
7: 8 the LORD s to me, "Amos, what do you see?"
7: 8 And I s, "A plumb line."
7: 8 Then the Lord s, "See, I am setting a plumb line in
7:11 For thus Amos has s, 'Jeroboam shall die by
7:12 And Amaziah s to Amos, "O seer, go,
7:15 and the LORD s to me, 'Go,
8: 2 He s, "Amos, what do you see?"
8: 2 And I s, "A basket of summer fruit."
8: 2 Then the LORD s to me, "The end has come
9: 1 the LORD standing beside the altar, and he s:
Jnh 1: 6 The captain came and s to him,
1: 7 The sailors s to one another, "Come,
1: 8 Then they s to him, "Tell us why this calamity has
1:10 Then the men were even more afraid, and s to him,
1:11 Then they s to him, "What shall we do to you,
1:12 He s to them, "Pick me up and throw me into
2: 4 Then I s, 'I am driven away from your sight;
3:10 about the calamity that he had s he would bring
4: 2 He prayed to the LORD and s, "O LORD!
4: 2 Is not this what I s while I was still
Jnh 4: 4 the LORD s, "Is it right for you to be angry?"
4: 8 He s, "It is better for me to die than to live."
4: 9 But God s to Jonah, "Is it right for you to be angry
4: 9 And he s, "Yes, angry enough to die."
4:10 the LORD s, "You are concerned about the bush,
Mic 2: 7 Should this be s, O house of Jacob?
3: 1 And I s: Listen, you heads of Jacob
7:10 and shame will cover her who s to me,
Hab 2: 2 Then the LORD answered me and s:
Zep 2:15 that s to itself, "I am, and there is no one else"?
3: 7 I s, "Surely the city will fear me,
3:16 On that day it shall be s to Jerusalem:
Hag 2:13 Then Haggai s, "If one who is unclean by contact
2:14 Haggai then s, So is it with this people,
Zec 1: 6 and s, "The LORD of hosts has dealt with us
1: 7 of Berechiah son of Iddo; and Zechariah s,
1: 9 Then I s, "What are these, my lord?"
1: 9 The angel who talked with me s to me,
1:12 Then the angel of the LORD s,
1:14 So the angel who talked with me s to me,
2: 4 and s to him, "Run, say to that young man:
2: 8 For thus s the LORD of hosts
3: 2 And the LORD s to Satan,
3: 4 angel s to those who were standing before him,
3: 4 to him he s, "See, I have taken your guilt away
3: 5 I s, "Let them put a clean turban on his head."
4: 2 He s to me, "What do you see?"
4: 2 And I s, "I see a lampstand all of gold,
4: 4 I s to the angel who talked with me,
4: 5 I s, "No, my lord."
4: 6 He s to me, "This is the word of the LORD
4:11 Then I s to him, "What are these two olive trees on
4:12 And a second time I s to him,
4:13 He s to me, "Do you not know what these are?"
4:13 I s, "No, my lord."
4:14 Then he s, "These are the two anointed ones who
5: 2 And he s to me, "What do you see?"
5: 3 Then he s to me, "This is the curse that goes out
5: 5 the angel who talked with me came forward and s
5: 6 I s, "What is it?"
5: 6 He s, "This is a basket coming out."
5: 6 And he s, "This is their iniquity in all the land."
5: 8 And he s, "This is Wickedness."
5:10 Then I s to the angel who talked with me,
5:11 He s to me, "To the land of Shinar,
6: 4 Then I s to the angel who talked with me,
6: 7 And he s, "Go, patrol the earth."
11: 4 Thus s the LORD my God:
11: 9 So I s, "I will not be your shepherd.
11:12 I then s to them, "If it seems right to you,
11:13 the LORD s to me, "Throw it into the treasury"—
11:15 Then the LORD s to me:
Mal 3:14 You have s, "It is vain to serve God.
Mt 1:20 of the Lord appeared to him in a dream and s,
2:13 to Joseph in a dream and s, "Get up, take the child
2:19 in a dream to Joseph in Egypt and s,
3: 3 the prophet Isaiah spoke when he s, "The voice
3: 7 he s to them, "You brood of vipers!
3:17 And a voice from heaven s, "This is my Son,
4: 3 The tempter came and s to him,
4: 7 Jesus s to him, "Again it is written,
4: 9 and he s to him, "All these I will give you,
4:10 Jesus s to him, "Away with you, Satan!
4:19 And he s to them, "Follow me,
5:21 that it was s to those of ancient times, 'You shall
5:27 "You have heard that it was s,
5:31 "It was also s, 'Whoever divorces his wife,
5:33 that it was s to those of ancient times,
5:38 "You have heard that it was s,
5:43 "You have heard that it was s,
8: 4 Then Jesus s to him, "See that you say nothing
8: 7 And he s to him, "I will come and cure him."
8:10 he was amazed and s to those who followed him,
8:13 And to the centurion Jesus s, "Go;
8:19 A scribe then approached and s, "Teacher,
8:20 And Jesus s to him, "Foxes have holes,
8:21 Another of his disciples s to him, "Lord,
8:22 But Jesus s to him, "Follow me,
8:26 And he s to them, "Why are you afraid,
8:32 And he s to them, "Go!"
9: 2 When Jesus saw their faith, he s to the paralytic,
9: 3 Then some of the scribes s to themselves,
9: 4 But Jesus, perceiving their thoughts, s,
9: 6 he then s to the paralytic—
9: 9 and he s to him, "Follow me."
9:11 the Pharisees saw this, they s to his disciples,
9:12 But when he heard this, he s,
9:15 And Jesus s to them, "The wedding guests cannot
9:21 for she s to herself, "If I only touch his cloak,
9:22 Jesus turned, and seeing her he s, "Take heart,
9:24 he s, "Go away; for the girl is
9:28 and Jesus s to them, "Do you believe
9:28 They s to him, "Yes, Lord."
9:29 Then he touched their eyes and s,
9:33 and the crowds were amazed and s,
9:34 But the Pharisees s, "By the ruler of the demons
9:37 Then he s to his disciples, "The harvest is
11: 3 and s to him, "Are you the one who is to come,
11:25 At that time Jesus s, "I thank you, Father,
12: 2 When the Pharisees saw it, they s to him, "Look,
12: 3 He s to them, "Have you not read what David did
12:11 He s to them, "Suppose one of you has
12:13 Then he s to the man, "Stretch out your hand."
12:23 All the crowds were amazed and s,
12:24 But when the Pharisees heard it, they s,
12:25 He knew what they were thinking and s to them,
12:38 Then some of the scribes and Pharisees s to him,
Mt 12:49 And pointing to his disciples, he s,
13:27 the slaves of the householder came and s to him,
13:28 The slaves s to him, 'Then do you want us to go
13:52 And he s to them, "Therefore every scribe
13:54 so that they were astounded and s,
13:57 But Jesus s to them, "Prophets are not
14: 2 and he s to his servants, "This is John the Baptist;
14: 8 Prompted by her mother, she s,
14:15 it was evening, the disciples came to him and s,
14:16 Jesus s to them, "They need not go away;
14:18 And he s, "Bring them here to me."
14:27 But immediately Jesus spoke to them and s,
14:29 He s, "Come." So Peter got out of the
15: 1 and scribes came to Jesus from Jerusalem and s,
15: 4 For God s, 'Honor your father and your mother,'
15: 7 Isaiah prophesied rightly about you when he s:
15:10 Then he called the crowd to him and s to them,
15:12 Then the disciples approached and s to him,
15:12 when they heard what you s?"
15:15 But Peter s to him, "Explain this parable to us."
15:16 he s, "Are you also still without understanding?
15:27 She s, "Yes, Lord, yet even the dogs eat
15:32 Then Jesus called his disciples to him and s,
15:33 The disciples s to him, "Where are we
15:34 They s, "Seven, and a few small fish."
16: 6 Jesus s to them, "Watch out,
16: 7 They s to one another, "It is
16: 8 And becoming aware of it, Jesus s,
16:14 And they s, "Some say John the Baptist,
16:15 He s to them, "But who do you say that I am?"
16:23 he turned and s to Peter, "Get behind me, Satan!
17: 4 Peter s to Jesus, "Lord, it is good for us to be here;
17: 5 and from the cloud a voice s, "This is my Son,
17:15 and s, "Lord, have mercy on my son, for he is
17:19 Then the disciples came to Jesus privately and s,
17:20 He s to them, "Because of your little faith.
17:22 As they were gathering in Galilee, Jesus s to them,
17:24 collectors of the temple tax came to Peter and s,
17:25 He s, "Yes, he does."
17:26 When Peter s, "From others," Jesus s to him,
18: 3 and s, "Truly I tell you, unless you change
18:21 Then Peter came and s to him, "Lord,
18:22 Jesus s to him, "Not seven times, but, I tell you,
18:28 and seizing him by the throat, he s,
18:32 Then his lord summoned him and s to him,
19: 5 and s, 'For this reason a man shall leave his father
19: 7 They s to him, "Why then did Moses command us
19: 8 He s to them, "It was because you were
19:10 His disciples s to him, "If such is the case of a man
19:11 But he s to them, "Not everyone can accept this
19:14 but Jesus s, "Let the little children come to me,
19:16 Then someone came to him and s, "Teacher,
19:17 And he s to him, "Why do you ask me
19:18 He s to him, "Which ones?"
19:18 And Jesus s, "You shall not murder;
19:20 The young man s to him, "I have kept all these;
19:21 Jesus s to him, "If you wish to be perfect, go,
19:23 Then Jesus s to his disciples, "Truly I tell you,
19:25 they were greatly astounded and s,
19:26 But Jesus looked at them and s,
19:27 Then Peter s in reply, "Look,
19:28 Jesus s to them, "Truly I tell you,
20: 4 and he s to them, 'You also go into the vineyard,
20: 6 found others standing around; and he s to them,
20: 7 They s to him, 'Because no one has hired us.'
20: 7 He s to them, 'You also go into the vineyard.'
20: 8 the owner of the vineyard s to his manager,
20:17 and s to them on the way,
20:21 And he s to her, "What do you want?"
20:21 She s to him, "Declare that these two sons
20:22 They s to him, "We are able."
20:23 He s to them, "You will indeed drink my cup,
20:25 But Jesus called them to him and s,
20:33 They s to him, "Lord, let our eyes be opened."
21:13 He s to them, "It is written,
21:16 and s to him, "Do you hear what these are saying?"
21:16 Jesus s to them, "Yes;
21:19 Then he s to it, "May no fruit ever come
21:23 the people came to him as he was teaching, and s,
21:24 Jesus s to them, "I will also ask you one question;
21:27 And he s to them, "Neither will I tell you
21:28 A man had two sons; he went to the first and s,
21:30 The father went to the second and s the same;
21:31 They s, "The first."
21:31 Jesus s to them, "Truly I tell you,
21:38 the tenants saw the son, they s to themselves,
21:41 They s to him, "He will put those wretches to
21:42 Jesus s to them, "Have you never read in
22: 8 Then he s to his slaves, 'The wedding is ready,
22:12 and he s to him, 'Friend, how did you get in here
22:13 Then the king s to the attendants,
22:15 and plotted to entrap him in what he s.
22:18 But Jesus, aware of their malice, s,
22:20 Then he s to them, "Whose head is this,
22:21 Then he s to them, "Give therefore to the emperor
22:24 Moses s, 'If a man dies childless,
22:31 have you not read what was s to you by God,
22:37 He s to him, " 'You shall love the Lord your God
22:42 They s to him, "The son of David."
22:43 He s to them, "How is it then that David by
22:44 'The Lord s to my Lord,
23: 1 Then Jesus s to the crowds and to his disciples,
25: 8 The foolish s to the wise,
25:21 His master s to him, 'Well done,
25:23 His master s to him, 'Well done,
26: 1 saying all these things, he s to his disciples,
26: 5 But they s, "Not during the festival,

Mt 26: 8 when the disciples saw it, they were angry and s,
26:10 But Jesus, aware of this, s to them,
26:15 and s, "What will you give me if I betray him
26:18 He s, "Go into the city to a certain man,
26:21 he s, "Truly I tell you, one of you will betray me."
26:25 Judas, who betrayed him, s, "Surely not I, Rabbi?"
26:25 He replied, "You have s so."
26:26 gave it to the disciples, and s, "Take, eat;
26:31 Then Jesus s to them, "You will all become
26:33 Peter s to him, "Though all become deserters
26:34 Jesus s to him, "Truly I tell you, this very night,
26:35 Peter s to him, "Even though I must die with you,
26:35 And so s all the disciples.
26:36 and he s to his disciples,
26:38 he s to them, "I am deeply grieved, even to death;
26:40 and he s to Peter, "So, could you not stay awake
26:45 Then he came to the disciples and s to them,
26:49 At once he came up to Jesus and s, "Greetings,
26:50 Jesus s to him, "Friend, do what you are here
26:52 Jesus s to him, "Put your sword back into its place;
26:55 At that hour Jesus s to the crowds,
26:61 and s, "This fellow s, 'I am able to destroy the
26:62 high priest stood up and s, "Have you no answer?
26:63 Then the high priest s to him,
26:64 Jesus s to him, "You have s so.
26:65 Then the high priest tore his clothes and s,
26:69 A servant-girl came to him and s,
26:71 and she s to the bystanders,
26:73 little while the bystanders came up and s to Peter,
26:75 Then Peter remembered what Jesus had s:
27: 4 He s, "I have sinned by betraying innocent blood."
27: 4 But they s, "What is that to us?
27: 6 But the chief priests, taking the pieces of silver, s,
27:11 Jesus s, "You say so."
27:13 Then Pilate s to him, "Do you not hear
27:17 So after they had gathered, Pilate s to them,
27:21 The governor again s to them,
27:21 And they s, "Barabbas."
27:22 Pilate s to them, "Then what should I do
27:22 All of them s, "Let him be crucified!"
27:43 for he s, 'I am God's Son.' "
27:47 When some of the bystanders heard it, they s,
27:49 But the others s, "Wait, let us see whether Elijah
27:54 and what took place, they were terrified and s,
27:63 and s, "Sir, we remember what that impostor said
27:63 that impostor s while he was still alive,
27:65 Pilate s to them, "You have a guard of soldiers;
28: 5 But the angel s to the women, "Do not be afraid;
28: 6 He is not here; for he has been raised, as he s.
28: 9 Suddenly Jesus met them and s, "Greetings!"
28:10 Then Jesus s to them, "Do not be afraid;
28:18 And Jesus came and s to them,
Mk 1:17 And Jesus s to them, "Follow me
1:37 When they found him, they s to him,
1:40 and kneeling he s to him, "If you choose,
1:41 and s to him, "I do choose.
2: 5 When Jesus saw their faith, he s to the paralytic,
2: 8 among themselves; and he s to them,
2:10 on earth to forgive sins"—he s to the paralytic—
2:14 and he s to him, "Follow me."
2:16 and tax collectors, they s to his disciples,
2:17 When Jesus heard this, he s to them,
2:18 and people came and s to him,
2:19 Jesus s to them, "The wedding guests cannot fast
2:24 The Pharisees s to him, "Look,
2:25 And he s to them, "Have you never read what
2:27 Then he s to them, "The sabbath was made
3: 3 And he s to the man who had the withered hand,
3: 4 Then he s to them, "Is it lawful to do good or
3: 5 he was grieved at their hardness of heart and s to
3:22 the scribes who came down from Jerusalem s,
3:30 for they had s, "He has an unclean spirit."
3:32 and they s to him, "Your mother and your brothers
3:34 And looking at those who sat around him, he s,
4: 2 and in his teaching he s to them:
4: 9 And he s, "Let anyone with ears to hear listen!"
4:11 And he s to them, "To you has been given
4:13 he s to them, "Do you not understand this parable?
4:21 He s to them, "Is a lamp brought in to be put under
4:24 And he s to them, "Pay attention to what you hear;
4:26 He also s, "The kingdom of God is as
4:30 also s, "With what can we compare the kingdom
4:35 he s to them, "Let us go across to the other side."
4:38 and they woke him up and s to him, "Teacher,
4:39 up and rebuked the wind, and s to the sea,
4:40 He s to them, "Why are you afraid?
4:41 And they were filled with great awe and s
5: 8 For he had s to him, "Come out of the man,
5:19 But Jesus refused, and s to him,
5:28 for she s, "If I but touch his clothes, I will
5:30 Jesus turned about in the crowd and s,
5:31 And his disciples s to him,
5:34 He s to her, "Daughter, your faith has made you
5:36 But overhearing what they s,
5:36 Jesus s to the leader of the synagogue,
5:39 When he had entered, he s to them,
5:41 He took her by the hand and s to her,
6: 2 They s, "Where did this man get all this?
6: 4 Then Jesus s to them, "Prophets are not
6:10 He s to them, "Wherever you enter a house,
6:15 But others s, "It is Elijah."
6:15 And others s, "It is a prophet,
6:16 But when Herod heard of it, he s, "John,
6:22 and the king s to the girl,
6:24 She went out and s to her mother,
6:31 He s to them, "Come away to a deserted place all
6:35 When it grew late, his disciples came to him and s,
Mk 6:37 They s to him, "Are we to go
6:38 And he s to them, "How many loaves have you?
6:38 they had found out, they s, "Five, and two fish."
6:50 But immediately he spoke to them and s,
7: 6 He s to them, "Isaiah prophesied rightly
7: 9 Then he s to them, "You have a fine way
7:10 Moses s, 'Honor your father and your mother';
7:14 Then he called the crowd again and s to them,
7:18 He s to them, "Then do you also fail
7:20 he s, "It is what comes out of a person that defiles.
7:27 He s to her, "Let the children be fed first,
7:29 Then he s to her, "For saying that, you may go—
7:34 looking up to heaven, he sighed and s to him,
8: 1 he called his disciples and s to them,
8: 5 "How many loaves do you have?" They s,
8:12 And he sighed deeply in his spirit and s,
8:16 They s to one another, "It is because
8:17 And becoming aware of it, Jesus s to them,
8:19 They s to him, "Twelve."
8:20 And they s to him, "Seven."
8:21 Then he s to them, "Do you not yet understand?"
8:24 And the man looked up and s, "I can see people,
8:32 He s all this quite openly.
8:33 he rebuked Peter and s, "Get behind me, Satan!
8:34 with his disciples, and s to them, "If any want
9: 1 And he s to them, "Truly I tell you,
9: 5 Then Peter s to Jesus, "Rabbi,
9:12 He s to them, "Elijah is indeed coming first
9:21 And he s, "From childhood.
9:23 Jesus s to him, "If you are able!—
9:26 so that most of them s, "He is dead."
9:29 He s to them, "This kind can come out only
9:35 He sat down, called the twelve, and s to them,
9:36 and taking it in his arms, he s to them,
9:38 John s to him, "Teacher, we saw someone casting
9:39 But Jesus s, "Do not stop him;
10: 4 They s, "Moses allowed a man to write
10: 5 But Jesus s to them, "Because of your hardness
10:11 He s to them, "Whoever divorces his wife
10:14 Jesus saw this, he was indignant and s to them,
10:18 Jesus s to him, "Why do you call me good?
10:20 He s to him, "Teacher, I have kept all these
10:21 Jesus, looking at him, loved him and s,
10:23 Then Jesus looked around and s to his disciples,
10:24 But Jesus s to them again, "Children,
10:26 They were greatly astounded and s to one another,
10:27 Jesus looked at them and s,
10:29 Jesus s, "Truly I tell you, there is no one who has
10:35 came forward to him and s to him, "Teacher,
10:36 And he s to them, "What is it you want me to do
10:37 And they s to him, "Grant us to sit,
10:38 But Jesus s to them, "You do
10:39 Then Jesus s to them, "The cup
10:42 So Jesus called them and s to them,
10:49 Jesus stood still and s, "Call him here."
10:51 Then Jesus s to him, "What do you want me to do
10:51 The blind man s to him, "My teacher,
10:52 Jesus s to him, "Go; your faith has made you well."
11: 2 and s to them, "Go into the village ahead of you,
11: 5 some of the bystanders s to them,
11: 6 They told them what Jesus had s;
11:14 He s to it, "May no one ever eat fruit
11:21 Peter remembered and s to him, "Rabbi, look!
11:28 and s, "By what authority are you doing these
11:29 Jesus s to them, "I will ask you one question;
11:33 And Jesus s to them, "Neither will I tell you
12: 7 those tenants s to one another, 'This is the heir;
12:13 and some Herodians to trap him in what he s.
12:14 And they came and s to him, "Teacher,
12:15 But knowing their hypocrisy, he s to them,
12:16 Then he s to them, "Whose head is this,
12:17 Jesus s to them, "Give to the emperor the things
12:24 Jesus s to them, "Is not this
12:26 how God s to him, 'I am the God of Abraham,
12:32 Then the scribe s to him, "You are right, Teacher;
12:32 you have truly s that 'he is one,
12:34 Jesus saw that he answered wisely, he s to him,
12:35 While Jesus was teaching in the temple, he s,
12:36 'The Lord s to my Lord, "Sit at my right hand,
12:38 As he taught, he s, "Beware of the scribes,
12:43 Then he called his disciples and s to them,
13: 1 one of his disciples s to him, "Look, Teacher,
14: 2 for they s, "Not during the festival, or there may
14: 4 some were there who s to one another in anger,
14: 6 Jesus s, "Let her alone; why do you trouble her?
14:12 the Passover lamb is sacrificed, his disciples s
14:18 and were eating, Jesus s, "Truly I tell you, one
14:20 He s to them, "It is one of the twelve,
14:22 gave it to them, and s, "Take; this is my body."
14:24 He s to them, "This is my blood of the covenant,
14:27 Jesus s to them, "You will all become deserters;
14:29 Peter s to him, "Even though all become deserters,
14:30 Jesus s to him, "Truly I tell you, this day,
14:31 But he s vehemently, "Even though I must die
14:31 And all of them s the same.
14:32 and he s to his disciples, "Sit here while I pray."
14:34 he s to them, "I am deeply grieved, even to death;
14:36 He s, "Abba, Father, for you all things are possible;
14:37 and he s to Peter, "Simon, are you asleep?
14:41 He came a third time and s to them,
14:45 when he came, he went up to him at once and s,
14:48 Then Jesus s to them, "Have you come out
14:62 Jesus s, "I am; and 'you will see the Son of Man
14:63 Then the high priest tore his clothes and s,
14:67 she stared at him and s,
14:70 after a little while the bystanders again s to Peter,
14:72 Then Peter remembered that Jesus had s to him,
Mk 15:35 When some of the bystanders heard it, they s,
15:39 saw that in this way he breathed his last, he s,
16: 6 But he s to them, "Do not be alarmed;
16: 8 and they s nothing to anyone, for they were afraid.
16:15 ⟦And he s to them, "Go into all the world⟧
Lk 1:13 But the angel s to him, "Do not be afraid,
1:18 Zechariah s to the angel, "How will I know
1:24 for five months she remained in seclusion. She s,
1:28 he came to her and s, "Greetings, favored one!
1:30 The angel s to her, "Do not be afraid, Mary,
1:34 Mary s to the angel, "How can this be,
1:35 The angel s to her, "The Holy Spirit will come
1:36 and this is the sixth month for her who was s to
1:38 Then Mary s, "Here am I, the servant of the Lord;
1:46 And Mary s, "My soul magnifies the Lord,
1:60 But his mother s, "No; he is to be called John."
1:61 They s to her, "None of your
1:66 All who heard them pondered them and s,
2:10 But the angel s to them, "Do not be afraid;
2:15 the shepherds s to one another,
2:33 and mother were amazed at what was being s
2:34 Simeon blessed them and s to his mother Mary,
2:48 and his mother s to him, "Child,
2:49 He s to them, "Why were you searching for me?
2:50 But they did not understand what he s to them.
3: 7 John s to the crowds that came out to be baptized
3:11 In reply he s to them,
3:13 He s to them, "Collect no more than
3:14 He s to them, "Do not extort money from anyone
4: 3 The devil s to him, "If you are the Son of God,
4: 6 the devil s to him, "To you I will give their glory
4:12 Jesus answered him, "It is s,
4:22 They s, "Is not this Joseph's son?"
4:23 He s to them, "Doubtless you will quote
4:24 And he s, "Truly I tell you,
4:43 But he s to them, "I must proclaim the good news
5: 4 When he had finished speaking, he s to Simon,
5:10 Then Jesus s to Simon, "Do not be afraid;
5:13 Jesus stretched out his hand, touched him, and s,
5:14 "Go," he s, "and show yourself to the priest, and,
5:20 When he saw their faith, he s, "Friend,
5:24 he s to the one who was paralyzed—
5:27 and he s to him, "Follow me."
5:33 Then they s to him, "John's disciples,
5:34 Jesus s to them, "You cannot make wedding guests
6: 2 But some of the Pharisees s,
6: 5 Then he s to them, "The Son of Man is lord of
6: 8 he s to the man who had the withered hand,
6: 9 Then Jesus s to them, "I ask you,
6:10 After looking around at all of them, he s to him,
6:20 Then he looked up at his disciples and s:
7: 9 and turning to the crowd that followed him, he s,
7:13 he had compassion for her and s to her,
7:14 And he s, "Young man, I say to you, rise!"
7:20 When the men had come to him, they s,
7:39 he s to himself, "If this man were a prophet,
7:40 Jesus spoke up and s to him, "Simon,
7:43 And Jesus s to him, "You have judged rightly."
7:44 Then turning toward the woman, he s to Simon,
7:48 Then he s to her, "Your sins are forgiven."
7:50 he s to the woman, "Your faith has saved you;
8: 4 and people from town after town came to him, he s
8: 8 As he s this, he called out,
8:10 He s, "To you it has been given to know
8:21 But he s to them, "My mother
8:22 into a boat with his disciples, and he s to them,
8:25 He s to them, "Where is your faith?"
8:25 and s to one another, "Who then is this,
8:30 "What is your name?" He s, "Legion";
8:45 When all denied it, Peter s, "Master,
8:46 But Jesus s, "Someone touched me;
8:48 He s to her, "Daughter, your faith has made you
8:52 but he s, "Do not weep;
9: 3 He s to them, "Take nothing for your journey,
9: 7 because it was s by some that John had been raised
9: 9 Herod s, "John I beheaded;
9:12 and the twelve came to him and s,
9:13 he s to them, "You give them something to eat."
9:13 They s, "We have no more than five loaves
9:14 And he s to his disciples,
9:20 He s to them, "But who do you say that I am?"
9:23 Then he s to them all,
9:33 Just as they were leaving him, Peter s to Jesus,
9:33 for Elijah"—not knowing what he s.
9:35 Then from the cloud came a voice that s,
9:43 at all that he was doing, he s to his disciples,
9:48 and s to them, "Whoever welcomes this child
9:50 But Jesus s to him, "Do not stop him;
9:54 When his disciples James and John saw it, they s,
9:57 they were going along the road, someone s to him,
9:58 And Jesus s to him, "Foxes have holes,
9:59 To another he s, "Follow me."
9:59 he s, "Lord, first let me go and bury my father."
9:60 Jesus s to him, "Let the dead bury their own dead;
9:61 Another s, "I will follow you, Lord;
9:62 Jesus s to him, "No one who puts a hand to
10: 2 He s to them, "The harvest is plentiful,
10:18 He s to them, "I watched Satan fall from heaven
10:21 in the Holy Spirit and s, "I thank you, Father, Lord
10:23 turning to the disciples, Jesus s to them privately,
10:25 he s, "what must I do to inherit eternal life?"
10:26 He s to him, "What is written in the law?
10:28 he s to him, "You have given the right answer;
10:35 gave them to the innkeeper, and s,
10:37 He s, "The one who showed him mercy."
10:37 Jesus s to him, "Go and do likewise."
11: 1 one of his disciples s to him, "Lord,

Lk 11: 2 He s to them, "When you pray, say:
11: 5 And he s to them, "Suppose one of you has
11:15 of them s, "He casts out demons by Beelzebul,
11:17 he knew what they were thinking and s to them,
11:27 woman in the crowd raised her voice and s to him,
11:28 But he s, "Blessed rather are those who hear
11:39 Then the Lord s to him,
11:46 And he s, "Woe also to you lawyers!
11:49 Therefore also the Wisdom of God s,
12: 3 Therefore whatever you have s in the dark will
12:13 Someone in the crowd s to him, "Teacher,
12:14 But he s to him, "Friend, who set me to be a judge
12:15 And he s to them, "Take care!
12:18 Then he s, 'I will do this:
12:20 But God s to him, 'You fool!
12:22 He s to his disciples, "Therefore I tell you,
12:41 Peter s, "Lord, are you telling this parable for us
12:42 And the Lord s, "Who then is the faithful
12:54 also s to the crowds, "When you see a cloud rising
13: 7 So he s to the gardener, 'See here!
13:12 When Jesus saw her, he called her over and s,
13:15 the Lord answered him and s, "You hypocrites!
13:17 he s this, all his opponents were put to shame;
13:18 He s therefore, "What is the kingdom of God like?
13:20 And again he s, "To what should I compare
13:23 will only a few be saved?" He s to them,
13:31 that very hour some Pharisees came and s to him,
13:32 He s to them, "Go and tell that fox for me, 'Listen,
14: 5 Then he s to them, "If one of you has a child or
14:12 He s also to the one who had invited him,
14:15 One of the dinner guests, on hearing this, s to him,
14:16 Then Jesus s to him, "Someone gave
14:18 The first s to him, 'I have bought a piece of land,
14:19 Another s, 'I have bought five yoke of oxen,
14:20 Another s, 'I have just been married,
14:21 Then the owner of the house became angry and s
14:22 the slave s, 'Sir, what you ordered has been done,
14:23 Then the master s to the slave,
14:25 and he turned and s to them,
15:11 Jesus s, "There was a man who had two sons.
15:12 The younger of them s to his father, 'Father,
15:17 But when he came to himself he s,
15:21 Then the son s to him, 'Father,
15:22 father s to his slaves, 'Quickly, bring out a robe—
15:31 Then the father s to him, 'Son,
16: 1 Then Jesus s to the disciples,
16: 2 So he summoned him and s to him,
16: 3 Then the manager s to himself, 'What will I do,
16: 6 He s to him, 'Take your bill, sit down quickly,
16: 7 He s to him, 'Take your bill and make it eighty.'
16:15 So he s to them, "You are those who justify
16:25 But Abraham s, 'Child, remember that
16:27 He s, 'Then, father, I beg you to send him
16:30 He s, 'No, father Abraham;
16:31 He s to him, 'If they do not listen to Moses and
17: 1 Jesus s to his disciples, "Occasions
17: 5 The apostles s to the Lord, "Increase our faith!"
17:14 When he saw them, he s to them,
17:19 Then he s to him, "Get up and go on your way;
17:22 Then he s to the disciples,
17:37 He s to them, "Where the corpse is,
18: 2 He s, "In a certain city there was
18: 4 For a while he refused; but later he s to himself,
18: 6 the Lord s, "Listen to what the unjust judge says.
18:16 But Jesus called for them and s,
18:19 Jesus s to him, "Why do you call me good?
18:22 When Jesus heard this, he s to him,
18:24 Jesus looked at him and s,
18:26 Those who heard it s, "Then who can be saved?"
18:28 Then Peter s, "Look, we have left our homes
18:29 And he s to them, "Truly I tell you,
18:31 Then he took the twelve aside and s to them, "See,
18:34 in fact, what he s was hidden from them,
18:34 and they did not grasp what was s.
18:41 He s, "Lord, let me see again."
18:42 Jesus s to him, "Receive your sight;
19: 5 Jesus came to the place, he looked up and s to him,
19: 7 All who saw it began to grumble and s,
19: 8 Zacchaeus stood there and s to the Lord, "Look,
19: 9 Then Jesus s to him, "Today salvation has come
19:12 So he s, "A nobleman went to a distant country
19:13 and gave them ten pounds, and s to them,
19:16 The first came forward and s, 'Lord,
19:17 He s to him, 'Well done, good slave!
19:19 He s to him, 'And you, rule over five cities.'
19:22 He s to him, 'I will judge you by your own words,
19:24 He s to the bystanders, 'Take the pound from him
19:25 (And they s to him, 'Lord, he has ten pounds!')
19:28 After he had s this, he went on ahead,
19:34 They s, "The Lord needs it."
19:39 Some of the Pharisees in the crowd s to him,
19:46 and he s, "It is written, 'My house shall be a house
20: 2 and s to him, "Tell us, by what
20: 8 Then Jesus s to them, "Neither will I tell you
20:13 the owner of the vineyard s, 'What shall I do?
20:14 they discussed it among themselves and s,
20:16 When they heard this, they s, "Heaven forbid!"
20:17 But he looked at them and s,
20:20 in order to trap him by what he s,
20:23 But he perceived their craftiness and s to them,
20:24 They s, "The emperor's."
20:25 He s to them, "Then give to the emperor the things
20:26 of the people to trap him by what he s;
20:34 Jesus s to them, "Those who belong
20:41 Then he s to them, "How can they say that
20:42 'The Lord s to my Lord, "Sit at my right hand,
20:45 the hearing of all the people he s to the disciples,

Lk 21: 3 He s, "Truly I tell you, this poor widow has put
21: 5 and gifts dedicated to God, he s,
21: 8 And he s, "Beware that you are not led astray;
21:10 Then he s to them, "Nation will rise against nation,
22:10 he s to them, "when you have entered the city,
22:15 He s to them, "I have eagerly desired
22:17 Then he took a cup, and after giving thanks he s,
22:25 But he s to them, "The kings of the Gentiles lord it
22:33 And he s to him, "Lord, I am ready to go with you
22:34 Jesus s, "I tell you, Peter, the cock will
22:35 He s to them, "When I sent you out without
22:35 They s, "No, not a thing."
22:36 He s to them, "But now, the one who has
22:38 They s, "Lord, look, here are two swords."
22:40 When he reached the place, he s to them,
22:46 and he s to them, "Why are you sleeping?
22:48 but Jesus s to him, "Judas, is it with a kiss
22:51 But Jesus s, "No more of this!"
22:52 Then Jesus s to the chief priests,
22:56 seeing him in the firelight, stared at him and s,
22:58 A little later someone else, on seeing him, s,
22:58 But Peter s, "Man, I am not!"
22:60 But Peter s, "Man, I do not know
22:61 how he had s to him,
22:67 They s, "If you are the Messiah, tell us."
22:70 He s to them, "You say that I am."
22:71 Then they s, "What further testimony do we need?
23: 4 Then Pilate s to the chief priests and the crowds,
23: 5 But they were insistent and s,
23:14 and s to them, "You brought me this man
23:22 A third time he s to them, "Why,
23:28 But Jesus turned to them and s,
23:34 ⟦Then Jesus s, "Father, forgive them;⟧
23:42 Then he s, "Jesus, remember me when you come
23:46 Then Jesus, crying with a loud voice, s, "Father,
23:46 Having s this, he breathed his last.
23:47 saw what had taken place, he praised God and s,
24: 5 but the men s to them,
24:17 And he s to them, "What are you discussing
24:23 that they had indeed seen a vision of angels who s
24:24 to the tomb and found it just as the women had s;
24:25 Then he s to them, "Oh, how foolish you are,
24:32 They s to each other, "Were not our hearts burning
24:36 Jesus himself stood among them and s to them,
24:38 He s to them, "Why are you frightened,
24:40 And when he had s this,
24:41 he s to them, "Have you anything here to eat?"
24:44 Then he s to them, "These are my words
24:46 and he s to them, "Thus it is written,
Jn 1:15 "This was he of whom I s,
1:21 He s, "I am not."
1:22 Then they s to him, "Who are you?
1:23 He s, "I am the voice of one crying out in
1:23 the way of the Lord,' " as the prophet Isaiah s.
1:30 This is he of whom I s,
1:33 the one who sent me to baptize with water s to me,
1:38 Jesus turned and saw them following, he s to them,
1:38 "What are you looking for?" They s to him,
1:39 He s to them, "Come and see."
1:41 He first found his brother Simon and s to him,
1:42 who looked at him and s,
1:43 He found Philip and s to him, "Follow me."
1:45 Philip found Nathanael and s to him,
1:46 Nathanael s to him, "Can anything good come out
1:46 Philip s to him, "Come and see."
1:47 toward him, he s of him, "Here is truly an Israelite
1:51 And he s to him, "Very truly, I tell you,
2: 3 the wine gave out, the mother of Jesus s to him,
2: 4 And Jesus s to her, "Woman,
2: 5 His mother s to the servants,
2: 7 Jesus s to them, "Fill the jars with water."
2: 8 He s to them, "Now draw some out,
2:10 and s to him, "Everyone serves
2:18 The Jews then s to him,
2:20 then s, "This temple has been under construction
2:22 his disciples remembered that he had s this;
3: 2 He came to Jesus by night and s to him, "Rabbi,
3: 4 Nicodemus s to him, "How can anyone be born
3: 7 Do not be astonished that I s to you,
3: 9 Nicodemus s to him, "How can these things be?"
3:26 They came to John and s to him, "Rabbi,
3:28 You yourselves are my witnesses that I s,
4: 7 and Jesus s to her, "Give me a drink."
4: 9 The Samaritan woman s to him,
4:11 The woman s to him, "Sir, you have no bucket,
4:13 Jesus s to her, "Everyone who drinks
4:15 The woman s to him, "Sir, give me this water,
4:16 Jesus s to her, "Go, call your husband,
4:17 Jesus s to her, "You are right in saying,
4:18 What you have s is true!"
4:19 woman s to him, "Sir, I see that you are a prophet.
4:21 Jesus s to her, "Woman, believe me,
4:25 The woman s to him, "I know
4:26 Jesus s to her, "I am he,
4:27 but no one s, "What do you want?"
4:28 She s to the people,
4:32 But he s to them, "I have food to eat that you do
4:33 So the disciples s to one another,
4:34 Jesus s to them, "My food is to do the will
4:42 They s to the woman, "It is no longer because of
what you s that we believe,
4:48 Then Jesus s to him, "Unless you see signs
4:49 The official s to him, "Sir,
4:50 Jesus s to him, "Go; your son will live."
4:52 to recover, and they s to him, "Yesterday at one in
4:53 that this was the hour when Jesus had s to him,
5: 6 he s to him, "Do you want to be made well?"

Jn 5: 8 Jesus s to him, "Stand up,
5:10 So the Jews s to the man who had been cured,
5:11 "The man who made me well s to me,
5:12 They asked him, "Who is the man who s to you,
5:14 Later Jesus found him in the temple and s to him,
5:19 Jesus s to them, "Very truly, I tell you,
6: 5 and saw a large crowd coming toward him, Jesus s
6: 6 He s this to test him,
6: 8 Andrew, Simon Peter's brother, s to him,
6:10 Jesus s, "Make the people sit down."
6:20 But he s to them, "It is I; do not be afraid."
6:25 they s to him, "Rabbi, when did you come here?"
6:28 Then they s to him, "What must we do to perform
6:30 So they s to him, "What sign are you going
6:32 Then Jesus s to them, "Very truly, I tell you,
6:34 They s to him, "Sir, give us this bread always."
6:35 Jesus s to them, "I am the bread of life.
6:36 But I s to you that you have seen me and yet do
6:41 Jews began to complain about him because he s,
6:53 So Jesus s to them, "Very truly, I tell you,
6:59 He s these things while he was teaching in
6:60 When many of his disciples heard it, they s,
6:61 s to them, "Does this offend you?
6:65 And he s, "For this reason I have told you
7: 3 So his brothers s to him, "Leave here and go
7: 6 Jesus s to them, "My time has not yet come,
7:33 then s, "I will be with you a little while longer,
7:35 The Jews s to one another,
7:38 As the scripture has s, 'Out of the believer's heart
7:39 Now he s this about the Spirit,
7:40 they heard these words, some in the crowd s,
7:41 Others s, "This is the Messiah."
7:42 not the scripture s that the Messiah is descended
8: 4 ⟦they s to him, "Teacher, this woman was caught⟧
8: 6 ⟦They s this to test him,⟧
8: 7 ⟦he straightened up and s to them,⟧
8:10 ⟦Jesus straightened up and s to her, "Woman,⟧
8:11 ⟦She s, "No one, sir."⟧
8:11 ⟦And Jesus s, "Neither do I condemn you.⟧
8:13 Then the Pharisees s to him,
8:19 Then they s to him, "Where is your Father?"
8:21 Again he s to them, "I am going away,
8:22 Then the Jews s, "Is he going to kill himself?
8:23 He s to them, "You are from below,
8:25 They s to him, "Who are you?"
8:25 Jesus s to them, "Why do I speak to you at all?
8:28 So Jesus s, "When you have lifted up the Son
8:31 Then Jesus s to the Jews who had believed in him,
8:39 Jesus s to them, "If you were Abraham's children,
8:41 They s to him, "We are not illegitimate children;
8:42 Jesus s to them, "If God were your Father,
8:52 The Jews s to him, "Now we know that you have
8:57 Then the Jews s to him,
8:58 Jesus s to them, "Very truly, I tell you,
9: 6 When he had s this, he spat on the ground
9:11 and s to me, 'Go to Siloam and wash.'
9:12 They s to him, "Where is he?"
9:12 He s, "I do not know."
9:15 He s to them, "He put mud on my eyes.
9:16 of the Pharisees s, "This man is not from God,
9:16 But others s, "How can a man who is
9:17 So they s again to the blind man,
9:17 He s, "He is a prophet."
9:22 His parents s this because they were afraid of
9:23 Therefore his parents s, "He is of age; ask him."
9:24 and they s to him, "Give glory to God!
9:26 They s to him, "What did he do to you?
9:35 he s, "Do you believe in the Son of Man?"
9:37 Jesus s to him, "You have seen him,
9:38 He s, "Lord, I believe." And he worshiped him.
9:39 Jesus s, "I came into this world for judgment so
9:40 of the Pharisees near him heard this and s to him,
9:41 Jesus s to them, "If you were blind,
10: 7 So again Jesus s to them, "Very truly, I tell you,
10:24 So the Jews gathered around him and s to him,
10:34 Jesus answered, "Is it not written in your law, 'I s,
10:36 and sent into the world is blaspheming because I s,
10:41 everything that John s about this man was true."
11: 4 But when Jesus heard it, he s,
11: 7 Then after this he s to the disciples,
11: 8 The disciples s to him, "Rabbi,
11:12 The disciples s to him, "Lord,
11:16 who was called the Twin, s to his fellow disciples,
11:21 Martha s to Jesus, "Lord, if you had been here,
11:23 Jesus s to her, "Your brother will rise again."
11:24 Martha s to him, "I know that he will rise again in
11:25 Jesus s to her, "I am the resurrection and the life.
11:27 She s to him, "Yes, Lord, I believe that you are
11:28 When she had s this, she went back
11:32 she knelt at his feet and s to him, "Lord,
11:34 He s, "Where have you laid him?"
11:34 They s to him, "Lord, come and see."
11:36 So the Jews s, "See how he loved him!"
11:37 of them s, "Could not he who opened the eyes of
11:39 Jesus s, "Take away the stone."
11:39 Martha, the sister of the dead man, s to him,
11:40 Jesus s to her, "Did I not tell you that
11:41 And Jesus looked upward and s, "Father,
11:42 but I have s this for the sake of
11:43 When he had s this, he cried with a loud voice,
11:44 Jesus s to them, "Unbind him, and let him go."
11:47 and s, "What are we to do?
11:49 Caiaphas, who was high priest that year, s to them,
12: 4 (the one who was about to betray him), s,
12: 6 (He s this not because he cared about the poor,
12: 7 Jesus s, "Leave her alone.
12:19 The Pharisees then s to one another, "You see,

Jn 12:21 who was from Bethsaida in Galilee, and **s** to him,
12:29 The crowd standing there heard it and **s**
12:29 Others **s**, "An angel has spoken to him."
12:33 He **s** this to indicate the kind of death he was
12:35 Jesus **s** to them, "The light is with you for
12:36 Jesus had **s** this, he departed and hid from them.
12:39 so they could not believe, because Isaiah also **s**,
12:41 Isaiah **s** this because he saw his glory and spoke
13: 6 He came to Simon Peter, who **s** to him, "Lord,
13: 8 Peter **s** to him, "You will never wash my feet."
13: 9 Simon Peter **s** to him, "Lord,
13:10 Jesus **s** to him, "One who has bathed does not need
13:11 for this reason he **s**, "Not all of you are clean."
13:12 and had returned to the table, he **s** to them,
13:27 Jesus **s** to him, "Do quickly what you are going
13:28 no one at the table knew why he **s** this to him.
13:31 When he had gone out, Jesus **s**,
13:33 and as I **s** to the Jews so now I say to you,
13:36 Simon Peter **s** to him, "Lord,
13:37 Peter **s** to him, "Lord, why can I
14: 5 Thomas **s** to him, "Lord, we do not know
14: 6 Jesus **s** to him, "I am the way, and the truth,
14: 8 Philip **s** to him, "Lord, show us the Father,
14: 9 Jesus **s** to him, "Have I been with you all this time,
14:22 Judas (not Iscariot) **s** to him, "Lord,
14:25 "I have **s** these things to you while I am still
14:26 and remind you of all that I have **s** to you.
15:11 I have **s** these things to you so that my joy may be
15:20 Remember the word that I **s** to you,
16: 1 "I have **s** these things to you to keep you
16: 4 But I have **s** these things to you so that
16: 6 But because I have **s** these things to you,
16:15 For this reason I **s** that he will take what is mine
16:17 Then some of his disciples **s** to one another,
16:18 They **s**, "What does he mean by this
16:19 to ask him, so he **s** to them, "Are you discussing
16:19 among yourselves what I meant when I **s**,
16:25 "I have **s** these things to you in figures of speech.
16:29 His disciples **s**, "Yes,
16:33 I have **s** this to you,
17: 1 he looked up to heaven and **s**, "Father,
18: 6 When Jesus **s** to them, "I am he,"
18: 7 And they **s**, "Jesus of Nazareth."
18:11 Jesus **s** to Peter, "Put your sword back
18:17 The woman **s** to Peter, "You are not also one
18:17 He **s**, "I am not."
18:20 I have **s** nothing in secret.
18:21 Ask those who heard what I **s** to them;
18:21 to them; they know what I **s**."
18:22 When he had **s** this, one of
18:25 He denied it and **s**, "I am not."
18:29 So Pilate went out to them and **s**,
18:31 Pilate **s** to them, "Take him yourselves
18:32 to fulfill what Jesus had **s** when he indicated
18:38 After he had **s** this, he went out to the Jews again
19: 4 Pilate went out again and **s** to them, "Look,
19: 5 Pilate **s** to them, "Here is the man!"
19: 6 Pilate **s** to them, "Take him yourselves
19:10 Pilate therefore **s** to him, "Do you refuse to speak
19:14 He **s** to the Jews, "Here is your King!"
19:21 Then the chief priests of the Jews **s** to Pilate,
19:21 but, 'This man **s**, I am King of the Jews.' "
19:24 So they **s** to one another, "Let us not tear it,
19:26 he **s** to his mother, "Woman, here is your son."
19:27 Then he **s** to the disciple, "Here is your mother."
19:28 he **s** (in order to fulfill the scripture),
19:30 Jesus had received the wine, he **s**, "It is finished."
20: 2 the one whom Jesus loved, and **s** to them,
20:13 They **s** to her, "Woman, why are you weeping?"
20:13 She **s** to them, "They have taken away my Lord,
20:14 When she had **s** this, she turned around
20:15 Jesus **s** to her, "Woman, why are you weeping?
20:15 Supposing him to be the gardener, she **s** to him,
20:16 Jesus **s** to her, "Mary!"
20:16 She turned and **s** to him in Hebrew, "Rabbouni!"
20:17 Jesus **s** to her, "Do not hold on to me,
20:18 and she told them that he had **s** these things to her.
20:19 Jesus came and stood among them and **s**,
20:20 he **s** this, he showed them his hands and his side.
20:21 Jesus **s** to them again, "Peace be with you.
20:22 When he had **s** this, he breathed on them and **s** to
20:25 But he **s** to them, "Unless I see the mark of
20:26 Jesus came and stood among them and **s**,
20:27 Then he **s** to Thomas, "Put your finger here
20:29 Jesus **s** to him, "Have you believed
21: 3 Simon Peter **s** to them, "I am going fishing."
21: 3 They **s** to him, "We will go with you."
21: 5 Jesus **s** to them, "Children, you have no fish,
21: 6 He **s** to them, "Cast the net to the right side of
21: 7 That disciple whom Jesus loved **s** to Peter,
21:10 Jesus **s** to them, "Bring some of the fish
21:12 Jesus **s** to them, "Come and have breakfast."
21:15 Jesus **s** to Simon Peter, "Simon son of John,
21:15 He **s** to him, "Yes, Lord;
21:15 Jesus **s** to him, "Feed my lambs."
21:16 A second time he **s** to him, "Simon son of John,
21:16 He **s** to him, "Yes, Lord;
21:16 Jesus **s** to him, "Tend my sheep."
21:17 He **s** to him the third time, "Simon son of John,
21:17 Peter felt hurt because he **s** to him the third time,
21:17 And he **s** to him, "Lord, you know everything;
21:17 Jesus **s** to him, "Feed my sheep.
21:19 (He **s** this to indicate the kind of death
21:19 After this he **s** to him, "Follow me."
21:20 to Jesus at the supper and had **s**,
21:21 When Peter saw him, he **s** to Jesus, "Lord,
21:22 Jesus **s** to him, "If it is my will that he remain

Ac 1: 4 "This," he **s**, "is what you have heard from me;
1: 9 When he had **s** this, as they were watching,
1:11 They **s**, "Men of Galilee, why do you stand
1:15 about one hundred twenty persons) and **s**,
1:24 Then they prayed and **s**, "Lord,
2:13 But others sneered and **s**, "They are filled
2:34 'The Lord **s** to my Lord, "Sit at my right hand,
2:37 to the heart and **s** to Peter and to the other apostles,
2:38 Peter **s** to them, "Repent,
3: 4 Peter looked intently at him, as did John, and **s**,
3: 6 But Peter **s**, "I have no silver or gold,
3:22 Moses **s**, 'The Lord your God will raise up for you
4: 8 Then Peter, filled with the Holy Spirit, **s** to them,
4:16 They **s**, "What will we do with them?
4:23 the chief priests and the elders had **s** to them.
4:24 they raised their voices together to God and **s**,
4:25 it is you who **s** by the Holy Spirit
5: 8 Peter **s** to her, "Tell me whether you
5: 8 And she **s**, "Yes, that was the price."
5: 9 Then Peter **s** to her, "How is it
5:19 the prison doors, brought them out, and **s**,
5:35 Then he **s** to them, "Fellow Israelites,
6: 2 the whole community of the disciples and **s**,
6: 5 What they **s** pleased the whole community,
6:13 They set up false witnesses who **s**,
7: 3 and **s** to him, 'Leave your country
7: 7 'But I will judge the nation that they serve,' **s** God,
7:33 Then the Lord **s** to him,
7:35 when they **s**, 'Who made you a ruler and
7:37 This is the Moses who **s** to the Israelites,
7:56 he **s**, "I see the heavens opened and the Son
7:60 When he had **s** this, he died.
8: 6 with one accord listened eagerly to what was **s**
8:20 But Peter **s** to him, "May your silver perish
8:24 nothing of what you have **s** may happen to me."
8:26 Then an angel of the Lord **s** to Philip,
8:29 Then the Spirit **s** to Philip,
8:36 and the eunuch **s**, "Look, here is water!
9:10 The Lord **s** to him in a vision, "Ananias."
9:11 The Lord **s** to him, "Get up and go to
9:15 But the Lord **s** to him, "Go,
9:17 He laid his hands on Saul and **s**, "Brother Saul,
9:21 All who heard him were amazed and **s**,
9:34 Peter **s** to him, "Aeneas, Jesus Christ heals you;
9:40 He turned to the body and **s**, "Tabitha, get up."
10: 4 He stared at him in terror and **s**, "What is it,
10:14 But Peter **s**, "By no means, Lord;
10:15 The voice **s** to him again, a second time,
10:19 the Spirit **s** to him, "Look,
10:21 So Peter went down to the men and **s**,
10:28 and he **s** to them, "You yourselves know
10:31 He **s**, 'Cornelius, your prayer has been heard
10:46 and extolling God. Then Peter **s**,
11:16 I remembered the word of the Lord, how he had **s**,
12: 8 The angel **s** to him, "Fasten your belt and put
12: 8 Then he **s** to him, "Wrap your cloak around you
12:11 Then Peter came to himself and **s**,
12:15 They **s** to her, "You are out of your mind!"
12:15 They **s**, "It is his angel."
13: 2 the Lord and fasting, the Holy Spirit **s**, "Set apart
13:10 and **s**, "You son of the devil, you enemy
13:22 In his testimony about him he **s**,
13:25 And as John was finishing his work, he **s**,
13:35 Therefore he has also **s** in another psalm,
13:40 that what the prophets **s** does not happen to you:
14:10 **s** in a loud voice, "Stand upright
15: 5 to the sect of the Pharisees stood up and **s**,
15: 7 Peter stood up and **s** to them, "My brothers,
15:24 have **s** things to disturb you
15:32 **s** much to encourage and strengthen the believers.
15:36 After some days Paul **s** to Barnabas, "Come,
16:14 to listen eagerly to what was **s** by Paul.
16:18 very much annoyed, turned and **s** to the spirit,
16:20 they **s**, "These men are disturbing our city;
16:30 Then he brought them outside and **s**, "Sirs,
17:18 Some **s**, "What does this babbler want to say?"
17:18 Others **s**, "He seems to be a proclaimer
17:22 Then Paul stood in front of the Areopagus and **s**,
17:28 as even some of your own poets have **s**,
17:32 but others **s**, "We will hear you again about this."
18: 6 in protest he shook the dust from his clothes and **s**
18: 9 One night the Lord **s** to Paul in a vision,
18:13 They **s**, "This man is persuading people
18:14 Gallio **s** to the Jews, "If it were a matter of crime
18:18 Paul **s** farewell to the believers and sailed
18:21 he **s**, "I will return to you, if God wills."
19: 2 He **s** to them, "Did you receive the Holy Spirit
19: 3 Then he **s**, "Into what then were you baptized?"
19: 4 Paul **s**, "John baptized with the baptism
19:15 But the evil spirit **s** to them in reply,
19:21 He **s**, "After I have gone there,
19:25 with the workers of the same trade, and **s**, "Men,
19:35 when the town clerk had quieted the crowd, he **s**,
19:41 When he had **s** this, he dismissed the assembly.
20:10 and bending over him took him in his arms, and **s**,
20:18 When they came to him, he **s** to them:
20:35 for he himself **s**, 'It is more blessed to give than
20:38 grieving especially because of what he had **s**,
21: 6 and **s** farewell to one another.
21:11 bound his own feet and hands with it, and **s**,
21:20 Then they **s** to him, "You see, brother,
21:37 he **s** to the tribune, "May I say something to you?"
22: 2 even more quiet. Then he **s**:
22: 8 Then he **s** to me, 'I am Jesus
22:10 The Lord **s** to me, 'Get up and go to Damascus;
22:13 and standing beside me, he **s**, 'Brother Saul,
22:14 Then he **s**, 'The God of our ancestors

Ac 22:19 And I **s**, 'Lord, they themselves know that
22:21 Then he **s** to me, 'Go, for I will send you far away
22:25 Paul **s** to the centurion who was standing by,
22:26 he went to the tribune and **s** to him,
22:27 are you a Roman citizen?" And he **s**, "Yes."
22:28 Paul **s**, "But I was born a citizen."
23: 1 Paul was looking intently at the council he **s**,
23: 3 At this Paul **s** to him, "God will strike you,
23: 4 Those standing nearby **s**, "Do you dare
23: 5 And Paul **s**, "I did not realize, brothers,
23: 7 When he **s** this, a dissension began between
23:11 That night the Lord stood near him and **s**,
23:14 They went to the chief priests and elders and **s**,
23:17 Paul called one of the centurions and **s**,
23:18 So he took him, brought him to the tribune, and **s**,
23:23 Then he summoned two of the centurions and **s**,
23:35 he **s**, "I will give you a hearing
24:25 Felix became frightened and **s**,
25: 5 "So," he **s**, "let those of you who have
25: 8 Paul **s** in his defense, "I have in no way committed
25:10 Paul **s**, "I am appealing to the emperor's tribunal;
25:22 Agrippa **s** to Festus, "I would like to hear
25:22 "Tomorrow," he **s**, "you will hear him."
25:24 And Festus **s**, "King Agrippa and all here present
26: 1 Agrippa **s** to Paul, "You have permission to speak
26:22 the prophets and Moses **s** would take place:
26:25 But Paul **s**, "I am not out of my mind,
26:28 Agrippa **s** to Paul, "Are you so quickly persuading
26:31 they **s** to one another, "This man is doing nothing
26:32 Agrippa **s** to Festus, "This man could have been
27:11 and to the owner of the ship than to what Paul **s**.
27:21 Paul then stood up among them and **s**, "Men,
27:24 and he **s**, 'Do not be afraid, Paul;
27:31 Paul **s** to the centurion and the soldiers,
27:35 After he had **s** this, he took bread;
28: 4 they **s** to one another, "This man must be
28:17 When they had assembled, he **s** to them,
28:24 Some were convinced by what he had **s**,
Ro 4:18 of many nations," according to what was **s**,
7: 7 to covet if the law had not **s**,
9: 9 For this is what the promise **s**,
9:26 "And in the very place where it was **s** to them,
1Co 6:16 For it is **s**, "The two shall be one flesh."
11:24 he broke it and **s**, "This is my body that is for you.
14: 9 how will anyone know what is being **s**?
14:29 and let the others weigh what is **s**.
2Co 2:13 So I **s** farewell to them and went on to Macedonia.
4: 6 For it is the God who **s**,
6:16 For we are the temple of the living God; as God **s**,
7: 3 for I **s** before that you are in our hearts,
7:14 but just as everything we **s** to you was true,
9: 3 so that you may be ready, as I **s** you would be;
12: 9 but he **s** to me, "My grace is sufficient for you,
Gal 1: 9 As we have **s** before, so now I repeat,
1:23 they only heard it **s**, "The one who formerly was
2:14 I **s** to Cephas before them all, "If you,
Eph 4: 8 Therefore it is **s**, "When he ascended
Tit 1:12 It was one of them, their very own prophet, who **s**,
Heb 1:13 But to which of the angels has he ever **s**,
3:10 I was angry with that generation, and I **s**,
3:15 As it is **s**, "Today, if you hear his voice,
4: 3 just as God has **s**, "As in my anger I swore,
5: 5 but was appointed by the one who **s** to him,
7:14 and in connection with that tribe Moses **s** nothing
7:21 because of the one who **s** to him,
10: 5 when Christ came into the world, he **s**,
10: 7 Then I **s**, 'See, God, I have come to do your will,
10: 8 When he **s** above, "You have neither desired
10:30 For we know the one who **s**, "Vengeance is mine,
12:21 Indeed, so terrifying was the sight that Moses **s**,
13: 5 he has **s**, "I will never leave you or forsake you."
Jas 2:11 the one who **s**, "You shall not commit adultery,"
2:11 "You shall not commit adultery," also **s**,
Jude 1: 9 but **s**, "The Lord rebuke you!"
1:18 for they **s** to you, "In the last time there will
Rev 4: 1 to me like a trumpet, **s**, "Come up here,
5: 5 Then one of the elders **s** to me, "Do not weep.
5:14 And the four living creatures **s**, "Amen!"
7:14 I **s** to him, "Sir, you are the one that knows."
7:14 Then he **s** to me, "These are they who have come
10: 4 "Seal up what the seven thunders have **s**,
10: 9 and he **s** to me, "Take it, and eat;
10:11 Then they **s** to me, "You must prophesy again
14: 7 He **s** in a loud voice, "Fear God
17: 1 the seven bowls came and **s** to me,
17: 7 But the angel **s** to me, "Why are you so amazed?
17:15 And he **s** to me, "The waters that you saw,
19: 3 Once more they **s**, "Hallelujah!
19: 9 And the angel **s** to me, "Write this:
19: 9 And he **s** to me, "These are true words of God."
19:10 but he **s** to me, "You must not do that!
21: 5 And the one who was seated on the throne **s**, "See,
I am making all things new." Also he **s**, "Write
21: 6 Then he **s** to me, "It is done!
21: 9 of the seven last plagues came and **s** to me,
22: 6 And he **s** to me, "These words are trustworthy
22: 9 but he **s** to me, "You must not do that!
22:10 And he **s** to me, "Do not seal up the words of
Tob 2: 2 I **s** to my son Tobias, "Go, my child,
2: 3 When he had returned he **s**, "Father!"
2: 6 the prophecy of Amos, how he **s** against Bethel,
2: 8 And my neighbors laughed and **s**,
2:13 I called her and **s**, "Where did you get this goat?
2:14 But she **s** to me, "It was given to me as a gift
3: 8 So the maid **s** to her,
3:10 But she thought it over and **s**,
3:11 she prayed and **s**, "Blessed are you, merciful God!

Tob 4: 2 and he s to himself, "Now I have asked
4: 3 and when he came to him he s, "My son,
5: 5 Tobias s to him, "Where do you come from,
5: 5 Then Tobias s to him, "Do you know the way
5: 7 Then Tobias s to him, "Wait for me, young man,
5: 9 Tobias went in to tell his father Tobit and s to him,
5:10 Then Tobias went out and called him, and s,
5:10 But the young man s, "Take courage;
5:10 Then Tobit s to him, "My son Tobias wishes to go
5:11 Then Tobit s to him, "Brother,
5:12 But Tobit s, "I want to be sure, brother,
5:14 Then Tobit s to him, "Welcome!
5:17 Tobit s to him, "Blessings be upon you, brother."
5:17 Then he called his son and s to him, "Son,
5:17 Tobit then s to him, "Have a safe journey."
5:18 But his mother began to weep, and s to Tobit,
5:21 Tobit s to her, "Do not worry;
6: 4 But the angel s to the young man,
6: 5 Then the angel s to him,
6: 7 the young man questioned the angel and s to him,
6:11 Raphael s to the young man,
6:11 Then Raphael s to him, "We must stay this night
6:14 Then Tobias s in answer to Raphael,
6:16 But Raphael s to him, "Do you
7: 1 Now when they entered Ecbatana, Tobias s to him,
7: 2 He s to his wife Edna,
7: 4 She s to them, "Do you know our kinsman Tobit?"
7: 9 Tobias s to Raphael, "Brother Azariah,
7:10 But Raguel overheard it and s to the lad,
7:11 But Tobias s, "I will neither eat nor drink anything
7:11 So Raguel s, "I will do so.
7:15 Raguel called his wife Edna and s to her, "Sister,
7:16 Then, wiping away the tears, she s to her,
8: 4 Tobias got out of bed and s to Sarah, "Sister,
8: 6 You s, 'It is not good that the man should
8: 8 And they both s, "Amen, Amen."
8:10 for he s, "It is possible that he will die
8:15 So they blessed the God of heaven, and Raguel s,
9: 1 Then Tobias called Raphael and s to him,
10: 2 he s, "Is it possible that he has been detained?
10: 4 His wife Anna s, "My child has perished
10: 7 Tobias came to him and s, "Send me back,
10: 8 Raguel s to Tobias, "Stay, my child, stay with me;
10: 9 But he s, "No! I beg you to send
10:11 he embraced Tobias and s, "Farewell, my child;
10:12 Then he kissed his daughter Sarah and s to her,
10:12 Then Edna s to Tobias, "My child
10:13 he blessed Raguel and his wife Edna, and s,
11: 1 which is opposite Nineveh, Raphael s,
11: 4 As they went on together Raphael s to him,
11: 6 she caught sight of him coming, she s to his father,
11: 7 Raphael s to Tobias, before he had approached
11:14 and he wept and s to him,
11:14 Then he s, "Blessed be God,
12: 1 Tobit called his son Tobias and s to him,
12: 4 Tobit s, "He deserves, my child,
12: 5 So Tobias called him and s,
12: 6 the two of them privately and s to them,
12:11 Already I have declared it to you when I s,
12:17 he s to them, "Do not be afraid; peace be with you.
13: 1 Then Tobit s: "Blessed be God
14: 4 and believe that whatever God has s will
14: 5 just as the prophets of Israel have s concerning it.
Jdt 2: 1 on the whole region, just as he had s.
2: 4 second only to himself, and s to him,
5: 3 and s to them, "Tell me, you Canaanites,
5: 5 Achior, the leader of all the Ammonites, s to him,
5:23 They s, "We are not afraid of the Israelites;
6: 1 s to Achior in the presence of all
6: 5 you have s these words in a moment of perversity;
6:17 and all that he had s in the presence of
7: 4 they were greatly terrified and s to one another,
7: 8 of the coastland came to him and s,
7:16 and he gave orders to do as they had s.
7:23 and s before all the elders,
7:30 But Uzziah s to them, "Courage,
8: 9 and when she heard all that Uzziah s to them,
8:11 They came to her, and she s to them,
8:11 What you have s to the people today is not right;
8:28 Then Uzziah s to her, "All that you have s was
8:32 Then Judith s to them, "Listen to me.
8:35 Uzziah and the rulers s to her, "Go in peace,
9: 1 to the Lord with a loud voice, and s,
9: 2 for you s, 'It shall not be done'—yet they did it.
9: 6 things you decided on presented themselves and s,
10: 7 at her beauty and s to her,
10: 9 Then she s to them, "Order the gate of the town to
10: 9 and accomplish the things you have just s to me."
10:14 in their eyes marvelously beautiful—they s to her,
10:16 but tell him what you have just s,
10:19 by her. They s to one another,
11: 1 Then Holofernes s to her, "Take courage, woman,
11: 9 and he told them all he had s to you.
11:10 lord and master, do not disregard what he s,
11:20 They marveled at her wisdom and s,
11:22 Then Holofernes s to her, "God has done well
11:23 If you do as you have s,
12: 2 But Judith s, "I cannot partake of them,
12: 3 Holofernes s to her, "If your supply runs out,
12:11 He s to Bagoas, the eunuch who had charge
12:13 and approached her and s,
12:17 So Holofernes s to her, "Have a drink and
12:18 Judith s, "I will gladly drink, my lord,
13: 3 for she s she would be going out for her prayers.
13: 3 She had s the same thing to Bagoas.
13: 4 Judith, standing beside his bed, s in her heart,
13: 7 took hold of the hair of his head, and s,

Jdt 13:14 Then she s to them with a loud voice, "Praise God,
13:15 and s, "See here, the head of Holofernes,
13:17 and s with one accord, "Blessed are you our God,
13:18 Then Uzziah s to her, "O daughter,
13:20 And all the people s, "Amen.
14: 1 Then Judith s to them, "Listen to me, my friends.
14: 7 and s, "Blessed are you in every tent of Judah!
14:13 They came to Holofernes' tent and s to the steward
15: 9 they all blessed her with one accord and s to her,
15:10 And all the people s, "Amen."
16: 1 And Judith s, Begin a song to my God
AdE 1:13 He s to his Friends, "This is how Vashti
1:16 Then Muchaeus s to the king and the governors,
1:17 the queen had s and how she had defied the king).
1:18 on hearing what she has s to the king,
2: 1 about Vashti or remembered what he had s and
2: 2 Then the king's servants s,
3: 3 Then the king's courtiers s to Mordecai,
3: 8 Then Haman s to King Artaxerxes,
4: 8 he s, "the days when you were an ordinary person,
4:10 And she s to him, "Go to Mordecai and say,
5: 3 The king s to her, "What do you wish, Esther?
5: 4 And Esther s, "Today is a special day for me.
5: 5 Then the king s, "Bring Haman quickly,
5: 6 they were drinking wine, the king s to Esther,
5: 7 She s, "My petition and request is:
5:12 And Haman s, "The queen did not invite anyone
5:14 His wife Zosara and his friends s to him,
6: 3 The king s, "What honor or dignity did we bestow
6: 3 on Mordecai?"The king's servants s,
6: 5 And the king s, "Summon him."
6: 6 Then the king s to Haman, "What shall I do
6: 6 And Haman s to himself, "Whom would
6: 7 So he s to the king, "For a person
6:10 Then the king s to Haman,
6:10 Do just as you have s for Mordecai the Jew,
6:13 His friends and his wife s to him,
7: 2 as they were drinking wine, the king s, "What is it,
7: 3 She answered and s, "If I have found favor with
7: 5 the king s, "Who is the person that would dare
7: 6 Esther s, "Our enemy is this evil man Haman!"
7: 8 The king s, "Will he dare even assault my wife
7: 9 Then Bugathan, one of the eunuchs, s to the king,
7: 9 So the king s, "Let Haman be hanged on that."
8: 5 Esther s, "If it pleases you,
8: 7 The king s to Esther, "Now that I have granted all
9:12 The king s to Esther, "In Susa, the capital,
9:13 And Esther s to the king,
10: 4 Mordecai s, "These things have come from God;
11: 1 Dositheus, who s that he was a priest and a Levite,
11: 1 which they s was authentic
13: 9 He s, "O Lord, Lord, you rule as King
14: 3 She prayed to the Lord God of Israel, and s:
15: 8 with soothing words, and s to her,
15:12 he embraced her, and s, "Speak to me."
15:13 She s to him, "I saw you, my lord,
Wis 1: 7 which holds all things together knows what is s,
8:21 and with my whole heart I s:
Sir 12:12 and be stung by what I have s.
17:14 He s to them, "Beware of all evil."
19:14 or if he s it, so that he may not repeat it.
24: 8 He s, 'Make your dwelling in Jacob,
24:31 I s, "I will water my garden
51:25 I opened my mouth and s,
Bar 1:10 They s: Here we send you money;
3:34 he called them, and they s, "Here we are!"
4: 9 that came upon you from God, and she s:
LtJ 6:20 the temple, but their hearts, it is s, are eaten away
Sus 1: 5 Concerning them the Lord had s:
1:13 One day they s to each other, "Let us go home,
1:17 She s to her maids, "Bring me olive oil
1:20 They s, "Look, the garden doors are shut,
1:22 Susanna groaned and s, "I am completely trapped.
1:27 nothing like this had ever been s about Susanna.
1:28 In the presence of the people they s,
1:36 The elders s, "While we were walking in
1:42 Then Susanna cried out with a loud voice, and s,
1:48 Taking his stand among them he s,
1:50 And the rest of the elders s to him, "Come,
1:51 Daniel s to them, "Separate them far
1:52 he summoned one of them and s to him,
1:53 though the Lord s, 'You shall not put an innocent
1:55 And Daniel s, "Very well!
1:56 And he s to him, "You offspring of Canaan and
1:59 Daniel s to him, "Very well!
Bel 1: 4 the king s to him, "Why do you not worship Bel?"
1: 6 The king s to him, "Do you not think that Bel is
1: 7 And Daniel laughed, and s, "Do not be deceived,
1: 8 and called the priests of Bel and s to them,
1: 9 Daniel s to the king, "Let it be done
1: 9 "Let it be done as you have s."
1:11 priests of Bel s, "See, we are now going outside;
1:17 The king s, "Are the seals unbroken, Daniel?"
1:19 he s, "and notice whose footprints these are."
1:20 The king s, "I see the footprints of men
1:24 The king s to Daniel, "You cannot deny that this is
1:25 Daniel s, "I worship the Lord my God,
1:26 The king s, "I give you permission."
1:27 Daniel s, "See what you have been worshiping!"
1:29 they s, "Hand Daniel over to us,
1:34 But the angel of the Lord s to Habakkuk,
1:35 Habakkuk s, "Sir, I have never seen Babylon,
1:38 Daniel s, "You have remembered me, O God,
1Mc 2: 7 and s, "Alas! Why was I born to see
2:19 But Mattathias answered and s in a loud voice:
2:33 They s to them, "Enough of this!
2:34 But they s, "We will not come out,

1Mc 2:37 for they s, "Let us all die in our innocence;
2:40 And all s to their neighbors:
2:49 And he s to his sons:
3:14 he s, "I will make a name for myself
3:17 they s to Judas, "How can we, few as we are,
3:41 the traders of the region heard what was s to them,
3:43 But they s to one another,
3:58 And Judas s, "Arm yourselves and be courageous.
4: 5 so he looked for them in the hills, because he s,
4: 8 But Judas s to those who were with him,
4:17 and he s to the people, "Do not be greedy
4:36 Then Judas and his brothers s, "See,
5:10 and sent to Judas and his brothers a letter that s,
5:15 they s that the people of Ptolemais and Tyre
5:17 Then Judas s to his brother Simon,
5:32 and he s to the men of his forces,
5:40 Timothy s to the officers of his forces,
5:57 So they s, "Let us also make a name for ourselves;
6:10 So he called all his Friends and s to them,
6:11 I s to myself, 'To what distress I have come!
6:22 They went to the king and s,
6:23 to live by what he s, and to follow his commands.
6:57 and s to the king, to the commanders of the forces,
7: 3 But when this act became known to him, he s,
7:14 for they s, "A priest of the line of Aaron has come
7:18 for they s, "There is no truth or justice in them,
7:36 and the temple; they wept and s,
7:40 Then Judas prayed and s,
9: 8 He became faint, but he s to those who were left,
9:10 But Judas s, "Far be it from us to do such a thing
9:20 they mourned many days and s,
9:28 the friends of Judas assembled and s to Jonathan,
9:44 And Jonathan s to those with him,
9:58 Then all the lawless plotted and s, "See!
9:71 He agreed, and did as he s;
10: 4 for he s to himself, "Let us act first to make peace
10:16 So he s, "Shall we find another such man?
10:22 of these things he was distressed and s,
10:55 Ptolemy the king replied and s,
10:56 I will become your father-in-law, as you have s."
10:63 and he s to his officers,
12: 3 to Rome and entered the senate chamber and s,
12:44 Then he s to Jonathan, "Why have you put all
12:46 Jonathan trusted him and did as he s;
12:53 for they s, "They have no leader or helper.
13:14 so he sent envoys to him and s,
13:46 they s, "Do not treat us according
14:22 We have recorded what they s
14:25 When the people heard these things they s,
15:33 Simon s to him in reply:
16: 2 in his two eldest sons Judas and John, and s
2Mc 2:11 And Moses s, "They were consumed because
2:32 to what has already been s;
3:12 And he s that it was utterly impossible
3:13 s that this money must in any case be confiscated
3:33 and s, "Be very grateful to the high priest Onias,
3:34 Having s this they vanished.
6:17 Let what we have s serve as a reminder;
6:24 not worthy of our time of life," he s,
6:28 When he had s this, he went at once to the rack.
6:30 to die under the blows, he groaned aloud and s:
7: 2 One of them, acting as their spokesman, s,
7: 6 against the people to their faces, when he s,
7: 8 He replied in the language of his ancestors and s
7: 9 And when he was at his last breath, he s,
7:11 and s nobly, "I got these from Heaven,
7:14 When he was near death, he s,
7:16 But he looked at the king, and s,
7:18 And when he was about to die, he s,
7:21 with a man's courage, and s to them,
7:30 While she was still speaking, the young man s,
8:18 "For they trust to arms and acts of daring," he s,
9: 4 For in his arrogance he s,
14:11 When he had s this, the rest of the king's Friends,
14:34 Having s this, he went away.
15: 2 the Jews who were compelled to follow him s,
15:33 and s that he would feed it piecemeal to the birds
1Es 1: 4 and he s, "You need no longer carry it
1:30 The king s to his servants,
3: 4 over the person of the king, s to one another
3: 9 and s, "When the king wakes, they will give him
3:16 He s, "Call the young men,
3:17 They s to them, "Explain to us
3:17 of the strength of wine, began and s:
3:24 When he had s this, he stopped speaking.
4:41 he stopped speaking, all the people shouted and s,
4:42 Then the king s to him, "Ask what you wish,
4:43 Then he s to the king,
5:68 the heads of the ancestral houses and s to them,
5:70 and the heads of the ancestral houses in Israel s
6: 3 and their associates came to them and s,
8:25 Then Ezra the scribe s, "Blessed be
8:52 for we had s to the king,
8:58 And I s to them, "You are holy to the Lord,
8:68 the leaders came to me and s,
8:74 I s, "O Lord, I am ashamed and confused
8:92 one of the men of Israel, called out, and s to Ezra,
9: 7 Then Ezra stood up and s to them,
9:10 all the multitude shouted and s with a loud voice,
9:10 "We will do as you have s.
9:49 Attharates s to Ezra the chief priest and reader,
3Mc 1:11 When they s that this was not permitted,
1:15 "But since this has happened," the king s,
4:20 when they s and proved that both the paper and
5:20 s that the Jews were benefited by today's sleep,
5:30 and with a threatening look he s,
5:35 Then the Jews, on hearing what the king had s,

3Mc 5:37 summoning Hermon he s in a threatening tone,
6:15 but just as you have s,
6:29 These then were the things he s;
6:35 The Jews, as we have s before,
7:12 admitting and approving the truth of what they s,
2Es 1:37 with the spirit they will believe the things I have s.
2:45 He answered and s to me,
2:46 Then I s to the angel,
2:47 He answered and s to me, "He is the Son of God,
2:48 Then the angel s to me, "Go,
3: 3 to speak anxious words to the Most High, and s,
3:28 "Then I s in my heart,
4: 2 and s to me, "Your understanding has utterly
4: 3 Then I s, "Yes, my lord."
4: 5 I s, "Speak, my lord."
4: 5 And he s to me, "Go, weigh for me the weight
4: 6 and s, "Who of those that have been born can do
4: 7 And he s to me, "If I had asked you,
4: 8 perhaps you would have s to me,
4:10 He s to me, "You cannot understand the things
4:12 and s to him, "It would have been better for us not
4:13 and s, "I went into a forest of trees of the plain,
4:14 and s, 'Come, let us go and make war against
4:15 the waves of the sea also made a plan and s,
4:19 I answered and s, "Each made a foolish plan,
4:20 He answered me and s, "You have judged rightly,
4:22 Then I answered and s, "I implore you, my lord,
4:26 He answered me and s, "If you are alive,
4:33 Then I answered and s, "How long?
4:34 and s, "Do not be in a greater hurry than
4:36 And the archangel Jeremiel answered and s,
4:38 Then I answered and s, "But, O sovereign Lord,
4:40 and s, "Go and ask a pregnant woman whether,
4:41 And I s, "No, lord, it cannot."
4:41 He s to me, "In Hades the chambers of
4:44 and s, "If I have found favor in your sight,
4:47 And he s to me, "Stand at my right side,
4:50 He s to me, "Consider it for yourself;
4:51 and s, "Do you think that I shall live
4:52 He answered me and s, "Concerning the signs
5:16 came to me and s, "Where have you been?
5:19 Then I s to him, "Go away from me and do
5:19 He heard what I s and left me.
5:23 I s, "O sovereign Lord, from every forest of
5:32 He s to me, "Listen to me, and I will instruct you;
5:33 Then I s, "Speak, my lord."
5:33 And he s to me, "Are you greatly disturbed
5:34 I s, "No, my lord,
5:35 He s to me, "You cannot."
5:35 And I s, "Why not, my lord?
5:36 He s to me, "Count up for me those who have not
5:38 I s, "O sovereign Lord, who is able
5:40 He s to me, "Just as you cannot do one of
5:41 I s, "Yet, O Lord, you have charge
5:42 He s to me, "I shall liken my judgment to a circle;
5:43 Then I answered and s, "Could you
5:44 He replied to me and s,
5:45 I s, "How have you said to your servant
5:45 "How have you s to your servant
5:46 He s to me, "Ask a woman's womb, and say to it,
5:47 I s, "Of course it cannot, but only each
5:48 He s to me, "Even so I have given the womb of
5:50 Then I inquired and s, "Since you have
5:56 I s, "I implore you, O Lord,
6: 1 He s to me, "At the beginning of the circle of
6: 7 I answered and s, "What will be the dividing of
6: 8 He s to me, "From Abraham to Isaac,
6:11 I answered and s, "O sovereign Lord,
6:13 He answered and s to me,
6:18 It s, "The days are coming when I draw near
6:30 And he s to me, "I have come
6:38 I s, "O Lord, you spoke at the beginning
6:38 and s on the first day,
6:55 because you have s that it was for us
6:56 you have s that they are nothing,
7: 2 He s to me, "Rise, Ezra, and listen to the words
7: 3 I s, "Speak, my lord."
7: 3 And he s to me, "There is a sea set in
7:10 I s, "That is right, lord."
7:10 He s to me, "So also is Israel's portion.
7:17 Then I answered and s, "O sovereign Lord,
7:19 He s to me, "You are not a better judge than
7:*45* I answered and s, "O sovereign Lord,
7:*45* "O sovereign Lord, I s then and I say now:
7:*49* He answered me and s, "Listen to me, Ezra,
7:*51* Inasmuch as you have s that the righteous are
7:*53* I s, "Lord, how could that be?"
7:*54* And he s to me, "Not only that,
7:*58* I s, "O sovereign Lord, what is plentiful is
7:*59* He answered me and s, "Consider
7:*62* and s, "O earth, what have you brought forth,
7:*70* and s, "When the Most High made the world
7:*71* for you have s that the mind grows with us.
7:*75* I answered and s, "If I have found favor
7:*76* He answered me and s, "I will show you that also,
7:*100* and s, "Will time therefore be given to the souls,
7:*101* He s to me, "They shall have freedom
7:*102* I answered and s, "If I have found favor
7:*104* and s, "Since you have found favor
7:*106* [36] I answered and s, "How then do we find
7:*112* [42] He answered me and s, "This present world is
7:*116* [46] and s, "This is my first and last comment:
7:*127* [57] He answered and s, "This is the significance
7:*128* [58] defeated they shall suffer what you have s,
7:*128* [58] victorious they shall receive what I have s.
7:*132* [62] I answered and s, "I know, O Lord,
8: 1 and s, "The Most High made this world for
2Es 8: 4 I answered and s, "Then drink your fill
8:19 before he was taken up. He s:
8:37 and s, "Some things you have spoken rightly,
8:42 I answered and s, "If I have found favor
8:46 and s, "Things that are present are
8:58 and s in their hearts that there is no God—
8:62 like you." Then I answered and s,
9: 1 and s, "Measure carefully in your mind,
9:14 I answered and s,
9:15 "I s before, and I say now, and will say it again:
9:17 He answered me and s, "As is the field,
9:28 and I began to speak before the Most High, and s,
9:30 and you s, 'Hear me, O Israel, and give heed
9:38 When I s these things in my heart,
9:40 and s to her, "Why are you weeping,
9:41 She s to me, "Let me alone, my lord,
9:42 I s to her, "What has happened to you? Tell me."
9:43 And she s to me, "Your servant was barren
10: 5 and answered her in anger and s,
10:18 She s to me, "I will not do so;
10:19 So I spoke again to her, and s,
10:27 I was afraid, and cried with a loud voice and s,
10:30 and strengthened me and set me on my feet, and s
10:32 I s, "It was because you abandoned me.
10:33 He s to me, "Stand up like a man,
10:34 I s, "Speak, my lord; only do
10:38 He answered me and s, "Listen to me,
12: 3 and I s to my spirit,
12: 7 Then I s, "O sovereign Lord,
12:10 He s to me, "This is the interpretation
12:45 Then I answered them and s,
13:13 and prayed to the Most High, and s,
13:20 in the last days." He answered me and s,
13:22 As for what you s about those who survive,
13:51 I s, "O sovereign Lord, explain this to me:
13:52 He s to me, "Just as no one can explore
14: 1 a voice came out of a bush opposite me and s,
14: 3 Then he s to me, "I revealed myself in a bush
14:19 Then I answered and s, "Let me speak
14:23 He answered me and s, "Go and gather the people,
14:27 and I gathered all the people together, and s,
16:55 He s, "Let the earth be made," and it was made,
4Mc 2:18 For, as I have s, the temperate mind is able to get
4: 2 governor of Syria, Phoenicia, and Cilicia, and s,
4: 6 He s that he had come with the king's authority
4:12 For he s that he had committed a sin deserving
5: 5 When Antiochus saw him he s,
6:13 some of the king's retinue came to him and s,
6:26 he lifted up his eyes to God and s,
6:30 he s this, the holy man died nobly in his tortures;
8: 4 and summoned them nearer and s,
8:12 When he had s these things,
8:27 neither s any of these things nor
8:29 all with one voice together, as from one mind, s:
9:10 When they had s these things,
9:16 when the guards s, "Agree to eat so that you may
9:23 "Imitate me, brothers," he s.
9:25 When he had s this, the saintly youth broke
9:28 But he steadfastly endured this agony and s,
9:30 To the tyrant he s, "Do you not think,
10: 9 When he was about to die, he s,
10:14 But he s to them, "You do not have
10:18 But he s, "Even if you remove my organ
11:12 he s, "Tyrant, they are splendid favors
11:13 to eat and be released, he s,
11:17 When he had s this, they led him to the wheel.
11:20 While being tortured he s,
12: 8 he s, "Let me loose, let me speak to the king and
12:11 he s, "You profane tyrant, most impious of all
12:15 Then because he too was about to die, he s,
13:11 one s, "Courage, brother," another s, "Bear up
13:13 cheerful and undaunted, s,
13:18 Those who were left behind s to each of
16:15 and s to your sons in the Hebrew language,
17: 1 Some of the guards s that when she also was about
18:15 who s, 'Many are the afflictions of the righteous.'

SAIL (22) [FORESAIL, SAILED, SAILING, SAILORS, SAILS]

Isa 33:23 the mast firm in its place, or keep the s spread out.
Eze 27: 7 Of fine embroidered linen from Egypt was your s,
Ac 13:13 Then Paul and his companions set s from Paphos
16:11 We set s from Troas and took a straight course
18:21 Then he set s from Ephesus.
20: 3 about to set s for Syria when a plot was made
20:13 We went ahead to the ship and set s for Assos,
20:16 For Paul had decided to s past Ephesus,
21: 1 When we had parted from them and set s,
21: 2 we went on board and set s.
27: 1 When it was decided that we were to s for Italy,
27: 2 on a ship of Adramyttium that was about to set s to
27:13 so they weighed anchor and began to s past Crete,
27:21 you should have listened to me and not have set s
28:10 and when we were about to s,
28:11 Three months later we set s on a ship
Wis 14: 1 to s and about to voyage over raging waves calls
Sir 43:24 Those who s the sea tell of its dangers,
1Mc 13:29 so that they could be seen by all who s the sea.
2Mc 5:21 that he could s on the land and walk on the sea,
1Es 4:23 and goes out to travel and rob and steal and to s
4Mc 13: 6 and make it calm for those who s into

SAILED (14) [SAIL]

Ac 13: 4 and from there they s to Cyprus.
14:26 From there they s back to Antioch,
Ac 15:39 Barnabas took Mark with him and s away
18:18 Paul said farewell to the believers and s for Syria,
20: 6 but we s from Philippi after the days
20:15 We s from there, and on the following day we
21: 3 we s to Syria and landed at Tyre,
27: 4 we s under the lee of Cyprus,
27: 5 After we had s across the sea that is off Cilicia
27: 7 We s slowly for a number of days and arrived
27: 7 we s under the lee of Crete off Salmone.
1Mc 7: 1 s with a few men to a town by the sea,
2Mc 14: 1 and his men that Demetrius son of Seleucus had s
4Mc 7: 3 the rudder of religion until he s into the haven

SAILING (4) [SAIL]

Lk 8:23 and while they were s he fell asleep.
Ac 27: 8 S past it with difficulty, we came to
27: 9 Since much time had been lost and s was
27:24 God has granted safety to all those who are s

SAILORS (5) [SAIL]

1Ki 9:27 s who were familiar with the sea,
Jnh 1: 7 The s said to one another, "Come, let us cast lots,
Ac 27:27 the s suspected that they were nearing land.
27:30 the s tried to escape from the ship and had lowered
Rev 18:17 s and all whose trade is on the sea,

SAILS (1) [SAIL]

Wis 5:10 like a ship that s through the billowy water,

SAINT (1) [SAINTED, SAINTLY, SAINTS, SAINTS']

Php 4:21 Greet every s in Christ Jesus.

SAINTED (1) [SAINT]

3Mc 6: 3 O Father, upon the children of the s Jacob,

SAINTLY (1) [SAINT]

4Mc 9:25 the s youth broke the thread of life.

SAINTS‡ (64) [SAINT]

Ps 31:23 Love the LORD, all you his s.
Mt 27:52 of the s who had fallen asleep were raised.
Ac 9:13 how much evil he has done to your s in Jerusalem;
9:32 he came down also to the s living in Lydda.
9:41 Then calling the s and widows,
26:10 I not only locked up many of the s in prison,
Ro 1: 7 who are called to be s:
8:27 because the Spirit intercedes for the s according to
12:13 Contribute to the needs of the s;
15:25 I am going to Jerusalem in a ministry to the s;
15:26 to share their resources with the poor among the s
15:31 to Jerusalem may be acceptable to the s,
16: 2 in the Lord as is fitting for the s,
16:15 and Olympas, and all the s who are with them.
1Co 1: 2 called to be s, together with all those who
6: 1 instead of taking it before the s?
6: 2 Do you not know that the s will judge the world?
14:33 (As in all the churches of the s,
16: 1 Now concerning the collection for the s:
16:15 to the service of the s;
2Co 1: 1 including all the s throughout Achaia:
8: 4 the privilege of sharing in this ministry to the s—
9: 1 for me to write you about the ministry to the s,
9:12 of this ministry not only supplies the needs of the s
13:12 All the s greet you.
Eph 1: 1 To the s who are in Ephesus and are faithful
1:15 in the Lord Jesus and your love toward all the s,
1:18 the riches of his glorious inheritance among the s,
2:19 the s and also members of the household of God,
3: 8 Although I am the very least of all the s,
3:18 to comprehend, with all the s, what is the breadth
4:12 to equip the s for the work of ministry,
5: 3 be mentioned among you, as is proper among s.
6:18 and always persevere in supplication for all the s.
Php 1: 1 To all the s in Christ Jesus who are in Philippi,
4:22 All the s greet you, especially those of
Col 1: 2 To the s and faithful brothers and sisters in Christ
1: 4 and of the love that you have for all the s,
1:12 to share in the inheritance of the s in the light.
1:26 but has now been revealed to his s.
1Th 3:13 at the coming of our Lord Jesus with all his s.
2Th 1:10 to be glorified by his s and to be marveled at on
Phm 1: 5 for all the s and your faith toward the Lord Jesus.
1: 7 hearts of the s have been refreshed through you,
Heb 6:10 that you showed for his sake in serving the s,
13:24 Greet all your leaders and all the s.
Jude 1: 3 for the faith that was once for all entrusted to the s.
Rev 5: 8 which are the prayers of the s.
5: 9 and by your blood you ransomed for God s
8: 3 of incense to offer with the prayers of all the s on
8: 4 the smoke of the incense, with the prayers of the s,
11:18 the prophets and s and all who fear your name,
13: 7 Also it was allowed to make war on the s and
13:10 Here is a call for the endurance and faith of the s.
14:12 Here is a call for the endurance of the s,
16: 6 because they shed the blood of s and prophets,
17: 6 that the woman was drunk with the blood of the s
18:20 O heaven, you s and apostles and prophets!
18:24 in you was found the blood of prophets and of s,
19: 8 for the fine linen is the righteous deeds of the s.
20: 9 of the earth and surrounded the camp of the s and
22:21 The grace of the Lord Jesus be with all the s.
Wis 5: 5 And why is their lot among the s?

Wis 18: 9 so that the s would share alike the same things,

SAINTS' (1) [SAINT]

1Ti 5:10 washed the s feet, helped the afflicted,

SAKAR See Index to Footnotes

SAKE‡ (193) [SAKES]

Ge 12:16 And for her s he dealt well with Abram;
18:26 I will forgive the whole place for their s."
18:29 He answered, "For the s of forty I will not do it."
18:31 "For the s of twenty I will not destroy it."
18:32 "For the s of ten I will not destroy it."
26: 7 of the place might kill me for the s of Rebekah,
26:24 for my servant Abraham's s."
39: 5 the Egyptian's house for Joseph's s;
Ex 18: 8 to Pharaoh and to the Egyptians for Israel's s,
Nu 11:29 Moses said to him, "Are you jealous for my s?
Jos 23: 3 to all these nations for your s,
1Sa 12:22 not cast away his people, for his great name's s,
2Sa 5:12 and that he had exalted his kingdom for the s
9: 1 to whom I may show kindness for Jonathan's s?"
9: 7 for I will show you kindness for the s
10:12 and let us be courageous for the s of our people,
18: 5 for my s with the young man Absalom."
18:12 For my s protect the young man Absalom!
1Ki 11:12 Yet for the s of your father David I will not do it
11:13 s of my servant David and for the s of Jerusalem,
11:32 s of my servant David and for the s of Jerusalem,
11:34 for the s of my servant David whom I chose
15: 4 for David's s the LORD his God gave him a lamp
2Ki 8:19 for the s of his servant David,
19:34 for my own s and for the s of my servant David."
20: 6 for my own s and for my servant David's s."
1Ch 14: 2 and that his kingdom was highly exalted for the s
17:19 For your servant's s, O LORD,
Ps 6: 4 deliver me for the s of your steadfast love.
23: 3 He leads me in right paths for his name's s.
25: 7 for your goodness' s, O LORD!
25:11 For your name's s, O LORD, pardon my guilt,
31: 3 for your name's s lead me and guide me,
44:26 Redeem us for the s of your steadfast love.
69: 7 It is for your s that I have borne reproach,
79: 9 deliver us, and forgive our sins, for your name's s.
106: 8 Yet he saved them for his name's s,
106:45 For their s he remembered his covenant,
109:21 act on my behalf for your name's s;
115: 1 the s of your steadfast love and your faithfulness.
122: 8 For the s of my relatives and friends I will say,
122: 9 For the s of the house of the LORD our God,
132:10 For your servant David's s do not turn away
143:11 For your name's s, O LORD, preserve my life.
Isa 37:35 my own s and for the s of my servant David."
42:21 LORD was pleased, for the s of his righteousness,
43:14 For your s I will send to Babylon and break
43:25 who blots out your transgressions for my own s,
45: 4 For the s of my servant Jacob,
48: 9 For my name's s I defer my anger,
48: 9 for the s of my praise I restrain it for you,
48:11 For my own s, for my own s, I do it,
62: 1 For Zion's s I will not keep silent,
62: 1 and for Jerusalem's s I will not rest,
63:17 Turn back for the s of your servants,
63:17 for the s of the tribes that are your heritage.
65: 8 so I will do for my servants' s,
66: 5 and reject you for my name's s have said, "Let
Jer 14: 7 act, O LORD, for your name's s;
14:21 Do not spurn us, for your name's s;
17:21 Thus says the LORD: For the s of your lives,
Eze 20: 9 But I acted for the s of my name,
20:14 But I acted for the s of my name,
20:22 and acted for the s of my name,
20:44 when I deal with you for my name's s,
28:17 you corrupted your wisdom for the s
36:22 It is not for your s, O house of Israel,
36:22 but for the s of my holy name,
36:32 It is not for your s that I will act,
Da 9:17 and for your own s, Lord,
9:19 For your own s, O my God,
Mt 5:10 for righteousness' s, for theirs is the kingdom
10:39 and those who lose their life for my s will find it.
15: 3 the commandment of God for the s
15: 6 So, for the s of your tradition,
16:25 and those who lose their life for my s will find it.
19:12 for the s of the kingdom of heaven.
19:29 for my name's s, will receive a hundredfold,
24:22 for the s of the elect those days will be cut short.
Mk 8:35 and those who lose their life for my s,
8:35 and for the s of the gospel, will save it.
10:29 for my s and for the s of the good news,
12:40 and for the s of appearance say long prayers.
13:20 but for the s of the elect, whom he chose,
Lk 9:24 and those who lose their life for my s will save it.
18:29 for the s of the kingdom of God,
20:47 and for the s of appearance say long prayers.
Jn 11:15 For your s I am glad I was not there,
11:42 for the s of the crowd standing here,
12:30 Jesus answered, "This voice has come for your s,
Ac 5:41 to suffer dishonor for the s of the name.
9:16 how much he must suffer for the s of my name."
15:26 who have risked their lives for the s
28:20 for the s of the hope of Israel that I am bound
Ro 1: 5 among all the Gentiles for the s of his name,
4:23 were written not for his s alone,
8:36 "For your s we are being killed all day long;
Ro 9: 3 from Christ for the s of my own people,
11:28 the gospel they are enemies of God for your s;
11:28 for the s of their ancestors;
14:20 Do not, for the s of food, destroy the work of God.
1Co 4:10 We are fools for the s of Christ,
9:10 Or does he not speak entirely for our s?
9:10 It was indeed written for our s,
9:23 I do it all for the s of the gospel,
10:28 and for the s of conscience—
11: 9 Neither was man created for the s of woman, but woman for the s of man.
2Co 2:10 has been for your s in the presence of Christ.
4: 5 as Lord and ourselves as your slaves for Jesus' s.
4:11 we are always being given up to death for Jesus' s,
4:15 Yes, everything is for your s, so that grace,
5:21 For our s he made him to be sin who knew no sin,
12:10 persecutions, and calamities for the s of Christ;
12:19 beloved, is for the s of building you up.
Eph 3: 1 that I Paul am a prisoner for Christ Jesus for the s
Php 3: 8 For his s I have suffered the loss of all things,
Col 1:24 I am now rejoicing in my sufferings for your s,
1:24 in Christ's afflictions for the s of his body,
1Th 1: 5 of persons we proved to be among you for your s.
3: 2 and encourage you for the s of your faith,
1Ti 5:23 the s of your stomach and your frequent ailments.
2Ti 1: 1 the s of the promise of life that is in Christ Jesus,
2:10 I endure everything for the s of the elect,
Tit 1: 1 the s of the faith of God's elect and the knowledge
Heb 1:14 for the s of those who are to inherit salvation?
6:10 and the love that you showed for his s in serving
12: 2 for the s of the joy that was set before him endured
12: 7 Endure trials for the s of discipline.
1Pe 1:20 but was revealed at the end of the ages for your s.
2:13 For the Lord's s accept the authority
4: 7 and discipline yourselves for the s of your prayers.
3Jn 1: 7 for they began their journey for the s of Christ,
Jude 1:11 to Balaam's error for the s of gain,
Rev 2: 3 and bearing up for the s of my name,
Sir 20:11 There are losses for the s of glory,
29: 9 Help the poor for the commandment's s,
29:10 Lose your silver for the s of a brother or a friend,
37: 5 a friend for their stomachs' s,
38:14 for the s of preserving life.
44:12 their children also, for their s.
44:22 To Isaac also he gave the same assurance for the s
Bar 2:14 and for your own s deliver us,
Aza 1:11 For your name's s do not give us up forever,
1:12 the s of Abraham your beloved and for the s of
1Mc 13: 4 of this all my brothers have perished for the s
2Mc 3:33 since for his s the Lord has granted you your life.
5:19 But the Lord did not choose the nation for the s of
5:19 but the place for the s of the nation.
6:25 for the s of living a brief moment longer,
7:23 you now forget yourselves for the s of his laws."
8:15 not for their own s, then for the s of the covenants
12:25 they let him go, for the s of saving their kindred.
13: 3 not for the s of his country's welfare,
3Mc 7:11 that those who for the belly's s had transgressed
2Es 1:10 For their s I have overthrown many kings;
7:11 For I made the world for their s,
7:*74* and not for their s, but because of the times
8: 1 Most High made this world for the s of many,
8: 1 but the world to come for the s of only a few.
8:44 and for whose s you have formed all things—
9:13 those to whom the age belongs and for whose s
4Mc 1: 8 from the noble bravery of those who died for the s
1:10 died for the s of nobility and goodness,
6:27 I am dying in burning torments for the s of
6:30 by virtue of reason, for the s of the law.
7:22 that it is blessed to endure any suffering for the s
9:30 by our endurance for the s of religion?
10:20 for the s of God, we let our bodily members
11: 2 tyrant, to be tortured for the s of virtue.
13: 9 let us die like brothers for the s of the law;
13:12 to being slain for the s of religion."
13:27 those who were left endured for the s of religion.
14: 6 agreed to go to death for its s.
15:12 the mother urged on to death for religion's s.
16:13 and urged them on to death for the s of religion.
16:17 while an aged man endures such agonies for the s
16:19 you ought to endure any suffering for the s of God.
16:20 For his s also our father Abraham was zealous
16:21 the fiery furnace and endured it for the s of God.
16:25 that those who die for the s of God live to God,
17: 7 to death for the s of religion?
17:20 then, who have been consecrated for the s of God,
18: 3 the s of religion were not only admired by mortals,

SAKES (3) [SAKE]

Jn 17:19 And for their s I sanctify myself,
2Co 8: 9 yet for your s he became poor,
4Mc 2:10 so that virtue is not abandoned for their s.

SAKKUTH (1)

Am 5:26 You shall take up S your king,

SALA (1) [=SALMON]

Lk 3:32 son of Boaz, son of S, son of Nahshon,

SALAH (KJV) See SHELAH

SALAMIEL (1)

Jdt 8: 1 of Nathanael son of S son of Sarasadai son

SALAMIS (1)

Ac 13: 5 When they arrived at S, they proclaimed the word

SALATHIEL‡ (3) [=SHEALTIEL]

Mt 1:12 Jechoniah was the father of S,
1:12 and S the father of Zerubbabel,
2Es 3: 1 I, S, who am also called Ezra.

SALATHIEL (KJV) See SHEALTIEL

SALCAH, SALCHAH (KJV) See SALECAH

SALE‡ (8) [SELL]

Lev 25:14 a s to your neighbor or buy from your neighbor,
25:27 the years since its s shall be computed and
25:29 be redeemed until a year has elapsed since its s;
25:50 the price of the s shall be applied to the number
Dt 18: 8 even though they have income from the s
28:68 for s to your enemies as male and female slaves,
Am 8: 5 the sabbath, so that we may offer wheat for s?
2Mc 11: 3 and to put up the high priesthood for s every year.

SALECAH (4)

Dt 3:10 and all of Bashan, as far as S and Edrei,
Jos 12: 5 over Mount Hermon and S and all Bashan to
13:11 and all Mount Hermon, and all Bashan to S;
1Ch 5:11 beside them in the land of Bashan as far as S:

SALEM (5) [=JERUSALEM]

Ge 14:18 And King Melchizedek of S brought out bread
Ps 76: 2 His abode has been established in S,
Heb 7: 1 This "King Melchizedek of S,
7: 2 next he is also king of S, that is, "king of peace."
Jdt 4: 4 and to Choba and Aesora, and the valley of S.

SALIM (1)

Jn 3:23 near S because water was abundant there;

SALIVA (2)

Mk 8:23 he had put s on his eyes and laid his hands on him,
Jn 9: 6 on the ground and made mud with the s and spread

SALLAI (2)

Ne 11: 8 his brothers Gabbai, S: nine hundred twenty-eight.
12:20 of S, Kallai; of Amok, Eber;

SALLIED (2) [SALLY]

1Mc 6:31 but the Jews s out and burned these with fire,
9:67 and his men s out from the town and set fire to

SALLU (3)

1Ch 9: 7 Of the Benjaminites: S son of Meshullam,
Ne 11: 7 S son of Meshullam son of Joed son
12: 7 S, Amok, Hilkiah, Jedaiah.

SALLY (1) [SALLIED]

1Mc 14:36 a citadel from which they used to s forth and defile

SALMA (4) [=SALMON]

1Ch 2:11 Nahshon became the father of S, S of Boaz,
2:51 S father of Bethlehem, and Hareph father
2:54 The sons of S: Bethlehem,

SALMON‡ (4) [=SALA, =SALMA]

Ru 4:20 Amminadab of Nahshon, Nahshon of S,
4:21 S of Boaz, Boaz of Obed,
Mt 1: 4 and Nahshon the father of S,
1: 5 and S the father of Boaz by Rahab,

SALMONE (1)

Ac 27: 7 we sailed under the lee of Crete off S.

SALOME (2)

Mk 15:40 of James the younger and of Joses, and S.
16: 1 the mother of James, and S bought spices,

SALT‡ (47) [SALTED, SALTINESS, SALTY]

Ge 19:26 looked back, and she became a pillar of s.
Ex 30:35 seasoned with s, pure and holy;
Lev 2:13 You shall not omit from your grain offerings the s
2:13 with all your offerings you shall offer s.
Nu 18:19 a covenant of s forever before the LORD for you
Dt 29:23 and s, nothing planted, nothing sprouting, unable
Jos 15:62 the City of S, and En-gedi:
Jdg 9:45 and he razed the city and sowed it with s.
2Sa 8:13 eighteen thousand Edomites in the Valley of S."
2Ki 2:20 He said, "Bring me a new bowl, and put s in it."
2:21 to the spring of water and threw the s into it,
14: 7 in the Valley of S and took Sela by storm;
1Ch 18:12 eighteen thousand Edomites in the Valley of S.
2Ch 13: 5 to David and his sons by a covenant of s?
25:11 he went to the Valley of S,
Ezr 4:14 Now because we share the s of the palace and it is
6: 9 for burnt offerings to the God of heaven, wheat, s,
7:22 one hundred baths of oil, and unlimited s.
Job 6: 6 Can that which is tasteless be eaten without s,
39: 6 the s land for its dwelling place?
Ps 60: T *twelve thousand Edomites the Valley of S.*

Jer 17: 6 of the wilderness, in an uninhabited **s** land.
48: 9 Set aside **s** for Moab, for she will surely fall;
Eze 16: 4 nor rubbed with **s**, nor wrapped in cloths.
43:24 the priests shall throw **s** on them and offer them up
47:11 they are to be left for **s**.
Zep 2: 9 a land possessed by nettles and **s** pits,
Mt 5:13 You are the **s** of the earth; but if **s** has lost its taste,
Mk 9:50 **S** is good; but if **s** has lost its saltiness,
9:50 Have **s** in yourselves, and be at peace
Lk 14:34 "**S** is good; but if **s** has lost its taste,
Col 4: 6 with **s**, so that you may know how you ought
Jas 3:12 No more can **s** water yield fresh.
Wis 10: 7 not ripen, and a pillar of **s** standing as a monument
Sir 22:15 **s**, and a piece of iron are easier to bear than
39:23 as when he turned a watered land into **s**.
39:26 and fire and iron and **s** and wheat flour and milk
43:19 He pours frost over the earth like **s**,
LtJ 6:28 of the meat with **s**, but give none to the poor
1Mc 10:29 the Jews from payment of tribute and **s** tax
11:35 and the **s** pits and the crown taxes due to us—
1Es 6:30 and likewise wheat and **s** and wine and oil,
8:20 a hundred baths of wine, and **s** in abundance.
2Es 5: 9 **S** waters shall be found in the sweet,

SALTED (2) [SALT]

Mk 9:49 "For everyone will be **s** with fire.
Tob 6: 6 and ate some of the fish, and kept some to be **s**.

SALTHAS (1)

1Es 9:22 Ishmael, and Nathanael, and Gedaliah, and **S**.

SALTINESS‡ (3) [SALT]

Mt 5:13 if salt has lost its taste, how can its **s** be restored?
Mk 9:50 but if salt has lost its **s**, how can you season it?
Lk 14:34 if salt has lost its taste, how can its **s** be restored?

SALTY (1) [SALT]

Ps 107:34 a fruitful land into a **s** waste,

SALU (2)

Nu 25:14 the Midianite woman, was Zimri son of **S**, head of
1Mc 2:26 just as Phinehas did against Zimri son of **S**.

SALUTATION, SALUTATIONS, SALUTE, SALUTED, SALUTETH

(KJV) See also GREET, GREETED, GREETING, GREETS, SALUTING, WELCOME, VISIT

SALUTE (3) [SALUTED, SALUTING]

1Sa 13:10 and Saul went out to meet him and **s** him.
25: 6 Thus you shall **s** him: 'Peace be to
25:14 of the wilderness to **s** our master;

SALUTED (1) [SALUTE]

1Sa 30:21 When David drew near to the people he **s** them.

SALUTING (1) [SALUTE]

Mk 15:18 And they began **s** him, "Hail, King of the Jews!"

SALVATION‡ (137) [SAVE]

Ge 49:18 I wait for your **s**, O LORD.
Ex 15: 2 and he has become my **s**;
Dt 32:15 and scoffed at the Rock of his **s**.
2Sa 22: 3 my shield and the horn of my **s**,
22:36 You have given me the shield of your **s**,
22:47 and exalted be my God, the rock of my **s**,
22:51 He is a tower of **s** for his king,
1Ch 16:23 Tell of his **s** from day to day.
16:35 Say also: "Save us, O God of our **s**,
2Ch 6:41 O LORD God, be clothed with **s**,
Job 13:16 This will be my **s**, that the godless shall not come
Ps 13: 5 my heart shall rejoice in your **s**.
18: 2 my shield, and the horn of my **s**, my stronghold.
18:35 You have given me the shield of your **s**,
18:46 and exalted be the God of my **s**,
24: 5 and vindication from the God of their **s**.
25: 5 and teach me, for you are the God of my **s**;
27: 1 The LORD is my light and my **s**;
27: 9 do not forsake me, O God of my **s**!
35: 3 say to my soul, "I am your **s**."
36:10 and your **s** to the upright of heart!
37:39 The **s** of the righteous is from the LORD;
38:22 make haste to help me, O Lord, my **s**.
40:10 I have spoken of your faithfulness and your **s**;
40:16 may those who love your **s** say continually,
50:23 to those who go the right way I will show the **s**
51:12 Restore to me the joy of your **s**,
51:14 O God, O God of my **s**,
62: 1 in silence; from him comes my **s**.
62: 2 He alone is my rock and my **s**, my fortress;
62: 6 He alone is my rock and my **s**, my fortress;
65: 5 with deliverance, O God of our **s**;
68:19 who daily bears us up; God is our **s**.
68:20 Our God is a God of **s**,
69:29 let your **s**, O God, protect me.
70: 4 Let those who love your **s** say evermore,
71:15 of your deeds of **s** all day long,
74:12 Yet God my King is from of old, working **s** in
79: 9 Help us, O God of our **s**,
Ps 85: 4 Restore us again, O God of our **s**,
85: 7 O LORD, and grant us your **s**.
85: 9 Surely his **s** is at hand for those who fear him,
88: 1 God of my **s**, when, at night,
89:26 my God, and the Rock of my **s**!'
91:16 long life I will satisfy them, and show them my **s**.
95: 1 let us make a joyful noise to the rock of our **s**!
96: 2 tell of his **s** from day to day.
116:13 the cup of **s** and call on the name of the LORD,
118:14 and my might; he has become my **s**.
118:21 that you have answered me and have become my **s**.
119:41 O LORD, your **s** according to your promise.
119:81 My soul languishes for your **s**;
119:123 My eyes fail from watching for your **s**,
119:155 **S** is far from the wicked,
119:166 I hope for your **s**, O LORD,
119:174 I long for your **s**, O LORD,
132:16 Its priests I will clothe with **s**,
Isa 12: 2 Surely God is my **s**; I will trust,
12: 2 and my might; he has become my **s**.
12: 3 With joy you will draw water from the wells of **s**.
17:10 For you have forgotten the God of your **s**,
25: 9 let us be glad and rejoice in his **s**.
33: 2 our **s** in the time of trouble.
33: 6 abundance of **s**, wisdom, and knowledge;
45: 8 let the earth open, that **s** may spring up,
45:17 Israel is saved by the LORD with everlasting **s**;
46:13 it is not far off, and my **s** will not tarry;
46:13 I will put **s** in Zion, for Israel my glory.
49: 6 that my **s** may reach to the end of the earth."
49: 8 on a day of **s** I have helped you;
51: 5 my **s** has gone out and my arms will rule
51: 6 but my **s** will be forever, and my deliverance will
51: 8 and my **s** to all generations.
52: 7 who brings good news, who announces **s**,
52:10 all the ends of the earth shall see the **s** of our God.
56: 1 for soon my **s** will come, and my deliverance be
59:11 for **s**, but it is far from us.
59:17 and a helmet of **s** on his head;
60:18 you shall call your walls **S**, and your gates Praise.
61:10 for he has clothed me with the garments of **s**,
62: 1 and her **s** like a burning torch.
62:11 Say to daughter Zion, "See, your **s** comes;
Jer 3:23 Truly in the LORD our God is the **s** of Israel.
La 3:26 It is good that one should wait quietly for the **s** of
Mic 7: 7 I will wait for the God of my **s**;
Hab 3:18 I will exult in the God of my **s**.
Mk 16: S ⟦and imperishable proclamation of eternal **s**.⟧
Lk 1:77 of **s** to his people by the forgiveness of their sins.
2:30 for my eyes have seen your **s**,
3: 6 and all flesh shall see the **s** of God.' "
19: 9 "Today **s** has come to this house,
Jn 4:22 we worship what we know, for **s** is from the Jews.
Ac 4:12 There is **s** in no one else,
13:26 to us the message of this **s** has been sent.
13:47 so that you may bring **s** to the ends of the earth.' "
16:17 who proclaim to you a way of **s**."
28:28 that this **s** of God has been sent to the Gentiles;
Ro 1:16 the power of God for **s** to everyone who has faith,
11:11 through their stumbling **s** has come to the Gentiles,
13:11 For **s** is nearer to us now than
2Co 1: 6 it is for your consolation and **s**;
6: 2 and on a day of **s** I have helped you."
6: 2 see, now is the day of **s**!
7:10 a repentance that leads to **s** and brings no regret,
Eph 1:13 the gospel of your **s**, and had believed in him,
6:17 Take the helmet of **s**, and the sword of the Spirit,
Php 1:28 of their destruction, but of your **s**.
2:12 work out your own **s** with fear and trembling;
1Th 5: 8 and for a helmet the hope of **s**.
5: 9 but for obtaining **s** through our Lord Jesus Christ,
2Th 2:13 as the first fruits for **s** through sanctification by
2Ti 2:10 they may also obtain the **s** that is in Christ Jesus,
3:15 to instruct you for **s** through faith in Christ Jesus.
Tit 2:11 the grace of God has appeared, bringing **s** to all,
Heb 1:14 to serve for the sake of those who are to inherit **s**?
2: 3 how can we escape if we neglect so great a **s**?
2:10 the pioneer of their **s** perfect through sufferings.
5: 9 the source of eternal **s** for all who obey him,
6: 9 in your case, things that belong to **s**.
1Pe 1: 5 of God through faith for a **s** ready to be revealed in
1: 9 the outcome of your faith, the **s** of your souls.
1:10 Concerning this **s**, the prophets who prophesied of
2: 2 spiritual milk, so that by it you may grow into **s**—
2Pe 3:15 and regard the patience of our Lord as **s**.
Jude 1: 3 to write to you about the **s** we share,
Rev 7:10 "**S** belongs to our God who is seated on
12:10 the **s** and the power and the kingdom of our God
19: 1 **S** and glory and power to our God,
Wis 5: 2 be amazed at the unexpected **s** of the righteous.
6:24 The multitude of the wise is the **s** of the world,
Bar 4:24 so they soon will see your **s** by God,
4:29 will bring you everlasting joy with your **s**.
2Es 6:25 to you shall be saved and shall see my **s** and
7:66 of any torment or **s** promised to them after death.
7:131 [61] much as joy over those to whom **s** is assured."
8:39 and their **s**, and their receiving their reward.
9: 8 will see my **s** in my land and within my borders,

SALVE (1)

Rev 3:18 and **s** to anoint your eyes so that you may see.

SAMARIA‡ (132) [SAMARIA'S, SAMARITAN, SAMARITANS, SHEMER]

1Ki 13:32 of the high places that are in the cities of **S**,
1Ki 16:24 the hill of **S** from Shemer for two talents of silver;
16:24 **S**, after the name of Shemer, the owner of the hill.
16:28 with his ancestors, and was buried in **S**;
16:29 of Omri reigned over Israel in **S** twenty-two years.
16:32 for Baal in the house of Baal, which he built in **S**.
18: 2 The famine was severe in **S**.
20: 1 He marched against **S**, laid siege to it,
20:10 if the dust of **S** will provide a handful for each of
20:17 "Men have come out from **S**."
20:34 for yourself in Damascus, as my father did in **S**."
20:43 resentful and sullen, and came to **S**.
21: 1 beside the palace of King Ahab of **S**.
21:18 to meet King Ahab of Israel, who rules in **S**;
22:10 at the entrance of the gate of **S**;
22:37 So the king died, and was brought to **S**;
22:37 they buried the king in **S**.
22:38 They washed the chariot by the pool of **S**;
22:51 in **S** in the seventeenth year of King Jehoshaphat
2Ki 1: 2 through the lattice in his upper chamber in **S**,
1: 3 go to meet the messengers of the king of **S**,
2:25 on to Mount Carmel, and then returned to **S**.
3: 1 of Ahab became king over Israel in **S**;
3: 6 So King Jehoram marched out of **S** at that time
5: 3 only my lord were with the prophet who is in **S**!
6:19 And he led them to **S**.
6:20 As soon as they entered **S**, Elisha said,
6:20 and they saw that they were inside **S**.
6:24 he marched against **S** and laid siege to it.
6:25 famine in **S** became so great that
7: 1 of barley for a shekel, at the gate of **S**."
7:18 about this time tomorrow in the gate of **S**,"
10: 1 Now Ahab had seventy sons in **S**.
10: 1 So Jehu wrote letters and sent them to **S**,
10:12 Then he set out and went to **S**.
10:17 When he came to **S**, he killed all who were left
10:17 he killed all who were left to Ahab in **S**,
10:35 and they buried him in **S**.
10:36 over Israel in **S** was twenty-eight years.
13: 1 of Jehu began to reign over Israel in **S**;
13: 6 the sacred pole also remained in **S**.
13: 9 and they buried him in **S**;
13:10 of Jehoahaz began to reign over Israel in **S**;
13:13 Joash was buried in **S** with the kings of Israel.
14:14 as hostages; then he returned to **S**.
14:16 and was buried in **S** with the kings of Israel;
14:23 of Joash of Israel began to reign in **S**;
15: 8 of Jeroboam reigned over Israel in **S** six months.
15:13 he reigned one month in **S**.
15:14 of Gadi came up from Tirzah and came to **S**;
15:14 down Shallum son of Jabesh in **S** and killed him;
15:17 he reigned ten years in **S**.
15:23 of Menahem began to reign over Israel in **S**;
15:25 in **S**, in the citadel of the palace along with Argob
15:27 of Remaliah began to reign over Israel in **S**;
17: 1 Hoshea son of Elah began to reign in **S**
17: 5 of Assyria invaded all the land and came to **S**;
17: 6 of Hoshea the king of Assyria captured **S**;
17:24 in the cities of **S** in place of the people of Israel;
17:24 they took possession of **S**, and settled in its cities.
17:26 and placed in the cities of **S** do not know the law
17:28 from **S** came and lived in Bethel;
17:29 of the high places that the people of **S** had made,
18: 9 King Shalmaneser of Assyria came up against **S**,
18:10 of King Hoshea of Israel, **S** was taken.
18:34 Have they delivered **S** out of my hand?
21:13 for **S**, and the plummet for the house of Ahab;
23:18 with the bones of the prophet who came out of **S**.
23:19 of **S**, which kings of Israel had made, provoking
2Ch 18: 2 After some years he went down to Ahab in **S**.
18: 9 at the entrance of the gate of **S**;
22: 9 while hiding in **S** and was brought to Jehu,
25:13 fell on the cities of Judah from **S** to Beth-horon;
25:24 also hostages; then he returned to **S**.
28: 8 from them and brought the booty to **S**.
28: 9 he went out to meet the army that came to **S**,
28:15 Then they returned to **S**.
Ezr 4:10 in the cities of **S** and in the rest of the province
4:17 of their associates who live in **S** and in the rest of
Ne 4: 2 of his associates and of the army of **S**,
Isa 7: 9 The head of Ephraim is **S**,
7: 9 and the head of **S** is the son of Remaliah.
8: 4 and the spoil of **S** will be carried away by the king
9: 9 Ephraim and the inhabitants of **S**—
10: 9 Is not **S** like Damascus?
10:10 images were greater than those of Jerusalem and **S**,
10:11 to Jerusalem and her idols what I have done to **S**
36:19 Have they delivered **S** out of my hand?
Jer 23:13 In the prophets of **S** I saw a disgusting thing:
31: 5 you shall plant vineyards on the mountains of **S**;
41: 5 from Shechem and Shiloh and **S**,
Eze 16:46 Your elder sister is **S**, who lived
16:51 **S** has not committed half your sins;
16:53 of Sodom and her daughters and the fortunes of **S**
16:55 **S** and her daughters shall return
23: 4 As for their names, Oholah is **S**,
23:33 and desolation is the cup of your sister **S**;
Hos 7: 1 and the wicked deeds of **S**;
8: 5 Your calf is rejected, O **S**.
8: 6 The calf of **S** shall be broken to pieces.
10: 5 inhabitants of **S** tremble for the calf of Beth-aven.
13:16 **S** shall bear her guilt, because she has rebelled
Am 3: 9 and say, "Assemble yourselves on Mount **S**,
3:12 shall the people of Israel who live in **S** be rescued,
4: 1 you cows of Bashan who are on Mount **S**,
6: 1 and for those who feel secure on Mount **S**,
8:14 Those who swear by Ashimah of **S**, and say,
Ob 1:19 the land of Ephraim and the land of **S**,

Mic 1: 1 which he saw concerning S and Jerusalem.
1: 5 What is the transgression of Jacob? Is it not **S**?
1: 6 I will make S a heap in the open country,
Lk 17:11 through the region between S and Galilee.
Jn 4: 4 But he had to go through **S.**
4: 9 a Jew, ask a drink of me, a woman of **S?"**
Ac 1: 8 in all Judea and **S,** and to the ends of the earth."
8: 1 throughout the countryside of Judea and **S.**
8: 5 the city of S and proclaimed the Messiah to them.
8: 9 in the city and amazed the people of **S,**
8:14 at Jerusalem heard that S had accepted the word
9:31 Galilee, and S had peace and was built up.
15: 3 and as they passed through both Phoenicia and **S,**
Tob 14: 4 even S and Jerusalem will be desolate.
Jdt 1: 9 and all who were in S and its towns,
4: 4 So they sent word to every district of **S,**
1Mc 3:10 and a large force from S to fight against Israel.
10:30 the three districts added to it from S and Galilee,
10:38 to Judea from the country of **S,**
11:28 the king to free Judea and the three districts of S
11:34 were added to Judea from **S.**
2Mc 15: 1 that Judas and his troops were in the region of **S,**
1Es 2:16 living in S and other places,
2:25 in S and Syria and Phoenicia, wrote as follows:

SAMARIA'S (1) [SAMARIA]

Hos 10: 7 S king shall perish like a chip on the face of

SAMARITAN (6) [SAMARIA]

Lk 10:33 But a S while traveling came near him;
17:16 And he was a **S.**
Jn 4: 5 So he came to a S city called Sychar,
4: 7 A S woman came to draw water,
4: 9 The S woman said to him, "How is it that you,
8:48 in saying that you are a S and have a demon?"

SAMARITANS (6) [SAMARIA]

Mt 10: 5 and enter no town of the **S,**
Lk 9:52 On their way they entered a village of the S
Jn 4: 9 (Jews do not share things in common with **S.**)
4:39 Many S from that city believed in him because of
4:40 S came to him, they asked him to stay with them;
Ac 8:25 the good news to many villages of the **S.**

SAMATUS (1)

1Es 9:34 Shashai, Azarel, Azael, S, Zambris, Joseph.

SAME‡ (344)

Ge 7:13 On the very s day Noah with his sons,
11: 1 the whole earth had one language and the s words.
26:12 and in the s year reaped a hundredfold.
26:32 That s day Isaac's servants came and told him
32:19 the s thing to Esau when you meet him,
32:22 The s night he got up and took his two wives,
39:17 and she told him the s story, saying,
41:11 We dreamed on the s night, he and I,
41:25 "Pharaoh's dreams are one and the **s;**
Ex 5: 6 That s day Pharaoh commanded the taskmasters of
5: 8 But you shall require of them the s quantity
5:13 s daily assignment as when you were given straw."
5:18 but you shall still deliver the s number of bricks."
6:26 It was this s Aaron and Moses to whom
6:27 the Israelites out of Egypt, the s Moses and Aaron.
7:11 magicians of Egypt, did the s by their secret arts.
7:22 magicians of Egypt did the s by their secret arts;
8: 7 But the magicians did the s by their secret arts,
12: 8 They shall eat the lamb that s night;
12:42 That s night is a vigil to be kept for the LORD
21:31 owner shall be dealt with according to this s rule.
22:30 the s with your oxen and with your sheep:
23:11 You shall do the s with your vineyard,
26: 2 all the curtains shall be of the s size.
26: 8 the eleven curtains shall be of the s size.
26:24 it shall be the s with both of them;
28: 8 on it shall be of the s workmanship and materials,
36: 9 all the curtains were of the s size.
36:15 the eleven curtains were of the s size.
39: 5 The decorated band on it was of the s materials
Lev 4:20 he shall do the s with this.
7: 7 there is the s ritual for them;
19: 6 It shall be eaten on the s day you offer it,
22:28 an animal with its young on the s day.
22:30 It shall be eaten on the s day;
23: 6 of the s month is the festival of unleavened bread
23:21 On that s day you shall make proclamation;
24:19 maims another shall suffer the s injury in return:
Nu 2:34 and they set out the s way, everyone by clans,
6:11 They shall sanctify the head that s day,
10:32 the s we will do for you."
15:16 with you shall have the s law and the s ordinance.
15:29 you shall have the s law for anyone who acts
18:27 the s as the grain of the threshing floor and
26: 9 These are the s Dathan and Abiram,
28:24 In the s way you shall offer daily, for seven days,
Dt 2:22 He did the s for the descendants of Esau,
7:19 the s to all the peoples of whom you are afraid.
9:20 I interceded also on behalf of Aaron at that s time.
10: 4 Then he wrote on the tablets the s words as before,
12:30 I also want to do the **s.**"
12:31 You must not do the **s** for the LORD your God,
15:17 the s with regard to your female slave.
21:23 you shall bury him that s day,
22: 3 You shall do the s with a neighbor's donkey;
22: 3 you shall do the s with a neighbor's garment;
Dt 22: 3 the s with anything else that your neighbor loses
27:11 The s day Moses charged the people as follows:
Jos 6:15 around the city in the s manner seven times.
Jdg 7: 9 That s night the LORD said to him, "Get up,
7:17 "Look at me, and do the **s;**
8: 8 and made the s request of them;
20:22 and again formed the battle line in the s place
1Sa 2:34 both of them shall die on the s day.
4:12 and came to Shiloh the s day,
6: 4 s plague was upon all of you and upon your lords.
17:23 and spoke the s words as before.
17:27 The people answered him in the s way,
17:30 from him toward another and spoke in the s way;
30:24 down into the battle shall be the s as the share of
31: 6 and all his men died together on the s day.
2Sa 1:11 and all the men who were with him did the **s.**
7: 4 s night the word of the LORD came to Nathan:
1Ki 3:17 my lord, this woman and I live in the s house;
6:25 cherubim had the s measure and the s form.
7: 8 of the hall, was of the s construction.
7:15 the second pillar was the **s.**
7:18 he did the s with the other capital.
7:37 with the s size and the s form.
8:64 The s day the king consecrated the middle of
11: 8 He did the s for all his foreign wives,
13: 3 He gave a sign the s day, saying,
22:12 the prophets were prophesying the s and saying,
2Ki 8:22 Libnah also revolted at the s time.
19:33 By the way that he came, by the s he shall return;
25:17 The second pillar had the **s,** with the latticework.
1Ch 17: 3 s night the word of the LORD came to Nathan,
2Ch 16:10 on some of the people at the s time.
18:11 the prophets were prophesying the s and saying,
27: 5 the s amount in the second and the third years.
28:22 to the LORD—this s King Ahaz.
32:12 not this s Hezekiah who took away his high places
32:30 This s Hezekiah closed the upper outlet of
35:12 And they did the s with the bulls.
Ezr 5: 3 At the s time Tattenai the governor of the province
Ne 5: 5 Now our flesh is the s as that of our kindred;
5: 5 our children are the s as their children;
6: 4 and I answered them in the s manner.
6: 5 In the s way Sanballat for the fifth time
Est 1: 1 the s Ahasuerus who ruled
9:21 and also the fifteenth day of the s month,
Job 4: 8 and sow trouble reap the **s.**
Ps 102:27 but you are the **s,** and your years have no end.
Ecc 2:14 Yet I perceived that the s fate befalls all of them.
3:19 the fate of humans and the fate of animals is the **s;**
3:19 They all have the s breath,
9: 2 since the s fate comes to all,
9: 3 that the s fate comes to everyone.
Isa 37:34 By the way that he came, by the s he shall return;
Jer 27:12 I spoke to King Zedekiah of Judah in the s way:
28: 1 In that s year, at the beginning of the reign
28:17 In that s year, in the seventh month,
39:10 and gave them vineyards and fields at the s time.
52:22 the second pillar had the **s,** with pomegranates.
Eze 1:16 and the four had the s form,
10:22 they were the s faces whose appearance I had seen
14:10 and the punishment of the prophet shall be the **s—**
18:24 and do the s abominable things that the wicked do,
21:19 both of them shall issue from the s land.
23:13 they both took the s way.
23:38 they have defiled my sanctuary on the s day
23:39 on the s day they came into my sanctuary
40:10 the three were of the s size;
40:10 and the pilasters on either side were of the s size.
40:21 and its pilasters and its vestibule were of the s size
40:22 of the s size as those of the gate that faced toward
40:24 they had the s dimensions as the others.
40:28 it was of the s dimensions as the others.
40:29 and its vestibule were of the s size as the others;
40:32 it was of the s size as the others.
40:33 and its vestibule were of the s dimensions as
40:35 it had the s dimensions as the others.
40:36 and its vestibule were of the s size as the others;
42:11 to the chambers on the north, of the s length
42:11 with the s exits and arrangements and doors.
44: 3 and shall go out by the s way.
45:11 The ephah and the bath shall be of the s measure,
45:20 You shall do the s on the seventh day of the month
45:25 he shall make the s provision for sin offerings,
46: 8 and he shall go out by the s way.
46:22 the four were of the s size.
Am 2: 4 by the s lies after which their ancestors walked.
2: 7 father and son go in to the s girl,
Zec 6:10 the s day to the house of Josiah son of Zephaniah.
Mt 5:12 the s way they persecuted the prophets who were
5:16 In the s way, let your light shine before others,
5:19 and teaches others to do the **s,**
5:46 Do not even the tax collectors do the **s?**
5:47 Do not even the Gentiles do the **s?**
7:17 In the s way, every good tree bears good fruit,
13: 1 That s day Jesus went out of the house and sat
18:28 But that s slave, as he went out,
20: 5 about noon and about three o'clock, he did the **s.**
20:14 I choose to give to this last the s as I give to you.
21:30 The father went to the second and said the **s;**
21:36 and they treated them in the s way.
22:23 The s day some Sadducees came to him,
22:26 The second did the **s,** so also the third,
25:17 In the s way, the one who had
26:44 and prayed for the third time, saying the s words.
27:41 In the s way the chief priests also,
27:44 with him also taunted him in the s way.
Mk 14:31 And all of them said the **s.**
Mk 14:39 and prayed, saying the s words.
15:31 In the s way the chief priests,
Lk 6:33 For even sinners do the **s.**
10: 7 Remain in the s house, eating
10:21 At that s hour Jesus rejoiced in the Holy Spirit
17: 4 if the s person sins against you seven times a day,
20:31 and so in the s way all seven died childless.
22:20 And he did the s with the cup after supper, saying,
23:12 That s day Herod and Pilate became friends
23:40 you are under the s sentence of condemnation?
24:13 Now on that s day two of them were going to
24:33 That s hour they got up and returned to Jerusalem;
Jn 21:13 and did the s with the fish.
Ac 1:11 in the s way as you saw him go into heaven."
11:17 If then God gave them the s gift that he gave us
14: 1 The s thing occurred in Iconium,
15:27 who themselves will tell you the s things by word
16:33 At the s hour of the night he took them
18: 3 because he was of the s trade, he stayed with them,
19:25 with the workers of the s trade, and said, "Men,
24:26 At the s time he hoped that money would
27:40 At the s time they loosened the ropes that tied
Ro 1:27 and in the s way also the men,
2: 1 the judge, are doing the very s things.
3:30 of faith and the uncircumcised through that s faith.
7: 4 In the s way, my friends, you have died to the law
9:21 the s lump one object for special use and another
10:12 the s Lord is Lord of all and is generous
12: 4 and not all the members have the s function,
13: 6 For the s reason you also pay taxes,
1Co 1:10 you be united in the s mind and the s purpose.
9: 8 Does not the law also say the **s?**
9:14 In the s way, the Lord commanded
10: 3 and all ate the s spiritual food,
10: 4 and all drank the s spiritual drink.
11: 5 it is one and the s thing as having her head shaved.
11:25 In the s way he took the cup also, after supper,
12: 4 Now there are varieties of gifts, but the s Spirit;
12: 5 and there are varieties of services, but the s Lord;
12: 6 the s God who activates all of them in everyone.
12: 8 of knowledge according to the s Spirit,
12: 9 to another faith by the s Spirit,
12:11 All these are activated by one and the s Spirit,
12:25 the members may have the s care for one another.
14: 7 It is the s way with lifeless instruments
2Co 1: 6 when you patiently endure the s sufferings
1:17 "Yes, yes" and "No, no" at the s time?
3:14 that s veil is still there,
3:18 the s image from one degree of glory to another;
4:13 as we have the s spirit of faith that is in accordance
8:16 of Titus the s eagerness for you that I myself have.
12:18 Did we not conduct ourselves with the s spirit?
12:18 Did we not take the s steps?
Gal 1:14 beyond many among my people of the s age,
Eph 3: 6 members of the s body, and sharers in the promise
4:10 the s one who ascended far above all the heavens,
5:28 In the s way, husbands should love their wives
6: 8 we will receive the s again from the Lord,
6: 9 And, masters, do the s to them.
6: 9 for you know that both of you have the s Master
Php 1:30 the s struggle that you saw I had and now hear
2: 2 be of the s mind, having the s love,
2: 5 Let the s mind be in you that was in Christ Jesus,
2:18 and in the s way you also must be glad and rejoice
3: 1 To write the s things to you is not troublesome
3:15 of us then who are mature be of the s mind;
4: 2 and I urge Syntyche to be of the s mind in
Col 4: 3 the s time pray for us as well that God will open
1Th 2:14 the s things from your own compatriots as they did
Heb 1:12 But you are the **s,** and your years will never end."
2:14 he himself likewise shared the s things,
6:11 the s diligence so as to realize the full assurance
6:17 In the s way, when God desired to show
9:21 the s way he sprinkled with the blood both the tent
10: 1 by the s sacrifices that are continually offered year
10:11 the s sacrifices that can never take away sins.
11: 9 who were heirs with him of the s promise.
13: 8 Jesus Christ is the s yesterday and today
Jas 1:11 It is the s way with the rich;
3:10 From the s mouth come blessing and cursing.
3:11 from the s opening both fresh and brackish water?
1Pe 3: 1 the s way, accept the authority of your husbands,
3: 7 in the s way, show consideration for your wives
4: 1 also with the s intention (for whoever has suffered
4: 4 that you no longer join them in the s excesses
5: 5 In the s way, you who are younger must accept
5: 9 the world are undergoing the s kinds of suffering.
2Pe 3: 7 But by the s word the present heavens
Jude 1: 7 which, in the s manner as they,
1: 8 in the s way these dreamers also defile the flesh,
Rev 21:16 city lies foursquare, its length the s as its width;
Tob 2: 9 That s night I washed myself and went
3: 7 On the s day, at Ecbatana in Media,
3:11 At that s time, with hands outstretched toward
3:17 the s time that Tobit returned from the courtyard
4: 1 That s day Tobit remembered the money
4: 4 when she dies, bury her beside me in the s grave.
12:14 And at the s time God sent me to heal you
Jdt 12: 3 where can we get you more of the **s?**
13: 3 She had said the s thing to Bagoas.
AdE 1: 1 the s Artaxerxes who ruled
8: 9 that is, Nisan, in the s year;
9: 2 On that s day the enemies of the Jews perished;
9:13 "Let the Jews be allowed to do the s tomorrow.
9:17 the fourteenth day they rested and made that s day
Wis 15: 7 of the s clay both the vessels that serve clean uses
15: 8 these workers form a futile god from the s clay—

Wis 17:14 they all slept the s sleep,
18: 8 For by the s means by which
18: 9 so that the saints would share alike the s things,
18:11 The slave was punished with the s penalty as
18:11 and the commoner suffered the s loss as the king;
19:16 those who had already shared the s rights.
19:18 while each note remains the s.
Sir Pr: 2 the s sense when translated into another language.
7:12 or do the s to a friend.
34:31 and goes again and does the s things,
42:21 he is from all eternity one and the s.
44:22 the s assurance for the sake of his father Abraham.
Bar 1: 8 At the s time, on the tenth day of Sivan,
3:14 at the s time discern where there is length of days,
LtJ 6:71 In the s way, their gods of wood,
1Mc 2:25 At the s time he killed
8:27 In the s way, if war comes first to the nation of
10:77 At the s time he advanced into the plain,
12: 2 also sent letters to the s effect to the Spartans and
15:22 The consul wrote the s thing to King Demetrius
2Mc 2: 4 It was also in the s document that the prophet,
2:13 The s things are reported in the records and in
2:14 In the s way Judas also collected all the books
3:33 the s young men appeared again
3:33 to Heliodorus dressed in the s clothing,
6: 8 that they should adopt the s policy toward the Jews
7:13 and tortured the fourth in the s way.
7:28 And in the s way the human race came into being.
8:14 and at the s time implored the Lord
10: 5 It happened that on the s day on which
10: 5 that is, on the twenty-fifth day of the s month,
10:36 in the s way wheeled around against the defenders
12: 8 in the s way to wipe out the Jews who were living
13:12 the s petition and had implored the merciful Lord
15:10 the s time pointing out the perfidy of the Gentiles
15:13 Then in the s fashion another appeared,
1Es 6: 3 At the s time Sisinnes the governor of Syria
9:48 at the s time explaining what was read.
3Mc 1:23 they resorted to the s posture of supplication as
3:11 in his s purpose, wrote this letter against them:
4:13 with in precisely the s fashion as the others,
5:20 the s way for the destruction of the lawless Jews!"
5:36 reconvened the party in the s manner and urged
6:30 in that s place in which they had expected
2Es 2:19 and the s number of springs flowing with milk
3:10 And the s fate befell all of them:
5:49 so I have made the s rule for the world
6:35 and fasted seven days in the s way as before,
11: 8 "Do not all watch at the s time;
13:12 the s man come down from the mountain and call
4Mc 2:22 the s time he enthroned the mind among the senses
8: 5 not to display the s madness as that of
10: 2 the s father begot me as well as those who died,
10: 2 and the s mother bore me,
10: 2 and that I was brought up on the s teachings?
10:13 do not give way to the s insanity as your brothers,
11:15 we ought likewise to die for the s principles.
12:13 like yours and are made of the s elements as you,
13: 9 in Assyria who despised the s ordeal of
13:20 There each of the brothers spent the s length
13:20 and was shaped during the s period of time;
13:20 from the s blood and through the s life,
13:21 they drank milk from the s fountains.
13:24 by the s law and trained in the s virtues
14:20 she was of the s mind as Abraham.
15:19 in his tortures gazing boldly at the s agonies,
16:22 You too must have the s faith in God and not

SAMGAR-NEBO (1)

Jer 39: 3 Nergal-sharezer, S, Sarsechim the Rabsaris,

SAMLAH (4)

Ge 36:36 and S of Masrekah succeeded him as king.
36:37 S died, and Shaul of Rehoboth on
1Ch 1:47 When Hadad died, S of Masrekah succeeded him.
1:48 When S died, Shaul of Rehoboth on

SAMOS (2)

Ac 20:15 The next day we touched at S,
1Mc 15:23 and to S, and to Pamphylia, and to Lycia,

SAMOTHRACE (1)

Ac 16:11 from Troas and took a straight course to S,

SAMOTHRACIA (KJV) See SAMOTHRACE

SAMPSAMES (1)

1Mc 15:23 and to S, and to the Spartans, and to Delos,

SAMSON (37) [SAMSON'S]

Jdg 13:24 The woman bore a son, and named him S.
14: 1 Once S went down to Timnah,
14: 3 But S said to his father, "Get her for me,
14: 5 Then S went down with his father and mother
14: 7 and talked with the woman, and she pleased S.
14:10 and S made a feast there as
14:12 S said to them, "Let me now put a riddle to you.
15: 1 S went to visit his wife, bringing along a kid.
15: 3 S said to them, "This time,
15: 4 So S went and caught three hundred foxes,
15: 6 And they said, "S, the son-in-law of the Timnite,
15: 7 S said to them, "If this is what you do,
15:10 They said, "We have come up to bind S,
Jdg 15:11 to the cleft of the rock of Etam, and they said to S,
15:12 S answered them, "Swear to me
15:16 And S said, "With the jawbone of a donkey,
16: 1 Once S went to Gaza, where he saw a prostitute
16: 2 The Gazites were told, "S has come here."
16: 3 But S lay only until midnight.
16: 6 to S, "Please tell me what makes your strength
16: 7 S said to her, "If they bind me
16: 9 she said to him, "The Philistines are upon you, S!"
16:10 Then Delilah said to S, "You have mocked me
16:12 and said to him, "The Philistines are upon you, S!"
16:13 to S, "Until now you have mocked me
16:14 she said to him, "The Philistines are upon you, S!"
16:20 Then she said, "The Philistines are upon you, S!"
16:23 "Our god has given S our enemy into our hand."
16:25 when their hearts were merry, they said, "Call S,
16:25 So they called S out of the prison,
16:26 S said to the attendant who held him by the hand,
16:27 who looked on while S performed.
16:28 Then S called to the LORD and said,
16:29 And S grasped the two middle pillars on which
16:30 Then S said, "Let me die with the Philistines."
1Sa 12:11 and S, and rescued you out of the hand
Heb 11:32 time would fail me to tell of Gideon, Barak, S,

SAMSON'S (4) [SAMSON]

Jdg 14:15 On the fourth day they said to S wife,
14:16 So S wife wept before him, saying, "You hate me;
14:20 And S wife was given to his companion,
15: 6 because he has taken S wife and given her

SAMUEL‡ (146)

1Sa 1:20 She named him S, for she said,
2:18 S was ministering before the LORD,
2:21 the boy S grew up in the presence of the LORD.
2:26 Now the boy S continued to grow both in stature
3: 1 boy S was ministering to the LORD under Eli.
3: 3 S was lying down in the temple of the LORD,
3: 4 Then the LORD called, "S! S!"
3: 6 The LORD called again, "S!"
3: 6 S got up and went to Eli, and said, "Here I am,
3: 7 Now S did not yet know the LORD,
3: 8 The LORD called S again, a third time.
3: 9 Therefore Eli said to S, "Go, lie down;
3: 9 So S went and lay down in his place.
3:10 and stood there, calling as before, "S! S!"
3:10 And S said, "Speak, for your servant is listening."
3:11 Then the LORD said to S, "See,
3:15 S lay there until morning;
3:15 S was afraid to tell the vision to Eli.
3:16 But Eli called S and said, "S, my son."
3:18 S told him everything and hid nothing from him.
3:19 As S grew up, the LORD was with him
3:20 that S was a trustworthy prophet of the LORD.
3:21 for the LORD revealed himself to S at Shiloh by
4: 1 And the word of S came to all Israel.
7: 3 Then S said to all the house of Israel,
7: 5 Then S said, "Gather all Israel at Mizpah,
7: 6 And S judged the people of Israel at Mizpah.
7: 8 The people of Israel said to S,
7: 9 So S took a sucking lamb and offered it as
7: 9 S cried out to the LORD for Israel,
7:10 As S was offering up the burnt offering,
7:12 Then S took a stone and set it up between Mizpah
7:13 against the Philistines all the days of S.
7:15 S judged Israel all the days of his life.
8: 1 When S became old, he made his sons judges
8: 4 of Israel gathered together and came to S
8: 6 But the thing displeased S when they said,
8: 6 a king to govern us." S prayed to the LORD,
8: 7 and the LORD said to S, "Listen to the voice of
8:10 So S reported all the words of the LORD to
8:19 But the people refused to listen to the voice of S;
8:21 When S had heard all the words of the people,
8:22 The LORD said to S, "Listen to their voice
8:22 S then said to the people of Israel,
9:14 they saw S coming out toward them on his way up
9:15 the LORD had revealed to S:
9:17 When S saw Saul, the LORD told him,
9:18 Then Saul approached S inside the gate, and said,
9:19 S answered Saul, "I am the seer;
9:22 Then S took Saul and his servant-boy
9:23 And S said to the cook,
9:24 S said, "See, what was kept is set before you.
9:24 So Saul ate with S that day.
9:26 the break of dawn S called to Saul upon the roof,
9:26 and both he and S went out into the street.
9:27 S said to Saul, "Tell the boy to go on before us,
10: 1 S took a vial of oil and poured it on his head,
10: 9 As he turned away to leave S,
10:14 we saw they were not to be found, we went to S."
10:15 Saul's uncle said, "Tell me what S said to you."
10:16 the matter of the kingship, of which S had spoken,
10:17 S summoned the people to the LORD at Mizpah
10:20 Then S brought all the tribes of Israel near,
10:24 S said to all the people,
10:25 S told the people the rights and duties of
10:25 Then S sent all the people back to their homes.
11: 7 "Whoever does not come out after Saul and S,
11:12 The people said to S, "Who is it that said,
11:14 S said to the people, "Come,
12: 1 S said to all Israel, "I have listened to you in all
12: 6 S said to the people, "The LORD is witness,
12:18 So S called upon the LORD,
12:18 all the people greatly feared the LORD and S.
12:19 to S, "Pray to the LORD your God
1Sa 12:20 And S said to the people, "Do not be afraid;
13: 8 He waited seven days, the time appointed by S;
13: 8 but S did not come to Gilgal,
13:10 the burnt offering, S arrived;
13:11 S said, "What have you done?"
13:13 S said to Saul, "You have done foolishly;
13:15 And S left and went on his way from Gilgal.
15: 1 S said to Saul, "The LORD sent me
15:10 The word of the LORD came to S:
15:11 S was angry; and he cried out to the LORD
15:12 S rose early in the morning to meet Saul, and S
15:13 When S came to Saul, Saul said to him,
15:14 But S said, "What then is this bleating of sheep
15:16 Then S said to Saul, "Stop!
15:17 S said, "Though you are little in your own eyes,
15:20 Saul said to S, "I have obeyed the voice of
15:22 And S said, "Has the LORD as great delight
15:24 Saul said to S, "I have sinned;
15:26 S said to Saul, "I will not return with you;
15:27 As S turned to go away,
15:28 And S said to him, "The LORD has torn
15:31 So S turned back after Saul;
15:32 Then S said, "Bring Agag king of the Amalekites
15:33 But S said, "As your sword has made women
15:33 And S hewed Agag in pieces before the LORD
15:34 Then S went to Ramah;
15:35 S did not see Saul again until the day of his death, but S grieved over Saul.
16: 1 The LORD said to S, "How long will you grieve
16: 2 S said, "How can I go?
16: 4 S did what the LORD commanded,
16: 7 But the LORD said to S,
16: 8 and made him pass before S.
16:10 made seven of his sons pass before S, and S said
16:11 S said to Jesse, "Are all your sons here?"
16:11 And S said to Jesse, "Send and bring him;
16:13 Then S took the horn of oil,
16:13 S then set out and went to Ramah.
19:18 he came to S at Ramah,
19:18 He and S went and settled at Naioth.
19:20 with S standing in charge of them,
19:22 he asked, "Where are S and David?"
19:24 and he too fell into a frenzy before S.
25: 1 Now S died; and all Israel assembled
28: 3 Now S had died, and all Israel had mourned
28:11 He answered, "Bring up S for me."
28:12 the woman saw S, she cried out with a loud voice;
28:14 So Saul knew that it was S,
28:15 Then S said to Saul, "Why have you disturbed me
28:16 S said, "Why then do you ask me,
28:20 filled with fear because of the words of S;
1Ch 6:28 sons of S: Joel his firstborn, the second Abijah.
6:33 Heman, the singer, son of Joel, son of S,
9:22 the seer S established them in their office of trust.
11: 3 according to the word of the LORD by S.
26:28 Also all that S the seer, and Saul son of Kish,
29:29 are written in the records of the seer S,
2Ch 35:18 in Israel since the days of the prophet S;
Ps 99: 6 S also was among those who called on his name.
Jer 15: 1 Though Moses and S stood before me,
Ac 3:24 from S and those after him,
13:20 until the time of the prophet S.
Heb 11:32 Jephthah, of David and S and the prophets—
Sir 46:13 S was beloved by his Lord;
46:19 S bore witness before the Lord and his anointed:
1Es 1:20 in Israel since the times of the prophet S;
2Es 7:*108* [38] and S in the days of Saul,

SANABASSAROS, SANABASSARUS

See Index to Footnotes

SANBALLAT (10)

Ne 2:10 When S the Horonite and Tobiah
2:19 S the Horonite and Tobiah the Ammonite official,
4: 1 when S heard that we were building the wall,
4: 7 But when S and Tobiah and the Arabs and
6: 1 to S and Tobiah and to Geshem the Arab and to
6: 2 S and Geshem sent to me,
6: 5 the same way S for the fifth time sent his servant
6:12 against me because Tobiah and S had hired him.
6:14 Remember Tobiah and S, O my God,
13:28 was the son-in-law of S the Horonite;

SANCTIFICATION (6) [SANCTIFY]

Ro 6:19 as slaves to righteousness for s.
6:22 the advantage you get is s.
1Co 1:30 and righteousness and s and redemption,
1Th 4: 3 For this is the will of God, your s:
2Th 2:13 the first fruits for salvation through s by the Spirit
Sir 7:31 the gift of the shoulders, the sacrifice of s,

SANCTIFIED‡ (30) [SANCTIFY]

Ex 29:43 and it shall be s by my glory;
Lev 22:32 that I may be s among the people of Israel:
1Sa 16: 5 And he s Jesse and his sons and invited them to
1Ch 15:14 the priests and the Levites s themselves to bring up
2Ch 5:11 the priests who were present had s themselves,
29:15 They gathered their brothers, s themselves,
29:17 then for eight days they s the house of the LORD,
29:19 we have made ready and s;
29:34 until other priests had s themselves, their kindred,
30: 3 because the priests had not s themselves
30: 8 and come to his sanctuary, which he has s forever,
30:15 and they s themselves and brought burnt offerings

2Ch 30:17 in the assembly who had not s themselves;
30:24 The priests s themselves in great numbers.
Jn 10:36 that the one whom the Father has s and sent into
17:19 so that they also may be s in truth.
Ac 20:32 to give you the inheritance among all who are s.
26:18 and a place among those who are s by faith in me.'
Ro 15:16 the offering of the Gentiles may be acceptable, s
1Co 1: 2 to those who are s in Christ Jesus,
6:11 But you were washed, you were s,
1Ti 4: 5 for it is s by God's word and by prayer.
Heb 2:11 and those who are s all have one Father.
10:10 And it is by God's will that we have been s
10:14 for all time those who are s.
10:29 the blood of the covenant by which they were s,
1Pe 1: 2 and destined by God the Father and s by the Spirit
3Mc 2: 9 chose this city and s this place for your name,
2:16 on your people Israel, you s this place.
2Es 9: 8 which I have s for myself from the beginning.

SANCTIFIES (2) [SANCTIFY]

Heb 2:11 For the one who s and those who are sanctified all
9:13 s those who have been defiled so that their flesh

SANCTIFY‡ (36) [SANCTIFICATION, SANCTIFIED, SANCTIFIES, SANCTIFYING, SANCTITY]

Ex 31:13 that you may know that I, the LORD, s you.
Lev 11:44 s yourselves therefore, and be holy, for I am holy.
20: 8 I am the LORD; I s you.
21: 8 for I the LORD, I who s you, am holy.
21:15 for I am the LORD; I s him.
21:23 for I am the LORD; I s them.
22: 9 I am the LORD; I s them.
22:16 for I am the LORD; I s them.
22:32 I am the LORD; I s you,
Nu 6:11 They shall s the head that same day,
Jos 3: 5 Then Joshua said to the people, "S yourselves;
7:13 Proceed to s the people, and say,
7:13 and say, 'S yourselves for tomorrow;
1Sa 16: 5 s yourselves and come with me to the sacrifice."
2Ki 10:20 Jehu decreed, "S a solemn assembly for Baal."
1Ch 15:12 s yourselves, you and your kindred,
2Ch 29: 5 S yourselves, and s the house of the LORD,
29:17 They began to s on the first day of the first month,
35: 6 Slaughter the passover lamb, s yourselves,
Job 1: 5 Job would send and s them,
Isa 29:23 they will s my name; they will s the Holy One
66:17 Those who s and purify themselves to go into
Eze 20:12 so that they might know that I the LORD s them.
36:23 I will s my great name, which has been profaned
37:28 the nations shall know that I the LORD s Israel,
Joel 1:14 S a fast, call a solemn assembly.
2:15 Blow the trumpet in Zion; s a fast;
2:16 S the congregation; assemble the aged;
Jn 17:17 S them in the truth; your word is truth.
17:19 And for their sakes I s myself,
1Th 5:23 May the God of peace himself s you entirely;
Heb 13:12 also suffered outside the city gate in order to s
1Pe 3:15 but in your hearts s Christ as Lord.
1Es 1: 3 that they should s themselves to the Lord and put

SANCTIFYING (1) [SANCTIFY]

2Ch 29:34 the priests in s themselves.

SANCTITY (1) [SANCTIFY]

2Mc 3:12 the s and inviolability of the temple that is honored

SANCTUARIES (6) [SANCTUARY]

Lev 21:23 that he may not profane my s;
26:31 will make your s desolate,
Eze 21: 2 toward Jerusalem and preach against the s;
27:18 of your trade, you profaned your s.
Am 7: 9 and the s of Israel shall be laid waste,
3Mc 2:28 of those who do not sacrifice shall enter their s,

SANCTUARY‡ (235) [SANCTUARIES, SANCTUARY'S]

Ex 15:17 the s, O LORD, that your hands have established.
25: 8 And have them make me a s,
30:13 to the shekel of the s (the shekel is twenty gerahs),
30:24 measured by the s shekel—
36: 1 the construction of the s shall work in accordance
36: 3 for doing the work on the s.
36: 4 doing every sort of task on the s came,
36: 6 to make anything else as an offering for the s."
38:24 in all the construction of the s,
38:24 shekels, measured by the s shekel.
38:25 shekels, measured by the s shekel;
38:26 half a shekel, measured by the s shekel),
38:27 of silver were for casting the bases of the s,
Lev 4: 6 before the LORD in front of the curtain of the s.
5:15 convertible into silver by the s shekel;
10: 4 the front of the s to a place outside the camp."
10:18 not brought into the inner part of the s.
10:18 You should certainly have eaten it in the s,
12: 4 not touch any holy thing, or come into the s,
16: 2 into the s inside the curtain before the mercy seat
16:16 Thus he shall make atonement for the s,
16:17 from the time he enters to make atonement in the s
16:33 He shall make atonement for the s,
19:30 You shall keep my sabbaths and reverence my s:
20: 3 defiling my s and profaning my holy name.
21:12 not go outside the s and thus profane the s of his
Lev 22: 9 so that they may not incur guilt and die in the s
26: 2 You shall keep my sabbaths and reverence my s:
27: 3 be fifty shekels of silver by the s shekel.
27:25 All assessments shall be by the s shekel:
Nu 3:28 attending to the duties of the s.
3:31 the vessels of the s with which the priests minister,
3:32 to have oversight of those who had charge of the s.
3:38 having charge of the rites within the s,
3:47 reckoning by the shekel of the s,
3:50 reckoned by the shekel of the s;
4:12 the utensils of the service that are used in the s,
4:15 and his sons have finished covering the s and all
4:15 the sanctuary and all the furnishings of the s,
4:16 in the s and in its utensils.
7:13 according to the shekel of the s,
7:19 according to the shekel of the s,
7:25 according to the shekel of the s,
7:31 according to the shekel of the s,
7:37 according to the shekel of the s,
7:43 according to the shekel of the s,
7:49 according to the shekel of the s,
7:55 according to the shekel of the s,
7:61 according to the shekel of the s,
7:67 according to the shekel of the s,
7:73 according to the shekel of the s,
7:79 according to the shekel of the s,
7:85 according to the shekel of the s,
7:86 according to the shekel of the s, all the gold of
8:19 among the Israelites for coming too close to the s.
18: 1 for offenses connected with the s,
18: 3 not approach either the utensils of the s or
18: 5 You yourselves shall perform the duties of the s
18:16 according to the shekel of the s (that is,
19:20 for they have defiled the s of the LORD.
28: 7 in the s you shall pour out a drink offering
31: 6 the vessels of the s and the trumpets for sounding
Jos 24:26 set it up there under the oak in the s of the LORD.
1Ki 6: 5 both the nave and the inner s;
6:16 and he built this within as an inner s,
6:17 The house, that is, the nave in front of the inner s,
6:19 The inner s he prepared in the innermost part of
6:20 The interior of the inner s was twenty cubits long,
6:21 in front of the inner s, and overlaid it with gold.
6:22 that belonged to the inner s he overlaid with gold.
6:23 the inner s he made two cherubim of olivewood,
6:31 For the entrance to the inner s he made doors
7:49 in front of the inner s;
8: 6 in the inner s of the house, in the most holy place,
8: 8 from the holy place in front of the inner s;
1Ch 22:19 and build the s of the LORD God so that the ark
23:32 of the tent of meeting and the s,
24: 5 for there were officers of the s and officers of God
28:10 LORD has chosen you to build a house as the s;
2Ch 4:20 to burn before the inner s, as prescribed;
5: 7 in the inner s of the house, in the most holy place,
5: 9 from the holy place in front of the inner s;
20: 8 and in it have built you a s for your name, saying,
26:18 to make offering. Go out of the s;
29:21 for a sin offering for the kingdom and for the s and
30: 8 yield yourselves to the LORD and come to his s,
36:17 of their s, and had no compassion on young man
Ne 10:39 oil to the storerooms where the vessels of the s are,
Ps 20: 2 May he send you help from the s,
28: 2 as I lift up my hands toward your most holy s.
60: 6 God has promised in his s:
63: 2 So I have looked upon you in the s,
68:24 the processions of my God, my King, into the s—
68:35 Awesome is God in his s, the God of Israel;
73:17 until I went into the s of God;
74: 3 the enemy has destroyed everything in the s.
74: 7 They set your s on fire;
78:69 He built his s like the high heavens, like the earth,
96: 6 strength and beauty are in his s.
108: 7 God has promised in his s:
114: 2 Judah became God's s, Israel his dominion.
150: 1 Praise God in his s; praise him in his mighty
Isa 8:14 He will become a s, a stone one strikes against;
16:12 when he comes to his s to pray, he will not prevail.
43:28 Therefore I profaned the princes of the s,
60:13 and the pine, to beautify the place of my s;
63:18 now our adversaries have trampled down your s.
Jer 17:12 exalted from the beginning, shrine of our s!
La 1:10 she has even seen the nations invade her s,
2: 7 The Lord has scorned his altar, disowned his s;
2:20 Should priest and prophet be killed in the s of
Eze 5:11 because you have defiled my s
8: 6 to drive me far from my s?
9: 6 And begin at my s."
11:16 among the countries, yet I have been a s to them
23:38 they have defiled my s on the same day
23:39 on the same day they came into my s to profane it.
24:21 I will profane my s, the pride of your power,
25: 3 over my s when it was profaned,
37:26 and will set my s among them forevermore.
37:28 when my s is among them forevermore.
44: 1 he brought me back to the outer gate of the s,
44: 5 and all those who are to be excluded from the s.
44: 7 uncircumcised in heart and flesh, to be in my s,
44: 8 to act for you in keeping my charge in my s.
44: 9 among the people of Israel, shall enter my s.
44:11 They shall be ministers in my s,
44:15 of my s when the people of Israel went astray
44:16 It is they who shall enter my s,
45: 2 by five hundred cubits shall be for the s,
45: 3 in which shall be the s, the most holy place.
45: 4 for the priests, who minister in the s and approach
45: 4 a place for their houses and a holy place for the s.
Eze 45:18 a young bull without blemish, and purify the s.
47:12 because the water for them flows from the s.
48: 8 with the s in the middle of it.
48:10 with the s of the LORD in the middle of it.
48:21 The holy portion with the s of the temple in
Da 8:11 from him and overthrew the place of his s.
8:13 the giving over of the s and host to be trampled?"
8:14 then the s shall be restored to its rightful state."
9:17 Lord, let your face shine upon your desolated s.
9:26 to come shall destroy the city and the s.
Am 7:13 for it is the king's s,
Mal 2:11 for Judah has profaned the s of the LORD,
Mt 23:16 'Whoever swears by the s is bound by nothing,
23:16 but whoever swears by the gold of the s is bound
23:17 the gold or the s that has made the gold sacred?
23:21 the s, swears by it and by the one who dwells in it;
23:35 whom you murdered between the s and the altar.
Lk 1: 9 to enter the s of the Lord and offer incense.
1:21 and wondered at his delay in the s.
1:22 and they realized that he had seen a vision in the s.
11:51 who perished between the altar and the s.
Heb 8: 2 a minister in the s and the true tent that the Lord,
8: 5 They offer worship in a s that is a sketch
9: 1 for worship and an earthly s.
9: 8 the Holy Spirit indicates that the way into the s has
9:24 For Christ did not enter a s made by human hands,
10:19 since we have confidence to enter the s by
13:11 of those animals whose blood is brought into the s
Jdt 4:12 and the s to be profaned and desecrated to
4:13 throughout Judea and in Jerusalem before the s of
5:19 and have occupied Jerusalem, where their s is,
8:21 be captured and our s will be plundered;
8:24 for their lives depend upon us, and the s—
9: 8 for they intend to defile your s,
16:20 in Jerusalem before the s,
Sir 36:18 Have pity on the city of your s,
45:24 that he should be leader of the s and of his people,
47:10 and the s resounded from early morning.
47:13 in his name and provide a s to stand forever.
49: 6 who set fire to the chosen city of the s,
50:11 he made the court of the s glorious.
51:12 *Give thanks to him who rebuilt his city and his s,*
1Mc 1:21 He arrogantly entered the s and took
1:36 for the citadel became an ambush against the s,
1:37 On every side of the s they shed innocent blood;
they even defiled the s.
1:39 Her s became desolate like a desert;
1:45 and sacrifices and drink offerings in the s,
1:46 to defile the s and the priests,
2: 7 the s given over to aliens?
3:43 and fight for our people and the s."
3:45 s was trampled down, and aliens held the citadel;
3:51 Your s is trampled down and profaned,
3:58 against us to destroy us and our s.
3:59 to see the misfortunes of our nation and of the s.
4:36 let us go up to cleanse the s and dedicate it."
4:38 There they saw the s desolate, the altar profaned,
4:41 in the citadel until he had cleansed the s.
4:43 the s and removed the defiled stones to
4:48 also rebuilt the s and the interior of the temple,
5: 1 that the altar had been rebuilt and the s dedicated
6: 7 and that they had surrounded the s with high walls
6:18 in the citadel kept hemming Israel in around the s.
6:26 they have fortified both the s and Beth-zur;
6:51 Then he encamped before the s for many days.
6:54 Only a few men were left in the s;
7:33 of the priests from the s and some of the elders of
7:42 that Nicanor has spoken wickedly against the s,
9:54 to tear down the wall of the inner court of the s.
10:39 the land adjoining it I have given as a gift to the s
10:39 to meet the necessary expenses of the s.
10:44 the structures of the s be paid from the revenues of
13: 3 of my father have done for the laws and the s;
13: 6 and the s and your wives and children,
14:15 the s glorious, and added to the vessels of the s.
14:29 that their s and the law might be preserved;
14:31 to invade their country and lay hands on their s,
14:36 to sally forth and defile the environs of the s,
14:42 over them and that he should take charge of the s
14:42 and that he should take charge of the s,
14:48 up in a conspicuous place in the precincts of the s,
15: 7 and I grant freedom to Jerusalem and the s.
2Mc 4:14 Despising the s and neglecting the sacrifices,
4:33 having first withdrawn to a place of s at Daphne
4:34 to come out from the place of s;
9:16 and the holy s, which he had formerly plundered,
10: 3 They purified the s, and made another altar
10: 5 the same day on which the s had been profaned by
10: 5 the purification of the s took place, that is,
13:23 the s and showed generosity to the holy place.
14:33 he stretched out his right hand toward the s,
15:17 the city and the s and the temple were in danger.
15:18 and first fear was for the consecrated s.
15:33 up these rewards of his folly opposite the s.
3Mc 1:10 and conceived a desire to enter the s.
2: 1 Then the high priest Simon, facing the s,
2:18 'We have trampled down the house of the s as
2Es 10:21 For you see how our s has been laid waste,
12:48 on account of the humiliation of our s.
15:25 Do not pollute my s.

SANCTUARY'S (1) [SANCTUARY]

2Ch 30:19 not in accordance with the s rules of cleanness."

SAND‡ (35) [SANDS, SANDY]

Ge 22:17 as numerous as the stars of heaven and as the s

Ge 32:12 and make your offspring as the s of the sea,
41:49 in such abundance—like the s of the sea—
Ex 2:12 the Egyptian and hid him in the s.
Lev 11:30 the lizard, the s lizard, and the chameleon.
Dt 33:19 of the seas and the hidden treasures of the s.
Jos 11: 4 a great army, in number like the s on the seashore,
Jdg 7:12 countless as the s on the seashore.
1Sa 13: 5 and troops like the s on the seashore in multitude;
2Sa 17:11 like the s by the sea for multitude,
1Ki 4:20 and Israel were as numerous as the s by the sea;
4:29 of understanding as vast as the s on the seashore,
Job 6: 3 For then it would be heavier than the s of the sea;
Ps 78:27 winged birds like the s of the seas;
139:18 I try to count them—they are more than the s;
Pr 27: 3 A stone is heavy, and s is weighty,
Isa 10:22 your people Israel were like the s of the sea,
35: 7 the burning s shall become a pool,
48:19 like the s, and your descendants like its grains;
Jer 5:22 I placed the s as a boundary for the sea,
15: 8 Their widows became more numerous than the s
Hos 1:10 of the people of Israel shall be like the s of the sea,
Hab 1: 9 they gather captives like s.
Mt 7:26 be like a foolish man who built his house on s.
Ro 9:27 the number of the children of Israel were like the s
Heb 11:12 of heaven and as the innumerable grains of s by
Rev 12:18 the dragon took his stand on the s of the seashore.
Wis 7: 9 because all gold is but a little s in her sight,
Sir 1: 2 The s of the sea, the drops of rain,
18:10 Like a drop of water from the sea and a grain of s,
22:15 S, salt, and a piece of iron are easier to bear than
Aza 1:13 like the stars of heaven and like the s on the shore
1Mc 11: 1 like the s by the seashore, and many ships;
Man 1: 9 in number than the s of the sea;
2Es 4:17 for the s stood firm and blocked it.

SANDAL (6) [SANDAL-THONG, SANDALS]

Dt 25: 9 pull his s off his foot, spit in his face, and declare,
25:10 as "the house of him whose s was pulled off."
Ru 4: 7 the one took off a s and gave it to the other;
4: 8 "Acquire it for yourself," he took off his s.
Jn 1:27 I am not worthy to untie the thong of his s."
Jdt 16: 9 Her s ravished his eyes, her beauty captivated his

SANDAL-THONG (2) [SANDAL, THONG]

Ge 14:23 not take a thread or a s or anything that is yours,
Isa 5:27 not a loincloth is loose, not a s broken;

SANDALS (27) [SANDAL]

Ex 3: 5 Remove the s from your feet,
12:11 your loins girded, your s on your feet,
Dt 29: 5 and the s on your feet have not worn out;
Jos 5:15 "Remove the s from your feet,
9: 5 patched s on their feet, and worn-out clothes;
9:13 and these garments and s of ours are worn out
1Ki 2: 5 and on the s on his feet.
2Ch 28:15 they clothed them, gave them s,
SS 7: 1 graceful are your feet in s, O queenly maiden!
Isa 20: 2 from your loins and take your s off your feet,"
Eze 16:10 with embroidered cloth and with s of fine leather;
24:17 Bind on your turban, and put your s on your feet;
24:23 Your turbans shall be on your heads and your s
Am 2: 6 and the needy for a pair of s—
8: 6 the poor for silver and the needy for a pair of s,
Mt 3:11 I am not worthy to carry his s.
10:10 or s, or a staff; for laborers deserve their food.
Mk 1: 7 to stoop down and untie the thong of his s.
6: 9 but to wear s and not to put on two tunics.
Lk 3:16 I am not worthy to untie the thong of his s.
10: 4 Carry no purse, no bag, no s;
15:22 put a ring on his finger and s on his feet.
22:35 "When I sent you out without a purse, bag, or s,
Ac 7:33 Lord said to him, 'Take off the s from your feet,
12: 8 "Fasten your belt and put on your s."
13:25 not worthy to untie the thong of the s on his feet.'
Jdt 10: 4 She put s on her feet, and put on her anklets,

SANDS (2) [SAND]

Jer 33:22 the host of heaven cannot be numbered and the s
Rev 20: 8 they are as numerous as the s of the sea.

SANDY (1) [SAND]

Sir 25:20 A s ascent for the feet of the aged—

SANG (19) [SING]

Ex 15: 1 Moses and the Israelites s this song to the LORD:
15:21 And Miriam s to them: "Sing to the LORD,
Nu 21:17 Then Israel s this song: "Spring up,
Jdg 5: 1 Deborah and Barak son of Abinoam s on that day,
1Sa 18: 7 the women s to one another as they made merry,
2Ch 29:28 The whole assembly worshiped, the singers s,
29:30 They s praises with gladness,
Ezr 3:11 and they s responsively, praising
Ne 12:42 And the singers s with Jezrahiah as their leader.
Job 38: 7 when the morning stars s together and
Ps 7: T *A Shiggaion of David, which he s to the LORD*
106:12 Then they believed his words; they s his praise.
Jdt 15:14 and all the people loudly s this song of praise.
Wis 10:20 they s hymns, O Lord, to your holy name,
Sir 47: 8 he s praise with all his heart,
1Mc 4:24 On their return they s hymns and praises
2Mc 1:30 Then the priests s the hymns.
1Es 5:61 they s hymns, giving thanks to the Lord,
4Mc 18:15 He s to you songs of the psalmist David, who said,

SANK‡ (10) [SINK]

Ex 15:10 they s like lead in the mighty waters.
Nu 21:18 the well that the leaders s,
Jdg 5:27 He s, he fell, he lay still at her feet; at her feet he s,
he fell; where he s, there he fell dead.
1Sa 17:49 the stone s into his forehead,
2Ki 9:24 and he s in his chariot.
Ps 76: 5 of their spoil; they s into sleep;
Jer 38: 6 but only mud, and Jeremiah s in the mud.
Hab 3: 6 the everlasting hills s low.

SANSANNAH (1)

Jos 15:31 Ziklag, Madmannah, S,

SAP (1)

Ps 92:14 they are always green and full of s,

SAPH (1)

2Sa 21:18 then Sibbecai the Hushathite killed S,

SAPHIR (KJV) See SHAPHIR

SAPPHIRA (1)

Ac 5: 1 with the consent of his wife S,

SAPPHIRE (11) [SAPPHIRES]

Ex 24:10 like a pavement of s stone,
28:18 the second row a turquoise, a s and a moonstone;
39:11 a turquoise, a s, and a moonstone;
Job 28:16 in the gold of Ophir, in precious onyx or s.
La 4: 7 were more ruddy than coral, their hair like s.
Eze 1:26 like a throne, in appearance like s;
10: 1 above them something like a s,
28:13 beryl, onyx, and jasper, s, turquoise, and emerald;
Rev 9:17 the color of fire and of s and of sulfur;
21:19 the first was jasper, the second s, the third agate,
Tob 13:16 of Jerusalem will be built with s and emerald,

SAPPHIRES (3) [SAPPHIRE]

Job 28: 6 Its stones are the place of s,
SS 5:14 His body is ivory work, encrusted with s.
Isa 54:11 and lay your foundations with s.

SAPPING (1) [SAPS]

La 1:14 they weigh on my neck, s my strength;

SAPS (1) [SAPPING]

Sir 38:18 and a sorrowful heart s one's strength.

SARA (KJV) See SARAH

SARAH (58) [=SARAI, SARAH'S]

Ge 17:15 not call her Sarai, but S shall be her name.
17:17 Can S, who is ninety years old, bear a child?"
17:19 "No, but your wife S shall bear you a son,
17:21 with Isaac, whom S shall bear to you
18: 6 And Abraham hastened into the tent to S,
18: 9 They said to him, "Where is your wife S?"
18:10 and your wife S shall have a son."
18:10 S was listening at the tent entrance behind him.
18:11 Now Abraham and S were old, advanced in age;
18:11 it had ceased to be with S after the manner
18:12 So S laughed to herself, saying,
18:13 The LORD said to Abraham, "Why did S laugh,
18:14 in due season, and S shall have a son."
18:15 But S denied, saying, "I did not laugh";
20: 2 Abraham said of his wife S,
20: 2 And King Abimelech of Gerar sent and took S.
20:14 and restored his wife S to him.
20:16 To S he said, "Look, I have given your brother
20:18 of the house of Abimelech because of S,
21: 1 The LORD dealt with S as he had said, and the
LORD did for S as he had promised.
21: 2 S conceived and bore Abraham a son
21: 3 the name Isaac to his son whom S bore him.
21: 6 Now S said, "God has brought laughter for me;
21: 7 to Abraham that S would nurse children?
21: 9 But S saw the son of Hagar the Egyptian,
21:12 whatever S says to you, do as she tells you,
23: 1 S lived one hundred twenty-seven years;
23: 2 And S died at Kiriath-arba (that is, Hebron)
23: 2 and Abraham went in to mourn for S and to weep
23:19 Abraham buried S his wife in the cave of the field
24:36 And S my master's wife bore a son to my master
25:10 There Abraham was buried, with his wife S.
49:31 There Abraham and his wife S were buried;
Isa 51: 2 to Abraham your father and to S who bore you;
Ro 9: 9 "About this time I will return and S shall have
Heb 11:11 and S herself was barren—
1Pe 3: 6 Thus S obeyed Abraham and called him lord.
Tob 3: 7 it also happened that S, the daughter of Raguel,
3:17 and S, daughter of Raguel,
3:17 S daughter of Raguel came down
6:11 and he has a daughter named S.
6:12 and no daughter except S only,
7: 8 and their daughter S likewise wept.
7: 9 ask Raguel to give me my kinswoman S."
7:10 brother, has the right to marry my daughter S.
7:12 Then Raguel summoned his daughter S.
7:16 the room as he had told her, and brought S there.
8: 4 Tobias got out of bed and said to S, "Sister,
10:10 So Raguel promptly gave Tobias his wife S,
10:11 The Lord of heaven prosper you and your wife S,
10:12 Then he kissed his daughter S and said to her,
10:12 to see children of you and of my daughter S
10:12 on I am your mother and S is your beloved wife.
11:15 that he had married Raguel's daughter S,
11:17 When Tobit met S the wife of his son Tobias,
12:12 So now when you and S prayed,
12:14 to heal you and S your daughter-in-law.

SARAH'S (4) [SARAH]

Ge 23: 1 this was the length of S life.
24:67 Then Isaac brought her into his mother S tent.
25:12 whom Hagar the Egyptian, S slave-girl,
Ro 4:19 or when he considered the barrenness of S womb.

SARAI (17) [=SARAH]

Ge 11:29 the name of Abram's wife was S,
11:30 Now S was barren; she had no child.
11:31 and his daughter-in-law S, his son Abram's wife,
12: 5 Abram took his wife S and his brother's son Lot,
12:11 he was about to enter Egypt, he said to his wife S,
12:17 and his house with great plagues because of S,
16: 1 Now S, Abram's wife, bore him no children.
16: 2 and S said to Abram, "You see that
16: 2 And Abram listened to the voice of S.
16: 3 S, Abram's wife, took Hagar the Egyptian,
16: 5 Then S said to Abram, "May the wrong done
16: 6 But Abram said to S, "Your slave-girl is
16: 6 Then S dealt harshly with her,
16: 8 And he said, "Hagar, slave-girl of S,
16: 8 She said, "I am running away from my mistress S."
17:15 "As for S your wife, you shall not call her S,

SARAPH (1)

1Ch 4:22 and the men of Cozeba, and Joash, and S,

SARASADAI (1)

Jdt 8: 1 of Nathanael son of Salamiel son of S son

SARBACHA (1)

AdE 9: 8 Pharadatha, Barea, S,

SARDINE (KJV) See CARNELIAN

SARDIS (3)

Rev 1:11 to Pergamum, to Thyatira, to S, to Philadelphia,
3: 1 "And to the angel of the church in S write:
3: 4 Yet you have still a few persons in S who have

SARDITES (KJV) See SEREDITES

SARDIUS (KJV) See CARNELIAN

SAREA (1)

2Es 14:24 and take with you S, Dabria, Selemia, Ethanus,

SAREPTA (KJV) See ZAREPHATH

SARGON (1)

Isa 20: 1 who was sent by King S of Assyria,

SARID (2)

Jos 19:10 boundary of its inheritance reached as far as S;
19:12 from S it goes in the other direction eastward

SARON (KJV) See SHARON

SAROTHIE (1)

1Es 5:34 the descendants of S, the descendants of Masiah,

SARSATHAEUS (2)

AdE 1:14 Arkesaeus, S, and Malesear,
1:14 Arkesaeus, S, and Malesear,

SARSECHIM (1)

Jer 39: 3 Nergal-sharezer, Samgar-nebo, S the Rabsaris,

SARUCH (KJV) See SERUG

SASH (9) [SASHES]

Ex 28: 4 a robe, a checkered tunic, a turban, and a s.
28:39 you shall make a s embroidered with needlework.
39:29 and the s of fine twisted linen, and of blue, purple,
Lev 8: 7 fastened the s around him,
16: 4 fasten the linen s, and wear the linen turban;
Job 12:18 He looses the s of kings,
Isa 3:24 and instead of a s, a rope;
22:21 and will clothe him with your robe and bind your s
Rev 1:13 a long robe and with a golden s across his chest.

SASHES (6) [SASH]

Ex 28:40 For Aaron's sons you shall make tunics and s
29: 9 and you shall gird them with s and tie headdresses
Lev 8:13 and fastened s around them,
Pr 31:24 she supplies the merchant with s.
Isa 3:20 the s, the perfume boxes, and the amulets;

Rev 15: 6 with golden s across their chests.

SAT (128) [SIT]

Ge 18: 1 as he s at the entrance of his tent in the heat of
21:16 she went and s down opposite him a good way off,
21:16 And as she s opposite him,
31:34 and put them in the camel's saddle, and s on them.
37:25 Then they s down to eat;
38:14 and s down at the entrance to Enaim,
48: 2 he summoned his strength and s up in bed.
Ex 2:15 and s down by a well.
12:29 from the firstborn of Pharaoh who s on his throne
16: 3 we s by the fleshpots and ate our fill of bread;
17:12 so they took a stone and put it under him, and he s
18:13 The next day Moses s as judge for the people,
32: 6 and the people s down to eat and drink,
Lev 15: 6 with the discharge has s shall wash their clothes,
Jdg 5:17 Asher s still at the coast of the sea,
6:11 the angel of the LORD came and s under the oak
13: 9 of God came again to the woman as she s in
19: 6 So the two men s and ate and drank together;
19:15 He went in and s down in the open square of
21: 2 and s there until evening before God,
Ru 2:14 So she s beside the reapers,
4: 1 to the gate and s down there than the next-of-kin,
4: 1 And he went over and s down.
4: 2 "Sit down here"; so they s down.
1Sa 19: 9 as he s in his house with his spear in his hand,
20:24 the new moon came, the king s at the feast to eat.
20:25 The king s upon his seat, as at other times,
20:25 Jonathan stood, while Abner s by Saul's side;
28:23 So he got up from the ground and s on the bed.
2Sa 2:13 One group s on one side of the pool,
2:13 while the other s on the other side of the pool.
7:18 Then King David went in and s before the LORD,
1Ki 2:12 So Solomon s on the throne of his father David;
2:19 then he s on his throne,
2:19 a throne brought for the king's mother, and she s
19: 4 and came and s down under a solitary broom tree.
21:13 The two scoundrels came in and s opposite him;
2Ki 4:20 the child s on her lap until noon, and he died.
13:13 and Jeroboam s upon his throne;
1Ch 17:16 Then King David went in and s before the LORD,
29:23 Then Solomon s on the throne of the LORD,
Ezr 9: 3 from my head and beard, and s appalled.
9: 4 while I s appalled until the evening sacrifice.
10: 9 the people s in the open square before the house
10:16 On the first day of the tenth month they s down
Ne 1: 4 When I heard these words I s down and wept,
Est 1: 2 when King Ahasuerus s on his royal throne in
1:14 and s first in the kingdom):
3:15 The king and Haman s down to drink;
Job 2: 8 a potsherd with which to scrape himself, and s
2:13 They s with him on the ground seven days
29:25 I chose their way, and s as chief,
Ps 9: 4 have s on the throne giving righteous judgment.
107:10 Some s in darkness and in gloom,
137: 1 there we s down and there we wept
SS 2: 3 With great delight I s in his shadow,
Isa 10:13 I have brought down those who s on thrones.
Jer 3: 2 By the waysides you have s waiting for lovers,
15:17 under the weight of your hand I s alone,
39: 3 the king of Babylon came and s in the middle gate:
Eze 3:15 I s there among them, stunned, for seven days.
8: 1 on the fifth day of the month, as I s in my house,
14: 1 Certain elders of Israel came to me and s down
20: 1 of Israel came to consult the LORD, and s down
23:41 you s on a stately couch,
Da 7:10 The court s in judgment, and the books were
Jnh 3: 6 covered himself with sackcloth, and s in ashes.
4: 5 Then Jonah went out of the city and s down east of
4: 5 He s under it in the shade,
Na 3: 8 Are you better than Thebes that s by the Nile,
Mt 4:16 people who s in darkness have seen a great light,
4:16 and for those who s in the region and shadow
5: 1 and after he s down, his disciples came to him.
9:10 And as he s at dinner in the house,
13: 1 That same day Jesus went out of the house and s
13: 2 around him that he got into a boat and s there,
13:48 they drew it ashore, s down,
15:29 and he went up the mountain, where he s down.
21: 7 and put their cloaks on them, and he s on them.
26: 7 and she poured it on his head as he s at the table.
26:55 Day after day I s in the temple teaching,
26:58 and going inside, he s with the guards in order
27:36 then they s down there and kept watch over him.
28: 2 came and rolled back the stone and s on it.
Mk 2:15 And as he s at dinner in Levi's house,
3:34 And looking at those who s around him, he said,
4: 1 that he got into a boat on the sea and s there,
6:40 they s down in groups of hundreds and of fifties.
9:35 He s down, called the twelve, and said to them,
11: 7 and threw their cloaks on it; and he s on it.
12:41 He s down opposite the treasury,
14: 3 as he s at the table,
16:19 ⟦into heaven and s down at the right hand of God.⟧
Lk 4:20 gave it back to the attendant, and s down.
5: 3 he s down and taught the crowds from the boat.
7:15 The dead man s up and began to speak,
10:39 who s at the Lord's feet and listened
22:55 and s down together, Peter s among them.
Jn 6: 3 the mountain and s down there with his disciples.
6:10 so they s down, about five thousand in all.
8: 2 ⟦the people came to him and he s down and began⟧
12:14 Jesus found a young donkey and s on it;
19:13 and s on the judge's bench at a place called
Ac 6:15 all who s in the council looked intently at him,
9:40 she opened her eyes, and seeing Peter, she s up.
13:14 into the synagogue and s down.
16:13 and we s down and spoke to
1Co 10: 7 it is written, "The people s down to eat and drink,
Heb 1: 3 he s down at the right hand of the Majesty on high,
10:12 "he s down at the right hand of God,"
Rev 3:21 as I myself conquered and s down with my Father
14:15 with a loud voice to the one who s on the cloud,
14:16 the one who s on the cloud swung his sickle over
20:11 I saw a great white throne and the one who s on it;
Tob 11: 5 Meanwhile Anna s looking intently down the road
AdE 1:14 who s beside him in the chief seats—
Bel 1:40 to the den he looked in, and there s Daniel!
1Mc 1:27 she who s in the bridal chamber was mourning.
11:52 King Demetrius s on the throne of his kingdom,
14: 9 Old men s in the streets;
14:12 the people s under their own vines and fig trees,
1Es 8:71 and s down in anxiety and grief.
8:72 and I s grief-stricken until the evening sacrifice.
9: 6 All the multitude s in the open square before
2Es 9:26 there I s among the flowers and ate of the plants of
12:51 But I s in the field seven days,
14:42 not know. They s forty days;

SATAN‡ (53) [SATAN'S]

1Ch 21: 1 S stood up against Israel, and incited David
Job 1: 6 and S also came among them.
1: 7 LORD said to S, "Where have you come from?"
1: 7 S answered the LORD, "From going to and fro
1: 8 The LORD said to S, "Have you considered my
1: 9 Then S answered the LORD, "Does Job fear God
1:12 The LORD said to S, "Very well,
1:12 So S went out from the presence of the LORD.
2: 1 and S also came among them to present himself
2: 2 LORD said to S, "Where have you come from?"
2: 2 S answered the LORD, "From going to and fro
2: 3 The LORD said to S, "Have you considered my
2: 4 Then S answered the LORD, "Skin for skin!
2: 6 The LORD said to S, "Very well,
2: 7 So S went out from the presence of the LORD,
Zec 3: 1 and S standing at his right hand to accuse him.
3: 2 the LORD said to S, "The LORD rebuke you, O S!
Mt 4:10 Jesus said to him, "Away with you, S!
12:26 If S casts out S, he is divided against himself;
16:23 he turned and said to Peter, "Get behind me, S!
Mk 1:13 in the wilderness forty days, tempted by S;
3:23 "How can S cast out S?
3:26 if S has risen up against himself and is divided,
4:15 S immediately comes and takes away the word
8:33 he rebuked Peter and said, "Get behind me, S!
Lk 10:18 "I watched S fall from heaven like a flash
11:18 If S also is divided against himself,
13:16 a daughter of Abraham whom S bound
22: 3 Then S entered into Judas called Iscariot,
22:31 S has demanded to sift all of you like wheat,
Jn 13:27 he received the piece of bread, S entered into him.
Ac 5: 3 "why has S filled your heart to lie to
26:18 from darkness to light and from the power of S
Ro 16:20 God of peace will shortly crush S under your feet.
1Co 5: 5 to hand this man over to S for the destruction of
7: 5 so that S may not tempt you because of your lack
2Co 2:11 we do this so that we may not be outwitted by S;
11:14 Even S disguises himself as an angel of light.
12: 7 a messenger of S to torment me,
1Th 2:18 again and again—but S blocked our way.
2Th 2: 9 of the lawless one is apparent in the working of S,
1Ti 1:20 whom I have turned over to S,
5:15 For some have already turned away to follow S.
Rev 2: 9 but are a synagogue of S.
2:13 who was killed among you, where S lives.
2:24 not learned what some call 'the deep things of S,'
3: 9 of the synagogue of S who say that they are Jews
12: 9 that ancient serpent, who is called the Devil and S,
20: 2 that ancient serpent, who is the Devil and S.
20: 7 S will be released from his prison

SATAN'S‡ (1) [SATAN]

Rev 2:13 where you are living, where S throne is.

SATED (10) [SATIATED]

Dt 33:23 O Naphtali, s with favor, full of the blessing of the
Job 31:31 'O that we might be s with his flesh!'—
Pr 1:31 of their way and be s with their own devices.
27: 7 The s appetite spurns honey,
Isa 34: 6 The LORD has a sword; it is s with blood,
Jer 46:10 The sword shall devour and be s,
50:10 all who plunder her shall be s, says the LORD.
La 3:15 he has s me with wormwood.
Hab 2:16 You will be s with contempt instead of glory.
3: 9 s were the arrows at your command.

SATHRABUZANES (4)

1Es 6: 3 and S and their associates came to them and said,
6: 7 and S, and their associates the local rulers in Syria
6:27 and S, and their associates,
7: 1 and S, and their associates,

SATIATE[D] (KJV) See also SATED, SATISFY, SATISFIED

SATIATED (1) [SATED]

3Mc 5:10 with a great abundance of wine and s

SATISFACTION (3) [SATISFY]

Pr 18:20 the yield of the lips brings s.
Isa 53:11 he shall find s through his knowledge.
Tit 2: 9 to be submissive to their masters and to give s

SATISFIED (46) [SATISFY]

Lev 26:26 and though you eat, you shall not be s.
Dt 21:14 But if you are not s with her,
Jos 22:30 the Gadites and the Manassites spoke, they were s.
Ru 2:14 She ate until she was s,
2:18 over after she herself had been s.
Job 19:22 like God, pursue me, never s with my flesh?
Ps 17:15 I awake I shall be s, beholding your likeness.
22:26 The poor shall eat and be s;
63: 5 My soul is s as with a rich feast,
65: 4 We shall be s with the goodness of your house,
78:30 But before they had s their craving,
104:13 the earth is s with the fruit of your work.
Pr 18:20 From the fruit of the mouth one's stomach is s;
27:20 Sheol and Abaddon are never s,
27:20 and human eyes are never s.
30:15 Three things are never s; four never say, "Enough"
Ecc 1: 8 the eye is not s with seeing,
4: 8 and their eyes are never s with riches.
5:10 The lover of money will not be s with money;
6: 7 yet the appetite is not s.
Isa 9:20 and they devoured on the left, but were not s;
43:24 or s me with the fat of your sacrifices.
44:16 over this half he roasts meat, eats it and is s.
66:11 you may nurse and be s from her consoling breast;
Jer 31:14 and my people shall be s with my bounty,
50:19 of Ephraim and in Gilead its hunger shall be s.
Eze 16:28 the whore with them, and still you were not s.
16:29 and even with this you were not s.
24:13 be cleansed until I have s my fury upon you.
27:33 from the seas, you s many peoples;
Hos 4:10 They shall eat, but not be s;
13: 6 When I fed them, they were s; they were s,
Joel 2:19 wine, and oil, and you will be s;
2:26 You shall eat in plenty and be s,
Am 4: 8 to one town to drink water, and were not s;
Mic 6:14 You shall eat, but not be s,
Lk 3:14 and be s with your wages."
Jn 6:12 When they were s, he told his disciples,
14: 8 "Lord, show us the Father, and we will be s."
Ac 27:38 After they had s their hunger,
Php 4:18 I am fully s, now that I have received
AdE 14: 8 now they are not s that we are in bitter slavery,
Sir 14: 9 eye of the greedy person is not s with his share;
1Es 3: 3 and when they were s they went away,
2Es 9:26 and the nourishment they afforded s me.

SATISFIES (2) [SATISFY]

Ps 103: 5 who s you with good as long as you live so
107: 9 For he s the thirsty, and the hungry he fills

SATISFY (23) [SATISFACTION, SATISFIED, SATISFIES, SATISFYING]

Job 38:27 to s the waste and desolate land,
38:39 or s the appetite of the young lions,
Ps 81:16 and with honey from the rock I would s you."
90:14 S us in the morning with your steadfast love,
91:16 With long life I will s them,
132:15 I will s its poor with bread.
Pr 5:19 May her breasts s you at all times;
6:30 not despised who steal only to s their appetite
13:25 The righteous have enough to s their appetite,
Isa 55: 2 and your labor for that which does not s?
58:10 to the hungry and s the needs of the afflicted,
58:11 and s your needs in parched places,
Jer 31:25 I will s the weary, and all who are faint I will
Eze 5:13 and I will vent my fury on them and s myself;
7:19 They shall not s their hunger or fill their stomachs
16:42 So I will s my fury on you,
21:17 I too will strike hand to hand, I will s my fury;
Mt 28:14 we will s him and keep you out of trouble."
Mk 15:15 So Pilate, wishing to s the crowd,
Lk 16:21 who longed to s his hunger with what fell from
Php 4:19 And my God will fully s every need of yours
Wis 16: 2 a delicacy to s the desire of appetite;
4Mc 3:10 he could not s his thirst from them.

SATISFYING (1) [SATISFY]

Ps 145:16 s the desire of every living thing.

SATRAP (1) [SATRAPIES, SATRAPS]

1Es 4:49 that no officer or s or governor

SATRAPIES (1) [SATRAP]

1Es 3: 2 the hundred twenty-seven s from India to Ethiopia.

SATRAPS (17) [SATRAP]

Ezr 8:36 to the king's s and to the governors of the province
Est 3:12 was written to the king's s and to the governors
8: 9 and to the s and the governors and the officials of
9: 3 of the provinces, the s and the governors,
Da 3: 2 Then King Nebuchadnezzar sent for the s,
3: 3 So the s, the prefects, and the governors,
3:27 And the s, the prefects, the governors,
6: 1 to set over the kingdom one hundred twenty s,
6: 2 to these the s gave account,
6: 3 and s because an excellent spirit was in him,

Da 6: 4 So the presidents and the s tried to find grounds
6: 6 So the presidents and s conspired and came to
6: 7 the kingdom, the prefects and the s, the counselors
1Es 3: 2 and all the s and generals and governors that were
3:14 and the s and generals and governors and prefects,
3:21 It makes all hearts feel rich, forgets kings and s,
4:47 the treasurers and governors and generals and s,

SATURATION See Index to Footnotes

SATYRS (KJV) See GOAT-DEMONS

SAUL‡ (398) [=PAUL, SAUL'S]

1Sa 9: 2 He had a son whose name was S,
9: 3 So Kish said to his son S,
9: 5 S said to the boy who was with him,
9: 7 Then S replied to the boy, "But if we go,
9: 8 The boy answered S again, "Here,
9:10 S said to the boy, "Good; come, let us go."
9:15 Now the day before S came,
9:17 When Samuel saw S, the LORD told him,
9:18 Then S approached Samuel inside the gate,
9:19 Samuel answered S, "I am the seer;
9:21 S answered, "I am only a Benjaminite,
9:22 Then Samuel took S and his servant-boy
9:24 and what went with it and set them before S.
9:24 So S ate with Samuel that day.
9:25 a bed was spread for S on the roof,
9:26 Then at the break of dawn Samuel called to S
9:26 S got up, and both he and Samuel went out into
9:27 the town, Samuel said to S, "Tell the boy to go on
10:11 Is S also among the prophets?"
10:12 "Is S also among the prophets?"
10:16 S said to his uncle, "He told us that
10:21 and S the son of Kish was taken by lot.
10:26 S also went to his home at Gibeah,
11: 4 When the messengers came to Gibeah of S,
11: 5 S was coming from the field behind the oxen;
11: 5 and S said, "What is the matter with the people,
11: 6 upon S in power when he heard these words,
11: 7 "Whoever does not come out after S and Samuel,
11:11 The next day S put the people in three companies.
11:12 "Who is it that said, 'Shall S reign over us?'
11:13 But S said, "No one shall be put to death this day,
11:15 and there they made S king before the LORD
11:15 and there S and all the Israelites rejoiced greatly.
13: 1 S was . . . years old when he began to reign;
13: 2 S chose three thousand out of Israel;
13: 2 two thousand were with S in Michmash and
13: 3 And S blew the trumpet throughout all the land,
13: 4 that S had defeated the garrison of the Philistines,
13: 4 the people were called out to join S at Gilgal.
13: 7 S was still at Gilgal, and all the people
13: 8 and the people began to slip away from S.
13: 9 So S said, "Bring the burnt offering here to me,
13:10 and S went out to meet him and salute him.
13:11 S replied, "When I saw that
13:13 Samuel said to S, "You have done foolishly;
13:15 The rest of the people followed S to join the army;
13:15 S counted the people who were present with him,
13:16 S, his son Jonathan, and the people who were
13:22 in the possession of any of the people with S
13:22 but S and his son Jonathan had them.
14: 1 of S said to the young man who carried his armor,
14: 2 S was staying in the outskirts of Gibeah under
14:17 Then S said to the troops that were with him,
14:18 S said to Ahijah, "Bring the ark of God here."
14:19 While S was talking to the priest,
14:19 and S said to the priest, "Withdraw your hand."
14:20 Then S and all the people who were
14:21 the Israelites who were with S and Jonathan.
14:23 and the troops with S numbered altogether
14:24 Now S committed a very rash act on that day.
14:33 Then it was reported to S, "Look,
14:34 S said, "Disperse yourselves among the troops,
14:35 And S built an altar to the LORD;
14:36 Then S said, "Let us go down after the Philistines
14:37 So S inquired of God, "Shall I go down after
14:38 S said, "Come here, all you leaders of the people;
14:40 people said to S, "Do what seems good to you."
14:41 Then S said, "O LORD God of Israel,
14:41 And Jonathan and S were indicated by the lot,
14:42 Then S said, "Cast the lot between me
14:43 S said to Jonathan, "Tell me what you have done."
14:44 S said, "God do so to me and more also;
14:45 Then the people said to S, "Shall Jonathan die,
14:46 Then S withdrew from pursuing the Philistines;
14:47 When S had taken the kingship over Israel,
14:49 sons of S were Jonathan, Ishvi, and Malchishua;
14:51 Kish was the father of S,
14:52 against the Philistines all the days of S;
14:52 and when S saw any strong or valiant warrior,
15: 1 to S, "The LORD sent me to anoint you king
15: 4 So S summoned the people,
15: 5 S came to the city of the Amalekites and lay
15: 6 S said to the Kenites, "Go!
15: 7 S defeated the Amalekites,
15: 9 S and the people spared Agag,
15:11 "I regret that I made S king,
15:12 Samuel rose early in the morning to meet S,
15:12 and Samuel was told, "S went to Carmel,
15:13 When Samuel came to S, S said to him,
15:15 S said, "They have brought them from
15:16 Then Samuel said to S, "Stop!
15:20 S said to Samuel, "I have obeyed the voice of

1Sa 15:24 S said to Samuel, "I have sinned;
15:26 Samuel said to S, "I will not return with you;
15:27 S caught hold of the hem of his robe, and it tore.
15:30 Then S said, "I have sinned;
15:31 So Samuel turned back after S;
15:31 and S worshiped the LORD.
15:34 and S went up to his house in Gibeah of S.
15:35 not see S again until the day of his death, but
Samuel grieved over S.
15:35 the LORD was sorry that he had made S king
16: 1 "How long will you grieve over S?
16: 2 If S hears of it, he will kill me."
16:14 Now the spirit of the LORD departed from S,
16:17 So S said to his servants,
16:19 So S sent messengers to Jesse, and said,
16:20 and a kid, and sent them by his son David to S.
16:21 And David came to S, and entered his service.
16:21 and entered his service. S loved him greatly,
16:22 S sent to Jesse, saying, "Let David remain
16:23 whenever the evil spirit from God came upon S,
16:23 and S would be relieved and feel better,
17: 2 S and the Israelites gathered and encamped in
17: 8 and are you not servants of S?
17:11 When S and all Israel heard these words of
17:12 of S the man was already old and advanced
17:13 The three eldest sons of Jesse had followed S to
17:14 the three eldest followed S,
17:15 from S to feed his father's sheep at Bethlehem.
17:19 Now S, and they, and all the men of Israel,
17:31 they repeated them before S; and he sent for him.
17:32 David said to S, "Let no one's heart fail because
17:33 S said to David, "You are not able to go
17:34 But David said to S, "Your servant used
17:37 So S said to David, "Go, and may the LORD be
17:38 S clothed David with his armor;
17:39 Then David said to S, "I cannot walk with these;
17:55 When S saw David go out against the Philistine,
17:57 Abner took him and brought him before S,
17:58 S said to him, "Whose son are you, young man?"
18: 1 When David had finished speaking to S,
18: 2 S took him that day and would not let him return
18: 5 and was successful wherever S sent him;
18: 5 as a result, S set him over the army.
18: 5 all the people, even the servants of S, approved.
18: 6 singing and dancing, to meet King S,
18: 7 "S has killed his thousands,
18: 8 S was very angry, for this saying displeased him.
18: 9 So S eyed David from that day on.
18:10 next day an evil spirit from God rushed upon S,
18:10 S had his spear in his hand;
18:11 and S threw the spear,
18:12 S was afraid of David, because the LORD was with
him but had departed from S.
18:13 So S removed him from his presence,
18:15 When S saw that he had great success,
18:17 Then S said to David, "Here is my elder daughter
18:17 S thought, "I will not raise a hand against him;
18:18 David said to S, "Who am I
18:20 S was told, and the thing pleased him.
18:21 S thought, "Let me give her to him that she may
18:21 Therefore S said to David a second time,
18:22 S commanded his servants,
18:24 servants of S told him, "This is what David said."
18:25 Then S said, "Thus shall you say to David,
18:25 Now S planned to make David fall by the hand of
18:27 S gave him his daughter Michal as a wife.
18:28 when S realized that the LORD was with David,
18:29 S was still more afraid of David.
18:29 So S was David's enemy from that time forward.
18:30 David had more success than all the servants of S,
19: 1 S spoke with his son Jonathan and
19: 2 "My father S is trying to kill you;
19: 4 Jonathan spoke well of David to his father S,
19: 6 S heeded the voice of Jonathan;
19: 6 Saul heeded the voice of Jonathan; S swore,
19: 7 Jonathan then brought David to S,
19: 9 Then an evil spirit from the LORD came upon S,
19:10 S sought to pin David to the wall with the spear;
19:10 but he eluded S, so that he struck the spear into
19:11 S sent messengers to David's house to keep watch
19:14 When S sent messengers to take David, she said,
19:15 Then S sent the messengers to see David
19:17 S said to Michal, "Why have you deceived me
19:17 Michal answered S, "He said to me, 'Let me go;
19:18 and told him all that S had done to him.
19:19 S was told, "David is at Naioth in Ramah."
19:20 Then S sent messengers to take David.
19:20 the spirit of God came upon the messengers of S,
19:21 When S was told, he sent other messengers,
19:21 S sent messengers again the third time,
19:24 it is said, "Is S also among the prophets?"
20:26 S did not say anything that day;
20:27 And S said to his son Jonathan,
20:28 Jonathan answered S, "David earnestly asked leave
20:32 Then Jonathan answered his father S,
20:33 But S threw his spear at him to strike him;
21: 7 Now a certain man of the servants of S was there
21:10 David rose and fled that day from S;
21:11 'S has killed his thousands,
22: 6 S heard that David and those who were
22: 6 S was sitting at Gibeah, under the tamarisk tree on
22: 7 S said to his servants who stood around him,
22:12 S said, "Listen now, son of Ahitub."
22:13 S said to him, "Why have you conspired
22:21 Abiathar told David that S had killed the priests of
22:22 that he would surely tell S.
23: 7 Now it was told S that David had come to Keilah.

1Sa 23: 7 And S said, "God has given him into my hand;
23: 8 S summoned all the people to war,
23: 9 David learned that S was plotting evil against him,
23:10 your servant has heard that S seeks to come
23:11 will S come down as your servant has heard?
23:12 and my men into the hand of S?"
23:13 S was told that David had escaped from Keilah,
23:14 S sought him every day, but the LORD did not
23:15 at Horesh when he learned that S had come out
23:17 for the hand of my father S shall not find you;
23:17 my father S also knows that this is so."
23:19 some Ziphites went up to S at Gibeah and said,
23:21 S said, "May you be blessed by the LORD
23:24 So they set out and went to Ziph ahead of S.
23:25 S and his men went to search for him.
23:25 When S heard that, he pursued David into
23:26 S went on one side of the mountain,
23:26 David was hurrying to get away from S,
23:26 while S and his men were closing in on David
23:27 a messenger came to S, saying, "Hurry and come;
23:28 So S stopped pursuing David,
24: 1 When S returned from following the Philistines,
24: 2 Then S took three thousand chosen men out
24: 3 and S went in to relieve himself.
24: 7 and did not permit them to attack S.
24: 7 S got up and left the cave, and went on his way.
24: 8 up and went out of the cave and called after S,
24: 8 When S looked behind him,
24: 9 David said to S, "Why do you listen to the words
24:16 David had finished speaking these words to S,
24:16 S said, "Is this your voice, my son David?"
24:16 S lifted up his voice and wept.
24:22 So David swore this to S. Then S went home;
25:44 S had given his daughter Michal, David's wife,
26: 1 Then the Ziphites came to S at Gibeah, saying,
26: 2 S rose and went down to the Wilderness of Ziph,
26: 3 S encamped on the hill of Hachilah,
26: 3 When he learned that S came after him into
26: 4 and learned that S had indeed arrived.
26: 5 and came to the place where S had encamped;
26: 5 and David saw the place where S lay,
26: 5 S was lying within the encampment,
26: 6 "Who will go down with me into the camp to S?"
26: 7 there S lay sleeping within the encampment,
26:17 S recognized David's voice, and said,
26:21 Then S said, "I have done wrong;
26:25 S said to David, "Blessed be you, my son David!
26:25 David went his way, and S returned to his place.
27: 1 "I shall now perish one day by the hand of S;
27: 1 then S will despair of seeking me any longer
27: 4 When S was told that David had fled to Gath,
28: 3 S had expelled the mediums and the wizards from
28: 4 S gathered all Israel, and they encamped
28: 5 When S saw the army of the Philistines,
28: 6 When S inquired of the LORD,
28: 7 Then S said to his servants,
28: 8 So S disguised himself and put on other clothes
28: 9 "Surely you know what S has done,
28:10 But S swore to her by the LORD,
28:12 woman said to S, "Why have you deceived me?
28:12 "Why have you deceived me? You are S!"
28:13 to S, "I see a divine being coming up out of
28:14 So S knew that it was Samuel,
28:15 to S, "Why have you disturbed me
28:15 S answered, "I am in great distress,
28:20 Immediately S fell full length on the ground,
28:21 The woman came to S, and when she saw
28:25 She put them before S and his servants,
29: 3 "Is this not David, the servant of King S of Israel,
29: 5 'S has killed his thousands,
31: 2 The Philistines overtook S and his sons;
31: 2 and Abinadab and Malchishua, the sons of S.
31: 3 The battle pressed hard upon S;
31: 4 Then S said to his armor-bearer,
31: 4 So S took his own sword and fell upon it.
31: 5 When his armor-bearer saw that S was dead,
31: 6 So S and his three sons and his armor-bearer
31: 7 that the men of Israel had fled and that S
31: 8 they found S and his three sons fallen
31:11 the Philistines had done to S,
31:12 and took the body of S and the bodies of his sons
2Sa 1: 1 After the death of S, when David had returned
1: 4 and S and his son Jonathan also died."
1: 5 do you know that S and his son Jonathan died?"
1: 6 and there was S leaning on his spear,
1:12 until evening for S and for his son Jonathan,
1:17 David intoned this lamentation over S
1:21 the shield of S, anointed with oil no more.
1:22 nor the sword of S return empty.
1:23 S and Jonathan, beloved and lovely!
1:24 O daughters of Israel, weep over S,
2: 4 "It was the people of Jabesh-gilead who buried S,"
2: 5 because you showed this loyalty to S your lord,
2: 7 for S your lord is dead,
2: 8 had taken Ishbaal son of S,
2:12 and the servants of Ishbaal son of S,
2:15 twelve for Benjamin and Ishbaal son of S,
3: 1 There was a long war between the house of S and
3: 1 while the house of S became weaker and weaker.
3: 6 While there was war between the house of S and
3: 6 was making himself strong in the house of S.
3: 7 Now S had a concubine whose name was Rizpah
3: 8 to the house of your father S, to his brothers,
3:10 to transfer the kingdom from the house of S,
4: 4 the news about S and Jonathan came from Jezreel.
4: 8 son of S, your enemy, who sought your life;
4: 8 the king this day on S and on his offspring."

2Sa 4:10 S is dead,' thought he was bringing good news,
5: 2 For some time, while S was king over us,
6:16 Michal daughter of S looked out of the window,
6:20 Michal the daughter of S came out to meet David,
6:23 And Michal the daughter of S had no child to
7:15 as I took it from S,
9: 1 of the house of S to whom I may show kindness
9: 2 a servant of the house of S whose name was Ziba,
9: 3 the house of S to whom I may show the kindness
9: 6 Mephibosheth son of Jonathan son of S came
9: 7 to you all the land of your grandfather S,
9: 9 to S and to all his house I have given
12: 7 and I rescued you from the hand of S;
16: 5 of S came out whose name was Shimei son
16: 8 the house of S, in whose place you have reigned;
19:17 And Ziba, the servant of the house of S,
19:24 Mephibosheth grandson of S came down to meet
21: 1 "There is bloodguilt on S and on his house,
21: 2 of Israel had sworn to spare them, S had tried
21: 4 of silver or gold between us and S or his house;
21: 7 between David and Jonathan son of S.
21: 8 whom she bore to S, Armoni and Mephibosheth;
21: 8 and the five sons of Merab daughter of S,
21:11 the concubine of S, had done,
21:12 David went and took the bones of S and the bones
21:12 on the day the Philistines killed S on Gilboa.
21:13 the bones of S and the bones of his son Jonathan;
21:14 the bones of S and of his son Jonathan in the land
22: 1 and from the hand of S.
1Ch 5:10 in the days of S they made war on the Hagrites,
8:33 Kish of S, S of Jonathan, Malchishua,
9:39 Kish of S, S of Jonathan, Malchishua,
10: 2 The Philistines overtook S and his sons;
10: 2 and Abinadab and Malchishua, sons of S.
10: 3 The battle pressed hard on S;
10: 4 Then S said to his armor-bearer,
10: 4 So S took his own sword and fell on it.
10: 5 When his armor-bearer saw that S was dead,
10: 6 Thus S died; he and his three sons
10: 7 in the valley saw that the army had fled and that S
10: 8 they found S and his sons fallen on Mount Gilboa.
10:11 that the Philistines had done to S,
10:12 and took away the body of S and the bodies of
10:13 So S died for his unfaithfulness;
11: 2 For some time now, even while S was king,
12: 1 not move about freely because of S son of Kish;
12:19 with the Philistines for the battle against S.
12:19 "He will desert to his master S at the cost
12:23 to David in Hebron to turn the kingdom of S over
12:29 Of the Benjaminites, the kindred of S,
12:29 to keep their allegiance to the house of S.
13: 3 for we did not turn to it in the days of S."
15:29 Michal daughter of S looked out of the window,
26:28 Also all that Samuel the seer, and S son of Kish,
Ps 18: T *and from the hand of S. He said:*
52: T *Doeg the Edomite came to S and said to him,*
54: T *the Ziphites went and told S, "David is in hiding*
57: T *A Miktam, when he fled from S, in the cave.*
59: T *S ordered his house to be watched in order to kill*
Isa 10:29 Ramah trembles, Gibeah of S has fled.
Ac 7:58 at the feet of a young man named S.
8: 1 And S approved of their killing him.
8: 3 But S was ravaging the church by entering house
9: 1 Meanwhile S, still breathing threats and murder
9: 4 "S, S, why do you persecute me?"
9: 8 S got up from the ground,
9:11 of Judas look for a man of Tarsus named S.
9:17 He laid his hands on S and said, "Brother S,
9:22 S became increasingly more powerful
9:24 but their plot became known to S.
11:25 Then Barnabas went to Tarsus to look for S,
11:30 sending it to the elders by Barnabas and S.
12:25 and S returned to Jerusalem and brought
13: 1 a member of the court of Herod the ruler, and S.
13: 2 and S for the work to which I have called them."
13: 7 who summoned Barnabas and S and wanted
13: 9 But S, also known as Paul,
13:21 and God gave them S son of Kish,
22: 7 'S, S, why are you persecuting me?'
22:13 and standing beside me, he said, 'Brother S,
26:14 'S, S, why are you persecuting me?
1Mc 4:30 the Philistines into the hands of Jonathan son of S,
2Es *7:108* [38] and Samuel in the days of S,

SAUL'S (32) [SAUL]

1Sa 9: 3 Now the donkeys of Kish, S father, had strayed.
10:14 S uncle said to him and to the boy,
10:15 S uncle said, "Tell me what Samuel said to you."
14:16 S lookouts in Gibeah of Benjamin were watching
14:50 of S wife was Ahinoam daughter of Ahimaaz.
14:50 of his army was Abner son of Ner, S uncle;
16:15 And S servants said to him, "See now,
17:39 David strapped S sword over the armor,
18:19 when S daughter Merab should have been given
18:20 Now S daughter Michal loved David.
18:23 So S servants reported these words to David
18:28 and that S daughter Michal loved him,
19: 1 But S son Jonathan took great delight in David.
20:25 Jonathan stood, while Abner sat by S side;
20:30 Then S anger was kindled against Jonathan.
21: 7 the Edomite, the chief of S shepherds.
22: 9 who was in charge of S servants, answered,
23:16 S son Jonathan set out and came to David
24: 4 and stealthily cut off a corner of S cloak.
24: 5 because he had cut off a corner of S cloak.
26:12 So David took the spear that was at S head and
2Sa 1: 2 On the third day, a man came from S camp,
2: 8 But Abner son of Ner, commander of S army,
2:10 S son, was forty years old when he began to reign
3:13 unless you bring S daughter Michal
3:14 Then David sent messengers to S son Ishbaal,
4: 1 When S son Ishbaal heard that Abner had died
4: 2 S son had two captains of raiding bands;
4: 4 S son Jonathan had a son who was crippled
9: 9 Then the king summoned S servant Ziba,
21: 7 Mephibosheth, the son of S son Jonathan,
1Ch 12: 2 they were Benjaminites, S kindred.

SAULITES See Index to Footnotes

SAVAGE (12) [SAVAGELY, SAVAGERY]

Da 8: 6 and it ran at it with s force.
Ac 20:29 s wolves will come in among you,
Wis 17:19 or the sound of the most s roaring beasts,
2Mc 4:25 of a cruel tyrant and the rage of a s wild beast.
10:35 and with s fury cut down everyone they met.
3Mc 5:31 a rich feast for the s animals instead of the Jews,
7: 5 with a cruelty more s than that of Scythian custom,
2Es 5:18 the flock in the power of s wolves."
4Mc 9:15 s of mind, you are mangling me in this manner,
9:30 "Do you not think, you most s tyrant,
12:13 a man, were you not ashamed, you most s beast,
16: 3 The lions surrounding Daniel were not so s,

SAVAGELY (1) [SAVAGE]

2Mc 15: 2 "Do not destroy so s and barbarously,

SAVAGERY (2) [SAVAGE]

2Mc 15:21 and the s of the elephants, stretched out his hands
3Mc 5:20 possessed by a s worse than that of Phalaris,

SAVE‡ (209) [LIFE-SAVING, SALVATION, SAVED, SAVES, SAVING, SAVIOR, SAVIORS]

Dt 23:14 to s you and to hand over your enemies to you,
Jos 10: 6 come up to us quickly, and s us, and help us;
1Sa 4: 3 so that he may come among us and s us from
7: 8 that he may s us from the hand of the Philistines."
9:16 He shall s my people from the hand of the
10: 1 the people of the LORD and you will s them from
10:27 "How can this man s us?"
11: 3 Then, if there is no one to s us,
12:21 after useless things that cannot profit or s,
17:37 will s me from the hand of this Philistine."
17:47 that the LORD does not s by sword and spear;
19:11 "If you do not s your life tonight,
23: 2 "Go and attack the Philistines and s Keilah."
2Sa 3:18 my servant David I will s my people Israel
22: 3 my savior; you s me from violence.
22:42 They looked, but there was no one to s them;
1Ki 1:12 so that you may s your own life and the life
2Ki 19:19 So now, O LORD our God, s us, I pray you,
19:34 For I will defend this city to s it,
1Ch 16:35 Say also: "S us, O God of our salvation,
2Ch 20: 9 and you will hear and s.'
32:11 'The LORD our God will s us from the hand of
32:13 of those lands at all able to s their lands out
32:14 has been able to s his people from my hand,
32:14 your God should be able to s you from my hand?
32:15 to s his people from my hand or from the hand
32:15 much less will your God s you out of my hand!"
Ne 6:11 a man like me go into the temple to s his life?
Job 2: 4 All that people have they will give to s their lives.
6:23 Or, 'S me from an opponent's hand'?
Ps 6: 4 Turn, O LORD, s my life;
7: 1 s me from all my pursuers, and deliver me,
18:41 but there was no one to s them;
22:21 S me from the mouth of the lion!
28: 9 O s your people, and bless your heritage;
31: 2 a strong fortress to s me.
31:16 s me in your steadfast love.
33:17 and by its great might it cannot s.
36: 6 you s humans and animals alike, O LORD.
44: 6 not in my bow do I trust, nor can my sword s me.
54: 1 S me, O God, by your name, and vindicate me
55:16 But I call upon God, and the LORD will s me.
57: 3 He will send from heaven and s me,
59: 2 from the bloodthirsty s me.
69: 1 S me, O God, for the waters have come up
69:35 God will s Zion and rebuild the cities of Judah;
71: 2 incline your ear to me and s me.
71: 3 to s me, for you are my rock and my fortress.
76: 9 to s all the oppressed of the earth.
80: 2 Stir up your might, and come to s us!
86: 2 s your servant who trusts in you.
86:16 s the child of your serving girl.
106:47 S us, O LORD our God, and gather us from
109:26 S me according to your steadfast love.
109:31 to s them from those who would condemn them
116: 4 "O LORD, I pray, s my life!"
118:25 S us, we beseech you, O LORD!
119:94 I am yours; s me, for I have sought your precepts.
119:146 s me, that I may observe your decrees.
142: 6 S me from my persecutors,
143: 9 S me, O LORD, from my enemies;
Pr 2:12 It will s you from the way of evil,
6: 3 So do this, my child, and s yourself,
6: 5 s yourself like a gazelle from the hunter,
23:14 you will s their lives from Sheol.
Isa 25: 9 we have waited for him, so that he might s us.
33:22 the LORD is our king; he will s us.
35: 4 He will come and s you.
36:18 by saying, The LORD will s us.
36:20 the LORD should s Jerusalem out of my hand?' "
37:20 So now, O LORD our God, s us from his hand,
37:35 For I will defend this city to s it,
38:20 The LORD will s me, and we will sing
44:17 he prays to it and says, "S me,
44:20 and he cannot s himself or say,
45:20 and keep on praying to a god that cannot s.
46: 2 they cannot s the burden, but themselves go
46: 4 I will carry and will s.
46: 7 it does not answer or s anyone from trouble.
47:13 stand up and s you, those who gaze at the stars,
47:15 there is no one to s you.
49:25 and I will s your children.
59: 1 See, the LORD's hand is not too short to s,
63: 1 "It is I, announcing vindication, mighty to s."
Jer 2:27 of their trouble they say, "Come and s us!"
2:28 Let them come, if they can s you,
11:12 they will never s them in the time of their trouble.
15:20 for I am with you to s you and deliver you,
17:14 s me, and I shall be saved; for you are my praise.
30:10 for I am going to s you from far away,
30:11 For I am with you, says the LORD, to s you;
31: 7 proclaim, give praise, and say, "S, O LORD,
39:17 But I will s you on that day, says the LORD,
39:18 surely s you, and you shall not fall by the sword;
42:11 to s you and to rescue you from his hand.
46:27 for I am going to s you from far away,
48: 6 S yourselves! Be like a wild ass in the
51: 6 Flee from the midst of Babylon, s your lives,
51:45 S your lives, each of you,
La 4:17 for a nation that could not s.
Eze 3:18 to s their life, those wicked persons shall die
7:19 and gold cannot s them on the day of the wrath of
13:21 and s my people from your hands;
13:22 not to turn from their wicked way and s their lives;
13:23 I will s my people from your hand.
14:14 they would s only their own lives
14:16 they would s neither sons nor daughters;
14:18 they would s neither sons nor daughters,
14:20 they would s neither son nor daughter;
14:20 they would s only their own lives
18:27 and right, they shall s their life.
33:12 The righteousness of the righteous shall not s them
34:22 I will s my flock, and they shall no longer
34:27 the bars of their yoke, and s them from the hands
36:29 I will s you from all your uncleannesses,
37:23 I will s them from all the apostasies
Da 6:14 He was determined to s Daniel,
Hos 1: 7 and I will s them by the LORD their God;
1: 7 I will not s them by bow, or by sword, or by war,
13:10 Where now is your king, that he may s you?
14: 3 Assyria shall not s us; we will
Am 2:14 nor shall the mighty s their lives;
2:15 those who are swift of foot shall not s themselves,
2:15 nor shall those who ride horses s their lives;
Jnh 4: 6 to s him from his discomfort;
Mic 6:14 you shall put away, but not s, and what you s,
Hab 1: 2 and you will not s?
3:13 came forth to s your people, to s your anointed.
Zep 1:18 nor their gold will be able to s them on the day of
3:19 And I will s the lame and gather the outcast,
Zec 8: 7 I will s my people from the east country and from
8:13 so I will s you and you shall be a blessing.
9:16 On that day the LORD their God will s them
10: 6 and I will s the house of Joseph.
Mt 1:21 for he will s his people from their sins."
8:25 they went and woke him up, saying, "Lord, s us!
14:30 and beginning to sink, he cried out, "Lord, s me!"
16:25 For those who want to s their life will lose it,
27:40 the temple and build it in three days, s yourself!
27:42 "He saved others; he cannot s himself.
27:49 let us see whether Elijah will come to s him."
Mk 3: 4 on the sabbath, to s life or to kill?"
8:35 For those who want to s their life will lose it,
8:35 and for the sake of the gospel, will s it.
15:30 s yourself, and come down from the cross!"
15:31 "He saved others; he cannot s himself.
Lk 6: 9 on the sabbath, to s life or to destroy it?"
9:24 For those who want to s their life will lose it,
9:24 and those who lose their life for my sake will s it.
19:10 the Son of Man came to seek out and to s the lost."
23:35 let him s himself if he is the Messiah of God,
23:37 "If you are the King of the Jews, s yourself!"
23:39 "Are you not the Messiah? S yourself and us!"
Jn 12:27 what should I say—'Father, s me from this hour'?
12:47 for I came not to judge the world, but to s
Ac 2:40 "S yourselves from this corrupt generation."
27:43 but the centurion, wishing to s Paul, kept them
Ro 11:14 and thus s some of them.
1Co 1:21 of our proclamation, to s those who believe.
7:16 Wife, for all you know, you might s your husband.
7:16 Husband, for all you know, you might s your wife.
9:22 that I might by all means s some.
16: 2 to put aside and s whatever extra you earn,
1Ti 1:15 Christ Jesus came into the world to s sinners—
4:16 in these things, for in doing this you will s
2Ti 4:18 and s me for his heavenly kingdom.
Heb 5: 7 to the one who was able to s him from death,
7:25 to s those who approach God through him,
9:28 but to s those who are eagerly waiting for him.
11: 7 the warning and built an ark to s his household;
Jas 1:21 that has the power to s your souls.
2:14 faith but do not have works? Can faith s you?
4:12 There is one lawgiver and judge who is able to s

Jas 5:15 The prayer of faith will s the sick,
5:20 from wandering will s the sinner's soul from death
Jude 1:23 s others by snatching them out of the fire;
Tob 1: 7 for six years I would s up a second tenth in money
5:14 to him, "Welcome! God s you,
6:18 You will s her, and she will go with you.
Jdt 6: 2 Their God will not s them;
AdE 4: 8 to the king in our behalf, and s us from death."
13: 9 when it is your will to s Israel,
13:13 to kiss the soles of his feet to s Israel!
14:14 But s us by your hand, and help me,
14:19 and s us from the hands of evildoers.
14:19 And s me from my fear!"
Wis 14: 4 showing that you can s from every danger,
Sir 42: 1 and do not sin to s face:
50: 4 He considered how to s his people from ruin,
51: 8 for you and s them from the hand of their enemies.
Bar 4:22 For I have put my hope in the Everlasting to s you,
LtJ 6:12 that cannot s themselves from rust and corrosion.
6:36 They cannot s anyone from death or rescue
6:49 they cannot s themselves from war or calamity?
6:57 and gold are unable to s themselves from thieves
1Mc 6:44 So he gave his life to s his people and to win
9: 9 Let us rather s our own lives now,
2Mc 7:25 and urged her to advise the youth to s himself.
11: 6 prayed the Lord to send a good angel to s Israel.
Man 1:14 you will s me according to your great mercy,
3Mc 2:32 for life they confidently attempted to s themselves
6:13 who have power to s the nation of Jacob.
4Mc 5: 6 I would advise you to s yourself by eating pork,
6:15 s yourself by pretending to eat pork."
10: 1 and many repeatedly urged him to s himself
10:13 but obey the king and s yourself."
12: 6 the surviving son to obey and s himself.

SAVED‡ (145) [SAVE]

Ge 19:20 and my life will be s!"
47:25 They said, "You have s our lives;
Ex 14:30 the LORD s Israel that day from the Egyptians;
Nu 10: 9 the LORD your God and be s from your enemies.
Dt 33:29 Who is like you, a people s by the LORD,
Jos 9:26 he s them from the Israelites;
22:31 now you have s the Israelites from the hand of
Jdg 8:19 as the LORD lives, if you had s them alive,
21:14 the women whom they had s alive of the women
1Sa 17:37 who s me from the paw of the lion and from
25:31 without cause or for having s himself.
2Sa 19: 5 of all your officers who have s your life today,
19: 9 and s us from the hand of the Philistines;
22: 4 and I am s from my enemies.
1Ki 1:29 who has s my life from every adversity,
2Ki 14:27 he s them by the hand of Jeroboam son of Joash.
1Ch 11:14 and the LORD s them by a great victory.
2Ch 32:22 So the LORD s Hezekiah and the inhabitants
Ne 9:27 great mercies you gave them saviors who s them
Est 7: 9 whose word s the king, stands at Haman's house,
Ps 18: 3 so I shall be s from my enemies.
22: 5 To you they cried, and were s;
33:16 A king is not s by his great army;
34: 6 and was s from every trouble.
44: 7 But you have s us from our foes,
80: 3 let your face shine, that we may be s.
80: 7 let your face shine, that we may be s.
80:19 let your face shine, that we may be s.
106: 8 Yet he s them for his name's sake,
106:10 So he s them from the hand of the foe,
107:13 and he s them from their distress;
107:19 and he s them from their distress;
116: 6 when I was brought low, he s me.
Pr 2:16 You will be s from the loose woman,
Isa 30:15 In returning and rest you shall be s;
36:18 the gods of the nations s their land out of the hand
36:20 of these countries have s their countries out
43:12 I declared and s and proclaimed,
45:17 But Israel is s by the LORD
45:22 Turn to me and be s, all the ends of the earth!
63: 9 or angel but his presence that s them;
Jer 4:14 of wickedness so that you may be s.
8:20 the summer is ended, and we are not s."
17:14 save me, and I shall be s; for you are my praise.
23: 6 In his days Judah will be s and Israel will live
33:16 be s and Jerusalem will live in safety.
Eze 3:19 but you will have s your life.
3:21 and you will have s your life.
14:16 they alone would be s, but the land would
14:18 but they alone would be s.
33: 5 they would have s their lives.
33: 9 but you will have s your life.
Da 6:27 for he has s Daniel from the power of the lions."
Joel 2:32 on the name of the LORD shall be s;
Ob 1:21 Those who have been s shall go up to Mount Zion
Mt 10:22 But the one who endures to the end will be s.
19:25 and said, "Then who can be s?"
24:13 But the one who endures to the end will be s.
24:22 not been cut short, no one would be s;
27:42 "He s others; he cannot save himself.
Mk 10:26 and said to one another, "Then who can be s?"
13:13 But the one who endures to the end will be s.
13:20 not cut short those days, no one would be s;
15:31 "He s others; he cannot save himself.
16:16 ⟦The one who believes and is baptized will be s;⟧
Lk 1:71 that we would be s from our enemies and from
7:50 And he said to the woman, "Your faith has s you;
8:12 so that they may not believe and be s.
8:50 Only believe, and she will be s."
13:23 Someone asked him, "Lord, will only a few be s?"
Lk 18:26 Those who heard it said, "Then who can be s?"
18:42 "Receive your sight; your faith has s you."
23:35 the leaders scoffed at him, saying, "He s others;
Jn 3:17 but in order that the world might be s through him.
5:34 but I say these things so that you may be s.
10: 9 Whoever enters by me will be s,
Ac 2:21 on the name of the Lord shall be s.'
2:47 to their number those who were being s.
4:12 among mortals by which we must be s."
11:14 by which you and your entire household will be s.'
15: 1 to the custom of Moses, you cannot be s."
15:11 we believe that we will be s through the grace of
16:30 "Sirs, what must I do to be s?"
16:31 "Believe on the Lord Jesus, and you will be s,
27:20 all hope of our being s was at last abandoned.
27:31 in the ship, you cannot be s."
Ro 5: 9 will we be s through him from the wrath of God.
5:10 having been reconciled, will we be s by his life.
8:24 For in hope we were s.
9:27 only a remnant of them will be s;
10: 1 and prayer to God for them is that they may be s.
10: 9 that God raised him from the dead, you will be s.
10:10 and one confesses with the mouth and so is s.
10:13 who calls on the name of the Lord shall be s."
11:26 And so all Israel will be s;
1Co 1:18 but to us who are being s it is the power of God.
3:15 the builder will be s, but only as through fire.
5: 5 so that his spirit may be s in the day of the Lord.
10:33 but that of many, so that they may be s.
15: 2 also you are being s, if you hold firmly to
2Co 2:15 of Christ to God among those who are being s and
Eph 2: 5 by grace you have been s—
2: 8 For by grace you have been s through faith,
1Th 2:16 to the Gentiles so that they may be s.
2Th 2:10 because they refused to love the truth and so be s.
1Ti 2: 4 to be s and to come to the knowledge of the truth.
2:15 Yet she will be s through childbearing,
2Ti 1: 9 who s us and called us with a holy calling,
Tit 3: 5 he s us, not because of any works of righteousness
Heb 10:39 but among those who have faith and so are s.
1Pe 3:20 that is, eight persons, were s through water.
4:18 And "If it is hard for the righteous to be s,
2Pe 2: 5 even though he s Noah, a herald of righteousness,
Jude 1: 5 who once for all s a people out of the land
Tob 14: 7 All the Israelites who are s in those days
Jdt 10:15 "You have s your life by hurrying down
AdE 10: 9 this is Israel, who cried out to God and were s.
10: 9 The Lord has s his people;
Wis 9:18 taught what pleases you, and were s by wisdom."
10: 4 wisdom again s it, steering the righteous man by
16: 7 For the one who turned toward it was s,
Sir 51:12 for you s me from destruction and rescued me
Aza 1:66 and s us from the power of death, and delivered us
1Mc 2:59 and Mishael believed and were s from the flame.
4: 9 how our ancestors were s at the Red Sea,
11:48 a large amount of spoil on that day, and s the king.
2Mc 1:11 Having been s by God out of grave dangers
2:17 It is God who has s all his people,
6:22 so that by doing this he might be s from death,
6:30 though I might have been s from death,
Man 1: 7 so that they may be s.
2Es 6:25 to you shall be s and shall see my salvation and
7:*60* for I will rejoice over the few who shall be s,
8: 3 have been created, but only a few shall be s."
8:41 in the world will not all be s."
9: 7 be that all who will be s and will be able to escape
9:13 but inquire how the righteous will be s,
9:15 there are more who perish than those who will be s,
9:21 and s for myself one grape out of a cluster,
9:22 but let my grape and my plant be s,
12:34 those who have been s throughout my borders,
12:42 and like a haven for a ship s from a storm.
13:48 who are found within my holy borders, shall be s.
4Mc 4:14 Apollonius, having been s beyond all expectations,
6:27 O God, that though I might have s myself,

SAVES (17) [SAVE]

1Sa 10:19 who s you from all your calamities
14:39 For as the LORD lives who s Israel,
Job 5:15 But he s the needy from the sword of their mouth,
22:29 you say it is pride; for he s the humble.
Ps 7:10 God is my shield, who s the upright in heart.
34:18 and s the crushed in spirit.
37:40 he rescues them from the wicked, and s them,
72:13 and s the lives of the needy.
145:19 he also hears their cry, and s them.
Pr 11: 6 The righteousness of the upright s them,
14:25 A truthful witness s lives,
1Pe 3:21 And baptism, which this prefigured, now s you—
Tob 12: 9 For almsgiving s from death and purges away
Sir 2:11 he forgives sins and s in time of distress.
34:15 for their hope is in him who s them.
Sus 1:60 who s those who hope in him.
1Mc 4:11 that there is one who redeems and s Israel."

SAVING (12) [SAVE]

Ge 19:19 you have shown me great kindness in s my life;
1Sa 12: 7 the s deeds of the LORD that he performed
14: 6 for nothing can hinder the LORD from s by many
Ps 28: 8 he is the s refuge of his anointed.
40:10 I have not hidden your s help within my heart,
67: 2 your s power among all nations.
78:22 and did not trust his s power.
88:12 or your s help in the land of forgetfulness?
Mic 6: 5 that you may know the s acts of the LORD."
Sir 39:18 and none can limit his s power.
1Mc 3:18 there is no difference between s by many or by few
2Mc 12:25 they let him go, for the sake of s their kindred.

SAVIOR (53) [SAVE]

2Sa 22: 3 my stronghold and my refuge, my s;
2Ki 13: 5 Therefore the LORD gave Israel a s,
Ps 17: 7 O s of those who seek refuge
106:21 They forgot God, their S,
Isa 19:20 because of oppressors, he will send them a s,
43: 3 the Holy One of Israel, your S.
43:11 I, I am the LORD, and besides me there is no s.
45:15 a God who hides himself, O God of Israel, the S.
45:21 a righteous God and a S;
49:26 all flesh shall know that I am the LORD your S,
60:16 the LORD, am your S and your Redeemer,
63: 8 not deal falsely"; and he became their s
Jer 14: 8 O hope of Israel, its s in time of trouble,
Hos 13: 4 and besides me there is no s.
Lk 1:47 and my spirit rejoices in God my S,
1:69 a mighty s for us in the house of his servant David,
2:11 to you is born this day in the city of David a S,
Jn 4:42 and we know that this is truly the S of the world."
Ac 5:31 God exalted him at his right hand as Leader and S
13:23 to Israel a S, Jesus, as he promised;
Eph 5:23 the body of which he is the S.
Php 3:20 and it is from there that we are expecting a S,
1Ti 1: 1 of Christ Jesus by the command of God our S and
2: 3 and is acceptable in the sight of God our S,
4:10 who is the S of all people,
2Ti 1:10 through the appearing of our S Christ Jesus,
Tit 1: 3 by the command of God our S,
1: 4 from God the Father and Christ Jesus our S.
2:10 be an ornament to the doctrine of God our S.
2:13 of the glory of our great God and S,
3: 4 and loving kindness of God our S appeared,
3: 6 on us richly through Jesus Christ our S,
2Pe 1: 1 the righteousness of our God and S Jesus Christ:
1:11 and S Jesus Christ will be richly provided for you.
2:20 the knowledge of our Lord and S Jesus Christ,
3: 2 and the commandment of the Lord and S spoken
3:18 and knowledge of our Lord and S Jesus Christ.
1Jn 4:14 the Father has sent his Son as the S of the world.
Jude 1:25 to the only God our S,
Jdt 9:11 protector of the forsaken, s of those without hope.
AdE 15: 2 after invoking the aid of the all-seeing God and S,
16:13 our s and perpetual benefactor, and of Esther,
Wis 16: 7 but by you, the S of all.
Sir 46: 1 as his name implies, a great s of God's elect,
51: 1 O Lord and King, and praise you, O God my S.
Bar 4:22 to you from your everlasting s.
1Mc 4:30 he prayed, saying, "Blessed are you, O S of Israel,
9:21 "How is the mighty fallen, the s of Israel!"
2Mc 3:35 to the Lord and made very great vows to the S
3Mc 6:29 praised their holy God and S,
6:32 praising God, their S and worker of wonders.
7:16 of their ancestors, the eternal S of Israel, in words
2Es 2:36 I publicly call on my s to witness.

SAVIORS‡ (1) [SAVE]

Ne 9:27 great mercies you gave them s who saved them

SAVORY (6)

Ge 27: 4 Then prepare for me s food, such as I like,
27: 7 and prepare for me s food to eat,
27: 9 I may prepare from them s food for your father,
27:14 and his mother prepared s food,
27:17 Then she handed the s food,
27:31 He also prepared s food, and brought it

SAVOUR (KJV) See AROMA, FRAGRANCE, FRAGRANT, ODOR, SMELL, TASTE

SAW‡ (747) [SAWED, SAWN, SAWS, SEE]

Ge 1: 4 And God s that the light was good;
1:10 And God s that it was good.
1:12 And God s that it was good.
1:18 And God s that it was good.
1:21 And God s that it was good.
1:25 And God s that it was good.
1:31 God s everything that he had made, and indeed,
3: 6 when the woman s that the tree was good for food,
6: 2 the sons of God s that they were fair;
6: 5 The LORD s that the wickedness
6:12 And God s that the earth was corrupt;
8:13 and s that the face of the ground was drying.
9:22 the father of Canaan, s the nakedness of his father,
12:14 the Egyptians s that the woman was very beautiful.
12:15 When the officials of Pharaoh s her,
13:10 and s that the plain of the Jordan
16: 4 and when she s that she had conceived,
16: 5 and when she s that she had conceived,
18: 2 He looked up and s three men standing near him.
18: 2 When he s them, he ran from the tent entrance
19: 1 When Lot s them, he rose to meet them,
19:28 the Plain and s the smoke of the land going up like
21: 9 But Sarah s the son of Hagar the Egyptian,
21:19 God opened her eyes and she s a well of water.
22: 4 On the third day Abraham looked up and s
22:13 And Abraham looked up and s a ram,
24:63 and looking up, he s camels coming.
24:64 And Rebekah looked up, and when she s Isaac,
26: 8 of a window and s him fondling his wife Rebekah.
28: 6 Now Esau s that Isaac had blessed Jacob

Ge 28: 8 So when Esau s that the Canaanite women did
29: 2 he s a well in the field and three flocks
29:10 Now when Jacob s Rachel,
29:31 When the LORD s that Leah was unloved,
30: 1 When Rachel s that she bore Jacob no children,
30: 9 When Leah s that she had ceased bearing children,
31: 2 And Jacob s that Laban did not regard him
31:10 in which I looked up and s that the male goats
31:42 God s my affliction and the labor of my hands,
32: 2 and when Jacob s them he said,
32:25 the man s that he did not prevail against Jacob,
33: 1 Now Jacob looked up and s Esau coming,
33: 5 Esau looked up and s the women and children,
34: 2 s her, he seized her and lay with her by force.
37: 4 his brothers s that their father loved him more
37:18 They s him from a distance,
37:25 up they s a caravan of Ishmaelites coming
37:29 to the pit and s that Joseph was not in the pit,
38: 2 There Judah s the daughter of a certain
38:14 She s that Shelah was grown up,
38:15 When Judah s her, he thought her to be
39: 3 His master s that the LORD was with him,
39:13 When she s that he had left his garment
40: 6 he s that they were troubled.
40:16 chief baker s that the interpretation was favorable,
41:22 a second time and I s in my dream seven ears
42: 7 When Joseph s his brothers, he recognized them,
42:21 we s his anguish when he pleaded with us,
42:27 he s his money at the top of the sack.
42:35 they and their father s their bundles of money,
43:16 When Joseph s Benjamin with them,
43:29 Then he looked up and s his brother Benjamin,
45:27 he s the wagons that Joseph had sent to carry him,
48: 8 Israel s Joseph's sons, he said, "Who are these?"
48:17 When Joseph s that his father laid his right hand
49:15 he s that a resting place was good,
50:11 of the land s the mourning on the threshing floor
50:23 Joseph s Ephraim's children of the third
Ex 2: 2 and when she s that he was a fine baby,
2: 5 She s the basket among the reeds
2: 6 When she opened it, she s the child.
2:11 he went out to his people and s their forced labor.
2:11 He s an Egyptian beating a Hebrew,
2:13 he s two Hebrews fighting;
3: 4 When the LORD s that he had turned aside to see,
5:19 The Israelite supervisors s that they were
8:15 But when Pharaoh s that there was a respite,
9:34 But when Pharaoh s that the rain and the hail and
14:30 and Israel s the Egyptians dead on the seashore.
14:31 Israel s the great work that the LORD did against
16:15 When the Israelites s it, they said to one another,
18:14 When Moses' father-in-law s all that he was doing
24:10 and they s the God of Israel.
32: 1 When the people s that Moses delayed to come
32: 5 When Aaron s this, he built an altar before it;
32:19 As soon as he came near the camp and s the calf
32:25 When Moses s that the people were running wild
33:10 When all the people s the pillar of cloud standing
34:30 When Aaron and all the Israelites s Moses,
39:43 When Moses s that they had done all the work just
Lev 9:24 and when all the people s it,
Nu 12:10 And Aaron turned towards Miriam and s
13:28 and besides, we s the descendants of Anak there.
13:32 and all the people that we s in it are of great size.
13:33 There we s the Nephilim (the Anakites come from
20:29 When all the congregation s that Aaron had died,
22: 2 Now Balak son of Zippor s all that Israel had done
22:23 The donkey s the angel of the LORD standing in
22:25 When the donkey s the angel of the LORD,
22:27 When the donkey s the angel of the LORD,
22:31 he s the angel of the LORD standing in the road,
22:33 The donkey s me, and turned away
24: 1 Balaam s that it pleased the LORD to bless Israel,
24: 2 Balaam looked up and s Israel camping tribe
25: 7 s it, he got up and left the congregation.
32: 1 When they s that the land of Jazer and the land
32: 9 they went up to the Wadi Eshcol and s the land,
Dt 1:19 that great and terrible wilderness that you s,
1:28 We actually s there the offspring of the Anakim!' "
1:31 you s how the LORD your God carried you,
4:12 You heard the sound of words but s no form;
4:15 Since you s no form when the LORD spoke
7:19 the great trials that your eyes s,
9:16 Then I s that you had indeed sinned against
26: 7 the LORD heard our voice and s our affliction,
29: 3 the great trials that your eyes s,
32:19 The LORD s it, and was jealous he spurned his sons
Jos 5:13 he looked up and s a man standing before him
7:21 I s among the spoil a beautiful mantle from Shinar,
8:14 When the king of Ai s this, he and all his people,
8:21 and all Israel s that the ambush had taken the city
24: 7 and your eyes s what I did to Egypt.
Jdg 1:24 When the spies s a man coming out of the city,
3:24 When they s that the doors of the roof chamber
9:36 And when Gaal s them, he said to Zebul, "Look,
9:43 he looked and s the people coming out of the city,
9:55 When the Israelites s that Abimelech was dead,
11:35 When he s her, he tore his clothes, and said, "Alas,
12: 3 When I s that you would not deliver me,
14: 1 and at Timnah he s a Philistine woman.
14: 2 "I s a Philistine woman at Timnah;
14:11 the people s him, they brought thirty companions
16: 1 where he s a prostitute and went in to her.
16:24 When the people s him, they praised their god;
18:26 When Micah s that they were too strong for him,
19: 3 girl's father s him and came with joy to meet him.
19:17 When the old man looked up and s the wayfarer in
Jdg 20:36 Then the Benjaminites s that they were defeated.
20:41 for they s that disaster was close upon them.
Ru 1:18 Naomi s that she was determined to go with her,
2:18 her mother-in-law s how much she had gleaned.
1Sa 5: 7 the inhabitants of Ashdod s how things were,
6:13 When they looked up and s the ark,
6:16 When the five lords of the Philistines s it,
9:14 they s Samuel coming out toward them on his way
9:17 When Samuel s Saul, the LORD told him,
10:11 before s how he prophesied with the prophets,
10:14 and when we s they were not to be found,
12:12 But when you s that King Nahash of
13: 6 When the Israelites s that they were in distress (for
13:11 I s that the people were slipping away from me,
14:52 and when Saul s any strong or valiant warrior,
17:24 All the Israelites, when they s the man,
17:42 When the Philistine looked and s David,
17:51 the Philistines s that their champion was dead,
17:55 When Saul s David go out against the Philistine,
18:15 When Saul s that he had great success,
19: 5 for all Israel. You s it, and rejoiced;
19:20 they s the company of the prophets in a frenzy,
22: 9 answered, "I s the son of Jesse coming to Nob,
25:23 When Abigail s David, she hurried and alighted
26: 5 and David s the place where Saul lay,
26:12 No one s it, or knew it, nor did anyone awake;
28: 5 When Saul s the army of the Philistines,
28:12 woman s Samuel, she cried out with a loud voice;
28:21 and when she s that he was terrified,
31: 5 When his armor-bearer s that Saul was dead,
31: 7 beyond the Jordan s that the men of Israel had fled
2Sa 1: 7 he looked behind him, he s me, and called to me.
6:16 and s King David leaping and dancing before
10: 6 the Ammonites s that they had become odious
10: 9 When Joab s that the battle was set against him
10:14 When the Ammonites s that the Arameans fled,
10:15 Arameans s that they had been defeated by Israel,
10:19 the kings who were servants of Hadadezer s
11: 2 that he s from the roof a woman bathing;
12:19 when David s that his servants were whispering
13:34 he s many people coming from the Horonaim road
17:18 But a boy s them, and told Absalom;
17:23 Ahithophel s that his counsel was not followed,
18:10 A man s it, and told Joab,
18:10 and told Joab, "I s Absalom hanging in an oak."
18:11 to the man who told him, "What, you s him!
18:24 and when he looked up, he s a man running alone.
18:26 Then the sentinel s another man running;
18:29 I s a great tumult, but I do not know what it was."
20:12 and the man s that all the people were stopping.
20:12 he s that all who came by him were stopping,
24:17 David s the angel who was destroying the people,
24:20 he s the king and his servants coming toward him;
1Ki 3:21 I s that he was dead;
11:28 Jeroboam was very able, and when Solomon s that
12:16 all Israel s that the king would not listen to them,
13:25 People passed by and s the body thrown in
16:18 When Zimri s that the city was taken,
18:17 When Ahab s Elijah, Ahab said to him, "Is it you,
18:39 When all the people s it, they fell on their faces
22:17 "I s all Israel scattered on the mountains,
22:19 I s the LORD sitting on his throne,
22:32 When the captains of the chariots s Jehoshaphat,
22:33 When the captains of the chariots s that it was not
2Ki 2:15 of prophets who were at Jericho s him at
2:24 When he turned around and s them,
3:22 the Moabites s the water opposite them as red
3:26 When the king of Moab s that the battle was going
4:25 When the man of God s her coming,
4:32 he s the child lying dead on his bed.
5:21 When Naaman s someone running after him,
6:17 LORD opened the eyes of the servant, and he s;
6:20 and they s that they were inside Samaria.
6:21 When the king of Israel s them he said to Elisha,
9:22 When Joram s Jehu, he said, "Is it peace, Jehu?"
9:26 and for the blood of his children that I s yesterday,
9:27 When King Ahaziah of Judah s this,
11: 1 Ahaziah's mother, s that her son was dead,
12:10 Whenever they s that there was a great deal
13: 4 for he s the oppression of Israel,
14:26 LORD s that the distress of Israel was very bitter;
16:10 he s the altar that was at Damascus.
23:16 Josiah turned, he s the tombs there on the mount;
1Ch 10: 5 When his armor-bearer s that Saul was dead,
10: 7 in the valley s that the army had fled and that Saul
15:29 and s King David leaping and dancing;
19: 6 When the Ammonites s that they had made
19:10 When Joab s that the line of battle was set
19:15 When the Ammonites s that the Arameans fled,
19:16 Arameans s that they had been defeated by Israel,
19:19 of Hadadezer s that they had been defeated
21:16 up and s the angel of the LORD standing
21:20 Ornan turned and s the angel;
21:21 David came to Ornan, Ornan looked and s David;
21:28 when David s that the LORD had answered him
2Ch 7: 3 When all the people of Israel s the fire come down
9: 6 the reports until I came and my own eyes s it.
10:16 all Israel s that the king would not listen to them,
12: 7 When the LORD s that they humbled themselves,
15: 9 when they s that the LORD his God was
18:16 "I s all Israel scattered on the mountains,
18:18 I s the LORD sitting on his throne,
18:31 When the captains of the chariots s Jehoshaphat,
18:32 when the captains of the chariots s that it was not
22:10 Ahaziah's mother, s that her son was dead,
24:11 when they s that there was a large amount
31: 8 Hezekiah and the officials came and s the heaps,
2Ch 32: 2 When Hezekiah s that Sennacherib had come
Ezr 3:12 wept with a loud voice when they s this house,
Ne 6:12 I perceived and s that God had not sent him at all,
9: 9 "And you s the distress of our ancestors in Egypt
13:15 In those days I s in Judah
13:23 also I s Jews who had married women of Ashdod,
Est 2:15 Now Esther was admired by all who s her.
3: 5 When Haman s that Mordecai did not bow down
5: 2 as the king s Queen Esther standing in the court,
5: 9 But when Haman s Mordecai in the king's gate,
7: 7 he s that the king had determined to destroy him.
Job 2:12 When they s him from a distance,
2:13 for they s that his suffering was very great.
20: 9 The eye that s them will see them no more,
28:27 then he s it and declared it;
29: 8 the young men s me and withdrew,
29:11 ear heard, it commended me, and when the eye s,
31:21 because I s I had supporters at the gate;
32: 5 But when Elihu s that there was no answer in
42:16 and s his children, and his children's children,
Ps 48: 5 As soon as they s it, they were astounded;
73: 3 I s the prosperity of the wicked.
77:16 When the waters s you, O God, when the waters s
107:24 they s the deeds of the LORD,
Pr 7: 7 and I s among the simple ones,
24:32 Then I s and considered it;
Ecc 1:14 I s all the deeds that are done under the sun;
2:13 Then I s that wisdom excels folly
2:24 This also, I s, is from the hand of God;
3:16 I s under the sun that in the place of justice,
3:22 So I s that there is nothing better than
4: 1 Again I s all the oppressions that are practiced
4: 4 Then I s that all toil and all skill in work come
4: 7 Again, I s vanity under the sun:
4:15 I s all the living who, moving about under the sun,
8:10 Then I s the wicked buried;
8:17 then I s all the work of God,
9:11 Again I s that under the sun the race is not to
SS 6: 9 The maidens s her and called her happy;
Isa 1: 1 which he s concerning Judah and Jerusalem in
2: 1 son of Amoz s concerning Judah and Jerusalem.
5: 7 he expected justice, but s bloodshed;
6: 1 I s the Lord sitting on a throne, high and lofty;
10:15 s magnify itself against the one who handles it?
13: 1 concerning Babylon that Isaiah son of Amoz s.
22: 9 and you s that there were many breaches in
59:15 The LORD s it, and it displeased him
59:16 He s that there was no one,
Jer 3: 7 she did not return, and her false sister Judah s it.
3: 8 She s that for all the adulteries of that faithless
23:13 In the prophets of Samaria I s a disgusting thing:
39: 4 the soldiers s them, they fled, going out of the city
41:13 the people who were with Ishmael s Johanan son
44:17 and prospered, and s no misfortune.
Eze 1: 1 the heavens were opened, and I s visions of God.
1:15 I s a wheel on the earth beside the living creatures,
1:27 like the loins I s something like gleaming amber,
1:27 like the loins I s something that looked like fire,
1:28 When I s it, I fell on my face,
10:15 the living creatures that I s by the river Chebar.
10:20 These were the living creatures that I s underneath
11: 1 among them I s Jaazaniah son of Azzur,
13:16 concerning Jerusalem and s visions of peace for it,
16: 6 and s you flailing about in your blood.
16:50 therefore I removed them when I s it.
19: 5 When she s that she was thwarted,
20:28 wherever they s any high hill or any leafy tree,
23:11 Her sister Oholibah s this,
23:13 And I s that she was defiled;
23:14 she s male figures carved on the wall,
23:16 When she s them she lusted after them,
28:18 to ashes on the earth in the sight of all who s you.
41: 8 I s also that the temple had a raised platform
43: 3 The vision I s was like the vision that I had seen
46:19 and there I s a place at the extreme western end
47: 7 I s on the bank of the river a great many trees on
Da 2:41 As you s the feet and toes partly of potter's clay
2:41 as you s the iron mixed with the clay.
2:43 As you s the iron mixed with clay,
2:45 as you s that a stone was cut from the mountain
3:27 the king's counselors gathered together and s that
4: 5 I s a dream that frightened me;
4: 9 Hear the dream that I s; tell me its interpretation.
4:10 Upon my bed this is what I s;
4:18 This is the dream that I, King Nebuchadnezzar, s.
4:20 The tree that you s, which grew great and strong,
4:23 And whereas the king s a holy watcher coming
7: 2 s in my vision by night the four winds
7: 7 After this I s in the visions by night a fourth beast,
7:13 I s one like a human being coming with the clouds
8: 2 In the vision I was looking and s myself in Susa
8: 3 I looked up and s a ram standing beside the river.
8: 4 I s the ram charging westward and northward
8: 7 I s it approaching the ram.
8:20 As for the ram that you s with the two horns,
10: 5 I looked up and s a man clothed in linen,
10: 7 I, Daniel, alone s the vision;
Hos 5:13 When Ephraim s his sickness,
9:10 in its first season, I s your ancestors.
9:13 Once I s Ephraim as a young palm planted in
Am 1: 1 which he s concerning Israel in the days
9: 1 I s the LORD standing beside the altar,
Jnh 3:10 When God s what they did,
Mic 1: 1 which he s concerning Samaria and Jerusalem.
Hab 1: 1 The oracle that the prophet Habakkuk s.
3: 7 I s the tents of Cushan under affliction;
3:10 The mountains s you, and writhed;

Hag 2: 3 among you that s this house in its former glory?
Zec 1: 8 In the night I s a man riding on a red horse!
1:18 And I looked up and s four horns.
2: 1 up and s a man with a measuring line in his hand.
5: 1 Again I looked up and s a flying scroll.
5: 9 I looked up and s two women coming forward.
6: 1 up and s four chariots coming out from
Mt 2:10 When they s that the star had stopped,
2:11 they s the child with Mary his mother;
2:16 Herod s that he had been tricked by the wise men,
3: 7 when he s many Pharisees and Sadducees coming
3:16 the heavens were opened to him and he s the Spirit
4:18 he walked by the Sea of Galilee, he s two brothers,
4:21 As he went from there, he s two other brothers,
5: 1 Jesus s the crowds, he went up the mountain;
8:14 he s his mother-in-law lying in bed with a fever;
8:18 Now when Jesus s great crowds around him,
8:34 and when they s him, they begged him
9: 2 When Jesus s their faith, he said to the paralytic,
9: 8 When the crowds s it, they were filled with awe,
9: 9 he s a man called Matthew sitting at the tax booth;
9:11 When the Pharisees s this,
9:23 to the leader's house and s the flute players and
9:36 When he s the crowds, he had compassion
12: 2 When the Pharisees s it, they said to him, "Look,
14:14 When he went ashore, he s a great crowd;
14:26 But when the disciples s him walking on the sea,
15:31 crowd was amazed when they s the mute speaking,
17: 8 they s no one except Jesus himself alone.
18:31 When his fellow slaves s what had happened,
20: 3 he s others standing idle in the marketplace;
21:15 and the scribes s the amazing things that he did,
21:20 When the disciples s it, they were amazed, saying,
21:32 and even after you s it, you did not change your
21:38 But when the tenants s the son,
25:37 was it that we s you hungry and gave you food,
25:38 was it that we s you a stranger and welcomed you,
25:39 that we s you sick or in prison and visited you?'
25:44 when was it that we s you hungry or thirsty or
26: 8 But when the disciples s it,
26:71 another servant-girl s him,
27: 3 Judas, his betrayer, s that Jesus was condemned,
27:24 So when Pilate s that he could do nothing,
27:54 s the earthquake and what took place,
28:17 When they s him, they worshiped him;
Mk 1:10 he s the heavens torn apart and
1:16 he s Simon and his brother Andrew casting a net
1:19 he s James son of Zebedee and his brother John,
2: 5 When Jesus s their faith, he said to the paralytic,
2:14 he s Levi son of Alphaeus sitting at the tax booth,
2:16 of the Pharisees s that he was eating with sinners
3:11 Whenever the unclean spirits s him,
5: 6 When he s Jesus from a distance,
5:15 to Jesus and s the demoniac sitting there, clothed
5:22 Jairus came and, when he s him, fell at his feet
5:38 the synagogue, he s a commotion, people weeping
6:33 Now many s them going and recognized them,
6:34 As he went ashore, he s a great crowd;
6:48 When he s that they were straining at the oars
6:49 But when they s him walking on the sea,
6:50 for they all s him and were terrified.
8:25 and he s everything clearly.
9: 8 they s no one with them any more, but only Jesus.
9:14 they s a great crowd around them,
9:15 When the whole crowd s him,
9:20 the spirit s him, immediately it convulsed the boy,
9:25 When Jesus s that a crowd came running together,
9:38 we s someone casting out demons in your name,
10:14 But when Jesus s this, he was indignant and said
11:20 they s the fig tree withered away to its roots.
12:34 When Jesus s that he answered wisely,
14:67 When she s Peter warming himself,
15:39 s that in this way he breathed his last, he said,
15:47 Mary Magdalene and Mary the mother of Joses s
16: 4 When they looked up, they s that the stone,
16: 5 As they entered the tomb, they s a young man,
16:14 ⟦not believed those who s him after he had risen.⟧
Lk 1:12 When Zechariah s him, he was terrified;
2:17 When they s this, they made known what had been
2:48 When his parents s him they were astonished;
5: 2 he s two boats there at the shore of the lake;
5: 8 But when Simon Peter s it,
5:12 When he s Jesus, he bowed with his face to
5:20 When he s their faith, he said, "Friend,
5:27 this he went out and s a tax collector named Levi,
7:13 the Lord s her, he had compassion for her and said
7:39 Now when the Pharisee who had invited him s it,
8:28 When he s Jesus, he fell down before him
8:34 When the swineherds s what had happened,
8:47 the woman s that she could not remain hidden,
9:30 Suddenly they s two men, Moses and Elijah,
9:32 since they had stayed awake, they s his glory and
9:49 we s someone casting out demons in your name,
9:54 When his disciples James and John s it, they said,
10:31 and when he s him, he passed by on the other side.
10:32 when he came to the place and s him,
10:33 and when he s him, he was moved with pity.
13:12 When Jesus s her, he called her over and said,
15:20 his father s him and was filled with compassion;
16:23 and s Abraham far away with Lazarus by his side.
17:14 When he s them, he said to them,
17:15 Then one of them, when he s that he was healed,
18:15 and when the disciples s it,
18:43 and all the people, when they s it, praised God.
19: 7 All who s it began to grumble and said,
19:41 As he came near and s the city, he wept over it,
20:14 But when the tenants s him,
Lk 21: 1 He looked up and s rich people putting their gifts
21: 2 also s a poor widow put in two small copper coins.
22:49 those who were around him s what was coming,
23: 8 When Herod s Jesus, he was very glad,
23:47 When the centurion s what had taken place,
23:48 for this spectacle s what had taken place,
23:55 and they s the tomb and how his body was laid.
24:12 he s the linen cloths by themselves;
Jn 1:29 The next day he s Jesus coming toward him
1:32 "I s the Spirit descending from heaven like a dove,
1:38 When Jesus turned and s them following,
1:39 They came and s where he was staying,
1:47 When Jesus s Nathanael coming toward him,
1:48 "I s you under the fig tree
1:50 because I told you that I s you under the fig tree?
2:23 because they s the signs that he was doing.
5: 6 When Jesus s him lying there and knew
6: 2 they s the signs that he was doing for the sick.
6: 5 When he looked up and s a large crowd coming
6:14 When the people s the sign that he had done,
6:19 they s Jesus walking on the sea and coming near
6:22 the sea s that there had been only one boat there.
6:22 They also s that Jesus had not got into the boat
6:24 So when the crowd s that neither Jesus
6:26 you are looking for me, not because you s signs,
8:56 he s it and was glad."
9: 1 As he walked along, he s a man blind from birth.
11:31 consoling her, s Mary get up quickly and go out.
11:32 When Mary came where Jesus was and s him,
11:33 When Jesus s her weeping,
12:41 Isaiah said this because he s his glory and spoke
19: 6 When the chief priests and the police s him,
19:26 When Jesus s his mother and
19:33 they came to Jesus and s that he was already dead,
19:35 (He who s this has testified so that you
20: 1 to the tomb and s that the stone had been removed
20: 5 to look in and s the linen wrappings lying there,
20: 6 He s the linen wrappings lying there,
20: 8 also went in, and he s and believed;
20:12 and she s two angels in white,
20:14 she turned around and s Jesus standing there,
20:20 Then the disciples rejoiced when they s the Lord.
21: 9 they had gone ashore, they s a charcoal fire there,
21:20 Peter turned and s the disciple whom Jesus loved
21:21 When Peter s him, he said to Jesus, "Lord,
Ac 1:11 in the same way as you s him go into heaven."
2:25 'I s the Lord always before me,
3: 3 he s Peter and John about to go into the temple,
3: 9 All the people s him walking and praising God,
3:12 When Peter s it, he addressed the people,
4:13 Now when they s the boldness of Peter and John
4:14 When they s the man who had been cured standing
6:15 they s that his face was like the face of an angel.
7:24 When he s one of them being wronged,
7:31 When Moses s it, he was amazed at the sight;
7:55 and s the glory of God and Jesus standing at
8:13 with Philip and was amazed when he s the signs
8:18 when Simon s that the Spirit was given through
8:39 the eunuch s him no more,
9: 7 because they heard the voice but s no one.
9:35 of Lydda and Sharon s him and turned to the Lord.
10: 3 in which he clearly s an angel of God coming in
10:11 He s the heaven opened and something like
11: 5 and in a trance I s a vision.
11: 6 As I looked at it closely I s four-footed animals,
11:23 When he came and s the grace of God, he rejoiced,
12: 3 After he s that it pleased the Jews,
12:16 they opened the gate, they s him and were amazed.
13:12 When the proconsul s what had happened,
13:45 Jews s the crowds, they were filled with jealousy;
14:11 When the crowds s what Paul had done,
16:19 But when her owners s that their hope
16:27 jailer woke up and s the prison doors wide open,
21:32 When they s the tribune and the soldiers,
22: 9 Now those who were with me s the light but did
22:13 In that very hour I regained my sight and s him.
22:18 and s Jesus saying to me,
26:13 I s a light from heaven, brighter than the sun,
28: 4 the natives s the creature hanging from his hand,
28: 6 and s that nothing unusual had happened to him,
Gal 2: 7 when they s that I had been entrusted with
2:14 But when I s that they were not acting consistently
Php 1:30 the same struggle that you s I had and now hear
Heb 11:13 but from a distance they s and greeted them.
11:23 because they s that the child was beautiful;
11:27 he persevered as though he s him who is invisible.
2Pe 2: 8 by their lawless deeds that he s and heard),
Rev 1: 2 even to all that he s.
1:12 and on turning I s seven golden lampstands,
1:13 in the midst of the lampstands I s one like the Son
1:17 When I s him, I fell at his feet as though dead.
1:20 of the seven stars that you s in my right hand,
5: 1 Then I s in the right hand of the one seated on
5: 2 I s a mighty angel proclaiming with a loud voice,
5: 6 Then I s between the throne and the four living
6: 1 Then I s the Lamb open one of the seven seals,
6: 9 I s under the altar the souls of those
7: 1 After this I s four angels standing at the four
7: 2 I s another angel ascending from the rising of
8: 2 And I s the seven angels who stand before God,
9: 1 and I s a star that had fallen from heaven to earth,
9:17 And this was how I s the horses in my vision:
10: 1 And I s another mighty angel coming down
10: 5 Then the angel whom I s standing on the sea and
11:11 and those who s them were terrified.
12:13 when the dragon s that he had been thrown down
13: 1 And I s a beast rising out of the sea
Rev 13: 2 And the beast that I s was like a leopard,
13:11 Then I s another beast that rose out of the earth;
14: 6 Then I s another angel flying in midheaven,
15: 1 I s another portent in heaven, great and amazing:
15: 2 And I s what appeared to be a sea of glass mixed
16:13 And I s three foul spirits like frogs coming from
17: 3 and I s a woman sitting on a scarlet beast
17: 6 And I s that the woman was drunk with the blood
17: 6 When I s her, I was greatly amazed.
17: 8 The beast that you s was, and is not,
17:12 the ten horns that you s are ten kings who have not
17:15 And he said to me, "The waters that you s,
17:16 And the ten horns that you s,
17:18 The woman you s is the great city that rules over
18: 1 this I s another angel coming down from heaven,
18:18 and cried out as they s the smoke of her burning,
19:11 I s heaven opened, and there was a white horse!
19:17 Then I s an angel standing in the sun,
19:19 Then I s the beast and the kings of the earth
20: 1 Then I s an angel coming down from heaven,
20: 4 Then I s thrones, and those seated
20: 4 I also s the souls of those who had been beheaded
20:11 I s a great white throne and the one who sat on it;
20:12 And I s the dead, great and small,
21: 1 Then I s a new heaven and a new earth;
21: 2 And I s the holy city, the new Jerusalem,
21:22 I s no temple in the city,
22: 8 I, John, am the one who heard and s these things.
22: 8 And when I heard and s them,
Tob 1:17 and if I s the dead body of any
10:11 Then he s them safely off;
10:12 Then she kissed them both and s them safely off.
11:13 Tobit s his son and threw his arms around him,
11:16 When the people of Nineveh s him coming,
12:19 but what you s was a vision.
14:15 and he s its prisoners being led into Media,
Jdt 6:12 When the men of the town s them,
7: 4 When the Israelites s their vast numbers,
10: 7 When they s her transformed in appearance
12:16 to seduce her from the day he first s her.
14: 6 and s the head of Holofernes in the hand of one of
14:10 When Achior s all that the God of Israel had done,
14:12 When the Assyrians s them they sent word
AdE 2:15 Esther found favor in the eyes of all who s her.
5: 9 But when he s Mordecai the Jew in the courtyard,
7: 7 for he s that he was in serious trouble.
11:12 Mordecai s in this dream what God had determined
15:13 She said to him, "I s you, my lord,
Wis 4:15 Yet the peoples s and did not understand,
12:27 they s and recognized as the true God
13:11 A skilled woodcutter may s down a tree easy
17: 6 and in terror they deemed the things that they s to
19:11 Afterward they s also a new kind of birds,
Sir 1: 9 he s her and took her measure;
17:13 Their eyes s his glorious majesty,
45:19 The Lord s it and was not pleased,
48:11 Happy are those who s you and were adorned
48:24 By his dauntless spirit he s the future,
49: 8 It was Ezekiel who s the vision of glory,
Bar 4: 9 For she s the wrath that came upon you from God,
Sus 1:33 with her and all who s her were weeping.
1:38 and when we s this wickedness we ran to them.
1:39 Although we s them embracing,
1:54 Now then, if you really s this woman, tell me this:
Bel 1:30 The king s that they were pressing him hard,
1Mc 1:16 Antiochus s that his kingdom was established,
2: 6 He s the blasphemies being committed in Judah
2:24 When Mattathias s it, he burned with zeal
3:17 But when they s the army coming to meet them,
3:29 he s that the money in the treasury was exhausted,
3:42 and his brothers s that misfortunes had increased
4: 7 And they s the camp of the Gentiles,
4:12 When the foreigners looked up and s them coming
4:20 They s that their army had been put to flight,
4:21 and when they also s the army of Judas drawn up
4:30 When he s that their army was strong, he prayed,
4:35 When Lysias s the rout of his troops and observed
4:38 There they s the sanctuary desolate,
4:38 the courts they s bushes sprung up as in a thicket,
4:38 They s also the chambers of the priests in ruins.
5:30 At dawn they looked out and s a large company,
5:31 So Judas s that the battle had begun and that
6:43 s that one of the animals was equipped
6:47 the Jews s the royal might and the fierce attack of
6:62 But when the king entered Mount Zion and s what
7:11 for they s that they had come with a large force.
7:23 And Judas s all the wrongs that Alcimus and those
7:25 When Alcimus s that Judas and those
7:44 When his army s that Nicanor had fallen,
8:18 for they s that the kingdom of the Greeks
9: 6 When they s the huge number of the enemy forces,
9: 7 When Judas s that his army had slipped away and
9:14 Judas s that Bacchides and the strength
9:16 on the left wing s that the right wing was crushed,
9:39 and s a tumultuous procession with a great amount
9:57 When Bacchides s that Alcimus was dead,
10:64 When his accusers s the honor that was paid him,
10:64 and s him clothed in purple, they all fled.
11:38 When King Demetrius s that the land was quiet
11:39 he s that all the troops were grumbling
11:49 of the city s that the Jews had gained control of
11:73 When his men who were fleeing s this,
12: 1 Jonathan s that the time was favorable for him,
12:29 for they s the fires burning.
12:42 Trypho s that he had come with a large army,
12:51 When their pursuers s that they would fight
13: 2 and he s that the people were trembling with fear.

1Mc 13:53 Simon s that his son John had reached manhood,
14:35 "The people s Simon's faithfulness and the glory
15:32 and when he s the splendor of Simon,
16: 6 He s that the soldiers were afraid to cross
16: 6 when his troops s him, they crossed over after him.
2Mc 4: 6 For he s that without the king's attention public
7:20 she s her seven sons perish within a single day,
8: 8 When Philip s that the man was gaining ground
15:12 What he s was this: Onias,
3Mc 3: 8 when they s an unexpected tumult
5:48 When the Jews s the dust raised by
6:23 and s them all fallen headlong to destruction,
2Es 2:42 s on Mount Zion a great multitude that I could
3: 2 because I s the desolation of Zion and the wealth
3:29 I came here I s ungodly deeds without number,
9:20 So I considered my world, and s that it was lost.
9:20 I s that my earth was in peril because of
9:21 And I s and spared some with great difficulty,
9:38 I looked around, and on my right I s a woman;
10:29 to me at first came to me, and when he s me
10:32 and lo, what I have seen I s, and can still see,
10:41 whom you s mourning and whom you began
10:44 The woman whom you s is Zion,
10:49 So you s her likeness, how she mourned
11: 1 I s rising from the sea an eagle
11: 2 I s it spread its wings over the whole earth,
11: 3 I s that out of its wings there grew opposing wings;
11: 5 Then I s that the eagle flew with its wings,
11: 6 And I s how all things
11: 7 Then I s the eagle rise upon its talons,
11:10 and s that the voice did not come from its heads,
11:22 And after this I looked and s that the twelve wings
11:24 As I kept looking I s that two little wings
11:25 Then I s that these little wings planned
11:30 And I s how it allied the two heads with itself,
11:33 and s the head in the middle suddenly disappear,
11:35 I s the head on the right side devour the one on
11:37 I s what seemed to be a lion roused from
12: 2 and s that the remaining head had disappeared.
12:11 The eagle that you s coming up from the sea is
12:16 the interpretation of the twelve wings that you s.
12:31 "And as for the lion whom you s rousing up out of
12:35 This is the dream that you s,
13: 3 I s that this man flew with the clouds of heaven;
13: 5 and s that an innumerable multitude
13: 6 And I looked and s that he carved out for himself
13: 8 and s that all who had gathered together
13: 9 he s the onrush of the approaching multitude,
13:10 but I s only how he sent forth
13:11 When I s it, I was amazed.
13:12 After this I s the same man come down from
13:32 whom you s as a man coming up from the sea.
13:34 as you s, wishing to come and conquer him.
13:36 as you s the mountain carved out without hands.
13:47 you s the multitude gathered together in peace.
13:53 This is the interpretation of the dream that you s.
14:18 that you s in the vision is already hurrying
4Mc 4:24 but s that all his threats and punishments
5: 5 When Antiochus s him he said,
6:24 When they s that he was so courageous in the face
8: 4 the tyrant s them, grouped about their mother as
8:15 But when they had heard the inducements and s
10: 8 he s his own flesh torn all around and drops
12: 2 he felt strong compassion for this child when he s
14: 9 they not only s what was happening,
15:14 who s them tortured and burned one by one,
15:19 and s in their nostrils the signs of the approach
15:20 When you s the flesh of children burned upon
15:20 when you s the place filled with many spectators
15:25 of her own soul she s mighty advocates—
16: 3 inflamed as she s her seven sons tortured
16:20 when Isaac s his father's hand wielding a knife
17: 7 as they s the mother of the seven children
17:23 when he s the courage of their virtue

SAWED‡ (1) [SAW]

1Ki 7: 9 cut according to measure, s with saws,

SAWN (1) [SAW]

Heb 11:37 They were stoned to death, they were s in two,

SAWS‡ (3) [SAW]

2Sa 12:31 to work with s and iron picks and iron axes,
1Ki 7: 9 cut according to measure, sawed with s,
1Ch 20: 3 set them to work with s and iron picks and axes.

SAY‡ (1030) [AFORESAID, SAID, SAYING, SAYINGS, SAYS]

Ge 3: 1 He said to the woman, "Did God s,
4:23 you wives of Lamech, listen to what I s:
12:12 they will s, 'This is his wife';
12:13 S you are my sister, so that it may go well
12:19 Why did you s, 'She is my sister,'
14:23 so that you might not s, 'I have made Abram rich.'
18:13 and s, 'Shall I indeed bear a child,
20: 5 Did he not himself s to me, 'She is my sister'?
20:13 at every place to which we come, s of me,
24:14 Let the girl to whom I shall s,
24:14 that I may drink,' and who shall s, 'Drink,
24:43 to draw, to whom I shall s,
24:44 and who will s to me, "Drink, and I will draw
26: 7 for he was afraid to s, "My wife," thinking,
26: 9 Why then did you s, 'She is my sister'?"
26:28 so we s, let there be an oath between you and us,
27: 6 "I heard your father s to your brother Esau,
30:27 Laban said to him, "If you will allow me to s so,
31:24 "Take heed that you s not a word to Jacob,
32: 4 "Thus you shall s to my lord Esau:
32:18 you shall s, 'They belong to your servant Jacob;
32:19 "You shall s the same thing to Esau
32:20 and you shall s, 'Moreover your servant Jacob is
34:11 and whatever you s to me I will give.
37:17 for I heard them s, 'Let us go to Dothan.' "
37:20 we shall s that a wild animal has devoured him,
43: 7 Could we in any way know that he would s,
44: 4 and when you overtake them, s to them,
44:16 And Judah said, "What can we s to my lord?
45: 9 Hurry and go up to my father and s to him,
45:17 Pharaoh said to Joseph, "S to your brothers,
45:19 You are further charged to s, 'Do this:
46:31 "I will go up and tell Pharaoh, and will s to him,
46:34 you shall s, 'Your servants have been keepers
50:17 'S to Joseph: I beg you, forgive the crime of your
Ex 3:13 "If I come to the Israelites and s to them,
3:13 what shall I s to them?"
3:14 He said further, "Thus you shall s to the Israelites,
3:15 "Thus you shall s to the Israelites, 'The LORD,
3:16 and s to them, 'The LORD,
3:18 of Israel shall go to the king of Egypt and s to him,
4: 1 but s, 'The LORD did not appear to you.' "
4:22 you shall s to Pharaoh, 'Thus says the LORD:
5:16 No straw is given to your servants, yet they s to us,
5:17 He said, "You are lazy, lazy; that is why you s,
6: 6 S therefore to the Israelites, 'I am the LORD,
7: 9 'Perform a wonder,' then you shall s to Aaron,
7:16 S to him, 'The LORD, the God of the Hebrews,
7:16 the God of the Hebrews, sent me to you to s,
7:19 The LORD said to Moses, "S to Aaron,
8: 1 "Go to Pharaoh and s to him,
8: 5 And the LORD said to Moses, "S to Aaron,
8:10 Moses said, "As you s!
8:16 Then the LORD said to Moses, "S to Aaron,
8:20 as he goes out to the water, and s to him,
9: 1 and s to him, 'Thus says the LORD,
9:13 and s to him, 'Thus says the LORD,
10:29 Moses said, "Just as you s!
12:27 you shall s, 'It is the passover sacrifice to
14: 3 Pharaoh will s of the Israelites,
16: 9 "S to the whole congregation of the Israelites,
16:12 s to them, 'At twilight you shall eat meat,
19: 3 saying, "Thus you shall s to the house of Jacob,
20:22 Thus you shall s to the Israelites:
23:22 attentively to his voice and do all that I s,
30:31 You shall s to the Israelites,
32:12 Why should the Egyptians s,
33: 5 the LORD had said to Moses, "S to the Israelites,
Lev 1: 2 Speak to the people of Israel and s to them:
9: 3 And s to the people of Israel,
15: 2 Speak to the people of Israel and s to them:
17: 2 and his sons and to all the people of Israel and s
17: 8 And s to them further: Anyone of the
18: 2 Speak to the people of Israel and s to them:
19: 2 to all the congregation of the people of Israel and s
20: 2 S further to the people of Israel:
21: 1 the sons of Aaron, and s to them:
21:17 Speak to Aaron and s: No one of your
22: 3 S to them: If anyone among all
22:18 and his sons and all the people of Israel and s
23: 2 Speak to the people of Israel and s to them:
23:10 Speak to the people of Israel and s to them:
25: 2 Speak to the people of Israel and s to them:
27: 2 Speak to the people of Israel and s to them:
Nu 5:12 Speak to the Israelites and s to them:
5:21 the woman take the oath of the curse and s to
5:22 And the woman shall s, "Amen.
6: 2 Speak to the Israelites and s to them:
6:23 Thus you shall bless the Israelites: You shall s to
8: 2 Speak to Aaron and s to him:
10:35 Whenever the ark set out, Moses would s, "Arise,
10:36 And whenever it came to rest, he would s,
11:12 Did I give birth to them, that you should s to me,
11:13 For they come weeping to me and s,
11:18 And s to the people: Consecrate yourselves
11:21 and you s, 'I will give them meat,
14:15 then the nations who have heard about you will s,
14:28 S to them, "As I live," says the LORD,
14:28 "I will do to you the very things I heard you s:
15: 2 Speak to the Israelites and s to them:
15:18 Speak to the Israelites and s to them:
16:24 S to the congregation: Get away from the
18:30 S also to them: When you have set apart the best
21:27 ballad singers s, "Come to Heshbon, let it be built;
22:17 and whatever you s to me I will do;
22:19 I may learn what more the LORD may s to me."
22:38 but do I have power to s just anything?
22:38 word God puts in my mouth, that is what I must s."
23: 5 "Return to Balak, and this is what you must s."
23:12 "Must I not take care to s what the LORD puts
23:16 "Return to Balak, and this is what you shall s."
24:13 what the LORD says, that is what I will s'?
25:12 s, 'I hereby grant him my covenant of peace.
27: 8 You shall also s to the Israelites, "If a man dies,
28: 2 the Israelites, and s to them:
28: 3 And you shall s to them, This is the offering
33:51 to the Israelites, and s to them:
34: 2 the Israelites, and s to them:
35:10 to the Israelites, and s to them:
Dt 1:42 The LORD said to me, "S to them,
4: 6 who, when they hear all these statutes, will s,
5:27 and hear all that the LORD our God will s.
5:30 Go s to them, 'Return to your tents.'
6:21 then you shall s to your children,
7:17 If you s to yourself, "These nations are more
8:17 Do not s to yourself, "My power and the might
9: 4 do not s to yourself, "It is because
9:28 the land from which you have brought us might s,
12:20 and you s, "I am going to eat some meat,"
13: 2 by them take place, and they s,
17:14 and you s, "I will set a king over me,
18:21 You may s to yourself, "How can we recognize
20: 3 and shall s to them: "Hear,
21:20 They shall s to the elders of his town,
22:16 father of the young woman shall s to the elders:
25: 7 at the gate and s, "My husband's brother refuses
26: 3 to the priest who is in office at that time, and s
26:13 then you shall s before the LORD your God:
27:16 All the people shall s, "Amen!"
27:17 All the people shall s, "Amen!"
27:18 All the people shall s, "Amen!"
27:19 All the people shall s, "Amen!"
27:20 All the people shall s, "Amen!"
27:21 All the people shall s, "Amen!"
27:22 All the people shall s, "Amen!"
27:23 All the people shall s, "Amen!"
27:24 All the people shall s, "Amen!"
27:25 All the people shall s, "Amen!"
27:26 All the people shall s, "Amen!"
28:67 In the morning you shall s,
28:67 and at evening you shall s,
30:12 It is not in heaven, that you should s,
30:13 Neither is it beyond the sea, that you should s,
31:17 In that day they will s,
32:27 for their adversaries might misunderstand and s,
32:37 Then he will s: Where are their gods,
Jos 7: 8 what can I s, now that Israel has turned their backs
7:13 Proceed to sanctify the people, and s,
8: 6 they will s, 'They are fleeing from us, as before.'
9:11 go to meet them, and s to them,
20: 2 "S to the Israelites, 'Appoint the cities of refuge,
22:24 to come your children might s to our children,
22:27 so that your children may never s to our children
22:28 or to our descendants in time to come, we could s,
Jdg 2: 3 So now I s, I will not drive them out before you;
4:20 and asks you, 'Is anyone here?' s, 'No.' "
6:32 that is to s, "Let Baal contend against him,"
7: 4 When I s, 'This one shall go with you,'
7: 4 and when I s, 'This one shall not go with you,'
7:11 and you shall hear what they s,
9: 2 "S in the hearing of all the lords of Shechem,
9:19 I s, you have acted in good faith and honor
9:29 I would s to him, 'Increase your army,
9:54 so people will not s about me,
11:10 we will surely do as you s."
12: 5 the men of Gilead would s to him,
12: 6 "Then s Shibboleth," and he said, "Sibboleth,"
16:15 Then she said to him, "How can you s,
19:30 saying, "Thus shall you s to all the Israelites,
21:22 we will s to them, 'Be generous and allow us
Ru 4: 4 So I thought I would tell you of it, and s:
1Sa 2:15 and s to the one who was sacrificing, "Give meat
2:16 and then take whatever you wish," he would s,
2:20 Then Eli would bless Elkanah and his wife, and s,
2:36 for a piece of silver or a loaf of bread, and shall s,
3: 9 and if he calls you, you shall s, 'Speak, LORD,
8: 7 "Listen to the voice of the people in all that they s
9: 9 anyone who went to inquire of God would s,
10: 2 they will s to you, 'The donkeys that you went
11: 9 "Thus shall you s to the inhabitants
14: 9 If they s to us, 'Wait until we come to you,'
14:10 But if they s, 'Come up to us,' then we will go up;
14:34 and s to them, 'Let all bring their oxen
16: 2 the LORD said, "Take a heifer with you, and s,
18:22 "Speak to David in private and s, 'See,
18:25 Then Saul said, "Thus shall you s to David,
20: 4 Then Jonathan said to David, "Whatever you s,
20: 6 If your father misses me at all, then s,
20:21 If I s to the boy, 'Look,
20:22 But if I s to the young man, 'Look,
20:26 Saul did not s anything that day;
24: 9 "Why do you listen to the words of those who s,
27:10 David would s, "Against the Negeb of Judah,"
27:11 thinking, "They might tell about us, and s,
2Sa 7: 8 therefore thus you shall s to my servant David:
7:20 And what more can David s to you?
11:21 then you shall s, 'Your servant Uriah
11:25 "Thus you shall s to Joab,
13: 5 and when your father comes to see you, s to him,
13:28 and when I s to you, 'Strike Amnon,'
14: 7 They s, 'Give up the man who struck his brother,
14:15 Now I have come to s this to my lord the king
15: 2 Absalom would call out and s,
15: 3 Absalom would s, "See, your claims are good
15:34 But if you return to the city and s to Absalom,
16:10 who then shall s, 'Why have you done so?' "
17: 5 and let us hear too what he has to s."
17: 9 at the first attack, whoever hears it will s,
19:10 therefore why do you s nothing about bringing
19:11 "S to the elders of Judah,
19:13 s to Amasa, 'Are you not my bone and my flesh?
20:18 Then she said, "They used to s in the old days,
21: 4 He said, "What do you s that I should do for you?"
24:12 "Go and s to David: Thus says the LORD:
1Ki 1:13 Go in at once to King David, and s to him,
1:34 then blow the trumpet, and s,
9: 8 and they will s, 'Why has the LORD done such
9: 9 Then they will s, 'Because they have forsaken
12:10 "Thus you should s to this people who spoke
12:10 thus you should s to them,

1Ki 12:23 **S** to King Rehoboam of Judah,
14: 5 Thus and thus you shall **s** to her."
18:10 and when they would **s**, 'He is not here,'
18:11 now you **s**, 'Go, tell your lord that Elijah is here.'
18:14 now you **s**, 'Go, tell your lord that Elijah is here';
18:44 Then he said, "Go **s** to Ahab,
20: 4 The king of Israel answered, "As you **s**, my lord,
21:19 You shall **s** to him, "Thus says the LORD:
21:19 You shall **s** to him, "Thus says the LORD:
22: 8 "Let the king not **s** such a thing."
22:27 and **s**, 'Thus says the king:
2Ki 1: 3 the messengers of the king of Samaria, and **s**
1: 6 'Go back to the king who sent you, and **s** to him:
2:18 he said to them, "Did I not **s** to you, Do not go?"
4:13 He said to him, "**S** to her,
4:26 and **s** to her, Are you all right?
4:28 Did I not **s**, Do not mislead me?"
5:22 He replied, "Yes, but my master has sent me to **s**,
7: 4 If we **s**, 'Let us enter the city,'
8:10 Elisha said to him, "Go, **s** to him,
8:14 who said to him, "What did Elisha **s** to you?"
9: 3 take the flask of oil, pour it on his head, and **s**,
9:17 send him to meet them, and let him **s**,
9:37 so that no one can **s**, This is Jezebel.' "
10: 5 we will do anything you **s**.
18:19 The Rabshakeh said to them, "**S** to Hezekiah:
18:22 But if you **s** to me,
19: 6 "**S** to your master, 'Thus says the LORD:
20: 5 and **s** to Hezekiah prince of my people,
20:14 and said to him, "What did these men **s**?
22:18 thus shall you **s** to him, Thus says the LORD,
1Ch 16:31 and let them **s** among the nations,
16:35 **S** also: "Save us, O God of our
17: 7 therefore thus you shall **s** to my servant David:
17:18 And what more can David **s** to you
21:10 "Go and **s** to David, 'Thus says the LORD:
2Ch 7:21 everyone passing by will be astonished, and **s**,
7:22 Then they will **s**, 'Because they abandoned
11: 3 **S** to King Rehoboam of Judah,
18: 7 "Let the king not **s** such a thing."
18:26 and **s**, 'Thus says the king:
25:19 You **s**, 'See, I have defeated Edom,'
34:26 thus shall you **s** to him:
Ezr 8:17 to **s** to Iddo and his colleagues the temple servants
9:10 "And now, our God, what shall we **s** after this?
Ne 5: 8 They were silent, and could not find a word to **s**.
5:12 We will do as you **s**."
6: 8 saying, "No such things as you **s** have been done;
Est 1:17 with contempt on their husbands, since they will **s**,
Job 7: 4 When I lie down I **s**, 'When shall I rise?'
7:13 When I **s**, 'My bed will comfort me,
8: 2 "How long will you **s** these things,
9:12 Who will **s** to him, 'What are you doing?'
9:22 I **s**, he destroys both the blameless and the wicked.
9:27 If I **s**, 'I will forget my complaint;
10: 2 I will **s** to God, Do not condemn me;
11: 4 For you **s**, 'My conduct is pure,
17:12 'The light,' they **s**, 'is near to the darkness.'
17:14 if I **s** to the Pit, 'You are my father,'
19:28 If you **s**, 'How we will persecute him!'
20: 7 those who have seen them will **s**,
21:14 They **s** to God, 'Leave us alone!
21:19 You **s**, 'God stores up their iniquity
21:28 For you **s**, 'Where is the house of the prince?
22:13 Therefore you **s**, 'What does God know?
22:29 When others are humiliated, you **s** it is pride;
23: 5 and understand what he would **s** to me.
24:25 and show that there is nothing in what I **s**?"
27: 5 Far be it from me to **s** that you are right;
28:22 Abaddon and Death **s**, 'We have heard a rumor
32:10 I **s**, 'Listen to me; let me also declare my opinion.'
32:11 while you searched out what to **s**.
32:13 Yet do not **s**, 'We have found wisdom;
32:15 they have not a word to **s**.
33: 9 You **s**, 'I am clean, without transgression;
33:32 If you have anything to **s**, answer me;
34:16 hear this; listen to what I **s**.
34:34 Those who have sense will **s** to me,
34:34 and the wise who hear me will **s**,
35: 2 You **s**, 'I am in the right before God.'
35:14 much less when you **s** that you do not see him,
36: 2 for I have yet something to **s** on God's behalf.
36:23 Who has prescribed for him his way, or who can **s**,
37:19 Teach us what we shall **s** to him;
38:35 so that they may go and **s** to you, 'Here we are'?
Ps 4: 6 There are many who **s**, "O that we might see
10: 4 In the pride of their countenance the wicked **s**,
10:13 the wicked renounce God, and **s** in their hearts,
11: 1 how can you **s** to me, "Flee like a bird to
12: 4 those who **s**, "With our tongues we will prevail;
13: 4 and my enemy will **s**, "I have prevailed";
14: 1 Fools **s** in their hearts, "There is no God."
16: 2 I **s** to the LORD, "You are my Lord;
29: 9 and in his temple all **s**, "Glory!"
31:14 I trust in you, O LORD; I **s**, "You are my God."
35: 3 **s** to my soul, "I am your salvation."
35:10 All my bones shall **s**, "O LORD, who is like you?
35:21 they **s**, "Aha, Aha, our eyes have seen it."
35:25 Do not let them **s** to themselves, "Aha,
35:25 Do not let them **s** "We have swallowed you up."
35:27 and **s** evermore, "Great is the LORD,
40:15 be appalled because of their shame who **s** to me,
40:16 may those who love your salvation **s** continually,
42: 3 while people **s** to me continually,
42: 9 I **s** to God, my rock, "Why have you forgotten me?
42:10 while they **s** to me continually,
53: 1 Fools **s** in their hearts, "There is no God."
Ps 55: 6 And I **s**, "O that I had wings like a dove!
58:11 People will **s**, "Surely there is a reward for
66: 3 **S** to God, "How awesome are your deeds!
70: 3 Let those who **s**, "Aha, Aha!"
70: 4 Let those who love your salvation **s** evermore,
71:11 They **s**, "Pursue and seize
73:11 And they **s**, "How can God know?
75: 4 I **s** to the boastful, "Do not boast,"
77:10 And I **s**, "It is my grief that the right hand of
79:10 Why should the nations **s**, "Where is their God?"
82: 6 I **s**, "You are gods, children of the Most High,
83: 4 They **s**, "Come, let us wipe them out as a nation;
87: 4 "This one was born there," they **s**.
87: 7 Singers and dancers alike **s**,
90: 3 You turn us back to dust, and **s**, "Turn back,
91: 2 will **s** to the LORD, "My refuge and my fortress;
94: 7 and they **s**, "The LORD does not see;
96:10 **S** among the nations, "The LORD is king!
102:24 I **s**, "do not take me away at the mid-point
106:48 And let all the people **s**, "Amen."
107: 2 Let the redeemed of the LORD **s** so,
109: 6 They **s**, "Appoint a wicked man against him;
115: 2 Why should the nations **s**, "Where is their God?"
118: 2 Let Israel **s**, "His steadfast love endures forever."
118: 3 Let the house of Aaron **s**,
118: 4 Let those who fear the LORD **s**,
122: 8 For the sake of my relatives and friends I will **s**,
124: 1 the LORD who was on our side—let Israel now **s**—
129: 1 attacked me from my youth"—let Israel now **s**—
129: 8 while those who pass by do not **s**,
139:11 If I **s**, "Surely the darkness shall cover me,
140: 6 I **s** to the LORD, "You are my God;
142: 5 I cry to you, O LORD; I **s**, "You are my refuge,
Pr 1:11 they **s**, "Come with us, let us lie in wait for blood;
3:28 Do not **s** to your neighbor, "Go, and come again,
5:12 and you **s**, "Oh, how I hated discipline,
7: 4 **S** to wisdom, "You are my sister,"
20: 9 Who can **s**, "I have made my heart clean;
20:22 Do not **s**, "I will repay evil";
20:25 It is a snare for one to **s** rashly, "It is holy,"
23: 7 they **s** to you; but they do not mean it.
23:35 "They struck me," you will **s**, "but I was not hurt;
24:12 if you **s**, "Look, we did not know this"—
24:29 not **s**, "I will do to others as they have done to me;
30: 9 and deny you, and **s**, "Who is the LORD?"
30:15 Three things are never satisfied; four never **s**,
Ecc 5: 6 not **s** before the messenger that it was a mistake;
6: 3 I **s** that a stillborn child is better off than he.
7:10 Do not **s**, "Why were the former days better than
7:21 Do not give heed to everything that people **s**,
8: 4 and who can **s** to him, "What are you doing?"
12: 1 and the years draw near when you will **s**,
SS 7: 8 I **s** I will climb the palm tree and lay hold
Isa 2: 3 Many peoples shall come and **s**, "Come,
5:19 who **s**, "Let him make haste,
6: 9 And he said, "Go and **s** to this people:
7: 4 and **s** to him, Take heed, be quiet, do not fear,
8:19 Now if people **s** to you, "Consult the ghosts and
12: 1 You will **s** in that day:
12: 4 And you will **s** in that day:
14:10 All of them will speak and **s** to you:
19:11 How can you **s** to Pharaoh, "I am one of the sages,
20: 6 In that day the inhabitants of this coastland will **s**,
22:15 who is master of the household, and **s** to him:
24:16 But I **s**, I pine away,
29:11 "Read this," they **s**, "We cannot, for it is sealed."
29:12 saying, "Read this," they **s**, "We cannot read."
29:15 whose deeds are in the dark, and who **s**,
29:16 Shall the thing made **s** of its maker,
29:16 or the thing formed **s** of the one who formed it,
30:10 who **s** to the seers, "Do not see";
30:22 you will **s** to them, "Away with you!"
33:24 And no inhabitant will **s**, "I am sick";
35: 4 **S** to those who are of a fearful heart, "Be strong,
36: 4 The Rabshakeh said to them, "**S** to Hezekiah:
36: 7 But if you **s** to me, 'We rely on the LORD
37: 6 "**S** to your master, 'Thus says the LORD:
38: 5 and **s** to Hezekiah, Thus says the LORD, the God
38:15 But what can I **s**?
39: 3 and said to him, "What did these men **s**?
40: 9 **s** to the cities of Judah, "Here is your God!"
40:27 Why do you **s**, O Jacob, and speak, O Israel,
41:13 it is I who **s** to you, "Do not fear, I will help you."
41:26 and beforehand, so that we might **s**, "He is right"?
42:17 who **s** to cast images, "You are our gods."
42:22 a spoil with no one to **s**, "Restore!"
43: 6 I will **s** to the north, "Give them up,"
43: 9 and let them hear and **s**, "It is true."
44: 5 This one will **s**, "I am the LORD's,"
44:19 nor is there knowledge or discernment to **s**,
44:20 and he cannot save himself or **s**,
45: 9 Does the clay **s** to the one who fashions it,
45:19 I did not **s** to the offspring of Jacob,
47: 8 who **s** in your heart, "I am, and there is no one
48: 5 so that you would not **s**, "My idol did them,
48: 7 so that you could not **s**, "I already knew them."
48:20 **s**, "The LORD has redeemed his servant Jacob!"
49:20 of your bereavement will yet **s** in your hearing:
49:21 Then you will **s** in your heart,
56: 3 Do not let the foreigner joined to the LORD **s**,
56: 3 and do not let the eunuch **s**, "I am just a dry tree."
56:12 "Come," they **s**, "let us get wine;
57:10 but you did not **s**, "It is useless."
58: 9 you shall cry for help, and he will **s**, Here I am.
62:11 **S** to daughter Zion, "See, your salvation comes;
65: 5 who **s**, "Keep to yourself, do not come near me,
65: 8 As the wine is found in the cluster, and they **s**,
Jer 1: 7 LORD said to me, "Do not **s**, 'I am only a boy';
2: 6 not **s**, "Where is the LORD who brought us up
2: 8 The priests did not **s**, "Where is the LORD?"
2:23 How can you **s**, "I am not defiled,
2:27 who **s** to a tree, "You are my father,"
2:27 But in the time of their trouble they **s**,
2:31 Why then do my people **s**, "We are free,
2:35 you **s**, "I am innocent;
3:12 and proclaim these words toward the north, and **s**:
3:16 says the LORD, they shall no longer **s**,
4: 5 and proclaim in Jerusalem, and **s**:
4: 5 shout aloud and **s**, "Gather together,
5: 2 Although they **s**, "As the LORD lives,"
5:15 nor can you understand what they **s**.
5:19 And when your people **s**, "Why has
5:19 you shall **s** to them, "As you have forsaken me
5:24 They do not **s** in their hearts,
7: 2 and **s**, Hear the word of the LORD,
7:10 which is called by my name, and **s**,
7:28 You shall **s** to them: This is the nation
8: 4 You shall **s** to them, Thus says the LORD:
8: 8 How can you **s**, "We are wise,
10:11 Thus shall you **s** to them:
11: 3 You shall **s** to them, Thus says the LORD,
11:21 who seek your life, and **s**,
13:12 And they will **s** to you,
13:13 Then you shall **s** to them:
13:18 **S** to the king and the queen mother;
13:21 What will you **s** when they set as head
13:22 And if you **s** in your heart,
14:15 and who **s**, "Sword and famine shall not come
14:17 You shall **s** to them this word:
15: 2 And when they **s** to you, "Where shall we go?"
15: 2 "Where shall we go?" you shall **s** to them:
16:10 and they **s** to you, "Why has
16:11 then you shall **s** to them:
16:19 the nations come from the ends of the earth and **s**:
17:15 See how they **s** to me,
17:20 and **s** to them: Hear the word of the
18:11 **s** to the people of Judah and the inhabitants
18:12 But they **s**, "It is no use!
18:19 O LORD, and listen to what my adversaries **s**!
19: 3 You shall **s**: Hear the word of the
19:11 and shall **s** to them: Thus says the LORD of hosts:
20: 9 If I **s**, "I will not mention him,
21: 4 Thus you shall **s** to Zedekiah:
21: 8 And to this people you shall **s**:
21:11 To the house of the king of Judah **s**:
21:13 you who **s**, "Who can come down against us,
22: 2 and **s**: Hear the word of the LORD,
22: 8 and all of them will **s** one to another,
23:17 they **s**, "No calamity shall come upon you."
23:31 says the LORD, who use their own tongues and **s**,
23:33 you shall **s** to them, "You are the burden,
23:34 And as for the prophet, priest, or the people who **s**,
23:35 Thus shall you **s** to one another,
23:38 But if you **s**, "the burden of the LORD,"
23:38 You shall not **s**, "the burden of the LORD,"
25:27 Then you shall **s** to them, Thus says the LORD
25:28 then you shall **s** to them:
25:30 against them all these words, and **s** to them:
26: 4 You shall **s** to them: Thus says the LORD:
27: 4 This is what you shall **s** to your masters:
29:24 To Shemaiah of Nehelam you shall **s**:
31: 7 proclaim, give praise, and **s**, "Save, O LORD,
31:10 **s**, "He who scattered Israel will gather him,
31:29 In those days they shall no longer **s**:
31:34 or **s** to each other, "Know the LORD,"
32: 3 Zedekiah had said, "Why do you prophesy and **s**:
32: 7 to come to you and **s**,
32:36 concerning this city of which you **s**,
33:10 In this place of which you **s**,
33:24 Have you not observed how these people **s**,
34: 2 and speak to King Zedekiah of Judah and **s** to him:
35:13 and **s** to the people of Judah and the inhabitants
36:14 of Nethaniah son of Shelemiah son of Cushi to **s**
36:29 concerning King Jehoiakim of Judah you shall **s**:
37: 7 This is what the two of you shall **s** to the king
38:20 Just obey the voice of the LORD in what I **s**
38:25 and they should come and **s** to you,
38:25 What did the king **s** to you?'
38:26 then you shall **s** to them,
39:16 Go and **s** to Ebed-melech the Ethiopian:
42:13 But if you continue to **s**,
43: 2 The LORD our God did not send you to **s**,
43:10 and **s** to them, Thus says the LORD of hosts,
45: 4 Thus you shall **s** to him, "Thus says the LORD:
46:14 **S**, "Take your stations and be ready,
48:14 can you **s**, "We are heroes and mighty warriors"?
48:17 **s**, "How the mighty scepter is broken,
48:19 Ask the man fleeing and the woman escaping; **s**,
50: 2 set up a banner and proclaim, do not conceal it, **s**:
51:35 the inhabitants of Zion shall **s**.
51:35 on the inhabitants of Chaldea," Jerusalem shall **s**.
51:62 and **s**, 'O LORD, you yourself threatened
51:64 and **s**, 'Thus shall Babylon sink, to rise no more,
La 2:13 What can I **s** for you, to what compare you,
3:18 so I **s**, "Gone is my glory, and all that I had hoped
Eze 2: 4 I am sending you to them, and you shall **s** to them,
2: 8 But you, mortal, hear what I **s** to you;
3:11 **S** to them, "Thus says the Lord GOD";
3:18 If I **s** to the wicked, "You shall surely die,"
3:27 I will open your mouth, and you shall **s** to them,
6: 3 and **s**, You mountains of Israel, hear the word of
6:11 Clap your hands and stamp your foot, and **s**,
8:12 For they **s**, 'The LORD does not see us,
9: 9 for they **s**, 'The LORD has forsaken the land,

Eze 11: 3 they **s,** 'The time is not near to build houses;
11: 5 and he said to me, "**S,** Thus says the LORD:
11:16 Therefore **s:** Thus says the Lord GOD:
11:17 Therefore **s:** Thus says the Lord GOD:
12:10 **S** to them, "Thus says the Lord GOD:
12:11 **S,** "I am a sign for you:
12:19 and **s** to the people of the land, Thus says
12:23 But **s** to them, The days are near,
12:28 Therefore **s** to them, Thus says the Lord GOD:
13: 2 **s** to those who prophesy out
13: 6 they **s,** "Says the LORD,"
13:11 **S** to those who smear whitewash on it
13:15 and I will **s** to you, The wall is no more,
13:18 and **s,** Thus says the Lord GOD:
14: 4 Therefore speak to them, and **s** to them,
14: 6 **s** to the house of Israel, Thus says the Lord GOD:
14:17 Or if I bring a sword upon that land and **s,**
16: 3 and **s,** Thus says the Lord GOD to Jerusalem:
17: 3 **S:** Thus says the Lord GOD:
17: 9 **S:** Thus says the Lord GOD: Will it prosper?
17:12 **S** now to the rebellious house:
18:19 Yet you **s,** "Why should not the son suffer for
18:25 Yet you **s,** "The way of the Lord is unfair."
19: 2 and **s:** What a lioness was your mother among
20: 3 speak to the elders of Israel, and **s** to them:
20: 5 and **s** to them: Thus says the Lord GOD:
20:27 mortal, speak to the house of Israel and **s** to them,
20:30 **s** to the house of Israel, Thus says the Lord GOD:
20:47 **s** to the forest of the Negeb, Hear the word of
21: 3 and **s** to the land of Israel, Thus says the LORD:
21: 7 And when they **s** to you, "Why do you moan?"
21: 7 you shall **s,** "Because of the news that has come.
21: 9 prophesy and **s:** Thus says the Lord; **S:** A sword,
21:28 As for you, mortal, prophesy, and **s,**
21:28 concerning their reproach; **s:**
22: 3 You shall **s,** Thus says the Lord GOD: A city!
22:24 **s** to it: You are a land that is not cleansed,
24: 3 And utter an allegory to the rebellious house and **s**
24:21 **S** to the house of Israel, Thus says
25: 3 **S** to the Ammonites, Hear the word of
26:17 And they shall raise a lamentation over you, and **s**
27: 3 and **s** to Tyre, which sits at the entrance to
28: 2 **s** to the prince of Tyre, Thus says the Lord GOD:
28: 9 Will you still **s,** "I am a god,"
28:12 and **s** to him, Thus says the Lord GOD:
28:22 and **s,** Thus says the Lord GOD:
29: 3 and **s,** Thus says the Lord GOD:
30: 2 prophesy, and **s,** Thus says the Lord GOD:
31: 2 **s** to Pharaoh king of Egypt and to his hordes:
32: 2 a lamentation over Pharaoh king of Egypt, and **s**
33: 2 speak to your people and **s** to them,
33: 8 If I **s** to the wicked, "O wicked ones,
33:10 Now you, mortal, **s** to the house of Israel,
33:11 **S** to them, As I live, says the Lord GOD,
33:12 And you, mortal, **s** to your people,
33:13 I **s** to the righteous that they shall surely live,
33:14 Again, though I **s** to the wicked,
33:17 Yet your people **s,** "The way of the Lord is
33:20 Yet you **s,** "The way of the Lord is not just."
33:25 Therefore **s** to them, Thus says the Lord GOD:
33:27 **S** this to them, Thus says the Lord GOD:
33:30 and at the doors of the houses, **s** to one another,
33:32 they hear what you **s,** but they will not do it.
34: 2 prophesy, and **s** to them—
35: 3 and **s** to it, Thus says the Lord GOD:
36: 1 mortal, prophesy to the mountains of Israel, and **s:**
36: 3 therefore prophesy, and **s:**
36: 6 and **s** to the mountains and hills,
36:13 Thus says the Lord GOD: Because they **s** to you,
36:22 **s** to the house of Israel, Thus says the Lord GOD:
36:35 And they will **s,** "This land
37: 4 "Prophesy to these bones, and **s** to them:
37: 9 prophesy, mortal, and **s** to the breath:
37:11 They **s,** 'Our bones are dried up,
37:12 Therefore prophesy, and **s** to them,
37:18 And when your people **s** to you,
37:19 **s** to them, Thus says the Lord GOD:
37:21 then **s** to them, Thus says the Lord GOD:
38: 3 and **s:** Thus says the Lord GOD:
38:11 You will **s,** "I will go up against the land
38:13 of Tarshish and all its young warriors will **s**
38:14 Therefore, mortal, prophesy, and **s** to Gog:
39: 1 And you, mortal, prophesy against Gog, and **s:**
44: 6 **S** to the rebellious house, to the house of Israel,
Da 4:35 There is no one who can stay his hand or **s** to him,
Hos 2: 1 **S** to your brother, Ammi, and to your sister,
2: 7 Then she shall **s,** "I will go and return
2:23 and I will **s** to Lo-ammi, "You are my people";
2:23 and he shall **s,** "You are my God."
10: 3 now they will **s:** "We have no king,
10: 8 They shall **s** to the mountains, Cover us,
13: 2 "Sacrifice to these," they **s.**
14: 2 **s** to him, "Take away all guilt;
14: 3 we will **s** no more, 'Our God,'
Joel 2:17 Let them **s,** "Spare your people, O LORD,
3:10 let the weakling **s,** "I am a warrior."
Am 3: 9 and to the strongholds in the land of Egypt, and **s,**
4: 1 who crush the needy, who **s** to their husbands,
5:16 and in all the streets they shall **s,** "Alas!
6:10 and shall **s** to someone in the innermost parts of
6:10 Then the relative shall **s,** "Hush!
6:13 in Lo-debar, who **s,** "Have we not
7:16 You **s,** 'Do not prophesy against Israel,
8:14 Those who swear by Ashimah of Samaria, and **s,**
9:10 who **s,** "Evil shall not overtake or meet us."
Ob 1: 3 You **s** in your heart, "Who will bring me down to
Mic 2: 4 and wail with bitter lamentation, and **s,**
3:11 yet they lean upon the LORD and **s,**
4: 2 and many nations shall come and **s:**
Na 3: 7 Then all who see you will shrink from you and **s,**
Hab 2: 1 I will keep watch to see what he will **s** to me,
2: 6 with mocking riddles, **s** about them,
2:19 Alas for you who **s** to the wood, "Wake up!"
Zep 1:12 those who **s** in their hearts,
Hag 1: 2 These people **s** the time has not yet come
2: 2 and to the remnant of the people, and **s,**
Zec 1: 3 **s** to them, Thus says the LORD of hosts:
2: 4 "Run, **s** to that young man:
6:12 **s** to him: Thus says the LORD of hosts:
7: 5 **S** to all the people of the land and the priests:
11: 5 and those who sell them **s,**
12: 5 Then the clans of Judah shall **s** to themselves,
13: 3 their fathers and mothers who bore them will **s**
13: 5 of them will **s,** "I am no prophet, I am a tiller of
13: 9 I will **s,** "They are my people";
13: 9 and they will **s,** "The LORD is our God."
Mal 1: 2 But you **s,** "How have you loved us?"
1: 5 Your own eyes shall see this, and you shall **s,**
1: 6 You **s,** "How have we despised your name?"
1: 7 And you **s,** "How have we polluted it?"
1:12 when you **s** that the Lord's table is polluted,
1:13 "What a weariness this is," you **s,**
2:17 Yet you **s,** "How have we wearied him?"
3: 7 But you **s,** "How shall we return?"
3: 8 But you **s,** "How are we robbing you?"
3:13 Yet you **s,** "How have we spoken against you?"
Mt 3: 9 Do not presume to **s** to yourselves,
5:22 But I **s** to you that if you are angry with a brother
5:22 if you **s,** 'You fool,' you will be liable to the hell
5:28 But I **s** to you that everyone who looks at a woman
5:32 But I **s** to you that anyone who divorces his wife,
5:34 But I **s** to you, Do not swear at all,
5:39 But I **s** to you, Do not resist an evildoer.
5:44 But I **s** to you, Love your enemies and pray
7: 4 Or how can you **s** to your neighbor,
7:22 On that day many will **s** to me, 'Lord, Lord,
8: 4 "See that you **s** nothing to anyone;
8: 9 and I **s** to one, 'Go,' and he goes, and to another,
9: 5 For which is easier, to **s,** 'Your sins are forgiven,'
or to **s,** 'Stand up and walk'?
10:19 about how you are to speak or what you are to **s;**
10:19 what you are to **s** will be given to you at that time;
10:27 What I **s** to you in the dark, tell in the light;
11:18 John came neither eating nor drinking, and they **s,**
11:19 and they **s,** 'Look, a glutton and a drunkard,
15: 5 But you **s** that whoever tells father or mother,
16: 2 He answered them, "When it is evening, you **s,**
16:13 "Who do people **s** that the Son of Man is?"
16:14 And they said, "Some **s** John the Baptist,
16:15 He said to them, "But who do you **s** that I am?"
17:10 then, do the scribes **s** that Elijah must come first?"
17:20 you will **s** to this mountain,
19: 9 And I **s** to you, whoever divorces his wife,
21: 3 If anyone says anything to you, just **s** this,
21:21 but even if you **s** to this mountain,
21:25 "If we **s,** 'From heaven,' he will **s** to us, 'Why then
21:26 But if we **s,** 'Of human origin,'
23:16 "Woe to you, blind guides, who **s,**
23:18 And you **s,** 'Whoever swears by the altar is bound
23:30 and you **s,** 'If we had lived in the days
23:39 I tell you, you will not see me again until you **s,**
24:26 So, if they **s** to you, 'Look! He is in the
24:26 If they **s,** 'Look! He is in the inner rooms,'
25:34 Then the king will **s** to those at his right hand,
25:41 Then he will **s** to those at his left hand,
26:18 and **s** to him, 'The Teacher says, My time is near;
26:22 And they became greatly distressed and began to **s**
26:54 which **s** it must happen in this way?"
27:11 Jesus said, "You **s** so."
28:13 "You must **s,** 'His disciples came by night
Mk 1:44 "See that you **s** nothing to anyone;
2: 9 Which is easier, to **s** to the paralytic, 'Your sins
2: 9 or to **s,** 'Stand up and take your mat and walk'?
2:11 "I **s** to you, stand up, take your mat and go
5:31 how can you **s,** 'Who touched me?' "
5:35 some people came from the leader's house to **s,**
7:11 But you **s** that if anyone tells father or mother,
8:27 "Who do people **s** that I am?"
8:29 He asked them, "But who do you **s** that I am?"
9: 6 He did not know what to **s,** for they were terrified.
9:11 the scribes **s** that Elijah must come first?"
10:28 Peter began to **s** to him, "Look,
10:47 he began to shout out and **s,** "Jesus, Son of David,
11: 3 just **s** this, 'The Lord needs it
11:23 Truly I tell you, if you **s** to this mountain,
11:23 but believe that what you **s** will come to pass,
11:31 "If we **s,** 'From heaven,' he will **s,** 'Why then did
11:32 But shall we **s,** 'Of human origin'?"—
12:18 Some Sadducees, who **s** there is no resurrection,
12:35 "How can the scribes **s** that the Messiah is the son
12:40 and for the sake of appearance **s** long prayers.
13: 5 Then Jesus began to **s** to them,
13: 6 Many will come in my name and **s,** 'I am he!'
13:11 do not worry beforehand about what you are to **s;**
13:11 but **s** whatever is given you at that time,
13:37 And what I **s** to you I **s** to all: Keep awake."
14:14 **s** to the owner of the house, 'The Teacher asks,
14:19 to be distressed and to **s** to him one after another,
14:40 and they did not know what to **s** to him.
14:58 "We heard him **s,** 'I will destroy this temple
14:69 on seeing him, began again to **s** to the bystanders,
15: 2 He answered him, "You **s** so."
Lk 3: 8 Do not begin to **s** to yourselves,
4:21 Then he began to **s** to them,
4:23 And you will **s,** 'Do here also in your hometown
5: 5 Yet if you **s** so, I will let down the nets."
5:23 Which is easier, to **s,** 'Your sins are forgiven you,'
or to **s,** 'Stand up and walk'?
5:24 "I **s** to you, stand up and take your bed and go
6:27 "But I **s** to you that listen, Love your enemies,
6:42 Or how can you **s** to your neighbor, 'Friend,
7: 6 the centurion sent friends to **s** to him, "Lord,
7: 8 and I **s** to one, 'Go,' and he goes, and to another,
7:14 And he said, "Young man, I **s** to you, rise!"
7:33 and you **s,** 'He has a demon';
7:34 and you **s,** 'Look, a glutton and a drunkard,
7:40 "Simon, I have something to **s** to you."
7:49 the table with him began to **s** among themselves,
8:49 someone came from the leader's house to **s,**
9:18 he asked them, "Who do the crowds **s** that I am?"
9:20 He said to them, "But who do you **s** that I am?"
9:61 but let me first **s** farewell to those at my home."
10: 5 Whatever house you enter, first **s,**
10: 9 and **s** to them, 'The kingdom of God has come
10:10 go out into its streets and **s,**
11: 2 He said to them, "When you pray, **s:**
11: 5 and you go to him at midnight and **s** to him,
11: 9 "So I **s** to you, Ask, and it will be given you;
11:18 you **s** that I cast out the demons by Beelzebul.
11:29 When the crowds were increasing, he began to **s,**
11:45 when you **s** these things, you insult us too."
11:54 to catch him in something he might **s.**
12:11 to defend yourselves or what you are to **s;**
12:12 at that very hour what you ought to **s."**
12:19 And I will **s** to my soul, 'Soul,
12:54 you immediately **s,** 'It is going to rain';
12:55 And when you see the south wind blowing, you **s,**
13:25 'Lord, open to us,' then in reply he will **s** to you,
13:26 Then you will begin to **s,**
13:27 he will **s,** 'I do not know where you come from;
13:35 not see me until the time comes when you **s,**
14: 9 the host who invited both of you may come and **s**
14:10 so that when your host comes, he may **s** to you,
14:17 At the time for the dinner he sent his slave to **s**
15:18 and I will **s** to him, "Father, I have sinned
17: 6 you could **s** to this mulberry tree,
17: 7 "Who among you would **s** to your slave
17: 8 Would you not rather **s** to him,
17:10 **s,** 'We are worthless slaves;
17:21 nor will they **s,** 'Look, here it is!'
17:23 They will **s** to you, 'Look there!'
19:31 just **s** this, 'The Lord needs it.' "
20: 5 "If we **s,** 'From heaven,' he will **s,** "Why did you
20: 6 But if we **s,** 'Of human origin,'
20:21 that you are right in what you **s** and teach,
20:27 those who **s** there is no resurrection,
20:41 "How can they **s** that the Messiah is David's son?
20:47 and for the sake of appearance **s** long prayers.
21: 8 for many will come in my name and **s,** 'I am he!'
22:11 and **s** to the owner of the house,
22:70 He said to them, "You **s** that I am."
23: 3 He answered, "You **s** so."
23:29 For the days are surely coming when they will **s,**
23:30 they will begin to **s** to the mountains, 'Fall on us';
Jn 1:22 What do you **s** about yourself?"
1:37 The two disciples heard him **s** this,
4:20 but you **s** that the place
4:35 Do you not **s,** 'Four months more,
5:34 but I **s** these things so that you may be saved.
5:47 how will you believe what I **s?"**
6:14 they began to **s,** "This is indeed the prophet who is
6:42 can he now **s,** 'I have come down from heaven'?"
7:26 speaking openly, but they **s** nothing to him!
8: 5 ⟦to stone such women. Now what do you **s?"**⟧
8:26 I have much to **s** about you and much to condemn;
8:43 Why do you not understand what I **s?**
8:52 Abraham died, and so did the prophets; yet you **s,**
8:54 he of whom you **s,** 'He is our God,'
8:55 if I would **s** that I do not know him,
9:17 "What do you **s** about him?
9:19 "Is this your son, who you **s** was born blind?
9:41 But now that you **s,** 'We see,' your sin remains.
10:36 can you **s** that the one whom
11:51 He did not **s** this on his own,
12:27 what should I **s**—'Father, save me from this hour'?
12:34 can you **s** that the Son of Man must be lifted up?
12:49 a commandment about what to **s** and what
13:33 and as I said to the Jews so now I **s** to you,
14: 9 How can you **s,** 'Show us the Father'?
14:10 words that I **s** to you I do not speak on my own;
14:28 You heard me **s** to you, 'I am going away,
16: 4 "I did not **s** these things to you from the beginning,
16:12 "I still have many things to **s** to you,
16:26 I do not **s** to you that I will ask the Father
18:37 Jesus answered, "You **s** that I am a king.
20:17 But go to my brothers and **s** to them,
21:23 Yet Jesus did not **s** to him that he would not die,
Ac 2:14 let this be known to you, and listen to what I **s.**
2:22 "You that are Israelites, listen to what I have to **s:**
2:29 I may **s** to you confidently of our ancestor David
4:14 they had nothing to **s** in opposition.
6:11 Then they secretly instigated some men to **s,**
6:14 for we have heard him **s** that this Jesus
8:34 may I ask you, does the prophet **s** this,
10:22 to his house and to hear what you have to **s."**
10:33 to all that the Lord has commanded you to **s."**
17:18 Some said, "What does this babbler want to **s?"**
21:14 we remained silent except to **s,**
21:37 "May I **s** something to you?"
23: 8 (The Sadducees **s** that there is no resurrection,
28: 6 they changed their minds and began to **s** that he

Ac 28:26 'Go to this people and s,
Ro 2: 2 You s, "We know that God's judgment
3: 5 to confirm the justice of God, what should we s?
3: 8 And why not s (as some people slander us
3: 8 (as some people slander us by saying that we s),
4: 1 What then are we to s was gained by Abraham,
4: 3 For what does the scripture s?
4: 9 We s, "Faith was reckoned to Abraham
6: 1 What then are we to s?
7: 7 What then should we s?
8:31 What then are we to s about these things?
9:14 What then are we to s?
9:19 You will s to me then,
9:20 Will what is molded s to the one who molds it,
9:30 What then are we to s?
10: 6 "Do not s in your heart,
10: 8 But what does it s?
10:20 Then Isaiah is so bold as to s,
11:19 You will s, "Branches were broken off so
12: 3 the grace given to me I s to everyone among you
1Co 1:15 no one can s that you were baptized in my name.
6: 3 to s nothing of ordinary matters?
6: 5 I s this to your shame.
7: 6 This I s by way of concession, not of command.
7: 8 To the unmarried and the widows I s that it is well
7:12 To the rest I s—I and not the Lord—
7:35 I s this for your own benefit,
9: 8 Do I s this on human authority?
9: 8 Does not the law also s the same?
10:15 judge for yourselves what I s.
11:22 What should I s to you?
12: 3 and no one can s "Jesus is Lord" except by
12:15 If the foot would s, "Because I am not a hand,
12:16 And if the ear would s, "Because I am not an eye,
12:21 The eye cannot s to the hand,
14:16 Otherwise, if you s a blessing with the spirit,
14:16 of an outsider s the "Amen" to your thanksgiving,
14:23 will they not s that you are out of your mind?
15:12 how can some of you s there is no resurrection of
15:34 I s this to your shame.
2Co 1:17 ready to s "Yes, yes" and "No,
1:20 this reason it is through him that we s the "Amen,"
7: 3 I do not s this to condemn you,
8: 8 I do not s this as a command,
9: 4 to s nothing of you—in this undertaking.
10:10 For they s, "His letters are weighty and strong,
10:11 Let such people understand that what we s
11:21 I must s, we were too weak for that!
12:16 (you s) since I was crafty, I took you in by deceit.
Gal 3:16 it does not s, "And to offsprings," as of many;
4:30 But what does the scripture s?
5:16 I s, and do not gratify the desires of the flesh.
Php 4: 4 Rejoice in the Lord always; again I will s, Rejoice.
Col 4:17 And s to Archippus, "See that you complete
1Th 5: 3 When they s, "There is peace and security,"
2Th 3:14 of those who do not obey what we s in this letter;
1Ti 5:13 saying what they should not s.
2Ti 2: 7 Think over what I s, for the Lord will give you
Tit 2: 8 having nothing evil to s of us.
Phm 1:19 I s nothing about your owing me
1:21 knowing that you will do even more than I s.
Heb 1: 5 For to which of the angels did God ever s,
5:11 About this we have much to s that is hard
7: 9 One might even s that Levi himself,
8:11 they shall not teach one another or s to each other,
11:32 And what more should I s?
13: 6 we can s with confidence, "The Lord is my helper;
Jas 1:13 No one, when tempted, should s,
2: 3 of the one wearing the fine clothes and s,
2: 3 while to the one who is poor you s, "Stand there,"
2:14 if you s you have faith but do not have works?
2:18 But someone will s, "You have faith
4:13 now, you who s, "Today or tomorrow we will go
4:15 Instead you ought to s, "If the Lord wishes,
1Jn 1: 6 If we s that we have fellowship with him
1: 8 If we s that we have no sin, we deceive ourselves,
1:10 If we s that we have not sinned,
4: 5 therefore what they s is from the world,
4:20 Those who s, "I love God,"
5:16 I do not s that you should pray about that.
Rev 2: 9 the part of those who s that they are Jews and are
2:24 to you I s, I do not lay on you any other burden;
3: 9 of the synagogue of Satan who s that they are Jews
3:17 For you s, 'I am rich, I have prospered,
16: 5 And I heard the angel of the waters s,
18:10 and s, "Alas, alas, the great city, Babylon,
22:17 The Spirit and the bride s, "Come."
22:17 And let everyone who hears s, "Come."
Tob 2: 3 Then he went on to s, "Look, father,
5:21 in good health. S no more!
6:16 brother, and s no more about this demon.
6:18 as brothers to you. Now s no more!"
Jdt 7: 9 "Listen to what we have to s,
7:31 and no help comes for us, I will do as you s."
11: 5 I will s nothing false to my lord this night.
AdE 4:10 And she said to him, "Go to Mordecai and s,
4:13 Mordecai told him to go back and s to her,
4:13 do not s to yourself that you alone among all
Wis 5: 3 and in anguish of spirit they will groan, and s,
12:12 For who will s, "What have you done?"
15:12 for they s one must get money however one can,
Sir 5: 1 Do not rely on your wealth, or s, "I have enough."
5: 3 Do not s, "Who can have power over me?"
5: 4 Do not s, "I sinned, yet what has happened
5: 6 Do not s, "His mercy is great,
5:12 If you know what to s, answer your neighbor;
7: 9 Do not s, "He will consider the great number
Sir 11:23 Do not s, "What do I need,
11:24 Do not s, "I have enough,
13: 6 he will speak to you kindly and s,
13:23 The poor person speaks and they s,
15:11 not s, "It was the Lord's doing that I fell away";
15:12 Do not s, "It was he who led me astray";
16:17 Do not s, "I am hidden from the Lord,
19:14 Question a neighbor; perhaps he did not s it;
20: 6 because they have nothing to s,
22:10 and at the end he will s, "What is it?"
31:12 Do not be greedy at it, and do not s,
32: 8 Be brief; s much in few words;
33: 4 Prepare what to s, and then you will be listened to;
36:12 Crush the heads of hostile rulers who s,
39:15 this is what you shall s in thanksgiving:
39:17 No one can s, 'What is this?'
39:21 No one can s, 'What is this?'
39:34 No one can s, "This is not as good as that,"
43:27 We could s more but could never s enough;
51:24 Why do you s you are lacking in these things,
Bar 1:15 And you shall s: The Lord our God is in the
LtJ 6: 6 But s in your heart, "It is you, O Lord,
1Mc 9:55 and he was paralyzed, so that he could no longer s
13: 9 and all that you s to us we will do."
13:17 among the people, who might s,
1Es 8:82 "And now, O Lord, what shall we s,
2Es 1:12 "But speak to them and s, Thus says the Lord:
2:34 Therefore I s to you, O nations that hear
5:46 He said to me, "Ask a woman's womb, and s to it,
5:52 S to her, 'Why are those whom you have borne
6:33 and to s to you: 'Believe and do not be afraid!
7:37 Then the Most High will s to the nations
7:45 "O sovereign Lord, I said then and I s now:
7:55 S to her, 'You produce gold and silver and bronze,
7:73 What, then, will they have to s in the judgment,
9:15 and I s now, and will s it again:
10:12 But if you s to me, 'My lamentation is not like
10:14 then I s to you, 'Just as you brought forth
14: 7 And now I s to you:
16:53 Sinners must not s that they have not sinned;
4Mc 2:24 How is it then, one might s,
4:26 I s, his decrees were despised by the people,
7:17 Some perhaps might s,
13: 2 we would s that they had been conquered

SAYING‡ (814) [SAY]

Ge 1:22 s, "Be fruitful and multiply and fill the waters in
4: 1 and she conceived and bore Cain, s,
5:29 s, "Out of the ground that
15:18 s, "To your descendants I give this land,
18:12 So Sarah laughed to herself, s,
18:15 But Sarah denied, s, "I did not laugh";
19:15 When morning dawned, the angels urged Lot, s,
24:37 My master made me swear, s,
26:11 So Abimelech warned all the people, s,
26:20 of Gerar quarreled with Isaac's herders, s,
26:22 so he called it Rehoboth, s,
28:20 Then Jacob made a vow, s,
30:24 s, "May the LORD add to me another son!"
31: 1 Now Jacob heard that the sons of Laban were s,
31:29 the God of your father spoke to me last night, s,
32: 6 The messengers returned to Jacob, s,
32:30 So Jacob called the place Peniel, s,
34: 4 So Shechem spoke to his father Hamor, s,
34: 8 But Hamor spoke with them, s,
34:20 of their city and spoke to the men of their city, s,
37: 9 s, "Look, I have had another dream:
37:21 he delivered him out of their hands, s,
38:28 s, "This one came out first."
39:12 she caught hold of his garment, s, "Lie with me!"
39:17 s, "The Hebrew servant, whom you have brought
39:19 s, "This is the way your servant treated me,"
42:28 s, "What is this that God has done to us?"
42:29 they told him all that had happened to them, s,
43: 3 "The man solemnly warned us, s,
43: 7 s, 'Is your father still alive?
44:19 My lord asked his servants, s,
44:32 s, 'If I do not bring him back to you,
48:20 So he blessed them that day, s,
48:20 saying, "By you Israel will invoke blessings, s,
49:29 Then he charged them, s to them,
50:16 So they approached Joseph, s,
50:25 So Joseph made the Israelites swear, s,
Ex 3:16 of Isaac, and of Jacob, has appeared to me, s:
5:13 The taskmasters were urgent, s,
9: 5 s, "Tomorrow the LORD will do this thing in
11: 8 and bow low to me, s, 'Leave us,
13:19 s, "God will surely take notice of you,
15:24 And the people complained against Moses, s,
17: 7 s, "Is the LORD among us or not?"
19: 3 the LORD called to him from the mountain, s,
19:12 You shall set limits for the people all around, s,
19:23 for you yourself warned us, s,
32:13 s to them, 'I will multiply your descendants like
33: 1 and Jacob, s, 'To your descendants I will give it.'
Lev 1: 1 and spoke to him from the tent of meeting, s:
4: 1 The LORD spoke to Moses, s,
4: 2 Speak to the people of Israel, s:
5:14 The LORD spoke to Moses, s:
6: 1 The LORD spoke to Moses, s:
6: 8 The LORD spoke to Moses, s:
6: 9 s: This is the ritual of the burnt offering.
6:19 The LORD spoke to Moses, s:
6:24 The LORD spoke to Moses, s:
6:25 s: This is the ritual of the sin offering.
7:22 The LORD spoke to Moses, s:
Lev 7:23 s: You shall eat no fat of ox or sheep or goat.
7:28 The LORD spoke to Moses, s:
7:29 Speak to the people of Israel, s:
8: 1 The LORD spoke to Moses, s:
11: 1 The LORD spoke to Moses and Aaron, s to them:
11: 2 Speak to the people of Israel, s:
12: 1 The LORD spoke to Moses, s:
12: 2 Speak to the people of Israel, s:
13: 1 The LORD spoke to Moses and Aaron, s:
14: 1 The LORD spoke to Moses, s:
14:33 The LORD spoke to Moses and Aaron, s:
14:35 s, "There seems to me to be some sort of disease
15: 1 The LORD spoke to Moses and Aaron, s:
18: 1 The LORD spoke to Moses, s:
19: 1 The LORD spoke to Moses, s:
20: 1 The LORD spoke to Moses, s:
21:16 The LORD spoke to Moses, s:
22: 1 The LORD spoke to Moses, s:
22:17 The LORD spoke to Moses, s:
22:26 The LORD spoke to Moses, s:
23: 1 The LORD spoke to Moses, s:
23:23 The LORD spoke to Moses, s:
23:24 Speak to the people of Israel, s:
23:26 The LORD spoke to Moses, s:
23:33 The LORD spoke to Moses, s:
23:34 Speak to the people of Israel, s:
24: 1 The LORD spoke to Moses, s:
24:13 The LORD said to Moses, s:
24:15 And speak to the people of Israel, s:
25: 1 The LORD spoke to Moses on Mount Sinai, s:
27: 1 The LORD spoke to Moses, s:
Nu 1: 1 after they had come out of the land of Egypt, s:
2: 1 The LORD spoke to Moses and Aaron, s:
3: 5 Then the LORD spoke to Moses, s:
3:11 Then the LORD spoke to Moses, s:
3:14 to Moses in the wilderness of Sinai, s:
3:44 Then the LORD spoke to Moses, s:
4: 1 The LORD spoke to Moses and Aaron, s:
4:17 Then the LORD spoke to Moses and Aaron, s:
4:21 Then the LORD spoke to Moses, s:
5: 1 The LORD spoke to Moses, s:
5: 5 The LORD spoke to Moses, s:
5:11 The LORD spoke to Moses, s:
5:19 Then the priest shall make her take an oath, s,
6: 1 The LORD spoke to Moses, s:
6:22 The LORD spoke to Moses, s:
6:23 s, Thus you shall bless the Israelites:
8: 1 The LORD spoke to Moses, s:
8: 5 The LORD spoke to Moses, s:
8:23 The LORD spoke to Moses, s:
9: 1 after they had come out of the land of Egypt, s:
9: 9 The LORD spoke to Moses, s:
9:10 Speak to the Israelites, s: Anyone of you
10: 1 The LORD spoke to Moses, s:
11:18 you have wailed in the hearing of the LORD, s,
11:20 s, 'Why did we ever leave Egypt?' "
13:32 s, "The land that we have gone through as spies is
14:17 in the way that you promised when you spoke, s,
14:26 And the LORD spoke to Moses and to Aaron, s:
14:40 and went up to the heights of the hill country, s,
15: 1 The LORD spoke to Moses, s:
15:17 The LORD spoke to Moses, s:
16:20 Then the LORD spoke to Moses and to Aaron, s:
16:23 And the LORD spoke to Moses, s:
16:36 Then the LORD spoke to Moses, s:
16:41 s, "You have killed the people of the LORD."
16:44 and the LORD spoke to Moses, s,
17: 1 The LORD spoke to Moses, s:
18:25 Then the LORD spoke to Moses, s:
18:26 You shall speak to the Levites, s:
19: 1 The LORD spoke to Moses and Aaron, s:
20: 7 The LORD spoke to Moses, s:
21:21 to King Sihon of the Amorites, s,
22: 5 in the land of Amaw, to summon him, s,
23: 7 Then Balaam uttered his oracle, s:
23:18 Then Balaam uttered his oracle, s:
24: 3 and he uttered his oracle, s:
24:15 So he uttered his oracle, s:
24:20 he looked on Amalek, and uttered his oracle, s:
24:21 he looked on the Kenite, and uttered his oracle, s:
24:23 Again he uttered his oracle, s:
25:10 The LORD spoke to Moses, s:
26: 3 of Moab by the Jordan opposite Jericho, s,
26:52 The LORD spoke to Moses, s:
27: 6 And the LORD spoke to Moses, s:
27: 7 of Zelophehad are right in what they are s;
27:15 Moses spoke to the LORD, s,
28: 1 The LORD spoke to Moses, s:
31: 1 The LORD spoke to Moses, s,
31:25 The LORD spoke to Moses, s,
32: 2 and to the leaders of the congregation, s,
32:10 on that day and he swore, s,
33:50 the LORD spoke to Moses, s:
34: 1 The LORD spoke to Moses, s:
34:13 Moses commanded the Israelites, s:
34:16 The LORD spoke to Moses, s:
35: 1 the LORD spoke to Moses, s:
35: 9 The LORD spoke to Moses, s:
36: 5 s, "The descendants of the tribe of Joseph are right
in what they are s.
Dt 1: 6 s, "You have stayed long enough at this mountain.
1:37 with me the LORD was angry on your account, s,
2:17 the LORD spoke to me, s,
3:21 And I charged Joshua as well at that time, s:
3:23 At that time, too, I entreated the LORD, s:
9:23 when the LORD sent you from Kadesh-barnea, s,
12:30 do not inquire concerning their gods, s,

Dt 13: 6 **s**, "Let us go worship other gods,"
13:13 **s**, "Let us go and worship other gods,"
20: 5 Then the officials shall address the troops, **s**,
20: 8 officials shall continue to address the troops, **s**,
22:14 slandering her by **s**, "I married this woman;
22:17 up charges against her, **s**, 'I did not find evidence
25: 8 If he persists, **s**, "I have no desire to marry her,"
27: 9 **s**: Keep silence and hear, O Israel!
27:15 All the people shall respond, **s**, "Amen!"
31:25 the ark of the covenant of the LORD, **s**,
34: 4 **s**, 'I will give it to your descendants';
Jos 1: 1 to Joshua son of Nun, Moses' assistant, **s**,
1:13 **s**, 'The LORD your God is providing you a place
2: 1 **s**, "Go, view the land, especially Jericho."
4:21 **s** to the Israelites, "When your children ask their
6:26 Joshua then pronounced this oath, **s**,
9:22 and said to them, "Why did you deceive us, **s**,
10: 3 and to King Debir of Eglon, **s**,
10: 6 Gibeonites sent to Joshua at the camp in Gilgal, **s**,
14: 9 And Moses swore on that day, **s**,
17:14 The tribe of Joseph spoke to Joshua, **s**,
18: 8 **s**, "Go throughout the land and write a description
20: 1 Then the LORD spoke to Joshua, **s**,
Jdg 5: 1 and Barak son of Abinoam sang on that day, **s**:
6:13 **s**, 'Did not the LORD bring us up from Egypt?'
7: 2 Israel would only take the credit away from me, **s**,
7:24 of Ephraim, **s**, "Come down against the Midianites
8:15 about whom you taunted me, **s**,
9:31 He sent messengers to Abimelech at Arumah, **s**,
10:10 So the Israelites cried to the LORD, **s**,
11: 2 they drove Jephthah away, **s** to him,
11:17 Israel then sent messengers to the king of Edom, **s**,
14:16 Samson's wife wept before him, **s**, "You hate me;
15:18 and he called on the LORD, **s**,
16:18 she sent and called the lords of the Philistines, **s**,
19:30 Then he commanded the men whom he sent, **s**,
20: 8 All the people got up as one, **s**,
20:12 **s**, "What crime is this that has been committed
20:28 ministered before it in those days), **s**,
21: 5 **s**, "That one shall be put to death."
21:20 And they instructed the Benjaminites, **s**,
Ru 3:17 **s**, "He gave me these six measures of barley,
4:17 women of the neighborhood gave him a name, **s**,
1Sa 6:21 of Kiriath-jearim, **s**, "The Philistines have returned
10: 2 **s**: What shall I do about my son?'
11: 7 by messengers, **s**, "Whoever does not come out
13: 3 Saul blew the trumpet throughout all the land, **s**,
14:12 and his armor-bearer, **s**, "Come up to us,
14:24 He had laid an oath on the troops, **s**,
14:28 **s**, 'Cursed be anyone who eats food this day.'
16:22 **s**, "Let David remain in my service,
18: 8 Saul was very angry, for this **s** displeased him.
19: 4 **s** to him, "The king should not sin
20:16 the house of David, **s**, "May the LORD seek out
20:21 Then I will send the boy, **s**, 'Go, find the arrows.'
20:42 **s**, 'The LORD shall be between me and you,
23:27 a messenger came to Saul, **s**, "Hurry and come;
26: 1 Then the Ziphites came to Saul at Gibeah, **s**,
26:14 to the army and to Abner son of Ner, **s**,
26:19 from my share in the heritage of the LORD, **s**,
30:26 **s**, "Here is a present for you from the spoil of
2Sa 1:16 for your own mouth has testified against you, **s**,
3:12 Abner sent messengers to David at Hebron, **s**,
3:14 David sent messengers to Saul's son Ishbaal, **s**,
3:17 Abner sent word to the elders of Israel, **s**,
3:33 The king lamented for Abner, **s**,
3:35 but David swore, **s**, "So may God do to me,
7: 7 **s**, "Why have you not built me a house of cedar?"
7:26 Thus your name will be magnified forever in the **s**,
7:27 have made this revelation to your servant, **s**,
13: 7 Then David sent home to Tamar, **s**,
15:10 **s**, "As soon as you hear the sound of the trumpet,
15:13 A messenger came to David, **s**,
18: 5 The king ordered Joab and Abishai and Ittai, **s**,
18:12 **s**: For my sake protect the young man Absalom!
19: 9 **s**, "The king delivered us from the hand
24: 1 **s**, "Go, count the people of Israel and Judah."
24:11 to the prophet Gad, David's seer, **s**,
1Ki 1: 5 Now Adonijah son of Haggith exalted himself, **s**,
1:13 my lord the king, swear to your servant, **s**:
1:17 to your servant by the LORD your God, **s**:
1:25 and **s**, 'Long live King Adonijah!'
1:29 The king swore, **s**, "As the LORD lives,
1:47 to congratulate our lord King David, **s**,
1:51 see, he has laid hold of the horns of the altar, **s**,
2: 1 he charged his son Solomon, **s**:
2:29 Solomon sent Benaiah son of Jehoiada, **s**, "Go,
2:30 Then Benaiah brought the king word again, **s**,
2:42 and solemnly adjure you, **s**,
5: 2 Solomon sent word to Hiram, **s**,
8:15 with his mouth to my father David, **s**,
8:25 **s**, 'There shall never fail you a successor
8:47 and plead with you in the land of their captors, **s**,
9: 5 as I promised your father David, **s**,
12: 6 **s**, "How do you advise me to answer this people?"
13: 3 He gave a sign the same day, **s**,
13: 4 Jeroboam stretched out his hand from the altar, **s**,
13:30 they mourned over him, **s**, "Alas, my brother!"
13:32 For the **s** that he proclaimed by the word of
15:18 who resided in Damascus, **s**,
16: 1 to Jehu son of Hanani against Baasha, **s**,
17: 2 The word of the LORD came to him, **s**,
17: 8 Then the word of the LORD came to him, **s**,
18: 1 in the third year of the drought, **s**, "Go,
18:27 At noon Elijah mocked them, **s**, "Cry aloud!
18:31 to whom the word of the LORD came, **s**,
19: 2 Then Jezebel sent a messenger to Elijah, **s**,
1Ki 19: 9 Then the word of the LORD came to him, **s**,
20: 5 **s**, 'Deliver to me your silver and gold,
21:10 and have them bring a charge against him, **s**,
21:13 **s**, "Naboth cursed God and the king."
21:14 they sent to Jezebel, **s**, "Naboth has been stoned;
21:17 word of the LORD came to Elijah the Tishbite, **s**:
22:12 All the prophets were prophesying the same and **s**,
22:21 and stood before the LORD, **s**,
2Ki 2:14 and struck the water, **s**, "Where is the LORD,
2:23 of the city and jeered at him, **s**,
5:10 Elisha sent a messenger to him, **s**, "Go,
5:11 But Naaman became angry and went away, **s**,
7:14 and the king sent them after the Aramean army, **s**,
8: 4 of the man of God, **s**, "Tell me all the great things
8: 6 So the king appointed an official for her, **s**,
8: 9 **s**, 'Shall I recover from this illness?' "
9: 6 young man poured the oil on his head, **s** to him,
9:18 **s**, "The messenger reached them,
9:23 Then Joram reined about and fled, **s** to Ahaziah,
9:27 Jehu pursued him, **s**, "Shoot him also!"
10: 1 and to the guardians of the sons of Ahab, **s**,
10: 6 Then he wrote them a second letter, **s**,
10:24 Now Jehu had stationed eighty men outside, **s**,
14: 8 **s**, "Come, let us look one another in the face."
14: 9 **s**, 'Give your daughter to my son for a wife';
16: 7 **s**, "I am your servant and your son.
16:15 King Ahaz commanded the priest Uriah, **s**,
17:13 and Judah by every prophet and every seer, **s**,
18:14 of Judah sent to the king of Assyria at Lachish, **s**,
18:22 **s** to Judah and to Jerusalem,
18:30 by **s**, The LORD will surely deliver us,
18:32 not listen to Hezekiah when he misleads you by **s**,
19: 9 he sent messengers again to Hezekiah, **s**,
19:20 Then Isaiah son of Amoz sent to Hezekiah, **s**,
22: 3 the secretary, to the house of the LORD, **s**,
22:12 and the king's servant Asaiah, **s**,
25:24 Gedaliah swore to them and their men, **s**,
1Ch 4: 9 and his mother named him Jabez, **s**,
4:10 Jabez called on the God of Israel, **s**,
12:19 the Philistines took counsel and sent him away, **s**,
16:18 **s**, "To you I will give the land of Canaan
16:22 **s**, "Do not touch my anointed ones;
17: 3 the word of the LORD came to Nathan, **s**:
17: 6 **s**, Why have you not built me a house of cedar?
17:24 be established and magnified forever in the **s**,
21: 9 The LORD spoke to Gad, David's seer, **s**,
22: 8 But the word of the LORD came to me, **s**,
22:17 the leaders of Israel to help his son Solomon, **s**,
2Ch 6: 4 with his mouth to my father David, **s**,
6:16 my father David, that which you promised him, **s**,
6:37 and plead with you in the land of their captivity, **s**,
7: 3 and worshiped and gave thanks to the LORD, **s**,
7:18 as I made covenant with your father David **s**,
10: 6 **s**, "How do you advise me to answer this people?"
12: 7 the word of the LORD came to Shemaiah, **s**:
16: 2 who resided in Damascus, **s**,
18:11 All the prophets were prophesying the same and **s**,
18:20 and stood before the LORD, **s**,
20: 8 in it have built you a sanctuary for your name, **s**,
20:21 as they went before the army, **s**,
20:37 **s**, "Because you have joined with Ahaziah,
21:12 A letter came to him from the prophet Elijah, **s**:
23:14 **s** to them, "Bring her out between the ranks;
25:17 **s**, "Come, let us look one another in the face."
25:18 **s**, 'Give your daughter to my son for a wife';
30: 6 **s**, "O people of Israel, return to the LORD,
30:18 But Hezekiah prayed for them, **s**,
32: 4 the land, **s**, "Why should the Assyrian kings come
32: 6 of the city and spoke encouragingly to them, **s**,
32: 9 the people of Judah that were in Jerusalem, **s**,
32:12 **s**, 'Before one altar you shall worship,
32:17 the God of Israel and to speak against him, **s**, "Just
35:21 But Neco sent envoys to him, **s**,
Ezr 9:11 the prophets, **s**, 'The land that you are entering
10: 2 of the descendants of Elam, addressed Ezra, **s**,
Ne 2:19 **s**, "What is this that you are doing?
6: 2 to me, **s**, "Come and let us meet together in one of
6: 3 So I sent messengers to them, **s**,
6: 8 **s**, "No such things as you say have been done;
8:11 So the Levites stilled all the people, **s**, "Be quiet
13:25 I made them take an oath in the name of God, **s**,
Est 4:10 and gave him a message for Mordecai, **s**,
Job 8:18 then it will deny them, **s**, 'I have never seen you.'
15:23 They wander abroad for bread, **s**, 'Where is it?'
22:20 **s**, 'Surely our adversaries are cut off,
24:15 eye of the adulterer also waits for the twilight, **s**,
33:13 Why do you contend against him, **s**,
Ps 2: 2 against the LORD and his anointed, **s**,
2: 5 and terrify them in his fury, **s**,
3: 2 many are **s** to me, "There is no help for you
22:31 **s** that he has done it.
52: 6 and fear, and will laugh at the evildoer, **s**,
78:19 They spoke against God, **s**,
105:11 **s**, "To you I will give the land of Canaan
105:15 **s**, "Do not touch my anointed ones;
137: 3 and our tormentors asked for mirth, **s**,
Isa 3: 6 a member of the clan, **s**, "You have a cloak;
3: 7 But the other will cry out on that day, **s**,
4: 1 **s**, "We will eat our own bread
6: 8 Then I heard the voice of the Lord **s**,
7: 5 has plotted evil against you, **s**,
7:10 Again the LORD spoke to Ahaz, **s**,
8:11 not to walk in the way of this people, **s**:
14: 8 **s**, "Since you were laid low,
19:25 **s**, "Blessed be Egypt my people,
20: 2 the LORD had spoken to Isaiah son of Amoz, **s**,
23: 4 for the sea has spoken, the fortress of the sea, **s**:
Isa 29:12 And if it is given to those who cannot read, **s**,
30:21 your ears shall hear a word behind you, **s**,
36: 7 **s** to Judah and to Jerusalem,
36:15 by **s**, The LORD will surely deliver us;
36:18 Do not let Hezekiah mislead you by **s**,
37: 9 he heard it, he sent messengers to Hezekiah, **s**,
37:15 And Hezekiah prayed to the LORD, **s**:
37:21 Then Isaiah son of Amoz sent to Hezekiah, **s**:
41: 6 Each one helps the other, **s** to one another,
41: 7 **s** of the soldering, "It is good";
41: 9 and called from its farthest corners, **s** to you,
45:14 They will make supplication to you, **s**,
46:10 **s**, "My purpose shall stand,
49: 9 **s** to the prisoners, "Come out," to those who are
51:16 and **s** to Zion, "You are my people."
Jer 1: 4 Now the word of the LORD came to me **s**,
1:11 The word of the LORD came to me, **s**, "Jeremiah,
1:13 word of the LORD came to me a second time, **s**,
2: 1 The word of the LORD came to me, **s**:
2:35 Now I am bringing you to judgment for **s**,
4:10 **s**, 'It shall be well with you,'
6:14 **s**, "Peace, peace," when there is no peace.
8: 6 no one repents of wickedness, **s**,
8:11 **s**, "Peace, peace," when there is no peace.
11: 4 from the iron-smelter, **s**, Listen to my voice,
11: 7 warning them persistently, even to this day, **s**,
11:19 **s**, "Let us destroy the tree with its fruit,
13: 3 word of the LORD came to me a second time, **s**,
14:13 Here are the prophets **s** to them,
20:15 **s**, "A child is born to you, a son,"
21: 1 and the priest Zephaniah son of Maaseiah, **s**,
22:18 They shall not lament for him, **s**, "Alas,
22:18 They shall not lament for him, **s**, "Alas, lord!"
23:17 They keep **s** to those who despise the word of
23:25 **s**, "I have dreamed, I have dreamed!"
23:38 "the burden of the LORD," when I sent to you, **s**,
26: 8 the prophets and all the people laid hold of him, **s**,
26: 9 **s**, 'This house shall be like Shiloh,
26:12 **s**, "It is the LORD who sent me to prophesy
27: 9 or your sorcerers, who are **s** to you,
27:16 Then I spoke to the priests and to all this people, **s**,
27:16 of your prophets who are prophesying to you, **s**,
28: 1 in the presence of the priests and all the people, **s**,
28:11 **s**, "Thus says the LORD:
29:25 of Maaseiah, and to all the priests, **s**,
29:28 For he has actually sent to us in Babylon, **s**,
29:31 **s**, Thus says the LORD concerning Shemaiah
32:13 In their presence I charged Baruch, **s**,
32:16 I prayed to the LORD, **s**:
32:43 in this land of which you are **s**, It is a desolation,
34: 5 for you and lament for you, **s**,
34:13 out of the house of slavery, **s**,
35:15 **s**, 'Turn now everyone of you from your evil way,
36: 5 And Jeremiah ordered Baruch, **s**,
36:29 You have dared to burn this scroll, **s**,
37: 3 of Maaseiah to the prophet Jeremiah **s**,
37: 9 Do not deceive yourselves, **s**,
37:13 of Hananiah arrested the prophet Jeremiah **s**,
37:19 are your prophets who prophesied to you, **s**,
38: 1 of Malchiah heard the words that Jeremiah was **s**
38:22 and **s**, 'Your trusted friends have seduced you
39:11 the captain of the guard, **s**,
40: 9 **s**, "Do not be afraid to serve the Chaldeans.
42:14 and **s**, 'No, we will go to the land of Egypt,
42:20 **s**, 'Pray for us to the LORD our God,
44: 4 to you all my servants the prophets, **s**, "I beg you
44:25 in deeds what you declared in words, **s**,
44:26 **s**, 'As the Lord GOD lives.'
49: 4 You trusted in your treasures, **s**,
Eze 9: 1 Then he cried in my hearing with a loud voice, **s**,
9:11 **s**, "I have done as you commanded me."
12:27 the house of Israel is **s**, "The vision that he sees is
13:10 in truth, because they have misled my people, **s**,
20: 5 I swore to them, **s**, I am the LORD your God.
20:49 they are **s** of me, 'Is he not a maker
22:28 seeing false visions and divining lies for them, **s**,
29: 3 **s**, "My Nile is my own; I made it for myself."
33:24 of these waste places in the land of Israel keep **s**,
35:12 **s**, "They are laid desolate,
Da 4:23 a holy watcher coming down from heaven and **s**,
6:13 but he is **s** his prayers three times a day."
9: 4 **s**, "Ah, Lord, great and awesome God,
Am 2:12 and commanded the prophets, **s**,
7:10 sent to King Jeroboam of Israel, **s**,
8: 5 **s**, "When will the new moon be over so
Jnh 1: 1 of the LORD came to Jonah son of Amittai, **s**,
2: 2 **s**, "I called to the LORD out of my distress,
3: 1 of the LORD came to Jonah a second time, **s**,
Mic 2:11 **s**, "I will preach to you of wine and strong drink,"
4:11 **s**, "Let her be profaned, and let our eyes gaze upon
Hag 1: 3 of the LORD came by the prophet Haggai, **s**:
1:13 spoke to the people with the LORD's message, **s**,
2: 1 of the LORD came by the prophet Haggai, **s**:
2:10 of the LORD came by the prophet Haggai, **s**:
2:21 **s**, I am about to shake the heavens and the earth,
Zec 1: 1 of Berechiah son of Iddo, **s**:
3: 6 Then the angel of the LORD assured Joshua, **s**
4: 8 Moreover the word of the LORD came to me, **s**,
7: 8 The word of the LORD came to Zechariah, **s**:
8: 1 The word of the LORD of hosts came to me, **s**:
8:18 The word of the LORD of hosts came to me, **s**:
8:21 **s**, "Come, let us go to entreat the favor of
8:23 grasping his garment and **s**, "Let us go with you,
Mal 2:17 By **s**, "All who do evil are good in the sight of
Mt 2: 8 Then he sent them to Bethlehem, **s**,
3:14 John would have prevented him, **s**,
4: 6 **s** to him, "If you are the Son of God,

Mt 5: 2 Then he began to speak, and taught them, s:
6:31 Therefore do not worry, s, 'What will we eat?'
7:28 Now when Jesus had finished s these things,
8: 2 s, "Lord, if you choose, you can make me clean."
8: 3 He stretched out his hand and touched him, s,
8: 6 and s, "Lord, my servant is lying
8:25 they went and woke him up, s, "Lord, save us!
8:27 They were amazed, s, "What sort of man is this,
9:14 Then the disciples of John came to him, s,
9:18 While he was s these things to them,
9:18 s, "My daughter has just died;
13: 3 he told them many things in parables, s: "Listen!
13:36 And his disciples approached him, s,
14:26 they were terrified, s, "It is a ghost!"
14:31 s to him, "You of little faith, why did you doubt?"
14:33 And those in the boat worshiped him, s,
15:23 And his disciples came and urged him, s,
15:25 But she came and knelt before him, s, "Lord,
16:22 Peter took him aside and began to rebuke him, s,
17: 7 But Jesus came and touched them, s,
18:26 So the slave fell on his knees before him, s,
19: 1 When Jesus had finished s these things,
20:12 s, 'These last worked only one hour,
20:32 Jesus stood still and called them, s,
21: 2 s to them, "Go into the village ahead of you,
21: 4 what had been spoken through the prophet, s,
21:11 The crowds were s, "This is the prophet Jesus
21:16 "Do you hear what these are s?"
21:20 When the disciples saw it, they were amazed, s,
21:37 Finally he sent his son to them, s,
22: 1 Once more Jesus spoke to them in parables, s:
22: 4 Again he sent other slaves, s,
22:16 s, "Teacher, we know that you are sincere,
22:23 to him, s there is no resurrection;
22:23 and they asked him a question, s,
22:43 then that David by the Spirit calls him Lord, s,
24: 3 the disciples came to him privately, s, "Tell us,
24: 5 For many will come in my name, s,
25:11 Later the other bridesmaids came also, s, 'Lord,
25:20 s, 'Master, you handed over to me five talents;
25:22 the one with the two talents also came forward, s,
25:24 s, 'Master, I knew that you were a harsh man,
26: 1 When Jesus had finished s all these things,
26:17 to Jesus, s, "Where do you want us to make
26:27 and after giving thanks he gave it to them, s,
26:44 and prayed for the third time, s the same words.
26:48 Now the betrayer had given them a sign, s,
26:68 s, "Prophesy to us, you Messiah!
26:70 But he denied it before all of them, s,
27:24 s, "I am innocent of this man's blood;
27:29 s, "Hail, King of the Jews!"
27:40 and s, "You who would destroy the temple
27:41 with the scribes and elders, were mocking him, s,
Mk 1:15 and s, "The time is fulfilled, and the kingdom
1:25 But Jesus rebuked him, s, "Be silent,
1:44 s to him, "See that you say nothing to anyone;
2:12 so that they were all amazed and glorified God, s,
3:21 for people were s, "He has gone out of his mind."
6:14 Some were s, "John the baptizer has been raised
6:46 After s farewell to them, he went up on
7:29 Then he said to her, "For s that, you may go—
7:37 They were astounded beyond measure, s,
8:15 And he cautioned them, s, "Watch out—
8:26 Then he sent him away to his home, s,
9:25 he rebuked the unclean spirit, s to it,
9:31 s to them, "The Son of Man is to be betrayed
9:32 not understand what he was s and were afraid
10:33 s, "See, we are going up to Jerusalem, and the Son
10:49 they called the blind man, s to him, "Take heart;
11:17 He was teaching and s, "Is it not written,
12: 6 Finally he sent him to them, s,
12:18 came to him and asked him a question, s,
14:13 So he sent two of his disciples, s to them,
14:39 again he went away and prayed, s the same words.
14:44 Now the betrayer had given them a sign, s,
14:57 up and gave false testimony against him, s,
14:65 to blindfold him, and to strike him, s to him,
14:68 But he denied it, s, "I do not know
15:29 shaking their heads and s, "Aha!
15:31 were also mocking him among themselves and s,
15:36 put it on a stick, and gave it to him to drink, s,
16: 3 They had been s to one another,
Lk 2:13 of the heavenly host, praising God and s,
2:28 Simeon took him in his arms and praised God, s,
3:16 John answered all of them by s, "I baptize you
4: 9 s to him, "If you are the Son of God,
4:35 But Jesus rebuked him, s, "Be silent,
4:36 They were all amazed and kept s to one another,
5: 8 he fell down at Jesus' knees, s,
5:26 s, "We have seen strange things today."
5:30 s, "Why do you eat and drink with tax collectors
7: 4 s, "He is worthy of having you do this for him,
7:16 Fear seized all of them; and they glorified God, s,
8:38 but Jesus sent him away, s,
9:22 s, "The Son of Man must undergo great suffering,
9:34 While he was s this, a cloud came
9:45 But they did not understand this s;
9:45 And they were afraid to ask him about this s.
10:17 The seventy returned with joy, s, "Lord,
10:39 at the Lord's feet and listened to what he was s.
11:27 While he was s this, a woman in
13:14 kept s to the crowd, "There are six days
13:25 to knock at the door, s, 'Lord, open to us,'
14:30 s, 'This fellow began to build and was not able
15: 2 Pharisees and the scribes were grumbling and s,
15: 6 s to them, 'Rejoice with me,
15: 9 she calls together her friends and neighbors, s,
Lk 17:13 s, "Jesus, Master, have mercy on us!"
18: 3 a widow who kept coming to him and s,
18:13 but was beating his breast and s, 'God,
19:14 s, 'We do not want this man to rule over us.'
19:18 Then the second came, s, 'Lord,
19:20 Then the other came, s, 'Lord, here is your pound.
19:30 s, "Go into the village ahead of you,
19:38 s, "Blessed is the king who comes in the name of
19:42 s, "If you, even you, had only recognized
20: 5 They discussed it with one another, s, "If we say,
22: 8 So Jesus sent Peter and John, s,
22:19 s, "This is my body, which is given for you.
22:20 And he did the same with the cup after supper, s,
22:57 But he denied it, s, "Woman, I do not know him."
23: 2 They began to accuse him, s,
23: 2 and s that he himself is the Messiah, a king."
23:35 but the leaders scoffed at him, s, "He saved others;
23:37 and s, "If you are the King of the Jews,
23:39 who were hanged there kept deriding him and s,
23:40 But the other rebuked him, s,
24:29 But they urged him strongly, s, "Stay with us,
24:34 They were s, "The Lord has risen indeed,
Jn 4:10 and who it is that is s to you, 'Give me a drink,'
4:17 Jesus said to her, "You are right in s,
4:37 For here the s holds true,
6:42 They were s, "Is not this Jesus, the son of Joseph,
6:52 The Jews then disputed among themselves, s,
7: 9 After s this, he remained in Galilee.
7:11 Jews were looking for him at the festival and s,
7:12 While some were s, "He is a good man,"
7:12 others were s, "No, he is deceiving the crowd."
7:15 The Jews were astonished at it, s,
7:25 Now some of the people of Jerusalem were s,
7:31 many in the crowd believed in him and were s,
7:36 What does he mean by s,
8:12 Again Jesus spoke to them, s,
8:22 Is that what he means by s, 'Where I am going,
8:30 As he was s these things, many believed in him.
8:33 What do you mean by s,
8:48 in s that you are a Samaritan and have a demon?"
9: 7 s to him, "Go, wash in the pool
9: 9 Some were s, "It is he."
9: 9 Others were s, "No, but it is someone like him."
9: 9 He kept s, "I am the man."
9:28 Then they reviled him, s, "You are his disciple,
10: 6 but they did not understand what he was s to them.
10:20 Many of them were s, "He has a demon and is out
10:21 Others were s, "These are not the words
10:41 Many came to him, and they were s,
11:11 After s this, he told them, "Our friend Lazarus has
13:21 After s this Jesus was troubled in spirit,
16:17 "What does he mean by s to us, 'A little while,
18:22 s, "Is that how you answer the high priest?"
19: 3 They kept coming up to him, s, "Hail,
Ac 2:12 All were amazed and perplexed, s to one another,
2:31 David spoke of the resurrection of the Messiah, s,
2:40 s, "Save yourselves from this corrupt generation."
3:25 of the covenant that God gave to your ancestors, s
5:28 s, "We gave you strict orders not to teach
6:13 "This man never stops s things
7:26 s, 'Men, you are brothers;
7:27 s, 'Who made you a ruler and a judge over us?
7:40 s to Aaron, 'Make gods for us who will lead
8: 9 s that he was someone great.
8:10 listened to him eagerly, s,
8:19 s, "Give me also this power so that anyone
9: 4 He fell to the ground and heard a voice s to him,
9:20 s, "He is the Son of God."
10: 3 an angel of God coming in and s to him,
10:13 he heard a voice s, "Get up, Peter; kill and eat."
10:26 But Peter made him get up, s, "Stand up;
11: 3 s, "Why did you go to uncircumcised men and eat
11: 4 Peter began to explain it to them, step by step, s,
11: 7 I also heard a voice s to me, 'Get up, Peter;
11:13 the angel standing in his house and s, 'Send
11:18 And they praised God, s, "Then God has given
12: 7 He tapped Peter on the side and woke him, s,
13:15 the synagogue sent them a message, s, "Brothers,
13:46 Then both Paul and Barnabas spoke out boldly, s,
13:47 For so the Lord has commanded us, s,
14:22 and encouraged them to continue in the faith, s,
16: 9 a man of Macedonia pleading with him and s,
16:15 and her household were baptized, she urged us, s,
16:35 morning came, the magistrates sent the police, s,
16:36 And the jailer reported the message to Paul, s,
17: 3 and s, "This is the Messiah,
17: 7 s that there is another king named Jesus."
19:13 over those who had evil spirits, s, "I adjure you by
19:26 of people by s that gods made with hands are
20: 1 and after encouraging them and s farewell,
21:40 he addressed them in the Hebrew language, s:
22: 7 I fell to the ground and heard a voice s to me,
22:18 and saw Jesus s to me,
24: 2 Tertullus began to accuse him, s:
25:14 Festus laid Paul's case before the king, s,
26:14 I heard a voice s to me in the Hebrew language,
26:22 s nothing but what the prophets
27:10 s, "Sirs, I can see that the voyage will be
27:33 Paul urged all of them to take some food, s,
28:25 in s to your ancestors through the prophet Isaiah,
Ro 3: 8 And why not say (as some people slander us by s
1Co 4: 6 you may learn through us the meaning of the s,
11:25 s, "This cup is the new covenant in my blood.
14:16 since the outsider does not know what you are s?
15:50 What I am s, brothers and sisters, is this:
15:54 then the s that is written will be fulfilled:
2Co 9: 2 s that Achaia has been ready since last year;
2Co 11:17 What I am s in regard to this boastful confidence,
11:17 I am s not with the Lord's authority, but as a fool;
Gal 3: 8 declared the gospel beforehand to Abraham, s,
Col 2: 4 I am s this so that no one may deceive you
1Ti 1: 7 without understanding either what they are s or
1:15 The s is sure and worthy of full acceptance,
3: 1 The s is sure: whoever aspires to the office of
4: 9 The s is sure and worthy of full acceptance.
5:13 s what they should not say.
2Ti 2:11 The s is sure: If we have died with him,
Tit 3: 8 The s is sure. I desire that you insist on these things
Heb 2:12 s, "I will proclaim your name to my brothers
4: 7 s through David much later, in the words already
6:14 s, "I will surely bless you and multiply you."
8: 1 Now the main point in what we are s is this:
9:20 s, "This is the blood of the covenant
10:15 And the Holy Spirit also testifies to us, for after s,
2Pe 1:17 s, "This is my Son, my Beloved,
3: 4 and s, "Where is the promise
Jude 1:14 the seventh generation from Adam, prophesied, s,
Rev 1:11 s, "Write in a book what you see and send it to
1:17 But he placed his right hand on me, s,
2: 7 an ear listen to what the Spirit is s to the churches.
2:11 an ear listen to what the Spirit is s to the churches.
2:17 an ear listen to what the Spirit is s to the churches.
2:29 an ear listen to what the Spirit is s to the churches.
3: 6 an ear listen to what the Spirit is s to the churches.
3:13 an ear listen to what the Spirit is s to the churches.
3:22 an ear listen to what the Spirit is s to the churches.
6: 6 a voice in the midst of the four living creatures s,
7: 3 s, "Do not damage the earth or the sea or the trees,
7:10 They cried out in a loud voice, s,
7:13 Then one of the elders addressed me, s,
9:14 s to the sixth angel who had the trumpet,
10: 4 but I heard a voice from heaven s,
10: 8 that I had heard from heaven spoke to me again, s,
11:12 they heard a loud voice from heaven s to them,
11:15 and there were loud voices in heaven, s,
13: 4 and they worshiped the beast, s,
14: 8 Then another angel, a second, followed, s, "Fallen,
14:13 And I heard a voice from heaven s, "Write this:
16:17 from the throne, s, "It is done!"
18: 4 Then I heard another voice from heaven s,
18:21 s, "With such violence Babylon the great city will
19: 1 be the loud voice of a great multitude in heaven, s,
19: 4 and worshiped God who is seated on the throne, s,
19: 5 And from the throne came a voice s,
21: 3 And I heard a loud voice from the throne s, "See,
Tob 3:10 "Never shall they reproach my father, s to him,
6:14 I have heard people s that it was a demon
7: 3 Then Edna questioned them, s,
7:12 by the hand and gave her to Tobias, s, "Take her
8: 5 Tobias began by s, "Blessed are you,
8:12 s, "Send one of the maids and have her go in
10: 4 And she began to weep and mourn for her son, s,
10: 6 But Tobit kept s to her, "Be quiet
11: 9 s, "Now that I have seen you, my child,
11:11 and holding him firmly, he blew into his eyes, s,
11:17 he blessed her s, "Come in, my daughter,
Jdt 5:22 When Achior had finished s these things,
AdE 6: 9 s, 'Thus shall it be done to everyone whom
Wis 2: 1 For they reasoned unsoundly, s to themselves,
Sir 21:15 When an intelligent person hears a wise s,
Bar 2:20 as you declared by your servants the prophets, s:
2:28 in the presence of the people of Israel, s,
Sus 1:47 "What is this you are s?"
Bel 1:28 s, "The king has become a Jew;
1Mc 1:11 from Israel and misled many, s, "Let us go
2:27 in the town with a loud voice, s:
3:50 s, "What shall we do with these?
4:30 he saw that their army was strong, he prayed, s,
9: 9 But they tried to dissuade him, s,
11: 9 He sent envoys to King Demetrius, s, "Come,
11:57 Then the young Antiochus wrote to Jonathan, s,
13: 3 he encouraged them, s to them,
15:28 one of his Friends, to confer with him, s,
2Mc 4: 1 s that it was he who had incited Heliodorus
7: 5 mother encouraged one another to die nobly, s,
12:14 and even blaspheming and s unholy things.
15:14 s, "This is a man who loves the family of Israel
15:34 blessed the Lord who had manifested himself, s,
1Es 1:26 And the king of Egypt sent word to him s,
1:58 s, "Until the land has enjoyed its sabbaths,
4:58 and praised the King of heaven, s,
8:82 which you gave by your servants the prophets, s,
9:53 The Levites commanded all the people, s,
3Mc 1:12 s, "Even if those men are deprived of this honor,
2:17 and exult in the arrogance of their tongue, s,
6:11 s, 'Not even their god has rescued them.'
6:23 he wept and angrily threatened his Friends, s,
2Es 1: 4 The word of the Lord came to me, s,
1:18 s, 'Why have you led us into this wilderness
4:35 s, 'How long are we to remain here?
7:*129* [59] s, 'Choose life for yourself, so that you may
10:48 And as for her s to you,
11: 7 and it uttered a cry to its wings, s,
11:15 And a voice sounded, s to it,
11:36 Then I heard a voice s to me,
11:37 a human voice to the eagle, and spoke, s,
12: 1 While the lion was s these words to the eagle,
12:40 and came to me and spoke to me, s,
14: 5 Then I commanded him, s,
14:38 And on the next day a voice called me, s, "Ezra,
14:45 the Most High spoke to me, s,
4Mc 2:19 s, "Cursed be their anger"?
9:14 member disjointed he denounced the tyrant, s,
9:19 While he was s these things,

4Mc 10:12 they dragged in the fourth, s,
11: 1 after being cruelly tortured, the fifth leaped up, s,
11: 9 While he was s these things,
12: 2 to come nearer and tried to persuade him, s,
13: 8 of religion and encouraged one another, s,

SAYINGS (12) [SAY]

Job 32:11 I waited for your words, I listened for your wise s,
Ps 78: 2 I will utter dark s from of old,
Pr 4:20 incline your ear to my s.
22:20 Have I not written for you thirty s of admonition
24:23 These also are s of the wise:
Ecc 12:11 The s of the wise are like goads, and like nails
12:11 the collected s that are given by one shepherd.
Lk 7: 1 After Jesus had finished all his s in the hearing of
9:28 after these s Jesus took with him Peter and John
Sir 1:25 In the treasuries of wisdom are wise s,
20:27 PROVERBIAL S The wise person advances
39: 2 he preserves the s of the famous

SAYS‡ (1084) [SAY]

A. SAYS THE †LORD (330)
B. THUS SAYS THE †LORD (283)
C. THUS SAYS THE *LORD †GOD (134)
D. SAYS THE *LORD †GOD (93)
E. SAYS THE *LORD (32)
F. THUS SAYS THE *LORD (11)

Ge 21:12 whatever Sarah s to you, do as she tells you,
22:16 "By myself I have sworn, s the LORD: A
32: 4 Thus s your servant Jacob,
41:55 to Joseph; what he s to you,
45: 9 'Thus s your son Joseph, God has made me lord
46:33 When Pharaoh calls you, and s,
Ex 4:22 you shall say to Pharaoh, 'Thus s the LORD: B
5: 1 "Thus s the LORD, the God of Israel, B
5:10 "Thus s Pharaoh, 'I will not give you straw.
7: 9 "When Pharaoh s to you, 'Perform a wonder,'
7:17 Thus s the LORD, "By this you shall know B
8: 1 to Pharaoh and say to him, 'Thus s the LORD: B
8:20 and say to him, 'Thus s the LORD: B
9: 1 'Thus s the LORD, the God of the Hebrews: B
9:13 'Thus s the LORD, the God of the Hebrews: B
10: 3 "Thus s the LORD, the God of the Hebrews, B
11: 4 Moses said, "Thus s the LORD: B
22: 9 clothing, or any other loss, of which one party s,
32:27 He said to them, "Thus s the LORD, B
Nu 14:28 Say to them, "As I live," s the LORD, A
20:14 "Thus s your brother Israel:
22:16 "Thus s Balak son of Zippor:
23:26 'Whatever the LORD s, that is what I must do'?"
24:13 what the LORD s, that is what I will say'?
30: 4 by which she has bound herself, and s nothing
30: 7 and her husband hears of it and s nothing to her at
30:14 if her husband s nothing to her from day to day,
Dt 15:16 But if he s to you, "I will not go out from you,"
Jos 7:13 for thus s the LORD, the God of Israel, B
22:16 "Thus s the whole congregation of the LORD,
24: 2 Joshua said to all the people, "Thus s the LORD, B
Jdg 5:23 "Curse Meroz, s the angel of the LORD,
6: 8 and he said to them, "Thus s the LORD, B
11:15 to him: "Thus s Jephthah:
1Sa 9: 6 Whatever he s always comes true.
10:18 "Thus s the LORD, the God of Israel, B
15: 2 Thus s the LORD of hosts, B
20: 7 If he s, 'Good!' it will be well
24:13 As the ancient proverb s, 'Out of
2Sa 7: 5 and tell my servant David: Thus s the LORD: B
7: 8 Thus s the LORD of hosts: B
11:20 if the king's anger rises, and if he s to you,
12: 7 Thus s the LORD, the God of Israel: B
12:11 Thus s the LORD: I will raise up trouble B
14:10 The king said, "If anyone s anything to you,
15:26 But if he s, 'I take no pleasure in you,' here I am,
24:12 to David: Thus s the LORD: B
1Ki 3:23 Then the king said, "The one s,
3:23 while the other s, 'Not so!
11:31 for thus s the LORD, the God of Israel, "See, B
12:24 "Thus s the LORD, You shall not go up or fight B
13: 2 and said, "O altar, altar, thus s the LORD: B
13:21 who came from Judah, "Thus s the LORD: B
14: 7 Go, tell Jeroboam, 'Thus s the LORD, B
17:14 For thus s the LORD the God of Israel: B
20: 2 to him: "Thus s Ben-hadad:
20: 5 and said: "Thus s Ben-hadad:
20:13 Ahab of Israel and said, "Thus s the LORD, B
20:14 He said, "Thus s the LORD, B
20:28 and said to the king of Israel, "Thus s the LORD: B
20:32 "Your servant Ben-hadad s, 'Please let me live.' "
20:42 Then he said to him, "Thus s the LORD, B
21:19 You shall say to him, "Thus s the LORD: B
21:19 You shall say to him, "Thus s the LORD: B
22:11 and he said, "Thus s the LORD: B
22:14 whatever the LORD s to me, that I will speak."
22:27 and say, 'Thus s the king:
2Ki 1: 4 Now therefore thus s the LORD, B
1: 6 to him: Thus s the LORD: B
1: 9 "O man of God, the king s, 'Come down.' "
1:16 and said to him, "Thus s the LORD: B
2:21 and said, "Thus s the LORD, B
3:16 And he said, "Thus s the LORD, B
3:17 For thus s the LORD, 'You shall see neither wind B
4:43 the people and let them eat, for thus s the LORD, B
7: 1 thus s the LORD, Tomorrow about this time B
9: 3 'Thus s the LORD: I anoint you king over Israel.' B
9: 6 "Thus s the LORD the God of Israel: B
2Ki 9:12 'Thus s the LORD, I anoint you king B
9:18 he said, "Thus s the king, 'Is it peace?' "
9:19 who came to them and said, "Thus s the king,
9:26 children that I saw yesterday, s the LORD, A
18:19 Thus s the great king, the king of Assyria:
18:29 Thus s the king: 'Do not let Hezekiah deceive you,
18:31 for thus s the king of Assyria:
19: 3 They said to him, "Thus s Hezekiah,
19: 6 "Say to your master, 'Thus s the LORD: B
19:20 saying, "Thus s the LORD, the God of Israel: B
19:32 thus s the LORD concerning the king of Assyria: B
19:33 he shall not come into this city, s the LORD. A
20: 1 and said to him, "Thus s the LORD: B
20: 5 Thus s the LORD, the God B
20:17 nothing shall be left, s the LORD. A
21:12 therefore thus s the LORD, B
22:15 She declared to them, "Thus s the LORD, B
22:16 Thus s the LORD, I will indeed bring disaster B
22:18 thus shall you say to him, Thus s the LORD, B
22:19 I also have heard you, s the LORD. A
1Ch 17: 4 and tell my servant David: Thus s the LORD: B
17: 7 Thus s the LORD of hosts: B
21:10 and say to David, 'Thus s the LORD: B
21:11 "Thus s the LORD, 'Take your choice: B
2Ch 11: 4 "Thus s the LORD: You shall B
12: 5 and said to them, "Thus s the LORD: B
18:10 and he said, "Thus s the LORD: B
18:13 "As the LORD lives, whatever my God s,
18:26 and say, 'Thus s the king:
20:15 Thus s the LORD to you: B
21:12 "Thus s the LORD, the God of your father David: B
24:20 above the people and said to them, "Thus s God:
32:10 "Thus s King Sennacherib of Assyria:
34:23 She declared to them, "Thus s the LORD, B
34:24 Thus s the LORD: I will indeed bring disaster B
34:26 Thus s the LORD, the God of Israel: B
34:27 I also have heard you, s the LORD. A
36:23 "Thus s King Cyrus of Persia:
Ezr 1: 2 "Thus s King Cyrus of Persia:
Ne 6: 6 among the nations—and Geshem also s it—
Job 28:14 The deep s, 'It is not in me,' and the sea s,
33:24 and s, 'Deliver him from going down into the Pit;
33:27 That person sings to others and s, 'I sinned,
34:18 who s to a king, 'You scoundrel!'
35:10 But no one s, 'Where is God my Maker,
37: 6 For to the snow he s, 'Fall on the earth';
39:25 When the trumpet sounds, it s 'Aha!'
Ps 12: 5 I will now rise up," s the LORD; A
27: 8 "Come," my heart s, "seek his face!"
50:16 But to the wicked God s:
110: 1 The LORD s to my lord,
Pr 7:13 and with impudent face she s to him:
9: 4 To those without sense she s,
9:16 And to those without sense she s,
20:14 bad," s the buyer, then goes away and boasts.
22:13 The lazy person s, "There is a lion outside!
24:24 Whoever s to the wicked, "You are innocent,"
26:13 The lazy person s, "There is a lion in the road!
26:19 so is one who deceives a neighbor and s,
28:24 Anyone who robs father or mother and s,
30: 1 An oracle. Thus s the man:
30:16 and the fire that never s, "Enough."
30:20 she eats, and wipes her mouth, and s,
Ecc 1: 2 Vanity of vanities, s the Teacher,
7:27 See, this is what I found, s the Teacher,
12: 8 Vanity of vanities, s the Teacher; all is vanity.
SS 2:10 My beloved speaks and s to me:
Isa 1:11 multitude of your sacrifices? s the LORD; A
1:18 Come now, let us argue it out, s the LORD: A
1:24 Therefore s the Sovereign, the LORD of hosts,
3:15 s the Lord GOD of hosts. D
7: 7 therefore thus s the Lord GOD: C
10: 8 For he s: "Are not my commanders all kings?
10:13 For he s: "By the strength of my
10:24 Therefore thus s the Lord GOD of hosts: C
14:22 I will rise up against them, s the LORD of hosts, A
14:22 offspring and posterity, s the LORD. A
14:23 with the broom of destruction, s the LORD of A
16:14 But now the LORD s, In three years,
17: 3 the glory of the children of Israel, s the LORD A
17: 6 s the LORD God of Israel. A
19: 4 a fierce king will rule over them, s the Sovereign,
21:12 sentinel s: "Morning comes, and also the night.
22:14 s the Lord GOD of hosts. D
22:15 Thus s the Lord GOD of hosts: C
22:25 On that day, s the LORD of hosts, A
28:16 therefore thus s the Lord GOD, See, I am laying C
29:22 Therefore thus s the LORD, B
30: 1 Oh, rebellious children, s the LORD, A
30:12 Therefore thus s the Holy One of Israel:
31: 9 s the LORD, whose fire is in Zion, A
33:10 "Now I will arise," s the LORD, A
36: 4 Thus s the great king, the king of Assyria:
36:14 Thus s the king: 'Do not let Hezekiah deceive you,
36:16 for thus s the king of Assyria:
37: 3 They said to him, "Thus s Hezekiah,
37: 6 "Say to your master, 'Thus s the LORD: B
37:21 "Thus s the LORD, the God of Israel: B
37:33 thus s the LORD concerning the king of Assyria: B
37:34 he shall not come into this city, s the LORD. A
38: 1 and said to him, "Thus s the LORD: B
38: 5 Thus s the LORD, the God B
39: 6 nothing shall be left, s the LORD. A
40: 1 Comfort, O comfort my people, s your God.
40: 6 A voice s, "Cry out!"
40:25 or who is my equal? s the Holy One.
41:14 I will help you, s the LORD; A
Isa 41:21 Set forth your case, s the LORD; A
41:21 bring your proofs, s the King of Jacob.
42: 5 Thus s God, the LORD, who created the heavens
43: 1 But now thus s the LORD, he who created you, B
43:10 You are my witnesses, s the LORD, A
43:12 and you are my witnesses, s the LORD. A
43:14 Thus s the LORD, your Redeemer, B
43:16 Thus s the LORD, who makes a way in the sea, B
44: 2 Thus s the LORD who made you, B
44: 6 Thus s the LORD, the King of Israel, B
44:16 He also warms himself and s, "Ah, I am warm,
44:17 he prays to it and s, "Save me,
44:24 Thus s the LORD, your Redeemer, B
44:26 who s of Jerusalem, "It shall be inhabited,"
44:27 who s to the deep, "Be dry—
44:28 who s of Cyrus, "He is my shepherd,
44:28 and who s of Jerusalem, "It shall be rebuilt,"
45: 1 Thus s the LORD to his anointed, to Cyrus, B
45:10 Woe to anyone who s to a father,
45:11 Thus s the LORD, the Holy One of Israel, B
45:13 not for price or reward, s the LORD of hosts. A
45:14 Thus s the LORD: The wealth of Egypt B
45:18 For thus s the LORD, who created B
48:17 Thus s the LORD, your Redeemer, B
48:22 "There is no peace," s the LORD, A
49: 5 now the LORD s, who formed me in the womb to
49: 6 he s, "It is too light a thing that you should
49: 7 Thus s the LORD, the Redeemer of Israel B
49: 8 Thus s the LORD: In a time of favor B
49:18 As I live, s the LORD, you shall put all of them A
49:22 Thus s the Lord GOD: I will soon lift up my C
49:25 But thus s the LORD: B
50: 1 Thus s the LORD: B
51:22 Thus s your Sovereign, the LORD,
52: 3 For thus s the LORD: You were sold B
52: 4 For thus s the Lord GOD: C
52: 5 therefore what am I doing here, s the LORD, A
52: 5 Their rulers howl, s the LORD, and continually, A
52: 7 who announces salvation, who s to Zion,
54: 1 the children of her that is married, s the LORD. A
54: 6 of a man's youth when she is cast off, s your God.
54: 8 s the LORD, your Redeemer. A
54:10 s the LORD, who has compassion on you. A
54:17 and their vindication from me, s the LORD. A
55: 8 nor are your ways my ways, s the LORD. A
56: 1 Thus s the LORD: Maintain justice, B
56: 4 For thus s the LORD: B
56: 8 Thus s the Lord GOD, who gathers the outcasts C
57:15 thus s the high and lofty one who inhabits eternity,
57:19 Peace, peace, to the far and the near, s the LORD; A
57:21 There is no peace, s my God, for the wicked.
59:20 who turn from transgression, s the LORD. A
59:21 me, this is my covenant with them, s the LORD: A
59:21 s the LORD, from now on and forever. A
65: 7 their ancestors' iniquities together, s the LORD; A
65: 8 Thus s the LORD: As the wine is found in the B
65:13 Therefore thus s the Lord GOD: C
65:25 or destroy on all my holy mountain, s the LORD. A
66: 1 Thus s the LORD: Heaven is my throne B
66: 2 and so all these things are mine, s the LORD. A
66: 9 and not deliver? s the LORD; A
66: 9 shut the womb? s your God.
66:12 For thus s the LORD: I will extend prosperity B
66:17 shall come to an end together, s the LORD. A
66:20 to my holy mountain Jerusalem, s the LORD, A
66:21 as priests and as Levites, s the LORD. A
66:22 shall remain before me, s the LORD; A
66:23 to worship before me, s the LORD. A
Jer 1: 8 for I am with you to deliver you, s the LORD." A
1:15 of the kingdoms of the north, s the LORD; A
1:19 for I am with you, s the LORD, to deliver you. A
2: 2 hearing of Jerusalem, Thus s the LORD: B
2: 3 disaster came upon them, s the LORD. A
2: 5 Thus s the LORD: What wrong did your B
2: 9 s the LORD, and I accuse your children's A
2:12 be shocked, be utterly desolate, s the LORD, A
2:19 s the Lord GOD of hosts. D
2:22 of your guilt is still before me, s the Lord GOD. D
2:29 You have all rebelled against me, s the LORD. A
3: 1 and would you return to me? s the LORD. A
3:10 but only in pretense, s the LORD. A
3:12 Return, faithless Israel, s the LORD. A
3:12 s the LORD; I will not be angry forever. A
3:13 and have not obeyed my voice, s the LORD. A
3:14 s the LORD, for I am your master; A
3:16 s the LORD, they shall no longer say, A
3:20 O house of Israel, s the LORD. A
4: 1 If you return, O Israel, s the LORD, A
4: 3 For thus s the LORD to the people of Judah and B
4: 9 On that day, s the LORD, A
4:17 because she has rebelled against me, s the LORD. A
4:27 For thus s the LORD: The whole land shall be a B
5: 9 s the LORD; and shall I not bring retribution A
5:11 have been utterly faithless to me, s the LORD. A
5:14 Therefore thus s the LORD, the God of hosts: B
5:15 O house of Israel, s the LORD. A
5:18 But even in those days, s the LORD, A
5:22 s the LORD; Do you not tremble before me? A
5:29 s the LORD, and shall I not bring retribution A
6: 6 For thus s the LORD of hosts: B
6: 9 Thus s the LORD of hosts: B
6:12 against the inhabitants of the land, s the LORD. A
6:15 they shall be overthrown, s the LORD. A
6:16 Thus s the LORD: Stand at the B
6:21 Therefore thus s the LORD: B
6:22 Thus s the LORD: See, a people is coming from B
7: 3 Thus s the LORD of hosts, the God of Israel: B

Jer 7:11 You know, I too am watching, s the LORD. A
7:13 you have done all these things, s the LORD, A
7:19 Is it I whom they provoke? s the LORD. A
7:20 Therefore thus s the Lord GOD: C
7:21 Thus s the LORD of hosts, the God of Israel: B
7:30 of Judah have done evil in my sight, s the LORD; A
7:32 the days are surely coming, s the LORD, A
8: 1 At that time, s the LORD, A
8: 3 the places where I have driven them, s the LORD A
8: 4 You shall say to them, Thus s the LORD: B
8:12 they shall be overthrown, s the LORD. A
8:13 When I wanted to gather them, s the LORD, A
8:17 and they shall bite you, s the LORD. A
9: 3 and they do not know me, s the LORD. A
9: 6 They refuse to know me, s the LORD. A
9: 7 Therefore thus s the LORD of hosts: B
9: 9 for these things? s the LORD; A
9:13 And the LORD s: Because they have forsaken
9:15 thus s the LORD of hosts, the God of Israel: B
9:17 Thus s the LORD of hosts: B
9:22 Thus s the LORD: "Human corpses shall fall B
9:23 Thus s the LORD: Do not let the wise boast B
9:24 for in these things I delight, s the LORD. A
9:25 The days are surely coming, s the LORD, A
10: 2 Thus s the LORD: Do not learn the way B
10:18 For thus s the LORD: I am going to sling B
11: 3 You shall say to them, Thus s the LORD, B
11:11 Therefore, thus s the LORD, B
11:21 Therefore thus s the LORD concerning the B
11:22 therefore thus s the LORD of hosts: B
12:14 Thus s the LORD concerning all B
12:17 uproot it and destroy it, s the LORD. A
13: 9 Thus s the LORD: Just so I will ruin B
13:11 s the LORD, in order that they might be for me A
13:12 Thus s the LORD, the God of Israel: B
13:13 Then you shall say to them: Thus s the LORD: B
13:14 parents and children together, s the LORD. A
13:25 s the LORD, because you have forgotten me A
14:10 Thus s the LORD concerning this people: B
14:15 Therefore thus s the LORD concerning B
15: 2 you shall say to them: Thus s the LORD: B
15: 3 over them four kinds of destroyers, s the LORD: A
15: 6 You have rejected me, s the LORD, A
15: 9 to the sword before their enemies, s the LORD. A
15:19 Therefore thus s the LORD: B
15:20 to save you and deliver you, s the LORD. A
16: 3 For thus s the LORD concerning the sons B
16: 5 For thus s the LORD: Do not enter B
16: 5 s the LORD, my steadfast love and mercy. A
16: 9 For thus s the LORD of hosts, the God of Israel: B
16:11 your ancestors have forsaken me, s the LORD, A
16:14 the days are surely coming, s the LORD, A
16:16 s the LORD, and they shall catch them; A
17: 5 Thus s the LORD: Cursed are those who trust B
17:21 Thus s the LORD: For the sake of your B
17:24 But if you listen to me, s the LORD, A
18: 6 as this potter has done? s the LORD. A
18:11 of Jerusalem: Thus s the LORD: B
18:13 Therefore thus s the LORD: B
19: 3 Thus s the LORD of hosts, the God of Israel: B
19: 6 the days are surely coming, s the LORD, A
19:11 Thus s the LORD of hosts: B
19:12 Thus will I do to this place, s the LORD, A
19:15 Thus s the LORD of hosts, the God of Israel: B
20: 4 For thus s the LORD: I am making you a terror B
21: 4 Thus s the LORD, the God of Israel: B
21: 7 s the LORD, I will give King Zedekiah of Judah, A
21: 8 to this people you shall say: Thus s the LORD: B
21:10 for evil and not for good, s the LORD: A
21:12 O house of David! Thus s the LORD: B
21:13 O rock of the plain, s the LORD; A
21:14 s the LORD; I will kindle a fire in its forest, A
22: 1 Thus s the LORD: Go down to B
22: 3 Thus s the LORD: Act with justice B
22: 5 I swear by myself, s the LORD, A
22: 6 For thus s the LORD concerning the house of B
22:11 For thus s the LORD concerning Shallum son B
22:14 who s, "I will build myself a spacious house
22:16 to know me? s the LORD. A
22:18 Therefore thus s the LORD B
22:24 As I live, s the LORD, even if King Coniah son A
22:30 Thus s the LORD: Record this man B
23: 1 of my pasture! s the LORD. A
23: 2 Therefore thus s the LORD, the God of Israel, B
23: 2 attend to you for your evil doings, s the LORD. A
23: 4 nor shall any be missing, s the LORD. A
23: 5 The days are surely coming, s the LORD, A
23: 7 the days are surely coming, s the LORD, A
23:11 I have found their wickedness, s the LORD. A
23:12 in the year of their punishment, s the LORD. A
23:15 Therefore thus s the LORD of hosts concerning B
23:16 Thus s the LORD of hosts: B
23:23 Am I a God near by, s the LORD, A
23:24 that I cannot see them? s the LORD. A
23:24 not fill heaven and earth? s the LORD. A
23:28 with wheat? s the LORD. A
23:29 Is not my word like fire, s the LORD, A
23:30 therefore, I am against the prophets, s the LORD, A
23:31 See, I am against the prophets, s the LORD, A
23:31 use their own tongues and say, "S the LORD." A
23:32 s the LORD, and who tell them, A
23:32 they do not profit this people at all, s the LORD. A
23:33 and I will cast you off, s the LORD." A
23:38 "the burden of the LORD," thus s the LORD: B
24: 5 Thus s the LORD, the God of Israel: B
24: 8 But thus s the LORD: B
25: 7 Yet you did not listen to me, s the LORD, A

Jer 25: 8 Therefore thus s the LORD of hosts: B
25: 9 s the LORD, even for King Nebuchadrezzar A
25:12 for their iniquity, s the LORD, A
25:27 you shall say to them, Thus s the LORD of hosts, B
25:28 Thus s the LORD of hosts: You must drink! B
25:29 the inhabitants of the earth, s the LORD of hosts. A
25:31 the guilty he will put to the sword, s the LORD. A
25:32 Thus s the LORD of hosts: B
26: 2 Thus s the LORD: Stand in the B
26: 4 You shall say to them: Thus s the LORD: B
26:18 'Thus s the LORD of hosts, B
27: 4 Thus s the LORD of hosts, the God of Israel: B
27: 8 with famine, and with pestilence, s the LORD, A
27:11 I will leave on its own land, s the LORD, A
27:15 I have not sent them, s the LORD, A
27:16 saying, Thus s the LORD: B
27:19 thus s the LORD of hosts concerning the pillars, B
27:21 thus s the LORD of hosts, the God of Israel, B
27:22 when I give attention to them, s the LORD. A
28: 2 "Thus s the LORD of hosts, the God of Israel: B
28: 4 Babylon, s the LORD, for I will break the yoke A
28:11 saying, "Thus s the LORD: B
28:13 tell Hananiah, Thus s the LORD: B
28:14 For thus s the LORD of hosts, the God of Israel: B
28:16 Therefore thus s the LORD: B
29: 4 Thus s the LORD of hosts, the God of Israel, B
29: 8 For thus s the LORD of hosts, the God of Israel: B
29: 9 I did not send them, s the LORD. A
29:10 For thus s the LORD: Only B
29:11 I know the plans I have for you, s the LORD, A
29:14 s the LORD, and I will restore your fortunes A
29:14 the places where I have driven you, s the LORD, A
29:16 Thus s the LORD concerning the king who sits B
29:17 Thus s the LORD of hosts, B
29:19 they did not heed my words, s the LORD, A
29:19 but they would not listen, s the LORD. A
29:21 Thus s the LORD of hosts, the God of Israel, B
29:23 one who knows and bears witness, s the LORD. A
29:25 Thus s the LORD of hosts, the God of Israel: B
29:31 Thus s the LORD concerning Shemaiah B
29:32 therefore thus s the LORD: B
29:32 that I am going to do to my people, s the LORD, A
30: 2 Thus s the LORD, the God of Israel: B
30: 3 For the days are surely coming, s the LORD, A
30: 3 Israel and Judah, s the LORD, A
30: 5 Thus s the LORD: We have heard a cry of panic, B
30: 8 On that day, s the LORD of hosts, A
30:10 you, have no fear, my servant Jacob, s the LORD, A
30:11 For I am with you, s the LORD, to save you; A
30:12 For thus s the LORD: Your hurt is incurable, B
30:17 and your wounds I will heal, s the LORD, A
30:18 Thus s the LORD: I am going to restore B
30:21 to approach me? s the LORD. A
31: 1 At that time, s the LORD, A
31: 2 Thus s the LORD: The people who survived the B
31: 7 For thus s the LORD: Sing aloud with gladness B
31:14 shall be satisfied with my bounty, s the LORD. A
31:15 Thus s the LORD: A voice is heard in Ramah, B
31:16 Thus s the LORD: Keep your voice from B
31:16 s the LORD: they shall come back from the land A
31:17 s the LORD: your children shall come back A
31:20 I will surely have mercy on him, s the LORD. A
31:23 Thus s the LORD of hosts, the God of Israel: B
31:27 The days are surely coming, s the LORD, A
31:28 over them to build and to plant, s the LORD. A
31:31 The days are surely coming, s the LORD, A
31:32 though I was their husband, s the LORD. A
31:33 the house of Israel after those days, s the LORD: A
31:34 the least of them to the greatest, s the LORD; A
31:35 Thus s the LORD, who gives the sun for light B
31:36 to cease from my presence, s the LORD, A
31:37 Thus s the LORD: If the heavens above can B
31:37 because of all they have done, s the LORD. A
31:38 The days are surely coming, s the LORD, A
32: 3 and say: Thus s the LORD: B
32: 5 he shall remain until I attend to him, s the LORD; A
32:14 Thus s the LORD of hosts, the God of Israel: B
32:15 For thus s the LORD of hosts, the God of Israel: B
32:28 Therefore, thus s the LORD: B
32:30 to anger by the work of their hands, s the LORD. A
32:36 Now therefore thus s the LORD, B
32:42 For thus s the LORD: Just as I have brought B
32:44 for I will restore their fortunes, s the LORD. A
33: 2 Thus s the LORD who made the earth, B
33: 4 For thus s the LORD, the God of Israel, B
33:10 Thus s the LORD: In this place B
33:11 the fortunes of the land as at first, s the LORD. A
33:12 Thus s the LORD of hosts: B
33:13 hands of the one who counts them, s the LORD. A
33:14 The days are surely coming, s the LORD, A
33:17 For thus s the LORD: David shall never lack B
33:20 Thus s the LORD: If any of you B
33:25 Thus s the LORD: Only if I had not B
34: 2 "Thus s the LORD, the God of Israel: B
34: 2 to him: Thus s the LORD: B
34: 4 Thus s the LORD concerning you: B
34: 5 For I have spoken the word, s the LORD. A
34:13 Thus s the LORD, the God of Israel: B
34:17 Therefore, thus s the LORD: B
34:17 to grant a release to you, s the LORD— A
34:22 I am going to command, s the LORD, A
35:13 Thus s the LORD of hosts, the God of Israel: B
35:13 and obey my words? s the LORD. A
35:17 Therefore, thus s the LORD, the God of hosts, B
35:18 Thus s the LORD of hosts, the God of Israel: B
35:19 thus s the LORD of hosts, the God of Israel: B
36:29 Thus s the LORD, You have dared B

Jer 36:30 Therefore thus s the LORD B
37: 7 Thus s the LORD, God of Israel: B
37: 9 Thus s the LORD: Do not deceive yourselves, B
38: 2 Thus s the LORD, Those who stay B
38: 3 Thus s the LORD, This city shall surely B
38:17 Jeremiah said to Zedekiah, "Thus s the LORD, B
39:16 Thus s the LORD of hosts, the God of Israel: B
39:17 But I will save you on that day, s the LORD, A
39:18 because you have trusted in me, s the LORD. A
42: 9 "Thus s the LORD, the God of Israel, B
42:11 do not be afraid of him, s the LORD, A
42:15 Thus s the LORD of hosts, the God of Israel: B
42:18 "For thus s the LORD of hosts, the God of Israel: B
42:20 and whatever the LORD our God s,
43:10 Thus s the LORD of hosts, the God of Israel: B
44: 2 Thus s the LORD of hosts, the God of Israel: B
44: 7 thus s the LORD God of hosts, the God of Israel: B
44:11 thus s the LORD of hosts, the God of Israel: B
44:25 Thus s the LORD of hosts, the God of Israel: B
44:26 Lo, I swear by my great name, s the LORD, A
44:29 This shall be the sign to you, s the LORD, A
44:30 Thus s the LORD, I am going B
45: 2 Thus s the LORD, the God of Israel, B
45: 4 Thus you shall say to him, "Thus s the LORD: B
45: 5 to bring disaster upon all flesh, s the LORD; A
46: 5 terror is all around! s the LORD. A
46:18 s the King, whose name is the LORD of hosts,
46:23 s the LORD, though it is impenetrable, A
46:26 be inhabited as in the days of old, s the LORD. A
46:28 s the LORD, for I am with you. A
47: 2 Thus s the LORD: See, waters are rising out of B
48: 1 Thus s the LORD of hosts, the God of Israel: B
48:12 the time is surely coming, s the LORD, A
48:15 s the King, whose name is the LORD of hosts.
48:25 and his arm is broken, s the LORD. A
48:30 I myself know his insolence, s the LORD; A
48:35 And I will bring to an end in Moab, s the LORD, A
48:38 like a vessel that no one wants, s the LORD. A
48:40 For thus s the LORD: Look, B
48:43 O inhabitants of Moab! s the LORD. A
48:44 in the year of their punishment, s the LORD. A
48:47 of Moab in the latter days, s the LORD. A
49: 1 Thus s the LORD: Has Israel no sons? B
49: 2 the time is surely coming, s the LORD, A
49: 2 those who dispossessed him, s the LORD. A
49: 5 s the Lord GOD of hosts, D
49: 6 the fortunes of the Ammonites, s the LORD. A
49: 7 Thus s the LORD of hosts: B
49:12 For thus s the LORD: If those who do B
49:13 For by myself I have sworn, s the LORD, A
49:16 from there I will bring you down, s the LORD. A
49:18 s the LORD, no one shall live there, A
49:26 be destroyed in that day, s the LORD of hosts. A
49:28 of Babylon defeated. Thus s the LORD: B
49:30 O inhabitants of Hazor! s the LORD. A
49:31 s the LORD, that has no gates or bars, A
49:32 against them from every side, s the LORD. A
49:35 Thus s the LORD of hosts: B
49:37 my fierce anger, s the LORD. A
49:38 and destroy their king and officials, s the LORD. A
49:39 I will restore the fortunes of Elam, s the LORD. A
50: 4 In those days and in that time, s the LORD, A
50:10 all who plunder her shall be sated, s the LORD. A
50:18 thus s the LORD of hosts, the God of Israel: B
50:20 In those days and at that time, s the LORD, A
50:21 s the LORD; do all that I have commanded you. A
50:30 be destroyed on that day, s the LORD. A
50:31 O arrogant one, s the Lord GOD of hosts; D
50:33 Thus s the LORD of hosts: B
50:35 A sword against the Chaldeans, s the LORD, A
50:40 s the LORD, so no one shall live there, A
51: 1 Thus s the LORD: I am going to stir B
51:24 wrong that they have done in Zion, s the LORD. A
51:25 s the LORD, that destroys the whole earth; A
51:26 but you shall be a perpetual waste, s the LORD. A
51:33 For thus s the LORD of hosts, the God of Israel: B
51:36 Therefore thus s the LORD: B
51:39 a perpetual sleep and never wake, s the LORD. A
51:48 against them out of the north, s the LORD. A
51:52 Therefore the time is surely coming, s the LORD, A
51:53 destroyers would come upon her, s the LORD. A
51:57 s the King, whose name is the LORD of hosts.
51:58 Thus s the LORD of hosts: B
La 3:24 "The LORD is my portion," s my soul,
Eze 2: 4 "Thus s the Lord GOD." C
3:11 Say to them, "Thus s the Lord GOD"; C
3:27 "Thus s the Lord GOD"; C
5: 5 Thus s the Lord GOD: This is Jerusalem; C
5: 7 Therefore thus s the Lord GOD: C
5: 8 therefore thus s the Lord GOD: C
5:11 Therefore, as I live, s the Lord GOD, surely, D
6: 3 Thus s the Lord GOD to the mountains and C
6:11 Thus s the Lord GOD: Clap your hands C
7: 2 thus s the Lord GOD to the land of Israel: C
7: 5 Thus s the Lord GOD: Disaster after disaster! C
11: 5 and he said to me, "Say, Thus s the LORD: B
11: 7 Therefore thus s the Lord GOD: C
11: 8 I will bring the sword upon you, s the Lord GOD. D
11:16 Therefore say: Thus s the Lord GOD: C
11:17 Therefore say: Thus s the Lord GOD: C
11:21 upon their own heads, s the Lord GOD. D
12:10 Say to them, "Thus s the Lord GOD: C
12:19 Thus s the Lord GOD concerning the inhabitants C
12:22 which s, "The days are prolonged,
12:23 Tell them therefore, "Thus s the Lord GOD: C
12:25 the word and fulfill it, s the Lord GOD. D
12:28 Therefore say to them, Thus s the Lord GOD: C

Eze 12:28 that I speak will be fulfilled, s the Lord GOD. D
13: 3 Thus s the Lord GOD, Alas for the senseless C
13: 6 they say, "S the LORD," A
13: 7 "S the LORD," even though I did not speak? A
13: 8 Therefore thus s the Lord GOD: C
13: 8 I am against you, s the Lord GOD. D
13:13 Therefore thus s the Lord GOD: C
13:16 when there was no peace, s the Lord GOD. D
13:18 and say, Thus s the Lord GOD: C
13:20 Therefore thus s the Lord GOD: C
14: 4 and say to them, Thus s the Lord GOD: C
14: 6 say to the house of Israel, Thus s the Lord GOD: C
14:11 and I will be their God, s the Lord GOD. D
14:14 by their righteousness, s the Lord GOD. D
14:16 as I live, s the Lord GOD, D
14:18 as I live, s the Lord GOD, D
14:20 and Job were in it, as I live, s the Lord GOD, D
14:21 For thus s the Lord GOD: C
14:23 all that I have done in it, s the Lord GOD. D
15: 6 Therefore thus s the Lord GOD: C
15: 8 they have acted faithlessly, s the Lord GOD. D
16: 3 Thus s the Lord GOD to Jerusalem: C
16: 8 s the Lord GOD, and you became mine. D
16:14 that I had bestowed on you, s the Lord GOD. D
16:19 and so it was, s the Lord GOD. D
16:23 to you! s the Lord GOD), D
16:30 How sick is your heart, s the Lord GOD, D
16:36 Thus s the Lord GOD, C
16:43 upon your head, s the Lord GOD. D
16:48 As I live, s the Lord GOD, D
16:58 lewdness and your abominations, s the LORD. A
16:59 Yes, thus s the Lord GOD: C
16:63 all that you have done, s the Lord GOD. D
17: 3 Say: Thus s the Lord GOD: C
17: 9 Say: Thus s the Lord GOD: Will it prosper? C
17:16 As I live, s the Lord GOD, D
17:19 Therefore thus s the Lord GOD: C
17:22 Thus s the Lord GOD: I myself will take a sprig C
18: 3 As I live, s the Lord GOD, D
18: 9 he shall surely live, s the Lord GOD. D
18:23 in the death of the wicked, s the Lord GOD, D
18:29 house of Israel s, "The way of the Lord is unfair."
18:30 of you according to your ways, s the Lord GOD. D
18:32 in the death of anyone, s the Lord GOD. D
20: 3 Thus s the Lord GOD: Why are you coming? C
20: 3 As I live, s the Lord GOD, D
20: 5 to them: Thus s the Lord GOD: C
20:27 of Israel and say to them, Thus s the Lord GOD: C
20:30 say to the house of Israel, Thus s the Lord GOD: C
20:31 As I live, s the Lord GOD, D
20:33 As I live, s the Lord GOD, D
20:36 enter into judgment with you, s the Lord GOD. D
20:39 for you, O house of Israel, thus s the Lord GOD: C
20:40 the mountain height of Israel, s the Lord GOD, D
20:44 O house of Israel, s the Lord GOD. D
20:47 Thus s the Lord GOD, I will kindle a fire in you, C
21: 3 and say to the land of Israel, Thus s the LORD: B
21: 7 and it will be fulfilled," s the Lord GOD. D
21: 9 prophesy and say: Thus s the Lord; F
21:13 not happen? s the Lord GOD. D
21:24 Therefore thus s the Lord GOD: C
21:26 thus s the Lord GOD: Remove the turban, C
21:28 Thus s the Lord GOD concerning C
22: 3 You shall say, Thus s the Lord GOD: A city! C
22:12 and you have forgotten me, s the Lord GOD. D
22:19 Therefore thus s the Lord GOD: C
22:28 saying, "Thus s the Lord GOD," C
22:31 their conduct upon their heads, s the Lord GOD. D
23:22 Therefore, O Oholibah, thus s the Lord GOD: C
23:28 For thus s the Lord GOD: C
23:32 Thus s the Lord GOD: You shall drink your C
23:34 for I have spoken, s the Lord GOD. D
23:35 Therefore thus s the Lord GOD: C
23:46 For thus s the Lord GOD: C
24: 3 and say to them, Thus s the Lord GOD: C
24: 6 Therefore thus s the Lord GOD: C
24: 9 thus s the Lord GOD: Woe to the bloody city! C
24:14 your doings I will judge you, s the Lord GOD. D
24:21 to the house of Israel, Thus s the Lord GOD: C
25: 3 Thus s the Lord GOD, Because you said, "Aha!" C
25: 6 For thus s the Lord GOD: C
25: 8 Thus s the Lord GOD: C
25:12 Thus s the Lord GOD: C
25:13 therefore thus s the Lord GOD, C
25:14 they shall know my vengeance, s the Lord GOD. D
25:15 Thus s the Lord GOD: C
25:16 therefore thus s the Lord GOD, C
26: 3 Therefore, thus s the Lord GOD: C
26: 5 I have spoken, s the Lord GOD. D
26: 7 For thus s the Lord GOD: C
26:14 for I the LORD have spoken, s the Lord GOD. D
26:15 Thus s the Lord GOD to Tyre: C
26:19 For thus s the Lord GOD: C
26:21 you will never be found again, s the Lord GOD. D
27: 3 on many coastlands, Thus s the Lord GOD: C
28: 2 say to the prince of Tyre, Thus s the Lord GOD: C
28: 6 Therefore thus s the Lord GOD: C
28:10 for I have spoken, s the Lord GOD. D
28:12 and say to him, Thus s the Lord GOD: C
28:22 and say, Thus s the Lord GOD: C
28:25 Thus s the Lord GOD: C
29: 3 and say, Thus s the Lord GOD: C
29: 8 Therefore, thus s the Lord GOD: C
29:13 Further, thus s the Lord GOD: C
29:19 Therefore thus s the Lord GOD: C
29:20 because they worked for me, s the Lord GOD. D
30: 2 Thus s the Lord GOD: Wail, "Alas for the day!" C

Eze 30: 6 Thus s the LORD: Those who support Egypt B
30: 6 shall fall within it by the sword, s the Lord GOD. D
30:10 Thus s the Lord GOD: I will put an end to the C
30:13 Thus s the Lord GOD: I will destroy the idols C
30:22 Therefore thus s the Lord GOD: C
31:10 Therefore thus s the Lord GOD: C
31:15 Thus s the Lord GOD: C
31:18 and all his horde, s the Lord GOD. D
32: 3 Thus s the Lord GOD: C
32: 8 and put darkness on your land, s the Lord GOD. D
32:11 For thus s the Lord GOD: C
32:14 streams to run like oil, s the Lord GOD. D
32:16 its hordes they shall chant it, s the Lord GOD. D
32:31 killed by the sword, s the Lord GOD. D
32:32 Pharaoh and all his multitude, s the Lord GOD. D
33:11 Say to them, As I live, s the Lord GOD, D
33:25 Therefore say to them, Thus s the Lord GOD: C
33:27 Say this to them, Thus s the Lord GOD: C
34: 2 to the shepherds: Thus s the Lord GOD: C
34: 8 s the Lord GOD, because my sheep have become D
34:10 Thus s the Lord GOD, I am against C
34:11 For thus s the Lord GOD: C
34:15 and I will make them lie down, s the Lord GOD. D
34:17 As for you, my flock, thus s the Lord GOD: C
34:20 Therefore, thus s the Lord GOD to them: C
34:30 are my people, s the Lord GOD. D
34:31 and I am your God, s the Lord GOD. D
35: 3 and say to it, Thus s the Lord GOD: C
35: 6 s the Lord GOD, I will prepare you for blood, D
35:11 as I live, s the Lord GOD, D
35:14 Thus s the Lord GOD: C
36: 2 Thus s the Lord GOD: C
36: 3 and say: Thus s the Lord GOD: C
36: 4 Thus s the Lord GOD to the mountains and C
36: 5 therefore thus s the Lord GOD: C
36: 6 watercourses and valleys, Thus s the Lord GOD: C
36: 7 therefore thus s the Lord GOD: C
36:13 Thus s the Lord GOD: C
36:14 bereave your nation of children, s the Lord GOD; D
36:15 to stumble, s the Lord GOD. D
36:22 say to the house of Israel, Thus s the Lord GOD: C
36:23 shall know that I am the LORD, s the Lord GOD, D
36:32 s the Lord GOD; let that be known to you. D
36:33 Thus s the Lord GOD: C
36:37 Thus s the Lord GOD: I will also let C
37: 5 Thus s the Lord GOD to these bones: C
37: 9 to the breath: Thus s the Lord GOD: C
37:12 and say to them, Thus s the Lord GOD: C
37:14 have spoken and will act," s the LORD. A
37:19 say to them, Thus s the Lord GOD: C
37:21 then say to them, Thus s the Lord GOD: C
38: 3 and say: Thus s the Lord GOD: C
38:10 Thus s the Lord GOD: C
38:14 to Gog: Thus s the Lord GOD: C
38:17 Thus s the Lord GOD: Are you he of whom C
38:18 s the Lord GOD, my wrath shall be aroused. D
38:21 in all my mountains, s the Lord GOD; D
39: 1 and say: Thus s the Lord GOD: C
39: 5 for I have spoken, s the Lord GOD. D
39: 8 It has happened, s the Lord GOD. D
39:10 those who plundered them, s the Lord GOD. D
39:13 the day that I show my glory, s the Lord GOD. D
39:17 As for you, mortal, thus s the Lord GOD: C
39:20 and all kinds of soldiers, s the Lord GOD. D
39:25 Therefore thus s the Lord GOD: C
39:29 upon the house of Israel, s the Lord GOD. D
43:18 Mortal, thus s the Lord GOD: C
43:19 s the Lord GOD, a bull for a sin offering. D
43:27 and I will accept you, s the Lord GOD. D
44: 6 to the house of Israel, Thus s the Lord GOD: C
44: 9 Thus s the Lord GOD: No foreigner, C
44:12 have sworn concerning them, s the Lord GOD, D
44:15 the fat and the blood, s the Lord GOD. D
44:27 he shall offer his sin offering, s the Lord GOD. D
45: 9 Thus s the Lord GOD: Enough, C
45: 9 of my people, s the Lord GOD. D
45:15 to make atonement for them, s the Lord GOD. D
45:18 Thus s the Lord GOD: In the first month C
46: 1 Thus s the Lord GOD: The gate of the inner C
46:16 Thus s the Lord GOD: If the prince C
47:13 Thus s the Lord GOD: These are the boundaries C
47:23 assign them their inheritance, s the Lord GOD. D
48:29 and these are their portions, s the Lord GOD. D
Hos 2:13 and forgot me, s the LORD. A
2:16 On that day, s the LORD, you will call me, A
2:21 On that day I will answer, s the LORD, A
11:11 I will return them to their homes, s the LORD. A
Joel 2:12 Yet even now, s the LORD, A
Am 1: 3 Thus s the LORD: For three transgressions of B
1: 5 Aram shall go into exile to Kir, s the LORD. A
1: 6 Thus s the LORD: For three transgressions of B
1: 8 of the Philistines shall perish, s the Lord GOD. D
1: 9 Thus s the LORD: For three transgressions of B
1:11 Thus s the LORD: For three transgressions of B
1:13 Thus s the LORD: For three transgressions of the B
1:15 he and his officials together, s the LORD. A
2: 1 Thus s the LORD: For three transgressions of B
2: 3 will kill all its officials with him, s the LORD. A
2: 4 Thus s the LORD: For three transgressions of B
2: 6 Thus s the LORD: For three transgressions of B
2:11 O people of Israel? s the LORD. A
2:16 shall flee away naked in that day, s the LORD. A
3:10 They do not know how to do right, s the LORD, A
3:11 Therefore thus s the Lord GOD: C
3:12 Thus s the LORD: As the shepherd rescues from B
3:13 s the Lord GOD, the God of hosts: D
3:15 great houses shall come to an end, s the LORD. A

Am 4: 3 you shall be flung out into Harmon, s the LORD. A
4: 5 O people of Israel! s the Lord GOD. D
4: 6 yet you did not return to me, s the LORD. A
4: 8 yet you did not return to me, s the LORD. A
4: 9 yet you did not return to me, s the LORD. A
4:10 yet you did not return to me, s the LORD. A
4:11 yet you did not return to me, s the LORD. A
5: 3 For thus s the Lord GOD: C
5: 4 For thus s the LORD to the house of Israel: B
5:16 thus s the LORD, the God of hosts, the Lord: B
5:17 will pass through the midst of you, s the LORD. A
5:27 s the LORD, whose name is the God of hosts. A
6: 8 Lord GOD has sworn by himself (s the LORD, A
6:14 O house of Israel, s the LORD, the God of hosts, A
7:17 Therefore thus s the LORD: B
8: 3 become wailings in that day," s the Lord GOD; D
8: 9 On that day, s the Lord GOD, D
8:11 The time is surely coming, s the Lord GOD, D
9: 7 O people of Israel? s the LORD. A
9: 8 utterly destroy the house of Jacob, s the LORD. A
9:12 s the LORD who does this. A
9:13 The time is surely coming, s the LORD, A
9:15 that I have given them, s the LORD your God. A
Ob 1: 1 Thus s the Lord GOD concerning Edom: C
1: 4 from there I will bring you down, s the LORD. A
1: 8 On that day, s the LORD, A
Mic 2: 3 Therefore thus s the LORD: B
3: 5 Thus s the LORD concerning B
4: 6 In that day, s the LORD, I will assemble the lame A
5:10 s the LORD, I will cut off your horses from A
6: 1 Hear what the LORD s: Rise,
Na 1:12 Thus s the LORD, "Though they are B
2:13 See, I am against you, s the LORD of hosts, A
3: 5 s the LORD of hosts, and will lift up your skirts A
Zep 1: 2 from the face of the earth, s the LORD. A
1: 3 from the face of the earth, s the LORD. A
1:10 On that day, s the LORD, A
2: 9 Therefore, as I live, s the LORD of hosts, A
3: 8 Therefore wait for me, s the LORD, A
3:20 your fortunes before your eyes, s the LORD. A
Hag 1: 2 Thus s the LORD of hosts: B
1: 5 Now therefore thus s the LORD of hosts: B
1: 7 Thus s the LORD of hosts: B
1: 8 take pleasure in it and be honored, s the LORD. A
1: 9 s the LORD of hosts. A
1:13 saying, I am with you, s the LORD. A
2: 4 now take courage, O Zerubbabel, s the LORD; A
2: 4 all you people of the land, s the LORD; A
2: 4 work, for I am with you, s the LORD of hosts, A
2: 6 For thus s the LORD of hosts: B
2: 7 I will fill this house with splendor, s the LORD A
2: 8 and the gold is mine, s the LORD of hosts. A
2: 9 be greater than the former, s the LORD of hosts; A
2: 9 in this place I will give prosperity, s the LORD A
2:11 Thus s the LORD of hosts: B
2:14 and with this nation before me, s the LORD; A
2:17 yet you did not return to me, s the LORD. A
2:23 On that day, s the LORD of hosts, I will take you, A
2:23 s the LORD, and make you like a signet ring; A
2:23 for I have chosen you, s the LORD of hosts. A
Zec 1: 3 say to them, Thus s the LORD of hosts: B
1: 3 Return to me, s the LORD of hosts, A
1: 3 and I will return to you, s the LORD of hosts. A
1: 4 "Thus s the LORD of hosts, B
1: 4 But they did not hear or heed me, s the LORD. A
1:14 Thus s the LORD of hosts; B
1:16 Therefore, thus s the LORD, B
1:16 my house shall be built in it, s the LORD A
1:17 Proclaim further: Thus s the LORD of hosts: B
2: 5 I will be a wall of fire all around it, s the LORD, A
2: 6 Flee from the land of the north, s the LORD; A
2: 6 like the four winds of heaven, s the LORD. A
2:10 I will come and dwell in your midst, s the LORD. A
3: 7 "Thus s the LORD of hosts: B
3: 9 s the LORD of hosts, and I will remove the guilt A
3:10 On that day, s the LORD of hosts, A
4: 6 but by my spirit, s the LORD of hosts. A
5: 4 I have sent it out, s the LORD of hosts, A
6:12 Thus s the LORD of hosts: B
7: 9 Thus s the LORD of hosts: B
7:13 I would not hear, s the LORD of hosts, A
8: 2 Thus s the LORD of hosts: B
8: 3 Thus s the LORD: I will return to Zion, B
8: 4 Thus s the LORD of hosts: B
8: 6 Thus s the LORD of hosts: B
8: 6 also seem impossible to me, s the LORD A
8: 7 Thus s the LORD of hosts: B
8: 9 Thus s the LORD of hosts: B
8:11 this people as in the former days, s the LORD A
8:14 For thus s the LORD of hosts: B
8:14 and I did not relent, s the LORD of hosts, A
8:17 for all these are things that I hate, s the LORD. A
8:19 Thus s the LORD of hosts: B
8:20 Thus s the LORD of hosts: B
8:23 Thus s the LORD of hosts: B
10:12 and they shall walk in his name, s the LORD. A
11: 6 on the inhabitants of the earth, s the LORD. A
12: 1 Thus s the LORD, who stretched out the heavens B
12: 4 On that day, s the LORD, A
13: 2 On that day, s the LORD of hosts, A
13: 7 the man who is my associate," s the LORD A
13: 8 In the whole land, s the LORD, A
Mal 1: 2 I have loved you, s the LORD. A
1: 2 not Esau Jacob's brother? s the LORD. A
1: 4 If Edom s, "We are shattered but we will rebuild
1: 4 the ruins," the LORD of hosts s:
1: 6 s the LORD of hosts to you, O priests, A

Mal 1: 8 s the LORD of hosts. A
1: 9 s the LORD of hosts. A
1:10 I have no pleasure in you, s the LORD of hosts, A
1:11 name is great among the nations, s the LORD A
1:13 and you sniff at me, s the LORD of hosts. A
1:13 from your hand? s the LORD. A
1:14 for I am a great King, s the LORD of hosts, A
2: 2 s the LORD of hosts, then I will send the curse A
2: 4 my covenant with Levi may hold, s the LORD A
2: 8 the covenant of Levi, s the LORD of hosts, A
2:16 For I hate divorce, s the LORD, the God of Israel, A
2:16 one's garment with violence, s the LORD A
3: 1 indeed, he is coming, s the LORD of hosts. A
3: 5 and do not fear me, s the LORD of hosts. A
3: 7 and I will return to you, s the LORD of hosts. A
3:10 and thus put me to the test, s the LORD of hosts; A
3:11 the field shall not be barren, s the LORD of hosts. A
3:12 for you will be a land of delight, s the LORD A
3:13 spoken harsh words against me, s the LORD. A
3:17 They shall be mine, s the LORD of hosts, A
4: 1 that comes shall burn them up, s the LORD A
4: 3 on the day when I act, s the LORD of hosts. A
Mt 7:21 "Not everyone who s to me, 'Lord, Lord,'
12:44 Then it s, 'I will return to my house
13:14 the prophecy of Isaiah that s:
21: 3 If anyone s anything to you, just say this,
24:23 Then if anyone s to you, 'Look!
24:48 But if that wicked slave s to himself,
26:18 and say to him, 'The Teacher s, My time is near;
Mk 11: 3 If anyone s to you, 'Why are you doing this?'
13:21 And if anyone s to you at that time, 'Look!
Lk 5:39 but s, 'The old is good.'"
11:24 but not finding any, it s, 'I will return to my house
12:45 But if that slave s to himself,
17: 4 and turns back to you seven times and s,
18: 6 the Lord said, "Listen to what the unjust judge s.
20:42 For David himself s in the book of Psalms,
Jn 19:24 This was to fulfill what the scripture s,
19:37 And again another passage of scripture s,
Ac 2:25 For David s concerning him,
2:34 but he himself s, 'The Lord said to my Lord,
7:48 with human hands; as the prophet s,
7:49 s the Lord, or what is the place of my rest? E
15:17 my name has been called. Thus s the Lord, F
21:11 and said, "Thus s the Holy Spirit,
Ro 3:19 Now we know that whatever the law s,
9:15 For he s to Moses, "I will have mercy
9:17 For the scripture s to Pharaoh,
9:25 As indeed he s in Hosea,
10: 6 But the righteousness that comes from faith s,
10:11 The scripture s, "No one who believes in him will
10:16 Isaiah s, "Lord, who has believed our message?"
10:19 First Moses s, "I will make you jealous
10:21 But of Israel he s, "All day long I have held out
11: 2 Do you not know what the scripture s of Elijah,
11: 9 And David s, "Let their table become a snare and
12:19 "Vengeance is mine, I will repay, s the Lord." E
14:11 For it is written, "As I live, s the Lord, E
15:10 again he s, "Rejoice, O Gentiles, with his people";
15:12 and again Isaiah s, "The root of Jesse shall come,
1Co 1:12 What I mean is that each of you s,
3: 4 For when one s, "I belong to Paul," and another,
10:28 But if someone s to you, "This has been offered
12: 3 by the Spirit of God ever s "Let Jesus be cursed!"
14:21 even then they will not listen to me," s the Lord. E
14:34 but should be subordinate, as the law also s.
15:27 But when it s, "All things are put in subjection,"
2Co 6: 2 For he s, "At an acceptable time I have listened
6:17 s the Lord, and touch nothing unclean; E
6:18 my sons and daughters, s the Lord Almighty." E
Gal 3:16 but it s, "And to your offspring," that is,
Eph 4: 9 (When it s, "He ascended,"
5:14 Therefore it s, "Sleeper, awake!
1Ti 4: 1 Now the Spirit expressly s that in later times
5:18 for the scripture s, "You shall not muzzle an ox
Heb 1: 6 when he brings the firstborn into the world, he s,
1: 7 Of the angels he s, "He makes his angels winds,
1: 8 But of the Son he s, "Your throne, O God,
3: 7 Therefore, as the Holy Spirit s, "Today,
4: 5 And again in this place it s,
5: 6 as he s also in another place,
8: 8 God finds fault with them when he s:
8: 8 "The days are surely coming, s the Lord, E
8: 9 and so I had no concern for them, s the Lord. E
8:10 the house of Israel after those days, s the Lord: E
10:16 make with them after those days, s the Lord: E
Jas 2:16 and one of you s to them, "Go in peace;
2:23 Thus the scripture was fulfilled that s,
4: 5 that it is for nothing that the scripture s,
4: 6 But he gives all the more grace; therefore it s,
1Jn 2: 4 Whoever s, "I have come to know him,"
2: 6 whoever s, "I abide in him," ought to walk just
2: 9 Whoever s, "I am in the light,"
Rev 1: 8 "I am the Alpha and the Omega," s the Lord E
14:13 s the Spirit, "they will rest from their labors,
18: 7 Since in her heart she s, 'I rule as a queen;
22:20 The one who testifies to these things s,
Jdt 2: 5 "Thus s the Great King, the lord of
6: 4 s King Nebuchadnezzar, lord of the whole earth.
Wis 2:20 for, according to what he s, he will be protected."
Sir 11:19 when he s, "I have found rest,
13:23 they extol to the clouds what he s.
20:16 The fool s, "I have no friends,
23:18 one who sins against his marriage bed s to himself,
37: 1 Every friend s, "I too am a friend";
Bar 2:21 Thus s the Lord: Bend your shoulders F
1Mc 11:31 so that you may know what it s.
1Mc 14:44 of these decisions or to oppose what he s,
1Es 2: 3 "Thus s Cyrus king of the Persians:
4: 3 and whatever he s to them they obey.
2Es 1:12 "But speak to them and say, Thus s the Lord: F
1:14 Yet you have forgotten me, s the Lord. E
1:15 "Thus s the Lord Almighty: F
1:21 What more can I do for you? s the Lord. E
1:22 Thus s the Lord Almighty: F
1:27 you have forsaken yourselves, s the Lord. E
1:28 "Thus s the Lord Almighty: F
1:32 I will require their blood of you, s the Lord. E
1:33 "Thus s the Lord Almighty: F
2: 1 "Thus s the Lord: I brought this people out of F
2: 2 The mother who bore them s to them, 'Go,
2: 9 not listened to me, s the Lord Almighty." E
2:10 Thus s the Lord to Ezra: F
2:14 for I am the Living One, s the Lord. E
2:15 because I have chosen you, s the Lord. E
2:17 for I have chosen you, s the Lord. E
2:28 be able to do anything against you, s the Lord. E
2:30 because I will deliver you, s the Lord. E
2:31 for I am merciful, s the Lord Almighty. E
11:38 The Most High s to you,
15: 1 that I will put in your mouth, s the Lord, E
15: 5 s the Lord, I am bringing evils upon the world, E
15: 7 Therefore, s the Lord, E
15: 9 I will surely avenge them, s the Lord, E
15:20 s God, from the rising sun and from the south,
15:21 into their bosom. Thus s the Lord God: F
15:24 not observe my commandments, s the Lord; E
15:48 Therefore God s,
15:52 with you so violently, s the Lord, E
15:56 As you will do to my chosen people, s the Lord, E
16:36 receive it and do not disbelieve what the Lord s.
16:48 I will be with them for their sins, s the Lord. E
16:53 of fire on the head of everyone who s,
16:74 Listen, my elect ones, s the Lord; E
16:76 s the Lord God, must not let your sins weigh E
4Mc 2: 5 Thus the law s, "You shall not covet
17:19 For Moses s, "All who are consecrated are
18:14 which s, 'Even though you go through the fire,
18:18 to teach you the song that Moses taught, which s,

SCAB, SCABBED (KJV) See ERUPTION, SCURVY, SPOT

SCABBARD (1)

Jer 47: 6 Put yourself into your s, rest and be still!

SCABS (3)

Lev 21:20 a blemish in his eyes or an itching disease or s
22:22 or maimed, or having a discharge or an itch or s—
Isa 3:17 with s the heads of the daughters of Zion,

SCAFFOLD (KJV) See PLATFORM

SCALE (5) [SCALES]

1Ki 22:34 of Israel between the s armor and the breastplate;
2Ch 18:33 of Israel between the s armor and the breastplate;
Joel 2: 7 like soldiers they s the wall.
Sir 1:22 for anger tips the s to one's ruin.
2Es 3:34 be found which way the turn of the s will incline.

SCALES (22) [SCALE]

Lev 11: 9 Everything in the waters that has fins and s,
11:10 and s, of the swarming creatures in the waters and
11:12 that does not have fins and s is detestable to you.
Dt 14: 9 whatever has fins and s you may eat.
14:10 And whatever does not have fins and s you shall
Pr 16:11 Honest balances and s are the LORD's;
20:23 and false s are not good.
Isa 40:12 and weighed the mountains in s and the hills in
40:15 and are accounted as dust on the s;
46: 6 and weigh out silver in the s—
Jer 32:10 got witnesses, and weighed the money on s.
Eze 29: 4 and make the fish of your channels stick to your s.
29: 4 the fish of your channels sticking to your s.
Da 5:27 you have been weighed on the s
Mic 6:11 Can I tolerate wicked s and a bag
Ac 9:18 immediately something like s fell from his eyes,
Rev 6: 5 Its rider held a pair of s in his hand,
9: 9 they had s like iron breastplates,
Wis 11:22 before you is like a speck that tips the s,
Sir 26:15 and no s can weigh the value of her chastity.
28:25 so make balances and s for your words.
42: 4 with s and weights, and of acquiring much

SCALL (KJV) See ITCH, ITCHING

SCALP (4) [SCALPED]

Dt 33:20 Gad lives like a lion; he tears at arm and s.
Jer 48:45 the s of the people of tumult.
2Mc 7: 4 be cut out and that they s him and cut off his hands
4Mc 9:28 up to his chin, and tore away his s.

SCALPED (2) [SCALP]

4Mc 10: 7 the instruments and s him with their fingernails in
15:20 severed hands upon hands, s heads upon heads,

SCANT (2)

Mic 6:10 and the s measure that is accursed?
1Mc 6:57 "Daily we grow weaker, our food supply is s,

SCAPEGOAT See Index to Footnotes

SCAR (2)

Lev 13:23 and does not spread, it is the s of the boil;
13:28 pronounce him clean; for it is the s of the burn.

SCARCELY (10) [SCARCITY]

Ge 27:30 when Jacob had s gone out from the presence
Ecc 5:20 For they will s brood over the days of their lives,
SS 3: 4 S had I passed them,
Isa 40:24 S are they planted, s sown, s has their stem taken
41: 3 s touching the path with his feet.
Lk 9:39 it mauls him and will s leave him.
Ac 14:18 they s restrained the crowds
27:16 a small island called Cauda we were s able to get

SCARCITY (1) [SCARCELY]

Dt 8: 9 a land where you may eat bread without s,

SCARE (1) [SCARED, SCARES]

Job 7:14 you s me with dreams and terrify me with visions,

SCARECROW (1) [SCARECROWS]

LtJ 6:70 Like a s in a cucumber bed, which guards nothing,

SCARECROWS (1) [SCARECROW]

Jer 10: 5 Their idols are like s in a cucumber field,

SCARED (1) [SCARE]

Wis 17: 9 s by the passing of wild animals and the hissing

SCARES (1) [SCARE]

Sir 22:20 One who throws a stone at birds s them away,

SCARFS (1)

Isa 3:19 the pendants, the bracelets, and the s;

SCARLET (7)

Isa 1:18 your sins are like s, they shall be like snow;
Mt 27:28 They stripped him and put a s robe on him,
Heb 9:19 with water and s wool and hyssop,
Rev 17: 3 on a s beast that was full of blasphemous names,
17: 4 The woman was clothed in purple and s,
18:12 jewels and pearls, fine linen, purple, silk and s,
18:16 in purple and s, adorned with gold, with jewels,

SCATTER (43) [SCATTERED, SCATTERING, SCATTERS]

Ge 49: 7 I will divide them in Jacob, and s them in Israel.
Lev 26:33 And you I will s among the nations,
Nu 16:37 then s the fire far and wide.
Dt 4:27 The LORD will s you among the peoples;
28:64 The LORD will s you among all peoples,
32:26 I thought to s them and blot out the memory
1Ki 14:15 and s them beyond the Euphrates,
Ne 1: 8 I will s you among the peoples;
Job 37:11 with moisture; the clouds s his lightning.
Ps 53: 5 For God will s the bones of the ungodly;
68:30 s the peoples who delight in war.
144: 6 Make the lightning flash and s them;
Isa 24: 1 and he will twist its surface and s its inhabitants.
28:25 they have leveled its surface, do they not s dill,
30:22 You will s them like filthy rags;
41:16 and the tempest shall s them.
Jer 9:16 I will s them among nations that neither they
13:24 I will s you like chaff driven by the wind from
18:17 I will s them before the enemy.
23: 1 Woe to the shepherds who destroy and s the sheep
49:32 I will s to every wind those who have shaven
49:36 and I will s them to all these winds,
Eze 5: 2 and one third you shall s to the wind,
5:10 and any of you who survive I will s to every wind.
5:12 and one third I will s to every wind
6: 5 and I will s your bones around your altars.
10: 2 and s them over the city."
12:14 I will s to every wind all who are around him,
12:15 the nations and s them through the countries.
20:23 to them in the wilderness that I would s them
22:15 I will s you among the nations and disperse you
29:12 I will s the Egyptians among the nations,
30:23 I will s the Egyptians among the nations,
30:26 and I will s the Egyptians among the nations
Da 4:14 strip off its foliage and s its fruit.
Hab 3:14 who came like a whirlwind to s us,
Zec 1:21 against the land of Judah to s its people."
Mt 25:24 and gathering where you did not s seed;
25:26 and gather where I did not s?
Mk 4:26 as if someone would s seed on the ground,
Sir 39:14 S the fragrance, and sing a hymn of praise;
Bar 2:29 among the nations, where I will s them.
2Mc 14:13 with orders to kill Judas and s his troops,

SCATTERED (92) [SCATTER]

Ge 11: 4 otherwise we shall be s abroad upon the face of
11: 8 the LORD s them abroad from there over the face
11: 9 from there the LORD s them abroad over the face
Ex 5:12 So the people s throughout the land of Egypt,
32:20 s it on the water, and made the Israelites drink it.
Nu 10:35 "Arise, O LORD, let your enemies be s,
Dt 30: 3 among whom the LORD your God has s you.

1Sa 11:11 and those who survived were s,
2Sa 22:15 He sent out arrows, and s them—lightning,
1Ki 22:17 Micaiah said, "I saw all Israel s on the mountains,
2Ki 25: 5 all his army was s, deserting him.
2Ch 18:16 Micaiah said, "I saw all Israel s on the mountains,
34: 4 he made dust of them and s it over the graves
Est 3: 8 "There is a certain people s and separated among
Job 4:11 and the whelps of the lioness are s.
18:15 sulfur is s upon their habitations.
38:24 or where the east wind is s upon the earth?
Ps 18:14 And he sent out his arrows, and s them;
44:11 and have s us among the nations.
68: 1 Let God rise up, let his enemies be s;
68:14 the Almighty s kings there, snow fell on Zalmon.
89:10 you s your enemies with your mighty arm.
92: 9 your enemies shall perish; all evildoers shall be s.
Pr 5:16 Should your springs be s abroad,
Isa 16: 2 Like fluttering birds, like s nestlings,
33: 3 before your majesty, nations s.
Jer 3:13 and s your favors among strangers
10:21 they have not prospered, and all their flock is s.
23: 2 It is you who have s my flock,
30:11 an end of all the nations among which I s you,
31:10 say, "He who s Israel will gather him,
40:12 the places to which they had been s and came to
40:15 around you would be s, and the remnant
49: 5 from all your neighbors, and you will be s,
52: 8 and all his army was s, deserting him.
La 4: 1 The sacred stones lie s at the head of every street.
4:16 The LORD himself has s them,
Eze 6: 8 among the nations and be s through the countries.
11:16 and though I s them among the countries,
11:17 of the countries where you have been s,
17:21 and the survivors shall be s to every wind;
20:34 the countries where you are s, with a mighty hand
20:41 of the countries where you have been s;
28:25 of Israel from the peoples among whom they are s,
29:13 from the peoples among whom they were s;
34: 5 So they were s, because there was no shepherd;
34: 5 and s, they became food for all the wild animals.
34: 6 My sheep were s, they wandered over all
34: 6 my sheep were s over all the face of the earth,
34:12 when they are among their s sheep,
34:12 from all the places to which they have been s on
34:21 with your horns until you s them far and wide,
36:19 I s them among the nations,
Joel 3: 2 because they have s them among the nations.
Na 3:18 Your people are s on the mountains with no one
Zep 3:10 my s ones, shall bring my offering.
Zec 1:19 "These are the horns that have s Judah, Israel,
1:21 He answered, "These are the horns that s Judah,
7:14 and I s them with a whirlwind among all
10: 9 Though I s them among the nations,
13: 7 Strike the shepherd, that the sheep may be s;
Mt 26:31 and the sheep of the flock will be s.'
Mk 14:27 the shepherd, and the sheep will be s.'
Lk 1:51 he has s the proud in the thoughts of their hearts.
Jn 16:32 when you will be s, each one to his home,
Ac 5:37 he also perished, and all who followed him were s.
8: 1 the apostles were s throughout the countryside
8: 4 Now those who were s went from place to place,
11:19 Now those who were s because of the persecution
Tob 13: 3 for he has s you among them.
13: 5 the nations among whom you have been s.
14: 4 will be s and taken as captives from the good land;
Jdt 5:19 from the places where they were s,
AdE 3: 8 a certain nation s among the other nations
9:19 On this account then the Jews who are s around
13: 4 that among all the nations in the world there is s
Wis 2: 4 be s like mist that is chased by the rays of the sun
11:20 at a single breath when pursued by justice and s by
17: 3 they were s, terribly alarmed,
Sir 28:14 and s them from nation to nation;
48:15 and were s over all the earth.
Bar 2: 4 where the Lord has s them.
2:13 among the nations where you have s us.
3: 8 we are today in our exile where you have s us,
Bel 1:14 and they s them throughout the whole temple in
1Mc 6:54 the rest s to their own homes,
2Mc 1:27 Gather together our s people,
2Es 1:11 and s in the east the peoples of two provinces,
2: 7 Let them be s among the nations;
5:28 and s your only one among the many?
5:36 and gather for me the s raindrops,
4Mc 15:15 their toes and fingers s on the ground,

SCATTERER See Index to Footnotes

SCATTERING (2) [SCATTER]
Job 37: 9 and cold from the s winds.
Ps 106:27 among the nations, s them over the lands.

SCATTERS (7) [SCATTER]
Job 36:30 he s his lightning around him and covers the roots
Ps 147:16 He gives snow like wool; he s frost like ashes.
Mt 12:30 and whoever does not gather with me s.
Lk 11:23 and whoever does not gather with me s.
Jn 10:12 and the wolf snatches them and s them.
2Co 9: 9 As it is written, "He s abroad, he gives to the poor;
Sir 43:17 He s the snow like birds flying down,

SCAVENGING (1)
Job 24: 5 s in the wasteland food for their young.

SCENT (4) [SCENTED]
Job 14: 9 at the s of water it will bud and put forth branches
SS 4:11 s of your garments is like the s of Lebanon.
7: 8 and the s of your breath like apples,

SCENTED (1) [SCENT]
Rev 18:12 purple, silk and scarlet, all kinds of s wood,

SCEPTER (29) [SCEPTERS]
Ge 49:10 The s shall not depart from Judah,
Nu 21:18 that the nobles of the people dug, with the s,
24:17 and a s shall rise out of Israel;
Est 4:11 if the king holds out the golden s to someone,
5: 2 and he held out to her the golden s that was
5: 2 Esther approached and touched the top of the s.
8: 4 The king held out the golden s to Esther,
Ps 45: 6 Your royal s is a s of equity;
60: 7 Ephraim is my helmet; Judah is my s.
89:44 You have removed the s from his hand,
108: 8 Ephraim is my helmet; Judah is my s.
110: 2 The LORD sends out from Zion your mighty s.
125: 3 For the s of wickedness shall not rest on
Isa 14: 5 the staff of the wicked, the s of rulers,
Jer 48:17 say, "How the mighty s is broken,
Eze 19:11 Its strongest stem became a ruler's s;
19:14 so that there remains in it no strong stem, no s
Am 1: 5 and the one who holds the s from Beth-eden;
1: 8 and the one who holds the s from Ashkelon;
Zec 10:11 and the s of Egypt shall depart.
Heb 1: 8 and the righteous s is the s of your kingdom.
AdE 4:11 the king stretches out the golden s is safe—
8: 4 The king extended his golden s to Esther,
14:11 do not surrender your s to what has no being;
15:11 Then he raised the golden s and touched her neck
Wis 10:14 the s of a kingdom and authority over his masters.
LtJ 6:14 One of them holds a s, like a district judge,

SCEPTERS‡ (3) [SCEPTER]
Wis 6:21 Therefore if you delight in thrones and s,
7: 8 I preferred her to s and thrones,
Sir 35:23 and breaks the s of the unrighteous;

SCEVA (1)
Ac 19:14 of a Jewish high priest named S were doing this.

SCHEDIA (1)
3Mc 4:11 the place called S, and the voyage was concluded

SCHEDULED (1)
Dt 31:10 "Every seventh year, in the s year of remission,

SCHEME (4) [SCHEMED, SCHEMER, SCHEMES, SCHEMING]
1Ki 2:23 Adonijah has devised this s at the risk of his life!
Ps 31:13 as they s together against me,
Eze 38:10 and you will devise an evil s.
AdE 16: 3 even undertake to s against their own benefactors.

SCHEMED (1) [SCHEME]
Bar 3:18 those who s to get silver,

SCHEMER (1) [SCHEME]
Pr 14:17 quick-tempered acts foolishly, and the s is hated.

SCHEMES (11) [SCHEME]
Job 5:13 and the s of the wily are brought to a quick end.
10: 3 to despise the work of your hands and favor the s
18: 7 and their own s throw them down.
21:27 I know your thoughts, and your s to wrong me.
Ps 10: 2 let them be caught in the s they have devised.
Pr 11: 6 but the treacherous are taken captive by their s.
Ecc 7:29 but they have devised many s.
Jer 4:14 How long shall your evil s lodge within you?
6:19 to bring disaster on this people, the fruit of their s,
11:19 not know it was against me that they devised s,
Hos 11: 6 and devours because of their s.

SCHEMING (2) [SCHEME]
Ps 64: 2 from the secret plots of the wicked, from the s
Eph 4:14 people's trickery, by their craftiness in deceitful s.

SCHISM (KJV) See DISSENSION

SCHOLAR (1)
Ezr 7:11 a s of the text of the commandments of the LORD

SCHOOL (KJV) See LECTURE HALL

SCHOOLMASTER (KJV) See DISCIPLINARIAN

SCIENCE (KJV) See KNOWLEDGE

SCOFF (8) [SCOFFED, SCOFFER, SCOFFERS, SCOFFING, SCOFFS]
Ps 10: 5 as for their foes, they s at them.
73: 8 They s and speak with malice;
74:10 How long, O God, is the foe to s?
74:22 remember how the impious s at you all day long.
Pr 9:12 if you s, you alone will bear it.
Isa 28:22 do not s, or your bonds will be made stronger;
Hab 1:10 At kings they s, and of rulers they make sport.
4Mc 5:22 You s at our philosophy as though living

SCOFFED (5) [SCOFF]
Dt 32:15 and s at the Rock of his salvation.
Zep 2:10 because they s and boasted against the people of
Lk 23:35 but the leaders s at him, saying, "He saved others;
Ac 17:32 they heard of the resurrection of the dead, some s;
1Es 1:51 the Lord spoke, they s at his prophets,

SCOFFER (10) [SCOFF]
Pr 9: 7 Whoever corrects a s wins abuse;
9: 8 A s who is rebuked will only hate you;
13: 1 but a s does not listen to rebuke.
14: 6 A s seeks wisdom in vain,
19:25 Strike a s, and the simple will learn prudence;
21:11 When a s is punished, the simple become wiser;
21:24 The proud, haughty person, named "S,"
22:10 Drive out a s, and strife goes out;
24: 9 and the s is an abomination to all.
Isa 29:20 tyrant shall be no more, and the s shall cease to be;

SCOFFERS (9) [SCOFF]
Ps 1: 1 or sit in the seat of s;
Pr 1:22 How long will s delight in their scoffing
15:12 S do not like to be rebuked;
19:29 Condemnation is ready for s,
29: 8 S set a city aflame, but the wise turn away wrath.
Isa 28:14 you s who rule this people in Jerusalem.
Ac 13:41 'Look, you s! Be amazed and perish,
2Pe 3: 3 that in the last days s will come,
Jude 1:18 "In the last time there will be s,

SCOFFING (5) [SCOFF]
2Ch 36:16 despising his words, and s at his prophets,
Job 34: 7 Who is there like Job, who drinks up s like water,
36:18 Beware that wrath does not entice you into s,
Pr 1:22 How long will scoffers delight in their s
2Pe 3: 3 s and indulging their own lusts

SCOFFS (1) [SCOFF]
Ps 74:18 Remember this, O LORD, how the enemy s,

SCOLDED (2) [SCOLDING]
1Sa 24: 7 So David s his men severely and did
Mk 14: 5 and the money given to the poor." And they s her.

SCOLDING (1) [SCOLDED]
Sir 29:28 for a sensible person to bear s about lodging and

SCOOP (1)
Lev 5:12 and the priest shall s up a handful of it

SCORCH (1) [SCORCHED, SCORCHING]
Rev 16: 8 and it was allowed to s them with fire;

SCORCHED (4) [SCORCH]
Eze 20:47 and all faces from south to north shall be s by it.
Mt 13: 6 But when the sun rose, they were s;
Mk 4: 6 And when the sun rose, it was s;
Rev 16: 9 they were s by the fierce heat,

SCORCHING (13) [SCORCH]
Ps 11: 6 a s wind shall be the portion of their cup.
Pr 6:28 Or can one walk on hot coals without s the feet?
16:27 and their speech is like a s fire.
Isa 11:15 will wave his hand over the River with his s wind;
49:10 neither s wind nor sun shall strike them down,
La 5:10 Our skin is black as an oven from the s heat
Mt 20:12 the burden of the day and the s heat.'
Lk 12:55 you say, 'There will be s heat'; and it happens.
Jas 1:11 the sun rises with its s heat and withers the field;
Rev 7:16 the sun will not strike them, nor any s heat;
Sir 18:16 Does not the dew give relief from the s heat?
34:19 from s wind and a shade from noonday sun,
43: 4 but three times as hot is the sun s the mountains;

SCORN (22) [SCORNED, SCORNERS, SCORNFUL, SCORNFULLY, SCORNS]
2Ch 30:10 but they laughed them to s, and mocked them.
Job 16:20 My friends s me; my eye pours out tears to God,
22:19 the innocent laugh them to s,
Ps 31:11 I am the s of all my adversaries,
39: 8 Do not make me the s of the fool.
44:13 the derision and s of those around us.
71:13 let those who seek to hurt me be covered with s
80: 6 You make us the s of our neighbors;
89:41 he has become the s of his neighbors.
109:25 I am an object of s to my accusers;
119:22 take away from me their s and contempt,
123: 4 Our soul has had more than its fill of the s
Jer 6:10 The word of the LORD is to them an object of s;
Mic 6:16 so you shall bear the s of my people.
Gal 4:14 you did not s or despise me,
Wis 4:18 but the Lord will laugh them to s.
Bar 2: 4 to be an object of s and a desolation among all
1Mc 2:49 "Arrogance and s have now become strong;

1Mc 3:14 who s the king's command."
2Mc 7:39 being exasperated at his s.
2Es 7:*76* not include yourself with those who have shown s,
7:*79* If it is one of those who have shown s and have

SCORNED (12) [SCORN]

Jdg 5:18 Zebulun is a people that s death;
2Sa 12:14 by this deed you have utterly s the LORD,
Ps 22: 6 s by others, and despised by the people.
SS 8: 7 the wealth of his house, it would be utterly s.
La 2: 7 The Lord has s his altar, disowned his sanctuary;
Eze 16:31 you were not like a whore, because you s payment.
23:32 you shall be s and derided, it holds so much.
Ac 19:27 the temple of the great goddess Artemis will be s,
2Es 7:24 They s his law, and denied his covenants;
7:*81* because they have s the law of the Most High.
9:11 as many as s my law while they still had freedom,
4Mc 6: 9 and s the punishment and endured the tortures.

SCORNERS (1) [SCORN]

Pr 3:34 Toward the s he is scornful,

SCORNFUL (1) [SCORN]

Pr 3:34 Toward the scorners he is s,

SCORNFULLY (1) [SCORN]

Wis 17: 7 and their boasted wisdom was s rebuked.

SCORNS (4) [SCORN]

2Ki 19:21 She despises you, she s you—
Job 39: 7 It s the tumult of the city;
Pr 30:17 a father and s to obey a mother will be pecked out
Isa 37:22 She despises you, she s you—

SCORPION (4) [SCORPIONS]

Lk 11:12 Or if the child asks for an egg, will give a s?
Rev 9: 5 like the torture of a s when it stings someone.
Sir 26: 7 taking hold of her is like grasping a s.
4Mc 11:10 so that he was completely curled back like a s,

SCORPIONS (10) [SCORPION]

Dt 8:15 an arid wasteland with poisonous snakes and s.
1Ki 12:11 but I will discipline you with s.' "
12:14 but I will discipline you with s."
2Ch 10:11 but I will discipline you with s.' "
10:14 but I will discipline you with s."
Eze 2: 6 and thorns surround you and you live among s;
Lk 10:19 to tread on snakes and s, and over all the power of
Rev 9: 3 like the authority of s of the earth.
9:10 They have tails like s, with stingers,
Sir 39:30 the fangs of wild animals and s and vipers,

SCOUNDREL (5) [SCOUNDRELS]

2Sa 16: 7 while he cursed, "Out! Out! Murderer! S!
20: 1 Now a s named Sheba son of Bichri,
Job 34:18 who says to a king, 'You s!'
Pr 6:12 A s and a villain goes around with crooked speech,
2Mc 13: 4 the anger of Antiochus against the s;

SCOUNDRELS (14) [SCOUNDREL]

Dt 13:13 that s from among you have gone out and led
Jdg 20:13 Now then, hand over those s in Gibeah,
1Sa 2:12 Now the sons of Eli were s;
2Sa 13:13 as for you, you would be as one of the s in Israel.
1Ki 21:10 seat two s opposite him, and have them bring
21:13 The two s came in and sat opposite him;
21:13 and the s brought a charge against Naboth,
2Ch 13: 7 and certain worthless s gathered around him
Pr 16:27 S concoct evil, and their speech is like
Jer 5:26 For s are found among my people;
Sir 11:33 Beware of s, for they devise evil,
Sus 1:32 she was veiled, the s ordered her to be unveiled,
1Mc 15: 3 Whereas certain s have gained control of
15:21 if any s have fled to you from their country,

SCOURED (1)

Lev 6:28 that shall be s and rinsed in water.

SCOURGE‡ (8) [SCOURGED, SCOURGES]

Jos 23:13 a s on your sides, and thorns in your eyes,
Job 5:21 You shall be hidden from the s of the tongue,
Ps 91:10 no evil shall befall you, no s come near your tent.
Isa 28:15 when the overwhelming s passes through it will
28:18 when the overwhelming s passes through you will
Wis 12:22 you s our enemies ten thousand times more,
Sir 23:11 and the s will not leave his house.
2Mc 9:11 and to come to his senses under the s of God,

SCOURGED (1) [SCOURGE]

3Mc 2:21 s him who had exalted himself in insolence

SCOURGES (6) [SCOURGE]

Ps 89:32 with the rod and their iniquity with s;
Jdt 8:27 but the Lord s those who are close to him in order
2Es 16:19 and anguish are sent as s for the correction
16:20 or ever be mindful of the s.
4Mc 6: 6 his flesh was being torn by s, his blood flowing,
9:12 they had worn themselves out beating him with s,

SCOURGES, SCOURGETH, SCOURGING, SCOURGINGS (KJV)
See also CHASTISES, FLOGGING

SCOUTS‡ (1)

1Ki 20:17 Ben-hadad had sent out s,

SCRAPE (2) [SCRAPED]

Job 2: 8 Job took a potsherd with which to s himself,
Eze 26: 4 I will s its soil from it and make it a bare rock.

SCRAPED (6) [SCRAPE]

Lev 14:41 He shall have the inside of the house s thoroughly,
14:41 and the plaster that is s off shall be dumped in
14:43 after he has taken out the stones and s the house
Nu 22:25 it s against the wall, and s Balaam's foot against
Jdg 14: 9 He s it out into his hands, and went on,

SCRAPS (1)

Jdg 1: 7 thumbs and big toes cut off used to pick up s under

SCRATCHED (1)

1Sa 21:13 He s marks on the doors of the gate,

SCREECH (1)

Zep 2:14 desert owl and the s owl shall lodge on its capitals;

SCREEN (21) [SCREENED, SCREENING]

Ex 26:36 You shall make a s for the entrance of the tent,
26:37 You shall make for the s five pillars of acacia,
27:16 of the court there shall be a s twenty cubits long,
35:12 the mercy seat, and the curtain for the s;
35:15 and the s for the entrance,
35:17 and the s for the gate of the court;
36:37 He also made a s for the entrance to the tent,
38:18 The s for the entrance to the court
39:34 and the curtain for the s;
39:38 and the s for the entrance of the tent;
39:40 and its bases, and the s for the gate of the court,
40: 3 and you shall s the ark with the curtain.
40: 5 and set up the s for the entrance of the tabernacle.
40: 8 and hang up the s for the gate of the court.
40:28 in place the s for the entrance of the tabernacle.
40:33 and put up the s at the gate of the court.
Nu 3:25 the s for the entrance of the tent of meeting,
3:26 the s for the entrance of the court that is around
3:31 and the s—all the service pertaining to these.
4:25 and the s for the entrance of the tent of meeting,
4:26 the s for the entrance of the gate of the court that is

SCREENED (1) [SCREEN]

Ex 40:21 and s the ark of the covenant;

SCREENING (2) [SCREEN]

Ex 40:21 and set up the curtain for s, and screened the ark
Nu 4: 5 and take down the s curtain, and cover the ark of

SCRIBE‡ (29) [SCRIBES]

1Ch 24: 6 The s Shemaiah son of Nethanel, a Levite,
27:32 being a man of understanding and a s;
Ezr 4: 8 and Shimshai the s wrote a letter against Jerusalem
4: 9 Shimshai the s, and the rest of their associates,
4:17 "To Rehum the royal deputy and Shimshai the s
4:23 and the s Shimshai and their associates,
7: 6 a s skilled in the law of Moses that the LORD
7:11 the s, a scholar of the text of the commandments
7:12 the s of the law of the God of heaven: Peace.
7:21 the s of the law of the God of heaven,
Ne 8: 1 the s Ezra to bring the book of the law of Moses,
8: 4 The s Ezra stood on a wooden platform
8: 9 who was the governor, and Ezra the priest and s,
8:13 the s Ezra in order to study the words of the law.
12:26 and of the priest Ezra, the s.
12:36 and the s Ezra went in front of them.
13:13 the s Zadok, and Pedaiah of the Levites,
Ps 45: 1 my tongue is like the pen of a ready s.
Mt 8:19 A s then approached and said, "Teacher,
13:52 "Therefore every s who has been trained for
Mk 12:32 Then the s said to him, "You are right, Teacher;
1Co 1:20 Where is the one who is wise? Where is the s?
Sir 38:24 The wisdom of the s depends on the opportunity
1Es 2:16 the s Shimshai, and the rest of their associates,
2:17 the recorder Rehum and the s Shimshai and
2:25 Beltethmus, the s Shimshai,
2:30 the s Shimshai and their associates went quickly
8: 3 This Ezra came up from Babylon as a s skilled in
8:25 Then Ezra the s said, "Blessed be the Lord alone,

SCRIBES‡ (65) [SCRIBE]

1Ch 2:55 The families also of the s that lived at Jabez:
2Ch 34:13 and some of the Levites were s, and officials,
Jer 8: 8 in fact, the false pen of the s has made it into a lie?
Na 3:17 your s like swarms of locusts settling on the fences
Mt 2: 4 and calling together all the chief priests and s of
5:20 unless your righteousness exceeds that of the s
7:29 as one having authority, and not as their s.
9: 3 Then some of the s said to themselves,
12:38 Then some of the s and Pharisees said to him,
15: 1 and s came to Jesus from Jerusalem and said,
16:21 at the hands of the elders and chief priests and s,
Mt 17:10 then, do the s say that Elijah must come first?"
20:18 the chief priests and s, and they will condemn him
21:15 the chief priests and the s saw the amazing things
23: 2 "The s and the Pharisees sit on Moses' seat;
23:13 "But woe to you, s and Pharisees, hypocrites!
23:15 Woe to you, s and Pharisees, hypocrites!
23:23 "Woe to you, s and Pharisees, hypocrites!
23:25 "Woe to you, s and Pharisees, hypocrites!
23:27 "Woe to you, s and Pharisees, hypocrites!
23:29 "Woe to you, s and Pharisees, hypocrites!
23:34 Therefore I send you prophets, sages, and s,
26:57 in whose house the s and the elders had gathered.
27:41 along with the s and elders, were mocking him,
Mk 1:22 as one having authority, and not as the s.
2: 6 Now some of the s were sitting there,
2:16 When the s of the Pharisees saw that he was eating
3:22 And the s who came down from Jerusalem said,
7: 1 of the s who had come from Jerusalem gathered
7: 5 So the Pharisees and the s asked him,
8:31 the chief priests, and the s, and be killed,
9:11 "Why do the s say that Elijah must come first?"
9:14 and some s arguing with them.
10:33 and the s, and they will condemn him to death;
11:18 And when the chief priests and the s heard it,
11:27 the chief priests, the s, and the elders came
12:28 One of the s came near and heard them disputing
12:35 can the s say that the Messiah is the son of David?
12:38 As he taught, he said, "Beware of the s,
14: 1 The chief priests and the s were looking for a way
14:43 from the chief priests, the s, and the elders.
14:53 the elders, and the s were assembled.
15: 1 with the elders and s and the whole council.
15:31 In the same way the chief priests, along with the s,
Lk 5:21 Then the s and the Pharisees began to question,
5:30 and their s were complaining to his disciples,
6: 7 The s and the Pharisees watched him
9:22 and be rejected by the elders, chief priests, and s,
11:53 the s and the Pharisees began to be very hostile
15: 2 Pharisees and the s were grumbling and saying,
19:47 the s, and the leaders of the people kept looking
20: 1 the chief priests and the s came with the elders
20:19 When the s and chief priests realized
20:39 Then some of the s answered, "Teacher,
20:46 of the s, who like to walk around in long robes,
22: 2 the s were looking for a way to put Jesus to death,
22:66 both chief priests and s, gathered together,
23:10 The chief priests and the s stood by,
Jn 8: 3 ⟦The s and the Pharisees brought a woman who⟧
Ac 4: 5 elders, and s assembled in Jerusalem,
6:12 up the people as well as the elders and the s;
23: 9 and certain s of the Pharisees' group stood up
1Mc 7:12 a group of s appeared in a body before Alcimus
2Mc 6:18 Eleazar, one of the s in high position,
3Mc 4:17 of time the s declared to the king

SCRIP (KJV) See BAG

SCRIPT‡ (4)

Est 1:22 to every province in its own s and to every people
3:12 in its own s and every people in its own language;
8: 9 to every province in its own s and to every people
8: 9 and also to the Jews in their s and their language.

SCRIPTURE‡ (34) [SCRIPTURES]

Mk 12:10 Have you not read this s:
Lk 4:21 "Today this s has been fulfilled in your hearing."
22:37 For I tell you, this s must be fulfilled in me,
Jn 2:22 the s and the word that Jesus had spoken.
7:38 As the s has said, 'Out of the believer's heart
7:42 Has not the s said that the Messiah is descended
10:35 and the s cannot be annulled—
13:18 But it is to fulfill the s,
17:12 so that the s might be fulfilled.
19:24 This was to fulfill what the s says,
19:28 he said (in order to fulfill the s), "I am thirsty."
19:36 These things occurred so that the s might
19:37 And again another passage of s says,
20: 9 for as yet they did not understand the s,
Ac 1:16 the s had to be fulfilled, which the Holy Spirit
8:32 the passage of the s that he was reading was this:
8:35 Philip began to speak, and starting with this s,
Ro 4: 3 For what does the s say?
9:17 For the s says to Pharaoh,
10:11 The s says, "No one who believes in him will
11: 2 Do you not know what the s says of Elijah,
2Co 4:13 same spirit of faith that is in accordance with s—
Gal 3: 8 And the s, foreseeing that God would justify
3:22 s has imprisoned all things under the power of sin,
4:30 But what does the s say?
1Ti 4:13 give attention to the public reading of s,
5:18 for the s says, "You shall not muzzle an ox
2Ti 3:16 All s is inspired by God and is useful for teaching,
Jas 2: 8 the royal law according to the s,
2:23 Thus the s was fulfilled that says,
4: 5 that it is for nothing that the s says,
1Pe 2: 6 For it stands in s: "See, I am laying in Zion
2Pe 1:20 of s is a matter of one's own interpretation,
4Mc 18:14 He reminded you of the s of Isaiah, which says,

SCRIPTURES (20) [SCRIPTURE]

Mt 21:42 Jesus said to them, "Have you never read in the s:
22:29 you know neither the s nor the power of God.
26:54 But how then would the s be fulfilled,
26:56 so that the s of the prophets may be fulfilled."
Mk 12:24 that you know neither the s nor the power of God?

Mk 14:49 But let the s be fulfilled.”
Lk 24:27 to them the things about himself in all the s.
24:32 while he was opening the s to us?”
24:45 Then he opened their minds to understand the s,
Jn 5:39 “You search the s because you think that
Ac 17: 2 on three sabbath days argued with them from the s,
17:11 and examined the s every day
18:24 He was an eloquent man, well-versed in the s.
18:28 showing by the s that the Messiah is Jesus.
Ro 1: 2 through his prophets in the holy s,
15: 4 the encouragement of the s we might have hope.
1Co 15: 3 Christ died for our sins in accordance with the s,
15: 4 on the third day in accordance with the s,
2Pe 3:16 to their own destruction, as they do the other s.
Sir Pr: 1 the s must not only themselves understand them,

SCROLL (53)

Ezr 6: 2 that a s was found on which this was written:
Ps 40: 7 in the s of the book it is written of me.
Isa 29:18 On that day the deaf shall hear the words of a s,
34: 4 and the skies roll up like a s.
Jer 36: 2 a s and write on it all the words that I have spoken
36: 4 and Baruch wrote on a s at Jeremiah's dictation all
36: 6 from the s that you have written at my dictation.
36: 8 about reading from the s the words of the LORD
36:10 Baruch read the words of Jeremiah from the s,
36:11 the words of the LORD from the s,
36:13 Baruch read the s in the hearing of the people.
36:14 the s that you read in the hearing of the people,
36:14 of Neriah took the s in his hand and came to them.
36:18 and I wrote them with ink on the s.”
36:20 the s in the chamber of Elishama the secretary,
36:21 Then the king sent Jehudi to get the s,
36:23 until the entire s was consumed in the fire that was
36:25 and Gemariah urged the king not to burn the s,
36:27 after the king had burned the s with the words
36:28 Take another s and write on it all the former words
36:28 on it all the former words that were in the first s,
36:29 You have dared to burn this s, saying,
36:32 Then Jeremiah took another s and gave it to
36:32 on it at Jeremiah's dictation all the words of the s
45: 1 a s at the dictation of Jeremiah, in the fourth year
51:60 a s all the disasters that would come on Babylon,
51:63 When you finish reading this s, tie a stone to it,
Eze 2: 9 and a written s was in it.
3: 1 eat this s, and go, speak to the house of Israel.
3: 2 I opened my mouth, and he gave me the s to eat.
3: 3 eat this s that I give you and fill your stomach
Zec 5: 1 Again I looked up and saw a flying s.
5: 2 I answered, “I see a flying s;
Lk 4:17 and the s of the prophet Isaiah was given to him.
4:17 the s and found the place where it was written:
4:20 And he rolled up the s,
Heb 9:19 and sprinkled both the s itself and all the people,
10: 7 O God' (in the s of the book it is written of me).”
Rev 5: 1 of the one seated on the throne a s written on the
5: 2 “Who is worthy to open the s and break its seals?”
5: 3 or under the earth was able to open the s or to look
5: 4 because no one was found worthy to open the s or
5: 5 so that he can open the s and its seven seals.”
5: 7 He went and took the s from the right hand of
5: 8 When he had taken the s,
5: 9 “You are worthy to take the s and to open its seals,
6:14 The sky vanished like a s rolling itself up,
10: 2 He held a little s open in his hand.
10: 8 take the s that is open in the hand of the angel
10: 9 to the angel and told him to give me the little s;
10:10 the little s from the hand of the angel and ate it;
Bar 1:14 you shall read aloud this s that we are sending you,
1Es 6:23 a s was found in which this was recorded:

SCRUB (1)

Isa 21:13 In the s of the desert plain you will lodge,

SCRUPLES (1) [SCRUPULOUSLY]

4Mc 4:13 although otherwise he had s about doing so,

SCRUPULOUSLY (2) [SCRUPLES]

1Es 6:29 of Coelesyria and Phoenicia a portion be s given
8:21 of God be s fulfilled for the Most High God,

SCRUTINY‡ (3)

1Co 2:15 and they are themselves subject to no one else's s.
Sir 18:20 and at the time of s you will find forgiveness.
23:10 for as a servant who is constantly under s will

SCULPTURED (2)

Jdg 3:19 he himself turned back at the s stones near Gilgal,
3:26 and passed beyond the s stones,

SCURVY (1)

Dt 28:27 s, and itch, of which you cannot be healed.

SCURVY (KJV) See also ITCH, ITCHING DISEASE

SCYTHES (1)

2Mc 13: 2 and three hundred chariots armed with s.

SCYTHIAN (3) [SCYTHIANS]

Col 3:11 circumcised and uncircumcised, barbarian, S,
3Mc 7: 5 with a cruelty more savage than that of S custom,
4Mc 10: 7 with their fingernails in a S fashion.

SCYTHIANS (1) [SCYTHIAN]

2Mc 4:47 if they had pleaded even before S.

SCYTHOPOLIS (3)

Jdt 3:10 he camped between Geba and S,
2Mc 12:29 Setting out from there, they hastened to S,
12:30 the goodwill that the people of S had shown them

SEA‡ (458) [SEA-BORN, SEA-MONSTERS, SEA-SERPENT, SEACOAST, SEAFARERS, SEAFOOD, SEAS, SEASHORE, SEASIDE]

A. RED SEA (30)
B. GREAT SEA (12)
C. DEAD SEA (10)

Ge 1:21 the great s monsters and every living creature
1:26 and let them have dominion over the fish of the s,
1:28 and have dominion over the fish of the s and over
9: 2 and on all the fish of the s;
14: 3 in the Valley of Siddim (that is, the Dead S). C
32:12 and make your offspring as the sand of the s,
41:49 like the sand of the s—
49:13 Zebulun shall settle at the shore of the s;
Ex 10:19 the locusts and drove them into the Red S; A
13:18 of the wilderness toward the Red S. A
14: 2 between Migdol and the s,
14: 2 you shall camp opposite it, by the s.
14: 9 they overtook them camped by the s,
14:16 and stretch out your hand over the s and divide it,
14:16 that the Israelites may go into the s on dry ground.
14:21 Then Moses stretched out his hand over the s.
14:21 the s back by a strong east wind all night,
14:21 and turned the s into dry land;
14:22 The Israelites went into the s on dry ground,
14:23 Egyptians pursued, and went into the s after them,
14:26 “Stretch out your hand over the s,
14:27 So Moses stretched out his hand over the s,
14:27 and at dawn the s returned to its normal depth.
14:27 the LORD tossed the Egyptians into the s.
14:28 of Pharaoh that had followed them into the s;
14:29 the Israelites walked on dry ground through the s,
15: 1 horse and rider he has thrown into the s.
15: 4 and his army he cast into the s;
15: 4 his picked officers were sunk in the Red S. A
15: 8 the deeps congealed in the heart of the s.
15:10 You blew with your wind, the s covered them;
15:19 went into the s, the LORD brought back the waters of the s upon them;
15:19 the Israelites walked through the s on dry ground.
15:21 horse and rider he has thrown into the s.”
15:22 Moses ordered Israel to set out from the Red S, A
20:11 the s, and all that is in them,
23:31 I will set your borders from the Red S to the sea A
23:31 from the Red Sea to the s of the Philistines,
Lev 11:16 the nighthawk, the s gull, the hawk of any kind;
Nu 11:22 Are there enough fish in the s to catch for them?”
11:31 and it brought quails from the s and let them fall
13:29 Canaanites live by the s, and along the Jordan.”
14:25 for the wilderness by the way to the Red S.” A
21: 4 by the way to the Red S, to go around the land A
33: 8 passed through the s into the wilderness,
33:10 set out from Elim and camped by the Red S. A
33:11 the Red S and camped in the wilderness of Sin. A
34: 3 from the end of the Dead S on the east; C
34: 5 and its termination shall be at the S.
34: 6 you shall have the Great S and its coast; B
34: 7 from the Great S you shall mark out your line B
34:11 and reach the eastern slope of the s of Chinnereth;
34:12 and its end shall be at the Dead S. C
Dt 1:40 in the direction of the Red S.” A
2: 1 in the direction of the Red S, A
3:17 from Chinnereth down to the s of the Arabah,
3:17 the Arabah, the Dead S, with the lower slopes C
4:49 on the east side of the Jordan as far as the S of
11: 4 the Red S flow over them as they pursued you, A
11:24 the river Euphrates, to the Western S
14:15 the nighthawk, the s gull, the hawk, of any kind;
30:13 Neither is it beyond the s, that you should say,
30:13 “Who will cross to the other side of the s for us,
34: 2 all the land of Judah as far as the Western S,
Jos 1: 4 to the Great S in the west shall be your territory. B
2:10 how the LORD dried up the water of the Red S A
3:16 while those flowing toward the s of the Arabah,
3:16 the Dead S, were wholly cut off. C
4:23 as the LORD your God did to the Red S, A
5: 1 and all the kings of the Canaanites by the s,
9: 1 along the coast of the Great S toward Lebanon— B
12: 3 the S of Chinneroth eastward, and in the direction
12: 3 to the s of the Arabah, the Dead Sea,
12: 3 to the sea of the Arabah, the Dead S, C
13:27 as far as the lower end of the S of Chinnereth,
15: 2 the Dead S, from the bay that faces southward; C
15: 4 and comes to its end at the s.
15: 5 And the east boundary is the Dead S, C
15: 5 from the bay of the s at the mouth of the Jordan;
15:11 then the boundary comes to an end at the s.
15:46 from Ekron to the s, all that were near Ashdod,
15:47 and the Great S with its coast. B
16: 3 then to Gezer, and it ends at the s.
16: 6 and the boundary goes from there to the s;
16: 8 to the Wadi Kanah, and ends at the s.
Jos 17: 9 along the north side of the wadi and ends at the s
17:10 with the s forming its boundary;
18:19 boundary ends at the northern bay of the Dead S, C
19:29 the boundary turns to Hosah, and it ends at the s;
23: 4 from the Jordan to the Great S in the west. B
24: 6 of Egypt, you came to the s;
24: 6 with chariots and horsemen to the Red S. A
24: 7 and made the s come upon them and cover them;
Jdg 5:17 Asher sat still at the coast of the s,
11:16 the wilderness to the Red S and came to Kadesh. A
2Sa 17:11 like the sand by the s for multitude,
22:16 Then the channels of the s were seen,
1Ki 4:20 and Israel were as numerous as the sand by the s;
5: 9 My servants shall bring it down to the s from
5: 9 into rafts to go by s to the place you indicate.
7:23 Then he made the molten s;
7:24 each of ten cubits, surrounding the s;
7:25 the s was set on them.
7:39 he set the s on the southeast corner of the house.
7:44 the one s, and the twelve oxen underneath the s.
9:26 which is near Eloth on the shore of the Red S, A
9:27 sailors who were familiar with the s,
10:22 the king had a fleet of ships of Tarshish at s with
18:43 “Go up now, look toward the s.”
18:44 a person's hand is rising out of the s.”
2Ki 14:25 from Lebo-hamath as far as the S of the Arabah,
16:17 he removed the s from the bronze oxen that were
25:13 the bronze s that were in the house of the LORD,
25:16 As for the two pillars, the one s, and the stands,
1Ch 16:32 Let the s roar, and all that fills it;
18: 8 with it Solomon made the bronze s and the pillars
2Ch 2:16 and bring it to you as rafts by s to Joppa;
4: 2 Then he made the molten s;
4: 3 each of ten cubits, surrounding the s;
4: 4 the s was set on them.
4: 6 The s was for the priests to wash in.
4:10 He set the s at the southeast corner of the house.
4:15 the one s, and the twelve oxen underneath it.
8:17 to Ezion-geber and Eloth on the shore of the s,
8:18 ships and servants familiar with the s.
20: 2 against you from Edom, from beyond the s;
Ezr 3: 7 to bring cedar trees from Lebanon to the s,
Ne 9: 9 in Egypt and heard their cry at the Red S. A
9:11 And you divided the s before them,
9:11 so that they passed through the s on dry land,
Est 10: 1 on the land and on the islands of the s.
Job 3: 8 Let those curse it who curse the S,
6: 3 then it would be heavier than the sand of the s;
7:12 Am I the S, or the Dragon,
9: 8 the heavens and trampled the waves of the S;
11: 9 the earth, and broader than the s.
12: 8 and the fish of the s will declare to you.
26:12 By his power he stilled the S;
28:14 The deep says, 'It is not in me,' and the s says,
36:30 around him and covers the roots of the s.
38: 8 “Or who shut in the s with doors when it burst out
38:16 “Have you entered into the springs of the s,
41:31 it makes the s like a pot of ointment.
Ps 8: 8 and the fish of the s,
18:15 Then the channels of the s were seen,
33: 7 He gathered the waters of the s as in a bottle;
46: 2 though the mountains shake in the heart of the s;
66: 6 He turned the s into dry land;
68:22 I will bring them back from the depths of the s,
72: 8 May he have dominion from s to s,
74:13 You divided the s by your might;
77:19 Your way was through the s, your path,
78:13 He divided the s and let them pass through it,
78:53 but the s overwhelmed their enemies.
80:11 it sent out its branches to the s,
89: 9 You rule the raging of the s;
89:25 I will set his hand on the s and his right hand on
93: 4 more majestic than the waves of the s,
95: 5 The s is his, for he made it, and the dry land,
96:11 let the s roar, and all that fills it;
98: 7 Let the s roar, and all that fills it;
104:25 Yonder is the s, great and wide,
106: 7 but rebelled against the Most High at the Red S. A
106: 9 He rebuked the Red S, and it became dry; A
106:22 and awesome deeds by the Red S. A
107:23 Some went down to the s in ships,
107:25 which lifted up the waves of the s.
107:29 and the waves of the s were hushed.
114: 3 The s looked and fled; Jordan turned back.
114: 5 Why is it, O s, that you flee?
136:13 who divided the Red S in two, A
136:15 overthrew Pharaoh and his army in the Red S, A
139: 9 and settle at the farthest limits of the s,
146: 6 the s, and all that is in them;
148: 7 you s monsters and all deeps,
Pr 8:29 when he assigned to the s its limit,
23:34 be like one who lies down in the midst of the s,
Ecc 1: 7 All streams run to the s, but the s is not full;
Isa 5:30 like the roaring of the s.
9: 1 of the s, the land beyond the Jordan, Galilee of
10:22 your people Israel were like the sand of the s,
10:26 his staff will be over the s,
11: 9 of the LORD as the waters cover the s.
11:11 from Hamath, and from the coastlands of the s.
11:15 the LORD will utterly destroy the tongue of the s
16: 8 shoots once spread abroad and crossed over the s.
17:12 they thunder like the thundering of the s!
21: 1 The oracle concerning the wilderness of the s.
23: 2 your messengers crossed over the s
23: 4 O Sidon, for the s has spoken, the fortress of the s,
23:11 He has stretched out his hand over the s,
24:15 in the coastlands of the s glorify the name of

Isa 27: 1 and he will kill the dragon that is in the s.
42:10 Let the s roar and all that fills it,
43:16 Thus says the LORD, who makes a way in the s,
48:18 and your success like the waves of the s;
50: 2 By my rebuke I dry up the s,
51:10 Was it not you who dried up the s,
51:10 of the s a way for the redeemed to cross over?
51:15 who stirs up the s so that its waves roar—
57:20 wicked are like the tossing s that cannot keep still;
60: 5 the abundance of the s shall be brought to you,
63:11 Where is the one who brought them up out of the s
Jer 5:22 I placed the sand as a boundary for the s,
6:23 their sound is like the roaring s;
25:22 and the kings of the coastland across the s;
27:19 the LORD of hosts concerning the pillars, the s,
31:35 who stirs up the s so that its waves roar—
33:22 and the sands of the s cannot be measured,
46:18 and like Carmel by the s.
48:32 Your branches crossed over the s,
49:21 the sound of their cry shall be heard at the Red S. A
49:23 they are troubled like the s that cannot be quiet.
50:42 The sound of them is like the roaring s;
51:36 I will dry up her s and make her fountain dry;
51:42 The s has risen over Babylon;
52:17 the bronze s that were in the house of the LORD,
52:20 As for the two pillars, the one s,
52:20 the twelve bronze bulls that were under the s,
La 2:13 For vast as the s is your ruin; who can heal you?
Eze 26: 3 as the s hurls its waves.
26: 5 It shall become, in the midst of the s,
26:16 Then all the princes of the s shall step down
26:17 once mighty on the s, you and your inhabitants,
26:18 coastlands by the s are dismayed at your passing.
27: 3 which sits at the entrance to the s,
27: 9 all the ships of the s with their mariners were
27:29 The mariners and all the pilots of the s stand on
27:32 like Tyre in the midst of the s?
38:20 the fish of the s, and the birds of the air,
39:11 the Valley of the Travelers east of the s;
47: 8 and when it enters the s,
47: 8 when it enters the sea, the s of stagnant waters,
47:10 beside the s from En-gedi to En-eglaim;
47:10 like the fish of the Great S. B
47:15 the Great S by way of Hethlon to Lebo-hamath, B
47:17 the boundary shall run from the s to Hazar-enon,
47:18 to the eastern s and as far as Tamar.
47:19 along the Wadi of Egypt to the Great S. B
47:20 the Great S shall be the boundary to B
48:28 along the Wadi of Egypt to the Great S. B
Da 7: 2 the four winds of heaven stirring up the great s, B
7: 3 and four great beasts came up out of the s,
11:45 He shall pitch his palatial tents between the s and
Hos 1:10 the people of Israel shall be like the sand of the s,
4: 3 even the fish of the s are perishing.
Joel 2:20 into the eastern s, and its rear into the western s;
Am 5: 8 who calls for the waters of the s,
6:12 Does one plow the s with oxen?
8:12 They shall wander from s to s,
9: 3 they hide from my sight at the bottom of the s,
9: 6 who calls for the waters of the s,
Jnh 1: 4 But the LORD hurled a great wind upon the s,
1: 4 upon the s that the ship threatened to break up.
1: 5 the cargo that was in the ship into the s,
1: 9 who made the s and the dry land."
1:11 that the s may quiet down for us?"
1:11 the s was growing more and more tempestuous.
1:12 "Pick me up and throw me into the s;
1:12 then the s will quiet down for you;
1:13 the s grew more and more stormy against them.
1:15 So they picked Jonah up and threw him into the s;
1:15 and the s ceased from its raging.
Mic 7:12 from s to s and from mountain to mountain.
7:19 You will cast all our sins into the depths of the s.
Na 1: 4 He rebukes the s and makes it dry,
3: 8 with water around her, her rampart a s,
Hab 1:14 You have made people like the fish of the s,
2:14 as the waters cover the s.
3: 8 or your rage against the s,
3:15 You trampled the s with your horses,
Zep 1: 3 the birds of the air and the fish of the s.
Hag 2: 6 I will shake the heavens and the earth and the s
Zec 9: 4 of its possessions and hurl its wealth into the s,
9:10 his dominion shall be from s to s,
10:11 They shall pass through the s of distress,
10:11 and the waves of the s shall be struck down,
14: 8 the eastern s and half of them to the western s;
Mt 4:13 and made his home in Capernaum by the s,
4:15 on the road by the s, across the Jordan,
4:18 As he walked by the S of Galilee,
4:18 casting a net into the s—for they were fishermen.
8:24 A windstorm arose on the s,
8:26 Then he got up and rebuked the winds and the s;
8:27 that even the winds and the s obey him?"
8:32 the steep bank into the s and perished in the water.
9: 1 a boat he crossed the s and came to his own town.
12:40 and three nights in the belly of the s monster,
13: 1 of the house and sat beside the s.
13:47 of heaven is like a net that was thrown into the s
14:25 morning he came walking toward them on the s.
14:26 But when the disciples saw him walking on the s,
15:29 he passed along the S of Galilee,
17:27 go to the s and cast a hook;
18: 6 and you were drowned in the depth of the s.
21:21 'Be lifted up and thrown into the s,'
23:15 For you cross s and land to make a single convert,
Mk 1:16 As Jesus passed along the S of Galilee,
1:16 and his brother Andrew casting a net into the s—

Mk 2:13 Jesus went out again beside the s;
3: 7 Jesus departed with his disciples to the s,
4: 1 Again he began to teach beside the s.
4: 1 that he got into a boat on the s and sat there,
4: 1 the whole crowd was beside the s on the land.
4:39 up and rebuked the wind, and said to the s,
4:41 that even the wind and the s obey him?"
5: 1 They came to the other side of the s,
5:13 rushed down the steep bank into the s,
5:13 and were drowned in the s.
5:21 and he was by the s.
6:47 When evening came, the boat was out on the s,
6:48 in the morning, walking on the s.
6:49 But when they saw him walking on the s,
7:31 went by way of Sidon towards the S of Galilee,
9:42 around your neck and you were thrown into the s.
11:23 'Be taken up and thrown into the s,'
Lk 17: 2 the s than for you to cause one of these little ones
17: 6 'Be uprooted and planted in the s,'
21:25 among nations confused by the roaring of the s
Jn 6: 1 After this Jesus went to the other side of the S of
Galilee, also called the S of Tiberias.
6:16 evening came, his disciples went down to the s,
6:17 and started across the s to Capernaum.
6:18 The s became rough because
6:19 they saw Jesus walking on the s and coming near
6:22 the s saw that there had been only one boat there.
6:25 When they found him on the other side of the s,
21: 1 to the disciples by the S of Tiberias;
21: 7 for he was naked, and jumped into the s.
Ac 4:24 who made the heaven and the earth, the s,
7:36 the Red S, and in the wilderness for forty years. A
10:32 in the home of Simon, a tanner, by the s.'
14:15 the heaven and the earth and the s and all that is
27: 2 we put to s, accompanied by Aristarchus,
27: 4 Putting out to s from there,
27: 5 After we had sailed across the s that is off Cilicia
27:12 majority was in favor of putting to s from there,
27:17 they lowered the s anchor and so were driven.
27:27 as we were drifting across the s of Adria,
27:30 from the ship and had lowered the boat into the s,
27:38 the ship by throwing the wheat into the s.
27:40 So they cast off the anchors and left them in the s.
28: 4 though he has escaped from the s,
Ro 9:27 of the children of Israel were like the sand of the s,
1Co 10: 1 and all passed through the s,
10: 2 into Moses in the cloud and in the s,
2Co 11:25 for a night and a day I was adrift at s;
11:26 danger at s, danger from false brothers and sisters;
Heb 11:29 By faith the people passed through the Red S as A
Jas 1: 6 for the one who doubts is like a wave of the s,
3: 7 and s creature, can be tamed and has been tamed
Jude 1:13 of the s, casting up the foam of their own shame;
Rev 4: 6 of the throne there is something like a s of glass,
5:13 and on earth and under the earth and in the s,
7: 1 the earth so that no wind could blow on earth or s
7: 2 who had been given power to damage earth and s,
7: 3 "Do not damage the earth or the s or the trees,
8: 8 burning with fire, was thrown into the s.
8: 9 A third of the s became blood,
8: 9 a third of the living creatures in the s died,
10: 2 Setting his right foot on the s and his left foot on
10: 5 Then the angel whom I saw standing on the s and
10: 6 and the s and what is in it:
10: 8 the hand of the angel who is standing on the s and
12:12 But woe to the earth and the s,
13: 1 a beast rising out of the s having ten horns
14: 7 the s and the springs of water."
15: 2 And I saw what appeared to be a s of glass mixed
15: 2 standing beside the s of glass with harps of God
16: 3 The second angel poured his bowl into the s,
16: 3 and every living thing in the s died.
18:17 sailors and all whose trade is on the s,
18:19 all who had ships at s grew rich by her wealth!
18:21 into the s, saying, "With such violence Babylon
20: 8 they are as numerous as the sands of the s.
20:13 And the s gave up the dead that were in it,
21: 1 and the s was no more.
Jdt 2:24 along the brook Abron, as far as the s.
5:13 Then God dried up the Red S before them, A
AdE 10: 1 a tax upon his kingdom both by land and s.
Wis 5:22 the water of the s will rage against them,
10:18 She brought them over the Red S, A
10:19 and cast them up from the depth of the s.
14: 3 because you have given it a path in the s,
14: 4 so that even a person who lacks skill may put to s.
19: 7 an unhindered way out of the Red S, A
19:12 for, to give them relief, quails came up from the s.
Sir 1: 2 The sand of the s, the drops of rain,
18:10 a drop of water from the s and a grain of sand,
24: 6 Over waves of the s, over all the earth,
24:29 For her thoughts are more abundant than the s,
24:31 And lo, my canal became a river, and my river a s.
29:18 and has tossed them about like waves of the s;
43:24 Those who sail the s tell of its dangers,
44:21 from s to s and from the Euphrates to the ends of
50: 3 a reservoir like the s in circumference.
Bar 3:30 Who has gone over the s, and found her,
Aza 1:13 of heaven and like the sand on the shore of the s.
1Mc 4: 9 how our ancestors were saved at the Red S, A
4:23 and cloth dyed blue and s purple, and great riches.
7: 1 sailed with a few men to a town by the s,
8:23 the Romans and with the nation of the Jews at s
8:32 we will defend their rights and fight you on s and
11: 8 of the coastal cities as far as Seleucia by the s,
13:29 so that they could be seen by all who sail the s.
14: 5 and opened a way to the isles of the s.

1Mc 14:34 He also fortified Joppa, which is by the s,
15: 1 sent a letter from the islands of the s to Simon,
15:11 in his flight to Dor, which is by the s;
15:14 and the ships joined battle from the s;
15:14 he pressed the town hard from land and s,
2Mc 5:21 that he could sail on the land and walk on the s,
9: 8 that he could command the waves of the s,
12: 4 of Joppa took them out to s and drowned them,
1Es 4: 2 who rule over land and s and all that is in them?
4:15 to the king and to every people that rules over s
4:23 and rob and steal and to sail the s and rivers;
Man 1: 3 who shackled the s by your word of command,
1: 9 in number than the sand of the s;
3Mc 2: 7 you overwhelmed him in the depths of the s,
6: 4 with his arrogant army by drowning them in the s,
7:20 by land and s and river to their own homes.
2Es 1:13 through the s, and made safe highways for you
4: 7 'How many dwellings are in the heart of the s,
4:14 'Come, let us go and make war against the s,
4:15 In like manner the waves of the s also made a plan
4:17 likewise also the plan of the waves of the s
4:19 and the locale of the s a place to carry its waves."
4:21 the land has been assigned to the forest and the s
5: 7 and the Dead S shall cast up fish; C
5:25 and from all the depths of the s you have filled
7: 3 a s set in a wide expanse so that it is deep and vast,
7: 5 If there are those who wish to reach the s,
9:34 when the ground has received seed, or the s a ship,
11: 1 the s an eagle that had twelve feathered wings
12:11 up from the s is the fourth kingdom that appeared
13: 2 wind arose from the s and stirred up all its waves.
13: 3 of a man come up out of the heart of the s.
13: 5 against the man who came up out of the s.
13:25 your seeing a man come up from the heart of the s,
13:32 whom you saw as a man coming up from the s.
13:51 the man coming up from the heart of the s?"
13:52 or know what is in the depths of the s,
16:12 the s is churned up from the depths,
16:57 he has measured the s and its contents;
16:58 he has confined the s in the midst of the waters;
4Mc 7: 1 the ship of religion over the s of the emotions,

SEA-BORN (1) [BEAR, SEA]

3Mc 6: 8 wasting away in the belly of a huge, s monster,

SEA-MONSTERS (1) [MONSTER, SEA]

Sir 43:25 all kinds of living things, and huge s.

SEA-SERPENT (1) [SERPENT, SEA]

Am 9: 3 there I will command the s, and it shall bite them.

SEACOAST (10) [COAST, SEA]

Dt 1: 7 the Shephelah, the Negeb, and the s—
Eze 25:16 and destroy the rest of the s.
Zep 2: 5 inhabitants of the s, you nation of the Cherethites!
2: 6 And you, O s, shall be pastures,
2: 7 The s shall become the possession of the remnant
Jdt 1: 7 and all who lived along the s,
2:28 upon all the people who lived along the s,
3: 6 to the s with his army and stationed garrisons in
5:22 Holofernes' officers and all the inhabitants of the s
2Mc 8:11 So he immediately sent to the towns on the s,

SEAFARERS (1) [SEA]

Rev 18:17 And all shipmasters and s,

SEAFOOD (1) [FOOD, SEA]

4Mc 1:34 Therefore when we crave s and fowl and animals

SEAHS See Index to Footnotes

SEAL‡ (38) [SEALED, SEALING, SEALS]

1Ki 21: 8 in Ahab's name and sealed them with his s;
Est 8: 8 and s it with the king's ring;
Job 38:14 It is changed like clay under the s,
41:15 shut up closely as with a s.
SS 8: 6 Set me as a s upon your heart,
8: 6 as a s upon your arm;
Isa 8:16 s the teaching among my disciples.
Da 8:26 As for you, s up the vision,
9:24 to s both vision and prophet,
Jn 6:27 For it is on him that God the Father has set his s."
Ro 4:11 the sign of circumcision as a s of the righteousness
1Co 9: 2 for you are the s of my apostleship in the Lord.
2Co 1:22 by putting his s on us and giving us his Spirit
Eph 1:13 with the s of the promised Holy Spirit;
4:30 with which you were marked with a s for the day
Rev 6: 3 When he opened the second s,
6: 5 When he opened the third s,
6: 7 When he opened the fourth s,
6: 9 When he opened the fifth s,
6:12 When he opened the sixth s, I looked,
7: 2 having the s of the living God,
7: 3 of our God with a s on their foreheads."
8: 1 When the Lamb opened the seventh s,
9: 4 but only those people who do not have the s
10: 4 "S up what the seven thunders have said,
22:10 not s up the words of the prophecy of this book,
AdE 3:10 and gave it to Haman to s the decree that was to
8: 8 Write in my name what you think best and s it
Sir 22:27 and an effective s upon my lips,
32: 5 A ruby s in a setting of gold is a concert of music
32: 6 A s of emerald in a rich setting of gold is

Sir 42: 6 there is an untrustworthy wife, a s is a good thing,
45:12 inscribed like a s with "Holiness,"
Bel 1:11 and shut the door and s it with your signet.
2Es 6:20 s is placed upon the age that is about to pass away,
7:*104* of judgment is decisive and displays to all the s
10:23 the s of Zion has been deprived of its glory,
4Mc 7:15 whom the faithful s of death has perfected!

SEALED‡ (34) [SEAL]

Dt 32:34 up in store with me, s up in my treasuries?
1Ki 21: 8 So she wrote letters in Ahab's name and s them
Ne 9:38 and on that s document are inscribed the names
10: 1 Upon the s document are the names of Nehemiah
Est 3:12 of King Ahasuerus and s with the king's ring.
8: 8 an edict written in the name of the king and s with
8:10 s them with the king's ring,
Job 14:17 my transgression would be s up in a bag,
SS 4:12 my bride, a garden locked, a fountain s.
Isa 29:11 for you like the words of a s document.
29:11 "Read this," they say, "We cannot, for it is s."
Jer 32:10 I signed the deed, s it, got witnesses,
32:11 Then I took the s deed of purchase,
32:14 both this s deed of purchase and this open deed,
32:44 and deeds shall be signed and s and witnessed,
Da 6:17 and the king s it with his own signet and with
12: 4 keep the words secret and the book s until the time
12: 9 the words are to remain secret and s until the time
Rev 5: 1 on the inside and on the back, s with seven seals;
7: 4 And I heard the number of those who were s,
7: 4 s out of every tribe of the people of Israel:
7: 5 From the tribe of Judah twelve thousand s,
7: 8 from the tribe of Benjamin twelve thousand s.
20: 3 and locked and s it over him,
AdE 8: 8 at the king's command and s with my ring cannot
8:10 with the king's authority and s with his ring,
Wis 2: 5 because it is s up and no one turns back.
Bel 1:14 shut the door and s it with the king's signet,
2Mc 2: 5 then he s up the entrance.
1Es 3: 8 and they s them and put them under the pillow
Man 1: 3 who confined the deep and s it with your terrible
2Es 2:38 of those who have been s at the feast of the Lord.
6: 5 those who stored up treasures of faith were s—
8:53 The root of evil is s up from you,

SEALING (1) [SEAL]

Mt 27:66 the guard and made the tomb secure by s the stone.

SEALS (10) [SEAL]

Job 9: 7 and it does not rise; who s up the stars;
Rev 5: 1 on the inside and on the back, sealed with seven s;
5: 2 to open the scroll and break its s?"
5: 5 so that he can open the scroll and its seven s."
5: 9 and to open its s, for you were slaughtered and
6: 1 Then I saw the Lamb open one of the seven s,
Tob 9: 5 to him the money bags, with their s intact;
Sir 38:27 those who cut the signets of s,
45:11 with precious stones engraved like s,
Bel 1:17 The king said, "Are the s unbroken, Daniel?"

SEAMLESS (1) [SEAMS]

Jn 19:23 the tunic was s, woven in one piece from the top.

SEAMS (1) [SEAMLESS]

Eze 27: 9 and its artisans were within you, caulking your s;

SEARCH (67) [SEARCHED, SEARCHERS, SEARCHES, SEARCHING, SEARCHINGS]

Dt 4:29 if you s after him with all your heart and soul.
Jos 2: 2 "Some Israelites have come here tonight to s out
2: 3 for they have come only to s out the whole land."
1Sa 23:23 I will s him out among all the thousands of Judah."
23:25 Saul and his men went to s for him.
2Sa 5:17 all the Philistines went up in s of David;
10: 3 Has not David sent his envoys to you to s the city,
1Ki 2:40 and went to Achish in Gath, to s for his slaves;
20: 6 and they shall s your house and the houses
2Ki 10:23 of Baal, "S and see that there is no worshiper of
1Ch 14: 8 all the Philistines went up in s of David;
19: 3 not his servants come to you to s and to overthrow
26:31 (In the fortieth year of David's reign s was made,
28: 8 observe and s out all the commandments of
29:17 I know, my God, that you s the heart,
Ezr 4:15 a s may be made in the annals of your ancestors.
5:17 a s made in the royal archives there in Babylon,
Job 10: 6 that you seek out my iniquity and s for my sin,
28: 3 and s out to the farthest bound the ore in gloom
Ps 64: 6 Who can s out our crimes?
77: 6 I meditate and s my spirit:
139: 3 You s out my path and my lying down,
139:23 S me, O God, and know my heart;
Pr 2: 4 and s for it as for hidden treasures—
25: 2 but the glory of kings is to s things out.
Ecc 1:13 to s out by wisdom all that is done under heaven;
7:25 to s out and to seek wisdom and the sum of things,
Jer 5: 1 S its squares and see if you can find one person
17:10 I the LORD test the mind and s the heart,
29:13 When you s for me, you will find me;
La 1:11 All her people groan as they s for bread;
Eze 34: 6 with no one to s or seek for them.
34:11 I myself will s for my sheep,
39:14 for seven months they shall make their s.
Am 9: 3 from there I will s out and take them;
Zep 1:12 At that time I will s Jerusalem with lamps,
Mt 2: 8 saying, "Go and s diligently for the child;
2:13 Herod is about to s for the child, to destroy him."
7: 7 "Ask, and it will be given you; s,
13:45 of heaven is like a merchant in s of fine pearls;
18:12 the ninety-nine on the mountains and go in s of
Lk 2:45 they returned to Jerusalem to s for him.
11: 9 "So I say to you, Ask, and it will be given you; s,
15: 8 sweep the house, and s carefully until she finds it?
Jn 5:39 "You s the scriptures because you think that
7:34 You will s for me, but you will not find me;
7:36 'You will s for me and you will not find me' and
7:52 S and you will see that no prophet is to arise
8:21 and you will s for me, but you will die in your sin.
Ac 17:27 so that they would s for God and perhaps grope
1Pe 1:10 that was to be yours made careful s and inquiry,
Jdt 8:14 how do you expect to s out God,
8:27 to s their hearts, nor has he taken vengeance on us;
Wis 6: 3 he will s out your works and inquire
Sir 1: 3 the abyss, and wisdom—who can s them out?
6:27 S out and seek, and she will become known
18: 4 and who can s out his mighty deeds?
51:14 and I will s for her until the end.
1Es 2:21 s may be made in the records of your ancestors.
2:26 So I ordered s to be made,
5:39 a s was made in the register and the genealogy
6:21 let s be made in the royal archives of our lord
6:23 Then Darius commanded that s be made in
2Es 5:34 the way of the Most High and to s out some part
12: 4 because you s out the ways of the Most High.
16:30 some clusters may be left by those who s carefully
16:31 be left by those who s their houses with the sword.

SEARCHED (23) [SEARCH]

Ge 31:35 So he s, but did not find the household gods.
44:12 He s, beginning with the eldest and ending with
Jos 2:22 The pursuers had s all along the way
2Sa 17:20 And when they had s and could not find them,
1Ki 1: 3 So they s for a beautiful girl throughout all
2Ki 2:17 So they sent fifty men who s for three days but did
2Ch 22: 9 He s for Ahaziah, who was captured while hiding
Ezr 4:19 and someone s and discovered
6: 1 and they s the archives where
Job 5:27 See, we have s this out; it is true.
28:27 he established it, and s it out.
32:11 while you s out what to say.
Ps 139: 1 O LORD, you have s me and known me.
Ecc 2: 3 I s with my mind how to cheer my body
Eze 20: 6 of the land of Egypt into a land that I had s out
34: 8 because my shepherds have not s for my sheep,
Ob 1: 6 How Esau has been pillaged, his treasures s out!
Ac 12:19 When Herod had s for him and could not find him,
2Ti 1:17 he eagerly s for me and found me
Tob 1:19 that the king knew about me and that I was being s
1Mc 3: 5 He s out and pursued those who broke the law;
9:26 They made inquiry and s for the friends of Judas,
2Es 13:54 and have s out my law;

SEARCHERS (1) [SEARCH]

Eze 39:15 As the s pass through the land,

SEARCHES‡ (13) [SEARCH]

1Ch 28: 9 for the LORD s every mind,
Job 13: 9 Will it be well with you when he s you out?
39: 8 and it s after every green thing.
Pr 11:27 but evil comes to the one who s for it.
Mt 7: 8 and everyone who s finds,
Lk 11:10 and everyone who s finds,
Ro 8:27 And God, who s the heart,
1Co 2:10 for the Spirit s everything, even the depths of God.
Rev 2:23 that I am the one who s minds and hearts,
Sir 42:18 He s out the abyss and the human heart;
2Es 16:50 the one who s out every sin on earth.
16:57 He s the abyss and its treasures;
16:62 who surely made all things and s out hidden things

SEARCHING (9) [SEARCH]

Jdg 6:29 After s and inquiring, they were told,
Pr 20:27 the lamp of the LORD, s every inmost part.
Mk 1:37 they said to him, "Everyone is s for you."
Lk 2:48 and I have been s for you in great anxiety."
2:49 He said to them, "Why were you s for me?
Ac 10:19 "Look, three men are s for you.
17: 5 While they were s for Paul and Silas
Wis 13: 7 For while they live among his works, they keep s,
4Mc 3:13 they went s throughout the enemy camp

SEARCHINGS (2) [SEARCH]

Jdg 5:15 the clans of Reuben there were great s of heart.
5:16 the clans of Reuben there were great s of heart.

SEARED (1)

1Ti 4: 2 of liars whose consciences are s with a hot iron.

SEAS‡ (30) [SEA]

Ge 1:10 the waters that were gathered together he called S.
1:22 and multiply and fill the waters in the s,
Lev 11: 9 whether in the s or in the streams—
11:10 But anything in the s or the streams that does
Dt 33:19 the affluence of the s and the hidden treasures of
Ne 9: 6 the s and all that is in them.
Ps 8: 8 whatever passes along the paths of the s.
24: 2 for he has founded it on the s,
65: 5 of all the ends of the earth and of the farthest s.
65: 7 You silence the roaring of the s,
69:34 the s and everything that moves in them.
78:27 winged birds like the sand of the s;
135: 6 in heaven and on earth, in the s and all deeps.
Pr 30:19 the way of a ship on the high s,
Jer 15: 8 became more numerous than the sand of the s;
Eze 26:17 How you have vanished from the s,
27: 4 Your borders are in the heart of the s;
27:25 and heavily laden in the heart of the s.
27:26 Your rowers have brought you into the high s.
27:26 east wind has wrecked you in the heart of the s.
27:27 sink into the heart of the s on the day of your ruin.
27:33 When your wares came from the s,
27:34 Now you are wrecked by the s,
28: 2 I sit in the seat of the gods, in the heart of the s,"
28: 8 you shall die a violent death in the heart of the s.
32: 2 but you are like a dragon in the s;
Jnh 2: 3 You cast me into the deep, into the heart of the s,
Jdt 1:12 as far as the coasts of the two s.
Aza 1:55 Bless the Lord, s and rivers;
1Mc 6:29 from other kingdoms and from islands of the s.

SEASHORE (10) [SEA, SHORE]

Ge 22:17 the stars of heaven and as the sand that is on the s.
Ex 14:30 and Israel saw the Egyptians dead on the s.
Jos 11: 4 a great army, in number like the sand on the s,
Jdg 7:12 countless as the sand on the s.
1Sa 13: 5 and troops like the sand on the s in multitude;
1Ki 4:29 of understanding as vast as the sand on the s,
Jer 47: 7 Against Ashkelon and against the s—
Heb 11:12 and as the innumerable grains of sand by the s."
Rev 12:18 the dragon took his stand on the sand of the s.
1Mc 11: 1 like the sand by the s, and many ships;

SEASIDE (1) [SEA]

Ac 10: 6 Simon, a tanner, whose house is by the s."

SEASON (32) [SEASONAL, SEASONED, SEASONS]

Ge 17:21 whom Sarah shall bear to you at this s next year."
18:10 one said, "I will surely return to you in due s,
18:14 At the set time I will return to you, in due s,
Lev 26: 4 I will give you your rains in their s,
Nu 13:20 Now it was the s of the first ripe grapes.
Dt 11:14 the rain for your land in its s, the early rain and
28:12 in its s and to bless all your undertakings.
2Ki 4:16 He said, "At this s, in due time,
4:17 The woman conceived and bore a son at that s,
Job 5:26 of grain comes up to the threshing floor in its s.
38:32 Can you lead forth the Mazzaroth in their s,
Ps 1: 3 which yield their fruit in its s,
104:27 to you to give them their food in due s;
145:15 and you give them their food in due s.
Pr 15:23 and a word in s, how good it is!
20: 4 The lazy person does not plow in s;
Ecc 3: 1 For everything there is a s,
Jer 5:24 who gives the rain in its s,
Eze 34:26 and I will send down the showers in their s;
Da 7:12 but their lives were prolonged for a s and a time.
Hos 2: 9 and my wine in its s;
9:10 Like the first fruit on the fig tree, in its first s,
Zec 10: 1 from the LORD in the s of the spring rain,
Mk 9:50 but if salt has lost its saltiness, how can you s it?
11:13 for it was not the s for figs.
12: 2 the s came, he sent a slave to the tenants to collect
Lk 20:10 the s came, he sent a slave to the tenants in order
Sir 50: 6 like the full moon at the festal s;
1Mc 4:54 At the very s and on the very day that
4:59 at that s the days of dedication of the altar should
2Es 8:41 not all that have been sown will come up in due s,
8:43 because it has not received your rain in due s,

SEASONAL (1) [SEASON]

Sir 37:11 with a s laborer about completing his work,

SEASONED (4) [SEASON]

Ex 30:35 s with salt, pure and holy;
1Ch 12:33 Of Zebulun, fifty thousand s troops,
12:36 Of Asher, forty thousand s troops ready for battle.
Col 4: 6 Let your speech always be gracious, s with salt,

SEASONING See Index to Footnotes

SEASONS‡ (16) [SEASON]

Ge 1:14 and let them be for signs and for s and for days
Est 9:31 of Purim should be observed at their appointed s,
Ps 104:19 You have made the moon to mark the s;
Eze 46:11 the festivals and the appointed s the grain offering
Da 2:21 He changes times and s, deposes kings and sets
7:25 shall attempt to change the sacred s and the law;
Zec 8:19 shall be s of joy and gladness,
Ac 14:17 giving you rains from heaven and fruitful s,
Gal 4:10 and months, and s, and years.
1Th 5: 1 Now concerning the times and the s,
Wis 7:18 of the solstices and the changes of the s,
8: 8 and wonders and of the outcome of s and times.
Sir 33: 8 and he appointed the different s and festivals.
43: 6 It is the moon that marks the changing s,
Bar 1:14 on the days of the festivals and at appointed s.
2Es 13:58 and whatever things come to pass in their s.

SEAT‡ (77) [SEATED, SEATING, SEATS]

Ex 25:17 Then you shall make a mercy s of pure gold;

Ex 25:18 at the two ends of the mercy s.
25:19 with the mercy s you shall make the cherubim
25:20 overshadowing the mercy s with their wings.
25:20 the cherubim shall be turned toward the mercy s.
25:21 You shall put the mercy s on the top of the ark;
25:22 and from above the mercy s,
26:34 the mercy s on the ark of the covenant in
30: 6 in front of the mercy s that is over the covenant,
31: 7 and the mercy s that is on it,
35:12 the mercy s, and the curtain for the screen;
37: 6 He made a mercy s of pure gold;
37: 7 at the two ends of the mercy s he made them,
37: 8 the mercy s he made the cherubim at its two ends.
37: 9 overshadowing the mercy s with their wings.
37: 9 of the cherubim were turned toward the mercy s.
39:35 ark of the covenant with its poles and the mercy s;
40:20 and set the mercy s above the ark;
Lev 16: 2 the sanctuary inside the curtain before the mercy s
16: 2 for I appear in the cloud upon the mercy s.
16:13 of the incense may cover the mercy s that is upon
16:14 with his finger on the front of the mercy s,
16:14 and before the mercy s he shall sprinkle the blood
16:15 upon the mercy s and before the mercy s.
Nu 7:89 to him from above the mercy s that was on the ark
21:15 the slopes of the wadis that extend to the s of Ar,
Jdg 3:20 So he rose from his s.
1Sa 1: 9 the priest was sitting on the s beside the doorpost
2: 8 to make them sit with princes and inherit a s
4:13 Eli was sitting upon his s by the road watching,
4:18 over backward from his s by the side of the gate;
20:25 The king sat upon his s, as at other times, upon the s by the wall.
2Sa 19: 8 Then the king got up and took his s in the gate.
1Ki 10:19 the s were arm rests and two lions standing beside
21: 9 and s Naboth at the head of the assembly;
21:10 s two scoundrels opposite him,
2Ki 11:19 He took his s on the throne of the kings.
25:28 a s above the other seats of the kings who were
1Ch 28:11 and of the room for the mercy s;
2Ch 9:18 the s were arm rests and two lions standing beside
19: 8 They had their s at Jerusalem.
Est 3: 1 and set his s above all the officials who were
Job 29: 7 when I took my s in the square,
Ps 1: 1 or sit in the s of scoffers;
7: 7 and over it take your s on high.
Pr 9:14 on a s at the high places of the town,
31:23 taking his s among the elders of the land.
SS 3:10 its s of purple; its interior was inlaid with love.
Jer 13:18 a lowly s, for your beautiful crown has come
26:10 and took their s in the entry of the New Gate of
52:32 a s above the seats of the other kings who were
Eze 8: 3 to the s of the image of jealousy,
28: 2 I sit in the s of the gods, in the heart of the seas,"
Mt 23: 2 "The scribes and the Pharisees sit on Moses' s;
27:19 While he was sitting on the judgment s,
Lk 11:43 the s of honor in the synagogues and to be greeted
Ac 12:21 took his s on the platform,
25: 6 the next day he took his s on the tribunal
25:17 the next day took my s on the tribunal and ordered
Ro 14:10 we will all stand before the judgment s of God.
2Co 5:10 of us must appear before the judgment s of Christ,
2Th 2: 4 so that he takes his s in the temple of God,
Heb 9: 5 the cherubim of glory overshadowing the mercy s.
12: 2 and has taken his s at the right hand of the throne
Jas 2: 3 the fine clothes and say, "Have a s here, please,"
Sir 7: 4 or the s of honor from the king.
12:12 or else he may try to take your own s,
38:33 They do not sit in the judge's s,
1Mc 7: 4 Demetrius took his s on the throne of his kingdom.
10:52 to my kingdom and have taken my s on the throne
10:53 and we have taken our s on the throne
10:55 to the land of your ancestors and took your s on
1Es 3:15 and he took his s in the council chamber,
2Es 7:*33* Most High shall be revealed on the s of judgment,
12:33 before his judgment s, and

SEATED‡ (41) [SEAT]

Ge 43:33 When they were s before him,
1Ki 16:11 as soon as he had s himself on his throne,
21:12 they proclaimed a fast and s Naboth at the head of
Ps 113: 5 Who is like the LORD our God, who is s on high,
Eze 1:26 and s above the likeness of a throne
Mt 19:28 the Son of Man is s on the throne of his glory,
23:22 the throne of God and by the one who is s upon it.
26:64 of Man s at the right hand of Power and coming on
Mk 14:62 the Son of Man s at the right hand of the Power,'
Lk 22:69 now on the Son of Man will be s at the right hand
Jn 2:14 and the money changers s at their tables.
6:11 he distributed them to those who were s;
Ac 8:28 s in his chariot, he was reading the prophet Isaiah.
26:30 and Bernice and those who had been s with them;
Eph 1:20 and s him at his right hand in the heavenly places,
2: 6 with him and s us with him in the heavenly places
Col 3: 1 where Christ is, s at the right hand of God.
Heb 8: 1 a high priest, one who is s at the right hand of
Rev 4: 2 with one s on the throne!
4: 3 the one s there looks like jasper and carnelian,
4: 4 and s on the thrones are twenty-four elders,
4: 9 and thanks to the one who is s on the throne,
4:10 before the one who is s on the throne and worship
5: 1 of the one s on the throne a scroll written on the
5: 7 the scroll from the right hand of the one who was s
5:13 "To the one s on the throne and to the Lamb
6:16 "Fall on us and hide us from the face of the one s
7:10 "Salvation belongs to our God who is s on
7:15 the one who is s on the throne will shelter them.
Rev 14:14 and s on the cloud was one like the Son of Man,
17: 1 of the great whore who is s on many waters,
17: 9 on which the woman is s;
17:15 "The waters that you saw, where the whore is s,
19: 4 down and worshiped God who is s on the throne,
20: 4 and those s on them were given authority to judge.
21: 5 And the one who was s on the throne said, "See,
AdE 15: 6 He was s on his royal throne,
Sir 1: 8 greatly to be feared, s upon his throne—the Lord.
31:12 Are you s at the table of the great?
31:18 If you are s among many persons,
1Mc 10:63 The king also s him at his side;

SEATING (2) [SEAT]

1Ki 10: 5 the food of his table, the s of his officials,
2Ch 9: 4 the food of his table, the s of his officials,

SEATS (10) [SEAT]

2Ki 25:28 above the other s of the kings who were with him
Jer 52:32 above the s of the other kings who were with him
Mt 21:12 the tables of the money changers and the s
23: 6 the place of honor at banquets and the best s in
Mk 11:15 the tables of the money changers and the s
12:39 the best s in the synagogues and places of honor
Lk 20:46 the best s in the synagogues and places of honor
AdE 1:14 and Malesear, who sat beside him in the chief s—
Sir 11: 1 and s them among the great.
2Mc 14:21 s of honor were set in place;

SEBA (4)

Ge 10: 7 S, Havilah, Sabtah, Raamah, and Sabteca.
1Ch 1: 9 S, Havilah, Sabta, Raama, and Sabteca.
Ps 72:10 may the kings of Sheba and S bring gifts.
Isa 43: 3 Ethiopia and S in exchange for you.

SEBAM (1)

Nu 32: 3 Dibon, Jazer, Nimrah, Heshbon, Elealeh, S, Nebo,

SEBAT (KJV) See SHEBAT

SECACAH (1)

Jos 15:61 In the wilderness, Beth-arabah, Middin, S,

SECHU (KJV) See SECU

SECLUDED (1) [SECLUSION]

3Mc 1:18 Young women who had been s in their chambers

SECLUSION (1) [SECLUDED]

Lk 1:24 and for five months she remained in s.

SECOND‡ (223) [SECOND-IN-COMMAND, TWO]

Ge 1: 8 and there was morning, the s day.
2:13 The name of the s river is Gihon;
6:16 make it with lower, s, and third decks.
7:11 the s month, on the seventeenth day of the month,
8:14 In the s month, on the twenty-seventh day of
22:15 of the LORD called to Abraham a s time
30: 7 and bore Jacob a s son.
30:12 Leah's maid Zilpah bore Jacob a s son.
32:19 He likewise instructed the s and the third
41: 5 Then he fell asleep and dreamed a s time;
41:22 I fell asleep a s time and I saw in my dream seven
41:52 The s he named Ephraim,
Ex 4: 8 they may believe the s sign.
16: 1 the s month after they had departed from the land
26: 4 on the edge of the outermost curtain in the s set.
26: 5 on the edge of the curtain that is in the s set;
26:10 of the curtain that is outermost in the s set.
26:20 and for the s side of the tabernacle,
28:18 the s row a turquoise, a sapphire and a moonstone;
36:11 on the edge of the outermost curtain of the s set;
36:12 on the edge of the curtain that was in the s set;
36:25 For the s side of the tabernacle, on the north side,
39:11 s row, a turquoise, a sapphire, and a moonstone;
40:17 In the first month in the s year,
Lev 5:10 the s he shall offer for a burnt offering according
8:22 Then he brought forward the s ram,
13:58 shall then be washed a s time, and it shall be clean.
Nu 1: 1 on the first day of the s month,
1: 1 in the s year after they had come out of the land
1:18 and on the first day of the s month they assembled
2:16 They shall set out s.
7:18 On the s day Nethanel son of Zuar,
9: 1 of the s year after they had come out of the land
9:11 In the s month on the fourteenth day, at twilight,
10: 6 when you blow a s alarm,
10:11 In the s year, in the s month,
29:17 On the s day: twelve young bulls,
Dt 22: 9 You shall not sow your vineyard with a s kind
24: 3 Then suppose the s man dislikes her,
24: 3 of his house (or the s man who married her dies);
Jos 5: 2 and circumcise the Israelites a s time."
6:14 the s day they marched around the city once and
10:32 and he took it on the s day,
19: 1 The s lot came out for Simeon,
Jdg 6:25 the s bull seven years old,
6:26 then take the s bull, and offer it as a burnt offering
6:28 s bull was offered on the altar that had been built.
20:24 against the Benjaminites the s day.
20:25 against them from Gibeah the s day,
1Sa 8: 2 and the name of his s, Abijah;
18:21 Therefore Saul said to David a s time,
20:27 But on the s day, the day after the new moon,
20:34 in fierce anger and ate no food on the s day of
23:17 and I shall be s to you;
2Sa 3: 3 his s, Chileab, of Abigail the widow of Nabal
14:29 He sent a s time, but Joab would not come.
20:10 He did not strike a s blow.
1Ki 6: 1 in the month of Ziv, which is the s month,
7:15 the s pillar was the same.
9: 2 the LORD appeared to Solomon a s time,
15:25 over Israel in the s year of King Asa of Judah;
18:34 Then he said, "Do it a s time";
18:34 and they did it a s time.
19: 7 The angel of the LORD came a s time,
2Ki 1:17 in the s year of King Jehoram son of Jehoshaphat
9:19 Then he sent out a s horseman,
10: 6 Then he wrote them a s letter, saying,
14: 1 In the s year of King Joash son of Joahaz of Israel,
15:32 In the s year of King Pekah son of Remaliah
19:29 and in the s year what springs from that;
22:14 she resided in Jerusalem in the S Quarter,
23: 4 of the s order, and the guardians of the threshold,
25:17 The s pillar had the same, with the latticework.
25:18 the s priest Zephaniah, and the three guardians of
1Ch 2:13 Abinadab the s, Shimea the third,
3: 1 the s Daniel, by Abigail the Carmelite;
3:15 Johanan the firstborn, the s Jehoiakim,
5:12 Shapham the s, Janai, and Shaphat in Bashan.
6:28 sons of Samuel: Joel his firstborn, the s Abijah.
7:15 And the name of the s was Zelophehad;
8: 1 Ashbel the s, Aharah the third,
8:39 Ulam his firstborn, Jeush the s,
12: 9 Ezer the chief, Obadiah s, Eliab third,
15:18 and with them their kindred of the s order,
16: 5 Asaph was the chief, and s to him Zechariah, Jeiel,
23:11 Jahath was the chief, and Zizah the s;
23:19 Jeriah the chief, Amariah the s, Jahaziel the third,
23:20 sons of Uzziel: Micah the chief and Isshiah the s.
24: 7 The first lot fell to Jehoiarib, the s to Jedaiah,
24:23 Jeriah the chief, Amariah the s, Jahaziel the third,
25: 9 the s to Gedaliah, to him and his brothers
26: 2 Zechariah the firstborn, Jediael the s,
26: 4 Shemaiah the firstborn, Jehozabad the s,
26:11 the s, Tebaliah the third, Zechariah the fourth:
27: 4 in charge of the division of the s month;
29:22 They made David's son Solomon king a s time;
2Ch 3: 2 on the s day of the s month of the fourth year
27: 5 The Ammonites paid him the same amount in the s
30: 2 to keep the passover in the s month
30:13 the festival of unleavened bread in the s month,
30:15 on the fourteenth day of the s month.
31:12 with his brother Shimei as s;
34:22 in Jerusalem in the S Quarter) and spoke to her to
35:24 and carried him in his s chariot and brought him
Ezr 3: 8 In the s year after their arrival at the house of God
3: 8 at the house of God at Jerusalem, in the s month,
4:24 and was discontinued until the s year of the reign
Ne 8:13 On the s day the heads of ancestral houses of all
11: 9 and Judah son of Hassenuah was s in charge of
11:17 and Bakbukiah, the s among his associates;
Est 2:14 then in the morning she came back to the s harem
7: 2 On the s day, as they were drinking wine,
9:29 confirming this s letter about Purim.
Job 42:14 He named the first Jemimah, the s Keziah,
Ps 109:13 may his name be blotted out in the s generation.
Isa 11:11 that day the Lord will extend his hand yet a s time
37:30 and in the s year what springs from that;
Jer 1:13 The word of the LORD came to me a s time,
13: 3 And the word of the LORD came to me a s time,
33: 1 word of the LORD came to Jeremiah a s time,
52:22 And the s pillar had the same, with pomegranates.
52:24 the s priest Zephaniah, and the three guardians of
Eze 4: 6 you shall lie down a s time, but on your right side,
10:14 the s face was that of a human being,
43:22 On the s day you shall offer a male goat
Da 2: 1 In the s year of Nebuchadnezzar's reign,
2: 7 a s time, "Let the king first tell his servants
7: 5 Another beast appeared, a s one,
8: 3 and the longer one came up s.
Jnh 3: 1 The word of the LORD came to Jonah a s time,
Zep 1:10 a wail from the S Quarter,
Hag 1: 1 In the s year of King Darius, in the sixth month,
1:15 In the s year of King Darius,
2:10 the s year of Darius, the word of the LORD came
2:20 The word of the LORD came a s time to Haggai
Zec 1: 1 In the eighth month, in the s year of Darius,
1: 7 the month of Shebat, in the s year of Darius,
4:12 And a s time I said to him,
6: 2 the s chariot black horses,
11:14 Then I broke my s staff Unity,
Mt 5:41 to go one mile, go also the s mile.
21:30 The father went to the s and said the same;
22:26 The s did the same, so also the third,
22:39 And a s is like it:
26:42 Again he went away for the s time and prayed,
Mk 12:21 the s married her and died, leaving no children;
12:31 The s is this, 'You shall love your neighbor
14:72 At that moment the cock crowed for the s time.
Lk 19:18 Then the s came, saying, 'Lord,
20:30 then the s
Jn 3: 4 a s time into the mother's womb and be born?"
4:54 the s sign that Jesus did after coming from Judea
9:24 the s time they called the man who had been blind,
21:16 A s time he said to him, "Simon son of John,
Ac 7:13 On the s visit Joseph made himself known
10:15 The voice said to him again, a s time,

Ac 11: 9 But a s time the voice answered from heaven,
12:10 After they had passed the first and the s guard,
13:33 also it is written in the s psalm, 'You are my Son;
28:13 and on the s day we came to Puteoli.
1Co 12:28 s prophets, third teachers;
15:47 the s man is from heaven.
2Co 13: 2 as I did when present on my s visit,
Tit 3:10 After a first and s admonition,
Heb 8: 7 there would have been no need to look for a s one.
9: 3 the s curtain was a tent called the Holy of Holies.
9: 7 but only the high priest goes into the s,
9:28 will appear a s time, not to deal with sin,
10: 9 He abolishes the first in order to establish the s.
2Pe 3: 1 beloved, the s letter I am writing to you;
Rev 2:11 not be harmed by the s death.
4: 7 the s living creature like an ox,
6: 3 When he opened the s seal,
6: 3 I heard the s living creature call out, "Come!"
8: 8 The s angel blew his trumpet,
11:14 The s woe has passed.
14: 8 Then another angel, a s, followed, saying, "Fallen,
16: 3 The s angel poured his bowl into the sea,
20: 6 Over these the s death has no power,
20:14 This is the s death, the lake of fire;
21: 8 with fire and sulfur, which is the s death."
21:19 the first was jasper, the s sapphire, the third agate,
Tob 1: 7 for six years I would save up a s tenth in money
Jdt 2: 4 the chief general of his army, s only to himself,
7: 6 On the s day Holofernes led out all his cavalry
AdE 2:14 the morning she departs to the s harem, where Gai
7: 2 And the s day, as they were drinking wine,
11: 2 In the s year of the reign of Artaxerxes the Great,
13: 3 and has attained the s place in the kingdom—
13: 6 who is in charge of affairs and is our s father,
16:11 down to by all as the person s to the royal throne.
Sir 6:11 you are prosperous, they become your s self,
23:23 s, she has committed an offense
50:21 and they bowed down in worship a s time,
1Mc 9: 1 and Alcimus into the land of Judah a s time,
9:54 in the s month, Alcimus gave orders to tear down
13:51 On the twenty-third day of the s month,
15:25 King Antiochus besieged Dor for the s time,
2Mc 5: 1 About this time Antiochus made his s invasion
7: 7 they brought forward the s for their sport.
13:22 The king negotiated a s time with the people
14: 8 s because I have regard also for my compatriots.
1Es 1:31 He got into his s chariot;
2:30 the temple in Jerusalem stopped until the s year of
3:11 The s wrote, "The king is strongest."
4: 1 Then the s, who had spoken of the strength of
5: 6 in the s year of his reign, in the month of Nisan,
5:56 the s year after their coming to the temple of God
5:56 in the s month, Zerubbabel son of Shealtiel
5:57 on the new moon of the s month in the s year
6: 1 Now in the s year of the reign of Darius,
2Es 5:16 Now on the s night Phaltiel, a chief of the people,
6:41 the s day, you created the spirit of the firmament,
7:*82* The s way, because they cannot now make
7:*93* The s order, because they see the perplexity
10: 2 I remained quiet until the evening of the s day.
11: 1 On the s night I had a dream:
11:27 a s also, and this disappeared more quickly than
12:15 But the s that is to reign shall hold sway for
4Mc 15:18 nor when the s in torments looked at you piteously

SECOND-IN-COMMAND (1) [COMMAND, SECOND]

Ge 41:43 He had him ride in the chariot of his s;

SECRET‡ (79) [SECRETLY, SECRETS]

Ex 7:11 did the same by their s arts.
7:22 magicians of Egypt did the same by their s arts;
8: 7 But the magicians did the same by their s arts,
8:18 magicians tried to produce gnats by their s arts,
Dt 27:15 the work of an artisan, and sets it up in s."
27:24 be anyone who strikes down a neighbor in s."
28:57 she is eating them in s for lack of anything else,
29:29 The s things belong to the LORD our God
Jdg 3:19 and said, "I have a s message for you, O king."
16: 9 So the s of his strength was not known.
16:17 So he told her his whole s, and said to her,
16:18 Delilah realized that he had told her his whole s,
16:18 for he has told his whole s to me."
1Sa 19: 2 stay in a s place and hide yourself.
2Sa 15:10 But Absalom sent s messengers throughout all
Job 13:10 surely rebuke you if in s you show partiality.
Ps 10: 9 they lurk in s like a lion in its covert;
51: 6 therefore teach me wisdom in my s heart.
64: 2 Hide me from the s plots of the wicked,
81: 7 I answered you in the s place of thunder;
90: 8 our s sins in the light of your countenance.
139:15 when I was being made in s,
Pr 9:17 and bread eaten in s is pleasant."
21:14 A gift in s averts anger;
25: 9 and do not disclose another's s;
Ecc 12:14 including every s thing, whether good or evil.
Isa 3:17 and the LORD will lay bare their s parts.
45: 3 of darkness and riches hidden in s places,
45:19 I did not speak in s, in a land of darkness;
48:16 From the beginning I have not spoken in s,
65: 4 and spend the night in s places;
Jer 13:17 my soul will weep in s for your pride;
23:24 in s places so that I cannot see them?
38:16 So King Zedekiah swore an oath in s to Jeremiah,
Eze 28: 3 no s is hidden from you;
Da 12: 4 the words s and the book sealed until the time of
12: 9 the words are to remain s and sealed until the time
Am 3: 7 without revealing his s to his servants
Mt 6: 4 so that your alms may be done in s;
6: 4 and your Father who sees in s will reward you.
6: 6 the door and pray to your Father who is in s;
6: 6 and your Father who sees in s will reward you.
6:18 not by others but by your Father who is in s;
6:18 and your Father who sees in s will reward you.
10:26 and nothing s that will not become known.
Mk 4:11 "To you has been given the s of the kingdom
4:22 nor is anything s, except to come to light.
Lk 8:17 nor is anything s that will not become known
12: 2 and nothing s that will not become known.
Jn 7: 4 no one who wants to be widely known acts in s.
7:10 then he also went, not publicly but as it were in s.
18:20 I have said nothing in s.
19:38 though a s one because of his fear of the Jews,
Ac 16:37 and now are they going to discharge us in s?
Ro 2:16 will judge the s thoughts of all.
16:25 to the revelation of the mystery that was kept s
1Co 2: 7 But we speak God's wisdom, s and hidden,
Php 4:12 In any and all circumstances I have learned the s
Tob 12: 7 It is good to conceal the s of a king,
12:11 'It is good to conceal the s of a king,
Jdt 2: 2 and set before them his s plan and recounted fully,
Wis 1:11 because no s word is without result,
2:22 the s purposes of God, nor hoped for the wages
7:21 I learned both what is s and what is manifest,
14:15 handed on to his dependents s rites and initiations.
14:23 or celebrate s mysteries, or hold frenzied revels
17: 3 that in their s sins they were unobserved behind
18: 9 For in s the holy children
Sir 8:17 for they cannot keep a s.
8:18 of strangers do nothing that is to be kept s,
42: 9 A daughter is a s anxiety to her father,
Sus 1:42 you know what is s and are aware of all things
Bel 1:21 the s doors through which they used to enter
2Mc 1:16 Opening a s door in the ceiling,
13:21 gave s information to the enemy;
3Mc 4:12 the city frequently went out in s to lament bitterly
2Es 12:36 And you alone were worthy to learn this s of
14: 6 and these you shall keep s.'
14:26 and some you shall deliver in s to the wise;

SECRETARIES (6) [SECRETARY]

1Ki 4: 3 Elihoreph and Ahijah sons of Shisha were s;
Est 3:12 the king's s were summoned on the thirteenth day
8: 9 The king's s were summoned at that time,
AdE 3:12 of the first month the king's s were summoned,
8: 9 The s were summoned on the twenty-third day of
9: 3 and the royal s were paying honor to the Jews,

SECRETARY (31) [SECRETARIES, SECRETARY'S]

2Sa 8:17 of Abiathar were priests; Seraiah was s;
20:25 Sheva was s; Zadok and Abiathar were priests;
2Ki 12:10 the king's s and the high priest went up,
18:18 and Shebnah the s, and Joah son of Asaph,
18:37 who was in charge of the palace, and Shebna the s,
19: 2 who was in charge of the palace, and Shebna the s,
22: 3 the s, to the house of the LORD, saying,
22: 8 The high priest Hilkiah said to Shaphan the s,
22: 9 Then Shaphan the s came to the king,
22:10 Shaphan the s informed the king,
22:12 Shaphan the s, and the king's servant Asaiah,
25:19 the s who was the commander of
1Ch 18:16 of Abiathar were priests; Shavsha was s;
2Ch 24:11 the king's s and the officer of
26:11 the numbers in the muster made by the s Jeiel and
34:15 Hilkiah said to the s Shaphan,
34:18 The s Shaphan informed the king,
34:20 the s Shaphan, and the king's servant Asaiah:
Isa 36: 3 who was in charge of the palace, and Shebna the s,
36:22 who was in charge of the palace, and Shebna the s,
37: 2 who was in charge of the palace, and Shebna the s,
Jer 36:10 in the chamber of Gemariah son of Shaphan the s.
36:12 Elishama the s, Delaiah son of Shemaiah,
36:20 in the chamber of Elishama the s, they went to
36:21 he took it from the chamber of Elishama the s;
36:26 to arrest the s Baruch and the prophet Jeremiah.
36:32 to the s Baruch son of Neriah, who wrote on it
37:15 and imprisoned him in the house of the s Jonathan,
37:20 not send me back to the house of the s Jonathan
52:25 the s of the commander of the army who mustered
AdE 6: 1 so he gave orders to his s to bring the book

SECRETARY'S (1) [SECRETARY]

Jer 36:12 down to the king's house, into the s chamber;

SECRETLY (25) [SECRET]

Ge 31:27 Why did you flee s and deceive me and
Dt 13: 6 If anyone s entices you—
Jos 2: 1 son of Nun sent two men s from Shittim as spies,
2Sa 12:12 For you did it s; but I will do this thing
2Ki 17: 9 of Israel s did things that were not right against
Job 31:27 and my heart has been s enticed,
Ps 64: 5 they talk of laying snares s, thinking,
101: 5 One who s slanders a neighbor I will destroy.
Jer 37:17 The king questioned him s in his house, and said,
40:15 Then Johanan son of Kareah spoke s to Gedaliah
Mt 2: 7 Then Herod s called for the wise men and learned
Ac 6:11 Then they s instigated some men to say,
Gal 2: 4 But because of false believers s brought in,
Eph 5:12 even to mention what such people do s;
2Pe 2: 1 who will s bring in destructive opinions.
Tob 1:18 but I would s remove the bodies and bury them.
LtJ 6:10 the priests s take gold and silver from their gods
1Mc 9:60 and s sent letters to all his allies in Judea,
10:79 Now Apollonius had s left a thousand cavalry
2Mc 1:19 the altar and s hid it in the hollow of a dry cistern,
6:11 in order to observe the seventh day s,
8: 1 and his companions s entered the villages
3Mc 3:23 they s suspect that we may soon alter our policy.
6:24 by s devising acts of no advantage to the kingdom.
2Es 3:14 to him alone you revealed the end of the times, s

SECRETS‡ (21) [SECRET]

Job 11: 6 and that he would tell you the s of wisdom!
Ps 44:21 For he knows the s of the heart.
Pr 11:13 A gossip goes about telling s,
20:19 A gossip reveals s;
Mt 13:11 "To you it has been given to know the s of
Lk 8:10 "To you it has been given to know the s of
1Co 14:25 After the s of the unbeliever's heart are disclosed,
Wis 6:22 and I will hide no s from you,
Sir 1:30 The Lord will reveal your s and overthrow you
4:18 and will reveal her s to them.
13:12 Cruel are those who do not keep your s;
14:21 in his heart on her ways and ponders her s,
22:22 But as for reviling, arrogance, disclosure of s,
27:16 Whoever betrays s destroys confidence,
27:17 but if you betray his s, do not follow after him.
27:21 but whoever has betrayed s is without hope.
42: 1 of repeating what you hear, and of betraying s.
42:18 he understands their innermost s.
2Es 10:38 for the Most High has revealed many s to you.
12:38 to comprehend and keep these s.
14: 5 the s of the times and declared to him the end of

SECT (6)

Ac 5:17 the s of the Sadducees), being filled with jealousy,
15: 5 But some believers who belonged to the s of
24: 5 and a ringleader of the s of the Nazarenes.
24:14 that according to the Way, which they call a s,
26: 5 to the strictest s of our religion and lived as
28:22 for with regard to this s we know

SECTION (13) [SECTIONS]

Ne 3:11 of Pahath-moab repaired another s and the Tower
3:19 repaired another s opposite the ascent to the
3:20 After him Baruch son of Zabbai repaired another s
3:21 of Uriah son of Hakkoz repaired another s from
3:24 him Binnui son of Henadad repaired another s,
3:27 After him the Tekoites repaired another s opposite
3:30 and Hanun sixth son of Zalaph repaired another s.
12:24 of David the man of God, s opposite to s.
Eze 45: 3 a s twenty-five thousand cubits long
45: 5 Another s, twenty-five thousand cubits long
Lk 1: 8 as priest before God and his s was on duty,
1Mc 12:37 and he repaired the s called Chaphenatha.

SECTIONS (1) [SECTION]

Sir 9: 7 or wander about in its deserted s.

SECTOR (1)

Nu 34: 3 your south s shall extend from the wilderness

SECU (1)

1Sa 19:22 He came to the great well that is in S;

SECUNDUS (1)

Ac 20: 4 by Aristarchus and S from Thessalonica,

SECURE (42) [SECURED, SECURELY, SECURITY]

Ex 9:19 in the open field brought to a s place;
9:20 and livestock off to a s place.
Dt 1:38 he is the one who will s Israel's possession of it.
3:28 of this people and who shall s their possession of
14:25 With the money s in hand,
2Sa 22:34 and set me s on the heights.
23: 5 ordered in all things and s.
2Ch 11:17 of Solomon s, for they walked for three years in
Job 11:15 you will be s, and will not fear.
12: 6 and those who provoke God are s,
21:23 being wholly at ease and s,
Ps 16: 9 and my soul rejoices; my body also rests s.
18:33 and set me s on the heights.
40: 2 and set my feet upon a rock, making my steps s.
102:28 The children of your servants shall live s;
112: 7 their hearts are firm, s in the LORD.
Pr 1:33 but those who listen to me will be s and will live
19:23 filled with it one rests s and suffers no harm.
29:25 but one who trusts in the LORD is s.
Isa 22:23 I will fasten him like a peg in a s place,
22:25 peg that was fastened in a s place will give way;
32:18 in s dwellings, and in quiet resting places.
47:10 You felt s in your wickedness;
Jer 49:31 advance against a nation at ease, that lives s,
Eze 27:24 bound with cords and made s;
34:27 They shall be s on their soil;
Am 6: 1 and for those who feel s on Mount Samaria,
Mic 5: 4 And they shall live s, for now he shall be great to
Zep 2:15 Is this the exultant city that lived s,
Mt 27:64 Therefore command the tomb to be made s until
27:65 go, make it as s as you can."

Mt 27:66 So they went with the guard and made the tomb s
Lk 17:33 Those who try to make their life s will lose it,
AdE 13: 7 and leave our government completely s
Sir 4:15 and all who listen to her will live s.
LtJ 6:18 so the priests make their temples s with doors
2Mc 1:14 to s most of its treasures as a dowry.
2:27 to s the gratitude of many we will gladly endure
3:22 and s for those who had entrusted it,
8:36 to s tribute for the Romans by the capture of
2Es 2:20 s justice for the ward, give to the needy,
16:59 like a dome and made it s upon the waters;

SECURED (3) [SECURE]

2Mc 4:11 s through John the father of Eupolemus,
4:24 and s the high priesthood for himself,
3Mc 4: 9 others had their feet s by unbreakable fetters,

SECURELY (15) [SECURE]

Lev 25:18 so that you may live on the land s.
25:19 and you will eat your fill and live on it s.
26: 5 you shall eat your bread to the full, and live s
Jdg 18: 7 they observed the people who were there living s,
Pr 3:23 on your way s and your foot will not stumble.
10: 9 Whoever walks in integrity walks s,
Isa 47: 8 hear this, you lover of pleasures, who sit s,
Eze 34:25 they may live in the wild and sleep in the woods s.
38:14 On that day when my people Israel are living s,
39: 6 I will send fire on Magog and on those who live s
39:26 when they live s in their land with no one
Ac 5:23 the prison s locked and the guards standing at
16:23 into prison and ordered the jailer to keep them s.
Col 1:23 that you continue s established and steadfast in
3Mc 3:25 and bound s with iron fetters,

SECURITY (16) [SECURE]

Ru 1: 9 The LORD grant that you may find s,
3: 1 "My daughter, I need to seek some s for you,
2Ki 20:19 if there will be peace and s in my days?"
Est 9:30 Letters were sent wishing peace and s to all
Job 24:23 He gives them s, and they are supported;
Ps 37: 3 so you will live in the land, and enjoy s.
122: 7 and s within your towers."
Pr 12: 3 No one finds s by wickedness,
Isa 38:14 O Lord, I am oppressed; be my s!
39: 8 "There will be peace and s in my days."
Jer 33: 6 and reveal to them abundance of prosperity and s.
Zec 14:11 Jerusalem shall abide in s.
1Th 5: 3 When they say, "There is peace and s,"
Sir 47:12 a wise son rose up who because of him lived in s:
2Mc 4:21 and he took measures for his own s.
9:21 to take thought for the general s of all.

SEDITION (3)

Ezr 4:15 and that s was stirred up in it from long ago.
4:19 and that rebellion and s have been made in it.
2Mc 14: 6 are keeping up war and stirring up s,

SEDITIONS (KJV) See JEALOUSY

SEDUCE (4) [SEDUCED, SEDUCER, SEDUCES, SEDUCTIVE]

Da 11:32 He shall s with intrigue those who violate
Jdt 12:12 If we do not s her, she will laugh at us."
12:16 for he had been waiting for an opportunity to s her
Sus 1:11 to disclose their lustful desire to s her.

SEDUCED (5) [SEDUCE]

Dt 11:16 Take care, or you will be s into turning away,
Jer 38:22 'Your trusted friends have s you
Jdt 13:16 that it was my face that s him to his destruction,
Sir 9: 8 many have been s by a woman's beauty,
42:10 be s and become pregnant in her father's house;

SEDUCER (1) [SEDUCE]

4Mc 18: 8 No s corrupted me on a desert plain,

SEDUCES (1) [SEDUCE]

Ex 22:16 a man s a virgin who is not engaged to be married,

SEDUCTIVE (1) [SEDUCE]

Pr 7:21 With much s speech she persuades him;

SEE‡ (1014) [ALL-SEEING, EYESIGHT, FORESEEING, FORESIGHT, NEAR-SIGHTED, SAW, SEEING, SEEN, SEER, SEERS, SEES, SIGHT, SIGHTS]

Ge 1:29 "S, I have given you every plant yielding seed
2:19 to the man to s what he would call them;
3:22 Then the LORD God said, "S, the man
8: 8 to s if the waters had subsided from the face of
9:16 I will s it and remember the everlasting covenant
9:23 and they did not s their father's nakedness.
11: 5 LORD came down to s the city and the tower,
12:12 Egyptians s you, they will say, 'This is his wife';
13:15 for all the land that you s I will give to you and
16: 2 "You s that the LORD has prevented me
18:21 and s whether they have done altogether according
24: 6 "S to it that you do not take my son back there.
26:28 "We s plainly that the LORD has been with you;
27: 1 so that he could not s, he called his elder son Esau
27: 2 "S, I am old; I do not know the day of my death.
27:39 Then his father Isaac answered him: "S,
31: 5 "I s that your father does not regard me
31:12 'Look up and s that all the goats that leap on
31:43 the flocks are my flocks, and all that you s is mine.
31:51 "S this heap and s the pillar,
32:20 and afterwards I shall s his face;
33:10 to s your face is like seeing the face of God—
37:14 s if it is well with your brothers and with the flock;
37:20 and we shall s what will become of his dreams."
37:32 s now whether it is your son's robe or not."
38:23 you s, I sent this kid, and you could not find her."
39:14 "S, my husband has brought among us a Hebrew
41:41 And Pharaoh said to Joseph, "S,
42: 9 you have come to s the nakedness of the land!"
42:12 you have come to s the nakedness of the land!"
43: 3 'You shall not s my face unless your brother is
43: 5 for the man said to us, 'You shall not s my face,
44:23 you shall s my face no more.'
44:26 for we cannot s the man's face
44:34 I fear to s the suffering that would come
45:12 of my brother Benjamin s that it is my own mouth
45:28 I must go and s him before I die."
48:10 and he could not s well.
48:11 "I did not expect to s your face;
48:11 and here God has let me s your children also."
Ex 1:16 and s them on the birthstool, if it is a boy, kill him;
2: 4 to s what would happen to him.
3: 3 and s why the bush is not burned up."
3: 4 the LORD saw that he had turned aside to s,
4:18 in Egypt and s whether they are still living."
4:21 s that you perform before Pharaoh all the wonders
6: 1 "Now you shall s what I will do to Pharaoh:
7: 1 The LORD said to Moses, "S,
7:17 S, with the staff that is in my hand I will strike
10: 5 so that no one will be able to s the land.
10:23 People could not s one another,
10:28 Take care that you do not s my face again,
10:28 for on the day you s my face you shall die."
10:29 I will never s your face again."
12:13 when I s the blood, I will pass over you,
14:13 not be afraid, stand firm, and s the deliverance that
14:13 whom you s today you shall never s again.
16: 7 in the morning you shall s the glory of the LORD,
16:29 S! The LORD has given you the sabbath,
16:32 that they may s the food with which I fed you in
23: 5 When you s the donkey of one
24: 8 "S the blood of the covenant that
25:40 And s that you make them according to the pattern
31: 2 S, I have called by name Bezalel son of Uri son
32:34 s, my angel shall go in front of you.
33:12 Moses said to the LORD, "S,
33:20 But," he said, "you cannot s my face;
33:20 for no one shall s me and live."
33:21 And the LORD continued, "S,
33:23 and you shall s my back;
34:10 the people among whom you live shall s the work
34:11 S, I will drive out before you the Amorites,
34:35 the Israelites would s the face of Moses,
35:30 Then Moses said to the Israelites: S,
Lev 10:19 And Aaron spoke to Moses, "S,
13:12 so far as the priest can s,
Nu 11:15 and do not let me s my misery."
11:23 Now you shall s whether my word will come true
13:18 and s what the land is like,
14:23 shall s the land that I swore to give
14:23 none of those who despised me shall s it.
15:39 You have the fringe so that, when you s it,
22:41 from there he could s part of the people of Israel.
23: 9 For from the top of the crags I s him,
23:13 to another place from which you may s them;
23:13 you shall s only part of them,
23:13 of them, and shall not s them all;
23:20 S, I received a command to bless;
23:23 of Jacob and Israel, 'S what God has done!'
24:17 I s him, but not now;
27:12 and s the land that I have given to the Israelites.
28:19 s that they are without blemish.
32: 8 I sent them from Kadesh-barnea to s the land.
32:11 shall s the land that I swore to give to Abraham,
Dt 1: 8 S, I have set the land before you;
1:21 S, the LORD your God has given the land
1:35 shall s the good land that I swore to give
1:36 He shall s it, and to him and
2:24 S, I have handed over to you King Sihon
2:31 The LORD said to me, "S,
3:25 Let me cross over to s the good land beyond
3:28 of the land that you will s."
4: 5 S, just as the LORD my God has charged me,
4:19 when you look up to the heavens and s the sun,
4:28 objects of wood and stone that neither s, nor hear,
11:26 S, I am setting before you today a blessing and
12:13 at any place you happen to s.
18:16 or ever again s this great fire, I will die."
20: 1 against your enemies, and s horses and chariots,
21:11 suppose you s among the captives
22: 4 not s your neighbor's donkey or ox fallen on
23:14 so that he may not s anything indecent among you
28:10 the earth shall s that you are called by the name of
28:34 and driven mad by the sight that your eyes shall s.
28:67 and the sights that your eyes shall s.
28:68 a route that I promised you would never s again;
29: 4 or eyes to s, or ears to hear.
29:22 will s the devastation of that land and
30:15 S, I have set before you today life and prosperity,
32:20 I will s what their end will be;
32:39 S now that I, even I, am he;
34: 4 I have let you s it with your eyes,
Jos 3: 3 "When you s the ark of the covenant of
5: 6 the LORD swore that he would not let them s
6: 2 The LORD said to Joshua, "S,
8: 1 S, I have handed over to you the king of Ai
8: 8 s, I have commanded you."
9:12 on the day we set out to come to you, but now, s,
9:13 when we filled them, and s, they are burst;
14:10 And now, as you s, the LORD has kept me alive,
24:27 Joshua said to all the people, "S,
Jdg 2: 2 S what you have done!
6:36 to s whether you will deliver Israel by my hand,
10:16 and he could no longer bear to s Israel suffer.
14: 8 and he turned aside to s the carcass of the lion,
19: 9 S, the day has drawn to a close.
Ru 1:15 "S, your sister-in-law has gone back to her people
3: 2 S, he is winnowing barley tonight at
1Sa 2:31 S, a time is coming when I will cut off
3: 2 that he could not s, was lying down in his room;
3:11 Then the LORD said to Samuel, "S,
4:15 so that he could not s.
9:24 Samuel said, "S, what was kept is set before you.
10: 7 these signs meet you, do whatever you s fit to do,
10:22 "S, he has hidden himself among the baggage."
10:24 "Do you s the one whom the LORD has chosen?
12: 2 S, it is the king who leads you now;
12:13 S, here is the king whom you have chosen,
12:13 s, the LORD has set a king over you.
12:16 therefore take your stand and s this great thing that
12:17 and s that the wickedness that you have done in
14:17 "Call the roll and s who has gone from us."
14:29 s how my eyes have brightened because I tasted
15:35 not s Saul again until the day of his death,
16: 7 for the LORD does not s as mortals s;
16:15 And Saul's servants said to him, "S now,
17:18 S how your brothers fare,
17:28 for you have come down just to s the battle."
18:22 "Speak to David in private and say, 'S,
19:15 the messengers to s David for themselves.
20:29 let me get away, and s my brothers.'
21:14 "Look, you s the man is mad;
24:11 S, my father, s the corner of your cloak in my
24:15 May he s to it, and plead my cause,
25:25 your servant, did not s the young men of my lord,
25:35 s, I have heeded your voice,
26:16 S now, where is the king's spear,
28:13 king said to her, "Have no fear; what do you s?"
28:13 "I s a divine being coming up out of the ground."
2Sa 3:13 when you come to s me."
4:10 when the one who told me, 'S,
7: 2 "S now, I am living in a house of cedar,
13: 5 and when your father comes to s you, say to him,
13: 5 so that I may s it and eat it from her hand.' "
13: 6 and when the king came to s him,
13:35 Jonadab said to the king, "S,
15: 3 "S, your claims are good and right;
15:25 and let me s both it and the place where it stays.
15:28 S, I will wait at the fords of the wilderness
16: 8 S, disaster has overtaken you;
18:26 the sentinel called to the gatekeeper and said, "S,
19: 8 The troops were all told, "S,
19:20 therefore, s, I have come this day,
24: 3 while the eyes of my lord the king can still s it!
1Ki 1:51 s, he has laid hold of the horns of the altar, saying,
9:12 But when Hiram came from Tyre to s the cities
11:31 for thus says the LORD, the God of Israel, "S,
14: 4 Now Ahijah could not s, for his eyes were dim
17:23 then Elijah said, "S, your son is alive."
20: 7 S how this man is seeking trouble;
22:23 So you s, the LORD has put a lying spirit in
2Ki 2:10 yet, if you s me as I am being taken from you,
2:12 But when he could no longer s him,
2:16 They said to him, "S now,
3:17 'You shall s neither wind nor rain,
5: 7 and s how he is trying to pick a quarrel with me."
6: 1 the company of prophets said to Elisha, "As you s,
6:17 "O LORD, please open his eyes that he may s."
6:20 open the eyes of these men so that they may s."
6:30 the people could s that he had sackcloth
6:32 s that you shut the door and hold it closed
7: 2 But he said, "You shall s it with your own eyes,
7:19 "You shall s it with your own eyes,
8:29 of Jehoram of Judah went down to s Joram son
9:17 and said, "I s a company."
9:34 he said, "S to that cursed woman and bury her;
10:16 "Come with me, and s my zeal for the LORD."
10:23 of Baal, "Search and s that there is no worshiper of
18:21 S, you are relying now on Egypt,
19: 9 "S, he has set out to fight against you,"
19:11 S, you have heard what the kings
19:16 open your eyes, O LORD, and s;
22:20 not s all the disaster that I will bring
23:17 Then he said, "What is that monument that I s?"
1Ch 11: 1 "S, we are your bone and flesh.
12:17 the God of our ancestors s and give judgment."
21:23 s, I present the oxen for burnt offerings,
22: 9 S, a son shall be born to you;
2Ch 13:12 S, God is with us at our head,
18:22 So you s, the LORD has put a lying spirit in
19:11 S, Amariah the chief priest is over you
20:10 S now, the people of Ammon, Moab,
20:17 and s the victory of the LORD on your behalf,
21:14 s, the LORD will bring a great plague
22: 6 of Judah went down to s Joram son of Ahab
24: 5 and s that you act quickly."
24:22 he said, "May the LORD s and avenge!"
25:19 You say, 'S, I have defeated Edom,'

2Ch 29: 8 and of hissing, as you **s** with your own eyes.
29:19 **s**, they are in front of the altar of the LORD."
30: 7 so that he made them a desolation, as you **s**.
34:28 not **s** all the disaster that I will bring on this place
Ezr 5:17 to **s** whether a decree was issued by King Cyrus
Ne 2:17 Then I said to them, "You **s** the trouble we are in,
4:11 "They will not know or **s** anything before we come
Est 3: 4 to **s** whether Mordecai's words would avail;
5:13 as I **s** the Jew Mordecai sitting at the king's gate."
8: 6 For how can I bear to **s** the calamity that is coming
8: 6 can I bear to **s** the destruction of my kindred?"
8: 7 **"S,** I have given Esther the house of Haman,
Job 3: 9 may it not **s** the eyelids of the morning—
3:23 Why is light given to one who cannot **s** the way,
4: 3 **S,** you have instructed many;
5:27 **S,** we have searched this out; it is true.
6:21 you **s** my calamity, and are afraid.
7: 7 my eye will never again **s** good.
7: 8 The eye that beholds me will **s** me no more;
8:19 **S,** these are their happy ways,
8:20 **"S,** God will not reject a blameless person,
9:11 Look, he passes by me, and I do not **s** him;
9:25 they flee away, they **s** no good.
10: 4 Do you **s** as humans **s**?
13:15 **S,** he will kill me; I have no hope;
17:15 where then is my hope? Who will **s** my hope?
19:26 then in my flesh I shall **s** God,
19:27 whom I shall **s** on my side,
20: 9 The eye that saw them will **s** them no more,
21:20 Let their own eyes **s** their destruction,
22:11 or darkness so that you cannot **s**;
22:12 **S** the highest stars, how lofty they are!
22:14 Thick clouds enwrap him, so that he does not **s**,
22:19 The righteous **s** it and are glad;
23: 9 I turn to the right, but I cannot **s** him.
24: 1 and why do those who know him never **s** his days?
24:15 'No eye will **s** me'; and he disguises his face.
28:10 and their eyes **s** every precious thing.
31: 4 Does he not **s** my ways, and number all my steps?
32:11 **"S,** I waited for your words,
33: 2 **S,** I open my mouth; the tongue in my
33: 6 **S,** before God I am as you are;
33:28 and my life shall **s** the light.'
33:30 so that they may **s** the light of life.
34:32 teach me what I do not **s**;
35: 5 Look at the heavens and **s**;
35:14 much less when you say that you do not **s** him,
36:22 **S,** God is exalted in his power;
36:30 **S,** he scatters his lightning around him and covers
39:29 its eyes **s** it from far away.
40: 4 **"S,** I am of small account;
Ps 4: 6 "O that we might **s** some good!
7:14 **S** how they conceive evil,
9:13 **S** what I suffer from those who hate me;
10:11 he has hidden his face, he will never **s** it."
10:14 But you do **s**! Indeed you note trouble
14: 2 on humankind to **s** if there are any who are wise,
16:10 or let your faithful one **s** the Pit.
17: 2 let your eyes **s** the right.
22: 7 All who **s** me mock at me;
27:13 I believe that I shall **s** the goodness of the LORD
31:11 those who **s** me in the street flee from me.
34: 8 O taste and **s** that the LORD is good;
36: 9 in your light we **s** light.
40: 3 will **s** and fear, and put their trust in the LORD.
40: 9 **s,** I have not restrained my lips, as you know,
40:12 my iniquities have overtaken me, until I cannot **s**;
41: 6 And when they come to **s** me,
46: 8 **s** what desolations he has brought on the earth.
49: 9 one should live on forever and never **s** the grave.
49:19 who will never again **s** the light.
50:18 You make friends with a thief when you **s** one,
52: 6 The righteous will **s**, and fear, and will laugh at
52: 7 **"S** the one who would not take refuge in God,
53: 2 God looks down from heaven on humankind to **s**
55: 9 for I **s** violence and strife in the city.
58:10 when they **s** vengeance done;
59: 4 Rouse yourself, come to my help and **s**!
64: 5 of laying snares secretly, thinking, "Who can **s** us?
64: 8 all who **s** them will shake with horror.
66: 5 Come and **s** what God has done:
69:23 Let their eyes be darkened so that they cannot **s**,
69:32 Let the oppressed **s** it and be glad;
71:20 You who have made me **s** many troubles
74: 9 We do not **s** our emblems;
80:14 look down from heaven, and **s**;
86:17 those who hate me may **s** it and be put to shame,
89:48 Who can live and never **s** death?
91: 8 You will only look with your eyes and **s**
94: 7 and they say, "The LORD does not **s**;
94: 9 He who formed the eye, does he not **s**?
106: 5 that I may **s** the prosperity of your chosen ones,
107:42 The upright **s** it and are glad;
109:25 when they **s** me, they shake their heads.
112:10 The wicked **s** it and are angry;
115: 5 not speak; eyes, but do not **s**.
119:40 **S,** I have longed for your precepts;
119:74 Those who fear you shall **s** me and rejoice,
128: 5 May you **s** the prosperity of Jerusalem all the days
128: 6 May you **s** your children's children.
135:16 they have eyes, but they do not **s**;
139:24 **S** if there is any wicked way in me,
142: 4 Look on my right hand and **s**—
Pr 22: 3 The clever **s** danger and hide;
22:29 Do you **s** those who are skillful in their work?
23:33 Your eyes will **s** strange things,
24:18 or else the LORD will **s** it and be displeased,
Pr 24:31 and **s**, it was all overgrown with thorns;
26:12 Do you **s** persons wise in their own eyes?
27:12 The clever **s** danger and hide;
29:20 Do you **s** someone who is hasty in speech?
Ecc 1:10 Is there a thing of which it is said, **"S,**
1:14 and **s**, all is vanity and a chasing after wind.
2: 3 on folly, until I might **s** what was good for mortals
3:22 who can bring them to **s** what will be after them?
5: 8 If you **s** in a province the oppression of the poor
5:11 and what gain has their owner but to **s** them
7:11 an advantage to those who **s** the sun.
7:27 **S,** this is what I found, says the Teacher,
7:29 **S,** this alone I found,
8:16 and to **s** the business that is done on earth,
8:16 how one's eyes **s** sleep neither day nor night,
11: 7 and it is pleasant for the eyes to **s** the sun.
12: 3 and those who look through the windows **s** dimly;
SS 2:14 let me **s** your face, let me hear your voice;
6:11 to **s** whether the vines had budded,
7:12 and **s** whether the vines have budded,
Isa 5:12 or **s** the work of his hands!
5:19 let him speed his work that we may **s** it;
8:18 **S,** I and the children whom
8:22 but will **s** only distress and darkness,
11: 3 He shall not judge by what his eyes **s**,
13: 9 **S,** the day of the LORD comes, cruel,
13:17 **S,** I am stirring up the Medes against them,
14:16 Those who **s** you will stare at you,
17: 1 **S,** Damascus will cease to be a city,
19: 1 **S,** the LORD is riding on a swift cloud
20: 6 the inhabitants of this coastland will say, **'S,**
21: 3 I am dismayed so that I cannot **s**.
26:10 of uprightness they deal perversely and do not **s**
26:11 your hand is lifted up, but they do not **s** it.
26:11 Let them **s** your zeal for your people,
28: 2 **S,** the Lord has one who is mighty and strong;
28:16 **S,** I am laying in Zion a foundation stone,
29:18 and darkness the eyes of the blind shall **s**.
30:10 who say to the seers, "Do not **s**";
30:20 but your eyes shall **s** your Teacher.
30:27 **S,** the name of the LORD comes from far away,
32: 1 **S,** a king will reign in righteousness,
33:17 Your eyes will **s** the king in his beauty;
33:19 No longer will you **s** the insolent people,
33:20 Your eyes will **s** Jerusalem, a quiet habitation,
35: 2 They shall **s** the glory of the LORD,
36: 6 **S,** you are relying on Egypt,
37:11 **S,** you have heard what the kings
37:17 open your eyes, O LORD, and **s**;
38: 8 **S,** I will make the shadow cast by
38:11 I shall not **s** the LORD in the land of the living;
40: 5 and all people shall **s** it together,
40:10 **S,** the Lord GOD comes with might,
40:15 **s**, he takes up the isles like fine dust.
40:26 Lift up your eyes on high and **s**:
41:20 so that all may **s** and know,
42: 9 **S,** the former things have come to pass,
42:18 and you that are blind, look up and **s**!
44: 9 their witnesses neither **s** nor know.
44:18 for their eyes are shut, so that they cannot **s**,
47:14 **S,** they are like stubble, the fire consumes them;
48: 6 now **s** all this; and will you not declare it?
48:10 **S,** I have refined you, but not like silver;
49: 7 the slave of rulers, "Kings shall **s** and stand up,
49:16 **S,** I have inscribed you on the palms of my hands;
49:18 Lift up your eyes all around and **s**;
51:22 **S,** I have taken from your hand the cup
52: 8 in plain sight they **s** the return of the LORD to Zion.
52:10 and all the ends of the earth shall **s** the salvation
52:13 **S,** my servant shall prosper;
52:15 for that which had not been told them they shall **s**,
53:10 he shall **s** his offspring, and shall prolong his days;
53:11 Out of his anguish he shall **s** light;
54:16 **S** it is I who have created the smith who blows
55: 4 **S,** I made him a witness to the peoples,
55: 5 **S,** you shall call nations that you do not know,
58: 3 "Why do we fast, but you do not **s**?
58: 7 when you **s** the naked, to cover them,
59: 1 **S,** the LORD's hand is not too short to save,
60: 5 Then you shall **s** and be radiant;
61: 9 all who **s** them shall acknowledge that they are
62: 2 The nations shall **s** your vindication,
62:11 Say to daughter Zion, **"S,** your salvation comes;
63:15 Look down from heaven and **s**,
65: 6 **S,** it is written before me:
66: 5 so that we may **s** your joy";
66:14 You shall **s**, and your heart shall rejoice;
66:18 and they shall come and shall **s** my glory,
Jer 1:10 **S,** today I appoint you over nations and
1:11 saying, "Jeremiah, what do you **s**?"
1:11 And I said, "I **s** a branch of an almond tree."
1:13 saying, "What do you **s**?"
1:13 And I said, "I **s** a boiling pot,
2:10 **s** if there has ever been such a thing.
2:19 and **s** that it is evil and bitter for you to forsake
3: 2 Look up to the bare heights, and **s**!
4:21 How long must I **s** the standard,
5: 1 Search its squares and **s** if you can find one person
5:12 and we shall not **s** sword or famine."
5:21 but do not **s**, who have ears, but do not hear.
6:10 **S,** their ears are closed, they cannot listen.
6:21 Therefore thus says the LORD: **S,**
6:22 **S,** a people is coming from the land of the north,
7:12 and **s** what I did to it for the wickedness
7:17 not **s** what they are doing in the towns of Judah
8:17 **S,** I am letting snakes loose among you,
11:20 let me **s** your retribution upon them,
Jer 12: 3 You **s** me and test me—my heart is with you.
13:20 Lift up your eyes and **s** those who come from
14:13 'You shall not **s** the sword,
17: 6 and shall not **s** when relief comes.
17:15 **S** how they say to me,
20:12 you **s** the heart and the mind;
20:12 let me **s** your retribution upon them,
20:18 Why did I come forth from the womb to **s** toil
21: 8 **S,** I am setting before you the way of life and
21:13 **S,** I am against you, O inhabitant of the valley,
22:10 for he shall return no more to **s** his native land.
22:12 and he shall never **s** this land again.
23:18 of the LORD so as to **s** and to hear his word?
23:24 in secret places so that I cannot **s** them?
23:30 **S,** therefore, I am against the prophets,
23:31 **S,** I am against the prophets, says the LORD,
23:32 **S,** I am against those who prophesy lying dreams,
24: 3 LORD said to me, "What do you **s**, Jeremiah?"
25:29 **S,** I am beginning to bring disaster on the city
25:32 **S,** disaster is spreading from nation to nation,
29:32 to **s** the good that I am going to do to my people,
30: 6 Ask now, and **s**, can a man bear a child?
30: 6 then do I **s** every man with his hands on his loins
31: 8 **S,** I am going to bring them from the land of
32: 4 with him face to face and **s** him eye to eye;
32:24 **S,** the siege ramps have been cast up against
32:24 you spoke has happened, as you yourself can **s**.
32:27 **S,** I am the LORD, the God of all flesh;
32:37 **S,** I am going to gather them from all the lands
34: 3 you shall **s** the king of Babylon eye to eye
40: 4 **S,** the whole land is before you;
42: 2 a few of us left out of many, as your eyes can **s**.
42:14 where we shall not **s** war,
42:18 You shall **s** this place no more.
43: 9 Let the Judeans **s** you do it,
46: 5 Why do I **s** them terrified?
46:25 The LORD of hosts, the God of Israel, said: **S,**
47: 2 **S,** waters are rising out of the north
51:61 **s** that you read all these words,
La 1:11 O LORD, and **s** how worthless I have become.
1:12 Look and **s** if there is any sorrow like my sorrow,
1:20 **S,** O LORD, how distressed I am;
3:36 one's case is subverted—does the Lord not **s** it?
3:63 **s**, I am the object of their taunt-songs.
5: 1 what has befallen us; look, and **s** our disgrace!
Eze 3: 8 **S,** I have made your face hard against their faces,
4: 8 **S,** I am putting cords on you so
4:15 to me, **"S,** I will let you have cow's dung instead
7: 5 Disaster after disaster! **S,**
7: 6 It has awakened against you; **s**, it comes!
7:10 **S,** the day! **S,** it comes! Your doom has gone out.
8: 6 "Mortal, do you **s** what they are doing,
8: 6 Yet you will **s** still greater abominations."
8: 9 and **s** the vile abominations
8:12 For they say, 'The LORD does not **s** us,
8:13 "You will **s** still greater abominations
8:15 You will **s** still greater abominations than these."
8:17 **S,** they are putting the branch to their nose!
9: 9 and the LORD does not **s**.'
12: 2 who have eyes to **s** but do not **s**,
12: 6 so that you may not **s** the land;
12:12 so that he may not **s** the land with his eyes.
12:13 the land of the Chaldeans, yet he shall not **s** it;
13: 9 be against the prophets who **s** false visions
13:23 therefore you shall no longer **s** false visions
14:22 When you **s** their ways and their deeds,
14:23 when you **s** their ways and their deeds,
16:37 so that they may **s** all your nakedness.
16:44 **S,** everyone who uses proverbs will use this
17: 7 And **s**! This vine stretched out
20:48 All flesh shall **s** that I the LORD have kindled it;
21: 7 **S,** it comes and it will be fulfilled,"
22:13 **S,** I strike my hands together at
26: 3 **S,** I am against you, O Tyre!
36: 9 **S** now, I am for you;
39:21 and all the nations shall **s** my judgment
40: 4 declare all that you **s** to the house of Israel."
Da 1:10 If he should **s** you in poorer condition than
2: 8 because you **s** I have firmly decreed:
3:25 He replied, "But I **s** four men unbound,
5:23 wood, and stone, which do not **s** or hear or know;
10: 7 the people who were with me did not **s** the vision,
10: 8 So I was left alone to **s** this great vision.
Joel 2:28 and your young men shall **s** visions.
Am 3: 9 and **s** what great tumults are within it,
6: 2 Cross over to Calneh, and **s**;
6:11 **S,** the LORD commands,
7: 8 the LORD said to me, "Amos, what do you **s**?"
7: 8 **"S,** I am setting a plumb line in the midst
8: 2 He said, "Amos, what do you **s**?"
Jnh 4: 5 waiting to **s** what would become of the city.
Mic 7: 9 to the light; I shall **s** his vindication.
7:10 Then my enemy will **s**,
7:10 My eyes will **s** her downfall;
7:16 nations shall **s** and be ashamed of all their might;
Na 2:13 **S,** I am against you, says the LORD of hosts,
3: 7 Then all who **s** you will shrink from you and say,
Hab 1: 3 Why do you make me **s** wrongdoing and look
1: 5 Look at the nations, and **s**!
2: 1 I will keep watch to **s** what he will say to me,
2:19 **S,** it is gold and silver plated,
Zec 2: 2 to **s** what is its width and what is its length."
2: 9 **S** now, I am going to raise my hand against them,
3: 4 **"S,** I have taken your guilt away from you,
4: 2 He said to me, "What do you **s**?"
4: 2 And I said, "I **s** a lampstand all of gold,
4:10 and shall **s** the plummet in the hand of Zerubbabel.

Zec 5: 2 And he said to me, "What do you s?"
5: 2 I answered, "I s a flying scroll;
5: 5 "Look up and s what this is that is coming out."
9: 5 Ashkelon shall s it and be afraid;
10: 2 teraphim utter nonsense, and the diviners s lies;
10: 7 Their children shall s it and rejoice,
12: 2 S, I am about to make Jerusalem a cup of reeling
14: 1 S, a day is coming for the LORD,
Mal 1: 5 Your own eyes shall s this, and you shall say,
3: 1 S, I am sending my messenger to prepare the way
3:10 s if I will not open the windows of heaven for you
3:18 Then once more you shall s the difference between
4: 1 S, the day is coming, burning like an oven,
Mt 5: 8 "Blessed are the pure in heart, for they will s God.
5:16 so that they may s your good works and give glory
7: 3 Why do you s the speck in your neighbor's eye,
7: 5 and then you will s clearly to take the speck out
8: 4 "S that you say nothing to anyone;
9:30 "S that no one knows of this."
10:16 "S, I am sending you out like sheep into the midst
11: 4 "Go and tell John what you hear and s:
11: 8 What then did you go out to s?
11: 9 What then did you go out to s?
11:10 This is the one about whom it is written, 'S,
12:22 that the one who had been mute could speak and s.
12:38 "Teacher, we wish to s a sign from you."
12:41 and s, something greater than Jonah is here!
12:42 and s, something greater than Solomon is here!
13:16 But blessed are your eyes, for they s,
13:17 and righteous people longed to s what you s, but
did not s it, and to hear what you hear,
15:17 not s that whatever goes into the mouth enters
16:28 before they s the Son of Man coming
18:10 for, I tell you, in heaven their angels continually s
20:18 "S, we are going up to Jerusalem, and the Son
22:11 "But when the king came in to s the guests,
23:38 S, your house is left to you, desolate.
23:39 I tell you, you will not s me again until you say,
24: 2 Then he asked them, "You s all these, do you not?
24: 6 s that you are not alarmed;
24:15 "So when you s the desolating sacrilege standing
24:30 and they will s 'the Son of Man coming on
24:33 So also, when you s all these things,
25:20 s, I have made five more talents.'
25:22 s, I have made two more talents.'
26:45 S, the hour is at hand, and the Son
26:46 S, my betrayer is at hand."
26:58 with the guards in order to s how this would end.
26:64 From now on you will s the Son of Man seated at
27: 4 "What is that to us? S to it yourself."
27:24 innocent of this man's blood; s to it yourselves."
27:49 let us s whether Elijah will come to save him."
28: 1 Mary Magdalene and the other Mary went to s
28: 6 Come, s the place where he lay.
28: 7 to Galilee; there you will s him.'
28:10 to Galilee; there they will s me."
Mk 1: 2 As it is written in the prophet Isaiah, "S,
1:44 "S that you say nothing to anyone;
3: 2 They watched him to s whether he would cure him
5:14 people came to s what it was that had happened.
5:31 "You s the crowd pressing in on you;
5:32 He looked all around to s who had done it.
6:38 "How many loaves have you? Go and s."
7:18 Do you not s that whatever goes into a person
8:18 Do you have eyes, and fail to s?
8:23 he asked him, "Can you s anything?"
8:24 And the man looked up and said, "I can s people,
9: 1 until they s that the kingdom of God has come
10:33 "S, we are going up to Jerusalem,
10:51 "My teacher, let me s again."
11:13 to s whether perhaps he would find anything on it.
12:15 Bring me a denarius and let me s it."
13: 2 Jesus asked him, "Do you s these great buildings?
13:14 "But when you s the desolating sacrilege set up
13:26 Then they will s 'the Son of Man coming
13:29 So also, when you s these things taking place,
14:42 S, my betrayer is at hand."
14:62 and 'you will s the Son of Man seated at
15: 4 S how many charges they bring against you."
15:32 so that we may s and believe."
15:36 let us s whether Elijah will come
16: 7 there you will s him, just as he told you."
Lk 2:10 the angel said to them, "Do not be afraid; for s—
2:15 to Bethlehem and s this thing that has taken place,
2:26 to him by the Holy Spirit that he would not s death
3: 6 and all flesh shall s the salvation of God.' "
6: 7 to s whether he would cure on the sabbath,
6:41 Why do you s the speck in your neighbor's eye,
6:42 you yourself do not s the log in your own eye?
6:42 and then you will s clearly to take the speck out
7:25 What then did you go out to s?
7:26 What then did you go out to s?
7:27 This is the one about whom it is written, 'S,
7:44 he said to Simon, "Do you s this woman?
8:16 so that those who enter may s the light.
8:20 brothers are standing outside, wanting to s you."
8:35 Then people came out to s what had happened,
9: 9 And he tried to s him.
9:27 not taste death before they s the kingdom of God."
10: 3 S, I am sending you out like lambs into the midst
10:19 S, I have given you authority to tread on snakes
10:23 "Blessed are the eyes that s what you s!
10:24 and kings desired to s what you s,
10:24 but did not s it, and to hear what you hear,
11:31 and s, something greater than Solomon is here!
11:32 and s, something greater than Jonah is here!
11:33 on the lampstand so that those who enter may s

Lk 11:38 to s that he did not first wash before dinner.
11:41 and s, everything will be clean for you.
12:54 "When you s a cloud rising in the west,
12:55 And when you s the south wind blowing, you say,
13: 7 So he said to the gardener, 'S here!
13:28 of teeth when you s Abraham and Isaac and Jacob
13:35 S, your house is left to you.
13:35 not s me until the time comes when you say,
14:18 and I must go out and s it;
14:28 to s whether he has enough to complete it?
14:29 all who s it will begin to ridicule him,
17:22 "The days are coming when you will long to s one
17:22 and you will not s it.
18:31 he took the twelve aside and said to them, "S,
18:41 He said, "Lord, let me s again."
19: 3 He was trying to s who Jesus was,
19: 4 ahead and climbed a sycamore tree to s him,
21: 6 "As for these things that you s, the days will come
21:20 "When you s Jerusalem surrounded by armies,
21:27 Then they will s 'the Son of Man coming in
21:30 as they sprout leaves you can s for yourselves
21:31 So also, when you s these things taking place,
22:21 But s, the one who betrays me is with me,
23: 8 for he had been wanting to s him for a long time,
23: 8 and was hoping to s him perform some sign.
24:24 but they did not s him."
24:39 s that it is I myself. Touch me and s; for a ghost
does not have flesh and bones as you s that I have."
24:49 And s, I am sending upon you
Jn 1:33 on whom you s the Spirit descend and remain is
1:39 He said to them, "Come and s."
1:46 Philip said to him, "Come and s."
1:50 You will s greater things than these."
1:51 you will s heaven opened and the angels
3: 3 no one can s the kingdom of God
3:36 whoever disobeys the Son will not s life,
4:19 "Sir, I s that you are a prophet.
4:29 "Come and s a man who told me everything I have
4:35 and s how the fields are ripe for harvesting.
4:48 you s signs and wonders you will not believe."
5:14 "S, you have been made well!
6:30 so that we may s it and believe you?
6:40 that all who s the Son and believe in him
6:62 if you were to s the Son of Man ascending to
7: 3 and go to Judea so that your disciples also may s
7:52 Search and you will s that no prophet is to arise
8:51 whoever keeps my word will never s death."
8:56 that he would s my day;
9: 7 he went and washed and came back able to s.
9:15 Then I washed, and now I s."
9:19 How then does he now s?"
9:25 that though I was blind, now I s."
9:39 for judgment so that those who do not s may s,
9:39 and those who do s may become blind."
9:41 But now that you say, 'We s,' your sin remains.
11: 9 because they s the light of this world.
11:34 They said to him, "Lord, come and s."
11:36 So the Jews said, "S how he loved him!"
11:40 you would s the glory of God?"
12: 9 not only because of Jesus but also to s Lazarus,
12:19 The Pharisees then said to one another, "You s,
12:21 and said to him, "Sir, we wish to s Jesus."
14:19 the world will no longer s me, but you will s me;
16:10 going to the Father and you will s me no longer;
16:16 "A little while, and you will no longer s me, and
again a little while, and you will s me."
16:17 'A little while, and you will no longer s me, and
again a little while, and you will s me';
16:19 'A little while, and you will no longer s me, and
again a little while, and you will s me'?
16:22 but I will s you again, and your hearts will rejoice,
17:24 may be with me where I am, to s my glory,
18:26 asked, "Did I not s you in the garden with him?"
19:24 but cast lots for it to s who will get it."
20:25 "Unless I s the mark of the nails in his hands,
20:27 "Put your finger here and s my hands.
Ac 2:17 and your young men shall s visions,
2:33 he has poured out this that you both s and hear.
3:16 has made this man strong, whom you s and know;
7:56 "I s the heavens opened and the Son
8:23 For I s that you are in the gall of bitterness and
9: 8 though his eyes were open, he could s nothing;
13:11 and you will be blind for a while, unable to s
15:36 where we proclaimed the word of the Lord and s
17:11 to s whether these things were so.
17:16 he was deeply distressed to s that the city was full
17:22 I s how extremely religious you are in every way.
18: 2 to leave Rome. Paul went to s them,
18:15 and names and your own law, s to it yourselves;
19:21 "After I have gone there, I must also s Rome."
19:26 You also s and hear that not only in Ephesus but
20:25 will ever s my face again.
20:38 that they would not s him again.
21:20 Then they said to him, "You s, brother,
22:11 Since I could not s because of the brightness of
22:14 to s the Righteous One and to hear his own voice;
25:24 you s this man about whom the whole Jewish
27:10 I can s that the voyage will be with danger
28:20 For this reason therefore I have asked to s you
Ro 1:11 For I am longing to s you so that I may share
1:28 And since they did not s fit to acknowledge God,
7:23 but I s in my members another law at war with
8:25 But if we hope for what we do not s,
9:33 as it is written, "S, I am laying in Zion a stone
11: 8 eyes that would not s and ears that would not hear,
11:10 let their eyes be darkened so that they cannot s,
15:21 "Those who have never been told of him shall s,

Ro 15:24 to s you on my journey and to be sent on by you,
1Co 8:10 For if others s you, who possess knowledge,
13:12 For now we s in a mirror, dimly, but then we will s
face to face.
16: 7 I do not want to s you now just in passing,
16:10 s that he has nothing to fear among you,
2Co 5:17 s, everything has become new!
6: 2 S, now is the acceptable time;
6: 2 s, now is the day of salvation!
6: 9 yet are well known; as dying, and s—
7: 8 for I s that I grieved you with that letter,
7:11 s what earnestness this godly grief has produced
13: 5 Examine yourselves to s whether you are living in
Gal 1:19 but I did not s any other apostle except James
3: 7 so, you s, those who believe are the descendants
6:11 S what large letters I make when I am writing
Eph 3: 9 and to make everyone s what is the plan of
Php 1:27 whether I come and s you or am absent and hear
2:23 therefore to send him as soon as I s how things go
Col 2: 5 to s your morale and the firmness of your faith
2: 8 S to it that no one takes you captive
4:16 and s that you read also the letter from Laodicea.
4:17 "S that you complete the task
1Th 2:17 we longed with great eagerness to s you face
3: 6 you always remember us kindly and long to s us—
3: 6 just as we long to s you.
3:10 that we may s you face to face
5:15 S that none of you repays evil for evil,
1Ti 4:15 so that all may s your progress.
6:16 whom no one has ever seen or can s;
2Ti 1: 4 I long to s you so that I may be filled with joy.
Tit 3:13 and s that they lack nothing.
Heb 2: 8 we do not yet s everything in subjection to them,
2: 9 but we do s Jesus, who for a little
3:19 So we s that they were unable to enter because
7: 4 S how great he is!
8: 5 the tent, was warned, "S that you make everything
10: 7 Then I said, 'S, God, I have come to do your will,
10: 9 "S, I have come to do your will."
10:25 and all the more as you s the Day approaching.
12:14 the holiness without which no one will s the Lord.
12:15 S to it that no one fails to obtain the grace of God;
12:16 S to it that no one becomes like Esau,
12:25 S that you do not refuse the one who is speaking;
13:23 he comes in time, he will be with me when I s you.
Jas 2:22 You s that faith was active along with his works,
2:24 You s that a person is justified by works and not
5: 9 S, the Judge is standing at the doors!
1Pe 1: 8 and even though you do not s him now,
2: 6 "S, I am laying in Zion a stone,
2:12 they may s your honorable deeds and glorify God
3: 2 when they s the purity and reverence of your lives.
3:10 "Those who desire life and desire to s good days,
1Jn 3: 1 S what love the Father has given us,
3: 2 we will be like him, for we will s him as he is.
4: 1 but test the spirits to s whether they are from God;
5:16 If you s your brother or sister committing what is
3Jn 1:14 instead I hope to s you soon,
Jude 1:14 "S, the Lord is coming with ten thousands
Rev 1: 7 every eye will s him, even those who pierced him;
1:11 "Write in a book what you s and send it to
1:12 I turned to s whose voice it was that spoke to me,
1:18 I was dead, and s, I am alive forever and ever;
3:18 and salve to anoint your eyes so that you may s.
5: 5 S, the Lion of the tribe of Judah,
9:20 which cannot s or hear or walk.
16:15 ("S, I am coming like a thief!
17: 8 will be amazed when they s the beast,
18: 7 I am no widow, and I will never s grief,'
18: 9 over her when they s the smoke of her burning;
21: 3 I heard a loud voice from the throne saying, "S,
21: 5 the one who was seated on the throne said, "S,
22: 4 they will s his face, and his name will be
22: 7 "S, I am coming soon!
22:12 "S, I am coming soon; my reward is with me,
Tob 2:10 For four years I remained unable to s.
3: 6 for me to die than to s so much distress in my life
3: 8 S, you have already been married
3: 9 May we never s a son or daughter of yours!"
3:17 so that he might s God's light with his eyes;
5:10 I cannot s the light of heaven,
5:10 in darkness like the dead who no longer s the light.
5:10 I hear people but I cannot s them."
5:21 Your eyes will s him on the day when he returns
8:12 of the maids and have her go in to s if he is alive.
9: 6 I s in Tobias the very image of my cousin Tobit."
10: 7 not believe that they will s me again.
10:11 and may I s children of yours before I die."
10:12 and may I live long enough to s children of you
11: 8 your father will regain his sight and s the light."
11:14 "I s you, my son, the light of my eyes!"
11:15 Now I s my son Tobias!"
12: 1 s to paying the wages of the man who went
12:20 S, I am ascending to him who sent me.
12:21 Then they stood up, and could s him no more.
13: 6 So now s what he has done for you;
13:16 of my descendants should survive to s your glory
14:10 For I s that there is much wickedness within it,
14:10 S, my son, what Nadab did
14:11 my children, s what almsgiving accomplishes,
Jdt 3: 3 S, our buildings and all our land
3: 4 come and deal with them as you s fit."
6: 5 you shall not s my face again from this day
6:19 s their arrogance, and have pity on our people
7:13 to keep watch to s that no one gets out of the town.
10: 4 to entice the eyes of all the men who might s her.
10:13 I am on my way to s Holofernes the commander

Jdt 10:15 by hurrying down to s our lord.
13:15 and said, "S here, the head of Holofernes,
14: 5 bring Achior the Ammonite to me so that he may s
15: 8 and to s Judith and to wish her well.
15:12 All the women of Israel gathered to s her,
AdE 2:11 to s what would happen to Esther.
5:13 as long as I s Mordecai the Jew in the courtyard."
Wis 2:17 Let us s if his words are true,
4:17 For they will s the end of the wise,
4:18 The unrighteous will s, and will have contempt
5: 2 When the unrighteous s them,
13: 7 they keep searching, and they trust in what they s,
15:15 these have neither the use of their eyes to s with,
18: 1 but did not s their forms,
Sir 2:10 Consider the generations of old and s:
6:36 you s an intelligent person, rise early to visit him;
13: 7 Should he s you afterwards,
15: 7 and sinners will not s her.
16:21 Like a tempest that no one can s,
23:18 says to himself, "Who can s me?
23:19 of human behavior and s into hidden corners.
25: 7 a man who lives to s the downfall of his foes.
31:14 Do not reach out your hand for everything you s,
36: 3 against foreign nations and let them s your might.
37: 9 and then stand aside to s what happens to you.
37:24 and all who s him will call him happy.
37:27 s what is bad for you and do not give in to it.
39:20 to the end of time he can s everything,
42:11 S that there is no lattice in her room,
42:22 and how sparkling they are to s!
46:10 so that all the Israelites might s how good it is
51:27 S with your own eyes that I have labored but little
Bar 2:17 O Lord, and s, for the dead who are in Hades,
3: 8 S, we are today in our exile
4:24 so they soon will s your salvation by God,
4:25 but you will soon s their destruction and will tread
4:36 and s the joy that is coming to you from God.
5: 5 and s your children gathered from west and east at
LtJ 6: 4 Now in Babylon you will s gods made of silver
6: 6 when you s the multitude before and
6:19 though their gods can s none of them.
6:40 for when they s someone who cannot speak,
6:49 How then can one fail to s that these are not gods,
Sus 1: 8 Every day the two elders used to s her,
1:12 Day after day they watched eagerly to s her.
1:18 they did not s the elders, because they were hiding.
1:20 the garden doors are shut, and no one can s us.
1:26 in at the side door to s what had happened to her.
1:54 Under what tree did you s them being intimate
Bel 1: 6 not s how much he eats and drinks every day?"
1:11 priests of Bel said, "S, we are now going outside;
1:20 "I s the footprints of men and women
1:27 Daniel said, "S what you have been worshiping!"
1Mc 2: 7 Why was I born to s this, the ruin of my people,
2:12 And s, our holy place, our beauty,
3:59 in battle than to s the misfortunes of our nation
4:10 to s whether he will favor us
4:36 Then Judas and his brothers said, "S,
6:26 And s, today they have encamped against
7: 3 he said, "Do not let me s their faces!"
7: 7 let him go and s all the ruin that Judas has brought
7:28 I shall come with a few men to s you face to face
9:58 Then all the lawless plotted and said, "S!
10:56 so that we may s one another,
2Mc 1: 9 And now s that you keep the festival of booths in
3:16 To s the appearance of the high priest was to
3:34 And s that you, who have been flogged by heaven,
5:26 to the sword all those who came out to s them,
6: 9 One could s, therefore, the misery that had come
7:17 and s how his mighty power will torture you
7:28 at the heaven and the earth and s everything that is
9:25 and waiting to s what will happen.
1Es 4:18 then s a woman lovely in appearance and beauty,
8:90 S, we are now before you in our iniquities;
Man 1: 9 not worthy to look up and s the height of heaven
3Mc 2:13 s now, O holy King, that because of our many
2Es 1:37 though they do not s me with bodily eyes,
1:38 with pride and s the people coming from the east;
2:29 so that your children may not s hell.
2:38 and s the number of those who have been sealed at
4: 4 then I will show you the way you desire to s,
4:26 "If you are alive, you will s, and if you live long,
4:43 the things that you desire to s will be disclosed
5: 2 be increased beyond what you yourself s,
5: 3 that you now s ruling shall be a trackless waste,
5: 3 and people shall s it desolate.
5: 4 you shall s it thrown into confusion after
5:35 not s the travail of Jacob and the exhaustion of
6:20 and all shall s my judgment together.
6:25 to you shall be saved and shall s my salvation and
6:26 And they shall s those who were taken up,
7:18 the difficult circumstances and will never s
7:27 the evils that I have foretold shall s my wonders.
7:*42* by which all shall s what has been destined.
7:*47* now I s that the world to come will bring delight
7:*83* they shall s the reward laid up
7:*85* they shall s how the habitations of
7:*86* they shall s how some of them will cross over
7:*91* they shall s with great joy the glory
7:*93* because they s the perplexity in which the souls of
7:*94* they s the witness that he who formed them bears
7:*96* and besides they s the straits and toil
7:*98* to s the face of him whom they served in life and
7:*100* to s what you have described to me?"
7:*101* that during these seven days they may s the things
8:17 for I s the failings of us who inhabit the earth;
9: 1 and when you s that some of the predicted signs
2Es 9: 8 and will s my salvation in my land and
10: 3 and I came to this field, as you s.
10: 6 do you not s our mourning,
10:21 For you s how our sanctuary has been laid waste,
10:32 and lo, what I have seen I saw, and can still s,
10:42 (you do not now s the form of a woman,
10:55 and s the splendor or the vastness of the building,
10:55 as far as it is possible for your eyes to s it,
11:36 "Look in front of you and consider what you s."
13: 7 And I tried to s the region or place from which
13:19 For they shall s great dangers and much distress,
13:20 and not to s what will happen in the last days."
13:51 Why did I s the man coming up from the heart of
13:52 on earth can s my Son or those who are with him,
15:10 S, my people are being led like a flock to
15:20 S how I am calling together all the kings of
15:34 S the clouds from the east,
15:37 those who s that wrath shall be horror-stricken,
16:27 a person will long to s another human being,
4Mc 1:24 as a person will s by reflecting on this experience,
9:30 as you s the arrogant design of your tyranny
10:19 S, here is my tongue; cut it off,
12: 3 "You s the result of your brothers' stupidity,
16: 9 I shall not s your children or have the happiness

SEED‡ (79) [SEEDLINGS, SEEDS, SEEDTIME]

Ge 1:11 plants yielding s, and fruit trees of every kind
1:11 of every kind on earth that bear fruit with the s
1:12 plants yielding s of every kind,
1:12 trees of every kind bearing fruit with the s in it.
1:29 I have given you every plant yielding s that is
1:29 and every tree with s in its fruit;
26:12 Isaac sowed s in that land,
47:19 just give us s, so that we may live and not die,
47:23 here is s for you; sow the land.
47:24 as s for the field and as food for yourselves
Ex 16:31 it was like coriander s, white,
Lev 11:37 upon any s set aside for sowing, it is clean;
11:38 on the s and any part of their carcass falls on it,
19:19 you shall not sow your field with two kinds of s;
26:16 You shall sow your s in vain,
27:16 be in accordance with its s requirements:
27:16 fifty shekels of silver to a homer of barley s.
27:30 the s from the ground or the fruit from the tree, are
Nu 11: 7 Now the manna was like coriander s,
24: 7 and his s shall have abundant water,
Dt 11:10 where you sow your s and irrigate by foot like
14:22 of all the yield of your s that is brought in yearly
22: 9 not sow your vineyard with a second kind of s,
28:38 You shall carry much s into the field
Jdg 6: 3 For whenever the Israelites put in s,
1Ki 18:32 large enough to contain two measures of s.
Ezr 9: 2 Thus the holy s has mixed itself with the peoples
Ps 126: 6 the s for sowing, shall come home with shouts
Ecc 11: 6 In the morning sow your s,
Isa 5:10 and a homer of s shall yield a mere ephah.
6:13 The holy s is its stump.
30:23 He will give rain for the s with which you sow
55:10 giving s to the sower and bread to the eater,
Jer 31:27 and the house of Judah with the s of humans and
the s of animals.
35: 7 nor shall you ever build a house, or sow s;
35: 9 We have no vineyard or field or s;
Eze 17: 5 he took a s from the land, placed it in fertile soil;
Joel 1:17 The s shrivels under the clods,
Am 9:13 and the treader of grapes the one who sows the s;
Hag 2:19 Is there any s left in the barn?
Mt 13:24 be compared to someone who sowed good s
13:27 'Master, did you not sow good s in your field?
13:31 of heaven is like a mustard s that someone took
13:37 "The one who sows the good s is the Son of Man;
13:38 and the good s are the children of the kingdom;
17:20 if you have faith the size of a mustard s,
25:24 and gathering where you did not scatter s;
Mk 4: 4 And as he sowed, some s fell on the path,
4: 5 Other s fell on rocky ground,
4: 7 Other s fell among thorns,
4: 8 Other s fell into good soil and brought forth grain,
4:26 as if someone would scatter s on the ground,
4:27 and the s would sprout and grow,
4:31 It is like a mustard s, which,
Lk 8: 5 "A sower went out to sow his s;
8:11 "Now the parable is this: The s is the word of God.
13:19 It is like a mustard s that someone took and sowed
17: 6 "If you had faith the size of a mustard s,
1Co 15:37 you do not sow the body that is to be, but a bare s,
15:38 and to each kind of s its own body.
2Co 9:10 He who supplies s to the sower and bread for food
will supply and multiply your s
1Pe 1:23 not of perishable but of imperishable s,
1Jn 3: 9 because God's s abides in them;
Wis 7: 2 from the s of a man and the pleasure of marriage.
14: 6 and guided by your hand left to the world the s of
Sir 26:20 *and sow it with your own s, trusting in your fine*
1Es 8:88 to destroy us without leaving a root or s or name?
2Es 4:30 a grain of evil s was sown in Adam's heart from
4:31 of ungodliness a grain of evil s has produced.
8: 6 and give us a s for our heart and cultivation
8:16 and about the s of Jacob, for whom I am troubled.
8:43 If the farmer's s does not come up,
8:44 have you also made them like the farmer's s?
9:17 "As is the field, so is the s;
9:34 when the ground has received s, or the sea a ship,
15:13 because their s shall fail to grow
4Mc 18: 1 O Israelite children, offspring of the s of Abraham,

SEEDLINGS (2) [SEED]

Wis 4: 3 none of their illegitimate s will strike a deep root or
2Es 8:41 of s, and yet not all that have been sown will come

SEEDS‡ (8) [SEED]

Nu 6: 4 not even the s or the skins.
Mt 13: 4 And as he sowed, some s fell on the path,
13: 5 Other s fell on rocky ground,
13: 7 Other s fell among thorns,
13: 8 Other s fell on good soil and brought forth grain,
13:32 it is the smallest of all the s,
Mk 4:31 is the smallest of all the s on earth;
2Es 8:41 "For just as the farmer sows many s in the ground

SEEDTIME (1) [SEED]

Ge 8:22 As long as the earth endures, s and harvest,

SEEING‡ (55) [SEE]

Ge 16:13 and remained alive after s him?"
18:18 s that Abraham shall become a great
26:27 s that you hate me and have sent me away
33:10 truly to see your face is like s the face of God—
Ex 2:12 and s no one he killed the Egyptian and hid him in
4:11 Who makes them mute or deaf, s or blind?
22:10 or is injured or is carried off, without anyone s it,
1Sa 18:23 s that I am a poor man and of no repute?"
2Sa 18:22 s that you have no reward for the tidings?"
Ezr 9:13 s that you, our God, have punsihed us less than
Job 21:22 s that he judges those that are on high?
Pr 20:12 The hearing ear and the s eye—
Ecc 1: 8 the eye is not satisfied with s,
2:16 of the wise or of fools, s that in the days
2:18 s that I must leave it to those who come after me
Isa 52: 5 s that my people are taken away without cause?
Eze 22:28 s false visions and divining lies for them, saying,
Mt 9:22 Jesus turned, and s her he said, "Take heart,
13:13 to them in parables is that 's they do not perceive,
15:31 the lame walking, and the blind s.
21:19 And s a fig tree by the side of the road,
Mk 11:13 S in the distance a fig tree in leaf,
12:28 and s that he answered them well, he asked him,
14:69 And the servant-girl, on s him,
Lk 22:56 Then a servant-girl, s him in the firelight,
22:58 A little later someone else, on s him, said,
24:37 and thought that they were s a ghost.
Ac 8: 6 hearing and s the signs that he did,
9:40 Then she opened her eyes, and s Peter, she sat up.
12: 9 he thought he was s a vision.
14: 9 at him intently and s that he had faith to be healed,
28:15 On s them, Paul thanked God and took courage.
2Co 3:18 s the glory of the Lord as though reflected in
4: 4 to keep them from s the light of the gospel of
Php 2:28 in order that you may rejoice at s him again,
Col 3: 9 s that you have stripped off the old self
AdE 8:15 The people in Susa rejoiced on s him.
Wis 16:18 but that s this they might know
Sir 42:25 Who could ever tire of s his glory?
2Mc 2: 2 or to be led astray in their thoughts on s the gold
3Mc 2:23 s the severe punishment that had overtaken him,
4: 8 s death immediately before them.
5:14 s that the guests were assembled,
2Es 7:15 why are you disturbed, s that you are to perish?
7:15 Why are you moved, s that you are mortal?
7:*87* and shall wither with fear at s the glory of
10:50 s that you are sincerely grieved
12:19 for your s eight little wings clinging to its wings,
12:22 your s three heads at rest, this is the interpretation:
12:26 As for your s that the large head disappeared,
12:29 As for your s two little wings passing over to
13:25 your s a man come up from the heart of the sea,
13:27 as for your s wind and fire and a storm coming out
13:39 for your s him gather to himself another multitude
4Mc 16: 1 endured s her children tortured to death,

SEEK‡ (234) [SEEKERS, SEEKING, SEEKS, SELF-SEEKING, SOUGHT]

Lev 13:36 the priest need not s for the yellow hair;
19:31 do not s them out, to be defiled by them:
Nu 10:33 to s out a resting place for them,
16:10 yet you s the priesthood as well!
Dt 1:33 who goes before you on the way to s out a place
4:29 From there you will s the LORD your God,
12: 5 But you shall s the place that
Ru 3: 1 "My daughter, I need to s some security for you,
1Sa 10: 2 'The donkeys that you went to s are found,
10:14 And he replied, "To s the donkeys;
20:16 "May the LORD s out the enemies of David."
23:15 that Saul had come out to s his life.
25:26 now let your enemies and those who s to do evil
25:29 to s your life, the life of my lord shall be bound in
26: 2 to s David in the Wilderness of Ziph.
26:20 the king of Israel has come out to s a single flea,
28: 7 "S out for me a woman who is a medium,
2Sa 17: 3 You s the life of only one man,
20:19 you s to destroy a city that is a mother in Israel;
1Ki 11:22 "What do you lack with me that you now s to go
18:10 or kingdom to which my lord has not sent to s you;
2Ki 2:16 please let them go and s your master;
6:19 and I will bring you to the man whom you s."
1Ch 4:39 to s pasture for their flocks,
10:14 and did not s guidance from the LORD.
16:10 let the hearts of those who s the LORD rejoice.
16:11 S the LORD and his strength,
16:11 s his presence continually.

1Ch 22:19 set your mind and heart to s the LORD your God.
28: 9 If you s him, he will be found by you;
2Ch 7:14 pray, s my face, and turn from their wicked ways,
11:16 to s the LORD God of Israel came after them
12:14 for he did not set his heart to s the LORD.
14: 4 and commanded Judah to s the LORD,
15: 2 If you s him, he will be found by you,
15:12 They entered into a covenant to s the LORD,
15:13 Whoever would not s the LORD,
16:12 yet even in his disease he did not s the LORD,
17: 3 he did not s the Baals,
19: 3 and have set your heart to s God."
20: 3 he set himself to s the LORD,
20: 4 Judah assembled to s help from the LORD;
20: 4 the towns of Judah they came to s the LORD.
26: 5 He set himself to s God in the days of Zechariah,
30:19 who set their hearts to s God,
31:21 to s his God, he did with all his heart;
34: 3 he began to s the God of his ancestor David,
Ezr 8:21 to s from him a safe journey for ourselves,
8:22 the hand of our God is gracious to all who s him,
9:12 and never s their peace or prosperity,
Ne 2:10 that someone had come to s the welfare of
Job 3: 4 May God above not s it, or light shine on it.
5: 8 "As for me, I would s God,
7:21 you will s me, but I shall not be."
8: 5 If you will s God and make supplication to
10: 6 that you s out my iniquity and search for my sin,
20:10 Their children will s the favor of the poor,
Ps 4: 2 long will you love vain words, and s after lies?
9:10 O LORD, have not forsaken those who s you.
10: 4 "God will not s it out";
10:15 s out their wickedness until you find none.
14: 2 if there are any who are wise, who s after God.
17: 7 of those who s refuge from their adversaries
22:26 those who s him shall praise the LORD.
24: 6 Such is the company of those who s him,
24: 6 who s the face of the God of Jacob.
27: 4 One thing I asked of the LORD, that will I s after:
27: 8 "Come," my heart says, "s his face!"
27: 8 Your face, LORD, do I s.
31: 1 In you, O LORD, I s refuge;
34:10 but those who s the LORD lack no good thing.
34:14 Depart from evil, and do good; s peace,
35: 4 be put to shame and dishonor who s after my life.
37:32 wicked watch for the righteous, and s to kill them.
38:12 Those who s my life lay their snares;
38:12 those who s to hurt me speak of ruin,
40:14 Let all those be put to shame and confusion who s
40:16 But may all who s you rejoice and be glad in you;
45:12 the people of Tyre will s your favor with gifts,
53: 2 if there are any who are wise, who s after God.
54: 3 against me, the ruthless s my life;
56: 5 All day long they s to injure my cause;
63: 1 you are my God, I s you, my soul thirsts for you;
63: 9 But those who s to destroy my life shall go down
69: 6 do not let those who s you be dishonored because
69:32 you who s God, let your hearts revive.
70: 2 be put to shame and confusion who s my life.
70: 4 Let all who s you rejoice and be glad in you.
71:13 let those who s to hurt me be covered with scorn
77: 2 In the day of my trouble I s the Lord;
83:16 so that they may s your name, O LORD.
105: 3 let the hearts of those who s the LORD rejoice.
105: 4 S the LORD and his strength;
105: 4 s his presence continually.
119: 2 who s him with their whole heart,
119:10 With my whole heart I s you;
119:155 for they do not s your statutes.
119:176 s out your servant, for I do
122: 9 of the LORD our God, I will s your good.
141: 8 in you I s refuge; do not leave me defenseless.
Pr 1:28 they will s me diligently, but will not find me.
2: 4 if you s it like silver, and search for it as
7:15 to s you eagerly, and I have found you!
8:17 and those who s me diligently find me.
17:11 Evil people s only rebellion,
19: 6 Many s the favor of the generous,
23:35 I will s another drink."
25:27 or to s honor on top of honor.
28: 5 those who s the LORD understand it completely.
29:10 and they s the life of the upright.
29:26 Many s the favor of a ruler,
Ecc 1:13 to s and to search out by wisdom all that is done
3: 6 a time to s, and a time to lose;
7:25 to know and to search out and to s wisdom and
SS 3: 2 I will s him whom my soul loves."
6: 1 that we may s him with you?
Isa 1: 5 Why do you s further beatings?
1:17 s justice, rescue the oppressed,
9:13 or s the LORD of hosts.
30: 2 and to s shelter in the shadow of Egypt;
34:16 S and read from the book of the LORD:
41:12 You shall s those who contend with you,
41:17 When the poor and needy s water,
45:19 not say to the offspring of Jacob, "S me in chaos."
51: 1 that pursue righteousness, you that s the LORD.
55: 6 S the LORD while he may be found,
58: 2 after day they s me and delight to know my ways,
65: 1 to be found by those who did not s me.
Jer 2:24 None who s her need weary themselves;
2:33 How well you direct your course to s lovers!
4:30 Your lovers despise you; they s your life.
11:21 who s your life, and say, "You shall not prophesy
19: 7 and by the hand of those who s their life.
19: 9 and those who s their life afflict them.
21: 7 into the hands of those who s their lives.
Jer 22:25 give you into the hands of those who s your life,
29: 7 But s the welfare of the city where I have sent you
29:13 if you s me with all your heart,
34:20 to their enemies and to those who s their lives.
34:21 to their enemies and to those who s their lives,
38:16 or hand you over to these men who s your life."
44:30 into the hands of his enemies, those who s his life,
45: 5 do you s great things for yourself? Do not s them;
46:26 I will hand them over to those who s their life,
49:37 and before those who s their life;
50: 4 they shall come weeping as they s
Eze 7:25 When anguish comes, they will s peace,
34: 6 with no one to search or s for them.
34:11 for my sheep, and will s them out.
34:12 As shepherds s out their flocks when they are
34:12 so I will s out my sheep.
34:16 I will s the lost, and I will bring back the strayed,
Da 2:18 and told them to s mercy from the God of heaven
9: 3 to s an answer by prayer and supplication
Hos 2: 7 and she shall s them, but shall not find them.
3: 5 and s the LORD their God, and David their king;
5: 6 With their flocks and herds they shall go to s
5:15 until they acknowledge their guilt and s my face.
7:10 not return to the LORD their God, or s him,
10:12 for it is time to s the LORD,
Am 5: 4 to the house of Israel: S me and live;
5: 5 not s Bethel, and do not enter into Gilgal or cross
5: 6 S the LORD and live, or he will break out against
5:14 S good and not evil, that you may live;
Na 3: 7 Where shall I s comforters for you?
3:11 you will s a refuge from the enemy.
Zep 2: 3 S the LORD, all you humble of the land,
2: 3 s righteousness, s humility;
3:12 They shall s refuge in the name of the LORD—
Zec 8:21 and to s the LORD of hosts; I myself am going."
8:22 Many peoples and strong nations shall come to s
11:16 or s the wandering, or heal the maimed,
12: 9 And on that day I will s to destroy all the nations
Mal 2: 7 and people should s instruction from his mouth,
3: 1 and the Lord whom you s will suddenly come
Lk 19:10 the Son of Man came to s out and to save the lost."
Jn 5:30 because I s to do not my own will but the will
5:44 from one another and do not s the glory that comes
7:18 Those who speak on their own s their own glory;
8:50 Yet I do not s my own glory;
Ac 15:17 so that all other peoples may s the Lord—
Ro 2: 7 to those who by patiently doing good s for glory
10:20 "I have been found by those who did not s me;
1Co 7:18 not s to remove the marks of circumcision.
7:18 Let him not s circumcision.
7:27 Are you bound to a wife? Do not s to be free.
7:27 Are you free from a wife? Do not s a wife.
10:24 Do not s your own advantage, but that of the other.
Php 4:17 Not that I s the gift, but I s the profit that
Col 3: 1 s the things that are above, where Christ is,
1Th 2: 6 nor did we s praise from mortals,
5:15 but always s to do good to one another and to all.
Heb 11: 6 that he exists and that he rewards those who s him.
1Pe 3:11 let them s peace and pursue it.
Rev 9: 6 And in those days people will s death but will
Tob 4:18 S advice from every wise person and do
AdE 16: 3 and not only s to injure our subjects,
Wis 1: 1 of the Lord in goodness and s him with sincerity
6:12 and is found by those who s her.
6:14 to s her will have no difficulty,
Sir 2:16 Those who fear the Lord s to please him,
3:21 Neither s what is too difficult for you,
4:11 and gives help to those who s her.
4:12 and those who s her from early morning are filled
6:27 Search out and s, and she will become known
7: 4 Do not s from the Lord high office,
7: 6 Do not s to become a judge,
24:34 but for all who s wisdom.
26:20 *S a fertile field within the whole plain,*
27: 1 and those who s to get rich will avert their eyes.
28: 4 can he then s pardon for his own sins?
32:14 and those who rise early to s him will find favor.
33:18 but for all who s instruction.
33:26 leave his hands idle, and he will s liberty.
33:33 which way will you go to s him?
39: 5 to rise early to s the Lord who made him,
40:26 and with it there is no need to s for help.
51:21 My heart was stirred to s her;
Bar 3:23 who s for understanding on the earth,
4:28 return with tenfold zeal to s him.
Aza 1:18 we fear you and s your presence.
1Mc 7:13 among the Israelites to s peace from them,
7:15 "We will not s to injure you or your Friends."
15:19 and countries that they should not s their harm
1Es 8:50 to s from him a prosperous journey for ourselves
8:52 power of our Lord will be with those who s him,
8:85 do not s ever to have peace with them,
2Es 6:10 s for nothing else, Ezra, between the heel and
12:48 the desolation of Zion, and to s mercy on account
14:23 and tell them not to s you for forty days.
14:36 and let no one s me for forty days."

SEEKERS‡ (1) [SEEK]

Bar 3:23 the story-tellers and the s for understanding,

SEEKING‡ (37) [SEEK]

Ge 37:15 the man asked him, "What are you s?"
37:16 "I am s my brothers," he said;
Ex 4:19 for all those who were s your life are dead."
Jdg 4:22 and I will show you the man whom you are s."
14: 4 for he was s a pretext to act against the Philistines.
Jdg 18: 1 of the Danites was s for itself a territory to live in;
1Sa 27: 1 then Saul will despair of s me any longer within
2Sa 3:17 past you have been s David as king over you.
1Ki 19:10 I alone am left, and they are s my life,
19:14 I alone am left, and they are s my life,
20: 7 See how this man is s trouble;
1Ch 10:13 moreover, he had consulted a medium, s guidance,
Ps 104:21 The young lions roar for their prey, s their food
Ecc 8:17 much they may toil in s, they will not find it out;
Jer 38: 4 For this man is not s the welfare of this people,
La 1:19 while s food to revive their strength.
Eze 7:26 they shall keep s a vision from the prophet;
Da 6:11 and found Daniel praying and s mercy
Am 8:12 they shall run to and fro, s the word of the LORD,
Mt 2:20 for those who were s the child's life are dead."
Jn 5:18 For this reason the Jews were s all the more
Ro 10: 3 and s to establish their own,
11: 3 I alone am left, and they are s my life."
11: 7 Israel failed to obtain what it was s.
1Co 10:33 not s my own advantage, but that of many,
Gal 1:10 Am I now s human approval, or God's approval?
Php 2:21 All of them are s their own interests,
Heb 11:14 in this way make it clear that they are s
AdE 11:12 s all day to understand it in every detail.
Wis 6:16 because she goes about s those worthy of her,
8:18 I went about s how to get her for myself.
13: 6 for perhaps they go astray while s God
Sir 51: 3 from the hand of those s my life,
1Mc 2:29 At that time many who were s righteousness
12:40 so he kept s to seize and kill him,
16:22 he had found out that they were s to destroy him.
4Mc 1: 2 to everyone who is s knowledge,

SEEKS (28) [SEEK]

Dt 18:11 or who s oracles from the dead.
1Sa 22:23 for the one who s my life s your life;
23:10 your servant has heard that Saul s to come
24: 9 'David s to do you harm'?
2Sa 16:11 "My own son s my life;
Ps 86:14 a band of ruffians s my life,
Pr 11:27 Whoever diligently s good s favor,
14: 6 A scoffer s wisdom in vain,
15:14 mind of one who has understanding s knowledge,
18:15 and the ear of the wise s knowledge.
31:13 She s wool and flax, and works
Ecc 3:15 and God s out what has gone by.
Isa 16: 5 ruler who s justice and is swift to do what is right.
26: 9 my spirit within me earnestly s you.
40:20 then s out a skilled artisan to set up an image
Jer 5: 1 can find one person who acts justly and s truth—
La 3:25 to the soul that s him.
Jn 4:23 for the Father s such as these to worship him.
7:18 one who s the glory of him who sent him is true,
8:50 there is one who s it and he is the judge.
Ro 3:11 there is no one who s God.
Sir 32:14 The one who s God will accept his discipline,
32:15 The one who s the law will be filled with it,
39: 1 He s out the wisdom of all the ancients,
39: 3 he s out the hidden meanings of proverbs and is
2Mc 2:27 for one who prepares a banquet and s the benefit

SEEM‡ (15) [SEEMED, SEEMS]

Ge 27:12 and I shall s to be mocking him,
1Sa 18:23 "Does it s to you a little thing to become
Job 10: 3 Does it s good to you to oppress,
Isa 5:28 all their bows bent, their horses' hoofs s like flint,
Eze 21:23 But to them it will s like a false divination;
Zec 8: 6 should it also s impossible to me,
Lk 8:18 even what they s to have will be taken away."
1Co 12:22 of the body that s to be weaker are indispensable,
2Co 10: 9 not want to s as though I am trying to frighten you
13: 7 though we may s to have failed.
Heb 4: 1 that none of you should s to have failed to reach it.
Sir Pr: 2 despite our diligent labor in translating, we may s
26:26 *A wife honoring her husband will s wise to all,*
30: 4 When the father dies he will not s to be dead,
4Mc 5: 7 it does not s to me that you are a philosopher

SEEMED‡ (26) [SEEM]

Ge 19:14 But he s to his sons-in-law to be jesting.
29:20 and they s to him but a few days because of
Nu 13:33 and to ourselves we s like grasshoppers, and so we s to them."
Dt 1:23 The plan s good to me,
2Sa 13: 2 for she was a virgin and it s impossible to Amnon
2Ch 30: 4 The plan s right to the king and all the assembly.
Ps 73:16 it s to me a wearisome task,
Ecc 9:13 and it s great to me.
Jer 18: 4 and he reworked it into another vessel, as s good
Eze 1:26 a throne was something that s like a human form.
Da 7:20 and that s greater than the others.
Lk 24:11 But these words s to them an idle tale,
Ac 15:28 For it has s good to the Holy Spirit and to us
Heb 12:10 For they disciplined us for a short time as s best
Rev 6: 6 and I heard what s to be a voice in the midst of
13: 3 One of its heads s to have received a death-blow,
19: 1 After this I heard what s to be the loud voice of
19: 6 I heard what s to be the voice of a great multitude,
Jdt 13:13 for it s unbelievable that she had returned.
Wis 3: 2 In the eyes of the foolish they s to have died,
Sir Pr: 3 s highly necessary that I should myself devote
1Mc 15:20 it has s good to us to accept the shield from them.
2Mc 1:13 with a force that s irresistible,
3Mc 1:29 for it s that not only the people but also the walls
2Es 11:37 I saw what s to be a lion roused from the forest,

SEEMLY (KJV) See FITTING

SEEMS (42) [SEEM]

A. SEEMS GOOD (23)

Lev 14:35 “There s to me to be some sort of disease
Jos 9:25 as it s good and right in your sight to do to us.” A
Jdg 10:15 do to us whatever s good to you; A
1Sa 1:23 “Do what s best to you, wait
3:18 let him do what s good to him.” A
11:10 and you may do to us whatever s good to you.” A
14:36 They said, “Do whatever s good to you.” A
14:40 people said to Saul, “Do what s good to you.” A
24: 4 and you shall do to him as it s good to you.’ ” A
29: 6 and to me it s right that you should march out and
2Sa 10:12 and may the LORD do what s good to him.” A
15:26 here I am, let him do to me what s good to him.” A
18: 4 “Whatever s best to you I will do.”
19:27 do therefore what s good to you. A
19:37 and do for him whatever s good to you.” A
19:38 and I will do for him whatever s good to you; A
24:22 the king take and offer up what s good to him; A
1Ki 21: 2 or, if it s good to you, A
1Ch 13: 2 “If it s good to you, A
19:13 and may the LORD do what s good to him.” A
21:23 and let my lord the king do what s good to him; A
Ezr 5:17 And now, if it s good to the king, A
7:18 Whatever s good to you and your colleagues A
Est 3:11 to do with them as it s good to you.” A
8: 5 and if the thing s right before the king,
Pr 14:12 There is a way that s right to a person,
16:25 Sometimes there is a way that s to be right,
18:17 The one who first states a case s right,
Jer 26:14 Do with me as s good and right to you. A
Hab 2: 3 If it s to tarry, wait for it; it will surely come,
Zec 8: 6 Even though it s impossible to the remnant
11:12 I then said to them, “If it s right to you,
Ac 17:18 “He s to be a proclaimer of foreign divinities.”
25:27 for it s to me unreasonable to send a prisoner
1Co 16: 4 If it s advisable that I should go also,
Heb 12:11 discipline always s painful rather than pleasant at
Sir 6:20 She s very harsh to the undisciplined;
1Es 2:21 in order that, if it s good to you, A
3: 5 and to the one whose statement s wisest,
6:21 Now therefore, O king, if it s wise to do so,
8:94 as s good to you and to all who obey the law of A
4Mc 5:10 It s to me that you will do something

SEEN‡ (293) [SEE]

Ge 7: 1 for I have s that you alone are righteous before me
9:14 over the earth and the bow is s in the clouds,
16:13 “Have I really s God and remained alive
24:30 As soon as he had s the nose-ring,
31:12 for I have s all that Laban is doing to you.
32:30 saying, “For I have s God face to face,
41:19 Never had I s such ugly ones in all the land
44:28 and I have never s him since.
45:13 and all that you have s.
46:30 having s for myself that you are still alive.”
Ex 3: 9 I have also s how the Egyptians oppress them.
4:31 to the Israelites and that he had s their misery,
10: 6 nor your grandparents have s,
13: 7 no leavened bread shall be s in your possession,
13: 7 and no leaven shall be s among you
19: 4 You have s what I did to the Egyptians,
20:22 “You have s for yourselves that I spoke with you
32: 9 The LORD said to Moses, “I have s this people,
33:23 but my face shall not be s.”
34: 3 do not let anyone be s throughout all the mountain;
Lev 5: 1 though able to testify as one who has s or learned
Nu 14:14 for you, O LORD, are s face to face,
14:22 of the people who have s my glory and the signs
23:21 nor has he s trouble in Israel.
27:13 When you have s it, you also shall be gathered
Dt 3:11 can still be s in Rabbah of the Ammonites.
3:21 “Your own eyes have s everything that
4: 3 You have s for yourselves what the LORD did
4: 9 the things that your eyes have s nor to let them slip
5:24 Today we have s that God may speak to someone
9:13 “I have s that this people is indeed
10:21 and awesome things that your own eyes have s.
11: 2 or s the discipline of the LORD your God),
11: 7 for it is your own eyes that have s every great deed
16: 4 No leaven shall be s with you in all your territory
29: 2 You have s all that the LORD did
29:17 You have s their detestable things,
Jos 23: 3 and you have s all that the LORD your God
Jdg 2: 7 who had s all the great work that
5: 8 Was shield or spear to be s among forty thousand
6:22 For I have s the angel of the LORD face to face.”
9:48 “What you have s me do, do quickly,
13:22 “We shall surely die, for we have s God.”
18: 9 for we have s the land, and it is very good.
1Sa 9:16 for I have s the suffering of my people,
16:18 “I have s a son of Jesse
17:25 “Have you s this man who has come up?
23:22 where he is, and who has s him there;
24:10 This very day your eyes have s how
2Sa 17:17 for they could not risk being s entering the city.
18:21 “Go, tell the king what you have s.”
22:11 he was s upon the wings of the wind.
22:16 Then the channels of the sea were s,
1Ki 6:18 all was cedar, no stone was s.
8: 8 of the poles were s from the holy place in front of
8: 8 but they could not be s from outside;
10: 7 the reports until I came and my own eyes had s it.
10:12 no such almug wood has come or been s
20:13 Have you s all this great multitude?
21:29 “Have you s how Ahab has humbled himself
2Ki 7:10 but there was no one to be s or heard there,
13:21 a marauding band was s and the man was thrown
20: 5 I have heard your prayer, I have s your tears;
20:15 He said, “What have they s in your house?”
20:15 “They have s all that is in my house;
23:24 that were s in the land of Judah and in Jerusalem,
1Ch 29:17 and now I have s your people,
2Ch 5: 9 of the poles were s from the holy place in front of
5: 9 but they could not be s from outside;
9:11 there never was s the like of them before in
Ezr 3:12 old people who had s the first house
Job 4: 8 As I have s, those who plow iniquity
5: 3 I have s fools taking root,
8:18 saying, ‘I have never s you.’
10:18 Would that I had died before any eye had s me,
13: 1 “Look, my eye has s all this,
15:17 what I have s I will declare—
20: 7 those who have s them will say, ‘Where are they?’
27:12 All of you have s it yourselves;
28: 7 and the falcon’s eye has not s it.
31:19 if I have s anyone perish for lack of clothing,
33:21 Their flesh is so wasted away that it cannot be s;
38:17 or have you s the gates of deep darkness?
38:22 or have you s the storehouses of the hail,
Ps 18:15 Then the channels of the sea were s,
31: 7 because you have s my affliction;
35:21 they say, “Aha, Aha, our eyes have s it.”
35:22 You have s, O LORD; do not be silent!
37:25 yet I have not s the righteous forsaken
37:35 I have s the wicked oppressing,
48: 8 so have we s in the city of the LORD of hosts,
68:24 Your solemn processions are s, O God,
84: 7 the God of gods will be s in Zion.
90:15 and as many years as we have s evil.
92:11 My eyes have s the downfall of my enemies;
95: 9 though they had s my work.
98: 3 the ends of the earth have s the victory of our God.
119:96 I have s a limit to all perfection,
Pr 25: 7 What your eyes have s
Ecc 3:10 I have s the business that God has given
4: 3 not s the evil deeds that are done under the sun.
5:13 There is a grievous ill that I have s under the sun:
5:18 This is what I have s to be good:
6: 1 There is an evil that I have s under the sun,
6: 5 moreover it has not s the sun or known anything;
7:15 In my vain life I have s everything;
9:13 also s this example of wisdom under the sun,
10: 5 There is an evil that I have s under the sun,
10: 7 I have s slaves on horseback,
SS 3: 3 “Have you s him whom my soul loves?”
Isa 6: 5 my eyes have s the King, the LORD of hosts!”
9: 2 The people who walked in darkness have s
30:30 and the descending blow of his arm to be s,
38: 5 I have heard your prayer, I have s your tears;
39: 4 He said, “What have they s in your house?”
39: 4 “They have s all that is in my house;
41: 5 The coastlands have s and are afraid,
47: 3 and your shame shall be s.
57:18 I have s their ways, but I will heal them;
64: 4 no eye has s any God besides you,
66: 8 Who has s such things?
66:19 that have not heard of my fame or s my glory;
Jer 1:12 Then the LORD said to me, “You have s well,
3: 6 Have you s what she did, that faithless one, Israel,
13:26 and your shame will be s.
13:27 I have s your abominations,
23:14 of Jerusalem I have s a more shocking thing:
44: 2 You yourselves have s all the disaster
La 1: 8 for they have s her nakedness;
1:10 she has even s the nations invade her sanctuary,
2:14 Your prophets have s for you false
2:14 to restore your fortunes, but have s oracles for you
2:16 at last we have s it!”
3: 1 I am one who has s affliction under the rod
3:59 You have s the wrong done to me, O LORD;
3:60 You have s all their malice,
Eze 3:23 like the glory that I had s by the river Chebar;
8: 4 like the vision that I had s in the valley.
8:12 have you s what the elders of the house
8:15 Then he said to me, “Have you s this, O mortal?
8:17 Then he said to me, “Have you s this, O mortal?
10:22 the same faces whose appearance I had s by
11:24 Then the vision that I had s left me.
13: 3 who follow their own spirit, and have s nothing!
13: 7 not s a false vision or uttered a lying divination,
43: 3 that I had s when he came to destroy the city,
43: 3 and like the vision that I had s by the river Chebar;
47: 6 He said to me, “Mortal, have you s this?”
Da 2:26 “Are you able to tell me the dream that I have s
8: 6 the two horns that I had s standing beside the river,
8:15 I, Daniel, had s the vision, I tried to understand it.
9:21 the man Gabriel, whom I had s before in a vision,
Hos 6:10 In the house of Israel I have s a horrible thing;
Zec 9: 8 for now I have s with my own eyes.
Mt 2: 9 went the star that they had s at its rising,
4:16 the people who sat in darkness have s a great light,
6: 1 before others in order to be s by them;
6: 5 so that they may be s by others.
6:18 so that your fasting may be s not by others but
9:33 “Never has anything like this been s in Israel.”
23: 5 They do all their deeds to be s by others;
Mk 2:12 saying, “We have never s anything like this!”
5:16 Those who had s what had happened to
9: 9 to tell no one about what they had s,
16:11 ⟦heard that he was alive and had been s by her,⟧
Lk 1:22 and they realized that he had s a vision in
2:20 and praising God for all they had heard and s,
2:26 not see death before he had s the Lord’s Messiah.
2:30 for my eyes have s your salvation,
5:26 saying, “We have s strange things today.”
7:22 “Go and tell John what you have s and heard:
8:36 Those who had s it told them how
9:36 of the things they had s.
19:37 for all the deeds of power that they had s,
24:23 that they had indeed s a vision of angels who said
Jn 1:14 and we have s his glory,
1:18 No one has ever s God.
1:34 And I myself have s and have testified that this is
3:11 of what we know and testify to what we have s;
3:21 be clearly s that their deeds have been done
3:32 He testifies to what he has s and heard,
4:45 since they had s all that he had done in Jerusalem
5:37 You have never heard his voice or s his form,
6:36 to you that you have s me and yet do not believe.
6:46 that anyone has s the Father except the one who is
from God; he has s the Father.
8:38 I declare what I have s in the Father’s presence;
8:57 and have you s Abraham?”
9: 8 and those who had s him before as a beggar began
9:37 Jesus said to him, “You have s him,
11:45 with Mary and had s what Jesus did,
14: 7 From now on you do know him and have s him.”
14: 9 Whoever has s me has s the Father.
15:24 now they have s and hated both me and my Father.
20:18 and announced to the disciples, “I have s
20:25 the other disciples told him, “We have s the Lord.”
20:29 “Have you believed because you have s me?
20:29 Blessed are those who have not s and
Ac 4:20 from speaking about what we have s and heard.”
7:34 surely s the mistreatment of my people who are
7:44 to make it according to the pattern he had s.
9:12 and he has s in a vision a man named Ananias
9:27 and described for them how on the road he had s
10:17 about what to make of the vision that he had s,
11:13 how he had s the angel standing in his house
16:10 When he had s the vision,
16:40 and when they had s and encouraged the brothers
21:27 the Jews from Asia, who had s him in the temple,
21:29 For they had previously s Trophimus the Ephesian
22:15 be his witness to all the world of what you have s
26:16 to the things in which you have s me and to those
Ro 1:20 and s through the things he has made.
8:24 Now hope that is s is not hope.
8:24 For who hopes for what is s?
1Co 2: 9 But, as it is written, “What no eye has s,
9: 1 Have I not s Jesus our Lord?
2Co 4:18 not at what can be s but at what cannot be s;
4:18 be s is temporary, but what cannot be s is eternal.
12: 6 that no one may think better of me than what is s
Php 4: 9 that you have learned and received and heard and s
Col 2: 1 and for all who have not s me face to face.
1Ti 3:16 s by angels, proclaimed among Gentiles,
6:16 whom no one has ever s or can see;
Heb 3: 9 though they had s my works
11: 1 the conviction of things not s.
11: 3 so that what is s was made from things that are
Jas 5:11 and you have s the purpose of the Lord,
1Pe 1: 8 Although you have not s him, you love him;
1Jn 1: 1 what we have s with our eyes,
1: 2 and we have s it and testify to it,
1: 3 we declare to you what we have s and heard so
3: 6 no one who sins has either s him or known him.
4:12 No one has ever s God;
4:14 And we have s and do testify that
4:20 not love a brother or sister whom they have s,
4:20 cannot love God whom they have not s.
3Jn 1:11 whoever does evil has not s God.
Rev 1:19 Now write what you have s, what is,
3:18 the shame of your nakedness from being s;
11:19 the ark of his covenant was s within his temple;
Tob 6:18 and will never be s near her any more.
11: 9 saying, “Now that I have s you, my child,
AdE 16: 7 be s, not so much from the more ancient records
Wis 13: 1 from the good things that are s to know
13: 7 because the things that are s are beautiful.
19: 7 The cloud was s overshadowing the camp,
Sir 16: 5 Many such things my eye has s,
34: 3 What is s in dreams is but a reflection,
34:12 I have s many things in my travels,
42:15 and will declare what I have s.
43:31 Who has s him and can describe him?
43:32 for I have s but few of his works.
Bar 3:20 Later generations have s the light of day,
3:22 not been heard of in Canaan, or s in Teman;
4:10 for I have s the exile of my sons and daughters,
4:24 as the neighbors of Zion have now s your capture,
LtJ 6:61 So also the lightning, when it flashes, is widely s;
Bel 1:35 Habakkuk said, “Sir, I have never s Babylon,
1Mc 4:20 the smoke that was s showed what had happened.
13: 3 and the difficulties that my brothers and I have s.
13:27 he made it high so that it might be s,
13:29 so that they could be s by all who sail the sea.
15:36 also the splendor of Simon and all that he had s.
2Mc 2: 4 the mountain where Moses had gone up and had s
3:25 Its rider was s to have armor and weapons of gold.
3:36 which he had s with his own eyes.
12: 9 so that the glow of the light was s in Jerusalem,
12:42 to keep themselves free from sin, for they had s
1Es 4:29 Yet I have s him with Apame,
5:63 old men who had s the former house,

3Mc 2: 8 And when they had s works of your hands,
2Es 1:36 They have s no prophets,
2:48 the wonders of the Lord God that you have s."
3:29 and my soul has s many sinners
3:30 because I have s how you endure those who sin,
3:33 the nations and have s that they abound in wealth,
6: 3 and before the beautiful flowers were s,
6:32 for the Mighty One has s your uprightness and has
6:40 so that your works could be s.
7:26 that the city that now is not s shall appear,
10:32 and lo, what I have s I saw, and can still see,
10:35 For I have s what I did not know,
10:39 He has s your righteous conduct,
11:19 after another and then were never s again.
12:10 the interpretation of this vision that you have s:
12:30 and full of tumult, as you have s.
12:37 write all these things that you have s in a book,
13:11 so that suddenly nothing was s of the innumerable
14: 8 the dreams that you have s,
14:16 now s happen shall take place hereafter.

SEER‡ (23) [SEE]

1Sa 9: 9 "Come, let us go to the s";
9: 9 now called a prophet was formerly called a s.)
9:11 and said to them, "Is the s here?"
9:18 "Tell me, please, where is the house of the s?"
9:19 Samuel answered Saul, "I am the s;
2Sa 24:11 of the LORD came to the prophet Gad, David's s,
2Ki 17:13 and Judah by every prophet and every s,
1Ch 9:22 and the s Samuel established them in their office
21: 9 The LORD spoke to Gad, David's s, saying,
25: 5 All these were the sons of Heman the king's s,
26:28 Also all that Samuel the s, and Saul son of Kish,
29:29 are written in the records of the s Samuel,
29:29 and in the records of the s Gad,
2Ch 9:29 the visions of the s Iddo concerning Jeroboam son
12:15 of the prophet Shemaiah and of the s Iddo,
16: 7 that time the s Hanani came to King Asa of Judah,
16:10 Then Asa was angry with the s,
19: 2 Jehu son of Hanani the s went out to meet him
29:25 and of Gad the king's s and of the prophet Nathan,
29:30 with the words of David and of the s Asaph.
35:15 and Asaph, and Heman, and the king's s Jeduthun.
Am 7:12 And Amaziah said to Amos, "O s, go,
Sir 46:15 by his words he became known as a trustworthy s.

SEERS‡ (5) [SEE]

2Ch 33:18 the words of the s who spoke to him in the name
33:19 these are written in the records of the s.
Isa 29:10 you prophets, and covered your heads, you s.
30:10 who say to the s, "Do not see";
Mic 3: 7 s shall be disgraced, and the diviners put to shame;

SEES‡ (53) [SEE]

Ge 44:31 when he s that the boy is not with us, he will die;
Ex 4:14 and when he s you his heart will be glad.
12:23 when he s the blood on the lintel and on
Lev 13: 5 and if he s that the disease is checked and
20:17 and s her nakedness, and she s his nakedness,
Nu 24: 4 who s the vision of the Almighty, who falls down,
24:16 who s the vision of the Almighty, who falls down,
Dt 32:36 when he s that their power is gone,
2Ki 2:19 "The location of this city is good, as my lord s;
Job 3:16 like an infant that never s the light?
11:11 when he s iniquity, will he not consider it?
28:24 and s everything under the heavens.
34:21 and he s all their steps.
42: 5 but now my eye s you;
Ps 33:13 looks down from heaven; he s all humankind.
37:13 for he s that their day is coming.
58: 8 like the untimely birth that never s the sun.
97: 4 light up the world; the earth s and trembles.
Pr 28:11 but an intelligent poor person s through the pose.
Isa 21: 6 "Go, post a lookout, let him announce what he s.
21: 7 When he s riders, horsemen in pairs,
28: 4 whoever s it, eats it up as soon as it comes to hand.
29:15 in the dark, and who say, "Who s us?
29:23 For when he s his children, the work of my hands,
42:20 He s many things, but does not observe them;
47:10 you said, "No one s me."
La 3:50 until the LORD from heaven looks down and s.
Eze 12:27 "The vision that he s is for many years ahead;
18:14 a son who s all the sins that his father has done,
32:31 When Pharaoh s them, he will be consoled
33: 3 if the sentinel s the sword coming upon the land
33: 6 the sentinel s the sword coming and does not blow
39:15 anyone who s a human bone shall set up a sign
Mt 6: 4 and your Father who s in secret will reward you.
6: 6 and your Father who s in secret will reward you.
6:18 and your Father who s in secret will reward you.
Jn 5:19 but only what he s the Father doing;
9:21 but we do not know how it is that now he s,
10:12 s the wolf coming and leaves the sheep
12:45 And whoever s me s him who sent me.
14:17 because it neither s him nor knows him.
1Co 4: 7 For who s anything different in you?
1Jn 3:17 the world's goods and s a brother or sister in need
AdE 16: 4 of God, who always s everything.
Sir 15:18 he is mighty in power and s everything;
18:12 He s and recognizes that their end is miserable;
23:18 the walls hide me, and no one s me.
30:20 he s with his eyes and groans as a eunuch groans
42:18 he s from of old the things that are to come.
2Mc 12:22 the manifestation to them of him who s all things.
15: 2 that he who s all things has honored and hallowed

SEETHE (1)

Eze 24: 5 boil its pieces, s also its bones in it.

SEGUB (3)

1Ki 16:34 set up its gates at the cost of his youngest son S,
1Ch 2:21 when he was sixty years old; and she bore him S;
2:22 and S became the father of Jair,

SEINE (2)

Hab 1:15 he gathers them in his s; so he rejoices and exults.
1:16 to his net and makes offerings to his s;

SEIR‡ (39)

Ge 14: 6 the hill country of S as far as El-paran on the edge
32: 3 before him to his brother Esau in the land of S,
33:14 until I come to my lord in S."
33:16 So Esau returned that day on his way to S.
36: 8 So Esau settled in the hill country of S;
36: 9 ancestor of the Edomites, in the hill country of S.
36:20 These are the sons of S the Horite,
36:21 the sons of S in the land of Edom.
36:30 clan by clan in the land of S.
Nu 24:18 S a possession of its enemies,
Dt 1: 2 (By the way of Mount S it takes eleven days
1:44 They beat you down in S as far as Hormah.
2: 1 as the LORD had told me and skirted Mount S
2: 4 the descendants of Esau, who live in S.
2: 5 I have given Mount S to Esau as a possession.
2: 8 the descendants of Esau who live in S,
2:12 Moreover, the Horim had formerly inhabited S,
2:22 of Esau, who live in S, by destroying the Horim
2:29 the descendants of Esau who live in S have done
33: 2 and dawned from S upon us;
Jos 11:17 from Mount Halak, which rises toward S, as far
12: 7 toward S (and Joshua gave their land to the tribes
15:10 the boundary circles west of Baalah to Mount S,
24: 4 I gave Esau the hill country of S to possess,
Jdg 5: 4 "LORD, when you went out from S,
1Ch 1:38 The sons of S: Lotan, Shobal,
4:42 went to Mount S, having as their leaders Pelatiah,
2Ch 20:10 the people of Ammon, Moab, and Mount S,
20:22 and Mount S, who had come against Judah,
20:23 and Moab attacked the inhabitants of Mount S,
20:23 they had made an end of the inhabitants of S,
25:11 and struck down ten thousand men of S.
25:14 he brought the gods of the people of S,
Isa 21:11 One is calling to me from S, "Sentinel,
Eze 35: 2 set your face against Mount S,
35: 3 I am against you, Mount S;
35: 7 I will make Mount S a waste and a desolation;
35:15 you shall be desolate, Mount S, and all Edom,
Sir 50:26 in S, and the Philistines, and the foolish people

SEIRAH (1)

Jdg 3:26 beyond the sculptured stones, and escaped to S.

SEIRATH (KJV) See SEIRAH

SEIZE (48) [SEIZED, SEIZES, SEIZING]

Ex 4: 4 "Reach out your hand, and s it by the tail"—
Jos 8: 7 you shall rise up from the ambush and s the city;
Jdg 7:24 the Midianites and s the waters against them,
2Sa 2:21 and s one of the young men, and take his spoil."
1Ki 13: 4 from the altar, saying, "S him!"
18:40 Elijah said to them, "S the prophets of Baal;
2Ki 6:13 I will send and s him."
Job 3: 6 That night—let thick darkness s it!
24: 2 they s flocks and pasture them.
36:17 judgment and justice s you.
Ps 10: 9 they lurk that they may s the poor;
10: 9 they s the poor and drag them off in their net.
71:11 "Pursue and s that person whom God has forsaken,
109: 8 May his days be few; may another s his position.
109:11 May the creditor s all that he has;
Pr 20:16 s the pledge given as surety for foreigners.
27:13 s the pledge given as surety for foreigners.
Isa 3: 6 Someone will even s a relative,
5:29 they growl and s their prey, they carry it off,
10: 6 to take spoil and s plunder,
13: 8 Pangs and agony will s them;
22:17 He will s firm hold on you,
Jer 20: 5 and s them, and carry them to Babylon.
Eze 23:25 They shall s your sons and your daughters,
38:12 to s spoil and carry off plunder;
38:13 "Have you come to s spoil?
38:13 to s a great amount of booty?"
Mic 2: 2 They covet fields, and s them;
Hab 1: 6 through the breadth of the earth to s dwellings
Zec 14:13 so that each will s the hand of a neighbor,
2Co 11:32 the city of Damascus in order to s me,
Heb 6:18 be strongly encouraged to s the hope set before us.
Rev 3:11 so that no one may s your crown.
Jdt 2:10 You shall go and s all their territory for me
4: 7 ordering them to s the mountain passes,
6:10 to s Achior and take him away to Bethulia
7: 1 and to s the passes up into the hill country
14: 3 Then they will s their arms and go into the camp
16: 4 and s my children as booty,
Sus 1:40 s this woman and asked who the young man was,
1Mc 4:18 and afterward s the plunder boldly."
6:56 that he was trying to s control of the government.
9:60 telling them to s Jonathan and his men;
12:40 so he kept seeking to s and kill him,
2Es 16:39 and pains will s it on every side.
4Mc 4: 6 with the king's authority to s the private funds in
4:10 up with his armed forces to s the money,
5: 2 to s each and every Hebrew and to compel them

SEIZED (95) [SEIZE]

Ge 19:16 the men s him and his wife and his two daughters
21:25 a well of water that Abimelech's servants had s,
34: 2 saw her, he s her and lay with her by force.
Ex 15:14 pangs s the inhabitants of Philistia.
15:15 trembling s the leaders of Moab;
Jdg 3:28 and s the fords of the Jordan against the Moabites,
7:24 and they s the waters as far as Beth-barah,
12: 6 Then they s him and killed him at the fords of
16:21 So the Philistines s him and gouged out his eyes.
19:25 the man s his concubine, and put her out to them.
2Sa 1: 9 for convulsions have s me,
4:10 I s him and killed him at Ziklag—
10: 4 So Hanun s David's envoys,
13:15 Amnon was s with a very great loathing for her;
1Ki 18:40 of them escape." Then they s them;
2Ki 14:14 He s all the gold and silver,
1Ch 19: 4 So Hanun s David's servants, shaved them,
2Ch 25:24 He s all the gold and silver,
25:24 he s also the treasuries of the king's house,
Job 16:12 he s me by the neck and dashed me to pieces;
20:19 they have s a house that they did not build.
Ps 56: T *when the Philistines s him in Gath.*
Isa 21: 3 pangs have s me, like the pangs of a woman
33:14 trembling has s the godless:
Jer 38:23 but shall be s by the king of Babylon;
48:41 the towns shall be taken and the strongholds s.
49:24 she turned to flee, and panic s her;
50:24 you were discovered and s,
50:43 anguish s him, pain like that of a woman in labor.
51:32 the fords have been s, the marshes have been
51:41 Sheshach is taken, the pride of the whole earth s!
Eze 23:10 they s her sons and her daughters;
Mic 4: 9 that pangs have s you like a woman in labor?
Mt 21:35 But the tenants s his slaves and beat one,
21:39 So they s him, threw him out of the vineyard,
22: 6 while the rest s his slaves,
Mk 12: 3 But they s him, and beat him,
12: 8 So they s him, killed him,
16: 8 for terror and amazement had s them;
Lk 5:26 Amazement s all of them,
7:16 Fear s all of them; and they glorified God,
8:29 (For many times it had s him;
8:37 for they were s with great fear.
22:54 Then they s him and led him away,
23:26 As they led him away, they s a man,
Ac 5: 5 And great fear s all who heard of it.
5:11 And great fear s the whole church
6:12 then they suddenly confronted him, s him,
12: 4 When he had s him, he put him in prison
16:19 they s Paul and Silas and dragged them into
18:17 Then all of them s Sosthenes,
21:27 stirred up the whole crowd. They s him,
21:30 They s Paul and dragged him out of the temple,
23:27 This man was s by the Jews and was about to
24: 6 even tried to profane the temple, and so we s him.
26:21 the Jews s me in the temple and tried to kill me.
Rev 20: 2 He s the dragon, that ancient serpent,
Jdt 2:25 He also s the territory of Cilicia,
4: 5 They immediately s all the high hilltops
6:12 they s their weapons and ran out of the town to
7: 5 Yet they all s their weapons,
7: 7 he s them and set guards of soldiers over them,
7:17 the valley and s the water supply and the springs
AdE 14: 1 Then Queen Esther, s with deadly anxiety,
Wis 17:17 they were s, and endured the inescapable fate;
Sir 23:21 and where he least suspects it, he will be s.
1Mc 1:32 the women and children, and s the livestock.
2:10 not inherited her palaces and has not s her spoils?
3:12 Then they s their spoils;
4:23 and they s a great amount of gold and silver,
5:28 then he s all its spoils and burned it with fire.
6:12 I s all its vessels of silver and gold,
6:24 and they have s our inheritances.
7: 2 army s Antiochus and Lysias to bring them to him.
7:16 but he s sixty of them and killed them in one day,
7:19 and s many of the men who had deserted to him,
7:47 Then the Jews s the spoils and the plunder;
9:36 of Jambri from Medeba came out and s John
9:61 And Jonathan's men s about fifty of the men of
11:46 the people of the city s the main streets of the city
11:48 the city and s a large amount of spoil on that day,
12:48 the people of Ptolemais closed the gates and s him,
12:50 that Jonathan had been s and had perished along
14: 3 and s him and took him to Arsaces,
15:30 that you have s and the tribute money of the places
15:33 nor s foreign property, but only the inheritance
16:22 he s the men who came to destroy him
2Mc 2:21 that though few in number they s the whole land
9: 5 As soon as he stopped speaking he was s with
1Es 1:38 and s his brother Zarius and brought him back
9: 4 be s for sacrifice and the men themselves expelled
3Mc 1: 1 that the regions that he had controlled had been s
2Es 5: 1 when those who inhabit the earth shall be s
15:37 and they shall be s with trembling.
4Mc 17: 1 about to be s and put to death she threw herself

SEIZES (10) [SEIZE]

Dt 22:25 and the man s her and lies with her,
22:28 and s her and lies with her,
Job 18: 9 trap s them by the heel; a snare lays hold of them.

Job 18:20 and horror s those of the east.
21: 6 and shuddering s my flesh.
30:18 With violence he s my garment;
Ps 119:53 Hot indignation s me because of the wicked,
Pr 7:13 She s him and kisses him,
Mk 9:18 and whenever it s him, it dashes him down;
Lk 9:39 Suddenly a spirit s him, and all at once he shrieks.

SEIZING (4) [SEIZE]
Dt 25:11 of his opponent by reaching out and s his genitals,
Mt 18:28 s him by the throat, he said, 'Pay what you owe.'
Ro 7: 8 But sin, s an opportunity in the commandment,
7:11 For sin, s an opportunity in the commandment,

SELA[‡] (6)
Jdg 1:36 from the ascent of Akrabbim, from S and upward.
2Ki 14: 7 in the Valley of Salt and took S by storm;
2Ch 25:12 took them to the top of S,
25:12 and threw them down from the top of S,
Isa 16: 1 Send lambs to the ruler of the land, from S,
42:11 let the inhabitants of S sing for joy,

SELA-HAMMAHLEKOTH (KJV) See ROCK OF ESCAPE

SELAH (74)
Ps 3: 2 "There is no help for you in God." *S*
3: 4 he answers me from his holy hill. *S*
3: 8 may your blessing be on your people! *S*
4: 2 will you love vain words, and seek after lies? *S*
4: 4 ponder it on your beds, and be silent. *S*
7: 5 and lay my soul in the dust. *S*
9:16 in the work of their own hands. *Higgaion. S*
9:20 the nations know that they are only human. *S*
20: 3 regard with favor your burnt sacrifices. *S*
21: 2 have not withheld the request of his lips. *S*
24: 6 who seek the face of the God of Jacob. *S*
24:10 he is the King of glory. *S*
32: 4 dried up as by the heat of summer. *S*
32: 5 you forgave the guilt of my sin. *S*
32: 7 surround me with glad cries of deliverance. *S*
39: 5 everyone stands as a mere breath. *S*
39:11 surely everyone is a mere breath. *S*
44: 8 we will give thanks to your name forever. *S*
46: 3 though the mountains tremble with its tumult. *S*
46: 7 the God of Jacob is our refuge. *S*
46:11 the God of Jacob is our refuge. *S*
47: 4 the pride of Jacob whom he loves. *S*
48: 8 which God establishes forever. *S*
49:13 the end of those who are pleased with their lot. *S*
49:15 for he will receive me. *S*
50: 6 for God himself is judge. *S*
52: 3 and lying more than speaking the truth. *S*
52: 5 he will uproot you from the land of the living. *S*
54: 3 they do not set God before them. *S*
55: 7 I would lodge in the wilderness; *S*
55:19 God, who is enthroned from of old, *S*
57: 3 he will put to shame those who trample on me. *S*
57: 6 but they have fallen into it themselves. *S*
59: 5 spare none of those who treacherously plot evil. *S*
59:13 that God rules over Jacob. *S*
60: 4 to rally to it out of bowshot. *S*
61: 4 find refuge under the shelter of your wings. *S*
62: 4 but inwardly they curse. *S*
62: 8 God is a refuge for us. *S*
66: 4 sing praises to your name." *S*
66: 7 let the rebellious not exalt themselves. *S*
66:15 I will make an offering of bulls and goats. *S*
67: 1 and bless us and make his face to shine upon us, *S*
67: 4 and guide the nations upon earth. *S*
68: 7 when you marched through the wilderness, *S*
68:19 God is our salvation. *S*
68:32 sing praises to the Lord, *S*
75: 3 it is I who keep its pillars steady. *S*
76: 3 and the weapons of war. *S*
76: 9 to save all the oppressed of the earth. *S*
77: 3 I meditate, and my spirit faints. *S*
77: 9 Has he in anger shut up his compassion?" *S*
77:15 the descendants of Jacob and Joseph. *S*
81: 7 I tested you at the waters of Meribah. *S*
82: 2 and show partiality to the wicked? *S*
83: 8 they are the strong arm of the children of Lot. *S*
84: 4 ever singing your praise. *S*
84: 8 give ear, O God of Jacob! *S*
85: 2 you pardoned all their sin. *S*
87: 3 O city of God. *S*
87: 6 "This one was born there." *S*
88: 7 your overwhelm me with all your waves. *S*
88:10 Do the shades rise up to praise you? *S*
89: 4 and build your throne for all generations.' " *S*
89:37 an enduring witness in the skies." *S*
89:45 you have covered him with shame. *S*
89:48 Who can escape the power of Sheol? *S*
140: 3 and under their lips is the venom of vipers. *S*
140: 5 along the road they have set snares for me. *S*
140: 8 do not further their evil plot. *S*
143: 6 my sould thirsts you like a parched land. *S*
Hab 3: 3 the Holy One from Mount Paran. *S*
3: 9 sated were the arrows at your command. *S*
3:13 bare from foundation to roof. *S*

SELDOM (1)
Pr 25:17 Let your foot be s in your neighbor's house,

SELECT (9) [SELECTED]
Ge 41:33 let Pharaoh s a man who is discerning and wise,
Ex 12:21 "Go, s lambs for your families,
Nu 35:11 you shall s cities to be cities of refuge for you,
Jos 3:12 So now s twelve men from the tribes of Israel,
4: 2 "S twelve men from the people,
2Ki 10: 3 s the son of your master who is the best qualified,
1Ch 7:40 heads of ancestral houses, s mighty warriors,
Ac 6: 3 s from among yourselves seven men
AdE 2: 3 and they shall s beautiful young virgins to

SELECTED (2) [SELECT]
Dt 1:23 plan seemed good to me, and I s twelve of you,
Ezr 10:16 Ezra the priest s men, heads of families,

SELED (2)
1Ch 2:30 S and Appaim; and S died childless.

SELEMIA (1)
2Es 14:24 and take with you Sarea, Dabria, S, Ethanus,

SELEUCIA (2)
Ac 13: 4 by the Holy Spirit, they went down to S;
1Mc 11: 8 of the coastal cities as far as S by the sea,

SELEUCUS (10)
1Mc 7: 1 of S set out from Rome,
2Mc 3: 3 even to the extent that King S of Asia defrayed
4: 7 When S died and Antiochus,
5:18 whom King S sent to inspect the treasury.
14: 1 that Demetrius son of S had sailed into the harbor
4Mc 3:20 so that even S Nicanor, king of Asia,
4: 3 the property of the temple but belong to King S."
4: 4 to the king and went up to S to inform him of
4:13 prayed for him so that King S would not suppose
4:15 When King S died, his son Antiochus Epiphanes

SELF (10) [SELFISH, SELFISHNESS, SELVES, YOURSELF, YOURSELVES]
Ex 32:13 how you swore to them by your own s,
Ro 6: 6 We know that our old s was crucified with him so
7:22 For I delight in the law of God in my inmost s,
Eph 4:22 your old s, corrupt and deluded by its lusts,
4:24 and to clothe yourselves with the new s,
Col 3: 9 seeing that you have stripped off the old s
3:10 and have clothed yourselves with the new s,
Phm 1:19 about your owing me even your own s.
1Pe 3: 4 be the inner s with the lasting beauty of a gentle
Sir 6:11 you are prosperous, they become your second s,

SELF-ABASEMENT (1) [ABASE]
Col 2:18 insisting on s and worship of angels,

SELF-CONDEMNED (2) [CONDEMN]
Gal 2:11 I opposed him to his face, because he stood s;
Tit 3:11 that such a person is perverted and sinful, being s.

SELF-CONTROL (19) [CONTROL]
Pr 25:28 without walls, is one who lacks s.
Ac 24:25 And as he discussed justice, s,
1Co 7: 5 not tempt you because of your lack of s.
7: 9 But if they are not practicing s, they should marry.
9:25 Athletes exercise s in all things;
Gal 5:23 gentleness, and s. There is no law against such
2Pe 1: 6 and knowledge with s, and s with endurance,
Wis 8: 7 she teaches s and prudence, justice and courage;
Sir 18:30 S Do not follow your base desires,
2Es 7:*125* [55] of those who practiced s shall shine more than
4Mc 1: 3 that reason rules over those emotions that hinder s,
1: 6 that are opposed to justice, courage, and s;
1:18 are rational judgment, justice, courage, and s.
1:30 by virtue of the restraining power of s.
1:31 S, then, is dominance over the desires.
5:23 but it teaches us s, so that we master all pleasures
5:34 nor will I renounce you, beloved s.
13:16 Therefore let us put on the full armor of s,

SELF-CONTROLLED (5) [CONTROL]
Tit 1: 8 prudent, upright, devout, and s.
2: 5 to be s, chaste, good managers of the household,
2: 6 Likewise, urge the younger men to be s.
2:12 and in the present age to live lives that are s,
4Mc 15:10 For they were righteous and s and brave

SELF-DENIAL (2) [DENY]
Lev 23:29 not practice s during that entire day shall be cut off
Sir 11:18 One becomes rich through diligence and s,

SELF-DISCIPLINE (2) [DISCIPLINE]
2Ti 1: 7 but rather a spirit of power and of love and of s.
Sir 26:14 and nothing is so precious as her s.

SELF-ESTEEM (2) [ESTEEM]
Pr 26:16 wiser in s than seven who can answer discreetly.
28:11 The rich is wise in s,

SELF-IMPORTANT (1) [IMPORTANT]
Pr 12: 9 than to be s and lack food.

SELF-IMPOSED (1) [IMPOSE]
Col 2:23 an appearance of wisdom in promoting s piety,

SELF-INDULGENCE (3) [INDULGE]
Mt 23:25 but inside they are full of greed and s.
Gal 5:13 not use your freedom as an opportunity for s,
Col 2:23 but they are of no value in checking s.

SELF-INDULGENT (1) [INDULGE]
Pr 18: 1 The one who lives alone is s,

SELF-KINDLED (1) [KINDLE]
Wis 17: 6 through to them except a dreadful, s fire,

SELF-RELIANT See Index to Footnotes

SELF-RESPECT (1) [RESPECT]
Sir 40:29 One loses s with another person's food,

SELF-SEEKING (1) [SEEK]
Ro 2: 8 for those who are s and who obey not the truth

SELFISH (5) [SELF]
Ps 119:36 Turn my heart to your decrees, and not to s gain.
Php 1:17 the others proclaim Christ out of s ambition,
2: 3 Do nothing from s ambition or conceit,
Jas 3:14 you have bitter envy and s ambition in your hearts,
3:16 For where there is envy and s ambition,

SELFISHNESS (1) [SELF]
2Co 12:20 anger, s, slander, gossip, conceit, and disorder.

SELFSAME (KJV) See SAME, THAT, VERY

SELL (33) [SALE, SELLER, SELLERS, SELLING, SELLS, SOLD]
Ge 25:31 Jacob said, "First s me your birthright."
37:27 Come, let us s him to the Ishmaelites,
47:22 therefore they did not s their land.
Ex 21: 8 he shall have no right to s her to a foreign people,
21:35 they shall s the live ox and divide the price of it;
Lev 25:39 so impoverished that they s themselves to you,
25:47 into difficulty with one of them and s themselves
Dt 2:28 You shall s me food for money, so that I may eat,
14:21 or you may s it to a foreigner.
21:14 you shall let her go free and not s her for money.
Jdg 4: 9 LORD will s Sisera into the hand of a woman."
2Ki 4: 7 and he said, "Go s the oil and pay your debts,
Ne 10:31 the sabbath day to s, we will not buy it from them
Pr 11:26 but a blessing is on the head of those who s it.
23:23 Buy truth, and do not s it;
Eze 30:12 and will s the land into the hand of evildoers;
48:14 They shall not s or exchange any of it;
Joel 3: 8 I will s your sons and your daughters into the hand
3: 8 and they will s them to the Sabeans,
Am 2: 6 because they s the righteous for silver,
8: 5 will the new moon be over so that we may s grain;
Zec 11: 5 and those who s them say,
Mt 19:21 "If you wish to be perfect, go, s your possessions,
Mk 10:21 s what you own, and give the money to the poor,
Lk 12:33 S your possessions, and give alms.
18:22 S all that you own and distribute the money to
22:36 And the one who has no sword must s his cloak
Ac 2:45 they would s their possessions and goods
Rev 13:17 no one can buy or s who does not have the mark,
LtJ 6:28 The priests s the sacrifices that are offered
1Mc 12:36 so that its garrison could neither buy nor s.
13:49 from going in and out to buy and s in the country.
2Mc 5:24 to kill all the grown men and to s the women

SELLER (3) [SELL]
Lev 25:15 the s shall charge you only for the remaining crop
Isa 24: 2 as with the buyer, so with the s;
Eze 7:12 let not the buyer rejoice, nor the s mourn,

SELLERS (2) [SELL]
Ne 13:20 and s of all kinds of merchandise spent
Eze 7:13 the s shall not return to what has been sold as long

SELLING (14) [SELL]
Dt 24: 7 enslaving or s the Israelite,
Ru 4: 3 is s the parcel of land that belonged
Ne 5: 8 but now you are s your own kin,
13:15 and I warned them at that time against s food.
Am 8: 6 and s the sweepings of the wheat."
Mt 21:12 and drove out all who were s and buying in
Mk 11:15 and began to drive out those who were s
Lk 17:28 they were eating and drinking, buying and s,
19:45 to drive out those who were s things there;
Jn 2:14 In the temple he found people s cattle, sheep,
2:16 He told those who were s the doves,
Sir 27: 2 so sin is wedged in between s and buying.
37:11 a merchant about business or with a buyer about s,
2Mc 8:10 by s the captured Jews into slavery.

SELLS[‡] (7) [SELL]
Ex 21: 7 When a man s his daughter as a slave,
22: 1 and slaughters it or s it,
Lev 25:25 If anyone of your kin falls into difficulty and s

Lev 25:29 If anyone **s** a dwelling house in a walled city,
Pr 31:24 She makes linen garments and **s** them;
Mt 13:44 in his joy he goes and **s** all that he has and buys
2Es 16:41 Let the one who **s** be like one who will flee;

SELVEDGE (KJV) See EDGE

SELVES (1) [SELF]
1Th 2: 8 not only the gospel of God but also our own **s**,

SEM (KJV) See SHEM

SEMACHIAH (1)
1Ch 26: 7 whose brothers were able men, Elihu and **S**.

SEMBLANCE (1) [RESEMBLED]
Isa 52:14 beyond human **s**, and his form beyond that

SEMEIN (1)
Lk 3:26 son of Mattathias, son of **S**, son of Josech,

SEMEIOS See Index to Footnotes

SEMEN (6)
Ge 38: 9 he spilled his **s** on the ground whenever he went in
Lev 15:16 If a man has an emission of **s**,
15:17 on which the **s** falls shall be washed with water,
15:18 a man lies with a woman and has an emission of **s**,
15:32 for him who has an emission of **s**,
22: 4 a corpse or a man who has had an emission of **s**,

SENAAH (3)
Ezr 2:35 Of **S**, three thousand six hundred thirty.
Ne 7:38 Of **S**, three thousand nine hundred thirty.
1Es 5:23 of **S**, three thousand three hundred thirty.

SENATE (8) [SENATOR, SENATORS]
Jdt 4: 8 and the **s** of the whole people of Israel,
1Mc 8:15 but they have built for themselves a **s** chamber,
8:19 they entered the **s** chamber and spoke as follows:
12: 3 So they went to Rome and entered the **s** chamber
12: 6 the **s** of the nation, the priests,
2Mc 1:10 The people of Jerusalem and of Judea and the **s**
4:44 three men sent by the **s** presented the case
11:27 "King Antiochus to the **s** of the Jews and to

SENATE (KJV) See also WHOLE BODY

SENATOR (1) [SENATE]
2Mc 6: 1 the king sent an Athenian **s** to compel the Jews

SENATORS (1) [SENATE]
1Mc 8:15 three hundred twenty **s** constantly deliberate

SEND (292) [SENDER, SENDING, SENDS, SENT]
Ge 7: 4 For in seven days I will **s** rain on the earth
24: 7 he will **s** his angel before you,
24:40 before whom I walk, will **s** his angel with you
24:54 he said, "**S** me back to my master."
27:45 then I will **s**, and bring you back from there.
30:25 Jacob said to Laban, "**S** me away,
37:13 Come, I will **s** you to them."
38:17 He answered, "I will **s** you a kid from the flock."
38:17 "Only if you give me a pledge, until you **s** it."
42: 4 not **s** Joseph's brother Benjamin with his brothers,
43: 4 If you will **s** our brother with us,
43: 5 but if you will not **s** him,
43: 8 Judah said to his father Israel, "**S** the boy with me,
43:14 he may **s** back your other brother and Benjamin.
45: 1 and he cried out, "**S** everyone away from me."
Ex 3:10 come, I will **s** you to Pharaoh to bring my people,
4:13 But he said, "O my Lord, please **s** someone else."
5:22 Why did you ever **s** me?
8:21 I will **s** swarms of flies on you, your officials,
9:14 this time I will **s** all my plagues upon you yourself,
9:19 **S**, therefore, and have your livestock
23:20 I am going to **s** an angel in front of you,
23:27 I will **s** my terror in front of you,
23:28 And I will **s** the pestilence in front of you,
33: 2 I will **s** an angel before you,
33:12 but you have not let me know whom you will **s**
Lev 26:25 I will **s** pestilence among you,
26:36 I will **s** faintness into their hearts in the lands
Nu 13: 2 "**S** men to spy out the land of Canaan,
13: 2 from each of their ancestral tribes you shall **s**
22:37 "Did I not **s** to summon you?
31: 4 You shall **s** a thousand from each of the tribes
35:25 Then the congregation shall **s** the slayer back to
Dt 1:22 "Let us **s** men ahead of us to explore the land
7:20 the LORD your God will **s** the pestilence
15:13 you **s** a male slave out from you a free person,
15:13 you shall not **s** him out empty-handed.
15:18 Do not consider it a hardship when you **s** them out
19:12 of the killer's city shall **s** to have the culprit taken
28:20 The LORD will **s** upon you disaster, panic,
28:48 the LORD will **s** against you,
32:24 The teeth of beasts I will **s** against them,
Jos 1:16 and wherever you **s** us we will go.
18: 4 and I will **s** them out that they may begin to go
1Sa 5:11 and said, "**S** away the ark of the God of Israel,
6: 2 Tell us what we should **s** with it to its place."
6: 3 "If you **s** away the ark of the God of Israel, do not
s it empty,
6: 8 Then **s** it off, and let it go its way.
9:16 about this time I will **s** to you a man from the land
9:26 "Get up, so that I may **s** you on your way."
11: 3 that we may **s** messengers through all the territory
12:17 that he may **s** thunder and rain;
16: 1 I will **s** you to Jesse the Bethlehemite,
16:11 And Samuel said to Jesse, "**S** and bring him;
16:19 "**S** me your son David who is with the sheep."
20:12 shall I not then **s** and disclose it to you?
20:13 and **s** you away, so that you may go in safety.
20:21 I will **s** the boy, saying, 'Go, find the arrows.'
20:31 **s** and bring him to me, for he shall surely die."
21: 2 of the matter about which I **s** you,
29: 4 of the Philistines said to him, "**S** the man back,
2Sa 11: 6 David sent word to Joab, "**S** me Uriah the Hittite."
11:12 and tomorrow I will **s** you back."
13: 9 Amnon said, "**S** out everyone from me."
14:29 Then Absalom sent for Joab to **s** him to the king;
14:32 that I may **s** you to the king with the question,
17:16 Therefore **s** quickly and tell David,
18: 3 it is better that you **s** us help from the city."
1Ki 8:44 by whatever way you shall **s** them,
18: 1 I will **s** rain on the earth."
20: 6 nevertheless I will **s** my servants to you tomorrow
2Ki 2:16 He responded, "No, do not **s** them."
2:17 until he was ashamed, he said, "**S** them."
4:22 "**S** me one of the servants and one of the donkeys,
5: 5 and I will **s** along a letter to the king of Israel."
6:13 I will **s** and seize him."
7:13 let us **s** and find out."
9:17 **s** him to meet them, and let him say,
15:37 In those days the LORD began to **s** King Rezin
17:27 "**S** there one of the priests whom you carried away
1Ch 13: 2 let us **s** abroad to our kindred who remain in all
2Ch 2: 7 So now **s** me an artisan skilled to work in gold,
2: 8 **S** me also cedar, cypress, and algum timber
2:15 let him **s** them to his servants.
6:27 and **s** down rain upon your land,
6:34 by whatever way you shall **s** them,
7:13 or **s** pestilence among my people,
28:11 and **s** back the captives whom you have taken
Ezr 4:11 of the province Beyond the River, **s** greeting.
4:14 therefore we **s** and inform the king,
5:17 Let the king **s** us his pleasure in this matter."
8:17 namely, to **s** us ministers for the house of our God.
10: 3 a covenant with our God to **s** away all these wives
10:19 They pledged themselves to **s** away their wives,
Ne 2: 5 I ask that you **s** me to Judah,
2: 6 So it pleased the king to **s** me, and I set him a date.
8:10 eat the fat and drink sweet wine and **s** portions
8:12 and to **s** portions and to make great rejoicing,
Est 9:19 on which they **s** gifts of food to one another.
Job 1: 4 and they would **s** and invite their three sisters
1: 5 Job would **s** and sanctify them,
14:20 you change their countenance, and **s** them away.
20:23 to the full God will **s** his fierce anger into them,
21:11 They **s** out their little ones like a flock,
30:12 they **s** me sprawling, and build roads for my ruin.
38:35 Can you **s** forth lightnings,
Ps 20: 2 May he **s** you help from the sanctuary,
43: 3 O **s** out your light and your truth;
57: 3 He will **s** from heaven and save me,
57: 3 God will **s** forth his steadfast love
104:30 When you **s** forth your spirit, they are created;
144: 6 **s** out your arrows and rout them.
Pr 25:13 are faithful messengers to those who **s** them;
26: 6 to **s** a message by a fool.
Ecc 11: 1 **S** out your bread upon the waters,
Isa 6: 8 "Whom shall I **s**, and who will go for us?"
6: 8 And I said, "Here am I; **s** me!"
10: 6 Against a godless nation I **s** him,
10:16 will **s** wasting sickness among his stout warriors,
16: 1 **S** lambs to the ruler of the land, from Sela,
19:20 the LORD because of oppressors, he will **s** them
42:19 or deaf like my messenger whom I **s**?
43:14 For your sake I will **s** to Babylon and break
48:20 proclaim it, **s** it forth to the end of the earth;
66:19 From them I will **s** survivors to the nations,
Jer 1: 7 for you shall go to all to whom I **s** you,
2:10 **s** to Kedar and examine with care;
9:16 and I will **s** the sword after them,
9:17 **s** for the skilled women to come;
14: 3 Her nobles **s** their servants for water;
14:14 I did not **s** them, nor did I command them or speak
14:15 not **s** them, and who say, "Sword and famine shall
15: 1 **S** them out of my sight, and let them go!
16:16 and afterward I will **s** for many hunters,
23:21 I did not **s** the prophets, yet they ran;
23:32 when I did not **s** them or appoint them;
24:10 And I will **s** sword, famine,
25: 9 to **s** for all the tribes of the north, says the LORD,
25:15 and make all the nations to whom I **s** you drink it.
26: 5 the words of my servants the prophets whom I **s**
27: 3 **S** word to the king of Edom, the king of Moab,
28:16 I am going to **s** you off the face of the earth.
29: 9 I did not **s** them, says the LORD.
29:31 **S** to all the exiles, saying, Thus says the LORD
29:31 to you, though I did not **s** him,
37:20 to my plea, and do not **s** me back to the house of
38:26 the king not to **s** me back to the house of Jonathan
43: 2 The LORD our God did not **s** you to say,
43:10 to **s** and take my servant King Nebuchadrezzar
48:12 when I shall **s** to him decanters to decant him,
Jer 49:37 I will **s** the sword after them,
51: 2 and I will **s** winnowers to Babylon,
Eze 5:17 I will **s** famine and wild animals against you,
14:13 and break its staff of bread and **s** famine upon it,
14:15 If I **s** wild animals through the land to ravage it,
14:19 Or if I **s** a pestilence into that land,
14:21 when I **s** upon Jerusalem my four deadly acts
28:23 for I will **s** pestilence into it, and bloodshed
32:18 wail over the hordes of Egypt, and **s** them down,
34:26 and I will **s** down the showers in their season;
39: 6 I will **s** fire on Magog and on those who
Da 11:20 "Then shall arise in his place one who shall **s**
Hos 8:14 but I will **s** a fire upon his cities,
Am 1: 4 So I will **s** a fire on the house of Hazael,
1: 7 So I will **s** a fire on the wall of Gaza,
1:10 So I will **s** a fire on the wall of Tyre,
1:12 So I will **s** a fire on Teman,
2: 2 So I will **s** a fire on Moab,
2: 5 So I will **s** a fire on Judah,
4: 7 I would **s** rain on one city,
4: 7 and **s** no rain on another city;
8:11 when I will **s** a famine on the land;
Mal 2: 2 then I will **s** the curse on you
4: 5 I will **s** you the prophet Elijah before the great
Mt 8:31 "If you cast us out, **s** us into the herd of swine."
9:38 of the harvest to **s** out laborers into his harvest."
13:41 The Son of Man will **s** his angels,
14:15 **s** the crowds away so that they may go into
15:23 "**S** her away, for she keeps shouting after us."
15:32 and I do not want to **s** them away hungry,
21: 3 And he will **s** them immediately."
23:34 Therefore I **s** you prophets, sages, and scribes,
24:31 he will **s** out his angels with a loud trumpet call,
26:53 and he will at once **s** me more than twelve legions
Mk 5:10 He begged him earnestly not to **s** them out of
5:12 "**S** us into the swine; let us enter them."
6: 7 He called the twelve and began to **s** them out two
6:36 **s** them away so that they may go into
8: 3 If I **s** them away hungry to their homes,
11: 3 and will **s** it back here immediately.' "
13:27 Then he will **s** out the angels,
Lk 9:12 "**S** the crowd away, so that they may go into
10: 2 of the harvest to **s** out laborers into his harvest.
11:49 'I will **s** them prophets and apostles,
16:24 and **s** Lazarus to dip the tip of his finger in water
16:27 father, I beg you to **s** him to my father's house—
20:13 I will **s** my beloved son;
Jn 3:17 not **s** the Son into the world to condemn the world,
13:20 whoever receives one whom I **s** receives me;
14:26 whom the Father will **s** in my name,
15:26 whom I will **s** to you from the Father,
16: 7 but if I go, I will **s** him to you.
20:21 As the Father has sent me, so I **s** you."
Ac 3:20 and that he may **s** the Messiah appointed for you,
7:34 Come now, I will **s** you to Egypt.'
10: 5 Now **s** men to Joppa for
10:22 a holy angel to **s** for you to come to his house and
10:32 **S** therefore to Joppa and ask for Simon,
11:13 '**S** to Joppa and bring Simon, who is called Peter;
11:29 each would **s** relief to the believers living in Judea;
15:22 and to **s** them to Antioch with Paul and Barnabas.
15:25 to choose representatives and **s** them to you,
22:21 'Go, for I will **s** you far away to the Gentiles.' "
24:25 when I have an opportunity, I will **s** for you."
24:26 and for that reason he used to **s** for him very often
25:21 to be held until I could **s** him to the emperor."
25:25 to his Imperial Majesty, I decided to **s** him.
25:27 for it seems to me unreasonable to **s** a prisoner
1Co 1:17 For Christ did not **s** me to baptize but to proclaim
16: 3 I will **s** any whom you approve with letters
16: 6 so that you may **s** me on my way, wherever I go.
16:11 **S** him on his way in peace,
16:19 The churches of Asia **s** greetings.
16:20 All the brothers and sisters **s** greetings.
2Co 1:16 from Macedonia and have you **s** me on to Judea.
Php 2:19 I hope in the Lord Jesus to **s** Timothy to you soon,
2:23 therefore to **s** him as soon as I see how things go
2:25 I think it necessary to **s** to you Epaphroditus—
2:28 I am the more eager to **s** him, therefore,
Tit 3:12 When I **s** Artemas to you, or Tychicus,
3:13 to **s** Zenas the lawyer and Apollos on their way,
3:15 All who are with me **s** greetings to you.
Heb 13:24 Those from Italy **s** you greetings.
2Jn 1:13 children of your elect sister **s** you their greetings.
3Jn 1: 6 You will do well to **s** them on in a manner worthy
1:15 The friends **s** you their greetings.
Rev 1:11 a book what you see and **s** it to the seven churches,
Tob 2:12 She used to **s** what she made to the owners
8:12 "**S** one of the maids and have her go in to see
10: 7 Tobias came to him and said, "**S** me back,
10: 8 I will **s** messengers to your father Tobit
10: 9 I beg you to **s** me back to my father."
Jdt 6: 2 He will **s** his forces and destroy them from
8:31 so that the Lord may **s** us rain to fill our cisterns.
9: 9 and **s** your wrath upon their heads.
11:22 "God has done well to **s** you ahead of the people,
16:17 he will **s** fire and worms into their flesh;
AdE 9:19 and **s** presents of food to one another,
Wis 9:10 **S** her forth from the holy heavens,
9:10 and from the throne of your glory **s** her,
11:17 did not lack the means to **s** upon them a multitude
Sir 29: 9 in their need do not **s** them away empty-handed.
39:14 **S** out fragrance like incense,
45: 9 to **s** forth a sound as he walked,
46:12 May their bones **s** forth new life from
49:10 the bones of the Twelve Prophets **s** forth new life
Bar 1:10 They said: Here we **s** you money;

Sus 1:29 "S for Susanna daughter of Hilkiah,
1Mc 3:35 to s a force against them to wipe out and destroy
7: 7 Now then s a man whom you trust;
11:43 you will do well to s me men who will help me,
12:10 we have undertaken to s to renew our family ties
12:18 And now please s us a reply to this."
13:16 S now one hundred talents of silver and two
13:18 "It was because Simon did not s him the money
13:21 by way of the wilderness and to s them food.
16:18 asking him to s troops to aid him and to turn over
2Mc 2:15 s people to get them for you.
3:37 be suitable to s on another mission to Jerusalem,
3:38 or plotter against your government, s him there,
6:23 telling them to s him to Hades.
11: 6 prayed the Lord to s a good angel to save Israel.
11:26 to s word to them and give them pledges
11:36 as you have considered them, s some one promptly
11:37 Therefore make haste and s messengers so
14:27 and commanding him to s Maccabeus to Antioch
15:23 s a good angel to spread terror and trembling
1Es 4:44 and to s back all the vessels that were taken
4:44 and vowed to s them back there.
6:22 let him s us directions concerning these things."
8:46 and the treasurers at that place to s us men to serve
9:51 and s portions to those who have none;
3Mc 3:25 you are to s to us those who live among you,
5:42 an irrevocable oath that he would s them to death
6:27 S them back to their homes in peace,
2Es 1:23 I did not s fire on you for your blasphemies,
2:18 I will s you help, my servants Isaiah and Jeremiah.
7:*104* Just as now a father does not s his son,
14:22 s the holy spirit into me, and I will write everything
15:49 I will s evils upon you:
16:60 as to s rivers from the heights to water the earth.

SENDER (1) [SEND]

2Mc 4:20 So this money was intended by the s for

SENDING‡ (40) [SEND]

Lev 16:21 and s it away into the wilderness by means
2Sa 13:16 in s me away is greater than the other that you did
1Ki 15:19 I am s you a present of silver and gold;
2Ki 1: 6 in Israel that you are s to inquire of Baal-zebub,
2Ch 16: 3 I am s to you silver and gold;
Est 9:22 days for s gifts of food to one another and presents
Isa 18: 2 s ambassadors by the Nile in vessels of papyrus on
Jer 16:16 I am now s for many fishermen, says the LORD,
17: 8 s out its roots by the stream.
25:16 of their minds because of the sword that I am s
25:27 because of the sword that I am s among you.
35:15 s them persistently, saying,
42: 6 of the LORD our God to whom we are s you,
Eze 2: 3 Mortal, I am s you to the people of Israel,
2: 4 I am s you to them, and you shall say to them,
17:15 But he rebelled against him by s ambassadors
31: 4 s forth its streams to all the trees of the field.
Joel 2:19 I am s you grain, wine, and oil,
Mal 3: 1 I am s my messenger to prepare the way
Mt 10:16 I am s you out like sheep into the midst of wolves;
11:10 'See, I am s my messenger ahead of you,
15:39 After s away the crowds, he got into the boat
Mk 1: 2 "See, I am s my messenger ahead of you,
Lk 7:27 'See, I am s my messenger ahead of you,
10: 3 I am s you out like lambs into the midst of wolves.
24:49 see, I am s upon you what my Father promised;
Ac 11:30 s it to the elders by Barnabas and Saul.
26:17 and from the Gentiles—to whom I am s you
Ro 8: 3 by s his own Son in the likeness of sinful flesh,
2Co 8:18 With him we are s the brother who is famous
8:22 we are s our brother whom we have often tested
9: 3 But I am s the brothers in order that our boasting
Gal 2: 8 the circumcised also worked through me in s me to
Eph 6:22 I am s him to you for this very purpose,
Phm 1:12 I am s him, that is, my own heart, back to you.
Rev 1: 1 by s his angel to his servant John,
AdE 9:19 also s presents to one another.
9:22 for feasting and gladness and for s presents of food
Bar 1:14 you shall read aloud this scroll that we are s you,
1Mc 13:21 in the citadel kept s envoys to Trypho urging him

SENDS (24) [SEND]

Dt 24: 1 puts it in her hand, and s her out of his house;
24: 3 and s her out of his house (or the second man who
1Ki 17:14 until the day that the LORD s rain on the earth."
2Ki 5: 7 that this man s word to me to cure a man
Job 5:10 He gives rain on the earth and s waters on
12:15 if he s them out, they overwhelm the land.
Ps 68:33 listen, he s out his voice, his mighty voice.
110: 2 The LORD s out from Zion your mighty scepter.
147:15 He s out his command to the earth;
147:18 He s out his word, and melts them;
Isa 6:12 until the LORD s everyone far away,
Jer 42: 5 to everything that the LORD your God s us
Mt 5:45 and s rain on the righteous and on the unrighteous.
Lk 14:32 he s a delegation and asks for the terms of peace.
2Th 2:11 For this reason God s them a powerful delusion,
2Ti 4:21 Eubulus s greetings to you,
Phm 1:23 in Christ Jesus, s greetings to you,
1Pe 5:13 s you greetings; and so does my son Mark.
Sir 43:13 By his command he s the driving snow and speeds
Bar 3:33 the one who s forth the light, and it goes;
2Mc 9:19 Antiochus their king and general s hearty greetings
1Es 4: 4 and if he s them out against the enemy, they go,
8:19 and reader of the law of the Most High God s for,
2Es 16: 8 The Lord God s calamities,

SENEH (1)

1Sa 14: 4 and the name of the other S.

SENIOR (3)

2Ki 19: 2 and Shebna the secretary, and the s priests,
Isa 37: 2 and Shebna the secretary, and the s priests,
Jer 19: 1 the elders of the people and some of the s priests,

SENIR (4) [=HERMON]

Dt 3: 9 while the Amorites call it S),
1Ch 5:23 from Bashan to Baal-hermon, S,
SS 4: 8 from the peak of S and Hermon,
Eze 27: 5 They made all your planks of fir trees from S;

SENNACHERIB (22) [SENNACHERIB'S]

2Ki 18:13 King S of Assyria came up against all
19:16 hear the words of S, which he has sent to mock
19:20 I have heard your prayer to me about King S
19:36 Then King S of Assyria left, went home,
2Ch 32: 1 King S of Assyria came and invaded Judah
32: 2 that S had come and intended to fight
32: 9 while King S of Assyria was at Lachish
32:10 "Thus says King S of Assyria:
32:22 the hand of King S of Assyria and from the hand
Isa 36: 1 King S of Assyria came up against all
37:17 hear all the words of S,
37:21 to me concerning King S of Assyria,
37:37 Then King S of Assyria left, went home,
Tob 1:15 and his son S reigned in his place,
1:18 I also buried any whom King S put to death
1:18 when S looked for them he could not find them.
1:22 of administrations of the accounts under King S
Sir 48:18 In his days S invaded the country;
2Mc 8:19 how, in the time of S,
15:22 one hundred eighty-five thousand in the camp of S.
3Mc 6: 5 S exulting in his countless forces,
2Es 7:*110* [40] and Hezekiah for the people in the days of S,

SENNACHERIB'S (1) [SENNACHERIB]

Tob 1:21 forty days passed before two of S sons killed him,

SENSE‡ (34) [SENSELESS, SENSES, SENSIBLE]

Dt 32:28 They are a nation void of s;
1Sa 25:33 Blessed be your good s, and blessed be you,
Ne 8: 8 They gave the s, so that the people understood
Job 34:10 "Therefore, hear me, you who have s,
34:34 Those who have s will say to me,
Pr 6:32 But he who commits adultery has no s;
7: 7 among the youths, a young man without s,
9: 4 To those without s she says,
9:16 And to those without s she says,
10:13 but a rod is for the back of one who lacks s.
10:21 but fools die for lack of s.
11:12 Whoever belittles another lacks s,
11:22 a pig's snout is a beautiful woman without good s.
12: 8 One is commended for good s,
12:11 but those who follow worthless pursuits have no s.
13:15 Good s wins favor, but the way of the faithless
15:21 Folly is a joy to one who has no s,
19:11 Those with good s are slow to anger,
Ecc 3:11 he has put a s of past and future into their minds,
10: 3 Even when fools walk on the road, they lack s,
Jer 5: 4 I said, "These are only the poor, they have no s;
Hos 7:11 like a dove, silly and without s;
1Co 12:17 where would the s of smell be?
2Co 10:12 they do not show good s.
Sir Pr: 2 the same s when translated into another language.
1:24 then the lips of many tell of their good s.
13:22 he talks s, but is not given a hearing.
22:13 and you will never be wearied by his lack of s.
26:25 *but one who has a s of shame will fear the Lord.*
29:14 the one who has lost all s of shame will fail him.
37:22 the fruits of his good s will be praiseworthy.
37:23 and the fruits of his good s will endure.
47:23 broad in folly and lacking in s, Rehoboam,
LtJ 6:41 and abandon them, for they have no s.

SENSELESS (17) [SENSE]

Dt 32: 6 thus repay the LORD, O foolish and s people?
Job 30: 8 A s, disreputable brood, they have been whipped
Pr 17:18 It is s to give a pledge,
Jer 5:21 O foolish and s people, who have eyes,
Eze 13: 3 for the s prophets who follow their own spirit,
Ro 1:21 and their s minds were darkened.
1Ti 6: 9 by many s and harmful desires that plunge people
2Ti 2:23 to do with stupid and s controversies;
Jas 2:20 Do you want to be shown, you s person,
Sir 16:23 a s and misguided person thinks foolishly.
21:19 To a s person education is fetters on his feet,
22:13 with a s person or visit an unintelligent person.
34: 1 The s have vain and false hopes,
3Mc 6:12 now and have mercy on us who by the s insolence
4Mc 5: 9 It is s not to enjoy delicious things that are
5:10 to me that you will do something even more s if,
8:17 "O wretches that we are and so s!

SENSES (5) [SENSE]

1Ki 8:47 yet if they come to their s in the land
2Ch 6:37 then if they come to their s in the land
Eph 2: 3 following the desires of flesh and s,
2Mc 9:11 to lose much of his arrogance and to come to his s
4Mc 2:22 the same time he enthroned the mind among the s

SENSIBLE (18) [SENSE]

Job 17:10 and I shall not find a s person among you.
1Co 10:15 I speak as to s people;
1Ti 3: 2 married only once, temperate, s, respectable,
Tob 6:12 Moreover, the girl is s, brave, and very beautiful,
Wis 6:24 and a s king is the stability of any people.
Sir 7:25 but give her to a s man.
19:29 and a s person is known when first met,
20:27 and one who is s pleases the great.
21: 7 when they slip, the s person knows it.
21:17 utterance of a s person is sought in the assembly,
21:21 the s person education is like a golden ornament,
22: 4 A s daughter obtains a husband of her own,
25: 8 Happy the man who lives with a s wife,
29:28 for a s person to bear scolding about lodging and
32:18 s person will not overlook a thoughtful suggestion;
33: 3 The s person will trust in the law;
38: 4 and the s will not despise them.
40:23 but a s wife is better than either.

SENSITIVITY (1)

Eph 4:19 They have lost all s and have abandoned

SENSUAL (1)

1Ti 5:11 for when their s desires alienate them from Christ,

SENT‡ (852) [SEND]

Ge 3:23 LORD God s him forth from the garden of Eden,
8: 7 and s out the raven; and it went to and
8: 8 Then he s out the dove from him,
8:10 and again he s out the dove from the ark;
8:12 he waited another seven days, and s out the dove;
19:13 and the LORD has s us to destroy it."
19:29 and s Lot out of the midst of the overthrow,
20: 2 And King Abimelech of Gerar s and took Sarah.
21:14 along with the child, and s her away.
24:59 So they s away their sister Rebekah and her nurse
25: 6 and he s them away from his son Isaac,
26:27 that you hate me and have s me away from you?"
26:29 to you nothing but good and have s you away
27:42 so she s and called her younger son Jacob and said
28: 5 Thus Isaac s Jacob away;
28: 6 and s him away to Paddan-aram to take a wife
31: 4 So Jacob s and called Rachel and Leah into
31:27 I would have s you away with mirth and songs,
31:42 now you would have s me away empty-handed.
32: 3 Jacob s messengers before him to his brother Esau
32: 5 and I have s to tell my lord,
32:18 they are a present s to my lord Esau;
32:23 He took them and s them across the stream,
37:14 So he s him from the valley of Hebron.
38:20 When Judah s the kid by his friend the Adullamite,
38:23 you see, I s this kid, and you could not find her."
38:25 she s word to her father-in-law,
41: 8 so he s and called for all the magicians of Egypt
41:14 Then Pharaoh s for Joseph,
44: 3 the men were s away with their donkeys.
45: 5 for God s me before you to preserve life.
45: 7 God s me before you to preserve for you a remnant
45: 8 So it was not you who s me here, but God;
45:23 To his father he s the following:
45:24 Then he s his brothers on their way,
45:27 he saw the wagons that Joseph had s to carry him,
46: 5 in the wagons that Pharaoh had s to carry him.
46:28 Israel s Judah ahead to Joseph to lead the way
Ex 2: 5 among the reeds and s her maid to bring it.
3:12 this shall be the sign for you that it is I who s you:
3:13 'The God of your ancestors has s me to you,'
3:14 'I AM has s me to you.' "
3:15 and the God of Jacob, has s me to you':
4:28 the words of the LORD with which he had s him,
7:16 the God of the Hebrews, s me to you to say,
9:23 and the LORD s thunder and hail,
15: 7 you s out your fury, it consumed them like stubble.
18: 2 After Moses had s away his wife Zipporah,
18: 6 He s word to Moses, "I, your father-in-law Jethro,
24: 5 He s young men of the people of Israel,
32:35 Then the LORD s a plague on the people,
Lev 10: 6 may mourn the burning that the LORD has s.
16:10 it may be s away into the wilderness to Azazel.
Nu 13: 3 So Moses s them from the wilderness of Paran,
13:16 These were the names of the men whom Moses s
13:17 Moses s them to spy out the land of Canaan,
13:27 "We came to the land to which you s us;
14:36 And the men whom Moses s to spy out the land,
16:12 Moses s for Dathan and Abiram sons of Eliab;
16:28 that the LORD has s me to do all these works;
16:29 then the LORD has not s me.
20:14 Moses s messengers from Kadesh to the king
20:16 and s an angel and brought us out of Egypt;
21: 6 LORD s poisonous serpents among the people,
21:21 Israel s messengers to King Sihon of the Amorites,
21:32 Moses s to spy out Jazer;
22: 5 He s messengers to Balaam son of Beor at Pethor,
22:10 of Zippor of Moab, has s me this message:
22:15 Once again Balak s officials,
22:40 and s them to Balaam and to the officials
24:12 "Did I not tell your messengers whom you s to me,
31: 6 Moses s them to the war,
32: 8 when I s them from Kadesh-barnea to see the land.
Dt 2:26 So I s messengers from the wilderness
9:23 And when the LORD s you from Kadesh-barnea,
24: 4 who s her away, is not permitted to take her again

Dt 34:11 the LORD s him to perform in the land of Egypt,
Jos 2: 1 of Nun s two men secretly from Shittim as spies,
2: 3 Then the king of Jericho s orders to Rahab,
2:21 She s them away and they departed.
6:17 because she hid the messengers we s.
6:25 the messengers whom Joshua s to spy out Jericho.
7: 2 Joshua s men from Jericho to Ai,
7:22 So Joshua s messengers, and they ran to the tent;
8: 3 and s them out by night
8: 9 So Joshua s them out;
10: 3 So King Adoni-zedek of Jerusalem s a message
10: 6 the Gibeonites s to Joshua at the camp in Gilgal,
11: 1 he s to King Jobab of Madon,
14: 7 of the LORD s me from Kadesh-barnea to spy out
14:11 as I was on the day that Moses s me;
22: 6 So Joshua blessed them and s them away,
22: 7 And when Joshua s them away to their tents
22:13 the Israelites s the priest Phinehas son of Eleazar
24: 5 Then I s Moses and Aaron,
24: 9 He s and invited Balaam son of Beor to curse you,
24:12 I s the hornet ahead of you,
24:28 So Joshua s the people away to their inheritances.
Jdg 1:23 The house of Joseph s out spies to Bethel
3:15 Israelites s tribute by him to King Eglon of Moab.
3:18 he s the people who carried the tribute
4: 6 She s and summoned Barak son of Abinoam
6: 8 the LORD s a prophet to the Israelites;
6:35 He s messengers throughout all Manasseh,
6:35 He also s messengers to Asher, Zebulun,
7: 8 he s all the rest of Israel back to their own tents,
7:24 Then Gideon s messengers throughout all
9:23 But God s an evil spirit between Abimelech and
9:31 He s messengers to Abimelech at Arumah, saying,
11:12 Then Jephthah s messengers to the king of
11:14 Once again Jephthah s messengers to the king of
11:17 Israel then s messengers to the king of Edom,
11:17 They also s to the king of Moab,
11:19 then s messengers to King Sihon of the Amorites,
11:28 not heed the message that Jephthah s him.
11:38 "Go," he said and s her away for two months.
13: 8 let the man of God whom you s come to us again
16:18 she s and called the lords of the Philistines, saying,
18: 2 So the Danites s five valiant men from
19:29 and s her throughout all the territory of Israel.
19:30 Then he commanded the men whom he s, saying,
20: 6 and s her throughout the whole extent
20:12 of Israel s men through all the tribe of Benjamin,
20:38 and the men in ambush was that when they s up
21:10 the congregation s twelve thousand soldiers there
21:13 Then the whole congregation s word to
1Sa 4: 4 So the people s to Shiloh,
5: 8 So they s and gathered together all the lords of
5:10 So they s the ark of the God of Israel to Ekron.
5:11 They s therefore and gathered together all
6:21 So they s messengers to the inhabitants
10:25 Then Samuel s all the people back to their homes.
11: 7 and cut them in pieces and s them throughout all
12: 8 to the LORD and the LORD s Moses and Aaron,
12:11 And the LORD s Jerubbaal and Barak,
12:18 and the LORD s thunder and rain that day;
13: 2 the rest of the people he s home to their tents.
15: 1 "The LORD s me to anoint you king
15:18 And the LORD s you on a mission, and said, 'Go,
15:20 on the mission on which the LORD s me,
16:12 He s and brought him in.
16:19 So Saul s messengers to Jesse, and said,
16:20 and a kid, and s them by his son David to Saul.
16:22 Saul s to Jesse, saying, "Let David remain
17:31 repeated them before Saul; and he s for him.
18: 5 and was successful wherever Saul s him;
19:11 Saul s messengers to David's house to keep watch
19:14 When Saul s messengers to take David, she said,
19:15 Saul s the messengers to see David for themselves.
19:20 Then Saul s messengers to take David.
19:21 When Saul was told, he s other messengers,
19:21 Saul s messengers again the third time,
20:22 for the LORD has s you away.
22:11 The king s for the priest Ahimelech son of Ahitub
24:19 and s the enemy safely away?
25: 5 So David s ten young men;
25:14 "David s messengers out of the wilderness
25:25 not see the young men of my lord, whom you s.
25:32 the God of Israel, who s you to meet me today!
25:39 David s and wooed Abigail, to make her his wife.
25:40 "David has s us to you to take you to him
26: 4 David s out spies, and learned
30:26 he s part of the spoil to his friends,
31: 9 and s messengers throughout the land of
2Sa 2: 5 David s messengers to the people of Jabesh-gilead,
3:12 Abner s messengers to David at Hebron, saying,
3:14 Then David s messengers to Saul's son Ishbaal,
3:15 Ishbaal s and took her from her husband Paltiel
3:17 Abner s word to the elders of Israel, saying,
3:26 he s messengers after Abner,
5:11 King Hiram of Tyre s messengers to David,
8:10 Toi s his son Joram to King David,
9: 5 Then King David s and brought him from
10: 2 So David s envoys to console him
10: 3 because he has s messengers with condolences
10: 3 not David s his envoys to you to search the city,
10: 4 in the middle at their hips, and s them away.
10: 5 When David was told, he s to meet them,
10: 6 the Ammonites s and hired the Arameans
10: 7 he s Joab and all the army with the warriors.
10:16 Hadadezer s and brought out
11: 1 David s Joab with his officers and all Israel
11: 3 David s someone to inquire about the woman.
2Sa 11: 4 So David s messengers to get her,
11: 5 and she s and told David, "I am pregnant."
11: 6 David s word to Joab, "Send me Uriah the Hittite."
11: 6 And Joab s Uriah to David.
11:14 and s it by the hand of Uriah.
11:18 Then Joab s and told David all the news about
11:22 came and told David all that Joab had s him to tell.
11:27 David s and brought her to his house,
12: 1 and the LORD s Nathan to David.
12:25 and s a message by the prophet Nathan;
12:27 Joab s messengers to David, and said,
12:31 or s them to the brickworks.
13: 7 Then David s home to Tamar, saying,
14: 2 Joab s to Tekoa and brought from there
14:29 Then Absalom s for Joab to send him to the king;
14:29 He s a second time, but Joab would not come.
14:32 Absalom answered Joab, "Look, I s word to you:
15:10 But Absalom s secret messengers throughout all
15:12 he s for Ahithophel the Gilonite,
18:29 Ahimaaz answered, "When Joab s your servant,
19:11 King David s this message to the priests Zadok
19:14 and they s word to the king, "Return,
22:15 He s out arrows, and scattered them—lightning,
24:13 answer I shall return to the one who s me."
24:15 So the LORD s a pestilence on Israel from
1Ki 1:44 the king has s with him the priest Zadok,
1:53 Then King Solomon s to have him brought down
2:25 So King Solomon s Benaiah son of Jehoiada;
2:29 Solomon s Benaiah son of Jehoiada, saying, "Go,
2:36 Then the king s and summoned Shimei,
2:42 the king s and summoned Shimei,
5: 1 King Hiram of Tyre s his servants to Solomon,
5: 2 Solomon s word to Hiram, saying,
5: 8 Hiram s word to Solomon,
5: 8 "I have heard the message that you have s to me;
5:14 He s them to the Lebanon,
8:66 On the eighth day he s the people away;
9:14 Hiram had s to the king one hundred twenty talents
9:27 Hiram s his servants with the fleet,
12: 3 And they s and called him;
12:18 When King Rehoboam s Adoram,
12:20 they s and called him to the assembly
15:18 King Asa s them to King Ben-hadad son
15:20 and s the commanders of his armies against
18:10 to which my lord has not s to seek you;
18:20 So Ahab s to all the Israelites,
19: 2 Then Jezebel s a messenger to Elijah, saying,
20: 2 Then he s messengers into the city to King Ahab
20: 5 I s to you, saying, 'Deliver to me your silver
20: 7 for he s to me for my wives, my children,
20:10 Ben-hadad s to him and said,
20:17 Ben-hadad had s out scouts,
21: 8 she s the letters to the elders and
21:11 did as Jezebel had s word to them.
21:11 Just as it was written in the letters that she had s
21:14 Then they s to Jezebel, saying,
2Ki 1: 2 so he s messengers, telling them, "Go,
1: 6 'Go back to the king who s you, and say to him:
1: 9 king s to him a captain of fifty with his fifty men.
1:11 Again the king s to him another captain of fifty
1:13 the king s the captain of a third fifty with his fifty.
1:16 you have s messengers to inquire of Baal-zebub,
2: 2 for the LORD has s me as far as Bethel."
2: 4 for the LORD has s me to Jericho."
2: 6 for the LORD has s me to the Jordan."
2:17 So they s fifty men who searched for three days
3: 7 he went he s word to King Jehoshaphat of Judah,
5: 6 know that I have s to you my servant Naaman,
5: 8 he s a message to the king,
5:10 Elisha s a messenger to him, saying, "Go,
5:22 He replied, "Yes, but my master has s me to say,
6: 9 But the man of God s word to the king of Israel,
6:10 The king of Israel s word to the place of which
6:14 So he s horses and chariots there and a great army;
6:23 after they ate and drank, he s them on their way,
6:32 "Are you aware that this murderer has s someone
7:14 and the king s them after the Aramean army,
8: 9 "Your son King Ben-hadad of Aram has s me
9:19 Then he s out a second horseman,
10: 1 So Jehu wrote letters and s them to Samaria,
10: 5 with the elders and the guardians, s word to Jehu:
10: 7 they put their heads in baskets and s them to him
10:21 Jehu s word throughout all Israel;
12:18 and s these to King Hazael of Aram.
14: 8 Then Amaziah s messengers to King Jehoash son
14: 9 King Jehoash of Israel s word to King Amaziah
14: 9 thornbush on Lebanon s to a cedar on Lebanon,
14:19 they s after him to Lachish, and killed him there.
16: 7 Ahaz s messengers to King Tiglath-pileser
16: 8 and s a present to the king of Assyria.
16:10 King Ahaz s to the priest Uriah a model of
16:11 with all that King Ahaz had s from Damascus,
17: 4 for he had s messengers to King So of Egypt,
17:13 and that I s to you by my servants the prophets."
17:25 therefore the LORD s lions among them,
17:26 therefore he has s lions among them;
18:14 King Hezekiah of Judah s to the king of Assyria
18:17 The king of Assyria s the Tartan, the Rabsaris,
18:27 "Has my master s me to speak these words
19: 2 And he s Eliakim, who was in charge of
19: 4 the king of Assyria has s to mock the living God,
19: 9 he s messengers again to Hezekiah, saying,
19:16 which he has s to mock the living God.
19:20 Then Isaiah son of Amoz s to Hezekiah, saying,
20:12 of Baladan of Babylon s envoys with letters and
22: 3 the king s Shaphan son of Azaliah,
22:15 Tell the man who s you to me,
2Ki 22:18 who s you to inquire of the LORD,
23:16 and he s and took the bones out of the tombs,
24: 2 The LORD s against him bands of the Chaldeans,
24: 2 he s them against Judah to destroy it,
1Ch 6:15 when the LORD s Judah and Jerusalem into exile
8: 8 after he had s away his wives Hushim and Baara.
10: 9 and s messengers throughout the land of
12:19 of the Philistines took counsel and s him away,
14: 1 King Hiram of Tyre s messengers to David,
18:10 he s his son Hadoram to King David,
18:10 He s all sorts of articles of gold, of silver,
19: 2 So David s messengers to console him
19: 3 because David has s consolers to you,
19: 4 in the middle at their hips, and s them away;
19: 5 about the men, he s messengers to them,
19: 6 and the Ammonites s a thousand talents of silver
19: 8 he s Joab and all the army of the warriors.
19:16 they s messengers and brought out
21:12 answer I shall return to the one who s me."
21:14 So the LORD s a pestilence on Israel;
21:15 And God s an angel to Jerusalem to destroy it;
2Ch 2: 3 Solomon s word to King Huram of Tyre:
2: 3 and s him cedar to build himself a house to live in.
2:11 of Tyre answered in a letter that he s to Solomon,
7:10 On the twenty-third day of the seventh month he s
8:18 Huram s him, in the care of his servants,
10: 3 They s and called him;
10:18 When King Rehoboam s Hadoram,
13:13 Jeroboam had s an ambush around to come
16: 2 and s them to King Ben-hadad of Aram,
16: 4 and s the commanders of his armies against
17: 7 In the third year of his reign he s his officials,
24:19 Yet he s prophets among them to bring them back
24:23 s all the booty they took to the king of Damascus.
25:13 But the men of the army whom Amaziah s back,
25:15 The LORD was angry with Amaziah and s to him
25:17 Then King Amaziah of Judah took counsel and s
25:18 King Joash of Israel s word to King Amaziah
25:18 thornbush on Lebanon s to a cedar on Lebanon,
25:27 they s after him to Lachish, and killed him there.
28:16 At that time King Ahaz s to the king of Assyria
30: 1 Hezekiah s word to all Israel and Judah,
32: 9 he s his servants to Jerusalem to King Hezekiah
32:21 And the LORD s an angel who cut off all
32:31 who had been s to him to inquire about the sign
34: 8 he s Shaphan son of Azaliah,
34:22 So Hilkiah and those whom the king had s went to
34:23 Tell the man who s you to me,
34:26 who s you to inquire of the LORD,
34:29 Then the king s word and gathered together all
35:21 But Neco s envoys to him, saying,
36:10 the year King Nebuchadnezzar s and brought him
36:15 s persistently to them by his messengers,
36:22 that he s a herald throughout all his kingdom and
Ezr 1: 1 that he s a herald throughout all his kingdom,
4:11 this is a copy of the letter that they s):
4:17 The king s an answer: "To Rehum
4:18 that you s to us has been read in translation
5: 6 in the province Beyond the River s to King Darius;
5: 7 they s him a report, in which was written
6:13 Then, according to the word s by King Darius,
7:14 For you are s by the king and his seven counselors
8:16 Then I s for Eliezer, Ariel, Shemaiah, Elnathan,
8:17 and s them to Iddo, the leader at
10:44 and they s them away with their children.
Ne 2: 9 the king had s officers of the army and cavalry
6: 2 Sanballat and Geshem s to me,
6: 3 So I s messengers to them, saying,
6: 4 They s to me four times in this way,
6: 5 for the fifth time s his servant to me with
6: 8 Then I s to him, saying, "No such things
6:12 I perceived and saw that God had not s him at all,
6:17 in those days the nobles of Judah s many letters
6:19 And Tobiah s letters to intimidate me.
Est 1:22 he s letters to all the royal provinces,
3:13 Letters were s by couriers to all the king's
4: 4 she s garments to clothe Mordecai,
5:10 he s and called for his friends and his wife Zeresh,
8:10 and s them by mounted couriers riding
9:20 and s letters to all the Jews who were in all
9:30 Letters were s wishing peace and security to all
Job 22: 9 You have s widows away empty-handed,
Ps 18:14 And he s out his arrows, and scattered them;
78:25 he s them food in abundance.
78:45 He s among them swarms of flies,
80:11 it s out its branches to the sea,
105:17 he had s a man ahead of them,
105:20 The king s and released him;
105:26 He s his servant Moses,
105:28 He s darkness, and made the land dark;
106:15 but s a wasting disease among them.
107:20 he s out his word and healed them,
111: 9 He s redemption to his people;
135: 9 he s signs and wonders into your midst,
Pr 9: 3 She has s out her servant-girls,
17:11 but a cruel messenger will be s against them.
22:21 you may give a true answer to those who s you?
Isa 9: 8 Lord s a word against Jacob, and it fell on Israel;
20: 1 who was s by King Sargon of Assyria,
36: 2 The king of Assyria s the Rabshakeh from Lachish
36:12 "Has my master s me to speak these words
37: 2 And he s Eliakim, who was in charge of
37: 4 the king of Assyria has s to mock the living God,
37: 9 When he heard it, he s messengers to Hezekiah,
37:17 which he has s to mock the living God.
37:21 Then Isaiah son of Amoz s to Hezekiah, saying:
39: 1 of Baladan of Babylon s envoys with letters and

Isa 48:16 And now the Lord GOD has **s** me and his spirit.
55:11 and succeed in the thing for which I **s** it.
57: 9 you **s** your envoys far away,
57: 9 and **s** down even to Sheol.
61: 1 he has **s** me to bring good news to the oppressed,
Jer 3: 8 Israel, I had **s** her away with a decree of divorce;
7:25 I have persistently **s** all my servants the prophets
19:14 where the LORD had **s** him to prophesy,
21: 1 when King Zedekiah **s** to him Pashhur son
23:38 "the burden of the LORD," when I **s** to you,
24: 5 whom I have **s** away from this place to the land of
25: 4 the LORD persistently **s** you all his servants
25:17 the nations to whom the LORD **s** me drink it:
26:12 "It is the LORD who **s** me to prophesy
26:15 the LORD **s** me to you to speak all these words
26:22 Then King Jehoiakim **s** Elnathan son of Achbor
27:15 I have not **s** them, says the LORD,
28: 9 be known that the LORD has truly **s** the prophet."
28:15 "Listen, Hananiah, the LORD has not **s** you,
29: 1 the words of the letter that the prophet Jeremiah **s**
29: 3 The letter was **s** by the hand of Elasah son
29: 3 of Judah **s** to Babylon to King Nebuchadnezzar
29: 4 the exiles whom I have **s** into exile from Jerusalem
29: 7 But seek the welfare of the city where I have **s** you
29:14 to the place from which I **s** you into exile.
29:19 I persistently **s** to you my servants the prophets,
29:20 all you exiles whom I **s** away from Jerusalem
29:25 In your own name you **s** a letter to all
29:28 For he has actually **s** to us in Babylon, saying,
35:15 I have **s** to you all my servants the prophets,
36:14 the officials **s** Jehudi son of Nethaniah son
36:21 Then the king **s** Jehudi to get the scroll,
37: 3 King Zedekiah **s** Jehucal son of Shelemiah and
37: 7 who **s** you to me to inquire of me, Pharaoh's army,
37:17 Then King Zedekiah **s** for him, and received him.
38:14 King Zedekiah **s** for the prophet Jeremiah
39:13 and all the chief officers of the king of Babylon **s**
40:14 of the Ammonites has **s** Ishmael son of Nethaniah
42: 9 to whom you **s** me to present your plea
42:20 For you yourselves **s** me to the LORD your God,
42:21 of the LORD your God in anything that he **s** me
43: 1 with which the LORD their God had **s** him
44: 4 I persistently **s** to you all my servants the prophets,
49:14 and a messenger has been **s** among the nations:
La 1:13 From on high he **s** fire;
Eze 3: 5 For you are not **s** to a people of obscure speech
3: 6 Surely, if I **s** you to them, they would listen to you.
13: 6 when the LORD has not **s** them,
20:28 there they **s** up their pleasing odors,
23:16 and **s** messengers to them in Chaldea.
23:40 They even **s** for men to come from far away,
23:40 to whom a messenger was **s**, and they came.
39:28 the LORD their God because I **s** them into exile
Da 3: 2 Then King Nebuchadnezzar **s** for the satraps,
3:28 and Abednego, who has **s** his angel
5:24 the hand was **s** and this writing was inscribed.
6:22 My God **s** his angel and shut the lions' mouths so
10:11 Stand on your feet, for I have now been **s** to you."
11:31 Forces **s** by him shall occupy and profane
Hos 5:13 and **s** to the great king.
Joel 2:25 my great army, which I **s** against you.
Am 4:10 I **s** among you a pestilence after the manner
7:10 the priest of Bethel, **s** to King Jeroboam of Israel,
Ob 1: 1 and a messenger has been **s** among the nations:
Mic 6: 4 and I **s** before you Moses, Aaron, and Miriam.
Hag 1:12 as the LORD their God had **s** him;
Zec 1:10 "They are those whom the LORD has **s** to patrol
2: 8 (after his glory **s** me) regarding the nations
2: 9 you will know that the LORD of hosts has **s** me.
2:11 that the LORD of hosts has **s** me to you.
4: 9 that the LORD of hosts has **s** me to you.
5: 4 I have **s** it out, says the LORD of hosts,
6:15 that the LORD of hosts has **s** me to you.
7: 2 of Bethel had **s** Sharezer and Regem-melech
7:12 that the LORD of hosts had **s** by his spirit through
Mal 2: 4 Know, then, that I have **s** this command to you,
Mt 2: 8 Then he **s** them to Bethlehem, saying,
2:16 and he **s** and killed all the children in and
10: 5 These twelve Jesus **s** out with the following
10:40 welcomes me welcomes the one who **s** me.
11: 2 he **s** word by his disciples
14:10 he **s** and had John beheaded in the prison.
14:35 they **s** word throughout the region
15:24 "I was **s** only to the lost sheep of the house
20: 2 he **s** them into his vineyard.
21: 1 at the Mount of Olives, Jesus **s** two disciples,
21:34 he **s** his slaves to the tenants to collect his produce.
21:36 Again he **s** other slaves, more than the first;
21:37 Finally he **s** his son to them, saying,
22: 3 He **s** his slaves to call those who had been invited
22: 4 Again he **s** other slaves, saying,
22: 7 He **s** his troops, destroyed those murderers,
22:16 So they **s** their disciples to him,
23:37 that kills the prophets and stones those who are **s**
27:19 his wife **s** word to him,
Mk 1:43 After sternly warning him he **s** him away at once,
3:14 and to be **s** out to proclaim the message,
3:31 and standing outside, they **s** to him and called him.
6:17 For Herod himself had **s** men who arrested John,
6:27 Immediately the king **s** a soldier of the guard
8: 9 And he **s** them away.
8:26 Then he **s** him away to his home, saying,
9:37 not me but the one who **s** me."
11: 1 he **s** two of his disciples
12: 2 he **s** a slave to the tenants to collect
12: 3 and beat him, and **s** him away empty-handed.
12: 4 And again he **s** another slave to them;
Mk 12: 5 Then he **s** another, and that one they killed
12: 6 Finally he **s** him to them, saying,
12:13 Then they **s** to him some Pharisees
14:13 So he **s** two of his disciples, saying to them,
16: S ⟦And afterward Jesus himself **s** out through them,⟧
Lk 1:19 and I have been **s** to speak to you and
1:26 In the sixth month the angel Gabriel was **s** by God
1:53 and **s** the rich away empty.
4:18 He has **s** me to proclaim release to the captives
4:26 yet Elijah was **s** to none of them except to a widow
4:43 for I was **s** for this purpose."
7: 3 he **s** some Jewish elders to him,
7: 6 the centurion **s** friends to say to him, "Lord,
7:10 When those who had been **s** returned to the house,
7:19 and **s** them to the Lord to ask,
7:20 they said, "John the Baptist has **s** us to you to ask,
8:38 but Jesus **s** him away, saying,
9: 2 and he **s** them out to proclaim the kingdom of God
9:48 welcomes me welcomes the one who **s** me;
9:52 And he **s** messengers ahead of him.
10: 1 and **s** them on ahead of him in pairs to every town
10:16 and whoever rejects me rejects the one who **s** me."
13:34 that kills the prophets and stones those who are **s**
14: 4 Jesus took him and healed him, and **s** him away.
14:17 At the time for the dinner he **s** his slave to say
15:15 who **s** him to his fields to feed the pigs.
19:14 But the citizens of his country hated him and **s**
19:29 he **s** two of the disciples,
19:32 So those who were **s** departed and found it
20:10 he **s** a slave to the tenants in order
20:10 tenants beat him and **s** him away empty-handed.
20:11 Next he **s** another slave;
20:11 and insulted and **s** away empty-handed.
20:12 And he **s** still a third;
20:20 So they watched him and **s** spies who pretended to
22: 8 So Jesus **s** Peter and John, saying,
22:35 "When I **s** you out without a purse, bag,
23: 7 he **s** him off to Herod,
23:11 then he put an elegant robe on him, and **s** him back
23:15 Neither has Herod, for he **s** him back to us.
Jn 1: 6 There was a man **s** from God,
1:19 the Jews **s** priests and Levites from Jerusalem
1:22 Let us have an answer for those who **s** us.
1:24 Now they had been **s** from the Pharisees.
1:33 the one who **s** me to baptize with water said to me,
3:28 but I have been **s** ahead of him.'
3:34 He whom God has **s** speaks the words of God,
4:34 "My food is to do the will of him who **s** me and
4:38 I **s** you to reap that for which you did not labor.
5:23 the Son does not honor the Father who **s** him.
5:24 and believes him who **s** me has eternal life,
5:30 not my own will but the will of him who **s** me.
5:33 You **s** messengers to John,
5:36 testify on my behalf that the Father has **s** me.
5:37 And the Father who **s** me has himself testified
5:38 because you do not believe him whom he has **s.**
6:29 that you believe in him whom he has **s."**
6:38 but the will of him who **s** me.
6:39 And this is the will of him who **s** me,
6:44 to me unless drawn by the Father who **s** me;
6:57 Just as the living Father **s** me,
7:16 "My teaching is not mine but his who **s** me.
7:18 one who seeks the glory of him who **s** him is true,
7:28 one who **s** me is true, and you do not know him.
7:29 I know him, because I am from him, and he **s** me."
7:32 and the chief priests and Pharisees **s** temple police
7:33 and then I am going to him who **s** me.
8:16 but I and the Father who **s** me.
8:18 and the Father who **s** me testifies on my behalf."
8:26 but the one who **s** me is true,
8:29 And the one who **s** me is with me;
8:42 I did not come on my own, but he **s** me.
9: 4 the works of him who **s** me while it is day;
9: 7 wash in the pool of Siloam" (which means **S**).
10:36 and **s** into the world is blaspheming because I said,
11: 3 So the sisters **s** a message to Jesus, "Lord,
11:42 so that they may believe that you **s** me."
12:44 in me believes not in me but in him who **s** me.
12:45 And whoever sees me sees him who **s** me.
12:49 but the Father who **s** me has himself given me
13:16 are messengers greater than the one who **s** them.
13:20 and whoever receives me receives him who **s** me."
14:24 but is from the Father who **s** me.
15:21 because they do not know him who **s** me.
16: 5 But now I am going to him who **s** me;
17: 3 and Jesus Christ whom you have **s.**
17: 8 and they have believed that you **s** me.
17:18 As you have **s** me into the world,
17:18 so I have **s** them into the world.
17:21 so that the world may believe that you have **s** me.
17:23 so that the world may know that you have **s** me
17:25 and these know that you have **s** me.
18:24 Annas **s** him bound to Caiaphas the high priest.
20:21 As the Father has **s** me, so I send you."
Ac 3:26 God raised up his servant, he **s** him first to you,
5:21 and **s** to the prison to have them brought.
7:12 he **s** our ancestors there on their first visit.
7:14 Then Joseph **s** and invited his father Jacob
7:35 and whom God now **s** as both ruler and liberator
8:14 they **s** Peter and John to them.
9:17 has **s** me so that you may regain your sight and
9:30 they brought him down to Caesarea and **s** him off
9:38 **s** two men to him with the request,
10: 8 after telling them everything, he **s** them to Joppa.
10:17 suddenly the men **s** by Cornelius appeared.
10:20 without hesitation; for I have **s** them."
10:29 So when I was **s** for, I came without objection.
Ac 10:29 Now may I ask why you **s** for me?
10:33 Therefore I **s** for you immediately,
10:36 You know the message he **s** to the people of Israel,
11:11 **s** to me from Caesarea, arrived at the house
11:22 and they **s** Barnabas to Antioch.
12:11 that the Lord has **s** his angel and rescued me from
13: 3 they laid their hands on them and **s** them off.
13: 4 So, being **s** out by the Holy Spirit,
13:15 the officials of the synagogue **s** them a message,
13:26 to us the message of this salvation has been **s.**
15: 3 So they were **s** on their way by the church,
15:22 They **s** Judas called Barsabbas, and Silas,
15:27 We have therefore **s** Judas and Silas,
15:30 So they were **s** off and went down to Antioch.
15:33 they were **s** off in peace by the believers to those who had **s** them.
16:35 When morning came, the magistrates **s** the police,
16:36 saying, "The magistrates **s** word to let you go;
17:10 That very night the believers **s** Paul and Silas off
17:14 the believers immediately **s** Paul away to the coast,
19:22 So he **s** two of his helpers, Timothy and Erastus,
19:31 **s** him a message urging him not to venture into
20: 1 the uproar had ceased, Paul **s** for the disciples;
20:17 From Miletus he **s** a message to Ephesus,
21:25 we have **s** a letter with our judgment
23:30 I **s** him to you at once,
24:24 he **s** for Paul and heard him speak concerning faith
28:28 to you then that this salvation of God has been **s** to
Ro 10:15 how are they to proclaim him unless they are **s?**
15:24 For I do hope to see you on my journey and to be **s**
1Co 4:17 For this reason I **s** you Timothy,
2Co 2:17 persons **s** from God and standing in his presence.
12:17 of you through any of those whom I **s** to you?
12:18 I urged Titus to go, and **s** the brother with him.
Gal 1: 1 **s** neither by human commission nor
4: 4 the fullness of time had come, God **s** his Son,
4: 6 God has **s** the Spirit of his Son into our hearts,
Php 4:16 you **s** me help for my needs more than once.
4:18 I have received from Epaphroditus the gifts you **s,**
Col 4: 8 I have **s** him to you for this very purpose,
1Th 3: 2 and we **s** Timothy, our brother and co-worker
3: 5 I **s** to find out about your faith;
2Ti 4:12 I have **s** Tychicus to Ephesus.
Heb 1:14 **s** to serve for the sake of those who are
Jas 2:25 the messengers and **s** them out by another road?
1Pe 1:12 by the Holy Spirit **s** from heaven—
2:14 as **s** by him to punish those who do wrong and
1Jn 4: 9 God **s** his only Son into the world so
4:10 and **s** his Son to be the atoning sacrifice
4:14 the Father has **s** his Son as the Savior of the world.
Rev 5: 6 which are the seven spirits of God **s** out into all
22: 6 of the spirits of the prophets, has **s** his angel
22:16 who **s** my angel to you with this testimony for
Tob 2:12 when she cut off a piece she had woven and **s** it to
3:17 So Raphael was **s** to heal both of them:
5:18 "Why is it that you have **s** my child away?
8:13 they **s** the maid, lit a lamp, and opened the door;
12:14 I was **s** to you to test you.
12:14 And at the same time God **s** me to heal you
12:20 See, I am ascending to him who **s** me.
14: 4 by the prophets of Israel, whom God **s,**
Jdt 1: 7 **s** messengers to all who lived in Persia and
1:11 So they **s** back his messengers empty-handed and
3: 1 therefore **s** messengers to him to sue for peace
4: 4 So they **s** word to every district of Samaria,
7:18 and they **s** some of their men toward the south and
7:32 The women and children he **s** home.
8:10 she **s** her maid, who was in charge
11: 7 of him who has **s** you to direct every living being!
11:14 they have **s** messengers there in order
11:16 God has **s** me to accomplish with you things
11:19 it was announced to me, and I was **s** to tell you."
12: 6 and **s** this message to Holofernes:
14: 5 of Israel and **s** him to us as if to his death."
14:12 When the Assyrians saw them they **s** word
15: 4 Uzziah **s** men to Betomasthaim and Choba
16:14 You **s** forth your spirit, and it formed them;
AdE 1:15 for not obeying the order that the king had **s** her by
1:22 The king **s** the decree into all his kingdom,
3:13 Instructions were **s** by couriers throughout all
4: 4 and **s** some clothes to Mordecai to put on instead
6: 5 be **s** rescinding the letters that Haman wrote
8: 5 the letters that Haman wrote and **s** to destroy
8:10 and sealed with his ring, and **s** out by couriers.
9:20 and **s** it to the Jews in the kingdom of Artaxerxes
16:17 not to put in execution the letters **s** by Haman son
Wis 9:17 and **s** your holy spirit from on high?
11:15 you **s** upon them a multitude of irrational creatures
12: 8 and **s** wasps as forerunners of your army
12:25 you **s** your judgment to mock them.
16: 3 of appetite because of the odious creatures **s**
16:18 so that it might not consume the creatures **s** against
19: 2 to depart and hastily **s** them out,
Sir 15: 9 for it has not been **s** from the Lord.
28:23 It will be **s** out against them like a lion;
34: 6 they are **s** by intervention from the Most High,
48: 6 You **s** kings down to destruction, and famous men,
48:18 he **s** his commander and departed;
51: 9 And I **s** up my prayer from the earth,
Bar 1: 7 and **s** it to Jerusalem to the high priest
1:21 in all the words of the prophets whom he **s** to us,
2:20 For you have **s** your anger and your wrath upon us,
4:11 but I **s** them away with weeping and sorrow.
4:23 For I **s** you out with sorrow and weeping,
4:37 your children are coming, whom you **s** away;
LtJ 6: 1 of a letter that Jeremiah **s** to those who were to
6:60 and when **s** to do a service, they are obedient.

LtJ 6:63 And the fire s from above to consume mountains
Sus 1:21 and this was why you s your maids away."
1:30 So they s for her.
Bel 1:37 Take the food that God has s you."
1Mc 1:29 the king s to the cities of Judah a chief collector
1:44 And the king s letters by messengers to Jerusalem
3:27 he s and gathered all the forces of his kingdom,
3:39 and s with them forty thousand infantry
5:10 and s to Judas and his brothers a letter that said,
5:38 Judas s men to spy out the camp,
5:48 Judas s them this friendly message,
6:12 and I s to destroy the inhabitants of Judah
6:60 and he s to the Jews an offer of peace,
7: 9 He s him, and with him he sent
7: 9 and with him he s the ungodly Alcimus,
7:10 and he s messengers to Judas and his brothers
7:19 And he s and seized many of the men
7:26 Then the king s Nicanor, one of his honored
7:27 and treacherously s to Judas
8:10 and they s a general against the Greeks
8:17 and s them to Rome to establish friendship
8:20 of the Jews have s us to you to establish alliance
8:22 and s to Jerusalem to remain with them there as
9: 1 he s Bacchides and Alcimus into the land of Judah
9:35 So Jonathan s his brother as leader of
9:60 and secretly s letters to all his allies in Judea,
9:63 and s orders to the men of Judea.
9:70 he s ambassadors to him to make peace with him
10: 3 Demetrius s Jonathan a letter in peaceable words
10:15 the promises that Demetrius had s to Jonathan,
10:17 And he wrote a letter and s it to him,
10:20 He also s him a purple robe and a golden crown.
10:25 So he s a message to them in the following words:
10:51 Then Alexander s ambassadors to Ptolemy king
10:69 Then he s the following message to the high priest
10:89 and he s to him a golden buckle,
11: 9 He s envoys to King Demetrius, saying, "Come,
11:17 the Arab cut off the head of Alexander and s it
11:41 Now Jonathan s to King Demetrius the request
11:42 And Demetrius s this message back to Jonathan:
11:44 So Jonathan s three thousand stalwart men to him
11:58 He also s him gold plate and a table service,
11:62 of their rulers as hostages and s them to Jerusalem.
12: 1 he chose men and s them to Rome to confirm
12: 2 also s letters to the same effect to the Spartans and
12: 3 and the Jewish nation have s us to renew
12: 7 in time past a letter was s to the high priest Onias
12:10 since you s your letter to us.
12:16 and have s them to Rome
12:19 This is a copy of the letter that they s to Onias:
12:26 He s spies to their camp,
12:34 the stronghold to those whom Demetrius had **s.**
12:46 he s away the troops, and they returned to the land
12:49 Then Trypho s troops and cavalry into Galilee and
13:11 He s Jonathan son of Absalom to Joppa,
13:14 so he s envoys to him and said,
13:17 but he s to get the money and the sons,
13:19 So he s the sons and the hundred talents,
13:25 Simon s and took the bones
13:34 and s them to King Demetrius with a request
13:35 King Demetrius s him a favorable reply
13:37 the gold crown and the palm branch that you **s,**
14: 2 he s one of his generals to take him alive.
14:20 This is a copy of the letter that the Spartans **s:**
14:21 The envoys who were s to our people have told us
14:23 And they have s a copy of this to
14:24 After this Simon s Numenius to Rome with
15: 1 s a letter from the islands of the sea to Simon,
15:17 They had been s by the high priest Simon and by
15:24 They also s a copy of these things to
15:26 Simon s to Antiochus two thousand picked troops,
15:28 He s to him Athenobius, one of his Friends,
16:18 a report about these things and s it to the king,
16:19 He s other troops to Gazara to do away with John;
16:19 he s letters to the captains asking them to come
16:20 and he s other troops to take possession
16:21 and that "he has s men to kill you also."
2Mc 1:20 s the descendants of the priests who had hidden
3: 7 and s him with commands to effect the removal of
4:19 the vile Jason s envoys, chosen
4:21 of Menestheus was s to Egypt for the coronation
4:23 After a period of three years Jason s Menelaus,
4:44 three men s by the senate presented the case
5:18 whom King Seleucus s to inspect the treasury.
5:24 Antiochus s Apollonius, the captain of
6: 1 the king s an Athenian senator to compel the Jews
8: 9 one of the king's chief Friends, and s him,
8:11 So he immediately s to the towns on the seacoast,
11:13 on their side. So he s to them
11:17 John and Absalom, who were s by you,
11:32 And I have also s Menelaus to encourage you.
11:34 The Romans also s them a letter, which read thus:
12:21 he s off the women and the children and also
12:43 and s it to Jerusalem to provide for a sin offering.
13:20 Judas s in to the garrison whatever was necessary.
14:12 appointed him governor of Judea, and s him off
14:19 Therefore he s Posidonius, Theodotus,
14:39 s more than five hundred soldiers to arrest him;
15:22 you s your angel in the time of King Hezekiah
15:31 he s for those who were in the citadel.
1Es 1:26 And the king of Egypt s word to him saying,
1:27 I was not s against you by the Lord God,
1:45 A year later Nebuchadnezzar s and removed him
1:50 The God of their ancestors s his messenger
2:26 "I have read the letter that you s me.
3:14 Then he s and summoned all the nobles of Persia
4:57 And he s back from Babylon all the vessels
1Es 4:57 he also commanded to be done and to be s
5: 2 And Darius s with them a thousand cavalry
6: 6 be s to Darius concerning them and a report made.
6: 7 the local rulers in Syria and Phoenicia, wrote and s
8:43 I s word to Eliezar, Iduel, Maasmas,
Pm 151: 4 It was he who s his messenger and took me
3Mc 1: 8 the Jews had s some of their council and elders
4: 4 a harsh and ruthless spirit were they being s off,
5:11 But the Lord s upon the king a portion of sleep,
2Es 1:32 I s you my servants the prophets,
4: 1 Then the angel that had been s to me,
4: 3 "I have been s to show you three ways,
4:52 but I was not s to tell you concerning your life,
5:31 to me on a previous night was s to me.
6:33 Therefore he s me to show you all these things,
7: 1 the angel who had been s to me on the former nights was s to me again.
13:10 how he s forth from his mouth something like
14: 4 and I s him and led my people out of Egypt;
15:50 like a flower when the heat shall rise that is s
16: 3 The sword has been s upon you,
16: 4 A fire has been s upon you,
16: 5 Calamities have been s upon you,
16:14 Calamities are s forth and shall not return
16:16 so the calamities that are s upon the earth shall
16:19 and anguish are s as scourges for the correction
4Mc 12: 6 he s for the boy's mother to show compassion

SENTENCE (25) [SENTENCED]

Nu 35:19 the avenger of blood shall execute the **s.**
Dt 17: 6 or three witnesses the death s shall be executed;
19: 6 although a death s was not deserved,
1Sa 24:15 and give s between me and you.
1Ki 2:38 And Shimei said to the king, "The s is fair;
2:42 And you said to me, 'The s is fair; I accept.'
2Ki 25: 6 up to the king of Babylon at Riblah, who passed s
Ps 51: 4 in your s and blameless when you pass judgment.
Ecc 8:11 s against an evil deed is not executed speedily,
Jer 26:11 the s of death because he has prophesied
26:16 "This man does not deserve the s of death,
39: 5 and he passed s on him.
52: 9 and he passed s on him.
Da 4:17 The s is rendered by decree of the watchers,
4:33 the s was fulfilled against Nebuchadnezzar.
Lk 23:22 I have found in him no ground for the s of death;
23:40 since you are under the same s of condemnation?
Ac 13:28 Even though they found no cause for a s of death,
24:21 unless it was this one s that I called out
25:15 the Jews informed me about him and asked for a s
Ro 9:28 for the Lord will execute his s on the earth quickly
2Co 1: 9 we felt that we had received the s of death so
Sir 41: 2 how welcome is your s to one who is needy
LtJ 6:18 as though under s of death,
Sus 1:55 for the angel of God has received the s from God

SENTENCED (3) [SENTENCE]

Mt 23:33 How can you escape being s to hell?
1Co 4: 9 as though s to death, because we have become
2Mc 4:47 while he s to death those unfortunate men,

SENTINEL (18) [SENTINEL'S, SENTINELS]

2Sa 18:24 The s went up to the roof of the gate by the wall,
18:25 The s shouted and told the king.
18:26 Then the s saw another man running;
18:26 and the s called to the gatekeeper and said, "See,
18:27 The s said, "I think the running of the first one is
2Ki 9:17 the s standing on the tower spied the company
9:18 The s reported, saying, "The messenger reached
9:20 Again the s reported, "He reached them,
Isa 21:11 **"S,** what of the night? **S,** what of the night?"
21:12 The s says: "Morning comes, and also the night.
Jer 37:13 a s there named Irijah son of Shelemiah son
Eze 3:17 I have made you a s for the house of Israel;
33: 2 of the land take one of their number as their **s;**
33: 3 and if the s sees the sword coming upon the land
33: 6 if the s sees the sword coming and does not blow
33: 7 mortal, I have made a s for the house of Israel;
Hos 9: 8 The prophet is a s for my God over Ephraim,

SENTINEL'S (1) [SENTINEL]

Eze 33: 6 but their blood I will require at the s hand.

SENTINELS (13) [SENTINEL]

Job 27:18 like booths made by s of the vineyard.
SS 3: 3 The s found me, as they went about in the city.
5: 7 Making their rounds in the city the s found me;
5: 7 they took away my mantle, those s of the walls.
Isa 52: 8 Your s lift up their voices,
56:10 Israel's s are blind, they are all
62: 6 Upon your walls, O Jerusalem, I have posted **s;**
Jer 6:17 Also I raised up s for you:
31: 6 when s will call in the hill country of Ephraim:
51:12 post **s;** prepare the ambushes;
Mic 7: 4 The day of their s, of their punishment, has come;
Sir 37:14 keeps us better informed than seven s sitting high
4Mc 3:13 Eluding the s at the gates,

SENTRIES (1)

Jdt 13:11 a distance Judith called out to the s at the gates,

SENUAH (KJV) See HASSENUAH

SEORIM (1)

1Ch 24: 8 the third to Harim, the fourth to **S,**

SEPARATE (37) [SEPARATED, SEPARATELY, SEPARATENESS, SEPARATES, SEPARATION]

Ge 1: 6 and let it s the waters from the waters."
1:14 in the dome of the sky to s the day from the night;
1:18 and to s the light from the darkness.
13: 9 the whole land before you? **S** yourself from me.
Ex 26:24 be s beneath, but joined at the top, at the first ring;
26:33 and the curtain shall s for you the holy place from
36:29 They were s beneath, but joined at the top,
Lev 15:31 the people of Israel s from their uncleanness,
Nu 4: 2 of the Kohathites s from the other Levites,
6: 2 to s themselves to the LORD,
6: 3 they shall s themselves from wine
6: 5 the time is completed for which they s themselves
6: 6 that they s themselves to the LORD they shall
6:12 and s themselves to the LORD for their days
8:14 Thus you shall s the Levites from among
16:21 **S** yourselves from this congregation,
2Ki 15: 5 and lived in a s house.
2Ch 26:21 and being leprous lived in a s house,
Ezr 10:11 s yourselves from the peoples of the land and from
Isa 56: 3 "The LORD will surely s me from his people";
Eze 14: 7 who s themselves from me,
Mt 13:49 The angels will come out and s the evil from
19: 6 what God has joined together, let no one **s."**
25:32 and he will s people one from another as
Mk 10: 9 what God has joined together, let no one **s."**
Ro 8:35 Who will s us from the love of Christ?
8:39 will be able to s us from the love of God
1Co 7:10 that the wife should not s from her husband
7:11 (but if she does **s,** let her remain unmarried or else
2Co 6:17 come out from them, and be s from them,
Gal 2:12 he drew back and kept himself s for fear of
Wis 1: 3 For perverse thoughts s people from God,
Sir 25:26 she does not go as you direct, s her from yourself.
Sus 1:51 Daniel said to them, **"S** them far from each other,
1Mc 12:36 between the citadel and the city to s it from
1Es 9: 9 s yourselves from the peoples of the land and
2Es 6:41 and commanded it to divide and s the waters,

SEPARATED[‡] (33) [SEPARATE]

Ge 1: 4 and God s the light from the darkness.
1: 7 So God made the dome and s the waters that were
13:11 thus they s from each other.
13:14 LORD said to Abram, after Lot had s from him,
30:40 Jacob s the lambs, and set the faces of the flocks
Lev 20:24 I have s you from the peoples.
20:26 I have s you from the other peoples to be mine.
Nu 16: 9 of Israel has s you from the congregation of Israel,
31:42 which Moses s from that of the troops,
Jdg 4:11 Heber the Kenite had s from the other Kenites,
1Ki 8:53 For you have s them from among all the peoples
2Ki 2:11 chariot of fire and horses of fire s the two of them,
Ezr 6:21 and s themselves from the pollutions of the nations
9: 1 the Levites have not s themselves from the peoples
Ne 4:19 and we are s far from one another on the wall.
9: 2 Then those of Israelite descent s themselves
10:28 and all who have s themselves from the peoples of
13: 3 they s from Israel all those of foreign descent.
Est 3: 8 a certain people scattered and s among the peoples
Job 41:17 they clasp each other and cannot be **s.**
1Th 2:17 we were made orphans by being s from you—
2Th 1: 9 s from the presence of the Lord and from the glory
Phm 1:15 Perhaps this is the reason he was s from you for a
Heb 7:26 s from sinners, and exalted above the heavens.
Sus 1:52 When they were s from each other,
1Mc 1:11 since we s from them many disasters have come
1Es 7:13 all those who had s themselves from
3Mc 2:33 they abhorred those who s themselves from them,
2Es 4: 9 and from which you cannot be **s,**
6:50 And you s one from the other,
7:88 when they shall be s from their mortal body.
7:*100* after they have been s from the bodies,
11:24 As I kept looking I saw that two little wings s from

SEPARATELY (1) [SEPARATE]

4Mc 15:12 But each child s and all of them together

SEPARATENESS (1) [SEPARATE]

3Mc 3: 4 they kept their s with respect to foods.

SEPARATES (3) [SEPARATE]

Pr 16:28 and a whisperer s close friends.
Mt 25:32 from another as a shepherd s the sheep from
1Co 7:15 But if the unbelieving partner **s,** let it be so;

SEPARATING See Index to Footnotes

SEPARATION (2) [SEPARATE]

Eze 42:20 to make a s between the holy and the common.
2Mc 14: 3 but had willfully defiled himself in the times of **s,**

SEPHAR (1)

Ge 10:30 from Mesha in the direction of **S,**

SEPHARAD (1)

Ob 1:20 of Jerusalem who are in S shall possess the towns

SEPHARVAIM (0) [SEPHARVITES]

2Ki 17:24 Cuthah, Avva, Hamath, and S,
17:31 to Adrammelech and Anammelech, the gods of S.
18:34 Where are the gods of S, Hena, and Ivvah?
19:13 the king of Arpad, the king of the city of S,
Isa 36:19 Where are the gods of S?
37:13 the king of Arpad, the king of the city of S,

SEPHARVITES (1) [SEPHARVAIM]

2Ki 17:31 the S burned their children in the fire

SEPULCHRE[S] (KJV) See also BURIAL PLACE[S], GRAVE[S], TOMB[S]

SEPULCHRES (1)

2Mc 12:39 to bring them back to lie with their kindred in the s

SERAH (3)

Ge 46:17 Imnah, Ishvah, Ishvi, Beriah, and their sister S.
Nu 26:46 And the name of the daughter of Asher was S.
1Ch 7:30 Imnah, Ishvah, Ishvi, Beriah, and their sister S.

SERAIAH (24)

2Sa 8:17 of Abiathar were priests; S was secretary;
2Ki 25:18 The captain of the guard took the chief priest S,
25:23 S son of Tanhumeth the Netophathite,
1Ch 4:13 The sons of Kenaz: Othniel and S;
4:14 and S became the father of Joab father
4:35 Joel, Jehu son of Joshibiah son of S son of Asiel,
6:14 Azariah of S, S of Jehozadak;
Ezr 2:2 S, Reelaiah, Mordecai, Bilshan, Mispar, Bigvai,
7:1 Ezra son of S, son of Azariah, son of Hilkiah,
Ne 10:2 S, Azariah, Jeremiah,
11:11 S son of Hilkiah son of Meshullam son
12:1 of Shealtiel, and Jeshua: S,
12:12 of ancestral houses, were: of S, Meraiah;
Jer 36:26 and S son of Azriel and Shelemiah son of Abdeel
40:8 Johanan son of Kareah, S son of Tanhumeth,
51:59 that the prophet Jeremiah commanded S son
51:59 S was the quartermaster.
51:61 And Jeremiah said to S:
52:24 The captain of the guard took the chief priest S,
1Es 5:5 Jeshua son of Jozadak son of S and Joakim son
5:8 Nehemiah, S, Resaiah, Eneneus, Mordecai,
8:1 of S son of Azariah son of Hilkiah son of Shallum
2Es 1:1 of the prophet Ezra son of S son of Azariah son

SERAPH‡ (1) [SERAPHS]

Isa 6:7 The s touched my mouth with it and said:

SERAPHIM See Index to Footnotes

SERAPHIMS (KJV) See SERAPHS

SERAPHS (2) [SERAPH]

Isa 6:2 S were in attendance above him;
6:6 Then one of the s flew to me,

SERAR (1)

1Es 5:32 the descendants of Barkos, the descendants of S,

SERED (2) [SEREDITES]

Ge 46:14 The children of Zebulun: S, Elon, and Jahleel
Nu 26:26 of S, the clan of the Seredites;

SEREDITES (1) [SERED]

Nu 26:26 of Sered, the clan of the S;

SERENITY (1)

Sir 51:27 but little and found for myself much s.

SERGIUS (1)

Ac 13:7 He was with the proconsul, S Paulus,

SERIOUS (9) [SERIOUSLY, SERIOUSNESS]

Dt 15:21 any s defect, such as lameness or blindness—
Ac 18:14 "If it were a matter of crime or s villainy,
25:7 bringing many s charges against him,
1Ti 3:8 Deacons likewise must be s, not double-tongued,
3:11 Women likewise must be s, not slanderers,
Tit 2:2 Tell the older men to be temperate, s, prudent,
1Pe 4:7 therefore be s and discipline yourselves for
AdE 7:7 for he saw that he was in s trouble.
2Mc 4:4 that the rivalry was s and that Apollonius son

SERIOUSLY (4) [SERIOUS]

Dt 17:1 or a sheep that has a defect, anything s wrong;
1Sa 25:25 My lord, do not take s this ill-natured fellow,
4Mc 8:21 let us s consider that if we disobey we are dead!
8:27 of these things nor even s considered them.

SERIOUSNESS (1) [SERIOUS]

4Mc 5:20 in matters either small or great is of equal s,

SERJEANTS (KJV) See MAGISTRATES

SERON (2)

1Mc 3:13 When S, the commander of the Syrian army,
3:23 he rushed suddenly against S and his army,

SERPENT (26) [SEA-SERPENT, SERPENTS]

Ge 3:1 the s was more crafty than any other wild animal
3:2 The woman said to the s, "We may eat of the fruit
3:4 But the s said to the woman, "You will not die;
3:13 The woman said, "The s tricked me, and I ate."
3:14 The LORD God said to the s,
Nu 21:8 the LORD said to Moses, "Make a poisonous s,
21:9 Moses made a s of bronze, and put it upon a pole; and whenever a s bit someone, that person would look at the s of bronze and live.
2Ki 18:4 in pieces the bronze s that Moses had made,
Job 26:13 his hand pierced the fleeing s.
Ps 58:4 They have venom like the venom of a s,
91:13 young lion and the s you will trample under foot.
Pr 23:32 At the last it bites like a s, and stings like an adder.
Isa 14:29 and its fruit will be a flying fiery s.
27:1 Leviathan the fleeing s, Leviathan the twisting s,
30:6 of lioness and roaring lion, of viper and flying s,
65:25 but the s—its food shall be dust!
Jn 3:14 And just as Moses lifted up the s in the wilderness,
2Co 11:3 But I am afraid that as the s deceived Eve
Rev 12:9 The great dragon was thrown down, that ancient s,
12:14 so that she could fly from the s into the wilderness,
12:15 the s poured water like a river after the woman,
20:2 He seized the dragon, that ancient s,
4Mc 18:8 the deceitful s, defile the purity of my virginity.

SERPENTS (9) [SERPENT]

Nu 21:6 the LORD sent poisonous s among the people,
21:7 pray to the LORD to take away the s from us."
Dt 32:33 their wine is the poison of s,
Mt 10:16 so be wise as s and innocent as doves.
1Co 10:9 as some of them did, and were destroyed by s.
Rev 9:19 their tails are like s, having heads;
Wis 11:15 to worship irrational s and worthless animals,
16:5 the bites of writhing s, your wrath did not continue
16:10 not conquered even by the fangs of venomous s,

SERUG (6)

Ge 11:20 he became the father of S;
11:21 after the birth of S two hundred seven years,
11:22 When S had lived thirty years,
11:23 S lived after the birth of Nahor two hundred years,
1Ch 1:26 S, Nahor, Terah;
Lk 3:35 son of S, son of Reu, son of Peleg, son of Eber,

SERVANT‡ (479) [SERVANT'S, SERVANT-BOY, SERVANT-GIRL, SERVANT-GIRLS, SERVANTS, SERVANTS']

A. SERVANT DAVID (32)
B. MOSES THE SERVANT (23)
C. SERVANT OF THE †LORD (23)
D. SERVANT MOSES (16)
E. SERVANT JACOB (11)
F. SERVANT OF *GOD (8)

Ge 18:3 if I find favor with you, do not pass by your s.
18:5 since you have come to your s."
18:7 and gave it to the s, who hastened to prepare it.
19:19 your s has found favor with you,
24:2 Abraham said to his s, the oldest of his house,
24:5 The s said to him, "Perhaps the woman may not
24:9 So the s put his hand under the thigh
24:10 the s took ten of his master's camels and departed,
24:14 the one whom you have appointed for your s Isaac.
24:17 Then the s ran to meet her and said,
24:34 So he said, "I am Abraham's s.
24:52 When Abraham's s heard their words,
24:53 the s brought out jewelry of silver and of gold,
24:59 and her nurse along with Abraham's s
24:61 thus the s took Rebekah, and went his way.
24:65 to the s, "Who is the man over there, walking in
24:65 The s said, "It is my master."
24:66 the s told Isaac all the things that he had done.
26:24 for my s Abraham's sake."
32:4 says your s Jacob, 'I have lived with Laban E
32:10 the faithfulness that you have shown to your s,
32:18 you shall say, 'They belong to your s Jacob; E
32:20 'Moreover your s Jacob is behind us.' " E
33:5 children whom God has graciously given your s."
33:14 Let my lord pass on ahead of his s,
39:17 "The Hebrew s, whom you have brought
39:19 saying, "This is the way your s treated me,"
41:12 a s of the captain of the guard.
43:28 They said, "Your s our father is well;
44:18 let your s please speak a word in my lord's ears,
44:18 and do not be angry with your s;
44:24 to your s my father we told him the words
44:27 Then your s my father said to us,
44:30 when I come to your s my father and the boy is not
44:31 the gray hairs of your s our father with sorrow
44:32 For your s became surety for the boy to my father,
44:33 please let your s remain as a slave to my lord
Ex 4:10 past nor even now that you have spoken to your s;
12:45 no bound or hired s may eat of it.
14:31 and believed in the LORD and in his s Moses. D
Lev 22:10 No bound or hired s of the priest shall eat of
Nu 11:11 "Why have you treated your s so badly?
12:7 Not so with my s Moses; D
12:8 not afraid to speak against my s Moses?" D
14:24 But my s Caleb, because he has a different spirit
Dt 3:24 to show your s your greatness and your might;
34:5 Then Moses, the s of the LORD, BC
Jos 1:1 After the death of Moses the s of the LORD, BC
1:2 "My s Moses is dead. D
1:7 with all the law that my s Moses commanded D
1:13 that Moses the s of the LORD commanded you, BC
1:15 land that Moses the s of the LORD gave you BC
5:14 "What do you command your s, my lord?"
8:31 as Moses the s of the LORD had commanded BC
8:33 as Moses the s of the LORD had commanded at BC
9:24 LORD your God had commanded his s Moses D
11:12 as Moses the s of the LORD had commanded. BC
11:15 As the LORD had commanded his s Moses, D
12:6 Moses, the s of the LORD, BC
12:6 and Moses the s of the LORD gave their land BC
13:8 as Moses the s of the LORD gave them: BC
14:7 Moses the s of the LORD sent me BC
18:7 which Moses the s of the LORD gave them." BC
22:2 that Moses the s of the LORD commanded you, BC
22:4 which Moses the s of the LORD gave you BC
22:5 and instruction that Moses the s of the LORD BC
24:29 Joshua son of Nun, the s of the LORD, died, C
Jdg 2:8 Joshua son of Nun, the s of the LORD, died C
7:10 go down to the camp with your s Purah;
7:11 with his s Purah to the outposts of the armed men
15:18 this great victory by the hand of your s.
19:3 He had with him his s and a couple of donkeys.
19:9 man with his concubine and his s got up to leave,
19:11 the day was far spent, and the s said to his master,
19:13 Then he said to his s, "Come,
Ru 2:5 Then Boaz said to his s who was in charge of
2:6 The s who was in charge of the reapers answered,
2:13 and spoken kindly to your s,
3:9 And she answered, "I am Ruth, your s;
3:9 spread your cloak over your s,
1Sa 1:11 the misery of your s, and remember me, and not forget your s, but will give to your s a male child,
1:16 Do not regard your s as a worthless woman,
1:18 And she said, "Let your s find favor in your sight."
2:13 the priest's s would come,
2:15 the priest's s would come and say to
3:9 'Speak, LORD, for your s is listening.' "
3:10 And Samuel said, "Speak, for your s is listening."
14:41 why have you not answered your s today?
17:32 your s will go and fight with this Philistine."
17:34 "Your s used to keep sheep for his father;
17:36 Your s has killed both lions and bears;
17:58 "I am the son of your s Jesse the Bethlehemite."
19:4 "The king should not sin against his s David, A
20:7 it will be well with your s;
20:8 Therefore deal kindly with your s,
20:8 for you have brought your s into a sacred covenant
22:8 or discloses to me that my son has stirred up my s
22:15 to his s or to any member of my father's house;
22:15 for your s has known nothing of all this,
23:10 your s has heard that Saul seeks to come to Keilah,
23:11 now, will Saul come down as your s has heard?
23:11 the God of Israel, I beseech you, tell your s."
25:24 please let your s speak in your ears,
25:24 and hear the words of your s.
25:25 your s, did not see the young men of my lord,
25:27 And now let this present that your s has brought
25:28 Please forgive the trespass of your s;
25:31 with my lord, then remember your s."
25:39 and has kept back his s from evil;
25:41 "Your s is a slave to wash the feet of the servants
26:18 And he added, "Why does my lord pursue his s?
26:19 let my lord the king hear the words of his s.
27:5 why should your s live in the royal city with you?"
27:12 therefore he shall always be my s."
28:2 then you shall know what your s can do."
28:21 she said to him, "Your s has listened to you;
28:22 Now therefore, you also listen to your s;
29:3 "Is this not David, the s of King Saul of Israel,
29:8 in your s from the day I entered your service until
30:13 "I am a young man of Egypt, s to an Amalekite.
2Sa 3:18 Through my s David I will save my people Israel A
7:5 Go and tell my s David: A
7:8 Now therefore thus you shall say to my s David: A
7:20 For you know your s, O Lord GOD!
7:21 so that your s may know it.
7:25 the word that you have spoken concerning your s
7:26 the house of your s David will be established A
7:27 have made this revelation to your s, saying,
7:27 therefore your s has found courage
7:28 and you have promised this good thing to your s;
7:29 of your s, so that it may continue forever
7:29 and with your blessing shall the house of your s
9:2 a s of the house of Saul whose name was Ziba,
9:6 He answered, "I am your s."
9:8 He did obeisance and said, "What is your s,
9:9 Then the king summoned Saul's s Ziba,
9:11 to all that my lord the king commands his s,
9:11 the king commands his servant, so your s will do."
11:21 'Your s Uriah the Hittite is dead too.' "
11:24 and your s Uriah the Hittite is dead also."
13:18 So his s put her out, and bolted the door after her.
13:24 and said, "Your s has sheepshearers;
13:24 the king and his servants please go with your s?"
13:35 as your s said, so it has come about."
14:6 Your s had two sons, and they fought
14:7 Now the whole family has risen against your s.
14:12 "Please let your s speak a word to my lord

2Sa 14:15 your s thought, 'I will speak to the king;
14:15 be that the king will perform the request of his s.
14:16 and deliver his s from the hand of
14:17 Your s thought, 'The word of my lord
14:19 For it was your s Joab who commanded me;
14:19 these words into the mouth of your s.
14:20 to change the course of affairs your s Joab did this.
14:22 "Today your s knows that I have found favor
14:22 in that the king has granted the request of his s."
15: 2 "Your s is of such and such a tribe in Israel,"
15: 8 For your s made a vow while I lived at Geshur
15:21 there also your s will be."
15:34 'I will be your s, O king; as I have been your
father's s in time past, so now I will be your s,'
16: 1 Ziba the s of Mephibosheth met him,
18:29 Ahimaaz answered, "When Joab sent your s,
19:17 And Ziba, the s of the house of Saul,
19:19 how your s did wrong on the day my lord
19:20 For your s knows that I have sinned;
19:26 "My lord, O king, my s deceived me;
19:26 for your s said to him, 'Saddle a donkey for me,
19:26 For your s is lame.
19:27 He has slandered your s to my lord the king.
19:28 you set your s among those who eat at your table.
19:35 Can your s taste what he eats or what he drinks?
19:35 then should your s be an added burden to my lord
19:36 Your s will go a little way over the Jordan with
19:37 Please let your s return, so that I may die
19:37 But here is your s Chimham;
20:17 she said to him, "Listen to the words of your s."
24:10 I pray you, take away the guilt of your s;
24:21 "Why has my lord the king come to his s?"
1Ki 1:13 'Did you not, my lord the king, swear to your s,
1:17 you swore to your s by the LORD your God,
1:19 but your s Solomon he has not invited.
1:26 But he did not invite me, your s,
1:26 and Benaiah son of Jehoiada, and your s Solomon.
1:51 that he will not kill his s with the sword.' "
2:38 as my lord the king has said, so will your s do."
3: 6 to your s my father David, because he walked
3: 7 you have made your s king in place
3: 8 And your s is in the midst of the people
3: 9 Give your s therefore an understanding mind
3:20 from beside me while your s slept.
8:24 for your s my father David as you declared to him;
8:25 keep for your s my father David
8:26 which you promised to your s my father David.
8:28 heeding the cry and the prayer that your s prays
8:29 that you may heed the prayer that your s prays
8:30 of your s and of your people Israel when they pray
8:52 Let your eyes be open to the plea of your s,
8:53 just as you promised through Moses, your s,
8:56 which he spoke through his s Moses. D
8:59 and may he maintain the cause of his s and
8:66 that the LORD had shown to his s David and A
11:11 the kingdom from you and give it to your s.
11:13 of my s David and for the sake of Jerusalem, A
11:26 an Ephraimite of Zeredah, a s of Solomon,
11:32 of my s David and for the sake of Jerusalem, A
11:34 for the sake of my s David whom I chose A
11:36 so that my s David may always have a lamp A
11:38 as David my s did, I will be with you,
12: 7 be a s to this people today and serve them,
14: 8 yet you have not been like my s David, A
14:18 which he spoke by his s the prophet Ahijah.
15:29 that he spoke by his s Ahijah the Shilonite—
16: 9 But his s Zimri, commander of half his chariots,
18: 9 that you would hand your s over to Ahab,
18:12 I your s have revered the LORD from my youth.
18:36 that you are God in Israel, that I am your s, and
18:43 He said to his s, "Go up now,
19: 3 to Judah; he left his s there.
19:21 he set out and followed Elijah, and became his s.
20: 9 All that you first demanded of your s I will do;
20:32 "Your s Ben-hadad says, 'Please let me live.' "
20:39 "Your s went out into the thick of the battle;
20:40 your s was busy here and there, he was gone."
2Ki 4: 1 "Your s my husband is dead;
4: 1 and you know that your s feared the LORD,
4: 2 She answered, "Your s has nothing in the house,
4:12 He said to his s Gehazi,
4:16 of God; do not deceive your s."
4:19 The father said to his s, "Carry him to his mother."
4:24 Then she saddled the donkey and said to her s,
4:25 he said to Gehazi his s, "Look,
4:38 he said to his s, "Put the large pot on,
4:43 But his s said, "How can I set this before
5: 6 know that I have sent to you my s Naaman,
5:15 please accept a present from your s."
5:17 be given to your s; for your s will no longer offer
5:18 But may the LORD pardon your s on this one count:
5:18 may the LORD pardon your s on this one count."
5:20 the s of Elisha the man of God, thought,
5:25 "Your s has not gone anywhere at all."
6:15 His s said, "Alas, master!
6:17 the LORD opened the eyes of the s, and he saw;
8: 4 the king was talking with Gehazi the s of the man
8:13 Hazael said, "What is your s, who is a mere dog,
8:19 for the sake of his s David, A
9:36 which he spoke by his s Elijah the Tishbite,
10:10 LORD has done what he said through his s Elijah."
14:25 which he spoke by his s Jonah son of Amittai,
16: 7 saying, "I am your s and your son.
18:12 that Moses the s of the LORD had commanded; BC
19:34 my own sake and for the sake of my s David." A
20: 6 for my own sake and for my s David's sake."
21: 8 all the law that my s Moses commanded them." D
2Ki 22:12 Shaphan the secretary, and the king's s Asaiah,
24: 1 Jehoiakim became his s for three years;
25: 8 a s of the king of Babylon, came to Jerusalem.
1Ch 6:49 to all that Moses the s of God had commanded. BF
16:13 O offspring of his s Israel,
17: 4 Go and tell my s David: A
17: 7 therefore thus you shall say to my s David: A
17:18 for honoring your s? You know your s.
17:23 the word that you have spoken concerning your s
17:24 the house of your s David will be established A
17:25 have revealed to your s that you will build a house
17:25 your s has found it possible to pray before you.
17:26 and you have promised this good thing to your s;
17:27 may it please you to bless the house of your s,
21: 8 now, I pray you, take away the guilt of your s;
2Ch 1: 3 which Moses the s of the LORD had made BC
6:15 you who have kept for your s,
6:16 O LORD, God of Israel, keep for your s,
6:17 which you promised to your s David. A
6:19 heeding the cry and the prayer that your s prays
6:20 and may you heed the prayer that your s prays
6:21 hear the plea of your s and of your people Israel,
6:42 Remember your steadfast love for your s David. A
13: 6 a s of Solomon son of David,
24: 6 tax levied by Moses, the s of the LORD, BC
24: 9 the tax that Moses the s of God laid on Israel BF
32:16 the Lord GOD and against his s Hezekiah.
34:20 the secretary Shaphan, and the king's s Asaiah:
Ne 1: 6 the prayer of your s that I now pray before you
1: 7 ordinances that you commanded your s Moses. D
1: 8 the word that you commanded your s Moses, D
1:11 let your ear be attentive to the prayer of your s,
1:11 Give success to your s today,
2: 5 and if your s has found favor with you,
4:22 and his s pass the night inside Jerusalem,
6: 5 the same way Sanballat for the fifth time sent his s
9:14 and statutes and a law through your s Moses. D
10:29 which was given by Moses the s of God, BF
Job 1: 8 "Have you considered my s Job?
2: 3 "Have you considered my s Job?
19:16 I call to my s, but he gives me no answer;
41: 4 a covenant with you to be taken as your s forever?
42: 7 not spoken of me what is right, as my s Job has.
42: 8 and go to my s Job, and offer up for yourselves
42: 8 and my s Job shall pray for you,
42: 8 of me what is right, as my s Job has done."
Ps 18: T *A Psalm of David the s of the LORD,* C
19:11 Moreover by them is your s warned;
19:13 Keep back your s also from the insolent;
27: 9 Do not turn your s away in anger,
31:16 Let your face shine upon your s;
35:27 who delights in the welfare of his s."
36: T *To the leader. Of David, the s of the LORD.* C
69:17 Do not hide your face from your s,
78:70 He chose his s David, and took him from A
86: 2 save your s who trusts in you.
86: 4 Gladden the soul of your s, for to you, O Lord,
86:16 give your strength to your s;
89: 3 I have sworn to my s David: A
89:20 I have found my s David; A
89:39 You have renounced the covenant with your s;
89:50 Remember, O Lord, how your s is taunted;
105: 6 O offspring of his s Abraham,
105:26 He sent his s Moses, and Aaron whom he had D
105:42 remembered his holy promise, and Abraham, his s.
109:28 to shame; may your s be glad.
116:16 O LORD, I am your s; I am your s, the child of
119:17 Deal bountifully with your s,
119:23 your s will meditate on your statutes.
119:38 Confirm to your s your promise,
119:49 Remember your word to your s,
119:65 You have dealt well with your s, O LORD,
119:76 according to your promise to your s.
119:84 How long must your s endure?
119:124 Deal with your s according to your steadfast love,
119:125 I am your s; give me understanding,
119:135 Make your face shine upon your s,
119:140 Your promise is well tried, and your s loves it.
119:176 seek out your s, for I do
132:10 For your s David's sake do not turn away the face
136:22 a heritage to his s Israel,
143: 2 Do not enter into judgment with your s,
143:12 and destroy all my adversaries, for I am your s.
144:10 gives victory to kings, who rescues his s David. A
Pr 11:29 and the fool will be s to the wise.
12: 9 Better to be despised and have a s,
14:35 A s who deals wisely has the king's favor,
30:10 Do not slander a s to a master,
30:10 or the s will curse you, and you will be held guilty.
Ecc 7:21 or you may hear your s cursing you;
10:16 Alas for you, O land, when your king is a s,
Isa 20: 3 as my s Isaiah has walked naked and barefoot
22:20 that day I will call my s Eliakim son of Hilkiah,
37:35 my own sake and for the sake of my s David." A
41: 8 But you, Israel, my s, Jacob, whom I have chosen,
41: 9 saying to you, "You are my s,
42: 1 Here is my s, whom I uphold, my chosen,
42:19 Who is blind but my s,
42:19 or blind like the s of the LORD? C
43:10 says the LORD, and my s whom I have chosen,
44: 1 hear, O Jacob my s, Israel whom I have chosen!
44: 2 Do not fear, O Jacob my s,
44:21 O Jacob, and Israel, for you are my s;
44:21 I formed you, you are my s;
44:26 who confirms the word of his s, and fulfills
45: 4 the sake of my s Jacob, and Israel my chosen, E
48:20 say, "The LORD has redeemed his s Jacob!" E
Isa 49: 3 And he said to me, "You are my s, Israel,
49: 5 who formed me in the womb to be his s,
49: 6 "It is too light a thing that you should be my s
50:10 the LORD and obeys the voice of his s,
52:13 my s shall prosper; he shall be exalted
53:11 my s, shall make many righteous,
63:11 they remembered the days of old, of Moses his s.
Jer 2:14 Is he a homeborn s?
25: 9 even for King Nebuchadrezzar of Babylon, my s,
27: 6 my s, and I have given him even the wild animals
30: 8 and strangers shall no more make a s of him.
30:10 But as for you, have no fear, my s Jacob, E
33:21 only then could my covenant with my s David A
33:22 so I will increase the offspring of my s David, A
33:26 of Jacob and of my s David and not choose any A
43:10 and take my s King Nebuchadrezzar of Babylon,
46:27 But as for you, have no fear, my s Jacob, E
46:28 As for you, have no fear, my s Jacob, E
Eze 28:25 on their own soil that I gave to my s Jacob. E
34:23 set up over them one shepherd, my s David, A
34:24 and my s David shall be prince among them; A
37:24 My s David shall be king over them; A
37:25 to my s Jacob, in which your ancestors lived; E
37:25 and my s David shall be their prince forever. A
Da 6:20 "O Daniel, s of the living God,
9:11 of Moses, the s of God, have been poured out BF
9:17 to the prayer of your s and to his supplication,
10:17 How can my lord's s talk with my lord?
Hag 2:23 O Zerubbabel my s, son of Shealtiel,
Zec 3: 8 I am going to bring my s the Branch.
Mal 4: 4 Remember the teaching of my s Moses, D
Mt 8: 6 "Lord, my s is lying at home paralyzed,
8: 8 but only speak the word, and my s will be healed.
8:13 And the s was healed in that hour.
12:18 "Here is my s, whom I have chosen, my beloved,
20:26 to be great among you must be your s,
23:11 The greatest among you will be your s.
Mk 9:35 to be first must be last of all and s of all."
10:43 to become great among you must be your s,
Lk 1:38 Then Mary said, "Here am I, the s of the Lord;
1:48 he has looked with favor on the lowliness of his s.
1:54 He has helped his s Israel,
1:69 mighty savior for us in the house of his s David, A
2:29 now you are dismissing your s in peace,
7: 7 But only speak the word, and let my s be healed.
Jn 12:26 and where I am, there will my s be also.
15:15 the s does not know what the master is doing;
Ac 3:13 the God of our ancestors has glorified his s Jesus,
3:26 When God raised up his s, he sent him first to you,
4:25 the Holy Spirit through our ancestor David, your s:
4:27 gathered together against your holy s Jesus,
4:30 through the name of your holy s Jesus."
Ro 1: 1 Paul, a s of Jesus Christ, called to be an apostle,
13: 4 for it is God's s for your good.
13: 4 the s of God to execute wrath on the wrongdoer. F
15: 8 that Christ has become a s of the circumcised
Gal 1:10 I would not be a s of Christ.
2:17 is Christ then a s of sin?
Eph 3: 7 Of this gospel I have become a s according to
Col 1: 7 from Epaphras, our beloved fellow s.
1:23 I, Paul, became a s of this gospel.
1:25 I became its s according to God's commission
4: 7 a faithful minister, and a fellow s in the Lord.
4:12 Epaphras, who is one of you, a s of Christ Jesus,
1Ti 4: 6 you will be a good s of Christ Jesus,
2Ti 2:24 the Lord's s must not be quarrelsome but kindly
Tit 1: 1 Paul, a s of God and an apostle of Jesus Christ, F
Heb 3: 5 Now Moses was faithful in all God's house as a s,
Jas 1: 1 James, a s of God and of the Lord Jesus Christ, F
2Pe 1: 1 Simeon Peter, a s and apostle of Jesus Christ,
Jude 1: 1 Jude, a s of Jesus Christ and brother of James,
Rev 1: 1 by sending his angel to his s John,
15: 3 And they sing the song of Moses, the s of God, BF
19:10 a fellow s with you and your comrades who hold
22: 9 I am a fellow s with you and your comrades
Jdt 5: 5 to a report from the mouth of your s,
9:10 the slave with the prince and the prince with his s;
11: 5 and let your s speak in your presence.
11: 6 If you follow out the words of your s,
11:17 Your s is indeed God-fearing and serves the God
11:17 but every night your s will go out into the valley
12: 4 your s will not use up the supplies I have with me
12: 6 "Let my lord now give orders to allow your s
AdE 14:17 And your s has not eaten at Haman's table,
14:18 Your s has had no joy since the day
Wis 9: 5 For I am your s the son of your serving girl,
10:16 She entered the soul of a s of the Lord,
18:21 showing that he was your s.
Sir 10:25 Free citizens will serve a wise s,
23:10 for as a s who is constantly under scrutiny will
37:11 with a lazy s about a big task—
Bar 1:20 Lord declared through his s Moses at the time D
2:28 as you spoke by your s Moses on the day D
3:36 and gave her to his s Jacob and to Israel, E
Aza 1:12 the sake of your s Isaac and Israel your holy one,
1Mc 4:30 the mighty warrior by the hand of your s David, A
1Es 4:59 and yours is the glory. I am your s.
6:27 the s of the Lord and governor of Judea,
2Es 3:23 and you raised up for yourself a s, named David.
5:45 to your s that you will certainly give life
5:56 if I have found favor in your sight, show your s
6:12 show your s the last of your signs
7:75 O Lord, show this also to your s:
7:*102* show further to me, your s,
7:*104* or a master his s, or a friend his dearest friend,
8: 6 grant to your s that we may pray before you,
8:24 O Lord, the prayer of your s,

2Es 9:43 "Your s was barren and had no child,
9:45 And after thirty years God heard your s,
10:37 therefore I beg you to give your s an explanation
12: 8 and show me, your s, the interpretation
13:14 beginning you have shown your s these wonders,

SERVANT'S (8) [SERVANT]

Ge 19: 2 turn aside to your s house and spend the night,
2Sa 7:19 you have spoken also of your s house for a great
1Ki 8:28 Regard your s prayer and his plea,
1Ch 17:17 you have also spoken of your s house for a great
17:19 For your s sake, O LORD,
2Ch 6:19 Regard your s prayer and his plea,
Ps 119:122 Guarantee your s well-being;
Jdt 5: 5 No falsehood shall come from your s mouth.

SERVANT-BOY (1) [BOY, SERVANT]

1Sa 9:22 Then Samuel took Saul and his s and brought them

SERVANT-GIRL (6) [GIRL, SERVANT]

2Sa 17:17 a s used to go and tell them,
Mt 26:69 A s came to him and said,
26:71 When he went out to the porch, another s saw him,
Mk 14:69 And the s, on seeing him,
Lk 22:56 Then a s, seeing him in the firelight,
Sir 41:22 of meddling with his s—

SERVANT-GIRLS (4) [GIRL, SERVANT]

Pr 9: 3 She has sent out her s,
27:27 of your household and nourishment for your s.
31:15 for her household and tasks for her s.
Mk 14:66 one of the s of the high priest came by.

SERVANTS‡ (433) [SERVANT]

A. ALL ... SERVANTS (32)
B. TEMPLE SERVANTS (24)
C. SERVANTS THE PROPHETS (23)
D. KING'S SERVANTS (13)

Ge 14:15 he and his s, and routed them and pursued them
20: 8 called all his s and told them all these things; A
21:25 a well of water that Abimelech's s had seized,
26:15 with earth all the wells that his father's s had dug
26:19 when Isaac's s dug in the valley and found there
26:25 And there Isaac's s dug a well.
26:32 That same day Isaac's s came and told him about
27:37 and I have given him all his brothers as s,
32:16 These he delivered into the hand of his s,
32:16 and said to his s, "Pass on ahead of me,
40:20 he made a feast for all his s, A
40:20 and the head of the chief baker among his s.
41:10 Once Pharaoh was angry with his s,
41:37 The proposal pleased Pharaoh and all his s. A
41:38 Pharaoh said to his s, "Can we find anyone else
42:10 your s have come to buy food.
42:11 your s have never been spies."
42:13 They said, "We, your s, are twelve brothers,
44: 7 be it from your s that they should do such a thing!
44: 9 Should it be found with any one of your s,
44:16 God has found out the guilt of your s;
44:19 My lord asked his s, saying,
44:21 Then you said to your s, 'Bring him down to me,
44:23 Then you said to your s,
44:31 and your s will bring down the gray hairs
45:16 Pharaoh and his s were pleased.
46:34 'Your s have been keepers of livestock
47: 3 And they said to Pharaoh, "Your s are shepherds,
47: 4 let your s settle in the land of Goshen."
50: 7 With him went up all the s of Pharaoh, A
50:17 Now therefore please forgive the crime of the s of
Ex 5:15 "Why do you treat your s like this?
5:16 No straw is given to your s, yet they say to us,
5:16 Look how your s are beaten!
32:13 Remember Abraham, Isaac, and Israel, your s,
Lev 25:42 For they are my s, whom I brought out of the land
25:55 For to me the people of Israel are s;
25:55 they are my s whom I brought out from the land
Nu 22:18 But Balaam replied to the s of Balak,
22:22 and his two s were with him.
31:49 "Your s have counted the warriors who are
32: 4 for cattle; and your s have cattle."
32: 5 let this land be given to your s for a possession;
32:25 "Your s will do as my lord commands.
32:27 but your s will cross over,
32:31 "As the LORD has spoken to your s,
Dt 9:27 Remember your s, Abraham, Isaac, and Jacob;
29: 2 to Pharaoh and to all his s and to all his land, A
32:36 have compassion on his s,
34:11 against Pharaoh and all his s and his entire land, A
Jos 9: 8 They said to Joshua, "We are your s."
9: 9 "Your s have come from a very far country,
9:11 go to meet them, and say to them, "We are your s;
9:24 "Because it was told to your s for a certainty that
10: 6 saying, "Do not abandon your s;
Jdg 3:24 After he had gone, the s came.
6:27 So Gideon took ten of his s,
19:19 We your s have straw and fodder for our donkeys,
Ru 2:13 even though I am not one of your s."
2:21 "He even said to me, 'Stay close by my s,
1Sa 12:19 "Pray to the LORD your God for your s,
16:15 And Saul's s said to him, "See now,
16:16 Let our lord now command the s who attend you
16:17 So Saul said to his s,
17: 8 Am I not a Philistine, and are you not s of Saul?
1Sa 17: 9 then we will be your s;
17: 9 then you shall be our s and serve us."
18: 5 And all the people, even the s of Saul, approved.
18:22 Saul commanded his s, "Speak to David in private
18:22 and all his s love you; A
18:23 Saul's s reported these words to David in private.
18:24 The s of Saul told him, "This is what David said."
18:26 When his s told David these words,
18:30 David had more success than all the s of Saul, A
19: 1 spoke with his son Jonathan and with all his s A
21: 7 a certain man of the s of Saul was there that day,
21:11 The s of Achish said to him,
21:14 Achish said to his s, "Look,
22: 6 and all his s were standing around him. A
22: 7 Saul said to his s who stood around him,
22: 9 Doeg the Edomite, who was in charge of Saul's s,
22:14 "Who among all your s is so faithful as David? A
22:17 But the s of the king would not raise their hand
25: 8 Please give whatever you have at hand to your s
25:10 But Nabal answered David's s, "Who is David?
25:10 There are many s today who are breaking away
25:40 When David's s came to Abigail at Carmel,
25:41 "Your servant is a slave to wash the feet of the s
28: 7 Then Saul said to his s,
28: 7 His s said to him, "There is a medium at Endor."
28:23 But his s, together with the woman, urged him;
28:25 She put them before Saul and his s, and they ate.
29:10 you and the s of your lord who came with you,
2Sa 2:12 Abner son of Ner, and the s of Ishbaal son of Saul,
2:13 Joab son of Zeruiah, and the s of David,
2:15 and twelve of the s of David.
2:17 the men of Israel were beaten by the s of David.
2:30 of David's s nineteen men besides Asahel.
2:31 But the s of David had killed
3:22 then the s of David arrived with Joab from a raid,
3:38 And the king said to his s,
8: 2 Moabites became s to David and brought tribute.
8: 6 Arameans became s to David and brought tribute.
8: 7 the gold shields that were carried by the s
8:14 and all the Edomites became David's s.
9:10 and your sons and your s shall till the land for him,
9:10 Now Ziba had fifteen sons and twenty s.
9:12 in Ziba's house became Mephibosheth's s.
10:19 When all the kings who were s of Hadadezer saw
11: 9 the entrance of the king's house with all the s A
11:11 and my lord Joab and the s of my lord are camping
11:13 to lie on his couch with the s of his lord,
11:17 and some of the s of David among the people fell.
11:24 Then the archers shot at your s from the wall;
11:24 some of the king's s are dead; D
12:18 And the s of David were afraid to tell him that
12:19 David saw that his s were whispering together,
12:19 and David said to his s, "Is the child dead?"
12:21 Then his s said to him,
13:24 the king and his s please go with your servant?"
13:28 Then Absalom commanded his s,
13:29 So the s of Absalom did to Amnon
13:31 all his s who were standing by tore their A
13:36 the king and all his s also wept very bitterly. A
14:30 Then he said to his s, "Look,
14:30 So Absalom's s set the field on fire.
14:31 "Why have your s set my field on fire?"
15:15 "Your s are ready to do whatever our lord
16: 6 He threw stones at David and at all the s A
16:11 David said to Abishai and to all his s, A
17:20 Absalom's s came to the woman at the house,
18: 7 of Israel were defeated there by the s of David,
18: 9 Absalom happened to meet the s of David.
19: 7 So go out at once and speak kindly to your s;
19:14 "Return, both you and all your s." A
19:17 with his fifteen sons and his twenty s,
20: 6 take your lord's s and pursue him,
21:15 and David went down together with his s.
21:22 they fell by the hands of David and his s.
24:20 he saw the king and his s coming toward him;
1Ki 1: 2 So his s said to him, "Let a young virgin be sought
1:27 and you have not let your s know who should sit
1:33 "Take with you the s of your lord,
1:47 the king's s came to congratulate our lord King D
3:15 and provided a feast for all his s. A
5: 1 Now King Hiram of Tyre sent his s to Solomon,
5: 6 My s will join your s, and I will give you whatever wages you set for your s;
5: 9 My s shall bring it down to the sea from
8:23 and steadfast love for your s who walk before you
8:32 and act, and judge your s,
8:36 and forgive the sin of your s, your people Israel,
9:27 Hiram sent his s with the fleet,
9:27 together with the s of Solomon.
10: 5 and the attendance of his s, their clothing,
10: 8 Happy are your wives! Happy are these your s,
10:13 Then she returned to her own land, with her s.
11:17 with some Edomites who were s of his father.
12: 7 then they will be your s forever."
15:18 and gave them into the hands of his s.
20: 6 I will send my s to you tomorrow about this time,
20: 6 and the houses of your s,
20:23 The s of the king of Aram said to him,
20:31 His s said to him, "Look, we have heard that
22: 3 The king of Israel said to his s,
22:49 "Let my s go with your s in the ships,"
2Ki 1:13 and the life of these fifty s of yours,
2:16 we have fifty strong men among your s;
3:11 Then one of the s of the king of Israel answered,
4:22 "Send me one of the s and one of the donkeys,
5:13 But his s approached and said to him, "Father,
5:23 and gave them to two of his s,
2Ki 6: 3 Then one of them said, "Please come with your s."
7:12 The king got up in the night, and said to his s,
7:13 One of his s said, "Let some men take five of
9: 7 on Jezebel the blood of my s the prophets, C
9: 7 and the blood of all the s of the LORD. A
10: 5 "We are your s; we will do anything you say.
12:20 His s arose, devised a conspiracy,
12:21 his s, who struck him down, so that he died.
14: 5 he killed his s who had murdered his father
17:13 and that I sent to you by my s the prophets." C
17:23 he had foretold through all his s the prophets. AC
18:24 a single captain among the least of my master's s,
18:26 "Please speak to your s in the Aramaic language,
19: 5 When the s of King Hezekiah came to Isaiah,
19: 6 the words that you have heard, with which the s of
21:10 The LORD said by his s the prophets, C
21:23 The s of Amon conspired against him,
22: 9 "Your s have emptied out the money
23:30 His s carried him dead in a chariot from Megiddo,
24: 2 of the LORD that he spoke by his s the prophets. C
24:10 the s of King Nebuchadnezzar of Babylon came
24:11 while his s were besieging it;
24:12 his s, his officers, and his palace officials.
1Ch 9: 2 priests, Levites, and temple s. B
18: 7 the gold shields that were carried by the s
19: 2 When David's s came to Hanun in the land of
19: 3 not his s come to you to search and to overthrow
19: 4 So Hanun seized David's s, shaved them,
19:19 When the s of Hadadezer saw
20: 8 they fell by the hand of David and his s.
21: 3 my lord the king, all of them my lord's s?
2Ch 2: 8 that your s are skilled in cutting Lebanon timber.
2: 8 My s will work with your s
2:10 I will provide for your s, those who cut the timber,
2:15 let him send them to his s.
6:14 in steadfast love with your s who walk before you
6:23 and act, and judge your s,
6:27 forgive the sin of your s, your people Israel,
8:18 Huram sent him, in the care of his s, ships and s familiar with the sea.
8:18 together with the s of Solomon,
9: 4 and the attendance of his s, and their clothing,
9: 7 Happy are your people! Happy are these your s,
9:10 Moreover the s of Huram and the s of Solomon
9:12 Then she returned to her own land, with her s.
9:21 king's ships went to Tarshish with the s of Huram;
10: 7 then they will be your s forever."
12: 8 Nevertheless they shall be his s,
24:25 his s conspired against him because of the blood of
25: 3 he killed his s who had murdered his father
32: 9 he sent his s to Jerusalem to King Hezekiah
32:16 His s said still more against the Lord GOD and
33:24 His s conspired against him and killed him
34:16 "All that was committed to your s they are doing.
35:23 and the king said to his s, "Take me away,
35:24 So his s took him out of the chariot
36:20 and they became s to him and to his sons until
Ezr 2:43 The temple s: the descendants of Ziha, B
2:55 The descendants of Solomon's s:
2:58 All the temple s and the descendants B
2:58 of Solomon's s were three hundred ninety-two.
2:65 besides their male and female s,
2:70 and the temple s lived in their towns, B
4:11 Your s, the people of the province Beyond
5:11 'We are the s of the God of heaven and earth,
7: 7 and the temple s also went up to Jerusalem, B
7:24 the singers, the doorkeepers, the temple s, B
7:24 or other s of this house of God.
8:17 to say to Iddo and his colleagues the temple s B
8:20 besides two hundred twenty of the temple s, B
9:11 which you commanded by your s the prophets, C
Ne 1: 6 now pray before you day and night for your s,
1:10 They are your s and your people,
1:11 of your s who delight in revering your name.
2:20 and we his s are going to start building;
3:26 and the temple s living on Ophel made repairs B
3:31 the house of the temple s and of the merchants, B
4:16 half of my s worked on construction,
4:23 So neither I nor my brothers nor my s nor the men
5:10 and my brothers and my s are lending them money
5:15 Even their s lorded it over the people.
5:16 and all my s were gathered there for the work. A
7:46 The temple s: the descendants of Ziha, B
7:57 The descendants of Solomon's s:
7:60 All the temple s and the descendants B
7:60 of Solomon's s were three hundred ninety-two.
7:73 the temple s, and all Israel settled in their towns. B
9:10 wonders against Pharaoh and all his s and all A
10:28 the gatekeepers, the singers, the temple s, B
11: 3 Israel, the priests, the Levites, the temple s, B
11: 3 and the descendants of Solomon's s.
11:21 But the temple s lived on Ophel; B
11:21 and Ziha and Gishpa were over the temple s. B
13:19 And I set some of my s over the gates,
Est 2: 2 Then the king's s who attended him said, D
3: 2 the king's s who were at the king's gate bowed D
3: 3 Then the king's s who were at the king's gate D
4:11 "All the king's s and the people of D
6: 3 The king's s who attended him said, D
6: 5 So the king's s told him, "Haman is there, D
Job 1: 3 five hundred donkeys, and very many s;
1:15 and killed the s with the edge of the sword;
1:16 from heaven and burned up the sheep and the s,
1:17 and killed the s with the edge of the sword;
4:18 Even in his s he puts no trust,
Ps 34:22 The LORD redeems the life of his s;
69:35 and his s shall live there and possess it;

Ps 69:36 the children of his **s** shall inherit it,
79: 2 the bodies of your **s** to the birds of the air for food,
79:10 of the outpoured blood of your **s** be known among
90:13 Have compassion on your **s**!
90:16 Let your work be manifest to your **s**,
102:14 For your **s** hold its stones dear,
102:28 The children of your **s** shall live secure;
105:25 to deal craftily with his **s**.
113: 1 Praise, O **s** of the LORD;
119:91 for all things are your **s**.
123: 2 As the eyes of **s** look to the hand of their master,
134: 1 bless the LORD, all you **s** of the LORD, A
135: 1 give praise, O **s** of the LORD,
135: 9 O Egypt, against Pharaoh and all his **s**. A
135:14 and have compassion on his **s**.
Pr 29:19 By mere words **s** are not disciplined,
Isa 36: 9 a single captain among the least of my master's **s**,
36:11 "Please speak to your **s** in Aramaic,
37: 5 When the **s** of King Hezekiah came to Isaiah,
37: 6 the words that you have heard, with which the **s** of
37:24 By your **s** you have mocked the Lord,
54:17 the **s** of the LORD and their vindication from me,
56: 6 to love the name of the LORD, and to be his **s**,
63:17 Turn back for the sake of your **s**,
65: 9 and my **s** shall settle there.
65:13 My **s** shall eat, but you shall be hungry;
65:13 my **s** shall drink, but you shall be thirsty;
65:13 my **s** shall rejoice, but you shall be put to shame;
65:14 my **s** shall sing for gladness of heart,
65:15 but to his **s** he will give a different name.
66:14 that the hand of the LORD is with his **s**,
Jer 7:25 I have persistently sent all my **s** the prophets AC
14: 3 Her nobles send their **s** for water;
21: 7 I will give King Zedekiah of Judah, and his **s**,
22: 2 and your **s**, and your people who enter these gates.
22: 4 riding in chariots and on horses, they, and their **s**,
25: 4 persistently sent you all his **s** the prophets, AC
25:19 his **s**, his officials, and all his people;
26: 5 the words of my **s** the prophets whom I send C
29:19 I persistently sent to you my **s** the prophets, C
35:15 I have sent to you all my **s** the prophets, AC
36:24 nor any of his **s** who heard all these words,
36:31 And I will punish him and his offspring and his **s**
37: 2 nor his **s** nor the people of the land listened to
37:18 "What wrong have I done to you or your **s**
44: 4 persistently sent to you all my **s** the prophets, AC
Eze 38:17 in former days by my **s** the prophets of Israel, C
46:17 to one of his **s**, it shall be his to the year of liberty;
Da 1:12 "Please test your **s** for ten days.
1:13 deal with your **s** according to what you observe."
2: 4 Tell your **s** the dream, and we will reveal
2: 7 "Let the king first tell his **s** the dream,
3:26 and Abednego, **s** of the Most High God, come out!
3:28 and delivered his **s** who trusted in him.
9: 6 We have not listened to your **s** the prophets, C
9:10 which he set before us by his **s** the prophets. C
Am 3: 7 without revealing his secret to his **s** the prophets. C
Zec 1: 6 which I commanded my **s** the prophets, C
Mal 1: 6 A son honors his father, and **s** their master.
Mt 14: 2 and he said to his **s**, "This is John the Baptist;
Lk 1: 2 from the beginning were eyewitnesses and **s** of
Jn 2: 5 His mother said to the **s**,
2: 9 where it came from (though the **s** who had drawn
13:16 I tell you, **s** are not greater than their master,
15:15 I do not call you **s** any longer,
15:20 '**S** are not greater than their master.'
Ac 4:29 to your **s** to speak your word with all boldness,
Ro 13: 6 for the authorities are God's **s**,
14: 4 Who are you to pass judgment on **s** of another?
1Co 3: 5 **S** through whom you came to believe,
3: 9 For we are God's **s**, working together;
4: 1 as **s** of Christ and stewards of God's mysteries.
2Co 6: 4 but as **s** of God we have commended ourselves
Php 1: 1 Paul and Timothy, **s** of Christ Jesus,
Heb 1: 7 and his **s** flames of fire."
1Pe 2:16 As **s** of God, live as free people,
Rev 1: 1 to show his **s** what must soon take place;
2:20 and beguiling my **s** to practice fornication and
6:11 of their fellow **s** and of their brothers and sisters,
7: 3 until we have marked the **s** of our God with a seal
10: 7 as he announced to his **s** the prophets." C
11:18 for rewarding your **s**, the prophets and saints
19: 2 and he has avenged on her the blood of his **s**."
19: 5 all you his **s**, and all who fear him, A
22: 3 and his **s** will worship him;
22: 6 to show his **s** what must soon take place."
Tob 8: 9 But Raguel arose and called his **s** to him,
8:18 Then he ordered his **s** to fill in the grave
9: 2 take four **s** and two camels with you and travel
9: 5 the four **s** and two camels went to Rages in Media
Jdt 3: 2 the **s** of Nebuchadnezzar, the Great King,
6: 3 we the king's **s** will destroy them as one man. D
6: 6 and the spear of my **s** shall pierce your sides,
7:12 let your **s** take possession of the spring of water
10:20 of Holofernes and all his **s** came out and led her A
10:23 into the presence of Holofernes and his **s**,
11: 4 they do the **s** of my lord King Nebuchadnezzar."
11:20 Her words pleased Holofernes and all his **s**. A
12: 5 Then the **s** of Holofernes brought her into the tent,
AdE 2: 2 king's **s** said, "Let beautiful and virtuous girls D
6: 3 The king's **s** said, "You have not done D
6: 5 The **s** of the king answered,
6: 8 let the king's **s** bring out the fine linen robe that D
15:16 and all his **s** tried to comfort her. A
Wis 6: 4 as **s** of his kingdom you did not rule rightly,
9: 4 and do not reject me from among your **s**.
12: 7 to you might receive a worthy colony of the **s**
Wis 12:20 the enemies of your **s** and those deserving
Sir 4:30 like a lion in your home, or suspicious of your **s**.
6:11 and lord it over your **s**;
36:22 Hear, O Lord, the prayer of your **s**,
Bar 2:20 as you declared by your **s** the prophets, saying: C
2:24 which you spoke by your **s** the prophets, C
Aza 1:10 we, your **s** who worship you,
1:21 Let all who do harm to your **s** be put to shame;
1:23 Now the king's **s** who threw them in kept D
1:63 Bless the Lord, you **s** of the Lord;
Sus 1:27 the **s** felt very much ashamed,
Bel 1:14 Then Daniel ordered his **s** to bring ashes,
1Mc 16:16 as well as some of his **s**.
2Mc 1: 2 with Abraham and Isaac and Jacob, his faithful **s**.
7: 6 'And he will have compassion on his **s**.' "
7:33 he will again be reconciled with his own **s**.
8:29 to be wholly reconciled with his **s**.
1Es 1: 3 He told the Levites, the temple **s** of Israel, B
1:30 The king said to his **s**,
1:30 And immediately his **s** took him out of the line
1:57 and they were **s** to him and to his sons until
2:17 your **s** the recorder Rehum and
5: 1 and their male and female **s**, and their livestock.
5:29 The temple **s**: the descendants of Esau, B
5:33 The descendants of Solomon's **s**:
5:35 All the temple **s** and the descendants B
5:35 of Solomon's **s** were three hundred seventy-two.
5:41 besides male and female **s**,
5:42 female **s** were seven thousand three hundred
6:13 'We are the **s** of the Lord who created the heaven
8: 5 temple singers and gatekeepers and temple **s**, B
8:22 or gatekeepers or temple **s** or persons employed B
8:49 and of the temple **s**, whom David and B
8:49 two hundred twenty temple **s**; B
8:82 which you gave by your **s** the prophets, saying, C
3Mc 5: 5 The **s** in charge of the Jews went out in
2Es 1:10 I struck down Pharaoh with his **s** and all his army.
1:32 I sent you my **s** the prophets, C
2: 1 commandments through my **s** the prophets; C
2:18 I will send you help, my **s** Isaiah and Jeremiah.
2:26 one of the **s** whom I have given you will perish,
16:35 and understand them, you who are **s** of the Lord.
4Mc 12:11 were you not ashamed to murder his **s** and torture

SERVANTS' (3) [SERVANT]

Ge 47: 4 for your **s** flocks because the famine is severe in
2Sa 6:20 before the eyes of his **s** maids,
Isa 65: 8 so I will do for my **s** sake,

SERVE‡ (226) [SERVED, SERVES, SERVICE, SERVICES, SERVING, SERVITUDE]

Ge 6:21 and it shall **s** as food for you and for them."
15:14 but I will bring judgment on the nation that they **s**,
25:23 the elder shall **s** the younger."
27:29 Let peoples **s** you, and nations bow down to you.
27:40 and you shall **s** your brother;
29:15 should you therefore **s** me for nothing?
29:18 so he said, "I will **s** you seven years
29:25 Did I not **s** with you for Rachel?
43:31 and controlling himself he said, "**S** the meal."
Ex 4:16 he shall **s** as a mouth for you,
4:16 and you shall **s** as God for him.
13: 9 It shall **s** for you as a sign on your hand and as
13:16 It shall **s** as a sign on your hand and as an emblem
14:12 'Let us alone and let us **s** the Egyptians'?
14:12 to **s** the Egyptians than to die in the wilderness."
21: 2 a male Hebrew slave, he shall **s** six years,
21: 6 and he shall **s** him for life.
28: 1 from among the Israelites, to **s** me as priests—
28: 4 for your brother Aaron and his sons to **s** me
28:41 so that they may **s** me as priests.
29: 1 so that they may **s** me as priests.
29:44 Aaron also and his sons I will consecrate, to **s** me
30:30 in order that they may **s** me as priests.
39:41 and the vestments of his sons to **s** as priests.
40:13 so that he may **s** me as priest.
40:15 that they may **s** me as priests:
Lev 7:35 once they have been brought forward to **s**
25:39 you shall not make them **s** as slaves.
25:40 They shall **s** with you until the year of the jubilee.
Nu 8:25 from the duty of the service and **s** no more.
10:10 they shall **s** as a reminder on your behalf before
10:31 and you will **s** as eyes for us.
16: 9 and to stand before the congregation and **s** them?
18: 2 and **s** you while you and your sons with you are
35:15 These six cities shall **s** as refuge for the Israelites,
Dt 4:19 be led astray and bow down to them and **s** them,
4:28 There you will **s** other gods made
6:13 you shall **s**, and by his name alone you shall swear.
7: 4 from following me, to **s** other gods.
7:16 you shall not **s** their gods,
8:19 the LORD your God and follow other gods to **s**
10:12 to **s** the LORD your God with all your heart and
13: 2 (whom you have not known) "and let us **s** them,"
13: 4 him you shall **s**, and to him you shall hold fast.
17: 3 by going to **s** other gods and worshiping them—
20:11 then all the people in it shall **s** you at forced labor.
28:14 following other gods to **s** them.
28:36 where you shall **s** other gods, of wood and stone.
28:47 not **s** the LORD your God joyfully and
28:48 therefore you shall **s** your enemies whom
28:64 and there you shall **s** other gods,
29:18 the LORD our God to **s** the gods of those nations.
30:17 to bow down to other gods and **s** them,
Dt 31:20 they will turn to other gods and **s** them,
Jos 22: 5 and to **s** him with all your heart and
23: 7 or **s** them, or bow yourselves down to them,
23:16 and go and **s** other gods and bow down to them,
24:14 and **s** him in sincerity and in faithfulness;
24:14 beyond the River and in Egypt, and **s** the LORD.
24:15 Now if you are unwilling to **s** the LORD,
24:15 choose this day whom you will **s**,
24:15 for me and my household, we will **s** the LORD."
24:16 that we should forsake the LORD to **s** other gods;
24:18 we also will **s** the LORD, for he is our God."
24:19 "You cannot **s** the LORD, for he is a holy God.
24:20 If you forsake the LORD and **s** foreign gods,
24:21 people said to Joshua, "No, we will **s** the LORD!"
24:22 that you have chosen the LORD, to **s** him."
24:24 "The LORD our God we will **s**,
Jdg 9:28 we of Shechem, that we should **s** him?
9:28 and Zebul his officer **s** the men of Hamor father
9:28 Why then should we **s** him?
9:38 'Who is Abimelech, that we should **s** him?'
1Sa 7: 3 Direct your heart to the LORD, and **s** him only,
11: 1 "Make a treaty with us, and we will **s** you."
12:10 of the hand of our enemies, and we will **s** you.'
12:14 and **s** him and heed his voice and not rebel against
12:20 but **s** the LORD with all your heart;
12:24 and **s** him faithfully with all your heart;
17: 9 then you shall be our servants and **s** us."
26:19 saying, 'Go, **s** other gods.'
2Sa 16:19 Moreover, whom should I **s**?
16:19 Just as I have served your father, so I will **s** you."
1Ki 9: 6 but go and **s** other gods and worship them,
12: 4 that he placed on us, and we will **s** you."
12: 7 be a servant to this people today and **s** them,
20:14 By the young men who **s** the district governors."
20:15 the young men who **s** the district governors,
20:17 The young men who **s** the district governors went
20:19 the young men who **s** the district governors,
2Ki 3:14 "As the LORD of hosts lives, whom I **s**,
4:41 and said, "**S** the people and let them eat."
5:16 But he said, "As the LORD lives, whom I **s**,
17:35 or bow yourselves to them or **s** them or sacrifice
18: 7 against the king of Assyria and would not **s** him.
25:24 live in the land, **s** the king of Babylon,
1Ch 28: 9 and **s** him with single mind and willing heart;
2Ch 7:19 and go and **s** other gods and worship them,
10: 4 that he placed on us, and we will **s** you."
19:11 and the Levites will **s** you as officers.
30: 8 and **s** the LORD your God,
33:16 and he commanded Judah to **s** the LORD the God
35: 3 Now **s** the LORD your God and his people Israel.
Ne 9:35 they did not **s** you and did not turn
Job 21:15 What is the Almighty, that we should **s** him?
36:11 and **s** him, they complete their days in prosperity,
39: 9 "Is the wild ox willing to **s** you?
Ps 2:11 **S** the LORD with fear, with trembling
22:30 Posterity will **s** him; future generations will be told
Pr 22:29 they will **s** kings; they will not **s** common people.
Isa 4: 6 It will **s** as a pavilion,
14: 3 the hard service with which you were made to **s**,
58: 3 Look, you **s** your own interest on your fast day,
59: 6 Their webs cannot **s** as clothing;
60:12 and kingdom that will not **s** you shall perish;
Jer 2:20 and you said, "I will not **s**!"
5:19 so you shall **s** strangers in a land that is not yours."
11:10 they have gone after other gods to **s** them;
13:10 after other gods to **s** them and worship them,
15:14 I will make you **s** your enemies in a land
15:19 you shall **s** as my mouth.
16:13 and there you shall **s** other gods day and night,
17: 4 and I will make you **s** your enemies in a land
25: 6 do not go after other gods to **s** and worship them,
25:11 and these nations shall **s** the king
27: 6 even the wild animals of the field to **s** him.
27: 7 All the nations shall **s** him and his son
27: 8 But if any nation or kingdom will not **s** this king,
27: 9 'You shall not **s** the king of Babylon.'
27:11 under the yoke of the king of Babylon and **s** him,
27:12 and **s** him and his people, and live.
27:13 concerning any nation that will not **s** the king
27:14 the prophets who are telling you not to **s** the king
27:17 **s** the king of Babylon and live.
28:14 that they may **s** King Nebuchadnezzar of Babylon,
28:14 and they shall indeed **s** him;
30: 9 But they shall **s** the LORD their God
35:15 and do not go after other gods to **s** them,
40: 9 saying, "Do not be afraid to **s** the Chaldeans.
40: 9 Stay in the land and **s** the king of Babylon,
44: 3 that they went to make offerings and **s** other gods
Eze 20:39 Go **s** your idols, everyone of you now
20:40 all of them, shall **s** me in the land;
41: 6 the temple to **s** as supports for the side chambers,
44:11 and they shall attend on them and **s** them.
44:13 They shall not come near to me, to **s** me as priest,
46:24 "These are the kitchens where those who **s** at
Da 1: 4 and competent to **s** in the king's palace;
3:12 They do not **s** your gods and they do not worship
3:14 that you do not **s** my gods and you do not worship
3:17 If our God whom we **s** is able to deliver us from
3:18 not **s** your gods and we will not worship
3:28 and yielded up their bodies rather than **s**
6:16 "May your God, whom you faithfully **s**,
6:20 has your God whom you faithfully **s** been able
7:14 nations, and languages should **s** him.
7:27 and all dominions shall **s** and obey them."
Zep 3: 9 of the LORD and **s** him with one accord.
Mal 3:14 You have said, "It is vain to **s** God.
3:17 as parents spare their children who **s** them.

Mal 3:18 and one who does not s him.
Mt 4:10 'Worship the Lord your God, and s only him.' "
6:24 "No one can s two masters;
6:24 You cannot s God and wealth.
8:15 and she got up and began to s him.
20:28 as the Son of Man came not to be served but to s,
Mk 1:31 Then the fever left her, and she began to s them.
10:45 For the Son of Man came not to be served but to s,
Lk 1:74 from the hands of our enemies, might s him
4:8 'Worship the Lord your God, and s only him.' "
4:39 Immediately she got up and began to s them.
12:37 and he will come and s them.
16:13 No slave can s two masters;
16:13 You cannot s God and wealth."
17:8 put on your apron and s me while I eat and drink;
Jn 12:48 on the last day the word that I have spoken will s
Ac 7:7 'But I will judge the nation that they s,' said God,
26:16 for this purpose, to appoint you to s and testify to
Ro 1:9 whom I s with my spirit by announcing the gospel
9:12 "The elder shall s the younger."
12:11 Do not lag in zeal, be ardent in spirit, s the Lord.
16:18 For such people do not s our Lord Christ,
1Co 9:13 and those who s at the altar share
10:11 These things happened to them to s as an example,
2Co 11:8 by accepting support from them in order to s you.
Col 3:24 as your reward; you s the Lord Christ.
1Th 1:9 to s a living and true God,
1Ti 3:10 if they prove themselves blameless, let them s
3:13 for those who s well as deacons gain
6:2 rather they must s them all the more,
Heb 1:14 sent to s for the sake of those who are
1Pe 4:10 s one another with whatever gift each
Jude 1:7 s as an example by undergoing a punishment
Tob 4:14 If you s God you will receive payment.
14:8,9 s God faithfully and do what is pleasing
Jdt 8:22 on our heads among the Gentiles, wherever we s
11:1 to s Nebuchadnezzar, king of all the earth.
11:7 Not only do human beings s him because of you,
12:13 of the Assyrian women who s in the palace
16:14 Let all your creatures s you, for you spoke,
AdE 12:5 And the king ordered Mordecai to s in the court,
Wis 15:7 of the same clay both the vessels that s clean uses
Sir 2:1 My child, when you come to s the Lord,
3:7 they will s their parents as their masters.
4:14 Those who s her minister to the Holy One;
8:8 you will learn discipline and how to s princes.
10:25 Free citizens will s a wise servant,
45:15 the heavens endure, to minister to the Lord and s
Bar 1:12 and we shall s them many days and find favor
2:21 Bend your shoulders and s the king of Babylon,
2:22 of the Lord and will not s the king of Babylon,
2:24 to s the king of Babylon;
LtJ 6:26 And those who s them are put to shame
6:30 Women s meals for gods of silver and gold
6:39 and those who s them will be put to shame.
1Mc 6:23 We were happy to s your father,
2Mc 6:17 Let what we have said s as a reminder;
1Es 1:4 worship the Lord your God and s his people Israel;
4:6 not s in the army or make war but till the soil;
8:46 and the treasurers at that place to send us men to s
3Mc 6:6 to the flames so as not to s vain things,
2Es 1:18 to s the Egyptians than to die in this wilderness.'
6:46 and you commanded them to s humankind,
8:26 but on those who s you in truth.
15:45 who survive shall s those who have destroyed it.

SERVED (80) [SERVE]

Ge 14:4 Twelve years they had s Chedorlaomer,
29:20 So Jacob s seven years for Rachel,
29:30 He s Laban for another seven years.
30:26 and my children for whom I have s you,
30:29 "You yourself know how I have s you,
31:6 that I have s your father with all my strength;
31:41 I s you fourteen years for your two daughters,
43:32 They s him by himself, and them by themselves,
Ex 38:8 the mirrors of the women who s at the entrance to
Nu 3:4 Eleazar and Ithamar s as priests in the lifetime
4:37 all who s at the tent of meeting,
4:41 all who s at the tent of meeting,
Dt 12:2 about to dispossess s their gods,
29:26 They turned and s other gods, worshiping them,
Jos 24:2 lived beyond the Euphrates and s other gods.
24:14 the gods that your ancestors s beyond the River
24:15 whether the gods your ancestors s in the region
24:31 Israel s the LORD all the days of Joshua,
Jdg 3:8 and the Israelites s Cushan-rishathaim eight years.
3:14 Israelites s King Eglon of Moab eighteen years.
1Sa 2:22 with the women who s at the entrance to the tent
7:4 and they s the LORD only.
12:10 and have s the Baals and the Astartes;
2Sa 13:17 He called the young man who s him and said,
16:19 Just as I have s your father, so I will serve you."
22:44 people whom I had not known s me.
1Ki 1:4 She became the king's attendant and s him,
4:21 they brought tribute and s Solomon all the days
16:31 and went and s Baal, and worshiped him.
22:53 He s Baal and worshiped him;
2Ki 4:40 They s some for the men to eat.
5:2 from the land of Israel, and she s Naaman's wife.
17:12 they s idols, of which the LORD had said
17:16 worshiped all the host of heaven, and s Baal.
17:33 the LORD but also s their own gods,
17:41 but also s their carved images;
21:3 worshiped all the host of heaven, and s them.
21:21 s the idols that his father s, and worshiped them;
1Ch 6:10 and Johanan of Azariah (it was he who s as priest
6:33 These are the men who s;
27:1 and their officers who s the king in all matters
28:1 the officers of the divisions that s the king,
2Ch 7:22 and worshiped them and s them;
24:18 and s the sacred poles and the idols.
33:3 worshiped all the host of heaven, and s them.
33:22 that his father Manasseh had made, and s them.
Ne 2:1 of King Artaxerxes, when wine was s him,
Est 1:7 Drinks were s in golden goblets,
Ps 18:43 people whom I had not known s me.
106:36 They s their idols, which became a snare to them.
Isa 40:2 that she has s her term, that her penalty is paid,
Jer 5:19 "As you have forsaken me and s foreign gods
8:2 which they have loved and s,
16:11 after other gods and have s and worshiped them,
22:9 and worshiped other gods and s them."
34:14 to you and have s you six years;
52:12 Nebuzaradan the captain of the bodyguard who s
Da 7:10 A thousand thousands s him,
Hos 12:12 there Israel s for a wife,
Mt 20:28 as the Son of Man came not to be s but to serve,
Mk 10:45 For the Son of Man came not to be s but to serve,
Jn 12:2 Martha s, and Lazarus was one of those at
Ac 10:7 from the ranks of those who s him,
13:36 he had s the purpose of God in his own generation,
17:25 nor is he s by human hands,
Ro 1:25 a lie and worshiped and s the creature rather than
Php 2:22 a father he has s with me in the work of the gospel.
Heb 7:13 from which no one has ever s at the altar.
AdE 1:10 the seven eunuchs who s King Artaxerxes,
Wis 10:9 Wisdom rescued from troubles those who s her.
16:25 it s your all-nourishing bounty,
Sir 25:8 and the one who has not s an inferior.
Bar 4:32 Wretched will be the cities that your children s
1Mc 10:14 for it s as a place of refuge.
11:38 So all the troops who had s under his predecessors
1Es 9:14 and Levi and Shabbethai s with them as judges.
2Es 7:*37* whom you have denied, whom you have not s,
7:89 they laboriously s the Most High,
7:*98* to see the face of him whom they s in life and

SERVES (16) [SERVE]

Job 37:7 s as a sign on everyone's hand,
Ps 76:10 Human wrath s only to praise you,
Mal 3:18 between one who s God and one who does
Lk 22:26 and the leader like one who s.
22:27 the one who is at the table or the one who s?
22:27 But I am among you as one who s.
Jn 2:10 "Everyone s the good wine first,
12:26 Whoever s me must follow me, and where I am,
12:26 Whoever s me, the Father will honor.
Ro 3:5 But if our injustice s to confirm the justice of God,
14:18 The one who thus s Christ is acceptable to God
1Pe 4:11 whoever s must do so with the strength
Jdt 11:17 Your servant is indeed God-fearing and s the God
Wis 13:11 a useful vessel that s life's needs,
Sir 39:4 He s among the great and appears before rulers;
LtJ 6:59 or a household utensil that s its owner's need,

SERVICE‡ (158) [SERVE]

Ge 30:26 for you know very well the s I have given you."
41:46 Joseph was thirty years old when he entered the s
50:2 the physicians in his s to embalm his father.
Ex 1:14 with hard s in mortar and brick and in every kind
14:5 "What have we done, letting Israel leave our s?"
30:16 from the Israelites and shall designate it for the s
31:10 and the vestments of his sons, for their s as priests,
32:29 "Today you have ordained yourselves for the s of
35:19 and the vestments of his sons, for their s as priests.
35:21 and for all its s, and for the sacred vestments.
39:40 and all the utensils for the s of the tabernacle,
Nu 3:7 of the tent of meeting, doing s at the tabernacle;
3:8 for the Israelites as they do s at the tabernacle.
3:26 all the s pertaining to these.
3:31 all the s pertaining to these.
3:36 all the s pertaining to these;
4:4 The s of the Kohathites relating to the tent
4:12 the utensils of the s that are used in the sanctuary,
4:14 which are used for the s there, the firepans,
4:24 This is the s of the clans of the Gershonites,
4:26 and their cords, and all the equipment for their s;
4:27 the s of the Gershonites shall be at the command
4:28 the s of the clans of the Gershonites relating to
4:31 as the whole of their s in the tent of meeting:
4:32 with all their equipment and all their related s;
4:33 This is the s of the clans of the Merarites,
4:33 the whole of their s relating to the tent of meeting,
4:47 of s and the work of bearing burdens relating to
7:5 that they may be used in doing the s of the tent
7:5 to each according to his s.
7:7 to the Gershonites, according to their s;
7:8 to their s, under the direction of Ithamar son
8:11 that they may do the s of the LORD.
8:15 Thereafter the Levites may go in to do s at the tent
8:19 to do the s for the Israelites at the tent of meeting,
8:22 in to do their s in the tent of meeting in attendance
8:24 and upward they shall begin to do duty in the s of
8:25 from the duty of the s and serve no more.
8:26 but they shall perform no s.
18:4 for all the s of the tent;
18:6 to perform the s of the tent of meeting.
18:21 a possession in return for the s that they perform,
18:21 the s in the tent of meeting.
18:23 Levites shall perform the s of the tent of meeting,
18:31 for it is your payment for your s in the tent
31:14 who had come from s in the war.
Jos 22:27 that we do perform the s of the LORD
1Sa 14:52 or valiant warrior, he took him into his s.
16:21 And David came to Saul, and entered his s.
16:22 saying, "Let David remain in my s,
19:4 and because his deeds have been of good s to you;
29:8 in your servant from the day I entered your s until
2Sa 9:2 And he said, "At your s!"
1Ki 12:4 Now therefore lighten the hard s of your father
2Ki 10:18 "Ahab offered Baal small s;
25:14 and all the bronze vessels used in the temple s,
1Ch 4:23 they lived there with the king in his s.
5:18 thousand seven hundred sixty, ready for s.
6:31 of the s of song in the house of the LORD,
6:32 and they performed their s in due order.
6:48 for all the s of the tabernacle of the house of God.
7:11 thousand two hundred, ready for s in war.
7:40 for s in war, was twenty-six thousand men.
9:13 qualified for the work of the s of the house of God.
9:19 the Korahites, were in charge of the work of the s,
9:28 Some of them had charge of the utensils of s,
9:33 in the chambers of the temple free from other s,
18:17 and David's sons were the chief officials in the s
23:24 and upward who were to do the work for the s of
23:26 carry the tabernacle or any of the things for its s"
23:28 the descendants of Aaron for the s of the house of
23:28 and any work for the s of the house of God;
23:32 for the s of the house of the LORD."
24:3 according to the appointed duties in their s.
24:19 as their appointed duty in their s to enter the house
25:1 the army also set apart for the s the sons of Asaph,
25:6 harps, and lyres for the s of the house of God.
26:8 were able men qualified for the s;
26:30 the work of the LORD and for the s of the king.
28:13 all the work of the s in the house of the LORD;
28:13 all the vessels for the s in the house of the LORD,
28:14 weight of gold for all golden vessels for each s,
28:14 the weight of silver vessels for each s,
28:15 according to the use of each in the s,
28:20 for the s of the house of the LORD is finished.
28:21 the priests and the Levites for all the s of the house
28:21 be every volunteer who has skill for any kind of s;
29:7 for the s of the house of God five thousand talents
2Ch 8:14 he appointed the divisions of the priests for their s,
10:4 Now therefore lighten the hard s of your father
13:10 of Aaron, and Levites for their s.
17:16 a volunteer for the s of the LORD,
17:19 These were in the s of the king,
24:14 utensils for the s and for the burnt offerings,
29:35 the s of the house of the LORD was restored.
30:22 to all the Levites who showed good skill in the s of
31:2 division by division, everyone according to his s,
31:16 for their s according to their offices,
31:21 that he undertook in the s of the house of God,
34:13 and directed all who did work in every kind of s;
35:2 to their offices and encouraged them in the s of
35:10 When the s had been prepared for,
35:15 they did not need to interrupt their s,
35:16 So all the s of the LORD was prepared that day,
Ezr 6:18 and the Levites in their courses for the s of God
7:19 The vessels that have been given you for the s of
Ne 10:32 of a shekel for the s of the house of our God:
12:9 Unno their associates stood opposite them in the s.
12:45 They performed the s of their God and the s
13:10 Levites and the singers, who had conducted the s,
13:14 for the house of my God and for his s.
Job 7:1 "Do not human beings have a hard s on earth,
14:14 All the days of my s I would wait
22:2 Can even the wisest be of s to him?
Ps 72:11 down before him, all nations give him s.
Isa 14:3 and the hard s with which you were made to serve,
41:2 a victor from the east, summoned him to his s?
Jer 17:16 not run away from being a shepherd in your s,
34:14 you must set them free from your s."
52:18 and all the vessels of bronze used in the temple s.
Mt 26:10 She has performed a good s for me.
Mk 14:6 She has performed a good s for me.
Lk 1:23 his time of s was ended, he went to his home.
Ro 15:16 the Gentiles in the priestly s of the gospel of God,
15:27 also to be of s to them in material things.
1Co 9:7 the expenses for doing military s?
9:13 in the temple s get their food from the temple,
16:15 and they have devoted themselves to the s of
16:16 to put yourselves at the s of such people,
2Co 8:23 Titus, he is my partner and co-worker in your s;
Eph 6:7 Render s with enthusiasm,
1Ti 1:12 he judged me faithful and appointed me to his s,
6:2 since those who benefit by their s are believers
2Ti 1:18 And you know very well how much s he rendered
Phm 1:13 of s to me in your place during my imprisonment
Heb 1:14 Are not all angels spirits in the divine s,
2:17 a merciful and faithful high priest in the s of God,
10:11 And every priest stands day after day at his s,
Rev 2:19 your love, faith, s, and patient endurance.
Wis 15:7 for our s, fashioning out of the same clay both
Sir 35:20 The one whose s is pleasing to the Lord will
39:31 always ready for his s on earth;
50:14 Finishing the s at the altars,
LtJ 6:60 and when sent to do a s, they are obedient.
1Mc 10:41 they shall give from now on for the s of
11:58 He also sent him gold plate and a table s,
2Mc 3:3 the expenses connected with the s of the sacrifices.
4:14 that the priests were no longer intent upon their s
8:9 a general and a man of experience in military s.
1Es 7:15 to strengthen their hands for the s of the Lord God
8:49 whom David and the leaders had given for the s of
3Mc 3:6 of other races paid no heed to their good s
2Es 6:42 be planted and cultivated and be of s before you.

4Mc 3:20 both appropriated money to them for the temple s
4:4 he praised Simon for his s to the king and went up
4:20 but also the temple s was abolished.
12:14 Surely they by dying nobly fulfilled their s to God,

SERVICES (7) [SERVE]

Dt 15:18 because for six years they have given you s worth
1Co 12:5 and there are varieties of s, but the same Lord;
Php 2:30 to make up for those s that you could not give me.
Sir 38:1 Honor physicians for their s,
1Mc 10:42 from the income of the s of the temple,
2Mc 9:26 to remember the public and private s rendered
1Es 7:9 the s of the Lord God of Israel in accordance with

SERVILE (KJV) See OCCUPATIONS, SERVILEWORK

SERVING‡ (30) [SERVE]

Ge 29:27 also in return for s me another seven years."
Nu 4:24 the service of the clans of the Gershonites, in s
4:49 to their several tasks of s or carrying;
Dt 11:13 s him with all your heart and with all your soul—
11:16 s other gods and worshiping them,
1Sa 8:8 forsaking me and s other gods,
1Ki 9:9 worshiping them and s them;
2Ch 11:14 and his sons had prevented them from s as priests
12:8 the difference between s me and s the kingdoms
Job 19:15 my s girls count me as a stranger;
Ps 86:16 save the child of your s girl.
116:16 I am your servant, the child of your s girl.
Isa 58:13 s your own interests, or pursuing your own affairs;
Eze 27:7 from Egypt was your sail, s as your ensign;
44:11 at the gates of the temple, and s in the temple;
Lk 1:8 Once when he was s as priest before God
Ac 6:4 will devote ourselves to prayer and to s the word."
20:19 s the Lord with all humility and with tears,
2Ti 2:4 No one s in the army gets entangled
Heb 6:10 and the love that you showed for his sake in s
1Pe 1:12 that they were s not themselves but you, in regard
Rev 1:6 priests s his God and Father,
5:10 to be a kingdom and priests s our God,
AdE 2:19 Meanwhile Mordecai was s in the courtyard.
11:3 a great man, s in the court of the king.
Wis 9:5 For I am your servant the son of your s girl,
16:24 For creation, s you who made it,
Bar 1:22 by s other gods and doing what is evil in the sight
1Es 5:39 they were excluded from s as priests.

SERVITOR (KJV) See SERVANT

SERVITUDE (2) [SERVE]

La 1:3 into exile with suffering and hard s;
1Es 8:79 and to give us food in the time of our s.

SESSION (1) [SESSIONS]

Jdt 4:8 and the senate of the whole people of Israel, in s

SESSIONS (1) [SESSION]

1Es 9:16 of the tenth month they began their s to investigate

SESTHEL (1)

1Es 9:31 Laccunus and Naidus, and Bescaspasmys and S,

SET‡ (907) [OFFSETS, SETS, SETTING, SETTINGS, SUNSET, WELL-SET]

Ge 1:17 God s them in the dome of the sky to give light
8:9 but the dove found no place to s its foot,
9:13 I have s my bow in the clouds,
12:5 and they s forth to go to the land of Canaan.
12:20 and they s him on the way,
18:8 and milk and the calf that he had prepared, and s it
18:14 At the s time I will return to you, in due season,
18:16 Then the men s out from there,
18:16 Abraham went with them to s them on their way.
21:28 Abraham s apart seven ewe lambs of the flock.
21:29 of these seven ewe lambs that you have s apart?"
22:3 the wood for the burnt offering, and s out and went
24:10 and he s out and went to Aram-naharaim,
24:33 Then food was s before him to eat;
26:31 and Isaac s them on their way,
28:11 for the night, because the sun had s.
28:12 that there was a ladder s up on the earth, the top
28:18 the stone that he had put under his head and s it up
28:22 which I have s up for a pillar,
30:36 and he s a distance of three days' journey
30:38 He s the rods that he had peeled in front of
30:40 and s the faces of the flocks toward the striped and
31:17 and s his children and his wives on camels;
31:21 and s his face toward the hill country of Gilead.
31:37 S it here before my kinsfolk and your kinsfolk,
31:45 So Jacob took a stone, and s it up as a pillar.
31:51 which I have s between you and me.
35:14 Jacob s up a pillar in the place
35:20 and Jacob s up a pillar at her grave;
41:33 and s him over the land of Egypt.
41:41 "See, I have s you over all the land of Egypt."
41:43 Thus he s him over all the land of Egypt.
43:9 not bring him back to you and s him before you,
44:21 so that I may s my eyes on him.'
45:22 To each one of them he gave a s of garments;
46:1 When Israel s out on his journey with all
46:5 Then Jacob s out from Beer-sheba;
Ge 49:26 of Joseph, on the brow of him who was s apart
Ex 1:11 Therefore they s taskmasters over them
5:14 whom Pharaoh's taskmasters had s over them,
8:22 But on that day I will s apart the land of Goshen,
9:5 The LORD s a time, saying,
13:12 you shall s apart to the LORD all that first opens
13:20 They s out from Succoth, and camped at Etham,
15:22 Moses ordered Israel to s out from the Red Sea,
16:1 The whole congregation of the Israelites s out
17:12 so his hands were steady until the sun s.
18:21 s such men over them as officers over thousands,
19:7 and s before them all these words that
19:12 You shall s limits for the people all around,
19:23 'S limits around the mountain and keep it holy.'"
21:1 the ordinances that you shall s before them:
23:5 you must help to s it free.
23:31 I will s your borders from the Red Sea to the sea
24:4 at the foot of the mountain, and s up twelve pillars,
24:13 So Moses s out with his assistant Joshua,
25:7 onyx stones and gems to be s in the ephod and for
25:30 And you shall s the bread of the Presence on
25:37 and the lamps shall be s up so as to give light on
26:4 on the edge of the outermost curtain in the first s;
26:4 the edge of the outermost curtain in the second s.
26:5 on the edge of the curtain that is in the second s;
26:10 the edge of the curtain that is outermost in one s,
26:10 of the curtain that is outermost in the second s.
26:35 You shall s the table outside the curtain,
27:5 You shall s it under the ledge of the altar so that
27:20 so that a lamp may be s up to burn regularly.
28:12 You shall s the two stones on the shoulder-pieces
28:17 You shall s in it four rows of stones.
28:20 they shall be s in gold filigree.
29:6 and you shall s the turban on his head,
35:9 and onyx stones and gems to be s in the ephod and
35:27 and gems to be s in the ephod and the breastpiece,
36:11 on the edge of the outermost curtain of the first s;
36:11 the edge of the outermost curtain of the second s;
36:12 the edge of the curtain that was in the second s;
36:17 on the edge of the outermost curtain of the one s,
39:7 He s them on the shoulder-pieces of the ephod,
39:10 They s in it four rows of stones.
39:37 with its lamps s on it and all its utensils,
40:2 of the first month you shall s up the tabernacle of
40:4 and you shall bring in the lampstand, and s up its
40:5 s up the screen for the entrance of the tabernacle.
40:6 You shall s the altar of burnt offering before
40:8 You shall s up the court all around,
40:17 the first day of the month, the tabernacle was s up.
40:18 Moses s up the tabernacle;
40:18 he laid its bases, and s up its frames,
40:20 and s the mercy seat above the ark;
40:21 and s up the curtain for screening,
40:23 and s the bread in order on it before the LORD;
40:25 and s up the lamps before the LORD;
40:29 He s the altar of burnt offering at the entrance of
40:30 He s the basin between the tent of meeting and
40:33 He s up the court around the tabernacle and
40:36 the Israelites would s out on each stage
40:37 not s out until the day that it was taken up.
Lev 8:9 And he s the turban on his head, and on the turban,
8:9 in front, he s the golden ornament, the holy crown,
11:37 upon any seed s aside for sowing, it is clean;
14:11 The priest who cleanses shall s the person to
16:7 and s them before the LORD at the entrance of
16:22 and the goat shall be s free in the wilderness.
17:10 I will s my face against
19:24 In the fourth year all their fruit shall be s apart
20:3 I myself will s my face against them,
20:5 I myself will s my face against them and
20:6 I will s my face against them,
20:25 which I have s apart for you to hold unclean.
24:3 Aaron shall s it up in the tent of meeting,
24:4 He shall s up the lamps on the lampstand
24:8 Every sabbath day Aaron shall s them in order
26:17 I will s my face against you,
Nu 1:51 When the tabernacle is to s out,
1:51 to be pitched, the Levites shall s it up.
2:9 They shall s out first on the march.
2:16 They shall s out second.
2:17 shall s out in the center of the camps;
2:17 they shall s out just as they camp, each in position,
2:24 They shall s out third on the march.
2:31 They shall s out last, by companies.
2:34 and they s out the same way, everyone by clans,
3:6 and s them before Aaron the priest,
4:5 When the camp is to s out,
5:16 and s her before the LORD;
5:18 The priest shall s the woman before the LORD,
5:30 then he shall s the woman before the LORD,
8:2 When you s up the lamps,
8:3 he s up its lamps to give light in front of
9:15 On the day the tabernacle was s up,
9:17 then the Israelites would s out;
9:18 of the LORD the Israelites would s out,
9:19 the charge of the LORD, and would not s out.
9:20 to the command of the LORD they would s out.
9:21 the cloud lifted in the morning, they would s out,
9:21 when the cloud lifted they would s out.
9:22 in camp and would not s out;
9:22 but when it lifted they would s out.
9:23 at the command of the LORD they would s out.
10:5 the camps on the east side shall s out;
10:6 the camps on the south side shall s out.
10:6 alarm is to be blown whenever they are to s out.
10:12 the Israelites s out by stages from the wilderness
10:13 They s out for the first time at the command of
Nu 10:14 The standard of the camp of Judah s out first,
10:17 who carried the tabernacle, s out.
10:18 Next the standard of the camp of Reuben s out,
10:21 the Kohathites, who carried the holy things, s out;
10:21 and the tabernacle was s up before their arrival.
10:22 Next the standard of the Ephraimite camp s out,
10:25 acting as the rear guard of all the camps, s out,
10:28 company by company, when they s out.
10:33 So they s out from the mount of the LORD
10:34 over them by day when they s out from the camp.
10:35 Whenever the ark s out, Moses would say, "Arise,
12:15 and the people did not s out on the march
12:16 After that the people s out from Hazeroth,
14:25 turn tomorrow and s out for the wilderness by
18:11 a perpetual due, whatever is s aside from the gifts
18:24 which they s apart as an offering to the LORD.
18:26 you shall s apart an offering from it to the LORD,
18:28 also shall s apart an offering to the LORD
18:29 you shall s apart every offering due to the LORD;
18:30 When you have s apart the best of it,
20:22 They s out from Kadesh, and the Israelites,
21:4 From Mount Hor they s out by the way to
21:8 "Make a poisonous serpent, and s it on a pole;
21:10 The Israelites s out, and camped in Oboth.
21:11 They s out from Oboth, and camped at Iye-abarim,
21:12 From there they s out, and camped in
21:13 From there they s out, and camped on
22:1 The Israelites s out, and camped in the plains
24:1 but s his face toward the wilderness.
24:21 and your nest is s in the rock;
31:28 s aside as tribute for the LORD,
33:3 They s out from Rameses in the first month,
33:5 So the Israelites s out from Rameses,
33:6 They s out from Succoth, and camped at Etham,
33:7 They s out from Etham, and turned back
33:8 They s out from Pi-hahiroth,
33:9 They s out from Marah and came to Elim;
33:10 They s out from Elim and camped by the Red Sea.
33:11 They s out from the Red Sea and camped in
33:12 They s out from the wilderness of Sin and camped
33:13 They s out from Dophkah and camped at Alush.
33:14 They s out from Alush and camped at Rephidim,
33:15 They s out from Rephidim and camped in
33:16 They s out from the wilderness of Sinai
33:17 They s out from Kibroth-hattaavah and camped
33:18 They s out from Hazeroth and camped at Rithmah.
33:19 They s out from Rithmah and camped
33:20 They s out from Rimmon-perez and camped
33:21 They s out from Libnah and camped at Rissah.
33:22 They s out from Rissah and camped at Kehelathah.
33:23 They s out from Kehelathah and camped
33:24 They s out from Mount Shepher and camped
33:25 They s out from Haradah and camped
33:26 They s out from Makheloth and camped at Tahath.
33:27 They s out from Tahath and camped at Terah.
33:28 They s out from Terah and camped at Mithkah.
33:29 They s out from Mithkah and camped
33:30 They s out from Hashmonah and camped
33:31 They s out from Moseroth and camped
33:32 They s out from Bene-jaakan and camped
33:33 They s out from Hor-haggidgad and camped
33:34 They s out from Jotbathah and camped
33:35 They s out from Abronah and camped
33:36 They s out from Ezion-geber and camped in
33:37 They s out from Kadesh and camped
33:41 They s out from Mount Hor and camped
33:42 They s out from Zalmonah and camped at Punon.
33:43 They s out from Punon and camped at Oboth.
33:44 They s out from Oboth and camped at Iye-abarim,
33:45 They s out from Iyim and camped at Dibon-gad.
33:46 They s out from Dibon-gad and camped
33:47 They s out from Almon-diblathaim and camped in
33:48 They s out from the mountains of Abarim
Dt 1:8 See, I have s the land before you;
1:19 we s out from Horeb and went through all
1:24 They s out and went up into the hill country,
1:36 the land on which he s foot,
4:41 Then Moses s apart on the east side of
4:44 This is the law that Moses s before the Israelites.
7:7 the LORD s his heart on you and chose you—
7:26 or you will be s apart for destruction like it.
7:26 for it is s apart for destruction.
10:8 At that time the LORD s apart the tribe of Levi
10:15 yet the LORD s his heart in love
11:24 Every place on which you s foot shall be yours;
11:25 of you on all the land on which you s foot,
11:29 you shall s the blessing on Mount Gerizim and
14:22 S apart a tithe of all the yield of your seed
14:24 to s his name is too far away from you,
15:12 in the seventh year you shall s that person free.
16:22 nor shall you s up a stone pillar—
17:14 and you say, "I will s a king over me,
17:15 you may indeed s over you a king whom
17:15 One of your own community you may s as king
19:2 you shall s apart three cities in the land that
19:7 I command you: You shall s apart three cities.
19:14 s up by former generations,
23:11 and when the sun has s,
26:10 You shall s it down before the LORD your God
26:19 to s you high above all nations that he has made,
27:2 you shall s up large stones and cover them
27:4 you shall s up these stones,
28:1 the LORD your God will s you high above all
28:36 and the king whom you s over you,
28:56 so gentle and refined that she does not venture to s
30:1 blessings and the curses that I have s before you,
30:15 See, I have s before you today life and prosperity,

Dt 30:19 and earth to witness against you today that I have s
32:13 He s him atop the heights of the land,
Jos 3: 1 in the morning Joshua rose and s out from Shittim
3: 3 then you shall s out from your place.
3:14 When the people s out from their tents to cross
4: 9 (Joshua s up twelve stones in the middle of
4:20 of the Jordan, Joshua s up in Gilgal,
6:23 and s them outside the camp of Israel.
6:26 at the cost of his youngest he shall s up its gates!"
8: 2 S an ambush against the city, behind it."
8: 3 and all the fighting men s out to go up against Ai.
8: 8 you have taken the city, you shall s the city on fire,
8:12 he s them in ambush between Bethel and Ai,
8:19 took it, and at once s the city on fire.
9:12 on the day we s out to come to you, but now, see,
9:17 So the Israelites s out and reached their cities on
10:13 and did not hurry to s for about a whole day.
10:18 and s men by it to guard them;
10:27 they s large stones against the mouth of the cave,
15:19 since you have s me in the land of the Negeb,
16: 9 the towns that were s apart for the Ephraimites
18: 1 and s up the tent of meeting there.
18: 9 the men went and traversed the land and s down in
20: 7 So they s apart Kedesh in Galilee in
24: 9 s out to fight against Israel.
24:26 and s it up there under the oak in the sanctuary of
Jdg 1: 8 They put it to the sword and s the city on fire.
1:15 since you have s me in the land of the Negeb,
5:14 From Ephraim they s out into the valley,
6:18 and bring out my present, and s it before you."
7:19 when they had just s the watch;
7:22 the LORD s every man's sword against his fellow
9:25 of Shechem s ambushes on the mountain tops.
9:49 and they s the stronghold on fire over them,
15: 5 When he had s fire to the torches,
17:10 a s of clothes, and your living."
18:11 s out from Zorah and Eshtaol,
18:30 Then the Danites s up the idol for themselves.
19: 3 Then her husband s out after her,
19:28 and the man s out for his home.
20:30 and s themselves in array against Gibeah,
20:48 Also the remaining towns they s on fire.
Ru 1: 7 So she s out from the place where she had been
1Sa 1:11 then I will s him before you as a nazirite until
2: 8 and on them he has s the world.
4:15 Eli was ninety-eight years old and his eyes were s,
6:15 and s them upon the large stone.
6:18 beside which they s down the ark of the LORD,
7:12 a stone and s it up between Mizpah and Jeshanah,
8:22 "Listen to their voice and s a king over them."
9: 6 about the journey on which we have s out."
9:24 and what went with it and s them before Saul.
9:24 Samuel said, "See, what was kept is s before you.
9:24 Eat; for it is s before you at the appointed time,
10:19 but s a king over us.'
12: 1 and have s a king over you.
12:13 see, the LORD has s a king over you.
15:12 where he s up a monument for himself,
16: 1 Fill your horn with oil and s out;
16:13 Samuel then s out and went to Ramah.
18: 5 as a result, Saul s him over the army.
23:13 who were about six hundred, s out and left Keilah;
23:16 Saul's son Jonathan s out and came to David
23:24 So they s out and went to Ziph ahead of Saul.
26: 5 Then David s out and came to the place
27: 2 So David s out and went over,
28:22 let me s a morsel of bread before you.
29:11 So David s out with his men early in the morning,
30: 9 So David s out, he and the six hundred men who
31:12 all the valiant men s out,
2Sa 3:10 and s up the throne of David over Israel and
4: 5 Rechab and Baanah, s out,
6: 2 David and all the people with him s out and went
6:17 and s it in its place, inside the tent
10: 9 that the battle was s against him both in front and
11:15 "S Uriah in the forefront of the hardest fighting,
12:20 when he asked, they s food before him and he ate.
12:31 and s them to work with saws and iron picks
13: 9 Then she took the pan and s them out before him,
14:17 'The word of my lord the king will s me at rest';
14:23 So Joab s off, went to Geshur,
14:30 go and s it on fire."
14:30 So Absalom's servants s the field on fire.
14:31 "Why have your servants s my field on fire?"
15:24 They s down the ark of God,
17: 1 and I will s out and pursue David tonight.
17:22 the people who were with him s out and crossed
17:23 He s his house in order, and hanged himself;
17:25 Now Absalom had s Amasa over the army in
18: 1 and s over them commanders of thousands
18:18 Now Absalom in his lifetime had taken and s up
19:28 but you s your servant among those who eat
20: 5 beyond the s time that had been appointed him.
22:34 and s me secure on the heights.
1Ki 5: 5 whom I will s on your throne in your place,
5: 6 and I will give you whatever wages you s
6:19 to s there the ark of the covenant of the LORD.
7:16 to s on the tops of the pillars;
7:21 He s up the pillars at the vestibule of the temple;
7:21 he s up the pillar on the south and called it Jachin;
7:21 he s up the pillar on the north and called it Boaz.
7:25 the sea was s on them.
7:29 on the borders that were s in the frames were lions,
7:39 He s five of the stands on the south side of
7:39 he s the sea on the southeast corner of the house.
9: 6 and my statutes that I have s before you,
10: 9 who has delighted in you and s you on the throne

1Ki 11:18 They s out from Midian and came to Paran;
12:29 He s one in Bethel, and the other he put in Dan.
14: 4 she s out and went to Shiloh,
14:12 Therefore s out, go to your house.
16:34 the cost of Abiram his firstborn, and s up its gates
17:10 So he s out and went to Zarephath.
19:19 So he s out from there,
19:21 Then he s out and followed Elijah,
20:43 The king of Israel s out toward home,
21:16 Ahab s out to go down to the vineyard of Naboth
2Ki 1:15 So he s out and went down with him to the king,
3: 9 the king of Judah, and the king of Edom s out;
4: 4 when each is full, s it aside."
4:25 So she s out, and came to the man of God
4:43 "How can I s this before a hundred people?"
4:44 He s it before them, they ate, and had some left,
6:22 S food and water before them so that they may eat
8: 3 she s out to appeal to the king for her house
8:12 you will s their fortresses on fire,
8:20 and s up a king of their own.
8:21 He s out by night and attacked the Edomites
9:21 of Israel and King Ahaziah of Judah s out, each
10: 3 s him on his father's throne,
10:12 Then he s out and went to Samaria.
11: 1 she s about to destroy all the royal family.
11:15 the captains who were s over the army,
12: 9 and s it beside the altar on the right side
12:17 when Hazael s his face to go up against Jerusalem,
17:10 they s up for themselves pillars and sacred poles
18:23 if you are able on your part to s riders on them.
19: 9 "See, he has s out to fight against you,"
19:35 That very night the angel of the LORD s out
20: 1 S your house in order, for you shall die;
21: 7 of Asherah that he had made he s in the house
25:26 the captains of the forces s out and went to Egypt;
1Ch 16: 1 s it inside the tent that David had pitched for it;
18: 3 he went to s up a monument at the river Euphrates.
19:10 the line of battle was s against him both in front
19:17 David s the battle in array against the Arameans,
20: 3 s them to work with saws and iron picks and axes.
22: 2 and he s stonecutters to prepare dressed stones
22:19 Now s your mind and heart to seek
23:13 Aaron was s apart to consecrate
25: 1 the officers of the army also s apart for the service
2Ch 3:17 He s up the pillars in front of the temple,
4: 4 the sea was s on them.
4: 6 and s five on the right side, and five on the left.
4: 7 and s them in the temple,
4:10 He s the sea at the southeast corner of the house.
6:11 There I have s the ark,
6:13 and three cubits high, and had s it in the court;
6:20 the place where you promised to s your name,
7:19 and my commandments that I have s before you,
9: 8 who has delighted in you and s you on his throne
11:16 Those who had s their hearts to seek
12:14 for he did not s his heart to seek the LORD.
13:11 s out the rows of bread on the table of pure gold,
17: 2 and s garrisons in the land of Judah,
19: 3 and have s your heart to seek God."
20: 3 he s himself to seek the LORD,
20:22 the LORD s an ambush against the Ammonites,
20:33 the people had not yet s their hearts upon the God
21: 8 the rule of Judah and s up a king of their own.
21: 9 He s out by night and attacked the Edomites,
22:10 she s about to destroy all the royal family of
23:10 and he s all the people as a guard for the king,
23:14 the captains who were s over the army, saying
23:20 They s the king on the royal throne.
24: 8 s it outside the gate of the house of the LORD.
25: 5 and s them by ancestral houses under commanders
25:14 s them up as his gods, and worshiped them,
26: 5 He s himself to seek God in the days of Zechariah,
26:15 In Jerusalem he s up machines,
30:14 They s to work and removed the altars that were
30:19 who s their hearts to seek God,
32: 5 Hezekiah s to work resolutely and built up
33: 7 The carved image of the idol that he had made he s
33:19 the sites on which he built high places and s up
35:12 They s aside the burnt offerings so
35:20 all this, when Josiah had s the temple in order,
Ezr 3: 2 and Zerubbabel son of Shealtiel with his kin s out
3: 3 They s up the altar on its foundation,
5: 2 of Jozadak s out to rebuild the house of God
6:18 Then they s the priests in their divisions and
7:10 For Ezra had s his heart to study the law of
8:20 whom David and his officials had s apart to attend
8:24 Then I s apart twelve of the leading priests:
9: 9 to give us new life to s up the house of our God,
Ne 2: 6 it pleased the king to send me, and I s him a date.
3: 1 Then the high priest Eliashib s to work
3: 1 They consecrated it and s up its doors;
3: 3 they laid its beams and s up its doors, its bolts,
3: 6 they laid its beams and s up its doors, its bolts,
3:13 they rebuilt it and s up its doors, its bolts,
3:14 he rebuilt it and s up its doors, its bolts,
3:15 he rebuilt it and covered it and s up its doors,
4: 9 and s a guard as a protection against them day
6: 1 (though up to that time I had not s up the doors in
6: 7 also s up prophets to proclaim in Jerusalem
7: 1 the wall had been built and I had s up the doors,
9:35 in the large and rich land that you s before them,
9:37 Its rich yield goes to the kings whom you have s
12:47 They s apart that which was for the Levites;
12:47 and the Levites s apart that which was for
13:11 And I gathered them together and s them
13:19 And I s some of my servants over the gates,
Est 2:17 and devotion, so that he s the royal crown

Est 3: 1 and s his seat above all the officials who were
8: 2 So Esther s Mordecai over the house of Haman.
Job 2:11 each of them s out from his home—
7:12 or the Dragon, that you s a guard over me?
7:17 that you s your mind on them,
13:27 you s a bound to the soles of my feet.
14:13 that you would appoint me a s time,
16:12 he s me up as his target;
19: 8 and he has s darkness upon my paths.
30: 1 whose fathers I would have disdained to s with
33: 5 s your words in order before me; take your stand.
36:16 and what was s on your table was full of fatness.
38:10 and prescribed bounds for it, and s bars and doors,
Ps 2: 2 The kings of the earth s themselves,
2: 6 "I have s my king on Zion, my holy hill."
3: 6 of ten thousands of people who have s themselves
4: 3 that the LORD has s apart the faithful for himself;
8: 1 You have s your glory above the heavens.
17:11 they s their eyes to cast me to the ground.
18:33 and s me secure on the heights.
19: 4 In the heavens he has s a tent for the sun,
20: 5 and in the name of our God s up our banners.
21: 3 you s a crown of fine gold on his head.
27: 5 he will s me high on a rock.
31: 8 you have s my feet in a broad place.
36: 4 they are s on a way that is not good;
40: 2 out of the miry bog, and s my feet upon a rock,
41:12 and s me in your presence forever.
44: 2 you afflicted the peoples, but them you s free;
54: 3 they do not s God before them.
55:21 but with a heart s on war;
57: 6 They s a net for my steps;
60: 4 You have s up a banner for those who fear you,
62:10 and s no vain hopes on robbery;
62:10 if riches increase, do not s your heart on them.
69:18 redeem me, s me free because of my enemies.
73: 9 They s their mouths against heaven,
73:18 Truly you s them in slippery places;
74: 4 they s up their emblems there.
74: 7 They s your sanctuary on fire;
75: 2 the s time that I appoint I will judge with equity.
78: 7 that they should s their hope in God, and not forget
86:14 and they do not s you before them.
89:19 "I have s the crown on one who is mighty,
89:25 I will s his hand on the sea and his right hand on
90: 8 You have s our iniquities before you,
101: 3 I will not s before my eyes anything that is base.
102:20 to s free those who were doomed to die;
104: 3 you s the beams of your chambers on the waters,
104: 5 You s the earth on its foundations,
104: 9 You s a boundary that they may not pass,
105:20 the ruler of the peoples s him free.
118: 5 LORD answered me and s me in a broad place.
119:30 I s your ordinances before me.
122: 5 For there the thrones for judgment were s up,
132:11 of the sons of your body I will s on your throne.
137: 6 if I do not s Jerusalem above my highest joy.
140: 5 along the road they have s snares for me.
141: 3 S a guard over my mouth, O LORD;
144: 7 s me free and rescue me from the mighty waters,
Pr 1:18 and s an ambush—for their own lives!
8:23 Ages ago I was s up, at the first,
9: 2 she has mixed her wine, she has also s her table.
19:18 do not s your heart on their destruction.
22:28 the ancient landmark that your ancestors s up.
29: 8 Scoffers s a city aflame,
Ecc 8:11 the human heart is fully s to do evil.
10: 6 folly is s in many high places,
SS 5:12 beside springs of water, bathed in milk, fitly s.
5:14 His arms are rounded gold, s with jewels.
5:15 legs are alabaster columns, s upon bases of gold.
6:12 my fancy s me in a chariot beside my prince.
8: 6 S me as a seal upon your heart,
Isa 14: 1 and will s them in their own land;
17:10 though you plant pleasant plants and s out slips of
29:21 who s a trap for the arbiter in the gate,
30: 2 who s out to go down to Egypt without asking
36: 8 if you are able on your part to s riders on them.
37: 9 "He has s out to fight against you."
37:36 Then the angel of the LORD s out and struck
38: 1 S your house in order, for you shall die;
40:20 then seeks out a skilled artisan to s up an image
41:19 I will s in the desert the cypress,
41:21 S forth your case, says the LORD;
42:25 it s him on fire all around,
43:26 s forth your case, so that you may be proved right.
44: 7 let them declare and s it forth before me.
44:13 with human beauty, to be s up in a shrine.
45:13 he shall build my city and s my exiles free,
46: 7 they s it in its place, and it stands there;
50: 7 therefore I have s my face like flint,
54:11 I am about to s your stones in antimony,
57: 7 a high and lofty mountain you have s your bed,
57: 8 and the doorpost you have s up your symbol;
65:11 who s a table for Fortune and fill cups of mixed
66:19 and I will s a sign among them.
Jer 1:15 and all of them shall s their thrones at the entrance
3:19 I thought how I would s you among my children,
4: 7 a destroyer of nations has s out;
5:26 Like fowlers they s a trap;
7:30 they have s their abominations in the house
9:13 they have forsaken my law that I s before them,
10:20 to spread my tent again, and to s up my curtains.
11:13 as the streets of Jerusalem are the altars you have s
11:16 with the roar of a great tempest he will s fire to it,
12: 3 and s them apart for the day of slaughter.
13:21 What will you say when they s as head

Jer 14:22 We s our hope on you, for it is you who do all this.
21:10 For I have s my face against this city for evil and
24: 6 I will s my eyes upon them for good,
26: 4 to walk in my law that I have s before you,
30:18 and the citadel s on its rightful site.
31:21 S up road markers for yourself,
31:29 and the children's teeth are s on edge."
31:30 of everyone who eats sour grapes shall be s
32:29 s it on fire, and burn it,
32:34 They s up their abominations in the house
34: 9 that all should s free their Hebrew slaves,
34:10 into the covenant that all would s free their slaves,
34:10 they obeyed and s them free.
34:11 the male and female slaves they had s free,
34:14 you must s free any Hebrews who have been sold
34:14 you must s them free from your service."
34:16 whom you had s free according to their desire,
35: 5 I s before the Rechabites pitchers full of wine,
37: 7 Pharaoh's army, which s out to help you,
37:12 Jeremiah s out from Jerusalem to go to the land
41:10 of Nethaniah took them captive and s out to cross
41:17 And they s out, and stopped at Geruth Chimham
43:10 and he will s his throne above these stones
44:10 in my law and my statutes that I s before you and
48: 9 S aside salt for Moab, for she will surely fall;
49:38 and I will s my throne in Elam,
50: 2 s up a banner and proclaim, do not conceal it, say:
50:24 You s a snare for yourself and you were caught,
50:42 s in array as a warrior for battle, against you,
51:30 her buildings are s on fire, her bars are broken.
51:39 I will s out their drink and make them drunk,
La 2: 4 with his right hand s like a foe;
3:12 he bent his bow and s me as a mark for his arrow.
Eze 2: 2 a spirit entered into me and s me on my feet;
3:24 The spirit entered into me, and s me on my feet;
4: 1 you, O mortal, take a brick and s it before you.
4: 2 s camps also against it, and plant battering rams
4: 3 s your face toward it, and let it be in a state
4: 7 You shall s your face toward the siege
5: 5 I have s her in the center of the nations,
6: 2 s your face toward the mountains of Israel,
13:17 s your face against the daughters of your people,
14: 8 I will s my face against them;
15: 7 I will s my face against them;
15: 7 when I s my face against them.
16:18 and s my oil and my incense before them.
16:19 you s it before them as a pleasing odor;
17: 4 s it in a city of merchants.
17: 5 he s it like a willow twig.
17:22 of a cedar; I will s it out.
18: 2 and the children's teeth are s on edge"?
19: 8 nations s upon him from the provinces all around;
20:24 and their eyes were s on their ancestors' idols.
20:46 s your face toward the south,
21: 2 s your face toward Jerusalem and preach against
21:15 At all their gates I have s the point of the sword.
21:22 to s battering rams, to call out for slaughter,
21:22 to s battering rams against the gates,
23:24 they shall s themselves against you on every side
24: 3 S on the pot, s it on, pour in water also;
25: 2 s your face toward the Ammonites and prophesy
25: 4 They shall s their encampments among you
26: 8 He shall s up a siege wall against you,
28:21 s your face toward Sidon, and prophesy against it,
29: 2 s your face against Pharaoh king of Egypt,
30: 8 when I have s fire to Egypt,
30:14 and will s fire to Zoan,
30:16 I will s fire to Egypt;
31:10 it towered high and s its top among the clouds,
31:14 the waters may grow to lofty height or s their tops
32:23 Their graves are s in the uttermost parts of the Pit.
33:31 but their heart is s on their gain.
34:23 I will s up over them one shepherd,
35: 2 s your face against Mount Seir,
37: 1 of the LORD and s me down in the middle of
37:26 and will s my sanctuary among them forevermore.
38: 2 s your face toward Gog, of the land of Magog,
39:14 They will s apart men to pass through
39:15 anyone who sees a human bone shall s up a sign
40: 2 and s me down upon a very high mountain,
40: 4 and s your mind upon all that I shall show you,
42: 6 for this reason the upper chambers were s back
45: 1 you shall s aside for the LORD a portion of
45: 6 Alongside the portion s apart as
48: 8 shall be the portion that you shall s apart,
48: 9 that you shall s apart for the LORD shall
48:20 The whole portion that you shall s apart shall
Da 1:18 the time that the king had s for them to be brought
2:44 in the days of those kings the God of heaven will s
3: 1 he s it up on the plain of Dura in the province
3: 2 of the statue that King Nebuchadnezzar had s up.
3: 3 of the statue that King Nebuchadnezzar had s up.
3: 3 before the statue that Nebuchadnezzar had s up,
3: 5 that King Nebuchadnezzar has s up.
3: 7 that King Nebuchadnezzar had s up.
3:12 not worship the golden statue that you have s up."
3:14 not worship the golden statue that I have s up?
3:18 not worship the golden statue that you have s up."
6: 1 to s over the kingdom one hundred twenty satraps,
7: 9 thrones were s in place, and an Ancient One took
8:18 then he touched me and s me on my feet.
9:10 which he s before us by his servants the prophets.
10:12 that you s your mind to gain understanding and
11:17 He shall s his mind to come with the strength
11:28 but his heart shall be s against the holy covenant.
11:31 They shall abolish the regular burnt offering and s
12:11 and the abomination that desolates is s up,

Hos 8: 1 S the trumpet to your lips!
8: 4 they s up princes, but without my knowledge.
Ob 1: 4 though your nest is s among the stars,
1: 7 those who ate your bread have s a trap for you—
Jnh 1: 3 But Jonah s out to flee to Tarshish from
3: 3 So Jonah s out and went to Nineveh,
Mic 2:12 I will s them together like sheep in a fold,
Na 2: 5 they hasten to the wall, and the mantelet is s up.
Zec 3: 9 For on the stone that I have s before Joshua,
5:11 they will s the basket down there on its base."
6: 8 toward the north country have s my spirit at rest in
6:11 and s it on the head of the high priest Joshua son
8:10 and I s them all against one other.
9:11 I will s your prisoners free from the waterless pit.
Mt 2: 9 When they had heard the king, they s out;
10:35 For I have come to s a man against his father,
27: 9 the price of the one on whom a price had been s,
27: 9 on whom some of the people of Israel had s
Mk 6:41 gave them to his disciples to s before the people;
7:24 From there he s out and went away to the region
13:14 the desolating sacrilege s up where it ought not to
14:16 So the disciples s out and went to the city,
Lk 1: 1 to s down an orderly account of the events
1:39 In those days Mary s out and went with haste to
7: 8 For I also am a man s under authority,
9:16 gave them to the disciples to s before the crowd.
9:51 he s his face to go to Jerusalem.
9:53 because his face was s toward Jerusalem.
10: 8 eat what is s before you;
11: 6 and I have nothing to s before him.'
12:14 who s me to be a judge or arbitrator over you?"
13:12 "Woman, you are s free from your ailment."
13:16 be s free from this bondage on the sabbath day?"
15:20 So he s off and went to his father.
17:23 Do not go, do not s off in pursuit.
19:35 after throwing their cloaks on the colt, they s Jesus
19:43 when your enemies will s up ramparts around you
Jn 5:45 on whom you have s your hope.
6:27 For it is on him that God the Father has s his seal."
13:15 For I have s you an example,
20: 3 the other disciple s out and went toward the tomb.
Ac 1: 7 to know the times or periods that the Father has s
6:13 They s up false witnesses who said,
13: 2 "S apart for me Barnabas and Saul for the work
13:13 Then Paul and his companions s sail from Paphos
13:39 by this Jesus everyone who believes is s free
13:47 saying, 'I have s you to be a light for the Gentiles,
15:16 from its ruins I will rebuild it, and I will s it up,
15:40 But Paul chose Silas and s out,
16:11 We s sail from Troas and took a straight course
16:34 He brought them up into the house and s food
17: 5 the marketplaces they formed a mob and s the city
18:21 Then he s sail from Ephesus.
20: 3 about to s sail for Syria when a plot was made
20:13 We went ahead to the ship and s sail for Assos,
20:18 the entire time from the first day that I s foot
21: 1 When we had parted from them and s sail,
21: 2 we went on board and s sail.
26:32 "This man could have been s free if he had
27: 2 that was about to s sail to the ports along the coast
27:21 you should have listened to me and not have s sail
27:32 the ropes of the boat and s it adrift.
28:11 Three months later we s sail on a ship
28:23 After they had s a day to meet with him,
Ro 1: 1 s apart for the gospel of God,
6:18 having been s free from sin,
8: 2 the Spirit of life in Christ Jesus has s you free from
8: 5 to the flesh s their minds on the things of the flesh,
8: 5 the Spirit s their minds on the things of the Spirit.
8: 6 To s the mind on the flesh is death,
8: 6 but to s the mind on the Spirit is life and peace.
8: 7 the mind that is s on the flesh is hostile to God;
8:21 be s free from its bondage to decay and will obtain
15:28 I will s out by way of you to Spain;
1Co 7: 5 by agreement for a s time,
10:27 eat whatever is s before you
2Co 1:10 on him we have s our hope
3: 7 of the glory of his face, a glory now s aside,
3:11 for if what was s aside came through glory,
3:13 at the end of the glory that was being s aside.
3:14 since only in Christ is it s aside.
7:13 because his mind has been s at rest by all of you.
Gal 1: 4 for our sins to s us free from the present evil age,
1:15 who had s me apart before I was born
4: 2 under guardians and trustees until the date s by
5: 1 For freedom Christ has s us free.
Eph 1: 9 according to his good pleasure that he s forth
1:12 who were the first to s our hope on Christ,
Php 3:19 their minds are s on earthly things.
Col 2:14 He s this aside, nailing it to the cross.
3: 2 S your minds on things that are above,
1Ti 4:10 because we have our hope s on the living God,
4:12 s the believers an example in speech and conduct,
5: 5 has s her hope on God and continues
6:17 or to s their hopes on the uncertainty of riches,
Heb 6:18 strongly encouraged to seize the hope s before us.
8: 2 and not any mortal, has s up.
9:10 until the time comes to s things right.
11: 8 when he was called to s out for a place that he was
11: 8 and he s out, not knowing where he was going.
12: 1 run with perseverance the race that is s before us,
12: 2 of the joy that was s before him endured the cross,
13:23 to know that our brother Timothy has been s free;
Jas 3: 5 How great a forest is s ablaze by a small fire!
3: 6 and is itself s on fire by hell.
1Pe 1:13 s all your hope on the grace
1:21 so that your faith and hope are s on God.

2Pe 3:12 because of which the heavens will be s ablaze
Rev 3: 8 Look, I have s before you an open door,
Tob 2: 2 When the table was s for me and an abundance
2: 7 sun had s, I went and dug a grave and buried him.
5:17 for the journey and s out with your brother.
6:18 for she was s apart for you before
10: 7 When the sun had s she would go in and mourn
13:12 all who overthrow your towers and s your homes
14:10 Ahikar escaped the fatal trap that Nadab had s
Jdt 2: 2 and all his nobles and s before them his secret plan
2:19 Then he s out with his whole army,
5: 1 the high hilltops and s up barricades in the plains.
6:16 They s Achior in the midst of all their people,
7: 7 he seized them and s guards of soldiers over them,
8: 5 at home where she s up a tent for herself on
8:12 and to s yourselves up in the place of God
8:24 my brothers, let us s an example for our kindred,
11:13 which they had consecrated and s aside for
11:19 there I will s your throne.
12: 1 and ordered them to s a table for her with some
14: 2 s a captain over them, as if you were going down
16: 6 nor did tall giants s upon him;
16:23 She s her maid free.
AdE 8: 2 and Esther s Mordecai over everything
8:14 on horseback s out with all speed to perform what
13:14 so that I might not s human glory above the glory
16: 5 And often many of those who are s in places
Wis 6:11 Therefore s your desire on my words;
9:18 And thus the paths of those on earth were s right,
13:10 But miserable, with their hopes s on dead things,
16:14 or s free the imprisoned soul.
Sir 2: 2 S your heart right and be steadfast,
22:18 Fences s on a high place will not stand firm
22:27 Who will s a guard over my mouth,
23: 2 Who will s whips over my thoughts,
28: 6 the end of your life, and s enmity aside;
31:16 Eat what is s before you like
33:26 S your slave to work, and you will find rest;
33:30 S him to work, as is fitting for him,
38:27 they s their heart on painting a lifelike image,
42:21 He has s in order the splendors of his wisdom;
47: 2 the fat is s apart from the offering of well-being,
47: 2 so David was s apart from the Israelites.
49: 6 who s fire to the chosen city of the sanctuary,
49:13 and s up gates and bars, and rebuilt our ruined
Bar 1:18 in the statutes of the Lord that he s before us.
2:10 in the statutes of the Lord that he s before us.
LtJ 6:18 so are their gods when they have been s up in
6:34 They cannot s up a king or depose one.
6:53 For they cannot s up a king over a country
Bel 1:11 O king, s out the food and prepare the wine,
1:14 they had gone out, the king s out the food for Bel.
1:36 the speed of the wind he s him down in Babylon,
1Mc 3:40 So they s out with their entire force,
6:17 he s up Antiochus the king's son to reign.
6:33 the king s out and took his army by a forced march
6:51 He s up siege towers, engines of war to throw fire
6:63 Then he s off in haste and returned to Antioch.
7: 1 of Seleucus s out from Rome,
9:67 and his men sallied out from the town and s fire to
10:33 of Judah into any part of my kingdom, I s free
10:50 He pressed the battle strongly until the sun s,
10:57 So Ptolemy s out from Egypt,
10:74 He chose ten thousand men and s out
11: 2 He s out for Syria with peaceable words,
11:22 soon as he heard it he s out and came to Ptolemais;
11:48 They s fire to the city and seized a large amount
11:57 and s you over the four districts and make you one
11:60 Then Jonathan s out and traveled beyond the river
11:66 and s a garrison over it.
11:68 they had s an ambush against him in
12:27 So when the sun had s,
15:10 one hundred seventy-fourth year Antiochus s out
2Mc 1: 8 and we lit the lamps and s out the loaves.
1:15 When the priests of the temple of Nanea had s out
1:27 s free those who are slaves among the Gentiles,
2:23 which has been s forth by Jason of Cyrene
3: 8 Heliodorus at once s out on his journey,
3:14 So he s a day and went in to direct the inspection
4:11 He s aside the existing royal concessions to
7:22 I who s in order the elements within each of you.
8: 6 he would s fire to towns and villages.
8:33 they burned those who had s fire to the sacred
10: 3 and lighted lamps and s out the bread of
10:19 and he himself s off for places
10:36 against the defenders and s fire to the towers;
12: 6 He s fire to the harbor by night, burned the boats,
12: 9 the Jamnites by night and s fire to the harbor and
12:20 s men in command of the divisions,
13:26 gained their goodwill, and s out for Antioch.
14:16 they s out from there immediately
14:21 leaders s a day on which to meet by themselves.
14:21 seats of honor were s in place;
1Es 4:44 which Cyrus s apart when he began
4:57 the vessels that Cyrus had s apart;
8:54 Then I s apart twelve of the leaders of the priests,
9: 1 Then Ezra s out and went from the court of
3Mc 2:27 and he s up a stone on the tower in the courtyard
6:38 and their destruction was s for the fifth to
2Es 2:14 I s aside evil and created good;
3:16 You s apart Jacob for yourself,
5:15 with me held me and strengthened me and s me
7: 3 a sea s in a wide expanse so that it is deep
7: 4 but it has an entrance s in a narrow place,
7: 6 There is a city built and s on a plain,
7: 7 to it is narrow and s in a precipitous place,
7:20 of God that is s before them be disregarded!

2Es 7:*61* they are s on fire and burn hotly,
9:47 I s a day for the marriage feast.
10:30 and strengthened me and s me on my feet,
11:25 that these little wings planned to s themselves up
11:26 As I kept looking, one was s up,
12: 2 that had gone over to it rose up and s themselves
12:34 in mercy he will s free the remnant of my people,
14:13 s your house in order, and reprove your people;
15:29 and from the day that they s out,
4Mc 6:15 We will s before you some cooked meat;
11:27 of the tyrant but those of the divine law that are s
17: 3 Nobly s like a roof on the pillars of your sons,
17: 5 before God and are firmly s in heaven with them.

SETH‡ (10)

Ge 4:25 and she bore a son and named him **S,** for she said,
4:26 To **S** also a son was born,
5: 3 according to his image, and named him **S.**
5: 4 the father of **S** were eight hundred years;
5: 6 When **S** had lived one hundred five years,
5: 7 **S** lived after the birth of Enosh
5: 8 the days of **S** were nine hundred twelve years;
1Ch 1: 1 Adam, **S,** Enosh;
Lk 3:38 son of Enos, son of **S,** son of Adam, son of God.
Sir 49:16 Shem and **S** and Enosh were honored,

SETHUR (1)

Nu 13:13 from the tribe of Asher, **S** son of Michael;

SETS (30) [SET]

Ge 45:22 of silver and five s of garments.
Ex 30: 8 and when Aaron s up the lamps in the evening,
Lev 16:26 The one who s the goat free
22: 7 When the sun s he shall be clean;
Nu 4:15 the furnishings of the sanctuary, as the camp s out,
Dt 26: 4 the priest takes the basket from your hand and s it
27:15 the work of an artisan, and s it up in secret."
32:22 and s on fire the foundations of the mountains.
2Ki 5: 5 of silver, six thousand shekels of gold, and ten s
Job 5:11 he s on high those who are lowly,
34:24 and s others in their place.
36: 7 but with kings on the throne he s them forever,
Ps 83:14 as the flame s the mountains ablaze,
146: 7 The LORD s the prisoners free;
Isa 26: 1 he s up victory like walls and bulwarks.
30:29 as when one s out to the sound of the flute to go to
Da 2:21 deposes kings and s up kings;
4:17 and s over it the lowliest of human beings.'
5:21 and s over it whomever he will.
Jn 19:12 Everyone who claims to be a king s himself
Heb 4: 7 again he s a certain day—
Jas 3: 6 s on fire the cycle of nature,
Jdt 16: 2 he s up his camp among his people;
Wis 13:15 and s it in the wall, and fastens it there with iron.
Sir 27:26 and whoever s a snare will be caught in it.
38:26 He s his heart on plowing furrows,
38:28 He s his heart on finishing his handiwork,
38:30 he s his heart to finish the glazing,
39: 5 He s his heart to rise early to seek
LtJ 6:27 If anyone s it upright, it cannot move itself;

SETTER (KJV) See PROCLAIMER

SETTING (38) [SET]

Ex 23: 5 and you would hold back from s it free,
31: 5 in cutting stones for s, and in carving wood,
35:33 in cutting stones for s, and in carving wood,
40: 4 You shall bring in the table, and arrange its s;
Nu 7: 1 when Moses had finished s up the tabernacle,
10:29 "We are s out for the place of which
Dt 4: 8 and ordinances as just as this entire law that I am s
11:26 I am s before you today a blessing and a curse:
11:32 and ordinances that I am s before you today.
1Sa 13:21 of a shekel for sharpening the axes and for s
1Ki 15: 4 s up his son after him, and establishing Jerusalem;
1Ch 29: 2 besides great quantities of onyx and stones for s,
Ps 50: 1 the earth from the rising of the sun to its s.
104:19 the sun knows its time for s.
113: 3 to its s the name of the LORD is to be praised.
Pr 25:11 A word fitly spoken is like apples of gold in a s
Jer 21: 8 See, I am s before you the way of life and the way
Am 7: 8 I am s a plumb line in the midst of my people
Hab 2: 9 s your nest on high to be safe from the reach
Mal 1:11 from the rising of the sun to its s my name is great
Mt 16:23 for you are s your mind not on divine things but
Mk 8:33 For you are s your mind not on divine things but
10:17 As he was s out on a journey,
Lk 4:40 the sun was s, all those who had any who were sick
Rev 10: 2 S his right foot on the sea and his left foot on
Tob 3:17 by s her free from the wicked demon Asmodeus.
Sir 32: 5 A ruby seal in a s of gold is a concert of music at
32: 6 A seal of emerald in a rich s of gold is the melody
45:11 in a s of gold, the work of a jeweler,
1Mc 13:29 For the pyramids he devised an elaborate s,
2Mc 5: 6 but imagining that he was s up trophies of victory
10:21 by s their enemies free to fight against them.
12:29 S out from there, they hastened to Scythopolis,
1Es 2:23 the Jews were rebels and kept s up blockades in it
Man 1:10 s up abominations and multiplying offenses.
3Mc 4:15 from the rising of the sun until its s,
4Mc 6:19 of impiety to the young by s them an example in
7: 5 For in s his mind firm like a jutting cliff,

SETTINGS (10) [SET]

Ex 28:11 you shall mount them in s of gold filigree.
28:13 You shall make s of gold filigree,
28:14 and you shall attach the corded chains to the s.
28:25 of the two cords you shall attach to the two s,
39: 6 enclosed in s of gold filigree and engraved like
39:13 they were enclosed in s of gold filigree.
39:16 and they made two s of gold filigree
39:18 of the two cords they had attached to the two s
2Ch 3: 6 He adorned the house with s of precious stones.
Eze 28:13 worked in gold were your s and your engravings.

SETTLE (52) [SETTLED, SETTLEMENT, SETTLEMENTS, SETTLES, SETTLING]

Ge 20:15 before you; s where it pleases you."
26: 2 s in the land that I shall show you.
35: 1 "Arise, go up to Bethel, and s there.
45:10 You shall s in the land of Goshen,
46:34 in order that you may s in the land of Goshen,
47: 4 let your servants s in the land of Goshen."
47: 6 s your father and your brothers in the best part of
49:13 Zebulun shall s at the shore of the sea;
Lev 20:22 so that the land to which I bring you to s in may
26:32 so that your enemies who come to s in it shall
Nu 14:30 into the land in which I swore to s you,
33:53 You shall take possession of the land and s in it,
Dt 2:21 so that they could dispossess them and s
2:22 that they could dispossess them and s in their place
26: 1 and you possess it, and s in it,
Jos 7: 7 that we had been content to s beyond the Jordan!
Ru 3:18 but will s the matter today."
2Sa 20:18 and so they would s a matter.
2Ki 8: 1 with your household, and s wherever you can;
Job 3: 5 Let clouds s upon it; let the blackness of the day
Ps 139: 9 the morning and s at the farthest limits of the sea,
Isa 7:19 And they will all come and s in the steep ravines,
16: 4 let the outcasts of Moab s among you;
23: 7 whose feet carried her to s far away?
49:20 make room for me to **s."**
54: 3 the nations and will s the desolate towns.
65: 9 and my servants shall s there.
Jer 32:37 and I will s them in safety.
42:15 to enter Egypt and go to s there,
42:17 to s there shall die by the sword, by famine,
42:22 in the place where you desire to go and **s."**
43: 2 'Do not go to Egypt to s there';
43: 5 the remnant of Judah who had returned to s in
44: 8 in the land of Egypt where you have come to **s?**
44:12 of Egypt to s, and they shall perish, everyone;
44:14 to s in the land of Egypt shall escape or survive
44:28 who have come to the land of Egypt to s,
49:18 no one shall live there, nor shall anyone s in it.
49:33 no one shall live there, nor shall anyone s in it.
50:40 nor shall anyone s in her.
Eze 28:25 in them in the sight of the nations, then they shall s
31:13 On its fallen trunk s all the birds of the air,
32: 4 and will cause all the birds of the air to s on you,
Zec 9: 6 a mongrel people shall s in Ashdod,
Mt 18:23 to a king who wished to s accounts with his slaves.
Lk 12:58 on the way make an effort to s the case,
Tob 7:11 "I will neither eat nor drink anything until you s
AdE 13: 2 to s the lives of my subjects in lasting tranquility
Sir 28:16 nor will they s down in peace.
1Mc 3:36 s aliens in all their territory,
2Mc 4:31 So the king went hurriedly to s the trouble,
11:14 and persuaded them to s everything on just terms,

SETTLED (76) [SETTLE]

Ge 4:16 and s in the land of Nod, east of Eden.
11: 2 upon a plain in the land of Shinar and s there.
11:31 but when they came to Haran, they s there.
13:12 Abram s in the land of Canaan,
13:12 while Lot s among the cities of the Plain
13:18 and came and s by the oaks of Mamre,
19:29 when he overthrew the cities in which Lot had s.
19:30 of Zoar and s in the hills with his two daughters,
20: 1 and s between Kadesh and Shur.
24:62 and was s in the Negeb.
25:11 And Isaac s at Beer-lahai-roi.
25:18 They s from Havilah to Shur,
25:18 he s down alongside of all his people.
26: 6 So Isaac s in Gerar.
26:17 and camped in the valley of Gerar and s there.
36: 8 Esau s in the hill country of Seir; Esau is Edom.
37: 1 Jacob s in the land where his father had lived as
38: 1 that Judah went down from his brothers and s near
47:11 Joseph s his father and his brothers,
47:27 Thus Israel s in the land of Egypt,
Ex 2:15 He s in the land of Midian,
10:14 The locusts came upon all the land of Egypt and s
24:16 The glory of the LORD s on Mount Sinai,
40:35 the tent of meeting because the cloud s upon it,
Nu 9:17 and in the place where the cloud s down,
10:12 and the cloud s down in the wilderness of Paran.
21:25 and Israel s in all the towns of the Amorites,
21:31 Thus Israel s in the land of the Amorites.
22: 5 and they have s next to me.
31:10 All their towns where they had s,
32:40 to Machir son of Manasseh, and he s there.
Dt 2:23 destroyed them and s in their place.)
17:14 and have taken possession of it and s in it,
19: 1 and s in their towns and in their houses,
21: 5 of dispute and assault shall be s.
Jos 19:47 they took possession of it and s in it,
19:50 he rebuilt the town, and s in it.
Jos 21:43 and having taken possession of it, they s there.
22:33 where the Reubenites and the Gadites were s.
Jdg 1:16 Then they went and s with the Amalekites.
1Sa 12: 8 and s them in this place.
19:18 He and Samuel went and s at Naioth.
2Sa 2: 3 and they s in the towns of Hebron.
7: 1 Now when the king was s in his house,
1Ki 11:24 they went to Damascus, s there,
2Ki 8: 2 she went with her household and s in the land of
17:24 they took possession of Samaria, and s in its cities.
17:25 they first s there, they did not worship the LORD;
18:11 s them in Halah, on the Habor, the river of Gozan,
1Ch 4:41 and exterminated them to this day, and s
17: 1 Now when David s in his house,
2Ch 8: 2 and s the people of Israel in them.
28:18 with its villages; and they s there.
Ezr 4:10 and noble Osnappar deported and s in the cities
Ne 7:73 the temple servants, and all Israel s in their towns.
7:73 the people of Israel being s in their towns—
11:23 and a s provision for the singers,
Ps 78:55 a possession and s the tribes of Israel in their tents.
Jer 48:11 s like wine on its dregs;
49: 1 and his people s in its towns?
Mt 25:19 of those slaves came and s accounts with them.
Ac 7: 4 Then he left the country of the Chaldeans and s
19:39 it must be s in the regular assembly.
Tob 14:12 and his wife and children returned to Media and s
Jdt 5: 9 There they s, and grew very prosperous in gold
5:19 and have s in the hill country,
Sir 22:17 A mind s on an intelligent thought is
1Mc 2: 1 moved from Jerusalem and s in Modein.
9:73 Jonathan s in Michmash and began to judge
13:48 and s in it those who observed the law.
14:34 He s Jews there, and provided
14:37 He s Jews in it and fortified it for the safety of
2Mc 13:23 s with them and offered sacrifice,
14:25 so Judas married, s down,
1Es 5:46 some of the people s in Jerusalem and its vicinity;
9:37 the Levites and the Israelites s in Jerusalem and in

SETTLEMENT‡ (1) [SETTLE]

2Mc 4: 6 public affairs could not again reach a peaceful s,

SETTLEMENTS‡ (19) [SETTLE]

Ge 36:43 according to their s in the land that they held.
Ex 12:20 in all your s you shall eat unleavened bread.
Lev 3:17 throughout your generations, in all your **s:**
7:26 either of bird or of animal, in any of your s.
23: 3 it is a sabbath to the LORD throughout your s.
23:14 throughout your generations in all your s.
23:17 You shall bring from your s two loaves of bread as
23:21 in all your s throughout your generations.
23:31 throughout your generations in all your s.
Dt 2:23 Avvim, who had lived in s in the vicinity of Gaza,
Jos 13:30 and all the s of Jair, which are in Bashan,
1Sa 27: 8 for these were the landed s from Telam on the way
1Ch 4:33 these towns as far as Baal. These were their s.
6:54 These are their dwelling places according to their s
7:28 Their possessions and s were Bethel and its towns,
2Ch 6:28 if their enemies besiege them in any of the s of
Eze 6:14 the land desolate and waste, throughout all their s,
1Es 9:12 in our s who have foreign wives come at
9:37 when the people of Israel were in their s,

SETTLERS See Index to Footnotes

SETTLES (1) [SETTLE]

Sir 43:20 it s on every pool of water,

SETTLING (5) [SETTLE]

Nu 33:55 they shall trouble you in the land where you are s.
Dt 2:12 destroying them and s in their place,
Jdg 5:17 at the coast of the sea, s down by his landings.
Ps 65:10 You water its furrows abundantly, s its ridges,
Na 3:17 s on the fences on a cold day—

SEVEN‡ (504) [SEVEN-TOWERED, SEVENFOLD, SEVENTH]

A. SEVEN DAYS (122)
B. SEVEN TIMES (33)
C. SEVEN YEARS (32)

Ge 5: 7 after the birth of Enosh eight hundred s years,
5:26 the birth of Lamech s hundred eighty-two years,
5:31 of Lamech were s hundred seventy-seven years;
7: 2 Take with you s pairs of all clean animals,
7: 3 and s pairs of the birds of the air also,
7: 4 For in s days I will send rain on the earth A
7:10 s days the waters of the flood came on the earth. A
8:10 He waited another s days, A
8:12 he waited another s days, and sent out the dove; A
11:21 after the birth of Serug two hundred s years,
21:28 Abraham set apart s ewe lambs of the flock.
21:29 of these s ewe lambs that you have set apart?"
21:30 "These s ewe lambs you shall accept
29:18 so he said, "I will serve you s years C
29:20 So Jacob served s years for Rachel, C
29:27 also in return for serving me another s years." C
29:30 He served Laban for another s years. C
31:23 and pursued him for s days until he caught up A
33: 3 bowing himself to the ground s times, B
41: 2 there came up out of the Nile s sleek and fat cows,
41: 3 Then s other cows, ugly and thin,

Ge 41: 4 ugly and thin cows ate up the s sleek and fat cows.
41: 5 s ears of grain, plump and good,
41: 6 Then s ears, thin and blighted by the east wind,
41: 7 thin ears swallowed up the s plump and full ears.
41:18 and s cows, fat and sleek, came up out of the Nile
41:19 Then s other cows came up after them, poor,
41:20 The thin and ugly cows ate up the first s fat cows,
41:22 a second time and I saw in my dream s ears
41:23 and s ears, withered, thin, and blighted by
41:24 and the thin ears swallowed up the s good ears.
41:26 The s good cows are seven years,
41:26 The seven good cows are s years, C
41:26 and the s good ears are seven years;
41:26 and the seven good ears are s years; C
41:27 The s lean and ugly cows that came up
41:27 ugly cows that came up after them are s years, C
41:27 as are the s empty ears blighted by the east wind.
41:27 They are s years of famine. C
41:29 There will come s years of great plenty C
41:30 After them there will arise s years of famine, C
41:34 of the land of Egypt during the s plenteous years.
41:36 reserve for the land against the s years of famine C
41:47 During the s plenteous years
41:48 the food of the s years when there was plenty in C
41:53 The s years of plenty that prevailed in the land C
41:54 and the s years of famine began to come, C
46:25 these she bore to Jacob—s persons in all).
50:10 a time of mourning for his father s days. A
Ex 2:16 The priest of Midian had s daughters.
7:25 S days passed after the LORD had struck A
12:15 S days you shall eat unleavened bread; A
12:19 s days no leaven shall be found in your houses; A
13: 6 S days you shall eat unleavened bread, A
13: 7 Unleavened bread shall be eaten for s days; A
22:30 s days it shall remain with its mother; A
23:15 for s days at the appointed time in the month A
25:37 You shall make the s lamps for it;
29:30 in his place shall wear them s days, A
29:35 through s days you shall ordain them. A
29:37 S days you shall make atonement for the altar, A
34:18 S days you shall eat unleavened bread, A
37:23 He made its s lamps and its snuffers and its trays
38:24 and s hundred thirty shekels,
38:25 and one thousand s hundred seventy-five shekels,
38:28 thousand s hundred seventy-five shekels he made
Lev 4: 6 of the blood s times before the LORD in front of B
4:17 and sprinkle it s times before the LORD, B
8:11 He sprinkled some of it on the altar s times, B
8:33 the entrance of the tent of meeting for s days, A
8:33 For it will take s days to ordain you; A
8:35 and night for s days, keeping the LORD's charge A
12: 2 she shall be ceremonially unclean s days; A
13: 4 shall confine the diseased person for s days. A
13: 5 then the priest shall confine him s days more. A
13:21 the priest shall confine him s days. A
13:26 the priest shall confine him s days. A
13:31 the person with the itching disease for s days. A
13:33 the person with the itch for s days more. A
13:50 and put the diseased article aside for s days. A
13:54 and he shall put it aside s days more. A
14: 7 He shall sprinkle it s times upon the one who B
14: 8 but shall live outside his tent s days. A
14:16 and sprinkle some oil with his finger s times B
14:27 that is in his left hand s times before the LORD. B
14:38 door of the house and shut up the house s days. A
14:51 and sprinkle the house s times. B
15:13 he shall count s days for his cleansing; A
15:19 she shall be in her impurity for s days, A
15:24 he shall be unclean s days; A
15:28 of her discharge, she shall count s days, A
16:14 the blood with his finger s times. B
16:19 of the blood on it with his finger s times, B
22:27 it shall remain s days with its mother, A
23: 6 s days you shall eat unleavened bread. A
23: 8 For s days you shall present A
23:15 you shall count off s weeks;
23:18 with the bread s lambs a year old without blemish,
23:34 of this seventh month, and lasting s days, A
23:36 S days you shall present the LORD's offerings A
23:39 the festival of the LORD, lasting s days; A
23:40 before the LORD your God for s days. A
23:41 shall keep it as a festival to the LORD s days A
23:42 You shall live in booths for s days; A
25: 8 You shall count off s weeks of years,
25: 8 of years, s times seven years, so that the period B
25: 8 of years, seven times s years, so that the period C
25: 8 period of s weeks of years gives forty-nine years.
Nu 1:39 of Dan were sixty-two thousand s hundred.
2:26 as enrolled of sixty-two thousand s hundred.
3:22 was s thousand five hundred.
4:36 by clans was two thousand s hundred fifty.
8: 2 s lamps shall give light in front of the lampstand.
12:14 would she not bear her shame for s days? A
12:14 Let her be shut out of the camp for s days, A
12:15 So Miriam was shut out of the camp for s days; A
13:22 (Hebron was built s years before Zoan in Egypt.) C
16:49 by the plague were fourteen thousand s hundred,
19: 4 sprinkle it s times towards the front of the tent B
19:11 of any human being shall be unclean s days. A
19:14 in the tent, shall be unclean s days. A
19:16 or a grave, shall be unclean s days. A
23: 1 Balaam said to Balak, "Build me s altars here, and prepare s bulls and s rams for me."
23: 4 Balaam said to him, "I have arranged the s altars,
23:14 He built s altars, and offered a bull and a ram
23:29 Balaam said to Balak, "Build me s altars here, and prepare s bulls and s rams for me."

Nu 26: 7 enrolled was forty-three thousand s hundred thirty.
26:34 of those enrolled was fifty-two thousand s hundred.
26:51 six hundred and one thousand s hundred thirty.
28:11 one ram, s male lambs a year old without blemish;
28:17 s days shall unleavened bread be eaten. A
28:19 one ram, and s male lambs a year old;
28:21 one-tenth shall you offer for each of the s lambs;
28:24 the same way you shall offer daily, for s days, A
28:27 two young bulls, one ram, s male lambs a year old.
28:29 one-tenth for each of the s lambs;
29: 2 one ram, s male lambs a year old without blemish.
29: 4 and one-tenth for each of the s lambs;
29: 8 one young bull, one ram, s male lambs a year old.
29:10 one-tenth for each of the s lambs;
29:12 shall celebrate a festival to the LORD s days. A
29:32 On the seventh day: s bulls, two rams,
29:36 one ram, s male lambs a year old without blemish,
31:19 Camp outside the camp s days; A
31:52 was sixteen thousand s hundred fifty shekels.
Dt 7: 1 s nations mightier and more numerous than you—
16: 3 s days you shall eat unleavened bread with it— A
16: 4 be seen with you in all your territory for s days; A
16: 9 You shall count s weeks; begin to count
16: 9 the s weeks from the time the sickle is first put to
16:13 You shall keep the festival of booths for s days, A
16:15 S days you shall keep the festival for A
28: 7 and flee before you s ways.
28:25 against them one way and flee before them s ways.
Jos 6: 4 with s priests bearing s trumpets
6: 4 around the city s times, the priests blowing B
6: 6 and have s priests carry s trumpets
6: 8 the s priests carrying the s trumpets
6:13 The s priests carrying the s trumpets
6:15 around the city in the same manner s times. B
6:15 day that they marched around the city s times. B
18: 2 among the Israelites s tribes whose inheritance
18: 5 They shall divide it into s portions,
18: 6 in s divisions and bring the description here to me;
18: 9 a book a description of it by towns in s divisions;
Jdg 6: 1 LORD gave them into the hand of Midian s years. C
6:25 the second bull s years old, C
8:26 he requested was one thousand s hundred shekels
12: 9 He judged Israel s years. C
14:12 If you can explain it to me within the s days of A
14:17 before him the s days that their feast lasted; A
16: 7 "If they bind me with s fresh bowstrings that are
16: 8 of the Philistines brought her s fresh bowstrings
16:13 "If you weave the s locks of my head with the web
16:14 the s locks of his head and wove them into
16:19 and had him shave off the s locks of his head.
20:16 were s hundred picked men who were left-handed;
Ru 4:15 who is more to you than s sons, has borne him."
1Sa 2: 5 The barren has borne s, but she who has many
6: 1 in the country of the Philistines s months.
10: 8 S days you shall wait, until I come to you A
10:27 But there were s thousand men who had escaped
11: 3 of Jabesh said to him, "Give us s days' respite
13: 8 waited s days, the time appointed by Samuel; A
16:10 Jesse made s of his sons pass before Samuel,
31:13 the tamarisk tree in Jabesh, and fasted s days. A
2Sa 2:11 the house of Judah was s years and six months. C
5: 5 At Hebron he reigned over Judah s years C
8: 4 from him one thousand s hundred horsemen,
10:18 of the Arameans s hundred chariot teams,
21: 6 let s of his sons be handed over to us,
21: 9 The s of them perished together.
1Ki 2:11 he reigned s years in Hebron, C
6: 6 and the third was s cubits wide;
6:38 He was s years in building it. C
7:17 s for the one capital, and s for the other capital.
8:65 before the LORD our God, s days. A
11: 3 Among his wives were s hundred princesses
16:15 Zimri reigned s days in Tirzah. A
18:43 Then he said, "Go again s times." B
19:18 Yet I will leave s thousand in Israel,
20:15 the people of Israel, s thousand.
20:29 They encamped opposite one another s days. A
2Ki 3: 9 they had made a roundabout march of s days, A
3:26 with him s hundred swordsmen to break through,
4:35 the child sneezed s times, B
5:10 saying, "Go, wash in the Jordan s times, B
5:14 So he went down and immersed himself s times B
8: 1 and it will come on the land for s years." C
8: 2 and settled in the land of the Philistines s years. C
8: 3 At the end of the s years, C
11:21 Jehoash was s years old when he began to reign. C
24:16 s thousand, the artisans and the smiths,
1Ch 3: 4 where he reigned for s years and six months. C
3:24 Pelaiah, Akkub, Johanan, Delaiah, and Anani, s.
5:13 Meshullam, Sheba, Jorai, Jacan, Zia, and Eber, s.
5:18 expert in war, forty-four thousand s hundred sixty,
9:13 one thousand s hundred sixty,
9:25 come in every s days, in turn, to be with them; A
10:12 under the oak in Jabesh, and fasted s days. A
12:25 mighty warriors, s thousand one hundred.
12:27 and with him three thousand s hundred.
15:26 they sacrificed s bulls and s rams.
18: 4 one thousand chariots, s thousand cavalry,
19:18 and David killed s thousand Aramean charioteers
26:30 one thousand s hundred men of ability,
26:32 two thousand s hundred men of ability,
29: 4 and s thousand talents of refined silver,
29:27 he reigned s years in Hebron, C
2Ch 7: 8 that time Solomon held the festival for s days, A
7: 9 of the altar s days and the festival seven days. A
7: 9 of the altar seven days and the festival s days. A
13: 9 to be consecrated with a young bull or s rams

2Ch 15:11 s hundred oxen and s thousand sheep.
17:11 also brought him s thousand s hundred rams
17:11 and s thousand s hundred male goats.
24: 1 Joash was s years old when he began to reign; C
26:13 an army of three hundred s thousand five hundred,
29:21 brought s bulls, s rams, s lambs, and s male goats
30:21 of unleavened bread s days with great gladness; A
30:22 the people ate the food of the festival for s days, A
30:23 to keep the festival for another s days; A
30:23 so they kept it for another s days with gladness. A
30:24 a thousand bulls and s thousand sheep
35:17 and the festival of unleavened bread s days. A
Ezr 2: 5 Of Arah, s hundred seventy-five.
2: 9 Of Zaccai, s hundred sixty.
2:25 Chephirah, and Beeroth, s hundred forty-three.
2:33 Of Lod, Hadid, and Ono, s hundred twenty-five.
2:65 there were s thousand three hundred thirty-seven;
2:66 They had s hundred thirty-six horses,
2:67 and six thousand s hundred twenty donkeys.
6:22 the festival of unleavened bread s days; A
7:14 and his s counselors to make inquiries about Judah
Ne 7:14 Of Zaccai, s hundred sixty.
7:29 Chephirah, and Beeroth, s hundred forty-three.
7:37 Of Lod, Hadid, and Ono, s hundred twenty-one.
7:67 there were s thousand three hundred thirty-seven;
7:68 They had s hundred thirty-six horses,
7:69 and six thousand s hundred twenty donkeys.
8:18 They kept the festival s days; A
Est 1: 5 great and small, a banquet lasting for s days, A
1:10 the s eunuchs who attended him,
1:14 and Memucan, the s officials of Persia and Media,
2: 9 and with s chosen maids from the king's palace,
Job 1: 2 to him s sons and three daughters.
1: 3 He had s thousand sheep, three thousand camels,
2:13 with him on the ground s days and seven nights, A
2:13 with him on the ground seven days and s nights,
5:19 in s no harm shall touch you.
42: 8 Now therefore take s bulls and s rams,
42:13 He also had s sons and three daughters.
Ps 12: 6 in a furnace on the ground, purified s times. B
119:164 S times a day I praise you B
Pr 6:16 s that are an abomination to him:
9: 1 she has hewn her s pillars.
24:16 for though they fall s times, they will rise again; B
26:16 in self-esteem than s who can answer discreetly.
26:25 for there are s abominations concealed within;
Ecc 11: 2 Divide your means s ways, or even eight,
Isa 4: 1 S women shall take hold of one man in that day,
11:15 and will split it into s channels,
30:26 like the light of s days, A
Jer 15: 9 She who bore s has languished;
52:25 and s men of the king's council who were found in
52:30 of the Judeans s hundred forty-five persons;
Eze 3:15 And I sat there among them, stunned, for s days. A
3:16 At the end of s days, the word of the LORD came A
39: 9 and they will make fires of them for s years. C
39:12 S months the house of Israel
39:14 for s months they shall make their search.
40:22 S steps led up to it;
40:26 There were s steps leading up to it;
41: 3 and the sidewalls of the entrance, s cubits.
43:25 For s days you shall provide daily a goat for A
43:26 S days shall they make atonement for the altar A
44:26 they shall count s days for him. A
45:21 and for s days unleavened bread shall be eaten. A
45:23 during the s days of the festival he shall provide A
45:23 offering to the LORD s young bulls and s rams
45:23 on each of the s days; A
45:25 fifteenth day of the month and for the s days A
Da 3:19 up s times more than was customary, B
4:16 And let s times pass over him. B
4:23 until s times pass over him'— B
4:25 and s times shall pass over you, B
4:32 and s times shall pass over you, B
9:25 of an anointed prince, there shall be s weeks;
Mic 5: 5 against them s shepherds and eight installed
Zec 3: 9 on a single stone with s facets,
4: 2 there are s lamps on it,
4: 2 with s lips on each of the lamps that are on the top
4:10 "These s are the eyes of the LORD,
Mt 12:45 along s other spirits more evil than itself,
15:34 They said, "**S**, and a few small fish."
15:36 he took the s loaves and the fish;
15:37 up the broken pieces left over, s baskets full.
16:10 Or the s loaves for the four thousand,
18:21 As many as s times?" B
18:22 Jesus said to him, "Not s times, but, I tell you, B
22:25 Now there were s brothers among us;
22:28 then, whose wife of the s will she be?
Mk 8: 5 "How many loaves do you have?" They said, "**S.**"
8: 6 the s loaves, and after giving thanks he broke them
8: 8 up the broken pieces left over, s baskets full.
8:20 "And the s for the four thousand,
8:20 And they said to him, "**S.**"
12:20 There were s brothers; the first married and,
12:22 none of the s left children.
12:23 For the s had married her."
16: 9 ⟦from whom he had cast out s demons.⟧
Lk 2:36 with her husband s years after her marriage, C
8: 2 from whom s demons had gone out,
11:26 and brings s other spirits more evil than itself,
17: 4 the same person sins against you s times a day, B
17: 4 turns back to you s times and says, 'I repent,' B
20:29 Now there were s brothers;
20:31 and so in the same way all s died childless.
20:33 For the s had married her."
24:13 about s miles from Jerusalem,

Ac 6: 3 from among yourselves s men of good standing,
13:19 he had destroyed s nations in the land of Canaan,
19:14 S sons of a Jewish high priest named Sceva
20: 6 where we stayed for s days. A
21: 4 up the disciples and stayed there for s days. A
21: 8 one of the s, and stayed with him.
21:27 When the s days were almost completed, A
28:14 and were invited to stay with them for s days. A
Ro 11: 4 "I have kept for myself s thousand who have
Heb 11:30 after they had been encircled for s days. A
2Pe 2: 5 a herald of righteousness, with s others,
Rev 1: 4 John to the s churches that are in Asia:
1: 4 and from the s spirits who are before his throne,
1:11 a book what you see and send it to the s churches,
1:12 and on turning I saw s golden lampstands,
1:16 In his right hand he held s stars,
1:20 of the s stars that you saw in my right hand,
1:20 and the s golden lampstands:
1:20 the s stars are the angels of the s churches,
1:20 and the s lampstands are the s churches.
2: 1 These are the words of him who holds the s stars
2: 1 who walks among the s golden lampstands:
3: 1 who has the s spirits of God and the s stars:
4: 5 and in front of the throne burn s flaming torches,
4: 5 which are the s spirits of God;
5: 1 on the inside and on the back, sealed with s seals;
5: 5 so that he can open the scroll and its s seals."
5: 6 having s horns and s eyes, which are the s spirits
6: 1 Then I saw the Lamb open one of the s seals,
8: 2 And I saw the s angels who stand before God,
8: 2 and s trumpets were given to them.
8: 6 Now the s angels who had the s trumpets made
10: 3 And when he shouted, the s thunders sounded.
10: 4 And when the s thunders had sounded,
10: 4 "Seal up what the s thunders have said,
11:13 s thousand people were killed in the earthquake,
12: 3 a great red dragon, with s heads and ten horns,
12: 3 and s diadems on his heads.
13: 1 rising out of the sea having ten horns and s heads;
15: 1 s angels with s plagues, which are the last,
15: 6 of the temple came the s angels with the s plagues,
15: 7 the s angels s golden bowls full of the wrath
15: 8 until the s plagues of the s angels were ended.
16: 1 a loud voice from the temple telling the s angels,
16: 1 and pour out on the earth the s bowls of the wrath
17: 1 of the s angels who had the s bowls came
17: 3 and it had s heads and ten horns.
17: 7 and of the beast with s heads and ten horns
17: 9 the s heads are s mountains on which the woman
is seated; also, they are s kings,
17:11 it is an eighth but it belongs to the s,
21: 9 of the s angels who had the s bowls full of the s
last plagues came
Tob 3: 8 For she had been married to s husbands,
3: 8 to s husbands and have not borne the name of
3:15 Already s husbands of mine have died.
6:14 that she already has been married to s husbands
7:11 I have given her to s men of our kinsmen,
11:18 for s days, and many gifts were given A
12:15 of the s angels who stand ready and enter before
14: 3 and the s sons of Tobias and gave this command:
Jdt 16:24 and the house of Israel mourned her for s days. A
AdE 1:10 the s eunuchs who served King Artaxerxes,
2: 9 as well as s maids chosen from the palace;
2:18 a banquet lasting s days for all his Friends and A
Sir 20:12 but pay for it s times over. B
22:12 Mourning for the dead lasts s days, A
37:14 keeps us better informed than s sentinels sitting
40: 8 human and animal, but to sinners s times more, B
LtJ 6: 3 for a long time, up to s generations;
Bel 1:32 There were s lions in the den,
1Mc 3:39 and s thousand cavalry to go into the land of Judah
13:28 He also erected s pyramids, opposite one another,
2Mc 7: 1 also that s brothers and their mother were arrested
7:20 she saw her s sons perish within a single day,
1Es 1: 9 the passover five thousand sheep and s hundred
1:19 and the festival of unleavened bread s days. A
4:63 feasted, with music and rejoicing, for s days. A
5:10 The descendants of Arah, s hundred fifty-six.
5:12 The descendants of Chorbe, s hundred five.
5:19 and Beeroth, s hundred forty-three.
5:22 and Ono, s hundred twenty-five.
5:42 were s thousand three hundred thirty-seven;
5:43 and s thousand thirty-six horses,
7:14 kept the festival of unleavened bread s days, A
8:11 the s Friends who are my counselors have decided,
3Mc 6:30 everything else needed for a festival of s days, A
7:17 accordance with the common desire, for s days. A
2Es 2:19 and s mighty mountains on which roses
5:13 and weep as you do now, and fast for s days, A
5:19 from me and do not come near me for s days; A
5:20 So I fasted s days, mourning and weeping, A
5:21 After s days the thoughts of my A
6:31 you will pray again and fast again for s days, A
6:35 Now after this I wept again and fasted s days in A
7:30 be turned back to primeval silence for s days, A
7:31 After s days the world that is not yet awake A
7:*80* always grieving and sad, in s ways.
7:*91* for they shall have rest in s orders.
7:*101* "They shall have freedom for s days, A
7:*101* that during these s days they may see the things A
9:23 "Now, if you will let s days more pass— A
9:27 After s days, while I lay on the grass, A
12:39 But as for you, wait here s days more, A
12:40 that the s days were past and I had not returned A
12:51 But I sat in the field s days, A
13: 1 After s days I dreamed a dream in the night. A
4Mc 1: 8 Eleazar and the s brothers and their mother.
8: 3 the tyrant had given these orders, s brothers—
13: 1 the s brothers despised sufferings even unto death,
14: 3 O sacred and harmonious concord of the s brothers
14: 4 the s youths proved coward or shrank from death,
14: 7 O most holy s, brothers in harmony!
14: 7 as the s days of creation move in choral dance A
14:12 for the mother of the s young men bore up under
15: 2 and that of preserving her s sons for a time,
15: 6 The mother of the s boys,
15: 6 In s pregnancies she had implanted
15:24 the destruction of s children and the ingenious
15:27 the deliverance that would preserve the s sons for
16: 1 a woman, advanced in years and mother of s sons,
16: 3 as she saw her s sons tortured in such varied ways.
16: 6 bearing s children, I am now the mother of none!
16: 7 O s childbirths all in vain,
16: 7 s profitless pregnancies, fruitless nurturings
16:24 the s encouraged and persuaded each of her sons
17: 2 who with your s sons nullified the violence of
17: 5 lighting the way of your star-like s sons to piety,
17: 7 of the s children enduring their varied tortures
17: 9 an aged priest and an aged woman and s sons,
17:13 the mother of the s sons entered the competition,
18: 6 of s sons expressed also these principles
18:20 and in his burning rage brought those s sons of

SEVEN-TOWERED (1) [SEVEN, TOWER]

4Mc 13: 7 so the s right reason of the youths,

SEVENFOLD (13) [SEVEN]

Ge 4:15 Whoever kills Cain will suffer a s vengeance."
4:24 is avenged s, truly Lamech seventy-sevenfold.
Lev 26:18 I will continue to punish you s for your sins.
26:21 I will continue to plague you s for your sins.
26:24 I myself will strike you s for your sins.
26:28 I in turn will punish you myself s for your sins.
Ps 79:12 Return s into the bosom of our neighbors
Pr 6:31 Yet if they are caught, they will pay s;
Isa 30:26 and the light of the sun will be s,
Sir 7: 3 and you will not reap a s crop.
20:14 for he looks for recompense s.
35:13 and he will repay you s.
4Mc 14: 8 encircled the s fear of tortures and dissolved it.

SEVENTEEN (12) [SEVENTEENTH]

Ge 37: 2 being s years old, was shepherding the flock
47:28 Jacob lived in the land of Egypt s years;
1Ki 14:21 and he reigned s years in Jerusalem,
2Ki 13: 1 in Samaria; he reigned s years.
1Ch 7:11 s thousand two hundred, ready for service in war.
2Ch 12:13 he reigned s years in Jerusalem,
Ezr 2:39 Of Harim, one thousand s.
Ne 7:42 Of Harim, one thousand s.
Jer 32: 9 and weighed out the money to him, s shekels
Tob 14:14 at the age of one hundred s years.
1Es 4:52 with the commandment to make s offerings;
5:25 The descendants of Charme, one thousand s.

SEVENTEENTH (7) [SEVENTEEN]

Ge 7:11 in the second month, on the s day of the month,
8: 4 on the s day of the month,
1Ki 22:51 in Samaria in the s year of King Jehoshaphat
2Ki 16: 1 In the s year of Pekah son of Remaliah,
1Ch 24:15 the s to Hezir, the eighteenth to Happizzez,
25:24 to the s, to Joshbekashah, his sons
Jdt 1:13 the s year he led his forces against King Arphaxad

SEVENTH‡ (142) [SEVEN]

A. SEVENTH DAY (58)
B. SEVENTH MONTH (31)
C. SEVENTH YEAR (23)

Ge 2: 2 s day God finished the work that he had done, A
2: 2 on the s day from all the work that he had done. A
2: 3 So God blessed the s day and hallowed it, A
8: 4 s month, on the seventeenth day of the month, B
Ex 12:15 from the first day until the s day shall be cut off A
12:16 and on the s day a solemn assembly; A
13: 6 the s day there shall be a festival to the LORD. A
16:26 Six days you shall gather it; but on the s day, A
16:27 the s day some of the people went out to gather, A
16:29 do not leave your place on the s day." A
16:30 So the people rested on the s day. A
20:10 the s day is a sabbath to the LORD your God; A
20:11 sea, and all that is in them, but rested the s day; A
21: 2 but in the s he shall go out a free person,
23:11 the s year you shall let it rest and lie fallow, C
23:12 but on the s day you shall rest, A
24:16 on the s day he called to Moses out of the cloud. A
31:15 but the s day is a sabbath of solemn rest, A
31:17 and on the s day he rested, and was refreshed." A
34:21 but on the s day you shall rest; A
35: 2 but on the s day you shall have a holy sabbath A
Lev 13: 5 The priest shall examine him on the s day, A
13: 6 The priest shall examine him again on the s day, A
13:27 The priest shall examine him the s day; A
13:32 On the s day the priest shall examine the itch; A
13:34 On the s day the priest shall examine the itch; A
13:51 He shall examine the disease on the s day. A
14: 9 On the s day he shall shave all his hair: A
14:39 The priest shall come again on the s day and A
16:29 In the s month, on the tenth day of the month, B
23: 3 but the s day is a sabbath of complete rest, A
Lev 23: 8 on the s day there shall be a holy convocation: A
23:16 You shall count until the day after the s sabbath,
23:24 In the s month, on the first day of the month, B
23:27 day of this s month is the day of atonement; B
23:34 On the fifteenth day of this s month, B
23:39 Now, the fifteenth day of the s month, B
23:41 shall keep it in the s month as a statute forever B
25: 4 s year there shall be a sabbath of complete rest C
25: 9 on the tenth day of the s month— B
25:20 Should you ask, What shall we eat in the s year, C
Nu 6: 9 on the s day they shall shave it. A
7:48 On the s day Elishama son of Ammihud, A
19:12 the water on the third day and on the s day, A
19:12 on the third day and on the s day, A
19:19 unclean ones on the third day and on the s day, A
19:19 thus purifying them on the s day. A
28:25 on the s day you shall have a holy convocation; A
29: 1 the s month you shall have a holy convocation; B
29: 7 this s month you shall have a holy convocation, B
29:12 On the fifteenth day of the s month you shall B
29:32 On the s day: seven bulls, A
31:19 and your captives on the third and on the s day. A
31:24 You must wash your clothes on the s day, A
Dt 5:14 the s day is a sabbath to the LORD your God; A
15: 1 s year you shall grant a remission of debts. C
15: 9 thinking, "The s year, the year of remission, C
15:12 in the s year you shall set that person free. C
16: 8 on the s day there shall be a solemn assembly A
31:10 Every s year, in the scheduled year of remission, C
Jos 6: 4 On the s day you shall march around A
6:15 On the s day they rose early, at dawn, A
6:16 And at the s time, when the priests had blown
19:40 The s lot came out for the tribe of Dan,
Jdg 14:17 she nagged him, on the s day he told her. A
14:18 to him on the s day before the sun went down, A
2Sa 12:18 On the s day the child died. A
1Ki 8: 2 in the month Ethanim, which is the s month. B
18:44 At the s time he said, "Look,
20:29 Then on the s day the battle began; A
2Ki 11: 4 in the s year Jehoiada summoned the captains C
12: 1 In the s year of Jehu, Jehoash began to reign; C
18: 9 was the s year of King Hoshea son of Elah C
25: 8 In the fifth month, on the s day of the month— A
25:25 But in the s month, Ishmael son of Nethaniah B
1Ch 2:15 Ozem the sixth, David the s;
12:11 Attai sixth, Eliel s,
24:10 the s to Hakkoz, the eighth to Abijah,
25:14 s to Jesarelah, his sons and his brothers, twelve;
26: 3 Jehohanan the sixth, Eliehoenai the s.
26: 5 Issachar the s, Peullethai the eighth;
27:10 S, for the seventh month, was Helez the Pelonite,
27:10 for the s month, was Helez the Pelonite, B
2Ch 5: 3 the king at the festival that is in the s month. B
7:10 On the twenty-third day of the s month he sent B
23: 1 But in the s year Jehoiada took courage, C
31: 7 and finished them in the s month. B
Ezr 3: 1 When the s month came, and the Israelites were B
3: 6 the s month they began to offer burnt offerings B
7: 7 in the s year of King Artaxerxes. C
7: 8 which was in the s year of the king. C
Ne 7:73 When the s month came— B
8: 2 This was on the first day of the s month. B
8:14 in booths during the festival of the s month, B
10:31 and we will forego the crops of the s year and C
Est 1:10 the s day, when the king was merry with wine, A
2:16 in the s year of his reign, C
Jer 28:17 In that same year, in the s month, B
34:14 "Every s year each of you C
41: 1 In the s month, Ishmael son of Nethaniah B
52:28 the s year, three thousand twenty-three Judeans; C
Eze 20: 1 In the s year, in the fifth month, C
30:20 in the first month, on the s day of the month, A
45:20 the s day of the month for anyone who has A
45:25 the s month, on the fifteenth day of the month B
Hag 2: 1 the s month, on the twenty-first day of the B
Zec 7: 5 and lamented in the fifth month and in the s,
8:19 and the fast of the s, and the fast of the tenth,
Mt 22:26 so also the third, down to the s.
Heb 4: 4 one place it speaks about the s day as follows, A
4: 4 God rested on the s day from all his works." A
Jude 1:14 in the s generation from Adam, prophesied,
Rev 8: 1 When the Lamb opened the s seal,
10: 7 the days when the s angel is to blow his trumpet,
11:15 Then the s angel blew his trumpet,
16:17 The s angel poured his bowl into the air,
21:20 the s chrysolite, the eighth beryl, the ninth topaz,
Tob 2:12 One day, the s of Dystrus,
AdE 1:10 On the s day, when the king was in good humor, A
2:16 which is Adar, in the s year of his reign. C
Bar 1: 2 on the s day of the month, A
Bel 1:40 On the s day the king came to mourn for Daniel. A
1Mc 6:53 because it was the s year; C
10:21 in the s month of the one hundred sixtieth year, B
2Mc 6:11 in order to observe the s day secretly, A
12:38 As the s day was coming on, A
15: 4 who ordered us to observe the s day," A
1Es 5:47 When the s month came, and the Israelites were B
5:53 from the new moon of the s month, B
8: 6 in the s year of the reign of Artaxerxes, C
8: 6 in the fifth month (this was the king's s year); C
9:37 On the new moon of the s month, B
9:40 on the new moon of the s month. B
3Mc 6:38 and their destruction was set for the fifth to the s
2Es 6:42 the waters to be gathered together in a s part of
6:47 "On the fifth day you commanded the s part,
6:50 from the other, for the s part where
6:52 to Leviathan you gave the s part, the watery part;

2Es 7:*87* The s way, which is worse than all the ways
7:*98* The s order, which is greater than all
4Mc 2: 8 and to cancel the debt when the s year arrives.
12: 1 the s and youngest of all came forward.

SEVENTIETH (1) [SEVENTY]

1Mc 13:41 In the one hundred s year the yoke of the Gentiles

SEVENTY‡ (78) [SEVENTIETH]

Ge 5:12 When Kenan had lived s years,
11:26 When Terah had lived s years,
46:27 of the house of Jacob who came into Egypt were s.
50: 3 And the Egyptians wept for him s days.
Ex 1: 5 The total number of people born to Jacob was s.
15:27 twelve springs of water and s palm trees;
24: 1 Nadab, and Abihu, and s of the elders of Israel,
24: 9 and Abihu, and s of the elders of Israel went up,
38:29 The bronze that was contributed was s talents,
Nu 7:13 one silver basin weighing s shekels,
7:19 one silver basin weighing s shekels,
7:25 one silver basin weighing s shekels,
7:31 one silver basin weighing s shekels,
7:37 one silver basin weighing s shekels,
7:43 one silver basin weighing s shekels,
7:49 one silver basin weighing s shekels,
7:55 one silver basin weighing s shekels,
7:61 one silver basin weighing s shekels,
7:67 one silver basin weighing s shekels,
7:73 one silver basin weighing s shekels,
7:79 one silver basin weighing s shekels,
7:85 and each basin s, all the silver of
11:16 "Gather for me s of the elders of Israel,
11:24 and he gathered s elders of the people,
11:25 that was on him and put it on the s elders;
33: 9 twelve springs of water and s palm trees,
Dt 10:22 Your ancestors went down to Egypt s persons;
Jdg 1: 7 "S kings with their thumbs and big toes cut off
8:30 Now Gideon had s sons, his own offspring,
9: 2 that all s of the sons of Jerubbaal rule over you,
9: 4 They gave him s pieces of silver out of the temple
9: 5 the sons of Jerubbaal, s men, on one stone;
9:18 s men on one stone, and have made Abimelech,
9:24 the violence done to the s sons of Jerubbaal might
9:56 against his father in killing his s brothers;
12:14 and thirty grandsons, who rode on s donkeys;
1Sa 6:19 and he killed s men of them.
11: 8 and those from Judah s thousand.
2Sa 24:15 and s thousand of the people died,
1Ki 5:15 Solomon also had s thousand laborers
2Ki 10: 1 Now Ahab had s sons in Samaria.
10: 6 Now the king's sons, s persons,
10: 7 the king's sons and killed them, s persons;
1Ch 21: 5 and in Judah four hundred s thousand who drew
21:14 and s thousand persons fell in Israel.
2Ch 2: 2 Solomon conscripted s thousand laborers
2:18 S thousand of them he assigned as laborers,
29:32 that the assembly brought was s bulls,
36:21 that it lay desolate it kept sabbath, to fulfill s years.
Ezr 8: 7 Jeshaiah son of Athaliah, and with him s males.
8:14 Uthai and Zaccur, and with them s males.
Ps 90:10 The days of our life are s years, or perhaps eighty,
Isa 23:15 From that day Tyre will be forgotten for s years,
23:15 At the end of s years, it will happen to Tyre as in
23:17 At the end of s years, the LORD will visit Tyre,
Jer 25:11 the king of Babylon s years.
25:12 Then after s years are completed,
29:10 Babylon's s years are completed will I visit you,
Eze 8:11 them stood s of the elders of the house of Israel,
41:12 on the west side was s cubits wide;
Da 9: 2 for the devastation of Jerusalem, namely, s years.
9:24 "S weeks are decreed for your people
Zec 1:12 with which you have been angry these s years?"
7: 5 for these s years, was it for me that you fasted?
Lk 10: 1 the Lord appointed s others and sent them on
10:17 The s returned with joy, saying, "Lord,
Ac 23:23 s horsemen, and two hundred spearmen.
Jdt 1: 2 the walls s cubits high and fifty cubits wide.
1: 4 He made its gates s cubits high
7: 2 forces numbered one hundred s thousand infantry
Bel 1:10 Now there were s priests of Bel,
2Mc 10:20 and on receiving s thousand drachmas let some
1Es 1:58 of its desolation until the completion of s years."
8:33 Jeshaiah son of Gotholiah, and with him s men.
8:34 Zeraiah son of Michael, and with him s men.
8:39 Jeuel, and Shemaiah, and with them s men.
8:40 Uthai son of Istalcurus, and with him s men.
2Es 14:46 but keep the s that were written last,

SEVENTY-FIRST (1)

1Mc 13:51 in the one hundred s year, the Jews entered it

SEVENTY-FIVE (10)

Ge 12: 4 Abram was s years old when he departed
25: 7 the length of Abraham's life, one hundred s years.
Ex 38:25 and one thousand seven hundred s shekels,
38:28 thousand seven hundred s shekels he made hooks
Nu 31:32 had taken totaled six hundred s thousand sheep,
31:37 of sheep and goats was six hundred s.
Ezr 2: 5 Of Arah, seven hundred s.
Est 9:16 and killed s thousand of those who hated them;
Ac 7:14 and all his relatives to come to him, s in all;
2Mc 12:29 which is s miles from Jerusalem.

SEVENTY-FOUR (5) [SEVENTY-FOURTH]

Nu 1:27 of the tribe of Judah were s thousand six hundred.
2: 4 a company as enrolled of s thousand six hundred.
Ezr 2:40 of the descendants of Hodaviah, s.
Ne 7:43 of Kadmiel of the descendants of Hodevah, s.
1Es 5:26 of Jeshua and Kadmiel and Bannas and Sudias, s.

SEVENTY-FOURTH (1) [SEVENTY-FOUR]

1Mc 15:10 In the one hundred s year Antiochus set out

SEVENTY-SECOND (2) [SEVENTY-TWO]

1Mc 14: 1 one hundred s year King Demetrius assembled his
14:27 in the one hundred s year,

SEVENTY-SEVEN (4) [SEVENTY-SEVENFOLD, SEVENTY-SEVENTH]

Ge 5:31 the days of Lamech were seven hundred s years;
Jdg 8:14 the officials and elders of Succoth, s people.
Ezr 8:35 s lambs, and as a sin offering twelve male goats;
Mt 18:22 "Not seven times, but, I tell you, s times.

SEVENTY-SEVENFOLD (1) [SEVENTY-SEVEN]

Ge 4:24 If Cain is avenged sevenfold, truly Lamech s."

SEVENTY-SEVENTH (1) [SEVENTY-SEVEN]

1Mc 16:14 in the one hundred s year, in the eleventh month,

SEVENTY-SIX (2)

Nu 26:22 of those enrolled was s thousand five hundred.
Ac 27:37 (We were in all two hundred s persons in the ship.)

SEVENTY-THREE (4)

Nu 3:43 was twenty-two thousand two hundred s.
3:46 of redemption of the two hundred s of the firstborn
Ezr 2:36 of the house of Jeshua, nine hundred s.
Ne 7:39 namely the house of Jeshua, nine hundred s.

SEVENTY-TWO‡ (12) [SEVENTY-SECOND]

Nu 31:33 s thousand oxen,
31:38 of which the LORD's tribute was s.
Ezr 2: 3 two thousand one hundred s.
2: 4 Of Shephatiah, three hundred s.
Ne 7: 8 two thousand one hundred s.
7: 9 Of Shephatiah, three hundred s.
11:19 who kept watch at the gates, were one hundred s.
1Es 5: 9 two thousand one hundred s.
5: 9 The descendants of Shephatiah, four hundred s.
5:24 of the descendants of Anasib, nine hundred s.
5:35 of Solomon's servants were three hundred s.
8:66 s lambs, and as a thank offering twelve male goats

SEVERAL (11)

Nu 4:49 through Moses they were appointed to their s tasks
Jos 19:49 the s territories of the land as inheritances,
21:33 of the s families of the Gershonites were
21:40 As for the towns of the s Merarite families, that is,
2Ch 8:14 the gatekeepers in their divisions for the s gates;
Ac 9:19 For s days he was with the disciples in Damascus,
10:48 Then they invited him to stay for s days.
21:10 While we were staying there for s days,
25:13 After s days had passed, King Agrippa
25:14 Since they were staying there s days,
3Mc 4: 4 all together, by the generals in the s cities,

SEVERE (32) [SEVERED, SEVERELY, SEVERITY]

Ge 12:10 for the famine was s in the land.
41:56 for the famine was s in the land of Egypt.
41:57 the famine became s throughout the world.
43: 1 Now the famine was s in the land.
47: 4 for your servants' flocks because the famine is s in
47:13 for the famine was very s.
47:20 because the famine was s upon them;
Dt 28:59 and your offspring with s and lasting afflictions
1Ki 17:17 his illness was so s that there was no breath left
18: 2 The famine was s in Samaria.
2Ki 25: 3 of the fourth month the famine became so s in
2Ch 16:12 and his disease became s;
21:15 and you yourself will have a s sickness with
Pr 15:10 There is s discipline for one who forsakes the way,
Jer 10:19 Woe is me because of my hurt! My wound is s.
52: 6 of the fourth month the famine became so s in
Lk 4:25 and there was a s famine over all the land;
12:47 or do what was wanted, will receive a s beating.
15:14 a s famine took place throughout that country,
Ac 8: 1 That day a s persecution began against the church
11:28 that there would be a s famine over all the world;
16:23 After they had given them a s flogging,
2Co 8: 2 for during a s ordeal of affliction,
13:10 I may not have to be s in using the authority that
Col 2:23 humility, and s treatment of the body,
Wis 6: 5 because s judgment falls on those in high places.
Sir 5:14 and s condemnation to the double-tongued.
31: 2 and a s illness carries off sleep.
1Mc 1:30 he suddenly fell upon the city, dealt it a s blow,
2Mc 14:45 and his wounds were s he ran through the crowd;
3Mc 2:23 seeing the s punishment that had overtaken him,
4Mc 9: 8 For we, through this s suffering and endurance,

SEVERED (3) [SEVERE]

Jdt 16: 9 and the sword s his neck!
4Mc 9:21 the ligaments joining his bones were already s,
15:20 s hands upon hands, scalped heads upon heads,

SEVERELY (10) [SEVERE]

Jdg 12: 2 with the Ammonites who oppressed us s.
1Sa 1: 6 Her rival used to provoke her s, to irritate her,
24: 7 So David scolded his men s and did
2Ch 24:25 they had withdrawn, leaving him s wounded,
Ps 118:18 The LORD has punished me s,
119:107 I am s afflicted; give me life,
Isa 64:12 Will you keep silent, and punish us so s?
Da 4:19 was s distressed for a while.
3Mc 4:19 After he had threatened them s,
7: 6 But we very s threatened them for these acts,

SEVERING (2)

Lev 1:17 He shall tear it open by its wings without s it.
5: 8 wringing its head at the nape without s it.

SEVERITY (2) [SEVERE]

Ro 11:22 Note then the kindness and the s of God: s toward those who have fallen,

SEW (2) [SEWED, SEWS]

Ecc 3: 7 a time to tear, and a time to s;
Eze 13:18 Woe to the women who s bands on all wrists,

SEWED (2) [SEW]

Ge 3: 7 and they s fig leaves together and made loincloths
Job 16:15 I have s sackcloth upon my skin,

SEWER (2)

Mt 15:17 and goes out into the s?
Mk 7:19 and goes out into the s?"

SEWS (3) [SEW]

Mt 9:16 No one s a piece of unshrunk cloth on
Mk 2:21 "No one s a piece of unshrunk cloth on
Lk 5:36 "No one tears a piece from a new garment and s it

SEX (2) [SEXUAL, SEXUALLY]

1Pe 3: 7 paying honor to the woman as the weaker s,
4Mc 15: 5 that mothers are the weaker s and give birth

SEXUAL (19) [SEX]

Lev 18:20 not have s relations with your kinsman's wife,
18:23 You shall not have s relations with any animal
18:23 to an animal to have s relations with it:
19:20 a man has s relations with a woman who is a slave,
20:15 If a man has s relations with an animal,
20:16 and has s relations with it, you shall kill the woman
Nu 25: 1 to have s relations with the women of Moab.
Eze 23:43 but they carry on their s acts with her.
Hos 4:18 their drinking is ended, they indulge in s orgies;
1Co 5: 1 It is actually reported that there is s immorality
7: 2 But because of cases of s immorality,
10: 8 not indulge in s immorality as some of them did,
2Co 12:21 of the impurity, s immorality, and licentiousness
Jude 1: 7 in s immorality and pursued unnatural lust,
Wis 14:26 s perversion, disorder in marriages, adultery,
Sir 41:17 Be ashamed of s immorality,
42: 8 or the aged who are guilty of s immorality.
4Mc 2: 2 because by mental effort he overcame s desire.
2: 4 to rule over the frenzied urge of s desire,

SEXUALLY (3) [SEX]

1Ki 1: 4 but the king did not know her s.
1Co 5: 9 not to associate with s immoral persons—
5:11 of brother or sister who is s immoral or greedy,

SHAALABBIN (1) [=SHAALBIM]

Jos 19:42 S, Aijalon, Ithlah,

SHAALBIM (2) [=SHAALABBIN]

Jdg 1:35 in Har-heres, in Aijalon, and in S, but the hand of
1Ki 4: 9 in Makaz, S, Beth-shemesh, and Elon-beth-hanan;

SHAALBON (2)

2Sa 23:32 Eliahba of S; the sons of Jashen: Jonathan
1Ch 11:33 Azmaveth of Baharum, Eliahba of S,

SHAALIM (1)

1Sa 9: 4 And they passed through the land of S,

SHAAPH (2)

1Ch 2:47 Regem, Jotham, Geshan, Pelet, Ephah, and S.
2:49 She also bore S father of Madmannah,

SHAARAIM (3)

Jos 15:36 S, Adithaim, Gederah, Gederothaim:
1Sa 17:52 the wounded Philistines fell on the way from S
1Ch 4:31 Hazar-susim, Beth-biri, and S.

SHAASHGAZ (1)

Est 2:14 of S, the king's eunuch, who was in charge of

SHABBETHAI (5)

Ezr 10:15 and Meshullam and S the Levites supported them.
Ne 8:7 Also Jeshua, Bani, Sherebiah, Jamin, Akkub, S,
11:16 and S and Jozabad, of the leaders of
1Es 9:14 and Meshullam and Levi and S served with them
9:48 Jadinus, Akkub, S, Hodiah, Maiannas and Kelita,

SHACKLED (1) [SHACKLES]

Man 1:3 who s the sea by your word of command,

SHACKLES (5) [SHACKLED]

Jdg 16:21 down to Gaza and bound him with bronze s;
Mk 5:4 for he had often been restrained with s and chains,
5:4 and the s he broke in pieces;
Lk 8:29 under guard and bound with chains and s,
3Mc 6:19 binding them with immovable s.

SHADDAI See Index to Footnotes

SHADE (20) [SHADED]

Jdg 9:15 then come and take refuge in my s;
Job 40:22 The lotus trees cover it for s;
Ps 80:10 The mountains were covered with its s,
121:5 the LORD is your s at your right hand.
Isa 4:6 a s by day from the heat,
16:3 make your s like night at the height of noon;
25:4 a shelter from the rainstorm and a s from the heat.
25:5 you subdued the heat with the s of clouds;
32:2 like the s of a great rock in a weary land.
Eze 17:23 in the s of its branches will nest winged creatures
31:3 with fair branches and forest s,
31:6 and in its s all great nations lived.
31:12 the peoples of the earth went away from its s
31:17 those who lived in its s among the nations.
Da 4:12 The animals of the field found s under it,
Hos 4:13 poplar, and terebinth, because their s is good.
Jnh 4:5 He sat under it in the s,
4:6 to give s over his head, to save him
Mk 4:32 so that the birds of the air can make nests in its s."
Sir 34:19 from scorching wind and a s from noonday sun,

SHADED (1) [SHADE]

Bar 5:8 The woods and every fragrant tree have s Israel

SHADES‡ (5)

Job 26:5 s below tremble, the waters and their inhabitants.
Ps 88:10 Do the s rise up to praise you?
Pr 2:18 and her paths to the s;
Isa 14:9 it rouses the s to greet you,
26:14 The dead do not live; s do not rise—

SHADOW‡ (42) [SHADOWS]

2Ki 20:9 the s has now advanced ten intervals;
20:10 "It is normal for the s to lengthen ten intervals;
rather let the s retreat ten intervals."
20:11 and he brought the s back the ten intervals,
1Ch 29:15 our days on the earth are like a s,
Job 7:2 Like a slave who longs for the s,
8:9 for our days on earth are but a s.
14:2 flees like a s and does not last.
17:7 and all my members are like a s.
Ps 17:8 hide me in the s of your wings,
36:7 All people may take refuge in the s of your wings.
39:6 Surely everyone goes about like a s.
57:1 in the s of your wings I will take refuge,
63:7 and in the s of your wings I sing for joy.
91:1 who abide in the s of the Almighty,
102:11 My days are like an evening s;
109:23 I am gone like a s at evening;
144:4 their days are like a passing s.
Ecc 6:12 which they pass like a s?
8:13 neither will they prolong their days like a s,
SS 2:3 With great delight I sat in his s,
Isa 30:2 and to seek shelter in the s of Egypt;
30:3 and the shelter in the s of Egypt your humiliation.
34:15 the owl nest and lay and hatch and brood in its s;
38:8 I will make the s cast by the declining sun on
49:2 in the s of his hand he hid me;
51:16 and hidden you in the s of my hand,
Jer 48:45 In the s of Heshbon fugitives stop exhausted;
La 4:20 "Under his s we shall live among the nations."
Hos 14:7 They shall again live beneath my s,
Mt 4:16 in the region and s of death light has dawned."
Lk 1:79 to those who sit in darkness and in the s of death,
Ac 5:15 in order that Peter's s might fall on some of them
Col 2:17 These are only a s of what is to come,
Heb 8:5 that is a sketch and s of the heavenly one;
10:1 the law has only a s of the good things to come
Jas 1:17 with whom there is no variation or s due
Wis 2:5 For our allotted time is the passing of a s,
5:9 "All those things have vanished like a s,
Sir 34:2 As one who catches at a s and pursues the wind,
2Es 2:36 Flee from the s of this age,
2:39 the s of this age have received glorious garments

SHADOWS (4) [SHADOW]

Jdg 9:36 "The s on the mountains look like people to you."
SS 2:17 Until the day breathes and the s flee, turn,
4:6 Until the day breathes and the s flee,
Jer 6:4 for the day declines, the s of evening lengthen!"

SHADRACH (15) [=HANANIAH]

Da 1:7 Hananiah he called S, Mishael he called Meshach,
2:49 and he appointed S, Meshach,
3:12 S, Meshach, and Abednego.
3:13 that S, Meshach, and Abednego be brought in;
3:14 Nebuchadnezzar said to them, "Is it true, O S,
3:16 S, Meshach, and Abednego answered the king,
3:19 Nebuchadnezzar was so filled with rage against S,
3:20 of the strongest guards in his army to bind S,
3:22 the raging flames killed the men who lifted S,
3:23 But the three men, S, Meshach, and Abednego,
3:26 "S, Meshach, and Abednego,
3:26 So S, Meshach, and Abednego came out from
3:28 Nebuchadnezzar said, "Blessed be the God of S,
3:29 of S, Meshach, and Abednego shall be torn limb
3:30 Then the king promoted S, Meshach,

SHAFT (12) [SHAFTS]

Ex 25:31 The base and the s of the lampstand shall be made
37:17 The base and the s of the lampstand were made
1Sa 17:7 The s of his spear was like a weaver's beam,
2Sa 5:8 let him get up the water s to attack the lame and
21:19 the s of whose spear was like a weaver's beam.
23:7 to touch them one uses an iron bar or the s of
1Ch 20:5 the s of whose spear was like a weaver's beam.
Rev 9:1 he was given the key to the s of the bottomless pit;
9:2 he opened the s of the bottomless pit,
9:2 the s rose smoke like the smoke of a great furnace,
9:2 the air were darkened with the smoke from the s.
Sir 38:25 and who glories in the s of a goad,

SHAFTS (3) [SHAFT]

Job 28:4 They open s in a valley away from human
Ps 7:13 his deadly weapons, making his arrows fiery s.
Wis 5:21 S of lightning will fly with true aim,

SHAGEE (1)

1Ch 11:34 Jonathan son of S the Hararite,

SHAGGY See Index to Footnotes

SHAHARAIM (1)

1Ch 8:8 And S had sons in the country of Moab

SHAHAZIMAH (KJV) See SHAHAZUMAH

SHAHAZUMAH (1)

Jos 19:22 S, and Beth-shemesh, and its boundary ends at

SHAKE‡ (34) [SHAKEN, SHAKES, SHAKING, SHOOK]

Jdg 16:20 "I will go out as at other times, and s myself free."
Ne 5:13 "So may God s out everyone from house and
Job 4:14 and trembling, which made all my bones s.
15:33 They will s off their unripe grape, like the vine,
16:4 against you, and s my head at you.
Ps 22:7 they make mouths at me, they s their heads;
46:2 though the mountains s in the heart of the sea;
64:8 all who see them will s with horror.
109:25 when they see me, they s their heads.
Isa 7:2 of his people shook as the trees of the forest s
10:32 he will s his fist at the mount of daughter Zion,
33:9 and Bashan and Carmel s off their leaves.
52:2 S yourself from the dust, rise up,
Jer 18:16 All who pass by it are horrified and s their heads.
23:9 My heart is crushed within me, all my bones s;
Eze 26:10 wheels, and chariots your very walls shall s,
26:15 Shall not the coastlands s at the sound of your fall,
Joel 3:16 and the heavens and the earth s.
Am 9:1 Strike the capitals until the thresholds s,
9:9 and s the house of Israel among all the nations
Hag 2:6 a little while, I will s the heavens and the earth and
2:7 and I will s all the nations,
2:21 saying, I am about to s the heavens and the earth,
Mt 10:14 s off the dust from your feet as you leave
Mk 6:11 s off the dust that is on your feet as a testimony
Lk 6:48 the river burst against that house but could not s it,
9:5 that town s the dust off your feet as a testimony
Heb 12:26 "Yet once more I will s not only the earth but also
Wis 4:19 and s them from the foundations;
Sir 12:18 Then he will s his head, and clap his hands,
13:7 he will pass you by and s his head at you.
22:2 anyone that picks it up will s it off his hand.
43:16 when he appears, the mountains s.
2Es 10:24 Therefore s off your great sadness

SHAKEN (42) [SHAKE]

1Ki 14:15 as a reed is s in the water;
Ne 5:13 Thus may they be s out and emptied."
Job 34:20 at midnight the people are s and pass away,
38:13 and the wicked be s out of it?
Ps 13:4 my foes will rejoice because I am s.
62:2 my fortress; I shall never be s.
62:6 my fortress; I shall not be s.
82:5 all the foundations of the earth are s.
104:5 so that it shall never be s.
109:23 I am s off like a locust.
Isa 13:13 and the earth will be s out of its place,
23:11 over the sea, he has s the kingdoms;
24:19 the earth is torn asunder, the earth is violently s.
Na 3:12 if s they fall into the mouth of the eater.
Mt 11:7 A reed s by the wind?
24:29 and the powers of heaven will be s.
Mk 13:25 and the powers in the heavens will be s.
Lk 6:38 A good measure, pressed down, s together,
7:24 A reed s by the wind?
21:26 for the powers of the heavens will be s.
Ac 2:25 for he is at my right hand so that I will not be s;
4:31 place in which they were gathered together was s;
16:26 violent that the foundations of the prison were s;
1Th 3:3 so that no one would be s by these persecutions.
2Th 2:2 not to be quickly s in mind or alarmed,
Heb 12:27 indicates the removal of what is s—
12:27 so that what cannot be s may remain.
12:28 since we are receiving a kingdom that cannot be s,
Rev 6:13 the fig tree drops its winter fruit when s by a gale.
Tob 12:16 The two of them were s;
Jdt 16:15 the mountains shall be s to their foundations with
AdE 15:13 and my heart was s with fear at your glory.
Wis 4:4 standing insecurely they will be s by the wind,
5:2 they will be s with dreadful fear,
Sir 27:4 When a sieve is s, the refuse appears;
28:14 Slander has s many, and scattered them
48:19 Then their hearts were s and their hands trembled,
1Mc 6:8 he was astounded and badly s.
9:13 The earth was s by the noise of the armies,
3Mc 2:22 He shook him on this side and that as a reed is s by
2Es 6:14 if the place where you are standing is greatly s
6:16 They will tremble and be s,

SHAKES (8) [SHAKE]

Job 9:6 who s the earth out of its place,
Ps 29:8 The voice of the LORD s the wilderness;
29:8 the LORD s the wilderness of Kadesh.
Eze 21:21 he s the arrows, he consults the teraphim,
27:28 of the cry of your pilots the countryside s,
Am 9:9 as one s with a sieve, but no pebble shall fall to the
Zep 2:15 Everyone who passes by it hisses and s the fist.
Sir 22:13 and be spattered when he s himself off.

SHAKING‡ (5) [SHAKE]

Ps 6:2 O LORD, heal me, for my bones are s with terror.
Eze 38:19 On that day there shall be a great s in the land
Da 10:17 For I am s, no strength remains in me,
Mt 27:39 Those who passed by derided him, s their heads
Mk 15:29 s their heads and saying, "Aha!

SHALIM (KJV) See SHAALIM

SHALISHAH (1) [BAAL-SHALISHAH]

1Sa 9:4 of Ephraim and passed through the land of S,

SHALL (6472) See Index of Articles Etc.

SHALLECHETH (1)

1Ch 26:16 at the gate of S on the ascending road.

SHALLOW (1)

Sir 19:4 One who trusts others too quickly has a s mind,

SHALLUM (33)

2Ki 15:10 S son of Jabesh conspired against him,
15:13 S son of Jabesh began to reign in
15:14 down S son of Jabesh in Samaria and killed him;
15:15 Now the rest of the deeds of S,
22:14 the wife of S son of Tikvah, son of Harhas, keeper
1Ch 2:40 the father of Sismai, and Sismai of S.
2:41 S became the father of Jekamiah,
3:15 the third Zedekiah, the fourth S.
4:25 S was his son, Mibsam his son, Mishma his son.
6:12 Ahitub of Zadok, Zadok of S,
6:13 S of Hilkiah, Hilkiah of Azariah,
7:13 Jahziel, Guni, Jezer, and S,
9:17 S, Akkub, Talmon, Ahiman;
9:17 and their kindred S was the chief,
9:19 S son of Kore, son of Ebiasaph, son of Korah,
9:31 one of the Levites, the firstborn of S the Korahite,
2Ch 28:12 Jehizkiah son of S, and Amasa son of Hadlai,
34:22 the wife of S son of Tokhath son of Hasrah,
Ezr 2:42 The descendants of the gatekeepers: of S, of Ater,
7:2 son of S, son of Zadok, son of Ahitub,
10:24 Of the gatekeepers: S, Telem, and Uri.
10:42 S, Amariah, and Joseph.
Ne 3:12 Next to him S son of Hallohesh,
3:15 And S son of Col-hozeh, ruler of the district
7:45 The gatekeepers: the descendants of S, of Ater,
Jer 22:11 the LORD concerning S son of King Josiah
32:7 of your uncle S is going to come to you and say,
35:4 above the chamber of Maaseiah son of S,
Bar 1:7 the high priest Jehoiakim son of Hilkiah son of S,
1Es 5:28 the descendants of S, the descendants of Ater,
8:1 of Seraiah son of Azariah son of Hilkiah son of S
9:25 Of the gatekeepers: S and Telem.
2Es 1:1 of Hilkiah son of S son of Zadok son of Ahitub

SHALMAI (1)

Ne 7:48 of Lebana, of Hagaba, of S,

SHALMAN (1)

Hos 10:14 as S destroyed Beth-arbel on the day of battle

SHALMANESER (7)
2Ki 17: 3 King S of Assyria came up against him;
18: 9 King S of Assyria came up against Samaria,
Tob 1: 2 in the days of King S of the Assyrians was taken
1:13 and good standing with S,
1:15 But when S died, and his son Sennacherib reigned
1:16 In the days of S I performed many acts of charity
2Es 13:40 whom S, king of the Assyrians, made captives;

SHALOM See Index to Footnotes

SHAMA‡ (1)
1Ch 11:44 S and Jeiel sons of Hotham the Aroerite,

SHAMBLES (KJV) See MEAT MARKET

SHAME‡ (182) [ASHAMED, SHAMED, SHAMEFUL, SHAMEFULLY, SHAMELESS, SHAMELESSLY, SHAMELESSNESS]
Nu 12:14 would she not bear her s for seven days?
1Sa 20:30 the son of Jesse to your own s,
20:30 and to the s of your mother's nakedness?
2Sa 13:13 As for me, where could I carry my s?
19: 5 "Today you have covered with s the faces
Ezr 9: 7 to plundering, and to utter s, as is now the case.
Ne 1: 3 who escaped captivity are in great trouble and s;
Job 8:22 Those who hate you will be clothed with s,
11: 3 and when you mock, shall no one s you?
36:14 They die in their youth, and their life ends in s.
Ps 4: 2 How long, you people, shall my honor suffer s?
6:10 they shall turn back, and in a moment be put to s.
22: 5 in you they trusted, and were not put to s.
25: 2 do not let me be put to s;
25: 3 Do not let those who wait for you be put to s;
25:20 do not let me be put to s, for I take refuge in you.
31: 1 do not let me ever be put to s;
31:17 Do not let me be put to s, O LORD,
31:17 let the wicked be put to s;
35: 4 be put to s and dishonor who seek after my life.
35:26 at my calamity be put to s and confusion;
35:26 against me be clothed with s and dishonor.
37:19 they are not put to s in evil times,
40:14 Let all those be put to s and confusion who seek
40:15 Let those be appalled because of their s who say
44:15 and s has covered my face
53: 5 they will be put to s, for God has rejected them.
57: 3 he will put to s those who trample on me.
69: 6 be put to s because of me, O Lord GOD of hosts;
69: 7 that s has covered my face.
69:19 the insults I receive, and my s and dishonor;
70: 2 be put to s and confusion who seek my life.
70: 3 turn back because of their s.
71: 1 let me never be put to s.
71:13 Let my accusers be put to s and consumed;
71:24 those who tried to do me harm have been put to s,
74:21 Do not let the downtrodden be put to s;
83:16 Fill their faces with s, so
83:17 Let them be put to s and dismayed forever;
86:17 that those who hate me may see it and be put to s,
89:45 you have covered him with s.
97: 7 All worshipers of images are put to s,
109:28 Let my assailants be put to s;
109:29 may they be wrapped in their own s as in a mantle.
119: 6 Then I shall not be put to s,
119:31 let me not be put to s.
119:46 and shall not be put to s;
119:78 Let the arrogant be put to s,
119:80 so that I may not be put to s.
119:116 and let me not be put to s in my hope.
127: 5 He shall not be put to s when he speaks with his
129: 5 May all who hate Zion be put to s
Pr 10: 5 but a child who sleeps in harvest brings s.
11:16 but she who hates virtue is covered with s.
12: 4 she who brings s is like rottenness in his bones.
18:13 one gives answer before hearing, it is folly and s.
19:26 chase away their mother are children who cause s
25: 8 when your neighbor puts you to s?
25:10 or else someone who hears you will bring s
28: 7 but companions of gluttons s their parents.
Isa 3:24 of sackcloth; instead of beauty, s.
20: 4 with buttocks uncovered, to the s of Egypt.
23: 9 to s all the honored of the earth.
30: 3 the protection of Pharaoh shall become your s,
30: 5 to s through a people that cannot profit them,
30: 5 that brings neither help nor profit, but s
42:17 They shall be turned back and utterly put to s—
44: 9 And so they will be put to s.
44:11 Look, all its devotees shall be put to s;
44:11 they shall be terrified, they shall all be put to s.
45:16 All of them are put to s and confounded,
45:17 not be put to s or confounded to all eternity.
47: 3 and your s shall be seen.
49:23 those who wait for me shall not be put to s.
50: 7 and I know that I shall not be put to s;
54: 4 for you will forget the s of your youth,
61: 7 Because their s was double,
65:13 but you shall be put to s;
66: 5 but it is they who shall be put to s.
Jer 2:36 You shall be put to s by Egypt as you were put to s
3:25 Let us lie down in our s,
8: 9 The wise shall be put to s,
10:14 goldsmiths are all put to s by their idols;
11:13 of Jerusalem are the altars you have set up to s,
13:26 and your s will be seen.
17:13 All who forsake you shall be put to s;
20:18 and spend my days in s?
23:40 upon you everlasting disgrace and perpetual s,
46:12 The nations have heard of your s,
46:24 Daughter Egypt shall be put to s;
48: 1 Kiriathaim is put to s, it is taken;
48: 1 the fortress is put to s and broken down;
48:20 Moab is put to s, for it is broken down;
48:39 How Moab has turned his back in s!
50: 2 Babylon is taken, Bel is put to s,
50: 2 Her images are put to s, her idols are dismayed.
51:17 goldsmiths are all put to s by their idols;
51:47 her whole land shall be put to s,
51:51 We are put to s, for we have heard insults;
Eze 7:18 S shall be on all faces, baldness on all their heads.
16:63 never open your mouth again because of your s,
32:24 They bear their s with those who go down to
32:25 and they bear their s with those who go down to
32:30 who have gone down in s with the slain,
32:30 and bear their s with those who go down to the Pit.
39:26 They shall forget their s, and all the treachery
44:13 but they shall bear their s,
Da 9: 7 O Lord, but open s, as at this day, falls on us,
9: 8 Open s, O LORD, falls on us, our kings,
12: 2 and some to s and everlasting contempt.
Hos 2:10 Now I will uncover her s in the sight of her lovers,
4: 7 they changed their glory into s.
9:10 and consecrated themselves to a thing of s,
10: 6 Ephraim shall be put to s,
Joel 2:26 And my people shall never again be put to s.
2:27 And my people shall never again be put to s.
Ob 1:10 s shall cover you, and you shall be cut off forever.
Mic 1:11 inhabitants of Shaphir, in nakedness and s;
3: 7 and the diviners put to s;
7:10 and s will cover her who said to me,
Na 3: 5 on your nakedness and kingdoms on your s.
Hab 2:10 You have devised s for your house
2:16 and s will come upon your glory!
Zep 3: 5 but the unjust knows no s.
3:11 On that day you shall not be put to s because of all
3:19 and I will change their s into praise and renown
Zec 10: 5 and they shall put to s the riders on horses.
Lk 13:17 When he said this, all his opponents were put to s;
Ro 9:33 and whoever believes in him will not be put to s."
10:11 "No one who believes in him will be put to s."
1Co 1:27 But God chose what is foolish in the world to s
1:27 God chose what is weak in the world to s
6: 5 I say this to your s.
15:34 I say this to your s.
2Co 11:21 To my s, I must say, we were too weak for that!
Php 1:20 and hope that I will not be put to s in any way,
3:19 and their glory is in their s;
Tit 2: 8 then any opponent will be put to s,
Heb 12: 2 the cross, disregarding its s, and has taken his seat
1Pe 2: 6 and whoever believes in him will not be put to s."
3:16 for your good conduct in Christ may be put to s.
1Jn 2:28 and not be put to s before him at his coming.
Jude 1:13 casting up the foam of their own s;
Rev 3:18 to clothe you and to keep the s of your nakedness
16:15 not going about naked and exposed to s.")
Tob 14:10 while the people are without s.
Jdt 9: 2 and exposed her thighs to put her to s,
13:16 committed no sin with me, to defile and s me."
AdE 7: 4 Our antagonist brings s on the king's court."
Sir 4:21 For there is a s that leads to sin,
4:21 and there is a s that is glory and favor.
5:14 for s comes to the thief, and severe condemnation
6: 1 for a bad name incurs s and reproach;
15: 4 and he will rely on her and not be put to s.
20:22 One may lose his life through s,
20:23 Another out of s makes promises to a friend,
20:26 and his s is ever with him.
24:22 Whoever obeys me will not be put to s,
26: 8 arouses great anger; she cannot hide her s.
26:25 *but one who has a sense of s will fear the Lord.*
29:14 the one who has lost all sense of s will fail him.
41:16 for it is not good to feel s in every circumstance,
42: 1 Then you will show proper s,
42:11 and put you to s in public gatherings.
42:14 it is woman who brings s and disgrace.
Bar 1:15 but there is open s on us today,
2: 6 but there is open s on us
LtJ 6:26 And those who serve them are put to s
6:39 and those who serve them will be put to s.
Aza 1:10 have become a s and a reproach.
1:17 for no s will come to those who trust in you.
1:19 Do not put us to s,
1:21 Let all who do harm to your servants be put to s;
1Mc 1:28 and all the house of Jacob was clothed with s.
4:45 a lasting s to them that the Gentiles had defiled it.
1Es 8:77 and exile and plundering, in s until this day.
2Es 7:87 in confusion and be consumed with s,
16:65 be put to s when your sins come out before others,
4Mc 5:35 I will not put you to s, philosophical reason,
9: 2 to s unless we should practice ready obedience to
13:18 "Do not put us to s, brother,

SHAMED (8) [SHAME]
Jer 2:26 As a thief is s when caught,
2:26 so the house of Israel shall be s—
9:19 We are utterly s, because we have left the land,
15: 9 she has been s and disgraced.
17:18 Let my persecutors be s, but do not let me be s;
20:11 They will be greatly s, for they will not succeed.
50:12 your mother shall be utterly s,

SHAMEFACEDNESS (KJV) See DECENTLY

SHAMEFUL (14) [SHAME]
Jer 3:24 "But from our youth the s thing has devoured all
1Co 14:35 For it is s for a woman to speak in church.
2Co 4: 2 We have renounced the s things that one hides;
Eph 5:12 For it is s even to mention
Tob 14:10 For God repaid him to his face for this s treatment.
Wis 2:20 Let us condemn him to a s death, for,
Sus 1:63 because she was found innocent of a s deed.
2Mc 9: 2 to flight by the inhabitants and beat a s retreat.
3Mc 3:25 to suffer the sure and s death that befits enemies.
4: 5 with which they were driven in such a s manner.
7:14 and put to a public and s death any whom they met
4Mc 5: 9 not to enjoy delicious things that are not s,
6:20 It would be s if we should survive for a little while
16:17 For it would be s if, while an aged man endures

SHAMEFULLY (8) [SHAME]
Pr 13: 5 but the wicked act s and disgracefully.
14:35 but his wrath falls on one who acts s.
17: 2 who deals wisely will rule over a child who acts s,
Jer 6:15 They acted s, they committed abomination;
8:12 They acted s, they committed abomination;
Hos 2: 5 she who conceived them has acted s.
1Th 2: 2 and been s mistreated at Philippi,
Sir 22: 4 but one who acts s is a grief to her father.

SHAMELESS (6) [SHAME]
Jer 13:27 your s prostitutions on the hills of the countryside.
Zep 2: 1 Gather together, gather, O s nation,
Ro 1:27 Men committed s acts with men and received
Sir 23: 6 and do not give me over to s passion.
26:24 *A s woman constantly acts disgracefully,*
40:30 In the mouth of the s begging is sweet,

SHAMELESSLY (1) [SHAME]
2Sa 6:20 as any vulgar fellow might s uncover himself!"

SHAMELESSNESS (1) [SHAME]
Sir 30:13 so that you may not be offended by his s.

SHAMER (KJV) See SHEMER

SHAMGAR (2)
Jdg 3:31 After him came S son of Anath,
5: 6 "In the days of S son of Anath, in the days of Jael,

SHAMHUTH (1)
1Ch 27: 8 The fifth commander, for the fifth month, was S,

SHAMIR (4)
Jos 15:48 And in the hill country, S, Jattir, Socoh,
Jdg 10: 1 who lived at S in the hill country of Ephraim,
10: 2 Then he died, and was buried at S.
1Ch 24:24 sons of Uzziel, Micah; of the sons of Micah, S.

SHAMLAI (1)
Ezr 2:46 Hagab, S, Hanan,

SHAMMA (1)
1Ch 7:37 Bezer, Hod, S, Shilshah, Ithran, and Beera.

SHAMMAH (8)
Ge 36:13 Nahath, Zerah, S, and Mizzah.
36:17 the clans Nahath, Zerah, S, and Mizzah;
1Sa 16: 9 Then Jesse made S pass by.
17:13 and next to him Abinadab, and the third S.
2Sa 23:11 Next to him was S son of Agee, the Hararite.
23:25 S of Harod; Elika of Harod;
23:33 son of S the Hararite; Ahiam son of Sharar
1Ch 1:37 The sons of Reuel: Nahath, Zerah, S, and Mizzah.

SHAMMAI (5) [SHAMMAI'S]
1Ch 2:28 The sons of Onam: S and Jada.
2:28 The sons of S: Nadab and Abishur.
2:44 and Rekem became the father of S.
2:45 The son of S: Maon; and Maon was the father of
4:17 and she conceived and bore Miriam, S,

SHAMMAI'S (1) [SHAMMAI]
1Ch 2:32 The sons of Jada, S brother:

SHAMMOTH (1)
1Ch 11:27 S of Harod, Helez the Pelonite,

SHAMMUA (5)
Nu 13: 4 From the tribe of Reuben, S son of Zaccur;
2Sa 5:14 S, Shobab, Nathan, Solomon,
1Ch 14: 4 in Jerusalem: S, Shobab, and Nathan;
Ne 11:17 and Abda son of S son of Galal son of Jeduthun.
12:18 of Bilgah, S; of Shemaiah, Jehonathan;

SHAMSHERAI (1)
1Ch 8:26 S, Shehariah, Athaliah,

SHAON See Index to Footnotes

SHAPED (10) [SHAPELY, SHAPES, SHAPING]

Ex 25:33 three cups s like almond blossoms, each
25:33 and three cups s like almond blossoms,
25:34 On the lampstand itself there shall be four cups s
37:19 three cups s like almond blossoms, each
37:19 and three cups s like almond blossoms,
37:20 On the lampstand itself there were four cups s
Pr 8:25 Before the mountains had been **s**, before the hills,
Hab 2:18 What use is an idol once its maker has s it—
2Mc 7:23 who s the beginning of humankind and devised
4Mc 13:20 of time and was s during the same period of time;

SHAPELY (2) [SHAPED]

Sir 9:8 Turn away your eyes from a s woman,
26:18 so are s legs and steadfast feet.

SHAPES (1) [SHAPED]

Wis 13:13 and s it with skill gained in idleness;

SHAPHAM (1)

1Ch 5:12 S the second, Janai, and Shaphat in Bashan.

SHAPHAN (30)

2Ki 22:3 the king sent S son of Azaliah, son of Meshullam,
22:8 The high priest Hilkiah said to S the secretary,
22:8 When Hilkiah gave the book to **S**, he read it.
22:9 Then S the secretary came to the king,
22:10 S the secretary informed the king,
22:10 S then read it aloud to the king.
22:12 Ahikam son of **S**, Achbor son of Micaiah,
22:12 S the secretary, and the king's servant Asaiah,
22:14 So the priest Hilkiah, Ahikam, Achbor, **S**,
25:22 of S as governor over the people who remained in
2Ch 34:8 he sent S son of Azaliah,
34:15 Hilkiah said to the secretary **S**,
34:15 and Hilkiah gave the book to **S**.
34:16 S brought the book to the king,
34:18 The secretary S informed the king,
34:18 S then read it aloud to the king.
34:20 the king commanded Hilkiah, Ahikam son of **S**,
34:20 the secretary **S**, and the king's servant Asaiah:
Jer 26:24 of S was with Jeremiah so that he was not given
29:3 The letter was sent by the hand of Elasah son of S
36:10 the chamber of Gemariah son of S the secretary,
36:11 When Micaiah son of Gemariah son of S heard all
36:12 Gemariah son of **S**, Zedekiah son of Hananiah,
39:14 of Ahikam son of S to be brought home.
40:5 then return to Gedaliah son of Ahikam son of **S**,
40:9 Gedaliah son of Ahikam son of S swore to them
40:11 of Ahikam son of S as governor over them,
41:2 and struck down Gedaliah son of Ahikam son of S
43:6 with Gedaliah son of Ahikam son of **S**;
Eze 8:11 with Jaazaniah son of S standing among them.

SHAPHAT (9)

Nu 13:5 from the tribe of Simeon, S son of Hori;
1Ki 19:16 of S of Abel-meholah as prophet in your place.
19:19 he set out from there, and found Elisha son of **S**,
2Ki 3:11 of the king of Israel answered, "Elisha son of **S**,
6:31 of Elisha son of S stays on his shoulders today."
1Ch 3:22 Hattush, Igal, Bariah, Neariah, and **S**, six.
5:12 Shapham the second, Janai, and S in Bashan.
27:29 Over the herds in the valleys was S son of Adlai.
1Es 5:34 the descendants of Barodis, the descendants of **S**,

SHAPHER (KJV) See SHEPHER

SHAPHIR (1)

Mic 1:11 Pass on your way, inhabitants of **S**,

SHAPING (2) [SHAPED]

Isa 44:12 s it with hammers, and forging it with his strong
Jer 18:11 I am a potter s evil against you and devising a plan

SHAQED See Index to Footnotes

SHARAI (1)

Ezr 10:40 Machnadebai, Shashai, **S**,

SHARAIM (KJV) See SHAARAIM

SHARAR (1)

2Sa 23:33 Ahiam son of S the Hararite;

SHARE‡ (80) [HALF-SHARE, SHARED, SHARERS, SHARES, SHARING]

Ge 14:24 and the s of the men who went with me—
14:24 Let them take their **s**."
Nu 18:20 nor shall you have any s among them; I am your s
31:28 From the s of the warriors who went out to battle,
Dt 32:9 own portion was his people, Jacob his allotted **s**.
1Sa 26:19 for they have driven me out today from my s in
30:24 For the s of the one who goes down into the battle shall be the same as the s of the one who stays by the baggage; they shall s alike."
2Sa 20:1 no s in the son of Jesse!
1Ki 12:16 "What s do we have in David?
2Ki 2:9 "Please let me inherit a double s of your spirit."
2Ch 10:16 "What s do we have in David?
Ezr 4:14 Now because we s the salt of the palace and it is
Ne 2:20 but you have no s or claim or historic right
Job 39:17 and given it no s in understanding.
Ps 68:23 so that the tongues of your dogs may have their s
Pr 17:2 and will s the inheritance as one of the family.
17:17 and kinsfolk are born to s adversity.
22:9 for they s their bread with the poor.
31:31 Give her a s in the fruit of her hands,
Ecc 9:6 never again will they have any s in all
Isa 58:7 Is it not to s your bread with the hungry,
Jer 37:12 to the land of Benjamin to receive his s of property
Mk 12:2 a slave to the tenants to collect from them his s of
Lk 3:11 "Whoever has two coats must s with anyone who
15:12 give me the s of the property that will belong
20:10 the tenants in order that they might give him his s
Jn 4:9 not s things in common with Samaritans.)
13:8 "Unless I wash you, you have no s with me."
Ac 1:17 among us and was allotted his s in this ministry."
8:21 You have no part or s in this,
Ro 1:11 so that I may s with you some spiritual gift
4:16 also to those who s the faith of Abraham (for he is
11:17 in their place to s the rich root of the olive tree,
15:26 to s their resources with the poor among the saints
15:27 Gentiles have come to s in their spiritual blessings,
1Co 9:10 and whoever threshes should thresh in hope of a s
9:12 If others s this rightful claim on you,
9:13 at the altar s in what is sacrificed on the altar?
9:23 so that I may s in its blessings.
2Co 1:7 for we know that as you s in our sufferings,
1:7 so also you s in our consolation.
6:15 Or what does a believer s with an unbeliever?
9:8 you may s abundantly in every good work.
Gal 4:30 for the child of the slave will not s the inheritance
6:6 Those who are taught the word must s
Eph 4:28 so as to have something to s with the needy.
Php 1:7 for all of you s in God's grace with me,
1:26 so that I may s abundantly in your boasting
4:14 In any case, it was kind of you to s my distress.
Col 1:12 to s in the inheritance of the saints in the light.
1Th 2:8 that we are determined to s with you not only
1Ti 6:18 to be rich in good works, generous, and ready to **s**,
2Ti 2:3 S in suffering like a good soldier of Christ Jesus.
2:6 the work who ought to have the first s of the crops.
Tit 1:4 my loyal child in the faith we **s**:
Heb 2:14 Since, therefore, the children s flesh and blood,
11:25 choosing rather to s ill-treatment with the people
12:8 not have that discipline in which all children **s**,
12:10 in order that we may s his holiness.
13:16 Do not neglect to do good and to s what you have,
Jude 1:3 to write to you about the salvation we **s**,
Rev 1:9 your brother who s with you in Jesus
18:4 and so that you do not s in her plagues;
20:6 and holy are those who s in the first resurrection.
22:19 God will take away that person's s in the tree
Tob 11:18 also present to s Tobit's joy.
Wis 2:9 Let none of us fail to s in our revelry;
18:9 so that the saints would s alike the same things,
Sir 14:9 of the greedy person is not satisfied with his **s**;
14:14 do not let your s of desired good pass by you.
22:23 so that you may s with him in his inheritance.
2Mc 5:27 so that they might not s in the defilement.
1Es 5:40 And Nehemiah and Attharias told them not to s in
3Mc 4:6 the bridal chamber to s married life exchanged joy
2Es 15:46 who s in the splendor of Babylon and the glory
4Mc 16:18 through God that you have had a s in the world
18:3 were deemed worthy to s in a divine inheritance.

SHARED (11) [SHARE]

1Ki 2:26 you s in all the hardships my father endured."
Pr 21:9 than in a house s with a contentious wife.
25:24 than in a house s with a contentious wife.
Php 4:15 no church s with me in the matter of giving
Heb 2:14 he himself likewise s the same things,
6:4 and have s in the Holy Spirit,
Wis 14:21 of stone or wood the name that ought not to be **s**.
19:16 with terrible sufferings those who had already s
2Mc 4:36 and the Greeks s their hatred of the crime.
5:20 the place itself s in the misfortunes that befell
14:25 settled down, and s the common life.

SHARERS (1) [SHARE]

Eph 3:6 s in the promise in Christ Jesus through the gospel.

SHARES (5) [SHARE]

2Sa 19:43 "We have ten s in the king,
Pr 14:10 and no stranger s its joy.
Lk 10:6 And if anyone is there who s in peace,
1Pe 5:1 as well as one who s in the glory to be revealed,
2Mc 8:30 and also to the aged, s equal to their own.

SHAREZER (3)

2Ki 19:37 his sons Adrammelech and S killed him with
Isa 37:38 his sons Adrammelech and S killed him with
Zec 7:2 of Bethel had sent S and Regem-melech

SHARING‡ (13) [SHARE]

Pr 5:17 and not for s with strangers.
Ro 5:2 and we boast in our hope of s the glory of God.
1Co 10:16 is it not a s in the blood of Christ?
10:16 is it not a s in the body of Christ?
2Co 8:4 the privilege of s in this ministry to the saints—
9:13 and by the generosity of your s with them and
Php 1:5 because of your s in the gospel from the first day
2:1 any s in the Spirit, any compassion and sympathy,
3:10 and the s of his sufferings by becoming like him
Phm 1:6 that the s of your faith may become effective
1Pe 4:13 But rejoice insofar as you are s Christ's sufferings,
Wis 8:18 understanding, and renown in s her words,
1Es 8:70 and the nobles have been s in this iniquity."

SHARON (7) [SHARONITE]

1Ch 5:16 and in all the pasture lands of S to their limits.
27:29 Over the herds that pastured in S was Shitrai
SS 2:1 I am a rose of **S**, a lily of the valleys.
Isa 33:9 S is like a desert; and Bashan and Carmel shake off
35:2 the majesty of Carmel and **S**.
65:10 S shall become a pasture for flocks,
Ac 9:35 the residents of Lydda and S saw him and turned

SHARONITE (1) [SHARON]

1Ch 27:29 that pastured in Sharon was Shitrai the **S**.

SHARP (27) [SHARPEN, SHARPENED, SHARPENING, SHARPENS, SHARPER, SHARPLY]

Job 41:30 Its underparts are like s potsherds;
Ps 45:5 Your arrows are s in the heart of
52:2 Your tongue is like a s razor,
57:4 and arrows, their tongues s swords.
59:7 with s words on their lips—
120:4 A warrior's s arrows, with glowing coals of
140:3 They make their tongue s as a snake's,
Pr 5:4 but in the end she is bitter as wormwood, s as
25:18 or a s arrow is one who bears false witness against
Isa 5:28 their arrows are **s**, all their bows bent,
41:15 Now, I will make of you a threshing sledge, **s**,
49:2 He made my mouth like a s sword,
Eze 5:1 And you, O mortal, take a s sword;
Ac 15:39 The disagreement became so s
Rev 1:16 and from his mouth came a **s**, two-edged sword,
2:12 the words of him who has the s two-edged sword:
14:14 and a s sickle in his hand!
14:17 and he too had a s sickle.
14:18 with a loud voice to him who had the s sickle,
14:18 "Use your s sickle and gather the clusters of
19:15 a s sword with which to strike down the nations,
Wis 18:16 carrying the s sword of your authentic command,
2Mc 9:5 and with s internal tortures—
3Mc 5:18 and with s threats demanded to know why
2Es 16:13 that he shoots are s and when they are shot to
4Mc 9:26 with iron gauntlets having s hooks,
11:19 To his back they applied s spits

SHARPEN (3) [SHARP]

1Sa 13:20 the Philistines to s their plowshare, mattocks, axes,
Jer 51:11 S the arrows! Fill the quivers!
Wis 5:20 and s stern wrath for a sword,

SHARPENED (3) [SHARP]

Eze 21:9 A sword, a sword is **s**, it is also polished;
21:10 It is s for slaughter, honed to flash
21:11 It is **s**, the sword is polished,

SHARPENING (1) [SHARP]

1Sa 13:21 of a shekel for s the axes and for setting the goads.

SHARPENS (3) [SHARP]

Job 16:9 my adversary s his eyes against me.
Pr 27:17 Iron s iron, and one person s the wits of another.

SHARPER (1) [SHARP]

Heb 4:12 living and active, s than any two-edged sword,

SHARPLY (1) [SHARP]

Tit 1:13 For this reason rebuke them **s**,

SHARPNESS (KJV) See SEVERE

SHARUHEN (1)

Jos 19:6 and **S**—thirteen towns with their villages;

SHASHAI (2)

Ezr 10:40 Machnadebai, **S**, Sharai,
1Es 9:34 **S**, Azarel, Azael, Samatus, Zambris, Joseph.

SHASHAK (2)

1Ch 8:14 and Ahio, **S**, and Jeremoth.
8:25 Iphdeiah, and Penuel were the sons of **S**.

SHATTER‡ (5) [SHATTERED, SHATTERER, SHATTERING, SHATTERS]

Ps 68:21 But God will s the heads of his enemies,
110:5 he will s kings on the day of his wrath.
110:6 he will s heads over the wide earth.
Da 2:40 it shall crush and s all these.
Am 9:1 and s them on the heads of all the people;

SHATTERED (14) [SHATTER]

Ex 9:25 and s every tree in the field.
15:6 your right hand, O LORD, s the enemy.

Jdg 5:26 she crushed his head, she s and pierced his temple.
1Sa 2:10 His adversaries shall be s;
Ps 105:33 and s the trees of their country.
Isa 7: 8 (Within sixty-five years Ephraim will be s,
21: 9 and all the images of her gods lie s on the ground."
Jer 51: 8 Suddenly Babylon has fallen and is s;
Am 6:11 and the great house shall be s to bits,
Ob 1: 9 Your warriors shall be s, O Teman,
Hab 3: 6 The eternal mountains were s;
Mal 1: 4 "We are s but we will rebuild the ruins,"
Rev 2:27 as when clay pots are s—
2Es 16:11 and who will not be utterly s at his presence?

SHATTERER (1) [SHATTER]
Na 2: 1 A s has come up against you.

SHATTERING (1) [SHATTER]
Da 12: 7 s of the power of the holy people comes to an end,

SHATTERS (7) [SHATTER]
Dt 33:27 He subdues the ancient gods, s the forces of old;
Job 34:24 He s the mighty without investigation,
Ps 46: 9 he breaks the bow, and s the spear;
48: 7 as when an east wind s the ships of Tarshish.
107:16 For he s the doors of bronze,
141: 7 Like a rock that one breaks apart and s on the land,
2Mc 12:28 upon the Sovereign who with power s the might

SHAUL‡ (9) [SHAULITES]
Ge 36:37 Samlah died, and S of Rehoboth on
36:38 S died, and Baal-hanan son
46:10 Jemuel, Jamin, Ohad, Jachin, Zohar, and S,
Ex 6:15 Jemuel, Jamin, Ohad, Jachin, Zohar, and S,
Nu 26:13 of S, the clan of the Shaulites.
1Ch 1:48 S of Rehoboth on the Euphrates succeeded him.
1:49 S died, Baal-hanan son of Achbor succeeded him.
4:24 Nemuel, Jamin, Jarib, Zerah, S;
6:24 Uriel his son, Uzziah his son, and S his son.

SHAULITES (1) [SHAUL]
Nu 26:13 of Shaul, the clan of the S.

SHAVE (15) [SHAVED, SHAVEN, SHAVING]
Lev 13:33 he shall s, but the itch he shall not s.
14: 8 and s off all his hair, and bathe himself in water,
14: 9 On the seventh day he shall s all his hair:
14: 9 he shall s all his hair.
21: 5 or s off the edges of their beards,
Nu 6: 9 they shall s the head on the day of their cleansing;
6: 9 on the seventh day they shall s it.
6:18 Then the nazirites shall s the consecrated head at
8: 7 on them, have them s their whole body with
Dt 14: 1 not lacerate yourselves or s your forelocks for
21:12 she shall s her head, pare her nails,
Jdg 16:19 and had him s off the seven locks of his head.
Isa 7:20 that day the Lord will s with a razor hired beyond
Eze 44:20 not s their heads or let their locks grow long;

SHAVED (12) [SHAVE]
Ge 41:14 When he had s himself and changed his clothes,
Nu 6:19 after they have s the consecrated head.
Jdg 16:17 my head were s, then my strength would leave me;
16:22 of his head began to grow again after it had been s.
2Sa 10: 4 s off half the beard of each,
1Ch 19: 4 So Hanun seized David's servants, s them,
Job 1:20 Then Job arose, tore his robe, s his head,
Jer 41: 5 with their beards s and their clothes torn,
48:37 For every head is s and every beard cut off;
1Co 11: 5 it is one and the same thing as having her head s.
11: 6 for a woman to have her hair cut off or to be s,
LtJ 6:31 with their clothes torn, their heads and beards s,

SHAVEH (1)
Ge 14:17 of Sodom went out to meet him at the Valley of S

SHAVEH-KIRIATHAIM (1)
Ge 14: 5 the Zuzim in Ham, the Emim in S,

SHAVEN (3) [SHAVE]
Jer 9:26 and all those with s temples who live in the desert.
25:23 Dedan, Tema, Buz, and all who have s temples;
49:32 to every wind those who have s temples,

SHAVING (2) [SHAVE]
Jer 16: 6 no s of the head for them.
Ac 21:24 and pay for the s of their heads.

SHAVSHA (1)
1Ch 18:16 of Abiathar were priests; S was secretary;

SHE (1296) [HER, HERS, HERSELF, SHE-BEAR, SHE-BEARS] See Index of Articles Etc.

SHE-BEAR (1) [BEAR, SHE]
Pr 17:12 to meet a s robbed of its cubs than to confront

SHE-BEARS (1) [BEAR, SHE]
2Ki 2:24 Then two s came out of the woods and mauled

SHEAF (7) [SHEAVES]
Ge 37: 7 Suddenly my s rose and stood upright;
37: 7 and bowed down to my s."
Lev 23:10 the s of the first fruits of your harvest to the priest.
23:11 He shall raise the s before the LORD,
23:12 On the day when you raise the s,
23:15 on which you bring the s of the elevation offering,
Dt 24:19 in your field and forget a s in the field, you shall

SHEAL (2)
Ezr 10:29 Meshullam, Malluch, Adaiah, Jashub, S,
1Es 9:30 Mamuchus, Adaiah, Jashub, and S and Jeremoth.

SHEALTIEL (15) [=SALATHIEL]
1Ch 3:17 and the sons of Jeconiah, the captive: S his son,
Ezr 3: 2 and Zerubbabel son of S with his kin set out
3: 8 of S and Jeshua son of Jozadak made a beginning,
5: 2 of S and Jeshua son of Jozadak set out to rebuild
Ne 12: 1 up with Zerubbabel son of S, and Jeshua:
Hag 1: 1 to Zerubbabel son of S, governor of Judah,
1:12 Then Zerubbabel son of S,
1:14 of Zerubbabel son of S, governor of Judah,
2: 2 Speak now to Zerubbabel son of S,
2:23 O Zerubbabel my servant, son of S,
Lk 3:27 son of Rhesa, son of Zerubbabel, son of S,
1Es 5: 5 and Joakim son of Zerubbabel son of S,
5:48 with his fellow priests, and Zerubbabel son of S,
5:56 of S and Jeshua son of Jozadak made a beginning,
6: 2 of S and Jeshua son of Jozadak began to build

SHEAR (3) [SHEARER, SHEARERS, SHEARING, SHEARINGS, SHEEPSHEARERS, SHORN]
Ge 31:19 Now Laban had gone to s his sheep,
38:13 up to Timnah to s his sheep,"
Dt 15:19 you shall not do work with your firstling ox nor s

SHEAR-JASHUB (1)
Isa 7: 3 Go out to meet Ahaz, you and your son S,

SHEARER (1) [SHEAR]
Ac 8:32 and like a lamb silent before its s,

SHEARERS (3) [SHEAR]
1Sa 25: 7 I hear that you have s;
25:11 and the meat that I have butchered for my s,
Isa 53: 7 and like a sheep that before its s is silent,

SHEARIAH (2)
1Ch 8:38 Azrikam, Bocheru, Ishmael, S, Obadiah,
9:44 Azrikam, Bocheru, Ishmael, S, Obadiah,

SHEARING (2) [SHEAR]
1Sa 25: 2 He was s his sheep in Carmel.
25: 4 in the wilderness that Nabal was s his sheep.

SHEARINGS (1) [SHEAR]
Tob 1: 6 the tithes of the cattle, and the first s of the sheep.

SHEATH‡ (8) [SHEATHED]
1Sa 17:51 he grasped his sword, drew it out of its s,
2Sa 20: 8 and over it was a belt with a sword in its s fastened
1Ch 21:27 and he put his sword back into its s.
Eze 21: 3 and will draw my sword out of its s,
21: 4 of its s against all flesh from south to north;
21: 5 the LORD have drawn my sword out of its s;
21:30 Return it to its s!
Jn 18:11 Jesus said to Peter, "Put your sword back into its s.

SHEATHED (1) [SHEATH]
Eze 21: 5 it shall not be s again.

SHEAVES (12) [SHEAF]
Ge 37: 7 There we were, binding s in the field.
37: 7 then your s gathered around it,
Ru 2: 7 and gather among the s behind the reapers.'
2:15 "Let her glean even among the standing s,
Job 24:10 though hungry, they carry the s;
Ps 126: 6 with shouts of joy, carrying their s.
129: 7 not fill their hands or binders of s their arms,
Jer 9:22 like s behind the reaper, and no one shall gather
Am 2:13 just as a cart presses down when it is full of s.
Mic 4:12 he has gathered them as s to the threshing floor.
Zec 12: 6 like a flaming torch among s;
Jdt 8: 3 as he stood overseeing those who were binding s

SHEBA (33)
Ge 10: 7 The descendants of Raamah: S and Dedan.
10:28 Obal, Abimael, S,
25: 3 Jokshan was the father of S and Dedan.
Jos 19: 2 It had for its inheritance Beer-sheba, S, Moladah,
2Sa 20: 1 Now a scoundrel named S son of Bichri,
20: 2 of Israel withdrew from David and followed S son
20: 6 David said to Abishai, "Now S son of Bichri
20: 7 they went out from Jerusalem to pursue S son
20:10 Then Joab and his brother Abishai pursued S son
20:13 all the people went on after Joab to pursue S son
20:14 S passed through all the tribes of Israel to Abel
20:21 called S son of Bichri, has lifted up his hand
2Sa 20:22 And they cut off the head of S son of Bichri,
1Ki 10: 1 the queen of S heard of the fame of Solomon,
10: 4 When the queen of S had observed all the wisdom
10:10 in such quantity as that which the queen of S gave
10:13 to the queen of S every desire that she expressed,
1Ch 1: 9 The descendants of Raamah: S and Dedan.
1:22 Ebal, Abimael, S,
1:32 The sons of Jokshan: S and Dedan.
5:13 Michael, Meshullam, S, Jorai, Jacan, Zia,
2Ch 9: 1 the queen of S heard of the fame of Solomon,
9: 3 queen of S had observed the wisdom of Solomon,
9: 9 that the queen of S gave to King Solomon.
9:12 the queen of S every desire that she expressed,
Job 6:19 caravans of Tema look, the travelers of S hope.
Ps 72:10 may the kings of S and Seba bring gifts.
72:15 May gold of S be given to him.
Isa 60: 6 all those from S shall come.
Jer 6:20 to me is frankincense that comes from S,
Eze 27:22 The merchants of S and Raamah traded with you;
27:23 Haran, Canneh, Eden, the merchants of S, Asshur,
38:13 S and Dedan and the merchants of Tarshish

SHEBAH (KJV) See SHIBAH

SHEBAM (KJV) See SEBAM

SHEBANIAH (7)
1Ch 15:24 S, Joshaphat, Nethanel, Amasai, Zechariah,
Ne 9: 4 Then Jeshua, Bani, Kadmiel, S, Bunni, Sherebiah,
9: 5 Sherebiah, Hodiah, S, and Pethahiah, said,
10: 4 Hattush, S, Malluch,
10:10 S, Hodiah, Kelita, Pelaiah, Hanan,
10:12 Zaccur, Sherebiah, S,
12:14 of Malluchi, Jonathan; of S, Joseph;

SHEBARIM (1)
Jos 7: 5 the gate as far as S and killing them on the slope.

SHEBAT (2)
Zec 1: 7 the month of S, in the second year of Darius,
1Mc 16:14 in the eleventh month, which is the month of S.

SHEBER (1)
1Ch 2:48 Maacah, Caleb's concubine, bore S and Tirhanah.

SHEBNA (7) [=SHEBNAH]
2Ki 18:37 and S the secretary, and Joah son of Asaph,
19: 2 and S the secretary, and the senior priests,
Isa 22:15 Come, go to this steward, to S,
36: 3 and S the secretary, and Joah son of Asaph,
36:11 Then Eliakim, S, and Joah said to the Rabshakeh,
36:22 and S the secretary, and Joah son of Asaph,
37: 2 and S the secretary, and the senior priests,

SHEBNAH (2) [=SHEBNA]
2Ki 18:18 and S the secretary, and Joah son of Asaph,
18:26 Then Eliakim son of Hilkiah, and S,

SHEBUEL (3)
1Ch 23:16 The sons of Gershom: S the chief.
25: 4 Bukkiah, Mattaniah, Uzziel, S, and Jerimoth,
26:24 S son of Gershom, son of Moses, was chief officer

SHECANIAH (13)
1Ch 3:21 his son Arnan, his son Obadiah, his son S.
3:22 The son of S: Shemaiah.
24:11 the ninth to Jeshua, the tenth to S,
2Ch 31:15 and S were faithfully assisting him in the cities of
Ezr 8: 3 of the descendants of S. Of Parosh,
8: 5 Of the descendants of Zattu, S son of Jahaziel,
10: 2 S son of Jehiel, of the descendants of Elam,
Ne 3:29 After him Shemaiah son of S,
6:18 because he was the son-in-law of S son of Arah:
12: 3 S, Rehum, Meremoth,
1Es 8:29 Of the descendants of David, Hattush son of S.
8:32 Of the descendants of Zattu, S son of Jahaziel,
8:92 Then S son of Jehiel, one of the men of Israel,

SHECHEM (68) [SHECHEM'S, SHECHEMITES]
Ge 12: 6 Abram passed through the land to the place at S,
33:18 Jacob came safely to the city of S,
34: 2 When S son of Hamor the Hivite,
34: 4 So S spoke to his father Hamor, saying,
34: 5 Jacob heard that S had defiled his daughter Dinah;
34: 6 And Hamor the father of S went out to Jacob
34: 8 "The heart of my son S longs for your daughter;
34:11 S also said to her father and to her brothers,
34:13 The sons of Jacob answered S
34:18 Their words pleased Hamor and Hamor's son S.
34:20 and his son S came to the gate of their city
34:24 of the city gate heeded Hamor and his son S;
34:26 They killed Hamor and his son S with the sword,
35: 4 and Jacob hid them under the oak that was near S.
37:12 to pasture their father's flock near S.
37:13 "Are not your brothers pasturing the flock at S?
37:14 sent him from the valley of Hebron. He came to S,
Nu 26:31 and of S, the clan of the Shechemites;
Jos 17: 2 Abiezer, Helek, Asriel, S, Hepher, and Shemida;
17: 7 from Asher to Michmethath, which is east of S;
20: 7 and S in the hill country of Ephraim,

Jos 21:21 To them were given S, the city of refuge for
24: 1 Then Joshua gathered all the tribes of Israel to S,
24:25 and made statutes and ordinances for them at S.
24:32 were buried at S, in the portion of ground
24:32 the father of S, for one hundred pieces of money;
Jdg 8:31 His concubine who was in S also bore him a son,
9: 1 to S to his mother's kinsfolk and said to them and
9: 2 "Say in the hearing of all the lords of S,
9: 3 on his behalf in the hearing of all the lords of S;
9: 6 the lords of S and all Beth-millo came together,
9: 6 by the oak of the pillar at S.
9: 7 you lords of S, so that God may listen to you.
9:18 over the lords of S, because he is your kinsman—
9:20 and devour the lords of S, and Beth-millo;
9:20 and let fire come out from the lords of S,
9:23 between Abimelech and the lords of S;
9:23 the lords of S dealt treacherously with Abimelech.
9:24 who killed them, and on the lords of S,
9:25 the lords of S set ambushes on the mountain tops.
9:26 Gaal son of Ebed moved into S with his kinsfolk,
9:26 the lords of S put confidence in him.
9:28 and who are we of S, that we should serve him?
9:28 the men of Hamor father of S?
9:31 of Ebed and his kinsfolk have come to S,
9:34 with him got up by night and lay in wait against S
9:39 So Gaal went out at the head of the lords of S,
9:41 so that they could not live on at S.
9:46 When all the lords of the Tower of S heard of it,
9:47 of the Tower of S were gathered together.
9:49 so that all the people of the Tower of S also died,
9:57 the wickedness of the people of S fall back
21:19 of the highway that goes up from Bethel to S,
1Ki 12: 1 Rehoboam went to S, for all Israel had come
12: 1 for all Israel had come to S to make him king.
12:25 Jeroboam built S in the hill country of Ephraim,
1Ch 6:67 S with its pasture lands in the hill country
7:19 The sons of Shemida were Ahian, S, Likhi,
7:28 S and its towns, as far as Ayyah and its towns;
2Ch 10: 1 Rehoboam went to S, for all Israel had come
10: 1 for all Israel had come to S to make him king.
Ps 60: 6 "With exultation I will divide up S,
108: 7 "With exultation I will divide up S,
Jer 41: 5 eighty men arrived from S and Shiloh
Hos 6: 9 they murder on the road to S,
Ac 7:16 and their bodies were brought back to S and laid
7:16 for a sum of silver from the sons of Hamor in S.
Sir 50:26 and the foolish people that live in S.

SHECHEM'S (2) [SHECHEM]

Ge 33:19 And from the sons of Hamor, S father,
34:26 and took Dinah out of S house, and went away.

SHECHEMITES (3) [SHECHEM]

Nu 26:31 and of Shechem, the clan of the S;
Jdt 5:16 the Jebusites, the S, and all the Gergesites,
4Mc 2:19 of the entire tribe of the S,

SHED (49) [BLOODSHED, SHEDDER, SHEDDING, SHEDS]

Ge 9: 6 by a human shall that person's blood be s;
37:22 Reuben said to them, "S no blood;
Lev 17: 4 he has s blood, and he shall be cut off from
Nu 35:33 for the blood that is s in it,
35:33 except by the blood of the one who s it.
Dt 19:10 of an innocent person may not be s in the land that
21: 7 "Our hands did not s this blood,
27:25 be anyone who takes a bribe to s innocent blood."
1Sa 25:31 for having s blood without cause or
1Ki 2: 5 in time of peace for blood that had been s in war,
2:31 the guilt for the blood that Joab s without cause.
2Ki 21:16 Moreover Manasseh s very much innocent blood,
24: 4 and also for the innocent blood that he had s;
1Ch 22: 8 to me, saying, 'You have s much blood
22: 8 you have s so much blood in my sight on the earth.
28: 3 for you are a warrior and have s blood.'
Ps 119:136 My eyes s streams of tears because your law is
Pr 1:16 for their feet run to evil, and they hurry to s blood.
6:17 a lying tongue, and hands that s innocent blood,
Isa 13:10 and the moon will not s its light.
26:21 the earth will disclose the blood s on it,
59: 7 and they rush to s innocent blood;
Jer 7: 6 and the widow, or s innocent blood in this place,
22: 3 and the widow, or s innocent blood in this place.
La 4:13 who s the blood of the righteous in the midst
Eze 16:38 and s blood are judged, and bring blood upon you
22: 4 the blood that you have s, and defiled by the idols
22: 9 In you are those who slander to s blood,
22:12 In you, they take bribes to s blood;
22:13 and at the blood that has been s within you.
24: 7 For the blood she s is inside it;
24: 8 I have placed the blood she s on a bare rock,
33:25 and lift up your eyes to your idols, and s blood;
36:18 upon them for the blood that they had s upon
Joel 3:19 in whose land they have s innocent blood.
Mt 23:35 that upon you may come all the righteous blood s
Lk 11:50 the blood of all the prophets s since the foundation
Ac 22:20 while the blood of your witness Stephen was s,
Ro 3:15 "Their feet are swift to s blood;
Rev 16: 6 because they s the blood of saints and prophets,
Sir 11:32 and a sinner lies in wait to s blood.
34:27 to deprive an employee of wages is to s blood.
1Mc 1:24 He s much blood, and spoke with great arrogance.
1:37 of the sanctuary they s innocent blood;
2Mc 1: 8 and burned the gate and s innocent blood.
3Mc 4: 4 of life and s tears at the most miserable expulsion
3Mc 5:26 The rays of the sun were not yet s abroad,
2Es 15:22 not cease from those who s innocent blood
4Mc 13:20 of the torturings, you did not s tears.

SHEDDER (1) [SHED]

Eze 18:10 If he has a son who is violent, a s of blood,

SHEDDING‡ (10) [SHED]

2Sa 3:27 he died for s the blood of Asahel, Joab's brother.
Jer 22:17 for s innocent blood, and for practicing oppression
Eze 22: 3 A city! S blood within itself;
22: 6 have been bent on s blood.
22:27 s blood, destroying lives to get dishonest gain.
Mt 23:30 not have taken part with them in s the blood of
Heb 9:22 and without the s of blood there is no forgiveness
12: 4 not yet resisted to the point of s your blood.
AdE 16: 5 in part responsible for the s of innocent blood,
Sus 1:46 "I want no part in s this woman's blood!"

SHEDEUR (5)

Nu 1: 5 From Reuben, Elizur son of S.
2:10 leader of the Reubenites shall be Elizur son of S,
7:30 On the fourth day Elizur son of S,
7:35 This was the offering of Elizur son of S.
10:18 and over the whole company was Elizur son of S.

SHEDS (5) [SHED]

Ge 9: 6 Whoever s the blood of a human,
Na 3:16 The locust s its skin and flies away.
Sir 14:18 a spreading tree that s some and puts forth others,
28:11 and a hasty dispute s blood.
31:13 Therefore it s tears for any reason.

SHEEP‡ (220) [MOUNTAIN-SHEEP, SHEEP'S, SHEEPFOLD, SHEEPFOLDS, SHEEPSHEARERS]

Ge 4: 2 Now Abel was a keeper of s,
12:16 and he had s, oxen, male donkeys,
20:14 Then Abimelech took s and oxen,
21:27 So Abraham took s and oxen and gave them
29: 2 the field and three flocks of s lying there beside it;
29: 3 of the well, and water the s, and put the stone back
29: 6 here is his daughter Rachel, coming with the s."
29: 7 Water the s, and go, pasture them."
29: 8 of the well; then we water the s."
29: 9 Rachel came with her father's s;
29:10 and the s of his mother's brother Laban,
30:32 removing from it every speckled and spotted s
31:19 Now Laban had gone to shear his s,
38:13 up to Timnah to shear his s,"
Ex 12: 5 you may take it from the s or from the goats.
13:13 every firstborn donkey you shall redeem with a s;
20:24 and your offerings of well-being, your s
22: 1 When someone steals an ox or a s,
22: 1 pay five oxen for an ox, and four s for a s.
22: 4 When the animal, whether ox or donkey or s,
22: 9 donkey, s, clothing, or any other loss,
22:10 someone delivers to another a donkey, ox, s,
22:30 the same with your oxen and with your s:
34:19 all your male livestock, the firstborn of cow and s.
Lev 1:10 from the s or goats, your offering shall be a male
3: 7 If you present a s as your offering,
4:32 If the offering you bring as a sin offering is a s,
4:35 the s is removed from the sacrifice of well-being,
5: 6 a female from the flock, a s or a goat,
5: 7 But if you cannot afford a s,
7:23 You shall eat no fat of ox or s or goat.
12: 8 a s, she shall take two turtledoves
22:19 of the cattle or the s or the goats.
22:27 When an ox or a s or a goat is born,
27:26 whether ox or s, it is the LORD's.
Nu 18:17 But the firstborn of a cow, or the firstborn of a s,
22:40 Balak sacrificed oxen and s,
27:17 the LORD may not be like s without a shepherd."
31:28 whether persons, oxen, donkeys, s, or goats.
31:30 whether persons, oxen, donkeys, s, or goats—
31:32 taken totaled six hundred seventy-five thousand s,
31:36 three hundred thirty-seven thousand five hundred s
31:37 of s and goats was six hundred seventy-five.
31:43 three hundred thirty-seven thousand five hundred s
32:36 and Beth-haran, fortified cities, and folds for s.
Dt 14: 4 These are the animals you may eat: the ox, the s,
14:26 oxen, s, wine, strong drink,
17: 1 or a s that has a defect, anything seriously wrong;
18: 3 whether an ox or a s:
18: 4 as well as the first of the fleece of your s,
22: 1 not watch your neighbor's ox or s straying away
28:31 Your s shall be given to your enemies,
Jos 6:21 both men and women, young and old, oxen, s,
7:24 donkeys, and s, and his tent and all that he had;
Jdg 6: 4 and no s or ox or donkey.
1Sa 14:32 and took s and oxen and calves,
14:34 'Let all bring their oxen or their s,
15: 3 child and infant, ox and s, camel and donkey.' "
15: 9 best of the s and of the cattle and of the fatlings,
15:14 "What then is this bleating of s in my ears,
15:15 the people spared the best of the s and the cattle,
15:21 But from the spoil the people took s and cattle,
16:11 but he is keeping the s."
16:19 "Send me your son David who is with the s."
17:15 from Saul to feed his father's s at Bethlehem.
17:20 left the s with a keeper, took the provisions,
17:28 With whom have you left those few s in
17:34 "Your servant used to keep s for his father;
1Sa 22:19 children and infants, oxen, donkeys, and s,
25: 2 he had three thousand s and a thousand goats.
25: 2 He was shearing his s in Carmel.
25: 4 in the wilderness that Nabal was shearing his s.
25:16 all the while we were with them keeping the s.
25:18 two skins of wine, five s ready dressed,
27: 9 but took away the s, the oxen, the donkeys,
2Sa 7: 8 from the pasture, from following the s to be prince
17:29 honey and curds, s, and cheese from the herd,
24:17 but these s, what have they done?
1Ki 1: 9 Adonijah sacrificed s, oxen,
1:19 fatted cattle, and s in abundance,
1:25 fatted cattle, and s in abundance,
4:23 one hundred s, besides deer, gazelles, roebucks,
8: 5 so many s and oxen that they could not be counted
8:63 and one hundred twenty thousand s.
22:17 like s that have no shepherd;
2Ki 3: 4 Now King Mesha of Moab was a s breeder,
5:26 olive orchards and vineyards, s and oxen,
1Ch 5:21 two hundred fifty thousand s,
12:40 wine, oil, oxen, and s, for there was joy in Israel.
17: 7 I took you from the pasture, from following the s,
21:17 But these s, what have they done?
2Ch 5: 6 sacrificing so many s and oxen that they could not
7: 5 and one hundred twenty thousand s.
14:15 and carried away s and goats in abundance,
15:11 seven hundred oxen and seven thousand s.
18: 2 of s and oxen for him and for the people who were
18:16 like s without a shepherd;
29:33 were six hundred bulls and three thousand s.
30:24 a thousand bulls and seven thousand s
30:24 the assembly a thousand bulls and ten thousand s.
31: 6 of Judah also brought in the tithe of cattle and s,
Ezr 6: 9 or s for burnt offerings to the God of heaven,
Ne 3: 1 with his fellow priests and rebuilt the S Gate.
3:32 of the corner and the S Gate the goldsmiths and
5:18 for one day was one ox and six choice s;
12:39 and the Tower of the Hundred, to the S Gate;
Job 1: 3 He had seven thousand s, three thousand camels,
1:16 from heaven and burned up the s and the servants,
31:20 and who was not warmed with the fleece of my s;
42:12 and he had fourteen thousand s,
Ps 8: 7 all s and oxen, and also the beasts of the field,
44:11 You have made us like s for slaughter,
44:22 and accounted as s for the slaughter.
49:14 Like s they are appointed for Sheol;
74: 1 Why does your anger smoke against the s
78:52 Then he led out his people like s,
95: 7 and the s of his hand.
100: 3 we are his people, and the s of his pasture.
119:176 I have gone astray like a lost s;
144:13 may our s increase by thousands,
Isa 7:21 a young cow and two s,
7:25 where cattle are let loose and where s tread.
13:14 or like s with no one to gather them,
22:13 killing oxen and slaughtering s,
40:11 and gently lead the mother s.
43:23 not brought me your s for burnt offerings,
53: 6 All we like s have gone astray;
53: 7 and like a s that before its shearers is silent,
Jer 12: 3 Pull them out like s for the slaughter,
23: 1 to the shepherds who destroy and scatter the s
50: 6 My people have been lost s;
50:17 Israel is a hunted s driven away by lions.
Eze 34: 2 Should not shepherds feed the s?
34: 3 but you do not feed the s.
34: 6 My s were scattered, they wandered over all
34: 6 my s were scattered over all the face of the earth,
34: 8 because my s have become a prey,
34: 8 my s have become food for all the wild animals,
34: 8 because my shepherds have not searched for my s,
34: 8 and have not fed my s;
34:10 and I will demand my s at their hand,
34:10 and put a stop to their feeding the s;
34:10 I will rescue my s from their mouths,
34:11 I myself will search for my s,
34:12 when they are among their scattered s,
34:12 so I will seek out my s.
34:15 I myself will be the shepherd of my s,
34:17 I shall judge between s and s,
34:19 And must my s eat what you have trodden
34:20 I myself will judge between the fat s and the lean s.
34:22 and I will judge between s and s.
34:31 are my s, the s of my pasture and I am your God,
45:15 and one s from every flock of two hundred,
Hos 12:12 and for a wife he guarded s.
Joel 1:18 even the flocks of s are dazed.
Mic 2:12 I will set them together like s in a fold,
5: 8 like a young lion among the flocks of s, which,
Zec 10: 2 Therefore the people wander like s;
11: 7 So, on behalf of the s merchants,
11: 7 the other I named Unity, and I tended the s.
11:11 it was annulled on that day, and the s merchants,
13: 7 Strike the shepherd, that the s may be scattered;
Mt 9:36 because they were harassed and helpless, like s
10: 6 but go rather to the lost s of the house of Israel.
10:16 I am sending you out like s into the midst
12:11 "Suppose one of you has only one s and it falls
12:12 much more valuable is a human being than a s!
15:24 "I was sent only to the lost s of the house
18:12 If a shepherd has a hundred s,
25:32 from another as a shepherd separates the s from
25:33 and he will put the s at his right hand and the goats
26:31 and the s of the flock will be scattered.'
Mk 6:34 because they were like s without a shepherd;
14:27 and the s will be scattered.'
Lk 15: 4 having a hundred s and losing one of them,

Lk 15: 6 for I have found my **s** that was lost.'
17: 7 in from plowing or tending **s** in the field,
Jn 2:14 In the temple he found people selling cattle, **s**,
2:15 both the **s** and the cattle.
5: 2 Now in Jerusalem by the **S** Gate there is a pool,
10: 2 one who enters by the gate is the shepherd of the **s**.
10: 3 and the **s** hear his voice.
10: 3 He calls his own **s** by name and leads them out.
10: 4 and the **s** follow him because they know his voice.
10: 7 "Very truly, I tell you, I am the gate for the **s**.
10: 8 but the **s** did not listen to them.
10:11 The good shepherd lays down his life for the **s**.
10:12 who is not the shepherd and does not own the **s**,
10:12 the wolf coming and leaves the **s** and runs away—
10:13 because a hired hand does not care for the **s**.
10:15 And I lay down my life for the **s**.
10:16 I have other **s** that do not belong to this fold.
10:26 because you do not belong to my **s**.
10:27 My **s** hear my voice.
21:16 Jesus said to him, "Tend my **s**."
21:17 Jesus said to him, "Feed my **s**.
Ac 8:32 "Like a **s** he was led to the slaughter,
Ro 8:36 we are accounted as **s** to be slaughtered."
Heb 11:37 they went about in skins of **s** and goats, destitute,
13:20 our Lord Jesus, the great shepherd of the **s**,
1Pe 2:25 For you were going astray like **s**,
Rev 18:13 olive oil, choice flour and wheat, cattle and **s**,
Tob 1: 6 and the first shearings of the **s**.
10:10 male and female slaves, oxen and **s**,
Jdt 2:17 and innumerable **s** and oxen and goats for food;
8:26 while he was tending the **s** of Laban,
11:19 You will drive them like **s** that have no shepherd,
Bel 1: 3 for it twelve bushels of choice flour and forty **s**
1:32 they had been given two human bodies and two **s**;
1Es 1: 8 for the passover two thousand six hundred **s**
1: 9 gave the Levites for the passover five thousand **s**
Pm 151: 1 in my father's house; I tended my father's **s**.
151: 4 and took me from my father's **s**,
2Es 5:26 you have provided for yourself one **s**,
16:32 because no **s** will go along them.

SHEEP'S (1) [SHEEP]

Mt 7:15 in **s** clothing but inwardly are ravenous wolves.

SHEEPCOTE (KJV) See PASTURE

SHEEPFOLD (1) [SHEEP]

Jn 10: 1 the **s** by the gate but climbs in by another way is

SHEEPFOLDS‡ (8) [SHEEP]

Ge 49:14 lying down between the **s**;
Nu 32:16 "We will build **s** here for our flocks,
Jdg 5:16 Why did you tarry among the **s**,
1Sa 24: 3 He came to the **s** beside the road,
2Ch 32:28 and stalls for all kinds of cattle, and **s**.
Ps 68:13 though they stay among the **s**—
78:70 and took him from the **s**;
Jdt 2:26 and burned their tents and plundered their **s**.

SHEEPMASTER (KJV) See SHEEP BREEDER

SHEEPSHEARERS (3) [SHEAR, SHEEP]

Ge 38:12 he went up to Timnah to his **s**,
2Sa 13:23 After two full years Absalom had **s** at Baal-hazor,
13:24 and said, "Your servant has **s**;

SHEER (4)

1Ki 19:12 and after the fire a sound of **s** silence.
Isa 28:19 and it will be **s** terror to understand the message.
Sir 40:15 they are unhealthy roots on **s** rock.
2Mc 6:29 in their opinion **s** madness.

SHEERAH (1)

1Ch 7:24 His daughter was **S**, who built both Lower

SHEET (3)

Isa 25: 7 the **s** that is spread over all nations;
Ac 10:11 and something like a large **s** coming down,
11: 5 There was something like a large **s** coming down

SHEHARIAH (1)

1Ch 8:26 Shamsherai, **S**, Athaliah,

SHEKEL (45) [SHEKELS]

Ge 24:22 the man took a gold nose-ring weighing a half **s**,
Ex 30:13 half a **s** according to the **s** of the sanctuary (the **s** is twenty gerahs), half a **s** as an offering to the LORD.
30:15 and the poor shall not give less, than the half **s**,
30:24 measured by the sanctuary **s**—
38:24 measured by the sanctuary **s**.
38:25 measured by the sanctuary **s**;
38:26 half a **s**, measured by the sanctuary **s**),
Lev 5:15 convertible into silver by the sanctuary **s**;
27: 3 be fifty shekels of silver by the sanctuary **s**.
27:25 All assessments shall be by the sanctuary **s**:
27:25 twenty gerahs shall make a **s**.
Nu 3:47 by the **s** of the sanctuary, a **s** of twenty gerahs.
3:50 reckoned by the **s** of the sanctuary;
7:13 according to the **s** of the sanctuary,
7:19 according to the **s** of the sanctuary,
Nu 7:25 according to the **s** of the sanctuary,
7:31 according to the **s** of the sanctuary,
7:37 according to the **s** of the sanctuary,
7:43 according to the **s** of the sanctuary,
7:49 according to the **s** of the sanctuary,
7:55 according to the **s** of the sanctuary,
7:61 according to the **s** of the sanctuary,
7:67 according to the **s** of the sanctuary,
7:73 according to the **s** of the sanctuary,
7:79 according to the **s** of the sanctuary,
7:85 according to the **s** of the sanctuary,
7:86 according to the **s** of the sanctuary, all the gold of
18:16 according to the **s** of the sanctuary (that is,
1Sa 9: 8 "Here, I have with me a quarter **s** of silver;
13:21 of a **s** for the plowshares and for the mattocks,
13:21 and one-third of a **s** for sharpening the axes and
2Ki 7: 1 a measure of choice meal shall be sold for a **s**, and two measures of barley for a **s**,
7:16 So a measure of choice meal was sold for a **s**, and two measures of barley for a **s**,
7:18 "Two measures of barley shall be sold for a **s**, and a measure of choice meal for a **s**,
Ne 10:32 to charge ourselves yearly one-third of a **s** for
Eze 45:12 The **s** shall be twenty gerahs.
Am 8: 5 We will make the ephah small and the **s** great,

SHEKELS (95) [SHEKEL]

Ge 23:15 a piece of land worth four hundred **s** of silver—
23:16 the hearing of the Hittites, four hundred **s** of silver,
24:22 two bracelets for her arms weighing ten gold **s**,
Ex 21:32 the owner shall pay to the slaveowner thirty **s**
30:23 of liquid myrrh five hundred **s**,
38:24 and seven hundred thirty **s**,
38:25 and one thousand seven hundred seventy-five **s**,
38:28 seven hundred seventy-five **s** he made hooks
38:29 and two thousand four hundred **s**;
Lev 27: 3 to sixty years of age the equivalent shall be fifty **s**
27: 4 If the person is a female, the equivalent is thirty **s**.
27: 5 twenty **s** for a male and ten **s** for a female.
27: 6 the equivalent for a male is five **s** of silver, and for a female the equivalent is three **s** of silver.
27: 7 for a male is fifteen **s**, and for a female ten **s**.
27:16 fifty **s** of silver to a homer of barley seed.
Nu 3:47 you shall accept five **s** apiece,
3:50 one thousand three hundred sixty-five **s**,
7:13 one silver plate weighing one hundred thirty **s**,
7:13 one silver basin weighing seventy **s**,
7:14 one golden dish weighing ten **s**, full of incense;
7:19 one silver plate weighing one hundred thirty **s**,
7:19 one silver basin weighing seventy **s**,
7:20 one golden dish weighing ten **s**, full of incense;
7:25 one silver plate weighing one hundred thirty **s**,
7:25 one silver basin weighing seventy **s**,
7:26 one golden dish weighing ten **s**, full of incense;
7:31 one silver plate weighing one hundred thirty **s**,
7:31 one silver basin weighing seventy **s**,
7:32 one golden dish weighing ten **s**, full of incense;
7:37 one silver plate weighing one hundred thirty **s**,
7:37 one silver basin weighing seventy **s**,
7:38 one golden dish weighing ten **s**, full of incense;
7:43 one silver plate weighing one hundred thirty **s**,
7:43 one silver basin weighing seventy **s**,
7:44 one golden dish weighing ten **s**, full of incense;
7:49 one silver plate weighing one hundred thirty **s**,
7:49 one silver basin weighing seventy **s**,
7:50 one golden dish weighing ten **s**, full of incense;
7:55 one silver plate weighing one hundred thirty **s**,
7:55 one silver basin weighing seventy **s**,
7:56 one golden dish weighing ten **s**, full of incense;
7:61 one silver plate weighing one hundred thirty **s**,
7:61 one silver basin weighing seventy **s**,
7:62 one golden dish weighing ten **s**, full of incense;
7:67 one silver plate weighing one hundred thirty **s**,
7:67 one silver basin weighing seventy **s**,
7:68 one golden dish weighing ten **s**, full of incense;
7:73 one silver plate weighing one hundred thirty **s**,
7:73 one silver basin weighing seventy **s**,
7:74 one golden dish weighing ten **s**, full of incense;
7:79 one silver plate weighing one hundred thirty **s**,
7:79 one silver basin weighing seventy **s**,
7:80 one golden dish weighing ten **s**, full of incense;
7:85 each silver plate weighing one hundred thirty **s**
7:85 the vessels two thousand four hundred **s** according
7:86 weighing ten **s** apiece according to the shekel of
7:86 the gold of the dishes being one hundred twenty **s**;
18:16 you shall fix at five **s** of silver,
31:52 was sixteen thousand seven hundred fifty **s**.
Dt 22:19 they shall fine him one hundred **s**
22:29 the man who lay with her shall give fifty **s**
Jos 7:21 and two hundred **s** of silver, and a bar of gold weighing fifty **s**,
Jdg 8:26 he requested was one thousand seven hundred **s**
1Sa 17: 5 weight of the coat was five thousand **s** of bronze.
17: 7 his spear's head weighed six hundred **s** of iron;
2Sa 14:26 two hundred **s** by the king's weight.
21:16 whose spear weighed three hundred **s** of bronze,
24:24 the threshing floor and the oxen for fifty **s**
1Ki 10:16 six hundred **s** of gold went into each large shield.
10:29 from Egypt for six hundred **s** of silver, and a horse
2Ki 5: 5 six thousand **s** of gold, and ten sets of garments.
6:25 so great that a donkey's head was sold for eighty **s**
6:25 and one-fourth of a kab of dove's dung for five **s**
15:20 fifty **s** of silver from each one,
1Ch 21:25 So David paid Ornan six hundred **s** of gold
2Ch 1:17 a chariot for six hundred **s** of silver,
3: 9 The weight of the nails was fifty **s** of gold.
2Ch 9:15 six hundred **s** of beaten gold went
9:16 three hundred **s** of gold went into each shield;
Ne 5:15 and took food and wine from them, besides forty **s**
Isa 7:23 worth a thousand **s** of silver,
Jer 32: 9 and weighed out the money to him, seventeen **s**
Eze 4:10 that you eat shall be twenty **s** a day by weight;
45:12 Twenty **s**, twenty-five **s**, and fifteen **s** shall make a mina for you.
Hos 3: 2 So I bought her for fifteen **s** of silver and a homer
Zec 11:12 So they weighed out as my wages thirty **s** of silver.
11:13 So I took the thirty **s** of silver and threw them into
1Mc 10:40 also grant fifteen thousand **s** of silver yearly out of
10:42 the five thousand **s** of silver

SHEKEM See Index to Footnotes

SHELAH (19) [SHELANITES]

Ge 10:24 the father of **S**; and **S** became the father of Eber.
11:12 he became the father of **S**;
11:13 after the birth of **S** four hundred three years,
11:14 When **S** had lived thirty years,
11:15 and **S** lived after the birth of Eber
38: 5 Yet again she bore a son, and she named him **S**.
38:11 in your father's house until my son **S** grows up"—
38:14 She saw that **S** was grown up,
38:26 since I did not give her to my son **S**."
46:12 The children of Judah: Er, Onan, **S**, Perez,
Nu 26:20 of **S**, the clan of the Shelanites;
1Ch 1:18 the father of **S**; and **S** became the father of Eber.
1:24 Shem, Arpachshad, **S**;
2: 3 The sons of Judah: Er, Onan, and **S**;
4:21 The sons of **S** son of Judah:
Ne 3:15 the wall of the Pool of **S** of the king's garden,
Lk 3:35 son of Reu, son of Peleg, son of Eber, son of **S**,

SHELANITES (1) [SHELAH]

Nu 26:20 of Shelah, the clan of the **S**;

SHELEMIAH (11)

1Ch 26:14 The lot for the east fell to **S**.
Ezr 10:39 **S**, Nathan, Adaiah,
10:41 Azarel, **S**, Shemariah,
Ne 3:30 After him Hananiah son of **S** and Hanun sixth son
13:13 as treasurers over the storehouses the priest **S**,
Jer 36:14 of Nethaniah son of **S** son of Cushi to say
36:26 the king's son and Seraiah son of Azriel and **S** son
37: 3 of **S** and the priest Zephaniah son of Maaseiah to
37:13 a sentinel there named Irijah son of **S** son
38: 1 Gedaliah son of Pashhur, Jucal son of **S**,
1Es 9:34 Eliasis, Binnui, Elialis, Shimei, **S**, Nethaniah.

SHELEPH (2)

Ge 10:26 Joktan became the father of Almodad, **S**,
1Ch 1:20 Joktan became the father of Almodad, **S**,

SHELESH (1)

1Ch 7:35 Zophah, Imna, **S**, and Amal.

SHELOMI (1)

Nu 34:27 of the Asherites a leader, Ahihud son of **S**.

SHELOMITH‡ (6)

Lev 24:11 now his mother's name was **S**, daughter of Dibri,
1Ch 3:19 Meshullam and Hananiah, and **S** was their sister;
23:18 The sons of Izhar: **S** the chief.
2Ch 11:20 who bore him Abijah, Attai, Ziza, and **S**.
Ezr 8:10 Of the descendants of Bani, **S** son of Josiphiah,
1Es 8:36 Of the descendants of Bani, **S** son of Josiphiah,

SHELOMOH See Index to Footnotes

SHELOMOTH (6)

1Ch 23: 9 The sons of Shimei: **S**, Haziel, and Haran, three.
24:22 Of the Izharites, **S**; of the sons of **S**, Jahath.
26:25 his son Joram, his son Zichri, and his son **S**.
26:26 This **S** and his brothers were in charge of all
26:28 all dedicated gifts were in the care of **S**

SHELTER (26) [SHELTERED, SHELTERING]

Ge 19: 8 for they have come under the **s** of my roof."
Ex 9:19 not brought under **s** will die when the hail comes
Job 24: 8 and cling to the rock for want of **s**.
Ps 27: 5 For he will hide me in his **s** in the day of trouble;
31:20 In the **s** of your presence you hide them
31:20 under your **s** from contentious tongues.
55: 8 a **s** for myself from the raging wind and tempest."
61: 4 find refuge under the **s** of your wings.
91: 1 You who live in the **s** of the Most High,
Isa 1: 8 like a **s** in a cucumber field, like a besieged city.
4: 6 and a refuge and a **s** from the storm and rain.
25: 4 a **s** from the rainstorm and a shade from the heat.
28:15 and in falsehood we have taken **s**";
28:17 and waters will overwhelm the **s**.
30: 2 and to seek **s** in the shadow of Egypt;
30: 3 and the **s** in the shadow of Egypt your humiliation.
Rev 7:15 the one who is seated on the throne will **s** them.
Jdt 6:13 So having taken **s** below the hill,
Wis 10:17 and became a **s** to them by day,
Sir 2:13 Therefore they will have no **s**.
6:14 Faithful friends are a sturdy **s**:

Sir 14:26 who places his children under her s, and lodges
22:25 I am not ashamed to s a friend,
34:19 a s from scorching wind and a shade
LtJ 6:68 for they can flee to s and help themselves.
3Mc 3:27 But those who s any of the Jews,

SHELTERED (2) [SHELTER]

Jer 46:19 Pack your bags for exile, s daughter Egypt!
Sir 14:27 who is s by her from the heat,

SHELTERING (1) [SHELTER]

3Mc 3:29 Every place detected s a Jew is to

SHELUMIEL (5)

Nu 1: 6 From Simeon, S son of Zurishaddai.
2:12 of the Simeonites shall be S son of Zurishaddai,
7:36 On the fifth day S son of Zurishaddai,
7:41 This was the offering of S son of Zurishaddai.
10:19 of the tribe of Simeon was S son of Zurishaddai,

SHEM (19)

Ge 5:32 Noah became the father of S, Ham, and Japheth.
6:10 And Noah had three sons, S, Ham, and Japheth.
7:13 the very same day Noah with his sons, S and Ham
9:18 The sons of Noah who went out of the ark were S,
9:23 Then S and Japheth took a garment,
9:26 "Blessed by the LORD my God be S;
9:27 and let him live in the tents of S;
10: 1 These are the descendants of Noah's sons, S,
10:21 To S also, the father of all the children of Eber,
10:22 The descendants of S: Elam,
10:31 These are the descendants of S, by their families,
11:10 These are the descendants of S.
11:10 When S was one hundred years old,
11:11 and S lived after the birth
1Ch 1: 4 Noah, S, Ham, and Japheth.
1:17 The descendants of S: Elam,
1:24 S, Arpachshad, Shelah;
Lk 3:36 son of Arphaxad, son of S, son of Noah,
Sir 49:16 S and Seth and Enosh were honored,

SHEMA (7)

Jos 15:26 Amam, S, Moladah,
1Ch 2:43 sons of Hebron: Korah, Tappuah, Rekem, and S.
2:44 S became father of Raham, father of Jorkeam;
5: 8 son of S, son of Joel, who lived in Aroer,
8:13 and S (they were heads of ancestral houses of
Ne 8: 4 and beside him stood Mattithiah, S, Anaiah,
1Es 9:43 S, Ananias, Azariah, Uriah, Hezekiah,

SHEMAAH (1)

1Ch 12: 3 then Joash, both sons of S of Gibeah;

SHEMAIAH‡ (45)

1Ki 12:22 But the word of God came to S the man of God:
1Ch 3:22 The son of Shecaniah: S. And the sons of S:
4:37 of Allon son of Jedaiah son of Shimri son of S—
5: 4 The sons of Joel: S his son, Gog his son,
9:14 Of the Levites: S son of Hasshub, son of Azrikam,
9:16 and Obadiah son of S, son of Galal, son
15: 8 S the chief, with two hundred of his kindred;
15:11 and the Levites Uriel, Asaiah, Joel, S, Eliel,
24: 6 The scribe S son of Nethanel, a Levite,
26: 4 S the firstborn, Jehozabad the second,
26: 6 his son S sons were born who exercised authority
26: 7 The sons of S: Othni, Rephael,
2Ch 11: 2 word of the LORD came to S the man of God:
12: 5 Then the prophet S came to Rehoboam and to
12: 7 the word of the LORD came to S, saying:
12:15 are they not written in the records of the prophet S
17: 8 With them were the Levites, S, Nethaniah,
29:14 and of the sons of Jeduthun, S and Uzziel.
31:15 Eden, Miniamin, Jeshua, S, Amariah,
35: 9 Conaniah also, and his brothers S and Nethanel,
Ezr 8:13 their names being Eliphelet, Jeuel, and S,
8:16 Then I sent for Eliezer, Ariel, S, Elnathan, Jarib,
10:21 Maaseiah, Elijah, S, Jehiel, and Uzziah.
10:31 Eliezer, Isshijah, Malchijah, S, Shimeon,
Ne 3:29 After him S son of Shecaniah,
6:10 the house of S son of Delaiah son of Mehetabel,
10: 8 Maaziah, Bilgai, S; these are the priests.
11:15 S son of Hasshub son of Azrikam son
12: 6 S, Joiarib, Jedaiah,
12:18 of Bilgah, Shammua; of S, Jehonathan;
12:34 Judah, Benjamin, S, and Jeremiah,
12:35 of Jonathan son of S son of Mattaniah son
12:36 S, Azarel, Milalai, Gilalai, Maai, Nethanel, Judah,
12:42 S, Eleazar, Uzzi, Jehohanan, Malchijah, Elam,
Jer 26:20 Uriah son of S from Kiriath-jearim.
29:24 To S of Nehelam you shall say:
29:31 Thus says the LORD concerning S of Nehelam:
29:31 Because S has prophesied to you,
29:32 to punish S of Nehelam and his descendants;
36:12 Elishama the secretary, Delaiah son of S,
1Es 1: 9 And Jeconiah and S and his brother Nethanel,
8:39 Jeuel, and S, and with them seventy men.
8:44 S, Jarib, Nathan, Elnathan, Zechariah,
9:21 and Zebadiah and Maaseiah and S and Jehiel

SHEMAMAH See Index to Footnotes

SHEMARIAH (4)

1Ch 12: 5 Jerimoth, Bealiah, S, Shephatiah the Haruphite;
2Ch 11:19 She bore him sons: Jeush, S, and Zaham.
Ezr 10:32 Benjamin, Malluch, and S.
10:41 Azarel, Shelemiah, S,

SHEMEBER (1)

Ge 14: 2 King S of Zeboiim, and the king of Bela (that is,

SHEMED (1)

1Ch 8:12 The sons of Elpaal: Eber, Misham, and S,

SHEMELIAH (1)

Tob 5:14 I knew Hananiah and Nathan, the two sons of S,

SHEMER (4) [SAMARIA]

1Ki 16:24 of Samaria from S for two talents of silver;
16:24 after the name of S, the owner of the hill.
1Ch 6:46 son of Amzi, son of Bani, son of S,
7:34 The sons of S: Ahi, Rohgah, Hubbah, and Aram.

SHEMIDA (3) [SHEMIDAITES]

Nu 26:32 and of S, the clan of the Shemidaites;
Jos 17: 2 Abiezer, Helek, Asriel, Shechem, Hepher, and S;
1Ch 7:19 The sons of S were Ahian, Shechem, Likhi,

SHEMIDAITES (1) [SHEMIDA]

Nu 26:32 and of Shemida, the clan of the S;

SHEMINITH (3)

1Ch 15:21 to lead with lyres according to the S.
Ps 6: T *with stringed instruments; according to The S.*
12: T *To the leader: according to The S.*

SHEMIRAMOTH (4)

1Ch 15:18 Jaaziel, S, Jehiel, Unni, Eliab, Benaiah, Maaseiah,
15:20 Aziel, S, Jehiel, Unni, Eliab, Maaseiah,
16: 5 S, Jehiel, Mattithiah, Eliab, Benaiah, Obed-edom,
2Ch 17: 8 Nethaniah, Zebadiah, Asahel, S, Jehonathan,

SHEMUEL (2)

Nu 34:20 Of the tribe of the Simeonites, S son of Ammihud.
1Ch 7: 2 Uzzi, Rephaiah, Jeriel, Jahmai, Ibsam, and S,

SHEN See Index to Footnotes

SHENAZZAR (1)

1Ch 3:18 Pedaiah, S, Jekamiah, Hoshama, and Nedabiah;

SHENIR (KJV) See SENIR

SHEOL (65)

Ge 37:35 "No, I shall go down to S to my son, mourning."
42:38 down my gray hairs with sorrow to S."
44:29 down my gray hairs in sorrow to S.'
44:31 of your servant our father with sorrow to S.
Nu 16:30 and they go down alive into S,
16:33 that belonged to them went down alive into S;
Dt 32:22 and burns to the depths of S;
1Sa 2: 6 he brings down to S and raises up.
2Sa 22: 6 the cords of S entangled me,
1Ki 2: 6 but do not let his gray head go down to S in peace.
2: 9 must bring his gray head down with blood to S."
Job 7: 9 so those who go down to S do not come up;
11: 8 Deeper than S—what can you know?
14:13 Oh that you would hide me in S,
17:13 If I look for S as my house,
17:16 Will it go down to the bars of S?
21:13 and in peace they go down to S.
24:19 so does S those who have sinned.
26: 6 S is naked before God,
Ps 6: 5 in S who can give you praise?
9:17 The wicked shall depart to S,
16:10 For you do not give me up to S,
18: 5 the cords of S entangled me;
30: 3 O LORD, you brought up my soul from S,
31:17 let them go dumbfounded to S.
49:14 Like sheep they are appointed for S;
49:14 their form shall waste away; S shall be their home.
49:15 God will ransom my soul from the power of S,
55:15 let them go down alive to S;
86:13 you have delivered my soul from the depths of S.
88: 3 and my life draws near to S.
89:48 Who can escape the power of S?
116: 3 the pangs of S laid hold on me;
139: 8 if I make my bed in S, you are there.
141: 7 so shall their bones be strewn at the mouth of S.
Pr 1:12 like S let us swallow them alive and whole,
5: 5 her steps follow the path to S.
7:27 Her house is the way to S,
9:18 that her guests are in the depths of S.
15:11 S and Abaddon lie open before the LORD,
15:24 in order to avoid S below.
23:14 you will save their lives from S.
27:20 S and Abaddon are never satisfied,
30:16 S, the barren womb, the earth ever thirsty
Ecc 9:10 or thought or knowledge or wisdom in S,
Isa 5:14 Therefore S has enlarged its appetite
7:11 let it be deep as S or high as heaven.
14: 9 S beneath is stirred up to meet you
14:11 Your pomp is brought down to S,
14:15 But you are brought down to S,
28:15 and with S we have an agreement;
28:18 and your agreement with S will not stand;
38:10 I am consigned to the gates of S for the rest
38:18 For S cannot thank you, death cannot praise you;
57: 9 and sent down even to S.
Eze 31:15 down to S I closed the deep over it and covered it;
31:16 when I cast it down to S with those who go down
31:17 They also went down to S with it,
32:21 with their helpers, out of the midst of S:
32:27 down to S with their weapons of war,
Hos 13:14 Shall I ransom them from the power of S?
13:14 O S, where is your destruction?
Am 9: 2 into S, from there shall my hand take them;
Jnh 2: 2 out of the belly of S I cried,
Hab 2: 5 They open their throats wide as S;

SHEPHAM (2)

Nu 34:10 your eastern boundary from Hazar-enan to S;
34:11 down from S to Riblah on the east side of Ain;

SHEPHATIAH (16)

2Sa 3: 4 the fifth, S son of Abital;
1Ch 3: 3 the fifth S, by Abital; the sixth Ithream,
9: 8 son of Michri, and Meshullam son of S,
12: 5 Jerimoth, Bealiah, Shemariah, S the Haruphite;
27:16 for the Simeonites, S son of Maacah;
2Ch 21: 2 Jehiel, Zechariah, Azariah, Michael, and S;
Ezr 2: 4 Of S, three hundred seventy-two.
2:57 S, Hattil, Pochereth-hazzebaim, and Ami.
8: 8 the descendants of S, Zebadiah son of Michael,
Ne 7: 9 Of S, three hundred seventy-two.
7:59 of S, of Hattil, of Pochereth-hazzebaim, of Amon.
11: 4 of Zechariah son of Amariah son of S son
Jer 38: 1 Now S son of Mattan, Gedaliah son of Pashhur,
1Es 5: 9 The descendants of S, four hundred seventy-two.
5:33 the descendants of Isdael, the descendants of S,
8:34 Of the descendants of S, Zeraiah son of Michael,

SHEPHELAH (13)

Dt 1: 7 the Arabah, the hill country, the S, the Negeb,
1Ki 10:27 as numerous as the sycamores of the S.
1Ch 27:28 and sycamore trees in the S was Baal-hanan
2Ch 1:15 as plentiful as the sycamore of the S.
9:27 and cedar as plentiful as the sycamore of the S.
26:10 both in the S and in the plain,
28:18 on the cities in the S and the Negeb of Judah,
Jer 17:26 from the land of Benjamin, from the S,
32:44 of the hill country, of the S, and of the Negeb;
33:13 In the towns of the hill country, of the S,
Ob 1:19 and those of the S the land of the Philistines;
Zec 7: 7 and when the Negeb and the S were inhabited?
1Mc 12:38 Simon also built Adida in the S;

SHEPHER (2)

Nu 33:23 from Kehelathah and camped at Mount S.
33:24 They set out from Mount S and camped

SHEPHERD‡ (64) [SHEPHERD'S, SHEPHERDING, SHEPHERDS, SHEPHERDS']

Ge 48:15 the God who has been my s all my life to this day,
49:24 by the name of the S, the Rock of Israel,
Nu 27:17 of the LORD may not be like sheep without a s."
2Sa 5: 2 It is you who shall be s of my people Israel,
7: 7 whom I commanded to s my people Israel, saying,
1Ki 22:17 like sheep that have no s;
1Ch 11: 2 It is you who shall be s of my people Israel,
17: 6 whom I commanded to s my people, saying,
2Ch 18:16 on the mountains, like sheep without a s;
Ps 23: 1 The LORD is my s, I shall not want.
28: 9 be their s, and carry them forever.
49:14 Death shall be their s,
78:71 the nursing ewes he brought him to be the s
80: 1 O S of Israel, you who lead Joseph like a flock!
Ecc 12:11 the collected sayings that are given by one s.
Isa 40:11 He will feed his flock like a s;
44:28 who says of Cyrus, "He is my s,
Jer 17:16 I have not run away from being a s in your service,
22:22 The wind shall s all your shepherds,
23: 2 concerning the shepherds who s my people:
23: 4 up shepherds over them who will s them,
31:10 and will keep him as a s a flock."
43:12 as a s picks his cloak clean of vermin;
49:19 Who is the s who can stand before me?
50:44 Who is the s who can stand before me?
Eze 34: 5 So they were scattered, because there was no s;
34: 8 for all the wild animals, since there was no s;
34:15 I myself will be the s of my sheep,
34:23 I will set up over them one s, my servant David,
34:23 he shall feed them and be their s.
37:24 and they shall all have one s.
Am 3:12 the s rescues from the mouth of the lion two legs,
Mic 7:14 S your people with your staff,
Zec 10: 2 they suffer for lack of a s.
11: 4 Be a s of the flock doomed to slaughter.
11: 7 I became the s of the flock doomed to slaughter.
11: 9 So I said, "I will not be your s.
11:15 Take once more the implements of a worthless s.
11:16 in the land a s who does not care for the perishing,
11:17 Oh, my worthless s, who deserts the flock!
13: 7 "Awake, O sword, against my s,
13: 7 Strike the s, that the sheep may be scattered;

Mt 2: 6 a ruler who is to s my people Israel.' "
9:36 and helpless, like sheep without a s.
18:12 If a s has a hundred sheep,
25:32 from another as a s separates the sheep from
26:31 'I will strike the s, and the sheep of the flock will
Mk 6:34 because they were like sheep without a s;
14:27 'I will strike the s, and the sheep will be scattered.'
Jn 10: 2 one who enters by the gate is the s of the sheep.
10:11 "I am the good s. The good s lays down his life for the sheep.
10:12 who is not the s and does not own the sheep,
10:14 I am the good s. I know my own and my own know
10:16 So there will be one flock, one s.
Ac 20:28 to s the church of God that he obtained with
Heb 13:20 the great s of the sheep,
1Pe 2:25 but now you have returned to the s and guardian
5: 4 And when the chief s appears,
Rev 7:17 the Lamb at the center of the throne will be their s,
Jdt 11:19 You will drive them like sheep that have no s,
Sir 18:13 and turns them back, as a s his flock.
2Es 2:34 that hear and understand, "Wait for your s;
5:18 like a s who leaves the flock in the power

SHEPHERD'S (3) [SHEPHERD]

Lev 27:32 every tenth one that passes under the s staff,
1Sa 17:40 and put them in his s bag, in the pouch;
Isa 38:12 up and removed from me like a s tent;

SHEPHERDING (1) [SHEPHERD]

Ge 37: 2 was s the flock with his brothers;

SHEPHERDS‡ (53) [SHEPHERD]

Ge 29: 3 s would roll the stone from the mouth of the well,
46:32 men are s, for they have been keepers of livestock;
46:34 because all s are abhorrent to the Egyptians."
47: 3 And they said to Pharaoh, "Your servants are s,
Ex 2:17 But some s came and drove them away.
2:19 They said, "An Egyptian helped us against the s;
Nu 14:33 And your children shall be s in the wilderness
1Sa 21: 7 the Edomite, the chief of Saul's s.
25: 7 now your s have been with us,
2Ki 10:12 On the way, when he was at Beth-eked of the S,
Isa 13:20 s will not make their flocks lie down there.
31: 4 when a band of s is called out against it—
56:11 The s also have no understanding;
63:11 out of the sea with the s of his flock?
Jer 3:15 I will give you s after my own heart,
6: 3 S with their flocks shall come against her.
10:21 the s are stupid, and do not inquire of the LORD;
12:10 Many s have destroyed my vineyard,
22:22 The wind shall shepherd all your s,
23: 1 Woe to the s who destroy and scatter the sheep
23: 2 concerning the s who shepherd my people:
23: 4 raise up s over them who will shepherd them,
25:34 you s, and cry out; roll in ashes,
25:35 Flight shall fail the s, and there shall be no escape
25:36 cry of the s, and the wail of the lords of the flock!
33:12 be pasture for s resting their flocks.
50: 6 their s have led them astray,
51:23 with you I smash s and their flocks;
Eze 34: 2 prophesy against the s of Israel: prophesy, and say to them—to the s:
34: 2 you s of Israel who have been feeding yourselves!
34: 2 Should not s feed the sheep?
34: 7 Therefore, you s, hear the word of the LORD:
34: 8 and because my s have not searched for my sheep, but the s have fed themselves,
34: 9 therefore, you s, hear the word of the LORD:
34:10 the Lord GOD, I am against the s;
34:10 no longer shall the s feed themselves.
34:12 As s seek out their flocks when they are
Am 1: 1 words of Amos, who was among the s of Tekoa,
1: 2 the pastures of the s wither,
Mic 5: 5 against them seven s and eight installed as rulers.
Na 3:18 Your s are asleep, O king of Assyria;
Zep 2: 6 meadows for s and folds for flocks.
Zec 10: 3 My anger is hot against the s,
11: 3 the wail of the s, for their glory is despoiled!
11: 5 and their own s have no pity on them.
11: 8 In one month I disposed of the three s,
Lk 2: 8 In that region there were s living in the fields,
2:15 the s said to one another, "Let us go now
2:18 who heard it were amazed at what the s told them.
2:20 The s returned, glorifying and praising God
Wis 17:17 or s or workers who toiled in the wilderness,

SHEPHERDS' (1) [SHEPHERD]

SS 1: 8 and pasture your kids beside the s tents.

SHEPHI (1) [=SHEPHO]

1Ch 1:40 Alian, Manahath, Ebal, S, and Onam.

SHEPHO (1) [=SHEPHI]

Ge 36:23 Alvan, Manahath, Ebal, S, and Onam.

SHEPHUPHAM (1) [SHUPHAMITES]

Nu 26:39 of S, the clan of the Shuphamites;

SHEPHUPHAN (1)

1Ch 8: 5 Gera, S, and Huram.

SHERAH (KJV) See SHEERAH

SHERD (1) [POTSHERD, POTSHERDS, SHERDS]

Isa 30:14 among its fragments not a s is found for taking fire

SHERDS (1) [SHERD]

Eze 23:34 and gnaw its s, and tear out your breasts;

SHEREBIAH (11)

Ezr 8:18 namely S, with his sons and kin, eighteen;
8:24 S, Hashabiah, and ten of their kin with them.
Ne 8: 7 Also Jeshua, Bani, S, Jamin, Akkub, Shabbethai,
9: 4 Jeshua, Bani, Kadmiel, Shebaniah, Bunni, S,
9: 5 Levites, Jeshua, Kadmiel, Bani, Hashabneiah, S,
10:12 Zaccur, S, Shebaniah,
12: 8 And the Levites: Jeshua, Binnui, Kadmiel, S,
12:24 And the leaders of the Levites: Hashabiah, S,
1Es 8:47 namely S with his descendants and kinsmen,
8:54 S and Hashabiah, and ten of their kinsmen
9:48 Jeshua and Anniuth and S, Jadinus, Akkub,

SHERESH (1)

1Ch 7:16 the name of his brother was S;

SHEREZER (KJV) See SHAREZER

SHERIFFS (KJV) See MAGISTRATES

SHESHACH (2)

Jer 25:26 And after them the king of S shall drink.
51:41 S is taken, the pride of the whole earth seized!

SHESHAI (3)

Nu 13:22 Ahiman, S, and Talmai, the Anakites, were there.
Jos 15:14 S, Ahiman, and Talmai, the descendants of Anak.
Jdg 1:10 and they defeated S and Ahiman and Talmai.

SHESHAN (5)

1Ch 2:31 The son of Ishi: S. The son of S: Ahlai.
2:34 Now S had no sons, only daughters;
2:34 S had an Egyptian slave, whose name was Jarha.
2:35 S gave his daughter in marriage to his slave Jarha;

SHESHBAZZAR (8)

Ezr 1: 8 who counted them out to S the prince of Judah.
1:11 All these S brought up,
5:14 and they were delivered to a man named S,
5:16 Then this S came and laid the foundations of
1Es 2:12 and by him they were given to S,
2:15 by S with the returning exiles from Babylon
6:18 and they were delivered to Zerubbabel and S
6:20 Then this S, after coming here,

SHETHAR (1)

Est 1:14 S, Admatha, Tarshish, Meres, Marsena,

SHETHAR-BOZENAI (4)

Ezr 5: 3 and S and their associates came to them and spoke
5: 6 and S and his associates the envoys who were in
6: 6 governor of the province Beyond the River, S,
6:13 the governor of the province Beyond the River, S,

SHETHITES (1)

Nu 24:17 and the territory of all the S.

SHEVA (2)

2Sa 20:25 S was secretary; Zadok and Abiathar were priests;
1Ch 2:49 S father of Machbenah and father of Gibea;

SHEWBREAD (KJV) See SHOWBREAD

SHIBAH (1)

Ge 26:33 He called it S; therefore the name of the city

SHIBBOLETH (1) [SIBBOLETH]

Jdg 12: 6 "Then say S," and he said, "Sibboleth,"

SHIBMAH (KJV) See SIBMAH

SHICRON (KJV) See SHIKKERON

SHIELD (66) [SHIELD-BEARER, SHIELDED, SHIELDING, SHIELDS]

Ge 15: 1 I am your s; your reward shall be very great."
Dt 13: 8 or compassion and do not s them.
33:29 the s of your help, and the sword of your triumph!
Jdg 5: 8 Was s or spear to be seen among forty thousand in
2Sa 1:21 For there the s of the mighty was defiled,
1:21 the s of Saul, anointed with oil no more.
22: 3 my s and the horn of my salvation,
22:31 he is a s for all who take refuge in him.
22:36 You have given me the s of your salvation,
1Ki 10:16 six hundred shekels of gold went into each large s.
10:17 three minas of gold went into each s;
2Ki 19:32 shoot an arrow there, come before it with a s,
1Ch 5:18 who carried s and sword, and drew the bow,
12: 8 with s and spear, whose faces were like the faces
12:24 The people of Judah bearing s and spear,
1Ch 12:34 were thirty-seven thousand armed with s and spear.
2Ch 9:15 of beaten gold went into each large s.
9:16 three hundred shekels of gold went into each s;
17:17 with two hundred thousand armed with bow and s,
25: 5 able to handle spear and s.
Job 15:26 against him with a thick-bossed s;
Ps 3: 3 O LORD, are a s around me, my glory,
5:12 you cover them with favor as with a s.
7:10 God is my s, who saves the upright in heart.
18: 2 my God, my rock in whom I take refuge, my s,
18:30 he is a s for all who take refuge in him.
18:35 You have given me the s of your salvation,
28: 7 The LORD is my strength and my s;
33:20 he is our help and s.
35: 2 Take hold of s and buckler, and rise up to help me!
59:11 and bring them down, O Lord, our s.
76: 3 There he broke the flashing arrows, the s,
84: 9 Behold our s, O God; look on the
84:11 For the LORD God is a sun and s;
89:18 For our s belongs to the LORD,
91: 4 his faithfulness is a s and buckler.
115: 9 He is their help and their s.
115:10 He is their help and their s.
115:11 He is their help and their s.
119:114 You are my hiding place and my s;
144: 2 my stronghold and my deliverer, my s,
Pr 2: 7 he is a s to those who walk blamelessly,
30: 5 he is a s to those who take refuge in him.
Isa 21: 5 Rise up, commanders, oil the s!
22: 6 with chariots and cavalry, and Kir uncovered the s.
37:33 shoot an arrow there, come before it with a s,
Jer 46: 3 Prepare buckler and s, and advance for battle!
46: 9 Ethiopia and Put who carry the s, the Ludim,
Eze 23:24 against you on every side with buckler, s,
27:10 they hung s and helmet in you;
38: 4 a great company, all of them with s and buckler,
Zec 12: 8 the LORD will s the inhabitants of Jerusalem so
Eph 6:16 With all of these, take the s of faith,
Jdt 9: 7 and trusting in s and spear, in bow and sling.
Wis 5:16 and with his arm he will s them.
5:19 he will take holiness as an invincible s,
18:21 he brought forward the s of his ministry,
Sir 29:13 better than a stout s and a sturdy spear,
34:19 a mighty s and strong support,
37: 5 yet in battle they will carry his s.
51:12 *Give thanks to the s of Abraham,*
1Mc 14:24 with a large gold s weighing one thousand minas,
15:18 a gold s weighing one thousand minas.
15:20 And it has seemed good to us to accept the s
4Mc 4: 9 to s the holy place that was being treated
7: 4 the besiegers with the s of his devout reason.

SHIELD-BEARER (2) [BEAR, SHIELD]

1Sa 17: 7 and his s went before him.
17:41 near to David, with his s in front of him.

SHIELDED (1) [SHIELD]

Dt 32:10 he s him, cared for him, guarded him as the apple

SHIELDING (2) [SHIELD]

2Mc 10:30 and s him with their own armor and weapons,
4Mc 7: 8 s it with their own blood and noble sweat

SHIELDS (32) [SHIELD]

2Sa 8: 7 the gold s that were carried by the servants
1Ki 10:16 King Solomon made two hundred large s
10:17 He made three hundred s of beaten gold;
14:26 the s of gold that Solomon had made;
14:27 so King Rehoboam made s of bronze instead,
2Ki 11:10 and s that had been King David's, which were in
1Ch 18: 7 the gold s that were carried by the servants
2Ch 9:15 King Solomon made two hundred large s
9:16 He made three hundred s of beaten gold;
11:12 He also put large s and spears in all the cities,
12: 9 the s of gold that Solomon had made;
12:10 but King Rehoboam made in place of them s
14: 8 armed with large s and spears,
14: 8 from Benjamin who carried s and drew bows;
23: 9 to the captains the spears and the large and small s
26:14 Uzziah provided for all the army the s, spears,
32: 5 and made weapons and s in abundance.
32:27 for spices, for s, and for all kinds of costly objects;
Ne 4:16 and half held the spears, s, bows, and body-armor;
Job 41:15 Its back is made of s in rows,
Ps 46: 9 he burns the s with fire.
47: 9 s of the earth belong to God; he is highly exalted.
SS 4: 4 a thousand bucklers, all of them s of warriors.
Eze 26: 8 and raise a roof of s against you.
32:27 and whose s are upon their bones;
39: 9 bucklers and s, bows and arrows,
Na 2: 3 The s of his warriors are red;
1Mc 4:57 of the temple with golden crowns and small s;
6: 2 Its temple was very rich, containing golden s,
6:39 When the sun shone on the s of gold and brass,
2Mc 5: 3 brandishing of s, massing of spears,
15:11 so much with confidence in s and spears as with

SHIFTED (1) [SHIFTING, SHIFTS]

2Mc 4:10 he at once s his compatriots over to the Greek way

SHIFTING (1) [SHIFTED]

Col 1:23 without s from the hope promised by the gospel

SHIFTS (1) [SHIFTED]
1Ki 5:14 sent them to Lebanon, ten thousand a month in s;

SHIGGAION (1)
Ps 7: T *A S of David, which he sang to the LORD*

SHIGIONOTH (1)
Hab 3: 1 A prayer of the prophet Habakkuk according to S.

SHIHON (KJV) See SHION

SHIHOR (3)
Jos 13: 3 (from the S, which is east of Egypt, northward to
1Ch 13: 5 So David assembled all Israel from the S of Egypt
Isa 23: 3 your revenue was the grain of S,

SHIHOR-LIBNATH (1)
Jos 19:26 on the west it touches Carmel and S,

SHIKKERON (1)
Jos 15:11 then the boundary bends around to S,

SHILHI (2)
1Ki 22:42 His mother's name was Azubah daughter of S.
2Ch 20:31 His mother's name was Azubah daughter of S.

SHILHIM (1)
Jos 15:32 S, Ain, and Rimmon: in all,

SHILLEM (2) [SHILLEMITES]
Ge 46:24 Jahzeel, Guni, Jezer, and S
Nu 26:49 of S, the clan of the Shillemites.

SHILLEMITES (1) [SHILLEM]
Nu 26:49 of Shillem, the clan of the S.

SHILOAH (1)
Isa 8: 6 the waters of S that flow gently, and melt in fear

SHILOH‡ (32)
Jos 18: 1 of the Israelites assembled at S,
18: 8 for you here before the LORD in S."
18: 9 then they came back to Joshua in the camp at S,
18:10 Joshua cast lots for them in S before the LORD;
19:51 of the tribes of the Israelites distributed by lot at S
21: 2 they said to them at S in the land of Canaan,
22: 9 parting from the Israelites at S,
22:12 the whole assembly of the Israelites gathered at S,
Jdg 18:31 as long as the house of God was at S.
21:12 with a man and brought them to the camp at S,
21:19 yearly festival of the LORD is taking place at S,
21:21 when the young women of S come out to dance in
21:21 a wife for himself from the young women of S,
1Sa 1: 3 and to sacrifice to the LORD of hosts at S,
1: 9 After they had eaten and drunk at S,
1:24 She brought him to the house of the LORD at S;
2:14 at S to all the Israelites who came there.
3:21 The LORD continued to appear at S,
3:21 for the LORD revealed himself to Samuel at S by
4: 3 of the covenant of the LORD here from S,
4: 4 So the people sent to S,
4:12 and came to S the same day,
14: 3 the priest of the LORD in S, carrying an ephod.
1Ki 2:27 concerning the house of Eli in S.
14: 2 that you are the wife of Jeroboam, and go to S;
14: 4 Jeroboam's wife did so; she set out and went to S,
Ps 78:60 He abandoned his dwelling at S,
Jer 7:12 Go now to my place that was in S,
7:14 just what I did to S.
26: 6 then I will make this house like S,
26: 9 saying, 'This house shall be like S,
41: 5 eighty men arrived from Shechem and S

SHILONI (KJV) See SHILONITE

SHILONITE (6) [SHILONITES]
1Ki 11:29 the prophet Ahijah the S found him on the road.
12:15 which the LORD had spoken by Ahijah the S
15:29 that he spoke by his servant Ahijah the S—
2Ch 9:29 and in the prophecy of Ahijah the S,
10:15 by Ahijah the S to Jeroboam son of Nebat.
Ne 11: 5 of Joiarib son of Zechariah son of the S.

SHILONITES (1) [SHILONITE]
1Ch 9: 5 And of the S: Asaiah the firstborn, and his sons.

SHILSHAH (1)
1Ch 7:37 Bezer, Hod, Shamma, S, Ithran, and Beera.

SHIMEA (5) [=SHIMEAH]
1Ch 2:13 Abinadab the second, S the third,
3: 5 These were born to him in Jerusalem: S, Shobab,
6:30 S his son, Haggiah his son, and Asaiah his son.
6:39 namely, Asaph son of Berechiah, son of S,
20: 7 When he taunted Israel, Jonathan son of S,

SHIMEAH (3) [=SHIMEA]
2Sa 13: 3 the son of David's brother S;
2Sa 13:32 But Jonadab, the son of David's brother S, said,
1Ch 8:32 who became the father of S.

SHIMEAM (1)
1Ch 9:38 and Mikloth became the father of S;

SHIMEATH (2) [SHIMEATHITES]
2Ki 12:21 It was Jozacar son of S and Jehozabad son
2Ch 24:26 against him were Zabad son of S the Ammonite,

SHIMEATHITES (1) [SHIMEATH]
1Ch 2:55 the Tirathites, the S, and the Sucathites.

SHIMEI‡ (49) [SHIMEI'S, SHIMEITES]
Ex 6:17 sons of Gershon: Libni and S, by their families.
Nu 3:18 by their clans: Libni and S.
2Sa 16: 5 of Saul came out whose name was S son of Gera;
16: 7 S shouted while he cursed, "Out!
16:13 while S went along on the hillside opposite him
19:16 S son of Gera, the Benjaminite, from Bahurim,
19:18 S son of Gera fell down before the king,
19:21 "Shall not S be put to death for this,
19:23 The king said to S, "You shall not die."
21:21 Jonathan son of David's brother S, killed him.
1Ki 1: 8 and the prophet Nathan, and S, and Rei,
2: 8 There is also with you S son of Gera,
2:36 Then the king sent and summoned S,
2:38 And S said to the king, "The sentence is fair;
2:38 So S lived in Jerusalem many days.
2:39 When it was told S, "Your slaves are in Gath,"
2:40 S arose and saddled a donkey, and went to Achish
2:40 S went and brought his slaves from Gath.
2:41 When Solomon was told that S had gone
2:42 the king sent and summoned S,
2:44 also said to S, "You know in your own heart all
4:18 S son of Ela, in Benjamin;
1Ch 3:19 of Pedaiah: Zerubbabel and S;
4:26 Hammuel his son, Zaccur his son, S his son.
4:27 S had sixteen sons and six daughters;
5: 4 Shemaiah his son, Gog his son, S his son,
6:17 of Gershom: Libni and S.
6:29 Mahli, Libni his son, S his son, Uzzah his son,
6:42 son of Ethan, son of Zimmah, son of S,
8:21 Adaiah, Beraiah, and Shimrath were the sons of S.
23: 7 The sons of Gershon were Ladan and S.
23: 9 sons of S: Shelomoth, Haziel, and Haran, three.
23:10 the sons of S: Jahath, Zina, Jeush, and Beriah.
23:10 These four were the sons of S.
25: 3 Gedaliah, Zeri, Jeshaiah, S, Hashabiah,
25:17 the tenth to S, his sons and his brothers, twelve;
27:27 Over the vineyards was S the Ramathite.
2Ch 29:14 and of the sons of Heman, Jehuel and S;
31:12 with his brother S as second;
31:13 and his brother S, by the appointment
Ezr 10:23 Jozabad, S, Kelaiah (that is, Kelita), Pethahiah,
10:33 Zabad, Eliphelet, Jeremai, Manasseh, and S.
10:38 Of the descendants of Binnui: S,
Est 2: 5 of Jair son of S son of Kish,
AdE 2: 5 of S son of Kish, of the tribe of Benjamin;
11: 2 Mordecai son of Jair son of S son of Kish,
1Es 9:23 And of the Levites: Jozabad and S and Kelaiah,
9:33 and Zabad and Eliphelet and Manasseh and S.
9:34 Eliasis, Binnui, Elialis, S, Shelemiah, Nethaniah.

SHIMEI'S (1) [SHIMEI]
1Ki 2:39 that two of S slaves ran away to King Achish son

SHIMEITES (2) [SHIMEI]
Nu 3:21 the clan of the Libnites and the clan of the S;
Zec 12:13 the family of the S by itself,

SHIMEON (1)
Ezr 10:31 Eliezer, Isshijah, Malchijah, Shemaiah, S,

SHIMHI, SHIMI (KJV) See SHIMEI

SHIMITES (KJV) See SHIMEITES

SHIMMA (KJV) See SHIMEA

SHIMON (1)
1Ch 4:20 sons of S: Amnon, Rinnah, Ben-hanan, and Tilon.

SHIMRATH (1)
1Ch 8:21 Adaiah, Beraiah, and S were the sons of Shimei.

SHIMRI (4)
1Ch 4:37 of Shiphi son of Allon son of Jedaiah son of S son
11:45 Jediael son of S, and his brother Joha the Tizite,
26:10 S the chief (for though he was not the firstborn,
2Ch 29:13 and of the sons of Elizaphan, S and Jeuel;

SHIMRITH (1) [=SHOMER]
2Ch 24:26 and Jehozabad son of S the Moabite.

SHIMRON (5) [SHIMRONITES]
Ge 46:13 children of Issachar: Tola, Puvah, Jashub, and S.
Nu 26:24 of S, the clan of the Shimronites.
Jos 11: 1 he sent to King Jobab of Madon, to the king of S,
19:15 Nahalal, S, Idalah, and Bethlehem—
1Ch 7: 1 sons of Issachar: Tola, Puah, Jashub, and S, four.

SHIMRON-MERON (1)
Jos 12:20 the king of S one the king of Achshaph one

SHIMRONITES (1) [SHIMRON]
Nu 26:24 of Shimron, the clan of the S.

SHIMSHAI (8)
Ezr 4: 8 and S the scribe wrote a letter against Jerusalem
4: 9 S the scribe, and the rest of their associates,
4:17 "To Rehum the royal deputy and S the scribe and
4:23 and the scribe S and their associates,
1Es 2:16 the scribe S, and the rest of their associates,
2:17 your servants the recorder Rehum and the scribe S
2:25 the scribe S, and the others associated with them
2:30 and the scribe S and their associates went quickly

SHINAB (1)
Ge 14: 2 King S of Admah, King Shemeber of Zeboiim,

SHINAR (8)
Ge 10:10 Erech, and Accad, all of them in the land of S.
11: 2 upon a plain in the land of S and settled there.
14: 1 In the days of King Amraphel of S,
14: 9 King Amraphel of S, and King Arioch of Ellasar,
Jos 7:21 I saw among the spoil a beautiful mantle from S,
Isa 11:11 from Ethiopia, from Elam, from S, from Hamath,
Da 1: 2 These he brought to the land of S,
Zec 5:11 He said to me, "To the land of S,

SHINE‡ (39) [SHINED, SHINES, SHINING, SHONE, SUNSHINE]
Nu 6:25 the LORD make his face to s upon you,
Job 3: 4 May God above not seek it, or light s on it.
18: 5 and the flame of their fire does not s.
22:28 and light will s on your ways.
37:15 and causes the lightning of his cloud to s?
Ps 4: 6 Let the light of your face s on us, O LORD!"
31:16 Let your face s upon your servant;
37: 6 He will make your vindication s like the light,
67: 1 to us and bless us and make his face to s upon us,
80: 1 upon the cherubim, s forth
80: 3 let your face s, that we may be saved.
80: 7 let your face s, that we may be saved.
80:19 let your face s, that we may be saved.
94: 1 you God of vengeance, s forth!
104:15 oil to make the face s, and bread to strengthen the
119:135 Make your face s upon your servant,
Ecc 8: 1 Wisdom makes one's face s,
Isa 60: 1 Arise, s; for your light has come,
Da 9:17 let your face s upon your desolated sanctuary.
12: 3 Those who are wise shall s like the brightness of
Zec 9:16 like the jewels of a crown they shall s on his land.
Mt 5:16 In the same way, let your light s before others,
13:43 the righteous will s like the sun in the kingdom
2Co 4: 6 "Let light s out of darkness,"
Eph 5:14 Rise from the dead, and Christ will s on you."
Php 2:15 in which you s like stars in the world.
Rev 18:23 and the light of a lamp will s in you no more;
21:23 And the city has no need of sun or moon to s on it,
Tob 13:11 A bright light will s to all the ends of the earth;
Wis 3: 7 In the time of their visitation they will s forth,
5: 6 and the light of righteousness did not s on us,
Sir 24:32 I will again make instruction s forth like the dawn,
LtJ 6:24 it will not s unless someone wipes off the tarnish;
6:67 or s like the sun or give light like the moon.
2Es 2:35 because perpetual light will s on you forevermore.
5: 4 and the sun shall suddenly begin to s at night,
7:97 it is shown them how their face is to s like the sun,
7:*125* [55] those who practiced self-control shall s more
10:25 her face suddenly began to s exceedingly;

SHINED (1) [SHINE]
Isa 9: 2 in a land of deep darkness—on them light has s.

SHINES (4) [SHINE]
Ps 50: 2 Out of Zion, the perfection of beauty, God s forth.
Pr 4:18 which s brighter and brighter until full day.
Isa 62: 1 until her vindication s out like the dawn,
Jn 1: 5 The light s in the darkness,

SHINING (21) [SHINE]
Ex 34:30 the skin of his face was s,
34:35 that the skin of his face was s;
Job 41:32 It leaves a s wake behind it;
Ps 148: 3 praise him, all you s stars!
Isa 4: 5 and smoke and the s of a flaming fire by night.
Eze 1:22 s like crystal, spread out above their heads.
32: 8 the s lights of the heavens I will darken above you,
Joel 2:10 and the stars withdraw their s.
3:15 and the stars withdraw their s.
Jn 5:35 He was a burning and s lamp,
Ac 26:13 than the sun, s around me and my companions.
2Pe 1:19 be attentive to this as to a lamp s in a dark place,
1Jn 2: 8 and the true light is already s.
Rev 1:16 and his face was like the sun s with full force.
8:12 a third of the day was kept from s,
Wis 17: 6 Nothing was s through to them except a dreadful,
Sir 26:17 Like the s lamp on the holy lampstand,
43: 8 s in the vault of the heavens!
50: 7 like the sun s on the temple of the Most High,

Bar 4: 2 walk toward the s of her light.
2Es 7:*42* or dawn or s or brightness or light,

SHION (1)
Jos 19:19 Hapharaim, S, Anaharath,

SHIP (34) [SHIP'S, SHIPMASTERS, SHIPS, SHIPWRECK, SHIPWRECKED, WARSHIPS]
Pr 30:19 the way of a s on the high seas,
Isa 33:21 with oars can go, nor stately s can pass.
Jnh 1: 3 down to Joppa and found a s going to Tarshish;
1: 4 upon the sea that the s threatened to break up.
1: 5 They threw the cargo that was in the s into the sea,
1: 5 had gone down into the hold of the s and had lain
1:13 the men rowed hard to bring the s back to land,
Ac 20:13 We went ahead to the s and set sail for Assos,
20:38 Then they brought him to the s.
21: 2 When we found a s bound for Phoenicia,
21: 3 because the s was to unload its cargo there.
21: 6 we went on board the s, and they returned home.
27: 2 on a s of Adramyttium that was about to set sail to
27: 6 There the centurion found an Alexandrian s bound
27:10 not only of the cargo and the s,
27:11 and to the owner of the s than to what Paul said.
27:15 the s was caught and could not be turned head-on
27:17 up they took measures to undergird the s;
27:22 be no loss of life among you, but only of the s.
27:30 to escape from the s and had lowered the boat into
27:31 "Unless these men stay in the s,
27:37 in all two hundred seventy-six persons in the s.)
27:38 they lightened the s by throwing the wheat into
27:39 on which they planned to run the s ashore,
27:41 But striking a reef, they ran the s aground;
27:44 some on planks and others on pieces of the s.
28:11 on a s that had wintered at the island,
28:11 an Alexandrian s with the Twin Brothers
Wis 5:10 like a s that sails through the billowy water,
14: 1 of wood more fragile than the s that carries him.
1Mc 15:37 Meanwhile Trypho embarked on a s and escaped
2Es 9:34 when the ground has received seed, or the sea a s,
12:42 and like a haven for a s saved from a storm.
4Mc 7: 1 of our father Eleazar steered the s of religion over

SHIP'S (2) [SHIP]
Ac 27:16 scarcely able to get the s boat under control.
27:19 their own hands they threw the s tackle overboard.

SHIPHI (1)
1Ch 4:37 of S son of Allon son of Jedaiah son of Shimri son

SHIPHMITE (1)
1Ch 27:27 the vineyards for the wine cellars was Zabdi the S.

SHIPHRAH (1)
Ex 1:15 one of whom was named S and the other Puah,

SHIPHTAN (1)
Nu 34:24 of the Ephraimites a leader, Kemuel son of S.

SHIPMASTER (KJV) See CAPTAIN

SHIPMASTERS (1) [MASTER, SHIP]
Rev 18:17 And all s and seafarers, sailors and all those

SHIPMEN (KJV) See SAILORS

SHIPPING (KJV) See BOATS

SHIPS (39) [SHIP]
Ge 49:13 he shall be a haven for s,
Nu 24:24 But s shall come from Kittim
Dt 28:68 The LORD will bring you back in s to Egypt,
Jdg 5:17 and Dan, why did he abide with the s?
1Ki 9:26 King Solomon built a fleet of s at Ezion-geber,
10:22 For the king had a fleet of s of Tarshish at sea with
10:22 of s of Tarshish used to come bringing gold,
22:48 Jehoshaphat made s of the Tarshish type to go
22:48 for the s were wrecked at Ezion-geber.
22:49 "Let my servants go with your servants in the s,"
2Ch 8:18 s and servants familiar with the sea.
9:21 For the king's s went to Tarshish with the servants
9:21 the s of Tarshish used to come bringing gold,
20:36 He joined him in building s to go to Tarshish;
20:36 they built the s in Ezion-geber.
20:37 And the s were wrecked and were not able to go
Ps 48: 7 as when an east wind shatters the s of Tarshish.
104:26 There go the s, and Leviathan that you formed
107:23 Some went down to the sea in s,
Pr 31:14 She is like the s of the merchant,
Isa 2:16 against all the s of Tarshish,
23: 1 O s of Tarshish, for your fortress is destroyed.
23:10 Cross over to your own land, O s of Tarshish;
23:14 O s of Tarshish, for your fortress is destroyed.
60: 9 coastlands shall wait for me, the s of Tarshish first,
Eze 27: 9 all the s of the sea with their mariners were
27:25 The s of Tarshish traveled for you in your trade.
27:29 and down from their s come all that handle the oar.
30: 9 messengers shall go out from me in s to terrify
Da 11:30 For s of Kittim shall come against him,
Da 11:40 with chariots and horsemen, and with many s.
Jas 3: 4 Or look at s: though they are so large
Rev 8: 9 and a third of the s were destroyed.
18:19 all who had s at sea grew rich by her wealth!
1Mc 8:26 arms, money, or s, just as Rome has decided;
8:28 arms, money, or s, just as Rome has decided;
11: 1 like the sand by the seashore, and many s;
13:29 and beside the suits of armor he carved s,
15:14 and the s joined battle from the sea;

SHIPWRECK (1) [SHIP, WRECKED]
1Ti 1:19 certain persons have suffered s in the faith;

SHIPWRECKED (1) [SHIP, WRECKED]
2Co 11:25 Once I received a stoning. Three times I was s;

SHIRT (1)
Lk 6:29 takes away your coat do not withhold even your s.

SHISHA (1)
1Ki 4: 3 Elihoreph and Ahijah sons of S were secretaries;

SHISHAK (7)
1Ki 11:40 but Jeroboam promptly fled to Egypt, to King S
14:25 King S of Egypt came up against Jerusalem;
2Ch 12: 2 King S of Egypt came up against Jerusalem
12: 5 who had gathered at Jerusalem because of S,
12: 5 so I have abandoned you to the hand of S."
12: 7 not be poured out on Jerusalem by the hand of S.
12: 9 So King S of Egypt came up against Jerusalem;

SHITRAI (1)
1Ch 27:29 Over the herds that pastured in Sharon was S

SHITTIM (6)
Nu 25: 1 While Israel was staying at S,
Jos 2: 1 of Nun sent two men secretly from S as spies,
3: 1 in the morning Joshua rose and set out from S
Hos 5: 2 and a pit dug deep in S;
Joel 3:18 the house of the LORD and water the Wadi S.
Mic 6: 5 and what happened from S to Gilgal,

SHIVERING (1)
1Es 9: 6 s because of the bad weather that prevailed.

SHIVERS (KJV) See SHATTERED

SHIZA (1)
1Ch 11:42 Adina son of S the Reubenite,

SHOA (1)
Eze 23:23 the Chaldeans, Pekod and S and Koa, and all

SHOBAB (4)
2Sa 5:14 Shammua, S, Nathan, Solomon,
1Ch 2:18 these were her sons: Jesher, S,
3: 5 These were born to him in Jerusalem: Shimea, S,
14: 4 Shammua, S, and Nathan;

SHOBACH (2)
2Sa 10:16 with S the commander of the army of Hadadezer
10:18 and wounded S the commander of their army,

SHOBAI (3)
Ezr 2:42 of Ater, of Talmon, of Akkub, of Hatita, and of S,
Ne 7:45 of Ater, of Talmon, of Akkub, of Hatita, of S,
1Es 5:28 the descendants of Hatita, the descendants of S,

SHOBAL (9)
Ge 36:20 the inhabitants of the land: Lotan, S,
36:23 These are the sons of S:
36:29 the clans Lotan, S, Zibeon, Anah,
1Ch 1:38 The sons of Seir: Lotan, S, Zibeon, Anah, Dishon,
1:40 The sons of S: Alian, Manahath,
2:50 S father of Kiriath-jearim,
2:52 S father of Kiriath-jearim had other sons:
4: 1 sons of Judah: Perez, Hezron, Carmi, Hur, and S.
4: 2 Reaiah son of S became the father of Jahath,

SHOBEK (1)
Ne 10:24 Hallohesh, Pilha, S,

SHOBI (1)
2Sa 17:27 S son of Nahash from Rabbah of the Ammonites,

SHOCHO, SHOCO (KJV) See SOCO

SHOCHOH (KJV) See SOCOH

SHOCK (2) [SHOCKED, SHOCKING, SHOCKS]
Job 5:26 as a s of grain comes up to the threshing floor
Eze 26: 9 the s of his battering rams against your walls

SHOCKED (3) [SHOCK]
Jer 2:12 Be appalled, O heavens, at this, be s,
Mk 10:22 he heard this, he was s and went away grieving,
1Mc 16:22 When he heard this, he was greatly s;

SHOCKING (2) [SHOCK]
Isa 29:14 with this people, s and amazing.
Jer 23:14 of Jerusalem I have seen a more s thing:

SHOCKS (1) [SHOCK]
Jdg 15: 5 and burned up the s and the standing grain,

SHOD (KJV) See GAVE THEM SANDALS, PUT ON, WEAR

SHOE (2) [SHOES]
Ps 60: 8 Moab is my washbasin; on Edom I hurl my s;
108: 9 Moab is my washbasin; on Edom I hurl my s;

SHOE, SHOE'S, SHOES (KJV) See also BARS, SANDAL[S], SANDAL-THONG

SHOELATCHET (KJV) See SANDAL-THONG

SHOES (2) [SHOE]
Eph 6:15 As s for your feet put on whatever will make you
Sir 46:19 "No property, not so much as a pair of s,

SHOHAM (1)
1Ch 24:27 of Jaaziah, Beno, S, Zaccur, and Ibri.

SHOMER (2) [=SHIMRITH]
2Ki 12:21 of Shimeath and Jehozabad son of S,
1Ch 7:32 Heber became the father of Japhlet, S, Hotham,

SHONE (18) [SHINE]
Ex 34:29 the skin of his face s because he had been talking
Dt 33: 2 he s forth from Mount Paran.
2Ki 3:22 and the sun s upon the water,
Job 29: 3 when his lamp s over my head,
31:26 if I have looked at the sun when it s,
Eze 40: 3 a man was there, whose appearance s like bronze,
43: 2 and the earth s with his glory.
Mt 17: 2 and his face s like the sun,
Lk 2: 9 and the glory of the Lord s around them,
Ac 12: 7 an angel of the Lord appeared and a light s in
22: 6 about noon a great light from heaven suddenly s
2Co 4: 6 who has s in our hearts to give the light of
Bar 3:34 the stars s in their watches, and were glad;
3:34 They s with gladness for him who made them.
1Mc 6:39 When the sun s on the shields of gold and brass,
2Mc 1:22 s out, a great fire blazed up, so that all marveled.
1:32 when the light from the altar s back, it went out.
2Es 6: 2 and before the flashes of lightning s,

SHOOK (20) [SHAKE]
Ex 19:18 while the whole mountain s violently.
2Sa 6: 6 of God and took hold of it, for the oxen s it.
1Ch 13: 9 to hold the ark, for the oxen s it.
Ne 5:13 I also s out the fold of my garment and said,
Ps 77:18 up the world; the earth trembled and s.
Isa 6: 4 the thresholds s at the voices of those who called,
7: 2 the heart of Ahaz and the heart of his people s as
14:16 the earth tremble, who s kingdoms,
Jer 48:27 but whenever you spoke of him you s your head!
Hab 3: 6 He stopped and s the earth;
Mt 27:51 The earth s, and the rocks were split.
28: 4 of him the guards s and became like dead men.
Ac 13:51 So they s the dust off their feet in protest
18: 6 in protest he s the dust from his clothes and said
28: 5 s off the creature into the fire
Heb 12:26 At that time his voice s the earth;
Sir 48:18 he s his fist against Zion, and made great boasts in
3Mc 2:22 He s him on this side and that as a reed is shaken
2Es 3:18 You bent down the heavens and s the earth,
10:26 so that the earth s at the sound.

SHOOT (19) [BOWSHOT, OFFSHOOTS, SHOOTING, SHOOTS, SHOT]
1Sa 20:20 I will s three arrows to the side of it,
20:36 "Run and find the arrows that I s."
2Sa 11:20 not know that they would s from the wall?
2Ki 9:27 Jehu pursued him, saying, "S him also!"
13:17 Elisha said, "S"; and he shot.
19:32 He shall not come into this city, s an arrow there,
1Ch 12: 2 and could s arrows and sling stones with either
Ps 11: 2 to s in the dark at the upright in heart.
64: 4 they s suddenly and without fear.
64: 7 But God will s his arrow at them;
Isa 11: 1 A s shall come out from the stump of Jesse,
37:33 He shall not come into this city, s an arrow there,
60:21 They are the s that I planted,
Jer 50:14 s at her, spare no arrows, for she has sinned
Eze 17: 4 broke off its topmost s; He carried it to a
36: 8 O mountains of Israel, shall s out your branches,
Ro 11:17 and you, a wild olive s, were grafted in their place
Sir 50: 8 like a green s on Lebanon on a summer day;
1Mc 6:51 machines to s arrows, and catapults.

SHOOTING‡ (2) [SHOOT]
2Ch 26:15 and the corners for s arrows and large stones.

Ps 64: 4 s from ambush at the blameless;

SHOOTS (14) [SHOOT]
Job 8:16 and their s spread over the garden.
14: 7 and that its s will not cease.
15:30 the flame will dry up their s,
Ps 80:11 and its s to the River.
128: 3 be like olive s around your table.
Pr 26:18 Like a maniac who s deadly firebrands and arrows,
Isa 16: 8 their s once spread abroad and crossed over
18: 5 he will cut off the s with pruning hooks,
27: 6 Israel shall blossom and put forth s,
61:11 For as the earth brings forth its s,
Eze 31: 5 from abundant water in its s.
Hos 14: 6 His s shall spread out; his beauty shall be like
Sir 40:22 but the green s of grain more than either.
2Es 16:13 that he s are sharp and when they are shot to

SHOPHACH (2)
1Ch 19:16 with S the commander of the army of Hadadezer
19:18 and also killed S the commander of their army.

SHOQED See Index to Footnotes

SHORE (9) [ASHORE, SEASHORE]
Ge 49:13 Zebulun shall settle at the s of the sea;
1Ki 9:26 which is near Eloth on the s of the Red Sea,
2Ch 8:17 to Ezion-geber and Eloth on the s of the sea,
Eze 27:29 mariners and all the pilots of the sea stand on the s
Lk 5: 2 he saw two boats there at the s of the lake;
5: 3 and asked him to put out a little way from the s.
5:11 When they had brought their boats to s,
Ac 27:13 and began to sail past Crete, close to the s.
Aza 1:13 like the stars of heaven and like the sand on the s

SHORN (4) [SHEAR]
2Ki 19:26 s of strength, are dismayed and confounded;
SS 4: 2 of s ewes that have come up from the washing,
Isa 15: 2 On every head is baldness, every beard is s;
37:27 s of strength, are dismayed and confounded;

SHORT‡ (33) [SHORT-LIVED, SHORTAGE, SHORTEN, SHORTENED, SHORTLY]
Ge 44: 4 they had gone only a s distance from the city,
Lev 22:23 that has a limb too long or too s you may present
2Ki 5:19 when Naaman had gone from him a s distance,
Job 20: 5 that the exulting of the wicked is s,
Ps 89:45 You have cut s the days of his youth;
89:47 Remember how s my time is—
Pr 10:27 but the years of the wicked will be s.
Isa 28:20 For the bed is too s to stretch oneself on it,
59: 1 See, the LORD's hand is not too s to save,
65:20 a youth, and one who falls s of a hundred will
Mt 24:22 And if those days had not been cut s,
24:22 for the sake of the elect those days will be cut s.
Mk 13:20 And if the Lord had not cut s those days,
13:20 whom he chose, he has cut s those days.
Lk 19: 3 because he was s in stature.
Ac 5:34 and ordered the men to be put outside for a s time.
Ro 3:23 all have sinned and fall s of the glory of God;
1Co 7:29 the appointed time has grown s;
1Th 2:17 As for us, brothers and sisters, when, for a s time,
Heb 12:10 For they disciplined us for a s time as seemed best
1Pe 5:12 I have written this s letter to encourage you and
Rev 12:12 because he knows that his time is s!"
Wis 2: 1 saying to themselves, "S and sorrowful is our life,
4:13 Being perfected in a s time,
15: 8 of earth a s time before and after a little while go
16: 3 while your people, after suffering want a s time,
2Mc 2:32 be foolish to lengthen the preface while cutting s
2Es 8: 5 for you have been given only a s time to live.
8:47 For you come far s of being able
12:20 whose times shall be s and their years swift;
16:52 For in a very s time iniquity will be removed from
4Mc 9: 5 a s time ago you learned nothing from Eleazar.
15:27 that would preserve the seven sons for a s time,

SHORT-LIVED (1) [LIVE, SHORT]
Wis 9: 5 a man who is weak and s, with little understanding

SHORTAGE (1) [SHORT]
Ex 16:18 and those who gathered little had no s;

SHORTEN (1) [SHORT]
Sir 30:24 Jealousy and anger s life, and anxiety brings

SHORTENED‡ (4) [SHORT]
Job 18: 7 Their strong steps are s,
Ps 102:23 my strength in midcourse; he has s my days.
Isa 50: 2 Is my hand s, that it cannot redeem?
2Es 2:13 that your days may be few, that they may be s.

SHORTLY (5) [SHORT]
Ge 41:32 and God will s bring it about.
Ac 25: 4 and that he himself intended to go there s.
Ro 16:20 God of peace will s crush Satan under your feet.
Wis 14:20 the one whom s before they had honored as
4Mc 1:12 I shall s have an opportunity to speak of this;

SHOT‡ (17) [SHOOT]
Ge 49:23 they s at him and pressed him hard.
Ex 19:13 but they shall be stoned or s with arrows;
1Sa 20:20 as though I s at a mark.
20:36 As the boy ran, he s an arrow beyond him.
2Sa 11:24 Then the archers s at your servants from the wall;
2Ki 9:24 and s Joram between the shoulders,
9:27 And they s him in the chariot at the ascent to Gur,
13:17 Elisha said, "Shoot"; and he s.
2Ch 35:23 The archers s King Josiah;
La 3:13 He s into my vitals the arrows of his quiver;
Eze 17: 7 It s out its branches toward him,
Wis 5:12 when an arrow is s at a target, the air, thus divided,
1Mc 10:80 and s arrows at his men from early morning
2Es 13:10 and from his tongue he s forth a storm of sparks.
16: 7 Can one turn back an arrow s by a strong archer?
16:13 and when they are s to the ends of the world will
16:16 as an arrow s by a mighty archer does not return,

SHOULD (534) See Index of Articles Etc.

SHOULDER (23) [SHOULDER-PIECES, SHOULDERS]
Ge 21:14 and gave it to Hagar, putting it on her s,
24:15 coming out with her water jar on her s.
24:45 with her water jar on her s;
24:46 She quickly let down her jar from her s, and said,
49:15 so he bowed his s to the burden,
Nu 6:19 The priest shall take the s of the ram,
Dt 18: 3 they shall give to the priest the s, the two jowls,
Jos 4: 5 and each of you take up a stone on his s,
Jdg 9:48 and took it up and laid it on his s.
Ne 9:29 They turned a stubborn s and stiffened their neck
Job 31:22 then let my s blade fall from my s,
31:36 Surely I would carry it on my s;
Ps 81: 6 "I relieved your s of the burden;
Isa 10:27 that day his burden will be removed from your s,
22:22 I will place on his s the key of the house of David;
Eze 12: 6 In their sight you shall lift the baggage on your s,
12: 7 carrying it on my s in their sight.
12:12 among them shall lift his baggage on his s in
24: 4 the thigh and the s; fill it with choice bones.
29:18 and every s was rubbed bare;
34:21 Because you pushed with flank and s,
Zec 7:11 But they refused to listen, and turned a stubborn s,

SHOULDER-PIECES (8) [PIECE, SHOULDER]
Ex 28: 7 It shall have two s attached to its two edges,
28:12 You shall set the two stones on the s of the ephod,
28:25 and so attach it in front to the s of the ephod.
28:27 in front to the lower part of the two s of the ephod,
39: 4 They made for the ephod s,
39: 7 He set them on the s of the ephod,
39:18 in this way they attached it in front to the s of
39:20 in front to the lower part of the two s of the ephod,

SHOULDERS (28) [SHOULDER]
Ge 9:23 on both their s, and walked backward and covered
Ex 12:34 up in their cloaks on their s.
28:12 before the LORD on his two s for remembrance.
Nu 7: 9 of the holy things that had to be carried on the s.
Dt 33:12 the beloved rests between his s.
Jdg 16: 3 pulled them up, bar and all, put them on his s,
1Sa 9: 2 he stood head and s above everyone else.
10:23 he was head and s taller than any of them.
17: 6 and a javelin of bronze slung between his s.
2Ki 6:31 of Elisha son of Shaphat stays on his s today."
9:24 and shot Joram between the s,
1Ch 15:15 the Levites carried the ark of God on their s with
2Ch 35: 3 you need no longer carry it on your s.
Ne 3: 5 but their nobles would not put their s to the work
Isa 9: 4 the yoke of their burden, and the bar across their s,
9: 6 authority rests upon his s; and he is named
14:25 and his burden from their s.
46: 7 They lift it to their s, they carry it,
49:22 and your daughters shall be carried on their s.
Eze 29: 7 you broke, and tore all their s;
Mt 23: 4 hard to bear, and lay them on the s of others;
Lk 15: 5 he has found it, he lays it on his s and rejoices.
Sir 6:25 Bend your s and carry her,
7:31 the first fruits, the guilt offering, the gift of the s,
Bar 2:21 Bend your s and serve the king of Babylon,
LtJ 6: 4 which people carry on their s,
6:26 Having no feet, they are carried on the s of others,
1Es 1: 4 "You need no longer carry it on your s.

SHOUT (60) [SHOUTED, SHOUTING, SHOUTINGS, SHOUTS, VINTAGE-SHOUT]
Jos 6: 5 then all the people shall s with a great s;
6:10 "You shall not s or let your voice be heard,
6:10 until the day I tell you to s. Then you shall s."
6:16 Joshua said to the people, "S!
6:20 they raised a great s, and the wall fell down flat;
Jdg 7:18 and s, 'For the LORD and for Gideon!' "
1Sa 4: 5 all Israel gave a mighty s,
17:52 with a s and pursued the Philistines as far as Gath
2Sa 15:10 then s: Absalom has become king at Hebron!"
1Ki 22:36 Then about sunset a s went through the army,
2Ch 13:15 Then the people of Judah raised the battle s.
Ezr 3:11 with a great s when they praised the LORD,
3:13 not distinguish the sound of the joyful s from
Job 30: 5 people s after them as after a thief.
Ps 20: 5 May we s for joy over your victory,
32:11 O righteous, and s for joy, all you upright in heart.
35:27 Let those who desire my vindication s for joy and
47: 1 s to God with loud songs of joy.
47: 5 God has gone up with a s,
60: 8 over Philistia I s in triumph."
65: 8 the gateways of the morning and the evening s
65:13 they s and sing together for joy.
71:23 My lips will s for joy when I sing praises to you;
81: 1 s for joy to the God of Jacob.
89:15 Happy are the people who know the festal s,
108: 9 over Philistia I s in triumph."
132: 9 and let your faithful s for joy.
132:16 and its faithful will s for joy.
Isa 12: 6 S aloud and sing for joy, O royal Zion,
16: 9 for the s over your fruit harvest
24:14 they s from the west over the majesty of
42:11 let them s from the tops of the mountains.
44:23 Sing, O heavens, for the LORD has done it; s,
48:20 flee from Chaldea, declare this with a s of joy,
54: 1 burst into song and s, you who have not been
58: 1 S out, do not hold back!
Jer 4: 5 s aloud and say, "Gather together,
4:16 they s against the cities of Judah.
20: 8 For whenever I speak, I must cry out, I must s,
25:30 he will roar mightily against his fold, and s,
48:33 the shouting is not the s of joy.
50:15 Raise a s against her from all sides,
51:14 and they shall raise a s of victory over you.
51:48 shall s for joy over Babylon;
Zep 3:14 Sing aloud, O daughter Zion; s, O Israel!
Zec 9: 9 S aloud, O daughter Jerusalem!
Mt 25: 6 But at midnight there was a s, 'Look!
Mk 10:47 he began to s out and say, "Jesus, Son of David,
Lk 19:40 if these were silent, the stones would s out."
Ac 7:57 and with a loud s all rushed together against him.
Gal 4:27 you who bear no children, burst into song and s,
1Pe 4:13 be glad and s for joy when his glory is revealed.
Rev 10: 3 he gave a great s, like a lion roaring.
Jdt 14: 9 the people raised a great s and made a joyful noise
LtJ 6:32 They howl and s before their gods as some do at
Sus 1:60 whole assembly raised a great s and blessed God,
1Mc 3:54 Then they sounded the trumpets and gave a loud s.
1Es 5:62 and shouted with a great s,

SHOUTED (55) [SHOUT]
Ex 32:17 Joshua heard the noise of the people as they s,
Lev 9:24 all the people saw it, they s and fell on their faces.
Jos 6:20 So the people s, and the trumpets were blown.
Jdg 18:23 They s to the Danites, who turned around and said
1Sa 10:24 And all the people s, "Long live the king!"
17: 8 He stood and s to the ranks of Israel,
25:14 and he s insults at them.
2Sa 16: 7 Shimei s while he cursed, "Out!
18:25 The sentinel s and told the king.
2Ki 11:12 they clapped their hands and s,
2Ch 13:15 And when the people of Judah s,
23:11 and they s, "Long live the king!"
32:18 They s it with a loud voice in the language
Ezr 3:12 though many s aloud for joy,
3:13 for the people s so loudly that
Est 8:15 while the city of Susa s and rejoiced.
Job 38: 7 and all the heavenly beings s for joy?
La 4:15 people s at them; "Away!
Mt 8:29 Suddenly they s, "What have you to do with us,
20:30 they heard that Jesus was passing by, they s,
20:31 but they s even more loudly, "Have mercy on us,
27:23 But they s all the more, "Let him be crucified!"
Mk 3:11 they fell down before him and s,
5: 7 and he s at the top of his voice,
15:13 They s back, "Crucify him!"
15:14 But they s all the more, "Crucify him!"
Lk 8:28 down before him and s at the top of his voice,
9:38 Just then a man from the crowd s, "Teacher,
18:38 he s, "Jesus, Son of David, have mercy on me!"
18:39 but he s even more loudly, "Son of David,
23:18 they all s out together, "Away with this fellow!
Jn 18:40 They s in reply, "Not this man, but Barabbas!"
19: 6 the chief priests and the police saw him, they s,
Ac 14:11 they s in the Lycaonian language,
16:28 But Paul s in a loud voice, "Do not harm yourself,
19:28 When they heard this, they were enraged and s,
19:34 for about two hours all of them s in unison,
21:34 Some in the crowd s one thing, some another;
22:22 to him, but then they s, "Away with such a fellow
Rev 10: 3 And when he s, the seven thunders sounded.
Jdt 14:16 with a loud voice and wept and groaned and s,
14:17 he rushed out to the people and s,
16:11 Then my oppressed people s;
Sir 50:16 Then the sons of Aaron s;
Sus 1:24 and the two elders s against her.
1:46 and he s with a loud voice,
Bel 1:18 the king looked at the table, and s in a loud voice,
1:37 Then Habakkuk s, "Daniel, Daniel!
1:41 The king s with a loud voice, "You are great,
1Es 4:41 he stopped speaking, all the people s and said,
5:62 And all the people sounded trumpets and s with
9:10 all the multitude s and said with a loud voice,
3Mc 1:23 They s to their compatriots to take arms
7:13 and the whole multitude s the Hallelujah
4Mc 10: 2 But he s, "Do you not know that the same father

SHOUTING (35) [SHOUT]
Jdg 15:14 the Philistines came s to meet him;
1Sa 4: 6 When the Philistines heard the noise of the s,
4: 6 "What does this great s in the camp of the Hebrews
17:20 as the army was going forth to the battle line, s
2Sa 6:15 of Israel brought up the ark of the LORD with s,

1Ch 15:28 up the ark of the covenant of the LORD with s,
2Ch 15:14 and with s, and with trumpets, and with horns.
Job 39:25 the thunder of the captains, and the s.
Ps 78:65 like a warrior s because of wine.
Ecc 9:17 the wise are more to be heeded than the s of a ruler
Isa 31: 4 is not terrified by their s or daunted at their noise,
43:14 s of the Chaldeans will be turned to lamentation.
Jer 48:33 the s is not the shout of joy.
Am 1:14 with s on the day of battle,
2: 2 amid s and the sound of the trumpet;
Mt 15:22 that region came out and started s, "Have mercy
15:23 saying, "Send her away, for she keeps s after us."
21: 9 that went ahead of him and that followed were s,
Mk 11: 9 ahead and those who followed were s,
Lk 4:41 Demons also came out of many, s,
8:24 They went to him and woke him up, s, "Master,
23:21 but they kept s, "Crucify, crucify him!"
Jn 12:13 of palm trees and went out to meet him, s,
Ac 12:22 The people kept s, "The voice of a god,
14:14 and rushed out into the crowd, s,
17: 6 and some believers before the city authorities, s,
19:32 Meanwhile, some were s one thing, some another;
21:28 s, "Fellow Israelites, help!
21:36 crowd that followed kept s, "Away with him!"
22:23 And while they were s, throwing off their cloaks,
25:24 s that he ought not to live any longer.
AdE 4: 1 he rushed through the street of the city, s loudly:
Sus 1:26 the people in the house heard the s in the garden,
2Mc 15:29 Then there was s and tumult,
3Mc 6:23 the s and saw them all fallen headlong

SHOUTINGS (1) [SHOUT]

Isa 22: 2 you that are full of s, tumultuous city,

SHOUTS (18) [SHOUT]

Job 8:21 and your lips with s of joy.
39: 7 it does not hear the s of the driver.
Ps 27: 6 and I will offer in his tent sacrifices with s of joy;
33: 3 play skillfully on the strings, with loud s.
42: 4 with glad s and songs of thanksgiving,
126: 2 and our tongue with s of joy;
126: 5 May those who sow in tears reap with s of joy.
126: 6 shall come home with s of joy,
Isa 16:10 in the vineyards no songs are sung, no s are raised;
42:13 he cries out, he s aloud, he shows himself mighty
Jer 31: 7 and raise s for the chief of the nations;
48:33 no one treads them with s of joy;
Zec 4: 7 he shall bring out the top stone amid s of 'Grace,
Lk 23:23 But they kept urgently demanding with loud s
Jdt 14:19 their loud cries and s rose up throughout the camp.
1Mc 5:31 up to Heaven, with trumpets and loud s,
2Mc 4:22 and ushered in with a blaze of torches and with s.
3Mc 4: 1 for the Gentiles with s and gladness,

SHOVEL (1) [SHOVELS]

Isa 30:24 which has been winnowed with s and fork.

SHOVELS (9) [SHOVEL]

Ex 27: 3 and s and basins and forks and firepans;
38: 3 the s, the basins, the forks, and the firepans:
Nu 4:14 the s, and the basins, all the utensils of the altar;
1Ki 7:40 Hiram also made the pots, the s, and the basins.
7:45 The pots, the s, and the basins,
2Ki 25:14 They took away the pots, the s, the snuffers,
2Ch 4:11 And Huram made the pots, the s, and the basins.
4:16 The pots, the s, the forks, and all the equipment
Jer 52:18 They took away the pots, the s, the snuffers,

SHOW‡ (218) [SHOWED, SHOWING, SHOWN, SHOWS]

Ge 12: 1 to the land that I will s you.
22: 2 on one of the mountains that I shall s you."
24:12 please grant me success today and s steadfast love
26: 2 settle in the land that I shall s you.
Ex 9:16 to s you my power, and to make my name resound
10: 1 of his officials, in order that I may s these signs
25: 9 In accordance with all that I s you concerning
33:13 I have found favor in your sight, s me your ways,
33:18 Moses said, "S me your glory, I pray."
33:19 and will s mercy on whom I will s mercy.
Lev 10: 3 those who are near me I will s myself holy,
Nu 20:12 to s my holiness before the eyes of the Israelites,
27:14 not s my holiness before their eyes at the waters."
Dt 1:33 to s you the route you should take."
3:24 to s your servant your greatness and your might;
4: 6 for this will s your wisdom and discernment to
7: 2 with them and s them no mercy.
13: 8 S them no pity or compassion and do
13:17 from his fierce anger and s you compassion,
16:19 not distort justice; you must not s partiality;
19:13 S no pity; you shall purge the guilt of innocent
19:21 S no pity: life for life, eye
25:12 you shall cut off her hand; s no pity.
Jdg 1:24 they said to him, "S us the way into the city,
4:22 and I will s you the man whom you are seeking."
6:17 then s me a sign that it is you who speak with me.
1Sa 8: 9 and s them the ways of the king who shall reign
10: 8 until I come to you and s you what you shall do."
14: 8 over to those men and will s ourselves to them.
14:12 "Come up to us, and we will s you something."
16: 3 and I will s you what you shall do;
20:14 s me the faithful love of the LORD;
2Sa 2: 6 the LORD s steadfast love and faithfulness
2:22 How then could I s my face to your brother Joab?"
2Sa 9: 1 to whom I may s kindness for Jonathan's sake?"
9: 3 of the house of Saul to whom I may s the kindness
9: 7 for I will s you kindness for the sake
15:20 the LORD s steadfast love and faithfulness
22:26 With the loyal you s yourself loyal;
22:26 with the blameless you s yourself blameless;
22:27 with the pure you s yourself pure,
22:27 and with the crooked you s yourself perverse.
1Ki 18:15 I will surely s myself to him today."
2Ki 20:13 or in all his realm that Hezekiah did not s them.
20:15 in my storehouses that I did not s them."
Est 1:11 to s the peoples and the officials her beauty;
4: 8 that he might s it to Esther, explain it to her,
Job 13: 8 Will you s partiality toward him,
13:10 surely rebuke you if in secret you s partiality.
15:17 "I will s you; listen to me;
24:25 and s that there is nothing in what I say?"
32:21 I will not s partiality to any person or use flattery
36: 2 a little, and I will s you, for I have yet something
Ps 16:11 You s me the path of life.
17: 7 Wondrously s your steadfast love,
18:25 With the loyal you s yourself loyal;
18:25 with the blameless you s yourself blameless;
18:26 with the pure you s yourself pure;
18:26 and with the crooked you s yourself perverse.
50:23 to those who go the right way I will s the salvation
68:28 Summon your might, O God; s your strength,
82: 2 "How long will you judge unjustly and s partiality
85: 7 S us your steadfast love, O LORD,
86:17 S me a sign of your favor,
91:16 life I will satisfy them, and s them my salvation.
106: 4 O LORD, when you s favor to your people;
109:16 For he did not remember to s kindness,
Pr 12:16 Fools s their anger at once,
22:21 to s you what is right and true,
28:21 To s partiality is not good—
Ecc 3:18 to human beings that God is testing them to s
10: 3 and s to everyone that they are fools.
Isa 27:11 he that formed them will s them no favor.
30:18 therefore he will rise up to s mercy to you.
39: 2 or in all his realm that Hezekiah did not s them.
39: 4 in my storehouses that I did not s them."
49: 9 to those who are in darkness, "S yourselves."
49:15 or s no compassion for the child of her womb?
Jer 16:13 for I will s you no favor.
18:17 I will s them my back, not my face,
32:18 You s steadfast love to the thousandth generation,
42: 3 Let the LORD your God s us where we should go
Eze 9: 5 your eye shall not spare, and you shall s no pity.
37:18 "Will you not s us what you mean by these?"
39:13 on the day that I s my glory,
40: 4 and set your mind upon all that I shall s you,
40: 4 for you were brought here in order that I might s it
44:23 and s them how to distinguish between the unclean
Da 2:27 or diviners can s to the king the mystery that
Joel 2:30 I will s portents in the heavens and on the earth,
Mic 7:15 of the land of Egypt, s us marvelous things.
7:20 You will s faithfulness to Jacob
Zec 1: 9 "I will s you what they are."
7: 9 s kindness and mercy to one another;
Mal 1: 8 will he be pleased with you or s you favor?
1: 9 Will he s favor to any of you?
Mt 6:16 for they disfigure their faces so as to s others
8: 4 but go, s yourself to the priest,
16: 1 and to test Jesus they asked him to s them a sign
16:21 to s his disciples that he must go to Jerusalem
22:16 and s deference to no one;
22:19 S me the coin used for the tax."
Mk 1:44 but go, s yourself to the priest,
12:14 and s deference to no one;
14: 7 you can s kindness to them whenever you wish;
14:15 He will s you a large room upstairs,
Lk 5:14 "Go," he said, "and s yourself to the priest, and,
6:47 I will s you what someone is like who comes
17:14 "Go and s yourselves to the priests."
20:21 and you s deference to no one,
20:24 "S me a denarius. Whose head and whose title
22:12 He will s you a large room upstairs,
Jn 2:18 "What sign can you s us for doing this?"
5:20 and he will s him greater works than these,
7: 4 If you do these things, s yourself to the world."
14: 8 Philip said to him, "Lord, s us the Father,
14: 9 How can you say, 'S us the Father'?
Ac 1:24 S us which one of these two you have chosen
2:19 And I will s portents in the heaven above
7: 3 and go to the land that I will s you.'
7:10 and to s wisdom when he stood before Pharaoh,
9:16 I myself will s him how much he must suffer for
Ro 2:15 They s that what the law requires is written
3:25 He did this to s his righteousness,
9:22 to s his wrath and to make known his power,
1Co 11:22 Or do you s contempt for the church of God
12:31 And I will s you a still more excellent way.
2Co 3: 3 and you s that you are a letter of Christ,
8:19 of the Lord himself and to s our goodwill.
8:24 s them the proof of your love and of our reason
10: 2 when I am present I need not s boldness by daring
10:12 they do not s good sense.
11:30 I will boast of the things that s my weakness.
Eph 2: 7 to come he might s the immeasurable riches
Php 4:10 but had no opportunity to s it.
Tit 2: 7 S yourself in all respects a model of good works,
2: 7 and in your teaching s integrity, gravity,
2:10 but to s complete and perfect fidelity,
3: 2 to be gentle, and to s every courtesy to everyone.
Heb 6:11 of you to s the same diligence so as to realize
6:17 to s even more clearly to the heirs of the promise
Heb 13: 2 Do not neglect to s hospitality to strangers,
Jas 2: 9 But if you s partiality, you commit sin
2:18 S me your faith apart from your works,
2:18 and I by my works will s you my faith.
3:13 S by your good life that your works are done
1Pe 3: 7 s consideration for your wives
Rev 1: 1 to s his servants what must soon take place;
4: 1 and I will s you what must take place after this."
17: 1 I will s you the judgment of the great whore
21: 9 I will s you the bride, the wife of the Lamb."
22: 6 to s his servants what must soon take place."
Tob 13: 5 but he will again s mercy on all of you.
13: 6 and s his power and majesty to a nation of sinners:
13: 6 with favor upon you and s you mercy.'
Jdt 2:11 But to those who resist s no mercy,
10:13 I will s him a way by which he can go
16:15 But to those who fear you you s mercy.
AdE 4: 8 in Susa for their destruction, to s to Esther;
Wis 5:13 ceased to be, and we had no sign of virtue to s,
6: 7 or s deference to greatness;
8:15 among the people I shall s myself capable,
11:21 For it is always in your power to s great strength,
12:17 For you s your strength when people doubt
Sir 4:22 Do not s partiality, to your own harm,
4:27 or s partiality to a ruler.
7:24 and do not s yourself too indulgent with them.
12:18 and whisper much, and s his true face.
17: 8 He put the fear of him into their hearts to s them
19:30 and the way he walks, s what he is.
35:11 With every gift s a cheerful face,
35:16 He will not s partiality to the poor;
36: 4 As you have used us to s your holiness to them,
36: 4 so use them to s your glory to us.
39: 8 He will s the wisdom of what he has learned,
41:16 Therefore s respect for my words;
42: 1 Then you will s proper shame,
42: 8 Then you will s your sound training,
Bar 5: 3 for God will s your splendor everywhere
LtJ 6:67 they cannot s signs in the heavens for the nations,
1Mc 2:50 Now, my children, s zeal for the law,
7:33 to s him the burnt offering that was being offered
11:33 because of the goodwill they s toward us.
2Mc 4:17 It is no light thing to s irreverence to
6:27 I will s myself worthy of my old age
7:37 to God to s mercy soon to our nation and by trials
8: 4 and to s his hatred of evil.
12:36 upon the Lord to s himself their ally and leader in
13: 9 with barbarous arrogance was coming to s
14: 9 with the gracious kindness that you s to all.
15: 2 but s respect for the day
3Mc 5:13 to s the might of his all-powerful hand to
2Es 1:25 When you beg mercy of me, I will s you no mercy.
2:31 and will s mercy to them;
4: 3 "I have been sent to s you three ways,
4: 4 then I will s you the way you desire to see,
4:45 s me this also: whether more time is to come
4:47 and I will s you the interpretation of a parable."
5:37 or s me the picture of a voice;
5:43 so that you might s your judgment the sooner?"
5:56 if I have found favor in your sight, s your servant
6:12 s your servant the last of your signs
6:20 then I will s these signs:
6:30 "I have come to s you these things this night.
6:33 Therefore he sent me to s you all these things,
7:*75* O Lord, s this also to your servant:
7:*76* He answered me and said, "I will s you that also,
7:*102* s further to me, your servant,
7:*104* I will s you this also.
10:59 and the Most High will s you
12: 8 and s me, your servant, the interpretation
12:39 the Most High to s you."
13:15 now s me the interpretation of this dream also.
13:19 and much distress, as these dreams s.
13:50 And then he will s them very many wonders."
4Mc 11:12 an opportunity to s our endurance for the law."
12: 6 to s compassion on her who had been bereaved of

SHOWED (70) [SHOW]

Ge 39:21 LORD was with Joseph and s him steadfast love;
Ex 15:25 and the LORD s him a piece of wood;
Nu 13:26 and s them the fruit of the land.
20:13 and by which he s his holiness.
Dt 4:36 On earth he s you his great fire,
34: 1 and the LORD s him the whole land:
Jdg 1:25 So he s them the way into the city;
1Sa 14:11 So both of them s themselves to the garrison of
15: 6 for you s kindness to all the people of Israel
2Sa 2: 5 because you s this loyalty to Saul your lord,
1Ki 13:12 And his sons s him the way that the man
16:27 and the power that he s,
22:45 and his power that he s, and how he waged war,
2Ki 6: 6 When he s him the place, he cut off a stick,
11: 4 then he s them the king's son.
20:13 he s them all his treasure house, the silver,
2Ch 30:22 to all the Levites who s good skill in the service of
Job 42:11 they s him sympathy and comforted him for all
Ps 106:45 and s compassion according to the abundance
Isa 39: 2 he s them his treasure house, the silver, the gold,
40:14 and s him the way of understanding?
47: 6 I gave them into your hand, you s them no mercy;
Jer 11:18 then you s me their evil deeds.
24: 1 The LORD s me two baskets of figs placed
32:20 You s signs and wonders in the land of Egypt,
52:31 s favor to King Jehoiachin of Judah
Eze 20:11 and s them my ordinances,
35:11 according to the anger and envy that you s because

Am 7: 1 This is what the Lord GOD s me:
7: 4 This is what the Lord GOD s me:
7: 7 This is what he s me:
8: 1 This is what the Lord GOD s me—
Zec 1:20 Then the LORD s me four blacksmiths.
3: 1 Then he s me the high priest Joshua standing
Mt 4: 8 a very high mountain and s him all the kingdoms
Lk 4: 5 the devil led him up and s him in an instant all
10:37 He said, "The one who s him mercy."
20:37 the fact that the dead are raised Moses himself **s,**
24:40 he had said this, he s them his hands and his feet.
Jn 20:20 After he said this, he s them his hands and his side.
21: 1 After these things Jesus s himself again to
21: 1 and he s himself in this way.
Ac 9:41 calling the saints and widows, he s her to be alive.
28: 2 The natives s us unusual kindness.
Heb 6:10 not overlook your work and the love that you s
Jas 5:11 Indeed we call blessed those who s endurance.
Rev 21:10 and s me the holy city Jerusalem coming down out
22: 1 Then the angel s me the river of the water of life,
22: 8 to worship at the feet of the angel who s them
Jdt 13:15 she pulled the head out of the bag and s it to them,
Wis 10:10 she s him the kingdom of God,
10:14 Those who accused him she s to be false,
16: 2 of this punishment you s kindness to your people,
Sir 16: 9 He s no pity on the doomed nation,
17: 7 and s them good and evil.
49: 8 God s him above the chariot of the cherubim.
Bar 4:13 or tread the paths his righteousness s them.
Bel 1:21 They s him the secret doors
1Mc 4:20 for the smoke that was seen s what had happened.
11: 4 they s him the burnt-out temple of Dagon,
2Mc 3:17 which plainly s to those who looked at him
13:23 the sanctuary and s generosity to the holy place.
15:32 He s them the vile Nicanor's head and
1Es 8: 4 and the king s him honor,
2Es 6:12 the last of your signs of which you s me a part on
9:29 you s yourself among us, to our ancestors in
10:27 and a place of huge foundations s itself.
13:32 and the signs occur that I s you before,
14: 5 and s him the secrets of the times and declared
4Mc 17: 2 and s the courage of your faith!

SHOWER (4) [SHOWERED, SHOWERS]

Job 37: 6 and the s of rain, his heavy s of rain,
Isa 45: 8 **S,** O heavens, from above, and let the skies rain
Am 7: 4 the Lord GOD was calling for a s of fire,

SHOWERED (2) [SHOWER]

Ps 68: 9 Rain in abundance, O God, you s abroad;
2Mc 10:30 They s arrows and thunderbolts on the enemy,

SHOWERS (11) [SHOWER]

Dt 32: 2 like gentle rain on grass, like s on new growth.
Ps 65:10 softening it with **s,** and blessing its growth.
72: 6 like s that water the earth.
Jer 3: 3 Therefore the s have been withheld,
14:22 Or can the heavens give **s?**
Eze 34:26 and I will send down the s in their season;
34:26 they shall be s of blessing.
Hos 6: 3 he will come to us like the **s,**
Mic 5: 7 be like dew from the LORD, like s on the grass,
Zec 10: 1 who gives s of rain to you,
Wis 16:22 that blazed in the hail and flashed in the s of rain;

SHOWING‡ (21) [SHOW]

Ex 20: 6 but s steadfast love to the thousandth generation
Dt 5:10 but s steadfast love to the thousandth generation
7:16 over to you, s them no pity;
28:50 a grim-faced nation s no respect to the old or favor
1Sa 23:21 be blessed by the LORD for s me compassion!
2Sa 3: 8 Today I keep s loyalty to the house
Ps 92:15 s that the LORD is upright;
Pr 18: 1 s contempt for all who have sound judgment.
Mic 7:18 because he delights in s clemency.
Ac 9:39 weeping and s tunics and other clothing
18:28 s by the scriptures that the Messiah is Jesus.
Ro 9:17 up for the very purpose of s my power in you,
12:10 outdo one another in s honor.
Gal 6:12 It is those who want to make a good s in the flesh
Jdt 13:11 still s his power in Israel and his strength
Wis 11: 8 s by their thirst at that time
14: 4 s that you can save from every danger,
18:21 s that he was your servant.
2Mc 4:49 even the Tyrians, s their hatred of the crime,
10:12 took the lead in s justice to the Jews because of
3Mc 6: 5 broke in pieces, s your power to many nations.

SHOWN (85) [SHOW]

Ge 19:19 you have s me great kindness in saving my life;
22: 3 to the place in the distance that God had s him.
22: 9 When they came to the place that God had s him,
24:14 By this I shall know that you have s steadfast love
32:10 the faithfulness that you have s to your servant,
41:28 God has s to Pharaoh what he is about to do.
41:39 "Since God has s you all this,
Ex 25:40 which is being s you on the mountain.
26:30 to the plan for it that you were s on the mountain.
27: 8 be made just as you were s on the mountain.
Lev 13: 7 in the skin after he has s himself to the priest
13:19 it shall be s to the priest.
13:49 it is a leprous disease and shall be s to the priest.
Nu 8: 4 to the pattern that the LORD had s Moses,
Dt 4:35 To you it was s so that you would acknowledge
5:24 LORD our God has s us his glory and greatness,
Jdg 13:23 or s us all these things,
1Ki 3: 6 "You have s great and steadfast love
8:66 because of all the goodness that the LORD had s
2Ki 8:10 the LORD has s me that he shall certainly die."
8:13 "The LORD has s me that you are to be king
2Ch 1: 8 "You have s great and steadfast love
7:10 the goodness that the LORD had s to David and
24:22 Zechariah's father, had s him, but killed his son.
Ezr 9: 8 But now for a brief moment favor has been s by
Ps 31:21 for he has wondrously s his steadfast love to me
48: 3 Within its citadels God has s himself
78:11 and the miracles that he had s them.
111: 6 He has s his people the power of his works,
Isa 26:10 If favor is s to the wicked,
63: 7 of Israel that he has s them according to his mercy,
Jer 3:11 Faithless Israel has s herself less guilty than false Judah.
38:21 this is what the LORD has s me—
44:10 They have s no contrition or fear to this day,
La 4:16 no honor was s to the priests,
5:12 no respect is s to the elders.
Eze 11:25 the exiles all the things that the LORD had s me.
Mal 2: 9 as you have not kept my ways but have s partiality
Mk 5:19 and what mercy he has s you."
Lk 1:51 He has s strength with his arm;
1:58 that the Lord had s his great mercy to her,
1:72 Thus he has s the mercy promised
7:47 hence she has s great love.
Jn 10:32 "I have s you many good works from the Father.
Ac 10:28 but God has s me that I should
Ro 1:19 because God has s it to them.
7:13 in order that sin might be s to be sin,
10:20 I have s myself to those who did not ask for me."
11:31 by the mercy s to you, they too may now receive
1Ti 5:10 as one who has brought up children, s hospitality,
Heb 8: 5 to the pattern that was s you on the mountain."
Jas 2:13 be without mercy to anyone who has s no mercy;
2:20 Do you want to be s, you senseless person,
Tob 13: 4 He has s you his greatness even there.
Jdt 8:29 not the first time your wisdom has been **s,**
AdE 1:22 so that in every house respect would be s
2:23 in the royal library in praise of the goodwill s
6: 4 While the king was inquiring about the goodwill s
Wis 3:14 for special favor will be s him for his faithfulness,
16: 4 while to these others it was merely s
Sir 3:23 for more than you can understand has been s you.
14:12 and the decree of Hades has not been s to you.
1Mc 14: 4 as was the honor s him, all his days.
2Mc 2: 8 as they were s in the case of Moses,
12:24 to whom no consideration would be **s.**
12:30 of Scythopolis had s them and their kind treatment
3Mc 6:15 Let it be s to all the Gentiles that you are with us,
2Es 1:35 I have s no signs will do what I have commanded.
3:31 and have not s to anyone how your way may
7:*44* and to you alone I have s these things."
7:*48* and has s us the paths of perdition
7:*76* not include yourself with those who have s scorn,
7:*77* but it will not be s to you until the last times.
7:*79* If it is one of those who have s scorn and have
7:*97* it is s them how their face is to shine like the sun,
8:62 I have not s this to all people,
8:63 you have already s me a great number of the signs
8:63 but you have not s me when you will do them."
10:50 has s you the brilliance of her glory,
12: 9 For you have judged me worthy to be s the end of
12:39 so that you may be s whatever it pleases
13:14 beginning you have s your servant these wonders,
13:56 Therefore I have s you these things;
14: 8 that I have s you, the dreams that you have seen,
4Mc 5:25 of the world in giving us the law has s sympathy

SHOWS (24) [SHOW]

Lev 13:49 if the disease s greenish or reddish in the garment,
Nu 23: 3 Whatever he s me I will tell you."
2Sa 22:51 and s steadfast love to his anointed,
Job 16:13 He slashes open my kidneys, and s no mercy;
34:19 who s no partiality to nobles,
Ps 18:50 and s steadfast love to his anointed,
59:17 are my fortress, the God who s me steadfast love.
Pr 3:34 but to the humble he s favor.
6:34 and he s no restraint when he takes revenge.
Isa 5:16 and the Holy God s himself holy by righteousness.
42:13 he s himself mighty against his foes.
Jn 5:20 the Son and s him all that he himself is doing;
Ac 10:34 "I truly understand that God s no partiality,
Ro 2:11 For God s no partiality.
3:12 there is no one who s kindness,
9:16 but on God who s mercy.
Gal 2: 6 makes no difference to me; God s no partiality)—
Tob 13: 2 For he afflicts, and he s mercy;
LtJ 6:59 So it is better to be a king who s his courage,
1Mc 5:41 he s fear and camps on the other side of the river,
12: 7 that you are our brothers, as the appended copy **s.**
2Mc 2: 7 gathers his people together again and s his mercy.
10:38 the Lord who s great kindness to Israel
2Es 7:*134* [64] he s patience toward those who have sinned,

SHRANK (3) [SHRINK]

1Mc 3: 6 Lawbreakers s back for fear of him;
2Mc 14:18 s from deciding the issue by bloodshed.
4Mc 14: 4 the seven youths proved coward or s from death,

SHREDS See Index to Footnotes

SHREWD (2) [SHREWDLY, SHREWDNESS]

Isa 5:21 and s in your own sight!
Lk 16: 8 for the children of this age are more s in dealing

SHREWDLY (2) [SHREWD]

Ex 1:10 Come, let us deal s with them,
Lk 16: 8 the dishonest manager because he had acted **s;**

SHREWDNESS (1) [SHREWD]

Pr 1: 4 to teach s to the simple, knowledge and prudence

SHRIEKS (2)

Lk 9:39 Suddenly a spirit seizes him, and all at once he **s.**
Ac 8: 7 crying with loud **s,** came out

SHRINE‡ (11) [SHRINES]

Jdg 17: 5 This man Micah had a **s,**
1Sa 9:12 because the people have a sacrifice today at the **s.**
9:13 you will find him, before he goes up to the s to eat.
9:14 toward them on his way up to the **s.**
9:19 go up before me to the **s,**
9:25 When they came down from the s into the town,
10: 5 the s with harp, tambourine, flute, and lyre playing
Isa 44:13 with human beauty, to be set up in a **s.**
Jer 17:12 exalted from the beginning, s of our sanctuary!
Heb 6:19 a hope that enters the inner s behind the curtain,
2Mc 14:33 over to me as a prisoner, I will level this s of God

SHRINES (8) [SHRINE]

2Ki 17:29 of its own and put them in the s of the high places
17:32 who sacrificed for them in the s of the high places.
23:19 the s of the high places that were in the towns
Eze 16:16 and made for yourself colorful **s,**
Ac 17:24 does not live in s made by human hands,
19:24 a silversmith who made silver s of Artemis,
Jdt 3: 8 Yet he demolished all their s and cut
1Mc 1:47 to build altars and sacred precincts and s for idols,

SHRINK (5) [SHRANK, SHRINKS]

Na 3: 7 Then all who see you will s from you and say,
Ac 20:20 I did not s from doing anything helpful,
20:27 not s from declaring to you the whole purpose
Heb 10:39 But we are not among those who s back and
Tob 11: 8 the white films s and peel off from his eyes,

SHRINKS (1) [SHRINK]

Heb 10:38 My soul takes no pleasure in anyone who s back."

SHRIVEL (1) [SHRIVELED, SHRIVELS]

Zep 2:11 he will s all the gods of the earth,

SHRIVELED (3) [SHRIVEL]

Job 16: 8 he has s me up, which is a witness against me;
Ps 22:16 My hands and feet have **s;**
La 4: 8 Their skin has s on their bones;

SHRIVELS (1) [SHRIVEL]

Joel 1:17 The seed s under the clods,

SHROUD (1) [SHROUDED]

Isa 25: 7 on this mountain the s that is cast over all peoples,

SHROUDED (1) [SHROUD]

Dt 4:11 blazing up to the very heavens, s in dark clouds.

SHRUB (1) [SHRUBS]

Jer 17: 6 They shall be like a s in the desert,

SHRUBS (2) [SHRUB]

Mt 13:32 but when it has grown it is the greatest of s
Mk 4:32 it grows up and becomes the greatest of all **s,**

SHUA (2) [SHUA'S]

Ge 38: 2 of a certain Canaanite whose name was **S;**
1Ch 7:32 Shomer, Hotham, and their sister **S.**

SHUA'S (1) [SHUA]

Ge 38:12 In course of time the wife of Judah, S daughter,

SHUAH (2)

Ge 25: 2 Jokshan, Medan, Midian, Ishbak, and **S.**
1Ch 1:32 Jokshan, Medan, Midian, Ishbak, and **S.**

SHUAL (2) [HAZAR-SHUAL]

1Sa 13:17 toward Ophrah, to the land of **S,**
1Ch 7:36 The sons of Zophah: Suah, Harnepher, **S,** Beri,

SHUBAEL (3)

1Ch 24:20 of the sons of Amram, **S;**
24:20 of the sons of **S,** Jehdeiah.
25:20 **S,** his sons and his brothers, twelve;

SHUDDER (7) [SHUDDERED, SHUDDERING]

Isa 32:10 In little more than a year you will **s,**
32:11 Tremble, you women who are at ease, **s,**
Eze 32:10 their kings shall s because of you.

Jas 2:19 Even the demons believe—and **s.**
Man 1: 4 at whom all things **s**, and tremble
3Mc 6:20 Even the king began to **s** bodily,
4Mc 14: 9 we ourselves **s** as we hear of the suffering

SHUDDERED (2) [SHUDDER]

2Es 5:14 Then I woke up, and my body **s** violently,
4Mc 17: 7 not those who first beheld it have **s** as they saw

SHUDDERING (1) [SHUDDER]

Job 21: 6 I think of it I am dismayed, and **s** seizes my flesh.

SHUFFLING (1)

Pr 6:13 winking the eyes, **s** the feet, pointing the fingers,

SHUHAH (1)

1Ch 4:11 the brother of **S** became the father of Mehir,

SHUHAM (1) [SHUHAMITES]

Nu 26:42 of **S**, the clan of the Shuhamites.

SHUHAMITES (2) [SHUHAM]

Nu 26:42 of Shuham, the clan of the **S.**
26:43 All the clans of the **S:**

SHUHITE (5)

Job 2:11 Eliphaz the Temanite, Bildad the **S**,
8: 1 Then Bildad the **S** answered:
18: 1 Then Bildad the **S** answered:
25: 1 Then Bildad the **S** answered:
42: 9 and Bildad the **S** and Zophar the Naamathite went

SHULAMMITE (2)

SS 6:13 Return, return, O **S!** Return, return,
6:13 Why should you look upon the **S**,

SHUMATHITES (1)

1Ch 2:53 Ithrites, the Puthites, the **S**, and the Mishraites;

SHUN (7) [SHUNNED]

Ps 88: 8 You have caused my companions to **s** me;
88:18 You have caused friend and neighbor to **s** me;
Ecc 9: 2 those who swear are like those who **s** an oath.
1Co 6:18 **S** fornication! Every sin that a person commits
1Ti 6:11 But as for you, man of God, **s** all this;
2Ti 2:22 **S** youthful passions and pursue righteousness,
Sir 32:17 The sinner will **s** reproof, and will find a decision

SHUNAMMITE (8) [SHUNEM]

1Ki 1: 3 and found Abishag the **S**,
1:15 Abishag the **S** was attending the king.
2:17 to give me Abishag the **S** as my wife."
2:21 Abishag the **S** be given to your brother Adonijah
2:22 why do you ask Abishag the **S** for Adonijah?
2Ki 4:12 to his servant Gehazi, "Call the **S** woman."
4:25 "Look, there is the **S** woman;
4:36 and said, "Call the **S** woman."

SHUNEM (3) [SHUNAMMITE]

Jos 19:18 Its territory included Jezreel, Chesulloth, **S**,
1Sa 28: 4 and came and encamped at **S.**
2Ki 4: 8 One day Elisha was passing through **S**,

SHUNI (2) [SHUNITES]

Ge 46:16 Ziphion, Haggi, **S**, Ezbon, Eri, Arodi, and Areli.
Nu 26:15 of **S**, the clan of the Shunites;

SHUNITES (1) [SHUNI]

Nu 26:15 of Shuni, the clan of the **S;**

SHUNNED (1) [SHUN]

Pr 19: 7 how much more are they **s** by their friends!

SHUPHAMITES (1) [SHEPHUPHAM]

Nu 26:39 of Shephupham, the clan of the **S;**

SHUPPIM (3)

1Ch 7:12 And **S** and Huppim were the sons of Ir,
7:15 And Machir took a wife for Huppim and for **S.**
26:16 For **S** and Hosah it came out for the west,

SHUR (6)

Ge 16: 7 the spring on the way to **S.**
20: 1 and settled between Kadesh and **S.**
25:18 They settled from Havilah to **S**,
Ex 15:22 and they went into the wilderness of **S.**
1Sa 15: 7 from Havilah as far as **S**, which is east of Egypt.
27: 8 from Telam on the way to **S** and on to the land

SHUSHAN (KJV) See SUSA

SHUT (83) [SHUTS, SHUTTING]

Ge 7:16 and the LORD **s** him in.
19: 6 of the door to the men, **s** the door after him,
19:10 and brought Lot into the house with them, and **s**
Lev 14:38 of the house and **s** up the house seven days.
14:46 while it is **s** up shall be unclean until the evening;
Nu 12:14 Let her be **s** out of the camp for seven days,
12:15 So Miriam was **s** out of the camp for seven days;
Dt 11:17 and he will **s** up the heavens, so that there will
Jos 2: 7 soon as the pursuers had gone out, the gate was **s.**
6: 1 Now Jericho was **s** up inside and out because of
Jdg 9:51 the lords of the city fled to it and **s** themselves in;
1Sa 6:10 and **s** up their calves at home.
23: 7 for he has **s** himself in by entering a town
2Sa 20: 3 So they were **s** up until the day of their death,
1Ki 8:35 "When heaven is **s** up and there is no rain
2Ki 4: 4 and **s** the door behind you and your children,
4: 5 and **s** the door behind her and her children;
6:32 that you **s** the door and hold it closed against him.
2Ch 6:26 "When heaven is **s** up and there is no rain
7:13 When I **s** up the heavens so that there is no rain,
28:24 He **s** up the doors of the house of the LORD
29: 7 They also **s** the doors of the vestibule and put out
Ne 7: 3 let them **s** and bar the doors.
13:19 that the doors should be **s** and gave orders
Job 3:10 it did not **s** the doors of my mother's womb,
24:16 by day they **s** themselves up;
38: 8 "Or who **s** in the sea with doors when it burst out
41:15 **s** up closely as with a seal.
Ps 77: 9 Has he in anger **s** up his compassion?"
88: 8 I am **s** in so that I cannot escape;
Ecc 12: 4 when the doors on the street are **s**, and the sound
Isa 6:10 and stop their ears, and **s** their eyes,
22:22 he shall open, and no one shall **s;** he shall **s**, and no one shall open.
24:10 every house is **s** up so that no one can enter.
24:22 they will be **s** up in a prison,
26:20 enter your chambers, and **s** your doors behind you;
33:15 of bloodshed and **s** their eyes from looking on evil,
44:18 for their eyes are **s**, so that they cannot see,
52:15 kings shall **s** their mouths because of him;
60:11 day and night they shall not be **s**,
66: 9 shall I, the one who delivers, **s** the womb?
Jer 13:19 of the Negeb are **s** up with no one to open them;
20: 9 within me there is something like a burning fire **s**
Eze 3:24 Go, **s** yourself inside your house.
44: 1 which faces east; and it was **s.**
44: 2 The LORD said to me: This gate shall remain **s;**
44: 2 therefore it shall remain **s.**
Da 6:22 My God sent his angel and **s** the lions' mouths so
Mal 1:10 someone among you would **s** the temple doors,
Mt 6: 6 and **s** the door and pray to your Father who is
13:15 and they have **s** their eyes;
25:10 into the wedding banquet; and the door was **s.**
Lk 4:25 the heaven was **s** up three years and six months,
13:25 the owner of the house has got up and **s** the door,
Jn 20:26 Although the doors were **s**,
Ac 21:30 and immediately the doors were **s.**
28:27 and they have **s** their eyes;
Heb 11:33 obtained promises, **s** the mouths of lions,
Rev 3: 7 who opens and no one will **s**,
3: 8 which no one is able to **s.**
11: 6 They have authority to **s** the sky,
21:25 Its gates will never be **s** by day—
Tob 8: 4 parents had gone out and **s** the door of the room,
Jdt 13: 1 Bagoas closed the tent from outside and **s** out
Wis 17: 2 and prisoners of long night, **s** in under their roofs,
17:16 thus was kept **s** up in a prison not made of iron;
Sir 48: 3 By the word of the Lord he **s** up the heavens,
LtJ 6:18 And just as the gates are **s** on every side
Sus 1:17 and **s** the garden doors so that I can bathe."
1:18 they **s** the doors of the garden and went out by
1:20 They said, "Look, the garden doors are **s**,
1:36 **s** the garden doors, and dismissed the maids.
Bel 1:11 and **s** the door and seal it with your signet.
1:14 **s** the door and sealed it with the king's signet,
1Mc 5: 5 They were **s** up by him in their towers;
5:26 of them have been **s** up in Bozrah and Bosor,
5:27 some have been **s** up in the other towns of Gilead;
5:47 But the people of the town **s** them out and blocked
11:61 but the people of Gaza **s** him out.
15:25 he **s** Trypho up and kept him from going out or in.
2Es 5:37 and bring out for me the winds **s** up in them,
16:78 It is **s** off and given up to be consumed by fire.

SHUTHELAH (4) [SHUTHELAHITES]

Nu 26:35 of **S**, the clan of the Shuthelahites;
26:36 And these are the descendants of **S:**
1Ch 7:20 The sons of Ephraim: **S**, and Bered his son,
7:21 **S** his son, and Ezer and Elead.

SHUTHELAHITES (1) [SHUTHELAH]

Nu 26:35 of Shuthelah, the clan of the **S;**

SHUTS (4) [SHUT]

Job 5:16 So the poor have hope, and injustice **s** its mouth.
12:14 if he **s** someone in, no one can open up.
La 3: 8 though I call and cry for help, he **s** out my prayer;
Rev 3: 7 of David, who opens and no one will shut, who **s**

SHUTTERS (1)

Eze 40:16 with **s** on the inside of the gateway all around,

SHUTTING (1) [SHUT]

Lk 3:20 added to them all by **s** up John in prison.

SHUTTLE (1)

Job 7: 6 My days are swifter than a weaver's **s**,

SIA (1) [=SIAHA]

Ne 7:47 of Keros, of **S**, of Padon,

SIAHA (1) [=SIA]

Ezr 2:44 Keros, **S**, Padon,

SIBBECAI (4)

2Sa 21:18 then **S** the Hushathite killed Saph,
1Ch 11:29 **S** the Hushathite, Ilai the Ahohite,
20: 4 then **S** the Hushathite killed Sippai,
27:11 for the eighth month, was **S** the Hushathite,

SIBBOLETH (1) [SHIBBOLETH]

Jdg 12: 6 "Then say Shibboleth," and he said, "**S**,"

SIBMAH (5)

Nu 32:38 Baal-meon (some names being changed), and **S;**
Jos 13:19 and **S**, and Zereth-shahar on the hill of the valley,
Isa 16: 8 the fields of Heshbon languish, and the vines of **S**,
16: 9 with the weeping of Jazer for the vines of **S;**
Jer 48:32 More than for Jazer I weep for you, O vine of **S!**

SIBRAIM (1)

Eze 47:16 **S** (which lies between the border of Damascus

SICHEM (KJV) See SHECHEM

SICK‡ (62) [SICKBED, SICKBEDS, SICKLY, SICKNESS]

1Sa 19:14 to take David, she said, "He is **s.**"
30:13 behind because I fell **s** three days ago.
1Ki 14: 1 At that time Abijah son of Jeroboam fell **s.**
14: 5 concerning her son; for he is **s.**
2Ki 13:14 Now when Elisha had fallen **s** with the illness
20: 1 In those days Hezekiah became **s** and was at
20:12 for he had heard that Hezekiah had been **s.**
2Ch 22: 6 of Ahab in Jezreel, because he was **s.**
32:24 In those days Hezekiah became **s** and was at
Ne 2: 2 "Why is your face sad, since you are not **s?**
Ps 35:13 But as for me, when they were **s**, I wore sackcloth;
107:17 Some were **s** through their sinful ways,
Pr 13:12 Hope deferred makes the heart **s**,
Isa 1: 5 The whole head is **s**, and the whole heart faint.
33:24 And no inhabitant will say, "I am **s**";
38: 1 In those days Hezekiah became **s** and was at
38: 9 after he had been **s** and had recovered
39: 1 for he heard that he had been **s** and had recovered.
Jer 8:18 My joy is gone, grief is upon me, my heart is **s.**
14:18 And if I enter the city, look—those **s** with famine!
La 5:17 Because of this our hearts are **s**,
Eze 16:30 How **s** is your heart, says the Lord GOD,
34: 4 you have not healed the **s**,
Da 8:27 I, Daniel, was overcome and lay **s** for some days;
Hos 7: 5 On the day of our king the officials became **s** with
Mal 1: 8 And when you offer those that are lame or **s**,
1:13 taken by violence or is lame or **s**,
Mt 4:24 and they brought to him all the **s**,
8:16 the spirits with a word, and cured all who were **s.**
9:12 of a physician, but those who are **s.**
10: 8 Cure the **s**, raise the dead, cleanse the lepers,
14:14 and he had compassion for them and cured their **s.**
14:35 throughout the region and brought all who were **s**
25:36 I was **s** and you took care of me,
25:39 that we saw you **s** or in prison and visited you?'
25:43 **s** and in prison and you did not visit me.'
25:44 or thirsty or a stranger or naked or **s** or in prison,
Mk 1:32 to him all who were **s** or possessed with demons.
1:34 he cured many who were **s** with various diseases,
2:17 of a physician, but those who are **s;**
6: 5 except that he laid his hands on a few **s** people
6:13 with oil many who were **s** and cured them.
6:55 that whole region and began to bring the **s** on mats
6:56 they laid the **s** in the marketplaces,
16:18 ⟦they will lay their hands on the **s**,⟧
Lk 4:40 all those who had any who were **s**
5:31 of a physician, but those who are **s;**
10: 9 cure the **s** who are there, and say to them,
Jn 5: 7 The **s** man answered him, "Sir,
6: 2 they saw the signs that he was doing for the **s.**
Ac 4: 9 of a good deed done to someone who was **s**
5:15 so that they even carried out the **s** into the streets,
5:16 the **s** and those tormented by unclean spirits,
19:12 that had touched his skin were brought to the **s**,
28: 8 so happened that the father of Publius lay **s** in bed
Jas 5:14 Are any among you **s?**
5:15 The prayer of faith will save the **s**,
Wis 17: 8 of a **s** soul were **s** themselves with ridiculous fear.
Sir 7:35 Do not hesitate to visit the **s**,
1Mc 1: 5 he fell **s** and perceived that he was dying.
6: 8 to his bed and became **s** from disappointment,

SICKBED (1) [BED, SICK]

Ps 41: 3 The LORD sustains them on their **s;**

SICKBEDS (1) [BED, SICK]

Sir 48: 6 and famous men, from their **s.**

SICKLE (12) [SICKLES]

Dt 16: 9 the seven weeks from the time the **s** is first put to
23:25 not put a **s** to your neighbor's standing grain.
Jer 50:16 and the wielder of the **s** in time of harvest;

Joel 3:13 Put in the **s,** for the harvest is ripe.
Mk 4:29 the grain is ripe, at once he goes in with his **s,**
Rev 14:14 and a sharp **s** in his hand!
14:15 on the cloud, "Use your **s** and reap, for the hour
14:16 So the one who sat on the cloud swung his **s** over
14:17 and he too had a sharp **s.**
14:18 with a loud voice to him who had the sharp **s,**
14:18 "Use your sharp **s** and gather the clusters of
14:19 the angel swung his **s** over the earth and gathered

SICKLES (1) [SICKLE]

1Sa 13:20 to sharpen their plowshare, mattocks, axes, or **s;**

SICKLY (1) [SICK]

Wis 6:23 nor will I travel in the company of **s** envy,

SICKNESS‡ (17) [SICK]

Ex 23:25 and I will take **s** away from among you.
Lev 20:18 If a man lies with a woman having her **s**
1Ki 8:37 whatever plague, whatever **s** there is;
2Ch 6:28 whatever suffering, whatever **s** there is;
21:15 and you yourself will have a severe **s** with
Pr 18:14 The human spirit will endure **s;**
Ecc 5:17 in much vexation and **s** and resentment.
Isa 10:16 will send wasting **s** among his stout warriors,
38:9 he had been sick and had recovered from his **s:**
Jer 6:7 **s** and wounds are ever before me.
Hos 5:13 When Ephraim saw his **s,** and Judah his wound,
Mt 4:23 the kingdom and curing every disease and every **s**
9:35 and curing every disease and every **s.**
10:1 and to cure every disease and every **s.**
Sir 30:17 and eternal sleep than chronic **s.**
31:22 and no **s** will overtake you.
37:30 overeating brings **s,** and gluttony leads to nausea.

SICKNESSES See Index to Footnotes

SICYON (1)

1Mc 15:23 and to Delos, and to Myndos, and to **S,**

SIDDIM (3)

Ge 14:3 All these joined forces in the Valley of **S** (that is,
14:8 and they joined battle in the Valley of **S**
14:10 Now the Valley of **S** was full of bitumen pits;

SIDE‡ (352) [ASIDE, FIVE-SIDED, FOUR-SIDED, MANY-SIDED, SIDEBOARD, SIDED, SIDES, SIDEWALLS]

A. OTHER SIDE (48)
B. ON EVERY SIDE (34)
C. EAST SIDE (31)

Ge 6:16 and put the door of the ark in its **s;**
31:42 had not been on my **s,**
38:16 He went over to her at the road **s,** and said,
Ex 17:12 Aaron and Hur held up his hands, one on one **s,**
17:12 one on one side, and the other on the other **s;** A
23:2 when you bear witness in a lawsuit, you shall not **s**
25:12 two rings on the one **s** of it,
25:12 and two rings on the other **s.** A
25:32 the lampstand out of one **s** of it and three branches
25:32 of the lampstand out of the other **s** of it; A
26:13 The cubit on the one **s,**
26:13 on the one side, and the cubit on the other **s,** A
26:13 on this **s** and that **s,** to cover it.
26:18 twenty frames for the south **s;**
26:20 and for the second **s** of the tabernacle,
26:20 on the north **s** twenty frames,
26:26 five for the frames of the one **s** of the tabernacle,
26:27 for the frames of the other **s** of the tabernacle, A
26:27 of the **s** of the tabernacle at the rear westward.
26:35 on the south **s** of the tabernacle opposite the table;
26:35 and you shall put the table on the north **s.**
27:9 On the south **s** the court shall have hangings
27:9 twisted linen one hundred cubits long for that **s;**
27:11 Likewise for its length on the north **s** there shall
27:12 of the court on the west **s** there shall be fifty cubits
27:14 be fifteen cubits of hangings on the one **s,**
27:15 be fifteen cubits of hangings on the other **s,** A
32:26 and said, "Who is on the LORD's **s?**
32:27 the God of Israel, 'Put your sword on your **s,**
36:23 twenty frames for the south **s;**
36:25 For the second **s** of the tabernacle,
36:25 the second side of the tabernacle, on the north **s,**
36:31 five for the frames of the one **s** of the tabernacle,
36:32 for the frames of the other **s** of the tabernacle, A
37:3 on its one **s** and two rings on its other side.
37:3 on its one side and two rings on its other **s.** A
37:18 the lampstand out of one **s** of it and three branches
37:18 of the lampstand out of the other **s** of it; A
38:9 for the south **s** the hangings of the court were
38:11 north **s** there were hangings one hundred cubits
38:12 the west **s** there were hangings fifty cubits long,
38:14 hangings for one **s** of the gate were fifteen cubits,
38:15 And so for the other **s;** A
38:15 on each **s** of the gate of the court were hangings
40:22 on the north **s** of the tabernacle,
40:24 opposite the table on the south **s** of the tabernacle,
Lev 1:11 It shall be slaughtered on the north **s** of the altar
1:15 and its blood shall be drained out against the **s** of
1:16 with its contents and throw it at the east **s** of C
5:9 the sin offering on the **s** of the altar, while the rest
Nu 2:2 the tent of meeting on every **s.** B
Nu 2:3 to camp on the east **s** toward the sunrise shall C
2:10 the south **s** shall be the regimental encampment
2:18 On the west **s** shall be the regimental encampment
2:25 On the north **s** shall be the regimental encampment
3:29 of the Kohathites were to camp on the south **s** of
3:35 they were to camp on the north **s** of the tabernacle.
10:5 the camps on the east **s** shall set out; C
10:6 the camps on the south **s** shall set out.
11:31 about a day's journey on this **s** and a day's journey
11:31 on this side and a day's journey on the other **s,** A
21:13 and camped on the other **s** of the Arnon, A
22:24 with a wall on either **s.**
32:19 with them on the other **s** of the Jordan and A
32:19 because our inheritance has come to us on this **s** of
32:32 of our inheritance shall remain with us on this **s** of
34:3 from the wilderness of Zin along the **s** of Edom.
34:11 from Shepham to Riblah on the east **s** of Ain; C
35:5 for the east **s** two thousand cubits, C
35:5 for the south **s** two thousand cubits,
35:5 for the west **s** two thousand cubits,
35:5 and for the north **s** two thousand cubits,
Dt 4:41 on the east **s** of the Jordan three cities C
4:47 the two kings of the Amorites on the eastern **s** of
4:49 the Arabah on the east **s** of the Jordan as far as C
30:13 "Who will cross to the other **s** of the sea for us, A
Jos 2:15 the outer **s** of the city wall and she resided within
8:11 and camped on the north **s** of Ai,
8:22 they were surrounded by Israelites, some on one **s,**
12:7 the Israelites defeated on the west **s** of the Jordan,
15:5 And the boundary on the north **s** runs from the bay
15:7 which is on the south **s** of the valley;
17:5 which is on the other **s** of the Jordan, A
17:9 the boundary of Manasseh goes along the north **s**
18:12 On the north **s** their boundary began at the Jordan;
18:14 on the western **s** southward from the mountain
18:14 This forms the western **s.**
18:15 southern **s** begins at the outskirts of Kiriath-jearim;
18:20 The Jordan forms its boundary on the eastern **s.**
21:44 rest on every **s** just as he had sworn to their B
22:4 the LORD gave you on the other **s** of the Jordan. A
22:11 on the **s** that belongs to the Israelites.
24:8 who lived on the other **s** of the Jordan; A
Jdg 7:5 as a dog laps, you shall put to one **s;**
7:5 you shall put to the other **s."** A
8:34 from the hand of all their enemies on every **s;** B
11:18 arrived on the east **s** of the land of Moab, C
11:18 and camped on the other **s** of the Arnon. A
Ru 2:1 Now Naomi had a kinsman on her husband's **s,**
1Sa 4:18 over backward from his seat by the **s** of the gate;
6:8 and put in a box at its **s** the figures of gold,
12:11 of the hand of your enemies on every **s;** B
14:1 over to the Philistine garrison on the other **s."** A
14:4 there was a rocky crag on one **s** and a rocky crag
14:40 He said to all Israel, "You shall be on one **s,**
14:40 I and my son Jonathan will be on the other **s."** A
14:47 he fought against all his enemies on every **s—** B
17:3 Philistines stood on the mountain on the one **s,**
17:3 and Israel stood on the mountain on the other **s,** A
20:20 I will shoot three arrows to the **s** of it,
20:21 the arrows are on this **s** of you, collect them,'
20:25 Jonathan stood, while Abner sat by Saul's **s;**
23:26 Saul went on one **s** of the mountain,
23:26 and his men on the other **s** of the mountain. A
26:13 Then David went over to the other **s,** A
31:7 the men of Israel who were on the other **s** of A
2Sa 2:13 One group sat on one **s** of the pool,
2:13 while the other sat on the other **s** of the pool. A
2:16 and thrust his sword in his opponent's **s;**
13:34 from the Horonaim road by the **s** of the mountain.
18:4 So the king stood at the **s** of the gate,
19:33 and I will provide for you in Jerusalem at my **s."**
1Ki 1:8 and David's own warriors did not **s** with Adonijah.
4:12 as far as the other **s** of Jokmeam; A
5:4 the LORD my God has given me rest on every **s;** B
6:5 and he made **s** chambers all around.
6:8 the middle story was on the south **s** of the house:
7:30 supports were cast with wreaths at the **s** of each.
7:39 the south **s** of the house, and five on the north **s** of
7:49 five on the south **s** and five on the north,
10:19 and on each **s** of the seat were arm rests
2Ki 2:8 the water was parted to the one **s** and to the other,
2:14 the water was parted to the one **s** and to the other,
9:25 and I rode **s** by **s** behind his father Ahab how
9:32 up to the window and said, "Who is on my **s?**
10:6 saying, "If you are on my **s,**
11:11 from the south **s** of the house to the north **s** of
11:11 to guard the king on every **s.** B
12:9 the right **s** as one entered the house of the LORD;
16:14 and put it on the north **s** of his altar.
1Ch 4:39 to the east **s** of the valley, C
5:9 the beginning of the desert this **s** of the Euphrates,
6:78 on the east **s** of the Jordan, C
9:18 in the king's gate on the east **s.** C
22:9 from all his enemies on every **s;** B
22:18 Has he not given you peace on every **s?** B
2Ch 4:6 and set five on the right **s,** and five on the left.
4:7 five on the south **s** and five on the north.
4:8 five on the right **s** and five on the left.
9:18 and on each **s** of the seat were arm rests
14:7 and he has given us peace on every **s."** B
23:10 from the south **s** of the house to the north **s** of
32:22 he gave them rest on every **s.** B
32:30 of Gihon and directed them down to the west **s** of
Ne 4:18 of the builders had his sword strapped at his **s**
Job 1:10 and his house and all that he has, on every **s?** B
15:10 The gray-haired and the aged are on our **s,**
18:11 Terrors frighten them on every **s,** B
Job 19:10 He breaks me down on every **s,** and I am gone, B
19:27 whom I shall see on my **s,**
Ps 12:8 On every **s** the wicked prowl, B
77:17 your arrows flashed on every **s.** B
91:7 A thousand may fall at your **s,**
97:3 and consumes his adversaries on every **s.** B
118:6 With the LORD on my **s** I do not fear.
118:7 The LORD is on my **s** to help me;
118:11 They surrounded me, surrounded me on every **s;** B
124:1 not been the LORD who was on our **s—**let Israel
124:2 if it had not been the LORD who was on our **s,**
Ecc 4:1 On the **s** of their oppressors there was power—
Jer 6:25 for the enemy has a sword, terror is on every **s."** B
49:32 I will bring calamity against them from every **s,**
51:2 against her from every **s** on the day of trouble.
Eze 1:10 the face of a lion on the right **s,**
1:10 the face of an ox on the left **s,**
4:4 Then lie on your left **s,** and place the punishment
4:6 but on your right **s,** and bear the punishment of
4:8 from one **s** to the other until you have completed
4:9 During the number of days that you lie on your **s,**
9:2 with a writing case at his **s.**
9:3 who had the writing case at his **s;**
9:11 man clothed in linen, with the writing case at his **s,**
10:3 Now the cherubim were standing on the south **s** of
10:16 the wheels at their **s** did not veer.
23:22 and I will bring them against you from every **s:**
23:24 they shall set themselves against you on every **s** B
28:23 by the sword that is against it on every **s.** B
40:10 There were three recesses on either **s** of
40:10 and the pilasters on either **s** were of the same size.
40:12 a barrier before the recesses, one cubit on either **s;**
40:12 and the recesses were six cubits on either **s.**
40:14 gate next to the pilaster on every **s** of the court. B
40:18 The pavement ran along the **s** of the gates,
40:21 Its recesses, three on either **s,**
40:26 It had palm trees on its pilasters, one on either **s.**
40:32 he brought me to the inner court on the east **s,** C
40:34 and it had palm trees on its pilasters, on either **s;**
40:37 and it had palm trees on its pilasters, on either **s;**
40:39 of the gate were two tables on either **s,**
40:40 and on the other **s** of the vestibule of A
40:41 and four tables on the outside of the **s** of the gate,
40:44 one at the **s** of the north gate facing south,
40:44 the other at the **s** of the east gate facing north.
40:48 of the vestibule, five cubits on either **s;**
40:48 sidewalls of the gate were three cubits on either **s.**
40:49 there were pillars beside the pilasters on either **s.**
41:1 on each **s** six cubits was the width of the pilasters.
41:2 of the entrance were five cubits on either **s.**
41:5 and the width of the **s** chambers, four cubits,
41:6 The **s** chambers were in three stories,
41:6 the temple to serve as supports for the **s** chambers,
41:7 of the **s** chambers widened from story to story;
41:8 the foundations of the **s** chambers measured
41:9 of the outer wall of the **s** chambers was five cubits;
41:9 free space between the **s** chambers of the temple
41:10 twenty cubits all around the temple on every **s.** B
41:11 The **s** chambers opened onto the area left free,
41:12 on the west **s** was seventy cubits wide;
41:15 together with its galleries on either **s,**
41:19 toward the palm tree on the one **s,**
41:19 toward the palm tree on the other **s.** A
41:26 and palm trees on either **s,**
42:2 that was on the north **s** was one hundred cubits,
42:4 of the chambers was a passage on the inner **s,**
42:16 He measured the east **s** with the measuring reed, C
42:17 Then he turned and measured the north **s,**
42:18 Then he turned and measured the south **s,**
42:19 Then he turned to the west **s** and measured,
46:19 which was at the **s** of the gate,
47:2 and the water was coming out on the south **s.**
47:7 of the river a great many trees on the one **s** and on
47:15 the north **s,** from the Great Sea by way of Hethlon
47:17 This shall be the north **s.**
47:18 On the east **s,** between Hauran and Damascus; C
47:18 This shall be the east **s.** C
47:19 On the south **s,** it shall run from Tamar as far as
47:19 This shall be the south **s.**
47:20 On the west **s,** the Great Sea shall be the boundary
47:20 This shall be the west **s.**
48:1 and extending from the east **s** to the west, Dan, C
48:2 the east **s** to the west, Asher, one portion. C
48:3 the east **s** to the west, Naphtali, one portion. C
48:4 the east **s** to the west, Manasseh, one portion. C
48:5 the east **s** to the west, Ephraim, one portion. C
48:6 the east **s** to the west, Reuben, one portion. C
48:7 the east **s** to the west, Judah, one portion. C
48:8 the east **s** to the west, shall be the portion C
48:8 the east **s** to the west, with the sanctuary C
48:10 on the northern **s,** ten thousand cubits in width on
48:10 ten thousand cubits in width on the western **s,**
48:10 ten thousand in width on the eastern **s,**
48:10 twenty-five thousand in length on the southern **s,**
48:16 the north **s** four thousand five hundred cubits,
48:16 the south **s** four thousand five hundred,
48:16 the east **s** four thousand five hundred, C
48:16 and the west **s** four thousand and five hundred.
48:23 the east **s** to the west, Benjamin, one portion. C
48:24 the east **s** to the west, Simeon, one portion. C
48:25 the east **s** to the west, Issachar, one portion. C
48:26 the east **s** to the west, Zebulun, one portion. C
48:27 the east **s** to the west, Gad, one portion. C
48:30 These shall be the exits of the city: On the north **s,**
48:32 On the east **s,** which is to be four thousand C
48:33 On the south **s,** which is to be four thousand
48:34 On the west **s,** which is to be four thousand

Da 7: 5 It was raised up on one **s**,
9: 7 "Righteousness is on your **s**, O Lord,
Mic 7: 9 until he takes my **s** and executes judgment for me.
Zec 5: 3 be cut off according to the writing on one **s**,
5: 3 cut off according to the writing on the other **s**. A
Mt 8:18 he gave orders to go over to the other **s**. A
8:28 When he came to the other **s**, A
14:22 into the boat and go on ahead to the other **s**, A
16: 5 When the disciples reached the other **s**, A
21:19 And seeing a fig tree by the **s** of the road,
Mk 4:35 said to them, "Let us go across to the other **s**." A
5: 1 They came to the other **s** of the sea, A
5:21 Jesus had crossed again in the boat to the other **s**, A
6:45 into the boat and go on ahead to the other **s**, A
8:13 he went across to the other **s**. A
16: 5 dressed in a white robe, sitting on the right **s**;
Lk 1:11 standing at the right **s** of the altar of incense.
8:22 "Let us go across to the other **s** of the lake." A
9:47 took a little child and put it by his **s**,
10:31 when he saw him, he passed by on the other **s**. A
10:32 passed by on the other **s**. A
16:23 and saw Abraham far away with Lazarus by his **s**.
17:24 and lights up the sky from one **s** to the other,
19:43 and hem you in on every **s**. B
Jn 6: 1 Jesus went to the other **s** of the Sea of Galilee, A
6:22 that had stayed on the other **s** of the sea saw A
6:25 When they found him on the other **s** of the sea, A
19:18 one on either **s**, with Jesus between them.
19:34 one of the soldiers pierced his **s** with a spear,
20:20 he said this, he showed them his hands and his **s**.
20:25 in the mark of the nails and my hand in his **s**,
20:27 Reach out your hand and put it in my **s**.
21: 6 "Cast the net to the right **s** of the boat,
Ac 12: 7 He tapped Peter on the **s** and woke him, saying,
Php 1:27 striving **s** by **s** with one mind for the faith of
Rev 4: 6 Around the throne, and on each **s** of the throne,
22: 2 On either **s** of the river is the tree of life
Wis 9:10 that she may labor at my **s**,
Sir 46: 5 when enemies pressed him on every **s**, B
46:16 when his enemies pressed him on every **s**, B
47: 7 For he wiped out his enemies on every **s**, B
47:19 But you brought in women to lie at your **s**,
51: 4 from choking fire on every **s**, B
51: 7 They surrounded me on every **s**, B
LtJ 6:18 on every **s** against anyone who has offended B
Sus 1:18 of the garden and went out by the **s** doors
1:26 in at the **s** door to see what had happened to her.
1:56 Then, putting him to one **s**,
1Mc 1:37 On every **s** of the sanctuary they shed innocent B
5:37 on the other **s** of the stream. A
5:41 But if he shows fear and camps on the other **s** A
6:38 The rest of the cavalry were stationed on either **s**,
9:24 and the country went over to their **s**.
9:45 the water of the Jordan is on this **s** and on that,
9:48 into the Jordan and swam across to the other **s**, A
10:20 and you are to take our **s** and keep friendship
10:63 The king also seated him at his **s**;
13:10 and he fortified it on every **s**. B
15:23 and to Phaselis, and to Cos, and to **S**,
2Mc 1:11 for taking our **s** against the king,
2:30 to discuss matters from every **s**,
3:26 on either **s** of him and flogged him continuously,
5: 3 attacks and counterattacks made on this **s** and on
10:16 and imploring God to fight on their **s**,
11:13 because the mighty God fought on their **s**.
3Mc 2:22 He shook him on this **s** and that as a reed is shaken
5: 7 they were forcibly confined on every **s**. B
2Es 4:47 And he said to me, "Stand at my right **s**,
7:*38* Look on this **s** and on that;
11:12 As I watched, one wing on the right **s** rose up,
11:20 the wings that followed also rose up on the right **s**,
11:24 under the head that was on the right **s**;
11:35 the head on the right **s** devour the one on the left.
12:29 over to the head which was on the right **s**,
14:15 to one **s** the thoughts that are most grievous to you,
16:39 and pains will seize it on every **s**. B
4Mc 3: 4 at our **s** so that we are not overcome by malice.
6: 3 they had tied his arms on each **s** they flogged him,
6: 8 and began to kick him in the **s** to make him get
9:11 and arms with thongs on each **s**.
15:32 from every **s** by the flood of your emotions and

SIDEBOARD (1) [BOARD, SIDE]

1Mc 15:32 and the **s** with its gold and silver plate,

SIDED (2) [SIDE]

Ac 14: 4 some **s** with the Jews, and some with the apostles.
1Mc 10:26 and have not **s** with our enemies,

SIDES‡ (49) [SIDE]

Ex 25:14 And you shall put the poles into the rings on the **s**
25:32 and there shall be six branches going out of its **s**,
26:13 shall hang over the **s** of the tabernacle,
27: 7 so that the poles shall be on the two **s** of the altar
29:16 and shall take its blood and dash it against all **s** of
29:20 dash the rest of the blood against all **s** of the altar.
30: 3 its top, and its **s** all around and its horns;
30: 4 on two opposite **s** of it you shall make them,
32:15 tablets that were written on both **s**,
37: 5 and put the poles into the rings on the **s** of the ark,
37:18 There were six branches going out of its **s**,
37:26 its top, and its **s** all around, and its horns;
37:27 on two opposite **s** of it,
38: 7 the rings on the **s** of the altar, to carry it with them;
Lev 1: 5 dashing the blood against all **s** of the altar that is at
Lev 1:11 the priests shall dash its blood against all **s** of
3: 2 the priests shall dash the blood against all **s** of
3: 8 and Aaron's sons shall dash its blood against all **s**
3:13 the sons of Aaron shall dash its blood against all **s**
7: 2 its blood shall be dashed against all **s** of the altar.
8:19 Moses dashed the blood against all **s** of the altar.
8:24 the rest of the blood against all **s** of the altar.
9:12 and he dashed it against all **s** of the altar.
9:18 which he dashed against all **s** of the altar,
Nu 33:55 be as barbs in your eyes and thorns in your **s**;
Jos 8:33 stood on opposite **s** of the ark in front of
23:13 a scourge on your **s**, and thorns in your eyes,
1Ki 4:24 and he had peace on all **s**.
2Ki 6:11 tell me who among us **s** with the king of Israel?"
1Ch 9:24 The gatekeepers were on the four **s**, east, west,
Ps 88:17 from all **s** they close in on me.
Jer 48:28 Be like the dove that nests on the **s** of the mouth of
50:15 Raise a shout against her from all **s**,
52:23 There were ninety-six pomegranates on the **s**;
Eze 1: 8 on their four **s** they had human hands.
36: 3 and crushed you from all **s**,
42:20 He measured it on the four **s**.
45: 7 And to the prince shall belong the land on both **s**
47:12 On the banks, on both **s** of the river,
48:21 on both **s** of the holy portion and of the property of
Heb 9: 4 the ark of the covenant overlaid on all **s** with gold,
Jdt 6: 6 and the spear of my servants shall pierce your **s**,
Sir 30:12 and beat his **s** while he is young,
1Mc 4:34 Then both **s** attacked, and there fell of the army
5:65 and burned its towers on all **s**.
6:45 and they parted before him on both **s**.
9:17 and many on both **s** were wounded and fell.
2Mc 13: 5 that on all **s** inclines precipitously into the ashes.
4Mc 6: 6 and his **s** were being cut to pieces.

SIDEWALLS (4) [SIDE, WALL]

Eze 40:48 the **s** of the gate were three cubits on either side.
41: 2 **s** of the entrance were five cubits on either side.
41: 3 and the **s** of the entrance, seven cubits.
41:26 on the **s** of the vestibule.

SIDON‡ (36) [SIDONIAN, SIDONIANS]

Ge 10:15 Canaan became the father of **S** his firstborn,
10:19 the territory of the Canaanites extended from **S**,
49:13 and his border shall be at **S**.
Jos 11: 8 as far as Great **S** and Misrephoth-maim,
19:28 Rehob, Hammon, Kanah, as far as Great **S**;
Jdg 1:31 or the inhabitants of **S**, or of Ahlab, or of Achzib,
10: 6 the gods of **S**, the gods of Moab,
18:28 from **S** and they had no dealings with Aram.
2Sa 24: 6 and from Dan they went around to **S**,
1Ki 17: 9 which belongs to **S**, and live there;
1Ch 1:13 Canaan became the father of **S** his firstborn,
Isa 23: 2 O inhabitants of the coast, O merchants of **S**,
23: 4 Be ashamed, O **S**, for the sea has spoken,
23:12 O oppressed virgin daughter **S**;
Jer 25:22 of **S**, and the kings of the coastland across the sea;
27: 3 of **S** by the hand of the envoys who have come
47: 4 from Tyre and **S** every helper that remains.
Eze 27: 8 The inhabitants of **S** and Arvad were your rowers;
28:21 set your face toward **S**, and prophesy against it,
28:22 I am against you, O **S**, and I will gain glory in
Joel 3: 4 What are you to me, O Tyre and **S**,
Zec 9: 2 Tyre and **S**, though they are very wise.
Mt 11:21 in you had been done in Tyre and **S**,
11:22 be more tolerable for Tyre and **S** than for you.
15:21 and went away to the district of Tyre and **S**.
Mk 3: 8 and the region around Tyre and **S**.
7:31 and went by way of **S** towards the Sea of Galilee,
Lk 4:26 of them except to a widow at Zarephath in **S**.
6:17 Jerusalem, and the coast of Tyre and **S**.
10:13 in you had been done in Tyre and **S**,
10:14 be more tolerable for Tyre and **S** than for you.
Ac 12:20 Herod was angry with the people of Tyre and **S**.
27: 3 The next day we put in at **S**;
Jdt 2:28 the seacoast, at **S** and Tyre, and those who lived
1Mc 5:15 that the people of Ptolemais and Tyre and **S**,
2Es 1:11 Tyre and **S**; I killed all their enemies.

SIDONIAN (1) [SIDON]

1Ki 11: 1 Moabite, Ammonite, Edomite, **S**,

SIDONIANS (16) [SIDON]

Dt 3: 9 (the **S** call Hermon Sirion,
Jos 13: 4 and Mearah that belongs to the **S**, to Aphek,
13: 6 to Misrephoth-maim, even all the **S**.
Jdg 3: 3 and all the Canaanites, and the **S**,
10:12 The **S** also, and the Amalekites, and the Maonites,
18: 7 after the manner of the **S**, quiet and unsuspecting,
18: 7 they were far from the **S** and had no dealings
1Ki 5: 6 how to cut timber like the **S**."
11: 5 Solomon followed Astarte the goddess of the **S**,
11:33 worshiped Astarte the goddess of the **S**,
16:31 of King Ethbaal of the **S**,
2Ki 23:13 for Astarte the abomination of the **S**,
1Ch 22: 4 for the **S** and Tyrians brought great quantities
Ezr 3: 7 to the **S** and the Tyrians to bring cedar trees
Eze 32:30 all of them, and all the **S**,
1Es 5:55 and carts to the **S** and the Tyrians,

SIEGE (48) [BESIEGE, BESIEGED, BESIEGERS, BESIEGES, BESIEGING, SIEGEWORKS]

Dt 20:19 that they should come under **s** from you?
Dt 28:53 to which the enemy **s** reduces you,
28:55 the enemy **s** will reduce you in all your towns.
28:57 the enemy **s** will reduce you in your towns.
Jos 10:31 and all Israel with him, to Lachish, and laid **s** to it,
10:34 and they laid **s** to it, and assaulted it;
2Sa 20:15 they threw up a **s** ramp against the city,
1Ki 15:27 Nadab and all Israel were laying **s** to Gibbethon.
20: 1 He marched against Samaria, laid **s** to it,
2Ki 6:24 he marched against Samaria and laid **s** to it.
6:25 As the **s** continued, famine in Samaria became
19:32 or cast up a **s** ramp against it.
25: 1 with all his army against Jerusalem, and laid **s**
2Ch 32:10 that you undergo the **s** of Jerusalem?
Ps 31:21 to me when I was beset as a city under **s**.
Isa 21: 2 Go up, O Elam, lay **s**, O Media;
23:13 They erected their **s** towers,
37:33 or cast up a **s** ramp against it.
Jer 6: 6 cast up a **s** ramp against Jerusalem.
10:17 O you who live under **s**!
19: 9 all shall eat the flesh of their neighbors in the **s**,
32:24 the **s** ramps have been cast up against the city
33: 4 to make a defense against the **s** ramps and before
52: 4 and they laid **s** to it;
Eze 4: 2 and build a **s** wall against it,
4: 3 let it be in a state of **s**, and press the **s** against it.
4: 7 You shall set your face toward the **s** of Jerusalem,
4: 8 until you have completed the days of your **s**.
5: 2 when the days of the **s** are completed;
17:17 up and **s** walls built to cut off many lives.
21:22 to cast up ramps, to build **s** towers.
24: 2 of Babylon has laid **s** to Jerusalem this very day.
26: 8 He shall set up a **s** wall against you,
Mic 5: 1 with a wall; **s** is laid against us;
Na 3:14 Draw water for the **s**, strengthen your forts;
Zec 12: 2 be against Judah also in the **s** against Jerusalem.
Sir 50: 4 and fortified the city against **s**.
1Mc 6:20 and he built **s** towers and other engines of war.
6:21 of the garrison escaped from the **s** and some of
6:49 to withstand a **s**, since it was a sabbatical year for
6:51 He set up **s** towers, engines of war to throw fire
11:22 and he wrote Jonathan not to continue the **s**,
11:23 he gave orders to continue the **s**.
13:43 He made a **s** engine, brought it up to the city,
13:44 The men in the **s** engine leaped out into the city,
2Mc 10:18 strong towers well equipped to withstand a **s**,
4Mc 17:24 and courageous for infantry battle and **s**,

SIEGEWORKS (8) [SIEGE]

Dt 20:20 in building **s** against the town that makes war
2Ki 25: 1 they built **s** against it all around.
Job 19:12 they have thrown up **s** against me,
Ecc 9:14 building great **s** against it.
Isa 29: 3 I will besiege you with towers and raise **s**
Jer 52: 4 they built **s** against it all around.
Eze 4: 2 and put **s** against it, and build a siege wall
Da 11:15 the king of the north shall come and throw up **s**,

SIEVE (3)

Isa 30:28 to sift the nations with the **s** of destruction,
Am 9: 9 as one shakes with a **s**, but no pebble shall fall to
Sir 27: 4 When a **s** is shaken, the refuse appears;

SIFT (3) [SIFTED]

Jdg 7: 4 take them down to the water and I will **s** them out
Isa 30:28 to **s** the nations with the sieve of destruction,
Lk 22:31 Satan has demanded to **s** all of you like wheat,

SIFTED (1) [SIFT]

Jdg 7: 3 Thus Gideon **s** them out; twenty-two thousand

SIGH‡ (4) [SIGHED, SIGHING, SIGHS]

Ps 90: 9 our years come to an end like a **s**.
Isa 24: 7 the vine languishes, all the merry-hearted **s**.
Eze 9: 4 of those who **s** and groan over all the abominations
24:17 **S**, but not aloud; make no mourning for the dead.

SIGHED (2) [SIGH]

Mk 7:34 Then looking up to heaven, he **s** and said to him,
8:12 And he **s** deeply in his spirit and said,

SIGHING (9) [SIGH]

Job 3:24 For my **s** comes like my bread,
Ps 5: 1 O LORD; give heed to my **s**.
31:10 my life is spent with sorrow, and my years with **s**;
38: 9 my **s** is not hidden from you.
Isa 21: 2 all the **s** she has caused I bring to an end.
35:10 and sorrow and **s** shall flee away.
51:11 and sorrow and **s** shall flee away.
Heb 13:17 Let them do this with joy and not with **s**—
Sir 25:18 and he cannot help **s** bitterly.

SIGHS‡ (1) [SIGH]

Ro 8:26 very Spirit intercedes with **s** too deep for words.

SIGHT‡ (359) [SEE]

A. EVIL IN THE SIGHT OF THE †LORD (53)

Ge 2: 9 that is pleasant to the **s** and good for food,
6: 8 But Noah found favor in the **s** of the LORD.
6:11 Now the earth was corrupt in God's **s**,
17:18 "O that Ishmael might live in your **s**!"
23: 4 so that I may bury my dead out of my **s**."

Ge 23: 8 that I should bury my dead out of my s,
32: 5 in order that I may find favor in your s.' "
38: 7 was wicked in the s of the LORD,
38:10 What he did was displeasing in the s of the LORD,
39: 4 So Joseph found favor in his s and attended him;
39:21 he gave him favor in the s of the chief jailer.
44:32 the blame in the s of my father all my life.'
47:18 in the s of my lord but our bodies and our lands.
Ex 3: 3 "I must turn aside and look at this great s,
4:30 and performed the signs in the s of the people.
7:20 In the s of Pharaoh and of his officials he lifted up
8:26 the s of the Egyptians sacrifices that are offensive
9: 8 let Moses throw it in the air in the s of Pharaoh.
11: 3 The LORD gave the people favor in the s of
11: 3 in the s of Pharaoh's officials and in the s of the
12:36 and the LORD had given the people favor in the s
15:26 and do what is right in his s,
17: 6 Moses did so, in the s of the elders of Israel.
19:11 down upon Mount Sinai in the s of all the people.
24:17 a devouring fire on the top of the mountain in the s
33:12 and you have also found favor in my s.'
33:13 Now if I have found favor in your s,
33:13 so that I may know you and find favor in your s.
33:16 shall it be known that I have found favor in your s,
33:17 for you have found favor in my s,
34: 9 He said, "If now I have found favor in your s,
Lev 20:17 and they shall be cut off in the s of their people;
25:53 however, rule with harshness over them in your s.
26:45 of Egypt in the s of the nations, to be their God:
Nu 11:11 Why have I not found favor in your s,
11:15 if I have found favor in your s—
19: 5 Then the heifer shall be burned in his s;
20:27 up Mount Hor in the s of the whole congregation.
25: 6 in the s of Moses and in the s of the whole
27:19 and commission him in their s.
32: 5 "If we have found favor in your s,
32:13 that had done evil in the s of the LORD A
33: 3 the passover the Israelites went out boldly in the s
Dt 4:25 thus doing what is evil in the s of the LORD A
6:18 Do what is right and good in the s of the LORD,
9:18 the LORD by doing what was evil in his s.
12:25 you do what is right in the s of the LORD.
12:28 and right in the s of the LORD your God.
13:18 in the s of the LORD your God.
17: 2 who does what is evil in the s of the LORD A
21: 9 you must do what is right in the s of the LORD.
25: 3 your neighbor will be degraded in your s.
28:34 and driven mad by the s that your eyes shall see.
31: 7 and said to him in the s of all Israel:
31:29 you will do what is evil in the s of the LORD, A
34: 7 his s was unimpaired and his vigor had not abated.
34:12 that Moses performed in the s of all Israel.
Jos 3: 7 "This day I will begin to exalt you in the s
4:14 the LORD exalted Joshua in the s of all Israel;
9:25 as it seems good and right in your s to do to us."
10:12 and he said in the s of Israel, "Sun,
23: 5 and drive them out of your s;
24:17 and who did those great signs in our s.
Jdg 2:11 was evil in the s of the LORD and worshiped A
3: 7 Israelites did what was evil in the s of the LORD, A
3:12 again did what was evil in the s of the LORD; A
3:12 had done what was evil in the s of the LORD. A
4: 1 again did what was evil in the s of the LORD, A
6: 1 Israelites did what was evil in the s of the LORD, A
6:21 and the angel of the LORD vanished from his s.
10: 6 again did what was evil in the s of the LORD, A
13: 1 again did what was evil in the s of the LORD, A
Ru 2: 2 behind someone in whose s I may find favor."
2:10 "Why have I found favor in your s,
2:13 she said, "May I continue to find favor in your s,
1Sa 1:18 she said, "Let your servant find favor in your s."
2:17 the sin of the young men was very great in the s of
12:17 in the s of the LORD is great in demanding a king
15:19 and do what was evil in the s of the LORD?" A
16:22 for he has found favor in my s."
20:29 So now, if I have found favor in your s,
25: 8 Therefore let my young men find favor in your s;
26:21 because my life was precious in your s today;
26:24 As your life was precious today in my s,
26:24 so may my life be precious in the s of the LORD,
27: 5 "If I have found favor in your s,
29: 9 that you are as blameless in my s as an angel
2Sa 12: 9 to do what is evil in his s?
12:11 with your wives in the s of this very sun.
13: 5 and prepare the food in my s,
13: 6 and make a couple of cakes in my s,
13: 8 She took dough, kneaded it, made cakes in his s,
14:22 that I have found favor in your s,
16: 4 let me find favor in your s, my lord the king."
16:22 in to his father's concubines in the s of all Israel.
22:25 according to my cleanness in his s.
1Ki 8:50 grant them compassion in the s of their captors,
9: 7 for my name I will cast out of my s;
11: 6 Solomon did what was evil in the s of the LORD, A
11:19 Hadad found great favor in the s of Pharaoh,
11:33 in my s and keeping my statutes
11:38 in my s by keeping my statutes
14: 8 doing only that which was right in my s,
14:22 Judah did what was evil in the s of the LORD; A
15: 5 David did what was right in the s of the LORD,
15:11 Asa did what was right in the s of the LORD,
15:26 He did what was evil in the s of the LORD, A
15:34 He did what was evil in the s of the LORD, A
16: 7 of all the evil that he did in the s of the LORD,
16:19 doing evil in the s of the LORD, A
16:25 Omri did what was evil in the s of the LORD; A
16:30 of Omri did evil in the s of the LORD more than A

1Ki 21:20 to do what is evil in the s of the LORD, A
21:25 to do what was evil in the s of the LORD, A
22:43 doing what was right in the s of the LORD;
22:52 He did what was evil in the s of the LORD, A
2Ki 1:13 of yours, be precious in your s.
1:14 but now let my life be precious in your s."
3: 2 He did what was evil in the s of the LORD, A
3:18 This is only a trifle in the s of the LORD,
8:18 He did what was evil in the s of the LORD. A
8:27 doing what was evil in the s of the LORD, A
12: 2 Jehoash did what was right in the s of the LORD
13: 2 He did what was evil in the s of the LORD, A
13:11 He also did what was evil in the s of the LORD; A
14: 3 He did what was right in the s of the LORD,
14:24 He did what was evil in the s of the LORD; A
15: 3 He did what was right in the s of the LORD,
15: 9 He did what was evil in the s of the LORD, A
15:18 He did what was evil in the s of the LORD; A
15:24 He did what was evil in the s of the LORD; A
15:28 He did what was evil in the s of the LORD; A
15:34 He did what was right in the s of the LORD,
16: 2 He did not do what was right in the s of the LORD
17: 2 He did what was evil in the s of the LORD, A
17:17 themselves to do evil in the s of the LORD, A
17:18 with Israel and removed them out of his s;
17:23 until the LORD removed Israel out of his s,
18: 3 He did what was right in the s of the LORD just
20: 3 and have done what is good in your s."
21: 2 He did what was evil in the s of the LORD, A
21: 6 He did much evil in the s of the LORD, A
21:15 because they have done what is evil in my s
21:16 that they did what was evil in the s of the LORD. A
21:20 He did what was evil in the s of the LORD, A
22: 2 He did what was right in the s of the LORD,
23:27 "I will remove Judah also out of my s,
23:32 He did what was evil in the s of the LORD, A
23:37 He did what was evil in the s of the LORD, A
24: 3 to remove them out of his s,
24: 9 He did what was evil in the s of the LORD, A
24:19 He did what was evil in the s of the LORD, A
1Ch 2: 3 was wicked in the s of the LORD,
17:17 And even this was a small thing in your s, O God;
22: 8 you have shed so much blood in my s on the earth.
28: 8 Now therefore in the s of all Israel,
29:25 The LORD highly exalted Solomon in the s
2Ch 7:20 I will cast out of my s,
14: 2 Asa did what was good and right in the s of
20:32 doing what was right in the s of the LORD.
21: 6 He did what was evil in the s of the LORD. A
22: 4 He did what was evil in the s of the LORD, A
24: 2 Joash did what was right in the s of the LORD all
25: 2 He did what was right in the s of the LORD,
26: 4 He did what was right in the s of the LORD,
27: 2 He did what was right in the s of the LORD just
28: 1 not do what was right in the s of the LORD,
29: 2 He did what was right in the s of the LORD,
29: 6 have done what was evil in the s of the LORD A
32:23 so that he was exalted in the s of all nations from
33: 2 He did what was evil in the s of the LORD, A
33: 6 He did much evil in the s of the LORD, A
33:22 He did what was evil in the s of the LORD, A
34: 2 He did what was right in the s of the LORD,
36: 5 He did what was evil in the s of the LORD A
36: 9 He did what was evil in the s of the LORD. A
36:12 He did what was evil in the s of the LORD A
Ne 1:11 and grant him mercy in the s of this man!"
4: 5 and do not let their sin be blotted out from your s;
8: 5 Ezra opened the book in the s of all the people,
Job 11: 4 'My conduct is pure, and I am clean in God's s.'
15:15 and the heavens are not clean in his s;
18: 3 Why are we stupid in your s?
25: 5 not bright and the stars are not pure in his s,
30:10 they do not hesitate to spit at the s of me.
41: 9 were not even the gods overwhelmed at the s of it?
Ps 10: 5 your judgments are on high, out of their s;
18:24 according to the cleanness of my hands in his s.
31:19 for those who take refuge in you, in the s
31:22 "I am driven far from your s."
39: 5 and my lifetime is as nothing in your s.
44:16 at the s of the enemy and the avenger.
51: 4 have I sinned, and done what is evil in your s,
72:14 and precious is their blood in his s.
78:12 In the s of their ancestors he worked marvels in
90: 4 For a thousand years in your s are like yesterday
98: 2 he has revealed his vindication in the s of
116:15 Precious in the s of the LORD is the death
Pr 3: 4 So you will find favor and good repute in the s
3:21 My child, do not let these escape from your s:
4:21 Do not let them escape from your s;
21: 2 All deeds are right in the s of the doer,
Ecc 6: 9 the s of the eyes than the wandering of desire;
Isa 5:21 and shrewd in your own s!
32: 3 the eyes of those who have s will not be closed,
38: 3 and have done what is good in your s."
43: 4 Because you are precious in my s, and honored,
49: 5 for I am honored in the s of the LORD,
52: 8 in plain s they see the return of the LORD to Zion.
65:12 but you did what was evil in my s,
65:16 and are hidden from my s.
66: 4 but they did what was evil in my s,
Jer 7:11 become a den of robbers in your s?
7:15 And I will cast you out of my s,
7:30 For the people of Judah have done evil in my s,
15: 1 Send them out of my s, and let them go!
16:17 nor is their iniquity concealed from my s.
18:10 but if it does evil in my s,
18:23 do not blot out their sin from your s.

Jer 19:10 the jug in the s of those who go with you,
32:30 of Judah have done nothing but evil in my s
32:31 so that I will remove it from my s
34:15 in my s by proclaiming liberty to one another,
44:22 the s of your evil doings, the abominations
52: 2 He did what was evil in the s of the LORD, A
Eze 4:12 baking it in their s on human dung.
5: 8 I will execute judgments among you in the s of
5:14 in the s of all that pass by.
6: 9 Then they will be loathsome in their own s for
10:19 the earth in my s as they went out with the wheels
12: 3 and go into exile by day in their s;
12: 3 from your place to another place in their s.
12: 4 by day in their s, as baggage for exile;
12: 4 and you shall go out yourself at evening in their s,
12: 5 Dig through the wall in their s,
12: 6 In their s you shall lift the baggage
12: 7 carrying it on my shoulder in their s.
16:41 and execute judgments on you in the s
20: 9 in the s of the nations among whom they lived, in whose s I made myself known to them
20:14 it should not be profaned in the s of the nations, in whose s I had brought them out.
20:22 it should not be profaned in the s of the nations, in whose s I had brought them out.
20:41 among you in the s of the nations.
22:16 be profaned through you in the s of the nations;
28:18 to ashes on the earth in the s of all who saw you.
28:25 and manifest my holiness in them in the s of
36:17 their conduct in my s was like the uncleanness of
36:34 instead of being the desolation that it was in the s
39:27 through them have displayed my holiness in the s
43:11 and write it down in their s,
Hos 2:10 I will uncover her shame in the s of her lovers,
Am 9: 3 they hide from my s at the bottom of the sea,
Jnh 2: 4 Then I said, 'I am driven away from your s;
Zep 3: 7 it will not lose s of all that I have brought upon it."
Hag 2: 3 Is it not in your s as nothing?
Mal 2:17 "All who do evil are good in the s of the LORD,
Mt 11: 5 the blind receive their s, the lame walk,
20:34 Immediately they regained their s
Mk 8:25 and he looked intently and his s was restored,
10:52 Immediately he regained his s and followed him
Lk 1:15 for he will be great in the s of the Lord.
4:18 to the captives and recovery of s to the blind,
7:21 and had given s to many who were blind.
7:22 the blind receive their s, the lame walk,
12: 6 Yet not one of them is forgotten in God's s.
16:15 "You are those who justify yourselves in the s
16:15 by human beings is an abomination in the s
18:42 Jesus said to him, "Receive your s;
18:43 Immediately he regained his s and followed him,
24:31 and he vanished from their s.
Jn 9:11 Then I went and washed and received my s."
9:15 also began to ask him how he had received his s.
9:18 and had received his s until they called the parents of the man who had received his s
Ac 1: 9 and a cloud took him out of their s.
4:19 in God's s to listen to you rather than to God,
7:31 When Moses saw it, he was amazed at the s;
9: 9 For three days he was without s,
9:12 on him so that he might regain his s."
9:17 so that you may regain your s and be filled with
9:18 from his eyes, and his s was restored.
21: 3 We came in s of Cyprus;
22:13 he said, 'Brother Saul, regain your s!'
22:13 In that very hour I regained my s and saw him.
Ro 2:13 of the law who are righteous in God's s,
3:20 justified in his s" by deeds prescribed by the law,
12:17 but take thought for what is noble in the s of all.
2Co 4: 2 to the conscience of everyone in the s of God.
5: 7 for we walk by faith, not by s.
8:21 to do what is right not only in the Lord's s but also
8:21 in the Lord's sight but also in the s of others.
Gal 1:22 by s to the churches of Judea that are in Christ;
1Ti 2: 3 and is acceptable in the s of God our Savior,
5: 4 for this is pleasing in God's s.
Heb 12:21 Indeed, so terrifying was the s that Moses said,
13:21 working among us that which is pleasing in his s,
1Pe 2: 4 by mortals yet chosen and precious in God's s,
3: 4 which is very precious in God's s.
Rev 3: 2 not found your works perfect in the s of my God.
13:13 down from heaven to earth in the s of all;
Tob 4:21 from every sin and do what is good in the s of
10:12 In the s of the Lord I entrust my daughter to you;
11: 6 When she caught s of him coming,
11: 8 and your father will regain his s and see the light."
11:17 to him and had restored his s.
14:8,9 and do what is pleasing in his s.
Jdt 5:12 So the Egyptians drove them out of their s.
10:10 where they lost s of her.
AdE 5: 8 if I have found favor in the s of the king,
Wis 2:15 the very s of him is a burden to us,
3: 4 For though in the s of others they were punished,
7: 9 because all gold is but a little sand in her s,
8:11 and in the s of rulers I shall be admired.
9: 9 she understands what is pleasing in your s
11:19 but the mere s of them could kill by fright.
17:17 They were stricken also with loss of s—
19:18 be clearly inferred from the s of what took place.
Sir 3:18 so you will find favor in the s of the Lord.
11:21 the s of the Lord to make the poor rich suddenly,
25: 1 they are beautiful in the s of God and of mortals:
43: 1 as glorious to behold as the s of the heavens.
44:23 who found favor in the s of all
46: 6 that he was fighting in the s of the Lord;
Bar 1:12 and find favor in their s.

Bar 1:22 and doing what is evil in the s of the Lord
2:14 in the s of those who have carried us into exile;
LtJ 6:37 They cannot restore s to the blind;
Aza 1:17 such may our sacrifice be in your s today,
Sus 1:23 rather than sin in the s of the Lord."
1Mc 2:23 a Jew came forward in the s of all to offer sacrifice
3:18 for in the s of Heaven there is no difference
11:51 So the Jews gained glory in the s of the king and
1Es 1:23 deeds of Josiah were upright in the s of the Lord,
1:39 he did what was evil in the s of the Lord.
1:44 He did what was evil in the s of the Lord.
1:47 He also did what was evil in the s of the Lord,
8:26 and who honored me in the s of the king
9:45 Then Ezra took up the book of the law in the s of
Man 1:10 and have done what is evil in your s,
3Mc 4:4 that at the s of their unusual punishments,
2Es 1:34 and have done what is evil in my s.
2:3 the Lord God and have done what is evil in my s.
3:8 in your s and rejected your commands,
3:13 when they were committing iniquity in your s,
3:35 the inhabitants of the earth not sinned in your s?
4:44 "If I have found favor in your s,
5:56 O Lord, if I have found favor in your s,
6:11 "O sovereign Lord, if I have found favor in your s,
7:*75* "If I have found favor in your s, O Lord,
7:*102* "If I have found favor in your s,
7:*104* "Since you have found favor in my s,
8:28 of those who have lived wickedly in your s,
8:42 "If I have found favor in your s, let me speak.
12:7 "O sovereign Lord, if I have found favor in your s,
15:28 What a terrifying s, appearing from the east!

SIGHTS (1) [SEE]

Dt 28:67 of the dread that your heart shall feel and the s

SIGN‡ (100) [SIGNATURE, SIGNED, SIGNPOST, SIGNS]

Ge 9:12 the s of the covenant that I make between me
9:13 and it shall be a s of the covenant between me and
9:17 the s of the covenant that I have established
17:11 it shall be a s of the covenant between me and you.
Ex 3:12 this shall be the s for you that it is I who sent you:
4:8 "If they will not believe you or heed the first s,
4:8 they may believe the second s.
8:23 This s shall appear tomorrow.' "
12:13 The blood shall be a s for you on the houses
13:9 It shall serve for you as a s on your hand and as
13:16 It shall serve as a s on your hand and as
31:13 "You shall keep my sabbaths, for this is a s
31:17 a s forever between me and the people of Israel
Nu 16:38 Thus they shall be a s to the Israelites.
Dt 6:8 Bind them as a s on your hand,
11:18 and you shall bind them as a s on your hand,
28:46 and your descendants as a s and a portent forever.
Jos 2:12 Give me a s of good faith
4:6 so that this may be a s among you.
Jdg 6:17 then show me a s that it is you who speak with me.
1Sa 2:34 Hophni and Phinehas, shall be the s to you—
10:1 the s to you that the LORD has anointed you ruler
14:10 That will be the s for us."
1Ki 13:3 He gave a s the same day, saying,
13:3 saying, "This is the s that the LORD has spoken:
13:5 the s that the man of God had given by the word of
2Ki 4:31 but there was no sound or s of life.
19:29 "And this shall be the s for you:
20:8 "What shall be the s that the LORD will heal me,
20:9 Isaiah said, "This is the s to you from the LORD,
2Ch 32:24 and he answered him and gave him a s.
32:31 to him to inquire about the s that had been done in
Job 37:7 serves as a s on everyone's hand,
Ps 86:17 Show me a s of your favor,
Isa 7:11 Ask a s of the LORD your God;
7:14 Therefore the Lord himself will give you a s.
19:20 a s and a witness to the LORD of hosts in the land
20:3 for three years as a s and a portent against Egypt
37:30 "And this shall be the s for you:
38:7 "This is the s to you from the LORD,
38:22 "What is the s that I shall go up to the house of
55:13 for an everlasting s that shall not be cut off.
66:19 and I will set a s among them.
Jer 44:29 This shall be the s to you, says the LORD,
Eze 4:3 This is a s for the house of Israel.
12:6 for I have made you a s for the house of Israel.
12:11 Say, "I am a s for you:
14:8 a s and a byword and cut them off from the midst
20:12 as a s between me and them,
20:20 and hallow my sabbaths that they may be a s
24:24 Thus Ezekiel shall be a s to you;
24:27 So you shall be a s to them;
39:15 anyone who sees a human bone shall set up a s
Da 6:8 O king, establish the interdict and s the document,
6:12 Did you not s an interdict,
Mt 12:38 "Teacher, we wish to see a s from you."
12:39 adulterous generation asks for a s, but no s will be given to it except the s of the prophet Jonah.
16:1 and to test Jesus they asked him to show them a s
16:4 An evil and adulterous generation asks for a s, but no s will be given to it except the s of Jonah."
24:3 the s of your coming and of the end of the age?"
24:30 the s of the Son of Man will appear in heaven,
26:48 Now the betrayer had given them a s, saying,
Mk 8:11 asking him for a s from heaven, to test him.
8:12 "Why does this generation ask for a s?
8:12 no s will be given to this generation."
13:4 and what will be the s that all these things are
14:44 Now the betrayer had given them a s, saying,
Lk 2:12 This will be a s for you:
2:34 and to be a s that will be opposed
11:16 kept demanding from him a s from heaven.
11:29 it asks for a s, but no s will be given to it except the s of Jonah.
11:30 just as Jonah became a s to the people of Nineveh,
21:7 what will be the s that this is about to take place?"
23:8 and was hoping to see him perform some s.
Jn 2:18 "What s can you show us for doing this?"
4:54 Now this was the second s that Jesus did
6:14 When the people saw the s that he had done,
6:30 "What s are you going to give us then,
10:41 and they were saying, "John performed no s,
12:18 that he had performed this s that the crowd went
Ac 4:16 that a notable s has been done through them;
4:22 For the man on whom this s
Ro 4:11 the s of circumcision as a seal of the righteousness
1Co 14:22 then, are a s not for believers but for unbelievers,
AdE 14:16 that I abhor the s of my proud position,
Wis 5:11 and afterward no s of its coming is found there;
5:13 ceased to be, and we had no s of virtue to show,
Sir 13:26 The s of a happy heart is a cheerful face,
43:6 governing the times, their everlasting s.
43:7 From the moon comes the s for festal days,
2Mc 6:13 a s of great kindness not to let the impious alone
15:35 a clear and conspicuous s to everyone of the help
3Mc 6:32 they formed choruses as a s of peaceful joy.
2Es 1:15 The quails were a s to you;

SIGNAL (11) [SIGNALED]

Isa 5:26 He will raise a s for a nation far away,
11:10 the root of Jesse shall stand as a s to the peoples;
11:12 He will raise a s for the nations,
13:2 On a bare hill raise a s, cry aloud to them;
18:3 when a s is raised on the mountains, look!
30:17 like a s on a hill.
49:22 and raise my s to the peoples;
Jer 6:1 and raise a s on Beth-haccherem;
Zec 10:8 I will s for them and gather them in,
1Mc 4:40 And when the s was given with the trumpets,
2Mc 4:14 in the wrestling arena after the s for

SIGNALED (1) [SIGNAL]

Lk 5:7 So they s their partners in the other boat to come

SIGNATURE (1) [SIGN]

Job 31:35 (Here is my s! let the Almighty answer me!)

SIGNED (7) [SIGN]

Jer 32:10 I s the deed, sealed it, got witnesses,
32:12 in the presence of the witnesses who s the deed
32:44 and deeds shall be s and sealed and witnessed,
Da 6:9 King Darius s the document and interdict.
6:10 Daniel knew that the document had been s,
6:13 O king, or to the interdict you have s,
2Mc 11:17 have delivered your s communication

SIGNET (23) [SIGNETS]

Ge 38:18 She replied, "Your s and your cord,
38:25 whose these are, the s and the cord and the staff."
41:42 Removing his s ring from his hand,
Ex 28:36 like the engraving of a s, "Holy to the LORD."
35:22 and earrings and s rings and pendants,
39:6 and engraved like the engravings of a s,
39:30 like the engraving of a s, "Holy to the LORD."
Nu 31:50 articles of gold, armlets and bracelets, s rings,
Est 3:10 the king took his s ring from his hand and gave it
8:2 Then the king took off his s ring,
Isa 3:21 the s rings and nose rings;
Jer 22:24 of Judah were the s ring on my right hand,
Eze 28:12 You were the s of perfection,
Da 6:17 with his own s and with the s of his lords,
Hag 2:23 says the LORD, and make you like a s ring;
Tob 1:22 Now Ahikar was chief cupbearer, keeper of the s,
AdE 3:10 the king took off his s ring and gave it to Haman
Sir 17:22 One's almsgiving is like a s ring with the Lord,
49:11 He was like a s ring on the right hand,
Bel 1:11 and shut the door and seal it with your s.
1:14 shut the door and sealed it with the king's s,
1Mc 6:15 He gave him the crown and his robe and the s,

SIGNETS (4) [SIGNET]

Ex 28:11 As a gem-cutter engraves s,
28:21 they shall be like s, each engraved with its name,
39:14 they were like s, each engraved with its name,
Sir 38:27 those who cut the s of seals,

SIGNIFICANCE (1)

2Es 7:*127* [57] "This is the s of the contest that all who are

SIGNIFICATION (KJV) See SOUND

SIGNIFY (KJV) See INDICATED, INDICATING, MAKING PUBLIC, NOTIFY

SIGNPOST (1) [POST, SIGN]

Eze 21:19 a s, make it for a fork in the road leading to a city;

SIGNS‡ (94) [SIGN]

Ge 1:14 and let them be for s and for seasons and for days
Ex 4:9 they will not believe even these two s or heed you,
4:17 with which you shall perform the s."
4:28 and all the s with which he had charged him.
4:30 and performed the s in the sight of the people.
7:3 and I will multiply my s and wonders in the land
10:1 of his officials, in order that I may show these s
10:2 of the Egyptians and what s I have done
Nu 14:11 in spite of all the s that I have done among them?
14:22 and the s that I did in Egypt and in the wilderness,
Dt 4:34 by trials, by s and wonders, by war,
6:22 before our eyes great and awesome s and wonders
7:19 the s and wonders, the mighty hand and
11:3 his s and his deeds that he did in Egypt to Pharaoh,
26:8 with a terrifying display of power, and with s
29:3 the s, and those great wonders.
34:11 for all the s and wonders that the LORD sent him
Jos 24:17 and who did those great s in our sight.
1Sa 10:7 Now when these s meet you,
10:9 and all these s were fulfilled that day.
Ne 9:10 You performed s and wonders against Pharaoh
Ps 65:8 at earth's farthest bounds are awed by your s;
78:43 when he displayed his s in Egypt,
105:27 They performed his s among them,
135:9 he sent s and wonders into your midst,
Isa 8:18 the children whom the LORD has given me are s
Jer 10:2 or be dismayed at the s of the heavens;
32:20 You showed s and wonders in the land of Egypt,
32:21 of Egypt with s and wonders, with a strong hand
Da 4:2 The s and wonders that the Most High God has
4:3 How great are his s, how mighty his wonders!
6:27 he works s and wonders in heaven and on earth;
Mt 16:3 but you cannot interpret the s of the times.
24:24 and false prophets will appear and produce great s
Mk 13:22 and false prophets will appear and produce s
16:17 ⟦And these s will accompany those who believe:⟧
16:20 ⟦with them and confirmed the message by the s⟧
Lk 21:11 and there will be dreadful portents and great s
21:25 "There will be s in the sun, the moon,
Jn 2:11 Jesus did this, the first of his s, in Cana of Galilee,
2:23 many believed in his name because they saw the s
3:2 for no one can do these s that you do apart from
4:48 you see s and wonders you will not believe."
6:2 they saw the s that he was doing for the sick.
6:26 you are looking for me, not because you saw s,
7:31 will he do more s than this man has done?"
9:16 "How can a man who is a sinner perform such s?"
11:47 This man is performing many s.
12:37 he had performed so many s in their presence,
20:30 Now Jesus did many other s in the presence
Ac 2:19 in the heaven above and s on the earth below,
2:22 and s that God did through him among you,
2:43 because many wonders and s were being done by
4:30 and s and wonders are performed through
5:12 Now many s and wonders were done among
6:8 did great wonders and s among the people.
7:36 having performed wonders and s in Egypt,
8:6 hearing and seeing the s that he did,
8:13 with Philip and was amazed when he saw the s
14:3 who testified to the word of his grace by granting s
15:12 the s and wonders that God had done through them
Ro 15:19 by the power of s and wonders,
1Co 1:22 For Jews demand s and Greeks desire wisdom,
2Co 12:12 The s of a true apostle were performed among you
12:12 s and wonders and mighty works.
2Th 2:9 who uses all power, s, lying wonders,
Heb 2:4 while God added his testimony by s and wonders
Rev 13:13 It performs great s, even making fire come down
13:14 and by the s that it is allowed to perform on behalf
16:14 These are demonic spirits, performing s,
19:20 prophet who had performed in its presence the s
AdE 10:9 God has done great s and wonders,
Wis 2:9 everywhere let us leave s of enjoyment,
8:8 of s and wonders and of the outcome of seasons
10:16 and withstood dread kings with wonders and s.
19:13 upon the sinners without prior s in the violence
Sir 36:6 Give new s, and work other wonders;
48:12 He performed twice as many s,
Bar 2:11 of the land of Egypt with a mighty hand and with s
LtJ 6:67 they cannot show s in the heavens for the nations,
2Es 1:35 I have shown no s will do what I have commanded.
4:52 "Concerning the s about which you ask me,
5:1 "Now concerning the s: lo,
5:13 These are the s that I am permitted to tell you,
6:12 the last of your s of which you showed me a part
6:20 then I will show these s:
7:26 the s that I have foretold to you will come to pass,
8:63 a great number of the s that you will do in
9:1 that some of the predicted s have occurred,
9:6 and the end in penalties and in s.
13:32 When these things take place and the s occur
13:44 at that time the Most High performed s for them,
14:8 Lay up in your heart the s that I have shown you,
4Mc 15:19 saw in their nostrils the s of the approach of death.

SIHON (37)

Nu 21:21 Israel sent messengers to King S of the Amorites,
21:23 But S would not allow Israel to pass
21:23 S gathered all his people together,
21:26 Heshbon was the city of King S of the Amorites,
21:27 let the city of S be established.
21:28 flame from the city of S.
21:29 and his daughters captives, to an Amorite king, S.
21:34 to him as you did to King S of the Amorites,
32:33 the kingdom of King S of the Amorites and
Dt 1:4 after he had defeated King S of the Amorites,
2:24 I have handed over to you King S the Amorite

Dt 2:26 the wilderness of Kedemoth to King S of Heshbon
2:30 But King S of Heshbon was not willing
2:31 I have begun to give S and his land over to you.
2:32 So when S came out against us,
3: 2 Do to him as you did to King S of the Amorites,
3: 6 as we had done to King S of Heshbon,
4:46 in the land of King S of the Amorites,
29: 7 King S of Heshbon and King Og
31: 4 LORD will do to them as he did to S and Og,
Jos 2:10 to S and Og, whom you utterly destroyed.
9:10 the Amorites who were beyond the Jordan, King S
12: 2 King S of the Amorites who lived at Heshbon,
12: 5 and over half of Gilead to the boundary of King S
13:10 the cities of King S of the Amorites, who reigned
13:21 and all the kingdom of King S of the Amorites,
13:21 as princes of S, who lived in the land.
13:27 the rest of the kingdom of King S of Heshbon,
Jdg 11:19 then sent messengers to King S of the Amorites,
11:20 S did not trust Israel to pass through his territory;
11:20 so S gathered all his people together,
11:21 gave S and all his people into the hand of Israel,
1Ki 4:19 of King S of the Amorites and of King Og
Ne 9:22 of King S of Heshbon and the land of King Og
Ps 135:11 S, king of the Amorites, and Og, king of Bashan,
136:19 S, king of the Amorites,
Jer 48:45 a flame from the house of S;

SIHOR (KJV) See NILE, SHIHOR

SILAGE (1)

Isa 30:24 oxen and donkeys that till the ground will eat s,

SILAS‡ (14) [=SILVANUS]

Ac 15:22 They sent Judas called Barsabbas, and S,
15:27 We have therefore sent Judas and S,
15:32 Judas and S, who were themselves prophets,
15:40 But Paul chose S and set out,
16:19 they seized Paul and S and dragged them into
16:25 and S were praying and singing hymns to God,
16:29 he fell down trembling before Paul and S.
17: 1 After Paul and S had passed through Amphipolis
17: 4 of them were persuaded and joined Paul and S,
17: 5 for Paul and S to bring them out to the assembly,
17:10 That very night the believers sent Paul and S off
17:14 but S and Timothy remained behind.
17:15 and after receiving instructions to have S
18: 5 When S and Timothy arrived from Macedonia,

SILENCE‡ (41) [SILENCED, SILENT, SILENTLY]

Ge 24:21 The man gazed at her in s to learn whether or not
Dt 27: 9 Keep s and hear, O Israel!
Jdg 3:19 So the king said, "S!"
1Ki 19:12 and after the fire a sound of sheer s.
Est 4:14 For if you keep s at such a time as this,
Job 4:16 there was s, then I heard a voice:
11: 3 Should your babble put others to s,
13:13 "Let me have s, and I will speak,
29:21 and waited, and kept s for my counsel.
31:34 so that I kept s, and did not go out of doors—
41:12 "I will not keep s concerning its limbs,
Ps 8: 2 to s the enemy and the avenger.
32: 3 While I kept s, my body wasted away
50: 3 Our God comes and does not keep s,
62: 1 For God alone my soul waits in s,
62: 5 For God alone my soul waits in s,
65: 7 You s the roaring of the seas,
83: 1 O God, do not keep s; do
94:17 my soul would soon have lived in the land of s.
115:17 nor do any that go down into s.
Ecc 3: 7 a time to keep s, and a time to speak;
Isa 41: 1 Listen to me in s, O coastlands;
47: 5 Sit in s, and go into darkness, daughter Chaldea!
Jer 48: 2 You also, O Madmen, shall be brought to s;
La 2:10 The elders of daughter Zion sit on the ground in s;
3:28 to sit alone in s when the Lord has imposed it,
Eze 26:13 I will s the music of your songs;
Hab 2:20 let all the earth keep s before him!
Ac 15:12 The whole assembly kept s,
19:33 And Alexander motioned for s and tried to make
21:40 on the steps and motioned to the people for s;
1Ti 2:11 Let a woman learn in s with full submission.
1Pe 2:15 that by doing right you should s the ignorance of
Rev 8: 1 there was s in heaven for about half an hour.
Wis 18:14 For while gentle s enveloped all things,
Sir 41:20 and of s, before those who greet you;
3Mc 3:23 both by speech and by s they abominate those few
5: 7 But with tears and a voice hard to s they all called
2Es 6:39 and darkness and s embraced everything;
7:30 Then the world shall be turned back to primeval s
7:32 and the dust those who rest there in s;

SILENCED (8) [SILENCE]

Jer 47: 5 Baldness has come upon Gaza, Ashkelon is s.
Mt 22:34 the Pharisees heard that he had s the Sadducees,
Ac 11:18 When they heard this, they were s.
Ro 3:19 so that every mouth may be s,
2Co 11:10 of mine will not be s in the regions of Achaia.
Tit 1:11 be s, since they are upsetting whole families
2Es 10:22 our harp has been laid low, our song has been s,
15:32 these shall be disorganized and s by their power,

SILENT‡ (66) [SILENCE]

Lev 10: 3 I will be glorified.' " And Aaron was s.
2Ki 2: 3 And he said, "Yes, I know; keep s."
2: 5 And he answered, "Yes, I know; be s."
7: 9 if we are s and wait until the morning light,
18:36 the people were s and answered him not a word,
Ne 5: 8 They were s, and could not find a word to say.
Job 6:24 "Teach me, and I will be s;
13: 5 If you would only keep s,
13:19 For then I would be s and die.
33:31 Pay heed, Job, listen to me; be s, and I will speak.
33:33 listen to me; be s, and I will teach you wisdom."
Ps 4: 4 ponder it on your beds, and be s.
28: 1 for if you are s to me, I shall be like those who go
30:12 so that my soul may praise you and not be s.
35:22 You have seen, O LORD; do not be s!
39: 2 I was s and still; I held my peace to no
39: 9 I am s; I do not open my mouth,
50:21 These things you have done and I have been s;
109: 1 Do not be s, O God of my praise.
Pr 11:12 but an intelligent person remains s.
17:28 Even fools who keep s are considered wise;
Isa 36:21 But they were s and answered him not a word,
53: 7 and like a sheep that before its shearers is s,
56:10 they are all s dogs that cannot bark;
57:11 Have I not kept s and closed my eyes,
62: 1 For Zion's sake I will not keep s,
62: 6 all day and all night they shall never be s.
64:12 Will you keep s, and punish us so severely?
65: 6 I will not keep s, but I will repay;
Jer 4:19 My heart is beating wildly; I cannot keep s;
Eze 24:27 and you shall speak and no longer be s.
Am 5:13 Therefore the prudent will keep s in such a time;
8: 3 cast out in every place. Be s!"
Hab 1:13 and are s when the wicked swallow those more
2:19 to s stone, "Rouse yourself!"
Zep 1: 7 Be s before the Lord GOD!
Zec 2:13 Be s, all people, before the LORD;
Mt 26:63 But Jesus was s. Then the high priest said to him,
Mk 1:25 But Jesus rebuked him, saying, "Be s,
3: 4 to save life or to kill?" But they were s.
9:34 But they were s, for on the way they had argued
14:61 But he was s and did not answer.
Lk 4:35 But Jesus rebuked him, saying, "Be s,
9:36 And they kept s and in those days told no one any
14: 4 But they were s. So Jesus took him and healed
19:40 He answered, "I tell you, if these were s,
20:26 and being amazed by his answer, they became s.
Ac 8:32 and like a lamb s before its shearer,
12:17 He motioned to them with his hand to be s,
18: 9 "Do not be afraid, but speak and do not be s;
21:14 we remained s except to say,
1Co 14:28 let them be s in church and speak to themselves
14:30 let the first person be s.
14:34 women should be s in the churches.
1Ti 2:12 or to have authority over a man; she is to keep s.
Wis 8:12 When I am s they will wait for me,
Sir 13:23 The rich person speaks and all are s;
20: 1 there is the person who is wise enough to keep s.
20: 5 Some people keep s and are thought to be wise,
20: 6 Some people keep s because they have nothing
20: 6 others keep s because they know when to speak.
20: 7 The wise remain s until the right moment,
26:14 A s wife is a gift from the Lord,
1Mc 11: 5 on him; but the king kept s.
2Es 14:43 me, I spoke in the daytime and was not s at night.
15: 8 I will be s no longer concerning their ungodly acts

SILENTLY (1) [SILENCE]

1Sa 1:13 Hannah was praying s; only her lips moved,

SILK‡ (1)

Rev 18:12 jewels and pearls, fine linen, purple, s and scarlet,

SILLA (1)

2Ki 12:20 on the way that goes down to S.

SILLY (3)

Hos 7:11 like a dove, s and without sense;
Eph 5: 4 Entirely out of place is obscene, s, and vulgar talk;
2Ti 3: 6 into households and captivate s women,

SILOAH (KJV) See SHELAH

SILOAM (3)

Lk 13: 4 when the tower of S fell on them—
Jn 9: 7 "Go, wash in the pool of S" (which means Sent).
9:11 and said to me, 'Go to S and wash.'

SILVANUS (4) [=SILAS]

2Co 1:19 S and Timothy and I, was not "Yes and No";
1Th 1: 1 S, and Timothy, To the church of
2Th 1: 1 S, and Timothy, To the church of
1Pe 5:12 Through S, whom I consider a faithful brother,

SILVER‡ (401) [SILVER-COVERED, SILVERSMITH]

A. SILVER ... GOLD (96)
B. GOLD ... SILVER (71)

Ge 13: 2 very rich in livestock, in s, and in gold. A
20:16 I have given your brother a thousand pieces of s;
23:15 a piece of land worth four hundred shekels of s—
23:16 for Ephron the s that he had named in the hearing
23:16 four hundred shekels of s,
24:35 he has given him flocks and herds, s and gold, A
24:53 the servant brought out jewelry of s and of gold, A
37:28 sold him to the Ishmaelites for twenty pieces of s.
44: 2 the s cup, in the top of the sack of the youngest,
44: 4 Why have you stolen my s cup?
44: 8 why then would we steal s or gold A
45:22 but to Benjamin he gave three hundred pieces of s
Ex 3:22 neighbor's house for jewelry of s and of gold, A
11: 2 to ask her neighbor for objects of s and gold." A
12:35 asked the Egyptians for jewelry of s and gold, A
20:23 You shall not make gods of s alongside me,
21:32 to the slaveowner thirty shekels of s,
25: 3 that you shall receive from them: gold, s, B
26:19 of s under the twenty frames, two bases under
26:21 and their forty bases of s, two bases under
26:25 there shall be eight frames, with their bases of s,
26:32 of gold and rest on four bases of s.
27:10 hooks of the pillars and their bands shall be of s.
27:11 hooks of the pillars and their bands shall be of s.
27:17 around the court shall be banded with s;
27:17 their hooks shall be of s, and their bases of bronze.
31: 4 to work in gold, s, and bronze, B
35: 5 bring the LORD's offering: gold, s, and bronze; B
35:24 of s or bronze brought it as the LORD's offering;
35:32 to work in gold, s, and bronze, B
36:24 he made forty bases of s under the twenty frames,
36:26 and their forty bases of s,
36:30 There were eight frames with their bases of s:
36:36 and he cast for them four bases of s.
38:10 the hooks of the pillars and their bands were of s.
38:11 the hooks of the pillars and their bands were of s.
38:12 the hooks of the pillars and their bands were of s.
38:17 the hooks of the pillars and their bands were of s;
38:17 the overlaying of their capitals was also of s,
38:17 and all the pillars of the court were banded with s.
38:19 their four bases were of bronze, their hooks of s,
38:19 overlaying of their capitals and their bands of s.
38:25 The s from those of the congregation who were
38:27 The hundred talents of s were for casting the bases
Lev 5:15 convertible into s by the sanctuary shekel;
27: 3 of age the equivalent shall be fifty shekels of s by
27: 6 the equivalent for a male is five shekels of s,
27: 6 for a female the equivalent is three shekels of s.
27:16 fifty shekels of s to a homer of barley seed.
Nu 7:13 one s plate weighing one hundred thirty shekels,
one s basin weighing seventy shekels,
7:19 one s plate weighing one hundred thirty shekels,
one s basin weighing seventy shekels,
7:25 one s plate weighing one hundred thirty shekels,
one s basin weighing seventy shekels,
7:31 one s plate weighing one hundred thirty shekels,
one s basin weighing seventy shekels,
7:37 one s plate weighing one hundred thirty shekels,
one s basin weighing seventy shekels,
7:43 one s plate weighing one hundred thirty shekels,
one s basin weighing seventy shekels,
7:49 one s plate weighing one hundred thirty shekels,
one s basin weighing seventy shekels,
7:55 one s plate weighing one hundred thirty shekels,
one s basin weighing seventy shekels,
7:61 one s plate weighing one hundred thirty shekels,
one s basin weighing seventy shekels,
7:67 one s plate weighing one hundred thirty shekels,
one s basin weighing seventy shekels,
7:73 one s plate weighing one hundred thirty shekels,
7:73 one s basin weighing seventy shekels,
7:79 one s plate weighing one hundred thirty shekels,
one s basin weighing seventy shekels,
7:84 twelve s plates, twelve s basins,
7:85 each s plate weighing one hundred thirty shekels
and each basin seventy, all the s of the vessels
10: 2 Make two s trumpets; you shall make them of
18:16 you shall fix at five shekels of s,
22:18 were to give me his house full of s and gold, A
24:13 of s and gold, I would not be able to go beyond A
31:22 gold, s, bronze, iron, tin, and lead— B
Dt 7:25 Do not covet the s or the gold that is on them A
8:13 and your s and gold is multiplied, A
17:17 also s and gold he must not acquire A
22:19 of s (which they shall give to
22:29 with her shall give fifty shekels of s to
29:17 the filthy idols of wood and stone, of s and gold, A
Jos 6:19 all s and gold, and vessels of bronze and iron, A
6:24 only the s and gold, and the vessels of bronze A
7:21 and two hundred shekels of s,
7:21 the ground inside my tent, with the s underneath."
7:22 hidden in his tent with the s underneath.
7:24 with the s, the mantle, and the bar of gold,
22: 8 and with very much livestock, with s, gold, A
Jdg 5:19 they got no spoils of s.
9: 4 They gave him seventy pieces of s out of
16: 5 we will each give you eleven hundred pieces of s."
17: 2 "The eleven hundred pieces of s that were taken
17: 2 that s is in my possession;
17: 3 Then he returned the eleven hundred pieces of s
17: 3 "I consecrate the s to the LORD from my hand
17: 4 his mother took two hundred pieces of s,
17:10 and I will give you ten pieces of s a year,
1Sa 2:36 to implore him for a piece of s or a loaf of bread,
9: 8 "Here, I have with me a quarter shekel of s;
2Sa 8:10 Joram brought with him articles of s, gold, A
8:11 together with the s and gold that he dedicated A
18:11 I would have been glad to give you ten pieces of s
18:12 a thousand pieces of s, I would not raise my hand

2Sa 21: 4 “It is not a matter of s or gold between us and A
24:24 and the oxen for fifty shekels of s.
1Ki 7:51 the s, the gold, and the vessels, A
10:21 of pure gold; none were of s—
10:22 bringing gold, s, ivory, apes, and peacocks. B
10:25 objects of s and gold, garments, weaponry, A
10:27 king made s as common in Jerusalem as stones,
10:29 from Egypt for six hundred shekels of s, and
15:15 and his own votive gifts—s, gold, A
15:18 Asa took all the s and the gold that were left A
15:19 I am sending you a present of s and gold; A
16:24 of Samaria from Shemer for two talents of s;
20: 3 Your s and gold are mine; A
20: 5 saying, ‘Deliver to me your s and gold, A
20: 7 for my wives, my children, my s, and my gold; A
20:39 or else you shall pay a talent of s.’
2Ki 5: 5 He went, taking with him ten talents of s,
5:22 please give them a talent of s and two changes
5:23 and tied up two talents of s in two bags,
6:25 a donkey’s head was sold for eighty shekels of s,
6:25 of a kab of dove’s dung for five shekels of s.
7: 8 into a tent, ate and drank, carried off s, gold, A
12:13 But for the house of the LORD no basins of s,
12:13 bowls, trumpets, or any vessels of gold, or of s, B
14:14 He seized all the gold and s, B
15:19 Menahem gave Pul a thousand talents of s,
15:20 fifty shekels of s from each one,
16: 8 Ahaz also took the s and gold found in the A
18:14 of Judah three hundred talents of s
18:15 the s that was found in the house of the LORD
20:13 all his treasure house, the s, the gold, the spices, A
23:33 on the land of one hundred talents of s and a talent
23:35 Jehoiakim gave the s and the gold to Pharaoh, A
23:35 He exacted the s and the gold from the people A
25:15 and what was made of s, for the silver.
25:15 and what was made of silver, for the s.
1Ch 18:10 He sent all sorts of articles of gold, of s, B
18:11 with the s and gold that he had carried off A
19: 6 a thousand talents of s to hire chariots and cavalry
22:14 one million talents of s, and bronze and iron
22:16 gold, s, bronze, and iron. B
28:14 the weight of s vessels for each service,
28:15 the weight of s for a lampstand and its lamps,
28:16 the s for the s tables,
28:17 for the s bowls and the weight of each;
29: 2 the s for the things of s,
29: 3 I have a treasure of my own of gold and s, B
29: 4 and seven thousand talents of refined s,
29: 5 and s for the things of s.
29: 7 ten thousand talents of s, eighteen thousand talents
2Ch 1:15 The king made s and gold as common A
1:17 a chariot for six hundred shekels of s,
2: 7 send me an artisan skilled to work in gold, s, B
2:14 He is trained to work in gold, s, bronze, iron, B
5: 1 and stored the s, the gold, A
9:14 the governors of the land brought gold and s B
9:20 s was not considered as anything in the days of
9:21 bringing gold, s, ivory, apes, and peacocks. B
9:24 objects of s and gold, garments, weaponry, A
9:27 king made s as common in Jerusalem as stone,
15:18 and his own votive gifts—s, gold, A
16: 2 Then Asa took s and gold from the treasures of A
16: 3 I am sending to you s and gold; A
17:11 Philistines brought Jehoshaphat presents, and s
21: 3 Their father gave them many gifts, of s, gold, A
24:14 and ladles, and vessels of gold and s. B
25: 6 from Israel for one hundred talents of s.
25:24 He seized all the gold and s, B
27: 5 that year one hundred talents of s,
32:27 he made for himself treasuries for s, for gold, A
36: 3 a tribute of one hundred talents of s and one talent
Ezr 1: 4 by the people of their place with s and gold, A
1: 6 All their neighbors aided them with s vessels,
1: 9 s basins, one thousand;
1:10 other s bowls, four hundred ten;
1:11 the gold and s vessels was five thousand four B
2:69 darics of gold, five thousand minas of s,
5:14 the gold and s vessels of the house of God, B
6: 5 let the gold and s vessels of the house of God, B
7:15 and also to convey the s and gold that the king A
7:16 with all the s and gold that you shall find in A
7:18 to do with the rest of the s and gold, A
7:22 up to one hundred talents of s,
8:25 the s and the gold and the vessels, the offering A
8:26 into their hand six hundred fifty talents of s, and
one hundred s vessels worth . . . talents,
8:28 and the s and the gold are a freewill offering A
8:30 priests and the Levites took over the s, the gold, A
8:33 within the house of our God, the s, the gold, A
Ne 5:15 besides forty shekels of s.
7:71 of gold and two thousand two hundred minas of s.
7:72 of gold, two thousand minas of s,
Est 1: 6 with cords of fine linen and purple to s rings
1: 6 gold and s on a mosaic pavement of porphyry, B
3: 9 of s into the hands of those who have charge of
Job 3:15 who fill their houses with s.
22:25 if the Almighty is your gold and your precious s,
27:16 Though they heap up s like dust,
27:17 and the innocent will divide the s.
28: 1 “Surely there is a mine for s,
28:15 and s cannot be weighed out as its price.
Ps 12: 6 s refined in a furnace on the ground,
66:10 you have tried us as s is tried.
68:13 the wings of a dove covered with s,
105:37 Then he brought Israel out with s and gold, A
115: 4 Their idols are s and gold, A
119:72 to me than thousands of gold and s pieces. B
Ps 135:15 The idols of the nations are s and gold, A
Pr 2: 4 like s, and search for it as for hidden treasures—
3:14 for her income is better than s,
8:10 Take my instruction instead of s,
8:19 even fine gold, and my yield than choice s.
10:20 The tongue of the righteous is choice s;
16:16 To get understanding is to be chosen rather than s.
17: 3 The crucible is for s, and the furnace is for gold,
22: 1 and favor is better than s or gold. A
25: 4 Take away the dross from the s,
25:11 like apples of gold in a setting of s.
27:21 The crucible is for s, and the furnace is for gold,
Ecc 2: 8 for myself s and gold and the treasure of kings A
12: 6 before the s cord is snapped,
SS 1:11 make you ornaments of gold, studded with s.
3:10 He made its posts of s, its back of gold,
8: 9 we will build upon her a battlement of s;
8:11 to bring for its fruit a thousand pieces of s.
Isa 1:22 Your s has become dross, your wine is mixed
2: 7 Their land is filled with s and gold, A
2:20 to the bats their idols of s and their idols of gold,
7:23 worth a thousand shekels of s,
13:17 who have no regard for s and do not delight
31: 7 all of you shall throw away your idols of s
39: 2 showed them his treasure house, the s, the gold, A
40:19 and casts for it s chains.
46: 6 and weigh out s in the scales—
48:10 See, I have refined you, but not like s;
60: 9 their s and gold with them, A
60:17 instead of iron I will bring s;
Jer 6:30 They are called “rejected s,”
10: 4 people deck it with s and gold; A
10: 9 Beaten s is brought from Tarshish,
32: 9 the money to him, seventeen shekels of s.
52:19 both those of gold and those of s. B
Eze 7:19 They shall fling their s into the streets,
7:19 Their s and gold cannot save them on the day A
16:13 You were adorned with gold and s, B
16:17 of my gold and my s that I had given you, B
22:18 all of them, s, bronze, tin, iron, and lead.
22:20 As one gathers s, bronze, iron, lead,
22:22 As s is melted in a smelter,
27:12 s, iron, tin, and lead they exchanged
28: 4 have gathered gold and s into your treasuries. B
38:13 to carry away s and gold, A
Da 2:32 its chest and arms of s,
2:35 the iron, the clay, the bronze, the s, and the gold, A
2:45 the bronze, the clay, the s, and the gold. A
5: 2 of gold and s that his father Nebuchadnezzar B
5: 3 the vessels of gold and s that had been taken B
5: 4 the wine and praised the gods of gold and s, B
5:23 You have praised the gods of s and gold, A
11: 8 and with their precious vessels of s and gold, A
11:38 not know he shall honor with gold and s, B
11:43 of the treasures of gold and of s, and all the B
Hos 2: 8 upon her s and gold that they used for Baal. A
3: 2 of s and a homer of barley and a measure of wine.
8: 4 With their s and gold they made idols A
9: 6 Nettles shall possess their precious things of s;
13: 2 idols of s made according to their understanding,
Joel 3: 5 For you have taken my s and my gold, A
Am 2: 6 because they sell the righteous for s,
8: 6 the poor for s and the needy for a pair of sandals,
Na 2: 9 “Plunder the s, plunder the gold!
Hab 2:19 See, it is gold and s plated, B
Zep 1:11 all who weigh out s are cut off.
1:18 Neither their s nor their gold will be able A
Hag 2: 8 The s is mine, and the gold is mine,
Zec 6:10 Collect s and gold from the exiles— A
6:11 Take the s and gold and make a crown, A
9: 3 and heaped up s like dust,
11:12 they weighed out as my wages thirty shekels of s.
11:13 of s and threw them into the treasury in the house
13: 9 refine them as one refines s,
14:14 gold, s, and garments in great abundance. B
Mal 3: 3 he will sit as a refiner and purifier of s,
3: 3 of Levi and refine them like gold and s, B
Mt 10: 9 Take no gold, or s, or copper in your belts, B
26:15 They paid him thirty pieces of s.
27: 3 he repented and brought back the thirty pieces of s
27: 5 Throwing down the pieces of s in the temple,
27: 6 But the chief priests, taking the pieces of s, said,
27: 9 “And they took the thirty pieces of s,
Lk 15: 8 “Or what woman having ten s coins,
Ac 3: 6 But Peter said, “I have no s or gold, A
7:16 the tomb that Abraham had bought for a sum of s
8:20 Peter said to him, “May your s perish with you,
17:29 to think that the deity is like gold, or s, or stone, B
19:19 it was found to come to fifty thousand s coins.
19:24 a silversmith who made s shrines of Artemis,
20:33 I coveted no one’s s or gold or clothing. A
1Co 3:12 if anyone builds on the foundation with gold, s, B
2Ti 2:20 not only of gold and s but also of wood and clay, B
Jas 5: 3 Your gold and s have rusted, B
1Pe 1:18 not with perishable things like s or gold, A
Rev 9:20 up worshiping demons and idols of gold and s B
18:12 of gold, s, jewels and pearls, fine linen, purple, B
Tob 1:14 of Media I left bags of s worth ten talents in trust
4:20 that I left ten talents of s in trust with Gabael son
Jdt 2:18 amount of gold and s from the royal palace. B
5: 9 and grew very prosperous in gold and s B
8: 7 Her husband Manasseh had left her gold and s, B
10:22 with s lamps carried before him.
12: 1 to bring her in where his s dinnerware was kept,
15:11 the tent of Holofernes and all his s dinnerware,
AdE 1: 6 to gold and s blocks on pillars of marble and B
1: 6 Gold and s couches were placed on a mosaic B
AdE 1: 7 The cups were of gold and s, B
3: 9 and I will pay ten thousand talents of s into
Wis 7: 9 and s will be accounted as clay before her.
13:10 gold and s fashioned with skill, B
15: 9 but they compete with workers in gold and s, B
Sir 26:18 Like golden pillars on s bases,
28:24 As you lock up your s and gold, A
29:10 Lose your s for the sake of a brother or a friend,
40:25 Gold and s make one stand firm, B
47:18 you gathered gold like tin and amassed s like lead.
51:28 and through me you will acquire s and gold. A
Bar 1: 8 the s vessels that Zedekiah son of Josiah,
3:17 hoarded up s and gold in which people trust, A
3:18 those who schemed to get s,
LtJ 6: 4 Babylon you will see gods made of s and gold A
6: 8 they themselves are overlaid with gold and s; B
6:10 priests secretly take gold and s from their gods B
6:11 these gods of s and gold and wood A
6:30 Women serve meals for gods of s and gold A
6:39 gold and s are like stones from the mountain, B
6:50 of wood and overlaid with gold and s, B
6:55 a temple of wooden gods overlaid with gold or s, B
6:57 wood and overlaid with s and gold are unable A
6:58 who can will strip them of their gold and s B
6:70 of wood, overlaid with gold and s. B
6:71 their gods of wood, overlaid with gold and s, B
1Mc 1:23 took the s and the gold, and the costly vessels; A
2:18 and your sons will be honored with s and gold A
3:41 they took s and gold in immense amounts, A
4:23 and they seized a great amount of gold and s, B
6: 1 was a city famed for its wealth in s and gold. A
6:12 I seized all its vessels of s and gold, A
8: 3 to get control of the s and gold mines there, A
10:40 I also grant fifteen thousand shekels of s yearly out
10:42 of s that my officials have received every year
10:60 and their Friends s and gold and many gifts, A
11:24 taking s and gold and clothing A
13:16 now one hundred talents of s and two of his sons
15:26 and s and gold and a large amount A
15:31 of s for the destruction that you have caused
15:32 and the sideboard with its gold and s plate, B
16:11 he had a large store of s and gold, A
16:19 so that he might give them s and gold and gifts; A
2Mc 2: 2 in their thoughts on seeing the gold and s statues B
3:11 and that it totaled in all four hundred talents of s
4: 8 at an interview three hundred sixty talents of s,
4:19 to carry three hundred s drachmas for the sacrifice
4:24 outbidding Jason by three hundred talents of s.
12:43 to the amount of two thousand drachmas of s,
1Es 1:36 the nation one hundred talents of s and one talent
2: 6 by the people of your place with gold and s, B
2: 9 with s and gold, with horses and cattle, A
2:13 one thousand s cups, twenty-nine s censers,
2:13 two thousand four hundred ten s bowls,
2:14 All the vessels were handed over, gold and s, B
4:18 gather gold and s or any other beautiful thing, B
4:19 to gold or s or any other beautiful thing. B
5:45 of gold, five thousand minas of s,
6:18 And the holy vessels of gold and of s, B
6:26 both of gold and of s, B
8:13 Jerusalem all the gold and s that may be found B
8:14 gold and s for bulls and rams and lambs B
8:16 do with the gold and s, perform it in accordance B
8:20 up to a hundred talents of s,
8:55 to them the s and the gold and the holy vessels A
8:56 and gave to them six hundred fifty talents of s,
and s vessels worth a hundred talents,
8:58 and the s and the gold are vowed to the Lord, A
8:60 and the Levites who took the s and the gold A
8:62 the s and the gold were weighed and delivered A
2Es *7:55* Say to her, ‘You produce gold and s and bronze, B
7:56 s is more abundant than gold, and bronze than s,

SILVER-COVERED (1) [COVER, SILVER]

Isa 30:22 Then you will defile your s idols

SILVERSMITH (2) [SILVER, SMITH]

Jdg 17: 4 to the s, who made it into an idol of cast metal;
Ac 19:24 a s who made silver shrines of Artemis,

SIMEON (53) [SIMEONITES, =SIMON]

Ge 29:33 has given me this son also”; and she named him S.
34:25 two of the sons of Jacob, S and Levi,
34:30 Then Jacob said to S and Levi,
35:23 The sons of Leah: Reuben (Jacob’s firstborn), S,
42:24 And he picked out S and had him bound
42:36 Joseph is no more, and S is no more,
43:23 Then he brought S out to them.
46:10 The children of S: Jemuel,
48: 5 Manasseh shall be mine, just as Reuben and S are.
49: 5 S and Levi are brothers; weapons of violence
Ex 1: 2 Reuben, S, Levi, and Judah,
6:15 The sons of S: Jemuel, Jamin,
6:15 these are the families of S.
Nu 1: 6 From S, Shelumiel son of Zurishaddai.
1:22 The descendants of S, their lineage, in their clans,
1:23 of S were fifty-nine thousand three hundred.
2:12 those to camp next to him shall be the tribe of S.
10:19 the company of the tribe of S was Shelumiel son
13: 5 from the tribe of S, Shaphat son of Hori;
26:12 The descendants of S by their clans:
Dt 27:12 S, Levi, Judah, Issachar, Joseph, and Benjamin.
Jos 19: 1 The second lot came out for S, for the tribe of S,
19: 8 the inheritance of the tribe of S according
19: 9 the tribe of S formed part of the territory of Judah;

Jos 19: 9 for them, the tribe of S obtained an inheritance
21: 4 by lot thirteen towns from the tribes of Judah, S,
21: 9 of the tribe of Judah and the tribe of S they gave
Jdg 1: 3 Judah said to his brother S,
1: 3 So S went with him.
1:17 Judah went with his brother S,
1Ch 2: 1 These are the sons of Israel: Reuben, S, Levi,
4:24 The sons of S: Nemuel, Jamin,
6:65 also gave them by lot out of the tribes of Judah, S,
2Ch 15: 9 and S who were residing as aliens with them,
34: 6 In the towns of Manasseh, Ephraim, and S,
Eze 48:24 from the east side to the west, S, one portion.
48:25 Adjoining the territory of S,
48:33 three gates, the gate of S, the gate of Issachar,
Lk 2:25 there was a man in Jerusalem whose name was S;
2:27 Guided by the Spirit, S came into the temple;
2:28 S took him in his arms and praised God, saying,
2:34 Then S blessed them and said to his mother Mary,
3:30 son of S, son of Judah, son of Joseph, son
Ac 13: 1 Barnabas, S who was called Niger,
15:14 S has related how God first looked favorably on
2Pe 1: 1 S Peter, a servant and apostle of Jesus Christ,
Rev 7: 7 from the tribe of S twelve thousand,
Jdt 6:15 of the tribe of S, and Chabris son of Gothoniel,
9: 2 of my ancestor S, to whom you gave a sword
1Mc 2: 1 In those days Mattathias son of John son of S,
2:65 "Here is your brother S who, I know,
4Mc 2:19 of S and Levi for their irrational slaughter of

SIMEONITES (8) [SIMEON]

Nu 2:12 of the S shall be Shelumiel son of Zurishaddai,
7:36 of Zurishaddai, the leader of the S:
25:14 head of an ancestral house belonging to the S.
26:14 These are the clans of the S,
34:20 Of the tribe of the S, Shemuel son of Ammihud.
1Ch 4:42 And some of them, five hundred men of the S,
12:25 Of the S, mighty warriors,
27:16 for the S, Shephatiah son of Maacah;

SIMILAR (6)

Jer 36:32 and many s words were added to them.
Eze 42:11 they were s to the chambers on the north,
Ro 9:10 something s happened to Rebecca
1Mc 5:14 came from Galilee and made a s report;
2Mc 2: 3 And with other s words he exhorted them that
2Es 7:*61* and are s to a flame and smoke—

SIMON‡ (154) [=PETER, =SIMEON, SIMON'S, =THASSI]

Mt 4:18 S, who is called Peter, and Andrew his brother,
10: 2 first, S, also known as Peter,
10: 4 S the Cananaean, and Judas Iscariot,
13:55 And are not his brothers James and Joseph and S
16:16 S Peter answered, "You are the Messiah,
16:17 "Blessed are you, S son of Jonah!
17:25 asking, "What do you think, S?
26: 6 Jesus was at Bethany in the house of S the leper,
27:32 they came upon a man from Cyrene named S;
Mk 1:16 he saw S and his brother Andrew casting a net
1:29 they entered the house of S and Andrew,
1:36 And S and his companions hunted for him.
3:16 S (to whom he gave the name Peter);
3:18 and Thaddaeus, and S the Cananaean,
6: 3 and brother of James and Joses and Judas and S,
14: 3 he was at Bethany in the house of S the leper,
14:37 and he said to Peter, "S, are you asleep?
15:21 it was S of Cyrene, the father of Alexander
Lk 5: 3 the one belonging to S, and asked him to put out
5: 4 When he had finished speaking, he said to S,
5: 5 S answered, "Master, we have worked all night
5: 8 But when S Peter saw it,
5:10 sons of Zebedee, who were partners with S.
5:10 Then Jesus said to S, "Do not be afraid;
6:14 S, whom he named Peter,
6:15 and Thomas, and James son of Alphaeus, and S,
7:40 Jesus spoke up and said to him, "S,
7:43 S answered, "I suppose the one
7:44 Then turning toward the woman, he said to S,
22:31 "S, S, listen! Satan has demanded to sift all of you
23:26 S of Cyrene, who was coming from the country,
24:34 and he has appeared to S!"
Jn 1:40 and followed him was Andrew, S Peter's brother.
1:41 He first found his brother S and said to him,
1:42 He brought S to Jesus, who looked at him
1:42 "You are S son of John.
6: 8 One of his disciples, Andrew, S Peter's brother,
6:68 S Peter answered him, "Lord,
6:71 He was speaking of Judas son of S Iscariot, for he,
13: 2 the heart of Judas son of S Iscariot to betray him.
13: 6 He came to S Peter, who said to him, "Lord,
13: 9 S Peter said to him, "Lord,
13:24 S Peter therefore motioned to him to ask Jesus
13:26 he gave it to Judas son of S Iscariot.
13:36 S Peter said to him, "Lord, where are you going?"
18:10 Then S Peter, who had a sword, drew it,
18:15 S Peter and another disciple followed Jesus.
18:25 Now S Peter was standing and warming himself.
20: 2 she ran and went to S Peter and the other disciple,
20: 6 Then S Peter came, following him,
21: 2 Gathered there together were S Peter,
21: 3 S Peter said to them, "I am going fishing."
21: 7 When S Peter heard that it was the Lord,
21:11 So S Peter went aboard and hauled the net ashore,
21:15 they had finished breakfast, Jesus said to S Peter,
21:15 "S son of John, do you love me more than these?"
Jn 21:16 A second time he said to him, "S son of John,
21:17 He said to him the third time, "S son of John,
Ac 1:13 and S the Zealot, and Judas son of James.
8: 9 man named S had previously practiced magic
8:13 Even S himself believed.
8:18 when S saw that the Spirit was given through
8:24 S answered, "Pray for me to the Lord,
9:43 in Joppa for some time with a certain S,
10: 5 to Joppa for a certain S who is called Peter;
10: 6 he is lodging with S, a tanner, whose house is by
10:18 They called out to ask whether S,
10:32 Send therefore to Joppa and ask for S,
10:32 he is staying in the home of S, a tanner,
11:13 'Send to Joppa and bring S, who is called Peter;
Sir 50: 1 S son of Onias, who in his life repaired the house,
50:20 Then S came down and raised his hands over
1Mc 2: 3 S called Thassi,
5:17 Then Judas said to his brother S,
5:20 Then three thousand men were assigned to S to go
5:21 So S went to Galilee and fought many battles
5:55 in Gilead and their brother S was in Galilee
9:19 and S took their brother Judas and buried him in
9:33 and his brother S and all who were with him heard
9:37 to Jonathan and his brother S,
9:62 Then Jonathan with his men, and S,
9:65 But Jonathan left his brother S in the town,
9:67 and S and his men sallied out from the town
10:74 and his brother S met him to help him.
10:82 Then S brought forward his force and engaged
11:59 He appointed Jonathan's brother S governor from
11:64 but left his brother S in the country.
11:65 S encamped before Beth-zur and fought against it
12:33 S also went out and marched through the country
12:38 S also built Adida in the Shephelah;
13: 1 S heard that Trypho had assembled a large army
13:13 S encamped in Adida, facing the plain.
13:14 Trypho learned that S had risen up in place
13:17 S knew that they were speaking deceitfully
13:18 "It was because S did not send him the money and
13:20 But S and his army kept marching
13:25 S sent and took the bones of his brother Jonathan,
13:27 And S built a monument over the tomb
13:33 But S built up the strongholds of Judea
13:34 S also chose emissaries and sent them
13:36 "King Demetrius to S, the high priest and friend
13:42 "In the first year of S the great high priest
13:43 In those days S encamped against Gazara
13:45 asking S to make peace with them;
13:47 So S reached an agreement with them
13:50 Then they cried to S to make peace with them,
13:52 S decreed that every year they should celebrate
13:53 S saw that his son John had reached manhood,
14: 4 The land had rest all the days of S.
14:17 that his brother S had become high priest
14:20 the city of the Spartans to the high priest S and to
14:23 they have sent a copy of this to the high priest S.' "
14:24 After this S sent Numenius to Rome with
14:25 "How shall we thank S and his sons?
14:27 which is the third year of the great high priest S,
14:29 S son of Mattathias, a priest of the sons of Joarib,
14:32 then S rose up and fought for his nation.
14:40 Romans had received the envoys of S with honor.
14:41 and their priests have resolved that S should
14:46 All the people agreed to grant S the right to act
14:47 So S accepted and agreed to be high priest,
14:49 so that S and his sons might have them.
15: 1 sent a letter from the islands of the sea to S,
15: 2 "King Antiochus to S the high priest and ethnarch
15:17 They had been sent by the high priest S and by
15:21 hand them over to the high priest S,
15:24 a copy of these things to the high priest S.
15:26 S sent to Antiochus two thousand picked troops,
15:27 the agreements he formerly had made with S,
15:32 and when he saw the splendor of S,
15:33 S said to him in reply:
15:36 and also the splendor of S and all that he had seen.
16: 1 to his father S what Cendebeus had done.
16: 2 S called in his two eldest sons Judas and John,
16:13 made treacherous plans against S and his sons,
16:14 Now S was visiting the towns of the country
16:16 When S and his sons were drunk,
16:16 in against S in the banquet hall and killed him
2Mc 3: 4 But a man named S, of the tribe of Benjamin,
3:11 an extent the impious S had misrepresented
4: 1 The previously mentioned S,
4: 4 was intensifying the malice of S.
4: 6 and that S would not stop his folly.
4:23 the brother of the previously mentioned S,
8:22 S and Joseph and Jonathan,
10:19 Maccabeus left S and Joseph, and also Zacchaeus
10:20 But those with S, who were money-hungry,
14:17 S, the brother of Judas, had encountered Nicanor,
1Es 9:32 and Melchias and Sabbaias and S Chosamaeus.
3Mc 2: 1 Then the high priest S, facing the sanctuary,
4Mc 4: 1 Now there was a certain S,
4: 4 he praised S for his service to the king and went
4: 5 to our country accompanied by the accursed S and

SIMON'S (6) [SIMON]

Mk 1:30 Now S mother-in-law was in bed with a fever,
Lk 4:38 After leaving the synagogue he entered S house.
4:38 S mother-in-law was suffering from a high fever,
Ac 10:17 They were asking for S house and were standing
1Mc 14:35 "The people saw S faithfulness and the glory
2Mc 4: 3 by one of S approved agents,

SIMPLE (18) [SIMPLE-MINDED, SIMPLY]

Job 5: 2 vexation kills the fool, and jealousy slays the s.
Ps 19: 7 of the LORD are sure, making wise the s;
116: 6 The LORD protects the s;
119:130 it imparts understanding to the s.
Pr 1: 4 to the s, knowledge and prudence to the young—
1:22 "How long, O s ones, will you love being s?
1:32 For waywardness kills the s,
7: 7 and I saw among the s ones,
8: 5 O s ones, learn prudence; acquire intelligence,
9: 4 "You that are s, turn in here!"
9:16 "You who are s, turn in here!"
14:15 The s believe everything,
14:18 The s are adorned with folly,
19:25 Strike a scoffer, and the s will learn prudence;
21:11 When a scoffer is punished, the s become wiser;
22: 3 but the s go on, and suffer for it.
27:12 but the s go on, and suffer for it.

SIMPLE-MINDED (1) [MIND, SIMPLE]

Ro 16:18 and flattery they deceive the hearts of the s.

SIMPLENESS See Index to Footnotes

SIMPLY (3) [SIMPLE]

Col 2:22 they are s human commands and teachings.
Wis 16:27 not destroyed by fire was melted when s warmed
1Mc 5:48 we will s pass by on foot."

SIMRI (KJV) See SHIMRI

SIN‡ (487) [SINFUL, SINFULLY, SINNED, SINNER, SINNER'S, SINNERS, SINNING, SINS]

A. SIN OFFERING (123)
B. SIN OFFERINGS (7)

Ge 4: 7 And if you do not do well, s is lurking at the door;
18:20 and Gomorrah and how very grave their s!
31:36 What is my s, that you have hotly pursued me?
39: 9 How then could I do this great wickedness, and s
Ex 10:17 Do forgive my s just this once,
16: 1 and Israel came to the wilderness of S,
17: 1 From the wilderness of S the whole congregation
20:20 the fear of him upon you so that you do not s."
23:33 or they will make you s against me;
29:14 with fire outside the camp; it is a s offering. A
29:36 a bull as a s offering for atonement. A
29:36 Also you shall offer a s offering for the altar, A
30:10 a year with the blood of the atoning s offering. A
32:21 that you have brought so great a s upon them?"
32:30 "You have sinned a great s.
32:30 perhaps I can make atonement for your s."
32:31 "Alas, this people has sinned a great s;
32:32 But now, if you will only forgive their s—
32:34 I will punish them for their s."
34: 7 forgiving iniquity and transgression and s,
34: 9 pardon our iniquity and our s,
Lev 4: 3 he shall offer for the s that he has committed a bull
4: 3 bull of the herd without blemish as a s offering A
4: 8 the fat from the bull of s offering: A
4:14 the s that they have committed becomes known,
4:14 for a s offering and bring it before the tent A
4:20 just as is done with the bull of s offering; A
4:21 it is the s offering for the assembly. A
4:23 the s that he has committed is made known to him,
4:24 before the LORD; it is a s offering. A
4:25 blood of the s offering with his finger and put it A
4:26 on his behalf for his s,
4:28 s that you have committed is made known to you,
4:28 for the s that you have committed.
4:29 on the head of the s offering; A
4:29 the s offering shall be slaughtered at the place A
4:32 the offering you bring as a s offering is a sheep, A
4:33 on the head of the s offering; A
4:33 be slaughtered as a s offering at the spot where A
4:34 blood of the s offering with his finger and put it A
4:35 on your behalf for the s that you have committed,
5: 1 of you s in that you have heard a public adjuration
5: 5 you shall confess the s that you have committed.
5: 6 as your penalty for the s that you have committed,
5: 6 a sheep or a goat, as a s offering; A
5: 6 on your behalf for your s.
5: 7 as your penalty for the s that you have committed,
5: 7 a s offering and the other for a burnt offering. A
5: 8 who shall offer first the one for the s offering, A
5: 9 the s offering on the side of the altar, A
5: 9 of the altar; it is a s offering. A
5:10 on your behalf for the s that you have committed,
5:11 for the s that you have committed one-tenth of
5:11 of an ephah of choice flour for a s offering; A
5:11 or lay frankincense on it, for it is a s offering. A
5:12 to the LORD; it is a s offering. A
5:17 If any of you s without knowing it,
6: 2 of you s and commit a trespass against the LORD
6: 3 the various things that one may do and s thereby—
6:17 like the s offering and the guilt offering. A
6:25 This is the ritual of the s offering. A
6:25 The s offering shall be slaughtered before A
6:26 priest who offers it as a s offering shall eat of it; A
6:30 But no s offering shall be eaten A
7: 7 The guilt offering is like the s offering, A
7:37 grain offering, the s offering, the guilt offering, A

Lev 8: 2 the anointing oil, the bull of s offering, A
8:14 He led forward the bull of s offering; A
8:14 upon the head of the bull of s offering, A
9: 2 "Take a bull calf for a s offering and a ram for A
9: 3 'Take a male goat for a s offering; A
9: 7 near to the altar and sacrifice your s offering A
9: 8 and slaughtered the calf of the s offering, A
9:10 the s offering he turned into smoke on the altar, A
9:15 the goat of the s offering that was for the people, A
9:15 and presented it as a s offering like the first one. A
9:22 he came down after sacrificing the s offering, A
10:16 about the goat of the s offering, and— A
10:17 not eat the s offering in the sacred area? A
10:19 today they offered their s offering A
10:19 If I had eaten the s offering today, A
12: 6 and a pigeon or a turtledove for a s offering. A
12: 8 a burnt offering and the other for a s offering; A
14:13 the lamb in the place where the s offering and A
14:13 for the guilt offering, like the s offering, A
14:19 the priest shall offer the s offering, A
14:22 a s offering and the other for a burnt offering. A
14:31 a s offering and the other for a burnt offering, A
15:15 a s offering and the other for a burnt offering; A
15:30 a s offering and the other for a burnt offering; A
16: 3 with a young bull for a s offering and a ram for A
16: 5 of Israel two male goats for a s offering, A
16: 6 Aaron shall offer the bull as a s offering A
16: 9 and offer it as a s offering; A
16:11 a s offering for himself, and shall make A
16:11 he shall slaughter the bull as a s offering A
16:15 He shall slaughter the goat of the s offering A
16:25 s offering he shall turn into smoke on the altar. A
16:27 of the s offering and the goat of the sin offering, A
16:27 of the sin offering and the goat of the s offering, A
19:22 before the LORD for his s that he committed;
19:22 and the s he committed shall be forgiven him.
23:19 shall also offer one male goat for a s offering, A
24:15 Anyone who curses God shall bear the s.
Nu 5: 7 and shall confess the s that has been committed.
6:11 and the priest shall offer one as a s offering and A
6:14 a year old without blemish as a s offering, A
6:16 and offer their s offering and burnt offering, A
7:16 one male goat for a s offering; A
7:22 one male goat as a s offering; A
7:28 one male goat for a s offering; A
7:34 one male goat for a s offering; A
7:40 one male goat for a s offering; A
7:46 one male goat for a s offering; A
7:52 one male goat for a s offering; A
7:58 one male goat for a s offering; A
7:64 one male goat for a s offering; A
7:70 one male goat for a s offering; A
7:76 one male goat for a s offering; A
7:82 one male goat for a s offering; A
7:87 and twelve male goats for a s offering; A
8: 8 shall take another young bull for a s offering. A
8:12 for a s offering and the other for a burnt offering A
8:21 The Levites purified themselves from s
9:13 such a one shall bear the consequences for the s.
12:11 for a s that we have so foolishly committed.
15:24 and one male goat for a s offering. A
15:25 and their s offering before the LORD, A
15:27 a female goat a year old for a s offering. A
16:22 shall one person s and you become angry with
18: 9 whether grain offering, s offering, A
27: 3 but died for his own s; and he had no sons.
28:15 And there shall be one male goat for a s offering A
28:22 also one male goat for a s offering, A
29: 5 with one male goat for a s offering, A
29:11 with one male goat for a s offering, A
29:11 in addition to the s offering of atonement, A
29:16 also one male goat for a s offering, A
29:19 also one male goat for a s offering, A
29:22 also one male goat for a s offering, A
29:25 also one male goat for a s offering, A
29:28 also one male goat for a s offering, A
29:31 also one male goat for a s offering, A
29:34 also one male goat for a s offering, A
29:38 also one male goat for a s offering, A
32:23 and be sure your s will find you out.
33:11 the Red Sea and camped in the wilderness of S.
33:12 They set out from the wilderness of S and camped
Dt 9:18 because of all the s you had committed,
9:27 their wickedness and their s,
20:18 and you thus s against the LORD your God.
Jos 22:17 not had enough of the s at Peor from which even
1Sa 2:17 the s of the young men was very great in the sight
12:23 be it from me that I should s against the LORD
14:34 and do not s against the LORD by eating with
14:38 and let us find out how this s has arisen today.
15:23 For rebellion is no less a s than divination,
15:25 Now therefore, I pray, pardon my s,
19: 4 "The king should not s against his servant David,
19: 5 why then will you s against an innocent person
20: 1 And what is my s against your father
2Sa 12:13 "Now the LORD has put away your s;
1Ki 8:34 forgive the s of your people Israel,
8:35 and turn from their s, because you punish them,
8:36 and forgive the s of your servants,
8:46 "If they s against you—
8:46 for there is no one who does not s—
12:30 And this thing became a s,
13:34 This matter became s to the house of Jeroboam,
15:26 of his ancestor and in the s that he caused Israel
15:34 of Jeroboam and in the s that he caused Israel
16: 2 and have caused my people Israel to s,
16:19 and for the s that he committed,
1Ki 16:19 for the sin that he committed, causing Israel to s.
17:18 to me to bring my s to remembrance,
21:22 to anger and have caused Israel to s.
22:52 of Jeroboam son of Nebat, who caused Israel to s.
2Ki 3: 3 he clung to the s of Jeroboam son of Nebat,
12:16 the s offerings was not brought into the house of B
13: 2 which he caused Israel to s;
13: 6 which he caused Israel to s, but walked in them;
13:11 which he caused Israel to s, but he walked in them.
14:24 which he caused Israel to s.
15: 9 which he caused Israel to s.
15:18 which he caused Israel to s.
15:24 which he caused Israel to s.
15:28 which he caused Israel to s.
17:21 the LORD and made them commit great s.
21:11 and has caused Judah also to s with his idols;
21:16 besides the s that he caused Judah to sin so
21:16 to s so that they did what was evil in the sight of
21:17 all that he did, and the s that he committed,
23:15 Jeroboam son of Nebat, who caused Israel to s—
2Ch 6:25 and forgive the s of your people Israel,
6:26 and turn from their s, because you punish them,
6:27 forgive the s of your servants, your people Israel,
6:36 "If they s against you—
6:36 for there is no one who does not s—
7:14 and will forgive their s and heal their land.
29:21 a s offering for the kingdom and for the A
29:23 the male goats for the s offering were brought A
29:24 priests slaughtered them and made a s offering A
29:24 that the burnt offering and the s offering should A
33:19 all his s and his faithlessness,
Ezr 6:17 and as a s offering for all Israel, A
8:35 and as a s offering twelve male goats; A
Ne 4: 5 do not let their s be blotted out from your sight;
6:13 to intimidate me and make me s by acting
10:33 and the s offerings to make atonement for Israel, B
13:26 Did not King Solomon of Israel s on account
13:26 nevertheless, foreign women made even him to s.
Job 1:22 not s or charge God with wrongdoing.
2:10 In all this Job did not s with his lips.
7:20 I s, what do I do to you, you watcher of humanity?
10: 6 that you seek out my iniquity and search for my s,
10:14 If I s, you watch me, and do not acquit me
13:23 Make me know my transgression and my s.
14:16 you would not keep watch over my s;
31:30 I have not let my mouth s by asking for their lives
34:37 For he adds rebellion to his s;
Ps 4: 4 When you are disturbed, do not s;
32: 1 transgression is forgiven, whose s is covered.
32: 5 Then I acknowledged my s to you, and I did
32: 5 and you forgave the guilt of my s.
38: 3 there is no health in my bones because of my s.
38:18 I confess my iniquity; I am sorry for my s.
39: 1 "I will guard my ways that I may not s
39:11 "You chastise mortals in punishment for s,
40: 6 Burnt offering and s offering you have not A
51: 2 and cleanse me from my s.
51: 3 and my s is ever before me.
59: 3 For no transgression or s of mine, O LORD,
59:12 For the s of their mouths, the words of their lips,
85: 2 of your people; you pardoned all their s.
109: 7 let his prayer be counted as s.
109:14 and do not let the s of his mother be blotted out.
119:11 so that I may not s against you.
Pr 5:22 and they are caught in the toils of their s.
10:16 the gain of the wicked to s.
13: 6 but s overthrows the wicked.
14:34 but s is a reproach to any people.
16:10 his mouth does not s in judgment.
20: 9 I am pure from my s"?
21: 4 the lamp of the wicked—are s.
24: 9 The devising of folly is s,
Ecc 5: 6 Do not let your mouth lead you into s,
Isa 3: 9 they proclaim their s like Sodom,
5:18 who drag s along as with cart ropes,
6: 7 your guilt has departed and your s is blotted out."
27: 9 this will be the full fruit of the removal of his s:
30: 1 but against my will, adding s to s;
53:10 When you make his life an offering for s,
53:12 yet he bore the s of many,
Jer 16:10 What is the s that we have committed against
16:18 And I will doubly repay their iniquity and their s,
17: 1 The s of Judah is written with an iron pen;
17: 3 as the price of your s throughout all your territory.
18:23 do not blot out their s from your sight.
31:34 and remember their s no more.
32:35 do this abomination, causing Judah to s.
33: 8 I will cleanse them from all the guilt of their s
33: 8 the guilt of their s and rebellion against me.
36: 3 so that I may forgive their iniquity and their s.
Eze 3:20 they shall die for their s, and their righteous deeds
3:21 If, however, you warn the righteous not to s,
3:21 and they do not s, they shall surely live,
18:24 and the s they have committed,
33:12 be able to live by their righteousness when they s.
33:14 yet if they turn from their s and do what is lawful
40:39 on which the burnt offering and the s offering A
42:13 the grain offering, the s offering, A
43:19 says the Lord GOD, a bull for a s offering. A
43:21 You shall also take the bull of the s offering, A
43:22 a male goat without blemish for a s offering; A
43:25 a goat for a s offering; A
44:27 he shall offer his s offering, says the Lord GOD. A
44:29 They shall eat the grain offering, the s offering, A
45:17 he shall provide the s offerings, grain offerings, B
45:19 of the s offering and put it on the doorposts of A
45:22 people of the land a young bull for a s offering. A
Eze 45:23 and a male goat daily for a s offering. A
45:25 he shall make the same provision for s offerings, B
46:20 the guilt offering and the s offering, A
Da 9:20 and confessing my s and the s of my people
9:24 to finish the transgression, to put an end to s,
Hos 4: 8 They feed on the s of my people;
8:11 When Ephraim multiplied altars to expiate s,
10: 8 The high places of Aven, the s of Israel,
12: 8 no offense has been found in me that would be s."
13:12 his s is kept in store.
Mic 1:13 it was the beginning of s to daughter Zion,
3: 8 to Jacob his transgression and to Israel his s.
6: 7 the fruit of my body for the s of my soul?"
Zec 13: 1 to cleanse them from s and impurity.
Mt 5:29 If your right eye causes you to s,
5:30 And if your right hand causes you to s,
12:31 people will be forgiven for every s and blasphemy,
13:41 of his kingdom all causes of s and all evildoers,
Mk 3:29 but is guilty of an eternal s"—
Jn 1:29 Lamb of God who takes away the s of the world!
5:14 Do not s any more, so that nothing worse happens
8: 7 ⟦among you who is without s be the first to throw⟧
8:11 ⟦Go your way, and from now on do not s again."⟧
8:21 but you will die in your s.
8:34 everyone who commits s is a slave to s.
8:46 Which of you convicts me of s?
9:41 "If you were blind, you would not have s.
9:41 But now that you say, 'We see,' your s remains.
15:22 come and spoken to them, they would not have s;
but now they have no excuse for their s.
15:24 that no one else did, they would not have s.
16: 8 the world wrong about s and righteousness
16: 9 about s, because they do not believe in me;
19:11 over to you is guilty of a greater s."
Ac 7:60 "Lord, do not hold this s against them."
Ro 3: 9 both Jews and Greeks, are under the power of s,
3:20 for through the law comes the knowledge of s.
4: 8 the one against whom the Lord will not reckon s."
5:12 just as s came into the world through one man, and
death came through s,
5:13 s was indeed in the world before the law, but s is
not reckoned when there is no law.
5:16 free gift is not like the effect of the one man's s.
5:20 but where s increased, grace abounded all
5:21 just as s exercised dominion in death,
6: 1 in s in order that grace may abound?
6: 2 How can we who died to s go on living in it?
6: 6 with him so that the body of s might be destroyed,
and we might no longer be enslaved to s.
6: 7 For whoever has died is freed from s.
6:10 The death he died, he died to s, once for all;
6:11 also must consider yourselves dead to s and alive
6:12 not let s exercise dominion in your mortal bodies,
6:13 No longer present your members to s
6:14 For s will have no dominion over you,
6:15 Should we s because we are not under law but
6:16 either of s, which leads to death, or of obedience,
6:17 having once been slaves of s,
6:18 having been set free from s,
6:20 When you were slaves of s,
6:22 you have been freed from s and enslaved to God,
6:23 For the wages of s is death,
7: 7 That the law is s? By no means!
7: 7 I would not have known s.
7: 8 But s, seizing an opportunity in the commandment,
7: 8 Apart from the law s lies dead.
7: 9 but when the commandment came, s revived
7:11 For s, seizing an opportunity in the commandment,
7:13 It was s, working death in me through what is
good, in order that s might be shown to be s,
7:14 but I am of the flesh, sold into slavery under s.
7:17 but s that dwells within me.
7:20 but s that dwells within me.
7:23 making me captive to the law of s that dwells
7:25 but with my flesh I am a slave to the law of s.
8: 2 in Christ Jesus has set you free from the law of s
8: 3 and to deal with s, he condemned s in the flesh,
8:10 though the body is dead because of s,
14:23 for whatever does not proceed from faith is s.
1Co 6:18 Every s that a person commits is outside the body;
7:28 But if you marry, you do not s,
7:28 and if a virgin marries, she does not s.
7:36 let him marry as he wishes; it is no s.
8:12 when you thus s against members of your family,
and wound their conscience when it is weak, you s
15:34 Come to a sober and right mind, and s no more;
15:56 sting of death is s, and the power of s is the law.
2Co 5:21 our sake he made him to be s who knew no s,
11: 7 a s by humbling myself so that you might
Gal 2:17 is Christ then a servant of s?
3:22 under the power of s, so that what was promised
Eph 4:26 Be angry but do not s;
1Ti 5:20 As for those who persist in s,
Heb 3:13 of you may be hardened by the deceitfulness of s.
4:15 has been tested as we are, yet without s.
9:26 of the age to remove s by the sacrifice of himself.
9:28 will appear a second time, not to deal with s,
10: 2 would no longer have any consciousness of s?
10: 3 But in these sacrifices there is a reminder of s
10: 6 and s offerings you have taken no pleasure. B
10: 8 and s offerings" (these are offered according to B
10:18 there is no longer any offering for s.
10:26 if we willfully persist in s after having received
11:25 of God than to enjoy the fleeting pleasures of s.
12: 1 also lay aside every weight and the s that clings
12: 4 In your struggle against s you have not yet resisted
13:11 as a sacrifice for s are burned outside the camp.

Jas 1:15 gives birth to s, and that s, when it is fully grown,
2: 9 you commit s and are convicted by the law
4:17 the right thing to do and fails to do it, commits s.
1Pe 2:22 "He committed no s, and no deceit was found
4: 1 suffered in the flesh has finished with s),
2Pe 2:14 They have eyes full of adultery, insatiable for s.
1Jn 1: 7 the blood of Jesus his Son cleanses us from all s.
1: 8 If we say that we have no s, we deceive ourselves,
2: 1 to you so that you may not s.
2: 1 But if anyone does s, we have an advocate with
3: 4 Everyone who commits s is guilty of lawlessness; s is lawlessness.
3: 5 and in him there is no s.
3: 8 Everyone who commits s is a child of the devil;
3: 9 Those who have been born of God do not s,
3: 9 they cannot s, because they have been born
5:16 committing what is not a mortal s, you will ask,
5:16 to those whose s is not mortal.
5:16 There is s that is mortal;
5:17 wrongdoing is s, but there is s that is not mortal.
5:18 We know that those who are born of God do not s,
Tob 4: 5 and refuse to s or to transgress his commandments.
4:21 from every s and do what is good in the sight of
12: 9 saves from death and purges away every s.
12:10 but those who commit s and do wrong
14: 7 but those who commit s and injustice will vanish
Jdt 5:17 as they did not s against their God they prospered,
5:20 if there is any oversight in this people and they s
11:10 unless they s against their God.
11:11 for a s has overtaken them by which they are about
13:16 and that he committed no s with me,
Wis 1: 4 or dwell in a body enslaved to s.
10:13 not desert him, but delivered him from s.
12: 2 and warn them of the things through which they s,
14:31 but the just penalty for those who s,
15: 2 even if we s we are yours, knowing your power;
15: 2 not s, because we know that you acknowledge us
15:13 know that they s when they make
Sir 3:27 and the sinner adds s to sins.
3:30 so almsgiving atones for s.
4:21 For there is a shame that leads to s,
5: 5 not be so confident of forgiveness that you add s
5: 5 so confident of forgiveness that you add sin to s.
7: 8 Do not commit a s twice;
7:36 and then you will never s.
8: 5 Do not reproach one who is turning away from s;
10:13 For the beginning of pride is s,
13:24 Riches are good if they are free from s;
14: 1 and need not suffer remorse for s.
15:20 and he has not given anyone permission to s.
18:27 s is all around, one guards against wrongdoing.
19: 8 and unless it would be a s for you, do not reveal it;
21: 2 Flee from s as from a snake;
21: 2 for if you approach s, it will bite you.
23:10 and utters the Name will never be cleansed from s.
23:11 If he swears in error, his s remains on him,
24:22 and those who work with me will not s."
25: 8 Happy is the one who does not s with the tongue,
25:24 From a woman s had its beginning,
26:28 a man who turns back from righteousness to s—
26:29 nor is a tradesman innocent of s.
27: 1 Many have committed s for gain,
27: 2 so s is wedged in between selling and buying.
27:10 A lion lies in wait for prey; so does s for evildoers.
32:12 but do not s through proud speech.
38:10 and cleanse your heart from all s.
42: 1 and do not s to save face:
46: 7 restrained the people from s,
47:23 son of Nebat led Israel into s and started Ephraim
Bar 1:10 with the money burnt offerings and s offerings B
Sus 1:23 rather than s in the sight of the Lord."
2Mc 2:11 "They were consumed because the s offering A
10: 4 but that, if they should ever s,
12:42 praying that the s that had been committed might
12:42 the people to keep themselves free from s,
12:42 as the result of the s of those who had fallen.
12:43 sent it to Jerusalem to provide for a s offering. A
12:45 so that they might be delivered from their s
1Es 7: 8 for the s of all Israel, according to the number of
8:76 and we are in great s to this day.
9: 7 and so have increased the s of Israel.
Man 1: 8 who did not s against you,
2Es 3:30 because I have seen how you endure those who s,
6: 5 now s were estranged, and before those who stored
15:24 Alas for those who s and do
15:26 For God knows all who s against him;
16:50 the one who searches out every s on earth.
16:63 Woe to those who s and want to hide their sins!
4Mc 4:12 For he said that he had committed a s deserving
5:19 Therefore do not suppose that it would be a petty s
17:21 as it were, a ransom for the s of our nation.

SINA (KJV) See SINAI

SINAI (44) [=HOREB]

A. MOUNT SINAI (23)

Ex 16: 1 which is between Elim and S,
19: 1 they came into the wilderness of S.
19: 2 entered the wilderness of S,
19:11 upon Mount S in the sight of all the people. A
19:18 Now Mount S was wrapped in smoke, A
19:20 When the LORD descended upon Mount S, A
19:23 people are not permitted to come up to Mount S; A
24:16 The glory of the LORD settled on Mount S, A
31:18 God finished speaking with Moses on Mount S, A
34: 2 the morning to Mount S and present yourself A
34: 4 in the morning and went up on Mount S, A
34:29 Moses came down from Mount S. A
34:32 that the LORD had spoken with him on Mount S. A
Lev 7:38 the LORD commanded Moses on Mount S, A
7:38 to the LORD, in the wilderness of S.
25: 1 The LORD spoke to Moses on Mount S, saying: A
26:46 the people of Israel on Mount S through Moses. A
27:34 to Moses for the people of Israel on Mount S. A
Nu 1: 1 LORD spoke to Moses in the wilderness of S,
1:19 So he enrolled them in the wilderness of S.
3: 1 when the LORD spoke with Moses on Mount S. A
3: 4 before the LORD in the wilderness of S,
3:14 LORD spoke to Moses in the wilderness of S,
9: 1 LORD spoke to Moses in the wilderness of S,
9: 5 at twilight, in the wilderness of S.
10:12 by stages from the wilderness of S,
26:64 the Israelites in the wilderness of S.
28: 6 ordained at Mount S for a pleasing odor, A
33:15 and camped in the wilderness of S.
33:16 They set out from the wilderness of S and camped
Dt 33: 2 He said: The LORD came from S,
33:16 and the favor of the one who dwells on S.
Jdg 5: 5 the One of S, before the LORD,
Ne 9:13 You came down also upon Mount S, A
Ps 68: 8 the God of S, at the presence of God,
68:17 the Lord came from S into the holy place.
Ac 7:30 to him in the wilderness of Mount S, A
7:38 with the angel who spoke to him at Mount S, A
Gal 4:24 One woman, in fact, is Hagar, from Mount S, A
4:25 Now Hagar is Mount S in Arabia and A
Jdt 5:14 he led them by the way of S and Kadesh-barnea.
Sir 48: 7 at S and judgments of vengeance at Horeb.
2Es 3:17 you brought them to Mount S. A
14: 4 and I led him up on Mount S, A

SINCE[‡] (317)

Ge 18: 5 s you have come to your servant."
22:12 s you have not withheld your son, your only son,
24:56 s the LORD has made my journey successful;
30:38 And s they bred when they came to drink,
33:10 s you have received me with such favor.
38: 9 s Onan knew that the offspring would not be his,
38:26 s I did not give her to my son Shelah."
41:39 "S God has shown you all this,
41:56 And s the famine had spread over all the land,
42:23 s he spoke with them through an interpreter.
44:28 and I have never seen him s.
45:11 s there are five more years of famine to come—
48:18 S this one is the firstborn,
Ex 5:23 S I first came to Pharaoh to speak in your name,
6:30 "S I am a poor speaker,
9:24 in all the land of Egypt s it became a nation.
21: 8 s he has dealt unfairly with her.
Lev 13:13 s it has all turned white, he is clean.
18:11 begotten by your father, s she is your sister.
19:20 s she has not been freed;
21: 8 s they offer the food of your God;
21:21 s he has a blemish, he shall not come near to offer
22:25 s they are mutilated, with a blemish in them,
25:15 you shall pay only for the number of years s
25:27 the years s its sale shall be computed and
25:29 be redeemed until a year has elapsed s its sale;
Nu 5:13 and there is no witness against her s she was
14:25 s the Amalekites and the Canaanites live in
19:13 S water for cleansing was not dashed on them,
19:20 S the water for cleansing has not been dashed
22: 6 curse this people for me, s they are stronger than I;
Dt 2: 5 s I have given Mount Seir to Esau as a possession.
2: 9 as a possession, s I have given Ar as a possession
4:15 S you saw no form when the LORD spoke to you
4:32 ever s the day that God created human beings on
12:12 (s they have no allotment or inheritance
15:11 S there will never cease to be some in need on
15:16 s he is well off with you,
17:16 s the LORD has said to you,
19: 6 s the two had not been at enmity before.
21:14 s you have dishonored her.
21:17 s he is the first issue of his virility,
22:27 S he found her in the open country,
34:10 Never s has there arisen a prophet in Israel
Jos 2:12 Now then, s I have dealt kindly with you,
6:25 Her family has lived in Israel ever s.
7: 3 S they are so few, do not make
10:14 There has been no day like it before or s,
14:10 these forty-five years s the time that
15:19 s you have set me in the land of the Negeb,
17:14 s we are a numerous people,
17:15 s the hill country of Ephraim is too narrow
21:10 s the lot fell to them first.
23:10 s it is the LORD your God who fights for you,
Jdg 1:15 s you have set me in the land of the Negeb,
19:23 S this man is my guest, do not do this vile thing.
19:30 'Has such a thing ever happened s the day that
21: 7 s we have sworn by the LORD that we will
21:16 s there are no women left in Benjamin?"
Ru 2:11 "All that you have done for your mother-in-law s
1Sa 9:13 s he must bless the sacrifice;
17:36 s he has defied the armies of the living God."
20:42 s both of us have sworn in the name of
25:26 s the LORD has restrained you from bloodguilt
28:16 s the LORD has turned from you
29: 3 S he deserted to me I have found no fault in him
2Sa 7: 6 a house s the day I brought up the people of Israel
19:30 s my lord the king has arrived home safely."
20:12 S he saw that all who came by him were stopping,
1Ki 8:16 'S the day that I brought my people Israel out
11:11 "S this has been your mind and you have
16: 2 "S I exalted you out of the dust
2Ki 4:13 S you have taken all this trouble for us,
6:30 now s he was walking on the city wall,
7:13 s those left here will suffer the fate of
8:19 s he had promised to give a lamp to him and
10: 2 "S your master's sons are with you and you have
21:15 s the day their ancestors came out of Egypt,
23:22 No such passover had been kept s the days of
1Ch 17: 5 not lived in a house s the day I brought out Israel
24: 4 S more chief men were found among the sons
2Ch 2: 6 But who is able to build him a house, s heaven,
6: 5 'S the day that I brought my people out of
21: 7 and s he had promised to give a lamp to him and
30:26 for s the time of Solomon son of King David
31:10 "S they began to bring the contributions into
35:18 No passover like it had been kept in Israel s
Ezr 4: 2 to him ever s the days of King Esar-haddon
8:18 S the gracious hand of our God was upon us,
8:22 s we had told the king that the hand
Ne 2: 2 "Why is your face sad, s you are not sick?
9:32 s the time of the kings of Assyria until today.
Est 1:17 with contempt on their husbands, s they will say,
2:12 s this was the regular period
Job 14: 5 S their days are determined,
17: 4 S you have closed their minds to understanding,
20: 4 ever s mortals were placed on earth,
38:12 "Have you commanded the morning s
Ps 22:10 and s my mother bore me you have been my God.
45:11 S he is your lord, bow to him;
Ecc 9: 2 s the same fate comes to all,
Isa 7:17 as have not come s the day that Ephraim departed
14: 8 S you were laid low, no one comes to cut us down.
Jer 8: 9 s they have rejected the word of the LORD,
Eze 23: 8 not give up her whorings that she had practiced s
34: 8 for all the wild animals, s there was no shepherd;
35: 6 s you did not hate bloodshed,
Da 4:18 s all the wise men of my kingdom are unable
12: 1 such as has never occurred s nations first came
Hos 4: 6 And s you have forgotten the law of your God,
10: 9 S the days of Gibeah you have sinned, O Israel;
13: 4 the LORD your God ever s the land of Egypt;
Hag 2:18 S the day that the foundation of
Zec 13: 5 for the land has been my possession s my youth."
Mal 3: 7 Ever s the days of your ancestors you have turned
Mt 13: 5 sprang up quickly, s they had no depth of soil.
13: 6 and s they had no root, they withered away.
27: 6 into the treasury, s they are blood money."
Mk 4: 5 and it sprang up quickly, s it had no depth of soil.
4: 6 and s it had no root, it withered away.
7:19 s it enters, not the heart but the stomach,
10:20 "Teacher, I have kept all these s my youth."
15:42 and s it was the day of Preparation, that is,
Lk 1: 1 S many have undertaken to set down
1:34 "How can this be, s I am a virgin?"
9:32 but s they had stayed awake,
11:50 the blood of all the prophets shed s the foundation
16:16 s then the good news of the kingdom
18:21 He replied, "I have kept all these s my youth."
23:40 s you are under the same sentence
24:21 it is now the third day s these things took place.
Jn 4:45 s they had seen all that he had done in Jerusalem at
9:32 Never s the world began has it been heard
12:11 s it was on account of him that many of
17: 2 s you have given him authority over all people,
18:15 S that disciple was known to the high priest,
19:31 S it was the day of Preparation,
Ac 2:30 S he was a prophet, he knew that God had sworn
9:38 S Lydda was near Joppa, the disciples,
13:46 S you reject it and judge yourselves to
15:24 S we have heard that certain persons who have
16:27 s he supposed that the prisoners had escaped.
17:25 s he himself gives to all mortals life and breath
17:29 S we are God's offspring,
18:15 but s it is a matter of questions about words
19:36 S these things cannot be denied,
19:40 s there is no cause that we can give
20: 7 s he intended to leave the next day,
21:14 S he would not be persuaded,
22:11 S I could not see because of the brightness of
22:30 S he wanted to find out what Paul was being
23:28 S I wanted to know the charge
24:11 not more than twelve days s I went up to worship
24:27 and s he wanted to grant the Jews a favor,
25:14 S they were staying there several days,
25:20 S I was at a loss how
26:11 and s I was so furiously enraged at them,
27: 9 S much time had been lost and sailing was
27:12 S the harbor was not suitable for spending
27:15 S the ship was caught and could not
27:21 S they had been without food for a long time,
28: 2 S it had begun to rain and was cold,
28:20 s it is for the sake of the hope of Israel
Ro 1:20 Ever s the creation of the world his eternal power
1:28 And s they did not see fit to acknowledge God,
3:23 s all have sinned and fall short of the glory of God;
3:30 s God is one; and he will justify the circumcised
5: 1 Therefore, s we are justified by faith,
6:14 s you are not under law but under grace.
8: 9 s the Spirit of God dwells in you.
14: 6 s they give thanks to God;
1Co 1:21 For s, in the wisdom of God,
5:10 s you would then need to go out of the world.
8: 7 S some have become so accustomed to idols until
8:10 might they not, s their conscience is weak,
11: 7 s he is the image and reflection of God;

1Co 14: 2 s they are speaking mysteries in the Spirit.
14:12 s you are eager for spiritual gifts,
14:16 s the outsider does not know what you are saying?
15:21 For s death came through a human being,
2Co 1:15 S I was sure of this, I wanted to come to you first,
3:12 **S,** then, we have such a hope,
3:14 s only in Christ is it set aside.
4: 1 s it is by God's mercy that we are engaged
5:20 s God is making his appeal through us;
7: 1 S we have these promises, beloved,
8:17 but s he is more eager than ever,
9: 2 saying that Achaia has been ready s last year;
11:18 s many boast according to human standards,
12:16 (you say) s I was crafty, I took you in by deceit.
13: 3 s you desire proof that Christ is speaking in me.
Php 1:25 S I am convinced of this,
1:30 s you are having the same struggle
Col 1: 9 For this reason, s the day we heard it,
3:24 s you know that from the Lord you will receive
1Th 4:14 For s we believe that Jesus died and rose again,
5: 8 But s we belong to the day, let us be sober,
1Ti 6: 2 s those who benefit by their service are believers
Tit 1:11 s they are upsetting whole families by teaching
3:11 s you know that such a person is perverted
Heb 2:14 **S,** therefore, the children share flesh and blood,
4: 6 S therefore it remains open for some to enter it,
4:14 **S,** then, we have a great high priest who has passed
5: 2 s he himself is subject to weakness;
5:11 s you have become dull in understanding.
6: 6 s on their own they are crucifying again the Son
7:25 s he always lives to make intercession for them.
8: 4 s there are priests who offer gifts according to
9:17 s it is not in force as long as
9:26 then he would have had to suffer again and again s
10: 1 S the law has only a shadow of the good things
10: 2 s the worshipers, cleansed once for all,
10:13 and s then has been waiting
10:19 s we have confidence to enter the sanctuary by
10:21 s we have a great priest over the house of God,
11:40 s God had provided something better so
12: 1 s we are surrounded by so great a cloud
12:28 s we are receiving a kingdom that cannot
1Pe 3: 7 s they too are also heirs of the gracious gift
4: 1 S therefore Christ suffered in the flesh,
2Pe 1:14 s I know that my death will come soon,
3: 4 For ever s our ancestors died,
3:11 S all these things are to be dissolved in this way,
3:17 You therefore, beloved, s you are forewarned,
1Jn 4:11 Beloved, s God loved us so much,
Rev 16:18 as had not occurred s people were upon the earth,
18: 7 S in her heart she says, 'I rule as a queen;
18:11 s no one buys their cargo anymore,
Tob 5: 2 s he does not know me and I do not know him?
5: 3 now twenty years have passed s I left this money
6:15 So now, s I am the only son my father has,
10:12 s from now on they are as much your parents
Jdt 4: 5 s their fields had recently been harvested.
4: 7 s by them Judea could be invaded;
5: 8 S they had abandoned the ways of their ancestors,
8:31 Now s you are a God-fearing woman, pray for us,
11:12 S their food supply is exhausted
11:14 S even the people in Jerusalem
12:20 in any one day s he was born.
15: 7 s there was a vast quantity of it.
AdE 4:11 now thirty days s I was called to go to the king.' "
14: 5 Ever s I was born I have heard in the tribe
14:18 Your servant has had no joy s the day
16:18 s he, the one who did these things,
Wis 12: 8 even these you spared, s they were but mortals,
14:17 s they lived at a distance,
15:17 s they have life, but the idols never had.
18:12 s in one instant their most valued children had been
Sir 17:30 s human beings are not immortal.
23:20 it was known to him, and so it is s its completion.
37:21 s he is lacking in all wisdom.
41:12 s it will outlive you longer than a thousand hoards
LtJ 6:29 S you know by these things that they are not gods,
6:50 S they are made of wood and overlaid with gold
6:65 S you know then that they are not gods,
1Mc 1:11 with the Gentiles around us, for s we separated
6:49 s it was a sabbatical year for the land.
9:27 not been s the time that prophets ceased to appear
9:29 **"S** the death of your brother Judas there has been
10:26 S you have kept your agreement with us
10:52 **"S** I have returned to my kingdom
11: 2 s he was Alexander's father-in-law.
12: 9 s we have as encouragement the holy books
12:10 for considerable time has passed s
14:29 **"S** wars often occurred in the country, Simon son
2Mc 1:18 S on the twenty-fifth day of Chislev
2:16 **S,** therefore, we are about to celebrate
3: 5 S he could not prevail over Onias,
3:33 s for his sake the Lord has granted you your life.
4:40 S the crowds were becoming aroused and filled
7:23 s you now forget yourselves for the sake
7:25 S the young man would not listen to him at all,
11:25 s we choose that this nation also should be free
14: 9 S you are acquainted, O king,
14:26 s he had appointed that conspirator against
14:29 S it was not possible to oppose the king,
1Es 1:20 No passover like it had been kept in Israel s
2:20 S the building of the temple is now going on,
3:24 s it forces people to do these things?"
4:12 s he is to be obeyed in this fashion?"
4:32 not women strong, s they do such things?"
5:69 to him ever s the days of King Esar-haddon of
3Mc 1: 8 S the Jews had sent some of their council
1:15 "But s this has happened," the king said,
2:22 s he was smitten by a righteous judgment.
2:31 s they expected to enhance their reputation
3: 5 but s they adorned their style of life with
3:20 s we treat all nations with benevolence.
3:22 S they incline constantly to evil,
5:13 the Jews, s they had escaped the appointed hour,
5:14 now, s it was nearly the middle of the tenth hour,
5:25 s the time had run out—
5:27 s he had been completely overcome
5:35 s this also was his aid that they had received.
6:29 s they now had escaped death.
7: 6 S we have come to realize that the God of heaven
7: 7 and s we have taken into account the friendly
7:15 s they had destroyed the profaners.
7:20 s at the king's command they had all
2Es 5:50 **"S** you have now given me the opportunity,
7:*104* **"S** you have found favor in my sight,
7:*134* [64] s they are his own creatures;
14:32 And s he is a righteous judge,
4Mc 1:19 s by means of it reason rules over the emotions.
2: 6 In fact, s the law has told us not to covet,
5:25 s we believe that the law was established by God,
7:19 s they believe that they, like our
8:17 S the king has summoned and exhorted us
10: 7 S they were not able in any way to break his spirit,
11:15 S to this end we were born and bred,
11:25 S you have not been able to persuade us
12:11 s you have received good things and
13: 1 **S,** then, the seven brothers despised sufferings
13:24 S they had been educated by the same law
14:11 s the mind of woman despised even more
14:19 s even bees at the time for making honeycombs
18: 5 S in no way whatever was he able to compel

SINCERE‡ (9) [SINCERELY, SINCERITY]

Mt 22:16 saying, "Teacher, we know that you are **s,**
Mk 12:14 "Teacher, we know that you are **s,**
2Co 11: 3 be led astray from a s and pure devotion to Christ.
1Ti 1: 5 a good conscience, and s faith.
2Ti 1: 5 I am reminded of your s faith,
2Pe 3: 1 in them I am trying to arouse your s intention
AdE 16: 6 of their evil natures beguile the s goodwill
Wis 6:17 of wisdom is the most s desire for instruction,
3Mc 3:19 and are unwilling to regard any action as s.

SINCERELY (5) [SINCERE]

Job 33: 3 and what my lips know they speak **s.**
Php 1:17 not s but intending to increase my suffering
Tob 14: 7 Those who s love God will rejoice,
3Mc 3:23 among them who are s disposed toward us;
2Es 10:50 that you are s grieved and profoundly distressed

SINCERITY‡ (7) [SINCERE]

Jos 24:14 and serve him in s and in faithfulness;
1Co 5: 8 but with the unleavened bread of s and truth.
2Co 1:12 with frankness and godly s, not by earthly wisdom
2:17 but in Christ we speak as persons of **s,**
Tob 8: 7 not because of lust, but with **s.**
14:8,9 of God and to bless his name at all times with s
Wis 1: 1 the Lord in goodness and seek him with s of heart;

SINEW (1) [SINEWS]

Isa 48: 4 and your neck is an iron s and your forehead brass,

SINEWS (7) [SINEW]

Job 10:11 and knit me together with bones and **s.**
40:17 the s of its thighs are knit together.
Eze 37: 6 I will lay s on you, and will cause flesh to come
37: 8 I looked, and there were s on them,
Col 2:19 nourished and held together by its ligaments and **s,**
4Mc 7:13 his muscles flabby, his s feeble,
9:28 These leopard-like beasts tore out his s with

SINFUL (22) [SIN]

Dt 9:21 Then I took the s thing you had made, the calf,
Ps 107:17 Some were sick through their s ways,
Isa 1: 4 Ah, s nation, people laden with iniquity,
Jer 9: 7 for what else can I do with my s people?
Eze 23:49 and you shall bear the penalty for your s idolatry;
Am 9: 8 eyes of the Lord GOD are upon the s kingdom,
Mk 8:38 of my words in this adulterous and s generation,
Lk 5: 8 "Go away from me, Lord, for I am a s man!"
Ro 7: 5 While we were living in the flesh, our s passions,
7:13 commandment might become s beyond measure.
8: 3 by sending his own Son in the likeness of s flesh,
1Ti 1: 9 for the godless and s, for the unholy and profane,
Tit 3:11 you know that such a person is perverted and **s,**
Wis 3:13 who has not entered into a s union;
Sir 10:23 and it is not proper to honor one who is **s.**
15:12 for he has no need of the s.
23:13 foul language, for it involves s speech.
27:13 and their laughter is wantonly **s.**
47:23 into sin and started Ephraim on its s ways.
1Mc 1:10 From them came forth a s root,
1:34 They stationed there a s people,
2Es 7:*114* [44] s indulgence has come to an end,

SINFULLY (1) [SIN]

Isa 31: 7 which your hands have s made for you.

SING‡ (166) [LOVE-SONG, SANG, SINGER, SINGERS, SINGING, SINGS, SONG, SONGS, SUNG, TAUNT-SONGS]

A. SING PRAISE (41)
B. SING PRAISES (31)
C. SING TO THE †LORD (15)

Ex 15: 1 "I will s to the LORD, for he has triumphed C
15:21 **"S** to the LORD, for he has triumphed gloriously; C
Nu 21:17 "Spring up, O well!—S to it!—
Jdg 5: 3 to the LORD I will **s,**
1Sa 21:11 Did they not s to one another of him in dances,
29: 5 of whom they s to one another in dances,
2Sa 22:50 among the nations, and s praises to your name. B
1Ch 16: 9 S to him, sing praises to him,
16: 9 Sing to him, s praises to him, B
16:23 S to the LORD, all the earth. C
16:33 the trees of the forest s for joy before the LORD,
2Ch 20:21 to s to the LORD and praise him in holy splendor, C
20:22 As they began to s and praise,
29:30 commanded the Levites to s praises to the LORD B
Job 21:12 They s to the tambourine and the lyre,
29:13 and I caused the widow's heart to s for joy.
Ps 5:11 let them ever s for joy.
7:17 and s praise to the name of the LORD, A
9: 2 I will s praise to your name, O Most High. A
9:11 S praises to the LORD, who dwells in Zion. B
13: 6 I will s to the LORD, C
18:49 among the nations, and s praises to your name. B
21:13 We will s and praise your power.
27: 6 I will s and make melody to the LORD.
30: 4 S praises to the LORD, O you his faithful ones, B
33: 3 S to him a new song;
47: 6 S praises to God, sing praises; B
47: 6 Sing praises to God, s praises; B
47: 6 s praises to our King, sing praises. B
47: 6 sing praises to our King, s praises. B
47: 7 king of all the earth; s praises with a psalm. B
51:14 and my tongue will s aloud of your deliverance.
57: 7 I will s and make melody.
57: 9 I will s praises to you among the nations. B
59:16 But I will s of your might;
59:16 I will s aloud of your steadfast love in
59:17 O my strength, I will s praises to you, B
61: 8 So I will always s praises to your name, B
63: 7 and in the shadow of your wings I s for joy.
65:13 they shout and s together for joy.
66: 2 s the glory of his name;
66: 4 they s praises to you, sing praises to your name." B
66: 4 they sing praises to you, s praises to your name." B
67: 4 Let the nations be glad and s for joy,
68: 4 S to God, sing praises to his name;
68: 4 Sing to God, s praises to his name; B
68:32 S to God, O kingdoms of the earth;
68:32 kingdoms of the earth; s praises to the Lord, B
71:22 I will s praises to you with the lyre, B
71:23 lips will shout for joy when I s praises to you; B
75: 9 I will s praises to the God of Jacob. B
81: 1 S aloud to God our strength;
84: 2 my heart and my flesh s for joy to the living God.
89: 1 I will s of your steadfast love, O LORD, forever;
92: 1 to s praises to your name, O Most High; B
92: 4 at the works of your hands I s for joy.
95: 1 O come, let us s to the LORD; C
96: 1 O s to the LORD a new song; C
96: 1 s to the LORD, all the earth. C
96: 2 S to the LORD, bless his name; C
96:12 Then shall all the trees of the forest s for joy
98: 1 O s to the LORD a new song, C
98: 4 break forth into joyous song and s praises. B
98: 5 S praises to the LORD with the lyre, B
98: 8 let the hills s together for joy
101: 1 I will s of loyalty and of justice;
101: 1 to you, O LORD, I will **s.**
104:12 they s among the branches.
104:33 I will s to the LORD as long as I live; C
104:33 I will s praise to my God while I have being. A
105: 2 S to him, sing praises to him;
105: 2 Sing to him, s praises to him; B
108: 1 I will s and make melody.
108: 3 and I will s praises to you among the nations. B
119:172 My tongue will s of your promise,
135: 3 s to his name, for he is gracious.
137: 3 saying, **"S** us one of the songs of Zion!"
137: 4 could we s the LORD's song in a foreign land?
138: 1 before the gods I s your praise;
138: 5 They shall s of the ways of the LORD,
144: 9 I will s a new song to you, O God;
145: 7 and shall s aloud of your righteousness.
146: 2 I will s praises to my God all my life long. B
147: 1 How good it is to s praises to our God; B
147: 7 S to the LORD with thanksgiving; C
149: 1 S to the LORD a new song, C
149: 5 let them s for joy on their couches.
Pr 29: 6 but the righteous s and rejoice.
Isa 5: 1 Let me s for my beloved my love-song
12: 5 S praises to the LORD, B
12: 6 Shout aloud and s for joy, O royal Zion,
23:16 Make sweet melody, s many songs,
24:14 They lift up their voices, they s for joy;
26:19 O dwellers in the dust, awake and s for joy!
27: 2 On that day: A pleasant vineyard, s about it!
35: 6 and the tongue of the speechless s for joy.
38:20 and we will s to stringed instruments all the days
42:10 S to the LORD a new song, C

Isa 42:11 let the inhabitants of Sela s for joy,
44:23 S, O heavens, for the LORD has done it;
49:13 S for joy, O heavens, and exult, O earth;
52: 8 up their voices, together they s for joy;
54: 1 S, O barren one who did not bear;
65:14 my servants shall s for gladness of heart,
Jer 20:13 S to the LORD; praise the LORD! C
31: 7 S aloud with gladness for Jacob,
31:12 They shall come and s aloud on the height of Zion,
33:11 the voices of those who s,
Am 6: 5 who s idle songs to the sound of the harp,
Zep 3:14 S aloud, O daughter Zion; shout, O Israel!
Zec 2:10 S and rejoice, O daughter Zion!
Ro 15: 9 and s praises to your name"; B
1Co 14:15 I will s praise with the spirit, A
14:15 but I will s praise with the mind also. A
Eph 5:19 as you s psalms and hymns and spiritual songs
Col 3:16 and with gratitude in your hearts s psalms, hymns,
Jas 5:13 They should s songs of praise.
Rev 4: 8 Day and night without ceasing they s, "Holy, holy,
5: 9 They s a new song: "You are worthy to take
14: 3 and they s a new song before the throne and before
15: 3 And they s the song of Moses, the servant of God,
Tob 12: 6 Bless and s praise to his name. A
12:18 Bless him each and every day; s his praises.
13:17 The gates of Jerusalem will s hymns of joy,
Jdt 16: 1 s to my Lord with cymbals.
16:13 I will s to my God a new song:
AdE 13:17 that we may live and s praise to your name, A
Sir 17:27 Who will s praises to the Most High in Hades B
17:28 those who are alive and well s the Lord's praises.
39:14 Scatter the fragrance, and s a hymn of praise;
39:35 So now s praise with all your heart and voice, A
44: 1 now s the praises of famous men,
51:11 and will s hymns of thanksgiving."
Aza 1:35 s praise to him and highly exalt him forever. A
1:36 s praise to him and highly exalt him forever. A
1:37 s praise to him and highly exalt him forever. A
1:38 s praise to him and highly exalt him forever. A
1:39 s praise to him and highly exalt him forever. A
1:40 s praise to him and highly exalt him forever. A
1:41 s praise to him and highly exalt him forever. A
1:42 s praise to him and highly exalt him forever. A
1:43 s praise to him and highly exalt him forever. A
1:44 s praise to him and highly exalt him forever. A
1:45 s praise to him and highly exalt him forever. A
1:46 s praise to him and highly exalt him forever. A
1:47 s praise to him and highly exalt him forever. A
1:48 s praise to him and highly exalt him forever. A
1:49 s praise to him and highly exalt him forever. A
1:50 s praise to him and highly exalt him forever. A
1:51 s praise to him and highly exalt him forever. A
1:52 s praise to him and highly exalt him forever. A
1:53 s praise to him and highly exalt him forever. A
1:54 s praise to him and highly exalt him forever. A
1:55 s praise to him and highly exalt him forever. A
1:56 s praise to him and highly exalt him forever. A
1:57 s praise to him and highly exalt him forever. A
1:58 s praise to him and highly exalt him forever. A
1:59 s praise to him and highly exalt him forever. A
1:60 s praise to him and highly exalt him forever. A
1:61 s praise to him and highly exalt him forever. A
1:62 s praise to him and highly exalt him forever. A
1:63 s praise to him and highly exalt him forever. A
1:64 s praise to him and highly exalt him forever. A
1:65 s praise to him and highly exalt him forever. A
1:66 s praise to him and highly exalt him forever. A
1:68 s praise to him and give thanks to him, A

SINGED (1)

Da 3:27 the hair of their heads was not s,

SINGER (2) [SING]

1Ch 6:33 Heman, the s, son of Joel, son of Samuel,
Eze 33:32 To them you are like a s of love songs,

SINGERS (48) [SING]

Nu 21:27 the ballad s say, "Come to Heshbon, let it be built;
1Ki 10:12 lyres also and harps for the s;
1Ch 9:33 Now these are the s, the heads of ancestral houses
15:16 the Levites to appoint their kindred as the s to play
15:19 The s Heman, Asaph, and Ethan were
15:27 and the the s, and Chenaniah the leader of the music of the s;
2Ch 5:12 and all the levitical s, Asaph, Heman,
5:13 and s to make themselves heard in unison in praise
9:11 lyres also and harps for the s;
23:13 and the s with their musical instruments leading in
29:28 The whole assembly worshiped, the s sang,
35:15 The s, the descendants of Asaph,
Ezr 2:41 The s: the descendants of Asaph,
2:65 and they had two hundred male and female s.
2:70 and the s, the gatekeepers,
7: 7 of Israel, and some of the priests and Levites, the s
7:24 or toll on any of the priests, the Levites, the s,
10:24 Of the s: Eliashib. Of the gatekeepers:
Ne 7: 1 the s, and the Levites had been appointed,
7:44 The s: the descendants of Asaph,
7:67 and they had two hundred forty-five s,
7:73 So the priests, the Levites, the gatekeepers, the s,
10:28 the priests, the Levites, the gatekeepers, the s,
10:39 and the gatekeepers and the s are.
11:22 the s, in charge of the work of the house of God.
11:23 and a settled provision for the s,
12:28 The companies of the s gathered together from
Ne 12:29 for the s had built for themselves villages
12:42 And the s sang with Jezrahiah as their leader.
12:45 as did the s and the gatekeepers,
12:46 and Asaph long ago there was a leader of the s,
12:47 the daily portions for the s and the gatekeepers.
13: 5 s, and gatekeepers, and the contributions for
13:10 so that the Levites and the s,
Ps 68:25 the s in front, the musicians last,
87: 7 S and dancers alike say, "All my springs are
Ecc 2: 8 I got s, both men and women,
Eze 40:44 of the inner gateway there were chambers for the s
Sir 47: 9 He placed s before the altar,
50:18 Then the s praised him with their voices in sweet
1Es 1:15 The temple s, the sons of Asaph,
5:27 The temple s: the descendants of Asaph,
5:42 there were two hundred forty-five musicians and s.
5:46 and the temple s, the gatekeepers,
8: 5 and temple s and gatekeepers and temple servants,
8:22 of the priests or Levites or temple s or gatekeepers
9:24 Of the temple s: Eliashib and Zaccur.

SINGING (35) [SING]

1Sa 18: 6 s and dancing, to meet King Saul,
2Sa 19:35 listen to the voice of s men and s women?
1Ch 16: 7 on that day David first appointed the s of praises
25: 7 who were trained in s to the LORD,
2Ch 23:18 with rejoicing and with s,
35:25 and all the s men and s women have spoken
Ne 12:27 with thanksgivings and with s, with cymbals,
Ps 26: 7 s aloud a song of thanksgiving,
84: 4 in your house, ever s your praise.
100: 2 come into his presence with s.
105:43 with joy, his chosen ones with s.
SS 2:12 the time of s has come,
Isa 14: 7 at rest and quiet; they break forth into s.
24: 9 No longer do they drink wine with s;
35: 2 and rejoice with joy and s.
35:10 and come to Zion with s;
44:23 break forth into s, O mountains, O forest,
49:13 break forth, O mountains, into s!
51:11 and come to Zion with s;
52: 9 Break forth together into s,
Zep 3:17 he will exult over you with loud s
Ac 16:25 and Silas were praying and s hymns to God,
Eph 5:19 s and making melody to the Lord in your hearts,
Rev 4:10 they cast their crowns before the throne, s,
5:12 s with full voice, "Worthy is the Lamb
5:13 and all that is in them, s,
7:12 s, "Amen! Blessing and glory
11:17 s, "We give you thanks, Lord God Almighty,
Tob 12:22 They kept blessing God and s his praises,
Jdt 15:13 and wearing garlands and s hymns.
Wis 18: 9 already they were s the praises of the ancestors.
Sir 9: 4 Do not dally with a s girl,
Aza 1: 1 s hymns to God and blessing the Lord.

SINGLE‡ (55) [SINGLE-HANDED, SINGLENESS]

Ex 10:19 not a s locust was left in all the country of Egypt.
21: 3 If he comes in s, he shall go out s;
33: 5 if for a s moment I should go up among you,
Lev 26:26 ten women shall bake your bread in a s oven,
Nu 13:23 and cut down from there a branch with a s cluster
15:15 be for both you and the resident alien a s statute,
35:30 be put to death on the testimony of a s witness.
Dt 2:34 We left not a s survivor.
3: 3 down until not a s survivor was left.
19:15 A s witness shall not suffice to convict a person
29:21 The LORD will s them out from all the tribes
Jos 3:13 they shall stand in a s heap."
3:16 rising up in a s heap far off at Adam,
1Sa 24:14 Whom do you pursue? A dead dog? A s flea?
26:20 for the king of Israel has come out to seek a s flea,
2Sa 2:25 around Abner and formed a s band;
1Ki 16:11 he did not leave him a s male of his kindred
2Ki 18:24 then can you repulse a s captain among the least
1Ch 12:38 of Israel were of a s mind to make David king.
23:11 so they were enrolled as a s family.
28: 9 and serve him with s mind and willing heart;
29: 9 with s mind they had offered freely to the LORD;
29:19 with s mind he may keep your commandments,
Est 8:12 on a s day throughout all the provinces
Isa 36: 9 then can you repulse a s captain among the least
Zec 3: 9 on a s stone with seven facets,
3: 9 and I will remove the guilt of this land in a s day.
Mt 6:27 by worrying add a s hour to your span of life?
23:15 For you cross sea and land to make a s convert,
27:14 But he gave him no answer, not even to a s charge,
Lk 12:25 by worrying add a s hour to your span of life?
Jn 12:24 it remains just a s grain; but if it dies,
18: 9 not lose a s one of those whom you gave me."
1Co 10: 8 and twenty-three thousand fell in a s day.
12:19 If all were a s member, where would the body be?
Gal 5:14 the whole law is summed up in a s commandment,
Heb 10:12 Christ had offered for all time a s sacrifice for sins,
10:14 For by a s offering he has perfected
12:16 who sold his birthright for a s meal.
Rev 18: 8 therefore her plagues will come in a s day—
21:21 each of the gates is a s pearl,
Tob 3: 8 and have not borne the name of a s one of them.
14: 4 not a s word of the prophecies will fail.
AdE 13: 7 and remain so may in a s day go down in violence
Wis 11:20 at a s breath when pursued by justice and scattered
1Mc 5:27 and destroy all these people in a s day."
2Mc 2:23 we shall attempt to condense into a s book.
2Mc 7:20 she saw her seven sons perish within a s day,
8:18 with a s nod to strike down those who are coming
1Es 5:47 they gathered with a s purpose in the square before
5:58 the work on the house of God with a s purpose.
Pm 151: T *after he fought in s combat with Goliath.*
3Mc 4:14 at the end to be destroyed in the space of a s day.
2Es 11: 6 not a s creature that was on the earth.

SINGLE-HANDED (1) [HAND, SINGLE]

3Mc 1: 2 intending s to kill him and thereby end the war.

SINGLENESS (2) [SINGLE]

1Ch 12:33 to help David with s of purpose.
Eph 6: 5 in s of heart, as you obey Christ;

SINGS (3) [SING]

Job 33:27 That person s to others and says, 'I sinned,
Pr 25:20 on a wound is one who s songs to a heavy heart.
Man 1:15 For all the host of heaven s your praise,

SINIM See Index to Footnotes

SINITES (2)

Ge 10:17 the Hivites, the Arkites, the S,
1Ch 1:15 the Hivites, the Arkites, the S,

SINK (11) [SANK, SINKING, SINKS, SUNK]

2Sa 22:40 you made my assailants s under me.
Ps 18:39 you made my assailants s under me.
44:25 For we s down to the dust;
69: 2 I s in deep mire, where there is no foothold;
Jer 51:64 'Thus shall Babylon s, to rise no more,
Eze 27:27 s into the heart of the seas on the day of your ruin.
Am 8: 8 and be tossed about and s again,
Mt 14:30 and beginning to s, he cried out, "Lord, save me!"
Lk 5: 7 so that they began to s.
9:44 "Let these words s into your ears:
Ac 20: 9 began to s off into a deep sleep

SINKING (1) [SINK]

Ps 69:14 rescue me from s in the mire;

SINKS (3) [SINK]

Ecc 10:18 Through sloth the roof s in,
Isa 5:24 and as dry grass s down in the flame,
Am 9: 5 and all of it rises like the Nile, and s again,

SINNED‡ (132) [SIN]

Ge 20: 9 How have I s against you,
Ex 9:27 and said to them, "This time I have s;
9:34 he s once more and hardened his heart,
10:16 "I have s against the LORD your God,
32:30 "You have s a great sin.
32:31 "Alas, this people has s a great sin;
32:33 "Whoever has s against me I will blot out
Lev 6: 4 when you have s and realize your guilt,
Nu 14:40 that the LORD has promised, for we have s."
21: 7 "We have s by speaking against the LORD and
22:34 Balaam said to the angel of the LORD, "I have s,
32:23 you do not do this, you have s against the LORD;
Dt 1:41 "We have s against the LORD!
9:16 Then I saw that you had indeed s against
Jos 7:11 Israel has s; they have transgressed my covenant
7:20 the one who s against the LORD God of Israel.
Jdg 10:10 saying, "We have s against you,
10:15 And the Israelites said to the LORD, "We have s;
11:27 It is not I who have s against you,
1Sa 7: 6 and said, "We have s against the LORD."
12:10 they cried to the LORD, and said, 'We have s,
15:24 Saul said to Samuel, "I have s;
15:30 Then Saul said, "I have s;
19: 4 because he has not s against you,
24:11 I have not s against you,
2Sa 12:13 "I have s against the LORD."
19:20 For your servant knows that I have s;
24:10 "I have s greatly in what I have done.
24:17 "I alone have s, and I alone have done wickedly;
1Ki 8:33 "When your people Israel, having s against you,
8:35 and there is no rain because they have s
8:47 saying, 'We have s, and have done wrong;
8:50 and forgive your people who have s against you,
14:16 which he s and which he caused Israel to commit."
18: 9 And he said, "How have I s,
2Ki 17: 7 This occurred because the people of Israel had s
1Ch 21: 8 "I have s greatly in that I have done this thing.
21:17 It is I who have s and done very wickedly.
2Ch 6:24 "When your people Israel, having s against you,
6:26 and there is no rain because they have s
6:37 saying, 'We have s, and have done wrong;
6:39 and forgive your people who have s against you.
Ne 1: 6 which we have s against you.
1: 6 Both I and my family have s.
9:29 but s against your ordinances,
Job 1: 5 for Job said, "It may be that my children have s,
8: 4 If your children s against him,
24:19 so does Sheol those who have s.
33:27 That person sings to others and says, 'I s,
35: 3 How am I better off than if I had s?'
35: 6 you have s, what do you accomplish against him?
Ps 41: 4 heal me, for I have s against you."
51: 4 Against you, you alone, have I s,
78:17 Yet they s still more against him,

Ps 78:32 In spite of all this they still **s;**
106: 6 Both we and our ancestors have **s;**
Isa 42:24 Was it not the LORD, against whom we have **s,**
43:27 Your first ancestor **s,** and your interpreters
64: 5 But you were angry, and we **s;**
Jer 2:35 to judgment for saying, "I have not **s.**"
3:25 for we have **s** against the LORD our God,
8:14 because we have **s** against the LORD.
14: 7 and we have **s** against you.
14:20 for we have **s** against you.
40: 3 because all of you **s** against the LORD and did
44:23 because you **s** against the LORD and did not obey
50: 7 because they have **s** against the LORD,
50:14 spare no arrows, for she has **s** against the LORD.
La 1: 8 Jerusalem **s** grievously, so she has become
5: 7 Our ancestors **s;** they are no more,
5:16 woe to us, for we have **s!**
Eze 28:16 with violence, and you **s;**
45:20 the seventh day of the month for anyone who has **s**
Da 9: 5 we have **s** and done wrong,
9: 8 and our ancestors, because we have **s** against you.
9:11 because we have **s** against you.
9:15 we have **s,** we have done wickedly.
Hos 4: 7 more they increased, the more they **s** against me;
10: 9 Since the days of Gibeah you have **s,** O Israel;
Mic 7: 9 because I have **s** against him,
Zep 1:17 because they have **s** against the LORD,
Mt 27: 4 He said, "I have **s** by betraying innocent blood."
Lk 15:18 "Father, I have **s** against heaven and before you;
15:21 'Father, I have **s** against heaven and before you;
Jn 9: 2 His disciples asked him, "Rabbi, who **s,**
9: 3 "Neither this man nor his parents **s;**
Ro 2:12 All who have **s** apart from the law will
2:12 and all who have **s** under the law will be judged by
3:23 since all have **s** and fall short of the glory of God;
5:12 and so death spread to all because all have **s—**
2Co 12:21 over many who previously **s** and have not repented
13: 2 I warned those who **s** previously and all the others,
Heb 3:17 Was it not those who **s,**
2Pe 2: 4 For if God did not spare the angels when they **s,**
1Jn 1:10 If we say that we have not **s,** we make him a liar,
Tob 3: 3 committed before you. They **s** against you,
AdE 14: 6 And now we have **s** before you,
Sir 5: 4 Do not say, "I **s,** yet what has happened to me?"
18:21 and when you have **s,** repent.
19:16 Who has not **s** with his tongue?
21: 1 Have you **s,** my child?
48:16 but others **s** more and more.
Bar 1:13 for we have **s** against the Lord our God,
1:17 because we have **s** before the Lord.
2: 5 because our nation **s** against the Lord our God,
2:12 we have **s,** we have been ungodly,
2:33 the ways of their ancestors, who **s** before the Lord.
3: 2 O Lord, and have mercy, for we have **s** before you.
3: 4 the children of those who **s** before you,
3: 7 the iniquity of our ancestors who **s** against you.
Aza 1: 6 For we have **s** and broken your law
1: 6 in all matters we have **s** grievously.
1Es 1:24 concerning those who **s** and acted wickedly toward
4:27 or stumbled, or **s** because of women.
6:15 But when our ancestors **s** against the Lord
8:92 and said to Ezra, "We have **s** against the Lord,
9:11 for we have **s** too much in these things.
Man 1: 7 and forgiveness to those who have **s** against you,
1:12 I have **s,** O Lord, I have **s,**
2Es 2: 3 and sorrow I have lost you, because you have **s**
3:35 the inhabitants of the earth not **s** in your sight?
7:*46* For who among the living is there that has not **s,**
7:*87* in whose presence they **s** while they were alive,
7:*106* [36] Moses for our ancestors who **s** in the desert,
7:*118* [48] For though it was you who **s,**
7:*134* [64] he shows patience toward those who have **s,**
8:38 about the fashioning of those who have **s,**
9:36 we who have received the law and **s** will perish,
15:27 because you have **s** against him.
16:53 Sinners must not say that they have not **s;**
16:53 "I have not **s** before God and his glory."

SINNER‡ (36) [SIN]

1Sa 2:25 someone can intercede for the **s** with the LORD;
Ps 51: 5 a **s** when my mother conceived me.
Pr 11:31 how much more the wicked and the **s!**
Ecc 2:26 the **s** he gives the work of gathering and heaping,
7:26 but the **s** is taken by her.
Lk 7:37 And a woman in the city, who was a **s,**
7:39 this is who is touching him—that she is a **s.**"
15: 7 be more joy in heaven over one **s** who repents than
15:10 of the angels of God over one **s** who repents."
18:13 'God, be merciful to me, a **s!**'
19: 7 "He has gone to be the guest of one who is a **s.**"
Jn 9:16 "How can a man who is a **s** perform such signs?"
9:24 We know that this man is a **s.**"
9:25 He answered, "I do not know whether he is a **s.**
Ro 3: 7 why am I still being condemned as a **s?**
Jas 5:20 you should know that whoever brings back a **s**
Sir 1:25 but godliness is an abomination to a **s.**
2:12 and to the **s** who walks a double path!
3:27 and the **s** adds sin to sins.
6: 1 so it is with the double-tongued **s.**
11:21 Do not wonder at the works of a **s,**
11:32 and a **s** lies in wait to shed blood.
12: 4 Give to the devout, but do not help the **s.**
12: 7 Give to the one who is good, but do not help the **s.**
12:14 with a **s** and becomes involved in the other's sins.
13:17 No more has a **s** with the devout.
15: 9 Praise is unseemly on the lips of a **s,**
16:13 The **s** will not escape with plunder,
27:30 yet a **s** holds on to them.
28: 9 and the **s** disrupts friendships and sows discord
29:16 A **s** wastes the property of his guarantor,
29:19 The **s** comes to grief through surety;
32:17 The **s** will shun reproof, and will find a decision
33:14 so the **s** is the opposite of the godly.
1Mc 2:48 and they never let the **s** gain the upper hand.
Man 1: 8 you have appointed repentance for me, who am a **s.**

SINNER'S (4) [SIN]

Pr 13:22 but the **s** wealth is laid up for the righteous.
Jas 5:20 the **s** soul from death and will cover a multitude
Sir 21: 6 Those who hate reproof walk in the **s** steps,
25:19 may a **s** lot befall her!

SINNERS‡ (85) [SIN]

Ge 13:13 of Sodom were wicked, great **s** against the LORD.
Nu 16:38 the censers of these **s** have become holy at the cost
32:14 And now you, a brood of **s,**
1Sa 15:18 'Go, utterly destroy the **s,** the Amalekites,
Ps 1: 1 or take the path that **s** tread,
1: 5 nor **s** in the congregation of the righteous;
25: 8 therefore he instructs **s** in the way.
26: 9 Do not sweep me away with **s,**
51:13 and **s** will return to you.
104:35 Let **s** be consumed from the earth,
Pr 1:10 My child, if **s** entice you, do not consent.
13:21 Misfortune pursues **s,** but prosperity rewards
14:21 Those who despise their neighbors are **s,**
23:17 Do not let your heart envy **s,**
Ecc 8:12 **s** do evil a hundred times and prolong their lives,
9: 2 As are the good, so are the **s;**
Isa 1:28 But rebels and **s** shall be destroyed together,
13: 9 and to destroy its **s** from it.
33:14 The **s** in Zion are afraid;
Am 9:10 All the **s** of my people shall die by the sword,
Mt 9:10 many tax collectors and **s** came and were sitting
9:11 with tax collectors and **s?"**
9:13 For I have come to call not the righteous but **s.**"
11:19 a friend of tax collectors and **s!'**
26:45 and the Son of Man is betrayed into the hands of **s.**
Mk 2:15 many tax collectors and **s** were also sitting
2:16 of the Pharisees saw that he was eating with **s**
2:16 "Why does he eat with tax collectors and **s?"**
2:17 I have come to call not the righteous but **s.**"
14:41 the Son of Man is betrayed into the hands of **s.**
Lk 5:30 and drink with tax collectors and **s?"**
5:32 to call not the righteous but **s** to repentance."
6:32 For even **s** love those who love them.
6:33 For even **s** do the same.
6:34 Even **s** lend to **s,** to receive as much again.
7:34 a friend of tax collectors and **s!'**
13: 2 they were worse **s** than all other Galileans?
15: 1 the tax collectors and **s** were coming near to listen
15: 2 "This fellow welcomes **s** and eats with them."
24: 7 that the Son of Man must be handed over to **s,**
Jn 9:31 We know that God does not listen to **s,**
Ro 5: 8 in that while we still were **s** Christ died for us.
5:19 one man's disobedience the many were made **s,**
Gal 2:15 We ourselves are Jews by birth and not Gentile **s;**
2:17 we ourselves have been found to be **s,**
1Ti 1:15 that Christ Jesus came into the world to save **s—**
Heb 7:26 separated from **s,** and exalted above the heavens.
12: 3 from **s,** so that you may not grow weary
Jas 4: 8 Cleanse your hands, you **s,** and purify your hearts,
1Pe 4:18 what will become of the ungodly and the **s?"**
Jude 1:15 of all the harsh things that ungodly **s** have spoken
Tob 4:17 on the grave of the righteous, but give none to **s.**
13: 6 and show his power and majesty to a nation of **s:**
13: 6 you **s,** and do what is right before him;
Wis 4:10 and while living among **s** were taken up.
19:13 upon the **s** without prior signs in the violence
Sir 5: 6 and his anger will rest on **s.**
7:16 Do not enroll in the ranks of **s;**
8:10 Do not kindle the coals of **s,**
9:11 Do not envy the success of **s,**
11: 9 and do not sit with **s** when they judge a case.
12: 6 also hates **s** and will inflict punishment on
15: 7 foolish will not obtain her, and **s** will not see her.
16: 6 In an assembly of **s** a fire is kindled,
19:22 nor is there prudence in the counsel of **s.**
21:10 The way of **s** is paved with smooth stones,
23: 8 **S** are overtaken through their lips;
39:25 but for **s** good things and bad.
39:27 but for **s** they turn into evils.
40: 8 human and animal, but to **s** seven times more,
41: 5 The children of **s** are abominable children,
41: 6 The inheritance of the children of **s** will perish,
49: 4 of them were great **s,** for they abandoned the law
1Mc 2:44 down **s** in their anger and renegades in their wrath;
2:62 Do not fear the words of **s,**
2Mc 12:23 putting the **s** to the sword,
14:42 to die nobly rather than to fall into the hands of **s**
Man 1: 5 and the wrath of your threat to **s** is unendurable;
1: 7 your mercies you have appointed repentance for **s,**
2Es 3:29 my soul has seen many **s** during these thirty years.
8:31 it is because of us **s** that you are called merciful.
15:22 My right hand will not spare the **s,**
15:23 consumed the foundations of the earth and the **s,**
16:53 **S** must not say that they have not sinned;

SINNING (9) [SIN]

Ge 20: 6 furthermore it was I who kept you from **s**
1Sa 14:33 the troops are **s** against the LORD by eating with
Ecc 7:20 on earth so righteous as to do good without ever **s.**
Hos 8:11 they became to him altars for **s.**
13: 2 And now they keep on **s** and make a cast image
1Jn 3: 8 for the devil has been **s** from the beginning.
Sir 19:28 Even if lack of strength keeps him from **s,**
20:21 One may be prevented from **s** by poverty;
2Es 7:*116* [46] had restrained him from **s.**

SINS‡ (265) [SIN]

A. SINS OF JEROBOAM (12)
B. FORGIVENESS OF SINS (10)

Lev 4: 2 When anyone **s** unintentionally in any of
4: 3 If it is the anointed priest who **s,**
4:22 When a ruler **s,** doing unintentionally any one
4:27 among you **s** unintentionally in doing any one of
5:13 for whichever of these **s** you have committed,
5:15 and **s** unintentionally in any of the holy things of
16:16 and because of their transgressions, all their **s;**
16:21 all their **s,** putting them on the head of the goat,
16:30 from all your **s** you shall be clean before
16:34 the people of Israel once in the year for all their **s.**
26:18 I will continue to punish you sevenfold for your **s.**
26:21 I will continue to plague you sevenfold for your **s.**
26:24 I myself will strike you sevenfold for your **s.**
26:28 in turn will punish you myself sevenfold for your **s.**
Nu 15:27 An individual who **s** unintentionally shall present
16:26 or you will be swept away for all their **s.**"
Jos 24:19 he will not forgive your transgressions or your **s.**
1Sa 2:25 If one person **s** against another,
2:25 but if someone **s** against the LORD,
12:19 to all our **s** the evil of demanding a king
1Ki 8:31 "If someone **s** against a neighbor and is given
14:16 give Israel up because of the **s** of Jeroboam, A
14:22 to jealousy with their **s** that they committed,
15: 3 He committed all the **s** that his father did
15:30 because of the **s** of Jeroboam that he committed A
16: 2 provoking me to anger with their **s,**
16:13 of all the **s** of Baasha and the **s** of his son Elah
16:19 because of the **s** that he committed,
16:26 and in the **s** that he caused Israel to commit,
16:31 to walk in the **s** of Jeroboam son of Nebat, A
2Ki 10:29 not turn aside from the **s** of Jeroboam son A
10:31 he did not turn from the **s** of Jeroboam, A
13: 2 and followed the **s** of Jeroboam son of Nebat, A
13: 6 not depart from the **s** of the house of Jeroboam,
13:11 not depart from all the **s** of Jeroboam son of A
14: 6 but all shall be put to death for their own **s.**"
14:24 not depart from all the **s** of Jeroboam son of A
15: 9 not depart from the **s** of Jeroboam son of Nebat, A
15:18 all his days from any of the **s** of Jeroboam A
15:24 he did not turn away from the **s** of Jeroboam A
15:28 not depart from the **s** of Jeroboam son of Nebat, A
17:22 The people of Israel continued in all the **s** that
24: 3 for the **s** of Manasseh, for all he had committed,
2Ch 6:22 "If someone **s** against another and is required
25: 4 but all shall be put to death for their own **s.**"
28:10 But what have you except **s** against
28:13 the LORD in addition to our present **s** and guilt.
Ne 1: 6 confessing the **s** of the people of Israel,
9: 2 and stood and confessed their **s** and the iniquities
9:37 over us because of our **s;**
Job 13:23 How many are my iniquities and my **s?**
Ps 25: 7 the **s** of my youth or my transgressions;
25:18 and my trouble, and forgive all my **s.**
51: 9 Hide your face from my **s,**
79: 9 deliver us, and forgive our **s,**
90: 8 our secret **s** in the light of your countenance.
103:10 He does not deal with us according to our **s,**
Isa 1:18 your **s** are like scarlet, they shall be like snow;
38:17 for you have cast all my **s** behind your back.
40: 2 from the LORD's hand double for all her **s.**
43:24 But you have burdened me with your **s;**
43:25 and I will not remember your **s.**
44:22 like a cloud, and your **s** like mist;
50: 1 No, because of your **s** you were sold,
58: 1 to the house of Jacob their **s.**
59: 2 and your **s** have hidden his face from you so
59:12 and our **s** testify against us.
Jer 5:25 and your **s** have deprived you of good.
14:10 he will remember their iniquity and punish their **s.**
15:13 for all your **s,** throughout all your territory.
30:14 because your **s** are so numerous.
30:15 because your **s** are so numerous,
31:30 But all shall die for their own **s;**
50:20 and the **s** of Judah, and none shall be found;
La 3:39 about the punishment of their **s?**
4:13 It was for the **s** of her prophets and the iniquities
4:22 he will punish, he will uncover your **s.**
Eze 14:13 when a land **s** against me by acting faithlessly,
16:51 Samaria has not committed half your **s;**
16:52 because of your **s** in which you acted more
18: 4 it is only the person who **s** that shall die.
18:14 a son who sees all the **s** that his father has done,
18:20 The person who **s** shall die.
18:21 But if the wicked turn away from all their **s**
21:24 so that in all your deeds your **s** appear—
33:10 "Our transgressions and our **s** weigh upon us,
33:16 None of the **s** that they have committed shall
Da 4:27 atone for your **s** with righteousness,
9:16 of our **s** and the iniquities of our ancestors,
Hos 8:13 and punish their **s;** they shall return to Egypt.
9: 9 will remember their iniquity, he will punish their **s.**
Am 5:12 and how great are your **s—**
Mic 1: 5 for the transgression of Jacob and for the **s** of
6:13 making you desolate because of your **s.**

Mic 7:19 You will cast all our s into the depths of the sea.
Mt 1:21 for he will save his people from their s."
3: 6 by him in the river Jordan, confessing their s.
9: 2 "Take heart, son; your s are forgiven."
9: 5 For which is easier, to say, 'Your s are forgiven,'
9: 6 the Son of Man has authority on earth to forgive s"
18:15 "If another member of the church s against you,
18:21 if another member of the church s against me,
26:28 poured out for many for the forgiveness of s. B
Mk 1: 4 a baptism of repentance for the forgiveness of s. B
1: 5 by him in the river Jordan, confessing their s.
2: 5 he said to the paralytic, "Son, your s are forgiven."
2: 7 Who can forgive s but God alone?"
2: 9 to say to the paralytic, 'Your s are forgiven,'
2:10 the Son of Man has authority on earth to forgive s"
3:28 for their s and whatever blasphemies they utter;
Lk 1:77 to his people by the forgiveness of their s.
3: 3 a baptism of repentance for the forgiveness of s, B
5:20 he said, "Friend, your s are forgiven you."
5:21 Who can forgive s but God alone?"
5:23 Which is easier, to say, 'Your s are forgiven you,'
5:24 the Son of Man has authority on earth to forgive s"
7:47 Therefore, I tell you, her s, which were many,
7:48 Then he said to her, "Your s are forgiven."
7:49 "Who is this who even forgives s?"
11: 4 And forgive us our s, for we ourselves forgive
17: 3 If another disciple s, you must rebuke
17: 4 if the same person s against you seven times a day,
24:47 forgiveness of s is to be proclaimed in his name B
Jn 8:24 I told you that you would die in your s,
8:24 for you will die in your s unless you believe
9:34 They answered him, "You were born entirely in s,
20:23 If you forgive the s of any, they are forgiven them;
20:23 if you retain the s of any, they are retained."
Ac 2:38 of Jesus Christ so that your s may be forgiven;
3:19 and turn to God so that your s may be wiped out,
5:31 give repentance to Israel and forgiveness of s. B
10:43 receives forgiveness of s through his name." B
13:38 this man forgiveness of s is proclaimed to you; B
13:39 from all those s from which you could not be freed
22:16 be baptized, and have your s washed away,
26:18 that they may receive forgiveness of s and B
Ro 3:25 over the s previously committed;
4: 7 iniquities are forgiven, and whose s are covered;
5:14 over those whose s were not like the transgression
11:27 when I take away their s."
1Co 6:18 but the fornicator s against the body itself.
15: 3 that Christ died for our s in accordance with
15:17 your faith is futile and you are still in your s.
Gal 1: 4 for our s to set us free from the present evil age,
Eph 2: 1 You were dead through the trespasses and s
Col 1:14 whom we have redemption, the forgiveness of s. B
1Th 2:16 filling up the measure of their s;
1Ti 5:22 and do not participate in the s of others;
5:24 The s of some people are conspicuous
5:24 while the s of others follow them there.
2Ti 3: 6 overwhelmed by their s and swayed by all kinds
Heb 1: 3 When he had made purification for s,
2:17 a sacrifice of atonement for the s of the people.
5: 1 to offer gifts and sacrifices for s.
5: 3 of this he must offer sacrifice for his own s as well
7:27 for his own s, and then for those of the people;
8:12 and I will remember their s no more."
9: 7 for the s committed unintentionally by the people.
9:22 shedding of blood there is no forgiveness of s. B
9:28 having been offered once to bear the s of many,
10: 4 for the blood of bulls and goats to take away s.
10:11 the same sacrifices that can never take away s.
10:12 for all time a single sacrifice for s,
10:17 also adds, "I will remember their s
10:26 there no longer remains a sacrifice for s,
Jas 5:15 and anyone who has committed s will be forgiven.
5:16 Therefore confess your s to one another,
5:20 from death and will cover a multitude of s.
1Pe 2:24 He himself bore our s in his body on the cross,
2:24 free from s, we might live for righteousness;
3:18 For Christ also suffered for s once for all,
4: 8 for love covers a multitude of s.
2Pe 1: 9 and is forgetful of the cleansing of past s.
1Jn 1: 9 If we confess our s, he who is faithful and just will forgive us our s
2: 2 and he is the atoning sacrifice for our s, and not for ours only but also for the s of the whole world.
2:12 your s are forgiven on account of his name.
3: 5 You know that he was revealed to take away s,
3: 6 No one who abides in him s; no one who s has either seen him or known him.
4:10 to be the atoning sacrifice for our s.
Rev 1: 5 To him who loves us and freed us from our s
18: 4 my people, so that you do not take part in her s,
18: 5 for her s are heaped high as heaven,
Tob 3: 3 for my s and for my unwitting offenses and those
3: 5 in exacting penalty from me for my s.
Jdt 7:28 for our s and the s of our ancestors;
11:17 He will tell me when they have committed their s.
Wis 2:12 he reproaches us for s against the law,
2:12 and accuses us of s against our training.
4:20 with dread when their s are reckoned up,
11:16 by the very things by which one s.
11:23 and you overlook people's s,
12:11 that you left them unpunished for their s.
12:19 because you give repentance for s.
17: 3 that in their secret s they were unobserved behind
Sir 2:11 he forgives s and saves in time of distress.
3: 3 Those who honor their father atone for s,
3:14 and will be credited to you against your s;
3:15 like frost in fair weather, your s will melt away.
3:27 and the sinner adds sin to s.
4:26 Do not be ashamed to confess your s,
5: 6 he will forgive the multitude of my s,"
12:14 a sinner and becomes involved in the other's s.
16: 9 on those dispossessed because of their s;
17:20 and all their s are before the Lord.
17:25 Turn back to the Lord and forsake your s;
19: 4 and one who s does wrong to oneself.
21: 1 Do so no more, but ask forgiveness for your past s.
23: 2 to spare me in my errors, and not overlook my s?
23: 3 and my s may abound, and I may fall
23:11 and if he disregards it, he s doubly;
23:12 and they will not wallow in s.
23:16 Two kinds of individuals multiply s,
23:18 The one who s against his marriage bed says
23:18 The Most High will not remember s."
26:11 and do not be surprised if she s against you.
28: 1 for he keeps a strict account of their s.
28: 2 and then your s will be pardoned when you pray.
28: 4 can he then seek pardon for his own s?
28: 5 who will make an atoning sacrifice for his s?
28: 8 Refrain from strife, and your s will be fewer;
34:23 nor for a multitude of sacrifices does he forgive s.
34:31 So if one fasts for his s,
38:15 He who s against his Maker,
39: 5 in prayer and asks pardon for his s.
47:11 The Lord took away his s,
47:24 Their s increased more and more,
48:15 nor did they forsake their s,
Bar 4:12 I was left desolate because of the s of my children,
LtJ 6: 2 of the s that you have committed before God,
Aza 1: 5 brought all this upon us because of our s.
1:14 in all the world because of our s.
Sus 1:52 your s have now come home,
2Mc 5:17 a little while because of the s of those who lived in
5:18 not happened that they were involved in many s,
6:14 until they have reached the full measure of their s;
6:15 when our s have reached their height.
7:18 because of our s against our own God.
7:32 For we are suffering because of our own s.
13: 8 because he had committed many s against
1Es 8:75 For our s have risen higher than our heads,
8:77 Because of our s and the s of our ancestors,
8:86 about because of our evil deeds and our great s.
8:86 For you, O Lord, lifted the burden of our s
Man 1: 9 the s I have committed are more in number than
1:10 so that I am rejected because of my s,
3Mc 2:13 because of our many and great s we are crushed
2:19 Wipe away our s and disperse our errors,
2Es 1: 6 that the s of their parents have increased in them,
4:39 on account of the s of those who inhabit the earth."
7:*68* and are full of s and burdened with transgressions.
7:*139* [69] and blot out the multitude of their s,
8:26 O do not look on the s of your people,
16:48 the more angry I will be with them for their s,
16:63 Woe to those who sin and want to hide their s!
16:65 You shall be put to shame when your s come out
16:66 will you hide your s before the Lord and his glory?
16:67 Cease from your s, and forget your iniquities,
16:76 must not let your s weigh you down,
16:77 by their s and overwhelmed by their iniquities!

SION (KJV) See SIRION, ZION; See also Index to Footnotes

SIP (1)

Ge 24:17 "Please let me s a little water from your jar."

SIPHMOTH (1)

1Sa 30:28 in Aroer, in S, in Eshtemoa,

SIPPAI (1)

1Ch 20: 4 then Sibbecai the Hushathite killed S,

SIR‡ (20) [SIRS]

Jdg 6:13 Gideon answered him, "But s,
6:15 He responded, "But s, how can I deliver Israel?
2Sa 1: 7 I answered, 'Here s.'
Mt 21:30 and he answered, 'I go, s'; but he did not go.
27:63 "S, we remember what that impostor said
Mk 7:28 But she answered him, "S, even the dogs
Lk 13: 8 He replied, 'S, let it alone for one more year,
14:22 'S, what you ordered has been done,
Jn 4:11 The woman said to him, "S, you have no bucket,
4:15 The woman said to him, "S, give me this water,
4:19 The woman said to him, "S, I see that you are
4:49 The official said to him, "S, come down before
5: 7 The sick man answered him, "S, I have no one
6:34 They said to him, "S, give us this bread always."
8:11 ⟦She said, "No one, s."⟧
9:36 He answered, "And who is he, s?
12:21 and said to him, "S, we wish to see Jesus."
20:15 she said to him, "S, if you have carried him away,
Rev 7:14 I said to him, "S, you are the one that knows."
Bel 1:35 Habakkuk said, "S, I have never seen Babylon,

SIRACH (2)

Sir 50:27 Jesus son of Eleazar son of S of Jerusalem,
51: 1 PRAYER OF JESUS SON OF S

SIRAH (1)

2Sa 3:26 and they brought him back from the cistern of S;

SIRENS (1)

4Mc 15:21 the melodies of s nor the songs of swans attract

SIRION (4) [=HERMON]

Dt 3: 9 (the Sidonians call Hermon S, while the Amorites
4:48 as far as Mount S (that is, Hermon),
Ps 29: 6 and S like a young wild ox.
Jer 18:14 Does the snow of Lebanon leave the crags of S?

SIRS (2) [SIR]

Ac 16:30 Then he brought them outside and said, "S,
27:10 "S, I can see that the voyage will be with danger

SISAMAI (KJV) See SISMAI

SISERA (21)

Jdg 4: 2 the commander of his army was S,
4: 7 I will draw out S, the general of Jabin's army,
4: 9 the LORD will sell S into the hand of a woman."
4:12 When S was told that Barak son of Abinoam
4:13 S called out all his chariots,
4:14 on which the LORD has given S into your hand.
4:15 And the LORD threw S and all his chariots
4:15 S got down from his chariot and fled away
4:16 All the army of S fell by the sword;
4:17 Now S had fled away on foot to the tent
4:18 Jael came out to meet S, and said to him,
4:22 Then, as Barak came in pursuit of S,
4:22 and there was S lying dead,
5:20 from their courses they fought against S.
5:26 she struck S a blow, she crushed his head,
5:28 the mother of S gazed through the lattice:
5:30 spoil of dyed stuffs for S,
1Sa 12: 9 and he sold them into the hand of S,
Ezr 2:53 Barkos, S, Temah,
Ne 7:55 of Barkos, of S, of Temah,
Ps 83: 9 as to S and Jabin at the Wadi Kishon,

SISINNES (4)

1Es 6: 3 At the same time S the governor of Syria
6: 7 A copy of the letter that S the governor of Syria
6:27 So Darius commanded S the governor of Syria
7: 1 Then S the governor of Coelesyria and Phoenicia,

SISMAI (2)

1Ch 2:40 Eleasah became the father of S, and S of Shallum.

SISTER‡ (132) [SISTER'S, SISTER-IN-LAW, SISTERS]

A. BROTHER ... SISTER (22)

Ge 4:22 The s of Tubal-cain was Naamah.
12:13 Say you are my s, so that it may go well with me
12:19 Why did you say, 'She is my s,'
20: 2 of his wife Sarah, "She is my s."
20: 5 Did he not himself say to me, 'She is my s'?
20:12 Besides, she is indeed my s,
24:30 and when he heard the words of his s Rebekah,
24:59 So they sent away their s Rebekah and her nurse
24:60 "May you, our s, become thousands of myriads;
25:20 of Bethuel the Aramean of Paddan-aram, s
26: 7 about his wife, he said, "She is my s";
26: 9 Why then did you say, 'She is my s'?"
28: 9 of Abraham's son Ishmael, and s of Nebaioth,
30: 1 that she bore Jacob no children, she envied her s;
30: 8 I have wrestled with my s, and have prevailed";
34:13 because he had defiled their s Dinah.
34:14 to give our s to one who is uncircumcised,
34:27 because their s had been defiled.
34:31 they said, "Should our s be treated like a whore?"
36: 3 and Basemath, Ishmael's daughter, s of Nebaioth.
36:22 and Lotan's s was Timna.
46:17 Imnah, Ishvah, Ishvi, Beriah, and their s Serah.
Ex 2: 4 His s stood at a distance,
2: 7 Then his s said to Pharaoh's daughter,
6:20 Amram married Jochebed his father's s
6:23 daughter of Amminadab and s of Nahshon,
15:20 Then the prophet Miriam, Aaron's s,
Lev 18: 9 You shall not uncover the nakedness of your s,
18:11 begotten by your father, since she is your s.
18:12 not uncover the nakedness of your father's s;
18:13 not uncover the nakedness of your mother's s,
18:18 And you shall not take a woman as a rival to her s,
18:18 uncovering her nakedness while her s is still alive.
20:17 If a man takes his s, a daughter of his father or
20:19 not uncover the nakedness of your mother's s or
20:19 of your mother's sister or of your father's s, for
21: 3 likewise, for a virgin s, close to him
Nu 6: 7 Even if their father or mother, brother or s, A
25:18 the daughter of a leader of Midian, their s;
26:59 Aaron, Moses, and their s Miriam.
Dt 27:22 "Cursed be anyone who lies with his s,
Jdg 15: 2 Is not her younger s prettier than she?
2Sa 13: 1 a beautiful s whose name was Tamar;
13: 2 that he made himself ill because of his s Tamar.
13: 4 "I love Tamar, my brother Absalom's s."
13: 5 'Let my s Tamar come and give me something
13: 6 the king, "Please let my s Tamar come and make
13:11 and said to her, "Come, lie with me, my s."
13:20 Be quiet for now, my s; he is your brother;
13:22 because he had raped his s Tamar.
13:32 from the day Amnon raped his s Tamar.

2Sa 17:25 of Nahash, s of Zeruiah, Joab's mother.
1Ki 11:19 sister-in-law for a wife, the s of Queen Tahpenes.
11:20 The s of Tahpenes gave birth by him
2Ki 11: 2 Jehosheba, King Joram's daughter, Ahaziah's s,
1Ch 1:39 and Lotan's s was Timna.
3: 9 of the concubines; and Tamar was their s.
3:19 and Shelomith was their s;
4: 3 and the name of their s was Hazzelelponi,
4:19 The sons of the wife of Hodiah, the s of Naham,
7:15 The name of his s was Maacah.
7:18 And his s Hammolecheth bore Ishhod, Abiezer,
7:30 Imnah, Ishvah, Ishvi, Beriah, and their s Serah.
7:32 Shomer, Hotham, and their s Shua.
2Ch 22:11 because she was a s of Ahaziah—
Job 17:14 and to the worm, 'My mother,' or 'My s,'
Pr 7: 4 Say to wisdom, "You are my s,"
SS 4: 9 You have ravished my heart, my s, my bride,
4:10 How sweet is your love, my s, my bride!
4:12 A garden locked is my s, my bride,
5: 1 I come to my garden, my s, my bride;
5: 2 "Open to me, my s, my love, my dove,
8: 8 We have a little s, and she has no breasts.
8: 8 What shall we do for our s,
Jer 3: 7 but she did not return, and her false s Judah saw it.
3: 8 yet her false s Judah did not fear,
3:10 for all this her false s Judah did not return to me
22:18 "Alas, my brother!" or "Alas, s!"
Eze 16:45 and you are the s of your sisters,
16:46 Your elder s is Samaria, who lived
16:46 and your younger s, who lived to the south of you,
16:48 your s Sodom and her daughters have not done
16:49 This was the guilt of your s Sodom:
16:56 Was not your s Sodom a byword in your mouth in
22:11 another in you defiles his s, his father's daughter.
23: 4 of the elder and Oholibah the name of her s.
23:11 Her s Oholibah saw this,
23:11 which were worse than those of her s.
23:18 as I had turned from her s.
23:31 You have gone the way of your s;
23:33 and desolation is the cup of your s Samaria;
44:25 brother or unmarried s they may defile themselves.
Hos 2: 1 Say to your brother, Ammi, and to your s,
Mt 5:22 a brother or s, you will be liable to judgment; A
5:22 and if you insult a brother or s, A
5:23 that your brother or s has something against you, A
5:24 first be reconciled to your brother or s, A
12:50 in heaven is my brother and s and mother." A
18:35 not forgive your brother or s from your heart." A
Mk 3:35 does the will of God is my brother and s A
Lk 10:39 She had a s named Mary,
10:40 that my s has left me to do all the work by myself?
Jn 11: the village of Mary and her s Martha.
11: 5 though Jesus loved Martha and her s and Lazarus,
11:28 she went back and called her s Mary,
11:39 Martha, the s of the dead man, said to him, "Lord,
19:25 and his mother's s, Mary the wife of Clopas,
Ac 23:16 Now the son of Paul's s heard about the ambush;
Ro 14:10 Why do you pass judgment on your brother or s? A
14:10 Or you, why do you despise your brother or s? A
14:15 brother or s is being injured by what you eat, A
14:21 that makes your brother or s stumble. A
16: 1 I commend to you our s Phoebe,
16:15 Greet Philologus, Julia, Nereus and his s,
1Co 5:11 brother or s who is sexually immoral or greedy, A
7:15 in such a case the brother or s is not bound. A
1Th 4: 6 that no one wrong or exploit a brother or s A
Phm 1: 2 to Apphia our s, to Archippus our fellow soldier,
Jas 2:15 If a brother or s is naked and lacks daily food, A
1Pe 5:13 Your s church in Babylon,
1Jn 2: 9 hating a brother or s, is still in the darkness. A
2:10 Whoever loves a brother or s lives in the light, A
3:15 All who hate a brother or s are murderers, A
3:17 world's goods and sees a brother or s in need A
4:20 not love a brother or s whom they have seen, A
5:16 If you see your brother or s committing what is A
2Jn 1:13 children of your elect s send you their greetings.
Tob 5:21 Do not fear for them, my s.
7:11 from now on you are her brother and she is your s.
7:15 Raguel called his wife Edna and said to her, "S,
8: 4 Tobias got out of bed and said to Sarah, "S,
3Mc 1: 1 took with him his s Arsinoë, and marched out

SISTER'S (4) [SISTER]

Ge 24:30 and the bracelets on his s arms,
29:13 When Laban heard the news about his s son Jacob,
Lev 20:17 he has uncovered his s nakedness,
Eze 23:32 You shall drink your s cup, deep and wide;

SISTER-IN-LAW (3) [SISTER]

Ru 1:15 "See, your s has gone back to her people and to her gods; return after your s."
1Ki 11:19 so that he gave him his s for a wife,

SISTERS‡ (111) [SISTER]

A. BROTHERS ... SISTERS (99)

Jos 2:13 my brothers and s, and all who belong to them, A
1Ch 2:16 and their s were Zeruiah and Abigail.
Job 1: 4 and invite their three s to eat and drink with them.
42:11 Then there came to him all his brothers and s A
Ps 22:22 I will tell of your name to my brothers and s; A
Eze 16:45 and you are the sister of your s,
16:51 and have made your s appear righteous by all
16:52 about for your s a more favorable judgment;
16:52 for you have made your s appear righteous.
Eze 16:55 for your s, Sodom and her daughters shall return
16:61 and be ashamed when I take your s,
Mt 5:47 And if you greet only your brothers and s, A
13:56 And are not all his s with us?
19:29 everyone who has left houses or brothers or s A
Mk 3:32 mother and your brothers and s are outside, A
6: 3 and are not his s here with us?"
10:29 no one who has left house or brothers or s A
10:30 houses, brothers and s, mothers and children, A
Lk 14:26 brothers and s, yes, and even life itself, A
Jn 11: 3 So the s sent a message to Jesus, "Lord,
Ac 16:40 and encouraged the brothers and s there, A
Ro 1:13 I want you to know, brothers and s, A
7: 1 Do you not know, brothers and s— A
8:12 So then, brothers and s, we are debtors, A
10: 1 Brothers and s, my heart's desire and prayer A
11:25 brothers and s, I want you to understand this A
12: 1 I appeal to you therefore, brothers and s, A
15:14 my brothers and s, that you yourselves are full A
15:30 I appeal to you, brothers and s, A
16:14 and the brothers and s who are with them. A
16:17 I urge you, brothers and s, A
1Co 1:10 Now I appeal to you, brothers and s, A
1:11 among you, my brothers and s. A
1:26 Consider your own call, brothers and s: A
2: 1 When I came to you, brothers and s, A
3: 1 brothers and s, I could not speak to you as A
4: 6 brothers and s, so that you may learn through us A
7:24 brothers and s, there remain with God. A
7:29 brothers and s, the appointed time has A
10: 1 I do not want you to be unaware, brothers and s, A
11:33 So then, my brothers and s, when you come A
12: 1 Now concerning spiritual gifts, brothers and s, A
14: 6 Now, brothers and s, if I come to you speaking A
14:20 Brothers and s, do not be children in your A
15: 1 Now I would remind you, brothers and s, A
15: 6 to more than five hundred brothers and s A
15:31 That is as certain, brothers and s, A
15:50 What I am saying, brothers and s, is this: A
16:15 brothers and s, you know that members of the A
16:20 All the brothers and s send greetings. A
2Co 1: 8 do not want you to be unaware, brothers and s, A
8: 1 We want you to know, brothers and s, A
11:26 danger at sea, danger from false brothers and s; A
13:11 Finally, brothers and s, farewell. A
Gal 1:11 For I want you to know, brothers and s, A
3:15 Brothers and s, I give an example from daily A
5:13 For you were called to freedom, brothers and s; A
6:18 be with your spirit, brothers and s. A
Php 1:14 and most of the brothers and s, A
3: 1 Finally, my brothers and s, rejoice in the Lord. A
3:17 Brothers and s, join in imitating me, A
4: 1 Therefore, my brothers and s, A
Col 1: 2 the saints and faithful brothers and s in Christ A
4:15 Give my greetings to the brothers and s A
1Th 1: 4 For we know, brothers and s beloved by God, A
2: 1 You yourselves know, brothers and s, A
2: 9 remember our labor and toil, brothers and s; A
2:14 brothers and s, became imitators of the churches A
2:17 As for us, brothers and s, when, for a short time, A
3: 7 For this reason, brothers and s, A
4: 1 brothers and s, we ask and urge you in the Lord A
4: 9 Now concerning love of the brothers and s, A
4:10 and indeed you do love all the brothers and s A
4:13 brothers and s, about those who have died, A
5: 1 the times and the seasons, brothers and s, A
5:12 But we appeal to you, brothers and s, A
5:26 Greet all the brothers and s with a holy kiss. A
2Th 1: 3 give thanks to God for you, brothers and s, A
2: 1 we beg you, brothers and s, A
2:13 brothers and s beloved by the Lord, A
2:15 So then, brothers and s, stand firm and hold fast A
3: 1 Finally, brothers and s, pray for us, A
3:13 Brothers and s, do not be weary A
1Ti 4: 6 the brothers and s, you will be a good servant A
5: 2 to younger women as s—with absolute purity.
2Ti 4:21 Linus and Claudia and all the brothers and s. A
Heb 2:11 not ashamed to call them brothers and s, A
2:12 "I will proclaim your name to my brothers and s, A
2:17 he had to become like his brothers and s A
3: 1 Therefore, brothers and s, holy partners in a A
3:12 Take care, brothers and s, that none of you A
13:22 I appeal to you, brothers and s, bear with my A
Jas 1: 2 My brothers and s, whenever you face trials A
2: 1 My brothers and s, do you with your acts A
2: 5 Listen, my beloved brothers and s. A
2:14 What good is it, my brothers and s, A
3: 1 should become teachers, my brothers and s, A
3:10 My brothers and s, this ought not to be so. A
3:12 Can a fig tree, my brothers and s, yield olives, A
4:11 speak evil against one another, brothers and s. A
5:19 brothers and s, if anyone among you wanders A
1Pe 5: 9 for you know that your brothers and s in all A
2Pe 1:10 Therefore, brothers and s, be all the more eager A
1Jn 3:10 are those who do not love their brothers and s. A
3:13 Do not be astonished, brothers and s, A
4:20 love God," and hate their brothers or s, are liars; A
4:21 who love God must love their brothers and s A
Rev 6:11 their fellow servants and of their brothers and s, A
Jdt 7:30 said to them, "Courage, my brothers and s! A
Sir 25: 1 agreement among brothers and s, A
2Mc 15:18 and also for brothers and s and relatives, A

SIT‡ (134) [SAT, SITS, SITTING]

Ge 27:19 now s up and eat of my game,
27:31 "Let my father s up and eat of his son's game,
Ex 18:14 Why do you s alone, while all the people stand
18:22 Let them s as judges for the people at all times;
Lev 15: 6 All who s on anything on which the one with
Nu 32: 6 "Shall your brothers go to war while you s here?
Jdg 4: 5 to s under the palm of Deborah between Ramah
5:10 you who s on rich carpets and you who walk by
Ru 4: 1 So Boaz said, "Come over, friend; s down here."
4: 2 and said, "S down here"; so they sat down.
1Sa 2: 8 from the ash heap, to make them s with princes
16:11 for we will not s down until he comes here."
20: 5 and I should not fail to s with the king at the meal;
1Ki 1:13 and he shall s on my throne?
1:17 and he shall s on my throne.
1:20 of all Israel are on you to tell them who shall s on
1:24 and he shall s on my throne'?
1:27 not let your servants know who should s on
1:30 and he shall s on my throne in my place,'
1:35 Let him enter and s on my throne;
1:48 who today has granted one of my offspring to s
3: 6 and have given him a son to s on his throne today.
8:20 I s on the throne of Israel, as the LORD promised,
8:25 a successor before me to s on the throne of Israel,
2Ki 7: 3 "Why should we s here until we die?
7: 4 but if we s here, we shall also die.
10:30 of the fourth generation shall s on the throne
15:12 "Your sons shall s on the throne of Israel to
1Ch 28: 5 to s upon the throne of the kingdom of the LORD
2Ch 6:10 and s on the throne of Israel,
6:16 a successor before me to s on the throne of Israel,
Ps 1: 1 or s in the seat of scoffers;
10: 8 They s in ambush in the villages;
26: 4 I do not s with the worthless,
26: 5 and will not s with the wicked.
50:20 You s and speak against your kin;
69:12 the subject of gossip for those who s in the gate,
110: 1 The LORD says to my lord, "S at my right hand
113: 8 to make them s with princes,
119:23 Even though princes s plotting against me,
132:12 forevermore, shall s on your throne."
139: 2 You know when I s down and when I rise up;
143: 3 making me s in darkness like those long dead.
Pr 3:24 If you s down, you will not be afraid;
23: 1 When you s down to eat with a ruler,
Ecc 10: 6 and the rich s in a low place.
Isa 3:26 ravaged, she shall s upon the ground.
14:13 I will s on the mount of assembly on the heights
16: 5 and on it shall s in faithfulness
42: 7 from the prison those who s in darkness.
47: 1 Come down and s in the dust,
47: 1 S on the ground without a throne,
47: 5 S in silence, and go into darkness,
47: 8 hear this, you lover of pleasures, who s securely,
47: 8 not s as a widow or know the loss of children"—
47:14 for warming oneself is this, no fire to s before!
65: 4 who s inside tombs, and spend the night
Jer 8:14 Why do we s still?
13:13 the kings who s on David's throne, the priests,
15:17 I did not s in the company of merrymakers,
16: 8 not go into the house of feasting to s with them,
17:25 by the gates of this city kings who s on the throne
22: 4 of this house shall enter kings who s on the throne
33:17 David shall never lack a man to s on the throne of
36:15 And they said to him, "S down and read it to us."
36:30 He shall have no one to s upon the throne
48:18 and s on the parched ground,
La 2:10 elders of daughter Zion s on the ground in silence;
3: 6 he has made me s in darkness like the dead
3:28 to s alone in silence when the Lord has imposed it,
3:63 Whether they s or rise—see,
Eze 26:16 and shall s on the ground;
28: 2 I s in the seat of the gods, in the heart of the seas,"
33:31 and they s before you as my people,
44: 3 may s in it to eat food before the LORD;
Da 7:26 Then the court shall s in judgment,
11:27 shall s at one table and exchange lies.
Joel 3:12 there I will s to judge all the neighboring nations.
Mic 4: 4 but they shall all s under their own vines and
7: 8 when I s in darkness, the LORD will be a light to
Zec 3: 8 you and your colleagues who s before you!
6:13 and shall s and rule on his throne.
8: 4 Old men and old women shall again s in the streets
Mal 3: 3 he will s as a refiner and purifier of silver,
Mt 14:19 he ordered the crowds to s down on the grass.
15:35 Then ordering the crowd to s down on the ground,
19:28 you who have followed me will also s
20:21 "Declare that these two sons of mine will s,
20:23 but to s at my right hand and at my left,
22:44 "S at my right hand, until I put your enemies
23: 2 "The scribes and the Pharisees s on Moses' seat;
25:31 then he will s on the throne of his glory.
26:36 "S here while I go over there and pray."
Mk 6:39 the people to s down in groups on the green grass.
8: 6 he ordered the crowd to s down on the ground;
10:37 And they said to him, "Grant us to s,
10:40 but to s at my right hand or at my left is not mine
12:36 "S at my right hand, until I put your enemies
14:32 and he said to his disciples, "S here while I pray."
Lk 1:79 to give light to those who s in darkness and in
9:14 "Make them s down in groups of about fifty each."
9:15 They did so and made them all s down.
12:37 he will fasten his belt and have them s down
14: 8 do not s down at the place of honor,
14:10 you are invited, go and s down at the lowest place,
14:10 be honored in the presence of all who s at the table
14:28 does not first s down and estimate the cost,
14:31 not s down first and consider whether he is able
16: 6 He said to him, 'Take your bill, s down quickly,

Lk 20:42 'The Lord said to my Lord, "S at my right hand,
22:30 and you will s on thrones judging the twelve tribes
Jn 6:10 Jesus said, "Make the people s down."
9: 8 "Is this not the man who used to s and beg?"
Ac 2:34 'The Lord said to my Lord, "S at my right hand,
3:10 and they recognized him as the one who used to s
8:31 And he invited Philip to get in and s beside him.
Heb 1:13 "S at my right hand until I make your enemies
Jas 2: 3 "Stand there," or, "S at my feet,"
Rev 11:16 Then the twenty-four elders who s on their thrones
Sir 6:10 And there are friends who s at your table,
11: 5 Many kings have had to s on the ground,
11: 9 and do not s with sinners when they judge a case.
12:12 Do not let him s at your right hand,
23:14 Remember your father and mother when you s
26:12 so she will s in front of every tent peg
32: 1 Take care of them first and then s down;
38:33 They do not s in the judge's seat,
LtJ 6:31 the priests s with their clothes torn,
6:42 s along the passageways, burning bran for incense.
Sus 1:50 "Come, s among us and inform us,
1Es 3: 7 of his wisdom he shall s next to Darius and shall
4:29 she would s at the king's right hand
4:42 You shall s next to me,
2Es 12:41 that you have forsaken us and s in this place?

SITE (15) [SITES]

Ge 49:30 from Ephron the Hittite as a burial s.
50:13 which Abraham bought as a burial s from Ephron
1Ch 21:22 the s of the threshing floor that I may build on it
21:25 of gold by weight for the s.
Ezr 2:68 to erect it on its s.
5:15 and let the house of God be rebuilt on its s."
6: 7 of the Jews rebuild this house of God on its s.
Isa 4: 5 over the whole s of Mount Zion and over its places
54: 2 Enlarge the s of your tent,
Jer 30:18 and the citadel set on its rightful s.
Zec 14:10 on its s from the Gate of Benjamin to the place of
1Es 5:44 they would erect the house on its s,
6:19 this temple of the Lord should be rebuilt on its s.
6:27 of the Jews to build this house of the Lord on its s.
3Mc 7:20 on a pillar and dedicating a place of prayer at the s

SITES (2) [SITE]

2Ki 23:14 and covered the s with human bones.
2Ch 33:19 the s on which he built high places and set up

SITH (KJV) See SINCE

SITHRI (1)

Ex 6:22 The sons of Uzziel: Mishael, Elzaphan, and S.

SITNAH (1)

Ge 26:21 that one also; so he called it S.

SITS (26) [SIT]

Ex 11: 5 from the firstborn of Pharaoh who s on his throne
Lev 15: 4 and everything on which he s shall be unclean.
15:20 everything also upon which she s shall be unclean.
15:22 upon which she s shall wash his clothes, and bathe
15:23 the bed or anything upon which she s,
15:26 and everything on which she s shall be unclean,
1Ki 1:46 Solomon now s on the royal throne.
Est 6:10 so to the Jew Mordecai who s at the king's gate.
Ps 2: 4 He who s in the heavens laughs;
9: 7 But the LORD s enthroned forever,
29:10 The LORD s enthroned over the flood;
29:10 the LORD s enthroned as king forever.
33:14 From where he s enthroned he watches all
47: 8 God s on his holy throne.
99: 1 He s enthroned upon the cherubim;
Pr 9:14 She s at the door of her house,
20: 8 A king who s on the throne
Isa 28: 6 a spirit of justice to the one who s in judgment,
30: 7 therefore I have called her, "Rahab who s still."
40:22 It is he who s above the circle of the earth,
Jer 29:16 concerning the king who s on the throne of David,
La 1: 1 How lonely s the city that once was full of people!
Eze 27: 3 which s at the entrance to the sea,
Wis 9: 4 give me the wisdom that s by your throne,
Sir 25:18 Her husband s among the neighbors,
40: 3 From the one who s on a splendid throne to

SITTING‡ (84) [SIT]

Ge 19: 1 and Lot was s in the gateway of Sodom.
23:10 Now Ephron was s among the Hittites;
Dt 22: 6 with the mother s on the fledglings or on the eggs,
Jdg 3:20 while he was s alone in his cool roof chamber,
20:26 s there before the LORD;
Ru 4: 4 Buy it in the presence of those s here,
1Sa 1: 9 the priest was s on the seat beside the doorpost of
4:13 Eli was s upon his seat by the road watching,
22: 6 Saul was s at Gibeah, under the tamarisk tree on
24: 3 and his men were s in the innermost parts of
2Sa 18:24 Now David was s between the two gates.
19: 8 "See, the king is s in the gate";
1Ki 13:14 and found him s under an oak tree.
13:20 As they were s at the table,
22:10 of Israel and King Jehoshaphat of Judah were s
22:19 I saw the LORD s on his throne,
2Ki 1: 9 who was s on the top of a hill, and said to him,
4:38 As the company of prophets was s before him,
6:32 Now Elisha was s in his house,
2Ki 6:32 and the elders were s with him.
18:27 and not to the people s on the wall,
19:27 "But I know your rising and your s,
2Ch 18: 9 of Israel and King Jehoshaphat of Judah were s
18: 9 and they were s at the threshing floor at
18:18 I saw the LORD s on his throne,
Ne 2: 6 king said to me (the queen also was s beside him),
Est 2:19 Mordecai was s at the king's gate.
2:21 while Mordecai was s at the king's gate,
5: 1 The king was s on his royal throne inside
5:13 as I see the Jew Mordecai s at the king's gate."
Isa 6: 1 I saw the Lord s on a throne, high and lofty;
36:12 and not to the people s on the wall,
37:28 I know your rising up and your s down,
Jer 22: 2 O King of Judah s on the throne of David—
22:30 of his offspring shall succeed in s on the throne
32:12 and in the presence of all the Judeans who were s
36:12 and all the officials were s there:
36:22 Now the king was s in his winter apartment
38: 7 The king happened to be s at the Benjamin Gate,
Eze 8: 1 with the elders of Judah s before me,
8:14 women were s there weeping for Tammuz.
Zec 5: 7 and there was a woman s in the basket!
Mt 9: 9 he saw a man called Matthew s at the tax booth;
9:10 many tax collectors and sinners came and were s
11:16 It is like children s in the marketplaces and calling
20:30 There were two blind men s by the roadside.
24: 3 When he was s on the Mount of Olives,
26:69 Now Peter was s outside in the courtyard.
27:19 While he was s on the judgment seat,
27:61 the other Mary were there, s opposite the tomb.
Mk 2: 6 Now some of the scribes were s there,
2:14 he saw Levi son of Alphaeus s at the tax booth,
2:15 many tax collectors and sinners were also s
3:32 A crowd was s around him;
5:15 They came to Jesus and saw the demoniac s there,
10:46 a blind beggar, was s by the roadside.
13: 3 When he was s on the Mount of Olives opposite
14:54 and he was s with the guards,
16: 5 dressed in a white robe, s on the right side;
16:14 ⟦the eleven themselves as they were s at the table;⟧
Lk 2:46 the temple, s among the teachers, listening to them
5:17 Pharisees and teachers of the law were s near
5:27 a tax collector named Levi, s at the tax booth;
5:29 a large crowd of tax collectors and others s at
7:32 like children s in the marketplace and calling
8:35 the man from whom the demons had gone s at
10:13 and Sidon, they would have repented long ago, s
18:35 a blind man was s by the roadside begging.
Jn 4: 6 tired out by his journey, was s by the well.
12:15 Look, your king is coming, s on a donkey's colt!"
20:12 s where the body of Jesus had been lying,
Ac 2: 2 and it filled the entire house where they were s.
14: 8 In Lystra there was a man s who could
20: 9 who was s in the window,
23: 3 Are you s there to judge me according to the law,
1Co 14:30 If a revelation is made to someone else s nearby,
Rev 17: 3 a woman s on a scarlet beast that was full
Tob 7: 1 where they found him s beside the courtyard door.
Wis 6:14 for she will be found s at the gate.
Sir 37:14 than seven sentinels s high on a watchtower.
38:28 So too is the smith, s by the anvil,
38:29 the potter s at his work and turning the wheel
2Es 14: 1 On the third day, while I was s under an oak,
4Mc 5: 1 s in state with his counselors on

SITUATION (7)

Tob 7:10 But let me explain to you the true s more fully,
2Mc 3: 9 and he inquired whether this really was the s.
3Mc 1:16 to aid in the present s and to avert the violence
3: 1 When the impious king comprehended this s,
3: 8 at the s, and expected that matters would change;
3:23 in every s, in accordance with their infamous way
5:15 and he gave him an account of the s.

SIVAN (2)

Est 8: 9 which is the month of S, on the twenty-third day;
Bar 1: 8 At the same time, on the tenth day of S,

SIX‡ (198) [ONE-SIXTH, SIXTH]

Ge 7: 6 Noah was s hundred years old when the flood
7:11 In the s hundredth year of Noah's life,
8:13 In the s hundred first year, in the first month,
30:20 because I have borne him s sons";
31:41 and s years for your flock,
Ex 12:37 about s hundred thousand men on foot,
14: 7 he took s hundred picked chariots and all
16:26 S days you shall gather it;
20: 9 S days you shall labor and do all your work.
20:11 For in s days the LORD made heaven and earth,
21: 2 a male Hebrew slave, he shall serve s years,
23:10 For s years you shall sow your land and gather
23:12 S days you shall do your work,
24:16 and the cloud covered it for s days;
25:32 and there shall be s branches going out of its sides,
25:33 so for the s branches going out of the lampstand.
25:35 so for the s branches that go out of the lampstand.
26: 9 and s curtains by themselves,
26:22 the tabernacle westward you shall make s frames.
28:10 s of their names on the one stone, the names of the remaining s on the other stone,
31:15 S days shall work be done,
31:17 between me and the people of Israel that in s days
34:21 S days you shall work,
35: 2 S days shall work be done,
Ex 36:16 and s curtains by themselves.
36:27 rear of the tabernacle westward he made s frames.
37:18 There were s branches going out of its sides,
37:19 so for the s branches going out of the lampstand.
38:26 for s hundred three thousand,
Lev 23: 3 S days shall work be done;
24: 6 You shall place them in two rows, s in a row,
25: 3 S years you shall sow your field,
25: 3 and s years you shall prune your vineyard,
Nu 1:25 of Gad were forty-five thousand s hundred fifty.
1:27 of Judah were seventy-four thousand s hundred.
1:46 was s hundred three thousand five hundred fifty.
2: 4 as enrolled of seventy-four thousand s hundred.
2:15 as enrolled of forty-five thousand s hundred fifty.
2:31 is one hundred fifty-seven thousand s hundred.
2:32 was s hundred three thousand five hundred fifty.
3:28 there were eight thousand s hundred,
3:34 was s thousand two hundred.
4:40 houses was two thousand s hundred thirty.
7: 3 s covered wagons and twelve oxen,
11:21 "The people I am with number s hundred thousand
26:41 those enrolled was forty-five thousand s hundred.
26:51 s hundred and one thousand seven hundred thirty.
31:32 totaled s hundred seventy-five thousand sheep,
31:37 of sheep and goats was s hundred seventy-five.
35: 6 to the Levites shall include the s cities of refuge,
35:13 The cities that you designate shall be s cities
35:15 These s cities shall serve as refuge for
Dt 5:13 S days you shall labor and do all your work.
15:12 is sold to you and works for you s years,
15:18 for s years they have given you services worth
16: 8 s days you shall continue to eat unleavened bread,
Jos 6: 3 Thus you shall do for s days,
6:14 They did this for s days.
15:59 s towns with their villages.
15:62 s towns with their villages.
Jdg 3:31 who killed s hundred of the Philistines with
12: 7 Jephthah judged Israel s years.
18:11 S hundred men of the Danite clan,
18:16 While the s hundred men of the Danites,
18:17 the s hundred men armed with weapons of war.
20:47 But s hundred turned and fled toward
Ru 3:15 and he measured out s measures of barley,
3:17 "He gave me these s measures of barley,
1Sa 13: 5 thirty thousand chariots, and s thousand horsemen,
13:15 with him, about s hundred men.
14: 2 that were with him were about s hundred men,
17: 4 of Gath, whose height was s cubits and a span.
17: 7 and his spear's head weighed s hundred shekels
23:13 David and his men, who were about s hundred,
27: 2 he and the s hundred men who were with him,
30: 9 he and the s hundred men who were with him.
2Sa 2:11 the house of Judah was seven years and s months.
5: 5 over Judah seven years and s months;
6:13 the ark of the LORD had gone s paces,
15:18 the s hundred Gittites who had followed him
21:20 who had s fingers on each hand,
21:20 and s toes on each foot, twenty-four in number;
1Ki 6: 6 the middle one was s cubits wide,
10:14 in one year was s hundred sixty-six talents of gold,
10:16 s hundred shekels of gold went
10:19 The throne had s steps.
10:20 one on each end of a step on the s steps.
10:29 from Egypt for s hundred shekels of silver,
11:16 (for Joab and all Israel remained there s months,
16:23 he reigned for twelve years, s of them in Tirzah.
2Ki 5: 5 s thousand shekels of gold,
11: 3 he remained with her s years,
13:19 and said, "You should have struck five or s times;
15: 8 reigned over Israel in Samaria s months.
1Ch 3: 4 s were born to him in Hebron,
3: 4 where he reigned for seven years and s months.
3:22 Hattush, Igal, Bariah, Neariah, and Shaphat, s.
4:27 Shimei had sixteen sons and s daughters;
7: 2 of David being twenty-two thousand s hundred.
8:38 Azel had s sons, and these are their names:
9: 6 Jeuel and their kin, s hundred ninety.
9:44 Azel had s sons, and these are their names:
12:24 numbered s thousand eight hundred armed troops.
12:26 Of the Levites four thousand s hundred.
12:35 twenty-eight thousand s hundred equipped
20: 6 had s fingers on each hand, and s toes on each foot,
21:25 So David paid Ornan s hundred shekels of gold
23: 4 s thousand shall be officers and judges,
25: 3 Jeshaiah, Shimei, Hashabiah, and Mattithiah, s,
26:17 On the east there were s Levites each day,
2Ch 1:17 a chariot for s hundred shekels of silver,
2: 2 with three thousand s hundred to oversee them.
2:17 to be one hundred fifty-three thousand s hundred.
2:18 and three thousand s hundred as overseers to make
3: 8 he overlaid it with s hundred talents of fine gold.
9:13 in one year was s hundred sixty-six talents of gold,
9:15 s hundred shekels of beaten gold went into each
9:18 The throne had s steps and a footstool of gold,
9:19 one on each end of a step on the s steps.
22:12 he remained with them s years,
26:12 of mighty warriors was two thousand s hundred.
29:33 The consecrated offerings were s hundred bulls
35: 8 passover offerings two thousand s hundred lambs
Ezr 2:10 Of Bani, s hundred forty-two.
2:11 Of Bebai, s hundred twenty-three.
2:13 Of Adonikam, s hundred sixty-six.
2:26 Of Ramah and Geba, s hundred twenty-one.
2:35 Of Senaah, three thousand s hundred thirty.
2:60 Tobiah, and Nekoda, s hundred fifty-two.
2:67 and s thousand seven hundred twenty donkeys.
8:26 into their hand s hundred fifty talents of silver,

Ne 5:18 for one day was one ox and s choice sheep;
7:10 Of Arah, s hundred fifty-two.
7:15 Of Binnui, s hundred forty-eight.
7:16 Of Bebai, s hundred twenty-eight.
7:18 Of Adonikam, s hundred sixty-seven.
7:20 Of Adin, s hundred fifty-five.
7:30 Of Ramah and Geba, s hundred twenty-one.
7:62 of Tobiah, of Nekoda, s hundred forty-two.
7:69 and s thousand seven hundred twenty donkeys.
Est 2:12 s months with oil of myrrh and s months with
Job 5:19 He will deliver you from s troubles;
42:12 s thousand camels, a thousand yoke of oxen,
Pr 6:16 There are s things that the LORD hates,
Isa 6:2 in attendance above him; each had s wings:
Jer 34:14 to you and have served you s years;
52:30 all the persons were four thousand s hundred.
Eze 9:2 s men came from the direction of the upper gate,
40:5 in the man's hand was s long cubits, each being
40:12 and the recesses were s cubits on either side.
41:1 on each side s cubits was the width of the pilasters.
41:3 and the width of the entrance, s cubits;
41:5 he measured the wall of the temple, s cubits thick;
41:8 a full reed of s long cubits.
46:1 east shall remain closed on the s working days;
46:4 to the LORD on the sabbath day shall be s lambs
46:6 and s lambs and a ram, which shall be without
Da 3:1 and whose width was s cubits;
Mt 17:1 S days later, Jesus took with him Peter and James
Mk 9:2 S days later, Jesus took with him Peter and James
Lk 4:25 the heaven was shut up three years and s months,
13:14 "There are s days on which work ought to
Jn 2:6 Now standing there were s stone water jars for
6:7 "S months' wages would not buy enough bread
12:1 S days before the Passover Jesus came
Ac 11:12 These s brothers also accompanied me,
18:11 He stayed there a year and s months,
Jas 5:17 and for three years and s months it did not rain on
Rev 4:8 four living creatures, each of them with s wings,
13:18 Its number is s hundred sixty-six.
Tob 1:7 Also for s years I would save up a second tenth
Jdt 1:2 hewn stones three cubits thick and s cubits long;
AdE 1:5 for s days in the courtyard of the royal palace,
2:12 s months while they are anointing themselves
2:12 s months with spices and ointments for women.
Sir 16:10 s hundred thousand foot soldiers who assembled
46:8 of s hundred thousand infantry,
Bel 1:3 of choice flour and forty sheep and s measures
1:31 and he was there for s days.
1Mc 6:42 and s hundred of the king's army fell.
2Mc 8:1 and so they gathered about s thousand.
8:16 to the number s thousand,
10:31 besides s hundred cavalry.
1Es 1:8 for the passover two thousand s hundred sheep
5:12 The descendants of Bani, s hundred forty-eight.
5:13 The descendants of Bebai, s hundred twenty-three.
5:14 descendants of Adonikam, s hundred sixty-seven.
5:20 from Kirama and Geba, s hundred twenty-one.
5:37 the descendants of Nekoda, s hundred fifty-two.
8:56 I weighed and gave to them s hundred fifty talents
2Es 6:42 s parts you dried up and kept so that some
11:23 the three heads that were at rest and s little wings.
11:24 from the s and remained under the head that was
4Mc 4:17 three thousand s hundred sixty talents annually.
11:24 We s boys have paralyzed your tyranny.

SIXTEEN‡ (22) [SIXTEENTH]

Ge 46:18 and these she bore to Jacob—s persons).
Ex 26:25 with their bases of silver, s bases;
36:30 s bases, under every frame two bases.
Nu 31:40 The persons were s thousand,
31:46 and s thousand persons.
31:52 was s thousand seven hundred fifty shekels.
Jos 15:41 s towns with their villages.
19:22 s towns with their villages.
2Ki 13:10 in Samaria; he reigned s years.
14:21 of Judah took Azariah, who was s years old,
15:2 He was s years old when he began to reign,
15:33 when he began to reign and reigned s years
16:2 he reigned s years in Jerusalem.
1Ch 4:27 Shimei had s sons and six daughters;
24:4 under s heads of ancestral houses of the sons
2Ch 13:21 the father of twenty-two sons and s daughters.
26:1 of Judah took Uzziah, who was s years old,
26:3 Uzziah was s years old when he began to reign,
27:1 he reigned s years in Jerusalem.
27:8 he reigned s years in Jerusalem.
28:1 he reigned s years in Jerusalem.
2Mc 11:11 of them and s hundred cavalry,

SIXTEENTH (3) [SIXTEEN]

1Ch 24:14 the fifteenth to Bilgah, the s to Immer,
25:23 to the s, to Hananiah, his sons
2Ch 29:17 and on the s day of the first month they finished.

SIXTH‡ (40) [SIX]

Ge 1:31 and there was morning, the s day.
30:19 Leah conceived again, and she bore Jacob a s son.
Ex 16:5 On the s day, when they prepare what they bring
16:22 On the s day they gathered twice as much food,
16:29 on the s day he gives you food for two days;
26:9 and the s curtain you shall double over at the front
Lev 25:21 I will order my blessing for you in the s year,
Nu 7:42 On the s day Eliasaph son of Deuel,
29:29 On the s day: eight bulls, two rams,
Jos 19:32 The s lot came out for the tribe of Naphtali,
2Sa 3:5 and the s, Ithream, of David's wife Eglah.
2Ki 18:10 In the s year of Hezekiah,
1Ch 2:15 Ozem the s, David the seventh;
3:3 the s Ithream, by his wife Eglah;
12:11 Attai s, Eliel seventh,
24:9 the fifth to Malchijah, the s to Mijamin,
25:13 the s to Bukkiah, his sons and his brothers, twelve;
26:3 Jehohanan the s, Eliehoenai the seventh.
26:5 Ammiel the s, Issachar the seventh, Peullethai the
27:9 S, for the s month, was Ira son of Ikkesh
Ezr 6:15 in the s year of the reign of King Darius.
Ne 3:30 of Shelemiah and Hanun s son of Zalaph
Eze 8:1 In the s year, in the s month,
Hag 1:1 In the second year of King Darius, in the s month,
1:15 day of the month, in the s month.
Lk 1:26 In the s month the angel Gabriel was sent by God
1:36 and this is the s month for her who was said to be
Rev 6:12 When he opened the s seal, I looked,
9:13 Then the s angel blew his trumpet,
9:14 saying to the s angel who had the trumpet,
16:12 The s angel poured his bowl on the great river
21:20 the s carnelian, the seventh chrysolite,
2Mc 7:18 After him they brought forward the s.
1Es 7:5 in the s year of King Darius.
2Es 6:53 the s day you commanded the earth to bring forth
7:86 The s way, they shall see how some
7:97 The s order, when it is shown them
4Mc 11:13 he too had died, the s, a mere boy, was led in.

SIXTIETH (2) [SIXTY]

1Mc 10:1 In the one hundred s year Alexander Epiphanes,
10:21 in the seventh month of the one hundred s year,

SIXTY‡ (50) [SIXTIETH]

Ge 25:26 Isaac was s years old when she bore them.
Lev 27:3 from twenty to s years of age the equivalent shall
27:7 And if the person is s years old or over,
Nu 7:88 the rams s, the male goats s, the male lambs a year old s.
26:27 of those enrolled was s thousand five hundred.
Dt 3:4 s towns, the whole region of Argob,
Jos 13:30 which are in Bashan, s towns,
2Sa 2:31 killed of Benjamin three hundred s of Abner's men
1Ki 4:13 s great cities with walls and bronze bars);
4:22 of choice flour, and s cors of meal,
6:2 for the LORD was s cubits long,
2Ki 25:19 and s men of the people of
1Ch 2:21 whom he married when he was s years old;
2:23 Kenath and its villages, s towns.
5:18 forty-four thousand seven hundred s,
9:13 one thousand seven hundred s,
2Ch 3:3 length, in cubits of the old standard, was s cubits,
11:21 and s concubines, and became the father of twenty-eight sons and s daughters).
12:3 twelve hundred chariots and s thousand cavalry.
Ezr 2:9 Of Zaccai, seven hundred s.
2:64 together was forty-two thousand three hundred s,
6:3 its height shall be s cubits and its width s cubits,
8:10 and with him one hundred s males.
8:13 Jeuel, and Shemaiah, and with them s males.
Ne 7:14 Of Zaccai, seven hundred s.
7:66 together was forty-two thousand three hundred s,
SS 3:7 Around it are s mighty men of the mighty men
6:8 There are s queens and eighty concubines,
Jer 52:25 and s men of the people of the land
Da 3:1 a golden statue whose height was s cubits
Mt 13:8 some a hundredfold, some s, some thirty.
13:23 in one case a hundredfold, in another s,
Mk 4:8 up and increasing and yielding thirty and s and
4:20 thirty and s and a hundredfold."
1Ti 5:9 be put on the list if she is not less than s years old
Rev 11:3 to prophesy for one thousand two hundred s days,
12:6 be nourished for one thousand two hundred s days.
Jdt 1:3 and s cubits wide at the foundations.
1Mc 4:28 next year he mustered s thousand picked infantry
7:16 but he seized s of them and killed them in one day,
2Mc 4:8 at an interview three hundred s talents of silver,
1Es 5:41 were forty-two thousand three hundred s;
6:25 its height to be s cubits and its width s cubits,
8:36 and with him a hundred s men.
4Mc 4:17 king three thousand six hundred s talents annually.

SIXTY-EIGHT (2)

1Ch 16:38 and also Obed-edom and his s kinsfolk;
Ne 11:6 in Jerusalem were four hundred s valiant warriors.

SIXTY-FIFTH (1) [SIXTY-FIVE]

1Mc 10:67 In the one hundred s year Demetrius son

SIXTY-FIVE (5) [SIXTY-FIFTH]

Ge 5:15 When Mahalalel had lived s years,
5:21 When Enoch had lived s years,
5:23 the days of Enoch were three hundred s years.
Nu 3:50 one thousand three hundred s shekels,
Isa 7:8 (Within s years Ephraim will be shattered,

SIXTY-FOUR (2)

Nu 26:25 s thousand three hundred enrolled.
26:43 s thousand four hundred enrolled.

SIXTY-NINE (2) [SIXTY-NINTH]

Ge 5:27 the days of Methuselah were nine hundred s years;
1Es 2:14 gold and silver, five thousand four hundred s,

SIXTY-NINTH (1) [SIXTY-NINE]

2Mc 1:7 in the one hundred s year, we Jews wrote to you,

SIXTY-ONE (3)

Nu 31:34 s thousand donkeys,
31:39 of which the LORD's tribute was s.
Ezr 2:69 to the building fund s thousand darics of gold,

SIXTY-SECOND (1) [SIXTY-TWO]

1Mc 10:57 and came to Ptolemais in the one hundred s year.

SIXTY-SEVEN (5) [SIXTY-SEVENTH]

Ne 7:18 Of Adonikam, six hundred s.
7:19 Of Bigvai, two thousand s.
7:72 two thousand minas of silver, and s priestly robes.
1Es 5:14 The descendants of Adonikam, six hundred s.
5:15 The descendants of Kilan and Azetas, s.

SIXTY-SEVENTH (1) [SIXTY-SEVEN]

1Mc 11:19 Demetrius became king in the one hundred s year.

SIXTY-SIX (7)

Ge 46:26 not including the wives of his sons, were s persons
Lev 12:5 her time of blood purification shall be s days.
1Ki 10:14 to Solomon in one year was six hundred s talents
2Ch 9:13 to Solomon in one year was six hundred s talents
Ezr 2:13 Of Adonikam, six hundred s.
Rev 13:18 Its number is six hundred s.
1Es 5:14 The descendants of Bigvai, two thousand s.

SIXTY-TWO (9) [SIXTY-SECOND]

Ge 5:18 Jared had lived one hundred s years he became
5:20 the days of Jared were nine hundred s years;
Nu 1:39 of the tribe of Dan were s thousand seven hundred.
2:26 as enrolled of s thousand seven hundred.
1Ch 26:8 for the service; s of Obed-edom.
Da 5:31 the kingdom, being about s years old.
9:25 and for s weeks it shall be built again with streets
9:26 After the s weeks, an anointed one shall be cut off
Tob 14:2 He was s years old when he lost his eyesight,

SIZE‡ (21)

Ex 26:2 all the curtains shall be of the same s.
26:8 the eleven curtains shall be of the same s.
36:9 all the curtains were of the same s.
36:15 the eleven curtains were of the same s.
Nu 13:32 and all the people that we saw in it are of great s.
Jos 22:10 an altar by the Jordan, an altar of great s.
2Sa 21:20 where there was a man of great s,
1Ki 7:37 with the same s and the same form.
1Ch 20:6 where there was a man of great s,
23:29 and all measures of quantity or s.
Eze 40:10 the three were of the same s;
40:10 and the pilasters on either side were of the same s.
40:21 and its vestibule were of the same s as those of
40:22 of the same s as those of the gate that faced toward
40:29 and its vestibule were of the same s as the others;
40:32 it was of the same s as the others.
40:36 and its vestibule were of the same s as the others;
46:22 the four were of the same s.
Mt 17:20 if you have faith the s of a mustard seed,
Lk 17:6 "If you had faith the s of a mustard seed,
1Mc 3:19 on the s of the army that victory in battle depends,

SKETCH (1) [SKETCHES]

Heb 8:5 They offer worship in a sanctuary that is a s

SKETCHES (1) [SKETCH]

Heb 9:23 for the s of the heavenly things to be purified

SKIES (15) [SKY]

Dt 33:26 the heavens to your help, majestic through the s.
Ne 1:9 though your outcasts are under the farthest s,
Job 36:28 which the s pour down and drop
37:18 Can you, like him, spread out the s,
37:21 on the light when it is bright in the s,
Ps 68:34 and whose power is in the s.
77:17 the s thundered; your arrows flashed on every side.
78:23 Yet he commanded the s above,
89:6 For who in the s can be compared to the LORD?
89:37 an enduring witness in the s."
Pr 8:28 when he made firm the s above,
Isa 34:4 and the s roll up like a scroll.
45:8 from above, and let the s rain down righteousness;
Jer 51:9 up to heaven and has been lifted up even to the s.
Zec 8:12 and the s shall give their dew;

SKIFFS (1)

Job 9:26 They go by like s of reed,

SKILL‡ (26) [SKILLED, SKILLFUL, SKILLFULLY]

Ex 28:3 whom I have endowed with s,
31:6 and I have given s to all the skillful,
35:26 to use their s spun the goats' hair.
35:31 with s, intelligence, and knowledge in every kind
35:35 with s to do every kind of work done by an artisan
36:1 the LORD has given s and understanding to know
36:2 to whom the LORD had given s,
36:8 with s among the workers made the tabernacle

1Ki 7:14 he was full of s, intelligence,
1Ch 28:21 in all the work will be every volunteer who has s
2Ch 30:22 the Levites who showed good s in the service of
Pr 1: 5 and the discerning acquire s,
Ecc 2:21 and knowledge and s must leave all to be enjoyed
4: 4 and all s in work come from one person's envy
Da 1:17 and s in every aspect of literature and wisdom;
Jdt 11: 8 For we have heard of your wisdom and s,
Wis 7:16 as are all understanding and s in crafts.
13:10 gold and silver fashioned with s,
13:13 and shapes it with s gained in idleness;
14: 4 so that even a person who lacks s may put to sea.
Sir Pr: 3 During that time I have applied my s day and night
9:17 A work is praised for the s of the artisan;
26:13 and her s puts flesh on his bones.
38: 3 The s of physicians makes them distinguished,
38: 6 And he gave s to human beings that he might
49: 1 of Josiah is like blended incense prepared by the s

SKILLED (25) [SKILL]
Ex 28:15 a breastpiece of judgment, in s work;
35:35 by any sort of artisan or s designer.
39: 3 and into the fine twisted linen, in s design.
39: 8 He made the breastpiece, in s work,
1Ch 22:15 and all kinds of artisans without number, s
2Ch 2: 7 So now send me an artisan s to work in gold,
2: 7 to join the s workers who are with me in Judah
2: 8 that your servants are s in cutting Lebanon timber.
2:13 "I have dispatched Huram-abi, a s artisan,
26:15 up machines, invented by s workers, on the towers
Ezr 7: 6 a scribe s in the law of Moses that the LORD
Job 3: 8 those who are s to rouse up Leviathan.
Isa 40:20 then seeks out a s artisan to set up an image
Jer 4:22 They are s in doing evil, but do not know how to
9:17 send for the s women to come;
10: 9 they are all the product of s workers.
50: 9 of a s warrior who does not return empty-handed.
Eze 27: 8 s men of Zemer were within you,
Da 8:23 of bold countenance shall arise, s in intrigue.
Am 5:16 and those s in lamentation, to wailing;
Mic 7: 3 Their hands are s to do evil;
1Co 3:10 like a s master builder I laid a foundation,
Wis 13:11 A s woodcutter may saw down a tree easy
Sir 18:29 Those who are s in words become wise themselves,
1Es 8: 3 a scribe s in the law of Moses, which was given by

SKILLFUL (18) [SKILL]
Ge 25:27 When the boys grew up, Esau was a s hunter,
Ex 31: 6 and I have given skill to all the s,
35:10 All who are s among you shall come and make all
35:25 All the s women spun with their hands,
36: 1 Bezalel and Oholiab and every s one to whom
36: 2 then called Bezalel and Oholiab and every s one
1Sa 16:16 to look for someone who is s in playing the lyre;
16:18 son of Jesse the Bethlehemite who is s in playing,
1Ch 25: 7 in singing to the LORD, all of whom were s,
2Ch 34:12 Other Levites, all s with instruments of music,
Ps 78:72 and guided them with s hand.
Pr 22:29 Do you see those who are s in their work?
Ecc 9:11 nor riches to the intelligent, nor favor to the s;
Isa 3: 3 counselor and s magician and expert enchanter.
Eze 21:31 into brutish hands, those s to destroy.
Sir 37:20 A s speaker may be hated;
38:31 and all are s in their own work.
4Mc 7: 1 For like a most s pilot,

SKILLFULLY (8) [SKILL]
Ex 26: 1 you shall make them with cherubim s worked
26:31 it shall be made with cherubim s worked into it.
28: 6 and of fine twisted linen, s worked.
36: 8 with cherubim s worked into them.
36:35 with cherubim s worked into it.
Ps 33: 3 play s on the strings, with loud shouts.
Wis 13:11 a tree easy to handle and s strip off all its bark,
14:19 s forced the likeness to take more beautiful form,

SKIN‡ (94) [LAMBSKINS, SKINNING, SKINS, WATERSKINS, WINESKIN, WINESKINS]
Ge 21:14 and took bread and a s of water,
21:15 When the water in the s was gone,
21:19 She went, and filled the s with water,
27:11 and I am a man of smooth s.
Ex 29:14 But the flesh of the bull, and its s, and its dung,
34:29 the s of his face shone because he had been talking
34:30 the s of his face was shining;
34:35 that the s of his face was shining;
Lev 4:11 But the s of the bull and all its flesh,
7: 8 the s of the burnt offering that he has offered.
8:17 But the bull itself, its s and flesh and its dung,
9:11 and the flesh and the s he burned with fire outside
11:32 whether an article of wood or cloth or s or sacking,
13: 2 When a person has on the s of his body a swelling
13: 2 it turns into a leprous disease on the s of his body,
13: 3 the disease on the s of his body, and if the hair in
13: 3 and the disease appears to be deeper than the s
13: 4 But if the spot is white in the s of his body,
13: 4 and appears no deeper than the s,
13: 5 and the disease has not spread in the s,
13: 6 in the s, the priest shall pronounce him clean;
13: 7 in the s after he has shown himself to the priest
13: 8 and if the eruption has spread in the s,
13:10 if there is a white swelling in the s that has turned
13:11 it is a chronic leprous disease in the s of his body.
Lev 13:12 But if the disease breaks out in the s,
13:12 so that it covers all the s of the diseased person
13:18 on the s of one's body a boil that has healed,
13:20 the s and its hair has turned white,
13:21 nor is it deeper than the s but has abated,
13:22 in the s, the priest shall pronounce him unclean;
13:24 the s and the raw flesh of the burn becomes a spot,
13:25 and it appears deeper than the s, it is
13:26 and it is no deeper than the s but has abated,
13:27 if it is spreading in the s,
13:28 the s but has abated, it is a swelling from the burn,
13:30 If it appears deeper than the s and the hair
13:31 the s and there is no black hair in it,
13:32 and the itch appears to be no deeper than the s,
13:34 if the itch has not spread in the s and it appears to
be no deeper than the s,
13:35 in the s after he was pronounced clean,
13:36 If the itch has spread in the s,
13:38 a man or a woman has spots on the s of the body,
13:39 if the spots on the s of the body are of a dull white,
13:39 it is a rash that has broken out on the s;
13:43 which resembles a leprous disease in the s of
13:48 or in a s or in anything made of s,
13:49 in warp or woof or in s or in anything made of s,
13:51 or in the s, whatever be the use of the s,
13:52 woolen or linen, or anything of s,
13:53 in warp or woof or in anything of s,
13:56 in warp or woof, or out of s.
13:57 in warp or woof, or in anything of s,
13:58 or anything of s from which the disease disappears
13:59 either in warp or woof, or in anything of s,
15:17 or of s on which the semen falls shall be washed
16:27 their s and their flesh and their dung shall
Nu 19: 5 Then the heifer shall be burned in his sight; its s,
31:20 You shall purify every garment, every article of s,
Dt 24: 8 Guard against an outbreak of a leprous s disease
Jdg 4:19 a s of milk and gave him a drink and covered him.
1Sa 1:24 an ephah of flour, and a s of wine.
10: 3 and another carrying a s of wine.
16:20 a s of wine, and a kid,
2Sa 16: 1 one hundred of summer fruits, and one s of wine.
2Ch 29:34 But the priests were too few and could not s all
Job 2: 4 Then Satan answered the LORD, "S for s!
7: 5 my s hardens, then breaks out again.
10:11 You clothed me with s and flesh,
16:15 I have sewed sackcloth upon my s,
18:13 By disease their s is consumed,
19:20 My bones cling to my s and to my flesh,
19:20 and I have escaped by the s of my teeth.
19:26 and after my s has been thus destroyed,
30:30 My s turns black and falls from me,
41: 7 Can you fill its s with harpoons,
Ps 102: 5 of my loud groaning my bones cling to my s.
Jer 13:23 Can Ethiopians change their s
La 3: 4 He has made my flesh and my s waste away,
4: 8 Their s has shriveled on their bones;
5:10 Our s is black as an oven from the scorching heat
Eze 37: 6 and cover you with s, and put breath in you,
37: 8 upon them, and s had covered them;
Mic 3: 2 who tear the s off my people,
3: 3 flay their s off them, break their bones in pieces,
Na 3:16 The locust sheds its s and flies away.
Ac 19:12 or aprons that had touched his s were brought to
Jdt 10: 5 She gave her maid a s of wine and a flask of oil,
2Mc 7: 7 They tore off the s of his head with the hair,

SKINNING (1) [SKIN]
2Ch 35:11 received from them, while the Levites did the s.

SKINS (18) [SKIN]
Ge 3:21 the LORD God made garments of s for the man
27:16 and she put the s of the kids on his hands and on
Ex 25: 5 tanned rams' s, fine leather, acacia wood,
26:14 a covering of tanned rams' s and an outer covering
35: 7 tanned rams' s, and fine leather, acacia wood,
35:23 of goats' hair or tanned rams' s or fine leather,
36:19 a covering of tanned rams' s and an outer covering
39:34 of tanned rams' s and the covering of fine leather,
Nu 6: 4 not even the seeds or the s.
1Sa 25:18 two s of wine, five sheep ready dressed,
Ne 5:18 and every ten days s of wine in abundance;
Mt 9:17 otherwise, the s burst, and the wine is spilled, and
the s are destroyed;
Mk 2:22 otherwise, the wine will burst the s, and the wine
is lost, and so are the s;
Lk 5:37 the new wine will burst the s and will be spilled,
and the s will be destroyed.
Heb 11:37 they went about in s of sheep and goats, destitute,

SKIP (2) [SKIPPED, SKIPS]
Ps 29: 6 He makes Lebanon s like a calf,
114: 6 O mountains, that you s like rams?

SKIPPED (1) [SKIP]
Ps 114: 4 The mountains s like rams, the hills like lambs.

SKIPS (1) [SKIP]
Sir 36:31 For who will trust a nimble robber that s from city

SKIRT See Index to Footnotes

SKIRTED (1) [SKIRTING]
Dt 2: 1 the LORD had told me and s Mount Seir for many

SKIRTING (1) [SKIRTED]
Dt 2: 3 "You have been s this hill country long enough.

SKIRTS (7)
Job 38:13 so that it might take hold of the s of the earth,
Jer 2:34 Also on your s is found the lifeblood of
13:22 the greatness of your iniquity that your s are lifted
13:26 I myself will lift up your s over your face,
La 1: 9 Her uncleanness was in her s;
Eze 5: 3 and bind them in the s of your robe.
Na 3: 5 and will lift up your s over your face;

SKULL‡ (6)
Jdg 9:53 on Abimelech's head, and crushed his s.
2Ki 9:35 they found no more of her than the s and the feet
Mt 27:33 place called Golgotha (which means Place of a S),
Mk 15:22 called Golgotha (which means the place of a s).
Lk 23:33 When they came to the place that is called The S,
Jn 19:17 he went out to what is called The Place of the S,

SKY (29) [SKIES]
Ge 1: 8 God called the dome S.
1: 9 "Let the waters under the s be gathered together
1:14 "Let there be lights in the dome of the s to separate
1:15 in the dome of the s to give light upon the earth."
1:17 in the dome of the s to give light upon the earth,
1:20 above the earth across the dome of the s."
Lev 26:19 and I will make your s like iron and your earth
Dt 11:11 watered by rain from the s,
28:23 The s over your head shall be bronze,
28:24 down upon you from the s until you are destroyed.
Jos 8:20 the smoke of the city was rising to the s.
Jdg 20:40 the whole city going up in smoke toward the s!
2Ki 7: 2 if the LORD were to make windows in the s,
7:19 if the LORD were to make windows in the s,
Ps 85:11 and righteousness will look down from the s.
Pr 30:19 the way of an eagle in the s,
Da 12: 3 like the brightness of the s,
Zec 5: 9 and they lifted up the basket between earth and s.
Mt 16: 2 you say, 'It will be fair weather, for the s is red.'
16: 3 for the s is red and threatening.'
16: 3 how to interpret the appearance of the s,
Lk 12:56 how to interpret the appearance of earth and s,
17:24 For as the lightning flashes and lights up the s
Rev 6:13 and the stars of the s fell to the earth as
6:14 The s vanished like a scroll rolling itself up,
11: 6 They have authority to shut the s,
Sir 43: 1 of the higher realms is the clear vault of the s,
43:12 It encircles the s with its glorious arc;
2Es 15:44 then the dust and smoke shall reach the s,

SLACK (7)
Jos 18: 3 be s about going in and taking possession of
Ezr 4:22 Moreover, take care not to be s in this matter;
Pr 10: 4 A s hand causes poverty, but the hand of
18: 9 One who is s in work is close kin to a vandal.
Jer 48:10 the one who is s in doing the work of the LORD;
Hab 1: 4 So the law becomes s and justice never prevails.
Sir 2:12 Woe to timid hearts and to s hands,

SLAIN‡ (50) [SLAY]
Ge 34:27 And the other sons of Jacob came upon the s,
Nu 19:18 and on whoever touched the bone, the s,
23:24 the prey and drunk the blood of the s."
25:14 The name of the s Israelite man,
31: 8 in addition to others who were s by them;
Dt 32:42 with the blood of the s and the captives,
Jos 11: 6 at this time I will hand over all of them, s,
Jdg 15:16 the jawbone of a donkey I have s a thousand men."
20:45 and two thousand of them were s.
2Sa 1:19 O Israel, lies s upon your high places!
1:22 From the blood of the s,
1:25 Jonathan lies s upon your high places.
1Ch 5:22 Many fell s, because the war was of God.
10: 1 and fell s on Mount Gilboa.
2Ch 13:17 five hundred thousand picked men of Israel fell s.
Job 39:30 and where the s are, there it is."
Ps 88: 5 like the s that lie in the grave,
Isa 10: 4 among the prisoners or fall among the s?
22: 2 Your s are not s by the sword,
26:21 and will no longer cover its s.
34: 3 Their s shall be cast out, and the stench
66:16 and those s by the LORD shall be many.
Jer 9: 1 so that I might weep day and night for the s
18:21 their youths be s by the sword in battle.
25:33 Those s by the LORD on that day shall extend
41:16 after he had s Gedaliah son of Ahikam—
51: 4 down s in the land of the Chaldeans,
51:47 and all her s shall fall in her midst.
51:49 Babylon must fall for the s of Israel,
51:49 s of all the earth have fallen because of Babylon.
Eze 6: 4 I will throw down your s in front of your idols.
6: 7 The s shall fall in your midst;
6:13 their s lie among their idols around their altars,
9: 7 "Defile the house, and fill the courts with the s.
11: 6 and have filled its streets with the s.
11: 7 s whom you have placed within it are the meat,
30: 4 the s fall in Egypt, and its wealth is carried away,
30:11 and fill the land with the s.
32:25 among the s with all its hordes, their graves all
32:25 they are placed among the s.
32:30 who have gone down in shame with the s,
32:32 with those who are s by the sword—
35: 8 I will fill its mountains with the s;

Eze 37: 9 and breathe upon these **s**, that they may live."
Da 11:26 be swept away, and many shall fall **s**.
Ac 7:42 to me **s** victims and sacrifices forty years in
Jdt 10:13 without losing one of his men, captured or **s**."
4Mc 13:12 to being **s** for the sake of religion."
18:11 He read to you about Abel **s** by Cain,

SLANDER (28) [SLANDERED, SLANDERER, SLANDERERS, SLANDERING, SLANDEROUS, SLANDERS]

Ps 15: 3 who do not **s** with their tongue, and do no evil
50:20 you **s** your own mother's child.
Pr 10:18 and whoever utters **s** is a fool.
30:10 Do not **s** a servant to a master,
Eze 22: 9 In you are those who **s** to shed blood,
36: 3 and you became an object of gossip and **s** among
Mt 15:19 adultery, fornication, theft, false witness, **s**.
Mk 7:22 wickedness, deceit, licentiousness, envy, **s**, pride,
Ro 3: 8 And why not say (as some people **s** us by saying
2Co 12:20 anger, selfishness, **s**, gossip, conceit, and disorder.
Eph 4:31 and wrath and anger and wrangling and **s**,
Col 3: 8 malice, **s**, and abusive language from your mouth.
1Ti 6: 4 From these come envy, dissension, **s**,
1Pe 2: 1 and all guile, insincerity, envy, and all **s**.
2Pe 2:10 they are not afraid to **s** the glorious ones,
2:12 They **s** what they do not understand,
Jude 1: 8 reject authority, and **s** the glorious ones.
1: 9 not dare to bring a condemnation of **s** against him,
1:10 these people **s** whatever they do not understand,
Rev 2: 9 I know the **s** on the part of those who say
Wis 1:11 and keep your tongue from **s**;
Sir 19:15 Question a friend, for often it is **s**;
26: 5 **S** in the city, the gathering of a mob,
28:14 **S** has shaken many, and scattered them
28:15 **S** has driven virtuous women from their homes,
28:16 Those who pay heed to **s** will not find rest,
51: 6 the **s** of an unrighteous tongue to the king.
4Mc 4: 1 of **s** he was unable to injure Onias in the eyes of

SLANDERED (4) [SLANDER]

Dt 22:19 to the young woman's father) because he has **s**
2Sa 19:27 He has **s** your servant to my lord the king.
1Co 4:13 when **s**, we speak kindly. We have become like the
2Mc 4: 1 about the money against his own country, **s** Onias,

SLANDERER‡ (3) [SLANDER]

Lev 19:16 You shall not go around as a **s** among your people,
Ps 140:11 Do not let the **s** be established in the land;
Jer 9: 4 and every neighbor goes around like a **s**.

SLANDERERS (4) [SLANDER]

Ro 1:30 **s**, God-haters, insolent, haughty, boastful,
1Ti 3:11 Women likewise must be serious, not **s**,
2Ti 3: 3 implacable, **s**, profligates, brutes, haters of good,
Tit 2: 3 not to be **s** or slaves to drink;

SLANDERING (1) [SLANDER]

Dt 22:14 **s** her by saying, "I married this woman;

SLANDEROUS (2) [SLANDER]

2Pe 2:11 do not bring against them a **s** judgment from
Sir 51: 2 and from the trap laid by a **s** tongue,

SLANDERS (3) [SLANDER]

Ps 101: 5 One who secretly **s** a neighbor I will destroy.
Jer 6:28 all stubbornly rebellious, going about with **s**;
3Mc 6: 7 who through envious **s** was thrown down into

SLANG (KJV) See SLUNG

SLAP‡ (2) [SLAPPED]

2Co 11:20 or puts on airs, or gives you a **s** in the face.
1Es 4:30 and **s** the king with her left hand.

SLAPPED (3) [SLAP]

1Ki 22:24 to Micaiah, **s** him on the cheek, and said,
2Ch 18:23 to Micaiah, **s** him on the cheek, and said,
Mt 26:67 spat in his face and struck him; and some **s** him,

SLASH (1) [SLASHES]

Jer 49: 3 lament, and **s** yourselves with whips!

SLASHES (1) [SLASH]

Job 16:13 He **s** open my kidneys, and shows no mercy;

SLAUGHTER‡ (84) [SLAUGHTERED, SLAUGHTERING, SLAUGHTERS]

Ge 43:16 and **s** an animal and make ready,
Ex 12: 6 of Israel shall **s** it at twilight.
12:21 to them, "Go, select lambs for your families, and **s**
29:11 and you shall **s** the bull before the LORD,
29:16 and you shall **s** the ram,
29:20 and you shall **s** the ram,
Lev 3: 2 on the head of the offering and **s** it at the entrance
7: 2 they shall **s** the guilt offering,
14:13 He shall **s** the lamb in the place where
14:19 Afterward he shall **s** the burnt offering;
14:25 The priest shall **s** the lamb of the guilt offering
Lev 14:50 and shall **s** one of the birds over fresh water in
16:11 he shall **s** the bull as a sin offering for himself.
16:15 He shall **s** the goat of the sin offering that is for
22:28 But you shall not **s**, from the herd or the flock,
Nu 11:22 Are there enough flocks and herds to **s** for them?
Dt 12:15 Yet whenever you desire you may **s** and eat meat
12:21 and you **s** as I have commanded you any
16: 4 and none of the meat of what you **s** on the evening
Jos 10:10 who inflicted a great **s** on them at Gibeon,
10:20 the Israelites had finished inflicting a very great **s**
Jdg 15: 8 He struck them down hip and thigh with great **s**;
1Sa 4:10 There was a very great **s**,
4:17 and there has also been a great **s** among the troops;
6:19 the LORD had made a great **s** among the people.
14:14 In that first **s** Jonathan and his armor-bearer killed
14:30 the **s** among the Philistines has not been great."
14:34 and **s** them here, and eat;
2Sa 17: 9 a **s** among the troops who follow Absalom.'
18: 7 and the **s** there was great on that day,
1Ki 11:24 and became leader of a marauding band, after the **s**
20:21 and defeated the Arameans with a great **s**.
2Ch 13:17 Abijah and his army defeated them with great **s**;
25:14 after Amaziah came from the **s** of the Edomites,
28: 5 who defeated him with great **s**.
30:17 therefore the Levites had to **s** the passover lamb
35: 6 **S** the passover lamb, sanctify yourselves,
Ps 44:11 You have made us like sheep for **s**,
44:22 and accounted as sheep for the **s**.
Pr 7:22 and goes like an ox to the **s**,
24:11 those who go staggering to the **s**;
Isa 13:18 Their bows will **s** the young men;
14:21 Prepare **s** for his sons because of the guilt
30:25 on a day of the great **s**, when the towers fall.
34: 2 he has doomed them, has given them over for **s**.
34: 6 a great **s** in the land of Edom.
53: 7 like a lamb that is led to the **s**,
57: 5 you that **s** your children in the valleys,
65:12 and all of you shall bow down to the **s**;
Jer 7:32 valley of the son of Hinnom, but the valley of **S**:
11:19 But I was like a gentle lamb led to the **s**.
12: 3 Pull them out like sheep for the **s**,
12: 3 and set them apart for the day of **s**.
19: 6 valley of the son of Hinnom, but the valley of **S**.
25:34 for the days of your **s** have come—
48:15 choicest of his young men have gone down to **s**,
50:27 Kill all her bulls, let them go down to the **s**.
51:40 I will bring them down like lambs to the **s**,
Eze 9: 2 each with his weapon for **s** in his hand;
21:10 It is sharpened for **s**, honed to flash
21:14 A sword for great **s**—it surrounds them;
21:15 It is made for flashing, it is polished for **s**.
21:22 to call out for **s**, for raising the battle cry,
21:28 A sword, a sword! Drawn for **s**
26:15 when **s** goes on within you?
34: 3 you **s** the fatlings; but you do not feed the sheep.
44:11 they shall **s** the burnt offering and the sacrifice for
Hos 9:13 but now Ephraim must lead out his children for **s**.
Ob 1:10 For the **s** and violence done to your brother Jacob,
Zec 11: 4 Be a shepherd of the flock doomed to **s**.
11: 7 I became the shepherd of the flock doomed to **s**.
Lk 19:27 bring them here and **s** them in my presence.' "
Ac 8:32 "Like a sheep he was led to the **s**,
Jas 5: 5 you have fattened your hearts in a day of **s**.
Rev 6: 4 so that people would **s** one another;
Jdt 2:11 to **s** and plunder throughout your whole region.
8:22 The **s** of our kindred and the captivity of the land
15: 5 and in Galilee outflanked them with great **s**,
15: 7 And the Israelites, when they returned from the **s**,
Wis 12: 5 their merciless **s** of children,
2Mc 5:13 and children, and **s** of young girls and infants.
2Es 15:10 See, my people are being led like a flock to the **s**;
15:26 therefore he will hand them over to death and **s**.
4Mc 2:19 and Levi for their irrational **s** of the entire tribe of

SLAUGHTERED (68) [SLAUGHTER]

Ge 37:31 Then they took Joseph's robe, **s** a goat,
Lev 1: 5 The bull shall be **s** before the LORD;
1:11 It shall be **s** on the north side of the altar before
3: 8 It shall be **s** before the tent of meeting,
3:13 it shall be **s** before the tent of meeting;
4: 4 the bull shall be **s** before the LORD.
4:15 and the bull shall be **s** before the LORD.
4:24 it shall be **s** at the spot where
4:24 where the burnt offering is **s** before the LORD;
4:29 and the sin offering shall be **s** at the place of
4:33 and it shall be **s** as a sin offering at the spot where
4:33 at the spot where the burnt offering is **s**.
6:25 The sin offering shall be **s** before the LORD at
6:25 at the spot where the burnt offering is **s**;
7: 2 at the spot where the burnt offering is **s**,
8:15 and it was **s**. Moses took the blood
8:19 and it was **s**. Moses dashed the blood against all
8:23 and it was **s**. Moses took some of its blood
9: 8 and **s** the calf of the sin offering,
9:12 Then he **s** the burnt offering.
9:15 that was for the people, and **s** it, and presented it as
9:18 He **s** the ox and the ram as a sacrifice
14: 5 the birds be **s** over fresh water in an earthen vessel.
14: 6 the living bird in the blood of the bird that was **s**
14:13 where the sin offering and the burnt offering are **s**
14:51 in the blood of the **s** bird and the fresh water,
Nu 14:16 to give them that he has **s** them in the wilderness.'
19: 3 be taken outside the camp and **s** in his presence.
1Sa 1:25 they **s** the bull, and they brought the child to Eli.
14:32 and **s** them on the ground;
14:34 with them that night, and **s** them there.
1Sa 28:24 She quickly **s** it, and she took flour, kneaded it,
1Ki 19:21 took the yoke of oxen, and **s** them;
2Ki 10:14 and **s** them at the pit of Beth-eked, forty-two in all;
23:20 He **s** on the altars all the priests of
25: 7 They **s** the sons of Zedekiah before his eyes,
2Ch 18: 2 Ahab **s** an abundance of sheep and oxen for him
29:22 So they **s** the bulls, and the priests received
29:22 they **s** the rams and their blood was dashed against
29:22 they also **s** the lambs and their blood was dashed
29:24 and the priests **s** them and made a sin offering
30:15 They **s** the passover lamb on the fourteenth day of
35: 1 they **s** the passover lamb on the fourteenth day of
35:11 They **s** the passover lamb,
Pr 9: 2 She has **s** her animals, she has mixed her wine,
Jer 39: 6 of Babylon **s** the sons of Zedekiah at Riblah
39: 6 also the king of Babylon **s** all the nobles of Judah.
41: 7 of Nethaniah and the men with him **s** them,
Eze 16:21 You **s** my children and delivered them up as
23:39 For when they had **s** their children for their idols,
40:39 the sin offering and the guilt offering were to be **s**.
40:41 eight tables, on which the sacrifices were to be **s**.
40:42 the burnt offerings and the sacrifices were **s**.
Mt 22: 4 my oxen and my fat calves have been **s**,
Ro 8:36 we are accounted as sheep to be **s**."
Rev 5: 6 the elders a Lamb standing as if it had been **s**,
5: 9 the scroll and to open its seals, for you were **s** and
5:12 "Worthy is the Lamb that was **s** to receive power
6: 9 of those who had been **s** for the word of God and
13: 8 in the book of life of the Lamb that was **s**.
18:24 and of all who have been **s** on earth."
Tob 7: 9 Then Raguel **s** a ram from the flock
8:19 and four rams and ordered them to be **s**.
Bel 1:28 and killed the dragon, and **s** the priests."
2Mc 10:17 and **s** those whom they encountered,
10:31 Twenty thousand five hundred were **s**,
12:16 and **s** untold numbers, so that the adjoining lake,
12:26 and **s** twenty-five thousand people.

SLAUGHTERERS See Index to Footnotes

SLAUGHTERING (6) [SLAUGHTER]

Jos 8:24 When Israel had finished **s** all the inhabitants of Ai
Jdg 20:42 and those who came out of the city were **s** them
Est 9: 5 with the sword, **s**, and destroying them, and did
Isa 22:13 and festivity, killing oxen and **s** sheep, eating meat
La 2:21 in the day of your anger you have killed them, **s**
2Mc 5: 6 But Jason kept relentlessly **s** his compatriots,

SLAUGHTERS (4) [SLAUGHTER]

Ex 22: 1 someone steals an ox or a sheep, and **s** it or sells it,
Lev 17: 3 of the house of Israel **s** an ox or a lamb or a goat in
17: 3 or **s** it outside the camp,
Isa 66: 3 Whoever **s** an ox is like one who kills a human

SLAVE‡ (147) [ENSLAVE, ENSLAVED, ENSLAVES, ENSLAVING, SLAVE'S, SLAVE-GIRL, SLAVEOWNER, SLAVERY, SLAVES]

Ge 9:26 and let Canaan be his **s**.
9:27 and let Canaan be his **s**."
15: 3 and so a **s** born in my house is to be my heir."
17:12 the **s** born in your house and the one bought
17:13 Both the **s** born in your house and the one bought
21:10 "Cast out this **s** woman with her son;
21:10 for the son of this **s** woman shall not inherit along
21:12 because of the boy and because of your **s** woman;
21:13 As for the son of the **s** woman,
44:10 he with whom it is found shall become my **s**,
44:17 the cup was found shall be my **s**;
44:33 please let your servant remain as a **s** to my lord
49:15 and became a **s** at forced labor.
Ex 11: 5 to the firstborn of the female **s** who is behind
12:44 but any **s** who has been purchased may eat of it
20:10 your son or your daughter, your male or female **s**,
20:17 or male or female **s**, or ox, or donkey,
21: 2 When you buy a male Hebrew **s**,
21: 5 But if the **s** declares, "I love my master, my wife,
21: 7 When a man sells his daughter as a **s**,
21:20 strikes a male or female **s** with a rod and the **s** dies
21:21 **s** survives a day or two, there is no punishment;
21:21 for the **s** is the owner's property.
21:26 a slaveowner strikes the eye of a male or female **s**,
21:26 the owner shall let the **s** go, a free person,
21:27 a tooth of a male or female **s**, the **s** shall be let go,
21:32 If the ox gores a male or female **s**,
23:12 and your homeborn **s** and the resident alien may
Lev 19:20 man has sexual relations with a woman who is a **s**,
Dt 5:14 or your daughter, or your male or female **s**,
5:14 your male and female **s** may rest as well as you.
5:15 Remember that you were a **s** in the land of Egypt,
5:21 or field, or male or female **s**, or ox, or donkey,
15:13 you send a male **s** out from you a free person,
15:15 Remember that you were a **s** in the land of Egypt,
15:17 and he shall be your **s** forever.
15:17 the same with regard to your female **s**.
16:12 Remember that you were a **s** in Egypt,
21:14 You must not treat her as a **s**,
24:18 Remember that you were a **s** in Egypt and
24:22 Remember that you were a **s** in the land of Egypt;
Jdg 9:18 of his **s** woman, king over the lords of Shechem,
1Sa 25:41 a **s** to wash the feet of the servants of my lord."
1Ki 9:21 these Solomon conscripted for **s** labor,
1Ch 2:34 but Sheshan had an Egyptian **s**,
2:35 in marriage to his **s** Jarha;

Job 7: 2 Like a s who longs for the shadow,
Ps 105:17 Joseph, who was sold as a s.
Pr 17: 2 A s who deals wisely will rule over
19:10 much less for a s to rule over princes.
22: 7 and the borrower is the s of the lender.
29:21 A s pampered from childhood will come to
30:22 a s when he becomes king, and a fool when glutted
Isa 24: 2 as with the s, so with his master;
49: 7 the s of rulers, "Kings shall see and stand up,
Jer 2:14 Is Israel a s? Is he a homeborn servant?
27: 7 and great kings shall make him their s.
Na 2: 7 the city be exiled, its s women led away, moaning
Mt 6:24 for a s will either hate the one and love the other,
8: 9 and to my s, 'Do this,' and the s does it."
10:24 nor a s above the master;
10:25 and the s like the master.
18:26 So the s fell on his knees before him, saying,
18:27 of that s released him and forgave him the debt.
18:28 But that same s, as he went out,
18:29 Then his fellow s fell down and pleaded with him,
18:32 and said to him, 'You wicked s!
18:33 Should you not have had mercy on your fellow s,
20:27 to be first among you must be your s;
24:45 "Who then is the faithful and wise s,
24:46 Blessed is that s whom his master will find
24:48 But if that wicked s says to himself,
24:50 of that s will come on a day when he does
25:21 'Well done, good and trustworthy s;
25:23 'Well done, good and trustworthy s;
25:26 But his master replied, 'You wicked and lazy s!
25:30 As for this worthless s, throw him into
26:51 drew it, and struck the s of the high priest,
Mk 10:44 to be first among you must be s of all.
12: 2 a s to the tenants to collect from them his share of
12: 4 And again he sent another s to them;
14:47 near drew his sword and struck the s of
Lk 7: 2 A centurion there had a s whom he valued highly,
7: 3 asking him to come and heal his s.
7: 8 and to my s, 'Do this,' and the s does it."
7:10 they found the s in good health.
12:43 Blessed is that s whom his master will find
12:45 But if that s says to himself,
12:46 of that s will come on a day when he does
12:47 That s who knew what his master wanted,
14:17 At the time for the dinner he sent his s to say
14:21 So the s returned and reported this to his master.
14:21 of the house became angry and said to his s,
14:22 the s said, 'Sir, what you ordered has been done,
14:23 Then the master said to the s,
15:29 For all these years I have been working like a s
16:13 No s can serve two masters; for a s will either hate
17: 7 among you would say to your s who has just come
17: 9 the s for doing what was commanded?
19:17 He said to him, 'Well done, good s!
19:22 by your own words, you wicked s!
20:10 he sent a s to the tenants in order
20:11 Next he sent another s;
22:50 Then one of them struck the s of the high priest
Jn 8:34 I tell you, everyone who commits sin is a s to sin.
8:35 The s does not have a permanent place in
18:10 struck the high priest's s, and cut off his right ear.
Ro 7:25 So then, with my mind I am a s to the law of God,
7:25 but with my flesh I am a s to the law of sin.
1Co 7:21 Were you a s when called?
7:22 called in the Lord as a s is a freed person
7:22 as whoever was free when called is a s of Christ.
9:19 I have made myself a s to all,
Gal 3:28 there is no longer s or free,
4: 7 So you are no longer a s but a child,
4:22 one by a s woman and the other by a free woman.
4:23 the child of the s, was born according to the flesh;
4:30 "Drive out the s and her child; for the child of the
s will not share the inheritance
4:31 not of the s but of the free woman.
Php 2: 7 taking the form of a s,
Col 3:11 Scythian, s and free; but Christ is all and in all!
1Ti 1:10 sodomites, s traders, liars, perjurers,
Phm 1:16 as a s but more than a s, a beloved brother—
Rev 6:15 s and free, hid in the caves and among the rocks of
13:16 both rich and poor, both free and s,
19:18 flesh of all, both free and s, both small and great."
Jdt 4:10 and hired laborer and purchased s—
9:10 of my lips strike down the s with the prince and
11: 5 Judith answered him, "Accept the words of your s,
11:16 when I, your s, learned all this, I fled from them.
Wis 18:11 The s was punished with the same penalty as
Sir 33:25 bread and discipline and work for a s.
33:26 Set your s to work, and you will find rest;
33:27 and for a wicked s there are racks and tortures.
33:31 If you have but one s, treat him like yourself,
33:31 If you have but one s, treat him like a brother,
42: 5 and of drawing blood from the back of a wicked s.
1Mc 2:11 no longer free, she has become a s.
2Mc 8:35 and made his way alone like a runaway s across
1Es 3:19 of the s and the free, of the poor and the rich.

SLAVE'S (1) [SLAVE]

Jn 18:10 The s name was Malchus.

SLAVE-GIRL (8) [GIRL, SLAVE]

Ge 16: 1 She had an Egyptian s whose name was Hagar,
16: 2 from bearing children; go in to my s;
16: 3 Abram's wife, took Hagar the Egyptian, her s,
16: 5 I gave my s to your embrace,
16: 6 But Abram said to Sarai, "Your s is in your power;
16: 8 And he said, "Hagar, s of Sarai,
25:12 whom Hagar the Egyptian, Sarah's s,
Ac 16:16 we met a s who had a spirit of divination

SLAVE-GIRLS (1)

Jdt 16:12 Sons of s pierced them through and wounded them

SLAVEOWNER (3) [OWN, SLAVE]

Ex 21:20 When a s strikes a male or female slave with a rod
21:26 When a s strikes the eye of a male or female slave,
21:32 the owner shall pay to the s thirty shekels of silver,

SLAVERY‡ (32) [SLAVE]

A. HOUSE OF SLAVERY (13)

Ex 2:23 The Israelites groaned under their s, and cried out.
2:23 Out of the s their cry for help rose up to God.
6: 6 of the Egyptians and deliver you from s to them.
6: 9 because of their broken spirit and their cruel s.
13: 3 out of Egypt, out of the house of s, A
13:14 out of Egypt, from the house of s. A
20: 2 out of the land of Egypt, out of the house of s; A
Dt 5: 6 out of the land of Egypt, out of the house of s; A
6:12 out of the land of Egypt, out of the house of s. A
7: 8 and redeemed you from the house of s, A
8:14 out of the land of Egypt, out of the house of s, A
13: 5 Egypt and redeemed you from the house of s— A
13:10 out of the land of Egypt, out of the house of s. A
Jos 24:17 from the land of Egypt, out of the house of s, A
Jdg 6: 8 and brought you out of the house of s; A
Ezr 9: 8 and grant us a little sustenance in our s.
9: 9 yet our God has not forsaken us in our s,
Ne 9:17 and determined to return to their s in Egypt.
Jer 34: 9 so that no one should hold another Judean in s.
34:13 out of the house of s, saying, A
Mic 6: 4 and redeemed you from the house of s; A
Ro 7:14 but I am of the flesh, sold into s under sin.
8:15 For you did not receive a spirit of s to fall back
Gal 4:24 is Hagar, from Mount Sinai, bearing children for s.
4:25 for she is in s with her children.
5: 1 therefore, and do not submit again to a yoke of s.
1Ti 6: 1 under the yoke of s regard their masters as worthy
Heb 2:15 and free those who all their lives were held in s by
Jdt 8:23 For our s will not bring us into favor,
AdE 14: 8 now they are not satisfied that we are in bitter s,
2Mc 5:14 and as many were sold into s as were killed.
8:10 by selling the captured Jews into s.

SLAVES‡ (161) [SLAVE]

Ge 9:25 lowest of s shall he be to his brothers."
12:16 male donkeys, male and female s, female donkeys,
15:13 and shall be s there, and they shall be oppressed
17:23 the s born in his house or bought with his money,
17:27 s born in the house and those bought with money
20:14 and oxen, and male and female s, and gave them
20:17 and also healed his wife and female s so
24:35 male and female s, camels and donkeys.
30:43 and male and female s, and camels and donkeys.
32: 5 donkeys, flocks, male and female s;
43:18 to make s of us and take our donkeys."
44: 9 moreover the rest of us will become my lord's s."
44:16 here we are then, my lord's s,
47:19 We with our land will become s to Pharaoh;
47:21 he made s of them from one end of Egypt to
47:25 may it please my lord, we will be s to Pharaoh."
50:18 and said, "We are here as your s."
Ex 6: 5 the Israelites whom the Egyptians are holding as s,
9:20 of the LORD hurried their s and livestock off to
9:21 the word of the LORD left their s and livestock in
21: 7 she shall not go out as the male s do.
Lev 25: 6 you, your male and female s,
25:39 you shall not make them serve as s.
25:42 they shall not be sold as s are sold.
25:44 As for the male and female s whom you may have,
25:44 that you may acquire male and female s.
25:46 These you may treat as s,
26:13 to be their s no more;
Dt 6:21 "We were Pharaoh's s in Egypt,
12:12 and your daughters, your male and female s, and
12:18 your male and female s, and the Levites resident
16:11 and female s, the Levites resident in your towns,
16:14 your male and female s, as well as the Levites,
23:15 S who have escaped to you
28:68 for sale to your enemies as male and female s,
Jos 9:23 you are cursed, and some of you shall always be s,
1Sa 2:27 of your ancestor in Egypt when they were s to
4: 9 not to become s to the Hebrews as they have been
8:16 He will take your male and female s,
8:17 and you shall be his s.
1Ki 2:39 of three years that two of Shimei's s ran away
2:39 When it was told Shimei, "Your s are in Gath,"
2:40 and went to Achish in Gath, to search for his s;
2:40 Shimei went and brought his s from Gath.
9:22 But of the Israelites Solomon made no s;
2Ki 4: 1 a creditor has come to take my two children as s."
5:26 sheep and oxen, and male and female s?
2Ch 8: 9 But of the people of Israel Solomon made no s
28:10 Judah and Jerusalem, male and female, as your s.
Ezr 9: 9 For we are s; yet our God has not forsaken us
Ne 5: 5 yet we are forcing our sons and daughters to be s,
7:67 besides their male and female s,
9:36 Here we are, s to this day—s in the land that you
Est 7: 4 If we had been sold merely as s, men and women,
Job 3:19 and the s are free from their masters.
31:13 I have rejected the cause of my male or female s,
Ecc 2: 7 I bought male and female s, and had s who were
10: 7 I have seen s on horseback, and princes walking
on foot like s.
Isa 14: 2 as male and female s in the LORD's land;
Jer 25:14 For many nations and great kings shall make s
34: 9 that all should set free their Hebrew s,
34:10 that all would set free their s, male or female,
34:11 the male and female s they had set free,
34:11 and brought them again into subjection as s.
34:16 of you took back your male and female s,
34:16 into subjection to be your s.
La 5: 8 S rule over us; there is no one to deliver
Joel 2:29 Even on the male and female s, in those days,
Zec 2: 9 and they shall become plunder for their own s.
Mt 13:27 the s of the householder came and said to him,
13:28 The s said to him, 'Then do you want us to go
18:23 to a king who wished to settle accounts with his s.
18:28 of his fellow s who owed him a hundred denarii;
18:31 When his fellow s saw what had happened,
21:34 he sent his s to the tenants to collect his produce.
21:35 But the tenants seized his s and beat one,
21:36 Again he sent other s, more than the first;
22: 3 He sent his s to call those who had been invited to
22: 4 Again he sent other s, saying,
22: 6 while the rest seized his s,
22: 8 Then he said to his s, 'The wedding is ready,
22:10 Those s went out into the streets
24:45 to give the other s their allowance of food at
24:49 and he begins to beat his fellow s,
25:14 summoned his s and entrusted his property
25:19 of those s came and settled accounts with them.
Mk 13:34 when he leaves home and puts his s in charge,
Lk 12:37 Blessed are those s whom the master finds alert
12:38 and finds them so, blessed are those s.
12:42 of his s, to give them their allowance of food at
12:45 and if he begins to beat the other s,
15:22 father said to his s, 'Quickly, bring out a robe—
15:26 of the s and asked what was going on.
17:10 say, 'We are worthless s;
19:13 He summoned ten of his s,
19:15 having received royal power, he ordered these s,
Jn 4:51 his s met him and told him that his child was alive.
8:33 of Abraham and have never been s to anyone.
18:18 Now the s and the police had made a charcoal fire
18:26 One of the s of the high priest,
Ac 2:18 Even upon my s, both men and women,
10: 7 he called two of his s and a devout soldier from
16:17 "These men are s of the Most High God,
Ro 6:16 if you present yourselves to anyone as obedient s,
6:16 you are s of the one whom you obey, either of sin,
6:17 having once been s of sin,
6:18 have become s of righteousness.
6:19 as s to impurity and to greater and greater iniquity,
6:19 now present your members as s to righteousness
6:20 When you were s of sin,
7: 6 so that we are s not under the old written code but
1Co 7:23 do not become s of human masters.
12:13 Jews or Greeks, s or free—
2Co 4: 5 as Lord and ourselves as your s for Jesus' sake.
11:20 you put up with it when someone makes s of you,
Gal 4: 1 as long as they are minors, are no better than s,
5:13 but through love become s to one another.
Eph 6: 5 S, obey your earthly masters with fear
6: 6 and in order to please them, but as s of Christ,
6: 8 whether we are s or free.
Col 3:22 S, obey your earthly masters in everything,
4: 1 Masters, treat your s justly and fairly,
Tit 2: 3 not to be slanderers or s to drink;
2: 9 Tell s to be submissive to their masters and
3: 3 led astray, s to various passions and pleasures,
1Pe 2:18 S, accept the authority of your masters
2Pe 2:19 but they themselves are s of corruption;
2:19 for people are s to whatever masters them.
Rev 18:13 horses and chariots, s—and human lives.
Tob 10:10 male and female s, oxen and sheep,
Jdt 3: 4 Our towns and their inhabitants are also your s;
6: 7 Now my s are going to take you back into
6:10 Then Holofernes ordered his s,
6:11 So the s took him and led him out of the camp into
7:27 We shall indeed become s,
8: 7 men and women s, livestock, and fields;
8:22 among the Gentiles, wherever we serve as s;
9: 3 and you struck down s along with princes
10:23 but his s raised her up.
13: 1 When evening came, his s quickly withdrew.
14:13 for the s have been so bold as to come down
14:18 "The s have tricked us! One Hebrew woman has
AdE 7: 4 and made s—we and our children—male and
female s.
Wis 19:14 these made s of guests who were their benefactors.
Sir 7:20 Do not abuse s who work faithfully,
7:21 Let your soul love intelligent s;
Bar 4:32 be the cities that your children served as s;
1Mc 3:41 and went to the camp to get the Israelites for s.
2Mc 1:27 set free those who are s among the Gentiles,
5:24 and to sell the women and boys as s.
8:11 inviting them to buy Jewish s and promising
8:11 and promising to hand over ninety s for a talent,
8:25 of those who had come to buy them as s.
1Es 4:26 and have become s because of them.
3Mc 2:28 involving poll tax and to the status of s.
7: 5 They also led them out with harsh treatment as s,
4Mc 13: 2 For if they had been s to their emotions

SLAY (1) [SLAIN, SLAYER, SLAYER'S, SLAYS]

Ge 18:25 do such a thing, to s the righteous with the wicked,

SLAYER (19) [SLAY]

Nu 35: 6 where you shall permit a s to flee,
35:11 s who kills a person without intent may flee there.
35:12 so that the s may not die until there is a trial before
35:24 then the congregation shall judge between the s
35:25 and the congregation shall rescue the s from
35:25 Then the congregation shall send the s back to
35:25 The s shall live in it until the death of
35:26 But if the s shall at any time go outside the bounds
35:28 For the s must remain in the city of refuge until
35:28 the death of the high priest the s may return home.
Jos 20: 4 The s shall flee to one of these cities
20: 5 they shall not give up the s,
20: 6 The s shall remain in that city until there is a trial
20: 6 then the s may return home,
21:13 the city of refuge for the s, with its pasture lands,
21:21 the city of refuge for the s,
21:27 the city of refuge for the s,
21:32 the city of refuge for the s,
21:38 the city of refuge for the s,

SLAYER'S (1) [SLAY]

Eze 21:11 the sword is polished, to be placed in the s hand.

SLAYS (1) [SLAY]

Job 5: 2 vexation kills the fool, and jealousy s the simple.

SLEDGE (3) [SLEDGES]

Job 41:30 it spreads itself like a threshing s on the mire.
Isa 28:27 Dill is not threshed with a threshing s,
41:15 Now, I will make of you a threshing s, sharp, new,

SLEDGES (3) [SLEDGE]

2Sa 24:22 the oxen for the burnt offering, and the threshing s
1Ch 21:23 and the threshing s for the wood,
Am 1: 3 they have threshed Gilead with threshing s of iron.

SLEEK (5)

Ge 41: 2 there came up out of the Nile seven s and fat cows,
41: 4 and thin cows ate up the seven s and fat cows.
41:18 and seven cows, fat and s, came up out of the Nile
Ps 73: 4 they have no pain; their bodies are sound and s.
Jer 5:28 they have grown fat and s.

SLEEP‡ (86) [ASLEEP, SLEEPER, SLEEPING, SLEEPLESS, SLEEPLESSNESS, SLEEPS, SLEPT]

Ge 2:21 LORD God caused a deep s to fall upon the man,
15:12 sun was going down, a deep s fell upon Abram,
28:16 Then Jacob woke from his s and said,
31:40 and the cold by night, and my s fled from my eyes.
Ex 22:27 in what else shall that person s?
Lev 14:47 and all who s in the house shall wash their clothes;
Dt 24:12 not s in the garment given you as the pledge.
24:13 your neighbor may s in the cloak and bless you;
Jos 2: 8 Before they went to s, she came up to them on
Jdg 16:14 But he awoke from his s, and pulled away the pin,
16:20 When he awoke from his s, he thought,
1Sa 9:25 and he lay down to s.
26:12 a deep s from the LORD had fallen upon them.
Est 6: 1 On that night the LORD could not s,
Job 4:13 when deep s falls on mortals,
14:12 they will not awake or be roused out of their s.
33:15 when deep s falls on mortals,
Ps 3: 5 I lie down and s; I wake again,
4: 8 I will both lie down and s in peace;
13: 3 or I will s the s of death,
22:29 indeed, shall all who s in the earth bow down;
44:23 Why do you s, O Lord?
76: 5 of their spoil; they sank into s;
78:65 Then the Lord awoke as from s,
121: 4 He who keeps Israel will neither slumber nor s.
127: 2 for he gives s to his beloved.
132: 4 not give s to my eyes or slumber to my eyelids,
Pr 3:24 when you lie down, your s will be sweet.
4:16 For they cannot s unless they have done wrong;
4:16 of s unless they have made someone stumble.
6: 4 Give your eyes no s and your eyelids no slumber;
6: 9 When will you rise from your s?
6:10 A little s, a little slumber,
19:15 Laziness brings on deep s;
20:13 Do not love s, or else you will come to poverty;
24:33 A little s, a little slumber,
Ecc 5:12 Sweet is the s of laborers,
5:12 but the surfeit of the rich will not let them s.
8:16 how one's eyes see s neither day nor night,
Isa 29:10 upon you a spirit of deep s;
38:15 my s has fled because of the bitterness of my soul.
Jer 31:26 and my s was pleasant to me.
51:39 and then s a perpetual s and never wake,
51:57 they shall s a perpetual s and never wake,
Eze 34:25 so that they may live in the wild and s in
Da 2: 1 that his spirit was troubled and his s left him.
6:18 no food was brought to him, and s fled from him.
12: 2 of those who s in the dust of the earth shall awake,
Zec 4: 1 and wakened me, as one is wakened from s.
Mt 1:24 When Joseph awoke from s,
Mk 4:27 and would s and rise night and day,
Lk 9:32 and his companions were weighed down with s;
Jn 11:13 but they thought that he was referring merely to s.
Ac 20: 9 into a deep s while Paul talked still longer.
20: 9 Overcome by s, he fell to the ground three floors
Ro 13:11 how it is now the moment for you to wake from s.
1Th 5: 7 for those who s s at night,
Tob 8: 9 Then they went to s for the night.
10: 7 in and mourn and weep all night long, getting no s
AdE 6: 1 That night the Lord took s from the king,
Wis 17:14 they all slept the same s,
Sir 30:17 and eternal s than chronic sickness.
31: 1 and anxiety about it drives away s.
31: 2 and a severe illness carries off s.
31:20 Healthy s depends on moderate eating;
40: 5 his s at night confuses his mind.
40: 6 he struggles in his s as he did by day.
42: 9 and worry over her robs him of s;
46:19 Before the time of his eternal s,
1Mc 6:10 "S has departed from my eyes
2Mc 2:26 but calls for sweat and loss of s,
1Es 3: 3 he went to s, but woke up again.
3: 6 and drink from gold cups, and s on a gold bed,
3Mc 1: 3 a certain insignificant man should s in the tent;
5:11 But the Lord sent upon the king a portion of s,
5:12 by so pleasant and deep a s that he quite failed
5:20 said that the Jews were benefited by today's s,
5:22 not so much employ the duration of the night in s
2Es 2:31 Remember your children that s,
7:35 and unrighteous deeds shall not s.
7:104 to be ill or s or eat or be healed in his place,
11: 8 let each s in its own place, and watch in its turn;

SLEEPER (2) [SLEEP]

Eph 5:14 "S, awake! Rise from the dead,
Sir 22: 9 or who rouses a s from deep slumber.

SLEEPERS See Index to Footnotes

SLEEPING (17) [SLEEP]

Nu 31:17 and kill every woman who has known a man by s
31:18 the young girls who have not known a man by s
31:35 women who had not known a man by s with him.
1Sa 26: 7 there Saul lay s within the encampment,
Mt 9:24 for the girl is not dead but s."
26:40 Then he came to the disciples and found them s;
26:43 Again he came and found them s,
26:45 "Are you still s and taking your rest?
Mk 5:39 The child is not dead but s."
14:37 He came and found them s;
14:40 And once more he came and found them s,
14:41 "Are you still s and taking your rest?
Lk 8:52 for she is not dead but s."
22:45 he came to the disciples and found them s because
22:46 and he said to them, "Why are you s?
Ac 12: 6 was s between two soldiers,
Jdt 14:14 for he supposed that he was s with Judith.

SLEEPLESS (2) [SLEEP]

2Co 6: 5 imprisonments, riots, labors, s nights, hunger;
11:27 through many a s night, hungry and thirsty,

SLEEPLESSNESS (1) [SLEEP]

Sir 31:20 The distress of s and of nausea and colic are with

SLEEPS (5) [SLEEP]

1Ki 1:21 when my lord the king s with his ancestors,
Pr 6:29 So is he who s with his neighbor's wife;
10: 5 but a child who s in harvest brings shame.
Isa 5:27 none slumbers or s, not a loincloth is loose,
1Es 4:10 Furthermore, he reclines, he eats and drinks and s,

SLEEVES (4)

Ge 37: 3 and he had made him a long robe with s.
37:23 the long robe with s that he wore;
37:32 They had the long robe with s taken to their father,
2Sa 13:18 (Now she was wearing a long robe with s;

SLEIGHT (KJV) See SCHEMING

SLEPT (48) [SLEEP]

Ge 2:21 a deep sleep to fall upon the man, and he s;
Jdg 11:39 She had never s with a man.
16:14 So while he s, Delilah took the seven locks
21:12 four hundred young virgins who had never s with
2Sa 11: 9 But Uriah s at the entrance of the king's house
1Ki 2:10 Then David s with his ancestors,
3:20 from beside me while your servant s.
11:21 that David s with his ancestors and that Joab
11:43 Solomon s with his ancestors and was buried in
14:20 then he s with his ancestors,
14:31 Rehoboam s with his ancestors and was buried
15: 8 Abijam s with his ancestors,
15:24 Then Asa s with his ancestors,
16: 6 Baasha s with his ancestors,
16:28 Omri s with his ancestors,
22:40 So Ahab s with his ancestors;
22:50 Jehoshaphat s with his ancestors and was buried
2Ki 8:24 So Joram s with his ancestors,
10:35 So Jehu s with his ancestors,
13: 9 So Jehoahaz s with his ancestors,
13:13 So Joash s with his ancestors,
14:16 Jehoash s with his ancestors,
14:22 after King Amaziah s with his ancestors.
14:29 Jeroboam s with his ancestors, the kings of Israel;
15: 7 Azariah s with his ancestors;
15:22 Menahem s with his ancestors,
15:38 Jotham s with his ancestors,
16:20 Ahaz s with his ancestors,
20:21 Hezekiah s with his ancestors;
21:18 Manasseh s with his ancestors,
24: 6 So Jehoiakim s with his ancestors;
2Ch 9:31 Solomon s with his ancestors and was buried in
12:16 Rehoboam s with his ancestors and was buried in
14: 1 So Abijah s with his ancestors,
16:13 Then Asa s with his ancestors,
21: 1 Jehoshaphat s with his ancestors and was buried
26: 2 after the king s with his ancestors.
26:23 Uzziah s with his ancestors;
27: 9 Jotham s with his ancestors,
28:27 Ahaz s with his ancestors,
32:33 Hezekiah s with his ancestors,
33:20 So Manasseh s with his ancestors,
SS 5: 2 I s, but my heart was awake.
Mt 25: 5 all of them became drowsy and s.
Tob 2: 9 and went into my courtyard and s by the wall of
Jdt 12: 5 of Holofernes brought her into the tent, and she s
Wis 17:14 they all s the same sleep,
2Es 10:59 So I s that night and the following one,

SLIDE (KJV) See SLIP, WAVERING

SLIGHT (2) [SLIGHTED]

2Co 4:17 For this s momentary affliction is preparing us for
Sir 8: 8 Do not s the discourse of the sages,

SLIGHTED (1) [SLIGHT]

Jdt 11: 2 in the hill country had not s me,

SLIME (1)

Ps 58: 8 Let them be like the snail that dissolves into s;

SLIMEPITS (KJV) See BITUMEN PITS

SLING (10) [SLINGERS, SLINGING, SLINGSTONES, SLUNG]

Jdg 20:16 every one could s a stone at a hair, and not miss.
1Sa 17:40 his s was in his hand, and he drew near to the
17:50 So David prevailed over the Philistine with a s and
25:29 but the lives of your enemies he shall s out as from the hollow of a s.
1Ch 12: 2 and s stones with either the right hand or the left;
Pr 26: 8 like binding a stone in a s to give honor to a fool.
Jer 10:18 to s out the inhabitants of the land at this time,
Jdt 9: 7 and trusting in shield and spear, in bow and s.
Sir 47: 4 in the s and struck down the boasting Goliath?

SLINGERS (4) [SLING]

2Ki 3:25 until the s surrounded and attacked it.
Zec 9:15 and they shall devour and tread down the s;
Jdt 6:12 and all the s kept them from coming up
1Mc 9:11 and the s and the archers went ahead of the army,

SLINGING (1) [SLING]

2Ch 26:14 helmets, coats of mail, bows, and stones for s.

SLINGSTONES‡ (1) [SLING, STONE]

Job 41:28 cannot make it flee; s, for it, are turned to chaff.

SLIP (13) [SLIPPED, SLIPPERY, SLIPPING, SLIPS]

Dt 4: 9 nor to let them s from your mind all the days
32:35 for the time when their foot shall s;
1Sa 13: 8 and the people began to s away from Saul.
2Sa 22:37 and my feet do not s;
2Ki 9:15 then let no one s out of the city to go and tell
Ps 18:36 and my feet did not s.
37:31 in their hearts; their steps do not s.
66: 9 and has not let our feet s.
Sir 19:16 A person may make a s without intending it.
20:18 A s on the pavement is better than a s of the tongue
21: 7 when they s, the sensible person knows it.
2Mc 10:20 thousand drachmas let some of them s away.

SLIPPED (7) [SLIP]

Ge 24:64 she s quickly from the camel,
Ps 17: 5 held fast to your paths; my feet have not s.
73: 2 feet had almost stumbled; my steps had nearly s.
Gal 2: 4 who s in to spy on the freedom we have
1Mc 9: 6 and many s away from the camp,
9: 7 When Judas saw that his army had s away and
3Mc 5:34 The king's Friends one by one sullenly s away

SLIPPERY (3) [SLIP]

Ps 35: 6 Let their way be dark and s,
73:18 Truly you set them in s places;
Jer 23:12 Therefore their way shall be to them like s paths in

SLIPPING (3) [SLIP]

1Sa 13:11 I saw that the people were s away from me,
Ps 94:18 When I thought, "My foot is s,"
3Mc 5:15 that the hour of the banquet was already s by,

SLIPS (5) [SLIP]

Dt 19: 5 the head s from the handle and strikes
Ps 38:16 those who boast against me when my foot s."
Isa 17:10 though you plant pleasant plants and set out s of

Sir 13:22 If the rich person **s**, many come to the rescue;
13:22 If the humble person **s**, they even criticize him;

SLOPE‡ (13) [SLOPES]

Nu 34:11 and reach the eastern **s** of the sea of Chinnereth;
Jos 7: 5 as far as Shebarim and killing them on the **s**.
10:11 while they were going down the **s** of Beth-horon,
15: 8 the southern **s** of the Jebusites (that is, Jerusalem);
15:10 the northern **s** of Mount Jearim (that is, Chesalon),
15:11 the boundary goes out to the **s** of the hill north
18:12 boundary goes up to the **s** of Jericho on the north,
18:13 to the **s** of Luz (that is, Bethel),
18:16 south of the **s** of the Jebusites,
18:18 to the north of the **s** of Beth-arabah it goes down to
18:19 then the boundary passes on to the north of the **s**
2Ch 13: 4 the **s** of Mount Zemaraim that is in the hill country
Sir 46: 6 and on the **s** he destroyed his opponents,

SLOPES (9) [SLOPE]

Nu 21:15 and the **s** of the wadis that extend to the seat of Ar,
Dt 3:17 with the lower **s** of Pisgah on the east.
4:49 as the Sea of the Arabah, under the **s** of Pisgah.
Jos 10:40 and the lowland and the **s**, and all their kings;
12: 3 southward to the foot of the **s** of Pisgah;
12: 8 in the **s**, in the wilderness, and in the Negeb,
13:20 and the **s** of Pisgah, and Beth-jeshimoth,
SS 4: 1 moving down the **s** of Gilead.
6: 5 moving down the **s** of Gilead.

SLOTH (1)

Ecc 10:18 Through **s** the roof sinks in,

SLOTHFUL (KJV) See BE SLOW, LAG, LAZY, SLACK, SLUGGISH

SLOW (23) [SLOWLY, SLOWNESS]

Ex 4:10 but I am **s** of speech and **s** of tongue."
34: 6 a God merciful and gracious, **s** to anger,
Nu 14:18 'The LORD is **s** to anger, and abounding in
Jdg 18: 9 Do not be **s** to go, but enter in and possess the land.
Ne 9:17 **s** to anger and abounding in steadfast love,
Ps 86:15 **s** to anger and abounding in steadfast love,
103: 8 **s** to anger and abounding in steadfast love.
145: 8 **s** to anger and abounding in steadfast love.
Pr 14:29 Whoever is **s** to anger has great understanding,
15:18 but those who are **s** to anger calm contention.
16:32 One who is **s** to anger is better than the mighty,
19:11 Those with good sense are **s** to anger,
Joel 2:13 **s** to anger, and abounding in steadfast love,
Jnh 4: 2 **s** to anger, and abounding in steadfast love,
Na 1: 3 The LORD is **s** to anger but great in power,
Lk 24:25 and how **s** of heart to believe all that
Jas 1:19 everyone be quick to listen, **s** to speak, **s** to anger;
2Pe 3: 9 The Lord is not **s** about his promise,
Tob 12: 6 Do not be **s** to acknowledge him.
Sir 5: 4 for the Lord is **s** to anger.
11:12 There are others who are **s** and need help,

SLOWLY‡ (2) [SLOW]

Ge 33:14 ahead of his servant, and I will lead on **s**,
Ac 27: 7 We sailed **s** for a number of days and arrived

SLOWNESS (2) [SLOW]

2Pe 3: 9 as some think of **s**, but is patient with you,
2Es 5:42 just as for those who are last there is no **s**,

SLUGGISH (4)

Ro 11: 8 "God gave them a **s** spirit,
Heb 6:12 so that you may not become **s**, but imitators of
Sir 4:29 or **s** and remiss in your deeds.
3Mc 4: 5 old men, **s** and bent with age, was being led away,

SLUMBER (11) [SLUMBERS]

Job 33:15 while they **s** on their beds,
Ps 121: 3 he who keeps you will not **s**.
121: 4 He who keeps Israel will neither **s** nor sleep.
132: 4 I will not give sleep to my eyes or **s** to my eyelids,
Pr 6: 4 Give your eyes no sleep and your eyelids no **s**;
6:10 a little **s**, a little folding of the hands to rest,
24:33 a little **s**, a little folding of the hands to rest,
Isa 56:10 dreaming, lying down, loving to **s**.
Na 3:18 of Assyria; your nobles **s**.
Sir 22: 9 or who rouses a sleeper from deep **s**.
31: 2 Wakeful anxiety prevents **s**,

SLUMBERS (1) [SLUMBER]

Isa 5:27 none **s** or sleeps, not a loincloth is loose,

SLUNG (2) [SLING]

1Sa 17: 6 and a javelin of bronze **s** between his shoulders.
17:49 **s** it, and struck the Philistine on his forehead;

SMALL (94) [SMALL-MINDED, SMALLER, SMALLEST]

Ge 19:11 the men who were at the door of the house, both **s**
30:15 a **s** matter that you have taken away my husband?
Ex 12: 4 If a household is too **s** for a whole lamb,
Nu 20:19 It is only a **s** matter;
26:54 and to a **s** tribe you shall give a **s** inheritance;
33:54 and to a **s** one you shall give a **s** inheritance;
Dt 1:17 hear out the **s** and the great alike;
25:13 in your bag two kinds of weights, large and **s**.
25:14 in your house two kinds of measures, large and **s**.
1Sa 20: 2 either great or **s** without disclosing it to me;
30: 2 the women and all who were in it, both **s**
30:19 Nothing was missing, whether **s** or great,
2Sa 7:19 yet this was a **s** thing in your eyes, O Lord GOD;
1Ki 2:20 she said, "I have one **s** request to make of you;
8:64 the LORD was too **s** to receive the burnt offerings
22:31 "Fight with no one **s** or great,
2Ki 2:23 up on the way, some **s** boys came out of the city
4:10 Let us make a **s** roof chamber with walls,
6: 1 the place where we live under your charge is too **s**
10:18 "Ahab offered Baal **s** service;
23: 2 the prophets, and all the people, both **s** and great;
1Ch 17:17 And even this was a **s** thing in your sight, O God;
25: 8 And they cast lots for their duties, **s** and great,
26:13 **s** and great alike, for their gates.
2Ch 18:30 "Fight with no one **s** or great,
23: 9 the large and **s** shields that had been King David's,
34:30 all the people both great and **s**;
36:18 All the vessels of the house of God, large and **s**,
Est 1: 5 both great and **s**, a banquet lasting for seven days,
Job 3:19 The **s** and the great are there,
8: 7 Though your beginning was **s**,
15:11 Are the consolations of God too **s** for you,
26:14 and how **s** a whisper do we hear of him!
40: 4 I am of **s** account; what shall I answer you?
Ps 104:25 living things both **s** and great.
115:13 the LORD, both **s** and great.
119:141 I am **s** and despised, yet I do not forget your
Pr 24:10 in the day of adversity, your strength being **s**;
30:24 Four things on earth are **s**,
Isa 22:24 every **s** vessel, from the cups to all the flagons.
29: 5 But the multitude of your foes shall be like **s** dust,
Jer 16: 6 Both great and **s** shall die in this land;
52:19 captain of the guard took away the **s** bowls also,
Eze 5: 3 Then you shall take from these a **s** number,
29:15 so **s** that they will never again rule over
46:22 in the four corners of the court were **s** courts,
Da 11:23 and become strong with a **s** party.
Am 7: 2 How can Jacob stand? He is so **s**!"
7: 5 How can Jacob stand? He is so **s**!"
8: 5 We will make the ephah **s** and the shekel great,
Jnh 3: 5 they proclaimed a fast, and everyone, great and **s**,
Zec 4:10 the day of **s** things shall rejoice,
Mt 15:34 They said, "Seven, and a few **s** fish."
Mk 8: 7 They had also a few **s** fish;
12:42 A poor widow came and put in two **s** copper coins,
Lk 12:26 If then you are not able to do so **s** a thing as that,
19:17 you have been trustworthy in a very **s** thing,
21: 2 also saw a poor widow put in two **s** copper coins.
Ac 12:18 there was no **s** commotion among the soldiers
15: 2 And after Paul and Barnabas had no **s** dissension
26:22 and so I stand here, testifying to both **s** and great,
27:16 of a **s** island called Cauda we were scarcely able
27:20 for many days, and no **s** tempest raged, all hope
1Co 4: 3 with me it is a very **s** thing that I should be judged
Jas 3: 4 yet they are guided by a very **s** rudder wherever
3: 5 So also the tongue is a **s** member,
3: 5 How great a forest is set ablaze by a **s** fire!
Rev 11:18 and all who fear your name, both **s** and great,
13:16 Also it causes all, both **s** and great,
19: 5 and all who fear him, **s** and great."
19:18 flesh of all, both free and slave, both **s** and great."
20:12 And I saw the dead, great and **s**,
Jdt 13: 4 everyone went out, and no one, either **s** or great,
13:13 They all ran together, both **s** and great,
16:16 every sacrifice as a fragrant offering is a **s** thing,
Wis 6: 7 because he himself made both **s** and great,
Sir 5:15 In great and **s** matters cause no harm,
11: 3 The bee is **s** among flying creatures,
19: 1 one who despises **s** things will fail little by little.
25:19 Any iniquity is **s** compared to a woman's iniquity;
Bar 1: 4 and to the elders, and to all the people, **s** and great,
2:29 surely turn into a **s** number among the nations,
1Mc 3:16 Judas went out to meet him with a **s** company.
3:29 that the revenues from the country were **s** because
4:57 of the temple with golden crowns and **s** shields,
5:45 the **s** and the great, with their wives and children
2Mc 10:24 the cavalry from Asia in no **s** number.
14: 8 our whole nation is now in no **s** misfortune.
1Es 1:54 great and **s**, the treasure chests of the Lord,
Pm 151: 1 I was **s** among my brothers, and the youngest
4Mc 5:20 in matters either **s** or great is of equal seriousness,
15: 4 upon the character of a **s** child a wondrous likeness

SMALL-MINDED (1) [MIND, SMALL]

Sir 14: 3 Riches are inappropriate for a **s** person;

SMALLER (6) [SMALL]

Nu 26:56 according to lot between the larger and the **s**.
35: 8 and from the **s** tribes you shall take few;
Eze 43:14 and from the **s** ledge to the larger ledge,
2Es 5:52 like those whom you bore before, but **s** in stature?'
5:54 that you and your contemporaries are **s**
5:55 and those who come after you will be **s** than you,

SMALLEST (4) [SMALL]

Isa 60:22 and the **s** one a mighty nation;
Mt 13:32 it is the **s** of all the seeds,
Mk 4:31 is the **s** of all the seeds on earth;
Wis 14: 5 people trust their lives even to the **s** piece of wood,

SMART (1)

Tob 11:12 and it made them **s**.

SMART (KJV) See also BRINGS TROUBLE

SMASH (11) [SMASHED, SMASHES, SMASHING]

Dt 7: 5 break down their altars, **s** their pillars,
12: 3 Break down their altars, **s** their pillars,
Jer 51:20 with you I **s** nations; with you I destroy kingdoms;
51:21 with you I **s** the horse and its rider;
51:21 with you I **s** the chariot and the charioteer;
51:22 with you I **s** man and woman;
51:22 with you I **s** the old man and the boy;
51:22 with you I **s** the young man and the girl;
51:23 with you I **s** shepherds and their flocks;
51:23 with you I **s** farmers and their teams;
51:23 with you I **s** governors and deputies.

SMASHED (5) [SMASH]

Dt 10: 2 which you **s**, and you shall put them in the ark."
Jdg 7:19 the trumpets and **s** the jars that were in their hands.
Ps 74: 6 they **s** all its carved work.
Isa 30:14 its breaking is like that of a potter's vessel that is **s**
Sir 13: 2 The pot will strike against it and be **s**.

SMASHES (1) [SMASH]

Da 2:40 just as iron crushes and **s** everything,

SMASHING (1) [SMASH]

Dt 9:17 from my two hands, **s** them before your eyes.

SMEAR (4) [SMEARED]

Ps 119:69 The arrogant **s** me with lies,
Eze 13:10 these prophets **s** whitewash on it.
13:11 to those who **s** whitewash on it that it shall fall.
Tob 11: 8 **S** the gall of the fish on his eyes;

SMEARED (6) [SMEAR]

Eze 13:12 "Where is the whitewash you **s** on it?"
13:14 down the wall that you have **s** with whitewash,
13:15 and upon those who have **s** it with whitewash;
13:15 The wall is no more, nor those who **s** it—
22:28 Its prophets have **s** whitewash on their behalf,
4Mc 9:20 The wheel was completely **s** with blood,

SMELL (12) [SMELLED, SMELLS, SWEET-SMELLING]

Ge 27:27 and he smelled the **s** of his garments,
27:27 "Ah, the **s** of my son is like the **s** of a field
Lev 26:31 and I will not **s** your pleasing odors.
Dt 4:28 and stone that neither see, nor hear, nor eat, nor **s**.
Ps 115: 6 not hear; noses, but do not **s**.
Da 3:27 and not even the **s** of fire came from them.
Joel 2:20 its stench and foul **s** will rise up.
1Co 12:17 where would the sense of **s** be?
Tob 6:18 the demon will **s** it and flee,
Sir 30:19 For it can neither eat nor **s**.
2Es 13:11 but only the dust of ashes and the **s** of smoke.

SMELLED (2) [SMELL]

Ge 8:21 And when the LORD **s** the pleasing odor,
27:27 and he **s** the smell of his garments,

SMELLS (1) [SMELL]

Job 39:25 From a distance it **s** the battle,

SMELT (1) [IRON-SMELTER, SMELTED, SMELTER]

Isa 1:25 I will **s** away your dross as with lye

SMELTED (1) [SMELT]

Job 28: 2 and copper is **s** from ore.

SMELTER (3) [SMELT]

Eze 22:18 In the **s** they have become dross.
22:20 bronze, iron, lead, and tin into a **s**,
22:22 silver is melted in a **s**, so you shall be melted in it;

SMILE (3) [SMILED, SMILES]

Ps 39:13 Turn your gaze away from me, that I may **s** again,
Sir 13: 6 and will **s** at you and encourage you;
21:20 when he laughs, but the wise **s** quietly.

SMILED (2) [SMILE]

Job 29:24 I **s** on them when they had no confidence;
4Mc 8: 4 he **s** at them, and summoned them nearer and said,

SMILES (2) [SMILE]

Sir 13:11 and while he **s** he will be examining you.
1Es 4:31 If she **s** at him, he laughs;

SMITER (1) [SMITTEN]

La 3:30 give one's cheek to the **s**, and be filled with insults.

SMITH (5) [BLACKSMITHS, COPPERSMITH, GOLDSMITH, GOLDSMITHS, IRONSMITH, SILVERSMITH, SMITHS]

1Sa 13:19 Now there was no s to be found throughout all
Pr 25: 4 and the s has material for a vessel;
Isa 54:16 the s who blows the fire of coals, and produces
Sir 31:26 As the furnace tests the work of the s,
38:28 So too is the s, sitting by the anvil,

SMITHS (4) [SMITH]

2Ki 24:14 ten thousand captives, all the artisans and the s;
24:16 seven thousand, the artisans and the s,
Jer 24: 1 and the s, and had brought them to Babylon.
29: 2 and the s had departed from Jerusalem.

SMITTEN (1) [SMITER]

3Mc 2:22 since he was s by a righteous judgment.

SMOKE (99) [SMOKING, SMOKY]

Ge 19:28 the s of the land going up like the s of a furnace.
Ex 19:18 Now Mount Sinai was wrapped in s,
19:18 the s went up like the s of a kiln,
29:13 and turn them into s on the altar.
29:18 and turn the whole ram into s on the altar;
29:25 into s on the altar on top of the burnt offering
Lev 1: 9 the priest shall turn the whole into s on the altar as
1:13 the priest shall offer the whole and turn it into s on
1:15 and turn it into s on the altar;
1:17 Then the priest shall turn it into s on the altar,
2: 2 the priest shall turn this token portion into s on
2: 9 and turn this into s on the altar,
2:11 for you must not turn any leaven or honey into s as
2:16 the priest shall turn a token portion of it into s—
3: 5 Aaron's sons shall turn these into s on the altar,
3:11 Then the priest shall turn these into s on the altar
3:16 Then the priest shall turn these into s on the altar
4:10 The priest shall turn them into s upon the altar
4:19 He shall remove all its fat and turn it into s on
4:26 All its fat he shall turn into s on the altar,
4:31 and the priest shall turn it into s on the altar for
4:35 and the priest shall turn it into s on the altar,
5:12 and turn this into s on the altar,
6:12 into s the fat pieces of the offerings of well-being.
6:15 and they shall turn its memorial portion into s on
6:22 to be turned entirely into s.
7: 5 The priest shall turn them into s on the altar as
7:31 The priest shall turn the fat into s on the altar,
8:16 and turned them into s on the altar.
8:20 and Moses turned into s the head and the parts and
8:21 Moses turned into s the whole ram on the altar;
8:28 from their hands and turned them into s on
9:10 from the sin offering he turned into s on the altar,
9:13 and the head, which he turned into s on the altar.
9:14 turned them into s on the altar.
9:17 he turned it into s on the altar,
9:20 and the fat was turned into s on the altar;
16:25 of the sin offering he shall turn into s on the altar.
17: 6 turn the fat into s as a pleasing odor to the LORD,
Nu 5:26 and turn it into s on the altar,
18:17 and shall turn their fat into s as an offering by fire
Dt 29:20 LORD's anger and passion will s against them.
Jos 8:20 the s of the city was rising to the sky.
8:21 that the ambush had taken the city and that the s of
Jdg 20:38 that when they sent up a cloud of s out of the city
20:40 But when the cloud, a column of s,
20:40 and there was the whole city going up in s toward
2Sa 22: 9 S went up from his nostrils,
Job 41:20 Out of its nostrils comes s,
Ps 18: 8 S went up from his nostrils,
37:20 they vanish—like s they vanish away.
66:15 with the s of the sacrifice of rams;
68: 2 As s is driven away, so drive them away;
74: 1 Why does your anger s against the sheep
102: 3 For my days pass away like s,
104:32 who touches the mountains and they s.
119:83 For I have become like a wineskin in the s,
144: 5 touch the mountains so that they s.
Pr 10:26 Like vinegar to the teeth, and s to the eyes,
SS 3: 6 from the wilderness, like a column of s, perfumed
Isa 4: 5 of assembly a cloud by day and s and the shining
6: 4 and the house filled with s.
9:18 and they swirled upward in a column of s.
14:31 For s comes out of the north,
30:27 burning with his anger, and in thick rising s;
34:10 its s shall go up forever.
51: 6 for the heavens will vanish like s,
65: 5 These are a s in my nostrils,
Hos 13: 3 from the threshing floor or like s from a window.
Joel 2:30 blood and fire and columns of s.
Na 2:13 and I will burn your chariots in s,
Rev 8: 4 And the s of the incense,
9: 2 the shaft rose s like the s of a great furnace,
9: 2 the sun and the air were darkened with the s from
9: 3 Then from the s came locusts on the earth,
9:17 and fire and s and sulfur came out of their mouths.
9:18 and s and sulfur coming out of their mouths.
14:11 the s of their torment goes up forever and ever.
15: 8 the temple was filled with s from the glory of God
18: 9 will weep and wail over her when they see the s
18:18 and cried out as they saw the s of her burning,
19: 3 The s goes up from her forever and ever."
Tob 6: 8 a s in the presence of a man or woman afflicted by
Wis 2: 2 for the breath in our nostrils is s,
Wis 5:14 it is dispersed like s before the wind,
11:18 or belch forth a thick pall of s,
Sir 22:24 The vapor and s of the furnace precede the fire;
LtJ 6:21 when their faces have been blackened by the s of
1Mc 4:20 for the s that was seen showed what had happened.
2Mc 7: 5 The s from the pan spread widely,
2Es 4:48 by I looked, and lo, the s remained.
4:50 and the fire is greater than the s,
4:50 but drops and s remained."
7:*61* and are similar to a flame and s—
13:11 but only the dust of ashes and the smell of s.
15:44 then the dust and s shall reach the sky,

SMOKING (3) [SMOKE]

Ge 15:17 a s fire pot and a flaming torch passed
Ex 20:18 the sound of the trumpet, and the mountain s,
Wis 10: 7 a continually s wasteland,

SMOKY (1) [SMOKE]

Ac 2:19 blood, and fire, and s mist.

SMOLDERING (2) [SMOLDERS]

Isa 7: 4 because of these two s stumps of firebrands,
Mt 12:20 not break a bruised reed or quench a s wick

SMOLDERS (1) [SMOLDERING]

Hos 7: 6 within them; all night their anger s;

SMOOTH (18) [SMOOTHED, SMOOTHER, SMOOTHLY, SMOOTHS]

Ge 27:11 and I am a man of s skin.
27:16 the kids on his hands and on the s part of his neck.
1Sa 17:40 and chose five s stones from the wadi,
Pr 2:16 from the adulteress with her s words,
6:24 from the s tongue of the adulteress.
7: 5 from the adulteress with her s words.
7:21 with her s talk she compels him.
26:23 Like the glaze covering an earthen vessel are s lips
Isa 18: 2 Go, you swift messengers, to a nation tall and s,
18: 7 to the LORD of hosts from a people tall and s,
26: 7 O Just One, you make s the path of the righteous.
30:10 speak to us s things, prophesy illusions,
57: 6 Among the s stones of the valley is your portion;
Lk 3: 5 and the rough ways made s;
Ro 16:18 and by s talk and flattery they deceive the hearts of
Sir 21:10 The way of sinners is paved with s stones,
22:17 like stucco decoration that makes a wall s.
32:21 Do not be overconfident on a s road,

SMOOTHED (1) [SMOOTH]

LtJ 6: 8 Their tongues are s by the carpenter,

SMOOTHER (2) [SMOOTH]

Ps 55:21 with speech s than butter, but with a heart set
Pr 5: 3 and her speech is s than oil;

SMOOTHLY (2) [SMOOTH]

Pr 23:31 when it sparkles in the cup and goes down s.
SS 7: 9 your kisses like the best wine that goes down s,

SMOOTHS (1) [SMOOTH]

Isa 41: 7 and the one who s with the hammer encourages

SMYRNA (2)

Rev 1:11 to Ephesus, to S, to Pergamum, to Thyatira,
2: 8 "And to the angel of the church in S write:

SNAIL (1)

Ps 58: 8 Let them be like the s that dissolves into slime;

SNAIL (KJV) See also SAND LIZARD

SNAKE (16) [SNAKE'S, SNAKES]

Ge 49:17 Dan shall be a s by the roadside,
Ex 4: 3 and it became a s; and Moses drew back from it.
7: 9 and it will become a s.' "
7:10 before Pharaoh and his officials, and it became a s.
7:15 take in your hand the staff that was turned into a s.
Pr 30:19 the way of a s on a rock,
Ecc 10: 8 through a wall will be bitten by a s.
10:11 If the s bites before it is charmed,
Isa 14:29 for from the root of the s will come forth an adder,
Jer 46:22 She makes a sound like a s gliding away;
Am 5:19 a hand against the wall, and was bitten by a s.
Mic 7:17 like a s, like the crawling things of the earth;
Mt 7:10 Or if the child asks for a fish, will give a s?
Lk 11:11 will give a s instead of a fish?
Sir 12:13 Who pities a s charmer when he is bitten,
21: 2 Flee from sin as from a s;

SNAKE'S (2) [SNAKE]

Ps 140: 3 They make their tongue sharp as a s,
Sir 25:15 There is no venom worse than a s venom,

SNAKES (7) [SNAKE]

Ex 7:12 down his staff, and they became s;
Dt 8:15 an arid wasteland with poisonous s and scorpions.
Jer 8:17 See, I am letting s loose among you,
Mt 23:33 You s, you brood of vipers!
Mk 16:18 ⟦they will pick up s in their hands,⟧
Lk 10:19 to tread on s and scorpions, and over all the power
Wis 17: 9 by the passing of wild animals and the hissing of s

SNAP (1) [SNAPPED, SNAPS]

Na 1:13 And now I will break off his yoke from you and s

SNAPPED (3) [SNAP]

Jdg 16: 9 But he s the bowstrings, as a strand of fiber snaps
16:12 But he s the ropes off his arms like a thread.
Ecc 12: 6 before the silver cord is s,

SNAPS (1) [SNAP]

Jdg 16: 9 as a strand of fiber s when it touches the fire.

SNARE‡ (42) [ENSNARE, ENSNARED, SNARED, SNARES]

Ex 10: 7 "How long shall this fellow be a s to us?
23:33 you worship their gods, it will surely be a s to you.
34:12 or it will become a s among you.
Dt 7:16 for that would be a s to you.
Jos 23:13 but they shall be a s and a trap for you,
Jdg 2: 3 and their gods shall be a s to you."
8:27 and it became a s to Gideon and to his family.
1Sa 18:21 a s for him and that the hand of the Philistines may
28: 9 Why then are you laying a s for my life to bring
Job 18: 9 trap seizes them by the heel; a s lays hold of them.
40:24 with hooks or pierce its nose with a s?
Ps 69:22 be a trap for them, a s for their allies.
91: 3 the s of the fowler and from the deadly pestilence;
106:36 They served their idols, which became a s to them.
119:110 The wicked have laid a s for me,
124: 7 We have escaped like a bird from the s of
124: 7 the s is broken, and we have escaped.
Pr 7:23 He is like a bird rushing into a s,
18: 7 and their lips a s to themselves.
20:25 It is a s for one to say rashly, "It is holy,"
21: 6 a lying tongue is a fleeting vapor and a s of death.
22:25 and entangle yourself in a s.
29: 6 In the transgression of the evil there is a s,
29:25 The fear of others lays a s,
Ecc 9:12 and like birds caught in a s,
Isa 8:14 a trap and a s for the inhabitants of Jerusalem.
24:17 Terror, and the pit, and the s are upon you,
24:18 of the pit shall be caught in the s.
Jer 50:24 You set a s for yourself and you were caught,
Eze 12:13 and he shall be caught in my s;
17:20 and he shall be caught in my s;
Hos 5: 1 for you have been a s at Mizpah,
9: 8 yet a fowler's s is on all his ways,
Am 3: 5 Does a bird fall into a s on the earth,
3: 5 Does a s spring up from the ground,
Ro 11: 9 David says, "Let their table become a s and a trap,
1Ti 3: 7 he may not fall into disgrace and the s of the devil.
2Ti 2:26 and that they may escape from the s of the devil,
Sir 27:20 and has escaped like a gazelle from a s.
27:26 and whoever sets a s will be caught in it.
27:29 in the fall of the godly will be caught in a s,
1Mc 5: 4 a trap and a s to the people and ambushed them on

SNARED (6) [SNARE]

Dt 12:30 take care that you are not s into imitating them,
Ps 9:16 the wicked are s in the work of their own hands.
Pr 6: 2 you are s by the utterance of your lips,
Ecc 9:12 so mortals are s at a time of calamity,
Isa 8:15 they shall be s and taken.
28:13 and fall backward, and be broken, and s,

SNARES (16) [SNARE]

2Sa 22: 6 the s of death confronted me.
Job 22:10 Therefore s are around you,
Ps 18: 5 the s of death confronted me.
38:12 Those who seek my life lay their s;
64: 5 they talk of laying s secretly, thinking,
116: 3 The s of death encompassed me;
140: 5 along the road they have set s for me.
141: 9 and from the s of evildoers.
Pr 13:14 so that one may avoid the s of death.
14:27 so that one may avoid the s of death.
22: 5 Thorns and s are in the way of the perverse;
Ecc 7:26 whose heart is s and nets, whose hands are fetters;
Jer 18:22 and laid s for my feet.
Wis 14:11 s for human souls and a trap for the feet of
Sir 9: 3 or you will fall into her s.
9:13 Know that you are stepping among s,

SNATCH (6) [SNATCHED, SNATCHES, SNATCHING]

Job 24: 9 "There are those who s the orphan child from
24:19 Drought and heat s away the snow waters;
Ps 40:14 and confusion who seek to s away my life;
52: 5 he will s and tear you from your tent;
Jn 10:28 No one will s them out of my hand.
10:29 and no one can s it out of the Father's hand.

SNATCHED (7) [SNATCH]

2Sa 23:21 s the spear out of the Egyptian's hand,
1Ch 11:23 s the spear out of the Egyptian's hand,
Job 22:16 They were s away before their time;
Am 4:11 and you were like a brand s from the fire;
Ac 8:39 the Spirit of the Lord s Philip away;
Rev 12: 5 But her child was s away and taken to God and

Sir 10: 3 and the reckless person will be s away.

SNATCHES (3) [SNATCH]
Job 9:12 He s away; who can stop him?
Mt 13:19 the evil one comes and s away what is sown in
Jn 10:12 and the wolf s them and scatters them.

SNATCHING (1) [SNATCH]
Jude 1:23 save others by s them out of the fire;

SNEERED (1)
Ac 2:13 others s and said, "They are filled with new wine."

SNEEZED (1) [SNEEZES]
2Ki 4:35 child s seven times, and the child opened his eyes.

SNEEZES (1) [SNEEZED]
Job 41:18 Its s flash forth light, and its eyes are like

SNIFF (1) [SNIFFING]
Mal 1:13 and you s at me, says the LORD of hosts.

SNIFFING (1) [SNIFF]
Jer 2:24 in her heat s the wind! Who can restrain her lust?

SNORTING (2)
Job 39:20 Its majestic s is terrible.
Jer 8:16 The s of their horses is heard from Dan;

SNOUT (1)
Pr 11:22 a pig's s is a beautiful woman without good sense.

SNOW (28) [SNOWS]
Ex 4: 6 he took it out, his hand was leprous, as white as s.
Nu 12:10 Miriam had become leprous, as white as s.
2Sa 23:20 a lion in a pit on a day when s had fallen.
2Ki 5:27 So he left his presence leprous, as white as s.
1Ch 11:22 a lion in a pit on a day when s had fallen.
Job 6:16 that run dark with ice, turbid with melting s.
24:19 Drought and heat snatch away the s waters;
37: 6 For to the s he says, 'Fall on the earth';
38:22 "Have you entered the storehouses of the s,
Ps 51: 7 wash me, and I shall be whiter than s.
68:14 Almighty scattered kings there, s fell on Zalmon.
147:16 He gives s like wool; he scatters frost like ashes.
148: 8 s and frost, stormy wind fulfilling his command!
Pr 25:13 of s in the time of harvest are faithful messengers
26: 1 Like s in summer or rain in harvest,
Isa 1:18 your sins are like scarlet, they shall be like s;
55:10 For as the rain and the s come down from heaven,
Jer 18:14 Does the s of Lebanon leave the crags of Sirion?
La 4: 7 Her princes were purer than s, whiter than milk;
Da 7: 9 his clothing was white as s,
Mt 28: 3 and his clothing white as s.
Rev 1:14 and his hair were white as white wool, white as s;
Wis 16:22 S and ice withstood fire without melting,
Sir 43:13 By his command he sends the driving s and speeds
43:17 He scatters the s like birds flying down,
Aza 1:46 Bless the Lord, dews and falling s;
1Mc 13:22 but that night a very heavy s fell,
13:22 and he did not go because of the s.

SNOWS (2) [SNOW]
Pr 31:21 She is not afraid for her household when it s,
Aza 1:50 Bless the Lord, frosts and s;

SNUFFDISHES (KJV) See TRAYS

SNUFFERS (8)
Ex 25:38 Its s and trays shall be of pure gold.
37:23 He made its seven lamps and its s and its trays
Nu 4: 9 with its lamps, its s, its trays,
1Ki 7:50 s, basins, dishes for incense, and firepans,
2Ki 12:13 for the house of the LORD no basins of silver, s,
25:14 They took away the pots, the shovels, the s,
2Ch 4:22 the s, basins, ladles, and firepans,
Jer 52:18 They took away the pots, the shovels, the s,

SO (1 of 3960) See Index of Articles Etc. for an Exhaustive Listing (See Introduction, page xi)
2Ki 17: 4 for he had sent messengers to King S of Egypt,

SO-CALLED (3) [CALL]
1Ch 4:14 s because they were artisans.
1Co 8: 5 there may be s gods in heaven or on earth—
2Th 2: 4 He opposes and exalts himself above every s god

SOAK (1) [SOAKED]
Ps 109:18 may it s into his body like water,

SOAKED (3) [SOAK]
Lev 6:21 you shall bring it well s,
7:12 and cakes of choice flour well s in oil.
Isa 34: 7 Their land shall be s with blood,

SOAP (3)
Job 9:30 If I wash myself with s and cleanse my hands
Jer 2:22 you wash yourself with lye and use much s,
Mal 3: 2 For he is like a refiner's fire and like fullers' s;

SOAR (1) [SOARS]
Ob 1: 4 Though you s aloft like the eagle,

SOARS (1) [SOAR]
Job 39:26 "Is it by your wisdom that the hawk s,

SOBER (6)
Ac 26:25 but I am speaking the s truth.
Ro 12: 3 but to think with s judgment,
1Co 15:34 Come to a s and right mind, and sin no more;
1Th 5: 6 but let us keep awake and be s;
5: 8 But since we belong to the day, let us be s,
2Ti 4: 5 As for you, always be s, endure suffering,

SOBRIETY (KJV) See DECENTLY, MODESTY, PROPRIETY

SOCHO (KJV) See SOCO

SOCHOH (KJV) See SOCOH

SOCIETY (5)
Job 30: 5 They are driven out from s;
Da 4:25 You shall be driven away from human s,
4:32 You shall be driven away from human s,
4:33 He was driven away from human s,
5:21 He was driven from human s,

SOCKET (4) [SOCKETS]
Ge 32:25 he struck him on the hip s;
32:32 not eat the thigh muscle that is on the hip s,
32:32 he struck Jacob on the hip s at the thigh muscle.
Job 31:22 and let my arm be broken from its s.

SOCKETS (3) [SOCKET]
1Ki 7:50 s for the doors of the innermost part of the house,
Zec 14:12 their eyes shall rot in their s,
4Mc 10: 5 by prying his limbs from their s,

SOCO (3) [=SOCOH]
1Ch 4:18 Heber father of S, and Jekuthiel father of Zanoah.
2Ch 11: 7 Beth-zur, S, Adullam,
28:18 S with its villages, Timnah with its villages,

SOCOH (5) [=SOCO]
Jos 15:35 Jarmuth, Adullam, S, Azekah,
15:48 And in the hill country, Shamir, Jattir, S,
1Sa 17: 1 they were gathered at S, which belongs to Judah,
17: 1 and encamped between S and Azekah,
1Ki 4:10 in Arubboth (to him belonged S and all the land

SOD, SODDEN (KJV) See BOILED, COOKING

SODI (1)
Nu 13:10 from the tribe of Zebulun, Gaddiel son of S;

SODOM‡ (51) [SODOMITES]
Ge 10:19 and in the direction of S, Gomorrah, Admah,
13:10 the LORD had destroyed S and Gomorrah.
13:12 of the Plain and moved his tent as far as S.
13:13 Now the people of S were wicked,
14: 2 these kings made war with King Bera of S,
14: 8 Then the king of S, the king of Gomorrah,
14:10 and as the kings of S and Gomorrah fled,
14:11 the enemy took all the goods of S and Gomorrah,
14:12 who lived in S, and his goods, and departed.
14:17 of S went out to meet him at the Valley of Shaveh
14:21 Then the king of S said to Abram,
14:22 But Abram said to the king of S,
18:16 and they looked toward S;
18:20 "How great is the outcry against S and Gomorrah
18:22 So the men turned from there, and went toward S,
18:26 "If I find at S fifty righteous in the city,
19: 1 The two angels came to S in the evening,
19: 1 and Lot was sitting in the gateway of S.
19: 4 they lay down, the men of the city, the men of S,
19:24 the LORD rained on S and Gomorrah sulfur
19:28 toward S and Gomorrah and toward all the land of
Dt 29:23 like the destruction of S and Gomorrah,
32:32 Their vine comes from the vinestock of S,
Isa 1: 9 we would have been like S,
1:10 Hear the word of the LORD, you rulers of S!
3: 9 they proclaim their sin like S, they do not hide it.
13:19 like S and Gomorrah when God overthrew them.
Jer 23:14 all of them have become like S to me,
49:18 As when S and Gomorrah
50:40 As when God overthrew S and Gomorrah
La 4: 6 the punishment of S, which was overthrown in
Eze 16:46 to the south of you, is S with her daughters.
16:48 your sister S and her daughters have not done
16:49 This was the guilt of your sister S:
16:53 the fortunes of S and her daughters and
16:55 S and her daughters shall return
16:56 Was not your sister S a byword in your mouth in
Am 4:11 as when God overthrew S and Gomorrah,
Zep 2: 9 Moab shall become like S and the Ammonites
Mt 10:15 be more tolerable for the land of S and Gomorrah
11:23 deeds of power done in you had been done in S,
11:24 be more tolerable for the land of S than for you."
Lk 10:12 on that day it will be more tolerable for S than for
17:29 but on the day that Lot left S,
Ro 9:29 we would have fared like S and been made
2Pe 2: 6 of S and Gomorrah to ashes he condemned them
Jude 1: 7 S and Gomorrah and the surrounding cities,
Rev 11: 8 of the great city that is prophetically called S
3Mc 2: 5 and sulfur the people of S who acted arrogantly,
2Es 2: 8 remember what I did to S and Gomorrah,
7:*106* [36] that first Abraham prayed for the people of S,

SODOMA (KJV) See SODOM

SODOMITE[S] (KJV) See also [MALE] TEMPLE PROSTITUTE[S]

SODOMITES (2) [SODOM]
1Co 6: 9 idolaters, adulterers, male prostitutes, s,
1Ti 1:10 fornicators, s, slave traders, liars, perjurers,

SOFT (7) [SOFTENED, SOFTENING, SOFTER, SOFTLY]
Job 41: 3 Will it speak s words to you?
Pr 15: 1 A s answer turns away wrath,
25:15 and a s tongue can break bones.
Mt 11: 8 Someone dressed in s robes?
11: 8 Look, those who wear s robes are in royal palaces.
Lk 7:25 Someone dressed in s robes?
Wis 15: 7 A potter kneads the s earth and laboriously molds

SOFT (KJV) See also FAINT, SOFTENING

SOFTENED (1) [SOFT]
Isa 1: 6 or bound up, or s with oil.

SOFTENING (1) [SOFT]
Ps 65:10 s it with showers, and blessing its growth.

SOFTER (1) [SOFT]
Ps 55:21 with words that were s than oil,

SOFTLY (1) [SOFT]
Jdg 4:21 went s to him and drove the peg into his temple,

SOIL (44) [SOILED]
Ge 4:14 Today you have driven me away from the s,
9:20 a man of the s, was the first to plant a vineyard.
Dt 29:23 all its s burned out by sulfur and salt,
30: 9 and in the fruit of your s.
2Ki 25:12 of the land to be vinedressers and tillers of the s.
1Ch 27:26 tilling the s, was Ezri son of Chelub.
2Ch 26:10 the hills and in the fertile lands, for he loved the s.
Ne 10:35 of our s and the first fruits of all fruit of every tree,
10:37 and to bring to the Levites the tithes from our s,
Job 14:19 the torrents wash away the s of the earth;
Pr 8:26 or the world's first bits of s.
SS 5: 3 I had bathed my feet; how could I s them?
Isa 32:13 s of my people growing up in thorns and briers;
34: 7 and their s made rich with fat.
34: 9 of Edom shall be turned into pitch, and her s
Jer 42:12 on you and restore you to your native s.
52:16 of the land to be vinedressers and tillers of the s.
Eze 17: 5 he took a seed from the land, placed it in fertile s;
17: 8 it was transplanted to good s by abundant waters,
26: 4 I will scrape its s from it and make it a bare rock.
26:12 Your stones and timber and s they shall cast into
28:25 of the nations, then they shall settle on their own s
34:27 They shall be secure on their s;
36:17 when the house of Israel lived on their own s,
37:14 and I will place you on your own s;
Joel 2:21 Do not fear, O s; be glad and rejoice,
Mic 5: 5 into our land and tread upon our s,
Hag 1:11 the new wine, the oil, on what the s produces,
Zec 13: 5 "I am no prophet, I am a tiller of the s;
Mal 3:11 so that it will not destroy the produce of your s;
Mt 13: 5 where they did not have much s,
13: 5 since they had no depth of s.
13: 8 Other seeds fell on good s and brought forth grain,
13:23 But as for what was sown on good s,
Mk 4: 5 where it did not have much s,
4: 5 since it had no depth of s.
4: 8 Other seed fell into good s and brought forth grain,
4:20 And these are the ones sown on the good s:
Lk 8: 8 Some fell into good s, and when it grew,
8:15 But as for that in the good s,
13: 7 Why should it be wasting the s?'
14:35 It is fit neither for the s nor for the manure pile;
Sir 20:28 Those who cultivate the s heap up their harvest,
1Es 4: 6 not serve in the army or make war but till the s;

SOILED (2) [SOIL]
Zep 3: 1 Ah, s, defiled, oppressing city!
Rev 3: 4 in Sardis who have not s their clothes;

SOJOURN (5)
Ge 47: 9 "The years of my earthly s are one hundred thirty;
47: 9 of the life of my ancestors during their long s."

Ps 5: 4 evil will not s with you.
Wis 19:10 For they still recalled the events of their s,
1Es 5: 7 These are the Judeans who came up out of their s

SOJOURN, SOJOURNED, SOJOURNER, SOJOURNERS, SOJOURNETH, SOJOURNING (KJV)
See also ALIEN, ALIENS, BOUND LABORERS, LIVE, LIVED, RESIDES, RESIDING, SETTLE, SETTLED, STAY, STAYED, STAYING, TRANSIENT ALIEN

SOLACE (1)
Job 16: 5 and the s of my lips would assuage your pain.

SOLACE (KJV) See also DELIGHT

SOLD (82) [SELL]
Ge 25:33 So he swore to him, and s his birthright to Jacob.
31:15 For he has s us, and he has been using up
37:28 and s him to the Ishmaelites for twenty pieces
37:36 the Midianites had s him in Egypt to Potiphar,
41:56 the land, Joseph opened all the storehouses, and s
42: 6 it was he who s to all the people of the land.
45: 4 Joseph, whom you s into Egypt.
45: 5 or angry with yourselves, because you s me here;
47:20 All the Egyptians s their fields,
Ex 21:16 that person has been s or is still held in possession,
22: 1 but if unable to do so, shall be s for the theft.
Lev 25:16 a certain number of harvests that are being s
25:23 The land shall not be s in perpetuity,
25:25 and redeem what the relative has s.
25:27 be refunded to the person to whom it was s,
25:28 what was s shall remain with the purchaser until
25:33 houses s in a city belonging to them—
25:34 the open land around their cities may not be s;
25:42 they shall not be s as slaves are s.
25:48 after they have s themselves they shall have
25:50 from the year when they s themselves to the alien
27:20 or if it has been s to someone else,
27:27 if it is not redeemed, it shall be s at its assessment.
27:28 or inherited landholding, may be s or redeemed;
Dt 15:12 is s to you and works for you six years,
32:30 unless their Rock had s them,
Jdg 2:14 and he s them into the power of their enemies all
3: 8 and he s them into the hand of King
4: 2 So the LORD s them into the hand of King Jabin
10: 7 and he s them into the hand of the Philistines and
1Sa 12: 9 and he s them into the hand of Sisera,
1Ki 21:20 Because you have s yourself to do what is evil in
21:25 who s himself to do what was evil in the sight of
2Ki 6:25 a donkey's head was s for eighty shekels of silver,
7: 1 about this time a measure of choice meal shall be s
7:16 So a measure of choice meal was s for a shekel,
7:18 "Two measures of barley shall be s for a shekel,
17:17 and they s themselves to do evil in the sight of
Ne 5: 8 bought back our Jewish kindred who had been s
13:16 in fish and all kinds of merchandise and s them on
Est 7: 4 For we have been s, I and my people,
7: 4 If we had been s merely as slaves,
Ps 44:12 You have s your people for a trifle,
105:17 Joseph, who was s as a slave.
Isa 50: 1 which of my creditors is it to whom I have s you?
50: 1 No, because of your sins you were s,
52: 3 For thus says the LORD: You were s for nothing,
Jer 34:14 of you must set free any Hebrews who have been s
Eze 7:13 For the sellers shall not return to what has been s
Joel 3: 3 and s girls for wine, and drunk it down.
3: 6 You have s the people of Judah and Jerusalem to
3: 7 to leave the places to which you have s them,
Mt 10:29 Are not two sparrows s for a penny?
13:46 he went and s all that he had and bought it.
18:25 as he could not pay, his lord ordered him to be s,
21:12 and the seats of those who s doves.
26: 9 this ointment could have been s for a large sum,
Mk 11:15 and the seats of those who s doves;
14: 5 For this ointment could have been s for more than
Lk 12: 6 Are not five sparrows s for two pennies?
Jn 12: 5 not s for three hundred denarii and
Ac 4:34 as owned lands or houses s them and brought
4:34 and brought the proceeds of what was s.
4:37 He s a field that belonged to him,
5: 1 with the consent of his wife Sapphira, s a piece
5: 4 it was s, were not the proceeds at your disposal?
5: 8 "Tell me whether you and your husband s the land
7: 9 patriarchs, jealous of Joseph, s him into Egypt;
Ro 7:14 but I am of the flesh, s into slavery under sin.
1Co 10:25 Eat whatever is s in the meat market
Heb 12:16 who s his birthright for a single meal.
Jdt 7:25 God has s us into their hands,
AdE 7: 4 For we have been s, I and my people,
Wis 10:13 When a righteous man was s,
Bar 4: 6 not for destruction that you were s to the nations,
1Mc 1:15 They joined with the Gentiles and s themselves
2Mc 4:32 he had s to Tyre and the neighboring cities.
5:14 and as many were s into slavery as were killed.
8:14 Others s all their remaining property,
8:14 the Lord to rescue those who had been s by
10:21 and accused these men of having s their kindred

SOLDERING (1)
Isa 41: 7 saying of the s, "It is good";

SOLDIER (12) [FOOT-SOLDIERS, SOLDIER'S, SOLDIERS, SOLDIERS']
1Ki 20:39 then a s turned and brought a man to me, and said,
Isa 3: 2 warrior and s, judge and prophet, diviner
42:13 The LORD goes forth like a s,
Mk 6:27 a s of the guard with orders to bring John's head.
Jn 19:23 and divided them into four parts, one for each s.
Ac 10: 7 he called two of his slaves and a devout s from
28:16 with the s who was guarding him.
Php 2:25 my brother and co-worker and fellow s,
2Ti 2: 3 Share in suffering like a good s of Christ Jesus.
Phm 1: 2 to Archippus our fellow s,
Jdt 15: 3 Then the Israelites, everyone that was a s,
4Mc 16:14 O mother, s of God in the cause of religion,

SOLDIER'S (2) [SOLDIER]
2Sa 20: 8 a s garment and over it was a belt with a sword
2Ti 2: 4 the s aim is to please the enlisting officer.

SOLDIERS‡ (81) [SOLDIER]
Jos 6: 2 along with its king and s.
Jdg 21:10 So the congregation sent twelve thousand s there
1Sa 4:10 for there fell of Israel thirty thousand foot s.
14:28 Then one of the s said,
15: 4 two hundred thousand foot s,
15: 4 and ten thousand s of Judah.
2Sa 8: 4 and twenty thousand foot s.
10: 6 the Arameans of Zobah, twenty thousand foot s,
19: 3 into the city that day as s steal in who are ashamed
24: 9 in Israel there were eight hundred thousand s able
1Ki 9:22 they were the s, they were his officials,
20:29 killed one hundred thousand Aramean foot s
2Ki 25: 4 the s fled by night by the way of the gate between
25:19 an officer who had been in command of the s,
1Ch 18: 4 and twenty thousand foot s.
19:18 and forty thousand foot s,
2Ch 8: 9 they were s, and his officers,
17:13 He had s, mighty warriors, in Jerusalem.
26:11 Moreover Uzziah had an army of s, fit for war,
Ezr 8:22 For I was ashamed to ask the king for a band of s
Jer 38: 4 he is discouraging the s who are left in this city,
39: 4 King Zedekiah of Judah and all the s saw them,
41: 3 and the Chaldean s who happened to be there.
41:16 s, women, children, and eunuchs,
49:26 and all her s shall be destroyed in that day,
50:30 and all her s shall be destroyed on that day,
51:32 and the s are in panic.
52: 7 the s fled and went out from the city by night by
52:25 an officer who had been in command of the s,
Eze 39:20 with warriors and all kinds of s,
Joel 2: 7 like s they scale the wall.
3: 9 Let all the s draw near, let them come up.
Na 2: 3 his s are clothed in crimson.
Mt 8: 9 I also am a man under authority, with s under me;
27:27 Then the s of the governor took Jesus into
27:65 Pilate said to them, "You have a guard of s;
28:12 a plan to give a large sum of money to the s,
Mk 15:16 s led him into the courtyard of the palace (that is,
Lk 3:14 S also asked him, "And we, what should we do?"
7: 8 For I also am a man set under authority, with s
23:11 Even Herod with his s treated him with contempt
23:36 The s also mocked him, coming up
Jn 18: 3 of s together with police from the chief priests and
18:12 So the s, their officer,
19: 2 s wove a crown of thorns and put it on his head,
19:23 When the s had crucified Jesus,
19:25 And that is what the s did.
19:32 Then the s came and broke the legs of the first and
19:34 Instead, one of the s pierced his side with a spear,
Ac 12: 4 in prison and handed him over to four squads of s
12: 6 was sleeping between two s,
12:18 among the s over what had become of Peter.
21:32 Immediately he took s and centurions and ran
21:32 When they saw the tribune and the s,
21:35 so great that he had to be carried by the s.
23:10 ordered the s to go down, take him by force,
23:23 for Caesarea with two hundred s,
23:31 So the s, according to their instructions,
27:31 Paul said to the centurion and the s,
27:32 s cut away the ropes of the boat and set it adrift.
Jdt 2: 5 one hundred twenty thousand foot s
2:19 with their chariots and cavalry and picked foot s.
7: 2 counting the baggage and the foot s handling it,
7: 7 he seized them and set guards of s over them,
9: 7 boasting in the strength of their foot s,
Sir 16:10 on the six hundred thousand foot s who assembled
1Mc 3:13 including a body of faithful s who stayed with him
6:30 of his forces was one hundred thousand foot s,
6:48 The s of the king's army went up to Jerusalem
9: 4 and went to Berea with twenty thousand foot s
12:49 and the Great Plain to destroy all Jonathan's s.
14:32 he armed the s of his nation and paid them wages.
16: 6 He saw that the s were afraid to cross the stream,
2Mc 5:12 He commanded his s to cut
14:39 sent more than five hundred s to arrest him;
1Es 8:51 for foot s and cavalry and an escort to keep us safe
3Mc 3:12 to his generals and s in Egypt and all its districts,
4Mc 3: 7 with the s of his nation had killed many of them.
3:12 two staunch young s, respecting the king's desire,
5: 1 and with his armed s standing around him,
17:23 to his s as an example for their own endurance,

SOLDIERS' (1) [SOLDIER]
Ac 27:42 The s plan was to kill the prisoners,

SOLE (10) [SOLES]
Dt 28:35 from the s of your foot to the crown of your head.
28:56 that she does not venture to set the s of her foot on
28:65 no resting place for the s of your foot.
Jos 1: 3 that the s of your foot will tread upon I have given
2Sa 14:25 from the s of his foot to the crown
2Ki 19:24 up with the s of my foot all the streams of Egypt.'
Job 2: 7 and inflicted loathsome sores on Job from the s
Isa 1: 6 From the s of the foot even to the head,
37:25 up with the s of my foot all the streams of Egypt.'
Eze 1: 7 soles of their feet were like the s of a calf's foot;

SOLEMN (21) [SOLEMNITY, SOLEMNLY]
Ex 12:16 On the first day you shall hold a s assembly,
12:16 and on the seventh day a s assembly;
13:19 the bones of Joseph who had required a s oath of
16:23 'Tomorrow is a day of s rest,
31:15 but the seventh day is a sabbath of s rest,
35: 2 a holy sabbath of s rest to the LORD;
Lev 23:36 by fire; it is a s assembly;
Nu 29:35 On the eighth day you shall have a s assembly;
Dt 16: 8 and on the seventh day there shall be a s assembly
Jdg 21: 5 a s oath had been taken concerning whoever did
2Ki 10:20 Jehu decreed, "Sanctify a s assembly for Baal."
2Ch 7: 9 On the eighth day they held a s assembly;
Ne 8:18 and on the eighth day there was a s assembly,
Ps 68:24 Your s processions are seen, O God,
Isa 1:13 I cannot endure s assemblies with iniquity.
Eze 21:23 like a false divination; they have sworn s oaths;
Joel 1:14 Sanctify a fast, call a s assembly.
2:15 sanctify a fast; call a s assembly;
Am 5:21 and I take no delight in your s assemblies.
2Mc 10:16 after making s supplication and imploring God
12:25 with many words he had confirmed his s promise

SOLEMNITIES, SOLEMNITY (KJV) See also APPOINTED FESTIVALS, FESTIVAL, SCHEDULED

SOLEMNITY (1) [SOLEMN]
Jn 19:31 because that sabbath was a day of great s.

SOLEMNLY (9) [SOLEMN]
Ge 43: 3 But Judah said to him, "The man s warned us,
Dt 8:19 I s warn you today that you shall surely perish.
1Sa 8: 9 you shall s warn them, and show them the ways of
1Ki 2:42 and s adjure you, saying, 'Know for certain that on
Jer 11: 7 For I s warned your ancestors
Mk 6:23 And he s swore to her, "Whatever you ask me,
1Th 4: 6 already told you beforehand and s warned you.
5:27 I s command you by the Lord that this letter
2Ti 4: 1 of his appearing and his kingdom, I s urge you:

SOLES (8) [SOLE]
Jos 3:13 the s of the feet of the priests who bear the ark of
4:18 and the s of the priests' feet touched dry ground,
1Ki 5: 3 until the LORD put them under the s of his feet.
Job 13:27 you set a bound to the s of my feet.
Eze 1: 7 s of their feet were like the sole of a calf's foot;
43: 7 of my throne and the place for the s of my feet,
Mal 4: 3 for they will be ashes under the s of your feet,
AdE 13:13 for I would have been willing to kiss the s

SOLICITED (1)
Eze 16:34 no one s you to play the whore;

SOLID (5)
1Co 3: 2 I fed you with milk, not s food, for you were not ready for s food.
Heb 5:12 You need milk, not s food;
5:14 But s food is for the mature,
3Mc 4:10 and in addition they were confined under a s deck,

SOLITARY (5) [SOLITUDE]
1Ki 19: 4 and came and sat down under a s broom tree.
Ecc 4: 8 the case of s individuals, without sons or brothers;
Isa 27:10 For the fortified city is s, a habitation deserted
4Mc 1:27 gluttony, and s gormandizing.
2: 7 that someone who is habitually a s gormandizer,

SOLITUDE (1) [SOLITARY]
2Es 16:26 For in all places there shall be great s;

SOLOMON (287) [=JEDIDIAH, SOLOMON'S]
2Sa 5:14 Shammua, Shobab, Nathan, S,
12:24 and she bore a son, and he named him S.
1Ki 1:10 or Benaiah or the warriors or his brother S.
1:12 and the life of your son S.
1:13 Your son S shall succeed me as king,
1:17 Your son S shall succeed me as king,
1:19 but your servant S he has not invited.
1:21 that my son S and I will be counted offenders."
1:26 and Benaiah son of Jehoiada, and your servant S.
1:30 'Your son S shall succeed me as king,
1:33 and have my son S ride on my own mule,
1:34 blow the trumpet, and say, 'Long live King S!'
1:37 with my lord the king, so may he be with S,
1:38 went down and had S ride on King David's mule,
1:39 the horn of oil from the tent and anointed S.

1Ki 1:39 and all the people said, "Long live King S!"
1:43 "No, for our lord King David has made S king;
1:46 S now sits on the royal throne.
1:47 the name of S more famous than yours,
1:50 fearing S, got up and went to grasp the horns of
1:51 S was informed, "Adonijah is afraid
1:51 "Adonijah is afraid of King S;
1:51 of the altar, saying, 'Let King S swear to me first
1:52 So S responded, "If he proves to be a worthy man,
1:53 Then King S sent to have him brought down from
1:53 He came to do obeisance to King S;
1:53 and S said to him, "Go home."
2:1 he charged his son S, saying:
2:12 So S sat on the throne of his father David;
2:17 He said, "Please ask King S—
2:19 So Bathsheba went to King S,
2:22 King S answered his mother,
2:23 Then King S swore by the LORD,
2:25 So King S sent Benaiah son of Jehoiada;
2:27 So S banished Abiathar from being priest to
2:29 When it was told King S,
2:29 S sent Benaiah son of Jehoiada, saying, "Go,
2:41 When S was told that Shimei had gone
2:45 But King S shall be blessed,
2:46 So the kingdom was established in the hand of S.
3:1 S made a marriage alliance with Pharaoh king
3:3 S loved the LORD, walking in the statutes
3:4 S used to offer a thousand burnt offerings on
3:5 At Gibeon the LORD appeared to S in a dream
3:6 And S said, "You have shown great
3:10 It pleased the Lord that S had asked this.
3:15 Then S awoke; it had been a dream.
4:1 King S was king over all Israel,
4:7 S had twelve officials over all Israel,
4:21 S was sovereign over all the kingdoms from
4:21 they brought tribute and served S all the days
4:26 S also had forty thousand stalls of horses
4:27 Those officials supplied provisions for King S and
4:29 God gave S very great wisdom, discernment,
4:34 from all the nations to hear the wisdom of S;
5:1 Now King Hiram of Tyre sent his servants to S,
5:2 S sent word to Hiram, saying,
5:7 When Hiram heard the words of S,
5:8 to S, "I have heard the message that you have sent
5:11 S in turn gave Hiram twenty thousand cors
5:11 S gave this to Hiram year by year.
5:12 the LORD gave S wisdom, as he promised him.
5:12 There was peace between Hiram and S;
5:13 King S conscripted forced labor out of all Israel;
5:15 S also had seventy thousand laborers
6:2 The house that King S built for
6:11 Now the word of the LORD came to S,
6:14 So S built the house, and finished it.
6:21 S overlaid the inside of the house with pure gold,
7:1 S was building his own house thirteen years,
7:8 S also made a house like this hall
7:13 King S invited and received Hiram from Tyre.
7:14 He came to King S, and did all his work.
7:40 that he did for King S on the house of the LORD:
7:45 all these vessels that Hiram made for King S for
7:47 S left all the vessels unweighed,
7:48 So S made all the vessels that were in the house of
7:51 Thus all the work that King S did on the house of
7:51 S brought in the things that his father David had
8:1 Then S assembled the elders of Israel and all
8:1 before King S in Jerusalem, to bring up the ark
8:2 All the people of Israel assembled to King S at
8:5 King S and all the congregation of Israel,
8:12 Then S said, "The LORD has said
8:22 Then S stood before the altar of the LORD in
8:54 Now when S finished offering all this prayer
8:63 S offered as sacrifices of well-being to
8:65 So S held the festival at that time,
9:1 When S had finished building the house of
9:1 the king's house and all that S desired to build,
9:2 the LORD appeared to S a second time,
9:10 in which S had built the two houses,
9:11 King Hiram of Tyre having supplied S with cedar
9:11 King S gave to Hiram twenty cities in the land
9:12 from Tyre to see the cities that S had given him,
9:15 the forced labor that King S conscripted to build
9:17 so S rebuilt Gezer), Lower Beth-horon,
9:19 and whatever S desired to build, in Jerusalem,
9:21 these S conscripted for slave labor,
9:22 But of the Israelites S made no slaves;
9:24 the city of David to her own house that S had built
9:25 a year S used to offer up burnt offerings
9:26 King S built a fleet of ships at Ezion-geber,
9:27 together with the servants of S.
9:28 which they delivered to King S.
10:1 When the queen of Sheba heard of the fame of S,
10:2 and when she came to S,
10:3 S answered all her questions;
10:4 queen of Sheba had observed all the wisdom of S,
10:10 as that which the queen of Sheba gave to King S.
10:13 Meanwhile King S gave to the queen
10:14 to S in one year was six hundred sixty-six talents
10:16 King S made two hundred large shields
10:21 it was not considered as anything in the days of S.
10:23 Thus King S excelled all the kings of the earth
10:24 The whole earth sought the presence of S
10:26 S gathered together chariots and horses;
11:1 King S loved many foreign women along with
11:2 S clung to these in love.
11:4 when S was old, his wives turned away his heart
11:5 S followed Astarte the goddess of the Sidonians,
11:6 So S did what was evil in the sight of the LORD,
1Ki 11:7 Then S built a high place for Chemosh
11:9 Then the LORD was angry with S,
11:11 Therefore the LORD said to S,
11:14 the LORD raised up an adversary against S,
11:23 God raised up another adversary against S,
11:25 He was an adversary of Israel all the days of S,
11:26 a servant of S, whose mother's name was Zeruah,
11:27 S built the Millo, and closed up the gap in the wall
11:28 The man Jeroboam was very able, and when S saw
11:31 about to tear the kingdom from the hand of S,
11:40 S sought therefore to kill Jeroboam;
11:40 and remained in Egypt until the death of S.
11:41 Now the rest of the acts of S,
11:41 are they not written in the Book of the Acts of S?
11:42 The time that S reigned in Jerusalem
11:43 S slept with his ancestors and was buried in
12:2 where he had fled from King S),
12:6 with the older men who had attended his father S
12:21 to restore the kingdom to Rehoboam son of S.
12:23 of S, and to all the house of Judah and Benjamin,
14:21 Now Rehoboam son of S reigned in Judah.
14:26 the shields of gold that S had made;
2Ki 21:7 to David and to his son S, "In this house,
23:13 which King S of Israel had built for Astarte
24:13 which King S of Israel had made,
25:16 which S had made for the house of the LORD,
1Ch 3:5 Shimea, Shobab, Nathan, and S,
3:10 The descendants of S: Rehoboam,
6:10 as priest in the house that S built in Jerusalem).
6:32 until S had built the house of the LORD
14:4 Shammua, Shobab, and Nathan; S,
18:8 with it S made the bronze sea and the pillars and
22:5 "My son S is young and inexperienced,
22:6 for his son S and charged him to build a house for
22:7 David said to S, "My son, I had planned to build
22:9 for his name shall be S, and I will give peace
22:17 the leaders of Israel to help his son S,
23:1 he made his son S king over Israel.
28:5 he has chosen my son S to sit upon the throne of
28:6 'It is your son S who shall build my house
28:9 my son S, know the God of your father,
28:11 Then David gave his son S the plan of
28:20 David said further to his son S,
29:1 "My son S, whom alone God has chosen,
29:19 Grant to my son S that with single mind he may
29:22 They made David's son S king a second time;
29:23 Then S sat on the throne of the LORD,
29:24 pledged their allegiance to King S.
29:25 LORD highly exalted S in the sight of all Israel,
29:28 and his son S succeeded him.
2Ch 1:1 S son of David established himself
1:2 S summoned all Israel, the commanders of
1:3 Then S, and the whole assembly with him,
1:5 And S and the assembly inquired at it.
1:6 S went up there to the bronze altar before
1:7 That night God appeared to S, and said to him,
1:8 S said to God, "You have shown great
1:11 God answered S, "Because this was in your heart,
1:13 So S came from the high place at Gibeon,
1:14 S gathered together chariots and horses;
2:1 S decided to build a temple for the name of
2:2 S conscripted seventy thousand laborers
2:3 S sent word to King Huram of Tyre:
2:11 of Tyre answered in a letter that he sent to S,
2:17 Then S took a census of all the aliens
3:1 S began to build the house of the LORD
3:14 And S made the curtain of blue and purple
4:11 the work that he did for King S on the house
4:16 of burnished bronze for King S for the house of
4:18 S made all these things in great quantities,
4:19 So S made all the things that were in the house
5:1 Thus all the work that S did for the house of
5:1 S brought in the things that his father David had
5:2 Then S assembled the elders of Israel and all
5:6 King S and all the congregation of Israel,
6:1 Then S said, "The LORD has said
6:12 Then S stood before the altar of the LORD in
6:13 S had made a bronze platform five cubits long,
7:1 When S had ended his prayer,
7:5 King S offered as a sacrifice twenty-two thousand
7:7 S consecrated the middle of the court that was
7:7 the bronze altar S had made could not hold
7:8 At that time S held the festival for seven days,
7:10 that the LORD had shown to David and to S and
7:11 Thus S finished the house of the LORD and
7:11 all that S had planned to do in the house of
7:12 LORD appeared to S in the night and said to him:
8:1 during which S had built the house of the LORD
8:2 S rebuilt the cities that Huram had given to him,
8:3 S went to Hamath-zobah, and captured it.
8:6 and whatever S desired to build, in Jerusalem,
8:8 these S conscripted for forced labor.
8:9 But of the people of Israel S made no slaves
8:10 These were the chief officers of King S,
8:11 S brought Pharaoh's daughter from the city
8:12 Then S offered up burnt offerings to the LORD
8:16 Thus all the work of S was accomplished from
8:17 Then S went to Ezion-geber and Eloth on
8:18 together with the servants of S,
8:18 of gold and brought it to King S.
9:1 When the queen of Sheba heard of the fame of S,
9:1 When she came to S, she discussed with him all
9:2 S answered all her questions;
9:2 there was nothing hidden from S that he could
9:3 queen of Sheba had observed the wisdom of S,
9:9 as those that the queen of Sheba gave to King S.
9:10 of Huram and the servants of S who brought gold
2Ch 9:12 Meanwhile King S granted the queen
9:13 to S in one year was six hundred sixty-six talents
9:14 of the land brought gold and silver to S.
9:15 King S made two hundred large shields
9:20 not considered as anything in the days of S.
9:22 Thus King S excelled all the kings of the earth
9:23 All the kings of the earth sought the presence of S
9:25 S had four thousand stalls for horses and chariots,
9:28 Horses were imported for S from Egypt and
9:29 Now the rest of the acts of S, from first to last,
9:30 S reigned in Jerusalem over all Israel forty years.
9:31 S slept with his ancestors and was buried in
10:2 where he had fled from King S),
10:6 with the older men who had attended his father S
11:3 son of S, and to all Israel in Judah and Benjamin,
11:17 three years they made Rehoboam son of S secure,
11:17 for three years in the way of David and S.
12:9 the shields of gold that S had made;
13:6 a servant of S son of David,
13:7 around him and defied Rehoboam son of S,
30:26 for since the time of S son of King David
33:7 of which God said to David and to his son S,
35:3 "Put the holy ark in the house that S son of David,
35:4 of Israel and the written directions of his son S.
Ne 12:45 according to the command of David and his son S.
13:26 Did not King S of Israel sin on account
Ps 72:T *Of S.*
127:T *A Song of Ascents. Of S.*
Pr 1:1 The proverbs of S son of David, king of Israel:
10:1 The proverbs of S. A wise child makes a glad
25:1 These are other proverbs of S that the officials
SS 1:5 like the tents of Kedar, like the curtains of S.
3:7 Look, it is the litter of S!
3:9 King S made himself a palanquin from the wood
3:11 Look, O daughters of Zion, at King S,
8:11 S had a vineyard at Baal-hamon;
8:12 you, O S, may have the thousand,
Jer 52:20 which King S had made for the house of
Mt 1:6 David was the father of S by the wife of Uriah,
1:7 and S the father of Rehoboam,
6:29 S in all his glory was not clothed like one of these.
12:42 the ends of the earth to listen to the wisdom of S,
12:42 and see, something greater than S is here!
Lk 11:31 the ends of the earth to listen to the wisdom of S,
11:31 and see, something greater than S is here!
12:27 S in all his glory was not clothed like one of these.
Jn 10:23 in the temple, in the portico of S.
Ac 7:47 But it was S who built a house for him.
Sir 47:13 S reigned in an age of peace,
47:23 S rested with his ancestors,
2Mc 2:8 and as S asked that the place should
2:9 that being possessed of wisdom S offered sacrifice
2:10 and consumed the sacrifices, so also S prayed,
2:12 Likewise S also kept the eight days.
1Es 1:3 the holy ark of the Lord in the house that King S,
1:5 of Israel and the magnificence of his son S.
2Es 7:*108* [38] and S for those at the dedication,
10:46 And after three thousand years S built the city,

SOLOMON'S (33) [SOLOMON]

1Ki 1:11 Then Nathan said to Bathsheba, S mother,
2:13 of Haggith came to Bathsheba, S mother.
4:11 in all Naphath-dor (he had Taphath, S daughter,
4:15 in Naphtali (he had taken Basemath, S daughter,
4:22 S provision for one day was thirty cors
4:25 During S lifetime Judah and Israel lived in safety,
4:27 and for all who came to King S table, each one
4:30 so that S wisdom surpassed the wisdom of all
5:10 So Hiram supplied S every need for timber
5:16 besides S three thousand three hundred supervisors
5:18 So S builders and Hiram's builders and
6:1 in the fourth year of S reign over Israel,
9:16 and had given it as dowry to his daughter, S wife;
9:19 as well as all of S storage cities,
9:23 the chief officers who were over S work:
10:13 as well as what he gave her out of S royal bounty.
10:21 All King S drinking vessels were of gold,
10:28 S import of horses was from Egypt and Kue,
2Ch 1:16 S horses were imported from Egypt and Kue;
3:3 These are S measurements for building the house
8:6 as well as all S storage towns,
9:20 All King S drinking vessels were of gold,
Ezr 2:55 The descendants of S servants:
2:58 of S servants were three hundred ninety-two.
Ne 7:57 The descendants of S servants:
7:60 of S servants were three hundred ninety-two.
11:3 and the descendants of S servants.
SS 1:1 The Song of Songs, which is S.
Ac 3:11 to them in the portico called S Portico,
5:12 And they were all together in S Portico.
1Es 5:33 The descendants of S servants:
5:35 of S servants were three hundred seventy-two.
4Mc 18:16 He recounted to you S proverb,

SOLSTICES (1)

Wis 7:18 the alternations of the s and the changes of

SOLUTIONS (1) [SOLVE]

Wis 8:8 she understands turns of speech and the s

SOLVE (4) [SOLUTIONS]

Ps 49:4 I will s my riddle to the music of the harp.
Da 5:12 and s problems were found in this Daniel,
5:16 that you can give interpretations and s problems.
2Es 4:4 If you can s one of them for me,

SOME‡ (568)

Ge 3: 6 and she also gave s to her husband,
9:21 He drank s of the wine and became drunk,
14:10 as the kings of Sodom and Gomorrah fled, s fell
25:30 Esau said to Jacob, "Let me eat s of that red stuff,
30:14 "Please give me s of your son's mandrakes."
33:15 "Let me leave with you s of the people who are
35:16 and when they were still s distance from Ephrath,
36: 6 to a land s distance from his brother Jacob.
37:28 When s Midianite traders passed by,
40: 1 S time after this, the cupbearer of the king
40: 4 and they continued for s time in custody.
43:11 take s of the choice fruits of the land in your bags,
48: 7 while there was still s distance to go to Ephrath;
Ex 2:17 But s shepherds came and drove them away.
4: 9 you shall take s water from the Nile and pour it on
10:10 Plainly, you have s evil purpose in mind.
10:26 a hoof shall be left behind, for we must choose s
12: 7 They shall take s of the blood and put it on
16:17 The Israelites did so, s gathering more, s less.
16:20 s left part of it until morning,
16:27 the seventh day s of the people went out to gather,
17: 5 and take s of the elders of Israel with you;
17: 9 "Choose s men for us and go out,
29:12 and shall take s of the blood of the bull and put it
29:20 and take s of its blood and put it on the lobe
29:21 you shall take s of the blood that is on the altar,
29:21 and s of the anointing oil, and sprinkle it on Aaron
30:36 and you shall beat s of it into powder, and put part
Lev 2:16 s of the coarse grain and oil with all its
4: 5 The anointed priest shall take s of the blood of
4: 6 the blood and sprinkle s of the blood seven times
4: 7 The priest shall put s of the blood on the horns of
4:16 The anointed priest shall bring s of the blood of
4:18 He shall put s of the blood on the horns of the altar
4:25 The priest shall take s of the blood of
4:30 The priest shall take s of its blood with his finger
4:34 The priest shall take s of the blood of
5: 9 He shall sprinkle s of the blood of the sin offering
8:11 He sprinkled s of it on the altar seven times,
8:12 He poured s of the anointing oil on Aaron's head
8:15 and with his finger put s on each of the horns of
8:23 Moses took s of its blood and put it on the lobe
8:24 Moses put s of the blood on the lobes
8:30 Then Moses took s of the anointing oil and s of the
blood that was on
14:14 The priest shall take s of the blood of
14:15 The priest shall take s of the log of oil and pour it
14:16 in the oil that is in his left hand and sprinkle s oil
14:17 S of the oil that remains in his hand
14:25 of the guilt offering and shall take s of the blood of
14:26 The priest shall pour s of the oil into the palm
14:27 and shall sprinkle with his right finger s of the oil
14:28 The priest shall put s of the oil that is in his hand
14:35 to me to be s sort of disease in my house."
16:14 He shall take s of the blood of the bull,
16:18 and shall take s of the blood of the bull and of
16:19 He shall sprinkle s of the blood on it
Nu 5:17 and take s of the dust that is on the floor of
5:20 s man other than your husband has had intercourse
11: 1 and consumed s outlying parts of the camp.
11:17 and I will take s of the spirit that is on you
11:25 and took s of the spirit that was on him and put it
13:20 Be bold, and bring s of the fruit of the land."
13:23 They also brought s pomegranates and figs.
19: 4 The priest Eleazar shall take s of its blood
19:17 For the unclean they shall take s ashes of
21: 1 against Israel and took s of them captive.
27:20 You shall give him s of your authority,
30:15 he nullifies them s time after he has heard of them,
31: 3 "Arm s of your number for the war,
32:38 and Baal-meon (s names being changed),
Dt 1:25 and gathered s of the land's produce,
11:30 they are beyond the Jordan, s distance to the west,
12:20 and you say, "I am going to eat s meat,"
15:11 there will never cease to be s in need on the earth,
15:14 thus giving to him s of the bounty with which
26: 2 you shall take s of the first of all the fruit of
Jos 2: 2 "S Israelites have come here tonight to search out
7: 1 of the tribe of Judah, took s of the devoted things;
7:11 They have taken s of the devoted things;
8:22 they were surrounded by Israelites, s on one side,
and s on the other;
9:23 and s of you shall always be slaves,
11:22 s remained only in Gaza, in Gath, and in Ashdod.
Jdg 8: 5 "Please give s loaves of bread to my followers,
14: 9 he gave s to them, and they ate it.
15: 4 and caught three hundred foxes, and took s torches;
18:22 they were s distance from the home of Micah,
19: 2 and was there s four months.
Ru 2:14 "Come here, and eat s of this bread,
2:14 and he heaped up for her s parched grain.
2:14 and she had s left over.
2:16 also pull out s handfuls for her from the bundles,
3: 1 "My daughter, I need to seek s security for you,
1Sa 7: 2 a long time passed, s twenty years,
8:12 and s to plow his ground and to reap his harvest,
9:11 they met s girls coming out to draw water,
10:27 But s worthless fellows said,
13: 7 S Hebrews crossed the Jordan to the land of Gad
17:18 and bring s token from them."
23:19 s Ziphites went up to Saul at Gibeah and said,
24:10 and s urged me to kill you, but I spared you.
2Sa 3:17 "For s time past you have been seeking David
5: 2 For s time, while Saul was king over us,
8: 1 S time afterward, David attacked the Philistines
2Sa 10: 1 S time afterward, the king of the Ammonites died,
10: 9 he chose s of the picked men of Israel,
11:17 s of the servants of David among the people fell.
11:24 s of the king's servants are dead;
12:18 He may do himself s harm."
13: 1 S time passed. David's son Absalom had a
17: 9 in one of the pits, or in s other place.
17: 9 And when s of our troops fall at the first attack,
1Ki 11:17 with s Edomites who were servants of his father.
13:15 "Come home with me and eat s food."
14: 3 Take with you ten loaves, s cakes,
18: 5 and not lose s of the animals."
21: 7 Get up, eat s food, and be cheerful;
2Ki 2: 7 and stood at s distance from them,
2:16 thrown him down on s mountain or into s valley."
2:23 up on the way, s small boys came out of the city
4:38 and make s stew for the company of prophets."
4:40 They served s for the men to eat.
4:41 He said, "Then bring s flour."
4:43 'They shall eat and have s left.' "
4:44 He set it before them, they ate, and had s left,
6:24 S time later King Ben-hadad
7:13 "Let s men take five of the remaining horses,
9:33 s of her blood spattered on the wall and on
17:25 the LORD sent lions among them, which killed s
20:18 S of your own sons who are born to you shall
25:12 the captain of the guard left s of the poorest people
1Ch 4:42 And s of them, five hundred men of
6:66 And s of the families of the sons
9: 3 And s of the people of Judah, Benjamin, Ephraim,
9:28 S of them had charge of the utensils of service,
9:32 Also s of their kindred of
11: 2 For s time now, even while Saul was king,
12:16 S Benjaminites and Judahites came to
12:19 S of the Manassites deserted to David
18: 1 S time afterward, David attacked the Philistines
19: 1 S time afterward, King Nahash of
19:10 he chose s of the picked men of Israel
2Ch 11:23 and distributed s of his sons through all
12: 7 but I will grant them s deliverance,
16:10 And Asa inflicted cruelties on s of the people at
17:11 S of the Philistines brought Jehoshaphat presents,
18: 2 After s years he went down to Ahab in Samaria.
19: 3 Nevertheless, s good is found in you,
20: 1 and with them s of the Meunites,
21: 4 and also s of the officials of Israel.
24: 4 S time afterward Joash decided to restore
32:21 s of his own sons struck him down there with
34:13 and s of the Levites were scribes, and officials,
36: 7 Nebuchadnezzar also carried s of the vessels of
Ezr 2:68 s of the heads of families made freewill offerings
2:70 s of the people lived in Jerusalem and its vicinity;
7: 7 S of the people of Israel, and s of the priests and
9: 2 For they have taken s of their daughters as wives
Ne 5: 5 and s of our daughters have been ravished;
7: 3 the inhabitants of Jerusalem, s at their watch posts,
7:70 Now s of the heads of ancestral houses contributed
7:71 And s of the heads of ancestral houses gave into
7:73 the singers, s of the people, the temple servants,
11: 4 And in Jerusalem lived s of the Judahites and of
11:25 s of the people of Judah lived in Kiriath-arba
12:35 and s of the young priests with trumpets:
13: 6 After s time I asked leave of the king
13:19 And I set s of my servants over the gates,
13:25 with them and cursed them and beat s of them
Ps 4: 6 "O that we might see s good!
20: 7 S take pride in chariots, and s in horses,
49:16 Do not be afraid when s become rich,
107: 4 S wandered in desert wastes,
107:10 S sat in darkness and in gloom,
107:17 S were sick through their sinful ways,
107:23 S went down to the sea in ships,
Pr 11:24 S give freely, yet grow all the richer;
13: 7 S pretend to be rich, yet have nothing;
18:24 S friends play at friendship but
Ecc 10:20 or s winged creature tell the matter.
Isa 39: 7 S of your own sons who are born to you shall
66:21 I will also take s of them as priests and as Levites,
Jer 19: 1 with you s of the elders of the people and s of the
26:17 And s of the elders of the land arose and said to all
35: 5 and I said to them, "Have s wine."
39:10 of Judah s of the poor people who owned nothing,
43: 9 Take s large stones in your hands,
44:14 they shall not go back, except s fugitives.
52:15 of the guard carried into exile s of the poorest of
52:16 the captain of the guard left s of the poorest people
Eze 5: 4 From these, again, you shall take s,
6: 8 But I will spare s.
6: 8 S of you shall escape the sword among the nations
10: 7 took s of it and put it into the hands of
16:16 You took s of your garments,
43:20 And you shall take s of its blood,
45:19 The priest shall take s of the blood of
Da 1: 2 as well as s of the vessels of the house of God.
1: 3 to bring s of the Israelites of the royal family and
2:41 but s of the strength of iron shall be in it,
3:20 and ordered s of the strongest guards in his army
8:10 It threw down to the earth s of the host and s of the
8:27 I, Daniel, was overcome and lay sick for s days;
11: 6 After s years they shall make an alliance,
11: 8 For s years he shall refrain from attacking the king
11:13 after s years he shall advance with a great army
11:33 for s days, however, they shall fall by sword
11:35 S of the wise shall fall,
12: 2 shall awake, s to everlasting life, and s to shame
Am 2:11 And I raised up s of your children to be prophets
and s of your youths to be nazirites.
Am 4:11 I overthrew s of you,
Mt 8:30 a large herd of swine was feeding at s distance
9: 2 then s people were carrying a paralyzed man lying
9: 3 Then s of the scribes said to themselves,
12:38 Then s of the scribes and Pharisees said to him,
13: 4 And as he sowed, s seeds fell on the path,
13: 8 forth grain, s a hundredfold, s sixty, s thirty.
16:14 And they said, "S say John the Baptist,
16:28 there are s standing here who will not taste death
19: 3 S Pharisees came to him,
22:23 The same day s Sadducees came to him,
23:34 and scribes, s of whom you will kill and crucify,
23:34 and s you will flog in your synagogues and pursue
25: 8 The foolish said to the wise, 'Give us s of your oil,
25: 9 you had better go to the dealers and buy s
26:67 and struck him; and s slapped him,
27: 9 on whom s of the people of Israel had set a price,
27:24 he took s water and washed his hands before
27:29 and after twisting s thorns into a crown,
27:47 When s of the bystanders heard it, they said,
28:11 s of the guard went into the city and told
28:17 they saw him, they worshiped him; but s doubted.
Mk 2: 1 When he returned to Capernaum after s days,
2: 3 Then s people came, bringing to him a paralyzed
2: 6 Now s of the scribes were sitting there,
2:26 and he gave s to his companions."
4: 4 And as he sowed, s seed fell on the path,
5:35 s people came from the leader's house to say,
6:14 S were saying, "John the baptizer has been raised
7: 1 the Pharisees and s of the scribes who had come
7: 2 they noticed that s of his disciples were eating
8: 3 and s of them have come from a great distance."
8:22 S people brought a blind man to him
9: 1 there are s standing here who will not taste death
9:14 and s scribes arguing with them.
10: 2 S Pharisees came, and to test him they asked,
11: 5 s of the bystanders said to them,
12: 5 s they beat, and others they killed.
12:13 to him s Pharisees and s Herodians to trap him
12:18 S Sadducees, who say there is no resurrection,
14: 4 But s were there who said to one another in anger,
14:57 S stood up and gave false testimony against him,
14:65 S began to spit on him, to blindfold him,
15:17 twisting s thorns into a crown, they put it on him.
15:35 When s of the bystanders heard it, they said,
15:44 he asked him whether he had been dead for s time.
Lk 5:18 Just then s men came, carrying a paralyzed man on
6: 1 his disciples plucked s heads of grain,
6: 2 But s of the Pharisees said,
6: 4 and gave s to his companions?"
7: 3 he sent s Jewish elders to him,
8: 2 as s women who had been cured of evil spirits
8: 5 he sowed, s fell on the path and was trampled on,
8: 6 S fell on the rock;
8: 7 S fell among thorns, and the thorns grew with it
8: 8 S fell into good soil, and when it grew,
9: 7 because it was said by s that John had been raised
9: 8 by s that Elijah had appeared,
9:27 there are s standing here who will not taste death
11:15 But s of them said, "He casts out demons
11:49 s of whom they will kill and persecute,'
13: 1 that very time there were s present who told him
13:30 Indeed, s are last who will be first, and s are first
who will be last."
13:31 that very hour s Pharisees came and said to him,
18: 9 He also told this parable to s who trusted
19:39 S of the Pharisees in the crowd said to him,
20:27 S Sadducees, those who say there is no resurrection
20:39 Then s of the scribes answered, "Teacher,
21: 5 When s were speaking about the temple,
21:16 and they will put s of you to death.
23: 8 and was hoping to see him perform s sign.
23: 9 He questioned him at s length,
24:22 Moreover, s women of our group astounded us.
24:24 S of those who were with us went to the tomb
Jn 2: 8 He said to them, "Now draw s out,
3:22 and he spent s time there with them and baptized.
6:23 Then s boats from Tiberias came near the place
6:64 But among you there are s who do not believe."
7:12 While s were saying, "He is a good man,"
7:25 Now s of the people of Jerusalem were saying,
7:40 When they heard these words, s in the crowd said,
7:41 But s asked, "Surely the Messiah does not come
7:44 S of them wanted to arrest him,
8: 6 ⟦they might have s charge to bring against him.⟧
9: 9 S were saying, "It is he."
9:16 S of the Pharisees said, "This man is not
9:40 S of the Pharisees near him heard this and said
11:18 Bethany was near Jerusalem, s two miles away,
11:37 But s of them said, "Could not he who opened
11:46 But s of them went to the Pharisees
12:20 up to worship at the festival were s Greeks.
13:29 S thought that, because Judas had
16:17 Then s of his disciples said to one another,
21: 6 to the right side of the boat, and you will find s."
21: 7 he put on s clothes, for he was naked,
21:10 "Bring s of the fish that you have just caught."
Ac 5: 2 he kept back s of the proceeds,
5:15 in order that Peter's shadow might fall on s
5:36 For s time ago Theudas rose up,
6: 9 Then s of those who belonged to the synagogue of
6:11 Then they secretly instigated s men to say,
7:26 to s of them as they were quarreling and tried
8:36 along the road, they came to s water;
9:19 after taking s food, he regained his strength.
9:23 After s time had passed, the Jews plotted
9:43 Meanwhile he stayed in Joppa for s time with

Ac 10:23 s of the believers from Joppa accompanied him.
11:20 But among them were s men of Cyprus
12: 1 upon s who belonged to the church.
14: 4 s sided with the Jews, and s with the apostles.
14:28 And they stayed there with the disciples for s time.
15: 2 and Barnabas and s of the others were appointed
15: 5 But s believers who belonged to the sect of
15:33 After they had been there for s time,
15:36 After s days Paul said to Barnabas, "Come,
16:12 We remained in this city for s days.
17: 4 S of them were persuaded and joined Paul
17: 5 of s ruffians in the marketplaces they formed
17: 6 and s believers before the city authorities,
17:18 Also s Epicurean and Stoic philosophers debated
17:18 S said, "What does this babbler want to say?"
17:28 as even s of your own poets have said,
17:32 of the resurrection of the dead, s scoffed;
17:34 But s of them joined him and became believers,
18:23 After spending s time there he departed and went
19: 1 where he found s disciples.
19: 9 When s stubbornly refused to believe
19:13 Then s itinerant Jewish exorcists tried to use
19:22 while he himself stayed for s time longer in Asia.
19:31 even s officials of the province of Asia,
19:32 Meanwhile, s were shouting one thing, s another;
19:33 S of the crowd gave instructions to Alexander,
20:30 S even from your own group will come distorting
21:16 S of the disciples from Caesarea also came along
21:34 S in the crowd shouted one thing, s another;
23: 6 that s were Sadducees and others were Pharisees,
24: 1 the high priest Ananias came down with s elders
24:17 after s years I came to bring alms to my nation and
24:19 But there were s Jews from Asia—
24:23 but to let him have s liberty and not to prevent any
24:24 S days later when Felix came
27: 1 they transferred Paul and s other prisoners to
27:26 But we will have to run aground on s island."
27:33 Paul urged all of them to take s food, saying,
27:34 Therefore I urge you to take s food,
27:44 s on planks and others on pieces of the ship.
28:24 S were convinced by what he had said,
Ro 1:11 with you s spiritual gift to strengthen you—
1:13 that I may reap s harvest among you as I have
3: 3 What if s were unfaithful?
3: 8 And why not say (as s people slander us by saying
11:14 and thus save s of them.
11:17 But if s of the branches were broken off, and you,
14: 2 S believe in eating anything,
14: 5 S judge one day to be better than another,
15:15 on s points I have written to you rather boldly
1Co 4:18 But s of you, thinking that I am not coming to you,
6:11 And this is what s of you used to be.
8: 7 s have become so accustomed to idols until now,
9:22 that I might by all means save s.
10: 7 Do not become idolaters as s of them did;
10: 8 not indulge in sexual immorality as s of them did,
10: 9 as s of them did, and were destroyed by serpents.
10:10 And do not complain as s of them did,
11:18 and to s extent I believe it.
11:30 of you are weak and ill, and s have died.
14: 6 unless I speak to you in s revelation or knowledge
15: 6 most of whom are still alive, though s have died.
15:12 how can s of you say there is no resurrection of
15:34 for s people have no knowledge of God.
15:37 perhaps of wheat or of s other grain.
16: 7 for I hope to spend s time with you,
2Co 2: 5 he has caused it not to me, but to s extent—
3: 1 Surely we do not need, as s do,
9: 4 if s Macedonians come with me and find
10:12 not dare to classify or compare ourselves with s
Gal 1: 7 but there are s who are confusing you and want
Eph 4:11 The gifts he gave were that s would be apostles, s
prophets, s evangelists, s pastors and teachers,
Php 1:15 S proclaim Christ from envy and rivalry,
2Th 3:11 For we hear that s of you are living in idleness,
1Ti 1: 6 S people have deviated from these and turned
4: 1 that in later times s will renounce the faith
4: 8 while physical training is of s value,
5: 4 to their own family and make s repayment
5:15 For s have already turned away to follow Satan.
5:24 of s people are conspicuous and precede them
6:10 in their eagerness to be rich s have wandered away
6:21 by professing it s have missed the mark as regards
2Ti 2:18 They are upsetting the faith of s.
2:20 s for special use, s for ordinary.
Heb 4: 6 Since therefore it remains open for s to enter it,
10:25 as is the habit of s, but encouraging one another,
13: 2 that s have entertained angels without knowing it.
1Pe 3: 1 so that, even if s of them do not obey the word,
2Pe 3: 9 as s think of slowness, but is patient with you,
3:16 There are s things in them hard to understand,
2Jn 1: 4 I was overjoyed to find s of your children walking
3Jn 1: 3 I was overjoyed when s of the friends arrived
Jude 1:22 And have mercy on s who are wavering;
Rev 2:10 the devil is about to throw s of you into prison so
2:14 you have s there who hold to the teaching
2:15 So you also have s who hold to the teaching of
2:17 To everyone who conquers I will give s of
2:24 not learned what s call 'the deep things of Satan,'
Tob 2: 3 So Tobias went to look for s poor person
4:16 Give s of your food to the hungry, and s of your
6: 6 then he roasted and ate s of the fish, and kept s to
6:17 take s of the fish's liver and heart,
Jdt 7:18 and they sent s of their men toward the south and
10:15 s of us will escort you and hand you over to him.
12: 1 to set a table for her with s of his own delicacies,
and with s of his own wine to drink.
Jdt 15:12 and s of them performed a dance in her honor.
AdE 4: 4 and sent s clothes to Mordecai to put on instead
Wis 4:10 There were s who pleased God and were loved
13:14 or makes it like s worthless animal, giving it a coat
19:15 but, while punishment of s sort will come upon
Sir Pr: 2 to have rendered s phrases imperfectly.
Pr: 3 of the reign of Euergetes and stayed for s time,
Pr: 3 that I should myself devote s diligence and labor
4: 6 for if in bitterness of soul s should curse you,
8: 6 for s of us are also growing old.
10:17 He removes s of them and destroys them,
14:18 a spreading tree that sheds s and puts forth others,
20: 5 S people keep silent and are thought to be wise,
20: 6 S people keep silent because they have nothing
20:11 and there are s who have raised their heads
20:12 S buy much for little, but pay for it seven times
33: 9 S days he exalted and hallowed,
33: 9 and s he made ordinary days.
33:12 S he blessed and exalted, and s he made holy
33:12 but s he cursed and brought low,
37: 1 but s friends are friends only in name.
37: 4 S companions rejoice in the happiness of a friend,
37: 5 S companions help a friend
37: 7 but s give counsel in their own interest.
37:19 S people may be clever enough to teach many,
44: 8 S of them have left behind a name,
48:16 S of them did what was right,
Bar 2: 3 S of us ate the flesh of their sons and others
LtJ 6:11 or even give s of it to the prostitutes on the terrace.
6:28 Likewise their wives preserve s of the meat
6:32 They howl and shout before their gods as s do at
6:33 The priests take s of the clothing of their gods
1Mc 1:13 and s of the people eagerly went to the king,
5:27 s have been shut up in the other towns of Gilead;
5:67 On that day s priests, who wished to do
6:21 But s of the garrison escaped from the siege and s
6:40 and s troops were on the plain,
7:19 of the men who had deserted to him, and s of
7:33 S of the priests from the sanctuary and s of the
8: 7 a heavy tribute and give hostages and surrender s
10:14 in Beth-zur did s remain who had forsaken the law
10:37 Let s of them be stationed in the great strongholds
10:37 and let s of them be put in positions of trust in
11:23 He chose s of the elders of Israel and s of the
16:16 as well as s of his servants.
2Mc 1:19 the pious priests of that time took s of the fire of
1:22 When this had been done and s time had passed,
2: 1 to take s of the fire,
2: 6 S of those who followed him came up intending
3:10 that there were s deposits belonging to widows
3:11 and also s money of Hyrcanus son of Tobias,
3:19 S of the young women who were kept indoors ran
3:19 and s to the walls, while others peered out of
3:31 S of Heliodorus's friends quickly begged Onias
3:32 the notion that s foul play had been perpetrated by
3:38 there is certainly s power of God about the place.
4:32 stole s of the gold vessels of the temple
4:41 s picked up stones, s blocks of wood,
4:42 a result, they wounded many of them, and killed s,
8:25 After pursuing them for s distance,
8:28 After the sabbath they gave s of the spoils
8:30 of s exceedingly high strongholds,
8:33 and s others, who had fled into one little house;
10:20 were bribed by s of those who were in the towers,
10:20 on receiving seventy thousand drachmas let s of
11:36 as you have considered them, send s one promptly
12: 2 But s of the governors in various places,
12:24 the brothers of s, to whom no consideration would
14: 4 a crown of gold and a palm, and besides these s of
1Es 1:41 Nebuchadnezzar also took s holy vessels of
4: 6 whenever they sow and reap, and bring s to
5:44 S of the heads of families,
5:46 and s of the people settled in Jerusalem
5:50 s joined them from the other peoples of the land.
5:63 S of the levitical priests and heads
8: 5 to Jerusalem s of the people of Israel and s of the
8:24 whether by death or s other punishment,
8:78 now in s measure mercy has come to us from you,
3Mc 1: 8 the Jews had sent s of their council and elders
1:20 s in houses and s in the streets,
2:31 Now s, however, with an obvious abhorrence of
3: 2 against the Jewish nation by s who conspired
3: 4 For this reason they appeared hateful to s;
3:10 And already s of their neighbors and friends and
business associates had taken s
4: 4 at the sight of their unusual punishments, even s
4: 9 s were fastened by the neck to the benches of
4:18 s still residing in their homes, and s at the place;
5:18 After the party had been going on for s time,
2Es 5:18 Rise therefore and eat s bread,
5:34 the way of the Most High and to search out s part
6:42 that s of them might be planted and cultivated and
7:86 how s of them will cross over into torments.
8:37 "S things you have spoken rightly,
9: 1 you see that s of the predicted signs have occurred,
9:21 And I saw and spared s with great difficulty,
11:20 There were s of them that ruled,
13:13 s of whom were joyful and s sorrowful; s of them
were bound, and s were bringing others as
14:26 you have finished, s things you shall make public,
14:26 and s you shall deliver in secret to the wise;
16:30 when a vineyard is gathered, s clusters may be left
16:68 they shall drag s of you away and force you
4Mc 1: 5 S might perhaps ask, "If reason rules
1:32 S desires are mental, others are physical,
2:18 to correct s, and to render others powerless.
5:13 if there is s power watching over this religion
4Mc 6:13 s of the king's retinue came to him and said,
6:15 We will set before you s cooked meat;
7:17 S perhaps might say, "Not all have full command
7:20 therefore arises when s persons appear to
8:16 if s of them had been cowardly and unmanly.
16: 9 Alas for my children, s unmarried,
17: 1 S of the guards said that when she also was about

SOMEBODY (2) [SOMEONE]

Pr 26:17 Like s who takes a passing dog by the ears
Ac 5:36 some time ago Theudas rose up, claiming to be s,

SOMEHOW (5)

Ac 27:12 on the chance that s they could reach Phoenix,
Ro 1:10 asking that by God's will I may s at last succeed
1Co 8: 9 of yours does not s become a stumbling block to
Php 3:11 if s I may attain the resurrection from the dead.
1Th 3: 5 I was afraid that s the tempter had tempted you

SOMEONE‡ (141) [SOMEBODY, SOMEONE'S]

Ex 4:13 But he said, "O my Lord, please send s else."
12:30 for there was not a house without s dead.
21:14 if s willfully attacks and kills another by treachery,
21:33 If s leaves a pit open,
22: 1 When s steals an ox or a sheep,
22: 5 s causes a field or vineyard to be grazed over,
22: 5 or lets livestock loose to graze in s else's field,
22: 7 When s delivers to a neighbor money or goods
22:10 When s delivers to another a donkey, ox, sheep,
22:14 When s borrows an animal from another
34:15 s among them will invite you,
Lev 16:21 into the wilderness by means of s designated for
27:20 or if it has been sold to s else,
27:22 If s consecrates to the LORD a field
Nu 6: 9 If s dies very suddenly nearby,
19: 9 Then s who is clean shall gather up the ashes of
19:14 This is the law when s dies in a tent:
21: 9 and whenever a serpent bit s,
27:16 appoint s over the congregation
35:20 Likewise, if s pushes another from hatred,
35:22 But if s pushes another suddenly without enmity,
Dt 4:42 s who unintentionally kills another person,
5:24 Today we have seen that God may speak to s and
19: 4 s who has killed another person unintentionally
19: 5 Suppose s goes into the forest with another
19:11 if s at enmity with another lies in wait and attacks
19:16 If a malicious witness comes forward to accuse s
21:18 If s has a stubborn and rebellious son who will
21:22 When s is convicted of a crime punishable
22:26 like that of s who attacks and murders a neighbor.
24: 7 If s is caught kidnaping another Israelite,
Ru 2: 2 behind s in whose sight I may find favor."
1Sa 2:25 s can intercede for the sinner with the LORD;
2:25 but if s sins against the LORD,
16:16 to look for s who is skillful in playing the lyre;
16:17 "Provide for me s who can play well,
19:22 And s said, "They are at Naioth in Ramah."
2Sa 11: 3 David sent s to inquire about the woman.
23:15 that s would give me water to drink from the well
1Ki 8:31 "If s sins against a neighbor and is given an oath
2Ki 5:21 When Naaman saw s running after him,
5:26 not go with you in spirit when s left his chariot
6:32 that this murderer has sent s to take off my head?
1Ch 11:17 that s would give me water to drink from the well
17:17 You regard me as s of high rank, O LORD God!
2Ch 6:22 "If s sins against another and is required to take
Ezr 4:19 and s searched and discovered
Ne 2:10 it displeased them greatly that s had come to seek
Est 4:11 Only if the king holds out the golden scepter to s,
Job 12:14 if he shuts s in, no one can open up.
Pr 4:16 of sleep unless they have made s stumble.
25:10 else s who hears you will bring shame upon you,
28:17 If s is burdened with the blood of another,
29:20 Do you see s who is hasty in speech?
Isa 3: 6 S will even seize a relative, a member of the clan,
Jer 14: 9 Why should you be like s confused,
Eze 1:28 and I heard the voice of s speaking.
33:21 s who had escaped from Jerusalem came to me
43: 6 I heard s speaking to me out of the temple.
Da 5:17 or give your rewards to s else!
8:15 Then s appeared standing before me,
Hos 6: 9 As robbers lie in wait for s,
Am 5:19 as if s fled from a lion, and was met by a bear;
6:10 shall say to s in the innermost parts of the house,
Mic 2:11 If s were to go about uttering empty falsehoods,
Mal 1:10 Oh, that s among you would shut the temple doors,
Mt 11: 8 S dressed in soft robes?
12:47 S told him, "Look, your mother
13:24 be compared to s who sowed good seed
13:31 a mustard seed that s took and sowed in his field;
13:44 like treasure hidden in a field, which s found
19:16 Then s came to him and said, "Teacher,
19:24 through the eye of a needle than for s who is rich
Mk 4:26 of God is as if s would scatter seed on the ground,
9:17 S from the crowd answered him, "Teacher,
9:38 we saw s casting out demons in your name,
10:25 through the eye of a needle than for s who is rich
15:36 And s ran, filled a sponge with sour wine,
Lk 6:47 I will show you what s is like who comes to me,
7:25 S dressed in soft robes?
8:46 But Jesus said, "S touched me;
8:49 s came from the leader's house to say,
9:49 we saw s casting out demons in your name,
9:57 As they were going along the road, s said to him,

Lk 12:13 S in the crowd said to him, "Teacher,
13:19 It is like a mustard seed that s took and sowed in
13:23 S asked him, "Lord, will only a few be saved?"
14: 8 "When you are invited by s to a wedding banquet,
14: 8 s more distinguished than you has been invited
14:16 "S gave a great dinner and invited many.
16:30 if s goes to them from the dead, they will repent.'
16:31 neither will they be convinced even if s rises from
18:25 through the eye of a needle than for s who is rich
22:58 A little later s else, on seeing him, said,
Jn 5: 7 making my way, s else steps down ahead of me."
9: 9 Others were saying, "No, but it is s like him."
18:39 But you have a custom that I release s for you at
21:18 and s else will fasten a belt around you
Ac 4: 9 a good deed done to s who was sick and are asked
5:25 Then s arrived and announced, "Look,
8: 9 saying that he was s great.
8:31 He replied, "How can I, unless s guides me?"
8:34 about himself or about s else?"
13:11 and he went about groping for s to lead him by
13:41 that you will never believe, even if s tells you.' "
Ro 5: 7 for a good person s might actually dare to die.
10:14 how are they to hear without s to proclaim him?
15:20 so that I do not build on s else's foundation,
1Co 3:10 and s else is building on it.
7:37 But if s stands firm in his resolve,
10:28 But if s says to you, "This has been offered
10:29 be subject to the judgment of s else's conscience?
14: 5 unless s interprets, so that the church may
14:30 If a revelation is made to s else sitting nearby,
15:35 But s will ask, "How are the dead raised?
2Co 10:16 of work already done in s else's sphere of action.
11: 4 For if s comes and proclaims another Jesus than
11:20 For you put up with it when s makes slaves of you,
1Ti 3: 5 for if s does not know how
Tit 1: 6 s who is blameless, married only once,
Heb 2: 6 But s has testified somewhere,
3: 4 (For every house is built by s,
5:12 you need s to teach you again the basic elements
6:16 of course, swear by s greater than themselves,
11:19 that God is able even to raise s from the dead—
Jas 2:18 But s will say, "You have faith and I have works."
1Pe 5: 8 the devil prowls around, looking for s to devour.
Rev 9: 5 like the torture of a scorpion when it stings s.
Tob 5: 4 s who was acquainted with the way.
Sir 19: 9 for s may have heard you and watched you,
29: 8 be patient with s in humble circumstances,
LtJ 6:24 it will not shine unless s wipes off the tarnish;
6:40 for when they see s who cannot speak,
6:73 Better, therefore, is s upright who has no idols;
1Mc 6: 5 Then s came to him in Persia and reported that
16:21 But s ran ahead and reported to John at Gazara
3Mc 1:14 And s answered thoughtlessly that it was wrong
2Es 7: 9 If now the city is given to s as an inheritance,
7:*115* [45] to have mercy on s who has been condemned
7:*115* [45] or to harm s who is victorious."
4Mc 2: 7 Otherwise how could it be that s who is habitually

SOMEONE'S (3) [SOMEONE]

Ex 21:35 If s ox hurts the ox of another, so that it dies,
Sir 41:21 of taking away s portion or gift,
LtJ 6:17 For just as s dish is useless when it is broken,

SOMETHING (108)

Ex 10: 6 s that neither your parents
24:10 Under his feet there was s like a pavement
Lev 6: 3 or have found s lost and lied about it—
Nu 16:30 But if the LORD creates s new,
35:20 or hurls s at another, lying in wait,
Dt 24: 1 not please him because he finds s objectionable
Jdg 14:14 He said to them, "Out of the eater came s to eat.
14:14 Out of the strong came s sweet."
1Sa 3:11 about to do s in Israel that will make both ears
14:12 saying, "Come up to us, and we will show you s."
20:26 for he thought, "S has befallen him;
2Sa 3:35 to persuade David to eat s while it was still day;
13: 5 'Let my sister Tamar come and give me s to eat,
1Ki 14:13 in him there is found s pleasing to the LORD,
17:13 and afterwards make s for yourself and your son.
2Ki 5:13 the prophet had commanded you to do s difficult,
5:20 I will run after him and get s out of him."
Job 36: 2 for I have yet s to say on God's behalf.
Ps 17:14 may they leave s over to their little ones.
Jer 2:11 But my people have changed their glory for s
20: 9 then within me there is s like a burning fire shut up
38:14 The king said to Jeremiah, "I have s to ask you;
Eze 1: 4 in the middle of the fire, s like gleaming amber.
1: 5 In the middle of it was s like four living creatures.
1:13 In the middle of the living creatures there was s
1:16 the same form, their construction being s like
1:22 Over the heads of the living creatures there was s
1:26 And above the dome over their heads there was s
1:26 of a throne was s that seemed like a human form.
1:27 Upward from what appeared like the loins I saw s
1:27 s that looked like fire enclosed all around;
1:27 from what looked like the loins I saw s that looked
10: 1 of the cherubim there appeared above them s like
10:10 s like a wheel within a wheel.
10:21 and underneath their wings s like human hands.
41:21 In front of the holy place was s resembling
Joel 3: 4 Are you paying me back for s?
Am 4: 1 who say to their husbands, "Bring s to drink!"
Mic 3: 5 who cry "Peace" when they have s to eat,
Mt 5:23 if you remember that your brother or sister has s
12: 6 I tell you, s greater than the temple is here.
12:41 and see, s greater than Jonah is here!
12:42 and see, s greater than Solomon is here!
14:16 you give them s to eat."
25:35 I was thirsty and you gave me s to drink,
25:37 or thirsty and gave you s to drink?
Mk 5:43 and told them to give her s to eat.
6:36 the surrounding country and villages and buy s
6:37 But he answered them, "You give them s to eat."
Lk 7:40 "Simon, I have s to say to you."
8:55 Then he directed them to give her s to eat.
9:13 But he said to them, "You give them s to eat."
11:31 and see, s greater than Solomon is here!
11:32 and see, s greater than Jonah is here!
11:54 to catch him in s he might say.
Jn 4:31 the disciples were urging him, "Rabbi, eat s."
4:33 "Surely no one has brought him s to eat?"
13:29 or, that he should give s to the poor.
Ac 3: 5 expecting to receive s from them.
9:18 And immediately s like scales fell from his eyes,
10:10 He became hungry and wanted s to eat;
10:11 the heaven opened and s like a large sheet coming
11: 5 There was s like a large sheet coming down
17:21 in nothing but telling or hearing s new.
21:37 he said to the tribune, "May I say s to you?"
23:17 for he has s to report to him."
23:18 he has s to tell you."
25:11 and have committed s for which I deserve to die,
25:26 I may have s to write—
Ro 2:28 nor is true circumcision s external and physical.
4: 2 he has s to boast about, but not before God.
4: 4 wages are not reckoned as a gift but as s due.
9:10 s similar happened to Rebecca
12:20 if they are thirsty, give them s to drink;
1Co 8: 2 Anyone who claims to know s does not yet have
11: 4 Any man who prays or prophesies with s
2Co 8:10 not only to do s but even to desire to do s—
Gal 6: 3 For if those who are nothing think they are s,
Eph 4:28 so as to have s to share with the needy.
Php 2: 6 not regard equality with God as s to be exploited,
Phm 1:14 good deed might be voluntary and not s forced.
Heb 8: 3 hence it is necessary for this priest also to have s
10:34 knowing that you yourselves possessed s better
11:40 God had provided s better so that they would not,
12:18 You have not come to s that can be touched,
Jas 4: 2 You want s and do not have it;
4: 2 And you covet s and cannot obtain it;
1Pe 4:12 as though s strange were happening to you.
3Jn 1: 9 I have written s to the church;
Rev 4: 6 in front of the throne there is s like a sea of glass,
8: 8 and s like a great mountain, burning with fire,
Tob 5:16 and I will add s to your wages."
10: 6 Probably s unexpected has happened there.
Jdt 8:32 to do s that will go down through all generations
11: 6 God will accomplish s through you,
Wis 2:16 We are considered by him as s base,
Sir Pr: 1 to write s pertaining to instruction and wisdom,
13: 5 If you own s, he will live with you;
19:10 Have you heard s? Let it die with you.
19:11 Having heard s, the fool suffers birth pangs like
34: 4 And from s false what can be true?
2Mc 3:21 There was s pitiable in the prostration of
3Mc 1:17 supposing that s mysterious was occurring.
2Es 13: 3 As I kept looking the wind made s like the figure
13:10 but I saw only how he sent forth from his mouth s
14:39 it was full of s like water,
4Mc 5:10 to me that you will do s even more senseless if,

SOMETIME (1) [SOMETIMES]

Jer 28:12 S after the prophet Hananiah had broken the yoke

SOMETIMES (8) [SOMETIME]

Nu 9:20 S the cloud would remain a few days over
9:21 S the cloud would remain from evening
Pr 16:25 S there is a way that seems to be right,
Ecc 2:21 because s one who has toiled with wisdom
Heb 10:33 s being publicly exposed to abuse and persecution,
10:33 and s being partners with those so treated.
Sir 37:14 our own mind s keeps us better informed than
LtJ 6:10 S the priests secretly take gold and silver

SOMEWHAT (1)

2Co 7:14 For if I have been s boastful about you to him,

SOMEWHERE (1) [WHERE]

Heb 2: 6 But someone has testified s, "What are human

SON‡ (2421) [GRANDSON, GRANDSONS, SON'S, SON-IN-LAW, SONS, SONS', SONS-IN-LAW]

A. MY SON (140)
B. SON OF MAN (85)
C. SON OF *GOD (40)
D. SON OF DAVID (24)
E. SON OF JESSE (21)
F. KING'S SON (14)
G. SON OF AARON (14)
H. ONLY SON (12)
I. BELOVED SON; SON, THE BELOVED (9)
J. GOD'S SON (4)
K. SON OF ABRAHAM (3)

Ge 4:17 and named it Enoch after his s Enoch.
4:25 and she bore a s and named him Seth, for she said,
4:26 To Seth also a s was born,
5: 3 he became the father of a s in his likeness,
5:28 he became the father of a s;
9:24 and knew what his youngest s had done to him,
11:31 Terah took his s Abram and his grandson Lot s of
11:31 and his daughter-in-law Sarai, his s Abram's wife,
12: 5 Abram took his wife Sarai and his brother's s Lot,
14:12 the s of Abram's brother, who lived in Sodom,
16:11 "Now you have conceived and shall bear a s;
16:15 Hagar bore Abram a s;
16:15 Abram named his s, whom Hagar bore, Ishmael.
17:16 and moreover I will give you a s by her.
17:19 "No, but your wife Sarah shall bear you a s,
17:23 Then Abraham took his s Ishmael and all
17:25 And his s Ishmael was thirteen years old
17:26 and his s Ishmael were circumcised;
18:10 and your wife Sarah shall have a s."
18:14 in due season, and Sarah shall have a s."
19:37 The firstborn bore a s, and named him Moab;
19:38 younger also bore a s and named him Ben-ammi;
21: 2 Sarah conceived and bore Abraham a s
21: 3 the name Isaac to his s whom Sarah bore him.
21: 4 And Abraham circumcised his s Isaac
21: 5 a hundred years old when his s Isaac was born
21: 7 Yet I have borne him a s in his old age."
21: 9 But Sarah saw the s of Hagar the Egyptian,
21: 9 to Abraham, playing with her s Isaac.
21:10 "Cast out this slave woman with her s;
21:10 the s of this slave woman shall not inherit along
21:10 not inherit along with my s Isaac." A
21:11 to Abraham on account of his s.
21:13 As for the s of the slave woman,
22: 2 He said, "Take your s, your only son Isaac,
22: 2 He said, "Take your son, your only s Isaac, H
22: 3 of his young men with him, and his s Isaac;
22: 6 of the burnt offering and laid it on his s Isaac,
22: 7 And he said, "Here I am, my s." A
22: 8 the lamb for a burnt offering, my s." A
22: 9 He bound his s Isaac, and laid him on the altar,
22:10 and took the knife to kill his s.
22:12 since you have not withheld your s, your only son,
22:12 you have not withheld your son, your only s, H
22:13 up as a burnt offering instead of his s.
22:16 you have done this, and have not withheld your s,
22:16 and have not withheld your son, your only s, H
23: 8 hear me, and entreat for me Ephron s of Zohar,
24: 3 for my s from the daughters of the Canaanites, A
24: 4 to my kindred and get a wife for my s Isaac." A
24: 5 must I then take your s back to the land
24: 6 "See to it that you do not take my s back there. A
24: 7 and you shall take a wife for my s from there. A
24: 8 only you must not take my s back there." A
24:15 who was born to Bethuel s of Milcah,
24:24 "I am the daughter of Bethuel s of Milcah,
24:36 And Sarah my master's wife bore a s to my master
24:37 for my s from the daughters of the Canaanites, A
24:38 to my kindred, and get a wife for my s.' A
24:40 You shall get a wife for my s from my kindred, A
24:44 the LORD has appointed for my master's s.'
24:47 She said, 'The daughter of Bethuel, Nahor's s,
24:48 the daughter of my master's kinsman for his s.
24:51 and let her be the wife of your master's s,
25: 6 and he sent them away from his s Isaac,
25: 9 in the field of Ephron s of Zohar the Hittite,
25:11 the death of Abraham God blessed his s Isaac.
25:12 Abraham's s, whom Hagar the Egyptian,
25:19 These are the descendants of Isaac, Abraham's s:
27: 1 he called his elder s Esau and said to him,
27: 1 "My s"; and he answered, "Here I am." A
27: 5 when Isaac spoke to his s Esau.
27: 6 Rebekah said to her s Jacob,
27: 8 my s, obey my word as I command you. A
27:13 "Let your curse be on me, my s; A
27:15 the best garments of her elder s Esau, which were
27:15 and put them on her younger s Jacob;
27:17 and the bread that she had prepared, to her s Jacob.
27:18 "Here I am; who are you, my s?" A
27:20 But Isaac said to his s,
27:20 that you have found it so quickly, my s?" A
27:21 "Come near, that I may feel you, my s, A
27:21 know whether you are really my s Esau or not." A
27:24 He said, "Are you really my s Esau?" A
27:26 "Come near and kiss me, my s." A
27:27 Ah, the smell of my s is like the smell of a field A
27:32 He answered, "I am your firstborn s, Esau."
27:37 What then can I do for you, my s?" A
27:42 words of her elder s Esau were told to Rebekah;
27:42 and called her younger s Jacob and said to him,
27:43 Now therefore, my s, obey my voice; A
28: 5 to Laban s of Bethuel the Aramean,
28: 9 of Abraham's s Ishmael, and sister of Nebaioth,
29: 5 "Do you know Laban s of Nahor?"
29:12 and that he was Rebekah's s;
29:13 Laban heard the news about his sister's s Jacob,
29:32 Leah conceived and bore a s,
29:33 She conceived again and bore a s, and said,
29:33 he has given me this s also";
29:34 Again she conceived and bore a s, and said,
29:35 She conceived again and bore a s, and said,
30: 5 And Bilhah conceived and bore Jacob a s.
30: 6 and has also heard my voice and given me a s";
30: 7 and bore Jacob a second s.
30:10 Then Leah's maid Zilpah bore Jacob a s.
30:12 Leah's maid Zilpah bore Jacob a second s.
30:17 and she conceived and bore Jacob a fifth s.
30:19 and she bore Jacob a sixth s.
30:23 She conceived and bore a s, and said,
30:24 saying, "May the LORD add to me another s!"
34: 2 When Shechem s of Hamor the Hivite,

Ge 34: 8 heart of my s Shechem longs for your daughter; A
34:18 words pleased Hamor and Hamor's s Shechem.
34:20 and his s Shechem came to the gate of their city
34:24 of the city gate heeded Hamor and his s Shechem;
34:26 They killed Hamor and his s Shechem with
35:17 for now you will have another s."
36: 2 the Hittite, Oholibamah daughter of Anah s
36:10 Eliphaz s of Adah the wife of Esau;
36:10 Reuel, the s of Esau's wife Basemath.
36:12 (Timna was a concubine of Eliphaz, Esau's s;
36:14 daughter of Anah s of Zibeon:
36:17 These are the sons of Esau's s Reuel:
36:32 Bela s of Beor reigned in Edom,
36:33 Jobab s of Zerah of Bozrah succeeded him as king.
36:35 Husham died, and Hadad s of Bedad,
36:38 Baal-hanan s of Achbor succeeded him as king.
36:39 Baal-hanan s of Achbor died,
37: 3 because he was the s of his old age;
37:34 and mourned for his s many days.
37:35 I shall go down to Sheol to my s, mourning." A
38: 3 She conceived and bore a s;
38: 4 and bore a s whom she named Onan.
38: 5 Yet again she bore a s, and she named him Shelah.
38:11 until my s Shelah grows up"— A
38:26 since I did not give her to my s Shelah." A
42:38 But he said, "My s shall not go down with you, A
43:29 up and saw his brother Benjamin, his mother's s,
43:29 God be gracious to you, my s!" A
45: 9 'Thus says your s Joseph, God has made me lord
45:28 My s Joseph is still alive. A
46:10 Zohar, and Shaul, the s of a Canaanite woman.
47:29 he called his s Joseph and said to him,
48: 2 Jacob was told, "Your s Joseph has come to you,"
48:19 But his father refused, and said, "I know, my s, A
49: 9 from the prey, my s, you have gone up. A
50:23 the children of Machir s of Manasseh were
Ex 2: 2 The woman conceived and bore a s;
2:10 and she took him as her s.
2:22 She bore a s, and he named him Gershom;
4:22 'Thus says the LORD: Israel is my firstborn s.
4:23 "Let my s go that he may worship me." A
4:23 now I will kill your firstborn s.' "
6:15 Zohar, and Shaul, the s of a Canaanite woman;
6:25 Aaron's s Eleazar married one of the daughters
20:10 you, your s or your daughter,
21: 9 If he designates her for his s,
29:30 The s who is priest in his
31: 2 I have called by name Bezalel s of Uri s of Hur,
31: 6 with him Oholiab s of Ahisamach, of the tribe
32:29 each one at the cost of a s or a brother,
33:11 but his young assistant, Joshua s of Nun,
35:30 has called by name Bezalel s of Uri s of Hur,
35:34 both him and Oholiab s of Ahisamach,
38:21 the Levites being under the direction of Ithamar s
38:22 Bezalel s of Uri s of Hur, of the tribe of Judah,
38:23 and with him was Oholiab s of Ahisamach,
Lev 12: 6 whether for a s or for a daughter,
21: 2 his mother, his father, his s, his daughter,
24:10 and the Israelite woman's s and
24:11 The Israelite woman's s blasphemed the Name in
25:49 or their uncle or their uncle's s may redeem them,
Nu 1: 5 From Reuben, Elizur s of Shedeur.
1: 6 From Simeon, Shelumiel s of Zurishaddai.
1: 7 From Judah, Nahshon s of Amminadab.
1: 8 From Issachar, Nethanel s of Zuar.
1: 9 From Zebulun, Eliab s of Helon.
1:10 from Ephraim, Elishama s of Ammihud;
1:10 from Manasseh, Gamaliel s of Pedahzur.
1:11 From Benjamin, Abidan s of Gideoni.
1:12 From Dan, Ahiezer s of Ammishaddai.
1:13 From Asher, Pagiel s of Ochran.
1:14 From Gad, Eliasaph s of Deuel.
1:15 From Naphtali, Ahira s of Enan.
2: 3 of Judah shall be Nahshon s of Amminadab,
2: 5 The leader of the Issacharites shall be Nethanel s
2: 7 leader of the Zebulunites shall be Eliab s of Helon,
2:10 of the Reubenites shall be Elizur s of Shedeur,
2:12 The leader of the Simeonites shall be Shelumiel s
2:14 leader of the Gadites shall be Eliasaph s of Reuel,
2:18 of Ephraim shall be Elishama s of Ammihud,
2:20 of the people of Manasseh shall be Gamaliel s
2:22 of the Benjaminites shall be Abidan s of Gideoni,
2:25 of the Danites shall be Ahiezer s of Ammishaddai,
2:27 leader of the Asherites shall be Pagiel s of Ochran,
2:29 leader of the Naphtalites shall be Ahira s of Enan,
3:24 with Eliasaph s of Lael as head of
3:30 with Elizaphan s of Uzziel as head of
3:32 Eleazar s of Aaron the priest was to be chief G
3:35 of the clans of Merari was Zuriel s of Abihail;
4:16 Eleazar s of Aaron the priest shall have charge G
4:28 to be under the oversight of Ithamar s of Aaron G
4:33 under the hand of Ithamar s of Aaron the priest. G
7: 8 the direction of Ithamar s of Aaron the priest. G
7:12 the first day was Nahshon s of Amminadab,
7:17 the offering of Nahshon s of Amminadab.
7:18 On the second day Nethanel s of Zuar,
7:23 This was the offering of Nethanel s of Zuar.
7:24 On the third day Eliab s of Helon,
7:29 This was the offering of Eliab s of Helon.
7:30 On the fourth day Elizur s of Shedeur,
7:35 This was the offering of Elizur s of Shedeur.
7:36 On the fifth day Shelumiel s of Zurishaddai,
7:41 the offering of Shelumiel s of Zurishaddai.
7:42 On the sixth day Eliasaph s of Deuel,
7:47 This was the offering of Eliasaph s of Deuel.
7:48 On the seventh day Elishama s of Ammihud,
7:53 This was the offering of Elishama s of Ammihud.

Nu 7:54 On the eighth day Gamaliel s of Pedahzur,
7:59 This was the offering of Gamaliel s of Pedahzur.
7:60 On the ninth day Abidan s of Gideoni,
7:65 This was the offering of Abidan s of Gideoni.
7:66 On the tenth day Ahiezer s of Ammishaddai,
7:71 the offering of Ahiezer s of Ammishaddai.
7:72 On the eleventh day Pagiel s of Ochran,
7:77 This was the offering of Pagiel s of Ochran.
7:78 On the twelfth day Ahira s of Enan,
7:83 This was the offering of Ahira s of Enan.
10:14 and over the whole company was Nahshon s
10:15 of the tribe of Issachar was Nethanel s of Zuar;
10:16 the company of the tribe of Zebulun was Eliab s
10:18 over the whole company was Elizur s of Shedeur.
10:19 of Simeon was Shelumiel s of Zurishaddai,
10:20 the company of the tribe of Gad was Eliasaph s
10:22 the whole company was Elishama s of Ammihud.
10:23 the tribe of Manasseh was Gamaliel s of Pedahzur,
10:24 of the tribe of Benjamin was Abidan s of Gideoni.
10:25 and over the whole company was Ahiezer s of
10:26 the company of the tribe of Asher was Pagiel s of
10:27 the company of the tribe of Naphtali was Ahira s of
10:29 Moses said to Hobab s of Reuel the Midianite,
11:28 And Joshua s of Nun, the assistant of Moses,
13: 4 From the tribe of Reuben, Shammua s of Zaccur;
13: 5 from the tribe of Simeon, Shaphat s of Hori;
13: 6 from the tribe of Judah, Caleb s of Jephunneh;
13: 7 from the tribe of Issachar, Igal s of Joseph;
13: 8 from the tribe of Ephraim, Hoshea s of Nun;
13: 9 from the tribe of Benjamin, Palti s of Raphu;
13:10 from the tribe of Zebulun, Gaddiel s of Sodi;
13:11 from the tribe of Manasseh), Gaddi s of Susi;
13:12 from the tribe of Dan, Ammiel s of Gemalli;
13:13 from the tribe of Asher, Sethur s of Michael;
13:14 from the tribe of Naphtali, Nahbi s of Vophsi;
13:15 from the tribe of Gad, Geuel s of Machi.
13:16 And Moses changed the name of Hoshea s of Nun
14: 6 And Joshua s of Nun and Caleb s of Jephunneh,
14:30 except Caleb s of Jephunneh and Joshua s of Nun.
14:38 But Joshua s of Nun and Caleb s of Jephunneh
16: 1 Now Korah s of Izhar s of Kohath s of Levi,
16: 1 Dathan and Abiram sons of Eliab, and On s of
16:37 Tell Eleazar s of Aaron the priest to take G
20:25 Take Aaron and his s Eleazar,
20:26 and put them on his s Eleazar.
20:28 and put them on his s Eleazar;
22: 2 Now Balak s of Zippor saw all that Israel had done
22: 4 Balak s of Zippor was king of Moab at that time.
22: 5 He sent messengers to Balaam s of Beor at Pethor,
22:10 "King Balak s of Zippor of Moab,
22:16 "Thus says Balak s of Zippor:
23:18 listen to me, O s of Zippor:
24: 3 "The oracle of Balaam s of Beor,
24:15 "The oracle of Balaam s of Beor,
25: 7 When Phinehas s of Eleazar,
25: 7 Phinehas son of Eleazar, s of Aaron the priest, G
25:11 "Phinehas s of Eleazar, son of Aaron the priest,
25:11 s of Aaron the priest, has turned back my wrath G
25:14 with the Midianite woman, was Zimri s of Salu,
26: 1 to Moses and to Eleazar s of Aaron the priest, G
26:33 Now Zelophehad s of Hepher had no sons,
26:65 except Caleb s of Jephunneh and Joshua s of Nun.
27: 1 Zelophehad was s of Hepher s of Gilead s of
Machir s of Manasseh s of Joseph,
27: 4 be taken away from his clan because he had no s?
27: 8 "If a man dies, and has no s,
27:18 the LORD said to Moses, "Take Joshua s of Nun,
31: 6 along with Phinehas s of Eleazar the priest,
31: 8 they also killed Balaam s of Beor with the sword.
32:12 none except Caleb s of Jephunneh the Kenizzite
32:12 of Jephunneh the Kenizzite and Joshua s of Nun,
32:28 concerning them to Eleazar the priest, to Joshua s
32:33 the Reubenites and to the half-tribe of Manasseh s
32:39 The descendants of Machir s of Manasseh went
32:40 so Moses gave Gilead to Machir s of Manasseh,
32:41 Jair s of Manasseh went and captured
34:17 the priest Eleazar and Joshua s of Nun.
34:19 Of the tribe of Judah, Caleb s of Jephunneh.
34:20 of the Simeonites, Shemuel s of Ammihud.
34:21 Of the tribe of Benjamin, Elidad s of Chislon.
34:22 the tribe of the Danites a leader, Bukki s of Jogli.
34:23 of the tribe of the Manassites a leader, Hanniel s of
34:24 of the Ephraimites a leader, Kemuel s of Shiphtan.
34:25 the Zebulunites a leader, Eli-zaphan s of Parnach.
34:26 Of the tribe of the Issacharites a leader, Paltiel s of
34:27 of the Asherites a leader, Ahihud s of Shelomi.
34:28 Of the tribe of the Naphtalites a leader, Pedahel s
36: 1 of the descendants of Gilead s of Machir s of
36:12 into the clans of the descendants of Manasseh s of
Dt 1:36 except Caleb s of Jephunneh.
1:38 Joshua s of Nun, your assistant, shall enter there;
5:14 you, or your s or your daughter,
10: 6 his s Eleazar succeeded him as priest.
11: 6 sons of Eliab s of Reuben,
12:18 you together with your s and your daughter,
13: 6 your father's s or your mother's s, or your own s or
18:10 No one shall be found among you who makes a s
21:15 the firstborn being the s of the one who is disliked,
21:16 to treat the s of the loved as the firstborn in
preference to the s of the disliked,
21:17 as firstborn the s of the one who is disliked,
21:18 and rebellious s who will not obey his father
21:20 "This s of ours is stubborn and rebellious.
23: 4 because they hired against you Balaam s of Beor,
25: 5 and one of them dies and has no s,
28:56 to her own s, and to her own daughter,
31:23 LORD commissioned Joshua s of Nun and said,

Dt 32:44 he and Joshua s of Nun.
34: 9 Joshua s of Nun was full of the spirit of wisdom,
Jos 1: 1 the LORD spoke to Joshua s of Nun,
2: 1 Then Joshua s of Nun sent two men secretly
2:23 They crossed over, came to Joshua s of Nun,
6: 6 So Joshua s of Nun summoned the priests and said
7: 1 Achan s of Carmi s of Zabdi s of Zerah,
7:18 and Achan s of Carmi s of Zabdi s of Zerah,
7:19 Then Joshua said to Achan, "My s, A
7:24 Then Joshua and all Israel with him took Achan s
13:22 Israelites also put to the sword Balaam s of Beor,
13:31 to the people of Machir s of Manasseh according
14: 1 which the priest Eleazar, and Joshua s of Nun,
14: 6 Caleb s of Jephunneh the Kenizzite said to him,
14:13 and gave Hebron to Caleb s of Jephunneh for
14:14 of Caleb s of Jephunneh the Kenizzite to this day,
15: 6 up to the Stone of Bohan, Reuben's s;
15: 8 the valley of the s of Hinnom at the southern slope
15:13 he gave to Caleb s of Jephunneh a portion among
15:17 Othniel s of Kenaz, the brother of Caleb, took it;
17: 2 these were the male descendants of Manasseh s
17: 3 Zelophehad s of Hepher s of Gilead s of Machir s
17: 4 before the priest Eleazar and Joshua s of Nun and
18:16 of the mountain that overlooks the valley of the s
18:17 it goes down to the Stone of Bohan, Reuben's s;
19:49 an inheritance among them to Joshua s of Nun.
19:51 and Joshua s of Nun and the heads of the families
21: 1 to Joshua s of Nun and to the heads of the families
21:12 town and its villages had been given to Caleb s of
22:13 the priest Phinehas s of Eleazar to the Reubenites
22:20 Did not Achan s of Zerah break faith in the matter
22:31 The priest Phinehas s of Eleazar said to
22:32 Then the priest Phinehas s of Eleazar and
24: 9 Then King Balak s of Zippor of Moab,
24: 9 He sent and invited Balaam s of Beor to curse you,
24:29 After these things Joshua s of Nun, died,
24:33 Eleazar s of Aaron died; G
24:33 the town of his s Phinehas,
Jdg 1:13 And Othniel s of Kenaz, Caleb's younger brother,
2: 8 Joshua s of Nun, the servant of the LORD, died
3: 9 Othniel s of Kenaz, Caleb's younger brother.
3:11 Then Othniel s of Kenaz died.
3:15 Ehud s of Gera, the Benjaminite,
3:31 After him came Shamgar s of Anath,
4: 6 and summoned Barak s of Abinoam from Kedesh
4:12 that Barak s of Abinoam had gone up
5: 1 and Barak s of Abinoam sang on that day, saying:
5: 6 "In the days of Shamgar s of Anath,
5:12 Barak, lead away your captives, O s of Abinoam.
6:11 as his s Gideon was beating out wheat in
6:29 they were told, "Gideon s of Joash did it."
6:30 the townspeople said to Joash, "Bring out your s,
7:14 the sword of Gideon s of Joash, a man of Israel;
8:13 When Gideon s of Joash returned from the battle
8:22 you and your s and your grandson also;
8:23 and my s will not rule over you; A
8:29 Jerubbaal s of Joash went to live in his own house.
8:31 in Shechem also bore him a s,
8:32 Then Gideon s of Joash died at a good old age,
9: 1 Now Abimelech s of Jerubbaal went to Shechem
9: 5 but Jotham, the youngest s of Jerubbaal, survived,
9:18 the s of his slave woman, king over the lords
9:26 When Gaal s of Ebed moved into Shechem
9:28 Gaal s of Ebed said, "Who is Abimelech,
9:28 not the s of Jerubbaal and Zebul his officer serve
9:30 of the city heard the words of Gaal s of Ebed,
9:31 Gaal s of Ebed and his kinsfolk have come
9:35 When Gaal s of Ebed went out and stood in
9:57 on them came the curse of Jotham s of Jerubbaal.
10: 1 After Abimelech, Tola s of Puah s of Dodo,
11: 1 Now Jephthah the Gileadite, the s of a prostitute,
11: 2 for you are the s of another woman."
11:25 Now are you any better than King Balak s
11:34 he had no s or daughter except her.
12:13 After him Abdon s of Hillel
12:15 Then Abdon s of Hillel the Pirathonite died,
13: 3 you shall conceive and bear a s.
13: 5 for you shall conceive and bear a s.
13: 7 'You shall conceive and bear a s.
13:24 The woman bore a s, and named him Samson.
17: 2 "May my s be blessed by the LORD!" A
17: 3 the silver to the LORD from my hand for my s, A
18:30 Jonathan s of Gershom, s of Moses,
20:28 and Phinehas s of Eleazar,
20:28 s of Aaron, ministered before it in those days), G
Ru 4:13 the LORD made her conceive, and she bore a s.
4:17 saying, "A s has been born to Naomi."
1Sa 1: 1 Elkanah s of Jeroham s of Elihu s of Tohu s of
1:20 In due time Hannah conceived and bore a s.
1:23 So the woman remained and nursed her s,
3: 6 he said, "I did not call, my s; lie down again." A
3:16 But Eli called Samuel and said, "Samuel, my s." A
4:16 He said, "How did it go, my s?" A
4:20 "Do not be afraid, for you have borne a s."
7: 1 They consecrated his s, Eleazar,
8: 2 The name of his firstborn s was Joel,
9: 1 Kish s of Abiel s of Zeror s of Becorath s of
9: 2 He had a s whose name was Saul,
9: 3 So Kish said to his s Saul,
10: 2 What shall I do about my s?' A
10:11 "What has come over the s of Kish?
10:21 and Saul the s of Kish was taken by lot.
13:16 his s Jonathan, and the people who were present
13:22 but Saul and his s Jonathan had them.
14: 1 One day Jonathan s of Saul said to
14: 3 along with Ahijah s of Ahitub,
14: 3 Ichabod's brother, s of Phinehas s of Eli,

1Sa 14:39 if it is in my s Jonathan, he shall surely die!" A
14:40 I and my s Jonathan will be on the other side." A
14:41 If this guilt is in me or in my s Jonathan, A
14:42 "Cast the lot between me and my s Jonathan." A
14:50 the commander of his army was Abner s of Ner,
14:51 and Ner the father of Abner was the s of Abiel.
16:18 a s of Jesse the Bethlehemite who is skillful E
16:19 "Send me your s David who is with the sheep."
16:20 and a kid, and sent them by his s David to Saul.
17:12 the s of an Ephrathite of Bethlehem in Judah,
17:17 Jesse said to his s David, "Take for your brothers
17:55 "Abner, whose s is this young man?"
17:56 The king said, "Inquire whose s the stripling is."
17:58 Saul said to him, "Whose s are you, young man?"
17:58 the s of your servant Jesse the Bethlehemite."
19: 1 with his s Jonathan and with all his servants
19: 1 But Saul's s Jonathan took great delight in David.
20:27 And Saul said to his s Jonathan,
20:27 "Why has the s of Jesse not come to the feast, E
20:30 He said to him, "You s of a perverse,
20:30 I not know that you have chosen the s of Jesse E
20:31 For as long as the s of Jesse lives upon the earth, E
22: 7 will the s of Jesse give every one of you fields E
22: 8 one discloses to me when my s makes a league A
22: 8 when my son makes a league with the s of Jesse, E
22: 8 that my s has stirred up my servant against me, A
22: 9 answered, "I saw the s of Jesse coming to Nob, E
22: 9 to Ahimelech s of Ahitub;
22:11 The king sent for the priest Ahimelech s of Ahitub
22:12 Saul said, "Listen now, s of Ahitub."
22:13 you and the s of Jesse, E
22:20 But one of the sons of Ahimelech s of Ahitub,
23: 6 Abiathar s of Ahimelech fled to David at Keilah,
23:16 Saul's s Jonathan set out and came to David
24:16 Saul said, "Is this your voice, my s David?" A
25: 8 at hand to your servants and to your s David.' "
25:10 Who is the s of Jesse? E
25:44 to Palti s of Laish, who was from Gallim.
26: 5 with Abner s of Ner, the commander of his army.
26: 6 and to Joab's brother Abishai s of Zeruiah,
26:14 David called to the army and to Abner s of Ner,
26:17 and said, "Is this your voice, my s David?" A
26:21 my s David, for I will never harm you again, A
26:25 said to David, "Blessed be you, my s David! A
27: 2 to King Achish s of Maoch of Gath.
30: 7 David said to the priest Abiathar s of Ahimelech,
2Sa 1: 4 and Saul and his s Jonathan also died."
1: 5 do you know that Saul and his s Jonathan died?"
1:12 until evening for Saul and for his s Jonathan,
1:13 He answered, "I am the s of a resident alien,
1:17 over Saul and his s Jonathan.
2: 8 But Abner s of Ner, commander of Saul's army,
2: 8 had taken Ishbaal s of Saul,
2:10 Saul's s, was forty years old when he began to
2:12 Abner s of Ner, and the servants of Ishbaal s of
2:13 Joab s of Zeruiah, and the servants of David,
2:15 twelve for Benjamin and Ishbaal s of Saul,
3: 3 the third, Absalom s of Maacah,
3: 4 the fourth, Adonijah s of Haggith; the fifth,
Shephatiah s of Abital;
3:14 Then David sent messengers to Saul's s Ishbaal,
3:15 and took her from her husband Paltiel the s
3:23 it was told Joab, "Abner s of Ner came to the king,
3:25 that Abner s of Ner came to deceive you,
3:28 before the LORD for the blood of Abner s of Ner.
3:37 that the king had no part in the killing of Abner s
4: 1 When Saul's s Ishbaal heard that Abner had died
4: 2 Saul's s had two captains of raiding bands;
4: 4 Saul's s Jonathan had a s who was crippled
4: 8 Ishbaal, s of Saul, your enemy, who sought your
7:14 I will be a father to him, and he shall be a s to me.
8: 3 also struck down King Hadadezer s of Rehob
8:10 Toi sent his s Joram to King David,
8:12 the spoil of King Hadadezer s of Rehob of Zobah.
8:16 Joab s of Zeruiah was over the army; Jehoshaphat
s of Ahilud was recorder;
8:17 Zadok s of Ahitub and Ahimelech s of Abiathar
8:18 Benaiah s of Jehoiada was over the Cherethites
9: 3 "There remains a s of Jonathan;
9: 4 "He is in the house of Machir s of Ammiel,
9: 5 and brought him from the house of Machir s of
9: 6 Mephibosheth s of Jonathan s of Saul came
9:12 a young s whose name was Mica.
10: 1 and his s Hanun succeeded him.
10: 2 "I will deal loyally with Hanun s of Nahash,
11:21 Who killed Abimelech s of Jerubbaal?
11:27 and she became his wife, and bore him a s.
12:24 and she bore a s, and he named him Solomon.
13: 1 David's s Absalom had a beautiful sister
13: 1 and David's s Amnon fell in love with her.
13: 3 the s of David's brother Shimeah;
13: 4 He said to him, "O s of the king,
13:21 but he would not punish his s Amnon,
13:25 But the king said to Absalom, "No, my s, A
13:32 But Jonadab, the s of David's brother Shimeah,
13:37 Absalom fled, and went to Talmai s of Ammihud,
13:37 David mourned for his s day after day.
14: 1 Now Joab s of Zeruiah perceived that
14:11 and my s not be destroyed." A
14:11 not one hair of your s shall fall to the ground."
14:16 the man who would cut both me and my s off A
15:27 Ahimaaz your s, and Jonathan s of Abiathar.
15:36 Zadok's s Ahimaaz and Abiathar's s Jonathan;
16: 3 The king said, "And where is your master's s?"
16: 5 of Saul came out whose name was Shimei s
16: 8 the kingdom into the hand of your s Absalom.
16: 9 Then Abishai s of Zeruiah said to the king,

2Sa 16:11 "My own s seeks my life;
16:19 Should it not be his s?
17:25 the s of a man named Ithra the Ishmaelite,
17:27 Shobi s of Nahash from Rabbah of the
Ammonites, and Machir s of Ammiel
18: 2 one third under the command of Abishai s of
18:12 I would not raise my hand against the king's s; F
18:18 "I have no s to keep my name in remembrance";
18:19 Then Ahimaaz s of Zadok said, "Let me run,
18:20 because the king's s is dead." F
18:22 Then Ahimaaz s of Zadok said again to Joab,
18:22 And Joab said, "Why will you run, my s, A
18:27 of the first one is like the running of Ahimaaz s
18:33 and as he went, he said, "O my s Absalom, A
18:33 as he went, he said, "O my son Absalom, my s, A
18:33 "O my son Absalom, my son, my s Absalom! A
18:33 O Absalom, my s, my son!" A
18:33 O Absalom, my son, my s!" A
19: 2 "The king is grieving for his s."
19: 4 my s Absalom, O Absalom, my son, my son!" A
19: 4 my son Absalom, O Absalom, my s, my son!" A
19: 4 my son Absalom, O Absalom, my son, my s!" A
19:16 Shimei s of Gera, the Benjaminite, from Bahurim,
19:18 Shimei s of Gera fell down before the king,
19:21 Abishai s of Zeruiah answered,
20: 1 Now a scoundrel named Sheba s of Bichri,
20: 1 no share in the s of Jesse! E
20: 2 from David and followed Sheba s of Bichri;
20: 6 to Abishai, "Now Sheba s of Bichri will do us
20: 7 they went out from Jerusalem to pursue Sheba s of
20:10 and his brother Abishai pursued Sheba s of Bichri.
20:13 all the people went on after Joab to pursue Sheba s
20:21 called Sheba s of Bichri, has lifted up his hand
20:22 And they cut off the head of Sheba s of Bichri,
20:23 Benaiah s of Jehoiada was in command of
20:24 Jehoshaphat s of Ahilud was the recorder;
21: 7 spared Mephibosheth, the s of Saul's s Jonathan,
21: 7 between David and Jonathan s of Saul.
21: 8 of Saul, whom she bore to Adriel s of Barzillai
21:12 of his s Jonathan from the people of Jabesh-gilead,
21:13 the bones of Saul and the bones of his s Jonathan;
21:14 the bones of Saul and of his s Jonathan in the land
21:17 But Abishai s of Zeruiah came to his aid,
21:19 and Elhanan s of Jaare-oregim, the Bethlehemite,
21:21 Jonathan s of David's brother Shimei, killed him.
23: 1 The oracle of David, s of Jesse, E
23: 9 among the three warriors was Eleazar s of Dodo s
23:11 Next to him was Shammah s of Agee, the Hararite.
23:18 Now Abishai s of Zeruiah, the brother of Joab,
23:20 Benaiah s of Jehoiada was a valiant warrior
23:22 Such were the things Benaiah s of Jehoiada did,
23:24 Elhanan s of Dodo of Bethlehem;
23:26 Helez the Paltite; Ira s of Ikkesh of Tekoa;
23:29 Heleb s of Baanah of Netophah; Ittai s of Ribai of
23:33 s of Shammah the Hararite; Ahiam s of Sharar the
23:34 Eliphelet s of Ahasbai of Maacah; Eliam s of
23:36 Igal s of Nathan of Zobah; Bani the Gadite;
23:37 the armor-bearer of Joab s of Zeruiah,
1Ki 1: 5 Now Adonijah s of Haggith exalted himself,
1: 7 He conferred with Joab s of Zeruiah and with
1: 8 But the priest Zadok, and Benaiah s of Jehoiada,
1:11 that Adonijah s of Haggith has become king
1:12 and the life of your s Solomon.
1:13 Your s Solomon shall succeed me as king,
1:17 Your s Solomon shall succeed me as king,
1:21 my s Solomon and I will be counted offenders." A
1:26 and the priest Zadok, and Benaiah s of Jehoiada,
1:30 'Your s Solomon shall succeed me as king,
1:32 the prophet Nathan, and Benaiah s of Jehoiada."
1:33 and have my s Solomon ride on my own mule, A
1:36 Benaiah s of Jehoiada answered the king, "Amen!
1:38 the prophet Nathan, and Benaiah s of Jehoiada,
1:42 Jonathan s of the priest Abiathar arrived.
1:44 the prophet Nathan, and Benaiah s of Jehoiada,
2: 1 he charged his s Solomon, saying:
2: 5 you know also what Joab s of Zeruiah did to me,
2: 5 Abner s of Ner, and Amasa s of Jether, whom he
2: 8 There is also with you Shimei s of Gera,
2:13 Then Adonijah s of Haggith came to Bathsheba,
2:22 for the priest Abiathar and for Joab s of Zeruiah!"
2:25 So King Solomon sent Benaiah s of Jehoiada;
2:29 Solomon sent Benaiah s of Jehoiada, saying, "Go,
2:32 Abner s of Ner, commander of the army of Israel,
2:32 of Israel, and Amasa s of Jether, commander of
2:34 Then Benaiah s of Jehoiada went up
2:35 The king put Benaiah s of Jehoiada over the army
2:39 of Shimei's slaves ran away to King Achish s of
2:46 Then the king commanded Benaiah s of Jehoiada;
3: 6 and have given him a s to sit on his throne today.
3:19 Then this woman's s died in the night,
3:20 in the middle of the night and took my s from A
3:20 and laid her dead s at my breast.
3:21 When I rose in the morning to nurse my s, A
3:21 clearly it was not the s I had borne."
3:22 "No, the living s is mine, and the dead s is yours."
3:22 "No, the dead s is yours, and the living s is mine."
3:23 'This is my s that is alive, and your son is dead'; A
3:23 and your s is dead'; while the other says, 'Not so!
3:23 Your s is dead, and my son is the living one.' "
3:23 Your son is dead, and my s is the living one.' " A
3:26 the woman whose s was alive said to the king—
3:26 because compassion for her s burned within her—
4: 2 Azariah s of Zadok was the priest;
4: 3 Jehoshaphat s of Ahilud was recorder;
4: 4 Benaiah s of Jehoiada was in command of
4: 5 Azariah s of Nathan was over the officials;
4: 5 Zabud s of Nathan was priest and king's friend;

1Ki 4: 6 and Adoniram s of Abda was in charge of
4:12 Baana s of Ahilud, in Taanach, Megiddo,
4:13 in Ramoth-gilead (he had the villages of Jair s of
4:14 Ahinadab s of Iddo, in Mahanaim;
4:16 Baana s of Hushai, in Asher and Bealoth;
4:17 Jehoshaphat s of Paruah, in Issachar;
4:18 Shimei s of Ela, in Benjamin;
4:19 Geber s of Uri, in the land of Gilead, the country
5: 5 as the LORD said to my father David, 'Your s,
5: 7 to David a wise s to be over this great people."
7:14 He was the s of a widow of the tribe of Naphtali,
8:19 but your s who shall be born to you shall build
11:12 I will tear it out of the hand of your s.
11:13 I will give one tribe to your s,
11:20 by him to his s Genubath, whom Tahpenes weaned
11:23 Rezon s of Eliada, who had fled from his master,
11:26 Jeroboam s of Nebat, an Ephraimite of Zeredah,
11:35 the kingdom away from his s and give it to you—
11:36 Yet to his s I will give one tribe,
11:43 and his s Rehoboam succeeded him.
12: 2 When Jeroboam s of Nebat heard of it
12:15 by Ahijah the Shilonite to Jeroboam s of Nebat.
12:16 We have no inheritance in the s of Jesse. E
12:21 the kingdom to Rehoboam s of Solomon.
12:23 to King Rehoboam of Judah, s of Solomon,
13: 2 'A s shall be born to the house of David,
14: 1 At that time Abijah s of Jeroboam fell sick.
14: 5 to inquire of you concerning her s;
14:20 and his s Nadab succeeded him.
14:21 Now Rehoboam s of Solomon reigned in Judah.
14:31 His s Abijam succeeded him.
15: 1 the eighteenth year of King Jeroboam s of Nebat,
15: 4 up his s after him, and establishing Jerusalem;
15: 8 Then his s Asa succeeded him.
15:18 to King Ben-hadad s of Tabrimmon s of Hezion
15:24 his s Jehoshaphat succeeded him.
15:25 Nadab s of Jeroboam began to reign over Israel in
15:27 Baasha s of Ahijah, of the house of Issachar,
15:33 Baasha s of Ahijah began to reign over all Israel
16: 1 The word of the LORD came to Jehu s of Hanani
16: 3 like the house of Jeroboam s of Nebat.
16: 6 and his s Elah succeeded him.
16: 7 the LORD came by the prophet Jehu s of Hanani
16: 8 Elah s of Baasha began to reign over Israel
16:13 of all the sins of Baasha and the sins of his s Elah
16:21 half of the people followed Tibni s of Ginath,
16:22 the people who followed Tibni s of Ginath;
16:26 he walked in all the way of Jeroboam s of Nebat,
16:28 his s Ahab succeeded him.
16:29 Ahab s of Omri began to reign over Israel;
16:29 Ahab s of Omri reigned over Israel
16:30 Ahab s of Omri did evil in the sight of the LORD
16:31 for him to walk in the sins of Jeroboam s of Nebat,
16:34 set up its gates at the cost of his youngest s Segub,
16:34 which he spoke by Joshua s of Nun.
17:12 go home and prepare it for myself and my s, A
17:13 make something for yourself and your s.
17:17 After this the s of the woman,
17:18 and to cause the death of my s!" A
17:19 But he said to her, "Give me your s."
17:20 with whom I am staying, by killing her s?"
17:23 then Elijah said, "See, your s is alive."
19:16 Also you shall anoint Jehu s of Nimshi as king
19:16 and you shall anoint Elisha s of Shaphat
19:19 and found Elisha s of Shaphat, who was plowing.
21:22 like the house of Jeroboam s of Nebat,
21:22 and like the house of Baasha s of Ahijah,
22: 8 inquire of the LORD, Micaiah s of Imlah;
22: 9 "Bring quickly Micaiah s of Imlah."
22:11 Zedekiah s of Chenaanah made for himself horns
22:24 Zedekiah s of Chenaanah came up to Micaiah,
22:26 governor of the city and to Joash the king's s, F
22:40 and his s Ahaziah succeeded him.
22:41 Jehoshaphat s of Asa began to reign over Judah in
22:49 Then Ahaziah s of Ahab said to Jehoshaphat,
22:50 his s Jehoram succeeded him.
22:51 Ahaziah s of Ahab began to reign over Israel
22:52 and in the way of Jeroboam s of Nebat,
2Ki 1:17 the second year of King Jehoram s of Jehoshaphat
1:17 because Ahaziah had no s.
3: 1 Jehoram s of Ahab became king over Israel
3: 3 he clung to the sin of Jeroboam s of Nebat,
3:11 of Israel answered, "Elisha s of Shaphat, who used
3:27 he took his firstborn s who was to succeed him,
4: 6 When the vessels were full, she said to her s,
4:14 Gehazi answered, "Well, she has no s,
4:16 in due time, you shall embrace a s."
4:17 The woman conceived and bore a s at that season,
4:28 Then she said, "Did I ask my lord for a s?
4:36 When she came to him, he said, "Take your s."
4:37 then she took her s and left.
6:28 "This woman said to me, 'Give up your s;
6:28 and we will eat my s tomorrow.' A
6:29 So we cooked my s and ate him. A
6:29 'Give up your s and we will eat him.'
6:29 But she has hidden her s."
6:31 if the head of Elisha s of Shaphat stays
8: 1 to the woman whose s he had restored to life,
8: 5 the woman whose s he had restored
8: 5 and here is her s whom Elisha restored to life."
8: 9 "Your s King Ben-hadad of Aram has sent me
8:16 In the fifth year of King Joram s of Ahab of Israel,
8:16 Jehoram s of King Jehoshaphat of Judah began
8:24 his s Ahaziah succeeded him.
8:25 the twelfth year of King Joram s of Ahab of Israel,
8:25 Ahaziah s of King Jehoram of Judah began
8:28 He went with Joram s of Ahab to wage war

2Ki 8:29 King Ahaziah s of Jehoram of Judah went down
8:29 of Jehoram of Judah went down to see Joram s
9: 2 look there for Jehu s of Jehoshaphat, s of Nimshi;
9: 9 the house of Ahab like the house of Jeroboam s of
9: 9 and like the house of Baasha s of Ahijah.
9:14 Thus Jehu s of Jehoshaphat s of Nimshi conspired
9:20 It looks like the driving of Jehu s of Nimshi;
9:29 In the eleventh year of Joram s of Ahab,
10: 3 the s of your master who is the best qualified,
10:15 he met Jehonadab s of Rechab coming
10:23 the temple of Baal with Jehonadab s of Rechab;
10:29 of Jeroboam s of Nebat, which he caused Israel
10:35 His s Jehoahaz succeeded him.
11: 1 Ahaziah's mother, saw that her s was dead,
11: 2 Ahaziah's sister, took Joash s of Ahaziah,
11: 4 then he showed them the king's s. F
11:12 Then he brought out the king's s, F
12:21 It was Jozacar s of Shimeath and Jehozabad s of
12:21 then his s Amaziah succeeded him.
13: 1 King Joash s of Ahaziah of Judah, Jehoahaz s of
13: 2 and followed the sins of Jeroboam s of Nebat,
13: 3 then into the hand of Ben-hadad s of Hazael.
13: 9 then his s Joash succeeded him.
13:10 Jehoash s of Jehoahaz began to reign over Israel
13:11 he did not depart from all the sins of Jeroboam s
13:24 his s Ben-hadad succeeded him.
13:25 Then Jehoash s of Jehoahaz took again from
Ben-hadad s of Hazael
14: 1 In the second year of King Joash s of Joahaz
14: 1 King Amaziah s of Joash of Judah, began to reign.
14: 8 King Jehoash s of Jehoahaz, s of Jehu, of Israel,
14: 9 saying, 'Give your daughter to my s for a wife'; A
14:13 King Amaziah of Judah s of Jehoash, s of Ahaziah,
14:16 then his s Jeroboam succeeded him.
14:17 King Amaziah s of Joash of Judah lived fifteen
14:17 the death of King Jehoash s of Jehoahaz of Israel.
14:23 In the fifteenth year of King Amaziah s of Joash
14:23 King Jeroboam s of Joash of Israel began to reign
14:24 he did not depart from all the sins of Jeroboam s of
14:25 which he spoke by his servant Jonah s of Amittai,
14:27 he saved them by the hand of Jeroboam s of Joash.
14:29 his s Zechariah succeeded him.
15: 1 of King Jeroboam of Israel King Azariah s of
15: 5 Jotham the king's s was in charge of the palace, F
15: 7 his s Jotham succeeded him.
15: 8 Zechariah s of Jeroboam reigned over Israel
15: 9 not depart from the sins of Jeroboam s of Nebat,
15:10 Shallum s of Jabesh conspired against him,
15:13 Shallum s of Jabesh began to reign in
15:14 Then Menahem s of Gadi came up from Tirzah
15:14 he struck down Shallum s of Jabesh in Samaria
15:17 Menahem s of Gadi began to reign over Israel;
15:18 from any of the sins of Jeroboam s of Nebat,
15:22 and his s Pekahiah succeeded him.
15:23 Pekahiah s of Menahem began to reign over Israel
15:24 he did not turn away from the sins of Jeroboam s
15:25 Pekah s of Remaliah, his captain,
15:27 Pekah s of Remaliah began to reign over Israel
15:28 not depart from the sins of Jeroboam s of Nebat,
15:30 Then Hoshea s of Elah made a conspiracy
15:30 against Pekah s of Remaliah, attacked him,
15:30 in the twentieth year of Jotham s of Uzziah.
15:32 In the second year of King Pekah s of Remaliah
15:32 King Jotham s of Uzziah of Judah began to reign.
15:37 of Aram and Pekah s of Remaliah against Judah.
15:38 his s Ahaz succeeded him.
16: 1 In the seventeenth year of Pekah s of Remaliah,
King Ahaz s of Jotham of Judah began to reign.
16: 3 He even made his s pass through fire,
16: 5 and King Pekah s of Remaliah of Israel came up
16: 7 saying, "I am your servant and your s.
16:20 his s Hezekiah succeeded him.
17: 1 Hoshea s of Elah began to reign in Samaria
17:21 they made Jeroboam s of Nebat king.
18: 1 the third year of King Hoshea s of Elah of Israel,
18: 1 Hezekiah s of King Ahaz of Judah began to reign.
18: 9 which was the seventh year of King Hoshea s of
18:18 there came out to them Eliakim s of Hilkiah,
18:18 and Shebnah the secretary, and Joah s of Asaph,
18:26 Then Eliakim s of Hilkiah, and Shebnah,
18:37 Then Eliakim s of Hilkiah,
18:37 and Shebna the secretary, and Joah s of Asaph,
19: 2 to the prophet Isaiah s of Amoz.
19:20 Then Isaiah s of Amoz sent to Hezekiah, saying,
19:37 His s Esar-haddon succeeded him.
20: 1 The prophet Isaiah s of Amoz came to him,
20:12 At that time King Merodach-baladan s of Baladan
20:21 and his s Manasseh succeeded him.
21: 6 He made his s pass through fire;
21: 7 to David and to his s Solomon, "In this house,
21:18 His s Amon succeeded him.
21:24 of the land made his s Josiah king in place of him.
21:26 then his s Josiah succeeded him.
22: 3 king sent Shaphan s of Azaliah, s of Meshullam,
22:12 Ahikam s of Shaphan, Achbor s of Micaiah,
22:14 wife of Shallum s of Tikvah, s of Harhas,
23:10 so that no one would make a s or a daughter pass
23:15 the high place erected by Jeroboam s of Nebat,
23:30 The people of the land took Jehoahaz s of Josiah,
23:34 Pharaoh Neco made Eliakim s of Josiah king
24: 6 then his s Jehoiachin succeeded him.
25:22 He appointed Gedaliah s of Ahikam s of Shaphan
25:23 Ishmael s of Nethaniah, Johanan s of Kareah,
Seraiah s of Tanhumeth the Netophathite, and
Jaazaniah s of the Maacathite.
25:25 Ishmael s of Nethaniah s of Elishama,
1Ch 1:43 Bela s of Beor, whose city was called Dinhabah.
1Ch 1:44 Jobab s of Zerah of Bozrah succeeded him.
1:46 When Husham died, Hadad s of Bedad,
1:49 Baal-hanan s of Achbor succeeded him.
2: 8 and Ethan's s was Azariah.
2:18 Caleb s of Hezron had children
2:31 The s of Appaim: Ishi. The s of Ishi: Sheshan.
The s of Sheshan: Ahlai.
2:45 The s of Shammai: Maon;
3: 2 Absalom, s of Maacah, daughter of King Talmai
3: 2 the fourth Adonijah, s of Haggith;
3:10 Abijah his s, Asa his s, Jehoshaphat his s,
3:11 Joram his s, Ahaziah his s, Joash his s,
3:12 Amaziah his s, Azariah his s, Jotham his s,
3:13 Ahaz his s, Hezekiah his s, Manasseh his s,
3:14 Amon his s, Josiah his s.
3:16 Jeconiah his s, Zedekiah his s;
3:17 the sons of Jeconiah the captive: Shealtiel his s,
3:21 his s Rephaiah, his s Arnan, his s Obadiah, his s
Shecaniah.
3:22 The s of Shecaniah: Shemaiah.
4: 2 Reaiah s of Shobal became the father of Jahath,
4: 8 Zobebah, and the families of Aharhel s of Harum.
4:15 The sons of Caleb s of Jephunneh:
4:15 and the s of Elah: Kenaz.
4:21 The sons of Shelah s of Judah:
4:25 Shallum his s, Mibsam his s, Mishma his s.
4:26 Hammuel his s, Zaccur his s, Shimei his s.
4:34 Meshobab, Jamlech, Joshah s of Amaziah,
4:35 Jehu s of Joshibiah s of Seraiah s of Asiel,
4:37 Ziza s of Shiphi s of Allon s of Jedaiah s of Shimri
s of Shemaiah—
5: 1 of Joseph s of Israel, so that he is not enrolled in
5: 4 of Joel: Shemaiah his s, Gog his s, Shimei his s,
5: 5 Micah his s, Reaiah his s, Baal his s,
5: 6 Beerah his s, whom King Tilgath-pilneser
5: 8 and Bela s of Azaz, s of Shema, s of Joel,
5:14 Abihail s of Huri, s of Jaroah, s of Gilead, s of
Michael, s of Jeshishai, s of Jahdo, s of Buz;
5:15 Ahi s of Abdiel, s of Guni, was chief in their clan;
6:20 Libni his s, Jahath his s, Zimmah his s,
6:21 Joah his s, Iddo his s, Zerah his s, Jeatherai his s.
6:22 Amminadab his s, Korah his s, Assir his s,
6:23 Elkanah his s, Ebiasaph his s, Assir his s,
6:24 his s, Uriel his s, Uzziah his s, and Shaul his s.
6:26 Elkanah his s, Zophai his s, Nahath his s,
6:27 Eliab his s, Jeroham his s, Elkanah his s.
6:29 Mahli, Libni his s, Shimei his s, Uzzah his s,
6:30 Shimea his s, Haggiah his s, and Asaiah his s.
6:33 Heman, the singer, s of Joel, s of Samuel,
6:34 s of Elkanah, s of Jeroham, s of Eliel, s of Toah,
6:35 s of Zuph, s of Elkanah, s of Mahath, s of Amasai,
6:36 s of Elkanah, s of Joel, s of Azariah, s of
Zephaniah,
6:37 s of Tahath, s of Assir, s of Ebiasaph, s of Korah,
6:38 s of Izhar, s of Kohath, s of Levi, s of Israel;
6:39 namely, Asaph s of Berechiah, s of Shimea,
6:40 s of Michael, s of Baaseiah, s of Malchijah,
6:41 s of Ethni, s of Zerah, s of Adaiah,
6:42 s of Ethan, s of Zimmah, s of Shimei,
6:43 s of Jahath, s of Gershom, s of Levi.
6:44 Ethan s of Kishi, s of Abdi, s of Malluch,
6:45 s of Hashabiah, s of Amaziah, s of Hilkiah,
6:46 s of Amzi, s of Bani, s of Shemer,
6:47 s of Mahli, s of Mushi, s of Merari, s of Levi;
6:50 Eleazar his s, Phinehas his s, Abishua his s,
6:51 Bukki his s, Uzzi his s, Zerahiah his s,
6:52 Meraioth his s, Amariah his s, Ahitub his s,
6:53 Zadok his s, Ahimaaz his s.
6:56 and its villages they gave to Caleb s of Jephunneh.
7: 3 The s of Uzzi: Izrahiah.
7:12 and Huppim were the sons of Ir, Hushim the s
7:16 Maacah the wife of Machir bore a s,
7:17 The s of Ulam: Bedan.
7:17 the sons of Gilead s of Machir, s of Manasseh.
7:20 and Bered his s, Tahath his s, Eleadah his s,
Tahath his s,
7:21 Zabad his s, Shuthelah his s, and Ezer and Elead.
7:23 and she conceived and bore a s;
7:25 Rephah was his s, Resheph his s, Telah his s,
Tahan his s,
7:26 Ladan his s, Ammihud his s, Elishama his s,
7:27 Nun his s, Joshua his s.
7:29 In these lived the sons of Joseph s of Israel.
8:30 His firstborn s: Abdon,
8:34 and the s of Jonathan was Merib-baal;
8:37 Raphah was his s, Eleasah his s, Azel his s.
9: 4 Uthai s of Ammihud, s of Omri, s of Imri, s of
Bani, from the sons of Perez s of Judah.
9: 7 s of Meshullam, s of Hodaviah, s of Hassenuah,
9: 8 Ibneiah s of Jeroham, Elah s of Uzzi, s of Michri,
and Meshullam s of Shephatiah, s of Reuel, s of
9:11 Azariah s of Hilkiah, s of Meshullam, s of Zadok,
s of Meraioth, s of Ahitub,
9:12 Adaiah s of Jeroham, s of Pashhur, s of Malchijah,
and Maasai s of Adiel, s of Jahzerah, s of
Meshullam, s of Meshillemith, s of Immer;
9:14 s of Hasshub, s of Azrikam, s of Hashabiah,
9:15 Mattaniah s of Mica, s of Zichri, s of Asaph;
9:16 and Obadiah s of Shemaiah, s of Galal, s of
Jeduthun, and Berechiah s of Asa, s of Elkanah,
9:19 Shallum s of Kore, s of Ebiasaph, s of Korah,
9:20 And Phinehas s of Eleazar was chief over them
9:21 Zechariah s of Meshelemiah was gatekeeper at
9:36 His firstborn s was Abdon, then Zur, Kish, Baal,
9:40 and the s of Jonathan was Merib-baal;
9:43 Rephaiah was his s, Eleasah his s, Azel his s.
10:14 and turned the kingdom over to David s of Jesse. E
1Ch 11: 6 And Joab s of Zeruiah went up first,
11:11 Jashobeam, s of Hachmoni,
11:12 among the three warriors was Eleazar s of Dodo,
11:22 Benaiah s of Jehoiada was a valiant man
11:24 Such were the things Benaiah s of Jehoiada did,
11:26 Elhanan s of Dodo of Bethlehem,
11:28 Ira s of Ikkesh of Tekoa, Abiezer of Anathoth,
11:30 Heled s of Baanah of Netophah,
11:31 Ithai s of Ribai of Gibeah of the Benjaminites,
11:34 Jonathan s of Shagee the Hararite,
11:35 Ahiam s of Sachar the Hararite, Eliphal s of Ur,
11:37 Hezro of Carmel, Naarai s of Ezbai,
11:38 Joel the brother of Nathan, Mibhar s of Hagri,
11:39 the armor-bearer of Joab s of Zeruiah,
11:41 Uriah the Hittite, Zabad s of Ahlai,
11:42 Adina s of Shiza the Reubenite,
11:43 Hanan s of Maacah, and Joshaphat the Mithnite,
11:45 Jediael s of Shimri, and his brother Joha the Tizite,
12: 1 not move about freely because of Saul s of Kish;
12:18 and with you, O s of Jesse! E
15:17 So the Levites appointed Heman s of Joel;
15:17 and of his kindred Asaph s of Berechiah;
15:17 their kindred, Ethan s of Kushaiah;
16:38 while Obed-edom s of Jeduthun and Hosah were
17:13 I will be a father to him, and he shall be a s to me.
18:10 he sent his s Hadoram to King David,
18:12 Abishai s of Zeruiah killed eighteen thousand
18:15 Joab s of Zeruiah was over the army; Jehoshaphat
s of Ahilud was recorder;
18:16 Zadok s of Ahitub and Ahimelech s of Abiathar
18:17 Benaiah s of Jehoiada was over the Cherethites
19: 1 of the Ammonites died, and his s succeeded him.
19: 2 "I will deal loyally with Hanun s of Nahash,
20: 5 and Elhanan s of Jair killed Lahmi the brother
20: 7 When he taunted Israel, Jonathan s of Shimea,
22: 5 "My s Solomon is young and inexperienced, A
22: 6 Then he called for his s Solomon and charged him
22: 7 David said to Solomon, "My s, I had planned A
22: 9 See, a s shall be born to you;
22:10 He shall be a s to me, and I will be a father to him,
22:11 Now, my s, the LORD be with you, A
22:17 the leaders of Israel to help his s Solomon,
23: 1 he made his s Solomon king over Israel.
24: 6 The scribe Shemaiah s of Nethanel, a Levite,
24: 6 and Ahimelech s of Abiathar,
26: 1 of the Korahites, Meshelemiah s of Kore,
26: 6 to his s Shemaiah sons were born who exercised
26:14 They cast lots also for his s Zechariah,
26:24 Shebuel s of Gershom, s of Moses, was chief
26:25 from Eliezer were his s Rehabiah, his s Jeshaiah,
his s Joram, his s Zichri, and his s Shelomoth.
26:28 and Saul s of Kish, and Abner s of Ner, and Joab s
27: 2 Jashobeam s of Zabdiel was in charge of
27: 5 was Benaiah s of the priest Jehoiada, as chief;
27: 6 his s Ammizabad was in charge of his division.
27: 7 for the fourth month, and his s Zebadiah after him;
27: 9 was Ira s of Ikkesh the Tekoite;
27:16 Eliezer s of Zichri was chief officer;
27:16 for the Simeonites, Shephatiah s of Maacah;
27:17 for Levi, Hashabiah s of Kemuel;
27:18 for Issachar, Omri s of Michael;
27:19 for Zebulun, Ishmaiah s of Obadiah;
27:19 for Naphtali, Jerimoth s of Azriel;
27:20 for the Ephraimites, Hoshea s of Azaziah;
27:20 for the half-tribe of Manasseh, Joel s of Pedaiah;
27:21 for the half-tribe of Manasseh in Gilead, Iddo s of
27:21 for Benjamin, Jaasiel s of Abner;
27:22 for Dan, Azarel s of Jeroham.
27:24 Joab s of Zeruiah began to count them,
27:25 the king's treasuries was Azmaveth s of Adiel.
27:25 was Jonathan s of Uzziah.
27:26 tilling the soil, was Ezri s of Chelub.
27:29 the herds in the valleys was Shaphat s of Adlai.
27:32 Jehiel s of Hachmoni attended the king's sons.
27:34 After Ahithophel came Jehoiada s of Benaiah,
28: 5 has chosen my s Solomon to sit upon the throne A
28: 6 'It is your s Solomon who shall build my house
28: 6 for I have chosen him to be a s to me,
28: 9 "And you, my s Solomon, know the God of A
28:11 Then David gave his s Solomon the plan of
28:20 David said further to his s Solomon,
29: 1 "My s Solomon, whom alone God has chosen, A
29:19 Grant to my s Solomon that with single mind A
29:22 They made David's s Solomon king
29:26 Thus David s of Jesse reigned over all Israel. E
29:28 and his s Solomon succeeded him.
2Ch 1: 1 Solomon s of David established himself D
1: 5 the bronze altar that Bezalel s of Uri, s of Hur,
2:12 who has given King David a wise s,
2:14 the s of one of the Danite women,
6: 9 but your s who shall be born to you shall build
9:29 the visions of the seer Iddo concerning Jeroboam s
9:31 and his s Rehoboam succeeded him.
10: 2 When Jeroboam s of Nebat heard of it
10:15 by Ahijah the Shilonite to Jeroboam s of Nebat.
10:16 We have no inheritance in the s of Jesse. E
11: 3 of Judah, s of Solomon, and to all Israel in Judah
11:17 and for three years they made Rehoboam s of
11:18 wife Mahalath daughter of Jerimoth s of David, D
11:18 and of Abihail daughter of Eliab s of Jesse. E
11:22 Rehoboam appointed Abijah s of Maacah
12:16 and his s Abijah succeeded him.
13: 6 Yet Jeroboam s of Nebat, a servant of Solomon
13: 6 a servant of Solomon s of David, D
13: 7 around him and defied Rehoboam s of Solomon,
14: 1 His s Asa succeeded him.
15: 1 The spirit of God came upon Azariah s of Oded.

2Ch 15: 8 the prophecy of Azariah s of Oded,
17: 1 His s Jehoshaphat succeeded him,
17:16 and next to him Amasiah s of Zichri,
18: 7 of the LORD, Micaiah s of Imlah;
18: 8 "Bring quickly Micaiah s of Imlah."
18:10 Zedekiah s of Chenaanah made for himself horns
18:23 Zedekiah s of Chenaanah came up to Micaiah,
18:25 governor of the city and to Joash the king's s; F
19: 2 Jehu s of Hanani the seer went out to meet him
19:11 and Zebadiah s of Ishmael,
20:14 of the LORD came upon Jahaziel s of Zechariah,
20:14 s of Benaiah, s of Jeiel, s of Mattaniah, a Levite
20:34 are written in the Annals of Jehu s of Hanani,
20:37 Then Eliezer s of Dodavahu of Mareshah
21: 1 his s Jehoram succeeded him.
21:17 so that no s was left to him except Jehoahaz, his youngest s.
22: 1 of Jerusalem made his youngest s Ahaziah king
22: 1 So Ahaziah s of Jehoram reigned as king of Judah.
22: 5 and went with Jehoram s of King Ahab of Israel
22: 6 And Ahaziah s of King Jehoram of Judah went
22: 6 of Judah went down to see Joram s of Ahab
22: 7 with Jehoram to meet Jehu s of Nimshi,
22:10 Ahaziah's mother, saw that her s was dead,
22:11 the king's daughter, took Joash s of Ahaziah,
23: 1 Azariah s of Jeroham, Ishmael s of Jehohanan, Azariah s of Obed, Maaseiah s of Adaiah, and Elishaphat s of Zichri.
23: 3 Jehoiada said to them, "Here is the king's s! F
23:11 Then he brought out the king's s, F
24:20 the spirit of God took possession of Zechariah s of
24:22 Zechariah's father, had shown him, but killed his s.
24:25 because of the blood of the s of the priest Jehoiada,
24:26 Those who conspired against him were Zabad s of
24:26 and Jehozabad s of Shimrith the Moabite.
24:27 And his s Amaziah succeeded him.
25:17 to King Joash s of Jehoahaz s of Jehu of Israel,
25:18 saying, 'Give your daughter to my s for a wife'; A
25:23 s of Joash, s of Ahaziah, at Beth-shemesh;
25:25 King Amaziah s of Joash of Judah, lived fifteen years after the death of King Joash s of Jehoahaz
26:21 His s Jotham was in charge of the palace of
26:22 the prophet Isaiah s of Amoz wrote.
26:23 His s Jotham succeeded him.
27: 9 and his s Ahaz succeeded him.
28: 3 and he made offerings in the valley of the s
28: 6 Pekah s of Remaliah killed one hundred twenty
28: 7 of Ephraim, killed the king's s Maaseiah, F
28:12 s of Johanan, Berechiah s of Meshillemoth, Jehizkiah s of Shallum, and Amasa s of Hadlai,
28:27 His s Hezekiah succeeded him.
29:12 Levites arose, Mahath s of Amasai, and Joel s of
29:12 sons of Merari, Kish s of Abdi, and Azariah s of
29:12 the Gershonites, Joah s of Zimmah, and Eden s of
30:26 for since the time of Solomon s of King David D
31:14 Kore s of Imnah the Levite,
32:20 and the prophet Isaiah s of Amoz prayed because
32:32 in the vision of the prophet Isaiah s of Amoz in
32:33 His s Manasseh succeeded him.
33: 6 He made his s pass through fire in the valley of the s of Hinnom,
33: 7 of which God said to David and to his s Solomon,
33:20 His s Amon succeeded him.
33:25 of the land made his s Josiah king to succeed him.
34: 8 he sent Shaphan s of Azaliah,
34: 8 and Joah s of Joahaz, the recorder,
34:20 Hilkiah, Ahikam s of Shaphan, Abdon s of Micah,
34:22 the wife of Shallum s of Tokhath s of Hasrah,
35: 3 holy ark in the house that Solomon s of David, D
35: 4 and the written directions of his s Solomon.
36: 1 The people of the land took Jehoahaz s of Josiah
36: 8 and his s Jehoiachin succeeded him.
Ezr 3: 2 Then Jeshua s of Jozadak, with his fellow priests, and Zerubbabel s of Shealtiel with his kin set out
3: 8 Zerubbabel s of Shealtiel and Jeshua s of Jozadak
5: 1 the prophets, Haggai and Zechariah s of Iddo,
5: 2 Then Zerubbabel s of Shealtiel and Jeshua s of
6:14 of the prophet Haggai and Zechariah s of Iddo.
7: 1 Ezra s of Seraiah, s of Azariah, s of Hilkiah,
7: 2 s of Shallum, s of Zadok, s of Ahitub,
7: 3 s of Amariah, s of Azariah, s of Meraioth,
7: 4 s of Zerahiah, s of Uzzi, s of Bukki,
7: 5 s of Abishua, s of Phinehas, s of Eleazar, s of the
8: 4 Of the descendants of Pahath-moab, Eliehoenai s
8: 5 the descendants of Zattu, Shecaniah s of Jahaziel,
8: 6 Of the descendants of Adin, Ebed s of Jonathan,
8: 7 the descendants of Elam, Jeshaiah s of Athaliah,
8: 8 Zebadiah s of Michael, and with him eighty males.
8: 9 Of the descendants of Joab, Obadiah s of Jehiel,
8:10 the descendants of Bani, Shelomith s of Josiphiah,
8:11 Of the descendants of Bebai, Zechariah s of Bebai,
8:12 the descendants of Azgad, Johanan s of Hakkatan,
8:18 of the descendants of Mahli s of Levi s of Israel,
8:33 Meremoth s of Uriah, and with him was Eleazar s
8:33 Jozabad s of Jeshua and Noadiah s of Binnui.
10: 2 Shecaniah s of Jehiel, of the descendants of Elam,
10: 6 went to the chamber of Jehohanan s of Eliashib,
10:15 Jonathan s of Asahel and Jahzeiah s of Tikvah
10:18 of the descendants of Jeshua s of Jozadak
Ne 1: 1 The words of Nehemiah s of Hacaliah.
3: 2 And next to them Zaccur s of Imri built.
3: 4 Next to them Meremoth s of Uriah s of Hakkoz
3: 4 Next to them Meshullam s of Berechiah s of
3: 4 Next to them Zadok s of Baana made repairs.
3: 6 Joiada s of Paseah and Meshullam s of Besodeiah
3: 8 Next to them Uzziel s of Harhaiah,
3: 9 Next to them Rephaiah s of Hur,
Ne 3:10 Next to them Jedaiah s of Harumaph
3:10 to him Hattush s of Hashabneiah made repairs.
3:11 Malchijah s of Harim and Hasshub s of
3:12 Next to him Shallum s of Hallohesh,
3:14 Malchijah s of Rechab, ruler of the district
3:15 And Shallum s of Col-hozeh,
3:16 After him Nehemiah s of Azbuk,
3:17 the Levites made repairs: Rehum s of Bani;
3:18 s of Henadad, ruler of half the district of Keilah;
3:19 next to him Ezer s of Jeshua,
3:20 After him Baruch s of Zabbai
3:21 After him Meremoth s of Uriah s of Hakkoz
3:23 After them Azariah s of Maaseiah s of Ananiah
3:24 Binnui s of Henadad repaired another section,
3:25 Palal s of Uzai repaired opposite the Angle and
3:25 After him Pedaiah s of Parosh
3:29 After them Zadok s of Immer
3:29 After him Shemaiah s of Shecaniah,
3:30 Hananiah s of Shelemiah and Hanun sixth s of
3:30 After him Meshullam s of Berechiah
6:10 the house of Shemaiah s of Delaiah s of Mehetabel,
6:18 Shecaniah s of Arah: and his s Jehohanan had married the daughter of Meshullam s of Berechiah.
8:17 the days of Jeshua s of Nun to that day the people
10: 1 s of Hacaliah, and Zedekiah;
10: 9 And the Levites: Jeshua s of Azaniah,
11: 4 Athaiah s of Uzziah s of Zechariah s of Amariah s of Shephatiah s of Mahalalel,
11: 5 Maaseiah s of Baruch s of Col-hozeh s of Hazaiah s of Adaiah s of Joiarib s of Zechariah s of the
11: 7 Sallu s of Meshullam s of Joed s of Pedaiah s of Kolaiah s of Maaseiah s of Ithiel s of Jeshaiah.
11: 9 Joel s of Zichri was their overseer; and Judah s of
11:10 Of the priests: Jedaiah s of Joiarib, Jachin,
11:11 Seraiah s of Hilkiah s of Meshullam s of Zadok s of Meraioth s of Ahitub,
11:12 and Adaiah s of Jeroham s of Pelaliah s of Amzi s of Zechariah s of Pashhur s of Malchijah,
11:13 and Amashsai s of Azarel s of Ahzai s of Meshillemoth s of Immer,
11:14 their overseer was Zabdiel s of Haggedolim.
11:15 Shemaiah s of Hasshub s of Azrikam s of Hashabiah s of Bunni;
11:17 and Mattaniah s of Mica s of Zabdi s of Asaph,
11:17 Abda s of Shammua s of Galal s of Jeduthun.
11:22 of the Levites in Jerusalem was Uzzi s of Bani s of Hashabiah s of Mattaniah s of Mica,
11:24 Pethahiah s of Meshezabel, of the descendants of Zerah s of Judah,
12: 1 and the Levites who came up with Zerubbabel s
12:23 the Book of the Annals until the days of Johanan s
12:24 Hashabiah, Sherebiah, and Jeshua s of Kadmiel,
12:26 in the days of Joiakim s of Jeshua s of Jozadak,
12:35 Zechariah s of Jonathan s of Shemaiah s of Mattaniah s of Micaiah s of Zaccur s of Asaph;
12:45 to the command of David and his s Solomon.
13:13 their assistant Hanan s of Zaccur s of Mattaniah,
13:28 sons of Jehoiada, s of the high priest Eliashib,
Est 2: 5 name was Mordecai s of Jair s of Shimei s of Kish,
3: 1 King Ahasuerus promoted Haman s of
3:10 to Haman s of Hammedatha the Agagite,
8: 5 the letters devised by Haman s of Hammedatha
9:10 Haman s of Hammedatha, the enemy of the Jews;
9:24 Haman s of Hammedatha the Agagite,
Job 32: 2 Then Elihu s of Barachel the Buzite,
32: 6 Elihu s of Barachel the Buzite answered:
Ps 2: 7 He said to me, "You are my s; A
3: T *of David, when he fled from his s Absalom.*
72: 1 O God, and your righteousness to a king's s. F
72:20 The prayers of David s of Jesse are ended. E
Pr 1: 1 proverbs of Solomon s of David, king of Israel: D
3:12 as a father the s in whom he delights.
4: 3 When I was a s with my father, tender,
5:20 Why should you be intoxicated, my s, A
23:24 he who begets a wise s will be glad in him.
30: 1 The words of Agur s of Jakeh.
31: 2 No, my s! No, son of my womb! A
31: 2 No, s of my womb! No, s of my vows!
Ecc 1: 1 The words of the Teacher, the s of David, D
Isa 1: 1 The vision of Isaiah s of Amoz,
2: 1 that Isaiah s of Amoz saw concerning Judah
7: 1 In the days of Ahaz s of Jotham s of Uzziah,
7: 1 and King Pekah s of Remaliah of Israel went up
7: 3 you and your s Shear-jashub,
7: 4 of the fierce anger of Rezin and Aram and the s
7: 5 with Ephraim and the s of Remaliah—
7: 6 for ourselves and make the s of Tabeel king in it;
7: 9 and the head of Samaria is the s of Remaliah.
7:14 the young woman is with child and shall bear a s,
8: 2 the priest Uriah and Zechariah s of Jeberechiah.
8: 3 and she conceived and bore a s.
8: 6 melt in fear before Rezin and the s of Remaliah;
9: 6 For a child has been born for us, a s given to us;
13: 1 concerning Babylon that Isaiah s of Amoz saw.
14:12 fallen from heaven, O Day Star, s of Dawn!
20: 2 at that time the LORD had spoken to Isaiah s of
22:20 On that day I will call my servant Eliakim s of
36: 3 And there came out to him Eliakim s of Hilkiah,
36: 3 and Shebna the secretary, and Joah s of Asaph,
36:22 Then Eliakim s of Hilkiah,
36:22 and Shebna the secretary, and Joah s of Asaph,
37: 2 to the prophet Isaiah s of Amoz.
37:21 Then Isaiah s of Amoz sent to Hezekiah, saying:
37:38 His s Esar-haddon succeeded him.
38: 1 The prophet Isaiah s of Amoz came to him,
39: 1 At that time King Merodach-baladan s of Baladan
66: 7 before her pain came upon her she delivered a s.
Jer 1: 1 The words of Jeremiah s of Hilkiah,
1: 2 of the LORD came in the days of King Josiah s of
1: 3 in the days of King Jehoiakim s of Josiah of Judah,
1: 3 of the eleventh year of King Zedekiah s of Josiah
7:31 which is in the valley of the s of Hinnom,
7:32 or the valley of the s of Hinnom,
15: 4 because of what King Manasseh s of Hezekiah
19: 2 the s of Hinnom at the entry of the Potsherd Gate,
19: 6 or the valley of the s of Hinnom,
20: 1 Now the priest Pashhur s of Immer,
20:15 "A child is born to you, a s," making him very
21: 1 King Zedekiah sent to him Pashhur s of Malchiah and the priest Zephaniah s of Maaseiah,
22:11 the LORD concerning Shallum s of King Josiah
22:18 the LORD concerning King Jehoiakim s of Josiah
22:24 even if King Coniah s of Jehoiakim of Judah were
24: 1 from Jerusalem King Jeconiah s of Jehoiakim
25: 1 of King Jehoiakim s of Josiah of Judah (that was
25: 3 from the thirteenth year of King Josiah s of Amon
26: 1 At the beginning of the reign of King Jehoiakim s
26:20 Uriah s of Shemaiah from Kiriath-jearim.
26:22 Then King Jehoiakim sent Elnathan s of Achbor
26:24 of Ahikam s of Shaphan was with Jeremiah so
27: 1 of the reign of King Zedekiah s of Josiah of Judah,
27: 7 and his s and his grandson, until the time
27:20 to Babylon King Jeconiah s of Jehoiakim of Judah,
28: 1 the prophet Hananiah s of Azzur, from Gibeon,
28: 4 I will also bring back to this place King Jeconiah s
29: 3 the hand of Elasah s of Shaphan and Gemariah s
29:21 Ahab s of Kolaiah and Zedekiah s of Maaseiah,
29:25 and to the priest Zephaniah s of Maaseiah,
31:20 Is Ephraim my dear s?
32: 7 Hanamel s of your uncle Shallum is going to come
32:12 the deed of purchase to Baruch s of Neriah s of
32:16 After I had given the deed of purchase to Baruch s
32:35 the high places of Baal in the valley of the s of
33:21 that he would not have a s to reign on his throne,
35: 1 from the LORD in the days of King Jehoiakim s
35: 3 I took Jaazaniah s of Jeremiah s of Habazziniah,
35: 4 the chamber of the sons of Hanan s of Igdaliah,
35: 4 above the chamber of Maaseiah s of Shallum,
35: 6 our ancestor Jonadab s of Rechab commanded us,
35: 8 the charge of our ancestor Jonadab s of Rechab
35:14 The command has been carried out that Jonadab s
35:16 of Jonadab s of Rechab have carried out
35:19 Jonadab s of Rechab shall not lack a descendant
36: 1 In the fourth year of King Jehoiakim s of Josiah
36: 4 Then Jeremiah called Baruch s of Neriah,
36: 8 And Baruch s of Neriah did all that the prophet
36: 9 In the fifth year of King Jehoiakim s of Josiah
36:10 in the chamber of Gemariah s of Shaphan
36:11 When Micaiah s of Gemariah s of Shaphan heard
36:12 Delaiah s of Shemaiah, Elnathan s of Achbor, Gemariah s of Shaphan, Zedekiah s of Hananiah,
36:14 the officials sent Jehudi s of Nethaniah s of Shelemiah s of Cushi to say
36:14 So Baruch s of Neriah took the scroll in his hand
36:26 the king commanded Jerahmeel the king's s F
36:26 Seraiah s of Azriel and Shelemiah s of Abdeel to
36:32 the secretary Baruch s of Neriah, who wrote on it
37: 1 Zedekiah s of Josiah, whom King Nebuchadrezzar
37: 1 succeeded Coniah s of Jehoiakim.
37: 3 King Zedekiah sent Jehucal s of Shelemiah and the priest Zephaniah s of Maaseiah to
37:13 a sentinel there named Irijah s of Shelemiah s of
38: 1 Shephatiah s of Mattan, Gedaliah s of Pashhur, Jucal s of Shelemiah, and Pashhur s of Malchiah
38: 6 the king's s, which was in the court of the guard, F
39:14 They entrusted him to Gedaliah s of Ahikam s of
40: 5 return to Gedaliah s of Ahikam s of Shaphan,
40: 6 Jeremiah went to Gedaliah s of Ahikam at Mizpah,
40: 7 that the king of Babylon had appointed Gedaliah s
40: 8 Ishmael s of Nethaniah, Johanan s of Kareah, Seraiah s of Tanhumeth,
40: 8 Jezaniah s of the Maacathite, they and their troops.
40: 9 Gedaliah s of Ahikam s of Shaphan swore to them
40:11 a remnant in Judah and had appointed Gedaliah s of Ahikam s of Shaphan as governor over them,
40:13 Now Johanan s of Kareah and all the leaders of
40:14 of the Ammonites has sent Ishmael s of Nethaniah
40:14 But Gedaliah s of Ahikam would not believe them.
40:15 Then Johanan s of Kareah spoke secretly
40:15 "Please let me go and kill Ishmael s of Nethaniah,
40:16 But Gedaliah s of Ahikam said to Johanan s
41: 1 Ishmael s of Nethaniah s of Elishama,
41: 1 came with ten men to Gedaliah s of Ahikam,
41: 2 Ishmael s of Nethaniah and the ten men
41: 2 struck down Gedaliah s of Ahikam s of Shaphan
41: 6 And Ishmael s of Nethaniah came out
41: 6 he said to them, "Come to Gedaliah s of Ahikam."
41: 7 Ishmael s of Nethaniah and the men
41: 9 Ishmael s of Nethaniah filled that cistern
41:10 had committed to Gedaliah s of Ahikam.
41:10 Ishmael s of Nethaniah took them captive
41:11 But when Johanan s of Kareah and all the leaders
41:11 the crimes that Ishmael s of Nethaniah had done,
41:12 and went to fight against Ishmael s of Nethaniah.
41:13 the people who were with Ishmael saw Johanan s
41:14 and went to Johanan s of Kareah.
41:15 But Ishmael s of Nethaniah escaped from Johanan
41:16 Then Johanan s of Kareah and all the leaders of
41:16 rest of the people whom Ishmael s of Nethaniah
41:16 after he had slain Gedaliah s of Ahikam—
41:18 for they were afraid of them, because Ishmael s of Nethaniah had killed Gedaliah s of Ahikam,
42: 1 Johanan s of Kareah and Azariah s of Hoshaiah,
42: 8 Then he summoned Johanan s of Kareah and all

Jer 43: 2 Azariah s of Hoshaiah and Johanan s of Kareah
43: 3 but Baruch s of Neriah is inciting you against us,
43: 4 So Johanan s of Kareah and all the commanders of
43: 5 But Johanan s of Kareah and all the commanders
43: 6 the guard had left with Gedaliah s of Ahikam s of
43: 6 also the prophet Jeremiah and Baruch s of Neriah.
45: 1 the prophet Jeremiah spoke to Baruch s of Neriah,
45: 1 in the fourth year of King Jehoiakim s of Josiah
46: 2 in the fourth year of King Jehoiakim s of Josiah
51:59 commanded Seraiah s of Neriah s of Mahseiah,
Eze 1: 3 of the LORD came to the priest Ezekiel s of Buzi,
8:11 with Jaazaniah s of Shaphan standing
11: 1 Jaazaniah s of Azzur, and Pelatiah s of Benaiah,
11:13 I was prophesying, Pelatiah s of Benaiah died.
14:20 they would save neither s nor daughter;
18:10 If he has a s who is violent, a shedder of blood,
18:14 a s who sees all the sins that his father has done,
18:19 "Why should not the s suffer for the iniquity of
18:19 When the s has done what is lawful and right,
44:25 father or mother, however, and for s or daughter,
Da 5:22 And you, Belshazzar his s,
9: 1 In the first year of Darius s of Ahasuerus,
Hos 1: 1 word of the LORD that came to Hosea s of Beeri,
1: 1 in the days of King Jeroboam s of Joash of Israel.
1: 3 and she conceived and bore him a s.
1: 8 she conceived and bore a s.
11: 1 I loved him, and out of Egypt I called my s. A
13:13 but he is an unwise s;
Joel 1: 1 word of the LORD that came to Joel s of Pethuel:
Am 1: 1 in the days of King Jeroboam s of Joash of Israel,
2: 7 father and s go in to the same girl,
7:14 "I am no prophet, nor a prophet's s;
8:10 I will make it like the mourning for an only s, H
Jnh 1: 1 word of the LORD came to Jonah s of Amittai,
Mic 6: 5 what Balaam s of Beor answered him,
7: 6 for the s treats the father with contempt,
Zep 1: 1 came to Zephaniah s of Cushi s of Gedaliah s of
Amariah s of Hezekiah, in the days of King Josiah
s of Amon of Judah.
Hag 1: 1 the prophet Haggai to Zerubbabel s of Shealtiel,
governor of Judah, and to Joshua s of Jehozadak,
1:12 Then Zerubbabel s of Shealtiel, and Joshua s of
1:14 stirred up the spirit of Zerubbabel s of Shealtiel,
1:14 and the spirit of Joshua s of Jehozadak,
2: 2 Speak now to Zerubbabel s of Shealtiel, governor
of Judah, and to Joshua s of Jehozadak,
2: 4 take courage, O Joshua, s of Jehozadak,
2:23 O Zerubbabel my servant, s of Shealtiel,
Zec 1: 1 the prophet Zechariah s of Berechiah s of Iddo,
1: 7 the prophet Zechariah s of Berechiah s of Iddo;
6:10 and go the same day to the house of Josiah s of
6:11 the head of the high priest Joshua s of Jehozadak;
6:14 Tobijah, Jedaiah, and Josiah s of Zephaniah,
Mal 1: 6 A s honors his father, and servants their master.
Mt 1: 1 the s of David, the son of Abraham. D
1: 1 the son of David, the s of Abraham. K
1:20 to him in a dream and said, "Joseph, s of David, D
1:21 She will bear a s, and you are to name him Jesus,
1:23 the virgin shall conceive and bear a s,
1:25 with her until she had borne a s;
2:15 "Out of Egypt I have called my s." A
3:17 from heaven said, "This is my S, the Beloved, AI
4: 3 "If you are the S of God, command these stones C
4: 6 "If you are the S of God, throw yourself down; C
4:21 James s of Zebedee and his brother John,
8:20 but the S of Man has nowhere to lay his head." B
8:29 "What have you to do with us, S of God? C
9: 2 "Take heart, s; your sins are forgiven."
9: 6 that the S of Man has authority on earth B
9:27 crying loudly, "Have mercy on us, S of David!" D
10: 2 James s of Zebedee, and his brother John;
10: 3 James s of Alphaeus, and Thaddaeus;
10:23 the towns of Israel before the S of Man comes. B
10:37 and whoever loves s or daughter more than me is
11:19 the S of Man came eating and drinking, B
11:27 and no one knows the S except the Father,
11:27 the Father except the S and anyone to whom
11:27 and anyone to whom the S chooses to reveal him.
12: 8 For the S of Man is lord of the sabbath." B
12:23 "Can this be the S of David?" D
12:32 Whoever speaks a word against the S of Man B
12:40 three nights the S of Man will be in the heart D
13:37 one who sows the good seed is the S of Man; B
13:41 The S of Man will send his angels, B
13:55 Is not this the carpenter's s?
14:33 saying, "Truly you are the S of God." C
15:22 "Have mercy on me, Lord, S of David; D
16:13 "Who do people say that the S of Man is?" B
16:16 "You are the Messiah, the S of the living God."
16:17 "Blessed are you, Simon s of Jonah!
16:27 "For the S of Man is to come with his angels in B
16:28 the S of Man coming in his kingdom." B
17: 5 a voice said, "This is my S, the Beloved; AI
17: 9 the S of Man has been raised from the dead." B
17:12 the S of Man is about to suffer at their hands." B
17:15 "Lord, have mercy on my s, A
17:22 "The S of Man is going to be betrayed B
19:28 the S of Man is seated on the throne of his glory, B
20:18 and the S of Man will be handed over to B
20:28 the S of Man came not to be served but to serve, B
20:30 "Lord, have mercy on us, S of David!" D
20:31 "Have mercy on us, Lord, S of David!" D
21: 9 "Hosanna to the S of David! D
21:15 "Hosanna to the S of David," D
21:28 he went to the first and said, 'S, go and work
21:37 Finally he sent his s to them, saying,
21:37 saying, 'They will respect my s.' A
Mt 21:38 But when the tenants saw the s,
22: 2 to a king who gave a wedding banquet for his s.
22:42 think of the Messiah? Whose s is he?"
22:42 They said to him, "The s of David." D
22:45 David thus calls him Lord, how can he be his s?"
23:35 of righteous Abel to the blood of Zechariah s
24:27 so will be the coming of the S of Man. B
24:30 the sign of the S of Man will appear in heaven, B
24:30 'the S of Man coming on the clouds of heaven' B
24:36 neither the angels of heaven, nor the S,
24:37 so will be the coming of the S of Man. B
24:39 so too will be the coming of the S of Man. B
24:44 the S of Man is coming at an unexpected hour. B
25:31 "When the S of Man comes in his glory, B
26: 2 S of Man will be handed over to be crucified." B
26:24 The S of Man goes as it is written of him, B
26:24 to that one by whom the S of Man is betrayed! B
26:45 S of Man is betrayed into the hands of sinners. B
26:63 tell us if you are the Messiah, the S of God." C
26:64 From now on you will see the S of Man seated B
27:40 are the S of God, come down from the cross." C
27:43 for he said, 'I am God's S.' " J
27:54 "Truly this man was God's S!" J
28:19 of the Father and of the S and of the Holy Spirit,
Mk 1: 1 of the good news of Jesus Christ, the S of God. C
1:11 from heaven, "You are my S, the Beloved; AI
1:19 he saw James s of Zebedee and his brother John,
2: 5 Jesus saw their faith, he said to the paralytic, "S,
2:10 that the S of Man has authority on earth B
2:14 he saw Levi s of Alphaeus sitting at the tax booth,
2:28 so the S of Man is lord even of the sabbath." B
3:11 "You are the S of God!" C
3:17 James s of Zebedee and John the brother of James
3:18 and James s of Alphaeus, and Thaddaeus,
5: 7 Jesus, S of the Most High God?
6: 3 the s of Mary and brother of James and Joses
8:31 that the S of Man must undergo great suffering, B
8:38 S of Man will also be ashamed when he comes B
9: 7 "This is my S, the Beloved; listen to him!" AI
9: 9 until after the S of Man had risen from the dead. B
9:12 How then is it written about the S of Man, B
9:17 "Teacher, I brought you my s; A
9:31 S of Man is to be betrayed into human hands, B
10:33 and the S of Man will be handed over to B
10:45 the S of Man came not to be served but to serve, B
10:46 Bartimaeus s of Timaeus, a blind beggar,
10:47 began to shout out and say, "Jesus, S of David, D
10:48 but he cried out even more loudly, "S of David, D
12: 6 He had still one other, a beloved s. I
12: 6 saying, 'They will respect my s.' A
12:35 scribes say that the Messiah is the s of David? D
12:37 so how can he be his s?"
13:26 'the S of Man coming in clouds' with great B
13:32 neither the angels in heaven, nor the S,
14:21 For the S of Man goes as it is written of him, B
14:21 to that one by whom the S of Man is betrayed! B
14:41 S of Man is betrayed into the hands of sinners. B
14:61 "Are you the Messiah, the S of the Blessed One?"
14:62 and 'you will see the S of Man seated at B
15:39 he said, "Truly this man was God's S!" J
Lk 1:13 Your wife Elizabeth will bear you a s,
1:31 you will conceive in your womb and bear a s,
1:32 and will be called the S of the Most High,
1:35 he will be called S of God. C
1:36 in her old age has also conceived a s;
1:57 for Elizabeth to give birth, and she bore a s.
2: 7 to her firstborn s and wrapped him in bands
3: 2 the word of God came to John s of Zechariah in
3:22 from heaven, "You are my S, the Beloved; AI
3:23 the s (as was thought) of Joseph s of Heli,
3:24 s of Matthat, s of Levi, s of Melchi, s of Jannai,
s of Joseph,
3:25 s of Mattathias, s of Amos, s of Nahum, s of Esli,
s of Naggai,
3:26 s of Maath, s of Mattathias, s of Semein, s of
Josech, s of Joda,
3:27 s of Joanan, s of Rhesa, s of Zerubbabel, s of
Shealtiel, s of Neri,
3:28 s of Melchi, s of Addi, s of Cosam, s of Elmadam,
s of Er,
3:29 s of Joshua, s of Eliezer, s of Jorim, s of Matthat,
s of Levi,
3:30 s of Simeon, s of Judah, s of Joseph, s of Jonam,
s of Eliakim,
3:31 s of Melea, s of Menna, s of Mattatha, s of Nathan,
3:31 son of Mattatha, son of Nathan, s of David, D
3:32 s of Jesse, son of Obed, son of Boaz, son E
3:32 s of Obed, s of Boaz, s of Sala, s of Nahshon,
3:33 s of Amminadab, s of Admin, s of Arni, s of
Hezron, s of Perez, s of Judah,
3:34 s of Jacob, s of Isaac, son of Abraham,
3:34 s of Abraham, son of Terah, son of Nahor, K
3:34 s of Terah, s of Nahor,
3:35 s of Serug, s of Reu, s of Peleg, s of Eber, s of
Shelah,
3:36 s of Cainan, s of Arphaxad, s of Shem, s of Noah,
s of Lamech,
3:37 s of Methuselah, s of Enoch, s of Jared, s of
Mahalaleel, s of Cainan,
3:38 s of Enos, s of Seth, s of Adam, son of God.
3:38 son of Enos, son of Seth, son of Adam, s of God. C
4: 3 The devil said to him, "If you are the S of God, C
4: 9 saying to him, "If you are the S of God, C
4:22 They said, "Is not this Joseph's s?"
4:41 shouting, "You are the S of God!" C
5:24 that the S of Man has authority on earth B
6: 5 "The S of Man is lord of the sabbath." B
Lk 6:15 and Thomas, and James s of Alphaeus, and Simon,
6:16 and Judas s of James,
6:22 and defame you on account of the S of Man. B
7:12 was his mother's only s, and she was a widow; H
7:34 the S of Man has come eating and drinking, B
8:28 Jesus, S of the Most High God?
9:22 "The S of Man must undergo great suffering, B
9:26 the S of Man will be ashamed when he comes B
9:35 "This is my S, my Chosen; listen to him!" A
9:38 I beg you to look at my s; he is my only child. A
9:41 and bear with you? Bring your s here."
9:44 The S of Man is going to be betrayed B
9:58 but the S of Man has nowhere to lay his head." B
10:22 and no one knows who the S is except the Father,
10:22 the Father is except the S and anyone to whom
10:22 the Son and anyone to whom the S chooses
11:30 so the S of Man will be to this generation. B
12: 8 the S of Man also will acknowledge before B
12:10 who speaks a word against the S of Man B
12:40 the S of Man is coming at an unexpected hour." B
12:53 father against s and s against father,
15:13 A few days later the younger s gathered all he had
15:19 I am no longer worthy to be called your s;
15:21 Then the s said to him, 'Father,
15:21 I am no longer worthy to be called your s.'
15:24 for this s of mine was dead and is alive again;
15:25 "Now his elder s was in the field;
15:30 But when this s of yours came back,
15:31 Then the father said to him, 'S,
17:22 to see one of the days of the S of Man, B
17:24 so will the S of Man be in his day. B
17:26 so too it will be in the days of the S of Man. B
17:30 that on the day that the S of Man is revealed. B
18: 8 the S of Man comes, will he find faith on earth?" B
18:31 everything that is written about the S of Man B
18:38 Then he shouted, "Jesus, S of David, D
18:39 but he shouted even more loudly, "S of David, D
19: 9 because he too is a s of Abraham. K
19:10 S of Man came to seek out and to save the lost." B
20:13 I will send my beloved s; I
20:41 "How can they say that the Messiah is David's s?
20:44 so how can he be his s?"
21:27 'the S of Man coming in a cloud' with power B
21:36 and to stand before the S of Man." B
22:22 the S of Man is going as it has been determined, B
22:48 with a kiss that you are betraying the S of Man?" B
22:69 the S of Man will be seated at the right hand of B
22:70 of them asked, "Are you, then, the S of God?" C
24: 7 the S of Man must be handed over to sinners, B
Jn 1:14 the glory as of a father's only s, H
1:18 It is God the only S, H
1:34 and have testified that this is the S of God." C
1:42 "You are Simon s of John.
1:45 Jesus s of Joseph from Nazareth."
1:49 Nathanael replied, "Rabbi, you are the S of God! C
1:51 ascending and descending upon the S of Man." B
3:13 who descended from heaven, the S of Man. B
3:14 so must the S of Man be lifted up, B
3:16 God so loved the world that he gave his only S, H
3:17 God did not send the S into the world to condemn
3:18 not believed in the name of the only S of God. CH
3:35 The Father loves the S and has placed all things
3:36 Whoever believes in the S has eternal life;
whoever disobeys the S will not see life,
4: 5 of ground that Jacob had given to his s Joseph.
4:46 Now there was a royal official whose s lay ill
4:47 and begged him to come down and heal his s,
4:50 Jesus said to him, "Go; your s will live."
4:53 when Jesus had said to him, "Your s will live."
5:19 I tell you, the S can do nothing on his own,
5:19 for whatever the Father does, the S does likewise.
5:20 the S and shows him all that he himself is doing;
5:21 so also the S gives life to whomever he wishes.
5:22 but has given all judgment to the S,
5:23 all may honor the S just as they honor the Father.
5:23 Anyone who does not honor the S does not honor
5:25 the dead will hear the voice of the S of God, C
5:26 he has granted the S also to have life in himself;
5:27 because he is the S of Man. B
6:27 which the S of Man will give you. B
6:40 the S and believe in him may have eternal life,
6:42 "Is not this Jesus, the s of Joseph,
6:53 the flesh of the S of Man and drink his blood, B
6:62 the S of Man ascending to where he was before? B
6:71 He was speaking of Judas s of Simon Iscariot,
8:28 "When you have lifted up the S of Man, B
8:35 the s has a place there forever.
8:36 if the S makes you free, you will be free indeed.
9:19 "Is this your s, who you say was born blind?
9:20 His parents answered, "We know that this is our s,
9:35 he said, "Do you believe in the S of Man?" B
10:36 because I said, 'I am God's S'? J
11: 4 that the S of God may be glorified through it." C
11:27 I believe that you are the Messiah, the S of God, C
12:23 hour has come for the S of Man to be glorified. B
12:34 can you say that the S of Man must be lifted up? B
12:34 Who is this S of Man?" B
13: 2 of Judas s of Simon Iscariot to betray him.
13:26 he gave it to Judas s of Simon Iscariot.
13:31 said, "Now the S of Man has been glorified, B
14:13 so that the Father may be glorified in the S.
17: 1 glorify your S so that the S may glorify you,
19: 7 die because he has claimed to be the S of God." C
19:26 he said to his mother, "Woman, here is your s."
20:31 believe that Jesus is the Messiah, the S of God, C
21:15 Jesus said to Simon Peter, "Simon s of John,
21:16 A second time he said to him, "Simon s of John,

Jn 21:17 He said to him the third time, "Simon s of John,
Ac 1:13 Bartholomew and Matthew, James s of Alphaeus,
1:13 and Simon the Zealot, and Judas s of James.
4:36 Barnabas (which means "s of encouragement").
7:21 and brought him up as her own s.
7:56 the heavens opened and the S of Man standing B
9:20 saying, "He is the S of God." C
13:10 and said, "You s of the devil, you enemy
13:21 and God gave them Saul s of Kish,
13:22 s of Jesse, to be a man after my heart, E
13:33 'You are my S; today I have begotten you.' A
16:1 the s of a Jewish woman who was a believer;
20:4 He was accompanied by Sopater s of Pyrrhus
20:28 that he obtained with the blood of his own S.
23:6 "Brothers, I am a Pharisee, a s of Pharisees.
23:16 Now the s of Paul's sister heard about the ambush;
Ro 1:3 the gospel concerning his S,
1:4 be S of God with power according to the spirit C
1:9 with my spirit by announcing the gospel of his S,
5:10 to God through the death of his S,
8:3 by sending his own S in the likeness
8:29 to be conformed to the image of his S,
8:32 He who did not withhold his own S,
9:9 and Sarah shall have a s."
1Co 1:9 into the fellowship of his S,
15:28 then the S himself will also be subjected to
2Co 1:19 For the S of God, Jesus Christ, C
Gal 1:16 to reveal his S to me,
2:20 live in the flesh I live by faith in the S of God, C
4:4 the fullness of time had come, God sent his S,
4:6 God has sent the Spirit of his S into our hearts,
Eph 4:13 the faith and of the knowledge of the S of God, C
Php 2:22 a s with a father he has served with me in the work
Col 1:13 into the kingdom of his beloved S, I
1Th 1:10 and to wait for his S from heaven, whom he raised
Heb 1:2 but in these last days he has spoken to us by a S,
1:5 "You are my S; today I have begotten you"? A
1:5 "I will be his Father, and he will be my S"? A
1:8 But of the S he says, "Your throne, O God,
3:6 however, was faithful over God's house as a s,
4:14 the S of God, let us hold fast to our confession. C
5:5 "You are my S, today I have begotten you"; A
5:8 Although he was a S, he learned obedience
6:6 they are crucifying again the S of God C
7:3 but resembling the S of God, C
7:28 appoints a S who has been made perfect forever.
10:29 by those who have spurned the S of God, C
11:17 the promises was ready to offer up his only s, H
11:24 refused to be called a s of Pharaoh's daughter,
Jas 2:21 by works when he offered his s Isaac on the altar?
1Pe 5:13 and so does my s Mark.
2Pe 1:17 saying, "This is my S, my Beloved, AI
2:15 following the road of Balaam s of Bosor,
1Jn 1:3 with the Father and with his S Jesus Christ.
1:7 the blood of Jesus his S cleanses us from all sin.
2:22 the one who denies the Father and the S.
2:23 No one who denies the S has the Father; everyone
who confesses the S has the Father also.
2:24 then you will abide in the S and in the Father.
3:8 The S of God was revealed for this purpose, C
3:23 of his S Jesus Christ and love one another,
4:9 God sent his only S into the world so H
4:10 and sent his S to be the atoning sacrifice
4:14 and do testify that the Father has sent his S as
4:15 in those who confess that Jesus is the S of God, C
5:5 the one who believes that Jesus is the S of God? C
5:9 the testimony of God that he has testified to his S.
5:10 who believe in the S of God have the testimony C
5:10 testimony that God has given concerning his S.
5:11 God gave us eternal life, and this life is in his S.
5:12 Whoever has the S has life;
5:12 whoever does not have the S of God does not C
5:13 to you who believe in the name of the S of God, C
5:20 And we know that the S of God has come C
5:20 we are in him who is true, in his S Jesus Christ.
2Jn 1:3 the Father's S, in truth and love.
1:9 in the teaching has both the Father and the S.
Rev 1:13 of the lampstands I saw one like the S of Man, B
2:18 These are the words of the S of God, C
12:5 And she gave birth to a s, a male child,
14:14 seated on the cloud was one like the S of Man, B
Tob 1:1 the story of Tobit s of Tobiel s of Hananiel s of
Aduel s of Gabael s of Raphael of the descendants
1:9 the father of a s whom I named Tobias.
1:15 and his s Sennacherib reigned in his place,
1:20 except my wife Anna and my s Tobias. A
1:21 and his s Esar-haddon reigned after him.
1:21 the s of my brother Hanael over all the accounts
2:1 my wife Anna and my s Tobias were restored A
2:2 I said to my s Tobias, "Go, my child, A
3:9 May we never see a s or daughter of yours!"
3:17 by giving her in marriage to Tobias s of Tobit,
4:2 Why do I not call my s Tobias and explain to A
4:3 Then he called his s Tobias,
4:3 "My s, when I die, give me a proper burial. A
4:4 my s, because she faced many dangers for you A
4:5 "Revere the Lord all your days, my s, A
4:12 "Beware, my s, of every kind of fornication. A
4:12 Remember, my s, that Noah, Abraham, Isaac, A
4:13 So now, my s, love your kindred, A
4:14 "Watch yourself, my s, in everything you do, A
4:20 my s, let me explain to you that I left ten talents A
4:20 I left ten talents of silver in trust with Gabael s
4:21 my s, because we have become poor. A
5:3 Then Tobit answered his s Tobias,
5:3 my s, find yourself a trustworthy man to go A
5:9 He replied, "Call the man in, my s, A
Tob 5:10 "My s Tobias wishes to go to Media. A
5:12 brother, whose s you are and what your name is."
5:13 the s of the great Hananiah, one of your relatives."
5:15 as well as expenses for yourself and my s. A
5:15 So go with my s, A
5:17 Then he called his s and said to him, "S,
5:17 my s, accompany you both for your safety." A
6:15 So now, since I am the only s my father has, H
6:15 and they have no other s to bury them."
7:7 my child, s of a good and noble father!"
9:5 that Tobit's s Tobias had married
9:6 "Good and noble s of a father good and noble,
10:1 when the days had passed and his s did not appear,
10:4 And she began to weep and mourn for her s,
10:7 and watch the road her s had taken,
11:5 down the road by which her s would come.
11:6 she said to his father, "Look, your s is coming,
11:9 Then Anna ran up to her s and threw her arms
11:13 Tobit saw his s and threw his arms around him,
11:14 "I see you, my s, the light of my eyes!" A
11:15 Now I see my s Tobias!" A
11:17 When Tobit met Sarah the wife of his s Tobias,
11:17 blessed be my s Tobias, and blessed be you, A
12:1 Tobit called his s Tobias and said to him,
14:3 called his s Tobias and the seven sons of Tobias
14:3 and gave this command: "My s, A
14:8,9 So now, my s, leave Nineveh; do not remain A
14:10 See, my s, what Nadab did A
Jdt 6:15 who in those days were Uzziah s of Micah,
6:15 of the tribe of Simeon, and Chabris s of Gothoniel,
6:15 and Charmis s of Melchiel.
8:1 the daughter of Merari s of Ox s of Joseph s of
Oziel s of Elkiah s of Ananias s of Gideon s of
Raphain s of Ahitub s of Elijah s of Hilkiah s of
Eliab s of Nathanael s of Salamiel s of Sarasadai s
AdE 2:5 name was Mordecai s of Jair s of Shimei s of Kish,
3:1 King Artaxerxes promoted Haman s of
9:10 of Haman s of Hammedatha, the Bougean,
9:24 —how Haman s of Hammedatha, the Macedonian,
11:1 and his s Ptolemy brought to Egypt
11:1 and had been translated by Lysimachus s
11:2 Mordecai s of Jair s of Shimei s of Kish,
12:6 But Haman s of Hammedatha, a Bougean,
16:10 For Haman s of Hammedatha, a Macedonian
16:17 not to put in execution the letters sent by Haman s
Wis 9:5 For I am your servant the s of your serving girl,
Sir 4:10 you will then be like a s of the Most High,
22:3 a disgrace to be the father of an undisciplined s,
30:1 He who loves his s will whip him often,
30:2 He who disciplines his s will profit by him,
30:3 who teaches his s will make his enemies envious,
30:7 Whoever spoils his s will bind up his wounds,
30:8 and an unchecked s turns out headstrong.
30:13 Discipline your s and make his yoke heavy,
33:20 To s or wife, to brother or friend,
34:24 Like one who kills a s before his father's eyes is
45:23 Phinehas s of Eleazar ranks third in glory
45:25 covenant was established with David s of Jesse E
45:25 that the king's heritage passes only from s to s,
46:1 Joshua s of Nun was mighty in war,
46:7 he and Caleb s of Jephunneh:
47:12 a wise s rose up who because of him lived
47:23 Then Jeroboam s of Nebat led Israel into sin
49:12 and so was Jeshua s of Jozadak;
50:1 of his people was the high priest, Simon s of
50:27 Jesus s of Eleazar s of Sirach of Jerusalem,
51:1 PRAYER OF JESUS S OF SIRACH
Bar 1:1 the words of the book that Baruch s of Neriah s of
Mahseiah s of Zedekiah s of Hasadiah s of Hilkiah
1:3 the words of this book to Jeconiah s of Jehoiakim,
1:7 to the high priest Jehoiakim s of Hilkiah s of
1:8 the silver vessels that Zedekiah s of Josiah,
1:11 and for the life of his s Belshazzar,
1:12 and under the protection of his s Belshazzar,
1Mc 1:1 After Alexander s of Philip, the Macedonian,
1:10 Antiochus Epiphanes, s of King Antiochus;
2:1 In those days Mattathias s of John s of Simeon,
2:26 just as Phinehas did against Zimri s of Salu.
3:1 Then his s Judas, who was called Maccabeus,
3:33 to take care of his s Antiochus until he returned.
3:38 Lysias chose Ptolemy s of Dorymenes,
4:30 the Philistines into the hands of Jonathan s of Saul,
5:18 But he left Joseph, s of Zechariah, and Azariah,
5:56 Joseph s of Zechariah, and Azariah,
6:2 and weapons left there by Alexander s of Philip,
6:15 that he might guide his s Antiochus and bring him
6:17 he set up Antiochus the king's s to reign. F
6:55 to bring up his s Antiochus to be king,
7:1 In the one hundred fifty-first year Demetrius s
8:17 So Judas chose Eupolemus s of John s of Accos,
8:17 of Accos, and Jason s of Eleazar, and sent them
10:1 s of Antiochus, landed and occupied Ptolemais.
10:67 In the one hundred sixty-fifth year Demetrius s
11:39 the young s of Alexander,
11:70 Mattathias s of Absalom and Judas s of Chalphi,
12:16 Numenius s of Antiochus and Antipater s of Jason,
13:11 He sent Jonathan s of Absalom to Joppa,
13:53 Simon saw that his s John had reached manhood,
14:22 'Numenius s of Antiochus and Antipater s of Jason
14:29 Simon s of Mattathias, a priest of the sons
15:1 Antiochus, s of King Demetrius, sent a letter
16:11 Now Ptolemy s of Abubus had been appointed
16:15 The s of Abubus received them treacherously in
2Mc 2:20 against Antiochus Epiphanes and his s Eupator,
3:11 and also some money of Hyrcanus s of Tobias,
4:4 that the rivalry was serious and that Apollonius s
4:21 When Apollonius s of Menestheus was sent
2Mc 4:45 to Ptolemy s of Dorymenes to win over the king.
7:26 she undertook to persuade her s.
7:27 "My s, have pity on me. I carried you nine A
8:9 Then Ptolemy promptly appointed Nicanor s of
9:25 So I have appointed my s Antiochus to be king, A
9:26 each of you, toward me and my s. A
9:29 then, fearing the s of Antiochus, he withdrew
10:10 who was the s of that ungodly man,
12:2 Timothy and Apollonius s of Gennaeus,
14:1 word came to Judas and his men that Demetrius s
1Es 1:3 in the house that King Solomon, s of David, D
1:5 of Israel and the magnificence of his s Solomon.
1:34 The men of the nation took Jeconiah s of Josiah,
1:43 His s Jehoiachin became king in his place;
5:5 the descendants of Phinehas s of Aaron; G
5:5 Jeshua s of Jozadak s of Seraiah and Joakim s of
Zerubbabel s of Shealtiel,
5:24 the descendants of Jedaiah s of Jeshua,
5:37 the descendants of Delaiah s of Tobiah,
5:48 Then Jeshua s of Jozadak, with his fellow priests,
and Zerubbabel s of Shealtiel, with his kinsmen,
5:56 Zerubbabel s of Shealtiel and Jeshua s of Jozadak
5:58 of Jeshua Emadabun and the sons of Joda s of
6:1 and Zechariah s of Iddo prophesied to the Jews
6:2 Zerubbabel s of Shealtiel and Jeshua s of Jozadak
8:1 s of Seraiah s of Azariah s of Hilkiah s of Shallum
8:2 s of Zadok s of Ahitub s of Amariah s of Uzzi s of
Bukki s of Abishua s of Phineas s of Eleazar son
8:2 son of Phineas son of Eleazar s of Aaron G
8:29 the descendants of David, Hattush s of Shecaniah.
8:31 Of the descendants of Pahath-moab, Eliehoenai s
8:32 the descendants of Zattu, Shecaniah s of Jahaziel,
8:32 Of the descendants of Adin, Obed s of Jonathan,
8:33 the descendants of Elam, Jeshaiah s of Gotholiah,
8:34 Zeraiah s of Michael, and with him seventy men.
8:35 Of the descendants of Joab, Obadiah s of Jehiel,
8:36 the descendants of Bani, Shelomith s of Josiphiah,
8:37 Of the descendants of Bebai, Zechariah s of Bebai,
8:38 the descendants of Azgad, Johanan s of Hakkatan,
8:40 Uthai s of Istalcurus, and with him seventy men.
8:47 of Mahli s of Levi, s of Israel, namely Sherebiah
8:62 in the house of our Lord to the priest Meremoth s
8:63 Eleazar s of Phinehas, and with them were
Jozabad s of Jeshua and Moeth s of Binnui,
8:92 Then Shecaniah s of Jehiel,
9:1 of the temple to the chamber of Jehohanan s
9:14 Jonathan s of Asahel and Jahzeiah s of Tikvah
9:19 of the descendants of Jeshua s of Jozadak
3Mc 1:3 But Dositheus, known as the s of Drimylus,
2Es 1:1 the prophet Ezra s of Seraiah s of Azariah s of
Hilkiah s of Shallum s of Zadok s of Ahitub
1:2 s of Ahijah s of Phinehas s of Eli s of Amariah s of
Azariah s of Meraimoth s of Arna s of Uzzi s of
Borith s of Abishua s of Phinehas s of Eleazar
1:3 s of Aaron, of the tribe of Levi, G
2:47 answered and said to me, "He is the S of God, C
7:28 For my s the Messiah shall be revealed A
7:29 After those years my s the Messiah shall die, A
7:*104* Just as now a father does not send his s,
7:*104* or a s his father, or a master his servant,
9:45 and considered my distress, and gave me a s.
10:1 that when my s entered his wedding chamber, A
10:8 you are sorrowing for one s, but we,
10:16 you will receive your s back in due time,
10:43 and who told you about the misfortune of her s—
10:46 then it was that the barren woman bore a s.
10:48 'My s died as he entered his wedding chamber,' A
10:49 you saw her likeness, how she mourned for her s,
13:32 then my S will be revealed, A
13:37 my S, will reprove the assembled nations A
13:52 can see my S or those who are with him, A
14:9 and henceforth you shall live with my S and A
4Mc 4:15 his s Antiochus Epiphanes succeeded to
12:6 and to influence her to persuade the surviving s
16:20 to sacrifice his s Isaac, the ancestor of our nation;

SON'S (13) [SON]

Ge 27:25 that I may eat of my s game and bless you."
27:31 "Let my father sit up and eat of his s game,
30:14 "Please give me some of your s mandrakes."
30:15 Would you take away my s mandrakes also?"
30:15 with you tonight for your s mandrakes."
30:16 for I have hired you with my s mandrakes."
37:32 see now whether it is your s robe or not."
37:33 He recognized it, and said, "It is my s robe!
Ex 4:25 Zipporah took a flint and cut off her s foreskin,
Lev 18:10 of your s daughter or of your daughter's daughter,
18:15 of your daughter-in-law: she is your s wife;
18:17 not take her s daughter or her daughter's daughter
1Ki 21:29 in his s days I will bring the disaster on his house."

SON-IN-LAW (14) [SON]

Jdg 15:6 And they said, "Samson, the s of the Timnite,
19:5 but the girl's father said to his s,
1Sa 18:18 that I should be s to the king?"
18:21 "You shall now be my s."
18:22 now then, become the king's s.'"
18:23 to you a little thing to become the king's s,
18:26 David was well pleased to be the king's s.
18:27 that he might become the king's s.
22:14 He is the king's s, and is quick to do your bidding,
2Ki 8:27 for he was s to the house of Ahab.
Ne 6:18 because he was the s of Shecaniah son of Arah:
13:28 was the s of Sanballat the Horonite;
1Mc 10:54 as my wife, and I will become your s,
16:12 for he was s of the high priest.

SONG‡ (92) [SING]

A. NEW SONG (10)

Ex 15: 1 Moses and the Israelites sang this s to the LORD:
Nu 21:17 Then Israel sang this s: "Spring up,
Dt 31:19 therefore write this s, and teach it to the Israelites;
31:19 in order that this s may be a witness for me against
31:21 this s will confront them as a witness,
31:22 That very day Moses wrote this s and taught it to
31:30 Then Moses recited the words of this s,
32:44 and recited all the words of this s in the hearing of
Jdg 5:12 Awake, awake, utter a s!
2Sa 1:18 (He ordered that The S of the Bow be taught to
22: 1 to the LORD the words of this s on the day when
1Ch 6:31 of the service of s in the house of the LORD,
6:32 with s before the tabernacle of the tent of meeting,
13: 8 with s and lyres and harps and tambourines
16:42 and instruments for sacred s.
2Ch 5:13 and when the s was raised,
29:27 the s to the LORD began also, and the trumpets,
Job 30: 9 now they mock me in s; I am a byword to them.
Ps 18: T *who addressed of this s to the LORD*
26: 7 singing aloud a s of thanksgiving,
28: 7 and with my s I give thanks to him.
30: T *A Psalm. A S at the dedication of the temple.*
33: 3 Sing to him a new s; A
40: 3 He put a new s in my mouth, A
40: 3 a s of praise to our God.
42: 8 and at night his s is with me,
45: T *Of the Korahites. A Maskil. A love s.*
46: T *Of the Korahites. According to Alamoth. A S.*
48: T *A S. A Psalm of the Korahites.*
65: T *To the leader. A Psalm of David. A S.*
66: T *To the leader. A S. A Psalm.*
67: T *with stringed instruments. A Psalm. A S.*
68: T *To the leader. Of David. A Psalm. A S.*
68: 4 lift up a s to him who rides upon the clouds—
69:30 I will praise the name of God with a s;
75: T *Do Not Destroy. A Psalm of Asaph. A S.*
76: T *with stringed instruments. A Psalm of Asaph. A S.*
78:63 and their girls had no marriage s.
81: 2 Raise a s, sound the tambourine,
83: T *A S. A Psalm of Asaph.*
87: T *Of the Korahites. A Psalm. A S.*
88: T *A S. A Psalm of the Korahites.*
92: T *A Psalm. A S for the Sabbath Day.*
96: 1 O sing to the LORD a new s; A
98: 1 O sing to the LORD a new s, A
98: 4 break forth into joyous s and sing praises.
108: T *A S. A Psalm of David.*
120: T *A S of Ascents.*
121: T *A S of Ascents.*
122: T *A S of Ascents. Of David.*
123: T *A S of Ascents.*
124: T *A S of Ascents. Of David.*
125: T *A S of Ascents.*
126: T *A S of Ascents.*
127: T *A S of Ascents. Of Solomon.*
128: T *A S of Ascents.*
129: T *A S of Ascents.*
130: T *A S of Ascents.*
131: T *A S of Ascents. Of David.*
132: T *A S of Ascents.*
133: T *A S of Ascents.*
134: T *A S of Ascents.*
137: 4 could we sing the LORD's s in a foreign land?
144: 9 I will sing a new s to you, O God; A
147: 1 for he is gracious, and a s of praise is fitting.
149: 1 Sing to the LORD a new s, A
Ecc 7: 5 the rebuke of the wise than to hear the s of fools.
12: 4 and all the daughters of s are brought low;
SS 1: 1 The S of Songs, which is Solomon's.
Isa 23:15 to Tyre as in the s about the prostitute:
25: 5 the s of the ruthless was stilled.
26: 1 that day this s will be sung in the land of Judah:
30:29 a s as in the night when a holy festival is kept;
42:10 Sing to the LORD a new s, A
51: 3 thanksgiving and the voice of s.
54: 1 burst into s and shout, you who have not been
55:12 and the hills before you shall burst into s,
Mic 2: 4 that day they shall take up a taunt s against you,
Gal 4:27 you who bear no children, burst into s and shout,
Rev 5: 9 They sing a new s: "You are worthy to take A
14: 3 and they sing a new s before the throne and A
14: 3 No one could learn that s except
15: 3 And they sing the s of Moses, the servant of God,
15: 3 the servant of God, and the s of the Lamb:
Jdt 15:14 and all the people loudly sang this s of praise.
16: 1 Begin a s to my God with tambourines,
16:13 I will sing to my God a new s: A
2Mc 7: 6 as Moses declared in his s that bore witness
3Mc 4: 6 a lament instead of a wedding s,
6:32 of dirges and took up the s of their ancestors,
2Es 10:22 our harp has been laid low, our s has been silenced,
4Mc 18:18 not forget to teach you the s that Moses taught,

SONGS‡ (39) [SING]

Ge 31:27 I would have sent you away with mirth and s,
1Sa 18: 6 with s of joy, and with musical instruments.
2Sa 6: 5 with s and lyres and harps and tambourines
1Ki 4:32 and his s numbered a thousand and five.
Ne 12: 8 who with his associates was in charge of the s
12:46 there were s of praise and thanksgiving to God.
Ps 42: 4 with glad shouts and s of thanksgiving,
47: 1 shout to God with loud s of joy.
69:12 and the drunkards make s about me.
95: 2 let us make a joyful noise to him with s of praise!
107:22 and tell of his deeds with s of joy.
118:15 There are glad s of victory in the tents of
119:54 have been my s wherever I make my home.
137: 3 For there our captors asked us for s,
137: 3 saying, "Sing us one of the s of Zion!"
Pr 25:20 on a wound is one who sings s to a heavy heart.
SS 1: 1 The Song of S, which is Solomon's.
Isa 16:10 and in the vineyards no s are sung,
23:16 Make sweet melody, sing many s,
24:16 From the ends of the earth we hear s of praise,
Eze 26:13 I will silence the music of your s;
33:32 To them you are like a singer of love s,
Am 5:23 Take away from me the noise of your s;
6: 5 who sing idle s to the sound of the harp,
8: 3 s of the temple shall become wailings in that day,"
8:10 and all your s into lamentation;
Eph 5:19 as you sing psalms and hymns and spiritual s
Col 3:16 hymns, and spiritual s to God.
Jas 5:13 They should sing s of praise.
Tob 2: 6 and all your s into lamentation."
Sir 39:15 with s on your lips, and with harps;
47:17 Your s, proverbs, and parables,
1Mc 4:54 it was dedicated with s and harps and lutes
13:51 and stringed instruments, and with hymns and s,
2Mc 15:25 with trumpets and battle s,
3Mc 7:16 in words of praise and all kinds of melodious s.
2Es 2:42 and they all were praising the Lord with s.
4Mc 15:21 the s of swans attract the attention of their hearers
18:15 He sang to you s of the psalmist David, who said,

SONS‡ (918) [SON]

A. SONS ... DAUGHTERS (84)
B. SONS OF AARON (20)
C. SONS OF MERARI (16)
D. AARON'S SONS (15)
E. KING'S SONS (15)
F. SONS OF ISRAEL (14)
G. SONS OF LEVI (13)

Ge 5: 4 and he had other s and daughters. A
5: 7 and had other s and daughters. A
5:10 and had other s and daughters. A
5:13 and had other s and daughters. A
5:16 and had other s and daughters. A
5:19 and had other s and daughters. A
5:22 and had other s and daughters. A
5:26 and had other s and daughters. A
5:30 and had other s and daughters. A
6: 2 the s of God saw that they were fair;
6: 4 the s of God went in to the daughters of humans,
6:10 And Noah had three s, Shem, Ham, and Japheth.
6:18 and you shall come into the ark, you, your s,
7: 7 with his s and his wife and his sons' wives went
7:13 On the very same day Noah with his s,
7:13 and the three wives of his s entered the ark,
8:16 and your s and your sons' wives with you.
8:18 with his s and his wife and his sons' wives.
9: 1 God blessed Noah and his s, and said to them,
9: 8 Then God said to Noah and to his s with him,
9:18 s of Noah who went out of the ark were Shem,
9:19 These three were the s of Noah;
10: 1 These are the descendants of Noah's s, Shem,
10:25 To Eber were born two s:
10:32 These are the families of Noah's s,
11:11 and had other s and daughters. A
11:13 and had other s and daughters. A
11:15 and had other s and daughters. A
11:17 and had other s and daughters. A
11:19 and had other s and daughters. A
11:21 and had other s and daughters. A
11:23 and had other s and daughters. A
11:25 and had other s and daughters. A
19:12 Sons-in-law, s, daughters, A
25: 3 The s of Dedan were Asshurim, Letushim,
25: 4 The s of Midian were Ephah, Epher, Hanoch,
25: 6 But to the s of his concubines Abraham gave gifts,
25: 9 His s Isaac and Ishmael buried him in the cave
25:13 These are the names of the s of Ishmael,
25:16 the s of Ishmael and these are their names,
27:29 and may your mother's s bow down to you.
29:34 because I have borne him three s";
30:20 because I have borne him six s";
30:35 and put them in charge of his s;
31: 1 Now Jacob heard that the s of Laban were saying,
31:28 not permit me to kiss my s and my daughters A
33:19 And from the s of Hamor, Shechem's father,
34: 5 but his s were with his cattle in the field,
34: 7 just as the s of Jacob came in from the field.
34:13 The s of Jacob answered Shechem
34:25 when they were still in pain, two of the s of Jacob,
34:27 And the other s of Jacob came upon the slain,
35:22 Now the s of Jacob were twelve.
35:23 The s of Leah: Reuben (Jacob's firstborn),
35:24 The s of Rachel: Joseph and Benjamin.
35:25 The s of Bilhah, Rachel's maid: Dan and Naphtali.
35:26 The s of Zilpah, Leah's maid: Gad and Asher.
35:26 These were the s of Jacob who were born to him
35:29 and his s Esau and Jacob buried him.
36: 5 These are the s of Esau who were born to him in
36: 6 Then Esau took his wives, his s, his daughters, A
36:10 These are the names of Esau's s:
36:11 The s of Eliphaz were Teman, Omar, Zepho,
36:12 These were the s of Adah, Esau's wife.
36:13 These were the s of Reuel:
36:13 These were the s of Esau's wife, Basemath.
Ge 36:14 These were the s of Esau's wife Oholibamah,
36:15 These are the clans of the s of Esau.
36:15 The s of Eliphaz the firstborn of Esau:
36:16 they are the s of Adah.
36:17 These are the s of Esau's son Reuel:
36:17 they are the s of Esau's wife Basemath.
36:18 These are the s of Esau's wife Oholibamah:
36:19 These are the s of Esau (that is, Edom),
36:20 These are the s of Seir the Horite,
36:21 the s of Seir in the land of Edom.
36:22 The s of Lotan were Hori and Heman;
36:23 These are the s of Shobal:
36:24 These are the s of Zibeon:
36:26 These are the s of Dishon:
36:27 These are the s of Ezer: Bilhan, Zaavan, and Akan.
36:28 These are the s of Dishan: Uz and Aran.
37: 2 he was a helper to the s of Bilhah and Zilpah,
37:35 All his s and all his daughters sought A
41:50 the years of famine came, Joseph had two s,
42: 1 that there was grain in Egypt, he said to his s,
42: 5 Thus the s of Israel were among the other F
42:11 We are all s of one man;
42:13 the s of a certain man in the land of Canaan;
42:32 We are twelve brothers, s of our father;
42:37 "You may kill my two s if I do not bring him back
44:27 'You know that my wife bore me two s;
45:21 The s of Israel did so. F
46: 5 and the s of Israel carried their father Jacob, F
46: 7 his s, and his sons' s with him, his daughters,
46:15 (these are the s of Leah, whom she bore to Jacob
46:15 all his s and his daughters numbered A
46:26 not including the wives of his s,
48: 1 So he took with him his two s,
48: 5 Therefore your two s, who were born to you in
48: 8 Israel saw Joseph's s, he said, "Who are these?"
48: 9 Joseph said to his father, "They are my s,
49: 1 Then Jacob called his s, and said:
49: 2 Assemble and hear, O s of Jacob;
49: 8 your father's s shall bow down before you.
49:33 When Jacob ended his charge to his s,
50:12 Thus his s did for him as he had instructed them.
Ex 1: 1 the s of Israel who came to Egypt with Jacob, F
3:22 put them on your s and on your daughters; A
4:20 So Moses took his wife and his s,
6:14 the s of Reuben, the firstborn of Israel:
6:15 The s of Simeon: Jemuel, Jamin,
6:16 of the s of Levi according to their genealogies: G
6:17 s of Gershon: Libni and Shimei, by their families.
6:18 The s of Kohath: Amram,
6:19 The s of Merari: Mahli and Mushi. C
6:21 The s of Izhar: Korah, Nepheg, and Zichri.
6:22 The s of Uzziel: Mishael, Elzaphan, and Sithri.
6:24 The s of Korah: Assir, Elkanah,
10: 9 with our s and daughters and with our flocks A
13:15 but every firstborn of my s I redeem.'
18: 3 along with her two s.
18: 5 bringing Moses' s and wife to him.
18: 6 am coming to you, with your wife and her two s."
21: 4 and she bears him s or daughters, A
22:29 The firstborn of your s you shall give to me.
27:21 and his s shall tend it from evening to morning
28: 1 and his s with him, from among the Israelites,
28: 1 Aaron and Aaron's s, Nadab and Abihu, D
28: 4 for your brother Aaron and his s to serve me
28: 9 and engrave on them the names of the s of Israel, F
28:11 the two stones with the names of the s of Israel; F
28:12 as stones of remembrance for the s of Israel; F
28:21 corresponding to the names of the s of Israel; F
28:29 So Aaron shall bear the names of the s of Israel F
28:40 For Aaron's s you shall make tunics and sashes D
28:41 and on his s with him,
28:43 Aaron and his s shall wear them when they go into
29: 4 You shall bring Aaron and his s to the entrance of
29: 8 Then you shall bring his s, and put tunics on them,
29: 9 You shall then ordain Aaron and his s.
29:10 Aaron and his s shall lay their hands on the head
29:15 and his s shall lay their hands on the head of
29:19 and his s shall lay their hands on the head of
29:20 and on the lobes of the right ears of his s,
29:21 and on his s and his sons' vestments with him;
29:21 as well as his s and his sons' vestments.
29:24 on the palms of Aaron and on the palms of his s,
29:27 from that which belonged to Aaron and his s.
29:28 and his s from the Israelites, for this is an offering;
29:29 of Aaron shall be passed on to his s after him;
29:32 and Aaron and his s shall eat the flesh of the ram
29:35 Thus you shall do to Aaron and to his s,
29:44 Aaron also and his s I will consecrate,
30:19 the water Aaron and his s shall wash their hands
30:30 You shall anoint Aaron and his s,
31:10 for the priest Aaron and the vestments of his s,
32: 2 your wives, your s, and your daughters, A
32:26 And all the s of Levi gathered around him. G
32:28 The s of Levi did as Moses commanded, G
34:16 from among their daughters for your s,
34:16 to their gods will make your s also prostitute
34:20 All the firstborn of your s you shall redeem.
35:19 and the vestments of his s,
39: 6 according to the names of the s of Israel. F
39: 7 to be stones of remembrance for the s of Israel; F
39:14 corresponding to the names of the s of Israel; F
39:27 woven of fine linen, for Aaron and his s,
39:41 and the vestments of his s to serve as priests.
40:12 and his s to the entrance of the tent of meeting,
40:14 You shall bring his s also and put tunics on them,
40:31 and his s washed their hands and their feet.
Lev 1: 5 and Aaron's s the priests shall offer the blood, D

Lev 1: 7 The **s** of the priest Aaron shall put fire on the altar
1: 8 Aaron's **s** the priests shall arrange the parts, D
1:11 and Aaron's **s** the priests shall dash its blood D
2: 2 and bring it to Aaron's **s** the priests. D
2: 3 of the grain offering shall be for Aaron and his **s**,
2:10 of the grain offering shall be for Aaron and his **s**;
3: 2 and Aaron's **s** the priests shall dash the blood D
3: 5 Aaron's **s** shall turn these into smoke on the D
3: 8 Aaron's **s** shall dash its blood against all sides D
3:13 **s** of Aaron shall dash its blood against all sides B
6: 9 Command Aaron and his **s**, saying:
6:14 The **s** of Aaron shall offer it before the LORD, B
6:16 Aaron and his **s** shall eat what is left of it;
6:20 This is the offering that Aaron and his **s** shall offer
6:25 Speak to Aaron and his **s**, saying:
7:10 shall belong to all the **s** of Aaron equally. B
7:31 but the breast shall belong to Aaron and his **s**.
7:33 one among the **s** of Aaron who offers the blood B
7:34 have given them to Aaron the priest and to his **s**,
7:35 This is the portion allotted to Aaron and to his **s**
8: 2 Take Aaron and his **s** with him, the vestments,
8: 6 Then Moses brought Aaron and his **s** forward,
8:13 And Moses brought forward Aaron's **s**, D
8:14 and Aaron and his **s** laid their hands upon the head
8:18 and his **s** laid their hands on the head of the ram,
8:22 and his **s** laid their hands on the head of the ram,
8:24 After Aaron's **s** were brought forward, D
8:27 on the palms of Aaron and on the palms of his **s**,
8:30 and also on his **s** and their vestments.
8:30 and also his **s** and their vestments.
8:31 And Moses said to Aaron and his **s**,
8:31 as I was commanded, 'Aaron and his **s** shall eat it';
8:36 Aaron and his **s** did all the things that
9: 1 the eighth day Moses summoned Aaron and his **s**
9: 9 The **s** of Aaron presented the blood to him, B
9:12 Aaron's **s** brought him the blood, D
9:18 Aaron's **s** brought him the blood, D
10: 1 Now Aaron's **s**, Nadab and Abihu, D
10: 4 **s** of Uzziel the uncle of Aaron, and said to them,
10: 6 to Aaron and to his **s** Eleazar and Ithamar, "Do
10: 9 nor your **s**, when you enter the tent of meeting,
10:12 Moses spoke to Aaron and to his remaining **s**,
10:14 you and your **s** and your daughters as well may eat A
10:16 Aaron's remaining **s**, and said,
13: 2 to Aaron the priest or to one of his **s** the priests.
16: 1 to Moses after the death of the two **s** of Aaron, B
17: 2 to Aaron and his **s** and to all the people of Israel
21: 1 Speak to the priests, the **s** of Aaron, B
21:24 Thus Moses spoke to Aaron and to his **s** and to all
22: 2 Direct Aaron and his **s** to deal carefully with
22:18 to Aaron and his **s** and all the people of Israel
26:29 You shall eat the flesh of your **s**,
Nu 1:10 From the **s** of Joseph: from Ephraim,
3: 2 These are the names of the **s** of Aaron: B
3: 3 these are the names of the **s** of Aaron, B
3:17 following were the **s** of Levi, by their names: G
3:18 the names of the **s** of Gershon by their clans:
3:19 The **s** of Kohath by their clans:
3:20 The **s** of Merari by their clans: Mahli and Mushi. C
3:25 The responsibility of the **s** of Gershon in the tent
3:36 The responsibility assigned to the **s** of Merari C
3:38 were Moses and Aaron and Aaron's **s**, D
3:48 and his **s** the money by which the excess number
3:51 the redemption money to Aaron and his **s**,
4: 5 Aaron and his **s** shall go in and take down
4:15 and his **s** have finished covering the sanctuary
4:19 Aaron and his **s** shall go in and assign each to
4:27 of Aaron and his **s**, in all that they are to carry,
6:23 to Aaron and his **s**, saying, Thus you shall bless
8:13 the Levites stand before Aaron and his **s**,
8:19 a gift to Aaron and his **s** from among the Israelites,
8:22 of meeting in attendance on Aaron and his **s**.
10: 8 **s** of Aaron, the priests, shall blow the trumpets; B
16: 1 along with Dathan and Abiram **s** of Eliab,
16:12 Moses sent for Dathan and Abiram **s** of Eliab;
18: 1 You and your **s** and your ancestral house
18: 1 and your **s** alone shall bear responsibility
18: 2 and serve you while you and your **s** with you are
18: 7 But you and your **s** with you
18: 8 to you and your **s** as a priestly portion due you
18: 9 or guilt offering, shall belong to you and your **s**.
18:11 together with your **s** and daughters, A
18:19 together with your **s** and daughters, A
21:29 He has made his **s** fugitives,
21:35 So they killed him, his **s**, and all his people,
26:11 Notwithstanding, the **s** of Korah did not die.
26:19 The **s** of Judah: Er and Onan;
26:28 **s** of Joseph by their clans: Manasseh and Ephraim.
26:33 Now Zelophehad son of Hepher had no **s**,
26:40 And the **s** of Bela were Ard and Naaman:
27: 3 for his own sin; and he had no **s**.
36:11 married **s** of their father's brothers.
Dt 7: 3 to their **s** or taking their daughters for your **s**,
11: 6 **s** of Eliab son of Reuben, how in the midst
12:12 you together with your **s** and your daughters, A
12:31 would even burn their **s** and their daughters A
16:11 you and your **s** and your daughters, A
16:14 you and your **s** and your daughters, A
18: 5 him and his **s** for all time.
21: 5 the priests, the **s** of Levi, shall come forward, G
21:15 both the loved and the disliked have borne him **s**,
21:16 on the day when he wills his possessions to his **s**,
23:17 of the **s** of Israel shall be a temple prostitute. F
28:32 Your **s** and daughters shall be given A
28:41 You shall have **s** and daughters, A
28:53 the flesh of your own **s** and daughters whom A
31: 9 and gave it to the priests, the **s** of Levi, G

Dt 32:19 and was jealous he spurned his **s** and daughters. A
33:24 And of Asher he said: Most blessed of **s** be Asher;
Jos 7:24 his **s** and daughters, with his oxen, donkeys, A
15:14 Caleb drove out from there the three **s** of Anak:
17: 3 of Manasseh had no **s**, but only daughters;
17: 6 an inheritance along with his **s**.
24: 2 Terah and his **s** Abraham and Nahor—
Jdg 1:20 and he drove out from it the three **s** of Anak.
3: 6 and their own daughters they gave to their **s**;
8:18 they resembled the **s** of a king."
8:19 "They were my brothers, the **s** of my mother;
8:30 Now Gideon had seventy **s**, his own offspring,
9: 2 that all seventy of the **s** of Jerubbaal rule over you,
9: 5 and killed his brothers the **s** of Jerubbaal,
9:18 and have killed his **s**, seventy men on one stone,
9:24 to the seventy **s** of Jerubbaal might be avenged
10: 4 He had thirty **s** who rode on thirty donkeys;
11: 2 Gilead's wife also bore him **s**;
11: 2 and when his wife's **s** grew up,
12: 9 He had thirty **s**. He gave his thirty daughters in
12: 9 thirty young women from outside for his **s**.
12:14 He had forty **s** and thirty grandsons,
17: 5 and installed one of his **s**, who became his priest.
17:11 the young man became to him like one of his **s**.
18:30 and his **s** were priests to the tribe of the Danites
Ru 1: 1 he and his wife and two **s**.
1: 2 the names of his two **s** were Mahlon and Chilion;
1: 3 died, and she was left with her two **s**.
1: 5 so that the woman was left without her two **s**
1:11 Do I still have **s** in my womb
1:12 even if I should have a husband tonight and bear **s**,
4:15 who is more to you than seven **s**, has borne him."
1Sa 1: 3 where the two **s** of Eli, Hophni and Phinehas,
1: 4 wife Peninnah and to all her **s** and daughters; A
1: 8 Am I not more to you than ten **s**?"
2:12 Now the **s** of Eli were scoundrels;
2:21 she conceived and bore three **s** and two daughters.
2:22 He heard all that his **s** were doing to all Israel,
2:24 my **s**; it is not a good report
2:29 and honor your **s** more than me
2:34 The fate of your two **s**, Hophni and Phinehas,
3:13 because his **s** were blaspheming God,
4: 4 The two **s** of Eli, Hophni and Phinehas,
4:11 and the two **s** of Eli, Hophni and Phinehas, died.
4:17 your two **s** also, Hophni and Phinehas, are dead,
8: 1 he made his **s** judges over Israel.
8: 3 Yet his **s** did not follow in his ways,
8: 5 and your **s** do not follow in your ways;
8:11 he will take your **s** and appoint them
12: 2 I am old and gray, but my **s** are with you.
14:49 **s** of Saul were Jonathan, Ishvi, and Malchishua;
16: 1 for I have provided for myself a king among his **s**."
16: 5 And he sanctified Jesse and his **s** and invited them
16:10 Jesse made seven of his **s** pass before Samuel,
16:11 Samuel said to Jesse, "Are all your **s** here?"
17:12 named Jesse, who had eight **s**.
17:13 The three eldest **s** of Jesse had followed Saul to
17:13 of his three **s** who went to the battle were Eliab
22:20 But one of the **s** of Ahimelech son of Ahitub,
28:19 and tomorrow you and your **s** shall be with me;
30: 3 their wives and **s** and daughters taken captive. A
30: 6 bitter in spirit for their **s** and daughters. A
30:19 whether small or great, **s** or daughters, A
31: 2 The Philistines overtook Saul and his **s**;
31: 2 and Abinadab and Malchishua, the **s** of Saul.
31: 6 So Saul and his three **s** and his armor-bearer
31: 7 and his **s** were dead, they forsook their towns
31: 8 and his three **s** fallen on Mount Gilboa.
31:12 and the bodies of his **s** from the wall of Beth-shan.
2Sa 2:18 The three **s** of Zeruiah were there, Joab, Abishai,
3: 2 **S** were born to David at Hebron:
3:39 these men, the **s** of Zeruiah, are too violent for me.
4: 2 They were **s** of Rimmon a Benjaminite
4: 5 Now the **s** of Rimmon the Beerothite,
4: 9 the **s** of Rimmon the Beerothite,
5:13 and more **s** and daughters were born to David. A
6: 3 Uzzah and Ahio, the **s** of Abinadab,
8:18 and David's **s** were priests.
9:10 You and your **s** and your servants shall till the land
9:10 Now Ziba had fifteen **s** and twenty servants.
9:11 like one of the king's **s**. E
13:23 and Absalom invited all the king's **s**. E
13:27 until he let Amnon and all the king's **s** go E
13:29 Then all the king's **s** rose, E
13:30 to David that Absalom had killed all the king's **s**, E
13:32 the young men the king's **s**; E
13:33 as if all the king's **s** were dead; E
13:35 "See, the king's **s** have come; E
13:36 king's **s** arrived, and raised their voices and E
14: 6 Your servant had two **s**, and they fought
14:27 There were born to Absalom three **s**,
15:27 with your two **s**, Ahimaaz your son,
15:36 Their two **s** are with them there,
16:10 "What have I to do with you, you **s** of Zeruiah?
19: 5 and the lives of your **s** and your daughters, A
19:17 with his fifteen **s** and his twenty servants,
19:22 "What have I to do with you, you **s** of Zeruiah,
21: 6 let seven of his **s** be handed over to us,
21: 8 king took the two **s** of Rizpah daughter of Aiah,
21: 8 and the five **s** of Merab daughter of Saul,
23:20 he struck down two **s** of Ariel of Moab.
23:32 Eliahba of Shaalbon; the **s** of Jashen: Jonathan
1Ki 1: 9 the king's **s**, and all the royal officials of Judah, E
2: 7 however, with the **s** of Barzillai the Gileadite,
4: 3 Elihoreph and Ahijah **s** of Shisha were secretaries;
13:11 One of his **s** came and told him all that the man
13:12 And his **s** showed him the way that the man

1Ki 13:13 Then he said to his **s**, "Saddle a donkey for me."
13:27 Then he said to his **s**, "Saddle a donkey for me."
13:31 After he had buried him, he said to his **s**,
18:31 the number of the tribes of the **s** of Jacob, to whom
2Ki 10: 1 Now Ahab had seventy **s** in Samaria.
10: 1 to the elders, and to the guardians of the **s** of Ahab,
10: 2 "Since your master's **s** are with you and you have
10: 6 take the heads of your master's **s** and come to me
10: 6 Now the king's **s**, seventy persons, E
10: 7 they took the king's **s** and killed them, E
10: 8 "They have brought the heads of the king's **s**," E
10:13 the royal princes and the **s** of the queen mother."
10:30 your **s** of the fourth generation shall sit on
15:12 "Your **s** shall sit on the throne of Israel to
17:17 They made their **s** and their daughters pass
19:37 his **s** Adrammelech and Sharezer killed him with
20:18 Some of your own **s** who are born to you shall
25: 7 the **s** of Zedekiah before his eyes, then put out
1Ch 1:19 To Eber were born two **s**:
1:28 The **s** of Abraham: Isaac and Ishmael.
1:31 These are the **s** of Ishmael.
1:32 The **s** of Keturah, Abraham's concubine:
1:32 The **s** of Jokshan: Sheba and Dedan.
1:33 The **s** of Midian: Ephah, Epher,
1:34 The **s** of Isaac: Esau and Israel.
1:35 The **s** of Esau: Eliphaz, Reuel,
1:36 The **s** of Eliphaz: Teman, Omar,
1:37 **s** of Reuel: Nahath, Zerah, Shammah, and Mizzah.
1:38 The **s** of Seir: Lotan, Shobal,
1:39 The **s** of Lotan: Hori and Homam;
1:40 The **s** of Shobal: Alian, Manahath,
1:40 The **s** of Zibeon: Aiah and Anah.
1:41 The **s** of Anah: Dishon.
1:41 **s** of Dishon: Hamran, Eshban, Ithran, and Cheran.
1:42 The **s** of Ezer: Bilhan, Zaavan, and Jaakan.
1:42 The **s** of Dishan: Uz and Aran.
2: 1 These are the **s** of Israel: F
2: 3 The **s** of Judah: Er, Onan,
2: 4 Judah had five **s** in all.
2: 5 The **s** of Perez: Hezron and Hamul.
2: 6 The **s** of Zerah: Zimri, Ethan,
2: 7 The **s** of Carmi: Achar, the troubler of Israel,
2: 9 The **s** of Hezron, who were born to him:
2:10 Nahshon, prince of the **s** of Judah.
2:16 The **s** of Zeruiah: Abishai, Joab, and Asahel, three.
2:18 these were her **s**: Jesher, Shobab, and Ardon.
2:25 The **s** of Jerahmeel, the firstborn of Hezron:
2:27 The **s** of Ram, the firstborn of Jerahmeel:
2:28 The **s** of Onam: Shammai and Jada.
2:28 The **s** of Shammai: Nadab and Abishur.
2:30 The **s** of Nadab: Seled
2:32 The **s** of Jada, Shammai's brother:
2:33 The **s** of Jonathan: Peleth and Zaza.
2:34 Now Sheshan had no **s**, only daughters;
2:42 The **s** of Caleb brother of Jerahmeel:
2:42 The **s** of Mareshah father of Hebron.
2:43 **s** of Hebron: Korah, Tappuah, Rekem, and Shema.
2:47 The **s** of Jahdai: Regem, Jotham,
2:50 The **s** of Hur the firstborn of Ephrathah:
2:52 Shobal father of Kiriath-jearim had other **s**:
2:54 The **s** of Salma: Bethlehem,
3: 1 the **s** of David who were born to him in Hebron:
3: 9 were David's **s**, besides the **s** of the concubines;
3:15 The **s** of Josiah: Johanan the firstborn,
3:17 and the **s** of Jeconiah, the captive:
3:19 The **s** of Pedaiah: Zerubbabel
3:19 and the **s** of Zerubbabel: Meshullam
3:21 The **s** of Hananiah: Pelatiah
3:22 And the **s** of Shemaiah: Hattush, Igal,
3:23 The **s** of Neariah: Elioenai,
3:24 The **s** of Elioenai: Hodaviah,
4: 1 The **s** of Judah: Perez, Hezron,
4: 3 These were the **s** of Etam:
4: 4 These were the **s** of Hur,
4: 6 These were the **s** of Naarah.
4: 7 The **s** of Helah: Zereth, Izhar, and Ethnan.
4:13 The **s** of Kenaz: Othniel
4:13 and the **s** of Othniel: Hathath and Meonothai.
4:15 The **s** of Caleb son of Jephunneh:
4:16 **s** of Jehallelel: Ziph, Ziphah, Tiria, and Asarel.
4:17 The **s** of Ezrah: Jether, Mered, Epher, and Jalon.
4:17 These are the **s** of Bithiah, daughter of Pharaoh,
4:19 The **s** of the wife of Hodiah, the sister of Naham,
4:20 The **s** of Shimon: Amnon,
4:20 The **s** of Ishi: Zoheth and Ben-zoheth.
4:21 The **s** of Shelah son of Judah:
4:24 The **s** of Simeon: Nemuel,
4:26 The **s** of Mishma: Hammuel his son,
4:27 Shimei had sixteen **s** and six daughters;
4:42 Neariah, Rephaiah, and Uzziel, **s** of Ishi;
5: 1 The **s** of Reuben the firstborn of Israel.
5: 1 birthright was given to the **s** of Joseph son of Israel
5: 3 The **s** of Reuben, the firstborn of Israel:
5: 4 The **s** of Joel: Shemaiah his son,
5:11 The **s** of Gad lived beside them in the land
5:14 These were the **s** of Abihail son of Huri,
6: 1 The **s** of Levi: Gershom, Kohath, and Merari. G
6: 2 **s** of Kohath: Amram, Izhar, Hebron, and Uzziel.
6: 3 **s** of Aaron: Nadab, Abihu, Eleazar, and Ithamar. B
6:16 The **s** of Levi: Gershom, Kohath, and Merari. G
6:17 These are the names of the **s** of Gershom:
6:18 **s** of Kohath: Amram, Izhar, Hebron, and Uzziel.
6:19 The **s** of Merari: Mahli and Mushi. C
6:22 The **s** of Kohath: Amminadab his son,
6:25 The **s** of Elkanah: Amasai and Ahimoth,
6:28 **s** of Samuel: Joel his firstborn, the second Abijah.
6:29 The **s** of Merari: Mahli, Libni his son, C

1Ch 6:33 These are the men who served; and their s were:
6:44 On the left were their kindred the s of Merari: C
6:49 But Aaron and his s made offerings on the altar
6:50 These are the s of Aaron: B
6:54 to the s of Aaron of the families of Kohathites— B
6:57 To the s of Aaron they gave the cities of refuge: B
6:66 the s of Kohath had towns of their territory out of
7: 1 The s of Issachar: Tola, Puah,
7: 2 The s of Tola: Uzzi, Rephaiah,
7: 3 And the s of Izrahiah: Michael, Obadiah,
7: 4 for they had many wives and s.
7: 6 s of Benjamin: Bela, Becher, and Jediael, three.
7: 7 The s of Bela: Ezbon, Uzzi,
7: 8 The s of Becher: Zemirah,
7: 8 All these were the s of Becher;
7:10 The s of Jediael: Bilhan. And the s of Bilhan:
7:11 All these were the s of Jediael according to
7:12 And Shuppim and Huppim were the s of Ir,
7:14 The s of Manasseh: Asriel,
7:16 and his s were Ulam and Rekem.
7:17 These were the s of Gilead son of Machir,
7:19 The s of Shemida were Ahian, Shechem, Likhi,
7:20 The s of Ephraim: Shuthelah,
7:29 In these lived the s of Joseph son of Israel.
7:30 The s of Asher: Imnah, Ishvah,
7:31 The s of Beriah: Heber
7:33 The s of Japhlet: Pasach, Bimhal, and Ashvath.
7:33 These are the s of Japhlet.
7:34 s of Shemer: Ahi, Rohgah, Hubbah, and Aram.
7:35 The s of Helem his brother:
7:36 The s of Zophah: Suah, Harnepher,
7:38 The s of Jether: Jephunneh, Pispa, and Ara.
7:39 The s of Ulla: Arah, Hanniel, and Rizia.
8: 3 And Bela had s: Addar, Gera, Abihud,
8: 6 the s of Ehud (they were heads of ancestral houses
8: 8 And Shaharaim had s in the country of Moab
8: 9 He had s by his wife Hodesh:
8:10 These were his s, heads of ancestral houses.
8:11 He also had s by Hushim: Abitub and Elpaal.
8:12 The s of Elpaal: Eber, Misham,
8:16 Michael, Ishpah, and Joha were s of Beriah.
8:18 Ishmerai, Izliah, and Jobab were the s of Elpaal.
8:21 Beraiah, and Shimrath were the s of Shimei.
8:25 Iphdeiah, and Penuel were the s of Shashak.
8:27 Elijah, and Zichri were the s of Jeroham.
8:35 The s of Micah: Pithon, Melech, Tarea, and Ahaz.
8:38 Azel had six s, and these are their names:
8:38 all these were the s of Azel.
8:39 The s of his brother Eshek:
8:40 The s of Ulam were mighty warriors, archers,
9: 4 son of Bani, from the s of Perez son of Judah.
9: 5 of the Shilonites: Asaiah the firstborn, and his s.
9: 6 Of the s of Zerah: Jeuel
9:14 son of Hashabiah, of the s of Merari; C
9:30 Others, of the s of the priests,
9:41 The s of Micah: Pithon, Melech,
9:44 Azel had six s, and these are their names:
9:44 these were the s of Azel.
10: 2 The Philistines overtook Saul and his s;
10: 2 and Abinadab and Malchishua, s of Saul.
10: 6 he and his three s and all his house died together.
10: 7 and his s were dead, they abandoned their towns
10: 8 they found Saul and his s fallen on Mount Gilboa.
10:12 the body of Saul and the bodies of his s,
11:22 he struck down two s of Ariel of Moab.
11:44 Shama and Jeiel s of Hotham the Aroerite,
11:46 and Jeribai and Joshaviah s of Elnaam,
12: 3 then Joash, both s of Shemaah of Gibeah;
12: 3 also Jeziel and Pelet s of Azmaveth;
12: 7 and Joelah and Zebadiah, s of Jeroham of Gedor.
14: 3 became the father of more s and daughters. A
15: 5 of the s of Kohath, Uriel the chief,
15: 6 of the s of Merari, Asaiah the chief, C
15: 7 of the s of Gershom, Joel the chief,
15: 8 of the s of Elizaphan, Shemaiah the chief,
15: 9 of the s of Hebron, Eliel the chief, with eighty
15:10 of the s of Uzziel, Amminadab the chief,
15:17 and of the s of Merari, their kindred, C
16:42 The s of Jeduthun were appointed to the gate.
17:11 up your offspring after you, one of your own s,
18:17 and David's s were the chief officials in
21:20 his four s who were with him hid themselves,
23: 6 in divisions corresponding to the s of Levi: G
23: 7 The s of Gershon were Ladan and Shimei.
23: 8 The s of Ladan: Jehiel the chief,
23: 9 s of Shimei: Shelomoth, Haziel, and Haran, three.
23:10 the s of Shimei: Jahath, Zina, Jeush, and Beriah.
23:10 These four were the s of Shimei.
23:11 but Jeush and Beriah did not have many s,
23:12 The s of Kohath: Amram,
23:13 The s of Amram: Aaron and Moses.
23:13 so that he and his s forever should make offerings
23:14 his s were to be reckoned among the tribe of Levi.
23:15 The s of Moses: Gershom and Eliezer.
23:16 The s of Gershom: Shebuel the chief.
23:17 The s of Eliezer: Rehabiah the chief;
23:17 Eliezer had no other s, but the s of Rehabiah were
23:18 The s of Izhar: Shelomith the chief.
23:19 The s of Hebron: Jeriah the chief,
23:20 The s of Uzziel: Micah the chief
23:21 The s of Merari: Mahli and Mushi. C
23:21 The s of Mahli: Eleazar and Kish.
23:22 Eleazar died having no s, but only daughters;
23:22 their kindred, the s of Kish, married them.
23:23 The s of Mushi: Mahli, Eder, and Jeremoth, three.
23:24 were the s of Levi by their ancestral houses, G
24: 1 s of Aaron: Nadab, Abihu, Eleazar, and Ithamar. B

1Ch 24: 2 and Abihu died before their father, and had no s;
24: 3 Along with Zadok of the s of Eleazar,
24: 3 and Ahimelech of the s of Ithamar,
24: 4 the s of Eleazar than among the s of Ithamar,
24: 4 under sixteen heads of ancestral houses of the s
24: 4 and eight of the s of Ithamar.
24: 5 among both the s of Eleazar and the s of Ithamar.
24:20 And of the rest of the s of Levi: G
24:20 of the s of Amram, Shubael; of the s of Shubael,
24:21 of the s of Rehabiah, Isshiah the chief.
24:22 of the s of Shelomoth, Jahath.
24:23 The s of Hebron: Jeriah the chief,
24:24 s of Uzziel, Micah; of the s of Micah, Shamir.
24:25 of the s of Isshiah, Zechariah.
24:26 The s of Merari: Mahli and Mushi. C
24:26 The s of Jaaziah: Beno.
24:27 The s of Merari: of Jaaziah, C
24:28 Of Mahli: Eleazar, who had no s.
24:29 Of Kish, the s of Kish: Jerahmeel.
24:30 The s of Mushi: Mahli, Eder, and Jerimoth.
24:30 These were the s of the Levites according
25: 1 of the army also set apart for the service the s
25: 2 Of the s of Asaph: Zaccur,
25: 2 Joseph, Nethaniah, and Asarelah, s of Asaph,
25: 3 Of Jeduthun, the s of Jeduthun:
25: 4 Of Heman, the s of Heman:
25: 5 All these were the s of Heman the king's seer,
25: 5 for God had given Heman fourteen s
25: 9 to him and his brothers and his s, twelve;
25:10 the third to Zaccur, his s and his brothers, twelve;
25:11 the fourth to Izri, his s and his brothers, twelve;
25:12 Nethaniah, his s and his brothers, twelve;
25:13 Bukkiah, his s and his brothers, twelve;
25:14 Jesarelah, his s and his brothers, twelve;
25:15 Jeshaiah, his s and his brothers, twelve;
25:16 Mattaniah, his s and his brothers, twelve;
25:17 the tenth to Shimei, his s and his brothers, twelve;
25:18 Azarel, his s and his brothers, twelve;
25:19 Hashabiah, his s and his brothers, twelve;
25:20 Shubael, his s and his brothers, twelve;
25:21 Mattithiah, his s and his brothers, twelve;
25:22 to Jeremoth, his s and his brothers, twelve;
25:23 to Hananiah, his s and his brothers, twelve;
25:24 to Joshbekashah, his s and his brothers, twelve;
25:25 to Hanani, his s and his brothers, twelve;
25:26 to Mallothi, his s and his brothers, twelve;
25:27 to Eliathah, his s and his brothers, twelve;
25:28 to Hothir, his s and his brothers, twelve;
25:29 to Giddalti, his s and his brothers, twelve;
25:30 to Mahazioth, his s and his brothers, twelve;
25:31 to Romamti-ezer, his s and his brothers, twelve.
26: 1 Meshelemiah son of Kore, of the s of Asaph.
26: 2 Meshelemiah had s: Zechariah the firstborn,
26: 4 Obed-edom had s: Shemaiah the firstborn,
26: 6 Shemaiah s were born who exercised authority
26: 7 The s of Shemaiah: Othni,
26: 8 s of Obed-edom with their s and brothers,
26: 9 Meshelemiah had s and brothers, able men,
26:10 Hosah, of the s of Merari, had sons: C
26:10 Hosah, of the sons of Merari, had s:
26:11 all the s and brothers of Hosah totaled thirteen.
26:15 and to his s was allotted the storehouse.
26:19 among the Korahites and the s of Merari. C
26:21 The s of Ladan, the s of the Gershonites
26:22 The s of Jehieli, Zetham and his brother Joel,
26:29 and his s were appointed to outside duties
27:32 Jehiel son of Hachmoni attended the king's s. E
28: 1 of all the property and cattle of the king and his s,
28: 4 and among my father's s he took delight
28: 5 And of all my s, for the LORD has given me many,
29:24 and also all the s of King David,
2Ch 5:12 Asaph, Heman, and Jeduthun, their s and kindred,
11:14 because Jeroboam and his s had prevented them
11:19 She bore him s: Jeush, Shemariah, and Zaham.
11:21 the father of twenty-eight s and sixty daughters).
11:23 and distributed some of his s through all
13: 5 the kingship over Israel forever to David and his s
13: 8 the kingdom of the LORD in the hand of the s
13:21 the father of twenty-two s and sixteen daughters
20:14 son of Mattaniah, a Levite of the s of Asaph,
21: 2 He had brothers, the s of Jehoshaphat:
21: 2 all these were the s of King Jehoshaphat of Judah.
21:17 along with his s and his wives,
22: 1 the Arabs to the camp had killed all the older s.
22: 8 of Judah and the s of Ahaziah's brothers,
23: 3 the LORD promised concerning the s of David.
23:11 and Jehoiada and his s anointed him;
24: 3 and he became the father of s and daughters. A
24:27 of his s, and of the many oracles against him,
28: 3 and made his s pass through fire,
28: 8 women, s, and daughters; A
29: 9 fallen by the sword and our s and our daughters A
29:11 My s, do not now be negligent,
29:12 Joel son of Azariah, of the s of the Kohathites;
29:12 and of the s of Merari, Kish son of Abdi, C
29:13 and of the s of Elizaphan, Shimri and Jeuel;
29:13 and of the s of Asaph, Zechariah and Mattaniah;
29:14 and of the s of Heman, Jehuel and Shimei;
29:14 and of the s of Jeduthun, Shemaiah and Uzziel.
31:18 their s, and their daughters, the whole multitude; A
32:21 some of his own s struck him down there with
34:12 Levites Jahath and Obadiah, of the s of Merari, C
34:12 of the s of the Kohathites, to have oversight.
36:20 and to his s until the establishment of the kingdom
Ezr 3: 9 And Jeshua with his s and his kin, and Kadmiel
and his s, Binnui and Hodaviah along with the s of
Henadad, the Levites, their s and kin,

Ezr 3:10 and the Levites, the s of Asaph, with cymbals,
8:18 namely Sherebiah, with his s and kin, eighteen;
8:19 with his kin and their s, twenty;
9: 2 as wives for themselves and for their s.
9:12 Therefore do not give your daughters to their s,
9:12 neither take their daughters for your s,
Ne 3: 3 The s of Hassenaah built the Fish Gate;
4:14 and fight for your kin, your s, your daughters, A
5: 2 "With our s and our daughters, we are many; A
5: 5 we are forcing our s and daughters to be slaves, A
10: 9 Binnui of the s of Henadad, Kadmiel;
10:28 their wives, their s, their daughters, A
10:30 of the land or take their daughters for our s;
10:36 the firstborn of our s and of our livestock,
10:39 s of Levi shall bring the contribution of grain, G
13:25 "You shall not give your daughters to their s, or
take their daughters for your s or for yourselves.
13:28 And one of the s of Jehoiada,
Est 5:11 the number of his s, all the promotions with which
9:10 the ten s of Haman son of Hammedatha,
9:12 and also the ten s of Haman.
9:13 let the ten s of Haman be hanged on the gallows."
9:14 and the ten s of Haman were hanged.
9:25 that he and his s should be hanged on the gallows.
Job 1: 2 to him seven s and three daughters.
1: 4 His s used to go and hold feasts
1:13 One day when his s and daughters were eating A
1:18 "Your s and daughters were eating A
42:13 He also had seven s and three daughters.
Ps 45:16 the place of ancestors you, O king, shall have s;
106:37 They sacrificed their s and their daughters to
106:38 the blood of their s and daughters, A
127: 3 S are indeed a heritage from the LORD,
127: 4 in the hand of a warrior are the s of one's youth.
132:11 of the s of your body I will set on your throne.
132:12 If your s keep my covenant and my decrees
132:12 their s also, forevermore, shall sit on your throne."
144:12 May our s in their youth be like plants full grown,
Ecc 4: 8 of solitary individuals, without s or brothers;
SS 1: 6 My mother's s were angry with me;
Isa 14:21 Prepare slaughter for his s because of the guilt
37:38 his s Adrammelech and Sharezer killed him with
39: 7 Some of your own s who are born to you shall
43: 6 bring my s from far away and my daughters from
49:22 and they shall bring your s in their bosom,
56: 5 and a name better than s and daughters; A
60: 4 your s shall come from far away,
Jer 3:24 their s and their daughters. A
5:17 they shall eat up your s and your daughters; A
7:31 to burn their s and their daughters in the fire— A
11:22 their s and their daughters shall die by famine; A
14:16 their wives, their s, and their daughters. A
16: 2 nor shall you have s or daughters in this place. A
16: 3 the s and daughters who are born in this place, A
19: 9 the flesh of their s and the flesh of their daughters,
29: 6 Take wives and have s and daughters; A
29: 6 for your s, and give your daughters in marriage,
29: 6 that they may bear s and daughters; A
32:35 to offer up their s and daughters to Molech, A
35: 3 and his brothers, and all his s,
35: 4 into the chamber of the s of Hanan son of Igdaliah,
35: 8 ourselves, our wives, our s, or our daughters, A
39: 6 of Babylon slaughtered the s of Zedekiah at Riblah
40: 8 the s of Ephai the Netophathite,
48:46 for your s have been taken captive,
49: 1 Has Israel no s? Has he no heir?
52:10 The king of Babylon killed the s of Zedekiah
Eze 14:16 they would save neither s nor daughters; A
14:18 they would save neither s nor daughters, A
14:22 s and daughters who will be brought out; A
16:20 You took your s and your daughters, A
23: 4 became mine, and they bore s and daughters. A
23:10 they seized her s and her daughters; A
23:25 They shall seize your s and your daughters, A
23:47 they shall kill their s and their daughters, A
24:21 and your s and your daughters whom you left A
24:25 and also their s and their daughters, A
46:16 If the prince makes a gift to any of his s out of his
inheritance, it shall belong to his s,
46:17 only his s may keep a gift from his inheritance.
46:18 he shall give his s their inheritance out
Da 11:10 "His s shall wage war and assemble a multitude
Joel 2:28 your s and your daughters shall prophesy,
3: 8 I will sell your s and your daughters into the hand
Am 7:17 your s and your daughters shall fall by the sword,
Zep 1: 8 and the king's s and all who dress themselves E
Zec 9:13 I will arouse your s, O Zion, against your s,
Mt 20:20 mother of the s of Zebedee came to him with her s,
20:21 "Declare that these two s of mine will sit,
21:28 "What do you think? A man had two s;
26:37 He took with him Peter and the two s of Zebedee,
27:56 and the mother of the s of Zebedee.
Mk 3:17 gave the name Boanerges, that is, S of Thunder);
10:35 James and John, the s of Zebedee,
Lk 5:10 s of Zebedee, who were partners with Simon.
15:11 Then Jesus said, "There was a man who had two s.
Jn 4:12 and with his s and his flocks drank from it?"
21: 2 the s of Zebedee, and two others of his disciples.
Ac 2:17 and your s and your daughters shall prophesy,
7:16 a sum of silver from the s of Hamor in Shechem.
7:29 There he became the father of two s.
19:14 Seven s of a Jewish high priest named Sceva
2Co 6:18 and you shall be my s and daughters, A
Gal 4:22 For it is written that Abraham had two s,
Heb 11:21 when dying, blessed each of the s of Joseph,
Tob 1: 7 I would give these to the priests, the s of Aaron, B
1: 7 to the s of Levi who ministered at Jerusalem. G

Tob 1:21 before two of Sennacherib's s killed him,
4:13 the s and daughters of your people, A
5:14 and Nathan, the two s of Shemeliah, and they used
14: 3 and the seven s of Tobias and gave this command:
Jdt 16: 6 nor did the s of the Titans strike him down,
16:12 S of slave-girls pierced them through
AdE 9:10 the ten s of Haman son of Hammedatha,
9:13 Also, hang up the bodies of Haman's ten **s."**
9:14 of the city the bodies of Haman's s to hang up.
9:25 and he and his s were hanged.
Wis 9: 7 and to be judge over your s and daughters. A
Sir 45:13 but only his s and his descendants in perpetuity.
47:23 and left behind him one of his **s,**
50:13 All the s of Aaron in their splendor held B
50:16 Then the s of Aaron shouted; B
51:12 *Give thanks to him who has chosen the s of Zadok*
Bar 2: 3 of their s and others the flesh of their daughters.
4:10 for I have seen the exile of my s and daughters, A
4:14 remember the capture of my s and daughters, A
4:16 They led away the widow's beloved **s,**
1Mc 1:48 and to leave their s uncircumcised.
2: 2 He had five **s,** John surnamed Gaddi,
2:14 Then Mattathias and his s tore their clothes,
2:16 and Mattathias and his s were assembled.
2:17 and supported by s and brothers.
2:18 and your s will be numbered among the Friends of
2:18 and your s will be honored with silver and gold
2:20 and my s and my brothers will continue to live by
2:28 and his s fled to the hills and left all that they had
2:30 their **s,** their wives, and their livestock,
2:49 and he said to his **s:**
5: 4 He also remembered the wickedness of the s
6:24 For this reason the s of our people besieged
9:53 And he took the s of the leading men of the land
11:62 the s of their rulers as hostages and sent them
13:16 now one hundred talents of silver and two of his s
13:17 but he sent to get the money and the **s,**
13:18 not send him the money and the **s,**
13:19 So he sent the s and the hundred talents,
14:25 "How shall we thank Simon and his **s?**
14:29 a priest of the s of Joarib, and his brothers,
14:49 so that Simon and his s might have them.
16: 2 Simon called in his two eldest s Judas and John,
16:13 made treacherous plans against Simon and his **s,**
16:14 and he went down to Jericho with his s Mattathias
16:16 When Simon and his s were drunk,
16:16 in the banquet hall and killed him and his two **s,**
2Mc 7:20 she saw her seven s perish within a single day,
7:41 Last of all, the mother died, after her **s.**
1Es 1:13 and for their kindred the priests, the s of Aaron, B
1:14 and for their kindred the priests, the s of Aaron. B
1:15 The temple singers, the s of Asaph,
1:57 and they were servants to him and to his s until
5: 1 with their wives and s and daughters, A
5:58 and his s and kindred and his brother Kadmiel and
the s of Jeshua Emadabun and the s of Joda son of
Iliadun, with their s and kindred,
5:59 and the Levites, the s of Asaph, with cymbals,
8:21 not come upon the kingdom of the king and his **s.**
2Es 1:28 a father entreats his s or a mother her daughters or
1:34 and your s will have no children,
7:*103* fathers for s or s for parents,
4Mc 4:25 because they had circumcised their **s,**
12: 6 on her who had been bereaved of so many s and
15: 2 and that of preserving her seven s for a time,
15: 9 of the nobility of her s and their ready obedience
15:22 the mother then suffered as her s were tortured on
15:27 the deliverance that would preserve the seven s for
15:32 the torture of your **s,** endured nobly and withstood
16: 1 woman, advanced in years and mother of seven **s,**
16: 3 inflamed as she saw her seven s tortured
16: 8 In vain, my **s,** I endured many birth pangs for you,
16:11 when I die, I shall have none of my s to bury me."
16:13 for immortality to the whole number of her **s,**
16:15 For when you and your s were arrested together,
16:15 and said to your s in the Hebrew language,
16:16 "My **s,** noble is the contest to which you are called
16:24 the seven encouraged and persuaded each of her s
17: 2 who with your seven s nullified the violence of
17: 3 Nobly set like a roof on the pillars of your **s,**
17: 5 lighting the way of your star-like seven s to piety,
17: 9 an aged priest and an aged woman and seven **s,**
17:13 the mother of the seven s entered the competition,
18: 6 of seven s expressed also these principles
18: 9 and when these s had grown up their father died.
18:20 and in his burning rage brought those seven s of
18:23 But the s of Abraham with their victorious mother

SONS-IN-LAW (3) [SON]

Ge 19:12 **S,** sons, daughters, or anyone you have in
19:14 So Lot went out and said to his **s,**
19:14 But he seemed to his s to be jesting.

SONS' (9) [SON]

Ge 6:18 your sons, your wife, and your s wives with you.
7: 7 with his sons and his wife and his s wives went
8:16 and your sons and your s wives with you.
8:18 with his sons and his wife and his s wives.
46: 7 s sons with him, his daughters, and his s daughters;
Ex 29:21 and on his sons and his s vestments with him;
29:21 as well as his sons and his s vestments.
Lev 10:13 because it is your due and your s due,

SOON (124) [SOONER]

Ge 24:30 As s as he had seen the nose-ring,
27:30 As s as Isaac had finished blessing Jacob,
39:18 but as s as I raised my voice and cried out,
40:10 As s as it budded, its blossoms came out and
44: 3 As s as the morning was light,
Ex 2:18 "How is it that you have come back so s today?"
8:29 Then Moses said, "As s as I leave you,
9:29 "As s as I have gone out of the city,
32:19 As s as he came near the camp and saw the calf
Nu 16:31 As s as he finished speaking all these words,
Dt 2:16 as s as all the warriors had died off from among
4:26 against you today that you will s utterly perish
31:16 **"S** you will lie down with your ancestors.
Jos 2: 7 s as the pursuers had gone out, the gate was shut.
2:11 As s as we heard it, our hearts melted,
4:11 As s as all the people had finished crossing over,
6: 5 as s as you hear the sound of the trumpet,
6:20 As s as the people heard the sound of the trumpets,
8:19 As s as he stretched out his hand,
Jdg 2:17 They s turned aside from the way
8:33 As s as Gideon died, the Israelites relapsed
9:33 Then early in the morning, as s as the sun rises,
1Sa 1:22 "As s as the child is weaned, I will bring him,
9:13 As s as you enter the town, you will find him,
13:10 As s as he had finished offering the burnt offering,
20:41 As s as the boy had gone,
29:10 and leave as s as you have light."
2Sa 13:36 As s as he had finished speaking,
15:10 saying, "As s as you hear the sound of the trumpet,
15:14 Hurry, or he will s overtake us,
22:45 as s as they heard of me, they obeyed me.
1Ki 15:29 As s as he was king, he killed all the house
16:11 as s as he had seated himself on his throne,
18:12 As s as I have gone from you,
20:36 as s as you have left me, a lion will kill you."
21:15 As s as Jezebel heard that Naboth had been stoned
21:16 As s as Ahab heard that Naboth was dead,
2Ki 6:20 As s as they entered Samaria, Elisha said,
10:25 s as he had finished presenting the burnt offering,
13:21 as s as the man touched the bones of Elisha,
14: 5 As s as the royal power was firmly
2Ch 25: 3 As s as the royal power was firmly
31: 5 As s as the word spread, the people of Israel gave
Ezr 2:68 As s as they came to the house of the LORD
Est 5: 2 As s as the king saw Queen Esther standing in
Job 32:22 or my Maker would s put an end to me!
Ps 18:44 As s as they heard of me they obeyed me;
37: 2 for they will s fade like the grass,
48: 5 As s as they saw it, they were astounded;
90:10 they are s gone, and we fly away.
94:17 my soul would s have lived in the land of silence.
106:13 But they s forgot his works;
Isa 28: 4 whoever sees it, eats it up as s as it comes to hand.
49:22 I will s lift up my hand to the nations,
56: 1 and do what is right, for s my salvation will come,
66: 8 s as Zion was in labor she delivered her children.
Jer 27:16 of the LORD's house will s be brought back
Eze 7: 8 S now I will pour out my wrath upon you;
36: 8 for they shall s come home.
Da 3: 7 as s as all the peoples heard the sound of the horn,
6: 3 S Daniel distinguished himself above all
Hos 8:10 They shall s writhe under the burden of kings and
Mt 24:32 as s as its branch becomes tender
Mk 1:29 As s as they left the synagogue,
9:39 in my name will be able s afterward to speak evil
13:28 as s as its branch becomes tender
15: 1 As s as it was morning,
Lk 1:44 For as s as I heard the sound of your greeting,
7:11 S afterwards he went to a town called Nain,
8: 1 S afterwards he went on through cities
12:36 the door for him as s as he comes and knocks.
21:30 as s as they sprout leaves you can see
Ac 12:12 As s as he realized this,
17:15 to have Silas and Timothy join him as s
27:14 But s a violent wind, called the northeaster,
1Co 4:19 But I will come to you **s,** if the Lord wills,
Php 2:19 I hope in the Lord Jesus to send Timothy to you **s,**
2:23 therefore to send him as s as I see how things go
2:24 and I trust in the Lord that I will also come **s.**
1Ti 3:14 I hope to come to you **s,**
2Ti 4: 9 Do your best to come to me **s,**
Heb 8:13 what is obsolete and growing old will s disappear.
13:19 so that I may be restored to you very **s.**
2Pe 1:14 since I know that my death will come **s,**
3Jn 1:14 instead I hope to see you **s,**
Rev 1: 1 to show his servants what must s take place;
2:16 I will come to you s and make war against them
3:11 I am coming **s;** hold fast to what you have,
6:11 who were s to be killed
11:14 The third woe is coming very **s.**
12: 4 that he might devour her child as s as it was born.
22: 6 to show his servants what must s take place."
22: 7 "See, I am coming **s!**
22:12 I am coming **s;** my reward is with me,
22:20 to these things says, "Surely I am coming **s."**
Tob 10: 6 Do not grieve for him, my dear; he will s be here."
Jdt 13: 9 S afterward she went out and gave Holofernes'
14: 2 As s as day breaks and the sun rises on the earth,
14:11 As s as it was dawn they hung the head
16:18 As s as the people were purified,
Wis 5:13 So we also, as s as we were born, ceased to be,
6:15 and one who is vigilant on her account will s
Sir 6:19 and s you will eat of her produce.
Bar 4:22 because of the mercy that will s come to you
4:24 so they s will see your salvation by God,
Bar 4:25 but you will s see their destruction and will tread
Bel 1:18 As s as the doors were opened,
1Mc 11:22 s as he heard it he set out and came to Ptolemais;
2Mc 1:15 they closed the temple as s as he entered it.
2:18 that he will s have mercy on us and will gather us
5:18 from his rash act as s as he came forward,
7:37 to God to show mercy s to our nation and by trials
8: 5 As s as Maccabeus got his army organized,
9: 5 As s as he stopped speaking he was seized with
11: 1 Very s after this, Lysias, the king's guardian
11:36 as s as you have considered them,
1Es 8:71 As s as I heard these things I tore my garments
3Mc 1: 8 the more eager to visit them as s as possible.
3:23 that we may s alter our policy.
3:25 as s as this letter arrives,
5:23 as s as the cock had crowed in the early morning,
2Es 7:*75* as s as everyone of us yields up the soul,
4Mc 2: 8 as s as one adopts a way of life in accordance with
8:29 that as s as the tyrant had ceased counseling them

SOONER (4) [SOON]

Ru 4: 1 No s had Boaz gone up to the gate and sat
Ps 58: 9 S than your pots can feel the heat of thorns,
Wis 13: 9 did they fail to find s the Lord of these things?
2Es 5:43 so that you might show your judgment the **s?"**

SOOT (3)

Ex 9: 8 "Take handfuls of s from the kiln,
9:10 So they took s from the kiln,
La 4: 8 Now their visage is blacker than **s;**

SOOTHING (1)

AdE 15: 8 He comforted her with s words, and said to her,

SOOTHSAYER (1) [SOOTHSAYERS, SOOTHSAYING]

Dt 18:10 or who practices divination, or is a **s,** or an augur,

SOOTHSAYERS (4) [SOOTHSAYER]

Dt 18:14 about to dispossess do give heed to s and diviners,
Isa 2: 6 from the east and of s like the Philistines,
Jer 27: 9 your **s,** or your sorcerers, who are saying to you,
Mic 5:12 and you shall have no more **s;**

SOOTHSAYING (2) [SOOTHSAYER]

2Ki 21: 6 he practiced s and augury,
2Ch 33: 6 practiced s and augury and sorcery,

SOP (KJV) See PIECE OF BREAD

SOPATER (1)

Ac 20: 4 He was accompanied by S son of Pyrrhus

SOPE (KJV) See SOAP

SOPHERETH (1)

Ne 7:57 of Solomon's servants: of Sotai, of **S,**

SORCERER (2) [SORCERY]

Ex 22:18 You shall not permit a female s to live.
Dt 18:10 or is a soothsayer, or an augur, or a **s,**

SORCERERS (6) [SORCERY]

Ex 7:11 Then Pharaoh summoned the wise men and the **s;**
Jer 27: 9 your dreamers, your soothsayers, or your **s,**
Da 2: 2 the **s,** and the Chaldeans be summoned to tell
Mal 3: 5 I will be swift to bear witness against the **s,**
Rev 21: 8 the murderers, the fornicators, the **s,** the idolaters,
22:15 and s and fornicators and murderers and idolaters,

SORCERESS (1) [SORCERY]

Isa 57: 3 But as for you, come here, you children of a **s,**

SORCERIES (5) [SORCERY]

2Ki 9:22 and s of your mother Jezebel continue?"
Isa 47: 9 in spite of your many s and the great power of
47:12 Stand fast in your enchantments and your many **s,**
Mic 5:12 and I will cut off s from your hand,
Rev 9:21 And they did not repent of their murders or their s

SORCERY (6) [SORCERER, SORCERERS, SORCERESS, SORCERIES]

2Ch 33: 6 practiced soothsaying and augury and **s,**
Na 3: 4 gracefully alluring, mistress of **s,**
3: 4 and peoples through her **s,**
Gal 5:20 **s,** enmities, strife, jealousy, anger, quarrels,
Rev 18:23 and all nations were deceived by your **s.**
Wis 12: 4 their works of s and unholy rites,

SORDID (2) [SORDIDNESS]

Tit 1:11 by teaching for s gain what it is not right to teach.
1Pe 5: 2 would have you do it—not for s gain but eagerly.

SORDIDNESS (1) [SORDID]

Jas 1:21 Therefore rid yourselves of all s and rank growth

SORE (1) [SORES]

Rev 16: 2 and painful s came on those who had the mark of

SOREK (1)
Jdg 16: 4 in love with a woman in the valley of **S**,

SORELY (KJV) See ANGUISH, FIERCELY

SORES (5) [SORE]
Job 2: 7 and inflicted loathsome **s** on Job from the sole
Isa 1: 6 but bruises and **s** and bleeding wounds;
Lk 16:20 a poor man named Lazarus, covered with **s**,
16:21 even the dogs would come and lick his **s**.
Rev 16:11 the God of heaven because of their pains and **s**,

SORREL (1)
Zec 1: 8 and behind him were red, **s**, and white horses.

SORROW‡ (52) [SORROWED, SORROWFUL, SORROWING, SORROWS]
Ge 42:38 you would bring down my gray hairs with **s**
44:29 you will bring down my gray hairs in **s** to Sheol.'
44:31 the gray hairs of your servant our father with **s**
Est 9:22 that had been turned for them from **s** into gladness
Ps 13: 2 and have **s** in my heart all day long?
31:10 my life is spent with **s**, and my years with sighing;
88: 9 my eye grows dim through **s**.
107:39 through oppression, trouble, and **s**,
119:28 My soul melts away for **s**;
Pr 10:22 and he adds no **s** with it.
15:13 but by **s** of heart the spirit is broken.
23:29 Who has woe? Who has **s**?
25:20 **s** gnaws at the human heart.
Ecc 1:18 and those who increase knowledge increase **s**.
7: 3 **S** is better than laughter, for by sadness
Isa 35:10 and **s** and sighing shall flee away.
51:11 and **s** and sighing shall flee away.
Jer 20:18 from the womb to see toil and **s**,
31:13 I will comfort them, and give them gladness for **s**.
45: 3 The LORD has added **s** to my pain;
La 1:12 Look and see if there is any **s** like my **s**,
Eze 23:33 You shall be filled with drunkenness and **s**.
Jn 16: 6 to you, **s** has filled your hearts.
Ro 9: 2 I have great **s** and unceasing anguish in my heart.
2Co 2: 7 that he may not be overwhelmed by excessive **s**.
Php 2:27 so that I would not have one **s** after another.
Tob 2: 5 I returned, I washed myself and ate my food in **s**.
3: 6 and great is the **s** within me.
3:10 in his old age down in **s** to Hades.
7:16 Lord of heaven grant you joy in place of your **s**.
AdE 9:22 from **s** into gladness and from a time of distress to
Sir 26: 6 But it is heartache and **s** when a wife is jealous of
30:10 or you will have **s** with him,
30:12 and you will have **s** of soul from him.
30:21 Do not give yourself over to **s**,
30:23 remove **s** far from you, for **s** has destroyed many,
37: 2 Is it not a **s** like that for death itself when
38:19 When a person is taken away, **s** is over;
Bar 4: 9 God has brought great **s** upon me;
4:11 but I sent them away with weeping and **s**.
4:23 For I sent you out with **s** and weeping,
5: 1 Take off the garment of your **s** and affliction,
1Es 3:20 and forgets all **s** and debt.
2Es 2: 3 but with mourning and **s** I have lost you,
7:*117* [47] what good is it to all that they live in **s** now
10:12 which I brought forth in pain and bore in **s**;
10:14 'Just as you brought forth in **s**,
10:15 Now, therefore, keep your **s** to yourself,
10:20 and be consoled because of the **s** of Jerusalem.
4Mc 1:23 Fear precedes pain and **s** comes after.

SORROWED (1) [SORROW]
2Es 10:39 and that you have **s** continually for your people

SORROWFUL (11) [SORROW]
Ge 50:10 they held there a very great and **s** lamentation,
2Co 6:10 as **s**, yet always rejoicing;
Wis 2: 1 saying to themselves, "Short and **s** is our life,
Sir 38:18 and a **s** heart saps one's strength.
1Es 9:52 and do not be **s**, for the Lord will exalt you."
9:53 "This day is holy; do not be **s**."
2Es 2:27 others shall weep and be **s**,
7:12 of this world were made narrow and **s**
10: 8 and to be **s**, because we are all sorrowing;
12:46 and do not be **s**, O house of Jacob;
13:13 some of whom were joyful and some **s**;

SORROWING (2) [SORROW]
2Es 10: 8 and to be sorrowful, because we are all **s**;
10: 8 you are **s** for one son, but we, the whole world,

SORROWS‡ (7) [SORROW]
2Ch 6:29 all knowing their own suffering and their own **s**
Ps 16: 4 Those who choose another god multiply their **s**;
Jer 49:24 anguish and **s** have taken hold of her,
2Es 8:54 **s** have passed away, and in the end the treasure
10:24 and lay aside your many **s**,
16:18 of **s**, when there shall be much lamentation;
4Mc 16:10 a widow and alone, with many **s**.

SORRY (8)
Ge 6: 6 the LORD was **s** that he had made humankind on
6: 7 for I am **s** that I have made them."
1Sa 15:35 And the LORD was **s** that he had made Saul king
22: 8 none of you is **s** for me or discloses to me
Ps 38:18 I confess my iniquity; I am **s** for my sin.
Jer 42:10 for I am **s** for the disaster that I have brought
2Co 7: 8 For even if I made you **s** with my letter,
Tob 2:10 All my kindred were **s** for me,

SORT (15) [SORTS]
Ex 35:35 by any **s** of artisan or skilled designer.
36: 4 that all the artisans who were doing every **s** of task
Lev 14:35 to me to be some **s** of disease in my house."
1Sa 4: 8 the gods who struck the Egyptians with every **s**
2Ki 1: 7 "What **s** of man was he who came to meet you
9:11 "You know the **s** and how they babble."
2Ch 15: 6 for God troubled them with every **s** of distress.
Mt 8:27 They were amazed, saying, "What **s** of man is this,
Lk 1:29 and pondered what **s** of greeting this might be.
1Co 3:13 and the fire will test what **s** of work each has done.
2Pe 3:11 what **s** of persons ought you to be in leading lives
Wis 19:15 but, while punishment of some **s** will come upon
2Mc 3:37 the king asked Heliodorus what **s** of person would
5:10 of any **s** and no place in the tomb of his ancestors.
15:11 a **s** of vision, which was worthy of belief.

SORTS (13) [SORT]
Ge 40:17 and in the uppermost basket there were all **s**
Ex 35:22 and signet rings and pendants, all **s** of gold objects,
Dt 6:11 houses filled with all **s** of goods that you did
2Ki 17:32 from among themselves all **s** of people as priests
1Ch 18:10 He sent all **s** of articles of gold, of silver,
29: 2 antimony, colored stones, all **s** of precious stones,
2Ch 2:14 to do all **s** of engraving and execute any design
Ne 9:25 and took possession of houses filled with all **s**
2Mc 7:31 who have contrived all **s** of evil against
12:13 and inhabited by all **s** of Gentiles.
3Mc 5:22 as in devising all **s** of insults for those they thought
7:16 crowned with all **s** of very fragrant flowers,
4Mc 1:34 and animals and all **s** of foods that are forbidden

SOSIPATER (3)
Ro 16:21 so do Lucius and Jason and **S**, my relatives.
2Mc 12:19 Dositheus and **S**, who were captains
12:24 into the hands of Dositheus and **S** and their men.

SOSTHENES (2)
Ac 18:17 Then all of them seized **S**,
1Co 1: 1 by the will of God, and our brother **S**,

SOSTRATUS (2)
2Mc 4:28 When **S** the captain of the citadel kept requesting
4:29 in the high priesthood, while **S** left Crates,

SOTAI (2)
Ezr 2:55 The descendants of Solomon's servants: **S**,
Ne 7:57 The descendants of Solomon's servants: of **S**,

SOTTISH (KJV) See STUPID

SOUGHT (69) [SEEK]
Ge 37:35 All his sons and all his daughters **s** to comfort him;
Ex 2:15 When Pharaoh heard of it, he **s** to kill Moses.
33: 7 And everyone who **s** the LORD would go out to
1Sa 10:21 But when they **s** him, he could not be found.
13:14 the LORD has **s** out a man after his own heart;
19:10 Saul **s** to pin David to the wall with the spear;
23:14 Saul **s** him every day, but the LORD did not
27: 4 he no longer **s** for him.
2Sa 4: 8 son of Saul, your enemy, who **s** your life;
1Ki 1: 2 "Let a young virgin be **s** for my lord the king,
10:24 The whole earth **s** the presence of Solomon
11:40 Solomon **s** therefore to kill Jeroboam;
2Ch 9:23 the kings of the earth **s** the presence of Solomon
14: 7 we have **s** the LORD our God; we have **s** him
15: 4 and **s** him, he was found by them.
15:15 and had **s** him with their whole desire,
16:12 but **s** help from physicians.
17: 4 but **s** the God of his father and walked
22: 9 who **s** the LORD with all his heart."
25:20 because they had **s** the gods of Edom.
26: 5 long as he **s** the LORD, God made him prosper.
Ne 7:64 These **s** their registration among those enrolled in
12:27 the dedication of the wall of Jerusalem they **s** out
Est 2: 2 "Let beautiful young virgins be **s** out for the king.
9: 2 to lay hands on those who had **s** their ruin;
10: 3 for he **s** the good of his people and interceded for
Ps 34: 4 I **s** the LORD, and he answered me,
37:36 though I **s** them, they could not be found.
52: 7 in abundant riches, and **s** refuge in wealth!"
78:34 When he killed them, they **s** for him;
78:34 they repented and **s** God earnestly.
119:45 I shall walk at liberty, for I have **s** your precepts.
119:94 I am yours; save me, for I have **s** your precepts.
Ecc 7:28 which my mind has **s** repeatedly,
12:10 The Teacher **s** to find pleasing words,
SS 3: 1 at night I **s** him whom my soul loves;
3: 1 I **s** him, but found him not;
3: 2 I **s** him, but found him not.
5: 6 I **s** him, but did not find him;
Isa 26:16 O LORD, in distress they **s** you,
62:12 and you shall be called, "**S** Out,
65: 1 I was ready to be **s** out by those who did not ask,
65:10 for my people who have **s** me.
Jer 26:21 heard his words, the king **s** to put him to death;
31: 2 in the wilderness; when Israel **s** for rest,
44:30 his enemy who **s** his life."
Jer 50:20 says the LORD, the iniquity of Israel shall be **s**,
Eze 22:30 And I **s** for anyone among them who would repair
26:21 though **s** for, you will never be found again,
34: 4 you have not **s** the lost,
Da 4:36 My counselors and my lords **s** me out,
Hos 12: 4 he wept and **s** his favor;
Zep 1: 6 who have not **s** the LORD or inquired of him.
Heb 12:17 even though he **s** the blessing with tears.
AdE 2: 2 "Let beautiful and virtuous girls be **s** out for
6: 2 on guard and **s** to lay hands on King Artaxerxes.
Wis 8: 2 I loved her and **s** her from my youth;
Sir 21:17 utterance of a sensible person is **s** in the assembly,
24: 7 Among all these I **s** a resting place;
38:32 Yet they are not **s** out for the council of the people,
47:25 For they **s** out every kind of wickedness,
51:13 I **s** wisdom openly in my prayer.
1Mc 14: 4 He **s** the good of his nation;
14:14 he **s** out the law, and did away with all
14:35 He **s** in every way to exalt his people.
2Mc 13:21 he was **s** for, caught, and put in prison.
1Es 7:13 the abominations of the peoples of the land and **s**
2Es 5:10 and it shall be **s** by many but shall not be found,

SOUL‡ (208) [SOUL'S, SOULS, SOULS']
Ge 34: 3 And his **s** was drawn to Dinah daughter of Jacob;
35:18 As her **s** was departing (for she died),
Dt 4:29 if you search after him with all your heart and **s**.
6: 5 and with all your **s**, and with all your might.
10:12 with all your heart and with all your **s**,
11:13 serving him with all your heart and with all your **s**
11:18 of mine in your heart and **s**,
13: 3 the LORD your God with all your heart and **s**.
26:16 with all your heart and with all your **s**.
30: 2 with all your heart and with all your **s**,
30: 6 with all your heart and with all your **s**,
30:10 with all your heart and with all your **s**.
Jos 22: 5 with all your heart and with all your **s**."
Jdg 5:21 March on, my **s**, with might!
1Sa 1:15 I have been pouring out my **s** before the LORD.
17:55 Abner said, "As your **s** lives, O king,
18: 1 the **s** of Jonathan was bound to the **s** of David,
18: 1 and Jonathan loved him as his own **s**.
18: 3 because he loved him as his own **s**.
2Sa 11:11 As you live, and as your **s** lives,
1Ki 2: 4 with all their heart and with all their **s**,
8:48 if they repent with all their heart and **s** in the land
11:37 and you shall reign over all that your **s** desires;
2Ki 23: 3 and his statutes, with all his heart and all his **s**,
23:25 with all his **s**, and with all his might,
2Ch 6:38 if they repent with all their heart and **s** in the land
15:12 with all their heart and with all their **s**.
34:31 and his statutes, with all his heart and all his **s**,
Job 3:20 and life to the bitter in **s**,
7:11 I will complain in the bitterness of my **s**.
10: 1 I will speak in the bitterness of my **s**.
21:25 Another dies in bitterness of **s**,
27: 2 and the Almighty, who has made my **s** bitter,
30:16 "And now my **s** is poured out within me;
30:25 Was not my **s** grieved for the poor?
33:28 He has redeemed my **s** from going down to the Pit,
Ps 6: 3 My **s** also is struck with terror, while you,
7: 5 and lay my **s** in the dust.
11: 5 and his **s** hates the lover of violence.
13: 2 How long must I bear pain in my **s**,
16: 9 Therefore my heart is glad, and my **s** rejoices;
19: 7 The law of the LORD is perfect, reviving the **s**;
22:20 Deliver my **s** from the sword,
23: 3 he restores my **s**. He leads me in right paths
25: 1 To you, O LORD, I lift up my **s**.
30: 3 O LORD, you brought up my **s** from Sheol,
30:12 so that my **s** may praise you and not be silent.
31: 9 my eye wastes away from grief, my **s**
33:19 to deliver their **s** from death,
33:20 Our **s** waits for the LORD;
34: 2 My **s** makes its boast in the LORD;
34: 6 This poor **s** cried, and was heard by the LORD,
35: 3 say to my **s**, "I am your salvation."
35: 9 Then my **s** shall rejoice in the LORD,
35:12 They repay me evil for good; my **s** is forlorn.
42: 1 so my **s** longs for you, O God.
42: 2 My **s** thirsts for God, for the living God.
42: 4 These things I remember, as I pour out my **s**:
42: 5 Why are you cast down, O my **s**,
42: 6 My **s** is cast down within me;
42:11 Why are you cast down, O my **s**,
43: 5 Why are you cast down, O my **s**,
49:15 God will ransom my **s** from the power of Sheol,
56:13 For you have delivered my **s** from death,
57: 1 be merciful to me, for in you my **s** takes refuge;
57: 6 for my steps; my **s** was bowed down.
57: 8 Awake, my **s**! Awake, O harp and lyre!
62: 1 For God alone my **s** waits in silence;
62: 5 For God alone my **s** waits in silence,
63: 1 you are my God, I seek you, my **s** thirsts for you;
63: 5 My **s** is satisfied as with a rich feast,
63: 8 My **s** clings to you; your right hand upholds me.
69:10 When I humbled my **s** with fasting,
71:23 my **s** also, which you have rescued.
73:21 When my **s** was embittered,
74:19 not deliver the **s** of your dove to the wild animals;
77: 2 my **s** refuses to be comforted.
84: 2 My **s** longs, indeed it faints for the courts of
86: 4 Gladden the **s** of your servant, for to you, O Lord,
86: 4 for to you, O Lord, I lift up my **s**.
86:13 you have delivered my **s** from the depths of Sheol.
88: 3 For my **s** is full of troubles,

Ps 94:17 my s would soon have lived in the land of silence.
94:19 your consolations cheer my s.
103: 1 O my s, and all that is within me,
103: 2 Bless the LORD, O my s,
103:22 Bless the LORD, O my s.
104: 1 Bless the LORD, O my s.
104:35 Bless the LORD, O my s.
107: 5 hungry and thirsty, their s fainted within them.
108: 1 I will sing and make melody. Awake, my s!
116: 7 Return, O my s, to your rest,
116: 8 For you have delivered my s from death,
119:20 My s is consumed with longing
119:25 My s clings to the dust;
119:28 My s melts away for sorrow;
119:81 My s languishes for your salvation;
119:129 therefore my s keeps them.
119:167 My s keeps your decrees; I love them exceedingly.
123: 4 Our s has had more than its fill of the scorn
130: 5 I wait for the LORD, my s waits,
130: 6 my s waits for the Lord more than those who watch
131: 2 But I have calmed and quieted my s,
131: 2 my s is like the weaned child that is with me.
138: 3 you answered me, you increased my strength of s.
143: 6 my s thirsts for you like a parched land.
143: 8 for to you I lift up my s.
146: 1 Praise the LORD! Praise the LORD, O my s!
Pr 2:10 and knowledge will be pleasant to your s;
3:22 be life for your s and adornment for your neck.
13:19 A desire realized is sweet to the s,
16:24 sweetness to the s and health to the body.
23:16 My s will rejoice when your lips speak what is
24:12 Does not he who keeps watch over your s know it?
24:14 Know that wisdom is such to your s;
25:25 Like cold water to a thirsty s,
27: 9 but the s is torn by trouble.
SS 1: 7 Tell me, you whom my s loves,
3: 1 at night I sought him whom my s loves;
3: 2 I will seek him whom my s loves."
3: 3 "Have you seen him whom my s loves?"
3: 4 when I found him whom my s loves.
5: 6 My s failed me when he spoke.
Isa 1:14 and your appointed festivals my s hates;
10:18 the LORD will destroy, both s and body,
15: 4 the loins of Moab quiver; his s trembles.
16:11 and my very s for Kir-heres.
26: 9 My s yearns for you in the night,
38:15 because of the bitterness of my s.
42: 1 my chosen, in whom my s delights;
Jer 13:17 my s will weep in secret for your pride;
32:41 with all my heart and all my s.
La 3:17 my s is bereft of peace;
3:20 My s continually thinks of it and is bowed down
3:24 "The LORD is my portion," says my s,
3:25 to the s that seeks him.
Eze 27:31 and they weep over you in bitterness of s,
Mic 6: 7 the fruit of my body for the sin of my s?"
Mt 10:28 who kill the body but cannot kill the s;
10:28 rather fear him who can destroy both s and body
12:18 my beloved, with whom my s is well pleased.
22:37 and with all your s, and with all your mind.'
Mk 12:30 and with all your s, and with all your mind,
Lk 1:46 And Mary said, "My s magnifies the Lord,
2:35 and a sword will pierce your own s too."
10:27 and with all your s, and with all your strength,
12:19 And I will say to my s, 'S, you have ample goods
Jn 12:27 "Now my s is troubled.
Ac 2:27 For you will not abandon my s to Hades,
4:32 of those who believed were of one heart and s,
1Th 5:23 and may your spirit and s and body be kept sound
Heb 4:12 piercing until it divides s from spirit,
6:19 a sure and steadfast anchor of the s,
10:38 s takes no pleasure in anyone who shrinks back."
Jas 5:20 from wandering will save the sinner's s from death
1Pe 2:11 the desires of the flesh that wage war against the s.
2Pe 2: 8 in his righteous s by their lawless deeds
3Jn 1: 2 just as it is well with your s.
Rev 18:14 fruit for which your s longed has gone from you,
Tob 13: 6 to him with all your heart and with all your s,
13: 7 and my s rejoices in the King of heaven.
13:15 My s blesses the Lord, the great King!
Wis 1: 4 because wisdom will not enter a deceitful s,
1:11 and a lying mouth destroys the s.
8:19 and a good s fell to my lot;
9: 3 and pronounce judgment in uprightness of s,
9:15 for a perishable body weighs down the s,
10: 7 as a monument to an unbelieving s.
10:16 She entered the s of a servant of the Lord,
16:14 or set free the imprisoned s.
17: 8 a sick s were sick themselves with ridiculous fear.
Sir 4: 6 for if in bitterness of s some should curse you,
6:26 Come to her with all your s,
7:21 Let your s love intelligent slaves;
7:29 With all your s fear the Lord,
14: 9 greedy injustice withers the s.
18:31 If you allow your s to take pleasure in base desire,
30:12 and you will have sorrow of s from him.
31:28 of heart and gladness of s.
34:17 Happy is the s that fears the Lord!
34:20 He lifts up the s and makes the eyes sparkle;
45:23 in the noble courage of his s;
50:25 Two nations my s detests,
51: 6 My s drew near to death, and my life was on the
51:19 My s grappled with wisdom,
51:20 I directed my s to her, and in purity I found her.
51:29 May your s rejoice in God's mercy,
Bar 2:18 with failing eyes and famished s,
3: 1 s in anguish and the wearied spirit cry out to you.
2Mc 3:16 in his color disclosed the anguish of his s.
6:30 but in my s I am glad to suffer these things
15:30 the man who was ever in body and s the defender
2Es 3:29 and my s has seen many sinners
5:14 and my s was so troubled that it fainted.
5:22 Then my s recovered the spirit of understanding,
6:37 and my s was in distress.
7:*75* as soon as everyone of us yields up the s,
8: 4 "Then drink your fill of understanding, O my s,
10:36 —or is my mind deceived, and my s dreaming?
12: 8 so that you may fully comfort my s.
4Mc 1:20 by nature concerned with both body and s.
1:26 In the s it is boastfulness, covetousness,
1:28 two plants growing from the body and the s,
3:15 considered it an altogether fearful danger to his s
13:15 of the s and the danger of eternal torment lying
15:25 of her own s she saw mighty advocates—

SOUL'S (1) [SOUL]

Isa 26: 8 your name and your renown are the s desire.

SOULS‡ (42) [SOUL]

Jos 23:14 and you know in your hearts and s, all of you,
Job 33:18 to spare their s from the Pit,
33:22 Their s draw near the Pit,
33:30 to bring back their s from the Pit,
Ps 24: 4 who do not lift up their s to what is false,
Pr 21:10 The s of the wicked desire evil;
Isa 57:16 even the s that I have made.
Jer 6:16 and walk in it, and find rest for your s.
Mt 11:29 and you will find rest for your s.
Lk 21:19 By your endurance you will gain your s.
Ac 14:22 There they strengthened the s of the disciples
Heb 13:17 for they are keeping watch over your s
Jas 1:21 that has the power to save your s.
1Pe 1: 9 the outcome of your faith, the salvation of your s.
1:22 that you have purified your s by your obedience to
2:25 to the shepherd and guardian of your s.
2Pe 2:14 insatiable for sin. They entice unsteady s.
Rev 6: 9 the altar the s of those who had been slaughtered
20: 4 I also saw the s of those who had been beheaded
Wis 2:22 nor discerned the prize for blameless s;
3: 1 But the s of the righteous are in the hand of God,
3:13 she will have fruit when God examines s.
4:11 their understanding or guile deceive their s.
4:14 for their s were pleasing to the Lord,
7:27 into holy s and makes them friends of God,
14:11 for human s and a trap for the feet of the foolish.
14:26 forgetfulness of favors, defiling of s,
15: 8 the time comes to return the s that were borrowed.
15:11 with active s and breathed a living spirit into them.
17: 1 therefore uninstructed s have gone astray.
Sir 51:26 and let your s receive instruction;
Aza 1:64 Bless the Lord, spirits and s of the righteous;
2Mc 15:17 in arousing valor and awaking courage in the s of
2Es 4:35 not the s of the righteous in their chambers ask
4:41 the chambers of the s are like the womb.
7:*32* up the s that have been committed to them.
7:*93* because they see the perplexity in which the s of
7:*99* This is the order of the s of the righteous,
7:*100* "Will time therefore be given to the s,
15: 8 and the s of the righteous cry out continually.
4Mc 13:21 such embraces brotherly-loving s are nourished;
18:23 and have received pure and immortal s from God,

SOULS' (1) [SOUL]

Wis 17:15 and now were paralyzed by their s surrender;

SOUND (170) [SOUNDED, SOUNDING, SOUNDINGS, SOUNDNESS, SOUNDS]

Ge 3: 8 the s of the LORD God walking in the garden at
3:10 He said, "I heard the s of you in the garden,
Ex 20:18 the s of the trumpet, and the mountain smoking,
28:35 and its s shall be heard when he goes into
32:18 But he said, "It is not the s made by victors,
32:18 or the s made by losers;
32:18 it is the s of revelers that I hear."
Lev 26:36 the s of a driven leaf shall put them to flight,
Nu 10: 7 you shall blow, but you shall not s an alarm.
10: 9 you shall s an alarm with the trumpets,
Dt 4:12 You heard the s of words but saw no form;
Jos 6: 5 as soon as you hear the s of the trumpet,
6:20 As soon as the people heard the s of the trumpets,
Jdg 5:11 To the s of musicians at the watering places,
1Sa 4:14 When Eli heard the s of the outcry, he said,
2Sa 5:24 the s of marching in the tops of the balsam trees,
6:15 and with the s of the trumpet.
15:10 saying, "As soon as you hear the s of the trumpet,
1Ki 1:41 When Joab heard the s of the trumpet, he said,
14: 6 But when Ahijah heard the s of her feet,
18:41 for there is a s of rushing rain."
19:12 and after the fire a s of sheer silence.
2Ki 4:31 but there was no s or sign of life.
6:32 Is not the s of his master's feet behind him?"
7: 6 the Aramean army to hear the s of chariots,
7: 6 and of horses, the s of a great army,
1Ch 14:15 the s of marching in the tops of the balsam trees,
15:19 Asaph, and Ethan were to s bronze cymbals;
15:28 to the s of the horn, trumpets, and cymbals,
16: 5 Asaph was to s the cymbals,
2Ch 13:12 and his priests have their battle trumpets to s
Ezr 3:13 not distinguish the s of the joyful shout from the s
3:13 so loudly that the s was heard far away.
Ne 4:20 Rally to us wherever you hear the s of the trumpet.
Job 21:12 and rejoice to the s of the pipe.
33: 8 and I have heard the s of your words.
39:24 it cannot stand still at the s of the trumpet.
Ps 5: 2 Listen to the s of my cry, my King and my God,
6: 8 for the LORD has heard the s of my weeping.
28: 6 for he has heard the s of my pleadings.
47: 5 the LORD with the s of a trumpet.
66: 8 O peoples, let the s of his praise be heard,
73: 4 For they have no pain; their bodies are s and sleek.
81: 2 Raise a song, s the tambourine,
98: 5 with the lyre and the s of melody.
98: 6 and the s of the horn make a joyful noise before
104: 7 at the s of your thunder they take to flight.
115: 7 they make no s in their throats.
150: 3 Praise him with trumpet s;
Pr 2: 7 he stores up s wisdom for the upright;
3:21 keep s wisdom and prudence,
8:14 I have good advice and s wisdom;
18: 1 showing contempt for all who have s judgment.
Ecc 12: 4 and the s of the grinding is low,
12: 4 and one rises up at the s of a bird,
Isa 14:11 and the s of your harps;
24:18 Whoever flees at the s of the terror shall fall into
30:19 surely be gracious to you at the s of your cry;
30:29 and gladness of heart, as when one sets out to the s
30:32 upon him will be to the s of timbrels and lyres;
33: 3 At the s of tumult, peoples fled;
65:19 no more shall the s of weeping be heard in it,
Jer 4:19 for I hear the s of the trumpet, the alarm of war.
4:21 and hear the s of the trumpet?
6:17 "Give heed to the s of the trumpet!"
6:23 their s is like the roaring sea;
7:34 I will bring to an end the s of mirth and gladness,
8:16 at the s of the neighing of their stallions
9:19 For a s of wailing is heard from Zion:
25:10 And I will banish from them the s of mirth and the s of gladness,
25:10 the s of the millstones and the light of the lamp.
30:19 and the s of merrymakers.
42:14 or hear the s of the trumpet,
46:22 She makes a s like a snake gliding away;
49: 2 when I will s the battle alarm against Rabbah of
49:21 At the s of their fall the earth shall tremble;
49:21 the s of their cry shall be heard at the Red Sea.
50:42 The s of them is like the roaring sea;
50:46 At the s of the capture of Babylon
51:55 the s of their clamor resounds;
Eze 1:24 the s of their wings like the s of mighty waters,
1:24 a s of tumult like the s of an army;
3:12 I heard behind me the s of loud rumbling;
3:13 the s of the wings of the living creatures brushing
3:13 and the s of the wheels beside them,
10: 5 The s of the wings of the cherubim was heard
19: 7 and all in it, at the s of his roaring.
23:42 The s of a raucous multitude was around her,
26:13 the s of your lyres shall be heard no more.
26:15 Shall not the coastlands shake at the s of your fall,
27:28 At the s of the cry of your pilots
31:16 I made the nations quake at the s of its fall,
33: 4 then if any who hear the s of the trumpet do
33: 5 the s of the trumpet and did not take warning;
43: 2 the s was like the s of mighty waters;
Da 3: 5 that when you hear the s of the horn,
3: 7 as soon as all the peoples heard the s of the horn,
3:10 that everyone who hears the s of the horn, pipe,
3:15 if you are ready when you hear the s of the horn,
10: 6 and the s of his words like the roar of a multitude.
10: 9 Then I heard the s of his words; and when I heard the s of his words,
Hos 5: 8 S the alarm at Beth-aven;
Joel 2: 1 s the alarm on my holy mountain!
Am 2: 2 amid shouting and the s of the trumpet;
6: 5 to the s of the harp, and like David improvise
Jnh 1: 6 "What are you doing s asleep?
Mic 6: 9 of the LORD cries to the city (it is s wisdom
Hab 3:16 my lips quiver at the s.
Zep 1:14 the s of the day of the LORD is bitter,
Zec 9:14 the Lord GOD will s the trumpet and march forth
Mt 6: 2 do not s a trumpet before you,
12:13 and it was restored, as s as the other.
Lk 1:44 For as soon as I heard the s of your greeting,
15:27 because he has got him back safe and s.'
Jn 3: 8 and you hear the s of it,
Ac 2: 2 And suddenly from heaven there came a s like
2: 6 at this s the crowd gathered and was bewildered,
1Co 14: 7 with lifeless instruments that produce s,
14: 8 And if the bugle gives an indistinct s,
14:10 of sounds in the world, and nothing is without s.
14:11 If then I do not know the meaning of a s,
15:52 For the trumpet will s, and the dead will
1Th 4:16 with the archangel's call and with the s
5:23 and may your spirit and soul and body be kept s
1Ti 1:10 and whatever else is contrary to the s teaching
4: 6 on the words of the faith and of the s teaching
6: 3 with the s words of our Lord Jesus Christ and
2Ti 1:13 to the standard of s teaching that you have heard
4: 3 when people will not put up with s doctrine,
Tit 1: 9 that he may be able both to preach with s doctrine
1:13 so that they may become s in the faith,
2: 1 as for you, teach what is consistent with s doctrine.
2: 2 prudent, and s in faith, in love, and in endurance.
2: 8 and s speech that cannot be censured;
Heb 12:19 and the s of a trumpet,
Rev 1:15 and his voice was like the s of many waters.
14: 2 like the s of many waters and like the s of loud thunder; the voice I heard was like the s of harpists
18:22 and the s of harpists and minstrels and of flutists

Rev 18:22 and the s of the millstone will be heard in you no
19: 6 like the s of many waters and like the s of mighty
Tob 8:13 and she went in and found them s asleep together.
AdE 13: 3 who excels among us in s judgment,
Wis 1:10 and the s of grumbling does not go unheard.
7: 3 my first s was a cry, as is true of all.
17:18 a melodious s of birds in wide-spreading branches,
17:19 or the s of the most savage roaring beasts,
Sir 25: 4 How attractive is s judgment in the gray-haired,
26:19 *My child, keep s the bloom of your youth,*
38:28 the s of the hammer deafens his ears,
42: 8 Then you will show your s training,
45: 9 to send forth a s as he walked,
46:17 and made his voice heard with a mighty s;
1Mc 9:12 the phalanx advanced to the s of the trumpets;
1Es 5:65 so that the s was heard far away;
5:66 to find out what the s of the trumpets meant.
2Es 6:17 and its s was like the s of mighty waters.
6:23 the trumpet shall s aloud,
6:39 the s of human voices was not yet there.
10:26 so that the earth shook at the s.
4Mc 1:15 Now reason is the mind that with s logic prefers

SOUNDED (25) [SOUND]
Lev 25: 9 Then you shall have the trumpet s loud;
25: 9 the trumpet s throughout all your land.
Jdg 3:27 he s the trumpet in the hill country of Ephraim;
6:34 of Gideon; and he s the trumpet,
1Sa 20:12 When I have s out my father,
2Sa 2:28 Joab s the trumpet and all the people stopped;
18:16 Then Joab s the trumpet, and the troops came back
20: 1 He s the trumpet and cried out,
2Ch 7: 6 Opposite them the priests s trumpets;
29:28 the singers sang, and the trumpeters s;
Ne 4:18 The man who s the trumpet was beside me.
Eze 3:13 that s like a loud rumbling.
19: 4 The nations s an alarm against him;
1Th 1: 8 the word of the Lord has s forth from you not only
Rev 10: 3 And when he shouted, the seven thunders s.
10: 4 And when the seven thunders had s,
Sir 50:16 they s a mighty fanfare as a reminder before the
1Mc 3:54 Then they s the trumpets and gave a loud shout.
5:33 who s their trumpets and cried aloud in prayer.
6:33 for battle and s their trumpets.
16: 8 They s the trumpets, and Cendebeus
1Es 5:62 And all the people s trumpets and shouted with
5:65 For the multitude s the trumpets loudly,
2Es 6: 2 and before the rumblings of thunder s,
11:15 And a voice s, saying to it,

SOUNDING (3) [SOUND]
Nu 31: 6 the vessels of the sanctuary and the trumpets for s
Sir 26:27 *and garrulous wife is like a trumpet s the charge,*
1Mc 7:45 and as they followed they kept s the battle call on

SOUNDINGS (2) [SOUND]
Ac 27:28 So they took s and found twenty fathoms;
27:28 on they took s again and found fifteen fathoms.

SOUNDNESS (3) [SOUND]
Ps 38: 3 There is no s in my flesh because
38: 7 and there is no s in my flesh.
Isa 1: 6 there is no s in it, but bruises and sores

SOUNDS (7) [SOUND]
Ex 19:13 When the trumpet s a long blast,
1Ch 15:16 to raise loud s of joy.
Job 15:21 Terrifying s are in their ears;
39:25 When the trumpet s, it says 'Aha!'
Ac 17:20 It s rather strange to us,
1Co 14:10 There are doubtless many different kinds of s in
Wis 17: 4 but terrifying s rang out around them,

SOUR (8)
Ru 2:14 and dip your morsel in the s wine."
Jer 31:29 "The parents have eaten s grapes,
31:30 the teeth of everyone who eats s grapes shall be set
Eze 18: 2 "The parents have eaten s grapes,
Mt 27:48 filled it with s wine, put it on a stick,
Mk 15:36 And someone ran, filled a sponge with s wine,
Lk 23:36 coming up and offering him s wine,
Jn 19:29 A jar full of s wine was standing there.

SOURCE‡ (7) [SOURCES]
Eze 36: 4 a s of plunder and an object of derision to the rest
1Co 1:30 He is the s of your life in Christ Jesus,
Gal 1:12 for I did not receive it from a human s,
Heb 5: 9 the s of eternal salvation for all who obey him,
Wis 12:16 For your strength is the s of righteousness,
2Mc 4: 8 and from another s of revenue eighty talents.
2Es 4: 7 or how many streams are at the s of the deep,

SOURCES‡ (2) [SOURCE]
Job 28:11 The s of the rivers they probe;
Isa 7:18 for the fly that is at the s of the streams of Egypt,

SOUTH‡ (122) [SOUTHEAST, SOUTHERN, SOUTHWARD, SOUTHWEST]
Ge 28:14 and to the east and to the north and to the s;
Ex 26:18 twenty frames for the s side;
26:35 on the s side of the tabernacle opposite the table;
27: 9 On the s side the court shall have hangings
Ex 36:23 twenty frames for the s side;
38: 9 for the s side the hangings of the court were
40:24 opposite the table on the s side of the tabernacle,
Nu 2:10 On the s side shall be the regimental encampment
3:29 of the Kohathites were to camp on the s side of
10: 6 the camps on the s side shall set out.
34: 3 your s sector shall extend from the wilderness
34: 4 your boundary shall turn s of the ascent
34: 4 and its outer limit shall be s of Kadesh-barnea;
35: 5 for the s side two thousand cubits,
Dt 3:27 to the north, to the s, and to the east.
33:23 possess the west and the s.
Jos 11: 2 and in the Arabah s of Chinneroth,
13: 4 in the s, all the land of the Canaanites, and Mearah
15: 1 to the wilderness of Zin at the farthest s.
15: 2 their s boundary ran from the end of the Dead Sea,
15: 3 and goes up s of Kadesh-barnea, along by Hezron,
15: 4 This shall be your s boundary.
15: 7 which is on the s side of the valley;
15:21 the tribe of the people of Judah in the extreme S,
17: 9 The towns here, to the s of the wadi,
17:10 The land to the s is Ephraim's and that to
18: 5 Judah continuing in its territory on the s,
18:13 on the mountain that lies s of Lower Beth-horon.
18:14 from the mountain that lies to the s,
18:16 s of the slope of the Jebusites,
18:19 at the s end of the Jordan:
19:34 touching Zebulun at the s, and Asher on the west,
Jdg 21:19 up from Bethel to Shechem, and s of Lebonah."
1Sa 14: 5 and the other on the s in front of Geba.
23:19 on the hill of Hachilah, which is s of Jeshimon.
23:24 in the Arabah to the s of Jeshimon.
1Ki 6: 8 The entrance for the middle story was on the s side
7:21 he set up the pillar on the s and called it Jachin;
7:25 three facing s, and three facing east;
7:39 He set five of the stands on the s side of the house,
7:49 five on the s side and five on the north,
2Ki 11:11 from the s side of the house to the north side of
23:13 to the s of the Mount of Destruction,
1Ch 9:24 on the four sides, east, west, north, and s;
26:15 Obed-edom's came out for the s,
26:17 on the north four each day, on the s four each day,
2Ch 4: 4 three facing s, and three facing east;
4: 7 five on the s side and five on the north.
23:10 from the s side of the house to the north side of
Job 9: 9 the Pleiades and the chambers of the s;
37:17 when the earth is still because of the s wind?
39:26 and spreads its wings toward the s?
Ps 78:26 and by his power he led out the s wind;
89:12 The north and the s—you created them;
107: 3 from the north and from the s.
Ecc 1: 6 wind blows to the s, and goes around to the north;
11: 3 whether a tree falls to the s or to the north,
SS 4:16 Awake, O north wind, and come, O s wind!
Isa 43: 6 "Give them up," and to the s, "Do not withhold;
Eze 10: 3 Now the cherubim were standing on the s side of
16:46 and your younger sister, who lived to the s of you,
20:46 set your face toward the s,
20:46 against the s, and prophesy against the forest land
20:47 all faces from s to north shall be scorched by it.
21: 4 of its sheath against all flesh from s to north;
40: 2 on which was a structure like a city to the s.
40:24 Then he led me toward the s,
40:24 and there was a gate on the s;
40:27 There was a gate on the s of the inner court;
40:27 and he measured from gate to gate toward the s,
40:28 he brought me to the inner court by the s gate,
40:28 and he measured the s gate;
40:44 one at the side of the north gate facing s,
40:45 that faces s is for the priests who have charge of
41:11 and another door toward the s;
42:10 the s also, opposite the vacant area and opposite
42:12 the entrances of the chambers to the s were entered
42:13 "The north chambers and the s chambers opposite
42:18 Then he turned and measured the s side,
46: 9 to worship shall go out by the s gate;
46: 9 and whoever enters by the s gate shall go out by
47: 1 the s end of the threshold of the temple, s of the
47: 2 and the water was coming out on the s side.
47:19 On the s side, it shall run from Tamar as far as
47:19 This shall be the s side.
48:16 the s side four thousand five hundred,
48:17 on the s two hundred fifty,
48:28 And adjoining the territory of Gad to the s,
48:33 On the s side, which is to
Da 8: 9 which grew exceedingly great toward the s,
11: 5 "Then the king of the s shall grow strong,
11: 6 of the s shall come to the king of the north to ratify
11: 9 latter shall invade the realm of the king of the s,
11:11 the king of the s shall go out and do battle against
11:14 many shall rise against the king of the s.
11:15 And the forces of the s shall not stand,
11:25 and determination against the king of the s with
11:25 of the s shall wage war with a much greater
11:29 and come into the s, but this time it shall not be
11:40 of the end the king of the s shall attack him.
Zec 6: 6 and the dappled ones go toward the s country."
9:14 and march forth in the whirlwinds of the s.
14:10 into a plain from Geba to Rimmon s of Jerusalem.
Mt 12:42 The queen of the S will rise up at the judgment
Lk 11:31 The queen of the S will rise at the judgment with
12:55 And when you see the s wind blowing, you say,
13:29 from east and west, from north and s, and will eat
Ac 8:26 up and go toward the s to the road that goes down
27:13 When a moderate s wind began to blow,
28:13 After one day there a s wind sprang up,
Rev 21:13 on the s three gates, and on the west three gates.
Tob 1: 2 to the s of Kedesh Naphtali in Upper Galilee
Jdt 2:25 s of the country of the Chelleans.
7:18 and they sent some of their men toward the s and
Sir 43:16 At his will the s wind blows;
1Mc 3:57 Then the army marched out and encamped to the s
5:65 the descendants of Esau in the land to the s.
2Es 15:20 says God, from the rising sun and from the s,
15:34 and from the north to the s!
15:38 heavy storm clouds shall be stirred up from the s,
15:39 the east wind shall be driven violently toward the s

SOUTHEAST (2) [EAST, SOUTH]
1Ki 7:39 he set the sea on the s corner of the house.
2Ch 4:10 He set the sea at the s corner of the house.

SOUTHERN (6) [SOUTH]
Nu 34: 3 Your s boundary shall begin from the end of
Jos 15: 8 of the son of Hinnom at the s slope of the Jebusites
18:15 The s side begins at the outskirts of Kiriath-jearim;
18:19 of the Jordan: this is the s border.
Eze 48:10 and twenty-five thousand in length on the s side,
Jdt 2:25 he came to the s borders of Japheth, facing Arabia.

SOUTHWARD (10) [SOUTH]
Ge 13:14 northward and s and eastward and westward;
Jos 12: 3 the Dead Sea, s to the foot of the slopes of Pisgah;
15: 1 of Judah according to their families reached s to
15: 2 from the bay that faces s;
15: 3 it goes out s of the ascent of Akrabbim,
17: 7 then the boundary goes along s to the inhabitants
18:13 the boundary passes along s in the direction
18:14 on the western side s from the mountain that lies
Da 8: 4 the ram charging westward and northward and s.
Zec 14: 4 shall withdraw northward, and the other half s.

SOUTHWEST (1) [SOUTH, WEST]
Ac 27:12 It was a harbor of Crete, facing s and northwest.

SOVEREIGN (47) [SOVEREIGNS, SOVEREIGNTY]
A. SOVEREIGN *LORD (13)

1Ki 4:21 Solomon was s over all the kingdoms from
Ps 8: 1 our S, how majestic is your name in all the earth!
8: 9 our S, how majestic is your name in all the earth!
Isa 1:24 Therefore says the S, the LORD of hosts,
3: 1 For now the S, the LORD of hosts,
10:16 Therefore the S, the LORD of hosts,
10:33 Look, the S, the LORD of hosts,
19: 4 a fierce king will rule over them, says the S,
51:22 Thus says your S, the LORD,
Da 4:17 that all who live may know that the Most High is s
4:26 from the time that you learn that Heaven is s.
Ac 4:24 "S Lord, who made the heaven and the earth, A
25:26 I have nothing definite to write to our s about him.
1Ti 6:15 he who is the blessed and only S,
Rev 6:10 "S Lord, holy and true, how long will it be A
Wis 12:18 Although you are s in strength,
2Mc 3:24 the S of spirits and of all authority caused so great
3:28 They recognized clearly the s power of God.
12:15 calling against the great S of the world,
12:28 upon the S who with power shatters the might
15: 3 a s in heaven who had commanded the keeping of
15: 4 "It is the living Lord himself, the S in heaven,
15: 5 "But I am a s also, on earth,
15:23 So now, O S of the heavens,
15:29 the S Lord in the language of their ancestors. A
3Mc 2: 2 and s of all creation, holy among the holy ones,
2Es 3: 4 "O s Lord, did you not speak at the beginning A
4:38 Then I answered and said, "But, O s Lord, A
5:23 "O s Lord, from every forest of the earth and A
5:38 I said, "O s Lord, who is able A
6:11 I answered and said, "O s Lord, A
7:17 Then I answered and said, "O s Lord, A
7:*45* I answered and said, "O s Lord, A
7:*58* "O s Lord, what is plentiful is of less worth, A
12: 7 "O s Lord, if I have found favor in your sight, A
13:51 I said, "O s Lord, explain this to me: A
4Mc 1: 1 whether devout reason is s over the emotions.
1: 5 why is it not s over forgetfulness and ignorance?"
1:13 is whether reason is s over the emotions.
1:30 but over the emotions it is s.
1:30 that rational judgment is s over the emotions
2:13 It is s over the relationship of friends,
2:16 for it is s over even this.
6:31 then, devout reason is s over the emotions.
8:28 For they were contemptuous of the emotions and s
13: 1 everyone must concede that devout reason is s
16: 1 it must be admitted that devout reason is s over

SOVEREIGNS (1) [SOVEREIGN]
AdE 16: 6 the sincere goodwill of their s.

SOVEREIGNTY (13) [SOVEREIGN]
Da 4: 3 and his s is from generation to generation.
4:22 and your s to the ends of the earth.
4:25 the Most High has s over the kingdom of mortals,
4:32 the Most High has s over the kingdom of mortals
4:34 For his s is an everlasting s,
5:21 until he learned that the Most High God has s over
Mic 4: 8 the s of daughter Jerusalem.
Wis 6: 3 and your s from the Most High;
12:16 and your s over all causes you to spare all.

Sir 10: 8 S passes from nation to nation on account
47:21 the s was divided and a rebel kingdom arose out
4Mc 13: 5 then can one fail to confess the s of right reason

SOW (54) [SOWED, SOWER, SOWING, SOWN, SOWS]

Ge 47:23 here is seed for you; s the land.
Ex 23:10 For six years you shall s your land and gather
23:16 of what you s in the field.
Lev 19:19 you shall not s your field with two kinds of seed;
25: 3 Six years you shall s your field,
25: 4 you shall not s your field or prune your vineyard.
25:11 you shall not s, or reap the aftergrowth,
25:20 if we may not s or gather in our crop?
25:22 When you s in the eighth year,
26:16 You shall s your seed in vain,
Dt 11:10 where you s your seed and irrigate by foot like
22: 9 You shall not s your vineyard with a second kind
2Ki 19:29 then in the third year s, reap, plant vineyards,
Job 4: 8 those who plow iniquity and s trouble reap
31: 8 then let me s, and another eat;
Ps 107:37 they s fields, and plant vineyards, and get
126: 5 May those who s in tears reap with shouts of joy.
Pr 11:18 but those who s righteousness get a true reward.
Ecc 11: 4 Whoever observes the wind will not s;
11: 6 In the morning s your seed,
Isa 17:11 make them blossom in the morning that you s;
28:25 do they not scatter dill, s cummin,
30:23 He will give rain for the seed with which you s
32:20 Happy will you be who s beside every stream,
37:30 then in the third year s, reap, plant vineyards,
Jer 4: 3 and do not s among thorns.
31:27 when I will s the house of Israel and the house
35: 7 nor shall you ever build a house, or s seed;
Hos 2:23 and I will s him for myself in the land.
8: 7 they s the wind, and they shall reap the whirlwind.
10:12 S for yourselves righteousness;
Mic 6:15 You shall s, but not reap;
Mt 6:26 they neither s nor reap nor gather into barns,
13: 3 A sower went out to s.
13:27 'Master, did you not s good seed in your field?
25:24 reaping where you did not s,
25:26 You knew, did you, that I reap where I did not s,
Mk 4: 3 "Listen! A sower went out to s.
Lk 8: 5 "A sower went out to s his seed;
12:24 Consider the ravens: they neither s nor reap,
19:21 and reap what you did not s.'
19:22 not deposit and reaping what I did not s?
1Co 15:36 What you s does not come to life unless it dies.
15:37 what you s, you do not s the body that is to be,
Gal 6: 7 God is not mocked, for you reap whatever you s.
6: 8 If you s to your own flesh, you will reap corruption
6: 8 but if you s to the Spirit, you will reap eternal life
2Pe 2:22 and, "The s is washed only to wallow in the mud."
Sir 7: 3 Do not s in the furrows of injustice,
26:20 *and s it with your own seed,*
1Es 4: 6 whenever they s and reap,
2Es 9:31 For I s my law in you,
16:24 No one shall be left to cultivate the earth or to s it.

SOWED (10) [SOW]

Ge 26:12 Isaac s seed in that land,
Jdg 9:45 and he razed the city and s it with salt.
Mt 13: 4 And as he s, some seeds fell on the path,
13:24 be compared to someone who s good seed
13:25 an enemy came and s weeds among the wheat,
13:31 like a mustard seed that someone took and s
13:39 and the enemy who s them is the devil;
Mk 4: 4 And as he s, some seed fell on the path,
Lk 8: 5 as he s, some fell on the path and was trampled
13:19 It is like a mustard seed that someone took and s in

SOWER (9) [SOW]

Isa 55:10 giving seed to the s and bread to the eater,
Jer 50:16 Cut off from Babylon the s,
Mt 13: 3 A s went out to sow.
13:18 "Hear then the parable of the s.
Mk 4: 3 "Listen! A s went out to sow.
4:14 The s sows the word.
Lk 8: 5 "A s went out to sow his seed;
Jn 4:36 so that s and reaper may rejoice together.
2Co 9:10 He who supplies seed to the s and bread

SOWING (7) [SOW]

Lev 11:37 of their carcass falls upon any seed set aside for s,
26: 5 and the vintage shall overtake the s;
Ps 126: 6 Those who go out weeping, bearing the seed for s,
Pr 6:14 perverted mind devising evil, continually s discord;
Isa 28:24 Do those who plow for s plow continually?
Zec 8:12 For there shall be a s of peace;
2Co 9:10 for food will supply and multiply your seed for s

SOWN‡ (39) [SOW]

Dt 21: 4 which is neither plowed nor s,
22: 9 that you have s and the yield of the vineyard itself.
Isa 19: 7 and all that is s by the Nile will dry up,
40:24 Scarcely are they planted, scarcely s,
61:11 and as a garden causes what is s in it to spring up,
Jer 2: 2 in the wilderness, in a land not s.
12:13 They have s wheat and have reaped thorns,
Eze 36: 9 I will turn to you, and you shall be tilled and s;
Hag 1: 6 You have s much, and harvested little;
Mt 13:19 the evil one comes and snatches away what is s in
13:19 this is what was s on the path.
13:20 As for what was s on rocky ground,
13:22 As for what was s among thorns,
13:23 But as for what was s on good soil,
Mk 4:15 These are the ones on the path where the word is s:
4:15 and takes away the word that is s in them.
4:16 And these are the ones s on rocky ground:
4:18 And others are those s among the thorns:
4:20 And these are the ones s on the good soil:
4:31 which, when s upon the ground,
4:32 when it is s it grows up and becomes the greatest
1Co 9:11 If we have s spiritual good among you,
15:42 What is s is perishable, what is raised is
15:43 It is s in dishonor, it is raised in glory.
15:43 It is s in weakness, it is raised in power.
15:44 It is s a physical body, it is raised a spiritual body.
Jas 3:18 And a harvest of righteousness is s in peace
2Es 4:28 For the evil about which you ask me has been s,
4:29 If therefore that which has been s is not reaped,
4:29 and if the place where the evil has been s does
4:29 the field where the good has been s will not come.
4:30 a grain of evil seed was s in Adam's heart from
4:32 When heads of grain without number are s,
5:48 the earth to those who from time to time are s in it.
6:22 S places shall suddenly appear unsown,
8:41 all that have been s will come up in due season,
8:41 so also those who have been s in the world will
9:33 they did not keep what had been s in them.
9:34 about that what was s or what was launched

SOWS‡ (12) [SOW]

Pr 6:19 and one who s discord in a family.
22: 8 Whoever s injustice will reap calamity,
Am 9:13 and the treader of grapes the one who s the seed;
Mt 13:37 "The one who s the good seed is the Son of Man;
Mk 4:14 The sower s the word.
Jn 4:37 'One s and another reaps.'
2Co 9: 6 the one who s sparingly will also reap sparingly,
9: 6 one who s bountifully will also reap bountifully.
Sir 6:19 Come to her like one who plows and s,
28: 9 and the sinner disrupts friendships and s discord
2Es 8:41 "For just as the farmer s many seeds in the ground
16:43 let the one who s be like one who will not reap;

SPACE (13) [SPACIOUS]

Ge 9:27 May God make s for Japheth,
32:16 and put a s between drove and drove."
Ex 25:37 be set up so as to give light on the s in front of it.
Jos 3: 4 Yet there shall be a s between you and it,
1Ki 7:36 where each had s, with wreaths all around.
Ne 4:13 So in the lowest parts of the s behind the wall,
Eze 40: 7 and the s between the recesses, five cubits;
41: 9 the free s between the side chambers of the temple
41:17 to the s above the door,
45: 2 with fifty cubits for an open s around it.
2Mc 14:44 a s opened and he fell in the middle of
14:44 and he fell in the middle of the empty s.
3Mc 4:11 at the end to be destroyed in the s of a single day.

SPACIOUS (3) [SPACE]

Ps 66:12 yet you have brought us out to a s place.
Jer 22:14 a s house with large upper rooms,"
2Es 7:*96* and the s liberty that they are to receive and enjoy

SPAIN (3)

Ro 15:24 when I go to S. For I do hope to see you on my
15:28 I will set out by way of you to S;
1Mc 8: 3 in the land of S to get control of the silver

SPAN‡ (11)

Ex 28:16 a s in length and a s in width.
39: 9 a s in length and a s in width when doubled.
1Sa 17: 4 of Gath, whose height was six cubits and a s.
Ps 90:10 even then their s is only toil and trouble;
Isa 40:12 of his hand and marked off the heavens with a s,
Eze 43:13 with a rim of one s around its edge.
Mt 6:27 by worrying add a single hour to your s of life?
Lk 12:25 by worrying add a single hour to your s of life?
Sir 30:22 and rejoicing lengthens one's life s.

SPARE (51) [SPARED, SPARES, SPARING, SPARINGLY]

Jos 2:13 that you will s my father and mother,
22:22 of faith toward the LORD, do not s us today
1Sa 15: 3 do not s them, but kill both man and woman,
2Sa 21: 2 although the people of Israel had sworn to s them,
1Ki 20:31 perhaps he will s your life."
2Ki 7: 4 if they s our lives, we shall live;
2Ch 31:10 we have had enough to eat and have plenty to s;
Ne 13:22 and s me according to the greatness
Job 2: 6 he is in your power; only s his life."
33:18 to s their souls from the Pit,
Ps 59: 5 s none of those who treacherously plot evil.
78:50 he did not s them from death,
119:88 In your steadfast love s my life,
Pr 13:24 Those who s the rod hate their children,
Isa 31: 5 he will protect and deliver it, he will s
47: 3 I will take vengeance, and I will s no one.
Jer 13:14 or s or have compassion when I destroy them.
21: 7 he shall not pity them, or s them,
50:14 shoot at her, s no arrows, for she has sinned
51: 3 Do not s her young men; utterly destroy her entire
Eze 5:11 my eye will not s, and I will have no pity.
6: 8 But I will s some.
7: 4 My eye will not s you, I will have no pity.
7: 9 My eye will not s; I will have no pity.
8:18 my eye will not s, nor will I have pity;
9: 5 your eye shall not s, and you shall show no pity.
9:10 As for me, my eye will not s, nor will I have pity,
24:14 I will not refrain, I will not s, I will not relent.
Joel 2:17 Let them say, "S your people, O LORD,
Jnh 1: 6 Perhaps the god will s us a thought so that we do
Mal 3:17 and I will s them as parents s their children who
Lk 15:17 and to s, but here I am dying of hunger!
Ro 11:21 For if God did not s the natural branches, perhaps
he will not s you.
1Co 7:28 and I would s you that.
2Co 1:23 to s you that I did not come again to Corinth.
2Pe 2: 4 For if God did not s the angels when they sinned,
2: 5 and if he did not s the ancient world,
AdE 13:15 God of Abraham, s your people;
Wis 2:10 let us not s the widow or regard the gray hairs of
11:26 You s all things, for they are yours, O Lord,
12:16 and your sovereignty over all causes you to s all.
Sir 13:12 they will not s you harm or imprisonment.
16: 8 He did not s the neighbors of Lot,
23: 2 so as not to s me in my errors,
1Mc 13: 5 be it from me to s my life in any time of distress,
1Es 1:53 and did not s young man or young woman,
2Es 8:45 s your people and have mercy on your inheritance,
15:22 My right hand will not s the sinners,
15:25 I will not s them. Depart, you faithless children!

SPARED‡ (29) [SPARE]

Ge 12:13 and that my life may be s on your account."
Ex 12:27 he struck down the Egyptians but s our houses.' "
Jos 6:25 and all who belonged to her, Joshua s.
1Sa 2:33 be s to weep out his eyes and grieve his heart;
15: 9 Saul and the people s Agag,
15:15 the people s the best of the sheep and the cattle,
24:10 and some urged me to kill you, but I s you.
2Sa 8: 2 and one length for those who were to be s.
21: 7 But the king s Mephibosheth,
2Ki 10:14 forty-two in all; he s none of them.
Job 21:30 that the wicked are s in the day of calamity,
Isa 9:19 like fuel for the fire; no one s another.
Jer 38:17 then your life shall be s,
38:20 and your life shall be s.
50:20 for I will pardon the remnant that I have s.
Eze 6:12 and any who are left and are s shall die of famine.
20:17 Nevertheless my eye s them,
Hos 10:11 and I s her fair neck;
Jdt 7:27 but our lives will be s,
11: 9 of Bethulia s him and he told them all he had said
Wis 12: 8 But even these you s, since they were but mortals,
Sir 46: 8 And these two alone were s out
Sus 1:62 Thus innocent blood was s that day.
1Es 1:50 he would have s them and his dwelling place.
3Mc 3:18 but they were s the exercise of our power because
7: 6 toward all people we barely s their lives.
2Es 3:30 and have s those who act wickedly,
9:21 And I saw and s some with great difficulty,
4Mc 4:12 that if he were s he would praise the blessedness

SPARES (1) [SPARE]

Pr 17:27 One who s words is knowledgeable;

SPARING (2) [SPARE]

Ac 20:29 wolves will come in among you, not s the flock.
2Es 16:71 They shall be like maniacs, s no one,

SPARINGLY (2) [SPARE]

2Co 9: 6 the one who sows s will also reap s,

SPARK (4) [SPARKS]

Isa 1:31 and their work like a s;
Wis 2: 2 reason is a s kindled by the beating of our hearts;
Sir 11:32 From a s many coals are kindled,
28:12 If you blow on a s, it will glow;

SPARKLE (1) [SPARKLED, SPARKLES, SPARKLING]

Sir 34:20 He lifts up the soul and makes the eyes s;

SPARKLED (1) [SPARKLE]

Eze 1: 7 and they s like burnished bronze.

SPARKLES (1) [SPARKLE]

Pr 23:31 when it s in the cup and goes down smoothly.

SPARKLING (1) [SPARKLE]

Sir 42:22 and how s they are to see!

SPARKS (5) [SPARK]

Job 5: 7 to trouble just as s fly upward.
41:19 its mouth go flaming torches; s of fire leap out.
Wis 3: 7 and will run like s through the stubble.
11:18 or flash terrible s from their eyes;
2Es 13:10 and from his tongue he shot forth a storm of s.

SPARROW (2) [SPARROWS]

Ps 84: 3 Even the s finds a home,
Pr 26: 2 Like a s in its flitting, like a swallow in its flying,

SPARROWS (5) [SPARROW]

Mt 10:29 Are not two s sold for a penny?
10:31 you are of more value than many s.
Lk 12: 6 Are not five s sold for two pennies?
12: 7 you are of more value than many s.
Tob 2:10 I did not know that there were s on the wall;

SPARTA (1) [SPARTANS]

1Mc 14:16 It was heard in Rome, and as far away as S,

SPARTANS (9) [SPARTA]

1Mc 12: 2 He also sent letters to the same effect to the S and
12: 5 a copy of the letter that Jonathan wrote to the S:
12: 6 rest of the Jewish people to their brothers the S,
12:20 "King Arius of the S, to the high priest Onias,
12:21 It has been found in writing concerning the S and
14:20 This is a copy of the letter that the S sent:
14:20 of the S to the high priest Simon and to the elders
14:23 the people of the S may have a record of them.
15:23 and to Sampsames, and to the S, and to Delos,

SPAT (6) [SPIT]

Mt 26:67 Then they s in his face and struck him;
27:30 They s on him, and took the reed and struck him
Mk 7:33 and he s and touched his tongue.
15:19 They struck his head with a reed, s upon him,
Lk 18:32 and he will be mocked and insulted and s upon.
Jn 9: 6 he s on the ground and made mud with the saliva

SPATTERED (4) [BESPATTERED]

Lev 6:27 and when any of its blood is s on a garment,
2Ki 9:33 some of her blood s on the wall and on the horses,
Isa 63: 3 their juice s on my garments,
Sir 22:13 and be s when he shakes himself off.

SPEAK‡ (466) [OUTSPOKEN, SPEAKER, SPEAKING, SPEAKS, SPEECH, SPEECHES, SPEECHLESS, SPOKE, SPOKEN, SPOKESMAN]

Ge 18:27 "Let me take it upon myself to s to the Lord,
18:30 he said, "Oh do not let the Lord be angry if I s.
18:31 "Let me take it upon myself to s to the Lord.
18:32 not let the Lord be angry if I s just once more.
24:33 until I have told my errand." He said, "S on."
24:50 we cannot s to you anything bad or good.
31:29 to me last night, saying, 'Take heed that you s
34: 6 of Shechem went out to Jacob to s with him,
37: 4 they hated him, and could not s peaceably to him.
44: 7 "Why does my lord s such words as these?
44:16 "What can we say to my lord? What can we s?
44:18 let your servant please s a word in my lord's ears,
50: 4 please s to Pharaoh as follows:
Ex 4:12 with your mouth and teach you what you are to s."
4:14 I know that he can s fluently;
4:15 You shall s to him and put the words in his mouth;
4:16 He indeed shall s for you to the people;
5:23 Since I first came to Pharaoh to s in your name,
7: 2 You shall s all that I command you,
19: 6 the words that you shall s to the Israelites."
19: 9 that the people may hear when I s with you and
19:19 Moses would s and God would answer him
20:19 "You s to us, and we will listen; but do not let God s to us, or we will die."
28: 3 And you shall s to all who have ability,
29:42 where I will meet with you, to s to you there.
31:13 You yourself are to s to the Israelites:
33: 9 and the LORD would s with Moses.
33:11 Thus the LORD used to s to Moses face to face,
34:34 in before the LORD to s with him, he would take
34:35 until he went in to s with him.
Lev 1: 2 S to the people of Israel and say to them:
4: 2 S to the people of Israel, saying:
5: 1 does not s up, you are subject to punishment.
6:25 S to Aaron and his sons, saying:
7:23 S to the people of Israel, saying:
7:29 S to the people of Israel, saying:
11: 2 S to the people of Israel, saying:
12: 2 S to the people of Israel, saying:
15: 2 S to the people of Israel and say to them:
17: 2 S to Aaron and his sons and to all the people
18: 2 S to the people of Israel and say to them:
19: 2 S to all the congregation of the people of Israel
21: 1 The LORD said to Moses: S to the priests,
21:17 S to Aaron and say: No one of your
22:18 S to Aaron and his sons and all the people
23: 2 S to the people of Israel and say to them:
23:10 S to the people of Israel and say to them:
23:24 S to the people of Israel, saying:
23:34 S to the people of Israel, saying:
24:15 And s to the people of Israel, saying:
25: 2 S to the people of Israel and say to them:
27: 2 S to the people of Israel and say to them:
Nu 5: 6 S to the Israelites: When a man
5:12 S to the Israelites and say to them:
6: 2 S to the Israelites and say to them:
6:23 S to Aaron and his sons,
7:89 of meeting to s with the LORD, he would hear
8: 2 S to Aaron and say to him:
9:10 S to the Israelites, saying:
12: 6 I s to them in dreams.
12: 8 With him I s face to face—
12: 8 not afraid to s against my servant Moses?"
15: 2 S to the Israelites and say to them:
Nu 15:18 S to the Israelites and say to them:
15:38 S to the Israelites, and tell them to make fringes
17: 2 S to the Israelites, and get twelve staffs
18:26 You shall s to the Levites, saying:
22:35 but s only what I tell you to speak."
22:35 but speak only what I tell you to s."
33:51 S to the Israelites, and say to them:
35:10 S to the Israelites, and say to them:
Dt 1: 3 as the LORD had commanded him to s to them.
3:26 Never s to me of this matter again!
5:24 Today we have seen that God may s to someone
18:18 who shall s to them everything that I command.
18:19 the words that the prophet shall s in my name,
18:20 or who presumes to s in my name a word
18:20 word that I have not commanded the prophet to s—
20: 2 the priest shall come forward and s to the troops,
25: 8 elders of his town shall summon him and s to him.
32: 1 Give ear, O heavens, and I will s;
Jos 10:21 no one dared to s against any of the Israelites.
Jdg 6:17 then show me a sign that it is you who s with me.
6:39 let me s one more time;
19: 3 to s tenderly to her and bring her back.
19:30 Consider it, take counsel, and s out.' "
1Sa 3: 9 and if he calls you, you shall say, 'S, LORD,
3:10 Samuel said, "S, for your servant is listening."
15:16 to me last night." He replied, "S."
18:22 "S to David in private and say, 'See,
19: 3 and I will s to my father about you;
25:17 he is so ill-natured that no one can s to him."
25:24 please let your servant s in your ears,
2Sa 3:27 Joab took him aside in the gateway to s
7: 7 did I ever s a word with any of the tribal leaders
13:13 Now therefore, I beg you, s to the king;
14: 3 Go to the king and s to him as follows."
14:12 "Please let your servant s a word to my lord
14:12 to my lord the king." He said, "S."
14:15 your servant thought, 'I will s to the king;
14:18 The woman said, "Let my lord the king s."
19: 7 So go out at once and s kindly to your servants;
19:29 king said to him, "Why s any more of your affairs?
19:43 not the first to s of bringing back our king?"
20:16 Tell Joab, 'Come here, I want to s to you.' "
1Ki 2:18 I will s to the king on your behalf."
2:19 to s to him on behalf of Adonijah.
4:33 He would s of trees, from the cedar that is in
4:33 he would s of animals, and birds, and reptiles,
12: 7 and s good words to them when you answer them,
22:13 be like the word of one of them, and s favorably."
22:14 whatever the LORD says to me, that I will s."
22:24 the spirit of the LORD pass from me to s to you?"
2Ki 6:12 who tells the king of Israel the words that you s
18:26 "Please s to your servants in the Aramaic
18:26 do not s to us in the language of Judah within
18:27 to s these words to your master and to you,
19:10 "Thus shall you s to King Hezekiah of Judah:
1Ch 17: 6 did I ever s a word with any of the judges of Israel,
2Ch 10: 7 and s good words to them,
10:10 "Thus should you s to the people who said to you,
18:12 be like the word of one of them, and s favorably."
18:13 whatever my God says, that I will s."
18:23 the spirit of the LORD pass from me to s to you?"
32:17 the LORD the God of Israel and to s against him,
Ne 13:24 and they could not s the language of Judah,
Est 6: 4 the outer court of the king's palace to s to the king
Job 2:10 "You s as any foolish woman would s.
7:11 I will s in the anguish of my spirit;
9:35 then I would s without fear of him,
10: 1 I will s in the bitterness of my soul.
11: 5 But oh, that God would s, and open his lips to you,
13: 3 But I would s to the Almighty,
13: 7 Will you s falsely for God,
13: 7 and s deceitfully for him?
13:13 "Let me have silence, and I will s,
13:22 or let me s, and you reply to me.
16: 6 "If I s, my pain is not assuaged, and if I forbear,
18: 2 Consider, and then we shall s.
21: 3 Bear with me, and I will s;
27: 4 my lips will not s falsehood,
29:22 After I spoke they did not s again,
32: 4 Now Elihu had waited to s to Job,
32: 7 I said, 'Let days s, and many years teach wisdom.'
32:16 And am I to wait, because they do not s,
32:20 I must s, so that I may find relief;
33: 3 and what my lips know they s sincerely.
33:31 Pay heed, Job, listen to me; be silent, and I will s.
33:32 s, for I desire to justify you.
37:20 Should he be told that I want to s?
41: 3 Will it s soft words to you?
42: 4 and I will s; I will question you,
Ps 2: 5 Then he will s to them in his wrath,
5: 6 You destroy those who s lies;
12: 2 with flattering lips and a double heart they s.
15: 2 and s the truth from their heart;
17:10 with their mouths they s arrogantly.
28: 3 who s peace with their neighbors,
31:18 Let the lying lips be stilled that s insolently against
35:20 For they do not s peace,
37:30 and their tongues s justice.
38:12 those who seek to hurt me s of ruin,
38:13 like the mute, who cannot s.
49: 3 My mouth shall s wisdom;
50: 7 and I will s, O Israel, I will testify against you.
50:20 You sit and s against your kin;
71:10 For my enemies s concerning me,
73: 8 They scoff and s with malice;
75: 5 up your horn on high, or s with insolent neck."
77: 4 I am so troubled that I cannot s.
Ps 85: 8 Let me hear what God the LORD will s,
85: 8 for he will s peace to his people, to his faithful,
109:20 of those who s evil against my life.
115: 5 They have mouths, but do not s;
119:46 I will also s of your decrees before kings,
120: 7 I am for peace; but when I s, they are for war.
135:16 They have mouths, but they do not s;
139:20 those who s of you maliciously,
144: 8 mouths s lies, and whose right hands are false.
144:11 mouths s lies, and whose right hands are false.
145:11 They shall s of the glory of your kingdom,
145:21 My mouth will s the praise of the LORD,
Pr 2:12 from those who s perversely,
8: 6 Hear, for I will s noble things,
16:13 and he loves those who s what is right.
23: 9 Do not s in the hearing of a fool,
23:16 My soul will rejoice when your lips s what is right.
31: 8 S out for those who cannot s,
31: 9 S out, judge righteously, defend the rights of
Ecc 3: 7 a time to keep silence, and a time to s;
Isa 8:10 s a word, but it will not stand, for God is with us.
8:20 Surely, those who s like this will have no dawn!
14:10 All of them will s and say to you:
19:18 that s the language of Canaan and swear allegiance
28:11 and with alien tongue he will s to this people,
29: 4 Then deep from the earth you shall s,
30:10 s to us smooth things, prophesy illusions,
32: 4 and the tongues of stammerers will s readily
32: 6 For fools s folly, and their minds plot iniquity:
33:15 Those who walk righteously and s uprightly,
36:11 "Please s to your servants in Aramaic,
36:11 do not s to us in the language of Judah within
36:12 to s these words to your master and to you,
37:10 "Thus shall you s to King Hezekiah of Judah:
40: 2 S tenderly to Jerusalem, and cry to her
40:27 Why do you say, O Jacob, and s, O Israel,
41: 1 let them approach, then let them s;
45:19 I did not s in secret, in a land of darkness;
45:19 I the LORD s the truth, I declare what is right.
52: 6 in that day they shall know that it is I who s;
59: 4 they rely on empty pleas, they s lies,
Jer 1: 6 Truly I do not know how to s,
1: 7 and you shall s whatever I command you,
4:12 Now it is I who s in judgment against them.
5: 5 Let me go to the rich and s to them;
6:10 To whom shall I s and give warning,
7:22 I did not s to them or command them
7:27 So you shall s all these words to them,
8: 6 but they do not s honestly;
9: 5 they have taught their tongues to s lies;
9: 8 They all s friendly words to their neighbors,
9:22 S! Thus says the LORD:
10: 5 scarecrows in a cucumber field, and they cannot s;
11: 2 and s to the people of Judah and the inhabitants
12: 6 though they s friendly words to you.
13:12 You shall s to them this word:
14:14 nor did I command them or s to them.
18:20 Remember how I stood before you to s good
20: 8 For whenever I s, I must cry out, I must shout,
20: 9 or s any more in his name,"
22: 1 of the king of Judah, and s there this word,
23:16 They s visions of their own minds,
23:21 I did not s to them, yet they prophesied.
23:28 let the one who has my word s my word faithfully.
26: 2 the LORD's house, and s to all the cities of Judah
26: 2 s to them all the words that I command you;
26: 8 that the LORD had commanded him to s to all
26:15 the LORD sent me to you to s all these words
28: 7 But listen now to this word that I s in your hearing
31:20 As often as I s against him, I still remember him.
32: 4 and shall s with him face to face and see him eye
34: 2 and s to King Zedekiah of Judah and say to him:
34: 3 the king of Babylon eye to eye and s with him face
35: 2 and s with them, and bring them to the house of
Eze 2: 1 stand up on your feet, and I will s with you.
2: 7 You shall s my words to them,
3: 1 eat this scroll, and go, s to the house of Israel.
3: 4 the house of Israel and s my very words to them.
3:10 that I shall s to you receive in your heart and hear
3:11 to your people, and s to them.
3:18 or s to warn the wicked from their wicked way,
3:22 go out into the valley, and there I will s with you.
3:27 But when I s with you, I will open your mouth,
12:25 But I the LORD will s the word that I s,
12:25 O rebellious house, I will s the word and fulfill it,
12:28 but the word that I s will be fulfilled,
13: 7 "Says the LORD," even though I did not s?
14: 4 Therefore s to them, and say to them,
17: 2 and s an allegory to the house of Israel.
20: 3 s to the elders of Israel, and say to them:
20:27 mortal, s to the house of Israel and say to them,
24:27 and you shall s and no longer be silent.
29: 3 s, and say, Thus says the Lord GOD:
32:21 The mighty chiefs shall s of them,
33: 2 s to your people and say to them,
33: 8 not s to warn the wicked to turn from their ways,
33:22 and I was no longer unable to s.
39:17 S to the birds of every kind and to all
Da 2: 9 You have agreed to s lying and misleading words
7:25 He shall s words against the Most High,
10:11 pay attention to the words that I am going to s
10:16 and I opened my mouth to s,
10:19 "Let my lord s, for you have strengthened me."
11:36 shall s horrendous things against the God of gods.
Hos 2:14 and bring her into the wilderness, and s tenderly
7:13 I would redeem them, but they s lies against me.
Mic 6:12 your inhabitants s lies, with tongues of deceit

Hab 2:18 though the product is only an idol that cannot s!
Hag 2: 2 S now to Zerubbabel son of Shealtiel,
2:21 S to Zerubbabel, governor of Judah, saying, I am
Zec 8:16 S the truth to one another,
13: 3 for you s lies in the name of the LORD";
Mt 5: 2 Then he began to s, and taught them, saying:
8: 8 only s the word, and my servant will be healed.
10:19 not worry about how you are to s or what you are
10:20 for it is not you who s,
11: 7 Jesus began to s to the crowds about John:
12:22 that the one who had been mute could s and see.
12:34 How can you s good things, when you are evil?
12:46 were standing outside, wanting to s to him.
12:47 brothers are standing outside, wanting to s to you."
13:10 "Why do you s to them in parables?"
13:13 The reason I s to them in parables is
13:35 "I will open my mouth to s in parables;
Mk 1:34 and he would not permit the demons to s,
2: 7 "Why does this fellow s in this way?
4:34 he did not s to them except in parables,
7:37 he even makes the deaf to hear and the mute to s."
9:17 he has a spirit that makes him unable to s;
9:39 in my name will be able soon afterward to s evil
12: 1 Then he began to s to them in parables.
13:11 for it is not you who s, but the Holy Spirit.
16:17 ⟦they will s in new tongues;⟧
Lk 1:19 to s to you and to bring you this good news.
1:20 unable to s, until the day these things occur."
1:22 When he did come out, he could not s to them,
1:22 to them and remained unable to s.
1:64 and he began to s, praising God.
2:38 and began to praise God and to s about the child
4:41 he rebuked them and would not allow them to s,
6:26 "Woe to you when all s well of you,
7: 7 But only s the word, and let my servant be healed.
7:15 The dead man sat up and began to s,
7:24 Jesus began to s to the crowds about John:
7:40 "Teacher," he replied, "S."
8:10 but to others I s in parables,
12: 1 he began to s first to his disciples,
Jn 1:40 One of the two who heard John s
3:11 we s of what we know and testify
7:13 Yet no one would s openly about him for fear of
7:18 Those who s on their own seek their own glory;
8:25 Jesus said to them, "Why do I s to you at all?
8:28 but I s these things as the Father instructed me.
9:21 He will s for himself."
12:49 a commandment about what to say and what to s.
12:50 What I s, therefore, I s just as the Father has told
14:10 The words that I say to you I do not s on my own;
16:13 will not s on his own, but will s whatever he hears,
16:25 The hour is coming when I will no longer s to you
17:13 and I s these things in the world so
19:10 "Do you refuse to s to me?
Ac 2: 4 the Holy Spirit and began to s in other languages,
4:17 let us warn them to s no more to anyone
4:18 So they called them and ordered them not to s
4:29 to your servants to s your word with all boldness,
5:40 they ordered them not to s in the name of Jesus,
6:11 "We have heard him s blasphemous words
8:35 to s, and starting with this scripture, he proclaimed
10:34 Then Peter began to s to them:
11:15 And as I began to s,
13:16 So Paul stood up and with a gesture began to s:
13:42 to s about these things again the next sabbath.
16: 6 having been forbidden by the Holy Spirit to s
18: 9 "Do not be afraid, but s and do not be silent;
18:14 Just as Paul was about to s,
18:26 He began to s boldly in the synagogue;
21:39 I beg you, let me s to the people."
23: 5 'You shall not s evil of a leader of your people.' "
24:10 the governor motioned to him to s, Paul replied:
24:24 he sent for Paul and heard him s concerning faith
26: 1 "You have permission to s for yourself."
26:26 and to him I s freely;
28:20 therefore I have asked to see you and s with you,
Ro 3: 5 (I s in a human way.)
15:18 For I will not venture to s of anything except
1Co 2: 6 Yet among the mature we do s wisdom,
2: 7 But we s God's wisdom, secret and hidden,
2:13 And we s of these things in words not taught
3: 1 I could not s to you as spiritual people,
4:13 when slandered, we s kindly.
9:10 Or does he not s entirely for our sake?
10:15 I s as to sensible people;
12: 2 and led astray to idols that could not s.
12:30 Do all s in tongues?
13: 1 If I s in the tongues of mortals and of angels,
14: 2 For those who s in a tongue do not s to other people but to God;
14: 3 those who prophesy s to other people
14: 4 Those who s in a tongue build up themselves,
14: 5 Now I would like all of you to s in tongues,
14: 6 unless I s to you in some revelation or knowledge
14:18 I thank God that I s in tongues more than all
14:19 church I would rather s five words with my mind,
14:21 I will s to this people; yet even then they will not
14:23 whole church comes together and all s in tongues,
14:28 be silent in church and s to themselves and to God.
14:29 Let two or three prophets s,
14:34 For they are not permitted to s,
14:35 For it is shameful for a woman to s in church.
2Co 2:17 but in Christ we s as persons of sincerity,
4:13 we also believe, and so we s,
6:13 I s as to children—open wide your hearts also.
Eph 4:25 let all of us s the truth to our neighbors,
6:19 Pray also for me, so that when I s,
6:20 Pray that I may declare it boldly, as I must s.
Php 1:14 dare to s the word with greater boldness and
1Th 1: 8 so that we have no need to s about it.
2: 4 even so we s, not to please mortals,
1Ti 5: 1 Do not s harshly to an older man, but s to him as to a father,
Tit 3: 2 to s evil of no one, to avoid quarreling,
Heb 4: 8 God would not s later about another day.
6: 9 Even though we s in this way, beloved,
7:11 to s of another priest arising according to the order
9: 5 Of these things we cannot s now in detail.
11:14 for people who s in this way make it clear
Jas 1:19 let everyone be quick to listen, slow to s,
2:12 So s and so act as those who are to be judged by
4:11 Do not s evil against one another,
2Pe 2:18 For they s bombastic nonsense,
Rev 13:15 the beast could even s and cause those who would
Tob 6:13 tonight I will s to her father about the girl,
6:13 and tonight we shall s concerning the girl
13: 8 Let all people s of his majesty,
13:12 Cursed are all who s a harsh word against you;
Jdt 11: 5 and let your servant s in your presence.
AdE 4: 8 then s to the king in our behalf,
6: 4 to s to the king about hanging Mordecai on
15:12 he embraced her, and said, "S to me."
Wis 5: 3 They will s to one another in repentance,
7:15 May God grant me to s with judgment,
8:12 and when I s they will give heed;
8:12 if I s at greater length,
10:21 and made the tongues of infants s clearly.
Sir 4:25 Never s against the truth, but be ashamed
13: 6 he will s to you kindly and say,
18:19 Before you s, learn;
20: 6 others keep silent because they know when to s.
21:25 The lips of babblers s of what is not their concern.
31:31 s no word of reproach to him,
32: 3 S, you who are older, for it is your right,
32: 7 S, you who are young, if you are obliged to,
39:10 Nations will s of his wisdom,
LtJ 6: 8 but they are false and cannot s.
6:40 for when they see someone who cannot s,
6:40 they bring Bel and pray that the mute may s,
1Mc 10:47 he had been the first to s peaceable words to them,
1Es 2:21 but to s to our lord the king,
4: 1 of the strength of the king, began to s:
4:13 and truth (and this was Zerubbabel), began to s:
4:33 and he began to s about truth:
3Mc 2:22 was unable even to s, since he was smitten by
5:45 of madness, so to s, by the very fragrant draughts
2Es 1:12 "But s to them and say, Thus says the Lord:
3: 3 and I began to s anxious words to the Most High,
3: 4 did you not s at the beginning when you planted
4: 5 I said, "S, my lord."
5:22 and I began once more to s words in the presence
5:33 Then I said, "S, my lord."
5:39 and how can I s concerning the things
5:50 now given me the opportunity, let me s
6:21 Children a year old shall s with their voices,
6:36 and I began to s in the presence of the Most High.
7: 2 listen to the words that I have come to s to you."
7: 3 I said, "S, my lord."
7:*38* Thus he will s to them on the day of judgment—
8:15 And now I will s out:
8:15 but I will s about your people,
8:19 and I will s before you."
8:25 For as long as I live I will s,
8:42 "If I have found favor in your sight, let me s.
9:28 and I began to s before the Most High, and said,
10:34 I said, "S, my lord; only do not forsake me,
11:38 "Listen and I will s to you.
12:32 and will come and s with them.
14:19 I answered and said, "Let me s in your presence,
15: 1 S in the ears of my people the words of
4Mc 1:12 I shall shortly have an opportunity to s of this;
5:15 When he had received permission to s,
12: 8 let me s to the king and to all his friends that are

SPEAKER (6) [SPEAK]

Ex 6:12 then shall Pharaoh listen to me, poor s that I am?"
6:30 "Since I am a poor s,
Ac 14:12 because he was the chief s.
1Co 14:11 be a foreigner to the s and the s a foreigner to me.
Sir 37:20 A skillful s may be hated;

SPEAKING‡ (150) [SPEAK]

Ge 18:33 when he had finished s to Abraham;
24:15 Before he had finished s, there was Rebekah,
24:45 "Before I had finished s in my heart,
29: 9 While he was still s with them,
50:21 In this way he reassured them, s kindly to them.
Ex 6:29 tell Pharaoh king of Egypt all that I am s to you."
31:18 When God finished s with Moses on Mount Sinai,
34:33 When Moses had finished s with them,
Nu 7:89 the voice s to him from above the mercy seat
16:31 As soon as he finished s all these words,
21: 7 "We have sinned by s against the LORD and
Dt 4:33 Has any people ever heard the voice of a god s out
5:26 that has heard the voice of the living God s out
31: 1 Moses had finished s all these words to all Israel,
Jdg 15:17 he had finished s, he threw away the jawbone;
1Sa 1:16 for I have been s out of my great anxiety
18: 1 When David had finished s to Saul,
24:16 When David had finished s these words to Saul,
2Sa 13:36 As soon as he had finished s,
1Ki 1:14 Then while you are still there s with the king,
1:22 While she was still s with the king,
1Ki 1:42 While he was still s, Jonathan son of the priest
2Ki 6:33 While he was still s with them,
2Ch 25:16 But as he was s the king said to him,
Job 1:16 While he was still s, another came and said,
1:17 While he was still s, another came and said,
1:18 While he was still s, another came and said,
4: 2 But who can keep from s?
Ps 34:13 and your lips from s deceit.
52: 3 and lying more than s the truth.
58: 3 they err from their birth, s lies.
109: 2 s against me with lying tongues.
Pr 26:24 in s while harboring deceit within;
Isa 58: 9 the pointing of the finger, the s of evil,
65:24 while they are yet s I will hear.
Jer 26: 7 and all the people heard Jeremiah s these words in
26: 8 And when Jeremiah had finished s all that
38: 4 and all the people, by s such words to them.
43: 1 When Jeremiah finished s to all
Eze 1:28 and I heard the voice of someone s.
2: 2 and I heard him s to me.
36: 5 I am s in my hot jealousy against the rest of
36: 6 I am s in my jealous wrath,
43: 6 I heard someone s to me out of the temple.
Da 7: 8 in this horn, and a mouth s arrogantly.
7:11 of the arrogant words that the horn was s.
8:13 Then I heard a holy one s,
8:18 As he was s to me, I fell into a trance,
9:20 While I was s, and was praying
9:21 while I was s in prayer,
10:11 he was s this word to me, I stood up trembling.
10:15 While he was s these words to me,
Mt 10:20 but the Spirit of your Father s through you.
12:46 While he was still s to the crowds,
15:31 the crowd was amazed when they saw the mute s,
16:11 How could you fail to perceive that I was not s
17: 5 While he was still s, suddenly
17:13 the disciples understood that he was s to them
21:45 they realized that he was s about them.
26:47 he was still s, Judas, one of the twelve, arrived;
Mk 2: 2 and he was s the word to them.
5:35 While he was still s, some people came from
9:25 "You spirit that keeps this boy from s and hearing,
14:43 Immediately, while he was still s, Judas,
Lk 5: 4 When he had finished s, he said to Simon,
5:21 "Who is this who is s blasphemies?
8:49 While he was still s, someone came from
9:31 in glory and were s of his departure,
11:37 he was s, a Pharisee invited him to dine with him;
21: 5 When some were s about the temple,
22:47 While he was still s, suddenly a crowd came,
22:60 At that moment, while he was still s,
Jn 2:21 But he was s of the temple of his body.
4:26 "I am he, the one who is s to you."
4:27 They were astonished that he was s with a woman,
4:27 or, "Why are you s with her?"
6:71 He was s of Judas son of Simon Iscariot, for he,
7:17 the teaching is from God or whether I am s
7:26 here he is, s openly, but they say nothing to him!
8:27 They did not understand that he was s to them
9:37 and the one s with you is he."
11:13 Jesus, however, had been s about his death,
13:18 I am not s of all of you;
13:22 uncertain of whom he was s.
13:24 to him to ask Jesus of whom he was s.
16:29 His disciples said, "Yes, now you are s plainly,
Ac 1: 3 during forty days and s about the kingdom of God.
2: 6 because each one heard them s in
2: 7 they asked, "Are not all these who are s Galileans?
2:11 in our own languages we hear them s
4: 1 While Peter and John were s to the people,
4:20 from s about what we have seen and heard."
9:28 s boldly in the name of the Lord.
10:44 While Peter was still s, the Holy Spirit fell
10:46 they heard them s in tongues and extolling God.
14: 3 for a long time, s boldly for the Lord, who testified
14: 9 He listened to Paul as he was s.
15:13 After they finished s, James replied, "My brothers,
20: 7 he continued s until midnight.
20:36 When he had finished s, he knelt down
22: 9 but did not hear the voice of the one who was s
26:25 most excellent Festus, but I am s the sober truth.
Ro 6:19 I am s in human terms because
7: 1 for I am s to those who know the law—
9: 1 I am s the truth in Christ—
11:13 Now I am s to you Gentiles.
1Co 12: 3 Therefore I want you to understand that no one s
14: 2 since they are s mysteries in the Spirit.
14: 6 brothers and sisters, if I come to you s in tongues,
14: 9 For you will be s into the air.
14:39 and do not forbid s in tongues;
2Co 11:21 I am s as a fool—I also dare to boast of that.
12: 6 I will not be a fool, for I will be s the truth.
12:19 We are s in Christ before God.
13: 3 since you desire proof that Christ is s in me.
Eph 4:15 But s the truth in love,
Php 1:20 but that by my s with all boldness,
1Th 2:16 from s to the Gentiles so that they may be saved.
Heb 2: 5 about which we are s, to angels.
8:13 In s of "a new covenant,"
11:19 and figuratively s, he did receive him back.
12:25 See that you do not refuse the one who is s;
Jas 3: 2 Anyone who makes no mistakes in s is perfect,
1Pe 3:10 from evil and their lips from s deceit;
4:11 Whoever speaks must do so as one s
2Pe 3:16 s of this as he does in all his letters.
Rev 4: 1 which I had heard s to me like a trumpet, said,
Jdt 14: 8 from the day she left until the moment she began s

AdE 15:15 And while she was **s**, she fainted and fell,
Sir 4:23 Do not refrain from **s** at the proper moment,
5:13 Honor and dishonor come from **s**,
11: 8 and do not interrupt when another is **s**.
23:12 There is a manner of **s** comparable to death;
29: 5 and is deferential in **s** of his neighbor's money;
32: 9 and when another is **s**, do not babble.
1Mc 2:23 When he had finished **s** these words,
3:23 When he finished **s**, he rushed suddenly
13:17 Simon knew that they were **s** deceitfully to him,
2Mc 7:30 While she was still **s**, the young man said,
9: 5 As soon as he stopped **s** he was seized with a pain
1Es 3:24 When he had said this, he stopped **s**.
4:12 in this fashion?" And he stopped **s**.
4:41 When he stopped **s**, all the people shouted
3Mc 6: 5 **s** grievous words with boasting and insolence, you,
2Es 6:15 while the voice is **s**, do not be terrified;
6:17 a voice was **s**, and its sound was like the sound
7: 1 When I had finished **s** these words,
10:29 While I was **s** these words,
12:31 up out of the forest and roaring and **s** to the eagle
4Mc 8:13 and wedges and bellows, the tyrant resumed **s**:

SPEAKS‡ (54) [SPEAK]

Ge 45:12 that it is my own mouth that **s** to you.
Ex 33:11 as one **s** to a friend.
Nu 22: 8 just as the LORD **s** to me";
Dt 18:20 But any prophet who **s** in the name of other gods,
18:22 If a prophet **s** in the name of the LORD but
2Sa 23: 2 The spirit of the LORD **s** through me,
Job 33: 2 See, I open my mouth; the tongue in my mouth **s**.
33:14 For God **s** in one way, and in two,
34:35 'Job **s** without knowledge,
Ps 36: 1 Transgression **s** to the wicked deep in their hearts;
50: 1 **s** and summons the earth from the rising of the sun
127: 5 not be put to shame when he **s** with his enemies in
Pr 1:21 at the entrance of the city gates she **s**:
12:17 Whoever **s** the truth gives honest evidence,
12:17 but a false witness **s** deceitfully.
26:25 when an enemy **s** graciously, do not believe it,
SS 2:10 My beloved **s** and says to me:
Jer 9: 5 and no one **s** the truth;
9: 8 it **s** deceit through the mouth.
10: 1 Hear the word that the LORD **s** to you,
Eze 10: 5 like the voice of God Almighty when he **s**.
14: 9 If a prophet is deceived and **s** a word, I,
Am 5:10 and they abhor the one who **s** the truth.
Hab 2: 3 it **s** of the end, and does not lie.
Mt 12:32 Whoever **s** a word against the Son of Man will
12:32 but whoever **s** against the Holy Spirit will not
12:34 For out of the abundance of the heart the mouth **s**.
15: 4 'Whoever **s** evil of father or mother must
Mk 7:10 and, 'Whoever **s** evil of father or mother must
Lk 6:45 of the abundance of the heart that the mouth **s**.
12:10 And everyone who **s** a word against the Son
20:37 where he **s** of the Lord as the God of Abraham,
Jn 3:31 to the earth and **s** about earthly things.
3:34 He whom God has sent **s** the words of God,
8:44 When he lies, he **s** according to his own nature,
Ro 3:19 it **s** to those who are under the law,
4: 6 So also David **s** of the blessedness of those
1Co 14: 5 prophesies is greater than one who **s** in tongues,
14:13 one who **s** in a tongue should pray for the power to
14:27 If anyone **s** in a tongue, let there be only two or
Heb 4: 4 in one place it **s** about the seventh day as follows,
11: 4 he died, but through his faith he still **s**.
12:24 and to the sprinkled blood that **s** a better word than
Jas 4:11 Whoever **s** evil against another or judges another,
4:11 **s** evil against the law and judges the law;
1Pe 4:11 Whoever **s** must do so as one speaking
Jdt 11:21 of the earth to the other looks so beautiful or **s**
Sir 12:16 An enemy **s** sweetly with his lips,
13:22 he **s** unseemly words, but they justify him.
13:23 The rich person **s** and all are silent;
13:23 poor person **s** and they say, "Who is this fellow?"
25: 9 and the one who **s** to attentive listeners.
27: 4 so do a person's faults when he **s**.
27: 7 Do not praise anyone before he **s**,

SPEAR‡ (59) [SPEARMEN, SPEAR'S, SPEARS]

Nu 25: 7 Taking a **s** in his hand,
Jdg 5: 8 Was shield or **s** to be seen among forty thousand
1Sa 13:22 of the battle neither sword nor **s** was to be found in
17: 7 The shaft of his **s** was like a weaver's beam,
17:45 "You come to me with sword and **s** and javelin;
17:47 that the LORD does not save by sword and **s**;
18:10 Saul had his **s** in his hand;
18:11 the **s**, for he thought, "I will pin David to
19: 9 as he sat in his house with his **s** in his hand,
19:10 Saul sought to pin David to the wall with the **s**;
19:10 so that he struck the **s** into the wall.
20:33 But Saul threw his **s** at him to strike him;
21: 8 "Is there no **s** or sword here with you?
22: 6 with his **s** in his hand,
26: 7 with his **s** stuck in the ground at his head;
26: 8 to the ground with one stroke of the **s**;
26:11 but now take the **s** that is at his head,
26:12 So David took the **s** that was at Saul's head and
26:16 See now, where is the king's **s**,
26:22 David replied, "Here is the **s**, O king!
2Sa 1: 6 and there was Saul leaning on his **s**,
2:23 in the stomach with the butt of his **s**,
2:23 so that the **s** came out at his back.
21:16 whose **s** weighed three hundred shekels of bronze,
21:19 the shaft of whose **s** was like a weaver's beam.
23: 7 an iron bar or the shaft of a **s**.
23: 8 wielded his **s** against eight hundred whom he killed
23:18 With his **s** he fought against three hundred men
23:21 The Egyptian had a **s** in his hand;
23:21 snatched the **s** out of the Egyptian's hand,
23:21 and killed him with his own **s**.
1Ch 11:11 wielded his **s** against three hundred whom he killed
11:20 With his **s** he fought against three hundred
11:23 Egyptian had in his hand a **s** like a weaver's beam;
11:23 snatched the **s** out of the Egyptian's hand,
11:23 and killed him with his own **s**.
12: 8 with shield and **s**, whose faces were like the faces
12:24 The people of Judah bearing shield and **s**
12:34 thirty-seven thousand armed with shield and **s**.
20: 5 the shaft of whose **s** was like a weaver's beam.
2Ch 25: 5 able to handle **s** and shield.
Job 39:23 Upon it rattle the quiver, the flashing **s**,
41:26 sword reaches it, it does not avail, nor does the **s**,
Ps 35: 3 Draw the **s** and javelin against my pursuers;
46: 9 he breaks the bow, and shatters the **s**;
Jer 50:42 They wield bow and **s**, they are cruel
Na 3: 3 flashing sword and glittering **s**, piles of dead,
Hab 3:11 at the gleam of your flashing **s**.
Jn 19:34 one of the soldiers pierced his side with a **s**,
Jdt 6: 6 Then at my return the sword of my army and the **s**
9: 7 and trusting in shield and **s**, in bow and sling.
11: 2 I would never have lifted my **s** against them.
AdE 16:24 accordingly shall be destroyed in wrath with **s**
Sir 29:13 better than a stout shield and a sturdy **s**,
3Mc 3:15 and Phoenicia by the power of the **s**,
5:43 and rapidly level it to the ground with fire and **s**,
6: 5 by the **s** and was lifted up against your holy city,
2Es 13: 9 he neither lifted his hand nor held a **s**
13:28 not holding a **s** or weapon of war, yet destroying

SPEAR'S (1) [SPEAR]

1Sa 17: 7 his **s** head weighed six hundred shekels of iron;

SPEARMEN (1) [MAN, SPEAR]

Ac 23:23 seventy horsemen, and two hundred **s**.

SPEARS (20) [SPEAR]

1Sa 13:19 "The Hebrews must not make swords or **s**
2Sa 18:14 He took three **s** in his hand,
2Ki 11:10 the **s** and shields that had been King David's,
2Ch 11:12 He also put large shields and **s** in all the cities,
14: 8 armed with large shields and **s**,
23: 9 The priest Jehoiada delivered to the captains the **s**
26:14 Uzziah provided for all the army the shields, **s**,
Ne 4:13 with their swords, their **s**, and their bows.
4:16 and half held the **s**, shields, bows,
4:21 the **s** from break of dawn until the stars came out.
Job 41: 7 or its head with fishing **s**?
Ps 57: 4 their teeth are **s** and arrows,
Isa 2: 4 and their **s** into pruning hooks;
Eze 39: 9 bows and arrows, handpikes and **s**—
Joel 3:10 and your pruning hooks into **s**;
Mic 4: 3 and their **s** into pruning hooks;
Jdt 1:15 of Ragau and struck him down with his **s**,
7:10 on their **s** but on the height of the mountains
2Mc 5: 3 brandishing of shields, massing of **s**,
15:11 so much with confidence in shields and **s** as with

SPECIAL (12) [ESPECIALLY, SPECIALLY]

Nu 6: 2 When either men or women make a **s** vow,
Eze 27:15 many coastlands were your own **s** markets;
48:12 as a **s** portion from the holy portion of the land,
Mal 3:17 my **s** possession on the day when I act,
Ro 9:21 to make out of the same lump one object for **s** use
Gal 4:10 You are observing **s** days, and months,
2Ti 2:20 some for **s** use, some for ordinary.
2:21 things I have mentioned will become **s** utensils,
AdE 2: 9 he treated her and her maids with **s** favor in
5: 4 And Esther said, "Today is a **s** day for me.
Wis 3:14 for **s** favor will be shown him for his faithfulness,
1Mc 6:37 they were fastened on each animal by **s** harness,

SPECIALLY (1) [SPECIAL]

2Mc 2: 8 that the place should be **s** consecrated."

SPECIES (2)

Jas 3: 7 For every **s** of beast and bird,
3: 7 can be tamed and has been tamed by the human **s**,

SPECIFICATIONS (1)

1Ki 6:38 in all its parts, and according to all its **s**.

SPECK (7)

Mt 7: 3 Why do you see the **s** in your neighbor's eye,
7: 4 'Let me take the **s** out of your eye,'
7: 5 and then you will see clearly to take the **s** out
Lk 6:41 Why do you see the **s** in your neighbor's eye,
6:42 'Friend, let me take out the **s** in your eye,'
6:42 and then you will see clearly to take the **s** out
Wis 11:22 Because the whole world before you is like a **s**

SPECKLED (9)

Ge 30:32 removing from it every **s** and spotted sheep
30:32 and the spotted and **s** among the goats;
30:33 that is not **s** and spotted among the goats and black
30:35 and all the female goats that were **s** and spotted,
30:39 so the flocks produced young that were striped, **s**,
31: 8 If he said, 'The **s** shall be your wages,'
31: 8 then all the flock bore **s**;
31:10 that leaped upon the flock were striped, **s**,
31:12 that leap on the flock are striped, **s**, and mottled;

SPECTACLE (7)

1Sa 1:14 "How long will you make a drunken **s** of yourself?
Na 3: 6 and treat you with contempt, and make you a **s**.
Lk 23:48 for this **s** saw what had taken place,
1Co 4: 9 because we have become a **s** to the world,
3Mc 4:11 to make them an obvious **s** to all coming back into
5:24 the city had been assembled for this most pitiful **s**
2Es 16:64 and will make a public **s** of all of you.

SPECTATORS (2)

4Mc 15:20 and when you saw the place filled with many **s** of
17:14 and the world and the human race were the **s**.

SPECTERS (2)

Wis 17: 3 terribly alarmed, and appalled by **s**.
17:15 and now were driven by monstrous **s**, and

SPECULATIONS (1)

1Ti 1: 4 and endless genealogies that promote **s** rather than

SPEECH (77) [SPEAK]

Ge 11: 7 so that they will not understand one another's **s**."
Ex 4:10 but I am slow of **s** and slow of tongue."
4:11 the LORD said to him, "Who gives **s** to mortals?
Dt 32: 2 my **s** condense like the dew;
1Sa 16:18 prudent in **s**, and a man of good presence;
Job 6:26 as if the **s** of the desperate were wind?
12:20 He deprives of **s** those who are trusted,
33: 1 now, hear my **s**, O Job, and listen to all my words.
Ps 19: 2 Day to day pours forth **s**,
19: 3 There is no **s**, nor are there words;
55: 9 Confuse, O Lord, confound their **s**;
55:21 with **s** smoother than butter, but with a heart set
Pr 4:24 Put away from you crooked **s**,
5: 3 and her **s** is smoother than oil;
6:12 and a villain goes around with crooked **s**,
7:21 With much seductive **s** she persuades him;
8:13 and the way of evil and perverted **s** I hate.
10:19 but the prudent are restrained in **s**.
12: 6 but the **s** of the upright delivers them.
16:21 and pleasant **s** increases persuasiveness.
16:23 The mind of the wise makes their **s** judicious,
16:27 and their **s** is like a scorching fire.
17: 7 Fine **s** is not becoming to a fool;
17: 7 still less is false **s** to a ruler.
19: 1 in integrity than one perverse of **s** who is a fool.
22:11 and are gracious in **s** will have the king as a friend.
29:20 Do you see someone who is hasty in **s**?
SS 5:16 His **s** is most sweet, and he is altogether desirable.
Isa 3: 8 their **s** and their deeds are against the LORD,
28:23 Pay attention, and hear my **s**.
29: 4 and your **s** shall whisper out of the dust.
32: 9 you complacent daughters, listen to my **s**.
33:19 of an obscure **s** that you cannot comprehend,
Eze 3: 5 a people of obscure **s** and difficult language,
3: 6 of obscure **s** and difficult language,
35:12 have heard all the abusive **s** that you uttered
Zep 3: 9 At that time I will change the **s** of the peoples to
3: 9 the speech of the peoples to a pure **s**,
Mk 7:32 a deaf man who had an impediment in his **s**;
Jn 10: 6 Jesus used this figure of **s** with them,
16:25 "I have said these things to you in figures of **s**.
16:29 not in any figure of **s**!
1Co 1: 5 in **s** and knowledge of every kind—
2: 4 My **s** and my proclamation were not
14: 9 if in a tongue you utter **s** that is not intelligible,
2Co 6: 7 truthful **s**, and the power of God;
8: 7 in faith, in **s**, in knowledge, in utmost eagerness,
10:10 bodily presence is weak, and his **s** contemptible."
11: 6 I may be untrained in **s**, but not in knowledge;
Col 4: 6 Let your **s** always be gracious, seasoned with salt,
1Ti 4:12 but set the believers an example in **s** and conduct,
Tit 2: 8 and sound **s** that cannot be censured;
1Jn 3:18 Little children, let us love, not in word or **s**,
Jude 1:16 they are bombastic in **s**, flattering people
Jdt 11: 9 "Now as for Achior's **s** in your council,
11:23 not only beautiful in appearance, but wise in **s**.
AdE 1:21 This **s** pleased the king and the governors,
14:13 Put eloquent **s** in my mouth before the lion,
Wis 8: 8 she understands turns of **s** and the solutions
Sir 4:24 For wisdom becomes known through **s**,
4:29 Do not be reckless in your **s**,
5:10 and let your **s** be consistent.
6: 5 Pleasant **s** multiplies friends,
9:18 and the one who is reckless in **s** is hated.
21: 7 The mighty in **s** are widely known;
21:16 but delight is found in the **s** of the intelligent.
23:13 foul language, for it involves sinful **s**.
25:25 and no boldness of **s** to an evil wife.
27: 6 a person's **s** discloses the cultivation of his mind.
27:23 but later he will twist his **s** and
32:12 but do not sin through proud **s**.
36:28 If kindness and humility mark her **s**,
1Mc 4:19 Just as Judas was finishing this **s**,
6:60 The **s** pleased the king and the commanders,
3Mc 3:23 both by **s** and by silence they abominate those few
2Es 6:16 that the **s** concerns them. They will tremble
4Mc 10:18 But he said, "Even if you remove my organ of **s**,

SPEECHES (1) [SPEAK]
Job 32:14 and I will not answer him with your s.

SPEECHLESS (10) [SPEAK]
Isa 35: 6 and the tongue of the s sing for joy.
Eze 3:26 so that you shall be s and unable to reprove them;
Da 10:15 I turned my face toward the ground and was s.
Mt 22:12 without a wedding robe?' And he was s.
Ac 9: 7 The men who were traveling with him stood s
2Pe 2:16 a s donkey spoke with a human voice
Wis 4:19 because he will dash them s to the ground,
2Mc 3:29 s because of the divine intervention and deprived
3Mc 4:16 praising s things that are not able even
4Mc 10:19 for in spite of this you will not make our reason s.

SPEED (4) [SPEEDILY, SPEEDING, SPEEDS, SPEEDY]
Ps 147:10 nor his pleasure in the s of a runner;
Isa 5:19 let him s his work that we may see it;
AdE 8:14 So the messengers on horseback set out with all s
Bel 1:36 the s of the wind he set him down in Babylon,

SPEEDILY (13) [SPEED]
Ps 31: 2 Incline your ear to me; rescue me s.
79: 8 let your compassion come s to meet us,
102: 2 answer me s in the day when I call.
140:11 let evil s hunt down the violent!
Ecc 8:11 sentence against an evil deed is not executed s,
Isa 5:26 Here they come, swiftly, s!
51:14 The oppressed shall s be released;
Joel 3: 4 upon your own heads swiftly and s.
AdE 16:18 for God, who rules over all things, has s inflicted
Sir 20:18 the downfall of the wicked will occur just as s.
21: 5 and his judgment comes s.
3Mc 2:20 S let your mercies overtake us,
4Mc 4:22 He s marched against them,

SPEEDING (1) [SPEED]
Hab 3:11 at the light of your arrows s by,

SPEEDS‡ (1) [SPEED]
Sir 43:13 By his command he sends the driving snow and s

SPEEDY (1) [SPEED]
Wis 14:14 and therefore their s end has been planned.

SPELLBOUND (3)
Mk 11:18 because the whole crowd was s by his teaching.
Lk 19:48 for all the people were s by what they heard.
2Es 2:43 And I was held s.

SPELLS (1)
Dt 18:11 or one who casts s, or who consults ghosts

SPELT (3)
Ex 9:32 But the wheat and the s were not ruined,
Isa 28:25 and barley in its proper place, and s as the border?
Eze 4: 9 beans and lentils, millet and s;

SPEND (45) [SPENDING, SPENT]
Ge 19: 2 turn aside to your servant's house and s the night,
19: 2 They said, "No; we will s the night in the square."
24:23 Is there room in your father's house for us to s
24:25 of straw and fodder and a place to s the night."
Dt 14:26 s the money for whatever you wish—
32:23 disasters upon them, s my arrows against them:
Jdg 19: 6 "Why not s the night and enjoy yourself?"
19: 9 until it is almost evening. S the night.
19: 9 S the night here and enjoy yourself.
19:10 But the man would not s the night;
19:11 and s the night in it."
19:13 and s the night at Gibeah or at Ramah."
19:15 to go in and s the night at Gibeah.
19:15 but no one took them in to s the night.
19:20 only do not s the night in the square."
20: 4 I and my concubine, to s the night.
2Sa 17: 8 he will not s the night with the troops.
1Ch 9:27 And they would s the night near the house of God;
Ne 13:21 "Why do you s the night in front of the wall?
Job 21:13 They s their days in prosperity,
39: 9 Will it s the night at your crib?
Isa 55: 2 Why do you s your money for that which is
65: 4 and s the night in secret places;
Jer 20:18 and s my days in shame?
Eze 5:13 My anger shall s itself, and I will vent my fury
5:13 when I s my fury on them.
6:12 Thus I will s my fury upon them.
7: 8 I will s my anger against you.
13:15 Thus I will s my wrath upon the wall,
20: 8 and s my anger against them in the midst of
20:21 and s my anger against them in the wilderness.
39:12 the house of Israel shall s burying them,
Lk 10:35 I will repay you whatever more you s.'
21:37 and at night he would go out and s the night on
Ac 17:21 and the foreigners living there would s their time
20:16 so that he might not have to s time in Asia;
27:12 where they could s the winter.
1Co 16: 6 perhaps I will stay with you or even s the winter,
16: 7 for I hope to s some time with you,
2Co 12:15 I will most gladly s and be spent for you.
Tit 3:12 for I have decided to s the winter there.
Jas 4: 3 in order to s what you get on your pleasures.
4:13 to such and such a town and s a year there,
Sir 42:12 or s her time among married women;
LtJ 6:10 and silver from their gods and s it on themselves,

SPENDING (2) [SPEND]
Ac 18:23 After s some time there he departed and went
27:12 Since the harbor was not suitable for s the winter,

SPENT‡ (40) [SPEND]
Ge 24:54 and they s the night there.
32:13 So he s that night there,
32:21 and he himself s that night in the camp.
47:15 of Egypt and from the land of Canaan was s,
47:18 not hide from my lord that our money is all s;
50: 3 they s forty days in doing this,
Ex 4:24 On the way, at a place where they s the night,
Lev 26:20 Your strength shall be s to no purpose:
Jos 2: 1 of a prostitute whose name was Rahab, and s
6:11 and s the night in the camp.
8: 9 but Joshua s that night in the camp.
8:13 But Joshua s that night in the valley.
Jdg 19: 7 his father-in-law kept urging him until he s
19:11 When they were near Jebus, the day was far s,
1Ki 19: 9 that place he came to a cave, and s the night there.
2Ch 20:25 They s three days taking the booty,
Ezr 10: 6 of Jehohanan son of Eliashib, where he s the night.
Ne 13:20 of merchandise s the night outside Jerusalem once
Ps 31:10 For my life is s with sorrow,
38: 8 I am utterly s and crushed;
71: 9 do not forsake me when my strength is s.
Ecc 2:11 that my hands had done and the toil I had s
Isa 49: 4 I have s my strength for nothing and vanity;
La 2:11 My eyes are s with weeping;
Da 6:18 the king went to his palace and s the night fasting;
Mt 21:17 of the city to Bethany, and s the night there.
Mk 5:26 and had s all that she had;
Lk 6:12 and he s the night in prayer to God.
8:43 and though she had s all she had on physicians,
15:14 When he had s everything,
Jn 3:22 and he s some time there with them and baptized.
Ac 2:46 as they s much time together in the temple,
26: 4 a life s from the beginning among my own people
2Co 12:15 I will most gladly spend and be s for you.
1Pe 4: 3 You have already s enough time in doing what
1Mc 11: 6 and they greeted one another and s the night there.
14:32 He s great sums of his own money;
1Es 9: 2 and s the night there; and he did eat bread or
3Mc 4: 8 s the remaining days of their marriage festival
4Mc 13:20 There each of the brothers s the same length

SPEWED (3)
Jer 51:34 with my delicacies, he has s me out.
Jnh 2:10 and it s Jonah out upon the dry land.
Wis 19:10 and instead of fish the river s out vast numbers

SPHERE (2)
2Co 10:15 but our hope is that, as your faith increases, our s
10:16 of work already done in someone else's s

SPICE (3) [SPICED, SPICES]
SS 4:10 and the fragrance of your oils than any s!
5: 1 I gather my myrrh with my s,
Rev 18:13 s, incense, myrrh, frankincense, wine, olive oil,

SPICED (1) [SPICE]
SS 8: 2 I would give you s wine to drink,

SPICERY (KJV) See GUM

SPICES (33) [SPICE]
Ex 25: 6 s for the anointing oil and for the fragrant incense,
30:23 Take the finest s: of liquid myrrh
30:34 Take sweet s, stacte, and onycha, and galbanum,
30:34 and galbanum, sweet s with pure frankincense
35: 8 s for the anointing oil and for the fragrant incense,
35:28 and s and oil for the light,
1Ki 10: 2 with camels bearing s, and very much gold,
10:10 a great quantity of s, and precious stones;
10:10 never again did s come in such quantity as
10:25 objects of silver and gold, garments, weaponry, s,
2Ki 20:13 the gold, the s, the precious oil, his armory,
1Ch 9:29 the wine, the oil, the incense, and the s.
9:30 prepared the mixing of the s,
2Ch 9: 1 having a very great retinue and camels bearing s
9: 9 a very great quantity of s, and precious stones:
9: 9 there were no s such as those that the queen
9:24 objects of silver and gold, garments, weaponry, s,
16:14 of s prepared by the perfumer's art;
32:27 for gold, for precious stones, for s, for shields,
SS 4:14 myrrh and aloes, with all chief s—
5:13 His cheeks are like beds of s, yielding fragrance.
6: 2 to the beds of s, to pasture his flock in the gardens,
8:14 a gazelle or a young stag upon the mountains of s!
Isa 39: 2 the gold, the s, the precious oil, his whole armory,
Jer 34: 5 And as s were burned for your ancestors,
34: 5 so they shall burn s for you and lament for you,
Eze 24:10 boil the meat well, mix in the s,
27:22 for your wares the best of all kinds of s,
Mk 16: 1 the mother of James, and Salome bought s, so
Lk 23:56 Then they returned, and prepared s and ointments.
24: 1 taking the s that they had prepared.
Jn 19:40 of Jesus and wrapped it with the s in linen cloths,
AdE 2:12 and six months with s and ointments for women.

SPIDER (KJV) See LIZARD; See also Index to Footnotes

SPIDER'S‡ (2)
Job 8:14 Their confidence is gossamer, a s house their trust.
Isa 59: 5 They hatch adders' eggs, and weave the s web;

SPIED (8) [SPY]
Nu 13:21 up and s out the land from the wilderness of Zin
13:32 of the land that they had s out, saying, "The land
14: 6 who were among those who had s out the land,
14:34 to the number of the days in which you s out
Dt 1:24 they reached the Valley of Eshcol they s it out
Jos 6:22 Joshua said to the two men who had s out the land,
7: 2 And the men went up and s out Ai.
2Ki 9:17 the sentinel standing on the tower s the company

SPIES (18) [SPY]
Ge 42: 9 He said to them, "You are s;
42:11 your servants have never been s."
42:14 as I have said to you; you are s!
42:16 or else, as Pharaoh lives, surely you are s."
42:31 we said to him, 'We are honest men, we are not s.
42:34 and I shall know that you are not s but honest men.
Nu 13:32 "The land that we have gone through as s is a land
14: 7 through as s is an exceedingly good land.
Jos 2: 1 of Nun sent two men secretly from Shittim as s,
6:23 So the young men who had been s went in
Jdg 1:23 The house of Joseph sent out s to Bethel (the name
1:24 When the s saw a man coming out of the city,
1Sa 26: 4 David sent out s, and learned
Job 39:29 From there it s the prey;
Lk 20:20 So they watched him and sent s who pretended to
Heb 11:31 because she had received the s in peace.
Sir 11:30 and like s they observe your weakness;
1Mc 12:26 He sent s to their camp,

SPIKENARD (KJV) See NARD

SPILLED (4)
Ge 38: 9 he s his semen on the ground whenever he went in
2Sa 14:14 We must all die; we are like water s on the ground,
Mt 9:17 otherwise, the skins burst, and the wine is s,
Lk 5:37 the new wine will burst the skins and will be s,

SPIN (2) [SPUN]
Mt 6:28 how they grow; they neither toil nor s,
Lk 12:27 how they grow: they neither toil nor s;

SPINDLE (2)
2Sa 3:29 or who holds a s, or who falls by the sword,
Pr 31:19 and her hands hold the s.

SPIRIT‡ (616) [SPIRITS, SPIRITUAL, SPIRITUALLY]
A. HOLY SPIRIT (95)
B. SPIRIT OF *GOD (23)
C. SPIRIT OF THE †LORD (22)
D. UNCLEAN SPIRIT (12)
E. EVIL SPIRIT (11)
F. SPIRIT OF THE *LORD (6)

Ge 6: 3 "My s shall not abide in mortals forever,
41: 8 In the morning his s was troubled;
41:38 one in whom is the s of God?" B
45:27 the s of their father Jacob revived.
Ex 6: 9 because of their broken s and their cruel slavery.
31: 3 and I have filled him with divine s,
35:21 and everyone whose s was willing,
35:31 he has filled him with divine s,
Nu 5:14 if a s of jealousy comes on him, and he is jealous
5:14 or if a s of jealousy comes on him,
5:30 a s of jealousy comes on a man and he is jealous
11:17 and I will take some of the s that is on you
11:25 and took some of the s that was on him and put it
11:25 and when the s rested upon them, they prophesied.
11:26 and the s rested on them;
11:29 and that the LORD would put his s on them!"
14:24 a different s and has followed me wholeheartedly,
24: 2 Then the s of God came upon him, B
27:18 "Take Joshua son of Nun, a man in whom is the s,
Dt 2:30 for the LORD your God had hardened his s
28:65 failing eyes, and a languishing s.
34: 9 Joshua son of Nun was full of the s of wisdom,
Jos 5: 1 and there was no longer any s in them,
Jdg 3:10 The s of the LORD came upon him, C
6:34 the s of the LORD took possession of Gideon; C
9:23 But God sent an evil s between Abimelech and E
11:29 Then the s of the LORD came upon Jephthah, C
13:25 s of the LORD began to stir him in Mahaneh-dan, C
14: 6 The s of the LORD rushed on him, C
14:19 Then the s of the LORD rushed on him, C
15:14 and the s of the LORD rushed on him, C
15:19 When he drank, his s returned, and he revived.
1Sa 10: 6 Then the s of the LORD will possess you, C
10:10 and the s of God possessed him, B
11: 6 And the s of God came upon Saul in power B
16:13 and the s of the LORD came mightily upon David C
16:14 Now the s of the LORD departed from Saul, C
16:14 and an evil s from the LORD tormented him. E

1Sa 16:15 "See now, an evil **s** from God is tormenting you. E
16:16 and when the evil **s** from God is upon you, E
16:23 whenever the evil **s** from God came upon Saul, E
16:23 and the evil **s** would depart from him. E
18:10 next day an evil **s** from God rushed upon Saul, E
19: 9 Then an evil **s** from the LORD came upon Saul, E
19:20 the **s** of God came upon the messengers of Saul, B
19:23 and the **s** of God came upon him. B
28: 8 And he said, "Consult a **s** for me,
30: 6 the people were bitter in **s** for their sons
30:12 When he had eaten, his **s** revived;
2Sa 23: 2 The **s** of the LORD speaks through me, C
1Ki 10: 5 there was no more **s** in her.
18:12 **s** of the LORD will carry you I know not where; C
22:21 a **s** came forward and stood before the LORD,
22:22 and be a lying **s** in the mouth of all his prophets.'
22:23 a lying **s** in the mouth of all these your prophets;
22:24 "Which way did the **s** of the LORD pass from me C
2Ki 2: 9 "Please let me inherit a double share of your **s**."
2:15 they declared, "The **s** of Elijah rests on Elisha."
2:16 it may be that the **s** of the LORD has caught him C
5:26 not go with you in **s** when someone left his chariot
19: 7 I myself will put a **s** in him,
1Ch 5:26 So the God of Israel stirred up the **s** of King Pul
5:26 the **s** of King Tilgath-pilneser of Assyria,
12:18 Then the **s** came upon Amasai, chief of the Thirty,
2Ch 9: 4 there was no more **s** left in her.
15: 1 The **s** of God came upon Azariah son of Oded. B
18:20 a **s** came forward and stood before the LORD,
18:21 and be a lying **s** in the mouth of all his prophets.'
18:22 a lying **s** in the mouth of these your prophets;
18:23 "Which way did the **s** of the LORD pass from me C
20:14 Then the **s** of the LORD came upon Jahaziel son C
24:20 the **s** of God took possession of Zechariah B
36:22 up the **s** of King Cyrus of Persia so that he sent
Ezr 1: 1 up the **s** of King Cyrus of Persia so that he sent
1: 5 everyone whose **s** God had stirred—
Ne 9:20 You gave your good **s** to instruct them,
9:30 and warned them by your **s** through your prophets;
Job 4:15 **s** glided past my face; the hair of my flesh bristled.
6: 4 my **s** drinks their poison;
7:11 I will speak in the anguish of my **s**;
10:12 and your care has preserved my **s**.
15:13 so that you turn your **s** against God,
17: 1 My **s** is broken, my days are extinct,
20: 3 and a **s** beyond my understanding answers me.
26: 4 and whose **s** has come forth from you?
27: 3 as long as my breath is in me and the **s** of God B
32: 8 But truly it is the **s** in a mortal,
32:18 I am full of words; the **s** within me constrains me.
33: 4 The **s** of God has made me, B
34:14 If he should take back his **s** to himself,
Ps 31: 5 Into your hand I commit my **s**;
32: 2 and in whose **s** there is no deceit.
34:18 and saves the crushed in **s**.
51:10 O God, and put a new and right **s** within me.
51:11 and do not take your holy **s** from me. A
51:12 and sustain in me a willing **s**.
51:17 The sacrifice acceptable to God is a broken **s**;
76:12 who cuts off the **s** of princes,
77: 3 I meditate, and my **s** faints.
77: 6 I meditate and search my **s**:
78: 8 whose **s** was not faithful to God.
104:30 When you send forth your **s**, they are created;
106:33 for they made his **s** bitter,
139: 7 Where can I go from your **s**?
142: 3 When my **s** is faint, you know my way.
143: 4 Therefore my **s** faints within me;
143: 7 Answer me quickly, O LORD; my **s** fails.
143:10 Let your good **s** lead me on a level path.
Pr 11:13 one who is trustworthy in **s** keeps a confidence.
15: 4 but perverseness in it breaks the **s**.
15:13 but by sorrow of heart the **s** is broken.
16: 2 but the LORD weighs the **s**.
16:18 and a haughty **s** before a fall.
16:19 It is better to be of a lowly **s** among the poor than
17:22 but a downcast **s** dries up the bones.
17:27 one who is cool in **s** has understanding.
18:14 The human **s** will endure sickness;
18:14 but a broken **s**—who can bear?
20:27 The human **s** is the lamp of the LORD,
25:13 they refresh the **s** of their masters.
29:23 but one who is lowly in **s** will obtain honor.
Ecc 3:21 Who knows whether the human **s** goes upward and
3:21 and the **s** of animals goes downward to the earth?
7: 8 the patient in **s** are better than the proud in **s**.
Isa 4: 4 of Jerusalem from its midst by a **s** of judgment and
4: 4 from its midst by a spirit of judgment and by a **s**
11: 2 The **s** of the LORD shall rest on him, C
11: 2 the **s** of wisdom and understanding,
11: 2 the **s** of counsel and might,
11: 2 the **s** of knowledge and the fear of the LORD.
19: 3 the **s** of the Egyptians within them will
19:14 LORD has poured into them a **s** of confusion;
26: 9 my **s** within me earnestly seeks you.
28: 6 and a **s** of justice to the one who sits in judgment,
29:10 LORD has poured out upon you a **s** of deep sleep;
29:24 those who err in **s** will come to understanding,
31: 3 their horses are flesh, and not **s**.
32:15 until a **s** from on high is poured out on us,
34:16 and his **s** has gathered them.
37: 7 I myself will put a **s** in him,
38:16 and in all these is the life of my **s**.
40:13 Who has directed the **s** of the LORD, C
42: 1 I have put my **s** upon him;
42: 5 to the people upon it and **s** to those who walk in it:
44: 3 I will pour my **s** upon your descendants,

Isa 48:16 And now the Lord GOD has sent me and his **s**.
54: 6 like a wife forsaken and grieved in **s**,
57:15 also with those who are contrite and humble in **s**,
57:15 to revive the **s** of the humble,
59:21 my **s** that is upon you, and my words
61: 1 The **s** of the Lord GOD is upon me, F
61: 3 the mantle of praise instead of a faint **s**.
63:10 But they rebelled and grieved his holy **s**; A
63:11 Where is the one who put within them his holy **s**, A
63:14 the **s** of the LORD gave them rest. C
65:14 and shall wail for anguish of **s**.
66: 2 to the humble and contrite in **s**,
Jer 51:11 The LORD has stirred up the **s** of the kings of
Eze 1:12 wherever the **s** would go, they went,
1:20 Wherever the **s** would go, they went,
1:20 for the **s** of the living creatures was in the wheels.
1:21 for the **s** of the living creatures was in the wheels.
2: 2 a **s** entered into me and set me on my feet;
3:12 Then the **s** lifted me up, and as the glory of
3:14 The **s** lifted me up and bore me away;
3:14 I went in bitterness in the heat of my **s**,
3:24 The **s** entered into me, and set me on my feet;
8: 3 and the **s** lifted me up between earth and heaven,
10:17 for the **s** of the living creatures was in them.
11: 1 The **s** lifted me up and brought me to the east gate
11: 5 Then the **s** of the LORD fell upon me, C
11:19 and put a new **s** within them;
11:24 The **s** lifted me up and brought me in a vision by
11:24 up and brought me in a vision by the **s** of God B
13: 3 for the senseless prophets who follow their own **s**,
18:31 and get yourselves a new heart and a new **s**!
21: 7 every **s** will faint and all knees will turn to water.
36:26 and a new **s** I will put within you;
36:27 I will put my **s** within you,
37: 1 the **s** of the LORD and set me down in the middle C
37:14 I will put my **s** within you, and you shall live,
39:29 when I pour out my **s** upon the house of Israel,
43: 5 **s** lifted me up, and brought me into the inner court;
Da 2: 1 that his **s** was troubled and his sleep left him.
2: 3 "I have had such a dream that my **s** is troubled by
4: 8 and who is endowed with a **s** of the holy gods—
4: 9 that you are endowed with a **s** of the holy gods and
4:18 for you are endowed with a **s** of the holy gods."
5:11 a man in your kingdom who is endowed with a **s**
5:12 an excellent **s**, knowledge, and understanding
5:14 I have heard of you that a **s** of the gods is in you,
5:20 and his **s** was hardened so that he acted proudly,
6: 3 and satraps because an excellent **s** was in him,
7:15 As for me, Daniel, my **s** was troubled within me,
Hos 4:12 For a **s** of whoredom has led them astray,
5: 4 For the **s** of whoredom is within them,
9: 7 "The prophet is a fool, the man of the **s** is mad!"
Joel 2:28 Then afterward I will pour out my **s** on all flesh;
2:29 in those days, I will pour out my **s**.
Mic 3: 8 I am filled with power, with the **s** of the LORD, C
Hab 2: 4 Their **s** is not right in them,
Hag 1:14 And the LORD stirred up the **s** of Zerubbabel son
1:14 and the **s** of Joshua son of Jehozadak,
1:14 and the **s** of all the remnant of the people;
2: 5 My **s** abides among you; do not fear.
Zec 4: 6 Not by might, nor by power, but by my **s**,
6: 8 toward the north country have set my **s** at rest in
7:12 that the LORD of hosts had sent by his **s** through
12: 1 the earth and formed the human **s** within:
12:10 a **s** of compassion and supplication on the house
13: 2 from the land the prophets and the unclean **s**. D
Mal 2:15 Both flesh and **s** are his.
Mt 1:18 she was found to be with child from the Holy **S**. A
1:20 the child conceived in her is from the Holy **S**. A
3:11 He will baptize you with the Holy **S** and fire. A
3:16 the **S** of God descending like a dove and B
4: 1 led up by the **S** into the wilderness to be tempted
5: 3 "Blessed are the poor in **s**,
10:20 but the **S** of your Father speaking through you.
12:18 I will put my **S** upon him,
12:28 if it is by the **S** of God that I cast out demons, B
12:31 but blasphemy against the **S** will not be forgiven.
12:32 but whoever speaks against the Holy **S** will not A
12:43 "When the unclean **s** has gone out of a person, D
22:43 is it then that David by the **S** calls him Lord,
26:41 the **s** indeed is willing, but the flesh is weak."
28:19 of the Father and of the Son and of the Holy **S**, A
Mk 1: 8 but he will baptize you with the Holy **S**." A
1:10 the heavens torn apart and the **S** descending like
1:12 **S** immediately drove him out into the wilderness.
1:23 in their synagogue a man with an unclean **s**, D
1:26 the unclean **s**, convulsing him and crying with D
2: 8 in his **s** that they were discussing these questions
3:29 against the Holy **S** can never have forgiveness, A
3:30 for they had said, "He has an unclean **s**." D
5: 2 man out of the tombs with an unclean **s** met him. D
5: 8 "Come out of the man, you unclean **s**!" D
7:25 an unclean **s** immediately heard about him, D
8:12 And he sighed deeply in his **s** and said,
9:17 he has a **s** that makes him unable to speak;
9:20 the **s** saw him, immediately it convulsed the boy,
9:25 he rebuked the unclean **s**, saying to it, D
9:25 "You **s** that keeps this boy from speaking
12:36 David himself, by the Holy **S**, declared, A
13:11 for it is not you who speak, but the Holy **S**. A
14:38 the **s** indeed is willing, but the flesh is weak."
Lk 1:15 before his birth he will be filled with the Holy **S**. A
1:17 the **s** and power of Elijah he will go before him,
1:35 "The Holy **S** will come upon you, A
1:41 And Elizabeth was filled with the Holy **S** A
1:47 and my **s** rejoices in God my Savior,
1:67 with the Holy **S** and spoke this prophecy: A

Lk 1:80 The child grew and became strong in **s**,
2:25 and the Holy **S** rested on him. A
2:26 by the Holy **S** that he would not see death A
2:27 Guided by the **S**, Simeon came into the temple;
3:16 He will baptize you with the Holy **S** and fire. A
3:22 the Holy **S** descended upon him in bodily form A
4: 1 full of the Holy **S**, returned from the Jordan A
4: 1 the Jordan and was led by the **S** in the wilderness,
4:14 Then Jesus, filled with the power of the **S**,
4:18 "The **S** of the Lord is upon me, F
4:33 a man who had the **s** of and unclean demon,
8:29 for Jesus had commanded the unclean **s** to come D
8:55 Her **s** returned, and she got up at once.
9:39 Suddenly a **s** seizes him, and all at once he shrieks.
9:42 But Jesus rebuked the unclean **s**, healed the boy, D
10:21 in the Holy **S** and said, "I thank you, Father, A
11:13 the heavenly Father give the Holy **S** A
11:24 "When the unclean **s** has gone out of a person, D
12:10 whoever blasphemes against the Holy **S** will not A
12:12 for the Holy **S** will teach you at that very hour A
13:11 with a **s** that had crippled her for eighteen years.
23:46 said, "Father, into your hands I commend my **s**."
Jn 1:32 "I saw the **S** descending from heaven like a dove,
1:33 'He on whom you see the **S** descend and remain is
1:33 the one who baptizes with the Holy **S**.' A
3: 5 of God without being born of water and **S**.
3: 6 and what is born of the **S** is **s**.
3: 8 So it is with everyone who is born of the **S**."
3:34 for he gives the **S** without measure.
4:23 the true worshipers will worship the Father in **s**
4:24 God is **s**, and those who worship him must
worship in **s** and truth."
6:63 It is the **s** that gives life; the flesh is useless.
6:63 The words that I have spoken to you are **s** and life.
7:39 Now he said this about the **S**,
7:39 for as yet there was no **S**,
11:33 he was greatly disturbed in **s** and deeply moved.
13:21 After saying this Jesus was troubled in **s**,
14:17 This is the **S** of truth,
14:26 But the Advocate, the Holy **S**, A
15:26 the **S** of truth who comes from the Father,
16:13 When the **S** of truth comes,
19:30 Then he bowed his head and gave up his **s**.
20:22 on them and said to them, "Receive the Holy **S**. A
Ac 1: 2 the Holy **S** to the apostles whom he had chosen. A
1: 5 with the Holy **S** not many days from now." A
1: 8 when the Holy **S** has come upon you; A
1:16 which the Holy **S** through David foretold A
2: 4 All of them were filled with the Holy **S** and A
2: 4 as the **S** gave them ability.
2:17 that I will pour out my **S** upon all flesh,
2:18 in those days I will pour out my **S**;
2:33 from the Father the promise of the Holy **S**, A
2:38 and you will receive the gift of the Holy **S**. A
4: 8 Then Peter, filled with the Holy **S**, said to them, A
4:25 by the Holy **S** through our ancestor David, A
4:31 and they were all filled with the Holy **S** and A
5: 3 the Holy **S** and to keep back part of the proceeds A
5: 9 together to put the **S** of the Lord to the test? F
5:32 and so is the Holy **S** whom God has given A
6: 3 full of the **S** and of wisdom,
6: 5 a man full of faith and the Holy **S**, A
6:10 the wisdom and the **S** with which he spoke.
7:51 you are forever opposing the Holy **S**, A
7:55 But filled with the Holy **S**, A
7:59 he prayed, "Lord Jesus, receive my **s**."
8:15 for them that they might receive the Holy **S** A
8:16 (for as yet the **S** had not come upon any of them;
8:17 and they received the Holy **S**. A
8:18 when Simon saw that the **S** was given through
8:19 whom I lay my hands may receive the Holy **S**." A
8:29 Then the **S** said to Philip,
8:39 the **S** of the Lord snatched Philip away; F
9:17 and be filled with the Holy **S**." A
9:31 of the Lord and in the comfort of the Holy **S**, A
10:19 the **S** said to him, "Look, three men are searching
10:38 of Nazareth with the Holy **S** and with power; A
10:44 the Holy **S** fell upon all who heard the word. A
10:45 the gift of the Holy **S** had been poured out even A
10:47 the Holy **S** just as we have?" A
11:12 The **S** told me to go with them and not to make
11:15 the Holy **S** fell upon them just as it had upon us A
11:16 but you will be baptized with the Holy **S**.' A
11:24 full of the Holy **S** and of faith. A
11:28 the **S** that there would be a severe famine over all
13: 2 the Lord and fasting, the Holy **S** said, "Set apart A
13: 4 So, being sent out by the Holy **S**, A
13: 9 Saul, also known as Paul, filled with the Holy **S**, A
13:52 were filled with joy and with the Holy **S**. A
15: 8 testified to them by giving them the Holy **S**, A
15:28 For it has seemed good to the Holy **S** and to us A
16: 6 having been forbidden by the Holy **S** to speak A
16: 7 but the **S** of Jesus did not allow them;
16:16 we met a slave-girl who had a **s** of divination
16:18 Paul, very much annoyed, turned and said to the **s**,
19: 2 the Holy **S** when you became believers?" A
19: 2 we have not even heard that there is a Holy **S**." A
19: 6 the Holy **S** came upon them, A
19:15 the evil **s** said to them in reply, "Jesus I know, E
19:16 Then the man with the evil **s** leaped on them, E
19:21 Paul resolved in the **S** to go through Macedonia
20:22 And now, as a captive to the **S**,
20:23 that the Holy **S** testifies to me in every city A
20:28 of which the Holy **S** has made you overseers, A
21: 4 the **S** they told Paul not to go on to Jerusalem.
21:11 and said, "Thus says the Holy **S**, A
23: 8 or **s**; but the Pharisees acknowledge all three.)

Ac 23: 9 What if a s or an angel has spoken to him?"
28:25 "The Holy S was right in saying to your A
Ro 1: 4 according to the s of holiness by resurrection from
1: 9 whom I serve with my s by announcing the gospel
5: 5 through the Holy S that has been given to us. A
7: 6 the old written code but in the new life of the S.
8: 2 the S of life in Christ Jesus has set you free from
8: 4 not according to the flesh but according to the S.
8: 5 to the S set their minds on the things of the S.
8: 6 but to set the mind on the S is life and peace.
8: 9 But you are not in the flesh; you are in the S,
8: 9 since the S of God dwells in you. B
8: 9 not have the S of Christ does not belong to him.
8:10 the S is life because of righteousness.
8:11 If the S of him who raised Jesus from
8:11 to your mortal bodies also through his S
8:13 if by the S you put to death the deeds of the body,
8:14 For all who are led by the S of God are children B
8:15 For you did not receive a s of slavery to fall back
8:15 but you have received a s of adoption.
8:16 it is that very S bearing witness with our s that we
8:23 who have the first fruits of the S,
8:26 Likewise the S helps us in our weakness;
8:26 very S intercedes with sighs too deep for words.
8:27 knows what is the mind of the S,
8:27 the S intercedes for the saints according to the will
9: 1 my conscience confirms it by the Holy S— A
11: 8 "God gave them a sluggish s,
12:11 Do not lag in zeal, be ardent in s, serve the Lord.
14:17 righteousness and peace and joy in the Holy S. A
15:13 in hope by the power of the Holy S. A
15:16 be acceptable, sanctified by the Holy S. A
15:19 by the power of the S of God, B
15:30 by our Lord Jesus Christ and by the love of the S,
1Co 2: 4 but with a demonstration of the S and of power,
2:10 these things God has revealed to us through the S;
2:10 the S searches everything, even the depths of God.
2:11 the human s that is within?
2:11 what is truly God's except the S of God. B
2:12 Now we have received not the s of the world,
2:12 but the S that is from God,
2:13 not taught by human wisdom but taught by the S,
2:14 not receive the gifts of God's S,
3:16 that you are God's temple and that God's S dwells
4:21 or with love in a s of gentleness?
5: 3 For though absent in body, I am present in s;
5: 4 my s is present with the power of our Lord Jesus,
5: 5 so that his s may be saved in the day of the Lord.
6:11 in the name of the Lord Jesus Christ and in the S
6:17 But anyone united to the Lord becomes one s
6:19 know that your body is a temple of the Holy S A
7:34 so that they may be holy in body and s;
7:40 And I think that I too have the S of God. B
12: 3 by the S of God ever says "Let Jesus be cursed!" B
12: 3 can say "Jesus is Lord" except by the Holy S. A
12: 4 Now there are varieties of gifts, but the same S;
12: 7 the manifestation of the S for the common good.
12: 8 one is given through the S the utterance of wisdom,
12: 8 utterance of knowledge according to the same S,
12: 9 to another faith by the same S, to another gifts of
healing by the one S,
12:11 All these are activated by one and the same S,
12:11 to each one individually just as the S chooses.
12:13 in the one S we were all baptized into one body—
12:13 and we were all made to drink of one S.
14: 2 since they are speaking mysteries in the S.
14:14 my s prays but my mind is unproductive.
14:15 with the s, but I will pray with the mind also;
14:15 I will sing praise with the s,
14:16 Otherwise, if you say a blessing with the s,
15:45 the last Adam became a life-giving s.
16:18 for they refreshed my s as well as yours.
2Co 1:22 by putting his seal on us and giving us his S
3: 3 not with ink but with the S of the living God,
3: 6 but of s; for the letter kills, but the S gives life.
3: 8 how much more will the ministry of the S come
3:17 Now the Lord is the S,
3:17 Lord is the Spirit, and where the S of the Lord is, F
3:18 for this comes from the Lord, the S.
4:13 as we have the same s of faith that is in accordance
5: 5 who has given us the S as a guarantee.
6: 6 patience, kindness, holiness of s, genuine love,
7: 1 from every defilement of body and of s,
11: 4 a different s from the one you received,
12:18 Did we not conduct ourselves with the same s?
13:13 the communion of the Holy S be with all of you. A
Gal 3: 2 Did you receive the S by doing the works of
3: 3 Having started with the S,
3: 5 the S and work miracles among you by your doing
3:14 so that we might receive the promise of the S
4: 6 God has sent the S of his Son into our hearts,
4:29 the child who was born according to the S,
5: 5 For through the S, by faith,
5:16 Live by the S, I say, and do not gratify the desires
5:17 For what the flesh desires is opposed to the S,
5:17 and what the S desires is opposed to the flesh;
5:18 But if you are led by the S,
5:22 By contrast, the fruit of the S is love, joy, peace,
5:25 If we live by the S, let us also be guided by the S.
6: 1 you who have received the S should restore such a
one in a s of gentleness.
6: 8 but if you sow to the S, you will reap eternal life
from the S.
6:18 the grace of our Lord Jesus Christ be with your s,
Eph 1:13 with the seal of the promised Holy S; A
1:17 may give you a s of wisdom and revelation
2: 2 the s that is now at work
Eph 2:18 him both of us have access in one S to the Father.
3: 5 to his holy apostles and prophets by the S:
3:16 in your inner being with power through his S,
4: 3 making every effort to maintain the unity of the S
4: 4 There is one body and one S,
4:23 and to be renewed in the s of your minds,
4:30 And do not grieve the Holy S of God, AB
5:18 but be filled with the S,
6:17 and the sword of the S, which is the word of God.
6:18 the S at all times in every prayer and supplication.
Php 1:19 the help of the S of Jesus Christ this will turn out
1:27 I will know that you are standing firm in one s,
2: 1 any consolation from love, any sharing in the S,
3: 3 in the S of God and boast in Christ Jesus B
4:23 The grace of the Lord Jesus Christ be with your s.
Col 1: 8 and he has made known to us your love in the S.
2: 5 I am absent in body, yet I am with you in s,
1Th 1: 5 and in the Holy S and with full conviction; A
1: 6 the word with joy inspired by the Holy S, A
4: 8 who also gives his Holy S to you. A
5:19 Do not quench the S.
5:23 and may your s and soul and body be kept sound
2Th 2: 2 either by s or by word or by letter,
2:13 through sanctification by the S and through belief
1Ti 3:16 He was revealed in flesh, vindicated in s,
4: 1 Now the S expressly says that
2Ti 1: 7 for God did not give us a s of cowardice,
1: 7 a s of power and of love and of self-discipline.
1:14 with the help of the Holy S living in us. A
4:22 The Lord be with your s. Grace be with you.
Tit 3: 5 the water of rebirth and renewal by the Holy S. A
3: 6 This S he poured out on us richly
Phm 1:25 The grace of the Lord Jesus Christ be with your s.
Heb 2: 4 and by gifts of the Holy S, A
3: 7 Therefore, as the Holy S says, "Today, A
4:12 piercing until it divides soul from s,
6: 4 and have shared in the Holy S, A
9: 8 By this the Holy S indicates that the way into A
9:14 the eternal S offered himself without blemish
10:15 And the Holy S also testifies to us, A
10:29 and outraged the S of grace?
Jas 2:26 For just as the body without the s is dead,
4: 5 "God yearns jealously for the s that he has made
1Pe 1: 2 the Father and sanctified by the S to be obedient
1:11 or time that the S of Christ within them indicated
1:12 by the Holy S sent from heaven— A
3: 4 with the lasting beauty of a gentle and quiet s,
3: 8 Finally, all of you, have unity of s, sympathy,
3:18 but made alive in the s,
4: 6 they might live in the s as God does.
4:14 because the s of glory, which is the Spirit of God,
4:14 the spirit of glory, which is the S of God, B
2Pe 1:21 men and women moved by the Holy S spoke A
1Jn 3:24 by the S that he has given us.
4: 1 Beloved, do not believe every s,
4: 2 By this you know the S of God: B
4: 2 every s that confesses that Jesus Christ has come
4: 3 and every s that does not confess Jesus is not
4: 3 And this is the s of the antichrist,
4: 6 From this we know the s of truth and the s of error.
4:13 because he has given us of his S.
5: 6 S is the one that testifies, for the S is the truth.
5: 8 the S and the water and the blood,
Jude 1:19 It is these worldly people, devoid of the S,
1:20 on your most holy faith; pray in the Holy S; A
Rev 1:10 I was in the s on the Lord's day,
2: 7 to what the S is saying to the churches.
2:11 to what the S is saying to the churches.
2:17 to what the S is saying to the churches.
2:29 to what the S is saying to the churches.
3: 6 to what the S is saying to the churches.
3:13 to what the S is saying to the churches.
3:22 to what the S is saying to the churches."
4: 2 At once I was in the s,
14:13 says the S, "they will rest from their labors,
17: 3 So he carried me away in the s into a wilderness,
18: 2 a haunt of every foul s, a haunt of every foul bird,
19:10 For the testimony of Jesus is the s of prophecy."
21:10 And in the s he carried me away to a great,
22:17 The S and the bride say, "Come."
Tob 3: 6 command my s to be taken from me,
3:10 On that day she was grieved in s and wept.
6: 8 a man or woman afflicted by a demon or evil s, E
Jdt 16:14 You sent forth your s, and it formed them;
AdE 15: 8 Then God changed the s of the king to gentleness,
Wis 1: 5 For a holy and disciplined s will flee from deceit,
1: 6 a kindly s, but will not free blasphemers from
1: 7 Because the s of the Lord has filled the world, F
2: 3 and the s will dissolve like empty air.
5: 3 and in anguish of s they will groan, and say,
7: 7 I called on God, and the s of wisdom came to me.
7:22 There is in her a s that is intelligent, holy, unique,
9:17 and sent your holy s from on high? A
12: 1 For your immortal s is in all things.
15:11 with active souls and breathed a living s into them.
15:16 and one whose s is borrowed formed them;
16:14 but cannot bring back the departed s,
Sir 7:11 Do not ridicule a person who is embittered in s,
31:29 Wine drunk to excess leads to bitterness of s,
34:14 The s of those who fear the Lord will live,
38:23 and be comforted for him when his s has departed.
39: 6 he will be filled with the s of understanding;
48:12 Elisha was filled with his s.
48:24 By his dauntless s he saw the future,
Bar 2:17 whose s has been taken from their bodies,
3: 1 soul in anguish and the wearied s cry out to you.
Aza 1:16 Yet with a contrite heart and a humble s may we
Sus 1:45 up the holy s of a young lad named Daniel, A
1Mc 9: 7 and the battle was imminent, he was crushed in s,
10:74 the words of Apollonius, his s was aroused.
13: 7 The s of the people was rekindled
2Mc 1: 3 to do his will with a strong heart and a willing s.
5:17 Antiochus was elated in s,
7:12 with him were astonished at the young man's s,
7:21 a noble s, she reinforced her woman's reasoning
9:11 Then it was that, broken in s,
14:46 upon the Lord of life and s to give them back
1Es 2: 2 the s of King Cyrus of the Persians, and he made
2: 8 and all whose s the Lord had stirred to go up
3Mc 2:20 of those who are downcast and broken in s,
2:32 a courageous s and did not abandon their religion;
3:22 in their innate malice they took this in a contrary s,
4: 4 a harsh and ruthless s were they being sent off,
2Es 1:37 with the s they will believe the things I have said.
3: 3 My s was greatly agitated,
5:22 Then my soul recovered the s of understanding,
6:26 be changed and converted to a different s.
6:37 My s was greatly aroused,
6:39 Then the s was blowing, and darkness
6:41 you created the s of the firmament,
7:*78* that a person shall die, as the s leaves the body
9:41 for I am greatly embittered in s
12: 3 and I said to my s,
12: 5 I am still weary in mind and very weak in my s,
14:22 send the holy s into me, A
14:40 for my s retained its memory,
16:62 and the s of Almighty God,
4Mc 6:11 he amazed even his torturers by his courageous s.
7:14 in s through reason; and by reason
9:26 While all were marveling at his courageous s,
10: 7 Since they were not able in any way to break his s,
14: 6 as though moved by an immortal s of devotion,

SPIRITS‡ (53) [SPIRIT]

Nu 16:22 and said, "O God, the God of the s of all flesh,
27:16 the God of the s of all flesh,
Dt 18:11 or who consults ghosts or s,
1Ki 8:66 to their tents, joyful and in good s because of all
2Ch 7:10 joyful and in good s because of the goodness that
Est 5: 9 Haman went out that day happy and in good s.
5:14 then go with the king to the banquet in good s."
Isa 8:19 the ghosts and the familiar s that chirp and mutter;
19: 3 the s of the dead and the ghosts and the familiar s;
57:16 for then the s would grow faint before me,
Mt 8:16 and he cast out the s with a word,
10: 1 and gave them authority over unclean s,
12:45 along seven other s more evil than itself,
Mk 1:27 He commands even the unclean s,
3:11 Whenever the unclean s saw him,
5:12 the unclean s begged him, "Send us into the swine;
5:13 And the unclean s came out and entered the swine;
6: 7 and gave them authority over the unclean s.
Lk 4:36 and power he commands the unclean s,
6:18 with unclean s were cured.
7:21 of diseases, plagues, and evil s,
8: 2 as some women who had been cured of evil s
10:20 do not rejoice at this, that the s submit to you,
11:26 and brings seven other s more evil than itself,
Ac 5:16 the sick and those tormented by unclean s,
8: 7 for unclean s, crying with loud shrieks, came out
19:12 and the evil s came out of them.
19:13 of the Lord Jesus over those who had evil s,
1Co 12:10 to another the discernment of s,
14:32 And the s of prophets are subject to the prophets,
Gal 4: 3 we were enslaved to the elemental s of the world.
4: 9 to the weak and beggarly elemental s?
Col 2: 8 according to the elemental s of the universe,
2:20 If with Christ you died to the elemental s of
1Ti 4: 1 by paying attention to deceitful s and teachings
Heb 1:14 Are not all angels s in the divine service,
12: 9 even more willing to be subject to the Father of s
12:23 and to the s of the righteous made perfect,
1Pe 3:19 also he went and made a proclamation to the s
1Jn 4: 1 but test the s to see whether they are from God;
Rev 1: 4 and from the seven s who are before his throne,
3: 1 the words of him who has the seven s of God and
4: 5 which are the seven s of God;
5: 6 which are the seven s of God sent out into all
16:13 And I saw three foul s like frogs coming from
16:14 These are demonic s, performing signs,
22: 6 for the Lord, the God of the s of the prophets,
Wis 7:20 the powers of s and the thoughts of human beings,
7:23 and penetrating through all s that are intelligent,
Aza 1:64 Bless the Lord, s and souls of the righteous;
2Mc 3:24 the Sovereign of s and of all authority caused
2Es 7:*80* such s shall not enter into habitations,

SPIRITUAL‡ (31) [SPIRIT]

Ro 1:11 to see you so that I may share with you some s gift
2:29 a matter of the heart—it is s and not literal.
7:14 For we know that the law is s;
12: 1 and acceptable to God, which is your s worship.
15:27 Gentiles have come to share in their s blessings,
1Co 1: 7 so that you are not lacking in any s gift as you wait
2:13 interpreting s things to those who are s.
2:15 Those who are s discern all things,
3: 1 I could not speak to you as s people,
9:11 If we have sown s good among you,
10: 3 and all ate the same s food,
10: 4 and all drank the same s drink.
10: 4 For they drank from the s rock that followed them,
12: 1 Now concerning s gifts, brothers and sisters,
14: 1 Pursue love and strive for the s gifts,

1Co 14:12 So with yourselves; since you are eager for s gifts,
14:37 a prophet, or to have s powers, must acknowledge
15:44 It is sown a physical body, it is raised a s body.
15:44 If there is a physical body, there is also a s body.
15:46 But it is not the s that is first, but the physical,
15:46 but the physical, and then the s.
Eph 1: 3 who has blessed us in Christ with every s blessing
5:19 as you sing psalms and hymns and s songs
6:12 against the s forces of evil in the heavenly places.
Col 1: 9 with the knowledge of God's will in all s wisdom
2:11 also you were circumcised with a s circumcision,
3:16 sing psalms, hymns, and s songs to God.
1Pe 2: 2 Like newborn infants, long for the pure, s milk,
2: 5 let yourselves be built into a s house,
2: 5 to offer s sacrifices acceptable to God

SPIRITUALLY‡ (2) [SPIRIT]

1Co 2:14 to understand them because they are s discerned.
Eph 2:22 also are built together s into a dwelling place

SPIT (8) [SPAT, SPITS, SPITTING, SPITTLE]

Nu 12:14 "If her father had but s in her face,
Dt 25: 9 pull his sandal off his foot, s in his face,
Job 17: 6 and I am one before whom people s.
30:10 they do not hesitate to s at the sight of me.
Mk 10:34 and s upon him, and flog him, and kill him;
14:65 Some began to s on him, to blindfold him,
Rev 3:16 I am about to s you out of my mouth.
Sir 28:12 if you s on it, it will be put out;

SPITE (14)

Lev 26:18 And if in s of this you will not obey me,
26:23 If in s of these punishments you have
Nu 14:11 in s of all the signs that I have done among them?
Dt 1:32 But in s of this, you have no trust in
Ezr 10: 2 but even now there is hope for Israel in s of this.
Job 34: 6 in s of being right I am counted a liar;
Ps 78:32 In s of all this they still sinned;
Isa 16:14 in s of all its great multitude;
47: 9 in full measure, in s of your many sorceries and
Jer 23: 4 Yet in s of all these things
1Th 1: 6 for in s of persecution you received the word
2: 2 to declare to you the gospel of God in s of great
Jdt 8:25 In s of everything let us give thanks to the Lord
4Mc 10:19 cut it off, for in s of this you will not make our

SPITS (2) [SPIT]

Lev 15: 8 one with the discharge s on persons who are clean,
4Mc 11:19 To his back they applied sharp s

SPITTING (2) [SPIT]

Isa 50: 6 I did not hide my face from insult and s.
2Mc 6:19 up to the rack of his own accord, s out the flesh,

SPITTLE (4) [SPIT]

1Sa 21:13 and let his s run down his beard.
Job 7:19 let me alone until I swallow my s?
Sir 26:22 *A prostitute is regarded as s,*
2Es 6:56 they are nothing, and that they are like s,

SPLENDID (13) [SPLENDOR]

Job 41:12 or its mighty strength, or its s frame.
Isa 22:18 and there your s chariots shall lie,
Eze 34:29 for them a s vegetation so that they shall no more
AdE 14: 2 She took off her s apparel and put on the garments
15: 1 and arrayed herself in s attire.
Sir 6:31 and put her on like a s crown.
40: 3 on a s throne to the one who grovels in dust
50: 7 like the rainbow gleaming in s clouds;
1Mc 14: 9 and the youths put on s military attire.
2Mc 8:35 took off his s uniform and made his way alone like
12:45 But if he was looking to the s reward that is laid
14:33 and build here a s temple to Dionysus."
4Mc 11:12 they are s favors that you grant us

SPLENDIDLY (2) [SPLENDOR]

Isa 63: 1 this so s robed, marching in his great might?"
2Mc 3:26 gloriously beautiful and s dressed,

SPLENDOR† (47) [SPLENDID, SPLENDIDLY, SPLENDORS]

Ex 15:11 majestic in holiness, awesome in s,
1Ch 16:29 Worship the LORD in holy s;
2Ch 20:21 to sing to the LORD and praise him in holy s,
Est 1: 4 of his kingdom and the s and pomp of his majesty
5:11 and Haman recounted to them the s of his riches,
Job 31:26 or the moon moving in s,
37:22 Out of the north comes golden s;
40:10 clothe yourself with glory and s.
Ps 21: 5 s and majesty you bestow on him.
29: 2 worship the LORD in holy s.
96: 9 Worship the LORD in holy s;
145: 5 On the glorious s of your majesty,
145:12 and the glorious s of your kingdom.
Isa 13:19 the s and pride of the Chaldeans,
La 2: 1 He has thrown down from heaven to earth the s
Eze 1:27 and there was a s all around.
1:28 such was the appearance of the s all around.
16:14 because of my s that I had bestowed on you,
27:10 and helmet in you; they gave you s.
28: 7 the beauty of your wisdom and defile your s.
28:17 you corrupted your wisdom for the sake of your s.
Da 4:36 and my majesty and s were restored to me for
Hag 2: 7 and I will fill this house with s,
2: 9 The latter s of this house shall be greater than
Mt 4: 8 the kingdoms of the world and their s;
Eph 5:27 so as to present the church to himself in s, without
Rev 18: 1 and the earth was made bright with his s.
18:14 and all your dainties and your s are lost to you,
Tob 14: 5 from their exile and will rebuild Jerusalem in s;
AdE 1: 4 the s of his bountiful celebration during the course
14:15 that I hate the s of the wicked and abhor the bed of
15: 7 Lifting his face, flushed with s,
Sir 45: 8 He clothed him in perfect s,
50:11 and clothed himself in perfect s,
50:13 in their s held the Lord's offering in their hands
Bar 4:24 with great glory and with the s of the Everlasting.
5: 3 God will show your s everywhere under heaven.
1Mc 2:62 for their s will turn into dung and worms.
15:32 and when he saw the s of Simon,
15:36 and also the s of Simon and all that he had seen.
1Es 1:33 and every one of the acts of Josiah, and his s,
6:10 in their hands and being completed with all s
Man 1: 5 for your glorious s cannot be borne, and the wrath
2Es 2:21 and let the blind have a vision of my s.
7:42 but only the s of the glory of the Most High,
10:55 go in and see the s or the vastness of the building,
15:46 in the s of Babylon and the glory of her person—

SPLENDORS (1) [SPLENDOR]

Sir 42:21 He has set in order the s of his wisdom;

SPLINTERED (1)

Joel 1: 7 It has laid waste my vines, and s my fig trees;

SPLIT (12) [SPLITS, SPLITTING]

Nu 16:31 the ground under them was s apart.
Jdg 15:19 So God s open the hollow place that is at Lehi,
1Sa 6:14 so they s up the wood of the cart and offered
Ps 78:15 He s rocks open in the wilderness,
Isa 11:15 and will s it into seven channels,
48:21 he s open the rock and the water gushed out.
Hab 3: 9 You s the earth with rivers.
Zec 14: 4 the Mount of Olives shall be s in two from east
Mt 27:51 The earth shook, and the rocks were s.
Rev 16:19 The great city was s into three parts,
Sus 1:59 the angel of God is waiting with his sword to s you
2Es 1:20 not s the rock so that waters flowed in abundance?

SPLITS (1) [SPLIT]

Ecc 10: 9 and whoever s logs will be endangered by them.

SPLITTING (1) [SPLIT]

1Ki 19:11 that it was s mountains and breaking rocks

SPOIL‡ (61) [SPOILED, SPOILER, SPOILERS, SPOILS]

Ge 49:27 and at evening dividing the s."
Ex 15: 9 'I will pursue, I will overtake, I will divide the s,
Nu 31:11 but they took all the s and all the booty,
31:12 the captives and the booty and the s to Moses,
31:32 The booty remaining from the s that
Dt 2:35 Only the livestock we kept as s for ourselves,
3: 7 and the plunder of the towns we kept as s
13:16 All of its s you shall gather into its public square;
13:16 then burn the town and all its s with fire,
20:14 livestock, and everything else in the town, all its s.
20:14 You may enjoy the s of your enemies,
Jos 7:21 I saw among the s a beautiful mantle from Shinar,
8: 2 only its s and its livestock you may take as booty
8:27 Only the livestock and the s of that city Israel took
11:14 All the s of these towns, and the livestock,
22: 8 divide the s of your enemies with your kindred."
Jdg 5:30 'Are they not finding and dividing the s?—
5:30 s of dyed stuffs for Sisera, s of dyed stuffs
5:30 of dyed work embroidered for my neck as s?'
14:19 He killed thirty men of the town, took their s,
1Sa 2: 5 but those who were hungry are fat with s.
14:30 if today the troops had eaten freely of the s taken
14:32 upon the s, and took sheep and oxen and calves
15:19 Why did you swoop down on the s,
15:21 But from the s the people took sheep and cattle,
30:16 of s they had taken from the land of the Philistines
30:19 s or anything that had been taken;
30:20 people said, "This is David's s."
30:22 not give them any of the s that we have recovered,
30:26 he sent part of the s to his friends,
30:26 for you from the s of the enemies of the LORD";
2Sa 2:21 and seize one of the young men, and take his s."
3:22 bringing much s with them.
8:12 the s of King Hadadezer son of Rehob of Zobah.
12:30 He also brought forth the s of the city,
2Ki 3:23 Now then, Moab, to the s!"
21:14 a prey and a s to all their enemies,
Ps 44:10 and our enemies have gotten s.
68:12 The women at home divide the s,
76: 5 The stouthearted were stripped of their s;
119:162 I rejoice at your word like one who finds great s.
Pr 16:19 a lowly spirit among the poor than to divide the s
Isa 3:14 the s of the poor is in your houses.
8: 4 the wealth of Damascus and the s of Samaria will
10: 2 that widows may be your s,
10: 6 to take s and seize plunder,
33: 4 S was gathered as the caterpillar gathers;
33:23 Then prey and s in abundance will be divided;
Isa 42:22 a s with no one to say, "Restore!"
53:12 and he shall divide the s with the strong;
Jer 17: 3 Your wealth and all your treasures I will give for s
49:32 their herds of cattle a s.
Eze 38:12 to seize s and carry off plunder;
38:13 "Have you come to seize s?
Da 11:24 lavishing plunder, s, and wealth on them.
Jdt 16: 4 and take my virgins as s.
Sir 18:15 or s your gift by harsh words.
1Mc 11:48 the city and seized a large amount of s on that day,
11:51 to Jerusalem with a large amount of s.
1Es 4: 5 whatever s they take and everything else.

SPOILED (1) [SPOIL]

Jer 18: 4 The vessel he was making of clay was s in the

SPOILER (1) [SPOIL]

Isa 42:24 Who gave up Jacob to the s,

SPOILERS (1) [SPOIL]

Jer 12:12 the bare heights in the desert s have come;

SPOILS (14) [SPOIL]

Jdg 5:19 they got no s of silver.
Da 11: 8 he shall carry off to Egypt as s of war.
Heb 7: 4 Abraham the patriarch gave him a tenth of the s.
Sir 30: 7 Whoever s his son will bind up his wounds,
37: 6 be unmindful of him when you distribute your s.
1Mc 1:35 the s of Jerusalem they stored them there,
2:10 and has not seized her s?
3:12 Then they seized their s;
5:28 then he seized all its s and burned it with fire.
6: 6 and abundant s that they had taken from
7:47 Then the Jews seized the s and the plunder;
2Mc 8:27 of the enemy and stripped them of their s,
8:28 of the s to those who had been tortured and to
8:31 the rest of the s they carried to Jerusalem.

SPOKE‡ (361) [SPEAK]

Ge 16:13 So she named the LORD who s to her,
18:29 Again he s to him, "Suppose forty are found there."
24: 7 and who s to me and swore to me,
24:30 "Thus the man s to me," he went to the man;
27: 5 Now Rebekah was listening when Isaac s
31:29 but the God of your father s to me last night,
34: 3 he loved the girl, and s tenderly to her.
34: 4 So Shechem s to his father Hamor, saying,
34: 8 But Hamor s with them, saying,
34:20 the gate of their city and s to the men of their city,
39:10 And although she s to Joseph day after day,
39:19 his master heard the words that his wife s to him,
42: 7 but he treated them like strangers and s harshly
42:23 since he s with them through an interpreter.
42:24 then he returned and s to them.
42:30 the lord of the land, s harshly to us,
43:19 up to the steward of Joseph's house and s with him
43:27 "Is your father well, the old man of whom you s?
43:29 your youngest brother, of whom you s to me?
46: 2 God s to Israel in visions of the night, and said,
50:17 Joseph wept when they s to him.
Ex 4:30 Aaron s all the words that the LORD had spoken
6: 2 God also s to Moses and said to him:
6:10 Then the LORD s to Moses,
6:12 But Moses s to the LORD,
6:13 Thus the LORD s to Moses and Aaron,
6:27 It was they who s to Pharaoh king of Egypt
6:28 when the LORD s to Moses in the land of Egypt,
7: 7 and Aaron eighty-three when they s to Pharaoh.
16:10 And as Aaron s to the whole congregation of
16:11 The LORD s to Moses and said,
20: 1 Then God s all these words:
20:22 "You have seen for yourselves that I s with you
30:11 The LORD s to Moses:
30:17 The LORD s to Moses:
30:22 The LORD s to Moses:
31: 1 The LORD s to Moses:
34:31 returned to him, and Moses s with them.
40: 1 The LORD s to Moses:
Lev 1: 1 The LORD summoned Moses and s to him from
4: 1 The LORD s to Moses, saying,
5:14 The LORD s to Moses, saying:
6: 1 The LORD s to Moses, saying:
6: 8 The LORD s to Moses, saying:
6:19 The LORD s to Moses, saying:
6:24 The LORD s to Moses, saying:
7:22 The LORD s to Moses, saying:
7:28 The LORD s to Moses, saying:
8: 1 The LORD s to Moses, saying:
10: 8 And the LORD s to Aaron:
10:12 Moses s to Aaron and to his remaining sons,
10:19 And Aaron s to Moses, "See,
11: 1 LORD s to Moses and Aaron, saying to them:
12: 1 The LORD s to Moses, saying:
13: 1 The LORD s to Moses and Aaron, saying:
14: 1 The LORD s to Moses, saying:
14:33 The LORD s to Moses and Aaron, saying:
15: 1 The LORD s to Moses and Aaron, saying:
16: 1 The LORD s to Moses after the death of the two
17: 1 The LORD s to Moses:
18: 1 The LORD s to Moses, saying:
19: 1 The LORD s to Moses, saying:
20: 1 The LORD s to Moses, saying:
21:16 The LORD s to Moses, saying:
21:24 Thus Moses s to Aaron and to his sons and to all

Lev 22: 1 The LORD s to Moses, saying:
22:17 The LORD s to Moses, saying:
22:26 The LORD s to Moses, saying:
23: 1 The LORD s to Moses, saying:
23: 9 The LORD s to Moses:
23:23 The LORD s to Moses, saying:
23:26 The LORD s to Moses, saying:
23:33 The LORD s to Moses, saying:
24: 1 The LORD s to Moses, saying:
24:23 Moses s thus to the people of Israel;
25: 1 The LORD s to Moses on Mount Sinai, saying:
27: 1 The LORD s to Moses, saying:
Nu 1: 1 The LORD s to Moses in the wilderness of Sinai,
2: 1 The LORD s to Moses and Aaron, saying:
3: 1 when the LORD s with Moses on Mount Sinai.
3: 5 Then the LORD s to Moses, saying:
3:11 Then the LORD s to Moses, saying:
3:14 the LORD s to Moses in the wilderness of Sinai,
3:44 Then the LORD s to Moses, saying:
4: 1 The LORD s to Moses and Aaron, saying:
4:17 Then the LORD s to Moses and Aaron, saying:
4:21 Then the LORD s to Moses, saying:
5: 1 The LORD s to Moses, saying:
5: 5 The LORD s to Moses, saying:
5:11 The LORD s to Moses, saying:
6: 1 The LORD s to Moses, saying:
6:22 The LORD s to Moses, saying:
7:89 between the two cherubim; thus it s to him.
8: 1 The LORD s to Moses, saying:
8: 5 The LORD s to Moses, saying:
8:23 The LORD s to Moses, saying:
9: 1 The LORD s to Moses in the wilderness of Sinai,
9: 8 Moses s to them, "Wait, so that I may hear what
9: 9 The LORD s to Moses, saying:
10: 1 The LORD s to Moses, saying:
11:25 the LORD came down in the cloud and s to him,
12: 1 Miriam and Aaron s against Moses because of
14:17 be great in the way that you promised when you **s,**
14:26 And the LORD s to Moses and to Aaron, saying:
15: 1 The LORD s to Moses, saying:
15:17 The LORD s to Moses, saying:
16:20 Then the LORD s to Moses and to Aaron, saying:
16:23 And the LORD s to Moses, saying:
16:36 Then the LORD s to Moses, saying:
16:44 and the LORD s to Moses, saying,
17: 1 The LORD s to Moses, saying:
17: 6 Moses s to the Israelites;
18: 8 The LORD s to Aaron: I have given you charge of
18:25 Then the LORD s to Moses, saying:
19: 1 The LORD s to Moses and Aaron, saying:
20: 7 The LORD s to Moses, saying:
21: 5 The people s against God and against Moses,
25:10 The LORD s to Moses, saying:
26: 3 and Eleazar the priest s with them in the plains
26:52 The LORD s to Moses, saying:
27: 6 And the LORD s to Moses, saying:
27:15 Moses s to the LORD, saying,
28: 1 The LORD s to Moses, saying:
31: 1 The LORD s to Moses, saying,
31:25 The LORD s to Moses, saying,
32: 2 Gadites and the Reubenites came and s to Moses,
33:50 the LORD s to Moses, saying:
34: 1 The LORD s to Moses, saying:
34:16 The LORD s to Moses, saying:
35: 1 the LORD s to Moses, saying:
35: 9 The LORD s to Moses, saying:
36: 1 came forward and s in the presence of Moses and
Dt 1: 1 that Moses s to all Israel beyond the Jordan—
1: 3 Moses s to the Israelites just as
1: 6 The LORD our God s to us at Horeb,
2:17 the LORD s to me, saying,
4:12 Then the LORD s to you out of the fire.
4:15 when the LORD s to you at Horeb out of the fire,
4:45 and the statutes and ordinances that Moses s to
5: 4 LORD s with you face to face at the mountain,
5:22 These words the LORD s with a loud voice
5:28 The LORD heard your words when you s to me,
27: 9 Then Moses and the levitical priests s to all Israel,
Jos 1: 1 the LORD s to Joshua son of Nun,
10:12 the Amorites over to the Israelites, Joshua s to
14:10 the time that the LORD s this word to Moses,
14:12 of which the LORD s on that day;
17:14 The tribe of Joseph s to Joshua, saying,
20: 1 Then the LORD s to Joshua, saying,
20: 2 of which I s to you through Moses,
22:30 and the Gadites and the Manassites **s,**
22:33 and the Israelites blessed God and s no more
24:27 the words of the LORD that he s to us;
Jdg 2: 4 When the angel of the LORD s these words to all
9: 3 So his mother's kinsfolk s all these words
9:37 Gaal s again and said, "Look,
11:11 and Jephthah s all his words before the LORD
13:11 "Are you the man who s to this woman?"
17: 2 and even s it in my hearing,—
1Sa 9:17 "Here is the man of whom I s to you.
17:23 and s the same words as before.
17:30 He turned away from him toward another and s in
17:31 When the words that David s were heard,
19: 1 Saul s with his son Jonathan and
19: 4 Jonathan s well of David to his father Saul,
28:17 The LORD has done to you just as he s by me;
30: 6 for the people s of stoning him,
2Sa 3:19 Abner also s directly to the Benjaminites;
7:17 and with all this vision, Nathan s to David.
12:18 "While the child was still alive, we s to him,
13:22 But Absalom s to Amnon neither good nor bad;
21: 2 So the king called the Gibeonites and s to them.
2Sa 22: 1 David s to the LORD the words of this song on
1Ki 2: 4 Then the LORD will establish his word that he s
8:56 which he s through his servant Moses.
12:10 "Thus you should say to this people who s to you,
12:14 and s to them according to the advice of
13:18 and an angel s to me by the word of the LORD:
13:26 according to the word that the LORD s to him."
14:18 which he s by his servant the prophet Ahijah.
15:29 that he s by his servant Ahijah the Shilonite—
16:12 which he s against Baasha by the prophet Jehu—
16:34 which he s by Joshua son of Nun.
17:16 according to the word of the LORD that he s
21: 6 I s to Naboth the Jezreelite and said to him,
2Ki 2:22 according to the word that Elisha **s.**
6:10 to the place of which the man of God **s.**
9:36 which he s by his servant Elijah the Tishbite,
10:10 which the LORD s concerning the house of Ahab;
10:17 according to the word of the LORD that he s
14:25 which he s by his servant Jonah son of Amittai,
22:19 when you heard how I s against this place,
24: 2 to the word of the LORD that he s by his servants
25:28 he s kindly to him, and gave him a seat above
1Ch 17:15 with all these words and all this vision, Nathan s
21: 9 The LORD s to Gad, David's seer, saying,
2Ch 10:14 he s to them in accordance with the advice of
30:22 Hezekiah s encouragingly to all the Levites
32: 6 at the gate of the city and s encouragingly to them,
32:19 They s of the God of Jerusalem as if he were like
33:10 The LORD s to Manasseh and to his people,
33:18 the words of the seers who s to him in the name of
34:22 in Jerusalem in the Second Quarter) and s to her to
36:12 before the prophet Jeremiah who s from the mouth
Ezr 5: 3 and their associates came to them and s
5: 9 Then we s to those elders and asked them,
Ne 6:19 Also they s of his good deeds in my presence,
9:13 and s with them from heaven,
13:24 half of their children s the language of Ashdod,
13:24 but s the language of various peoples.
Est 3: 4 When they s to him day after day and he would
4:10 Then Esther s to Hathach and gave him a message
8: 3 Then Esther s again to the king;
Job 2:13 and no one s a word to him,
29:22 After I s they did not speak again,
Ps 33: 9 For he **s,** and it came to be;
39: 3 then I s with my tongue:
78:19 They s against God, saying,
89:19 you s in a vision to your faithful one, and said:
99: 7 He s to them in the pillar of cloud;
105:31 He s, and there came swarms of flies,
105:34 He **s,** and the locusts came,
106:33 and he s words that were rash.
SS 5: 6 My soul failed me when he **s.**
Isa 7:10 Again the LORD s to Ahaz, saying,
8: 5 The LORD s to me again:
8:11 the LORD s thus to me while his hand was strong
9:17 and an evildoer, and every mouth s folly.
16:13 the word that the LORD s concerning Moab in
65:12 when I called, you did not answer, when I **s,**
66: 4 when I called, no one answered, when I **s,**
Jer 7:13 says the LORD, and when I s to you persistently,
22:21 I s to you in your prosperity, but you said,
25: 2 the prophet Jeremiah s to all the people of Judah
26:12 Jeremiah s to all the officials and all the people,
27:12 I s to King Zedekiah of Judah in the same way:
27:16 Then I s to the priests and to all this people,
28: 1 from Gibeon, s to me in the house of the LORD,
28: 5 the prophet Jeremiah s to the prophet Hananiah in
28:11 And Hananiah s in the presence of all the people,
30: 4 that the LORD s concerning Israel and Judah:
32:24 What you s has happened, as you yourself can see.
34: 6 Then the prophet Jeremiah s all these words
36: 2 from the day I s to you,
37: 2 the LORD that he s through the prophet Jeremiah.
38: 8 So Ebed-melech left the king's house and s to
40:15 Then Johanan son of Kareah s secretly to Gedaliah
45: 1 the prophet Jeremiah s to Baruch son of Neriah,
46:13 that the LORD s to the prophet Jeremiah about
48:27 but whenever you s of him you shook your head!
50: 1 The word that the LORD s concerning Babylon,
51:12 the LORD has both planned and done what he s
52:32 he s kindly to him, and gave him a seat above
Eze 2: 2 And when he s to me, a spirit entered into me
3:24 and he s with me and said to me:
24:18 So I s to the people in the morning,
38:17 of whom I s in former days by my servants
Da 1:19 and the king s with them.
7:20 horn that had eyes and a mouth that s arrogantly,
8:13 and another holy one said to the one that **s,**
9: 6 who s in your name to our kings, our princes,
9:12 which he s against us and against our rulers,
10:19 When he s to me, I was strengthened and said,
Hos 1: 2 When the LORD first s through Hosea,
12: 4 he met him at Bethel, and there he s with him.
12:10 I s to the prophets; it was I who multiplied visions,
13: 1 When Ephraim **s,** there was trembling;
Jnh 2:10 Then the LORD s to the fish,
Hag 1:13 s to the people with the LORD's message,
Zec 1:11 Then they s to the angel of the LORD
Mal 3:16 those who revered the LORD s with one another.
Mt 3: 3 the prophet Isaiah s when he said, "The voice
9:33 the one who had been mute **s;**
14:27 But immediately Jesus s to them and said,
17:25 And when he came home, Jesus s of it first,
19:13 The disciples s sternly to those who brought them;
22: 1 Once more Jesus s to them in parables, saying:
Mk 3:23 he called them to him, and s to them in parables,
4:33 With many such parables he s the word to them,
Mk 6:50 But immediately he s to them and said,
7:35 his tongue was released, and he s plainly.
10:13 and the disciples s sternly to them.
15:12 Pilate s to them again, "Then what do you wish me
Lk 1:67 with the Holy Spirit and s this prophecy:
1:70 as he s through the mouth of his holy prophets
4:22 All s well of him and were amazed at the gracious
4:32 because he s with authority.
7:40 Jesus s up and said to him, "Simon,
9:11 and s to them about the kingdom of God,
11:14 the one who had been mute **s,**
24:44 that I s to you while I was still with you—
Jn 4:50 The man believed the word that Jesus s to him
8:12 Again Jesus s to them, saying,
8:20 He s these words while he was teaching in
12:41 Isaiah said this because he saw his glory and s
18:16 went out, s to the woman who guarded the gate,
Ac 2:31 David s of the resurrection of the Messiah, saying,
4:31 and they were all filled with the Holy Spirit and s
6:10 the wisdom and the Spirit with which he **s.**
7: 6 And God s in these terms,
7:38 with the angel who s to him at Mount Sinai,
7:44 as God directed when he s to Moses,
9:29 He s and argued with the Hellenists;
10: 7 When the angel who s to him had left,
11:19 and they s the word to no one except Jews.
11:20 on coming to Antioch, s to the Hellenists also,
13:43 who s to them and urged them to continue in
13:46 Then both Paul and Barnabas s out boldly, saying,
14: 1 into the Jewish synagogue and s in such a way that
16:13 down and s to the women who had gathered there.
16:32 They s the word of the Lord to him and
18:25 and he s with burning enthusiasm
19: 6 and they s in tongues and prophesied—
19: 8 the synagogue and for three months s out boldly,
19: 9 and s evil of the Way before the congregation,
1Co 13:11 When I was a child, I s like a child,
2Co 4:13 "I believed, and so I **s"**—
Heb 1: 1 Long ago God s to our ancestors in many
13: 7 those who s the word of God to you;
Jas 5:10 take the prophets who s in the name of the Lord.
2Pe 1:21 and women moved by the Holy Spirit s from God.
2:16 a speechless donkey s with a human voice
Rev 1:12 I turned to see whose voice it was that s to me,
10: 8 voice that I had heard from heaven s to me again,
13:11 it had two horns like a lamb and it s like a dragon.
Tob 7: 7 He also s to him as follows, "Blessings on you,
14: 4 the word of God that Nahum s about Nineveh,
Jdt 8: 8 No one s ill of her, for she feared God
16:14 Let all your creatures serve you, for you **s,**
AdE 3: 4 Day after day they s to him,
8: 3 Then she s once again to the king and,
Sir 44: 3 those who s in prophetic oracles;
Bar 2: 1 So the Lord carried out the threat he s against us:
2:24 which you s by your servants the prophets,
2:28 as you s by your servant Moses on the day
1Mc 1:24 He shed much blood, and s with great arrogance.
1:30 Deceitfully he s peaceable words to them,
2:17 Then the king's officers s to Mattathias as follows:
7:15 Alcimus s peaceable words to them
7:34 and defiled them and s arrogantly,
7:41 "When the messengers from the king s blasphemy,
8:19 they entered the senate chamber and s as follows:
2Mc 7:27 she s in their native language as follows,
15:12 one who s fittingly and had been trained
15:14 And Onias **s,** saying, "This is a man who loves
1Es 1:51 and whenever the Lord **s,** they scoffed
5: 6 who s wise words before King Darius of
2Es 6:29 While he s to me, little by little the place
6:38 I said, "O Lord, you s at the beginning of creation,
7:22 they were not obedient, and s against him;
7:*129* [59] s to the people, saying, 'Choose life for
9: 4 the Most High s from the days that were of old,
10:19 So I s again to her, and said,
11: 6 and no one s against it—
11:37 how it uttered a human voice to the eagle, and **s,**
12:17 "As for your hearing a voice that **s,**
12:34 of which I s to you at the beginning.
12:40 and came to me and s to me, saying,
14: 3 and s to Moses when my people were in bondage
14:43 me, I s in the daytime and was not silent at night.
14:45 the forty days were ended, the Most High s to me,

SPOKEN‡ (229) [SPEAK]

Ge 19:21 will not overthrow the city of which you have **s.**
21: 2 at the time of which God had s to him.
24:51 the wife of your master's son, as the LORD has **s."**
35:13 up from him at the place where he had s with him.
35:14 up a pillar in the place where he had s with him,
35:15 the place where God had s with him Bethel.
Ex 4:10 past nor even now that you have s to your servant;
4:30 Aaron spoke all the words that the LORD had s
9:12 just as the LORD had s to Moses.
9:35 just as the LORD had s through Moses.
19: 8 "Everything that the LORD has s we will do."
24: 3 "All the words that the LORD has s we will do."
24: 7 they said, "All that the LORD has s we will do,
32:34 lead the people to the place about which I have s
34:32 that the LORD had s with him on Mount Sinai.
Lev 10:11 that the LORD has s to them through Moses.
Nu 5: 4 as the LORD had s to Moses, so the Israelites did.
12: 2 "Has the LORD s only through Moses?
12: 2 Has he not s through us also?"
14:35 I the LORD have **s;**
15:22 that the LORD has s to Moses—
23:19 Has he **s,** and will he not fulfill it?

Nu 32:31 "As the LORD has s to your servants,
Dt 5:28 the words of this people, which they have s to you;
5:28 they are right in all that they have s.
9:10 on them were all the words that the LORD had s
10: 4 that the LORD had s to you on the mountain out
13: 5 be put to death for having s treason against
18:21 a word that the LORD has not s?"
18:22 it is a word that the LORD has not s.
18:22 The prophet has s it presumptuously;
Jos 11:23 according to all that the LORD had s to Moses;
Ru 2:13 for you have comforted me and s kindly
4: 1 of whom Boaz had s, came passing by.
1Sa 3:12 against Eli all that I have s concerning his house,
9:21 Why then have you s to me in this way?"
10:16 the matter of the kingship, of which Samuel had s,
20:23 As for the matter about which you and I have s,
25:30 to my lord according to all the good that he has s
2Sa 2:27 Joab said, "As God lives, if you had not s,
6:22 but by the maids of whom you have s,
7:19 you have s also of your servant's house for a great
7:25 the word that you have s concerning your servant
7:29 for you, O Lord GOD, have s,
23: 3 of Israel has s, the Rock of Israel has said to me:
1Ki 2:27 thus fulfilling the word of the LORD that he had s
12:15 which the LORD had s by Ahijah the Shilonite
13: 3 saying, "This is the sign that the LORD has s:
13:11 the words also that he had s to the king,
14:11 of the air shall eat; for the LORD has s.'
18:24 All the people answered, "Well s!"
22:28 the LORD has not s by me."
22:38 according to the word of the LORD that he had s.
2Ki 1:17 to the word of the LORD that Elijah had s.
4:13 Would you have a word s on your behalf to
19:21 the word that the LORD has s concerning him:
20:19 "The word of the LORD that you have s is good."
1Ch 17:17 you have also s of your servant's house for a great
17:23 the word that you have s concerning your servant
21:19 which he had s in the name of the LORD.
22:11 as he has s concerning you.
2Ch 2:15 barley, oil, and wine, of which my lord has s,
10:15 which he had s by Ahijah the Shilonite
18:27 the LORD has not s by me."
35:25 and all the singing men and singing women have s
36:22 the LORD s by Jeremiah, the LORD stirred up
Ne 2:18 and also the words that the king had s to me.
Job 21: 3 then after I have s, mock on.
33: 8 "Surely, you have s in my hearing,
40: 5 I have s once, and I will not answer;
42: 7 After the LORD had s these words to Job,
42: 7 for you have not s of me what is right,
42: 8 for you have not s of me what is right,
Ps 40:10 I have s of your faithfulness and your salvation;
62:11 Once God has s; twice have I heard this:
87: 3 Glorious things are s of you, O city of God.
103:20 ones who do his bidding, obedient to his s word.
Pr 25:11 A word fitly s is like apples of gold in a setting
Ecc 10:12 Words s by the wise bring them favor,
SS 8: 8 on the day when she is s for?
Isa 1: 2 O earth; for the LORD has s:
1:20 for the mouth of the LORD has s.
20: 2 at that time the LORD had s to Isaiah son of Amoz,
21:17 for the LORD, the God of Israel, has s.
22:25 that was on it will perish, for the LORD has s.
23: 4 Be ashamed, O Sidon, for the sea has s,
24: 3 for the LORD has s this word.
25: 8 from all the earth, for the LORD has s.
37:22 the word that the LORD has s concerning him:
38:15 For he has s to me, and he himself has done it.
39: 8 "The word of the LORD that you have s is good."
40: 5 for the mouth of the LORD has s."
46:11 I have s, and I will bring it to pass;
48:15 I, even I, have s and called him,
48:16 From the beginning I have not s in secret,
58:14 for the mouth of the LORD has s.
59: 3 lips have s lies, your tongue mutters wickedness.
Jer 3: 5 This is how you have s, but you have done all the
4:28 for I have s, I have purposed;
5:12 They have s falsely of the LORD, and have said,
5:14 Because they have s this word,
9:12 To whom has the mouth of the LORD s,
13:15 do not be haughty, for the LORD has s.
18: 8 concerning which I have s, turns from its evil,
23:35 or "What has the LORD s?"
23:37 or "What has the LORD s?"
25: 3 and I have s persistently to you,
26:16 he has s to us in the name of the LORD our God."
27:13 the LORD has s concerning any nation that will
28:16 because you have s rebellion against the LORD."
29:23 and have s in my name lying words that I did
29:32 for he has s rebellion against the LORD.
30: 2 Write in a book all the words that I have s to you.
34: 5 For I have s the word, says the LORD.
35:14 But I myself have s to you persistently,
35:17 I have s to them and they have not listened,
36: 2 that I have s to you against Israel and Judah and all
36: 4 the words of the LORD that he had s to him.
38:25 If the officials should hear that I have s with you,
44:16 "As for the word that you have s to us in the name
48: 8 the plain shall be destroyed, as the LORD has s.
Eze 5:13 the LORD, have s in my jealousy,
5:15 with furious punishments—I, the LORD, have s—
5:17 I, the LORD, have s.
17:21 and you shall know that I, the LORD, have s.
17:24 I the LORD have s; I will accomplish it.
21:17 I will satisfy my fury; I the LORD have s.
21:32 be remembered no more, for I the LORD have s.
22:14 I the LORD have s, and I will do it.
22:28 when the LORD has not s.
23:34 for I have s, says the Lord GOD.
24:14 I the LORD have s; the time is coming,
26: 5 I have s, says the Lord GOD.
26:14 for I the LORD have s, says the Lord GOD.
28:10 for I have s, says the Lord GOD.
30:12 of foreigners; I the LORD have s.
34:24 among them; I, the LORD, have s.
36:36 I, the LORD, have s, and I will do it.
37:14 the LORD, have s and will act," says the LORD.
39: 5 for I have s, says the Lord GOD.
39: 8 This is the day of which I have s.
Joel 3: 8 to a nation far away; for the LORD has s.
Am 3: 1 Hear this word that the LORD has s against you,
3: 8 The Lord GOD has s; who can but prophesy?
Ob 1:18 of Esau; for the LORD has s.
Mic 4: 4 for the mouth of the LORD of hosts has s.
Mal 3:13 You have s harsh words against me,
3:13 Yet you say, "How have we s against you?"
Mt 1:22 All this took place to fulfill what had been s by
2:15 This was to fulfill what had been s by the Lord
2:17 Then was fulfilled what had been s through
2:23 so that what had been s through the prophets might
4:14 so that what had been s through the prophet
8:17 This was to fulfill what had been s through
12:17 This was to fulfill what had been s through
13:35 to fulfill what had been s through the prophet:
21: 4 This took place to fulfill what had been s through
24:15 as was s of by the prophet Daniel
27: 9 Then was fulfilled what had been s through
Mk 16:19 ⟦So then the Lord Jesus, after he had s to them,⟧
Lk 1:45 be a fulfillment of what was s to her by the Lord."
9:36 When the voice had s, Jesus was found alone.
20:39 "Teacher, you have s well."
Jn 2:22 the scripture and the word that Jesus had s.
6:63 The words that I have s to you are spirit and life.
7:46 police answered, "Never has anyone s like this!"
9:29 We know that God has s to Moses,
12:29 Others said, "An angel has s to him."
12:38 to fulfill the word s by the prophet Isaiah:
12:48 on the last day the word that I have s will serve
12:49 for I have not s on my own,
15: 3 by the word that I have s to you.
15:22 If I had not come and s to them,
17: 1 After Jesus had s these words,
18: 1 After Jesus had s these words,
18: 9 This was to fulfill the word that he had s,
18:20 Jesus answered, "I have s openly to the world;
18:23 Jesus answered, "If I have s wrongly,
18:23 But if I have s rightly, why do you strike me?"
Ac 2:16 No, this is what was s through the prophet Joel:
3:24 And all the prophets, as many as have s,
8:25 after Peter and John had testified and s the word of
9:27 how on the road he had seen the Lord, who had s
9:27 in Damascus he had s boldly in the name of Jesus.
10:22 who is well s of by the whole Jewish nation,
13:34 he has s in this way,
13:45 they contradicted what was s by Paul.
13:46 that the word of God should be s first to you.
14:25 When they had s the word in Perga,
16: 2 He was well s of by the believers in Lystra
22:12 the law and well s of by all the Jews living there,
23: 9 What if a spirit or an angel has s to him?"
28:21 or s anything evil about you.
28:22 that everywhere it is s against."
Ro 14:16 So do not let your good be s of as evil.
2Co 6:11 We have s frankly to you Corinthians;
Heb 1: 2 but in these last days he has s to us by a Son,
3: 5 to testify to the things that would be s later.
7:13 Now the one of whom these things are s belonged
12:19 the hearers beg that not another word be s to them.
2Pe 3: 2 that you should remember the words s in the past
3: 2 and the commandment of the Lord and Savior s
Jude 1:15 of all the harsh things that ungodly sinners have s
Tob 14: 4 everything that was s by the prophets of Israel,
Jdt 2:12 what I have s I will accomplish by my own hand.
6: 4 For he has s; none of his words shall be in vain.
6: 9 I have s, and none of my words shall fail
8: 9 When Judith heard the harsh words s by the people
8:28 "All that you have said was s out of a true heart,
AdE 4: 8 has s against us and demands our death.
5: 5 both came to the dinner that Esther had s about.
Sir Pr: 1 of learning be able through the s and written word
36:20 and fulfill the prophecies s in your name.
Bel 1: 9 because he has s blasphemy against Bel."
1Mc 7:42 that Nicanor has s wickedly against the sanctuary,
2Mc 4:48 so those who had s for the city and the villages and
1Es 1:47 the words that were s by the prophet Jeremiah
3:17 Then the first, who had s of the strength of wine,
4: 1 the second, who had s of the strength of the king,
4:13 who had s of women and truth
3Mc 5:21 When the king had s, all those present readily
2Es 5:31 When I had s these words,
5:34 "No, my lord, but because of my grief I have s;
6:55 "All this I have s before you, O Lord,
7:*130* [60] or even myself who have s to them.
8:37 "Some things you have s rightly,
8:40 As I have s, therefore, so it shall be.
4Mc 2:20 he would not have s thus.
16: 5 she would have mourned over them and perhaps s

SPOKES (2)

1Ki 7:33 their axles, their rims, their s,
Eze 10:12 Their entire body, their rims, their s, their wings,

SPOKESMAN (2) [MAN, SPEAK]

2Mc 7: 2 One of them, acting as their s, said,
7: 4 and he commanded that the tongue of their s

SPONGE (3)

Mt 27:48 At once one of them ran and got a s,
Mk 15:36 And someone ran, filled a s with sour wine,
Jn 19:29 So they put a s full of the wine on a branch

SPOON[S] (KJV) See DISH[ES], LADLES

SPORT (10)

1Sa 31: 4 not come and thrust me through, and make s
1Ch 10: 4 not come and make s of me."
Job 30: 1 "But now they make s of me,
Ps 104:26 and Leviathan that you formed to s in it.
Pr 10:23 Doing wrong is like s to a fool,
Hab 1:10 At kings they scoff, and of rulers they make s.
Bar 3:17 those who make s of the birds of the air,
1Mc 9:26 who took vengeance on them and made s of them.
2Mc 7: 7 they brought forward the second for their s.
7:10 After him, the third was the victim of their s.

SPORTING (KJV) See FONDLING, REVELING

SPOT (24) [SPOTLESS, SPOTS, SPOTTED]

Lev 4:24 at the s where the burnt offering is slaughtered
4:33 and it shall be slaughtered as a sin offering at the s
6:25 be slaughtered before the LORD at the s where
7: 2 at the s where the burnt offering is slaughtered,
13: 2 of his body a swelling or an eruption or a s,
13: 4 But if the s is white in the skin of his body,
13:19 a white swelling or a reddish-white s,
13:23 if the s remains in one place and does not spread,
13:24 the skin and the raw flesh of the burn becomes a s,
13:25 the s has turned white and it appears deeper than
13:26 priest examines it and the hair in the s is not white,
13:28 if the s remains in one place and does not spread in
13:42 or the bald forehead a reddish-white diseased s,
13:55 If the diseased s has not changed color,
13:55 you shall burn it in fire, whether the leprous s is on
13:56 he shall tear the s out of the cloth,
14:56 and for a swelling or an eruption or a s,
2Sa 23: 7 And they are entirely consumed in fire on the s.
2Ki 5:11 and would wave his hand over the s,
Job 31: 7 and if any s has clung to my hands;
Eph 5:27 without a s or wrinkle or anything of the kind—
1Ti 6:14 to keep the commandment without s or blame until
2Pe 3:14 to be found by him at peace, without s or blemish;
Sir 42:11 no s that overlooks the approaches to the house.

SPOTLESS (1) [SPOT]

Wis 7:26 a s mirror of the working of God,

SPOTS (6) [SPOT]

Lev 13:38 a man or a woman has s on the skin of the body,
13:38 on the skin of the body, white s,
13:39 if the s on the skin of the body are of a dull white,
14:37 the walls of the house with greenish or reddish s,
21: 5 They shall not make bald s upon their heads,
Jer 13:23 Ethiopians change their skin or leopards their s?

SPOTTED (6) [SPOT]

Ge 30:32 and s sheep and every black lamb, and the s and
30:33 and s among the goats and black among the lambs,
30:35 and s, and all the female goats that were speckled
30:35 and all the female goats that were speckled and s,
30:39 that were striped, speckled, and s.

SPOUSE (KJV) See BRIDE

SPRANG (10) [SPRING]

Jdg 6:21 and fire s up from the rock and consumed the meat
Mt 13: 5 and they s up quickly, since they had no depth
Mk 4: 5 and it s up quickly, since it had no depth of soil.
10:50 throwing off his cloak, he s up and came to Jesus.
Ac 14:10 And the man s up and began to walk.
28:13 After one day there a south wind s up,
Tob 2: 4 Then I s up, left the dinner before even tasting it,
9: 6 He s up and greeted Gabael,
AdE 15: 8 and in alarm he s from his throne and took her
2Es 3: 7 From him there s nations and tribes,

SPRAWLED (2) [SPRAWLING]

Jer 2:20 and under every green tree you s and played
Jdt 14:15 the bedchamber and found him s on the floor dead,

SPRAWLING (2) [SPRAWLED]

Job 30:12 they send me s, and build roads for my ruin.
Eze 29: 3 the great dragon s in the midst of its channels,

SPREAD (166) [OUTSPREAD, SPREADING, SPREADS, WIDE-SPREADING, WIDESPREAD]

Ge 10: 5 From these the coastland peoples s.
10:18 Afterward the families of the Canaanites s abroad.
10:32 from these the nations s abroad on the earth after
28:14 and you shall s abroad to the west and to the east

Ge 41:56 And since the famine had s over all the land,
Ex 1:12 the more they multiplied and s,
23: 1 You shall not s a false report.
25:20 The cherubim shall s out their wings above,
29: 2 and unleavened wafers s with oil.
37: 9 The cherubim s out their wings above,
40:19 and he s the tent over the tabernacle, and put
Lev 2: 4 or unleavened wafers s with oil.
7:12 unleavened wafers s with oil,
13: 5 the disease is checked and the disease has not s in
13: 6 the disease has abated and the disease has not s in
13: 8 and if the eruption has s in the skin,
13:23 if the spot remains in one place and does not s,
13:28 But if the spot remains in one place and does not s
13:32 if the itch has not s,
13:34 if the itch has not s in the skin and it appears to
13:36 If the itch has s in the skin,
13:51 If the disease has s in the cloth, in warp or woof,
13:53 and the disease has not s in the clothing,
13:55 though the disease has not s, it is unclean;
14:39 if the disease has s in the walls of the house,
14:44 if the disease has s in the house,
14:48 not s in the house after the house was plastered,
Nu 4: 6 and s over that a cloth all of blue,
4: 7 the Presence they shall s a blue cloth, and put on it
4: 8 then they shall s over them a crimson cloth,
4:11 Over the golden altar they shall s a blue cloth,
4:13 and s a purple cloth over it;
4:14 and they shall s on it a covering of fine leather,
6:15 with oil and unleavened wafers s with oil,
11:32 and they s them out for themselves all around
21:30 and we laid waste until fire s to Medeba."
22: 5 they have s over the face of the earth,
22:11 'A people has come out of Egypt and has s over
Dt 22:17 Then they shall s out the cloth before the elders of
Jos 7:23 and they s them out before the LORD.
Jdg 8:25 So they s a garment, and each threw into it
Ru 3: 9 s your cloak over your servant,
1Sa 9:25 a bed was s for Saul on the roof,
14:23 The battle s out over the hill country of Ephraim.
30:16 they were s out all over the ground,
2Sa 5:18 the Philistines had come and s out in the valley
5:22 and were s out in the valley of Rephaim.
17:19 and s out grain on it; and nothing was known of it.
18: 8 The battle s over the face of all the country;
21:10 and s it on a rock for herself,
1Ki 4:31 his fame s throughout all the surrounding nations.
6:27 the wings of the cherubim were s out so that
6:32 and s gold on the cherubim and on the palm trees.
8: 7 For the cherubim s out their wings over the place
8:22 and s out his hands to heaven.
2Ki 8:15 and dipped it in water and s it over the king's face,
9:13 and s them for him on the bare steps;
19:14 up to the house of the LORD and s it before
1Ch 28:18 of the cherubim that s their wings and covered
2Ch 5: 8 For the cherubim s out their wings over the place
6:12 the whole assembly of Israel, and s out his hands.
6:13 and s out his hands toward heaven.
26: 8 and his fame s even to the border of Egypt,
26:15 And his fame s far, for he was marvelously helped
31: 5 the word s, the people of Israel gave in abundance
Ezr 9: 5 s out my hands to the LORD my God,
Ne 4:19 "The work is great and widely s out,
Est 9: 4 and his fame s throughout all the provinces as
Job 8:16 and their shoots s over the garden.
17:13 if I s my couch in darkness,
29:19 my roots s out to the waters, with the dew all night
37:18 Can you, like him, s out the skies,
Ps 5:11 S your protection over them,
44:20 or s out our hands to a strange god,
78:19 saying, "Can God s a table in the wilderness?
88: 9 I s out my hands to you.
105:39 He s a cloud for a covering,
136: 6 who s out the earth on the waters,
140: 5 and with cords they have s a net,
Pr 15: 7 The lips of the wise s knowledge;
Isa 16: 8 their shoots once s abroad and crossed over
19: 8 and those who s nets on the water will languish.
21: 5 They prepare the table, they s the rugs, they eat,
25: 7 the sheet that is s over all nations;
25:11 Though they s out their hands in the midst of it,
25:11 as swimmers s out their hands to swim,
33:23 the mast firm in its place, or keep the sail s out.
37:14 up to the house of the LORD and s it before
42: 5 who s out the earth and what comes from it,
44:24 who by myself s out the earth;
48:13 and my right hand s out the heavens;
54: 3 For you will s out to the right and to the left,
Jer 8: 2 be s before the sun and the moon and all the host
10:20 there is no one to s my tent again,
23:15 from the prophets of Jerusalem ungodliness has s
43:10 and he will s his royal canopy over them.
48:40 and s his wings against Moab;
49:22 and s his wings against Bozrah,
La 1:13 he s a net for my feet; he turned me back;
Eze 1:11 Their wings were s out above;
1:22 shining like crystal, s out above their heads.
2:10 He s it before me; it had writing on the
12:13 I will s my net over him,
16: 8 I s the edge of my cloak over you,
16:14 Your fame s among the nations on account
17:20 I will s my net over him,
19: 8 they s their net over him; he was caught in their pit.
23:41 with a table s before it
32:23 who s terror in the land of the living.
32:24 who s terror in the land of the living.
32:25 for terror of them was s in the land of the living,
Eze 32:26 for they s terror in the land of the living.
32:32 For he s terror in the land of the living;
Hos 5: 1 for you have been a snare at Mizpah, and a net s
14: 6 His shoots shall s out; his beauty shall be like
Joel 2: 2 Like blackness s upon the mountains a great
Zec 2: 6 I have s you abroad like the four winds of heaven,
Mal 2: 3 and s dung on your faces,
Mt 4:24 So his fame s throughout all Syria,
9:26 And the report of this s throughout that district.
9:31 and s the news about him throughout that district.
21: 8 A very large crowd s their cloaks on the road,
21: 8 and others cut branches from the trees and s them
Mk 1:28 to s throughout the surrounding region of Galilee.
1:45 to s the word, so that Jesus could no longer go into
11: 8 people s their cloaks on the road, and others s leafy
Lk 4:14 about him s through all the surrounding country.
5:15 more than ever the word about Jesus s abroad;
7:17 This word about him s throughout Judea and all
Jn 9: 6 on the ground and made mud with the saliva and s
9:11 "The man called Jesus made mud, s it on my eyes,
21:23 So the rumor s in the community
Ac 6: 7 The word of God continued to s;
10:37 That message s throughout Judea,
13:49 Thus the word of the Lord s throughout the region.
Ro 5:12 and so death s to all because all have sinned—
Php 1:12 to me has actually helped to s the gospel,
2Th 3: 1 so that the word of the Lord may s rapidly and
2Ti 2:17 and their talk will s like gangrene.
Jdt 4:11 on their heads and s out their sackcloth before
5:10 a famine s over the land of Canaan they went
7: 3 and they s out in breadth over Dothan as far
7:18 Their tents and supply trains s out in great number,
12:15 Her maid went ahead and s for her on the ground
16:25 No one ever again s terror among the Israelites
Wis 17:21 while over those people alone heavy night was s,
18:10 for their children was s abroad.
Sir 24:15 and like choice myrrh I s my fragrance,
24:16 Like a terebinth I s out my branches,
47:15 Your influence s throughout the earth,
51:19 I s out my hands to the heavens,
Aza 1:25 and s out and burned those Chaldeans who were
1Mc 6:40 part of the king's army was s out on the high hills,
11:47 and they all rallied around him and then s out
14:10 until his renown s to the ends of the earth.
2Mc 4:39 and when report of them had s abroad,
7: 5 The smoke from the pan s widely,
8: 7 And talk of his valor s everywhere.
15:23 a good angel to s terror and trembling before us.
2Es 11: 2 I saw it s its wings over the whole earth,
15: 6 because iniquity has s throughout every land,
15:29 their hissing shall s over the earth,
16:59 He has s out the heaven like a dome
4Mc 4:22 that a rumor of his death had s and that the people
9:19 he was saying these things, they s fire under him,

SPREADING (19) [SPREAD]

Lev 13:27 if it is s in the skin,
13:51 this is a s leprous disease; it is unclean.
13:52 or anything of skin, for it is a s leprous disease;
13:57 in warp or woof, or in anything of skin, it is s;
14:44 it is a s leprous disease in the house; it is unclean.
1Sa 2:24 that I hear the people of the LORD s abroad.
Job 36:29 Can anyone understand the s of the clouds,
Pr 29: 5 a neighbor is s a net for the neighbor's feet.
Isa 18: 5 and the s branches he will hew away.
Jer 25:32 See, disaster is s from nation to nation,
Eze 17: 6 It sprouted and became a vine s out, but low;
26: 5 in the midst of the sea, a place for s nets.
26:14 you shall be a place for s nets.
47:10 it will be a place for the s of nets;
Lk 19:36 people kept s their cloaks on the road.
Ac 4:17 But to keep it from s further among the people,
3Jn 1:10 to what he is doing in s false charges against us.
Sir 14:18 on a s tree that sheds some and puts forth others,
48:20 s out their hands toward him.

SPREADS (13) [SPREAD]

Lev 13: 7 But if the eruption s in the skin after he has shown
13:22 If it s in the skin, the priest shall pronounce him
13:35 itch s in the skin after he was pronounced clean,
Dt 32:11 as it s its wings, takes them up,
Job 26: 9 and s over it his cloud.
39:18 When it s its plumes aloft,
39:26 and s its wings toward the south?
41:30 it s itself like a threshing sledge on the mire.
Pr 7:16 colored s of Egyptian linen;
16:28 A perverse person s strife,
Isa 40:22 and s them like a tent to live in;
2Co 2:14 and through us s in every place the fragrance
Sir 38: 8 and from him health s over all the earth.

SPRIG (1)

Eze 17:22 I myself will take a s from the lofty top of a cedar;

SPRING‡ (64) [SPRANG, SPRINGS, SPRUNG]

Ge 16: 7 The angel of the LORD found her by a s of water
16: 7 the s on the way to Shur.
24:13 I am standing here by the s of water,
24:16 She went down to the s, filled her jar,
24:29 and Laban ran out to the man, to the s.
24:30 and there he was, standing by the camels at the s.
24:42 "I came today to the s, and said, 'O LORD,
24:43 I am standing here by the s of water;
Ge 24:45 and she went down to the s, and drew.
26:19 in the valley and found there a well of s water,
35:11 and kings shall s from you.
49:22 Joseph is a fruitful bough, a fruitful bough by a s;
Lev 11:36 But a s or a cistern holding water shall be clean,
Nu 21:17 Then Israel sang this song: "S up, O well!—
Jos 15: 9 from the top of the mountain to the s of the Waters
18:15 to the s of the Waters of Nephtoah;
Jdg 7: 1 with him rose early and encamped beside the s
2Sa 11: 1 In the s of the year, the time when kings go out
1Ki 20:22 the s the king of Aram will come up against you."
20:26 the s Ben-hadad mustered the Arameans and went
2Ki 2:21 he went to the s of water and threw the salt into it,
3:25 every s of water they stopped up,
13:20 of Moabites used to invade the land in the s of
1Ch 20: 1 In the s of the year, the time when kings go out
2Ch 36:10 In the s of the year King Nebuchadnezzar sent
Ne 2:13 by night by the Valley Gate past the Dragon's S
Job 8:19 and out of the earth still others will s.
29:23 they opened their mouths as for the s rain.
Ps 85:11 Faithfulness will s up from the ground,
114: 8 the flint into a s of water.
Pr 16:15 his favor is like the clouds that bring the s rain.
25:26 Like a muddied s or a polluted fountain are
Isa 42: 9 before they s forth, I tell you of them.
44: 4 They shall s up like a green tamarisk,
45: 8 let the earth open, that salvation may s up,
58: 8 and your healing shall s up quickly;
58:11 like a s of water, whose waters never fail.
61:11 and as a garden causes what is sown in it to s up,
61:11 and praise to s up before all the nations.
Jer 3: 3 and the s rain has not come;
5:24 the autumn rain and the s rain,
9: 1 O that my head were a s of water,
33:15 at that time I will cause a righteous Branch to s up
Hos 6: 3 like the s rains that water the earth."
13:15 his fountain shall dry up, his s shall be parched.
Am 3: 5 Does a snare s up from the ground,
Zec 10: 1 from the LORD in the season of the s rain,
Jn 4:14 The water that I will give will become in them a s
1Th 2: 3 not s from deceit or impure motives or trickery,
Jas 3:11 a s pour forth from the same opening both fresh
Rev 21: 6 To the thirsty I will give water as a gift from the s
Jdt 7: 3 the s, and they spread out in breadth over Dothan
7:12 let your servants take possession of the s of water
12: 7 and bathed at the s in the camp.
AdE 10: 6 There was the little s that became a river,
11:10 and at their outcry, as though from a tiny s,
Wis 2: 7 and let no flower of s pass us by.
Sir 21:13 and their counsel like a life-giving s.
50: 8 like lilies by a s of water,
2Mc 14:30 that this austerity did not s from the best motives.
2Es 7:*41* or summer or s or heat or winter or frost or cold,
14:47 For in them is the s of understanding,
16:21 and then calamities shall s up on the earth—
4Mc 3:14 and found the s, and from it boldly brought

SPRINGS (44) [SPRING]

Ge 36:24 he is the Anah who found the s in the wilderness,
Ex 15:27 where there were twelve s of water
Nu 33: 9 at Elim there were twelve s of water
Dt 8: 7 with s and underground waters welling up
Jos 15:19 give me s of water as well."
15:19 Caleb gave her the upper s and the lower s.
1Ki 18: 5 "Go through the land to all the s of water and to all
2Ki 3:19 all s of water you shall stop up,
19:29 and in the second year what s from that;
2Ch 32: 3 to stop the flow of the s that were outside the city;
32: 4 and they stopped all the s and the wadi that flowed
Job 38:16 "Have you entered into the s of the sea,
Ps 74:15 You cut openings for s and torrents;
84: 6 the valley of Baca they make it a place of s;
87: 7 "All my s are in you."
104:10 You make s gush forth in the valleys;
107:33 s of water into thirsty ground,
107:35 a parched land into s of water.
Pr 4:23 for from it flow the s of life.
5:16 Should your s be scattered abroad,
8:24 when there were no s abounding with water.
SS 5:12 His eyes are like doves beside s of water,
Isa 35: 7 and the thirsty ground s of water;
37:30 and in the second year what s from that;
41:18 and the dry land s of water.
43:19 now it s forth, do you not perceive it?
49:10 and by s of water will guide them.
Hos 10: 4 so litigation s up like poisonous weeds in
Heb 12:15 that no root of bitterness s up and causes trouble,
2Pe 2:17 These are waterless s and mists driven by a storm;
Rev 7:17 and he will guide them to s of the water of life,
8:10 it fell on a third of the rivers and on the s of water.
14: 7 made heaven and earth, the sea and the s of water."
16: 4 into the rivers and the s of water,
Jdt 6:11 the hill country and came to the s below Bethulia.
7: 7 and visited the s that supplied their water;
7:17 the valley and seized the water supply and the s of
Aza 1:56 Bless the Lord, you s; sing praise to him
2Es 2:19 and the same number of s flowing with milk
2:32 my s run over, and my grace will not fail."
6:24 and the s of the fountains shall stand still,
16:60 he has put s of water in the desert,
4Mc 3:10 and though s were plentiful there,

SPRINKLE (17) [SPRINKLED, SPRINKLES, SPRINKLING]

Ex 29:21 and s it on Aaron and his vestments and

Lev 4: 6 in the blood and s some of the blood seven times
4:17 the blood and s it seven times before the LORD,
5: 9 He shall s some of the blood of the sin offering on
14: 7 He shall s it seven times upon the one who is to
14:16 and s some oil with his finger seven times before
14:27 and shall s with his right finger some of the oil
14:51 and s the house seven times.
16:14 s it with his finger on the front of the mercy seat,
16:14 and before the mercy seat he shall s the blood
16:19 He shall s some of the blood on it
Nu 8: 7 s the water of purification on them,
19: 4 and s it seven times towards the front of the tent
19:18 and s it on the tent, on all the furnishings,
19:19 The clean person shall s the unclean ones on
Eze 36:25 I will s clean water upon you,
2Mc 1:21 to s the liquid on the wood and on the things laid

SPRINKLED‡ (15) [SPRINKLE]
Lev 8:11 He s some of it on the altar seven times,
8:30 the altar and s them on Aaron and his vestments,
Hos 7: 9 gray hairs are s upon him, but he does not know it.
Heb 9:19 and s both the scroll itself and all the people,
9:21 in the same way he s with the blood both the tent
10:22 with our hearts s clean from an evil conscience
12:24 and to the s blood that speaks a better word than
1Pe 1: 2 the Spirit to be obedient to Jesus Christ and to be s
AdE 4: 1 put on sackcloth, and s himself with ashes;
1Mc 3:47 put on sackcloth and s ashes on their heads,
4:39 they s themselves with ashes
2Mc 10:25 Maccabeus and his men s dust on their heads
14:15 they s dust on their heads and prayed
3Mc 1:18 with their mothers, s their hair with dust, and filled
4: 6 their myrrh-perfumed hair s with ashes,

SPRINKLES (1) [SPRINKLE]
Nu 19:21 The one who s the water for cleansing shall wash

SPRINKLING (3) [SPRINKLE]
Lev 16:15 s it upon the mercy seat and before the mercy seat.
Heb 9:13 with the s of the ashes of a heifer,
11:28 By faith he kept the Passover and the s of blood,

SPROUT (12) [SPROUTED, SPROUTING, SPROUTS]
Nu 17: 5 And the staff of the man whom I choose shall s;
Job 5: 6 nor does trouble s from the ground;
14: 7 if it is cut down, that it will s again,
Ps 92: 7 the wicked s like grass and all evildoers flourish,
132:17 There I will cause a horn to s up for David;
Isa 45: 8 and let it cause righteousness to s up also;
55:10 making it bring forth and s,
Eze 29:21 that day I will cause a horn to s up for the house
Am 7: 1 at the time the latter growth began to s (it was
Mk 4:27 and the seed would s and grow,
Lk 21:30 as soon as they s leaves you can see for yourselves
Sir 51:12 *him who makes a horn to s for the house of David.*

SPROUTED (3) [SPROUT]
Ge 41: 6 thin and blighted by the east wind, s after them.
Nu 17: 8 the staff of Aaron for the house of Levi had s.
Eze 17: 6 It s and became a vine spreading out, but low;

SPROUTING (4) [SPROUT]
Ge 41:23 thin, and blighted by the east wind, s after them;
Dt 29:18 among you a root s poisonous and bitter growth.
29:23 nothing s, unable to support any vegetation,
Eze 17: 9 its fresh s leaves to fade?

SPROUTS (1) [SPROUT]
Sir 37:18 it s four branches, good and evil, life and death;

SPRUNG (3) [SPRING]
Ge 2: 5 in the earth and no herb of the field had yet s up—
Tob 8: 6 From the two of them the human race has s.
1Mc 4:38 In the courts they saw bushes s up as in a thicket,

SPUE[D] (KJV) See SPIT, VOMIT[ED]

SPUN (3) [SPIN]
Ex 35:25 All the skillful women s with their hands,
35:25 and brought what they had s in blue and purple
35:26 to use their skill s the goats' hair.

SPUNGE (KJV) See SPONGE

SPURN (9) [SPURNED, SPURNS]
Lev 26:15 if you s my statutes, and abhor my ordinances,
26:43 because they dared to s my ordinances,
26:44 I will not s them, or abhor them so as
Ps 77: 7 "Will the Lord s forever, and never again
119:118 You s all who go astray from your statutes;
Jer 14:21 Do not s us, for your name's sake;
3Mc 3:23 not only s the priceless citizenship,
4Mc 3:18 and by nobility of reason s all domination by
5: 9 and wrong to s the gifts of nature.

SPURNED (6) [SPURN]
Dt 32:19 and was jealous he s his sons and daughters.
Ps 89:38 But now you have s and rejected him;
107:11 and s the counsel of the Most High.
La 2: 6 and in his fierce indignation has s king and priest.
Hos 8: 3 Israel has s the good; the enemy shall pursue him.
Heb 10:29 be deserved by those who have s the Son of God,

SPURNS (1) [SPURN]
Pr 27: 7 The sated appetite s honey,

SPY (16) [SPIED, SPIES, SPYING]
Nu 13: 2 to s out the land of Canaan, which I am giving to
13:16 the names of the men whom Moses sent to s out
13:17 Moses sent them to s out the land of Canaan,
14:36 And the men whom Moses sent to s out the land,
14:38 of those men who went to s out the land.
21:32 Moses sent to s out Jazer;
Jos 6:25 the messengers whom Joshua sent to s out Jericho.
7: 2 and said to them, "Go up and s out the land."
14: 7 the LORD sent me from Kadesh-barnea to s out
Jdg 18: 2 to s out the land and to explore it;
18:14 five men who had gone to s out the land
18:17 to s out the land proceeded to enter and take
2Sa 10: 3 to s it out, and to overthrow it?"
1Ch 19: 3 to search and to overthrow and to s out the land?"
Gal 2: 4 in to s on the freedom we have in Christ Jesus,
1Mc 5:38 Judas sent men to s out the camp,

SPYING (2) [SPY]
Ge 42:30 and charged us with s on the land.
Nu 13:25 At the end of forty days they returned from s out

SQUADS (1)
Ac 12: 4 he put him in prison and handed him over to four s

SQUANDER (1) [SQUANDERED, SQUANDERING]
Pr 29: 3 company with prostitutes is to s one's substance.

SQUANDERED (1) [SQUANDER]
Lk 15:13 and there he s his property in dissolute living.

SQUANDERING (1) [SQUANDER]
Lk 16: 1 brought to him that this man was s his property.

SQUARE‡ (40) [FOURSQUARE, SQUARED, SQUARES]
Ge 19: 2 They said, "No; we will spend the night in the s."
Ex 27: 1 altar shall be s, and it shall be three cubits high.
28:16 It shall be s and doubled,
30: 2 it shall be s, and shall be two cubits high;
37:25 it was s, and was two cubits high;
38: 1 it was s, and three cubits high.
39: 9 It was s; the breastpiece was made double,
Dt 13:16 All of its spoil you shall gather into its public s;
Jdg 19:15 He went in and sat down in the open s of the city,
19:17 up and saw the wayfarer in the open s of the city,
19:20 only do not spend the night in the s."
2Sa 21:12 who had stolen them from the public s
2Ch 29: 4 and the Levites and assembled them in the s on
32: 6 and gathered them together to him in the s at
Ezr 10: 9 All the people sat in the open s before the house
Ne 8: 1 all the people gathered together into the s before
8: 3 He read from it facing the s before the Water Gate
8:16 and in the s at the Water Gate and in the s at
Est 4: 6 in the open s of the city in front of the king's gate,
6: 9 the open s of the city, proclaiming before him:
6:11 and led him riding through the open s of the city,
Job 29: 7 when I took my seat in the s,
Isa 59:14 for truth stumbles in the public s,
Eze 16:24 and made yourself a lofty place in every s;
16:31 and making your lofty place in every s!
40:47 a s; and the altar was in front of the temple.
41:21 The doorposts of the nave were s.
43:16 The altar hearth shall be s,
43:17 The ledge also shall be s,
45: 2 a s plot of five hundred by five hundred cubits
48:20 be twenty-five thousand cubits s,
Tob 2: 4 and removed the body from the s and laid it in one
AdE 6: 9 let it be proclaimed through the open s of the city,
6:11 and made him ride through the open s of the city,
2Mc 10: 2 down the altars that had been built in the public s
1Es 5:47 they gathered with a single purpose in the s before
9: 6 the multitude sat in the open s before the temple,
9:38 with one accord in the open s before the east gate
9:41 He read aloud in the open s before the gate of

SQUARED (1) [SQUARE]
1Mc 10:11 the walls and encircle Mount Zion with s stones,

SQUARES (11) [SQUARE]
Pr 1:20 in the s she raises her voice.
7:12 now in the s, and at every corner she lies in wait.
SS 3: 2 in the streets and in the s;
Isa 15: 3 and in the s everyone wails and melts in tears.
Jer 5: 1 Search its s and see if you can find one person
9:21 from the streets and the young men from the s."
48:38 and in the s there is nothing but lamentation;
49:26 Therefore her young men shall fall in her s,
50:30 Therefore her young men shall fall in her s,
Am 5:16 In all the s there shall be wailing;
Na 2: 4 they rush to and fro through the s;

SQUEEZED (1)
Jdg 6:38 When he rose early next morning and s the fleece,

STABBED (3)
2Sa 3:27 and there he s him in the stomach.
1Mc 6:46 He got under the elephant, s it from beneath,
2Mc 13:15 He s the leading elephant and its rider.

STABILITY (6)
Pr 29: 4 By justice a king gives s to the land,
Isa 33: 6 he will be the s of your times, abundance
2Pe 3:17 with the error of the lawless and lose your own s.
AdE 13: 5 so that our kingdom may not attain s.
Wis 6:24 and a sensible king is the s of any people.
3Mc 6:28 until now has granted an unimpeded and notable s

STABLE (KJV) See FIRMLY ESTABLISHED, PASTURE

STABLISH, STABLISHED, STABLISHETH (KJV) See CONFIRM, ENJOINING, ESTABLISH, ESTABLISHED, ESTABLISHES, FOUND, SET UP, STRENGTHEN

STACHYS (1)
Ro 16: 9 our co-worker in Christ, and my beloved S.

STACKED (1)
Ex 22: 6 in thorns so that the s grain or the standing grain or

STACKS (KJV) See STACKED

STACTE (2)
Ex 30:34 Take sweet spices, s, and onycha, and galbanum,
Sir 24:15 and s, and like the odor of incense in the tent.

STADIA‡ (1)
2Mc 11: 5 a fortified place about five s from Jerusalem,

STAFF (78) [STAFFS]
Ge 32:10 for with only my s I crossed this Jordan;
38:18 and the s that is in your hand."
38:25 whose these are, the signet and the cord and the s."
49:10 nor the ruler's s from between his feet,
Ex 4: 2 in your hand?" He said, "A s."
4: 3 So he threw the s on the ground,
4: 4 and it became a s in his hand—
4:17 Take in your hand this s,
4:20 and Moses carried the s of God in his hand.
7: 9 'Take your s and throw it down before Pharaoh,
7:10 down his s before Pharaoh and his officials,
7:12 Each one threw down his s,
7:12 but Aaron's s swallowed up theirs.
7:15 and take in your hand the s that was turned into
7:17 with the s that is in my hand I will strike the water
7:19 'Take your s and stretch out your hand over
7:20 of Pharaoh and of his officials he lifted up the s
8: 5 'Stretch out your hand with your s over the rivers,
8:16 'Stretch out your s and strike the dust of the earth,
8:17 Aaron stretched out his hand with his s and struck
9:23 Then Moses stretched out his s toward heaven,
10:13 Moses stretched out his s over the land of Egypt,
12:11 your sandals on your feet, and your s in your hand;
14:16 But you lift up your s,
17: 5 in your hand the s with which you struck the Nile,
17: 9 the top of the hill with the s of God in my hand."
21:19 and walks around outside with the help of a s,
Lev 26:26 When I break your s of bread,
27:32 every tenth one that passes under the shepherd's s,
Nu 17: 2 Write each man's name on his s,
17: 3 and write Aaron's name on the s of Levi.
17: 3 be one s for the head of each ancestral house.
17: 5 And the s of the man whom I choose shall sprout;
17: 6 and the s of Aaron was among theirs.
17: 8 the s of Aaron for the house of Levi had sprouted.
17: 9 and they looked, and each man took his s.
17:10 "Put back the s of Aaron before the covenant,
20: 8 Take the s, and assemble the congregation, you
20: 9 So Moses took the s from before the LORD,
20:11 up his hand and struck the rock twice with his s;
21:18 with the scepter, with the s."
22:27 and he struck the donkey with his s.
Jdg 5:14 and from Zebulun those who bear the marshal's s;
6:21 the angel of the LORD reached out the tip of the s
1Sa 14:27 so he extended the s that was in his hand,
14:43 "I tasted a little honey with the tip of the s that was
17:40 Then he took his s in his hand,
2Sa 23:21 but Benaiah went against him with a s,
2Ki 4:29 "Gird up your loins, and take my s in your hand,
4:29 and lay my s on the face of the child."
4:31 Gehazi went on ahead and laid the s on the face of
18:21 that broken reed of a s,
1Ch 11:23 but Benaiah went against him with a s,
Ps 23: 4 your rod and your s—they comfort me.
105:16 and broke every s of bread,
Isa 3: 1 support and s—all support of bread,
10:15 or as if a s should lift the one who is not wood!
10:24 and lift up their s against you as the Egyptians did.
10:26 his s will be over the sea,

Isa 14: 5 The LORD has broken the s of the wicked,
30:32 And every stroke of the s of punishment that
36: 6 you are relying on Egypt, that broken reed of a s,
Jer 48:17 How the mighty scepter is broken, the glorious s!"
Eze 4:16 I am going to break the s of bread in Jerusalem;
5:16 and break your s of bread.
14:13 and break its s of bread and send famine upon it,
20:37 I will make you pass under the s,
29: 6 because you were a s of reed to the house of Israel;
Mic 7:14 Shepherd your people with your s,
Zec 8: 4 each with s in hand because of their great age.
11:10 I took my s Favor and broke it,
11:14 Then I broke my second s Unity,
Mt 10:10 or sandals, or a s; for laborers deserve their food.
Mk 6: 8 to take nothing for their journey except a s;
Lk 9: 3 "Take nothing for your journey, no s, nor bag,
Heb 11:21 "bowing in worship over the top of his s."
Rev 11: 1 Then I was given a measuring rod like a s,
Tob 5:18 the s of our hand as he goes in and out before us?

STAFFS (6) [STAFF]
Nu 17: 2 and get twelve s from them,
17: 6 and all their leaders gave him s,
17: 6 twelve s; and the staff of Aaron was among theirs.
17: 7 the s before the LORD in the tent of the covenant.
17: 9 the s from before the LORD to all the Israelites;
Zec 11: 7 I took two s; one I named Favor,

STAG (4) [STAGS]
Pr 7:22 or bounds like a s toward the trap
SS 2: 9 My beloved is like a gazelle or a young s.
2:17 like a gazelle or a young s on the cleft mountains.
8:14 or a young s upon the mountains of spices!

STAGE (4) [STAGES]
Ex 40:36 Israelites would set out on each s of their journey;
40:38 of all the house of Israel at each s of their journey.
Nu 33: 2 Moses wrote down their starting points, s by s,

STAGES (6) [STAGE]
Ge 12: 9 And Abram journeyed on by s toward the Negeb.
13: 3 He journeyed on by s from the Negeb as far
Ex 17: 1 of the Israelites journeyed by s,
Nu 10:12 Israelites set out by s from the wilderness of Sinai,
33: 1 These are the s by which the Israelites went out of
33: 2 these are their s according to their starting places.

STAGGER (8) [STAGGERED, STAGGERING, STAGGERS]
Job 12:25 he makes them s like a drunkard.
Isa 19:14 and they have made Egypt s in all its doings as
28: 7 These also reel with wine and s with strong drink;
28: 7 confused with wine, they s with strong drink;
29: 9 s, but not from strong drink!
Jer 25:16 They shall drink and s and go out of their minds
La 5:13 and boys s under loads of wood.
Hab 2:16 Drink, you yourself, and s!

STAGGERED (1) [STAGGER]
Ps 107:27 they reeled and s like drunkards,

STAGGERING (3) [STAGGER]
Pr 24:11 those who go s to the slaughter;
Isa 51:17 who have drunk to the dregs the bowl of s.
51:22 See, I have taken from your hand the cup of s;

STAGGERS (2) [STAGGER]
Isa 19:14 in all its doings as a drunkard s around in vomit.
24:20 The earth s like a drunkard, it sways like a hut;

STAGNANT (1)
Eze 47: 8 and when it enters the sea, the sea of s waters,

STAGS (1) [STAG]
La 1: 6 Her princes have become like s

STAIN‡ (2) [BLOODSTAIN, STAINED, STAINS]
Jer 2:22 the s of your guilt is still before me,
Sir 33:23 bring no s upon your honor.

STAINED (5) [STAIN]
Isa 63: 1 from Bozrah in garments s crimson?
63: 3 on my garments, and s all my robes.
Jdt 9: 3 of the deceit they had practiced, was s with blood,
Wis 15: 4 a figure s with varied colors,
Sir 47:20 You s your honor, and defiled your family line,

STAINS (1) [STAIN]
Jas 3: 6 it s the whole body, sets on fire the cycle of nature,

STAIRS (4) [STAIRWAY]
1Ki 6: 8 one went up by winding s to the middle story,
Ne 3:15 far as the s that go down from the City of David.
9: 4 the s of the Levites and cried out with a loud voice
12:37 they went straight up by the s of the city of David,

STAIRWAY‡ (4) [STAIRS]
Eze 40:31 and its s had eight steps.
40:34 and its s had eight steps.
40:37 and its s had eight steps.
41: 7 for the structure was supplied with a s all around

STAKE (3) [STAKES]
Ezr 9: 8 and given us a s in his holy place,
Job 6:29 Turn now, my vindication is at s.
Sir 27: 2 a s is driven firmly into a fissure between stones,

STAKES (2) [STAKE]
Isa 33:20 whose s will never be pulled up,
54: 2 lengthen your cords and strengthen your s.

STALK (3) [STALKS]
Ge 41: 5 plump and good, were growing on one s.
41:22 full and good, growing on one s.
Mk 4:28 The earth produces of itself, first the s,

STALKS (3) [STALK]
Jos 2: 6 with the s of flax that she had laid out on the roof.
Ps 91: 6 or the pestilence that s in darkness,
Pr 6:26 but the wife of another s a man's very life.

STALL (2) [STALLS]
Am 6: 4 from the flock, and calves from the s;
Mal 4: 2 You shall go out leaping like calves from the s.

STALLION (1) [STALLIONS]
Sir 33: 6 like a s that neighs no matter who the rider is.

STALLIONS (5) [STALLION]
Jer 5: 8 They were well-fed lusty s,
8:16 of the neighing of their s the whole land quakes.
47: 3 At the noise of the stamping of the hoofs of his s,
50:11 about like a heifer on the grass, and neigh like s,
Eze 23:20 and whose emission was like that of s.

STALLS (4) [STALL]
1Ki 4:26 also had forty thousand s of horses for his chariots,
2Ch 9:25 Solomon had four thousand s for horses
32:28 and s for all kinds of cattle, and sheepfolds.
Hab 3:17 from the fold and there is no herd in the s,

STALWART (2)
1Mc 11:44 So Jonathan sent three thousand s men to him
2Mc 12:27 S young men took their stand before the walls

STAMMERERS (1) [STAMMERING]
Isa 32: 4 the tongues of s will speak readily and distinctly.

STAMMERING (2) [STAMMERERS]
Isa 28:11 with s lip and with alien tongue he will speak
33:19 s in a language that you cannot understand.

STAMP (1) [STAMPED, STAMPING]
Eze 6:11 Clap your hands and s your foot, and say,

STAMPED (3) [STAMP]
2Sa 22:43 I crushed them and s them down like the mire of
Eze 25: 6 and s your feet and rejoiced with all the malice
Da 7:19 and s what was left with its feet;

STAMPING (2) [STAMP]
Jer 47: 3 At the noise of the s of the hoofs of his stallions,
Da 7: 7 and s what was left with its feet.

STANCHED (KJV) See STOPPED

STAND‡ (301) [BYSTANDERS, STANDING, STANDS, STOOD]
Ge 19: 9 But they replied, "S back!"
24:31 Why do you s outside when I have prepared
Ex 7:15 s by at the river bank to meet him,
9:11 The magicians could not s before Moses because
14:13 s firm, and see the deliverance that
17: 9 Tomorrow I will s on the top of the hill with
18:14 while all the people s around you from morning
19:17 They took their s at the foot of the mountain.
30:18 You shall make a bronze basin with a bronze s
30:28 and the basin with its s,
31: 9 and the basin with its s,
33: 8 all the people would rise and s, each of them,
33: 9 of cloud would descend and s at the entrance of
33:21 a place by me where you shall s on the rock;
35:16 its poles, and all its utensils, the basin with its s;
38: 8 He made the basin of bronze with its s of bronze,
39:39 and all its utensils; the basin with its s;
40:11 You shall also anoint the basin with its s,
Lev 26:37 you shall have no power to s against your enemies.
27:14 as the priest assesses it, so it shall s.
27:17 as of the year of jubilee, that assessment shall s;
Nu 8:13 Then you shall have the Levites s before Aaron
16: 9 and to s before the congregation and serve them?
22:22 the LORD took his s in the road as his adversary.
23:15 "S here beside your burnt offerings,
27:19 have him s before Eleazar the priest and all
27:21 But he shall s before Eleazar the priest,
27:22 He took Joshua and had him s before Eleazar
30: 4 then all her vows shall s,
Nu 30: 4 any pledge by which she has bound herself shall s.
30: 5 by which she has bound herself, shall s;
30: 7 at the time that he hears, then her vows shall s,
30: 7 by which she has bound herself shall s.
30:11 then all her vows shall s,
30:11 and any pledge by which she bound herself shall s.
30:12 or concerning her pledge of herself, shall not s.
30:13 her husband may allow to s,
Dt 5:31 But you, s here by me, and I will tell you all
7:24 no one will be able to s against you,
9: 2 "Who can s up to the Anakim?"
10: 8 to s before the LORD to minister to him,
11:25 No one will be able to s against you;
18: 5 to s and minister in the name of the LORD,
18: 7 like all his fellow-Levites who s to minister there
27:12 these shall s on Mount Gerizim for the blessing of
27:13 And these shall s on Mount Ebal for the curse:
29:10 You s assembled today, all of you,
29:14 not only with you who s here with us today before
Jos 1: 5 No one shall be able to s against you all the days
3: 8 you shall s still in the Jordan.' "
3:13 they shall s in a single heap."
5:15 for the place where you s is holy."
7:10 The LORD said to Joshua, "S up!
7:12 the Israelites are unable to s before their enemies;
7:13 to s before your enemies until you take away
10: 8 not one of them shall s before you."
10:12 "Sun, s still at Gibeon, and Moon, in the valley of
20: 4 to one of these cities and shall s at the entrance of
Jdg 4:20 He said to her, "S at the entrance of the tent,
16:25 They made him s between the pillars;
1Sa 6:20 "Who is able to s before the LORD,
10:23 When he took his s among the people,
12: 7 Now therefore take your s,
12:16 Now therefore take your s and see this great thing
14: 9 then we will s still in our place,
17:16 the Philistine came forward and took his s,
19: 3 and s beside my father in the field where you are,
2Sa 1: 9 He said to me, 'Come, s over me and kill me;
2:25 they took their s on the top of a hill.
15: 2 Absalom used to rise early and s beside the road
18:30 The king said, "Turn aside, and s here."
20:11 And one of Joab's men took his s by Amasa,
23:12 But he took his s in the middle of the plot,
1Ki 7:27 each s was four cubits long, four cubits wide,
7:30 Each s had four bronze wheels and axles
7:34 at the four corners of each s;
7:35 of the s there was a round band half a cubit high;
7:35 on the top of the s,
8:11 so that the priests could not s to minister because
17: 1 before whom I s, there shall be neither dew
18:15 "As the LORD of hosts lives, before whom I s,
19:11 "Go out and s on the mountain before the LORD,
2Ki 5:11 and s and call on the name of the LORD his God,
10: 4 not withstand him; how then can we s?"
1Ch 11:14 and David took their s in the middle of the plot,
23:30 And they shall s every morning,
2Ch 5:14 so that the priests could not s to minister because
20: 9 we will s before this house, and before you,
20:17 take your position, s still, and see the victory of
29:11 for the LORD has chosen you to s in his presence
Ezr 10:13 we cannot s in the open.
Ne 9: 5 "S up and bless the LORD your God
Job 8:15 If one leans against its house, it will not s;
19:25 and that at the last he will s upon the earth;
30:20 I s, and you merely look at me.
30:28 I s up in the assembly and cry for help.
32:16 because they do not speak, because they s there,
33: 5 in order before me; take your s.
39:24 it cannot s still at the sound of the trumpet.
40:12 tread down the wicked where they s.
41:10 Who can s before it?
Ps 1: 5 Therefore the wicked will not s in the judgment,
5: 5 The boastful will not s before your eyes;
10: 1 O LORD, do you s far off?
15: 4 who s by their oath even to their hurt;
20: 8 but we shall rise and s upright.
22:23 s in awe of him, all you offspring of Israel!
24: 3 And who shall s in his holy place?
33: 8 let all the inhabitants of the world s in awe of him.
38:11 and companions s aloof from my affliction,
38:11 and my neighbors s far off.
76: 7 can s before you when once your anger is
78:13 and made the waters s like a heap.
89:28 and my covenant with him will s firm.
109: 6 let an accuser s on his right.
119:91 By your appointment they s today,
130: 3 should mark iniquities, Lord, who could s?
134: 1 who s by night in the house of the LORD!
135: 2 you that s in the house of the LORD,
147:17 who can s before his cold?
Pr 8: 2 beside the way, at the crossroads she takes her s;
12: 7 but the house of the righteous will s.
25: 6 in the king's presence or s in the place of the great;
27: 4 but who is able to s before jealousy?
Ecc 3:14 so that all should s in awe before him.
8:12 because they s in fear before him,
8:13 because they do not s in fear before God.
Isa 7: 7 It shall not s, and it shall not come to pass.
7: 9 If you do not s firm in faith, you shall not s at all.
8:10 speak a word, but it will not s, for God is with us.
11:10 the root of Jesse shall s as a signal to the peoples;
21: 8 "Upon a watchtower I s, O Lord,
22: 7 and the cavalry took their s at the gates.
28:18 and your agreement with Sheol will not s;
29:23 and will s in awe of the God of Israel.
32: 8 and by noble things they s.

Isa 40: 8 but the word of our God will s forever.
44:11 Let them all assemble, let them s up;
46:10 saying, "My purpose shall s,
47:12 S fast in your enchantments
47:13 s up and save you, those who gaze at the stars,
48:13 when I summon them, they s at attention.
49: 7 the slave of rulers, "Kings shall see and s up,
50: 8 Let us s up together.
51:17 S up, O Jerusalem, you who have drunk at
61: 5 Strangers shall s and feed your flocks,
Jer 1:17 s up and tell them everything that I command you.
6:16 Thus says the LORD: S at the crossroads,
7: 2 S in the gate of the LORD's house,
7:10 and s before me in this house, which is called
14: 6 The wild asses s on the bare heights,
15:19 I will take you back, and you shall s before me.
17:19 Go and s in the People's Gate,
26: 2 S in the court of the LORD's house,
35:19 not lack a descendant to s before me for all time.
44:28 shall know whose words will s, mine or theirs!
46:15 Why did your bull not s?
46:21 and fled together, they did not s;
48:19 S by the road and watch, you inhabitant of Aroer!
49:19 Who is the shepherd who can s before me?
50:44 Who is the shepherd who can s before me?
51:29 for the LORD's purposes against Babylon s,
Eze 2: 1 He said to me: O mortal, s up on your feet,
13: 5 that it might s in battle on the day of the LORD.
17:14 and that by keeping his covenant it might s.
22:30 the wall and s in the breach before me on behalf of
24:11 S it empty upon the coals,
27:29 mariners and all the pilots of the sea s on the shore
46: 2 and shall take his s by the post of the gate.
47:10 People will s fishing beside the sea from En-gedi
Da 2:44 and bring them to an end, and it shall s forever;
7: 4 and it was lifted up from the ground and made to s
10:11 S on your feet, for I have now been sent to you."
11:15 And the forces of the south shall not s,
11:32 the people who are loyal to their God shall s firm
Am 2:15 the bow shall not s, and those who are swift
7: 2 I beg you! How can Jacob s?
7: 5 I beg you! How can Jacob s?
Mic 5: 4 And he shall s and feed his flock in the strength of
7:17 and they shall s in fear of you.
Na 1: 6 Who can s before his indignation?
Hab 2: 1 I will s at my watchpost, and station myself on
3: 2 I have heard of your renown, and I s in awe,
Zec 4:14 the two anointed ones who s by the Lord of
14: 4 that day his feet shall s on the Mount of Olives,
Mal 3: 2 and who can s when he appears?
Mt 6: 5 for they love to s and pray in the synagogues and
9: 5 or to say, 'S up and walk'?
9: 6 "S up, take your bed and go to your home."
12:25 and no city or house divided against itself will s.
12:26 how then will his kingdom s?
Mk 2: 9 or to say, 'S up and take your mat and walk'?
2:11 s up, take your mat and go to your home."
3:24 against itself, that kingdom cannot s.
3:25 that house will not be able to s.
3:26 he cannot s, but his end has come.
9:27 and he was able to s.
11:25 "Whenever you s praying, forgive,
13: 9 and you will s before governors and kings because
Lk 1:19 I s in the presence of God,
5:23 or to say, 'S up and walk'?
5:24 s up and take your bed and go to your home."
6: 8 the withered hand, "Come and s here."
11:18 how will his kingdom s?
13:11 She was bent over and was quite unable to s
13:25 you begin to s outside and to knock at the door,
21:28 s up and raise your heads,
21:36 and to s before the Son of Man."
Jn 5: 8 Jesus said to him, "S up, take your mat and walk."
8: 3 ⟦and making her s before all of them,⟧
8:44 a murderer from the beginning and does not s in
Ac 1:11 why do you s looking up toward heaven?
3: 6 in the name of Jesus Christ of Nazareth, s up
4: 7 When they had made the prisoners s in their midst,
4:26 The kings of the earth took their s,
5:20 s in the temple and tell the people
5:27 they had them s before the council.
6: 6 They had these men s before the apostles,
10:26 But Peter made him get up, saying, "S up;
14:10 in a loud voice, "S upright on your feet."
22:30 He brought Paul down and had him s before them.
26: 6 And now I s here on trial on account of my hope
26:16 But get up and s on your feet;
26:22 and so I s here, testifying to both small and great,
27:24 you must s before the emperor;
Ro 5: 2 to this grace in which we s;
11:20 but you s only through faith.
11:20 So do not become proud, but s in awe.
14: 4 It is before their own lord that they s or fall.
14: 4 for the Lord is able to make them s.
14:10 For we will all s before the judgment seat of God.
1Co 15: 1 which you in turn received, in which also you s,
16:13 Keep alert, s firm in your faith, be courageous,
2Co 1:24 because you s firm in the faith.
Gal 5: 1 S firm, therefore, and do not submit again to
Eph 6:11 you may be able to s against the wiles of the devil.
6:13 and having done everything, to s firm.
6:14 S therefore, and fasten the belt of truth
Php 4: 1 my joy and crown, s firm in the Lord in this way,
Col 4:12 so that you may s mature and fully assured
1Th 3: 8 we now live, if you continue to s firm in the Lord.
2Th 2:15 s firm and hold fast to the traditions
1Ti 5:20 so that the rest also may s in fear.
Jas 2: 3 while to the one who is poor you say, "S there,"
1Pe 5:12 that this is the true grace of God. S fast in it.
Jude 1:24 and to make you s without blemish in the presence
Rev 6:17 and who is able to s?"
8: 2 And I saw the seven angels who s before God,
11: 4 the two olive trees and the two lampstands that s
12:18 the dragon took his s on the sand of the seashore.
18:10 they will s far off, in fear of her torment,
18:15 who gained wealth from her, will s far off,
Tob 6:18 both of you must first s up and pray,
12:15 of the seven angels who s ready and enter before
Jdt 8:33 S at the town gate tonight so that I may go out
10:16 When you s before him, have no fear
13: 3 to s outside the bedchamber and to wait for her
AdE 16: 3 but in their inability to s prosperity,
Wis 5: 1 Then the righteous will s with great confidence in
6: 7 For the Lord of all will not s in awe of anyone,
Sir 5:10 S firm for what you know,
6: 8 but they will not s by you in time of trouble.
6:10 but they will not s by you in time of trouble.
6:34 S in the company of the elders.
11:20 S by your agreement and attend to it,
13:10 do not s aloof, or you will be forgotten.
22:18 Fences set on a high place will not s firm against
22:18 a timid mind with a fool's resolve will not s firm
22:23 S by him in time of distress,
27:14 Their cursing and swearing make one's hair s
37: 9 and then s aside to see what happens to you.
40:25 Gold and silver make one s firm,
42:17 so that the universe may s firm in his glory.
43:10 of the Holy One they s in their appointed places;
44:12 Their descendants s by the covenants;
47:13 in his name and provide a sanctuary to s forever.
Bar 5: 5 Arise, O Jerusalem, s upon the height;
Sus 1:48 Taking his s among them he said,
1Mc 4:18 But s now against our enemies and fight them,
5:44 they could s before Judas no longer.
9:11 from the camp and took its s for the encounter.
10:72 People will tell you that you cannot s before us,
2Mc 12:27 Stalwart young men took their s before the walls
13:12 Judas exhorted them and ordered them to s ready.
1Es 1: 5 S in order in the temple according to
1:27 S aside, and do not oppose the Lord."
8:90 for we can no longer s in your presence because
9:11 and we are not able to s in the open air.
2Es 2:38 s erect and see the number
4:47 And he said to me, "S at my right side,
6:24 and the springs of the fountains shall s still,
7:*34* Only judgment shall remain, truth shall s,
8:21 before whom the hosts of angels s trembling
10:33 He said to me, "S up like a man,
13:35 But he shall s on the top of Mount Zion.
16:65 and your own iniquities shall s as your accusers on
4Mc 1: 4 and those that s in the way of courage,
17: 5 with the stars, does not s so august as you, who,
17: 5 s in honor before God and are firmly set in heaven
17:18 now s before the divine throne and live the life

STANDARD (12) [STANDARDS]

Nu 10:14 The s of the camp of Judah set out first,
10:18 Next the s of the camp of Reuben set out,
10:22 Next the s of the Ephraimite camp set out,
10:25 Then the s of the camp of Dan,
2Ch 3: 3 the length, in cubits of the old s, was sixty cubits,
Isa 31: 9 and his officers desert the s in panic,"
Jer 4: 6 Raise a s toward Zion, flee for safety,
4:21 How long must I see the s,
51:12 Raise a s against the walls of Babylon;
51:27 Raise a s in the land, blow the trumpet among
Eze 45:11 the homer shall be the s measure.
2Ti 1:13 to the s of sound teaching that you have heard

STANDARDBEARER (KJV) See INVALID

STANDARDS (6) [STANDARD]

Jn 8:15 You judge by human s; I judge no one.
1Co 1:26 not many of you were wise by human s,
2Co 1:17 according to ordinary human s,
10: 2 who think we are acting according to human s.
10: 3 but we do not wage war according to human s;
11:18 since many boast according to human s,

STANDING (163) [STAND]

Ge 18: 2 He looked up and saw three men s near him.
18:22 while Abraham remained s before the LORD.
24:13 I am s here by the spring of water,
24:30 and there he was, s by the camels at the spring.
24:43 I am s here by the spring of water;
41: 1 Pharaoh dreamed that he was s by the Nile,
41:17 "In my dream I was s on the banks of the Nile;
Ex 3: 5 for the place on which you are s is holy ground."
17: 6 be s there in front of you on the rock at Horeb.
22: 6 in thorns so that the stacked grain or the s grain or
33:10 the people saw the pillar of cloud s at the entrance
Nu 22:23 donkey saw the angel of the LORD s in the road,
22:31 and he saw the angel of the LORD s in the road,
22:34 for I did not know that you were s in the road
23: 6 who was s beside his burnt offerings with all
23:17 he was s beside his burnt offerings with
Dt 5: 5 (At that time I was s between the LORD and you
16: 9 from the time the sickle is first put to the s grain.
23:25 If you go into your neighbor's s grain,
23:25 not put a sickle to your neighbor's s grain.
Jos 4:10 the ark remained s in the middle of the Jordan,
5:13 and saw a man s before him with a drawn sword
Jdg 15: 5 the foxes go into the s grain of the Philistines,
15: 5 and burned up the shocks and the s grain,
18:17 The priest was s by the entrance of the gate with
Ru 2:15 "Let her glean even among the s sheaves,
1Sa 1:26 I am the woman who was s here in your presence,
19:20 with Samuel s in charge of them,
22: 6 and all his servants were s around him.
2Sa 13:31 all his servants who were s by tore their garments.
1Ki 10:19 of the seat were arm rests and two lions s beside
10:20 while twelve lions were s,
13: 1 Jeroboam was s by the altar to offer incense,
13:25 with the lion s by the body.
13:28 with the donkey and the lion s beside the body.
22:19 the host of heaven s beside him to the right and to
2Ki 2: 7 as they both were s by the Jordan.
9:17 the sentinel s on the tower spied the company
11:14 there was the king s by the pillar,
1Ch 21:15 then s by the threshing floor of Ornan the Jebusite.
21:16 and saw the angel of the LORD s between earth
2Ch 9:18 of the seat were arm rests and two lions s beside
9:19 while twelve lions were s,
18:18 with all the host of heaven s to the right and to
23:13 there was the king s by his pillar at the entrance,
Ne 7: 3 while the gatekeepers are still s guard,
8: 5 for he was s above all the people;
12:25 and Akkub were gatekeepers s guard at
Est 5: 2 soon as the king saw Queen Esther s in the court,
6: 5 "Haman is there, s in the court."
Ps 122: 2 Our feet are s within your gates, O Jerusalem.
Isa 6:13 an oak whose stump remains s when it is felled."
17: 5 when reapers gather s grain and their arms harvest
27: 9 no sacred poles or incense altars will remain s.
Jer 28: 5 the people who were s in the house of the LORD;
Eze 8:11 with Jaazaniah son of Shaphan s among them.
10: 3 the cherubim were s on the south side of the house
40: 3 and he was s in the gateway.
43: 6 While the man was s beside me,
Da 2:31 its brilliance extraordinary; it was s before you,
3: 3 When they were s before the statue
8: 3 I looked up and saw a ram s beside the river.
8: 6 the ram with the two horns that I had seen s beside
8:15 Then someone appeared s before me,
10: 4 as I was s on the bank of the great river (that is,
12: 5 one s on this bank of the stream and one on
Hos 8: 7 The s grain has no heads, it shall yield no meal;
Am 7: 7 Lord was s beside a wall built with a plumb line,
9: 1 I saw the LORD s beside the altar, and he said:
Zec 1: 8 He was s among the myrtle trees in the glen;
1:10 man who was s among the myrtle trees answered,
1:11 of the LORD who was s among the myrtle trees,
3: 1 Then he showed me the high priest Joshua s before
3: 1 and Satan s at his right hand to accuse him.
3: 4 The angel said to those who were s before him,
3: 5 and the angel of the LORD was s by.
3: 7 the right of access among those who are s here.
Mt 12:46 his mother and his brothers were s outside,
12:47 your mother and your brothers are s outside,
16:28 there are some s here who will not taste death
20: 3 he saw others s idle in the marketplace;
20: 6 and found others s around;
20: 6 he said to them, 'Why are you s here idle all day?'
24:15 "So when you see the desolating sacrilege s in
Mk 3:31 and s outside, they sent to him and called him.
9: 1 there are some s here who will not taste death
Lk 1:11 s at the right side of the altar of incense.
5: 1 while Jesus was s beside the lake of Gennesaret,
8:20 "Your mother and your brothers are s outside,
9:27 there are some s here who will not taste death
18:11 The Pharisee, s by himself, was praying thus,
18:13 But the tax collector, s far off,
Jn 1:35 The next day John again was s with two
2: 6 Now s there were six stone water jars for
7:37 the great day, while Jesus was s there, he cried out,
8: 9 ⟦Jesus was left alone with the woman s before⟧
11:42 I have said this for the sake of the crowd s here,
12:29 crowd s there heard it and said that it was thunder.
18: 5 Judas, who betrayed him, was s with them.
18:16 but Peter was s outside at the gate.
18:18 they were s around it and warming themselves.
18:18 Peter also was s with them and warming himself.
18:22 one of the police s nearby struck Jesus on the face,
18:25 Now Simon Peter was s and warming himself.
19:25 s near the cross of Jesus were his mother,
19:26 and the disciple whom he loved s beside her,
19:29 A jar full of sour wine was s there.
20:14 she turned around and saw Jesus s there,
Ac 2:14 But Peter, s with the eleven,
4:10 that this man is s before you in good health by
4:14 When they saw the man who had been cured s
5:23 the prison securely locked and the guards s at
5:25 in prison are s in the temple and teaching
6: 3 from among yourselves seven men of good s,
7:33 for the place where you are s is holy ground.
7:55 into heaven and saw the glory of God and Jesus s
7:56 "I see the heavens opened and the Son of Man s at
10:17 They were asking for Simon's house and were s
11:13 the angel s in his house and saying, 'Send to Joppa
12:14 in and announced that Peter was s at the gate.
13:50 But the Jews incited the devout women of high s
17:12 not a few Greek women and men of high s.
22:13 and s beside me, he said, 'Brother Saul,
22:20 of your witness Stephen was shed, I myself was s
22:25 Paul said to the centurion who was s by,
23: 2 the high priest Ananias ordered those s near him
23: 4 Those s nearby said, "Do you dare
24:21 that I called out while s before them,
1Co 6: 4 do you appoint as judges those who have no s in

1Co 10:12 you think you are s, watch out that you do not fall.
2Co 2:17 as persons sent from God and s in his presence.
Php 1:27 I will know that you are s firm in one spirit,
1Ti 3:13 for those who serve well as deacons gain a good s
Heb 9:8 yet been disclosed as long as the first tent is still s.
Jas 5:9 See, the Judge is s at the doors!
Rev 3:20 I am s at the door, knocking;
5:6 the elders a Lamb s as if it had been slaughtered,
7:1 After this I saw four angels s at the four corners of
7:9 s before the throne and before the Lamb,
10:5 Then the angel whom I saw s on the sea and
10:8 in the hand of the angel who is s on the sea and on
14:1 and there was the Lamb, s on Mount Zion!
15:2 s beside the sea of glass with harps of God
19:17 Then I saw an angel s in the sun,
20:12 s before the throne, and books were opened.
Tob 1:13 the Most High gave me favor and good s
5:4 and found the angel Raphael s in front of him;
Jdt 5:22 all the people s around the tent began to complain;
10:6 the town gate of Bethulia and found Uzziah s there
13:4 Then Judith, s beside his bed, said in her heart,
AdE 6:5 "Haman is s in the courtyard."
7:9 it is s at Haman's house,
Wis 4:4 s insecurely they will be shaken by the wind,
10:7 a pillar of salt s as a monument to an unbelieving
18:16 and touched heaven while s on the earth.
Sir 8:14 for the decision will favor him because of his s.
45:23 and s firm, when the people turned away,
Sus 1:50 for God has given you the s of an elder."
2Mc 14:45 and s upon a steep rock,
2Es 6:14 And if the place where you are s is greatly shaken
6:29 little by little the place where I was s began to rock
4Mc 5:1 and with his armed soldiers s around him,
6:1 the guards who were s by dragged him violently to

STANDS (53) [STAND]

Ge 47:26 and it s to this day,
Nu 14:14 and your cloud s over them and you go in front
Jos 8:29 a great heap of stones, which s there to this day.
22:19 where the LORD's tabernacle now s, and take
22:29 the LORD our God that s before his tabernacle!"
Jdg 6:24 To this day it still s at Ophrah,
1Ki 7:27 He also made the ten s of bronze;
7:28 This was the construction of the s:
7:32 the axles of the wheels were in the s;
7:34 the supports were of one piece with the s.
7:37 In this way he made the ten s;
7:38 there was a basin for each of the ten s.
7:39 He set five of the s on the south side of the house,
7:43 the ten s, the ten basins on the s;
2Ki 16:17 Then King Ahaz cut off the frames of the s,
25:13 the s and the bronze sea that were in the house of
25:16 As for the two pillars, the one sea, and the s,
2Ch 4:14 He made the s, the basins on the s,
Est 7:9 whose word saved the king, s at Haman's house,
Job 23:13 But he s alone and who can dissuade him?
Ps 26:12 My foot s on level ground;
33:11 The counsel of the LORD s forever,
39:5 Surely everyone s as a mere breath.
45:9 at your right hand s the queen in gold of Ophir.
87:1 On the holy mount s the city he founded;
94:16 Who s up for me against evildoers?
109:31 For he s at the right hand of the needy,
119:90 you have established the earth, and it s fast.
119:161 but my heart s in awe of your words.
SS 2:9 Look, there he s behind our wall,
Isa 3:13 he s to judge the peoples.
46:7 they carry it, they set it in its place, and it s there;
59:14 and righteousness s at a distance;
Jer 27:19 the pillars, the sea, the s, and the rest of the vessels
52:17 and the s and the bronze sea that were in the house
52:20 the sea, and the s, which King Solomon had made
Eze 6:4 and your incense s shall be broken;
6:6 and destroyed, your incense s cut down,
21:21 the king of Babylon s at the parting of the way,
41:22 "This is the table that s before the LORD."
Da 6:12 The king answered, "The thing s fast,
Jn 1:26 Among you s one whom you do not know,
3:29 friend of the bridegroom, who s and hears him,
1Co 7:37 But if someone s firm in his resolve,
2Ti 2:19 God's firm foundation s, bearing this inscription:
Heb 10:11 And every priest s day after day at his service,
1Pe 2:6 For it s in scripture: "See, I am laying in Zion a
4:5 to give an accounting to him who s ready to judge
AdE 4:8 for Haman, who s next to the king,
13:5 s constantly in opposition to every nation,
Sir 12:15 He s by you for a while, but if you falter,

STANK (2) [STINK]

Ex 7:21 The river s so that the Egyptians could
8:14 gathered them together in heaps, and the land s.

STAR (16) [STAR-GOD, STAR-LIKE, STARRY, STARS]

Nu 24:17 a s shall come out of Jacob,
Isa 14:12 How you are fallen from heaven, O Day S,
Mt 2:2 For we observed his s at its rising,
2:7 from them the exact time when the s had appeared.
2:9 went the s that they had seen at its rising,
2:10 When they saw that the s had stopped,
Ac 7:43 and the s of your god Rephan,
1Co 15:41 indeed, s differs from s in glory.
2Pe 1:19 until the day dawns and the morning s rises
Rev 2:28 one who conquers I will also give the morning s.
8:10 and a great s fell from heaven, blazing like a torch,
Rev 8:11 The name of the s is Wormwood.
9:1 and I saw a s that had fallen from heaven to earth,
22:16 the descendant of David, the bright morning s."
Sir 50:6 Like the morning s among the clouds,

STAR-GOD (1) [*GOD, STAR]

Am 5:26 and Kaiwan your s, your images,

STAR-LIKE (1) [STAR]

4Mc 17:5 lighting the way of your s seven sons to piety,

STARE (5) [STARED]

Ps 22:17 They s and gloat over me;
Isa 14:16 Those who see you will s at you,
Ac 3:12 why do you wonder at this, or why do you s at us,
Sir 26:9 The haughty s betrays an unchaste wife;
1Es 4:19 and gape at her, and with open mouths s at her,

STARED (5) [STARE]

2Ki 8:11 He fixed his gaze and s at him,
Isa 63:5 I s, but there was no one to sustain me;
Mk 14:67 she s at him and said, "You also were with Jesus,
Lk 22:56 s at him and said, "This man also was with him."
Ac 10:4 He s at him in terror and said, "What is it, Lord?"

STARRY (1) [STAR]

Wis 10:17 and a s flame through the night.

STARS (71) [STAR]

Ge 1:16 to rule the night—and the s.
15:5 "Look toward heaven and count the s,
22:17 as numerous as the s of heaven and as the sand
26:4 I will make your offspring as numerous as the s
37:9 the moon, and eleven s were bowing down to me."
Ex 32:13 'I will multiply your descendants like the s
Dt 1:10 that today you are as numerous as the s of heaven.
4:19 the moon, and the s, all the host of heaven,
10:22 as numerous as the s in heaven.
28:62 once you were as numerous as the s in heaven,
Jdg 5:20 The s fought from heaven,
1Ch 27:23 to make Israel as numerous as the s of heaven.
Ne 4:21 from break of dawn until the s came out.
9:23 You multiplied their descendants like the s
Job 3:9 Let the s of its dawn be dark;
9:7 not rise; who seals up the s;
22:12 See the highest s, how lofty they are!
25:5 even the moon is not bright and the s are not pure
38:7 when the morning s sang together and all
Ps 8:3 the moon and the s that you have established;
136:9 the moon and s to rule over the night,
147:4 He determines the number of the s;
148:3 praise him, all you shining s!
Ecc 12:2 the light and the moon and the s are darkened and
Isa 13:10 the s of the heavens and their constellations will
14:13 I will raise my throne above the s of God;
47:13 up and save you, those who gaze at the s,
Jer 31:35 and the s for light by night, who stirs up the sea so
Eze 32:7 I will cover the heavens, and make their s dark;
Da 8:10 to the earth some of the host and some of the s,
12:3 like the s forever and ever.
Joel 2:10 and the s withdraw their shining.
3:15 and the s withdraw their shining.
Ob 1:4 though your nest is set among the s,
Na 3:16 You increased your merchants more than the s of
Mt 24:29 the s will fall from heaven,
Mk 13:25 and the s will be falling from heaven,
Lk 21:25 be signs in the sun, the moon, and the s, and on
Ac 27:20 When neither sun nor s appeared for many days,
1Co 15:41 and another glory of the s;
Php 2:15 in which you shine like s in the world.
Heb 11:12 as the s of heaven and as the innumerable grains
Jude 1:13 wandering s, for whom the deepest darkness
Rev 1:16 In his right hand he held seven s,
1:20 of the seven s that you saw in my right hand,
1:20 the seven s are the angels of the seven churches,
2:1 These are the words of him who holds the seven s
3:1 the seven spirits of God and the seven s:
6:13 and the s of the sky fell to the earth as
8:12 and a third of the moon, and a third of the s,
12:1 and on her head a crown of twelve s.
12:4 down a third of the s of heaven and threw them to
Wis 7:19 cycles of the year and the constellations of the s,
7:29 and excels every constellation of the s.
13:2 or the circle of the s, or turbulent water,
17:5 the brilliant flames of the s avail to illumine
Sir 43:9 The glory of the s is the beauty of heaven,
44:21 and exalt his offspring like the s,
Bar 3:34 the s shone in their watches, and were glad;
LtJ 6:60 For sun and moon and s are bright,
Aza 1:13 like the s of heaven and like the sand on the shore
1:41 Bless the Lord, s of heaven;
2Mc 9:10 while before had thought that he could touch the s
2Es 5:5 the peoples shall be troubled, and the s shall fall.
6:45 and the arrangement of the s to come into being;
7:*39* a day that has no sun or moon or s,
7:*97* and how they are to be made like the light of the s,
7:*125* [55] self-control shall shine more than the s,
16:56 At his word the s were fixed in their places,
16:56 and he knows the number of the s.
4Mc 17:5 The moon in heaven, with the s,

START (6) [STARTED, STARTING, STARTS]

1Sa 29:10 S early in the morning, and leave as soon
2Ki 4:4 and s pouring into all these vessels;
Ne 2:18 Then they said, "Let us s building!"
2:20 and we his servants are going to s building;
Lk 14:9 in disgrace you would s to take the lowest place.
Tob 5:17 Before he went out to s his journey,

STARTED (18) [START]

Ex 22:6 the one who s the fire shall make full restitution.
Jos 18:8 So the men s on their way;
Jdg 19:22 surrounded the house, and s pounding on the door.
Ru 1:6 Then she s to return with her daughters-in-law
Mt 14:29 Peter got out of the boat, s walking on the water,
15:22 that region came out and s shouting, "Have mercy
Lk 2:43 When the festival was ended and they s to return,
2:44 Then they s to look for him among their relatives
Jn 4:3 he left Judea and s back to Galilee.
4:50 the word that Jesus spoke to him and s on his way.
5:16 Therefore the Jews s persecuting Jesus,
6:17 and s across the sea to Capernaum.
Ac 21:15 After these days we got ready and s to go up
Gal 3:3 Having s with the Spirit, are you now ending with
Sir 47:23 of Nebat led Israel into sin and s Ephraim
1Mc 9:60 He s to come with a large force,
16:5 the morning they s out and marched into the plain,
2Es 16:6 quench a fire in the stubble once it has s to burn?

STARTING (4) [START]

Ge 31:21 s out he crossed the Euphrates, and set his face
Nu 33:2 Moses wrote down their s points, stage by stage,
33:2 these are their stages according to their s places.
Ac 8:35 Philip began to speak, and s with this scripture,

STARTLE (1) [STARTLED]

Isa 52:15 so he shall s many nations;

STARTLED (2) [STARTLE]

Ru 3:8 At midnight the man was s, and turned over,
Lk 24:37 They were s and terrified,

STARTS (1) [START]

Pr 26:27 a stone will come back on the one who s it rolling.

STARVING (1)

2Ki 7:12 They know that we are s;

STATE‡ (17) [STATED, STATEMENT, STATEMENTS, STATES, STATING]

Lev 7:20 a s of uncleanness shall be cut off from their kin.
22:3 while he is in a s of uncleanness,
Eze 4:3 set your face toward it, and let it be in a s of siege,
16:55 and her daughters shall return to their former s,
16:55 and her daughters shall return to their former s,
16:55 and your daughters shall return to your former s.
Da 8:14 the sanctuary shall be restored to its rightful s."
Mt 12:45 and the last s of that person is worse than the first.
Lk 11:26 the last s of that person is worse than the first."
Ac 23:30 also to s before you what they have against him."
2Pe 2:20 the last s has become worse for them than the first.
2Mc 4:30 While such was the s of affairs,
1Es 3:5 "Let each of us s what one thing is strongest;
3Mc 3:26 for ourselves in good order and in the best s.
5:45 when the animals had been brought virtually to a s
2Es 1:36 yet will recall their former s.
4Mc 5:1 in s with his counselors on a certain high place,

STATED (2) [STATE]

Lk 2:24 and they offered a sacrifice according to what is s
2Mc 3:9 that had been made and s why he had come,

STATELINESS (1) [STATELY]

Sir 45:7 He blessed him with s, and put a glorious robe on

STATELY (6) [STATELINESS]

Pr 30:29 things are s in their stride; four are s in their gait:
SS 7:7 You are s as a palm tree,
Isa 33:21 with oars can go, nor s ship can pass.
Eze 23:41 you sat on a s couch, with a table spread before it
Sir 26:17 so is a beautiful face on a s figure.

STATEMENT (5) [STATE]

Ac 28:25 and as they were leaving, Paul made one further s:
2Co 4:2 by the open s of the truth we commend ourselves
1Es 3:5 and to the one whose s seems wisest,
3:8 Then each wrote his own s,
3:9 to the one whose s the king and the three nobles

STATEMENTS (1) [STATE]

1Es 3:16 and they shall explain their s."

STATER See Index to Footnotes

STATES (1) [STATE]

Pr 18:17 The one who first s a case seems right,

STATING (4) [STATE]

1Mc 12:7 s that you are our brothers,
2Mc 9:13 who would no longer have mercy on him, s
14:27 s that he was displeased with the covenant
4Mc 1:12 I shall begin by s my main principle,

STATION (2) [STATIONED, STATIONS]

Hab 2: 1 and s myself on the rampart;
1Mc 10:32 he may s in it men of his own choice to guard it.

STATIONED (30) [STATION]

Jos 8:13 So they s the forces, the main encampment
Jdg 20:29 So Israel s men in ambush around Gibeah.
20:36 in ambush that they had s against Gibeah.
1Ki 10:26 which he s in the chariot cities and with the king
2Ki 10:24 Now Jehu had s eighty men outside, saying,
1Ch 9:18 s previously in the king's gate on the east side.
2Ch 1:14 which he s in the chariot cities and with the king
9:25 which he s in the chariot cities and with the king
23:19 He s the gatekeepers at the gates of the house of
29:25 He s the Levites in the house of the LORD
Ezr 3:10 in their vestments were s to praise the LORD
Ne 4:13 I s the people according to their families,
Isa 21: 8 and at my post I am s throughout the night.
Da 1: 5 so that at the end of that time they could be s in
1:19 therefore they were s in the king's court.
6: 1 s throughout the whole kingdom,
Jdt 3: 6 with his army and s garrisons in the fortified towns
1Mc 1:34 They s there a sinful people,
4:61 Judas s a garrison there to guard it;
5:42 he s the officers of the army at the stream
6:35 with each elephant they s a thousand men armed
6:38 The rest of the cavalry were s on either side,
6:50 king took Beth-zur and s a guard there to hold it.
10:37 Let some of them be s in the great strongholds of
11: 3 But when Ptolemy entered the towns he s forces as
12:27 and he s outposts around the camp.
12:34 And he s a garrison there to guard it.
15:41 up Kedron and s horsemen and troops there,
2Mc 15:20 the elephants strategically s and
15:31 and had called his compatriots together and s

STATIONS (3) [STATION]

Ne 13:11 I gathered them together and set them in their s.
Jer 46: 4 Take your s with your helmets, whet your lances,
46:14 Say, "Take your s and be ready,

STATISTICS (1)

2Mc 2:24 the flood of s involved and the difficulty there is

STATUE (17) [STATUES]

Da 2:31 and lo! there was a great s. This s was huge,
2:32 The head of that s was of fine gold,
2:34 the s on its feet of iron and clay and broke them
2:35 the stone that struck the s became a great mountain
3: 1 a golden s whose height was sixty cubits
3: 2 to assemble and come to the dedication of the s
3: 3 of the s that King Nebuchadnezzar had set up.
3: 3 before the s that Nebuchadnezzar had set up.
3: 5 the golden s that King Nebuchadnezzar has set up.
3: 7 the golden s that King Nebuchadnezzar had set up.
3:10 shall fall down and worship the golden s,
3:12 not worship the golden s that you have set up."
3:14 not worship the golden s that I have set up?
3:15 to fall down and worship the s that I have made,
3:18 not worship the golden s that you have set up."
Ac 19:35 the temple keeper of the great Artemis and of the s

STATUES (1) [STATUE]

2Mc 2: 2 in their thoughts on seeing the gold and silver s

STATURE‡ (10)

1Sa 2:26 to grow both in s and in favor with the LORD and
16: 7 on the height of his s, because I have rejected him;
1Ch 11:23 And he killed an Egyptian, a man of great s,
Isa 45:14 tall of s, shall come over to you and be yours,
Lk 19: 3 because he was short in s.
Eph 4:13 to maturity, to the measure of the full s of Christ.
Bar 3:26 who were famous of old, great in s, expert in war.
2Es 2:43 In their midst was a young man of great s,
5:52 whom you bore before, but smaller in s?'
5:54 in s than those who were before you,

STATUS (2)

3Mc 2:28 to a registration involving poll tax and to the s
2:29 shall also be reduced to their former limited s."

STATUTE (30) [STATUTES]

Ge 47:26 Joseph made it a s concerning the land of Egypt,
Ex 15:25 the LORD made for them a s and an ordinance
Lev 3:17 be a perpetual s throughout your generations,
10: 9 it is a s forever throughout your generations.
16:29 This shall be a s to you forever:
16:31 and you shall deny yourselves; it is a s forever.
16:34 This shall be an everlasting s for you,
17: 7 a s forever to them throughout their generations.
23:14 it is a s forever throughout your generations
23:21 This is a s forever in all your settlements
23:31 it is a s forever throughout your generations
23:41 as a s forever throughout your generations.
24: 3 it shall be a s forever throughout your generations.
Nu 9:12 to all the s for the passover they shall keep it.
9:14 so according to the s of the passover and according
9:14 you shall have one s for both the resident alien and
15:15 and the resident alien a single s, a perpetual statute
15:15 a perpetual s throughout your generations;
18:23 be a perpetual s throughout your generations.
19: 2 a s of the law that the LORD has commanded:
Nu 19:10 This shall be a perpetual s for the Israelites and for
19:21 It shall be a perpetual s for them.
27:11 It shall be for the Israelites a s and ordinance,
31:21 "This is the s of the law that
35:29 These things shall be a s and ordinance for you
1Sa 30:25 that day forward he made it a s and an ordinance
1Ch 16:17 which he confirmed to Jacob as a s,
Ps 81: 4 For it is a s for Israel,
94:20 those who contrive mischief by s?
105:10 which he confirmed to Jacob as a s,

STATUTES (142) [STATUTE]

Ge 26: 5 my commandments, my s, and my laws."
Ex 15:26 give heed to his commandments and keep all his s,
18:16 and I make known to them the s and instructions
18:20 teach them the s and instructions and make known
Lev 10:11 and you are to teach the people of Israel all the s
18: 3 You shall not follow their s.
18: 4 and my s you shall keep, following them:
18: 5 You shall keep my s and my ordinances;
18:26 But you shall keep my s and my ordinances
19:19 You shall keep my s.
19:37 You shall keep all my s and all my ordinances,
20: 8 Keep my s, and observe them;
20:22 You shall keep all my s and all my ordinances,
25:18 You shall observe my s
26: 3 If you follow my s and keep my commandments
26:15 if you spurn my s, and abhor my ordinances,
26:43 to spurn my ordinances, and they abhorred my s.
26:46 These are the s and ordinances and laws that
Nu 9: 3 to all its s and all its regulations you shall keep it.
30:16 the s that the LORD commanded Moses
Dt 4: 1 to the s and ordinances that I am teaching you
4: 5 now teach you s and ordinances for you to observe
4: 6 who, when they hear all these s, will say,
4: 8 And what other great nation has s and ordinances
4:14 to teach you s and ordinances for you to observe in
4:40 Keep his s and his commandments,
4:45 These are the decrees and the s and ordinances
5: 1 the s and ordinances that I am addressing
5:31 the s and the ordinances, that you shall teach them,
6: 1 the s and the ordinances—
6:17 and his s that he has commanded you.
6:20 "What is the meaning of the decrees and the s and
6:24 the LORD commanded us to observe all these s,
7:11 the s, and the ordinances—
8:11 and his s, which I am commanding you today.
11:32 the s and ordinances that I am setting
12: 1 These are the s and ordinances
16:12 and diligently observe these s.
17:19 the words of this law and these s,
26:16 to observe these s and ordinances;
26:17 and for you to walk in his ways, to keep his s,
27:10 and his s that I am commanding you today.
Jos 24:25 and made s and ordinances for them at Shechem.
2Sa 22:23 and from his s I did not turn aside.
1Ki 2: 3 walking in his ways and keeping his s,
3: 3 walking in the s of his father David;
3:14 keeping my s and my commandments,
6:12 if you will walk in my s, obey my ordinances,
8:58 and to keep his commandments, his s,
8:61 walking in his s and keeping his commandments,
9: 4 and keeping my s and my ordinances,
9: 6 and do not keep my commandments and my s
11:11 and you have not kept my covenant and my s
11:33 in my sight and keeping my s and my ordinances,
11:34 and who did keep my commandments and my s;
11:38 and do what is right in my sight by keeping my s
2Ki 17:13 and keep my commandments and my s,
17:15 They despised his s, and his covenant
17:34 and they do not follow the s or the ordinances or
17:37 The s and the ordinances and the law and
23: 3 keeping his commandments, his decrees, and his s,
1Ch 22:13 to observe the s and the ordinances that
29:19 your decrees, and your s, performing all of them,
2Ch 7:17 that I have commanded you and keeping my s
7:19 and forsake my s and my commandments
19:10 s or ordinances, then you shall instruct them,
33: 8 the s, and the ordinances given through Moses."
34:31 keeping his commandments, his decrees, and his s,
Ezr 7:10 and to teach the s and ordinances in Israel.
7:11 of the commandments of the LORD and his s
Ne 1: 7 failing to keep the commandments, the s,
9:13 good s and commandments,
9:14 to them and gave them commandments and s and
10:29 the LORD our Lord and his ordinances and his s.
Ps 18:22 and his s I did not put away from me.
50:16 "What right have you to recite my s,
89:31 if they violate my s and do
99: 7 they kept his decrees, and the s that he gave them.
105:45 that they might keep his s and observe his laws.
119: 5 that my ways may be steadfast in keeping your s!
119: 8 I will observe your s; do not utterly forsake me.
119:12 Blessed are you, O LORD; teach me your s.
119:16 I will delight in your s;
119:23 your servant will meditate on your s.
119:26 you answered me; teach me your s.
119:33 Teach me, O LORD, the way of your s,
119:48 which I love, and I will meditate on your s.
119:54 Your s have been my songs wherever I make my
119:64 of your steadfast love; teach me your s.
119:68 You are good and do good; teach me your s.
119:71 so that I might learn your s.
119:80 May my heart be blameless in your s,
119:83 yet I have not forgotten your s.
119:112 I incline my heart to perform your s forever,
Ps 119:117 be safe and have regard for your s continually.
119:118 You spurn all who go astray from your s;
119:124 to your steadfast love, and teach me your s.
119:135 upon your servant, and teach me your s.
119:145 I will keep your s.
119:155 for they do not seek your s.
119:171 because you teach me your s.
147:19 his s and ordinances to Israel.
Isa 10: 1 make iniquitous decrees, who write oppressive s,
24: 5 for they have transgressed laws, violated the s,
Jer 44:10 nor have they walked in my law and my s that I set
44:23 or walk in his law and in his s and in his decrees,
Eze 5: 6 she has rebelled against my ordinances and my s,
5: 6 rejecting my ordinances and not following my s.
5: 7 have not followed my s or kept my ordinances,
11:12 whose s you have not followed,
11:20 that they may follow my s and keep my ordinances
18: 9 follows my s, and is careful
18:17 observes my ordinances, and follows my s;
18:19 and has been careful to observe all my s,
18:21 and keep all my s and do what is lawful and right,
20:11 I gave them my s and showed them my ordinances,
20:13 not observe my s but rejected my ordinances,
20:16 not observe my s, and profaned my sabbaths;
20:18 Do not follow the s of your parents,
20:19 I the LORD am your God; follow my s,
20:21 they did not follow my s, and were not careful
20:24 but had rejected my s and profaned my sabbaths,
20:25 Moreover I gave them s that were not good
33:15 and walk in the s of life, committing no iniquity—
36:27 and make you follow my s and be careful
37:24 and be careful to observe my s.
44:24 and my s regarding all my appointed festivals,
Am 2: 4 the law of the LORD, and have not kept his s,
Mic 6:16 For you have kept the s of Omri and all the works
Zec 1: 6 But my words and my s,
Mal 3: 7 of your ancestors you have turned aside from my s
4: 4 the s and ordinances that I commanded him
Sir 6:37 Reflect on the s of the Lord,
45:17 In his commandments he gave him authority and s
Bar 1:18 to walk in the s of the Lord that he set before us.
2:10 to walk in the s of the Lord that he set before us.
4:13 They had no regard for his s;
2Es 1:24 so that they may keep my s.
7:11 and when Adam transgressed my s,
7:24 they have been unfaithful to his s,
9:32 they did not keep it and did not observe the s;
13:42 at least they might keep their s that they had

STAUNCH (1)

4Mc 3:12 two s young soldiers, respecting the king's desire,

STAVES (KJV) See ARROWS, CLUBS, POLES, STAFF, STAFFS, STICKS

STAY (84) [STAYED, STAYING, STAYS]

Ge 19:30 for he was afraid to s in Zoar;
22: 5 Then Abraham said to his young men, "S here
27:44 and s with him a while,
29:19 to any other man; s with me."
42:19 of your brothers s here where you are imprisoned.
Ex 2:21 Moses agreed to s with the man,
9:28 I will let you go; you need s no longer."
16:29 each of you s where you are;
Nu 20:19 Israelites said to him, "We will s on the highway;
22: 8 He said to them, "S here tonight,
23: 3 "S here beside your burnt offerings
32:17 Meanwhile our little ones will s in the fortified
Dt 3:19 shall s behind in the towns that I have given
Jos 8: 4 not go very far from the city, but all of you s alert.
10:19 but do not s there yourselves;
Jdg 6:18 And he said, "I will s until you return."
17:10 Then Micah said to him, "S with me,
17:11 The Levite agreed to s with the man;
19: 4 His father-in-law, the girl's father, made him s,
Ru 2:21 "He even said to me, 'S close by my servants,
1Sa 19: 2 s in a secret place and hide yourself.
22:23 S with me, and do not be afraid;
2Sa 15:19 Go back, and s with the king;
19: 7 not a man will s with you this night;
22:19 but the LORD was my s.
24:16 "It is enough; now s your hand."
2Ki 2: 2 Elijah said to Elisha, "S here;
2: 4 Elijah said to him, "Elisha, s here;
2: 6 Then Elijah said to him, "S here;
4:10 so that he can s there whenever he comes to us."
14:10 Be content with your glory, and s at home;
15:20 and did not s there in the land.
1Ch 21:15 to the destroying angel, "Enough! S your hand."
2Ch 23: 7 S with the king in his comings and goings."
25:19 Now s at home; why should you provoke trouble
Ne 5: 2 we must get grain, so that we may eat and s alive."
Job 24:13 and do not s in its paths.
Ps 32: 9 else it will not s near you.
68:13 though they s among the sheepfolds—
Pr 7:11 her feet do not s at home;
Jer 17: 8 and its leaves shall s green;
21: 9 Those who s in this city shall die by the sword,
27:22 be carried to Babylon, and there they shall s, until
38: 2 Those who s in this city shall die by the sword,
40: 5 and s with him among the people;
40: 9 S in the land and serve the king of Babylon,
42:13 if you continue to say, 'We will not s in this land,'
42:14 or be hungry for bread, and there we will s,'
43: 4 to s in the land of Judah.

La 4:15 "They shall s here no longer."
Da 4:35 There is no one who can s his hand or say to him,
Mt 10:11 and s there until you leave.
26:38 remain here, and s awake with me."
26:40 "So, could you not s awake with me one hour?
26:41 S awake and pray that you may not come into
Mk 6:10 s there until you leave the place.
Lk 9: 4 Whatever house you enter, s there,
19: 5 for I must s at your house today."
24:29 But they urged him strongly, saying, "S with us,
24:29 So he went in to s with them.
24:49 so s here in the city until you have been clothed
Jn 4:40 they asked him to s with them;
Ac 10:48 Then they invited him to s for several days.
13:17 the people great during their s in the land of Egypt,
16:15 come and s at my home."
18:20 When they asked him to s longer, he declined;
21:16 an early disciple, with whom we were to s.
27:31 "Unless these men s in the ship,
28:14 and were invited to s with them for seven days.
1Co 16: 6 perhaps I will s with you or even spend the winter,
16: 8 But I will s in Ephesus until Pentecost,
Tob 5: 6 and would s with our kinsman Gabael who lives
6:11 "We must s this night in the home of Raguel.
8:20 but shall s here eating and drinking with me;
10: 8 Raguel said to Tobias, "S, my child, s with me;
14:10 do not s overnight within the confines of the city.
Sir 1:23 Those who are patient s calm until
7: 2 S away from wrong, and it will turn away
22:13 S clear of him, or you may have trouble,
1Mc 12:45 and choose for yourself a few men to s with you,
1Es 9:12 So let the leaders of the multitude s,
3Mc 7:19 as a joyous festival during the time of their s.
2Es 10: 4 I intend not to return to the town, but to s here;

STAYED (58) [STAY]

Ge 28:11 to a certain place and s there for the night,
29:14 And he s with him a month.
32: 4 with Laban as an alien, and s until now;
45: 1 So no one s with him
Nu 20: 1 and the people s in Kadesh.
22: 8 so the officials of Moab s with Balaam.
Dt 1: 6 saying, "You have s long enough at this mountain.
1:46 you had s at Kadesh as many days as you did,
10:10 I s on the mountain forty days and forty nights,
Jos 2:22 into the hill country and s there three days,
Jdg 5:17 Gilead s beyond the Jordan;
15: 8 and he went down and s in the cleft of the rock
18: 2 to the house of Micah, they s there.
19: 4 so they ate and drank, and he s there.
Ru 2:23 So she s close to the young women of Boaz,
1Sa 13:16 the people who were present with them s in Geba
22: 4 and they s with him all the time that David was in
23:25 down to the rock and s in the wilderness of Maon.
27: 3 David s with Achish at Gath, he and his troops,
30: 9 where those s who were left behind.
30:10 two hundred s behind, too exhausted to cross
2Sa 13:38 having fled to Geshur, s there three years.
19:32 He had provided the king with food while he s
Est 7: 7 but Haman s to beg his life from Queen Esther,
Jer 39:14 So he s with his own people.
40: 6 and s with him among the people who were left in
Mt 24:43 the thief was coming, he would have s awake
Mk 1:45 but s out in the country;
Lk 2:43 the boy Jesus s behind in Jerusalem,
9:32 but since they had s awake,
Jn 4:40 and he s there two days.
6:22 The next day the crowd that had s on the other side
11: 6 he s two days longer in the place where he was.
11:20 she went and met him, while Mary s at home.
Ac 8:13 he s constantly with Philip and was amazed
9:43 Meanwhile he s in Joppa for some time with
12:19 down from Judea to Caesarea and s there.
14:28 And they s there with the disciples for some time.
18: 3 because he was of the same trade, he s with them,
18:11 He s there a year and six months,
19:22 while he himself s for some time longer in Asia.
20: 3 where he s for three months.
20: 6 where we s for seven days.
21: 4 up the disciples and s there for seven days.
21: 7 and we greeted the believers and s with them
21: 8 one of the seven, and s with him.
25: 6 After he had s among them not more than eight
28:12 We put in at Syracuse and s there for three days;
Gal 1:18 to visit Cephas and s with him fifteen days;
Heb 11: 9 By faith he s for a time in
Tob 9: 5 and two camels went to Rages in Media and s
Jdt 12: 9 Then she returned purified and s in the tent
14:17 Then he went to the tent where Judith had s,
Sir Pr: 3 of the reign of Euergetes and s for some time,
1Mc 3:13 of faithful soldiers who s with him and went out
11:40 and he s there many days.
2Mc 14:23 Nicanor s on in Jerusalem and did nothing out of
2Es 13:58 And I s there three days.

STAYING (14) [STAY]

Ge 36: 7 the land where they were s could not support them
Nu 25: 1 While Israel was s at Shittim,
1Sa 14: 2 Saul was s in the outskirts of Gibeah under
1Ki 17:20 even upon the widow with whom I am s,
Jer 40:10 I am s at Mizpah to represent you before
Jn 1:38 translated means Teacher), "where are you s?"
1:39 They came and saw where he was s,
Ac 1: 4 While s with them, he ordered them not
1:13 they went to the room upstairs where they were s,
10:18 who was called Peter, was s there.
10:32 he is s in the home of Simon, a tanner, by the sea.'
18:18 After s there for a considerable time,
21:10 While we were s there for several days,
25:14 Since they were s there several days,

STAYS (8) [STAY]

1Sa 30:24 as the share of the one who s by the baggage;
2Sa 7: 2 but the ark of God s in a tent."
15:25 and let me see both it and the place where it s.
1Ki 7:35 its s and its borders were of one piece with it.
7:36 of its s and on its borders he carved cherubim,
2Ki 6:31 of Elisha son of Shaphat s on his shoulders today."
Rev 16:15 Blessed is the one who s awake and is clothed,
Wis 5:14 like the remembrance of a guest who s but a day.

STEAD (1)

1Mc 14:17 in his s, and that he was ruling over the country

STEADFAST‡ (193) [STEADFASTLY, STEADFASTNESS]

A. STEADFAST LOVE (172)
B. STEADFAST LOVE ENDURES FOREVER (43)
C. STEADFAST LOVE AND ... FAITHFULNESS (16)

Ge 24:12 please grant me success today and show s love A
24:14 By this I shall know that you have shown s love A
24:27 not forsaken his s love and his faithfulness AC
32:10 least of all the s love and all the faithfulness AC
39:21 LORD was with Joseph and showed him s love; A
Ex 15:13 "In your s love you led the people A
20: 6 but showing s love to the thousandth generation A
34: 6 and abounding in s love and faithfulness, AC
34: 7 keeping s love for the thousandth generation, A
Nu 14:18 in s love, forgiving iniquity and transgression, A
14:19 according to the greatness of your s love, A
Dt 5:10 but showing s love to the thousandth generation A
Jos 23: 6 be very s to observe and do all that is written in
2Sa 2: 6 may the LORD show s love and faithfulness AC
7:15 But I will not take my s love from him, A
15:20 may the LORD show s love and faithfulness AC
22:51 and shows s love to his anointed, A
1Ki 3: 6 and s love to your servant my father David, A
3: 6 and you have kept for him this great and s love, A
8:23 s love for your servants who walk before you A
1Ch 16:34 for his s love endures forever. AB
16:41 for his s love endures forever. AB
17:13 I will not take my s love from him, A
2Ch 1: 8 "You have shown great and s love A
5:13 For he is good, for his s love endures forever, AB
6:14 s love with your servants who walk before you A
6:42 Remember your s love for your servant David." A
7: 3 For he is good, for his s love endures forever. AB
7: 6 for his s love endures forever— AB
20:21 for his s love endures forever." AB
Ezr 3:11 for his s love endures forever toward Israel." AB
7:28 to me s love before the king and his counselors, A
9: 9 has extended to us his s love before the kings A
Ne 1: 5 awesome God who keeps covenant and s love A
9:17 slow to anger and abounding in s love, A
9:32 keeping covenant and s love— A
13:22 according to the greatness of your s love. A
Job 10:12 You have granted me life and s love, A
Ps 5: 7 But I, through the abundance of your s love, A
6: 4 deliver me for the sake of your s love. A
13: 5 But I trusted in your s love; A
17: 7 Wondrously show your s love, A
18:50 and shows s love to his anointed, A
21: 7 s love of the Most High he shall not be moved. A
25: 6 of your s love, for they have been from of old. A
25: 7 according to your s love remember me, A
25:10 paths of the LORD are s love and faithfulness, AC
26: 3 For your s love is before my eyes, A
31: 7 I will exult and rejoice in your s love, A
31:16 save me in your s love. A
31:21 for he has wondrously shown his s love to me A
32:10 s love surrounds those who trust in the LORD. A
33: 5 the earth is full of the s love of the LORD. A
33:18 on those who hope in his s love, A
33:22 Let your s love, O LORD, be upon us, A
36: 5 Your s love, O LORD, extends to the heavens, A
36: 7 How precious is your s love, O God! A
36:10 O continue your s love to those who know you, A
40:10 not concealed your s love and your faithfulness AC
40:11 your s love and your faithfulness keep me safe AC
42: 8 By day the LORD commands his s love, A
44:26 Redeem us for the sake of your s love. A
48: 9 We ponder your s love, O God, in the midst A
51: 1 O God, according to your s love; A
52: 8 I trust in the s love of God forever and ever. A
57: 3 will send forth his s love and his faithfulness. AC
57: 7 My heart is s, O God, my heart is s.
57:10 For your s love is as high as the heavens; A
59:10 My God in his s love will meet me; A
59:16 I will sing aloud of your s love in the morning. A
59:17 are my fortress, the God who shows me s love. A
61: 7 s love and faithfulness to watch over him! AC
62:12 and s love belongs to you, A
63: 3 Because your s love is better than life, A
66:20 not rejected my prayer or removed his s love A
69:13 in the abundance of your s love, answer me. A
69:16 Answer me, O LORD, for your s love is good; A
77: 8 Has his s love ceased forever? A
78: 8 a generation whose heart was not s,
78:37 Their heart was not s toward him;
85: 7 Show us your s love, O LORD, A
Ps 85:10 S love and faithfulness will meet; AC
86: 5 abounding in s love to all who call on you. A
86:13 For great is your s love toward me; A
86:15 and abounding in s love and faithfulness. AC
88:11 Is your s love declared in the grave, A
89: 1 I will sing of your s love, O LORD, forever; A
89: 2 I declare that your s love is established forever; A
89:14 s love and faithfulness go before you. AC
89:24 My faithfulness and s love shall be with him; A
89:28 Forever I will keep my s love for him, A
89:33 but I will not remove from him my s love, A
89:49 where is your s love of old, A
90:14 Satisfy us in the morning with your s love, A
92: 2 to declare your s love in the morning, A
94:18 I thought, "My foot is slipping," your s love, A
98: 3 He has remembered his s love and faithfulness AC
100: 5 the LORD is good; his s love endures forever, AB
103: 4 who crowns you with s love and mercy, A
103: 8 slow to anger and abounding in s love. A
103:11 so great is his s love toward those who fear him; A
103:17 But the s love of the LORD is from everlasting A
106: 1 for his s love endures forever. AB
106: 7 not remember the abundance of your s love, A
106:45 according to the abundance of his s love. A
107: 1 for his s love endures forever. AB
107: 8 Let them thank the LORD for his s love, A
107:15 Let them thank the LORD for his s love, A
107:21 Let them thank the LORD for his s love, A
107:31 Let them thank the LORD for his s love, A
107:43 and consider the s love of the LORD. A
108: 1 My heart is s, O God, my heart is s;
108: 4 For your s love is higher than the heavens, A
109:21 because your s love is good, deliver me. A
109:26 Save me according to your s love. A
115: 1 the sake of your s love and your faithfulness. AC
117: 2 For great is his s love toward us, A
118: 1 his s love endures forever! AB
118: 2 Let Israel say, "His s love endures forever." AB
118: 3 "His s love endures forever." AB
118: 4 "His s love endures forever." AB
118:29 for he is good, for his s love endures forever. AB
119: 5 O that my ways may be s in keeping your statutes!
119:41 Let your s love come to me, O LORD, A
119:64 The earth, O LORD, is full of your s love; A
119:76 Let your s love become my comfort according A
119:88 In your s love spare my life, A
119:124 Deal with your servant according to your s love, A
119:149 In your s love hear my voice; A
119:159 preserve my life according to your s love. A
130: 7 For with the LORD there is s love, A
136: 1 for he is good, for his s love endures forever. AB
136: 2 for his s love endures forever. AB
136: 3 for his s love endures forever; AB
136: 4 for his s love endures forever; AB
136: 5 for his s love endures forever; AB
136: 6 for his s love endures forever; AB
136: 7 for his s love endures forever; AB
136: 8 for his s love endures forever; AB
136: 9 for his s love endures forever; AB
136:10 for his s love endures forever; AB
136:11 for his s love endures forever; AB
136:12 for his s love endures forever; AB
136:13 for his s love endures forever; AB
136:14 for his s love endures forever; AB
136:15 for his s love endures forever; AB
136:16 for his s love endures forever; AB
136:17 for his s love endures forever; AB
136:18 for his s love endures forever; AB
136:19 for his s love endures forever; AB
136:20 for his s love endures forever; AB
136:21 for his s love endures forever; AB
136:22 for his s love endures forever. AB
136:23 for his s love endures forever; AB
136:24 for his s love endures forever; AB
136:25 for his s love endures forever. AB
136:26 for his s love endures forever. AB
138: 2 for your s love and your faithfulness; AC
138: 8 your s love, O LORD, endures forever. AB
143: 8 Let me hear of your s love in the morning, A
143:12 In your s love cut off my enemies, A
145: 8 slow to anger and abounding in s love. A
147:11 in those who hope in his s love. A
Pr 11:19 Whoever is s in righteousness will live,
Isa 16: 5 a throne shall be established in s love in the tent A
26: 3 Those of s mind you keep in peace—
54:10 but my s love shall not depart from you, A
55: 3 my s, sure love for David.
63: 7 according to the abundance of his s love. A
Jer 9:24 s love, justice, and righteousness in the earth, A
16: 5 says the LORD, my s love and mercy. A
32:18 You show s love to the thousandth generation, A
33:11 for his s love endures forever!" AB
La 3:22 The s love of the LORD never ceases, A
3:32 according to the abundance of his s love; A
Da 9: 4 and s love with those who love you A
Hos 2:19 in righteousness and in justice, in s love, A
6: 6 For I desire s love and not sacrifice, A
10:12 Sow for yourselves righteousness; reap s love; A
Joel 2:13 slow to anger, and abounding in s love, A
Jnh 4: 2 slow to anger, and abounding in s love, A
Ac 11:23 to remain faithful to the Lord with s devotion;
1Co 15:58 Therefore, my beloved, be s, immovable,
Col 1:23 that you continue securely established and s in
Heb 6:19 We have this hope, a sure and s anchor of the soul,
1Pe 5: 9 Resist him, s in your faith,
AdE 13: 3 and s fidelity, and has attained the second place in
Wis 7:23 humane, s, sure, free from anxiety, all-powerful,

Sir 2: 2 Set your heart right and be s,
26:18 so are shapely legs and s feet.
27: 3 If a person is not s in the fear of the Lord,

STEADFASTLY (2) [STEADFAST]

2Sa 20: 2 but the people of Judah followed their king s from
4Mc 9:28 But he s endured this agony and said,

STEADFASTNESS (8) [STEADFAST]

Ro 15: 4 so that by s and by the encouragement of
15: 5 the God of s and encouragement grant you to live
1Th 1: 3 of love and s of hope in our Lord Jesus Christ.
2Th 1: 4 for your s and faith during all your persecutions
3: 5 to the love of God and to the s of Christ.
2Ti 3:10 my faith, my patience, my love, my s,
4Mc 15:30 O more noble than males in s,
16:14 By s you have conquered even a tyrant,

STEADILY (3) [STEADY]

2Ch 17:12 Jehoshaphat grew s greater.
1Mc 6:40 and they advanced s and in good order.
2Es 15:43 They shall go on s to Babylon and blot it out.

STEADY (4) [STEADILY]

Ex 17:12 so his hands were s until the sun set.
Ps 75: 3 with all its inhabitants, it is I who keep its pillars s.
112: 8 Their hearts are s, they will not be afraid;
119:133 Keep my steps s according to your promise,

STEAL (24) [STEALING, STEALS, STOLE, STOLEN]

Ge 31:30 why did you s my gods?"
44: 8 why then would we s silver or gold
Ex 20:15 You shall not s.
Lev 19:11 You shall not s; you shall not deal falsely;
19:13 not defraud your neighbor; you shall not s;
Dt 5:19 Neither shall you s.
2Sa 19: 3 The troops stole into the city that day as soldiers s
Ps 69: 4 What I did not s must I now restore?
Pr 6:30 not despised who s only to satisfy their appetite
30: 9 be poor, and s, and profane the name of my God.
Jer 7: 9 Will you s, murder, commit adultery,
23:30 who s my words from one another.
Ob 1: 5 would they not s only what they wanted?
Mt 6:19 and where thieves break in and s;
6:20 and where thieves do not break in and s.
19:18 You shall not commit adultery; You shall not s;
27:64 otherwise his disciples may go and s him away,
Mk 10:19 You shall not commit adultery; You shall not s;
Lk 18:20 You shall not murder; You shall not s;
Jn 10:10 The thief comes only to s and kill and destroy.
12: 6 the common purse and used to s what was put
Ro 2:21 While you preach against stealing, do you s?
13: 9 You shall not murder; You shall not s;
1Es 4:23 and goes out to travel and rob and s and to sail

STEALING (4) [STEAL]

Job 4:12 "Now a word came s to me,
Hos 4: 2 lying, and murder, and s and adultery break out;
Ro 2:21 While you preach against s, do you steal?
Eph 4:28 Thieves must give up s; rather let them labor

STEALS (3) [STEAL]

Ex 22: 1 When someone s an ox or a sheep,
Zec 5: 3 for everyone who s shall be cut off according to
1Es 4:24 and when he s and robs and plunders,

STEALTH (2) [STEALTHILY]

Mt 26: 4 they conspired to arrest Jesus by s and kill him.
Mk 14: 1 for a way to arrest Jesus by s and kill him;

STEALTH (KJV) See also STOLE

STEALTHILY (3) [STEALTH]

Ru 3: 7 she came s and uncovered his feet, and lay down.
1Sa 24: 4 David went and s cut off a corner of Saul's cloak.
Ps 10: 8 Their eyes s watch for the helpless;

STEDFAST (KJV) See ENDURING, FIRM, SECURE, STEADFAST, UNSHAKEN, VALID

STEEDS (8)

Jdg 5:22 with the galloping, galloping of his s.
1Ki 4:28 and straw for the horses and swift s,
Est 8:10 by mounted couriers riding on fast s bred from
8:14 So the couriers, mounted on their swift royal s,
Isa 30:16 and, "We will ride upon swift s"—
Jer 46: 4 Harness the horses; mount the s!
Mic 1:13 Harness the s to the chariots,
Zec 6: 7 the s came out, they were impatient to get off

STEEL (KJV) See BRONZE; See also Index to Footnotes

STEEP (6)

Isa 7:19 And they will all come and settle in the s ravines,
Mic 1: 4 like waters poured down a s place.
Mt 8:32 the s bank into the sea and perished in the water.
Mk 5:13 rushed down the s bank into the sea,
Lk 8:33 and the herd rushed down the s bank into the lake
2Mc 14:45 and standing upon a s rock,

STEERED (1) [STEERING, STEERING-OARS, STEERS]

4Mc 7: 1 of our father Eleazar s the ship of religion over

STEERING (1) [STEERED]

Wis 10: 4 s the righteous man by a paltry piece of wood.

STEERING-OARS (1) [OAR, STEERED]

Ac 27:40 the ropes that tied the s;

STEERS‡ (3) [STEERED]

Isa 34: 7 and young s with the mighty bulls.
Tob 8:19 and brought two s and four rams and ordered them
Wis 14: 3 it is your providence, O Father, that s its course,

STELE See Index to Footnotes

STEM (5)

Isa 40:24 scarcely has their s taken root in the earth,
Eze 19:11 Its strongest s became a ruler's scepter;
19:12 its strong s was withered; the fire consumed it.
19:14 And fire has gone out from its s,
19:14 so that there remains in it no strong s,

STEM (KJV) See also STUMP

STEMS See Index to Footnotes

STENCH (8)

Isa 3:24 Instead of perfume there will be a s;
34: 3 and the s of their corpses shall rise;
Joel 2:20 its s and foul smell will rise up.
Am 4:10 I made the s of your camp go up into your nostrils;
Jn 11:39 a s because he has been dead four days."
2Mc 9: 9 of the s the whole army felt revulsion at his decay.
9:10 Because of his intolerable s no one was able
9:12 And when he could not endure his own s,

STEP (10) [DOORSTEP, FOOTSTEPS, OVERSTEPPING, STEPPED, STEPPING, STEPS]

1Sa 5: 5 and all who enter the house of Dagon do not s on
20: 3 there is but a s between me and death."
1Ki 10:20 one on each end of a s on the six steps.
2Ch 9:19 one on each end of a s on the six steps.
Job 31: 7 if my s has turned aside from the way,
Pr 4:12 When you walk, your s will not be hampered;
Eze 26:16 Then all the princes of the sea shall s down
Ac 11: 4 Then Peter began to explain it to them, s by s,
Wis 13:18 a prosperous journey, a thing that cannot take a s;

STEPHANAS (3)

1Co 1:16 (I did baptize also the household of S;
16:15 of the household of S were the first converts
16:17 at the coming of S and Fortunatus and Achaicus,

STEPHEN (9)

Ac 6: 5 pleased the whole community, and they chose S,
6: 8 S, full of grace and power, did great wonders
6: 9 stood up and argued with S.
7: 2 And S replied: "Brothers and fathers, listen to me.
7:54 they became enraged and ground their teeth at S.
7:59 While they were stoning S, he prayed,
8: 2 Devout men buried S and made loud lamentation
11:19 that took place over S traveled as far as Phoenicia,
22:20 And while the blood of your witness S was shed,

STEPPE (2)

1Ch 6:78 Bezer in the s with its pasture lands,
Job 39: 6 to which I have given the s for its home,

STEPPED‡ (4) [STEP]

Ge 44:18 Then Judah s up to him and said, "O my lord,
Mk 5: 2 And when he had s out of the boat,
Lk 8:27 As he s out on land,
Jn 18: 6 "I am he," they s back and fell to the ground.

STEPPING (1) [STEP]

Sir 9:13 Know that you are s among snares,

STEPS‡ (54) [STEP]

Ex 20:26 You shall not go up by s to my altar,
1Ki 10:19 The throne had six s.
10:20 one on each end of a step on the six s.
2Ki 9:13 and spread them for him on the bare s;
2Ch 9:11 the king made s for the house of the LORD and
9:18 The throne had six s and a footstool of gold,
9:19 one on each end of a step on the six s.
Job 14:16 For then you would not number my s,
18: 7 Their strong s are shortened,
23:11 My foot has held fast to his s;
29: 6 when my s were washed with milk,
31: 4 Does he not see my ways, and number all my s?
31:37 I would give him an account of all my s;
34:21 and he sees all their s.
Ps 17: 5 My s have held fast to your paths;
18:36 You gave me a wide place for my s under me,
37:23 Our s are made firm by the LORD,
37:31 of their God is in their hearts; their s do not slip.
40: 2 and set my feet upon a rock, making my s secure.
44:18 nor have our s departed from your way,
56: 6 They stir up strife, they lurk, they watch my s.
57: 6 They set a net for my s;
73: 2 feet had almost stumbled; my s had nearly slipped.
74: 3 Direct your s to the perpetual ruins;
85:13 and will make a path for his s.
119:128 Truly I direct my s by all your precepts;
119:133 Keep my s steady according to your promise,
Pr 5: 5 her s follow the path to Sheol.
14:15 but the clever consider their s.
16: 9 but the LORD directs the s.
20:24 All our s are ordered by the LORD;
Ecc 5: 1 Guard your s when you go to the house of God;
Isa 26: 6 the feet of the poor, the s of the needy.
38: 8 on the dial of Ahaz turn back ten s."
38: 8 on the dial the ten s by which it had declined.
Jer 10:23 that mortals as they walk cannot direct their s.
La 4:18 They dogged our s so that we could not walk
Eze 40: 6 going up its s, and measured the threshold of
40:22 Seven s led up to it;
40:26 There were seven s leading up to it;
40:31 and its stairway had eight s.
40:34 and its stairway had eight s.
40:37 and its stairway had eight s.
40:49 ten s led up to it;
43:17 Its s shall face east.
Hab 3:16 and my s tremble beneath me.
Jn 5: 7 someone else s down ahead of me."
Ac 21:35 When Paul came to the s,
21:40 on the s and motioned to the people for silence;
2Co 12:18 Did we not take the same s?
1Pe 2:21 so that you should follow in his s.
Sir 21: 6 Those who hate reproof walk in the sinner's s,
51:15 from my youth I followed her s.
2Mc 10:26 Falling upon the s before the altar,

STERILITY (1)

Dt 7:14 with neither s nor barrenness among you

STERN (8) [STERNLY]

Isa 21: 2 A s vision is told to me;
Mk 4:38 But he was in the s, asleep on the cushion;
Ac 27:29 they let down four anchors from the s and prayed
27:41 s was being broken up by the force of the waves.
Wis 5:20 and sharpen s wrath for a sword,
11:10 but you examined the ungodly as a s king does
12: 9 at one blow by dread wild animals or your s word.
18:15 the midst of the land that was doomed, a s warrior

STERNLY (12) [STERN]

Mt 9:30 Then Jesus s ordered them, "See that no one knows
16:20 Then he s ordered the disciples not to tell anyone
19:13 The disciples spoke s to those who brought them;
20:31 The crowd s ordered them to be quiet;
Mk 1:43 After s warning him he sent him away at once,
3:12 But he s ordered them not to make him known.
8:30 he s ordered them not to tell anyone about him.
10:13 and the disciples spoke s to them.
10:48 Many s ordered him to be quiet,
Lk 9:21 He s ordered and commanded them not
18:15 disciples saw it, they s ordered them not to do it.
18:39 Those who were in front s ordered him to be quiet;

STEW (7)

Ge 25:29 Once when Jacob was cooking a s,
25:34 Then Jacob gave Esau bread and lentil s,
2Ki 4:38 and make some s for the company of prophets."
4:39 and came and cut them up into the pot of s,
4:40 But while they were eating the s, they cried out,
Hag 2:12 and with the fold touches bread, or s, or wine,
Bel 1:33 he had made a s and had broken bread into a bowl,

STEWARD (13) [STEWARDS]

Ge 43:16 he said to the s of his house,
43:19 up to the s of Joseph's house and spoke with him
43:24 the s had brought the men into Joseph's house,
44: 1 Then he commanded the s of his house,
44: 4 Joseph said to his s, "Go, follow after the men;
2Ki 10: 5 So the s of the palace, and the governor of the city,
Isa 22:15 Come, go to this s, to Shebna,
Lk 8: 3 the wife of Herod's s Chuza, and Susanna,
Jn 2: 8 "Now draw some out, and take it to the chief s."
2: 9 When the s tasted the water that had become wine,
2: 9 the s called the bridegroom
Tit 1: 7 For a bishop, as God's s, must be blameless;
Jdt 14:13 They came to Holofernes' tent and said to the s

STEWARDS (7) [STEWARD]

1Ch 27:31 All these were s of King David's property.
28: 1 the s of all the property and cattle of the king
1Co 4: 1 as servants of Christ and s of God's mysteries.
4: 2 it is required of s that they be found trustworthy.
1Pe 4:10 Like good s of the manifold grace of God,
AdE 1: 8 to have it so, and he commanded his s to comply
1Es 8:67 They delivered the king's orders to the royal s and

STICK (19) [STICKING, STICKS, STUCK]

Dt 13:17 Do not let anything devoted to destruction **s**
2Ki 6: 6 When he showed him the place, he cut off a **s**,
Job 33:21 and their bones, once invisible, now **s** out.
Isa 28:27 dill is beaten out with a **s**, and cummin with a rod.
57: 4 you open your mouth wide and **s** out your tongue?
Eze 29: 4 make the fish of your channels **s** to your scales.
37:16 take a **s** and write on it, "For Judah,
37:16 another **s** and write on it, "For Joseph (the **s** of
37:17 and join them together into one **s**,
37:19 about to take the **s** of Joseph (which is in the hand
37:19 put the **s** of Judah upon it, and make them one **s**,
Mt 27:48 put it on a **s**, and gave it to him to drink.
Mk 15:36 put it on a **s**, and gave it to him to drink, saying,
1Co 4:21 Am I to come to you with a **s**,
Wis 13:13 useful for nothing, a **s** crooked and full of knots,
Sir 13:16 and people **s** close to those like themselves.
33:25 Fodder and a **s** and burdens for a donkey;

STICKING (1) [STICK]

Eze 29: 4 with all the fish of your channels **s** to your scales.

STICKS (9) [STICK]

Nu 15:32 they found a man gathering **s** on the sabbath day.
15:33 Those who found him gathering **s** brought him
1Sa 17:43 "Am I a dog, that you come to me with **s**?"
1Ki 17:10 a widow was there gathering **s**;
17:12 I am now gathering a couple of **s**,
Ps 22:15 and my tongue **s** to my jaws;
Pr 18:24 but a true friend **s** closer than one's nearest kin.
La 4: 4 The tongue of the infant **s** to the roof of its mouth
Eze 37:20 When the **s** on which you write are in your hand

STIFF (1) [STIFF-NECKED, STIFFENED]

Job 40:17 It makes its tail **s** like a cedar;

STIFF-NECKED (8) [NECK, STIFF]

Ex 32: 9 "I have seen this people, how **s** they are.
33: 3 on the way, for you are a **s** people."
33: 5 "Say to the Israelites, 'You are a **s** people;
34: 9 Although this is a **s** people,
2Ch 30: 8 Do not now be **s** as your ancestors were,
Ac 7:51 "You **s** people, uncircumcised in heart and ears,
Sir 16:11 Even if there were only one **s** person,
Bar 2:30 for they are a **s** people.

STIFFENED (8) [STIFF]

2Ch 36:13 he **s** his neck and hardened his heart
Ne 9:16 and **s** their necks and did
9:17 but they **s** their necks and determined to return
9:29 They turned a stubborn shoulder and **s** their neck
Jer 7:26 or pay attention, but they **s** their necks.
17:23 they **s** their necks and would not hear
19:15 because they have **s** their necks,
1Es 1:48 he **s** his neck and hardened his heart

STIFFHEARTED (KJV) See STUBBORN

STILL‡ (314) [STILLBORN, STILLED, STILLING]

Ge 8: 9 the waters were **s** on the face of the whole earth.
25: 6 while he was **s** living, and he sent them away
29: 7 He said, "Look, it is **s** broad daylight;
29: 9 While he was **s** speaking with them,
34:25 On the third day, when they were **s** in pain,
35:16 and when they were **s** some distance from Ephrath,
41:21 for they were **s** as ugly as before.
43: 7 saying, 'Is your father **s** alive?
43:27 old man of whom you spoke? Is he **s** alive?"
43:28 "Your servant our father is well; he is **s** alive."
44:14 to Joseph's house while he was **s** there;
45: 3 Is my father **s** alive?"
45:26 And they told him, "Joseph is **s** alive!
45:28 My son Joseph is **s** alive.
46:30 having seen for myself that you are **s** alive."
48: 7 while there was **s** some distance to go to Ephrath;
50:15 "What if Joseph **s** bears a grudge against us
Ex 4:18 in Egypt and see whether they are **s** living."
5:18 but you shall **s** deliver the same number of bricks."
7:13 **S** Pharaoh's heart was hardened,
9: 2 For if you refuse to let them go and **s** hold them,
9:17 You are **s** exalting yourself against my people,
14:14 and you have only to keep **s**."
15:16 they became **s** as a stone until your people,
21:16 whether that person has been sold or is **s** held
36: 3 They **s** kept bringing him freewill offerings every
Lev 18:18 while her sister is **s** alive.
Nu 9:10 shall **s** keep the passover to the LORD.
11:33 But while the meat was **s** between their teeth,
19:13 their uncleanness is **s** on them.
30:16 and a father and his daughter while she is **s** young
Dt 3:11 can **s** be seen in Rabbah of the Ammonites.
4:38 for a possession, as it is **s** today.
5:24 to someone and the person may **s** live.
31:27 so rebellious toward the LORD while I am **s** alive
Jos 3: 8 you shall stand **s** in the Jordan.' "
3:16 the waters flowing from above stood **s**,
9:12 it was **s** warm when we took it from our houses
10:12 "Sun, stand **s** at Gibeon, and Moon, in the valley
10:13 And the sun stood **s**, and the moon stopped,
13: 1 very much of the land **s** remains to be possessed.
13: 2 This is the land that **s** remains:
Jos 14:11 I am **s** as strong today as I was on the day
Jdg 3:25 he **s** did not open the doors of the roof chamber,
5:17 Asher sat **s** at the coast of the sea,
5:27 He sank, he fell, he lay **s** at her feet;
6:24 To this day it **s** stands at Ophrah,
7: 4 "The troops are **s** too many;
8:20 for he was afraid, because he was **s** a boy.
Ru 1:11 Do I **s** have sons in my womb
1Sa 12:25 But if you **s** do wickedly, you shall be swept away,
13: 7 Saul was **s** at Gilgal, and all the people
14: 9 then we will stand **s** in our place,
18:29 Saul was **s** more afraid of David.
20:14 If I am **s** alive, show me the faithful love of
2Sa 1: 9 and yet my life **s** lingers.'
2:23 where Asahel had fallen and died, stood **s**.
3:35 to eat something while it was **s** day;
9: 1 "Is there **s** anyone left of the house of Saul
12:18 for they said, "While the child was **s** alive,
12:22 He said, "While the child was **s** alive,
14:32 It would be better for me to be there **s**.'
18:14 while he was **s** alive in the oak.
18:30 So he turned aside, and stood **s**.
19:34 "How many years have I **s** to live,
19:35 Can I **s** listen to the voice of singing men
24: 3 while the eyes of my lord the king can **s** see it!
1Ki 1:14 Then while you are **s** there speaking with the king,
1:22 While she was **s** speaking with the king,
1:42 While he was **s** speaking, Jonathan son of
9:21 their descendants who were **s** left in the land,
12: 2 of Nebat heard of it (for he was **s** in Egypt,
12: 6 while he was **s** alive, saying,
20:32 And he said, "Is he **s** alive?
22: 8 "There is **s** one other by whom we may inquire of
22:43 and the people **s** sacrificed and offered incense on
22:46 the male temple prostitutes who were **s** in the land
2Ki 6:33 While he was **s** speaking with them,
14: 4 the people **s** sacrificed and made offerings on
15: 4 the people **s** sacrificed and made offerings on
15:35 the people **s** sacrificed and made offerings on
17:29 But every nation **s** made gods of its own
23:26 **S** the LORD did not turn from the fierceness
2Ch 8: 8 from their descendants who were **s** left in the land,
8: 8 conscripted for forced labor, as is **s** the case today.
10: 6 while he was **s** alive, saying,
14: 7 the land is **s** ours because we have sought
18: 7 "There is **s** one other by whom we may inquire of
20:17 take your position, stand **s**,
27: 2 But the people **s** followed corrupt practices.
32:16 His servants said **s** more against the Lord GOD
33:17 people, however, **s** sacrificed at the high places,
34: 3 eighth year of his reign, while he was **s** a boy,
Ne 7: 3 while the gatekeepers are **s** standing guard,
Est 6:14 While they were **s** talking with him,
Job 1:16 While he was **s** speaking, another came and said,
1:17 While he was **s** speaking, another came and said,
1:18 While he was **s** speaking, another came and said,
2: 3 He **s** persists in his integrity,
2: 9 "Do you **s** persist in your integrity?
4:16 It stood **s**, but I could not discern its appearance.
8:19 and out of the earth **s** others will spring.
29: 5 when the Almighty was **s** with me,
30:27 My inward parts are in turmoil, and are never **s**;
37:17 you whose garments are hot when the earth is **s**
39:24 it cannot stand **s** at the sound of the trumpet.
Ps 23: 2 he leads me beside **s** waters;
37: 7 Be **s** before the LORD, and wait patiently
39: 2 I was silent and **s**; I held my peace to no
46:10 "Be **s**, and know that I am God!
69:26 whom you have wounded, they attack **s** more.
71:17 and I **s** proclaim your wondrous deeds.
76: 8 the earth feared and was **s**
78:17 Yet they sinned **s** more against him,
78:30 while the food was **s** in their mouths,
78:32 In spite of all this they **s** sinned;
83: 1 do not hold your peace or be **s**, O God!
89: 9 when its waves rise, you **s** them.
92:14 In old age they **s** produce fruit;
107:29 he made the storm be **s**,
139:18 to the end—I am **s** with you.
Pr 9: 9 and they will become wiser **s**;
17: 7 **s** less is false speech to a ruler.
31:15 She rises while it is **s** night and provides food
Ecc 2: 3 my mind **s** guiding me with wisdom—
4: 2 more fortunate than the living, who are **s** alive;
Isa 5:25 and his hand is stretched out **s**.
9:12 his hand is stretched out **s**.
9:17 his hand is stretched out **s**.
9:20 They gorged on the right, but **s** were hungry,
9:21 his hand is stretched out **s**.
10: 4 his hand is stretched out **s**.
23: 2 Be **s**, O inhabitants of the coast,
29: 8 dreams of eating and wakes up **s** hungry,
29: 8 dreams of drinking, and wakes up faint, **s** thirsty,
30: 7 therefore I have called her, "Rahab who sits **s**."
42:14 I have kept **s** and restrained myself;
57:20 wicked are like the tossing sea that cannot keep **s**;
Jer 2:22 the stain of your guilt is **s** before me,
8:14 Why do we sit **s**?
31:20 As often as I speak against him, I **s** remember him.
33: 1 while he was **s** confined in the court of the guard:
37: 4 Now Jeremiah was **s** going in and out among
44: 6 a waste and a desolation, as they **s** are today.
44:23 disaster has befallen you, as is **s** evident today."
47: 6 Put yourself into your scabbard, rest and be **s**!
49:12 If those who do not deserve to drink the cup **s** have
Eze 8: 6 Yet you will see **s** greater abominations."
8:13 "You will see **s** greater abominations
Eze 8:15 You will see **s** greater abominations than these."
8:17 and provoke my anger **s** further?
15: 7 the fire shall **s** consume them;
16:28 and **s** you were not satisfied.
28: 9 Will you **s** say, "I am a god,"
32:21 "They have come down, they lie **s**,
Da 3:21 So the men were bound, **s** wearing their tunics,
4:31 While the words were **s** in the king's mouth,
4:36 and **s** more greatness was added to me.
11: 4 And while **s** rising in power,
11:35 for there is **s** an interval until the time appointed.
Hos 11:12 but Judah **s** walks with God,
Am 4: 7 the rain from you when there were **s** three months
Jnh 4: 2 Is not this what I said while I was **s**
Hab 2: 3 For there is **s** a vision for the appointed time;
3:11 the moon stood **s** in its exalted place,
Hag 2:19 and the olive tree **s** yield nothing?
Zec 14:12 their flesh shall rot while they are **s** on their feet;
Mt 12:46 While he was **s** speaking to the crowds,
15:16 he said, "Are you also **s** without understanding?
16: 9 Do you **s** not perceive?
16:14 and **s** others Jeremiah or one of the prophets."
17: 5 While he was **s** speaking, suddenly
19:20 "I have kept all these; what do I **s** lack?"
20:32 Jesus stood **s** and called them, saying,
26:45 "Are you **s** sleeping and taking your rest?
26:47 While he was **s** speaking, Judas, one of the twelve,
26:65 Why do we **s** need witnesses?
27:63 that impostor said while he was **s** alive,
28:15 And this story is **s** told among the Jews to this day.
Mk 1:35 In the morning, while it was **s** very dark,
4:24 and **s** more will be given you.
4:39 and said to the sea, "Peace! Be **s**!"
4:40 Have you **s** no faith?"
5:35 While he was **s** speaking, some people came from
8:17 Do you **s** not perceive or understand?
8:28 and **s** others, one of the prophets."
10:49 Jesus stood **s** and said, "Call him here."
12: 6 He had **s** one other, a beloved son.
13: 7 this must take place, but the end is **s** to come.
14:41 "Are you **s** sleeping and taking your rest?
14:43 Immediately, while he was **s** speaking, Judas,
14:63 "Why do we **s** need witnesses?
Lk 7:14 and touched the bier, and the bearers stood **s**.
8:49 While he was **s** speaking, someone came from
9:19 Elijah; and **s** others, that one of
13: 7 for fruit on this fig tree, and **s** I find none.
14:22 you ordered has been done, and there is **s** room.'
14:32 If he cannot, then, while the other is **s** far away,
15:20 But while he was **s** far off,
18:22 he said to him, "There is **s** one thing lacking.
18:40 Jesus stood **s** and ordered the man to be brought
20:12 And he sent **s** a third;
22:47 While he was **s** speaking, suddenly a crowd came,
22:59 Then about an hour later **s** another kept insisting,
22:60 At that moment, while he was **s** speaking,
24: 6 while he was **s** in Galilee,
24:17 They stood **s**, looking sad.
24:41 their joy they were disbelieving and **s** wondering,
24:44 that I spoke to you while I was **s** with you—
Jn 5:17 Jesus answered them, "My Father is **s** working,
11:30 but was **s** at the place where Martha had met him.
14: 9 Philip, and you **s** do not know me?
14:25 "I have said these things to you while I am **s**
16:12 "I **s** have many things to say to you,
20: 1 on the first day of the week, while it was **s** dark,
Ac 9: 1 **s** breathing threats and murder against
10:19 While Peter was **s** thinking about the vision,
10:44 While Peter was **s** speaking,
20: 9 into a deep sleep while Paul talked **s** longer.
Ro 3: 7 why am I **s** being condemned as a sinner?
4:11 that he had by faith while he was **s** uncircumcised.
5: 6 For while we were **s** weak,
5: 8 in that while we **s** were sinners Christ died for us.
9:19 "Why then does he **s** find fault?
1Co 3: 2 Even now you are **s** not ready,
3: 3 for you are **s** of the flesh.
8: 7 they **s** think of the food they eat as food offered to
9:12 on you, do not we **s** more?
12:31 And I will show you a **s** more excellent way.
15: 6 most of whom are **s** alive, though some have died.
15:17 your faith is futile and you are **s** in your sins.
2Co 3:14 that same veil is **s** there,
5: 4 For while we are **s** in this tent,
7: 7 your zeal for me, so that I rejoiced **s** more.
7:13 we rejoiced **s** more at the joy of Titus,
Gal 1:10 If I were **s** pleasing people,
1:22 and I was **s** unknown by sight to the churches
5:11 why am I **s** being persecuted
5:11 if I am **s** preaching circumcision?
Php 1:30 that you saw I had and now hear that I **s** have.
2:25 **S**, I think it necessary to send
Col 2:20 why do you live as if you **s** belonged to the world?
2Th 2: 5 that I told you these things when I was **s** with you?
Heb 4: 1 while the promise of entering his rest is **s** open,
4: 9 a sabbath rest **s** remains for the people of God;
5:13 on milk, being **s** an infant, is unskilled in the word
6:10 for his sake in serving the saints, as you **s** do.
7:10 for he was **s** in the loins of his ancestor
9: 8 as long as the first tent is **s** standing.
11: 4 he died, but through his faith he **s** speaks.
1Jn 2: 9 in the light," while hating a brother or sister, is **s** in
Jude 1:23 and have mercy on **s** others with fear,
Rev 3: 4 Yet you have **s** a few persons in Sardis who have
9:12 There are **s** two woes to come.
22:11 Let the evildoer **s** do evil, and the filthy **s** be filthy, and the righteous **s** do right, and the holy **s** be holy.

Tob 1: 4 in the land of Israel, while I was s a young man,
2: 8 And my neighbors laughed and said, "Is he s
3:15 Why should I s live?
5:10 Although s alive, I am among the dead.
11: 3 and prepare the house while they are s on
14:10 Was he not, while s alive,
Jdt 13:11 s showing his power in Israel and his strength
AdE 6:14 While they were s talking,
Wis 10: 7 Evidence of their wickedness s remains:
16:17 the fire had s greater effect,
17:21 s heavier than darkness were they to themselves.
19: 3 For while they were s engaged in mourning,
19: 4 up the punishment that their torments s lacked,
19:10 For they s recalled the events of their sojourn,
Sir 6:18 when you have gray hair you will s find wisdom.
18: 7 and when they stop, they are s perplexed.
32: 8 be as one who knows and can s hold his tongue.
33:21 While you are s alive and have breath in you,
41: 1 and s is vigorous enough to enjoy food!
46: 4 that the sun stood s and one day become as long
51:13 While I was s young, before I went
Aza 1: 2 Then Azariah stood s in the fire and prayed aloud:
1Mc 1: 6 among them while he was s alive.
4: 4 while the division was s absent from the camp.
5:14 While the letter was s being read,
6:27 they will do s greater things,
6:55 while s living had appointed to bring
10:27 Now continue s to keep faith with us,
10:88 he honored Jonathan s more;
12:36 to build the walls of Jerusalem s higher,
2Mc 4:34 he persuaded him, though s suspicious,
7: 5 s breathing, and to fry him in a pan.
7:24 The youngest brother being s alive,
7:30 While she was s speaking, the young man said,
9: 9 and while he was s living in anguish and pain,
11: 8 And there, while they were s near Jerusalem,
14:11 quickly inflamed Demetrius s more.
14:45 S alive and aflame with anger, he rose,
3Mc 3: 1 but was s more bitterly hostile toward those in
4:15 to an end after forty days but s uncompleted.
4:18 s in the country, some s residing in their homes,
5:19 while it was s night he had carried out completely
2Es 1:16 but to this day you s complain.
4:49 drops s remained in the cloud.
5:50 of whom you have told me, s young?
6:24 and the springs of the fountains shall stand s,
8:11 and afterwards you will s guide it in your mercy.
9:11 as scorned my law while they s had freedom,
9:11 an opportunity of repentance was s open to them,
10: 5 the reflections with which I was s engaged,
10:32 and lo, what I have seen I saw, and can s see,
12: 5 I am s weary in mind and very weak in my spirit,
13:16 And s more, alas for those who are not left!
15:31 remembering their origin, shall become s stronger;
4Mc 18:10 While he was s with you,

STILLBORN (3) [BEAR, STILL]
Nu 12:12 Do not let her be like one s,
Job 3:16 Or why was I not buried like a s child,
Ecc 6: 3 I say that a s child is better off than he.

STILLED (8) [STILL]
Ne 8:11 So the Levites s all the people, saying, "Be quiet,
Job 26:12 By his power he s the Sea;
Ps 31:18 Let the lying lips be s that speak insolently against
Isa 24: 8 The mirth of the timbrels is s,
24: 8 the mirth of the lyre is s.
25: 5 the song of the ruthless was s.
Sir 43:23 By his plan he s the deep and planted islands in it.
46: 7 and s their wicked grumbling.

STILLING (1) [STILL]
Jer 51:55 laying Babylon waste, and s her loud clamor.

STING (3) [STINGERS, STINGS, STUNG]
1Co 15:55 Where, O death, is your s?"
15:56 s of death is sin, and the power of sin is the law.
4Mc 14:19 s those who approach their hive and defend it even

STINGERS (1) [STING]
Rev 9:10 They have tails like scorpions, with s,

STINGINESS (1) [STINGY]
Sir 31:24 and their testimony to his s is accurate.

STINGS (2) [STING]
Pr 23:32 the last it bites like a serpent, and s like an adder.
Rev 9: 5 like the torture of a scorpion when it s someone.

STINGY (2) [STINGINESS]
Pr 23: 6 Do not eat the bread of the s;
Sir 31:24 The city complains of the one who is s with food,

STINK (2) [STANK, STINKING]
Ex 7:18 fish in the river shall die, the river itself shall s,
Isa 50: 2 their fish s for lack of water, and die of thirst.

STINKING (1) [STINK]
4Mc 6:25 and poured s liquids into his nostrils.

STINT (1)
Sir 35:10 and do not s the first fruits of your hands.

STIR‡ (21) [BESTIR, STIRRED, STIRRING, STIRS]
Jdg 13:25 of the LORD began to s him in Mahaneh-dan,
Job 17: 8 the innocent s themselves up against the godless.
41:10 No one is so fierce as to dare to s it up.
Ps 56: 6 They s up strife, they lurk, they watch my steps.
59: 3 the mighty s up strife against me.
78:38 and did not s up all his wrath.
80: 2 S up your might, and come to save us!
140: 2 who plan evil things in their minds and s up wars
Pr 15:18 Those who are hot-tempered s up strife,
SS 2: 7 do not s up or awaken love until it is ready!
3: 5 do not s up or awaken love until it is ready!
8: 4 do not s up or awaken love until it is ready!
Isa 19: 2 I will s up Egyptians against Egyptians,
Jer 50: 9 For I am going to s up and bring against Babylon
51: 1 to s up a destructive wind against Babylon and
Da 11: 2 he shall s up all against the kingdom of Greece.
11:25 He shall s up his power and determination against
Hos 7: 4 whose baker does not need to s the fire,
Joel 3: 9 Prepare war, s up the warriors.
Ac 17:13 they came there too, to s up and incite the crowds.
Sir 11:34 into your home and they will s up trouble for you,

STIRRED‡ (33) [STIR]
Ex 35:21 And they came, everyone whose heart was s,
36: 2 everyone whose heart was s to come to do
Ru 1:19 the whole town was s because of them;
1Sa 22: 8 or discloses to me that my son has s up my servant
26:19 If it is the LORD who has s you up against me,
1Ch 5:26 So the God of Israel s up the spirit of King Pul
2Ch 36:22 the LORD s up the spirit of King Cyrus of Persia
Ezr 1: 1 the LORD s up the spirit of King Cyrus of Persia
1: 5 everyone whose spirit God had s—
4:15 and that sedition was s up in it from long ago.
Isa 9:11 the LORD raised adversaries against them, and s
14: 9 Sheol beneath is s up to meet you when you come;
41:25 I s up one from the north, and he has come,
Jer 51:11 The LORD has s up the spirit of the kings of
Hag 1:14 And the LORD s up the spirit of Zerubbabel son
Mk 15:11 But the chief priests s up the crowd
Jn 5: 7 to put me into the pool when the water is s up;
Ac 6:12 They s up the people as well as the elders and
13:50 and s up persecution against Paul and Barnabas,
14: 2 But the unbelieving Jews s up the Gentiles
21:27 from Asia, who had seen him in the temple, s up
21:38 not the Egyptian who recently s up a revolt and led
2Co 9: 2 and your zeal has s up most of them.
Wis 11: 6 s up and defiled with blood
Sir 51:21 My heart was s to seek her;
Sus 1:45 God s up the holy spirit of a young lad
1Mc 2:24 he burned with zeal and his heart was s.
3:49 and the first fruits and the tithes, and they s up
1Es 2: 2 the Lord s up the spirit of King Cyrus of
2: 8 and all whose spirit the Lord had s to go up
2: 9 from many whose hearts were s.
2Es 13: 2 a wind arose from the sea and s up all its waves.
15:38 heavy storm clouds shall be s up from the south,

STIRRING‡ (8) [STIR]
Jdg 9:31 and they are s up the city against you.
Isa 13:17 See, I am s up the Medes against them,
Jer 6:22 the north, a great nation is s from the farthest parts
25:32 tempest is s from the farthest parts of the earth!
50:41 and many kings are s from the farthest parts of
Da 7: 2 in my vision by night the four winds of heaven s
Ac 24:12 with anyone in the temple or s up a crowd either in
2Mc 14: 6 are keeping up war and s up sedition,

STIRS (11) [STIR]
Dt 32:11 an eagle s up its nest, and hovers over its young;
Pr 10:12 Hatred s up strife, but love covers all offenses.
15: 1 but a harsh word s up anger.
28:25 The greedy person s up strife,
29:22 One given to anger s up strife,
Isa 42:13 like a warrior he s up his fury;
51:15 who s up the sea so that its waves roar—
54:15 If anyone s up strife, it is not from me;
54:15 whoever s up strife with you shall fall because
Jer 31:35 who s up the sea so that its waves roar—
Lk 23: 5 "He s up the people by teaching

STOCK (5)
Ps 80:15 the s that your right hand planted.
Jer 2:21 I planted you as a choice vine, from the purest s.
Eze 44:22 but only a virgin of the s of the house of Israel,
Tob 5:14 kindred are good people; you come of good s.
Sir 26:20 *sow it with your own seed, trusting in your fine s.*

STOCKS (7)
2Ch 16:10 Asa was angry with the seer, and put him in the s,
Job 13:27 You put my feet in the s, and watch all my paths;
33:11 he puts my feet in the s,
Jer 20: 2 in the s that were in the upper Benjamin Gate of
20: 3 when Pashhur released Jeremiah from the s,
29:26 to put him in the s and the collar.
Ac 16:24 the innermost cell and fastened their feet in the s.

STOIC (1)
Ac 17:18 Also some Epicurean and S philosophers debated

STOKING (1)
Aza 1:23 Now the king's servants who threw them in kept s

STOLE (7) [STEAL]
Ge 31:19 and Rachel s her father's household gods.
2Sa 15: 6 so Absalom s the hearts of the people of Israel.
19: 3 The troops s into the city that day as soldiers steal
2Ki 11: 2 and s him away from among the king's children
2Ch 22:11 and s him away from among the king's children
Mt 28:13 by night and s him away while we were asleep.'
2Mc 4:32 s some of the gold vessels of the temple

STOLEN‡ (17) [STEAL]
Ge 30:33 if found with me, shall be counted s."
31:32 Jacob did not know that Rachel had s the gods.
31:39 whether s by day or s by night.
40:15 For in fact I was s out of the land of the Hebrews;
44: 4 Why have you s my silver cup?
Ex 22: 7 and they are s from the neighbor's house,
22:12 if it was s, restitution shall be made to its owner.
Dt 28:31 Your donkey shall be s in front of you,
Jos 7:11 they have s, they have acted deceitfully,
2Sa 19:41 the people of Judah s you away,
21:12 who had s them from the public square
Pr 9:17 "S water is sweet, and bread eaten
Jude 1: 4 For certain intruders have s in among you,
Tob 2:13 It is surely not s, is it?
2:13 for we have no right to eat anything s."
2Mc 4:39 many of the gold vessels had already been s.

STOMACH‡ (17) [STOMACHS, STOMACHS']
Dt 18: 3 to the priest the shoulder, the two jowls, and the s.
2Sa 2:23 So Abner struck him in the s with the butt
3:27 and there he stabbed him in the s.
4: 6 and they struck him in the s;
Pr 18:20 From the fruit of the mouth one's s is satisfied;
La 1:20 See, O LORD, how distressed I am; my s churns,
2:11 My eyes are spent with weeping; my s churns;
Eze 3: 3 eat this scroll that I give you and fill your s with it.
Mt 15:17 that whatever goes into the mouth enters the s,
Mk 7:19 not the heart but the s,
1Co 6:13 "Food is meant for the s and the s
1Ti 5:23 for the sake of your s and your frequent ailments.
Rev 10: 9 it will be bitter to your s,
10:10 but when I had eaten it, my s was made bitter.
Sir 36:23 The s will take any food,
4Mc 7: 6 nor profaned your s, which had room only

STOMACHS (2) [STOMACH]
Job 20:14 yet their food is turned in their s;
Eze 7:19 They shall not satisfy their hunger or fill their s

STOMACHS' (1) [STOMACH]
Sir 37: 5 Some companions help a friend for their s sake,

STONE‡ (201) [CHALKSTONES, CORNERSTONE, CORNERSTONES, MILLSTONE, MILLSTONES, MOONSTONE, SLINGSTONES, STONE'S, STONECUTTERS, STONECUTTING, STONED, STONEHEAP, STONES, STONING]
Ge 2:12 bdellium and onyx s are there.
11: 3 And they had brick for s, and bitumen for mortar.
28:18 the s that he had put under his head and set it up
28:22 and this s, which I have set up for a pillar, shall
29: 2 The s on the well's mouth was large,
29: 3 the shepherds would roll the s from the mouth of
29: 3 put the s back in its place on the mouth of the well.
29: 8 and the s is rolled from the mouth of the well,
29:10 up and rolled the s from the well's mouth,
31:45 So Jacob took a s, and set it up as a pillar.
35:14 where he had spoken with him, a pillar of s;
Ex 7:19 even in vessels of wood and in vessels of s.' "
8:26 that are offensive to them, will they not s us?
15: 5 they went down into the depths like a s.
15:16 they became still as a s until your people,
17: 4 They are almost ready to s me."
17:12 they took a s and put it under him, and he sat on it.
20:25 But if you make for me an altar of s,
21:18 the other with a s or fist so that the injured party,
24:10 like a pavement of sapphire s,
24:12 and I will give you the tablets of s,
28:10 six of their names on the one s,
28:10 and the names of the remaining six on the other s,
31:18 tablets of s, written with the finger of God.
34: 1 "Cut two tablets of s like the former ones,
34: 4 So Moses cut two tablets of s like the former ones;
34: 4 and took in his hand the two tablets of s.
Lev 20: 2 the people of the land shall s them to death.
24:14 and let the whole congregation s him.
24:16 the whole congregation shall s the blasphemer.
Nu 14:10 But the whole congregation threatened to s them.
15:35 all the congregation shall s him outside the camp."
35:17 Or anyone who strikes another with a s in hand
35:23 while handling any s that could cause death,
Dt 4:13 and he wrote them on two s tablets.
4:28 objects of wood and s that neither see, nor hear,
5:22 He wrote them on two s tablets,
9: 9 I went up the mountain to receive the s tablets,

Dt 9:10 the LORD gave me the two s tablets written with
9:11 the LORD gave me the two s tablets,
10: 1 "Carve out two tablets of s like the former ones,
10: 3 cut two tablets of s like the former ones,
13:10 S them to death for trying to turn you away from
16:22 nor shall you set up a s pillar—
17: 5 and you shall s the man or woman to death.
21:21 Then all the men of the town shall s him to death.
22:21 and the men of her town shall s her to death,
22:24 both of them to the gate of that town and s them
28:36 where you shall serve other gods, of wood and s.
28:64 there you shall serve other gods, of wood and s,
29:17 the filthy idols of wood and s, of silver and gold,
Jos 4: 5 and each of you take up a s on his shoulder,
15: 6 and the boundary goes up to the S of Bohan,
18:17 it goes down to the S of Bohan, Reuben's son;
24:26 and he took a large s,
24:27 "See, this s shall be a witness against us;
Jdg 9: 5 the sons of Jerubbaal, seventy men, on one s;
9:18 seventy men on one s, and have made Abimelech,
20:16 every one could sling a s at a hair, and not miss.
1Sa 6:14 A large s was there; so they split up the wood
6:15 and set them upon the large s.
6:18 The great s, beside which they set down the ark of
7:12 a s and set it up between Mizpah and Jeshanah,
14:33 roll a large s before me here."
17:49 David put his hand in his bag, took out a s,
17:49 the s sank into his forehead,
17:50 a s, striking down the Philistine and killing him;
20:19 and remain beside the s there.
20:41 the s heap and prostrated himself with his face to
25:37 his heart died within him; he became like a s.
2Sa 12:30 and in it was a precious s;
20: 8 When they were at the large s that is in Gibeon,
1Ki 1: 9 oxen, and fatted cattle by the s Zoheleth,
5:18 the stonecutting and prepared the timber and the s
6: 7 The house was built with s finished at the quarry,
6:18 all was cedar, no s was seen.
6:36 the inner court with three courses of dressed s
7:12 The great court had three courses of dressed s
8: 9 the two tablets of s that Moses had placed there
21:10 Then take him out, and s him to death."
2Ki 3:25 on every good piece of land everyone threw a s,
3:25 Only at Kir-hareseth did the s walls remain,
12:12 to buy timber and quarried s for making repairs on
16:17 and put it on a pediment of s.
19:18 wood and s—and so they were destroyed.
22: 6 to buy timber and quarried s to repair the house.
1Ch 20: 2 and in it was a precious s;
22:14 timber and s too I have provided.
2Ch 1:15 and gold as common in Jerusalem as s,
2:14 silver, bronze, iron, s, and wood, and in purple,
9:27 king made silver as common in Jerusalem as s,
34:11 the carpenters and the builders to buy quarried s,
Ezr 5: 8 It is being built of hewn s,
Ne 4: 3 and he said, "That s wall they are building—
9:11 like a s into mighty waters.
Job 38:30 The waters become hard like s,
41:24 Its heart is as hard as s,
Ps 91:12 so that you will not dash your foot against a s.
118:22 The s that the builders rejected has become
Pr 17: 8 like a magic s in the eyes of those who give it;
24:31 and its s wall was broken down.
26: 8 like binding a s in a sling to give honor to a fool.
26:27 a s will come back on the one who starts it rolling.
27: 3 A s is heavy, and sand is weighty,
Isa 8:14 a sanctuary, a s one strikes against;
28:16 I am laying in Zion a foundation s, a tested s,
37:19 wood and s—and so they were destroyed.
Jer 2:27 and to a s, "You gave me birth."
3: 9 committing adultery with s and tree.
51:26 No s shall be taken from you for a corner
51:26 from you for a corner and no s for a foundation,
51:63 When you finish reading this scroll, tie a s to it,
Eze 3: 9 Like the hardest s, harder than flint,
11:19 heart of s from their flesh and give them a heart of
16:40 and they shall s you and cut you to pieces
20:32 of the countries, and worship wood and s."
23:47 The assembly shall s them and
28:13 every precious s was your covering, carnelian,
36:26 from your body the heart of s and give you a heart
40:42 also four tables of hewn s for the burnt offering,
Da 2:34 As you looked on, a s was cut out,
2:35 But the s that struck the statue became
2:45 just as you saw that a s was cut from the mountain
5: 4 bronze, iron, wood, and s.
5:23 wood, and s, which do not see or hear or know;
6:17 A s was brought and laid on the mouth of the den,
Hos 12:11 so their altars shall be like s heaps on the furrows
Am 5:11 you have built houses of hewn s,
Hab 2:19 to silent s, "Rouse yourself!"
Hag 2:15 a s was placed upon a s in the LORD's temple,
Zec 3: 9 For on the s that I have set before Joshua,
3: 9 on a single s with seven facets,
4: 7 he shall bring out the top s amid shouts of 'Grace,
12: 3 On that day I will make Jerusalem a heavy s for all
Mt 4: 6 so that you will not dash your foot against a s.' "
7: 9 if your child asks for bread, will give a s?
21:42 'The s that the builders rejected has become
21:44 one who falls on this s will be broken to pieces;
24: 2 not one s will be left here upon another;
27:60 a great s to the door of the tomb and went away.
27:66 and made the tomb secure by sealing the s.
28: 2 came and rolled back the s and sat on it.
Mk 12:10 'The s that the builders rejected has become
13: 2 Not one s will be left here upon another;
15:46 He then rolled a s against the door of the tomb.
Mk 16: 3 "Who will roll away the s for us from the entrance
16: 4 When they looked up, they saw that the s,
Lk 4: 3 command this s to become a loaf of bread."
4:11 so that you will not dash your foot against a s.' "
19:44 they will not leave within you one s upon another;
20: 6 we say, 'Of human origin,' all the people will s us;
20:17 'The s that the builders rejected has become
20:18 Everyone who falls on that s will be broken
21: 6 the days will come when not one s will be left
24: 2 They found the s rolled away from the tomb,
Jn 2: 6 Now standing there were six s water jars for
8: 5 ⟦the law Moses commanded us to s such women.⟧
8: 7 ⟦without sin be the first to throw a s at her."⟧
10:31 The Jews took up stones again to s him.
10:32 For which of these are you going to s me?"
10:33 not for a good work that we are going to s you,
11: 8 "Rabbi, the Jews were just now trying to s you,
11:38 It was a cave, and a s was lying against it.
11:39 Jesus said, "Take away the s."
11:41 So they took away the s.
19:13 at a place called The S Pavement,
20: 1 to the tomb and saw that the s had been removed
Ac 4:11 This Jesus is 'the s that was rejected by you,
7:58 of the city and began to s him;
14: 5 with their rulers, to mistreat them and to s them,
17:29 or s, an image formed by the art and imagination
Ro 9:32 They have stumbled over the stumbling s,
9:33 laying in Zion a s that will make people stumble,
2Co 3: 3 not on tablets of s but on tablets of human hearts.
3: 7 ministry of death, chiseled in letters on s tablets,
1Pe 2: 4 a living s, though rejected by mortals yet chosen
2: 6 "See, I am laying in Zion a s,
2: 7 but for those who do not believe, "The s that
2: 8 and "A s that makes them stumble,
Rev 2:17 and I will give a white s, and on the white s is written a new name
9:20 of gold and silver and bronze and s and wood,
18:21 a s like a great millstone and threw it into the sea,
Wis 11: 4 and from hard s a remedy for their thirst.
13:10 or a useless s, the work of an ancient hand.
14:21 on objects of s or wood the name that ought not to
Sir 6:21 She will be like a heavy s to test them,
22: 1 The idler is like a filthy s,
22:20 One who throws a s at birds scares them away,
27:25 a s straight up throws it on his own head,
29:10 and do not let it rust under a s and be lost.
47: 4 when he whirled the s in the sling and struck down
1Mc 2:36 or hurl a s at them or block up their hiding places,
10:73 where there is no s or pebble, or place to flee."
13:27 with polished s at the front and back.
1Es 6: 9 of hewn s, with costly timber laid in the walls.
6:25 of hewn s and one course of new native timber;
3Mc 2:27 and he set up a s on the tower in the courtyard
2Es 5: 5 and the s shall utter its voice;

STONE'S (1) [STONE]

Lk 22:41 Then he withdrew from them about a s throw,

STONECUTTERS (6) [CUT, STONE]

1Ki 5:15 and eighty thousand s in the hill country,
2Ki 12:12 to the masons and the s,
1Ch 22: 2 and he set s to prepare dressed stones for building
22:15 You have an abundance of workers: s, masons,
2Ch 2: 2 and eighty thousand s in the hill country,
2:18 eighty thousand as s in the hill country,

STONECUTTING (1) [CUT, STONE]

1Ki 5:18 the Gebalites did the s and prepared the timber and

STONED (19) [STONE]

Ex 19:13 but they shall be s or shot with arrows;
21:28 the ox shall be s, and its flesh shall not be eaten;
21:29 and it kills a man or a woman, the ox shall be s,
21:32 and the ox shall be s.
Lev 20:27 they shall be s to death, their blood is upon them.
24:23 the blasphemer outside the camp, and s him
Nu 15:36 the camp and s him to death,
Jos 7:25 And all Israel s him to death;
1Ki 12:18 all Israel s him to death.
21:13 they took him outside the city, and s him to death.
21:14 they sent to Jezebel, saying, "Naboth has been s;
21:15 that Naboth had been s and was dead, Jezebel said
2Ch 10:18 the people of Israel s him to death.
24:21 and by command of the king they s him to death in
Mt 21:35 killed another, and s another.
Ac 5:26 for they were afraid of being s by the people.
14:19 Then they s Paul and dragged him out of the city,
Heb 11:37 They were s to death, they were sawn in two,
12:20 touches the mountain, it shall be s to death."

STONEHEAP (1) [HEAP, STONE]

Job 8:17 Their roots twine around the s;

STONES‡ (156) [STONE]

Ge 28:11 Taking one of the s of the place,
31:46 And Jacob said to his kinsfolk, "Gather s,"
31:46 and they took s, and made a heap;
Ex 20:25 do not build it of hewn s,
25: 7 onyx s and gems to be set in the ephod and for
28: 9 You shall take two onyx s,
28:11 so you shall engrave the two s with the names of
28:12 You shall set the two s on the shoulder-pieces of
28:12 as s of remembrance for the sons of Israel;
28:17 You shall set in it four rows of s.
Ex 28:21 There shall be twelve s with names corresponding
31: 5 in cutting s for setting, and in carving wood,
35: 9 and onyx s and gems to be set in the ephod and
35:27 And the leaders brought onyx s and gems to be set
35:33 in cutting s for setting, and in carving wood,
39: 6 The onyx s were prepared,
39: 7 to be s of remembrance for the sons of Israel;
39:10 They set in it four rows of s.
39:14 There were twelve s with names corresponding to
Lev 14:40 that the s in which the disease appears be taken out
14:42 take other s and put them in the place of those s,
14:43 after he has taken out the s and scraped the house
14:45 its s and timber and all the plaster of the house,
26: 1 and you shall not place figured s in your land,
Nu 33:52 destroy all their figured s,
Dt 8: 9 a land whose s are iron and
27: 2 you shall set up large s and cover them
27: 4 you shall set up these s,
27: 5 altar of s on which you have not used an iron tool.
27: 6 the altar of the LORD your God of unhewn s.
27: 8 on the s all the words of this law very clearly.
Jos 4: 3 'Take twelve s from here out of the middle of
4: 6 'What do those s mean to you?'
4: 7 So these s shall be to the Israelites
4: 8 took up twelve s out of the middle of the Jordan,
4: 9 set up twelve s in the middle of the Jordan,
4:20 Those twelve s, which they had taken out of
4:21 in time to come, 'What do these s mean?'
7:25 they burned them with fire, cast s on them,
7:26 over him a great heap of s that remains to this day.
8:29 and raised over it a great heap of s,
8:31 of the law of Moses, "an altar of unhewn s,
8:32 Joshua wrote on the s a copy of the law of Moses,
10:11 the LORD threw down huge s from heaven
10:18 "Roll large s against the mouth of the cave,
10:27 they set large s against the mouth of the cave,
Jdg 3:19 But he himself turned back at the sculptured s
3:26 and passed beyond the sculptured s,
1Sa 17:40 and chose five smooth s from the wadi,
2Sa 16: 6 He threw s at David and at all the servants
16:13 throwing s and flinging dust at him.
18:17 and raised over him a very great heap of s.
1Ki 5:17 costly s in order to lay the foundation of the house
5:17 to lay the foundation of the house with dressed s.
7: 9 All these were made of costly s,
7:10 The foundation was of costly s, huge s, s of eight and ten cubits.
7:11 There were costly s above, cut to measure,
10: 2 and very much gold, and precious s;
10:10 a great quantity of spices, and precious s;
10:11 a great quantity of almug wood and precious s.
10:27 king made silver as common in Jerusalem as s,
15:22 they carried away the s of Ramah and its timber,
18:31 Elijah took twelve s, according to the number of
18:32 the s he built an altar in the name of the LORD.
18:38 the wood, the s, and the dust,
19: 6 and there at his head was a cake baked on hot s,
2Ki 3:19 every good piece of land you shall ruin with s."
1Ch 12: 2 and sling s with either the right hand or the left;
22: 2 to prepare dressed s for building the house of God.
29: 2 besides great quantities of onyx and s for setting, antimony, colored s, all sorts of precious s,
29: 8 Whoever had precious s gave them to the treasury
2Ch 3: 6 He adorned the house with settings of precious s.
9: 1 and very much gold and precious s.
9: 9 a very great quantity of spices, and precious s:
9:10 from Ophir brought algum wood and precious s.
16: 6 they carried away the s of Ramah and its timber,
26:14 helmets, coats of mail, bows, and s for slinging.
26:15 and the corners for shooting arrows and large s.
32:27 for gold, for precious s, for spices, for shields,
Ezr 6: 4 with three courses of hewn s and one course
Ne 4: 2 Will they revive the s out of the heaps
Est 1: 6 marble, mother-of-pearl, and colored s.
Job 5:23 For you shall be in league with the s of the field,
6:12 Is my strength the strength of s,
14:19 the waters wear away the s;
22:24 and gold of Ophir like the s of the torrent-bed,
28: 6 Its s are the place of sapphires,
Ps 102:14 For your servants hold its s dear,
Pr 20:15 There is gold, and abundance of costly s;
Ecc 3: 5 a time to throw away s, and a time to gather s
10: 9 Whoever quarries s will be hurt by them;
Isa 5: 2 He dug it and cleared it of s,
9:10 but we will build with dressed s;
14:19 who go down to the s of the Pit,
27: 9 the s of the altars like chalkstones crushed
54:11 I am about to set your s in antimony,
54:12 and all your wall of precious s.
57: 6 Among the smooth s of the valley is your portion;
60:17 instead of wood, bronze, instead of s, iron.
62:10 build up, build up the highway, clear it of s,
Jer 43: 9 Take some large s in your hands,
43:10 and he will set his throne above these s
La 3: 9 he has blocked my ways with hewn s,
3:53 they flung me alive into a pit and hurled s on me;
4: 1 sacred s lie scattered at the head of every street.
Eze 26:12 Your s and timber and soil they shall cast into
27:22 and all precious s, and gold.
28:14 you walked among the s of fire.
28:16 from among the s of fire.
Da 11:38 with precious s and costly gifts.
Mic 1: 6 I will pour down her s into the valley,
Hab 2:11 The very s will cry out from the wall,
Zec 5: 4 in that house and consume it, both timber and s."
Mt 3: 9 for I tell you, God is able from these s to raise
4: 3 command these s to become loaves of bread."

Mt 23:37 that kills the prophets and s those who are sent
Mk 5: 5 and bruising himself with s.
13: 1 Teacher, what large s and what large buildings!"
Lk 3: 8 for I tell you, God is able from these s to raise
13:34 that kills the prophets and s those who are sent
19:40 if these were silent, the s would shout out."
21: 5 with beautiful s and gifts dedicated to God,
Jn 8:59 So they picked up s to throw at him,
10:31 The Jews took up s again to stone him.
1Co 3:12 silver, precious s, wood, hay, straw—
1Pe 2: 5 like living s, let yourselves be built into
Tob 13:16 and all your walls with precious s.
13:16 of Jerusalem will be paved with ruby and with s
Jdt 1: 2 with hewn s three cubits thick and six cubits long;
6:12 from coming up by throwing s at them.
10:21 emeralds and other precious s.
AdE 1: 6 and silver blocks on pillars of marble and other s.
15: 6 all covered with gold and precious s.
Wis 18:24 the ancestors were engraved on the four rows of s,
Sir 21: 8 like one who gathers s for his burial mound.
21:10 The way of sinners is paved with smooth s,
27: 2 a stake is driven firmly into a fissure between s,
45:11 with precious s engraved like seals,
50: 9 with all kinds of precious s;
LtJ 6:39 with gold and silver are like s from the mountain,
1Mc 4:43 and removed the defiled s to an unclean place.
4:46 the s in a convenient place on the temple hill until
4:47 Then they took unhewn s, as the law directs,
5:47 and blocked up the gates with s.
6:51 engines of war to throw fire and s,
10:11 the walls and encircle Mount Zion with squared s,
2Mc 1:16 they threw s and struck down the leader
1:31 that was left should be poured on large s.
4:41 some picked up s, some blocks of wood,
2Es 7:52 "If you have just a few precious s,

STONING (3) [STONE]

1Sa 30: 6 for the people spoke of s him,
Ac 7:59 While they were s Stephen, he prayed,
2Co 11:25 Once I received a s.

STONY See Index to Footnotes

STOOD‡ (260) [STAND]

Ge 18: 8 and he s by them under the tree while they ate.
19:27 in the morning to the place where he had s before
28:13 And the LORD s beside him and said,
37: 7 Suddenly my sheaf rose and s upright;
41: 3 and s by the other cows on the bank of the Nile.
43:15 Then they went on their way down to Egypt, and s
45: 1 before all those who s by him,
Ex 2: 4 His sister s at a distance,
9:10 they took soot from the kiln, and s before Pharaoh,
15: 8 the floods s up in a heap;
18:13 people s around him from morning until evening.
20:18 they were afraid and trembled and s at a distance,
20:21 Then the people s at a distance,
32:26 then Moses s in the gate of the camp,
34: 5 The LORD descended in the cloud and s
Lev 9: 5 the whole congregation drew near and s before
Nu 12: 5 and s at the entrance of the tent,
16:18 and they s at the entrance of the tent of meeting
16:27 and Abiram came out and s at the entrance
16:48 He s between the dead and the living;
22:24 Then the angel of the LORD s in a narrow path
22:26 and s in a narrow place,
27: 2 They s before Moses, Eleazar the priest,
Dt 4:10 how you once s before the LORD your God
4:11 you approached and s at the foot of the mountain
31:15 the pillar of cloud s at the entrance to the tent.
Jos 3:16 the waters flowing from above s still,
3:17 of the covenant of the LORD s on dry ground in
4: 3 from the place where the priests' feet s,
4: 9 the priests bearing the ark of the covenant had s;
4:14 they s in awe of him, as they had s in awe of Moses
8:33 s on opposite sides of the ark in front of
10:13 And the sun s still, and the moon stopped,
11:13 of the towns that s on mounds except Hazor,
Jdg 7:21 Every man s in his place all around the camp,
9: 7 he went and s on the top of Mount Gerizim,
9:35 of Ebed went out and s in the entrance of the gate
9:44 with him rushed forward and s at the entrance of
18:16 s by the entrance of the gate,
1Sa 3:10 Now the LORD came and s there,
9: 2 he s head and shoulders above everyone else.
17: 3 The Philistines s on the mountain on the one side,
and Israel s on the mountain on the other side,
17: 8 He s and shouted to the ranks of Israel,
17:26 David said to the men who s by him,
17:51 Then David ran and s over the Philistine;
18:15 he s in awe of him.
20:25 Jonathan s, while Abner sat by Saul's side;
22: 7 Saul said to his servants who s around him,
22:17 The king said to the guard who s around him,
26:13 and s on top of a hill far away,
2Sa 1:10 So I s over him, and killed him,
2:23 the place where Asahel had fallen and died, s still.
12:17 The elders of his house s beside him,
18: 4 So the king s at the side of the gate,
18:13 then you yourself would have s aloof."
18:30 So he turned aside, and s still.
20:15 and it s against the rampart.
23:10 but he s his ground. He struck down the Philistines
1Ki 1:28 So she came into the king's presence, and s before
3:15 He came to Jerusalem where he s before the ark of
1Ki 3:16 to the king and s before him.
3:28 and they s in awe of the king,
7:25 It s on twelve oxen, three facing north,
8:14 while all the assembly of Israel s.
8:22 Then Solomon s before the altar of the LORD in
8:55 he s and blessed all the assembly of Israel with
13:24 and the donkey s beside it;
13:24 the lion also s beside the body.
19:13 in his mantle and went out and s at the entrance of
22:21 a spirit came forward and s before the LORD,
2Ki 2: 7 and s at some distance from them,
2:13 and went back and s on the bank of the Jordan.
4:12 When he had called her, she s before him.
4:15 When he had called her, she s at the door.
5:15 he came and s before him and said,
5:25 He went in and s before his master;
8: 9 When he entered and s before him, he said,
10: 9 he s and said to all the people, "You are innocent.
11:11 the guards s, every man with his weapons
13:21 he came to life and s on his feet.
18:17 they came and s by the conduit of the upper pool,
18:28 the Rabshakeh s and called out in a loud voice in
23: 3 The king s by the pillar and made a covenant
23:16 when Jeroboam s by the altar at the festival;
1Ch 6:39 who s on his right, namely,
21: 1 Satan s up against Israel, and incited David
2Ch 3:13 the cherubim s on their feet, facing the nave.
4: 4 It s on twelve oxen, three facing north,
5:12 in fine linen, with cymbals, harps, and lyres, s east
6: 3 while all the assembly of Israel s.
6:12 Then Solomon s before the altar of the LORD in
6:13 had set it in the court; and he s on it.
7: 6 The priests s at their posts;
7: 6 the priests sounded trumpets; and all Israel s.
13: 4 Then Abijah s on the slope of Mount Zemaraim
18:20 a spirit came forward and s before the LORD,
20: 5 Jehoshaphat s in the assembly of Judah
20:13 Meanwhile all Judah s before the LORD,
20:19 s up to praise the LORD, the God of Israel,
20:20 and as they went out, Jehoshaphat s and said,
24:20 he s above the people and said to them,
28:12 s up against those who were coming from the war,
29:26 The Levites s with the instruments of David,
30:27 priests and the Levites s up and blessed the people,
34: 4 he demolished the incense altars that s above them.
34:31 The king s in his place and made a covenant
35:10 the priests s in their place,
Ezr 10: 5 Then Ezra s up and made the leading priests,
10:10 Then Ezra the priest s up and said to them,
Ne 4:14 I s up and said to the nobles and the officials and
8: 4 The scribe Ezra s on a wooden platform
8: 4 and beside him s Mattithiah, Shema, Anaiah,
8: 5 and when he opened it, all the people s up.
9: 2 and s and confessed their sins and the iniquities
9: 3 They s up in their place and read from the book of
9: 4 and Chenani s on the stairs of the Levites
12: 9 and Unno their associates s opposite them in
12:40 So both companies of those who gave thanks s in
Est 5: 1 the third day Esther put on her royal robes and s in
8: 5 and Esther rose and s before the king.
Job 4:16 It s still, but I could not discern its appearance.
29: 8 and the aged rose up and s;
31:34 because I s in great fear of the multitude,
Ps 33: 9 he commanded, and it s firm.
104: 6 the waters s above the mountains.
106:23 his chosen one, s in the breach before him,
106:30 Then Phinehas s up and interceded,
Isa 36: 2 He s by the conduit of the upper pool on
36:13 the Rabshakeh s and called out in a loud voice in
Jer 15: 1 Though Moses and Samuel s before me,
18:20 Remember how I s before you to speak good
19:14 he s in the court of the LORD's house and said
23:18 For who has s in the council of the LORD so as
23:22 But if they had s in my council,
36:21 the king and all the officials who s beside the king.
44:15 and all the women who s by, a great assembly,
Eze 3:23 and the glory of the LORD s there,
8:11 them s seventy of the elders of the house of Israel,
9: 2 They went in and s beside the bronze altar.
10: 6 he went in and s beside a wheel.
17: 6 its roots remained where it s.
19:11 it s out in its height with its mass of branches.
37:10 and s on their feet, a vast multitude.
Da 2: 2 When they came in and s before the king,
7:10 ten thousand times ten thousand s attending him.
8:17 So he came near where I s;
10:11 he was speaking this word to me, I s up trembling.
10:16 and said to the one who s before me, "My lord,
11: 1 I s up to support and strengthen him.
Ob 1:11 On the day that you s aside,
1:14 not have s at the crossings to cut off his fugitives;
Hab 3:11 the moon s still in its exalted place,
Zec 3: 3 Now Joshua was dressed with filthy clothes as he s
Mal 2: 5 and he revered me and s in awe of my name.
Mt 9: 7 And he s up and went to his home.
13: 2 while the whole crowd s on the beach.
20:32 Jesus s still and called them, saying,
26:62 high priest s up and said, "Have you no answer?
27:11 Now Jesus s before the governor;
Mk 2:12 And he s up, and immediately took the mat
10:49 Jesus s still and said, "Call him here."
14:47 of those who s near drew his sword and struck
14:57 Some s up and gave false testimony against him,
14:60 the high priest s up before them and asked Jesus,
15:39 Now when the centurion, who s facing him,
Lk 2: 9 Then an angel of the Lord s before them,
4:16 as was his custom. He s up to read,
Lk 4:39 he s over her and rebuked the fever, and it left her.
5:25 Immediately he s up before them,
6: 8 He got up and s there.
6:17 He came down with them and s on a level place,
7:14 and touched the bier, and the bearers s still.
7:38 She s behind him at his feet, weeping,
9:32 they saw his glory and the two men who s with him
10:25 Just then a lawyer s up to test Jesus.
13:13 immediately she s up straight
18:40 Jesus s still and ordered the man to be brought
19: 8 Zacchaeus s there and said to the Lord, "Look,
22:28 "You are those who have s by me in my trials;
23:10 The chief priests and the scribes s by,
23:35 And the people s by, watching;
23:49 s at a distance, watching these things.
24: 4 two men in dazzling clothes s beside them.
24:17 They s still, looking sad.
24:36 Jesus himself s among them and said to them,
Jn 11:56 for Jesus and were asking one another as they s in
20:11 But Mary s weeping outside the tomb.
20:19 Jesus came and s among them and said,
20:26 Jesus came and s among them and said,
21: 4 Just after daybreak, Jesus s on the beach;
Ac 1:10 suddenly two men in white robes s by them.
1:15 In those days Peter s up among
3: 8 Jumping up, he s and began to walk,
5:34 s up and ordered the men to be put outside for
6: 9 s up and argued with Stephen.
7:10 and to show wisdom when he s before Pharaoh,
9: 7 with him s speechless because they heard
9:39 All the widows s beside him,
10:30 suddenly a man in dazzling clothes s before me.
11:28 One of them named Agabus s up and predicted by
13:16 So Paul s up and with a gesture began to speak:
15: 5 to the sect of the Pharisees s up and said,
15: 7 Peter s up and said to them, "My brothers,
16: 9 there s a man of Macedonia pleading with him
17:22 Then Paul s in front of the Areopagus and said,
21:40 Paul s on the steps and motioned to the people
23: 9 and certain scribes of the Pharisees' group s up
23:11 That night the Lord s near him and said,
24:20 when I s before the council,
25:18 When the accusers s up, they did not charge him
27:21 Paul then s up among them and said, "Men,
27:23 For last night there s by me an angel of the God
Gal 2:11 because he s self-condemned;
Col 2:14 the record that s against us with its legal demands.
2Ti 4:17 But the Lord s by me and gave me strength,
Heb 9: 4 In it s the golden altar of incense and the ark of
Jas 1:12 a one has s the test and will receive the crown
Rev 4: 1 this I looked, and there in heaven a door s open!
4: 2 and there in heaven s a throne,
7:11 And all the angels s around the throne and around
8: 3 Another angel with a golden censer came and s at
11:11 and they s on their feet,
12: 4 the dragon s before the woman who was about
18:17 and all whose trade is on the sea, s far off
Tob 12:21 Then they s up, and could see him no more.
Jdt 4:14 the priests who s before the Lord and ministered to
8: 3 he s overseeing those who were binding sheaves
10:18 around her as she s outside the tent of Holofernes,
AdE 8: 4 and she rose and s before the king.
15: 6 When she had gone through all the doors, she s
Wis 10:11 she s by him and made him rich.
18:16 and s and filled all things with death,
19: 7 and dry land emerging where water had s before,
Sir 39:17 At his word the waters s in a heap,
46: 3 Who before him ever s so firm?
46: 4 the sun s still and one day become as long as two?
50:12 as he s by the hearth of the altar with a garland
Aza 1: 2 Then Azariah s still in the fire and prayed aloud:
Sus 1:34 Then the two elders s up before the people
1Mc 1:62 in Israel s firm and were resolved in their hearts
7:36 At this the priests went in and s before the altar
10:81 But his men s fast, as Jonathan had commanded,
14:26 and the house of his father have s firm;
2Mc 3:26 who s on either side of him
3:33 in the same clothing, and they s and said,
1Es 1:10 s in proper order according to kindred
5:59 And the priests s arrayed in their vestments
7: 9 the Levites s arrayed in their vestments,
9: 7 Then Ezra s up and said to them,
9:42 and reader of the law s on the wooden platform
9:43 and beside him s Mattathiah,
9:46 When he opened the law, they all s erect.
3Mc 5:51 as they s now at the gates of death.
6:31 or rather, who s at its gates,
2Es 2:47 to praise those who had s valiantly for the name of
4:17 for the sand s firm and blocked it.
4:48 So I s and looked, and lo,
4Mc 16:15 you s and watched Eleazar being tortured,

STOOP (3) [STOOPING, STOOPS]

Ps 10:10 They s, they crouch, and the helpless fall
Isa 46: 2 They s, they bow down together;
Mk 1: 7 I am not worthy to s down and untie the thong

STOOPING (1) [STOOP]

Lk 24:12 s and looking in, he saw the linen cloths

STOOPS (1) [STOOP]

Isa 46: 1 Nebo s, their idols are on beasts and cattle;

STOP (55) [STOPPED, STOPPING, STOPS]

Ge 19:17 do not look back or s anywhere in the Plain;

Ex 5: 5 of the land and yet you want them to s working!"
Nu 11:28 said, "My lord Moses, s them!"
17: 5 thus I will put a s to the complaints of
Jdg 9: 9 'Shall I s producing my rich oil by which gods
9:11 'Shall I s producing my sweetness
9:13 'Shall I s producing my wine that cheers gods
15: 7 I swear I will not s until I have taken revenge
1Sa 9: 5 or my father will s worrying about the donkeys
9:27 s here yourself for a while,
15:16 Then Samuel said to Saul, **"S!**
2Ki 3:19 all springs of water you shall s up,
4: 8 he would s there for a meal.
2Ch 25:16 "Have we made you a royal counselor? **S!**
32: 3 with his officers and his warriors to s the flow of
Ezr 5: 5 not s them until a report reached Darius and
Ne 4:11 before we come upon them and kill them and s
5:10 Let us s this taking of interest.
6: 3 the work s while I leave it to come down to you?"
Job 9:12 He snatches away; who can s him?
37:14 s and consider the wondrous works of God.
Pr 17:14 so s before the quarrel breaks out.
Isa 6:10 Make the mind of this people dull, and s their ears,
33:15 who s their ears from hearing of bloodshed
Jer 48:45 In the shadow of Heshbon fugitives s exhausted;
Eze 16:41 I will s you from playing the whore,
34:10 and put a s to their feeding the sheep;
Mt 19:14 the little children come to me, and do not s them;
23:13 and when others are going in, you s them.
Mk 9:38 and we tried to s him,
9:39 But Jesus said, "Do not s him;
10:14 "Let the little children come to me; do not s them;
Lk 9:49 and we tried to s him,
9:50 But Jesus said to him, "Do not s him;
18:16 the little children come to me, and do not s them;
19:39 "Teacher, order your disciples to **s."**
Jn 2:16 S making my Father's house a marketplace!"
Ac 8:38 He commanded the chariot to s, and both of them,
13:10 will you not s making crooked the straight paths of
Eph 6: 9 S threatening them, for you know that both
Tob 10: 6 Tobit kept saying to her, "Be quiet and s worrying,
10: 7 S trying to deceive me!
Jdt 4: 7 and it would be easy to s any who tried to enter,
AdE 14: 9 to s the mouths of those who praise you and
Sir 4:26 and do not try to s the current of a river.
18: 7 they are just beginning, and when they **s,**
20:29 like a muzzle on the mouth they s reproofs.
27:14 and their quarrels make others s their ears.
31:17 Be the first to s, as befits good manners,
1Mc 6:27 and you will not be able to s them."
11:50 make the Jews s fighting against us and our city."
2Mc 4: 6 and that Simon would not s his folly.
9: 7 Yet he did not in any way s his insolence,
3Mc 6: 1 directed the elders around him to s calling upon
2Es 13:47 Most High will s the channels of the river again,

STOPPED (61) [STOP]

Ge 26:15 the Philistines had s up and filled with earth all
26:18 for the Philistines had s them up after the death
41:49 that he s measuring it; it was beyond measure.
Lev 15: 3 or his member is s from discharging,
Nu 16:48 and the living; and the plague was **s.**
16:50 When the plague was **s,** Aaron returned to Moses
25: 8 So the plague was s among the people of Israel.
Jos 10:13 And the sun stood still, and the moon **s,**
10:13 The sun s in midheaven, and did not hurry to set
1Sa 6:14 the field of Joshua of Beth-shemesh, and s there.
10: 2 and now your father has s worrying about them
23:28 So Saul s pursuing David,
2Sa 2:28 Joab sounded the trumpet and all the people **s;**
15:17 and they s at the last house.
1Ki 15:21 he s building Ramah and lived in Tirzah.
2Ki 3:25 every spring of water they s up,
4: 6 Then the oil s flowing.
13:18 he struck three times, and **s.**
2Ch 16: 5 When Baasha heard of it, he s building Ramah,
25:16 So the prophet **s,** but said,
32: 4 and they s all the springs and the wadi that flowed
Ezr 4:24 of God in Jerusalem s and was discontinued until
Job 38:11 and here shall your proud waves be **s'?**
Ps 63:11 for the mouths of liars will be **s.**
106:30 up and interceded, and the plague was **s.**
Isa 33: 1 and when you have s dealing treacherously,
Jer 38:27 So they s questioning him,
41:17 and s at Geruth Chimham near Bethlehem,
44:18 from the time we s making offerings to the queen
48:33 I have s the wine from the wine presses;
Eze 1:21 when they **s,** the others **s;**
1:24 when they **s,** they let down their wings.
1:25 when they **s,** they let down their wings.
10:17 When they **s,** the others **s,**
10:18 from the threshold of the house and s above
10:19 They s at the entrance of the east gate of the house
11:23 and s on the mountain east of the city.
Hab 3: 6 He s and shook the earth;
Zec 7:11 and s their ears in order not to hear.
Mt 2: 9 until it s over the place where the child was.
2:10 When they saw that the star had **s,**
Mk 5:29 Immediately her hemorrhage **s;**
Lk 7:45 the time I came in she has not s kissing my feet.
8:44 and immediately her hemorrhage **s.**
Ac 21:32 the tribune and the soldiers, they s beating Paul.
Tob 6: 1 So she s weeping. The young man went out
Jdt 10: 1 When Judith had s crying out to the God of Israel,
AdE 4: 2 He got as far as the king's gate, and there he **s,**
1Mc 9:55 his mouth was s and he was paralyzed,
13:47 an agreement with them and s fighting

2Mc 9: 5 As soon as he s speaking he was seized with a pain
1Es 2:30 And the building of the temple in Jerusalem s until
3:24 When he had said this, he s speaking.
4:12 to be obeyed in this fashion?" And he s speaking.
4:41 When he s speaking, all the people shouted
3Mc 1:13 no one there had s him.
6:32 They s their chanting of dirges and took up
2Es 10: 3 But when all of them had s consoling me,
13:44 and s the channels of the river

STOPPING (4) [STOP]

2Sa 2:27 to pursue their kinsmen, not s until morning."
20:12 and the man saw that all the people were **s.**
20:12 Since he saw that all who came by him were **s,**
2Mc 9: 4 to drive without s until he completed the journey.

STOPS‡ (4) [STOP]

1Ki 18:44 and go down before the rain s you.' "
Ps 58: 4 like the deaf adder that s its ear,
107:42 and all wickedness s its mouth.
Ac 6:13 "This man never s saying things against this holy

STORAGE (5) [STORE]

1Ki 9:19 as well as all of Solomon's s cities,
2Ch 8: 4 in the wilderness and all the s towns that he built
8: 6 as well as all Solomon's s towns,
17:12 He built fortresses and s cities in Judah.
1Mc 6:53 But they had no food in **s,**

STORE (18) [STORAGE, STORE-CHAMBERS, STORE-CITIES, STORED, SHOREHOUSE, STOREHOUSES, STOREROOMS, STORES, STORING]

Ge 6:21 every kind of food that is eaten, and s it up;
Dt 14:28 and s it within your towns;
32:34 Is not this laid up in s with me,
Pr 7: 1 keep my words and s up my commandments
Jer 40:10 and s them in your vessels,
Hos 13:12 Ephraim's iniquity is bound up; his sin is kept in **s.**
Am 3:10 those who s up violence and robbery
Mt 6:19 "Do not s up for yourselves treasures on earth,
6:20 but s up for yourselves treasures in heaven,
Lk 12:17 for I have no place to s my crops?'
12:18 and there I will s all my grain and my goods.
12:21 with those who s up treasures for themselves
Wis 6: 8 But a strict inquiry is in s for the mighty.
Sir 29:12 S up almsgiving in your treasury,
1Mc 9:35 for permission to s with them the great amount
16:11 he had a large s of silver and gold,
Man 1:13 not be angry with me forever or s up evil for me;
2Es 8:36 when you are merciful to those who have no s

STORE-CHAMBERS (2) [CHAMBER, STORE]

2Ch 31:11 Then Hezekiah commanded them to prepare s in
2Es 6:40 a ray of light to be brought out from your **s,**

STORE-CITIES (1) [CITY, STORE]

2Ch 16: 4 Dan, Abel-maim, and all the s of Naphtali.

STORED‡ (24) [STORE]

Ge 41:48 and s up food in the cities;
41:48 he s up in every city the food from the fields
41:49 So Joseph s up grain in such abundance—
Lev 26:10 You shall eat old grain long **s,**
1Ki 7:51 and s them in the treasuries of the house of
2Ki 5:24 he took the bags from them, and s them inside;
20:17 that which your ancestors have s up until this day,
2Ch 5: 1 and s the silver, the gold, and all the vessels in
Ezr 6: 1 the archives where the documents were s
Ps 17:14 May their bellies be filled with what you have s up
Isa 23:18 her profits will not be s or hoarded,
39: 6 that which your ancestors have s up until this day,
Jdt 4: 5 the villages on them and s up food in preparation
1Mc 1:35 they s up arms and food,
1:35 the spoils of Jerusalem they s them there,
4:46 and s the stones in a convenient place on
13:33 and he s food in the strongholds.
14:33 where formerly the arms of the enemy had been **s,**
2Mc 8:31 and carefully s all of them in strategic places;
1Es 1:41 and s them in his temple in Babylon.
2:10 from Jerusalem and s in his temple of idols.
6:18 of the house in Jerusalem and s in his own temple,
2Es 6: 5 those who s up treasures of faith were sealed—
7:77 a treasure of works s up with the Most High,

STOREHOUSE (7) [HOUSE, STORE]

Dt 28:12 The LORD will open for you his rich **s,**
1Ch 26:15 and to his sons was allotted the **s.**
26:17 as well as two and two at the **s;**
Ne 10:38 to the house of our God, to the chambers of the **s.**
Jer 38:11 to a wardrobe of the **s,**
Mal 3:10 Bring the full tithe into the **s,**
Lk 12:24 they have neither s nor barn,

STOREHOUSES (20) [HOUSE, STORE]

Ge 41:56 Joseph opened all the **s,** and sold to the Egyptians,
2Ki 20:13 his armory, all that was found in his **s;**
20:15 there is nothing in my s that I did not show them."
2Ch 32:28 s also for the yield of grain, wine, and oil;

Ne 12:25 at the s of the gates.
13:12 the tithe of the grain, wine, and oil into the **s.**
13:13 over the s the priest Shelemiah, the scribe Zadok,
Job 38:22 "Have you entered the s of the snow,
38:22 or have you seen the s of the hail,
Ps 33: 7 he put the deeps in **s.**
135: 7 for the rain and brings out the wind from his **s.**
Isa 39: 2 his whole armory, all that was found in his **s.**
39: 4 there is nothing in my s that I did not show them."
Jer 10:13 and he brings out the wind from his **s.**
51:16 and he brings out the wind from his **s.**
Joel 1:17 seed shrivels under the clods, the s are desolate;
Sir 1:17 and their s with her produce.
43:14 the s are opened, and the clouds fly out like birds.
Bar 3:15 And who has entered her **s?**
2Es 6:22 and full s shall suddenly be found to be empty;

STOREROOMS (1) [ROOM, STORE]

Ne 10:39 oil to the s where the vessels of the sanctuary are,

STORES (12) [STORE]

1Ch 22: 3 also provided great s of iron for nails for the doors
27:28 Over the s of oil was Joash.
2Ch 11:11 and put commanders in them, and s of food, oil,
Ne 12:44 for the s, the contributions, the first fruits,
Job 21:19 'God s up their iniquity for their children.'
Pr 2: 7 he s up sound wisdom for the upright;
Isa 10:28 at Michmash he s his baggage;
Jer 41: 8 "Do not kill us, for we have s of wheat, barley, oil,
1Mc 6:53 from the Gentiles had consumed the last of the **s.**
9:52 and in them he put troops and s of food.
2Mc 12:27 and great s of war engines and missiles were there.
1Es 1:54 the treasure chests of the Lord, and the royal **s,**

STORIES (3) [STORY]

Eze 41: 6 The side chambers were in three **s,**
42: 3 the chambers rose gallery by gallery in three **s.**
42: 6 in three **s,** and they had no pillars like the pillars of

STORING (2) [STORE]

Ro 2: 5 But by your hard and impenitent heart you are s
1Ti 6:19 thus s up for themselves the treasure of

STORK (5)

Lev 11:19 the **s,** the heron of any kind, the hoopoe,
Dt 14:18 the **s,** the heron, of any kind;
Ps 104:17 the s has its home in the fir trees.
Jer 8: 7 Even the s in the heavens knows its times;
Zec 5: 9 they had wings like the wings of a **s,**

STORM‡ (33) [RAINSTORM, STORM-TOSSED, STORMED, STORMINGS, STORMS, STORMY, WINDSTORM]

2Ki 14: 7 in the Valley of Salt and took Sela by **s;**
Job 21:18 and like chaff that the s carries away?
30:22 and you toss me about in the roar of the **s.**
Ps 107:29 he made the s be still,
Pr 1:27 when panic strikes you like a **s,**
3:25 or of the s that strikes the wicked;
Isa 4: 6 and a refuge and a shelter from the s and rain.
17:13 before the wind and whirling dust before the **s.**
28: 2 like a s of hail, a destroying tempest, like a s of mighty, overflowing waters;
Jer 23:19 Look, the s of the LORD!
30:23 Look, the s of the LORD!
Eze 38: 9 You shall advance, coming on like a **s;**
Am 1:14 with a s on the day of the whirlwind;
Jnh 1: 4 and such a mighty s came upon the sea that
1:12 of me that this great s has come upon you."
Na 1: 3 His way is in whirlwind and **s,**
Zec 10: 1 from the LORD who makes the s clouds,
Ac 27:18 We were being pounded by the s so violently that
2Pe 2:17 and mists driven by a **s;**
Wis 5:14 and like a light frost driven away by a **s;**
Sir 33: 2 about it is like a boat in a **s.**
40:13 and crash like a loud clap of thunder in a **s.**
43:17 so do the s from the north and the whirlwind.
2Mc 5:11 he left Egypt and took the city by **s.**
10:24 He came on, intending to take Judea by **s.**
2Es 12:42 and like a haven for a ship saved from a **s.**
13:10 and from his tongue he shot forth a s of sparks.
13:11 of fire and the flaming breath and the great **s,**
13:27 for your seeing wind and fire and a s coming out
13:37 their ungodliness (this was symbolized by the **s),**
15:34 exceedingly threatening, full of wrath and **s.**
15:38 heavy s clouds shall be stirred up from the south,

STORM-TOSSED (1) [STORM, TOSS]

Isa 54:11 O afflicted one, **s,** and not comforted,

STORMED (1) [STORM]

2Mc 10:35 bravely s the wall and with savage fury cut down

STORMINGS (1) [STORM]

4Mc 7: 2 by the s of the tyrant and overwhelmed by

STORMS (3) [STORM]

Ps 57: 1 until the destroying s pass by.
Wis 16:16 pursued by unusual rains and hail and relentless **s,**
4Mc 15:32 and withstood the wintry s that assail religion.

STORMY (7) [STORM]
Ps 107:25 For he commanded and raised the s wind,
148: 8 snow and frost, s wind fulfilling his command!
Eze 1: 4 As I looked, a s wind came out of the north:
13:11 and a s wind will break out.
13:13 In my wrath I will make a s wind break out,
Jnh 1:13 for the sea grew more and more s against them.
Mt 16: 3 And in the morning, 'It will be s today,

STORY‡ (29) [STORIES, STORY-TELLERS]
Ge 37: 2 This is the s of the family of Jacob.
39:17 and she told him the same s, saying,
1Ki 6: 6 The lowest s was five cubits wide,
6: 8 the middle s was on the south side of the house:
one went up by winding stairs to the middle s, and
from the middle s to the third.
6:10 against the whole house, each s five cubits high,
2Ch 13:22 are written in the s of the prophet Iddo.
Eze 41: 6 one over another, thirty in each s.
41: 7 of the side chambers widened from s to s;
41: 7 this reason the structure became wider from s to s.
41: 7 from the bottom s to the uppermost s by way
Mt 8:33 they told the whole s about what had happened to
28:15 And this s is still told among the Jews to this day.
Mk 12:26 in the s about the bush, how God said to him,
Lk 20:37 the s about the bush, where he speaks of the Lord
Tob 1: 1 the s of Tobit son of Tobiel son of Hananiel son
Sir 20:19 A coarse person is like an inappropriate s,
22:10 Whoever tells a s to a fool tells it to a drowsy man;
Sus 1:27 And when the elders told their s,
2Mc 2:19 The s of Judas Maccabeus and his brothers,
6:17 we must go on briefly with the s.
15:37 So I will here end my s.
15:39 the s delights the ears of those who read the work.
4Mc 1:12 and then I shall turn to their s,
3: 6 Now this can be explained more clearly by the s

STORY-TELLERS (1) [STORY, TELL]
Bar 3:23 the s and the seekers for understanding,

STOUT (3) [STOUTHEARTED, STOUTLY]
Isa 10:16 will send wasting sickness among his s warriors,
Am 2:16 and those who are s of heart among
Sir 29:13 better than a s shield and a sturdy spear,

STOUT (KJV) See also ARROGANT BOASTING, GREATER, HARSH, STRONG

STOUTHEARTED (2) [HEART, STOUT]
Ps 76: 5 The s were stripped of their spoil;
1Mc 9:14 then all the s men went with him,

STOUTLY (1) [STOUT]
4Mc 15:31 in the universal flood, s endured the waves,

STOVE (1)
Lev 11:35 whether an oven or s, it shall be broken in pieces;

STRAGGLER (1)
Isa 14:31 and there is no s in its ranks.

STRAIGHT (51) [STRAIGHTEN, STRAIGHTENED, STRAIGHTFORWARD]
Jos 6: 5 and all the people shall charge s ahead."
6:20 so the people charged s ahead into the city
1Sa 6:12 The cows went s in the direction of Beth-shemesh
Ne 12:37 they went s up by the stairs of the city of David,
Ps 5: 8 make your way s before me.
49:14 s to the grave they descend,
107: 7 he led them by a s way,
Pr 3: 6 and he will make s your paths.
4:25 and your gaze be s before you.
4:26 Keep s the path of your feet,
5: 6 She does not keep s to the path of life;
8: 9 They are all s to one who understands and right
9:15 who are going s on their way,
11: 5 righteousness of the blameless keeps their ways s,
15:21 but a person of understanding walks s ahead.
Ecc 1:15 What is crooked cannot be made s,
7:13 who can make s what he has made crooked?
Isa 40: 3 make s in the desert a highway for our God.
45:13 and I will make all his paths s;
Jer 31: 9 in a s path in which they shall not stumble;
31:39 s to the hill Gareb, and shall then turn to Goah.
Eze 1: 7 Their legs were s, and the soles of their feet were
1: 9 each of them moved s ahead, without turning
1:12 Each moved s ahead; wherever the spirit would go,
1:23 Under the dome their wings were stretched out s,
10:22 Each one moved s ahead.
46: 9 by which they entered, but shall go out s ahead.
Am 4: 3 in the wall you shall leave, each one s ahead;
Mt 3: 3 'Prepare the way of the Lord, make his paths s.'"
Mk 1: 3 'Prepare the way of the Lord, make his paths s.'"
Lk 3: 4 'Prepare the way of the Lord, make his paths s.
3: 5 and the crooked shall be made s,
13:11 over and was quite unable to stand up s.
13:13 she stood up s and began praising God.
Jn 1:23 'Make s the way of the Lord,'"
Ac 9:11 "Get up and go to the street called S,
13:10 not stop making crooked the s paths of the Lord?
16:11 from Troas and took a s course to Samothrace,
21: 1 we came by a s course to Cos,
Heb 12:13 and make s paths for your feet,
2Pe 2:15 They have left the s road and have gone astray,
Tob 4:19 and ask him that your ways may be made s and
7: 1 take me s to our brother Raguel."
Jdt 10:11 As the women were going s on through the valley,
13:20 walking in the s path before our God."
Wis 10:10 she guided him on s paths;
Sir 2: 6 make your ways s, and hope in him.
4:18 Then she will come s back to them again
27:25 a stone s up throws it on his own head,
39:24 To the faithful his ways are s,
51:15 my foot walked on the s path;

STRAIGHTEN (1) [STRAIGHT]
LtJ 6:27 and if it is tipped over, it cannot s itself.

STRAIGHTENED (2) [STRAIGHT]
Jn 8: 7 ⟦questioning him, he s up and said to them,⟧
8:10 ⟦Jesus s up and said to her, "Woman,⟧

STRAIGHTFORWARD (1) [FORWARD, STRAIGHT]
Ecc 7:29 this alone I found, that God made human beings s,

STRAIGHTWAY (KJV) See AS SOON AS, AT ONCE, IMMEDIATELY, JUST AS, RIGHT AWAY, SUDDENLY, THEN, WITHOUT DELAY

STRAIN (3) [STRAINED, STRAINING]
Dt 28:32 you will s your eyes looking for them all day but
Ecc 2:22 the toil and s with which they toil under the sun?
Mt 23:24 You s out a gnat but swallow a camel!

STRAINED (2) [STRAIN]
Jdg 16:30 He s with all his might;
Isa 25: 6 filled with marrow, of well-aged wines s clear.

STRAINING (2) [STRAIN]
Mk 6:48 When he saw that they were s at the oars against
Php 3:13 forgetting what lies behind and s forward

STRAITS (4)
Dt 28:53 In the desperate s to which the enemy siege
28:55 in the desperate s to which the enemy siege
28:57 in the desperate s to which the enemy siege
2Es 7:*96* and besides they see the s and toil from which

STRAND (1)
Jdg 16: 9 as a s of fiber snaps when it touches the fire.

STRANGE‡ (26) [STRANGER, STRANGERS]
Dt 32:16 They made him jealous with s gods,
Ps 44:20 or spread out our hands to a s god,
81: 9 There shall be no s god among you;
114: 1 the house of Jacob from a people of s language,
Pr 23:33 Your eyes will see s things,
Isa 28:21 to do his deed—s is his deed!
43:12 when there was no s god among you;
Hos 8:12 they are regarded as a s thing.
Lk 5:26 saying, "We have seen s things today."
Ac 17:20 It sounds rather s to us,
1Co 14:21 "By people of s tongues and by the lips of
2Co 11:15 not s if his ministers also disguise themselves
Heb 13: 9 Do not be carried away by all kinds of s teachings;
1Pe 4:12 as though something s were happening to you.
AdE 13: 5 perversely following a s manner of life and laws,
Wis 2:15 of life is unlike that of others, and his ways are s.
14:23 or hold frenzied revels with s customs,
19: 5 but they themselves might meet a s death.
Sir 43:25 In it are s and marvelous creatures,
Bar 4:15 a nation ruthless and of a s language,
1Mc 1:38 she became s to her offspring,
1:44 he directed them to follow customs s to the land,
6:13 perishing of bitter disappointment in a s land."
2Mc 9: 6 the bowels of others with many and s inflictions.
9:28 among the mountains in a s land.
2Es 1: 6 and have offered sacrifices to s gods.

STRANGER‡ (25) [STRANGE]
Ge 23: 4 "I am a s and an alien residing among you;
Dt 10:19 You shall also love the s,
25: 5 not be married outside the family to a s.
Job 15:19 and no s passed among them.
19:15 my serving girls count me as a s;
29:16 and I championed the cause of the s.
31:32 the s has not lodged in the street;
Ps 69: 8 I have become a s to my kindred,
94: 6 They kill the widow and the s,
Pr 11:15 To guarantee loans for a s brings trouble,
14:10 and no s shares its joy.
20:16 the garment of one who has given surety for a s;
27: 2 a s, and not your own lips.
27:13 the garment of one who has given surety for a s;
Ecc 6: 2 to enjoy these things, but a s enjoys them.
Jer 14: 8 why should you be like a s in the land,
Mt 25:35 I was a s and you welcomed me,
25:38 was it that we saw you a s and welcomed you,
25:43 I was a s and you did not welcome me,
25:44 that we saw you hungry or thirsty or a s or naked
Lk 24:18 the only s in Jerusalem who does not know
Jn 10: 5 They will not follow a s,
Sir 11:34 and will make you a s to your own family.
29:26 "Come here, s, prepare the table;
29:27 "Be off, s, for an honored guest is here;

STRANGERS‡ (40) [STRANGE]
Ge 42: 7 he treated them like s and spoke harshly to them.
Dt 10:18 the orphan and the widow, and who loves the s,
10:19 for you were s in the land of Egypt.
16:11 the Levites resident in your towns, as well as the s,
16:14 as well as the Levites, the s, the orphans,
1Ch 16:19 of little account, and s in the land,
Ps 105:12 of little account, and s in it,
109:11 may s plunder the fruits of his toil.
146: 9 The LORD watches over the s;
Pr 5:10 and s will take their fill of your wealth,
5:17 and not for sharing with s.
Isa 61: 5 S shall stand and feed your flocks,
Jer 2:25 But you said, "It is hopeless, for I have loved s,
3:13 and scattered your favors among s
5:19 so you shall serve s in a land that is not yours."
30: 8 and s shall no more make a servant of him.
La 5: 2 Our inheritance has been turned over to s,
Eze 7:21 I will hand it over to s as booty,
16:32 who receives s instead of her husband!
28: 7 I will bring s against you, the most terrible of
Joel 3:17 and s shall never again pass through it.
Ob 1:11 on the day that s carried off his wealth,
Jn 10: 5 because they do not know the voice of s."
Ro 12:13 to the needs of the saints; extend hospitality to s.
Eph 2:12 and s to the covenants of promise,
2:19 So then you are no longer s and aliens,
Heb 11:13 They confessed that they were s and foreigners on
13: 2 Do not neglect to show hospitality to s,
3Jn 1: 5 even though they are s to you;
Jdt 9: 2 on those s who had torn off a virgin's clothing
Wis 19:13 for they practiced a more bitter hatred of s.
19:14 Others had refused to receive s when they came
19:15 the former for having received s with hostility,
Sir 8:18 In the presence of s do nothing that is to
11:34 Receive s into your home and they will stir
26:19 *and do not give your strength to s.*
1Mc 1:38 she became a dwelling of s;
3Mc 2:25 who were s to everything just.
2Es 16:40 in the midst of the calamities be like s on the earth.
16:46 for s shall gather their fruits,

STRANGLE‡ (1) [STRANGLED, STRANGLING]
4Mc 9:17 your wheel is not so powerful as to s my reason.

STRANGLED‡ (5) [STRANGLE]
Na 2:12 The lion has torn enough for his whelps and s prey
Ac 15:20 from fornication and from whatever has been s
15:29 to idols and from blood and from what is s and
21:25 to idols and from blood and from what is s and
Tob 2: 3 and now he lies there s."

STRANGLES See Index to Footnotes

STRANGLING (1) [STRANGLE]
Job 7:15 I would choose s and death rather than this body.

STRAP (1) [STRAPPED, STRAPS]
1Sa 25:13 "Every man s on his sword!"

STRAPPED (5) [STRAP]
Dt 1:41 So all of you s on your battle gear,
1Sa 17:39 David s Saul's sword over the armor,
25:13 And every one of them s on his sword;
25:13 David also s on his sword;
Ne 4:18 of the builders had his sword s at his side

STRAPS (1) [STRAP]
Jer 27: 2 Make yourself a yoke of s and bars,

STRATAGEM (1) [STRATEGY]
2Mc 14:29 for an opportunity to accomplish this by a s.

STRATEGIC (2) [STRATEGY]
2Mc 8: 6 He captured s positions and put to flight not a few
8:31 and carefully stored all of them in s places;

STRATEGICALLY (1) [STRATEGY]
2Mc 15:20 the elephants s stationed and the cavalry deployed

STRATEGY (4) [STRATAGEM, STRATEGIC, STRATEGICALLY]
2Ki 18:20 Do you think that mere words are s and power
Isa 36: 5 Do you think that mere words are s and power
Jdt 11: 8 and the most astounding in military s.
2Mc 13:18 tried s in attacking their positions.

STRAW‡ (22)
Ge 24:25 of s and fodder and a place to spend the night."
24:32 and gave him s and fodder for the camels,
Ex 5: 7 "You shall no longer give the people s to make

Ex 5: 7 let them go and gather s for themselves.
5:10 "Thus says Pharaoh, 'I will not give you s.
5:11 Go and get s yourselves, wherever you can find it;
5:12 the land of Egypt, to gather stubble for s.
5:13 same daily assignment as when you were given s."
5:16 No s is given to your servants, yet they say to us,
5:18 Go now, and work; for no s shall be given you,
Jdg 19:19 We your servants have s and fodder
1Ki 4:28 also brought to the required place barley and s for
Job 21:18 How often are they like s before the wind,
41:27 It counts iron as s, and bronze as rotten wood.
Isa 11: 7 and the lion shall eat s like the ox.
25:10 in their place as s is trodden down in a dung-pit.
65:25 the lion shall eat s like the ox;
Jer 23:28 What has s in common with wheat?
Na 1:10 they are consumed like dry s.
1Co 3:12 silver, precious stones, wood, hay, s—
2Es 1:33 I will drive you out as the wind drives s;
15:23 of the earth and the sinners, like burnt s.

STRAWED (KJV) See SCATTER, SCATTERED, SPREAD

STRAY (6) [ASTRAY, STRAYED, STRAYING, STRAYS]

Ps 119:10 do not let me s from your commandments.
119:110 but I do not s from your precepts.
Pr 7:25 do not s into her paths.
22: 6 and when old, they will not s.
Isa 63:17 do you make us s from your ways
Sir 2: 7 do not s, or else you may fall.

STRAYED (7) [STRAY]

1Sa 9: 3 Now the donkeys of Kish, Saul's father, had s.
Isa 16: 8 reached to Jazer and s to the desert;
Eze 34: 4 you have not brought back the s,
34:16 I will seek the lost, and I will bring back the s,
Hos 7:13 Woe to them, for they have s from me!
Wis 5: 6 So it was we who s from the way of truth,
Bar 3:21 Their descendants have s far from her way.

STRAYING (2) [STRAY]

Dt 22: 1 not watch your neighbor's ox or sheep s away
Pr 19:27 Cease s, my child, from the words of knowledge,

STRAYS (2) [STRAY]

Pr 27: 8 a bird that s from its nest is one who s from home.

STREAKS (1)

Ge 30:37 and almond and plane, and peeled white s in them,

STREAM (32) [STREAMS]

Ge 2: 6 but a s would rise from the earth, and water
32:23 He took them and sent them across the s,
Dt 9:21 and I threw the dust of it into the s that runs down
Ps 110: 7 He will drink from the s by the path;
Pr 18: 4 the fountain of wisdom is a gushing s.
21: 1 The king's heart is a s of water in the hand of
Isa 2: 2 all the nations shall s to it.
30:28 like an overflowing s that reaches up to the neck—
30:33 breath of the LORD, like a s of sulfur, kindles it.
32:20 Happy will you be who sow beside every s,
59:19 a pent-up s that the wind of the LORD drives on.
66:12 the wealth of the nations like an overflowing s;
Jer 17: 8 sending out its roots by the s.
51:44 The nations shall no longer s to him;
La 2:18 Let tears s down like a torrent day and night!
Da 7:10 s of fire issued and flowed out from his presence.
12: 5 one standing on this bank of the s and one on
Joel 3:18 and all the s beds of Judah shall flow with water;
Am 5:24 and righteousness like an ever-flowing s.
Mic 4: 1 Peoples shall s to it,
Sir 39:13 and blossom like a rose growing by a s of water.
1Mc 5:37 on the other side of the s.
5:39 and they are encamped across the s,
5:40 as Judas and his army drew near to the s of water,
5:42 When Judas approached the s of water,
5:42 of the army at the s and gave them this command,
16: 5 and a s lay between them.
16: 6 He saw that the soldiers were afraid to cross the s,
2Es 1:22 When you were in the wilderness, at the bitter s,
1:23 threw a tree into the water and made the s sweet.
13:10 from his mouth something like a s of fire,
13:11 the s of fire and the flaming breath and

STREAMS (35) [STREAM]

Lev 11: 9 whether in the seas or in the s—such you may eat.
11:10 the seas or the s that does not have fins and scales,
Dt 8: 7 a good land, a land with flowing s, with springs
10: 7 to Jotbathah, a land with flowing s.
2Ki 19:24 up with the sole of my foot all the s of Egypt.'
Job 20:17 the s flowing with honey and curds.
29: 6 and the rock poured out for me s of oil!
Ps 1: 3 They are like trees planted by s of water,
42: 1 As a deer longs for flowing s,
46: 4 There is a river whose s make glad the city
74:15 you dried up ever-flowing s.
78:16 He made s come out of the rock,
78:44 so that they could not drink of their s.
104:12 By the s the birds of the air have their habitation;
119:136 My eyes shed s of tears because your law is
Pr 5:16 be scattered abroad, s of water in the streets?
Ecc 1: 7 All s run to the sea, but the sea is not full;
1: 7 to the place where the s flow, there they continue
SS 4:15 and flowing s from Lebanon.
Isa 7:18 for the fly that is at the sources of the s of Egypt,
32: 2 like s of water in a dry place,
33:21 be for us a place of broad rivers and s,
34: 9 And the s of Edom shall be turned into pitch,
35: 6 in the wilderness, and s in the desert;
37:25 up with the sole of my foot all the s of Egypt.'
44: 3 and s on the dry ground;
44: 4 like willows by flowing s.
Jer 18:14 the mountain waters run dry, the cold flowing s?
Eze 31: 4 sending forth its s to all the trees of the field.
32: 2 you thrash about in your s,
32: 2 trouble the water with your feet, and foul your s.
32:14 and cause their s to run like oil,
2Es 4: 7 or how many s are at the source of the deep,
4: 7 or how many s are above the firmament,
15:41 that all the fields and all the s shall be filled with

STREET‡ (28) [STREETS]

Dt 32:25 In the s the sword shall bereave,
Jos 2:19 of you go out of the doors of your house into the s,
1Sa 9:26 and both he and Samuel went out into the s.
Job 18:17 and they have no name in the s.
31:32 the stranger has not lodged in the s;
Ps 31:11 those who see me in the s flee from me.
Pr 1:20 Wisdom cries out in the s;
7: 8 passing along the s near her corner,
7:12 now in the s, now in the squares,
Ecc 12: 4 the s are shut, and the sound of the grinding is low,
Isa 42: 2 or make it heard in the s;
51:20 they lie at the head of every s like an antelope in
51:23 like the ground and like the s for them to walk on.
Jer 6:11 Pour it out on the children in the s,
37:21 of bread was given him daily from the bakers' s,
La 1:20 In the s the sword bereaves;
2:19 who faint for hunger at the head of every s.
4: 1 sacred stones lie scattered at the head of every s.
Eze 16:25 at the head of every s you built your lofty place
16:31 building your platform at the head of every s,
Na 3:10 in pieces at the head of every s;
Mt 6: 5 and pray in the synagogues and at the s corners,
Mk 11: 4 and found a colt tied near a door, outside in the s.
Ac 9:11 "Get up and go to the s called Straight,
Rev 11: 8 and their dead bodies will lie in the s of the great
21:21 and the s of the city is pure gold,
22: 2 through the middle of the s of the city.
AdE 4: 1 then he rushed through the s of the city,

STREETS (71) [STREET]

2Sa 1:20 proclaim it not in the s of Ashkelon;
22:43 and stamped them down like the mire of the s.
Ps 18:42 I cast them out like the mire of the s.
144:14 no exile, and no cry of distress in our s.
Pr 5:16 be scattered abroad, streams of water in the s?
22:13 I shall be killed in the s!"
26:13 There is a lion in the s!"
Ecc 12: 5 and the mourners will go about the s;
SS 3: 2 in the s and in the squares;
Isa 5:25 and their corpses were like refuse in the s.
10: 6 and to tread them down like the mire of the s.
15: 3 in the s they bind on sackcloth;
24:11 There is an outcry in the s for lack of wine;
33: 7 the valiant cry in the s;
58:12 the restorer of s to live in.
Jer 5: 1 Run to and fro through the s of Jerusalem,
7:17 in the towns of Judah and in the s of Jerusalem?
7:34 in the cities of Judah and in the s of Jerusalem;
9:21 from the s and the young men from the squares."
11: 6 in the cities of Judah, and in the s of Jerusalem:
11:13 as the s of Jerusalem are the altars you have set up
14:16 be thrown out into the s of Jerusalem,
33:10 of Judah and the s of Jerusalem that are desolate,
44: 6 in the towns of Judah and in the s of Jerusalem;
44: 9 in the land of Judah and in the s of Jerusalem?
44:17 in the towns of Judah and in the s of Jerusalem.
44:21 that you made in the towns of Judah and in the s
51: 4 the land of the Chaldeans, and wounded in her s.
La 2:11 because infants and babes faint in the s of the city.
2:12 as they faint like the wounded in the s of the city,
2:21 and the old are lying on the ground in the s;
4: 5 Those who feasted on delicacies perish in the s;
4: 8 they are not recognized in the s.
4:14 Blindly they wandered through the s,
4:18 so that we could not walk in our s;
Eze 7:19 They shall fling their silver into the s,
11: 6 and have filled its s with the slain.
26:11 the hoofs of his horses he shall trample all your s.
28:23 into it, and bloodshed into its s;
Da 9:25 for sixty-two weeks it shall be built again with s
Am 5:16 and in all the s they shall say, "Alas!
Mic 7:10 she will be trodden down like the mire of the s.
Na 2: 4 The chariots race madly through the s,
Zep 3: 6 I have laid waste their s so that no one walks in
Zec 8: 4 Old men and old women shall again sit in the s
8: 5 And the s of the city shall be full of boys and girls
playing in its s.
9: 3 and gold like the dirt of the s.
10: 5 trampling the foe in the mud of the s;
Mt 6: 2 the hypocrites do in the synagogues and in the s,
12:19 nor will anyone hear his voice in the s.
22: 9 Go therefore into the main s,
22:10 the s and gathered all whom they found, both good
Lk 10:10 go out into its s and say,
13:26 and drank with you, and you taught in our s.'
Lk 14:21 at once into the s and lanes of the town and bring
Ac 5:15 so that they even carried out the sick into the s,
Tob 13:16 The s of Jerusalem will be paved with ruby and
Jdt 7:14 be strewn about in the s where they live.
7:22 and were collapsing in the s of the town and in
Sir 9: 7 Do not look around in the s of a city,
23:21 This man will be punished in the s of the city,
49: 6 and made its s desolate, as Jeremiah had foretold.
1Mc 1:55 at the doors of the houses and in the s.
2: 9 Her infants have been killed in her s,
11:46 the people of the city seized the main s of the city
14: 9 Old men sat in the s;
2Mc 3:19 with sackcloth under their breasts, thronged the s.
3Mc 1:18 and filled the s with groans and lamentations.
1:20 some in houses and some in the s,
4: 3 or what s were not filled with mourning

STRENGTH‡ (226) [STRONG]

Ge 4:12 it will no longer yield to you its s;
31: 6 that I have served your father with all my s;
48: 2 he summoned his s and sat up in bed.
Ex 13: 3 LORD brought you out from there by s of hand;
13:14 'By s of hand the LORD brought us out of Egypt,
13:16 by s of hand the LORD brought us out of Egypt."
15: 2 The LORD is my s and my might,
15:13 you guided them by your s to your holy abode.
Lev 26:20 Your s shall be spent to no purpose:
Nu 11: 6 but now our s is dried up,
Dt 11: 8 that you may have s to go in and occupy the land
33:25 and as your days, so is your s.
Jos 14:11 my s now is as my s was then, for war,
Jdg 8:21 for as the man is, so is his s."
16: 5 "Coax him, and find out what makes his s so great,
16: 6 "Please tell me what makes your s so great,
16: 9 So the secret of his s was not known.
16:15 and have not told me what makes your s so great."
16:17 my head were shaved, then my s would leave me;
16:19 He began to weaken, and his s left him.
1Sa 2: 1 my s is exalted in my God.
2: 4 but the feeble gird on s.
2:10 he will give s to his king,
2:31 a time is coming when I will cut off your s and
2:31 when I will cut off your strength and the s
28:20 and there was no s in him,
28:22 that you may have s when you go on your way."
30: 4 until they had no more s to weep.
2Sa 15:12 The conspiracy grew in s,
22:33 with s has opened wide my path.
22:40 For you girded me with s for the battle;
1Ki 19: 8 in the s of that food forty days and forty nights
2Ki 9:24 Jehu drew his bow with all his s,
19: 3 and there is no s to bring them forth.
19:26 shorn of s, are dismayed and confounded;
1Ch 16:11 Seek the LORD and his s,
16:27 s and joy are in his place.
16:28 ascribe to the LORD glory and s.
29:12 it is in your hand to make great and to give s to all.
Ne 4:10 Judah said, "The s of the burden bearers is failing,
8:10 for the joy of the LORD is your s."
Job 6:11 What is my s, that I should wait?
6:12 Is my s the s of stones,
9: 4 and mighty in s—who has resisted him,
9:19 If it is a contest of s, he is the strong one!
12:13 "With God are wisdom and s;
12:16 With him are s and wisdom;
16:15 and have laid my s in the dust.
18:12 Their s is consumed by hunger,
26: 2 How you have assisted the arm that has no s!
30: 2 What could I gain from the s of their hands?
35:10 who gives s in the night,
36: 5 he is mighty in s of understanding.
36:19 or will all the force of your s?
39:11 Will you depend on it because its s is great,
40:16 Its s is in its loins,
41:12 or its mighty s, or its splendid frame.
41:22 In its neck abides s, and terror dances before it.
Ps 18: 1 I love you, O LORD, my s.
18:32 the God who girded me with s,
18:39 For you girded me with s for the battle;
21: 1 In your s the king rejoices,
21:13 Be exalted, O LORD, in your s!
28: 7 The LORD is my s and my shield;
28: 8 The LORD is the s of his people;
29: 1 ascribe to the LORD glory and s.
29:11 May the LORD give s to his people!
31:10 my s fails because of my misery,
32: 4 my s was dried up as by the heat of summer.
33:16 a warrior is not delivered by his great s.
38:10 My heart throbs, my s fails me;
46: 1 God is our refuge and s,
59: 9 O my s, I will watch for you;
59:17 O my s, I will sing praises to you, for you, O God,
65: 6 By your s you established the mountains;
68:28 Summon your might, O God; show your s, O God,
68:35 he gives power and s to his people.
71: 9 do not forsake me when my s is spent.
73:26 God is the s of my heart and my portion forever.
78:51 the first issue of their s in the tents of Ham.
81: 1 Sing aloud to God our s;
84: 5 Happy are those whose s is in you,
84: 7 They go from s to s;
86:16 give your s to your servant;
89:17 For you are the glory of their s;
93: 1 the LORD is robed, he is girded with s.
96: 6 s and beauty are in his sanctuary.
96: 7 ascribe to the LORD glory and s.

Ps 102:23 He has broken my s in midcourse;
105: 4 Seek the LORD and his s;
105:36 the first issue of all their s.
118:14 The LORD is my s and my might;
138: 3 you answered me, you increased my s of soul.
147:10 His delight is not in the s of the horse,
Pr 8:14 I have insight, I have s.
14: 4 abundant crops come by the s of the ox.
20:29 The glory of youths is their s,
24: 5 those who have knowledge than those who have s;
24:10 in the day of adversity, your s being small;
30:25 a people without s, yet they provide their food in
31: 3 Do not give your s to women,
31:17 She girds herself with s,
31:25 S and dignity are her clothing,
Ecc 7:19 Wisdom gives s to the wise more than ten rulers
10:10 then more s must be exerted;
10:17 for s, and not for drunkenness!
Isa 10:13 For he says: "By the s of my hand I have done it,
12: 2 for the LORD GOD is my s and my might;
28: 6 and s to those who turn back the battle at the gate.
30:15 in quietness and in trust shall be your s.
37: 3 and there is no s to bring them forth.
37:27 shorn of s, are dismayed and confounded;
40: 9 lift up your voice with s, O Jerusalem, herald of
40:26 because he is great in s, mighty in power,
40:31 those who wait for the LORD shall renew their s,
41: 1 let the peoples renew their s;
44:12 he becomes hungry and his s fails,
45:24 it shall be said of me, are righteousness and s;
49: 4 I have spent my s for nothing and vanity;
49: 5 and my God has become my s—
51: 9 Awake, awake, put on s, O arm of the LORD!
52: 1 Awake, awake, put on your s, O Zion!
Jer 16:19 O LORD, my s and my stronghold,
17: 5 in mere mortals and make mere flesh their s,
49: 4 Why do you boast in your s?
49: 4 Your s is ebbing, O faithless daughter.
51:30 their s has failed, they have become women;
La 1: 6 they fled without s before the pursuer.
1:11 they trade their treasures for food to revive their s.
1:14 they weigh on my neck, sapping my s;
1:19 in the city while seeking food to revive their s.
Da 2:41 but some of the s of iron shall be in it,
10: 8 My s left me, and complexion grew deathly pale,
and I retained no s.
10:16 upon me that I retain no s.
10:17 For I am shaking, no s remains in me,
11:15 for there shall be no s to resist.
11:17 to come with the s of his whole kingdom,
Hos 7: 9 Foreigners devour his s, but he does not know it;
Am 2:14 and the strong shall not retain their s,
6:13 not by our own s taken Karnaim for ourselves?"
Mic 5: 4 stand and feed his flock in the s of the LORD,
Na 1:12 "Though they are at full s and many,
2: 1 gird your loins; collect all your s.
3: 9 Ethiopia was her s, Egypt too,
Hab 3:19 GOD, the Lord, is my s;
Hag 2:22 to destroy the s of the kingdoms of the nations,
Zec 12: 5 of Jerusalem have s through the LORD of hosts,
Mk 5: 4 and no one had the s to subdue him.
12:30 and with all your mind, and with all your s.'
12:33 and with all the understanding, and with all the s,'
Lk 1:51 He has shown s with his arm;
10:27 and with all your s, and with all your mind;
21:36 the s to escape all these things that will take place,
22:43 ⟦from heaven appeared to him and gave him s.⟧
Ac 9:19 and after taking some food, he regained his s.
1Co 1:25 and God's weakness is stronger than human s.
10:13 and he will not let you be tested beyond your s,
Eph 6:10 be strong in the Lord and in the s of his power.
Col 1:11 May you be made strong with all the s that comes
2Ti 4:17 But the Lord stood by me and gave me s,
Heb 11:34 won s out of weakness, became mighty in war,
1Pe 4:11 whoever serves must do so with the s
Tob 14:8,9 at all times with sincerity and with all their s.
Jdt 2: 5 and take with you men confident in their s,
5: 3 and in what does their power and s consist?
5:23 a people with no s or power for making war.
7:22 they no longer had any s.
9: 7 boasting in the s of their foot soldiers,
9: 8 Break their s by your might,
9:11 "For your s does not depend on numbers,
13: 7 "Give me s today, O Lord God of Israel!"
13:11 still showing his power in Israel and his s
16:13 you are great and glorious, wonderful in s,
Wis 10: 2 and gave him s to rule all things.
11:21 For it is always in your power to show great s,
12:16 For your s is the source of righteousness,
12:17 For you show your s when people doubt
12:18 Although you are sovereign in s,
13:19 he asks s of a thing whose hands have no s.
16:16 were flogged by the s of your arm,
18:22 He conquered the wrath not by s of body,
Sir 5: 2 Do not follow your inclination and s in pursuing
9: 2 to a woman and let her trample down your s.
11:12 who lack s and abound in poverty;
17: 3 He endowed them with s like his own,
19:28 Even if lack of s keeps him from sinning,
26:19 *and do not give your s to strangers.*
28:10 in proportion to a person's s will be his anger,
31:25 Do not try to prove your s by wine-drinking,
31:30 reducing his s and adding wounds.
38:18 and a sorrowful heart saps one's s.
39:28 on the day of reckoning they will pour out their s
40:26 Riches and s build up confidence,
41: 2 to one who is needy and failing in s, worn down
Sir 43:15 In his majesty he gives the clouds their s,
43:28 Where can we find the s to praise him?
43:30 When you exalt him, summon all your s,
46: 9 The Lord gave Caleb s, which remained with him
47: 5 and he gave s to his right arm to strike down
Bar 1:12 The Lord will give us s, and light to our eyes;
3:14 Learn where there is wisdom, where there is s,
Aza 1:21 and deprived of all power, and let their s
1Mc 2:61 of those who put their trust in him will lack s.
3:19 but s comes from Heaven.
3:35 against them to wipe out and destroy the s of Israel
4:32 melt the boldness of their s;
9: 8 We may have the s to fight them."
9: 9 saying, "We do not have the s.
9:14 that Bacchides and the s of his army were on
10:71 and let us match s with each other there,
2Mc 10:34 The men within, relying on the s of the place,
12:14 relying on the s of the walls and on their supply
12:35 by main s, wishing to take the accursed man alive,
1Es 3:17 Then the first, who had spoken of the s of wine,
4: 1 the second, who had spoken of the s of the king,
4:40 To it belongs the s and the kingship and the power
3Mc 2: 4 even giants who trusted in their s and boldness,
2Es 5:53 the s of youth are different from those born during
5:55 creation that already is aging and passing the s of
12: 5 and not even a little s is left in me,
15:50 the glory of your s shall wither like a flower

STRENGTHEN‡ (41) [STRONG]

Dt 3:28 But charge Joshua, and encourage and s him,
33: 7 s his hands for him, and be a help against his
Jdg 16:28 remember me and s me only this once, O God,
1Ki 20:22 s yourself, and consider well what you have to do;
2Ch 16: 9 to s those whose heart is true to him.
Ne 6: 9 But now, O God, s my hands.
Ps 10:17 you will s their heart, you will incline your ear
89:21 my arm also shall s him.
104:15 and bread to s the human heart.
119:28 s me according to your word.
Isa 35: 3 S the weak hands, and make firm the feeble knees.
41:10 I will s you, I will help you,
54: 2 lengthen your cords and s your stakes.
Jer 23:14 they s the hands of evildoers,
Eze 30:24 I will s the arms of the king of Babylon,
30:25 I will s the arms of the king of Babylon,
34:16 and I will s the weak,
Da 11: 1 I stood up to support and s him.
Na 3:14 Draw water for the siege, s your forts;
Zec 10: 6 I will s the house of Judah,
Lk 22:32 when once you have turned back, s your brothers."
Ac 15:32 said much to encourage and s the believers.
Ro 1:11 with you some spiritual gift to s you—
16:25 Now to God who is able to s you according
1Co 1: 8 He will also s you to the end,
1Th 3: 2 to s and encourage you for the sake of your faith,
3:13 so s your hearts in holiness that you may
2Th 2:17 and s them in every good work and word.
3: 3 he will s you and guard you from the evil one.
Heb 12:12 lift your drooping hands and s your weak knees,
Jas 5: 8 S your hearts, for the coming of the Lord is near.
1Pe 5:10 will himself restore, support, s, and establish you.
Rev 3: 2 and s what remains and is on the point of death,
Jdt 11:22 to s our hands and bring destruction
1Mc 6:18 They were trying in every way to harm them and s
10:23 in forming a friendship with the Jews to s himself.
1Es 7:15 to s their hands for the service of the Lord God
2Es 2:15 s their feet, because I have chosen you,
2:25 "Good nurse, nourish your children; s their feet.
12: 6 now entreat the Most High that he may s me to
12: 8 s me and show me, your servant, the interpretation

STRENGTHENED (33) [STRONG]

Jdg 3:12 the LORD s King Eglon of Moab against Israel,
7:11 and afterward your hands shall be s to attack
9:24 who s his hands to kill his brothers.
1Sa 23:16 there he s his hand through the LORD.
30: 6 But David s himself in the LORD his God.
2Sa 16:21 and the hands of all who are with you will be s."
2Ch 11:17 They s the kingdom of Judah,
17: 1 and s himself against Israel.
24:13 the house of God to its proper condition and s it.
32: 5 he also s the Millo in the city of David,
Job 4: 3 you have s the weak hands.
Eze 34: 4 You have not s the weak,
Da 10:18 Again one in human form touched me and s me.
10:19 When he spoke to me, I was s and said,
10:19 "Let my lord speak, for you have s me."
Hos 7:15 It was I who trained and s their arms,
Ac 14:22 There they s the souls of the disciples
16: 5 So the churches were s in the faith and increased
1Co 1: 6 as the testimony of Christ has been s among you—
Eph 3:16 he may grant that you may be s in your inner being
1Ti 1:12 who has s me, because he judged me faithful
Heb 13: 9 for it is well for the heart to be s by grace,
Sir 45: 8 and s him with the symbols of authority,
1Mc 1:34 men who were renegades. These s their position;
13:48 He also s its fortifications and built in it a house
13:52 He s the fortifications of the temple hill alongside
2Mc 11: 9 the merciful God, and were s in heart, ready
3Mc 1: 7 he s the morale of his subjects.
2Es 5:15 with me held me and s me and set me on my feet.
10:30 he grasped my right hand and s me and set me
4Mc 7: 9 You, father, s our loyalty to the law
13:25 for nobility s their goodwill toward one another,
15:23 s her to disregard, for the time, her parental love.

STRENGTHENING (3) [STRONG]

2Ch 28:20 and oppressed him instead of s him.
Ac 15:41 He went through Syria and Cilicia, s the churches.
18:23 through the region of Galatia and Phrygia, s all

STRENGTHENS (4) [STRONG]

Ps 147:13 For he s the bars of your gates;
Isa 40:29 He gives power to the faint, and s the powerless.
Php 4:13 I can do all things through him who s me.
Sir 3: 9 For a father's blessing s the houses of the children,

STRESS (2)

Isa 21:15 from the bent bow, and from the s of battle.
Lk 12:50 and what s I am under until it is completed!

STRETCH (49) [OUTSTRETCHED, STRETCHED, STRETCHER, STRETCHES, STRETCHING]

Ex 3:20 So I will s out my hand and strike Egypt
7: 5 when I s out my hand against Egypt and bring
7:19 and s out your hand over the waters of Egypt—
8: 5 'S out your hand with your staff over the rivers,
8:16 'S out your staff and strike the dust of the earth,
9:22 "S out your hand toward heaven so that hail
9:29 I will s out my hands to the LORD;
10:12 "S out your hand over the land of Egypt,
10:21 "S out your hand toward heaven so that there may
14:16 and s out your hand over the sea and divide it,
14:26 "S out your hand over the sea,
Nu 24: 6 Like palm groves that s far away,
Jos 8:18 "S out the sword that is in your hand toward Ai;
1Ki 8:38 of their own hearts so that they s out their hands
2Ki 21:13 I will s over Jerusalem the measuring line
2Ch 6:29 so that they s out their hands toward this house;
Job 1:11 But s out your hand now, and touch all that he has,
1:12 only do not s out your hand against him!"
2: 5 But s out your hand now and touch his bone
11:13 you will s out your hands toward him.
Ps 68:31 let Ethiopia hasten to s out its hands to God.
104: 2 You s out the heavens like a tent,
125: 3 righteous might not s out their hands to do wrong.
138: 7 you s out your hand, and your right hand delivers
143: 6 I s out my hands to you;
144: 7 S out your hand from on high;
Isa 1:15 When you s out your hands,
28:20 For the bed is too short to s oneself on it,
34:11 He shall s the line of confusion over it,
Jer 6:12 for I will s out my hand against the inhabitants of
51:25 I will s out my hand against you,
Eze 6:14 I will s out my hand against them,
14: 9 and I will s out my hand against him,
14:13 and I s out my hand against it,
25:13 I will s out my hand against Edom,
25:16 I will s out my hand against the Philistines,
30:25 He shall s it out against the land of Egypt,
35: 3 I s out my hand against you to make you
Da 11:42 He shall s out his hand against the countries,
Zep 1: 4 I will s out my hand against Judah,
2:13 And he will s out his hand against the north,
Mt 12:13 Then he said to the man, "S out your hand."
Mk 3: 5 of heart and said to the man, "S out your hand."
Lk 6:10 he said to him, "S out your hand."
Jn 21:18 But when you grow old, you will s out your hands,
Ac 4:30 while you s out your hand to heal,
Sir 7:32 S out your hand to the poor,
15:16 s out your hand for whichever you choose.
1Es 6:33 and nation that shall s out their hands to hinder

STRETCHED (76) [STRETCH]

Ge 48:14 But Israel s out his right hand and laid it on
Ex 8: 6 So Aaron s out his hand over the waters of Egypt;
8:17 Aaron s out his hand with his staff and struck
9:15 by now I could have s out my hand and struck you
9:23 Then Moses s out his staff toward heaven,
9:33 and s out his hands to the LORD;
10:13 So Moses s out his staff over the land of Egypt,
10:22 So Moses s out his hand toward heaven,
14:21 Then Moses s out his hand over the sea.
14:27 So Moses s out his hand over the sea,
15:12 You s out your right hand,
Jos 8:18 And Joshua s out the sword that was in his hand
8:19 As soon as he s out his hand,
8:26 with which he s out the sword,
2Sa 17:19 s it over the well's mouth,
24:16 when the angel s out his hand toward Jerusalem
1Ki 13: 4 Jeroboam s out his hand from the altar, saying,
13: 4 that he s out against him withered so that he could
17:21 Then he s himself upon the child three times,
1Ch 21:16 in his hand a drawn sword s out over Jerusalem.
Job 9: 8 who alone s out the heavens and trampled
15:25 Because they s out their hands against God,
38: 5 Or who s the line upon it?
Ps 77: 2 in the night my hand is s out without wearying;
Pr 1:24 have s out my hand and no one heeded,
Isa 5:25 he s out his hand against them and struck them;
5:25 and his hand is s out still.
9:12 his hand is s out still.
9:17 his hand is s out still.
9:21 his hand is s out still.
10: 4 his hand is s out still.
14:26 this is the hand that is s out over all the nations.
14:27 His hand is s out, and who will turn it back?
23:11 He has s out his hand over the sea,

Isa 42: 5 who created the heavens and s them out,
44:24 who made all things, who alone s out the heavens,
45:12 it was my hands that s out the heavens,
51:13 who s out the heavens and laid the foundations of
54: 2 and let the curtains of your habitations be s out;
Jer 10:12 and by his understanding s out the heavens.
15: 6 so I have s out my hand against you
51:15 and by his understanding s out the heavens.
La 1:10 Enemies have s out their hands
2: 8 he s the line; he did not withhold his hand from
Eze 1:23 Under the dome their wings were s out straight,
2: 9 I looked, and a hand was s out to me,
8: 3 It s out the form of a hand,
10: 7 a cherub s out his hand from among the cherubim
16:27 Therefore I s out my hand against you,
17: 7 This vine s out its roots toward him;
25: 7 therefore I have s out my hand against you,
Hos 7: 5 he s out his hand with mockers.
Zec 1:16 the measuring line shall be s out over Jerusalem.
12: 1 the LORD, who s out the heavens and founded
Mt 8: 3 He s out his hand and touched him, saying,
12:13 He s it out, and it was restored,
Mk 1:41 Jesus s out his hand and touched him,
3: 5 He s it out, and his hand was restored.
Lk 5:13 Then Jesus s out his hand, touched him, and said,
Ac 26: 1 Paul s out his hand and began to defend himself:
Jdt 13: 2 with Holofernes s out on his bed,
Sir 4:31 Do not let your hand be s out to receive and closed
43:12 the hands of the Most High have s it out.
1Mc 6:25 against us alone that they have s out their hands;
7:47 and the right hand that he had so arrogantly s out,
9:47 and Jonathan s out his hand to strike Bacchides,
2Mc 7:10 and courageously s forth his hands,
14:33 he s out his right hand toward the sanctuary,
14:34 Then the priests s out their hands toward heaven
15:15 Jeremiah s out his right hand and gave to Judas
15:21 s out his hands toward heaven and called upon
15:32 which had been boastfully s out against
3Mc 5:25 s their hands toward heaven and
4Mc 4:11 s out his hands toward heaven,
9:13 When the noble youth was s out around this,
11:18 He was carefully s tight upon it,

STRETCHER (1) [STRETCH]

2Mc 3:27 his men took him up, put him on a s,

STRETCHES (8) [STRETCH]

Ge 49: 9 He crouches down, he s out like a lion,
Job 26: 7 He s out Zaphon over the void,
Isa 31: 3 When the LORD s out his hand,
33:17 they will behold a land that s far away.
40:22 who s out the heavens like a curtain,
44:13 The carpenter s a line, marks it out with a stylus,
La 1:17 Zion s out her hands, but there is no one
AdE 4:11 the king s out the golden scepter is safe—

STRETCHING (3) [STRETCH]

Isa 51:16 s out the heavens and laying the foundations of the
Jer 4:31 s out her hands, "Woe is me!
1Es 8:73 and kneeling down and s out my hands to the Lord

STREW (1) [STREWN]

Eze 32: 5 I will s your flesh on the mountains,

STREWN (3) [STREW]

Ps 141: 7 so shall their bones be s at the mouth of Sheol.
Jdt 7:14 before the sword reaches them they will be s about
7:25 to be s before them in thirst and exhaustion.

STRICKEN‡ (10) [STRIKE]

1Sa 5:12 those who did not die were s with tumors,
24: 5 Afterward David was s to the heart
2Sa 24:10 David was s to the heart because he had numbered
Ps 102: 4 My heart is s and withered like grass;
Isa 16: 7 Mourn, utterly s, for the raisin cakes of
53: 4 yet we accounted him s, struck down by God,
53: 8 s for the transgression of my people.
Hos 9:16 Ephraim is s, their root is dried up,
Wis 19:17 They were s also with loss of sight—
1Mc 9:55 for at that time Alcimus was s and his work

STRICT (6) [STRICTEST, STRICTLY, STRICTNESS]

Ac 5:28 "We gave you s orders not to teach in this name,
Wis 6: 8 But a s inquiry is in store for the mighty.
Sir 26:10 Keep s watch over a headstrong daughter, or else,
28: 1 for he keeps a s account of their sins.
42:11 Keep s watch over a headstrong daughter,
51:19 and in my conduct I was s;

STRICTEST (1) [STRICT]

Ac 26: 5 to the s sect of our religion and lived as a Pharisee.

STRICTLY (9) [STRICT]

1Sa 14:28 "Your father s charged the troops with an oath,
Ezr 7:26 let judgment be s executed on them,
Mk 5:43 He s ordered them that no one should know this,
Ac 22: 3 educated s according to our ancestral law,
23:14 "We have s bound ourselves by an oath
2Mc 3: 1 and the laws were s observed because of the piety
1Es 8:24 or the law of the kingdom shall be s punished,
2Es 7:21 For the Lord s commanded those who came into
2Es 16:64 The Lord will s examine all their works,

STRICTNESS (2) [STRICT]

Jas 3: 1 that we who teach will be judged with greater s.
Wis 12:21 with what s you have judged your children,

STRIDE (2) [STRIDING]

2Sa 22:37 You have made me s freely,
Pr 30:29 Three things are stately in their s;

STRIDING (1) [STRIDE]

Pr 30:31 the he-goat, and a king s before his people.

STRIFE‡ (36) [STRIVE]

Ge 13: 7 and there was s between the herders
13: 8 "Let there be no s between you and me,
2Sa 22:44 You delivered me from s with the peoples;
Job 33:19 and with continual s in their bones,
Ps 18:43 You delivered me from s with the peoples;
55: 9 for I see violence and s in the city.
56: 6 They stir up s, they lurk, they watch my steps.
59: 3 the mighty stir up s against me.
Pr 10:12 Hatred stirs up s, but love covers all offenses.
13:10 By insolence the heedless make s,
15:18 Those who are hot-tempered stir up s,
16:28 A perverse person spreads s,
17: 1 with quiet than a house full of feasting with s.
17:14 The beginning of s is like letting out water;
17:19 One who loves transgression loves s;
18: 6 A fool's lips bring s, and a fool's mouth invites
20: 3 It is honorable to refrain from s,
22:10 Drive out a scoffer, and s goes out;
23:29 Who has sorrow? Who has s?
26:21 so is a quarrelsome person for kindling s.
28:25 The greedy person stirs up s,
29:22 One given to anger stirs up s,
30:33 so pressing anger produces s.
Isa 54:15 If anyone stirs up s, it is not from me;
54:15 whoever stirs up s with you shall fall because
Jer 15:10 a man of s and contention to the whole land!
Hab 1: 3 before me; s and contention arise.
Ro 1:29 Full of envy, murder, s, deceit, craftiness,
Gal 5:20 enmities, s, jealousy, anger, quarrels, dissensions,
Wis 14:22 but though living in great s due to ignorance,
Sir 27:15 The s of the proud leads to bloodshed,
28: 8 Refrain from s, and your sins will be fewer;
28: 8 for the hot-tempered kindle s,
28:10 in proportion to the obstinacy, so will s increase;
40: 5 and fear of death, and fury and s.
40: 9 come death and bloodshed and s and sword,

STRIKE‡ (99) [STRICKEN, STRIKES, STRIKING, STRUCK, TERROR-STRICKEN]

Ge 3:15 he will s your head, and you will s his heel."
Ex 2:13 "Why do you s your fellow Hebrew?"
3:20 So I will stretch out my hand and s Egypt
7:17 the staff that is in my hand I will s the water that is
8:16 'Stretch out your staff and s the dust of the earth,
9: 3 the hand of the LORD will s with
12:12 I will s down every firstborn in the land of Egypt,
12:13 over you, and no plague shall destroy you when I s
12:23 LORD will pass through to s down the Egyptians;
12:23 the destroyer to enter your houses to s you down.
17: 6 S the rock, and water will come out of it,
Lev 10: 6 you will die and wrath will s all the congregation;
26:24 I myself will s you sevenfold for your sins.
Nu 14:12 I will s them with pestilence and disinherit them,
24: 8 He shall s with his arrows.
Dt 28:35 The LORD will s you on the knees and on
Jdg 6:16 and you shall s down the Midianites,
1Sa 17:35 I would catch it by the jaw, s it down, and kill it.
17:46 and I will s you down and cut off your head;
20:33 But Saul threw his spear at him to s him;
26: 8 I will not s him twice."
26:10 the LORD will s him down;
2Sa 1:15 "Come here and s him down."
2:22 why should I s you to the ground?
5: 8 "Whoever would s down the Jebusites,
5:24 before you to s down the army of the Philistines."
13:28 and when I say to you, 'S Amnon,' then kill him.
17: 2 I will s down only the king,
18:11 Why then did you not s him there to the ground?
20:10 He did not s a second blow.
1Ki 2:29 saying, "Go, s him down."
2:31 "Do as he has said, s him down and bury him;
14:15 "The LORD will s Israel,
20:35 of a company of prophets said to another, "S me!"
20:35 But the man refused to s him.
20:37 Then he found another man and said, "S me!"
2Ki 6:18 and said, "S this people, please, with blindness."
9: 7 You shall s down the house of your master Ahab,
13:18 "S the ground with them";
13:19 but now you will s down Aram only three times."
1Ch 14:15 before you to s down the army of the Philistines."
Job 15:29 nor will they s root in the earth;
20:24 a bronze arrow will s them through.
36:32 and commands it to s the mark.
Ps 3: 7 For you s all my enemies on the cheek;
10:18 so that those from earth may s terror no more.
89:23 before him and s down those who hate him.
121: 6 sun shall not s you by day, nor the moon by night.
141: 5 Let the righteous s me; let the faithful correct me.
Pr 19:25 S a scoffer, and the simple will learn prudence;
Isa 11: 4 he shall s the earth with the rod of his mouth,
19:22 The LORD will s Egypt, striking and healing;
49:10 neither scorching wind nor sun shall s them down,
58: 4 to quarrel and to fight and to s with a wicked fist.
Jer 21: 6 And I will s down the inhabitants of this city,
21: 7 He shall s them down with the edge of the sword;
33: 5 with the dead bodies of those whom I shall s down
Eze 5: 2 one third you shall take and s with the sword all
7: 9 Then you shall know that it is I the LORD who s.
21:12 Ah! S the thigh!
21:14 And you, mortal, prophesy; S hand to hand.
21:17 I too will s hand to hand, I will satisfy my fury;
22:13 I s my hands together at the dishonest gain
32:15 when I s down all who live in it,
39: 3 I will s your bow from your left hand,
Hos 14: 5 he shall s root like the forests of Lebanon.
Am 9: 1 S the capitals until the thresholds shake,
Mic 5: 1 with a rod they s the ruler of Israel upon the cheek.
6:13 Therefore I have begun to s you down,
Zec 1:21 to terrify them, to s down the horns of the nations
11:17 May the sword s his arm and his right eye!
12: 4 says the LORD, I will s every horse with panic,
12: 4 I s every horse of the peoples with blindness.
13: 7 S the shepherd, that the sheep may be scattered;
14:12 the LORD will s all the peoples that wage war
Mal 4: 6 so that I will not come and s the land with a curse.
Mt 26:31 'I will s the shepherd, and the sheep of the flock
Mk 14:27 'I will s the shepherd, and the sheep will be
14:65 to blindfold him, and to s him, saying to him,
Lk 22:49 they asked, "Lord, should we s with the sword?"
Jn 18:23 But if I have spoken rightly, why do you s me?"
Ac 23: 2 near him to s him on the mouth.
23: 3 At this Paul said to him, "God will s you,
Rev 2:23 and I will s her children dead.
7:16 the sun will not s them, nor any scorching heat;
11: 6 and to s the earth with every kind of plague,
19:15 to s down the nations, and he will rule them with
Jdt 9:10 of my lips s down the slave with the prince and
16: 6 nor did the sons of the Titans s him down,
Wis 4: 3 of their illegitimate seedlings will s a deep root
Sir 8:16 where no help is at hand, they will s you down.
13: 2 The pot will s against it and be smashed.
47: 5 and he gave strength to his right arm to s down
1Mc 4:33 S them down with the sword
9:47 Jonathan stretched out his hand to s Bacchides,
2Mc 8:18 with a single nod to s down those who are coming
15:16 with which you will s down your adversaries."
2Es 15:11 and will s Egypt with plagues, as before,

STRIKER (KJV) See VIOLENT

STRIKES (24) [STRIKE]

Ex 21:12 Whoever s a person mortally shall be put to death.
21:15 Whoever s father or mother shall be put to death.
21:18 When individuals quarrel and one s the other with
21:20 When a slaveowner s a male or female slave with
21:26 a slaveowner s the eye of a male or female slave,
Nu 35:16 But anyone who s another with an iron object,
35:17 Or anyone who s another with a stone in hand
35:18 Or anyone who s another with a weapon of wood
35:21 or in enmity s another with the hand,
Dt 19: 5 the handle and s the other person who then dies;
27:24 be anyone who s down a neighbor in secret."
Job 5:18 For he wounds, but he binds up; he s,
34:26 He s them for their wickedness while others look
Pr 1:26 I will mock when panic s you,
1:27 when panic s you like a storm,
3:25 or of the storm that s the wicked;
17:10 A rebuke s deeper into a discerning person than
Isa 8:14 He will become a sanctuary, a stone one s against;
30:31 when he s with his rod.
41: 7 the hammer encourages the one who s the anvil,
Eze 17:10 When the east wind s it, will it not utterly wither,
Mt 5:39 But if anyone s you on the right cheek,
Lk 6:29 If anyone s you on the cheek, offer the other also;
2Mc 3:39 he s and destroys those who come to do it injury."

STRIKING‡ (9) [STRIKE]

Ge 4:23 a man for wounding me, a young man for s me.
1Sa 17:50 s down the Philistine and killing him;
1Ki 20:37 So the man hit him, s and wounding him.
Isa 19:22 The LORD will strike Egypt, s and healing;
Jn 19: 3 "Hail, King of the Jews!" and s him on the face.
Ac 7:24 the oppressed man and avenged him by s down
27:41 But s a reef, they ran the ship aground;
Sir 16: 5 and my ear has heard things more s than these.
2Mc 10: 3 then, s fire out of flint, they offered sacrifices,

STRING (1) [BOWSTRING, STRINGED, STRINGS, STRUNG, TEN-STRINGED]

Ps 11: 2 they have fitted their arrow to the s,

STRINGED (11) [STRING]

Ps 4: T *To the leader: with s instruments.*
6: T *To the leader: with s instruments;*
45: 8 From ivory palaces s instruments make you glad;
54: T *To the leader: with s instruments.*
55: T *To the leader: with s instruments.*
61: T *To the leader: with s instruments.*
67: T *To the leader: with s instruments.*
76: T *To the leader: with s instruments.*
Isa 38:20 and we will sing to s instruments all the days
Hab 3:19 To the leader: with s instruments.
1Mc 13:51 and with harps and cymbals and s instruments,

STRINGS (4) [STRING]
Ps 33: 2 make melody to him with the harp of ten s.
33: 3 play skillfully on the s, with loud shouts.
150: 4 praise him with s and pipe!
SS 1:10 your neck with s of jewels.

STRIP (25) [STRIPPED, STRIPS]
Lev 19:10 You shall not s your vineyard bare,
Nu 20:26 s Aaron of his vestments, and put them
Dt 24:20 you beat your olive trees, do not s what is left;
1Sa 31: 8 next day, when the Philistines came to s the dead,
2Sa 23:10 people came back to him—but only to s the dead.
1Ch 10: 8 next day when the Philistines came to s the dead,
Job 41:13 Who can s off its outer garment?
Isa 27:10 there they lie down, and s its branches.
32:11 s, and make yourselves bare,
45: 1 to subdue nations before him and s kings
47: 2 s off your robe, uncover your legs,
Jer 5:10 s away her branches, for they are not the LORD's.
La 4:21 you shall become drunk and s yourself bare.
Eze 16:39 they shall s you of your clothes
23:26 They shall also s you of your clothes
26:16 and s off their embroidered garments.
Da 4:14 s off its foliage and scatter its fruit.
Hos 2: 3 or I will s her naked and expose her as in
13:15 It shall s his treasury of every precious thing.
Am 3:11 and s you of your defense;
Mic 2: 8 you s the robe from the peaceful,
Zec 9: 4 the Lord will s it of its possessions
Jdt 7: 4 "They will now s clean the whole land;
Wis 13:11 to handle and skillfully s off all its bark,
LtJ 6:58 Anyone who can will s them of their gold

STRIPE (2) [STRIPED]
Ex 21:25 burn for burn, wound for wound, s for s.

STRIPE[S] (KJV) See also BEATING[S], BLOWS, BRUISES, FLOGGING[S], LASHES, SCOURGES, WOUNDS

STRIPED (7) [STRIPE]
Ge 30:35 that day Laban removed the male goats that were s
30:39 and so the flocks produced young that were s,
30:40 the s and the completely black animals in the flock
31: 8 and if he said, 'The s shall be your wages,' then all the flock bore s.
31:10 the male goats that leaped upon the flock were s,
31:12 that leap on the flock are s, speckled, and mottled;

STRIPLING (1)
1Sa 17:56 The king said, "Inquire whose son the s is."

STRIPPED (30) [STRIP]
Ge 37:23 they s him of his robe, the long robe with sleeves
Ex 33: 6 the Israelites s themselves of their ornaments,
Nu 20:28 Moses s Aaron of his vestments,
1Sa 18: 4 Jonathan s himself of the robe
19:24 He too s off his clothes, and he too fell in a frenzy
31: 9 They cut off his head, s off his armor,
2Ki 18:16 At that time Hezekiah s the gold from the doors of
1Ch 10: 9 They s him and took his head and his armor,
Job 12:17 He leads counselors away s,
12:19 He leads priests away s, and overthrows
19: 9 He has s my glory from me,
22: 6 and s the naked of their clothing.
Ps 76: 5 The stouthearted were s of their spoil;
Jer 49:10 But as for me, I have s Esau bare,
Eze 12:19 because their land shall be s of all it contains,
19:12 its fruit was s off, its strong stem was withered;
32:15 the land of Egypt desolate and when the land is s
Da 5:20 and his glory was s from him.
Joel 1: 7 it has s off their bark and thrown it down;
Mt 27:28 They s him and put a scarlet robe on him,
27:31 they s him of the robe and put his own clothes
Mk 15:20 they s him of the purple cloak
Lk 10:30 and fell into the hands of robbers, who s him,
Ac 16:22 and the magistrates had them s of their clothing
Col 3: 9 that you have s off the old self with its practices
1Mc 1:22 on the front of the temple; he s it all off.
2Mc 4:38 he immediately s off the purple robe
8:27 the arms of the enemy and s them of their spoils,
11:12 Most of them got away s and wounded,
4Mc 6: 2 First they s the old man,

STRIPS (3) [STRIP]
Job 12:24 He s understanding from the leaders of the earth,
Ps 29: 9 of the LORD causes the oaks to whirl, and s
Jn 11:44 his hands and feet bound with s of cloth,

STRIVE (16) [STRIFE, STRIVEN, STRIVING, STROVE]
Isa 41:11 those who s against you shall be as nothing
45: 9 Woe to you who s with your Maker,
Mt 6:32 For it is the Gentiles who s for all these things;
6:33 But s first for the kingdom of God
Lk 12:30 of the world that s after all these things,
12:31 Instead, s for his kingdom,
13:24 "S to enter through the narrow door;
Ro 9:30 Gentiles, who did not s for righteousness,
9:31 who did s for the righteousness that is based on
9:32 Because they did not s for it on the basis of faith,
1Co 12:31 But s for the greater gifts.
14: 1 Pursue love and s for the spiritual gifts,
14:12 s to excel in them for building up the church.
2Pe 3:14 s to be found by him at peace,
2Mc 2:31 the narrative should be allowed to s for brevity
2Es 5:34 while I s to understand the way of the Most High

STRIVEN (2) [STRIVE]
Ge 32:28 for you have s with God and with humans,
2Es 7:92 because they have s with great effort to overcome

STRIVES See Index to Footnotes

STRIVING (2) [STRIVE]
Lk 12:29 And do not keep s for what you are to eat
Php 1:27 s side by side with one mind for the faith of

STROKE (5)
1Sa 26: 8 therefore let me pin him to the ground with one s
Ps 39:10 Remove your s from me; I am worn down by
Isa 30:32 And every s of the staff of punishment that
Mt 5:18 not one letter, not one s of a letter,
Lk 16:17 than for one s of a letter in the law to be dropped.

STROKES (KJV) See FLOGGING

STRONG‡ (255) [STRENGTH, STRENGTHEN, STRENGTHENED, STRENGTHENING, STRENGTHENS, STRONGER, STRONGEST, STRONGHOLD, STRONGHOLDS, STRONGLY]
A. STRONG DRINK (21)

Ge 49:14 a s donkey, lying down between the sheepfolds;
Ex 1: 7 they multiplied and grew exceedingly s,
1:20 and the people multiplied and became very s.
10:19 LORD changed the wind into a very s west wind,
13: 9 a s hand the LORD brought you out of Egypt.
14:21 the sea back by a s east wind all night, and turned
Lev 10: 9 Drink no wine or s drink, neither you A
Nu 6: 3 shall separate themselves from wine and s drink; A
11: 4 The rabble among them had a s craving;
13:18 whether the people who live in it are s or weak,
13:28 Yet the people who live in the land are s,
21:24 for the boundary of the Ammonites was s.
28: 7 a drink offering of s drink to the LORD. A
Dt 2:21 a s and numerous people, as tall as the Anakim.
9: 2 a s and tall people, the offspring of the Anakim,
14:26 sheep, wine, s drink, or whatever you desire. A
29: 6 and you have not drunk wine or s drink— A
31: 6 Be s and bold; have no fear
31: 7 "Be s and bold, for you are the one who will go
31:23 "Be s and bold, for you shall bring the Israelites
Jos 1: 6 Be s and courageous; for you shall put this people
1: 7 Only be s and very courageous,
1: 9 I hereby command you: Be s and courageous;
1:18 Only be s and courageous."
10:25 or dismayed; be s and courageous;
14:11 as s today as I was on the day that Moses sent me;
17:13 But when the Israelites grew s,
17:18 of iron, and though they are s."
23: 9 before you great and s nations;
Jdg 1:28 When Israel grew s, they put the Canaanites
3:29 all s, able-bodied men; no one escaped.
9:51 But there was a s tower within the city,
13: 4 Now be careful not to drink wine or s drink, A
13: 7 So then drink no wine or s drink, A
13:14 She is not to drink wine or s drink, A
14:14 Out of the s came something sweet."
18:26 When Micah saw that they were too s for him,
1Sa 1:15 I have drunk neither wine nor s drink, A
14:52 and when Saul saw any s or valiant warrior,
2Sa 2: 7 Therefore let your hands be s, and be valiant;
3: 6 Abner was making himself s in the house of Saul.
10:11 He said, "If the Arameans are too s for me,
10:11 but if the Ammonites are too s for you,
10:12 Be s, and let us be courageous for the sake
22:18 He delivered me from my s enemy,
23: 1 the favorite of the S One of Israel:
1Ki 2: 2 to go the way of all the earth. Be s,
19:11 so s that it was splitting mountains
2Ki 2:16 we have fifty s men among your servants;
24:16 one thousand, all of them s and fit for war.
1Ch 11:10 who gave him s support in his kingdom,
19:12 He said, "If the Arameans are too s for me,
19:12 Ammonites are too s for you, then I will help you.
19:13 Be s, and let us be courageous for our people and
22:13 Be s and of good courage.
28:10 to build a house as the sanctuary; be s,
28:20 "Be s and of good courage, and act.
2Ch 11:11 He made the fortresses s, and put commanders
11:12 and spears in all the cities, and made them very s.
12: 1 rule of Rehoboam was established and he grew s,
13:21 But Abijah grew s. He took fourteen wives,
25: 8 Rather, go by yourself and act; be s in battle,
26: 8 even to the border of Egypt, for he became very s.
26:15 for he was marvelously helped until he became s.
26:16 he had become s he grew proud, to his destruction.
27: 6 So Jotham became s because he ordered his ways
32: 7 "Be s and of good courage.
Ezr 9:12 so that you may be s and eat the good of the land
Ezr 10: 4 and we are with you; be s,
Ne 1:10 by your great power and your s hand.
Job 4:11 The s lion perishes for lack of prey,
9:19 If it is a contest of strength, he is the s one!
12:21 and looses the belt of the s.
18: 7 Their s steps are shortened,
39: 4 Their young ones become s,
Ps 18:17 He delivered me from my s enemy,
19: 5 and like a s man runs its course with joy.
22:12 s bulls of Bashan surround me;
24: 8 The LORD, s and mighty, the LORD,
27:14 be s, and let your heart take courage;
30: 7 you had established me as a s mountain;
31: 2 Be a rock of refuge for me, a s fortress to save me.
31:24 Be s, and let your heart take courage,
35:10 You deliver the weak from those too s for them,
61: 3 a s tower against the enemy.
71: 3 Be to me a rock of refuge, a s fortress, to save me,
71: 7 but you are my s refuge.
77:15 With your s arm you redeemed your people,
80:17 the one whom you made s for yourself.
83: 8 they are the s arm of the children of Lot.
89:13 s is your hand, high your right hand.
90:10 or perhaps eighty, if we are s;
136:12 with a s hand and an outstretched arm,
140: 7 O LORD, my Lord, my s deliverer,
142: 6 for they are too s for me.
Pr 14:26 In the fear of the LORD one has s confidence,
18:10 The name of the LORD is a s tower;
18:11 The wealth of the rich is their s city;
20: 1 Wine is a mocker, s drink a brawler, A
21:14 and a concealed bribe in the bosom, s wrath.
23:11 for their redeemer is s; he will plead their cause
24: 5 Wise warriors are mightier than s ones,
31: 4 or for rulers to desire s drink; A
31: 6 Give s drink to one who is perishing, A
31:17 with strength, and makes her arms s.
Ecc 9:11 nor the battle to the s, nor bread to the wise,
12: 3 and the s men are bent,
SS 8: 6 for love is s as death, passion fierce as the grave.
Isa 1:31 The s shall become like tinder,
5:11 in the morning in pursuit of s drink, A
8:11 while his hand was s upon me, and warned me not
17: 9 On that day their s cities will be like
24: 9 s drink is bitter to those who drink it. A
25: 3 Therefore s peoples will glorify you;
26: 1 We have a s city; he sets up victory
27: 1 and great and s sword will punish Leviathan
28: 2 See, the Lord has one who is mighty and s;
28: 7 also reel with wine and stagger with s drink; A
28: 7 the priest and the prophet reel with s drink, A
28: 7 with wine, they stagger with s drink; A
29: 9 stagger, but not from s drink! A
31: 1 and in horsemen because they are very s,
35: 4 Say to those who are of a fearful heart, "Be s,
44:12 and forging it with his s arm;
44:14 or chooses a holm tree or an oak and lets it grow s
53:12 and he shall divide the spoil with the s;
56:12 let us fill ourselves with s drink. A
58:11 in parched places, and make your bones s;
Jer 4:12 a wind too s for that.
9: 3 they have grown s in the land for falsehood,
31:11 and has redeemed him from hands too s for him.
32:21 with a s hand and outstretched arm,
50:34 Their Redeemer is s; the LORD of hosts
51:12 of Babylon; make the watch s;
51:53 and though she should fortify her s height,
Eze 3:14 the hand of the LORD being s upon me.
7:24 I will put an end to the arrogance of the s,
17: 9 No s arm or mighty army will be needed to pull it
19:12 its s stem was withered; the fire consumed it.
19:14 so that there remains in it no s stem,
22:14 or can your hands remain s in the days
26:11 and your s pillars shall fall to the ground.
30:21 so that it may become s to wield the sword.
30:22 both the s arm and the one that was broken;
34:16 but the fat and the s I will destroy.
Da 2:40 And there shall be a fourth kingdom, s as iron;
2:42 so the kingdom shall be partly s and partly brittle.
4:11 The tree grew great and s,
4:20 The tree that you saw, which grew great and s,
4:22 You have grown great and s.
7: 7 terrifying and dreadful and exceedingly s.
8: 4 it did as it pleased and became s.
8:24 He shall grow s in power,
9:27 a s covenant with many for one week, and for half
10:19 you are safe. Be s and courageous!"
11: 2 and when he has become s through his riches,
11: 5 "Then the king of the south shall grow s,
11:23 he shall act deceitfully and become s with
Am 2: 9 and who was as s as oaks;
2:14 and the s shall not retain their strength,
5: 9 who makes destruction flash out against the s,
Mic 2:11 "I will preach to you of wine and s drink," A
4: 3 and shall arbitrate between s nations far away;
4: 7 and those who were cast off, a s nation;
Zec 8: 9 says the LORD of hosts: Let your hands be s—
8:13 Do not be afraid, but let your hands be s.
8:22 Many peoples and s nations shall come to seek
10:12 I will make them s in the LORD,
Mt 12:29 enter a s man's house and plunder his property, without first tying up the s man?
14:30 But when he noticed the s wind,
Mk 3:27 enter a s man's house and plunder his property without first tying up the s man;
Lk 1:15 He must never drink wine or s drink; A
1:80 The child grew and became s in spirit,

Lk 2:40 The child grew and became s, filled with wisdom;
11:21 When a s man, fully armed, guards his castle,
16: 3 I am not s enough to dig,
Jn 6:18 sea became rough because a s wind was blowing.
Ac 3: 7 and immediately his feet and ankles were made s.
3:16 his name itself has made this man s,
Ro 4:20 but he grew s in his faith as he gave glory to God,
15: 1 We who are s ought to put up with the failings of
1Co 1:27 in the world to shame the s;
4:10 We are weak, but you are s.
7:36 if his passions are s, and so it has to be,
16:13 stand firm in your faith, be courageous, be s.
2Co 10:10 For they say, "His letters are weighty and s,
12:10 for whenever I am weak, then I am s.
13: 9 For we rejoice when we are weak and you are s.
Eph 6:10 be s in the Lord and in the strength of his power.
Col 1:11 be made s with all the strength that comes
2Ti 2: 1 my child, be s in the grace that is in Christ Jesus;
Jas 3: 4 though they are so large that it takes s winds
1Jn 2:14 you are s and the word of God abides in you,
Jdt 9: 9 Give to me, a widow, the s hand to do what I plan.
Wis 10: 5 and kept him s in the face of his compassion
14:16 Then the ungodly custom, grown s with time,
Sir 6:29 Then her fetters will become for you a s defense,
28:14 it has destroyed s cities, and overturned the houses
34:19 a mighty shield and s support,
LtJ 6:36 from death or rescue the weak from the s.
1Mc 1: 4 a very s army and ruled over countries,
1:17 So he invaded Egypt with a s force,
1:20 and came to Jerusalem with a s force.
1:33 city of David with a great s wall and s towers,
2:49 "Arrogance and scorn have now become s;
2:64 My children, be courageous and grow s in the law,
3:15 Once again a s army of godless men went up
3:17 fight against so great and so s a multitude?
3:27 the forces of his kingdom, a very s army.
4: 7 they saw the camp of the Gentiles, s and fortified,
4:30 When he saw that their army was s, he prayed,
4:60 with high walls and s towers all around,
5: 6 where he found a s band and many people,
5:26 all these towns were s and large—
5:46 This was a large and very s town on the road,
6: 6 a s force, but had turned and fled before the Jews;
6: 6 that the Jews had grown s from the arms, supplies,
6:37 the elephants were wooden towers, s and covered;
6:41 trembled, for the army was very large and s.
6:57 the place against which we are fighting is s,
6:62 and saw what a s fortress the place was,
7:25 that Judas and those with him had grown s,
8: 1 that they were very s and were well-disposed
8: 2 and that they were very s.
9:50 to Jerusalem and built s cities in Judea:
11:15 Ptolemy marched out and met him with a s force,
2Mc 1: 3 to do his will with a s heart and a willing spirit.
1:24 you are awe-inspiring and s and just and merciful,
3:26 to him, remarkably s, gloriously beautiful
10:18 in two very s towers well equipped to withstand
12:18 though in one place he had left a very s garrison.
12:35 who was on horseback and was a s man,
13:19 a s fortress of the Jews, was turned back,
14: 1 the harbor of Tripolis with a s army and a fleet,
1Es 4:14 and are not men many, and is not wine s?
4:32 Gentlemen, why are not women s,
4:34 are not women s? The earth is vast,
4:38 But truth endures and is s forever,
6:14 by a king of Israel who was great and s,
8:85 so that you may be s and eat the good things of
8:95 and we are with you to take s measures."
3Mc 3: 8 were not s enough to help them,
2Es 7:*34* truth shall stand, and faithfulness shall grow s.
7:*112* [42] those who were s prayed for the weak.
8:22 whose utterances are certain, whose command is s
10:22 and our s men made powerless.
15:16 growing s against one another,
16: 7 Can one turn back an arrow shot by a s archer?
16:13 For his right hand that bends the bow is s,
4Mc 4: 5 by the accursed Simon and a very s military force.
12: 2 he felt s compassion for this child when he saw
15:11 of none of them were the various tortures s enough

STRONGER (33) [STRONG]

Ge 25:23 the one shall be s than the other,
30:41 Whenever the s of the flock were breeding,
30:42 so the feebler were Laban's, and the s Jacob's.
49:26 of your father are s than the blessings of
Nu 13:31 for they are s than we."
22: 6 curse this people for me, since they are s than I;
Dt 1:28 'The people are s and taller than we;
Jdg 14:18 What is s than a lion?"
2Sa 1:23 were swifter than eagles, they were s than lions.
3: 1 David grew s and s,
13:14 being s than she, he forced her and lay with her.
1Ki 20:23 and so they were s than we;
20:23 and surely we shall be s than they.
20:25 and surely we shall be s than they."
Job 17: 9 they that have clean hands grow s and s.
Ps 105:24 and made them s than their foes,
Pr 18:19 An ally offended is s than a city;
Ecc 6:10 they are not able to dispute with those who are s.
Isa 28:22 do not scoff, or your bonds will be made s;
Da 11: 5 of his officers shall grow s than he and shall rule
11:25 with a much greater and s army.
Lk 11:22 one s than he attacks him and overpowers him,
1Co 1:25 and God's weakness is s than human strength.
10:22 Are we s than he?
Sir 8:12 Do not lend to one who is s than you;
Sus 1:39 because he was s than we,
1Es 4: 3 But the king is s; he is their lord
4:35 But truth is great, and s than all things.
5:50 the land were hostile to them and were s than they;
2Es 15:31 remembering their origin, shall become still s;
4Mc 13:22 and they grow s from this common nurture

STRONGEST (13) [STRONG]

Ps 78:31 of God rose against them and he killed the s
Eze 19:11 Its s stem became a ruler's scepter;
Da 3:20 and ordered some of the s guards in his army
11:39 with the s fortresses by the help of a foreign god.
1Es 3: 5 "Let each of us state what one thing is s;
3:10 The first wrote, "Wine is s."
3:11 The second wrote, "The king is s."
3:12 The third wrote, "Women are s,
3:18 how is wine the s? It leads astray the minds of all
3:24 Gentlemen, is not wine the s,
4: 2 are not men s, who rule over land and sea and all
4:12 Gentlemen, why is not the king the s,
4:41 "Great is truth, and s of all!"

STRONGHOLD (44) [STRONG]

Jdg 6:26 to the LORD your God on the top of the s here,
9:46 they entered the s of the temple of El-berith.
9:49 and following Abimelech put it against the s,
9:49 and they set the s on fire over them,
1Sa 22: 4 with him all the time that David was in the s.
22: 5 "Do not remain in the s;
24:22 but David and his men went up to the s.
2Sa 5: 7 Nevertheless David took the s of Zion,
5: 9 David occupied the s, and named it the city
5:17 but David heard about it and went down to the s.
22: 3 my s and my refuge, my savior;
23:14 David was then in the s;
1Ch 11: 5 David took the s of Zion, now the city of David.
11: 7 David resided in the s;
11:16 David was then in the s;
12: 8 From the Gadites there went over to David at the s
12:16 Some Benjaminites and Judahites came to the s
Ps 9: 9 The LORD is a s for the oppressed,
9: 9 a s in times of trouble.
18: 2 my shield, and the horn of my salvation, my s.
27: 1 The LORD is the s of my life;
94:22 But the LORD has become my s,
144: 2 my s and my deliverer, my shield,
Pr 10:29 The way of the LORD is a s for the upright,
21:22 against a city of warriors and brought down the s
Isa 29: 7 all that fight against her and her s,
Jer 16:19 O LORD, my strength and my s,
Eze 24:25 mortal, on the day when I take from them their s,
30:15 the s of Egypt, and cut off the hordes of Thebes.
Joel 3:16 a s for the people of Israel.
Na 1: 7 The LORD is good, a s in a day of trouble;
Zec 9:12 Return to your s, O prisoners of hope;
1Mc 4:61 that the people might have a s that faced Idumea.
5: 9 But they fled to the s of Dathema,
5:11 to come and capture the s to which we have fled,
5:29 and they went all the way to the s of Dathema.
5:30 and engines of war to capture the s,
6:61 On these conditions the Jews evacuated the s.
12:34 over the s to those whom Demetrius had sent.
16: 8 of them fell wounded and the rest fled into the s.
16:15 in the little s called Dok, which he had built;
2Mc 10:32 Timothy himself fled to a s called Gazara,
12:19 destroyed those whom Timothy had left in the s,
1Es 8:81 to give us a s in Judea and Jerusalem.

STRONGHOLDS (55) [STRONG]

Jdg 6: 2 in the mountains, caves and s.
1Sa 23:14 David remained in the s in the wilderness,
23:19 "David is hiding among us in the s of Horesh,
23:29 and lived in the s of En-gedi.
2Sa 22:46 and came trembling out of their s.
Ps 18:45 and came trembling out of their s.
89:40 you have laid his s in ruins.
Isa 34:13 Thorns shall grow over its s,
Jer 48: 7 because you trusted in your s and your treasures,
48:18 against you; he has destroyed your s.
48:41 the towns shall be taken and the s seized.
49:27 and it shall devour the s of Ben-hadad.
51:30 have given up fighting, they remain in their s;
La 2: 2 in his wrath he has broken down the s
2: 5 He has destroyed all its palaces, laid in ruins its s,
Eze 19: 7 And he ravaged their s, and laid waste their towns;
33:27 and those who are in s and in caves shall die
Da 11:24 He shall devise plans against s,
Hos 8:14 a fire upon his cities, and it shall devour his s.
Am 1: 4 and it shall devour the s of Ben-hadad.
1: 7 fire that shall devour its s.
1:10 fire that shall devour its s.
1:12 and it shall devour the s of Bozrah.
1:14 fire that shall devour its s,
2: 2 and it shall devour the s of Kerioth,
2: 5 and it shall devour the s of Jerusalem.
3: 9 Proclaim to the s in Ashdod,
3: 9 and to the s in the land of Egypt, and say,
3:10 those who store up violence and robbery in their s.
3:11 and your s shall be plundered.
6: 8 I abhor the pride of Jacob and hate his s;
Mic 5:11 the cities of your land and throw down all your s;
2Co 10: 4 but they have divine power to destroy s.
1Mc 1: 2 He fought many battles, conquered s,
5:27 to attack the s tomorrow and capture
5:65 down its s and burned its towers on all sides.
8:10 tore down their s, and enslaved them to this day.
10:12 Then the foreigners who were in the s
10:37 Let some of them be stationed in the great s of
11:18 in the s were killed by the inhabitants of the s.
11:41 and the troops in the s;
12:33 as far as Askalon and the neighboring s.
12:35 of the people and planned with them to build s
12:45 I will hand it over to you as well as the other s and
13:33 up the s of Judea and walled them all around,
13:33 and he stored food in the s.
13:38 let the s that you have built be your possession.
14:42 and over the country and the weapons and the s,
15: 7 All the weapons that you have prepared and the s
2Mc 8:30 and got possession of some exceedingly high s,
10:15 the Idumeans, who had control of important s,
10:16 rushed to the s of the Idumeans.
10:23 destroyed more than twenty thousand in the two s.
11: 6 that Lysias was besieging the s,

STRONGLY‡ (7) [STRONG]

Ge 19: 3 But he urged them s; so they turned aside to him
Lk 24:29 But they urged him s, saying, "Stay with us,
1Co 16:12 I s urged him to visit you with the other brothers,
2Ti 4:15 for he s opposed our message.
Heb 6:18 we who have taken refuge might be s encouraged
1Mc 10:50 He pressed the battle s until the sun set,
2Mc 12:13 He also attacked a certain town that was s fortified

STROVE (2) [STRIVE]

Hos 12: 3 and in his manhood he s with God.
12: 4 He s with the angel and prevailed,

STRUCK‡ (192) [STRIKE]

Ge 19:11 And they s with blindness the men who were at
32:25 he s him on the hip socket;
32:32 he s Jacob on the hip socket at the thigh muscle.
Ex 7:20 of his officials he lifted up the staff and s the water
7:25 Seven days passed after the LORD had s the Nile.
8:17 Aaron stretched out his hand with his staff and s
9:15 now I could have stretched out my hand and s you
9:25 The hail s down everything that was in
9:25 the hail also s down all the plants of the field,
12:27 he s down the Egyptians but spared our houses.' "
12:29 At midnight the LORD s down all the firstborn in
17: 5 in your hand the staff with which you s the Nile,
Lev 26:17 and you shall be s down by your enemies;
Nu 8:17 the day that I s down all the firstborn in the land
11:33 the LORD s the people with a very great plague.
14:42 not let yourselves be s down before your enemies.
20:11 Then Moses lifted up his hand and s the rock twice
22:23 Balaam s the donkey, to turn it back onto the road.
22:25 against the wall; so he s it again.
22:27 and he s the donkey with his staff.
22:28 that you have s me these three times?"
22:32 "Why have you s your donkey these three times?
24:10 and he s his hands together.
33: 4 whom the LORD had s down among them.
35:21 then the one who s the blow shall be put to death;
Dt 2:33 and we s him down, along with his offspring
3: 3 We s him down until not a single survivor
21: 1 and it is not known who s the person down,
25:18 and s down all who lagged behind you;
Jos 8:21 then they turned back and s down the men of Ai.
8:22 on the other; and Israel s them down
10:10 and s them down as far as Azekah and Makkedah.
10:26 Afterward Joshua s them down and put them
10:28 and s it and its king with the edge of the sword;
10:30 and he s it with the edge of the sword,
10:32 and s it with the edge of the sword,
10:33 and Joshua s him and his people,
10:35 and s it with the edge of the sword;
10:37 and s it with the edge of the sword,
10:39 they s them with the edge of the sword,
11: 8 They s them down, until they had left no one
11:10 and s its king down with the sword.
11:12 and s them with the edge of the sword,
11:14 the people they s down with the edge of the sword,
11:17 He took all their kings, s them down,
Jdg 5:26 she s Sisera a blow, she crushed his head,
7:13 and came to the tent, and s it so that it fell;
15: 8 He s them down hip and thigh
20:21 and s down on that day twenty-two thousand of
20:25 and s down eighteen thousand of the Israelites,
1Sa 4: 8 the gods who s the Egyptians with every sort
5: 6 and he terrified and s them with tumors,
5: 9 he s the inhabitants of the city,
6: 9 then we shall know that it is not his hand that s us;
7:11 and s them down as far as beyond Beth-car.
14:31 After they had s down the Philistines that day
14:48 He did valiantly, and s down the Amalekites,
17:35 and s it down, rescuing the lamb from its mouth;
17:49 slung it, and s the Philistine on his forehead;
19:10 he eluded Saul, so that he s the spear into the wall.
25:38 About ten days later the LORD s Nabal,
27: 9 David s the land, leaving neither man
2Sa 1:15 So he s him down and he died.
2:23 So Abner s him in the stomach with the butt of his
4: 6 and they s him in the stomach;
5:25 and he s down the Philistines from Geba all
6: 7 against Uzzah; and God s him there
8: 3 David also s down King Hadadezer son of Rehob
11:15 so that he may be s down and die.
12: 9 You have s down Uriah the Hittite with the sword,
12:15 The LORD s the child that Uriah's wife bore
14: 6 and one s the other and killed him.

2Sa 14: 7 They say, 'Give up the man who s his brother,
18:15 surrounded Absalom and s him, and killed him.
20:10 Joab s him in the belly so
22:39 I s them down, so that they did not rise;
23:10 s down the Philistines until his arm grew weary,
23:20 he s down two sons of Ariel of Moab.
1Ki 2:25 he s him down, and he died.
2:34 Then Benaiah son of Jehoiada went up and s him
2:46 and he went out and s him down, and he died.
15:27 and Baasha s him down at Gibbethon,
16:10 Zimri came in and s him down and killed him,
22:34 a certain man drew his bow and unknowingly s
2Ki 2: 8 Then Elijah took his mantle and rolled it up, and s
2:14 and s the water, saying, "Where is the LORD,
2:14 When he had s the water,
6:18 So he s them with blindness as Elisha had asked.
10: 9 but who s down all these?
12:21 his servants, who s him down, so that he died.
13:18 he s three times, and stopped.
13:19 and said, "You should have s five or six times;
13:19 then you would have s down Aram
15: 5 The LORD s the king, so that he was leprous to
15:10 and s him down in public and killed him,
15:14 he s down Shallum son of Jabesh in Samaria
19:35 and s down one hundred eighty-five thousand in
25:21 The king of Babylon s them down and put them
25:25 they s down Gedaliah so that he died,
1Ch 11:22 he s down two sons of Ariel of Moab.
13:10 he s him down because he put out his hand to
14:16 and they s down the Philistine army from Gibeon
18: 3 David also s down King Hadadezer of Zobah,
21: 7 with this thing, and he s Israel.
2Ch 13:20 the LORD s him down, and he died.
18:33 a certain man drew his bow and unknowingly s
21:18 After all this the LORD s him in his bowels with
25:11 and s down ten thousand men of Seir.
26:20 because the LORD had s him.
32:21 of his own sons s him down there with the sword.
Est 9: 5 the Jews s down all their enemies with the sword,
Job 1:19 s the four corners of the house,
16:10 they have s me insolently on the cheek;
26:12 by his understanding he s down Rahab.
Ps 6: 3 My soul also is s with terror, while you,
6:10 All my enemies shall be ashamed and s
18:38 I s them down, so that they were not able to rise;
69:26 For they persecute those whom you have s down,
78:20 Even though he s the rock so that water gushed out
78:51 He s all the firstborn in Egypt,
105:33 He s their vines and fig trees,
105:36 He s down all the firstborn in their land,
135: 8 He it was who s down the firstborn of Egypt,
135:10 He s down many nations
136:10 who s Egypt through their firstborn,
136:17 who s down great kings,
Pr 23:35 "They s me," you will say, "but I was not hurt;
Isa 5:25 he stretched out his hand against them and s them;
9:13 The people did not turn to him who s them,
10:20 of Jacob will no more lean on the one who s them,
10:26 as when he s Midian at the rock of Oreb;
14: 6 s down the peoples in wrath with unceasing blows,
14:29 that the rod that s you is broken,
27: 7 he s them down as he s down those who s them?
37:36 and s down one hundred eighty-five thousand in
50: 6 I gave my back to those who s me,
53: 4 yet we accounted him stricken, s down by God,
57:17 I s them, I hid and was angry;
60:10 for in my wrath I s you down,
Jer 2:30 In vain I have s down your children;
5: 3 You have s them, but they felt no anguish;
14:17 is s down with a crushing blow,
14:19 Why have you s us down so that there is no healing
20: 2 Then Pashhur s the prophet Jeremiah,
26:23 who s him down with the sword
31:19 and after I was discovered, I s my thigh;
41: 2 up and s down Gedaliah son of Ahikam son
41: 9 the men whom he had s down was the large cistern
52:27 And the king of Babylon s them down,
Eze 40: 1 in the fourteenth year after the city was s down,
Da 2:34 and it s the statue on its feet of iron and clay
2:35 the stone that s the statue became a great mountain
8: 7 It was enraged against it and s the ram,
Hos 6: 1 he has s down, and he will bind us up.
Am 4: 9 I s you with blight and mildew;
Hag 2:17 I s you and all the products of your toil with blight
Zec 10:11 and the waves of the sea shall be s down,
Mt 26:51 drew it, and s the slave of the high priest,
26:67 Then they spat in his face and s him;
26:68 Who is it that s you?"
27:30 and took the reed and s him on the head.
Mk 14:47 of those who stood near drew his sword and s
15:19 They s his head with a reed, spat upon him,
Lk 22:50 Then one of them s the slave of the high priest
22:64 Who is it that s you?"
Jn 18:10 who had a sword, drew it, s the high priest's slave,
18:22 of the police standing nearby s Jesus on the face,
Ac 12:23 an angel of the Lord s him down,
23: 3 yet in violation of the law you order me to be s?"
1Co 10: 5 and they were s down in the wilderness.
2Co 4: 9 s down, but not destroyed;
Rev 8:12 and a third of the sun was s,
Jdt 1:15 in the mountains of Ragau and s him down
9: 3 and you s down slaves along with princes,
13: 8 Then she s his neck twice with all her might,
13:15 The Lord has s him down by the hand of a woman.
Sir 47: 4 when he whirled the stone in the sling and s down
48:21 The Lord s down the camp of the Assyrians,
1Mc 2:44 and s down sinners in their anger and renegades
5: 7 before him; he s them down.
5:65 He s Hebron and its villages and tore
7:41 and s down one hundred eighty-five thousand of
9:66 He s down Odomera and his kindred and
2Mc 1:16 they threw stones and s down the leader
3:25 at Heliodorus and s at him with its front hoofs.
9: 5 s him with an incurable and invisible blow.
15:24 against your holy people be s down."
3Mc 5:27 the report and being s by the unusual invitation
2Es 1:10 I s down Pharaoh with his servants
4Mc 8: 4 And s by their appearance and nobility,

STRUCTURE‡ (10) [STRUCTURES]

1Ki 6: 5 He also built a s against the wall of the house,
6:10 He built the s against the whole house,
Ezr 5: 3 a decree to build this house and to finish this s?"
5: 9 a decree to build this house and to finish this s?'
Eze 40: 2 on which was a s like a city to the south.
41: 7 for the s was supplied with a stairway all around
41: 7 this reason the s became wider from story to story.
Eph 2:21 In him the whole s is joined together and grows
Wis 7:17 the s of the world and the activity of the elements;
1Es 6:11 and laying the foundations of this s?'

STRUCTURES (1) [STRUCTURE]

1Mc 10:44 the s of the sanctuary be paid from the revenues of

STRUGGLE (14) [STRUGGLED, STRUGGLES, STRUGGLING]

Pr 28: 4 but those who keep the law s against them.
Isa 25:11 their pride will be laid low despite the s
Eph 6:12 For our s is not against enemies of blood and flesh,
Php 1:30 since you are having the same s that you saw I had
Col 1:29 For this I toil and s with all the energy
1Ti 4:10 For to this end we toil and s,
Heb 10:32 you endured a hard s with sufferings,
12: 4 In your s against sin you have not yet resisted to
Sir 11:11 There are those who work and s and hurry,
2Mc 14:43 But in the heat of the s he did not hit exactly,
2Es 12:47 the Mighty One has not forgotten you in your s.
4Mc 8:24 not s against compulsion or take hollow pride
9:23 in my s or renounce our courageous family ties.
13:15 for great is the s of the soul and the danger

STRUGGLED (5) [STRUGGLE]

Ge 25:22 The children s together within her;
Ps 60: T *when he s with Aram-naharaim and with*
Isa 27: 8 By expulsion, by exile you s against them;
Php 4: 3 they have s beside me in the work of the gospel,
1Mc 7:21 Alcimus s to maintain his high priesthood,

STRUGGLES (4) [STRUGGLE]

Sir 38:28 and he s with the heat of the furnace;
40: 6 he s in his sleep as he did by day.
2Mc 15: 9 and reminding them also of the s they had won,
2Es 12:18 of that kingdom great s shall arise, and it shall be

STRUGGLING (1) [STRUGGLE]

Col 2: 1 For I want you to know how much I am s for you,

STRUNG (1) [STRING]

Ps 7:12 he has bent and s his bow;

STRUTTING (1)

Pr 30:31 the s rooster, the he-goat, and a king striding

STUBBLE (13)

Ex 5:12 throughout the land of Egypt, to gather s for straw.
15: 7 you sent out your fury, it consumed them like s.
Isa 5:24 Therefore, as the tongue of fire devours the s,
33:11 You conceive chaff, you bring forth s;
40:24 and the tempest carries them off like s.
41: 2 like driven s with his bow.
47:14 See, they are like s, the fire consumes them;
Joel 2: 5 the crackling of a flame of fire devouring the s,
Ob 1:18 and the house of Esau s;
Mal 4: 1 when all the arrogant and all evildoers will be s;
Wis 3: 7 and will run like sparks through the s.
2Es 15:61 You shall be broken down by them like s,
16: 6 quench a fire in the s once it has started to burn?

STUBBORN (27) [STUBBORNLY, STUBBORNNESS]

Dt 9: 6 for you are a s people.
9:13 "I have seen that this people is indeed a s people.
10:16 and do not be s any longer.
21:18 a s and rebellious son who will not obey his father
21:20 "This son of ours is s and rebellious.
29:19 we go our own s ways" (thus bringing disaster
31:27 For I know well how rebellious and s you are.
Jdg 2:19 not drop any of their practices or their s ways.
2Ki 17:14 They would not listen but were s,
Ne 9:29 They turned a s shoulder and stiffened their neck
Ps 78: 8 a s and rebellious generation,
81:12 So I gave them over to their s hearts,
Pr 3:35 The wise will inherit honor, but s fools, disgrace.
29: 1 One who is often reproved, yet remains s,
Isa 46:12 Listen to me, you s of heart,
Jer 5:23 But this people has a s and rebellious heart;
16:12 following your s evil will, refusing to listen to me.
23:17 to all who stubbornly follow their own s hearts,
Eze 2: 4 The descendants are impudent and s.
3: 7 of Israel have a hard forehead and a s heart.
Hos 4:16 Like a s heifer, Israel is s;
Zec 7:11 But they refused to listen, and turned a s shoulder,
Sir 3:26 A s mind will fare badly at the end,
3:27 A s mind will be burdened by troubles,
30: 8 An unbroken horse turns out s,
30:12 or else he will become s and disobey you,

STUBBORNLY (8) [STUBBORN]

Ex 13:15 When Pharaoh s refused to let us go,
Job 15:26 running s against him with a thick-bossed shield;
Jer 3:17 they shall no longer s follow their own evil will.
6:28 They are all s rebellious, going about
9:14 but have s followed their own hearts
13:10 who s follow their own will and have gone
23:17 and to all who s follow their own stubborn hearts,
Ac 19: 9 When some s refused to believe and spoke evil of

STUBBORNNESS (9) [STUBBORN]

Dt 9:27 pay no attention to the s of this people,
1Sa 15:23 and s is like iniquity and idolatry.
Jer 7:24 but, in the s of their evil will,
11: 8 but everyone walked in the s of an evil will.
18:12 of us will act according to the s of our evil will."
Mk 16:14 ⟦he upbraided them for their lack of faith and s,⟧
Sir 16:10 foot soldiers who assembled in their s.
Bar 2:33 and turn from their s and their wicked deeds;
4Mc 8:26 and such a fatal s please us,

STUCCO (1)

Sir 22:17 on an intelligent thought is like s decoration

STUCK (5) [STICK]

1Sa 26: 7 with his spear s in the ground at his head;
Job 29:10 and their tongues s to the roof of their mouths.
Jer 38:22 that your feet are s in the mud, they desert you.'
Ac 27:41 the bow s and remained immovable,
Sir 19:12 Like an arrow s in a person's thigh,

STUDDED (2)

SS 1:11 We will make you ornaments of gold, s with silver.
Sir 50: 9 like a vessel of hammered gold s with all kinds

STUDENTS (1) [STUDY]

Mt 23: 8 for you have one teacher, and you are all s.

STUDIED (1) [STUDY]

Ps 111: 2 s by all who delight in them.

STUDY (6) [STUDENTS, STUDIED, STUDYING]

Ezr 7:10 Ezra had set his heart to s the law of the LORD,
Ne 8:13 the scribe Ezra in order to s the words of the law.
Ps 101: 2 I will s the way that is blameless.
Ecc 12:12 and much s is a weariness of the flesh.
Isa 47:13 let those who s the heavens stand up and save you,
Sir 38:34 the one who devotes himself to the s of the law of

STUDY (KJV) See also DO YOUR BEST, LIVE

STUDYING (1) [STUDY]

Ecc 12: 9 weighing and s and arranging many proverbs.

STUFF (1) [STUFFS]

Ge 25:30 Esau said to Jacob, "Let me eat some of that red s,

STUFF (KJV) See also BAGGAGE, BELONGINGS, GOODS, HOUSEHOLD FURNITURE, POSSESSIONS

STUFFS (2) [STUFF]

Jdg 5:30 of dyed s for Sisera, spoil of dyed s embroidered,

STUMBLE‡ (51) [STUMBLED, STUMBLES, STUMBLING]

Lev 26:37 They shall s over one another,
Ps 27: 2 and foes—they shall s and fall.
37:24 though we s, we shall not fall headlong,
119:165 nothing can make them s.
Pr 3:23 on your way securely and your foot will not s.
4:12 and if you run, you will not s.
4:16 of sleep unless they have made someone s.
4:19 they do not know what they s over.
24:17 and do not let your heart be glad when they s,
Isa 8:15 And many among them shall s;
28: 7 they err in vision, they s in giving judgment.
31: 3 LORD stretches out his hand, the helper will s,
59:10 we s at noon as in the twilight,
63:13 Like a horse in the desert, they did not s.
Jer 6:21 against which they shall s;
13:16 and before your feet s on the mountains at twilight;
20:10 All my close friends are watching for me to s.
20:11 my persecutors will s, and they will not prevail.
31: 9 in a straight path in which they shall not s;
50:32 The arrogant one shall s and fall,
Eze 21:15 therefore hearts melt and many s.

Eze 33:12 it shall not make them s when they turn
36:15 and no longer shall you cause your nation to s,
44:12 before their idols and made the house of Israel s
Da 11:19 but he shall s and fall, and shall not be found.
Hos 4: 5 You shall s by day; the prophet also shall s with
14: 9 but transgressors s in them.
Na 2: 5 He calls his officers; they s as they come forward;
3: 3 without end—they s over the bodies!
Zep 1: 3 I will make the wicked s. I will cut off humanity
Mal 2: 8 you have caused many to s by your instruction;
Mt 18: 8 "If your hand or your foot causes you to s,
18: 9 And if your eye causes you to s,
Mk 9:43 If your hand causes you to s, cut it off;
9:45 And if your foot causes you to s, cut it off;
9:47 And if your eye causes you to s, tear it out;
Lk 17: 2 for you to cause one of these little ones to s.
Jn 11: 9 Those who walk during the day do not s,
11:10 But those who walk at night s,
Ro 9:33 in Zion a stone that will make people s,
14:21 or do anything that makes your brother or sister s.
2Co 11:29 Who is made to s, and I am not indignant?
1Pe 2: 8 and "A stone that makes them s,
2: 8 They s because they disobey the word,
2Pe 1:10 for if you do this, you will never s.
Sir 9: 5 or you may s and incur penalties for her.
13:23 And should he s, they even push him down.
32:15 but the hypocrite will s at it.
32:20 and do not s at an obstacle twice.
41: 9 When you s, there is lasting joy;

STUMBLED‡ (12) [STUMBLE]

Ps 9: 3 they s and perished before you.
73: 2 But as for me, my feet had almost s;
105:37 and there was no one among their tribes who s.
Isa 3: 8 For Jerusalem has s and Judah has fallen,
Jer 18:15 they have s in their ways, in the ancient roads,
46: 6 in the north by the river Euphrates they have s
46:12 for warrior has s against warrior;
46:16 Your multitude s and fell, and one said to another,
Hos 14: 1 for you have s because of your iniquity.
Ro 9:32 They have s over the stumbling stone,
11:11 So I ask, have they s so as to fall?
1Es 4:27 Many have perished, or s,

STUMBLES‡ (5) [STUMBLE]

Isa 5:27 None of them is weary, none s,
8:14 of Israel he will become a rock one s over—
59:14 for truth s in the public square,
Hos 5: 5 Ephraim s in his guilt; Judah also s with them.

STUMBLING‡ (32) [STUMBLE]

Lev 19:14 You shall not revile the deaf or put a s block
Job 4: 4 Your words have supported those who were s,
18:12 and calamity is ready for their s.
Ps 35:15 But at my s they gathered in glee,
116: 8 my eyes from tears, my feet from s.
Jer 6:21 See, I am laying before this people s blocks
Eze 3:20 and I lay a s block before them, they shall die;
7:19 For it was the s block of their iniquity.
14: 3 and placed their iniquity as a s block before them;
14: 4 and place their iniquity as a s block before them,
14: 7 and placing their iniquity as a s block before them,
Mt 16:23 You are a s block to me;
18: 6 "If any of you put a s block before one
18: 7 Woe to the world because of s blocks!
18: 7 Occasions for s are bound to come,
18: 7 but woe to the one by whom the s block comes!
Mk 9:42 "If any of you put a s block before one
Lk 17: 1 "Occasions for s are bound to come,
Jn 16: 1 to you to keep you from s.
Ro 9:32 They have stumbled over the s stone,
11: 9 a s block and a retribution for them;
11:11 through their s salvation has come to the Gentiles,
11:12 Now if their s means riches for the world,
14:13 to put a s block or hindrance in the way of another.
1Co 1:23 a s block to Jews and foolishness to Gentiles,
8: 9 of yours does not somehow become a s block to
1Jn 2:10 and in such a person there is no cause for s.
Rev 2:14 of Balaam, who taught Balak to put a s block
Tob 11:10 up and came s out through the courtyard door.
Sir 31: 7 It is a s block to those who are avid for it,
31:29 to bitterness of spirit, to quarrels and s.
34:19 a guard against s and a help against falling.

STUMBLINGBLOCK (KJV) See STUMBLING BLOCK

STUMBLINGSTONE (KJV) See STONE, STUMBLING STONE

STUMP (7) [STUMPS]

Job 14: 8 and its s dies in the ground,
Isa 6:13 a terebinth or an oak whose s remains standing
6:13 The holy seed is its s.
11: 1 A shoot shall come out from the s of Jesse,
Da 4:15 But leave its s and roots in the ground,
4:23 but leave its s and roots in the ground,
4:26 As it was commanded to leave the s and roots of

STUMPS (1) [STUMP]

Isa 7: 4 because of these two smoldering s of firebrands,

STUNG (1) [STING]

Sir 12:12 and be s by what I have said.

STUNNED (4)

Ge 45:26 He was s; he could not believe them.
Ps 76: 6 O God of Jacob, both rider and horse lay s.
La 1:13 he has left me s, faint all day long.
Eze 3:15 And I sat there among them, s, for seven days.

STUPEFY (1) [STUPOR]

Isa 29: 9 S yourselves and be in a stupor,

STUPID‡ (19) [STUPIDITY]

Job 11:12 But a s person will get understanding,
18: 3 Why are we s in your sight?
Ps 73:22 I was s and ignorant; I was like a brute beast
92: 6 dullard cannot know, the s cannot understand this:
Pr 12: 1 but those who hate to be rebuked are s.
19:13 A s child is ruin to a father,
24:30 by the vineyard of a s person;
30: 2 Surely I am too s to be human;
Isa 19:11 the wise counselors of Pharaoh give s counsel.
Jer 4:22 they are s children, they have no understanding.
10: 8 They are both s and foolish;
10:14 Everyone is s and without knowledge;
10:21 shepherds are s, and do not inquire of the LORD;
51:17 Everyone is s and without knowledge;
2Ti 2:23 to do with s and senseless controversies;
Tit 3: 9 But avoid s controversies, genealogies,
Sir 22:15 a piece of iron are easier to bear than a s person.
27:12 Among s people limit your time,
42: 8 Do not be ashamed to correct the s or foolish or

STUPIDITY (1) [STUPID]

4Mc 12: 3 "You see the result of your brothers' s,

STUPOR (2) [STUPEFY]

Isa 29: 9 Stupefy yourselves and be in a s,
Jdt 13:15 the canopy beneath which he lay in his drunken s.

STURDY (2)

Sir 6:14 Faithful friends are a s shelter:
29:13 better than a stout shield and a s spear,

STYLE (3)

Ex 28:15 you shall make it in the s of the ephod;
2Mc 15:39 so also the s of the story delights the ears
3Mc 3: 5 but since they adorned their s of life with

STYLUS (1)

Isa 44:13 carpenter stretches a line, marks it out with a s,

SUA (1)

1Es 5:29 the descendants of S, the descendants of Padon,

SUAH (1)

1Ch 7:36 The sons of Zophah: S, Harnepher, Shual, Beri,

SUBAI (1)

1Es 5:30 the descendants of Hagab, the descendants of S,

SUBAS (1)

1Es 5:34 the descendants of S, the descendants of Apherra,

SUBDUE (12) [SUBDUED, SUBDUES, SUBDUING]

Ge 1:28 and fill the earth and s it;
Dt 9: 3 he will defeat them and s them before you,
Jdg 16: 5 so that we may bind him in order to s him;
16: 6 so that one could s you."
1Ch 17:10 and I will s all your enemies.
Ps 74: 8 They said to themselves, "We will utterly s them";
81:14 Then I would quickly s their enemies,
Isa 45: 1 to s nations before him and strip kings of their
Mk 5: 4 and no one had the strength to s him.
Sir 12: 5 for by means of it they might s you;
1Mc 4:28 and five thousand cavalry to s them.
2Es 4:15 up and s the forest of the plain so that there

SUBDUED (25) [SUBDUE]

Ge 14: 5 and the kings who were with him came and s
14: 7 and s all the country of the Amalekites,
Nu 32: 4 the land that the LORD s before the congregation
32:22 and the land is s before the LORD—
32:29 be s before you, then you shall give them the land
Jos 18: 1 The land lay s before them.
Jdg 3:30 So Moab was s that day under the hand of Israel.
4:23 So on that day God s King Jabin of Canaan before
8:28 So Midian was s before the Israelites,
11:33 the Ammonites were s before the people of Israel.
1Sa 7:13 So the Philistines were s and did not again enter
2Sa 8: 1 David attacked the Philistines and s them;
8:11 that he dedicated from all the nations he s,
1Ch 18: 1 David attacked the Philistines and s them;
20: 4 and the Philistines were s.
22:18 and the land is s before the LORD and his people.
2Ch 13:18 Thus the Israelites were s at that time,
Ne 9:24 and you s before them the inhabitants of the land,
Ps 18:47 the God who gave me vengeance and s peoples
47: 3 He s peoples under us, and nations under our feet.
Isa 25: 5 you s the heat with the shade of clouds;
Wis 18:22 but by his word he s the avenger,
Sir 46:18 he s the leaders of the enemy and all the rulers of
1Mc 8: 4 They also s the kings who came against them from
8:12 They have s kings far and near,

SUBDUES (2) [SUBDUE]

Dt 33:27 He s the ancient gods, shatters the forces of old;
Ps 144: 2 who s the peoples under me.

SUBDUING (1) [SUBDUE]

1Mc 1:20 After s Egypt, Antiochus returned in

SUBJECT (44) [SUBJECTED, SUBJECTING, SUBJECTION, SUBJECTS]

Lev 5: 1 does not speak up, you are s to punishment.
5:17 you have incurred guilt, and are s to punishment.
19: 8 All who eat it shall be s to punishment,
20:17 he shall be s to punishment.
20:19 they shall be s to punishment.
20:20 they shall be s to punishment;
Nu 35:31 the life of a murderer who is s to the death penalty;
Jdg 1:30 and became s to forced labor.
1:33 of Beth-anath became s to forced labor for them.
1:35 and they became s to forced labor.
2Sa 10:19 with Israel, and became s to them.
1Ch 18: 2 Moabites became s to David and brought tribute.
18: 6 Arameans became s to David, and brought tribute.
18:13 and all the Edomites became s to David.
19:19 they made peace with David, and became s to him.
Ps 69:12 I am the s of gossip for those who sit in the gate,
Ro 13: 1 Let every person be s to the governing authorities;
13: 5 be s, not only because of wrath but also because
1Co 2:15 they are themselves s to no one else's scrutiny.
10:29 For why should my liberty be s to the judgment
14:32 And the spirits of prophets are s to the prophets,
2Co 9: 2 the s of my boasting about you to the people
Gal 3:25 we are no longer s to a disciplinarian,
4:21 Tell me, you who desire to be s to the law,
5:18 you are led by the Spirit, you are not s to the law.
Eph 5:21 Be s to one another out of reverence for Christ.
5:22 be s to your husbands as you are to the Lord.
5:24 Just as the church is s to Christ,
Php 3:21 also enables him to make all things s to himself.
Col 3:18 Wives, be s to your husbands,
Tit 3: 1 Remind them to be s to rulers and authorities,
Heb 2: 5 Now God did not s the coming world,
5: 2 since he himself is s to weakness;
7:28 the law appoints as high priests those who are s
12: 9 be even more willing to be s to the Father of spirits
1Pe 3:22 authorities, and powers made s to him.
Wis 8:14 I shall govern peoples, and nations will be s to me;
Sir 4:27 Do not s yourself to a fool,
Bar 2: 4 He made them s to all the kingdoms around us,
2Mc 9:12 he uttered these words, "It is right to be s to God;
3Mc 7:21 not s at all to confiscation of their belongings
4Mc 1: 1 s that I am about to discuss is most philosophical,
1: 2 For the s is essential to everyone
2:23 and one who lives s to this will rule a kingdom

SUBJECTED (7) [SUBJECT]

Ro 8:20 for the creation was s to futility,
8:20 of its own will but by the will of the one who s it,
1Co 15:28 When all things are s to him,
15:28 be s to the one who put all things in subjection
3Mc 2:13 s to our enemies, and overtaken by helplessness.
2:28 be s to a registration involving poll tax and to
2Es 11: 6 I saw how all things under heaven were s to it,

SUBJECTING (2) [SUBJECT]

Heb 2: 8 s all things under their feet." Now in s all things to them, God left nothing outside their control.

SUBJECTION (9) [SUBJECT]

Ps 106:42 and they were brought into s under their power.
Jer 34:11 and brought them again into s as slaves.
34:16 you brought them again into s to be your slaves.
1Co 15:27 For "God has put all things in s under his feet."
15:27 But when it says, "All things are put in s,"
15:27 not include the one who put all things in s
15:28 also be subjected to the one who put all things in s
Heb 2: 8 As it is, we do not yet see everything in s to them,
Sir 47:19 and through your body you were brought into s.

SUBJECTION (KJV) See also ACCEPT THE AUTHORITY, ACCEPTING THE AUTHORITY, ENSLAVE, OBEDIENCE, SUBJECT, SUBJECTING, SUBMISSION, SUBMISSIVE, SUBMIT

SUBJECTS (5) [SUBJECT]

AdE 13: 2 to settle the lives of my s in lasting tranquility and,
15:10 for our law applies only to our s.
16: 3 and not only seek to injure our s,
2Mc 11:23 we desire that the s of the kingdom be undisturbed
3Mc 1: 7 he strengthened the morale of his s.

SUBJUGATE (1)

2Ch 28:10 you intend to s the people of Judah and Jerusalem,

SUBMISSION (2) [SUBMIT]

1Ti 2:11 Let a woman learn in silence with full **s**.
Heb 5: 7 and he was heard because of his reverent **s**.

SUBMISSIVE (3) [SUBMIT]

1Ti 3: 4 keeping his children **s** and respectful
Tit 2: 5 kind, being **s** to their husbands,
2: 9 to be **s** to their masters and to give satisfaction

SUBMIT (13) [SUBMISSION, SUBMISSIVE, SUBMITTED]

Ge 16: 9 "Return to your mistress, and **s** to her."
Dt 20:12 If it does not **s** to you peacefully,
22:15 of the young woman and her mother shall then **s**
Ps 81:11 Israel would not **s** to me.
Lk 10:17 "Lord, in your name even the demons **s** to us!"
10:20 do not rejoice at this, that the spirits **s** to you,
Ro 8: 7 it does not **s** to God's law—
2Co 11: 4 you **s** to it readily enough.
Gal 2: 5 we did not **s** to them even for a moment,
5: 1 therefore, and do not **s** again to a yoke of slavery.
Col 2:20 Why do you **s** to regulations,
Heb 13:17 Obey your leaders and **s** to them,
Jas 4: 7 **S** yourselves therefore to God.

SUBMITTED (2) [SUBMIT]

Ro 10: 3 they have not **s** to God's righteousness.
4Mc 13:12 and the father by whose hand Isaac would have **s**

SUBORDINATE (1)

1Co 14:34 they are not permitted to speak, but should be **s**,

SUBORNED (KJV) See SECRETLY INSTIGATED

SUBSCRIBE (KJV) See SIGNED, WRITE

SUBSEQUENT (1)

1Pe 1:11 the sufferings destined for Christ and the **s** glory.

SUBSIDED (4)

Ge 8: 1 a wind blow over the earth, and the waters **s**;
8: 8 if the waters had **s** from the face of the ground;
8:11 so Noah knew that the waters had **s** from the earth.
Jdg 8: 3 When he said this, their anger against him **s**.

SUBSTANCE (6) [SUBSTANTIAL]

Ex 16:14 on the surface of the wilderness was a fine flaky **s**,
Dt 33:11 O LORD, his **s**, and accept the work of his hands;
Ps 139:16 Your eyes beheld my unformed **s**.
Pr 3: 9 the LORD with your **s** and with the first fruits
29: 3 with prostitutes is to squander one's **s**.
Col 2:17 but the **s** belongs to Christ.

SUBSTANTIAL (1) [SUBSTANCE]

2Mc 4:45 a **s** bribe to Ptolemy son of Dorymenes to win over

SUBSTITUTE (2) [SUBSTITUTED, SUBSTITUTES, SUBSTITUTION]

Lev 27:10 both that one and its **s** shall be holy.
27:33 it and the **s** shall be holy and cannot be redeemed.

SUBSTITUTED (2) [SUBSTITUTE]

Lev 27:10 Another shall not be exchanged or **s** for it,
27:10 and if one animal is **s** for another,

SUBSTITUTES (5) [SUBSTITUTE]

Nu 3:12 from among the Israelites as **s** for all the firstborn
3:41 as **s** for all the firstborn among the Israelites,
3:41 the livestock of the Levites as **s** for all the firstborn
3:45 Accept the Levites as **s** for all the firstborn among
3:45 the livestock of the Levites as **s** for their livestock;

SUBSTITUTION (2) [SUBSTITUTE]

Lev 27:33 or make **s** for it; if one makes **s** for it, then both it

SUBTIL (KJV) See CRAFTY, WILY

SUBTLE (2) [SUBTLETIES]

Wis 7:22 **s**, mobile, clear, unpolluted, distinct, invulnerable,
7:23 that are intelligent, pure, and altogether **s**.

SUBTLETIES (2) [SUBTLE]

Sir 1: 6 Her **s**—who knows them?
39: 2 of the famous and penetrates the **s** of parables;

SUBURBS (2)

1Mc 11: 4 and Azotus and its **s** destroyed,
11:61 and burned its **s** with fire and plundered them.

SUBURBS (KJV) See also COMMON LAND[S], COUNTRYSIDE, OPEN COUNTRY, OPEN LAND, OPEN SPACE, PASTURE LANDS, PRECINCTS

SUBVERT (1) [SUBVERTED, SUBVERTS]

Pr 18: 5 or to **s** the innocent in judgment.

SUBVERT (KJV) See also SUBVERTED, UPSETTING

SUBVERTED (2) [SUBVERT]

Ps 119:78 because they have **s** me with guile;
La 3:36 when one's case is **s**—does the Lord not see it?

SUBVERTS (2) [SUBVERT]

Ex 23: 8 and **s** the cause of those who are in the right.
Dt 16:19 a bribe blinds the eyes of the wise and **s** the cause

SUCATHITES (1)

1Ch 2:55 the Tirathites, the Shimeathites, and the **S**.

SUCCEED (38) [SUCCEEDED, SUCCEEDING, SUCCEEDS, SUCCESS, SUCCESSES, SUCCESSFUL, SUCCESSFULLY, SUCCESSION, SUCCESSIVE, SUCCESSOR]

Nu 14:41 the command of the LORD? That will not **s**.
Dt 25: 6 the firstborn whom she bears shall **s** to the name of
29: 9 in order that you may **s** in everything that you do.
Jdg 18: 5 the mission we are undertaking will **s**."
1Sa 26:25 You will do many things and will **s** in them."
1Ki 1:13 Your son Solomon shall **s** me as king,
1:17 Your son Solomon shall **s** me as king,
1:24 have you said, 'Adonijah shall **s** me as king,
1:30 'Your son Solomon shall **s** me as king,
22:22 'You are to entice him, and you shall **s**;
2Ki 3:27 Then he took his firstborn son who was to **s** him,
14:21 and made him king to **s** his father Amaziah.
1Ch 22:11 so that you may **s** in building the house of
2Ch 1: 8 and have made me **s** him as king.
13:12 of your ancestors; for you cannot **s**."
18:21 'You are to entice him, and you shall **s**;
26: 1 and made him king to **s** his father Amaziah.
33:25 of the land made his son Josiah king to **s** him.
36: 1 and made him king to **s** his father in Jerusalem.
Ps 21:11 if they devise mischief, they will not **s**.
Pr 15:22 plans go wrong, but with many advisers they **s**.
Ecc 7:18 for the one who fears God shall **s** with both.
10:10 but wisdom helps one to **s**.
Isa 47:12 perhaps you may be able to **s**,
55:11 and **s** in the thing for which I sent it.
Jer 20:11 They will be greatly shamed, for they will not **s**.
22:30 a man who shall not **s** in his days;
22:30 of his offspring shall **s** in sitting on the throne
32: 5 you fight against the Chaldeans, you shall not **s**?"
Eze 17:15 horses and a large army. Will he **s**?
Da 8:24 and shall **s** in what he does.
11:17 but it shall not **s** or be to his advantage.
11:25 But he shall not **s**, for plots shall be devised
11:27 But it shall not **s**, for there remains an end at
Ro 1:10 asking that by God's will I may somehow at last **s**
9:31 did not **s** in fulfilling that law.
Sir 48: 8 to inflict retribution, and prophets to **s** you.
2Mc 15: 5 he did not **s** in carrying out his abominable design.

SUCCEEDED (72) [SUCCEED]

Ge 36:33 and Jobab son of Zerah of Bozrah **s** him as king.
36:34 and Husham of the land of the Temanites **s** him
36:35 **s** him as king, the name of his city being Avith.
36:36 and Samlah of Masrekah **s** him as king.
36:37 Shaul of Rehoboth on the Euphrates **s** him as king.
36:38 and Baal-hanan son of Achbor **s** him as king.
36:39 and Hadar **s** him as king, the name
Dt 10: 6 his son Eleazar **s** him as priest.
2Sa 10: 1 and his son Hanun **s** him.
1Ki 11:43 and his son Rehoboam **s** him.
14:20 with his ancestors, and his son Nadab **s** him.
14:31 His son Abijam **s** him.
15: 8 Then his son Asa **s** him.
15:24 his son Jehoshaphat **s** him.
15:28 in the third year of King Asa of Judah, and **s** him.
16: 6 and his son Elah **s** him.
16:10 year of King Asa of Judah, and **s** him.
16:28 in Samaria; his son Ahab **s** him.
22:40 and his son Ahaziah **s** him.
22:50 of his father David; his son Jehoram **s** him.
2Ki 1:17 Jehoram **s** him as king in the second year
8:15 until he died. And Hazael **s** him.
8:24 of David; his son Ahaziah **s** him.
10:35 His son Jehoahaz **s** him.
12:21 then his son Amaziah **s** him.
13: 9 then his son Joash **s** him.
13:24 of Aram died, his son Ben-hadad **s** him.
14:16 then his son Jeroboam **s** him.
14:29 of Israel; his son Zechariah **s** him.
15: 7 of David; his son Jotham **s** him.
15:22 and his son Pekahiah **s** him.
15:38 his ancestor; his son Ahaz **s** him.
16:20 of David; his son Hezekiah **s** him.
19:37 His son Esar-haddon **s** him.
20:21 and his son Manasseh **s** him.
21:18 His son Amon **s** him.
21:26 then his son Josiah **s** him.
24: 6 then his son Jehoiachin **s** him.
1Ch 1:44 Bela died, Jobab son of Zerah of Bozrah **s** him.
1:45 Husham of the land of the Temanites **s** him.
1:46 **s** him; and the name of his city was Avith.
1:47 When Hadad died, Samlah of Masrekah **s** him.
1:48 Shaul of Rehoboth on the Euphrates **s** him.
1:49 Shaul died, Baal-hanan son of Achbor **s** him.
1:50 When Baal-hanan died, Hadad **s** him;
19: 1 of the Ammonites died, and his son **s** him.
29:28 and his son Solomon **s** him.
2Ch 6:10 for I have **s** my father David,
9:31 and his son Rehoboam **s** him.
12:16 and his son Abijah **s** him.
14: 1 His son Asa **s** him.
17: 1 His son Jehoshaphat **s** him,
21: 1 of David; his son Jehoram **s** him.
24:27 And his son Amaziah **s** him.
26:23 His son Jotham **s** him.
27: 9 and his son Ahaz **s** him.
28:27 His son Hezekiah **s** him.
32:33 His son Manasseh **s** him.
33:20 His son Amon **s** him.
36: 8 and his son Jehoiachin **s** him.
Job 9: 4 in strength—who has resisted him, and **s**?—
Isa 37:38 His son Esar-haddon **s** him.
Jer 22:11 who **s** his father Josiah, and who went away
37: 1 **s** Coniah son of Jehoiakim.
Ac 24:27 Felix was **s** by Porcius Festus;
Wis 7:30 for it is **s** by the night,
Bel 1: 1 Cyrus the Persian **s** to his kingdom.
1Mc 1: 1 of the Persians and the Medes, he **s** him as king.
2Mc 4: 7 who was called Epiphanes, **s** to the kingdom,
8:35 having **s** chiefly in the destruction
10:11 This man, when he **s** to the kingdom,
4Mc 4:15 his son Antiochus Epiphanes **s** to the throne,

SUCCEEDING (1) [SUCCEED]

1Ch 29:23 **s** his father David as king;

SUCCEEDS (2) [SUCCEED]

Pr 30:23 and a maid when she **s** her mistress.
Sir 43:26 Because of him each of his messengers **s**,

SUCCESS (20) [SUCCEED]

Ge 24:12 please grant me **s** today and show steadfast love
27:20 "Because the LORD your God granted me **s**."
1Sa 18:14 David had **s** in all his undertakings;
18:15 When Saul saw that he had great **s**,
18:30 David had more **s** than all the servants of Saul,
Ne 1:11 Give **s** to your servant today,
2:20 "The God of heaven is the one who will give us **s**,
Job 5:12 so that their hands achieve no **s**.
Ps 118:25 O LORD, we beseech you, give us **s**!
Isa 48:18 and your **s** like the waves of the sea;
Tob 10:13 because he had made his journey a **s**.
Wis 13:19 and work and **s** with his hands he asks strength of
Sir 9:11 Do not envy the **s** of sinners,
10: 5 Human **s** is in the hand of the Lord,
11:17 and his favor brings lasting **s**.
38:14 for they too pray to the Lord that he grant them **s**
2Mc 5: 6 not realizing that **s** at the cost of one's kindred is
10: 7 of thanksgiving to him who had given **s** to
10:23 Having **s** at arms in everything he undertook,
10:28 as pledge of **s** and victory not only their valor but

SUCCESSES (1) [SUCCEED]

2Mc 8: 8 that he was pushing ahead with more frequent **s**,

SUCCESSFUL (10) [SUCCEED]

Ge 24:21 or not the LORD had made his journey **s**.
24:40 will send his angel with you and make your way **s**.
24:42 if now you will only make **s** the way I am going!
24:56 since the LORD has made my journey **s**;
39: 2 LORD was with Joseph, and he became a **s** man;
Jos 1: 7 so that you may be **s** wherever you go.
1: 8 and then you shall be **s**.
1Sa 18: 5 David went out and was **s** wherever Saul sent him;
Tob 5:22 his journey will be **s**, and he will come back
11:15 to his father that his journey had been **s**,

SUCCESSFULLY (2) [SUCCEED]

2Ch 7:11 and in his own house he **s** accomplished.
Pr 21:28 but a good listener will testify **s**.

SUCCESSION (1) [SUCCEED]

1Es 1:34 and made him king in **s** to his father Josiah.

SUCCESSIVE (1) [SUCCEED]

Jdg 3: 2 that **s** generations of Israelites might know war,

SUCCESSOR (10) [SUCCEED]

Lev 6:22 anointed from among Aaron's descendants as a **s**,
1Ki 2: 4 there shall not fail you a **s** on the throne of Israel.'
8:25 'There shall never fail you a **s** before me to sit on
9: 5 'There shall not fail you a **s** on the throne
2Ch 6:16 'There shall never fail you a **s** before me to sit on
7:18 'You shall never lack a **s** to rule over Israel.'
22: 1 made his youngest son Ahaziah king as his **s**;
Sir 46: 1 and was the **s** of Moses in the prophetic office.
2Mc 9:23 into the upper country, appointed his **s**,
14:26 against the kingdom, Judas, to be his **s**.

SUCCOTH‡ (18)

Ge 33:17 But Jacob journeyed to **S**,

Ge 33:17 therefore the place is called S.
Ex 12:37 The Israelites journeyed from Rameses to S,
13:20 They set out from S, and camped at Etham,
Nu 33: 5 Israelites set out from Rameses, and camped at S.
33: 6 They set out from S, and camped at Etham,
Jos 13:27 Beth-nimrah, S, and Zaphon,
Jdg 8: 5 So he said to the people of S,
8: 6 But the officials of S said,
8: 8 as the people of S had answered.
8:14 one of the people of S, and questioned him;
8:14 and he listed for him the officials and elders of S,
8:15 Then he came to the people of S, and said,
8:16 and with them he trampled the people of S.
1Ki 7:46 in the clay ground between S and Zarethan.
2Ch 4:17 in the clay ground between S and Zeredah.
Ps 60: 6 and portion out the Vale of S.
108: 7 and portion out the Vale of S.

SUCCOTH-BENOTH (1)

2Ki 17:30 the people of Babylon made S, the people

SUCCOUR, SUCCOURED, SUCCOURER (KJV) See HELP, HELPED

SUCH‡ (337)

Ge 18:25 Far be it from you to do s a thing,
20: 9 that you have brought s great guilt on me
27: 4 Then prepare for me savory food, s as I like,
27: 9 savory food for your father, s as he likes;
27:14 his mother prepared savory food, s as his father
27:46 Jacob marries one of the Hittite women s as these,
30:32 and s shall be my wages.
33:10 since you have received me with s favor.
34: 7 for s a thing ought not to be done.
41:19 Never had I seen s ugly ones in all the land
41:49 So Joseph stored up grain in s abundance—
44: 7 "Why does my lord speak s words as these?
44: 7 Far be it from your servants that they should do s
44:15 not know that one s as I can practice divination?"
Ex 3:21 I will bring this people into s favor with
9:24 s heavy hail as had never fallen in all the land
10:14 s a dense swarm of locusts as had never been
11: 6 s as has never been or will ever be again.
18:21 set s men over them as officers over thousands,
34:10 s as have not been performed in all the earth or
Lev 7:19 for other flesh, all who are clean may eat s flesh.
10: 1 s as he had not commanded them.
10:19 and yet s things as these have befallen me!
11: 3 and chews the cud—s you may eat.
11: 9 in the streams—s you may eat.
11:34 be unclean if water from any s vessel comes
11:34 be drunk shall be unclean if it was in any s vessel.
14:22 s as he can afford, one for a sin offering and
14:30 of the turtledoves or pigeons s as he can afford,
15:10 all who carry s a thing shall wash their clothes,
19: 5 in s a way that it is acceptable on your behalf.
19: 8 and any s person shall be cut off from the people.
22: 6 the person who touches any s shall be unclean
22:24 s you shall not do within your land,
22:25 nor shall you accept any s animals from
23:30 s a one I will destroy from the midst of the people.
25:33 S property as may be redeemed from
27: 9 any s that may be given to the LORD shall
Nu 9:13 s a one shall bear the consequences for the sin.
15: 4 then whoever presents s an offering to
15:31 s a person shall be utterly cut off and bear
19:13 s persons shall be cut off from Israel.
25:11 by manifesting s zeal among them on my behalf
Dt 5:29 If only they had s a mind as this,
12: 4 not worship the LORD your God in s ways.
13: 8 you must not yield to or heed any s persons.
13:11 and never again do any s wickedness.
13:14 that s an abhorrent thing has been done
15:21 any serious defect, s as lameness or blindness—
17: 4 that s an abhorrent thing has occurred in Israel,
17: 8 any s matters of dispute in your towns—
18:12 it is because of s abhorrent practices that
18:15 you shall heed s a prophet.
19:20 a crime s as this shall never again be committed
22: 5 for whoever does s things is abhorrent to
25:16 For all who do s things, all who act dishonestly,
33:17 s are the myriads of Ephraim,
33:17 s the thousands of Manasseh.
Jos 16: 8 S is the inheritance of the tribe of the Ephraimites
Jdg 13:23 or now announced to us s things as these."
18: 4 He said to them, "Micah did s and s for me,
18:23 the matter that you come with s a company?"
19:24 but against this man do not do s a vile thing."
19:30 'Has s a thing ever happened since the day that
1Sa 2:23 He said to them, "Why do you do s things?
21: 2 an appointment with the young men for s and s
27:11 S was his practice all the time he lived in
2Sa 7:14 I will punish him with a rod s as mortals use,
9: 8 that you should look upon a dead dog s as I?"
11:11 and as your soul lives, I will not do s a thing."
13:12 for s a thing is not done in Israel;
14:13 then have you planned s a thing against the people
15: 2 "Your servant is of s and s a tribe in Israel,"
19:36 Why should the king recompense me with s
23:22 S were the things Benaiah son of Jehoiada did,
1Ki 2: 7 for with s loyalty they met me when I fled
9: 8 'Why has the LORD done s a thing to this land
10:10 never again did spices come in s quantity as
10:12 no s almug wood has come or been seen
22: 8 Jehoshaphat said, "Let the king not say s a thing."
2Ki 6: 8 He said, "At s and s a place shall be my camp."
6:10 More than once or twice he warned s a place so
7: 2 to make windows in the sky, could s a thing
7:19 to make windows in the sky, could s a thing
18:21 S is Pharaoh king of Egypt to all who rely on him.
21:12 I am bringing upon Jerusalem and Judah s evil that
23:22 No s passover had been kept since the days of
1Ch 11:24 S were the things Benaiah son of Jehoiada did,
29:18 keep forever s purposes and thoughts in the hearts
29:25 and bestowed upon him s royal majesty as had
2Ch 1:12 s as none of the kings had who were before you,
7:21 'Why has the LORD done s a thing to this land
9: 9 there were no spices s as those that the queen
18: 7 Jehoshaphat said, "Let the king not say s a thing."
35:18 none of the kings of Israel had kept s a passover
Ezr 7:27 who put s a thing as this into the heart of the king
9:13 and have given us s a remnant as this,
Ne 4:17 The burden bearers carried their loads in s a way
6: 8 saying, "No s things as you say have been done;
13:26 of Israel sin on account of s women?
Est 4:14 For if you keep silence at s a time as this,
4:14 Perhaps you have come to royal dignity for just s
Job 6:21 S you have now become to me;
8:13 S are the paths of all who forget God;
12: 3 Who does not know s things as these?
14: 3 Do you fix your eyes on s a one?
15:13 and let s words go out of your mouth?
16: 2 "I have heard many s things;
18:21 Surely s are the dwellings of the ungodly,
18:21 s is the place of those who do not know God."
23:14 and many s things are in his mind.
Ps 24: 6 S is the company of those who seek him,
49:13 S is the fate of the foolhardy,
53: 5 in terror s as has not been.
73:12 S are the wicked; always at ease,
139: 6 S knowledge is too wonderful for me;
144:15 Happy are the people to whom s blessings fall;
Pr 1:19 S is the end of all who are greedy for gain;
6:15 on s a one calamity will descend suddenly;
18:19 s quarreling is like the bars of a castle.
24:14 Know that wisdom is s to your soul;
29: 7 the wicked have no s understanding.
Ecc 8:10 in the city where they had done s things.
Isa 7:17 on your people and on your ancestral house s days
36: 6 S is Pharaoh king of Egypt to all who rely on him.
47:15 S to you are those with whom you have labored,
58: 4 S fasting as you do today will not make your voice
58: 5 Is s the fast that I choose, a day to humble oneself?
66: 8 Who has heard of s a thing?
66: 8 Who has seen s things?
Jer 2:10 see if there has ever been s a thing.
3: 1 Would not s a land be greatly polluted?
5: 9 shall I not bring retribution on a nation s as this?
5:29 shall I not bring retribution on a nation s as this?
9: 9 shall I not bring retribution on a nation s as this?
16:20 for themselves gods? S are no gods!
19: 3 I am going to bring s disaster upon this place that
33:24 in s contempt that they no longer regard them as
38: 4 and all the people, by speaking s words to them.
40:16 "Do not do s a thing,
44: 7 Why are you doing s great harm to yourselves,
Eze 1:11 s were their faces. Their wings were spread out
1:28 s was the appearance of the splendor all around.
17:15 Can one escape who does s things?
18: 9 acting faithfully—s a one is righteous;
21:27 I will make it! (S has never occurred.)
41:25 s as were carved on the walls;
Da 2: 1 Nebuchadnezzar dreamed s dreams
2: 3 "I have had s a dream that my spirit is troubled by
2:10 has ever asked s a thing of any magician
10:16 because of the vision s pains have come upon me
12: 1 s as has never occurred since nations first came
Hos 9: 4 S sacrifices shall be like mourners' bread;
Joel 1: 2 Has s a thing happened in your days,
Am 5:13 Therefore the prudent will keep silent in s a time;
Jnh 1: 4 and s a mighty storm came upon the sea that
Mic 2: 6 "one should not preach of s things;
2:11 s a one would be the preacher for this people!
Hab 2: 6 Shall not everyone taunt s people and,
Zep 1:17 I will bring s distress upon people
Zec 14:19 S shall be the punishment of Egypt and
Mt 8:10 in no one in Israel have I found s faith.
9: 8 who had given s authority to human beings.
11:26 yes, Father, for s was your gracious will.
13: 2 S great crowds gathered around him that he got
13:21 yet s a person has no root,
18: 5 Whoever welcomes one s child
18:17 to listen even to the church, let s a one be to you as
19:10 "If s is the case of a man with his wife,
19:14 to s as these that the kingdom of heaven belongs."
24:21 s as has not been from the beginning of the world
Mk 2: 8 "Why do you raise s questions in your hearts?
4: 1 S a very large crowd gathered around him
4:33 With many s parables he spoke the word to them,
9: 3 s as no one on earth could bleach them.
9:37 "Whoever welcomes one s child
10:14 it is to s as these that the kingdom of God belongs.
13:19 s as has not been from the beginning of
Lk 5:22 "Why do you raise s questions in your hearts?
7: 9 "I tell you, not even in Israel have I found s faith."
9: 9 but who is this about whom I hear s things?"
10:21 yes, Father, for s was your gracious will.
18:16 it is to s as these that the kingdom of God belongs.
Jn 4:23 for the Father seeks s as these to worship him.
5:16 because he was doing s things on the sabbath.
5:34 Not that I accept s human testimony,
7:15 saying, "How does this man have s learning,
Jn 7:32 The Pharisees heard the crowd muttering s things
8: 5 ⟦the law Moses commanded us to stone s women.⟧
9:16 "How can a man who is a sinner perform s signs?"
15: 6 s branches are gathered, thrown into the fire,
Ac 5: 8 and your husband sold the land for s and s
14: 1 into the Jewish synagogue and spoke in s a way
20:35 an example that by s work we must support
22:22 "Away with s a fellow from the earth!
26:29 to me today might become s as I am—
Ro 1:32 that those who practice s things deserve to die—
2: 2 that God's judgment on those who do s things is
2: 3 that when you judge those who do s things and
2:29 S a person receives praise not from others but
4: 5 s faith is reckoned as righteousness.
16:18 For s people do not serve our Lord Christ,
1Co 5: 4 the Lord Jesus on the man who has done s a thing.
5:11 Do not even eat with s a one.
7:15 in s a case the brother or sister is not bound.
9:24 Run in s a way that you may win it.
11:16 we have no s custom, nor do the churches of God.
14: 7 s as the flute or the harp.
16:16 to put yourselves at the service of s people,
16:18 So give recognition to s persons.
2Co 2: 6 This punishment by the majority is enough for s
3: 4 S is the confidence that we have through Christ
3:12 Since, then, we have s a hope,
10:11 Let s people understand that what we say by letter
11:13 For s boasters are false apostles, deceitful workers,
12: 3 And I know that s a person—
12: 5 On behalf of s a one I will boast,
Gal 5: 8 S persuasion does not come from
5:21 those who do s things will not inherit the kingdom
5:23 There is no law against s things.
6: 1 you who have received the Spirit should restore s
Eph 5:12 even to mention what s people do secretly;
Php 2:29 then in the Lord with all joy, and honor s people,
Col 3: 8 But now you must get rid of all s things—
2Th 3:12 Now s persons we command and exhort in
1Ti 1: 5 the aim of s instruction is love that comes from
Tit 3:11 you know that s a person is perverted and sinful,
Heb 4:11 no one may fall through s disobedience as theirs.
7:26 it was fitting that we should have s a high priest,
8: 1 we have s a high priest,
9: 6 S preparations having been made,
12: 3 Consider him who endured s hostility
13:16 for s sacrifices are pleasing to God.
Jas 1:12 S a one has stood the test and will receive
3:15 S wisdom does not come down from above,
4:13 "Today or tomorrow we will go to s and s
4:16 in your arrogance; all s boasting is evil.
1Jn 2: 4 is a liar, and in s a person the truth does not exist;
2:10 and in s a person there is no cause for stumbling.
5:16 you will ask, and God will give life to s a one—
2Jn 1: 7 any s person is the deceiver and the antichrist!
1:11 to welcome is to participate in the evil deeds of s
3Jn 1: 8 Therefore we ought to support s people,
Jude 1:15 that they have committed in s an ungodly way,
Rev 16:18 s as had not occurred since people were upon
18:21 "With s violence Babylon the great city will
Tob 3:13 the earth and not listen to s reproaches any more.
7: 7 "O most miserable of calamities that s an upright
Jdt 12:12 if we let s a woman go without having intercourse
AdE 1: 7 s as the king himself drank.
2:20 s were the instructions of Mordecai;
4:14 For if you keep quiet at s a time as this,
4:14 who knows whether it was not for s a time as this
10: 3 His way of life was s as to make him beloved
Wis 4:15 or take s a thing to heart,
11:18 or s as breathe out fiery breath,
12:19 Through s works you have taught your people that
12:20 if you punished with s great care and indulgence
14:22 they call s great evils peace.
15: 6 for s objects of hope are those who either make
16: 1 through s creatures, and were tormented by
16: 9 because they deserved to be punished by s things.
Sir 6: 8 For there are friends who are s when it suits them,
6:34 Attach yourself to s a one.
7:35 because for s deeds you will be loved.
15:13 s things are not loved by those who fear him.
16: 5 Many s things my eye has seen,
16:23 S are the thoughts of one devoid of understanding;
20:15 s a one is hateful to God and humans.
23:12 S conduct will be far from the godly,
25:20 s is a garrulous wife to a quiet husband.
33: 1 in trials s a one will be rescued again and again.
33: 3 s a one the law is as dependable as a divine oracle.
34: 8 Without s deceptions the law will be fulfilled,
39:17 for at the appointed time all s questions will
45:13 Before him s beautiful things did not exist.
51:24 and why do you endure s great thirst?
LtJ 6:73 s a person will be far above reproach.
Aza 1:17 s may our sacrifice be in your sight today,
Sus 1:48 "Are you s fools, O Israelites,
1Mc 1:51 In s words he wrote to his whole kingdom.
3:30 He feared that he might not have s funds as he had
4: 6 not have armor and swords s as they desired.
9:10 be it from us to do s a thing as to flee from them.
9:27 s as had not been since the time
10:16 So he said, "Shall we find another s man?
10:73 not be able to withstand my cavalry and s an army
10:89 s as it is the custom to give to the King's Kinsmen.
15: 8 to the royal treasury and any s future debts shall
2Mc 1:19 where they took s precautions that
2:29 s in my judgment is the case with us.
3:11 s an extent the impious Simon had misrepresented
4: 3 to s a degree that even murders were committed
4:13 There was s an extreme of Hellenization

2Mc 4:30 While s was the state of affairs,
6:12 not to be depressed by s calamities,
6:24 "S pretense is not worthy of our time of life,"
8:7 the nights most advantageous for s attacks.
9:28 s as he had inflicted on others,
10:4 that they might never again fall into s misfortunes,
10:9 S then was the end of Antiochus,
11:20 And concerning s matters and their details,
13:7 By s a fate it came about that Menelaus
1Es 1:21 none of the kings of Israel had kept s a passover
2:20 we think it best not to neglect s a matter,
2:29 and that s wicked proceedings go no further to
4:32 not women strong, since they do s things?"
4:37 all their works are unrighteous, and all s things.
8:87 and gave us s a root as this;
3Mc 2:26 with s audacity that he framed evil reports in
3:9 for s a great community ought not be left to its fate
4:4 For with s a harsh and ruthless spirit were they
4:5 by the violence with which they were driven in s
7:9 and inescapably as an antagonist to avenge s acts.
2Es 1:9 on whom I have bestowed s great benefits?
4:6 that you should ask me about s things?"
7:*80* s spirits shall not enter into habitations,
4Mc 1:4 that hinder one from justice, s as malice, and those
5:27 but also to eat in s a way that you may deride us
5:28 But you shall have no s occasion to laugh at me,
6:18 in accordance with law the reputation of s a life,
7:8 S should be those who are administrators of
8:5 the beauty and the number of s brothers.
8:26 Why does s contentiousness excite us and such
8:26 Why does such contentiousness excite us and s
13:21 From s embraces brotherly-loving souls are
15:17 who alone gave birth to s complete devotion!
16:3 as she saw her seven sons tortured in s varied
16:4 so many and s great emotions by devout reason.
16:12 and God-fearing mother did not wail with s
16:17 while an aged man endures s agonies for the sake

SUCHATHITES (KJV) See SUCATHITES

SUCK (6) [SUCKING, SUCKLING]

Dt 33:19 for they s the affluence of the seas and
Job 3:12 or breasts for me to s?
20:16 They will s the poison of asps;
39:30 Its young ones s up blood;
Isa 60:16 You shall s the milk of nations,
60:16 you shall s the breasts of kings;

SUCK, SUCKED, SUCKING (KJV) See also AT [THE BREAST], DRAIN, INFANT, NURSE, NURSED, NURSING

SUCKING (2) [SUCK]

Nu 11:12 as a nurse carries a s child,'
1Sa 7:9 a s lamb and offered it as a whole burnt offering to

SUCKLING (1) [SUCK]

Sir 46:16 and he offered in sacrifice a s lamb.

SUCKLING[S] (KJV) See also BABES, INFANT[S], NURSING CHILD

SUD (1)

Bar 1:4 all who lived in Babylon by the river S.

SUDDEN‡ (8) [SUDDENLY]

Job 9:23 When disaster brings s death,
22:10 and s terror overwhelms you,
Pr 3:25 Do not be afraid of s panic,
1Th 5:3 then s destruction will come upon them,
Wis 17:15 for s and unexpected fear overwhelmed them.
2Mc 14:17 of the s consternation created by the enemy.
14:22 in readiness at key places to prevent s treachery on
3Mc 3:24 if a s disorder later arises against us,

SUDDENLY (88) [SUDDEN]

Ge 37:7 S my sheaf rose and stood upright;
Nu 6:9 If someone dies very s nearby,
12:4 S the LORD said to Moses, Aaron, and Miriam,
35:22 But if someone pushes another s without enmity,
Jos 10:9 So Joshua came upon them s,
11:7 So Joshua came s upon them
Jdg 14:5 s a young lion roared at him.
1Ki 1:18 But now s Adonijah has become king, though you,
19:5 S an angel touched him and said to him,
2Ki 3:20 s water began to flow from the direction of Edom,
2Ch 29:36 for the thing had come about s.
Job 1:19 and s a great wind came across the desert, struck
5:3 but s I cursed their dwelling.
Ps 64:4 they shoot s and without fear.
64:7 at them; they will be wounded s.
Pr 6:15 on such a one calamity will descend s;
23:5 for s it takes wings to itself,
24:22 for disaster comes from them s,
29:1 will s be broken beyond healing.
Ecc 9:12 when it s falls upon them.
Isa 29:5 like flying chaff. And in an instant, s,
30:13 and about to collapse, whose crash comes s,
47:11 and ruin shall come on you s,
48:3 then s I did them and they came to pass.
Jer 4:20 S my tents are destroyed, my curtains in a moment.
6:26 for s the destroyer will come upon us.
15:8 I have made anguish and terror fall upon her s.
18:22 when you bring the marauder s upon them!
49:19 I will s chase Edom away from it;
50:44 I will s chase them away from her;
51:8 S Babylon has fallen and is shattered;
Eze 37:7 and as I prophesied, s there was a noise, a rattling,
Hab 2:7 Will not your own creditors s rise,
Mal 3:1 Lord whom you seek will s come to his temple.
Mt 2:19 the Lord s appeared in a dream to Joseph in Egypt
3:16 s the heavens were opened to him and he saw
4:11 and s angels came and waited on him.
8:29 S they shouted, "What have you to do with us,
8:32 So they came out and entered the swine; and s,
9:18 s a leader of the synagogue came in and knelt
9:20 Then s a woman who had been suffering
17:3 S there appeared to them Moses and Elijah,
17:5 s a bright cloud overshadowed them,
26:51 S, one of those with Jesus put his hand
28:2 And s there was a great earthquake;
28:9 S Jesus met them and said, "Greetings!"
Mk 9:8 S when they looked around,
13:36 or else he may find you asleep when he comes s.
Lk 2:13 And s there was with the angel a multitude of
9:30 S they saw two men, Moses and Elijah,
9:39 S a spirit seizes him, and all at once he shrieks.
22:47 While he was still speaking, s a crowd came,
24:4 s two men in dazzling clothes stood beside them.
Ac 1:10 s two men in white robes stood by them.
2:2 And s from heaven there came a sound like
6:12 then they s confronted him, seized him,
9:3 s a light from heaven flashed around him.
10:16 and the thing was s taken up to heaven.
10:17 s the men sent by Cornelius appeared.
10:30 when s a man in dazzling clothes stood before me.
12:7 S an angel of the Lord appeared and a light shone
12:10 when s the angel left him.
16:26 S there was an earthquake,
22:6 about noon a great light from heaven s shone
Tob 6:3 S a large fish leaped up from the water and tried
Wis 14:15 who had been s taken from him;
Sir 5:7 for s the wrath of the Lord will come upon you,
11:21 in the sight of the Lord to make the poor rich s,
1Mc 1:30 but he s fell upon the city, dealt it a severe blow,
3:23 he rushed s against Seron and his army,
4:2 upon the camp of the Jews and attack them s.
2Mc 3:27 When he s fell to the ground
5:5 a thousand men and s made an assault on the city.
3Mc 3:8 and the crowds that s were forming,
4:2 the unexpected destruction that had s been decreed
2Es 5:4 and the sun shall s begin to shine at night,
6:22 Sown places shall s appear unsown,
6:22 and full storehouses shall s be found to be empty;
6:23 and when all hear it, they shall s be terrified.
8:14 If then you will s and quickly destroy what with
10:25 her face s began to shine exceedingly;
10:26 she s uttered a loud and fearful cry,
11:20 of them that ruled, yet disappeared s;
11:26 I kept looking, one was set up, but s disappeared;
11:29 at rest (the one that was in the middle) s awoke;
11:33 and saw the head in the middle s disappear,
13:11 so that s nothing was seen of
14:1 s a voice came out of a bush opposite me and said,

SUDIAS (1)

1Es 5:26 of Jeshua and Kadmiel and Bannas and S,

SUE (2) [LAWSUIT, LAWSUITS]

Mt 5:40 and if anyone wants to s you and take your coat,
Jdt 3:1 therefore sent messengers to him to s for peace

SUET (3)

Lev 1:8 the head and the s, on the wood that is on the fire
1:12 and its s, and the priest shall arrange them on
8:20 into smoke the head and the parts and the s.

SUFFER‡ (76) [SUFFERED, SUFFERING, SUFFERINGS, SUFFERS]

Ge 4:15 Whoever kills Cain will s a sevenfold vengeance."
Lev 24:19 Anyone who maims another shall s the same injury
Nu 14:33 and shall s for your faithlessness,
Jdg 10:16 and he could no longer bear to see Israel s.
2Ki 7:13 since those left here will s the fate of
Ne 2:17 so that we may no longer s disgrace."
9:27 into the hands of their enemies, who made them s.
Job 24:11 they tread the wine presses, but s thirst.
Ps 4:2 How long, you people, shall my honor s shame?
9:13 See what I s from those who hate me;
34:10 The young lions s want and hunger,
60:3 You have made your people s hard things;
88:15 I s your terrors; I am desperate.
Pr 11:24 others withhold what is due, and only s want.
19:15 an idle person will s hunger.
21:17 Whoever loves pleasure will s want;
22:3 but the simple go on, and s for it.
27:12 but the simple go on, and s for it.
Isa 24:6 and its inhabitants s for their guilt;
54:4 do not be discouraged, for you will not s disgrace;
Jer 15:15 know that on your account I s insult.
La 1:5 the LORD has made her s for the multitude
Eze 18:19 "Why should not the son s for the iniquity of
18:20 A child shall not s for the iniquity of a parent,
18:20 nor a parent s for the iniquity of a child;
34:29 and no longer s the insults of the nations.
36:7 that are all around you shall themselves s insults.
36:30 that you may never again s the disgrace of famine
Da 6:2 so that the king might s no loss.
11:33 and s captivity and plunder.
Zec 10:2 they s for lack of a shepherd.
Mt 17:12 also the Son of Man is about to s at their hands."
Lk 22:15 to eat this Passover with you before I s;
24:26 the Messiah should s these things and then enter
24:46 that the Messiah is to s and to rise from the dead
Ac 3:18 through all the prophets, that his Messiah would s.
5:41 that they were considered worthy to s dishonor for
9:16 I myself will show him how much he must s for
17:3 for the Messiah to s and to rise from the dead,
26:23 the Messiah must s, and that, by being the first
Ro 8:17 we s with him so that we may also be glorified
1Co 3:15 If the work is burned up, the builder will s loss;
12:26 If one member suffers, all s together with it;
2Co 2:3 as I did, so that when I came, I might not s pain
1Th 3:4 that we were to s persecution;
2Th 1:9 These will s the punishment of eternal destruction,
2Ti 1:12 and for this reason I s as I do.
2:9 for which I s hardship, even to the point
Heb 9:26 then he would have had to s again and again since
1Pe 1:6 for a little while you have had to s various trials,
2:20 But if you endure when you do right and s for it,
3:14 if you do s for doing what is right, you are blessed.
3:17 For it is better to s for doing good,
3:17 than to s for doing evil.
4:15 But let none of you s as a murderer, a thief,
Rev 2:10 Do not fear what you are about to s.
Jdt 7:9 my lord, and your army will s no losses.
Wis 4:19 and barren, and they will s anguish,
14:29 and expect to s no harm.
Sir 14:1 and need not s remorse for sin.
30:7 and will s heartache at every cry.
32:24 and the one who trusts the Lord will not s loss.
41:7 for they s disgrace because of him.
2Mc 6:30 but in my soul I am glad to s these things
14:42 into the hands of sinners and s outrages unworthy
3Mc 3:25 to s the sure and shameful death
2Es 4:12 and to s and not understand why."
5:34 for every hour I s agonies of heart,
7:*99* not give heed shall s hereafter."
7:*126* [56] not consider what we should s after death."
7:*128* [58] are defeated they shall s what you have said,
15:59 you shall come and s fresh miseries.
4Mc 4:25 they had known beforehand that they would s this
9:8 and shall be with God, on whose account we s;
9:32 but you s torture by the threats that come
15:11 though so many factors influenced the mother to s

SUFFERED (38) [SUFFER]

Lev 24:20 the injury inflicted is the injury to be s.
1Sa 25:15 the men were very good to us, and we s no harm,
2Ki 5:1 The man, though a mighty warrior, s from leprosy.
Ps 116:3 on me; I s distress and anguish.
Eze 36:6 because you have s the insults of the nations;
Mt 11:12 until now the kingdom of heaven has s violence,
27:19 for today I have s a great deal because of a dream
Lk 13:2 "Do you think that because these Galileans s
Ac 28:5 shook off the creature into the fire and s no harm.
Php 3:8 For his sake I have s the loss of all things,
1Th 2:2 but though we had already s
2:14 for you s the same things
1Ti 1:19 certain persons have s shipwreck in the faith;
Heb 2:18 Because he himself was tested by what he s,
5:8 he learned obedience through what he s;
11:26 He considered abuse s for the Christ to
11:36 Others s mocking and flogging,
13:12 also s outside the city gate in order to sanctify
1Pe 2:21 because Christ also s for you,
2:23 when he s, he did not threaten;
3:18 For Christ also s for sins once for all,
4:1 Since therefore Christ s in the flesh,
4:1 also with the same intention (for whoever has s in
5:10 And after you have s for a little while,
Jdt 8:19 so they s a great catastrophe before our enemies.
Wis 18:1 and counted them happy for not having s,
18:11 and the commoner s the same loss as the king;
18:19 not perish without knowing why they s.
19:13 for they justly s because of their wicked acts;
1Mc 5:61 Thus the people s a great rout because,
2Mc 4:48 and the holy vessels quickly s the unjust penalty.
9:21 from the region of Persia I s an annoying illness,
3Mc 5:33 So Hermon s an unexpected and dangerous threat,
2Es 7:18 but those who have done wickedly have s
10:22 our children have s abuse,
4Mc 15:7 and because of the many pains she s with each
15:16 even the birth pangs you s for them!
15:22 then s as her sons were tortured on the wheel and

SUFFERING‡ (62) [SUFFER]

Ge 44:34 to see the s that would come upon my father."
1Sa 9:16 for I have seen the s of my people,
2Ch 6:28 whatever s, whatever sickness there is;
6:29 all knowing their own s and their own sorrows so
Ne 9:27 of their s they cried out to you and you heard them
Job 2:13 for they saw that his s was very great.
9:28 I become afraid of all my s,
Isa 49:13 and will have compassion on his s ones.
53:3 a man of s and acquainted with infirmity;
La 1:3 into exile with s and hard servitude;
1:18 but hear, all you peoples, and behold my s;
Mt 9:20 a woman who had been s from hemorrhages
16:21 that he must go to Jerusalem and undergo great s
24:21 For at that time there will be great s,

Mt 24:29 "Immediately after the **s** of those days the sun will
Mk 5:25 a woman who had been **s** from hemorrhages
8:31 that the Son of Man must undergo great **s,**
13:19 For in those days there will be **s,**
13:24 "But in those days, after that **s,**
Lk 4:38 Simon's mother-in-law was **s** from a high fever,
8:43 a woman who had been **s** from hemorrhages
9:22 "The Son of Man must undergo great **s,**
17:25 But first he must endure much **s** and be rejected
Ac 1: 3 After his **s** he presented himself alive to them
7:11 and great **s,** and our ancestors could find no food.
Ro 5: 3 knowing that **s** produces endurance,
12:12 Rejoice in hope, be patient in **s,**
2Co 1: 6 the same sufferings that we are also **s.**
Php 1:17 not sincerely but intending to increase my **s**
1:29 but of **s** for him as well—
2Th 1: 5 for which you are also **s.**
2Ti 1: 8 but join with me in **s** for the gospel,
2: 3 Share in **s** like a good soldier of Christ Jesus.
3:11 and **s** the things that happened to me in Antioch,
4: 5 As for you, always be sober, endure **s,**
Heb 2: 9 with glory and honor because of the **s** of death,
Jas 5:10 As an example of **s** and patience, beloved,
5:13 Are any among you **s?**
1Pe 2:19 you endure pain while **s** unjustly.
3:17 if **s** should be God's will,
4:19 Therefore, let those **s** in accordance
5: 9 the world are undergoing the same kinds of **s.**
2Pe 2:13 **s** the penalty for doing wrong.
Wis 12:27 in their **s** they became incensed at those creatures
16: 3 while your people, after **s** want a short time,
Sir 25:14 Any **s,** but not **s** from those who hate!
2Mc 7:18 For we are **s** these things on our own account,
7:32 For we are **s** because of our own sins.
7:36 a brief **s** have drunk of ever-flowing life,
9:28 having endured the more intense **s,**
Man 1: 7 and very merciful, and you relent at human **s.**
3Mc 2: 2 give attention to us who are **s** grievously from
2:13 of our many and great sins we are crushed with **s,**
4Mc 5:23 so that we endure any **s** willingly;
7:22 and knows that it is blessed to endure any **s** for
9: 8 For we, through this severe **s** and endurance,
10:10 are **s** because of our godly training and virtue,
14: 9 we ourselves shudder as we hear of the **s**
15:13 nurture and indomitable **s** by mothers!
16:19 you ought to endure any **s** for the sake of God.
18: 3 in **s** for the sake of religion were not only admired

SUFFERINGS (26) [SUFFER]

Ex 3: 7 of their taskmasters. Indeed, I know their **s,**
Mk 9:12 through many **s** and be treated with contempt?
Ro 5: 3 And not only that, but we also boast in our **s,**
8:18 the **s** of this present time are not worth comparing
2Co 1: 5 For just as the **s** of Christ are abundant for us,
1: 6 when you patiently endure the same **s** that we are
1: 7 for we know that as you share in our **s,**
Eph 3:13 therefore that you may not lose heart over my **s**
Php 3:10 and the sharing of his **s** by becoming like him
Col 1:24 I am now rejoicing in my **s** for your sake,
Heb 2:10 the pioneer of their salvation perfect through **s.**
10:32 you endured a hard struggle with **s,**
1Pe 1:11 the **s** destined for Christ and the subsequent glory.
4:13 But rejoice insofar as you are sharing Christ's **s,**
5: 1 as an elder myself and a witness of the **s** of Christ,
Wis 19:16 with terrible **s** those who had already shared
2Mc 6:30 from death, I am enduring terrible **s** in my body
7:12 for he regarded his **s** as nothing.
9:18 But when his **s** did not in any way abate,
4Mc 1: 9 All of these, by despising **s** that bring death,
7: 8 with their own blood and noble sweat in **s** even
11:12 through these noble **s** you give us an opportunity
11:20 to an arena of **s** for religion,
13: 1 the seven brothers despised **s** even unto death,
14: 9 but also bore the **s** patiently,
18: 2 not only of **s** from within,

SUFFERS (9) [SUFFER]

Lev 22: 4 or **s** a discharge may eat of the sacred donations
Pr 13:20 but the companion of fools **s** harm.
19:23 filled with it one rests secure and **s** no harm.
Eze 22: 7 the alien residing within you **s** extortion;
Mt 17:15 for he is an epileptic and he **s** terribly;
1Co 12:26 If one member **s,** all suffer together with it;
1Pe 4:16 Yet if any of you **s** as a Christian,
Sir 13: 3 a poor person **s** wrong, and must add apologies.
19:11 the fool **s** birth pangs like a woman in labor with

SUFFICE (4) [SUFFICIENCY, SUFFICIENT]

Dt 19:15 A single witness shall not **s** to convict a person
Jdg 21:14 but they did not **s** for them.
Ps 49: 8 For the ransom of life is costly, and can never **s**
4Mc 6:28 and let our punishment **s** for them.

SUFFICE, SUFFICED, SUFFICETH

(KJV) See also END, ENOUGH, PROVIDE, SATISFIED

SUFFICIENCY (1) [SUFFICE]

Job 20:22 In full **s** they will be in distress;

SUFFICIENT (7) [SUFFICE]

Lev 25:26 but then prospers and finds **s** means to do so,
25:28 But if there is not **s** means to recover it,
2Ch 30: 3 not sanctified themselves in **s** number,
2Co 2:16 Who is **s** for these things?
12: 9 "My grace is **s** for you,
Wis 18:12 For the living were not **s** even to bury them,
2Mc 10:19 a force **s** to besiege them;

SUGGESTION (3) [SUGGESTS]

AdE 6:10 "You have made an excellent **s!**
Sir 32:18 sensible person will not overlook a thoughtful **s;**
2Mc 6: 8 At the **s** of the people of Ptolemais

SUGGESTS (1) [SUGGESTION]

Sir 43: 8 The new moon, as its name **s,** renews itself;

SUIT (6) [SUITABLE, SUITED, SUITS]

2Sa 15: 2 anyone brought a **s** before the king for judgment,
15: 4 Then all who had a **s** or cause might come to me,
Job 34:33 Will he then pay back to **s** you,
Isa 59: 4 No one brings **s** justly, no one goes
2Ti 4: 3 for themselves teachers to **s** their own desires,
Wis 16:21 was changed to **s** everyone's liking.

SUITABLE (9) [SUIT]

Ge 49:28 blessing each one of them with a **s** blessing.
Ecc 3:11 He has made everything **s** for its time;
Ac 27:12 Since the harbor was not **s** for spending the winter,
1Ti 2: 9 and decently in **s** clothing,
Wis 13:15 then he makes a **s** niche for it,
2Mc 2:29 and decoration has to consider only what is **s**
3:37 of person would be **s** to send on another mission
4:32 thinking he had obtained a **s** opportunity,
4Mc 5:26 He has permitted us to eat what will be most **s**

SUITED (2) [SUIT]

Wis 16:20 providing every pleasure and **s** to every taste.
3Mc 4:11 that was well **s** to make them an obvious spectacle

SUITS (3) [SUIT]

Sir 6: 8 For there are friends who are such when it **s** them,
1Mc 13:29 and on the columns he put **s** of armor for
13:29 and beside the **s** of armor he carved ships,

SUKKIIM (1)

2Ch 12: 3 Libyans, **S,** and Ethiopians.

SULFUR (16)

Ge 19:24 the LORD rained on Sodom and Gomorrah **s**
Dt 29:23 all its soil burned out by **s** and salt,
Job 18:15 **s** is scattered upon their habitations.
Ps 11: 6 On the wicked he will rain coals of fire and **s;**
Isa 30:33 breath of the LORD, like a stream of **s,** kindles it.
34: 9 be turned into pitch, and her soil into **s;**
Eze 38:22 down torrential rains and hailstones, fire and **s,**
Lk 17:29 it rained fire and **s** from heaven and destroyed all
Rev 9:17 the color of fire and of sapphire and of **s;**
9:17 fire and smoke and **s** came out of their mouths.
9:18 and smoke and **s** coming out of their mouths.
14:10 with fire and **s** in the presence of the holy angels
19:20 into the lake of fire that burns with **s.**
20:10 into the lake of fire and **s,**
21: 8 be in the lake that burns with fire and **s,**
3Mc 2: 5 and **s** the people of Sodom who acted arrogantly,

SULLEN (3) [SULLENLY]

1Ki 20:43 king of Israel set out toward home, resentful and **s,**
21: 4 Ahab went home resentful and **s** because
3Mc 6:20 and he forgot his **s** insolence.

SULLENLY (1) [SULLEN]

3Mc 5:34 The king's Friends one by one **s** slipped away

SULTRY (1)

Jnh 4: 8 When the sun rose, God prepared a **s** east wind,

SUM‡ (11) [SUMMARY, SUMMED, SUMS]

2Ki 22: 4 the entire **s** of the money that has been brought
Est 4: 7 the exact **s** of money that Haman had promised
Ps 119:160 The **s** of your word is truth;
139:17 How vast is the **s** of them!
Ecc 7:25 and to search out and to seek wisdom and the **s**
7:27 adding one thing to another to find the **s,**
Mt 26: 9 this ointment could have been sold for a large **s,**
28:12 they devised a plan to give a large **s** of money to
Ac 7:16 the tomb that Abraham had bought for a **s** of silver
22:28 a large **s** of money to get my citizenship."
2Es 12:25 because it is they who shall **s** up his wickedness

SUMMARY (1) [SUM]

2Mc 10:10 and will give a brief **s** of the principal calamities

SUMMED (2) [SUM]

Ro 13: 9 any other commandment, are **s** up in this word,
Gal 5:14 the whole law is **s** up in a single commandment,

SUMMER (27)

Ge 8:22 seedtime and harvest, cold and heat, **s** and winter,
2Sa 16: 1 one hundred of **s** fruits, and one skin of wine.
16: 2 the bread and **s** fruit for the young men to eat,
Ps 32: 4 my strength was dried up as by the heat of **s.**
74:17 of the earth; you made **s** and winter.
Pr 6: 8 it prepares its food in **s,**
10: 5 A child who gathers in **s** is prudent,
26: 1 Like snow in **s** or rain in harvest,
30:25 yet they provide their food in the **s;**
Isa 18: 6 And the birds of prey will **s** on them,
28: 4 will be like a first-ripe fig before the **s;**
Jer 8:20 "The harvest is past, the **s** is ended,
40:10 but as for you, gather wine and **s** fruits and oil,
40:12 they gathered wine and **s** fruits in great abundance.
48:32 upon your **s** fruits and your vintage
Da 2:35 and became like the chaff of the **s** threshing floors;
Am 3:15 down the winter house as well as the **s** house;
8: 1 the Lord GOD showed me—a basket of **s** fruit.
8: 2 And I said, "A basket of **s** fruit."
Mic 7: 1 after the **s** fruit has been gathered,
Zec 14: 8 it shall continue in **s** as in winter.
Mt 24:32 and puts forth its leaves, you know that **s** is near.
Mk 13:28 and puts forth its leaves, you know that **s** is near.
Lk 21:30 for yourselves and know that **s** is already near.
Sir 50: 8 like a green shoot on Lebanon on a **s** day;
Aza 1:45 Bless the Lord, winter cold and **s** heat;
2Es 7:*41* or **s** or spring or heat or winter or frost or cold,

SUMMIT (3)

2Sa 15:32 When David came to the **s,**
16: 1 When David had passed a little beyond the **s,**
Jer 22: 6 You are like Gilead to me, like the **s** of Lebanon;

SUMMON (23) [SUMMONED, SUMMONING, SUMMONS]

Nu 22: 5 in the land of Amaw, to **s** him, saying,
22:20 "If the men have come to **s** you,
22:37 Balak said to Balaam, "Did I not send to **s** you?
Dt 25: 8 elders of his town shall **s** him and speak to him.
2Sa 20: 5 So Amasa went to **s** Judah;
1Ki 1:28 King David answered, "**S** Bathsheba to me."
1:32 King David said, "**S** to me the priest Zadok,
22:13 messenger who had gone to **s** Micaiah said to him,
2Ki 10:19 Now therefore **s** to me all the prophets of Baal,
2Ch 18:12 messenger who had gone to **s** Micaiah said to him,
Job 9:19 If it is a matter of justice, who can **s** him?
Ps 68:28 **S** your might, O God; show your strength,
Isa 48:13 when I **s** them, they stand at attention.
Jer 49:19 For who is like me? Who can **s** me?
50:29 **S** archers against Babylon, all who bend the bow.
50:44 For who is like me? Who can **s** me?
51:27 **s** against her the kingdoms, Ararat, Minni,
Eze 36:29 and I will **s** the grain and make it abundant
38:21 I will **s** the sword against Gog
Jdt 7:26 Now **s** them and surrender the whole town
8:10 to **s** Uzziah and Chabris and Charmis,
AdE 6: 5 And the king said, "**S** him."
Sir 43:30 When you exalt him, **s** all your strength,

SUMMONED (91) [SUMMON]

Ge 48: 2 he **s** his strength and sat up in bed.
Ex 1:18 the king of Egypt **s** the midwives and said to them,
7:11 Then Pharaoh **s** the wise men and the sorcerers;
8:25 Then Pharaoh **s** Moses and Aaron, and said, "Go,
9:27 Then Pharaoh **s** Moses and Aaron,
10:16 Pharaoh hurriedly **s** Moses and Aaron and said,
10:24 Then Pharaoh **s** Moses, and said, "Go,
12:31 Then he **s** Moses and Aaron in the night, and said,
19: 7 So Moses came, **s** the elders of the people,
19:20 the LORD **s** Moses to the top of the mountain,
Lev 1: 1 The LORD **s** Moses and spoke to him from
9: 1 On the eighth day Moses **s** Aaron and his sons and
10: 4 Moses **s** Mishael and Elzaphan,
Nu 24:10 "I **s** you to curse my enemies,
Dt 29: 2 Moses **s** all Israel and said to them:
31: 7 Then Moses **s** Joshua and said to him in the sight
Jos 4: 4 Then Joshua **s** the twelve men from the Israelites,
6: 6 Joshua son of Nun **s** the priests and said to them,
9:22 Joshua **s** them, and said to them,
10:24 Joshua **s** all the Israelites, and said to the chiefs of
22: 1 Then Joshua **s** the Reubenites, the Gadites,
23: 2 Joshua **s** all Israel, their elders
24: 1 and **s** the elders, the heads, the judges,
Jdg 4: 6 and **s** Barak son of Abinoam from Kedesh
4:10 Barak **s** Zebulun and Naphtali to Kedesh;
1Sa 10:17 Samuel **s** the people to the LORD at Mizpah
15: 4 So Saul **s** the people, and numbered them
23: 8 Saul **s** all the people to war, to go down to Keilah,
28:15 so I have **s** you to tell me what I should do."
2Sa 9: 2 and he was **s** to David.
9: 9 Then the king **s** Saul's servant Ziba,
14:33 and told him; and he **s** Absalom.
1Ki 2:36 Then the king sent and **s** Shimei, and said to him,
2:42 the king sent and **s** Shimei,
18: 3 Ahab **s** Obadiah, who was in charge of the palace.
22: 9 Then the king of Israel **s** an officer and said,
2Ki 3:10 The LORD has **s** us, three kings,
3:13 it is the LORD who has **s** us, three kings,
4:36 Elisha **s** Gehazi and said, "Call
11: 4 But in the seventh year Jehoiada **s** the captains of
12: 7 Therefore King Jehoash **s** the priest Jehoiada with
1Ch 15:11 David **s** the priests Zadok and Abiathar,
2Ch 1: 2 Solomon **s** all Israel, the commanders of
18: 8 Then the king of Israel **s** an officer and said,
24: 6 So the king **s** Jehoiada the chief, and said to him,
Est 2:14 the king delighted in her and she was **s** by name.
3:12 the king's secretaries were **s** on the thirteenth day
8: 9 The king's secretaries were **s** at that time,
Job 9:16 If I **s** him and he answered me,
Ps 105:16 When he **s** famine against the land,

Isa 13: 3 have s my warriors, my proudly exulting ones,
41: 2 a victor from the east, s him to his service?
41:25 from the rising of the sun he was s by name.
Jer 42: 8 Then he s Johanan son of Kareah and all
Da 2: 2 and the Chaldeans be s to tell the king his dreams.
Mt 10: 1 Then Jesus s his twelve disciples
18:32 his lord s him and said to him, 'You wicked slave!
25:14 s his slaves and entrusted his property to them;
Lk 7:18 So John s two of his disciples
16: 2 So he s him and said to him,
19:13 He s ten of his slaves, and gave them ten pounds,
19:15 be s so that he might find out what they had gained
Jn 18:33 Pilate entered the headquarters again, s Jesus,
Ac 13: 7 who s Barnabas and Saul and wanted to hear
23:23 Then he s two of the centurions and said,
24: 2 When Paul had been s, Tertullus began
Tob 7:12 Then Raguel s his daughter Sarah.
Jdt 2: 2 He s all his ministers and all his nobles and set
2:14 and s all the commanders, generals,
13:12 down to the town gate and s the elders of the town.
14: 6 So they s Achior from the house of Uzziah.
AdE 2:14 not go in to the king again unless she is s by name.
3:12 of the first month the king's secretaries were s,
4: 5 Then Esther s Hachratheus,
5:10 and s his friends and his wife Zosara.
8: 1 Mordecai was s by the king,
8: 9 The secretaries were s on the twenty-third day of
Wis 1:16 But the ungodly by their words and deeds s death;
Sus 1:52 he s one of them and said to him,
1Mc 1: 6 So he s his most honored officers,
2Mc 4:28 the two of them were s by the king on account
8: 1 the villages and s their kindred
1Es 3:14 and s all the nobles of Persia and Media and
3:16 So they were s, and came in.
3Mc 5: 1 so he s Hermon, keeper of the elephants,
5:18 on for some time, the king s Hermon and
6:30 s the official in charge of the revenues
4Mc 8: 4 he smiled at them, and s them nearer and said,
8:17 Since the king has s and exhorted us
11:20 of us brothers have been s to an arena of sufferings
12: 2 He s him to come nearer and tried

SUMMONING (5) [SUMMON]

Nu 10: 2 and you shall use them for s the congregation,
Jer 25:29 for I am s a sword against all the inhabitants of
Mk 15:44 if he were already dead; and s the centurion,
Lk 16: 5 So, s his master's debtors one by one,
3Mc 5:37 After s Hermon he said in a threatening tone,

SUMMONS (2) [SUMMON]

Ps 50: 1 speaks and s the earth from the rising of the sun
Jdt 1:11 the s of Nebuchadnezzar, king of the Assyrians,

SUMPTUOUS (1) [SUMPTUOUSLY]

Sir 29:22 own crude roof than s food in the house of others.

SUMPTUOUSLY (1) [SUMPTUOUS]

Lk 16:19 and fine linen and who feasted s every day.

SUMS (3) [SUM]

Mk 12:41 Many rich people put in large s.
1Mc 14:32 He spent great s of his own money;
2Mc 3: 6 that the treasury in Jerusalem was full of untold s

SUN‡ (185) [SUN'S, SUNDOWN, SUNLESS, SUNRISE, SUNSET, SUNSHINE]

Ge 15:12 As the s was going down,
15:17 When the s had gone down and it was dark,
19:23 s had risen on the earth when Lot came to Zoar.
28:11 for the night, because the s had set.
32:31 The s rose upon him as he passed Penuel,
37: 9 the s, the moon, and eleven stars were bowing
Ex 16:21 but when the s grew hot, it melted.
17:12 so his hands were steady until the s set.
22:26 you shall restore it before the s goes down;
Lev 22: 7 When the s sets he shall be clean;
Nu 25: 4 and impale them in the s before the LORD,
Dt 4:19 when you look up to the heavens and see the s,
17: 3 the s or the moon or any of the host of heaven,
23:11 and when the s has set,
33:14 with the choice fruits of the s, and the rich yield of
Jos 10:12 "S, stand still at Gibeon, and Moon, in the valley
10:13 And the s stood still, and the moon stopped,
10:13 The s stopped in midheaven,
Jdg 5:31 But may your friends be like the s as it rises
9:33 Then early in the morning, as soon as the s rises,
14:18 to him on the seventh day before the s went down,
19:14 and the s went down on them near Gibeah,
1Sa 11: 9 'Tomorrow, by the time the s is hot,
2Sa 2:24 s was going down they came to the hill of Ammah,
3:35 or anything else before the s goes down!"
12:11 with your wives in the sight of this very s.
12:12 before all Israel, and before the s."
23: 4 like the s rising on a cloudless morning,
2Ki 3:22 and the s shone upon the water,
20:11 by which the s had declined on the dial of Ahaz.
23: 5 those also who made offerings to Baal, to the s,
23:11 the kings of Judah had dedicated to the s,
23:11 then he burned the chariots of the s with fire.
Ne 7: 3 of Jerusalem are not to be opened until the s is hot;
Job 8:16 The wicked thrive before the s,
9: 7 who commands the s, and it does not rise;
31:26 if I have looked at the s when it shone,
Ps 19: 4 In the heavens he has set a tent for the s,
50: 1 and summons the earth from the rising of the s
58: 8 like the untimely birth that never sees the s.
72: 5 May he live while the s endures,
72:17 his fame continue as long as the s.
74:16 you established the luminaries and the s.
84:11 For the LORD God is a s and shield;
89:36 and his throne endure before me like the s.
104:19 the s knows its time for setting.
104:22 s rises, they withdraw and lie down in their dens.
113: 3 of the s to its setting the name of the LORD is to
121: 6 The s shall not strike you by day,
136: 8 the s to rule over the day,
148: 3 s and moon; praise him, all you shining stars!
Ecc 1: 3 from all the toil at which they toil under the s?
1: 5 The s rises and the s goes down,
1: 9 there is nothing new under the s.
1:14 I saw all the deeds that are done under the s;
2:11 and there was nothing to be gained under the s.
2:17 what is done under the s was grievous to me;
2:18 in which I had toiled under the s,
2:19 and used my wisdom under the s.
2:20 concerning all the toil of my labors under the s,
2:22 and strain with which they toil under the s?
3:16 I saw under the s that in the place of justice,
4: 1 the oppressions that are practiced under the s.
4: 3 not seen the evil deeds that are done under the s.
4: 7 Again, I saw vanity under the s:
4:15 I saw all the living who, moving about under the s,
5:13 There is a grievous ill that I have seen under the s:
5:18 under the s the few days of the life God gives us;
6: 1 There is an evil that I have seen under the s,
6: 5 moreover it has not seen the s or known anything;
6:12 be after them under the s?
7:11 an advantage to those who see the s.
8: 9 applying my mind to all that is done under the s,
8:15 for people under the s than to eat,
8:15 the days of life that God gives them under the s.
8:17 no one can find out what is happening under the s.
9: 3 This is an evil in all that happens under the s,
9: 6 in all that happens under the s.
9: 9 of your vain life that are given you under the s,
9: 9 and in your toil at which you toil under the s.
9:11 I saw that under the s the race is not to the swift,
9:13 also seen this example of wisdom under the s,
10: 5 There is an evil that I have seen under the s,
11: 7 and it is pleasant for the eyes to see the s.
12: 2 before the s and the light and the moon and
SS 1: 6 because the s has gazed on me.
6:10 bright as the s, terrible as an army with banners?"
Isa 13:10 the s will be dark at its rising,
19:18 One of these will be called the City of the S.
24:23 the moon will be abashed, and the s ashamed;
30:26 the light of the moon will be like the light of the s,
30:26 and the light of the s will be sevenfold,
38: 8 I will make the shadow cast by the declining s on
38: 8 So the s turned back on the dial the ten steps
41:25 the rising of the s he was summoned by name.
45: 6 from the rising of the s and from the west,
49:10 neither scorching wind nor s shall strike them
60:19 The s shall no longer be your light by day,
60:20 Your s shall no more go down,
Jer 8: 2 and they shall be spread before the s and the moon
15: 9 her s went down while it was yet day;
31:35 the s for light by day and the fixed order of
Eze 8:16 prostrating themselves to the s toward the east.
32: 7 I will cover the s with a cloud,
Da 6:14 and until the s went down he made every effort
Joel 2:10 The s and the moon are darkened,
2:31 The s shall be turned to darkness,
3:15 The s and the moon are darkened,
Am 8: 9 I will make the s go down at noon,
Jnh 4: 8 When the s rose, God prepared a sultry east wind,
4: 8 and the s beat down on the head of Jonah so
Mic 3: 6 The s shall go down upon the prophets,
Na 3:17 when the s rises, they fly away;
Hab 3: 4 The brightness was like the s;
3:10 The s raised high its hands;
Mal 1:11 the rising of the s to its setting my name is great
4: 2 But for you who revere my name the s
Mt 5:45 for he makes his s rise on the evil and on the good,
13: 6 But when the s rose, they were scorched;
13:43 the righteous will shine like the s in the kingdom
17: 2 and his face shone like the s,
24:29 the s will be darkened, and the moon will not give
Mk 4: 6 And when the s rose, it was scorched;
13:24 the s will be darkened, and the moon will not give
16: 2 when the s had risen, they went to the tomb.
Lk 4:40 As the s was setting, all those who had any who
21:25 "There will be signs in the s, the moon,
Ac 2:20 The s shall be turned to darkness and the moon
13:11 be blind for a while, unable to see the s."
26:13 I saw a light from heaven, brighter than the s,
27:20 When neither s nor stars appeared for many days,
1Co 15:41 There is one glory of the s,
Eph 4:26 do not let the s go down on your anger,
Jas 1:11 For the s rises with its scorching heat and withers
Rev 1:16 and his face was like the s shining with full force.
6:12 the s became black as sackcloth,
7: 2 from the rising of the s,
7:16 the s will not strike them, nor any scorching heat;
8:12 and a third of the s was struck,
9: 2 the s and the air were darkened with the smoke
10: 1 his face was like the s,
12: 1 a woman clothed with the s,
16: 8 The fourth angel poured his bowl on the s,
19:17 Then I saw an angel standing in the s,
Rev 21:23 the city has no need of s or moon to shine on it,
22: 5 they need no light of lamp or s,
Tob 2: 7 s had set, I went and dug a grave and buried him.
10: 7 When the s had set she would go in and mourn
Jdt 14: 2 As soon as day breaks and the s rises on the earth,
AdE 10: 6 and there was light and s and abundant water—
11:11 and the s rose, and the lowly were exalted
Wis 2: 4 that is chased by the rays of the s and overcome
5: 6 and the s did not rise upon us.
7:29 She is more beautiful than the s,
16:27 when simply warmed by a fleeting ray of the s,
16:28 that one must rise before the s to give you thanks,
18: 3 and a harmless s for their glorious wandering.
Sir 17:19 All their works are as clear as the s before him,
17:31 What is brighter than the s?
23:19 are ten thousand times brighter than the s;
26:16 Like the s rising in the heights of the Lord,
33: 7 when all the daylight in the year is from the s?
34:19 from scorching wind and a shade from noonday s,
42:16 The s looks down on everything with its light,
43: 2 The s, when it appears, proclaims as it rises what
43: 4 three times as hot is the s scorching the mountains;
46: 4 that the s stood still and one day become as long
48:23 In Isaiah's days the s went backward,
50: 7 like the s shining on the temple of the Most High,
LtJ 6:60 For s and moon and stars are bright,
6:67 or shine like the s or give light like the moon.
Aza 1:40 Bless the Lord, s and moon;
1Mc 6:39 When the s shone on the shields of gold and brass,
10:50 He pressed the battle strongly until the s set,
12:27 So when the s had set,
2Mc 1:22 and when the s, which had been clouded over,
1Es 4:34 and heaven is high, and the s is swift in its course,
3Mc 4:15 and zealous intensity from the rising of the s
5:26 The rays of the s were not yet shed abroad,
2Es 5: 4 and the s shall suddenly begin to shine at night,
6:45 the brightness of the s, the light of the moon,
7:39 a day that has no s or moon or stars,
7:97 how their face is to shine like the s,
15:20 says God, from the rising s and from the south,

SUN'S (1) [SUN]

Lk 23:45 the s light failed; and the curtain of the temple

SUNDER (KJV) See ASUNDER, CUTS IN TWO, PIECES, SHATTERS, SNAP

SUNDOWN (1) [SUN]

Mk 1:32 at s, they brought to him all who were sick

SUNDRY (KJV) See MANY

SUNG (6) [SING]

Job 36:24 to extol his work, of which mortals have s.
Isa 16:10 and in the vineyards no songs are s,
26: 1 that day this song will be s in the land of Judah:
Mt 26:30 When they had s the hymn,
Mk 14:26 When they had s the hymn,
Aza 1:34 and to be s and glorified forever.

SUNK (6) [SINK]

Ex 15: 4 his picked officers were s in the Red Sea.
Job 38: 6 On what were its bases s,
Ps 9:15 The nations have s in the pit that they made;
38: 2 For your arrows have s into me,
La 2: 9 Her gates have s into the ground;
Eze 27:34 your merchandise and all your crew have s

SUNLESS (1) [SUN]

Job 30:28 I go about in s gloom;

SUNRISE (6) [RISE, SUN]

Ex 22: 3 but if it happens after s, bloodguilt is incurred.
Nu 2: 3 Those to camp on the east side toward the s shall
21:11 in the wilderness bordering Moab toward the s.
34:15 the Jordan at Jericho eastward, toward the s.
Jos 19:12 toward the s to the boundary of Chisloth-tabor;
19:13 the east toward the s to Gath-hepher, to Eth-kazin,

SUNSET (8) [SET, SUN]

Dt 16: 6 the passover sacrifice, in the evening at s, the time
24:13 You shall give the pledge back by s,
24:15 You shall pay them their wages daily before s,
Jos 8:29 and at s Joshua commanded,
10:27 At s Joshua commanded, and they took them down
1Ki 22:36 Then about s a shout went through the army,
2Ch 18:34 until evening; then at s he died.
Tob 2: 4 in one of the rooms until s when I might bury it.

SUNSHINE (1) [SHINE, SUN]

Isa 18: 4 from my dwelling like clear heat in s,

SUP (KJV) See EAT, PRESSING FORWARD

SUPER-APOSTLES (2) [APOSTLE]

2Co 11: 5 I think that I am not in the least inferior to these s.
12:11 for I am not at all inferior to these s,

SUPERFLUITY, SUPERFLUOUS (KJV) See NOT NECESSARY, RANK GROWTH

SUPERFLUOUS (1)
2Mc 12:44 it would have been s and foolish to pray for

SUPERHUMAN (1) [HUMAN]
2Mc 9: 8 a little while before had thought in his s arrogance

SUPERIOR (5)
Heb 1: 4 having become as much s to angels as
7: 7 beyond dispute that the inferior is blessed by the s.
Wis 7:29 Compared with the light she is found to be s,
Sir 25:10 But none is s to the one who fears the Lord.
4Mc 2:11 It is s to love for one's wife,

SUPERSCRIPTION (KJV) See INSCRIPTION, TITLE

SUPERVISED (1) [SUPERVISION]
1Es 7: 2 s the holy work with very great care,

SUPERVISION (1) [SUPERVISED, SUPERVISORS]
3Mc 7:12 and without royal authority or s,

SUPERVISOR See Index to Footnotes

SUPERVISORS (6) [SUPERVISION]
Ex 5: 6 the taskmasters of the people, as well as their s,
5:10 the s of the people went out and said to the people,
5:14 And the s of the Israelites,
5:15 Then the Israelite s came to Pharaoh and cried,
5:19 The Israelite s saw that they were in trouble
1Ki 5:16 besides Solomon's three thousand three hundred s

SUPH (1)
Dt 1: 1 in the wilderness, on the plain opposite S,

SUPHAH (1)
Nu 21:14 "Waheb in S and the wadis.

SUPPER‡ (10)
Lk 17: 8 'Prepare s for me, put on your apron and serve me
22:20 And he did the same with the cup after s, saying,
Jn 13: 2 son of Simon Iscariot to betray him. And during s
21:20 the one who had reclined next to Jesus at the s
1Co 11:20 it is not really to eat the Lord's s.
11:21 each of you goes ahead with your own s,
11:25 In the same way he took the cup also, after s,
Rev 19: 9 Blessed are those who are invited to the marriage s
19:17 "Come, gather for the great s of God,
4Mc 3: 9 Now all the rest were at s,

SUPPLANT (1) [SUPPLANTED, SUPPLANTERS, SUPPLANTING]
Hos 12: 3 In the womb he tried to s his brother,

SUPPLANTED (2) [SUPPLANT]
Ge 27:36 For he has s me these two times.
2Mc 4:26 who after supplanting his own brother was s

SUPPLANTERS (1) [SUPPLANT]
Jer 9: 4 for all your kin are s, and every neighbor goes

SUPPLANTING (1) [SUPPLANT]
2Mc 4:26 who after s his own brother was supplanted

SUPPLANTS See Index to Footnotes

SUPPLE (KJV) See CLEANSE

SUPPLEMENT See Index to Footnotes

SUPPLEMENTS (1)
Sir 42:25 Each s the virtues of the other.

SUPPLIANT (1) [SUPPLICATION]
Sir 4: 4 Do not reject a s in distress,

SUPPLIANTS (1) [SUPPLICATION]
Zep 3:10 From beyond the rivers of Ethiopia my s,

SUPPLICATION‡ (33) [SUPPLIANT, SUPPLIANTS, SUPPLICATIONS]
2Sa 24:25 So the LORD answered his s for the land,
Est 4: 8 to go to the king to make s to him and entreat him
Job 8: 5 If you will seek God and make s to the Almighty,
Ps 6: 9 The LORD has heard my s;
28: 2 Hear the voice of my s, as I cry to you for help,
30: 8 O LORD, I cried, and to the LORD I made s:
55: 1 do not hide yourself from my s.
86: 6 listen to my cry of s.
119:170 Let my s come before you;
142: 1 with my voice I make s to the LORD.
Isa 45:14 They will make s to you, saying,
Da 9: 3 to seek an answer by prayer and s with fasting
9:17 listen to the prayer of your servant and to his s,
9:18 We do not present our s before you on the ground
9:20 and presenting my s before the LORD my God
Zec 12:10 And I will pour out a spirit of compassion and s on
Eph 6:18 Pray in the Spirit at all times in every prayer and s.
6:18 To that end keep alert and always persevere in s
Php 4: 6 and s with thanksgiving let your requests
Sir 35:17 He will not ignore the s of the orphan,
Bar 2:14 Hear, O Lord, our prayer and our s,
4:20 the robe of peace and put on sackcloth for my s;
1Mc 7:37 and to be for your people a house of prayer and s.
2Mc 3:18 a general s because the holy place was about to
3:20 holding up their hands to heaven, they all made s.
8:29 they made common s and implored the merciful
9:18 the following letter, in the form of a s.
10:16 after making solemn s and imploring God to fight
10:25 and girded their loins with sackcloth, in s to God.
12:42 and they turned to s, praying that the sin
3Mc 1:23 they resorted to the same posture of s as the others.
2:21 having heard the lawful s,
5:25 with most tearful s and mournful dirges implored

SUPPLICATIONS‡ (13) [SUPPLICATION]
2Sa 21:14 After that, God heeded s for the land.
Job 41: 3 Will it make many s to you?
Ps 31:22 you heard my s when I cried out to you for help.
116: 1 because he has heard my voice and my s.
130: 2 Let your ears be attentive to the voice of my s!
140: 6 give ear, O LORD, to the voice of my s."
143: 1 give ear to my s in your faithfulness;
Isa 19:22 and he will listen to their s and heal them.
Da 9:23 At the beginning of your s a word went out,
1Ti 2: 1 First of all, then, I urge that s, prayers,
5: 5 and continues in s and prayers night and day;
Heb 5: 7 Jesus offered up prayers and s,
3Mc 1:21 Various were the s of those gathered there because

SUPPLIED (14) [SUPPLY]
Ge 47:17 That year he s them with food in exchange
Nu 4: 9 and all the vessels for oil with which it is s;
1Ki 4:27 Those officials s provisions for King Solomon and
5:10 So Hiram s Solomon's every need for timber
9:11 King Hiram of Tyre having s Solomon with cedar
Pr 13: 4 while the appetite of the diligent is richly s.
Isa 33:16 their food will be s, their water assured.
Eze 41: 7 for the structure was s with a stairway all around
2Co 11: 9 for my needs were s by the friends who came
Jdt 7: 7 and visited the springs that s their water;
Wis 16:20 and without their toil you s them from heaven
1Mc 14:10 He s the towns with food,
2Es 8:10 the fruit of the breasts, should be s,
9:19 which is s both with an unfailing table and

SUPPLIES (10) [SUPPLY]
Pr 31:24 she s the merchant with sashes.
Da 11:13 with a great army and abundant s.
2Co 9:10 He who s seed to the sower and bread
9:12 the rendering of this ministry not only s the needs
1Pe 4:11 so with the strength that God s,
Tob 5:17 prepare s for the journey and set out
Jdt 3:10 for a whole month in order to collect all the s
12: 4 up the s I have with me before the Lord carries out
1Mc 6: 6 that the Jews had grown strong from the arms, s,
1Es 5:72 cut off their s, and hindered their building;

SUPPLY (16) [SUPPLIED, SUPPLIES]
Ex 1:11 They built s cities, Pithom and Rameses,
Dt 2:28 and s me water for money, so that I may drink.
2Ch 31:10 so that we have this great s left over."
Isa 23:18 but her merchandise will s abundant food
2Co 9:10 for food will s and multiply your seed for sowing
Gal 3: 5 does God s you with the Spirit and work miracles
Jas 2:16 and yet you do not s their bodily needs,
Jdt 7:17 the valley and seized the water s and the springs of
7:18 Their tents and s trains spread out in great number,
11:12 Since their food s is exhausted
12: 3 Holofernes said to her, "If your s runs out,
Sir 39:33 and he will s every need in its time.
1Mc 6:57 men, "Daily we grow weaker, our food s is scant,
8:26 not give or s grain, arms, money, or ships, just
2Mc 12:14 relying on the strength of the walls and on their s
15:21 that were in front of him and the varied s of arms

SUPPORT‡ (35) [SUPPORTED, SUPPORTERS, SUPPORTING, SUPPORTS]
Ge 13: 6 the land could not s both of them living together;
36: 7 the land where they were staying could not s them
Lev 25:35 and become dependent on you, you shall s them;
Dt 29:23 nothing sprouting, unable to s any vegetation,
2Sa 3:12 and I will give you my s to bring all Israel over
1Ch 11:10 who gave him strong s in his kingdom,
Ps 18:18 but the LORD was my s.
20: 2 and give you s from Zion.
Isa 3: 1 s and staff—all s of bread, and all s of water—
Eze 30: 6 Those who s Egypt shall fall,
Da 11: 1 I stood up to s and strengthen him.
Mic 1:11 Beth-ezel is wailing and shall remove its s
Mt 15: 5 'Whatever s you might have had from me is given
Mk 7:11 'Whatever s you might have had
Ac 20:34 that I worked with my own hands to s myself
20:35 an example that by such work we must s the weak,
Ro 11:18 remember that it is not you that s the root,
2Co 11: 8 I robbed other churches by accepting s from them
2Ti 4:16 At my first defense no one came to my s,
1Pe 5:10 will himself restore, s, strengthen,
2Pe 1: 5 you must make every effort to s your faith
3Jn 1: 7 accepting no s from non-believers.
1: 8 Therefore we ought to s such people,
Tob 8: 6 for him you made his wife Eve as a helper and s.
AdE 15: 3 on one she leaned gently for s,
Sir 3:31 when they fall they will find s.
34:18 To whom does he look? And who is his s?
34:19 a mighty shield and strong s,
36:29 a helper fit for him and a pillar of s.
1Es 4:54 also concerning their s and the priests' vestments
4:55 that the s for the Levites should be provided until
8:52 and will s them in every way."
2Es 5:45 it might even now be able to s all of them present

SUPPORTED (13) [SUPPORT]
1Ki 1: 7 and with the priest Abiathar, and they s Adonijah.
2:28 Joab had s Adonijah though he had not s Absalom
Ezr 8:36 and they s the people and the house of God.
10:15 and Meshullam and Shabbethai the Levites s them.
Job 4: 4 Your words have s those who were stumbling,
24:23 He gives them security, and they are s;
Ps 18:35 and your right hand has s me;
89:43 and you have not s him in battle.
Eze 41: 6 that they should not be s by the wall of the temple.
Da 11: 6 and her child and the one who s her.
Sir 13:21 When the rich person totters, he is s by friends,
1Mc 2:17 and s by sons and brothers.

SUPPORTERS (2) [SUPPORT]
Job 31:21 because I saw I had s at the gate;
1Mc 11:39 Trypho had formerly been one of Alexander's s;

SUPPORTING (2) [SUPPORT]
1Ki 6: 6 the s beams should not be inserted into the walls
Est 9: 3 and the royal officials were s the Jews,

SUPPORTS‡ (9) [SUPPORT]
1Ki 7:30 at the four corners were s for a basin.
7:30 The s were cast with wreaths at the side of each.
7:34 There were four s at the four corners of each stand;
7:34 the s were of one piece with the stands.
10:12 the king made s for the house of the LORD,
Eze 41: 6 of the temple to serve as s for the side chambers,
Ro 11:18 but the root that s you.
Sir 25:22 and great disgrace when a wife s her husband.
1Mc 2:27 for the law and s the covenant come out with me!"

SUPPOSE (27) [SUPPOSED, SUPPOSING]
Ge 18:24 S there are fifty righteous within the city;
18:28 S five of the fifty righteous are lacking?
18:29 Again he spoke to him, "S forty are found there."
18:30 S thirty are found there."
18:31 S twenty are found there."
18:32 S ten are found there."
Ex 4: 1 "But s they do not believe me or listen to me,
Dt 19: 5 S someone goes into the forest with another
21:11 s you see among the captives
22:13 S a man marries a woman,
24: 1 S a man enters into marriage with a woman,
24: 3 Then s the second man dislikes her,
25: 1 S two persons have a dispute and enter
2Sa 13:32 "Let not my lord s that they have killed all
Mt 12:11 "S one of you has only one sheep and it falls into
Lk 7:43 "I s the one for whom he canceled
11: 5 And he said to them, "S one of you has a friend,
Jn 21:25 I s that the world itself could not contain the books
Ac 2:15 Indeed, these are not drunk, as you s,
13:25 he said, 'What do you s that I am?
Jas 4: 5 Or do you s that it is for nothing that
AdE 9:12 What do you s they have done in
2Mc 6:24 "for many of the young might s that Eleazar
4Mc 4:13 prayed for him so that King Seleucus would not s
5:18 Even if, as you s, our law were not truly divine
5:19 Therefore do not s that it would be a petty sin
9: 7 do not s that you can injure us by torturing us.

SUPPOSED (11) [SUPPOSE]
Lk 19:11 and because they s that the kingdom of God was
Ac 7:25 He s that his kinsfolk would understand that God
16:13 where we s there was a place of prayer;
16:27 since he s that the prisoners had escaped.
21:29 they s that Paul had brought him into the temple.
Gal 2: 6 And from those who were s to
Jdt 14:14 for he s that he was sleeping with Judith.
Wis 13: 2 but they s that either fire or wind or swift air,
17: 2 For when lawless people s that they held
Sus 1: 5 who were s to govern the people."
1Mc 6:43 and he s that the king was on it.

SUPPOSING (3) [SUPPOSE]
Jn 20:15 S him to be the gardener, she said to him, "Sir,
Ac 14:19 dragged him out of the city, s that he was dead.
3Mc 1:17 s that something mysterious was occurring.

SUPPRESS (1) [SUPPRESSED]
Ro 1:18 of those who by their wickedness s the truth.

SUPPRESSED (1) [SUPPRESS]
Sus 1: 9 They s their consciences

SUPREMACY (1) [SUPREME]

4Mc 13: 4 s of the mind over these cannot be overlooked,

SUPREME (10) [SUPREMACY]

1Pe 2:13 whether of the emperor as s,
2Mc 3:36 to all concerning the deeds of the s God,
3Mc 1: 9 to the s God and made thank offerings
1:16 the s God to aid in the present situation and
3:11 and not considering the might of the s God,
4:16 and uttering improper words against the s God.
5:25 and mournful dirges implored the s God
7:22 So the s God perfectly performed great deeds
4Mc 1:19 Rational judgment is s over all of these,
7:10 O s king over the passions, Eleazar!

SUR (2)

2Ki 11: 6 (another third being at the gate S and a third at
Jdt 2:28 in S and Ocina and all who lived in Jamnia.

SURE (48) [SURELY, SURETY]

Nu 32:23 and be s your sin will find you out.
Dt 12:23 Only be s that you do not eat the blood;
15: 4 because the LORD is s to bless you in the land
Jdg 15: 2 Her father said, "I was s that you had rejected her;
1Sa 2:35 I will build him a s house,
23:22 Go and make s once more;
23:23 and come back to me with s information.
25:28 the LORD will certainly make my lord a s house,
2Sa 7:16 and your kingdom shall be made s forever
2Ki 4: 9 to her husband, "Look, I am s
Ps 19: 7 the decrees of the LORD are s,
48: 3 its citadels God has shown himself a s defense.
93: 5 decrees are very s; holiness befits your house,
132:11 a s oath from which he will not turn back:
Pr 4:26 and all your ways will be s.
28:22 a hurry to get rich and does not know that loss is s
Isa 25: 1 plans formed of old, faithful and s.
28:16 a s foundation: "One who trusts will not panic."
55: 3 my steadfast, s love for David.
Hos 5: 9 among the tribes of Israel I declare what is s.
6: 3 his appearing is as s as the dawn;
Ac 12:11 "Now I am s that the Lord has sent his angel
Ro 2:19 and if you are s that you are a guide to the blind,
2Co 1:15 Since I was s of this, I wanted to come to you first,
Gal 2: 2 in order to make s that I was not running,
Eph 5: 5 Be s of this, that no fornicator or impure person,
1Ti 1:15 The saying is s and worthy of full acceptance,
3: 1 The saying is s: whoever aspires to the
4: 9 The saying is s and worthy of full acceptance.
2Ti 1: 5 and your mother Eunice and now, I am s, lives
1:12 and I am s that he is able to guard until
2:11 The saying is s: If we have died with him,
Tit 3: 8 The saying is s. I desire that you insist on these
Heb 6:19 a s and steadfast anchor of the soul,
13:18 we are s that we have a clear conscience,
1Jn 2: 3 Now by this we may be s that we know him,
2: 5 By this we may be s that we are in him:
2:29 be s that everyone who does right has been born
Tob 5:12 But Tobit said, "I want to be s, brother,
5:14 because I wanted to be s about your ancestry.
Wis 7:23 s, free from anxiety, all-powerful, overseeing all,
18: 6 that they might rejoice in s knowledge of the oaths
Sir 12:11 to be s it does not become completely tarnished.
42: 7 be s it is counted and weighed,
2Mc 9:27 For I am s that he will follow my policy
3Mc 3:25 the s and shameful death that befits enemies.
3:26 we are s that for the remaining time
2Es 8:22 whose word is s and whose utterances are certain,

SURELY‡ (235) [SURE]

Ge 9: 5 your own lifeblood I will s require a reckoning:
18:10 one said, "I will s return to you in due season,
20: 7 if you do not restore her, know that you shall s die,
28:16 "S the LORD is in this place—
28:22 and of all that you give me I will s give one tenth
29:14 "S you are my bone and my flesh!"
29:32 s now my husband will love me."
31:42 had not been on my side, s now you would have
32:12 Yet you have said, 'I will s do you good,
42:16 or else, as Pharaoh lives, s you are spies."
44:28 and I said, S he has been torn to pieces;
50:24 but God will s come to you,
Ex 2:14 Then Moses was afraid and thought, "S
13:19 saying, "God will s take notice of you,
18:18 You will s wear yourself out,
22:23 when they cry out to me, I will s heed their cry;
23:33 you worship their gods, it will s be a snare to you.
Nu 11:18 S it was better for us in Egypt.'
14:35 s I will do thus to all this wicked congregation
22:17 for I will s do you great honor,
22:33 s just now I would have killed you and let it live."
23:23 S there is no enchantment against Jacob,
32:11 'S none of the people who came up out of Egypt,
Dt 2: 7 S the LORD your God has blessed you
4: 6 "S this great nation is a wise
8:19 I solemnly warn you today that you shall s perish.
13: 9 But you shall s kill them;
16:15 in all your undertakings, and you shall s celebrate.
23:21 for the LORD your God will s require it of you,
30:11 S, this commandment that I am commanding you
31:18 On that day I will s hide my face on account of all
31:29 I know that after my death you will s act corruptly,
Jos 14: 9 'S the land on which your foot has trodden shall
Jdg 4: 9 And she said, "I will s go with you;
11:10 we will s do as you say."
13:22 And Manoah said to his wife, "We shall s die,
20:39 so they thought, "S they are defeated before us,
1Sa 14:39 even if it is in my son Jonathan, he shall s die!"
14:44 you shall s die, Jonathan!"
15:22 S, to obey is better than sacrifice,
15:32 Agag said, "S this is the bitterness of death."
16: 6 "S the LORD's anointed is now before
17:25 S he has come up to defy Israel.
20:26 he is not clean, s he is not clean."
20:31 Now send and bring him to me, for he shall s die."
22:16 The king said, "You shall s die, Ahimelech,
22:22 that he would s tell Saul.
24:20 Now I know that you shall s be king,
25:21 "S it was in vain that I protected all
25:34 For as s as the LORD the God of Israel lives,
28: 9 "S you know what Saul has done,
30: 8 for you shall s overtake and shall s rescue."
2Sa 14:19 The woman answered and said, "As s as you live,
1Ki 1:42 you are a worthy man and s you bring good news."
11: 2 they will s incline your heart to follow their gods";
11:11 I will s tear the kingdom from you and give it
13:32 in the cities of Samaria, shall s come to pass."
18:14 that Elijah is here'; he will s kill me."
18:15 I will s show myself to him today."
18:27 "Cry aloud! S he is a god;
20:23 and s we shall be stronger than they.
20:25 and s we shall be stronger than they."
22:32 they said, "It is s the king of Israel."
2Ki 1: 4 bed to which you have gone, but you shall s die.' "
1: 6 the bed to which you have gone, but shall s die.' "
1:16 bed to which you have gone, but you shall s die."
5:11 "I thought that for me he would s come out,
18:30 The LORD will s deliver us,
24: 3 S this came upon Judah at the command of the
Est 6:13 but will s fall before him."
Job 5: 2 S vexation kills the fool, and jealousy slays
8: 6 s then he will rouse himself for you and restore
11:15 S then you will lift up your face without blemish;
13:10 He will s rebuke you if in secret you show
16: 7 S now God has worn me out;
17: 2 S there are mockers around me,
18: 5 "S the light of the wicked is put out,
18:21 S such are the dwellings of the ungodly,
22:20 'S our adversaries are cut off, and what they left,
28: 1 "S there is a mine for silver,
30:24 "S one does not turn against the needy,
31:36 S I would carry it on my shoulder;
33: 8 "S, you have spoken in my hearing,
35:13 S God does not hear an empty cry,
36: 5 "S God is mighty and does not despise any;
36:26 S God is great, and we do not know him;
38: 5 Who determined its measurements—s you know!
38:21 S you know, for you were born then,
Ps 23: 6 S goodness and mercy shall follow me all the days
39: 5 S everyone stands as a mere breath.
39: 6 S everyone goes about like a shadow.
39: 6 S for nothing they are in turmoil;
39:11 s everyone is a mere breath.
54: 4 But s, God is my helper;
58:11 "S there is a reward for the righteous;
58:11 s there is a God who judges on earth."
85: 9 S his salvation is at hand for those who fear him,
139:11 If I say, "S the darkness shall cover me,
140:13 S the righteous shall give thanks to your name;
Pr 21: 5 The plans of the diligent lead s to abundance,
23:18 S there is a future, and your hope will not
30: 2 S I am too stupid to be human;
30: 4 name of the person's child? S you know!
Ecc 4:16 S this also is vanity and a chasing after wind.
7: 7 S oppression makes the wise foolish,
7:20 S there is no one on earth so righteous as
Isa 5: 9 S many houses shall be desolate,
8:20 S, those who speak like this will have no dawn!
12: 2 S God is my salvation; I will trust,
22:14 S this iniquity will not be forgiven you
30:19 He will s be gracious to you at the sound
36:15 The LORD will s deliver us;
38:17 S it was for my welfare that I had great bitterness,
40: 7 upon it; s the people are grass.
49: 4 yet s my cause is with the LORD,
49:19 S your waste and your desolate places
49:19 s now you will be too crowded
53: 4 S he has borne our infirmities
56: 3 "The LORD will s separate me from his people";
63: 8 For he said, "S they are my people,
Jer 2:35 s his anger has turned from me."
5: 5 s they know the way of the LORD,
7:32 Therefore, the days are s coming, says the LORD,
9:25 The days are s coming, says the LORD,
15:11 S I have intervened in your life for good, s I have
16:14 Therefore, the days are s coming, says the LORD,
16:21 "Therefore I am s going to teach them,
19: 6 Therefore the days are s coming, says the LORD,
23: 5 The days are s coming, says the LORD,
23: 7 Therefore, the days are s coming, says the LORD,
23:39 I will s lift you up and cast you away
29:11 For s I know the plans I have for you,
30: 3 For the days are s coming, says the LORD,
31:20 I will s have mercy on him, says the LORD.
31:27 The days are s coming, says the LORD,
31:31 The days are s coming, says the LORD,
31:38 The days are s coming, says the LORD,
32: 4 but shall s be given into the hands of the king
33:14 The days are s coming, says the LORD,
34: 3 but shall s be captured and handed over to him;
37: 9 saying, "The Chaldeans will s go away from us,"
38: 3 This city shall s be handed over to the army of
39:18 For I will s save you, and you shall not fall by
44:29 that my words against you will s be carried out:
48: 7 S, because you trusted in your strongholds
48: 9 Set aside salt for Moab, for she will s fall;
48:12 Therefore, the time is s coming, says the LORD,
49: 2 Therefore, the time is s coming, says the LORD,
49:20 S the little ones of the flock shall
49:20 s their fold shall be appalled at their fate.
50:34 He will s plead their cause,
50:45 S the little ones of the flock shall
50:45 s their fold shall be appalled at their fate.
51:14 S I will fill you with troops like a swarm
51:52 Therefore the time is s coming, says the LORD,
Eze 3: 6 S, if I sent you to them, they would listen to you.
3:18 If I say to the wicked, "You shall s die,"
3:21 they shall s live, because they took warning;
5:10 S, parents shall eat their children in your midst,
5:11 Therefore, as I live, says the Lord GOD, s,
17:16 As I live, says the Lord GOD, s in the place
17:19 As I live, I will s return upon his head my oath
18: 9 he shall s live, says the Lord GOD.
18:13 he shall s die; his blood shall be upon himself.
18:17 for his father's iniquity; he shall s live.
18:19 to observe all my statutes, he shall s live.
18:21 they shall s live; they shall not die.
18:28 they shall s live; they shall not die.
20:33 s with a mighty hand and an outstretched arm,
33: 8 "O wicked ones, you shall s die,"
33:13 Though I say to the righteous that they shall s live,
33:14 though I say to the wicked, "You shall s die,"
33:15 they shall s live, they shall not die.
33:16 and right, they shall s live.
33:24 the land is s given us to possess."
33:27 s those who are in the waste places shall fall by
Hos 12:11 they shall s come to nothing.
Joel 1:12 s, joy withers away among the people.
2:20 S he has done great things!
Am 3: 7 S the Lord GOD does nothing,
4: 2 The time is s coming upon you,
5: 5 for Gilgal shall s go into exile,
7:17 Israel shall s go into exile away from its land.' "
8: 7 S I will never forget any of their deeds.
8:11 The time is s coming, says the Lord GOD,
9:13 The time is s coming, says the LORD,
Ob 1: 2 I will s make you least among the nations;
Mic 2:12 I will s gather all of you, O Jacob,
3:11 "S the LORD is with us!
Hab 2: 3 it will s come, it will not delay.
Zep 3: 7 I said, "S the city will fear me,
Mt 15: 4 'Whoever speaks evil of father or mother must s
26:22 began to say to him one after another, "S, not I,
26:25 Judas, who betrayed him, said, "S not I, Rabbi?"
Mk 7:10 'Whoever speaks evil of father or mother must s
14:19 and to say to him one after another, "S, not I?"
Lk 1:48 S, from now on all generations will call me blessed
6:23 for s your reward is great in heaven;
22:59 "S this man also was with him;
23:29 For the days are s coming when they will say,
Jn 4:33 "S no one has brought him something to eat?"
7:41 "S the Messiah does not come from Galilee,
7:47 "S you have not been deceived too, have you?
7:52 They replied, "S you are not also from Galilee,
9:40 "S we are not blind, are we?"
11:56 S he will not come to the festival, will he?"
Ac 7:34 I have s seen the mistreatment
Ro 5: 9 Much more s then, now that we have been justified
5:10 much more s, having been reconciled,
5:15 much more s have the grace of God and
5:17 much more s will those who receive
2Co 1:18 As s as God is faithful,
3: 1 S we do not need, as some do,
Eph 3: 2 for s you have already heard of the commission
4:21 For s you have heard about him and were taught
Heb 6:14 saying, "I will s bless you and multiply you."
8: 8 "The days are s coming, says the Lord,
Rev 22:20 The one who testifies to these things says, "S I am
Tob 2:13 It is s not stolen, is it?
Jdt 12: 4 Judith replied, "As s as you live, my lord,
AdE 6:13 to be humiliated before him, you will s fall.
Sir 5: 3 for the Lord will s punish you.
48:11 For we also shall s live.
Bar 2:29 this very great multitude will s turn into
1Mc 5:40 for he will s defeat us.
3Mc 7: 6 to realize that the God of heaven s defends
2Es 1:13 S it was I who brought you through the sea,
6:32 your voice has s been heard by the Most High;
8:45 S not, O Lord above!
11:45 Therefore you, eagle, will s disappear,
15: 9 I will s avenge them, says the Lord,
16:62 the spirit of Almighty God, who s made all things
4Mc 12:14 S they by dying nobly fulfilled their service

SURETY (14) [SURE]

Ge 43: 9 I myself will be s for him;
44:32 your servant became s for the boy to my father,
Job 17: 3 who is there that will give s for me?
Pr 17:18 to become s for a neighbor.
20:16 the garment of one who has given s for a stranger;
seize the pledge given as s for foreigners.
22:26 be one of those who give pledges, who become s
27:13 the garment of one who has given s for a stranger;
seize the pledge given as s for foreigners.
Sir 8:13 Do not give s beyond your means; but if you give
s, be prepared to pay.
29:14 A good person will be s for his neighbor,

Sir 29:18 Being s has ruined many who were prosperous,
29:19 The sinner comes to grief through s;

SURETY (KJV) See also CERTAIN, GUARANTEE, INDEED, PLEDGE, SURE

SURFACE (13) [SURFACES]

Ex 10: 5 They shall cover the s of the land,
10:15 They covered the s of the whole land,
16:14 the s of the wilderness was a fine flaky substance,
Lev 14:37 and if it appears to be deeper than the s,
Isa 24: 1 and he will twist its s and scatter its inhabitants.
28:25 When they have leveled its s,
Jer 8: 2 they shall be like dung on the s of the ground.
16: 4 they shall become like dung on the s of the ground.
25:33 they shall become dung on the s of the ground.
Am 5: 8 and pours them out on the s of the earth,
9: 6 and pours them out upon the s of the earth—
Wis 13:14 and coloring its s red and covering every blemish
Sir 16:30 With all kinds of living beings he covered its s,

SURFACES (1) [SURFACE]

1Ki 7:36 On the s of its stays and on its borders he carved

SURFEIT (1)

Ecc 5:12 but the s of the rich will not let them sleep.

SURFEITING (KJV) See DISSIPATION

SURGE (2) [SURGING]

Jer 46: 7 rising like the Nile, like rivers whose waters s?
46: 8 like rivers whose waters s,

SURGING (1) [SURGE]

1Sa 14:16 as the multitude was s back and forth.

SURLINESS (1) [SURLY]

Sir 41:19 of s in receiving or giving,

SURLY (1) [SURLINESS]

1Sa 25: 3 but the man was s and mean; he was a Calebite.

SURMISINGS (KJV) See SUSPICIONS

SURNAME (1) [NAME]

Isa 45: 4 I s you, though you do not know me.

SURNAME (KJV) See also CALLED, NAME

SURNAMED (1) [NAME]

1Mc 2: 2 He had five sons, John s Gaddi,

SURPASS (6) [SURPASSED, SURPASSES, SURPASSING]

1Ki 10: 7 and prosperity far s the report that I had heard.
2Ch 9: 6 you far s the report that I had heard.
Pr 31:29 women have done excellently, but you s them all."
Eze 15: 2 how does the wood of the vine s all other wood—
32:19 "Whom do you s in beauty?
Sir 18:17 Indeed, does not a word s a good gift?

SURPASSED (2) [SURPASS]

1Ki 4:30 so that Solomon's wisdom s the wisdom of all
Ecc 2: 9 So I became great and s all who were before me

SURPASSES (4) [SURPASS]

Eph 3:19 and to know the love of Christ that s knowledge,
Php 4: 7 And the peace of God, which s all understanding,
Sir 25:11 Fear of the Lord s everything;
43:30 exalt him as much as you can, for he s even that.

SURPASSING (6) [SURPASS]

Ps 150: 2 praise him according to his s greatness!
Ecc 1:16 s all who were over Jerusalem before me;
2Co 9:14 for you and pray for you because of the s grace
Php 3: 8 I regard everything as loss because of the s value
2Mc 4:13 of foreign ways because of the s wickedness
3Mc 6:24 "You are committing treason and s tyrants

SURPLUS (1)

Tob 4:16 Give all your s as alms,

SURPRISE (2) [SURPRISED]

1Th 5: 4 for that day to s you like a thief;
1Mc 12:33 He turned aside to Joppa and took it by s,

SURPRISED (3) [SURPRISE]

1Pe 4: 4 They are s that you no longer join them in
4:12 do not be s at the fiery ordeal that is taking place
Sir 26:11 and do not be s if she sins against you.

SURRENDER‡ (15) [SURRENDERED, SURRENDERS]

1Sa 23:12 the men of Keilah s me and my men into the hand
23:12 The LORD said, "They will s you."
23:20 and our part will be to s him into the king's hand."
Jer 21: 9 but those who go out and s to
38:17 If you will only s to the officials of the king
38:18 But if you do not s to the officials of the king
38:21 But if you are determined not to s,
Jdt 7:13 thirst will destroy them, and they will s their town.
7:26 Now summon them and s the whole town as booty
8: 9 how he promised them under oath to s the town to
8:11 to s the town to our enemies unless the Lord turns
8:33 within the days after which you have promised to s
AdE 14:11 do not s your scepter to what has no being;
Wis 17:15 and now were paralyzed by their souls' s;
1Mc 8: 7 a heavy tribute and give hostages and s some

SURRENDERED‡ (2) [SURRENDER]

Jer 50:15 a shout against her from all sides, "She has s;
3Mc 6: 6 in Babylon who had voluntarily s their lives to

SURRENDERS (1) [SURRENDER]

Dt 20:11 If it accepts your terms of peace and s to you,

SURROUND (21) [SURROUNDED, SURROUNDING, SURROUNDS]

Jos 7: 9 and s us, and cut off our name from the earth.
2Ki 11: 8 shall s the king, each with weapons in hand;
2Ch 14: 7 and s them with walls and towers, gates and bars;
23: 7 The Levites shall s the king,
Job 16:13 his archers s me. He slashes open my kidneys,
40:22 the willows of the wadi s it.
Ps 17: 9 my deadly enemies who s me.
17:11 They track me down; now they s me;
22:12 strong bulls of Bashan s me;
32: 7 you s me with glad cries of deliverance.
88:17 They s me like a flood all day long;
125: 2 As the mountains s Jerusalem,
140: 9 Those who s me lift up their heads;
142: 7 The righteous will s me, for you will deal
Eze 2: 6 and thorns s you and you live among scorpions;
Hos 7: 2 Now their deeds s them, they are before my face.
Am 3:11 An adversary shall s the land,
Hab 1: 4 The wicked s the righteous—
Lk 8:45 "Master, the crowds s you and press in on you."
19:43 up ramparts around you and s you,
2Es 15:44 They shall come to it and s it;

SURROUNDED‡ (36) [SURROUND]

Ge 19: 4 all the people to the last man, s the house;
Jos 8:22 so they were s by Israelites, some on one side,
Jdg 19:22 the men of the city, a perverse lot, s the house,
20: 5 and s the house at night.
2Sa 18:15 Joab's armor-bearers, s Absalom and struck him,
1Ki 5: 3 of the warfare with which his enemies s him,
2Ki 3:25 until the slingers s and attacked it.
6:14 they came by night, and s the city.
8:21 and their chariot commanders who had s him;
2Ch 21: 9 who had s him and his chariot commanders.
Ps 118:10 All nations s me; in the name of the
118:11 They s me, s me on every side;
118:12 They s me like bees; they blazed like a
Hos 11:12 Ephraim has s me with lies,
Jnh 2: 3 into the heart of the seas, and the flood s me;
2: 5 The waters closed in over me; the deep s me;
Mic 5: 7 Then the remnant of Jacob, s by many peoples,
5: 8 the remnant of Jacob, s by many peoples, shall be
Lk 21:20 "When you see Jerusalem s by armies,
Ac 14:20 disciples s him, he got up and went into the city.
25: 7 Jews who had gone down from Jerusalem s him,
Heb 12: 1 since we are s by so great a cloud of witnesses,
Rev 20: 9 up over the breadth of the earth and s the camp of
Jdt 2:26 He s all the Midianites, and burned their tents
7:19 because all their enemies had s them,
7:20 chariots, and cavalry, s them for thirty-four days,
Wis 19:17 when, s by yawning darkness,
Sir 50: 5 How glorious he was, s by the people,
50:12 like a young cedar on Lebanon s by the trunks
51: 7 They s me on every side, and there was no one
1Mc 6: 7 they had s the sanctuary with high walls as before,
10:80 for they s his army and shot arrows at his men
13:43 against Gazara and s it with troops.
15:14 He s the town, and the ships joined battle from
2Mc 14:41 Being s, Razis fell upon his own sword,

SURROUNDING‡ (31) [SURROUND]

Nu 32:33 with the territories of the s towns.
35: 2 also give to the Levites pasture lands s the towns.
Jos 15:12 the boundary s the people of Judah according
1Ki 4:31 his fame spread throughout all the s nations.
7:24 each of ten cubits, s the sea;
1Ch 6:55 in the land of Judah and its s pasture lands,
28:12 of the LORD, all the s chambers, the treasuries of
2Ch 4: 3 each of ten cubits, s the sea;
Ne 3:22 After him the priests, the men of the s area,
Jer 1:15 of the gates of Jerusalem, against all its s walls and
Eze 43:17 a rim around it half a cubit wide, and its s base,
Zec 12: 2 a cup of reeling for all the s peoples;
12: 6 to the right and to the left all the s peoples,
14:14 the wealth of all the s nations shall be collected—
Mk 1:28 to spread throughout the s region of Galilee.
6:36 so that they may go into the s country and villages
Lk 4:14 report about him spread through all the s country.
7:17 throughout Judea and all the s country.
8:37 of the s country of the Gerasenes asked Jesus
9:12 they may go into the s villages and countryside,
Ac 14: 6 cities of Lycaonia, and to the s country;
Jude 1: 7 Likewise, Sodom and Gomorrah and the s cities,
Rev 5:11 and I heard the voice of many angels s the throne
AdE 9:12 you suppose they have done in the s countryside?
Bar 2: 4 of scorn and a desolation among all the s peoples,
1Mc 1:31 and tore down its houses and its s walls.
1:54 They also built altars in the s towns of Judah,
7:24 So Judas went out into all the s parts of Judea,
7:46 People came out of all the s villages of Judea,
10:84 But Jonathan burned Azotus and the s towns
4Mc 16: 3 The lions s Daniel were not so savage,

SURROUNDS (7) [SURROUND]

Dt 33:12 the High God s him all day long—
Ps 32:10 but steadfast love s those who trust in the LORD.
49: 5 when the iniquity of my persecutors s me,
89: 8 mighty as you, O LORD? Your faithfulness s you.
125: 2 so the LORD s his people,
Eze 21:14 A sword for great slaughter—it s them;
Sir 23:18 Darkness s me, the walls hide me,

SURVEYS (1)

Job 41:34 It s everything that is lofty;

SURVIVAL (1) [SURVIVE]

Sir 16: 3 Do not trust in their s, or rely on their numbers;

SURVIVE‡ (20) [SURVIVAL, SURVIVED, SURVIVES, SURVIVING, SURVIVOR, SURVIVORS]

Lev 26:36 And as for those of you who s,
26:39 And those of you who s shall languish in the land
2Sa 17:12 and he will not s, nor will any of those with him.
Job 27:15 Those who s them the pestilence buries,
Isa 16:14 and those who s will be very few and feeble.
Jer 21: 7 those who s the pestilence, sword, and famine—
44:14 in the land of Egypt shall escape or s or return to
Eze 5:10 and any of you who s I will scatter to every wind.
Hab 2: 8 all that s of the peoples shall plunder you—
Zec 14:16 Then all who s of the nations that have come
Ac 27:34 for it will help you s;
Tob 13:16 of my descendants should s to see your glory
Jdt 6: 4 Not even their footprints will s our attack;
Sir 23:27 Those who s her will recognize
2Es 9: 8 will s the dangers that have been predicted,
13:22 As for what you said about those who s,
13:22 and concerning those who do not s,
15:45 who s shall serve those who have destroyed it.
16:22 and those who s the famine shall die by the sword.
4Mc 6:20 be shameful if we should s for a little while and

SURVIVED (6) [SURVIVE]

Jos 8:22 down until no one was left who s or escaped.
Jdg 9: 5 but Jotham, the youngest son of Jerubbaal, s,
1Sa 11:11 and those who s were scattered,
Ne 1: 2 and I asked them about the Jews that s,
Jer 31: 2 The people who s the sword found grace in
La 2:22 of the anger of the LORD no one escaped or s;

SURVIVES (4) [SURVIVE]

Ex 21:21 if the slave s a day or two, there is no punishment;
1Co 3:14 If what has been built on the foundation s,
2Mc 3:38 will get him back thoroughly flogged, if he s at all;
2Es 9:37 however, does not perish but s in its glory."

SURVIVING (3) [SURVIVE]

2Ki 19:30 The s remnant of the house of Judah shall again
Isa 37:31 The s remnant of the house of Judah shall again
4Mc 12: 6 and to influence her to persuade the s son to obey

SURVIVOR (8) [SURVIVE]

Nu 21:35 and all his people, until there was no s left;
Dt 2:34 We left not a single s.
3: 3 We struck him down until not a single s was left.
2Ki 10:11 close friends, and priests, until he left him no s.
Ezr 9:14 until you destroy us without remnant or s?
Job 18:19 and no s where they used to live.
Jer 42:17 they shall have no remnant or s from the disaster
Ob 1:18 and there shall be no s of the house of Esau;

SURVIVORS (32) [SURVIVE]

Ge 45: 7 and to keep alive for you many s.
Nu 24:19 and destroy the s of Ir."
Dt 7:20 until even the s and the fugitives are destroyed.
Jos 10:20 when the s had entered into the fortified towns,
10:33 and his people, leaving him no s.
13:12 in Edrei (he alone was left of the s of the Rephaim)
23:12 and join the s of these nations left here among you,
Jdg 21:17 "There must be heirs for the s of Benjamin,
2Ki 19:31 and from Mount Zion a band of s.
Ezr 1: 4 and let all s, in whatever place they reside,
Ne 1: 3 They replied, "The s there in the province
Isa 1: 9 If the LORD of hosts had not left us a few s,
4: 2 of the land shall be the pride and glory of the s
10:20 and the s of the house of Jacob will no more lean
37:32 and from Mount Zion a band of s.
45:20 draw near, you s of the nations!
49: 6 up the tribes of Jacob and to restore the s of Israel;
66:19 From them I will send s to the nations, to Tarshish,
Jer 51:50 You s of the sword, go, do not linger!
Eze 7:16 If any s escape, they shall be found on
14:22 Yet, s shall be left in it,
17:21 and the s shall be scattered to every wind;
23:25 and your s shall fall by the sword.

Eze 23:25 and your s shall be devoured by fire.
Joel 2:32 among the s shall be those whom the LORD calls.
Ob 1:14 you should not have handed over his s on the day
Mic 2:12 O Jacob, I will gather the s of Israel;
Zep 2: 9 and the s of my nation shall possess them.
Ro 9:29 "If the Lord of hosts had not left s to us,
Sir 36:11 Let s be consumed in the fiery wrath,
1Mc 2:44 the s fled to the Gentiles for safety.
1Es 1:56 The s he led away to Babylon with the sword,

SUSA (40)
Ezr 4: 9 the Babylonians, the people of **S**, that is,
Ne 1: 1 in the twentieth year, while I was in **S** the capital,
Est 1: 2 on his royal throne in the citadel of **S**,
1: 5 for all the people present in the citadel of **S**,
2: 3 to the harem in the citadel of **S** under custody
2: 5 in the citadel of **S** whose name was Mordecai son
2: 8 in the citadel of **S** in custody of Hegai,
3:15 and the decree was issued in the citadel of **S**.
3:15 but the city of **S** was thrown into confusion.
4: 8 the written decree issued in **S** for their destruction,
4:16 gather all the Jews to be found in **S**,
8:14 The decree was issued in the citadel of **S**.
8:15 while the city of **S** shouted and rejoiced.
9: 6 In the citadel of **S** the Jews killed
9:11 of those killed in the citadel of **S** was reported to
9:12 of **S** the Jews have killed five hundred people and
9:13 the Jews who are in **S** be allowed tomorrow also
9:14 a decree was issued in **S**,
9:15 in **S** gathered also on the fourteenth day of
9:15 and they killed three hundred persons in **S**;
9:18 in **S** gathered on the thirteenth day and on
Da 8: 2 In the vision I was looking and saw myself in **S**
AdE 1: 2 King Artaxerxes was enthroned in the city of **S**,
2: 3 to be brought to the harem in **S**,
2: 5 in **S** the capital whose name was Mordecai son
2: 8 and many girls were gathered in **S** the capital
3:15 The matter was expedited also in **S**.
3:15 the city of **S** was thrown into confusion.
4: 8 also gave him a copy of what had been posted in **S**
4:16 "Go and gather all the Jews who are in **S** and fast
8:14 and the decree was published also in **S**.
8:15 The people in **S** rejoiced on seeing him.
9: 6 the city of **S** the Jews killed five hundred people,
9:11 the number of those killed in **S** was reported to
9:12 The king said to Esther, "In **S**, the capital,
9:15 The Jews who were in **S** gathered on
9:18 The Jews who were in **S**, the capital,
9:19 the country outside **S** keep the fourteenth of Adar
11: 3 He was a Jew living in the city of **S**, a great man,
16:18 at the gate of **S** with all his household—

SUSANCHITES (KJV) See SUSA

SUSANNA (11)
Lk 8: 3 the wife of Herod's steward Chuza, and **S**,
Sus 1: 2 He married the daughter of Hilkiah, named **S**,
1: 7 **S** would go into her husband's garden to walk.
1:22 **S** groaned and said, "I am completely trapped.
1:24 Then **S** cried out with a loud voice,
1:27 for nothing like this had ever been said about **S**.
1:28 full of their wicked plot to have **S** put to death.
1:29 "Send for **S** daughter of Hilkiah,
1:31 Now **S** was a woman of great refinement
1:42 Then **S** cried out with a loud voice, and said,
1:63 and his wife praised God for their daughter **S**,

SUSI (1)
Nu 13:11 from the tribe of Manasseh), Gaddi son of **S**;

SUSPECT (1) [SUSPECTED, SUSPECTS]
3Mc 3:23 they secretly **s** that we may soon alter our policy.

SUSPECTED (2) [SUSPECT]
Ac 27:27 the sailors **s** that they were nearing land.
2Mc 12: 4 they wished to live peaceably and **s** nothing,

SUSPECTS (1) [SUSPECT]
Sir 23:21 and where he least **s** it, he will be seized.

SUSPENDED (2)
Job 28: 4 they are forgotten by travelers, they sway **s**,
2Es 16:58 and by his word he has **s** the earth over the water.

SUSPENSE (3)
Jn 10:24 "How long will you keep us in **s**?
Ac 27:33 the fourteenth day that you have been in **s**
3Mc 5:49 the end of their most miserable **s**,

SUSPICION (1) [SUSPICIONS, SUSPICIOUS]
Sir 37:10 Do not consult the one who regards you with **s**;

SUSPICIONS (1) [SUSPICION]
1Ti 6: 4 From these come envy, dissension, slander, base **s**,

SUSPICIOUS (3) [SUSPICION]
Sir 4:30 be like a lion in your home, or **s** of your servants.
2Mc 4:34 he persuaded him, though still **s**,
7:24 and he was **s** of her reproachful tone.

SUSTAIN (6) [SUSTAINED, SUSTAINS, SUSTENANCE]
Ps 51:12 and **s** in me a willing spirit.
55:22 on the LORD, and he will **s** you;
SS 2: 5 **S** me with raisins, refresh me with apples;
Isa 50: 4 that I may know how to **s** the weary with a word.
63: 5 I stared, but there was no one to **s** me;
2Es 5:45 at one time and the creation will **s** them,

SUSTAINED (6) [SUSTAIN]
Ge 27:37 and with grain and wine I have **s** him.
Dt 19:15 of two or three witnesses shall a charge be **s**.
32:10 He **s** him in a desert land,
Ne 9:21 Forty years you **s** them in the wilderness so
Isa 63: 5 own arm brought me victory, and my wrath **s** me.
2Co 13: 1 be **s** by the evidence of two or three witnesses."

SUSTAINS (4) [SUSTAIN]
Ps 3: 5 I wake again, for the LORD **s** me.
41: 3 The LORD **s** them on their sickbed;
Heb 1: 3 and he **s** all things by his powerful word.
Wis 16:26 but that your word **s** those who trust in you.

SUSTENANCE (4) [SUSTAIN]
Jdg 6: 4 and leave no **s** in Israel,
Ezr 9: 8 that he may brighten our eyes and grant us a little **s**
Pr 6: 8 and gathers its **s** in harvest.
Wis 16:21 For your **s** manifested your sweetness

SUSTENANCE (KJV) See also FOOD

SWADDLED, SWADDLING, SWADDLINGBAND (KJV) See also BANDS OF CLOTH, BORE, IN CLOTHS

SWADDLING (2)
Job 38: 9 and thick darkness its **s** band,
Wis 7: 4 I was nursed with care in **s** cloths.

SWALLOW (19) [SWALLOWED, SWALLOWS]
Nu 16:34 for they said, "The earth will **s** us too!"
2Sa 20:19 why will you **s** up the heritage of the LORD?"
20:20 far be it, that I should **s** up or destroy!
Job 7:19 let me alone until I **s** my spittle?
20:15 They **s** down riches and vomit them up again;
20:18 and will not **s** it down;
Ps 21: 9 The LORD will **s** them up in his wrath,
69:15 or the deep **s** me up,
84: 3 sparrow finds a home, and the **s** a nest for herself,
Pr 1:12 like Sheol let us **s** them alive and whole,
26: 2 Like a sparrow in its flitting, like a **s** in its flying,
Isa 25: 7 he will **s** up death forever.
38:14 Like a **s** or a crane I clamor, I moan like a dove.
Jer 8: 7 **s**, and crane observe the time of their coming;
Jnh 1:17 the LORD provided a large fish to **s** up Jonah;
Hab 1:13 the wicked **s** those more righteous than they?
Mt 23:24 You strain out a gnat but **s** a camel!
Tob 6: 3 from the water and tried to **s** the young man's foot,
Jdt 5:24 and your vast army will **s** them up."

SWALLOWED (20) [SWALLOW]
Ge 41: 7 The thin ears **s** up the seven plump and full ears.
41:24 and the thin ears **s** up the seven good ears.
Ex 7:12 but Aaron's staff **s** up theirs.
15:12 You stretched out your right hand, the earth **s** them.
Nu 16:32 The earth opened its mouth and **s** them up,
21:28 and **s** up the heights of the Arnon.
26:10 the earth opened its mouth and **s** them up along
Dt 11: 6 of all Israel the earth opened its mouth and **s** them
2Sa 17:16 the people who are with him will be **s** up.'"
Job 37:20 Did anyone ever wish to be **s** up?
Ps 35:25 Do not let them say, "We have **s** you up."
106:17 The earth opened and **s** up Dathan,
124: 3 then they would have **s** us up alive,
Isa 49:19 and those who **s** you up will be far away.
Jer 51:34 he has **s** me like a monster;
51:44 and make him disgorge what he has **s**.
Hos 8: 8 Israel is **s** up; now they are among the
1Co 15:54 "Death has been **s** up in victory."
2Co 5: 4 so that what is mortal may be **s** up by life.
Rev 12:16 and **s** the river that the dragon had poured

SWALLOWS (3) [SWALLOW]
Nu 16:30 and the ground opens its mouth and **s** them up,
Job 39:24 With fierceness and rage it **s** the ground;
LtJ 6:22 Bats, **s**, and birds alight on their bodies and heads;

SWAM (1) [SWIM]
1Mc 9:48 and the men with him leaped into the Jordan and **s**

SWAMP (1) [SWAMPED, SWAMPS]
Isa 35: 7 the haunt of jackals shall become a **s**,

SWAMPED (2) [SWAMP]
Mt 8:24 so great that the boat was being **s** by the waves;
Mk 4:37 so that the boat was already being **s**.

SWAMPS (1) [SWAMP]
Eze 47:11 But its **s** and marshes will not become fresh;

SWAN (KJV) See DESERT OWL, WHITE OWL

SWANS (1)
4Mc 15:21 the songs of **s** attract the attention of their hearers

SWARE (KJV) See EXCHANGED AN OATH, HAS SWORN, MADE AN OATH, PLEDGED, PROMISED, PROMISED AN OATH, SAID, SWEAR, SWORE, SWORN, TOOK AN OATH, VOWED

SWARM (11) [SWARMED, SWARMING, SWARMS]
Ge 1:21 of every kind, with which the waters **s**,
7:21 all swarming creatures that **s** on the earth,
Ex 8: 3 The river shall **s** with frogs;
10:14 such a dense **s** of locusts as had never been before,
Lev 11:29 for you among the creatures that **s** upon the earth:
11:31 These are unclean for you among all that **s**;
11:41 All creatures that **s** upon the earth are detestable;
11:42 all the creatures that **s** upon the earth,
Jdg 14: 8 and there was a **s** of bees in the body of the lion,
Jer 51:14 Surely I will fill you with troops like a **s** of locusts,
Jdt 2:20 with them went a mixed crowd like a **s** of locusts,

SWARMED (2) [SWARM]
Ps 105:30 Their land **s** with frogs, even in the chambers
2Mc 9: 9 And so the ungodly man's body **s** with worms,

SWARMING (8) [SWARM]
Ge 7:21 all **s** creatures that swarm on the earth,
Lev 5: 2 or the carcass of an unclean **s** thing—
11:10 of the **s** creatures in the waters and among all
11:44 You shall not defile yourselves with any **s** creature
22: 5 and whoever touches any **s** thing by which he may
Joel 1: 4 What the cutting locust left, the **s** locust has eaten.
1: 4 What the **s** locust left, the hopping locust has eaten,
2:25 for the years that the **s** locust has eaten,

SWARMS (13) [SWARM]
Ge 1:20 "Let the waters bring forth **s** of living creatures,
Ex 8:21 I will send **s** of flies on you, your officials,
8:21 the houses of the Egyptians shall be filled with **s**
8:22 so that no **s** of flies shall be there,
8:24 and great **s** of flies came into the house of Pharaoh
8:29 the LORD that the **s** of flies may depart tomorrow
8:31 he removed the **s** of flies from Pharaoh,
Lev 11:43 yourselves detestable with any creature that **s**;
11:46 the waters and every creature that **s** upon the earth,
Ps 78:45 He sent among them **s** of flies,
105:31 He spoke, and there came **s** of flies,
Eze 47: 9 every living creature that **s** will live,
Na 3:17 your scribes like **s** of locusts settling on the fences

SWAY (8) [SWAYED, SWAYS]
Jdg 9: 9 and go to **s** over the trees?'
9:11 and go to **s** over the trees?'
9:13 and go to **s** over the trees?'
Job 28: 4 they are forgotten by travelers, they **s** suspended,
Sir 24: 6 and over every people and nation I have held **s**.
2Es 11:40 you have held **s** over the world with great terror,
12:15 But the second that is to reign shall hold **s** for
4Mc 14:20 But sympathy for her children did not **s** the mother

SWAYED (2) [SWAY]
2Sa 19:14 Amasa **s** the hearts of all the people of Judah
2Ti 3: 6 overwhelmed by their sins and **s** by all kinds

SWAYS (1) [SWAY]
Isa 24:20 The earth staggers like a drunkard, it **s** like a hut;

SWEAR (68) [SWEARING, SWEARS, SWORE, SWORN]
Ge 21:23 now therefore **s** to me here by God that you will
21:24 And Abraham said, "I **s** it."
24: 3 and I will make you **s** by the LORD,
24:37 My master made me **s**, saying,
25:33 Jacob said, "**S** to me first."
47:31 And he said, "**S** to me"; and he swore to him.
50: 5 My father made me **s** an oath;
50: 6 and bury your father, as he made you **s** to do."
50:25 So Joseph made the Israelites **s**, saying,
Lev 6: 3 if you **s** falsely regarding any of the various things
19:12 And you shall not **s** falsely by my name,
Dt 6:13 and by his name alone you shall **s**.
10:20 and by his name you shall **s**.
32:40 For I lift up my hand to heaven, and **s**:
Jos 2:12 **s** to me by the LORD that you
2:17 be released from this oath that you have made us **s**
2:20 be released from this oath that you made us **s**
23: 7 or **s** by them, or serve them,
Jdg 15: 7 I **s** I will not stop until I have taken revenge
15:12 "**S** to me that you yourselves will not attack me."
1Sa 3:14 Therefore I **s** to the house of Eli that the iniquity

1Sa 20:17 Jonathan made David s again by his love for him;
24:21 S to me therefore by the LORD that you will
30:15 "S to me by God that you will not kill me,
2Sa 19:7 for I s by the LORD, if you do not go,
1Ki 1:13 'Did you not, my lord the king, s to your servant,
1:51 the horns of the altar, saying, 'Let King Solomon s
2:42 "Did I not make you s by the LORD,
8:31 against a neighbor and is given an oath to s,
22:16 "How many times must I make you s
2Ki 9:26 I s I will repay you on this very plot of ground.'
2Ch 18:15 "How many times must I make you s
36:13 who had made him s by God;
Ezr 10:5 all Israel s that they would do as had been said.
Ps 24:4 to what is false, and do not s deceitfully.
63:11 all who s by him shall exult,
Ecc 9:2 those who s are like those who shun an oath.
Isa 19:18 that speak the language of Canaan and s allegiance
45:23 To me every knee shall bow, every tongue shall s."
48:1 who s by the name of the LORD,
65:16 and whoever takes an oath in the land shall s by
Jer 4:2 if you s, "As the LORD lives!"
5:2 they say, "As the LORD lives," yet they s falsely.
7:9 Will you steal, murder, commit adultery, s falsely,
12:16 to s by my name, "As the LORD lives,"
12:16 as they taught my people to s by Baal,
22:5 if you will not heed these words, I s by myself,
22:6 but I s that I will make you a desert,
44:26 Lo, I s by my great name, says the LORD,
Eze 36:7 I s that the nations that are all
Da 12:7 And I heard him s by the one who lives forever
Hos 4:15 and do not s, "As the LORD lives."
Am 8:14 Those who s by Ashimah of Samaria, and say,
Zep 1:5 and s to the LORD, but also s by Milcom;
Mal 3:5 against the adulterers, against those who s falsely,
Mt 5:33 to those of ancient times, 'You shall not s falsely,
5:34 But I say to you, Do not s at all, either by heaven,
5:36 And do not s by your head,
Heb 3:18 And to whom did he s that they would
6:13 because he had no one greater by whom to s,
6:16 of course, s by someone greater than themselves,
Jas 5:12 Above all, my beloved, do not s,
Jdt 13:16 I s that it was my face that seduced him
Wis 14:29 in lifeless idols they s wicked oaths and expect
14:31 it is not the power of the things by which people s,
1Es 1:48 Although King Nebuchadnezzar had made him s
8:96 the leaders of the priests and Levites of all Israel s

SWEARING (2) [SWEAR]

Hos 4:2 S, lying, and murder, and stealing
Sir 27:14 Their cursing and s make one's hair stand on end,

SWEARS (19) [SWEAR]

Nu 30:2 or s an oath to bind himself by a pledge,
1Ki 8:31 and comes and s before your altar in this house,
2Ch 6:22 to take an oath and comes and s before your altar
Zec 5:3 on one side, and everyone who s falsely shall
5:4 the house of anyone who s falsely by my name;
Mt 23:16 'Whoever s by the sanctuary is bound by nothing, but whoever s by the gold of the sanctuary is
23:18 'Whoever s by the altar is bound by nothing, but whoever s by the gift that is on the altar is bound
23:20 whoever s by the altar, s by it and by everything
23:21 whoever s by the sanctuary, s by it and by the one
23:22 and whoever s by heaven, s by the throne of God
Sir 23:10 also the person who always s and utters the Name
23:11 The one who s many oaths is full of iniquity,
23:11 If he s in error, his sin remains on him,
23:11 if he s a false oath, he will not be justified,

SWEAT (6) [SWEATING]

Ge 3:19 By the s of your face you shall eat bread
Eze 44:18 not bind themselves with anything that causes s.
Lk 22:44 ⟦his s became like great drops of blood falling⟧
2Mc 2:26 it is no light matter but calls for s and loss of sleep,
4Mc 6:11 with his face bathed in s,
7:8 with their own blood and noble s in sufferings

SWEATING (1) [SWEAT]

4Mc 3:8 when evening fell, he came, s and quite exhausted,

SWEEP (17) [SWEEPINGS, SWEEPS, SWEPT]

Ge 18:23 "Will you indeed s away the righteous with
18:24 will you then s away the place and not forgive it
Ps 26:9 Do not s me away with sinners,
58:9 whether green or ablaze, may he s them away!
69:15 Do not let the flood s over me,
90:5 You s them away; they are like a
Pr 21:7 The violence of the wicked will s them away,
Isa 8:8 it will s on into Judah as a flood, and, pouring
14:23 and I will s it with the broom of destruction,
21:1 As whirlwinds in the Negeb s on,
28:17 hail will s away the refuge of lies,
Hab 1:11 Then they s by like the wind;
Zep 1:2 I will utterly s away everything from the face of
1:3 I will s away humans and animals; I will s away the birds of the air and the fish of the sea.
Lk 15:8 s the house, and search carefully until she finds it?
Rev 12:15 to s her away with the flood.

SWEEPINGS (1) [SWEEP]

Am 8:6 and selling the s of the wheat."

SWEEPS (2) [SWEEP]

Job 27:21 it s them out of their place.
Ps 69:2 I have come into deep waters, and the flood s over

SWEET (50) [SWEET-SMELLING, SWEETER, SWEETLY, SWEETNESS]

Ex 15:25 he threw it into the water, and the water became s.
30:34 Take s spices, stacte, and onycha, and galbanum, s spices with pure frankincense
Lev 16:12 and two handfuls of crushed s incense,
Jdg 14:14 Out of the strong came something s."
Ne 8:10 the fat and drink s wine and send portions of them
Job 20:12 "Though wickedness is s in their mouth,
21:33 The clods of the valley are s to them;
24:20 The womb forgets them; the worm finds them s;
Ps 81:2 sound the tambourine, the s lyre with the harp.
119:103 How s are your words to my taste,
Pr 3:24 when you lie down, your sleep will be s.
9:17 "Stolen water is s, and bread eaten
13:19 A desire realized is s to the soul,
20:17 Bread gained by deceit is s,
24:13 the drippings of the honeycomb are s to your taste.
27:7 but to a ravenous appetite even the bitter is s.
Ecc 5:12 S is the sleep of laborers, whether they eat little
11:7 Light is s, and it is pleasant for the eyes to see
SS 2:3 and his fruit was s to my taste.
2:14 for your voice is s, and your face is lovely.
4:10 How s is your love, my sister, my bride!
5:16 His speech is most s, and he is altogether desirable.
Isa 5:20 who put bitter for s and s for bitter!
23:16 Make s melody, sing many songs,
43:24 You have not bought me s cane with money,
Jer 6:20 or s cane from a distant land?
Eze 3:3 I ate it; and in my mouth it was as s as honey.
27:19 and s cane were bartered for your merchandise.
Joel 1:5 over the s wine, for it is cut off from your mouth.
3:18 In that day the mountains shall drip s wine,
Am 9:13 the mountains shall drip s wine,
Rev 10:9 but s as honey in your mouth."
10:10 it was s as honey in my mouth,
AdE 1:7 There was abundant s wine,
Sir 11:3 but what it produces is the best of s things.
23:17 To a fornicator all bread is s;
38:5 Was not water made s with a tree in order
40:18 Wealth and wages make life s,
40:21 The flute and the harp make s melody,
40:30 In the mouth of the shameless begging is s,
47:9 to make s melody with their voices.
49:1 his memory is as s as honey to every mouth,
50:18 Then the singers praised him with their voices in s
2Mc 15:39 while wine mixed with water is s and delicious
1Es 9:51 eat the fat and drink the s,
2Es 1:23 threw a tree into the water and made the stream s.
5:9 Salt waters shall be found in the s,
4Mc 9:29 "How s is any kind of death for the religion

SWEET-SMELLING (2) [SMELL, SWEET]

Ex 30:23 and of s cinnamon half as much, that is,
Sir 38:11 Offer a s sacrifice, and a memorial portion

SWEETER (6) [SWEET]

Jdg 14:18 before the sun went down, "What is s than honey?
Ps 19:10 s also than honey, and drippings of the honeycomb.
119:103 s than honey to my mouth!
Sir 23:27 and nothing s than to heed the commandments of
24:20 For the memory of me is s than honey,
24:20 and the possession of me s than the honeycomb.

SWEETLY (1) [SWEET]

Sir 12:16 An enemy speaks s with his lips,

SWEETNESS‡ (4) [SWEET]

Jdg 9:11 'Shall I stop producing my s and my delicious
Pr 16:24 s to the soul and health to the body.
Wis 16:21 For your sustenance manifested your s toward
Sir 27:23 In your presence his mouth is all s,

SWEETSMELLING (KJV) See FRAGRANT

SWELL (4) [SWELLED, SWELLING, SWOLLEN]

Dt 8:4 and your feet did not s these forty years.
Ne 9:21 not wear out and their feet did not s.
Ps 73:7 Their eyes s out with fatness;
Ac 28:6 They were expecting him to s up or drop dead,

SWELLED (4) [SWELL]

Ge 7:18 The waters s and increased greatly on the earth;
7:19 The waters s so mightily on the earth that all
7:20 the waters s above the mountains,
7:24 waters s on the earth for one hundred fifty days.

SWELLING‡ (8) [SWELL]

Lev 13:2 on the skin of his body a s or an eruption or a spot,
13:10 a white s in the skin that has turned the hair white,
13:10 and there is quick raw flesh in the s,
13:19 and in the place of the boil there appears a white s
13:28 it is a s from the burn,
13:43 the diseased s is reddish-white on his bald head or
14:56 and for a s or an eruption or a spot,
Jdt 2:8 and the s river shall be filled with their dead.

SWELLINGS See Index to Footnotes

SWEPT‡ (20) [SWEEP]

Ge 1:2 a wind from God s over the face of the waters.
Nu 16:26 or you will be s away for all their sins."
Jdg 5:21 The torrent Kishon s them away,
1Sa 12:25 But if you still do wickedly, you shall be s away,
Job 15:30 and their blossom will be s away by the wind.
Ps 73:19 in a moment, s away utterly by terrors!
88:16 Your wrath has s over me;
124:4 then the flood would have s us away,
Pr 13:23 but it is s away through injustice.
Isa 44:22 I have s away your transgressions like a cloud,
Jer 12:4 in it the animals and the birds are s away,
Da 11:22 Armies shall be utterly s away and broken
11:26 They shall break him, his army shall be s away,
Hab 3:10 a torrent of water s by;
Mt 12:44 it comes, it finds it empty, s, and put in order.
24:39 until the flood came and s them all away,
Lk 8:23 A windstorm s down on the lake,
11:25 When it comes, it finds it s and put in order.
Rev 12:4 His tail s down a third of the stars of heaven
2Mc 5:16 and s away with profane hands

SWERVE (3) [SWERVED]

Ps 119:157 yet I do not s from your decrees.
Pr 4:27 Do not s to the right or to the left;
Joel 2:7 they do not s from their paths.

SWERVED (1) [SWERVE]

2Ti 2:18 who have s from the truth by claiming that

SWIFT (28) [SWIFTER, SWIFTLY, SWIFTNESS]

2Sa 2:18 Now Asahel was as s of foot as a wild gazelle.
1Ki 4:28 and straw for the horses and s steeds,
1Ch 12:8 and who were s as gazelles on the mountains:
Est 8:14 So the couriers, mounted on their s royal steeds,
Job 24:18 "S are they on the face of the waters;
39:5 Who has loosed the bonds of the s ass,
Ecc 9:11 under the sun the race is not to the s, nor the battle
Isa 16:5 in faithfulness a ruler who seeks justice and is s
18:2 Go, you s messengers, to a nation tall and smooth,
19:1 LORD is riding on a s cloud and comes to Egypt;
30:16 and, "We will ride upon s steeds"—
30:16 therefore your pursuers shall be s!
Jer 46:6 s cannot flee away, nor can the warrior escape;
Da 9:21 in s flight at the time of the evening sacrifice.
Am 2:14 Flight shall perish from the s,
2:15 those who are s of foot shall not save themselves,
Hab 1:8 they fly like an eagle s to devour.
Mal 3:5 I will be s to bear witness against the sorcerers,
Ro 3:15 "Their feet are s to shed blood;
2Pe 2:1 bringing s destruction on themselves.
Wis 13:2 but they supposed that either fire or wind or s air,
18:14 and night in its s course was now half gone,
Sir 45:3 By his words he performed s miracles;
1Es 4:34 and heaven is high, and the sun is s in its course,
3Mc 4:5 forced to march at a s pace by the violence
2Es 1:26 and your feet are s to commit murder.
12:20 whose times shall be short and their years s;
4Mc 14:10 For the power of fire is intense and s,

SWIFTER (6) [SWIFT]

2Sa 1:23 were s than eagles, they were stronger than lions.
Job 7:6 My days are s than a weaver's shuttle,
9:25 "My days are s than a runner;
Jer 4:13 his horses are s than eagles—
La 4:19 Our pursuers were s than the eagles in the heavens;
Hab 1:8 Their horses are s than leopards,

SWIFTLY‡ (11) [SWIFT]

Dt 32:35 of their calamity is at hand, their doom comes s.
Ps 18:10 he came s upon the wings of the wind.
147:15 to the earth; his word runs s.
Isa 5:26 Here they come, s, speedily!
51:5 I will bring near my deliverance s,
Jer 48:16 near at hand and his doom approaches s.
Joel 3:4 I will turn your deeds back upon your own heads s
Wis 6:5 he will come upon you terribly and s,
Sir 18:26 all things move s before the Lord.
2Es 4:26 because the age is hurrying s to its end.
4Mc 10:21 God will visit you s, for you are cutting out

SWIFTNESS (1) [SWIFT]

2Es 8:18 and now also I have heard of the s of the judgment

SWIM (6) [SWAM, SWIMMERS]

Isa 25:11 as swimmers spread out their hands to s,
Eze 47:5 it was deep enough to s in,
Ac 27:42 so that none might s away and escape;
27:43 He ordered those who could s to jump overboard
Wis 19:19 and creatures that s moved over to the land.
Aza 1:57 you whales and all that s in the waters;

SWIMMERS (1) [SWIM]

Isa 25:11 as s spread out their hands to swim,

SWINE (11) [SWINE'S, SWINEHERDS]

Mt 7:6 and do not throw your pearls before s,
8:30 a large herd of s was feeding at some distance

Mt 8:31 "If you cast us out, send us into the herd of s."
8:32 So they came out and entered the s;
Mk 5:11 there on the hillside a great herd of s was feeding;
5:12 "Send us into the s; let us enter them."
5:13 the unclean spirits came out and entered the s;
5:16 to the demoniac and to the s reported it.
Lk 8:32 there on the hillside a large herd of s was feeding;
8:33 the demons came out of the man and entered the s,
1Mc 1:47 to sacrifice s and other unclean animals,

SWINE (KJV) See also PIG

SWINE'S (4) [SWINE]

Isa 65: 4 who eat s flesh, with broth of abominable things
66: 3 like one who offers s blood;
2Mc 6:18 was being forced to open his mouth to eat s flesh.
7: 1 to partake of unlawful s flesh.

SWINEHERDS (3) [SWINE]

Mt 8:33 The s ran off, and on going into the town,
Mk 5:14 s ran off and told it in the city and in the country.
Lk 8:34 When the s saw what had happened,

SWINGING (1) [SWINGS]

Eze 41:24 two s leaves for each door.

SWINGS (1) [SWINGING, SWUNG]

Dt 19: 5 and when one of them s the ax to cut down a tree,

SWIRLED (1) [SWIRLS]

Isa 9:18 and they s upward in a column of smoke.

SWIRLS (1) [SWIRLED]

Hos 13: 3 that s from the threshing floor or like smoke from

SWOLLEN (1) [SWELL]

2Ti 3: 4 s with conceit, lovers of pleasure rather than lovers

SWOON[ED] (KJV) See FAINT

SWOONED (1)

Jer 15: 9 who bore seven has languished; she has s away;

SWOOP (5) [SWOOPING]

Dt 28:49 to s down on you like an eagle,
1Sa 15:19 Why did you s down on the spoil,
Isa 11:14 they shall s down on the backs of the Philistines
Jer 48:40 Look, he shall s down like an eagle,
49:22 Look, he shall mount up and s down like an eagle,

SWOOPING (1) [SWOOP]

Job 9:26 like an eagle s on the prey.

SWORD‡ (474) [SWORDS, SWORDSMEN]

Ge 3:24 the cherubim, and a s flaming and turning to guard
27:40 By your s you shall live,
31:26 carried away my daughters like captives of the s.
34:26 and his son Shechem with the s,
48:22 of the Amorites with my s and with my bow."
Ex 5: 3 or he will fall upon us with pestilence or s."
5:21 and have put a s in their hand to kill us."
15: 9 I will draw my s, my hand shall destroy them.'
17:13 Joshua defeated Amalek and his people with the s.
18: 4 and delivered me from the s of Pharaoh").
22:24 and I will kill you with the s,
32:27 the God of Israel, 'Put your s on your side,
Lev 26: 6 and no s shall go through your land.
26: 7 and they shall fall before you by the s.
26: 8 your enemies shall fall before you by the s.
26:25 I will bring the s against you,
26:33 and I will unsheathe the s against you,
26:36 and they shall flee as one flees from the s,
26:37 as if to escape a s, though no one pursues;
Nu 14: 3 into this land to fall by the s?
14:43 and you shall fall by the s;
19:16 a s, or who has died naturally, or a human bone,
20:18 or we will come out with the s against you."
21:24 to the s, and took possession of his land from
22:23 with a drawn s in his hand;
22:29 I wish I had a s in my hand!
22:31 with his drawn s in his hand;
31: 8 they also killed Balaam son of Beor with the s.
Dt 13:15 to the s, utterly destroying it and everything in it—
13:15 even putting its livestock to the s.
20:13 you shall put all its males to the s.
32:25 In the street the s shall bereave,
32:41 when I whet my flashing s,
32:42 and my s shall devour flesh—
33:29 the shield of your help, and the s of your triumph!
Jos 5:13 and saw a man standing before him with a drawn s
6:21 to destruction by the edge of the s all in the city,
8:18 "Stretch out the s that is in your hand toward Ai;
8:18 And Joshua stretched out the s that was in his hand
8:24 to the very last had fallen by the edge of the s,
8:24 and attacked it with the edge of the s.
8:26 with which he stretched out the s,
10:11 the hailstones than the Israelites killed with the s.
10:28 and struck it and its king with the edge of the s;
10:30 and he struck it with the edge of the s,
10:32 and struck it with the edge of the s,
10:35 and struck it with the edge of the s;
Jos 10:37 and struck it with the edge of the s,
10:39 they struck them with the edge of the s,
11:10 and struck its king down with the s.
11:11 And they put to the s all who were in it,
11:12 and struck them with the edge of the s,
11:14 down with the edge of the s,
13:22 the Israelites also put to the s Balaam son of Beor,
19:47 and after capturing it and putting it to the s,
24:12 it was not by your s or by your bow.
Jdg 1: 8 They put it to the s and set the city on fire.
1:25 and they put the city to the s,
3:16 Ehud made for himself a s with two edges,
3:21 took the s from his right thigh,
3:22 for he did not draw the s out of his belly;
4:16 All the army of Sisera fell by the s;
7:14 the s of Gideon son of Joash, a man of Israel;
7:20 they cried, "A s for the LORD and for Gideon!"
7:22 the LORD set every man's s against his fellow
8:20 But the boy did not draw his s, for he was afraid,
9:54 "Draw your s and kill me,
18:27 put them to the s, and burned down the city.
20:37 Then they put the whole city to the s.
20:48 and put them to the s—
21:10 "Go, put the inhabitants of Jabesh-gilead to the s,
1Sa 2:33 the members of your household shall die by the s.
13:22 of the battle neither s nor spear was to be found in
14:20 and every s was against the other,
15: 8 the people with the edge of the s.
15:33 "As your s has made women childless,
17:39 David strapped Saul's s over the armor,
17:45 "You come to me with s and spear and javelin;
17:47 that the LORD does not save by s and spear;
17:50 there was no s in David's hand.
17:51 he grasped his s, drew it out of its sheath,
18: 4 and even his s and his bow and his belt.
21: 8 "Is there no spear or s here with you?
21: 8 I did not bring my s or my weapons with me,
21: 9 The priest said, "The s of Goliath the Philistine,
22:10 and gave him the s of Goliath the Philistine."
22:13 by giving him bread and a s,
22:19 Nob, the city of the priests, he put to the s;
22:19 oxen, donkeys, and sheep, he put to the s.
25:13 David said to his men, "Every man strap on his s!"
25:13 And every one of them strapped on his s;
25:13 David also strapped on his s;
31: 4 "Draw your s and thrust me through with it,
31: 4 So Saul took his own s and fell upon it.
31: 5 he also fell upon his s and died with him.
2Sa 1:12 because they had fallen by the s.
1:22 nor the s of Saul return empty.
2:16 and thrust his s in his opponent's side;
2:26 "Is the s to keep devouring forever?
3:29 or who holds a spindle, or who falls by the s,
11:25 for the s devours now one and now another;
12: 9 You have struck down Uriah the Hittite with the s,
12: 9 and have killed him with the s of the Ammonites.
12:10 therefore the s shall never depart from your house,
15:14 and attack the city with the edge of the s."
18: 8 forest claimed more victims that day than the s.
20: 8 a soldier's garment and over it was a belt with a s
20:10 But Amasa did not notice the s in Joab's hand;
23:10 though his hand clung to the s.
24: 9 eight hundred thousand soldiers able to draw the s,
1Ki 1:51 that he will not kill his servant with the s.' "
2: 8 'I will not put you to death with the s.'
2:32 and killed with the s two men more righteous
3:24 So the king said, "Bring me a s,"
3:24 and they brought a s before the king.
19: 1 and how he had killed all the prophets with the s.
19:10 and killed your prophets with the s.
19:14 and killed your prophets with the s.
19:17 Whoever escapes from the s of Hazael,
19:17 and whoever escapes from the s of Jehu,
2Ki 6:22 with your s and your bow those whom you want
8:12 you will kill their young men with the s,
10:25 So they put them to the s,
11:15 and kill with the s anyone who follows her."
11:20 after Athaliah had been killed with the s at
19: 7 I will cause him to fall by the s in his own land.' "
19:37 and Sharezer killed him with the s,
1Ch 5:18 who carried shield and s, and drew the bow,
10: 4 Then Saul said to his armor-bearer, "Draw your s,
10: 4 So Saul took his own s and fell on it.
10: 5 he also fell on his s and died.
21: 5 million one hundred thousand men who drew the s,
21: 5 four hundred seventy thousand who drew the s.
21:12 while the s of your enemies overtakes you;
21:12 or three days of the s of the LORD,
21:16 in his hand a drawn s stretched out over Jerusalem.
21:27 and he put his s back into its sheath.
21:30 he was afraid of the s of the angel of the LORD.
2Ch 20: 9 the s, judgment, or pestilence, or famine,
21: 4 he put all his brothers to the s,
23:14 anyone who follows her is to be put to the s."
23:21 after Athaliah had been killed with the s.
29: 9 Our fathers have fallen by the s and our sons
32:21 of his own sons struck him down there with the s.
36:17 who killed their youths with the s in the house
36:20 in Babylon those who had escaped from the s,
Ezr 9: 7 to the s, to captivity, to plundering,
Ne 4:18 of the builders had his s strapped at his side
Est 9: 5 the Jews struck down all their enemies with the s,
Job 1:15 and killed the servants with the edge of the s;
1:17 and killed the servants with the edge of the s;
5:15 But he saves the needy from the s of their mouth,
5:20 and in war from the power of the s.
15:22 and they are destined for the s.
Job 19:29 be afraid of the s, for wrath brings the punishment of the s,
27:14 If their children are multiplied, it is for the s;
36:12 But if they do not listen, they shall perish by the s,
39:22 it does not turn back from the s.
40:19 only its Maker can approach it with the s.
41:26 Though the s reaches it, it does not avail,
Ps 7:12 If one does not repent, God will whet his s;
17:13 By your s deliver my life from the wicked,
22:20 Deliver my soul from the s,
37:14 the s and bend their bows to bring down the poor
37:15 their s shall enter their own heart,
44: 3 for not by their own s did they win the land,
44: 6 not in my bow do I trust, nor can my s save me.
45: 3 Gird your s on your thigh, O mighty one,
63:10 they shall be given over to the power of the s,
76: 3 the shield, the s, and the weapons of war.
78:62 He gave his people to the s,
78:64 Their priests fell by the s,
89:43 Moreover, you have turned back the edge of his s,
144:11 Rescue me from the cruel s,
Pr 5: 4 as wormwood, sharp as a two-edged s.
12:18 Rash words are like s thrusts,
25:18 Like a war club, a s, or a sharp arrow
SS 3: 8 with his s at his thigh because of alarms by night.
Isa 1:20 you shall be devoured by the s;
2: 4 nation shall not lift up s against nation,
3:25 Your men shall fall by the s and your warriors
13:15 and whoever is caught will fall by the s.
14:19 clothed with the dead, those pierced by the s,
21:15 they have fled from the swords, from the drawn s,
22: 2 Your slain are not slain by the s,
27: 1 and great and strong s will punish Leviathan
31: 8 the Assyrian shall fall by a s, not of mortals;
31: 8 and a s, not of humans, shall devour him;
31: 8 he shall flee from the s, and his young men shall
34: 5 When my s has drunk its fill in the heavens, lo,
34: 6 The LORD has a s; it is sated with blood,
37: 7 I will cause him to fall by the s in his own land.' "
37:38 and Sharezer killed him with the s,
41: 2 he makes them like dust with his s,
49: 2 He made my mouth like a sharp s,
51:19 devastation and destruction, famine and s—
65:12 I will destine you to the s, and all of you shall bow
66:16 and by his s, on all flesh;
Jer 2:30 Your own s devoured your prophets like
4:10 even while the s is at the throat!"
5:12 and we shall not see s or famine."
5:17 with the s your fortified cities in which you trust.
6:25 for the enemy has a s, terror is on every side."
9:16 and I will send the s after them,
11:22 the young men shall die by the s;
12:12 for the s of the LORD devours from one end of
14:12 but by the s, by famine, and by pestilence
14:13 'You shall not see the s,
14:15 "S and famine shall not come on this land":
14:15 By s and famine those prophets shall
14:16 the streets of Jerusalem, victims of famine and s.
14:18 I go out into the field, look—those killed by the s!
15: 2 and those destined for the s, to the s;
15: 3 the s to kill, the dogs to drag away,
15: 9 of them I will give to the s before their enemies,
16: 4 They shall perish by the s and by famine,
18:21 hurl them out to the power of the s,
18:21 their youths be slain by the s in battle.
19: 7 will make them fall by the s before their enemies,
20: 4 by the s of their enemies while you look on.
20: 4 and shall kill them with the s.
21: 7 those who survive the pestilence, s, and famine—
21: 7 He shall strike them down with the edge of the s;
21: 9 Those who stay in this city shall die by the s,
24:10 And I will send s, famine,
25:16 of their minds because of the s that I am sending
25:27 because of the s that I am sending among you.
25:29 for I am summoning a s against all the inhabitants
25:31 and the guilty he will put to the s,
25:38 of the cruel s, and because of his fierce anger.
26:23 the s and threw his dead body into the burial place
27: 8 then I will punish that nation with the s,
27:13 Why should you and your people die by the s,
29:17 I am going to let loose on them s, famine,
29:18 I will pursue them with the s, with famine,
31: 2 The people who survived the s found grace in
32:24 and the city, faced with s, famine, and pestilence,
32:36 of the king of Babylon by the s, by famine,
33: 4 a defense against the siege ramps and before the s:
34: 4 You shall not die by the s;
34:17 a release to the s, to pestilence, and to famine.
38: 2 Those who stay in this city shall die by the s,
39:18 and you shall not fall by the s;
41: 2 of Shaphan with the s and killed him,
42:16 then the s that you fear shall overtake you there,
42:17 to settle there shall die by the s, by famine,
42:22 Be well aware, then, that you shall die by the s,
43:11 and those who are destined for the s, to the s.
44:12 by the s and by famine they shall perish;
44:12 they shall die by the s and by famine;
44:13 with the s, with famine, and with pestilence,
44:18 and have perished by the s and by famine."
44:27 of Egypt shall perish by the s and by famine,
44:28 And those who escape the s shall return from
46:10 The s shall devour and be sated,
46:14 for the s shall devour those around you."
46:16 because of the destroying s."
47: 6 Ah, s of the LORD!
48: 2 to silence; the s shall pursue you.
48:10 the one who keeps back the s from bloodshed.

Jer 49:37 I will send the s after them,
50:16 because of the destroying s all of them shall return
50:35 A s against the Chaldeans, says the LORD,
50:36 A s against the diviners, so that they may become
50:36 A s against her warriors, so that they may be
50:37 A s against her horses and against her chariots,
50:37 A s against all her treasures, that they may be
51:50 You survivors of the s, go, do not linger!
La 1:20 In the street the s bereaves;
2:21 and my young men have fallen by the s;
4: 9 by the s than those pierced by hunger,
5: 9 because of the s in the wilderness.
Eze 5: 1 And you, O mortal, take a sharp s;
5: 2 one third you shall take and strike with the s all
5: 2 and I will unsheathe the s after them.
5:12 one third shall fall by the s around you;
5:12 to every wind and will unsheathe the s after them.
5:17 and I will bring the s upon you.
6: 3 I, I myself will bring a s upon you,
6: 8 Some of you shall escape the s among the nations
6:11 For they shall fall by the s, by famine,
6:12 those nearby shall fall by the s;
7:15 The s is outside, pestilence and famine are inside;
7:15 those in the field die by the s;
11: 8 You have feared the s;
11: 8 I will bring the s upon you, says the Lord GOD.
11:10 You shall fall by the s;
12:14 and I will unsheathe the s behind them.
12:16 But I will let a few of them escape from the s,
14:17 Or if I bring a s upon that land and say,
14:17 'Let a s pass through the land,'
14:21 s, famine, wild animals, and pestilence,
17:21 All the pick of his troops shall fall by the s,
21: 3 and will draw my s out of its sheath,
21: 4 therefore my s shall go out of its sheath
21: 5 the LORD have drawn my s out of its sheath;
21: 9 A s, a s is sharpened, it is also polished;
21:11 The s is given to be polished,
21:11 It is sharpened, the s is polished,
21:12 they are thrown to the s, together with my people.
21:14 Let the s fall twice, thrice; it is a s for killing.
21:14 A s for great slaughter—it surrounds them;
21:15 At all their gates I have set the point of the s.
21:19 for the s of the king of Babylon to come;
21:20 for the s to come to Rabbah of the Ammonites or
21:28 concerning their reproach; say: A s, a s!
23:10 and they killed her with the s.
23:25 and your survivors shall fall by the s.
24:21 behind shall fall by the s.
25:13 from Teman even to Dedan they shall fall by the s.
26: 6 in the country shall be killed by the s.
26: 8 in the country he shall put to the s.
26:11 He shall put your people to the s,
28:23 by the s that is against it on every side.
29: 8 I will bring a s upon you,
30: 4 A s shall come upon Egypt,
30: 5 of the allied land shall fall with them by the s.
30: 6 to Syene they shall fall within it by the s,
30:17 of On and of Pi-beseth shall fall by the s;
30:21 so that it may become strong to wield the s.
30:22 and I will make the s fall from his hand.
30:24 and put my s in his hand;
30:25 I put my s into the hand of the king of Babylon.
31:17 to those killed by the s, along with its allies,
31:18 with those who are killed by the s.
32:10 When I brandish my s before them,
32:11 s of the king of Babylon shall come against you.
32:20 among those who are killed by the s.
32:20 Egypt has been handed over to the s;
32:21 they lie still, the uncircumcised, killed by the s."
32:22 all of them killed, fallen by the s.
32:23 all of them killed, fallen by the s,
32:24 all of them killed, fallen by the s,
32:25 all of them uncircumcised, killed by the s;
32:26 all of them uncircumcised, killed by the s;
32:28 with those who are killed by the s.
32:29 with those who are killed by the s;
32:30 with those who are killed by the s,
32:31 Pharaoh and all his army, killed by the s,
32:32 with those who are slain by the s—
33: 2 If I bring the s upon a land,
33: 3 and if the sentinel sees the s coming upon the land
33: 4 and the s comes and takes them away,
33: 6 if the sentinel sees the s coming and does not blow
33: 6 and the s comes and takes any of them,
33:27 in the waste places shall fall by the s;
35: 5 to the power of the s at the time of their calamity,
35: 8 those killed with the s shall fall.
38:21 the s against Gog in all my mountains,
39:23 and they all fell by the s.
Da 11:33 however, they shall fall by s and flame,
Hos 1: 7 I will not save them by bow, or by s, or by war,
2:18 and I will abolish the bow, the s,
7:16 their officials shall fall by the s because of the rage
11: 6 The s rages in their cities,
13:16 they shall fall by the s, their little ones shall be
Am 1:11 because he pursued his brother with the s
4:10 I killed your young men with the s;
7: 9 against the house of Jeroboam with the s."
7:11 thus Amos has said, 'Jeroboam shall die by the s,
7:17 your sons and your daughters shall fall by the s,
9: 1 and those who are left I will kill with the s;
9: 4 there I will command the s, and it shall kill them;
9:10 All the sinners of my people shall die by the s,
Mic 4: 3 nation shall not lift up s against nation,
5: 6 They shall rule the land of Assyria with the s,
5: 6 and the land of Nimrod with the drawn s;
Mic 6:14 and what you save, I will hand over to the s.
Na 2:13 and the s shall devour your young lions;
3: 3 flashing s and glittering spear, piles of dead,
3:15 the s will cut you off.
Zep 2:12 You also, O Ethiopians, shall be killed by my s.
Hag 2:22 every one by the s of a comrade.
Zec 9:13 O Greece, and wield you like a warrior's s.
11:17 May the s strike his arm and his right eye!
13: 7 "Awake, O s, against my shepherd,
Mt 10:34 I have not come to bring peace, but a s.
26:51 one of those with Jesus put his hand on his s,
26:52 Jesus said to him, "Put your s back into its place;
for all who take the s will perish by the s.
Mk 14:47 of those who stood near drew his s and struck
Lk 2:35 and a s will pierce your own soul too."
21:24 by the edge of the s and be taken away as captives
22:36 one who has no s must sell his cloak and buy one.
22:49 they asked, "Lord, should we strike with the s?"
Jn 18:10 Then Simon Peter, who had a s, drew it,
18:11 "Put your s back into its sheath.
Ac 12: 2 the brother of John, killed with the s.
16:27 he drew his s and was about to kill himself,
Ro 8:35 or famine, or nakedness, or peril, or s?
13: 4 for the authority does not bear the s in vain!
Eph 6:17 and the s of the Spirit, which is the word of God.
Heb 4:12 sharper than any two-edged s,
11:34 escaped the edge of the s,
11:37 they were sawn in two, they were killed by the s;
Rev 1:16 and from his mouth came a sharp, two-edged s,
2:12 the words of him who has the sharp two-edged s:
2:16 to you soon and make war against them with the s
6: 4 and he was given a great s.
6: 8 to kill with s, famine, and pestilence,
13:10 if you kill with the s, with the s you must be killed.
13:14 for the beast that had been wounded by the s and
19:15 a sharp s with which to strike down the nations,
19:21 rest were killed by the s of the rider on the horse,
19:21 the s that came from his mouth;
Jdt 1:12 that he would kill with his s also all the inhabitants
2:27 and put all their young men to the s.
6: 6 Then at my return the s of my army and the spear
7:14 and before the s reaches them they will be strewn
8:19 over to the s and to pillage,
9: 2 to whom you gave a s to take revenge
9: 8 and to break off the horns of your altar with the s.
11:10 nor can the s prevail against them,
13: 6 and took down his s that hung there.
16: 4 and kill my young men with the s,
16: 9 and the s severed his neck!
Wis 5:20 and sharpen stern wrath for a s,
18:16 carrying the sharp s of your authentic command,
Sir 21: 3 All lawlessness is like a two-edged s;
22:21 Even if you draw your s against a friend,
26:28 the Lord will prepare him for the s!
28:18 Many have fallen by the edge of the s,
39:30 the s that punishes the ungodly with destruction.
40: 9 come death and bloodshed and strife and s,
46: 2 when he lifted his hands and brandished his s
Bar 2:25 by famine and s and pestilence.
Sus 1:59 the angel of God is waiting with his s to split you
Bel 1:26 and I will kill the dragon without s or club."
1Mc 2: 9 her youths by the s of the foe.
3: 3 protecting the camp by his s.
3:12 and Judas took the s of Apollonius,
4:15 and all those in the rear fell by the s.
4:33 down with the s of those who love you,
5:28 and killed every male by the edge of the s;
5:51 He destroyed every male by the edge of the s,
7:38 and let them fall by the s;
7:46 so that they all fell by the s;
8:23 and may s and enemy be far from them.
9:73 Thus the s ceased from Israel.
10:85 The number of those who fell by the s,
12:48 and they killed with the s all who had entered
2Mc 5:26 He put to the s all those who came out to see them,
12:23 putting the sinners to the s,
14:41 Being surrounded, Razis fell upon his own s,
15:15 and gave to Judas a golden s, and
15:16 "Take this holy s, a gift from God,
1Es 1:53 These killed their young men with the s
1:56 The survivors he led away to Babylon with the s,
4:23 A man takes his s, and goes out to travel and rob
8:77 to the s and exile and plundering,
Pm 151: 7 But I drew his own s;
2Es 12:27 for the two who remained, the s shall devour them.
12:28 the s of one shall devour him who was with him;
12:28 but he also shall fall by the s in the last days.
15: 5 the s and famine, death and destruction,
15:15 For the s and misery draw near them,
15:19 shall make an assault upon their houses with the s,
15:22 and my s will not cease
15:35 and there shall be blood from the s as high as
15:49 widowhood, poverty, famine, s, and pestilence,
15:57 and you shall fall by the s;
15:57 in the open country shall fall by the s.
16: 3 The s has been sent upon you,
16:21 the s, famine, and great confusion.
16:22 those who survive the famine shall die by the s.
16:31 be left by those who search their houses with the s.

SWORD-EDGES See Index to Footnotes

SWORDS‡ (37) [SWORD]

Ge 34:25 took their s and came against the city unawares,
49: 5 weapons of violence are their s.
1Sa 13:19 "The Hebrews must not make s or spears
1Ki 18:28 with s and lances until the blood gushed out
Ne 4:13 with their s, their spears, and their bows.
Ps 55:21 that were softer than oil, but in fact were drawn s.
57: 4 and arrows, their tongues sharp s.
64: 3 who whet their tongues like s,
149: 6 be in their throats and two-edged s in their hands,
Pr 30:14 There are those whose teeth are s,
SS 3: 8 all equipped with s and expert in war,
Isa 2: 4 they shall beat their s into plowshares,
21:15 For they have fled from the s,
Eze 16:40 and cut you to pieces with their s.
23:47 and with their s they shall cut them down;
28: 7 they shall draw their s against the beauty
30:11 and they shall draw their s against Egypt,
32:12 I will cause your hordes to fall by the s
32:27 whose s were laid under their heads,
33:26 You depend on your s, you commit abominations,
38: 4 all of them with shield and buckler, wielding s.
38:21 the s of all will be against their comrades.
Joel 3:10 Beat your plowshares into s,
Mic 4: 3 they shall beat their s into plowshares,
Mt 26:47 with him was a large crowd with s and clubs,
26:55 "Have you come out with s and clubs to arrest me
Mk 14:43 and with him there was a crowd with s and clubs,
14:48 "Have you come out with s and clubs to arrest me
Lk 22:38 They said, "Lord, look, here are two s."
22:52 "Have you come out with s and clubs as if I were
AdE 13: 6 be utterly destroyed by the s of their enemies,
1Mc 4: 6 they did not have armor and s such as they desired.
2Mc 5: 2 companies fully armed with lances and drawn s—
12:22 and pierced by the points of their own s.
1Es 3:22 and before long they draw their s.
2Es 15:15 up to fight against nation, with s in their hands.
15:41 fire and hail and flying s and floods of water,

SWORDSMEN (1) [MAN, SWORD]

2Ki 3:26 with him seven hundred s to break through,

SWORE (98) [SWEAR]

Ge 21:31 because there both of them s an oath.
24: 7 and who spoke to me and s to me,
24: 9 the thigh of Abraham his master and s to him
25:33 So he s to him, and sold his birthright to Jacob.
26: 3 the oath that I s to your father Abraham.
31:53 So Jacob s by the Fear of his father Isaac,
47:31 And he said, "Swear to me"; and he s to him.
50:24 of this land to the land that he s to Abraham,
Ex 6: 8 into the land that I s to give to Abraham, Isaac,
13: 5 which he s to your ancestors to give you,
13:11 as he s to you and your ancestors,
32:13 how you s to them by your own self,
33: 1 and go to the land of which I s to Abraham, Isaac,
Nu 14:16 to bring this people into the land he s to give them
14:23 shall see the land that I s to give to their ancestors;
14:30 shall come into the land in which I s to settle you,
32:10 LORD's anger was kindled on that day and he s,
32:11 shall see the land that I s to give to Abraham,
Dt 1: 8 go in and take possession of the land that I s to
1:34 LORD heard your words, he was wrathful and s:
1:35 the good land that I s to give to your ancestors,
4:31 the covenant with your ancestors that he s to them.
6:10 that he s to your ancestors, to Abraham, to Isaac,
6:18 the good land that the LORD s to your ancestors
7: 8 the LORD loved you and kept the oath that he s to
7:12 the covenant loyalty that he s to your ancestors;
7:13 in the land that he s to your ancestors to give you.
8:18 so that he may confirm his covenant that he s to
10:11 the land that I s to their ancestors to give them."
11: 9 that the LORD s to your ancestors to give them
11:21 that the LORD s to your ancestors to give them,
13:17 as he s to your ancestors,
19: 8 as he s to your ancestors—
26: 3 that I have come into the land that the LORD s to
26:15 as you s to our ancestors—
28:11 that the LORD s to your ancestors to give you.
29:13 as he promised you and as he s to your ancestors,
30:20 so that you may live in the land that the LORD s to
34: 4 "This is the land of which I s to Abraham, to Isaac,
Jos 1: 6 in possession of the land that I s to their ancestors
5: 6 the LORD s that he would not let them see
6:22 of it and all who belong to her, as you s to her."
9:15 the leaders of the congregation s an oath to them.
9:20 because of the oath that we s to them."
14: 9 And Moses s on that day, saying,
21:43 to Israel all the land that he s to their ancestors
1Sa 19: 6 Saul heeded the voice of Jonathan; Saul s,
20: 3 also s, "Your father knows well that you like me;
24:22 So David s this to Saul.
28:10 But Saul s to her by the LORD,
2Sa 3:35 but David s, saying, "So may God do to me,
21:17 Then David's men s to him,
1Ki 1:17 you s to your servant by the LORD your God,
1:29 The king s, saying, "As the LORD lives,
1:30 as I s to you by the LORD,
2: 8 I s to him by the LORD,
2:23 Then King Solomon s by the LORD,
2Ki 25:24 Gedaliah s to them and their men, saying,
Ezr 10: 5 they would do as had been said. So they s.
Ne 9:15 to go in to possess the land that you s to give them.
Ps 89:49 which by your faithfulness you s to David?
95:11 in my anger I s, "They shall not enter my rest."
106:26 and s to them that he would make them fall in
132: 2 how he s to the LORD and vowed to the Mighty
132:11 The LORD s to David a sure oath
Isa 54: 9 Just as I s that the waters of Noah
Jer 11: 5 I may perform the oath that I s to your ancestors,

Jer 32:22 which you s to their ancestors to give them,
38:16 So King Zedekiah s an oath in secret to Jeremiah,
40: 9 Gedaliah son of Ahikam son of Shaphan s to them
Eze 20: 5 I s to the offspring of the house of Jacob—
20: 5 I s to them, saying, I am the LORD your God.
20: 6 On that day I s to them that I would bring them out
20:15 Moreover I s to them in the wilderness
20:23 Moreover I s to them in the wilderness
20:28 For when I had brought them into the land that I s
20:42 the country that I s to give to your ancestors.
47:14 I s to give it to your ancestors,
Mt 26:74 Then he began to curse, and he s an oath,
Mk 6:23 And he solemnly s to her, "Whatever you ask me,
14:71 But he began to curse, and he s an oath,
Lk 1:73 the oath that he s to our ancestor Abraham,
Heb 3:11 As in my anger I s, 'They will not enter my rest.' "
4: 3 just as God has said, "As in my anger I s,
6:13 by whom to swear, he s by himself,
Rev 10: 6 and s by him who lives forever and ever,
Tob 8:20 for Tobias and s on oath to him in these words:
Jdt 1:12 and s by his throne and kingdom
Wis 14:30 to idols, and because in deceit they s unrighteously
Bar 2:34 I will bring them again into the land that I s to give
1Mc 7:15 to them and s this oath to them,
7:18 the agreement and the oath that they s."
7:35 and in anger he s this oath,
9:71 and he s to Jonathan that he would not try
2Mc 13:23 yielded and s to observe all their rights,
14:33 toward the sanctuary, and s this oath:
1Es 8:96 And they s to it.
3Mc 5:42 and he firmly s an irrevocable oath that he would

SWORN (47) [SWEAR]

Ge 14:22 "I have s to the LORD, God Most High,
22:16 "By myself I have s, says the LORD:
Lev 6: 5 or anything else about which you have s falsely,
Dt 2:14 as the LORD had s concerning them.
28: 9 as his holy people, as he has s to you,
29:12 into the covenant of the LORD your God, s by
29:14 I am making this covenant, s by an oath,
31: 7 with this people into the land that the LORD has s
Jos 5: 6 the land that he had s to their ancestors to give us,
9:18 of the congregation had s to them by the LORD,
9:19 "We have s to them by the LORD,
21:44 on every side just as he had s to their ancestors;
Jdg 2:15 as the LORD had warned them and s to them;
21: 1 Now the Israelites had s at Mizpah,
21: 7 since we have s by the LORD that we will
21:18 the Israelites had s, "Cursed be anyone who gives
1Sa 20:42 since both of us have s in the name of the LORD,
2Sa 3: 9 For just what the LORD has s to David,
21: 2 although the people of Israel had s to spare them,
1Ch 16:16 that he made with Abraham, his s promise
2Ch 15:15 for they had s with all their heart,
Ps 89: 3 I have s to my servant David:
89:35 Once and for all I have s by my holiness;
105: 9 that he made with Abraham, his s promise
110: 4 The LORD has s and will not change his mind,
119:106 I have s an oath and confirmed it,
Isa 5: 9 The LORD of hosts has s in my hearing:
14:24 The LORD of hosts has s:
45:23 By myself I have s, from my mouth has gone forth
54: 9 over the earth, so I have s that I will not be angry
62: 8 The LORD has s by his right hand and
Jer 5: 7 and have s by those who are no gods.
49:13 For by myself I have s, says the LORD,
51:14 The LORD of hosts has s by himself:
Eze 21:23 they have s solemn oaths;
44:12 therefore I have s concerning them,
Am 4: 2 The Lord GOD has s by his holiness:
6: 8 Lord GOD has s by himself (says the LORD,
8: 7 The LORD has s by the pride of Jacob:
Mic 7:20 you have s to our ancestors from the days of old.
Ac 2:30 he knew that God had s with an oath to him
Heb 7:21 "The Lord has s and will not change his mind,
Tob 9: 3 You are witness to the oath Raguel has s,
10: 7 that Raguel had s to observe for his daughter,
Jdt 8:11 even s and pronounced this oath between God
1Mc 6:62 he broke the oath he had s and gave orders to tear
2Mc 4:34 offered him s pledges and gave him his right hand,

SWUNG (3) [SWINGS]

Eze 26: 2 the gateway of the peoples; it has s open to me;
Rev 14:16 So the one who sat on the cloud s his sickle over
14:19 the angel s his sickle over the earth and gathered

SYCAMINE (KJV) See MULBERRY

SYCAMORE (5) [SYCAMORES]

1Ch 27:28 and s trees in the Shephelah was Baal-hanan
2Ch 1:15 and he made cedar as plentiful as the s of
9:27 and cedar as plentiful as the s of the Shephelah.
Am 7:14 but I am a herdsman, and a dresser of s trees,
Lk 19: 4 So he ran ahead and climbed a s tree to see him,

SYCAMORES (3) [SYCAMORE]

1Ki 10:27 and he made cedars as numerous as the s of
Ps 78:47 with hail, and their s with frost.
Isa 9:10 the s have been cut down,

SYCHAR (1)

Jn 4: 5 So he came to a Samaritan city called S,

SYCHEM (KJV) See SHECHEM

SYCOMORE (KJV) See SYCAMORE, SYCAMORES

SYENE (3)

Isa 49:12 and these from the land of S.
Eze 29:10 from Migdol to S, as far as the border of Ethiopia.
30: 6 Migdol to S they shall fall within it by the sword,

SYMBOL‡ (5) [SYMBOLIZED, SYMBOLS]

Isa 57: 8 the door and the doorpost you have set up your s;
1Co 11:10 For this reason a woman ought to have a s
Heb 9: 9 This is a s of the present time,
Wis 16: 6 and received a s of deliverance to remind them
3Mc 2:29 on their bodies by fire with the ivy-leaf s

SYMBOLIZED (3) [SYMBOL]

2Es 13:37 for their ungodliness (this was s by the storm),
13:38 with which they are to be tortured (which were s
13:38 without effort by means of the law (which was s

SYMBOLS (1) [SYMBOL]

Sir 45: 8 and strengthened him with the s of authority,

SYMEON See Index to Footnotes

SYMPATHETIC (1) [SYMPATHY]

4Mc 13:23 the brothers were the more s to one another.

SYMPATHIZE (1) [SYMPATHY]

Heb 4:15 For we do not have a high priest who is unable to s

SYMPATHY (11) [SYMPATHETIC, SYMPATHIZE]

Job 42:11 they showed him s and comforted him for all
Php 2: 1 any sharing in the Spirit, any compassion and s,
1Pe 3: 8 Finally, all of you, have unity of spirit, s,
4Mc 5:25 of the world in giving us the law has shown s
6:13 partly out of s from their acquaintance with him,
13:23 s and brotherly affection had been so established,
14:14 have a s and parental love for their offspring.
14:18 to demonstrate s for children by the example
14:20 But s for her children did not sway the mother of
15: 4 who because of their birth pangs have a deeper s
15: 7 with each of them she had s for them;

SYNAGOGUE‡ (42) [SYNAGOGUES]

Mt 9:18 a leader of the s came in and knelt before him,
12: 9 He left that place and entered their s;
13:54 and began to teach the people in their s,
Mk 1:21 the sabbath came, he entered the s and taught.
1:23 Just then there was in their s a man with
1:29 As soon as they left the s,
3: 1 the s, and a man was there who had
5:22 one of the leaders of the s named Jairus came and,
5:36 Jesus said to the leader of the s, "Do not fear,
5:38 they came to the house of the leader of the s,
6: 2 On the sabbath he began to teach in the s,
Lk 4:16 he went to the s on the sabbath day,
4:20 The eyes of all in the s were fixed on him.
4:28 they heard this, all in the s were filled with rage.
4:33 In the s there was a man who had the spirit of
4:38 After leaving the s he entered Simon's house.
6: 6 On another sabbath he entered the s and taught,
7: 5 and it is he who built our s for us."
8:41 a man named Jairus, a leader of the s.
13:14 of the s, indignant because Jesus had cured on
Jn 6:59 He said these things while he was teaching in the s
9:22 to be the Messiah would be put out of the s.
12:42 for fear that they would be put out of the s;
Ac 6: 9 of those who belonged to the s of the Freedmen
13:14 the sabbath day they went into the s and sat down.
13:15 the officials of the s sent them a message, saying,
13:43 When the meeting of the s broke up,
14: 1 where Paul and Barnabas went into the Jewish s
17: 1 where there was a s of the Jews.
17:10 and when they arrived, they went to the Jewish s.
17:17 in the s with the Jews and the devout persons,
18: 4 the s and would try to convince Jews and Greeks.
18: 7 Then he left the s and went to the house of
18: 7 his house was next door to the s.
18: 8 Crispus, the official of the s,
18:17 all of them seized Sosthenes, the official of the s,
18:19 into the s and had a discussion with the Jews.
18:26 He began to speak boldly in the s;
19: 8 the s and for three months spoke out boldly,
22:19 they themselves know that in every s I imprisoned
Rev 2: 9 are Jews and are not, but are a s of Satan.
3: 9 the s of Satan who say that they are Jews and are

SYNAGOGUES (25) [SYNAGOGUE]

Mt 4:23 teaching in their s and proclaiming the good news
6: 2 as the hypocrites do in the s and in the streets,
6: 5 to stand and pray in the s and at the street corners,
9:35 about all the cities and villages, teaching in their s,
10:17 over to councils and flog you in their s;
23: 6 of honor at banquets and the best seats in the s,
23:34 and some you will flog in your s and pursue
Mk 1:39 the message in their s and casting out demons.
12:39 to have the best seats in the s and places of honor
13: 9 and you will be beaten in s;
Lk 4:15 to teach in their s and was praised by everyone.
4:44 So he continued proclaiming the message in the s
11:43 to have the seat of honor in the s and to be greeted
12:11 When they bring you before the s, the rulers,
13:10 he was teaching in one of the s on the sabbath.
20:46 to have the best seats in the s and places of honor
21:12 they will hand you over to s and prisons,
Jn 16: 2 They will put you out of the s.
18:20 I have always taught in s and in the temple,
Ac 9: 2 and asked him for letters to the s at Damascus,
9:20 immediately he began to proclaim Jesus in the s,
13: 5 they proclaimed the word of God in the s of
15:21 for he has been read aloud every sabbath in the s."
24:12 or stirring up a crowd either in the s or throughout
26:11 in all the s I tried to force them to blaspheme;

SYNTYCHE (1)

Php 4: 2 I urge Euodia and I urge S to be of the same mind

SYRACUSE (1)

Ac 28:12 We put in at S and stayed there for three days;

SYRIA (22) [SYRIAN, SYROPHOENICIAN]

Mt 4:24 So his fame spread throughout all S,
Lk 2: 2 and was taken while Quirinius was governor of S.
Ac 15:23 to the believers of Gentile origin in Antioch and S
15:41 He went through S and Cilicia,
18:18 to the believers and sailed for S,
20: 3 to set sail for S when a plot was made against him
21: 3 we sailed to S and landed at Tyre,
Gal 1:21 Then I went into the regions of S and Cilicia,
Jdt 1:12 of Cilicia and Damascus and S,
1Mc 3:41 from S and the land of the Philistines joined
11: 2 He set out for S with peaceable words,
11:60 and all the army of S gathered to him as allies.
1Es 2:25 in Samaria and S and Phoenicia, wrote as follows:
6: 3 At the same time Sisinnes the governor of S
6: 7 that Sisinnes the governor of S and Phoenicia,
6: 7 their associates the local rulers in S and Phoenicia,
6:27 So Darius commanded Sisinnes the governor of S
6:27 and those who were appointed as local rulers in S
8:19 of S and Phoenicia that whatever Ezra the priest
8:23 throughout all S and Phoenicia;
2Es 16: 1 Woe to you, Egypt and S!
4Mc 4: 2 So he came to Apollonius, governor of S,

SYRIA-DAMASCUS (KJV) See ARAM OF DAMASCUS

SYRIA-MAACHAH (KJV) See ARAM-MAACAH

SYRIACK (KJV) See ARAMAIC

SYRIAN (4) [SYRIA]

Lk 4:27 none of them was cleansed except Naaman the S."
Jdt 8:26 and what happened to Jacob in S Mesopotamia,
1Mc 3:13 When Seron, the commander of the S army,
7:39 and the S army joined him.

SYRIANS (KJV) See ARAM, ARAMEAN[S], EDOMITES

SYROPHOENICIAN (1) [PHOENICIA, SYRIA]

Mk 7:26 Now the woman was a Gentile, of S origin.

SYRTIS (1)

Ac 27:17 then, fearing that they would run on the S,

SYZYGUS See Index to Footnotes

T

TAANACH (7)

Jos 12:21 the king of T one the king of Megiddo one
17:11 the inhabitants of T and its villages,
21:25 T with its pasture lands, and Gath-rimmon
Jdg 1:27 or T and its villages, or the inhabitants of Dor
5:19 then fought the kings of Canaan, at T,
1Ki 4:12 in T, Megiddo, and all Beth-shean,
1Ch 7:29 Beth-shean and its towns, T and its towns,

TAANATH-SHILOH (1)

Jos 16: 6 on the east the boundary makes a turn toward T,

TABBAOTH (3)

Ezr 2:43 the descendants of Ziha, Hasupha, T,
Ne 7:46 the descendants of Ziha, of Hasupha, of T,
1Es 5:29 the descendants of T, the descendants of Keros,

TABBATH (1)

Jdg 7:22 as far as the border of Abel-meholah, by T.

TABBUR-EREZ (1)

Jdg 9:37 "Look, people are coming down from T,

TABEEL (3)

Ezr 4: 7 Bishlam and Mithredath and T and the rest
Isa 7: 6 for ourselves and make the son of T king in it;
1Es 2:16 Bishlam, Mithridates, T, Rehum, Beltethmus,

TABERAH (2)

Nu 11: 3 So that place was called T, because the fire
Dt 9:22 At T also, and at Massah, and at Kibroth-hattaavah

TABERING (KJV) See BEATING

TABERNACLE‡ (112)

Ex 25: 9 that I show you concerning the pattern of the t
26: 1 Moreover you shall make the t with ten curtains
26: 6 so that the t may be one whole.
26: 7 of goats' hair for a tent over the t;
26:12 shall hang over the back of the t.
26:13 shall hang over the sides of the t,
26:15 of acacia wood for the t.
26:17 you shall make these for all the frames of the t.
26:18 You shall make the frames for the t:
26:20 and for the second side of the t,
26:22 rear of the t westward you shall make six frames.
26:23 You shall make two frames for corners of the t in
26:26 five for the frames of the one side of the t,
26:27 five bars for the frames of the other side of the t,
26:27 and five bars for the frames of the side of the t at
26:30 Then you shall erect the t according to the plan
26:35 the lampstand on the south side of the t opposite
27: 9 You shall make the court of the t.
27:19 All the utensils of the t for every use,
35:10 that the LORD has commanded: the t,
35:15 the screen for the entrance, the entrance of the t;
35:18 of the t and the pegs of the court, and their cords;
36: 8 All those with skill among the workers made the t
36:13 so the t was one whole.
36:14 of goats' hair for a tent over the t;
36:20 the upright frames for the t of acacia wood.
36:22 he did this for all the frames of the t.
36:23 The frames for the t he made in this way:
36:25 For the second side of the t, on the north side,
36:27 For the rear of the t westward he made six frames.
36:28 He made two frames for corners of the t in
36:31 five for the frames of the one side of the t,
36:32 five bars for the frames of the other side of the t,
36:32 for the frames of the t at the rear westward.
38:20 the pegs for the t and for the court all around were
38:21 the records of the t, the t of the covenant,
38:31 all the pegs of the t,
39:32 of the t of the tent of meeting was finished;
39:33 Then they brought the t to Moses,
39:40 and all the utensils for the service of the t,
40: 2 of the first month you shall set up the t of the tent
40: 5 and set up the screen for the entrance of the t.
40: 6 before the entrance of the t of the tent of meeting,
40: 9 and anoint the t and all that is in it,
40:17 on the first day of the month, the t was set up.
40:18 Moses set up the t; he laid its bases,
40:19 the tent over the t, and put the covering of the tent
40:21 into the t, and set up the curtain for screening,
40:22 on the north side of the t, outside the curtain,
40:24 opposite the table on the south side of the t,
40:28 in place the screen for the entrance of the t.
40:29 the altar of burnt offering at the entrance of the t
40:33 He set up the court around the t and the altar,
40:34 and the glory of the LORD filled the t.
40:35 and the glory of the LORD filled the t.
40:36 Whenever the cloud was taken up from the t,
40:38 For the cloud of the LORD was on the t by day,
Lev 8:10 the anointing oil and anointed the t and all
15:31 not die in their uncleanness by defiling my t
17: 4 to the LORD before the t of the LORD, he shall
Nu 1:50 Rather you shall appoint the Levites over the t of
1:50 they are to carry the t and all its equipment,
1:50 and shall camp around the t.
1:51 the t is to set out, the Levites shall take it down;
1:51 the t is to be pitched, the Levites shall set it up.
1:53 the t of the covenant, that there may be no wrath
1:53 the Levites shall perform the guard duty of the t
3: 7 of the tent of meeting, doing service at the t;
3: 8 for the Israelites as they do service at the t.
3:23 of the Gershonites were to camp behind the t on
3:25 of Gershon in the tent of meeting was to be the t,
3:26 that is around the t and the altar, and its cords—
3:29 to camp on the south side of the t,
3:35 they were to camp on the north side of the t.
3:36 the frames of the t, the bars, the pillars, the bases,
3:38 Those who were to camp in front of the t on
4:16 the oversight of all the t and all that is in it,
4:25 They shall carry the curtains of the t,
4:26 around the t and the altar, and their cords, and all
4:31 the frames of the t, with its bars, pillars,
Nu 5:17 the dust that is on the floor of the t and put it into
7: 1 the day when Moses had finished setting up the t,
7: 3 they presented them before the t.
9:15 the day the t was set up, the cloud covered the t,
9:15 and from evening until morning it was over the t,
9:18 As long as the cloud rested over the t,
9:19 when the cloud continued over the t many days,
9:20 the cloud would remain a few days over the t, and
9:22 that the cloud continued over the t,
10:11 the cloud lifted from over the t of the covenant.
10:17 Then the t was taken down,
10:17 who carried the t, set out.
10:21 and the t was set up before their arrival.
16: 9 in order to perform the duties of the LORD's t,
17:13 Everyone who approaches the t of
19:13 defile the t of the LORD;
31:30 to the Levites who have charge of the t of
31:47 to the Levites who had charge of the t of
Jos 22:19 into the LORD's land where the LORD's t
22:29 of the LORD our God that stands before his t!"
2Sa 7: 6 but I have been moving about in a tent and a t.
1Ch 6:32 They ministered with song before the t of the tent
6:48 for all the service of the t of the house of God.
16:39 the t of the LORD in the high place that was
17: 5 but I have lived in a tent and a t.
21:29 For the t of the LORD, which Moses had made
23:26 so the Levites no longer need to carry the t or any
2Ch 1: 5 was there in front of the t of the LORD.
La 2: 6 like a garden, he has destroyed his t;
Jdt 9: 8 to pollute the t where your glorious name resides,

TABERNACLES See Index to Footnotes

TABITHA (2) [=DORCAS]

Ac 9:36 in Joppa there was a disciple whose name was T,
9:40 He turned to the body and said, "T, get up."

TABLE (103) [TABLES]

Ge 43:34 Portions were taken to them from Joseph's t,
Ex 25:23 You shall make a t of acacia wood,
25:27 the poles used for carrying the t shall be close to
25:28 and the t shall be carried with these.
25:30 of the Presence on the t before me always.
26:35 You shall set the t outside the curtain,
26:35 on the south side of the tabernacle opposite the t;
26:35 and you shall put the t on the north side.
30:27 and the t and all its utensils,
31: 8 the t and its utensils, and the pure lampstand
35:13 the t with its poles and all its utensils,
37:10 He also made the t of acacia wood,
37:14 the poles used for carrying the t were close to
37:15 He made the poles of acacia wood to carry the t,
37:16 the vessels of pure gold that were to be on the t,
39:36 the t with all its utensils, and the bread of
40: 4 You shall bring in the t, and arrange its setting;
40:22 He put the t in the tent of meeting,
40:24 opposite the t on the south side of the tabernacle,
Lev 24: 6 six in a row, on the t of pure gold.
Nu 3:31 Their responsibility was to be the ark, the t,
4: 7 Over the t of the bread of the Presence
Jdg 1: 7 to pick up scraps under my t;
1Sa 20:29 For this reason he has not come to the king's t."
20:34 from the t in fierce anger and ate no food on
2Sa 9: 7 and you yourself shall eat at my t always."
9:10 Mephibosheth shall always eat at my t."
9:11 Mephibosheth ate at David's t,
9:13 for he always ate at the king's t.
19:28 among those who eat at your t.
1Ki 2: 7 and let them be among those who eat at your t;
4:27 for all who came to King Solomon's t, each one
7:48 the golden t for the bread of the Presence,
10: 5 the food of his t, the seating of his officials,
13:20 As they were sitting at the t,
18:19 prophets of Asherah, who eat at Jezebel's t."
2Ki 4:10 and put there for him a bed, a t, a chair,
1Ch 28:16 weight of gold for each t for the rows of bread,
2Ch 9: 4 the food of his t, the seating of his officials,
13:11 set out the rows of bread on the t of pure gold,
29:18 and the t for the rows of bread and all its utensils.
Ne 5:17 there were at my t one hundred fifty people,
Job 36:16 and what was set on your t was full of fatness.
Ps 23: 5 a t before me in the presence of my enemies;
69:22 Let their t be a trap for them,
78:19 saying, "Can God spread a t in the wilderness?
128: 3 be like olive shoots around your t.
Pr 9: 2 she has mixed her wine, she has also set her t.
Isa 21: 5 They prepare the t, they spread the rugs, they eat,
65:11 who set a t for Fortune and fill cups of mixed wine
Jer 52:33 of his life he dined regularly at the king's t.
Eze 23:41 with a t spread before it
39:20 be filled at my t with horses and charioteers,
41:22 "This is the t that stands before the LORD."
44:16 it is they who shall approach my t,
Da 11:27 shall sit at one t and exchange lies.
Mal 1: 7 By thinking that the LORD's t may be despised.
1:12 when you say that the Lord's t is polluted,
Mt 15:27 dogs eat the crumbs that fall from their masters' t."
26: 7 and she poured it on his head as he sat at the t.
Mk 7:28 the dogs under the t eat the children's crumbs."
14: 3 as he sat at the t, a woman came with an alabaster
16:14 ⟦as they were sitting at the t;⟧
Lk 5:29 of tax collectors and others sitting at the t
7:36 the Pharisee's house and took his place at the t.
7:49 But those who were at the t with him began to say
11:37 so he went in and took his place at the t.
Lk 14:10 be honored in the presence of all who sit at the t
16:21 with what fell from the rich man's t;
17: 7 'Come here at once and take your place at the t'?
22:14 When the hour came, he took his place at the t,
22:21 betrays me is with me, and his hand is on the t.
22:27 the one who is at the t or the one who serves?
22:27 Is it not the one at the t?
22:30 you may eat and drink at my t in my kingdom,
24:30 When he was at the t with them, he took bread,
Jn 12: 2 and Lazarus was one of those at the t with him.
13: 4 got up from the t, took off his outer robe, and tied
13:12 had put on his robe, and had returned to the t,
13:28 Now no one at the t knew why he said this to him.
Ro 11: 9 "Let their t become a snare and a trap,
1Co 10:21 of the t of the Lord and the table of demons.
10:21 of the table of the Lord and the t of demons.
Heb 9: 2 the first one, in which were the lampstand, the t,
Tob 2: 2 When the t was set for me and an abundance
9: 6 Raguel's house they found Tobias reclining at t.
Jdt 12: 1 to set a t for her with some of his own delicacies,
AdE 14:17 And your servant has not eaten at Haman's t,
Sir 6:10 And there are friends who sit at your t,
14:10 A miser begrudges bread, and it is lacking at his t.
29:26 prepare the t; let me eat what you have there."
30:25 Those who are cheerful and merry at t will benefit
31:12 Are you seated at the t of the great?
40:29 When one looks to the t of another,
Bel 1:13 beneath the t they had made a hidden entrance,
1:18 the king looked at the t,
1:21 to enter to consume what was on the t.
1Mc 1:22 He took also the t for the bread of the Presence,
4:49 the altar of incense, and the t into the temple.
4:51 They placed the bread on the t and hung up
11:58 He also sent him gold plate and a t service,
3Mc 5:39 But the officials who were at t with him,
2Es 9:19 with an unfailing t and an inexhaustible pasture,

TABLELAND (8) [LAND]

Dt 3:10 all the towns of the t,
4:43 Bezer in the wilderness on the t belonging to
Jos 13: 9 and all the t from Medeba as far as Dibon;
13:16 and all the t by Medeba;
13:17 and all its towns that are in the t;
13:21 all the towns of the t,
20: 8 they appointed Bezer in the wilderness on the t,
Jer 48:21 Judgment has come upon the t, upon Holon,

TABLES (17) [TABLE]

1Ch 28:16 the silver for the silver t,
2Ch 4: 8 He also made ten t and placed them in the temple,
4:19 golden altar, the t for the bread of the Presence,
Isa 28: 8 All t are covered with filthy vomit;
Eze 40:39 the vestibule of the gate were two t on either side,
40:40 at the entrance of the north gate were two t;
40:40 of the vestibule of the gate were two t.
40:41 Four t were on the inside,
40:41 and four t on the outside of the side of the gate,
40:41 of the gate, eight t, on which the sacrifices were
40:42 also four t of hewn stone for the burnt offering,
40:43 on the t the flesh of the offering was to be laid.
Mt 21:12 and he overturned the t of the money changers
Mk 11:15 and he overturned the t of the money changers
Jn 2:14 and the money changers seated at their t.
2:15 of the money changers and overturned their t.
Ac 6: 2 the word of God in order to wait on t.

TABLET (6) [TABLETS]

Pr 3: 3 write them on the t of your heart.
7: 3 write them on the t of your heart.
Isa 8: 1 a large t and write on it in common characters,
30: 8 Go now, write it before them on a t,
Jer 17: 1 with a diamond point it is engraved on the t
Lk 1:63 He asked for a writing t and wrote,

TABLETS (43) [TABLET]

Ex 24:12 and I will give you the t of stone,
31:18 he gave him the two t of the covenant,
31:18 t of stone, written with the finger of God.
32:15 carrying the two t of the covenant in his hands,
32:15 t that were written on both sides,
32:16 The t were the work of God,
32:16 the writing of God, engraved upon the t.
32:19 and he threw the t from his hands and broke them
34: 1 "Cut two t of stone like the former ones,
34: 1 on the t the words that were on the former t,
34: 4 So Moses cut two t of stone like the former ones;
34: 4 and took in his hand the two t of stone.
34:28 And he wrote on the t the words of the covenant,
34:29 from the mountain with the two t of the covenant
Dt 4:13 and he wrote them on two stone t.
5:22 He wrote them on two stone t,
9: 9 to receive the stone t, the t of the covenant that
9:10 the LORD gave me the two stone t written with
9:11 the LORD gave me the two stone t, the t of the
9:15 the two t of the covenant were in my two hands.
9:17 of the two t and flung them from my two hands,
10: 1 "Carve out two t of stone like the former ones,
10: 2 on the t the words that were on the former tablets,
10: 2 on the tablets the words that were on the former t,
10: 3 cut two t of stone like the former ones,
10: 3 went up the mountain with the two t in my hand.
10: 4 Then he wrote on the t the same words as before,
10: 5 and put the t in the ark that I had made;
1Ki 8: 9 the two t of stone that Moses had placed there
2Ch 5:10 in the ark except the two t that Moses put there

Hab 2: 2 make it plain on **t**, so that a runner may read it.
2Co 3: 3 not on **t** of stone but on **t** of human hearts.
3: 7 ministry of death, chiseled in letters on stone **t**,
Heb 9: 4 and the **t** of the covenant;
1Mc 8:22 on bronze **t**, and sent to Jerusalem to remain
14:18 they wrote to him on bronze **t** to renew with him
14:27 on bronze **t** and put it on pillars on Mount Zion.
14:48 to inscribe this decree on bronze **t**,
2Es 14:24 But prepare for yourself many writing **t**,

TABOR (10) [AZNOTH-TABOR, CHISLOTH-TABOR]

Jos 19:22 also touches **T**, Shahazumah, and Beth-shemesh,
Jdg 4: 6 commands you, 'Go, take position at Mount **T**,
4:12 of Abinoam had gone up to Mount **T**,
4:14 So Barak went down from Mount **T**
8:18 "What about the men whom you killed at **T**?"
1Sa 10: 3 on from there further and come to the oak of **T**;
1Ch 6:77 with its pasture lands, **T** with its pasture lands,
Ps 89:12 **T** and Hermon joyously praise your name.
Jer 46:18 one is coming like **T** among the mountains,
Hos 5: 1 a snare at Mizpah, and a net spread upon **T**,

TABRET[S] (KJV) See BYWORD, TAMBOURINE[S], TIMBRELS, SETTINGS

TABRIMMON (1)

1Ki 15:18 to King Ben-hadad son of **T** son of Hezion

TACHES (KJV) See CLASP, CLASPS, HOOKS

TACHMONITE (KJV) See TAHCHEMONITE

TACKLE (1)

Ac 27:19 their own hands they threw the ship's **t** overboard.

TADMOR (1)

2Ch 8: 4 He built **T** in the wilderness and all

TAHAN (2) [TAHANITES]

Nu 26:35 of **T**, the clan of the Tahanites.
1Ch 7:25 Resheph his son, Telah his son, **T** his son,

TAHANITES (1) [TAHAN]

Nu 26:35 of Tahan, the clan of the **T**.

TAHAPANES (KJV) See TAHPANHES

TAHASH (1)

Ge 22:24 bore Tebah, Gaham, **T**, and Maacah.

TAHATH (6)

Nu 33:26 They set out from Makheloth and camped at **T**.
33:27 They set out from **T** and camped at Terah.
1Ch 6:24 **T** his son, Uriel his son, Uzziah his son,
6:37 son of **T**, son of Assir, son of Ebiasaph, son
7:20 his son, **T** his son, Eleadah his son, **T** his son,

TAHCHEMONITE (1)

2Sa 23: 8 warriors whom David had: Josheb-basshebeth a **T**;

TAHPANHES (7) [=TEHAPHNEHES]

Jer 2:16 and **T** have broken the crown of your head.
43: 7 And they arrived at **T**.
43: 8 the word of the LORD came to Jeremiah in **T**:
43: 9 that is at the entrance to Pharaoh's palace in **T**.
44: 1 at **T**, at Memphis, and in the land of Pathros,
46:14 proclaim in Memphis and **T**;
Jdt 1: 9 **T** and Raamses and the whole land of Goshen,

TAHPENES (3)

1Ki 11:19 for a wife, the sister of Queen **T**.
11:20 sister of **T** gave birth by him to his son Genubath,
11:20 whom **T** weaned in Pharaoh's house;

TAHREA (1) [=TAREA]

1Ch 9:41 The sons of Micah: Pithon, Melech, **T**, and Ahaz;

TAHTIM-HODSHI See Index to Footnotes

TAIL (15) [TAILS]

Ex 4: 4 "Reach out your hand, and seize it by the **t**"—
29:22 You shall also take the fat of the ram, the fat **t**,
Lev 3: 9 the whole broad **t**, which shall be removed close
7: 3 the broad **t**, the fat that covers the entrails,
8:25 He took the fat—the broad **t**,
9:19 the broad **t**, the fat that covers the entrails,
Dt 28:13 LORD will make you the head, and not the **t**;
28:44 they shall be the head and you shall be the **t**.
Jdg 15: 4 and he turned the foxes **t** to **t**,
Job 40:17 It makes its **t** stiff like a cedar;
Isa 9:14 So the LORD cut off from Israel head and **t**,
9:15 and prophets who teach lies are the **t**;
19:15 Neither head nor **t**, palm branch or reed,
Rev 12: 4 His **t** swept down a third of the stars of heaven

TAILS (5) [TAIL]

Jdg 15: 4 and put a torch between each pair of **t**.
Rev 9:10 They have **t** like scorpions, with stingers,
9:10 and in their **t** is their power to harm people
9:19 of the horses is in their mouths and in their **t**;
9:19 their **t** are like serpents, having heads;

TAKE‡ (977) [TAKEN, TAKES, TAKING, TOOK]

Ge 3:22 now, he might reach out his hand and **t** also from
6:21 Also **t** with you every kind of food that is eaten,
7: 2 **T** with you seven pairs of all clean animals,
12:19 Now then, here is your wife, **t** her, and be gone."
13: 9 If you **t** the left hand, then I will go to the right;
13: 9 if you **t** the right hand, then I will go to the left."
14:21 but **t** the goods for yourself."
14:23 that I would not **t** a thread or a sandal-thong
14:24 I will **t** nothing but what the young men have eaten
14:24 Let them **t** their share."
18:27 "Let me **t** it upon myself to speak to the Lord,
18:31 "Let me **t** it upon myself to speak to the Lord.
19:15 **t** your wife and your two daughters who are here,
22: 2 He said, "**T** your son, your only son Isaac,
24: 5 must I then **t** your son back to the land
24: 6 "See to it that you do not **t** my son back there.
24: 7 and you shall **t** a wife for my son from there.
24: 8 only you must not **t** my son back there."
24:37 not **t** a wife for my son from the daughters of
24:51 Look, Rebekah is before you, **t** her and go,
27: 3 Now then, **t** your weapons,
27:10 and you shall **t** it to your father to eat,
28: 2 and **t** as wife from there one of the daughters
28: 4 that you may **t** possession of the land where you
28: 6 and sent him away to Paddan-aram to **t** a wife
30:15 Would you **t** away my son's mandrakes also?"
31:24 "**T** heed that you say not a word to Jacob,
31:29 to me last night, saying, '**T** heed that you speak
31:31 for I thought that you would **t** your daughters
31:32 point out what I have that is yours, and **t** it."
31:50 or if you **t** wives in addition to my daughters,
34: 9 and **t** our daughters for yourselves.
34:16 and we will **t** your daughters for ourselves,
34:17 then we will **t** our daughter and be gone."
34:21 let us **t** their daughters in marriage,
37:21 saying, "Let us not **t** his life."
38:25 And she said, "**T** note, please, whose these are,
41:34 and **t** one-fifth of the produce of the land of Egypt
42:33 **t** grain for the famine of your households,
42:36 and now you would **t** Benjamin.
43:11 **t** some of the choice fruits of the land
43:12 **T** double the money with you.
43:13 **T** your brother also, and be on your way again to
43:18 to make slaves of us and **t** our donkeys."
44:29 If you **t** this one also from me,
45:18 **T** your father and your households and come
45:19 **t** wagons from the land of Egypt
Ex 2: 9 "**T** this child and nurse it for me,
4: 9 you shall **t** some water from the Nile and pour it
4: 9 that you shall **t** from the Nile will become blood
4:17 **T** in your hand this staff,
6: 7 I will **t** you as my people, and I will be your God.
7: 9 '**T** your staff and throw it down before Pharaoh,
7:15 at the river bank to meet him, and **t** in your hand
7:19 '**T** your staff and stretch out your hand over
7:23 and he did not **t** even this to heart.
8: 8 "Pray to the LORD to **t** away the frogs from me
9: 8 "**T** handfuls of soot from the kiln,
10:28 **T** care that you do not see my face again,
12: 3 that on the tenth of this month they are to **t** a lamb
12: 5 you may **t** it from the sheep or from the goats.
12: 7 They shall **t** some of the blood and put it on
12:22 **T** a bunch of hyssop, dip it in the blood that is in
12:32 **T** your flocks and your herds, as you said,
12:46 not **t** any of the animal outside the house,
13:19 saying, "God will surely **t** notice of you,
16:33 And Moses said to Aaron, "**T** a jar,
17: 5 and **t** some of the elders of Israel with you;
17: 5 **t** in your hand the staff with which you struck
21:14 you shall **t** the killer from my altar for execution.
22:26 If you **t** your neighbor's cloak in pawn,
23: 8 You shall **t** no bribe, for a bribe blinds
23:25 and I will **t** sickness away from among you.
25: 2 Tell the Israelites to **t** for me an offering;
28: 9 You shall **t** two onyx stones,
28:38 and Aaron shall **t** on himself any guilt incurred in
29: 1 **T** one young bull and two rams without blemish,
29: 5 Then you shall **t** the vestments,
29: 7 You shall **t** the anointing oil,
29:12 and shall **t** some of the blood of the bull and put it
29:13 You shall **t** all the fat that covers the entrails,
29:15 Then you shall **t** one of the rams,
29:16 and shall **t** its blood and dash it against all sides of
29:19 You shall **t** the other ram;
29:20 and **t** some of its blood and put it on the lobe
29:21 you shall **t** some of the blood that is on the altar,
29:22 You shall also **t** the fat of the ram, the fat tail,
29:25 Then you shall **t** them from their hands,
29:26 You shall **t** the breast of the ram
29:31 You shall **t** the ram of ordination,
30:12 you **t** a census of the Israelites to register them,
30:16 You shall **t** the atonement money from
30:23 **T** the finest spices: of liquid myrrh
30:34 **T** sweet spices, stacte, and onycha, and galbanum,
32: 2 "**T** off the gold rings that are on the ears
32:24 So I said to them, 'Whoever has gold, **t** it off';
Ex 33: 5 So now **t** off your ornaments,
33: 7 Now Moses used to **t** the tent and pitch it outside
33:23 I will **t** away my hand, and you shall see my back;
34: 9 and **t** us for your inheritance."
34:12 **T** care not to make a covenant with the inhabitants
34:16 And you will **t** wives from among their daughters
34:34 he would **t** the veil off, until he came out;
35: 5 **T** from among you an offering to the LORD;
40: 9 Then you shall **t** the anointing oil,
Lev 2: 8 he shall **t** it to the altar.
4: 5 The anointed priest shall **t** some of the blood of
4:25 The priest shall **t** some of the blood of
4:30 The priest shall **t** some of its blood with his finger
4:34 The priest shall **t** some of the blood of
6:10 and he shall **t** up the ashes to which
6:11 Then he shall **t** off his vestments and put
6:15 They shall **t** from it a handful of the choice flour
8: 2 **T** Aaron and his sons with him, the vestments,
8:33 For it will **t** seven days to ordain you;
9: 2 "**T** a bull calf for a sin offering and a ram for
9: 3 '**T** a male goat for a sin offering;
10:12 **T** the grain offering that is left from
12: 8 she shall **t** two turtledoves or two pigeons,
14: 6 He shall **t** the living bird with the cedarwood and
14:10 On the eighth day he shall **t** two male lambs
14:12 The priest shall **t** one of the lambs,
14:14 The priest shall **t** some of the blood of
14:15 The priest shall **t** some of the log of oil
14:21 he shall **t** one male lamb for a guilt offering to
14:24 and the priest shall **t** the lamb of the guilt offering
14:25 and shall **t** some of the blood of the guilt offering,
14:42 They shall **t** other stones and put them in
14:42 and **t** other plaster and plaster the house.
14:49 the cleansing of the house he shall **t** two birds,
14:51 and shall **t** the cedarwood and the hyssop and
15:14 On the eighth day he shall **t** two turtledoves
15:29 On the eighth day she shall **t** two turtledoves
16: 5 He shall **t** from the congregation of the people
16: 7 He shall **t** the two goats and set them before
16:12 He shall **t** a censer full of coals of fire from
16:14 He shall **t** some of the blood of the bull,
16:18 and shall **t** some of the blood of the bull and of
16:23 and shall **t** off the linen vestments that he put on
18:17 and you shall not **t** her son's daughter
18:18 you shall not **t** a woman as a rival to her sister,
19:18 not **t** vengeance or bear a grudge against any
23:40 the first day you shall **t** the fruit of majestic trees,
24: 5 You shall **t** choice flour, and bake twelve loaves
24:14 **T** the blasphemer outside the camp;
25:36 Do not **t** interest in advance or otherwise make
Nu 1: 2 **T** a census of the whole congregation of Israelites,
1:49 not **t** a census of them with the other Israelites.
1:51 tabernacle is to set out, the Levites shall **t** it down;
4: 2 **T** a census of the Kohathites separate from
4: 5 in and **t** down the screening curtain, and cover
4: 9 They shall **t** a blue cloth, and cover the lampstand
4:12 and they shall **t** all the utensils of the service
4:13 They shall **t** away the ashes from the altar,
4:22 **T** a census of the Gershonites also,
5:17 the priest shall **t** holy water in an earthen vessel,
5:17 and **t** some of the dust that is on the floor of
5:19 Then the priest shall make her **t** an oath, saying,
5:21 the priest make the woman **t** the oath of the curse
5:25 The priest shall **t** the grain offering
5:26 the priest shall **t** a handful of the grain offering,
6:18 and shall **t** the hair from the consecrated head
6:19 The priest shall **t** the shoulder of the ram,
6:21 This is the law for the nazirites who **t** a vow.
6:21 In accordance with whatever vow they **t**,
8: 6 **T** the Levites from among the Israelites
8: 8 Then let them **t** a young bull and its grain offering
8: 8 you shall **t** another young bull for a sin offering.
11:16 and have them **t** their place there with you.
11:17 and I will **t** some of the spirit that is on you
16: 6 Do this: **t** censers, Korah and all your company,
16:17 of you **t** his censer, and put incense on it,
16:37 the priest to **t** the censers out of the blaze;
16:46 Moses said to Aaron, "**T** your censer,
18: 6 It is I who now **t** your brother Levites from
19: 4 The priest Eleazar shall **t** some of its blood
19: 6 The priest shall **t** cedarwood, hyssop,
19:17 For the unclean they shall **t** some ashes of
19:18 then a clean person shall **t** hyssop,
20: 8 **T** the staff, and assemble the congregation, you
20:25 **T** Aaron and his son Eleazar,
21: 7 to the LORD to **t** away the serpents from us."
23:12 "Must I not **t** care to say what the LORD puts
23:27 "Come now, I will **t** you to another place;
24:22 How long shall Asshur **t** you away captive?"
25: 4 "**T** all the chiefs of the people,
26: 2 "**T** a census of the whole congregation of
26: 4 "**T** a census of the people,
27:18 the LORD said to Moses, "**T** Joshua son of Nun,
28: 2 by fire, my pleasing odor, you shall **t** care to offer
31:29 **T** it from their half and give it to Eleazar the priest
31:30 But from the Israelites' half you shall **t** one out
32:17 but we will **t** up arms as a vanguard before
32:20 if you **t** up arms to go before the LORD for
33:53 You shall **t** possession of the land and settle in it,
34:18 You shall **t** one leader of every tribe to apportion
35: 8 from the larger tribes you shall **t** many, and from the smaller tribes you shall **t** few;
Dt 1: 8 go in and **t** possession of the land that I swore
1:21 go up, **t** possession, as the LORD,
1:33 to show you the route you should **t**."
1:39 and they shall **t** possession of it.
2:24 Begin to **t** possession by engaging him in battle.

Dt 2:31 Begin now to t possession of his land."
3: 4 there was no citadel that we did not t
4: 2 to what I command you nor t away anything
4: 9 But t care and watch yourselves closely,
4:15 t care and watch yourselves closely,
4:22 but you are going to cross over to t possession of
4:34 to go and t a nation for himself from the midst
4:39 and t to heart that the LORD is God in heaven
6:12 t care that you do not forget the LORD,
7:25 on them and t it for yourself, because you could
8:11 T care that you do not forget
11:16 T care, or you will be seduced into turning away,
12:13 T care that you do not offer your burnt offerings
12:19 T care that you do not neglect the Levite as long
12:30 t care that you are not snared into imitating them,
12:32 do not add to it or t anything from it.
13: 2 omens or the portents declared by them t place,
15:17 then you shall t an awl and thrust it
18:22 of the LORD but the thing does not t place
20: 9 then the commanders shall t charge of them.
20:14 You may, however, t as your booty the women,
20:19 making war against it in order to t it,
20:19 Although you may t food from them,
21: 3 The elders of the town nearest the body shall t
21:10 over to you and you t them captive,
21:19 then his father and his mother shall t hold of him
22: 1 you shall t them back to their owner.
22: 6 you shall not t the mother with the young.
22:18 of that town shall t the man and punish him;
24: 4 is not permitted to t her again to be his wife
24: 6 No one shall t a mill or an upper millstone
24:10 you shall not go into the house to t the pledge.
24:17 you shall not t a widow's garment in pledge.
26: 2 you shall t some of the first of all the fruit of
28:42 the fruit of your ground the cicada shall t over.
28:63 the LORD will t delight in bringing you to ruin
30: 9 the LORD will again t delight in prospering you,
31:26 "T this book of the law and put it beside the ark of
32:41 I will t vengeance on my adversaries,
32:43 and t vengeance on his adversaries;
32:46 "T to heart all the words that I am giving
Jos 1:11 the Jordan, to go in to t possession of the land that
1:15 and they too t possession of the land that
1:15 to your own land and t possession of it,
3: 6 "T up the ark of the covenant,
4: 3 'T twelve stones from here out of the middle of
4: 5 and each of you t up a stone on his shoulder,
6: 6 "T up the ark of the covenant,
6:18 to covet and t any of the devoted things and make
7:13 to stand before your enemies until you t away
8: 1 t all the fighting men with you,
8: 2 only its spoil and its livestock you may t as booty
9:11 'T provisions in your hand for the journey;
17:12 Manassites could not t possession of those towns;
22: 5 T good care to observe the commandment
22:19 and t for yourselves a possession among us;
22:23 may the LORD himself t vengeance.
Jdg 2: 6 to their own inheritances to t possession of
2:22 or not they would t care to walk in the way of
4: 6 commands you, 'Go, t position at Mount Tabor,
6:20 "T the meat and the unleavened cakes,
6:25 the LORD said to him, "T your father's bull,
6:26 then t the second bull, and offer it as
7: 2 Israel would only t the credit away from me,
7: 4 t them down to the water and I will sift them out
9:15 then come and t refuge in my shade;
11:15 Israel did not t away the land of Moab or the land
11:23 Do you intend to t their place?
11:35 and I cannot t back my vow."
14: 3 to t a wife from the uncircumcised Philistines?"
15: 2 Why not t her instead?"
18:17 to spy out the land proceeded to enter and t
18:24 He replied, "You t my gods that I made,
19:18 Nobody has offered to t me in.
19:30 Consider it, t counsel, and speak out.' "
20:10 We will t ten men of a hundred throughout all
Ru 2:10 that you should t notice of me,
4: 6 T my right of redemption yourself,
1Sa 2:14 the fork brought up the priest would t for himself.
2:16 burn the fat first, and then t whatever you wish,"
2:16 if not, I will t it by force."
2:19 for him a little robe and t it to him each year,
4: 9 T courage, and be men, O Philistines,
6: 7 but t their calves home, away from them.
6: 8 T the ark of the LORD and place it on the cart,
6:21 Come down and t it up to you."
8:11 he will t your sons and appoint them
8:13 He will t your daughters to be perfumers
8:14 He will t the best of your fields and vineyards
8:15 He will t one-tenth of your grain and
8:16 He will t your male and female slaves,
8:17 He will t one-tenth of your flocks,
9: 3 "T one of the boys with you;
12: 7 Now therefore t your stand,
12:16 therefore t your stand and see this great thing that
16: 2 And the LORD said, "T a heifer with you,
17:17 "T for your brothers an ephah
17:18 also t these ten cheeses to the commander
19:14 When Saul sent messengers to t David, she said,
19:20 Then Saul sent messengers to t David.
20: 1 against your father that he is trying to t my life?"
21: 9 if you will t that, t it,
24:11 though you are hunting me to t my life.
25:11 Shall I t my bread and my water and the meat
25:25 My lord, do not t seriously this ill-natured fellow,
25:40 "David has sent us to you to t you to him
26:11 but now t the spear that is at his head,
1Sa 29:10 As for the evil report, do not t it to heart,
30:15 "Will you t me down to this raiding party?"
30:15 and I will t you down to them."
30:22 except that each man may t his wife and children,
2Sa 2:21 and seize one of the young men, and t his spoil."
4: 6 They came inside the house as though to t wheat,
6:10 So David was unwilling to t the ark of the LORD
7:15 But I will not t my steadfast love from him,
12: 4 and he was loath to t one of his own flock or herd
12:11 and I will t your wives before your eyes,
12:28 and encamp against the city, and t it;
12:28 or I myself will t the city,
13:20 do not t this to heart."
13:33 therefore, do not let my lord the king t it to heart,
14:14 But God will not t away a life;
15: 5 he would put out his hand and t hold of them,
15:20 Go back, and t your kinsfolk with you;
15:26 But if he says, 'I t no pleasure in you,' here I am,
16: 9 Let me go over and t off his head."
19:30 Mephibosheth said to the king, "Let him t it all,
20: 6 t your lord's servants and pursue him,
22: 3 my rock, in whom I t refuge,
22:31 he is a shield for all who t refuge in him.
24: 2 and t a census of the people,
24: 4 of the king to t a census of the people of Israel.
24:10 I pray you, t away the guilt of your servant;
24:22 the king t and offer up what seems good to him;
1Ki 1:33 "T with you the servants of your lord,
2: 4 'If your heirs t heed to their way,
2:31 and thus t away from me and
5: 9 up there for you to t away.
11:31 T for yourself ten pieces;
11:34 Nevertheless I will not t the whole kingdom away
11:35 but I will t the kingdom away from his son
11:37 I will t you, and you shall reign over all
14: 3 T with you ten loaves, some cakes,
19: 4 now, O LORD, t away my life,
19:10 and they are seeking my life, to t it away."
19:14 and they are seeking my life, to t it away."
20: 6 on whatever pleases them, and t it away."
20:12 he said to his men, "T your positions!"
20:18 "If they have come out for peace, t them alive;
20:18 if they have come out for war, t them alive."
21:10 Then t him out, and stone him to death."
21:15 t possession of the vineyard of Naboth
21:16 of Naboth the Jezreelite, to t possession of it.
21:18 where he has gone to t possession.
22: 3 yet we are doing nothing to t it out of the hand of
22:26 The king of Israel then ordered, "T Micaiah,
2Ki 2: 1 the LORD was about to t Elijah up to heaven by
2: 3 the LORD will t your master away from you?"
2: 5 the LORD will t your master away from you?"
4: 1 creditor has come to t my two children as slaves."
4:29 "Gird up your loins, and t my staff in your hand,
4:36 When she came to him, he said, "T your son."
6: 9 "T care not to pass this place,
6:32 this murderer has sent someone to t off my head?
7:12 we shall t them alive and get into the city.' "
7:13 "Let some men t five of the remaining horses,
8: 8 "T a present with you and go to meet the man
9: 1 t this flask of oil in your hand,
9: 2 and t him into an inner chamber.
9: 3 Then t the flask of oil, pour it on his head,
9:17 Joram said, "T a horseman;
10: 6 t the heads of your master's sons and come to me
10:14 He said, "T them alive."
13:15 Elisha said to him, "T a bow and arrows";
13:18 He continued, "T the arrows"; and he took them.
18:32 and t you away to a land like your own land,
19:30 the house of Judah shall again t root downward,
20: 7 Let them t it and apply it to the boil,
1Ch 13:13 not t the ark into his care into the city of David;
17:13 I will not t my steadfast love from him,
21: 8 now, I pray you, t away the guilt of your servant;
21:11 "Thus says the LORD, 'T your choice:
21:23 Then Ornan said to David, "T it;
21:24 I will not t for the LORD what is yours,
28:10 T heed now, for the LORD has chosen you
29:17 and t pleasure in uprightness;
2Ch 2:16 you will t it up to Jerusalem."
6:22 and is required to t an oath and comes and swears
15: 7 But you, t courage!
18:25 The king of Israel then ordered, "T Micaiah,
19: 7 t care what you do, for there is no perversion
20:17 This battle is not for you to fight; t your position,
20:25 and his people came to t the booty from them,
24:11 the chest and t it and return it to its place.
32:18 in order that they might t the city.
35: 5 T position in the holy place according to
35:23 and the king said to his servants, "T me away,
36: 6 and bound him with fetters to t him to Babylon.
Ezr 4:22 Moreover, t care not to be slack in this matter;
5:15 He said to him, "T these vessels;
9:12 neither t their daughters for your sons,
10: 4 T action, for it is your duty, and we are with you;
Ne 5:12 made them t an oath to do as they had promised.
10:30 to the peoples of the land or t their daughters
13:25 and I made them t an oath in the name of God,
13:25 t their daughters for your sons or for yourselves.
Est 2:13 to t with her from the harem to the king's palace.
4: 4 so that he might t off his sackcloth;
6:10 t the robes and the horse, as you have said,
8:13 the Jews were to be ready on that day to t revenge
Job 5: 5 and they t it even out of the thorns;
7:21 pardon my transgression and t away my iniquity?
8:20 nor t the hand of evildoers.
9:34 If he would t his rod away from me,
Job 11:18 you will be protected and t your rest in safety.
13:14 I will t my flesh in my teeth,
23:10 But he knows the way that I t;
24: 3 they t the widow's ox for a pledge.
24: 9 and t as a pledge the infant of the poor.
27:10 Will they t delight in the Almighty?
33: 5 in order before me; t your stand.
34: 9 'It profits one nothing to t delight in God.'
34:14 If he should t back his spirit to himself,
38:13 so that it might t hold of the skirts of the earth,
38:20 that you may t it to its territory and
40:24 Can one t it with hooks or pierce its nose with
42: 8 Now therefore t seven bulls and seven rams,
Ps 1: 1 or t the path that sinners tread,
2: 2 and the rulers t counsel together,
2:12 Happy are all who t refuge in him.
5:11 But let all who t refuge in you rejoice;
7: 1 O LORD my God, in you I t refuge;
7: 7 and over it t your seat on high.
10:14 that you may t it into your hands;
11: 1 In the LORD I t refuge;
15: 3 nor t up a reproach against their neighbors;
15: 5 and do not t a bribe against the innocent.
16: 1 Protect me, O God, for in you I t refuge.
16: 4 I will not pour out or t their names upon my lips.
18: 2 my God, my rock in whom I t refuge, my shield,
18:30 he is a shield for all who t refuge in him.
20: 7 Some t pride in chariots, and some in horses,
25:20 not let me be put to shame, for I t refuge in you.
27:10 the LORD will t me up.
27:14 be strong, and let your heart t courage;
31: 4 t me out of the net that is hidden for me,
31:13 as they plot to t my life.
31:19 and accomplished for those who t refuge in you,
31:24 Be strong, and let your heart t courage,
34: 8 happy are those who t refuge in him.
34:22 of those who t refuge in him will be condemned.
35: 2 T hold of shield and buckler,
36: 7 All people may t refuge in the shadow
37: 4 T delight in the LORD, and he will give you
37:40 and saves them, because they t refuge in him.
43: 2 For you are the God in whom I t refuge;
50:16 or t my covenant on your lips?
51:11 and do not t your holy spirit from me.
52: 7 "See the one who would not t refuge in God,
57: 1 in the shadow of your wings I will t refuge,
62: 4 They t pleasure in falsehood;
64:10 the righteous rejoice in the LORD and t refuge
71: 1 In you, O LORD, I t refuge;
83:12 "Let us t the pastures of God
102:24 "do not t me away at the mid-point of my life,
104: 7 at the sound of your thunder they t to flight.
104:29 when you t away their breath,
118: 8 to t refuge in the LORD than to put confidence
118: 9 to t refuge in the LORD than to put confidence
119:22 t away from me their scorn and contempt,
119:43 not t the word of truth utterly out of my mouth,
119:52 of your ordinances from of old, I t comfort,
137: 9 be who t your little ones and dash them against
139: 9 If I t the wings of the morning and settle at
144: 2 my shield, in whom I t refuge,
Pr 5:10 and strangers will t their fill of your wealth,
7:18 Come, let us t our fill of love until morning;
8:10 T my instruction instead of silver,
13:10 but wisdom is with those who t advice.
20:16 T the garment of one who has given surety for
25: 4 T away the dross from the silver,
25: 5 t away the wicked from the presence of the king,
27:13 T the garment of one who has given surety for
30: 5 he is a shield to those who t refuge in him.
Ecc 3:13 that all should eat and drink and t pleasure
4:13 who will no longer t advice.
5:15 they shall t nothing for their toil,
7:18 It is good that you should t hold of the one,
Isa 3:18 the Lord will t away the finery of the anklets,
4: 1 Seven women shall t hold of one man in that day,
4: 1 be called by your name; t away our disgrace."
7: 4 T heed, be quiet, do not fear,
7:20 and it will t off the beard as well.
8: 1 T a large tablet and write on it
8:10 T counsel together, but it shall be brought
10: 6 to t spoil and seize plunder,
14: 2 nations will t them and bring them to their place,
14: 2 they will t captive those who were their captors,
14: 4 you will t up this taunt against the king
20: 2 from your loins and t your sandals off your feet,"
23:16 T a harp, go about the city,
25: 8 the disgrace of his people he will t away from all
27: 6 In days to come Jacob shall t root,
28:19 As often as it passes through, it will t you;
30: 2 to t refuge in the protection of Pharaoh,
36:17 and t you away to a land like your own land,
37:31 the house of Judah shall again t root downward,
38:21 Now Isaiah had said, "Let them t a lump of figs,
41: 6 saying to one another, "T courage!"
42:25 it burned him, but he did not t it to heart.
45:21 let them t counsel together!
47: 2 T the millstones and grind meal,
47: 3 I will t vengeance, and I will spare no one.
51:18 there is no one to t her by the hand among all
57:13 a breath will t them away.
58:14 then you shall t delight in the LORD,
62: 6 You who remind the LORD, t no rest,
64: 6 and our iniquities, like the wind, t us away.
64: 7 or attempts to t hold of you;
66: 3 and in their abominations they t delight;
66:21 also t some of them as priests and as Levites,

Jer 3:14 I will **t** you, one from a city and two from
5: 1 the streets of Jerusalem, look around and **t** note!
5: 3 but they refused to **t** correction.
5:26 they **t** over the goods of others.
6: 8 **T** warning, O Jerusalem, or I shall turn from you
6:10 they **t** no pleasure in it.
9:10 **T** up weeping and wailing for the mountains,
12: 2 You plant them, and they **t** root;
13: 4 "**T** the loincloth that you bought and are wearing,
13: 6 and **t** from there the loincloth
13:18 and the queen mother; "**T** a lowly seat,
13:21 Will not pangs **t** hold of you,
15:15 In your forbearance do not **t** me away;
15:19 If you turn back, I will **t** you back,
16: 2 You shall not **t** a wife,
17:21 of your lives, **t** care that you do not bear a burden
19: 1 **T** with you some of the elders of the people
20:10 and **t** our revenge on him."
25:15 **T** from my hand this cup of the wine of wrath,
27:20 of Babylon did not **t** away when he took into exile
29: 6 **T** wives and have sons and daughters;
29: 6 **t** wives for your sons, and give your daughters
30: 3 to their ancestors and they shall **t** possession of it.
31: 4 Again you shall **t** your tambourines,
32: 3 the hand of the king of Babylon, and he shall **t** it;
32: 5 and he shall **t** Zedekiah to Babylon,
32:14 **T** these deeds, both this sealed deed of purchase
32:24 have been cast up against the city to **t** it,
32:28 Nebuchadrezzar of Babylon, and he shall **t** it.
34:22 and they will fight against it, and **t** it,
36: 2 **T** a scroll and write on it all the words
36:28 **T** another scroll and write on it all the former
37: 8 they shall **t** it and burn it with fire.
38:10 "**T** three men with you from here,
39: 7 and bound him in fetters to **t** him to Babylon.
39:12 "**T** him, look after him well and do him no harm,
40: 4 come, and I will **t** good care of you;
40:14 Ishmael son of Nethaniah to **t** your life?"
40:15 Why should he **t** your life,
43: 3 in order that they may kill us or **t** us into exile
43: 9 **T** some large stones in your hands,
43:10 to send and **t** my servant King Nebuchadrezzar
44:12 I will **t** the remnant of Judah who are determined
46: 4 **T** your stations with your helmets,
46:11 Go up to Gilead, and **t** balm,
46:14 Say, "**T** your stations and be ready,
49:29 **T** their tents and their flocks,
50:14 **T** up your positions around Babylon,
50:15 **t** vengeance on her, do to her as she has done.
51:36 I am going to defend your cause and **t** vengeance
Eze 4: 1 And you, O mortal, **t** a brick and set it before you.
4: 3 Then **t** an iron plate and place it as an iron wall
4: 9 And you, **t** wheat and barley, beans and lentils,
5: 1 And you, O mortal, **t** a sharp sword;
5: 1 then **t** balances for weighing, and divide the hair.
5: 2 one third you shall **t** and strike with the sword all
5: 3 Then you shall **t** from these a small number,
5: 4 From these, again, you shall **t** some,
7:24 of the nations to **t** possession of their houses.
10: 6 "**T** fire from within the wheelwork,
11: 9 I will **t** you out of it and give you over to
14: 4 of those of the house of Israel who **t** their idols
14: 5 that I may **t** hold of the hearts of the house
15: 3 Does one **t** a peg from it on which
16:39 and **t** your beautiful objects and leave you naked
16:61 and be ashamed when I **t** your sisters,
17:22 I myself will **t** a sprig from the lofty top of a cedar;
18: 8 does not **t** advance or accrued interest,
21:26 Remove the turban, **t** off the crown;
22:12 In you, they **t** bribes to shed blood;
22:12 you **t** both advance interest and accrued interest,
23:26 of your clothes and **t** away your fine jewels.
23:29 and **t** away all the fruit of your labor,
23:48 so that all women may **t** warning and
24: 5 **T** the choicest one of the flock,
24: 8 To rouse my wrath, to **t** vengeance,
24:16 about to **t** away from you the delight of your eyes;
24:25 on the day when I **t** from them their stronghold,
33: 2 of the land **t** one of their number as their sentinel;
33: 4 the sound of the trumpet do not **t** warning,
33: 5 the sound of the trumpet and did not **t** warning;
35:10 and we will **t** possession of them,"—
36:24 I will **t** you from the nations,
37:16 **t** a stick and write on it, "For Judah,
37:16 then **t** another stick and write on it,
37:19 about to **t** the stick of Joseph (which is in the hand
37:21 I will **t** the people of Israel from the nations
38:13 to **t** away cattle and goods,
39:10 to **t** wood out of the field or cut down any trees in
43:20 And you shall **t** some of its blood,
43:21 You shall also **t** the bull of the sin offering,
45:18 you shall **t** a young bull without blemish,
45:19 The priest shall **t** some of the blood of
46: 2 and shall **t** his stand by the post of the gate.
46:18 The prince shall not **t** any of the inheritance of
Da 2: 9 and misleading words to me until things **t** a turn.
8:19 and I will tell you what will **t** place later in
11: 3 who shall rule with great dominion and **t** action
11: 7 and he shall **t** action against them and prevail.
11:15 and **t** a well-fortified city.
11:16 against him shall **t** the actions he pleases,
11:16 He shall **t** a position in the beautiful land,
11:30 be enraged and **t** action against the holy covenant.
11:32 to their God shall stand firm and **t** action.
Hos 1: 2 **t** for yourself a wife of whoredom
1:11 and they shall **t** possession of the land,
2: 9 Therefore I will **t** back my grain in its time,
Hos 2: 9 and I will **t** away my wool and my flax,
2:19 And I will **t** you for my wife forever;
2:19 I will **t** you for my wife in righteousness and
2:20 I will **t** you for my wife in faithfulness;
4:11 Wine and new wine **t** away the understanding.
14: 2 **T** words with you and return to the LORD;
14: 2 say to him, "**T** away all guilt;
Am 4: 2 when they shall **t** you away with hooks,
5: 1 Hear this word that I **t** up over you in lamentation,
5:11 Therefore because you trample on the poor and **t**
5:12 you who afflict the righteous, who **t** a bribe,
5:21 and I **t** no delight in your solemn assemblies.
5:23 **T** away from me the noise of your songs;
5:26 You shall **t** up Sakkuth your king,
5:27 therefore I will **t** you into exile beyond Damascus,
6:10 shall **t** up the body to bring it out of the house,
9: 2 from there shall my hand **t** them;
9: 3 from there I will search out and **t** them;
Ob 1:17 and the house of Jacob shall **t** possession
Jnh 4: 3 And now, O LORD, please **t** my life from me,
Mic 2: 2 houses, and **t** them away;
2: 4 that day they shall **t** up a taunt song against you,
2: 9 from their young children you **t** away my glory
Na 1: 7 he protects those who **t** refuge in him,
3:14 tread the mortar, **t** hold of the brick mold!
Hab 1:10 and heap up earth to **t** it.
Hag 1: 8 so that I may **t** pleasure in it and be honored,
2: 4 now **t** courage, O Zerubbabel, says the LORD;
2: 4 **t** courage, O Joshua, son of Jehozadak,
2: 4 **t** courage, all you people of the land,
2:23 I will **t** you, O Zerubbabel my servant,
Zec 3: 4 "**T** off his filthy clothes."
6:11 **T** the silver and gold and make a crown,
8:23 nations of every language shall **t** hold of a Jew,
9: 7 I will **t** away its blood from its mouth,
11:15 **T** once more the implements of
Mal 2:16 So **t** heed to yourselves and do not be faithless.
Mt 1:20 do not be afraid to **t** Mary as your wife,
2:13 **t** the child and his mother, and flee to Egypt,
2:20 **t** the child and his mother, and go to the land
5:40 and if anyone wants to sue you and **t** your coat,
7: 4 'Let me **t** the speck out of your eye,'
7: 5 You hypocrite, first **t** the log out of your own eye,
and then you will see clearly to **t** the speck out
7:13 and there are many who **t** it.
9: 2 "**T** heart, son; your sins are forgiven."
9: 6 "Stand up, **t** your bed and go to your home."
9:22 Jesus turned, and seeing her he said, "**T** heart,
10: 9 **T** no gold, or silver, or copper in your belts,
10:38 not **t** up the cross and follow me is not worthy
11:12 and the violent **t** it by force.
11:29 **T** my yoke upon you, and learn from me;
14:27 "**T** heart, it is I; do not be afraid."
15:26 "It is not fair to **t** the children's food and throw it
16:24 let them deny themselves and **t** up their cross
17:25 From whom do kings of the earth **t** toll or tribute?
17:27 **t** the first fish that comes up;
17:27 **t** that and give it to them for you and me."
18:10 "**T** care that you do not despise one
18:16 **t** one or two others along with you,
20:14 **T** what belongs to you and go;
24: 6 for this must **t** place, but the end is not yet.
24:17 on the housetop must not go down to **t** what is in
24:25 **T** note, I have told you beforehand.
25:28 So **t** the talent from him,
25:44 and did not **t** care of you?'
26:26 gave it to the disciples, and said, "**T**, eat;
26:52 for all who **t** the sword will perish by the sword.
Mk 2: 9 or to say, 'Stand up and **t** your mat and walk'?
2:11 stand up, **t** your mat and go to your home."
6: 8 to **t** nothing for their journey except a staff;
6:50 immediately he spoke to them and said, "**T** heart,
7:27 to **t** the children's food and throw it to the dogs."
8:34 let them deny themselves and **t** up their cross
10:49 they called the blind man, saying to him, "**T** heart;
11: 6 and they allowed them to **t** it.
13: 7 this must **t** place, but the end is still to come.
13:15 down or enter the house to **t** anything away;
14:22 gave it to them, and said, "**T**; this is my body."
15:23 but he did not **t** it.
15:24 casting lots to decide what each should **t**.
15:36 let us see whether Elijah will come to **t** him down."
Lk 5:24 stand up and **t** your bed and go to your home."
6:42 'Friend, let me **t** out the speck in your eye,'
6:42 You hypocrite, first **t** the log out of your own eye,
6:42 and then you will see clearly to **t** the speck out
9: 3 He said to them, "**T** nothing for your journey,
9:23 and **t** up their cross daily and follow me.
10:35 to the innkeeper, and said, '**T** care of him;
12:15 And he said to them, "**T** care!
14: 9 in disgrace you would start to **t** the lowest place.
16: 6 He said to him, '**T** your bill, sit down quickly,
16: 7 He said to him, '**T** your bill and make it eighty.'
17: 7 'Come here at once and **t** your place at the table'?
17:31 in the house must not come down to **t** them away;
19:17 in a very small thing, **t** charge of ten cities.'
19:21 you **t** what you did not deposit,
19:24 '**T** the pound from him and give it to
21: 7 what will be the sign that this is about to **t** place?"
21: 9 for these things must **t** place first,
21:28 Now when these things begin to **t** place,
21:36 to escape all these things that will **t** place,
22:17 "**T** this and divide it among yourselves;
22:36 "But now, the one who has a purse must **t** it,
Jn 2: 8 and **t** it to the chief steward."
2:16 "**T** these things out of here!
5: 8 "Stand up, **t** your mat and walk."
Jn 5:11 '**T** up your mat and walk.' "
5:12 the man who said to you, '**T** it up and walk'?"
6:15 that they were about to come and **t** him by force
6:21 Then they wanted to **t** him into the boat,
10:17 I lay down my life in order to **t** it up again.
10:18 and I have power to **t** it up again.
11:39 Jesus said, "**T** away the stone."
14: 3 I will come again and will **t** you to myself,
16:14 he will **t** what is mine and declare it to you.
16:15 that he will **t** what is mine and declare it to you.
16:22 and no one will **t** your joy from you.
16:33 But **t** courage; I have conquered the world!"
17:15 I am not asking you to **t** them out of the world,
18:31 "**T** him yourselves and judge him according
19: 6 "**T** him yourselves and crucify him;
19:38 asked Pilate to let him **t** away the body of Jesus.
20:15 and I will **t** him away."
21:18 around you and **t** you where you do not wish
Ac 1:20 and 'Let another **t** his position of overseer.'
1:25 to **t** the place in this ministry and apostleship
4:28 and your plan had predestined to **t** place.
7:33 '**T** off the sandals from your feet,
15:14 to **t** from among them a people for his name.
15:37 to **t** with them John called Mark.
15:38 not to **t** with them one who had deserted them
16:37 Let them come and **t** us out themselves."
20:13 intending to **t** Paul on board there;
23:10 ordered the soldiers to go down, **t** him by force,
23:17 "**T** this young man to the tribune,
23:24 and **t** him safely to Felix the governor."
26:22 the prophets and Moses said would **t** place:
27:33 Paul urged all of them to **t** some food, saying,
27:34 Therefore I urge you to **t** some food,
Ro 11:27 when I **t** away their sins."
12:17 but **t** thought for what is noble in the sight of all.
1Co 6: 1 do you dare to **t** it to court before the unrighteous,
6:15 Should I therefore **t** the members of Christ
8: 9 But **t** care that this liberty of yours does
16: 3 with letters to **t** your gift to Jerusalem.
2Co 10: 5 and we **t** every thought captive to obey Christ.
12:17 Did I **t** advantage of you through any
12:18 Titus did not **t** advantage of you, did he?
12:18 Did we not **t** the same steps?
Gal 5:15 **t** care that you are not consumed by one another.
6: 1 **T** care that you yourselves are not tempted.
Eph 5:11 **T** no part in the unfruitful works of darkness,
6:13 Therefore **t** up the whole armor of God,
6:16 With all of these, **t** the shield of faith,
6:17 **T** the helmet of salvation,
2Th 3:14 **T** note of those who do not obey what we say
1Ti 3: 5 how can he **t** care of God's church?
5:23 but **t** a little wine for the sake of your stomach
6: 7 so that we can **t** nothing out of it;
6:12 **t** hold of the eternal life,
6:19 that they may **t** hold of the life that really is life.
Heb 3:12 **T** care, brothers and sisters,
4: 1 let us **t** care that none of you should seem
5: 4 And one does not presume to **t** this honor,
10: 4 for the blood of bulls and goats to **t** away sins.
10:11 the same sacrifices that can never **t** away sins.
Jas 2: 3 if you **t** notice of the one wearing the fine clothes
5:10 **t** the prophets who spoke in the name of the Lord.
1Jn 3: 5 You know that he was revealed to **t** away sins,
Rev 1: 1 to show his servants what must soon **t** place;
1:19 what is, and what is to **t** place after this.
4: 1 and I will show you what must **t** place after this."
5: 9 "You are worthy to **t** the scroll and
6: 4 its rider was permitted to **t** peace from the earth,
10: 8 **t** the scroll that is open in the hand of
10: 9 and he said to me, "**T** it, and eat;
18: 4 my people, so that you do not **t** part in her sins,
22: 6 to show his servants what must soon **t** place."
22:17 Let anyone who wishes **t** the water of life as
22:19 God will **t** away that person's share in the tree
Tob 3:15 if it is not pleasing to you, O Lord, to **t** my life,
4:13 to **t** a wife for yourself from among them.
5: 8 but do not **t** too long."
5:10 But the young man said, "**T** courage;
5:10 for God to heal you; **t** courage."
6: 5 "Cut open the fish and **t** out its gall, heart,
6:13 "You have every right to **t** her in marriage.
6:13 so that we may **t** her to be your bride.
6:13 And when we return from Rages we will **t** her
6:16 to **t** a wife from your father's house?
6:16 and say no more about this demon. **T** her.
6:17 **t** some of the fish's liver and heart,
7: 1 **t** me straight to our brother Raguel."
7:11 to you. **T** your kinswoman;
7:12 "**T** her to be your wife in accordance with the law
7:12 **T** her and bring her safely to your father.
7:15 "Sister, get the other room ready, and **t** her there."
7:16 she said to her, "**T** courage, my daughter;
7:16 **T** courage, my daughter."
8:21 **T** at once half of what I own and return in safety
8:21 when my wife and I die. **T** courage, my child.
8:21 to your wife now and forever. **T** courage, my child.
9: 2 **t** four servants and two camels with you
11:11 he blew into his eyes, saying, "**T** courage, father."
12: 5 "**T** for your wages half of all
14: 3 gave this command: "My son, **t** your children
14: 4 that all these things will **t** place
Jdt 1:12 that he would **t** revenge on the whole territory
2: 5 Leave my presence and **t** with you men confident
2:13 **t** care not to transgress any
6: 5 until I **t** revenge on this race that came out
6: 7 to **t** you back into the hill country and put you
6:10 and **t** him away to Bethulia and hand him over to

Jdt 7:12 let your servants t possession of the spring
8:30 and made us t an oath that we cannot break.
8:35 to t vengeance on our enemies."
9: 2 to t revenge on those strangers who had torn off
11: 1 Then Holofernes said to her, "T courage, woman,
11: 3 you have come to safety. T courage!
14: 1 T this head and hang it upon the parapet
14: 2 each of you t up your weapons,
16: 4 and t my virgins as spoil.
16:17 The Lord Almighty will t vengeance on them in
AdE 4:15 the messenger this answer to t back to Mordecai:
15: 9 I am your husband. T courage;
16: 4 They not only t away thankfulness from others,
16: 8 In the future we will t care
Wis 2: 7 Let us t our fill of costly wine and perfumes,
4: 3 a deep root or t a firm hold.
4:15 or t such a thing to heart,
5:17 The Lord will t his zeal as his whole armor,
5:19 he will t holiness as an invincible shield,
8: 2 I desired to t her for my bride,
8: 9 Therefore I determined to t her to live with me,
13:18 a prosperous journey, a thing that cannot t a step;
14:19 the likeness to t more beautiful form,
Sir 12:11 t care to be on your guard against him.
12:12 or he may overthrow you and t your place.
12:12 or else he may try to t your own seat,
13: 8 T care not to be led astray and humiliated
14:16 Give, and t, and indulge yourself,
18:19 and before you fall ill, t care of your health.
18:31 If you allow your soul to t pleasure in base desire,
19: 3 Decay and worms will t possession of him,
19:17 and let the law of the Most High t its course.
19:27 he will t advantage of you.
22:22 in these cases any friend will t to flight.
23:25 Her children will not t root,
25: 1 I t pleasure in three things,
28:26 T care not to err with your tongue,
30:23 Indulge yourself and t comfort,
32: 1 T care of them first and then sit down;
32: 2 t your place, so that you may be merry along
33:21 do not let anyone t your place.
34:26 To t away a neighbor's living is to commit murder;
36:23 The stomach will t any food,
37: 8 for he will t thought for himself.
39:31 They t delight in doing his bidding,
46: 1 to t vengeance on the enemies that rose
47: 4 and t away the people's disgrace,
Bar 4: 2 Turn, O Jacob, and t her;
4: 5 T courage, my people, who perpetuate Israel's
4:21 T courage, my children, cry to God,
4:27 T courage, my children, and cry to God,
4:30 T courage, O Jerusalem,
4:34 I will t away her pride in her great population,
5: 1 T off the garment of your sorrow and affliction,
LtJ 6: 9 People t gold and make crowns for the heads
6:10 Sometimes the priests secretly t gold and silver
6:33 The priests t some of the clothing of their gods
6:38 They cannot t pity on a widow or do good to
Bel 1:33 and was going into the field to t it to the reapers.
1:34 "T the food that you have to Babylon, to Daniel,
1:37 T the food that God has sent you."
1Mc 3:15 to t vengeance on the Israelites.
3:33 to t care of his son Antiochus until he returned.
3:50 Where shall we t them?
5:19 and he gave them this command, "T charge
6: 3 So he came and tried to t the city and plunder it,
6:26 against the citadel in Jerusalem to t it;
7: 9 and he commanded him to t vengeance on
7:38 T vengeance on this man and on his army,
9:30 therefore we have chosen you today to t his place
10:20 and you are to t our side and keep friendship
10:43 And all who t refuge at the temple in Jerusalem,
10:62 The king gave orders to t off Jonathan's garments
11:37 Now therefore t care to make a copy of this,
14: 2 he sent one of his generals to t him alive.
14:42 be governor over them and that he should t charge
14:42 and that he should t charge of the sanctuary,
15:40 to provoke the people and invade Judea and t
16: 3 T my place and my brother's,
16:20 to t possession of Jerusalem and the temple hill.
2Mc 2: 1 to t some of the fire,
2:30 and to t trouble with details,
4:14 they hurried to t part in the unlawful proceedings
6:15 that he may not t vengeance on us afterward
7: 5 the king ordered them to t him to the fire,
7:24 that he would t him for his Friend and entrust him
9:21 and I have deemed it necessary to t thought for
10:24 He came on, intending to t Judea by storm.
11: 7 Maccabeus himself was the first to t up arms,
12:35 wishing to t the accursed man alive,
12:39 and his men went to t up the bodies of the fallen
13: 4 he ordered them to t him to Beroea and to put him
14: 9 may it please you to t thought for our country
15: 5 to t up arms and finish the king's business."
15:16 "T this holy sword, a gift from God,
1Es 1:30 "T me away from the battle, for I am very weak."
2:28 the city and to t care that nothing more be done
4: 5 whatever spoil they t and everything else.
4:30 and t the crown from the king's head and put it
5: 2 a thousand cavalry to t them back to Jerusalem
6:19 that he should t all these vessels back
8:19 they shall t care to give him,
8:83 'The land that you are entering to t possession
8:84 and do not t their daughters for your descendants;
8:93 Let us t an oath to the Lord about this,
8:95 Rise up and t action, for it is your task,
8:95 and we are with you to t strong measures."
3Mc 1:14 that it was wrong to t that as a portent.
1:23 They shouted to their compatriots to t arms
4:17 that they were no longer able to t the census of
2Es 2:11 Moreover, I will t back to myself their glory,
2:40 T again your full number, O Zion,
3:20 you did not t away their evil heart from them,
7:*135* [65] because he would rather give than t away;
8:27 Do not t note of the endeavors
8:41 and not all that were planted will t root;
9:47 when he grew up and I came to t a wife for him,
12:46 "T courage, O Israel;
13:32 When these things t place and the signs occur
14:16 now seen happen shall t place hereafter.
14:24 and t with you Sarea, Dabria, Selemia, Ethanus,
16:46 and t their children captive;
4Mc 6:29 and t my life in exchange for theirs."
8:10 Therefore t pity on yourselves.
8:18 why do we t pleasure in vain resolves and venture
8:20 Let us t pity on our youth and have compassion
8:24 against compulsion or t hollow pride in being put
9: 7 and if you t our lives because of our religion,
9:24 and t vengeance on the accursed tyrant."
12:18 but on you he will t vengeance both
17: 4 T courage, therefore, O holy-minded mother,

TAKEN‡ (344) [TAKE]

Ge 2:22 the LORD God had t from the man he made into
2:23 for out of Man this one was t."
3:19 for out of it you were t;
3:23 to till the ground from which he was t.
12:15 And the woman was t into Pharaoh's house.
14:14 Abram heard that his nephew had been t captive,
20: 3 to die because of the woman whom you have t;
27:35 and he has t away your blessing."
27:36 and look, now he has t away my blessing."
30:15 a small matter that you have t away my husband?
30:23 and said, "God has t away my reproach";
31: 1 "Jacob has t all that was our father's;
31: 9 Thus God has t away the livestock of your father,
31:16 that God has t away from our father belongs to us
31:34 Now Rachel had t the household gods
37:32 the long robe with sleeves t to their father,
39: 1 Now Joseph was t down to Egypt, and Potiphar,
43:34 Portions were t to them from Joseph's table,
Ex 14:11 that you have t us away to die in the wilderness?
25:15 they shall not be t from it.
40:36 Whenever the cloud was t up from the tabernacle,
40:37 but if the cloud was not t up,
40:37 they did not set out until the day that it was t up.
Lev 7:34 For I have t the breast of the elevation offering,
14:40 be t out and thrown into an unclean place outside
14:43 after he has t out the stones and scraped the house
14:45 and t outside the city to an unclean place.
16:27 shall be t outside the camp;
25:37 not lend them your money at interest t in advance,
Nu 8:16 I have t them for myself,
8:18 but I have t the Levites in place of all the firstborn
10:17 Then the tabernacle was t down,
16:15 I have not t one donkey from them,
19: 3 and it shall be t outside the camp and slaughtered
27: 4 be t away from his clan because he had no son?
31:32 had t totaled six hundred seventy-five thousand
31:53 (The troops had all t plunder for themselves.)
34:14 by their ancestral houses have t their inheritance,
34:15 and the half-tribe have t their inheritance beyond
36: 3 be t from the inheritance of our ancestors
36: 3 so it will be t away from the allotted portion
36: 4 be t from the inheritance of our ancestral tribe."
Dt 4:20 But the LORD has t you and brought you out of
17:14 and have t possession of it and settled in it,
17:18 When he has t the throne of his kingdom,
19:12 of the killer's city shall send to have the culprit t
Jos 4:20 which they had t out of the Jordan,
7:11 They have t some of the devoted things;
7:15 And the one who is t as having
7:16 and the tribe of Judah was t.
7:17 and the clan of the Zerahites was t;
7:17 family by family, and Zabdi was t.
7:18 of the tribe of Judah, was t.
8: 8 And when you have t the city,
8:21 that the ambush had t the city and that the smoke
8:23 the king of Ai was t alive and brought to Joshua.
10: 1 of Jerusalem heard how Joshua had t Ai,
11:19 of Gibeon; all were t in battle.
20: 4 then the fugitive shall be t into the city,
21:43 and having t possession of it, they settled there.
22: 9 of which they had t possession by command of
Jdg 8:24 each of you give me an earring he has t as booty."
8:25 each threw into it an earring he had t as booty.
14: 9 But he did not tell them that he had t the honey
15: 6 because he has t Samson's wife and given her
15: 7 I swear I will not stop until I have t revenge
17: 2 "The eleven hundred pieces of silver that were t
18:27 The Danites, having t what Micah had made,
21: 5 a solemn oath had been t concerning whoever did
1Sa 7:14 that the Philistines had t from Israel were restored
10:20 and the tribe of Benjamin was t by lot.
10:21 and the family of the Matrites was t by lot.
10:21 and Saul the son of Kish was t by lot.
12: 3 Whose ox have I t?
12: 3 Or whose donkey have I t?
12: 3 from whose hand have I t a bribe to blind my eyes
12: 4 not defrauded us or oppressed us or t anything
14:30 if today the troops had eaten freely of the spoil t
14:42 and my son Jonathan." And Jonathan was t.
14:47 When Saul had t the kingship over Israel,
1Sa 21: 6 be replaced by hot bread on the day it is t away.
28:21 I have t my life in my hand,
30: 2 and t captive the women and all who were in it,
30: 3 and their wives and sons and daughters t captive.
30: 5 David's two wives also had been t captive,
30:16 When he had t him down,
30:16 of spoil they had t from the land of the Philistines
30:18 David recovered all that the Amalekites had t;
30:19 spoil or anything that had been t;
2Sa 2: 8 had t Ishbaal son of Saul, and brought him over
12: 9 and have t his wife to be your wife,
12:10 and have t the wife of Uriah the Hittite to
12:27 moreover, I have t the water city.
18:18 in his lifetime had t and set up for himself a pillar
19:24 he had not t care of his feet, or trimmed his beard,
1Ki 4:15 (he had t Basemath, Solomon's daughter, as his
7: 8 whom he had t in marriage.
8:47 to which they have been t captive, and repent,
15:14 But the high places were not t away.
16:18 When Zimri saw that the city was t,
21:19 Have you killed, and also t possession?"
22:43 yet the high places were not t away,
2Ki 2: 9 before I am t from you."
2:10 yet, if you see me as I am being t from you,
4:13 Since you have t all this trouble for us,
5: 2 on one of their raids had t a young girl captive
12: 3 Nevertheless the high places were not t away;
13:25 the towns that he had t from his father Jehoahaz
15: 4 Nevertheless the high places were not t away;
18:10 of King Hoshea of Israel, Samaria was t.
20:18 to you shall be t away;
24: 7 the king of Babylon had t over all that belonged
1Ch 9: 1 And Judah was t into exile in Babylon because
9:28 when they were brought in and t out.
2Ch 2:17 after the census that his father David had t;
6:37 to which they have been t captive, and repent,
6:38 to which they were t captive,
15: 8 and Benjamin and from the towns that he had t in
15:17 But the high places were not t out of Israel.
17: 2 in the cities of Ephraim that his father Asa had t.
20:21 When he had t counsel with the people,
28:11 the captives whom you have t from your kindred,
28:18 and had t Beth-shemesh, Aijalon, Gederoth,
30: 2 in Jerusalem had t counsel to keep the passover in
Ezr 5:14 which Nebuchadnezzar had t out of the temple
9: 2 For they have t some of their daughters as wives
10:14 in our towns who have t foreign wives come
Est 2: 8 Esther also was t into the king's palace and put
2:16 When Esther was t to King Ahasuerus
8: 2 which he had t from Haman,
Job 1:21 the LORD gave, and the LORD has t away;
19: 9 and t the crown from my head.
27: 2 who has t away my right, and the Almighty,
28: 2 Iron is t out of the earth,
30:16 days of affliction have t hold of me.
34: 5 'I am innocent, and God has t away my right;
34:20 and the mighty are t away by no human hand.
41: 4 with you to be t as your servant forever?
Ps 30:11 you have t off my sackcloth and clothed me
31: 7 you have t heed of my adversities,
82: 1 God has t his place in the divine council;
Pr 11: 6 but the treacherous are t captive by their schemes.
22:27 why should your bed be t from under you?
24:11 if you hold back from rescuing those t away
Ecc 3:14 nothing can be added to it, nor anything t from it;
7:26 but the sinner is t by her.
9:12 Like fish t in a cruel net,
Isa 6: 6 that had been t from the altar with a pair of tongs.
8:15 they shall be snared and t.
16:10 and gladness are t away from the fruitful field;
22: 8 He has t away the covering of Judah.
28: 9 from milk, those t from the breast?
28:13 and be broken, and snared, and t.
28:15 and in falsehood we have t shelter";
39: 7 to you shall be t away;
40:24 scarcely has their stem t root in the earth,
42: 6 I have t you by the hand and kept you;
49:24 Can the prey be t from the mighty,
49:25 Even the captives of the mighty shall be t,
51:22 I have t from your hand the cup of staggering;
52: 5 seeing that my people are t away without cause?
53: 8 By a perversion of justice he was t away.
57: 1 the devout are t away, while no one understands.
57: 1 For the righteous are t away from calamity,
Jer 6:11 both husband and wife shall be t,
6:24 anguish has t hold of us, pain as of a woman in
8: 9 they shall be dismayed and t;
8:21 I mourn, and dismay has t hold of me.
13:17 because the LORD's flock has been t captive.
13:19 all Judah is t into exile, wholly t into exile.
16: 5 for I have t away my peace from this people,
24: 1 after King Nebuchadrezzar of Babylon had t
29: 1 whom Nebuchadnezzar had t into exile
38: 3 over to the army of the king of Babylon and be t.
38:28 of the guard until the day that Jerusalem was t.
39: 3 When Jerusalem was t, all the officials of
39: 5 and when they had t him,
40: 7 the land who had not been t into exile to Babylon,
40:10 and live in the towns that you have t over."
48: 1 Kiriathaim is put to shame, it is t;
48: 7 and your treasures, you also shall be t;
48:33 and joy have been t away from the fruitful land
48:41 the towns shall be t and the strongholds seized.
48:46 for your sons have been t captive,
49:24 anguish and sorrows have t hold of her,
50: 2 Babylon is t, Bel is put to shame,
50: 9 from there she shall be t.

Jer 51:26 be t from you for a corner and no stone for
51:31 the king of Babylon that his city is t from end
51:41 Sheshach is t, the pride of the whole earth seized!
51:56 her warriors are t, their bows are broken;
La 3:58 You have t up my cause, O Lord,
4:20 the breath of our life, was t in their pits—
Eze 11: 7 but you shall be t out of it.
14: 3 these men have t their idols into their hearts,
15: 3 Is wood t from it to make anything?
17:13 under oath (he had t away the chief men of
21:24 to remembrance, you shall be t in hand.
22:25 they have t treasure and precious things;
33: 5 But if they had t warning,
33: 6 they are t away in their iniquity,
33:15 give back what they have t by robbery,
Da 5: 2 that his father Nebuchadnezzar had t out of
5: 3 the vessels of gold and silver that had been t out
6:23 and commanded that Daniel be t up out of
6:23 So Daniel was t up out of the den,
7:12 the rest of the beasts, their dominion was t away,
7:26 and his dominion shall be t away,
12:11 the time that the regular burnt offering is t away
Joel 3: 5 For you have t my silver and my gold,
Am 2: 8 down beside every altar on garments t in pledge;
3: 5 up from the ground, when it has t nothing?
6:13 by our own strength t Karnaim for ourselves?"
Hab 2: 6 How long will you load yourselves with goods t
Zep 3:15 LORD has t away the judgments against you,
Zec 3: 4 "See, I have t your guilt away from you,
14: 1 plunder t from you will be divided in your midst.
14: 2 be t and the houses looted and the women raped;
Mal 1:13 You bring what has been t by violence or is lame
Mt 9:15 when the bridegroom is t away from them,
13:12 even what they have will be t away.
18:31 and reported to their lord all that had t place.
21:43 the kingdom of God will be t away from you
23:30 not have t part with them in shedding the blood of
24:34 not pass away until all these things have t place.
24:40 one will be t and one will be left.
24:41 one will be t and one will be left.
25:29 even what they have will be t away.
26:56 But all this has t place,
Mk 2:20 when the bridegroom is t away from them,
4:25 even what they have will be t away."
11:23 'Be t up and thrown into the sea,'
13:30 not pass away until all these things have t place.
14:18 And when they had t their places and were eating,
16:19 ⟦was t up into heaven and sat down at the right⟧
Lk 2: 2 and was t while Quirinius was governor of Syria.
2:15 to Bethlehem and see this thing that has t place,
5: 9 at the catch of fish that they had t;
5:35 when the bridegroom will be t away from them,
8:18 even what they seem to have will be t away."
9: 7 Herod the ruler heard about all that had t place,
9:51 When the days drew near for him to be t up,
10:42 which will not be t away from her."
11:52 For you have t away the key of knowledge;
17:34 one will be t and the other left.
17:35 one will be t and the other left."
19:26 even what they have will be t away.
21:24 the edge of the sword and be t away as captives
21:32 not pass away until all things have t place.
23:19 in prison for an insurrection that had t place in
23:47 When the centurion saw what had t place,
23:48 for this spectacle saw what had t place,
24:18 the things that have t place there in these days?"
Jn 20: 2 "They have t the Lord out of the tomb,
20:13 She said to them, "They have t away my Lord,
Ac 1: 2 until the day when he was t up to heaven,
1:11 who has been t up from you into heaven,
1:22 of John until the day when he was t up from us—
8:33 For his life is t away from the earth."
10:16 and the thing was suddenly t up to heaven.
17: 9 after they had t bail from Jason and the others,
20:12 Meanwhile they had t the boy away alive
1Co 16: 2 so that collections need not be t when I come.
2Co 5: 3 when we have t it off we will not be found naked.
7: 2 we have t advantage of no one.
1Ti 3:16 believed in throughout the world, t up in glory.
2Ti 2:18 that the resurrection has already t place
Heb 6:18 we who have t refuge might
10: 6 and sin offerings you have t no pleasure.
10: 8 "You have neither desired nor t pleasure
11: 5 By faith Enoch was t so that he did
11: 5 and "he was not found, because God had t him."
11: 5 before he was t away that "he had pleased God."
12: 2 and has t his seat at the right hand of the throne
Rev 5: 8 When he had t the scroll,
11:17 you have t your great power and begun to reign.
12: 5 But her child was snatched away and t to God and
13:10 If you are to be t captive, into captivity you go;
Tob 1: 2 of the Assyrians was t into captivity from Thisbe,
1:20 not t into the royal treasury except my wife Anna
3: 6 command my spirit to be t from me,
10: 7 and watch the road her son had t,
14: 4 be scattered and t as captives from the good land;
14:15 those whom King Cyaxares of Media had t captive.
Jdt 4:12 to be carried off and their wives to be t as booty,
6: 9 in your heart that they will not be t,
6:13 So having t shelter below the hill,
6:17 He answered and told them what had t place at
8:27 nor has he t vengeance on us;
15: 4 to tell what had t place and to urge all to rush out
16:19 and the canopy that she had t for herself
AdE 2: 6 he had been t captive from Jerusalem
8: 2 king took the ring that had been t from Haman,
Wis 4:10 and while living among sinners were t up.
14:15 who had been suddenly t from him;
15: 8 while go to the earth from which all mortals are t,
Sir 3:28 for an evil plant has t root in him.
31: 7 and every fool will be t captive by it.
31:27 Wine is very life to human beings if t
38:19 When a person is t away, sorrow is over;
42:21 Nothing can be added or t away,
44:16 Enoch pleased the Lord and was t up,
46:19 as a pair of shoes, have I t from anyone!"
48: 9 You were t up by a whirlwind of fire,
49:14 for he was t up from the earth.
Bar 2:17 whose spirit has been t from their bodies,
3:29 Who has gone up into heaven, and t her,
4:20 I have t off the robe of peace and put on sackcloth
4:26 they were t away like a flock carried off by
LtJ 6: 1 to those who were to be t to Babylon as exiles by
6: 2 be t to Babylon as exiles by Nebuchadnezzar,
6:43 of them is led off by one of the passers-by and is t
1Mc 2:11 All her adornment has been t away;
2:58 of great zeal for the law, was t up into heaven.
3:45 Joy was t from Jacob; the flute and the harp ceased
6: 6 and abundant spoils that they had t from
9:72 to him the captives whom he had t previously
10:33 of the Jews t as a captive from the land of Judah
10:52 and have t my seat on the throne of my ancestors,
10:53 we have t our seat on the throne of his kingdom—
10:84 and those who had t refuge in it,
15:29 and you have t possession of many places
15:33 "We have neither t foreign land
15:33 at one time had been unjustly t by our enemies.
2Mc 5: 5 and at last the city was being t,
6: 7 the Jews were t, under bitter constraint,
7:27 and have t care of you.
12: 6 and massacred those who had t refuge there.
14: 2 and had t possession of the country,
1Es 4:44 and to send back all the vessels that were t
6:18 which Nebuchadnezzar had t out of the house
6:32 be t out of the house of the perpetrator,
3Mc 1: 5 and many captives also were t.
2:28 Those who object to this are to be t by force
3:10 and friends and business associates had t some
3:24 we have t precautions so that,
7: 7 and since we have t into account the friendly
2Es 1:32 but you have t and killed them
6:26 And they shall see those who were t up,
8:19 of the words of Ezra's prayer, before he was t up.
13:40 that were t away from their own land into exile in
13:40 and they were t into another land.
14: 9 for you shall be t up from among humankind,

TAKES‡ (75) [TAKE]

Ex 21:10 If he t another wife to himself,
Lev 20:14 man t a wife and her mother also, it is depravity;
20:17 If a man t his sister, a daughter of his father or
20:21 If a man t his brother's wife, it is impurity;
Nu 15:14 or who t up permanent residence among you,
Dt 1: 2 (By the way of Mount Seir it t eleven days
10:17 who is not partial and t no bribe,
19:11 with another lies in wait and attacks and t the life
26: 4 the priest t the basket from your hand and sets it
27:25 be anyone who t a bribe to shed innocent blood."
32:11 as it spreads its wings, t them up,
32:41 and my hand t hold on judgment;
Jos 7:14 tribe that the LORD t shall come near by clans,
7:14 that the LORD t shall come near by households,
7:14 and the household that the LORD t shall come
15:16 "Whoever attacks Kiriath-sepher and t it,
Jdg 1:12 "Whoever attacks Kiriath-sepher and t it,
1Sa 17:26 and t away the reproach from Israel?
1Ki 20:11 on armor should not brag like one who t it off."
Job 5:13 He t the wise in their own craftiness;
12:20 and t away the discernment of the elders.
27: 8 when God t away their lives?
30:17 and the pain that gnaws me t no rest.
Ps 40:17 but the Lord t thought for me.
57: 1 be merciful to me, for in you my soul t refuge;
142: 4 there is no one who t notice of me;
147:11 but the LORD t pleasure in those who fear him,
149: 4 For the LORD t pleasure in his people;
Pr 1:19 it t away the life of its possessors.
6:34 and he shows no restraint when he t revenge.
8: 2 beside the way, at the crossroads she t her stand;
11:30 but violence t lives away.
18: 2 A fool t no pleasure in understanding,
23: 5 for suddenly it t wings to itself,
26:17 Like somebody who t a passing dog by
27:18 anyone who t care of a master will be honored.
Ecc 8:14 There is a vanity that t place on earth,
Isa 40:15 see, he t up the isles like fine dust.
44:15 Part of it he t and warms himself;
57: 1 The righteous perish, and no one t it to heart;
57:13 But whoever t refuge in me shall possess the land
65:16 and whoever t an oath in the land shall swear by
Jer 4:29 At the noise of horseman and archer every town t
Eze 18:13 t advance or accrued interest;
18:17 t no advance or accrued interest,
33: 4 and the sword comes and t them away,
33: 6 and the sword comes and t any of them,
Mic 7: 9 until he t my side and executes judgment for me.
Na 1: 2 the LORD t vengeance on his adversaries
Mt 11: 6 And blessed is anyone who t no offense at me."
Mk 4:15 Satan immediately comes and t away the word
Lk 6:29 and from anyone who t away your coat do
6:30 and if anyone t away your goods,
7:23 And blessed is anyone who t no offense at me."
8:12 then the devil comes and t away the word
11:22 he t away his armor in which he trusted
Jn 1:29 the Lamb of God who t away the sin of the world!
10:18 No one t it from me,
2Co 11:20 or preys upon you, or t advantage of you,
Eph 3:15 in heaven and on earth t its name.
Col 2: 8 to it that no one t you captive through philosophy
2Th 2: 4 so that he t his seat in the temple of God,
Heb 5: 4 but t it only when called by God,
9:17 For a will t effect only at death,
10:38 soul t no pleasure in anyone who shrinks back."
Jas 3: 4 though they are so large that it t strong winds
Rev 22:19 if anyone t away from the words of the book
Wis 5:15 the Most High t care of them.
6: 7 and he t thought for all alike.
13:13 he t and carves with care in his leisure,
13:16 He t thought for it, so that it may not fall,
Sir 38: 7 By them the physician heals and t away pain;
38:30 and he t care in firing the kiln.
1Es 4:23 A man t his sword, and goes out to travel and rob
4Mc 2:12 It t precedence over love for children,

TAKING (69) [TAKE]

Ge 24:10 t all kinds of choice gifts from his master;
28:11 T one of the stones of the place,
38:19 and t off her veil she put on the garments
Ex 5: 4 why are you t the people away from their work?
Lev 2: 2 t from it a handful of the choice flour and oil,
9:17 and, t a handful of it, he turned it into smoke on
Nu 25: 7 T a spear in his hand,
Dt 7: 3 to their sons or t their daughters for your sons,
22: 7 Let the mother go, t only the young for yourself,
24: 6 for that would be t a life in pledge.
25: 5 to her, t her in marriage, and performing the duty
Jos 8:12 T about five thousand men,
18: 3 in and t possession of the land that the LORD,
Jdg 21:19 yearly festival of the LORD is t place at Shiloh,
1Sa 25:26 and from t vengeance with your own hand,
2Sa 4: 5 while he was t his noonday rest.
19:18 while the crossing was t place,
2Ki 5: 5 He went, t with him ten talents of silver,
8: 9 So Hazael went to meet him, t a present with him,
2Ch 19: 7 or partiality, or t of bribes."
20:25 They spent three days t the booty,
Ne 5: 7 "You are all t interest from your own people."
5:10 Let us stop this t of interest.
13: 6 While this was t place I was not in Jerusalem,
Job 5: 3 I have seen fools t root,
Pr 7: 8 t the road to her house
20:18 Plans are established by t advice;
31:23 t his seat among the elders of the land.
Isa 3: 1 is t away from Jerusalem and from Judah support
30:14 among its fragments not a sherd is found for t fire
Eze 14: 7 t their idols into their hearts
25:12 and has grievously offended in t vengeance
Zec 5:10 "Where are they t the basket?"
Mt 14:19 T the five loaves and the two fish,
26:45 "Are you still sleeping and t your rest?
27: 6 But the chief priests, t the pieces of silver, said,
Mk 6:41 T the five loaves and the two fish,
9:36 and t it in his arms, he said to them,
13:29 So also, when you see these things t place,
14:41 "Are you still sleeping and t your rest?
15:46 Joseph bought a linen cloth, and t down the body,
Lk 9:16 And t the five loaves and the two fish,
16: 3 that my master is t the position away from me?
19:22 t what I did not deposit and reaping what I did
21:31 So also, when you see these things t place,
24: 1 t the spices that they had prepared.
Ac 9:19 after t some food, he regained his strength.
18:21 but on t leave of them,
19: 9 he left them, t the disciples with him,
24:23 and not to prevent any of his friends from t care
1Co 6: 1 instead of t it before the saints?
Gal 2: 1 up again to Jerusalem with Barnabas, t Titus
Php 2: 7 but emptied himself, t the form of a slave,
Heb 9: 7 without t the blood that he offers for himself and
1Pe 4:12 not be surprised at the fiery ordeal that is t place
Tob 8: 7 I now am t this kinswoman of mine,
AdE 3: 7 t the days and the months one by one,
Sir 26: 7 t hold of her is like grasping a scorpion.
41:21 of t away someone's portion or gift,
Sus 1:48 T his stand among them he said,
1Mc 1:24 T them all, he went into his own land.
7:24 t vengeance on those who had deserted
11:24 t silver and gold and clothing
2Mc 1:11 for t our side against the king,
4:34 Therefore Menelaus, t Andronicus aside,
4:46 t the king aside into a colonnade as if
12:43 t account of the resurrection.
3Mc 7: 6 always t their part as a father does
4Mc 3:12 t a pitcher climbed over the enemy's ramparts.

TALE (1) [TALES]

Lk 24:11 But these words seemed to them an idle t,

TALE (KJV) See also COUNT THEM, FULL NUMBER, SAME NUMBER, QUANTITY

TALEBEARER (KJV) See GOSSIP, SLANDERER, WHISPERER

TALENT‡ (15) [TALENTS]

Ex 25:39 shall be made from a t of pure gold.
37:24 He made it and all its utensils of a t of pure gold.

Ex 38:27 one hundred bases for the hundred talents, a **t** for
2Sa 12:30 the weight of it was a **t** of gold,
1Ki 20:39 or else you shall pay a **t** of silver.'
2Ki 5:22 please give them a **t** of silver and two changes
23:33 on the land of one hundred talents of silver and a **t**
1Ch 20: 2 he found that it weighed a **t** of gold,
2Ch 36: 3 a tribute of one hundred talents of silver and one **t**
Mt 25:18 But the one who had received the one **t** went off
25:24 Then the one who had received the one **t**
25:25 and I went and hid your **t** in the ground.
25:28 So take the **t** from him,
2Mc 8:11 and promising to hand over ninety slaves for a **t,**
1Es 1:36 the nation one hundred talents of silver and one **t**

TALENTS‡ (78) [TALENT]

Ex 38:24 the gold from the offering, was twenty-nine **t**
38:25 congregation who were counted was one hundred **t**
38:27 The hundred **t** of silver were for casting the bases
38:27 one hundred bases for the hundred **t,**
38:29 The bronze that was contributed was seventy **t,**
1Ki 9:14 to the king one hundred twenty **t** of gold.
9:28 and imported from there four hundred twenty **t**
10:10 she gave the king one hundred twenty **t** of gold,
10:14 in one year was six hundred sixty-six **t** of gold,
16:24 of Samaria from Shemer for two **t** of silver;
2Ki 5: 5 He went, taking with him ten **t** of silver,
5:23 Naaman said, "Please accept two **t.**"
5:23 and tied up two **t** of silver in two bags,
15:19 Menahem gave Pul a thousand **t** of silver,
18:14 of King Hezekiah of Judah three hundred **t** of silver and thirty **t** of gold.
23:33 on the land of one hundred **t** of silver and a talent
1Ch 19: 6 a thousand **t** of silver to hire chariots and cavalry
22:14 for the house of the LORD one hundred thousand **t** of gold, one million **t** of silver,
29: 4 three thousand **t** of gold, of the gold of Ophir, and seven thousand **t** of refined silver,
29: 7 the service of the house of God five thousand **t**
29: 7 ten thousand **t** of silver, eighteen thousand **t** of bronze, and one hundred thousand **t** of iron.
2Ch 3: 8 he overlaid it with six hundred **t** of fine gold.
8:18 and imported from there four hundred fifty **t**
9: 9 she gave the king one hundred twenty **t** of gold,
9:13 in one year was six hundred sixty-six **t** of gold,
25: 6 from Israel for one hundred **t** of silver.
25: 9 about the hundred **t** that I have given to the army
27: 5 The Ammonites gave him that year one hundred **t**
36: 3 a tribute of one hundred **t** of silver and one talent
Ezr 7:22 up to one hundred **t** of silver,
8:26 into their hand six hundred fifty **t** of silver, and one hundred silver vessels worth . . . **t,** and one hundred **t** of gold,
Est 3: 9 and I will pay ten thousand **t** of silver into
Mt 18:24 one who owed him ten thousand **t** was brought
25:15 to one he gave five **t,**
25:16 received the five **t** went off at once and traded with them, and made five more **t.**
25:17 the one who had the two **t** made two more **t.**
25:20 the one who had received the five **t** came forward, bringing five more **t,** saying, 'Master, you handed over to me five **t;** see, I have made five more **t.**'
25:22 And the one with the two **t** also came forward, saying, 'Master, you handed over to me two **t;** see, I have made two more **t.**'
25:28 and give it to the one with the ten **t.**
Tob 1:14 of Media I left bags of silver worth ten **t** in trust
4:20 that I left ten **t** of silver in trust with Gabael son
AdE 1: 7 made of ruby, worth thirty thousand **t.**
3: 9 and I will pay ten thousand **t** of silver into
4: 7 how Haman had promised to pay ten thousand **t**
1Mc 11:28 and promised him three hundred **t.**
13:16 now one hundred **t** of silver and two of his sons
13:19 So he sent the sons and the hundred **t,**
15:31 or else pay me five hundred **t** of silver for
15:31 that you have caused and five hundred **t** more for
15:35 for them we will give you one hundred **t.**"
2Mc 3:11 and that it totaled in all four hundred **t** of silver
4: 8 at an interview three hundred sixty **t** of silver,
4: 8 and from another source of revenue eighty **t.**
4:24 outbidding Jason by three hundred **t** of silver.
5:21 So Antiochus carried off eighteen hundred **t** from
8:10 the tribute due to the Romans, two thousand **t,**
1Es 1:36 the nation one hundred **t** of silver and one talent
4:51 that twenty **t** a year should be given for
4:52 and an additional ten **t** a year for burnt offerings
8:20 up to a hundred **t** of silver,
8:56 to them six hundred fifty **t** of silver, and silver vessels worth a hundred **t,** and a hundred **t** of gold,
4Mc 4:17 king three thousand six hundred sixty **t** annually.

TALES (1) [TALE]

1Ti 4: 7 to do with profane myths and old wives' **t.**

TALITHA (1)

Mk 5:41 He took her by the hand and said to her, "**T** cum,"

TALK (45) [TALKATIVE, TALKED, TALKERS, TALKING, TALKS]

Nu 11:17 I will come down and **t** with you there;
Dt 6: 7 to your children and **t** about them when you are
1Sa 2: 3 **T** no more so very proudly,
2Sa 19:11 The **t** of all Israel has come to the king.
Job 11: 2 and should one full of **t** be vindicated?
15: 3 Should they argue in unprofitable **t,**
16: 4 I also could **t** as you do, if you were in my place;
19:18 when I rise, they **t** against me.
35:16 Job opens his mouth in empty **t,**
Ps 64: 5 they **t** of laying snares secretly, thinking,
71:24 All day long my tongue will **t**
73:15 If I had said, "I will **t** on in this way,"
Pr 4:24 and put devious **t** far from you.
6:22 and when you awake, they will **t** with you.
7:21 with her smooth **t** she compels him.
14: 3 The **t** of fools is a rod for their backs,
14:23 but mere **t** leads only to poverty.
24: 2 and their lips **t** of mischief.
Ecc 10:13 and their **t** ends in wicked madness;
10:14 yet fools **t** on and on.
Eze 33:30 your people who **t** together about you by
Da 10:17 How can my lord's servant **t** with my lord?
Jn 14:30 I will no longer **t** much with you,
Ro 16:18 by smooth **t** and flattery they deceive the hearts of
1Co 4:19 not the **t** of these arrogant people but their power.
4:20 kingdom of God depends not on **t** but on power.
Eph 4:29 Let no evil **t** come out of your mouths,
5: 4 of place is obscene, silly, and vulgar **t;**
1Ti 1: 6 from these and turned to meaningless **t,**
2Ti 2:17 and their **t** will spread like gangrene.
Tit 2: 9 in every respect; they are not to **t** back,
2Jn 1:12 instead I hope to come to you and **t** with you face
3Jn 1:14 and we will **t** together face to face.
Tob 3: 4 exile, and death, to become the **t,** the byword,
Jdt 2: 1 there was **t** in the palace of Nebuchadnezzar,
Sir 13:11 for he will test you by prolonged **t,**
21:18 knowledge is **t** that has no meaning.
22:13 Do not **t** much with a senseless person or visit
27:13 The **t** of fools is offensive,
32: 4 Where there is entertainment, do not pour out **t;**
38:25 and whose **t** is about bulls?
2Mc 8: 7 And **t** of his valor spread everywhere.
1Es 3:21 and makes everyone **t** in millions.
3Mc 3: 6 which was common **t** among all;
2Es 9:25 Then I will come and **t** with you."

TALKATIVE (1) [TALK]

Sir 20: 5 while others are detested for being **t.**

TALKED (21) [TALK]

Ge 45:15 and after that his brothers **t** with him.
Jdg 14: 7 Then he went down and **t** with the woman,
1Sa 17:23 As he **t** with them, the champion,
Zec 1: 9 The angel who **t** with me said to me,
1:13 and comforting words to the angel who **t** with me.
1:14 So the angel who **t** with me said to me,
1:19 I asked the angel who **t** with me,
2: 3 Then the angel who **t** with me came forward,
4: 1 The angel who **t** with me came again,
4: 4 I said to the angel who **t** with me,
4: 5 Then the angel who **t** with me answered me,
5: 5 the angel who **t** with me came forward and said
5:10 Then I said to the angel who **t** with me,
6: 4 Then I said to the angel who **t** with me,
Lk 1:65 and all these things were **t** about throughout
Ac 10:27 And as he **t** with him, he went in and found
20: 9 into a deep sleep while Paul **t** still longer.
Rev 21:15 The angel who **t** to me had a measuring rod
1Mc 3:26 and the Gentiles **t** of the battles of Judas.
14: 9 they all **t** together of good things,
2Es 5:15 the angel who had come and **t** with me held me

TALKERS (1) [TALK]

Tit 1:10 idle **t** and deceivers, especially those of

TALKING (30) [TALK]

Ge 17:22 And when he had finished **t** with him,
Ex 34:29 of his face shone because he had been **t** with God.
Dt 11:19 **t** about them when you are at home and
1Sa 14:19 While Saul was **t** to the priest,
17:28 His eldest brother Eliab heard him **t** to the men;
2Ki 2:11 As they continued walking and **t,**
8: 4 the king was **t** with Gehazi the servant of the man
Est 6:14 While they were still **t** with him,
Job 16: 3 Or what provokes you that you keep on **t?**
29: 9 the nobles refrained from **t,** and laid their hands
Isa 59:13 **t** oppression and revolt, conceiving lying words
Mt 16: 8 why are you **t** about having no bread?
17: 3 to them Moses and Elijah, **t** with him.
26:70 saying, "I do not know what you are **t** about."
Mk 8:17 "Why are you **t** about having no bread?
9: 4 to them Elijah with Moses, who were **t**
14:68 not know or understand what you are **t** about."
14:71 "I do not know this man you are **t** about."
Lk 9:30 Moses and Elijah, **t** to him.
22:60 "Man, I do not know what you are **t** about!"
24:14 and **t** with each other about all these things
24:15 While they were **t** and discussing,
24:32 not our hearts burning within us while he was **t**
24:36 While they were **t** about this,
Jn 16:18 We do not know what he is **t** about."
2Co 11:23 I am **t** like a madman—
AdE 6:14 While they were still **t,** the eunuchs arrived
Sir 34: 9 with much experience knows what he is **t** about.
2Es 10:25 While I was **t** to her, her face suddenly began
15:53 and clapping your hands and **t** about their death

TALKS (2) [TALK]

Sir 13:22 he **t** sense, but is not given a hearing.
20: 8 Whoever **t** too much is detested,

TALL (15) [TALLER, TALLEST]

Dt 2:10 large and numerous people, as **t** as the Anakim—
2:21 and numerous people, as **t** as the Anakim.
9: 2 a strong and **t** people, the offspring of
1Ch 11:23 a man of great stature, five cubits **t.**
Isa 18: 2 you swift messengers, to a nation **t** and smooth,
18: 7 be brought to the LORD of hosts from a people **t**
45:14 **t** of stature, shall come over to you and be yours,
Eze 1:18 Their rims were **t** and awesome,
16: 7 up and became **t** and arrived at full womanhood;
31: 4 The waters nourished it, the deep made it grow **t,**
Jdt 16: 6 nor did **t** giants set upon him;
Sir 24:13 "I grew **t** like a cedar in Lebanon,
24:14 I grew **t** like a palm tree in En-gedi,
24:14 and like a plane tree beside water I grew **t.**
Pm 151: 5 My brothers were handsome and **t,**

TALLER (4) [TALL]

Dt 1:28 'The people are stronger and **t** than we;
1Sa 10:23 he was head and shoulders **t** than any of them.
1Mc 6:43 It was **t** than all the others,
2Es 2:43 **t** than any of the others,

TALLEST (3) [TALL]

2Ki 19:23 I felled its **t** cedars, its choicest cypresses;
Isa 10:33 the **t** trees will be cut down,
37:24 I felled its **t** cedars, its choicest cypresses;

TALMAI (6)

Nu 13:22 Ahiman, Sheshai, and **T,** the Anakites, were there.
Jos 15:14 Ahiman, and **T,** the descendants of Anak.
Jdg 1:10 and they defeated Sheshai and Ahiman and **T.**
2Sa 3: 3 daughter of King **T** of Geshur;
13:37 Absalom fled, and went to **T** son of Ammihud,
1Ch 3: 2 son of Maacah, daughter of King **T** of Geshur;

TALMON (6)

1Ch 9:17 Shallum, Akkub, **T,** Ahiman;
Ezr 2:42 of Shallum, of Ater, of **T,** of Akkub, of Hatita,
Ne 7:45 the descendants of Shallum, of Ater, of **T,**
11:19 The gatekeepers, Akkub, **T** and their associates,
12:25 Mattaniah, Bakbukiah, Obadiah, Meshullam, **T,**
1Es 5:28 the descendants of **T,** the descendants of Akkub,

TALONS (2)

2Es 11: 7 Then I saw the eagle rise upon its **t,**
11:45 your most evil **t,** and your whole worthless body,

TAMAH (KJV) See TEMAH

TAMAR (27)

Ge 38: 6 for Er his firstborn; her name was **T.**
38:11 Then Judah said to his daughter-in-law **T,**
38:11 So **T** went to live in her father's house.
38:13 When **T** was told, "Your father-in-law is going up
38:24 "Your daughter-in-law **T** has played the whore;
Ru 4:12 like the house of Perez, whom **T** bore to Judah."
2Sa 13: 1 a beautiful sister whose name was **T;**
13: 2 that he made himself ill because of his sister **T,**
13: 4 Amnon said to him, "I love **T,**
13: 5 'Let my sister **T** come and give me something
13: 6 the king, "Please let my sister **T** come and make
13: 7 Then David sent home to **T,** saying,
13: 8 So **T** went to her brother Amnon's house,
13:10 Then Amnon said to **T,** "Bring the food into
13:10 So **T** took the cakes she had made,
13:19 But **T** put ashes on her head,
13:20 So **T** remained, a desolate woman,
13:22 because he had raped his sister **T.**
13:32 from the day Amnon raped his sister **T.**
14:27 and one daughter whose name was **T;**
1Ki 9:18 Baalath, **T** in the wilderness, within the land,
1Ch 2: 4 His daughter-in-law **T** also bore him Perez
3: 9 of the concubines; and **T** was their sister.
Eze 47:18 to the eastern sea and as far as **T.**
47:19 from **T** as far as the waters of Meribath-kadesh,
48:28 the boundary shall run from **T** to the waters
Mt 1: 3 and Judah the father of Perez and Zerah by **T,**

TAMARISK (4)

Ge 21:33 Abraham planted a **t** tree in Beer-sheba,
1Sa 22: 6 under the **t** tree on the height,
31:13 and buried them under the **t** tree in Jabesh,
Isa 44: 4 They shall spring up like a green **t,**

TAMBOURINE (8) [TAMBOURINES]

Ge 31:27 with mirth and songs, with **t** and lyre.
Ex 15:20 Aaron's sister, took a **t** in her hand;
1Sa 10: 5 **t,** flute, and lyre playing in front of them;
Job 21:12 They sing to the **t** and the lyre,
Ps 81: 2 Raise a song, sound the **t,**
149: 3 making melody to him with **t** and lyre.
150: 4 Praise him with **t** and dance;
Isa 5:12 of lyre and harp, **t** and flute and wine, but who do

TAMBOURINES (9) [TAMBOURINE]

Ex 15:20 and all the women went out after her with **t** and
1Sa 18: 6 singing and dancing, to meet King Saul, with **t,**
2Sa 6: 5 with songs and lyres and harps and **t** and castanets
1Ch 13: 8 with song and lyres and harps and **t** and cymbals
Ps 68:25 the musicians last, between them girls playing **t:**

Jer 31: 4 Again you shall take your **t**,
Jdt 3: 7 with garlands and dances and **t**.
16: 1 And Judith said, Begin a song to my God with **t**,
1Mc 9:39 with **t** and musicians and many weapons.

TAME (2) [TAMED, TAMES]
Jas 3: 8 but no one can **t** the tongue—
4Mc 14:15 the ones that are **t** protect their young by building

TAMED (2) [TAME]
Jas 3: 7 can be **t** and has been **t** by the human species,

TAMES (1) [TAME]
4Mc 1:29 and so **t** the jungle of habits and emotions.

TAMMUZ (1)
Eze 8:14 women were sitting there weeping for **T**.

TANACH (KJV) See TAANACH

TANGLED (1) [ENTANGLE]
AdE 14: 2 to adorn she covered with her **t** hair.

TANHUMETH (2)
2Ki 25:23 Seraiah son of **T** the Netophathite,
Jer 40: 8 Johanan son of Kareah, Seraiah son of **T**,

TANIS (1)
Jdt 1:10 even beyond **T** and Memphis,

TANNED (6) [TANNER]
Ex 25: 5 **t** rams' skins, fine leather, acacia wood,
26:14 a covering of **t** rams' skins and an outer covering
35: 7 **t** rams' skins, and fine leather; acacia wood,
35:23 or goats' hair or **t** rams' skins or fine leather,
36:19 a covering of **t** rams' skins and an outer covering
39:34 of **t** rams' skins and the covering of fine leather,

TANNER (3) [TANNED]
Ac 9:43 in Joppa for some time with a certain Simon, a **t**.
10: 6 with Simon, a **t**, whose house is by the seaside."
10:32 he is staying in the home of Simon, a **t**,

TAPHATH (1)
1Ki 4:11 in all Naphath-dor (he had **T**, Solomon's daughter,

TAPPED (1)
Ac 12: 7 He **t** Peter on the side and woke him, saying,

TAPPUAH (6) [BETH-TAPPUAH, EN-TAPPUAH]
Jos 12:17 the king of **T** one the king of Hepher one
15:34 Zanoah, En-gannim, **T**, Enam,
16: 8 From **T** the boundary goes westward to
17: 8 The land of **T** belonged to Manasseh,
17: 8 of **T** on the boundary of Manasseh belonged to
1Ch 2:43 sons of Hebron: Korah, **T**, Rekem, and Shema.

TARAH (KJV) See TERAH

TARALAH (1)
Jos 18:27 Rekem, Irpeel, **T**,

TARE (KJV) See CONVULSED, CONVULSIONS, MAULED, TORE

TAREA (1) [=TAHREA]
1Ch 8:35 The sons of Micah: Pithon, Melech, **T**, and Ahaz.

TARES (KJV) See WEEDS

TARGET (4)
Job 7:20 Why have you made me your **t**?
16:12 he set me up as his **t**;
Wis 5:12 when an arrow is shot at a **t**, the air, thus divided,
5:21 and will leap from the clouds to the **t**,

TARNISH (1) [TARNISHED]
LtJ 6:24 it will not shine unless someone wipes off the **t**;

TARNISHED (1) [TARNISH]
Sir 12:11 to be sure it does not become completely **t**.

TARPELITES (KJV) See OFFICIALS

TARRIED, TARRIEST, TARRIETH, TARRY, TARRYING (KJV) See also BEEN THERE, CONTINUE[D], DELAY[ED], LINGER[ED], LIVE, REMAIN[ED], SPEND TIME, SPENT THE NIGHT, SPENT TIME, STAY, STAYED, STAYING, STAYS, STOPPED, SUSPENSE, WAIT, WAITED, WAITING, WASTE TIME

TARRIED (1) [TARRY]
Ge 31:54 they ate bread and **t** all night in the hill country.

TARRY (5) [TARRIED]
Jdg 5:16 Why did you **t** among the sheepfolds,
5:28 Why **t** the hoofbeats of his chariots?'
Isa 46:13 it is not far off, and my salvation will not **t**;
Hab 2: 3 If it seems to **t**, wait for it;
Sir 14:12 Remember that death does not **t**,

TARSHISH (28)
Ge 10: 4 Elishah, **T**, Kittim, and Rodanim.
1Ki 10:22 a fleet of ships of **T** at sea with the fleet of Hiram.
10:22 Once every three years the fleet of ships of **T** used
22:48 Jehoshaphat made ships of the **T** type to go
1Ch 1: 7 Elishah, **T**, Kittim, and Rodanim.
7:10 Jeush, Benjamin, Ehud, Chenaanah, Zethan, **T**,
2Ch 9:21 For the king's ships went to **T** with the servants
9:21 the ships of **T** used to come bringing gold,
20:36 He joined him in building ships to go to **T**;
20:37 ships were wrecked and were not able to go to **T**.
Est 1:14 Admatha, **T**, Meres, Marsena, and Memucan,
Ps 48: 7 as when an east wind shatters the ships of **T**.
72:10 the kings of **T** and of the isles render him tribute,
Isa 2:16 against all the ships of **T**,
23: 1 Wail, O ships of **T**, for your fortress is destroyed.
23: 6 Cross over to **T**—wail, O inhabitants of the coast!
23:10 Cross over to your own land, O ships of **T**;
23:14 Wail, O ships of **T**, for your fortress is destroyed.
60: 9 coastlands shall wait for me, the ships of **T** first,
66:19 to the nations, to **T**, Put, and Lud—
Jer 10: 9 Beaten silver is brought from **T**,
Eze 27:12 **T** did business with you out of the abundance
27:25 The ships of **T** traveled for you in your trade.
38:13 of **T** and all its young warriors will say to you,
Jnh 1: 3 But Jonah set out to flee to **T** from the presence of
1: 3 down to Joppa and found a ship going to **T**;
1: 3 and went on board, to go with them to **T**,
4: 2 That is why I fled to **T** at the beginning;

TARSUS (7)
Ac 9:11 of Judas look for a man of **T** named Saul.
9:30 down to Caesarea and sent him off to **T**.
11:25 Then Barnabas went to **T** to look for Saul,
21:39 Paul replied, "I am a Jew, from **T** in Cilicia,
22: 3 born in **T** in Cilicia, but brought up in this city at
2Mc 3: 5 he went to Apollonius of **T**,
4:30 that the people of **T** and of Mallus revolted

TARTAK (1)
2Ki 17:31 the Avvites made Nibhaz and **T**;

TARTAN (1)
2Ki 18:17 The king of Assyria sent the **T**, the Rabsaris,

TARTAN (KJV) See also COMMANDER-IN-CHIEF

TARTAROS See Index to Footnotes

TASK (17) [TASKMASTER, TASKMASTERS, TASKS]
Ex 18:18 the **t** is too heavy for you; you cannot do it alone.
36: 4 that all the artisans who were doing every sort of **t**
36: 4 each from the **t** being performed,
Lev 16:21 by means of someone designated for the **t**.
Nu 4:19 in and assign each to a particular **t** or burden.
Ezr 10:13 Nor is this a **t** for one day or for two,
Ps 73:16 it seemed to me a wearisome **t**,
Jer 50:25 of hosts has a **t** to do in the land of the Chaldeans.
Ac 6: 3 whom we may appoint to this **t**,
Col 3:23 Whatever your **t**, put yourselves into it,
4:17 that you complete the **t** that you have received in
1Ti 3: 1 to the office of bishop desires a noble **t**.
Sir 7:20 hired laborers who devote themselves to their **t**.
7:25 and you complete a great **t**;
37:11 with a lazy servant about a big **t**—
1Es 8:95 Rise up and take action, for it is your **t**,
3Mc 4:18 the **t** was impossible for all the generals in Egypt.

TASKMASTER (4) [MASTER, TASK]
1Ki 12:18 who was **t** over the forced labor,
2Ch 10:18 who was **t** over the forced labor,
Job 3:18 they do not hear the voice of the **t**.
Isa 60:17 as your overseer and Righteousness as your **t**.

TASKMASTERS (6) [MASTER, TASK]
Ex 1:11 Therefore they set **t** over them to oppress them
3: 7 I have heard their cry on account of their **t**.
5: 6 That same day Pharaoh commanded the **t** of
5:10 the **t** and the supervisors of the people went out
5:13 The **t** were urgent, saying, "Complete your work,
5:14 whom Pharaoh's **t** had set over them,

TASKS‡ (8) [TASK]
Ex 1:13 The Egyptians became ruthless in imposing **t** on
1:14 They were ruthless in all the **t** that they imposed
Nu 4:49 to their several **t** of serving or carrying;
Pr 31:15 for her household and **t** for her servant-girls.
Lk 10:40 But Martha was distracted by her many **t**;
Sir 3:17 My child, perform your **t** with humility;
16:27 and they do not abandon their **t**.
1Mc 14:42 the sanctuary and appoint officials over its **t** and

TASSELS (1)
Dt 22:12 You shall make **t** on the four corners of the cloak

TASTE (26) [TASTED, TASTELESS, TASTES, TASTING]
Ex 16:31 and the **t** of it was like wafers made with honey.
Nu 11: 8 the **t** of it was like the **t** of cakes baked with oil.
2Sa 3:35 "So may God do to me, and more, if I **t** bread
19:35 Can your servant **t** what he eats
Job 6:30 Cannot my **t** discern calamity?
Ps 34: 8 O **t** and see that the LORD is good;
119:103 How sweet are your words to my **t**,
Pr 24:13 drippings of the honeycomb are sweet to your **t**.
SS 2: 3 and his fruit was sweet to my **t**.
Jnh 3: 7 no herd or flock, shall **t** anything.
Mt 5:13 but if salt has lost its **t**,
16:28 there are some standing here who will not **t** death
Mk 9: 1 there are some standing here who will not **t** death
Lk 9:27 there are some standing here who will not **t** death
14:24 of those who were invited will **t** my dinner.' "
14:34 "Salt is good; but if salt has lost its **t**,
Jn 8:52 'Whoever keeps my word will never **t** death.'
Ac 23:14 by an oath to **t** no food until we have killed Paul.
Col 2:21 "Do not handle, Do not **t**, Do not touch"?
Heb 2: 9 the grace of God he might **t** death for everyone.
Wis 16:20 providing every pleasure and suited to every **t**.
2Mc 6:20 the courage to refuse things that it is not right to **t**,
13:18 The king, having had a **t** of the daring of the Jews,
2Es 6:44 and of varied appeal to the **t**,
9:24 and **t** no meat and drink no wine,

TASTED (10) [TASTE]
1Sa 14:24 So none of the troops **t** food.
14:29 how my eyes have brightened because I **t** a little
14:43 "I **t** a little honey with the tip of the staff that was
Job 21:25 in bitterness of soul, never having **t** of good.
Mt 27:34 but when he **t** it, he would not drink it.
Jn 2: 9 the steward **t** the water that had become wine,
Heb 6: 4 and have **t** the heavenly gift,
6: 5 and have **t** the goodness of the word of God and
1Pe 2: 3 if indeed you have **t** that the Lord is good.
2Es 6:26 who from their birth have not **t** death;

TASTELESS (1) [TASTE]
Job 6: 6 Can that which is **t** be eaten without salt,

TASTES (3) [TASTE]
Job 12:11 Does not the ear test words as the palate **t** food?
34: 3 for the ear tests words as the palate **t** food.
Sir 36:24 As the palate **t** the kinds of game,

TASTING (2) [TASTE]
Tob 2: 4 Then I sprang up, left the dinner before even **t** it,
4Mc 10: 1 urged him to save himself by **t** the meat.

TATTENAI (4)
Ezr 5: 3 At the same time **T** the governor of the province
5: 6 of the letter that **T** the governor of the province
6: 6 **T**, governor of the province Beyond the River,
6:13 according to the word sent by King Darius, **T**,

TATTLERS (KJV) See GOSSIPS

TATTOO (1)
Lev 19:28 in your flesh for the dead or **t** any marks upon you:

TAUGHT‡ (67) [TEACH]
Dt 31:22 That very day Moses wrote this song and **t** it to
2Sa 1:18 The Song of the Bow be **t** to the people of Judah;
2Ki 17:28 he **t** them how they should worship the LORD.
2Ch 17: 9 They **t** in Judah, having the book of the law of
17: 9 around through all the cities of Judah and **t** among
35: 3 the Levites who **t** all Israel and who were holy to
Ne 8: 9 the Levites who **t** the people said to all the people,
Ps 71:17 O God, from my youth you have **t** me,
119:102 from your ordinances, for you have **t** me.
Pr 4: 4 he **t** me, and said to me,
4:11 I have **t** you the way of wisdom;
31: 1 An oracle that his mother **t** him:
Ecc 12: 9 the Teacher also **t** the people knowledge,
Isa 40:14 and who **t** him the path of justice?
40:14 Who **t** him knowledge, and showed him the way
50: 4 wakens my ear to listen as those who are **t**.
54:13 All your children shall be **t** by the LORD,
Jer 2:33 that even to wicked women you have **t** your ways.
9: 5 they have **t** their tongues to speak lies;
9:14 after the Baals, as their ancestors **t** them.
12:16 as they **t** my people to swear by Baal,
32:33 though I have **t** them persistently,
Eze 22:26 the common, neither have they **t** the difference
Da 1: 4 be **t** the literature and language of the Chaldeans.
Hos 11: 3 Yet it was I who **t** Ephraim to walk,
Mt 5: 2 Then he began to speak, and **t** them, saying:
7:29 for he **t** them as one having authority,
Mk 1:21 the sabbath came, he entered the synagogue and **t**.
1:22 for he **t** them as one having authority,
2:13 whole crowd gathered around him, and he **t** them.
6:30 and told him all that they had done and **t**.

Mk 10: 1 and, as was his custom, he again t them.
12:38 As he t, he said, "Beware of the scribes,
Lk 5: 3 Then he sat down and t the crowds from the boat.
6: 6 the synagogue and t, and there was
11: 1 "Lord, teach us to pray, as John t his disciples."
13:26 and you t in our streets.'
Jn 6:45 'And they shall all be t by God.'
7:15 when he has never been t?"
18:20 I have always t in synagogues and in the temple,
Ac 1: 1 about all that Jesus did and t from the beginning
11:26 for an entire year they met with the church and t
15:35 they t and proclaimed the word of the Lord.
18:25 and t accurately the things concerning Jesus,
1Co 2:13 words not t by human wisdom but t by the Spirit,
Gal 1:12 not receive it from a human source, nor was I t it,
6: 6 Those who are t the word must share
Eph 4:21 you have heard about him and were t in him,
4:22 You were t to put away your former way of life,
Col 2: 7 just as you were t, abounding in thanksgiving.
1Th 4: 9 for you yourselves have been t by God
2Th 2:15 and hold fast to the traditions that you were t
1Jn 2:27 and is true and is not a lie, and just as it has t you,
Rev 2:14 of Balaam, who t Balak to put a stumbling block
Wis 6:10 those who have been t them will find a defense.
7:22 the fashioner of all things, t me.
9:18 and people were t what pleases you,
12:19 Through such works you have t your people that
Sir 21:12 The one who is not clever cannot be t,
1Es 8: 7 but t all Israel all the ordinances and judgments.
9:48 Hanan, Pelaiah, the Levites, t the law of the Lord,
9:55 by the words which they had been t.
2Es 8:29 but regard those who have gloriously t your law.
4Mc 18:10 he t you the law and the prophets.
18:12 and he t you about Hananiah, Azariah,
18:18 not forget to teach you the song that Moses t,

TAUNT (15) [TAUNT-SONGS, TAUNTED, TAUNTERS, TAUNTS]

1Ki 9: 7 and Israel will become a proverb and a t
Ne 4: 4 turn their t back on their own heads,
6:13 a bad name, in order to t me.
Ps 42:10 a deadly wound in my body, my adversaries t me,
44:13 You have made us the t of our neighbors,
55:12 It is not enemies who t me—
79: 4 We have become a t to our neighbors,
89:51 with which your enemies t,
102: 8 All day long my enemies t me;
119:42 Then I shall have an answer for those who t me,
Isa 14: 4 you will take up this t against the king
Jer 24: 9 a disgrace, a byword, a t,
Eze 5:15 You shall be a mockery and a t,
Mic 2: 4 that day they shall take up a t song against you,
Hab 2: 6 Shall not everyone t such people and,

TAUNT-SONGS (2) [SING, TAUNT]

La 3:14 the object of their t all day long.
3:63 see, I am the object of their t.

TAUNTED (9) [TAUNT]

Jdg 8:15 about whom you t me, saying,
2Sa 21:21 When he t Israel, Jonathan son
1Ch 20: 7 When he t Israel, Jonathan son of Shimea,
Ps 79:12 of our neighbors the taunts with which they t you,
89:50 Remember, O Lord, how your servant is t;
89:51 with which they t the footsteps of your anointed.
Zep 2: 8 how they have t my people and made boasts
Mt 27:44 with him also t him in the same way.
Mk 15:32 Those who were crucified with him also t him.

TAUNTERS (1) [TAUNT]

Ps 44:16 at the words of the t and revilers,

TAUNTS (4) [TAUNT]

Ne 5: 9 to prevent the t of the nations our enemies?
Ps 79:12 into the bosom of our neighbors the t
La 3:61 You have heard their t, O LORD,
Zep 2: 8 the t of Moab and the revilings of the Ammonites,

TAUT (1)

Ge 49:24 Yet his bow remained t,

TAUTNESS See Index to Footnotes

TAVERNS (1)

Ac 28:15 came as far as the Forum of Appius and Three T

TAX (41) [TAXED, TAXES]

2Ch 24: 6 to bring in from Judah and Jerusalem the t levied
24: 9 the t that Moses the servant of God laid on Israel
24:10 and brought their t and dropped it into the chest
Ne 5: 4 on our fields and vineyards to pay the king's t.
Mt 5:46 Do not even the t collectors do the same?
9: 9 a man called Matthew sitting at the t booth;
9:10 many t collectors and sinners came
9:11 "Why does your teacher eat with t collectors
10: 3 Thomas and Matthew the t collector;
11:19 a friend of t collectors and sinners!'
17:24 collectors of the temple t came to Peter and said,
17:24 "Does your teacher not pay the temple t?"
18:17 a one be to you as a Gentile and a t collector.
21:31 the t collectors and the prostitutes are going into
21:32 the t collectors and the prostitutes believed him;
Mt 22:19 Show me the coin used for the t."
Mk 2:14 he saw Levi son of Alphaeus sitting at the t booth,
2:15 many t collectors and sinners were also sitting
2:16 that he was eating with sinners and t collectors,
2:16 "Why does he eat with t collectors and sinners?"
Lk 3:12 Even t collectors came to be baptized,
5:27 this he went out and saw a t collector named Levi,
5:27 a tax collector named Levi, sitting at the t booth;
5:29 a large crowd of t collectors and others sitting at
5:30 "Why do you eat and drink with t collectors
7:29 including the t collectors,
7:34 a friend of t collectors and sinners!'
15: 1 Now all the t collectors and sinners were coming
18:10 one a Pharisee and the other a t collector.
18:11 rogues, adulterers, or even like this t collector.
18:13 But the t collector, standing far off,
19: 2 he was a chief t collector and was rich.
AdE 10: 1 a t upon his kingdom both by land and sea.
1Mc 10:29 the Jews from payment of tribute and salt t
10:31 shall be holy and free from t.
13:39 and cancel the crown t that you owe;
13:39 and whatever other t has been collected
15: 5 therefore I confirm to you all the t remissions that
1Es 8:22 that no tribute or any other t is to be laid on any
8:22 that no one has authority to impose any t on them.
3Mc 2:28 be subjected to a registration involving poll t and

TAXED (1) [TAX]

2Ki 23:35 but he t the land in order to meet Pharaoh's

TAXES (13) [TAX]

Mt 22:17 Is it lawful to pay t to the emperor, or not?"
Mk 12:14 Is it lawful to pay t to the emperor, or not?
Lk 20:22 Is it lawful for us to pay t to the emperor, or not?"
23: 2 forbidding us to pay t to the emperor,
Ro 13: 6 For the same reason you also pay t,
13: 7 what is due them—t to whom t are due,
AdE 2:18 and he granted a remission of t to those who were
1Mc 10:33 let all officials cancel also the t on their livestock.
11:34 from the royal t that the king formerly received
11:35 the t due to us, and the salt pits and the crown t due
1Es 4: 6 and they compel one another to pay t to the king.

TAXING (KJV) See CENSUS, REGISTRATION

TEACH‡ (124) [TAUGHT, TEACHER, TEACHERS, TEACHES, TEACHING, TEACHINGS]

Ex 4:12 be with your mouth and t you what you are
4:15 and will t you what you shall do.
18:20 t them the statutes and instructions
35:34 And he has inspired him to t,
Lev 10:11 to t the people of Israel all the statutes that
Dt 4: 5 I now t you statutes and ordinances for you
4:10 and may t their children so";
4:14 that time to t you statutes and ordinances for you
5:31 that you shall t them, so that they may do them in
6: 1 to t you to observe in the land that you are about
11:19 T them to your children, talking about them
20:18 not t you to do all the abhorrent things
31:19 therefore write this song, and t it to the Israelites;
33:10 They t Jacob your ordinances,
Jdg 3: 2 to t those who had no experience of it before):
13: 8 to us again and t us what we are to do concerning
1Ki 8:36 when you t them the good way
2Ki 17:27 and t them the law of the god of the land."
2Ch 6:27 when you t them the good way
17: 7 Nethanel, and Micaiah, to t in the cities of Judah.
Ezr 7:10 and to t the statutes and ordinances in Israel.
7:25 and you shall t those who do not know them.
Job 6:24 "T me, and I will be silent;
8:10 not t you and tell you and utter words out
12: 7 "But ask the animals, and they will t you;
12: 8 the plants of the earth, and they will t you;
21:22 Will any t God knowledge,
27:11 I will t you concerning the hand of God;
32: 7 'Let days speak, and many years t wisdom.'
33:33 listen to me; be silent, and I will t you wisdom."
34:32 t me what I do not see;
37:19 T us what we shall say to him;
Ps 25: 4 O LORD; t me your paths.
25: 5 Lead me in your truth, and t me,
25:12 He will t them the way that they should choose.
27:11 T me your way, O LORD,
32: 8 and t you the way you should go;
34:11 I will t you the fear of the LORD.
45: 4 let your right hand t you dread deeds.
51: 6 therefore t me wisdom in my secret heart.
51:13 Then I will t transgressors your ways,
78: 5 commanded our ancestors to t to their children;
86:11 T me your way, O LORD,
90:12 So t us to count our days that we may gain
94:12 O LORD, and whom you t out of your law,
105:22 and to t his elders wisdom.
119:12 Blessed are you, O LORD; t me your statutes.
119:26 you answered me; t me your statutes.
119:29 and graciously t me your law.
119:33 T me, O LORD, the way of your statutes,
119:64 of your steadfast love; t me your statutes.
119:66 T me good judgment and knowledge,
119:68 You are good and do good; t me your statutes.
119:108 O LORD, and t me your ordinances.
119:124 to your steadfast love, and t me your statutes.
Ps 119:135 upon your servant, and t me your statutes.
119:171 because you t me your statutes.
132:12 and my decrees that I shall t them,
143: 8 T me the way I should go,
143:10 T me to do your will, for you are my God.
Pr 1: 4 to t shrewdness to the simple, knowledge
9: 9 t the righteous and they will gain in learning.
Isa 2: 3 that he may t us his ways and that we may walk
9:15 and prophets who t lies are the tail;
28: 9 "Whom will he t knowledge,
Jer 9:20 t to your daughters a dirge,
16:21 "Therefore I am surely going to t them,
16:21 this time I am going to t them my power
31:34 No longer shall they t one another,
Eze 44:23 They shall t my people the difference between
Mic 3:11 its priests t for a price, its prophets give oracles
4: 2 that he may t us his ways and that we may walk
Hab 2:19 "Rouse yourself!" Can it t?
Mt 11: 1 to t and proclaim his message in their cities.
13:54 and began to t the people in their synagogue,
22:16 and t the way of God in accordance with truth,
23: 3 do whatever they t you and follow it;
23: 3 for they do not practice what they t.
Mk 4: 1 Again he began to t beside the sea.
4: 2 He began to t them many things in parables,
6: 2 On the sabbath he began to t in the synagogue,
6:34 and he began to t them many things.
8:31 Then he began to t them that the Son of Man
12:14 but t the way of God in accordance with truth.
Lk 4:15 He began to t in their synagogues and was praised
11: 1 "Lord, t us to pray, as John taught his disciples."
12:12 for the Holy Spirit will t you at
20:21 we know that you are right in what you say and t,
20:21 but t the way of God in accordance with truth.
Jn 7:14 Jesus went up into the temple and began to t.
7:35 to go to the Dispersion among the Greeks and t
8: 2 ⟦to him and he sat down and began to t them.⟧
9:34 and are you trying to t us?"
14:26 will t you everything, and remind you of all
Ac 4:18 not to speak or t at all in the name of Jesus.
5:28 "We gave you strict orders not to t in this name,
5:42 at home they did not cease to t and proclaim Jesus
21:21 that you t all the Jews living among the Gentiles
Ro 2:21 then, that t others, will you not t yourself?
1Co 4:17 as I t them everywhere in every church.
11:14 Does not nature itself t you that if
Col 3:16 t and admonish one another in all wisdom;
1Ti 1: 3 not to t any different doctrine,
2:12 I permit no woman to t or to have authority over
4:11 These are the things you must insist on and t.
6: 2 T and urge these duties.
2Ti 2: 2 to faithful people who will be able to t others
Tit 1:11 for sordid gain what it is not right to t.
2: 1 for you, t what is consistent with sound doctrine.
2: 3 they are to t what is good,
Heb 5:12 to t you again the basic elements of the oracles
8:11 they shall not t one another or say to each other,
Jas 3: 1 for you know that we who t will be judged
1Jn 2:27 and so you do not need anyone to t you.
Sir 9: 1 or you will t her an evil lesson to your own hurt.
37:19 Some people may be clever enough to t many,
45: 5 so that he might t Jacob the covenant,
45:17 to t Jacob the testimonies,
1Es 8:23 and you shall t it to those who do not know it.
2Es 4: 4 and will t you why the heart is evil."
10:38 "Listen to me, and I will t you,
12:38 you shall t them to the wise among your people,
4Mc 18:18 not forget to t you the song that Moses taught,

TEACHER (71) [TEACH]

1Ch 25: 8 small and great, t and pupil alike.
Job 36:22 who is a t like him?
Ecc 1: 1 The words of the T, the son of David,
1: 2 Vanity of vanities, says the T, vanity of vanities!
1:12 I, the T, when king over Israel in Jerusalem,
7:27 See, this is what I found, says the T,
12: 8 Vanity of vanities, says the T; all is vanity.
12: 9 the T also taught the people knowledge,
12:10 The T sought to find pleasing words,
Isa 30:20 yet your T will not hide himself any more, but
your eyes shall see your T.
50: 4 The Lord GOD has given me the tongue of a t,
Hab 2:18 a cast image, a t of lies?
Mt 8:19 A scribe then approached and said, "T,
9:11 "Why does your t eat with tax collectors
10:24 "A disciple is not above the t,
10:25 it is enough for the disciple to be like the t,
12:38 some of the scribes and Pharisees said to him, "T,
17:24 "Does your t not pay the temple tax?"
19:16 Then someone came to him and said, "T,
22:16 saying, "T, we know that you are sincere,
22:24 "T, Moses said, 'If a man dies childless,
22:36 "T, which commandment in the law is the greatest
23: 8 you are not to be called rabbi, for you have one t,
26:18 and say to him, 'The T says, My time is near;
Mk 4:38 and they woke him up and said to him, "T,
5:35 Why trouble the t any further?"
9:17 Someone from the crowd answered him, "T,
9:38 to him, "T, we saw someone casting out demons
10:17 "Good T, what must I do to inherit eternal life?"
10:20 "T, I have kept all these since my youth."
10:35 came forward to him and said to him, "T,
10:51 blind man said to him, "My t, let me see again."
12:14 And they came and said to him, "T,
12:19 "T, Moses wrote for us that 'if
12:32 Then the scribe said to him, "You are right, T;

Mk 13: 1 T, what large stones and what large buildings!"
14:14 say to the owner of the house, 'The T asks,
Lk 3:12 and they asked him, "T, what should we do?"
6:40 A disciple is not above the t,
6:40 everyone who is fully qualified will be like the t.
7:40 I have something to say to you." "T,"
8:49 do not trouble the t any longer."
9:38 Just then a man from the crowd shouted, "T,
10:25 "T," he said, "what must I do
11:45 One of the lawyers answered him, "T,
12:13 Someone in the crowd said to him, "T,
18:18 A certain ruler asked him, "Good T,
19:39 "T, order your disciples to stop."
20:21 "T, we know that you are right in what you say
20:28 and asked him a question, "T, Moses wrote for us
20:39 Then some of the scribes answered, "T,
21: 7 They asked him, "T, when will this be,
22:11 'The t asks you, "Where is the guest room,
Jn 1:38 "Rabbi" (which translated means T),
3: 2 that you are a t who has come from God;
3:10 Jesus answered him, "Are you a t of Israel,
8: 4 ⟦"T, this woman was caught in the very act⟧
11:28 "The T is here and is calling for you."
13:13 You call me T and Lord—
13:14 So if I, your Lord and T, have washed your feet,
20:16 "Rabbouni!" (which means T).
Ac 5:34 a t of the law, respected by all the people,
Ro 2:20 a t of children, having in the law the embodiment
12: 7 ministry, in ministering; the t, in teaching;
Gal 6: 6 in all good things with their t.
1Ti 2: 7 a t of the Gentiles in faith and truth.
3: 2 sensible, respectable, hospitable, an apt t,
2Ti 1:11 a herald and an apostle and a t,
2:24 be quarrelsome but kindly to everyone, an apt t,
2Mc 1:10 t of King Ptolemy, and to the Jews in Egypt,

TEACHERS (14) [TEACH]

Ps 119:99 I have more understanding than all my t,
Pr 5:13 not listen to the voice of my t or incline my ear
Lk 2:46 the temple, sitting among the t, listening to them
5:17 Pharisees and t of the law were sitting near
Ac 13: 1 the church at Antioch there were prophets and t:
1Co 12:28 the church first apostles, second prophets, third t;
12:29 Are all apostles? Are all prophets? Are all t?
Eph 4:11 some evangelists, some pastors and t,
1Ti 1: 7 desiring to be t of the law,
2Ti 4: 3 for themselves t to suit their own desires,
Heb 5:12 For though by this time you ought to be t,
Jas 3: 1 Not many of you should become t,
2Pe 2: 1 just as there will be false t among you,
2: 2 of these t the way of truth will be maligned.

TEACHES (18) [TEACH]

Job 15: 5 For your iniquity t your mouth,
35:11 who t us more than the animals of the earth,
Ps 25: 9 and t the humble his way.
94:10 he who t knowledge to humankind,
Isa 28:26 For they are well instructed; their God t them.
48:17 who t you for your own good,
Mt 5:19 and t others to do the same,
5:19 and t them will be called great in the kingdom
1Ti 6: 3 Whoever t otherwise and does not agree with
1Jn 2:27 But as his anointing t you about all things,
Wis 8: 7 for she t self-control and prudence,
Sir 4:11 Wisdom t her children and gives help
18:13 He rebukes and trains and t them,
22: 9 Whoever t a fool is like one who glues potsherds
30: 3 He who t his son will make his enemies envious,
33:29 for idleness t much evil.
4Mc 5:23 but it t us self-control, so that we master all
5:24 and it t us piety, so that with proper reverence

TEACHING‡ (102) [TEACH]

Ex 13: 9 so that the t of the LORD may be on your lips;
Dt 4: 1 to the statutes and ordinances that I am t you
32: 2 May my t drop like the rain,
2Ch 15: 3 and without a t priest, and without law;
Ps 78: 1 Give ear, O my people, to my t;
Pr 1: 8 and do not reject your mother's t;
3: 1 My child, do not forget my t,
4: 2 for I give you good precepts: do not forsake my t.
6:20 and do not forsake your mother's t.
6:23 For the commandment is a lamp and the t a light,
13:14 The t of the wise is a fountain of life,
22:17 and apply your mind to my t;
31:26 and the t of kindness is on her tongue.
Isa 1:10 Listen to the t of our God,
8:16 seal the t among my disciples.
8:20 for t and for instruction?"
42: 4 and the coastlands wait for his t.
42:21 to magnify his t and make it glorious.
51: 4 for a t will go out from me,
51: 7 you people who have my t in your hearts;
Jer 6:19 and as for my t, they have rejected it.
Eze 22:26 to my t and have profaned my holy things;
Mal 4: 4 Remember the t of my servant Moses,
Mt 4:23 t in their synagogues and proclaiming
7:28 the crowds were astounded at his t,
9:35 Then Jesus went about all the cities and villages, t
15: 9 t human precepts as doctrines.'"
16:12 but of the t of the Pharisees and Sadducees.
19:11 he said to them, "Not everyone can accept this t,
21:23 the elders of the people came to him as he was t,
22:33 the crowd heard it, they were astounded at his t.
26:55 Day after day I sat in the temple t,
Mt 28:20 and t them to obey everything
Mk 1:22 They were astounded at his t,
1:27 A new t—with authority!
4: 2 and in his t he said to them:
6: 6 Then he went about among the villages t.
7: 7 t human precepts as doctrines.'
9:31 for he was t his disciples,
11:17 He was t and saying, "Is it not written,
11:18 because the whole crowd was spellbound by his t.
12:35 While Jesus was t in the temple, he said,
14:49 Day after day I was with you in the temple t,
Lk 4:31 a city in Galilee, and was t them on the sabbath.
4:32 They were astounded at his t,
5:17 One day, while he was t,
13:10 he was t in one of the synagogues on the sabbath.
13:22 t as he made his way to Jerusalem.
19:47 Every day he was t in the temple.
20: 1 as he was t the people in the temple and telling
21:37 Every day he was t in the temple,
23: 5 "He stirs up the people by t throughout all Judea,
Jn 6:59 while he was t in the synagogue at Capernaum.
6:60 they said, "This t is difficult; who can accept it?"
7:16 "My t is not mine but his who sent me.
7:17 to do the will of God will know whether the t is
7:28 Then Jesus cried out as he was t in the temple,
8:20 while he was t in the treasury of the temple,
18:19 about his disciples and about his t.
Ac 2:42 They devoted themselves to the apostles' t
4: 2 because they were t the people and proclaiming
5:21 the temple at daybreak and went on with their t.
5:25 in prison are standing in the temple and t
5:28 yet here you have filled Jerusalem with your t
13:12 for he was astonished at the t about the Lord.
15: 1 down from Judea and were t the brothers,
17:19 "May we know what this new t is
18:11 t the word of God among them.
20:20 and t you publicly and from house to house,
21:28 This is the man who is t everyone everywhere
28:31 proclaiming the kingdom of God and t about
Ro 6:17 to the form of t to which you were entrusted,
12: 7 ministry, in ministering; the teacher, in t;
16:17 in opposition to the t that you have learned;
1Co 14: 6 or knowledge or prophecy or t?
Col 1:28 warning everyone and t everyone in all wisdom,
1Ti 1:10 and whatever else is contrary to the sound t
4: 6 on the words of the faith and of the sound t
4:13 the public reading of scripture, to exhorting, to t.
4:16 Pay close attention to yourself and to your t;
5:17 especially those who labor in preaching and t;
6: 1 name of God and the t may not be blasphemed.
6: 3 and the t that is in accordance with godliness,
2Ti 1:13 to the standard of sound t that you have heard
3:10 Now you have observed my t, my conduct,
3:16 by God and is useful for t,
4: 2 and encourage, with the utmost patience in t.
Tit 1: 9 that is trustworthy in accordance with the t,
1:11 by t for sordid gain what it is not right to teach.
2: 7 and in your t show integrity, gravity,
Heb 6: 1 leaving behind the basic t about Christ,
2Jn 1: 9 Everyone who does not abide in the t of Christ,
1: 9 whoever abides in the t has both the Father and
1:10 to you and does not bring this t;
Rev 2:14 you have some there who hold to the t of Balaam,
2:15 So you also have some who hold to the t of
2:20 a prophet and is t and beguiling my servants
2:24 who do not hold this t, who have
Sir 24:33 I will again pour out t like prophecy,
1Es 9:49 and to the Levites who were t the multitude,
2Es 7:78 Now concerning death, the t is:
7:*90* Therefore this is the t concerning them:

TEACHINGS (6) [TEACH]

Pr 7: 2 keep my t as the apple of your eye;
Col 2:22 they are simply human commands and t.
1Ti 4: 1 by paying attention to deceitful spirits and t
Heb 13: 9 Do not be carried away by all kinds of strange t;
Sir Pr: 1 Many great t have been given to us through
4Mc 10: 2 and that I was brought up on the same t?

TEAMS (2)

2Sa 10:18 of the Arameans seven hundred chariot t,
Jer 51:23 with you I smash farmers and their t;

TEAR (47) [TEARFUL, TEARING, TEARS, TORE, TORN]

Ex 34:13 You shall t down their altars, break their pillars,
Lev 1:17 He shall t it open by its wings without severing it.
10: 6 and do not t your vestments,
13:56 he shall t the spot out of the cloth,
21:10 shall not dishevel his hair, nor t his vestments.
Jdg 2: 2 of this land; t down their altars.'
14: 6 the lion apart barehanded as one might t apart
2Sa 3:31 "T your clothes, and put on sackcloth,
1Ki 11:11 I will surely t the kingdom from you and give it
11:12 I will t it out of the hand of your son.
11:13 I will not, however, t away the entire kingdom;
11:31 of Israel, "See, I am about to t the kingdom from
Job 18: 4 You who t yourself in your anger—
Ps 7: 2 or like a lion they will t me apart;
17:12 They are like a lion eager to t,
50:22 then, you who forget God, or I will t you apart,
52: 5 he will snatch and t you from your tent;
58: 6 t out the fangs of the young lions, O LORD!
137: 7 how they said, "T it down! T it down!
Ecc 3: 7 a time to t, and a time to sew;
Isa 64: 1 O that you would t open the heavens and come
Jer 22:24 even from there I would t you off
24: 6 I will build them up, and not t them down;
36:24 was alarmed, nor did they t their garments.
Eze 13:20 I will t them from your arms,
13:21 I will t off your veils, and save my people
23:34 and gnaw its sherds, and t out your breasts;
Hos 5:14 I myself will t and go away;
13: 8 and will t open the covering of their heart;
Am 3:15 I will t down the winter house as well as
Mic 3: 2 who t the skin off my people,
Mal 1: 4 They may build, but I will t down,
Mt 5:29 t it out and throw it away;
9:16 and a worse t is made.
18: 9 t it out and throw it away;
Mk 2:21 the new from the old, and a worse t is made.
9:47 And if your eye causes you to stumble, t it out;
Jn 19:24 So they said to one another, "Let us not t it,
Ac 23:10 fearing that they would t Paul to pieces,
Rev 7:17 and God will wipe away every t from their eyes."
21: 4 he will wipe every t from their eyes.
1Mc 4:45 And they thought it best to t it down,
6:62 the oath he had sworn and gave orders to t down
9:54 Alcimus gave orders to t down the wall of
9:55 But he only began to t it down,
2Mc 14:33 shrine of God to the ground and t down the altar,

TEARFUL (2) [TEAR]

3Mc 4: 2 was incessant mourning, lamentation, and t cries;
5:25 toward heaven and with most t supplication

TEARING (5) [TEAR]

Eze 22:25 Its princes within it are like a roaring lion t
22:27 Its officials within it are like wolves t the prey,
Zec 11:16 the flesh of the fat ones, t off even their hoofs.
2Co 10: 8 for building you up and not for t you down,
13:10 for building up and not for t down.

TEARS‡ (61) [TEAR]

Dt 33:20 Gad lives like a lion; he t at arm and scalp.
2Ki 20: 5 I have heard your prayer, I have seen your t;
Job 12:14 If he t down, no one can rebuild;
16:20 My friends scorn me; my eye pours out t to God,
Ps 6: 6 every night I flood my bed with t;
39:12 do not hold your peace at my t.
42: 3 My t have been my food day and night,
56: 8 put my t in your bottle.
80: 5 You have fed them with the bread of t,
80: 5 and given them t to drink in full measure.
102: 9 I eat ashes like bread, and mingle t with my drink,
116: 8 my eyes from t, my feet from stumbling.
119:136 My eyes shed streams of t because your law is
126: 5 May those who sow in t reap with shouts of joy.
Pr 14: 1 but the foolish t it down with her own hands.
15:25 The LORD t down the house of the proud,
Ecc 4: 1 Look, the t of the oppressed—
Isa 15: 3 and in the squares everyone wails and melts in t.
16: 9 I drench you with my t, O Heshbon and Elealeh;
22: 4 Look away from me, let me weep bitter t;
25: 8 Lord GOD will wipe away the t from all faces,
38: 5 I have heard your prayer, I have seen your t;
Jer 9: 1 and my eyes a fountain of t,
9:18 so that our eyes may run down with t,
13:17 my eyes will weep bitterly and run down with t,
14:17 Let my eyes run down with t night and day,
31:16 from weeping, and your eyes from t;
La 1: 2 in the night, with t on her cheeks;
1:16 For these things I weep; my eyes flow with t;
2:18 Let t stream down like a torrent day and night!
3:48 of t because of the destruction of my people.
Eze 24:16 nor shall your t run down.
Mic 5: 8 when it goes through, treads down and t in pieces,
Mal 2:13 You cover the LORD's altar with t,
Lk 5:36 "No one t a piece from a new garment and sews it
7:38 to bathe his feet with her t and to dry them
7:44 for my feet, but she has bathed my feet with her t
Ac 20:19 serving the Lord with all humility and with t,
20:31 not cease night or day to warn everyone with t.
2Co 2: 4 and anguish of heart and with many t,
Php 3:18 and now I tell you even with t.
2Ti 1: 4 Recalling your t, I long to see you so that I may
Heb 5: 7 with loud cries and t, to the one who was able
12:17 even though he sought the blessing with t.
Tob 7:16 Then, wiping away the t, she said to her,
Sir 12:16 an enemy may have t in his eyes,
22:19 One who pricks the eye brings t,
31:13 Therefore it sheds t for any reason.
34:28 When one builds and another t down,
35:18 Do not the t of the widow run down her cheek
38:16 My child, let your t fall for the dead,
Sus 1:35 Through her t she looked up toward Heaven,
2Mc 11: 6 they and all the people, with lamentations and t,
3Mc 1: 4 Arsinoë went to the troops with wailing and t,
1:16 and they filled the temple with cries and t;
4: 4 of life and shed t at the most miserable expulsion
5: 7 with t and a voice hard to silence they all called
6:14 of infants and their parents entreat you with t.
6:22 the king's anger was turned to pity and t because
4Mc 4:11 and with t begged the Hebrews to pray for him
15:20 of the torturings, you did not shed t.

TEATS (KJV) See BREASTS

TEBAH (1)
Ge 22:24 his concubine, whose name was Reumah, bore **T**,

TEBALIAH (1)
1Ch 26:11 **T** the third, Zechariah the fourth:

TEBETH (1)
Est 2:16 which is the month of **T**,

TEDIOUS (KJV) See DETAIN

TEEMS (1)
Lev 20:25 by bird or by anything with which the ground **t**,

TEETH (52) [TOOTH]
Ge 49:12 and his **t** whiter than milk.
Nu 11:33 But while the meat was still between their **t**,
Dt 32:24 The **t** of beasts I will send against them,
Job 4:10 and the **t** of the young lions are broken.
13:14 I will take my flesh in my **t**,
16: 9 he has gnashed his **t** at me;
19:20 and I have escaped by the skin of my **t**.
29:17 and made them drop their prey from their **t**.
41:14 There is terror all around its **t**.
Ps 3: 7 you break the **t** of the wicked.
35:16 gnashing at me with their **t**.
37:12 and gnash their **t** at them;
57: 4 their **t** are spears and arrows,
58: 6 O God, break the **t** in their mouths;
112:10 they gnash their **t** and melt away;
124: 6 who has not given us as prey to their **t**.
Pr 10:26 Like vinegar to the **t**, and smoke to the eyes,
30:14 There are those whose **t** are swords,
30:14 whose **t** are knives, to devour the poor from off
SS 4: 2 Your **t** are like a flock of shorn ewes
6: 6 Your **t** are like a flock of ewes,
7: 9 that goes down smoothly, gliding over lips and **t**.
Isa 41:15 sharp, new, and having **t**;
Jer 31:29 and the children's **t** are set on edge."
31:30 the **t** of everyone who eats sour grapes shall be set
La 2:16 they hiss, they gnash their **t**, they cry:
3:16 He has made my **t** grind on gravel,
Eze 18: 2 and the children's **t** are set on edge"?
Da 7: 5 had three tusks in its mouth among its **t**
7: 7 It had great iron **t** and was devouring,
7:19 with its **t** of iron and claws of bronze,
Joel 1: 6 its **t** are lions' **t**, and it has the fangs of a lioness.
Am 4: 6 I gave you cleanness of **t** in all your cities,
Zec 9: 7 and its abominations from between its **t**;
Mt 8:12 where there will be weeping and gnashing of **t**."
13:42 where there will be weeping and gnashing of **t**.
13:50 where there will be weeping and gnashing of **t**.
22:13 where there will be weeping and gnashing of **t**.'
24:51 where there will be weeping and gnashing of **t**.
25:30 where there will be weeping and gnashing of **t**.'
Mk 9:18 and he foams and grinds his **t** and becomes rigid;
Lk 13:28 weeping and gnashing of **t** when you see Abraham
Ac 7:54 they became enraged and ground their **t**
Rev 9: 8 hair like women's hair, and their **t** like lions' **t**;
Sir 21: 2 Its **t** are lion's **t**, and can destroy human lives.
30:10 and in the end you will gnash your **t**.
51: 3 from grinding **t** about to devour me,
2Es 15:30 a portion of the land of the Assyrians with their **t**.
4Mc 7: 6 you neither defiled your sacred **t**

TEHAPHNEHES (1) [=TAHPANHES]
Eze 30:18 At **T** the day shall be dark,

TEHINNAH (1)
1Ch 4:12 Paseah, and **T** the father of Ir-nahash.

TEIL (KJV) See TEREBINTH

TEKEL (2)
Da 5:25 that was inscribed: MENE, MENE, **T**, and PARSIN.
5:27 **T**, you have been weighed on the scales

TEKOA (12) [TEKOITE, TEKOITES]
2Sa 14: 2 to **T** and brought from there a wise woman.
14: 4 When the woman of **T** came to the king,
14: 9 The woman of **T** said to the king,
23:26 Helez the Paltite; Ira son of Ikkesh of **T**;
1Ch 2:24 of Hezron bore him Ashhur, father of **T**.
4: 5 Ashhur father of **T** had two wives,
11:28 Ira son of Ikkesh of **T**, Abiezer of Anathoth,
2Ch 11: 6 He built up Bethlehem, Etam, **T**,
20:20 and went out into the wilderness of **T**;
Jer 6: 1 Blow the trumpet in **T**, and raise a signal on
Am 1: 1 who was among the shepherds of **T**,
1Mc 9:33 and they fled into the wilderness of **T** and camped

TEKOITE (1) [TEKOA]
1Ch 27: 9 for the sixth month, was Ira son of Ikkesh the **T**;

TEKOITES (2) [TEKOA]
Ne 3: 5 Next to them the **T** made repairs;
3:27 After him the **T** repaired another section opposite

TEL-ABIB (1)
Eze 3:15 I came to the exiles at **T**,

TEL-HARSHA (3)
Ezr 2:59 **T**, Cherub, Addan, and Immer,
Ne 7:61 **T**, Cherub, Addon, and Immer,
1Es 5:36 up from Tel-melah and **T**,

TEL-MELAH (3)
Ezr 2:59 The following were those who came up from **T**,
Ne 7:61 The following were those who came up from **T**,
1Es 5:36 The following are those who came up from **T**

TELAH (1)
1Ch 7:25 Rephah was his son, Resheph his son, **T** his son,

TELAIM (1)
1Sa 15: 4 and numbered them in **T**,

TELAM (1)
1Sa 27: 8 the landed settlements from **T** on the way to Shur

TELASSAR (2)
2Ki 19:12 Rezeph, and the people of Eden who were in **T**?
Isa 37:12 Rezeph, and the people of Eden who were in **T**?

TELEM (3)
Jos 15:24 Ziph, **T**, Bealoth,
Ezr 10:24 Of the gatekeepers: Shallum, **T**, and Uri.
1Es 9:25 Of the gatekeepers: Shallum and **T**.

TELL‡ (484) [FORETOLD, FORTUNE-TELLING, STORY-TELLERS, TELLING, TELLS, TOLD]
Ge 12:18 Why did you not **t** me that she was your wife?
21:26 you did not **t** me, and I have not heard of it
24:23 "**T** me whose daughter you are.
24:49 and truly with my master, **t** me;
24:49 **t** me, so that I may turn either to the right hand or
29:15 **T** me, what shall your wages be?"
31:20 in that he did not **t** him that he intended to flee.
31:27 and deceive me and not **t** me?
32: 5 and I have sent to **t** my lord,
32:29 Then Jacob asked him, "Please **t** me your name."
37:16 "**t** me, please, where they are pasturing the flock."
40: 8 Please **t** them to me."
42:22 "Did I not **t** you not to wrong the boy?
43: 6 "Why did you treat me so badly as to **t** the man
45:13 You must **t** my father how greatly I am honored
46:31 "I will go up and **t** Pharaoh, and will say to him,
49: 1 around, that I may **t** you what will happen to you
Ex 6:11 "Go and **t** Pharaoh king of Egypt to let
6:29 **t** Pharaoh king of Egypt all that I am speaking
7: 2 and your brother Aaron shall **t** Pharaoh to let
8: 9 "Kindly **t** me when I am to pray for you and
10: 2 that you may **t** your children and grandchildren
11: 2 **T** the people that every man is to ask his neighbor
12: 3 **T** the whole congregation of Israel that on
13: 8 You shall **t** your child on that day,
14: 2 **T** the Israelites to turn back and camp in front
14:15 **T** the Israelites to go forward.
19: 3 say to the house of Jacob, and **t** the Israelites:
25: 2 **T** the Israelites to take for me an offering;
Lev 14:35 the owner of the house shall come and **t** the priest,
16: 2 **T** your brother Aaron not to come just at any time
Nu 14:14 and they will **t** the inhabitants of this land.
15:38 and **t** them to make fringes on the corners
16:37 **T** Eleazar son of Aaron the priest to take
19: 2 **T** the Israelites to bring you a red heifer
22:20 but do only what I **t** you to do."
22:35 but speak only what I **t** you to speak."
23: 3 Whatever he shows me I will **t** you."
23:26 But Balaam answered Balak, "Did I not **t** you,
24:12 "Did I not **t** your messengers whom you sent
Dt 5:27 **t** us everything that the LORD our God tells you,
5:31 and I will **t** you all the commandments,
32: 7 your elders, and they will **t** you.
Jos 2:14 If you do not **t** this business of ours,
2:20 But if you **t** this business of ours,
4: 7 then you shall **t** them that the waters of
4:10 the LORD commanded Joshua to **t** the people,
6:10 until the day I **t** you to shout.
7:19 **T** me now what you have done;
Jdg 5:10 "**T** of it, you who ride on white donkeys,
13: 6 and he did not **t** me his name;
14: 6 not **t** his father or his mother what he had done.
14: 9 But he did not **t** them that he had taken the honey
14:16 Why should I **t** you?"
16: 6 "Please **t** me what makes your strength so great,
16:10 please **t** me how you could be bound."
16:13 **t** me how you could be bound."
20: 3 And the Israelites said, "**T** us,
Ru 3: 4 and he will **t** you what to do."
3: 5 She said to her, "All that you **t** me I will do."
4: 4 So I thought I would **t** you of it, and say:
4: 4 but if you will not, **t** me, so that I may know;
1Sa 3:15 Samuel was afraid to **t** the vision to Eli.
6: 2 **T** us what we should send with it to its place."
9: 6 perhaps he will **t** us about the journey
9: 8 I will give it to the man of God, to **t** us our way."
9:18 "**T** me, please, where is the house of the seer?"
9:19 in the morning I will let you go and will **t** you all
9:27 "**T** the boy to go on before us,
10:15 "**T** me what Samuel said to you."
10:16 he did not **t** him anything.
1Sa 14: 1 But he did not **t** his father.
14:43 "**T** me what you have done."
15:16 I will **t** you what the LORD said
19: 3 if I learn anything I will **t** you."
20: 9 upon you, would I not **t** you?"
20:10 Then David said to Jonathan, "Who will **t** me
22:22 that he would surely **t** Saul.
23:11 the God of Israel, I beseech you, **t** your servant."
25: 8 Ask your young men, and they will **t** you.
25:19 But she did not **t** her husband Nabal.
27:11 thinking, "They might **t** about us, and say,
28:15 I have summoned you to **t** me what I should do."
2Sa 1: 4 "How did things go? **T** me!"
1:20 **T** it not in Gath, proclaim it not in the streets
3:19 then Abner went to **t** David at Hebron all
7: 5 Go and **t** my servant David:
11:22 and told David all that Joab had sent him to **t**.
12:18 And the servants of David were afraid to **t** him
12:18 how then can we **t** him the child is dead?
13: 4 Will you not **t** me?"
15:35 **t** it to the priests Zadok and Abiathar.
17: 6 If not, you **t** us."
17:16 Therefore send quickly and **t** David,
17:17 a servant-girl used to go and **t** them,
17:17 and they would go and **t** King David;
18:21 "Go, **t** the king what you have seen."
20:16 **T** Joab, 'Come here, I want to speak to you.' "
1Ki 1:20 of all Israel are on you to **t** them who shall sit on
14: 3 he will **t** you what shall happen to the child."
14: 7 Go, **t** Jeroboam, 'Thus says the LORD,
18: 8 Go, **t** your lord that Elijah is here."
18:11 now you say, 'Go, **t** your lord that Elijah is here.'
18:12 when I come and **t** Ahab and he cannot find you,
18:14 now you say, 'Go, **t** your lord that Elijah is here';
20: 9 to the messengers of Ben-hadad, "**T** my lord
20:11 The king of Israel answered, "**T** him:
22:16 to **t** me nothing but the truth in the name of
22:18 "Did I not **t** you that he would
2Ki 2: 9 "**T** me what I may do for you,
4: 2 **T** me, what do you have in the house?"
4:24 do not hold back for me unless I **t** you."
6:11 **t** me who among us sides with the king of Israel?"
7: 9 therefore let us go and **t** the king's household."
7:12 "I will **t** you what the Arameans have prepared
8: 4 "**T** me all the great things that Elisha has done."
9:12 They said, "Liar! Come on, **t** us!"
9:15 then let no one slip out of the city to go and **t**
22:15 **T** the man who sent you to me,
1Ch 16: 9 sing praises to him, **t** of all his wonderful works.
16:23 **T** of his salvation from day to day.
17: 4 Go and **t** my servant David:
21:18 to **t** David that he should go up and erect an altar
2Ch 10:10 but you must lighten it for us'; **t** them,
18:15 to **t** me nothing but the truth in the name of
18:17 "Did I not **t** you that he would
34:23 **T** the man who sent you to me,
Est 2:10 for Mordecai had charged her not to **t**.
5:14 the morning **t** the king to have Mordecai hanged
Job 1:15 I alone have escaped to **t** you."
1:16 I alone have escaped to **t** you."
1:17 I alone have escaped to **t** you."
1:19 I alone have escaped to **t** you."
8:10 not teach you and **t** you and utter words out
11: 6 and that he would **t** you the secrets of wisdom!
12: 7 the birds of the air, and they will **t** you;
38: 4 **T** me, if you have understanding.
Ps 2: 7 I will **t** of the decree of the LORD:
9: 1 I will **t** of all your wonderful deeds.
22:22 I will **t** of your name to my brothers and sisters;
30: 9 Will it **t** of your faithfulness?
35:28 Then my tongue shall **t** of your righteousness and
40: 5 Were I to proclaim and **t** of them,
41: 6 when they go out, they **t** it abroad.
48:13 go through its citadels, that you may **t** the next
50:12 "If I were hungry, I would not **t** you,
64: 9 they will **t** what God has brought about,
66:16 and I will **t** what he has done for me.
71:15 My mouth will **t** of your righteous acts,
73:28 the Lord GOD my refuge, to **t** of all your works.
75: 1 People **t** of your wondrous deeds.
78: 4 we will **t** to the coming generation
78: 6 and rise up and **t** them to their children,
96: 2 **t** of his salvation from day to day.
105: 2 **t** of all his wonderful works.
107:22 and **t** of his deeds with songs of joy.
142: 2 I **t** my trouble before him.
145:11 the glory of your kingdom, and **t** of your power,
Ecc 6:12 For who can **t** them what will be after them under
8: 7 for who can **t** them how it will be?
10:14 and who can **t** anyone what the future holds?
10:20 or some winged creature **t** the matter.
SS 1: 7 **T** me, you whom my soul loves,
5: 8 **t** him this: I am faint with love.
Isa 3:10 **T** the innocent how fortunate they are,
5: 5 now I will **t** you what I will do to my vineyard.
19:12 Let them **t** you and make known what the LORD
41:22 Let them bring them, and **t** us what is to happen.
41:22 **T** us the former things, what they are,
41:23 **T** us what is to come hereafter,
42: 9 before they spring forth, I **t** you of them.
44: 7 Let them **t** us what is yet to be.
Jer 1:17 up and **t** them everything that I command you.
4:16 **T** the nations, "Here they are!"
16:10 And when you **t** this people all these words,
19: 2 and proclaim there the words that I **t** you.
23:27 by their dreams that they **t** one another,
23:28 Let the prophet who has a dream **t** the dream,

Jer 23:32 says the LORD, and who t them,
28:13 t Hananiah, Thus says the LORD:
33: 3 and will t you great and hidden things
36:17 Then they questioned Baruch, "T us now,
38:15 Jeremiah said to Zedekiah, "If I t you,
38:25 'Just t us what you said to the king;
42: 4 whatever the LORD answers you I will t you;
42:20 t us and we will do it.'
42:21 in anything that he sent me to t you.
48:20 T it by the Arnon, that Moab is laid waste.
51:31 to t the king of Babylon that his city is taken from
Eze 12:16 that they may t of all their abominations among
12:23 T them therefore, "Thus says the Lord GOD:
17:12 not know what these things mean? T them:
24:19 "Will you not t us what these things mean for us,
44: 5 that I shall t you concerning all the ordinances of
Da 2: 2 Chaldeans be summoned to t the king his dreams.
2: 4 T your servants the dream,
2: 5 not t me both the dream and its interpretation,
2: 6 if you do t me the dream and its interpretation,
2: 6 Therefore t me the dream and its interpretation."
2: 7 "Let the king first t his servants the dream,
2: 9 if you do not t me the dream,
2: 9 Therefore, t me the dream,
2:16 the king give him time and he would t the king
2:25 the exiles from Judah a man who can t the king
2:26 "Are you able to t me the dream that I have seen
2:36 now we will t the king its interpretation.
4: 6 in order that they might t me the interpretation of
4: 7 but they could not t me its interpretation.
4: 9 Hear the dream that I saw; t me its interpretation.
4:18 the wise men of my kingdom are unable to t me
5: 7 and t me its interpretation shall be clothed
5: 8 but they could not read the writing or t the king
5:15 to read this writing and t me its interpretation,
5:16 to read the writing and t me its interpretation,
8:19 and I will t you what will take place later in
10:21 But I am to t you what is inscribed in the book
Joel 1: 3 T your children of it,
1: 3 and let your children t their children,
Jnh 1: 8 "T us why this calamity has come upon us.
3: 2 and proclaim to it the message that I t you."
Mic 1:10 T it not in Gath, weep not at all;
Zec 10: 2 the dreamers t false dreams,
Mt 2:13 and flee to Egypt, and remain there until I t you;
3: 9 for I t you, God is able from these stones to raise
5:18 For truly I t you, until heaven
5:20 For I t you, unless your righteousness exceeds
5:26 Truly I t you, you will never get out
6: 2 Truly I t you, they have received their reward.
6: 5 Truly I t you, they have received their reward.
6:16 Truly I t you, they have received their reward.
6:25 "Therefore I t you, do not worry about your life,
6:29 yet I t you, even Solomon in all his glory was
8:10 to those who followed him, "Truly I t you,
8:11 I t you, many will come from east and west
10:15 Truly I t you, it will be more tolerable for the land
10:23 for truly I t you, you will not have gone
10:27 What I say to you in the dark, t in the light;
10:42 truly I t you, none of these will lose their reward."
11: 4 "Go and t John what you hear and see:
11: 9 Yes, I t you, and more than a prophet.
11:11 Truly I t you, among those born
11:22 But I t you, on the day of judgment it will
11:24 But I t you that on the day of judgment it will
12: 6 I t you, something greater than the temple is here.
12:31 Therefore I t you, people will be forgiven
12:36 I t you, on the day of judgment you will have
13:17 Truly I t you, many prophets
13:30 and at harvest time I will t the reapers,
16:18 And I t you, you are Peter,
16:20 not to t anyone that he was the Messiah.
16:28 Truly I t you, there are some standing here who
17: 9 "T no one about the vision until after the Son
17:12 but I t you that Elijah has already come,
17:20 For truly I t you, if you have faith the size of
18: 3 "Truly I t you, unless you change and become
18:10 for, I t you, in heaven their angels continually see
18:13 And if he finds it, truly I t you,
18:17 If the member refuses to listen to them, t it to
18:18 Truly I t you, whatever you bind on earth will
18:19 truly I t you, if two of you agree on earth
18:22 Jesus said to him, "Not seven times, but, I t you,
19:23 Then Jesus said to his disciples, "Truly I t you,
19:24 Again I t you, it is easier for a camel to go
19:28 Jesus said to them, "Truly I t you,
21: 5 "T the daughter of Zion, Look,
21:21 Jesus answered them, "Truly I t you,
21:24 if you t me the answer, then I will also t you
21:27 And he said to them, "Neither will I t you
21:31 Jesus said to them, "Truly I t you,
21:43 Therefore I t you, the kingdom of God will
22: 4 saying, 'T those who have been invited:
22:17 T us, then, what you think.
23:36 Truly I t you, all this will come
23:39 For I t you, you will not see me again
24: 2 Truly I t you, not one stone will be left here
24: 3 the disciples came to him privately, saying, "T us,
24:34 Truly I t you, this generation will not pass away
24:47 Truly I t you, he will put that one in charge
25:12 But he replied, 'Truly I t you, I do not know you.'
25:40 And the king will answer them, 'Truly I t you,
25:45 Then he will answer them, 'Truly I t you,
26:13 Truly I t you, wherever this good news is
26:21 "Truly I t you, one of you will betray me."
26:29 I t you, I will never again drink of this fruit of
26:34 Jesus said to him, "Truly I t you, this very night,
Mt 26:63 t us if you are the Messiah, the Son of God."
26:64 But I t you, From now on you will see the Son
27:64 and steal him away, and t the people,
28: 7 Then go quickly and t his disciples,
28: 8 and ran to t his disciples.
28:10 go and t my brothers to go to Galilee;
Mk 3:28 "Truly I t you, people will be forgiven
5:19 and t them how much the Lord has done for you,
7:36 Then Jesus ordered them to t no one;
8:12 Truly I t you, no sign will be given
8:30 And he sternly ordered them not to t anyone
9: 1 And he said to them, "Truly I t you,
9: 9 to t no one about what they had seen,
9:13 But I t you that Elijah has come,
9:41 For truly I t you, whoever gives you a cup
10:15 Truly I t you, whoever does not receive
10:29 Jesus said, "Truly I t you,
10:32 and began to t them what was to happen to him,
11:23 Truly I t you, if you say to this mountain,
11:24 So I t you, whatever you ask for in prayer,
11:29 I will t you by what authority I do these things.
11:33 And Jesus said to them, "Neither will I t you
12:43 to them, "Truly I t you, this poor widow has put
13: 4 "T us, when will this be, and what will be the sign
13:30 Truly I t you, this generation will not pass away
14: 9 Truly I t you, wherever the good news is
14:18 "Truly I t you, one of you will betray me,
14:25 Truly I t you, I will never again drink of the fruit
14:30 Jesus said to him, "Truly I t you, this day,
16: 7 t his disciples and Peter that he is going ahead
Lk 3: 8 for I t you, God is able from these stones to raise
4:24 And he said, "Truly I t you,
5:14 And he ordered him to t no one.
6:46 Lord,' and do not do what I t you?
7: 9 the crowd that followed him, he said, "I t you,
7:22 "Go and t John what you have seen and heard:
7:26 Yes, I t you, and more than a prophet.
7:28 I t you, among those born
7:47 Therefore, I t you, her sins, which were many,
8:56 he ordered them to t no one what had happened.
9:21 and commanded them not to t anyone,
9:27 But truly I t you, there are some standing here who
10:12 I t you, on that day it will be more tolerable
10:24 For I t you that many prophets and kings desired
10:40 T her then to help me."
11: 8 I t you, even though he will not get up
11:51 I t you, it will be charged against this generation.
12: 4 "I t you, my friends, do not fear those who kill
12: 5 Yes, I t you, fear him!
12: 8 "And I t you, everyone who acknowledges me
12:13 t my brother to divide the family inheritance
12:22 He said to his disciples, "Therefore I t you,
12:27 yet I t you, even Solomon in all his glory was
12:37 truly I t you, he will fasten his belt
12:44 Truly I t you, he will put that one in charge
12:51 No, I t you, but rather division!
12:59 I t you, you will never get out until you have paid
13: 3 I t you; but unless you repent,
13: 5 I t you; but unless you repent,
13:24 I t you, will try to enter and will not be able.
13:32 He said to them, "Go and t that fox for me,
13:35 And I t you, you will not see me until
14:24 For I t you, none of those
15: 7 so, I t you, there will be more joy in heaven
15:10 I t you, there is joy in the presence of the angels
16: 9 And I t you, make friends for yourselves
17:34 I t you, on that night there will be two in one bed;
18: 8 I t you, he will quickly grant justice to them.
18:14 I t you, this man went down
18:17 Truly I t you, whoever does not receive
18:29 And he said to them, "Truly I t you,
19:11 he went on to t a parable,
19:26 'I t you, to all those who have,
19:40 He answered, "I t you, if these were silent,
20: 2 and said to him, "T us, by what authority
20: 3 "I will also ask you a question, and you t me:
20: 8 Then Jesus said to them, "Neither will I t you
20: 9 He began to t the people this parable:
21: 3 "Truly I t you, this poor widow has put
21:32 Truly I t you, this generation will not pass away
22:16 for I t you, I will not eat it until it is fulfilled in
22:18 for I t you that from now on I will not drink of
22:34 Jesus said, "I t you, Peter,
22:37 For I t you, this scripture must be fulfilled in me,
22:67 They said, "If you are the Messiah, t us."
22:67 He replied, "If I t you, you will not believe;
23:43 He replied, "Truly I t you,
Jn 1:51 And he said to him, "Very truly, I t you,
3: 3 Jesus answered him, "Very truly, I t you,
3: 5 Jesus answered, "Very truly, I t you,
3:11 I t you, we speak of what we know and testify
3:12 can you believe if I t you about heavenly things?
4:35 But I t you, look around you,
5:19 Jesus said to them, "Very truly, I t you,
5:24 I t you, anyone who hears my word
5:25 "Very truly, I t you, the hour is coming,
6:26 Jesus answered them, "Very truly, I t you,
6:32 Then Jesus said to them, "Very truly, I t you,
6:47 I t you, whoever believes has eternal life.
6:53 So Jesus said to them, "Very truly, I t you,
8:34 Jesus answered them, "Very truly, I t you,
8:45 But because I t the truth, you do not believe me.
8:46 If I t the truth, why do you not believe me?
8:51 Very truly, I t you, whoever keeps my word will
8:58 Jesus said to them, "Very truly, I t you,
9:36 T me, so that I may believe in him."
10: 1 I t you, anyone who does not enter the sheepfold
Jn 10: 7 So again Jesus said to them, "Very truly, I t you,
10:24 If you are the Messiah, t us plainly."
11:40 "Did I not t you that if you believed,
12:24 I t you, unless a grain of wheat falls into the earth
13:16 I t you, servants are not greater than their master,
13:19 I t you this now, before it occurs,
13:20 Very truly, I t you, whoever receives one whom I
13:21 "Very truly, I t you, one of you will betray me."
13:38 Very truly, I t you, before the cock crows,
14:12 I t you, the one who believes in me will also do
16: 7 Nevertheless I t you the truth:
16:20 Very truly, I t you, you will weep and mourn,
16:23 I t you, if you ask anything of the Father
16:25 but will t you plainly of the Father.
18:34 or did others t you about me?"
20:15 t me where you have laid him,
21:18 Very truly, I t you, when you were younger,
Ac 5: 8 "T me whether you and your husband sold
5:20 in the temple and t the people the whole message
5:38 So in the present case, I t you,
12:17 he added, "T this to James and to the believers."
15:27 who themselves will t you the same things
21:21 that you t them not to circumcise their children
21:23 So do what we t you.
22:27 The tribune came and asked Paul, "T me,
23:18 he has something to t you."
23:22 "T no one that you have informed me of this."
24:20 Or let these men here t what crime they had found
Ro 15: 8 For I t you that Christ has become a servant of
1Co 15:51 Listen, I will t you a mystery!
Gal 4:21 T me, you who desire to be subject to the law,
Eph 6:21 Tychicus will t you everything.
Php 3:18 and now I t you even with tears.
Col 4: 7 Tychicus will t you all the news about me;
4: 9 They will t you about everything here.
Tit 2: 2 T the older men to be temperate, serious, prudent,
2: 3 t the older women to be reverent in behavior,
2: 9 T slaves to be submissive to their masters and
Heb 11:32 For time would fail me to t of Gideon, Barak,
Rev 17: 7 I will t you the mystery of the woman,
Tob 5: 7 young man, until I go in and t my father;
5: 9 So Tobias went in to t his father Tobit and said
5:11 of what family are you and from what tribe? T me,
Jdt 2: 7 T them to prepare earth and water,
5: 3 "T me, you Canaanites, what people is this
5: 5 and I will t you the truth about this people
6: 2 as you have done today and t us not to make war
8:34 for I will not t you until I have finished what I am
10:16 but t him what you have just said,
11: 3 But now t me why you have fled from them
11:17 will t me when they have committed their sins.
11:18 Then I will come and t you,
11:19 it was announced to me, and I was sent to t you."
14: 8 t me what you have done during these days."
15: 4 to t what had taken place and to urge all
AdE 5:14 the morning t the king to have Mordecai hanged
Wis 6:22 I will t you what wisdom is and how she came to
Sir 1:24 then the lips of many t of their good sense.
6: 9 and t of the quarrel to your disgrace.
20:20 for he does not t it at the proper time.
37: 9 and t you, "Your way is good,"
43:24 Those who sail the sea t of its dangers,
Sus 1:10 but they did not t each other of their distress,
1:41 but she would not t us.
1:54 then, if you really saw this woman, t me this:
1:58 Now then, t me: Under what tree did you catch
Bel 1: 8 you do not t me who is eating these provisions,
1Mc 4:46 a prophet should come to t what to do with them.
10:72 People will t you that you cannot stand before us,
2Mc 10:10 Now we will t what took place
1Es 8:46 and ordered them to t Iddo and his kindred and
Pm 151: 3 And who will t my Lord?
2Es 1: 5 so that they may t their children's children
2:10 "T my people that I will give them the kingdom
2:48 t my people how great and how many are
4:52 I can t you in part;
4:52 but I was not sent to t you concerning your life,
5:13 These are the signs that I am permitted to t you,
5:32 pay attention to me, and I will t you more."
5:51 a woman who bears children, and she will t you.
7:*54* but ask the earth and she will t you;
8: 2 But I t you a parable, Ezra.
8: 2 it will t you that it provides a large amount of clay
9:42 I said to her, "What has happened to you? T me."
10: 9 and she will t you that it is she who ought
10:38 and t you about the things that you fear;
11:42 you have hated those who t the truth,
13:21 "I will t you the interpretation of the vision,
13:56 after three more days I will t you other things,
14:23 and t them not to seek you for forty days.
4Mc 12: 7 as we shall t a little later,

TELLING (34) [TELL]

Jdg 7:13 there was a man t a dream to his comrade;
7:15 the t of the dream and its interpretation,
2Sa 11:19 "When you have finished t the king all the news
2Ki 1: 2 so he sent messengers, t them, "Go,
8: 5 While he was t the king how Elisha had restored
Ezr 8:17 t them what to say to Iddo and his colleagues
Ps 19: 1 The heavens are t the glory of God;
26: 7 and t all your wondrous deeds.
Pr 11:13 A gossip goes about t secrets,
Jer 27:14 the prophets who are t you not to serve the king
40:16 for you are t a lie about Ishmael."
43: 2 to Jeremiah, "You are t a lie.
Mt 14: 4 because John had been t him,

Mt 28:13 t them, "You must say, 'His disciples came
Mk 6:18 For John had been t Herod,
Lk 12:41 are you t this parable for us or for everyone?"
20: 1 as he was teaching the people in the temple and t
Jn 13:29 Jesus was t him, "Buy what we need for
Ac 10: 8 and after t them everything,
17:18 because he was t the good news about Jesus and
17:21 in nothing but t or hearing something new.
19: 4 t the people to believe in the one who was
Gal 4:16 now become your enemy by t you the truth?
5: 2 am t you that if you let yourselves
1Ti 2: 7 a herald and an apostle (I am t the truth,
Rev 13:14 t them to make an image for the beast
16: 1 a loud voice from the temple t the seven angels,
AdE 9:21 t them that they should keep the fourteenth
9:25 in to the king, t him to hang Mordecai;
Bel 1:12 otherwise Daniel will, who is t lies about us."
1Mc 9:60 t them to seize Jonathan and his men;
2Mc 6:23 t them to send him to Hades.
2Es 10:45 for her t you that she was barren for thirty years,
10:47 her t you that she brought him up with much care,

TELLS (24) [TELL]

Ge 21:12 whatever Sarah says to you, do as she t you,
Dt 5:27 tell us everything that the LORD our God t you,
2Ki 6:12 who t the king of Israel the words that you speak
2Ch 32:11 when he t you, 'The LORD our God will save us
Job 36:33 Its crashing t about him; he is jealous with anger
Mt 15: 5 But you say that whoever t father or mother,
Mk 7:11 But you say that if anyone t father or mother,
Jn 2: 5 to the servants, "Do whatever he t you."
19:35 and he knows that he t the truth.)
Ac 3:22 You must listen to whatever he t you.
13:41 even if someone t you.' "
Tob 1: 1 This book t the story of Tobit son of Tobiel son
Sir 22:10 Whoever t a story to a fool t it to a drowsy man;
24: 1 and t of her glory in the midst of her people.
24: 2 and in the presence of his hosts she t of her glory:
1Es 4: 4 he t them to make war on one another, they do it;
4: 7 If he t them to kill, they kill;
4: 7 if he t them to release, they release;
4: 8 if he t them to attack, they attack;
4: 8 if he t them to lay waste, they lay waste;
4: 8 if he t them to build, they build;
4: 9 if he t them to cut down, they cut down;
4: 9 if he t them to plant, they plant.

TEMA (5)

Ge 25:15 Hadad, T, Jetur, Naphish, and Kedemah.
1Ch 1:30 Mishma, Dumah, Massa, Hadad, T,
Job 6:19 caravans of T look, the travelers of Sheba hope.
Isa 21:14 O inhabitants of the land of T.
Jer 25:23 Dedan, T, Buz, and all who have shaven temples;

TEMAH (3)

Ezr 2:53 Barkos, Sisera, T,
Ne 7:55 of Barkos, of Sisera, of T,
1Es 5:32 the descendants of T, the descendants of Neziah,

TEMAN (13) [TEMANITE, TEMANITES]

Ge 36:11 The sons of Eliphaz were T, Omar, Zepho,
36:15 the clans T, Omar, Zepho, Kenaz,
36:42 Kenaz, T, Mibzar,
1Ch 1:36 The sons of Eliphaz: T, Omar, Zephi, Gatam,
1:53 Kenaz, T, Mibzar,
Jer 49: 7 Is there no longer wisdom in T?
49:20 that he has formed against the inhabitants of T:
Eze 25:13 from T even to Dedan they shall fall by the sword.
Am 1:12 So I will send a fire on T,
Ob 1: 9 Your warriors shall be shattered, O T,
Hab 3: 3 God came from T, the Holy One
Bar 3:22 not been heard of in Canaan, or seen in T;
3:23 the merchants of Merran and T,

TEMANITE (6) [TEMAN]

Job 2:11 Eliphaz the T, Bildad the Shuhite,
4: 1 Then Eliphaz the T answered:
15: 1 Then Eliphaz the T answered:
22: 1 Then Eliphaz the T answered:
42: 7 the LORD said to Eliphaz the T:
42: 9 So Eliphaz the T and Bildad the Shuhite and

TEMANITES (2) [TEMAN]

Ge 36:34 and Husham of the land of the T succeeded him
1Ch 1:45 Husham of the land of the T succeeded him.

TEMENI (1)

1Ch 4: 6 Hepher, T, and Haahashtari.

TEMPER (5) [HOT-TEMPERED, QUICK-TEMPERED, TEMPERATE, TEMPERED, TEMPERS]

Ps 32: 9 whose t must be curbed with bit and bridle,
Pr 14:29 but one who has a hasty t exalts folly.
16:32 one whose t is controlled than one who captures
2Mc 4:25 but having the hot t of a cruel tyrant and the rage
1Es 4:31 if she loses her t with him, he flatters her,

TEMPERANCE (KJV) See SELF-CONTROL

TEMPERATE (10) [TEMPER]

1Ti 3: 2 t, sensible, respectable, hospitable, an apt teacher,
3:11 not slanderers, but t, faithful in all things.
Tit 2: 2 Tell the older men to be t, serious, prudent,
4Mc 1:35 checked by the t mind, and all the impulses of
2: 2 certainly, that the t Joseph is praised,
2:16 the t mind repels all these malicious emotions,
2:18 t mind is able to get the better of the emotions,
2:23 to this will rule a kingdom that is t,
3:17 the t mind can conquer the drives of the emotions
3:19 to a narrative demonstration of t reason.

TEMPERED (1) [TEMPER]

Pr 19:19 A violent t person will pay the penalty;

TEMPERED (KJV) See also ARRANGED, BLENDED, MIXED

TEMPERS (1) [TEMPER]

Wis 7:20 the natures of animals and the t of wild animals,

TEMPEST (27) [TEMPESTUOUS]

Job 9:17 For he crushes me with a t,
Ps 50: 3 and a mighty t all around him.
55: 8 a shelter for myself from the raging wind and t."
83:15 with your t and terrify them with your hurricane.
Pr 10:25 When the t passes, the wicked are no more,
Isa 28: 2 like a storm of hail, a destroying t,
29: 6 and great noise, with whirlwind and t, and
30:30 with a cloudburst and t and hailstones.
32: 2 a hiding place from the wind, a covert from the t,
40:24 and the t carries them off like stubble.
41:16 and the t shall scatter them.
Jer 11:16 but with the roar of a great t he will set fire to it,
23:19 a whirling t; it will burst upon the head of the
25:32 and a great t is stirring from the farthest parts of
30:23 a whirling t; it will burst upon the head of the
Ac 27:20 for many days, and no small t raged, all hope
Heb 12:18 a blazing fire, and darkness, and gloom, and a t,
Wis 5:23 and like a t it will winnow them away.
Sir 16:21 Like a t that no one can see,
2Es 15:13 be ruined by blight and hail and by a terrible t.
15:35 pour out a heavy t on the earth, and their own t;
15:39 and the t that was to cause destruction by
15:40 Great and mighty clouds, full of wrath and t,
15:40 upon every high and lofty place a terrible t,
15:44 they shall pour out on it the t and all its fury;
4Mc 13: 7 conquered the t of the emotions.

TEMPESTUOUS (1) [TEMPEST]

Jnh 1:11 For the sea was growing more and more t.

TEMPLE‡ (436) [TEMPLES]

A. TEMPLE OF THE †LORD (24)
B. TEMPLE SERVANTS (24)
C. HOLY TEMPLE (14)
D. TEMPLE OF *GOD (12)
E. TEMPLE OF THE *LORD (10)

Ge 38:21 "Where is the t prostitute who was at Enaim by
Dt 23:17 of the daughters of Israel shall be a t prostitute;
23:17 none of the sons of Israel shall be a t prostitute.
Jdg 4:21 went softly to him and drove the peg into his t,
4:22 with the tent peg in his t.
5:26 she shattered and pierced his t.
9: 4 of silver out of the t of Baal-berith
9:27 Then they went into the t of their god,
9:46 they entered the stronghold of the t of El-berith.
1Sa 1: 9 beside the doorpost of the t of the LORD. A
3: 3 Samuel was lying down in the t of the LORD, A
31:10 They put his armor in the t of Astarte;
2Sa 22: 7 From his t he heard my voice,
1Ki 6: 7 of iron was heard in the t while it was being built.
7:21 He set up the pillars at the vestibule of the t;
7:50 and for the doors of the nave of the t, of gold.
14:24 there were also male t prostitutes in the land.
15:12 He put away the male t prostitutes out of the land,
22:46 of the male t prostitutes who were still in the land
2Ki 10:21 They entered the t of Baal,
10:21 until the t of Baal was filled from wall to wall.
10:23 the t of Baal with Jehonadab son of Rechab;
10:25 and then went into the citadel of the t of Baal.
10:26 They brought out the pillar that was in the t
10:27 and destroyed the t of Baal,
18:16 the gold from the doors of the t of the LORD, A
23: 4 the t of the LORD all the vessels made for Baal, A
23: 7 of the male t prostitutes that were in the house of
24:13 all the vessels of gold in the t of the LORD, A
25:14 and all the bronze vessels used in the t service,
1Ch 9: 2 priests, Levites, and t servants. B
9:33 in the chambers of the t free from other service,
10:10 They put his armor in the t of their gods,
10:10 and fastened his head in the t of Dagon.
28:11 the plan of the vestibule of the t, and
29: 1 t will not be for mortals but for the LORD God.
29:19 the t for which I have made provision."
2Ch 2: 1 Solomon decided to build a t for the name of
2:12 who will build a t for the LORD,
3:17 He set up the pillars in front of the t,
4: 7 and set them in the t,
4: 8 He also made ten tables and placed them in the t,
4:22 As for the entrance to the t:
4:22 and the doors of the nave of the t were of gold.
2Ch 7: 1 and the glory of the LORD filled the t.
7: 3 down and the glory of the LORD on the t,
26:16 and entered the t of the LORD to make offering A
27: 2 only he did not invade the t of the LORD. A
29:16 the t of the LORD into the court of the house of A
35:20 After all this, when Josiah had set the t in order,
Ezr 2:43 The t servants: the descendants of Ziha, B
2:58 All the t servants and the descendants B
2:70 and the t servants lived in their towns, B
3: 6 But the foundation of the t of the LORD was not A
3:10 the foundation of the t of the LORD, the priests A
4: 1 that the returned exiles were building a t to
5:14 the t in Jerusalem and had brought into the t of
5:14 these King Cyrus took out of the t of Babylon,
5:15 go and put them in the t in Jerusalem,
6: 5 of the t in Jerusalem and brought to Babylon,
6: 5 and brought back to the t in Jerusalem,
7: 7 and the t servants also went up to Jerusalem, B
7:24 the singers, the doorkeepers, the t servants, B
8:17 to say to Iddo and his colleagues the t servants B
8:20 besides two hundred twenty of the t servants, B
Ne 2: 8 to make beams for the gates of the t fortress,
3:26 the t servants living on Ophel made repairs B
3:31 made repairs as far as the house of the t servants B
6:10 the t, and let us close the doors of the temple,
6:10 and let us close the doors of the t,
6:11 a man like me go into the t to save his life?
7:46 The t servants: the descendants of Ziha, B
7:60 All the t servants and the descendants B
7:73 t servants, and all Israel settled in their towns. B
10:28 the gatekeepers, the singers, the t servants, B
11: 3 Israel, the priests, the Levites, the t servants, B
11:21 But the t servants lived on Ophel; B
11:21 and Ziha and Gishpa were over the t servants. B
Ps 5: 7 I will bow down toward your holy t in awe C
11: 4 The LORD is in his holy t; C
18: 6 From his t he heard my voice,
27: 4 the beauty of the LORD, and to inquire in his t.
29: 9 and in his t all say, "Glory!"
30: T *A Song at the dedication of the t. Of David.*
48: 9 O God, in the midst of your t.
65: 4 with the goodness of your house, your holy t. C
68:29 of your t at Jerusalem kings bear gifts to you.
79: 1 they have defiled your holy t; C
138: 2 toward your holy t and give thanks to your name C
Isa 6: 1 and the hem of his robe filled the t.
15: 2 Dibon has gone up to the t,
44:28 and of the t, "Your foundation shall be laid."
66: 6 A voice from the t!
Jer 7: 4 "This is the t of the LORD, A
7: 4 the t of the LORD, the temple of the LORD." A
7: 4 the temple of the LORD, the t of the LORD." A
24: 1 of figs placed before the t of the LORD. A
38:14 at the third entrance of the t of the LORD. A
41: 5 and incense to present at the t of the LORD. A
50:28 of the LORD our God, vengeance for his t.
51:11 the vengeance of the LORD, vengeance for his t.
52:18 and all the vessels of bronze used in the t service.
Eze 8:16 there, at the entrance of the t of the LORD, A
8:16 with their backs to the t of the LORD, A
40: 5 a wall all around the outside of the t area.
40:45 for the priests who have charge of the t,
40:47 and the altar was in front of the t.
40:48 the vestibule of the t and measured the pilasters of
41: 5 he measured the wall of the t, six cubits thick;
41: 5 four cubits, all around the t.
41: 6 of the t to serve as supports for the side chambers,
41: 6 they should not be supported by the wall of the t.
41: 7 with a stairway all around the t.
41: 8 also that the t had a raised platform all around;
41: 9 the free space between the side chambers of the t
41:10 of twenty cubits all around the t on every side.
41:12 The building that was facing the t yard on
41:13 Then he measured the t, one hundred cubits deep;
41:14 the width of the east front of the t and the yard,
41:15 of the t and the inner room and the outer vestibule
41:16 the threshold the t was paneled with wood all
41:19 They were carved on the whole t all around;
42: 1 the t yard and opposite the building on the north.
42: 8 those opposite the t were one hundred cubits long.
42:15 the interior of the t area,
42:15 and measured the t area all around.
43: 4 the LORD entered the t by the gate facing east,
43: 5 and the glory of the LORD filled the t.
43: 6 I heard someone speaking to me out of the t.
43:10 you, mortal, describe the t to the house of Israel,
43:11 make known to them the plan of the t,
43:12 This is the law of the t:
43:12 This is the law of the t.
43:21 be burnt in the appointed place belonging to the t,
44: 4 by way of the north gate to the front of the t;
44: 4 the glory of the LORD filled the t of the LORD; A
44: 5 all the ordinances of the t of the LORD A
44: 5 and mark well those who may be admitted to the t
44: 7 profaning my t when you offer to me my food,
44:11 having oversight at the gates of the t,
44:11 at the gates of the temple, and serving in the t;
44:14 Yet I will appoint them to keep charge of the t,
45: 5 shall be for the Levites who minister at the t,
45:19 and put it on the doorposts of the t,
45:20 so you shall make atonement for the t.
46:24 at the t shall boil the sacrifices of the people."
47: 1 Then he brought me back to the entrance of the t;
47: 1 from below the threshold of the t toward the east
47: 1 the temple toward the east (for the t faced east);
47: 1 the south end of the threshold of the t,
48:21 The holy portion with the sanctuary of the t in

Da 5: 2 of the **t** in Jerusalem, so that the king
5: 3 of gold and silver that had been taken out of the **t**,
5:23 vessels of his **t** have been brought in before you,
11:31 Forces sent by him shall occupy and profane the **t**
Hos 4:14 and sacrifice with **t** prostitutes;
Am 7:13 and it is a **t** of the kingdom."
8: 3 songs of the **t** shall become wailings in that day,"
Jnh 2: 4 how shall I look again upon your holy **t**?' C
2: 7 and my prayer came to you, into your holy **t**. C
Mic 1: 2 a witness against you, the Lord from his holy **t**. C
Hab 2:20 But the LORD is in his holy **t**; C
Hag 2:15 stone was placed upon a stone in the LORD's **t**,
2:18 that the foundation of the LORD's **t** was laid,
Zec 6:12 and he shall build the **t** of the LORD. A
6:13 It is he that shall build the **t** of the LORD; A
6:14 as a memorial in the **t** of the LORD. A
6:15 and help to build the **t** of the LORD; A
8: 9 the foundation was laid for the rebuilding of the **t**,
Mal 1:10 that someone among you would shut the **t** doors,
3: 1 Lord whom you seek will suddenly come to his **t**.
Mt 4: 5 and placed him on the pinnacle of the **t**,
12: 5 the sabbath the priests in the **t** break the sabbath
12: 6 I tell you, something greater than the **t** is here.
17:24 the collectors of the **t** tax came to Peter and said,
17:24 "Does your teacher not pay the **t** tax?"
21:12 the **t** and drove out all who were selling
21:12 and buying in the **t**, and he overturned the tables
21:14 The blind and the lame came to him in the **t**,
21:15 and heard the children crying out in the **t**,
21:23 When he entered the **t**, the chief priests and
24: 1 As Jesus came out of the **t** and was going away,
24: 1 to point out to him the buildings of the **t**.
26:55 Day after day I sat in the **t** teaching,
26:61 'I am able to destroy the **t** of God and to build it D
27: 5 Throwing down the pieces of silver in the **t**,
27:40 "You who would destroy the **t** and build it
27:51 that moment the curtain of the **t** was torn in two,
Mk 11:11 Then he entered Jerusalem and went into the **t**;
11:15 And he entered the **t** and began
11:15 in the **t**, and he overturned the tables of
11:16 not allow anyone to carry anything through the **t**.
11:27 As he was walking in the **t**, the chief priests,
12:35 While Jesus was teaching in the **t**, he said,
13: 1 As he came out of the **t**,
13: 3 on the Mount of Olives opposite the **t**,
14:49 Day after day I was with you in the **t** teaching,
14:58 'I will destroy this **t** that is made with hands,
15:29 You who would destroy the **t** and build it
15:38 And the curtain of the **t** was torn in two,
Lk 2:27 Guided by the Spirit, Simeon came into the **t**;
2:37 She never left the **t** but worshiped there
2:46 After three days they found him in the **t**,
4: 9 and placed him on the pinnacle of the **t**,
18:10 "Two men went up to the **t** to pray,
19:45 Then he entered the **t** and began
19:47 Every day he was teaching in the **t**.
20: 1 as he was teaching the people in the **t** and telling
21: 5 When some were speaking about the **t**,
21:37 Every day he was teaching in the **t**,
21:38 up early in the morning to listen to him in the **t**.
22: 4 the chief priests and officers of the **t** police about
22:52 the officers of the **t** police,
22:53 When I was with you day after day in the **t**,
23:45 and the curtain of the **t** was torn in two.
24:53 and they were continually in the **t** blessing God.
Jn 2:14 In the **t** he found people selling cattle, sheep,
2:15 he drove all of them out of the **t**,
2:19 Jesus answered them, "Destroy this **t**,
2:20 "This **t** has been under construction
2:21 But he was speaking of the **t** of his body.
5:14 Later Jesus found him in the **t** and said to him,
7:14 the middle of the festival Jesus went up into the **t**
7:28 Then Jesus cried out as he was teaching in the **t**,
7:32 and the chief priests and Pharisees sent **t** police
7:45 Then the **t** police went back to the chief priests
8: 2 ⟦Early in the morning he came again to the **t**.⟧
8:20 while he was teaching in the treasury of the **t**,
8:59 but Jesus hid himself and went out of the **t**
10:23 and Jesus was walking in the **t**,
11:56 as they stood in the **t**,
18:20 I have always taught in synagogues and in the **t**,
Ac 2:46 as they spent much time together in the **t**,
3: 1 One day Peter and John were going up to the **t** at
3: 2 at the gate of the **t** called the Beautiful Gate so
3: 2 ask for alms from those entering the **t**.
3: 3 he saw Peter and John about to go into the **t**,
3: 8 and he entered the **t** with them,
3:10 and ask for alms at the Beautiful Gate of the **t**;
4: 1 the priests, the captain of the **t**,
5:20 in the **t** and tell the people the whole message
5:21 the **t** at daybreak and went on with their teaching.
5:22 But when the **t** police went there,
5:24 of the **t** and the chief priests heard these words,
5:25 in prison are standing in the **t** and teaching
5:26 captain went with the **t** police and brought them,
5:42 in the **t** and at home they did not cease to teach
14:13 priest of Zeus, whose **t** was just outside the city,
19:27 of ours may come into disrepute but also that the **t**
19:35 the **t** keeper of the great Artemis and of the statue
19:37 brought these men here who are neither **t** robbers
21:26 he entered the **t** with them,
21:27 the Jews from Asia, who had seen him in the **t**,
21:28 that, he has actually brought Greeks into the **t**
21:29 that Paul had brought him into the **t**.
21:30 They seized Paul and dragged him out of the **t**,
22:17 to Jerusalem and while I was praying in the **t**,
24: 6 He even tried to profane the **t**,
Ac 24:12 with anyone in the **t** or stirring up a crowd either
24:18 While I was doing this, they found me in the **t**,
25: 8 or against the **t**, or against the emperor."
26:21 the Jews seized me in the **t** and tried to kill me.
1Co 3:16 that you are God's **t** and that God's Spirit dwells
3:17 If anyone destroys God's **t**, God will destroy that
3:17 For God's **t** is holy, and you are that **t**.
6:19 that your body is a **t** of the Holy Spirit within you,
8:10 who possess knowledge, eating in the **t** of an idol,
9:13 in the **t** service get their food from the temple,
9:13 in the temple service get their food from the **t**,
2Co 6:16 What agreement has the **t** of God with idols? D
6:16 For we are the **t** of the living God;
Eph 2:21 and grows into a holy **t** in the Lord; C
2Th 2: 4 so that he takes his seat in the **t** of God, D
Rev 3:12 I will make you a pillar in the **t** of my God; D
7:15 and worship him day and night within his **t**,
11: 1 "Come and measure the **t** of God and the altar D
11: 2 but do not measure the court outside the **t**;
11:19 Then God's **t** in heaven was opened, and the ark
of his covenant was seen within his **t**;
14:15 Another angel came out of the **t**,
14:17 Then another angel came out of the **t** in heaven,
15: 5 the **t** of the tent of witness in heaven was opened,
15: 6 and out of the **t** came the seven angels with
15: 8 and the **t** was filled with smoke from the glory of God
15: 8 and no one could enter the **t** until
16: 1 a loud voice from the **t** telling the seven angels,
16:17 and a loud voice came out of the **t**,
21:22 I saw no **t** in the city, for its **t** is the Lord God the
Almighty and the Lamb.
Tob 1: 4 of Israel should offer sacrifice and where the **t**,
14: 4 the **t** of God in it will be burned to the ground, D
14: 5 and they will rebuild the **t** of God, D
14: 5 and in it the **t** of God will be rebuilt, D
Jdt 4: 2 Jerusalem and for the **t** of the Lord their God. E
4: 3 the **t** had been consecrated after their profanation.
4:11 at Jerusalem prostrated themselves before the **t**
5:18 The **t** of their God was razed to the ground,
8:24 both the **t** and the altar—rests upon us.
Wis 3:14 and a place of great delight in the **t** of the Lord. E
9: 8 You have given command to build a **t**
Sir 36:19 and your **t** with your glory.
45: 9 to make their ringing heard in the **t** as a reminder
49:12 the house and raised a **t** holy to the Lord,
50: 1 and in his time fortified the **t**.
50: 2 the high retaining walls for the **t** enclosure.
50: 7 the **t** of the Most High, like the rainbow gleaming
51:14 Before the **t** I asked for her,
Bar 1: 8 which had been carried away from the **t**,
LtJ 6:13 because of the dust from the **t**,
6:20 They are just like a beam of the **t**, but their hearts,
6:21 by the smoke of the **t**.
6:55 in a **t** of wooden gods overlaid with gold or silver,
Aza 1:31 Blessed are you in the **t** of your holy glory,
Bel 1:10 So the king went with Daniel into the **t** of Bel.
1:14 and they scattered them throughout the whole **t** in
1:22 who destroyed it and its **t**.
1Mc 1:22 and the gold decoration on the front of the **t**;
2: 8 Her **t** has become like a person without honor;
4:46 the stones in a convenient place on the **t** hill until
4:48 also rebuilt the sanctuary and the interior of the **t**,
4:49 the altar of incense, and the table into the **t**.
4:50 and these gave light in the **t**.
4:57 of the **t** with golden crowns and small shields;
6: 2 Its **t** was very rich, containing golden shields,
7:36 in and stood before the altar and the **t**;
10:41 from now on for the service of the **t**.
10:42 from the income of the services of the **t**,
10:43 And all who take refuge at the **t** in Jerusalem,
10:83 the **t** of their idol, for safety.
10:84 the **t** of Dagon, and those who had taken refuge
11: 4 they showed him the burnt-out **t** of Dagon,
13:52 the fortifications of the **t** hill alongside the citadel,
15: 9 on you and your nation and the **t**,
16:20 to take possession of Jerusalem and the **t** hill.
2Mc 1:13 in the **t** of Nanea by a deception employed by
1:15 When the priests of the **t** of Nanea had set out
1:15 they closed the **t** as soon as he entered it.
1:18 the purification of the **t**, we thought it necessary
1:18 who built the **t** and the altar, offered sacrifices.
2: 9 for the dedication and completion of the **t**.
2:19 and the purification of the great **t**,
2:22 the **t** famous throughout the world, and liberated
3: 2 and glorified the **t** with the finest presents,
3: 4 who had been made captain of the **t**,
3:12 the **t** that is honored throughout the whole world.
3:30 the **t**, which a little while before was full of fear
4:32 of the gold vessels of the **t** and gave them
4:42 **t** robber himself they killed close by the treasury.
5:15 Antiochus dared to enter the most holy **t** in all C
5:21 from the **t**, and hurried away to Antioch, thinking
6: 2 also to pollute the **t** in Jerusalem and to call it
6: 2 in Jerusalem and to call it the **t** of Olympian Zeus,
6: 2 in Gerizim the **t** of Zeus-the-Friend-of-Strangers,
6: 4 For the **t** was filled with debauchery and reveling
8: 2 and to have pity on the **t** that had been profaned
10: 1 recovered the **t** and the city;
11: 3 on the **t** as he did on the sacred places of
11:25 our decision is that their **t** be restored to them and
12:26 Then Judas marched against Carnaim and the **t** of
13:10 of the law and their country and the holy **t**, C
13:14 **t**, city, country, and commonwealth,
14: 4 of the customary olive branches from the **t**.
14:13 and to install Alcimus as high priest of the great **t**.
14:31 and holy **t** while the priests were offering C
14:33 and build here a splendid **t** to Dionysus."
2Mc 14:35 that there should be a **t** for your habitation
15:17 city and the sanctuary and the **t** were in danger.
1Es 1: 2 arrayed in their vestments, in the **t** of the Lord. E
1: 3 He told the Levites, the **t** servants of Israel, B
1: 5 Stand in order in the **t** according to the groupings
1: 8 Zechariah, and Jehiel, the chief officers of the **t**,
1:15 The **t** singers, the sons of Asaph,
1:41 and stored them in his **t** in Babylon.
1:49 and polluted the **t** of the Lord in Jerusalem— E
1:49 the **t** that God had made holy.
1:53 with the sword around their holy **t**, C
2: 7 added as votive offerings for the **t** of the Lord E
2:10 from Jerusalem and stored in his **t** of idols.
2:18 and walls and laying the foundations for a **t**.
2:20 Since the building of the **t** is now going on,
2:30 the **t** in Jerusalem stopped until the second year of
4:45 You also vowed to build the **t**,
4:51 for the building of the **t** until it was completed,
4:55 when the **t** would be finished and Jerusalem built.
4:63 up and build Jerusalem and the **t** that is called
5:27 The **t** singers: the descendants of Asaph,
5:29 The **t** servants: the descendants of Esau, B
5:35 All the **t** servants and the descendants B
5:44 they came to the **t** of God that is in Jerusalem, D
5:46 and the **t** singers, the gatekeepers,
5:53 though the **t** of God was not yet built. D
5:56 after their coming to the **t** of God in Jerusalem, D
5:57 the foundation of the **t** of God on the new moon D
5:58 So the builders built the **t** of the Lord. E
5:67 from exile were building the **t** for the Lord God
6:18 of the house in Jerusalem and stored in his own **t**,
6:18 these King Cyrus took out again from the **t**
6:19 and put them in the **t** at Jerusalem,
6:19 this **t** of the Lord should be rebuilt on its site. E
7: 2 of the Jews and the chief officers of the **t**.
7: 7 offered at the dedication of the **t** of the Lord E
8: 5 and some of the priests and Levites and **t** singers
8: 5 and gatekeepers and **t** servants, B
8:14 together with what is given by the nation for the **t**
8:17 that are given you for the use of the **t** of your God
8:18 to you as necessary for the **t** of your God,
8:22 be laid on any of the priests or Levites or **t** singers
8:22 gatekeepers or **t** servants or persons employed B
8:22 or temple servants or persons employed in this **t**,
8:49 and of the **t** servants, whom David and B
8:49 two hundred twenty **t** servants; B
8:60 in Jerusalem carried them to the **t** of the Lord. E
8:67 honored the people and the **t** of the Lord. E
8:81 and glorified the **t** of our Lord,
8:91 weeping and lying on the ground before the **t**,
9: 1 the **t** to the chamber of Jehohanan son of Eliashib,
9: 6 the multitude sat in the open square before the **t**,
9:24 Of the **t** singers: Eliashib and Zaccur.
9:38 in the open square before the east gate of the **t**;
9:41 the gate of the **t** from early morning until midday,
3Mc 1:10 he marveled at the good order of the **t**,
1:13 he inquired why, when he entered every other **t**,
1:16 and they filled the **t** with cries and tears;
1:20 they crowded together at the most high **t**.
3:16 went up to honor the **t** of those wicked people,
3:17 to enter their inner **t** and honor it with magnificent
5:43 and by burning to the ground the **t** inaccessible
2Es 10:21 our altar thrown down, our **t** destroyed;
4Mc 3:20 both appropriated money to them for the **t** service
4: 3 which are not the property of the **t** but belong
4: 8 But, uttering threats, Apollonius went on to the **t**.
4: 9 and children were imploring God in the **t** to shield
4:11 Then Apollonius fell down half dead in the **t** area
4:20 but also the **t** service was abolished.

TEMPLES (15) [TEMPLE]

Lev 13:41 If he loses the hair from his forehead and **t**,
19:27 the hair on your **t** or mar the edges of your beard.
Jer 9:26 and all those with shaven **t** who live in the desert.
25:23 Dedan, Tema, Buz, and all who have shaven **t**;
43:12 He shall kindle a fire in the **t** of the gods
43:13 the **t** of the gods of Egypt he shall burn with fire.
49:32 to every wind those who have shaven **t**,
Joel 3: 5 and have carried my rich treasures into your **t**.
Ro 2:22 You that abhor idols, do you rob **t**?
Jdt 4: 1 how he had plundered and destroyed all their **t**,
LtJ 6:18 are their gods when they have been set up in the **t**.
6:18 so the priests make their **t** secure with doors
6:31 and in their **t** the priests sit with their clothes torn,
2Mc 9: 2 and attempted to rob the **t** and control the city.
3Mc 3:16 when we had granted very great revenues to the **t**

TEMPORAL (KJV) See TEMPORARY

TEMPORARILY (1) [TEMPORARY]

2Mc 14:17 but had been **t** checked because of the sudden

TEMPORARY (2) [TEMPORARILY]

2Co 4:18 for what can be seen is **t**,
4Mc 15: 8 of God she disdained the **t** safety of her children.

TEMPT (1) [TEMPTATION, TEMPTED, TEMPTER, TEMPTS]

1Co 7: 5 so that Satan may not **t** you because of your lack

TEMPTATION‡ (2) [TEMPT]

1Ti 6: 9 rich fall into **t** and are trapped by many senseless
Jas 1:12 Blessed is anyone who endures **t**.

TEMPTED‡ (9) [TEMPT]

Mt 4: 1 the Spirit into the wilderness to be **t** by the devil.
Mk 1:13 He was in the wilderness forty days, **t** by Satan;
Lk 4: 2 where for forty days he was **t** by the devil.
Gal 6: 1 Take care that you yourselves are not **t**.
1Th 3: 5 the tempter had **t** you and that our labor had been
Jas 1:13 No one, when **t**, should say, "I am being **t** by God"
1:13 be **t** by evil and he himself tempts no one.
1:14 But one is **t** by one's own desire,

TEMPTER (2) [TEMPT]

Mt 4: 3 The **t** came and said to him,
1Th 3: 5 the **t** had tempted you and that our labor had been

TEMPTS (1) [TEMPT]

Jas 1:13 be tempted by evil and he himself **t** no one.

TEN‡ (240) [NINE-TENTHS, ONE-TENTH, TEN-STRINGED, TEN-THOUSANDTH, TENFOLD, TENS, TENTH, THREE-TENTHS, TWO-TENTHS]

Ge 5:14 the days of Kenan were nine hundred and **t** years;
16: 3 Abram had lived **t** years in the land of Canaan,
18:32 Suppose **t** are found there."
18:32 "For the sake of **t** I will not destroy it."
24:10 Then the servant took **t** of his master's camels
24:22 for her arms weighing **t** gold shekels,
24:55 at least **t** days; after that she may go."
31: 7 and changed my wages **t** times.
31:41 and you have changed my wages **t** times.
32:15 **t** bulls, twenty female donkeys and **t** male donkeys.
42: 3 So **t** of Joseph's brothers went down to buy grain
45:23 **t** donkeys loaded with the good things of Egypt,
45:23 and **t** female donkeys loaded with grain, bread,
50:22 and Joseph lived one hundred **t** years.
50:26 And Joseph died, being one hundred **t** years old;
Ex 26: 1 the tabernacle with **t** curtains of fine twisted linen,
26:16 **T** cubits shall be the length of a frame,
27:12 with **t** pillars and **t** bases.
34:28 the words of the covenant, the **t** commandments.
36: 8 the workers made the tabernacle with **t** curtains;
36:21 **T** cubits was the length of a frame,
38:12 with **t** pillars and **t** bases;
Lev 26: 8 a hundred of you shall give chase to **t** thousand;
26:26 **t** women shall bake your bread in a single oven,
27: 5 for a male and **t** shekels for a female.
27: 7 and for a female **t** shekels.
Nu 7:14 one golden dish weighing **t** shekels, full of incense;
7:20 one golden dish weighing **t** shekels, full of incense;
7:26 one golden dish weighing **t** shekels, full of incense;
7:32 one golden dish weighing **t** shekels, full of incense;
7:38 one golden dish weighing **t** shekels, full of incense;
7:44 one golden dish weighing **t** shekels, full of incense;
7:50 one golden dish weighing **t** shekels, full of incense;
7:56 one golden dish weighing **t** shekels, full of incense;
7:62 one golden dish weighing **t** shekels, full of incense;
7:68 one golden dish weighing **t** shekels, full of incense;
7:74 one golden dish weighing **t** shekels, full of incense;
7:80 one golden dish weighing **t** shekels, full of incense;
7:86 weighing **t** shekels apiece according to the shekel
10:36 O LORD of the **t** thousand thousands of Israel."
11:19 or five days, or **t** days, or twenty days,
11:32 the least anyone gathered was **t** homers;
14:22 and yet have tested me these **t** times and have
29:23 On the fourth day: **t** bulls, two rams,
Dt 4:13 that is, the **t** commandments;
10: 4 the **t** commandments that the LORD had spoken
Jos 15:57 **t** towns with their villages.
17: 5 Thus there fell to Manasseh **t** portions,
21: 5 The rest of the Kohathites received by lot **t** towns
21:26 of the families of the rest of the Kohathites were **t**
22:14 and with him **t** chiefs, one from each of
24:29 died, being one hundred **t** years old.
Jdg 1: 4 and they defeated **t** thousand of them at Bezek.
2: 8 died at the age of one hundred **t** years.
3:29 At that time they killed about **t** thousand of
4: 6 bringing **t** thousand from the tribe of Naphtali and
4:10 and **t** thousand warriors went up behind him;
4:14 with **t** thousand warriors following him.
6:27 So Gideon took **t** of his servants,
7: 3 and **t** thousand remained.
12:11 and he judged Israel **t** years.
17:10 and I will give you **t** pieces of silver a year,
20:10 We will take **t** men of a hundred throughout all
20:10 and a thousand of **t** thousand,
20:34 against Gibeah **t** thousand picked men out
Ru 1: 4 When they had lived there about **t** years,
4: 2 Then Boaz took **t** men of the elders of the city,
1Sa 1: 8 Am I not more to you than **t** sons?"
14:23 numbered altogether about **t** thousand men.
15: 4 and **t** thousand soldiers of Judah.
17:17 an ephah of this parched grain and these **t** loaves,
17:18 also take these **t** cheeses to the commander
18: 7 and David his **t** thousands."
18: 8 "They have ascribed to David **t** thousands,
21:11 and David his **t** thousands'?"
25: 5 So David sent **t** young men;
25:38 About **t** days later the LORD struck Nabal,
29: 5 and David his **t** thousands'?"
2Sa 15:16 except **t** concubines whom he left behind to look
18: 3 But you are worth **t** thousand of us;
18:11 I would have been glad to give you **t** pieces
18:15 And **t** young men, Joab's armor-bearers,
19:43 "We have **t** shares in the king,
20: 3 the king took the **t** concubines whom he had left
1Ki 4:23 **t** fat oxen, and twenty pasture-fed cattle,
5:14 **t** thousand a month in shifts;
6: 3 Its depth was **t** cubits in front of the house.
6:23 of olivewood, each **t** cubits high.
6:24 it was **t** cubits from the tip of one wing to the tip
6:25 The other cherub also measured **t** cubits;
6:26 The height of one cherub was **t** cubits,
7:10 huge stones, stones of eight and **t** cubits.
7:23 it was round, **t** cubits from brim to brim,
7:24 each of **t** cubits, surrounding the sea;
7:27 He also made the **t** stands of bronze;
7:37 In this way he made the **t** stands;
7:38 He made **t** basins of bronze;
7:38 there was a basin for each of the **t** stands.
7:43 the **t** stands, the **t** basins on the stands;
11:31 Take for yourself **t** pieces;
11:31 and will give you **t** tribes.
11:35 to you—that is, the **t** tribes.
14: 3 Take with you **t** loaves, some cakes,
2Ki 5: 5 taking with him **t** talents of silver, six thousand shekels of gold, and **t** sets of garments.
13: 7 **t** chariots and **t** thousand footmen;
14: 7 He killed **t** thousand Edomites in the Valley
15:17 he reigned **t** years in Samaria.
20: 9 the shadow has now advanced **t** intervals; shall it retreat **t** intervals?"
20:10 for the shadow to lengthen **t** intervals; rather let the shadow retreat **t** intervals."
20:11 and he brought the shadow back the **t** intervals,
24:14 all the warriors, **t** thousand captives,
25:25 of the royal family, came with **t** men;
1Ch 6:61 the half of Manasseh, **t** towns.
29: 7 and **t** thousand darics of gold, **t** thousand talents of
2Ch 4: 1 twenty cubits wide, and **t** cubits high.
4: 2 it was round, **t** cubits from rim to rim,
4: 3 Under it were panels all around, each of **t** cubits,
4: 6 He also made **t** basins in which to wash,
4: 7 He made **t** golden lampstands as prescribed,
4: 8 also made **t** tables and placed them in the temple,
14: 1 In his days the land had rest for **t** years.
25:11 and struck down **t** thousand men of Seir.
25:12 of Judah captured another **t** thousand alive,
27: 5 **t** thousand cors of wheat and **t** thousand of barley.
30:24 a thousand bulls and **t** thousand sheep.
36: 9 he reigned three months and **t** days in Jerusalem.
Ezr 1:10 other silver bowls, four hundred **t**;
8:12 and with him one hundred **t** males.
8:24 Hashabiah, and **t** of their kin with them.
Ne 4:12 they said to us **t** times,
5:18 and every **t** days skins of wine in abundance;
11: 1 of the people cast lots to bring one out of **t** to live
Est 3: 9 and I will pay **t** thousand talents of silver into
9:10 the **t** sons of Haman son of Hammedatha,
9:12 and also the **t** sons of Haman.
9:13 the **t** sons of Haman be hanged on the gallows."
9:14 and the **t** sons of Haman were hanged.
Job 19: 3 These **t** times you have cast reproach upon me;
Ps 3: 6 of **t** thousands of people who have set themselves
33: 2 make melody to him with the harp of **t** strings.
68:17 With mighty chariotry, twice **t** thousand,
91: 7 **t** thousand at your right hand,
Ecc 7:19 to the wise more than **t** rulers that are in a city.
SS 5:10 distinguished among **t** thousand.
Isa 5:10 For **t** acres of vineyard shall yield but one bath,
38: 8 on the dial of Ahaz turn back **t** steps."
38: 8 on the dial the **t** steps by which it had declined.
Jer 41: 1 came with **t** men to Gedaliah son of Ahikam,
41: 2 of Nethaniah and the **t** men with him got up
41: 8 But there were **t** men among them who said
42: 7 At the end of **t** days the word of the LORD came
Eze 40:11 the width of the opening of the gateway, **t** cubits;
40:49 **t** steps led up to it;
41: 2 The width of the entrance was **t** cubits;
42: 4 **t** cubits wide and one hundred cubits deep,
45: 3 and **t** thousand wide, in which shall be
45: 5 and **t** thousand cubits wide,
45:14 like the homer, contains **t** baths);
48:10 **t** thousand cubits in width on the western side,
48:10 **t** thousand in width on the eastern side,
48:13 in length and **t** thousand in width.
48:18 the holy portion shall be **t** thousand cubits to
48:18 and **t** thousand to the west,
Da 1:12 "Please test your servants for **t** days.
1:14 to this proposal and tested them for **t** days.
1:15 of **t** days it was observed that they appeared better
1:20 he found them **t** times better than all
7: 7 the beasts that preceded it, and it had **t** horns.
7:10 **t** thousand times **t** thousand stood attending him.
7:20 and concerning the **t** horns that were on its head,
7:24 the **t** horns, out of this kingdom **t** kings shall arise,
Am 5: 3 which marched out a hundred shall have **t** left.
6: 9 If **t** people remain in one house, they shall die.
Mic 6: 7 with **t** thousands of rivers of oil?
Hag 2:16 to a heap of twenty measures, there were but **t**;
Zec 5: 2 its length is twenty cubits, and its width **t** cubits."
8:23 In those days **t** men from nations
Mt 18:24 one who owed him **t** thousand talents was brought
20:24 **t** heard it, they were angry with the two brothers.
25: 1 **T** bridesmaids took their lamps and went to meet
25:28 and give it to the one with the **t** talents.
Mk 10:41 When the **t** heard this, they began to be angry
Lk 14:31 and consider whether he is able with **t** thousand
15: 8 "Or what woman having **t** silver coins,
17:12 As he entered a village, **t** lepers approached him.
17:17 Then Jesus asked, "Were not **t** made clean?
19:13 summoned **t** of his slaves, and gave them **t** pounds,
Lk 19:16 'Lord, your pound has made **t** more pounds.'
19:17 in a very small thing, take charge of **t** cities.'
19:24 and give it to the one who has **t** pounds.'
19:25 (And they said to him, 'Lord, he has **t** pounds!')
Ac 25: 6 not more than eight or **t** days, he went down
1Co 4:15 you might have **t** thousand guardians in Christ,
14:19 than **t** thousand words in a tongue.
Jude 1:14 Lord is coming with **t** thousands of his holy ones,
Rev 2:10 and for **t** days you will have affliction.
12: 3 a great red dragon, with seven heads and **t** horns,
13: 1 a beast rising out of the sea having **t** horns
13: 1 and on its horns were **t** diadems,
17: 3 and it had seven heads and **t** horns.
17: 7 and of the beast with seven heads and **t** horns
17:12 the **t** horns that you saw are **t** kings who have not
17:16 And the **t** horns that you saw,
Tob 1:14 of silver worth **t** talents in trust with Gabael,
4:20 let me explain to you that I left **t** talents of silver
AdE 3: 9 and I will pay **t** thousand talents of silver into
4: 7 to pay **t** thousand talents into the royal treasury
9:10 the **t** sons of Haman son of Hammedatha,
9:13 Also, hang up the bodies of Haman's **t** sons."
Wis 7: 2 within the period of **t** months,
12:22 you scourge our enemies **t** thousand times more,
Sir 23:19 of the Lord are **t** thousand times brighter than
41: 4 Whether life lasts for **t** years or a hundred or
1Mc 4:29 and Judas met them with **t** thousand men.
10:74 He chose **t** thousand men and set out
2Mc 11: 4 but was elated with his **t** thousands of infantry,
12:19 more than **t** thousand men.
13: 2 a Greek force of one hundred **t** thousand infantry,
1Es 1:44 he reigned three months and **t** days in Jerusalem.
2:13 two thousand four hundred **t** silver bowls,
4:52 an additional **t** talents a year for burnt offerings to
8:38 and with him a hundred **t** men.
8:54 and **t** of their kinsmen with them;
2Es 5:46 'If you bear **t** children, why one after another?'
5:46 Request it therefore to produce **t** at one time."
16:28 For **t** shall be left out of a city;

TEN-STRINGED (1) [STRING, TEN]

Ps 144: 9 upon a **t** harp I will play to you,

TEN-THOUSANDTH (1) [TEN, THOUSAND]

2Es 7:*138* [68] not one **t** of humankind could have life;

TENANTS (16)

Lev 25:23 with me you are but aliens and **t**.
Mt 21:33 Then he leased it to **t** and went to another country.
21:34 he sent his slaves to the **t** to collect his produce.
21:35 But the **t** seized his slaves and beat one,
21:38 But when the **t** saw the son,
21:40 what will he do to those **t**?"
21:41 vineyard to other **t** who will give him the produce
Mk 12: 1 then he leased it to **t** and went to another country.
12: 2 the **t** to collect from them his share of the produce
12: 7 But those **t** said to one another, 'This is the heir;
12: 9 and destroy the **t** and give the vineyard to others.
Lk 20: 9 "A man planted a vineyard, and leased it to **t**,
20:10 the **t** in order that they might give him his share of
20:10 the **t** beat him and sent him away empty-handed.
20:14 But when the **t** saw him, they discussed it
20:16 He will come and destroy those **t** and give

TEND‡ (4) [TENDED, TENDING, TENDS]

Ex 27:21 and his sons shall **t** it from evening to morning
Nu 1:50 and all its equipment, and they shall **t** it,
Jn 21:16 Jesus said to him, "**T** my sheep."
1Pe 5: 2 to **t** the flock of God that is in your charge,

TENDED (3) [TEND]

Ps 78:72 With upright heart he **t** them,
Zec 11: 7 the other I named Unity, and I **t** the sheep.
Pm 151: 1 in my father's house; I **t** my father's sheep.

TENDENCY (1)

4Mc 1:25 In pleasure there exists even a malevolent **t**,

TENDER (14) [TENDERHEARTED, TENDERLY, TENDERNESS]

Ge 18: 7 **t** and good, and gave it to the servant,
2Ki 19:26 like plants of the field and like **t** grass,
Pr 4: 3 When I was a son with my father, **t**,
Isa 37:27 like plants of the field and like **t** grass,
47: 1 For you shall no more be called **t** and delicate.
Eze 17:22 I will break off a **t** one from the topmost of its
Da 4:15 in the **t** grass of the field.
Hos 11: 8 my compassion grows warm and **t**.
Mt 24:32 as its branch becomes **t** and puts forth its leaves,
Mk 13:28 as its branch becomes **t** and puts forth its leaves,
Lk 1:78 By the **t** mercy of our God,
1Pe 3: 8 sympathy, love for one another, a **t** heart,
Sir 43:21 and withers the **t** grass like fire.
4Mc 15: 6 in herself **t** love toward them,

TENDERHEARTED (1) [HEART, TENDER]

Eph 4:32 be kind to one another, **t**, forgiving one another,

TENDERHEARTED (KJV) See also IRRESOLUTE

TENDERLY (6) [TENDER]
Ge 34:3 he loved the girl, and spoke **t** to her
Jdg 19:3 to speak **t** to her and bring her back.
Isa 40:2 Speak **t** to Jerusalem, and cry to her
Hos 2:14 and bring her into the wilderness, and speak **t**
Eph 5:29 but he nourishes and **t** cares for it,
1Th 2:7 like a nurse **t** caring for her own children.

TENDERNESS (1) [TENDER]
4Mc 15:9 she felt a greater **t** toward them.

TENDING (4) [TEND]
Ps 78:71 from **t** the nursing ewes he brought him to be
Lk 17:7 in from plowing or **t** sheep in the field,
Jdt 8:26 while he was **t** the sheep of Laban,
Sir 43:4 A man **t** a furnace works in burning heat,

TENDS (2) [TEND]
Pr 27:18 Anyone who **t** a fig tree will eat its fruit,
1Co 9:7 Or who **t** a flock and does not get any of its milk?

TENFOLD (1) [TEN]
Bar 4:28 return with **t** zeal to seek him.

TENONS (KJV) See PEGS

TENS (10) [TEN]
Ex 18:21 as officers over thousands, hundreds, fifties and **t**.
18:25 over thousands, hundreds, fifties, and **t**.
Dt 1:15 commanders of fifties, commanders of **t**,
Ps 144:13 by **t** of thousands in our fields,
Da 11:12 and he shall overthrow **t** of thousands,
11:41 and **t** of thousands shall fall victim,
Sir 47:6 for the **t** of thousands he conquered,
Aza 1:17 or with **t** of thousands of fat lambs;
1Mc 3:55 of thousands and hundreds and fifties and **t**.
4Mc 4:3 in the Jerusalem treasuries there are deposited **t**

TENSE (1)
4Mc 7:13 his body no longer **t** and firm, his muscles flabby,

TENT‡ (326) [TENT-CORD, TENT-CURTAINS, TENT-DWELLING, TENTMAKERS, TENTS]
A. TENT OF MEETING (146)

Ge 9:21 and he lay uncovered in his **t**.
12:8 and pitched his **t**, with Bethel on the west and Ai
13:3 to the place where his **t** had been at the beginning,
13:12 of the Plain and moved his **t** as far as Sodom.
13:18 So Abram moved his **t**, and came and settled by
18:1 as he sat at the entrance of his **t** in the heat of
18:2 he ran from the **t** entrance to meet them,
18:6 And Abraham hastened into the **t** to Sarah,
18:9 And he said, "There, in the **t**."
18:10 Sarah was listening at the **t** entrance behind him.
24:67 Then Isaac brought her into his mother Sarah's **t**.
26:25 the name of the LORD, and pitched his **t** there.
31:25 Now Jacob had pitched his **t** in the hill country,
31:33 So Laban went into Jacob's **t**, and into Leah's **t**, and into the **t** of the two maids,
31:33 he went out of Leah's **t**, and entered Rachel's.
31:34 Laban felt all about in the **t**,
33:19 the plot of land on which he had pitched his **t**.
35:21 and pitched his **t** beyond the tower of Eder.
Ex 18:7 after the other's welfare, and they went into the **t**.
26:7 You shall also make curtains of goats' hair for a **t**
26:9 over at the front of the **t**.
26:11 the clasps into the loops, and join the **t** together,
26:12 The part that remains of the curtains of the **t**,
26:13 in the length of the curtains of the **t**,
26:14 for the **t** a covering of tanned rams' skins and
26:36 You shall make a screen for the entrance of the **t**,
27:21 the **t** of meeting, outside the curtain that is A
28:43 **t** of meeting, or when they come near the altar A
29:4 and his sons to the entrance of the **t** of meeting, A
29:10 shall bring the bull in front of the **t** of meeting. A
29:11 at the entrance of the **t** of meeting, A
29:30 the **t** of meeting to minister in the holy place. A
29:32 at the entrance of the **t** of meeting. A
29:42 at the entrance of the **t** of meeting before A
29:44 I will consecrate the **t** of meeting and the altar; A
30:16 designate it for the service of the **t** of meeting; A
30:18 You shall put it between the **t** of meeting and A
30:20 When they go into the **t** of meeting, A
30:26 With it you shall anoint the **t** of meeting and A
30:36 in the **t** of meeting where I shall meet with you; A
31:7 the **t** of meeting, and the ark of the covenant, A
31:7 and all the furnishings of the **t**,
33:7 Now Moses used to take the **t** and pitch it outside
33:7 he called it the **t** of meeting. A
33:7 the LORD would go out to the **t** of meeting, A
33:8 Whenever Moses went out to the **t**,
33:8 and watch Moses until he had gone into the **t**.
33:9 When Moses entered the **t**,
33:9 and stand at the entrance of the **t**,
33:10 of cloud standing at the entrance of the **t**,
33:10 all of them, at the entrance of their **t**.
33:11 Joshua son of Nun, would not leave the **t**.
35:11 its **t** and its covering, its clasps
35:21 LORD's offering to be used for the **t** of meeting, A
36:14 He also made curtains of goats' hair for a **t** over
Ex 36:18 of bronze to join the **t** together so that it might
36:19 for the **t** a covering of tanned rams' skins and
36:37 He also made a screen for the entrance to the **t**,
38:8 who served at the entrance to the **t** of meeting. A
38:30 the bases for the entrance of the **t** of meeting, A
39:32 the tabernacle of the **t** of meeting was finished; A
39:33 the **t** and all its utensils, its hooks, its frames,
39:38 and the screen for the entrance of the **t**;
39:40 service of the tabernacle, for the **t** of meeting; A
40:2 set up the tabernacle of the **t** of meeting. A
40:6 entrance of the tabernacle of the **t** of meeting, A
40:7 place the basin between the **t** of meeting and A
40:12 and his sons to the entrance of the **t** of meeting, A
40:19 the **t** over the tabernacle, and put the covering of
40:19 and put the covering of the **t** over it;
40:22 He put the table in the **t** of meeting, A
40:24 He put the lampstand in the **t** of meeting, A
40:26 He put the golden altar in the **t** of meeting A
40:29 entrance of the tabernacle of the **t** of meeting, A
40:30 the basin between the **t** of meeting and the altar, A
40:32 When they went into the **t** of meeting, A
40:34 Then the cloud covered the **t** of meeting, A
40:35 **t** of meeting because the cloud settled upon it, A
Lev 1:1 and spoke to him from the **t** of meeting, saying: A
1:3 bring it to the entrance of the **t** of meeting, A
1:5 altar that is at the entrance of the **t** of meeting. A
3:2 slaughter it at the entrance of the **t** of meeting; A
3:8 It shall be slaughtered before the **t** of meeting, A
3:13 it shall be slaughtered before the **t** of meeting; A
4:4 the bull to the entrance of the **t** of meeting A
4:5 of the bull and bring it into the **t** of meeting. A
4:7 that is in the **t** of meeting before the LORD; A
4:7 which is at the entrance of the **t** of meeting. A
4:14 sin offering and bring it before the **t** of meeting. A
4:16 of the blood of the bull into the **t** of meeting, A
4:18 that is before the LORD in the **t** of meeting; A
4:18 that is at the entrance of the **t** of meeting. A
6:16 in the court of the **t** of meeting they shall eat it. A
6:26 in the court of the **t** of meeting. A
6:30 the **t** of meeting for atonement in the holy place; A
8:3 congregation at the entrance of the **t** of meeting A
8:4 at the entrance of the **t** of meeting, A
8:31 Boil the flesh at the entrance of the **t** of meeting, A
8:33 the entrance of the **t** of meeting for seven days, A
8:35 of the **t** of meeting day and night for seven days, A
9:5 to the front of the **t** of meeting; A
9:23 Moses and Aaron entered the **t** of meeting, A
10:7 the entrance of the **t** of meeting, or you will die; A
10:9 when you enter the **t** of meeting, A
12:6 to the priest at the entrance of the **t** of meeting A
14:8 but shall live outside his **t** seven days.
14:11 at the entrance of the **t** of meeting. A
14:23 to the entrance of the **t** of meeting, A
15:14 the entrance of the **t** of meeting and give them A
15:29 to the priest to the entrance of the **t** of meeting. A
16:7 the LORD at the entrance of the **t** of meeting; A
16:16 and so he shall do for the **t** of meeting, A
16:17 be in the **t** of meeting from the time he enters A
16:20 the holy place and the **t** of meeting and the altar, A
16:23 Then Aaron shall enter the **t** of meeting, A
16:33 he shall make atonement for the **t** of meeting A
17:4 to the entrance of the **t** of meeting, to present it A
17:5 to the priest at the entrance of the **t** of meeting, A
17:6 of the LORD at the entrance of the **t** of meeting, A
17:9 not bring it to the entrance of the **t** of meeting, A
19:21 at the entrance of the **t** of meeting, A
24:3 Aaron shall set it up in the **t** of meeting, A
Nu 1:1 in the **t** of meeting, on the first day of the A
2:2 they shall camp facing the **t** of meeting A
2:17 The **t** of meeting, with the camp of the Levites, A
3:7 the **t** of meeting, doing service at the tabernacle; A
3:8 charge of all the furnishings of the **t** of meeting, A
3:25 of the sons of Gershon in the **t** of meeting A
3:25 the **t** with its covering, the screen for the entrance
3:25 the screen for the entrance of the **t** of meeting, A
3:38 in front of the **t** of meeting toward the east— A
4:3 qualify to do work relating to the **t** of meeting. A
4:4 the **t** of meeting concerns the most holy things. A
4:15 the **t** of meeting that the Kohathites are to carry. A
4:23 all who qualify to do work in the **t** of meeting. A
4:25 and the **t** of meeting with its covering, A
4:25 the screen for the entrance of the **t** of meeting, A
4:28 of the Gershonites relating to the **t** of meeting. A
4:30 who qualifies to do the work of the **t** of meeting. A
4:31 as the whole of their service in the **t** of meeting: A
4:33 of their service relating to the **t** of meeting, A
4:35 qualified for work relating to the **t** of meeting; A
4:37 all who served at the **t** of meeting, A
4:39 qualified for work relating to the **t** of meeting— A
4:41 all who served at the **t** of meeting, A
4:43 qualified for work relating to the **t** of meeting— A
4:47 of bearing burdens relating to the **t** of meeting, A
6:10 to the priest at the entrance of the **t** of meeting, A
6:13 be brought to the entrance of the **t** of meeting, A
6:18 head at the entrance of the **t** of meeting, A
7:5 be used in doing the service of the **t** of meeting, A
7:89 When Moses went into the **t** of meeting to speak A
8:9 shall bring the Levites before the **t** of meeting, A
8:15 may go in to do service at the **t** of meeting, A
8:19 the service for the Israelites at the **t** of meeting, A
8:22 went in to do their service in the **t** of meeting A
8:24 to do duty in the service of the **t** of meeting; A
8:26 may assist their brothers in the **t** of meeting A
9:15 the cloud covered the tabernacle, the **t** of the
9:17 Whenever the cloud lifted from over the **t**,
10:3 before you at the entrance of the **t** of meeting. A
11:16 bring them to the **t** of meeting, A
Nu 11:24 and placed them all around the **t**.
11:26 but they had not gone out to the **t**,
12:4 "Come out, you three, to the **t** of meeting." A
12:5 and stood at the entrance of the **t**,
12:10 When the cloud went away from over the **t**,
14:10 glory of the LORD appeared at the **t** of meeting A
16:18 they stood at the entrance of the **t** of meeting A
16:19 against them at the entrance of the **t** of meeting. A
16:42 and Aaron turned toward the **t** of meeting; A
16:43 and Aaron came to the front of the **t** of meeting, A
16:50 to Moses at the entrance of the **t** of meeting. A
17:4 in the **t** of meeting before the covenant, A
17:7 before the LORD in the **t** of the covenant.
17:8 When Moses went into the **t** of the covenant on
18:2 and your sons with you are in front of the **t** of
18:3 for you and for the whole **t**.
18:4 the duties of the **t** of meeting, for all the service A
18:4 for all the service of the **t**;
18:6 to perform the service of the **t** of meeting. A
18:21 the service in the **t** of meeting. A
18:22 shall no longer approach the **t** of meeting, A
18:23 **t** of meeting, and they shall bear responsibility A
18:31 payment for your service in the **t** of meeting A
19:4 the front of the **t** of meeting. A
19:14 This is the law when someone dies in a **t**:
19:14 everyone who comes into the **t**,
19:14 and everyone who is in the **t**,
19:18 and sprinkle it on the **t**, on all the furnishings,
20:6 the assembly to the entrance of the **t** of meeting; A
25:6 were weeping at the entrance of the **t** of meeting. A
25:8 he went after the Israelite man into the **t**,
27:2 the entrance of the **t** of meeting, and they said, A
31:54 brought it into the **t** of meeting as a memorial A
Dt 31:14 and present yourselves in the **t** of meeting, A
31:14 and presented themselves in the **t** of meeting, A
31:15 the LORD appeared at the **t** in a pillar of cloud;
31:15 the pillar of cloud stood at the entrance to the **t**.
Jos 7:21 They now lie hidden in the ground inside my **t**,
7:22 So Joshua sent messengers, and they ran to the **t**;
7:22 hidden in his **t** with the silver underneath.
7:23 They took them out of the **t** and brought them
7:24 donkeys, and sheep, and his **t** and all that he had;
18:1 and set up the **t** of meeting there. A
19:51 at the entrance of the **t** of meeting. A
Jdg 4:17 on foot to the **t** of Jael wife of Heber the Kenite;
4:18 So he turned aside to her into the **t**,
4:20 He said to her, "Stand at the entrance of the **t**,
4:21 But Jael wife of Heber took a **t** peg,
4:22 So he went into her **t**;
4:22 with the **t** peg in his temple.
5:26 She put her hand to the **t** peg and her right hand to
7:13 and came to the **t**, and struck it so that it fell;
7:13 it turned upside down, and the **t** collapsed."
1Sa 2:22 who served at the entrance to the **t** of meeting. A
17:54 but he put his armor in his **t**.
2Sa 6:17 inside the **t** that David had pitched for it;
7:2 but the ark of God stays in a **t**."
7:6 I have been moving about in a **t** and a tabernacle.
16:22 So they pitched a **t** for Absalom upon the roof;
1Ki 1:39 the horn of oil from the **t** and anointed Solomon.
2:28 to the **t** of the LORD and grasped the horns of
2:29 the **t** of the LORD and now is beside the altar,"
2:30 So Benaiah came to the **t** of the LORD and said
8:4 the ark of the LORD, the **t** of meeting, A
8:4 and all the holy vessels that were in the **t**;
2Ki 7:8 they went into a **t**, ate and drank,
7:8 Then they came back, entered another **t**,
1Ch 6:32 of the **t** of meeting, until Solomon had built A
9:19 guardians of the thresholds of the **t**,
9:21 at the entrance of the **t** of meeting. A
9:23 that is, the house of the **t**, as guards.
15:1 a place for the ark of God and pitched a **t** for it.
16:1 and set it inside the **t** that David had pitched for it;
17:1 the ark of the covenant of the LORD is under a **t**."
17:5 but I have lived in a **t** and a tabernacle.
23:32 Thus they shall keep charge of the **t** of meeting A
2Ch 1:3 God's **t** of meeting, which Moses the servant A
1:4 for he had pitched a **t** for it in Jerusalem.)
1:6 which was at the **t** of meeting, A
1:13 from the **t** of meeting, to Jerusalem. A
5:5 So they brought up the ark, the **t** of meeting, A
5:5 and all the holy vessels that were in the **t**;
24:6 on the congregation of Israel for the **t** of
Job 5:24 You shall know that your **t** is safe,
8:22 and the **t** of the wicked will be no more."
18:6 The light is dark in their **t**,
18:14 They are torn from the **t** in which they trusted,
19:12 and encamp around my **t**.
20:26 what is left in their **t** will be consumed.
21:28 Where is the **t** in which the wicked lived?'
29:4 when the friendship of God was upon my **t**;
31:31 of my **t** ever said, 'O that we might be sated
Ps 15:1 who may abide in your **t**?
19:4 In the heavens he has set a **t** for the sun,
27:5 he will conceal me under the cover of his **t**;
27:6 I will offer in his **t** sacrifices with shouts of joy;
52:5 he will snatch and tear you from your **t**;
61:4 Let me abide in your **t** forever,
78:60 the **t** where he dwelt among mortals,
78:67 He rejected the **t** of Joseph,
91:10 no scourge come near your **t**.
104:2 You stretch out the heavens like a **t**,
Pr 14:11 but the **t** of the upright flourishes.
Isa 16:5 be established in steadfast love in the **t** of David,
33:20 a quiet habitation, an immovable **t**,
38:12 up and removed from me like a shepherd's **t**;
40:22 and spreads them like a **t** to live in;

Isa 54: 2 Enlarge the site of your **t**,
Jer 10:20 My **t** is destroyed, and all my cords are broken;
10:20 there is no one to spread my **t** again,
La 2: 4 in whom we took pride in the **t** of daughter Zion;
Zec 10: 4 out of them the **t** peg, out of them the battle bow,
Ac 7:43 No; you took along the **t** of Moloch,
7:44 "Our ancestors had the **t** of testimony in
2Co 5: 1 that if the earthly **t** we live in is destroyed,
5: 2 For in this **t** we groan, longing to be clothed
5: 4 For while we are still in this **t**,
Heb 8: 2 a minister in the sanctuary and the true **t** that
8: 5 for Moses, when he was about to erect the **t**,
9: 2 For a **t** was constructed, the first one,
9: 3 Behind the second curtain was a **t** called the Holy
9: 6 into the first **t** to carry out their ritual duties;
9: 8 as long as the first **t** is still standing.
9:11 the greater and perfect **t** (not made with hands,
9:21 with the blood both the **t** and all the vessels used
13:10 in the **t** have no right to eat.
Rev 15: 5 temple of the **t** of witness in heaven was opened,
Tob 13:10 so that his **t** may be rebuilt in you in joy.
Jdt 5:22 all the people standing around the **t** began
6:10 who waited on him in his **t**,
8: 5 at home where she set up a **t** for herself on
8:36 they returned from the **t** and went to their posts.
10:15 Go at once to his **t**;
10:17 and they brought them to the **t** of Holofernes.
10:18 for her arrival was reported from **t** to **t**.
10:18 and gathered around her as she stood outside the **t**
10:20 and led her into the **t**.
10:22 they told him of her, he came to the front of the **t**,
12: 5 the servants of Holofernes brought her into the **t**,
12: 9 in the **t** until she ate her food toward evening.
13: 1 Bagoas closed the **t** from outside and shut out
13: 2 But Judith was left alone in the **t**,
14: 3 They will rush into the **t** of Holofernes and will
14: 7 and said, "Blessed are you in every **t** of Judah!
14:13 to Holofernes' **t** and said to the steward in charge
14:14 Bagoas went in and knocked at the entry of the **t**,
14:17 Then he went to the **t** where Judith had stayed,
15:11 the **t** of Holofernes and all his silver dinnerware,
Wis 9: 8 the holy **t** that you prepared from the beginning.
9:15 and this earthy **t** burdens the thoughtful mind.
Sir 14:24 near her house and fastens his **t** peg to her walls;
14:25 who pitches his **t** near her, and so occupies
24: 8 and my Creator chose the place for my **t**.
24:10 In the holy **t** I ministered before him,
24:15 and stacte, and like the odor of incense in the **t**.
26:12 of every **t** peg and open her quiver to the arrow.
2Mc 2: 4 that the **t** and the ark should follow with him,
2: 5 and he brought there the **t** and the ark and
3Mc 1: 2 and crossed over by night to the **t** of Ptolemy,
1: 3 a certain insignificant man should sleep in the **t**;
4Mc 3: 8 sweating and quite exhausted, to the royal **t**,

TENT-CORD (1) [CORD, TENT]

Job 4:21 Their **t** is plucked up within them,

TENT-CURTAINS (1) [CURTAIN, TENT]

Hab 3: 7 the **t** of the land of Midian trembled.

TENT-DWELLING (1) [DWELL, TENT]

Jdg 5:24 wife of Heber the Kenite, of **t** women most blessed

TENTH‡ (51) [TEN]

Ge 8: 5 The waters continued to abate until the **t** month;
8: 5 in the **t** month, on the first day of the month,
14:20 And Abram gave him one **t** of everything.
28:22 and of all that you give me I will surely give one **t**
Ex 12: 3 Tell the whole congregation of Israel that on the **t**
16:36 An omer is a **t** of an ephah.
Lev 16:29 In the seventh month, on the **t** day of the month,
23:27 the **t** day of this seventh month is the day
25: 9 on the **t** day of the seventh month—
27:32 every **t** one that passes under the shepherd's staff,
Nu 7:66 On the **t** day Ahiezer son of Ammishaddai,
29: 7 On the **t** day of this seventh month you shall have
Dt 23: 2 to the **t** generation, none of their descendants shall
23: 3 to the **t** generation, none of their descendants shall
Jos 4:19 The people came up out of the Jordan on the **t** day
2Ki 25: 1 And in the ninth year of his reign, in the **t** month,
25: 1 in the tenth month, on the **t** day of the month,
1Ch 12:13 Jeremiah **t**, Machbannai eleventh.
24:11 the ninth to Jeshua, the **t** to Shecaniah,
25:17 the **t** to Shimei, his sons and his brothers, twelve;
27:13 **T**, for the **t** month, was Maharai of Netophah,
Ezr 10:16 the **t** month they sat down to examine the matter.
Est 2:16 in his royal palace in the **t** month,
Isa 6:13 Even if a **t** part remain in it,
Jer 32: 1 from the LORD in the **t** year of King Zedekiah
39: 1 in the **t** month, King Nebuchadrezzar of Babylon
52: 4 in the **t** month, on the **t** day of the month,
52:12 In the fifth month, on the **t** day of the month—
Eze 20: 1 in the fifth month, on the **t** day of the month,
24: 1 in the **t** month, on the **t** day of the month,
29: 1 In the **t** year, in the **t** month,
33:21 In the twelfth year of our exile, in the **t** month,
40: 1 on the **t** day of the month,
Zec 8:19 and the fast of the seventh, and the fast of the **t**,
Lk 18:12 I fast twice a week; I give a **t** of all my income.'
Heb 7: 4 Abraham the patriarch gave him a **t** of the spoils.
Rev 11:13 and a **t** of the city fell;
21:20 the **t** chrysoprase, the eleventh jacinth,
Tob 1: 7 likewise the **t** of the grain, wine, olive oil,
1: 7 for six years I would save up a second **t** in money
1: 8 A third **t** I would give to the orphans and widows
Sir 25: 7 and a **t** my tongue proclaims:
Bar 1: 8 At the same time, on the **t** day of Sivan,
1Es 9:16 of the **t** month they began their sessions
3Mc 5:14 now, since it was nearly the middle of the **t** hour,
2Es 14:12 as well as half of the **t** part; so two of its parts
remain, besides half of the **t** part.

TENTMAKERS (1) [MAKE, TENT]

Ac 18: 3 and they worked together—by trade they were **t**.

TENTS‡ (72) [TENT]

Ge 4:20 he was the ancestor of those who live in **t**
9:27 and let him live in the **t** of Shem;
13: 5 also had flocks and herds and **t**,
25:27 while Jacob was a quiet man, living in **t**.
Ex 16:16 all providing for those in their own **t**.' "
33: 8 of their **t** and watch Moses until he had gone into
Nu 11:10 all at the entrances of their **t**.
16:26 "Turn away from the **t** of these wicked men,
16:27 and stood at the entrance of their **t**,
24: 5 how fair are your **t**, O Jacob,
Dt 1:27 you grumbled in your **t** and said,
5:30 Go say to them, 'Return to your **t**.'
11: 6 their **t**, and every living being in their company;
16: 7 the next morning you may go back to your **t**.
33:18 in your going out; and Issachar, in your **t**.
Jos 3:14 When the people set out from their **t** to cross over
22: 4 to your **t** in the land where your possession lies,
22: 6 and they went to their **t**.
22: 7 And when Joshua sent them away to their **t**
22: 8 "Go back to your **t** with much wealth,
Jdg 6: 5 and they would even bring their **t**,
7: 8 he sent all the rest of Israel back to their own **t**,
20: 8 saying, "We will not any of us go to our **t**,
1Sa 13: 2 the rest of the people he sent home to their **t**.
2Sa 20: 1 Everyone to your **t**, O Israel!"
1Ki 8:66 and they blessed the king, and went to their **t**,
12:16 To your **t**, O Israel! Look now to your own house,
12:16 So Israel went away to their **t**.
2Ki 7: 7 in the twilight and abandoned their **t**,
7:10 the donkeys tied, and the **t** as they were."
1Ch 4:41 of King Hezekiah of Judah, and attacked their **t**
5:10 in their **t** throughout all the region east of Gilead.
2Ch 10:16 Each of you to your **t**, O Israel!
10:16 So all Israel departed to their **t**.
14:15 also attacked the **t** of those who had livestock,
Job 11:14 and do not let wickedness reside in your **t**.
12: 6 The **t** of robbers are at peace,
15:34 and fire consumes the **t** of bribery.
18:15 In their **t** nothing remains;
22:23 if you remove unrighteousness from your **t**,
Ps 69:25 let no one live in their **t**.
78:51 the first issue of their strength in the **t** of Ham.
78:55 and settled the tribes of Israel in their **t**.
83: 6 the **t** of Edom and the Ishmaelites,
84:10 of my God than live in the **t** of wickedness.
106:25 They grumbled in their **t**,
118:15 There are glad songs of victory in the **t** of
120: 5 that I must live among the **t** of Kedar.
SS 1: 5 like the **t** of Kedar, like the curtains of Solomon.
1: 8 and pasture your kids beside the shepherds' **t**.
Isa 13:20 Arabs will not pitch their **t** there,
Jer 4:20 Suddenly my **t** are destroyed,
6: 3 They shall pitch their **t** around her;
30:18 I am going to restore the fortunes of the **t**
35: 7 but you shall live in **t** all your days,
35:10 but we have lived in **t**,
37:10 of them only wounded men in their **t**,
49:29 Take their **t** and their flocks,
Eze 25: 4 among you and pitch their **t** in your midst;
Da 11:45 He shall pitch his palatial **t** between the sea and
Hos 9: 6 thorns shall be in their **t**.
12: 9 I will make you live in **t** again,
Hab 3: 7 I saw the **t** of Cushan under affliction;
Zec 12: 7 LORD will give victory to the **t** of Judah first,
Mal 2:12 from the **t** of Jacob anyone who does this—
Heb 11: 9 living in **t**, as did Isaac and Jacob,
Jdt 2:26 and burned their **t** and plundered their sheepfolds.
7:18 Their **t** and supply trains spread out
15: 1 When the men in the **t** heard it,
Wis 11: 2 and pitched their **t** in untrodden places.
1Mc 9:66 and the people of Phasiron in their **t**.
2Mc 12:12 receiving his pledges they went back to their **t**.

TEPHON (1)

1Mc 9:50 and Bethel, and Timnath, and Pharathon, and **T**,

TERAH (14)

Ge 11:24 he became the father of **T**;
11:25 after the birth of **T** one hundred nineteen years,
11:26 When **T** had lived seventy years,
11:27 the descendants of **T**. **T** was the father of Abram,
11:28 before his father **T** in the land of his birth,
11:31 **T** took his son Abram and his grandson Lot son
11:32 days of **T** were two hundred five years; and **T** died
Nu 33:27 They set out from Tahath and camped at **T**.
33:28 They set out from **T** and camped at Mithkah.
Jos 24: 2 **T** and his sons Abraham and Nahor—
1Ch 1:26 Serug, Nahor, **T**;
Lk 3:34 son of Abraham, son of **T**, son of Nahor,

TERAPHIM‡ (9)

Jdg 17: 5 and he made an ephod and **t**,
18:14 **t**, and an idol of cast metal?
18:17 the idol of cast metal, the ephod, and the **t**.
18:18 the ephod, and the **t**, the priest said to them,
18:20 He took the ephod, the **t**, and the idol,
2Ki 23:24 Josiah put away the mediums, wizards, **t**,
Eze 21:21 he shakes the arrows, he consults the **t**,
Hos 3: 4 without sacrifice or pillar, without ephod or **t**.
Zec 10: 2 For the **t** utter nonsense, and the diviners see lies;

TEREBINTH‡ (3) [TEREBINTHS]

Isa 6:13 like a **t** or an oak whose stump remains standing
Hos 4:13 oak, poplar, and **t**, because their shade is good.
Sir 24:16 Like a **t** I spread out my branches,

TEREBINTHS‡ (1) [TEREBINTH]

Ps 56: T *according to The Dove on Far-off* **T**. *Of David.*

TERESH (2)

Est 2:21 Bigthan and **T**, two of the king's eunuchs,
6: 2 how Mordecai had told about Bigthana and **T**,

TERM‡ (1) [TERMED, TERMS]

Isa 40: 2 that she has served her **t**, that her penalty is paid,

TERMED (2) [TERM]

Isa 62: 4 You shall no more be **t** Forsaken,
62: 4 and your land shall no more be **t** Desolate;

TERMINATION (1)

Nu 34: 5 and its **t** shall be at the Sea.

TERMS (20) [TERM]

Dt 2:26 to King Sihon of Heshbon with the following **t**
20:10 to a town to fight against it, offer it **t** of peace.
20:11 If it accepts your **t** of peace and surrenders to you,
1Ki 20:34 "I will let you go on those **t**."
Jer 32:11 containing the **t** and conditions,
34:18 the **t** of the covenant that they made before me,
Da 11:17 and he shall bring **t** of peace and perform them.
Mt 5:25 to **t** quickly with your accuser while you are on
Lk 14:32 he sends a delegation and asks for the **t** of peace.
Ac 7: 6 And God spoke in these **t**,
Ro 6:19 in human **t** because of your natural limitations.
1Mc 6:58 Now then let us come to **t** with these people,
7:12 before Alcimus and Bacchides to ask for just **t**.
8:29 Thus on these **t** the Romans make a treaty with
8:30 If after these **t** are in effect both parties shall
11:66 Then they asked him to grant them **t** of peace,
2Mc 11:14 and persuaded them to settle everything on just **t**,
13:25 so angry that they wanted to annul its **t**.
14:20 When the **t** had been fully considered,
1Es 9:14 of Tikvah undertook the matter on these **t**,

TERRACE (1) [TERRACES]

LtJ 6:11 or even give some of it to the prostitutes on the **t**.

TERRACES (1) [TERRACE]

Job 24:11 between their **t** they press out oil;

TERRESTRIAL (KJV) See EARTHLY

TERRIBLE‡ (30) [TERROR]

Dt 1:19 and went through all that great and **t** wilderness
8:15 who led you through the great and **t** wilderness,
31:17 and many **t** troubles will come upon them.
31:21 And when many **t** troubles come upon them,
1Ki 2: 8 a **t** curse on the day when I went to Mahanaim;
1Ch 17:21 making for yourself a name for great and **t** things,
Job 39:20 Its majestic snorting is **t**.
SS 6: 4 comely as Jerusalem, **t** as an army with banners.
6:10 bright as the sun, **t** as an army with banners?"
Isa 21: 1 it comes from the desert, from a **t** land.
35: 4 with **t** recompense. He will come and save you."
Eze 28: 7 the most **t** of the nations;
30:11 the most **t** of the nations, shall be brought in
31:12 from the most **t** of the nations have cut it down
32:12 all of them most **t** among the nations.
Joel 2:11 Truly the day of the LORD is great; **t** indeed—
2:31 before the great and **t** day of the LORD comes.
Zep 1:18 a full, a **t** end he will make of all the inhabitants of
2:11 The LORD will be **t** against them;
Mal 4: 5 before the great and **t** day of the LORD comes.
Mt 8: 6 at home paralyzed, in **t** distress."
Wis 11:18 or flash **t** sparks from their eyes;
16: 5 the **t** rage of wild animals came upon your people
19:16 with **t** sufferings those who had already shared
2Mc 6:30 from death, I am enduring **t** sufferings in my body
Man 1: 3 who confined the deep and sealed it with your **t**
2Es 8:22 and whose ordinance is **t**,
15:13 be ruined by blight and hail and by a **t** tempest.
15:40 upon every high and lofty place a **t** tempest,
4Mc 4:15 to the throne, an arrogant and **t** man,

TERRIBLY (6) [TERROR]

Mt 17:15 for he is an epileptic and he suffers **t**;
Mk 9:26 After crying out and convulsing him **t**,
AdE 11: 6 both ready to fight, and they roared **t**.
Wis 6: 5 he will come upon you **t** and swiftly,
17: 3 **t** alarmed, and appalled by specters.
2Mc 10:34 kept blaspheming **t** and uttering wicked words.

TERRIFIED‡ (47) [TERROR]

1Sa 5: 6 and he t and struck them with tumors,
28:21 and when she saw that he was t, she said to him,
31: 4 But his armor-bearer was unwilling; for he was t.
2Ki 10: 4 But they were utterly t and said, "Look,
1Ch 10: 4 But his armor-bearer was unwilling, for he was t.
Est 7: 6 Then Haman was t before the king and the queen.
Job 23:15 Therefore I am t at his presence;
23:16 has made my heart faint; the Almighty has t me;
31:34 and the contempt of families t me,
Ecc 8: 3 Do not be t; go from his presence,
Isa 31: 4 is not t by their shouting or daunted at their noise,
41:23 do good, or do harm, that we may be afraid and t.
44:11 they shall be t, they shall all be put to shame.
Jer 46: 5 Why do I see them t?
Da 4: 5 in bed and the visions of my head t me.
4:19 for a while. His thoughts t him.
5: 6 king's face turned pale, and his thoughts t him.
5: 9 Then King Belshazzar became greatly t
7:15 and the visions of my head t me.
7:28 As for me, Daniel, my thoughts greatly t me,
Mt 14:26 they were t, saying, "It is a ghost!"
27:54 the earthquake and what took place, they were t
Mk 6:50 for they all saw him and were t.
9: 6 He did not know what to say, for they were t.
Lk 1:12 When Zechariah saw him, he was t;
2: 9 of the Lord shone around them, and they were t.
9:34 and they were t as they entered the cloud.
21: 9 you hear of wars and insurrections, do not be t;
24: 5 The women were t and bowed their faces to
24:37 They were startled and t,
Jn 6:19 the sea and coming near the boat, and they were t.
Rev 11:11 and those who saw them were t.
11:13 rest were t and gave glory to the God of heaven.
Jdt 4: 2 they were therefore greatly t at his approach;
7: 4 they were greatly t and said to one another,
AdE 7: 6 Haman was t in the presence of the king
1Mc 12:28 they were afraid and were t at heart;
2Es 6:15 while the voice is speaking, do not be t;
6:23 and when all hear it, they shall suddenly be t.
6:24 the earth and those who inhabit it shall be t,
10:25 to approach her, and my heart was t.
10:55 do not be afraid, and do not let your heart be t;
12: 3 and the earth was exceedingly t.
12: 5 of the great fear with which I have been t tonight.
16:10 He will thunder, and who will not be t?
16:18 beginning of wars, when the powers shall be t;
4Mc 16:17 you young men were to be t by tortures.

TERRIFIES (1) [TERROR]

Job 33:16 he opens their ears, and t them with warnings,

TERRIFY (19) [TERROR]

2Ch 32:18 on the wall, to frighten and t them, in order
Job 3: 5 let the blackness of the day t it.
7:14 you scare me with dreams and t me with visions,
9:34 and not let dread of him t me,
13:11 Will not his majesty t you,
13:21 and do not let dread of you t me.
15:24 distress and anguish t them;
33: 7 No fear of me need t you;
Ps 2: 5 and t them in his fury, saying,
83:15 with your tempest and t them with your hurricane.
Isa 2:19 when he rises to t the earth.
2:21 when he rises to t the earth.
Jer 49:37 I will t Elam before their enemies,
Eze 30: 9 from me in ships to t the unsuspecting Ethiopians;
Da 4:19 do not let the dream or the interpretation t you."
5:10 Do not let your thoughts t you
Hab 2:17 the destruction of the animals will t you—
Zec 1:21 but these have come to t them,
4Mc 9: 5 to t us by threatening us with death by torture,

TERRIFYING (15) [TERROR]

Ge 15:12 and a deep and t darkness descended upon him.
Dt 4:34 and by t displays of power,
26: 8 with a t display of power,
34:12 and for all the mighty deeds and all the t displays
Job 15:21 T sounds are in their ears;
Isa 10:33 will lop the boughs with t power;
Da 7: 7 t and dreadful and exceedingly strong.
7:19 exceedingly t, with its teeth of iron and claws
Heb 12:21 Indeed, so t was the sight that Moses said,
AdE 15: 6 with gold and precious stones. He was most t.
Wis 17: 4 but t sounds rang out around them,
2Es 11:45 you and your t wings, your most evil little wings,
12: 8 the interpretation and meaning of this t vision so
12:13 be more t than all the kingdoms that have been
15:28 What a t sight, appearing from the east!

TERRITORIES (4) [TERRITORY]

Nu 32:33 with the t of the surrounding towns.
Jos 19:49 When they had finished distributing the several t
Jdg 21:24 and they went out from there to their own t.
2Ch 11:13 presented themselves to him from all their t.

TERRITORY‡ (108) [TERRITORIES]

Ge 10:19 And the t of the Canaanites extended from Sidon,
10:30 The t in which they lived extended from Mesha in
Ex 13: 7 no leaven shall be seen among you in all your t.
Nu 20:16 a town on the edge of your t.
20:17 or to the left until we have passed through your t."
20:21 to give Israel passage through their t;
21:22 until we have passed through your t."
21:23 not allow Israel to pass through his t.
24:17 and the t of all the Shethites.
33:44 from Oboth and camped at Iye-abarim, in the t
Dt 2: 4 about to pass through the t of your kindred,
3:12 the Reubenites and Gadites the t north of Aroer,
3:16 and the Gadites I gave the t from Gilead as far as
11:24 your t shall extend from the wilderness to
12:20 When the LORD your God enlarges your t,
16: 4 No leaven shall be seen with you in all your t
19: 8 If the LORD your God enlarges your t,
28:40 You shall have olive trees throughout all your t,
Jos 1: 4 to the Great Sea in the west shall be your t.
13:16 Their t was from Aroer, which is on the edge of
13:25 Their t was Jazer, and all the towns of Gilead,
13:26 and from Mahanaim to the t of Debir,
13:30 Their t extended from Mahanaim,
16: 2 it passes along to Ataroth, the t of the Archites;
16: 3 to the t of the Japhletites, as far as the t of Lower
16: 5 The t of the Ephraimites by their families was
17: 7 The t of Manasseh reached from Asher
18: 5 Judah continuing in its t on the south,
18: 5 and the house of Joseph in their t on the north.
18:11 the t allotted to it fell between the tribe of Judah
19: 9 the tribe of Simeon formed part of the t of Judah;
19:18 Its t included Jezreel, Chesulloth, Shunem,
19:41 The t of its inheritance included Zorah, Eshtaol,
19:47 When the t of the Danites was lost to them,
Jdg 1: 3 "Come up with me into the t allotted to me,
1: 3 I too will go with you into the t allotted to you."
1:18 with its t, Ashkelon with its t, and Ekron with its t.
11:18 They did not enter the t of Moab,
11:20 Sihon did not trust Israel to pass through his t;
11:22 They occupied all the t of the Amorites from
18: 1 of the Danites was seeking for itself a t to live in;
18: 1 for until then no t among the tribes
19:29 and sent her throughout all the t of Israel.
20: 6 sent her throughout the whole extent of Israel's t;
21:23 Then they went and returned to their t,
1Sa 5: 6 both in Ashdod and in its t.
7:13 and did not again enter the t of Israel;
7:14 and Israel recovered their t from the hand of
10: 2 by Rachel's tomb in the t of Benjamin at Zelzah;
11: 3 that we may send messengers through all the t
11: 7 throughout all the t of Israel by messengers,
2Sa 21: 5 we should have no place in all the t of Israel—
1Ki 1: 3 for a beautiful girl throughout all the t of Israel,
2Ki 9:10 The dogs shall eat Jezebel in the t of Jezreel,
9:36 'In the t of Jezreel the dogs shall eat the flesh
9:37 of Jezebel shall be like dung on the field in the t
10:32 Hazael defeated them throughout the t of Israel:
15:16 all who were in it and its t from Tirzah on;
18: 8 the Philistines as far as Gaza and its t,
1Ch 5:22 And they lived in their t until the exile.
6:66 of the sons of Kohath had towns of their t out of
21:12 of the LORD destroying throughout all the t
2Ch 16: 1 from going out or coming into the t of King Asa
26: 6 he built cities in the t of Ashdod and elsewhere
34:33 from all the t that belonged to the people of Israel,
Job 38:20 to its t and that you may discern the paths
Jer 15:13 for all your sins, throughout all your t.
17: 3 as the price of your sin throughout all your t.
Eze 43:12 the whole t on the top of the mountain all
48: 2 Adjoining the t of Dan, from the east side
48: 3 Adjoining the t of Asher, from the east side
48: 4 Adjoining the t of Naphtali, from the east side
48: 5 Adjoining the t of Manasseh, from the east side
48: 6 Adjoining the t of Ephraim, from the east side
48: 7 Adjoining the t of Reuben, from the east side
48: 8 Adjoining the t of Judah, from the east side
48:12 a most holy place, adjoining the t of the Levites.
48:13 Alongside the t of the priests,
48:22 of the prince shall lie between the t of Judah and
48:22 the territory of Judah and the t of Benjamin.
48:24 Adjoining the t of Benjamin, from the east side
48:25 Adjoining the t of Simeon, from the east side
48:26 Adjoining the t of Issachar, from the east side
48:27 Adjoining the t of Zebulun, from the east side
48:28 And adjoining the t of Gad to the south,
Am 1:13 in Gilead in order to enlarge their t.
6: 2 Or is your t greater than their territory,
6: 2 Or is your territory greater than their t,
Zep 2: 8 and made boasts against their t.
Mt 4:13 in the t of Zebulun and Naphtali,
Jdt 1:12 on the whole t of Cilicia and Damascus and Syria,
2:10 You shall go and seize all their t for me
2:25 He also seized the t of Cilicia,
16: 4 He boasted that he would burn up my t,
Sir 24: 7 in whose t should I abide?
Bar 3:24 how vast the t that he possesses!
1Mc 3:36 settle aliens in all their t,
3:42 and that the forces were encamped in their t.
5: 9 against the Israelites who lived in their t,
9:72 and did not come again into their t.
11:34 the t of Judea and the three districts of Aphairema
14: 2 that Demetrius had invaded his t,
15:29 You have devastated their t,
2Es 4:15 that there also we may gain more t for ourselves.'
4Mc 3:11 in the enemy's t tormented and inflamed him,

TERROR‡ (73) [TERRIBLE, TERRIBLY, TERRIFIED, TERRIFIES, TERRIFY, TERRIFYING, TERROR-ALL-AROUND, TERROR-STRICKEN, TERRORIZE, TERRORS]

Ge 35: 5 a t from God fell upon the cities all around them,
Ex 15:16 T and dread fell upon them;
23:27 I will send my t in front of you,
Lev 26:16 I will bring t on you;
Dt 32:25 the sword shall bereave, and in the chambers t,
Job 22:10 and sudden t overwhelms you,
31:23 For I was in t of calamity from God,
41:14 There is t all around its teeth.
41:22 In its neck abides strength, and t dances before it.
Ps 6: 2 heal me, for my bones are shaking with t.
6: 3 My soul also is struck with t, while you,
6:10 be ashamed and struck with t;
10:18 so that those from earth may strike t no more.
14: 5 There they shall be in great t,
31:13 the whispering of many—t all around!—
53: 5 There they shall be in great t,
53: 5 in t such as has not been.
78:33 like a breath, and their years in t.
91: 5 You will not fear the t of the night,
Isa 2:10 and hide in the dust from the t of the LORD,
2:19 from the t of the LORD,
2:21 from the t of the LORD,
17:14 At evening time, lo, t!
19:17 land of Judah will become a t to the Egyptians;
24:17 T, and the pit, and the snare are upon you,
24:18 Whoever flees at the sound of the t shall fall into
28:19 and it will be sheer t to understand the message.
31: 9 His rock shall pass away in t,
33:18 Your mind will muse on the t:
47:12 perhaps you may inspire t.
54:14 and from t, for it shall not come near you.
Jer 6:25 for the enemy has a sword, t is on every side."
8:15 for a time of healing, but there is t instead.
14:19 for a time of healing, but there is t instead.
15: 8 I have made anguish and t fall upon her suddenly.
17:17 Do not become a t to me;
20: 4 a t to yourself and to all your friends;
20:10 For I hear many whispering: "T is all around!
30: 5 We have heard a cry of panic, of t, and no peace.
32:21 and outstretched arm, and with great t;
46: 5 They do not look back—t is all around!
48:43 T, pit, and trap are before you,
48:44 Everyone who flees from the t shall fall into
49: 5 I am going to bring t upon you,
49:16 The t you inspire and the pride
49:29 and a cry shall go up: "T is all around!"
Eze 23:46 and make them an object of t and of plunder.
26:17 who imposed your t on all the mainland!
32:23 who spread t in the land of the living.
32:24 who spread t in the land of the living.
32:25 for t of them was spread in the land of the living,
32:26 for they spread t in the land of the living.
32:27 the t of the warriors was in the land of the living.
32:30 for all the t that they caused by their might;
32:32 For he spread t in the land of the living;
Mk 16: 8 for t and amazement had seized them;
Ac 10: 4 He stared at him in t and said, "What is it, Lord?"
Ro 13: 3 For rulers are not a t to good conduct, but to bad.
Jdt 16:25 No one ever again spread t among the Israelites
Wis 17: 6 and in t they deemed the things that they saw to
17:19 of the mountains, it paralyzed them with t.
Sir 45: 2 and made him great, to the t of his enemies.
1Mc 3:25 and t fell on the Gentiles all around them.
2Mc 3:17 t and bodily trembling had come over the man,
3:24 by the power of God, and became faint with t.
12:22 t and fear came over the enemy at
13:16 the end they filled the camp with t and confusion
15:23 a good angel to spread t and trembling before us.
3Mc 6:17 with them and brought an uncontrollable t upon
6:19 the enemy and filled them with confusion and t,
2Es 5: 1 the earth shall be seized with great t,
11:40 you have held sway over the world with great t,
13:13 Then I woke up in great t,

TERROR-ALL-AROUND (1) [AROUND, TERROR]

Jer 20: 3 The LORD has named you not Pashhur but "T,"

TERROR-STRICKEN (1) [STRIKE, TERROR]

Isa 30:31 The Assyrian will be t at the voice of the LORD,

TERRORIZE (1) [TERROR]

Sir 30: 9 Pamper a child, and he will t you;

TERRORS (11) [TERROR]

Job 6: 4 the t of God are arrayed against me.
18:11 T frighten them on every side,
18:14 and are brought to the king of t.
20:25 of their gall; t come upon them.
24:17 for they are friends with the t of deep darkness.
27:20 T overtake them like a flood;
30:15 T are turned upon me; my honor is pursued
Ps 55: 4 the t of death have fallen upon me.
73:19 in a moment, swept away utterly by t!
88:15 I suffer your t; I am desperate.
Ecc 12: 5 and t are in the road;

TERTIUS (1)

Ro 16:22 I T, the writer of this letter, greet you in the Lord.

TERTULLUS (2)

Ac 24: 1 with some elders and an attorney, a certain T,
24: 2 Paul had been summoned, T began to accuse him,

TEST‡ (77) [TESTED, TESTER, TESTING, TESTS]

Ex 15:25 and an ordinance and there he put them to the t.
16: 4 In that way I will t them,
17: 2 Why do you t the LORD?"
20:20 for God has come only to t you and to put the fear
Dt 6:16 Do not put the LORD your God to the t,
8:16 to humble you and to t you,
Jdg 2:22 to t Israel, whether or not they would take care
3: 1 to t all those in Israel who had no experience
1Ki 10: 1 she came to t him with hard questions.
2Ch 9: 1 to Jerusalem to t him with hard questions,
32:31 to t him and to know all that was in his heart.
Job 7:18 visit them every morning, t them every moment?
12:11 Does not the ear t words as the palate tastes food?
Ps 7: 9 you who t the minds and hearts, O righteous God.
17: 3 if you t me, you will find no wickedness in me;
26: 2 and try me; t my heart and mind.
106:14 and put God to the t in the desert;
139:23 t me and know my thoughts.
Ecc 2: 1 I will make a t of pleasure; enjoy yourself."
Isa 7:12 and I will not put the LORD to the t.
Jer 6:27 so that you may know and t their ways.
9: 7 I will now refine and t them,
12: 3 You see me and t me—my heart is with you.
17:10 I the LORD t the mind and search the heart,
20:12 O LORD of hosts, you t the righteous,
La 3:40 Let us t and examine our ways,
Da 1:12 "Please t your servants for ten days.
Zec 13: 9 and t them as gold is tested.
Mal 3:10 and thus put me to the t,
3:15 but when they put God to the t they escape."
Mt 4: 7 'Do not put the Lord your God to the t.' "
16: 1 and to t Jesus they asked him to show them a sign
19: 3 and to t him they asked,
22:18 said, "Why are you putting me to the t,
22:35 a lawyer, asked him a question to t him.
Mk 8:11 asking him for a sign from heaven, to t him.
10: 2 Some Pharisees came, and to t him they asked,
12:15 "Why are you putting me to the t?
Lk 4:12 'Do not put the Lord your God to the t.' "
4:13 When the devil had finished every t,
10:25 Just then a lawyer stood up to t Jesus.
11:16 to t him, kept demanding from him a sign
Jn 6: 6 He said this to t him,
8: 6 ⟦They said this to t him,⟧
Ac 5: 9 to put the Spirit of the Lord to the t?
15:10 Now therefore why are you putting God to the t
1Co 3:13 the fire will t what sort of work each has done.
10: 9 We must not put Christ to the t,
2Co 2: 9 to t you and to know whether you are obedient
13: 5 whether you are living in the faith. T yourselves.
13: 5 unless, indeed, you fail to meet the t!
13: 7 not that we may appear to have met the t,
Gal 4:14 though my condition put you to the t,
6: 4 All must t their own work;
1Th 5:21 but t everything; hold fast to what is good;
Heb 3: 9 where your ancestors put me to the t,
11:17 By faith Abraham, when put to the t,
Jas 1:12 a one has stood the t and will receive the crown
1Pe 4:12 that is taking place among you to t you,
1Jn 4: 1 but t the spirits to see whether they are from God;
Rev 3:10 the whole world to t the inhabitants of the earth.
Tob 12:14 I was sent to you to t you.
Jdt 8:12 Who are you to put God to the t today,
8:13 You are putting the Lord Almighty to the t,
8:25 who is putting us to the t as he did our ancestors.
Wis 1: 2 he is found by those who do not put him to the t,
2:17 and let us t what will happen at the end of his life;
2:19 Let us t him with insult and torture,
18:25 for merely to t the wrath was enough.
Sir 4:17 and she will t them with her ordinances.
6:21 She will be like a heavy stone to t them,
13:11 for he will t you by prolonged talk,
18:23 do not be like one who puts the Lord to the t.
27: 5 so the t of a person is in his conversation.
37:27 My child, t yourself while you live;
3Mc 5:40 how long will you put us to the t,
4Mc 9: 7 Therefore, tyrant, put us to the t;

TESTAMENT See Index to Footnotes

TESTATOR (KJV) See ONE WHO MADE IT

TESTED‡ (42) [TEST]

Ge 22: 1 After these things God t Abraham.
42:15 Here is how you shall be t:
42:16 in order that your words may be t,
Ex 17: 7 because the Israelites quarreled and t the LORD,
Nu 14:22 and yet have t me these ten times and have
Dt 6:16 as you t him at Massah.
33: 8 whom you t at Massah, with whom you contended
Job 23:10 when he has t me, I shall come out like gold.
Ps 66:10 For you, O God, have t us;
78:18 They t God in their heart by demanding
78:41 They t God again and again,
78:56 Yet they t the Most High God,
81: 7 I t you at the waters of Meribah.
95: 9 when your ancestors t me,
Pr 27:21 so a person is t by being praised.
Ecc 7:23 All this I have t by wisdom;
Isa 28:16 I am laying in Zion a foundation stone, a t stone,
48:10 I have t you in the furnace of adversity.
Da 1:14 he agreed to this proposal and t them for ten days.
Zec 13: 9 and test them as gold is t.
1Co 10:13 and he will not let you be t beyond your strength,
2Co 8:22 we are sending our brother whom we have often t
1Ti 3:10 And let them first be t;
Heb 2:18 Because he himself was t by what he suffered,
2:18 he is able to help those who are being t.
4:15 but we have one who in every respect has been t
1Pe 1: 7 though perishable, is t by fire—
Rev 2: 2 you have t those who claim to be apostles but are
2:10 of you into prison so that you may be t,
Jdt 8:26 and how he t Isaac, and what happened to Jacob
Wis 1: 3 and when his power is t, it exposes the foolish;
3: 5 God t them and found them worthy of himself;
6: 6 but the mighty will be mightily t.
11:10 For you t them as a parent does in warning,
Sir 2: 5 For gold is t in the fire,
27: 7 for this is the way people are t.
31:10 Who has been t by it and been found perfect?
44:20 and when he was t he proved faithful.
1Mc 2:52 Was not Abraham found faithful when t,
2Es 16:73 Then the t quality of my elect shall be manifest,
16:73 like gold that is t by fire.
4Mc 17:12 for on that day virtue gave the awards and t them

TESTER (1) [TEST]

Jer 6:27 I have made you a t and a refiner among my people

TESTICLES (3)

Lev 21:20 or an itching disease or scabs or crushed t.
22:24 that has its t bruised or crushed or torn or cut,
Dt 23: 1 No one whose t are crushed

TESTIFIED‡ (28) [TESTIFY]

Dt 19:18 having t falsely against another,
2Sa 1:16 for your own mouth has t against you, saying,
2Ch 24:19 they t against them, but they would not listen.
Jn 1:15 (John t to him and cried out,
1:32 And John t, "I saw the Spirit descending
1:34 And I myself have seen and have t that this is
3:26 to whom you t, here he is baptizing,
4:44 (for Jesus himself had t that a prophet has no honor
5:33 sent messengers to John, and he t to the truth.
5:37 Father who sent me has himself t on my behalf.
19:35 (He who saw this has t so that you
Ac 2:40 And he t with many other arguments
8:25 after Peter and John had t and spoken the word of
14: 3 who t to the word of his grace by granting signs
15: 8 t to them by giving them the Holy Spirit,
20:21 as I t to both Jews and Greeks about repentance
23:11 For just as you have t for me in Jerusalem,
1Co 15:15 because we t of God that he raised Christ—
Heb 2: 6 But someone has t somewhere,
7: 8 in the other, by one of whom it is t that he lives.
1Pe 1:11 when it t in advance to the sufferings destined
1Jn 5: 9 the testimony of God that he has t to his Son.
3Jn 1: 3 of the friends arrived and t to your faithfulness to
1: 6 they have t to your love before the church.
1:12 Everyone has t favorably about Demetrius,
Rev 1: 2 who t to the word of God and to the testimony
1Mc 2:56 Caleb, because he t in the assembly,
4Mc 6:32 we would have t to their domination.

TESTIFIES (11) [TESTIFY]

Job 16: 8 has risen up against me, and it t to my face.
Pr 6:19 a lying witness who t falsely,
Hos 5: 5 Israel's pride t against him;
7:10 Israel's pride t against him;
Jn 3:32 He t to what he has seen and heard,
5:32 There is another who t on my behalf,
8:18 and the Father who sent me t on my behalf."
Ac 20:23 except that the Holy Spirit t to me in every city
Heb 10:15 And the Holy Spirit also t to us, for after saying,
1Jn 5: 6 Spirit is the one that t, for the Spirit is the truth.
Rev 22:20 The one who t to these things says,

TESTIFY‡ (50) [TESTIFIED, TESTIFIES, TESTIFYING, TESTIMONIES, TESTIMONY]

Lev 5: 1 that you have heard a public adjuration to t and—
5: 1 though able to t as one who has seen or learned of
1Sa 12: 3 t against me before the LORD and
12: 3 T against me and I will restore it to you."
Job 15: 6 your own lips t against you.
Ps 50: 7 and I will speak, O Israel, I will t against you.
Pr 21:28 but a good listener will t successfully.
Isa 59:12 and our sins t against us.
Jer 14: 7 Although our iniquities t against us, act,
Am 3:13 Hear, and t against the house of Jacob,
Mt 23:31 Thus you t against yourselves
26:62 What is it that they t against you?"
Mk 14:60 What is it that they t against you?"
Lk 21:13 This will give you an opportunity to t.
Jn 1: 7 He came as a witness to t to the light,
1: 8 but he came to t to the light.
2:25 and needed no one to t about anyone;
3:11 of what we know and t to what we have seen;
5:31 "If I t about myself, my testimony is not true.
5:36 t on my behalf that the Father has sent me.
5:39 and it is they that t on my behalf.
7: 7 because I t against it that its works are evil.
8:14 Jesus answered, "Even if I t on my own behalf,
8:18 I t on my own behalf,
10:25 The works that I do in my Father's name t to me;
12:17 and raised him from the dead continued to t.
15:26 he will t on my behalf.
15:27 also are to t because you have been with me from
18:23 "If I have spoken wrongly, t to the wrong.
18:37 and for this I came into the world, to t to the truth.
Ac 10:42 He commanded us to preach to the people and to t
10:43 All the prophets t about him
20:24 to t to the good news of God's grace.
22: 5 and the whole council of elders can t about me.
26: 5 if they are willing to t,
26:16 and t to the things in which you have seen me and
Ro 10: 2 I can t that they have a zeal for God,
2Co 8: 3 For, as I can t, they voluntarily gave according
Gal 4:15 For I t that, had it been possible,
5: 3 Once again I t to every man who lets himself
Col 4:13 For I t for him that he has worked hard for you
Heb 3: 5 to t to the things that would be spoken later.
1Pe 5:12 and to t that this is the true grace of God.
1Jn 1: 2 and we have seen it and t to it,
4:14 and do t that the Father has sent his Son as
5: 7 There are three that t:
3Jn 1:12 We also t for him, and you know
Sus 1:21 we will t against you that a young man was
1:41 she would not tell us. These things we t."
1Mc 2:37 and earth t for us that you are killing us unjustly."

TESTIFYING (5) [TESTIFY]

Jn 8:13 "You are t on your own behalf;
21:24 This is the disciple who is t to these things
Ac 18: 5 t to the Jews that the Messiah was Jesus.
26:22 and so I stand here, t to both small and great,
28:23 t to the kingdom of God and trying

TESTIMONIES (2) [TESTIFY]

1Ki 2: 3 his commandments, his ordinances, and his t,
Sir 45:17 to teach Jacob the t, and to enlighten Israel with

TESTIMONY‡ (65) [TESTIFY]

Nu 35:30 be put to death on the t of a single witness.
Job 21:29 and do you not accept their t,
Isa 8:16 Bind up the t, seal the teaching
Mt 8: 4 the gift that Moses commanded, as a t to them."
10:18 as a t to them and the Gentiles.
24:14 as a t to all the nations;
26:59 for false t against Jesus so that they might put him
Mk 1:44 for your cleansing what Moses commanded, as a t
6:11 the dust that is on your feet as a t against them."
13: 9 before governors and kings because of me, as a t
14:55 the whole council were looking for t against Jesus
14:56 For many gave false t against him,
14:56 and their t did not agree.
14:57 Some stood up and gave false t against him,
14:59 But even on this point their t did not agree.
Lk 5:14 an offering for your cleansing, for a t to them."
9: 5 that town shake the dust off your feet as a t
22:71 Then they said, "What further t do we need?
Jn 1:19 the t given by John when the Jews sent priests
3:11 yet you do not receive our t.
3:32 yet no one accepts his t.
3:33 Whoever has accepted his t has certified this,
4:39 in him because of the woman's t,
5:31 "If I testify about myself, my t is not true.
5:32 and I know that his t to me is true.
5:34 Not that I accept such human t,
5:36 But I have a t greater than John's.
8:13 on your own behalf; your t is not valid."
8:14 my t is valid because I know where I have come
8:17 that the t of two witnesses is valid.
19:35 His t is true, and he knows that he tells the truth.)
21:24 and we know that his t is true.
Ac 4:33 the apostles gave their t to the resurrection of
7:44 "Our ancestors had the tent of t in the wilderness,
13:22 In his t about him he said, 'I have found David,
22:18 because they will not accept your t about me.'
1Co 1: 6 just as the t of Christ has been strengthened
2Co 1:12 Indeed, this is our boast, the t of our conscience:
2Th 1:10 because our t to you was believed.
1Ti 6:13 who in his t before Pontius Pilate made
2Ti 1: 8 of the t about our Lord or of me his prisoner,
Tit 1:13 That t is true. For this reason rebuke them sharply,
Heb 2: 4 while God added his t by signs and wonders
10:28 the law of Moses dies without mercy "on the t
1Jn 5: 9 If we receive human t, the t of God is greater; for
this is the t of God that he has testified to his Son.
5:10 Those who believe in the Son of God have the t
5:10 a liar by not believing in the t that God has given
5:11 And this is the t: God gave us eternal life,
3Jn 1:12 and you know that our t is true.
Rev 1: 2 to the word of God and to the t of Jesus Christ,
1: 9 because of the word of God and the t of Jesus.
6: 9 for the word of God and for the t they had given;
11: 7 When they have finished their t,
12:11 the blood of the Lamb and by the word of their t,
12:17 the commandments of God and hold the t
19:10 with you and your comrades who hold the t
19:10 For the t of Jesus is the spirit of prophecy."
20: 4 for their t to Jesus and for the word of God.
22:16 who sent my angel to you with this t for
Wis 17:11 condemned by its own t;
Sir 31:23 and their t to his generosity is trustworthy.
31:24 and their t to his stinginess is accurate.
2Mc 3:36 He bore t to all concerning the deeds of

TESTING (14) [TEST]

Dt 8: 2 t you to know what was in your heart,
13: 3 for the LORD your God is t you,

Jdg 3: 4 They were for the **t** of Israel,
Ps 105:19 the word of the LORD kept **t** him.
Ecc 3:18 with regard to human beings that God is **t** them
Lk 8:13 for a while and in a time of **t** fall away.
1Co 10:13 No **t** has overtaken you that is not common
10:13 but with the **t** he will also provide the way out so
2Co 8: 8 but I am **t** the genuineness of your love against
9:13 Through the **t** of this ministry you glorify God
Heb 3: 8 as on the day of **t** in the wilderness,
Jas 1: 3 that the **t** of your faith produces endurance;
Sir 2: 1 to serve the Lord, prepare yourself for **t**.
6: 7 When you gain friends, gain them through **t**,

TESTS (7) [TEST]

Job 34: 3 for the ear **t** words as the palate tastes food.
Ps 11: 5 The LORD **t** the righteous and the wicked,
Pr 17: 3 but the LORD **t** the heart.
1Th 2: 4 but to please God who **t** our hearts.
Sir 27: 5 The kiln **t** the potter's vessels;
31:26 As the furnace **t** the work of the smith,
31:26 so wine **t** hearts when the insolent quarrel.

TETRARCH See Index to Footnotes

TEXT (2)

Ezr 7:11 of the **t** of the commandments of the LORD
Lk 20:17 "What then does this **t** mean:

THA See Index to Footnotes

THADDAEUS (2) [=JUDAS]

Mt 10: 3 James son of Alphaeus, and **T**;
Mk 3:18 and Thomas, and James son of Alphaeus, and **T**,

THAHASH (KJV) See TAHASH

THAMAH (KJV) See TEMAH

THAMAR (KJV) See TAMAR

THAN‡ (720)

Ge 3: 1 serpent was more crafty **t** any other wild animal
4:13 "My punishment is greater **t** I can bear!
19: 9 Now we will deal worse with you **t** with them."
25:23 the one shall be stronger **t** the other,
28:17 This is none other **t** the house of God,
29:19 to you **t** that I should give her to any other man;
29:30 and he loved Rachel more **t** Leah.
37: 3 Now Israel loved Joseph more **t** any other
37: 4 that their father loved him more **t** all his brothers,
38:26 "She is more in the right **t** I,
39: 9 He is not greater in this house **t** I am,
41:40 with regard to the throne will I be greater **t** you."
48:19 his younger brother shall be greater **t** he,
48:22 to you one portion more **t** to your brothers,
49:12 eyes are darker **t** wine, and his teeth whiter **t** milk.
49:26 of your father are stronger **t** the blessings of
Ex 1: 9 are more numerous and more powerful **t** we.
5: 5 "Now they are more numerous **t** the people of
14:12 to serve the Egyptians **t** to die in the wilderness."
18:11 Now I know that the LORD is greater **t** all gods,
22:20 other **t** the LORD alone,
30:15 and the poor shall not give less, **t** the half shekel,
36: 5 "The people are bringing much more **t** enough
36: 7 what they had already brought was more **t** enough
Lev 13: 3 and the disease appears to be deeper **t** the skin
13: 4 and appears no deeper **t** the skin,
13:20 and if it appears deeper **t** the skin
13:21 nor is it deeper **t** the skin but has abated,
13:25 the spot has turned white and it appears deeper **t**
13:26 and it is no deeper **t** the skin but has abated,
13:30 If it appears deeper **t** the skin and the hair
13:31 and it appears no deeper **t** the skin
13:32 and the itch appears to be no deeper **t** the skin,
13:34 the skin and it appears to be no deeper **t** the skin,
14:37 and if it appears to be deeper **t** the surface,
Nu 5:20 some man other **t** your husband has had intercourse
12: 3 more so **t** anyone else on the face of the earth.
13:31 for they are stronger **t** we."
14: 9 for they are no more **t** bread for us;
14:12 of you a nation greater and mightier **t** they."
22: 6 since they are stronger **t** I;
22:15 more numerous and more distinguished **t** these.
24: 7 his king shall be higher **t** Agag,
Dt 1:28 'The people are stronger and taller **t** we;
4:38 and mightier **t** yourselves,
7: 1 and more numerous **t** you—
7: 7 you were more numerous **t** any other people
7:17 "These nations are more numerous **t** I;
9: 1 and dispossess nations larger and mightier **t** you,
9:14 a nation mightier and more numerous **t** they."
11:23 and mightier **t** yourselves.
20: 1 an army larger **t** your own,
25: 3 if more lashes **t** these are given,
30: 5 and numerous **t** your ancestors.
Jos 10: 2 and was larger **t** Ai, and all its men were warriors.
10:11 because of the hailstones **t** the Israelites killed
22:19 by building yourselves an altar other **t** the altar of
22:29 other **t** the altar of the LORD our God that stands
Jdg 2:19 and behave worse **t** their ancestors,
7:14 "This is no other **t** the sword of Gideon son
8: 2 not the gleaning of the grapes of Ephraim better **t**
Jdg 11:25 Now are you any better **t** King Balak son
14:18 What is sweeter **t** honey? What is stronger **t** a lion?
15: 2 Is not her younger sister prettier **t** she?
16:30 at his death were more **t** those he had killed
Ru 1:13 it has been far more bitter for me **t** for you,
3:10 this last instance of your loyalty is better **t**
3:12 there is another kinsman more closely related **t** I.
4: 1 to the gate and sat down there **t** the next-of-kin,
4:15 who is more to you **t** seven sons, has borne him."
1Sa 1: 8 Am I not more to you **t** ten sons?"
2:29 and honor your sons more **t** me
9: 2 among the people of Israel more handsome **t** he;
10:23 he was head and shoulders taller **t** any of them.
15:22 Surely, to obey is better **t** sacrifice, and to heed **t**
the fat of rams.
15:23 For rebellion is no less a sin **t** divination,
15:28 to a neighbor of yours, who is better **t** you.
18:30 David had more success **t** all the servants of Saul,
24:17 He said to David, "You are more righteous **t** I;
27: 1 for me **t** to escape to the land of the Philistines;
2Sa 1:23 were swifter **t** eagles, they were stronger **t** lions.
6:22 I will make myself yet more contemptible **t** this,
13:14 and being stronger **t** she, he forced her and lay
13:15 his loathing was even greater **t** the lust he had felt
13:16 for this wrong in sending me away is greater **t**
17:14 the Archite is better **t** the counsel of Ahithophel."
18: 8 forest claimed more victims that day **t** the sword.
19: 7 for you **t** any disaster that has come upon you
19:43 and in David also we have more **t** you.
19:43 of the people of Judah were fiercer **t** the words of
20: 6 of Bichri will do us more harm **t** Absalom;
1Ki 1:37 and make his throne greater **t** the throne
1:47 the name of Solomon more famous **t** yours, and
make his throne greater **t** your throne.'
2:32 and better **t** himself, Abner son
4:31 He was wiser **t** anyone else,
4:31 wiser **t** Ethan the Ezrahite, and Heman, Calcol,
12:10 'My little finger is thicker **t** my father's loins.
14:22 more **t** all that their ancestors had done.
16:25 he did more evil **t** all who were before him.
16:30 of the LORD more **t** all who were before him.
16:33 **t** had all the kings of Israel who were before him.
18:44 a little cloud no bigger **t**
19: 4 for I am no better **t** my ancestors."
20:23 and so they were stronger **t** we;
20:23 and surely we shall be stronger **t** they.
20:25 and surely we shall be stronger **t** they."
2Ki 5:12 better **t** all the waters of Israel?
6:10 More **t** once or twice he warned such a place so
6:16 for there are more with us **t** there are with them."
9:35 they found no more of her **t** the skull and the feet
13: 7 an army of not more **t** fifty horsemen, ten chariots
21: 9 to do more evil **t** the nations had done that
21:11 has done things more wicked **t** all that
1Ch 4: 9 Jabez was honored more **t** his brothers;
24: 4 the sons of Eleazar **t** among the sons of Ithamar,
2Ch 2: 5 for our God is greater **t** other gods.
10:10 'My little finger is thicker **t** my father's loins.
11:21 of Absalom more **t** all his other wives
21:13 who were better **t** yourself,
25: 9 LORD is able to give you much more **t** this."
29:34 the Levites were more conscientious **t** the priests
30:18 they ate the passover otherwise **t** as prescribed.
32: 7 for there is one greater with us **t** with him.
33: 9 so that they did more evil **t** the nations whom
Ezr 9: 6 for our iniquities have risen higher **t** our heads,
9:13 have punished us less **t** our iniquities deserved
Ne 7: 2 a faithful man and feared God more **t** many.
Est 1:19 to another who is better **t** she.
2:17 the king loved Esther more **t** all the other women;
4:13 in the king's palace you will escape any more **t** all
6: 6 the king wish to honor more **t** me?"
Job 3:21 and dig for it more **t** for hidden treasures;
6: 3 For then it would be heavier **t** the sand of the sea;
7: 6 My days are swifter **t** a weaver's shuttle,
7:15 and death rather **t** this body.
9:25 "My days are swifter **t** a runner;
11: 6 that God exacts of you less **t** your guilt deserves.
11: 8 It is higher **t** heaven—what can you do?
11: 8 Deeper **t** Sheol—what can you know?
11: 9 measure is longer **t** the earth, and broader **t** the sea.
11:17 And your life will be brighter **t** the noonday;
15:10 the aged are on our side, those older **t** your father.
30: 1 they make sport of me, those who are younger **t** I,
32: 2 at Job because he justified himself rather **t** God;
32: 4 because they were older **t** he.
33:12 I will answer you: God is greater **t** any mortal.
34:19 nor regards the rich more **t** the poor,
35: 3 How am I better off **t** if I had sinned?'
35: 5 observe the clouds, which are higher **t** you.
35:11 who teaches us more **t** the animals of the earth,
35:11 and makes us wiser **t** the birds of the air?'
42:12 the latter days of Job more **t** his beginning;
Ps 4: 7 You have put gladness in my heart more **t**
8: 5 Yet you have made them a little lower **t** God,
17:14 may their children have more **t** enough;
19:10 More to be desired are they **t** gold,
19:10 sweeter also **t** honey, and drippings of the
37:16 Better is a little that the righteous person has **t**
40: 5 they would be more **t** can be counted.
40:12 they are more **t** the hairs of my head,
51: 7 wash me, and I shall be whiter **t** snow.
52: 3 You love evil more **t** good,
52: 3 and lying more **t** speaking the truth.
55:21 with speech smoother **t** butter, but with a heart set
55:21 with words that were softer **t** oil,
58: 9 Sooner **t** your pots can feel the heat of thorns,
Ps 61: 2 Lead me to the rock that is higher **t** I;
62: 9 they are together lighter **t** a breath.
63: 3 Because your steadfast love is better **t** life,
69: 4 More in number **t** the hairs
69:31 This will please the LORD more **t** an ox or a bull
73:25 there is nothing on earth that I desire other **t** you.
76: 4 more majestic **t** the everlasting mountains.
84:10 in your courts is better **t** a thousand elsewhere.
84:10 be a doorkeeper in the house of my God **t** live in
87: 2 the LORD loves the gates of Zion more **t** all
93: 4 More majestic **t** the thunders of mighty waters,
93: 4 more majestic **t** the waves of the sea,
105:24 and made them stronger **t** their foes,
108: 4 For your steadfast love is higher **t** the heavens,
118: 8 to take refuge in the LORD **t** to put confidence
118: 9 to take refuge in the LORD **t** to put confidence
119:72 The law of your mouth is better to me **t** thousands
119:98 commandment makes me wiser **t** my enemies,
119:99 I have more understanding **t** all my teachers,
119:100 I understand more **t** the aged,
119:103 sweeter **t** honey to my mouth!
119:127 Truly I love your commandments more **t** gold,
more **t** fine gold.
123: 3 for we have had more **t** enough of contempt.
123: 4 Our soul has had more **t** its fill of the scorn
130: 6 the Lord more **t** those who watch for the morning,
more **t** those who watch for the morning.
139:18 I try to count them—they are more **t** the sand;
Pr 3:14 for her income is better **t** silver, and her revenue
better **t** gold.
3:15 She is more precious **t** jewels,
5: 3 and her speech is smoother **t** oil;
8:10 and knowledge rather **t** choice gold;
8:11 for wisdom is better **t** jewels,
8:19 My fruit is better **t** gold, even fine gold,
8:19 even fine gold, and my yield **t** choice silver.
12: 9 **t** to be self-important and lack food.
15:16 a little with the fear of the LORD **t** great treasure
15:17 a dinner of vegetables where love is **t** a fatted ox
16: 8 Better is a little with righteousness **t** large income
16:16 How much better to get wisdom **t** gold!
16:16 to be chosen rather **t** silver.
16:19 It is better to be of a lowly spirit among the poor **t**
16:32 One who is slow to anger is better **t** the mighty,
16:32 one whose temper is controlled **t** one who captures
17: 1 a dry morsel with quiet **t** a house full of feasting
17:10 A rebuke strikes deeper into a discerning person **t**
17:12 to meet a she-bear robbed of its cubs **t** to confront
18:19 An ally offended is stronger **t** a city;
18:24 but a true friend sticks closer **t** one's nearest kin.
19: 1 in integrity **t** one perverse of speech who is a fool.
19:22 and it is better to be poor **t** a liar.
21: 3 to the LORD **t** sacrifice.
21: 9 a corner of the housetop **t** in a house shared with
21:19 a desert land **t** with a contentious and fretful wife.
22: 1 A good name is to be chosen rather **t** great riches,
22: 1 and favor is better **t** silver or gold.
24: 5 Wise warriors are mightier **t** strong ones,
24: 5 who have knowledge **t** those who have strength;
25: 7 **t** to be put lower in the presence of a noble.
25:24 a corner of the housetop **t** in a house shared with
26:12 There is more hope for fools **t** for them.
26:16 in self-esteem **t** seven who can answer discreetly.
27: 3 but a fool's provocation is heavier **t** both.
27: 5 Better is open rebuke **t** hidden love.
27:10 neighbor who is nearby **t** kindred who are far
28: 6 to be poor and walk in integrity **t** to be crooked
28:23 will afterward find more favor **t** one who flatters
29:20 There is more hope for a fool **t** for anyone
31:10 She is far more precious **t** jewels.
Ecc 1: 8 All things are wearisome; more **t** one can express;
2: 7 more **t** any who had been before me in Jerusalem.
2:24 There is nothing better for mortals **t** to eat
3:12 that there is nothing better for them **t** to be happy
3:22 So I saw that there is nothing better **t**
4: 2 more fortunate **t** the living, who are still alive;
4: 3 but better **t** both is the one who has not yet been,
4: 6 a handful with quiet **t** two handfuls with toil,
4: 9 Two are better **t** one, because they have
4:13 a poor but wise youth **t** an old but foolish king,
5: 1 to listen is better **t** the sacrifice offered by fools;
5: 5 not vow **t** that you should vow and not fulfill it.
6: 3 I say that a stillborn child is better off **t** he.
6: 5 yet it finds rest rather **t** he.
6: 9 the sight of the eyes **t** the wandering of desire;
7: 1 A good name is better **t** precious ointment,
7: 1 and the day of death, **t** the day of birth.
7: 2 It is better to go to the house of mourning **t** to go
7: 3 Sorrow is better **t** laughter,
7: 5 It is better to hear the rebuke of the wise **t** to hear
7: 8 Better is the end of a thing **t** its beginning;
7: 8 the patient in spirit are better **t** the proud in spirit.
7:10 "Why were the former days better **t** these?"
7:19 to the wise more **t** ten rulers that are in a city.
7:26 I found more bitter **t** death the woman who is
8:15 for people under the sun **t** to eat,
9: 4 for a living dog is better **t** a dead lion.
9:16 So I said, "Wisdom is better **t** might;
9:17 the wise are more to be heeded **t** the shouting of
9:18 Wisdom is better **t** weapons of war,
SS 1: 2 For your love is better **t** wine,
1: 4 we will extol your love more **t** wine;
4:10 how much better is your love **t** wine,
4:10 and the fragrance of your oils **t** any spice!
5: 9 What is your beloved more **t** another beloved,
5: 9 What is your beloved more **t** another beloved,
Isa 10:10 of the idols whose images were greater **t** those

Isa 13:12 I will make mortals more rare **t** fine gold,
13:12 and humans **t** the gold of Ophir.
32:10 In little more **t** a year you will shudder,
40:17 they are accounted by him as less **t** nothing
54: 1 of the desolate woman will be more **t** the children
55: 9 For as the heavens are higher **t** the earth, so are my ways higher **t** your ways and my thoughts **t** your
56: 5 and a name better **t** sons and daughters;
Jer 3:11 Israel has shown herself less guilty **t** false Judah.
4:13 his horses are swifter **t** eagles—
5: 3 They have made their faces harder **t** rock;
7:24 and looked backward rather **t** forward.
7:26 They did worse **t** their ancestors did.
10: 8 the instruction given by idols is no better **t** wood!
15: 8 Their widows became more numerous **t** the sand
16:12 you have behaved worse **t** your ancestors,
46:23 because they are more numerous **t** locusts;
48:32 More **t** for Jazer I weep for you,
La 4: 6 the chastisement of my people has been greater **t**
4: 7 Her princes were purer **t** snow, whiter **t** milk; their bodies were more ruddy **t** coral,
4: 8 Now their visage is blacker **t** soot;
4: 9 by the sword **t** those pierced by hunger,
4:19 Our pursuers were swifter **t** the eagles in
Eze 3: 9 Like the hardest stone, harder **t** flint,
5: 6 becoming more wicked **t** the nations and
5: 7 Because you are more turbulent **t** the nations
8:15 You will see still greater abominations **t** these."
16:47 a very little time you were more corrupt **t** they
16:51 you have committed more abominations **t** they,
16:52 in which you acted more abominably **t** they,
16:52 they are more in the right **t** you.
23:11 yet she was more corrupt **t** she in her lusting and
23:11 which were worse **t** those of her sister.
28: 3 You are indeed wiser **t** Daniel;
36:11 and will do more good to you **t** ever before.
42: 5 from them **t** from the lower and middle chambers
42: 6 the ground more **t** the lower and the middle ones.
Da 1:10 in poorer condition **t** the other young men
1:15 that they appeared better and fatter **t** all
1:20 he found them ten times better **t** all the magicians
2:30 that I have more **t** any other living being,
3:19 up seven times more **t** was customary,
3:28 and yielded up their bodies rather **t** serve
7:20 and that seemed greater **t** the others.
8: 3 horns were long, but one was longer **t** the other,
11: 2 The fourth shall be far richer **t** all of them,
11: 5 but one of his officers shall grow stronger **t** he
11: 5 and shall rule a realm greater **t** his own realm.
11:13 of the north shall again raise a multitude, larger **t**
11:36 and consider himself greater **t** any god,
11:37 for he shall consider himself greater **t** all.
Hos 2: 7 for it was better with me then **t** now."
4:18 they love lewdness more **t** their glory.
6: 6 the knowledge of God rather **t** burnt offerings.
Am 6: 2 Are you better **t** these kingdoms?
6: 2 Or is your territory greater **t** their territory,
Jnh 4: 3 for it is better for me to die **t** to live."
4: 8 He said, "It is better for me to die **t** to live."
4:11 in which there are more **t** a hundred
Na 3: 8 Are you better **t** Thebes that sat by the Nile,
3:16 You increased your merchants more **t** the stars of
Hab 1: 8 Their horses are swifter **t** leopards, more menacing **t** wolves at dusk;
1:13 the wicked swallow those more righteous **t** they?
Hag 2: 9 The latter splendor of this house shall be greater **t**
Mt 3:11 one who is more powerful **t** I is coming after me;
5:29 it is better for you to lose one of your members **t**
5:30 it is better for you to lose one of your members **t**
5:37 anything more **t** this comes from the evil one.
5:47 what more are you doing **t** others?
6:25 Is not life more **t** food,
6:25 and the body more **t** clothing?
6:26 Are you not of more value **t** they?
10:15 of Sodom and Gomorrah on the day of judgment **t**
10:31 you are of more value **t** many sparrows.
10:37 Whoever loves father or mother more **t** me is
10:37 and whoever loves son or daughter more **t** me is
11: 9 Yes, I tell you, and more **t** a prophet.
11:11 born of women no one has arisen greater **t** John
11:11 the least in the kingdom of heaven is greater **t** he.
11:22 be more tolerable for Tyre and Sidon **t** for you.
11:24 be more tolerable for the land of Sodom **t** for you."
12: 6 I tell you, something greater **t** the temple is here.
12:12 much more valuable is a human being **t** a sheep!
12:41 and see, something greater **t** Jonah is here!
12:42 and see, something greater **t** Solomon is here!
12:45 along seven other spirits more evil **t** itself,
12:45 and the last state of that person is worse **t** the first.
18: 8 to enter life maimed or lame **t** to have two hands
18: 9 with one eye **t** to have two eyes and to be thrown
18:13 he rejoices over it more **t** over the ninety-nine
19:24 for a camel to go through the eye of a needle **t**
21:36 Again he sent other slaves, more **t** the first;
26:53 and he will at once send me more **t** twelve legions
27:64 and the last deception would be worse **t** the first."
Mk 1: 7 one who is more powerful **t** I is coming after me;
9:43 to enter life maimed **t** to have two hands and to go
9:45 for you to enter life lame **t** to have two feet and to
9:47 with one eye **t** to have two eyes and to be thrown
10:25 for a camel to go through the eye of a needle **t**
12:31 There is no other commandment greater **t** these."
12:33 much more important **t** all whole burnt offerings
12:43 in more **t** all those who are contributing to
14: 5 for more **t** three hundred denarii,
Lk 3:13 "Collect no more **t** the amount prescribed
3:16 but one who is more powerful **t** I is coming;

Lk 5:15 more **t** ever the word about Jesus spread abroad;
7:26 Yes, I tell you, and more **t** a prophet.
7:28 of women no one is greater **t** John;
7:28 the least in the kingdom of God is greater **t** he."
9:13 "We have no more **t** five loaves and two fish—
10:12 that day it will be more tolerable for Sodom **t** for
10:14 be more tolerable for Tyre and Sidon **t** for you.
11:22 But when one stronger **t** he attacks him
11:26 and brings seven other spirits more evil **t** itself,
11:26 the last state of that person is worse **t** the first."
11:31 and see, something greater **t** Solomon is here!
11:32 and see, something greater **t** Jonah is here!
12: 7 you are of more value **t** many sparrows.
12:23 For life is more **t** food,
12:23 and the body more **t** clothing.
12:24 Of how much more value are you **t** the birds!
13: 2 they were worse sinners **t** all other Galileans?
13: 4 do you think that they were worse offenders **t** all
14: 8 someone more distinguished **t** you has been invited
15: 7 more joy in heaven over one sinner who repents **t**
16: 8 with their own generation **t** are the children
16:17 **t** for one stroke of a letter in the law to
17: 2 the sea **t** for you to cause one of these little ones
18:14 this man went down to his home justified rather **t**
18:25 for a camel to go through the eye of a needle **t**
21: 3 this poor widow has put in more **t** all of them;
Jn 1:50 You will see greater things **t** these."
3:19 and people loved darkness rather **t** light
4: 1 and baptizing more disciples **t** John"
4:12 Are you greater **t** our ancestor Jacob,
5:20 and he will show him greater works **t** these,
5:36 But I have a testimony greater **t** John's.
7:31 will he do more signs **t** this man has done?"
8:53 Are you greater **t** our father Abraham, who died?
10:29 What my Father has given me is greater **t** all else,
11:50 the people **t** to have the whole nation destroyed."
12:43 for they loved human glory more **t** the glory
13:16 I tell you, servants are not greater **t** their master,
13:16 are messengers greater **t** the one who sent them.
14:12 in fact, will do greater works **t** these,
14:28 because the Father is greater **t** I.
15:13 No one has greater love **t** this,
15:20 'Servants are not greater **t** their master.'
19: 8 when Pilate heard this, he was more afraid **t** ever.
21:15 do you love me more **t** these?"
Ac 4:19 to listen to you rather **t** to God, you must judge;
4:22 healing had been performed was more **t** forty
5:14 Yet more **t** ever believers were added to the Lord,
5:29 "We must obey God rather **t** any human authority.
15:28 on you no further burden **t** these essentials:
17:11 These Jews were more receptive **t** those
20:35 'It is more blessed to give **t** to receive.' "
21:28 more **t** that, he has actually brought Greeks into
23:13 There were more **t** forty who joined
23:21 for more **t** forty of their men are lying in ambush
24:11 not more **t** twelve days since I went up to worship
25: 6 among them not more **t** eight or ten days, he went
26:13 I saw a light from heaven, brighter **t** the sun,
27:11 and to the owner of the ship **t** to what Paul said.
Ro 1:25 and worshiped and served the creature rather **t**
5:11 But more **t** that, we even boast in God
8:37 in all these things we are more **t** conquerors
11:25 So that you may not claim to be wiser **t** you are,
12: 3 not to think of yourself more highly **t** you ought
12:16 do not claim to be wiser **t** you are.
13:11 to us now **t** when we became believers;
14: 5 Some judge one day to be better **t** another,
1Co 1:25 For God's foolishness is wiser **t** human wisdom,
1:25 and God's weakness is stronger **t** human strength.
3:11 For no one can lay any foundation other **t** the one
7: 9 it is better to marry **t** to be aflame with passion.
7:21 of your present condition now more **t** ever.
9:12 but we endure anything rather **t** put an obstacle in
9:15 Indeed, I would rather die **t** that—
10:22 Are we stronger **t** he?
14: 5 One who prophesies is greater **t** one who speaks
14:18 I thank God that I speak in tongues more **t** all
14:19 **t** ten thousand words in a tongue.
15: 6 Then he appeared to more **t** five hundred brothers
15:10 On the contrary, I worked harder **t** any of them—
2Co 1:13 we write you nothing other **t** what you can read
8:17 but since he is more eager **t** ever,
8:22 but who is now more eager **t** ever because
11: 4 if someone comes and proclaims another Jesus **t**
12: 6 that no one may think better of me **t** what is seen
12:13 have you been worse off **t** the other churches,
Gal 3:20 Now a mediator involves more **t** one party;
4: 1 as long as they are minors, are no better **t** slaves,
4:27 of the desolate woman are more numerous **t**
6: 4 then that work, rather **t** their neighbor's work,
Eph 3:20 to accomplish abundantly far more **t** all we can ask
Php 2: 3 in humility regard others as better **t** yourselves.
3: 8 More **t** that, I regard everything as loss because of
4:16 you sent me help for my needs more **t** once.
4:18 I have been paid in full and have more **t** enough;
1Ti 1: 4 that promote speculations rather **t**
5: 8 has denied the faith and is worse **t** an unbeliever.
5: 9 be put on the list if she is not less **t** sixty years old
2Ti 3: 4 lovers of pleasure rather **t** lovers of God,
Phm 1:16 as a slave but more **t** a slave, a beloved brother—
1:21 knowing that you will do even more **t** I say.
Heb 1: 4 name he has inherited is more excellent **t** theirs.
2: 7 You have made them for a little while lower **t**
2: 9 for a little while was made lower **t** the angels,
3: 3 Yet Jesus is worthy of more glory **t** Moses,
3: 3 just as the builder of a house has more honor **t**
4:12 sharper **t** any two-edged sword,

Heb 6:16 of course, swear by someone greater **t** themselves,
7:11 rather **t** one according to the order of Aaron?
7:28 which came later **t** the law,
9:23 things themselves need better sacrifices **t** these.
11: 4 to God a more acceptable sacrifice **t** Cain's.
11:25 the people of God **t** to enjoy the fleeting pleasures
11:26 for the Christ to be greater wealth **t** the treasures
12:11 discipline always seems painful rather **t** pleasant
12:24 to the sprinkled blood that speaks a better word **t**
1Pe 1: 7 being more precious **t** gold that,
3:17 **t** to suffer for doing evil.
2Pe 2:20 last state has become worse for them **t** the first.
2:21 to have known the way of righteousness **t**,
1Jn 3:20 for God is greater **t** our hearts,
4: 4 the one who is in you is greater **t** the one who is
3Jn 1: 4 I have no greater joy **t** this,
Rev 2:19 I know that your last works are greater **t** the first.
Tob 3: 6 For it is better for me to die **t** to live,
3: 6 for me to die **t** to see so much distress in my life
6:13 Indeed he knows that you, rather **t** any other man,
7:10 at liberty to give her to any other man **t** yourself,
12: 8 but better **t** both is almsgiving with righteousness.
12: 8 A little with righteousness is better **t** wealth
12: 8 It is better to give alms **t** to lay up gold.
14: 4 it will be safer in Media **t** in Assyria and Babylon.
Jdt 12:20 much more **t** he had ever drunk in any one day
AdE 1:19 to a woman better **t** she.
6: 6 the king wish to honor more **t** me?"
Wis 4: 1 Better **t** this is childlessness with virtue,
7:10 I loved her more **t** health and beauty,
7:10 and I chose to have her rather **t** light,
7:24 For wisdom is more mobile **t** any motion;
7:29 She is more beautiful **t** the sun,
8: 5 in life, what is richer **t** wisdom, the active cause
8: 6 who more **t** she is fashioner of what exists?
8: 7 in life is more profitable for mortals **t** these.
10:12 that godliness is more powerful **t** anything else.
13: 3 how much better **t** these is their Lord,
14: 1 of wood more fragile **t** the ship that carries him.
15:10 Their heart is ashes, their hope is cheaper **t** dirt,
15:10 and their lives are of less worth **t** clay,
15:13 For these persons, more **t** all others,
15:14 But most foolish, and more miserable **t** an infant,
15:17 for they are better **t** the objects they worship,
15:18 which are worse **t** all others when judged
16:19 the midst of water it burned more intensely **t** fire,
17: 6 to be worse **t** that unseen appearance.
17:21 still heavier **t** darkness were they to themselves.
Sir 3:23 more **t** you can understand has been shown you.
4:10 and he will love you more **t** does your mother.
7:19 for her charm is worth more **t** gold.
8:12 Do not lend to one who is stronger **t** you;
10:24 of them is greater **t** the one who fears the Lord.
10:27 Better is the worker who has goods in plenty **t**
13: 2 or associate with one mightier and richer **t** you.
14: 6 No one is worse **t** one who is grudging to himself;
16: 3 for one can be better **t** a thousand,
16: 3 to die childless better **t** to have ungodly children.
16: 5 and my ear has heard things more striking **t** these.
17:31 What is brighter **t** the sun?
18:16 So a word is better **t** a gift.
19:24 the God-fearing who lack understanding **t**
20: 2 How much better it is to rebuke **t** to fume!
20:18 on the pavement is better **t** a slip of the tongue;
20:31 Better are those who hide their folly **t** those who
22:11 but the life of the fool is worse **t** death.
22:14 What is heavier **t** lead?
22:15 a piece of iron are easier to bear **t** a stupid person.
23:19 the Lord are ten thousand times brighter **t** the sun;
23:27 that nothing is better **t** the fear of the Lord,
23:27 and nothing sweeter **t** to heed the commandments
24:20 For the memory of me is sweeter **t** honey,
24:20 the possession of me sweeter **t** the honeycomb.
24:29 For her thoughts are more abundant **t** the sea,
24:29 and her counsel deeper **t** the great abyss.
25:15 There is no venom worse **t** a snake's venom,
25:15 and no anger worse **t** a woman's wrath.
25:16 I would rather live with a lion and a dragon **t** live
26: 5 all these are worse **t** death.
29:11 and it will profit you more **t** gold.
29:13 better **t** a stout shield and a sturdy spear,
29:22 under their own crude roof **t** sumptuous food in
30:14 healthy, and fit **t** rich and afflicted in body.
30:15 Health and fitness are better **t** any gold,
30:15 and a robust body **t** countless riches.
30:16 There is no wealth better **t** health of body,
30:17 Death is better **t** a life of misery,
30:17 and eternal sleep **t** chronic sickness.
31:13 What has been created more greedy **t** the eye?
32: 7 if you are obliged to, but no more **t** twice,
33: 7 Why is one day more important **t** another,
33:22 from you **t** that you should look to the hand
34:12 and I understand more **t** I can express.
36:23 yet one food is better **t** another.
36:28 her husband is more fortunate **t** other men.
37:13 for no one is more faithful to you **t** it is.
37:14 keeps us better informed **t** seven sentinels sitting
39:11 he will leave a name greater **t** a thousand,
40:18 but better **t** either is finding a treasure.
40:19 but better **t** either is the one who finds wisdom.
40:19 but a blameless wife is accounted better **t** either.
40:20 but the love of friends is better **t** either.
40:21 but a pleasant voice is better **t** either.
40:22 but the green shoots of grain more **t** either.
40:23 but a sensible wife is better **t** either.
40:24 but almsgiving rescues better **t** either.
40:25 but good counsel is esteemed more **t** either.

Sir 40:26 but the fear of the Lord is better **t** either.
40:27 and covers a person better **t** any glory.
40:28 it is better to die **t** to beg.
41:12 since it will outlive you longer **t**
41:15 Better are those who hide their folly **t** those who
42:14 of a man **t** a woman who does good;
43:28 For he is greater **t** all his works.
43:32 Many things greater **t** these lie hidden,
LtJ 6:19 They light more lamps for them **t** they light
6:59 **t** to be these false gods;
6:59 that protects its contents, **t** these false gods;
6:59 a wooden pillar in a palace, **t** these false gods.
6:68 The wild animals are better **t** they are,
Aza 1:14 O Lord, have become fewer **t** any other nation,
Sus 1:23 rather **t** sin in the sight of the Lord."
1:39 because he was stronger **t** we,
1Mc 1:63 They chose to die rather **t** to be defiled by food or
3:30 to give more lavishly **t** preceding kings.
3:59 in battle **t** to see the misfortunes of our nation and
6:43 It was taller **t** all the others,
7:23 it was more **t** the Gentiles had done.
9:6 until no more **t** eight hundred of them were left.
10:38 be under one ruler and obey no other authority **t**
12:24 with a larger force **t** before,
13:5 for I am not better **t** my brothers.
2Mc 5:5 Jason took no fewer **t** a thousand men
5:22 a Phrygian and in character more barbarous **t**
5:23 over his compatriots worse **t** the others did.
6:19 welcoming death with honor rather **t** life
7:2 For we are ready to die rather **t** transgress
7:7 "Will you eat rather **t** have your body punished
7:39 and handled him worse **t** the others,
8:9 of no fewer **t** twenty thousand Gentiles
8:24 they killed more **t** nine thousand of the enemy,
8:30 and Bacchides they killed more **t** twenty thousand
10:17 killing no fewer **t** twenty thousand.
10:23 he destroyed more **t** twenty thousand in
12:10 When they had gone more **t** a mile from there,
12:19 more **t** ten thousand men.
13:9 to show the Jews things far worse **t** those
14:30 meeting him more rudely **t** had been his custom,
14:39 sent more **t** five hundred soldiers to arrest him;
14:42 preferring to die nobly rather **t** to fall into
1Es 4:25 A man loves his wife more **t** his father
4:35 But truth is great, and stronger **t** all things.
5:50 to them and were stronger **t** they;
8:75 For our sins have risen higher **t** our heads,
Man 1:9 the sins I have committed are more in number **t**
3Mc 5:20 possessed by a savagery worse **t** that of Phalaris,
7:5 a cruelty more savage **t** that of Scythian custom,
7:15 to death more **t** three hundred men;
2Es 1:18 to serve the Egyptians **t** to die in this wilderness.'
2:43 taller **t** any of the others,
2:43 but he was more exalted **t** they.
3:12 to be more ungodly **t** were their ancestors.
3:31 Are the deeds of Babylon better **t** those of Zion?
4:12 to be here **t** to come here and live in ungodliness,
4:34 "Do not be in a greater hurry **t** the Most High.
4:45 whether more time is to come **t** has passed,
4:50 for just as the rain is more **t** the drops,
4:50 and the fire is greater **t** the smoke,
5:13 you shall hear yet greater things **t** these."
5:33 Or do you love him more **t** his Maker does?"
5:44 "The creation cannot move faster **t** the Creator,
5:54 in stature **t** those who were before you,
5:55 those who come after you will be smaller **t** you,
6:31 I will again declare to you greater things **t** these,
7:16 rather **t** what is now present?"
7:19 "You are not a better judge **t** the Lord,
7:19 or wiser **t** the Most High!
7:20 rather **t** that the law of God that is set before them
7:56 silver is more abundant **t** gold, and bronze **t** silver,
and iron **t** bronze, and lead **t** iron, and clay **t** lead.'
7:59 who has what is hard to get rejoices more **t**
7:66 It is much better with them **t** with us;
7:87 which is worse **t** all the ways
7:98 which is greater **t** all that have been mentioned,
7:*125* [55] who practiced self-control shall shine more **t**
7:*125* [55] but our faces shall be blacker **t** darkness?
7:*135* [65] because he would rather give **t** take away;
8:30 with those who are deemed worse **t** wild animals,
8:47 of being able to love my creation more **t** I love it.
9:15 there are more who perish **t** those who will
9:16 as a wave is greater **t** a drop of water."
10:57 For you are more blessed **t** many,
11:4 the middle head was larger **t** the other heads,
11:27 and this disappeared more quickly **t** the first.
11:29 it was greater **t** the other two heads.
11:32 it had greater power over the world **t** all the wings
12:13 and it shall be more terrifying **t** all the kingdoms
12:15 for a longer time **t** any other one of the twelve.
12:24 its inhabitants more oppressively **t** all who were
12:45 For we are no better **t** those who died there."
13:20 **t** to pass from the world like a cloud,
13:24 are left are more blessed **t** those who have died.
14:16 For evils worse **t** those that you have
4Mc 5:16 no compulsion more powerful **t** our obedience
7:10 O aged man, more powerful **t** tortures;
7:10 more powerful than tortures; O elder, fiercer **t** fire;
9:1 die rather **t** transgress our ancestral commandments
9:3 for us do not pity us more **t** we pity ourselves.
9:4 to be more grievous **t** death itself.
9:30 that you are being tortured more **t** I,
11:14 "I am younger in age **t** my brothers,
14:2 more royal **t** kings and freer **t** the free!
14:10 What could be more excruciatingly painful **t** this?
15:1 more desirable to the mother **t** her children!
4Mc 15:4 a deeper sympathy toward their offspring **t** do
15:6 more **t** any other mother, loved her children.
15:16 tried now by more bitter pains **t** even
15:30 O more noble **t** males in steadfastness,
15:30 and more courageous **t** men in endurance!
16:14 and deed you have proved more powerful **t**
16:24 to die rather **t** violate God's commandment.

THANK‡ (35) [THANKED, THANKFUL, THANKFULNESS, THANKING, THANKS, THANKSGIVING, THANKSGIVINGS]

Lev 7:12 the **t** offering unleavened cakes mixed with oil,
1Ch 16:4 to **t**, and to praise the LORD, the God of Israel.
2Ch 29:31 near, bring sacrifices and **t** offerings to the house
29:31 The assembly brought sacrifices and **t** offerings;
Ps 35:18 Then I will **t** you in the great congregation;
52:9 I will **t** you forever,
56:12 I will render **t** offerings to you.
107:8 Let them **t** the LORD for his steadfast love,
107:15 Let them **t** the LORD for his steadfast love,
107:21 Let them **t** the LORD for his steadfast love,
107:31 Let them **t** the LORD for his steadfast love,
118:21 I **t** you that you have answered me
Isa 38:18 For Sheol cannot **t** you, death cannot praise you;
38:19 The living, the living, they **t** you, as I do this day;
Jer 17:26 bringing **t** offerings to the house of the LORD.
33:11 they bring **t** offerings to the house of the LORD:
Am 4:5 bring a **t** offering of leavened bread,
Mt 11:25 At that time Jesus said, "I **t** you, Father,
Lk 10:21 "I **t** you, Father, Lord of heaven and earth,
17:9 you **t** the slave for doing what was commanded?
18:11 'God, I **t** you that I am not like other people:
Jn 11:41 "Father, I **t** you for having heard me.
Ro 1:8 I **t** my God through Jesus Christ for all of you,
1Co 1:14 I **t** God that I baptized none of you except Crispus
14:18 I **t** God that I speak in tongues more than all
Php 1:3 I **t** my God every time I remember you,
Col 1:3 In our prayers for you we always **t** God,
1Th 3:9 How can we **t** God enough for you in return
Phm 1:4 in my prayers, I always **t** my God
Sir 35:4 and one who gives alms sacrifices a **t** offering.
51:12 For this reason I **t** you and praise you,
1Mc 14:25 "How shall we **t** Simon and his sons?
2Mc 1:11 by God out of grave dangers we **t** him greatly
1Es 8:66 and as a **t** offering twelve male goats—
3Mc 1:9 and made **t** offerings and did what was fitting for

THANKED (5) [THANK]

Lk 17:16 He prostrated himself at Jesus' feet and **t** him.
Ac 28:15 On seeing them, Paul **t** God and took courage.
Sir 12:1 and you will be **t** for your good deeds.
29:25 the host and provide drink without being **t**,
2Mc 12:31 they **t** them and exhorted them to be well disposed

THANKFUL‡ (2) [THANK]

Col 3:15 you were called in the one body. And be **t**.
Wis 18:2 and were **t** that your holy ones,

THANKFULNESS (2) [THANK]

1Co 10:30 If I partake with **t**, why should I be denounced
AdE 16:4 They not only take away **t** from others, but,

THANKING (1) [THANK]

1Ch 23:30 stand every morning, **t** and praising the LORD,

THANKS‡ (122) [THANK]

1Ch 16:8 O give **t** to the LORD, call on his name,
16:34 O give **t** to the LORD, for he is good;
16:35 that we may give **t** to your holy name,
16:41 of those chosen and expressly named to render **t**
29:13 we give **t** to you and praise your glorious name.
2Ch 7:3 and worshiped and gave **t** to the LORD, saying,
7:6 that King David had made for giving **t** to
20:21 "Give **t** to the LORD, for his steadfast love endures
30:22 sacrificing offerings of well-being and giving **t** to
31:2 the gates of the camp of the LORD and to give **t**
Ezr 3:11 praising and giving **t** to the LORD,
Ne 12:24 over against them, to praise and to give **t**,
12:31 and appointed two great companies that gave **t**
12:38 The other company of those who gave **t** went to
12:40 So both companies of those who gave **t** stood in
Ps 7:17 to the LORD the **t** due to his righteousness,
9:1 I will give **t** to the LORD with my whole heart;
28:7 and with my song I give **t** to him.
30:4 and give **t** to his holy name.
30:12 O LORD my God, I will give **t** to you forever.
44:8 and we will give **t** to your name forever.
54:6 I will give **t** to your name, O LORD,
57:9 I will give **t** to you, O Lord, among the peoples;
75:1 give **t** to you, O God; we give **t**; your name is near.
79:13 will give **t** to you forever;
86:12 I give **t** to you, O Lord my God,
92:1 It is good to give **t** to the LORD, to sing praises
97:12 O you righteous, and give **t** to his holy name!
100:4 Give **t** to him, bless his name.
105:1 O give **t** to the LORD, call on his name,
106:1 O give **t** to the LORD, for he is good;
106:47 that we may give **t** to your holy name and glory
107:1 O give **t** to the LORD, for he is good;
108:3 I will give **t** to you, O LORD,
109:30 With my mouth I will give great **t** to the LORD;
111:1 I will give **t** to the LORD with my whole heart,
118:1 O give **t** to the LORD, for he is good;
Ps 118:19 that I may enter through them and give **t** to
118:28 You are my God, and I will give **t** to you;
118:29 O give **t** to the LORD, for he is good,
122:4 to give **t** to the name of the LORD.
136:1 O give **t** to the LORD, for he is good,
136:2 O give **t** to the God of gods,
136:3 O give **t** to the Lord of lords,
136:26 O give **t** to the God of heaven,
138:1 I give you **t**, O LORD, with my whole heart;
138:2 toward your holy temple and give **t** to your name
140:13 Surely the righteous shall give **t** to your name;
142:7 so that I may give **t** to your name.
145:10 All your works shall give **t** to you, O LORD,
Isa 12:1 You will say in that day: I will give **t** to you,
12:4 Give **t** to the LORD, call on his name;
Jer 33:11 "Give **t** to the LORD of hosts,
Da 2:23 O God of my ancestors, I give **t** and praise,
Mt 15:36 and after giving **t** he broke them and gave them to
26:27 and after giving **t** he gave it to them, saying,
Mk 8:6 the seven loaves, and after giving **t** he broke them
14:23 and after giving **t** he gave it to them,
Lk 22:17 Then he took a cup, and after giving **t** he said,
22:19 he took a loaf of bread, and when he had given **t**,
Jn 6:11 Jesus took the loaves, and when he had given **t**,
6:23 the bread after the Lord had given **t**.
Ac 27:35 and giving **t** to God in the presence of all,
Ro 1:21 they did not honor him as God or give **t** to him,
6:17 But **t** be to God that you,
7:25 **T** be to God through Jesus Christ our Lord!
14:6 eat in honor of the Lord, since they give **t** to God;
14:6 abstain in honor of the Lord and give **t** to God.
16:4 to whom not only I give **t**,
1Co 1:4 I give **t** to my God always for you because of
10:30 be denounced because of that for which I give **t**?
11:24 and when he had given **t**,
14:17 For you may give **t** well enough,
15:57 But **t** be to God, who gives us the victory
2Co 1:11 so that many will give **t** on our behalf for
2:14 But **t** be to God, who in Christ always leads us
8:16 But **t** be to God who put in the heart of Titus
9:15 **T** be to God for his indescribable gift!
Eph 1:16 I do not cease to give **t** for you as I remember you
5:20 giving **t** to God the Father at all times and
Col 1:12 giving **t** to the Father, who has enabled you
3:17 giving **t** to God the Father through him.
1Th 1:2 We always give **t** to God for all of you
2:13 We also constantly give **t** to God for this,
5:18 give **t** in all circumstances;
2Th 1:3 We must always give **t** to God for you,
2:13 But we must always give **t** to God for you,
Heb 12:28 let us give **t**, by which we offer to God
Rev 4:9 the living creatures give glory and honor and **t** to
11:17 "We give you **t**, Lord God Almighty,
Jdt 8:25 of everything let us give **t** to the Lord our God,
Wis 16:28 before the sun to give you **t**, and must pray to you
Sir 17:27 in Hades in place of the living who give **t**?
20:16 and I get no **t** for my good deeds.
39:6 of wisdom of his own and give **t** to the Lord
39:15 Ascribe majesty to his name and give **t** to him
47:8 In all that he did he gave **t** to the Holy One,
51:1 PRAYER OF JESUS SON OF SIRACH I give you **t**,
51:1 I give **t** to your name,
51:12 *Give t to the LORD, for he is good,*
51:12 *Give t to the God of praise,*
51:12 *Give t to the guardian of Israel,*
51:12 *Give t to him who formed all things,*
51:12 *Give t to the redeemer of Israel,*
51:12 *Give t to him who gathers the dispersed of Israel,*
51:12 *Give t to him who rebuilt his city*
51:12 *Give t to him who makes a horn to sprout for*
51:12 *Give t to him who has chosen the sons of Zadok*
51:12 *Give t to the shield of Abraham,*
51:12 *Give t to the rock of Isaac,*
51:12 *Give t to the mighty one of Jacob,*
51:12 *Give t to him who has chosen Zion,*
51:12 *Give t to the King of the kings of kings,*
Aza 1:67 Give **t** to the Lord, for he is good,
1:68 sing praise to him and give **t** to him,
2Mc 8:27 giving great praise and **t** to the Lord,
1Es 4:60 I give you **t**, O Lord of our ancestors."
5:61 giving **t** to the Lord, "For his goodness
3Mc 6:33 gave **t** to heaven unceasingly and lavishly for
7:16 joyfully and loudly giving **t** to the one God
2Es 2:37 giving **t** to him who has called you to

THANKSGIVING (42) [THANK]

Lev 7:12 If you offer it for **t**,
7:13 With your **t** sacrifice of well-being
7:15 of your **t** sacrifice of well-being shall be eaten on
22:29 When you sacrifice a **t** offering to the LORD,
1Ch 25:3 who prophesied with the lyre in **t** and praise to
2Ch 5:13 in unison in praise and **t** to the LORD,
33:16 on it sacrifices of well-being and of **t**;
Ne 11:17 who was the leader to begin the **t** in prayer,
12:8 in charge of the songs of **t**.
12:46 and there were songs of praise and **t** to God.
Ps 26:7 singing aloud a song of **t**,
42:4 with glad shouts and songs of **t**,
50:14 Offer to God a sacrifice of **t**,
50:23 Those who bring **t** as their sacrifice honor me;
69:30 I will magnify him with **t**.
95:2 Let us come into his presence with **t**;
100:T *A Psalm of t.*
100:4 Enter his gates with **t**, and his courts with praise.
107:22 And let them offer **t** sacrifices,
116:17 a **t** sacrifice and call on the name of the LORD.

Ps 147: 7 Sing to the LORD with t;
Isa 51: 3 and gladness will be found in her, t and the voice
Jer 30:19 Out of them shall come t,
Jnh 2: 9 But I with the voice of t will sacrifice to you;
1Co 14:16 of an outsider say the "Amen" to your t,
2Co 4:15 may increase t, to the glory of God.
9:11 which will produce t to God through us;
Eph 5: 4 but instead, let there be t.
Php 4: 6 by prayer and supplication with t let your requests
Col 2: 7 just as you were taught, abounding in t.
4: 2 keeping alert in it with t.
1Ti 4: 3 be received with t by those who believe and know
4: 4 provided it is received with t;
Rev 7:12 and wisdom and t and honor and power and might
Jdt 15:14 Judith began this t before all Israel,
Sir 17:28 as from one who does not exist, t has ceased;
39:15 this is what you shall say in t:
51:11 and will sing hymns of t."
1Mc 4:56 a sacrifice of well-being and a t offering.
2Mc 10: 7 of t to him who had given success to the purifying
3Mc 6:35 to the accompaniment of joyous t and psalms.
7:19 they had all landed in peace with appropriate t,

THANKSGIVINGS (4) [THANK]

Ne 12:27 with t and with singing, with cymbals, harps,
2Co 9:12 the saints but also overflows with many t to God.
1Ti 2: 1 intercessions, and t be made for everyone,
2Mc 10:38 with hymns and t they blessed the Lord

THANKWORTHY (KJV) See CREDIT

THARA (KJV) See TERAH

THARABA (1)

AdE 1:10 Tharra, Boraze, Zatholtha, Abataza, and T,

THARRA (2)

AdE 1:10 he told Haman, Bazan, T, Boraze, Zatholtha,
12: 1 in the courtyard with Gabatha and T,

THARSEAS See Index to Footnotes

THARSHISH (KJV) See TARSHISH

THASSI (1) [=SIMON]

1Mc 2: 3 Simon called T,

THAT (9652) [THOSE] See Index of Articles Etc.

THE (70930) See Index of Articles Etc.

THEATER (2)

Ac 19:29 and people rushed together to the t,
19:31 a message urging him not to venture into the t.

THEBES (5)

Jer 46:25 See, I am bringing punishment upon Amon of T,
Eze 30:14 and will execute acts of judgment on T.
30:15 and cut off the hordes of T.
30:16 T shall be breached, and Memphis face adversaries
Na 3: 8 Are you better than T that sat by the Nile,

THEBEZ (3)

Jdg 9:50 Abimelech went to T, and encamped against T,
2Sa 11:21 so that he died at T?

THEFT (5) [THIEF]

Ex 22: 1 but if unable to do so, shall be sold for the t.
Mt 15:19 adultery, fornication, t, false witness, slander.
Mk 7:21 that evil intentions come: fornication, t,
Wis 14:25 t and deceit, corruption, faithlessness, tumult,
Sir 41:19 and of t, in the place where you live.

THEFTS (1) [THIEF]

Rev 9:21 or their sorceries or their fornication or their t.

THEIR (5688) [THEY] See Index of Articles Etc.

THEIRS (25) [THEY] See Index of Articles Etc.

THELASAR (KJV) See TEL ASSAR

THEM (7051) [THEY] See Index of Articles Etc.

THEME (1)

Ps 45: 1 My heart overflows with a goodly t;

THEMSELVES (457) [THEY] See Index of Articles Etc.

THEN (3602) See Index of Articles Etc.

THEODOTUS (2)

2Mc 14:19 Therefore he sent Posidonius, T,
3Mc 1: 2 But a certain T, determined to carry out

THEOPHILUS (2)

Lk 1: 3 an orderly account for you, most excellent T,
Ac 1: 1 T, I wrote about all that Jesus did and taught from

THERAS (2)

1Es 8:41 I assembled them at the river called T,
8:61 the river T on the twelfth day of the first month;

THERE (2448) See Index of Articles Etc.

THEREAFTER (4)

Nu 8:15 T the Levites may go in to do service at the tent
8:22 T the Levites went in to do their service in the tent
15:23 the day the LORD gave commandment and t,
1Es 5:52 and t the regular offerings and sacrifices

THEREBY (10)

Lev 6: 3 of the various things that one may do and sin t—
6: 7 of the things that one may do and incur guilt t.
15:32 an emission of semen, becoming unclean t,
Dt 19:10 t bringing bloodguilt upon you.
22:30 t violating his father's rights.
Jn 5:18 t making himself equal to God.
Ac 27:21 from Crete and t avoided this damage and loss.
1Co 4: 4 but I am not t acquitted.
3Mc 1: 2 intending single-handed to kill him and t end
4Mc 9:24 T the just Providence of our ancestors may

THEREFORE‡ (866)

Ge 2:24 T a man leaves his father and his mother
3:23 t the LORD God sent him forth from the garden
10: 9 t it is said, "Like Nimrod a mighty hunter before
11: 9 T it was called Babel, because there
16:14 T the well was called Beer-lahai-roi;
19:22 T the city was called Zoar.
20: 6 T I did not let you touch her.
21:23 now t swear to me here by God that you will
21:31 T that place was called Beer-sheba;
25:30 (T he was called Edom.)
26:33 t the name of the city is Beer-sheba to this day.
27: 8 t, my son, obey my word as I command you.
27:43 Now t, my son, obey my voice;
29:15 should you t serve me for nothing?
29:34 have borne him three sons"; t he was named Levi.
29:35 t she named him Judah; then she ceased bearing.
30: 6 and given me a son"; t she named him Dan.
31:48 and me today." T he called it Galeed,
32:32 T to this day the Israelites do not eat
33:17 t the place is called Succoth.
38:29 T he was named Perez.
41:33 Now t let Pharaoh select a man who is discerning
44:30 Now t, when I come to your servant my father
44:33 Now t, please let your servant remain as a slave
47:22 t they did not sell their land.
48: 5 T your two sons, who were born to you in
50: 5 Now t let me go up, so that I may bury my father;
50:11 T the place was named Abel-mizraim;
50:17 Now t please forgive the crime of the servants of
Ex 1:11 T they set taskmasters over them to oppress them
6: 6 Say t to the Israelites, 'I am the LORD,
9:19 t, and have your livestock and everything
13:15 T I sacrifice to the LORD every male
16:29 t on the sixth day he gives you food for two days;
19: 5 Now t, if you obey my voice
20:11 t the LORD blessed the sabbath day
22:31 t you shall not eat any meat that is mangled
31:16 T the Israelites shall keep the sabbath,
33: 6 T the Israelites stripped themselves of their
Lev 11:44 sanctify yourselves t, and be holy, for I am holy.
17:12 T I have said to the people of Israel:
17:14 t I have said to the people of Israel:
20: 7 Consecrate yourselves t, and be holy;
20:25 You shall t make a distinction between
21: 6 of their God; t they shall be holy.
Nu 11:18 T the LORD will give you meat,
14:17 t, let the power of the LORD be great in the way
16:11 T you and all your company have gathered
18:24 T I have said of them
20:12 t you shall not bring this assembly into the land
21:27 T the ballad singers say, "Come to Heshbon,
22:34 t, if it is displeasing to you, I will return home."
25:12 T say, 'I hereby grant him my covenant of peace.
31:17 Now t, kill every male among the little ones,
Dt 5:15 t the LORD your God commanded you to keep
5:32 You must t be careful to do as the LORD
6: 3 Hear t, O Israel, and observe them diligently,
7: 9 Know t that the LORD your God is God,
7:11 T, observe diligently the commandment—
8: 6 T keep the commandments of the LORD
10: 9 T Levi has no allotment or inheritance
11: 1 You shall love the LORD your God, t,
15: 9 and t view your needy neighbor with hostility
15:11 to be some in need on the earth, I t command you,
19: 7 T I command you: You shall set apart three cities.
23:14 t your camp must be holy,
24:18 t I command you to do this.
24:22 t I am commanding you to do this.
25:19 T when the LORD your God has given you rest
27:10 T obey the LORD your God,
Dt 28:48 t you shall serve your enemies whom
29: 9 T diligently observe the words of this covenant,
31:19 t write this song, and teach it to the Israelites;
Jos 4:17 Joshua t commanded the priests,
7:12 T the Israelites are unable to stand
7:14 In the morning t you shall come forward tribe
7:26 T that place to this day is called the Valley
9:23 Now t you are cursed, and some
13: 7 Now t divide this land for an inheritance to
22: 4 t turn and go to your tents in the land
22:26 T we said, 'Let us now build an altar,
23: 6 T be very steadfast to observe and do all
23:11 Be very careful, t, to love the LORD your God.
24:10 t he blessed you; so I rescued you out of his hand.
24:14 "Now t revere the LORD,
24:18 T we also will serve the LORD,
24:27 t it shall be a witness against you,
Jdg 3: 8 T the anger of the LORD was kindled
6:32 T on that day Gideon was called Jerubbaal,
7: 3 Now t proclaim this in the hearing of the troops,
9:16 "Now t, if you acted in good faith and honor
9:32 Now t, go by night, you and the troops that are
10:13 t I will deliver you no more.
11:13 now t restore it peaceably."
15:19 T it was named En-hakkore,"
18:14 Now t consider what you will do."
20:42 T they turned away from the Israelites in
1Sa 1: 7 T Hannah wept and would not eat.
1:13 t Eli thought she was drunk.
1:28 T I have lent him to the LORD;
2:30 T the LORD the God of Israel declares:
3: 9 T Eli said to Samuel, "Go, lie down;
3:14 T I swear to the house of Eli that the iniquity
5:11 They sent t and gathered together all the lords of
10:12 T it became a proverb, "Is Saul also among
10:19 Now t present yourselves before the LORD
12: 7 Now t take your stand, so that I may enter
12:16 Now t take your stand and see this great thing that
15: 1 now t listen to the words of the LORD.
15:25 Now t, I pray, pardon my sin, and return with me,
18:21 T Saul said to David a second time,
19: 2 t be on guard tomorrow morning;
19:24 T it is said, "Is Saul also among the prophets?"
20: 8 T deal kindly with your servant,
23:28 t that place was called the Rock of Escape.
24:15 May the LORD t be judge,
24:21 Swear to me t by the LORD that you will
25: 8 T let my young men find favor in your sight;
25:17 t know this and consider what you should do;
26: 8 now t let me pin him to the ground
26:19 Now t let my lord the king hear the words
26:20 Now t, do not let my blood fall to the ground,
27: 6 t Ziklag has belonged to the kings of Judah
27:12 t he shall always be my servant."
28:18 t the LORD has done this thing to you today.
28:22 Now t, you also listen to your servant;
2Sa 2: 7 T let your hands be strong, and be valiant;
2:16 T that place was called Helkath-hazzurim,
5: 8 T it is said, "The blind and the lame shall
5:20 T that place is called Baal-perazim.
7: 8 Now t thus you shall say to my servant David:
7:22 T you are great, O LORD God;
7:27 t your servant has found courage
7:29 now t may it please you to bless the house
12:10 t the sword shall never depart from your house,
12:16 David t pleaded with God for the child;
13:13 Now t, I beg you, speak to the king;
13:33 Now t, do not let my lord the king take it to heart,
17:16 T send quickly and tell David,
18: 3 t it is better that you send us help from the city."
19:10 Now t why do you say nothing about bringing
19:20 For your servant knows that I have sinned; t, see,
19:27 do t what seems good to you.
22:25 T the LORD has recompensed me according
23:17 T he would not drink it.
1Ki 1:12 Now t come, let me give you advice,
2: 6 Act t according to your wisdom,
2: 9 T do not hold him guiltless,
2:24 Now t as the LORD lives,
3: 9 Give your servant t an understanding mind
5: 6 T command that cedars from the Lebanon be cut
8:25 T, O LORD, God of Israel, keep for your servant
8:26 T, O God of Israel, let your word be confirmed,
8:61 T devote yourselves completely to
9: 9 t the LORD has brought this disaster
9:13 T he said, "What kind of cities are these
11:11 T the LORD said to Solomon,
11:40 Solomon sought t to kill Jeroboam;
12: 4 Now t lighten the hard service of your father
13:26 t the LORD has given him to the lion,
14:10 t, I will bring evil upon the house
14:12 T set out, go to your house.
16: 3 t, I will consume Baasha and his house,
16:16 t all Israel made Omri, the commander of
18:19 Now t have all Israel assemble for me
20:28 the valleys,' t I will give all this great multitude
20:42 t your life shall be for his life,
22:19 Micaiah said, "T hear the word of the LORD:
2Ki 1: 4 Now t thus says the LORD,
1: 6 T you shall not leave the bed
1:16 t you shall not leave the bed
5:27 T the leprosy of Naaman shall cling to you,
7: 4 T, let us desert to the Aramean camp;
7: 9 t let us go and tell the king's household."
9:26 t lift him out and throw him on the plot of ground,
10:19 Now t summon to me all the prophets of Baal,
12: 7 T King Jehoash summoned the priest Jehoiada

2Ki 12: 7 Now **t** do not accept any more money
13: 5 **T** the LORD gave Israel a savior,
17: 4 **t** the king of Assyria confined him
17:18 **T** the LORD was very angry with Israel
17:25 **t** the LORD sent lions among them,
17:26 **t** he has sent lions among them;
19: 4 **t** lift up your prayer for the remnant that is left."
19:32 "**T** thus says the LORD concerning the king
21:12 **t** thus says the LORD, the God
22:17 **t** my wrath will be kindled against this place,
22:20 **T,** I will gather you to your ancestors,
1Ch 10:14 **T** the LORD put him to death and turned
11: 7 **t** it was called the city of David.
11:19 **T** he would not drink it.
14:11 **T** that place is called Baal-perazim.
17: 7 Now **t** thus you shall say to my servant David:
17:25 **t** your servant has found it possible to pray
17:27 **t** may it please you to bless the house
22: 5 I will **t** make preparation for it."
28: 8 Now **t** in the sight of all Israel,
2Ch 6:16 **T,** O LORD, God of Israel,
6:17 **T,** O LORD, God of Israel,
7:22 **t** he has brought all this calamity upon them.' "
10: 4 Now **t** lighten the hard service of your father
17: 5 **T** the LORD established the kingdom
18:18 Micaiah said, "**T** hear the word of the LORD:
20:26 **t** that place has been called the Valley of Beracah
28: 5 **T** the LORD his God gave him into the hand of
29: 8 **T** the wrath of the LORD came upon Judah
30:17 **t** the Levites had to slaughter the passover lamb
32:15 Now **t** do not let Hezekiah deceive you
32:25 **T** wrath came upon him and upon Judah
33:11 **T** the LORD brought against them
36:17 **T** he brought up against them the king of
Ezr 4:14 **t** we send and inform the king,
4:21 **T** issue an order that these people be made
9:12 **T** do not give your daughters to their sons,
Ne 6: 7 So come, **t,** and let us confer together."
9:27 **T** you gave them into the hands of their enemies,
9:30 **T** you handed them over to the peoples of
9:32 "Now **t,** our God—the great
Est 9:19 **T** the Jews of the villages,
9:26 **T** these days are called Purim, from the word Pur.
Job 5:17 **t** do not despise the discipline of the Almighty.
6: 3 **t** my words have been rash.
7:11 "**T** I will not restrain my mouth;
9:22 It is all one; **t** I say, he destroys both
17: 4 **t** you will not let them triumph.
20:21 **t** their prosperity will not endure.
22:10 **T** snares are around you,
22:13 **T** you say, 'What does God know?
23:15 **T** I am terrified at his presence;
32: 6 **t** I was timid and afraid to declare my opinion to
32:10 **T** I say, 'Listen to me;
34:10 "**T,** hear me, you who have sense,
34:33 **t** declare what you know.
37:24 **T** mortals fear him; he does not regard any who
42: 3 **T** I have uttered what I did not understand,
42: 6 **t** I despise myself, and repent in dust and ashes."
42: 8 Now **t** take seven bulls and seven rams,
Ps 1: 5 **T** the wicked will not stand in the judgment,
2:10 Now **t,** O kings, be wise;
16: 9 **T** my heart is glad, and my soul rejoices;
18:24 **T** the LORD has recompensed me according
25: 8 **t** he instructs sinners in the way.
32: 6 **T** let all who are faithful offer prayer to you;
42: 6 **t** I remember you from the land of Jordan and
45: 2 **t** God has blessed you forever.
45: 7 **T** God, your God, has anointed you with the oil
45:17 **t** the peoples will praise you forever and ever.
46: 2 **T** we will not fear,
51: 6 **t** teach me wisdom in my secret heart.
73: 6 **T** pride is their necklace; violence covers them
73:10 **T** the people turn and praise them,
78:21 **T,** when the LORD heard, he was full of rage;
95:11 **T** in my anger I swore,
106:23 **T** he said he would destroy them—
106:26 **T** he raised his hand and swore to them
110: 7 **t** he will lift up his head.
116: 2 **t** I will call on him as long as I live.
119:104 **t** I hate every false way.
119:119 you count as dross; **t** I love your decrees.
119:129 Your decrees are wonderful; **t** my soul keeps them.
143: 4 **T** my spirit faints within me;
Pr 1:31 **t** they shall eat the fruit of their way and be sated
2:20 **T** walk in the way of the good,
20:19 **t** do not associate with a babbler.
Ecc 5: 2 **t** let your words be few.
SS 1: 3 perfume poured out; **t** the maidens love you.
Isa 1:24 **T** says the Sovereign, the LORD of hosts,
5:13 **T** my people go into exile without knowledge;
5:14 **T** Sheol has enlarged its appetite
5:24 **T,** as the tongue of fire devours the stubble,
5:25 **T** the anger of the LORD was kindled
7: 7 **t** thus says the Lord GOD:
7:14 **T** the Lord himself will give you a sign.
8: 7 **t,** the Lord is bringing up against it
10:16 **T** the Sovereign, the LORD of hosts,
10:24 **T** thus says the Lord GOD of hosts:
13: 7 **T** all hands will be feeble,
13:13 **T** I will make the heavens tremble,
15: 4 **t** the loins of Moab quiver; his soul trembles.
15: 7 **T** the abundance they have gained
16: 7 **T** let Moab wail, let everyone wail for Moab.
16: 9 **T** I weep with the weeping of Jazer for the vines
16:11 **T** my heart throbs like a harp for Moab,
17:10 **t,** though you plant pleasant plants

Isa 21: 3 **T** my loins are filled with anguish;
22: 4 **T** I said: Look away from me,
24: 6 **T** a curse devours the earth,
24: 6 **t** the inhabitants of the earth dwindled,
24:15 **T** in the east give glory to the LORD;
25: 3 **T** strong peoples will glorify you;
27: 9 **T** by this the guilt of Jacob will be expiated,
27:11 **t** he that made them will not have compassion
28:13 **T** the word of the LORD will be to them,
28:14 **T** hear the word of the LORD,
28:16 **t** thus says the Lord GOD, See, I am laying
28:22 Now **t** do not scoff, or your bonds will
29:22 **T** thus says the LORD, who redeemed Abraham,
30: 3 **T** the protection of Pharaoh
30: 7 **t** I have called her, "Rahab who sits still."
30:12 **T** thus says the Holy One of Israel:
30:13 **t** this iniquity shall become for you like a break in
30:16 We will flee upon horses"—**t** you shall flee!
30:16 **t** your pursuers shall be swift!
30:18 **T** the LORD waits to be gracious to you;
30:18 **t** he will rise up to show mercy to you.
37: 4 **t** lift up your prayer for the remnant that is left."
37:33 "**T** thus says the LORD concerning the king
43:28 **T** I profaned the princes of the sanctuary,
47: 8 Now **t** hear this, you lover of pleasures,
50: 7 **t** I have not been disgraced;
50: 7 **t** I have set my face like flint,
51:21 **T** hear this, you who are wounded, who are drunk,
52: 5 Now **t** what am I doing here, says the LORD,
52: 6 **T** my people shall know my name;
52: 6 **t** in that day they shall know
53:12 **T** I will allot him a portion with the great,
59: 9 **T** justice is far from us, and righteousness does
61: 7 **t** they shall possess a double portion;
63:10 **t** he became their enemy;
65:13 **T** thus says the Lord GOD:
Jer 2: 9 **T** once more I accuse you, says the LORD,
3: 3 **T** the showers have been withheld,
5: 6 **T** a lion from the forest shall kill them,
5:14 **T** thus says the LORD, the God of hosts:
5:27 **t** they have become great and rich,
6:15 **T** they shall fall among those who fall;
6:18 **T** hear, O nations, and know, O congregation,
6:21 **T** thus says the LORD: See,
7:14 **t** I will do to the house that is called by my name,
7:20 **T** thus says the Lord GOD:
7:32 **T,** the days are surely coming, says the LORD,
8:10 **T** I will give their wives to others and their fields
8:12 **T** they shall fall among those who fall;
9: 7 **T** thus says the LORD of hosts:
9:15 **T** thus says the LORD of hosts,
10:21 **t** they have not prospered,
11:11 **T,** thus says the LORD, assuredly I am going
11:21 **T** thus says the LORD concerning the people
11:22 **t** thus says the LORD of hosts:
12: 8 her voice against me—**t** I hate her.
14:10 **t** the LORD does not accept them,
14:15 **T** thus says the LORD concerning
15:19 **T** thus says the LORD:
16:13 **T** I will hurl you out of this land into a land
16:14 **T,** the days are surely coming, says the LORD,
16:21 "**T** I am surely going to teach them,
18:11 **t,** say to the people of Judah and the inhabitants
18:13 **T** thus says the LORD: Ask among the
18:21 **T** give their children over to famine;
19: 6 **T** the days are surely coming, says the LORD,
20:11 **t** my persecutors will stumble,
22:18 **T** thus says the LORD concerning King
23: 2 **T** thus says the LORD, the God of Israel,
23: 7 **T,** the days are surely coming, says the LORD,
23:12 **T** their way shall be to them like slippery paths in
23:15 **T** thus says the LORD of hosts concerning
23:30 See, **t,** I am against the prophets,
23:39 **t,** I will surely lift you up and cast you away
25: 8 **T** thus says the LORD of hosts:
25:30 **t,** shall prophesy against them all these words,
26:13 Now **t** amend your ways and your doings,
27: 9 You, **t,** must not listen to your prophets,
28:16 **T** thus says the LORD: I am going to send
29:32 **t** thus says the LORD: I am going to punish
30:16 **T** all who devour you shall be devoured,
31: 3 **t** I have continued my faithfulness to you.
31:20 **T** I am deeply moved for him;
32:23 **T** you have made all these disasters come
32:28 **T,** thus says the LORD: I am going to give
32:36 Now **t** thus says the LORD, the God of Israel,
34:17 **T,** thus says the LORD: You have
35:17 **T,** thus says the LORD, the God of hosts,
35:19 **t** thus says the LORD of hosts, the God of Israel:
36:30 **T** thus says the LORD concerning King
40: 3 **T** this thing has come upon you.
44:11 **T** thus says the LORD of hosts,
44:22 **t** your land became a desolation and a waste and
44:26 **T** hear the word of the LORD,
48:11 **t** his flavor has remained and his aroma is
48:12 **T,** the time is surely coming, says the LORD,
48:31 **T** I wail for Moab; I cry out
48:36 **T** my heart moans for Moab like a flute,
49: 2 **T,** the time is surely coming, says the LORD,
49:20 **T** hear the plan that the LORD has made
49:26 **T** her young men shall fall in her squares,
50:18 **T,** thus says the LORD of hosts,
50:30 **T** her young men shall fall in her squares,
50:39 **T** wild animals shall live with hyenas in Babylon,
50:45 **T** hear the plan that the LORD has made
51:36 **T** thus says the LORD: I am going to defend
51:52 **T** the time is surely coming, says the LORD,

La 3:21 But this I call to mind, and **t** I have hope:
3:24 says my soul, "**t** I will hope in him."
Eze 5: 7 **T** thus says the Lord GOD:
5: 8 **t** thus says the Lord GOD:
5:11 **T,** as I live, says the Lord GOD, surely,
5:11 **t** I will cut you down;
7:20 **t** I will make of it an unclean thing to them.
8:18 **T** I will act in wrath;
11: 4 **T** prophesy against them; prophesy, O mortal."
11: 7 **T** thus says the Lord GOD:
11:16 **T** say: Thus says the Lord GOD:
11:17 **T** say: Thus says the Lord GOD:
12: 3 **T,** mortal, prepare for yourself an exile's baggage,
12:23 Tell them **t,** "Thus says the Lord GOD:
12:28 **T** say to them, Thus says the Lord GOD:
13: 8 **T** thus says the Lord GOD:
13:13 **T** thus says the Lord GOD:
13:20 **T** thus says the Lord GOD:
13:23 **t** you shall no longer see false visions
14: 4 **T** speak to them, and say to them,
14: 6 **T** say to the house of Israel,
15: 6 **T** thus says the Lord GOD:
16:27 **T** I stretched out my hand against you,
16:35 **T,** O whore, hear the word of the LORD:
16:37 **t,** I will gather all your lovers,
16:43 **t,** I have returned your deeds upon your head,
16:50 **t** I removed them when I saw it.
17:19 **T** thus says the Lord GOD:
18:30 **T** I will judge you, O house of Israel,
20:27 **T,** mortal, speak to the house of Israel and say
20:30 **T** say to the house of Israel,
21: 4 **t** my sword shall go out of its sheath
21: 6 Moan **t,** mortal; moan with breaking
21:15 **t** hearts melt and many stumble.
21:24 **T** thus says the Lord GOD:
22: 4 **T** I have made you a disgrace before the nations,
22:19 **T** thus says the Lord GOD:
22:31 **T** I have poured out my indignation upon them;
23: 9 **T** I delivered her into the hands of her lovers,
23:22 **T,** O Oholibah, thus says the Lord GOD:
23:31 **t** I will give her cup into your hand.
23:35 **T** thus says the Lord GOD:
23:35 behind your back, **t** bear the consequences
24: 6 **T** thus says the Lord GOD:
24: 9 **T** thus says the Lord GOD:
25: 4 **t** I am handing you over to the people of the east
25: 7 **t** I have stretched out my hand against you,
25: 9 **t** I will lay open the flank of Moab from the towns
25:13 **t** thus says the Lord GOD,
25:16 **t** thus says the Lord GOD,
26: 3 **T,** thus says the Lord GOD:
28: 6 **T** thus says the Lord GOD:
28: 7 **t,** I will bring strangers against you,
29: 8 **T,** thus says the Lord GOD:
29:10 **t,** I am against you, and against your channels,
29:19 **T** thus says the Lord GOD:
30:22 **T** thus says the Lord GOD:
31:10 **T** thus says the Lord GOD:
32:32 **t** he shall be laid to rest among the uncircumcised,
33:25 **T** say to them, Thus says the Lord GOD:
34: 7 **T,** you shepherds, hear the word of the LORD:
34: 9 **t,** you shepherds, hear the word of the LORD:
34:20 **T,** thus says the Lord GOD to them:
35: 6 **t,** as I live, says the Lord GOD,
35:11 **t,** as I live, says the Lord GOD, I will deal
36: 3 **t** prophesy, and say: Thus says the Lord GOD:
36: 4 **t,** O mountains of Israel, hear the word of
36: 5 **t** thus says the Lord GOD:
36: 6 **T** prophesy concerning the land of Israel,
36: 7 **t** thus says the Lord GOD:
36:14 **t** you shall no longer devour people
36:22 **T** say to the house of Israel,
37:12 **T** prophesy, and say to them,
38:14 **T,** mortal, prophesy, and say to Gog:
39:25 **T** thus says the Lord GOD:
43: 8 **t** I have consumed them in my anger.
44: 2 by it; **t** it shall remain shut.
44:12 **t** I have sworn concerning them,
Da 1:19 **t** they were stationed in the king's court.
2: 6 **T** tell me the dream and its interpretation."
2: 9 **T,** tell me the dream, and I shall know
2:24 **T** Daniel went to Arioch, whom
3: 7 **T,** as soon as all the peoples heard the sound of
3:29 **T** I make a decree: Any people,
4:27 **T,** O king, may my counsel be acceptable to you:
6: 9 **T** King Darius signed the document and interdict.
9:17 Now **t,** O our God, listen to the prayer
9:25 Know **t** and understand:
Hos 2: 6 **T** I will hedge up her way with thorns;
2: 9 **T** I will take back my grain in its time,
2:14 **T,** I will now allure her, and bring her into
4: 3 **T** the land mourns, and all who live in it languish;
4:13 **T** your daughters play the whore,
5:12 **T** I am like maggots to Ephraim,
6: 5 **T** I have hewn them by the prophets,
10:14 **t** the tumult of war shall rise against your people,
13: 3 **T** they shall be like the morning mist or like
13: 6 and their heart was proud; **t** they forgot me.
Am 3: 2 **t** I will punish you for all your iniquities.
3:11 **T** thus says the Lord GOD:
4:12 **T** thus I will do to you, O Israel;
5:11 **T** because you trample on the poor and take
5:13 **T** the prudent will keep silent in such a time;
5:16 **T** thus says the LORD, the God of hosts,
5:27 **t** I will take you into exile beyond Damascus,
6: 7 **T** they shall now be the first to go into exile,
7:16 "Now **t** hear the word of the LORD.

Am 7:17 T thus says the LORD: 'Your wife shall become a
Mic 1: 6 T I will make Samaria a heap in the open country,
1:14 T you shall give parting gifts to Moresheth-gath;
2: 3 T thus says the LORD: Now,
2: 5 T you will have no one to cast the line by lot in
3: 6 T it shall be night to you, without vision,
3:12 T because of you Zion shall be plowed as a field;
5: 3 T he shall give them up until the time
6:13 T I have begun to strike you down,
6:16 T I will make you a desolation,
Hab 1: 4 t judgment comes forth perverted.
1:16 T he sacrifices to his net and makes offerings
Zep 2: 9 T, as I live, says the LORD of hosts,
3: 8 T wait for me, says the LORD,
Hag 1: 5 Now t thus says the LORD of hosts:
1:10 T the heavens above you have withheld the dew,
Zec 1: 3 T say to them, Thus says the LORD of hosts:
1:16 T, thus says the LORD, I have returned
7:12 T great wrath came from the LORD of hosts.
8:19 for the house of Judah: t love truth and peace.
10: 2 T the people wander like sheep;
Mal 3: 6 t you, O children of Jacob, have not perished.
Mt 3:10 every tree t that does not bear good fruit is cut
5:19 T, whoever breaks one of the least
5:48 Be perfect, t, as your heavenly Father is perfect.
6:25 "T I tell you, do not worry about your life,
6:31 T do not worry, saying, 'What will we eat?'
9:38 t ask the Lord of the harvest to send out laborers
10:32 "Everyone t who acknowledges me before others,
12:27 T they will be your judges.
12:31 T I tell you, people will be forgiven for every sin
13:52 "T every scribe who has been trained for
19: 6 T what God has joined together,
21:43 T I tell you, the kingdom of God will
22: 9 Go t into the main streets,
22:21 "Give t to the emperor the things that are
23: 3 t, do whatever they teach you and follow it;
23:34 T I send you prophets, sages, and scribes,
24:42 Keep awake t, for you do not know
24:44 T you also must be ready,
25:13 Keep awake t, for you know neither the day nor
27:64 T command the tomb to be made secure until
28:19 Go t and make disciples of all nations,
Mk 10: 9 T what God has joined together,
13:35 T, keep awake—for you do
Lk 1:35 t the child to be born will be holy;
3: 9 every tree t that does not bear good fruit is cut
7: 7 t I did not presume to come to you.
7:47 T, I tell you, her sins, which were many,
10: 2 t ask the Lord of the harvest to send out laborers
11:19 T they will be your judges.
11:35 T consider whether the light in you is
11:49 T also the Wisdom of God said,
12: 3 T whatever you have said in the dark will
12:22 He said to his disciples, "T I tell you,
13:18 He said t, "What is the kingdom of God like?
14:20 'I have just been married, and t I cannot come.'
14:33 So t, none of you can become my disciple
20:33 t, whose wife will the woman be?
23:16 I will t have him flogged and release him."
23:22 I will t have him flogged and then release him."
Jn 5:16 T the Jews started persecuting Jesus,
9:23 T his parents said, "He is of age; ask him."
11:45 Many of the Jews t, who had come with Mary
11:54 Jesus t no longer walked about openly among
12:50 t, I speak just as the Father has told me."
13:24 Simon Peter t motioned to him to ask Jesus
15:19 you out of the world—t the world hates you.
19:10 Pilate t said to him, "Do you refuse to speak
19:11 t the one who handed me over to you is guilty of
Ac 2:26 t my heart was glad, and my tongue rejoiced;
2:33 Being t exalted at the right hand of God,
2:36 T let the entire house of Israel know
3:19 Repent t, and turn to God so that your sins may
6: 3 T, friends, select from among yourselves
8:22 Repent t of this wickedness of yours,
10:32 Send t to Joppa and ask for Simon,
10:33 T I sent for you immediately,
13:35 T he has also said in another psalm,
13:38 Let it be known to you t, my brothers,
13:40 t, that what the prophets said does not happen
15:10 Now t why are you putting God to the test
15:19 T I have reached the decision that we should
15:27 We have t sent Judas and Silas,
16:36 t come out now and go in peace."
17:12 Many of them t believed,
17:23 What t you worship as unknown,
19:38 If t Demetrius and the artisans with him have
20:26 T I declare to you this day that I am
20:31 T be alert, remembering that for three years I did
24:16 T I do my best always to have a clear conscience
25:26 T I have brought him before all of you,
26: 3 t I beg of you to listen to me patiently.
27:34 T I urge you to take some food,
28:20 For this reason t I have asked to see you
Ro 1:24 T God gave them up in the lusts of their hearts
2: 1 T you have no excuse, whoever you are,
4:22 T his faith "was reckoned to him
5: 1 T, since we are justified by faith,
5:12 T, just as sin came into the world through one man,
5:18 T just as one man's trespass led to condemnation
6: 4 T we have been buried with him by baptism
6:12 T, do not let sin exercise dominion
8: 1 There is t now no condemnation for those who
12: 1 I appeal to you t, brothers and sisters,
13: 2 T whoever resists authority resists what God has
13: 5 T one must be subject, not only because of wrath
Ro 13:10 t, love is the fulfilling of the law.
14:13 Let us t no longer pass judgment on one another,
15: 7 t, just as Christ has welcomed you,
15: 9 "T I will confess you among the Gentiles,
1Co 4: 5 T do not pronounce judgment before the time,
5: 8 T, let us celebrate the festival,
6:15 Should I t take the members of Christ
6:20 t glorify God in your body.
8:13 T, if food is a cause of their falling,
10:14 T, my dear friends, flee from the worship of idols.
11:27 T, eats the bread or drinks the cup of the Lord in
12: 3 T I want you to understand that no one speaking
14:13 T, one who speaks in a tongue should pray for
14:23 t, the whole church comes together and all speak
15:58 T, my beloved, be steadfast, immovable,
16:11 t let no one despise him.
2Co 4: 1 T, since it is by God's mercy that we are engaged
5:11 T, knowing the fear of the Lord,
5:14 that one has died for all; t all have died.
5:16 t, we regard no one from a human point of view;
6:17 T come out from them, and be separate
8:24 T openly before the churches,
12: 7 T, to keep me from being too elated,
12:10 T I am content with weaknesses, insults,
Gal 3:24 T the law was our disciplinarian
5: 1 t, and do not submit again to a yoke of slavery.
Eph 3:13 I pray t that you may not lose heart
4: 1 I t, the prisoner in the Lord,
4: 8 T it is said, "When he ascended
5: 1 T be imitators of God, as beloved children,
5: 7 T do not be associated with them.
5:14 T it says, "Sleeper, awake!
6:13 T take up the whole armor of God,
6:14 Stand t, and fasten the belt of truth
Php 2: 9 T God also highly exalted him and gave him
2:12 T, my beloved, just as you have always obeyed
2:23 I hope t to send him as soon as I see
2:28 I am the more eager to send him, t,
4: 1 T, my brothers and sisters,
Col 2: 6 As you t have received Christ Jesus the Lord,
2:16 T do not let anyone condemn you in matters
3: 5 Put to death, t, whatever in you is earthly:
1Th 3: 1 T when we could bear it no longer,
4: 8 T whoever rejects this rejects not human authority
4:18 T encourage one another with these words.
5:11 T encourage one another and build up each other,
2Th 1: 4 T we ourselves boast of you among the churches
2Ti 2:10 T I endure everything for the sake of the elect,
Heb 1: 9 t God, your God, has anointed you with the oil
2: 1 T we must pay greater attention
2:14 Since, t, the children share flesh and blood,
2:17 T he had to become like his brothers and sisters
3: 1 T, brothers and sisters, holy partners in
3: 7 T, as the Holy Spirit says, "Today,
3:10 T I was angry with that generation, and I said,
4: 1 T, while the promise of entering
4: 6 Since t it remains open for some to enter it,
4:11 Let us t make every effort to enter that rest,
4:16 Let us t approach the throne of grace
6: 1 T let us go on toward perfection,
10:19 T, my friends, since we have confidence to enter
10:35 Do not, t, abandon that confidence of yours;
11:12 T from one person, and this one as good as dead,
11:16 T God is not ashamed to be called their God;
12: 1 T, since we are surrounded by so great a cloud
12:12 T lift your drooping hands
12:28 T, since we are receiving a kingdom that cannot
13:12 T Jesus also suffered outside the city gate in order
Jas 1:21 T rid yourselves of all sordidness and rank growth
4: 4 T whoever wishes to be a friend of the world
4: 6 But he gives all the more grace; t it says,
4: 7 Submit yourselves t to God.
5: 7 t, beloved, until the coming of the Lord.
5:16 T confess your sins to one another,
1Pe 1:13 T prepare your minds for action;
2: 1 Rid yourselves, t, of all malice, and all guile,
4: 1 Since t Christ suffered in the flesh,
4: 7 t be serious and discipline yourselves for the sake
4:19 T, let those suffering in accordance
5: 6 Humble yourselves t under the mighty hand
2Pe 1:10 T, brothers and sisters, be all the more eager
1:12 T I intend to keep on reminding you
3:14 T, beloved, while you are waiting
3:17 You t, beloved, since you are forewarned,
1Jn 4: 5 t what they say is from the world,
3Jn 1: 8 T we ought to support such people,
Rev 3:18 T I counsel you to buy from me gold refined
3:19 Be earnest, t, and repent.
18: 8 t her plagues will come in a single day—
Jdt 3: 1 They t sent messengers to him to sue for peace
4: 2 they were t greatly terrified at his approach;
5:24 T let us go ahead, Lord Holofernes,
7:11 T, my lord, do not fight against them
8:17 T, while we wait for his deliverance,
8:24 "T, my brothers, let us set an example
11:10 T, lord and master, do not disregard what he said,
AdE 1:13 Give t your ruling and judgment on this matter."
1:19 If t it pleases the king, let him issue
9:26 T these days were called "Purim,"
13: 6 "T we have decreed that those indicated to you in
16:17 "You will t do well not to put in execution
16:19 "T post a copy of this letter publicly
16:22 "T you shall observe this with all good cheer as
Wis 1: 8 t those who utter unrighteous things will
2: 6 "Come, t, let us enjoy the good things that exist,
4:14 t he took them quickly from the midst
5:16 T they will receive a glorious crown and
Wis 6: 1 Listen t, O kings, and understand;
6:11 T set your desire on my words;
6:21 T if you delight in thrones and scepters,
6:25 T be instructed by my words, and you will profit.
7: 7 T I prayed, and understanding was given me;
7:25 t nothing defiled gains entrance into her.
8: 9 T I determined to take her to live with me,
10:20 T the righteous plundered the ungodly;
12: 2 T you correct little by little those who trespass,
12:23 T those who lived unrighteously, in a life of folly,
12:25 T, as though to children who cannot reason,
12:27 T the utmost condemnation came upon them.
14: 5 t people trust their lives even to the smallest piece
14:11 T there will be a visitation also upon
14:14 and t their speedy end has been planned.
16: 1 T those people were deservedly punished
16:25 T at that time also, changed into all forms,
17: 1 t uninstructed souls have gone astray.
18: 3 T you provided a flaming pillar of fire as a guide
Sir Pr: 2 You are invited t to read it with goodwill
2:13 T they will have no shelter.
10:13 T the Lord brings upon them unheard-of calamities
18:12 t he grants them forgiveness all the more.
31:13 T it sheds tears for any reason.
41:16 T show respect for my words;
43:14 T the storehouses are opened,
44:17 t a remnant was left on the earth when
44:21 T the Lord assured him with an oath that
45:24 T a covenant of friendship was established
51:20 t I will never be forsaken.
51:21 t I have gained a prize possession.
LtJ 6: 3 T when you have come to Babylon
6:64 T one must not think that they are gods,
6:69 that they are gods; t do not fear them.
6:73 Better, t, is someone upright who has no idols;
Bel 1:22 T the king put them to death,
1Mc 6:19 Judas t resolved to destroy them,
9:30 Now t we have chosen you today to take his place
10:54 now t let us establish friendship with one another;
11:37 Now t take care to make a copy of this,
12: 9 T, though we have no need of these things,
12:11 We t remember you constantly on every occasion,
12:16 We t have chosen Numenius son of Antiochus
12:23 We t command that our envoys report
12:53 Now t let us make war on them and blot out
15: 5 now t I confirm to you all the tax remissions that
15:19 We t have decided to write to the kings
15:21 T if any scoundrels have fled to you
2Mc 2:16 t, we are about to celebrate the purification,
2:16 Will you t please keep the days?
2:32 At this point t let us begin our narrative,
4:21 T upon arriving at Joppa he proceeded
4:34 T Menelaus, taking Andronicus aside,
4:37 T Antiochus was grieved at heart and filled
4:46 T Ptolemy, taking the king aside into a colonnade
4:49 T even the Tyrians, showing their hatred of
5: 4 T everyone prayed that the apparition might prove
5:20 T the place itself shared in the misfortunes
6: 9 t, the misery that had come upon them.
6:16 T he never withdraws his mercy from us.
6:27 T, by bravely giving up my life now,
7: 8 T he in turn underwent tortures as
7:18 T astounding things have happened.
7:23 T the Creator of the world,
8:36 and that t the Jews were invulnerable,
9: 2 T the people rushed to the rescue with arms,
9:26 I t urge and beg you to remember the public
10: 7 T, carrying ivy-wreathed wands
11:26 t, to send word to them and give them pledges
11:30 T those who go home by the thirtieth
11:37 T make haste and send messengers so
12:45 T he made atonement for the dead,
14: 7 T I have laid aside my ancestral glory—
14:19 T he sent Posidonius, Theodotus,
1Es 2: 5 If any of you, t, are of his people,
2:24 T we now make known to you, O lord and king,
2:28 T I have now issued orders
4:22 T you must realize that women rule over you!
4:46 I pray t that you fulfill the vow
6:21 Now t, O king, if it seems wise to do so,
6:33 "T may the Lord, whose name is there called
8:11 Let as many as are so disposed, t, leave with you,
8:84 T do not give your daughters in marriage
Man 1: 8 T you, O Lord, God of the righteous,
3Mc 3:24 T, fully convinced by these indications
3:25 T we have given orders that,
4:15 of these people was t conducted with bitter haste
2Es 2:34 T I say to you, O nations that hear
3:34 Now t weigh in a balance our iniquities and those
4:29 If t that which has been sown is not reaped,
5:18 Rise t and eat some bread, and do not forsake us,
5:45 If t all creatures will live at one time and
5:46 Request it t to produce ten at one time."
5:54 T you also should consider that you
6:31 If t you will pray again and fast again
6:33 T he sent me to show you all these things,
6:48 t the nations might declare your wondrous works.
7:14 T unless the living pass through the difficult
7:15 Now t why are you disturbed,
7:18 t, can endure difficult circumstances
7:*57* Judge t which things are precious and desirable,
7:*64* the mind grows with us, and t we are tormented,
7:*72* t, those who live on earth shall be tormented,
7:*90* T this is the teaching concerning them:
7:*100* "Will time t be given to the souls,
7:*112* [42] t those who were strong prayed for the weak.
7:*115* [45] T no one will then be able to have mercy

2Es 7:*131* [61] T there shall not be grief at their destruction,
8:17 T I will pray before you for myself and for them,
8:19 T hear my voice and understand my words
8:40 As I have spoken, t, so it shall be.
8:55 T do not ask any more questions about
8:61 T my judgment is now drawing near;
9:13 T, do not continue to be curious about how
10:15 Now, t, keep your sorrow to yourself,
10:17 T go into the town to your husband."
10:24 T shake off your great sadness
10:37 Now t I beg you to give your servant
10:40 This t is the meaning of the vision.
10:51 T I told you to remain in the field
10:53 T I told you to go into the field
10:55 "T do not be afraid, and do not let your heart
11:45 T you, eagle, will surely disappear,
12:6 T I will now entreat the Most High
12:24 T they are called the heads of the eagle,
12:37 T write all these things that you have seen in
12:44 T if you forsake us, how much better it would
13:24 Understand t that those who are left are more
13:47 T you saw the multitude gathered together
13:49 T when he destroys the multitude of the nations
13:56 T I have shown you these things;
14:13 Now t, set your house in order,
15:7 T, says the Lord,
15:26 t he will hand them over to death and slaughter.
15:48 in all her deeds and devices. T God says,
15:55 t you shall receive your recompense.
16:51 T do not be like her or her works.
4Mc 1:34 T when we crave seafood and fowl and animals
3:16 T, opposing reason to desire,
5:17 T we consider that we should not transgress it
5:19 T do not suppose that it would be a petty sin
5:25 "T we do not eat defiling food;
5:32 T get your torture wheels ready and fan
6:22 T, O children of Abraham,
7:16 t, because of piety an aged man despised tortures
7:20 No contradiction t arises
8:10 T take pity on yourselves.
9:7 T, tyrant, put us to the test;
11:27 t, unconquered, we hold fast to reason."
13:16 T let us put on the full armor of self-control,
13:23 T, when sympathy and brotherly affection had
16:19 and t you ought to endure any suffering for
17:4 Take courage, t, O holy-minded mother,
18:3 T those who gave over their bodies in suffering

THEREUPON (2)
Jer 31:26 T I awoke and looked, and my sleep was pleasant
3Mc 2:21 T God, who oversees all things,

THESE (1438) [THIS] See Index of Articles Etc.

THESSALONIANS (2) [THESSALONICA]
1Th 1:1 the T in God the Father and the Lord Jesus Christ:
2Th 1:1 the T in God our Father and the Lord Jesus Christ:

THESSALONICA (7) [THESSALONIANS]
Ac 17:1 they came to T, where there was a synagogue of
17:11 These Jews were more receptive than those in T,
17:13 But when the Jews of T learned that the word
20:4 by Aristarchus and Secundus from T,
27:2 by Aristarchus, a Macedonian from T.
Php 4:16 For even when I was in T,
2Ti 4:10 has deserted me and gone to T;

THEUDAS (1)
Ac 5:36 For some time ago T rose up,

THEY (8792) [THEIR, THEIRS, THEM, THEMSELVES] See Index of Articles Etc.

THICK‡ (37) [THICK-BOSSED, THICKER, THICKNESS]
Ex 19:16 as well as a t cloud on the mountain,
20:21 while Moses drew near to the t darkness
Dt 5:22 out of the fire, the cloud, and the t darkness,
Jdg 6:5 up, and they would even bring their tents, as t
7:12 of the east lay along the valley as t as locusts;
2Sa 18:9 the mule went under the t branches of a great oak.
22:10 t darkness was under his feet.
22:12 He made darkness around him a canopy, t clouds,
1Ki 8:12 that he would dwell in t darkness.
20:39 "Your servant went out into the t of the battle;
2Ch 6:1 that he would reside in t darkness.
Job 3:6 That night—let t darkness seize it!
22:14 T clouds enwrap him, so that he does not see,
23:17 and t darkness would cover my face!
26:8 He binds up the waters in his t clouds,
37:11 He loads the t cloud with moisture;
38:9 and t darkness its swaddling band,
Ps 18:9 t darkness was under his feet.
18:11 his canopy t clouds dark with water.
97:2 Clouds and t darkness are all around him;
Isa 8:22 and they will be thrust into t darkness.
30:27 burning with his anger, and in t rising smoke;
60:2 and t darkness the peoples;
Jer 2:31 or a land of t darkness?
Eze 19:11 it towered aloft among the t boughs;
24:12 its t rust does not depart.
34:12 on a day of clouds and t darkness.
41:5 he measured the wall of the temple, six cubits t;
41:12 wall of the building was five cubits t all around,
Joel 2:2 a day of clouds and t darkness!
Zep 1:15 a day of clouds and t darkness,
Zec 11:2 oaks of Bashan, for the t forest has been felled!
Jdt 1:2 around Ecbatana with hewn stones three cubits t
Wis 11:18 or belch forth a t pall of smoke,
LtJ 6:13 of the dust from the temple, which is t upon them.
2Mc 1:20 that they had not found fire but only a t liquid,
2Es 16:28 those who have hidden themselves in t groves

THICK-BOSSED (1) [THICK]
Job 15:26 running stubbornly against him with a t shield;

THICKEN See Index to Footnotes

THICKER (2) [THICK]
1Ki 12:10 'My little finger is t than my father's loins.
2Ch 10:10 'My little finger is t than my father's loins.

THICKET (4) [THICKETS]
Ge 22:13 caught in a t by its horns.
Jer 4:7 A lion has gone up from its t,
1Mc 4:38 In the courts they saw bushes sprung up as in a t,
9:45 with marsh and t; there is no place to turn.

THICKETS (7) [THICKET]
Isa 9:18 it kindled the t of the forest,
10:34 He will hack down the t of the forest with an ax,
Jer 4:29 and archer every town takes to flight; they enter t;
12:5 how will you fare in the t of the Jordan?
49:19 a lion coming up from the t of the Jordan against
50:44 a lion coming up from the t of the Jordan against
Zec 11:3 for the t of the Jordan are destroyed!

THICKNESS (5) [THICK]
1Ki 7:26 Its t was a handbreadth; its brim was made like the
2Ch 4:5 Its t was a handbreadth; its rim was made like the
Jer 52:21 it was hollow and its t was four fingers.
Eze 40:5 so he measured the t of the wall, one reed;
41:9 The t of the outer wall of the side chambers

THIEF (28) [THEFT, THEFTS, THIEF'S, THIEVES]
Ex 22:1 the t shall pay five oxen for an ox,
22:1 The t shall make restitution,
22:2 If a t is found breaking in, and is beaten to death,
22:4 in the thief's possession, the t shall pay double.
22:7 then the t, if caught, shall pay double.
22:8 If the t is not caught,
Job 24:14 and in the night is like a t.
30:5 people shout after them as after a t.
Ps 50:18 You make friends with a t when you see one,
Pr 29:24 To be a partner of a t is to hate one's own life;
Jer 2:26 As a t is shamed when caught,
Hos 7:1 for they deal falsely, the t breaks in,
Joel 2:9 they enter through the windows like a t.
Zec 5:4 and it shall enter the house of the t,
Mt 24:43 in what part of the night the t was coming,
Lk 12:33 where no t comes near and no moth destroys.
12:39 at what hour the t was coming,
Jn 10:1 but climbs in by another way is a t and a bandit.
10:10 The t comes only to steal and kill and destroy.
12:6 but because he was a t;
1Th 5:2 the day of the Lord will come like a t in the night.
5:4 for that day to surprise you like a t;
1Pe 4:15 But let none of you suffer as a murderer, a t,
2Pe 3:10 But the day of the Lord will come like a t,
Rev 3:3 If you do not wake up, I will come like a t,
16:15 ("See, I am coming like a t!
Sir 5:14 for shame comes to the t,
20:25 A t is preferable to a habitual liar,

THIEF'S (1) [THIEF]
Ex 22:4 found alive in the t possession, the thief shall pay

THIEVES (12) [THIEF]
Pr 6:30 T are not despised who steal only
Isa 1:23 Your princes are rebels and companions of t.
Jer 48:27 though he was not caught among t;
49:9 If t came by night, even they would pillage only
Ob 1:5 If t came to you, if plunderers by night
Mt 6:19 and rust consume and where t break in and steal;
6:20 nor rust consumes and where t do not break in
Lk 18:11 t, rogues, adulterers,
Jn 10:8 All who came before me are t and bandits;
1Co 6:10 t, the greedy, drunkards, revilers, robbers—
Eph 4:28 T must give up stealing; rather let them labor
LtJ 6:57 and gold are unable to save themselves from t

THIGH (29) [THIGHS]
Ge 24:2 "Put your hand under my t
24:9 the t of Abraham his master and swore to him
32:32 to this day the Israelites do not eat the t muscle
32:32 he struck Jacob on the hip socket at the t muscle.
47:29 under my t and promise to deal loyally and truly
Ex 29:22 and the right t (for it is a ram of ordination),
29:27 the t that was raised as an elevation offering from
Lev 7:32 And the right t from your sacrifices
7:33 of the offering of well-being shall have the right t
7:34 and the t that is offered, from the people of Israel,
8:25 with their fat—and the right t.
8:26 and placed them on the fat and on the right t.
9:21 the right t Aaron raised as an elevation offering
10:14 the breast that is elevated and the t that is raised,
10:15 The t that is raised and the breast
Nu 6:20 the breast that is elevated and the t that is offered.
18:18 that is elevated and as the right t are yours.
Jdg 3:16 and he fastened it on his right t under his clothes.
3:21 took the sword from his right t,
15:8 down hip and t with great slaughter;
1Sa 9:24 The cook took up the t and what went with it
Ps 45:3 Gird your sword on your t, O mighty one,
SS 3:8 with his sword at his t because of alarms by night.
Jer 31:19 and after I was discovered, I struck my t;
Eze 21:12 Ah! Strike the t!
24:4 the t and the shoulder; fill it with choice bones.
Rev 19:16 On his robe and on his t he has a name inscribed,
Sir 19:12 Like an arrow stuck in a person's t,
2Es 15:36 and a man's t and a camel's hock.

THIGHS (6) [THIGH]
Ex 28:42 they shall reach from the hips to the t;
Dt 28:57 the afterbirth that comes out from between her t,
Job 40:17 the sinews of its t are knit together.
SS 7:1 Your rounded t are like jewels,
Da 2:32 its middle and t of bronze,
Jdt 9:2 and exposed her t to put her to shame,

THIMNATHAH (KJV) See TIMNAH

THIN (9)
Ge 41:3 Then seven other cows, ugly and t,
41:4 and t cows ate up the seven sleek and fat cows.
41:6 Then seven ears, t and blighted by the east wind,
41:7 The t ears swallowed up the seven plump
41:19 up after them, poor, very ugly, and t.
41:20 t and ugly cows ate up the first seven fat cows,
41:23 withered, t, and blighted by the east wind,
41:24 and the t ears swallowed up the seven good ears.
Lev 13:30 and t, the priest shall pronounce him unclean;

THING‡ (218) [ANYTHING, EVERYTHING, THINGS]
A. SUCH A THING (23)
B. LIVING THING (9)

Ge 1:26 over every creeping t that creeps upon the earth."
1:28 and over every living t that moves upon B
6:19 And of every living t, of all flesh, B
6:20 of every creeping t of the ground according
7:4 every living t that I have made I will blot out B
7:14 and every creeping t that creeps on the earth,
7:23 He blotted out every living t that was on the B
8:17 Bring out with you every living t that is with B
8:17 birds and animals and every creeping t that creeps
8:19 And every animal, every creeping t,
9:3 Every moving t that lives shall be food for you;
18:25 Far be it from you to do such a t, A
20:10 "What were you thinking of, that you did this t?"
24:50 "The t comes from the LORD;
32:19 the same t to Esau when you meet him,
34:7 for such a t ought not to be done. A
34:14 They said to them, "We cannot do this t,
34:19 And the young man did not delay to do the t,
41:32 of Pharaoh's dream means that the t is fixed
44:7 from your servants that they should do such a t! A
Ex 2:14 and thought, "Surely the t is known."
9:5 "Tomorrow the LORD will do this t in the land."
10:17 that at the least he remove this deadly t from me."
14:12 Is this not the very t we told you in Egypt,
33:17 "I will do the very t that you have asked;
34:10 for it is an awesome t that I will do with you.
35:4 This is the t that the LORD has commanded:
Lev 5:2 Or when any of you touch any unclean t—
5:2 or the carcass of an unclean swarming t—
5:16 And you shall make restitution for the holy t
6:4 or the lost t that you found,
7:19 that touches any unclean t shall not be eaten;
7:21 When any one of you touches any unclean t—
9:6 "This is the t that the LORD commanded you
12:4 she shall not touch any holy t,
15:10 all who carry such a t shall wash their clothes, A
22:5 and whoever touches any swarming t
27:28 every devoted t is most holy to the LORD.
Nu 18:9 of theirs that they render to me as a most holy t,
18:10 As a most holy t you shall eat it;
18:14 Every devoted t in Israel shall be yours.
Dt 7:26 Do not bring an abhorrent t into your house,
9:21 Then I took the sinful t you had made, the calf,
12:31 because every abhorrent t that
13:14 an abhorrent t has been done among you,
14:3 You shall not eat any abhorrent t.
17:4 that such an abhorrent t has occurred in Israel,
18:22 of the LORD but the t does not take place
Jos 7:12 a t devoted for destruction themselves.
7:15 and for having done an outrageous t in Israel.' "
9:24 for our lives because of you, and did this t.
23:14 that not one t has failed of all the good things that
Jdg 11:37 she said to her father, "Let this t be done for me:
13:14 or strong drink, or eat any unclean t.
19:23 Since this man is my guest, do not do this vile t.
19:24 but against this man do not do such a vile t."
19:30 'Has such a t ever happened since the day that A
1Sa 8:6 But the t displeased Samuel when they said,

1Sa 12:16 Now therefore take your stand and see this great **t**
18:20 Saul was told, and the **t** pleased him.
18:23 to you a little **t** to become the king's son-in-law,
24: 6 LORD forbid that I should do this **t** to my lord,
26:16 This **t** that you have done is not good.
28:10 no punishment shall come upon you for this **t.**"
28:18 therefore the LORD has done this **t** to you today.
2Sa 2: 6 because you have done this **t.**
3:13 But one **t** I require of you:
7:19 this was a small **t** in your eyes, O Lord GOD;
7:28 you have promised this good **t** to your servant;
11:11 and as your soul lives, I will not do such a **t.**" A
11:27 the **t** that David had done displeased the LORD,
12: 6 the lamb fourfold, because he did this **t,** and
12:12 but I will do this **t** before all Israel,
12:21 "What is this **t** that you have done?
13:12 for such a **t** is not done in Israel; A
14:13 have you planned such a **t** against the people A
1Ki 1:27 Has this **t** been brought about by my lord the king
9: 8 'Why has the LORD done such a **t** to this land A
12:24 Let everyone go home, for this **t** is from me."
12:30 And this **t** became a sin,
16:31 if it had been a light **t** for him to walk in the sins
20: 9 but this **t** I cannot do."
22: 8 Jehoshaphat said, "Let the king not say such a **t.** A
22:20 Then one said one **t,** and another said another,
2Ki 2:10 He responded, "You have asked a hard **t;**
7: 2 in the sky, could such a **t** happen?" A
7:19 in the sky, could such a **t** happen?" A
8:13 who is a mere dog, that he should do this great **t?**"
20: 9 the LORD will do the **t** that he has promised:
1Ch 2: 7 who transgressed in the matter of the devoted **t;**
13: 4 for the **t** pleased all the people.
17:17 And even this was a small **t** in your sight, O God;
17:26 you have promised this good **t** to your servant;
21: 7 But God was displeased with this **t,**
21: 8 "I have sinned greatly in that I have done this **t.**
2Ch 7:21 'Why has the LORD done such a **t** to this land A
11: 4 Let everyone return home, for this **t** is from me."
18: 7 Jehoshaphat said, "Let the king not say such a **t.** A
18:19 Then one said one **t,** and another said another,
29:36 for the **t** had come about suddenly.
Ezr 7:27 put such a **t** as this into the heart of the king A
Ne 5: 9 So I said, "The **t** that you are doing is not good.
13:17 "What is this evil **t** that you are doing,
Est 8: 5 and if the **t** seems right before the king,
Job 3:25 Truly the **t** that I fear comes upon me,
12:10 In his hand is the life of every living **t** and B
13:28 One wastes away like a rotten **t,**
14: 4 Who can bring a clean **t** out of an unclean?
28:10 and their eyes see every precious **t.**
39: 8 and it searches after every green **t.**
Ps 27: 4 One **t** I asked of the LORD, that will I seek after:
34:10 but those who seek the LORD lack no good **t.**
41: 8 They think that a deadly **t** has fastened on me,
84:11 No good **t** does the LORD withhold
88: 8 you have made me a **t** of horror to them.
145:16 satisfying the desire of every living **t.** B
Pr 18:22 He who finds a wife finds a good **t,**
Ecc 1:10 Is there a **t** of which it is said, "See, this is new"?
7: 8 Better is the end of a **t** than its beginning;
7:27 adding one **t** to another to find the sum,
8: 1 And who knows the interpretation of a **t?**
12:14 including every secret **t,** whether good or evil.
Isa 29:16 Shall the **t** made say of its maker,
29:16 or the **t** formed say of the one who formed it,
38: 7 the LORD will do this **t** that he has promised:
43:19 I am about to do a new **t;**
44:20 "Is not this **t** in my right hand a fraud?"
49: 6 "It is too light a **t** that you should be my servant
52:11 from there! Touch no unclean **t;**
55:11 and succeed in the **t** for which I sent it.
66: 8 Who has heard of such a **t?** A
Jer 2:10 see if there has ever been such a **t.** A
3:24 from our youth the shameful **t** has devoured all
5:30 appalling and horrible **t** has happened in the land:
18:13 The virgin Israel has done a most horrible **t.**
18:16 a **t** to be hissed at forever.
19: 8 I will make this city a horror, a **t** to be hissed at;
23:13 In the prophets of Samaria I saw a disgusting **t:**
23:14 of Jerusalem I have seen a more shocking **t:**
24: 9 I will make them a horror, an evil **t,**
31:22 For the LORD has created a new **t** on the earth:
40: 3 Therefore this **t** has come upon you.
40:16 "Do not do such a **t,** A
44: 4 not to do this abominable **t** that I hate!"
La 1:17 Jerusalem has become a filthy **t** among them.
Eze 7:20 therefore I will make of it an unclean **t** to them.
28:16 so I cast you as a profane **t** from the mountain
44:29 and every devoted **t** in Israel shall be theirs.
Da 2:10 asked such a **t** of any magician or enchanter A
2:11 The **t** that the king is asking is too difficult,
6:12 The king answered, "The **t** stands fast,
Hos 6:10 In the house of Israel I have seen a horrible **t;**
8:12 they are regarded as a strange **t.**
9:10 and consecrated themselves to a **t** of shame,
9:10 and became detestable like the **t** they loved.
10: 6 The **t** itself shall be carried to Assyria as tribute to
13:15 It shall strip his treasury of every precious **t.**
Joel 1: 2 Has such a **t** happened in your days, A
Na 2: 9 An abundance of every precious **t!**"
Mk 10:21 loved him and said, "You lack one **t;**
16:18 ⟦and if they drink any deadly **t,** it will not hurt⟧
Lk 2:15 to Bethlehem and see this **t** that has taken place,
10:42 there is need of only one **t.**
12:26 If then you are not able to do so small a **t** as that,
18:22 he said to him, "There is still one **t** lacking.
Lk 19:17 you have been trustworthy in a very small **t,**
22:35 They said, "No, not a **t.**"
Jn 1: 3 and without him not one **t** came into being.
9:25 One **t** I do know, that though I was blind,
9:30 The man answered, "Here is an astonishing **t!**
Ac 10:16 and the **t** was suddenly taken up to heaven.
14: 1 The same **t** occurred in Iconium,
19:32 Meanwhile, some were shouting one **t,**
21:34 Some in the crowd shouted one **t,** some another;
Ro 7:15 I do not do what I want, but I do the very **t** I hate.
13: 6 are God's servants, busy with this very **t.**
1Co 4: 3 with me it is a very small **t** that I should be judged
5: 4 Lord Jesus on the man who has done such a **t.** A
5: 6 Your boasting is not a good **t.**
11: 5 and the same **t** as having her head shaved.
15:40 but the glory of the heavenly is one **t,**
2Co 5: 5 He who has prepared us for this very **t** is God,
Gal 2:10 They asked only one **t,** that we remember
3: 2 The only **t** I want to learn from you is this:
5: 6 only **t** that counts is faith working through love.
Php 3:13 but this one **t** I do: forgetting what lies behind
Phm 1:22 One **t** more—prepare a guest room
Heb 10:31 a fearful **t** to fall into the hands of the living God.
Jas 4:17 who knows the right **t** to do and fails to do it,
Rev 16: 3 and every living **t** in the sea died. B
Jdt 13: 3 She had said the same **t** to Bagoas.
16:16 every sacrifice as a fragrant offering is a small **t,**
16:16 to you is a very little **t;**
AdE 7: 5 "Who is the person that would dare to do this **t?**"
13:10 and earth and every wonderful **t** under heaven.
Wis 4:15 or take such a **t** to heart, A
13:17 he is not ashamed to address a lifeless **t.**
13:18 For health he appeals to a **t** that is weak;
13:18 for life he prays to a **t** that is dead;
13:18 for aid he entreats a **t** that is utterly inexperienced;
13:18 a prosperous journey, a **t** that cannot take a step;
13:19 of a **t** whose hands have no strength.
14: 8 and the perishable **t** because it was named a god.
15: 9 they count it a glorious **t** to mold counterfeit gods.
16: 7 not by the **t** that was beheld, but by you,
17:11 For wickedness is a cowardly **t,**
Sir 18:13 the compassion of the Lord is for every living **t.** B
31:13 Remember that a greedy eye is a bad **t.**
34: 4 From an unclean **t** what can be clean?
41:11 The human body is a fleeting **t,**
42: 6 there is an untrustworthy wife, a seal is a good **t;**
Bel 1: 7 for this **t** is only clay inside and bronze outside,
1Mc 9:10 be it from us to do such a **t** as to flee from them. A
15:22 The consul wrote the same **t** to King Demetrius
2Mc 4:17 It is no light **t** to show irreverence to
1Es 3: 5 "Let each of us state what one **t** is strongest;
4:18 and silver or any other beautiful **t,**
4:19 to gold or silver or any other beautiful **t.**

THINGS‡ (926) [THING]

A. ALL THINGS (146)
B. ALL THESE THINGS (55)
C. GOOD THINGS (33)
D. HOLY THINGS (16)
E. GREAT THINGS (15)
F. THINGS TO COME (6)

Ge 1:24 cattle and creeping **t** and wild animals of the earth
6: 7 with animals and creeping **t** and birds of the air,
7:23 and animals and creeping **t** and birds of the air;
15: 1 After these **t** the word of the LORD came
20: 8 called all his servants and told them all these **t;** B
20: 9 You have done **t** to me that ought not to be done."
22: 1 After these **t** God tested Abraham.
22:20 Now after these **t** it was told Abraham,
24: 1 and the LORD had blessed Abraham in all **t.** A
24:28 and told her mother's household about these **t.**
24:66 the servant told Isaac all the **t** that he had done.
29:13 Jacob told Laban all these **t,** B
38:23 Judah replied, "Let her keep the **t** as her own,
45:23 ten donkeys loaded with the good **t** of Egypt, C
Ex 18:20 to them the way they are to go and the **t** they are
21:11 And if he does not do these three **t** for her,
29:28 These **t** shall be a perpetual ordinance for Aaron
35: 1 the **t** that the LORD has commanded you to do:
Lev 4: 2 about **t** not to be done, and does any one of them:
4:13 the **t** that by the LORD's commandments ought
4:22 doing unintentionally any one of all the **t** that
4:27 the **t** that by the LORD's commandments ought
5:15 and sins unintentionally in any of the holy **t** of D
5:17 the **t** that by the LORD's commandments ought
6: 3 of the various **t** that one may do and sin thereby—
6: 7 of the **t** that one may do and incur guilt thereby.
8:36 the **t** that the LORD commanded through Moses.
10:19 and yet such **t** as these have befallen me!
14:11 along with these **t,** before the LORD,
15:27 Whoever touches these **t** shall be unclean,
20:23 Because they did all these **t,** I abhorred them. B
Nu 4: 4 to the tent of meeting concerns the most holy **t.** D
4:15 but they must not touch the holy **t,** D
4:15 the **t** of the tent of meeting that the Kohathites are
4:19 not die when they come near to the most holy **t:** D
4:20 go in to look on the holy **t** even for a moment; D
7: 9 holy **t** that had to be carried on the shoulders. D
10:21 the Kohathites, who carried the holy **t,** set out; D
14:28 "I will do to you the very **t** I heard you say:
15:13 Every native Israelite shall do these **t** in this way,
18: 9 This shall be yours from the most holy **t,** D
35:29 These **t** shall be a statute and ordinance for you
Dt 1:18 at that time with all the **t** that you should do.
4: 9 the **t** that your eyes have seen nor to let them slip
Dt 4:19 **t** that the LORD your God has allotted to all
4:30 all these **t** have happened to you in time to come, B
10:21 who has done for you these great and awesome **t**
16:22 **t** that the LORD your God hates.
18:12 whoever does these **t** is abhorrent to the LORD;
20:18 not teach you to do all the abhorrent **t** that they do
22: 5 for whoever does such **t** is abhorrent to
25:16 For all who do such **t,** all who act dishonestly,
29:17 You have seen their detestable **t,**
29:29 The secret **t** belong to the LORD our God,
29:29 but the revealed **t** belong to us and
30: 1 When all these **t** have happened to you, B
32:16 with abhorrent **t** they provoked him.
32:24 with venom of **t** crawling in the dust.
Jos 1:17 Just as we obeyed Moses in all **t,** A
6:18 you, keep away from the **t** devoted to destruction,
6:18 and take any of the devoted **t** and make the camp
7: 1 Israelites broke faith in regard to the devoted **t:**
7: 1 of the tribe of Judah, took some of the devoted **t;**
7:11 They have taken some of the devoted **t;**
7:12 unless you destroy the devoted **t** from among you.
7:13 "There are devoted **t** among you, O Israel;
7:13 until you take away the devoted **t** from
7:15 the one who is taken as having the devoted **t** shall
22:20 in the matter of the devoted **t,**
23:14 not one thing has failed of all the good **t** that C
23:15 the good **t** that the LORD your God promised C
23:15 so the LORD will bring upon you all the bad **t,**
24:29 After these **t** Joshua son of Nun,
Jdg 13:23 or shown us all these **t,** B
13:23 or now announced to us such **t** as these."
Ru 3:16 who said, "How did **t** go with you, my daughter?"
1Sa 2:23 He said to them, "Why do you do such **t?**
5: 7 when the inhabitants of Ashdod saw how **t** were,
12:21 not turn aside after useless **t** that cannot profit
12:24 for consider what great **t** he has done for you. E
15:21 the best of the **t** devoted to destruction,
17:22 the **t** in charge of the keeper of the baggage,
19: 7 So Jonathan called David and related all these **t** B
25:37 his wife told him these **t,**
26:25 You will do many **t** and will succeed in them."
2Sa 1: 4 David said to him, "How did **t** go?
7:23 doing great and awesome **t** for them,
13:21 When King David heard of all these **t,** B
14:20 the wisdom of the angel of God to know all **t** A
23: 5 ordered in all **t** and secure. A
23:17 The three warriors did these **t.**
23:22 Such were the **t** Benaiah son of Jehoiada did,
24:12 Thus says the LORD: Three **t** I offer you;
1Ki 7:51 in the **t** that his father David had dedicated,
18:36 and that I have done all these **t** at your bidding. B
2Ki 1: 7 to meet you and told you these **t?**"
7: 8 carried off **t** from it, and went and hid them.
8: 4 "Tell me all the great **t** that Elisha has done." E
14: 3 in all **t** he did as his father Joash had done. A
17: 9 of Israel secretly did **t** that were not right against
17:11 They did wicked **t,** provoking the LORD
21:11 has done **t** more wicked than all that
23:16 of the man of God who had predicted these **t.**
23:17 and predicted these **t** that you have done against
1Ch 11:19 The three warriors did these **t.**
11:24 Such were the **t** Benaiah son of Jehoiada did,
17:19 making known all these great **t.** E
17:21 for yourself a name for great and terrible **t,**
21:10 'Thus says the LORD: Three **t** I offer you;
23:13 was set apart to consecrate the most holy **t,** D
23:26 the tabernacle or any of the **t** for its service"—
29: 2 the gold for the **t** of gold, the silver for the **t** of
silver, and the bronze for the **t** of bronze, the iron
for the **t** of iron, and wood for the **t** of wood,
29: 5 gold for the **t** of gold and silver for the **t** of silver.
29:14 For all **t** come from you, A
29:17 of my heart I have freely offered all these **t,** B
2Ch 4:18 Solomon made all these **t** in great quantities, B
4:19 So Solomon made all the **t** that were in the house
5: 1 in the **t** that his father David had dedicated,
20:25 goods, clothing, and precious **t,**
24: 7 and had even used all the dedicated **t** of the house
29:16 the unclean **t** that they found in the temple of
31: 6 of the dedicated **t** that had been consecrated to
31:12 the tithes and the dedicated **t.**
32: 1 After these **t** and these acts of faithfulness,
32:23 in Jerusalem and precious **t** to King Hezekiah
Ezr 9: 1 After these **t** had been done,
Ne 4: 2 are these feeble Jews doing? Will they restore **t?**
4:14 After I looked these **t** over,
6: 8 saying, "No such **t** as you say have been done;
6:14 O my God, according to these **t** that they did,
Est 2: 1 After these **t,** when the anger
3: 1 these **t** King Ahasuerus promoted Haman son
9:20 Mordecai recorded these **t,**
Job 5: 9 He does great **t** and unsearchable, E
5: 9 marvelous **t** without number.
8: 2 "How long will you say these **t,**
9:10 who does great **t** beyond understanding, E
9:10 and marvelous **t** without number.
10:13 Yet these **t** you hid in your heart;
11: 7 "Can you find out the deep **t** of God?
12: 3 Who does not know such **t** as these?
13:20 Only grant two **t** to me, then I will
13:26 For you write bitter **t** against me,
16: 2 "I have heard many such **t;**
22:18 Yet he filled their houses with good **t**— C
23:14 and many such **t** are in his mind.
28:11 hidden **t** they bring to light.
33:29 "God indeed does all these **t,** twice, three times, B
37: 5 he does great **t** that we cannot comprehend. E

Job 42: 2 "I know that you can do all **t**, A
42: 3 **t** too wonderful for me, which I did not know.
Ps 8: 6 you have put all **t** under their feet, A
15: 5 Those who do these **t** shall never be moved.
35:11 they ask me about **t** I do not know.
42: 4 These **t** I remember, as I pour out my soul:
50:21 These **t** you have done and I have been silent;
60: 3 You have made your people suffer hard **t**;
71:19 You who have done great **t**, O God, E
72:18 the God of Israel, who alone does wondrous **t**.
78: 3 **t** that we have heard and known,
86:10 For you are great and do wondrous **t**;
87: 3 Glorious **t** are spoken of you, O city of God.
98: 1 for he has done marvelous **t**.
104:25 great and wide, creeping **t** innumerable are there,
104:25 living **t** both small and great.
104:28 you open your hand, they are filled with good **t**. C
106:21 their Savior, who had done great **t** in Egypt, E
107: 9 and the hungry he fills with good **t**. C
107:43 Let those who are wise give heed to these **t**,
119:18 so that I may behold wondrous **t** out of your law.
119:91 for all **t** are your servants. A
126: 2 "The LORD has done great **t** for them." E
126: 3 LORD has done great **t** for us, and we rejoiced. E
131: 1 with **t** too great and too marvelous for me.
140: 2 who plan evil **t** in their minds and stir
148:10 creeping **t** and flying birds!
Pr 1:13 We shall find all kinds of costly **t**;
6:16 There are six **t** that the LORD hates,
8: 6 Hear, for I will speak noble **t**,
12:14 the fruit of the mouth one is filled with good **t**, C
13: 2 the fruit of their words good persons eat good **t**, C
13:16 The clever do all **t** intelligently, A
16:30 One who winks the eyes plans perverse **t**;
23:33 Your eyes will see strange **t**,
23:33 and your mind utter perverse **t**.
25: 2 It is the glory of God to conceal **t**,
25: 2 but the glory of kings is to search **t** out.
30: 7 Two **t** I ask of you;
30:15 Three **t** are never satisfied;
30:18 Three **t** are too wonderful for me;
30:21 Under three **t** the earth trembles;
30:24 Four **t** on earth are small,
30:29 Three **t** are stately in their stride;
Ecc 1: 8 All **t** are wearisome; more than one can express; A
5: 9 all **t** considered, this is an advantage for a land: A
6: 2 yet God does not enable them to enjoy these **t**,
6: 3 if he does not enjoy life's good **t**, or has no C
7:25 and to seek wisdom and the sum of **t**,
8:10 in the city where they had done such **t**.
11: 9 for all these **t** God will bring you into judgment. B
Isa 25: 1 for you have done wonderful **t**,
29:14 so I will again do amazing **t** with this people,
29:16 You turn **t** upside down!
30:10 speak to us smooth **t**, prophesy illusions,
32: 8 But those who are noble plan noble **t**,
32: 8 and by noble **t** they stand.
38:16 O Lord, by these **t** people live,
41:22 Tell us the former **t**, what they are,
41:22 or declare to us the **t** to come. F
42: 9 See, the former **t** have come to pass,
42: 9 and new **t** I now declare;
42:16 These are the **t** I will do, and I will not forsake
42:20 He sees many **t**, but does not observe them;
43: 9 and foretold to us the former **t**?
43:18 Do not remember the former **t**,
43:18 or consider the **t** of old.
44: 7 Who has announced from of old the **t** to come? F
44: 9 and the **t** they delight in do not profit;
44:21 Remember these **t**, O Jacob, and Israel,
44:24 I am the LORD, who made all **t**, A
45: 7 I the LORD do all these **t**. B
46: 1 these **t** you carry are loaded as burdens
46: 9 remember the former **t** of old;
46:10 from the beginning and from ancient times **t** not
47: 7 not lay these **t** to heart or remember their end.
47: 9 both these **t** shall come upon you in a moment,
48: 3 The former **t** I declared long ago,
48: 6 From this time forward I make you hear new **t**,
48: 6 hidden **t** that you have not known.
48:14 Who among them has declared these **t**?
51:19 These two **t** have befallen you—who will grieve
56: 4 the **t** that please me and hold fast my covenant,
57: 6 Shall I be appeased for these **t**?
65: 4 with broth of abominable **t** in their vessels;
65:17 the former **t** shall not be remembered or come
66: 2 All these **t** my hand has made, B
66: 2 and so all these **t** are mine, says the LORD. B
66: 8 Who has seen such **t**?
Jer 2: 5 and went after worthless **t**,
2: 7 a plentiful land to eat its fruits and its good **t**. C
2: 8 and went after **t** that do not profit.
2:34 Yet in spite of all these **t** B
5: 9 Shall I not punish them for these **t**?
5:19 "Why has the LORD our God done all these **t** B
5:29 Shall I not punish them for these **t**?
7:13 And now, because you have done all these **t**, B
9: 9 Shall I not punish them for these **t**?
9:24 for in these **t** I delight, says the LORD.
10:16 for he is the one who formed all **t**, A
13:22 "Why have these **t** come upon me?"
16:19 worthless **t** in which there is no profit.
20: 1 heard Jeremiah prophesying these **t**.
26:10 When the officials of Judah heard these **t**,
30:15 I have done these **t** to you.
33: 3 and will tell you great and hidden **t** that you have
45: 5 And you, do you seek great **t** for yourself? E

Jer 48:44 For I will bring these **t** upon Moab in the year
51:19 for he is the one who formed all **t**, A
La 1: 7 all the precious **t** that were hers in days of old.
1:10 stretched out their hands over all her precious **t**;
1:16 For these **t** I weep; my eyes flow with tears;
5:17 because of these **t** our eyes have grown dim:
Eze 5:11 with all your detestable **t** and
7:20 made their abominable images, their detestable **t**;
8:10 were all kinds of creeping **t**,
11: 5 I know the **t** that come into your mind.
11:18 from it all its detestable **t** and all its abominations.
11:21 for those whose heart goes after their detestable **t**
11:25 the exiles all the **t** that the LORD had shown me.
16: 5 to do any of these **t** for you out of compassion
16:30 says the Lord GOD, that you did all these **t**, B
16:43 but have enraged me with all these **t**; B
16:50 and did abominable **t** before me;
17:12 Do you not know what these **t** mean?
17:15 Can one escape who does such **t**?
17:18 because he gave his hand and yet did all these **t**, B
18:11 of these **t** (though his father does none of them),
18:13 He has done all these abominable **t**;
18:24 and do the same abominable **t** that the wicked do,
20: 7 Cast away the detestable **t** your eyes feast on,
20: 8 the detestable **t** their eyes feasted on,
20:30 and go astray after their detestable **t**?
20:40 the choicest of your gifts, with all your sacred **t**.
21:26 **t** shall not remain as they are.
22: 8 You have despised my holy **t**, D
22:25 they have taken treasure and precious **t**;
22:26 to my teaching and have profaned my holy **t**; D
24:19 "Will you not tell us what these **t** mean for us,
37:23 with their idols and their detestable **t**,
38:20 and all creeping **t** that creep on the ground,
44:13 the **t** that are most sacred;
Da 2: 9 and misleading words to me until **t** take a turn.
2:22 He reveals deep and hidden **t**;
11:36 shall speak horrendous **t** against the God of gods.
12: 7 all these **t** would be accomplished. B
12: 8 "My lord, what shall be the outcome of these **t**?"
Hos 2:18 and the creeping **t** of the ground;
9: 6 Nettles shall possess their precious **t** of silver;
14: 9 Those who are wise understand these **t**;
Joel 2:20 Surely he has done great **t**! E
2:21 for the LORD has done great **t**! E
Mic 2: 6 "one should not preach of such **t**;
7:15 of the land of Egypt, show us marvelous **t**.
7:17 like the crawling **t** of the earth;
Hab 1:14 like crawling **t** that have no ruler.
Zec 3: 8 For they are an omen of **t** to come: F
4:10 the day of small **t** shall rejoice,
8:12 the remnant of this people to possess all these **t**. B
8:16 These are the **t** that you shall do:
8:17 for all these are **t** that I hate, says the LORD.
Mt 6:32 For it is the Gentiles who strive for all these **t**; B
6:32 that you need all these **t**. B
6:33 and all these **t** will be given to you as well. B
7:11 in heaven give good **t** to those who ask him! C
7:28 Now when Jesus had finished saying these **t**,
9:18 While he was saying these **t** to them,
11:25 because you have hidden these **t** from the wise
11:27 All **t** have been handed over to me by my Father; A
12:34 How can you speak good **t**, when you are evil? C
12:35 good person brings good **t** out of a good treasure, C
12:35 evil person brings evil **t** out of an evil treasure.
13: 3 he told them many **t** in parables, saying: "Listen!
13:34 Jesus told the crowds all these **t** in parables; B
16:23 for you are setting your mind not on divine **t** but
16:23 not on divine things but on human **t**."
17:11 "Elijah is indeed coming and will restore all **t**; A
19: 1 When Jesus had finished saying these **t**,
19:26 but for God all **t** are possible." A
19:28 "Truly I tell you, at the renewal of all **t**, A
21:15 the chief priests and the scribes saw the amazing **t**
21:23 "By what authority are you doing these **t**,
21:24 I will also tell you by what authority I do these **t**.
21:27 by what authority I am doing these **t**.
22:21 "Give therefore to the emperor the **t** that are
22:21 and to God the **t** that are God's."
24:33 So also, when you see all these **t**, B
24:34 not pass away until all these **t** have taken place. B
25:21 you have been trustworthy in a few **t**,
25:21 I will put you in charge of many **t**;
25:23 you have been trustworthy in a few **t**,
25:23 I will put you in charge of many **t**;
26: 1 When Jesus had finished saying all these **t**, B
Mk 4: 2 He began to teach them many **t** in parables,
4:19 the desire for other **t** come in and choke the word,
6:34 and he began to teach them many **t**.
7:13 And you do many **t** like this."
7:15 but the **t** that come out are what defile."
7:23 All these evil **t** come from within,
8:33 For you are setting your mind not on divine **t** but
8:33 not on divine things but on human **t**."
9:12 "Elijah is indeed coming first to restore all **t**. A
9:23 All **t** can be done for the one who believes." A
10:27 for God all **t** are possible." A
11:28 "By what authority are you doing these **t**?
11:29 and I will tell you by what authority I do these **t**.
11:33 by what authority I am doing these **t**."
12:17 "Give to the emperor the **t** that are the emperor's,
12:17 and to God the **t** that are God's."
13: 4 and what will be the sign that all these **t** are B
13:29 So also, when you see these **t** taking place,
13:30 not pass away until all these **t** have taken place. B
14:36 said, "Abba, Father, for you all **t** are possible; A
15: 3 Then the chief priests accused him of many **t**.

Lk 1: 4 so that you may know the truth concerning the **t**
1:20 unable to speak, until the day these **t** occur."
1:49 for the Mighty One has done great **t** for me, E
1:53 he has filled the hungry with good **t**, C
1:65 and all these **t** were talked about throughout B
2:51 His mother treasured all these **t** in her heart. B
3:19 and because of all the evil **t** that Herod had done,
4:23 the **t** that we have heard you did at Capernaum.' "
5:26 saying, "We have seen strange **t** today."
7:18 The disciples of John reported all these **t** to him. B
9: 9 but who is this about whom I hear such **t**?"
9:36 told no one any of the **t** they had seen.
10:21 because you have hidden these **t** from the wise
10:22 All **t** have been handed over to me by my Father; A
10:41 you are worried and distracted by many **t**;
11:41 So give for alms those **t** that are within;
11:45 when you say these **t**, you insult us too."
11:53 and to cross-examine him about many **t**,
12:20 the **t** you have prepared, whose will they be?'
12:30 of the world that strive after all these **t**, B
12:31 and these **t** will be given to you as well.
13:17 at all the wonderful **t** that he was doing.
16:25 during your lifetime you received your good **t**, C
16:25 and Lazarus in like manner evil **t**;
17:20 of God is not coming with **t** that can be observed;
18:34 But they understood nothing about all these **t**; B
19:42 had only recognized on this day the **t** that make
19:45 to drive out those who were selling **t** there;
20: 2 by what authority are you doing these **t**?
20: 8 by what authority I am doing these **t**."
20:25 give to the emperor the **t** that are the emperor's,
20:25 and to God the **t** that are God's."
21: 6 for these **t** that you see, the days will come when
21: 9 for these **t** must take place first,
21:28 Now when these **t** begin to take place,
21:31 So also, when you see these **t** taking place,
21:32 not pass away until all **t** have taken place. A
21:36 to escape all these **t** that will take place, B
23:49 stood at a distance, watching these **t**.
24:14 and talking with each other about all these **t** B
24:18 the **t** that have taken place there in these days?"
24:19 He asked them, "What **t**?"
24:19 They replied, "The **t** about Jesus of Nazareth,
24:21 it is now the third day since these **t** took place.
24:26 the Messiah should suffer these **t** and then enter
24:27 to them the **t** about himself in all the scriptures.
24:48 You are witnesses of these **t**.
Jn 1: 3 All **t** came into being through him, A
1:50 You will see greater **t** than these."
2:16 "Take these **t** out of here!
3: 9 Nicodemus said to him, "How can these **t** be?"
3:10 and yet you do not understand these **t**?
3:12 If I have told you about earthly **t** and you do
3:12 can you believe if I tell you about heavenly **t**?
3:31 to the earth and speaks about earthly **t**.
3:35 The Father loves the Son and has placed all **t** A
4: 9 (Jews do not share **t** in common with Samaritans.)
4:25 "When he comes, he will proclaim all **t** to us." A
5:16 because he was doing such **t** on the sabbath.
5:34 but I say these **t** so that you may be saved.
6:59 He said these **t** while he was teaching in
7: 4 If you do these **t**, show yourself to the world."
7:32 The Pharisees heard the crowd muttering such **t**
8:28 but I speak these **t** as the Father instructed me.
8:30 As he was saying these **t**, many believed in him.
12:16 His disciples did not understand these **t** at first;
12:16 that these **t** had been written of him
13: 3 that the Father had given all **t** into his hands, A
13:17 you know these **t**, you are blessed if you do them.
14:25 "I have said these **t** to you while I am still
15:11 I have said these **t** to you so that my joy may be
15:21 But they will do all these **t** to you on account B
16: 1 "I have said these **t** to you to keep you
16: 4 But I have said these **t** to you so that
16: 4 "I did not say these **t** to you from the beginning,
16: 6 But because I have said these **t** to you,
16:12 "I still have many **t** to say to you,
16:13 and he will declare to you the **t** that are to come.
16:25 "I have said these **t** to you in figures of speech.
16:30 Now we know that you know all **t**, A
17:13 and I speak these **t** in the world so
19:36 These **t** occurred so that the scripture might
19:38 After these **t**, Joseph of Arimathea,
20:18 and she told them that he had said these **t** to her.
21: 1 After these **t** Jesus showed himself again to
21:24 This is the disciple who is testifying to these **t**
21:25 But there are also many other **t** that Jesus did;
Ac 2:44 All who believed were together and had all **t** A
4:25 and the peoples imagine vain **t**?
5:11 the whole church and all who heard of these **t**.
5:32 And we are witnesses to these **t**,
6:13 "This man never stops saying **t** against this holy
7: 1 Then the high priest asked him, "Are these **t** so?"
7:50 Did not my hand make all these **t**?' B
7:54 When they heard these **t**,
13:42 to speak about these **t** again the next sabbath.
14:15 that you should turn from these worthless **t** to
15:17 who has been making these **t**
15:20 from **t** polluted by idols and from fornication and
15:24 have said **t** to disturb you
15:27 who themselves will tell you the same **t** by word
17:11 to see whether these **t** were so.
17:25 to all mortals life and breath and all **t**. A
18:17 But Gallio paid no attention to any of these **t**.
18:25 and taught accurately the **t** concerning Jesus,
19:21 Now after these **t** had been accomplished,
19:36 Since these **t** cannot be denied,

Ac 21:19 he related one by one the **t** that God had done
26: 9 I myself was convinced that I ought to do many **t**
26:16 and testify to the **t** in which you have seen me and
26:26 Indeed the king knows about these **t**,
26:26 that none of these **t** has escaped his notice,
Ro 1:20 and seen through the **t** he has made.
1:28 a debased mind and to **t** that should not be done.
1:32 that those who practice such **t** deserve to die—
2: 1 because you, the judge, are doing the very same **t**.
2: 2 that God's judgment on those who do such **t** is
2: 3 that when you judge those who do such **t** and
4:17 to the dead and calls into existence the **t** that do
6:21 So what advantage did you then get from the **t**
6:21 The end of those **t** is death.
8: 5 according to the flesh set their minds on the **t** of
8: 5 to the Spirit set their minds on the **t** of the Spirit.
8:28 We know that all **t** work together for good A
8:31 What then are we to say about these **t**?
8:37 in all these **t** we are more than conquerors B
8:38 nor **t** present, nor things to come, nor powers,
8:38 nor things present, nor **t** to come, nor powers, F
10: 5 "the person who does these **t** will live by them."
11:36 from him and through him and to him are all **t**. A
15:27 also to be of service to them in material **t**.
1Co 1:28 **t** that are not, to reduce to nothing **t** that are,
2:10 these **t** God has revealed to us through the Spirit;
2:13 of these **t** in words not taught by human wisdom
2:13 interpreting spiritual **t** to those who are spiritual.
2:15 Those who are spiritual discern all **t**, A
3:21 about human leaders. For all **t** are yours, A
4: 5 the **t** now hidden in darkness and will disclose
4:13 the dregs of all **t**, to this very day. A
6:12 "All **t** are lawful for me," A
6:12 but not all **t** are beneficial. A
6:12 "All **t** are lawful for me," but I will not be A
8: 6 from whom are all **t** and for whom we exist, A
8: 6 whom are all **t** and through whom we exist. A
9:22 I have become all **t** to all people, A
9:25 Athletes exercise self-control in all **t**; A
10: 6 Now these **t** occurred as examples for us,
10:11 These **t** happened to them to serve as an example,
10:23 "All **t** are lawful," A
10:23 but not all **t** are beneficial. A
10:23 "All **t** are lawful," but not all things build up. A
10:23 "All things are lawful," but not all **t** build up. A
11:12 but all **t** come from God. A
11:34 the other **t** I will give instructions when I come.
13: 7 bears all **t**, believes all things, hopes all things, A
13: 7 bears all things, believes all **t**, hopes all things, A
13: 7 bears all things, believes all things, hopes all **t**, A
13: 7 hopes all things, endures all **t**. A
14:26 Let all **t** be done for building up. A
14:40 but all **t** should be done decently and in order. A
15:27 "God has put all **t** in subjection under his feet." A
15:27 But when it says, "All **t** are put in subjection," A
15:27 that this does not include the one who put all **t** A
15:28 When all **t** are subjected to him, A
15:28 subjected to the one who put all **t** in subjection A
2Co 2:16 Who is sufficient for these **t**?
4: 2 We have renounced the shameful **t** that one hides;
11: 6 and in all **t** we have made this evident to you. A
11:28 besides other **t**, I am under daily pressure because
11:30 I will boast of the **t** that show my weakness.
12: 4 was caught up into Paradise and heard **t** that are
13:10 So I write these **t** while I am away from you,
13:11 Put **t** in order, listen to my appeal,
Gal 2:18 I build up again the very **t** that I once tore down,
3:10 and obey all the **t** written in the book of the law."
3:22 has imprisoned all **t** under the power of sin, A
5:21 drunkenness, carousing, and **t** like these.
5:21 those who do such **t** will not inherit the kingdom
5:23 There is no law against such **t**.
6: 6 the word must share in all good **t** C
Eph 1:10 to gather up all **t** in him, A
1:10 **t** in heaven and **t** on earth.
1:11 to the purpose of him who accomplishes all **t** A
1:22 And he has put all **t** under his feet A
1:22 has made him the head over all **t** for the church, A
3: 9 for ages in God who created all **t**; A
4:10 so that he might fill all **t**.) A
5: 6 for because of these **t** the wrath of God comes
Php 2:14 Do all **t** without murmuring and arguing, A
2:23 therefore to send him as soon as I see how **t** go
3: 1 To write the same **t** to you is not troublesome
3: 8 For his sake I have suffered the loss of all **t**, A
3:19 their minds are set on earthly **t**.
3:21 enables him to make all **t** subject to himself. A
4: 8 of praise, think about these **t**.
4: 9 the **t** that you have learned and received and heard
4:13 I can do all **t** through him who strengthens me. A
Col 1:16 in him all **t** in heaven and on earth were created, A
1:16 **t** visible and invisible, whether thrones
1:16 all **t** have been created through him and for him. A
1:17 He himself is before all **t**, A
1:17 and in him all **t** hold together. A
1:20 God was pleased to reconcile to himself all **t**, A
2:22 All these regulations refer to **t** that perish
3: 1 seek the **t** that are above, where Christ is,
3: 2 Set your minds on **t** that are above, not on **t** that
are on earth,
3: 8 But now you must get rid of all such **t**—
1Th 2:14 the same **t** from your own compatriots as they did
4: 6 because the Lord is an avenger in all these **t**, B
2Th 2: 5 that I told you these **t** when I was still with you?
3: 4 and will go on doing the **t** that we command.
1Ti 1: 7 or the **t** about which they make assertions.
3:11 not slanderers, but temperate, faithful in all **t**. A
1Ti 4:11 These are the **t** you must insist on and teach.
4:15 Put these **t** into practice, devote yourself to them,
4:16 continue in these **t**, for in doing this you will save
6:13 In the presence of God, who gives life to all **t**, A
2Ti 2: 7 for the Lord will give you understanding in all **t**. A
2:21 **t** I have mentioned will become special utensils,
3:11 my persecutions and suffering the **t** that happened
Tit 1:15 To the pure all **t** are pure, A
2:15 Declare these **t**; exhort and reprove with all
3: 8 I desire that you insist on these **t**,
3: 8 these **t** are excellent and profitable to everyone.
Heb 1: 2 whom he appointed heir of all **t**, A
1: 3 and he sustains all **t** by his powerful word. A
2: 8 subjecting all **t** under their feet." A
2: 8 Now in subjecting all **t** to them, A
2:10 for whom and through whom all **t** exist, A
2:14 he himself likewise shared the same **t**,
3: 4 but the builder of all **t** is God.) A
3: 5 to testify to the **t** that would be spoken later.
5: 1 in charge of **t** pertaining to God on their behalf,
6: 9 beloved, we are confident of better **t** in your case,
t that belong to salvation.
6:18 so that through two unchangeable **t**,
7:13 the one of whom these **t** are spoken belonged
9: 5 Of these **t** we cannot speak now in detail.
9:10 until the time comes to set **t** right.
9:11 when Christ came as a high priest of the good **t** C
9:23 of the heavenly **t** to be purified with these rites,
9:23 heavenly **t** themselves need better sacrifices than
10: 1 law has only a shadow of the good **t** to come CF
11: 1 Now faith is the assurance of **t** hoped for, the
conviction of **t** not seen.
11: 3 what is seen was made from **t** that are not visible.
12:27 of what is shaken—that is, created **t**—
13:18 desiring to act honorably in all **t**. A
1Pe 1:12 in regard to the **t** that have now been announced
1:12 **t** into which angels long to look!
1:18 not with perishable **t** like silver or gold,
4: 7 The end of all **t** is near; A
4:11 God may be glorified in all **t** through Jesus A
2Pe 1: 4 Thus he has given us, through these **t**,
1: 8 if these **t** are yours and are increasing among you,
1: 9 anyone who lacks these **t** is nearsighted and blind,
1:12 I intend to keep on reminding you of these **t**,
1:15 be able at any time to recall these **t**.
3: 4 all **t** continue as they were from the beginning A
3:11 Since all these **t** are to be dissolved in this way, B
3:14 beloved, while you are waiting for these **t**,
3:16 There are some **t** in them hard to understand,
1Jn 1: 4 We are writing these **t** so that our joy may
2: 1 I am writing these **t** to you so that you may not sin.
2:15 Do not love the world or the **t** in the world.
2:26 I write these **t** to you concerning those who
2:27 But as his anointing teaches you about all **t**, A
5:13 I write these **t** to you who believe in the name of
Jude 1:10 and they are destroyed by those **t** that,
1:15 of all the harsh **t** that ungodly sinners have spoken
Rev 2:14 But I have a few **t** against you:
2:24 not learned what some call 'the deep **t** of Satan,'
4:11 you created all **t**, and by your will they existed A
16: 5 who are and were, for you have judged these **t**;
21: 4 for the first **t** have passed away."
21: 5 "See, I am making all **t** new." A
21: 7 Those who conquer will inherit these **t**,
22: 8 I, John, am the one who heard and saw these **t**.
22:20 The one who testifies to these **t** says,
Tob 2:14 These **t** are known about you!"
7:11 until you settle the **t** that pertain to me."
12: 6 the living for the good **t** he has done for you. C
12:20 down all these **t** that have happened to you." B
14: 4 that all these **t** will take place B
Jdt 5:22 When Achior had finished saying these **t**,
7:28 do today the **t** that we have described!"
8: 1 Now in those days Judith heard about these **t**:
8:14 to search out God, who made all these **t**, B
9: 5 "For you have done these **t** and those that went
9: 5 You have designed the **t** that are now,
9: 6 **t** you decided on presented themselves and said,
9:13 and bruise on those who have planned cruel **t**
10: 9 and accomplish the **t** you have just said to me."
11:13 **t** it is not lawful for any of the people even
11:16 to accomplish with you **t** that will astonish
12: 2 I will have enough with the **t** I brought with me."
15: 8 in Jerusalem came to witness the good **t** that C
15:11 and hitched up her carts and piled the **t** on them.
AdE 1: 1 after this that the following **t** happened in the days
2: 1 After these **t**, the king's anger abated,
2:15 she neglected none of the **t** that Gai,
4: 9 Hachratheus went in and told Esther all these **t**. B
5:13 But these **t** give me no pleasure as long
9:20 Mordecai recorded these **t** in a book,
10: 4 Mordecai said, "These **t** have come from God;
12: 4 The king made a permanent record of these **t**,
12: 5 and rewarded him for these **t**.
13: 9 "O Lord, Lord, you rule as King over all **t**, A
13:12 You know all **t**; you know, A
13:14 and I will not do these **t** in pride.
14:15 You have knowledge of all **t**, A
16:18 the one who did these **t**, has been hanged at
16:18 for God, who rules over all **t**, A
16:21 For God, who rules over all **t**, A
Wis 1: 7 which holds all **t** together knows what is said, A
1: 8 therefore those who utter unrighteous **t** will
1:10 because a jealous ear hears all **t**, A
1:14 For he created all **t** so that they might exist; A
2: 6 therefore, let us enjoy the good **t** that exist, C
3:14 who has not devised wicked **t** against the Lord;
Wis 5: 9 "All those **t** have vanished like a shadow,
6:10 For they will be made holy who observe holy **t** D
7:11 All good **t** came to me along with her, C
7:22 the fashioner of all **t**, taught me. A
7:24 her pureness she pervades and penetrates all **t**. A
7:27 Although she is but one, she can do all **t**, A
7:27 and while remaining in herself, she renews all **t**; A
8: 1 and she orders all **t** well. A
8: 5 the active cause of all **t**? A
8: 8 she knows the **t** of old, and infers the things
8: 8 and infers the **t** to come; F
8:17 When I considered these **t** inwardly,
9: 1 who have made all **t** by your word, A
9:11 For she knows and understands all **t**, A
10: 2 and gave him strength to rule all **t**. A
10:10 and gave him knowledge of holy **t**; D
11: 5 the very **t** by which their enemies were punished,
11:16 that one is punished by the very **t**
11:20 But you have arranged all **t** by measure A
11:23 But you are merciful to all, for you can do all **t**, A
11:24 For you love all **t** that exist, A
11:24 and detest none of the **t** that you have made,
11:26 You spare all **t**, for they are yours, O Lord, A
12: 1 For your immortal spirit is in all **t**. A
12: 2 and warn them of the **t** through which they sin,
12:15 You are righteous and you rule all **t** righteously, A
13: 1 and they were unable from the good **t** C
13: 3 in the beauty of these **t** people assumed them to
13: 5 from the greatness and beauty of created **t** comes
13: 7 because the **t** that are seen are beautiful.
13: 9 did they fail to find sooner the Lord of these **t**?
13:10 But miserable, with their hopes set on dead **t**,
14:31 it is not the power of the **t** by which people swear,
15: 1 patient, and ruling all **t** in mercy. A
15: 6 Lovers of evil **t** and fit for such objects
16: 9 because they deserved to be punished by such **t**.
16:17 in water, which quenches all **t**, A
16:20 of these **t** you gave your people food of angels,
17: 6 and in terror they deemed the **t** that they saw to
18: 9 so that the saints would share alike the same **t**,
18:14 For while gentle silence enveloped all **t**, A
18:16 and stood and filled all **t** with death, A
Sir 1: 4 Wisdom was created before all other **t**,
2: 9 You who fear the Lord, hope for good **t**, C
7:31 and the first fruits of the holy **t**. D
11: 3 but what it produces is the best of sweet **t**.
11:14 Good **t** and bad, life and death, C
15:13 such **t** are not loved by those who fear him.
16: 5 Many such **t** my eye has seen,
16: 5 and my ear has heard **t** more striking than these.
16:29 and filled it with his good **t**. C
18:26 all **t** move swiftly before the Lord. A
19: 1 one who despises small **t** will fail little by little.
24: 8 "Then the Creator of all **t** gave me a command, A
25: 1 I take pleasure in three **t**,
26: 5 Of three **t** my heart is frightened,
26:28 At two **t** my heart is grieved,
27:24 I have hated many **t**, but him above all;
30:18 Good **t** poured out upon a mouth that is closed C
34: 9 An educated person knows many **t**,
34:10 An inexperienced person knows few **t**,
34:12 I have seen many **t** in my travels,
34:31 and goes again and does the same **t**,
39:25 the beginning good **t** were created for the good, C
39:25 but for sinners good **t** and bad. C
42: 1 Of the following **t** do not be ashamed,
42: 6 and where there are many hands, lock **t** up.
42:18 he sees from of old the **t** that are to come.
42:19 and he reveals the traces of hidden **t**.
42:23 All these **t** live and remain forever; B
42:24 All **t** come in pairs, one opposite the other, A
43:22 A mist quickly heals all **t**; A
43:25 all kinds of living **t**, and huge sea-monsters.
43:26 and by his word all **t** hold together. A
43:32 Many **t** greater than these lie hidden,
43:33 For the Lord has made all **t**, A
45:13 Before him such beautiful **t** did not exist.
48:25 and the hidden **t** before they happened.
50:28 with these **t**, and those who lay them
51:12 *Give thanks to him who formed all* ***t***, A
51:24 Why do you say you are lacking in these **t**,
Bar 3:32 But the one who knows all **t** knows her, A
LtJ 6:29 Since you know by these **t** that they are not gods,
6:39 These **t** that are made of wood and overlaid
6:47 then can the **t** that are made by them be gods?
Sus 1:41 not tell us. These **t** we testify."
1:42 you know what is secret and are aware of all **t** A
1:43 the wicked **t** that they have charged against me!"
1Mc 4:27 **t** had not happened to Israel as he had intended,
5:37 After these **t** Timothy gathered another army
6: 8 **t** had not turned out for him as he had planned.
6:27 they will do still greater **t**,
6:59 that they became angry and did all these **t**." B
9:37 After these **t** it was reported to Jonathan
9:44 for today **t** are not as they were before.
10:22 of these **t** he was distressed and said,
10:88 When King Alexander heard of these **t**,
11:29 and wrote a letter to Jonathan about all these **t**; B
11:42 only will I do these **t** for you and your nation,
12: 9 Therefore, though we have no need of these **t**,
13: 3 "You yourselves know what great **t** my brothers E
14: 9 they all talked together of good **t**, C
14:25 When the people heard these **t** they said,
14:35 because he had done all these **t** and because of B
14:36 In his days **t** prospered in his hands,
14:38 of these **t** King Demetrius confirmed him in
15:24 a copy of these **t** to the high priest Simon.

1Mc 16: 2 until this day, and **t** have prospered in our hands
16:18 a report about these **t** and sent it to the king,
2Mc 1:21 the liquid on the wood and on the **t** laid upon it.
1:24 O Lord, Lord God, Creator of all **t**, A
2: 8 Then the Lord will disclose these **t**,
2:13 The same **t** are reported in the records and in
6: 4 besides brought in **t** for sacrifice that were unfit.
6:20 the courage to refuse **t** that it is not right to taste,
6:30 but in my soul I am glad to suffer these **t**
7:18 For we are suffering these **t** on our own account,
7:18 Therefore astounding **t** have happened.
7:23 of humankind and devised the origin of all **t**, A
7:28 that God did not make them out of **t** that existed.
10:38 When they had accomplished these **t**,
12:14 and even blaspheming and saying unholy **t**.
12:22 the manifestation to them of him who sees all **t**. A
12:41 who reveals the **t** that are hidden;
13: 9 the Jews **t** far worse than those that had been done
15: 2 that he who sees all **t** has honored and hallowed A
1Es 1:17 So the **t** that had to do with the sacrifices to
1:33 These **t** are written in the book of the histories of
1:33 and the **t** that he had done before,
1:42 But the **t** that are reported about Jehoiakim,
1:56 and utterly destroyed all its glorious **t**.
2: 7 besides the other **t** added as votive offerings for
3:12 but above all **t** truth is victor." A
3:24 since it forces people to do these **t**?"
4:19 they let all those **t** go,
4:32 why are not women strong, since they do such **t**?"
4:35 Is not the one who does these **t** great?
4:35 But truth is great, and stronger than all **t**. A
4:37 all their works are unrighteous, and all such **t**.
5:40 Attharias told them not to share in the holy **t** D
6: 4 and this roof and finishing all the other **t**?
6: 4 who are the builders that are finishing these **t**?"
6:22 let him send us directions concerning these **t**."
6:32 or nullify any of the **t** herein written,
8: 1 After these **t**, when Artaxerxes,
8:21 Let all **t** prescribed in the law of God A
8:53 And again we prayed to our Lord about these **t**,
8:68 After these **t** had been done,
8:71 As soon as I heard these **t** I tore my garments
8:82 what shall we say, when we have these **t**?
8:85 so that you may be strong and eat the good **t** of C
8:90 in your presence because of these **t**."
9:11 for we have sinned too much in these **t**.
Man 1: 4 at whom all **t** shudder, and tremble A
3Mc 2: 3 you, the creator of all **t** and the governor of all, A
2:21 Thereupon God, who oversees all **t**, A
3:21 Among other **t**, we made known
4:16 praising speechless **t** that are not able even
5:28 This was the act of God who rules over all **t**, A
5:28 a forgetfulness of the **t** he had previously devised.
5:37 must I give you orders about these **t**?
6: 6 to the flames so as not to serve vain **t**,
6:22 because of the **t** that he had devised beforehand.
6:29 These then were the **t** he said;
6:36 a public rite for these **t** in their whole community
7: 8 at all or reproaching them for the irrational **t**
7:18 the king had generously provided all **t** to them A
2Es 1:37 with the spirit they will believe the **t** I have said.
3: 8 they did ungodly **t** in your sight
4: 6 that you should ask me about such **t**?"
4: 9 **t** that you have experienced and
4:10 the **t** with which you have grown up;
4:23 but about those **t** that we daily experience:
4:25 It is about these **t** that I have asked."
4:27 not be able to bring the **t** that have been promised
4:33 When will these **t** be?
4:42 so also do these places hasten to give back those **t**
4:43 **t** that you desire to see will be disclosed to you."
5:13 you shall hear yet greater **t** than these."
5:38 to know these **t** except he whose dwelling is not
5:39 concerning the **t** that you have asked me?"
5:40 "Just as you cannot do one of the **t**
6: 6 then I planned these **t**, and they were made
6:30 "I have come to show you these **t** this night.
6:31 I will again declare to you greater **t** than these,
6:33 Therefore he sent me to show you all these **t**, B
6:53 wild animals, and creeping **t**;
7: 6 and it is full of all good **t**; C
7:14 they can never receive those **t**
7:17 in your law that the righteous shall inherit these **t**,
7:25 empty **t** are for the empty, and full **t** are for the full.
7:*44* and to you alone I have shown these **t**."
7:57 therefore which **t** are precious and desirable,
7:*62* of the dust like the other created **t**?
7:*70* he first prepared the judgment and the **t**
7:*101* so that during these seven days they may see the **t**
8:37 "Some **t** you have spoken rightly,
8:44 and for whose sake you have formed all **t**— A
8:46 "**T** that are present are for those who live now,
and **t** that are future are for those who will live
8:59 For just as the **t** that I have predicted await you,
9:35 but the **t** that held them remain;
9:38 When I said these **t** in my heart, I looked around,
10:22 our holy **t** have been polluted, D
10:38 and tell you about the **t** that you fear;
10:52 that the Most High would reveal these **t** to you.
11: 6 I saw how all **t** under heaven were subjected to A
12:23 and they shall renew many **t** in it,
12:37 write all these **t** that you have seen in a book, B
13:18 because they understand the **t** that are reserved for
13:20 Yet it is better to come into these **t**,
13:21 also explain to you the **t** that you have mentioned.
13:32 When these **t** take place and the signs occur
13:56 Therefore I have shown you these **t**;
2Es 13:56 that after three more days I will tell you other **t**,
13:58 and whatever **t** come to pass in their seasons.
14: 5 I told him many wondrous **t**,
14:21 and so no one knows the **t** which have been done
14:22 the **t** that were written in your law,
14:26 you have finished, some **t** you shall make public,
16:35 Listen now to these **t**, and understand them,
16:62 surely made all **t** and searches out hidden things A
16:62 surely made all things and searches out hidden **t**
4Mc 4: 4 When Apollonius learned the details of these **t**,
5: 9 not to enjoy delicious **t** that are not shameful,
5:25 that in the nature of **t** the Creator of the world
6:14 destroying yourself through these evil **t**?
8:12 When he had said these **t**,
8:27 of these **t** nor even seriously considered them.
9:10 When they had said these **t**,
9:19 While he was saying these **t**,
11: 5 of all **t** and live according to his virtuous law? A
11: 9 While he was saying these **t**,
12:11 since you have received good **t** and C

THINK‡ (103) [THINKING, THINKS, THOUGHT, THOUGHTFUL, THOUGHTLESS, THOUGHTLESSLY, THOUGHTS]

Nu 36: 6 'Let them marry whom they **t** best;
2Sa 10: 3 to their lord Hanun, "Do you really **t** that David
18:27 "I **t** the running of the first one is like the running
2Ki 10: 5 do whatever you **t** right."
18:20 Do you **t** that mere words are strategy and power
1Ch 19: 3 "Do you **t**, because David has sent consolers
2Ch 13: 8 now you **t** that you can withstand the kingdom of
Est 4:13 to reply to Esther, "Do not **t** that in
Job 4: 7 "**T** now, who that was innocent ever perished?
6:26 Do you **t** that you can reprove words,
21: 6 When I **t** of it I am dismayed,
35: 2 "Do you **t** this to be just?
41: 8 **t** of the battle; you will not do it again!
41:32 one would **t** the deep to be white-haired.
Ps 10: 6 They **t** in their heart, "We shall not be moved;
10:11 They **t** in their heart, "God has forgotten,
41: 8 They **t** that a deadly thing has fastened on me,
59: 7 for "Who," they **t**, "will hear us?"
63: 6 when I **t** of you on my bed, and meditate on you
77: 3 I **t** of God, and I moan;
119:52 When I **t** of your ordinances from of old,
119:59 I **t** of your ways, I turn my feet to your decrees;
143: 5 I **t** about all your deeds,
144: 3 or mortals that you **t** of them?
Pr 12:15 Fools **t** their own way is right,
Isa 36: 5 Do you **t** that mere words are strategy and power
Jer 13:12 "Do you **t** we do not know
40: 4 go wherever you **t** it good and right to go.
40: 5 or go wherever you **t** it right to go."
44:19 do you **t** that we made cakes for her,
Eze 11: 5 This is what you **t**, O house of Israel;
Mt 5:17 "Do not **t** that I have come to abolish the law or
6: 7 for they **t** that they will be heard because
9: 4 said, "Why do you **t** evil in your hearts?
10:34 not **t** that I have come to bring peace to the earth;
17:25 Jesus spoke of it first, asking, "What do you **t**,
18:12 What do you **t**? If a shepherd has a hundred sheep,
21:28 "What do you **t**? A man had two sons;
22:17 Tell us, then, what you **t**.
22:42 "What do you **t** of the Messiah?
26:53 Do you **t** that I cannot appeal to my Father,
Lk 10:36 Which of these three, do you **t**,
12:51 Do you **t** that I have come to bring peace to
13: 2 "Do you **t** that because these Galileans suffered
13: 4 do you **t** that they were worse offenders than all
Jn 5:39 because you **t** that in them you have eternal life;
5:45 Do not **t** that I will accuse you before the Father;
11:56 as they stood in the temple, "What do you **t**?
16: 2 an hour is coming when those who kill you will **t**
Ac 17:29 we ought not to **t** that the deity is like gold,
28:22 But we would like to hear from you what you **t**,
Ro 12: 3 not to **t** of yourself more highly than you ought to
t, but to **t** with sober judgment,
1Co 3:18 If you **t** that you are wise in this age,
4: 1 **T** of us in this way,
4: 9 I **t** that God has exhibited us apostles as last of all,
7:26 I **t** that, in view of the impending crisis,
7:40 And I **t** that I too have the Spirit of God.
8: 7 they still **t** of the food they eat as food offered to
10:12 So if you **t** you are standing,
12:23 of the body that we **t** less honorable we clothe
2Co 10: 2 to oppose those who **t** we are acting according
11: 5 I **t** that I am not in the least inferior
11:16 I repeat, let no one **t** that I am a fool;
12: 6 that no one may **t** better of me than what is seen
Gal 5:10 in the Lord that you will not **t** otherwise.
6: 3 For if those who are nothing **t** they are something,
Php 1: 7 It is right for me to **t** this way about all of you,
2:25 I **t** it necessary to send to you Epaphroditus—
3:15 and if you **t** differently about anything,
4: 8 and if there is anything worthy of praise, **t** about
2Ti 2: 7 **T** over what I say, for the Lord will give you
Heb 10:29 How much worse punishment do you **t** will
Jas 1:26 If any **t** they are religious,
2Pe 1:13 I **t** it right, as long as I am in this body,
3: 9 as some **t** of slowness, but is patient with you,
AdE 8: 8 Write in my name what you **t** best and seal it
Wis 1: 1 **t** of the Lord in goodness and seek him
Sir 15: 8 and liars will never **t** of her.
18:24 **T** of his wrath on the day of death,
Sir 18:25 In the time of plenty **t** of the time of hunger;
18:25 in days of wealth **t** of poverty and need.
25: 7 I can **t** of nine whom I would call blessed,
LtJ 6:40 Why then must anyone **t** that they are gods,
6:44 Why then must anyone **t** that they are gods,
6:56 then must anyone admit or **t** that they are gods?
6:64 Therefore one must not **t** that they are gods,
Bel 1: 6 "Do you not **t** that Bel is a living god?
2Mc 7:16 But do not **t** that God has forsaken our people.
7:19 not **t** that you will go unpunished for having tried
9:12 mortals should not **t** that they are equal to God."
1Es 2:20 we **t** it best not to neglect such a matter,
2Es 4: 2 and do you **t** you can comprehend the way of
4:51 "Do you **t** that I shall live until those days?
6:34 to **t** vain thoughts concerning the former times;
8:28 Do not **t** of those who have lived wickedly
8:51 But **t** of your own case,
16:63 He knows your imaginations and what you **t**
4Mc 1:33 I for one **t** so.
5:16 to govern our lives by the divine law, **t**
6:17 **t** so basely that out of cowardice we feign
9:30 To the tyrant he said, "Do you not **t**,

THINKING (34) [THINK]

Ge 20:10 "What were you **t** of, that you did this thing?"
26: 7 for he was afraid to say, "My wife," **t**,
32: 8 **t**, "If Esau comes to the one company
Dt 15: 9 **t**, "The seventh year, the year of remission,
29:19 **t** in their hearts, "We are safe even
Jdg 16: 2 They kept quiet all night, **t**,
1Sa 27:11 **t**, "They might tell about us, and say,
27:12 **t**, "He has made himself utterly abhorrent
2Sa 5: 6 **t**, "David cannot come in here."
2Ki 7:12 **t**, 'When they come out of the city,
2Ch 32: 1 **t** to win them for himself.
Ne 5: 7 After **t** it over, I brought charges against
6: 9 **t**, "Their hands will drop from the work,
Ps 64: 5 they talk of laying snares secretly, **t**,
Mal 1: 7 By **t** that the LORD's table may be despised.
Mt 12:25 He knew what they were **t** and said to them,
Lk 6: 8 Even though he knew what they were **t**,
11:17 But he knew what they were **t** and said to them,
Ac 10:19 While Peter was still **t** about the vision,
Ro 1:21 but they became futile in their **t**,
1Co 4:18 But some of you, **t** that I am not coming to you,
14:20 Brothers and sisters, do not be children in your **t**;
14:20 rather, be infants in evil, but in **t** be adults.
2Co 12:19 Have you been **t** all along
Col 2:18 puffed up without cause by a human way of **t**,
Heb 11:15 If they had been **t** of the land that they had left
Wis 12:10 and that their way of **t** would never change.
17: 3 For **t** that in their secret sins they were unobserved
Sir 13:26 but to devise proverbs requires painful **t**.
17: 6 ears and a mind for **t** he gave them.
1Mc 5:61 **t** to do a brave deed,
2Mc 4:32 **t** he had obtained a suitable opportunity,
5:21 **t** in his arrogance that he could sail on the land
14:14 **t** that the misfortunes and calamities of

THINKS (6) [THINK]

1Sa 20: 3 and he **t**, 'Do not let Jonathan know this,
La 3:20 My soul continually **t** of it and is bowed down
Ro 14:14 but it is unclean for anyone who **t** it unclean.
1Co 7:36 If anyone **t** that he is not behaving properly
Sir 16:23 a senseless and misguided person **t** foolishly.
4Mc 13:14 Let us not fear him who **t** he is killing us,

THIRD‡ (195) [THREE]

A. THE THIRD DAY (53)
B. THIRD OF (19)

Ge 1:13 and there was morning, the **t** day. A
2:14 The name of the **t** river is Tigris,
6:16 make it with lower, second, and **t** decks.
22: 4 On the **t** day Abraham looked up and saw A
31:22 On the **t** day Laban was told that Jacob had fled. A
32:19 He likewise instructed the second and the **t**
34:25 On the **t** day, when they were still in pain, A
40:20 On the **t** day, which was Pharaoh's birthday, A
42:18 On the **t** day Joseph said to them, A
50:23 Joseph saw Ephraim's children of the **t** generation;
Ex 19: 1 the **t** new moon after the Israelites had gone out
19:11 and prepare for the **t** day, A
19:11 because on the **t** day the LORD will come down A
19:15 he said to the people, "Prepare for the **t** day; A
19:16 On the morning of the **t** day there was thunder A
20: 5 of parents, to the **t** and the fourth generation
28:19 and the **t** row a jacinth, an agate, and an amethyst;
34: 7 to the **t** and the fourth generation."
39:12 the **t** row, a jacinth, an agate, and an amethyst;
Lev 7:17 of the sacrifice shall be burned up on the **t** day. A
7:18 eaten on the **t** day, it shall not be acceptable, A
19: 6 over until the **t** day shall be consumed in fire. A
19: 7 is eaten at all on the **t** day, it is an abomination; A
Nu 2:24 They shall set out **t** on the march.
7:24 On the **t** day Eliab son of Helon, A
14:18 the children to the **t** and the fourth generation.'
19:12 the water on the **t** day and on the seventh day, A
19:12 if they do not purify themselves on the **t** day A
19:19 the unclean ones on the **t** day and on A
29:20 On the **t** day: eleven bulls, A
31:19 and your captives on the **t** and on the seventh day.
Dt 5: 9 of parents, to the **t** and fourth generation
14:28 Every **t** year you shall bring out the full tithe
23: 8 The children of the **t** generation that are born

Dt 26:12 of your produce in the **t** year (which is the year of
Jos 9:17 and reached their cities on the **t** day. A
17:11 of Megiddo and its villages (the **t** is Naphath).
19:10 The **t** lot came up for the tribe of Zebulun,
Jdg 20:30 up against the Benjaminites on the **t** day, A
1Sa 3:8 The LORD called Samuel again, a **t** time.
17:13 and next to him Abinadab, and the **t** Shammah.
19:21 Saul sent messengers again the **t** time,
20:5 so that I may hide in the field until the **t** evening.
20:12 about this time tomorrow, or on the **t** day, A
30:1 David and his men came to Ziklag on the **t** day, A
2Sa 1:2 On the **t** day, a man came from Saul's camp, A
3:3 the **t**, Absalom son of Maacah,
18:2 one **t** under the command of Joab, one **t** under the
18:2 and one **t** under the command of Ittai the Gittite.
1Ki 3:18 Then on the **t** day after I gave birth, A
6:6 and the **t** was seven cubits wide;
6:8 and from the middle story to the **t**.
12:12 and all the people came to Rehoboam the **t** day, A
12:12 "Come to me again the **t** day." A
15:28 So Baasha killed Nadab in the **t** year of King Asa
15:33 In the **t** year of King Asa of Judah,
18:1 in the **t** year of the drought, saying, "Go,
18:34 Again he said, "Do it a **t** time";
18:34 and they did it a **t** time,
22:2 But in the **t** year King Jehoshaphat of Judah came
2Ki 1:13 the king sent the captain of a **t** fifty with his fifty.
1:13 So the **t** captain of fifty went up,
11:6 (another **t** being at the gate Sur and a third at
11:6 the gate Sur and a **t** at the gate behind the guards),
18:1 In the **t** year of King Hoshea son of Elah of Israel,
19:29 then in the **t** year sow, reap, plant vineyards,
20:5 on the **t** day you shall go up to the house of A
20:8 up to the house of the LORD on the **t** day?" A
1Ch 2:13 Abinadab the second, Shimea the **t**,
3:2 the **t** Absalom, son of Maacah, daughter
3:15 the second Jehoiakim, the **t** Zedekiah,
8:1 Ashbel the second, Aharah the **t**,
8:39 Jeush the second, and Eliphelet the **t**.
12:9 Ezer the chief, Obadiah second, Eliab **t**,
23:19 Jahaziel the **t**, and Jekameam the fourth.
24:8 the **t** to Harim, the fourth to Seorim,
24:23 Jahaziel the **t**, Jekameam the fourth.
25:10 the **t** to Zaccur, his sons and his brothers, twelve;
26:2 Zebadiah the **t**, Jathniel the fourth,
26:4 Joah the **t**, Sachar the fourth, Nethanel the fifth,
26:11 Tebaliah the **t**, Zechariah the fourth:
27:5 The **t** commander, for the **t** month,
2Ch 10:12 and all the people came to Rehoboam the **t** day, A
10:12 "Come to me again the **t** day." A
15:10 They were gathered at Jerusalem in the **t** month
17:7 In the **t** year of his reign he sent his officials,
23:4 This is what you are to do: one **t** of you, B
23:5 one **t** shall be at the king's house, and one **t** at
27:5 the same amount in the second and the **t** years.
31:7 In the **t** month they began to pile up the heaps,
Ezr 6:15 and this house was finished on the **t** day of A
Est 1:3 in the **t** year of his reign,
5:1 the **t** day Esther put on her royal robes and A
8:9 in the **t** month, which is the month of Sivan,
Job 42:14 the second Keziah, and the **t** Keren-happuch.
Isa 19:24 On that day Israel will be the **t** with Egypt
37:30 then in the **t** year sow, reap, plant vineyards,
Jer 38:14 and received him at the **t** entrance of the temple
Eze 5:2 One **t** of the hair you shall burn in the fire inside B
5:2 one **t** you shall take and strike with the sword all
5:2 and one **t** you shall scatter to the wind,
5:12 One **t** of you shall die of pestilence or B
5:12 one **t** shall fall by the sword around you;
5:12 and one **t** I will scatter to every wind
10:14 the **t** that of a lion, and the fourth that of an eagle.
31:1 In the eleventh year, in the **t** month,
Da 1:1 In the **t** year of the reign of King Jehoiakim
2:39 and yet a **t** kingdom of bronze,
5:7 and rank **t** in the kingdom."
5:16 and rank **t** in the kingdom."
5:29 concerning him that he should rank **t** in
8:1 In the **t** year of the reign of King Belshazzar
10:1 In the **t** year of King Cyrus of Persia
Hos 6:2 on the **t** day he will raise us up, A
Zec 6:3 the **t** chariot white horses,
13:9 And I will put this **t** into the fire,
Mt 16:21 and be killed, and on the **t** day be raised. A
17:23 and on the **t** day he will be raised." A
20:19 and on the **t** day he will be raised." A
22:26 The second did the same, so also the **t**,
26:44 he went away and prayed for the **t** time,
27:64 the tomb to be made secure until the **t** day; A
Mk 12:21 leaving no children; and the **t** likewise;
14:41 He came a **t** time and said to them,
Lk 9:22 and be killed, and on the **t** day be raised." A
13:32 and on the **t** day I finish my work. A
18:33 and on the **t** day he will rise again." A
20:12 And he sent still a **t**;
20:31 and the **t** married her,
23:22 A **t** time he said to them, "Why,
24:7 and be crucified, and on the **t** day rise again." A
24:21 it is now the **t** day since these things took place. A
24:46 to suffer and to rise from the dead on the **t** day, A
Jn 2:1 On the **t** day there was a wedding in Cana A
21:14 now the **t** time that Jesus appeared to the disciples
21:17 He said to him the **t** time, "Simon son of John,
21:17 Peter felt hurt because he said to him the **t** time,
Ac 10:40 God raised him on the **t** day and allowed him A
27:19 on the **t** day with their own hands they threw A
1Co 12:28 second prophets, **t** teachers;
15:4 he was raised on the **t** day in accordance with A
2Co 12:2 fourteen years ago was caught up to the **t** heaven—
12:14 Here I am, ready to come to you this **t** time.
13:1 This is the **t** time I am coming to you.
Rev 4:7 the **t** living creature with a face like a human face,
6:5 When he opened the **t** seal,
6:5 I heard the **t** living creature call out, "Come!"
8:7 and a **t** of the earth was burned up, B
8:7 and a **t** of the trees were burned up, B
8:9 A **t** of the sea became blood, B
8:9 a **t** of the living creatures in the sea died, B
8:9 and a **t** of the ships were destroyed. B
8:10 The **t** angel blew his trumpet,
8:10 and it fell on a **t** of the rivers and on the springs B
8:11 A **t** of the waters became wormwood, B
8:12 and a **t** of the sun was struck, B
8:12 and a **t** of the moon, and a third of the stars, B
8:12 and a third of the moon, and a **t** of the stars, B
8:12 so that a **t** of their light was darkened; B
8:12 a **t** of the day was kept from shining, B
9:15 month, and the year, to kill a **t** of humankind. B
9:18 a **t** of humankind was killed, B
11:14 The **t** woe is coming very soon.
12:4 a **t** of the stars of heaven and threw them to B
14:9 Then another angel, a **t**, followed them,
16:4 The **t** angel poured his bowl into the rivers and
21:19 first was jasper, the second sapphire, the **t** agate,
Tob 1:8 A **t** tenth I would give to the orphans and widows
1:8 I would bring it and give it to them in the **t** year,
AdE 1:3 in the **t** year of his reign,
15:1 On the **t** day, when she ended her prayer, A
Sir 23:16 of individuals multiply sins, and a **t** incurs wrath.
23:23 against her husband; and **t**,
26:28 and because of a **t** anger comes over me:
45:23 of Eleazar ranks **t** in glory for being zealous in
50:25 and the **t** is not even a people:
1Mc 10:30 and instead of collecting the **t** of the grain and B
14:27 which is the **t** year of the great high priest Simon,
2Mc 7:10 After him, the **t** was the victim of their sport.
1Es 3:12 The **t** wrote, "Women are strongest,
4:13 Then the **t**, who had spoken of women and truth
3Mc 5:40 ordering now for a **t** time that they be destroyed,
2Es 5:4 into confusion after the **t** period;
6:42 "On the **t** day you commanded the waters to A
6:44 These were made on the **t** day. A
6:51 that had been dried up on the **t** day, to live in it, A
7:*83* The **t** way, they shall see the reward laid up
7:*94* The **t** order, they see the witness
11:18 Then the **t** wing raised itself up,
14:1 On the **t** day, while I was sitting under an oak, A
4Mc 10:1 the **t** was led in, and many repeatedly urged him
15:18 at you piteously nor when the **t** expired;

THIRST‡ (36) [THIRSTED, THIRSTS, THIRSTY]

Ex 17:3 to kill us and our children and livestock with **t**?"
Dt 28:48 against you, in hunger and **t**, in nakedness
Jdg 15:18 Am I now to die of **t**,
2Ch 32:11 handing you over to die by famine and by **t**,
Ne 9:15 their **t** you brought water for them out of the rock,
9:20 and gave them water for their **t**.
Job 24:11 they tread the wine presses, but suffer **t**.
Ps 69:21 and for my **t** they gave me vinegar to drink.
104:11 the wild asses quench their **t**.
Isa 5:13 and their multitude is parched with **t**.
41:17 and their tongue is parched with **t**,
48:21 not **t** when he led them through the deserts;
49:10 they shall not hunger or **t**,
50:2 their fish stink for lack of water, and die of **t**.
Jer 2:25 from going unshod and your throat from **t**.
La 4:4 of the infant sticks to the roof of its mouth for **t**;
Hos 2:3 into a parched land, and kill her with **t**.
Am 8:11 not a famine of bread, or a **t** for water,
8:13 and the young men shall faint for **t**.
Mt 5:6 "Blessed are those who hunger and **t**
Rev 7:16 They will hunger no more, and **t** no more;
Jdt 7:13 of Bethulia get their water. So **t** will destroy them,
7:22 and the women and young men fainted from **t**
7:25 to be strewn before them in **t** and exhaustion.
8:31 Then we will no longer feel faint from **t**."
Wis 11:4 and from hard stone a remedy for their **t**.
11:8 showing by their **t** at that time
11:14 they felt **t** in a different way from the righteous.
Sir 24:21 and those who drink of me will **t** for more.
51:24 and why do you endure such great **t**?
2Es 8:59 so the **t** and torment that are prepared await them.
15:58 for bread and drink their own blood in **t** for water.
4Mc 1:26 covetousness, **t** for honor, rivalry, and malice;
3:6 by the story of King David's **t**.
3:10 he could not satisfy his **t** from them.
3:15 But David, though he was burning with **t**,

THIRSTED (1) [THIRST]

Ex 17:3 But the people **t** there for water;

THIRSTS (4) [THIRST]

Ps 42:2 My soul **t** for God, for the living God.
63:1 you are my God, I seek you, my soul **t** for you;
143:6 my soul **t** for you like a parched land.
Isa 55:1 Ho, everyone who **t**, come to the waters;

THIRSTY‡ (41) [THIRST]

Jdg 4:19 "Please give me a little water to drink; for I am **t**."
15:18 By then he was very **t**,
Ru 2:9 If you get **t**, go to the vessels and drink from what
2Sa 17:29 "The troops are hungry and weary and **t** in
Job 5:5 and the **t** pant after their wealth.
Ps 107:5 hungry and **t**, their soul fainted within them.
107:9 For he satisfies the **t**, and the hungry he fills
107:33 springs of water into **t** ground,
Pr 25:21 and if they are **t**, give them water to drink;
25:25 Like cold water to a **t** soul,
30:16 the barren womb, the earth ever **t** for water,
Isa 21:14 Bring water to the **t**, meet the fugitive with bread,
29:8 a **t** person dreams of drinking and wakes up faint,
still **t**, so shall the multitude of all the nations be
32:6 and to deprive the **t** of drink.
35:7 and the **t** ground springs of water;
44:3 For I will pour water on the **t** land,
65:13 my servants shall drink, but you shall be **t**;
Eze 19:13 into the wilderness, into a dry and **t** land.
Mt 25:35 I was **t** and you gave me something to drink,
25:37 or **t** and gave you something to drink?
25:42 I was **t** and you gave me nothing to drink,
25:44 or **t** or a stranger or naked or sick or in prison,
Jn 4:13 of this water will be **t** again,
4:14 of the water that I will give them will never be **t**.
4:15 that I may never be **t** or have to keep coming here
6:35 and whoever believes in me will never be **t**.
7:37 he cried out, "Let anyone who is **t** come to me,
19:28 he said (in order to fulfill the scripture), "I am **t**."
Ro 12:20 if they are **t**, give them something to drink;
1Co 4:11 To the present hour we are hungry and **t**,
2Co 11:27 hungry and **t**, often without food, cold and naked.
Rev 21:6 To the **t** I will give water as a gift from the spring
22:17 And let everyone who is **t** come.
Jdt 8:30 the people were so **t** that they compelled us to do
Wis 11:4 When they were **t**, they called upon you,
Sir 26:12 As a **t** traveler opens his mouth and drinks
2Es 1:17 When you were hungry and **t** in the wilderness,
1:20 When you were **t**, did I not split the rock so
1:22 at the bitter stream, **t** and blaspheming my name,
4Mc 3:10 but the king was extremely **t**,

THIRTEEN (13) [THIRTEENTH]

Ge 17:25 And his son Ishmael was **t** years old
Nu 29:13 **t** young bulls, two rams, fourteen male lambs
29:14 three-tenths of an ephah for each of the **t** bulls,
Jos 19:6 **t** towns with their villages;
21:4 the priest received by lot **t** towns from the tribes
21:6 The Gershonites received by lot **t** towns from
21:19 were **t** in all, with their pasture lands.
21:33 of the Gershonites were in all **t**,
1Ki 7:1 Solomon was building his own house **t** years,
1Ch 6:60 All their towns throughout their families were **t**.
6:62 to their families were allotted **t** towns out of
26:11 all the sons and brothers of Hosah totaled **t**.
Eze 40:11 and the width of the gateway, **t** cubits.

THIRTEENTH‡ (19) [THIRTEEN]

Ge 14:4 but in the **t** year they rebelled.
1Ch 24:13 the **t** to Huppah, the fourteenth to Jeshebeab,
25:20 the **t**, Shubael, his sons and his brothers, twelve;
Est 3:7 and the lot fell on the **t** day of the twelfth month,
3:12 on the **t** day of the first month, and an edict,
3:13 in one day, the **t** day of the twelfth month,
8:12 on the **t** day of the twelfth month,
9:1 which is the month of Adar, on the **t** day,
9:17 This was on the **t** day of the month of Adar,
9:18 the Jews who were in Susa gathered on the **t** day
Jer 1:2 in the **t** year of his reign.
25:3 the **t** year of King Josiah son of Amon of Judah,
AdE 3:12 So on the **t** day of the first month
8:12 the **t** of the twelfth month, which is Adar,
9:1 Now on the **t** day of the twelfth month,
16:20 so that on the **t** day of the twelfth month, Adar,
1Mc 7:43 the armies met in battle on the **t** day of the month
7:49 be celebrated each year on the **t** day of Adar.
2Mc 15:36 but to celebrate the **t** day of the twelfth month—

THIRTIETH‡ (3) [THIRTY]

Eze 1:1 In the **t** year, in the fourth month,
2Mc 11:30 by the **t** of Xanthicus will have our pledge
2Es 3:1 In the **t** year after the destruction of the city,

THIRTY‡ (133) [THIRTIETH]

Ge 5:3 When Adam had lived one hundred **t** years,
5:5 that Adam lived were nine hundred **t** years;
5:16 after the birth of Jared eight hundred **t** years,
6:15 its width fifty cubits, and its height **t** cubits.
11:14 When Shelah had lived **t** years,
11:17 after the birth of Peleg four hundred **t** years,
11:18 When Peleg had lived **t** years,
11:22 When Serug had lived **t** years,
18:30 Suppose **t** are found there."
18:30 He answered, "I will not do it, if I find **t** there."
32:15 **t** milch camels and their colts,
41:46 Joseph was **t** years old when he entered
47:9 years of my earthly sojourn are one hundred **t**;
Ex 12:40 in Egypt was four hundred **t** years.
12:41 At the end of four hundred **t** years,
21:32 the owner shall pay to the slaveowner **t** shekels
26:8 The length of each curtain shall be **t** cubits,
36:15 The length of each curtain was **t** cubits,
38:24 and seven hundred **t** shekels,
Lev 27:4 the person is a female, the equivalent is **t** shekels.
Nu 4:3 from **t** years old up to fifty years old,
4:23 from **t** years old up to fifty years old
4:30 from **t** years old up to fifty years old
4:35 from **t** years old up to fifty years old,

Nu 4:39 from **t** years old up to fifty years old,
4:40 ancestral houses was two thousand six hundred **t.**
4:43 from **t** years old up to fifty years old,
4:47 from **t** years old up to fifty years old,
7:13 one silver plate weighing one hundred **t** shekels,
7:19 one silver plate weighing one hundred **t** shekels,
7:25 one silver plate weighing one hundred **t** shekels,
7:31 one silver plate weighing one hundred **t** shekels,
7:37 one silver plate weighing one hundred **t** shekels,
7:43 one silver plate weighing one hundred **t** shekels,
7:49 one silver plate weighing one hundred **t** shekels,
7:55 one silver plate weighing one hundred **t** shekels,
7:61 one silver plate weighing one hundred **t** shekels,
7:67 one silver plate weighing one hundred **t** shekels,
7:73 one silver plate weighing one hundred **t** shekels,
7:79 one silver plate weighing one hundred **t** shekels,
7:85 each silver plate weighing one hundred **t** shekels
20:29 all the house of Israel mourned for Aaron **t** days.
26:7 enrolled was forty-three thousand seven hundred **t.**
26:51 six hundred and one thousand seven hundred **t.**
31:39 The donkeys were **t** thousand five hundred,
31:45 **t** thousand five hundred donkeys,
Dt 34:8 for Moses in the plains of Moab **t** days;
Jos 8:3 Joshua chose **t** thousand warriors
Jdg 10:4 He had **t** sons who rode on **t** donkeys; and they had **t** towns, which are in the land of Gilead,
12:9 He had **t** sons. He gave his **t** daughters in marriage outside his clan and brought in **t** young women
12:14 He had forty sons and **t** grandsons,
14:11 they brought **t** companions to be with him.
14:12 then I will give you **t** linen garments and **t** festal
14:13 give me **t** linen garments and **t** festal garments."
14:19 He killed **t** men of the town, took their spoil,
20:31 killing about **t** men of Israel.
20:39 on the Israelites, killing about **t** of them;
1Sa 4:10 for there fell of Israel **t** thousand foot soldiers.
9:22 of whom there were about **t.**
13:5 **t** thousand chariots, and six thousand horsemen,
2Sa 5:4 David was **t** years old when he began to reign,
6:1 the chosen men of Israel, **t** thousand.
23:13 the beginning of harvest three of the **t** chiefs went
23:18 the brother of Joab, was chief of the **T.**
23:19 He was the most renowned of the **T,**
23:23 He was renowned among the **T,**
23:24 Among the **T** were Asahel brother of Joab;
1Ki 4:22 Solomon's provision for one day was **t** cors
5:13 the levy numbered **t** thousand men.
6:2 twenty cubits wide, and **t** cubits high.
7:2 fifty cubits wide, and **t** cubits high,
7:6 of Pillars fifty cubits long and **t** cubits wide.
7:23 A line of **t** cubits would encircle it completely.
2Ki 18:14 of silver and **t** talents of gold.
1Ch 11:15 of the **t** chiefs went down to the rock to David at
11:20 Abishai, the brother of Joab, was chief of the **T.**
11:21 He was the most renowned of the **T,**
11:25 He was renowned among the **T,**
11:42 a leader of the Reubenites, and **t** with him,
12:4 warrior among the **T** and a leader over the **T;**
12:18 Then the spirit came upon Amasai, chief of the **T,**
15:7 Joel the chief, with one hundred **t** of his kindred;
23:3 The Levites, **t** years old and upward,
27:6 a mighty man of the **T** and in command of the **T;**
2Ch 4:2 A line of **t** cubits would encircle it completely.
24:15 he was one hundred **t** years old at his death.
35:7 from the flock to the number of **t** thousand,
Ezr 1:9 And this was the inventory: gold basins, **t;**
1:10 gold bowls, **t;** other silver bowls,
2:35 Of Senaah, three thousand six hundred **t.**
Ne 7:38 Of Senaah, three thousand nine hundred **t.**
7:70 fifty basins, and five hundred **t** priestly robes.
Est 4:11 not been called to come in to the king for **t** days."
Pr 22:20 for you **t** sayings of admonition and knowledge,
Eze 40:17 **t** chambers fronted on the pavement.
41:6 one over another, **t** in each story.
46:22 forty cubits long and **t** wide;
Da 6:7 divine or human, for **t** days, except to you,
6:12 divine or human, within **t** days except to you,
Zec 11:12 they weighed out as my wages **t** shekels of silver.
11:13 So I took the **t** shekels of silver and threw them
Mt 13:8 some a hundredfold, some sixty, some **t.**
13:23 in another sixty, and in another **t.**"
26:15 They paid him **t** pieces of silver.
27:3 the **t** pieces of silver to the chief priests and
27:9 "And they took the **t** pieces of silver,
Mk 4:8 up and increasing and yielding **t** and sixty and
4:20 **t** and sixty and a hundredfold."
Lk 3:23 about **t** years old when he began his work.
Jn 2:6 each holding twenty or **t** gallons.
Gal 3:17 the law, which came four hundred **t** years later,
Jdt 15:11 All the people plundered the camp for **t** days.
AdE 1:7 made of ruby, worth **t** thousand talents.
4:11 now **t** days since I was called to go to the king.' "
1Mc 10:36 to the number of **t** thousand men,
2Mc 12:9 of the light was seen in Jerusalem, **t** miles distant.
12:23 and destroyed as many as **t** thousand.
1Es 1:7 who were present Josiah gave **t** thousand lambs
2:13 twenty-nine silver censers, **t** gold bowls,
5:23 three thousand three hundred **t.**
2Es 3:29 soul has seen many sinners during these **t** years.
9:43 though I lived with my husband for **t** years.
9:44 during those **t** years I prayed to the Most High,
9:45 And after **t** years God heard your servant,
10:45 for her telling you that she was barren for **t** years,

THIRTY-EIGHT (4) [THIRTY-EIGHTH]

Dt 2:14 until we crossed the Wadi Zered was **t** years,
1Ch 23:3 were counted, and the total was **t** thousand.
Ne 7:45 of Akkub, of Hatita, of Shobai, one hundred **t.**
Jn 5:3 One man was there who had been ill for **t** years.

THIRTY-EIGHTH (3) [THIRTY-EIGHT]

1Ki 16:29 In the **t** year of King Asa of Judah,
2Ki 15:8 In the **t** year of King Azariah of Judah,
Sir Pr:3 in the **t** year of the reign of Euergetes and stayed

THIRTY-FIFTH (1) [THIRTY-FIVE]

2Ch 15:19 And there was no more war until the **t** year of

THIRTY-FIRST (1) [THIRTY-ONE]

1Ki 16:23 In the **t** year of King Asa of Judah,

THIRTY-FIVE (11) [THIRTY-FIFTH]

Ge 11:12 When Arpachshad had lived **t** years,
Nu 1:37 of Benjamin were **t** thousand four hundred.
2:23 as enrolled of **t** thousand four hundred.
1Ki 22:42 Jehoshaphat was **t** years old when he began
2Ch 3:15 of the house he made two pillars **t** cubits high,
20:31 He was **t** years old when he began to reign;
Ezr 2:67 four hundred **t** camels,
Ne 7:69 four hundred **t** camels,
Da 12:12 and attain the thousand three hundred **t** days.
2Mc 15:27 they laid low at least **t** thousand,
1Es 5:43 There were four hundred **t** camels,

THIRTY-FOUR (3)

Ge 11:16 When Eber had lived **t** years,
1Ch 7:7 by genealogies was twenty-two thousand **t.**
Jdt 7:20 chariots, and cavalry, surrounded them for **t** days,

THIRTY-NINE (2) [THIRTY-NINTH]

Ezr 2:42 of Hatita, and of Shobai, in all one hundred **t.**
1Es 5:28 the descendants of Shobai, in all one hundred **t.**

THIRTY-NINTH (3) [THIRTY-NINE]

2Ki 15:13 Shallum son of Jabesh began to reign in the **t** year
15:17 In the **t** year of King Azariah of Judah,
2Ch 16:12 In the **t** year of his reign Asa was diseased

THIRTY-ONE (3) [THIRTY-FIRST]

Jos 12:24 the king of Tirzah one **t** kings in all.
2Ki 22:1 he reigned **t** years in Jerusalem.
2Ch 34:1 he reigned **t** years in Jerusalem.

THIRTY-SECOND (2) [THIRTY-TWO]

Ne 5:14 from the twentieth year to the **t** year
13:6 the **t** year of King Artaxerxes of Babylon I went

THIRTY-SEVEN (10) [THIRTY-SEVENTH]

Ge 25:17 of the life of Ishmael, one hundred **t** years;
Ex 6:16 the length of Levi's life was one hundred **t** years.
6:20 length of Amram's life was one hundred **t** years.
Nu 31:36 three hundred **t** thousand five hundred sheep
31:43 three hundred **t** thousand five hundred sheep
2Sa 23:39 Uriah the Hittite—**t** in all.
1Ch 12:34 with whom there were **t** thousand armed
Ezr 2:65 there were seven thousand three hundred **t;**
Ne 7:67 there were seven thousand three hundred **t;**
1Es 5:42 were seven thousand three hundred **t;**

THIRTY-SEVENTH (4) [THIRTY-SEVEN]

2Ki 13:10 In the **t** year of King Joash of Judah,
25:27 In the **t** year of the exile of King Jehoiachin
Jer 52:31 In the **t** year of the exile of King Jehoiachin
1Mc 1:10 to reign in the one hundred **t** year of the kingdom

THIRTY-SIX (7) [THIRTY-SIXTH]

Nu 31:38 The oxen were **t** thousand,
31:44 **t** thousand oxen,
Jos 7:5 The men of Ai killed about **t** of them,
1Ch 7:4 **t** thousand, for they had many wives and sons.
Ezr 2:66 They had seven hundred **t** horses,
Ne 7:68 They had seven hundred **t** horses,
1Es 5:43 and seven thousand **t** horses,

THIRTY-SIXTH (1) [THIRTY-SIX]

2Ch 16:1 In the **t** year of the reign of Asa,

THIRTY-THREE (7)

Ge 46:15 in all his sons and his daughters numbered **t**).
Ex 6:18 length of Kohath's life was one hundred **t** years.
Lev 12:4 Her time of blood purification shall be **t** days;
2Sa 5:5 over all Israel and Judah **t** years.
1Ki 2:11 he reigned seven years in Hebron, and **t** years
1Ch 3:4 And he reigned **t** years in Jerusalem.
29:27 he reigned seven years in Hebron, and **t** years

THIRTY-TWO‡ (17) [THIRTY-SECOND]

Ge 11:20 When Reu had lived **t** years,
Nu 1:35 of Manasseh were **t** thousand two hundred.
2:21 a company as enrolled of **t** thousand two hundred.
26:37 of those enrolled was **t** thousand five hundred.
31:35 and **t** thousand persons in all,
31:40 of which the LORD's tribute was **t** persons.
1Ki 20:1 **t** kings were with him, along with horses
20:15 the district governors, two hundred **t;**
20:16 he and the **t** kings allied with him.
1Ki 22:31 the king of Aram had commanded the **t** captains
2Ki 8:17 He was **t** years old when he became king,
1Ch 19:7 They hired **t** thousand chariots and the king
2Ch 21:5 Jehoram was **t** years old when he began to reign;
21:20 He was **t** years old when he began to reign;
Jer 52:29 into exile from Jerusalem eight hundred **t** persons;
1Mc 6:30 and **t** elephants accustomed to war.
1Es 5:15 The descendants of Azaru, four hundred **t.**

THIS (3373) [THESE] See Index of Articles Etc.

THISBE (1)

Tob 1:2 of the Assyrians was taken into captivity from **T,**

THISTLE (1) [THISTLEDOWN, THISTLES]

Hos 10:8 Thorn and **t** shall grow up on their altars.

THISTLEDOWN (1) [THISTLE]

Wis 5:14 hope of the ungodly is like **t** carried by the wind,

THISTLES (4) [THISTLE]

Ge 3:18 thorns and **t** it shall bring forth for you;
Isa 34:13 nettles and **t** in its fortresses.
Mt 7:16 Are grapes gathered from thorns, or figs from **t?**
Heb 6:8 But if it produces thorns and **t,**

THOCANOS See Index to Footnotes

THOMAS (11)

Mt 10:3 **T** and Matthew the tax collector;
Mk 3:18 and Matthew, and **T,** and James son of Alphaeus,
Lk 6:15 and **T,** and James son of Alphaeus, and Simon,
Jn 11:16 **T,** who was called the Twin,
14:5 **T** said to him, "Lord, we do not know
20:24 But **T** (who was called the Twin),
20:26 in the house, and **T** was with them.
20:27 Then he said to **T,** "Put your finger here
20:28 **T** answered him, "My Lord and my God!"
21:2 **T** called the Twin, Nathanael of Cana in Galilee,
Ac 1:13 and John, and James, and Andrew, Philip and **T,**

THONG (5) [SANDAL-THONG, THONGS]

Mk 1:7 I am not worthy to stoop down and untie the **t**
Lk 3:16 I am not worthy to untie the **t** of his sandals.
Jn 1:27 I am not worthy to untie the **t** of his sandal."
Ac 13:25 I am not worthy to untie the **t** of the sandals
Sir 33:27 Yoke and **t** will bow the neck,

THONGS (4) [THONG]

Isa 58:6 to undo the **t** of the yoke,
Ac 22:25 But when they had tied him up with **t,**
2Mc 7:1 under torture with whips and **t,**
4Mc 9:11 they bound his hands and arms with **t**

THORN (6) [THORNBUSH, THORNBUSHES, THORNS]

Isa 55:13 Instead of the **t** shall come up the cypress;
Eze 28:24 a pricking brier or a piercing **t**
Hos 10:8 **T** and thistle shall grow up on their altars.
Mic 7:4 the most upright of them a **t** hedge.
2Co 12:7 a **t** was given me in the flesh,
Sir 24:15 Like cassia and camel's **t** I gave forth perfume,

THORNBUSH (6) [BUSH, THORN]

2Ki 14:9 "A **t** on Lebanon sent to a cedar on Lebanon,
14:9 of Lebanon passed by and trampled down the **t.**
2Ch 25:18 "A **t** on Lebanon sent to a cedar on Lebanon,
25:18 of Lebanon passed by and trampled down the **t.**
Pr 26:9 Like a **t** brandished by the hand of a drunkard is
LtJ 6:71 like a **t** in a garden on which every bird perches;

THORNBUSHES (1) [BUSH, THORN]

Isa 7:19 and in the clefts of the rocks, and on all the **t,**

THORNS (51) [THORN]

Ge 3:18 **t** and thistles it shall bring forth for you;
Ex 22:6 in **t** so that the stacked grain or the standing grain
Nu 33:55 be as barbs in your eyes and **t** in your sides;
Jos 23:13 a scourge on your sides, and **t** in your eyes,
Jdg 8:7 I will trample your flesh on the **t** of the wilderness
8:16 the city and he took **t** of the wilderness and briers
2Sa 23:6 the godless are all like **t** that are thrown away;
Job 5:5 and they take it even out of the **t;**
31:40 let **t** grow instead of wheat,
Ps 58:9 Sooner than your pots can feel the heat of **t,**
118:12 they blazed like a fire of **t;**
Pr 15:19 The way of the lazy is overgrown with **t,**
22:5 **T** and snares are in the way of the perverse;
24:31 it was all overgrown with **t;**
Ecc 7:6 For like the crackling of **t** under a pot,
Isa 5:6 and it shall be overgrown with briers and **t;**
7:23 will become briers and **t.**
7:24 for all the land will be briers and **t;**
7:25 you will not go there for fear of briers and **t;**
9:18 like a fire, consuming briers and **t;**
10:17 it will burn and devour his **t** and briers in one day.
27:4 If it gives me **t** and briers,
32:13 the soil of my people growing up in **t** and briers;
33:12 like **t** cut down, that are burned in the fire."

Isa 34:13 T shall grow over its strongholds,
Jer 4: 3 up your fallow ground, and do not sow among t.
12:13 They have sown wheat and have reaped t,
Eze 2: 6 and t surround you and you live among scorpions;
Hos 2: 6 Therefore I will hedge up her way with t;
9: 6 t shall be in their tents.
Na 1:10 Like t they are entangled,
Mt 7:16 Are grapes gathered from t, or figs from thistles?
13: 7 Other seeds fell among t, and the t grew up and
13:22 As for what was sown among t,
27:29 and after twisting some t into a crown,
Mk 4: 7 Other seed fell among t, and the t grew up and
4:18 And others are those sown among the t:
15:17 twisting some t into a crown, they put it on him.
Lk 6:44 Figs are not gathered from t,
8: 7 Some fell among t, and the t grew with it and
8:14 As for what fell among the t,
Jn 19: 2 soldiers wove a crown of t and put it on his head,
19: 5 wearing the crown of t and the purple robe.
Heb 6: 8 But if it produces t and thistles,
Sir 28:24 As you fence in your property with t,
43:19 and icicles form like pointed t.
2Es 16:32 and its roads and all its paths shall bring forth t,
16:77 with underbrush and its path overwhelmed with t,

THOROUGH (4) [THOROUGHLY]

Dt 13:14 then you shall inquire and make a t investigation.
17: 4 and you make a t inquiry,
19:18 and the judges shall make a t inquiry.
Ac 23:15 that you want to make a more t examination

THOROUGHLY (9) [THOROUGH]

Ge 11: 3 "Come, let us make bricks, and burn them t."
Lev 14:41 He shall have the inside of the house scraped t,
Dt 9:21 grinding it t, until it was reduced to dust;
Ps 51: 2 Wash me t from my iniquity,
Jer 6: 9 Glean t as a vine the remnant of Israel;
Mk 7: 3 do not eat unless they t wash their hands,
Ac 23:20 they were going to inquire more t into his case.
2Mc 3:38 for you will get him back t flogged,
4Mc 1:29 and prunes and ties up and waters and t irrigates,

THOSE (2220) [THAT] See Index of Articles Etc.

THOUGH‡ (394) [ALTHOUGH]

Ge 31:30 Even t you had to go because you longed greatly
31:50 t no one else is with us,
50:20 Even t you intended to do harm to me,
Ex 21:18 t not dead, is confined to bed,
Lev 5: 1 t able to testify as one who has seen or learned of
11: 4 the camel, for even t it chews the cud,
11: 5 The rock badger, for even t it chews the cud,
11: 6 The hare, for even t it chews the cud,
11: 7 for even t it has divided hoofs and is cleft-footed,
13:55 t the disease has not spread, it is unclean;
25:35 they shall live with you as t resident aliens.
26:17 and you shall flee t no one pursues you.
26:26 and t you eat, you shall not be satisfied.
26:36 and they shall fall t no one pursues.
26:37 as if to escape a sword, t no one pursues;
Nu 5:13 so that she is undetected t she has defiled herself,
5:14 t she has not defiled herself;
14:44 even t the ark of the covenant of the LORD,
35:23 and death ensues, t they were not enemies,
Dt 2:11 t the Moabites call them Emim.
2:20 t the Ammonites call them Zamzummim,
18: 8 even t they have income from the sale
28:61 even t not recorded in the book of this law,
29:19 in their hearts, "We are safe even t
33: 6 and not die out, even t his numbers are few.
Jos 17:18 for t it is a forest, you shall clear it and possess it
17:18 t they have chariots of iron, and t they are strong."
Ru 2:13 even t I am not one of your servants."
3:12 But now, t it is true that I am a near kinsman,
1Sa 1: 5 t the LORD had closed her womb.
12:12 t the LORD your God was your king.
15:17 Samuel said, "T you are little in your own eyes,
20:20 as t I shot at a mark.
24:11 t you are hunting me to take my life.
2Sa 3:39 Today I am powerless, even t anointed king;
4: 6 They came inside the house as t to take wheat,
23:10 t his hand clung to the sword.
1Ki 1:18 now suddenly Adonijah has become king, t you,
2:28 for Joab had supported Adonijah t he had
2Ki 3: 2 t not like his father and mother,
5: 1 man, t a mighty warrior, suffered from leprosy.
19:18 t they were no gods but the work
25: 4 t the Chaldeans were all around the city.
1Ch 5: 2 t Judah became prominent among his brothers
12:17 t my hands have done no wrong,
26:10 Shimri the chief (for t he was not the firstborn,
2Ch 30:19 even t not in accordance with
Ezr 2:59 t they could not prove their families
3:12 t many shouted aloud for joy,
9:15 t no one can face you because of this."
Ne 1: 9 t your outcasts are under the farthest skies,
6: 1 in it (t up to that time I had not set up the doors in
Est 4:16 that I will go to the king, t it is against the law;
Job 8: 7 T your beginning was small,
9:15 T I am innocent, I cannot answer him;
9:20 T I am innocent, my own mouth would condemn
9:20 t I am blameless, he would prove me perverse.
10:19 and were as t I had not been,
Job 14: 8 T its root grows old in the earth,
16:17 t there is no violence in my hands,
20: 6 Even t they mount up high as the heavens,
20:12 "T wickedness is sweet in their mouth,
20:12 t they hide it under their tongues,
20:13 t they are loath to let it go,
24:10 t hungry, they carry the sheaves;
27:16 T they heap up silver like dust,
32: 3 t they had declared Job to be in the wrong.
33:14 and in two, t people do not perceive it.
34: 6 t I am without transgression.'
39:13 t its pinions lack plumage.
39:16 t its labor should be in vain, yet it has no fear;
40:23 it is confident t Jordan rushes against its mouth.
41:26 T the sword reaches it, it does not avail,
Ps 23: 4 t I walk through the darkest valley, I fear no evil;
27: 3 T an army encamp against me,
27: 3 t war rise up against me, yet I will be confident.
35:14 as t I grieved for a friend or a brother;
37:10 t you look diligently for their place,
37:24 t we stumble, we shall not fall headlong,
37:36 t I sought them, they could not be found.
46: 2 we will not fear, t the earth should change,
46: 2 t the mountains shake in the heart of the sea;
46: 3 t its waters roar and foam,
46: 3 t the mountains tremble with its tumult.
49:11 t they named lands their own.
49:18 T in their lifetime they count themselves happy
68:13 t they stay among the sheepfolds—
71:15 t their number is past my knowledge.
78:20 Even t he struck the rock so that water gushed out
92: 7 t the wicked sprout like grass
95: 9 and put me to the proof, t they had seen my work.
119:23 Even t princes sit plotting against me,
119:61 T the cords of the wicked ensnare me,
138: 6 For t the LORD is high, he regards the lowly;
138: 7 T I walk in the midst of trouble,
Pr 24:16 for t they fall seven times, they will rise again;
26:26 t hatred is covered with guile,
28: 6 to be crooked in one's ways even t rich.
29:19 for t they understand, they will not give heed.
Ecc 4:12 And t one might prevail against another,
4:14 even t born poor in the kingdom.
5:14 t they are parents of children,
6: 6 Even t he should live a thousand years twice over,
8:12 T sinners do evil a hundred times
8:17 even t those who are wise claim to know,
Isa 1:15 even t you make many prayers, I will not listen;
1:18 t your sins are like scarlet,
1:18 t they are red like crimson,
10:22 t your people Israel were like the sand of the sea,
12: 1 O LORD, for t you were angry with me,
17:10 t you plant pleasant plants and set out slips of
17:11 t you make them grow on the day
22: 3 t they had fled far away.
25:11 T they spread out their hands in the midst of it,
30: 4 For t his officials are at Zoan
30:20 T the Lord may give you the bread of adversity
37:19 t they were no gods, but the work
45: 4 I surname you, t you do not know me.
45: 5 I arm you, t you do not know me,
46: 5 and compare me, as t we were alike?
59:10 among the vigorous as t we were dead.
63:16 t Abraham does not know us and Israel does
Jer 2:11 even t they are no gods?
2:22 T you wash yourself with lye and use much soap,
2:34 t you did not catch them breaking in.
5:22 t the waves toss, they cannot prevail,
5:22 the waves toss, they cannot prevail, t they roar,
11:11 t they cry out to me, I will not listen to them.
12: 6 t they speak friendly words to you.
14:15 the prophets who prophesy in my name t I did
15: 1 T Moses and Samuel stood before me,
25: 4 t the LORD persistently sent you all his servants
26: 5 to you urgently—t you have not heeded—
29:31 Because Shemaiah has prophesied to you, t I did
31:32 a covenant that they broke, t I was their husband,
32: 5 t you fight against the Chaldeans,
32:25 t the city has been given into the hands of
32:33 t I have taught them persistently,
32:35 t I did not command them,
46:23 says the LORD, t it is impenetrable,
48:27 t he was not caught among thieves;
50:11 T you rejoice, t you exult,
50:11 t you frisk about like a heifer on the grass,
51: 5 t their land is full of guilt before the Holy One
51:53 T Babylon should mount up to heaven,
51:53 and t she should fortify her strong height,
52: 7 t the Chaldeans were all around the city.
La 3: 8 t I call and cry for help, he shuts out my prayer;
4: 6 t no hand was laid on it.
Eze 2: 6 t briers and thorns surround you and you live
8:18 and t they cry in my hearing with a loud voice,
11:16 T I removed them far away among the nations,
11:16 and t I scattered them among the countries,
12: 3 t they are a rebellious house.
13: 7 "Says the LORD," even t I did not speak?
14:18 t these three men were in it,
18:11 of these things (t his father does none of them),
26:21 t sought for, you will never be found again,
28: 2 t you compare your mind with the mind of a god.
28: 9 t you are but a mortal, and no god,
33:13 T I say to the righteous that they shall surely live,
33:14 Again, t I say to the wicked,
Da 5:22 even t you knew all this!
10: 7 t a great trembling fell upon them,
11:20 t not in anger or in battle.
Hos 3: 1 t they turn to other gods and love raisin cakes."
4:15 T you play the whore, O Israel,
8:10 T they bargain with the nations,
8:12 T I write for him the multitude of my instructions,
8:13 T they offer choice sacrifices,
8:13 they offer choice sacrifices, t they eat flesh,
9:16 Even t they give birth, I will kill the cherished
Am 5:22 Even t you offer me your burnt offerings
9: 2 T they dig into Sheol, from there
9: 2 t they climb up to heaven,
9: 3 T they hide themselves on the top of Carmel,
9: 3 t they hide from my sight at the bottom of the sea,
9: 4 t they go into captivity in front of their enemies,
Ob 1: 4 T you soar aloft like the eagle,
1: 4 t your nest is set among the stars,
1:16 and shall be as t they had never been.
Na 1:12 "T they are at full strength and many,
1:12 T I have afflicted you, I will afflict you no more.
2: 2 t ravagers have ravaged them
Hab 2:18 t the product is only an idol that cannot speak!
3:17 T the fig tree does not blossom,
3:17 t the produce of the olive fails and
3:17 t the flock is cut off from the fold
Zep 1:13 T they build houses, they shall not inhabit them;
1:13 t they plant vineyards, they shall not drink wine
Zec 8: 6 Even t it seems impossible to the remnant
9: 2 Tyre and Sidon, t they are very wise.
10: 6 and they shall be as t I had not rejected them;
10: 9 T I scattered them among the nations,
Mal 2:14 t she is your companion and your wife
Mt 14: 5 T Herod wanted to put him to death,
26:33 "T all become deserters because of you,
26:35 Peter said to him, "Even t I must die with you,
26:55 with swords and clubs to arrest me as t I were
26:60 t many false witnesses came forward.
Mk 14:29 Peter said to him, "Even t all become deserters,
14:31 he said vehemently, "Even t I must die with you,
14:48 with swords and clubs to arrest me as t I were
Lk 6: 8 Even t he knew what they were thinking,
8:43 and t she had spent all she had on physicians,
11: 8 even t he will not get up and give him anything
18: 4 but later he said to himself, 'T I have no fear
23:50 who, t a member of the council,
Jn 2: 9 where it came from (t the servants who had drawn
6:71 t one of the twelve, was going to betray him.
8:55 t you do not know him.
9:25 One thing I do know, that t I was blind,
10:33 t only a human being, are making yourself God."
10:38 But if I do them, even t you do not believe me,
11: 5 t Jesus loved Martha and her sister and Lazarus,
11:25 Those who believe in me, even t they die,
13:10 And you are clean, t not all of you."
19:38 t a secret one because of his fear of the Jews,
21:11 and t there were so many, the net was not torn.
Ac 3:12 as t by our own power
3:13 t he had decided to release him.
7: 5 even t he had no child.
9: 8 and t his eyes were open, he could see nothing;
13:28 t they found no cause for a sentence of death,
15:24 t with no instructions from us,
17:25 as t he needed anything, since he himself gives
17:27 t indeed he is not far from each one of us.
18:25 t he knew only the baptism of John.
23:20 as t they were going to inquire more thoroughly
28: 4 t he has escaped from the sea,
28:17 t I had done nothing against our people or
28:19 even t I had no charge to bring against my nation.
Ro 1:20 invisible t they are, have been understood
1:21 for t they knew God, they did not honor him
2:14 t not having the law, are a law to themselves.
5: 7 t perhaps for a good person someone might
8:10 Christ is in you, t the body is dead because of sin,
9: 6 It is not as t the word of God had failed.
9:27 "T the number of the children of Israel were like
1Co 2: 6 t it is not a wisdom of this age or of the rulers
4: 9 as t sentenced to death, because we have become
4:15 For t you might have ten thousand guardians
5: 3 For t absent in body, I am present in spirit;
7:29 even those who have wives be as t they had none,
7:30 those who mourn as t they were not mourning,
7:30 those who rejoice as t they were not rejoicing,
7:30 and those who buy as t they had no possessions,
7:31 with the world as t they had no dealings with it.
8: 5 even t there may be so-called gods in heaven or
9:19 For t I am free with respect to all,
9:20 under the law (t I myself am not under the law) so
9:21 the law I became as one outside the law (t I am
9:26 nor do I box as t beating the air;
12:12 t many, are one body, so it is with Christ.
15: 6 most of whom are still alive, t some have died.
15:10 t it was not I, but the grace of God that is
2Co 3:18 as t reflected in a mirror, are being transformed
4:16 Even t our outer nature is wasting away,
5: 6 even t we know that while we are at home in
5:16 even t we once knew Christ from a human point
7: 8 I do not regret it (t I did regret it,
7: 8 that I grieved you with that letter, t only briefly).
8: 9 the generous act of our Lord Jesus Christ, that t
10: 9 not want to seem as t I am trying to frighten you
12:11 not at all inferior to these super-apostles, even t
13: 7 t we may seem to have failed.
Gal 2: 2 before them (t only in a private meeting with
2: 3 with me, was not compelled to be circumcised, t
2:14 I said to Cephas before them all, "If you, t a Jew,
4: 1 t they are the owners of all the property;
4:14 t my condition put you to the test,
Php 2: 6 t he was in the form of God,

Php 3: 4 even **t** I, too, have reason for confidence in
Col 2: 5 For **t** I am absent in body,
1Th 2: 2 but **t** we had already suffered
2: 7 **t** we might have made demands as apostles
2Th 2: 2 by letter, as **t** from us, to the effect that the day of
1Ti 1:13 even **t** I was formerly a blasphemer,
Phm 1: 8 **t** I am bold enough in Christ to command you
Heb 3: 9 **t** they had seen my works
4: 3 **t** his works were finished at the foundation of
5:12 For **t** by this time you ought to be teachers,
6: 9 Even **t** we speak in this way, beloved,
7: 5 **t** these also are descended from Abraham.
11:11 even **t** he was too old—
11:27 he persevered as **t** he saw him who is invisible.
11:39 all these, **t** they were commended for their faith,
12:17 even **t** he sought the blessing with tears.
13: 3 as **t** you were in prison with them;
13: 3 as **t** you yourselves were being tortured.
Jas 3: 4 **t** they are so large that it takes strong winds
1Pe 1: 7 being more precious than gold that, **t** perishable,
1: 8 and even **t** you do not see him now,
2: 4 **t** rejected by mortals yet chosen and precious
2:12 so that, **t** they malign you as evildoers,
4: 6 **t** they had been judged in the flesh
4:12 as **t** something strange were happening to you.
2Pe 1:12 **t** you know them already and are established in
2: 5 even **t** he saved Noah, a herald of righteousness,
2:11 **t** greater in might and power,
2Jn 1: 5 but not as **t** I were writing you a new commandment,
3Jn 1: 5 even **t** they are strangers to you;
Jude 1: 5 I desire to remind you, **t** you are fully informed,
Rev 1:17 When I saw him, I fell at his feet as **t** dead.
2: 9 and your poverty, even **t** you are rich.
Tob 11:15 **T** he afflicted me, he has had mercy upon me.
AdE 11:10 and at their outcry, as **t** from a tiny spring,
Wis 2: 2 and hereafter we shall be as **t** we had never been,
3: 4 For **t** in the sight of others they were punished,
4: 7 But the righteous, **t** they die early, will be at rest.
8:10 in the presence of the elders, **t** I am young.
11: 9 **t** they were being disciplined in mercy,
11:14 For **t** they had mockingly rejected him who long
12: 9 **t** you were not unable to give the ungodly into
12:10 **t** you were not unaware that their origin was evil
12:25 Therefore, as **t** to children who cannot reason,
14:11 because, **t** part of what God created,
14:17 by their zeal they might flatter the absent one as **t**
14:22 but **t** living in great strife due to ignorance,
15:15 **t** these have neither the use of their eyes to see
17:10 **t** it nowhere could be avoided.
18: 2 **t** previously wronged, were doing them no injury;
18:13 For **t** they had disbelieved everything because
19: 2 **t** they themselves had permitted your people
Sir 42:10 or, **t** married, for fear she may be barren.
44: 9 they have perished as **t** they had never existed;
44: 9 they have become as **t** they had never been born,
47: 3 He played with lions as **t** they were young goats,
47: 3 and with bears as **t** they were lambs of the flock.
LtJ 6:18 as **t** under sentence of death,
6:19 **t** their gods can see none of them.
6:40 as **t** Bel were able to understand!
Aza 1:17 as **t** it were with burnt offerings of rams and bulls,
1:27 of the furnace as **t** a moist wind were whistling
Sus 1:43 **t** I have done none of the wicked things
1:53 **t** the Lord said, 'You shall not put an innocent
1Mc 8: 4 even **t** the place was far distant from them.
10:77 and went to Azotus as **t** he were going farther.
12: 9 Therefore, **t** we have no need of these things,
2Mc 2:21 that **t** few in number they seized the whole land
4:34 he persuaded him, **t** still suspicious,
6:30 **t** I might have been saved from death,
7:16 **t** you also are mortal, you do what you please.
12: 3 as **t** there were no ill will to the Jews;
12:18 **t** in one place he had left a very strong garrison.
14:35 **t** you have need of nothing,
14:45 and **t** his blood gushed forth
1Es 5:37 **t** they could not prove by their ancestral houses
5:53 **t** the temple of God was not yet built.
Pm 151: T *as his own composition (**t** it is outside the number),*
3Mc 2: 9 **t** you have no need of anything;
2:24 a while he recovered, and **t** he had been punished,
3: 8 The Greeks in the city, **t** wronged in no way,
4:18 **t** most of them were still in the country,
5:40 as **t** we are idiots, ordering now for a third time
2Es 1:27 It is not as **t** you had forsaken me;
1:37 **t** they do not see me with bodily eyes,
3:33 **t** they are unmindful of your commandments.
7:*43* It will last as **t** for a week of years.
7:72 because **t** they had understanding,
7:*72* and **t** they received the commandments,
7:*72* and **t** they obtained the law,
7:*118* [48] For **t** it was you who sinned,
8:58 **t** they knew well that they must die.
9:10 **t** they received my benefits,
9:32 But **t** our ancestors received the law,
9:43 **t** I lived with my husband for thirty years.
13:20 **t** incurring peril, than to pass from the world like
4Mc 2: 8 even **t** a lover of money,
3:10 and **t** springs were plentiful there,
3:15 But David, **t** he was burning with thirst,
4:25 **t** they had known beforehand
5:22 at our philosophy as **t** living by it were irrational,
6: 2 **t** he remained adorned with the gracefulness
6: 5 was unmoved, as **t** being tortured in a dream;
6:16 as **t** more bitterly tormented by this counsel,
6:27 O God, that **t** I might have saved myself,
7: 2 and **t** buffeted by the stormings of the tyrant
7:12 Eleazar, **t** being consumed by the fire,
4Mc 7:13 Most amazing, indeed, **t** he was an old man,
8: 4 grouped about their mother as **t** a chorus,
8:27 But the youths, **t** about to be tortured,
9: 5 as **t** a short time ago you learned nothing
9:22 but as **t** transformed by fire into immortality,
12: 2 Even **t** the tyrant had been vehemently reproached
14: 5 as **t** running the course toward immortality,
14: 6 as **t** moved by an immortal spirit of devotion,
14:19 as **t** with an iron dart,
15:11 **t** so many factors influenced the mother to suffer
16: 5 If this woman, **t** a mother, had been fainthearted,
16:13 as **t** having a mind like adamant
18:14 which says, 'Even **t** you go through the fire,

THOUGHT (115) [THINK]

Ge 20:11 Abraham said, "I did it because I **t**,
26: 9 "Because I **t** I might die because of her."
31:31 for I **t** that you would take your daughters
32:20 For he **t**, "I may appease him with the present
38:15 When Judah saw her, he **t** her to be a prostitute,
45:20 Give no **t** to your possessions,
Ex 2:14 Then Moses was afraid and **t**,
13:17 for God **t**, "If the people face war,
Nu 33:56 And I will do to you as I **t** to do to them.
Dt 1:39 your little ones, who you **t** would become booty,
1:41 and **t** it easy to go up into the hill country.
15: 9 Be careful that you do not entertain a mean **t**,
32:26 I **t** to scatter them and blot out the memory
Jos 22:28 And we **t**, If this should be said to us or
Jdg 3:24 the doors of the roof chamber were locked, they **t**,
16:20 When he awoke from his sleep, he **t**,
20:32 The Benjaminites **t**, "They are being routed
20:39 so they **t**, "Surely they are defeated before us,
Ru 1:12 Even if I **t** there was hope for me,
4: 4 So I **t** I would tell you of it, and say:
1Sa 1:13 therefore Eli **t** she was drunk.
9:20 give no further **t** to them,
16: 6 When they came, he looked on Eliab and **t**,
18:11 for he **t**, "I will pin David to the wall."
18:17 For Saul **t**, "I will not raise a hand against him;
18:21 Saul **t**, "Let me give her to him that she may be
20:26 for he **t**, "Something has befallen him;
2Sa 4:10 'See, Saul is dead,' **t** he was bringing good news,
14:15 your servant **t**, 'I will speak to the king;
14:17 Your servant **t**, 'The word of my lord
2Ki 5:11 saying, "I **t** that for me he would surely come out,
5:20 the servant of Elisha the man of God, **t**,
20:19 For he **t**, "Why not, if there will be peace
1Ch 28: 9 and understands every plan and **t**.
Est 3: 6 But he **t** it beneath him to lay hands
Job 9:35 for I know I am not what I am **t** to be.
29:18 Then I **t**, 'I shall die in my nest,
Ps 40:17 I am poor and needy, but the Lord takes **t** for me.
50:21 you **t** that I was one just like yourself.
64: 6 We have **t** out a cunningly conceived plot."
73:16 But when I **t** how to understand this,
94:18 When I **t**, "My foot is slipping,"
Pr 21:29 but the upright give **t** to their ways.
Ecc 4: 2 And I **t** the dead, who have already died,
9:10 for there is no work or **t** or knowledge or wisdom
Isa 39: 8 For he **t**, "There will be peace and security
57:11 and did not remember me or give me a **t**?
Jer 3: 7 And I **t**, "After she has done all this she will return
3:19 I **t** how I would set you among my children,
3:19 And I **t** you would call me, My Father,
La 1: 9 she took no **t** of her future;
3:19 The **t** of my affliction and my homelessness
Eze 20: 8 Then I **t** I would pour out my wrath upon them
20:13 Then I **t** I would pour out my wrath upon them
20:21 Then I **t** I would pour out my wrath upon them
20:32 What is in your mind shall never happen—the **t**,
Jnh 1: 6 the god will spare us a **t** so that we do not perish."
Mic 2: 8 from those who pass by trustingly with no **t**
Mal 3:16 before him of those who revered the LORD and **t**
Mt 20:10 the first came, they **t** they would receive more;
Mk 6:49 they **t** it was a ghost and cried out;
Lk 3:23 He was the son (as was **t**) of Joseph son of Heli,
12:17 And he **t** to himself, 'What should I do,
24:37 and **t** that they were seeing a ghost.
Jn 11:13 but they **t** that he was referring merely to sleep.
11:31 because they **t** that she was going to the tomb
13:29 Some **t** that, because Judas had
Ac 8:20 you **t** you could obtain God's gift with money!
12: 9 he **t** he was seeing a vision.
26: 8 Why is it **t** incredible by any of you
27:13 they **t** they could achieve their purpose;
Ro 12:17 but take **t** for what is noble in the sight of all.
1Co 13:11 I was a child, I spoke like a child, I **t** like a child,
2Co 9: 5 So I **t** it necessary to urge the brothers to go on
10: 5 and we take every **t** captive to obey Christ.
1Ti 3: 7 Moreover, he must be well **t** of by outsiders,
Tob 3:10 But she **t** it over and said,
Jdt 8:14 and find out his mind or comprehend his **t**?
AdE 16:14 He **t** that by these methods he would catch us
Wis 3: 2 and their departure was **t** to be a disaster,
5: 4 We **t** that their lives were madness and
6: 7 and he takes **t** for all alike.
6:15 To fix one's **t** on her is perfect understanding,
6:16 and meets them in every **t**.
12:27 at those creatures that they had **t** to be gods,
13:16 He takes **t** for it, so that it may not fall,
14:30 because they **t** wrongly about God
15:15 For they **t** that all their heathen idols were gods,
Sir 3:31 Those who repay favors give **t** to the future;
11: 5 but one who was never **t** of has worn a crown.
20: 5 Some people keep silent and are **t** to be wise,
Sir 22:17 on an intelligent **t** is like stucco decoration
37: 8 for he will take **t** for himself.
39:32 of all this and have **t** it out and left it in writing:
40: 2 and anxious **t** of the day of their death.
41: 1 how bitter is the **t** of you to the one at peace
42:20 No **t** escapes him, and nothing is hidden
Bar 3:23 or given **t** to her paths.
1Mc 4:45 And they **t** it best to tear it down,
2Mc 1:18 we **t** it necessary to notify you,
4:19 however, **t** best not to use it for sacrifice,
9: 8 while before had **t** in his superhuman arrogance
9:10 to carry the man who a little while before had **t**
9:21 and I have deemed it necessary to take **t** for
12:45 it was a holy and pious **t**.
13: 3 he **t** that he would be established in office.
14: 9 may it please you to take **t** for our country
14:37 and was very well **t** of and
14:40 for he **t** that by arresting him he would do them
1Es 3:20 It turns every **t** to feasting and mirth,
4:21 with no **t** of his father or his mother
3Mc 5:22 as in devising all sorts of insults for those they **t**
5:49 they **t** that this was their last moment of life,
2Es 7:*59* "Consider within yourself what you have **t**,
7:*92* to overcome the evil **t** that was formed with them,

THOUGHTFUL (4) [THINK]

Wis 9:15 and this earthy tent burdens the **t** mind.
Sir 27:12 but among **t** people linger on.
31:15 and in every matter be **t**.
32:18 sensible person will not overlook a **t** suggestion;

THOUGHTLESS (2) [THINK]

Nu 30: 6 while obligated by her vows or any **t** utterance
30: 8 or the **t** utterance of her lips,

THOUGHTLESSLY (1) [THINK]

3Mc 1:14 And someone answered **t** that it was wrong

THOUGHTS‡ (69) [THINK]

Ge 6: 5 of the **t** of their hearts was only evil continually.
1Ch 29:18 keep forever such purposes and **t** in the hearts
Job 4:13 Amid **t** from visions of the night,
20: 2 My **t** urge me to answer,
21:27 I know your **t**, and your schemes to wrong me.
Ps 10: 4 all their **t** are, "There is no God."
33:11 the **t** of his heart to all generations.
40: 5 your wondrous deeds and your **t** toward us;
56: 5 all their **t** are against me for evil.
92: 5 Your **t** are very deep!
94:11 The LORD knows our **t**,
139: 2 you discern my **t** from far away.
139:17 How weighty to me are your **t**, O God!
139:23 test me and know my **t**.
Pr 1:23 I will pour out my **t** to you;
12: 5 The **t** of the righteous are just;
Ecc 10:20 Do not curse the king, even in your **t**,
Isa 55: 7 and the unrighteous their **t**;
55: 8 For my **t** are not your **t**,
55: 9 and my **t** than your **t**.
59: 7 their **t** are **t** of iniquity,
66:18 For I know their works and their **t**,
Eze 38:10 On that day **t** will come into your mind,
Da 2:29 came **t** of what would be hereafter,
2:30 and that you may understand the **t** of your mind.
4:19 distressed for a while. His **t** terrified him.
5: 6 the king's face turned pale, and his **t** terrified him.
5:10 not let your **t** terrify you or your face grow pale.
7:28 As for me, Daniel, my **t** greatly terrified me,
Am 4:13 creates the wind, reveals his **t** to mortals,
Mic 4:12 But they do not know the **t** of the LORD;
Mt 9: 4 But Jesus, perceiving their **t**, said,
Lk 1:51 he has scattered the proud in the **t** of their hearts.
2:35 so that the inner **t** of many will be revealed—
9:47 But Jesus, aware of their inner **t**,
Ro 2:15 and their conflicting **t** will accuse
2:16 through Jesus Christ, will judge the secret **t** of all.
1Co 3:20 "The Lord knows the **t** of the wise,
2Co 11: 3 your **t** will be led astray from a sincere
Heb 4:12 it is able to judge the **t** and intentions of the heart.
Jas 2: 4 and become judges with evil **t**?
Wis 1: 3 For perverse **t** separate people from God,
1: 5 and will leave foolish **t** behind,
2:14 He became to us a reproof of our **t**;
7:15 and to have **t** worthy of what I have received;
7:20 the powers of spirits and the **t** of human beings,
11:15 In return for their foolish and wicked **t**,
Sir 8:19 Do not reveal your **t** to anyone,
16:23 Such are the **t** of one devoid of understanding;
21:11 Whoever keeps the law controls his **t**,
23: 2 Who will set whips over my **t**,
24:29 For her **t** are more abundant than the sea,
33: 5 and his **t** like a turning axle.
35:24 and the works of all according to their **t**;
Bar 2: 8 each of us, from the **t** of our wicked hearts.
2Mc 2: 2 or to be led astray in their **t** on seeing the gold
2Es 3: 1 and my **t** welled up in my heart,
5:21 the **t** of my heart were very grievous to me again.
6:34 to think vain **t** concerning the former times;
7:22 they devised for themselves vain **t**,
9:39 I dismissed the **t** with which I had been engaged,
10:31 And why are your understanding and the **t**
13:38 to their face with their evil **t** and the torments
14:14 and put away from you mortal **t**;
14:15 lay to one side the **t** that are most grievous to you,
16:54 he knows their imaginations and their **t**

THOUSAND‡ (627) [TEN-THOUSANDTH, THOUSANDS, THOUSANDTH]

Ge 20:16 I have given your brother a **t** pieces of silver;
Ex 12:37 about six hundred **t** men on foot, besides children.
32:28 and about three **t** of the people fell on that day.
38:25 and one **t** seven hundred seventy-five shekels,
38:26 for six hundred three **t**, five hundred fifty men.
38:28 **t** seven hundred seventy-five shekels he made
38:29 and two **t** four hundred shekels;
Lev 26: 8 and a hundred of you shall give chase to ten **t**;
Nu 1:21 the tribe of Reuben were forty-six **t** five hundred.
1:23 of Simeon were fifty-nine **t** three hundred.
1:25 of Gad were forty-five **t** six hundred fifty.
1:27 of Judah were seventy-four **t** six hundred.
1:29 of Issachar were fifty-four **t** four hundred.
1:31 of Zebulun were fifty-seven **t** four hundred.
1:33 of the tribe of Ephraim were forty **t** five hundred.
1:35 of Manasseh were thirty-two **t** two hundred.
1:37 of Benjamin were thirty-five **t** four hundred.
1:39 the tribe of Dan were sixty-two **t** seven hundred.
1:41 the tribe of Asher were forty-one **t** five hundred.
1:43 of Naphtali were fifty-three **t** four hundred.
1:46 number was six hundred three **t** five hundred fifty.
2: 4 as enrolled of seventy-four **t** six hundred.
2: 6 as enrolled of fifty-four **t** four hundred.
2: 8 as enrolled of fifty-seven **t** four hundred.
2: 9 is one hundred eighty-six **t** four hundred.
2:11 a company as enrolled of forty-six **t** five hundred.
2:13 as enrolled of fifty-nine **t** three hundred.
2:15 as enrolled of forty-five **t** six hundred fifty.
2:16 is one hundred fifty-one **t** four hundred fifty.
2:19 a company as enrolled of forty **t** five hundred.
2:21 as enrolled of thirty-two **t** two hundred.
2:23 as enrolled of thirty-five **t** four hundred.
2:24 is one hundred eight **t** one hundred.
2:26 as enrolled of sixty-two **t** seven hundred.
2:28 as enrolled of forty-one **t** five hundred.
2:30 as enrolled of fifty-three **t** four hundred.
2:31 of Dan is one hundred fifty-seven **t** six hundred.
2:32 was six hundred three **t** five hundred fifty.
3:22 was seven **t** five hundred.
3:28 there were eight **t** six hundred,
3:34 a month old and upward, was six **t** two hundred.
3:39 from a month old and upward, was twenty-two **t**.
3:43 was twenty-two **t** two hundred seventy-three.
3:50 one **t** three hundred sixty-five shekels,
4:36 by clans was two **t** seven hundred fifty.
4:40 their ancestral houses was two **t** six hundred thirty.
4:44 by their clans was three **t** two hundred.
4:48 their enrollment was eight **t** five hundred eighty.
7:85 the vessels two **t** four hundred shekels according
10:36 O LORD of the ten **t** thousands of Israel."
11:21 people I am with number six hundred **t** on foot;
16:49 by the plague were fourteen **t** seven hundred,
25: 9 those that died by the plague were twenty-four **t**.
26: 7 enrolled was forty-three **t** seven hundred thirty.
26:14 Simeonites, twenty-two **t** two hundred.
26:18 of those enrolled was forty **t** five hundred.
26:22 of those enrolled was seventy-six **t** five hundred.
26:25 sixty-four **t** three hundred enrolled.
26:27 of those enrolled was sixty **t** five hundred.
26:34 of those enrolled was fifty-two **t** seven hundred.
26:37 of those enrolled was thirty-two **t** five hundred.
26:41 of those enrolled was forty-five **t** six hundred.
26:43 sixty-four **t** four hundred enrolled.
26:47 of those enrolled was fifty-three **t** four hundred.
26:50 of those enrolled was forty-five **t** four hundred.
26:51 six hundred and one **t** seven hundred thirty.
26:62 The number of those enrolled was twenty-three **t**,
31: 4 You shall send a **t** from each of the tribes of Israel
31: 5 a **t** from each tribe were conscripted,
31: 5 twelve **t** armed for battle.
31: 6 Moses sent them to the war, a **t** from each tribe,
31:32 had taken totaled six hundred seventy-five **t** sheep,
31:33 seventy-two **t** oxen,
31:34 sixty-one **t** donkeys,
31:35 and thirty-two **t** persons in all,
31:36 three hundred thirty-seven **t** five hundred sheep
31:38 The oxen were thirty-six **t**,
31:39 The donkeys were thirty **t** five hundred,
31:40 The persons were sixteen **t**,
31:43 three hundred thirty-seven **t** five hundred sheep
31:44 thirty-six **t** oxen,
31:45 thirty **t** five hundred donkeys,
31:46 and sixteen **t** persons.
31:52 was sixteen **t** seven hundred fifty shekels.
35: 4 the wall of the town outward a **t** cubits all around.
35: 5 for the east side two **t** cubits, for the south side two **t** cubits, for the west side two **t** cubits, and for the north side two **t** cubits,
Dt 1:11 increase you a **t** times more and bless you,
7: 9 and keep his commandments, to a **t** generations,
32:30 How could one have routed a **t**,
Jos 3: 4 a distance of about two **t** cubits;
4:13 About forty **t** armed for war crossed over before
7: 3 or three **t** men should go up and attack Ai.
7: 4 So about three **t** of the people went up there;
8: 3 Joshua chose thirty **t** warriors and sent them out
8:12 Taking about five **t** men, he set them in ambush
8:25 both men and women, was twelve **t**—
23:10 One of you puts to flight a **t**,
Jdg 1: 4 and they defeated ten **t** of them at Bezek.
3:29 that time they killed about ten **t** of the Moabites,
4: 6 bringing ten **t** from the tribe of Naphtali and
4:10 and ten **t** warriors went up behind him;
4:14 with ten **t** warriors following him.
Jdg 5: 8 Was shield or spear to be seen among forty **t**
7: 3 twenty-two **t** returned, and ten **t** remained.
8:10 about fifteen **t** men, all who were left of all
8:10 one hundred twenty **t** men bearing arms had fallen.
8:26 that he requested was one **t** seven hundred shekels
9:49 about a **t** men and women.
12: 6 Forty-two **t** of the Ephraimites fell at that time.
15:11 Then three **t** men of Judah went down to the cleft
15:15 and with it he killed a **t** men.
15:16 the jawbone of a donkey I have slain a **t** men."
16:27 the roof there were about three **t** men and women,
20: 2 four hundred **t** foot-soldiers bearing arms.
20:10 and a hundred of a **t**, and a **t** of ten **t**,
20:15 Benjaminites mustered twenty-six **t** armed men
20:17 mustered four hundred **t** armed men,
20:21 down on that day twenty-two **t** of the Israelites.
20:25 and struck down eighteen **t** of the Israelites,
20:34 against Gibeah ten **t** picked men out of all Israel,
20:35 Israelites destroyed twenty-five **t** one hundred men
20:44 Eighteen **t** Benjaminites fell,
20:45 five **t** of them were cut down on the main roads,
20:45 and two **t** of them were slain.
20:46 of Benjamin were twenty-five **t** arms-bearing men,
21:10 So the congregation sent twelve **t** soldiers there
1Sa 4: 2 who killed about four **t** men on the field of battle.
4:10 for there fell of Israel thirty **t** foot soldiers.
10:27 But there were seven **t** men who had escaped
11: 8 those from Israel were three hundred **t**, and those from Judah seventy **t**.
13: 2 Saul chose three **t** out of Israel; two **t** were with
13: 2 a **t** were with Jonathan in Gibeah of Benjamin;
13: 5 thirty **t** chariots, and six **t** horsemen,
14:23 with Saul numbered altogether about ten **t** men.
15: 4 two hundred **t** foot soldiers, and ten **t** soldiers of
17: 5 weight of the coat was five **t** shekels of bronze.
17:18 to the commander of their **t**.
18:13 and made him a commander of a **t**;
24: 2 Saul took three **t** chosen men out of all Israel,
25: 2 he had three **t** sheep and a **t** goats.
26: 2 with three **t** chosen men of Israel,
2Sa 6: 1 the chosen men of Israel, thirty **t**.
8: 4 from him one **t** seven hundred horsemen,
8: 4 and twenty **t** foot soldiers.
8: 5 David killed twenty-two **t** men of the Arameans.
8:13 he killed eighteen **t** Edomites in the Valley
10: 6 twenty **t** foot soldiers, as well as the king of Maacah, one **t** men, and the men of Tob, twelve **t**
10:18 and forty **t** horsemen, and wounded Shobach
17: 1 "Let me choose twelve **t** men,
18: 3 But you are worth ten **t** of us;
18: 7 on that day, twenty **t** men.
18:12 I felt in my hand the weight of a **t** pieces of silver,
19:17 with him were a **t** people from Benjamin.
24: 9 in Israel there were eight hundred **t** soldiers able
24: 9 and those of Judah were five hundred **t**.
24:15 and seventy **t** of the people died,
1Ki 3: 4 Solomon used to offer a **t** burnt offerings on
4:26 also had forty **t** stalls of horses for his chariots, and twelve **t** horsemen.
4:32 He composed three **t** proverbs, and his songs numbered a **t** and five.
5:11 in turn gave Hiram twenty **t** cors of wheat as food
5:13 the levy numbered thirty **t** men.
5:14 ten **t** a month in shifts;
5:15 had seventy **t** laborers and eighty **t** stonecutters
5:16 Solomon's three **t** three hundred supervisors who
7:26 like the flower of a lily; it held two **t** baths.
8:63 of well-being to the LORD twenty-two **t** oxen
8:63 and one hundred twenty **t** sheep.
10:26 and twelve **t** horses, which he stationed in
12:21 one hundred eighty **t** chosen troops to fight
19:18 Yet I will leave seven **t** in Israel,
20:15 them he mustered all the people of Israel, seven **t**.
20:29 killed one hundred **t** Aramean foot soldiers
20:30 the wall fell on twenty-seven **t** men that were left.
2Ki 3: 4 to the king of Israel one hundred **t** lambs,
3: 4 and the wool of one hundred **t** rams.
5: 5 six **t** shekels of gold, and ten sets of garments.
13: 7 ten chariots and ten **t** footmen;
14: 7 He killed ten **t** Edomites in the Valley of Salt
15:19 Menahem gave Pul a **t** talents of silver,
18:23 I will give you two **t** horses,
19:35 down one hundred eighty-five **t** in the camp of
24:14 all the officials, all the warriors, ten **t** captives,
24:16 seven **t**, the artisans and the smiths, one **t**,
1Ch 5:18 expert in war, forty-four **t** seven hundred sixty,
5:21 fifty **t** of their camels, two hundred fifty **t** sheep, two **t** donkeys, and one hundred **t** captives.
7: 2 the days of David being twenty-two **t** six hundred.
7: 4 thirty-six **t**, for they had many wives and sons.
7: 5 in all eighty-seven **t** mighty warriors,
7: 7 by genealogies was twenty-two **t** thirty-four.
7: 9 mighty warriors, was twenty **t** two hundred.
7:11 seventeen **t** two hundred, ready for service in war.
7:40 for service in war, was twenty-six **t** men.
9:13 one **t** seven hundred sixty,
12:14 the least equal to a hundred and the greatest to a **t**.
12:24 spear numbered six **t** eight hundred armed troops.
12:25 mighty warriors, seven **t** one hundred.
12:26 Of the Levites four **t** six hundred.
12:27 and with him three **t** seven hundred.
12:29 Of the Benjaminites, the kindred of Saul, three **t**,
12:30 Of the Ephraimites, twenty **t** eight hundred,
12:31 Of the half-tribe of Manasseh, eighteen **t**,
12:33 Of Zebulun, fifty **t** seasoned troops,
12:34 Of Naphtali, a **t** commanders, with whom there were thirty-seven **t** armed
1Ch 12:35 twenty-eight **t** six hundred equipped for battle.
12:36 Of Asher, forty **t** seasoned troops ready for battle.
12:37 one hundred twenty **t** armed with all the weapons
16:15 the word that he commanded, for a **t** generations,
18: 4 David took from him one **t** chariots, seven **t** cavalry, and twenty **t** foot soldiers.
18: 5 David killed twenty-two **t** Arameans.
18:12 Abishai son of Zeruiah killed eighteen **t** Edomites
19: 6 a **t** talents of silver to hire chariots and cavalry
19: 7 They hired thirty-two **t** chariots and the king
19:18 and David killed seven **t** Aramean charioteers
19:18 and forty **t** foot soldiers, and also killed Shophach
21: 5 all Israel there were one million one hundred **t** men
21: 5 in Judah four hundred seventy **t** who drew the
21:14 and seventy **t** persons fell in Israel.
22:14 for the house of the LORD one hundred **t** talents
23: 3 were counted, and the total was thirty-eight **t**.
23: 4 "Twenty-four **t** of these," David said,
23: 4 six **t** shall be officers and judges,
23: 5 four **t** gatekeepers, and four **t** shall offer praises to
26:30 one **t** seven hundred men of ability,
26:32 two **t** seven hundred men of ability,
27: 1 each division numbering twenty-four **t**:
27: 2 in his division were twenty-four **t**.
27: 4 In his division were twenty-four **t**.
27: 5 in his division were twenty-four **t**.
27: 7 in his division were twenty-four **t**.
27: 8 in his division were twenty-four **t**.
27: 9 in his division were twenty-four **t**.
27:10 in his division were twenty-four **t**.
27:11 in his division were twenty-four **t**.
27:12 in his division were twenty-four **t**.
27:13 in his division were twenty-four **t**.
27:14 in his division were twenty-four **t**.
27:15 in his division were twenty-four **t**.
29: 4 three **t** talents of gold, of the gold of Ophir, and seven **t** talents of refined silver,
29: 7 service of the house of God five **t** talents and ten **t** darics of gold, ten **t** talents of silver, eighteen **t** talents of bronze, and one hundred **t** talents of iron.
29:21 a **t** bulls, a **t** rams, and a **t** lambs,
2Ch 1: 6 and offered a **t** burnt offerings on it.
1:14 and twelve **t** horses, which he stationed in
2: 2 seventy **t** laborers and eighty **t** stonecutters in the hill country, with three **t** six hundred to oversee
2:10 twenty **t** cors of crushed wheat, twenty **t** cors of barley, twenty **t** baths of wine, and twenty **t** baths
2:17 to be one hundred fifty-three **t** six hundred.
2:18 Seventy **t** of them he assigned as laborers, eighty **t** as stonecutters in the hill country, and three **t** six hundred as overseers
4: 5 like the flower of a lily; it held three **t** baths.
7: 5 twenty-two **t** oxen and one hundred twenty **t** sheep.
9:25 Solomon had four **t** stalls for horses and chariots, and twelve **t** horses,
11: 1 he assembled one hundred eighty **t** chosen troops
12: 3 with twelve hundred chariots and sixty **t** cavalry.
13: 3 four hundred **t** picked men;
13: 3 with eight hundred **t** picked mighty warriors.
13:17 five hundred **t** picked men of Israel fell slain.
14: 8 Asa had an army of three hundred **t** from Judah,
14: 8 and two hundred eighty **t** troops
15:11 seven hundred oxen and seven **t** sheep.
17:11 also brought him seven **t** seven hundred rams and seven **t** seven hundred male goats.
17:14 with three hundred **t** mighty warriors,
17:15 with two hundred eighty **t**,
17:16 with two hundred **t** mighty warriors.
17:17 with two hundred **t** armed with bow and shield,
17:18 with one hundred eighty **t** armed for war.
25: 5 that they were three hundred **t** picked troops fit
25: 6 He also hired one hundred **t** mighty warriors
25:11 and struck down ten **t** men of Seir.
25:12 The people of Judah captured another ten **t** alive,
25:13 they killed three **t** people in them,
26:12 of mighty warriors was two **t** six hundred.
26:13 an army of three hundred seven **t** five hundred,
27: 5 ten **t** cors of wheat and ten **t** of barley.
28: 6 of Remaliah killed one hundred twenty **t** in Judah
28: 8 of Israel took captive two hundred **t** of their kin,
29:33 offerings were six hundred bulls and three **t** sheep.
30:24 a **t** bulls and seven **t** sheep for offerings,
30:24 the assembly a **t** bulls and ten **t** sheep.
35: 7 flock to the number of thirty **t**, and three **t** bulls;
35: 8 the passover offerings two **t** six hundred lambs
35: 9 the Levites for the passover offerings five **t** lambs
Ezr 1: 9 silver basins, one **t**;
1:10 other vessels, one **t**;
1:11 and silver vessels was five **t** four hundred.
2: 3 two **t** one hundred seventy-two.
2: 6 two **t** eight hundred twelve.
2: 7 Of Elam, one **t** two hundred fifty-four.
2:12 Of Azgad, one **t** two hundred twenty-two.
2:14 Of Bigvai, two **t** fifty-six.
2:31 Of the other Elam, one **t** two hundred fifty-four.
2:35 Of Senaah, three **t** six hundred thirty.
2:37 Of Immer, one **t** fifty-two.
2:38 Of Pashhur, one **t** two hundred forty-seven.
2:39 Of Harim, one **t** seventeen.
2:64 together was forty-two **t** three hundred sixty,
2:65 there were seven **t** three hundred thirty-seven;
2:67 and six **t** seven hundred twenty donkeys.
2:69 sixty-one **t** darics of gold, five **t** minas of silver,
8:27 twenty gold bowls worth a **t** darics,
Ne 3:13 and its bars, and repaired a **t** cubits of the wall,
7: 8 two **t** one hundred seventy-two.
7:11 two **t** eight hundred eighteen.

Ne 7:12 Of Elam, one **t** two hundred fifty-four.
7:17 Of Azgad, two **t** three hundred twenty-two.
7:19 Of Bigvai, two **t** sixty-seven.
7:34 one **t** two hundred fifty-four.
7:38 Of Senaah, three **t** nine hundred thirty.
7:40 Of Immer, one **t** fifty-two.
7:41 Of Pashhur, one **t** two hundred forty-seven.
7:42 Of Harim, one **t** seventeen.
7:66 together was forty-two **t** three hundred sixty,
7:67 there were seven **t** three hundred thirty-seven;
7:69 and six **t** seven hundred twenty donkeys.
7:70 governor gave to the treasury one **t** darics of gold,
7:71 twenty **t** darics of gold and two **t** two hundred
7:72 twenty **t** darics of gold, two **t** minas of silver,
Est 3:9 and I will pay ten **t** talents of silver into the hands
9:16 and killed seventy-five **t** of those who hated them;
Job 1:3 He had seven **t** sheep, three **t** camels,
9:3 one could not answer him once in a **t.**
33:23 one of a **t,** one who declares a person upright,
42:12 and he had fourteen **t** sheep, six **t** camels, a **t** yoke
of oxen, and a **t** donkeys.
Ps 50:10 the cattle on a **t** hills.
60:T *when Joab on his return killed twelve t Edomites*
68:17 With mighty chariotry, twice ten **t,**
84:10 a day in your courts is better than a **t** elsewhere.
90:4 a **t** years in your sight are like yesterday when it is
91:7 A **t** may fall at your side, ten **t** at your right hand,
105:8 the word that he commanded, for a **t** generations,
Ecc 6:6 Even though he should live a **t** years twice over,
7:28 One man among a **t** I found,
SS 4:4 hang a **t** bucklers, all of them shields of warriors.
5:10 distinguished among ten **t.**
8:11 each one was to bring for its fruit a **t** pieces
8:12 you, O Solomon, may have the **t,**
Isa 7:23 where there used to be a **t** vines,
7:23 worth a **t** shekels of silver,
30:17 A **t** shall flee at the threat of one,
36:8 I will give you two **t** horses,
37:36 down one hundred eighty-five **t** in the camp of
Jer 52:28 in the seventh year, three **t** twenty-three Judeans;
52:30 all the persons were four **t** six hundred.
Eze 45:1 twenty-five **t** cubits long and twenty **t** cubits wide;
45:3 a section twenty-five **t** cubits long and ten **t** wide,
45:5 twenty-five **t** cubits long and ten **t** cubits wide,
45:6 five **t** cubits wide, and twenty-five **t** cubits long;
47:3 the man measured one **t** cubits,
47:4 Again he measured one **t,**
47:4 Again he measured one **t,**
47:5 Again he measured one **t,**
48:8 twenty-five **t** cubits in width,
48:9 twenty-five **t** cubits in length, and twenty **t** in
48:10 measuring twenty-five **t** cubits on the northern
side, ten **t** cubits in width on the western side, ten **t**
in width on the eastern side, and twenty-five **t** in
48:13 twenty-five **t** cubits in length and ten **t** in width.
48:13 be twenty-five **t** cubits and the width twenty **t.**
48:15 five **t** cubits in width and twenty-five **t** in length,
48:16 the north side four **t** five hundred cubits, the south
side four **t** five hundred, the east side four **t** five
hundred, and the west side four **t** and five hundred.
48:18 be ten **t** cubits to the east, and ten **t** to the west,
48:20 be twenty-five **t** cubits square,
48:21 from the twenty-five **t** cubits of the holy portion
48:21 from the twenty-five **t** cubits to the west border,
48:30 to be four **t** five hundred cubits by measure,
48:32 which is to be four **t** five hundred cubits,
48:33 to be four **t** five hundred cubits by measure,
48:34 which is to be four **t** five hundred cubits,
48:35 of the city shall be eighteen **t** cubits.
Da 5:1 King Belshazzar made a great festival for a **t**
5:1 and he was drinking wine in the presence of the **t.**
7:10 A **t** thousands served him, and ten **t** times ten **t**
stood attending him.
8:14 "For two **t** three hundred evenings and mornings;
12:11 there shall be one **t** two hundred ninety days.
12:12 and attain the **t** three hundred thirty-five days.
Am 5:3 city that marched out a **t** shall have a hundred left,
Jnh 4:11 a hundred and twenty **t** persons who do
Mt 14:21 And those who ate were about five **t** men,
15:38 Those who had eaten were four **t** men,
16:9 not remember the five loaves for the five **t,**
16:10 Or the seven loaves for the four **t,**
18:24 one who owed him ten **t** talents was brought
Mk 5:13 and the herd, numbering about two **t,**
6:44 the loaves numbered five **t** men.
8:9 Now there were about four **t** people.
8:19 When I broke the five loaves for the five **t,**
8:20 "And the seven for the four **t,**
Lk 9:14 For there were about five **t** men.
14:31 consider whether he is able with ten **t** to oppose
the one who comes against him with twenty **t?**
Jn 6:10 so they sat down, about five **t** in all.
Ac 2:41 and that day about three **t** persons were added.
4:4 and they numbered about five **t.**
19:19 it was found to come to fifty **t** silver coins.
21:38 up a revolt and led the four **t** assassins out into
Ro 11:4 for myself seven **t** who have not bowed the knee
1Co 4:15 though you might have ten **t** guardians in Christ,
10:8 and twenty-three **t** fell in a single day.
14:19 than ten **t** words in a tongue.
2Pe 3:8 that with the Lord one day is like a **t** years, and a **t**
years are like one day.
Rev 7:4 one hundred forty-four **t,** sealed out of every tribe
7:5 From the tribe of Judah twelve **t** sealed,
7:5 from the tribe of Reuben twelve **t,**
7:5 from the tribe of Gad twelve **t,**
7:6 from the tribe of Asher twelve **t,**
Rev 7:6 from the tribe of Naphtali twelve **t,**
7:6 from the tribe of Manasseh twelve **t,**
7:7 from the tribe of Simeon twelve **t,**
7:7 from the tribe of Levi twelve **t,**
7:7 from the tribe of Issachar twelve **t,**
7:8 from the tribe of Zebulun twelve **t,**
7:8 from the tribe of Joseph twelve **t,**
7:8 from the tribe of Benjamin twelve **t** sealed.
11:3 to prophesy for one **t** two hundred sixty days,
11:13 seven **t** people were killed in the earthquake,
12:6 be nourished for one **t** two hundred sixty days.
14:1 with him were one hundred forty-four **t** who had
14:3 one hundred forty-four **t** who have been redeemed
20:2 and bound him for a **t** years,
20:3 until the **t** years were ended.
20:4 to life and reigned with Christ a **t** years.
20:5 not come to life until the **t** years were ended.)
20:6 and they will reign with him a **t** years.
20:7 When the **t** years are ended,
Jdt 2:5 twenty **t** foot soldiers and twelve **t** cavalry.
2:15 one hundred twenty **t** of them, together with
twelve **t** archers on horseback,
7:2 forces numbered one hundred seventy **t** infantry
7:2 and twelve **t** cavalry, not counting the baggage
7:17 together with five **t** Assyrians,
AdE 1:7 made of ruby, worth thirty **t** talents.
3:9 and I will pay ten **t** talents of silver into
4:7 how Haman had promised to pay ten **t** talents into
9:16 They destroyed fifteen **t** of them,
Wis 12:22 you scourge our enemies ten **t** times more,
Sir 6:6 but let your advisers be one in a **t.**
16:3 for one can be better than a **t,**
16:10 on the six hundred **t** foot soldiers who assembled
23:19 the eyes of the Lord are ten **t** times brighter than
39:11 he will leave a name greater than a **t,**
41:4 for ten years or a hundred or a **t,**
41:12 it will outlive you longer than a **t** hoards of gold.
46:8 of six hundred **t** infantry,
1Mc 2:38 to the number of a **t** persons.
3:39 sent with them forty **t** infantry and seven **t** cavalry
4:1 took five **t** infantry and one **t** picked cavalry,
4:6 in the plain with three **t** men,
4:15 and three **t** of them fell.
4:28 mustered sixty **t** picked infantry and five **t** cavalry
4:29 and Judas met them with ten **t** men.
4:34 and there fell of the army of Lysias five **t** men;
5:13 and have destroyed about a **t** persons there."
5:20 Then three **t** men were assigned to Simon to go
5:20 and eight **t** to Judas for Gilead.
5:22 as many as three **t** of the Gentiles fell,
5:34 As many as eight **t** of them fell that day.
5:60 many as two **t** of the people of Israel fell that day.
6:30 one hundred **t** foot soldiers, twenty **t** horsemen,
6:35 with each elephant they stationed a **t** men armed
7:40 Judas encamped in Adasa with three **t** men.
7:41 down one hundred eighty-five **t** of the Assyrians.
9:4 with twenty **t** foot soldiers and two **t** cavalry.
9:5 and with him were three **t** picked men.
9:49 And about one **t** of Bacchides' men fell that day.
10:36 in the king's forces to the number of thirty **t** men,
10:40 I also grant fifteen **t** shekels of silver yearly out of
10:42 the five **t** shekels of silver
10:74 He chose ten **t** men and set out from Jerusalem,
10:77 he mustered three **t** cavalry and a large army,
10:79 Now Apollonius had secretly left a **t** cavalry
10:85 with those burned alive, came to eight **t.**
11:44 So Jonathan sent three **t** stalwart men to him
11:45 to the number of a hundred and twenty **t,**
11:47 and they killed on that day about one hundred **t.**
11:74 As many as three **t** of the foreigners fell that day.
12:41 to meet him with forty **t** picked warriors,
12:47 He kept with himself three **t** men, two **t** of whom
he left in Galilee, while one **t** accompanied him.
14:24 with a large gold shield weighing one **t** minas,
15:13 one hundred twenty **t** warriors and eight **t** cavalry.
15:18 have brought a gold shield weighing one **t** minas.
15:26 And Simon sent to Antiochus two **t** picked troops,
16:4 of the country twenty **t** warriors and cavalry,
16:10 and about two **t** of them fell.
2Mc 4:40 about three **t** men and launched an unjust attack,
5:5 a **t** men and suddenly made an assault on the city.
5:14 the total of three days eighty **t** were destroyed,
forty **t** in hand-to-hand fighting,
5:24 with an army of twenty-two **t,**
8:1 and so they gathered about six **t.**
8:9 of no fewer than twenty **t** Gentiles of all nations,
8:10 the tribute due to the Romans, two **t** talents,
8:16 to the number six **t,** and exhorted them not to
8:19 when one hundred eighty-five **t** perished,
8:20 eight **t** Jews fought along with four **t** Macedonians;
8:20 the Macedonians were hard pressed, the eight **t,**
8:20 destroyed one hundred twenty **t** Galatians
8:24 they killed more than nine **t** of the enemy,
8:30 and Bacchides they killed more than twenty **t**
8:34 who had brought the **t** merchants to buy the Jews,
10:17 killing no fewer than twenty **t.**
10:18 When at least nine **t** took refuge
10:20 and on receiving seventy **t** drachmas let some
10:23 he destroyed more than twenty **t** in
10:31 Twenty **t** five hundred were slaughtered,
11:2 about eighty **t** infantry and all his cavalry
11:11 and laid low eleven **t** of them
12:10 against Timothy, at least five **t** Arabs
12:19 in the stronghold, more than ten **t** men.
12:20 one hundred twenty **t** infantry and two **t** five
hundred cavalry.
12:23 and destroyed as many as thirty **t.**
2Mc 12:26 and slaughtered twenty-five **t** people.
12:28 as many as twenty-five **t** of those who were in it.
12:33 with three **t** infantry and four hundred cavalry.
12:43 to the amount of two **t** drachmas of silver,
13:2 a Greek force of one hundred ten **t** infantry,
13:2 five **t** three hundred cavalry,
13:15 and killed as many as two **t** men in the camp.
15:22 and he killed fully one hundred eighty-five **t** in
15:27 they laid low at least thirty-five **t,**
1Es 1:7 gave thirty **t** lambs and kids, and three **t** calves;
1:8 for the passover two **t** six hundred sheep
1:9 gave the Levites for the passover five **t** sheep
2:13 one **t** gold cups, one **t** silver cups,
2:13 two **t** four hundred ten silver bowls, and one **t** other
2:14 gold and silver, five **t** four hundred sixty-nine,
5:2 a **t** cavalry to take them back to Jerusalem
5:9 two **t** one hundred seventy-two.
5:11 two **t** eight hundred twelve.
5:12 one **t** two hundred fifty-four.
5:13 one **t** three hundred twenty-two.
5:14 The descendants of Bigvai, two **t** sixty-six.
5:17 The descendants of Baiterus, three **t** five.
5:23 three **t** three hundred thirty.
5:24 The descendants of Immer, one **t** and fifty-two.
5:25 one **t** two hundred forty-seven.
5:25 The descendants of Charme, one **t** seventeen.
5:41 were forty-two **t** three hundred sixty;
5:42 servants were seven **t** three hundred thirty-seven;
5:43 and seven **t** thirty-six horses,
5:43 and five **t** five hundred twenty-five donkeys.
5:45 the work a **t** minas of gold, five **t** minas of silver,
3Mc 3:28 and also two **t** drachmas from the royal treasury,
2Es 6:51 to live in it, where there are a **t** mountains;
10:45 the reason is that there were three **t** years in
10:46 And after three **t** years Solomon built the city,
4Mc 4:17 the king three **t** six hundred sixty talents annually.

THOUSANDS‡ (59) [THOUSAND]

Ge 24:60 "May you, our sister, become **t** of myriads;
Ex 18:21 set such men over them as officers over **t,**
18:25 as officers over **t,** hundreds, fifties, and tens.
Nu 10:36 O LORD of the ten thousand **t** of Israel."
31:5 So out of the **t** of Israel,
31:14 the commanders of **t** and the commanders
31:48 the officers who were over the **t** of the army,
31:48 the commanders of **t** and the commanders
31:52 from the commanders of **t** and the commanders
31:54 from the commanders of **t** and of hundreds,
Dt 1:15 commanders of **t,** commanders of hundreds,
33:17 the myriads of Ephraim, such the **t** of Manasseh.
1Sa 8:12 and he will appoint for himself commanders of **t**
18:7 "Saul has killed his **t,** and David his ten **t."**
18:8 to David ten **t,** and to me they have ascribed **t;**
21:11 'Saul has killed his **t,** and David his ten **t'?"**
22:7 will he make you all commanders of **t** and
23:23 I will search him out among all the **t** of Judah."
29:2 were passing on by hundreds and by **t,**
29:5 'Saul has killed his **t,** and David his ten **t'?"**
2Sa 18:1 over them commanders of **t** and commanders
18:4 all the army marched out by hundreds and by **t.**
1Ch 12:20 Elihu, and Zillethai, chiefs of the **t** in Manasseh.
13:1 David consulted with the commanders of the **t**
15:25 and the commanders of the **t,**
26:26 and the officers of the **t** and the hundreds,
27:1 the commanders of the **t** and the hundreds,
28:1 the commanders of the **t,** the commanders of
29:6 the commanders of the **t** and of the hundreds,
2Ch 1:2 the commanders of the **t** and of the hundreds,
17:14 Of Judah, the commanders of the **t:**
25:5 under commanders of the **t** and of the hundreds
Ps 3:6 of ten **t** of people who have set themselves
68:17 twice ten thousand, **t** upon **t,**
119:72 The law of your mouth is better to me than **t**
144:13 may our sheep increase by **t,** by tens of **t** in our
Da 7:10 A thousand **t** served him,
11:12 and he shall overthrow tens of **t,**
11:41 and tens of **t** shall fall victim,
Mic 6:7 Will the LORD be pleased with **t** of rams, with ten **t**
of rivers of oil?
Lk 12:1 Meanwhile, when the crowd gathered by the **t,**
Ac 21:20 many **t** of believers there are among the Jews,
Jude 1:14 the Lord is coming with ten **t** of his holy ones,
Rev 5:11 they numbered myriads of myriads and **t** of **t,**
Sir 47:6 they glorified him for the tens of **t** he conquered,
Aza 1:17 or with tens of **t** of fat lambs;
1Mc 3:55 in charge of **t** and hundreds and fifties and tens.
2Mc 11:4 with his ten **t** of infantry, and his **t** of cavalry,
1Es 1:9 and Joram, captains over **t,** gave the Levites for
4Mc 4:3 of **t** in private funds, which are not the property of

THOUSANDTH (4) [THOUSAND]

Ex 20:6 but showing steadfast love to the **t** generation
34:7 keeping steadfast love for the **t** generation,
Dt 5:10 but showing steadfast love to the **t** generation
Jer 32:18 You show steadfast love to the **t** generation,

THRACIAN (1)

2Mc 12:35 when one of the **T** cavalry bore down on him

THRASH (1) [THRASHING]

Eze 32:2 you **t** about in your streams,

THRASHING (1) [THRASH]

Sir 22:6 but a **t** and discipline are at all times wisdom.

THREAD‡ (7) [THREADS]

Ge 14:23 a **t** or a sandal-thong or anything that is yours,
38:28 midwife took and bound on his hand a crimson **t**,
38:30 Afterward his brother came out with the crimson **t**
Jdg 16:12 But he snapped the ropes off his arms like a **t**.
SS 4: 3 Your lips are like a crimson **t**,
Jer 51:13 your end has come, the **t** of your life is cut.
4Mc 9:25 the saintly youth broke the **t** of life.

THREADS (1) [THREAD]

Ex 39: 3 Gold leaf was hammered out and cut into **t**

THREAT (7) [THREATEN, THREATENED, THREATENING, THREATENS, THREATS]

Isa 30:17 A thousand shall flee at the **t** of one, at the **t** of five you shall flee,
La 2:17 he has carried out his **t**;
Bar 2: 1 So the Lord carried out the **t** he spoke against us:
Man 1: 5 and the wrath of your **t** to sinners is unendurable;
3Mc 5:33 Hermon suffered an unexpected and dangerous **t**,
4Mc 14: 9 not only heard the direct word of **t**,

THREATEN (5) [THREAT]

Ps 73: 8 with malice; loftily they **t** oppression.
Eze 6:10 I did not **t** in vain to bring this disaster upon them.
1Pe 2:23 when he suffered, he did not **t**;
Sir 19:17 Question your neighbor before you **t** him;
2Es 16:11 The Lord will **t**, and who will not

THREATENED (11) [THREAT]

Nu 14:10 But the whole congregation **t** to stone them.
Jer 36:31 all the disasters with which I have **t** them—
40: 2 LORD your God **t** this place with this disaster;
51:62 you yourself **t** to destroy this place so
Jnh 1: 4 a mighty storm came upon the sea that the ship **t**
Jdt 8:16 for God is not like a human being, to be **t**,
AdE 11: 9 they feared the evils that **t** them,
Bar 2: 7 with which the Lord **t** us have come upon us.
3Mc 4:19 After he had **t** them severely,
6:23 he wept and angrily **t** his Friends, saying,
7: 6 But we very severely **t** them for these acts,

THREATENING (8) [THREAT]

Mt 16: 3 'It will be stormy today, for the sky is red and **t**.'
Ac 4:21 After **t** them again, they let them go,
Eph 6: 9 Stop **t** them, for you know that both of you have
3Mc 5:30 and with a **t** look he said,
5:37 After summoning Hermon he said in a **t** tone,
2Es 15:34 Their appearance is exceedingly **t**,
4Mc 9: 5 You are trying to terrify us by **t** us with death
13: 6 the **t** waves and make it calm for those who sail

THREATENS (1) [THREAT]

4Mc 8:19 up this vain opinion and this arrogance that **t**

THREATS (12) [THREAT]

Pr 13: 8 but the poor get no **t**.
Lk 3:14 "Do not extort money from anyone by **t**
Ac 4:29 And now, Lord, look at their **t**,
9: 1 still breathing **t** and murder against the disciples
Bar 2: 2 with the **t** that were written in the law of Moses.
2:24 and you have carried out your **t**,
3Mc 2:24 but went away uttering bitter **t**.
5:18 and with sharp **t** demanded to know why
4Mc 4: 8 But, uttering **t**, Apollonius went on to the temple.
4:24 but saw that all his **t** and punishments
8:19 the instruments of torture and consider the **t**
9:32 but you suffer torture by the **t** that come

THREE‡ (544) [ONE-THIRD, THIRD, THREE-PRONGED, THREE-TENTHS, THREE-YEAR-OLD, THREEFOLD, THRICE, THRICE-ACCURSED, TWO-THIRDS]

A. THREE DAYS (66)
B. THREE TIMES (34)
C. THREE YEARS (34)
D. THREE MONTHS (20)
E. THREE DAYS' (10)

Ge 5:22 after the birth of Methuselah **t** hundred years,
5:23 of Enoch were **t** hundred sixty-five years.
6:10 And Noah had **t** sons, Shem, Ham, and Japheth.
6:15 the length of the ark **t** hundred cubits,
7:13 and the **t** wives of his sons entered the ark,
9:19 These **t** were the sons of Noah;
9:28 After the flood Noah lived **t** hundred fifty years.
11:13 after the birth of Shelah four hundred **t** years,
11:15 after the birth of Eber four hundred **t** years,
14:14 born in his house, **t** hundred eighteen of them,
15: 9 He said to him, "Bring me a heifer **t** years old, C
15: 9 a female goat **t** years old, a ram three years old, C
15: 9 a female goat three years old, a ram **t** years old, C
18: 2 He looked up and saw **t** men standing near him.
18: 6 "Make ready quickly **t** measures of choice flour,
29: 2 a well in the field and **t** flocks of sheep lying there
29:34 because I have borne him **t** sons";
30:36 of **t** days' journey between himself and Jacob, E
38:24 About **t** months later Judah was told, D
40:10 and on the vine there were **t** branches.
40:12 the **t** branches are three days;
40:12 the three branches are **t** days; A
40:13 within **t** days Pharaoh will lift up your head A
40:16 there were **t** cake baskets on my head,
40:18 the **t** baskets are three days;
40:18 the three baskets are **t** days; A
40:19 within **t** days Pharaoh will lift up your head— A
42:17 he put them all together in prison for **t** days. A
45:22 to Benjamin he gave **t** hundred pieces of silver
Ex 2: 2 that he was a fine baby, she hid him **t** months. D
3:18 now go a **t** days' journey into the wilderness, E
5: 3 **t** days' journey into the wilderness to sacrifice E
8:27 **t** days' journey into the wilderness and sacrifice E
10:22 in all the land of Egypt for **t** days. A
10:23 and for **t** days they could not move from A
15:22 They went **t** days in the wilderness A
21:11 And if he does not do these **t** things for her,
23:14 **T** times in the year you shall hold a festival B
23:17 **T** times in the year all your males shall appear B
25:32 **t** branches of the lampstand out of one side of it
25:32 the lampstand out of one side of it and **t** branches
25:33 **t** cups shaped like almond blossoms, each
25:33 and **t** cups shaped like almond blossoms,
27: 1 altar shall be square, and it shall be **t** cubits high.
27:14 with **t** pillars and **t** bases.
27:15 with **t** pillars and **t** bases.
32:28 about **t** thousand of the people fell on that day.
34:23 **T** times in the year all your males shall appear B
34:24 up to appear before the LORD your God **t** times B
37:18 **t** branches of the lampstand out of one side of it and **t** branches of the lampstand out of
37:19 **t** cups shaped like almond blossoms, each
37:19 and **t** cups shaped like almond blossoms,
38: 1 it was square, and **t** cubits high.
38:14 with **t** pillars and **t** bases.
38:15 with **t** pillars and **t** bases.
38:26 for six hundred **t** thousand,
Lev 19:23 **t** years it shall be forbidden to you, C
25:21 so that it will yield a crop for **t** years. C
27: 6 for a female the equivalent is **t** shekels of silver.
Nu 1:23 of Simeon were fifty-nine thousand **t** hundred.
1:46 was six hundred **t** thousand five hundred fifty.
2:13 as enrolled of fifty-nine thousand **t** hundred.
2:32 was six hundred **t** thousand five hundred fifty.
3:50 one thousand **t** hundred sixty-five shekels,
4:44 by their clans was **t** thousand two hundred.
10:33 from the mount of the LORD **t** days' journey E
10:33 of the LORD going before them **t** days' journey, E
12: 4 "Come out, you **t**, to the tent of meeting."
12: 4 So the **t** of them came out.
22:28 that you have struck me these **t** times?" B
22:32 Why have you struck your donkey these **t** times? B
22:33 and turned away from me these **t** times. B
24:10 but instead you have blessed them these **t** times. B
26:25 sixty-four thousand **t** hundred enrolled.
31:36 **t** hundred thirty-seven thousand five hundred sheep
31:43 **t** hundred thirty-seven thousand five hundred sheep
33: 8 a **t** days' journey in the wilderness of Etham, E
35:14 you shall designate **t** cities beyond the Jordan,
35:14 and **t** cities in the land of Canaan,
Dt 4:41 on the east side of the Jordan **t** cities
16:16 **T** times a year all your males shall appear B
17: 6 of two or **t** witnesses the death sentence shall
19: 2 you shall set apart **t** cities in the land that
19: 3 the distances and divide into **t** regions the land
19: 7 I command you: You shall set apart **t** cities.
19: 9 then you shall add **t** more cities to these **t**,
19:15 of two or **t** witnesses shall a charge be sustained.
Jos 1:11 for in **t** days you are to cross over the Jordan, A
2:16 Hide yourselves there **t** days, A
2:22 into the hill country and stayed there **t** days, A
3: 2 At the end of **t** days the officers went through A
7: 3 or **t** thousand men should go up and attack Ai.
7: 4 So about **t** thousand of the people went up there;
9:16 But when **t** days had passed after they had made A
15:14 Caleb drove out from there the **t** sons of Anak:
18: 4 Provide **t** men from each tribe,
21:32 with its pasture lands—**t** towns.
Jdg 1:20 and he drove out from it the **t** sons of Anak.
7: 6 The number of those that lapped was **t** hundred;
7: 7 "With the **t** hundred that lapped I will deliver you,
7: 8 but retained the **t** hundred.
7:16 the **t** hundred men into **t** companies,
7:20 **t** companies blew the trumpets and broke the jars,
7:22 When they blew the **t** hundred trumpets,
8: 4 he and the **t** hundred who were with him,
9:22 Abimelech ruled over Israel **t** years. C
9:43 and divided them into **t** companies,
11:26 **t** hundred years, why did you not recover them
14:14 But for **t** days they could not explain the riddle. A
15: 4 So Samson went and caught **t** hundred foxes,
15:11 Then **t** thousand men of Judah went down to
16:15 You have mocked me **t** times now and have B
16:27 and on the roof there were about **t** thousand men
19: 4 him stay, and he remained with him **t** days; A
1Sa 2:21 she conceived and bore **t** sons and two daughters.
9:20 As for your donkeys that were lost **t** days ago, A
10: 3 **t** men going up to God will meet you there, one carrying **t** kids, another carrying **t** loaves of bread,
11: 8 those from Israel were **t** hundred thousand,
11:11 The next day Saul put the people in **t** companies.
13: 2 Saul chose **t** thousand out of Israel;
13:17 of the camp of the Philistines in **t** companies;
17:13 The **t** eldest sons of Jesse had followed Saul to
17:13 of his **t** sons who went to the battle were Eliab
17:14 the **t** eldest followed Saul,
20:20 I will shoot **t** arrows to the side of it,
1Sa 20:41 He bowed **t** times, and they kissed each other, B
24: 2 Saul took **t** thousand chosen men out of all Israel,
25: 2 he had **t** thousand sheep and a thousand goats.
26: 2 with **t** thousand chosen men of Israel,
30:12 or drunk water for **t** days and three nights. A
30:12 or drunk water for three days and **t** nights.
30:13 behind because I fell sick **t** days ago. A
31: 6 So Saul and his **t** sons and his armor-bearer
31: 8 and his **t** sons fallen on Mount Gilboa.
2Sa 2:18 The **t** sons of Zeruiah were there, Joab, Abishai,
2:31 of David had killed of Benjamin **t** hundred sixty
6:11 in the house of Obed-edom the Gittite **t** months; D
13:38 having fled to Geshur, stayed there **t** years. C
14:27 There were born to Absalom **t** sons,
18: 2 And David divided the army into **t** groups:
18:14 He took **t** spears in his hand,
20: 4 the men of Judah together to me within **t** days, A
21: 1 in the days of David for **t** years, year after year; C
21:16 whose spear weighed **t** hundred shekels
23: 8 he was chief of the **T**;
23: 9 Next to him among the **t** warriors was Eleazar son
23:13 the beginning of harvest **t** of the thirty chiefs went
23:16 Then the **t** warriors broke through the camp of
23:17 The **t** warriors did these things.
23:18 With his spear he fought against **t** hundred men
23:18 and won a name beside the **T**.
23:19 but he did not attain to the **T**.
23:22 and won a name beside the **t** warriors.
23:23 but he did not attain to the **T**.
24:12 Thus says the LORD: **T** things I offer you;
24:13 he asked him, "Shall **t** years of famine come C
24:13 Or will you flee **t** months before your foes D
24:13 Or shall there be **t** days' pestilence in your land? E
1Ki 2:39 of **t** years that two of Shimei's slaves ran away C
4:32 He composed **t** thousand proverbs,
5:16 Solomon's **t** thousand **t** hundred supervisors who
6:36 the inner court with **t** courses of dressed stone
7: 4 There were window frames in the **t** rows, facing each other in the **t** rows.
7: 5 opposite, facing each other in the **t** rows.
7:12 The great court had **t** courses of dressed stone
7:25 It stood on twelve oxen, **t** facing north, **t** facing west, **t** facing south, and **t** facing east; the sea was
7:27 four cubits wide, and **t** cubits high.
9:25 **T** times a year Solomon used to offer B
10:17 He made **t** hundred shields of beaten gold;
10:17 **t** minas of gold went into each shield;
10:22 Once every **t** years the fleet of ships C
11: 3 and **t** hundred concubines;
12: 5 He said to them, "Go away for **t** days, A
15: 2 He reigned for **t** years in Jerusalem. C
17:21 Then he stretched himself upon the child **t** times, B
22: 1 **t** years Aram and Israel continued without war. C
2Ki 2:17 So they sent fifty men who searched for **t** days A
3:10 The LORD has summoned us, **t** kings,
3:13 it is the LORD who has summoned us, **t** kings,
9:32 Two or **t** eunuchs looked out at him.
13:18 he struck **t** times, and stopped. B
13:19 now you will strike down Aram only **t** times." B
13:25 **T** times Joash defeated him and recovered B
17: 5 for **t** years he besieged it. C
18:10 and at the end of **t** years, C
18:14 of King Hezekiah of Judah **t** hundred talents
23:31 he reigned **t** months in Jerusalem. D
24: 1 Jehoiakim became his servant for **t** years; C
24: 8 he reigned **t** months in Jerusalem. D
25:17 the height of the capital was **t** cubits;
25:18 and the **t** guardians of the threshold;
1Ch 2: 3 these **t** the Canaanite woman Bath-shua bore
2:16 The sons of Zeruiah: Abishai, Joab, and Asahel, **t**.
3:23 Elioenai, Hizkiah, and Azrikam, **t**.
7: 6 sons of Benjamin: Bela, Becher, and Jediael, **t**.
10: 6 he and his **t** sons and all his house died together.
11:11 Jashobeam, son of Hachmoni, was chief of the **T**;
11:11 against **t** hundred whom he killed at one time.
11:12 among the **t** warriors was Eleazar son of Dodo,
11:15 **T** of the thirty chiefs went down to the rock
11:18 the **T** broke through the camp of the Philistines,
11:19 The **t** warriors did these things.
11:20 With his spear he fought against **t** hundred
11:20 and won a name beside the **T**.
11:21 but he did not attain to the **T**.
11:24 and he won a name beside the **t** warriors.
11:25 but he did not attain to the **T**.
12:27 and with him **t** thousand seven hundred.
12:29 the kindred of Saul, **t** thousand,
12:39 They were there with David for **t** days, A
13:14 of Obed-edom in his house **t** months, D
21:10 'Thus says the LORD: **T** things I offer you;
21:12 either **t** years of famine; C
21:12 or **t** months of devastation by your foes, D
21:12 or **t** days of the sword of the LORD, A
23: 8 Jehiel the chief, Zetham, and Joel, **t**.
23: 9 sons of Shimei: Shelomoth, Haziel, and Haran, **t**.
23:23 The sons of Mushi: Mahli, Eder, and Jeremoth, **t**.
25: 5 had given Heman fourteen sons and **t** daughters.
29: 4 **t** thousand talents of gold,
2Ch 2: 2 with **t** thousand six hundred to oversee them.
2:18 and **t** thousand six hundred as overseers to make
4: 4 It stood on twelve oxen, **t** facing north, **t** facing west, **t** facing south, and **t** facing east; the sea was
4: 5 like the flower of a lily; it held **t** thousand baths.
6:13 and **t** cubits high, and had set it in the court;
8:13 the new moons, and the **t** annual festivals—
9:16 He made **t** hundred shields of beaten gold;
9:16 **t** hundred shekels of gold went into each shield;
9:21 once every **t** years the ships of Tarshish used C

2Ch 10: 5 He said to them, "Come to me again in t days." A
11:17 and for t years they made Rehoboam son C
11:17 for they walked for t years in the way of David C
13: 2 He reigned for t years in Jerusalem. C
14: 8 an army of t hundred thousand from Judah, armed
14: 9 an army of a million men and t hundred chariots,
17:14 with t hundred thousand mighty warriors,
20:25 They spent t days taking the booty, A
25: 5 they were t hundred thousand picked troops fit
25:13 they killed t thousand people in them,
26:13 of t hundred seven thousand five hundred,
29:33 were six hundred bulls and t thousand sheep.
31:16 males from t years old and upwards, C
35: 7 of thirty thousand, and t thousand bulls;
35: 8 and kids and t hundred bulls.
36: 2 he reigned t months in Jerusalem. D
36: 9 he reigned t months and ten days in Jerusalem. D
Ezr 2: 4 Of Shephatiah, t hundred seventy-two.
2:17 Of Bezai, t hundred twenty-three.
2:32 Of Harim, t hundred twenty.
2:34 Of Jericho, t hundred forty-five.
2:35 Of Senaah, t thousand six hundred thirty.
2:58 of Solomon's servants were t hundred ninety-two.
2:64 together was forty-two thousand t hundred sixty,
2:65 there were seven thousand t hundred thirty-seven;
6: 4 with t courses of hewn stones and one course
8: 5 and with him t hundred males.
8:15 and there we camped t days. A
8:32 came to Jerusalem and remained there t days. A
10: 8 and that if any did not come within t days, A
10: 9 at Jerusalem within the t days; A
Ne 2:11 So I came to Jerusalem and was there for t days. A
7: 9 Of Shephatiah, t hundred seventy-two.
7:17 Of Azgad, two thousand t hundred twenty-two.
7:22 Of Hashum, t hundred twenty-eight.
7:23 Of Bezai, t hundred twenty-four.
7:35 Of Harim, t hundred twenty.
7:36 Of Jericho, t hundred forty-five.
7:38 Of Senaah, t thousand nine hundred thirty.
7:60 of Solomon's servants were t hundred ninety-two.
7:66 together was forty-two thousand t hundred sixty,
7:67 there were seven thousand t hundred thirty-seven;
Est 4:16 and neither eat nor drink for t days, night or day. A
9:15 of Adar and they killed t hundred persons in Susa;
Job 1: 2 to him seven sons and t daughters.
1: 3 He had seven thousand sheep, t thousand camels,
1: 4 and they would send and invite their t sisters
1:17 "The Chaldeans formed t columns,
2:11 when Job's t friends heard of all these troubles
32: 1 So these t men ceased to answer Job,
32: 3 he was angry also at Job's t friends
32: 5 in the mouths of these t men,
33:29 "God indeed does all these things, twice, t times, B
42:13 He also had seven sons and t daughters.
Pr 30:15 T things are never satisfied;
30:18 T things are too wonderful for me;
30:21 Under t things the earth trembles;
30:29 T things are stately in their stride;
Isa 16:14 But now the LORD says, In t years, C
17: 6 two or t berries in the top of the highest bough,
20: 3 for t years as a sign and a portent against Egypt C
Jer 36:23 As Jehudi read t or four columns,
38:10 "Take t men with you from here,
52:24 and the t guardians of the threshold;
52:28 t thousand twenty-three Judeans;
Eze 4: 5 t hundred ninety days, equal to the number of
4: 9 t hundred ninety days, you shall eat it.
14:14 Daniel, and Job, these t, were in it,
14:16 even if these t men were in it, as I live, says
14:18 though these t men were in it,
40:10 There were t recesses on either side of
40:10 the t were of the same size;
40:21 Its recesses, t on either side,
40:48 sidewalls of the gate were t cubits on either side.
41: 6 The side chambers were in t stories,
41:16 all t had windows with recessed frames.
41:22 t cubits high, two cubits long,
42: 3 the chambers rose gallery by gallery in t stories.
42: 6 For they were in t stories,
48:31 t gates, the gate of Reuben, the gate of Judah,
48:32 t gates, the gate of Joseph, the gate of Benjamin,
48:33 t gates, the gate of Simeon, the gate of Issachar,
48:34 t gates, the gate of Gad, the gate of Asher,
Da 1: 5 They were to be educated for t years, C
3:23 But the t men, Shadrach, Meshach,
3:24 not t men that we threw bound into the fire?"
6: 2 and over them t presidents, including Daniel;
6:10 to get down on his knees t times a day to pray B
6:13 but he is saying his prayers t times a day." B
7: 5 had t tusks in its mouth among its teeth
7: 8 for it, t of the earlier horns were plucked up by
7:20 and to make room for which t of them fell out—
7:24 and shall put down t kings.
8:14 two thousand t hundred evenings and mornings;
10: 2 Daniel, had been mourning for t weeks.
10: 3 not anointed myself at all, for the full t weeks.
11: 2 T more kings shall arise in Persia.
12:12 and attain the thousand t hundred thirty-five days.
Am 1: 3 For t transgressions of Damascus, and for four,
1: 6 For t transgressions of Gaza, and for four,
1: 9 For t transgressions of Tyre, and for four,
1:11 For t transgressions of Edom, and for four,
1:13 For t transgressions of the Ammonites,
2: 1 For t transgressions of Moab, and for four,
2: 4 For t transgressions of Judah, and for four,
2: 6 For t transgressions of Israel, and for four,
4: 4 every morning, your tithes every t days; A
Am 4: 7 the rain from you when there were still t months D
4: 8 so t towns wandered to one town to drink water,
Jnh 1:17 in the belly of the fish t days and three nights. A
1:17 in the belly of the fish three days and t nights.
3: 3 an exceedingly large city, a t days' walk across. E
Zec 11: 8 In one month I disposed of the t shepherds,
Mt 12:40 as Jonah was t days and three nights in the belly A
12:40 as Jonah was three days and t nights in the belly
12:40 for t days and three nights the Son of Man will A
12:40 and t nights the Son of Man will be in the heart of
13:33 that a woman took and mixed in with t measures
15:32 with me now for t days and have nothing to eat; A
17: 4 if you wish, I will make t dwellings here,
18:16 by the evidence of two or t witnesses.
18:20 For where two or t are gathered in my name,
20: 5 he went out again about noon and about t o'clock,
26:34 the cock crows, you will deny me t times." B
26:61 the temple of God and to build it in t days.'" A
26:75 the cock crows, you will deny me t times." B
27:40 the temple and build it in t days, A
27:45 darkness came over the whole land until t in
27:46 And about t o'clock Jesus cried with a loud voice,
27:63 'After t days I will rise again.' A
Mk 8: 2 with me now for t days and have nothing to eat. A
8:31 and be killed, and after t days rise again. A
9: 5 let us make t dwellings, one for you,
9:31 and t days after being killed, he will rise again." A
10:34 and after t days he will rise again." A
14: 5 for more than t hundred denarii,
14:30 you will deny me t times." B
14:58 and in t days I will build another, A
14:72 you will deny me t times." B
15:29 the temple and build it in t days, A
15:33 darkness came over the whole land until t in
15:34 At t o'clock Jesus cried out with a loud voice,
Lk 1:56 And Mary remained with her about t months D
2:46 After t days they found him in the temple, A
4:25 the heaven was shut up t years and six months, C
9:33 let us make t dwellings, one for you,
10:36 Which of these t, do you think,
11: 5 'Friend, lend me t loaves of bread;
12:52 t against two and two against t;
13: 7 For t years I have come looking for fruit C
13:21 that a woman took and mixed in with t measures
22:34 you have denied t times that you know me." B
22:61 you will deny me t times." B
23:44 and darkness came over the whole land until t in
Jn 2:19 and in t days I will raise it up." A
2:20 and will you raise it up in t days?" A
6:19 When they had rowed about t or four miles,
12: 5 for t hundred denarii and the money given to
13:38 you will have denied me t times. B
Ac 2:41 that day about t thousand persons were added.
3: 1 at t o'clock in the afternoon.
5: 7 an interval of about t hours his wife came in,
7:20 t months he was brought up in his father's D
9: 9 For t days he was without sight, A
10: 3 One afternoon at about t o'clock he had a vision
10:16 This happened t times, B
10:19 "Look, t men are searching for you.
10:30 "Four days ago at this very hour, at t o'clock,
11:10 This happened t times; B
11:11 At that very moment t men,
17: 2 and on t sabbath days argued with them from
19: 8 synagogue and for t months spoke out boldly, D
20: 3 where he stayed for t months. D
20: 9 to the ground t floors below and was picked
20:31 remembering that for t years I did not cease C
23: 8 but the Pharisees acknowledge all t.)
25: 1 T days after Festus had arrived in the province, A
28: 7 and entertained us hospitably for t days. A
28:11 T months later we set sail on a ship D
28:12 put in at Syracuse and stayed there for t days; A
28:15 as the Forum of Appius and T Taverns to meet us.
28:17 T days later he called together the local leaders A
1Co 13:13 And now faith, hope, and love abide, these t;
14:27 let there be only two or at most t,
14:29 Let two or t prophets speak,
2Co 11:25 T times I was beaten with rods. B
11:25 T times I was shipwrecked; B
12: 8 T times I appealed to the Lord about this, B
13: 1 by the evidence of two or t witnesses."
Gal 1:18 Then after t years I did go up to Jerusalem C
1Ti 5:19 on the evidence of two or t witnesses.
Heb 10:28 "on the testimony of two or t witnesses."
11:23 for t months after his birth, because they saw D
Jas 5:17 t years and six months it did not rain on the C
1Jn 5: 7 There are t that testify:
5: 8 and the water and the blood, and these t agree.
Rev 6: 6 and t quarts of barley for a day's pay,
8:13 of the other trumpets that the t angels are about
9:18 By these t plagues a third
11: 9 For t and a half days members of the peoples
11:11 But after the t and a half days,
16:13 And I saw t foul spirits like frogs coming from
16:19 The great city was split into t parts,
21:13 on the east t gates, on the north t gates, on the
south t gates, and on the west t gates.
Jdt 1: 2 around Ecbatana with hewn stones t cubits thick
2:21 t days from Nineveh to the plain of Bectileth, A
8: 4 as a widow for t years and four months C
12: 7 She remained in the camp t days. A
16:20 For t months the people continued feasting D
AdE 4:16 for t days and nights do not eat or drink, A
9:15 on the fourteenth and killed t hundred people,
Sir 13: 7 until he has drained you two or t times, B
25: 1 I take pleasure in t things,
Sir 25: 2 I hate t kinds of people, and I loathe their manner
26: 5 Of t things my heart is frightened,
43: 4 t times as hot is the sun scorching the mountains; B
48: 3 and also t times brought down fire. B
Aza 1:28 Then the t with one voice praised and glorified
1Mc 4: 6 in the plain with t thousand men,
4:15 and t thousand of them fell.
5:20 Then t thousand men were assigned to Simon
5:22 as many as t thousand of the Gentiles fell,
5:24 and made t days' journey into the wilderness. E
5:33 Then he came up behind them in t companies,
7:40 Judas encamped in Adasa with t thousand men.
8:15 every day t hundred twenty senators constantly
9: 5 and with him were t thousand picked men.
10:30 the land of Judah or from the t districts added to it
10:34 the t days before a festival and the three after A
10:34 and the three days before a festival and the t after
10:38 the t districts that have been added to Judea from
10:77 he mustered t thousand cavalry and a large army,
11:18 But King Ptolemy died t days later, A
11:28 to free Judea and the t districts of Samaria
11:28 and promised him t hundred talents.
11:34 both the territory of Judea and the t districts
11:44 So Jonathan sent t thousand stalwart men to him
11:74 many as t thousand of the foreigners fell that day.
12:47 He kept with himself t thousand men,
2Mc 4: 8 at an interview t hundred sixty talents of silver,
4:19 to carry t hundred silver drachmas for
4:23 After a period of t years Jason sent Menelaus, C
4:24 outbidding Jason by t hundred talents of silver.
4:40 Lysimachus armed about t thousand men
4:44 t men sent by the senate presented the case
5:14 of t days eighty thousand were destroyed, A
7:27 and nursed you for t years, C
12:33 who came out with t thousand infantry
13: 2 five thousand t hundred cavalry,
13: 2 and t hundred chariots armed with scythes.
13:12 and lying prostrate for t days without ceasing, A
14: 1 T years later, word came to Judas and his men C
1Es 1: 7 and kids, and t thousand calves;
1: 8 thousand six hundred sheep and t hundred calves.
1:35 He reigned t months in Judah and Jerusalem. D
1:44 he reigned t months and ten days in Jerusalem. D
3: 4 Then the t young men of the bodyguard,
3: 9 the one whose statement the king and the t nobles
5:13 one thousand t hundred twenty-two.
5:16 descendants of Bezai, t hundred twenty-three.
5:17 The descendants of Baiterus, t thousand five.
5:22 The descendants of Jerechus, t hundred forty-five.
5:23 t thousand three hundred thirty.
5:23 three thousand t hundred thirty.
5:35 of Solomon's servants were t hundred seventy-two.
5:41 were forty-two thousand t hundred sixty;
5:42 were seven thousand t hundred thirty-seven;
6:25 with t courses of hewn stone and one course
8:32 and with him t hundred men.
8:41 and we encamped there t days, A
8:62 When we had been there t days, A
9: 4 if any did not meet there within two or t days, A
9: 5 at Jerusalem within t days; A
3Mc 6: 6 The t companions in Babylon
6:38 for the fifth to the seventh of Epeiph, the t days A
7:15 to death more than t hundred men;
2Es 4: 3 "I have been sent to show you t ways,
4: 3 and to put before you t problems.
6:21 to premature children at t and four months,
6:24 so that for t hours they shall not flow.
6:35 to complete the t weeks that had been prescribed
10:45 the reason is that there were t thousand years in
10:46 And after t thousand years Solomon built the city,
11: 1 that had twelve feathered wings and t heads.
11:23 on the eagle's body except the t heads that were
12:22 "As for your seeing t heads at rest,
12:23 the Most High will raise up t kings,
13:56 that after t more days I will tell you other things,
13:58 And I stayed there t days. A
16:29 as in an olive orchard t or four olives may be left
16:31 so in those days t or four shall be left
16:38 around her womb for two or t hours beforehand,
4Mc 4:17 king t thousand six hundred sixty talents annually.
13: 9 let us imitate the t youths in Assyria who despised

THREE TAVERNS See TAVERNS, THREE

THREE-PRONGED (1) [THREE]

1Sa 2:13 with a t fork in his hand,

THREE-STRINGED See Index to Footnotes

THREE-TENTHS (8) [TEN, THREE]

Lev 14:10 of t of an ephah of choice flour mixed with oil,
Nu 15: 9 t of an ephah of choice flour,
28:12 also t of an ephah of choice flour for
28:20 t of an ephah shall you offer for a bull,
28:28 t of an ephah for each bull,
29: 3 t of one ephah for the bull, two-tenths for the ram,
29: 9 t of an ephah for the bull,
29:14 t of an ephah for each of the thirteen bulls,

THREE-YEAR-OLD (1) [OLD, THREE, YEAR]

1Sa 1:24 she took him up with her, along with a t bull,

THREEFOLD (1) [THREE]

Ecc 4:12 A t cord is not quickly broken.

THREESCORE (KJV) See SIXTY

THRESH (7) [THRESHED, THRESHES, THRESHING]

1Ch 21:20 Ornan continued to t wheat.
Isa 27:12 On that day the LORD will t from the channel of
28:28 but one does not t it forever;
41:15 you shall t the mountains and crush them,
Hos 10:11 Ephraim was a trained heifer that loved to t,
Mic 4:13 Arise and t, O daughter Zion,
1Co 9:10 in hope and whoever threshes should t in hope of

THRESHED (3) [THRESH]

Isa 21:10 O my t and winnowed one,
28:27 Dill is not t with a threshing sledge,
Am 1: 3 they have t Gilead with threshing sledges of iron.

THRESHES (1) [THRESH]

1Co 9:10 and whoever t should thresh in hope of a share in

THRESHING‡ (51) [THRESH]

Ge 50:10 When they came to the t floor of Atad,
50:11 the land saw the mourning on the t floor of Atad,
Lev 26: 5 Your t shall overtake the vintage,
Nu 15:20 as you present a donation from the t floor.
18:27 of the t floor and the fullness of the wine press.
18:30 to the Levites as produce of the t floor,
Dt 15:14 Provide liberally out of your flock, your t floor,
16:13 from your t floor and your wine press.
Jdg 6:37 I am going to lay a fleece of wool on the t floor;
Ru 3: 2 See, he is winnowing barley tonight at the t floor.
3: 3 on your best clothes and go down to the t floor;
3: 6 So she went down to the t floor and did just
3:14 be known that the woman came to the t floor."
1Sa 23: 1 and are robbing the t floors."
2Sa 6: 6 When they came to the t floor of Nacon,
24:16 of the LORD was then by the t floor of Araunah
24:18 up and erect an altar to the LORD on the t floor
24:21 the t floor from you in order to build an altar to
24:22 t sledges and the yokes of the oxen for the wood.
24:24 the t floor and the oxen for fifty shekels of silver.
1Ki 22:10 the t floor at the entrance of the gate of Samaria;
2Ki 6:27 From the t floor or from the wine press?"
13: 7 and made them like the dust at t.
1Ch 13: 9 When they came to the t floor of Chidon,
21:15 then standing by the t floor of Ornan the Jebusite.
21:18 to the LORD on the t floor of Ornan the Jebusite.
21:21 he went out from the t floor,
21:22 the site of the t floor that I may build on it an altar
21:23 and the t sledges for the wood,
21:28 that the LORD had answered him at the t floor
2Ch 3: 1 on the t floor of Ornan the Jebusite.
18: 9 and they were sitting at the t floor at the entrance
Job 5:26 of grain comes up to the t floor in its season.
39:12 and bring your grain to your t floor?
41:30 it spreads itself like a t sledge on the mire.
Isa 28:27 Dill is not threshed with a t sledge,
41:15 Now, I will make of you a t sledge, sharp, new,
Jer 51:33 Daughter Babylon is like a t floor at the time
Da 2:35 and became like the chaff of the summer t floors;
Hos 9: 1 You have loved a prostitute's pay on all t floors.
9: 2 T floor and wine vat shall not feed them,
13: 3 from the t floor or like smoke from a window.
Joel 2:24 The t floors shall be full of grain,
Am 1: 3 they have threshed Gilead with t sledges of iron.
Mic 4:12 he has gathered them as sheaves to the t floor.
Mt 3:12 and he will clear his t floor
Lk 3:17 to clear his t floor and to gather the wheat
2Es 4:30 and will produce until the time of t comes!
4:32 how great a t floor they will fill!"
4:39 on account of us that the time of t is delayed for
9:17 and as is the farmer, so is the t floor.

THRESHOLD‡ (27) [THRESHOLDS]

Jdg 19:27 with her hands on the t.
1Sa 5: 4 and both his hands were lying cut off upon the t;
5: 5 of Dagon do not step on the t of Dagon in Ashdod
1Ki 14:17 As she came to the t of the house, the child died.
2Ki 12: 9 the t put in it all the money that was brought into
22: 4 which the keepers of the t have collected from
23: 4 and the guardians of the t,
25:18 and the three guardians of the t;
2Ch 34: 9 which the Levites, the keepers of the t,
Est 2:21 two of the king's eunuchs, who guarded the t,
6: 2 two of the king's eunuchs, who guarded the t,
Pr 17:19 one who builds a high t invites broken bones.
Jer 35: 4 of Maaseiah son of Shallum, keeper of the t.
52:24 and the three guardians of the t;
Eze 9: 3 the cherub on which it rested to the t of the house.
10: 4 of the LORD rose up from the cherub to the t of
10:18 Then the glory of the LORD went out from the t
40: 6 going up its steps, and measured the t of the gate,
40: 7 and the t of the gate by the vestibule of the gate at
41:16 Facing the t the temple was paneled with wood all
43: 8 When they placed their t by my threshold
43: 8 by my t and their doorposts beside my doorposts,
46: 2 and he shall bow down at the t of the gate.
47: 1 water was flowing from below the t of the temple
47: 1 from below the south end of the t of the temple,
Zep 1: 9 On that day I will punish all who leap over the t,
Zep 2:14 the raven croak on the t;

THRESHOLDS‡ (5) [THRESHOLD]

1Ch 9:19 guardians of the t of the tent,
9:22 who were chosen as gatekeepers at the t,
2Ch 3: 7 its beams, its t, its walls, and its doors;
Isa 6: 4 on the t shook at the voices of those who called,
Am 9: 1 Strike the capitals until the t shake,

THREW‡ (87) [THROW]

Ge 37:24 and they took him and t him into a pit.
50: 1 Then Joseph t himself on his father's face
Ex 4: 3 So he t the staff on the ground,
7:10 Aaron t down his staff before Pharaoh
7:12 Each one t down his staff,
9:10 and Moses t it in the air,
14:24 and t the Egyptian army into panic.
15:25 he t it into the water, and the water became sweet.
32:19 and he t the tablets from his hands
32:24 so they gave it to me, and I t it into the fire,
Dt 9:21 and I t the dust of it into the stream that runs
Jos 8:29 t it down at the entrance of the gate of the city,
10:10 And the LORD t them into a panic before Israel,
10:11 the LORD t down huge stones from heaven
10:27 down from the trees and t them into the cave
Jdg 4:15 And the LORD t Sisera and all his chariots
8:12 and t all the army into a panic.
8:25 each t into it an earring he had taken as booty.
9:53 But a certain woman t an upper millstone
15:17 he had finished speaking, he t away the jawbone;
1Sa 7:10 against the Philistines and t them into confusion;
18:11 and Saul t the spear, for he thought,
20:33 But Saul t his spear at him to strike him;
2Sa 16: 6 He t stones at David and at all the servants
18:17 t him into a great pit in the forest,
20:12 and t a garment over him.
20:15 they t up a siege ramp against the city,
20:22 and t it out to Joab.
1Ki 19:19 Elijah passed by him and t his mantle over him.
2Ki 2:21 of water and t the salt into it, and said, "Thus says
3:25 on every good piece of land everyone t a stone,
4:41 He t it into the pot, and said,
6: 6 and t it in there, and made the iron float.
9:33 "Throw her down." So they t her down;
10:25 The guards and the officers t them out,
23: 6 beat it to dust and t the dust of it upon the graves
23:12 and t the rubble into the Wadi Kidron.
2Ch 25:12 and t them down from the top of Sela,
30:14 for offering incense they took away and t into
33:15 and he t them out of the city.
Ne 9:11 but you t their pursuers into the depths,
13: 8 and I t all the household furniture of Tobiah out
Job 2:12 they tore their robes and t dust in the air
Jer 26:23 down with the sword and t his dead body into
38: 6 So they took Jeremiah and t him into the cistern
41: 7 and t them into a cistern.
Da 3:24 not three men that we t bound into the fire?"
8: 7 it t the ram down to the ground and trampled
8:10 It t down to the earth some of the host and some
Jnh 1: 5 They t the cargo that was in the ship into the sea,
1:15 So they picked Jonah up and t him into the sea;
Zec 11:13 of silver and t them into the treasury in the house
Mt 13:48 and put the good into baskets but t out the bad.
18:30 and t him into prison until he would pay the debt.
21:39 So they seized him, t him out of the vineyard,
26:39 he t himself on the ground and prayed,
Mk 11: 7 the colt to Jesus and t their cloaks on it;
12: 8 killed him, and t him out of the vineyard.
14:35 he t himself on the ground and prayed that,
Lk 20:12 this one also they wounded and t out.
20:15 So they t him out of the vineyard and killed him.
Ac 16:23 they t them into prison and ordered the jailer
27:19 and on the third day with their own hands they t
Rev 8: 5 and filled it with fire from the altar and t it on
12: 4 down a third of the stars of heaven and t them to
14:19 and he t it into the great wine press of the wrath
18:19 And they t dust on their heads,
18:21 like a great millstone and t it into the sea, saying,
20: 3 and t him into the pit,
Tob 11: 9 Then Anna ran up to her son and t her arms
11:13 Tobit saw his son and t his arms around him,
Jdt 14: 7 they raised him up he t himself at Judith's feet,
Aza 1:23 the king's servants who t them in kept stoking
Bel 1:31 They t Daniel into the lions' den,
1:42 Then he pulled Daniel out, and t into
1Mc 5:43 and they t away their arms and fled into
7:19 and killed them and t them into a great pit.
7:44 they t down their arms and fled.
11:11 He t blame on Alexander
11:51 And they t down their arms and made peace.
2Mc 1:16 they t stones and struck down the leader
1:16 and cut off their heads and t them to the people
4:41 and t them in wild confusion at Lysimachus
14:43 and bravely t himself down into the crowd.
2Es 1:23 t a tree into the water and made the stream sweet.
4Mc 6:25 with maliciously contrived instruments, t him
17: 1 about to be seized and put to death she t herself

THRICE (1) [THREE]

Eze 21:14 Let the sword fall twice, t;

THRICE (KJV) See also THREE TIMES

THRICE-ACCURSED (3) [CURSE, THREE]

AdE 16:15 who were consigned to annihilation by this t man,
2Mc 8:34 The t Nicanor, who had brought
15: 3 the t wretch asked if there were a sovereign

THRILL (1)

Isa 60: 5 your heart shall t and rejoice,

THRIVE (3)

Job 8:16 The wicked t before the sun,
Jer 12: 1 Why do all who are treacherous t?
Eze 17:10 When it is transplanted, will it t?

THRIVES See Index to Footnotes

THROAT (7) [THROATS]

Job 24:12 and the t of the wounded cries for help;
Ps 69: 3 I am weary with my crying; my t is parched.
Pr 23: 2 put a knife to your t if you have a big appetite.
23: 7 for like a hair in the t,
Jer 2:25 Keep your feet from going unshod and your t
4:10 even while the sword is at the t!"
Mt 18:28 seizing him by the t, he said, 'Pay what you owe.'

THROATS (5) [THROAT]

Ps 5: 9 their t are open graves; they flatter with their
115: 7 they make no sound in their t.
149: 6 be in their t and two-edged swords in their hands,
Hab 2: 5 They open their t wide as Sheol;
Ro 3:13 "Their t are opened graves;

THROBS (2)

Ps 38:10 My heart t, my strength fails me;
Isa 16:11 Therefore my heart t like a harp for Moab,

THRONE (196) [ENTHRONED, ENTHRONES, THRONES]

Ge 41:40 with regard to the t will I be greater than you."
Ex 11: 5 on his t to the firstborn of the female slave who is
12:29 on his t to the firstborn of the prisoner who was in
Dt 17:18 When he has taken the t of his kingdom,
2Sa 3:10 set up the t of David over Israel and over Judah,
7:13 and I will establish the t of his kingdom forever.
7:16 your t shall be established forever.
14: 9 let the king and his t be guiltless."
1Ki 1:13 and he shall sit on my t?
1:17 and he shall sit on my t.
1:20 to tell them who shall sit on the t of my lord
1:24 and he shall sit on my t'?
1:27 not let your servants know who should sit on the t
1:30 and he shall sit on my t in my place,'
1:35 Let him enter and sit on my t;
1:37 and make his t greater than the t of my lord
1:46 Solomon now sits on the royal t.
1:47 and make his t greater than your t.'
1:48 of my offspring to sit on my t and permitted me
2: 4 there shall not fail you a successor on the t
2:12 So Solomon sat on the t of his father David;
2:19 then he sat on his t, and had a t brought for the
2:24 who has established me and placed me on the t
2:33 and to his house, and to his t,
2:45 and the t of David shall be established before
3: 6 and have given him a son to sit on his t today.
5: 5 whom I will set on your t in your place,
7: 7 of the T where he was to pronounce judgment,
8:20 I sit on the t of Israel, as the LORD promised,
8:25 a successor before me to sit on the t of Israel,
9: 5 I will establish your royal t over Israel forever,
9: 5 'There shall not fail you a successor on the t
10: 9 who has delighted in you and set you on the t
10:18 The king also made a great ivory t,
10:19 The t had six steps.
10:19 The top of the t was rounded in the back,
16:11 as soon as he had seated himself on his t,
22:19 I saw the LORD sitting on his t,
2Ki 10: 3 set him on his father's t,
10:30 the fourth generation shall sit on the t of Israel."
11:19 He took his seat on the t of the kings.
13:13 and Jeroboam sat upon his t;
15:12 on the t of Israel to the fourth generation."
1Ch 17:12 and I will establish his t forever.
17:14 and his t shall be established forever.
22:10 and I will establish his royal t in Israel forever.'
28: 5 he has chosen my son Solomon to sit upon the t
29:23 Then Solomon sat on the t of the LORD,
2Ch 6:10 and sit on the t of Israel, as the LORD promised,
6:16 a successor before me to sit on the t of Israel,
7:18 then I will establish your royal t,
9: 8 who has delighted in you and set you on his t
9:17 The king also made a great ivory t,
9:18 The t had six steps and a footstool of gold,
9:18 which were attached to the t,
18:18 I saw the LORD sitting on his t,
21: 4 When Jehoram had ascended the t of his father
23:20 They set the king on the royal t.
Est 1: 2 when King Ahasuerus sat on his royal t in
5: 1 The king was sitting on his royal t inside
Job 36: 7 but with kings on the t he sets them forever,
Ps 9: 4 you have sat on the t giving righteous judgment.
9: 7 he has established his t for judgment.
11: 4 the LORD's t is in heaven.
45: 6 Your t, O God, endures forever and ever.

Ps 47: 8 God sits on his holy **t**.
89: 4 and build your **t** for all generations.' "
89:14 and justice are the foundation of your **t**;
89:29 and his **t** as long as the heavens endure.
89:36 and his **t** endure before me like the sun.
89:44 and hurled his **t** to the ground.
93: 2 your **t** is established from of old;
97: 2 and justice are the foundation of his **t**.
103:19 The LORD has established his **t** in the heavens,
132:11 "One of the sons of your body I will set on your **t**.
132:12 their sons also, forevermore, shall sit on your **t**."
Pr 16:12 for the **t** is established by righteousness.
20: 8 the **t** of judgment winnows all evil with his eyes.
20:28 and his **t** is upheld by righteousness.
25: 5 and his **t** will be established in righteousness.
29:14 his **t** will be established forever.
Isa 6: 1 I saw the Lord sitting on a **t**, high and lofty;
9: 7 and there shall be endless peace for the **t** of David
14:13 I will raise my **t** above the stars of God;
16: 5 a **t** shall be established in steadfast love in the tent
22:23 he will become a **t** of honor to his ancestral house.
47: 1 Sit on the ground without a **t**, daughter Chaldea!
66: 1 Heaven is my **t** and the earth is my footstool;
Jer 3:17 At that time Jerusalem shall be called the **t** of
13:13 the kings who sit on David's **t**, the priests,
14:21 do not dishonor your glorious **t**;
17:12 O glorious **t**, exalted from the beginning,
17:25 of this city kings who sit on the **t** of David, riding
22: 2 O King of Judah sitting on the **t** of David—
22: 4 of this house shall enter kings who sit on the **t**
22:30 of his offspring shall succeed in sitting on the **t**
29:16 the LORD concerning the king who sits on the **t**
33:17 David shall never lack a man to sit on the **t** of
33:21 so that he would not have a son to reign on his **t**,
36:30 He shall have no one to sit upon the **t** of David,
43:10 and he will set his **t** above these stones
49:38 and I will set my **t** in Elam,
La 5:19 your **t** endures to all generations.
Eze 1:26 over their heads there was something like a **t**,
1:26 a **t** was something that seemed like a human form.
10: 1 like a sapphire, in form resembling a **t**.
43: 7 this is the place of my **t** and the place for the soles
Da 5:20 he was deposed from his kingly **t**,
7: 9 and an Ancient One took his **t**,
7: 9 his **t** was fiery flames, and its wheels were burning
Jnh 3: 6 he rose from his **t**, removed his robe,
Hag 2:22 and to overthrow the **t** of kingdoms;
Zec 6:13 and shall sit and rule on his **t**.
6:13 There shall be a priest by his **t**,
Mt 5:34 either by heaven, for it is the **t** of God,
19:28 the Son of Man is seated on the **t** of his glory,
23:22 the **t** of God and by the one who is seated upon it.
25:31 then he will sit on the **t** of his glory.
Lk 1:32 and the Lord God will give to him the **t**
Ac 2:30 that he would put one of his descendants on his **t**.
7:49 'Heaven is my **t**, and the earth is my footstool.
Heb 1: 8 But of the Son he says, "Your **t**, O God,
4:16 therefore approach the **t** of grace with boldness,
8: 1 one who is seated at the right hand of the **t** of
12: 2 and has taken his seat at the right hand of the **t**
Rev 1: 4 and from the seven spirits who are before his **t**,
2:13 where you are living, where Satan's **t** is.
3:21 a place with me on my **t**,
3:21 and sat down with my Father on his **t**.
4: 2 there in heaven stood a **t**, with one seated on the **t**!
4: 3 the **t** is a rainbow that looks like an emerald.
4: 4 Around the **t** are twenty-four thrones,
4: 5 Coming from the **t** are flashes of lightning,
4: 5 and in front of the **t** burn seven flaming torches,
4: 6 and in front of the **t** there is something like a sea
4: 6 Around the **t**, and on each side of the **t**,
4: 9 and thanks to the one who is seated on the **t**,
4:10 before the one who is seated on the **t** and worship
4:10 they cast their crowns before the **t**, singing,
5: 1 of the one seated on the **t** a scroll written on the
5: 6 between the **t** and the four living creatures and
5: 7 the right hand of the one who was seated on the **t**.
5:11 the voice of many angels surrounding the **t** and
5:13 on the **t** and to the Lamb be blessing and honor
6:16 from the face of the one seated on the **t** and from
7: 9 standing before the **t** and before the Lamb,
7:10 to our God who is seated on the **t**,
7:11 And all the angels stood around the **t** and around
7:11 on their faces before the **t** and worshiped God,
7:15 For this reason they are before the **t** of God,
7:15 the one who is seated on the **t** will shelter them.
7:17 Lamb at the center of the **t** will be their shepherd,
8: 3 the saints on the golden altar that is before the **t**.
12: 5 and taken to God and to his **t**;
13: 2 And the dragon gave it his power and his **t**
14: 3 and they sing a new song before the **t** and before
16:10 fifth angel poured his bowl on the **t** of the beast,
16:17 from the **t**, saying, "It is done!"
19: 4 down and worshiped God who is seated on the **t**,
19: 5 And from the **t** came a voice saying,
20:11 I saw a great white **t** and the one who sat on it;
20:12 standing before the **t**, and books were opened.
21: 3 And I heard a loud voice from the **t** saying, "See,
21: 5 And the one who was seated on the **t** said, "See,
22: 1 flowing from the **t** of God and of the Lamb
22: 3 But the **t** of God and of the Lamb will be in it,
Jdt 1:12 by his **t** and kingdom that he would take revenge
11:19 there I will set your **t**.
AdE 15: 6 He was seated on his royal **t**,
15: 8 from his **t** and took her in his arms until she came
16:11 down to by all as the person second to the royal **t**.
Wis 9: 4 give me the wisdom that sits by your **t**,
Wis 9:10 and from the **t** of your glory send her,
9:12 and shall be worthy of the **t** of my father.
18:15 from heaven, from the royal **t**, into the midst of
Sir 1: 8 greatly to be feared, seated upon his **t**—the Lord.
24: 4 and my **t** was in a pillar of cloud.
40: 3 on a splendid **t** to the one who grovels in dust
47:11 a covenant of kingship and a glorious **t** in Israel.
Bar 5: 6 carried in glory, as on a royal **t**.
Aza 1:32 into the depths from your **t** on the cherubim,
1:33 Blessed are you on the **t** of your kingdom,
1Mc 2:57 inherited the **t** of the kingdom forever.
7: 4 Demetrius took his seat on the **t** of his kingdom.
10:52 and have taken my seat on the **t** of my ancestors,
10:53 we have taken our seat on the **t** of his kingdom—
10:55 and took your seat on the **t** of their kingdom.
11:52 So King Demetrius sat on the **t** of his kingdom,
2Es 8:21 whose **t** is beyond measure and whose glory is
4Mc 4:15 his son Antiochus Epiphanes succeeded to the **t**,
17:18 now stand before the divine **t** and live the life

THRONES‡ (22) [THRONE]

1Ki 22:10 of Judah were sitting on their **t**, arrayed
2Ch 18: 9 of Judah were sitting on their **t**, arrayed
Ps 122: 5 For there the **t** for judgment were set up,
122: 5 the **t** of the house of David.
Isa 10:13 a bull I have brought down those who sat on **t**.
14: 9 from their **t** all who were kings of the nations.
Jer 1:15 and all of them shall set their **t** at the entrance of
Eze 26:16 of the sea shall step down from their **t**;
Da 7: 9 **t** were set in place, and an Ancient One took his
Mt 19:28 also sit on twelve **t**, judging the twelve tribes
Lk 1:52 He has brought down the powerful from their **t**,
22:30 and you will sit on **t** judging the twelve tribes
Col 1:16 whether **t** or dominions or rulers or powers—
Rev 4: 4 Around the throne are twenty-four **t**, and seated on
the **t** are twenty-four elders,
11:16 Then the twenty-four elders who sit on their **t**
20: 4 Then I saw **t**, and those seated
Jdt 9: 3 along with princes, and princes on their **t**.
Wis 5:23 and evildoing will overturn the **t** of rulers.
6:21 Therefore if you delight in **t** and scepters,
7: 8 I preferred her to scepters and **t**,
Sir 10:14 The Lord overthrows the **t** of rulers,

THRONG (6) [THRONGED]

Ps 35:18 in the mighty **t** I will praise you.
42: 4 how I went with the **t**, and led them in procession
55:14 we walked in the house of God with the **t**.
109:30 I will praise him in the midst of the **t**.
Isa 5:14 her **t** and all who exult in her.
3Mc 6:14 The whole **t** of infants

THRONGED (1) [THRONG]

2Mc 3:19 with sackcloth under their breasts, **t** the streets.

THROUGH‡ (743) [THROUGHOUT]

Ge 12: 6 Abram passed **t** the land to the place at Shechem,
13:17 walk **t** the length and the breadth of the land,
19:32 so that we may preserve offspring **t** our father."
19:34 so that we may preserve offspring **t** our father."
21:12 it is **t** Isaac that offspring shall be named for you.
26: 4 of the earth shall gain blessing for themselves **t**
30: 3 upon my knees and that I too may have children **t**
30:32 let me pass **t** all your flock today, removing
31:37 Although you have felt about **t** all my goods,
41:36 so that the land may not perish **t** the famine."
41:46 and went **t** all the land of Egypt.
42:23 since he spoke with them **t** an interpreter.
Ex 9:16 and to make my name resound **t** all the earth.
9:35 just as the LORD had spoken **t** Moses.
11: 4 About midnight I will go out **t** Egypt.
12:12 For I will pass **t** the land of Egypt that night,
12:23 LORD will pass **t** to strike down the Egyptians;
14:29 But the Israelites walked on dry ground **t** the sea,
15:19 but the Israelites walked **t** the sea on dry ground.
19:21 and warn the people not to break **t** to the LORD
19:24 either the priests or the people break **t** to come up
26:28 shall pass **t** from end to end.
27: 7 the poles shall be put **t** the rings,
29:35 **t** seven days you shall ordain them.
36:33 the middle bar to pass **t** from end to end halfway
38: 7 And he put the poles **t** the rings on the sides of
Lev 8:36 the things that the LORD commanded **t** Moses.
10: 3 the LORD meant when he said, '**T** those who are
10:11 the statutes that the LORD has spoken to them **t**
11:46 and every living creature that moves **t** the waters
21: 9 daughter of a priest profanes herself **t** prostitution,
26: 6 and no sword shall go **t** your land.
26:46 and the people of Israel on Mount Sinai **t** Moses.
Nu 4:49 According to the commandment of the LORD **t**
5: 2 everyone who is unclean **t** contact with a corpse;
9: 6 there were certain people who were unclean **t**
9: 7 "Although we are unclean **t** touching a corpse,
9:10 or your descendants who is unclean **t** touching
12: 2 "Has the LORD spoken only **t** Moses?
12: 2 Has he not spoken **t** us also?"
13:32 "The land that we have gone **t** as spies is a land
14: 7 "The land that we went **t** as spies is
16:40 just as the LORD had said to him **t** Moses.
20:17 Now let us pass **t** your land.
20:17 We will not pass **t** field or vineyard,
20:17 the right hand or to the left until we have passed **t**
20:18 But Edom said to him, "You shall not pass **t**,
20:19 just let us pass **t** on foot."
20:20 But he said, "You shall not pass **t**."
Nu 20:21 Thus Edom refused to give Israel passage **t**
21:22 "Let me pass **t** your land;
21:22 by the King's Highway until we have passed **t**
21:23 But Sihon would not allow Israel to pass **t**
25: 8 the Israelite and the woman, **t** the belly.
27:23 as the LORD had directed **t** Moses.
31:23 shall be passed **t** fire, and it shall be clean.
31:23 shall be passed **t** the water.
33: 8 passed **t** the sea into the wilderness,
36:13 and the ordinances that the LORD commanded **t**
Dt 1:19 and went **t** all that great and terrible wilderness
2: 4 about to pass **t** the territory of your kindred,
2: 7 he knows your going **t** this great wilderness.
2:27 "If you let me pass **t** your land, I will travel only
2:28 Only allow me to pass **t** on foot—
2:30 of Heshbon was not willing to let us pass **t**,
8:15 who led you **t** the great and terrible wilderness,
15:17 an awl and thrust it **t** his earlobe into the door,
18:10 among you who makes a son or daughter pass **t**
29:16 and how we came **t** the midst of the nations
29:16 how we came through the midst of the nations **t**
31:29 to anger **t** the work of your hands."
32:47 **t** it you may live long in the land
33:26 who rides **t** the heavens to your help, majestic **t**
the skies.
Jos 1:11 "Pass **t** the camp, and command the people:
2:15 Then she let them down by a rope **t** the window,
2:18 not tie this crimson cord in the window **t**
3: 2 the end of three days the officers went **t** the camp
5: 4 had died during the journey **t** the wilderness
5: 5 the people born on the journey **t** the wilderness
13:30 from Mahanaim, **t** all Bashan, the whole kingdom
14:10 while Israel was journeying **t** the wilderness;
18:12 then up **t** the hill country westward;
20: 2 of which I spoke to you **t** Moses,
21: 2 "The LORD commanded **t** Moses that we
21: 8 as the LORD had commanded **t** Moses.
22: 9 by command of the LORD **t** Moses.
24: 3 from beyond the River and led him **t** all the land
24:17 and among all the peoples **t** whom we passed;
Jdg 5:28 the mother of Sisera gazed **t** the lattice:
9:54 So the young man thrust him **t**, and he died.
11:16 Israel went **t** the wilderness to the Red Sea
11:17 saying, 'Let us pass **t** your land';
11:18 Then they journeyed **t** the wilderness,
11:19 'Let us pass **t** your land to our country.'
11:20 Sihon did not trust Israel to pass **t** his territory;
11:29 and he passed **t** Gilead and Manasseh.
19:25 and abused her all **t** the night until the morning.
20:12 of Israel sent men **t** all the tribe of Benjamin,
Ru 4:12 **t** the children that the LORD will give you
1Sa 9: 4 He passed **t** the hill country of Ephraim and
passed **t** the land
9: 4 And they passed **t** the land of Shaalim,
9: 4 Then he passed **t** the land of Benjamin,
11: 3 that we may send messengers **t** all the territory
19:12 So Michal let David down **t** the window;
23:16 there he strengthened his hand **t** the LORD.
31: 4 "Draw your sword and thrust me **t** with it,
31: 4 uncircumcised may not come and thrust me **t**,
2Sa 2:29 and his men traveled all that night **t** the Arabah;
3:18 **T** my servant David I will save my people Israel
20:14 Sheba passed **t** all the tribes of Israel to Abel
23: 2 The spirit of the LORD speaks **t** me,
23:16 three warriors broke **t** the camp of the Philistines,
24: 2 who were with him, "Go **t** all the tribes of Israel,
24: 8 So when they had gone **t** all the land,
1Ki 8:53 to be your heritage, just as you promised **t** Moses,
8:56 which he spoke **t** his servant Moses.
10:29 so **t** the king's traders they were exported to all
18: 5 "Go **t** the land to all the springs of water and to all
18: 6 they divided the land between them to pass **t** it;
22:36 Then about sunset a shout went **t** the army,
2Ki 1: 2 Ahaziah had fallen **t** the lattice
3:11 **t** whom we may inquire of the LORD?"
3:26 with him seven hundred swordsmen to break **t**,
4: 8 One day Elisha was passing **t** Shunem,
8: 8 Inquire of the LORD **t** him,
10:10 for the LORD has done what he said **t**
11:16 she went **t** the horses' entrance to
11:19 from the house of the LORD, marching **t** the gate
16: 3 He even made his son pass **t** fire,
17:17 They made their sons and their daughters pass **t**
17:23 as he had foretold **t** all his servants the prophets.
21: 6 He made his son pass **t** fire;
23:10 that no one would make a son or a daughter pass **t**
1Ch 10: 4 "Draw your sword, and thrust me **t** with it,
11:18 the Three broke **t** the camp of the Philistines,
2Ch 1:17 so **t** them these were exported to all the kings of
11:23 and distributed some of his sons **t** all the districts
17: 9 around **t** all the cities of Judah and taught among
22: 7 that the downfall of Ahaziah should come about **t**
23: 2 around **t** Judah and gathered the Levites from all
23:20 marching **t** the upper gate to the king's house.
28: 3 and made his sons pass **t** fire,
29:25 for the commandment was from the LORD **t**
30:10 the couriers went from city to city **t** the country
32: 4 the springs and the wadi that flowed **t** the land,
33: 6 He made his son pass **t** fire in the valley of
33: 8 the statutes, and the ordinances given **t** Moses."
34:14 the book of the law of the LORD given **t** Moses.
Ezr 6:14 **t** the prophesying of the prophet Haggai
Ne 9:11 so that they passed **t** the sea on dry land,
9:14 and statutes and a law **t** your servant Moses.
9:30 and warned them by your spirit **t** your prophets;
Est 4: 1 went **t** the city, wailing with a loud and bitter cry;
6: 9 and let him conduct the man on horseback **t**

Est 6:11 the horse and robed Mordecai and led him riding **t**
Job 11:10 If he passes **t**, and imprisons,
15:20 **t** all the years that are laid up for the ruthless.
20:24 a bronze arrow will strike them **t.**
22:13 Can he judge **t** the deep darkness?
24:16 In the dark they dig **t** houses;
29: 3 and by his light I walked **t** darkness;
30: 3 **T** want and hard hunger they gnaw the dry
30:14 As **t** a wide breach they come;
Ps 5: 7 But I, **t** the abundance of your steadfast love,
18:12 Out of the brightness before him there broke **t**
19: 4 yet their voice goes out **t** all the earth,
21: 5 His glory is great **t** your help;
21: 7 and **t** the steadfast love of the Most High he shall
23: 4 though I walk **t** the darkest valley, I fear no evil;
32: 3 my body wasted away **t** my groaning all day long.
44: 5 **T** you we push down our foes;
44: 5 **t** your name we tread down our assailants.
48:13 go **t** its citadels, that you may tell
66: 6 they passed **t** the river on foot.
66:12 we went **t** fire and **t** water;
68: 7 when you marched **t** the wilderness,
77:19 way was **t** the sea, your path, **t** the mighty waters;
78:13 He divided the sea and let them pass **t** it,
84: 6 As they go **t** the valley of Baca they make it
88: 9 my eye grows dim **t** sorrow.
89:40 You have broken **t** all his walls;
105:32 and lightning that flashed **t** their land.
105:41 it flowed **t** the desert like a river.
106: 9 he led them **t** the deep as **t** a desert.
106:43 and were brought low **t** their iniquity.
107:17 Some were sick **t** their sinful ways,
107:39 they are diminished and brought low **t** oppression,
109:24 My knees are weak **t** fasting;
118:19 I may enter **t** them and give thanks to the LORD.
118:20 the righteous shall enter **t** it.
119:104 **T** your precepts I get understanding;
136:10 who struck Egypt **t** their firstborn,
136:14 and made Israel pass **t** the midst of it,
136:16 who led his people **t** the wilderness,
Pr 7: 6 the window of my house I looked out **t** my lattice,
13:23 but it is swept away **t** injustice.
28:11 but an intelligent poor person sees **t** the pose.
28:26 but those who walk in wisdom come **t** safely.
Ecc 8:15 in their toil **t** the days of life that God gives them
10: 8 whoever breaks **t** a wall will be bitten by a snake.
10:18 **T** sloth the roof sinks in, and **t** indolence the house leaks.
12: 3 and those who look **t** the windows see dimly;
SS 2: 9 gazing in at the windows, looking **t** the lattice.
Isa 8:21 They will pass **t** the land,
9:19 **T** the wrath of the LORD of hosts
10:28 he has passed **t** Migron, at Michmash he stores his
13:15 Whoever is found will be thrust **t,**
28:15 when the overwhelming scourge passes **t** it will
28:18 when the overwhelming scourge passes **t** you will
28:19 As often as it passes **t**, it will take you;
28:19 for morning by morning it will pass **t,**
30: 5 to shame **t** a people that cannot profit them,
30: 6 **T** a land of trouble and distress,
34:10 no one shall pass **t** it forever and ever.
43: 2 When you pass **t** the waters, I will be with you;
43: 2 and **t** the rivers, they shall not overwhelm you;
43: 2 when you walk **t** fire you shall not be burned,
45: 2 I will break in pieces the doors of bronze and cut **t**
47: 2 uncover your legs, pass **t** the rivers.
48:21 They did not thirst when he led them **t** the deserts;
53:10 **t** him the will of the LORD shall prosper.
53:11 he shall find satisfaction **t** his knowledge.
60:15 and hated, with no one passing **t,**
62:10 Go **t**, go **t** the gates,
63:13 who led them **t** the depths?
Jer 2: 6 in a land that no one passes **t,**
2:37 and you will not prosper **t** them.
4: 5 Blow the trumpet **t** the land;
5: 1 Run to and fro **t** the streets of Jerusalem,
5:10 Go up **t** her vine-rows and destroy,
9: 8 it speaks deceit **t** the mouth.
9:10 they are laid waste so that no one passes **t,**
9:12 so that no one passes **t?**
17:27 and to carry in no burden **t** the gates of Jerusalem
22: 4 if you will indeed obey this word, then **t** the gates
37: 2 the LORD that he spoke **t** the prophet Jeremiah.
39: 4 of the city at night by way of the king's garden **t**
39:11 of Babylon gave command concerning Jeremiah **t**
42: 5 to everything that the LORD your God sends us **t**
51:43 and **t** which no mortal passes.
51:52 and **t** all her land the wounded shall groan.
La 3:44 with a cloud so that no prayer can pass **t.**
4:14 Blindly they wandered **t** the streets,
Eze 5:17 pestilence and bloodshed shall pass **t** you;
6: 8 the sword among the nations and be scattered **t**
8: 8 Then he said to me, "Mortal, dig **t** the wall";
8: 8 and when I dug **t** the wall, there was an entrance.
9: 4 "Go **t** the city, **t** Jerusalem,
9: 5 "Pass **t** the city after him, and kill;
12: 5 Dig **t** the wall in their sight,
12: 5 and carry the baggage **t** it.
12: 7 the evening I dug **t** the wall with my own hands;
12:12 he shall dig **t** the wall and carry it **t;**
12:15 the nations and scatter them **t** the countries.
14: 5 all of whom are estranged from me **t** their idols.
14:15 If I send wild animals **t** the land to ravage it,
14:15 and no one may pass **t** because of the animals;
14:17 'Let a sword pass **t** the land,'
20:23 the nations and disperse them **t** the countries,
20:26 I defiled them **t** their very gifts,
Eze 20:31 and make your children pass **t** the fire,
22:15 the nations and disperse you **t** the countries,
22:16 be profaned **t** you in the sight of the nations;
29:11 No human foot shall pass **t** it, and no animal foot shall pass **t** it;
33:28 be so desolate that no one will pass **t.**
36:19 and they were dispersed **t** the countries;
36:23 **t** you I display my holiness before their eyes.
38:16 so that the nations may know me, when **t** you,
39:14 They will set apart men to pass **t**
39:15 As the searchers pass **t** the land,
39:27 and **t** them have displayed my holiness in
42:12 the south were entered **t** the entrance at the head
45:20 for anyone who has sinned **t** error or ignorance;
46:19 Then he brought me **t** the entrance,
47: 3 and then led me **t** the water;
47: 4 and led me **t** the water; and it was knee-deep.
47: 4 and led me **t** the water; and it was up to the waist.
Da 10:20 and when I am **t** with him,
11: 2 and when he has become strong **t** his riches,
11:10 which shall advance like a flood and pass **t,**
11:21 in without warning and obtain the kingdom **t**
11:40 He shall advance against countries and pass **t** like
Hos 1: 2 When the LORD first spoke **t** Hosea,
8: 4 They made kings, but not **t** me;
12:10 and **t** the prophets I will bring destruction.
13: 1 but he incurred guilt **t** Baal and died.
Joel 2: 8 they burst **t** the weapons and are not halted.
2: 9 they enter **t** the windows like a thief.
3:17 and strangers shall never again pass **t** it.
Am 4: 3 **T** breaches in the wall you shall leave,
5:17 for I will pass **t** the midst of you,
Mic 2:13 they will break **t** and pass the gate,
5: 8 when it goes **t**, treads down and tears in pieces,
Na 2: 4 The chariots race madly **t** the streets,
2: 4 they rush to and fro **t** the squares;
3: 4 who enslaves nations **t** her debaucheries,
3: 4 and peoples **t** her sorcery,
Hab 1: 6 who march **t** the breadth of the earth
Zec 4:10 which range **t** the whole earth."
4:12 which pour out the oil **t** the two golden pipes?"
7:12 that the LORD of hosts had sent by his spirit **t**
10:11 They shall pass **t** the sea of distress,
12: 5 of Jerusalem have strength **t** the LORD of hosts,
13: 3 their mothers who bore them shall pierce them **t**
Mt 1:22 to fulfill what had been spoken by the Lord **t**
2:15 to fulfill what had been spoken by the Lord **t**
2:17 Then was fulfilled what had been spoken **t**
2:23 so that what had been spoken **t** the prophets might
4:14 so that what had been spoken **t**
7:13 "Enter **t** the narrow gate;
8:17 This was to fulfill what had been spoken **t**
10:20 but the Spirit of your Father speaking **t** you.
10:23 for truly I tell you, you will not have gone **t** all
12: 1 At that time Jesus went **t** the grainfields on
12:17 This was to fulfill what had been spoken **t**
12:43 it wanders **t** waterless regions looking for
13:35 to fulfill what had been spoken **t** the prophet:
19:24 for a camel to go **t** the eye of a needle than
21: 4 This took place to fulfill what had been spoken **t**
27: 9 Then was fulfilled what had been spoken **t**
Mk 2: 4 and after having dug **t** it,
2:23 One sabbath he was going **t** the grainfields;
7:13 thus making void the word of God **t** your tradition
9:12 that he is to go **t** many sufferings and be treated
9:29 "This kind can come out only **t** prayer."
9:30 They went on from there and passed **t** Galilee.
10:25 for a camel to go **t** the eye of a needle than
11:16 not allow anyone to carry anything **t** the temple.
16: S ⟦And afterward Jesus himself sent out **t** them.⟧
Lk 1:70 as he spoke **t** the mouth of his holy prophets from
4:14 about him spread **t** all the surrounding country.
4:30 But he passed **t** the midst of them and went
5:19 the roof and let him down with his bed **t** the tiles
6: 1 while Jesus was going **t** the grainfields,
8: 1 Soon afterwards he went on **t** cities and villages,
9: 6 They departed and went **t** the villages,
11:24 it wanders **t** waterless regions looking for
13:22 Jesus went **t** one town and village after another,
13:24 "Strive to enter **t** the narrow door;
17:11 the way to Jerusalem Jesus was going **t** the region
18:25 for a camel to go **t** the eye of a needle than
19: 1 He entered Jericho and was passing **t** it.
Jn 1: 3 All things came into being **t** him,
1: 7 so that all might believe **t** him.
1:10 and the world came into being **t** him;
1:17 The law indeed was given **t** Moses; grace and truth came **t** Jesus Christ.
3:17 but in order that the world might be saved **t** him.
4: 4 But he had to go **t** Samaria.
11: 4 so that the Son of God may be glorified **t** it."
14: 6 No one comes to the Father except **t** me.
17:20 also on behalf of those who will believe in me **t**
20:31 that **t** believing you may have life in his name.
Ac 1: 2 after giving instructions **t** the Holy Spirit to
1:16 the Holy Spirit **t** David foretold concerning Judas,
2:16 No, this is what was spoken **t** the prophet Joel:
2:22 and signs that God did **t** him among you,
3:16 that is **t** Jesus has given him this perfect health in
3:18 In this way God fulfilled what he had foretold **t**
3:21 that God announced long ago **t** his holy prophets.
4:16 in Jerusalem that a notable sign has been done **t**
4:25 the Holy Spirit **t** our ancestor David, your servant:
4:30 and signs and wonders are performed **t** the name
5:12 and wonders were done among the people **t**
7:25 that his kinsfolk would understand that God **t**
7:35 both ruler and liberator **t** the angel who appeared
Ac 8:18 Now when Simon saw that the Spirit was given **t**
8:40 and as he was passing **t** the region,
9:25 and let him down **t** an opening in the wall,
10:43 in him receives forgiveness of sins **t** his name."
13: 6 they had gone **t** the whole island as far as Paphos,
13:38 that **t** this man forgiveness of sins is proclaimed
14: 3 by granting signs and wonders to be done **t** them.
14:22 "It is **t** many persecutions that we must enter
14:24 they passed **t** Pisidia and came to Pamphylia.
15: 3 and as they passed **t** both Phoenicia and Samaria,
15: 7 be the one **t** whom the Gentiles would hear
15:11 we believe that we will be saved **t** the grace of
15:12 of all the signs and wonders that God had done **t**
15:41 He went **t** Syria and Cilicia,
16: 6 They went **t** the region of Phrygia and Galatia,
17: 1 and Silas had passed **t** Amphipolis and Apollonia,
17:23 For as I went **t** the city and looked carefully at
18:23 to place **t** the region of Galatia and Phrygia,
18:27 On his arrival he greatly helped those who **t**
19: 1 Paul passed **t** the interior regions and came
19:11 God did extraordinary miracles **t** Paul,
19:21 Paul resolved in the Spirit to go **t** Macedonia
20: 2 When he had gone **t** those regions and had given
20: 3 and so he decided to return **t** Macedonia.
20:19 the trials that came to me **t** the plots of the Jews.
21: 4 **T** the Spirit they told Paul not to go on
21:19 the things that God had done among the Gentiles **t**
21:24 go **t** the rite of purification with them,
28:25 in saying to your ancestors **t** the prophet Isaiah,
Ro 1: 2 which he promised beforehand **t** his prophets in
1: 5 **t** whom we have received grace and apostleship
1: 8 First, I thank my God **t** Jesus Christ for all of you,
1:17 in it the righteousness of God is revealed **t** faith
1:20 and seen **t** the things he has made.
2:16 according to my gospel, God, **t** Jesus Christ,
3: 7 But if **t** my falsehood God's truthfulness abounds
3:20 for **t** the law comes the knowledge of sin.
3:22 of God **t** faith in Jesus Christ for all who believe.
3:24 **t** the redemption that is in Christ Jesus,
3:25 a sacrifice of atonement by his blood, effective **t**
3:30 of faith and the uncircumcised **t** that same faith.
4:13 to Abraham or to his descendants **t** the law but **t** the righteousness of faith.
5: 1 we have peace with God **t** our Lord Jesus Christ,
5: 2 **t** whom we have obtained access to this grace
5: 5 into our hearts **t** the Holy Spirit
5: 9 will we be saved **t** him from the wrath of God.
5:10 we were reconciled to God **t** the death of his Son,
5:11 we even boast in God **t** our Lord Jesus Christ, **t** whom we have now received reconciliation.
5:12 just as sin came into the world **t** one man, and death came **t** sin, and so death spread to all
5:15 For if the many died **t** the one man's trespass,
5:17 death exercised dominion **t** that one,
5:17 exercise dominion in life **t** the one man, Jesus
5:21 also exercise dominion **t** justification leading to eternal life **t** Jesus Christ
7: 4 you have died to the law **t** the body of Christ,
7:11 deceived me and **t** it killed me.
7:13 It was sin, working death in me **t** what is good,
7:13 and **t** the commandment might become sinful
7:25 Thanks be to God **t** Jesus Christ our Lord!
8:11 the dead will give life to your mortal bodies also **t**
8:37 in all these things we are more than conquerors **t**
9: 7 but "It is **t** Isaac that descendants shall be named
9:30 have attained it, that is, righteousness **t** faith;
10:17 and what is heard comes **t** the word of Christ.
11:11 But **t** their stumbling salvation has come to
11:20 but you stand only **t** faith.
11:36 For from him and **t** him and to him are all things.
15:18 of anything except what Christ has accomplished **t**
16:26 and **t** the prophetic writings is made known to all
16:27 **t** Jesus Christ, to whom be the glory forever!
1Co 1:21 the world did not know God **t** wisdom, God decided, **t** the foolishness of our proclamation,
2:10 these things God has revealed to us **t** the Spirit;
3: 5 Servants **t** whom you came to believe,
3:15 the builder will be saved, but only as **t** fire.
4: 6 that you may learn **t** us the meaning of the saying,
4:15 in Christ Jesus I became your father **t** the gospel.
7:14 the unbelieving husband is made holy **t** his wife,
7:14 the unbelieving wife is made holy **t** her husband.
8: 6 **t** whom are all things and **t** whom we exist.
10: 1 and all passed **t** the sea,
11:12 as woman came from man, so man comes **t**
12: 8 To one is given **t** the Spirit the utterance
15: 2 **t** which also you are being saved,
15:21 For since death came **t** a human being, the resurrection of the dead has also come **t** a human
15:57 who gives us the victory **t** our Lord Jesus Christ.
16: 5 I will visit you after passing **t** Macedonia—for I intend to pass **t** Macedonia—
2Co 1: 5 so also our consolation is abundant **t** Christ.
1:11 for the blessing granted us **t** the prayers of many.
1:20 For this reason it is **t** him that we say the "Amen,"
2:14 and **t** us spreads in every place the fragrance
3: 4 the confidence that we have **t** Christ toward God.
3:11 for if what was set aside came **t** glory,
5:18 who reconciled us to himself **t** Christ,
5:20 since God is making his appeal **t** us;
6: 4 **t** great endurance, in afflictions, hardships,
9:11 which will produce thanksgiving to God **t** us;
9:13 **T** the testing of this ministry you glorify God
11:27 **t** many a sleepless night, hungry and thirsty,
11:33 I was let down in a basket **t** a window in the wall,
12:17 of you **t** any of those whom I sent to you?
Gal 1: 1 but **t** Jesus Christ and God the Father,

Gal 1:12 but I received it **t** a revelation of Jesus Christ.
1:15 before I was born and called me **t** his grace,
2: 8 (for he who worked **t** Peter making him an apostle
2: 8 also worked **t** me in sending me to the Gentiles),
2:16 by the works of the law but **t** faith in Jesus Christ.
2:19 For **t** the law I died to the law,
2:21 for if justification comes **t** the law,
3:14 we might receive the promise of the Spirit **t** faith.
3:18 but God granted it to Abraham **t** the promise.
3:19 and it was ordained **t** angels by a mediator.
3:21 then righteousness would indeed come **t** the law.
3:22 so that what was promised **t** faith
3:26 in Christ Jesus you are all children of God **t** faith.
4: 7 and if a child then also an heir, **t** God.
4:23 the other, the child of the free woman, was born **t**
5: 5 For **t** the Spirit, by faith, we eagerly wait for
5: 6 the only thing that counts is faith working **t** love.
5:13 but **t** love become slaves to one another.
Eph 1: 5 He destined us for adoption as his children **t** Jesus
1: 7 In him we have redemption **t** his blood,
2: 1 You were dead **t** the trespasses and sins
2: 5 even when we were dead **t** our trespasses,
2: 8 For by grace you have been saved **t** faith,
2:16 both groups to God in one body **t** the cross,
2:16 thus putting to death that hostility **t** it.
2:18 for **t** him both of us have access in one Spirit to
3: 6 sharers in the promise in Christ Jesus **t** the gospel.
3:10 so that **t** the church the wisdom of God
3:12 to God in boldness and confidence **t** faith in him.
3:16 be strengthened in your inner being with power **t**
3:17 and that Christ may dwell in your hearts **t** faith,
4: 6 who is above all and **t** all and in all.
Php 1:11 that comes **t** Jesus Christ for the glory and praise
1:19 for I know that **t** your prayers and the help of
3: 9 but one that comes **t** faith in Christ,
4:13 I can do all things **t** him who strengthens me.
Col 1:16 all things have been created **t** him and for him.
1:20 and **t** him God was pleased to reconcile
1:20 by making peace **t** the blood of his cross.
1:22 he has now reconciled in his fleshly body **t** death,
2: 8 to it that no one takes you captive **t** philosophy
2:12 you were also raised with him **t** faith in the power
3:17 giving thanks to God the Father **t** him.
1Th 3: 7 we have been encouraged about you **t** your faith.
4: 2 For you know what instructions we gave you **t**
4:14 and rose again, even so, **t** Jesus, God will bring
5: 9 for obtaining salvation **t** our Lord Jesus Christ,
2Th 2:13 as the first fruits for salvation **t** sanctification by
the Spirit and **t** belief in the truth.
2:14 For this purpose he called you **t** our proclamation
2:16 who loved us and **t** grace gave us eternal comfort
1Ti 2:15 Yet she will be saved **t** childbearing,
4: 2 **t** the hypocrisy of liars whose consciences are
4:14 to you **t** prophecy with the laying on of hands by
2Ti 1: 6 the gift of God that is within you **t** the laying on
1:10 but it has now been revealed **t** the appearing
1:10 and brought life and immortality to light **t**
2: 2 and what you have heard from me **t**
3:15 to instruct you for salvation **t** faith in Christ Jesus.
4:17 that **t** me the message might be fully proclaimed
Tit 1: 3 in due time he revealed his word **t**
3: 5 **t** the water of rebirth and renewal by
3: 6 This Spirit he poured out on us richly **t**
Phm 1: 7 the hearts of the saints have been refreshed **t** you,
1:22 I am hoping **t** your prayers to be restored to you.
Heb 1: 2 **t** whom he also created the worlds.
2: 2 For if the message declared **t** angels was valid,
2: 3 It was declared at first **t** the Lord,
2:10 for whom and **t** whom all things exist,
2:10 the pioneer of their salvation perfect **t** sufferings.
2:14 so that **t** death he might destroy the one who has
4: 7 "today"—saying **t** David much later,
4:11 that no one may fall **t** such disobedience as theirs.
4:14 a great high priest who has passed **t** the heavens,
5: 8 he learned obedience **t** what he suffered;
6:12 of those who **t** faith and patience inherit
6:18 so that **t** two unchangeable things,
7: 9 who receives tithes, paid tithes **t** Abraham,
7:11 Now if perfection had been attainable **t**
7:16 **t** a legal requirement concerning physical descent,
7:16 but **t** the power of an indestructible life.
7:19 **t** which we approach God.
7:25 for all time to save those who approach God **t**
8: 6 which has been enacted **t** better promises.
9:11 then **t** the greater and perfect tent (not made
9:14 who **t** the eternal Spirit offered himself
10:10 that we have been sanctified **t** the offering of
10:20 by the new and living way that he opened for us **t**
10:20 that he opened for us through the curtain (that is, **t**
11: 4 **T** this he received approval as righteous,
11: 4 he died, but **t** his faith he still speaks.
11:18 "It is **t** Isaac that descendants shall be named
11:29 By faith the people passed **t** the Red Sea as
11:33 who **t** faith conquered kingdoms,
12:15 and **t** it many become defiled.
13:15 **T** him, then, let us continually offer a sacrifice
13:21 that which is pleasing in his sight, **t** Jesus Christ,
1Pe 1: 3 a new birth into a living hope **t** the resurrection
1: 5 of God **t** faith for a salvation ready to be revealed
1:12 the things that have now been announced to you **t**
1:21 **T** him you have come to trust in God,
1:23 **t** the living and enduring word of God.
2: 5 to offer spiritual sacrifices acceptable to God **t**
3:20 that is, eight persons, were saved **t** water.
3:21 **t** the resurrection of Jesus Christ,
4:11 God may be glorified in all things **t** Jesus Christ.
5:12 **T** Silvanus, whom I consider a faithful brother,
2Pe 1: 1 as precious as ours **t** the righteousness of our God
1: 3 **t** the knowledge of him who called us
1: 4 Thus he has given us, **t** these things,
1: 4 that **t** them you may escape from the corruption
2:20 the defilements of the world **t** the knowledge
3: 2 of the Lord and Savior spoken **t** your apostles.
3: 6 **t** which the world of that time was deluged
1Jn 4: 9 into the world so that we might live **t** him.
Jude 1:25 **t** Jesus Christ our Lord, be glory, majesty, power,
Rev 22: 2 **t** the middle of the street of the city.
Tob 6:18 related **t** his father's lineage,
11:10 up and came stumbling out **t** the courtyard door.
Jdt 2:24 Then he followed the Euphrates and passed **t**
8:32 I am about to do something that will go down **t**
10:10 down the mountain and passed **t** the valley,
10:11 As the women were going straight on **t** the valley,
11: 6 God will accomplish something **t** you,
11:19 Then I will lead you **t** Judea,
13:10 They passed **t** the camp, circled around the valley,
15: 2 and fled by every path across the plain and **t**
16:12 of slave-girls pierced them **t** and wounded them
AdE 4: 1 he rushed **t** the street of the city, shouting loudly:
6: 9 let it be proclaimed **t** the open square of the city,
6:11 on Mordecai and made him ride **t** the open square
15: 6 When she had gone **t** all the doors,
16: 7 "What has been wickedly accomplished **t**
Wis 2:24 but **t** the devil's envy death entered the world,
3: 7 and will run like sparks **t** the stubble.
5: 7 and we journeyed **t** trackless deserts,
5:10 like a ship that sails **t** the billowy water,
5:11 when a bird flies **t** the air,
7:23 and penetrating **t** all spirits that are intelligent,
10:17 and a starry flame **t** the night.
10:18 and led them **t** deep waters;
11: 2 They journeyed **t** an uninhabited wilderness,
11: 5 For **t** the very things by which
11:13 For when they heard that **t** their own punishments
12: 2 and you remind and warn them of the things **t**
12:11 not **t** fear of anyone that you left them unpunished
12:19 **T** such works you have taught your people that
12:23 you tormented **t** their own abominations.
13: 3 If **t** delight in the beauty of these things
14: 3 and a safe way **t** the waves,
14: 5 even to the smallest piece of wood, and passing **t**
14:14 For **t** human vanity they entered the world,
14:30 and because in deceit they swore unrighteously **t**
16: 1 those people were deservedly punished **t**
17: 6 Nothing was shining **t** to them except a dreadful,
18: 4 **t** whom the imperishable light of the law was to
19: 8 where those protected by your hand passed **t**
19:17 all of them tried to find the way **t** their own doors.
Sir Pr: 1 to us **t** the Law and the Prophets and the others
Pr: 1 of learning be able **t** the spoken and written word
4:24 For wisdom becomes known **t** speech,
4:24 and education **t** the words of the tongue.
6: 7 When you gain friends, gain them **t** testing,
8:15 and **t** their folly you will perish with them.
8:16 and do not journey with them **t** lonely country,
10: 3 a city becomes fit to live in **t** the understanding
11:18 One becomes rich **t** diligence and self-denial,
14:23 who peers **t** her windows and listens at her doors;
16: 4 For **t** one intelligent person a city can be filled
16: 4 but **t** a clan of outlaws it becomes desolate.
20:22 One may lose his life **t** shame,
23: 8 Sinners are overtaken **t** their lips;
23:14 and behave like a fool **t** bad habit;
23:23 **t** her fornication she has committed adultery
26:28 a warrior in want **t** poverty,
29:19 The sinner comes to grief **t** surety;
32:12 but do not sin **t** proud speech.
39: 9 and his name will live **t** all generations.
44:21 that the nations would be blessed **t** his offspring;
45:26 that their glory may endure **t** all their generations.
46: 4 Was it not **t** him that the sun stood still
47:19 and **t** your body you were brought into subjection.
48:20 and delivered them **t** Isaiah.
51:28 and **t** me you will acquire silver and gold.
Bar 1:20 the Lord declared **t** his servant Moses at the time
3:28 they perished **t** their folly.
Aza 1:27 as though a moist wind were whistling **t** it.
Sus 1:35 **T** her tears she looked up toward Heaven,
1:57 and they were intimate with you **t** fear;
Bel 1:13 **t** which they used to go in regularly and consume
1:21 the secret doors **t** which they used to enter
1Mc 3: 8 He went **t** the cities of Judah;
3:37 He crossed the Euphrates river and went **t**
5:46 they had to go **t** it.
5:48 "Let us pass **t** your land to get to our land.
5:51 he passed **t** the town over the bodies of the dead.
5:62 of those men **t** whom deliverance was given
5:66 to go into the land of the Philistines, and passed **t**
6: 1 King Antiochus was going **t** the upper provinces
6:31 They came **t** Idumea and encamped
11:47 around him and then spread out **t** the city;
11:62 And he passed **t** the country as far as Damascus.
12:32 and marched **t** all that region.
12:33 and marched **t** the country as far as Askalon and
2Mc 2:18 as he promised **t** the law.
4:11 secured **t** John the father of Eupolemus,
5: 2 over all the city golden-clad cavalry charging **t**
6:25 and **t** my pretense, for the sake of living
7:30 the law that was given to our ancestors **t** Moses.
7:38 and **t** me and my brothers to bring to an end
14: 8 For **t** the folly of those whom I have mentioned
14:43 and the crowd was now rushing in **t** the doors.
14:45 and his wounds were severe he ran **t** the crowd;
3Mc 2: 7 in the depths of the sea, but carried **t**
3Mc 5: 5 and arranged for their continued custody **t**
5:18 the Jews had been allowed to remain alive **t**
6: 7 who **t** envious slanders was thrown down into
6:36 of the deliverance that had come to them **t** God.
7:23 Blessed be the Deliverer of Israel **t** all times!
2Es 1:13 Surely it was I who brought you **t** the sea,
2: 1 and I gave them commandments **t** my servants
3:19 Your glory passed **t** the four gates of fire
5:11 or anyone who does right, passed **t** you?'
5:56 in your sight, show your servant **t**
6: 6 they were made **t** me alone and not **t** another; just
as the end shall come **t** me alone and not **t** another.
7: 5 the broad part unless they pass **t** the narrow part?
7: 9 unless by passing **t** the appointed danger?"
7:14 living pass **t** the difficult and futile experiences,
7:*60* and **t** them my name has now been honored.
9:31 and you shall be glorified **t** it forever.'
11:39 so that the end of my times might come **t** them?
13:45 **T** that region there was a long way to go,
14:17 For the weaker the world becomes **t** old age,
16:30 by those who search carefully **t** the vineyard,
16:77 so that no one can pass **t**.
4Mc 1:11 and thus their native land was purified **t** them.
2: 9 by the law **t** reason so that one neither gleans
2:14 **t** the law, can prevail even over enmity.
4:26 he himself tried **t** torture to compel everyone in
5:38 either by words or **t** deeds."
6:14 why are you so irrationally destroying yourself **t**
7: 9 to the law **t** your glorious endurance,
7:11 ran **t** the multitude of the people and conquered
7:14 in spirit **t** reason; and by reason
7:22 not be able to overcome the emotions **t** godliness?
8: 9 and every one of you with dreadful punishments **t**
9: 4 which insures our safety **t** transgression of
9: 8 For we, **t** this severe suffering and endurance,
9:18 **t** all these tortures I will convince you
11:12 because **t** these noble sufferings you give us
11:19 pierced his ribs so that his entrails were burned **t**.
13:19 and all-wise Providence has bequeathed **t**
13:20 growing from the same blood and **t** the same life,
16:18 Remember that it is **t** God that you have had
17:22 And **t** the blood of those devout ones
18:14 which says, 'Even though you go **t** the fire,

THROUGHLY (KJV) See SURELY, THOROUGHLY, TRULY

THROUGHOUT‡ (191) [THROUGH]

Ge 17: 7 and your offspring after you **t** their generations,
17: 9 and your offspring after you **t** their generations.
17:12 **T** your generations every male among you shall
23:17 the trees that were in the field, **t** its whole area,
41:29 There will come seven years of great plenty **t** all
41:54 but **t** the land of Egypt there was bread.
41:57 because the famine became severe **t** the world.
Ex 5:12 So the people scattered **t** the land of Egypt,
7:19 there shall be blood **t** the whole land of Egypt,
7:21 and there was blood **t** the whole land of Egypt.
8:16 it may become gnats **t** the whole land of Egypt.' "
8:17 of the earth turned into gnats **t** the whole land
9: 9 on humans and animals **t** the whole land
9:25 the open field **t** all the land of Egypt, both human
11: 6 there will be a loud cry **t** the whole land of Egypt,
12:14 **t** your generations you shall observe it as
12:17 you shall observe this day **t** your generations as
12:42 to be kept for the LORD by all the Israelites **t**
16:32 'Let an omer of it be kept **t** your generations,
16:33 to be kept **t** your generations."
27:21 It shall be a perpetual ordinance to be observed **t**
29:42 be a regular burnt offering **t** your generations at
30: 8 a regular incense offering before the LORD **t**
30:10 **T** your generations he shall perform
30:21 him and for his descendants **t** their generations.
30:31 be my holy anointing oil **t** your generations.
31:13 a sign between me and you **t** your generations,
31:16 observing the sabbath **t** their generations,
32:27 Go back and forth from gate to gate **t** the camp,
34: 3 and do not let anyone be seen **t** all the mountain;
36: 6 and word was proclaimed **t** the camp:
40:15 a perpetual priesthood **t** all generations to come.
Lev 3:17 It shall be a perpetual statute **t** your generations,
6:18 as their perpetual due **t** your generations,
7:36 as a perpetual due from the people of Israel **t**
10: 9 it is a statute forever **t** your generations.
17: 7 be a statute forever to them **t** their generations.
21:17 of your offspring **t** their generations who has
22: 3 If anyone among all your offspring **t**
23: 3 it is a sabbath to the LORD **t** your settlements.
23:14 it is a statute forever **t** your generations
23:21 This is a statute forever in all your settlements **t**
23:31 it is a statute forever **t** your generations
23:41 in the seventh month as a statute forever **t**
24: 3 it shall be a statute forever **t** your generations.
25: 9 you shall have the trumpet sounded **t**
25:10 the fiftieth year and you shall proclaim liberty **t**
25:24 **T** the land that you hold,
25:30 in perpetuity to the purchaser, **t** the generations;
Nu 10: 8 a perpetual institution for you **t** your generations.
11:10 Moses heard the people weeping **t** their families,
15:15 a perpetual statute **t** your generations;
15:21 **T** your generations you shall give to the LORD
15:23 the LORD gave commandment and thereafter, **t**
15:38 to make fringes on the corners of their garments **t**
18:23 it shall be a perpetual statute **t** your generations.
28:14 the burnt offering of every month **t** the months of

Nu 35:29 for you t your generations wherever you live.
Dt 1:15 commanders of tens, and officials, t your tribes.
9:25 T the forty days and forty nights
16:18 You shall appoint judges and officials t
25:10 T Israel his family shall be known as "the house
28:40 You shall have olive trees t all your territory,
28:52 in which you trusted, come down t your land;
28:52 it shall besiege you in all your towns t the land
Jos 3:15 Now the Jordan overflows all its banks t the time
18: 4 that they may begin to go t the land,
18: 8 "Go t the land and write a description of it,
Jdg 6:35 He sent messengers t all Manasseh,
7:24 Then Gideon sent messengers t all
19:29 and sent her t all the territory of Israel.
20: 6 sent her t the whole extent of Israel's territory;
20:10 We will take ten men of a hundred t all the tribes
1Sa 5:11 For there was a deathly panic t the whole city.
11: 7 in pieces and sent them t all the territory of Israel
13: 3 And Saul blew the trumpet t all the land, saying,
13:19 Now there was no smith to be found t all the land
31: 9 and sent messengers t the land of the Philistines
2Sa 8:14 t all Edom he put garrisons,
15:10 But Absalom sent secret messengers t all
19: 9 the people were disputing t all the tribes of Israel,
1Ki 1: 3 for a beautiful girl t all the territory of Israel,
4:31 his fame spread t all the surrounding nations.
2Ki 10:21 Jehu sent word t all Israel;
10:32 Hazael defeated them t the territory of Israel:
1Ch 5:10 and they lived in their tents t all the region east
6:60 All their towns t their families were thirteen.
10: 9 and sent messengers t the land of the Philistines
21: 4 So Joab departed and went t all Israel,
21:12 the LORD destroying t all the territory of Israel.'
22: 5 famous and glorified t all lands;
27: 1 month after month t the year,
2Ch 16: 9 the eyes of the LORD range t the entire earth,
17:19 the king had placed in the fortified cities t
20: 3 and proclaimed a fast t all Judah.
24: 9 A proclamation was made t Judah and Jerusalem
30: 5 they decreed to make a proclamation t all Israel,
30: 6 So couriers went t all Israel and Judah with letters
31: 1 and pulled down the high places and the altars t
31:20 Hezekiah did this t all Judah;
34: 7 and demolished all the incense altars t all the land
36:22 of Persia so that he sent a herald t all his kingdom
Ezr 1: 1 so that he sent a herald t all his kingdom,
4: 5 and they bribed officials to frustrate their plan t
10: 7 They made a proclamation t Judah and Jerusalem
Est 1:20 when the decree made by the king is proclaimed t
3: 6 t the whole kingdom of Ahasuerus.
8:12 on a single day t all the provinces
9: 2 the Jews gathered in their cities t all the provinces
9: 4 and his fame spread t all the provinces as
9:28 These days should be remembered and kept t
Ps 10: 6 t all generations we shall not meet adversity."
72: 5 and as long as the moon, t all generations.
102:24 you whose years endure t all generations."
105:31 and gnats t their country.
135:13 your renown, O LORD, t all ages.
145:13 and your dominion endures t all generations.
Isa 21: 8 and at my post I am stationed t the night.
62: 7 and makes it renowned t the earth.
Jer 14:18 both prophet and priest ply their trade t the land,
15:13 without price, for all your sins, t all your territory.
17: 3 as the price of your sin t all your territory.
23:15 of Jerusalem ungodliness has spread t the land."
Eze 6:14 the land desolate and waste, t all their settlements,
30:23 and disperse them t the lands.
30:26 the nations and disperse them t the countries.
45: 1 it shall be holy t its entire extent.
Da 4: 1 nations, and languages that live t the earth:
6: 1 stationed t the whole kingdom,
6:25 and nations of every language t the whole world:
Mt 4:23 Jesus went t Galilee, teaching in their synagogues
4:24 So his fame spread t all Syria,
9:26 And the report of this spread t that district.
9:31 and spread the news about him t that district.
14:35 they sent word t the region
24:14 of the kingdom will be proclaimed t the world,
Mk 1:28 to spread t the surrounding region of Galilee.
1:39 And he went t Galilee, proclaiming the message
Lk 1:65 and all these things were talked about t
7:17 This word about him spread t Judea and all
8:39 proclaiming t the city how much Jesus had done
15:14 a severe famine took place t that country,
23: 5 "He stirs up the people by teaching t all Judea,
Ac 7:11 Now there came a famine t Egypt and Canaan,
8: 1 the apostles were scattered t the countryside
9:31 Meanwhile the church t Judea, Galilee,
9:42 This became known t Joppa,
10:37 That message spread t Judea,
13:49 Thus the word of the Lord spread t the region.
24: 5 an agitator among all the Jews t the world,
24:12 up a crowd either in the synagogues or t the city.
26:20 then in Jerusalem and t the countryside of Judea,
Ro 1: 8 because your faith is proclaimed t the world.
2Co 1: 1 including all the saints t Achaia:
Php 1:13 so that it has become known t
Col 1:26 that has been hidden t the ages and generations
1Th 4:10 the brothers and sisters t Macedonia.
1Ti 3:16 believed in t the world, taken up in glory.
Tob 11:14 May his holy name be blessed t all the ages.
13: 1 because his kingdom lasts t all ages.
Jdt 2:11 over to slaughter and plunder t your whole region.
4:13 for the people fasted many days t Judea and
7:29 and general lamentation arose t the assembly,
11: 8 and it is reported t the whole world
Jdt 11:23 of King Nebuchadnezzar and be renowned t
14:19 and their loud cries and shouts rose up t the camp.
16:21 of her life she was honored t the whole country.
AdE 3:13 Instructions were sent by couriers t all the empire
8:12 which is Adar, t all the kingdom of Artaxerxes.
9: 4 that Mordecai's name be held in honor t
13: 2 and open to travel t all its extent,
Wis 4: 2 t all time it marches, crowned in triumph,
17:14 But t the night, which was really powerless
Sir 47:10 and arranged their times t the year,
47:15 Your influence spread t the earth,
Bel 1:14 and they scattered them t the whole temple in
2Mc 2:22 and regained possession of the temple famous t
3:12 of the temple that is honored t the whole world.
3:14 There was no little distress t the whole city.
9:24 the people t the realm would not be troubled,
14:14 And the Gentiles t Judea,
1Es 1:32 that this should always be done t the whole nation
2: 2 and he made a proclamation t all his kingdom and
8:23 t all Syria and Phoenicia;
9: 3 a proclamation was made t Judea and Jerusalem
3Mc 6: 1 and t his life had been adorned with every virtue,
2Es 7:*94* that t their life they kept the law
12:34 those who have been saved t my borders,
15: 6 because iniquity has spread t every land,
4Mc 3:13 they went searching t the enemy camp
12:12 and these t all time will never let you go.

THROW (65) [DISCUS-THROWING, THREW, THROWING, THROWN, THROWS]

Ge 37:20 let us kill him and t him into one of the pits;
37:22 t him into this pit here in the wilderness,
Ex 1:22 "Every boy that is born to the Hebrews you shall t
4: 3 And he said, "T it on the ground."
7: 9 'Take your staff and t it down before Pharaoh,
9: 8 let Moses t it in the air in the sight of Pharaoh.
22:31 you shall t it to the dogs.
23:27 and will t into confusion all the people
Lev 1:16 He shall remove its crop with its contents and t it
Nu 19: 6 t them into the fire in which the heifer is burning.
Dt 7:23 and t them into great panic,
2Sa 11:21 not a woman t an upper millstone on him from
17: 2 and t him into a panic;
2Ki 9:25 and t him on the plot of ground belonging
9:26 lift him out and t him on the plot of ground,
9:33 He said, "T her down."
2Ch 32:17 to t contempt on the LORD the God of Israel and
Job 18: 7 and their own schemes t them down.
Pr 1:14 T in your lot among us;
Ecc 3: 5 a time to t away stones, and a time
3: 6 a time to keep, and a time to t away;
Isa 2:20 On that day people will t away to the moles and
22:18 and t you like a ball into a wide land;
31: 7 For on that day all of you shall t away your idols
Jer 7:29 Cut off your hair and t it away;
36:23 a penknife and t them into the fire in the brazier,
51:63 and t it into the middle of the Euphrates,
Eze 5: 4 t them into the fire and burn them up;
6: 4 and I will t down your slain in front of your idols.
16:39 and they shall t down your platform and break
27:30 They t dust on their heads and wallow in ashes;
32: 3 In an assembly of many peoples I will t my net
32: 4 I will t you on the ground,
43:24 and the priests shall t salt on them and offer them
Da 3:20 and to t them into the furnace of blazing fire.
11:15 king of the north shall come and t up siegeworks,
Jnh 1:12 "Pick me up and t me into the sea;
Mic 5:11 of your land and t down all your strongholds;
Na 3: 6 I will t filth at you and treat you with contempt,
Zec 11:13 the LORD said to me, "T it into the treasury"—
Mt 4: 6 "If you are the Son of God, t yourself down;
5:29 tear it out and t it away;
5:30 cut it off and t it away;
7: 6 and do not t your pearls before swine,
13:42 and they will t them into the furnace of fire,
13:50 and t them into the furnace of fire,
15:26 "It is not fair to take the children's food and t it to
18: 8 cut it off and t it away;
18: 9 tear it out and t it away;
22:13 and t him into the outer darkness,
25:30 this worthless slave, t him into the outer darkness,
Mk 7:27 for it is not fair to take the children's food and t it
Lk 4: 9 t yourself down from here,
12:58 and the officer t you in prison.
14:35 for the manure pile; they t it away.
22:41 Then he withdrew from them about a stone's t,
Jn 8: 7 ⟦who is without sin be the first to t a stone at her.⟧
8:59 So they picked up stones to t at him,
Ac 27:18 the next day they began to t the cargo overboard,
Rev 2:10 the devil is about to t some of you into prison so
Tob 6: 5 Keep them with you, but t away the intestines.
Sir 12:16 but in his heart he plans to t you into a pit;
1Mc 6:51 engines of war to t fire and stones,
11: 5 to t blame on him; but the king kept silent.
2Mc 9:15 to t out with their children for the wild animals

THROWING (12) [THROW]

2Sa 16:13 t stones and flinging dust at him.
Ezr 10: 1 weeping and t himself down before the house
Jer 38: 9 to the prophet Jeremiah by t him into the cistern
Mt 27: 5 T down the pieces of silver in the temple,
Mk 10:50 t off his cloak, he sprang up and came to Jesus.
Lk 19:35 after t their cloaks on the colt, they set Jesus on it.
Ac 22:23 And while they were shouting, t off their cloaks,
Ac 27:38 they lightened the ship by t the wheat into the sea.
Rev 2:22 Beware, I am t her on a bed,
2:22 and those who commit adultery with her I am t
Jdt 6:12 the slingers kept them from coming up by t stones
1Mc 15:25 continually t his forces against it

THROWN (89) [THROW]

Ex 15: 1 horse and rider he has t into the sea.
15:21 horse and rider he has t into the sea."
Lev 14:40 be taken out and t into an unclean place outside
2Sa 20:21 "His head shall be t over the wall to you."
23: 6 But the godless are all like thorns that are t away;
1Ki 13:24 His body was t in the road,
13:25 People passed by and saw the body t in the road,
13:28 and he went and found the body t in the road,
18:30 the altar of the LORD that had been t down;
19:10 for the Israelites have forsaken your covenant, t
19:14 for the Israelites have forsaken your covenant, t
2Ki 2:16 of the LORD has caught him up and t him down
7:15 and equipment that the Arameans had t away
13:21 a marauding band was seen and the man was t
Est 3:15 but the city of Susa was t into confusion.
7: 8 Haman had t himself on the couch
Job 19:12 they have t up siegeworks against me,
Ps 102:10 for you have lifted me up and t me aside.
Jer 14:16 the people to whom they prophesy shall be t out
22:19 and t out beyond the gates of Jerusalem.
41: 9 the cistern into which Ishmael had t all the bodies
50:15 her bulwarks have fallen, her walls are t down."
La 2: 1 He has t down from heaven to earth the splendor
2:10 they have t dust on their heads and put
Eze 16: 5 but you were t out in the open field,
21:12 they are t to the sword, together with my people.
38:20 and the mountains shall be t down,
Da 3: 6 and worship shall immediately be t into a furnace
3:11 down and worship shall be t into a furnace
3:15 you shall immediately be t into a furnace
3:21 and they were t into the furnace of blazing fire.
6: 7 O king, shall be t into a den of lions.
6:12 O king, shall be t into a den of lions?"
6:16 Daniel was brought and t into the den of lions.
6:24 and t into the den of lions—
Joel 1: 7 it has stripped off their bark and t it down;
Mt 3:10 not bear good fruit is cut down and t into the fire.
5:13 but is t out and trampled under foot.
5:25 and you will be t into prison.
5:29 of your members than for your whole body to be t
6:30 which is alive today and tomorrow is t into
7:19 not bear good fruit is cut down and t into the fire.
8:12 of the kingdom will be t into the outer darkness,
13:47 the kingdom of heaven is like a net that was t into
18: 8 to have two hands or two feet and to be t into
18: 9 to have two eyes and to be t into the hell of fire.
21:21 'Be lifted up and t into the sea,' it will be done.
24: 2 upon another; all will be t down."
Mk 9:42 around your neck and you were t into the sea.
9:45 to enter life lame than to have two feet and to be t
9:47 with one eye than to have two eyes and to be t
11:23 'Be taken up and t into the sea,'
13: 2 upon another; all will be t down."
Lk 3: 9 that does not bear good fruit is cut down and t
4:35 When the demon had t him down before them,
12:28 which is alive today and tomorrow is t into
13:28 and you yourselves t out.
17: 2 around your neck and you were t into the sea than
21: 6 upon another; all will be t down."
Jn 3:24 —John, of course, had not yet been t into prison.
15: 6 Whoever does not abide in me is t away like
15: 6 such branches are gathered, t into the fire,
Ac 16:37 and have t us into prison;
Rev 8: 8 burning with fire, was t into the sea.
12: 9 The great dragon was t down,
12: 9 he was t down to the earth, and his angels were t down with him.
12:10 for the accuser of our comrades has been t down,
12:13 dragon saw that he had been t down to the earth,
18:21 be t down, and will be found no more;
19:20 These two were t alive into the lake of fire
20:10 And the devil who had deceived them was t into
20:14 Then Death and Hades were t into the lake of fire.
20:15 not found written in the book of life was t into
Tob 1:17 if I saw the dead body of any of my people t out
2: 3 of our own people has been murdered and t into
AdE 3:15 the city of Susa was t into confusion.
7: 8 Haman had t himself on the couch,
Wis 17:19 or an echo t back from a hollow of the mountains,
Bar 2:25 and indeed they have been t out to the heat of day
LtJ 6:71 or like a corpse t out in the darkness.
2Mc 10:30 they were t into disorder and cut to pieces.
3Mc 6: 7 who through envious slanders was t down into
2Es 5: 4 you shall see it t into confusion after
10:21 our altar t down, our temple destroyed;
16:23 And the dead shall be t out like dung,
4Mc 4:25 were t headlong from heights along
12: 1 When he too, t into the caldron,
16:21 Daniel the righteous was t to the lions,

THROWS (5) [THROW]

Pr 14:16 but the fool t off restraint and is careless.
Sir 21:15 he laughs at it and t it behind his back.
22:20 One who t a stone at birds scares them away,
27:25 Whoever t a stone straight up t it on his own head,

THRUST (23) [THRUSTING, THRUSTS]

Dt 15:17 an awl and t it through his earlobe into the door,

Jdg 3:21 and **t** it into Eglon's belly;
9:54 So the young man **t** him through, and he died.
1Sa 2:14 and he would **t** it into the pan, or kettle,
31: 4 "Draw your sword and **t** me through with it,
31: 4 that these uncircumcised may not come and **t** me
2Sa 2:16 and **t** his sword in his opponent's side;
18:14 and **t** them into the heart of Absalom,
1Ki 14: 9 and have **t** me behind your back;
1Ch 10: 4 "Draw your sword, and **t** me through with it,
Job 18: 8 For they are **t** into a net by their own feet,
18:18 They are **t** from light into darkness,
24: 4 They **t** the needy off the road;
Ps 36:12 they are **t** down, unable to rise.
SS 5: 4 My beloved **t** his hand into the opening,
Isa 8:22 and they will be **t** into thick darkness.
13:15 Whoever is found will be **t** through,
22:19 I will **t** you from your office,
Jer 46:15 —because the LORD **t** him down.
Eze 26:20 then I will **t** you down with those who descend
28: 8 They shall **t** you down to the Pit,
Zec 5: 8 So he **t** her back into the basket,
Mal 3: 5 against those who **t** aside the alien,

THRUSTING (2) [THRUST]

Dt 6:19 **t** out all your enemies from before you,
Eze 46:18 **t** them out of their holding;

THRUSTS (2) [THRUST]

Dt 9: 4 the LORD your God **t** them out before you,
Pr 12:18 Rash words are like sword **t**,

THUG (1)

Pr 28:24 "That is no crime," is partner to a **t**.

THUMB (5) [THUMBS, THUMBSCREWS]

Lev 8:23 of Aaron's right ear and on the **t** of his right hand
14:14 and on the **t** of the right hand,
14:17 and on the **t** of the right hand,
14:25 and on the **t** of the right hand,
14:28 and on the **t** of the right hand,

THUMBS (4) [THUMB]

Ex 29:20 and on the **t** of their right hands,
Lev 8:24 of their right ears and on the **t** of their right hands
Jdg 1: 6 and caught him, and cut off his **t** and big toes.
1: 7 with their **t** and big toes cut off used to pick

THUMBSCREWS (1) [THUMB]

4Mc 8:13 and **t** and iron claws and wedges and bellows,

THUMMIM (8)

Ex 28:30 of judgment you shall put the Urim and the **T**,
Lev 8: 8 and in the breastpiece he put the Urim and the **T**.
Dt 33: 8 Give to Levi your **T**, and your Urim to your loyal
1Sa 14:41 but if this guilt is in your people Israel, give **T**."
Ezr 2:63 be a priest to consult Urim and **T**.
Ne 7:65 until a priest with Urim and **T** should come.
Sir 45:10 with the oracle of judgment, Urim and **T**;
1Es 5:40 a high priest should appear wearing Urim and **T**.

THUNDER (38) [THUNDERBOLT, THUNDERBOLTS, THUNDERED, THUNDERING, THUNDERINGS, THUNDERPEALS, THUNDERS]

Ex 9:23 and the LORD sent **t** and hail,
9:28 Enough of God's **t** and hail!
9:29 the **t** will cease, and there will be no more hail,
9:33 then the **t** and the hail ceased,
9:34 that the rain and the hail and the **t** had ceased,
19:16 On the morning of the third day there was **t**
19:19 and God would answer him in **t**.
20:18 When all the people witnessed the **t** and lightning,
1Sa 2:10 the Most High will **t** in heaven
12:17 that he may send **t** and rain;
12:18 and the LORD sent **t** and rain that day;
Job 26:14 But the **t** of his power who can understand?"
37: 2 to the **t** of his voice and the rumbling that comes
39:25 the **t** of the captains, and the shouting.
40: 9 and can you **t** with a voice like his?
Ps 42: 7 Deep calls to deep at the **t** of your cataracts;
77:18 The crash of your **t** was in the whirlwind;
81: 7 I answered you in the secret place of **t**;
104: 7 at the sound of your **t** they take to flight.
Isa 17:12 Ah, the **t** of many peoples, they **t** like the thundering of the sea!
29: 6 you will be visited by the LORD of hosts with **t**
Eze 1:24 like the **t** of the Almighty,
Mk 3:17 the name Boanerges, that is, Sons of **T**);
Jn 12:29 and said that it was **t**.
Rev 4: 5 and rumblings and peals of **t**,
6: 1 as with a voice of **t**, "Come!"
8: 5 and there were peals of **t**, rumblings,
11:19 peals of **t**, an earthquake, and heavy hail.
14: 2 of many waters and like the sound of loud **t**;
16:18 rumblings, peals of **t**, and a violent earthquake,
Wis 19:13 the violence of **t**, for they justly suffered because
Sir 32:10 Lightning travels ahead of the **t**,
40:13 and crash like a loud clap of **t** in a storm.
43:17 The voice of his **t** rebukes the earth;
2Es 6: 2 and before the rumblings of **t** sounded,
7:*40* or cloud or **t** or lightning,
16:10 He will **t**, and who will not be terrified?

THUNDERBOLT (2) [THUNDER]

Job 28:26 and a way for the **t**;
38:25 and a way for the **t**,

THUNDERBOLTS (2) [THUNDER]

Ps 78:48 over their cattle to the hail, and their flocks to **t**.
2Mc 10:30 They showered arrows and **t** on the enemy,

THUNDERED (5) [THUNDER]

1Sa 7:10 the LORD **t** with a mighty voice that day against
2Sa 22:14 The LORD **t** from heaven;
Ps 18:13 The LORD also **t** in the heavens,
77:17 the skies **t**; your arrows flashed on every side.
Sir 46:17 Then the Lord **t** from heaven,

THUNDERING (1) [THUNDER]

Isa 17:12 they thunder like the **t** of the sea!

THUNDERINGS (1) [THUNDER]

Job 36:29 the spreading of the clouds, the **t** of his pavilion?

THUNDERPEALS (1) [PEALS, THUNDER]

Rev 19: 6 of many waters and like the sound of mighty **t**,

THUNDERS (8) [THUNDER]

Job 37: 4 he **t** with his majestic voice and he does
37: 5 God **t** wondrously with his voice;
Ps 29: 3 God of glory **t**, the LORD, over mighty waters.
93: 4 More majestic than the **t** of mighty waters,
Rev 10: 3 And when he shouted, the seven **t** sounded.
10: 4 And when the seven **t** had sounded,
10: 4 "Seal up what the seven **t** have said,
AdE 11: 5 **t** and earthquake, tumult on the earth!

THUS‡ (746)

A. THUS SAYS THE †LORD (283)
B. THUS SAYS THE *LORD †GOD (134)
C. THUS SAYS THE *LORD (11)

Ge 2: 1 **T** the heavens and the earth were finished,
5: 5 **T** all the days that Adam lived were nine hundred
5: 8 **T** all the days of Seth were nine hundred twelve
5:11 **T** all the days of Enosh were nine hundred five
5:14 **T** all the days of Kenan were nine hundred
5:17 **T** all the days of Mahalalel were eight hundred
5:20 **T** all the days of Jared were nine hundred sixty-two
5:23 **T** all the days of Enoch were three hundred
5:27 **T** all the days of Methuselah were nine hundred
5:31 **T** all the days of Lamech were seven hundred
13:11 **t** they separated from each other.
19:36 **T** both the daughters of Lot became pregnant
24:30 "**T** the man spoke to me," he went to the man;
24:61 **t** the servant took Rebekah, and went his way.
25:34 **T** Esau despised his birthright.
28: 5 **T** Isaac sent Jacob away;
30:43 **T** the man grew exceedingly rich,
31: 9 **T** God has taken away the livestock
32: 4 "**T** you shall say to my lord Esau:
32: 4 **T** says your servant Jacob,
37:35 **T** his father bewailed him.
41:43 **T** he set him over all the land of Egypt.
41:45 **T** Joseph gained authority over the land of Egypt.
42: 5 **T** the sons of Israel were among
42:20 **T** your words will be verified,
45: 9 '**T** says your son Joseph, God has made me lord
47:27 **T** Israel settled in the land of Egypt,
50:12 **T** his sons did for him as he had instructed them.
Ex 3:14 He said further, "**T** you shall say to the Israelites,
3:15 "**T** you shall say to the Israelites, 'The LORD,
4:22 you shall say to Pharaoh, '**T** says the LORD: A
5: 1 "**T** says the LORD, the God of Israel, A
5:10 "**T** says Pharaoh, 'I will not give you straw.
6:13 **T** the LORD spoke to Moses and Aaron
7:17 **T** says the LORD, "By this you shall know A
8: 1 to Pharaoh and say to him, '**T** says the LORD: A
8:20 and say to him, '**T** says the LORD: A
8:23 **T** I will make a distinction between my people
9: 1 '**T** says the LORD, the God of the Hebrews: A
9:13 '**T** says the LORD, the God of the Hebrews: A
10: 3 "**T** says the LORD, the God of the Hebrews, A
11: 4 Moses said, "**T** says the LORD: A
14:30 **T** the LORD saved Israel that day from
19: 3 saying, "**T** you shall say to the house of Jacob,
20:22 **T** you shall say to the Israelites:
28:30 **t** Aaron shall bear the judgment of the Israelites
29:35 **T** you shall do to Aaron and to his sons,
32:27 He said to them, "**T** says the LORD, A
33:11 **T** the LORD used to speak to Moses face to face,
Lev 4: 3 **t** bringing guilt on the people,
4:26 **T** the priest shall make atonement on his behalf
4:31 **T** the priest shall make atonement on your behalf,
4:35 **T** the priest shall make atonement on your behalf
5:10 **T** the priest shall make atonement on your behalf
5:13 **T** the priest shall make atonement on your behalf
8:15 **T** he consecrated it, to make atonement for it.
8:30 **T** he consecrated Aaron and his vestments,
14:20 **T** the priest shall make atonement on his behalf
14:52 **T** he shall cleanse the house with the blood of
15:31 **T** you shall keep the people of Israel separate
16: 3 **T** shall Aaron come into the holy place:
16:16 **T** he shall make atonement for the sanctuary,
18:25 **T** the land became defiled;
21:12 not go outside the sanctuary and **t** profane
Lev 21:24 **T** Moses spoke to Aaron and to his sons and to all
22:31 **T** you shall keep my commandments
23:44 **T** Moses declared to the people of Israel
24:23 Moses spoke **t** to the people of Israel;
25:52 until the jubilee year, they shall compute **t**:
Nu 4:49 **t** they were enrolled by him,
6:23 saying, **T** you shall bless the Israelites:
7:89 between the two cherubim; **t** it spoke to him.
8: 7 **T** you shall do to them, to cleanse them:
8:14 **T** you shall separate the Levites from among
8:26 **T** you shall do with the Levites
14:35 I the LORD have spoken; surely I will do **t**
15:11 **T** it shall be done for each ox or ram,
16:38 **T** they shall be a sign to the Israelites.
17: 5 **t** I will put a stop to the complaints of
18:28 **T** you also shall set apart an offering to
19:19 **t** purifying them on the seventh day.
20: 8 **T** you shall bring water out of the rock for them;
20: 8 **t** you shall provide drink for the congregation
20:14 "**T** says your brother Israel:
20:21 **T** Edom refused to give Israel passage
21:31 **T** Israel settled in the land of the Amorites.
22:16 "**T** says Balak son of Zippor:
25: 3 **T** Israel yoked itself to the Baal of Peor,
Dt 4:25 **t** doing what is evil in the sight of
12: 3 and **t** blot out their name from their places.
15:14 **t** giving to him some of the bounty with which
20:15 **T** you shall treat all the towns that are very far
20:18 and you **t** sin against the LORD your God.
29:19 we go our own stubborn ways" (**t** bringing disaster
29:24 "Why has the LORD done **t** to this land?
32: 6 Do you **t** repay the LORD,
Jos 6: 3 **T** you shall do for six days,
7:13 for **t** says the LORD, the God of Israel, A
10:25 for **t** the LORD will do to all the enemies
17: 5 **T** there fell to Manasseh ten portions,
21:43 **T** the LORD gave to Israel all the land
22:16 "**T** says the whole congregation of the LORD,
24: 2 Joshua said to all the people, "**T** says the LORD, A
Jdg 6: 6 **T** Israel was greatly impoverished because
6: 8 and he said to them, "**T** says the LORD, A
7: 3 **T** Gideon sifted them out;
9:56 **T** God repaid Abimelech for
10: 6 **T** they abandoned the LORD,
11:15 to him: "**T** says Jephthah:
19:30 saying, "**T** shall you say to all the Israelites,
Ru 1:17 May the LORD do **t** and so to me,
1Sa 2:17 **T** the sin of the young men was very great in
2:27 to him, "**T** the LORD has said, 'I revealed myself
7:12 for he said, "**T** far the LORD has helped us."
10:18 "**T** says the LORD, the God of Israel, A
11: 2 and **t** put disgrace upon all Israel."
11: 9 "**T** shall you say to the inhabitants
15: 2 **T** says the LORD of hosts, A
18:25 Then Saul said, "**T** shall you say to David,
20:16 **T** Jonathan made a covenant with the house
23: 5 **T** David rescued the inhabitants of Keilah.
25: 6 **T** you shall salute him: 'Peace be to
2Sa 7: 5 and tell my servant David: **T** says the LORD: A
7: 8 therefore **t** you shall say to my servant David:
7: 8 **T** says the LORD of hosts: A
7:18 that you have brought me **t** far?
7:26 **T** your name will be magnified forever in
11:25 "**T** you shall say to Joab, 'Do
12: 7 **T** says the LORD, the God of Israel: A
12:11 **T** says the LORD: I will raise up trouble A
12:31 **T** he did to all the cities of the Ammonites.
14: 7 **T** they would quench my one remaining ember,
15: 6 **T** Absalom did to every Israelite who came to
17:15 "**T** and so did Ahithophel counsel Absalom and
17:15 and **t** and so I have counseled.
17:21 **t** and so has Ahithophel counseled against you."
24:12 to David: **T** says the LORD: A
1Ki 1: 6 "Why have you done **t** and so?"
1:48 and went on to pray **t**,
2:27 **t** fulfilling the word of the LORD
2:30 saying, "**T** said Joab, and **t** he answered me."
2:31 and **t** take away from me and
7:22 **T** the work of the pillars was finished.
7:51 **T** all the work that King Solomon did on
10:23 **T** King Solomon excelled all the kings of
11:31 for **t** says the LORD, the God of Israel, "See, A
12:10 "**T** you should say to this people who spoke
12:10 **t** you should say to them,
12:24 "**T** says the LORD, You shall not go up or fight A
13: 2 and said, "O altar, altar, **t** says the LORD: A
13: 9 **t** I was commanded by the word of the LORD:
13:21 who came from Judah, "**T** says the LORD: A
14: 5 **T** and **t** you shall say to her."
14: 7 Go, tell Jeroboam, '**T** says the LORD, A
16:12 **T** Zimri destroyed all the house of Baasha,
17:14 For **t** says the LORD the God of Israel: A
20: 2 to him: "**T** says Ben-hadad:
20: 5 and said: "**T** says Ben-hadad:
20:13 King Ahab of Israel and said, "**T** says the LORD, A
20:14 He said, "**T** says the LORD, A
20:28 and said to the king of Israel, "**T** says the LORD: A
20:42 Then he said to him, "**T** says the LORD, A
21:19 You shall say to him, "**T** says the LORD: A
21:19 You shall say to him, "**T** says the LORD: A
22:11 and he said, "**T** says the LORD: A
22:27 and say, '**T** says the king:
2Ki 1: 4 Now therefore **t** says the LORD, A
1: 6 to him: **T** says the LORD: A
1:16 and said to him, "**T** says the LORD: A
2:21 and said, "**T** says the LORD, A
3:16 And he said, "**T** says the LORD, A

2Ki 3:17 For t says the LORD, 'You shall see neither wind A
4:43 the people and let them eat, for t says the LORD, A
7: 1 t says the LORD, Tomorrow about this time A
9: 3 pour it on his head, and say, 'T says the LORD: A
9: 6 "T says the LORD the God of Israel: A
9:12 'T says the LORD, I anoint you king A
9:14 T Jehu son of Jehoshaphat son
9:18 he said, "T says the king, 'Is it peace?' "
9:19 who came to them and said, "T says the king,
10:28 T Jehu wiped out Baal from Israel.
11: 2 T she hid him from Athaliah,
18:19 T says the great king, the king of Assyria:
18:29 T says the king: 'Do not let Hezekiah deceive you,
18:31 for t says the king of Assyria:
19: 3 They said to him, "T says Hezekiah,
19: 6 "Say to your master, 'T says the LORD: A
19:10 "T shall you speak to King Hezekiah of Judah:
19:20 saying, "T says the LORD, the God of Israel: A
19:32 t says the LORD concerning the king of Assyria: A
20: 1 and said to him, "T says the LORD: A
20: 5 T says the LORD, the God A
21:12 therefore t says the LORD, A
22:15 She declared to them, "T says the LORD, A
22:16 T says the LORD, I will indeed bring disaster A
22:18 t shall you say to him, Thus says the LORD,
22:18 thus shall you say to him, T says the LORD, A
1Ch 10: 6 T Saul died; he and his three sons
17: 4 and tell my servant David: T says the LORD: A
17: 7 therefore t you shall say to my servant David:
17: 7 T says the LORD of hosts: A
17:16 that you have brought me t far?
17:24 T your name will be established
20: 3 T David did to all the cities of the Ammonites.
21:10 and say to David, 'T says the LORD: A
21:11 "T says the LORD, 'Take your choice: A
23:32 T they shall keep charge of the tent of meeting
29:26 T David son of Jesse reigned over all Israel.
2Ch 4:11 T Huram finished the work that he did
5: 1 T all the work that Solomon did for the house of
6:31 T may they fear you and walk in your ways all
7:11 T Solomon finished the house of the LORD and
8:16 T all the work of Solomon was accomplished
9:22 T King Solomon excelled all the kings of
10:10 "T should you speak to the people who said
11: 4 "T says the LORD: You shall A
12: 5 and said to them, "T says the LORD: A
13:13 t his troops were in front of Judah,
13:18 T the Israelites were subdued at that time,
18:10 and he said, "T says the LORD: A
18:26 and say, 'T says the king:
20:15 T says the LORD to you: A
21:12 "T says the LORD, the God A
22:11 T Jehoshabeath, daughter of King Jehoram
24:20 above the people and said to them, "T says God:
24:24 T they executed judgment on Joash.
29:35 T the service of the house of
32:10 "T says King Sennacherib of Assyria:
34:23 She declared to them, "T says the LORD, A
34:24 T says the LORD: I will indeed bring disaster A
34:26 t shall you say to him:
34:26 T says the LORD, the God of Israel: A
36:23 "T says King Cyrus of Persia:
Ezr 1: 2 "T says King Cyrus of Persia:
5: 3 to them and spoke to them t,
9: 2 T the holy seed has mixed itself with the peoples
Ne 5:13 T may they be shaken out and emptied."
13:30 T I cleansed them from everything foreign,
Est 6: 9 'T shall it be done for the man whom
6:11 "T shall it be done for the man whom
9:26 T because of all that was written in this letter,
Job 19:26 and after my skin has been t destroyed,
34:25 T, knowing their works, he overturns them in
38:11 'T far shall you come, and no farther,
Ps 106:39 T they became unclean by their acts,
128: 4 T shall the man be blessed who fears the LORD.
147:20 He has not dealt t with any other nation;
Pr 30: 1 An oracle. T says the man:
SS 5: 9 more than another beloved, that you t adjure us?
Isa 7: 7 therefore t says the Lord GOD: B
8:11 For the LORD spoke t to me
10:24 Therefore t says the Lord GOD of hosts: B
18: 4 For t the LORD said to me:
21: 6 For t the Lord said to me:
21:16 For t the Lord said to me:
22:15 T says the Lord GOD of hosts: B
24:13 t it shall be on the earth and among the nations,
28:16 therefore t says the Lord GOD, See, I am laying B
29:22 Therefore t says the LORD, A
30:12 Therefore t says the Holy One of Israel:
30:15 For t said the Lord GOD, the Holy One of Israel:
31: 4 For t the LORD said to me,
36: 4 T says the great king, the king of Assyria:
36:14 T says the king: 'Do not let Hezekiah deceive you,
36:16 for t says the king of Assyria:
37: 3 They said to him, "T says Hezekiah,
37: 6 "Say to your master, 'T says the LORD: A
37:10 "T shall you speak to King Hezekiah of Judah:
37:21 "T says the LORD, the God of Israel: A
37:33 t says the LORD concerning the king of Assyria: A
38: 1 and said to him, "T says the LORD: A
38: 5 T says the LORD, the God A
42: 5 T says God, the LORD, who created the heavens
43: 1 But now t says the LORD, he who created you, A
43:14 T says the LORD, your Redeemer, A
43:16 T says the LORD, who makes a way in the sea, A
44: 2 T says the LORD who made you, A
44: 6 T says the LORD, the King of Israel, A

Isa 44:24 T says the LORD, your Redeemer, A
45: 1 T says the LORD to his anointed, to Cyrus, A
45:11 T says the LORD, the Holy One of Israel, A
45:14 T says the LORD: The wealth of Egypt A
45:18 For t says the LORD, who created A
48:17 T says the LORD, your Redeemer, A
49: 7 T says the LORD, the Redeemer of Israel A
49: 8 T says the LORD: In a time of favor A
49:22 T says the Lord GOD: I will soon lift up my B
49:25 But t says the LORD: A
50: 1 T says the LORD: A
51:22 T says your Sovereign, the LORD,
52: 3 For t says the LORD: You were sold A
52: 4 For t says the Lord GOD: B
56: 1 T says the LORD: Maintain justice, A
56: 4 For t says the LORD: A
56: 8 T says the Lord GOD, who gathers the outcasts B
57:15 For t says the high and lofty one who inhabits
63:14 T you led your people, to make for yourself a
65: 8 T says the LORD: As the wine is found in the A
65:13 Therefore t says the Lord GOD: B
66: 1 T says the LORD: Heaven is my throne A
66:12 For t says the LORD: I will extend prosperity A
Jer 2: 2 in the hearing of Jerusalem, T says the LORD: A
2: 5 T says the LORD: What wrong did your A
4: 3 For t says the LORD to the people of Judah and A
4:27 For t says the LORD: The whole land shall be a A
5:13 T shall it be done to them!
5:14 Therefore t says the LORD, the God of hosts: A
6: 6 For t says the LORD of hosts: A
6: 9 T says the LORD of hosts: A
6:16 T says the LORD: Stand at the A
6:21 Therefore t says the LORD: A
6:22 T says the LORD: See, a people is coming A
7: 3 T says the LORD of hosts, the God of Israel: A
7:20 Therefore t says the Lord GOD: B
7:21 T says the LORD of hosts, the God of Israel: A
8: 4 You shall say to them, T says the LORD: A
9: 7 Therefore t says the LORD of hosts: A
9:15 t says the LORD of hosts, the God of Israel: A
9:17 T says the LORD of hosts: A
9:22 T says the LORD: "Human corpses shall fall A
9:23 T says the LORD: Do not let the wise boast A
10: 2 T says the LORD: Do not learn the way of A
10:11 T shall you say to them:
10:18 For t says the LORD: I am going to sling A
11: 3 You shall say to them, T says the LORD, A
11:11 Therefore, t says the LORD, A
11:21 Therefore t says the LORD concerning A
11:22 therefore t says the LORD of hosts: A
12:14 T says the LORD concerning all A
13: 1 T said the LORD to me,
13: 9 T says the LORD: Just so I will ruin A
13:12 T says the LORD, the God of Israel: A
13:13 Then you shall say to them: T says the LORD: A
14:10 T says the LORD concerning this people: A
14:15 Therefore t says the LORD concerning A
15: 2 you shall say to them: T says the LORD: A
15:19 Therefore t says the LORD: A
16: 3 For t says the LORD concerning the sons A
16: 5 For t says the LORD: Do not enter the house A
16: 9 For t says the LORD of hosts, the God of Israel: A
17: 5 T says the LORD: Cursed are those who trust A
17:19 T said the LORD to me:
17:21 T says the LORD: For the sake of your A
18:11 T says the LORD: Look, I am a potter A
18:13 Therefore t says the LORD: A
19: 1 T said the LORD: Go and buy a potter's
19: 3 T says the LORD of hosts, the God of Israel: A
19:11 T says the LORD of hosts: A
19:12 T will I do to this place, says the LORD,
19:15 T says the LORD of hosts, the God of Israel: A
20: 4 For t says the LORD: I am making you a terror A
21: 4 T you shall say to Zedekiah:
21: 4 T says the LORD, the God of Israel: A
21: 8 to this people you shall say: T says the LORD: A
21:12 O house of David! T says the LORD: A
22: 1 T says the LORD: Go down to A
22: 3 T says the LORD: Act with justice A
22: 6 For t says the LORD concerning the house of A
22:11 For t says the LORD concerning Shallum son A
22:18 Therefore t says the LORD A
22:30 T says the LORD: Record this man A
23: 2 Therefore t says the LORD, the God of Israel, A
23:15 Therefore t says the LORD of hosts concerning A
23:16 T says the LORD of hosts: A
23:35 T shall you say to one another, among yourselves,
23:37 T you shall ask the prophet,
23:38 "the burden of the LORD," t says the LORD: A
24: 5 T says the LORD, the God of Israel: A
24: 8 But t says the LORD: A
25: 8 Therefore t says the LORD of hosts: A
25:15 For t the LORD, the God of Israel, said to me:
25:27 you shall say to them, T says the LORD of hosts, A
25:28 T says the LORD of hosts: You must drink! A
25:32 T says the LORD of hosts: A
26: 2 T says the LORD: Stand in the A
26: 4 You shall say to them: T says the LORD: A
26:18 'T says the LORD of hosts, A
27: 2 T the LORD said to me:
27: 4 T says the LORD of hosts, the God of Israel: A
27:16 saying, T says the LORD: A
27:19 t says the LORD of hosts concerning the pillars, A
27:21 t says the LORD of hosts, the God of Israel, A
28: 2 "T says the LORD of hosts, the God of Israel: A
28:11 saying, "T says the LORD: A
28:13 tell Hananiah, T says the LORD: A

Jer 28:14 For t says the LORD of hosts, the God of Israel: A
28:16 Therefore t says the LORD: A
29: 4 T says the LORD of hosts, the God of Israel, A
29: 8 For t says the LORD of hosts, the God of Israel: A
29:10 For t says the LORD: Only when Babylon's A
29:16 T says the LORD concerning the king who sits A
29:17 T says the LORD of hosts, A
29:21 T says the LORD of hosts, the God of Israel, A
29:25 T says the LORD of hosts, the God of Israel: A
29:31 T says the LORD concerning Shemaiah A
29:32 therefore t says the LORD: A
30: 2 T says the LORD, the God of Israel: A
30: 5 T says the LORD: We have heard a cry of panic, A
30:12 For t says the LORD: Your hurt is incurable, A
30:18 T says the LORD: I am going to restore A
31: 2 T says the LORD: The people who survived A
31: 7 For t says the LORD: Sing aloud with gladness A
31:15 T says the LORD: A voice is heard in Ramah, A
31:16 T says the LORD: Keep your voice from A
31:23 T says the LORD of hosts, the God of Israel: A
31:35 T says the LORD, who gives the sun for light A
31:37 T says the LORD: If the heavens above can A
32: 3 prophesy and say: T says the LORD: A
32:14 T says the LORD of hosts, the God of Israel: A
32:15 For t says the LORD of hosts, the God of Israel: A
32:28 Therefore, t says the LORD: A
32:36 Now therefore t says the LORD, A
32:42 For t says the LORD: Just as I have brought A
33: 2 T says the LORD who made the earth, A
33: 4 For t says the LORD, the God of Israel, A
33:10 T says the LORD: In this place A
33:12 T says the LORD of hosts: A
33:17 For t says the LORD: David shall never lack A
33:20 T says the LORD: If any of you A
33:25 T says the LORD: Only if I had not established A
34: 2 "T says the LORD, the God of Israel: A
34: 2 and say to him: T says the LORD: A
34: 4 T says the LORD concerning you: A
34:13 T says the LORD, the God of Israel: A
34:17 Therefore, t says the LORD: A
35:13 T says the LORD of hosts, the God of Israel: A
35:17 Therefore, t says the LORD, the God of hosts, A
35:18 T says the LORD of hosts, the God of Israel: A
35:19 t says the LORD of hosts, the God of Israel: A
36:29 T says the LORD, You have dared A
36:30 Therefore t says the LORD concerning A
37: 7 T says the LORD, God of Israel: A
37: 9 T says the LORD: Do not deceive yourselves, A
37:16 T Jeremiah was put in the cistern house,
38: 2 T says the LORD, Those who stay A
38: 3 T says the LORD, This city shall surely A
38:17 Jeremiah said to Zedekiah, "T says the LORD, A
39:16 T says the LORD of hosts, the God of Israel: A
42: 9 "T says the LORD, the God of Israel, A
42:13 t disobeying the voice of the LORD your God
42:15 T says the LORD of hosts, the God of Israel: A
42:18 "For t says the LORD of hosts, the God of Israel: A
43:10 T says the LORD of hosts, the God of Israel: A
44: 2 T says the LORD of hosts, the God of Israel: A
44: 7 t says the LORD God of hosts, the God of Israel: A
44:11 t says the LORD of hosts, the God of Israel: A
44:25 T says the LORD of hosts, the God of Israel: A
44:30 T says the LORD, I am going A
45: 2 T says the LORD, the God of Israel, A
45: 4 T you shall say to him, "Thus says the LORD:
45: 4 Thus you shall say to him, "T says the LORD: A
47: 2 T says the LORD: See, waters are rising out of A
48: 1 T says the LORD of hosts, the God of Israel: A
48:40 For t says the LORD: Look, he shall swoop A
48:47 T far is the judgment on Moab.
49: 1 T says the LORD: Has Israel no sons? A
49: 7 T says the LORD of hosts: A
49:12 For t says the LORD: If those who do A
49:28 of Babylon defeated. T says the LORD: A
49:35 T says the LORD of hosts: A
50:18 t says the LORD of hosts, the God of Israel: A
50:33 T says the LORD of hosts: A
51: 1 T says the LORD: I am going to stir A
51:33 For t says the LORD of hosts, the God of Israel: A
51:36 Therefore t says the LORD: A
51:58 T says the LORD of hosts: A
51:64 'T shall Babylon sink, to rise no more,
51:64 T far are the words of Jeremiah.
Eze 1: 8 And the four had their faces and their wings t:
2: 4 "T says the Lord GOD." B
3:11 Say to them, "T says the Lord GOD"; B
3:27 "T says the Lord GOD"; B
4:13 "T shall the people of Israel eat their bread,
5: 5 T says the Lord GOD: This is Jerusalem; B
5: 7 Therefore t says the Lord GOD: B
5: 8 therefore t says the Lord GOD: B
6: 3 T says the Lord GOD to the mountains and B
6:11 T says the Lord GOD: Clap your hands B
6:12 T I will spend my fury upon them.
7: 2 t says the Lord GOD to the land of Israel: B
7: 5 T says the Lord GOD: Disaster after disaster! B
11: 5 and he said to me, "Say, T says the LORD: A
11: 7 Therefore t says the Lord GOD: B
11:16 Therefore say: T says the Lord GOD: B
11:17 Therefore say: T says the Lord GOD: B
12:10 Say to them, "T says the Lord GOD: B
12:19 T says the Lord GOD concerning the inhabitants B
12:23 Tell them therefore, "T says the Lord GOD: B
12:28 Therefore say to them, T says the Lord GOD: B
13: 3 T says the Lord GOD, Alas for B
13: 8 Therefore t says the Lord GOD: B
13:13 Therefore t says the Lord GOD: B

Eze 13:15 **T** I will spend my wrath upon the wall,
13:18 and say, **T** says the Lord GOD: B
13:20 Therefore **t** says the Lord GOD: B
14: 4 and say to them, **T** says the Lord GOD: B
14: 6 say to the house of Israel, **T** says the Lord GOD: B
14:21 For **t** says the Lord GOD: B
15: 6 Therefore **t** says the Lord GOD: B
16: 3 **T** says the Lord GOD to Jerusalem: B
16:36 **T** says the Lord GOD, B
16:59 Yes, **t** says the Lord GOD: B
17: 3 Say: **T** says the Lord GOD: B
17: 9 Say: **T** says the Lord GOD: Will it prosper? B
17:19 Therefore **t** says the Lord GOD: B
17:22 **T** says the Lord GOD: I myself will take a sprig B
20: 3 **T** says the Lord GOD: Why are you coming? B
20: 5 to them: **T** says the Lord GOD: B
20:27 of Israel and say to them, **T** says the Lord GOD: B
20:30 say to the house of Israel, **T** says the Lord GOD: B
20:39 for you, O house of Israel, **t** says the Lord GOD: B
20:47 **T** says the Lord GOD, I will kindle a fire in you, B
21: 3 and say to the land of Israel, **T** says the LORD: A
21: 9 and say: **T** says the Lord; C
21:24 Therefore **t** says the Lord GOD: B
21:26 **t** says the Lord GOD: Remove the turban, B
21:28 **T** says the Lord GOD concerning B
22: 3 You shall say, **T** says the Lord GOD: A city! B
22:19 Therefore **t** says the Lord GOD: B
22:28 saying, "**T** says the Lord GOD," B
23:21 **T** you longed for the lewdness of your youth,
23:22 Therefore, O Oholibah, **t** says the Lord GOD: B
23:28 For **t** says the Lord GOD: B
23:32 **T** says the Lord GOD: You shall drink your B
23:35 Therefore **t** says the Lord GOD: B
23:44 **T** they went in to Oholah and to Oholibah,
23:46 For **t** says the Lord GOD: B
23:48 **T** will I put an end to lewdness in the land,
24: 3 and say to them, **T** says the Lord GOD: B
24: 6 Therefore **t** says the Lord GOD: B
24: 9 **t** says the Lord GOD: Woe to the bloody city! B
24:21 to the house of Israel, **T** says the Lord GOD: B
24:24 **T** Ezekiel shall be a sign to you;
25: 3 **T** says the Lord GOD, Because you said, "Aha!" B
25: 6 For **t** says the Lord GOD: B
25: 8 **T** says the Lord GOD: B
25:10 **T** Ammon shall be remembered no more among
25:12 **T** says the Lord GOD: B
25:13 therefore **t** says the Lord GOD, B
25:15 **T** says the Lord GOD: B
25:16 therefore **t** says the Lord GOD, B
26: 3 Therefore, **t** says the Lord GOD: B
26: 7 For **t** says the Lord GOD: B
26:15 **T** says the Lord GOD to Tyre: B
26:19 For **t** says the Lord GOD: B
27: 3 on many coastlands, **T** says the Lord GOD: B
28: 2 say to the prince of Tyre, **T** says the Lord GOD: B
28: 6 Therefore **t** says the Lord GOD: B
28:12 and say to him, **T** says the Lord GOD: B
28:22 and say, **T** says the Lord GOD: B
28:25 **T** says the Lord GOD: B
29: 3 and say, **T** says the Lord GOD: B
29: 8 Therefore, **t** says the Lord GOD: B
29:13 Further, **t** says the Lord GOD: B
29:19 Therefore **t** says the Lord GOD: B
30: 2 **T** says the Lord GOD: Wail, "Alas for the day!" B
30: 6 **T** says the LORD: Those who support Egypt A
30:10 **T** says the Lord GOD: I will put an end to the B
30:13 **T** says the Lord GOD: I will destroy the idols B
30:19 **T** I will execute acts of judgment on Egypt.
30:22 Therefore **t** says the Lord GOD: B
31:10 Therefore **t** says the Lord GOD: B
31:15 **T** says the Lord GOD: B
32: 3 **T** says the Lord GOD: B
32:11 For **t** says the Lord GOD: B
33:10 say to the house of Israel, **T** you have said:
33:25 Therefore say to them, **T** says the Lord GOD: B
33:27 Say this to them, **T** says the Lord GOD: B
34: 2 to the shepherds: **T** says the Lord GOD: B
34:10 **T** says the Lord GOD, I am against B
34:11 For **t** says the Lord GOD: B
34:17 As for you, my flock, **t** says the Lord GOD: B
34:20 Therefore, **t** says the Lord GOD to them: B
35: 3 and say to it, **T** says the Lord GOD: B
35:14 **T** says the Lord GOD: B
36: 2 **T** says the Lord GOD: B
36: 3 and say: **T** says the Lord GOD: B
36: 4 **T** says the Lord GOD to the mountains and B
36: 5 therefore **t** says the Lord GOD: B
36: 6 watercourses and valleys, **T** says the Lord GOD: B
36: 7 therefore **t** says the Lord GOD: B
36:13 **T** says the Lord GOD: B
36:22 say to the house of Israel, **T** says the Lord GOD: B
36:33 **T** says the Lord GOD: On the day B
36:37 **T** says the Lord GOD: I will B
37: 5 **T** says the Lord GOD to these bones: B
37: 9 to the breath: **T** says the Lord GOD: B
37:12 and say to them, **T** says the Lord GOD: B
37:19 say to them, **T** says the Lord GOD: B
37:21 then say to them, **T** says the Lord GOD: B
38: 3 and say: **T** says the Lord GOD: B
38:10 **T** says the Lord GOD: On that day B
38:14 to Gog: **T** says the Lord GOD: B
38:17 **T** says the Lord GOD: Are you he of whom B
39: 1 and say: **T** says the Lord GOD: B
39:16 **T** they shall cleanse the land.
39:17 As for you, mortal, **t** says the Lord GOD: B
39:25 Therefore **t** says the Lord GOD: B
43:18 Mortal, **t** says the Lord GOD: B
Eze 43:20 **t** you shall purify it and make atonement for it.
44: 6 to the house of Israel, **T** says the Lord GOD: B
44: 9 **T** says the Lord GOD: No foreigner, B
45: 9 **T** says the Lord GOD: Enough, O princes B
45:18 **T** says the Lord GOD: In the first month, B
46: 1 **T** says the Lord GOD: The gate of the inner B
46:15 **T** the lamb and the grain offering and the oil
46:16 **T** says the Lord GOD: If the prince B
47:13 **T** says the Lord GOD: These are the boundaries B
Hos 4:14 **t** a people without understanding comes to ruin.
10:15 **T** it shall be done to you, O Bethel,
Am 1: 3 **T** says the LORD: For three transgressions of A
1: 6 **T** says the LORD: For three transgressions of A
1: 9 **T** says the LORD: For three transgressions of A
1:11 **T** says the LORD: For three transgressions of A
1:13 **T** says the LORD: For three transgressions of A
2: 1 **T** says the LORD: For three transgressions of A
2: 4 **T** says the LORD: For three transgressions of A
2: 6 **T** says the LORD: For three transgressions of A
3:11 Therefore **t** says the Lord GOD: B
3:12 **T** says the LORD: As the shepherd rescues A
4:12 Therefore **t** I will do to you, O Israel;
5: 3 For **t** says the Lord GOD: B
5: 4 For **t** says the LORD to the house of Israel: A
5:16 **t** says the LORD, the God of hosts, the Lord: A
7:11 For **t** Amos has said, 'Jeroboam shall die by
7:17 Therefore **t** says the LORD: A
Ob 1: 1 **T** says the Lord GOD concerning Edom: B
Mic 2: 3 Therefore **t** says the LORD: A
2: 6 "Do not preach"—**t** they preach—
3: 5 **T** says the LORD concerning A
7: 3 dictate what they desire; **t** they pervert justice.
Na 1:12 **T** says the LORD, "Though they are A
Hag 1: 2 **T** says the LORD of hosts: A
1: 5 Now therefore **t** says the LORD of hosts: A
1: 7 **T** says the LORD of hosts: A
2: 6 For **t** says the LORD of hosts: A
2:11 **T** says the LORD of hosts: A
Zec 1: 3 say to them, **T** says the LORD of hosts: A
1: 4 "**T** says the LORD of hosts, A
1:14 **T** says the LORD of hosts; A
1:16 Therefore, **t** says the LORD, A
1:17 Proclaim further: **T** says the LORD of hosts: A
2: 8 For **t** said the LORD of hosts
3: 7 "**T** says the LORD of hosts: A
6:12 **T** says the LORD of hosts: A
7: 9 **T** says the LORD of hosts: A
7:14 **T** the land they left was desolate,
8: 2 **T** says the LORD of hosts: A
8: 3 **T** says the LORD: I will return to Zion, A
8: 4 **T** says the LORD of hosts: A
8: 6 **T** says the LORD of hosts: A
8: 7 **T** says the LORD of hosts: A
8: 9 **T** says the LORD of hosts: A
8:14 For **t** says the LORD of hosts: A
8:19 **T** says the LORD of hosts: A
8:20 **T** says the LORD of hosts: A
8:23 **T** says the LORD of hosts: A
11: 4 **T** said the LORD my God:
12: 1 **T** says the LORD, who stretched out the heavens A
Mal 3:10 and **t** put me to the test, says the LORD of hosts;
Mt 7:20 **T** you will know them by their fruits.
22:45 David **t** calls him Lord, how can he be his son?"
23:31 **T** you testify against yourselves
Mk 7: 3 **t** observing the tradition of the elders;
7:13 **t** making void the word of God
7:19 (**T** he declared all foods clean.)
Lk 1:72 **T** he has shown the mercy promised
12:58 **T**, when you go with your accuser before
18:11 The Pharisee, standing by himself, was praying **t**,
20:44 David **t** calls him Lord;
24:46 "**T** it is written, that the Messiah is to suffer and
Ac 13:49 **T** the word of the Lord spread throughout
15:17 my name has been called. **T** says the Lord, C
21:11 and said, "**T** says the Holy Spirit,
21:24 **T** all will know that there is nothing
Ro 1:13 to come to you (but **t** far have been prevented),
4:11 and who **t** have righteousness reckoned to them,
7: 2 **T** a married woman is bound by the law
11:14 and **t** save some of them.
14:18 The one who **t** serves Christ is acceptable to God
15:20 **T** I make it my ambition to proclaim
1Co 8:12 when you **t** sin against members of your family,
15:45 **T** it is written, "The first man, Adam,
Eph 2:15 in place of the two, **t** making peace,
2:16 **t** putting to death that hostility through it.
1Th 2:16 **T** they have constantly been filling up
1Ti 6:19 **t** storing up for themselves the treasure of
Heb 6:15 And **t** Abraham, having patiently endured,
9:12 **t** obtaining eternal redemption.
9:23 **T** it was necessary for the sketches of
Jas 2:23 **T** the scripture was fulfilled that says,
1Pe 3: 6 **T** Sarah obeyed Abraham and called him lord.
2Pe 1: 4 **T** he has given us, through these things,
Jdt 1: 6 **T**, many nations joined the forces of
1:14 **T** he took possession of his towns and came
1:15 **t** destroying him once and for all.
2: 5 "**T** says the Great King, the lord of
7:15 **T** you will pay them back with evil,
10: 4 **T** she made herself very beautiful,
AdE 1:20 **t** all women will give honor to their husbands,
6: 9 '**T** shall it be done to everyone whom
6:11 of the city, proclaiming, "**T** shall it be done
Wis 2:21 **T** they reasoned, but they were led astray,
5:12 the air, **t** divided, comes together at once,
9:18 And **t** the paths of those on earth were set right,
17:16 **t** was kept shut up in a prison not made of iron;
Sir 21: 4 **t** the house of the proud will be laid waste.
24:11 **T** in the beloved city he gave me a resting place,
Bar 2:21 **T** says the Lord: Bend your shoulders C
Sus 1:62 **T** innocent blood was spared that day.
1Mc 2:26 **T** he burned with zeal for the law,
3: 8 **t** he turned away wrath from Israel.
4:25 **T** Israel had a great deliverance that day.
4:51 **T** they finished all the work they had undertaken.
5:44 **T** Carnaim was conquered;
5:61 **T** the people suffered a great rout because,
6:16 **T** King Antiochus died there in
8:29 **T** on these terms the Romans make a treaty with
9:73 **T** the sword ceased from Israel.
10:65 **T** the king honored him and enrolled him
11:13 **T** he put two crowns on his head,
2Mc 4:38 The Lord **t** repaid him with
9: 8 **T** he who only a little while before had thought
11:22 The king's letter ran **t**: "King Antiochus to his
11:34 The Romans also sent them a letter, which read **t**:
15:15 and as he gave it he addressed him **t**:
1Es 2: 3 "**T** says Cyrus king of the Persians:
2Es 1:12 "But speak to them and say, **T** says the Lord: C
1:15 "**T** says the Lord Almighty: C
1:22 **T** says the Lord Almighty: C
1:28 "**T** says the Lord Almighty: C
1:33 "**T** says the Lord Almighty: C
2: 1 "**T** says the Lord: I brought this people out of C
2:10 **T** says the Lord to Ezra: C
3:22 **T** the disease became permanent;
7:38 **T** he will speak to them on the day of judgment—
15:21 repay into their bosom. **T** says the Lord God: C
4Mc 1:11 and **t** their native land was purified through them.
1:22 **T** desire precedes pleasure and delight follows it.
2: 5 **T** the law says, "You shall not covet
2: 8 **T**, as soon as one adopts a way of life
2:20 he would not have spoken **t**.
12: 6 When he had **t** appealed to him,
16: 2 **T** I have demonstrated not only

THWART (1) [THWARTED, THWARTS]
1Co 1:19 and the discernment of the discerning I will **t**."

THWARTED (2) [THWART]
Job 42: 2 and that no purpose of yours can be **t**.
Eze 19: 5 When she saw that she was **t**,

THWARTS (1) [THWART]
Pr 10: 3 but he **t** the craving of the wicked.

THYATIRA (4)
Ac 16:14 from the city of **T** and a dealer in purple cloth.
Rev 1:11 to **T**, to Sardis, to Philadelphia, and to Laodicea."
2:18 "And to the angel of the church in **T** write:
2:24 But to the rest of you in **T**,

THYINE (KJV) See SCENTED

TIARA (2)
Jdt 10: 3 She combed her hair, put on a **t**,
16: 8 with a **t** and put on a linen gown to beguile him.

TIBERIAS (3)
Jn 6: 1 the Sea of Galilee, also called the Sea of **T**.
6:23 from **T** came near the place where they had eaten
21: 1 to the disciples by the Sea of **T**;

TIBERIUS‡ (1)
Lk 3: 1 In the fifteenth year of the reign of Emperor **T**,

TIBHATH (1)
1Ch 18: 8 From **T** and from Cun, cities of Hadadezer,

TIBNI (3)
1Ki 16:21 half of the people followed **T** son of Ginath,
16:22 the people who followed **T** son of Ginath;
16:22 so **T** died, and Omri became king.

TIDAL (2)
Ge 14: 1 of Elam, and King **T** of Goiim,
14: 9 King **T** of Goiim, King Amraphel of Shinar,

TIDINGS (16)
2Sa 18:19 and carry **t** to the king that the LORD
18:20 Joab said to him, "You are not to carry **t** today; you may carry **t** another day,
18:22 seeing that you have no reward for the **t**?"
18:25 "If he is alone, there are **t** in his mouth."
18:26 The king said, "He also is bringing **t**."
18:27 "He is a good man, and comes with good **t**."
18:31 the Cushite said, "Good **t** for my lord the king!
1Ki 14: 6 For I am charged with heavy **t** for you.
Ps 68:11 great is the company of those who bore the **t**:
112: 7 They are not afraid of evil **t**;
Isa 40: 9 O Zion, herald of good **t**;
40: 9 O Jerusalem, herald of good **t**, lift it up,
41:27 and I give to Jerusalem a herald of good **t**.
Jer 49:14 I have heard **t** from the LORD,
Na 1:15 the mountains the feet of one who brings good **t**,

TIE (6) [TIED, TIES, TYING]
Ex 29: 9 with sashes and **t** headdresses on them;

Jos 2:18 and you do not **t** this crimson cord in the window
Job 39:10 Can you **t** it in the furrow with ropes,
Pr 6:21 **t** them around your neck.
Jer 51:63 When you finish reading this scroll, **t** a stone to it,
Mt 23: 4 They **t** up heavy burdens, hard to bear,

TIED (19) [TIE]

Ex 39:31 They **t** to it a blue cord,
Lev 8:13 and **t** headdresses on them,
Jos 2:21 Then she **t** the crimson cord in the window.
1Ki 20:32 So they **t** sackcloth around their waists,
2Ki 5:23 and **t** up two talents of silver in two bags,
7:10 nothing but the horses **t**, the donkeys **t**,
12:10 and **t** it up in bags.
Est 1: 6 and blue hangings **t** with cords of fine linen
Mt 21: 2 and immediately you will find a donkey **t**,
Mk 11: 2 you will find **t** there a colt
11: 4 They went away and found a colt **t** near a door,
Lk 19:30 and as you enter it you will find **t** there a colt
Jn 13: 4 and **t** a towel around himself.
13: 5 and to wipe them with the towel that was **t**
Ac 22:25 But when they had **t** him up with thongs,
27:40 At the same time they loosened the ropes that **t**
4Mc 6: 3 they had **t** his arms on each side they flogged him,
11:10 they **t** him to it on his knees,

TIES (8) [TIE]

Zec 11:14 annulling the family **t** between Judah and Israel.
1Mc 12:10 we have undertaken to send to renew our family **t**
12:17 from us concerning the renewal of our family **t**.
4Mc 1:29 and **t** up and waters and thoroughly irrigates,
9:23 or renounce our courageous family **t**.
10:15 I will not renounce our noble family **t**.
13:19 You are not ignorant of the affection of family **t**,
13:27 of family **t**, those who were left endured for

TIGHT‡ (3) [TIGHT-FISTED, TIGHTENED]

Jdg 16:13 of my head with the web and make it **t** with
16:14 and made them **t** with the pin.
4Mc 11:18 He was carefully stretched **t** upon it,

TIGHT-FISTED (1) [FIST, TIGHT]

Dt 15: 7 be hard-hearted or **t** toward your needy neighbor.

TIGHTENED (1) [TIGHT]

4Mc 9:19 while fanning the flames they **t** the wheel further.

TIGLATH-PILESER (3) [=PUL, =TILGATH-PILNESER]

2Ki 15:29 King **T** of Assyria came and captured Ijon,
16: 7 Ahaz sent messengers to King **T** of Assyria,
16:10 to Damascus to meet King **T** of Assyria,

TIGRIS (6)

Ge 2:14 The name of the third river is **T**,
Da 10: 4 on the bank of the great river (that is, the **T**),
Tob 6: 2 night overtook them they camped by the **T** river.
6: 3 down to wash his feet in the **T** river.
Jdt 1: 6 the **T**, and the Hydaspes, and, on the plain,
Sir 24:25 and like the **T** at the time of the first fruits.

TIKVAH (3)

2Ki 22:14 of Shallum son of **T**, son of Harhas, keeper of
Ezr 10:15 of Asahel and Jahzeiah son of **T** opposed this,
1Es 9:14 and Jahzeiah son of **T** undertook the matter

TIKVATH (KJV) See also TOKHATH

TILES (1)

Lk 5:19 through the **t** into the middle of the crowd in front

TILGATH-PILNESER (3) [=TIGLATH-PILESER]

1Ch 5: 6 whom King **T** of Assyria carried away into exile;
5:26 the spirit of King **T** of Assyria,
2Ch 28:20 So King **T** of Assyria came against him,

TILL (11) [TILLED, TILLER, TILLERS, TILLING, TILLS]

Ge 2: 5 and there was no one to **t** the ground;
2:15 the man and put him in the garden of Eden to **t** it
3:23 to **t** the ground from which he was taken.
4:12 When you **t** the ground, it will no longer yield
2Sa 9:10 and your sons and your servants shall **t** the land
Pr 12:11 Those who **t** their land will have plenty of food,
Isa 30:24 and donkeys that **t** the ground will eat silage,
61: 5 foreigners shall **t** your land and dress your vines;
Jer 27:11 says the LORD, to **t** it and live there.
1Es 4: 6 not serve in the army or make war but **t** the soil;
2Es 15:13 Let the farmers that **t** the ground mourn,

TILLAGE (KJV) See FIELD, FROM OUR SOIL, WORK

TILLED (3) [TILL]

Eze 36: 9 I will turn to you, and you shall be **t** and sown;
36:34 The land that was desolate shall be **t**,
1Mc 14: 8 They **t** their land in peace;

TILLER (2) [TILL]

Ge 4: 2 and Cain a **t** of the ground.
Zec 13: 5 "I am no prophet, I am a **t** of the soil;

TILLERS (2) [TILL]

2Ki 25:12 of the land to be vinedressers and **t** of the soil.
Jer 52:16 of the land to be vinedressers and **t** of the soil.

TILLING (1) [TILL]

1Ch 27:26 **t** the soil, was Ezri son of Chelub.

TILLS (1) [TILL]

Pr 28:19 Anyone who **t** the land will have plenty of bread,

TILON (1)

1Ch 4:20 Amnon, Rinnah, Ben-hanan, and **T**.

TILT (1) [TILTED]

Job 38:37 Or who can **t** the waterskins of the heavens,

TILTED (1) [TILT]

Jer 1:13 "I see a boiling pot, **t** away from the north."

TIMAEUS (1)

Mk 10:46 Bartimaeus son of **T**, a blind beggar,

TIMBER (25) [TIMBERS]

Lev 14:45 its stones and **t** and all the plaster of the house,
1Ki 5: 6 among us who knows how to cut **t** like
5: 8 in the matter of cedar and cypress **t**.
5:10 So Hiram supplied Solomon's every need for **t**
5:18 the stonecutting and prepared the **t** and the stone
9:11 with cedar and cypress **t** and gold,
15:22 they carried away the stones of Ramah and its **t**,
2Ki 12:12 to buy **t** and quarried stone for making repairs on
22: 6 to buy **t** and quarried stone to repair the house.
1Ch 22:14 **t** and stone too I have provided.
2Ch 2: 8 cypress, and algum **t** from Lebanon,
2: 8 that your servants are skilled in cutting Lebanon **t**.
2: 9 to prepare **t** for me in abundance,
2:10 those who cut the **t**, twenty thousand cors
2:16 We will cut whatever **t** you need from Lebanon,
16: 6 they carried away the stones of Ramah and its **t**,
34:11 and **t** for binders, and beams for the buildings that
Ezr 5: 8 and **t** is laid in the walls;
6: 4 of hewn stones and one course of **t**;
Ne 2: 8 directing him to give me **t** to make beams for
Eze 26:12 Your stones and **t** and soil they shall cast into
Zec 5: 4 in that house and consume it, both **t** and stones."
1Es 4:48 to bring cedar **t** from Lebanon to Jerusalem,
6: 9 of hewn stone, with costly **t** laid in the walls.
6:25 of hewn stone and one course of new native **t**;

TIMBERS (2) [TIMBER]

1Ki 6:10 and it was joined to the house with **t** of cedar.
LtJ 6:55 but the gods will be burned up like **t**.

TIMBREL (KJV) See TAMBOURINE

TIMBRELS (3)

Jdg 11:34 to meet him with **t** and with dancing.
Isa 24: 8 The mirth of the **t** is stilled,
30:32 upon him will be to the sound of **t** and lyres;

TIME‡ (880) [DAYTIME, ILL-TIMED, TIMES]

A. LONG TIME (29)
B. FOR ALL TIME (20)
C. APPOINTED TIME (19)
D. TIME OF TROUBLE (12)
E. TIME OF ... DISTRESS (11)
F. TIME TO COME (11)
G. TIME IS [SURELY] COMING (9)
H. TIME APPOINTED (8)

Ge 3: 8 the LORD God walking in the garden at the **t** of
4: 3 of **t** Cain brought to the LORD an offering of
4:26 At that **t** people began to invoke the name of
12: 6 At that **t** the Canaanites were in the land.
13: 7 At that **t** the Canaanites and the Perizzites lived in
18:14 At the set **t** I will return to you, in due season,
21: 2 at the **t** of which God had spoken to him.
21:22 At that **t** Abimelech, with Phicol the commander
22:15 of the LORD called to Abraham a second **t**
24:11 the **t** when women go out to draw water.
25:24 When her **t** to give birth was at hand,
26: 8 When Isaac had been there a long **t**, A
29: 7 it is not **t** for the animals to be gathered together.
29:21 that I may go in to her, for my **t** is completed."
29:34 "Now this **t** my husband will be joined to me,
29:35 and said, "This **t** I will praise the LORD";
38: 1 at that **t** that Judah went down from his brothers
38:12 In course of **t** the wife of Judah, Shua's daughter,
38:12 when Judah's **t** of mourning was over,
38:27 When the **t** of her delivery came,
39: 5 From the **t** that he made him overseer in his house
39: 7 after a **t** his master's wife cast her eyes on Joseph
40: 1 Some **t** after this, the cupbearer of the king
40: 4 and they continued for some **t** in custody.
41: 5 Then he fell asleep and dreamed a second **t**;
41:22 a second **t** and I saw in my dream seven ears
43:18 replaced in our sacks the first **t**,
Ge 43:20 my lord, we came down the first **t** to buy food;
47:29 When the **t** of Israel's death drew near,
50: 3 for that is the **t** required for embalming.
50:10 a **t** of mourning for his father seven days.
Ex 2:23 After a long **t** the king of Egypt died. A
8:32 But Pharaoh hardened his heart this **t** also,
9: 5 The LORD set a **t**, saying,
9:14 For this **t** I will send all my plagues
9:18 Tomorrow at this **t** I will cause the heaviest hail
9:27 and said to them, "This **t** I have sinned;
12:40 The **t** that the Israelites had lived
13:10 You shall keep this ordinance at its proper **t**
21:19 except to pay for the loss of **t**,
23:15 for seven days at the appointed **t** in the month C
34:18 at the **t** appointed in the month of Abib; H
34:21 in plowing **t** and in harvest **t** you shall rest.
Lev 12: 2 at the **t** of her menstruation, she shall be unclean.
12: 4 Her **t** of blood purification shall
12: 5 her **t** of blood purification shall be sixty-six days.
13:58 shall then be washed a second **t**,
14: 2 for the leprous person at the **t** of his cleansing:
15:25 not at the **t** of her impurity,
15:25 she has a discharge beyond the **t** of her impurity,
16: 2 not to come just at any **t** into the sanctuary inside
16:17 the **t** he enters to make atonement in the sanctuary
23: 4 which you shall celebrate at the **t** appointed H
25:34 for that is their possession for all **t**. B
25:50 the **t** they were with the owner shall be rated as the
t of a hired laborer.
Nu 3: 1 This is the lineage of Aaron and Moses at the **t**
6: 5 the **t** is completed for which they separate
6:12 The former **t** shall be void,
6:13 the **t** of their consecration has been completed:
7:10 of the altar at the **t** when it was anointed;
7:84 at the **t** when it was anointed,
9: 2 the Israelites keep the passover at its appointed **t**. C
9: 3 at twilight, you shall keep it at its appointed **t**; C
9: 7 the LORD's offering at its appointed **t** among C
9:13 the LORD's offering at its appointed **t**; C
9:22 or a month, or a longer **t**,
10:13 They set out for the first **t** at the command of
14:15 Now if you kill this people all at one **t**,
20:15 and we lived in Egypt a long **t**; A
22: 4 Balak son of Zippor was king of Moab at that **t**.
28: 2 to offer to me at its appointed **t**. C
30: 5 if her father expresses disapproval to her at the **t**
30: 7 of it and says nothing to her at the **t** that he hears,
30: 8 But if, at the **t** that her husband hears of it,
30:12 But if her husband nullifies them at the **t**
30:14 because he said nothing to her at the **t**
30:15 But if he nullifies them some **t** after he has heard
35:26 at any **t** go outside the bounds of the original city
Dt 1: 9 At that **t** I said to you,
1:16 I charged your judges at that **t**:
1:18 at that **t** with all the things that you should do.
2:14 of **t** we had traveled from Kadesh-barnea
2:34 At that **t** we captured all his towns,
3: 4 At that **t** we captured all his towns;
3: 8 that **t** we took from the two kings of the Amorites
3:12 for the land that we took possession of at that **t**,
3:18 At that **t**, I charged you as follows:
3:21 And I charged Joshua as well at that **t**, saying:
3:23 At that **t**, too, I entreated the LORD, saying:
4:14 that **t** to teach you statutes and ordinances for you
4:30 these things have happened to you in **t** to come, F
4:40 that the LORD your God is giving you for all **t**. B
5: 5 that **t** I was standing between the LORD and you
6:20 When your children ask you in **t** to come, F
9:19 But the LORD listened to me that **t** also.
9:20 also on behalf of Aaron at that same **t**.
10: 1 At that **t** the LORD said to me,
10: 8 At that **t** the LORD set apart the tribe of Levi
10:10 as I had done the first **t**.
16: 6 the **t** of day when you departed from Egypt.
16: 9 the seven weeks from the **t** the sickle is first put to
18: 5 him and his sons for all **t**. B
20:19 If you besiege a town for a long **t**, A
26: 3 to the priest who is in office at that **t**,
31:14 The LORD said to Moses, "Your **t** to die is near;
31:29 In **t** to come trouble will befall you, F
32:35 for the **t** when their foot shall slip;
Jos 2: 5 And when it was **t** to close the gate at dark,
3:15 the Jordan overflows all its banks throughout the **t**
4: 6 When your children ask in **t** to come, F
4:21 your children ask their parents in **t** to come, F
5: 2 At that **t** the LORD said to Joshua,
5: 2 and circumcise the Israelites a second **t**."
6:16 And at the seventh **t**, when the priests had blown
10:42 Joshua took all these kings and their land at one **t**,
11: 6 for tomorrow at this **t** I will hand over all of them,
11:10 Joshua turned back at that **t**, and took Hazor,
11:10 that **t** Hazor was the head of all those kingdoms.
11:18 Joshua made war a long **t** with all those kings. A
11:21 At that **t** Joshua came and wiped out the Anakim
14:10 the **t** that the LORD spoke this word to Moses,
20: 6 the death of the one who is high priest at the **t**:
22:24 that in **t** to come your children might say F
22:27 to our children in **t** to come, F
22:28 be said to us or to our descendants in **t** to come, F
23: 1 A long **t** afterward, when the LORD had given A
24: 7 Afterwards you lived in the wilderness a long **t**. A
Jdg 3:29 At that **t** they killed about ten thousand of
4: 4 At that **t** Deborah, a prophetess,
6:39 let me speak one more **t**;
10:14 let them deliver you in the **t** of your distress." E
11: 4 After a **t** the Ammonites made war against Israel.
11:26 why did you not recover them within that **t**?

Jdg 12: 6 of the Ephraimites fell at that **t**.
14: 4 At that **t** the Philistines had dominion over Israel.
15: 1 After a while, at the **t** of the wheat harvest,
15: 3 Samson said to them, "This **t**,
16:18 "This **t** come up, for he has told his whole secret
18:30 the Danites until the **t** the land went into captivity.
21:14 Benjamin returned at that **t**;
21:24 So the Israelites departed from there at that **t**
1Sa 1:16 of my great anxiety and vexation all this **t**."
1:20 In due **t** Hannah conceived and bore a son.
1:22 I will offer him as a nazirite for all **t**." B
2:31 a **t** is coming when I will cut off your strength G
3: 2 that **t** Eli, whose eyesight had begun to grow dim
3: 8 The LORD called Samuel again, a third **t**.
7: 2 a long **t** passed, some twenty years, A
9:16 about this **t** I will send to you a man from the land
9:24 Eat; for it is set before you at the appointed **t**, C
11: 9 'Tomorrow, by the **t** the sun is hot,
13: 8 waited seven days, the **t** appointed by Samuel; H
14:18 at that **t** the ark of God went with the Israelites.
18:19 But at the **t** when Saul's daughter Merab should
18:21 Therefore Saul said to David a second **t**,
18:26 be the king's son-in-law. Before the **t** had expired,
18:29 So Saul was David's enemy from that **t** forward.
19:21 Saul sent messengers again the third **t**,
20:12 about this **t** tomorrow, or on the third day,
22: 4 and they stayed with him all the **t** that David was
22:15 the first **t** that I have inquired of God for him?
25: 7 all the **t** they were in Carmel.
27: 7 The length of **t** that David lived in the country of
27:11 the **t** he lived in the country of the Philistines.
2Sa 2:11 The **t** that David was king in Hebron over
3:17 "For some **t** past you have been seeking David
5: 2 For some **t**, while Saul was king over us,
7:11 from the **t** that I appointed judges
8: 1 Some **t** afterward, David attacked the Philistines
10: 1 Some **t** afterward, the king of the Ammonites died,
11: 1 the **t** when kings go out to battle,
13: 1 Some **t** passed. David's son Absalom had a
14:29 He sent a second **t**, but Joab would not come.
15:34 as I have been your father's servant in **t** past,
17: 7 "This **t** the counsel that Ahithophel has given is
18:14 Joab said, "I will not waste **t** like this with you."
20: 5 beyond the set **t** that had been appointed him.
23: 8 against eight hundred whom he killed at one **t**.
24:15 Israel from that morning until the appointed **t**; C
1Ki 1: 6 His father had never at any **t** displeased him
2: 1 When David's **t** to die drew near,
2: 5 in **t** of peace for blood that had been shed in war,
2:11 **t** that David reigned over Israel was forty years;
2:26 But I will not at this **t** put you to death,
8:65 So Solomon held the festival at that **t**,
9: 2 the LORD appeared to Solomon a second **t**,
9: 3 my eyes and my heart will be there for all **t**. B
11:17 He was a young boy at that **t**.
11:29 that **t**, when Jeroboam was leaving Jerusalem,
11:42 The **t** that Solomon reigned in Jerusalem
14: 1 At that **t** Abijah son of Jeroboam fell sick.
14:20 **t** that Jeroboam reigned was twenty-two years;
18:29 on until the **t** of the offering of the oblation,
18:34 said, "Do it a second **t**"; and they did it a second **t**.
18:34 he said, "Do it a third **t**"; and they did it a third **t**,
18:36 At the **t** of the offering of the oblation,
18:44 At the seventh **t** he said, "Look,
19: 2 like the life of one of them by this **t** tomorrow."
19: 7 The angel of the LORD came a second **t**,
20: 6 to you tomorrow about this **t**,
2Ki 3: 6 So King Jehoram marched out of Samaria at that **t**
3:20 The next day, about the **t** of the morning offering,
4:16 He said, "At this season, in due **t**,
4:17 in due **t**, as Elisha had declared to her.
5:26 Is this a **t** to accept money and to accept clothing,
6:24 Some **t** later King Ben-hadad
7: 1 the LORD, Tomorrow about this **t** a measure
7:18 about this **t** tomorrow in the gate of Samaria,"
8:22 Libnah also revolted at the same **t**.
10: 6 and come to me at Jezreel tomorrow at this **t**."
10:36 The **t** that Jehu reigned over Israel
12:17 At that **t** King Hazael of Aram went up,
15:16 At that **t** Menahem sacked Tiphsah,
16: 6 At that **t** the king of Edom recovered Elath
18:16 that **t** Hezekiah stripped the gold from the doors
20:12 At that **t** King Merodach-baladan son of Baladan
24:10 At that **t** the servants of King Nebuchadnezzar
1Ch 11: 2 For some **t** now, even while Saul was king,
11:11 against three hundred whom he killed at one **t**.
15:13 Because you did not carry it the first **t**,
17:10 from the **t** that I appointed judges
18: 1 Some **t** afterward, David attacked the Philistines
19: 1 Some **t** afterward, King Nahash of the Ammonites
20: 1 the **t** when kings go out to battle,
21:28 At that **t**, when David saw that
21:29 of burnt offering were at that **t** in the high place
29:22 They made David's son Solomon king a second **t**;
2Ch 7: 8 At that **t** Solomon held the festival for seven days,
7:16 my eyes and my heart will be there for all **t**. B
13:18 Thus the Israelites were subdued at that **t**,
15: 3 For a long **t** Israel was without the true God, A
16: 7 that **t** the seer Hanani came to King Asa of Judah,
16:10 on some of the people at the same **t**.
21:10 At that **t** Libnah also revolted against his rule,
21:19 In course of **t**, at the end of two years,
24: 4 Some **t** afterward Joash decided to restore
25:27 From the **t** that Amaziah turned away from
28:16 At that **t** King Ahaz sent to the king of Assyria
28:22 the **t** of his distress he became yet more faithless E
30: 3 (for they could not keep it at its proper **t** because
30:26 for since the **t** of Solomon son of King David
32:23 in the sight of all nations from that **t** onward.
35:17 the passover at that **t**, and the festival
Ezr 4:24 At that **t** the work on the house of God
5: 3 the same **t** Tattenai the governor of the province
5:16 that **t** until now it has been under construction,
8:35 At that **t** those who had come from captivity,
10:13 the people are many, and it is a **t** of heavy rain;
Ne 1:11 At the **t**, I was cupbearer to the king.
4:22 I also said to the people at that **t**,
5:14 the **t** that I was appointed to be their governor in
6: 1 up to that **t** I had not set up the doors in the gates),
6: 5 for the fifth **t** sent his servant to me with
9:27 in the **t** of their suffering they cried out to you
9:32 since the **t** of the kings of Assyria until today.
13: 6 After some **t** I asked leave of the king
13:15 and I warned them at that **t** against selling food.
13:21 From that **t** on they did not come on the sabbath.
Est 4:14 For if you keep silence at such a **t** as this,
4:14 to royal dignity for just such a **t** as this."
8: 9 The king's secretaries were summoned at that **t**,
9:27 as it was written and at the **t** appointed. H
Job 6:17 In **t** of heat they disappear;
14:13 that you would appoint me a set **t**,
15:32 It will be paid in full before their **t**,
22:16 They were snatched away before their **t**;
34:23 not appointed a **t** for anyone to go before God
38:23 which I have reserved for the **t** of trouble, D
39: 2 and do you know the **t** when they give birth,
Ps 32: 6 at a **t** of distress, the rush of mighty waters shall E
37:39 he is their refuge in the **t** of trouble. D
69:13 At an acceptable **t**, O God,
71: 9 Do not cast me off in the **t** of old age;
75: 2 At the set **t** that I appoint I will judge with equity.
77: 8 Are his promises at an end for all **t**? B
89:47 Remember how short my **t** is—
102:13 for it is **t** to favor it; the appointed time has come.
102:13 the appointed **t** has come. C
104:19 the sun knows its **t** for setting.
113: 2 Blessed be the name of the LORD from this **t** on
115:18 But we will bless the LORD from this **t** on
119:126 It is **t** for the LORD to act,
121: 8 in from this **t** on and forevermore.
125: 2 from this **t** on and forevermore.
131: 3 in the LORD from this **t** on and forevermore.
Pr 7: 9 in the evening, at the **t** of night and darkness.
25:13 of snow in the **t** of harvest are faithful messengers
25:19 trust in a faithless person in **t** of trouble. D
31:25 and she laughs at the **t** to come. F
Ecc 3: 1 and a **t** for every matter under heaven:
3: 2 a **t** to be born, and a **t** to die;
3: 2 a **t** to plant, and a **t** to pluck up what is planted;
3: 3 a **t** to kill, and a **t** to heal;
3: 3 a **t** to break down, and a **t** to build up;
3: 4 a **t** to weep, and a **t** to laugh;
3: 4 a **t** to mourn, and a **t** to dance;
3: 5 a **t** to throw away stones, and a **t** to gather stones
3: 5 a **t** to embrace, and a **t** to refrain from embracing;
3: 6 a **t** to seek, and a **t** to lose;
3: 6 a **t** to keep, and a **t** to throw away;
3: 7 a **t** to tear, and a **t** to sew;
3: 7 a **t** to keep silence, and a **t** to speak;
3: 8 a **t** to love, and a **t** to hate;
3: 8 a **t** for war, and a **t** for peace.
3:11 He has made everything suitable for its **t**;
3:17 for he has appointed a **t** for every matter,
7:17 why should you die before your **t**?
8: 5 and the wise mind will know the **t** and way.
8: 6 For every matter has its **t** and way,
9:11 but **t** and chance happen to them all.
9:12 For no one can anticipate the **t** of disaster.
9:12 so mortals are snared at a **t** of calamity,
10:17 and your princes feast at the proper **t**—
SS 2:12 the **t** of singing has come,
Isa 7:15 the **t** he knows how to refuse the evil and choose
9: 1 In the former **t** he brought into contempt the land
9: 1 but in the latter **t** he will make glorious the way of
9: 7 and with righteousness from this **t** onward
11:11 yet a second **t** to recover the remnant that is left
13:22 its **t** is close at hand, and its days will not be
17:14 At evening **t**, lo, terror!
18: 7 that **t** gifts will be brought to the LORD of hosts
20: 2 at that **t** the LORD had spoken to Isaiah son
26:17 near her **t**, so were we because of you, O LORD;
30: 8 it may be for the **t** to come as a witness forever. F
33: 2 our salvation in the **t** of trouble. D
39: 1 At that **t** King Merodach-baladan son of Baladan
42:14 For a long **t** I have held my peace, A
42:23 who will attend and listen for the **t** to come? F
48: 6 From this **t** forward I make you hear new things,
48:16 from the **t** it came to be I have been there.
49: 8 In a **t** of favor I have answered you,
49:20 in the **t** of your bereavement will yet say
60:22 in its **t** I will accomplish it quickly.
Jer 1:13 The word of the LORD came to me a second **t**,
2:27 But in the **t** of their trouble they say,
2:28 if they can save you, in your **t** of trouble; D
3:17 At that **t** Jerusalem shall be called the throne of
4:11 At that **t** it will be said to this people and
6:15 at the **t** that I punish them,
8: 1 At that **t**, says the LORD,
8: 7 swallow, and crane observe the **t** of their coming;
8:12 at the **t** when I punish them,
8:15 for a **t** of healing, but there is terror instead.
10:15 at the **t** of their punishment they shall perish.
10:18 to sling out the inhabitants of the land at this **t**,
11:12 they will never save them in the **t** of their trouble.
11:14 for I will not listen when they call to me in the **t**
13: 3 the word of the LORD came to me a second **t**,
14: 8 O hope of Israel, its savior in **t** of trouble, D
14:19 for a **t** of healing, but there is terror instead.
15:11 on you in a **t** of trouble and in a time of distress. D
15:11 on you in a time of trouble and in a **t** of distress. E
16:21 this **t** I am going to teach them my power
27: 7 until the **t** of his own land comes;
29:28 saying, "It will be a long **t**; A
30: 7 it is a **t** of distress for Jacob; E
31: 1 At that **t**, says the LORD,
32: 2 At that **t** the army of the king
32:14 in order that they may last for a long **t**. A
32:39 that they may fear me for all **t**, B
33: 1 word of the LORD came to Jeremiah a second **t**,
33:15 that **t** I will cause a righteous Branch to spring up
33:18 and to make sacrifices for all **t**. B
33:20 and night would not come at their appointed **t**, C
35:19 lack a descendant to stand before me for all **t**. B
39:10 and gave them vineyards and fields at the same **t**.
44:18 the **t** we stopped making offerings to the queen
46:21 the **t** of their punishment.
48:12 Therefore, the **t** is surely coming, G
49: 2 Therefore, the **t** is surely coming, G
49: 8 the **t** when I punish him.
50: 4 In those days and in that **t**, says the LORD,
50:16 and the wielder of the sickle in **t** of harvest;
50:20 In those days and at that **t**, says the LORD,
50:27 their day has come, the **t** of their punishment!
50:31 your day has come, the **t** when I will punish you.
51: 6 for this is the **t** of the LORD's vengeance;
51:18 at the **t** of their punishment they shall perish.
51:33 Daughter Babylon is like a threshing floor at the **t**
51:33 a little while and the **t** of her harvest will come.
51:52 Therefore the **t** is surely coming, says the LORD, G
La 1:15 a **t** against me to crush my young men;
Eze 4: 6 you shall lie down a second **t**,
7: 7 The **t** has come, the day is near—
7:12 The **t** has come, the day draws near;
11: 3 'The **t** is not near to build houses;
16:47 a very little **t** you were more corrupt than they
21:25 the **t** of final punishment,
21:29 the **t** of final punishment.
22: 3 its **t** has come; making its idols, defiling itself.
22: 4 the appointed **t** of your years has come. C
24:14 the **t** is coming, I will act. G
30: 3 a **t** of doom for the nations.
33:22 by the **t** the fugitive came to me in the morning;
35: 5 of the sword at the **t** of their calamity, at the time
35: 5 at the **t** of their final punishment;
46:14 this is the ordinance for all **t**. B
48:35 And the name of the city from that **t** on shall be,
Da 1: 5 so that at the end of that **t** they could be stationed
1:18 the **t** that the king had set for them to be brought
2: 7 They answered a second **t**,
2: 8 to gain **t**, because you see I have firmly decreed:
2:16 that the king give him **t** and he would tell the king
3: 8 at this **t** certain Chaldeans came forward
4:26 from the **t** that you learn that Heaven is sovereign.
4:36 At that **t** my reason returned to me;
7:12 their lives were prolonged for a season and a **t**.
7:22 the holy ones of the Most High, and the **t** arrived
7:25 and they shall be given into his power for a **t**,
7:25 into his power for a time, two times, and half a **t**.
8:17 O mortal, that the vision is for the **t** of the end."
8:19 for it refers to the appointed **t** of the end. C
9:21 in swift flight at the **t** of the evening sacrifice.
9:25 from the **t** that the word went out to restore
9:25 rebuild Jerusalem until the **t** of a anointed prince,
9:25 with streets and moat, but in a troubled **t**.
10: 2 At that **t** I, Daniel, had been mourning
11:24 against strongholds, but only for a **t**.
11:27 for there remains an end at the **t** appointed. H
11:29 "At the **t** appointed he shall return and come H
11:29 but this **t** it shall not be as it was before.
11:35 purified, and cleansed, until the **t** of the end,
11:35 for there is still an interval until the **t** appointed. H
11:40 "At the **t** of the end the king of the south
12: 1 "At that **t** Michael, the great prince,
12: 1 There shall be a **t** of anguish,
12: 1 But at that **t** your people shall be delivered,
12: 4 the words secret and the book sealed until the **t** of
12: 7 the one who lives forever that it would be for a **t**,
12: 7 for a time, two times, and half a **t**, and that when
12: 9 to remain secret and sealed until the **t** of the end.
12:11 the **t** that the regular burnt offering is taken away
Hos 2: 9 Therefore I will take back my grain in its **t**,
2:15 at the **t** when she came out of the land of Egypt.
10:12 for it is **t** to seek the LORD,
13:13 for at the proper **t** he does not present himself at
Joel 3: 1 For then, in those days and at that **t**,
Am 4: 2 The **t** is surely coming upon you, G
5:13 Therefore the prudent will keep silent in such a **t**;
for it is an evil **t**.
7: 1 at the **t** the latter growth began to sprout (it was
8:11 The **t** is surely coming, says the Lord GOD, G
9:13 The **t** is surely coming, says the LORD, G
Jnh 3: 1 word of the LORD came to Jonah a second **t**,
Mic 2: 3 for it will be an evil **t**.
3: 4 he will hide his face from them at that **t**,
5: 3 the **t** when she who is in labor has brought forth;
Hab 2: 3 For there is still a vision for the appointed **t**; C
3: 2 In our own **t** revive it; in our own **t** make it known;
Zep 1:12 At that **t** I will search Jerusalem with lamps,
3: 9 At that **t** I will change the speech of the peoples to
3:19 I will deal with all your oppressors at that **t**.
3:20 that **t** I will bring you home, at the **t** when I gather

Hag 1: 2 These people say the **t** has not yet come to rebuild
1: 4 Is it a **t** for you yourselves to live
2:20 a second **t** to Haggai on the twenty-fourth day of
Zec 4:12 And a second **t** I said to him,
14: 7 for at evening **t** there shall be light.
Mt 1:11 at the **t** of the deportation to Babylon.
2: 1 In the **t** of King Herod,
2: 7 from them the exact **t** when the star had appeared.
2:16 to the **t** that he had learned from the wise men.
4:17 From that **t** Jesus began to proclaim, "Repent,
6:13 And do not bring us to the **t** of trial,
8:29 Have you come here to torment us before the **t**?"
10:19 what you are to say will be given to you at that **t**;
11:25 At that **t** Jesus said, "I thank you, Father,
12: 1 At that **t** Jesus went through the grainfields on
13:30 and at harvest **t** I will tell the reapers,
14: 1 that **t** Herod the ruler heard reports about Jesus;
14:24 but by this **t** the boat,
16:21 From that **t** on, Jesus began to show his disciples
18: 1 At that **t** the disciples came to Jesus and asked,
21:34 When the harvest **t** had come,
21:41 the produce at the harvest **t**."
24:21 For at that **t** there will be great suffering,
24:45 their allowance of food at the proper **t**?
25:19 After a long **t** the master of those slaves came A
26:18 and say to him, 'The Teacher says, My **t** is near;
26:41 and pray that you may not come into the **t** of trial;
26:42 Again he went away for the second **t** and prayed,
26:44 he went away and prayed for the third **t**,
27:16 At that **t** they had a notorious prisoner,
Mk 1:15 "The **t** is fulfilled, and the kingdom
13:11 but say whatever is given you at that **t**,
13:21 And if anyone says to you at that **t**, 'Look!
13:33 for you do not know when the **t** will come.
14:38 and pray that you may not come into the **t** of trial;
14:41 He came a third **t** and said to them,
14:72 At that moment the cock crowed for the second **t**.
15:44 he asked him whether he had been dead for some **t**.
Lk 1:10 Now at the **t** of the incense offering,
1:20 which will be fulfilled in their **t**,
1:23 his **t** of service was ended, he went to his home.
1:57 Now the **t** came for Elizabeth to give birth,
2: 6 the **t** came for her to deliver her child.
2:21 it was **t** to circumcise the child;
2:22 When the **t** came for their purification according
4:13 he departed from him until an opportune **t**.
4:25 in the **t** of Elijah, when the heaven was shut
4:27 There were also many lepers in Israel in the **t** of
7:45 but from the **t** I came in she has
8:13 for a while and in a **t** of testing fall away.
8:27 For a long **t** he had worn no clothes, A
11: 4 And do not bring us to the **t** of trial."
12:42 of food at the proper **t**?
12:56 not know how to interpret the present **t**?
13: 1 that very **t** there were some present who told him
13:35 not see me until the **t** comes when you say,
14:17 At the **t** for the dinner he sent his slave to say
19:44 not recognize the **t** of your visitation from God."
20: 9 and went to another country for a long **t**. A
21: 8 and, 'The **t** is near!'
22:40 "Pray that you may not come into the **t** of trial."
22:46 Get up and pray that you may not come into the **t**
23: 7 who was himself in Jerusalem at that **t**.
23: 8 for he had been wanting to see him for a long **t**, A
23:22 A third **t** he said to them, "Why,
Jn 3: 4 a second **t** into the mother's womb and be born?"
3:22 and he spent some **t** there with them and baptized.
5: 6 and knew that he had been there a long **t**, A
7: 6 "My **t** has not yet come, but your **t** is always here.
7: 8 for my **t** has not yet fully come."
9:24 second **t** they called the man who had been blind,
10:22 At that **t** the festival of the Dedication took place
14: 9 "Have I been with you all this **t**, Philip,
21:14 now the third **t** that Jesus appeared to the disciples
21:16 A second **t** he said to him, "Simon son of John,
21:17 He said to him the third **t**, "Simon son of John,
21:17 Peter felt hurt because he said to him the third **t**,
Ac 1: 6 is this the **t** when you will restore the kingdom
1:21 during all the **t** that the Lord Jesus went in and out
2:46 as they spent much **t** together in the temple,
3:21 in heaven until the **t** of universal restoration
5:34 the men to be put outside for a short **t**.
5:36 For some **t** ago Theudas rose up,
5:37 the **t** of the census and got people to follow him;
7:17 the **t** drew near for the fulfillment of the promise
7:20 At this **t** Moses was born,
7:41 At that **t** they made a calf,
7:45 And it was there until the **t** of David,
8:11 for a long **t** he had amazed them with his magic. A
9:23 After some **t** had passed, the Jews plotted
9:37 At that **t** she became ill and died.
9:43 Meanwhile he stayed in Joppa for some **t** with
10:15 The voice said to him again, a second **t**,
11: 9 But a second **t** the voice answered from heaven,
11:27 At that **t** prophets came down from Jerusalem
12: 1 About that **t** King Herod laid violent hands
13:20 After that he gave them judges until the **t** of
14: 3 So they remained for a long **t**, A
14:28 they stayed there with the disciples for some **t**.
15:33 After they had been there for some **t**,
17:21 and the foreigners living there would spend their **t**
18:18 After staying there for a considerable **t**,
18:23 After spending some **t** there he departed and went
19:22 while he himself stayed for some **t** longer in Asia.
19:23 that **t** no little disturbance broke out concerning
20:16 so that he might not have to spend **t** in Asia;
20:18 the entire **t** from the first day that I set foot
Ac 24:26 At the same **t** he hoped that money would
25:17 So when they met here, I lost no **t**,
26: 5 They have known for a long **t**, A
27: 9 Since much **t** had been lost and sailing was
27:21 Since they had been without food for a long **t**, A
27:40 At the same **t** they loosened the ropes that tied
28: 6 but after they had waited a long **t** and saw A
Ro 3:26 at the present **t** that he himself is righteous and
5: 6 at the right **t** Christ died for the ungodly.
8:18 I consider that the sufferings of this present **t** are
9: 9 "About this **t** I will return and Sarah shall have
11: 5 So too at the present **t** there is a remnant,
13:11 Besides this, you know what **t** it is,
1Co 4: 5 do not pronounce judgment before the **t**,
7: 5 by agreement for a set **t**,
7:18 at the **t** of his call already circumcised?
7:18 Was anyone at the **t** of his call uncircumcised?
7:29 the appointed **t** has grown short; C
9: 7 Who at any **t** pays the expenses
11:21 For when the **t** comes to eat,
15: 6 and sisters at one **t**, most of whom are still alive,
16: 7 for I hope to spend some **t** with you,
2Co 1:17 yes" and "No, no" at the same **t**?
6: 2 "At an acceptable **t** I have listened to you,
6: 2 See, now is the acceptable **t**;
12:14 Here I am, ready to come to you this third **t**.
13: 1 This is the third **t** I am coming to you.
Gal 4: 4 But when the fullness of **t** had come,
4:29 as at that **t** the child who was born according to
6: 9 for we will reap at harvest **t**, if we do not give up.
Eph 1:10 as a plan for the fullness of **t**,
2:11 remember that at one **t** you Gentiles by birth,
2:12 remember that you were at that **t** without Christ,
5:16 making the most of the **t**,
Php 1: 3 I thank my God every **t** I remember you,
Col 4: 3 the same **t** pray for us as well that God will open
4: 5 making the most of the **t**.
1Th 2:17 As for us, brothers and sisters, when, for a short **t**,
2Th 2: 6 so that he may be revealed when his **t** comes.
1Ti 2: 6 a ransom for all—this was attested at the right **t**.
6:15 which he will bring about at the right **t**—
2Ti 4: 2 be persistent whether the **t** is favorable
4: 3 For the **t** is coming when people will not put up G
4: 6 and the **t** of my departure has come.
Tit 1: 3 in due **t** he revealed his word through
Heb 4:16 and find grace to help in **t** of need.
5:12 For though by this **t** you ought to be teachers,
7:25 for all **t** to save those who approach God B
9: 9 This is a symbol of the present **t**,
9:10 for the body imposed until the **t** comes
9:28 will appear a second **t**, not to deal with sin,
10:12 Christ had offered for all **t** a single sacrifice B
10:14 for all **t** those who are sanctified. B
11: 9 for a **t** in the land he had been promised,
11:32 For **t** would fail me to tell of Gideon, Barak,
12:10 for a short **t** as seemed best to them,
12:11 at the **t**, but later it yields the peaceful fruit
12:26 At that **t** his voice shook the earth;
13:23 he comes in **t**, he will be with me when I see you.
1Pe 1: 5 for a salvation ready to be revealed in the last **t**.
1:11 or **t** that the Spirit of Christ within them indicated
1:17 live in reverent fear during the **t** of your exile.
4: 3 You have already spent enough **t** in doing what
4:17 For the **t** has come for judgment to begin with
5: 6 so that he may exalt you in due **t**.
2Pe 1:15 that after my departure you may be able at any **t**
3: 6 through which the world of that **t** was deluged
Jude 1:18 "In the last **t** there will be scoffers,
1:25 and authority, before all **t** and now and forever.
Rev 1: 3 who keep what is written in it; for the **t** is near.
2:21 I gave her **t** to repent,
11:18 and the **t** for judging the dead,
12:12 because he knows that his **t** is short!"
12:14 she is nourished for a **t**, and times, and half a **t**.
22:10 of the prophecy of this book, for the **t** is near.
Tob 2:11 At that **t**, also, my wife Anna earned money
3:11 At that same **t**, with hands outstretched toward
3:17 the same **t** that Tobit returned from the courtyard
5:10 the **t** is near for God to heal you; take courage."
12:13 And that **t** when you did not hesitate to get up
12:14 And at the same **t** God sent me to heal you
Jdt 4: 6 Joakim, who was in Jerusalem at the **t**,
4: 7 wide enough for only two at a **t** to pass.
5: 7 At one **t** they lived in Mesopotamia,
5: 8 and lived there for a long **t**. A
5:16 and all the Gergesites, and lived there a long **t**. A
7:30 by that **t** the Lord our God will turn his mercy
8:15 he has power to protect us within any **t** he pleases,
8:29 not the first **t** your wisdom has been shown,
9: 1 very **t** when the evening incense was being offered
13: 5 Now indeed is the **t** to help your heritage and
16:25 or for a long **t** after her death. A
AdE 2:12 this **t** the days of beautification are completed—
2:15 **t** was fulfilled for Esther daughter of Aminadab,
4:14 For if you keep quiet at such a **t** as this,
4:14 who knows whether it was not for such a **t** as this
9:22 gladness and from a **t** of distress to a holiday, E
9:22 be celebrated as a **t** for feasting and gladness and
9:28 days of Purim were to be observed for all **t**, B
14:12 make yourself known in this **t** of our affliction,
16:20 against those who attack them at the **t**
16:24 most hateful to wild animals and birds for all **t**. B
Wis 2: 4 Our name will be forgotten in **t**,
2: 5 For our allotted **t** is the passing of a shadow,
3: 7 In the **t** of their visitation they will shine forth,
4: 2 throughout all **t** it marches, crowned in triumph,
4: 8 For old age is not honored for length of **t**,
Wis 4:13 Being perfected in a short **t**,
11: 8 at that **t** how you punished their enemies.
12:20 granting them **t** and opportunity to give
14:16 Then the ungodly custom, grown strong with **t**,
15: 8 mortals who were made of earth a short **t** before
15: 8 when the **t** comes to return the souls
16: 3 while your people, after suffering want a short **t**,
16:18 At one **t** the flame was restrained,
16:19 and at another **t** even in the midst
16:25 Therefore at that **t** also, changed into all forms,
Sir Pr: 3 of the reign of Euergetes and stayed for some **t**,
Pr: 3 During that **t** I have applied my skill day and night
2: 2 and do not be impetuous in **t** of calamity.
2:11 he forgives sins and saves in **t** of distress. E
4:20 Watch for the opportune **t**, and beware of evil,
4:31 be stretched out to receive and closed when it is **t**
5: 7 and at the **t** of punishment you will perish.
6: 8 but they will not stand by you in **t** of trouble. D
6:10 but they will not stand by you in **t** of trouble. D
10: 4 over it he will raise up the right leader for the **t**.
18:20 and at the **t** of scrutiny you will find forgiveness.
18:25 In the **t** of plenty think of the **t** of hunger;
19: 9 and in **t** will hate you.
20:20 for he does not tell it at the proper **t**.
22: 6 in **t** of mourning is ill-timed conversation,
22:23 Stand by him in **t** of distress, E
24:25 and like the Tigris at the **t** of the first fruits.
24:26 and like the Jordan at harvest **t**.
24:27 like the Gihon at the **t** of vintage.
27:12 Among stupid people limit your **t**,
29: 2 Lend to your neighbor in his **t** of need;
29: 5 but at the **t** for repayment he delays, and finds
fault with the **t**.
31:28 at the proper **t** and in moderation is rejoicing
32: 4 do not display your cleverness at the wrong **t**.
32:11 Leave in good **t** and do not be the last;
33:24 At the **t** when you end the days of your life,
35:26 mercy is as welcome in **t** of distress as clouds E
35:26 of distress as clouds of rain in **t** of drought.
36:10 Hasten the day, and remember the appointed **t**, C
37: 4 but in **t** of trouble they are against him. D
38:13 a **t** when recovery lies in the hands of physicians,
39:16 be done at the appointed **t**. C
39:17 for at the appointed **t** all such questions will C
39:20 to the end of **t** he can see everything,
39:31 their **t** comes they never disobey his command."
39:33 and he will supply every need in its **t**.
39:34 for everything proves good in its appointed **t**. C
40:24 Kindred and helpers are for a **t** of trouble, D
42:12 or spend her **t** among married women;
44:17 in the **t** of wrath he kept the race alive;
46:19 Before the **t** of his eternal sleep,
48:10 At the appointed **t**, it is written, C
48:25 He revealed what was to occur to the end of **t**,
50: 1 and in his **t** fortified the temple.
50:21 and they bowed down in worship a second **t**,
51:12 from destruction and rescued me in **t** of trouble. D
51:30 Do your work in good **t**, and in his own **t** God will
give you your reward.
Bar 1: 2 at the **t** when the Chaldeans took Jerusalem
1: 8 At the same **t**, on the tenth day of Sivan,
1:19 the **t** when the Lord brought our ancestors out of
1:20 at the **t** when he brought our ancestors out of
3:14 the same **t** discern where there is length of days,
3:32 The one who prepared the earth for all **t** filled it B
4:35 for a long **t** she will be inhabited by demons. A
LtJ 6: 3 for a long **t**, up to seven generations; A
Sus 1:13 "Let us go home, for it is **t** for lunch."
1:14 for a **t** when they could find her alone.
1Mc 2:25 At the same **t** he killed
2:29 At that **t** many who were seeking righteousness
2:49 it is a **t** of ruin and furious anger.
2:53 in the **t** of his distress kept the commandment, E
4:60 that **t** they fortified Mount Zion with high walls
7:35 and his army are delivered into my hands this **t**,
9: 1 and Alcimus into the land of Judah a second **t**,
9: 7 for he had no **t** to assemble them.
9:10 If our **t** has come, let us die bravely
9:27 not been since the **t** that prophets ceased to appear
9:31 So Jonathan accepted the leadership at that **t**
9:55 for at that **t** Alcimus was stricken
9:56 And Alcimus died at that **t** in great agony.
10:30 from this day and for all **t**. B
10:77 At the same **t** he advanced into the plain,
11:14 Now King Alexander was in Cilicia at that **t**,
11:36 of these grants shall be canceled from this **t**
12: 1 Jonathan saw that the **t** was favorable for him,
12: 7 in **t** past a letter was sent to the high priest Onias
12:10 for considerable **t** has passed
13: 5 from me to spare my life in any **t** of distress, E
15: 8 canceled for you from henceforth and for all **t**. B
15:25 King Antiochus besieged Dor for the second **t**,
15:33 at one **t** had been unjustly taken by our enemies.
16: 9 At that **t** Judas the brother of John was wounded,
16:24 the **t** that he became high priest after his father.
2Mc 1: 5 and may he not forsake you in **t** of evil.
1:19 the pious priests of that **t** took some of the fire of
1:22 When this had been done and some **t** had passed,
3: 5 that **t** was governor of Coelesyria and Phoenicia,
5: 1 About this **t** Antiochus made his second invasion
6:24 "Such pretense is not worthy of our **t** of life,"
8:14 and at the same **t** implored the Lord
8:19 how, in the **t** of Sennacherib,
8:20 and the **t** of the battle against the Galatians
9: 1 About that **t**, as it happened,
12:36 and his men had been fighting for a long **t** A
13: 9 that had been done in his father's **t**.

2Mc 13:22 The king negotiated a second **t** with the people
15:10 the same **t** pointing out the perfidy of the Gentiles
15:22 you sent your angel in the **t** of King Hezekiah
15:37 and from that **t** the city has been in the possession
1Es 1:19 at that **t** kept the passover and the festival
1:58 it shall keep sabbath all the **t** of its desolation
2:16 In the **t** of King Artaxerxes of the Persians,
6: 3 At the same **t** Sisinnes the governor of Syria
6:20 in process of construction from that **t** until now,
8:64 weight of everything was recorded at that very **t.**
8:79 and to give us food in the **t** of our servitude.
9:12 who have foreign wives come at the **t** appointed, H
9:16 at the same **t** explaining what was read.
3Mc 1:29 because indeed all at that **t** preferred death to
3:26 that for the remaining **t** the government will
3:29 and shall become useless for all **t** B
4:17 But after the previously mentioned interval of **t**
5:18 After the party had been going on for some **t,**
5:25 since the **t** had run out—
5:40 ordering now for a third **t** that they be destroyed,
6:28 from the **t** of our ancestors until now has granted
6:35 and passed the **t** in feasting to the accompaniment
7:19 as a joyous festival during the **t** of their stay.
2Es 3: 9 in its **t** you brought the flood upon the inhabitants
4:30 and will produce until the **t** of threshing comes!
4:39 on account of us that the **t** of threshing is delayed
4:45 whether more **t** is to come than has passed,
5:12 At that **t** people shall hope but not obtain;
5:43 at one **t** those who have been and those who are
5:44 at one **t** those who have been created in it."
5:45 that you will certainly give life at one **t**
5:45 If therefore all creatures will live at one **t** and
5:45 be able to support all of them present at one **t."**
5:46 Request it therefore to produce ten at one **t."**
5:47 "Of course it cannot, but only each in its own **t."**
5:48 of the earth to those who from **t** to **t** are sown
5:53 of youth are different from those born during the **t**
6:24 At that **t** friends shall make war on friends
7:26 "For indeed the **t** will come,
7:*89* During the **t** that they lived in it,
7:*100* "Will **t** therefore be given to the souls,
7:*119* [49] if an immortal **t** has been promised to us,
8: 5 for you have been given only a short **t** to live.
8:11 what has been fashioned may be nourished for a **t;**
9: 2 that it is the very **t** when the Most High is about
9:18 a **t** in this age when I was preparing for those who
10:16 you will receive your son back in due **t,**
10:34 so that I may not die before my **t.**
11: 8 "Do not all watch at the same **t;**
11:13 And after a **t** its reign came to an end,
11:13 and it continued to reign a long **t.** A
11:16 you who have ruled the earth all this **t;**
11:20 and in due **t** the wings that followed also rose up
12:15 for a longer **t** than any other one of the twelve.
12:18 the **t** of that kingdom great struggles shall arise,
12:21 when the middle of its **t** draws near;
12:21 be kept for the **t** when its end approaches,
13:23 at that **t** will protect those who fall into peril,
13:44 at that **t** the Most High performed signs for them,
13:52 except in the **t** of his day.
13:57 Most High for the wonders that he does from **t** to **t,**
14:32 in due **t** he took from you what he had given.
16:38 the ninth month when the **t** of her delivery draws
16:52 in a very short **t** iniquity will be removed from
4Mc 2:22 but at the same **t** he enthroned the mind among
3:20 At a **t** when our ancestors were enjoying profound
3:21 at that **t** certain persons attempted a revolution
5: 7 Although you have had them for so long a **t,**
6:20 that **t** be a laughingstock to all for our cowardice,
9: 5 a short **t** ago you learned nothing from Eleazar.
12: 4 will be miserably tortured and die before your **t,**
12:12 and these throughout all **t** will never let you go.
13:20 of **t** and was shaped during the same period of **t;**
13:21 When they were born after an equal **t** of gestation,
14:19 the **t** for making honeycombs defend themselves
15: 2 and that of preserving her seven sons for a **t,**
15:23 strengthened her to disregard, for the **t,**
15:27 that would preserve the seven sons for a short **t,**
18: 9 the **t** of my maturity I remained with my husband,

TIMES‡ (209) [TIME]

A. THREE TIMES (34)
B. SEVEN TIMES (33)
C. AT ALL TIMES (22)
D. FORMER TIMES (7)
E. LAST TIMES (7)
F. APPOINTED TIMES (5)

Ge 27:36 For he has supplanted me these two **t.**
31: 7 and changed my wages ten **t,**
31:41 and you have changed my wages ten **t.**
33: 3 bowing himself to the ground seven **t,** B
43:34 but Benjamin's portion was five **t** as much as any
Ex 18:22 Let them sit as judges for the people at all **t;** C
18:26 And they judged the people at all **t;** C
23:14 Three **t** in the year you shall hold a festival A
23:17 Three **t** in the year all your males shall appear A
34:23 Three **t** in the year all your males shall appear A
34:24 to appear before the LORD your God three **t** A
Lev 4: 6 of the blood seven **t** before the LORD in front of B
4:17 and sprinkle it seven **t** before the LORD, B
8:11 He sprinkled some of it on the altar seven **t,** B
14: 7 He shall sprinkle it seven **t** upon the one who B
14:16 and sprinkle some oil with his finger seven **t** B
14:27 that is in his left hand seven **t** before the LORD. B
14:51 and sprinkle the house seven **t.** B
Lev 16:14 the blood with his finger seven **t.** B
16:19 of the blood on it with his finger seven **t,** B
23:37 as **t** of holy convocation, for presenting to
25: 8 seven **t** seven years, so that the period B
Nu 14:22 and yet have tested me these ten **t** and have
19: 4 with his finger and sprinkle it seven **t** towards B
22:28 that you have struck me these three **t?"** A
22:32 have you struck your donkey these three **t?** A
22:33 and turned away from me these three **t.** A
24: 1 so he did not go, as at other **t,** to look for omens,
24:10 but instead you have blessed them these three **t.** A
Dt 1:11 increase you a thousand **t** more and bless you,
16:16 Three **t** a year all your males shall appear before A
Jos 6: 4 around the city seven **t,** the priests blowing B
6:15 around the city in the same manner seven **t.** B
6:15 that they marched around the city seven **t.** B
Jdg 16:15 You have mocked me three **t** now and have A
16:20 he thought, "I will go out as at other **t,**
Ru 4: 7 Now this was the custom in former **t** in Israel D
1Sa 20:25 The king sat upon his seat, as at other **t,**
20:41 He bowed three **t,** and they kissed each other, A
2Sa 13:18 of the king were clothed in earlier **t.)**
1Ki 9:25 Three **t** a year Solomon used to offer A
17:21 he stretched himself upon the child three **t,** A
18:43 Then he said, "Go again seven **t."** B
22:16 "How many **t** must I make you swear
2Ki 4:35 the child sneezed seven **t,** B
5:10 saying, "Go, wash in the Jordan seven **t,** B
5:14 and immersed himself seven **t** in the Jordan, B
13:18 he struck three **t,** and stopped. A
13:19 and said, "You should have struck five or six **t;**
13:19 now you will strike down Aram only three **t."** A
13:25 Three **t** Joash defeated him and recovered A
1Ch 9:20 of Eleazar was chief over them in former **t;** D
12:32 those who had understanding of the **t,**
2Ch 15: 5 In those **t** it was not safe for anyone to go
18:15 "How many **t** must I make you swear
Ezr 10:14 at appointed **t,** and with them the elders F
Ne 4:12 they said to us ten **t,**
6: 4 They sent to me four **t** in this way,
9:28 from heaven, and many **t** you rescued them
10:34 by ancestral houses, at appointed **t,** year by year, F
13:31 at appointed **t,** and for the first fruits. F
Job 19: 3 These ten **t** you have cast reproach upon me;
24: 1 "Why are **t** not kept by the Almighty,
27:10 Will they call upon God at all **t?** C
33:29 "God indeed does all these things, twice, three **t,** A
Ps 9: 9 a stronghold in **t** of trouble.
10: 1 Why do you hide yourself in **t** of trouble?
10: 5 Their ways prosper at all **t;** C
12: 6 in a furnace on the ground, purified seven **t.** B
31:15 My **t** are in your hand;
34: 1 I will bless the LORD at all **t;** C
37:19 they are not put to shame in evil **t,**
49: 5 Why should I fear in **t** of trouble,
62: 8 Trust in him at all **t,** O people; C
106: 3 who do righteousness at all **t.** C
106:43 Many **t** he delivered them,
119:20 with longing for your ordinances at all **t.** C
119:164 Seven **t** a day I praise you B
Pr 5:19 May her breasts satisfy you at all **t;** C
17:17 A friend loves at all **t,** C
24:16 for though they fall seven **t,** they will rise again; B
Ecc 7:22 that many **t** you have yourself cursed others.
8:12 a hundred **t** and prolong their lives,
Isa 33: 6 he will be the stability of your **t,** abundance
46:10 from the beginning and from ancient **t** things not
Jer 8: 7 Even the stork in the heavens knows its **t;**
28: 8 and me from ancient **t** prophesied war,
Eze 4:10 at fixed **t** you shall eat it.
4:11 at fixed **t** you shall drink.
12:27 he prophesies for distant **t."**
36:11 to be inhabited as in your former **t,** D
Da 1:20 he found them ten **t** better than all the magicians
2:21 He changes **t** and seasons,
3:19 up seven **t** more than was customary, B
4:16 And let seven **t** pass over him. B
4:23 until seven **t** pass over him'— B
4:25 and seven **t** shall pass over you, B
4:32 and seven **t** shall pass over you, B
6:10 on his knees three **t** a day to pray to his God A
6:13 but he is saying his prayers three **t** a day." A
7:10 ten thousand **t** ten thousand stood attending him.
7:25 be given into his power for a time, two **t,**
11: 6 and the one who supported her. "In those **t**
11:14 "In those **t** many shall rise against the king of
12: 7 that it would be for a time, two **t,** and half a time,
Mt 5:21 that it was said to those of ancient **t,** 'You shall not
5:33 that it was said to those of ancient **t,** 'You shall not
16: 3 but you cannot interpret the signs of the **t.**
18:21 As many as seven **t?"** B
18:22 Jesus said to him, "Not seven **t,** but, I tell you, B
18:22 "Not seven times, but, I tell you, seventy-seven **t.**
26:34 the cock crows, you will deny me three **t."** A
26:75 the cock crows, you will deny me three **t."** A
Mk 14:30 you will deny me three **t."** A
14:72 you will deny me three **t."** A
Lk 8:29 (For many **t** it had seized him;
17: 4 the same person sins against you seven **t** a day, B
17: 4 turns back to you seven **t** and says, 'I repent,' B
19: 8 I will pay back four **t** as much."
21:24 until the **t** of the Gentiles are fulfilled.
21:36 at all **t,** praying that you may have the strength C
22:34 until you have denied three **t** that you know me." A
22:61 you will deny me three **t."** A
Jn 13:38 you will have denied me three **t.** A
Ac 1: 7 to know the **t** or periods that the Father has set
Ac 3:20 that **t** of refreshing may come from the presence
10:16 This happened three **t,** and the thing was A
11:10 This happened three **t;** then everything was A
17:26 the **t** of their existence and the boundaries of
17:30 God has overlooked the **t** of human ignorance,
2Co 11:24 Five **t** I have received from the Jews
11:25 Three **t** I was beaten with rods. A
11:25 Three **t** I was shipwrecked; A
12: 8 Three **t** I appealed to the Lord about this, A
Gal 4:18 to be made much of for a good purpose at all **t,** C
Eph 5:20 the Father at all **t** and for everything in the name C
6:18 Spirit at all **t** in every prayer and supplication. C
1Th 5: 1 Now concerning the **t** and the seasons,
2Th 3:16 Lord of peace himself give you peace at all **t** C
1Ti 4: 1 that in later **t** some will renounce the faith
2Ti 3: 1 that in the last days distressing **t** will come.
1Pe 3:20 who in former **t** did not obey, D
Rev 12:14 where she is nourished for a time, and **t,** and half
Tob 4:19 At all **t** bless the Lord God, C
5: 6 "Yes," he replied, "I have been there many **t;**
14: 4 but all will come true at their appointed **t.** F
14: 5 the period when the **t** of fulfillment shall come.
14:8,9 and to bless his name at all **t** with sincerity C
Wis 7:18 the beginning and end and middle of **t,**
8: 8 and wonders and of the outcome of seasons and **t.**
12:22 you scourge our enemies ten thousand **t** more,
19:22 and you have not neglected to help them at all **t** C
Sir 2: 4 and in **t** of humiliation be patient.
6:37 and meditate at all **t** on his commandments. C
13: 7 until he has drained you two or three **t,** A
20:12 but pay for it seven **t** over. B
22: 6 a thrashing and discipline are at all **t** wisdom. C
23:19 the Lord are ten thousand **t** brighter than the sun;
26: 4 and at all **t** his face is cheerful. C
40: 8 human and animal, but to sinners seven **t** more, B
43: 4 three **t** as hot is the sun scorching the mountains; A
43: 6 governing the **t,** their everlasting sign.
44: 7 and were the pride of their **t.**
47:10 and arranged their **t** throughout the year,
48: 3 and also three **t** brought down fire. A
49: 3 in lawless **t** he made godliness prevail.
1Mc 1:36 an evil adversary of Israel at all **t.** C
16: 2 so that we have delivered Israel many **t.**
2Mc 9:16 the holy vessels he would give back, many **t** over;
12:30 and their kind treatment of them in **t**
14: 3 but had willfully defiled himself in the **t**
14:38 In former **t,** when there was no mingling with D
15: 8 the former **t** when help had come to them D
1Es 1:20 like it had been kept in Israel since the **t** of
1:24 In ancient **t** the events of his reign
5:50 and they offered sacrifices at the proper **t**
8:76 from the **t** of our ancestors,
3Mc 5:37 "How many **t,** you poor wretch,
7:23 Blessed be the Deliverer of Israel through all **t!**
2Es 3:14 and to him alone you revealed the end of the **t,**
3:18 the depths to tremble, and troubled the **t.**
3:23 So the **t** passed and the years were completed,
4:27 to the righteous in their appointed **t,** F
4:37 and measured the **t** by measure, and numbered
4:37 and numbered the **t** by number;
6: 7 "What will be the dividing of the **t?**
6:34 to think vain thoughts concerning the former **t;** D
6:34 then you will not act hastily in the last **t.'"** E
7:*73* or how will they answer in the last **t?** E
7:*74* but because of the **t** that he has foreordained."
7:*75* in rest until those **t** come when you will renew
7:*77* but it will not be shown to you until the last **t.** E
7:*87* to be judged in the last **t.** E
8:50 who inhabit the world in the last **t,** E
8:63 of the signs that you will do in the last **t,** E
9: 6 so also are the **t** of the Most High:
11:39 so that the end of my **t** might come through them?
11:44 The Most High has looked at his **t;**
12: 9 to be shown the end of the **t** and the last events of
12: 9 the end of the times and the last events of the **t."**
12:20 whose **t** shall be short and their years swift;
13:46 "Then they lived there until the last **t;** E
13:58 the **t** and whatever things come to pass
14: 5 secrets of the **t** and declared to him the end of the **t.**
14: 9 with those who are like you, until the **t** are ended.
14:10 age has lost its youth, and the **t** begin to grow old.
14:15 and hurry to escape from these **t.**
4Mc 16: 6 "O how wretched am I and many **t** unhappy!

TIMID‡ (5)

Job 32: 6 I was **t** and afraid to declare my opinion to you.
Pr 11:16 The **t** become destitute, but the aggressive gain
Sir 2:12 Woe to **t** hearts and to slack hands,
22:18 a **t** mind with a fool's resolve will not stand firm
34:16 Those who fear the Lord will not be **t,**

TIMNA (6)

Ge 36:12 (**T** was a concubine of Eliphaz, Esau's son;
36:22 and Lotan's sister was **T.**
36:40 the clans **T,** Alvah, Jetheth,
1Ch 1:36 Teman, Omar, Zephi, Gatam, Kenaz, **T,**
1:39 and Lotan's sister was **T.**
1:51 The clans of Edom were: clans **T,** Aliah, Jetheth,

TIMNAH (12) [TIMNITE]

Ge 38:12 he went up to **T** to his sheepshearers,
38:13 "Your father-in-law is going up to **T**
38:14 which is on the road to **T.**
Jos 15:10 down to Beth-shemesh, and passes along by **T;**
15:57 Gibeah, and **T:** ten towns with their villages.

Jos 19:43 Elon, T, Ekron,
Jdg 14: 1 Once Samson went down to T, and at T he saw a
14: 2 "I saw a Philistine woman at T;
14: 5 down with his father and mother to T.
14: 5 When he came to the vineyards of T,
2Ch 28:18 T with its villages, and Gimzo with its villages;

TIMNATH (1)
1Mc 9:50 and Emmaus, and Beth-horon, and Bethel, and T,

TIMNATH-HERES (1) [=TIMNATH-SERAH]
Jdg 2: 9 within the bounds of his inheritance in T,

TIMNATH-SERAH (2) [=TIMNATH-HERES]
Jos 19:50 T in the hill country of Ephraim;
24:30 They buried him in his own inheritance at T,

TIMNITE (1) [TIMNAH]
Jdg 15: 6 And they said, "Samson, the son-in-law of the T,

TIMON (1)
Ac 6: 5 Prochorus, Nicanor, T, Parmenas, and Nicolaus,

TIMOTHEUS (KJV) See TIMOTHY

TIMOTHY (42) [TIMOTHY'S]
Ac 16: 1 where there was a disciple named T,
16: 3 Paul wanted T to accompany him;
17:14 but Silas and T remained behind.
17:15 to have Silas and T join him as soon as possible,
18: 5 When Silas and T arrived from Macedonia,
19:22 So he sent two of his helpers, T and Erastus,
20: 4 by Gaius from Derbe, and by T,
Ro 16:21 T, my co-worker, greets you;
1Co 4:17 For this reason I sent you T,
16:10 If T comes, see that he has nothing to fear
2Co 1: 1 and T our brother, To the church of God that is
1:19 Silvanus and T and I, was not "Yes and No";
Php 1: 1 Paul and T, servants of Christ Jesus,
2:19 I hope in the Lord Jesus to send T to you soon,
Col 1: 1 by the will of God, and T our brother,
1Th 1: 1 and T, To the church of the Thessalonians in God
3: 2 and we sent T, our brother and co-worker for God
3: 6 But T has just now come to us from you,
2Th 1: 1 and T, To the church of the Thessalonians
1Ti 1: 2 To T, my loyal child in the faith:
1:18 I am giving you these instructions, T, my child,
6:20 T, guard what has been entrusted to you.
2Ti 1: 2 To T, my beloved child: Grace,
Phm 1: 1 Paul, a prisoner of Christ Jesus, and T our brother,
Heb 13:23 to know that our brother T has been set free;
1Mc 5: 6 and many people, with T as their leader.
5:11 and T is leading their forces.
5:34 the army of T realized that it was Maccabeus,
5:37 After these things T gathered another army
5:40 T said to the officers of his forces,
2Mc 8:30 In encounters with the forces of T
9: 3 to Nicanor and the forces of T.
10:24 Now T, who had been defeated by the Jews
10:32 T himself fled to a stronghold called Gazara,
10:37 They killed T, who was hiding in a cistern,
12: 2 T and Apollonius son of Gennaeus,
12:10 on their march against T,
12:18 They did not find T in that region,
12:19 marched out and destroyed those whom T had left
12:20 in command of the divisions, and hurried after T,
12:21 When T learned of the approach of Judas,
12:24 T himself fell into the hands of Dositheus

TIMOTHY'S (2) [TIMOTHY]
Php 2:22 But T worth you know, how like a son with
2Mc 8:32 They killed the commander of T forces,

TIN (5)
Nu 31:22 gold, silver, bronze, iron, t, and lead—
Eze 22:18 all of them, silver, bronze, t, iron, and lead.
22:20 bronze, iron, lead, and t into a smelter,
27:12 iron, t, and lead they exchanged for your wares.
Sir 47:18 gathered gold like t and amassed silver like lead.

TINDER (1)
Isa 1:31 The strong shall become like t,

TINGLE (3)
1Sa 3:11 both ears of anyone who hears of it t.
2Ki 21:12 that the ears of everyone who hears of it will t.
Jer 19: 3 that the ears of everyone who hears of it will t.

TINKLING (1)
Isa 3:16 mincing along as they go, t with their feet;

TINKLING (KJV) See also ANKLETS, CLANGING

TINY (1)
AdE 11:10 and at their outcry, as though from a t spring,

TIP (6) [TIPPED, TIPS]
Jdg 6:21 the t of the staff that was in his hand, and touched
1Sa 14:27 and dipped the t of it in the honeycomb,
14:43 "I tasted a little honey with the t of the staff
1Ki 6:24 it was ten cubits from the t of one wing to the t of
Lk 16:24 the t of his finger in water and cool my tongue;

TIPHSAH (2)
1Ki 4:24 the region west of the Euphrates from T to Gaza,
2Ki 15:16 At that time Menahem sacked T,

TIPPED (1) [TIP]
LtJ 6:27 and if it is t over, it cannot straighten itself.

TIPS (2) [TIP]
Wis 11:22 the whole world before you is like a speck that t
Sir 1:22 for anger t the scale to one's ruin.

TIRAS (2)
Ge 10: 2 Magog, Madai, Javan, Tubal, Meshech, and T.
1Ch 1: 5 Magog, Madai, Javan, Tubal, Meshech, and T.

TIRATHITES (1)
1Ch 2:55 the T, the Shimeathites, and the Sucathites.

TIRE (1) [TIRED]
Sir 42:25 Who could ever t of seeing his glory?

TIRED (5) [TIRE]
Jdg 16:16 and pestered him, he was t to death.
Pr 26:15 and is too t to bring it back to the mouth.
Jer 12:13 they have t themselves out but profit nothing.
Jn 4: 6 t out by his journey, was sitting by the well.
1Mc 10:81 and the enemy's horses grew t.

TIRES (KJV) See CRESCENTS, TURBANS

TIRHAKAH (2)
2Ki 19: 9 the king heard concerning King T of Ethiopia,
Isa 37: 9 the king heard concerning King T of Ethiopia,

TIRHANAH (1)
1Ch 2:48 Maacah, Caleb's concubine, bore Sheber and T.

TIRIA (1)
1Ch 4:16 sons of Jehallelel: Ziph, Ziphah, T, and Asarel.

TIRSHATHA (KJV) See GOVERNOR

TIRZAH (18)
Nu 26:33 Noah, Hoglah, Milcah, and T.
27: 1 Mahlah, Noah, Hoglah, Milcah, and T.
36:11 Mahlah, T, Hoglah, Milcah, and Noah,
Jos 12:24 the king of T one thirty-one kings in all.
17: 3 Mahlah, Noah, Hoglah, Milcah, and T.
1Ki 14:17 got up and went away, and she came to T.
15:21 he stopped building Ramah and lived in T.
15:33 of Ahijah began to reign over all Israel at T;
16: 6 with his ancestors, and was buried at T;
16: 8 of Baasha began to reign over Israel in T;
16: 9 When he was at T, drinking himself drunk in
16: 9 who was in charge of the palace at T,
16:15 Zimri reigned seven days in T.
16:17 and all Israel with him, and they besieged T.
16:23 he reigned for twelve years, six of them in T.
2Ki 15:14 of Gadi came up from T and came to Samaria;
15:16 all who were in it and its territory from T on;
SS 6: 4 You are beautiful as T, my love,

TISHBE (1) [TISHBITE]
1Ki 17: 1 Now Elijah the Tishbite, of T in Gilead,

TISHBITE (6) [TISHBE]
1Ki 17: 1 Now Elijah the T, of Tishbe in Gilead,
21:17 word of the LORD came to Elijah the T, saying:
21:28 the word of the LORD came to Elijah the T:
2Ki 1: 3 But the angel of the LORD said to Elijah the T,
1: 8 He said, "It is Elijah the T."
9:36 which he spoke by his servant Elijah the T,

TITANS (1)
Jdt 16: 6 nor did the sons of the T strike him down,

TITHE (20) [TITHES]
Nu 18:21 To the Levites I have given every t in Israel for
18:24 the Levites as their portion the t of the Israelites,
18:26 from the Israelites the t that I have given you
18:26 an offering from it to the LORD, a t of the t.
Dt 12:17 within your towns the t of your grain, your wine,
14:22 a t of all the yield of your seed that is brought
14:23 you shall eat the t of your grain, your wine,
14:28 Every third year you shall bring out the full t
26:12 the t of your produce in the third year (which is the year of the t),
2Ch 31: 5 they brought in abundantly the t of everything.
31: 6 in the cities of Judah also brought in the t of cattle
31: 6 and the t of the dedicated things
Ne 10:38 and the Levites shall bring up a t of the tithes to
13:12 Then all Judah brought the t of the grain, wine,
Mal 3:10 Bring the full t into the storehouse,
Mt 23:23 For you t mint, dill, and cummin,
Lk 11:42 For you t mint and rue and herbs of all kinds,
Sir 35:11 and dedicate your t with gladness.

TITHES (25) [TITHE]
Lev 27:30 All t from the land, whether the seed from
27:31 If persons wish to redeem any of their t,
27:32 All t of herd and flock,
Nu 18:28 to the LORD from all the t that you receive from
Dt 12: 6 your t and your donations, your votive gifts,
12:11 your t and your donations,
2Ch 31:12 the t and the dedicated things.
Ne 10:37 and to bring to the Levites the t from our soil,
10:37 for it is the Levites who collect the t
10:38 with the Levites when the Levites receive the t;
10:38 and the Levites shall bring up a tithe of the t to
12:44 the contributions, the first fruits, and the t,
13: 5 the frankincense, the vessels, and the t of grain,
Am 4: 4 sacrifices every morning, your t every three days;
Mal 3: 8 are we robbing you?" In your t and offerings!
Heb 7: 5 a commandment in the law to collect t from
7: 6 collected t from Abraham and blessed him
7: 8 t are received by those who are mortal;
7: 9 who receives t, paid t through Abraham,
Tob 1: 6 the flock, the t of the cattle, and the first shearings
Jdt 11:13 to consume the first fruits of the grain and the t of
1Mc 3:49 and the first fruits and the t, and they stirred up
10:31 Jerusalem and its environs, its t and its revenues,
11:35 the other payments henceforth due to us of the t,

TITIUS (1)
Ac 18: 7 the house of a man named T Justus, a worshiper

TITLE (4)
Ex 3:15 and this my t for all generations.
Mt 22:20 "Whose head is this, and whose t?"
Mk 12:16 "Whose head is this, and whose t?"
Lk 20:24 Whose head and whose t does it bear?"

TITTLE (KJV) See STROKE OF A LETTER

TITUS‡ (14)
2Co 2:13 not rest because I did not find my brother T there.
7: 6 consoled us by the arrival of T,
7:13 we rejoiced still more at the joy of T,
7:14 so our boasting to T has proved true as well.
8: 6 so that we might urge T that,
8:16 But thanks be to God who put in the heart of T
8:23 T, he is my partner and co-worker in your service;
12:18 I urged T to go, and sent the brother with him.
12:18 T did not take advantage of you, did he?
Gal 2: 1 up again to Jerusalem with Barnabas, taking T
2: 3 But even T, who was with me,
2Ti 4:10 Crescens has gone to Galatia, T to Dalmatia.
Tit 1: 4 To T, my loyal child in the faith we share:
2Mc 11:34 "Quintus Memmius and T Manius,

TIZITE (1)
1Ch 11:45 Jediael son of Shimri, and his brother Joha the T,

TO (25824) See Index of Articles Etc.

TOAH (1)
1Ch 6:34 son of Jeroham, son of Eliel, son of T,

TOB (5)
Jdg 11: 3 from his brothers and lived in the land of T.
11: 5 to bring Jephthah from the land of T.
2Sa 10: 6 and the men of T, twelve thousand men.
10: 8 and the men of T and Maacah,
1Mc 5:13 in the land of T have been killed;

TOB-ADONIJAH (1)
2Ch 17: 8 Jehonathan, Adonijah, Tobijah, and T;

TOBIAH (16) [TOBIAH'S]
Ezr 2:60 T, and Nekoda, six hundred fifty-two.
Ne 2:10 and T the Ammonite official heard this,
2:19 the Horonite and T the Ammonite official,
4: 3 T the Ammonite was beside him, and he said,
4: 7 and T and the Arabs and the Ammonites and
6: 1 to Sanballat and T and to Geshem the Arab and to
6:12 because T and Sanballat had hired him.
6:14 Remember T and Sanballat, O my God,
6:17 the nobles of Judah sent many letters to T,
6:19 And T sent letters to intimidate me.
7:62 of T, of Nekoda, six hundred forty-two.
13: 4 and who was related to T,
13: 5 for T a large room where they had previously put
13: 7 the wrong that Eliashib had done on behalf of T,
13: 8 and I threw all the household furniture of T out of
1Es 5:37 the descendants of Delaiah son of T,

TOBIAH'S (1) [TOBIAH]
Ne 6:17 and T letters came to them.

TOBIAS‡ (54) [TOBIAS'S]
Tob 1: 9 the father of a son whom I named T.
1:20 royal treasury except my wife Anna and my son T.
2: 1 my wife Anna and my son T were restored to me.
2: 2 I said to my son T, "Go, my child,
2: 3 So T went to look for some poor person

Tob 3:17 by giving her in marriage to **T** son of Tobit,
3:17 For **T** was entitled to have her
4: 2 Why do I not call my son **T** and explain to him
4: 3 Then he called his son **T**,
5: 1 Then **T** answered his father Tobit,
5: 3 Then Tobit answered his son **T**,
5: 4 So **T** went out to look for a man to go with him
5: 5 **T** said to him, "Where do you come from,
5: 5 Then **T** said to him, "Do you know the way to go
5: 7 Then **T** said to him, "Wait for me, young man,
5: 9 **T** went in to tell his father Tobit and said to him,
5:10 Then **T** went out and called him, and said,
5:10 "My son **T** wishes to go to Media.
6:11 to the young man, "Brother **T**."
6:14 Then **T** said in answer to Raphael,
6:18 When **T** heard the words of Raphael and learned
7: 1 Now when they entered Ecbatana, **T** said to him,
7: 5 And **T** added, "He is my father!"
7: 7 He then embraced his kinsman **T** and wept.
7: 9 **T** said to Raphael, "Brother Azariah,
7:11 But **T** said, "I will neither eat nor drink anything
7:12 to him he took her by the hand and gave her to **T**,
8: 2 Then **T** remembered the words of Raphael,
8: 4 **T** got out of bed and said to Sarah, "Sister, get up,
8: 5 **T** began by saying, "Blessed are you,
8:20 for **T** and swore on oath to him in these words:
9: 1 Then **T** called Raphael and said to him,
9: 5 and informed him that Tobit's son **T** had married
9: 6 into Raguel's house they found **T** reclining
9: 6 for I see in **T** the very image of my cousin Tobit."
10: 1 Tobit kept counting how many days **T** would need
10: 7 **T** came to him and said, "Send me back,
10: 8 Raguel said to **T**, "Stay, my child, stay with me;
10:10 So Raguel promptly gave **T** his wife Sarah,
10:11 he embraced **T** and said, "Farewell, my child;
10:12 Then Edna said to **T**, "My child and dear brother,
10:13 **T** parted from Raguel with happiness and joy,
11: 7 Raphael said to **T**, before he had approached his
11:10 through the courtyard door. **T** went up to him,
11:15 Now I see my son **T**!"
11:15 **T** reported to his father that his journey had been
11:17 When Tobit met Sarah the wife of his son **T**,
11:17 blessed be my son **T**, and blessed be you,
12: 1 Tobit called his son **T** and said to him, "My child,
12: 5 So **T** called him and said,
14: 3 he called his son **T** and the seven sons of **T** and
14:15 **T** praised God for all he had done to the people
2Mc 3:11 and also some money of Hyrcanus son of **T**,

TOBIAS'S (2) [TOBIAS]

Tob 11:18 With merriment they celebrated **T** wedding feast
14:12 **T** mother died, he buried her beside his father.

TOBIEL (2)

Tob 1: 1 the story of Tobit son of **T** son of Hananiel son
1: 8 the mother of my father **T**, for my father had died

TOBIJAH (3)

2Ch 17: 8 Asahel, Shemiramoth, Jehonathan, Adonijah, **T**,
Zec 6:10 from Heldai, **T**, and Jedaiah—
6:14 And the crown shall be in the care of Heldai, **T**,

TOBIT‡ (36) [TOBIT'S]

Tob 1: 1 the story of **T** son of Tobiel son of Hananiel son
1: 3 **T**, walked in the ways of truth
3:17 **T**, by removing the white films from his eyes,
3:17 by giving her in marriage to Tobias son of **T**,
3:17 that **T** returned from the courtyard into his house,
4: 1 That same day **T** remembered the money
5: 1 Then Tobias answered his father **T**,
5: 3 Then **T** answered his son Tobias,
5: 9 Tobias went in to tell his father **T** and said to him,
5:10 So he went in to him, and **T** greeted him first.
5:10 But **T** retorted, "What joy is left for me any more?
5:10 Then **T** said to him, "My son Tobias wishes to go
5:11 Then **T** said to him, "Brother,
5:12 But **T** said, "I want to be sure, brother,
5:14 Then **T** said to him, "Welcome!
5:17 **T** said to him, "Blessings be upon you, brother."
5:17 **T** then said to him, "Have a safe journey."
5:18 But his mother began to weep, and said to **T**,
5:21 **T** said to her, "Do not worry;
7: 2 much the young man resembles my kinsman **T**!"
7: 4 She said to them, "Do you know our kinsman **T**?"
9: 6 for I see in Tobias the very image of my cousin **T**."
10: 1 Now, day by day, **T** kept counting
10: 6 But **T** kept saying to her, "Be quiet
10: 8 to your father **T** and they will inform him
11:10 Then **T** got up and came stumbling out through
11:13 **T** saw his son and threw his arms around him,
11:15 So **T** went in rejoicing and praising God at the top
11:16 Then **T**, rejoicing and praising God,
11:17 **T** acknowledged that God had been merciful
11:17 When **T** met Sarah the wife of his son Tobias,
12: 1 **T** called his son Tobias and said to him,
12: 4 **T** said, "He deserves, my child,
13: 1 Then **T** said: "Blessed be God
14: 2 **T** died in peace when he was one hundred twelve
14:13 the property of Raguel and that of his father **T**.

TOBIT'S (3) [TOBIT]

Tob 9: 5 and informed him that **T** son Tobias had married
11:18 also present to share **T** joy.
14: 1 So ended **T** words of praise.

TOCHEN (1)

1Ch 4:32 And their villages were Etam, Ain, Rimmon, **T**,

TODAY‡ (253) [TODAY'S]

Ge 4:14 **T** you have driven me away from the soil,
21:26 and I have not heard of it until **t**."
24:12 please grant me success **t** and show steadfast love
24:42 "I came **t** to the spring, and said, 'O LORD,
30:32 let me pass through all your flock **t**, removing
31:43 what can I do **t** about these daughters of mine,
31:48 "This heap is a witness between you and me **t**."
40: 7 "Why are your faces downcast **t**?"
41: 9 to Pharaoh, "I remember my faults **t**.
50:20 to preserve a numerous people, as he is doing **t**.
Ex 2:18 "How is it that you have come back so soon **t**?"
5:14 the required quantity of bricks yesterday and **t**,
13: 4 **T**, in the month of Abib, you are going out.
14:13 that the LORD will accomplish for you **t**;
14:13 whom you see **t** you shall never see again.
16:25 "Eat it **t**, for **t** is a sabbath to the LORD; **t** you will not find it in the field.
19:10 the people and consecrate them **t** and tomorrow.
32:29 "**T** you have ordained yourselves for the service
34:11 Observe what I command you **t**.
Lev 8:34 as has been done **t**, the LORD has commanded
9: 4 For **t** the LORD will appear to you.' "
10:19 **t** they offered their sin offering
10:19 If I had eaten the sin offering **t**,
Dt 1:10 that **t** you are as numerous as the stars of heaven.
1:39 who **t** do not yet know right from wrong,
2:18 "**T** you are going to cross the boundary of Moab
4: 4 to the LORD your God are all alive **t**.
4: 8 as this entire law that I am setting before you **t**?
4:26 I call heaven and earth to witness against you **t**
4:38 for a possession, as it is still **t**.
4:39 So acknowledge **t** and take to heart that
4:40 which I am commanding you **t**
5: 1 and ordinances that I am addressing to you **t**;
5: 3 but with us, who are all of us here alive **t**.
5:24 **T** we have seen that God may speak to someone
6: 6 Keep these words that I am commanding you **t**
7:11 that I am commanding you **t**.
8: 1 I command you **t** you must diligently observe,
8:11 and his statutes, which I am commanding you **t**.
8:18 that he swore to your ancestors, as he is doing **t**.
8:19 I solemnly warn you **t** that you shall surely perish.
9: 1 You are about to cross the Jordan **t**,
9: 3 Know then **t** that the LORD your God is the one
10:13 and his decrees that I am commanding you **t**,
10:15 out of all the peoples, as it is **t**.
11: 2 Remember **t** that it was not your children
11: 8 that I am commanding you **t**,
11:13 that I am commanding you **t**—
11:26 I am setting before you **t** a blessing and a curse:
11:27 that I am commanding you **t**;
11:28 turn from the way that I am commanding you **t**,
11:32 and ordinances that I am setting before you **t**.
12: 8 You shall not act as we are acting here **t**,
12:28 to obey all these words that I command you **t**,
13:18 that I am commanding you **t**,
15: 5 this entire commandment that I command you **t**.
15:15 for this reason I lay this command upon you **t**.
19: 9 that I command you **t**, by loving
20: 3 **T** you are drawing near to do battle
26: 3 "**T** I declare to the LORD your God
26:17 **T** you have obtained the LORD's agreement:
26:18 **T** the LORD has obtained your agreement:
27: 1 that I am commanding you **t**.
27: 4 about which I am commanding you **t**,
27:10 and his statutes that I am commanding you **t**.
28: 1 that I am commanding you **t**,
28:13 which I am commanding you **t**,
28:14 of the words that I am commanding you **t**,
28:15 which I am commanding you **t**,
29:10 You stand assembled **t**, all of you,
29:12 the LORD your God is making with you **t**,
29:13 in order that he may establish you **t** as his people,
29:14 not only with you who stand here with us **t** before
29:15 but also with those who are not here with us **t**.
30: 2 just as I am commanding you **t**,
30: 8 that I am commanding you **t**,
30:11 that I am commanding you **t** is not too hard
30:15 See, I have set before you **t** life and prosperity,
30:16 that I am commanding you **t**,
30:18 I declare to you **t** that you shall perish;
30:19 and earth to witness against you **t** that I have set
32:46 that I am giving in witness against you **t**;
Jos 5: 9 "**T** I have rolled away from you the disgrace
7:25 The LORD is bringing trouble on you **t**."
14:10 and here I am **t**, eighty-five years old.
14:11 I am still as strong **t** as I was on the day
22:16 in turning away **t** from following the LORD,
22:16 by building yourselves an altar **t** in rebellion
22:18 you must turn away **t** from following the LORD!
22:18 If you rebel against the LORD **t**,
22:22 of faith toward the LORD, do not spare us **t**
22:31 "**T** we know that the LORD is among us,
Jdg 11:27 decide **t** for the Israelites or for the Ammonites."
21: 3 that **t** there should be one tribe lacking in Israel?"
Ru 2:19 "Where did you glean **t**?
2:19 name of the man with whom I worked **t** is Boaz."
3:18 but will settle the matter **t**."
4: 9 "**T** you are witnesses that I have acquired from
4:10 of his native place; **t** you are witnesses."
1Sa 4: 3 the LORD put us to rout **t** before the Philistines?
4:16 I fled from the battle **t**."
1Sa 9:12 because the people have a sacrifice **t** at the shrine.
9:19 for **t** you shall eat with me,
10: 2 from me **t** you will meet two men
10:19 But **t** you have rejected your God,
11:13 **t** the LORD has brought deliverance to Israel."
12:17 Is it not the wheat harvest **t**?
14:30 How much better if **t** the troops had eaten freely
14:38 and let us find out how this sin has arisen **t**.
14:41 why have you not answered your servant **t**?
14:45 for he has worked with God **t**."
17:10 the Philistine said, "**T** I defy the ranks of Israel!
20:27 not come to the feast, either yesterday or **t**?"
21: 5 how much more **t** will their vessels be holy?"
22: 8 to lie in wait, as he is doing **t**."
22:13 to lie in wait, as he is doing **t**?"
22:15 Is **t** the first time that I have inquired of God
24:18 **T** you have explained how you have dealt well
25:10 There are many servants **t** who are breaking away
25:32 the God of Israel, who sent you to meet me **t**!
25:33 who have kept me **t** from bloodguilt and
26: 8 "God has given your enemy into your hand **t**;
26:19 before the LORD, for they have driven me out **t**
26:21 because my life was precious in your sight **t**;
26:23 for the LORD gave you into my hand **t**,
26:24 As your life was precious **t** in my sight,
27:10 "Against whom have you made a raid **t**?"
28:18 therefore the LORD has done this thing to you **t**.
29: 6 in you from the day of your coming to me until **t**.
2Sa 3: 8 **T** I keep showing loyalty to the house
3:39 **T** I am powerless, even though anointed king;
6:20 "How the king of Israel honored himself **t**, uncovering himself **t** before the eyes
11:12 Then David said to Uriah, "Remain here **t** also,
14:22 "**T** your servant knows that I have found favor
15:20 and shall I **t** make you wander about with us,
16: 3 for he said, '**T** the house
16:12 with good for this cursing of me **t**."
18:20 Joab said to him, "You are not to carry tidings **t**;
18:20 but **t** you shall not do so,
19: 5 "**T** you have covered with shame the faces of all your officers who have saved your life **t**,
19: 6 You have made it clear **t** that commanders
19: 6 if Absalom were alive and all of us were dead **t**,
19:22 that you should **t** become an adversary to me?
19:35 **T** I am eighty years old;
1Ki 1:25 For **t** he has gone down and has sacrificed oxen,
1:48 who **t** has granted one of my offspring to sit
2:24 **t** Adonijah shall be put to death."
3: 6 and have given him a son to sit on his throne **t**.
5: 7 and said, "Blessed be the LORD **t**,
8:28 and the prayer that your servant prays to you **t**;
12: 7 be a servant to this people **t** and serve them,
14:14 who shall cut off the house of Jeroboam **t**,
18:15 I will surely show myself to him **t**."
20:13 Look, I will give it into your hand **t**;
2Ki 2: 3 that **t** the LORD will take your master away
2: 5 that **t** the LORD will take your master away
4:23 He said, "Why go to him **t**?
6:28 up your son; we will eat him **t**,
6:31 of Elisha son of Shaphat stays on his shoulders **t**."
1Ch 28: 7 and my ordinances, as he is **t**.'
29: 5 consecrating themselves **t** to the LORD?"
2Ch 8: 8 for forced labor, as is still the case **t**.
35:21 I am not coming against you **t**,
Ne 1:11 Give success to your servant **t**,
9:32 since the time of the kings of Assyria until **t**.
Est 5: 4 let the king and Haman come **t** to a banquet
Job 23: 2 "**T** also my complaint is bitter;
Ps 2: 7 "You are my son; **t** I have begotten you.
95: 7 O that **t** you would listen to his voice!
119:91 By your appointment they stand **t**,
Pr 7:14 and **t** I have paid my vows;
22:19 I have made them known to you **t**—yes, to you.
Isa 48: 7 before **t** you have never heard of them,
56:12 tomorrow will be like **t**, great beyond measure."
58: 4 Such fasting as you do **t** will not make your voice
Jer 1:10 **t** I appoint you over nations and over kingdoms,
1:18 I for my part have made you **t** a fortified city,
25:18 an object of hissing and of cursing, as they are **t**;
36: 2 from the days of Josiah until **t**.
40: 4 I have just released you **t** from the fetters
42:19 Be well aware that I have warned you **t**
42:21 So I have told you **t**,
44: 2 Look at them; **t** they are a desolation,
44: 6 a waste and a desolation, as they still are **t**.
44:23 this disaster has befallen you, as is still evident **t**."
Zec 9:12 **t** I declare that I will restore to you double.
Mt 6:30 which is alive **t** and tomorrow is thrown into
6:34 Today's trouble is enough for **t**.
16: 3 And in the morning, 'It will be stormy **t**,
21:28 'Son, go and work in the vineyard **t**.'
27:19 for **t** I have suffered a great deal because of
Lk 4:21 "**T** this scripture has been fulfilled
5:26 saying, "We have seen strange things **t**."
12:28 which is alive **t** and tomorrow is thrown into
13:32 I am casting out demons and performing cures **t**
13:33 Yet **t**, tomorrow, and the next day I must be
19: 5 for I must stay at your house **t**."
19: 9 "**T** salvation has come to this house,
22:61 how he had said to him, "Before the cock crows **t**,
23:43 **t** you will be with me in Paradise."
Ac 4: 9 if we are questioned **t** because of
13:33 'You are my Son; **t** I have begotten you.'
19:40 we are in danger of being charged with rioting **t**,
22: 3 being zealous for God, just as all of you are **t**.
24:21 of the dead that I am on trial before you **t**.' "
26: 2 to make my defense **t** against all the accusations

Ac 26:29 to me t might become such as I am—
27:33 "T is the fourteenth day that you have been
Heb 1: 5 "You are my Son; t I have begotten you"?
3: 7 Therefore, as the Holy Spirit says, "T, if you hear
3:13 as long as it is called "t," so that none of you
3:15 As it is said, "T, if you hear his voice,
4: 7 "t"—saying through David much later, in the
words already quoted, "T, if you hear his voice,
5: 5 "You are my Son, t I have begotten you";
13: 8 Christ is the same yesterday and t and forever.
Jas 4:13 "T or tomorrow we will go to such and such
Tob 7:11 She is given to you from t and forever.
Jdt 6: 2 as you have done t and tell us not to make war
6:19 and look kindly t on the faces
7:28 do t the things that we have described!"
8:11 What you have said to the people t is not right;
8:12 Who are you to put God to the test t,
8:29 T is not the first time your wisdom has been shown
12:13 and to become t like one of the Assyrian women
12:18 because t is the greatest day in my whole life."
13: 7 "Give me strength t, O Lord God of Israel!"
13:11 against our enemies, as he has done t!"
AdE 5: 4 And Esther said, "T is a special day for me.
5: 4 to the dinner that I shall prepare t."
5: 8 and tomorrow I will do as I have done t."
Sir 10:10 the king of t will die tomorrow.
20:15 T he lends and tomorrow he asks it back;
38:22 yesterday it was his, and t it is yours.
Bar 1:15 but there is open shame on us t,
1:19 of the land of Egypt until t,
2:26 by your name you have made as it is t,
3: 8 we are t in our exile where you have scattered us,
Aza 1:17 such may our sacrifice be in your sight t,
1Mc 2:63 T they will be exalted, but tomorrow they will not
3:17 And we are faint, for we have eaten nothing t."
4:10 and crush this army before us t.
5:32 "Fight t for your kindred!"
6:26 t they have encamped against the citadel
7:42 So also crush this army before us t;
9:30 therefore we have chosen you t to take his place
9:44 for t things are not as they were before.
10:20 so we have appointed you t to be the high priest
3Mc 6:13 And let the Gentiles cower t in fear

TODAY'S (2) [TODAY]

Mt 6:34 T trouble is enough for today.
3Mc 5:20 said that the Jews were benefited by t sleep,

TOE (5) [TOES]

Lev 8:23 of his right hand and on the big t of his right foot.
14:14 and on the big t of the right foot.
14:17 and on the big t of the right foot,
14:25 and on the big t of the right foot.
14:28 and the big t of the right foot,

TOES (9) [TOE]

Ex 29:20 and on the big t of their right feet,
Lev 8:24 on the thumbs of their right hands and on the big t
Jdg 1: 6 and caught him, and cut off his thumbs and big t.
1: 7 with their thumbs and big t cut off used to pick
2Sa 21:20 and six t on each foot, twenty-four in number;
1Ch 20: 6 and six t on each foot, twenty-four in number;
Da 2:41 As you saw the feet and t partly of potter's clay
2:42 As the t of the feet were part iron and part clay,
4Mc 15:15 their t and fingers scattered on the ground,

TOGARMAH (2)

Ge 10: 3 descendants of Gomer: Ashkenaz, Riphath, and T.
1Ch 1: 6 Ashkenaz, Diphath, and T.

TOGETHER‡ (423) [ALTOGETHER]

Ge 1: 9 "Let the waters under the sky be gathered t
1:10 the waters that were gathered t he called Seas.
3: 7 and they sewed fig leaves t and made loincloths
6: 7 people t with animals and creeping things
11:31 and they went out t from Ur of the Chaldeans
13: 6 the land could not support both of them living t;
13: 6 so great that they could not live t,
22: 6 So the two of them walked on t.
22: 8 So the two of them walked on t.
22:19 and they arose and went t to Beer-sheba;
25:22 The children struggled t within her;
29: 7 it is not time for the animals to be gathered t.
29: 8 "We cannot until all the flocks are gathered t,
29:22 So Laban gathered t all the people of the place,
36: 7 their possessions were too great for them to live t;
42:17 And he put them all t in prison for three days.
46:15 t with his daughter Dinah;
Ex 8:14 they gathered them t in heaps, and the land stank.
26:11 and join the tent t, so that it may be one whole.
26:17 be two pegs in each frame to fit the frames t;
28: 7 so that it may be joined t.
36:18 He made fifty clasps of bronze to join the tent t so
36:22 Each frame had two pegs for fitting t;
Lev 10:15 t with the offerings by fire of the fat,
23:20 as an elevation offering before the LORD, t with
Nu 1:18 the whole congregation t.
6:20 for the priest, t with the breast that is elevated and
14:35 to all this wicked congregation gathered t
15:24 t with its grain offering and its drink offering,
16:11 and all your company have gathered t against
16:27 t with their wives, their children,
18:11 t with your sons and daughters,
18:19 t with your sons and daughters,
Nu 20: 2 they gathered t against Moses and against Aaron.
20:10 Moses and Aaron gathered the assembly t before
21:16 "Gather the people t, and I will give them water."
21:23 Sihon gathered all his people t,
24:10 and he struck his hands t.
27: 3 the company of those who gathered themselves t
Dt 4:49 t with all the Arabah on the east side of the Jordan
12: 7 you and your households t,
12:12 you t with your sons and your daughters,
12:18 you t with your son and your daughter,
14:26 you and your household rejoicing t.
15:20 You shall eat it, you t with your household,
22:10 not plow with an ox and a donkey yoked t.
22:11 not wear clothes made of wool and linen woven t.
25: 5 When brothers reside t, and one of them dies
26:11 t with the Levites and the aliens who reside
32:14 t with the choicest wheat—
Jos 7:15 t with all that he has,
8:16 the people who were in the city were called t
9: 2 they gathered t with one accord to fight Joshua
11: 5 and came and camped t at the waters of Merom,
16: 9 t with the towns that were set apart for
19: 8 t with all the villages all around these towns as far
Jdg 6:33 the Amalekites and the people of the east came t,
9: 6 the lords of Shechem and all Beth-millo came t,
9:47 of the Tower of Shechem were gathered t.
10:17 Israelites came t, and they encamped at Mizpah.
11:20 so Sihon gathered all his people t,
19: 6 So the two men sat and ate and drank t;
20:14 Benjaminites came t out of the towns to Gibeah,
Ru 1:22 So Naomi returned t with Ruth the Moabite,
4:11 who t built up the house of Israel.
4:13 and she became his wife. When they came t,
1Sa 5: 8 and gathered t all the lords of the Philistines,
5:11 They sent therefore and gathered t all the lords of
8: 4 the elders of Israel gathered t and came to Samuel
11:11 so that no two of them were left t.
17:10 Give me a man, that we may fight t."
28:23 But his servants, t with the woman, urged him;
31: 6 and his armor-bearer and all his men died t on
2Sa 2:16 in his opponent's side; so they fell down t.
2:30 and when he had gathered all the people t,
8:11 t with the silver and gold that he dedicated
10:15 they gathered themselves t.
10:17 When it was told David, he gathered all Israel t,
12:19 David saw that his servants were whispering t,
12:28 Now, then, gather the rest of the people t,
12:29 So David gathered all the people t and went
20: 4 "Call the men of Judah t to me within three days,
21: 9 The seven of them perished t.
21:15 and David went down t with his servants.
23:11 The Philistines gathered t at Lehi,
1Ki 3:18 also gave birth. We were t;
9:27 t with the servants of Solomon.
10:26 Solomon gathered t chariots and horses;
20: 1 King Ben-hadad of Aram gathered all his army t;
22: 6 Then the king of Israel gathered the prophets t,
2Ki 3:23 kings must have fought t, and killed one another.
8: 6 t with all the revenue of the fields from the day
1Ch 10: 6 he and his three sons and all his house died t.
11: 1 all Israel gathered t to David at Hebron and said,
11:10 t with all Israel, to make him king,
13: 2 that they may come t to us.
15: 4 Then David gathered t the descendants of Aaron
18:11 t with the silver and gold that he had carried off
19:17 David was informed, he gathered all Israel t,
22: 2 to gather t the aliens who were residing in
28: 1 t with the palace officials, the mighty warriors,
2Ch 1:14 Solomon gathered t chariots and horses;
3:11 wings of the cherubim t extended twenty cubits:
8:18 t with the servants of Solomon,
18: 5 Then the king of Israel gathered the prophets t,
21: 3 t with fortified cities in Judah;
28:24 Ahaz gathered t the utensils of the house of God,
30:13 Many people came t in Jerusalem to keep
30:23 the whole assembly agreed t to keep the festival
32: 6 and gathered them t to him in the square at
34:29 the king sent word and gathered t all the elders
Ezr 2:64 t was forty-two thousand three hundred sixty,
3: 1 the people gathered t in Jerusalem.
3: 8 t with the rest of their people,
3: 9 t took charge of the workers in the house of God.
Ne 4: 6 and all the wall was joined t to half its height;
4: 8 and all plotted t to come and fight
6: 2 and let us meet t in one of the villages in the plain
6: 7 So come, therefore, and let us confer t."
6:10 he said, "Let us meet t in the house of God,
7:66 t was forty-two thousand three hundred sixty,
8: 1 all the people gathered t into the square before
8:13 came t to the scribe Ezra in order to study
12:28 The companies of the singers gathered t from
13:11 I gathered them t and set them in their stations.
Est 2:19 When the virgins were being gathered t,
5:12 also I am invited by her, t with the king.
Job 2:11 They met t to go and console and comfort him.
3:18 There the prisoners are at ease t;
9:32 that we should come to trial t.
10:11 and knit me t with bones and sinews.
16: 4 I could join words t against you,
16:10 they mass themselves t against me.
17:16 Shall we descend t into the dust?"
19:12 His troops come on t; they have thrown
30: 7 under the nettles they huddle t.
31:38 and its furrows have wept t;
34:15 all flesh would perish t, and all mortals return
38: 7 when the morning stars sang t and all
38:38 the dust runs into a mass and the clods cling t?
Job 40:13 Hide them all in the dust t;
40:17 the sinews of its thighs are knit t.
41:23 The folds of its flesh cling t;
Ps 2: 2 and the rulers take counsel t,
31:13 as they scheme t against me,
34: 3 and let us exalt his name t.
35:15 they gathered t against me;
41: 7 All who hate me whisper t about me;
48: 4 Then the kings assembled, they came on t.
49: 2 both low and high, rich and poor t.
49:10 and dolt perish t and leave their wealth to others.
62: 9 they are t lighter than a breath.
65:13 they shout and sing t for joy.
71:10 and those who watch for my life consult t.
83: 3 they consult t against those you protect.
94:21 They band t against the life of the righteous,
98: 8 let the hills sing t for joy
102:22 when peoples gather t, and kingdoms, to worship
122: 3 Jerusalem—built as a city that is bound firmly t.
133: 1 and pleasant it is when kindred live t in unity!
139:13 you knit me t in my mother's womb.
148:12 Young men and women alike, old and young t!
Ecc 3: 5 and a time to gather stones t;
4:11 Again, if two lie t, they keep warm;
Isa 1:28 But rebels and sinners shall be destroyed t,
1:31 they and their work shall burn t,
8: 9 Band t, you peoples, and be dismayed;
8:10 Take counsel t, but it shall be brought to naught;
9:21 and t they were against Judah.
11: 6 the calf and the lion and the fatling t,
11: 7 their young shall lie down t;
11:14 t they shall plunder the people of the east.
13: 4 an uproar of kingdoms, of nations gathering t!
22: 3 Your rulers have all fled t;
24: 4 the heavens languish t with the earth.
24:22 They will be gathered t like prisoners in a pit;
31: 3 and they will all perish t.
40: 5 and all people shall see it t,
41: 1 let us t draw near for judgment.
41:19 in the desert the cypress, the plane and the pine t,
43: 9 Let all the nations gather t,
45:16 the makers of idols go in confusion t.
45:20 Assemble yourselves and come t, draw near,
45:21 and present your case; let them take counsel t!
46: 2 They stoop, they bow down t;
50: 8 Let us stand up t.
52: 8 lift up their voices, t they sing for joy;
52: 9 Break forth t into singing, you ruins of Jerusalem;
60: 4 they all gather t, they come to you;
65: 7 and their ancestors' iniquities t, says the LORD;
65:25 The wolf and the lamb shall feed t,
66:17 vermin, and rodents, shall come to an end t,
Jer 3:18 and t they shall come from the land of the north to
4: 5 "Gather t, and let us go into the fortified cities!"
6:12 be turned over to others, their fields and wives t;
6:21 parents and children t, neighbor and friend shall
8:14 Gather t, let us go into the fortified cities
13:14 parents and children t, says the LORD.
21: 4 and I will bring them t into the center of this city.
24: 1 t with the officials of Judah, the artisans,
31: 8 t; a great company, they shall return here.
31:24 And Judah and all its towns shall live there t,
41: 1 As they ate bread t there at Mizpah,
46:12 against warrior; both have fallen t.
46:21 they too have turned and fled t,
49:14 "Gather yourselves t and come against her,
50: 4 they and the people of Judah t;
51:38 Like lions they shall roar t;
52:15 t with the rest of the artisans.
La 1:14 by his hand they were fastened t;
2: 8 to lament; they languish t.
Eze 21:12 they are thrown to the sword, t with my people.
22:13 I strike my hands t at the dishonest gain
26: 7 king of kings, t with horses, chariots, cavalry,
33:30 your people who talk t about you by the walls,
37: 7 a rattling, and the bones came t, bone to its bone.
37:17 and join them t into one stick,
41:15 t with its galleries on either side,
46: 5 t with a hin of oil to each ephah.
46: 7 t with a hin of oil to each ephah.
46:11 t with a hin of oil to an ephah.
48:20 the holy portion t with the property of the city.
Da 2:43 but they will not hold t,
3:27 and the king's counselors gathered t and saw that
5: 6 His limbs gave way, and his knees knocked t.
8:12 over to it t with the regular burnt offering;
Hos 1:11 and the people of Israel shall be gathered t,
4: 3 t with the wild animals and the birds of the air,
6: 9 so the priests are banded t;
Am 1:15 he and his officials t, says the LORD.
3: 3 Do two walk t unless they have made an
Mic 2:12 I will set them t like sheep in a fold,
Zep 2: 1 Gather t, gather, O shameless nation,
Zec 10: 5 T they shall be like warriors in battle,
12: 3 all the nations of the earth shall come t against it.
Mt 1:18 to Joseph, but before they lived t, she was found
2: 4 and calling t all the chief priests and scribes of
13:30 Let both of them grow t until the harvest;
18:25 t with his wife and children
19: 6 what God has joined t, let no one separate."
22:34 that he had silenced the Sadducees, they gathered t,
22:41 Now while the Pharisees were gathered t,
23:37 How often have I desired to gather your children t
24:41 Two women will be grinding meal t;
27: 1 the elders of the people conferred t against Jesus
27: 7 After conferring t, they used them to buy
Mk 3:20 and the crowd came t again,

Mk 9:25 When Jesus saw that a crowd came running **t**,
10: 9 what God has joined **t**, let no one separate."
15:16 and they called **t** the whole cohort.
Lk 6:38 A good measure, pressed down, shaken **t**,
9: 1 the twelve **t** and gave them power and authority
13:34 How often have I desired to gather your children **t**
15: 6 he calls **t** his friends and neighbors,
15: 9 she calls **t** her friends and neighbors, saying,
17:35 There will be two women grinding meal **t**;
22:55 in the middle of the courtyard and sat down **t**,
22:66 gathered **t**, and they brought him to their council.
23:13 Pilate then called **t** the chief priests, the leaders,
23:18 they all shouted out **t**, "Away with this fellow!
24:33 the eleven and their companions gathered **t**.
Jn 4:36 so that sower and reaper may rejoice **t**.
18: 3 of soldiers **t** with police from the chief priests and
18:20 where all the Jews come **t**.
20: 4 The two were running **t**, but the other disciple
21: 2 Gathered there **t** were Simon Peter,
Ac 1: 6 So when they had come **t**, they asked him, "Lord,
1:14 **t** with certain women, including Mary the mother
1:15 up among the believers (**t** the crowd numbered
2: 1 they were all **t** in one place.
2:44 All who believed were **t** and had all things
2:46 as they spent much time **t** in the temple,
3:11 all the people ran **t** to them in
4:24 they raised their voices **t** to God and said,
4:26 and the rulers have gathered **t** against the Lord
4:27 gathered **t** against your holy servant Jesus,
4:31 place in which they were gathered **t** was shaken;
5: 9 that you have agreed **t** to put the Spirit of the Lord
5:12 And they were all **t** in Solomon's Portico.
5:21 they called **t** the council and the whole body of
6: 2 And the twelve called **t** the whole community of
6: 5 **t** with Philip, Prochorus, Nicanor, Timon,
7:57 and with a loud shout all rushed **t** against him.
10:24 and had called **t** his relatives and close friends.
14:27 the church **t** and related all that God had done
15: 6 and the elders met **t** to consider this matter.
15:30 When they gathered the congregation **t**,
18: 3 and they worked **t**—by trade they were tentmakers.
18: 8 became a believer in the Lord, **t** with all his
19:25 These he gathered **t**, with the workers of
19:29 and people rushed **t** to the theater,
19:32 most of them did not know why they had come **t**.
21:30 all the city was aroused, and the people rushed **t**.
28:17 Three days later he called **t** the local leaders of
Ro 3:12 **t** they have become worthless;
8:28 We know that all things work **t** for good
15: 6 so that **t** you may with one voice glorify the God
1Co 1: 2 **t** with all those who in every place call on
3: 9 For we are God's servants, working **t**;
7: 5 and then come **t** again, so that Satan may
11:17 because when you come **t** it is not for the better
11:18 For, to begin with, when you come **t** as a church,
11:20 When you come **t**, it is not really to eat
11:33 my brothers and sisters, when you come **t** to eat,
11:34 eat at home, so that when you come **t**,
12:26 If one member suffers, all suffer **t** with it;
12:26 if one member is honored, all rejoice **t** with it.
14:23 whole church comes **t** and all speak in tongues,
14:26 When you come **t**, each one has a hymn, a lesson,
16:19 **t** with the church in their house,
2Co 6: 1 As we work **t** with him,
7: 3 you are in our hearts, to die **t** and to live **t**.
Eph 2: 5 made us alive **t** with Christ—
2:21 In him the whole structure is joined **t** and grows
2:22 also are built **t** spiritually into a dwelling place
4:16 joined and knit **t** by every ligament
4:31 and wrath and anger and wrangling and slander, **t**
Php 4: 3 **t** with Clement and the rest of my co-workers,
Col 1:17 and in him all things hold **t**.
2:13 God made you alive **t** with him,
2:19 nourished and held **t** by its ligaments and sinews,
3:14 which binds everything **t** in perfect harmony.
1Th 4:17 the clouds **t** with them to meet the Lord in the air;
2Th 2: 1 of our Lord Jesus Christ and our being gathered **t**
Heb 10:25 not neglecting to meet **t**, as is the habit of some,
1Pe 3: 7 show consideration for your wives in your life **t**,
5:13 Your sister church in Babylon, chosen **t** with you,
3Jn 1:14 and we will talk **t** face to face.
Rev 17:12 to receive authority as kings for one hour, **t** with
Tob 2: 2 and he shall eat **t** with me.
6: 6 the fish the young man gathered **t** the gall, heart,
6: 6 The two continued on their way **t** until they were
8: 7 and I may find mercy and that we may grow old **t**."
8:13 and she went in and found them sound asleep **t**.
10:12 May we all prosper **t** all the days of our lives."
11: 4 As they went on **t** Raphael said to him,
13:13 be gathered **t** and will praise the Lord of the ages.
14: 7 and are truly mindful of God will be gathered **t**;
Jdt 2:15 **t** with twelve thousand archers on horseback,
4: 3 all the people of Judea had just now gathered **t**,
5: 2 In great anger he called **t** all the princes of Moab
6:16 They called **t** all the elders of the town,
7:17 **t** with five thousand Assyrians,
13:10 Then the two of them went out **t**,
13:13 They all ran **t**, both small and great,
AdE 3:15 And while the king and Haman caroused **t**,
9:18 came **t** also on the fourteenth, but did not rest.
16:13 **t** with their whole nation.
Wis 1: 7 that which holds all things **t** knows what is said,
5:12 the air, thus divided, comes **t** at once,
14:10 for what was done will be punished **t** with
18: 5 and you destroyed them all **t** by a mighty flood.
18:12 and they all **t**, by the one form
Sir 22: 9 a fool is like one who glues potsherds **t**,
Sir 25: 8 and the one who does not plow with ox and ass **t**.
43:26 and by his word all things hold **t**.
50:17 Then all the people **t** quickly fell to the ground
LtJ 6:48 the priests consult **t** as to where they can hide
Sus 1:14 Then **t** they arranged for a time
Bel 1:27 fat, and hair, and boiled them **t** and made cakes,
1Mc 3:10 now gathered **t** Gentiles and a large force
3:46 Then they gathered **t** and went to Mizpah,
5: 9 Now the Gentiles in Gilead gathered **t** against
5:10 Gentiles around us have gathered **t** to destroy us.
5:15 had gathered **t** against them "to annihilate us."
5:44 **t** with all who were in them.
5:45 Then Judas gathered **t** all the Israelites in Gilead,
6:20 They gathered **t** and besieged the citadel in
10:61 renegades, gathered **t** against him to accuse him;
12:37 So they gathered **t** to rebuild the city;
13: 2 and gathering the people **t**
13: 6 for all the nations have gathered **t** out of hatred
14: 9 they all talked **t** of good things,
2Mc 1:14 Antiochus came to the place **t** with his Friends,
1:27 Gather **t** our scattered people,
2: 7 until God gathers his people **t** again
3:19 of the young women who were kept indoors ran **t**
6:11 were betrayed to Philip and were all burned **t**,
8:16 But Maccabeus gathered his forces **t**,
11: 7 Then they eagerly rushed off **t**.
11: 9 And **t** they all praised the merciful God,
15:31 and had called his compatriots **t** and stationed
1Es 5:56 **t** with their kindred and the levitical priests
7:10 after the priests and the Levites were purified **t**.
7:11 but the Levites were all purified **t**,
8:14 **t** with what is given by the nation for the temple
9:36 and they put them away **t** with their children.
9:55 which they had been taught. And they came **t**.
3Mc 1:19 in a disorderly rush flocked **t** in the city.
1:20 and without a backward look they crowded **t** at
1:27 they turned, **t** with our people,
3:25 **t** with their wives and children,
3:27 the most hateful torments, **t** with their families.
4: 4 all **t**, by the generals in the several cities,
4: 6 all **t** raising a lament instead of a wedding song,
5: 3 **t** with those of his Friends and of the army
6: 4 you destroyed **t** with his arrogant army
6:39 and rescued them all **t** and unharmed.
7: 3 to gather **t** the Jews of the kingdom in a body and
2Es 5: 6 and the birds shall fly away **t**;
6: 3 the innumerable hosts of angels were gathered **t**,
6:20 and all shall see my judgment **t**.
6:42 the waters to be gathered **t** in a seventh part of
6:47 where the water had been gathered **t**,
6:50 where the water had been gathered **t** could
11:28 between themselves to reign **t**;
12:40 they all gathered **t**, from the least to the greatest,
13: 5 of people were gathered **t** from the four winds
13: 8 and saw that all who had gathered **t** against him,
13:11 All these were mingled **t**,
13:34 and an innumerable multitude shall be gathered **t**,
13:47 you saw the multitude gathered **t** in peace.
13:49 the multitude of the nations that are gathered **t**,
14:27 and I gathered all the people **t**, and said,
15:20 See how I am calling **t** all the kings of the earth
4Mc 3: 7 the Philistines all day long, and **t** with the soldiers
4: 9 While the priests **t** with women
8:29 all with one voice **t**, as from one mind, said:
13:13 of them and all of them **t** looking at one another,
15:12 and all of them **t** the mother urged on to death
16:15 For when you and your sons were arrested **t**,
18:23 with their victorious mother are gathered **t** into

TOHU (1)

1Sa 1: 1 of Jeroham son of Elihu son of **T** son of Zuph,

TOI (3) [=TOU]

2Sa 8: 9 When King **T** of Hamath heard
8:10 **T** sent his son Joram to King David,
8:10 Now Hadadezer had often been at war with **T**.

TOIL[‡] (58) [TOILED, TOILING, TOILS, TOILSOME]

Ge 3:17 in **t** you shall eat of it all the days of your life;
5:29 from our work and from the **t** of our hands."
Dt 26: 7 our **t**, and our oppression.
Jos 7: 3 do not make the whole people **t** up there."
Job 20:18 They will give back the fruit of their **t**,
24: 5 Like wild asses in the desert they go out to their **t**,
Ps 90:10 even then their span is only **t** and trouble;
109:11 may strangers plunder the fruits of his **t**.
127: 2 eating the bread of anxious **t**;
Pr 14:23 In all **t** there is profit,
Ecc 1: 3 gain from all the **t** at which they **t** under the sun?
2:10 for my heart found pleasure in all my **t**, and this
was my reward for all my **t**.
2:11 that my hands had done and the **t** I had spent
2:18 I hated all my **t** in which I had toiled under
2:20 to despair concerning all the **t** of my labors under
2:21 to be enjoyed by another who did not **t** for it.
2:22 get from all the **t** and strain with which they **t**
2:24 and find enjoyment in their **t**.
3: 9 What gain have the workers from their **t**?
3:13 and drink and take pleasure in all their **t**.
4: 4 Then I saw that all **t** and all skill in work come
4: 6 a handful with quiet than two handfuls with **t**,
4: 8 yet there is no end to all their **t**,
4: 9 because they have a good reward for their **t**.
5:15 they shall take nothing for their **t**,
Ecc 5:18 to eat and drink and find enjoyment in all the **t**
5:19 to accept their lot and find enjoyment in their **t**—
6: 7 All human **t** is for the mouth,
8:15 with them in their **t** through the days of life
8:17 However much they may **t** in seeking,
9: 9 and in your **t** at which you **t** under the sun.
10:15 The **t** of fools wears them out,
Jer 20:18 Why did I come forth from the womb to see **t**
Hag 2:17 the products of your **t** with blight and mildew
Mt 6:28 how they grow; they neither **t** nor spin,
Lk 12:27 how they grow: they neither **t** nor spin;
2Co 11:27 in **t** and hardship, through many a sleepless night,
Col 1:29 For this I **t** and struggle with all the energy
1Th 2: 9 You remember our labor and **t**,
2Th 3: 8 but with **t** and labor we worked night and day,
1Ti 4:10 For to this end we **t** and struggle,
Rev 2: 2 your **t** and your patient endurance.
Wis 10:10 and increased the fruit of his **t**.
15: 4 nor the fruitless **t** of painters,
15: 8 With misspent **t**, these workers form a futile god
16:20 without their **t** you supplied them from heaven
Sir 6:19 For when you cultivate her you will **t** but little,
14:15 and what you acquired by **t** to be divided by lot?
28:15 and deprived them of the fruit of their **t**.
2Mc 2:26 For us who have undertaken the **t** of abbreviating,
2:27 of many we will gladly endure the uncomfortable **t**,
1Es 4:22 "Do you not labor and **t**,
2Es 2:12 and they shall neither **t** nor become weary.
7:96 and **t** from which they have been delivered,

TOILED (4) [TOIL]

Ecc 2:18 I hated all my toil in which I had **t** under the sun,
2:19 for which I **t** and used my wisdom under the sun.
2:21 because sometimes one who has **t** with wisdom
Wis 17:17 or shepherds or workers who **t** in the wilderness,

TOILING (2) [TOIL]

Ecc 4: 8 "For whom am I **t**," they ask,
5:16 and what gain do they have from **t** for the wind?

TOILS (5) [TOIL]

Pr 5:22 and they are caught in the **t** of their sin.
Ecc 5:18 and find enjoyment in all the toil with which one **t**
1Co 16:16 and of everyone who works and **t** with them.
Sir 31: 3 The rich person **t** to amass a fortune,
31: 4 The poor person **t** to make a meager living,

TOILSOME (1) [TOIL]

2Es 7:12 of this world were made narrow and sorrowful and **t**;

TOKEN (5) [TOKENS]

Lev 2: 2 the priest shall turn this **t** portion into smoke on
2: 9 from the grain offering its **t** portion and turn this
2:16 the priest shall turn a **t** portion of it into smoke—
24: 7 to be a **t** offering for the bread,
1Sa 17:18 and bring some **t** from them."

TOKENS (1) [TOKEN]

2Mc 12:40 of each one of the dead they found sacred **t** of

TOKHATH (1)

2Ch 34:22 the wife of Shallum son of **T** son of Hasrah,

TOLA (6) [TOLAITES]

Ge 46:13 **T**, Puvah, Jashub, and Shimron.
Nu 26:23 of **T**, the clan of the Tolaites;
Jdg 10: 1 After Abimelech, **T** son of Puah son of Dodo,
1Ch 7: 1 **T**, Puah, Jashub, and Shimron, four.
7: 2 The sons of **T**: Uzzi, Rephaiah,
7: 2 namely of **T**, mighty warriors of their generations,

TOLAD (1)

1Ch 4:29 Bilhah, Ezem, **T**,

TOLAITES (1) [TOLA]

Nu 26:23 of Tola, the clan of the **T**;

TOLBANES See Index to Footnotes

TOLD[‡] (385) [TELL]

Ge 3:11 He said, "Who **t** you that you were naked?
9:22 and **t** his two brothers outside.
12: 4 So Abram went, as the LORD had **t** him;
14:13 Then one who had escaped came and **t** Abram
20: 8 called all his servants and **t** them all these things;
22:20 Now after these things it was **t** Abraham,
24:28 and **t** her mother's household about these things.
24:33 he said, "I will not eat until I have **t** my errand."
24:66 the servant **t** Isaac all the things that he had done.
26:32 That same day Isaac's servants came and **t** him
27:19 I have done as you **t** me;
27:42 words of her elder son Esau were **t** to Rebekah;
29:12 Jacob **t** Rachel that he was her father's kinsman,
29:12 and she ran and **t** her father.
29:13 Jacob **t** Laban all these things,
31:22 On the third day Laban was **t** that Jacob had fled.
37: 5 and when he **t** it to his brothers,
37: 9 He had another dream, and **t** it to his brothers,
37:10 But when he **t** it to his father and to his brothers,
38:13 When Tamar was **t**, "Your father-in-law is going

Ge 38:24 About three months later Judah was **t**,
39:17 and she **t** him the same story, saying,
40: 9 So the chief cupbearer **t** his dream to Joseph,
41: 8 Pharaoh **t** them his dreams,
41:12 When we **t** him, he interpreted our dreams to us,
41:24 But when I **t** it to the magicians,
41:28 It is as I **t** Pharaoh;
42:29 they **t** him all that had happened to them, saying,
43: 7 What we **t** him was in answer to these questions.
44: 2 And he did as Joseph **t** him.
44:24 to your servant my father we **t** him the words
45:26 And they **t** him, "Joseph is still alive!
45:27 But when they **t** him all the words of Joseph
47: 1 So Joseph went and **t** Pharaoh,
48: 1 After this Joseph was **t**, "Your father is ill."
48: 2 When Jacob was **t**, "Your son Joseph has come
Ex 4:28 Moses **t** Aaron all the words of the LORD
5:19 that they were in trouble when they were **t**,
6: 9 Moses **t** this to the Israelites;
12:35 The Israelites had done as Moses **t** them;
14: 5 the king of Egypt was **t** that the people had fled,
14:12 Is this not the very thing we **t** you in Egypt,
16:22 the leaders of the congregation came and **t** Moses,
17:10 So Joshua did as Moses **t** him,
18: 8 Then Moses **t** his father-in-law all that the LORD
19: 9 When Moses had **t** the words of the people to
19:25 So Moses went down to the people and **t** them.
24: 3 Moses came and **t** the people all the words of
34:34 and **t** the Israelites what he had been commanded,
Nu 9: 4 So Moses **t** the Israelites that they should keep
11:24 So Moses went out and **t** the people the words of
11:27 And a young man ran and **t** Moses,
13:27 And they **t** him, "We came to the land
14:39 When Moses **t** these words to all the Israelites,
29:40 So Moses **t** the Israelites everything just as
Dt 1:43 Although I **t** you, you would not listen.
2: 1 as the LORD had **t** me and skirted Mount Seir
31: 2 and the LORD has **t** me,
Jos 2: 2 The king of Jericho was **t**,
2:23 and **t** him all that had happened to them.
4: 8 the tribes of the Israelites, as the LORD **t** Joshua,
9:24 "Because it was **t** to your servants for a certainty
10:17 it was **t** Joshua, "The five kings have been found,
Jdg 4:12 When Sisera was **t** that Barak son
6:27 and did as the LORD had **t** him;
6:29 After searching and inquiring, they were **t**,
9: 7 When it was **t** to Jotham,
9:42 into the fields. When Abimelech was **t**,
9:47 Abimelech was **t** that all the lords of the Tower
13: 6 Then the woman came and **t** her husband,
13:10 So the woman ran quickly and **t** her husband,
14: 2 Then he came up, and **t** his father and mother,
14:16 "Look, I have not **t** my father or my mother.
14:17 she nagged him, on the seventh day he **t** her.
16: 2 The Gazites were **t**, "Samson has come here."
16:10 "You have mocked me and **t** me lies;
16:13 "Until now you have mocked me and **t** me lies;
16:15 now and have not **t** me what makes your strength
16:17 So he **t** her his whole secret, and said to her,
16:18 Delilah realized that he had **t** her his whole secret,
16:18 for he has **t** his whole secret to me."
Ru 2:11 the death of your husband has been fully **t** me,
2:19 So she **t** her mother-in-law
3:16 Then she **t** her all that the man had done for her,
1Sa 3:13 For I have **t** him that I am about
3:17 Eli said, "What was it that he **t** you?
3:17 if you hide anything from me of all that he **t** you."
3:18 So Samuel **t** him everything and hid nothing
4:13 When the man came into the city and **t** the news,
4:14 Then the man came quickly and **t** Eli.
9:17 When Samuel saw Saul, the LORD **t** him,
10:16 "He **t** us that the donkeys had been found."
10:25 Samuel **t** the people the rights and duties of
11: 5 So they **t** him the message from the inhabitants
11: 9 messengers came and **t** the inhabitants of Jabesh,
14:43 Jonathan **t** him, "I tasted a little honey with the tip
15:12 and Samuel was **t**, "Saul went to Carmel,
18:20 Saul was **t**, and the thing pleased him.
18:24 servants of Saul **t** him, "This is what David said."
18:26 When his servants **t** David these words,
19: 2 Jonathan **t** David, "My father Saul is trying
19:11 David's wife Michal **t** him,
19:18 and **t** him all that Saul had done to him.
19:19 Saul was **t**, "David is at Naioth in Ramah."
19:21 When Saul was **t**, he sent other messengers,
22:21 Abiathar **t** David that Saul had killed the priests
23: 1 Now they **t** David, "The Philistines are fighting
23: 7 Now it was **t** Saul that David had come to Keilah.
23:13 Saul was **t** that David had escaped from Keilah,
23:22 for I am **t** that he is very cunning.
23:25 When David was **t**, he went down to the rock
24: 1 he was **t**, "David is in the wilderness of En-gedi."
25:12 and came back and **t** him all this.
25:14 But one of the young men **t** Abigail, Nabal's wife,
25:36 so she **t** him nothing at all until the morning light.
25:37 his wife **t** him these things,
27: 4 When Saul was **t** that David had fled to Gath,
2Sa 2: 4 When they **t** David, "It was the people
3:23 it was **t** Joab, "Abner son of Ner came to the king,
4:10 when the one who **t** me,
6:12 It was **t** King David, "The LORD has blessed
10: 5 When David was **t**, he sent to meet them,
10:17 When it was **t** David, he gathered all Israel
11: 5 and she sent and **t** David, "I am pregnant."
11:10 When they **t** David, "Uriah did not go down
11:18 Then Joab sent and **t** David all the news about
11:22 and came and **t** David all that Joab had sent him
2Sa 14:33 Then Joab went to the king and **t** him;
15:31 David was **t** that Ahithophel was among
17:18 But a boy saw them, and **t** Absalom;
17:21 and went and **t** King David.
18:10 A man saw it, and **t** Joab,
18:11 Joab said to the man who **t** him, "What,
18:25 The sentinel shouted and **t** the king.
19: 1 It was **t** Joab, "The king is weeping and mourning
19: 8 The troops were all **t**, "See,
21:11 When David was **t** what Rizpah daughter of Aiah,
24:13 So Gad came to David and **t** him;
1Ki 1:23 The king was **t**, "Here is the prophet Nathan."
2:29 When it was **t** King Solomon,
2:39 When it was **t** Shimei, "Your slaves are in Gath,"
2:41 When Solomon was **t** that Shimei had gone
10: 2 she **t** him all that was on her mind.
10: 7 Not even half had been **t** me;
13:11 One of his sons came and **t** him all that the man
13:11 also that he had spoken to the king, they **t** to their
13:25 and **t** it in the town where the old prophet lived.
18:13 not been **t** my lord what I did when Jezebel killed
18:16 So Obadiah went to meet Ahab, and **t** him;
19: 1 Ahab **t** Jezebel all that Elijah had done,
2Ki 1: 7 to meet you and **t** you these things?"
4: 7 She came and **t** the man of God, and he said,
4:27 LORD has hidden it from me and has not **t** me."
4:31 He came back to meet him and **t** him,
5: 4 in and **t** his lord just what the girl from the land
6:13 He was **t**, "He is in Dothan."
7:10 and **t** them, "We went to the Aramean camp,
7:15 So the messengers returned, and **t** the king.
8: 6 When the king questioned the woman, she **t** him.
8: 7 When it was **t** him, "The man
8:14 "He **t** me that you would certainly recover."
9:36 When they came back and **t** him, he said,
10: 8 When the messenger came and **t** him,
17:26 So the king of Assyria was **t**,
18:37 with their clothes torn and **t** him the words of
23:17 The people of the city **t** him,
1Ch 19: 5 When David was **t** about the men,
2Ch 9: 6 of the greatness of your wisdom had been **t** to me;
20: 2 Messengers came and **t** Jehoshaphat,
Ezr 2:63 the governor **t** them that they were not to partake
8:22 since we had **t** the king that the hand
Ne 2:12 I **t** no one what my God had put into my heart
2:16 I had not yet **t** the Jews, the priests, the nobles,
2:18 I **t** them that the hand of my God had been gracious
7:65 the governor **t** them that they were not to partake
8: 1 They **t** the scribe Ezra to bring the book of the law
9:15 and you **t** them to go in to possess the land
9:23 into the land that you had **t** their ancestors to enter
Est 2:22 and he **t** it to Queen Esther, and Esther **t** the king
3: 4 and he would not listen to them, they **t** Haman,
3: 4 for he had **t** them that he was a Jew.
3: 6 So, having been **t** who Mordecai's people were,
4: 4 Esther's maids and her eunuchs came and **t** her,
4: 7 and Mordecai **t** him all that had happened to him,
4: 9 and **t** Esther what Mordecai had said.
4:12 When they **t** Mordecai what Esther had said,
4:13 Mordecai **t** them to reply to Esther,
6: 2 how Mordecai had **t** about Bigthana and Teresh,
6: 5 So the king's servants **t** him, "Haman is there,
6:13 When Haman **t** his wife Zeresh
8: 1 for Esther had **t** what he was to her.
Job 15:18 what sages have **t**, and their ancestors have
37:20 Should he be **t** that I want to speak?
42: 9 and did what the LORD had **t** them;
Ps 22:30 future generations will be **t** about the Lord,
40: 9 I have **t** the glad news of deliverance in
44: 1 O God, our ancestors have **t** us,
54: T *the Ziphites went and* **t** *Saul, "David is in hiding*
78: 3 that our ancestors have **t** us.
119:26 When I **t** of my ways, you answered me;
Pr 25: 7 for it is better to be **t**,
Isa 21: 2 A stern vision is **t** to me;
36:22 and **t** him the words of the Rabshakeh.
40:21 Has it not been **t** you from the beginning?
44: 8 have I not **t** you from of old and declared it?
45:21 Who **t** this long ago? Who declared it of old?
52:15 for that which had not been **t** them they shall see,
Jer 36:13 Micaiah **t** them all the words that he had heard,
42:21 So I have **t** you today,
Eze 11:25 And I **t** the exiles all the things that
Da 2:18 and **t** them to seek mercy from the God of heaven
4: 7 and the diviners came in, and I **t** them the dream,
4: 8 and I **t** him the dream:
7: 5 in its mouth among its teeth and was **t**,
8:26 and the mornings that has been **t** is true.
Jnh 1:10 because he had **t** them so.
Mic 6: 8 He has **t** you, O mortal, what is good;
Hab 1: 5 that you would not believe if you were **t**.
Mt 2: 5 They **t** him, "In Bethlehem of Judea;
8:33 they **t** the whole story about what had happened
12:47 Someone **t** him, "Look, your mother
12:48 But to the one who had **t** him this, Jesus replied,
13: 3 And he **t** them many things in parables, saying:
13:33 He **t** them another parable:
13:34 Jesus **t** the crowds all these things in parables;
13:34 without a parable he **t** them nothing.
14:12 then they went and **t** Jesus.
16:12 that he had not **t** them to beware of the yeast
16:24 Then Jesus **t** his disciples,
24:25 Take note, I have **t** you beforehand.
26:13 what she has done will be **t** in remembrance
28:11 into the city and **t** the chief priests everything
28:15 this story is still **t** among the Jews to this day.
Mk 1:30 and they **t** him about her at once.
Mk 3: 9 He **t** his disciples to have a boat ready for him
5:14 The swineherds ran off and **t** it in the city and in
5:33 fell down before him, and **t** him the whole truth.
5:43 and **t** them to give her something to eat.
6:30 and **t** him all that they had done and taught.
11: 6 They **t** them what Jesus had said;
12:12 When they realized that he had **t** this parable
13:23 But be alert; I have already **t** you everything.
14: 9 what she has done will be **t** in remembrance
14:16 and found everything as he had **t** them;
16: 7 there you will see him, just as he **t** you."
16:10 ⟦She went out and **t** those who had been with him⟧
16:13 ⟦And they went back and **t** the rest,⟧
16: S ⟦that had been commanded them they **t** briefly⟧
Lk 2:17 they made known what had been **t** them
2:18 were amazed at what the shepherds **t** them.
2:20 they had seen and heard, as it had been **t** them.
5:36 He also **t** them a parable: "No one tears a piece
6:39 He also **t** them a parable: "Can a blind person
8:20 And he was **t**, "Your mother
8:34 they ran off and **t** it in the city and in the country.
8:36 Those who had seen it **t** them how
9:10 the apostles **t** Jesus all they had done.
9:36 and in those days **t** no one any of
12:16 Then he **t** them a parable: "The land of a rich man
13: 1 that very time there were some present who **t** him
13: 6 Then he **t** this parable: "A man had a fig tree
14: 7 the guests chose the places of honor, he **t** them
15: 3 So he **t** them this parable:
18: 1 Then Jesus **t** them a parable about their need
18: 9 He also **t** this parable to some who trusted
18:37 They **t** him, "Jesus of Nazareth is passing by."
19:32 and found it as he had **t** them.
20:19 and chief priests realized that he had **t** this parable
21:29 Then he **t** them a parable:
22:13 they went and found everything as he had **t** them;
24: 6 Remember how he **t** you,
24: 9 they **t** all this to the eleven and to all the rest.
24:10 other women with them who **t** this to the apostles.
24:23 they came back and **t** us that they had indeed seen
24:35 Then they **t** what had happened on the road,
Jn 1:50 because I **t** you that I saw you under the fig tree?
2:16 He **t** those who were selling the doves,
3:12 If I have **t** you about earthly things and you do
4:29 a man who **t** me everything I have ever done!
4:39 "He **t** me everything I have ever done."
4:51 and **t** him that his child was alive.
5:15 The man went away and **t** the Jews
6:12 When they were satisfied, he **t** his disciples,
6:65 "For this reason I have **t** you
8:24 I **t** you that you would die in your sins,
8:40 a man who has **t** you the truth that I heard
9:27 He answered them, "I have **t** you already,
10:25 Jesus answered, "I have **t** you,
11:11 After saying this, he **t** them,
11:14 Then Jesus **t** them plainly, "Lazarus is dead.
11:28 and called her sister Mary, and **t** her privately,
11:46 to the Pharisees and **t** them what he had done.
12:22 Philip went and **t** Andrew; then Andrew and Philip went and **t** Jesus.
12:50 therefore, I speak just as the Father has **t** me."
14: 2 would I have **t** you that I go to prepare a place
14:29 And now I have **t** you this before it occurs,
16: 4 that I **t** you about them.
18: 8 Jesus answered, "I **t** you that I am he.
18:38 he went out to the Jews again and **t** them,
20:18 she **t** them that he had said these things to her.
20:25 other disciples **t** him, "We have seen the Lord."
Ac 9: 6 and you will be **t** what you are to do."
11:12 The Spirit **t** me to go with them and not to make
11:13 He **t** us how he had seen the angel standing
15:12 and listened to Barnabas and Paul as they **t** of all
21: 4 the Spirit they **t** Paul not to go on to Jerusalem.
21:21 They have been **t** about you that you teach all
21:24 that there is nothing in what they have been **t**
22:10 be **t** everything that has been assigned to you
23:16 and gained entrance to the barracks and **t** Paul.
25:16 I **t** them that it was not the custom of the Romans
27:25 in God that it will be exactly as I have been **t**.
Ro 9:12 not by works but by his call) she was **t**,
15:21 "Those who have never been **t** of him shall see,
2Co 7: 7 as he **t** us of your longing, your mourning,
12: 4 into Paradise and heard things that are not to be **t**,
Php 3:18 I have often **t** you of them,
1Th 3: 4 we **t** you beforehand that we were
3: 6 has **t** us also that you always remember us kindly
4: 6 just as we have already **t** you beforehand
2Th 2: 5 Do you not remember that I **t** you these things
Heb 9:19 For when every commandment had been **t** to all
11:18 of whom he had been **t**,
Rev 6:11 They were each given a white robe and **t** to rest
9: 4 They were **t** not to damage the grass of the earth
10: 9 to the angel and **t** him to give me the little scroll;
11: 1 a measuring rod like a staff, and I was **t**, "Come
Tob 2:14 and **t** her to return it to the owners.
7:13 Then he called her mother and **t** her
7:16 and made the bed in the room as he had **t** her,
Jdt 3: 5 The men came to Holofernes and **t** him all this.
6:17 He answered and **t** them what had taken place at
10:18 waiting until they **t** him about her.
10:22 When they **t** him of her,
11: 9 and he **t** them all he had said to you.
11:19 For this was **t** me to give me foreknowledge;
13: 3 Now Judith had **t** her maid to stand outside
14: 8 So Judith **t** him in the presence of the people all
15: 5 for they were **t** what had happened in the camp of
AdE 1:10 when the king was in good humor, he **t** Haman,

AdE 1:15 and **t** him what must be done to Queen Vashti for
3:4 Mordecai had **t** them that he was a Jew.
3:11 The king **t** Haman, "Keep the money,
4:4 the queen's maids and eunuchs came and **t** her,
4:7 So Mordecai **t** him what had happened and
4:8 and he **t** him to charge her to go in to the king
4:9 Hachratheus went in and **t** Esther all these things.
4:13 Mordecai **t** him to go back and say to her,
4:17 and did what Esther had **t** him to do.
5:11 And he **t** them about his riches and the honor that
6:2 how he had **t** the king about the two royal eunuchs
6:13 Haman **t** his wife Zosara
8:1 Esther had **t** the king that he was related to her.
Sus 1:18 They did as she **t** them:
1:27 And when the elders **t** their story,
1Mc 3:56 he **t** to go home again, according to the law.
5:25 and **t** them all that had happened to their kindred
8:2 He had been **t** of their wars and of the brave deeds
11:5 They also **t** the king what Jonathan had done,
11:40 to Imalkue what Demetrius had done and **t** of
14:21 The envoys who were sent to our people have **t** us
2Mc 3:7 he **t** him of the money
3:9 he **t** about the disclosure that had been made
8:12 he **t** his companions of the arrival of the army,
8:19 he **t** them of the occasions when help came
14:26 He **t** him that Nicanor was disloyal to
15:38 If it is well **t** and to the point,
1Es 1:3 He **t** the Levites, the temple servants of Israel,
1:33 that he had done before, and these that are now **t**,
4:61 and went to Babylon and **t** this to all his kindred.
5:40 And Nehemiah and Attharias **t** them not to share
8:45 I **t** them to go to Iddo,
9:39 they **t** Ezra the chief priest and reader to bring
2Es 5:50 Is our mother, of whom you have **t** me,
7:*101* the things of which you have been **t**,
10:43 and about who **t** you about the misfortune of her son—
10:51 Therefore I **t** you to remain in the field
10:53 Therefore I **t** you to go into the field
10:59 that night and the following one, as he had **t** me.
12:50 So the people went into the city, as I **t** them to do.
14:5 I **t** him many wondrous things,
4Mc 2:6 In fact, since the law has **t** us not to covet,
18:12 He **t** you of the zeal of Phinehas,

TOLERABLE (5) [TOLERATE]

Mt 10:15 be more **t** for the land of Sodom and Gomorrah
11:22 on the day of judgment it will be more **t** for Tyre
11:24 the day of judgment it will be more **t** for the land
Lk 10:12 on that day it will be more **t** for Sodom than for
10:14 But at the judgment it will be more **t** for Tyre

TOLERATE (9) [TOLERABLE]

Est 3:8 so that it is not appropriate for the king to **t** them.
Ps 101:5 A haughty look and an arrogant heart I will not **t**.
Mic 6:11 Can I **t** wicked scales and a bag
Rev 2:2 I know that you cannot **t** evildoers;
2:20 you **t** that woman Jezebel,
AdE 3:8 It is not expedient for the king to **t** them.
Sus 1:57 a daughter of Judah would not **t** your wickedness.
3Mc 1:22 not **t** the completion of his plans or the fulfillment
2Es 15:8 neither will I **t** their wicked practices.

TOLL (4)

Ezr 4:13 or **t**, and the royal revenue will be reduced.
4:20 to whom tribute, custom, and **t** were paid.
7:24 or **t** on any of the priests, the Levites, the singers,
Mt 17:25 From whom do kings of the earth take **t** or tribute?

TOMB (70) [TOMBS]

Ge 35:20 it is the pillar of Rachel's **t**,
50:5 In the **t** that I hewed out for myself in the land
Jdg 8:32 and was buried in the **t** of his father Joash
16:31 and Eshtaol in the **t** of his father Manoah.
1Sa 10:2 by Rachel's **t** in the territory of Benjamin
2Sa 2:32 up Asahel and buried him in the **t** of his father,
4:12 of Ishbaal they took and buried in the **t** of Abner
17:23 he died and was buried in the **t** of his father
21:14 in the **t** of his father Kish;
1Ki 13:22 your body shall not come to your ancestral **t**."
2Ki 9:28 in his **t** with his ancestors in the city of David.
21:26 He was buried in his **t** in the garden of Uzza;
23:16 he turned and looked up at the **t** of the man
23:17 the **t** of the man of God who came from Judah
23:30 and buried him in his own **t**.
2Ch 16:14 the **t** that he had hewn out for himself in the city
Job 21:32 a watch is kept over their **t**.
Isa 14:18 of the nations lie in glory, each in his own **t**;
22:16 that you have cut out a **t** here for yourself,
22:16 cutting a **t** on the height,
53:9 They made his grave with the wicked and his **t**
Jer 5:16 Their quiver is like an open **t**;
Mt 27:60 and laid it in his own new **t**,
27:60 a great stone to the door of the **t** and went away.
27:61 the other Mary were there, sitting opposite the **t**.
27:64 Therefore command the **t** to be made secure until
27:66 with the guard and made the **t** secure by sealing
28:1 and the other Mary went to see the **t**.
28:8 So they left the **t** quickly with fear and great joy,
Mk 6:29 they came and took his body, and laid it in a **t**.
15:46 laid it in a **t** that had been hewn out of the rock.
15:46 He then rolled a stone against the door of the **t**.
16:2 when the sun had risen, they went to the **t**.
16:3 the stone for us from the entrance to the **t**?"
16:5 As they entered the **t**, they saw a young man,
16:8 So they went out and fled from the **t**,
Lk 23:53 in a rock-hewn **t** where no one had ever been laid.
23:55 and they saw the **t** and how his body was laid.
24:1 at early dawn, they came to the **t**,
24:2 They found the stone rolled away from the **t**,
24:9 returning from the **t**, they told all this to the eleven
24:12 But Peter got up and ran to the **t**;
24:22 They were at the **t** early this morning,
24:24 to the **t** and found it just as the women had said;
Jn 11:17 that Lazarus had already been in the **t** four days.
11:31 because they thought that she was going to the **t**
11:38 Then Jesus, again greatly disturbed, came to the **t**.
12:17 of the **t** and raised him from the dead continued
19:41 a new **t** in which no one had ever been laid.
19:42 and the **t** was nearby, they laid Jesus there.
20:1 to the **t** and saw that the stone had been removed
from the **t**.
20:2 "They have taken the Lord out of the **t**,
20:3 the other disciple set out and went toward the **t**.
20:4 other disciple outran Peter and reached the **t** first.
20:6 following him, and went into the **t**.
20:8 Then the other disciple, who reached the **t** first,
20:11 But Mary stood weeping outside the **t**.
20:11 As she wept, she bent over to look into the **t**;
Ac 2:29 and his **t** is with us to this day.
7:16 the **t** that Abraham had bought for a sum of silver
13:29 down from the tree and laid him in a **t**.
Rev 11:9 and refuse to let them be placed in a **t**;
1Mc 2:70 and was buried in the **t** of his ancestors
9:19 and buried him in the **t** of their ancestors
13:27 And Simon built a monument over the **t**
13:30 This is the **t** that he built in Modein;
2Mc 5:10 he had no funeral of any sort and no place in the **t**
1Es 1:31 and was buried in the **t** of his ancestors.
4Mc 17:8 to inscribe on their **t** these words as a reminder to

TOMBS (22) [TOMB]

1Sa 13:6 and in holes and in rocks and in **t** and in cisterns.
2Ki 23:16 As Josiah turned, he saw the **t** there on the mount;
23:16 and he sent and took the bones out of the **t**,
2Ch 21:20 but not in the **t** of the kings.
24:25 but they did not bury him in the **t** of the kings.
28:27 but they did not bring him into the **t** of the kings
32:33 on the ascent to the **t** of the descendants of David;
35:24 and was buried in the **t** of his ancestors.
Isa 65:4 inside **t**, and spend the night in secret places;
Jer 8:1 of Jerusalem shall be brought out of their **t**;
Mt 8:28 two demoniacs coming out of the **t** met him.
23:27 For you are like whitewashed **t**,
23:29 For you build the **t** of the prophets and decorate
27:52 The **t** also were opened, and many bodies of
27:53 of the **t** and entered the holy city and appeared
Mk 5:2 a man out of the **t** with an unclean spirit met him.
5:3 He lived among the **t**;
5:5 Night and day among the **t** and on
Lk 8:27 and he did not live in a house but in the **t**.
11:47 the **t** of the prophets whom your ancestors killed.
11:48 for they killed them, and you build their **t**.
2Es 2:16 and bring them out from their **t**,

TOMORROW‡ (68)

Ex 8:10 And he said, "**T**." Moses said,
8:23 This sign shall appear **t**.' "
8:29 the LORD that the swarms of flies may depart **t**
9:5 "**T** the LORD will do this thing in the land."
9:18 **T** at this time I will cause the heaviest hail to fall
10:4 **t** I will bring locusts into your country.
16:23 '**T** is a day of solemn rest,
17:9 **T** I will stand on the top of the hill with the staff
19:10 to the people and consecrate them today and **t**.
32:5 "**T** shall be a festival to the LORD."
Nu 11:18 Consecrate yourselves for **t**,
14:25 turn **t** and set out for the wilderness by the way to
16:7 and **t** put fire in them, and lay incense on them
16:16 be present **t** before the LORD,
Jos 3:5 for **t** the LORD will do wonders among you."
7:13 and say, 'Sanctify yourselves for **t**;
11:6 for **t** at this time I will hand over all of them,
22:18 be angry with the whole congregation of Israel **t**.
Jdg 19:9 **T** you can get up early in the morning
20:28 "Go up, for **t** I will give them into your hand."
1Sa 9:16 "**T** about this time I will send to you a man from
11:9 '**T**, by the time the sun is hot,
11:10 "**T** we will give ourselves up to you,
19:2 therefore be on guard **t** morning;
19:11 not save your life tonight, **t** you will be killed."
20:5 David said to Jonathan, "**T** is the new moon,
20:12 I have sounded out my father, about this time **t**,
20:18 Jonathan said to him, "**T** is the new moon;
20:19 On the day after **t**, you shall go a long way down;
28:19 and **t** you and your sons shall be with me;
2Sa 11:12 and **t** I will send you back."
1Ki 19:2 like the life of one of them by this time **t**."
20:6 I will send my servants to you **t** about this time,
2Ki 6:28 we will eat him today, and we will eat my son **t**.'
7:1 thus says the LORD, **T** about this time a measure
7:18 about this time **t** in the gate of Samaria,"
10:6 of your master's sons and come to me at Jezreel **t**
2Ch 20:16 **T** go down against them; they will come up by
20:17 Do not fear or be dismayed; **t** go out against them,
Est 5:8 let the king and Haman come **t** to the banquet
5:12 **T** also I am invited by her, together with the king.
9:13 the Jews who are in Susa be allowed **t** also to do
Pr 3:28 **t** I will give it"—when you have it with you.
27:1 Do not boast about **t**, for you do not know what
Isa 22:13 "Let us eat and drink, for **t** we die."
56:12 And **t** will be like today, great beyond measure."
Mt 6:30 which is alive today and **t** is thrown into the oven,
6:34 "So do not worry about **t**,
6:34 for **t** will bring worries of its own.
Lk 12:28 which is alive today and **t** is thrown into the oven,
13:32 and performing cures today and **t**,
13:33 **t**, and the next day I must be on my way,
Ac 23:20 to ask you to bring Paul down to the council **t**,
25:22 "**T**," he said, "you will hear him."
1Co 15:32 "Let us eat and drink, for **t** we die."
Jas 4:13 or **t** we will go to such and such a town and spend
4:14 Yet you do not even know what **t** will bring.
AdE 5:8 and **t** I will do as I have done today."
5:12 and I am invited again **t**.
9:13 "Let the Jews be allowed to do the same **t**.
Sir 10:10 the king of today will die **t**.
20:15 Today he lends and **t** he asks it back;
1Mc 2:63 but **t** they will not be found,
5:27 to attack the strongholds **t** and capture
3Mc 5:20 "**t** without delay prepare the elephants in
5:38 now once more for the destruction of the Jews **t**!"
2Es 10:58 But **t** night you shall remain here,
14:26 **t** at this hour you shall begin to write."

TONE (3)

Gal 4:20 with you now and could change my **t**,
2Mc 7:24 and he was suspicious of her reproachful **t**.
3Mc 5:37 summoning Hermon he said in a threatening **t**,

TONGS (3)

1Ki 7:49 the flowers, the lamps, and the **t**, of gold;
2Ch 4:21 the flowers, the lamps, and the **t**, of purest gold;
Isa 6:6 that had been taken from the altar with a pair of **t**.

TONGUE‡ (117) [DOUBLE-TONGUED, EVIL-TONGUED, TONGUE-LASHING, TONGUES]

Ex 4:10 but I am slow of speech and slow of **t**."
2Sa 23:2 his word is upon my **t**.
Job 5:21 You shall be hidden from the scourge of the **t**,
6:30 Is there any wrong on my **t**?
15:5 and you choose the **t** of the crafty.
20:16 the **t** of a viper will kill them.
27:4 and my **t** will not utter deceit.
33:2 See, I open my mouth; the **t** in my mouth speaks.
41:1 or press down its **t** with a cord?
Ps 12:3 the **t** that makes great boasts,
15:3 who do not slander with their **t**, and do no evil
22:15 and my **t** sticks to my jaws;
34:13 Keep your **t** from evil, and your lips
35:28 Then my **t** shall tell of your righteousness and
39:1 that I may not sin with my **t**;
39:3 then I spoke with my **t**:
45:1 my **t** is like the pen of a ready scribe.
50:19 for evil, and your **t** frames deceit.
51:14 and my **t** will sing aloud of your deliverance.
52:2 Your **t** is like a sharp razor,
52:4 You love all words that devour, O deceitful **t**.
64:8 Because of their **t** he will bring them to ruin;
66:17 and he was extolled with my **t**.
71:24 All day long my **t** will talk of your righteous help,
119:172 My **t** will sing of your promise,
120:2 O LORD, from lying lips, from a deceitful **t**."
120:3 what more shall be done to you, you deceitful **t**?
126:2 and our **t** with shouts of joy;
137:6 Let my **t** cling to the roof of my mouth,
139:4 Even before a word is on my **t**, O LORD,
140:3 They make their **t** sharp as a snake's,
Pr 6:17 a lying **t**, and hands that shed innocent blood,
6:24 from the smooth **t** of the adulteress.
10:20 The **t** of the righteous is choice silver;
10:31 but the perverse **t** will be cut off.
12:18 but the **t** of the wise brings healing.
12:19 but a lying **t** lasts only a moment.
15:2 The **t** of the wise dispenses knowledge,
15:4 A gentle **t** is a tree of life,
16:1 but the answer of the **t** is from the LORD.
17:4 and a liar gives heed to a mischievous **t**.
17:20 and the perverse of **t** fall into calamity.
18:21 Death and life are in the power of the **t**,
21:6 a lying **t** is a fleeting vapor and a snare of death.
21:23 over mouth and **t** is to keep out of trouble.
25:15 and a soft **t** can break bones.
25:23 The north wind produces rain, and a backbiting **t**,
26:28 A lying **t** hates its victims,
28:23 find more favor than one who flatters with the **t**.
31:26 and the teaching of kindness is on her **t**.
SS 4:11 honey and milk are under your **t**;
Isa 5:24 Therefore, as the **t** of fire devours the stubble,
11:15 the LORD will utterly destroy the **t** of the sea
28:11 with stammering lip and with alien **t** he will speak
30:27 and his **t** is like a devouring fire;
35:6 and the **t** of the speechless sing for joy.
41:17 and their **t** is parched with thirst,
45:23 "To me every knee shall bow, every **t** shall swear."
50:4 The Lord GOD has given me the **t** of a teacher,
54:17 and you shall confute every **t** that rises
57:4 do you open your mouth wide and stick out your **t**?
59:3 your **t** mutters wickedness.
Jer 9:8 Their **t** is a deadly arrow;
La 4:4 The **t** of the infant sticks to the roof of its mouth
Eze 3:26 I will make your **t** cling to the roof of your mouth,
Hos 7:16 by the sword because of the rage of their **t**.
Zep 3:13 nor shall a deceitful **t** be found in their mouths.
Mk 7:33 and he spat and touched his **t**.

Mk 7:35 his **t** was released, and he spoke plainly.
Lk 1:64 and his **t** freed, and he began
16:24 to dip the tip of his finger in water and cool my **t;**
Ac 2: 3 and a **t** rested on each of them.
2:26 therefore my heart was glad, and my **t** rejoiced;
Ro 14:11 and every **t** shall give praise to God."
1Co 14: 2 in a **t** do not speak to other people but to God;
14: 4 Those who speak in a **t** build up themselves,
14: 9 if in a **t** you utter speech that is not intelligible,
14:13 one who speaks in a **t** should pray for the power
14:14 For if I pray in a **t,**
14:19 than ten thousand words in a **t.**
14:26 each one has a hymn, a lesson, a revelation, a **t,**
14:27 If anyone speaks in a **t,** let there be only two or
Php 2:11 every **t** should confess that Jesus Christ is Lord,
Jas 3: 5 So also the **t** is a small member,
3: 6 And the **t** is a fire.
3: 6 The **t** is placed among our members as a world
3: 8 but no one can tame the **t—**
Wis 1:11 and keep your **t** from slander;
Sir 4:24 and education through the words of the **t.**
5:13 and the **t** of mortals may be their downfall.
5:14 and do not lay traps with your **t;**
6: 5 and a gracious **t** multiplies courtesies.
17: 6 Discretion and **t** and eyes,
19:16 Who has not sinned with his **t?**
20:18 slip on the pavement is better than a slip of the **t;**
22:27 and my **t** may not destroy me?
23: 7 DISCIPLINE OF THE T Listen, my children,
25: 7 and a tenth my **t** proclaims:
25: 8 Happy is the one who does not sin with the **t,**
28:17 but a blow of the **t** crushes the bones.
28:18 but not as many as have fallen because of the **t.**
28:26 Take care not to err with your **t,**
32: 8 be as one who knows and can still hold his **t.**
37:18 and it is the **t** that continually rules them.
51: 2 and from the trap laid by a slanderous **t,**
51: 5 from an unclean **t** and lying words—
51: 6 the slander of an unrighteous **t** to the king.
51:22 The Lord gave me my **t** as a reward,
2Mc 7: 4 and he commanded that the **t** of their spokesman
7:10 he quickly put out his **t** and courageously
15:33 He cut out the **t** of the ungodly Nicanor and said
3Mc 2:17 in their wrath and exult in the arrogance of their **t,**
6: 4 exalted with lawless insolence and boastful **t,**
2Es 13:10 and from his **t** he shot forth a storm of sparks.
4Mc 10:17 abominable Antiochus gave orders to cut out his **t.**
10:19 here is my **t;** cut it off,
10:21 for you are cutting out a **t** that has been melodious

TONGUE-LASHING (1) [TONGUE]

Sir 26: 6 and a **t** makes it known to all.

TONGUES (48) [TONGUE]

Jdg 7: 5 "All those who lap the water with their **t,**
Job 20:12 though they hide it under their **t,**
29:10 and their **t** stuck to the roof of their mouths.
Ps 5: 9 throats are open graves; they flatter with their **t.**
10: 7 under their **t** are mischief and iniquity.
12: 4 "With our **t** we will prevail;
31:20 under your shelter from contentious **t.**
37:30 righteous utter wisdom, and their **t** speak justice.
57: 4 and arrows, their **t** sharp swords.
64: 3 who whet their **t** like swords,
68:23 **t** of your dogs may have their share from the foe."
73: 9 and their **t** range over the earth.
78:36 they lied to him with their **t.**
109: 2 speaking against me with lying **t.**
Isa 32: 4 **t** of stammerers will speak readily and distinctly.
66:18 and I am coming to gather all nations and **t;**
Jer 9: 3 They bend their **t** like bows;
9: 5 they have taught their **t** to speak lies;
23:31 who use their own **t** and say, "Says the LORD."
Mic 6:12 with **t** of deceit in their mouths.
Zec 14:12 and their **t** shall rot in their mouths.
Mk 16:17 ⟦they will speak in new **t;**⟧
Ac 2: 3 Divided **t,** as of fire, appeared among them,
10:46 they heard them speaking in **t** and extolling God.
19: 6 and they spoke in **t** and prophesied—
Ro 3:13 they use their **t** to deceive."
1Co 12:10 to another various kinds of **t,** to another the
interpretation of **t.**
12:28 forms of leadership, various kinds of **t.**
12:30 Do all speak in **t?**
13: 1 If I speak in the **t** of mortals and of angels,
13: 8 as for **t,** they will cease;
14: 5 Now I would like all of you to speak in **t,** but even
14: 5 prophesies is greater than the one who speaks in **t,**
14: 6 if I come to you speaking in **t,**
14:18 I thank God that I speak in **t** more than all of you;
14:21 By people of strange **t** and by the lips of foreigners
14:22 **T,** then, are a sign not for believers but
14:23 whole church comes together and all speak in **t,**
14:39 and do not forbid speaking in **t;**
Jas 1:26 and do not bridle their **t** but deceive their hearts,
1Pe 3:10 let them keep their **t** from evil and their lips
Rev 16:10 people gnawed their **t** in agony,
Wis 1: 6 true observer of their hearts, and a hearer of their **t.**
10:21 and made the **t** of infants speak clearly.
LtJ 6: 8 Their **t** are smoothed by the carpenter,
4Mc 12:13 the **t** of men who have feelings like yours
18:21 pierced the pupils of their eyes and cut out their **t,**

TONIGHT (19)

Ge 19: 5 "Where are the men who came to you **t?**
19:34 let us make him drink wine **t** also;
30:15 he may lie with you **t** for your son's mandrakes."
Nu 22: 8 He said to them, "Stay here **t,**
Jos 2: 2 "Some Israelites have come here **t** to search out
4: 3 lay them down in the place where you camp **t.'** "
Ru 1:12 even if I should have a husband **t** and bear sons,
3: 2 he is winnowing barley **t** at the threshing floor.
1Sa 19:11 "If you do not save your life **t,**
2Sa 17: 1 and I will set out and pursue David **t.**
17:16 'Do not lodge **t** at the fords of the wilderness,
Ne 6:10 indeed, **t** they are coming to kill you."
Ac 23:23 "Get ready to leave by nine o'clock **t** for Caesarea
Tob 6:13 **t** I will speak to her father about the girl,
6:13 and **t** we shall speak concerning the girl
7:10 "Eat and drink, and be merry **t.**
Jdt 8:33 Stand at the town gate **t** so that I may go out
11: 3 You will live **t** and ever after.
2Es 12: 5 the great fear with which I have been terrified **t.**

TOO (192) See Index of Articles Etc.

TOOK‡ (840) [TAKE]

Ge 2:15 The LORD God **t** the man and put him in
2:21 then he **t** one of his ribs and closed up its place
3: 6 she **t** of its fruit and ate;
4:19 Lamech **t** two wives; the name of the
5:24 then he was no more, because God **t** him.
6: 2 they **t** wives for themselves of all that they chose.
8: 9 So he put out his hand and **t** it and brought it into
8:20 **t** of every clean animal and of every clean bird,
9:23 Then Shem and Japheth **t** a garment,
11:29 Abram and Nahor **t** wives;
11:31 Terah **t** his son Abram and his grandson Lot son
12: 5 Abram **t** his wife Sarai and his brother's son Lot,
12:19 'She is my sister,' so that I **t** her for my wife?
14:11 enemy **t** all the goods of Sodom and Gomorrah,
14:12 also **t** Lot, the son of Abram's brother, who lived
16: 3 Sarai, Abram's wife, **t** Hagar the Egyptian,
17:23 Then Abraham **t** his son Ishmael and all
18: 7 Abraham ran to the herd, and **t** a calf,
18: 8 Then he **t** curds and milk and the calf
20: 2 And King Abimelech of Gerar sent and **t** Sarah.
20:14 Then Abimelech **t** sheep and oxen,
21:14 and **t** bread and a skin of water,
21:27 So Abraham **t** sheep and oxen and gave them
22: 3 and **t** two of his young men with him,
22: 6 Abraham **t** the wood of the burnt offering
22:10 Then Abraham reached out his hand and **t**
22:13 Abraham went and **t** the ram and offered it up as
24: 7 who **t** me from my father's house and from
24:10 servant **t** ten of his master's camels and departed,
24:22 the man **t** a gold nose-ring weighing a half shekel,
24:61 thus the servant **t** Rebekah, and went his way.
24:65 So she **t** her veil and covered herself.
24:67 He **t** Rebekah, and she became his wife;
25: 1 Abraham **t** another wife, whose name was Keturah.
27:15 Then Rebekah **t** the best garments
27:36 He **t** away my birthright;
28: 9 Esau went to Ishmael and **t** Mahalath daughter
28:18 and he **t** the stone that he had put under his head
29:23 But in the evening he **t** his daughter Leah
30: 9 she **t** her maid Zilpah and gave her to Jacob as
30:37 Then Jacob **t** fresh rods of poplar and almond
31:23 So he **t** his kinsfolk with him and pursued him
31:45 So Jacob **t** a stone, and set it up as a pillar.
31:46 and they **t** stones, and made a heap;
32:13 and from what he had with him he **t** a present
32:22 The same night he got up and **t** his two wives,
32:23 He **t** them and sent them across the stream,
33:11 So he urged him, and he **t** it.
34:25 **t** their swords and came against the city unawares,
34:26 and **t** Dinah out of Shechem's house,
34:28 They **t** their flocks and their herds, their donkeys,
36: 2 Esau **t** his wives from the Canaanites:
36: 6 Then Esau **t** his wives, his sons, his daughters,
37:24 and they **t** him and threw him into a pit.
37:28 And they **t** Joseph to Egypt.
37:31 Then they **t** Joseph's robe, slaughtered a goat,
38: 6 Judah **t** a wife for Er his firstborn;
38:28 and the midwife **t** and bound on his hand
39:20 Joseph's master **t** him and put him into the prison,
40:11 and I **t** the grapes and pressed them
43:15 the men **t** the present, and they **t** double the money
46: 6 They also **t** their livestock and the goods
47: 2 From among his brothers he **t** five men
48: 1 So he **t** with him his two sons,
48:13 Joseph **t** them both, Ephraim in his right hand
48:17 so he **t** his father's hand,
48:22 the portion that I **t** from the hand of the Amorites
Ex 2: 6 He was crying, and she **t** pity on him,
2: 9 So the woman **t** the child and nursed it.
2:10 and she **t** him as her son.
2:25 and God **t** notice of them.
4: 6 and when he **t** it out, his hand was leprous,
4: 7 and when he **t** it out, it was restored like the rest
4:20 So Moses **t** his wife and his sons,
4:25 Zipporah **t** a flint and cut off her son's foreskin,
9:10 So they **t** soot from the kiln,
12:34 the people **t** their dough before it was leavened,
13:19 And Moses **t** with him the bones of Joseph
14: 6 and **t** his army with him;
14: 7 he **t** six hundred picked chariots and all
14:19 from in front of them and **t** its place behind them.
15:20 Aaron's sister, **t** a tambourine in her hand;
17:12 so they **t** a stone and put it under him,
18: 2 his father-in-law Jethro **t** her back,
Ex 19:17 They **t** their stand at the foot of the mountain.
24: 6 Moses **t** half of the blood and put it in basins,
24: 7 Then he **t** the book of the covenant,
24: 8 Moses **t** the blood and dashed it on the people,
32: 3 all the people **t** off the gold rings from their ears,
32: 4 He **t** the gold from them, formed it in a mold,
32:20 He **t** the calf that they had made,
34: 4 and **t** in his hand the two tablets of stone.
40:20 He **t** the covenant and put it into the ark,
Lev 6: 4 and would restore what you **t** by robbery or
8:10 Then Moses **t** the anointing oil and anointed
8:15 Moses **t** the blood and with his finger put some
8:16 Moses **t** all the fat that was around the entrails,
8:23 Moses **t** some of its blood and put it on the lobe
8:25 He **t** the fat—the broad tail,
8:26 he **t** one cake of unleavened bread,
8:28 Then Moses **t** them from their hands
8:29 Moses **t** the breast and raised it as an elevation
8:30 Then Moses **t** some of the anointing oil and some
9:15 He **t** the goat of the sin offering that was for
10: 1 Nadab and Abihu, each **t** his censer, put fire in it,
24:23 and they **t** the blasphemer outside the camp,
Nu 1:17 and Aaron **t** these men who had been designated
3:49 So Moses **t** the redemption money
3:50 from the firstborn of the Israelites he **t** the money,
7: 6 So Moses **t** the wagons and the oxen,
11:25 and **t** some of the spirit that was on him and put it
16: 1 and On son of Peleth—descendants of Reuben—**t**
16:18 So each man **t** his censer,
16:39 So Eleazar the priest **t** the bronze censers
16:47 So Aaron **t** it as Moses had ordered,
17: 9 and they looked, and each man **t** his staff.
20: 9 So Moses **t** the staff from before the LORD,
21: 1 against Israel and **t** some of them captive.
21:24 and **t** possession of his land from the Arnon to
21:25 Israel **t** all these towns, and Israel settled in all
21:35 and they **t** possession of his land.
22:22 and the angel of the LORD **t** his stand in the road
22:41 On the next day Balak **t** Balaam and brought him
23:14 So he **t** him to the field of Zophim,
23:28 So Balak **t** Balaam to the top of Peor,
27:22 He **t** Joshua and had him stand before Eleazar
31: 9 The Israelites **t** the women of Midian
31: 9 and they **t** all their cattle, their flocks,
31:11 but they **t** all the spoil and all the booty,
31:47 the Israelites' half Moses **t** one of every fifty,
Dt 1:15 So I **t** the leaders of your tribes,
3: 8 that time we **t** from the two kings of the Amorites
3:12 for the land that we **t** possession of at that time,
9:17 So I **t** hold of the two tablets and flung them
9:21 Then I **t** the sinful thing you had made, the calf,
28:63 as the LORD **t** delight in making you prosperous
29: 8 We **t** their land and gave it as an inheritance to
30: 7 and on the adversaries who **t** advantage of you.
32:37 are their gods, the rock in which they **t** refuge,
Jos 2: 4 But the woman **t** the two men and hid them.
3: 6 So they **t** up the ark of the covenant and went
4: 8 They **t** up twelve stones out of the middle of
6:12 and the priests **t** up the ark of the LORD.
7: 1 **t** some of the devoted things;
7:21 then I coveted them and **t** them.
7:23 They **t** them out of the tent and brought them
7:24 and all Israel with him **t** Achan son of Zerah,
8:19 They entered the city, **t** it,
8:27 and the spoil of that city Israel **t** as their booty,
8:29 and they **t** his body down from the tree,
9: 4 and **t** worn-out sacks for their donkeys,
9:12 it was still warm when we **t** it from our houses
10:13 until the nation **t** vengeance on their enemies.
10:27 and they **t** them down from the trees
10:28 Joshua **t** Makkedah on that day,
10:32 and he **t** it on the second day,
10:35 and they **t** it that day, and struck it with the edge
10:37 and **t** it, and struck it with the edge of the sword,
10:39 and he **t** it with its king and all its towns;
10:42 Joshua **t** all these kings and their land at one time,
11:10 Joshua turned back at that time, and **t** Hazor,
11:12 and all their kings, Joshua **t,**
11:14 and the livestock, the Israelites **t** for their booty;
11:16 So Joshua **t** all that land:
11:17 He **t** all their kings, struck them down,
11:23 So Joshua **t** the whole land,
15:17 Othniel son of Kenaz, the brother of Caleb, **t** it;
19:47 they **t** possession of it and settled in it,
24: 3 Then I **t** your father Abraham from beyond
24: 8 and you **t** possession of their land,
24:26 and he **t** a large stone,
Jdg 1: 8 people of Judah fought against Jerusalem and **t** it.
1:13 **t** it; and he gave him his daughter Achsah as wife.
1:18 Judah **t** Gaza with its territory,
1:19 and he **t** possession of the hill country,
3: 6 and they **t** their daughters as wives
3:13 and they **t** possession of the city of palms.
3:21 **t** the sword from his right thigh,
3:25 they **t** the key and opened them.
4:21 But Jael wife of Heber **t** a tent peg,
4:21 and **t** a hammer in her hand,
6:27 So Gideon **t** ten of his servants,
6:34 the spirit of the LORD **t** possession of Gideon;
7: 8 So he **t** the jars of the troops from their hands,
8:12 he pursued them and **t** the two kings of Midian,
8:16 So he **t** the elders of the city and he **t** thorns of
8:21 and he **t** the crescents that were on the necks
9:43 he **t** his troops and divided them
9:45 he **t** the city, and killed the people that were in it;
9:48 Abimelech **t** an ax in his hand,
9:48 and **t** it up and laid it on his shoulder.

Jdg 9:50 and encamped against Thebez, and **t** it.
11:13 **t** away my land from the Arnon to the Jabbok and
12: 3 I **t** my life in my hand,
12: 5 the Gileadites **t** the fords of the Jordan against
13:19 So Manoah **t** the kid with the grain offering,
14:19 He killed thirty men of the town, **t** their spoil,
15: 4 caught three hundred foxes, and **t** some torches;
15:15 reached down and **t** it, and with it he killed
16: 3 **t** hold of the doors of the city gate and
16:12 So Delilah **t** new ropes and bound him with them,
16:14 Delilah **t** the seven locks of his head
16:31 and **t** him and brought him up and buried him
17: 2 I **t** it; but now I will return it to you."
17: 4 his mother **t** two hundred pieces of silver,
18:18 the men went into Micah's house and **t** the idol
18:20 He **t** the ephod, the teraphim, and the idol,
19: 1 **t** to himself a concubine from Bethlehem
19:15 but no one **t** them in to spend the night.
19:29 When he had entered his house, he **t** a knife,
20: 6 Then I **t** my concubine and cut her into pieces,
20:22 The Israelites **t** courage, and again formed
21:23 they **t** wives for each of them from
Ru 1: 4 These **t** Moabite wives; the name of the
2:18 Then she **t** out and gave her what was left over
2:19 Blessed be the man who **t** notice of you."
4: 2 Then Boaz **t** ten men of the elders of the city,
4: 7 the one **t** off a sandal and gave it to the other;
4: 8 "Acquire it for yourself," he **t** off his sandal.
4:13 So Boaz **t** Ruth and she became his wife.
4:16 Naomi **t** the child and laid him in her bosom,
1Sa 1:24 When she had weaned him, she **t** him up with her,
2:21 And the LORD **t** note of Hannah;
5: 2 then the Philistines **t** the ark of God and brought it
5: 3 So they **t** Dagon and put him back in his place.
6:10 they **t** two milch cows and yoked them to the cart,
6:15 The Levites **t** down the ark of the LORD and
7: 1 the people of Kiriath-jearim came and **t** up the ark
7: 9 So Samuel **t** a sucking lamb and offered it as
7:12 Then Samuel **t** a stone and set it up
8: 3 they **t** bribes and perverted justice.
9:22 Then Samuel **t** Saul and his servant-boy
9:24 The cook **t** up the thigh and what went with it
10: 1 Samuel **t** a vial of oil and poured it on his head,
10:23 When he **t** his stand among the people,
11: 7 He **t** a yoke of oxen,
14:32 and **t** sheep and oxen and calves,
14:52 or valiant warrior, he **t** him into his service.
15: 8 He **t** King Agag of the Amalekites alive,
15:21 But from the spoil the people **t** sheep and cattle,
16:13 Then Samuel **t** the horn of oil,
16:20 Jesse **t** a donkey loaded with bread,
16:23 David **t** the lyre and played it with his hand,
17:16 the Philistine came forward and **t** his stand,
17:20 left the sheep with a keeper, **t** the provisions,
17:34 and **t** a lamb from the flock,
17:40 Then he **t** his staff in his hand,
17:49 David put his hand in his bag, **t** out a stone,
17:54 David **t** the head of the Philistine and brought it
17:57 Abner **t** him and brought him before Saul,
18: 2 Saul **t** him that day and would not let him return
19: 1 But Saul's son Jonathan **t** great delight in David.
19: 5 for he **t** his life in his hand when he attacked
19:13 Michal **t** an idol and laid it on the bed;
21:12 David **t** these words to heart
24: 2 Saul **t** three thousand chosen men out of all Israel,
25:18 Then Abigail hurried and **t** two hundred loaves,
26:12 So David **t** the spear that was at Saul's head and
27: 9 but **t** away the sheep, the oxen, the donkeys,
28:24 She quickly slaughtered it, and she **t** flour,
31: 4 So Saul **t** his own sword and fell upon it.
31:12 and **t** the body of Saul and the bodies of his sons
31:13 Then they **t** their bones and buried them under
2Sa 1:10 I **t** the crown that was on his head and the armlet
1:11 Then David **t** hold of his clothes and tore them;
2:25 they **t** their stand on the top of a hill.
2:32 They **t** up Asahel and buried him in the tomb
3:15 Ishbaal sent and **t** her from her husband Paltiel
3:27 Joab **t** him aside in the gateway to speak
3:30 All the people **t** notice of it, and it pleased them;
4: 7 Then they **t** his head and traveled by way of
4:12 of Ishbaal they **t** and buried in the tomb of Abner
5: 7 Nevertheless David **t** the stronghold of Zion,
5:13 David **t** more concubines and wives;
6: 6 to the ark of God and **t** hold of it,
6:10 instead David **t** it to the house of Obed-edom
7: 8 I **t** you from the pasture, from following the sheep
7:15 my steadfast love from him, as I **t** it from Saul,
8: 1 David **t** Metheg-ammah out of the hand of
8: 4 David **t** from him one thousand seven hundred
8: 7 David **t** the gold shields that were carried by
8: 8 King David **t** a great amount of bronze.
12: 4 but he **t** the poor man's lamb,
12:26 against Rabbah of the Ammonites, and **t**
12:29 and fought against it and **t** it.
12:30 He **t** the crown of Milcom from his head;
13: 8 She **t** dough, kneaded it, made cakes in his sight,
13: 9 Then she **t** the pan and set them out before him,
13:10 So Tamar **t** the cakes she had made,
13:11 she brought them near him to eat, he **t** hold of her,
17:19 The man's wife **t** a covering,
18:14 He **t** three spears in his hand,
18:17 They **t** Absalom, threw him into a great pit in
19: 8 Then the king got up and **t** his seat in the gate.
20: 3 the king **t** the ten concubines whom he had left
20: 9 And Joab **t** Amasa by the beard
20:11 And one of Joab's men **t** his stand by Amasa,
21: 8 king **t** the two sons of Rizpah daughter of Aiah,

2Sa 21:10 Then Rizpah the daughter of Aiah **t** sackcloth,
21:12 David went and **t** the bones of Saul and the bones
21:18 this a battle **t** place with the Philistines, at Gob;
22:17 He reached from on high, he **t** me,
23:12 But he **t** his stand in the middle of the plot,
1Ki 1:39 the priest Zadok **t** the horn of oil from the tent
3: 1 he **t** Pharaoh's daughter and brought her into
3:20 She got up in the middle of the night and **t** my son
8:48 who **t** them captive, and pray to you
11:18 they **t** people with them from Paran and came
12: 6 Then King Rehoboam **t** counsel with
12:28 the king **t** counsel, and made two calves of gold.
13:29 The prophet **t** up the body of the man of God,
14:26 he **t** away the treasures of the house of the LORD
14:26 of the king's house; he **t** everything.
14:26 He also **t** away all the shields of gold
15:18 Then Asa **t** all the silver and the gold
16:31 he **t** as his wife Jezebel daughter of King Ethbaal
17:19 He **t** him from her bosom,
17:23 Elijah **t** the child, brought him down from
18: 4 Obadiah **t** a hundred prophets,
18:26 So they **t** the bull that was given them,
18:31 Elijah **t** twelve stones, according to the number of
19:21 **t** the yoke of oxen, and slaughtered them;
20:12 And they **t** their positions against the city.
20:33 they quickly **t** it up from him and said, "Yes,
20:34 the towns that my father **t** from your father;
20:41 he quickly **t** the bandage away from his eyes.
21: 1 Later the following events **t** place:
21:13 So they **t** him outside the city,
2Ki 2: 8 Then Elijah **t** his mantle and rolled it up,
2:14 He **t** the mantle of Elijah that had fallen from him,
3:26 he **t** with him seven hundred swordsmen to break
3:27 he **t** his firstborn son who was to succeed him,
4:37 then she **t** her son and left.
5:24 he came to the citadel, he **t** the bags from them,
6: 7 So he reached out his hand and **t** it.
6: 8 he **t** counsel with his officers.
7:14 So they **t** two mounted men,
8:15 But the next day he **t** the bed-cover and dipped it
9:13 Then hurriedly they all **t** their cloaks
10: 7 they **t** the king's sons and killed them,
10:14 They **t** them alive, and slaughtered them at the pit
10:15 Jehu **t** him up with him into the chariot.
11: 2 Ahaziah's sister, **t** Joash son of Ahaziah,
11:19 He **t** the captains, the Carites, the guards,
11:19 He **t** his seat on the throne of the kings.
12: 9 Then the priest Jehoiada **t** a chest,
12:17 fought against Gath, and **t** it.
12:18 of Judah **t** all the votive gifts that Jehoshaphat,
13:15 so he **t** a bow and arrows.
13:18 He continued, "Take the arrows"; and he **t** them.
13:25 of Jehoahaz **t** again from Ben-hadad son
14: 7 in the Valley of Salt and **t** Sela by storm;
14:21 All the people of Judah **t** Azariah,
16: 8 Ahaz also **t** the silver and gold found in the house
16: 9 and **t** it, carrying its people captive to Kir;
17:24 they **t** possession of Samaria,
18:10 and at the end of three years, **t** it.
22:20 They **t** the message back to the king.
23:16 and he sent and **t** the bones out of the tombs,
23:30 The people of the land **t** Jehoahaz son of Josiah,
23:34 to Jehoiakim. But he **t** Jehoahaz away;
24:12 of Babylon **t** him prisoner in the eighth year
24:15 he **t** into captivity from Jerusalem to Babylon.
25: 7 they bound him in fetters and **t** him to Babylon.
25:14 They **t** away the pots, the shovels, the snuffers,
25:15 the captain of the guard **t** away for the gold,
25:18 The captain of the guard **t** the chief priest Seraiah,
25:19 the city he **t** an officer who had been in command
25:20 Nebuzaradan the captain of the guard **t** them,
1Ch 2:23 But Geshur and Aram **t** from them Havvoth-jair,
7:15 Machir **t** a wife for Huppim and for Shuppim.
10: 4 So Saul **t** his own sword and fell on it.
10: 9 They stripped him and **t** his head and his armor,
10:12 the valiant warriors got up and **t** away the body
11: 5 Nevertheless David **t** the stronghold of Zion,
11:14 and David **t** their stand in the middle of the plot,
12:19 of the Philistines **t** counsel and sent him away,
13:13 he **t** it instead to the house of Obed-edom
14: 3 David **t** more wives in Jerusalem,
17: 7 I **t** you from the pasture, from following
17:13 as I **t** it from him who was before you,
18: 1 he **t** Gath and its villages from the Philistines.
18: 4 David **t** from him one thousand chariots,
18: 7 David **t** the gold shields that were carried by
18: 8 David **t** a vast quantity of bronze;
20: 2 David **t** the crown of Milcom from his head;
21:15 about to destroy it, the LORD **t** note and relented
28: 4 and among my father's sons he **t** delight
2Ch 2:17 Then Solomon **t** a census of all
10: 6 Then King Rehoboam **t** counsel with
11:18 Rehoboam **t** as his wife Mahalath daughter
11:20 After her he **t** Maacah daughter of Absalom,
11:21 and concubines (he **t** eighteen wives
12: 4 He **t** the fortified cities of Judah and came as far
12: 9 he **t** away the treasures of the house of
12: 9 of the king's house; he **t** everything.
12: 9 He also **t** away the shields of gold
13:19 Abijah pursued Jeroboam, and **t** cities from him:
13:21 He **t** fourteen wives, and became the father
14: 3 He **t** away the foreign altars and the high places,
15: 8 he **t** courage, and put away the abominable idols
15:14 They **t** an oath to the LORD with a loud voice,
16: 2 Then Asa **t** silver and gold from the treasures of
20:25 which they **t** for themselves
22:11 the king's daughter, **t** Joash son of Ahaziah,

2Ch 23: 1 But in the seventh year Jehoiada **t** courage,
23:20 And he **t** the captains, the nobles,
24:20 the spirit of God **t** possession of Zechariah son of
24:23 sent all the booty they **t** to the king of Damascus.
25:11 Amaziah **t** courage, and led out his people;
25:12 **t** them to the top of Sela,
25:13 in them, and **t** much booty.
25:17 Then King Amaziah of Judah **t** counsel and sent
26: 1 Then all the people of Judah **t** Uzziah,
28: 5 who defeated him and **t** captive a great number
28: 8 of Israel **t** captive two hundred thousand
28: 8 they also **t** much booty from them and brought
28:15 by name got up and **t** the captives,
29:16 and the Levites **t** them and carried them out to
30:14 and all the altars for offering incense they **t** away
30:16 They **t** their accustomed posts according to
32:12 this same Hezekiah who **t** away his high places
33:11 who **t** Manasseh captive in manacles,
33:15 He **t** away the foreign gods and the idol from
34:28 They **t** the message back to the king.
34:33 Josiah **t** away all the abominations from all
35:24 So his servants **t** him out of the chariot
36: 1 The people of the land **t** Jehoahaz son of Josiah
36: 4 but Neco **t** his brother Jehoahaz and carried him
36:20 He **t** into exile in Babylon those who had escaped
Ezr 3: 9 together **t** charge of the workers in the house
5:14 these King Cyrus **t** out of the temple of Babylon,
6: 5 which Nebuchadnezzar **t** out of the temple
7:28 I **t** courage, for the hand of the LORD my God
8:30 So the priests and the Levites **t** over the silver,
Ne 2:12 The only animal I **t** was the animal I rode.
4:23 the guard who followed me ever **t** off our clothes;
5:15 and **t** food and wine from them,
9:22 so they **t** possession of the land of King Sihon
9:25 and **t** possession of houses filled with all sorts
Est 3:10 So the king **t** his signet ring from his hand
6:11 So Haman **t** the robes and the horse
8: 2 Then the king **t** off his signet ring,
Job 2: 8 Job **t** a potsherd with which to scrape himself,
27: 1 Job again **t** up his discourse and said:
29: 1 Job again **t** up his discourse and said:
29: 7 when I **t** my seat in the square,
Ps 18:16 He reached down from on high, he **t** me;
22: 9 Yet it was you who **t** me from the womb;
48: 5 they were in panic, they **t** to flight;
48: 6 trembling **t** hold of them there,
71: 6 it was you who **t** me from my mother's womb.
78:70 and **t** him from the sheepfolds;
80: 9 it **t** deep root and filled the land.
105:44 and they **t** possession of the wealth of the peoples,
Pr 7:20 He **t** a bag of money with him;
SS 5: 7 they wounded me, they **t** away my mantle,
Isa 20: 1 came to Ashdod and fought against it and **t** it—
22: 7 and the cavalry **t** their stand at the gates.
41: 9 you whom I **t** from the ends of the earth,
63:18 Your holy people **t** possession for a little while;
Jer 3: 9 Because she **t** her whoredom so lightly,
13: 7 and I **t** the loincloth from the place
25:17 So I **t** the cup from the LORD's hand,
26:10 and **t** their seat in the entry of the New Gate of
26:23 and they **t** Uriah from Egypt and brought him
27:20 of Babylon did not take away when he **t** into exile
28: 3 which King Nebuchadnezzar of Babylon **t** away
28:10 the prophet Hananiah **t** the yoke from the neck of
31:18 "You disciplined me, and I **t** the discipline;
31:32 that I made with their ancestors when I **t** them by
32:11 Then I **t** the sealed deed of purchase,
32:23 and they entered and **t** possession of it.
34:11 But afterward they turned around and **t** back
34:16 of you **t** back your male and female slaves,
35: 3 I **t** Jaazaniah son of Jeremiah son of Habazziniah,
36:14 So Baruch son of Neriah **t** the scroll in his hand
36:21 and he **t** it from the chamber of Elishama
36:32 Then Jeremiah **t** another scroll and gave it to
38: 6 So they **t** Jeremiah and threw him into the cistern
38:11 So Ebed-melech **t** the men with him and went to
38:11 and **t** from there old rags and worn-out clothes,
39:14 and **t** Jeremiah from the court of the guard.
40: 1 when he **t** him bound in fetters along with all
40: 2 captain of the guard **t** Jeremiah and said to him,
41:10 Then Ishmael **t** captive all the rest of
41:10 of Nethaniah **t** them captive and set out to cross
41:12 they **t** all their men and went to fight
41:16 the leaders of the forces with him **t** all the rest of
43: 5 the commanders of the forces **t** all the remnant
52:11 and the king of Babylon **t** him to Babylon,
52:18 They **t** away the pots, the shovels, the snuffers,
52:19 captain of the guard **t** away the small bowls also,
52:24 The captain of the guard **t** the chief priest Seraiah,
52:25 the city he **t** an officer who had been in command
52:26 Nebuzaradan the captain of the guard **t** them,
52:28 the number of the people whom Nebuchadrezzar **t**
52:29 in the eighteenth year of Nebuchadrezzar he **t**
52:30 Nebuzaradan the captain of the guard **t** into exile
La 1: 9 she **t** no thought of her future;
2: 4 in whom we **t** pride in the tent of daughter Zion;
Eze 3:21 they shall surely live, because they **t** warning;
7:20 their beautiful ornament, in which they **t** pride,
8: 3 and **t** me by a lock of my head;
10: 7 **t** some of it and put it into the hands of the man
10: 7 who **t** it and went out.
16:16 You **t** some of your garments,
16:17 You also **t** your beautiful jewels of my gold
16:18 you **t** your embroidered garments to cover them,
16:20 You **t** your sons and your daughters,
16:37 with whom you **t** pleasure,
17: 3 He **t** the top of the cedar,

Eze 17: 5 he **t** a seed from the land, placed it in fertile soil;
17:12 **t** its king and its officials,
17:13 He **t** one of the royal offspring and made
19: 5 she **t** another of her cubs and made him a young
23:13 they both **t** the same way.
25:15 and with malice of heart **t** revenge in destruction;
27: 5 they **t** a cedar from Lebanon to make a mast
36: 5 **t** my land as their possession,
42: 5 for the galleries **t** more away from them than from
Da 7: 9 and an Ancient One **t** his throne,
8:11 it **t** the regular burnt offering away from him
Hos 1: 3 So he went and **t** Gomer daughter of Diblaim,
11: 3 I **t** them up in my arms;
13:11 and I **t** him away in my wrath.
Am 7:15 and the LORD **t** me from following the flock,
Zec 11: 7 to slaughter. I **t** two staffs;
11:10 I **t** my staff Favor and broke it,
11:13 So I **t** the thirty shekels of silver and threw them
Mal 3:16 The LORD **t** note and listened,
Mt 1:18 the birth of Jesus the Messiah **t** place in this way.
1:22 All this **t** place to fulfill what had been spoken by
1:24 commanded him; he **t** her as his wife,
2:14 Joseph got up, **t** the child and his mother by night,
2:21 Then Joseph got up, **t** the child and his mother,
4: 5 the devil **t** him to the holy city and placed him on
4: 8 the devil **t** him to a very high mountain
8:17 "He **t** our infirmities and bore our diseases."
9:25 he went in and **t** her by the hand,
13:31 of heaven is like a mustard seed that someone **t**
13:33 that a woman **t** and mixed in with three measures
13:57 And they **t** offense at him.
14:12 His disciples came and **t** the body and buried it;
14:20 they **t** up what was left over of the broken pieces,
15:12 "Do you know that the Pharisees **t** offense
15:36 he **t** the seven loaves and the fish;
15:37 and they **t** up the broken pieces left over,
16:22 And Peter **t** him aside and began to rebuke him,
17: 1 Jesus **t** with him Peter and James
20:17 he **t** the twelve disciples aside by themselves,
21: 4 This **t** place to fulfill what had been spoken
25: 1 Ten bridesmaids **t** their lamps and went to meet
25: 3 foolish **t** their lamps, they **t** no oil with them;
25: 4 but the wise **t** flasks of oil with their lamps.
25:36 I was sick and you **t** care of me,
26:20 it was evening, he **t** his place with the twelve;
26:26 While they were eating, Jesus **t** a loaf of bread,
26:27 Then he **t** a cup, and after giving thanks he gave it
26:37 He **t** with him Peter and the two sons of Zebedee,
26:57 Those who had arrested Jesus **t** him to Caiaphas
27: 9 "And they **t** the thirty pieces of silver,
27:24 he **t** some water and washed his hands before
27:27 Then the soldiers of the governor **t** Jesus into
27:30 and **t** the reed and struck him on the head.
27:54 saw the earthquake and what **t** place,
27:59 So Joseph **t** the body and wrapped it in
28: 9 And they came to him, **t** hold of his feet,
28:15 they **t** the money and did as they were directed.
Mk 1:31 He came and **t** her by the hand and lifted her up.
2:12 and immediately **t** the mat and went out before all
4:36 they **t** him with them in the boat, just as he was.
5:40 and **t** the child's father and mother
5:41 He **t** her by the hand and said to her,
6: 3 And they **t** offense at him.
6:29 they came and **t** his body, and laid it in a tomb.
6:43 and they **t** up twelve baskets full of broken pieces
7:33 He **t** him aside in private, away from the crowd,
8: 6 and he **t** the seven loaves,
8: 8 and they **t** up the broken pieces left over,
8:23 He **t** the blind man by the hand and led him out of
8:32 And Peter **t** him aside and began to rebuke him.
9: 2 Jesus **t** with him Peter and James and John,
9:27 But Jesus **t** him by the hand and lifted him up,
9:36 Then he **t** a little child and put it among them;
10:16 And he **t** them up in his arms,
10:32 He **t** the twelve aside again and began
14:22 While they were eating, he **t** a loaf of bread,
14:23 Then he **t** a cup, and after giving thanks he gave it
14:33 He **t** with him Peter and James and John,
14:53 They **t** Jesus to the high priest;
14:65 The guards also **t** him over and beat him.
Lk 1:25 on me and **t** away the disgrace I have endured
2:28 Simeon **t** him in his arms and praised God,
4: 9 Then the devil **t** him to Jerusalem,
5:25 **t** what he had been lying on,
6: 4 of God and **t** and ate the bread of the Presence,
7:36 the Pharisee's house and **t** his place at the table.
8:54 But he **t** her by the hand and called out, "Child,
9:10 He **t** them with him and withdrew privately to
9:28 Now about eight days after these sayings Jesus **t**
9:47 **t** a little child and put it by his side,
10:34 brought him to an inn, and **t** care of him.
10:35 The next day he **t** out two denarii,
11:37 so he went in and **t** his place at the table.
13:19 It is like a mustard seed that someone **t** and sowed
13:21 that a woman **t** and mixed in with three measures
14: 4 Jesus **t** him and healed him, and sent him away.
15:14 a severe famine **t** place throughout that country,
18:31 Then he **t** the twelve aside and said to them, "See,
22:14 When the hour came, he **t** his place at the table,
22:17 Then he **t** a cup, and after giving thanks he said,
22:19 Then he **t** a loaf of bread,
23:53 Then he **t** it down, wrapped it in a linen cloth,
24:21 it is now the third day since these things **t** place.
24:30 When he was at the table with them, he **t** bread,
24:43 and he **t** it and ate in their presence.
Jn 1:28 This **t** place in Bethany across the Jordan
2: 8 and take it to the chief steward." So they **t** it.
Jn 5: 9 and he **t** up his mat and began to walk.
6:11 Then Jesus **t** the loaves,
10:22 the festival of the Dedication **t** place in Jerusalem.
10:31 The Jews **t** up stones again to stone him.
11:41 So they **t** away the stone.
12: 3 Mary **t** a pound of costly perfume made
12:13 So they **t** branches of palm trees and went out
13: 4 up from the table, **t** off his outer robe, and tied
18:13 First they **t** him to Annas,
18:28 Then they **t** Jesus from Caiaphas
19: 1 Then Pilate **t** Jesus and had him flogged.
19:16 be crucified. So they **t** Jesus;
19:23 they **t** his clothes and divided them
19:23 They also **t** his tunic;
19:27 that hour the disciple **t** her into his own home.
19:40 They **t** the body of Jesus and wrapped it with
21:13 Jesus came and **t** the bread and gave it to them,
Ac 1: 9 and a cloud **t** him out of their sight.
3: 7 And he **t** him by the right hand and raised him up;
4:26 The kings of the earth **t** their stand,
5:17 Then the high priest **t** action;
7:43 No; you **t** along the tent of Moloch,
8:13 the signs and great miracles that **t** place.
9:25 but his disciples **t** him by night and let him down
9:27 But Barnabas **t** him, brought him to the apostles,
9:39 when he arrived, they **t** him to the room upstairs.
11:19 the persecution that **t** place over Stephen traveled
11:28 and this **t** place during the reign of Claudius.
12:21 **t** his seat on the platform,
13:29 they **t** him down from the tree and laid him in
15:39 Barnabas **t** Mark with him and sailed away
16: 3 and he **t** him and had him circumcised because of
16:11 from Troas and **t** a straight course to Samothrace,
16:33 of the night he **t** them and washed their wounds;
16:39 they **t** them out and asked them to leave the city.
17:19 So they **t** him and brought him to the Areopagus
18:26 they **t** him aside and explained the Way of God
20:10 and bending over him **t** him in his arms, and said,
20:14 we **t** him on board and went to Mitylene.
21:11 He came to us and **t** Paul's belt,
21:26 Then Paul **t** the men, and the next day,
21:32 Immediately he **t** soldiers and centurions and ran
22:11 those who were with me **t** my hand and led me
23:18 So he **t** him, brought him to the tribune, and said,
23:19 The tribune **t** him by the hand,
23:31 **t** Paul and brought him during the night
25: 6 the next day he **t** his seat on the tribunal
25:17 the next day I **t** my seat on the tribunal and ordered
27:17 After hoisting it up they **t** measures to undergird
27:28 So they **t** soundings and found twenty fathoms;
27:28 a little farther on they **t** soundings again
27:35 After he had said this, he **t** bread;
27:36 Then all of them were encouraged and **t** food
28:15 On seeing them, Paul thanked God and **t** courage.
1Co 11:23 the night when he was betrayed **t** a loaf of bread,
11:25 In the same way he **t** the cup also, after supper,
2Co 12:16 (you say) since I was crafty, I **t** you in by deceit.
2Th 2:12 the truth but **t** pleasure in unrighteousness will
Heb 7:20 for others who became priests **t** their office
8: 9 when I **t** them by the hand to lead them out of
9:19 he **t** the blood of calves and goats,
Rev 5: 7 He went and **t** the scroll from the right hand of
8: 5 Then the angel **t** the censer and filled it with fire
10:10 So I **t** the little scroll from the hand of the angel
12:18 the dragon **t** his stand on the sand of the seashore.
18:21 a mighty angel **t** up a stone like a great millstone
Tob 2:10 and Ahikar **t** care of me for two years
4:12 all **t** wives from among their kindred.
5: 3 we each **t** one part, and I put one with the money.
7: 1 So he **t** him to Raguel's house,
7:12 When she came to him he **t** her by the hand
8: 1 so they **t** the young man and brought him into
8: 2 and he **t** the fish's liver and heart out of the bag
Jdt 1:14 Thus he **t** possession of his towns and came
2:17 He **t** along a vast number of camels and donkeys
2:22 From there Holofernes **t** his whole army,
3: 6 in the fortified towns and **t** picked men from them
5:15 and **t** up residence in the land of the Amorites,
5:15 and crossing over the Jordan they **t** possession
6:11 the slaves **t** him and led him out of the camp into
6:21 Uzziah **t** him from the assembly to his own house
8: 3 and **t** to his bed and died in his town Bethulia.
10: 3 **t** off her widow's garments,
10:12 and **t** her into custody. They asked her,
12:19 Then she **t** what her maid had prepared and ate
13: 6 and **t** down his sword that hung there.
13: 7 **t** hold of the hair of his head, and said,
14:11 Then they all **t** their weapons,
15: 3 in the hills around Bethulia also **t** to flight.
15: 7 **t** possession of what remained.
15:11 She **t** them and loaded her mules and hitched
15:12 She **t** ivy-wreathed wands in her hands
AdE 3:10 the king **t** off his signet ring and gave it to Haman
6: 1 That night the Lord **t** sleep from the king,
8: 2 king **t** the ring that had been taken from Haman,
9:15 and killed three hundred people, but **t** no plunder.
9:27 and the Jews **t** upon themselves,
12: 1 Now Mordecai **t** his rest in the courtyard
14: 2 She **t** off her splendid apparel and put on
14: 5 O Lord, **t** Israel out of all the nations,
15: 1 the third day, when she ended her prayer, she **t** off
15: 2 she **t** two maids with her;
15: 8 and in alarm he sprang from his throne and **t** her
Wis 4:14 he **t** them quickly from the midst of wickedness.
5: 7 We **t** our fill of the paths of lawlessness
14: 6 the hope of the world **t** refuge on a raft,
16:21 ministering to the desire of the one who **t** it,
Wis 18: 5 you in punishment **t** away a multitude
19:18 be clearly inferred from the sight of what **t** place.
Sir 1: 9 he saw her and **t** her measure;
24:12 I **t** root in an honored people,
47:11 The Lord **t** away his sins,
Bar 1: 2 the Chaldeans **t** Jerusalem and burned it with fire.
1: 8 Baruch **t** the vessels of the house of the Lord,
Sus 1:61 And they **t** action against the two elders,
Bel 1:27 Then Daniel **t** pitch, fat, and hair,
1:36 Then the angel of the Lord **t** him by the crown
1Mc 1:21 He arrogantly entered the sanctuary and **t**
1:22 He **t** also the table for the bread of the Presence,
1:23 He **t** the silver and the gold,
1:23 he **t** also the hidden treasures that he found.
1:27 Every bridegroom **t** up the lament;
1:32 They **t** captive the women and children,
3: 1 was called Maccabeus, **t** command in his place.
3:12 and Judas **t** the sword of Apollonius,
3:37 Then the king **t** the remaining half of his forces
3:41 they **t** silver and gold in immense amounts,
4: 1 Now Gorgias **t** five thousand infantry
4:47 Then they **t** unhewn stones, as the law directs,
5: 8 He also **t** Jazer and its villages;
5:23 Then he **t** the Jews of Galilee and Arbatta,
5:28 and he **t** the town, and killed every male by
5:35 and fought against it and **t** it;
5:36 From there he marched on and **t** Chaspho, Maked,
5:44 But he **t** the town and burned the sacred precincts
6: 8 He **t** to his bed and became sick
6:33 the king set out and **t** his army by a forced march
6:36 These **t** their position beforehand wherever
6:50 So the king **t** Beth-zur and stationed a guard there
6:63 but he fought against him, and **t** the city by force.
7: 4 Demetrius **t** his seat on the throne of his kingdom.
8: 7 they **t** him alive and decreed that he
8: 8 These they **t** from him and gave
8:10 the Romans **t** captive their wives and children;
9: 2 and they **t** it and killed many people.
9:11 from the camp and **t** its stand for the encounter.
9:19 and Simon **t** their brother Judas and buried him in
9:26 who **t** vengeance on them and made sport
9:40 and the Jews **t** all their goods.
9:53 And he **t** the sons of the leading men of the land
10:10 And Jonathan **t** up residence in Jerusalem
10:55 to the land of your ancestors and **t** your seat on
11:12 So he **t** his daughter away from him and gave her
11:62 and **t** the sons of their rulers as hostages
11:66 from there, **t** possession of the town, and set
12:33 He turned aside to Joppa and **t** it by surprise,
13:25 and **t** the bones of his brother Jonathan,
14: 3 and seized him and **t** him to Arsaces,
14: 5 To crown all his honors he **t** Joppa for a harbor,
16:16 Ptolemy and his men rose up, **t** their weapons,
2Mc 1:19 the pious priests of that time **t** some of the fire of
1:19 where they **t** such precautions that
3:27 his men **t** him up, put him on a stretcher,
4:12 He **t** delight in establishing a gymnasium right
4:21 and he **t** measures for his own security.
4:41 and others **t** handfuls of the ashes that were lying
5: 5 Jason **t** no fewer than a thousand men
5: 5 Menelaus **t** refuge in the citadel.
5:11 he **t** it to mean that Judea was in revolt.
5:11 he left Egypt and **t** the city by storm.
5:16 He **t** the holy vessels with his polluted hands,
6:21 of that unlawful sacrifice **t** the man aside because
8:20 against the Galatians that **t** place in Babylonia,
8:20 and **t** a great amount of booty.
8:35 **t** off his splendid uniform and made his way alone
9:29 And Philip, one of his courtiers, **t** his body home;
10: 5 the purification of the sanctuary **t** place, that is,
10:10 Now we will tell what **t** place
10:12 **t** the lead in showing justice to the Jews because
10:13 he **t** poison and ended his life.
10:18 When at least nine thousand **t** refuge
10:27 And rising from their prayer they **t** up their arms
10:30 Two of them **t** Maccabeus between them,
11: 4 He **t** no account whatever of the power of God,
12: 4 of Joppa **t** them out to sea and drowned them,
12:16 They **t** the town by the will of God,
12:27 Stalwart young men **t** their stand before the walls
12:43 He also **t** up a collection, man by man,
13:26 Lysias **t** the public platform,
14:26 he **t** the covenant that had been made and went
14:46 **t** them in both hands and hurled them at
1Es 1:10 This is what **t** place.
1:30 And immediately his servants **t** him out of the line
1:34 The men of the nation **t** Jeconiah son of Josiah,
1:40 a chain of bronze and **t** him away to Babylon.
1:41 Nebuchadnezzar also **t** some holy vessels of
1:54 They **t** all the holy vessels of the Lord,
3:13 king awoke, they **t** the writing and gave it to him,
3:15 and he **t** his seat in the council chamber,
4:61 So he **t** the letters, and went to Babylon
5:48 **t** their places and prepared the altar of the God
6:18 these King Cyrus **t** out again from the temple
6:26 which Nebuchadnezzar **t** out of the house
8:60 So the priests and the Levites who **t** the silver and
9:45 Then Ezra **t** up the book of the law in the sight of
Pm 151: 4 It was he who sent his messenger and **t** me
151: 7 and **t** away disgrace from the people of Israel.
3Mc 1: 1 **t** with him his sister Arsinoë,
1: 2 **t** with him the best of the Ptolemaic arms
1:26 But he, in his arrogance, **t** heed of nothing,
3:14 When our expedition **t** place in Asia,
3:22 But in their innate malice they **t** this in a
5:42 **t** no account of the changes of mind
6:32 They stopped their chanting of dirges and **t** up

2Es 13:40 he **t** them across the river,
14:32 in due time he **t** from you what he had given.
14:37 So I **t** the five men, as he commanded me,
14:40 I **t** it and drank;

TOOL‡ (3) [TOOLS]

Dt 27: 5 of stones on which you have not used an iron **t.**
Jos 8:31 on which no iron **t** has been used";
1Ki 6: 7 nor ax nor any **t** of iron was heard in the temple

TOOLS (2) [TOOL]

Ge 4:22 who made all kinds of bronze and iron **t.**
Sir 48:17 he tunneled the rock with iron **t,**

TOOTH (11) [TEETH]

Ex 21:24 **t** for **t,** hand for hand, foot for foot,
21:27 owner knocks out a **t** of a male or female slave,
21:27 a free person, to compensate for the **t.**
Lev 24:20 for fracture, eye for eye, **t** for **t;**
Dt 19:21 life for life, eye for eye, **t** for **t,**
Pr 25:19 a bad **t** or a lame foot is trust in a faithless person
Mt 5:38 'An eye for an eye and a **t** for a **t.'**

TOP‡ (78) [ATOP, TOPMOST, TOPS]

Ge 11: 4 and a tower with its **t** in the heavens,
22: 9 and laid him on the altar, on **t** of the wood.
28:12 the **t** of it reaching to heaven;
28:18 and set it up for a pillar and poured oil on the **t**
42:27 he saw his money at the **t** of the sack.
43:12 with you the money that was returned in the **t**
43:21 there was each one's money in the **t** of his sack,
44: 1 and put each man's money in the **t** of his sack.
44: 2 the silver cup, in the **t** of the sack of the youngest,
44: 8 the money that we found at the **t** of our sacks,
Ex 17: 9 the **t** of the hill with the staff of God in my hand."
17:10 Aaron, and Hur went up to the **t** of the hill.
19:20 upon Mount Sinai, to the **t** of the mountain,
19:20 LORD summoned Moses to the **t** of the mountain,
24:17 on the **t** of the mountain in the sight of the people
25:21 You shall put the mercy seat on the **t** of the ark;
26:24 but joined at the **t,** at the first ring;
29:25 on **t** of the burnt offering of pleasing odor before
30: 3 You shall overlay it with pure gold, its **t,**
34: 2 on the **t** of the mountain.
36:29 They were separate beneath, but joined at the **t,**
37:26 He overlaid it with pure gold, its **t,**
Lev 14:17 on **t** of the blood of the guilt offering.
Nu 4:25 the outer covering of fine leather that is on **t** of it,
20:28 and Aaron died there on the **t** of the mountain.
21:20 to the valley lying in the region of Moab by the **t**
23: 9 For from the **t** of the crags I see him,
23:14 So he took him to the field of Zophim, to the **t**
23:28 So Balak took Balaam to the **t** of Peor,
Dt 3:27 the **t** of Pisgah and look around you to the west,
28:13 you shall be only at the **t,** and not at the bottom—
34: 1 to the **t** of Pisgah, which is opposite Jericho,
Jos 15: 8 and the boundary goes up to the **t** of the mountain
15: 9 the boundary extends from the **t** of the mountain
Jdg 6:26 on the **t** of the stronghold here, in proper order;
9: 7 he went and stood on the **t** of Mount Gerizim,
16: 3 and carried them to the **t** of the hill that is in front
1Sa 26:13 and stood on **t** of a hill far away,
2Sa 2:25 they took their stand on the **t** of a hill.
1Ki 7:35 On the **t** of the stand there was a round band half
7:35 on the **t** of the stand,
10:19 The **t** of the throne was rounded in the back,
18:42 Elijah went up to the **t** of Carmel;
2Ki 1: 9 who was sitting on the **t** of a hill, and said to him,
2Ch 3:15 with a capital of five cubits on the **t** of each.
4:12 and the two capitals on the **t** of the pillars;
4:12 the two bowls of the capitals that were on the **t** of
25:12 took them to the **t** of Sela, and threw them down from the **t** of Sela,
Est 5: 2 Then Esther approached and touched the **t** of
Pr 23:34 like one who lies on the **t** of a mast.
25:27 or to seek honor on **t** of honor.
Isa 17: 6 two or three berries in the **t** of the highest bough,
30:17 until you are left like a flagstaff on the **t** of
Jer 52:22 all of bronze, encircled the **t** of the capital.
Eze 17: 3 He took the **t** of the cedar,
17:22 I myself will take a sprig from the lofty **t** of
31: 3 and of great height, its **t** among the clouds.
31:10 it towered high and set its **t** among the clouds,
43:12 the whole territory on the **t** of the mountain all
Da 4:11 The tree grew great and strong, its **t** reached
4:20 so that its **t** reached to heaven and was visible to
Am 1: 2 and the **t** of Carmel dries up.
9: 3 Though they hide themselves on the **t** of Carmel,
Zec 4: 2 with a bowl on the **t** of it;
4: 2 on each of the lamps that are on the **t** of it.
4: 7 and he shall bring out the **t** stone amid shouts
Mt 27:51 the curtain of the temple was torn in two, from **t**
Mk 5: 7 and he shouted at the **t** of his voice,
15:38 the curtain of the temple was torn in two, from **t**
Lk 8:28 down before him and shouted at the **t** of his voice,
Jn 19:23 woven in one piece from the **t.**
Heb 11:21 "bowing in worship over the **t** of his staff."
Tob 11:15 in rejoicing and praising God at the **t** of his voice.
13: 6 acknowledge him at the **t** of your voice.
Jdt 6:12 and ran out of the town to the **t** of the hill,
1Mc 1:59 that was on **t** of the altar of burnt offering.
2Es 13:35 But he shall stand on the **t** of Mount Zion.

TOPAZ (1)

Rev 21:20 the ninth **t,** the tenth chrysoprase,

TOPHEL (1)

Dt 1: 1 on the plain opposite Suph, between Paran and **T,**

TOPHETH‡ (9)

2Ki 23:10 He defiled **T,** which is in the valley
Jer 7:31 And they go on building the high place of **T,**
7:32 when it will no more be called **T,**
7:32 they will bury in **T** until there is no more room.
19: 6 when this place shall no more be called **T,**
19:11 In **T** they shall bury until there is no more room
19:12 and to its inhabitants, making this city like **T.**
19:13 of Judah shall be defiled like the place of **T—**
19:14 When Jeremiah came from **T,**

TOPMOST (2) [TOP]

Eze 17: 4 broke off its **t** shoot; He carried it to a land of trade
17:22 a tender one from the **t** of its young twigs;

TOPPLE (1)

Isa 40:20 a skilled artisan to set up an image that will not **t.**

TOPS (23) [TOP]

Ge 8: 5 the **t** of the mountains appeared.
Jdg 9:25 of Shechem set ambushes on the mountain **t.**
9:36 people are coming down from the mountain **t!"**
2Sa 5:24 the sound of marching in the **t** of the balsam trees,
1Ki 7:16 to set on the **t** of the pillars;
7:17 chain work for the capitals on the **t** of the pillars;
7:19 Now the capitals that were on the **t** of the pillars
7:22 On the **t** of the pillars was lily-work.
7:41 the two bowls of the capitals that were on the **t** of
7:41 the two bowls of the capitals that were on the **t** of
1Ch 14:15 the sound of marching in the **t** of the balsam trees,
2Ch 3:16 He made encircling chains and put them on the **t**
Ps 72:16 may it wave on the **t** of the mountains;
Isa 14:14 I will ascend to the **t** of the clouds,
42:11 let them shout from the **t** of the mountains.
Eze 6:13 on all the mountain **t,** under every green tree,
31:14 the waters may grow to lofty height or set their **t**
Hos 4:13 They sacrifice on the **t** of the mountains,
Joel 2: 5 they leap on the **t** of the mountains,
Jdt 7:10 for it is not easy to reach the **t** of their mountains.
7:13 to the **t** of the nearby mountains and camp there
2Es 16:60 and pools on the **t** of the mountains,
4Mc 14:16 in precipitous chasms and in holes and **t** of trees,

TORCH (6) [TORCHES]

Ge 15:17 and a flaming **t** passed between these pieces.
Jdg 15: 4 and put a **t** between each pair of tails.
Isa 62: 1 and her salvation like a burning **t.**
Zec 12: 6 like a flaming **t** among sheaves;
Rev 8:10 and a great star fell from heaven, blazing like a **t,**
Sir 48: 1 a prophet like fire, and his word burned like a **t.**

TORCHES (12) [TORCH]

Jdg 7:16 and empty jars, with **t** inside the jars,
7:20 holding in their left hands the **t,**
15: 4 and caught three hundred foxes, and took some **t;**
15: 5 When he had set fire to the **t,**
Job 41:19 From its mouth go flaming **t;**
Eze 1:13 like **t** moving to and fro among
Da 10: 6 his face like lightning, his eyes like flaming **t,**
Na 2: 4 their appearance is like **t,** they dart like lightning.
Jn 18: 3 They came there with lanterns and **t** and weapons.
Rev 4: 5 and in front of the throne burn seven flaming **t,**
1Mc 6:39 with them and gleamed like flaming **t.**
2Mc 4:22 and ushered in with a blaze of **t** and with shouts.

TORE‡ (61) [TEAR]

Ge 37:29 that Joseph was not in the pit, he **t** his clothes.
37:34 Then Jacob **t** his garments,
44:13 At this they **t** their clothes.
Nu 14: 6 those who had spied out the land, **t** their clothes
Jos 7: 6 Then Joshua **t** his clothes,
Jdg 11:35 When he saw her, he **t** his clothes, and said,
14: 6 and he **t** the lion apart barehanded
1Sa 15:27 Saul caught hold of the hem of his robe, and it **t.**
2Sa 1:11 Then David took hold of his clothes and **t** them;
13:19 and **t** the long robe that she was wearing;
13:31 king rose, **t** his garments, and lay on the ground;
13:31 his servants who were standing by **t** their garments.
1Ki 11:30 of the new garment he was wearing and **t** it
14: 8 and **t** the kingdom away from the house of David
21:27 he **t** his clothes and put sackcloth
2Ki 2:12 he grasped his own clothes and **t** them
5: 7 he **t** his clothes and said, "Am I God,
6:30 the words of the woman he **t** his clothes—
11:14 Athaliah **t** her clothes and cried, "Treason!
11:18 the land went to the house of Baal, and **t** it down;
19: 1 When King Hezekiah heard it, he **t** his clothes,
22:11 the words of the book of the law, he **t** his clothes.
2Ch 23:13 Athaliah **t** her clothes, and cried, "Treason!
23:17 to the house of Baal, and **t** it down;
34:19 king heard the words of the law he **t** his clothes.
Ezr 9: 3 When I heard this, I **t** my garment and my mantle,
Est 4: 1 Mordecai **t** his clothes and put on sackcloth
Job 1:20 Then Job arose, **t** his robe, shaved his head,
2:12 they **t** their robes and threw dust in the air
Ps 35:15 ruffians whom I did not know **t** at me
Isa 23:13 they **t** down her palaces, they made her a ruin.
37: 1 When King Hezekiah heard it, he **t** his clothes,
La 3:11 he led me off my way and **t** me to pieces;
Eze 29: 7 you broke, and **t** all their shoulders;
Mt 26:65 Then the high priest **t** his clothes and said,
Mk 14:63 Then the high priest **t** his clothes and said,
Ac 14:14 they **t** their clothes and rushed out into the crowd,
Gal 2:18 But if I build up again the very things that I once **t**
Jdt 14:16 and groaned and shouted, and **t** his clothes.
14:19 they **t** their tunics and were greatly dismayed,
AdE 4: 1 he **t** his clothes, put on sackcloth,
1Mc 1:31 and **t** down its houses and its surrounding walls.
1:56 The books of the law that they found they **t**
2:14 Then Mattathias and his sons **t** their clothes,
2:25 and he **t** down the altar.
2:45 and his friends went around and **t** down the altars;
3:47 on their heads, and **t** their clothes.
4:39 Then they **t** their clothes and mourned
4:45 So they **t** down the altar,
5:65 and **t** down its strongholds and burned its towers
5:68 he **t** down their altars, and the carved images
8:10 conquered the land, **t** down their strongholds,
9:54 He **t** down the work of the prophets!
11:71 Jonathan **t** his clothes, put dust on his head,
2Mc 4:38 **t** off his purple robe, and led him around
7: 7 They **t** off the skin of his head with the hair,
10: 2 they **t** down the altars that had been built in
14:46 he **t** out his entrails, took them in both hands
1Es 8:71 As soon as I heard these things I **t** my garments
4Mc 9:28 These leopard-like beasts **t** out his sinews with
9:28 up to his chin, and **t** away his scalp.

TORMAH See Index to Footnotes

TORMENT‡ (23) [TORMENTED, TORMENTING, TORMENTORS, TORMENTS]

Job 19: 2 "How long will you **t** me,
Isa 50:11 you shall lie down in **t.**
Mt 8:29 Have you come here to **t** us before the time?"
Mk 5: 7 I adjure you by God, do not **t** me."
Lk 8:28 I beg you, do not **t** me"—
16:28 that they will not also come into this place of **t.'**
2Co 12: 7 a messenger of Satan to **t** me,
Rev 11:10 because these two prophets had been a **t** to
14:11 the smoke of their **t** goes up forever and ever.
18: 7 so give her a like measure of **t** and grief.
18:10 in fear of her **t,** and say, "Alas, alas,
18:15 in fear of her **t,** weeping and mourning aloud,
Wis 3: 1 and no **t** will ever touch them.
17:13 prefers ignorance of what causes the **t.**
Sir 4:17 will **t** them by her discipline until she trusts them,
2Es 7:*36* of **t** shall appear, and opposite it shall be the place
7:*66* of any **t** or salvation promised to them after death.
7:*84* they shall consider the **t** laid up for themselves in
7:*99* and the previously mentioned are the ways of **t**
8:59 so the thirst and **t** that are prepared await them.
9:12 these must in **t** acknowledge it after death.
4Mc 9: 9 from the divine justice eternal **t** by fire."
13:15 of eternal **t** lying before those who transgress

TORMENTED (20) [TORMENT]

1Sa 16:14 and an evil spirit from the LORD **t** him.
2Sa 13: 2 Amnon was so **t** that he made himself ill because
Mt 15:22 my daughter is **t** by a demon."
Lk 16:23 In Hades, where he was being **t,**
Ac 5:16 bringing the sick and those **t** by unclean spirits,
Heb 11:37 of sheep and goats, destitute, persecuted, **t—**
2Pe 2: 8 was **t** in his righteous soul by their lawless deeds
Rev 14:10 be **t** with fire and sulfur in the presence of
20:10 and they will be **t** day and night forever and ever.
Wis 11: 9 they learned how the ungodly were **t** when judged
12:23 you **t** through their own abominations
16: 1 and were **t** by a multitude of animals.
16: 4 how their enemies were being **t.**
2Es 7:*64* the mind grows with us, and therefore we are **t,**
7:*67* that we shall be preserved alive but cruelly **t?**
7:*72* therefore, those who live on earth shall be **t,**
7:*75* or whether we shall be **t** at once?"
7:*76* or number yourself among those who are **t.**
4Mc 3:11 in the enemy's territory **t** and inflamed him,
6:16 Eleazar, as though more bitterly **t** by this counsel,

TORMENTING (1) [TORMENT]

1Sa 16:15 "See now, an evil spirit from God is **t** you.

TORMENTORS (2) [TORMENT]

Ps 137: 3 and our **t** asked for mirth, saying,
Isa 51:23 And I will put it into the hand of your **t,**

TORMENTS (15) [TORMENT]

Ps 32:10 Many are the **t** of the wicked,
Wis 19: 4 up the punishment that their **t** still lacked,
3Mc 3:27 will be tortured to death with the most hateful **t,**
2Es 7:*38* here are delight and rest, and there are fire and **t.'**
7:*47* the world to come will bring delight to few, but **t**
7:*80* but shall immediately wander about in **t,**
7:*86* how some of them will cross over into **t.**
9: 9 with contempt shall live in **t.**
13:38 to their face with their evil thoughts and the **t**
4Mc 6:27 I am dying in burning **t** for the sake of the law.
8:19 of torture and consider the threats of **t,**
10:11 will undergo unceasing **t."**

4Mc 12: 3 for they died in **t** because of their disobedience.
15:18 nor when the second in **t** I looked at you piteously
15:22 and how many **t** the mother then suffered

TORN (66) [TEAR]

Ge 31:39 which was **t** by wild beasts I did not bring to you;
37:33 Joseph is without doubt **t** to pieces."
44:28 and I said, Surely he has been **t** to pieces;
Ex 28:32 so that it may not be **t.**
39:23 so that it might not be **t.**
Lev 7:24 an animal that died or was **t** by wild animals may
13:45 the leprous disease shall wear **t** clothes and let
14:45 He shall have the house **t** down,
17:15 who eat what dies of itself or what has been **t**
22: 8 That which died or was **t** by wild animals he shall
22:24 that has its testicles bruised or crushed or **t** or cut,
Jos 9: 4 and wineskins, worn-out and **t** and mended,
1Sa 4:12 with his clothes **t** and with earth upon his head.
15:28 "The LORD has **t** the kingdom of Israel
28:17 the LORD has **t** the kingdom out of your hand,
2Sa 1: 2 with his clothes **t** and dirt on his head.
15:32 to meet him with his coat **t** and earth on his head.
1Ki 13: 3 'The altar shall be **t** down,
13: 5 The altar also was **t** down,
13:26 which has **t** him and killed him according to
2Ki 5: 8 that the king of Israel had **t** his clothes,
5: 8 "Why have you **t** your clothes?
17:21 When he had **t** Israel from the house of David,
18:37 with their clothes **t** and told him the words of
22:19 you have **t** your clothes and wept before me,
2Ch 34:27 and have **t** your clothes and wept before me,
Ezr 9: 5 with my garments and my mantle **t,**
Job 16: 9 He has **t** me in his wrath, and hated me;
18:14 They are **t** from the tent in which they trusted,
26: 8 and the cloud is not **t** open by them.
Ps 60: 2 to quake; you have **t** it open;
Pr 27: 9 but the soul is **t** by trouble.
Isa 24:19 The earth is utterly broken, the earth is **t** asunder,
36:22 came to Hezekiah with their clothes **t,**
Jer 5: 6 everyone who goes out of them shall be **t**
33: 4 the houses of the kings of Judah that were **t** down
41: 5 with their beards shaved and their clothes **t,**
51:35 May my **t** flesh be avenged on Babylon,"
Eze 4:14 never eaten what died of itself or was **t** by animals,
30: 4 and its foundations are **t** down.
44:31 that died of itself or was **t** by animals.
Da 2: 5 you shall be **t** limb from limb,
3:29 and Abednego shall be **t** limb from limb,
Hos 6: 1 for it is he who has **t,** and he will heal us;
Na 2:12 The lion has **t** enough for his whelps
2:12 with prey and his dens with **t** flesh.
Mt 27:51 At that moment the curtain of the temple was **t**
Mk 1:10 the heavens **t** apart and the Spirit descending like
15:38 And the curtain of the temple was **t** in two,
Lk 5:36 otherwise the new will be **t,**
23:45 and the curtain of the temple was **t** in two.
Jn 21:11 and though there were so many, the net was not **t.**
Gal 4:15 you would have **t** out your eyes and given them
Jdt 9: 2 to take revenge on those strangers who had **t** off
Sir 6: 2 or you may be **t** apart as by a bull.
LtJ 6:31 in their temples the priests sit with their clothes **t,**
1Mc 5:14 other messengers, with their garments **t,**
6: 7 that they had **t** down the abomination
13:45 went up on the wall with their clothes **t,**
1Es 8:73 with my garments and my holy mantle **t,**
3Mc 4: 6 they were **t** by the harsh treatment of the heathen.
2Es 1:32 and killed them and **t** their bodies in pieces;
9:38 her clothes were **t,** and there were ashes
4Mc 6: 6 his flesh was being **t** by scourges,
9:11 and having **t** off his tunic,
10: 8 he saw his own flesh **t** all around and drops

TORRENT (7) [TORRENT-BED, TORRENTIAL, TORRENTS]

Jdg 5:21 The **t** Kishon swept them away, the onrushing **t,** the **t** Kishon.
Ps 124: 4 the **t** would have gone over us;
Jer 47: 2 of the north and shall become an overflowing **t;**
La 2:18 Let tears stream down like a **t** day and night!
Hab 3:10 a **t** of water swept by;

TORRENT-BED (2) [TORRENT]

Job 6:15 My companions are treacherous like a **t,**
22:24 and gold of Ophir like the stones of the **t,**

TORRENTIAL (1) [TORRENT]

Eze 38:22 and I will pour down **t** rains and hailstones,

TORRENTS (7) [TORRENT]

2Sa 22: 5 the **t** of perdition assailed me;
23:30 Benaiah of Pirathon; Hiddai of the **t** of Gaash;
Job 14:19 the **t** wash away the soil of the earth;
38:25 "Who has cut a channel for the **t** of rain,
Ps 18: 4 the **t** of perdition assailed me;
74:15 You cut openings for springs and **t;**
78:20 so that water gushed out and **t** overflowed,

TORTOISE (KJV) See GREAT LIZARD

TORTUOUS (1) [TORTURE]

Sir 4:17 For at first she will walk with them on **t** paths;

TORTURE‡ (28) [TORTUOUS, TORTURED, TORTURERS, TORTURES, TORTURING, TORTURINGS]

Rev 9: 5 They were allowed to **t** them for five months,
9: 5 and their **t** was like the **t** of a scorpion
Wis 2:19 Let us test him with insult and **t,**
2Mc 7: 1 under **t** with whips and thongs,
7:17 and see how his mighty power will **t** you
8:17 and the **t** of the derided city, and besides,
9: 7 the fall was so hard as to **t** every limb of his body.
4Mc 4:26 he himself tried through **t** to compel everyone in
5: 6 "Before I begin to **t** you,
5:32 Therefore get your **t** wheels ready and fan
6: 1 by dragged him violently to the instruments of **t.**
8: 1 over the most painful instruments of **t.**
8:12 the instruments of **t** to be brought forward so as
8:19 the instruments of **t** and consider the threats
8:25 to death for fearing the instruments of **t.**
9: 5 to terrify us by threatening us with death by **t,**
9: 6 of their religion lived piously while enduring **t,**
9:26 they bound him to the **t** machine and catapult.
9:32 but you suffer **t** by the threats that come
11:16 if you intend to **t** me for not eating defiling foods,
12:11 and **t** on the wheel those who practice religion?
12:13 and to maltreat and **t** them in this way?
14: 1 Furthermore, they encouraged them to face the **t,**
14: 5 toward immortality, hastened to death by **t.**
15:21 as did the voices of the children in **t** calling
15:32 the **t** of your sons, endured nobly and withstood
17:10 looking to God and enduring **t** even to death."

TORTURED (29) [TORTURE]

Mt 18:34 over to be **t** until he would pay his entire debt.
24: 9 over to be **t** and will put you to death,
Heb 11:35 Others were **t,** refusing to accept release,
13: 3 those who are being **t,** as though you yourselves were being **t.**
2Mc 7:13 they maltreated and **t** the fourth in the same way.
8:28 of the spoils to those who had been **t** and to
8:30 giving to those who had been **t** and to the orphans
9: 6 for he had **t** the bowels of others with many
9:11 for he was **t** with pain every moment.
3Mc 3:27 will be **t** to death with the most hateful torments,
4:14 but to be **t** with the outrages that he had ordered,
2Es 13:38 to be **t** (which were symbolized by the flames),
4Mc 6: 5 was unmoved, as though being **t** in a dream;
8: 2 they would be **t** even more cruelly.
8: 5 as that of the old man who has just been **t,**
8:27 But the youths, though about to be **t,**
9:30 that you are being **t** more than I,
10:16 a brother to those who have just now been **t."**
11: 1 When he too died, after being cruelly **t,**
11: 2 tyrant, to be **t** for the sake of virtue.
11:20 being **t** he said, "O contest befitting holiness,
12: 4 will be miserably **t** and die before your time,
13:27 their brothers being maltreated and **t** to death.
15:14 who saw them **t** and burned one by one,
15:22 then suffered as her sons were **t** on the wheel and
16: 1 endured seeing her children **t** to death,
16: 3 as she saw her seven sons **t** in such varied ways.
16:15 you stood and watched Eleazar being **t,**

TORTURERS (3) [TORTURE]

4Mc 1:11 even their **t,** marveled at their courage
6:10 while being beaten, was victorious over his **t;**
6:11 he amazed even his **t** by his courageous spirit.

TORTURES (30) [TORTURE]

Sir 33:27 and for a wicked slave there are racks and **t.**
2Mc 7: 8 in turn underwent **t** as the first brother had done.
7:42 about the eating of sacrifices and the extreme **t.**
9: 5 there was no relief, and with sharp internal **t**—
4Mc 6: 9 and scorned the punishment and endured the **t.**
6:30 he said this, the holy man died nobly in his **t;**
6:30 even in the **t** of death he resisted,
7: 2 and overwhelmed by the mighty waves of **t,**
7: 4 his sacred life was consumed by **t** and racks,
7:10 O aged man, more powerful than **t;**
7:16 of piety an aged man despised **t** even to death,
8: 9 of you with dreadful punishments through **t.**
9: 6 young men should die despising your coercive **t,**
9: 7 to eat so that you may be released from the **t,"**
9:18 through all these **t** I will convince you
10:16 Contrive **t,** tyrant, so that you may learn
11: 6 But these deeds deserve honors, not **t."**
11:23 of **t** and enemy of those who are truly devout.
12:12 up for you intense and eternal fire and **t,**
14: 8 encircled the sevenfold fear of **t** and dissolved it.
14:11 over these men in their **t,**
15:11 of none of them were the various **t** strong enough
15:19 at the eyes of each one in his **t** gazing boldly at
16: 2 but also that a woman has despised the fiercest **t.**
16:17 you young men were to be terrified by **t.**
17: 3 and unswerving against the earthquake of the **t.**
17: 7 the seven children enduring their varied **t** to death
17:23 of their virtue and their endurance under the **t,**
18:20 to the catapult and back again to more **t,**
18:21 and put them to death with various **t.**

TORTURING (3) [TORTURE]

4Mc 9: 7 do not suppose that you can injure us by **t** us.
9:27 Before **t** him, they inquired if he were willing
11:16 for not eating defiling foods, go on **t!"**

TORTURINGS (1) [TORTURE]

4Mc 15:20 the place filled with many spectators of the **t,**

TOSS (3) [STORM-TOSSED, TOSSED, TOSSES, TOSSING, TOSSINGS]

Job 30:22 and you **t** me about in the roar of the storm.
Isa 57:20 its waters **t** up mire and mud.
Jer 5:22 though the waves **t,** they cannot prevail,

TOSSED (5) [TOSS]

Ex 14:27 the LORD **t** the Egyptians into the sea.
Am 8: 8 and be **t** about and sink again,
Eph 4:14 **t** to and fro and blown about by every wind
Jas 1: 6 driven and **t** by the wind;
Sir 29:18 and has **t** them about like waves of the sea;

TOSSES (2) [TOSS]

2Ki 19:21 virgin daughter Zion; she **t** her head—
Isa 37:22 virgin daughter Zion; she **t** her head—

TOSSING (3) [TOSS]

Job 7: 4 the night is long, and I am full of **t** until dawn.
Isa 57:20 the wicked are like the **t** sea that cannot keep still;
Ac 22:23 throwing off their cloaks, and **t** dust into the air,

TOSSINGS (1) [TOSS]

Ps 56: 8 You have kept count of my **t;**

TOTAL (17) [TOTALED, TOTALLY]

Ex 1: 5 **t** number of people born to Jacob was seventy.
Lev 25:50 They shall compute with the purchaser the **t** from
Nu 2: 9 The **t** enrollment of the camp of Judah,
2:16 The **t** enrollment of the camp of Reuben,
2:24 The **t** enrollment of the camp of Ephraim,
2:31 The **t** enrollment of the camp of Dan
2:32 the **t** enrollment in the camps by their companies
3:39 The **t** enrollment of the Levites whom Moses
3:43 The **t** enrollment, all the firstborn males from
35: 7 that you give to the Levites shall **t** forty-eight,
Jos 8:25 The **t** of those who fell that day,
1Ch 21: 5 Joab gave the **t** count of the people to David.
23: 3 were counted, and the **t** was thirty-eight thousand.
Ezr 1:11 the **t** of the gold and silver vessels was five
8:34 The **t** was counted and weighed,
2Mc 5:14 Within the **t** of three days eighty thousand were
3Mc 4:10 so that, with their eyes in **t** darkness,

TOTALED (3) [TOTAL]

Nu 31:32 taken **t** six hundred seventy-five thousand sheep,
1Ch 26:11 all the sons and brothers of Hosah **t** thirteen.
2Mc 3:11 and that it **t** in all four hundred talents of silver

TOTALLY (1) [TOTAL]

Da 7:26 to be consumed and **t** destroyed.

TOTTER‡ (2) [TOTTERING, TOTTERS]

Ps 46: 6 The nations are in an uproar, the kingdoms **t;**
59:11 make them **t** by your power,

TOTTERING (2) [TOTTER]

Ps 60: 2 repair the cracks in it, for it is **t.**
62: 3 all of you, as you would a leaning wall, a **t** fence?

TOTTERS (2) [TOTTER]

Ps 75: 3 When the earth **t,** with all its inhabitants,
Sir 13:21 the rich person **t,** he is supported by friends,

TOU (2) [=TOI]

1Ch 18: 9 When King **T** of Hamath heard that David had
18:10 Now Hadadezer had often been at war with **T.**

TOUBIANI (1)

2Mc 12:17 came to Charax, to the Jews who are called **T.**

TOUCH‡ (56) [TOUCHED, TOUCHES, TOUCHING]

Ge 3: 3 nor shall you **t** it, or you shall die.' "
20: 6 Therefore I did not let you **t** her.
Ex 12:22 and **t** the lintel and the two doorposts with
19:12 not to go up the mountain or to **t** the edge of it.
19:12 Any who **t** the mountain shall be put to death.
19:13 No hand shall **t** them, but they shall be stoned
Lev 5: 2 Or when any of you **t** any unclean thing—
5: 3 Or when you **t** human uncleanness—
11: 8 and their carcasses you shall not **t;**
12: 4 she shall not **t** any holy thing,
15: 7 All who **t** the body of the one with the discharge
15:10 All who **t** anything that was under him shall
Nu 4:15 but they must not **t** the holy things,
16:26 and **t** nothing of theirs, or you will be swept away
19:11 Those who **t** the dead body of any human being
19:13 All who **t** a corpse, the body of a human being
Dt 14: 8 and you shall not **t** their carcasses.
Jos 9:19 the God of Israel, and now we must not **t** them.
1Sa 1:11 and no razor shall **t** his head."
2Sa 14:10 bring him to me, and he shall never **t** you again."
23: 7 to **t** them one uses an iron bar or the shaft of
1Ch 16:22 "Do not **t** my anointed ones;
Est 9:10 but they did not **t** the plunder.

Est 9:15 but they did not **t** the plunder.
Job 1:11 stretch out your hand now, and **t** all that he has,
2: 5 But stretch out your hand now and **t** his bone
5:19 in seven no harm shall **t** you.
6: 7 My appetite refuses to **t** them;
Ps 105:15 "Do not **t** my anointed ones;
144: 5 **t** the mountains so that they smoke.
Isa 52:11 **T** no unclean thing; go out from the midst of it,
Jer 12:14 concerning all my evil neighbors who **t**
La 4:14 that no one was able to **t** their garments.
4:15 "Away! Away! Do not **t**!"
Eze 9: 6 but **t** no one who has the mark.
Mt 9:21 "If I only **t** his cloak, I will be made well."
14:36 and begged him that they might **t** even the fringe
Mk 3:10 all who had diseases pressed upon him to **t** him.
5:28 "If I but **t** his clothes, I will be made well."
6:56 and begged him that they might **t** even the fringe
8:22 a blind man to him and begged him to **t** him.
10:13 to him in order that he might **t** them;
Lk 6:19 And all in the crowd were trying to **t** him,
18:15 even infants to him that he might **t** them;
24:39 **T** me and see; a ghost does not have flesh and
1Co 7: 1 "It is well for a man not to **t** a woman."
2Co 6:17 and **t** nothing unclean; then I will welcome you,
Col 2:21 "Do not handle, Do not taste, Do not **t**"?
Heb 11:28 of the firstborn would not **t** the firstborn of Israel.
1Jn 5:18 and the evil one does not **t** them.
Jdt 11:13 for any of the people even to **t** with their hands.
Wis 3: 1 and no torment will ever **t** them.
Aza 1:27 not **t** them at all and caused them no pain
2Mc 9:10 while before had thought that he could **t** the stars
1Es 4:28 Do not all lands fear to **t** him?
4Mc 17: 1 into the flames so that no one might **t** her body.

TOUCHED (52) [TOUCH]

Ge 26:29 not **t** you and have done to you nothing but good
Ex 4:25 and **t** Moses' feet with it, and said,
Nu 19:18 and on whoever **t** the bone, the slain, the corpse,
31:19 of you has killed any person or **t** a corpse,
Jos 4:18 and the soles of the priests' feet **t** dry ground,
Jdg 6:21 and **t** the meat and the unleavened cakes;
1Sa 10:26 with him went warriors whose hearts God had **t**.
1Ki 19: 5 Suddenly an angel **t** him and said to him,
19: 7 angel of the LORD came a second time, **t** him,
2Ki 13:21 as soon as the man **t** the bones of Elisha,
2Ch 3:11 **t** the wall of the house, and its other wing,
3:11 five cubits long, **t** the wing of the other cherub;
3:12 one wing, five cubits long, **t** the wall of the house,
Est 5: 2 Esther approached and **t** the top of the scepter.
Job 19:21 O you my friends, for the hand of God has **t** me!
Isa 6: 7 The seraph **t** my mouth with it and said:
6: 7 "Now that this has **t** your lips,
Jer 1: 9 the LORD put out his hand and **t** my mouth;
Eze 1: 9 their wings **t** one another;
1:11 each of which **t** the wing of another,
Da 8:18 then he **t** me and set me on my feet.
10:10 hand **t** me and roused me to my hands and knees.
10:16 Then one in human form **t** my lips,
10:18 in human form **t** me and strengthened me.
Mt 8: 3 He stretched out his hand and **t** him, saying,
8:15 he **t** her hand, and the fever left her, and she got
9:20 up behind him and **t** the fringe of his cloak,
9:29 Then he **t** their eyes and said,
14:36 and all who **t** it were healed.
17: 7 But Jesus came and **t** them, saying,
20:34 Moved with compassion, Jesus **t** their eyes.
Mk 1:41 Jesus stretched out his hand and **t** him,
5:27 came up behind him in the crowd and **t** his cloak,
5:30 about in the crowd and said, "Who **t** my clothes?"
5:31 how can you say, 'Who **t** me?' "
6:56 and all who **t** it were healed.
7:33 and he spat and **t** his tongue.
Lk 5:13 Then Jesus stretched out his hand, **t** him, and said,
7:14 Then he came forward and **t** the bier,
8:44 up behind him and **t** the fringe of his clothes,
8:45 Then Jesus asked, "Who **t** me?"
8:46 But Jesus said, "Someone **t** me;
8:47 the presence of all the people why she had **t** him,
22:51 And he **t** his ear and healed him.
Ac 19:12 or aprons that had **t** his skin were brought to
20:15 The next day we **t** at Samos,
Heb 12:18 You have not come to something that can be **t**,
1Jn 1: 1 what we have looked at and **t** with our hands,
AdE 15:11 Then he raised the golden scepter and **t** her neck
Wis 18:16 and **t** heaven while standing on the earth.
18:20 The experience of death **t** also the righteous,
LtJ 6:29 to them may even be **t** by women in their periods

TOUCHES (45) [TOUCH]

Ge 26:11 "Whoever **t** this man or his wife shall be put
Ex 29:37 whatever **t** the altar shall become holy.
30:29 whatever **t** them will become holy.
Lev 6:18 anything that **t** them shall become holy.
6:27 Whatever **t** its flesh shall become holy;
7:19 Flesh that **t** any unclean thing shall not be eaten;
7:21 When any one of you **t** any unclean thing—
11:24 whoever **t** the carcass of any of them shall
11:26 everyone who **t** one of them shall be unclean.
11:27 whoever **t** the carcass of any of them shall
11:31 whoever **t** one of them when they are dead shall
11:36 while whatever **t** the carcass in it shall be unclean.
11:39 anyone who **t** its carcass shall be unclean until
15: 5 Anyone who **t** his bed shall wash his clothes,
15:11 All those whom the one with the discharge **t**
15:12 that the one with the discharge **t** shall be broken;
15:19 whoever **t** her shall be unclean until the evening.
Lev 15:21 Whoever **t** her bed shall wash his clothes,
15:22 Whoever **t** anything upon which
15:23 when he **t** it he shall be unclean until the evening.
15:27 Whoever **t** these things shall be unclean,
22: 4 Whoever **t** anything made unclean by a corpse or
22: 5 and whoever **t** any swarming thing
22: 6 the person who **t** any such shall be unclean
Nu 19:16 in the open field **t** one who has been killed by
19:21 and whoever **t** the water for cleansing shall
19:22 Whatever the unclean person **t** shall be unclean,
19:22 anyone who **t** it shall be unclean until evening.
Jos 16: 7 and **t** Jericho, ending at the Jordan.
19:11 and on to Maralah, and **t** Dabbesheth,
19:22 also **t** Tabor, Shahazumah, and Beth-shemesh,
19:26 on the west it **t** Carmel and Shihor-libnath,
19:27 and **t** Zebulun and the valley
Jdg 16: 9 as a strand of fiber snaps when it **t** the fire.
Job 4: 5 it **t** you, and you are dismayed.
Ps 104:32 who **t** the mountains and they smoke.
Pr 6:29 no one who **t** her will go unpunished.
Am 9: 5 GOD of hosts, he who **t** the earth and it melts,
Hag 2:12 and with the fold **t** bread, or stew, or wine, or oil,
2:13 by contact with a dead body **t** any of these,
Zec 2: 8 one who **t** you **t** the apple of my eye.
Heb 12:20 "If even an animal **t** the mountain,
Sir 13: 1 Whoever **t** pitch gets dirty,
34:30 one washes after touching a corpse, and **t** it again,

TOUCHING (11) [TOUCH]

Nu 9: 6 through **t** a corpse, so that they could not keep
9: 7 "Although we are unclean through **t** a corpse,
9:10 or your descendants who is unclean through **t**
Jos 19:34 **t** Zebulun at the south, and Asher on the west,
1Ki 6:27 that a wing of one was **t** the one wall, and a wing of the other cherub was **t** the other wall;
6:27 the center of the house were **t** wing to wing.
Isa 41: 3 scarcely **t** the path with his feet.
Da 8: 5 the face of the whole earth without **t** the ground.
Lk 7:39 and what kind of woman this is who is **t** him—
Sir 34:30 If one washes after **t** a corpse,

TOUR (1)

2Mc 3: 8 ostensibly to make a **t** of inspection of the cities

TOW (2)

Sir 21: 9 An assembly of the wicked is like a bundle of **t**,
Aza 1:23 in kept stoking the furnace with naphtha, pitch, **t**,

TOW (KJV) See also FIBER, TINDER, WICK

TOWARD‡ (273) [TOWARDS]

Ge 12: 9 And Abram journeyed on by stages **t** the Negeb.
15: 5 "Look **t** heaven and count the stars,
18:16 men set out from there, and they looked **t** Sodom;
18:22 So the men turned from there, and went **t** Sodom,
19:28 he looked down **t** Sodom and Gomorrah and **t** all
20: 1 From there Abraham journeyed **t** the region of
24:11 it was **t** evening, the time when women go out
24:27 and his faithfulness **t** my master.
28:10 Jacob left Beer-sheba and went **t** Haran.
30:40 and set the faces of the flocks **t** the striped and
31:21 and set his face **t** the hill country of Gilead.
48:13 Ephraim in his right hand **t** Israel's left, and Manasseh in his left hand **t** Israel's right,
Ex 9:22 "Stretch out your hand **t** heaven so
9:23 Then Moses stretched out his staff **t** heaven,
10:21 "Stretch out your hand **t** heaven so that there may
10:22 So Moses stretched out his hand **t** heaven,
13:18 by the roundabout way of the wilderness **t**
14: 5 and his officials were changed **t** the people,
16:10 they looked **t** the wilderness,
25:20 of the cherubim shall be turned **t** the mercy seat.
34: 8 And Moses quickly bowed his head **t** the earth,
37: 9 of the cherubim were turned **t** the mercy seat.
Lev 9:22 Aaron lifted his hands **t** the people
Nu 2: 3 Those to camp on the east side **t** the sunrise shall
3:38 in front of the tent of meeting **t** the east—
16:42 Moses and Aaron turned **t** the tent of meeting;
21:11 in the wilderness bordering Moab **t** the sunrise.
24: 1 but set his face **t** the wilderness.
34:15 the Jordan at Jericho eastward, **t** the sunrise.
Dt 15: 7 do not be hard-hearted or tight-fisted **t**
31:27 so rebellious **t** the LORD while I am still alive
Jos 2:16 She said to them, "Go **t** the hill country,
3:16 while those flowing **t** the sea of the Arabah,
8:18 "Stretch out the sword that is in your hand **t** Ai;
8:18 the sword that was in his hand **t** the city.
9: 1 the lowland all along the coast of the Great Sea **t**
11:17 which rises **t** Seir, as far as Baal-gad in the valley
12: 1 whose land they occupied beyond the Jordan **t**
12: 7 that rises **t** Seir (and Joshua gave their land to
13: 5 and all Lebanon, **t** the east,
15: 7 and so northward, turning **t** Gilgal,
15:21 **t** the boundary of Edom, were Kabzeel, Eder,
16: 6 then on the east the boundary makes a turn **t**
19:12 in the other direction eastward **t** the sunrise to
19:13 the east **t** the sunrise to Gath-hepher, to Eth-kazin,
19:13 and going on to Rimmon it bends **t** Neah;
22:22 in rebellion or in breach of faith **t** the LORD,
Jdg 7:22 and the army fled as far as Beth-shittah **t** Zererah,
13:20 When the flame went up **t** heaven from the altar,
20:32 and draw them away from the city **t** the roads."
20:40 and there was the whole city going up in smoke **t**
20:45 and fled **t** the wilderness to the rock of Rimmon,
Jdg 20:47 and fled **t** the wilderness to the rock of Rimmon,
1Sa 9:14 they saw Samuel coming out **t** them on his way
13:15 they went up from Gilgal **t** Gibeah of Benjamin.
13:17 one company turned **t** Ophrah,
13:18 another company turned **t** Beth-horon, and another company turned **t** the mountain that looks down upon the valley of Zeboim **t** the wilderness.
17:30 He turned away from him **t** another and spoke in
17:48 David ran quickly **t** the battle line to meet
19:23 He went there, **t** Naioth in Ramah;
20:12 or on the third day, if he is well disposed **t** David,
25:20 David and his men came down **t** her;
2Sa 15:23 and all the people moved on **t** the wilderness.
24: 5 **t** Gad and on to Jazer.
24:16 when the angel stretched out his hand **t** Jerusalem
24:20 he saw the king and his servants coming **t** him;
1Ki 3: 6 and in uprightness of heart **t** you;
6:27 their other wings **t** the center of the house
7:25 The hindquarters of each were **t** the inside.
8:29 your eyes may be open night and day **t** this house,
8:29 the prayer that your servant prays **t** this place.
8:30 of your people Israel when they pray **t** this place;
8:35 and then they pray **t** this place,
8:38 so that they stretch out their hands **t** this house;
8:42 when a foreigner comes and prays **t** this house,
8:44 to the LORD **t** the city that you have chosen and
8:48 and pray to you **t** their land,
8:54 he had knelt with hands outstretched **t** heaven;
18:43 "Go up now, look **t** the sea."
20:43 The king of Israel set out **t** home,
2Ki 13:23 he turned **t** them, because of his covenant
1Ch 18: 3 **t** Hamath, as he went to set up a monument at
19:14 and the troops who were with him advanced **t**
29:18 and direct their hearts **t** you.
2Ch 4: 4 The hindquarters of each were **t** the inside.
6:13 and spread out his hands **t** heaven.
6:20 May your eyes be open day and night **t** this house,
6:20 the prayer that your servant prays **t** this place.
6:21 when they pray **t** this place;
6:26 and then they pray **t** this place,
6:29 so that they stretch out their hands **t** this house;
6:32 when they come and pray **t** this house,
6:34 to you **t** this city that you have chosen and
6:38 to which they were taken captive, and pray **t**
20:24 they looked **t** the multitude;
Ezr 3:11 for his steadfast love endures forever **t** Israel."
Est 1:13 the king's procedure **t** all who were versed in law
Job 10:17 and increase your vexation **t** me;
11:13 you will stretch out your hands **t** him.
13: 8 Will you show partiality **t** him,
24:18 no treader turns **t** their vineyards.
32:21 not show partiality to any person or use flattery **t**
39:26 and spreads its wings **t** the south?
Ps 5: 7 I will bow down **t** your holy temple in awe
25:15 My eyes are ever **t** the LORD,
28: 2 as I lift up my hands **t** your most holy sanctuary.
40: 5 your wondrous deeds and your thoughts **t** us;
73:22 I was like a brute beast **t** you.
78:37 Their heart was not steadfast **t** him;
85: 4 and put away your indignation **t** us.
86:13 For great is your steadfast love **t** me;
103:11 so great is his steadfast love **t** those who fear him;
117: 2 For great is his steadfast love **t** us,
119:132 as is your custom **t** those who love your name.
138: 2 I bow down **t** your holy temple and give thanks
141: 8 But my eyes are turned **t** you, O GOD, my Lord;
Pr 3:34 **T** the scorners he is scornful,
7:10 Then a woman comes **t** him,
7:22 or bounds like a stag **t** the trap
23: 5 flying like an eagle **t** heaven.
SS 2: 4 and his intention **t** me was love.
Jer 3:12 Go, and proclaim these words **t** the north,
4: 6 Raise a standard **t** Zion, flee for safety,
4:11 of the bare heights in the desert **t** my poor people,
15: 1 yet my heart would not turn **t** this people.
31:40 to the corner of the Horse Gate **t** the east,
39: 4 and they went **t** the Arabah.
50: 5 with faces turned **t** it, and they shall come
Eze 1:23 wings were stretched out straight, one **t** another;
4: 3 set your face **t** it, and let it be in a state of siege,
4: 7 You shall set your face **t** the siege of Jerusalem,
6: 2 set your face **t** the mountains of Israel,
8: 5 So I lifted up my eyes **t** the north, and there,
8:16 to the temple of the LORD, and their faces **t** the east, prostrating themselves to the sun **t** the east.
17: 6 Its branches turned **t** him,
17: 7 This vine stretched out its roots **t** him;
17: 7 It shot out its branches **t** him,
20:46 set your face **t** the south, preach against the south,
21: 2 set your face **t** Jerusalem and preach against
25: 2 set your face **t** the Ammonites and prophesy
28:21 set your face **t** Sidon, and prophesy against it,
38: 2 set your face **t** Gog, of the land of Magog,
40:22 of the same size as those of the gate that faced **t**
40:24 Then he led me **t** the south,
40:27 and he measured from gate to gate **t** the south,
41:11 one door **t** the north, and another door **t** the south;
41:19 human face turned **t** the palm tree on the one side,
41:19 and the face of a young lion turned **t** the palm tree
42: 1 he led me out into the outer court, **t** the north,
42: 7 **t** the outer court, opposite the chambers,
47: 1 from below the threshold of the temple **t** the east
47: 2 around on the outside to the outer gate that faces **t**
47: 8 "This water flows **t** the eastern region and goes
Da 6:10 which had windows in its upper room open **t**
8: 6 It came **t** the ram with the two horns
8: 8 in its place there came up four prominent horns **t**

Da 8: 9 t the south, t the east, and t the beautiful land.
10:15 I turned my face t the ground and was speechless.
11: 4 be broken and divided t the four winds of heaven,
11:19 he shall turn back t the fortresses of his own land,
12: 7 raised his right hand and his left hand t heaven.
Zec 6: 6 with the black horses goes t the north country,
6: 6 the white ones go t the west country,
6: 6 and the dappled ones go t the south country."
6: 8 Then he cried out to me, "Lo, those who go t
Mt 14:25 And early in the morning he came walking t them
14:29 started walking on the water, and came t Jesus.
Lk 7:44 Then turning t the woman, he said to Simon,
9:53 because his face was set t Jerusalem.
11:53 to be very hostile t him and to cross-examine him
12:21 up treasures for themselves but are not rich t
Jn 1:29 next day he saw Jesus coming t him and declared,
1:47 When Jesus saw Nathanael coming t him,
6: 5 up and saw a large crowd coming t him,
6:21 and immediately the boat reached the land t
20: 3 and the other disciple set out and went t the tomb.
Ac 1:10 he was going and they were gazing up t heaven,
1:11 why do you stand looking up t heaven?
8:26 up and go t the south to the road that goes down
20:21 about repentance t God and faith t our Lord Jesus.
24:16 to have a clear conscience t God and all people.
Ro 1:30 boastful, inventors of evil, rebellious t parents,
11:22 severity t those who have fallen, but God's kindness t you,
1Co 7:36 If anyone thinks that he is not behaving properly t
15:10 and his grace t me has not been in vain.
2Co 1:12 and all the more t you.
3: 4 the confidence that we have through Christ t God.
10: 1 but bold t you when I am away!—
Eph 1:14 this is the pledge of our inheritance t redemption
1:15 of your faith in the Lord Jesus and your love t all
2: 7 the immeasurable riches of his grace in kindness t
Php 3:14 on t the goal for the prize of the heavenly call
Col 4: 5 Conduct yourselves wisely t outsiders,
1Th 2:10 and blameless our conduct was t you believers.
4:12 so that you may behave properly t outsiders and
Phm 1: 5 for all the saints and your faith t the Lord Jesus.
Heb 6: 1 Therefore let us go on t perfection,
6: 1 repentance from dead works and faith t God,
8:12 For I will be merciful t their iniquities,
Tob 1: 2 above Asher t the west, and north of Phogor.
3:11 with hands outstretched t the window,
3:12 I turn my face to you, and raise my eyes t you.
5:14 Do not feel bitter t me, brother,
Jdt 3: 9 Then he came t Esdraelon, near Dothan,
7:18 of their men t the south and the east, t Egrebeh,
12: 5 T the morning watch she got up
12: 9 and stayed in the tent until she ate her food t
Wis 16: 7 For the one who turned t it was saved,
16:21 For your sustenance manifested your sweetness t
Sir 28: 4 If one has no mercy t another like himself,
33:30 Do not be overbearing t anyone,
36:22 according to your goodwill t your people,
38:15 will be defiant t the physician.
48:20 spreading out their hands t him.
Bar 4: 2 walk t the shining of her light.
4:36 Look t the east, O Jerusalem,
5: 5 look t the east, and see your children gathered
Sus 1:35 Through her tears she looked up t Heaven,
1Mc 8: 1 and were well-disposed t all who made
11:33 because of the goodwill they show t us.
14:35 of the justice and loyalty that he had maintained t
2Mc 3:15 the altar in their priestly vestments and called t
5:23 In his malice t the Jewish citizens,
6: 8 the same policy t the Jews and make them partake
6:29 a little before had acted t him with goodwill
9:26 each of you, t me and my son.
11:19 you will maintain your goodwill t the government,
12:14 behaved most insolently t Judas and his men,
14:33 he stretched out his right hand t the sanctuary,
14:34 Then the priests stretched out their hands t heaven
15:21 stretched out his hands t heaven and called upon
15:30 the man who maintained his youthful goodwill t
1Es 1:24 and acted wickedly t the Lord
4:58 he lifted up his face to heaven t Jerusalem,
5:47 in the square before the first gate t the east.
3Mc 3: 1 but was still more bitterly hostile t those in
3: 3 to maintain goodwill and unswerving loyalty t
3:18 because of the benevolence that we have t all.
3:19 By maintaining their manifest ill-will t us,
3:21 to all our amnesty t their compatriots here,
3:23 among them who are sincerely disposed t us;
3:24 by these indications that they are ill-disposed t us
5: 3 the army who were especially hostile t the Jews.
5:25 stretched their hands t heaven and
6:26 from all nations in their goodwill t us
7: 4 of the ill-will that these people had t all nations.
7: 6 in accordance with the clemency that we have t
7: 7 the friendly and firm goodwill that they had t us
7:11 be favorably disposed t the king's government.
2Es 7:*134* [64] he shows patience t those who have sinned,
13:23 who have works and faith t the Almighty.
15:39 the east wind shall be driven violently t the south
4Mc 4:11 stretched out his hands t heaven,
5:25 in giving us the law has shown sympathy t us.
9: 9 because of your bloodthirstiness t us,
13:25 for nobility strengthened their goodwill t
14: 5 as though running the course t immortality,
14:13 which draws everything t an emotion felt
15: 4 of their birth pangs have a deeper sympathy t their
15: 6 in herself tender love t them,
15: 9 she felt a greater tenderness t them.
15:13 yearning of parents t offspring,

TOWARDS (6) [TOWARD]

Nu 12:10 And Aaron turned t Miriam and saw
19: 4 and sprinkle it seven times t the front of the tent
2Sa 23:13 T the beginning of harvest three of the thirty
Isa 11:13 and Judah shall not be hostile t Ephraim.
Mk 6:48 he came t them early in the morning,
7:31 and went by way of Sidon t the Sea of Galilee,

TOWEL (2)

Jn 13: 4 and tied a t around himself.
13: 5 to wipe them with the t that was tied around him.

TOWER (39) [SEVEN-TOWERED, TOWERED, TOWERING, TOWERS, WATCHTOWER]

Ge 11: 4 and a t with its top in the heavens,
11: 5 The LORD came down to see the city and the t,
35:21 and pitched his tent beyond the t of Eder.
Jdg 8: 9 I will break down this t."
8:17 He also broke down the t of Penuel,
9:46 all the lords of the T of Shechem heard of it,
9:47 Abimelech was told that all the lords of the T
9:49 that all the people of the T of Shechem also died,
9:51 But there was a strong t within the city,
9:51 and they went to the roof of the t.
9:52 Abimelech came to the t, and fought against it,
9:52 and came near to the entrance of the t to burn it
2Sa 22:51 He is a t of salvation for his king,
2Ki 9:17 the sentinel standing on the t spied the company
Ne 3: 1 they consecrated it as far as the T of the Hundred and as far as the T of Hananel.
3:11 and the T of the Ovens.
3:25 the t projecting from the upper house of the king
3:26 the Water Gate on the east and the projecting t.
3:27 the great projecting t as far as the wall of Ophel.
12:38 above the T of the Ovens, to the Broad Wall,
12:39 and the T of Hananel and the T of the Hundred,
Ps 61: 3 a strong t against the enemy.
Pr 18:10 The name of the LORD is a strong t;
SS 4: 4 Your neck is like the t of David, built in courses;
7: 4 Your neck is like an ivory t.
7: 4 Your nose is like a t of Lebanon,
Isa 2:15 against every high t, and against every
Jer 31:38 be rebuilt for the LORD from the t of Hananel to
Mic 4: 8 And you, O t of the flock, hill of daughter Zion,
Zec 14:10 from the T of Hananel to the king's wine presses.
Lk 13: 4 Or those eighteen who were killed when the t
14:28 For which of you, intending to build a t,
Sir 26:22 *a married woman as a t of death to her lovers.*
1Mc 13:43 and battered and captured one t.
2Mc 13: 5 For there is a t there, fifty cubits high,
14:41 the t and were forcing the door of the courtyard,
3Mc 2:27 and he set up a stone on the t in the courtyard

TOWERED (3) [TOWER]

Eze 19:11 it t aloft among the thick boughs;
31: 5 So it t high above all the trees of the field;
31:10 Because it t high and set its top among the clouds,

TOWERING (2) [TOWER]

Ps 37:35 and t like a cedar of Lebanon.
Sir 50:10 and like a cypress t in the clouds.

TOWERS (42) [TOWER]

1Ch 27:25 in the cities, in the villages and in the t,
2Ch 14: 7 and surround them with walls and t,
26: 9 Uzziah built t in Jerusalem at the Corner Gate,
26:10 He built t in the wilderness
26:15 on the t and the corners for shooting arrows
27: 4 and forts and t on the wooded hills.
32: 5 raised t on it, and outside it he built another wall;
Ps 48:12 Walk about Zion, go all around it, count its t,
122: 7 and security within your t."
SS 8:10 I was a wall, and my breasts were like t;
Isa 13:22 in its t, and jackals in the pleasant palaces;
23:13 They erected their siege t,
29: 3 I will besiege you with t and raise siegeworks
30:25 on a day of the great slaughter, when the t fall.
33:18 Where is the one who counted the t?"
Eze 21:22 to cast up ramps, to build siege t.
26: 4 the walls of Tyre and break down its t.
26: 9 against your walls and break down your t
27:11 men of Gamad were at your t.
Tob 13:12 all who overthrow your t and set your homes
13:16 The t of Jerusalem will be built with gold,
Jdt 1: 3 At its gates he raised t one hundred cubits high
1:14 captured its t, plundered its markets,
7: 5 and when they had kindled fires on their t,
7:32 and they went up on the walls and t of their town.
1Mc 1:33 of David with a great strong wall and strong t,
4:60 with high walls and strong t all around,
5: 5 They were shut up by him in their t;
5: 5 burned with fire their t and all who were in them.
5:65 down its strongholds and burned its t on all sides.
6:20 and he built siege t and other engines of war.
6:37 On the elephants were wooden t,
6:51 He set up siege t, engines of war to throw fire
13:33 with high t and great walls and gates and bolts,
16:10 They also fled into the t that were in the fields
2Mc 10:18 in two very strong t well equipped to withstand
10:20 were bribed by some of those who were in the t,
10:22 and immediately captured the two t.
10:36 around against the defenders and set fire to the t;
1Es 1:55 the walls of Jerusalem, burned their t with fire,
4: 4 they go, and conquer mountains, walls, and t.
4Mc 13: 6 For just as t jutting out over harbors hold back

TOWN‡ (177) [DAUGHTER-TOWNS, HOMETOWN, TOWNS, TOWNSPEOPLE]

Nu 20:16 a t on the edge of your territory.
35: 4 of the t outward a thousand cubits all around.
35: 5 You shall measure, outside the t,
35: 5 with the t in the middle;
Dt 2:34 and in each t we utterly destroyed men, women,
2:36 on the edge of the Wadi Arnon (including the t
13:13 and led the inhabitants of the t astray,
13:15 you shall put the inhabitants of that t to the sword,
13:16 then burn the t and all its spoil with fire,
20:10 When you draw near to a t to fight against it,
20:14 and everything else in the t, all its spoil.
20:19 If you besiege a t for a long time,
20:20 down for use in building siegeworks against the t
21: 3 The elders of the t nearest the body shall take
21: 4 the elders of that t shall bring the heifer down to
21: 6 that t nearest the body shall wash their hands over
21:19 and bring him out to the elders of his t at the gate
21:20 They shall say to the elders of his t,
21:21 Then all the men of the t shall stone him to death.
22:17 the cloth before the elders of the t.
22:18 elders of that t shall take the man and punish him;
22:21 and the men of her t shall stone her to death,
22:23 and a man meets her in the t and lies with her,
22:24 both of them to the gate of that t and stone them
22:24 because she did not cry for help in the t and
25: 8 the elders of his t shall summon him and speak
Jos 11:19 not a t that made peace with the Israelites, except
13: 9 and the t that is in the middle of the valley,
13:16 and the t that is in the middle of the valley,
17: 8 but the t of Tappuah on the boundary
18:14 a t belonging to the tribe of Judah.
19:50 the LORD they gave him the t that he asked for,
19:50 he rebuilt the t, and settled in it.
20: 6 to the t in which the deed was done.' "
21:12 the t and its villages had been given to Caleb son
24:33 the t of his son Phinehas,
Jdg 8:27 Gideon made an ephod of it and put it in his t,
12: 7 and was buried in his t in Gilead.
14:18 The men of the t said to him on the seventh day
14:19 He killed thirty men of the t, took their spoil,
17: 8 This man left the t of Bethlehem in Judah,
Ru 1:19 the whole t was stirred because of them;
2:18 She picked it up and came into the t,
1Sa 1: 3 by year from his t to worship and to sacrifice to
9: 6 he said to him, "There is a man of God in this t;
9:10 So they went to the t where the man of God was.
9:11 As they went up the hill to the t,
9:12 Hurry; he has come just now to the t,
9:13 As soon as you enter the t, you will find him,
9:14 they went up to the t. As they were entering the t,
9:25 When they came down from the shrine into the t,
9:27 As they were going down to the outskirts of the t,
10: 5 there, as you come to the t,
23: 7 in by entering a t that has gates and bars."
2Sa 19:37 so that I may die in my own t,
1Ki 13:25 and told it in the t where the old prophet lived.
17:10 When he came to the gate of the t,
2Ch 31:19 to their towns, t by t, the people designated
Ezr 10:14 and with them the elders and judges of every t,
Ne 7: 6 to Jerusalem and Judah, each to his t.
Ps 107: 4 finding no way to an inhabited t;
107: 7 until they reached an inhabited t.
107:36 and they establish a t to live in;
Pr 8: 3 the t, at the entrance of the portals she cries out:
9: 3 she calls from the highest places in the t,
9:14 on a seat at the high places of the t,
Ecc 10:15 for they do not even know the way to t.
Isa 22: 2 tumultuous city, exultant t?
Jer 4:29 At the noise of horseman and archer every t takes
48: 8 The destroyer shall come upon every t, and no t shall escape;
49:25 How the famous city is forsaken, the joyful t!
Am 4: 8 or three towns wandered to one t to drink water,
Hab 2:12 "Alas for you who build a t by bloodshed,
Mt 2:23 There he made his home in a t called Nazareth,
8:33 The swineherds ran off, and on going into the t,
8:34 Then the whole t came out to meet Jesus;
9: 1 a boat he crossed the sea and came to his own t.
10: 5 and enter no t of the Samaritans,
10:11 Whatever t or village you enter,
10:14 from your feet as you leave that house or t.
10:15 on the day of judgment than for that t.
10:23 they persecute you in one t, flee to the next;
23:34 in your synagogues and pursue from t to t,
Mk 1:45 so that Jesus could no longer go into a t openly,
Lk 1:26 by God to a t in Galilee called Nazareth,
1:39 with haste to a Judean t in the hill country,
2: 4 Joseph also went from the t of Nazareth in Galilee
2:39 to their own t of Nazareth.
4:29 They got up, drove him out of the t,
4:29 to the brow of the hill on which their t was built,
7:11 Soon afterwards he went to a t called Nain,
7:12 As he approached the gate of the t,
7:12 and with her was a large crowd from the t.
8: 4 and people from t after t came to him, he said
9: 5 that t shake the dust off your feet as a testimony
10: 1 and sent them on ahead of him in pairs to every t
10: 8 a t and its people welcome you, eat what is set
10:10 But whenever you enter a t and they do
10:11 'Even the dust of your t that clings to our feet,

Lk 10:12 be more tolerable for Sodom than for that **t.**
13:22 through one **t** and village after another,
14:21 at once into the streets and lanes of the **t** and bring
23:51 He came from the Jewish **t** of Arimathea,
Jn 11:54 from there to a **t** called Ephraim in the region near
Ac 16: 4 As they went from **t** to **t,**
19:35 But when the **t** clerk had quieted the crowd,
Tit 1: 5 and should appoint elders in every **t,**
Jas 4:13 or tomorrow we will go to such and such a **t**
Jdt 6:12 When the men of the **t** saw them, they seized their weapons and ran out of the **t** to
6:14 Israelites came down from their **t** and found him;
6:14 and placed him before the magistrates of their **t,**
6:16 They called together all the elders of the **t,**
7: 7 He reconnoitered the approaches to their **t,**
7:13 and they will surrender their **t.**
7:13 to keep watch to see that no one gets out of the **t.**
7:22 and were collapsing in the streets of the **t** and in
7:23 the rulers of the **t** and cried out with a loud voice,
7:26 the whole **t** as booty to the army of Holofernes
7:32 they went up on the walls and towers of their **t.**
7:32 In the **t** they were in great misery.
8: 3 and took to his bed and died in his **t** Bethulia.
8: 9 to surrender the **t** to the Assyrians after five days,
8:10 and Chabris and Charmis, the elders of her **t.**
8:11 promising to surrender the **t** to our enemies unless
8:18 or **t** of ours that worships gods made with hands,
8:33 Stand at the **t** gate tonight so that I may go out
8:33 after which you have promised to surrender the **t**
10: 6 Then they went out to the **t** gate of Bethulia
10: 6 with the elders of the **t,**
10: 9 of the **t** to be opened for me so that I may go out
10:10 The men of the **t** watched her until she had gone
13:12 When the people of her **t** heard her voice,
13:12 the **t** gate and summoned the elders of the **t.**
14: 2 and let every able-bodied man go out of the **t;**
14: 9 a great shout and made a joyful noise in their **t.**
Sir 20:15 he opens his mouth like a **t** crier.
1Mc 1:51 the towns of Judah to offer sacrifice, **t** by **t.**
2:15 to the **t** of Modein to make them offer sacrifice.
2:17 "You are a leader, honored and great in this **t,**
2:27 Mattathias cried out in the **t** with a loud voice,
2:28 to the hills and left all that they had in the **t.**
5:28 and he took the **t,** and killed every male by
5:31 the battle had begun and that the cry of the **t** went
5:44 But he took the **t** and burned the sacred precincts
5:46 This was a large and very strong **t** on the road,
5:47 But the people of the **t** shut them out and blocked
5:50 and he fought against the **t** all that day and all
5:50 and the **t** was delivered into his hands.
5:51 and razed and plundered the **t.**
5:51 Then he passed through the **t** over the bodies of
5:59 and his men came out of the **t** to meet them
6: 7 with high walls as before, and also Beth-zur, his **t.**
6:49 the **t** because they had no provisions there
7: 1 sailed with a few men to a **t** by the sea,
9:52 He also fortified the **t** of Beth-zur, and Gazara,
9:65 But Jonathan left his brother Simon in the **t,**
9:67 and his men sallied out from the **t** and set fire to
11: 3 as a garrison in each **t.**
11:66 took possession of the **t,** and set a garrison over it.
15:14 He surrounded the **t,** and the ships joined battle
15:14 he pressed the **t** hard from land and sea,
2Mc 12:13 also attacked a certain **t** that was strongly fortified
12:16 They took the **t** by the will of God,
12:27 a fortified **t** where Lysias lived with multitudes
12:28 and they got the **t** into their hands,
1Es 5: 8 and the rest of Judea, each to his own **t.**
2Es 10: 4 I intend not to return to the **t,** but to stay here;
10:17 Therefore go into the **t** to your husband."

TOWNCLERK (KJV) See TOWN CLERK

TOWNS‡ (312) [TOWN]

Ex 20:10 your livestock, or the alien resident in your **t.**
Nu 13:19 and whether the **t** that they live in are unwalled
13:28 and the **t** are fortified and very large;
21: 2 then we will utterly destroy their **t."**
21: 3 and they utterly destroyed them and their **t,**
21:25 Israel took all these **t,** and Israel settled in all the **t** of the Amorites,
31:10 All their **t** where they had settled,
32:16 and **t** for our little ones,
32:17 in the fortified **t** because of the inhabitants of
32:24 Build **t** for your little ones,
32:26 and all our livestock shall remain there in the **t**
32:33 of King Og of Bashan, the land and its **t,**
32:33 with the territories of the surrounding **t.**
32:38 and they gave names to the **t** that they rebuilt.
35: 2 **t** for the Levites to live in;
35: 2 to the Levites pasture lands surrounding the **t.**
35: 3 The **t** shall be theirs to live in,
35: 4 The pasture lands of the **t,**
35: 5 to them as pasture land for their **t.**
35: 6 The **t** that you give to the Levites shall include
35: 6 and in addition to them you shall give forty-two **t.**
35: 7 The **t** that you give to the Levites
35: 8 for the **t** that you shall give from the possession of
35: 8 shall give of its **t** to the Levites.
Dt 2:34 At that time we captured all his **t,**
2:35 well as the plunder of the **t** that we had captured.
2:37 of the Wadi Jabbok as well as the **t** of
3: 4 At that time we captured all his **t;**
3: 4 sixty **t,** the whole region of Argob,
3: 5 All these were fortress **t** with high walls,
3: 7 the plunder of the **t** we kept as spoil for ourselves.
Dt 3:10 all the **t** of the tableland,
3:10 **t** of Og's kingdom in Bashan.
3:12 well as half the hill country of Gilead with its **t,**
3:19 shall stay behind in the **t** that I have given to you.
5:14 or the resident alien in your **t,**
12:12 in your **t** (since they have no allotment
12:15 and eat meat within any of your **t,** according to
12:17 may you eat within your **t** the tithe of your grain,
12:18 and the Levites resident in your **t,**
12:21 you may eat within your **t** whenever you desire.
13:12 of the **t** that the LORD your God is giving you
14:21 you may give it to aliens residing in your **t**
14:27 As for the Levites resident in your **t,**
14:28 and store it within your **t;**
14:29 the orphans, and the widows in your **t,**
15: 7 a member of your community in any of your **t**
15:22 within your **t** you may eat it,
16: 5 to offer the passover sacrifice within any of your **t**
16:11 the Levites resident in your **t,**
16:14 the orphans, and the widows resident in your **t.**
16:18 and officials throughout your tribes, in all your **t**
17: 2 of your **t** that the LORD your God is giving you,
17: 8 any such matters of dispute in your **t—**
18: 6 If a Levite leaves any of your **t,**
19: 1 and settled in their **t** and in their houses,
20:15 Thus you shall treat all the **t** that are very far
20:15 which are not **t** of the nations here.
20:16 But as for the **t** of these peoples that
21: 2 to measure the distances to the **t** that are near
23:16 in any place they choose in any one of your **t,**
24:14 or aliens who reside in your land in one of your **t.**
26:12 so that they may eat their fill within your **t,**
28:52 It shall besiege you in all your **t** until your high
28:52 it shall besiege you in all your **t** throughout
28:55 the enemy siege will reduce you in all your **t.**
28:57 the enemy siege will reduce you in your **t.**
31:12 as well as the aliens residing in your **t—**
Jos 10:19 Do not let them enter their **t,**
10:20 the survivors had entered into the fortified **t,**
10:37 and its king and its **t,** and every person in it;
10:39 and he took it with its king and all its **t;**
11:12 And all the **t** of those kings, and all their kings,
11:13 of the **t** that stood on mounds except Hazor,
11:14 All the spoil of these **t,** and the livestock,
11:21 Joshua utterly destroyed them with their **t.**
13:17 and all its **t** that are in the tableland;
13:21 all the **t** of the tableland,
13:23 to their families with their **t** and villages.
13:25 Their territory was Jazer, and all the **t** of Gilead,
13:28 according to their clans, with their **t** and villages.
13:30 which are in Bashan, sixty **t,**
13:31 and Edrei, the **t** of the kingdom of Og in Bashan;
14: 4 to the Levites in the land, but only **t** to live in,
15: 9 and from there to the **t** of Mount Ephron;
15:21 The **t** belonging to the tribe of the people of Judah
15:32 in all, twenty-nine **t,** with their villages.
15:36 fourteen **t** with their villages.
15:41 sixteen **t** with their villages.
15:44 nine **t** with their villages.
15:47 Ashdod, its **t** and its villages;
15:47 Gaza, its **t** and its villages;
15:51 eleven **t** with their villages.
15:54 nine **t** with their villages.
15:57 and Timnah: ten **t** with their villages.
15:59 and Eltekon: six **t** with their villages.
15:60 and Rabbah: two **t** with their villages.
15:62 and En-gedi: six **t** with their villages.
16: 9 the **t** that were set apart for the Ephraimites within
16: 9 all those **t** with their villages.
17: 9 The **t** here, to the south of the wadi,
17: 9 among the **t** of Manasseh, belong to Ephraim.
17:12 Manassites could not take possession of those **t;**
18: 9 a book a description of it by **t** in seven divisions;
18:21 Now the **t** of the tribe of Benjamin according
18:24 twelve **t** with their villages:
18:28 fourteen **t** with their villages.
19: 6 thirteen **t** with their villages;
19: 7 four **t** with their villages;
19: 8 together with all the villages all around these **t**
19:15 twelve **t** with their villages.
19:16 these **t** with their villages.
19:22 sixteen **t** with their villages.
19:23 to its families—the **t** with their villages.
19:30 twenty-two **t** with their villages.
19:31 these **t** with their villages.
19:35 The fortified **t** are Ziddim, Zer, Hammath,
19:38 nineteen **t** with their villages.
19:39 to its families—the **t** with their villages.
19:48 these **t** with their villages.
21: 2 through Moses that we be given **t** to live in,
21: 3 the Levites the following **t** and pasture lands out
21: 4 the priest received by lot thirteen **t** from the tribes
21: 5 The rest of the Kohathites received by lot ten **t**
21: 6 The Gershonites received by lot thirteen **t** from
21: 7 according to their families received twelve **t** from
21: 8 These **t** and their pasture lands the Israelites gave
21: 9 of Simeon they gave the following **t** mentioned
21:16 nine **t** out of these two tribes.
21:18 with its pasture lands—four **t.**
21:19 The **t** of the descendants of Aaron—
21:20 the **t** allotted to them were out of the tribe
21:22 with its pasture lands—four **t.**
21:24 with its pasture lands—four **t.**
21:25 with its pasture lands—two **t.**
21:26 The **t** of the families of the rest of
21:27 with its pasture lands—two **t.**
21:29 with its pasture lands—four **t;**
Jos 21:31 with its pasture lands—four **t.**
21:32 with its pasture lands—three **t.**
21:33 The **t** of the several families of
21:35 with its pasture lands—four **t.**
21:37 with its pasture lands—four **t.**
21:39 with its pasture lands—four **t** in all.
21:40 As for the **t** of the several Merarite families,
21:41 The **t** of the Levites within the holdings of
21:41 in all forty-eight **t** with their pasture lands.
21:42 Each of these **t** had its pasture lands around it;
21:42 so it was with all these **t.**
24:13 and **t** that you had not built, and you live in them;
Jdg 10: 4 and they had thirty **t,** which are in the land
11:26 and in all the **t** that are along the Arnon,
11:33 twenty **t,** and as far as Abel-keramim.
20:14 The Benjaminites came together out of the **t**
20:15 from their **t,** besides the inhabitants
20:48 Also the remaining **t** they set on fire.
21:23 and rebuilt the **t,** and lived in them.
1Sa 7:14 The **t** that the Philistines had taken
18: 6 the women came out of all the **t** of Israel,
27: 5 let a place be given me in one of the country **t,**
30:29 in the **t** of the Jerahmeelites, in the **t** of the Kenites,
31: 7 they forsook their **t** and fled;
2Sa 2: 3 and they settled in the **t** of Hebron.
8: 8 From Betah and from Berothai, **t** of Hadadezer,
1Ki 12:17 the Israelites who were living in the **t** of Judah.
20:34 the **t** that my father took from your father;
2Ki 13:25 the **t** that he had taken from his father Jehoahaz
13:25 and recovered the **t** of Israel.
17: 9 at all their **t,** from watchtower to fortified city;
23: 8 He brought all the priests out of the **t** of Judah,
23:19 of the high places that were in the **t** of Samaria,
1Ch 2:22 who had twenty-three **t** in the land of Gilead.
2:23 Kenath and its villages, sixty **t.**
4:31 These were their **t** until David became king.
4:32 Ain, Rimmon, Tochen, and Ashan, five **t,**
4:33 with all their villages that were around these **t**
5:16 in Bashan and in its **t,**
6:60 All their **t** throughout their families were thirteen.
6:61 out of the half-tribe, the half of Manasseh, ten **t.**
6:62 to their families were allotted thirteen **t** out of
6:63 to their families were allotted twelve **t** out of
6:64 So the people of Israel gave the Levites the **t**
6:65 and Benjamin these **t** that are mentioned by name.
6:66 of Kohath had **t** of their territory out of the tribe
7:28 and settlements were Bethel and its **t,**
7:28 and westward Gezer and its **t,** Shechem and its **t,** as far as Ayyah and its **t;**
7:29 Beth-shean and its **t,** Taanach and its **t,** Megiddo and its **t,** Dor and its **t.**
8:12 and Shemed, who built Ono and Lod with its **t,**
9: 2 in their possessions in their **t** were Israelites,
10: 7 they abandoned their **t** and fled;
2Ch 8: 4 in the wilderness and all the storage **t** that he built
8: 6 as well as all Solomon's storage **t,** and all the **t** for his chariots, the **t** for his cavalry,
15: 8 and from the **t** that he had taken in the hill country
20: 4 the **t** of Judah they came to seek the LORD.
23: 2 and gathered the Levites from all the **t** of Judah,
31:19 in the fields of common land belonging to their **t,**
34: 6 In the **t** of Manasseh, Ephraim, and Simeon,
Ezr 2: 1 to Jerusalem and Judah, all to their own **t.**
2:70 servants lived in their **t,** and all Israel in their **t.**
3: 1 and the Israelites were in the **t,**
10:14 in our **t** who have taken foreign wives come
Ne 7:73 and all Israel settled in their **t.**
7:73 the people of Israel being settled in their **t—**
8:15 that they should publish and proclaim in all their **t**
10:37 the Levites who collect the tithes in all our rural **t.**
11: 1 while nine-tenths remained in the other **t.**
11: 3 the **t** of Judah all lived on their property in their **t:**
11:20 were in all the **t** of Judah,
12:44 for the Levites from the fields belonging to the **t;**
Est 9:19 the Jews of the villages, who live in the open **t,**
Ps 48:11 the **t** of Judah rejoice because of your judgments.
97: 8 Zion hears and is glad, and the **t** of Judah rejoice,
Isa 17: 2 Her **t** will be deserted forever;
42:11 Let the desert and its **t** lift up their voice,
54: 3 the nations and will settle the desolate **t.**
Jer 2:28 you have as many gods as you have **t,** O Judah.
4:29 all the **t** are forsaken, and no one lives in them.
7:17 not see what they are doing in the **t** of Judah and
9:11 and I will make the **t** of Judah a desolation,
11:13 For your gods have become as many as your **t,**
13:19 The **t** of the Negeb are shut up with no one
17:26 the **t** of Judah and the places around Jerusalem,
19:15 now bringing upon this city and upon all its **t** all
25:18 and the **t** of Judah, its kings and officials,
31:23 of Judah and in its **t** when I restore their fortunes:
31:24 And Judah and all its **t** shall live there together,
33:10 in the **t** of Judah and the streets of Jerusalem
33:12 or animals, and in all its **t** there shall again
33:13 In the **t** of the hill country, of the Shephelah,
33:13 and in the **t** of Judah,
34:22 The **t** of Judah I will make a desolation
36: 6 the people of Judah who come up from their **t.**
36: 9 from the **t** of Judah to Jerusalem proclaimed a fast
40: 5 of Babylon appointed governor of the **t** of Judah,
40:10 and live in the **t** that you have taken over."
44: 2 that I have brought on Jerusalem and on all the **t**
44: 6 in the **t** of Judah and in the streets of Jerusalem;
44:17 in the **t** of Judah and in the streets of Jerusalem.
44:21 the offerings that you made in the **t** of Judah and
48: 9 her **t** shall become a desolation,
48:15 The destroyer of Moab and his **t** has come up,
48:24 and all the **t** of the land of Moab, far and near.

Jer 48:28 Leave the **t**, and live on the rock,
48:41 the **t** shall be taken and the strongholds seized.
49: 1 and his people settled in its **t**?
49:13 and all her **t** shall be perpetual wastes.
La 5:11 virgins in the **t** of Judah.
Eze 6: 6 your **t** shall be waste and your high places ruined,
19: 7 he ravaged their strongholds, and laid waste their **t**;
25: 9 the flank of Moab from the **t** on its frontier,
35: 4 I lay your **t** in ruins;
36: 4 the desolate wastes and the deserted **t**,
36:10 **t** shall be inhabited and the waste places rebuilt;
36:33 I will cause the **t** to be inhabited,
36:35 and ruined **t** are now inhabited and fortified."
36:38 shall the ruined **t** be filled with flocks of people.
39: 9 Then those who live in the **t** of Israel will go out
Am 4: 8 or three **t** wandered to one town to drink water,
Ob 1:20 in Sepharad shall possess the **t** of the Negeb.
Mic 5:14 from among you and destroy your **t**.
Zec 7: 7 along with the **t** around it,
Mt 10:23 you will not have gone through all the **t** of Israel
14:13 they followed him on foot from the **t**.
Mk 1:38 He answered, "Let us go on to the neighboring **t**,
6:33 on foot from all the **t** and arrived ahead of them.
Lk 2: 3 All went to their own **t** to be registered.
Ac 5:16 also gather from the **t** around Jerusalem,
8:40 he proclaimed the good news to all the **t**
Jdt 1: 9 and all who were in Samaria and its **t**,
1:14 Thus he took possession of his **t** and came
2:24 the fortified **t** along the brook Abron,
2:27 and sacked their **t** and ravaged their lands
3: 4 Our **t** and their inhabitants are also your slaves;
3: 6 in the fortified **t** and took picked men from them
4:12 and the **t** they had inherited to be destroyed,
5: 3 What **t** do they inhabit?
5:18 and their **t** were occupied by their enemies.
6: 7 the hill country and put you in one of the **t** beside
15: 7 Even the villages and **t** in the hill country and in
Bar 2:23 I will make to cease from the **t** of Judah and from
1Mc 1:44 by messengers to Jerusalem and the **t** of Judah;
1:51 over all the people and commanded the **t** of Judah
1:54 also built altars in the surrounding **t** of Judah,
1:58 those who were found month after month in the **t**.
5:26 all these **t** were strong and large—
5:27 some have been shut up in the other **t** of Gilead;
5:36 Maked, and Bosor, and the other **t** of Gilead.
5:68 he plundered the **t** and returned to the land
10:84 and the surrounding **t** and plundered them;
11: 2 and the people of the **t** opened their gates to him
11: 3 when Ptolemy entered the **t** he stationed forces as
11:60 and traveled beyond the river and among the **t**,
14:10 He supplied the **t** with food,
14:17 that he was ruling over the country and the **t** in it,
14:33 He fortified the **t** of Judea,
14:34 and provided in those **t** whatever was necessary
16:14 the **t** of the country and attending to their needs,
16:18 and to turn over to him the **t** and the country.
2Mc 8: 6 he would set fire to **t** and villages.
8:11 So he immediately sent to the **t** on the seacoast,
1Es 5:46 the gatekeepers, and all Israel in their **t**.

TOWNSPEOPLE (6) [PEOPLE, TOWN]
Ge 24:13 daughters of the **t** are coming out to draw water.
38:21 the **t**, "Where is the temple prostitute who was
38:22 the **t** said, 'No prostitute has been here.' "
Jdg 6:27 because he was too afraid of his family and the **t**
6:28 When the **t** rose early in the morning,
6:30 Then the **t** said to Joash, "Bring out your son,

TRACE (5) [TRACED, TRACES]
Da 2:35 so that not a **t** of them could be found.
Jas 3:17 without a **t** of partiality or hypocrisy.
Wis 5:10 and when it has passed no **t** can be found,
6:22 I will **t** her course from the beginning of creation,
Bar 3:18 and were anxious, but there is no **t** of their works?

TRACED (1) [TRACE]
Wis 9:16 but who has **t** out what is in the heavens?

TRACES (2) [TRACE]
Wis 2: 4 our life will pass away like the **t** of a cloud,
Sir 42:19 and he reveals the **t** of hidden things.

TRACHONITIS (1)
Lk 3: 1 of the region of Ituraea and **T**,

TRACK (3) [TRACKED, TRACKLESS, TRACKS]
Ps 17:11 They **t** me down; now they surround me;
Joel 2: 8 each keeps to its own **t**;
Wis 5:10 no **t** of its keel in the waves;

TRACKED (1) [TRACK]
Hos 6: 8 Gilead is a city of evildoers, **t** with blood.

TRACKLESS (3) [TRACK]
Ps 107:40 on princes and makes them wander in **t** wastes;
Wis 5: 7 and we journeyed through **t** deserts,
2Es 5: 3 land that you now see ruling shall be a **t** waste,

TRACKS (4) [TRACK]
Ps 65:11 your wagon **t** overflow with richness.
SS 1: 8 follow the **t** of the flock, and pasture your kids
Jer 2:23 a restive young camel interlacing her **t**,
Jdt 14: 4 and cut them down in their **t**.

TRADE (19) [TRADED, TRADER, TRADERS, TRADESMAN, TRADING]
Ge 34:10 live and **t** in it, and get property in it."
34:21 let them live in the land and **t** in it,
42:34 and you may **t** in the land.' "
Isa 23:17 and she will return to her **t**,
Jer 14:18 prophet and priest ply their **t** throughout the land,
La 1:11 they **t** their treasures for food
Eze 17: 4 He carried it to a land of **t**,
27:19 Vedan and Javan from Uzal entered into **t**
27:25 The ships of Tarshish traveled for you in your **t**.
28: 5 in **t** you have increased your wealth,
28:16 In the abundance of your **t** you were filled
28:18 in the unrighteousness of your **t**,
Ac 18: 3 because he was of the same **t**,
18: 3 by **t** they were tentmakers.
19:25 with the workers of the same **t**, and said, "Men,
19:27 that this **t** of ours may come into disrepute but
Rev 18:17 sailors and all whose **t** is on the sea,
18:22 an artisan of any **t** will be found in you no more;
Sir 38:34 and their concern is for the exercise of their **t**.

TRADED (11) [TRADE]
Eze 27:13 Javan, Tubal, and Meshech **t** with you;
27:15 The Rhodians **t** with you;
27:17 Judah and the land of Israel **t** with you;
27:18 Damascus **t** with you for your abundant goods—
27:20 Dedan **t** with you in saddlecloths for riding.
27:22 The merchants of Sheba and Raamah **t** with you;
27:23 Asshur, and Chilmad **t** with you.
27:24 These **t** with you in choice garments,
27:24 in these they **t** with you.
Joel 3: 3 and **t** boys for prostitutes, and sold girls for wine,
Mt 25:16 the five talents went off at once and **t** with them,

TRADER (1) [TRADE]
Hos 12: 7 A **t**, in whose hands are false balances,

TRADERS (12) [TRADE]
Ge 37:28 When some Midianite **t** passed by,
1Ki 10:15 that which came from the **t** and from the business
10:28 the king's **t** received them from Kue at a price.
10:29 the king's **t** they were exported to all the kings of
2Ch 1:16 the king's **t** received them from Kue at a price.
9:14 besides that which the **t** and merchants brought;
Job 41: 6 Will **t** bargain over it?
Isa 23: 8 whose **t** were the honored of the earth?
Zep 1:11 for all the **t** have perished;
Zec 14:21 And there shall no longer be **t** in the house of
1Ti 1:10 sodomites, slave **t**, liars, perjurers,
1Mc 3:41 the **t** of the region heard what was said to them,

TRADESMAN (1) [MAN, TRADE]
Sir 26:29 nor is a **t** innocent of sin.

TRADING (2) [TRADE]
Job 20:18 the profit of their **t** they will get no enjoyment.
Lk 19:15 that he might find out what they had gained by **t**.

TRADITION (11) [TRADITIONAL, TRADITIONS]
Mt 15: 2 "Why do your disciples break the **t** of the elders?
15: 3 the commandment of God for the sake of your **t**?
15: 6 sake of your **t**, you make void the word of God.
Mk 7: 3 thus observing the **t** of the elders;
7: 5 "Why do your disciples not live according to the **t**
7: 8 the commandment of God and hold to human **t**."
7: 9 the commandment of God in order to keep your **t**!
7:13 thus making void the word of God through your **t**
Col 2: 8 to human **t**, according to the elemental spirits of
2Th 3: 6 not according to the **t** that they received from us.
4Mc 8: 7 the ancestral **t** of your national life.

TRADITIONAL (1) [TRADITION]
3Mc 3:18 they were carried away by their **t** arrogance,

TRADITIONS (5) [TRADITION]
Mk 7: 4 and there are also many other **t** that they observe,
1Co 11: 2 and maintain the **t** just as I handed them on
Gal 1:14 I was far more zealous for the **t** of my ancestors.
2Th 2:15 and hold fast to the **t** that you were taught by us,
3Mc 1: 3 and apostatized from the ancestral **t**, had led

TRAFFICK[ERS] (KJV) See TRADE, TRADERS

TRAFFICKED (1)
Isa 47:15 who have **t** with you from your youth;

TRAILS See Index to Footnotes

TRAIN (5) [TRAINED, TRAINING, TRAINS]
Ps 68:18 leading captives in your **t** and receiving gifts
Pr 22: 6 **T** children in the right way, and when old,
Da 11:43 Libyans and the Ethiopians shall follow in his **t**.
1Ti 4: 7 and old wives' tales. **T** yourself in godliness,
AdE 15: 4 while the other followed, carrying her **t**.

TRAINED (17) [TRAIN]
Ge 14:14 he led forth his **t** men, born in his house,
1Ch 25: 7 who were **t** in singing to the LORD,
2Ch 2: 7 crimson, and blue fabrics, **t** also in engraving,
2:14 He is **t** to work in gold, silver, bronze, iron, stone,
Jer 13:21 as head over you those whom you have **t** to
Hos 7:15 It was I who **t** and strengthened their arms,
10:11 Ephraim was a **t** heifer that loved to thresh,
Mt 13:52 "Therefore every scribe who has been **t** for
Heb 5:14 for those whose faculties have been **t** by practice
12:11 of righteousness to those who have been **t** by it.
2Pe 2:14 They have hearts **t** in greed.
Sus 1: 3 and had **t** their daughter according to the law
1Mc 4: 7 and these men were **t** in war.
2Mc 15:12 and had been **t** from childhood in all that belongs
2Es 14:24 these five, who are **t** to write rapidly;
4Mc 5:34 I will not play false to you, O law that **t** me,
13:24 by the same law and **t** in the same virtues

TRAINING (9) [TRAIN]
1Ti 1: 4 that promote speculations rather than the divine **t**
4: 8 while physical **t** is of some value,
2Ti 3:16 for correction, and for **t** in righteousness,
Tit 2:12 **t** us to renounce impiety and worldly passions,
Wis 2:12 and accuses us of sins against our **t**.
Sir 33: 4 draw upon your **t**, and give your answer.
41:14 My children, be true to your **t** and be at peace;
42: 8 Then you will show your sound **t**,
4Mc 10:10 are suffering because of our godly **t** and virtue,

TRAINS (6) [TRAIN]
2Sa 22:35 He **t** my hands for war,
Ps 18:34 He **t** my hands for war,
144: 1 my rock, who **t** my hands for war,
Jdt 7:18 and supply **t** spread out in great number,
Sir 18:13 He rebukes and **t** and teaches them,
4Mc 5:23 and it also **t** us in courage,

TRAITOR (4) [TREASON]
Lk 6:16 and Judas Iscariot, who became a **t**.
2Mc 5:15 who had become a **t** both to the laws and
10:13 He heard himself called a **t** at every turn,
10:22 Then he killed these men who had turned **t**,

TRAITORS (6) [TREASON]
Jer 9: 2 For they are all adulterers, a band of **t**.
3Mc 3:24 behind our backs as **t** and barbarous enemies.
4:10 they would undergo treatment befitting **t** during
6:12 of life in the manner of **t**.
7: 3 and to punish them with barbarous penalties as **t**;
7: 5 as slaves, or rather as **t**, and, girding themselves

TRAMPING (1) [TRAMPLE]
Isa 9: 5 all the boots of the **t** warriors and all the garments

TRAMPLE (20) [TRAMPING, TRAMPLED, TRAMPLES, TRAMPLING]
Jdg 8: 7 I will **t** your flesh on the thorns of the wilderness
Job 39:15 and that a wild animal may **t** them.
Ps 7: 5 **t** my life to the ground,
56: 1 O God, for people **t** on me;
56: 2 my enemies **t** on me all day long,
57: 3 he will put to shame those who **t** on me.
68:30 **T** under foot those who lust after tribute;
91:13 young lion and the serpent you will **t** under foot.
Isa 1:12 from your hand? **T** my courts no more;
14:25 and on my mountains **t** him under foot;
41:25 He shall **t** on rulers as on mortar,
Eze 26:11 the hoofs of his horses he shall **t** all your streets.
Da 7:23 it shall devour the whole earth, and **t** it down,
Am 2: 7 they who **t** the head of the poor into the dust of
5:11 Therefore because you **t** on the poor and take
8: 4 Hear this, you that **t** on the needy,
Na 3:14 **t** the clay, tread the mortar,
Mt 7: 6 before swine, or they will **t** them under foot
Rev 11: 2 for it is given over to the nations, and they will **t**
Sir 9: 2 Do not give yourself to a woman and let her **t**

TRAMPLED (30) [TRAMPLE]
Jdg 8:16 briers and with them he **t** the people of Succoth.
2Ki 7:17 the people **t** him to death in the gate,
7:20 the people **t** him to death in the gate.
9:33 on the wall and on the horses, which **t** on her.
14: 9 of Lebanon passed by and **t** down the thornbush.
2Ch 25:18 of Lebanon passed by and **t** down the thornbush.
Job 9: 8 who alone stretched out the heavens and **t**
Isa 5: 5 I will break down its wall, and it shall be **t** down.
14:19 like a corpse **t** underfoot.
28: 3 **T** under foot will be the proud garland of
63: 3 I trod them in my anger and **t** them in my wrath;
63: 6 I **t** down peoples in my anger,
63:18 now our adversaries have **t** down your sanctuary.
Jer 12:10 they have **t** down my portion,
Da 8: 7 it threw the ram down to the ground and **t** upon it,
8:10 of the host and some of the stars, and **t** on them.
8:13 the giving over of the sanctuary and host to be **t**?"
Hab 3:12 In fury you trod the earth, in anger you **t** nations.
3:15 You **t** the sea with your horses,
Mt 5:13 but is thrown out and **t** under foot.
Lk 8: 5 as he sowed, some fell on the path and was **t** on,
12: 1 so that they **t** on one another,
21:24 and Jerusalem will be **t** on by the Gentiles,

1Mc 3:45 sanctuary was **t** down, and aliens held the citadel;
3:51 Your sanctuary is **t** down and profaned,
3Mc 2:18 'We have **t** down the house of the sanctuary as
2:18 as the houses of the abominations are **t** down.'
2Es 5:29 And those who opposed your promises have **t**
8:57 Moreover, they have even **t** on his righteous ones,
16:69 and shall be **t** under foot.

TRAMPLES (2) [TRAMPLE]
Isa 26: 6 The foot **t** it, the feet of the poor,
41: 2 delivers up nations to him, and **t** kings under foot;

TRAMPLING‡ (6) [TRAMPLE]
Isa 22: 5 the Lord GOD of hosts has a day of tumult and **t**
58:13 If you refrain from **t** the sabbath,
Zec 10: 5 **t** the foe in the mud of the streets;
1Mc 4:60 to keep the Gentiles from coming and **t** them
3Mc 5:48 as well as by the **t** of the crowd,
6:21 the armed forces following them and began **t**

TRANCE (5)
Da 8:18 As he was speaking to me, I fell into a **t,**
10: 9 I heard the sound of his words, I fell into a **t,**
Ac 10:10 and while it was being prepared, he fell into a **t.**
11: 5 and in a **t** I saw a vision.
22:17 while I was praying in the temple, I fell into a **t**

TRANQUIL (2) [TRANQUILITY]
Pr 14:30 A **t** mind gives life to the flesh,
Sir 47:13 because God made all his borders **t,**

TRANQUILITY (2) [TRANQUIL]
AdE 13: 2 to settle the lives of my subjects in lasting **t** and,
2Mc 14: 6 and will not let the kingdom attain **t.**

TRANSACTION (1)
Ru 4: 7 to confirm a **t,** the one took off a sandal and gave

TRANSFER (3) [TRANSFERRED]
2Sa 3:10 to **t** the kingdom from the house of Saul,
Eze 48:14 they shall not **t** this choice portion of the land,
AdE 16:14 and would **t** the kingdom of the Persians to

TRANSFERRED (5) [TRANSFER]
Nu 36: 7 the Israelites shall be **t** from one tribe to another;
36: 9 No inheritance shall be **t** from one tribe
Ac 25: 3 against Paul, to have him **t** to Jerusalem.
27: 1 they **t** Paul and some other prisoners to a centurion
Col 1:13 darkness and **t** us into the kingdom of his beloved

TRANSFIGURED (2)
Mt 17: 2 And he was **t** before them,
Mk 9: 2 And he was **t** before them,

TRANSFORM (1) [TRANSFORMED]
Php 3:21 He will **t** the body of our humiliation that it may

TRANSFORMED (5) [TRANSFORM]
Ro 12: 2 but be **t** by the renewing of your minds,
2Co 3:18 are being **t** into the same image from one degree
Jdt 10: 7 When they saw her **t** in appearance
Wis 19:19 For land animals were **t** into water creatures,
4Mc 9:22 but as though **t** by fire into immortality,

TRANSGRESS (26) [TRANSGRESSED, TRANSGRESSES, TRANSGRESSING, TRANSGRESSION, TRANSGRESSIONS, TRANSGRESSOR, TRANSGRESSORS]
Nu 14:41 "Why do you continue to **t** the command of
Jos 23:16 If you **t** the covenant of the LORD your God,
2Ch 24:20 Why do you **t** the commandments of the LORD,
Ps 17: 3 in me; my mouth does not **t.**
Pr 8:29 so that the waters might not **t** his command,
Eze 20:38 and those who **t** against me;
33:12 of the righteous shall not save them when they **t;**
Am 4: 4 Come to Bethel—and **t;**
Hab 1:11 they **t** and become guilty;
Tob 4: 5 and refuse to sin or to **t** his commandments.
Jdt 2:13 take care not to **t** any of your lord's commands,
Wis 6: 9 so that you may learn wisdom and not **t.**
Sir 19:24 the highly intelligent who **t** the law.
31:10 the power to **t** and did not **t,**
2Mc 7: 2 to die rather than **t** the laws of our ancestors."
1Es 6:32 that if anyone should **t** or nullify any of
8:24 All who **t** the law of your God or the law of
8:87 but we turned back again to **t** your law by mixing
4Mc 5:17 we consider that we should not **t** it in any respect.
5:20 to **t** the law in matters either small or great is
5:27 be tyrannical for you to compel us not only to **t**
5:29 nor will I **t** the sacred oaths of my ancestors
8:14 to you when you **t** under compulsion."
9: 1 to die rather than **t** our ancestral commandments;
13:15 before those who **t** the commandment of God.

TRANSGRESSED (30) [TRANSGRESS]
Dt 26:13 I have neither **t** nor forgotten any of your
Jos 7:11 they have **t** my covenant that I imposed on them.
7:15 for having **t** the covenant of the LORD,
Jdg 2:20 "Because this people have **t** my covenant
1Sa 15:24 for I have **t** the commandment of the LORD
2Ki 18:12 of the LORD their God but **t** his covenant—
1Ch 2: 7 who **t** in the matter of the devoted thing;
5:25 But they **t** against the God of their ancestors,
Ezr 10:13 for many of us have **t** in this matter.
Isa 24: 5 for they have **t** laws, violated the statutes,
43:27 and your interpreters **t** against me.
64: 5 because you hid yourself we **t.**
Jer 2: 8 the rulers **t** against me; the prophets prophesied by
34:18 And those who **t** my covenant and did not keep
La 3:42 We have **t** and rebelled, and you have
Eze 2: 3 they and their ancestors have **t** against me
Da 9:11 "All Israel has **t** your law and turned aside,
Hos 6: 7 But at Adam they **t** the covenant;
8: 1 they have broken my covenant, and **t** my law.
1Es 1:48 and hardened his heart and **t** the laws of the Lord,
8:82 For we have **t** your commandments,
3Mc 7:10 of the Jewish nation who had willfully **t** against
7:11 that those who for the belly's sake had **t**
7:12 in his kingdom who had **t** the law of God.
2Es 3: 7 but he **t** it, and immediately you appointed death
3:21 burdened with an evil heart, **t** and was overcome,
3:25 but the inhabitants of the city **t,**
7:11 and when Adam **t** my statutes,
7:46 among mortals that has not **t** your covenant?
14:30 which you also have **t** after them.

TRANSGRESSES (1) [TRANSGRESS]
Dt 17: 2 sight of the LORD your God, and **t** his covenant

TRANSGRESSING (1) [TRANSGRESS]
Isa 59:13 **t,** and denying the LORD, and turning away

TRANSGRESSION‡ (41) [TRANSGRESS]
Ex 23:21 for he will not pardon your **t;**
34: 7 forgiving iniquity and **t** and sin,
Nu 14:18 forgiving iniquity and **t,** but by no means clearing
Job 7:21 not pardon my **t** and take away my iniquity?
8: 4 he delivered them into the power of their **t.**
13:23 Make me know my **t** and my sin.
14:17 my **t** would be sealed up in a bag,
33: 9 You say, 'I am clean, without **t;**
34: 6 my wound is incurable, though I am without **t.**'
35:15 and he does not greatly heed **t,**
Ps 19:13 Then I shall be blameless, and innocent of great **t.**
32: 1 Happy are those whose **t** is forgiven,
36: 1 **T** speaks to the wicked deep in their hearts;
59: 3 For no **t** or sin of mine, O LORD,
89:32 then I will punish their **t** with the rod
Pr 10:19 When words are many, **t** is not lacking,
12:13 The evil are ensnared by the **t** of their lips,
17:19 One who loves **t** loves strife;
29: 6 In the **t** of the evil there is a snare,
29:16 When the wicked are in authority, **t** increases,
29:22 and the hothead causes much **t.**
Isa 24:20 its **t** lies heavy upon it, and it falls, and will not rise
53: 8 stricken for the **t** of my people.
57: 4 Are you not children of **t,**
59:20 to those in Jacob who turn from **t,**
Da 8:13 the **t** that makes desolate,
9:24 to finish the **t,** to put an end to sin,
Am 4: 4 to Gilgal—and multiply **t;**
Mic 1: 5 All this is for the **t** of Jacob and for the sins of
1: 5 What is the **t** of Jacob? Is it not Samaria?
3: 8 to declare to Jacob his **t** and to Israel his sin.
6: 7 Shall I give my firstborn for my **t,**
7:18 over the **t** of the remnant of your possession?
Ro 5:14 even over those whose sins were not like the **t**
Gal 6: 1 My friends, if anyone is detected in a **t,**
Heb 2: 2 every **t** or disobedience received a just penalty,
2Pe 2:16 but was rebuked for his own **t;**
Wis 10: 1 she delivered him from his **t,**
14:31 that always pursues the **t** of the unrighteous.
4Mc 5:13 it will excuse you from any **t** that arises out
9: 4 which insures our safety through **t** of the law,

TRANSGRESSIONS (53) [TRANSGRESS]
Lev 16:16 and because of their **t,** all their sins;
16:21 and all their **t,** all their sins,
Jos 24:19 he will not forgive your **t** or your sins.
1Ki 8:50 all their **t** that they have committed against you;
Job 31:33 if I have concealed my **t** as others do,
35: 6 if your **t** are multiplied, what do you do to him?
36: 9 then he declares to them their work and their **t,**
Ps 5:10 because of their many **t** cast them out,
25: 7 Do not remember the sins of my youth or my **t;**
32: 5 I said, "I will confess my **t** to the LORD,"
39: 8 Deliver me from all my **t.**
51: 1 according to your abundant mercy blot out my **t.**
51: 3 For I know my **t,** and my sin is ever before me.
65: 3 of iniquity overwhelm us, you forgive our **t.**
103:12 so far he removes our **t** from us.
Pr 28:13 No one who conceals **t** will prosper,
Isa 43:25 I, I am He who blots out your **t** for my own sake,
44:22 I have swept away your **t** like a cloud,
50: 1 and for your **t** your mother was put away.
53: 5 But he was wounded for our **t,**
59:12 For our **t** before you are many,
59:12 Our **t** indeed are with us, and we know our
Jer 5: 6 their **t** are many, their apostasies are great.
La 1: 5 for the multitude of her **t;**
1:14 My **t** were bound into a yoke;
1:22 as you have dealt with me because of all my **t;**
Eze 14:11 nor defile themselves any more with all their **t.**
18:22 None of the **t** that they have committed shall
18:28 from all the **t** that they had committed, they shall
18:30 Repent and turn from all your **t;**
18:31 from you all the **t** that you have committed
21:24 in that your **t** are uncovered,
33:10 "Our **t** and our sins weigh upon us,
37:23 or with any of their **t.**
39:24 according to their uncleanness and their **t,**
Da 8:23 when the **t** have reached their full measure,
Am 1: 3 For three **t** of Damascus, and for four, I will not
1: 6 For three **t** of Gaza, and for four, I will not revoke
1: 9 For three **t** of Tyre, and for four, I will not revoke
1:11 For three **t** of Edom, and for four, I will not revoke
1:13 For three **t** of the Ammonites, and for four,
2: 1 For three **t** of Moab, and for four, I will not revoke
2: 4 For three **t** of Judah, and for four, I will not revoke
2: 6 For three **t** of Israel, and for four, I will not revoke
3:14 On the day I punish Israel for its **t,**
5:12 For I know how many are your **t,**
Mic 1:13 for in you were found the **t** of Israel.
Gal 3:19 It was added because of **t,**
Heb 9:15 a death has occurred that redeems them from the **t**
Man 1: 9 my **t** are multiplied, O Lord, they are multiplied!
1:12 O Lord, I have sinned, and I acknowledge my **t.**
1:13 Do not destroy me with my **t!**
2Es *7:68* and are full of sins and burdened with **t.**

TRANSGRESSOR (3) [TRANSGRESS]
Gal 2:18 then I demonstrate that I am a **t.**
1Ti 2:14 but the woman was deceived and became a **t.**
Jas 2:11 you have become a **t** of the law.

TRANSGRESSORS (8) [TRANSGRESS]
Ps 37:38 But **t** shall be altogether destroyed;
51:13 Then I will teach **t** your ways,
Isa 46: 8 and consider, recall it to mind, you **t,**
53:12 and was numbered with the **t;**
53:12 and made intercession for the **t.**
Hos 14: 9 the upright walk in them, but **t** stumble in them.
Jas 2: 9 you commit sin and are convicted by the law as **t.**
3Mc 2:17 otherwise the **t** will boast in their wrath and exult

TRANSIENT (1) [TRANSIENTS]
Nu 35:15 for the resident or **t** alien among them,

TRANSIENTS (1) [TRANSIENT]
1Ch 29:15 For we are aliens and **t** before you,

TRANSLATE (KJV) See TRANSFER

TRANSLATED (6) [TRANSLATION]
Ezr 4: 7 the letter was written in Aramaic and **t.**
Jn 1:38 "Rabbi" (which **t** means Teacher),
1:41 the Messiah" (which is **t** Anointed).
1:42 You are to be called Cephas" (which is **t** Peter).
AdE 11: 1 and had been **t** by Lysimachus son of Ptolemy,
Sir Pr: 2 the same sense when **t** into another language.

TRANSLATING (1) [TRANSLATION]
Sir Pr: 2 despite our diligent labor in **t,** we may seem to

TRANSLATION (3) [TRANSLATED, TRANSLATING]
Ezr 4:18 that you sent to us has been read in **t** before me.
Ac 13: 8 the **t** of his name) opposed them and tried to turn
Sir Pr: 3 and labor to the **t** of this book.

TRANSLATION (KJV) See also TAKEN

TRANSPARENT (1)
Rev 21:21 and the street of the city is pure gold, **t** as glass.

TRANSPLANTED (4) [PLANT]
Eze 17: 8 it was **t** to good soil by abundant waters,
17:10 When it is **t,** will it thrive?
19:10 Your mother was like a vine in a vineyard **t** by
19:13 Now it is **t** into the wilderness,

TRANSPORT (2) [TRANSPORTED]
Dt 14:24 the distance is so great that you are unable to **t** it,
Jdt 2:17 and mules for **t,** and innumerable sheep and oxen

TRANSPORTED (1) [TRANSPORT]
2Mc 9: 4 **T** with rage, he conceived the idea of turning

TRAP (26) [ENTRAP, TRAPPED, TRAPS]
Jos 23:13 but they shall be a snare and a **t** for you,
Job 18: 9 A **t** seizes them by the heel;
18:10 a **t** for them in the path.
Ps 69:22 Let their table be a **t** for them,
140: 5 The arrogant have hidden a **t** for me,
141: 9 Keep me from the **t** that they have laid for me,
142: 3 In the path where I walk they have hidden a **t**
Pr 7:22 or bounds like a stag toward the **t**
Ecc 7:26 the woman who is a **t,** whose heart is snares
Isa 8:14 a **t** and a snare for the inhabitants of Jerusalem.
29:21 who set a **t** for the arbiter in the gate,
Jer 5:26 Like fowlers they set a **t;**
48:43 Terror, pit, and **t** are before you,
48:44 of the pit shall be caught in the **t.**
Am 3: 5 when there is no **t** for it?
Ob 1: 7 those who ate your bread have set a **t** for you—

Mk 12:13 and some Herodians to t him in what he said.
Lk 20:20 in order to t him by what he said,
20:26 not able in the presence of the people to t him
21:35 like a t. For it will come upon all who live
Ro 11: 9 "Let their table become a snare and a t,
Tob 14:10 Ahikar escaped the fatal t that Nadab had set
Wis 14:11 for human souls and a t for the feet of the foolish.
14:21 And this became a hidden t for humankind,
Sir 51: 2 and from the t laid by a slanderous tongue,
1Mc 5: 4 a t and a snare to the people and ambushed them

TRAPPED (4) [TRAP]

Ps 59:12 the words of their lips, let them be t in their pride.
Isa 42:22 all of them are t in holes and hidden in prisons;
1Ti 6: 9 and are t by many senseless and harmful desires
Sus 1:22 Susanna groaned and said, "I am completely t.

TRAPPINGS (1)

2Mc 5: 3 the flash of golden t, and armor of all kinds.

TRAPS (1) [TRAP]

Sir 5:14 and do not lay t with your tongue;

TRAVAIL (2)

2Es 5:35 the t of Jacob and the exhaustion of the people
5:37 and then I will explain to you the t that you ask

TRAVAIL, TRAVAILED, TRAVAILEST, TRAVAILETH (KJV) See also ADVERSITY, ANGUISH, BIRTH, BUSINESS, CONCEIVE, DELIVERY, HARDSHIP, LABOR, TOIL, TRIBULATION, VENTURE, WORK, WRITHE

TRAVEL (11) [TRAVELED, TRAVELER, TRAVELER'S, TRAVELERS, TRAVELING, TRAVELS]

Ex 13:21 so that they might t by day and by night.
Dt 2:27 I will t only along the road;
Job 21:29 Have you not asked those who t the roads,
Isa 35: 8 the unclean shall not t on it,
Ac 19:29 Macedonians who were Paul's t companions.
2Co 8:19 also been appointed by the churches to t with us
Tob 5: 7 for I do need you to t with me,
9: 2 take four servants and two camels with you and t
AdE 13: 2 to make my kingdom peaceable and open to t
Wis 6:23 nor will I t in the company of sickly envy,
1Es 4:23 and goes out to t and rob and steal and to sail

TRAVELED‡ (14) [TRAVEL]

Dt 1:31 all the way that you t until you reached this place.
2:14 the length of time we had t from Kadesh-barnea
Jos 5: 6 For the Israelites t forty years in the wilderness,
1Sa 31:12 the valiant men set out, t all night long, and took
2Sa 2:29 and his men t all that night through the Arabah;
4: 7 and t by way of the Arabah all night long.
Eze 27:25 The ships of Tarshish t for you in your trade.
Lk 15:13 the younger son gathered all he had and t to
Ac 11:19 that took place over Stephen t as far as Phoenicia,
Tob 5: 6 I have often t to Media,
Sir 34:11 but he that has t acquires much cleverness.
Bar 4:26 My pampered children have t rough roads;
1Mc 11:60 Then Jonathan set out and t beyond the river and
2Es 3:33 For I have t widely among the nations

TRAVELER (5) [TRAVEL]

2Sa 12: 4 Now there came a t to the rich man,
Job 31:32 I have opened my doors to the t—
Isa 35: 8 no t, not even fools, shall go astray.
Jer 14: 8 like a t turning aside for the night?
Sir 26:12 As a thirsty t opens his mouth and drinks

TRAVELER'S (1) [TRAVEL]

Jer 9: 2 O that I had in the desert a t lodging place,

TRAVELERS‡ (7) [TRAVEL]

Jdg 5: 6 caravans ceased and t kept to the byways.
Job 6:19 The caravans of Tema look, the t of Sheba hope.
28: 4 they are forgotten by t, they sway suspended,
Isa 33: 8 The highways are deserted, t have quit the road.
Eze 39:11 the Valley of the T east of the sea;
39:11 it shall block the path of the t,
Lk 2:44 Assuming that he was in the group of t,

TRAVELING (6) [TRAVEL]

Lk 10:33 But a Samaritan while t came near him;
14:25 Now large crowds were t with him;
Ac 9: 7 The men who were t with him stood speechless
26:12 I was t to Damascus with the authority
Sir 8:15 Do not go t with the reckless,
42: 3 a partner or with t companions, and of dividing

TRAVELS (5) [TRAVEL]

Dt 23:14 the LORD your God t along with your camp,
Sir 32:10 Lightning t ahead of the thunder,
34:12 I have seen many things in my t,
39: 4 he t in foreign lands and learns what is good
51:13 before I went on my t,

TRAVERSED (3) [TRAVERSING]

Jos 18: 9 So the men went and t the land and set down in
Wis 5:11 is t by the movement of its wings,
Sir 24: 5 the vault of heaven and t the depths of the abyss.

TRAVERSING (1) [TRAVERSED]

Job 33:18 their lives from t the River.

TRAVERSING (KJV) See INTERLACING

TRAYS (3)

Ex 25:38 Its snuffers and t shall be of pure gold.
37:23 He made its seven lamps and its snuffers and its t
Nu 4: 9 with its lamps, its snuffers, its t,

TREACHEROUS (22) [TREASON]

Job 6:15 My companions are t like a torrent-bed,
Ps 25: 3 let them be ashamed who are wantonly t.
35:19 Do not let my t enemies rejoice over me,
55:23 bloodthirsty and t shall not live out half their days.
78:57 they twisted like a t bow.
Pr 2:22 and the t will be rooted out of it.
11: 3 but the crookedness of the t destroys them.
11: 6 but the t are taken captive by their schemes.
12: 5 the advice of the wicked is t.
13: 2 but the desire of the t is for wrongdoing.
Isa 24:16 For the t deal treacherously, the t deal very treacherously.
33: 1 t one, with whom no one has dealt treacherously!
Jer 12: 1 Why do all who are t thrive?
Hab 1:13 why do you look on the t,
2: 5 wealth is t; the arrogant do not endure.
2Ti 3: 4 t, reckless, swollen with conceit, lovers
Sir 22:22 arrogance, disclosure of secrets, or a t blow—
27:25 and a t blow opens up many wounds.
1Mc 7:10 and his brothers with peaceable but t words.
7:30 that Nicanor had come to him with t intent,
16:13 and made t plans against Simon and his sons,

TREACHEROUSLY (20) [TREASON]

Nu 31:16 the Israelites act t against the LORD in the affair
Jdg 9:23 and the lords of Shechem dealt t with Abimelech.
1Sa 14:33 And he said, "You have dealt t;
2Sa 18:13 if I had dealt t against his life
Ne 13:27 and do all this great evil and act t against our God
Ps 59: 5 spare none of those who t plot evil.
Isa 24:16 the treacherous deal t, the treacherous deal very t.
33: 1 with whom no one has dealt t!
33: 1 and when you have stopped dealing t, you will be dealt with t.
48: 8 For I knew that you would deal very t,
Jer 12: 6 even they have dealt t with you;
La 1: 2 all her friends have dealt t with her,
Eze 20:27 ancestors blasphemed me, by dealing t with me.
39:23 because they dealt t with me.
Wis 14:24 but they either t kill one another,
1Mc 7:27 to Jerusalem with a large force, and t sent
13:31 Trypho dealt t with the young King Antiochus;
16:15 The son of Abubus received them t in

TREACHERY (17) [TREASON]

Ex 21:14 someone willfully attacks and kills another by t,
Lev 26:40 in that they committed t against me and,
Jos 22:16 'What is this t that you have committed against
22:31 you have not committed this t against the LORD;
2Ki 17: 4 But the king of Assyria found t in Hoshea;
Ps 38:12 and meditate t all day long.
52: 2 Your tongue is like a sharp razor, you worker of t.
Jer 5:27 their houses are full of t;
Eze 18:24 for the t of which they are guilty and
39:26 and all the t they have practiced against me,
Da 9: 7 of the t that they have committed against you.
Hos 7: 3 and the officials by their t.
1Mc 9:61 the men of the country who were leaders in this t,
16:17 an act of great t and returned evil for good.
2Mc 4:34 Andronicus came to Onias, and resorting to t,
14:22 in readiness at key places to prevent sudden t on
4Mc 4:13 that Apollonius had been overcome by human t

TREAD (31) [DOWNTRODDEN, TREADER, TREADING, TREAD, TROD, TRODDEN]

Dt 33:29 and you shall t on their backs.
Jos 1: 3 that the sole of your foot will t upon I have given
Job 24:11 they t the wine presses, but suffer thirst.
40:12 t down the wicked where they stand.
Ps 1: 1 or take the path that sinners t,
36:11 Do not let the foot of the arrogant t on me,
44: 5 through your name we t down our assailants.
60:12 it is he who will t down our foes.
91:13 You will t on the lion and the adder,
108:13 it is he who will t down our foes.
Isa 7:25 where cattle are let loose and where sheep t.
10: 6 and to t them down like the mire of the streets.
63: 2 your garments like theirs who t the wine press?"
Jer 25:30 and shout, like those who t grapes,
Eze 34:18 but you must t down with your feet the rest
Joel 3:13 Go in, t, for the wine press is full.
Mic 1: 3 and will come down and t upon the high places of
5: 5 Assyrians come into our land and t upon our soil,
5: 6 from the Assyrians if they come into our land or t
6:15 you shall t olives, but not anoint yourselves with
6:15 you shall t grapes, but not drink wine.
Mic 7:19 he will t our iniquities under foot.
Na 3:14 trample the clay, t the mortar,
Hab 3:19 and makes me t upon the heights.
Zec 9:15 and they shall devour and t down the slingers;
Mal 4: 3 And you shall t down the wicked,
Lk 10:19 given you authority to t on snakes and scorpions,
Rev 19:15 he will t the wine press of the fury of the wrath
Bar 4:13 or t the paths his righteousness showed them.
4:25 but you will soon see their destruction and will t
2Es 16:26 The grapes shall ripen, but who will t them?

TREADER (3) [TREAD]

Job 24:18 no t turns toward their vineyards.
Isa 16:10 no t treads out wine in the presses;
Am 9:13 and the t of grapes the one who sows the seed;

TREADING (4) [TREAD]

Dt 25: 4 You shall not muzzle an ox while it is t out
Ne 13:15 In those days I saw in Judah people t wine presses
1Co 9: 9 "You shall not muzzle an ox while it is t out
1Ti 5:18 "You shall not muzzle an ox while it is t out

TREADS (5) [TREAD]

Isa 16:10 no treader t out wine in the presses;
41:25 on rulers as on mortar, as the potter t clay.
Jer 48:33 no one t them with shouts of joy;
Am 4:13 and t on the heights of the earth—
Mic 5: 8 t down and tears in pieces, with no one to deliver.

TREASON (9) [TRAITOR, TRAITORS, TREACHEROUS, TREACHEROUSLY, TREACHERY]

Dt 13: 5 be put to death for having spoken t against
1Sa 24:11 that there is no wrong or t in my hands.
2Ki 9:23 saying to Ahaziah, "T, Ahaziah!"
11:14 Athaliah tore her clothes and cried, "T! T!"
2Ch 23:13 Athaliah tore her clothes, and cried, "T! T!"
Eze 17:20 with him there for the t he has committed
3Mc 6:24 "You are committing t and surpassing tyrants

TREASURE (43) [TREASURED, TREASURER, TREASURERS, TREASURES, TREASURIES, TREASURY]

Ge 43:23 of your father must have put t in your sacks
2Ki 20:13 he showed them all his t house, the silver,
1Ch 29: 3 I have a t of my own of gold and silver,
Ps 119:11 I t your word in my heart,
Pr 2: 1 and t up my commandments within you,
15: 6 In the house of the righteous there is much t,
15:16 a little with the fear of the LORD than great t
21:20 Precious t remains in the house of the wise,
Ecc 2: 8 also gathered for myself silver and gold and the t
Isa 33: 6 the fear of the LORD is Zion's t.
39: 2 he showed them his t house, the silver, the gold,
Eze 22:25 they have taken t and precious things;
Na 2: 9 There is no end of t! An abundance of every
Hag 2: 7 so that the t of all nations shall come,
Mt 2:11 Then, opening their t chests,
6:21 For where your t is, there your heart will be also.
12:35 good person brings good things out of a good t,
12:35 the evil person brings evil things out of an evil t.
13:44 kingdom of heaven is like t hidden in a field,
13:52 a household who brings out of his t what is new
19:21 and you will have t in heaven;
Mk 10:21 and you will have t in heaven;
Lk 6:45 of the good t of the heart produces good,
6:45 and the evil person out of evil t produces evil;
12:33 for yourselves that do not wear out, an unfailing t
12:34 For where your t is, there your heart will be also.
18:22 and you will have t in heaven;
2Co 4: 7 But we have this t in clay jars,
1Ti 6:19 up for themselves the t of a good foundation for
2Ti 1:14 Guard the good t entrusted to you,
Jas 5: 3 You have laid up t for the last days.
Tob 4: 9 a good t for yourself against the day of necessity.
Wis 7:14 for it is an unfailing t for mortals;
Sir 3: 4 like those who lay up t.
6:14 whoever finds one has found a t.
20:30 Hidden wisdom and unseen t,
29:11 Lay up your t according to the commandments of
40:18 but better than either is finding a t.
41:14 hidden wisdom and unseen t—
1Es 1:54 the t chests of the Lord, and the royal stores,
2Es 7:77 a t of works stored up with the Most High,
8:54 in the end the t of immortality is made manifest.
4Mc 4: 4 up to Seleucus to inform him of the rich t.

TREASURED (8) [TREASURE]

Ex 19: 5 be my t possession out of all the peoples.
Dt 7: 6 on earth to be his people, his t possession.
14: 2 on earth to be his people, his t possession.
26:18 to be his t people, as he promised you,
Job 23:12 I have t in my bosom the words of his mouth.
Eze 7:22 so that they may profane my t place;
Lk 2:19 But Mary t all these words and pondered them
2:51 His mother t all these things in her heart.

TREASURER (4) [TREASURE]

Ezr 1: 8 into the charge of Mithredath the t,
Ro 16:23 Erastus, the city t, and our brother Quartus,
1Es 2:11 he gave them to Mithridates, his t,
1Es 4:49 or governor or t should forcibly enter their doors;

TREASURERS (7) [TREASURE]
Ezr 7:21 to all the t in the province Beyond the River:
Ne 13:13 as t over the storehouses the priest Shelemiah,
Da 3: 2 the counselors, the t, the justices, the magistrates,
3: 3 the counselors, the t, the justices, the magistrates,
1Es 4:47 for him to all the t and governors and generals
8:19 the t of Syria and Phoenicia that whatever Ezra
8:46 to tell Iddo and his kindred and the t at that place

TREASURES (45) [TREASURE]
Dt 33:19 affluence of the seas and the hidden t of the sand.
1Ki 14:26 the t of the house of the LORD and the t of the
15:18 the t of the house of the LORD and the t of the
2Ki 16: 8 of the LORD and in the t of the king's house,
24:13 the t of the house of the LORD, and the t of the
1Ch 9:26 in charge of the chambers and the t of the house
2Ch 12: 9 the t of the house of the LORD and the t of the
16: 2 and gold from the t of the house of the LORD
36:18 the t of the house of the LORD, and the t of the king
Job 3:21 and dig for it more than for hidden t;
20:26 Utter darkness is laid up for their t;
Pr 2: 4 and search for it as for hidden t—
10: 2 T gained by wickedness do not profit,
21: 6 of t by a lying tongue is a fleeting vapor and
Isa 2: 7 and there is no end to their t;
10:13 and have plundered their t;
30: 6 and their t on the humps of camels,
45: 3 I will give you the t of darkness and riches hidden
Jer 15:13 Your wealth and your t I will give as plunder,
17: 3 Your wealth and all your t I will give for spoil as
20: 5 and all the t of the kings of Judah into the hand
48: 7 you trusted in your strongholds and your t,
49: 4 You trusted in your t, saying,
50:37 A sword against all her t,
51:13 You who live by mighty waters, rich in t,
La 1:11 they trade their t for food to revive their strength.
Da 11:43 of the t of gold and of silver, and all the riches
Joel 3: 5 and have carried my rich t into your temples.
Ob 1: 6 How Esau has been pillaged, his t searched out!
Mic 6:10 Can I forget the t of wickedness in the house of
Mt 6:19 "Do not store up for yourselves t on earth,
6:20 but store up for yourselves t in heaven,
Lk 12:21 up t for themselves but are not rich toward God."
Col 2: 3 in whom are hidden all the t of wisdom
Heb 11:26 the Christ to be greater wealth than the t of Egypt,
1Mc 1:23 he took also the hidden t that he found.
2Mc 1:14 to secure most of its t as a dowry.
1:15 the priests of the temple of Nanea had set out the t
2Es 6: 5 those who stored up t of faith were sealed—
16:57 He searches the abyss and its t;

TREASURIES (25) [TREASURE]
Dt 32:34 up in store with me, sealed up in my t?
1Ki 7:51 stored them in the t of the house of the LORD.
2Ki 12:18 that was found in the t of the house of the LORD
14:14 in the t of the king's house, as well as hostages;
18:15 of the LORD and in the t of the king's house.
1Ch 26:20 the t of the house of God and the t of the dedicated
26:20 in charge of the t of the house of the LORD.
26:22 in charge of the t of the house of the LORD.
26:24 son of Moses, was chief officer in charge of the t.
26:26 of all the t of the dedicated gifts that King David,
27:25 Over the king's t was Azmaveth son of Adiel.
27:25 Over the t in the country, in the cities,
28:11 its t, its upper rooms, and its inner chambers,
28:12 the t of the house of God, and the t for dedicated
2Ch 5: 1 and all the vessels in the t of the house of God.
8:15 regarding anything at all, or regarding the t.
25:24 he seized also the t of the king's house,
32:27 and he made for himself t for silver, for gold,
Est 3: 9 so that they may put it into the king's t."
4: 7 that Haman had promised to pay into the king's t
Pr 8:21 with wealth those who love me, and filling their t.
Eze 28: 4 and have gathered gold and silver into your t.
Sir 1:25 In the t of wisdom are wise sayings,
4Mc 4: 3 that in the Jerusalem t there are deposited tens

TREASURY (39) [TREASURE]
Jos 6:19 they shall go into the t of the LORD."
6:24 they put into the t of the house of the LORD
1Ch 29: 8 Whoever had precious stones gave them to the t
Ezr 6: 4 let the cost be paid from the royal t.
7:20 you may provide out of the king's t.
Ne 7:70 The governor gave to the t one thousand darics
Da 1: 2 and placed the vessels in the t of his gods.
Hos 13:15 It shall strip his t of every precious thing.
Zec 11:13 Then the LORD said to me, "Throw it into the t"—
11:13 and threw them into the t in the house of the LORD.
Mt 27: 6 said, "It is not lawful to put them into the t,
Mk 12:41 He sat down opposite the t, and watched the crowd putting money into the t.
12:43 in more than all those who are contributing to the t.
Lk 21: 1 and saw rich people putting their gifts into the t;
Jn 8:20 while he was teaching in the t of the temple,
Ac 8:27 queen of the Ethiopians, in charge of her entire t.
Tob 1:20 not taken into the royal t except my wife Anna
AdE 3: 9 of silver into the king's t."
4: 7 into the royal t to bring about the destruction of
Sir 29:12 Store up almsgiving in your t,
1Mc 3:29 he saw that the money in the t was exhausted,
13:15 that your brother Jonathan owed the royal t,
14:49 and to deposit copies of them in the t,
15: 8 to the royal t and any such future debts shall
2Mc 3: 6 that the t in Jerusalem was full of untold sums
3:13 in any case be confiscated for the king's t.
3:24 But when he arrived at the t with his bodyguard,
3:28 this man who had just entered the aforesaid t with
3:40 of Heliodorus and the protection of the t.
4:42 temple robber himself they killed close by the t.
5:18 whom King Seleucus sent to inspect the t.
1Es 5:45 that they would give to the sacred t for the work
6:25 the cost to be paid from the t of King Cyrus;
8:18 you may provide out of the royal t.
8:45 who was the leading man at the place of the t,
3Mc 3:28 and also two thousand drachmas from the royal t,
4Mc 4: 6 to seize the private funds in the t.
4: 7 to the sacred t should be deprived of them,

TREAT‡ (26) [ILL-TREAT, ILL-TREATMENT, TREATED, TREATING, TREATMENT, TREATMENTS, TREATS]
Ge 43: 6 "Why did you t me so badly as to tell the man
Ex 5:15 "Why do you t your servants like this?
Lev 21: 8 and you shall t them as holy, since they offer
25:46 These you may t as slaves,
Nu 10:29 come with us, and we will t you well;
11:15 If this is the way you are going to t me,
Dt 20:15 Thus you shall t all the towns that are very far
21:14 You must not t her as a slave,
21:16 he is not permitted to t the son of the loved as
Ne 9:32 do not t lightly all the hardship that has come
Job 22:24 if you t gold like dust,
Jer 24: 8 so will I t King Zedekiah of Judah, his officials,
Hos 11: 8 How can I t you like Zeboiim?
Na 3: 6 I will throw filth at you and t you with contempt,
Lk 15:19 t me like one of your hired hands." '
Col 3:19 love your wives and never t them harshly.
4: 1 Masters, t your slaves justly and fairly,
Jdt 10:16 and he will t you well."
11: 4 Rather, all will t you well,
Sir 13:11 Do not try to t him as an equal,
14:11 My child, t yourself well,
33:31 If you have but one slave, t him like yourself,
33:31 If you have but one slave, t him like a brother,
1Mc 13:46 "Do not t us according to our wicked acts but
2Mc 9:27 and will t you with moderation and kindness."
3Mc 3:20 since we t all nations with benevolence.

TREATED (36) [TREAT]
Ge 34:31 they said, "Should our sister be t like a whore?"
39:19 saying, "This is the way your servant t me,"
42: 7 but he t them like strangers and spoke harshly
Lev 15:26 during all the days of her discharge shall be t as
Nu 11:11 "Why have you t your servant so badly?
Dt 26: 6 When the Egyptians t us harshly and afflicted us,
1Sa 2:17 they t the offerings of the LORD with contempt.
2:30 those who despise me shall be t with contempt.
Ecc 8:14 that there are righteous people who are t
8:14 and there are wicked people who are t according
Jer 6:14 They have t the wound of my people carelessly,
8:11 They have t the wound of my people carelessly,
Eze 7:19 their gold shall be t as unclean.
22: 7 Father and mother are t with contempt in you;
28:24 among all their neighbors who have t them
28:26 upon all their neighbors who have t them
Mt 21:36 and they t them in the same way.
Mk 9:12 through many sufferings and be t with contempt?
Lk 2:48 "Child, why have you t us like this?
23:11 Even Herod with his soldiers t him with contempt
Ac 27: 3 and Julius t Paul kindly, and allowed him to go
1Co 12:23 and our less respectable members are t
2Co 6: 8 We are t as impostors, and yet are true;
Heb 10:33 and sometimes being partners with those so t.
Tob 2:10 but the more they t me with ointments
14:13 He t his parents-in-law with great respect
AdE 2: 9 he t her and her maids with special favor in
Sir 26:28 intelligent men who are t contemptuously,
1Mc 11:26 king t him as his predecessors had t him;
11:53 that Jonathan had done him, but t him very harshly.
2Mc 6:22 and be t kindly on account of his old friendship
7:24 Antiochus felt that he was being t with contempt,
3Mc 6: 9 who are being outrageously t by the abominable
6:31 those disgracefully t and near to death,
4Mc 4: 9 to shield the holy place that was being t

TREATING (4) [TREAT]
Nu 22:30 Have I been in the habit of t you this way?"
Heb 12: 7 God is t you as children;
Sus 1:57 how you have been t the daughters of Israel,
3Mc 3:15 and great benevolence, gladly t them well.

TREATISE (KJV) See BOOK

TREATMENT (11) [TREAT]
Est 2:12 this was the regular period of their cosmetic t,
Col 2:23 humility, and severe t of the body,
Tob 14:10 God repaid him to his face for this shameful t.
2Mc 2:31 of expression and to forego exhaustive t.
12:30 of Scythopolis had shown them and their kind t
3Mc 3:25 with insulting and harsh t,
4: 6 as they were torn by the harsh t of the heathen.
4:10 they would undergo t befitting traitors during
6:26 with outrageous t those who from the beginning
7: 5 They also led them out with harsh t as slaves,
4Mc 8:17 and exhorted us to accept kind t if we obey him,

TREATMENTS (2) [TREAT]
Est 2: 3 let their cosmetic t be given them.
2: 9 and he quickly provided her with her cosmetic t

TREATS (1) [TREAT]
Mic 7: 6 for the son t the father with contempt,

TREATY‡ (13)
Jos 9: 6 so now make a t with us."
9: 7 then how can we make a t with you?"
9:11 come now, make a t with us." '
9:15 guaranteeing their lives by a t;
9:16 after they had made a t with them,
1Sa 11: 1 "Make a t with us, and we will serve you."
11: 2 "On this condition I will make a t with you,
1Ki 5:12 and the two of them made a t.
20:34 So he made a t with him and let him go.
Isa 33: 8 The t is broken, its oaths are despised,
Hos 12: 1 they make a t with Assyria,
1Mc 8:29 Thus on these terms the Romans make a t with
2Mc 13:25 people of Ptolemais were indignant over the t;

TREE‡ (187) [TREES]
A. TREE OF LIFE (14)
B. EVERY TREE (12)
C. EVERY GREEN TREE (11)

Ge 1:29 and every t with seed in its fruit; B
2: 9 the ground the LORD God made to grow every t B
2: 9 the t of life also in the midst of the garden, A
2: 9 and the t of the knowledge of good and evil.
2:16 "You may freely eat of every t of the garden; B
2:17 the t of the knowledge of good and evil you shall
3: 1 'You shall not eat from any t in the garden'?"
3: 3 not eat of the fruit of the t that is in the middle of
3: 6 the woman saw that the t was good for food,
3: 6 and that the t was to be desired to make one wise,
3:11 from the t of which I commanded you not to eat?"
3:12 she gave me fruit from the t, and I ate."
3:17 the t about which I commanded you, 'You shall
3:22 from the t of life, and eat, and live forever"— A
3:24 and turning to guard the way to the t of life. A
18: 4 and rest yourselves under the t.
18: 8 and he stood by them under the t while they ate.
21:33 Abraham planted a tamarisk t in Beer-sheba,
Ex 9:25 and shattered every t in the field. B
10: 5 they shall devour every t of yours that grows B
10:15 nothing green was left, no t, no plant in the field,
Lev 27:30 the seed from the ground or the fruit from the t,
Dt 12: 2 on the hills, and under every leafy t.
16:21 You shall not plant any t as a sacred pole beside
19: 5 when one of them swings the ax to cut down a t,
21:22 and you hang him on a t,
21:23 his corpse must not remain all night upon the t;
21:23 for anyone hung on a t is under God's curse.
22: 6 in any t or on the ground, with fledglings or eggs,
Jos 8:29 he hanged the king of Ai on a t until evening;
8:29 and they took his body down from the t,
Jdg 9: 8 So they said to the olive t, 'Reign over us.'
9: 9 The olive t answered them,
9:10 Then the trees said to the fig t,
9:11 But the fig t answered them,
1Sa 14: 2 the outskirts of Gibeah under the pomegranate t
22: 6 under the tamarisk t on the height,
31:13 and buried them under the tamarisk t in Jabesh,
1Ki 13:14 and found him sitting under an oak t.
14:23 on every high hill and under every green t; C
19: 4 and came and sat down under a solitary broom t.
19: 5 he lay down under the broom t and fell asleep.
2Ki 3:19 every good t you shall fell,
3:25 and every good t they felled.
16: 4 on the hills, and under every green t. C
17:10 on every high hill and under every green t; C
18:31 from your own vine and your own fig t,
2Ch 28: 4 on the hills, and under every green t. C
Ne 10:35 of all fruit of every t, year by year, to the house B
10:37 and our contributions, the fruit of every t, B
Job 14: 7 "For there is hope for a t, if it is cut down,
15:33 and cast off their blossoms, like the olive t.
19:10 and I am gone, he has uprooted my hope like a t.
24:20 so wickedness is broken like a t.
Ps 52: 8 But I am like a green olive t in the house of God.
92:12 The righteous flourish like the palm t,
120: 4 with glowing coals of the broom t!
Pr 3:18 She is a t of life to those who lay hold of her; A
11:30 The fruit of the righteous is a t of life, A
13:12 but a desire fulfilled is a t of life. A
15: 4 A gentle tongue is a t of life, A
27:18 Anyone who tends a fig t will eat its fruit,
Ecc 11: 3 whether a t falls to the south or to the north,
11: 3 in the place where the t falls, there it will lie.
12: 5 the almond t blossoms, the grasshopper drags itself
SS 2: 3 As an apple t among the trees of the wood,
2:13 The fig t puts forth its figs,
7: 7 You are stately as a palm t,
7: 8 I say I will climb the palm t and lay hold
8: 5 Under the apple t I awakened you.
Isa 17: 6 as when an olive t is beaten—
17: 6 four or five on the branches of a fruit t,
24:13 as when an olive t is beaten,
34: 4 or fruit withering on a fig t.
36:16 from your own vine and your own fig t
44:14 a holm t or an oak and lets it grow strong among
44:23 O mountains, O forest, and every t in it! B
56: 3 and do not let the eunuch say, "I am just a dry t."
57: 5 with lust among the oaks, under every green t; C
65:22 like the days of a t shall the days of my people be,
Jer 1:11 And I said, "I see a branch of an almond t."
2:20 under every green t you sprawled and played C

Jer 2:27 who say to a **t**, "You are my father,"
3: 6 up on every high hill and under every green **t**, C
3: 9 committing adultery with stone and **t**.
3:13 among strangers under every green **t**, C
8:13 nor figs on the fig **t**;
10: 3 a **t** from the forest is cut down,
11:16 The LORD once called you, "A green olive **t**,
11:19 saying, "Let us destroy the **t** with its fruit,
17: 2 beside every green **t**, and on the high hills, C
17: 8 They shall be like a **t** planted by water,
Eze 6:13 under every green **t**, and under every leafy oak, C
17:24 I bring low the high **t**, I make high the low **t**;
17:24 I dry up the green **t** and make the dry **t** flourish.
20:28 wherever they saw any high hill or any leafy **t**,
20:47 and it shall devour every green **t** in you C
20:47 in you and every dry **t**;
31: 8 no **t** in the garden of God was like it in beauty.
36:30 I will make the fruit of the **t** and the produce of
41:18 a palm **t** between cherub and cherub.
41:19 a human face turned toward the palm **t** on
41:19 the face of a young lion turned toward the palm **t**
Da 4:10 there was a **t** at the center of the earth,
4:11 The **t** grew great and strong,
4:14 'Cut down the **t** and chop off its branches,
4:20 The **t** that you saw, which grew great and strong,
4:23 'Cut down the **t** and destroy it,
4:26 to leave the stump and roots of the **t**,
Hos 9:10 Like the first fruit on the fig **t**, in its first season,
14: 6 his beauty shall be like the olive **t**,
Joel 1:12 The vine withers, the fig **t** droops.
2:22 the **t** bears its fruit, the fig **t** and vine give their full
Hab 3:17 Though the fig **t** does not blossom,
Hag 2:19 Do the vine, the fig **t**, the pomegranate, and the olive **t** still yield nothing?
Zec 3:10 to come under your vine and fig **t**."
Mt 3:10 every **t** therefore that does B
7:17 In the same way, every good **t** bears good fruit, but the bad **t** bears bad fruit.
7:18 A good **t** cannot bear bad fruit, nor can a bad **t** bear good fruit.
7:19 Every **t** that does not bear good fruit is cut down B
12:33 make the **t** good, and its fruit good; or make the **t** bad, and its fruit bad; for the **t** is known by its fruit.
13:32 the greatest of shrubs and becomes a **t**,
21:19 And seeing a fig **t** by the side of the road,
21:19 And the fig **t** withered at once.
21:20 saying, "How did the fig **t** wither at once?"
21:21 only will you do what has been done to the fig **t**,
24:32 "From the fig **t** learn its lesson:
Mk 11:13 Seeing in the distance a fig **t** in leaf,
11:20 they saw the fig **t** withered away to its roots.
11:21 The fig **t** that you cursed has withered."
13:28 "From the fig **t** learn its lesson:
Lk 3: 9 every **t** therefore that does B
6:43 "No good **t** bears bad fruit, nor again does a bad **t** bear good fruit;
6:44 for each **t** is known by its own fruit.
13: 6 "A man had a fig **t** planted in his vineyard;
13: 7 I have come looking for fruit on this fig **t**,
13:19 it grew and became a **t**,
17: 6 you could say to this mulberry **t**,
19: 4 ahead and climbed a sycamore **t** to see him,
21:29 "Look at the fig **t** and all the trees;
Jn 1:48 under the fig **t** before Philip called you."
1:50 because I told you that I saw you under the fig **t**?
Ac 5:30 whom you had killed by hanging him on a **t**.
10:39 They put him to death by hanging him on a **t**;
13:29 they took him down from the **t** and laid him in
Ro 11:17 in their place to share the rich root of the olive **t**,
11:24 a wild olive **t** and grafted, contrary to nature, into a cultivated olive **t**,
11:24 be grafted back into their own olive **t**.
Gal 3:13 "Cursed is everyone who hangs on a **t**"—
Jas 3:12 Can a fig **t**, my brothers and sisters, yield olives,
Rev 2: 7 from the **t** of life that is in the paradise of God. A
6:13 as the fig **t** drops its winter fruit when shaken by
7: 1 on earth or sea or against any **t**.
9: 4 of the earth or any green growth or any **t**,
22: 2 of the river is the **t** of life with its twelve kinds A
22: 2 leaves of the **t** are for the healing of the nations.
22:14 the **t** of life and may enter the city by the gates. A
22:19 take away that person's share in the **t** of life A
AdE 8: 7 and have hanged him on a **t** because he acted
Wis 13:11 A skilled woodcutter may saw down a **t** easy
Sir 6: 3 and you will be left like a withered **t**.
14:18 Like abundant leaves on a spreading **t**
24:14 I grew tall like a palm **t** in En-gedi,
24:14 like a fair olive **t** in the field, and like a plane **t**
27: 6 Its fruit discloses the cultivation of a **t**;
38: 5 with a **t** in order that its power might be known?
50:10 like an olive **t** laden with fruit,
Bar 5: 8 and every fragrant **t** have shaded Israel
Sus 1:54 Under what **t** did you see them being intimate
1:54 He answered, "Under a mastic **t**."
1:58 Under what **t** did you catch them being intimate
2Es 1:23 a **t** into the water and made the stream sweet.
2:12 The **t** of life shall give them fragrant perfume, A
8:52 the **t** of life is planted, A
16:29 or four olives may be left on every **t**, B
4Mc 18:16 'There is a **t** of life for those who do his will.' A

TREES (147) [TREE]

Ge 1:11 and fruit **t** of every kind on earth that bear fruit
1:12 **t** of every kind bearing fruit with the seed in it.
3: 2 "We may eat of the fruit of the **t** in the garden;
3: 8 from the presence of the LORD God among the **t**
23:17 with the cave that was in it and all the **t** that were
Ex 10:15 the plants in the land and all the fruit of the **t** that
15:27 of water and seventy palm **t**;
Lev 19:23 into the land and plant all kinds of **t** for food,
23:40 the first day you shall take the fruit of majestic **t**,
23:40 branches of palm **t**, boughs of leafy trees,
23:40 boughs of leafy **t**, and willows of the brook;
26: 4 and the **t** of the field shall yield their fruit.
26:20 and the **t** of the land shall not yield their fruit.
Nu 13:20 and whether there are **t** in it or not.
24: 6 like cedar **t** beside the waters.
33: 9 twelve springs of water and seventy palm **t**,
Dt 8: 8 fig **t** and pomegranates, a land of olive **t** and
20:19 not destroy its **t** by wielding an ax against them.
20:19 Are **t** in the field human beings
20:20 You may destroy only the **t** that you know do
24:20 you beat your olive **t**, do not strip what is left;
28:40 You shall have olive **t** throughout all
28:42 All your **t** and the fruit of your ground
34: 3 that is, the valley of Jericho, the city of palm **t**—
Jos 10:26 and he hung them on five **t**.
10:26 And they hung on the **t** until evening.
10:27 down from the **t** and threw them into the cave
Jdg 9: 8 **t** once went out to anoint a king over themselves.
9: 9 and go to sway over the **t**?'
9:10 Then the **t** said to the fig tree,
9:11 and go to sway over the **t**?'
9:12 **t** said to the vine, 'You come and reign over us.'
9:13 and go to sway over the **t**?'
9:14 So all the **t** said to the bramble,
9:15 And the bramble said to the **t**,
2Sa 5:11 to David, along with cedar **t**, and carpenters
5:23 and come upon them opposite the balsam **t**.
5:24 the sound of marching in the tops of the balsam **t**,
1Ki 4:25 all of them under their vines and fig **t**.
4:33 He would speak of **t**, from the cedar that is in
6:29 palm **t**, and open flowers,
6:32 palm **t**, and open flowers;
6:32 spread gold on the cherubim and on the palm **t**.
6:35 He carved cherubim, palm **t**, and open flowers,
7:36 lions, and palm **t**, where each had space,
2Ki 6: 4 When they came to the Jordan, they cut down **t**.
1Ch 14:14 around and come on them opposite the balsam **t**.
14:15 the sound of marching in the tops of the balsam **t**,
16:33 the **t** of the forest sing for joy before the LORD,
27:28 and sycamore **t** in the Shephelah was Baal-hanan
2Ch 28:15 to their kindred at Jericho, the city of palm **t**.
Ezr 3: 7 and the Tyrians to bring cedar **t** from Lebanon to
Ne 8:15 and other leafy **t** to make booths, as it is written."
9:25 olive orchards, and fruit **t** in abundance;
Job 40:22 The lotus **t** cover it for shade;
Ps 1: 3 They are like **t** planted by streams of water,
96:12 Then shall all the **t** of the forest sing for joy
104:16 The **t** of the LORD are watered abundantly,
104:17 the stork has its home in the fir **t**.
105:33 struck their vines and fig **t**, and shattered the **t** of
148: 9 Mountains and all hills, fruit **t** and all cedars!
Ecc 2: 5 and planted in them all kinds of fruit **t**.
2: 6 from which to water the forest of growing **t**.
SS 2: 3 As an apple tree among the **t** of the wood,
4:14 calamus and cinnamon, with all **t** of frankincense,
Isa 7: 2 of Ahaz and the heart of his people shook as the **t**
10:19 The remnant of the **t** of his forest will be so few
10:33 the tallest **t** will be cut down,
10:34 and Lebanon with its majestic **t** will fall.
44:14 and lets it grow strong among the **t** of the forest.
55:12 and all the **t** of the field shall clap their hands.
Jer 5:17 they shall eat up your vines and your fig **t**;
6: 6 Cut down her **t**; cast up a siege ramp against
7:20 on the **t** of the field and the fruit of the ground;
46:22 against her with axes, like those who fell **t**.
Eze 15: 2 the vine branch that is among the **t** of the forest?
15: 6 the wood of the vine among the **t** of the forest,
17:24 the **t** of the field shall know that I am the LORD.
27: 5 They made all your planks of fir **t** from Senir;
31: 4 sending forth its streams to all the **t** of the field.
31: 5 So it towered high above all the **t** of the field;
31: 8 nor the fir **t** equal its boughs; the plane **t** were as
31: 9 the **t** of Eden that were in the garden of God.
31:14 that no **t** by the waters may grow to lofty height
31:14 that no **t** that drink water may reach up to them
31:15 and all the **t** of the field fainted because of it.
31:16 and all the **t** of Eden,
31:18 Which among the **t** of Eden was like you in glory
31:18 down with the **t** of Eden to the world below;
34:27 The **t** of the field shall yield their fruit,
39:10 to take wood out of the field or cut down any **t** in
40:16 and on the pilasters were palm **t**.
40:22 and its palm **t** were of the same size as those of
40:26 It had palm **t** on its pilasters, one on either side.
40:31 and palm **t** were on its pilasters,
40:34 and it had palm **t** on its pilasters, on either side;
40:37 and it had palm **t** on its pilasters, on either side;
41:18 It was formed of cherubim and palm **t**,
41:20 cherubim and palm **t** were carved on the wall.
41:25 the nave were carved cherubim and palm **t**, such
41:26 And there were recessed windows and palm **t** on
47: 7 of the river a great many **t** on the one side and on
47:12 there will grow all kinds of **t** for food.
Hos 2:12 I will lay waste her vines and her fig **t**,
Joel 1: 7 It has laid waste my vines, and splintered my fig **t**;
1:12 all the **t** of the field are dried up;
1:19 and flames have burned all the **t** of the field.
Am 4: 9 locust devoured your fig **t** and your olive **t**;
7:14 but I am a herdsman, and a dresser of sycamore **t**,
Mic 4: 4 under their own vines and under their own fig **t**,
Na 3:12 All your fortresses are like fig **t**
Zec 1: 8 He was standing among the myrtle **t** in the glen;
1:10 among the myrtle **t** answered,
1:11 the myrtle **t**, "We have patrolled the earth, and lo,
4: 3 And by it there are two olive **t**,
4:11 "What are these two olive **t** on the right and
4:12 "What are these two branches of the olive **t**,
11: 2 for the glorious **t** are ruined!
Mt 3:10 Even now the ax is lying at the root of the **t**;
21: 8 from the **t** and spread them on the road.
Mk 8:24 "I can see people, but they look like **t**, walking."
Lk 3: 9 Even now the ax is lying at the root of the **t**;
21:29 "Look at the fig tree and all the **t**;
Jn 12:13 So they took branches of palm **t** and went out
Jude 1:12 autumn **t** without fruit, twice dead, uprooted;
Rev 7: 3 "Do not damage the earth or the sea or the **t**,
8: 7 and a third of the **t** were burned up,
11: 4 the two olive **t** and the two lampstands that stand
Sir 50:12 on Lebanon surrounded by the trunks of palm **t**.
1Mc 10:30 the half of the fruit of the **t** that I should receive,
11:34 from the crops of the land and the fruit of the **t**.
14: 8 and the **t** of the plains their fruit.
14:12 All the people sat under their own vines and fig **t**,
2Es 1:20 of the heat I clothed you with the leaves of **t**.
2:18 for you twelve **t** loaded with various fruits,
4:13 "I went into a forest of **t** of the plain,
5:23 and from all its **t** you have chosen one vine,
15:13 and their **t** shall be ruined by blight and hail and
15:42 **t** of the forests, and grass of the meadows,
15:62 with fire all your forests and your fruitful **t**.
16:25 The **t** shall bear fruit, but who will gather it?
4Mc 2:14 The fruit **t** of the enemy are not cut down,
14:16 in precipitous chasms and in holes and tops of **t**,

TRELLIS (1)

Ps 74: 5 At the upper entrance they hacked the wooden **t**

TREMBLE (50) [TREMBLED, TREMBLES, TREMBLING]

Dt 2:25 they will **t** and be in anguish because of you."
1Ch 16:30 **t** before him, all the earth.
Ezr 10: 3 of those who **t** at the commandment of our God;
Job 9: 6 the earth out of its place, and its pillars **t**;
26: 5 shades below **t**, the waters and their inhabitants.
26:11 The pillars of heaven **t**, and are astounded
Ps 46: 3 though the mountains **t** with its tumult.
69:23 and make their loins **t** continually.
96: 9 **t** before him, all the earth.
99: 1 The LORD is king; let the peoples **t**!
114: 7 **T**, O earth, at the presence of the LORD,
Ecc 12: 3 of the house **t**, and the strong men are bent,
Isa 13:13 Therefore I will make the heavens **t**,
14:16 "Is this the man who made the earth **t**,
19: 1 the idols of Egypt will **t** at his presence,
19:16 and **t** with fear before the hand that the LORD
24:18 and the foundations of the earth **t**.
32:11 **T**, you women who are at ease, shudder,
41: 5 the ends of the earth **t**;
64: 2 so that the nations might **t** at your presence!
66: 5 you who **t** at his word:
Jer 5:22 says the LORD; Do you not **t** before me?
33: 9 they shall fear and **t** because of all the good
49:21 At the sound of their fall the earth shall **t**;
50:46 of the capture of Babylon the earth shall **t**,
Eze 7:27 and the hands of the people of the land shall **t**.
26:16 they shall **t** every moment,
26:18 Now the coastlands **t** on the day of your fall;
32:10 they shall **t** every moment for their lives,
Da 6:26 in all my royal dominion people should **t** and fear
Hos 10: 5 inhabitants of Samaria **t** for the calf of Beth-aven.
Joel 2: 1 Let all the inhabitants of the land **t**,
2:10 The earth quakes before them, the heavens **t**.
Am 8: 8 Shall not the land **t** on this account,
Na 2:10 Hearts faint and knees **t**, all loins quake,
Hab 2: 7 and those who make you **t** wake up?
3: 6 he looked and made the nations **t**.
3:16 I hear, and I **t** within; my lips quiver at the sound.
3:16 and my steps **t** beneath me.
Ac 7:32 Moses began to **t** and did not dare to look.
Heb 12:21 so terrifying was the sight that Moses said, "I **t**
Sir 16:18 the abyss and the earth, **t** at his visitation!
48:12 Never in his lifetime did he **t** before any ruler,
1Mc 4:32 let them **t** in their destruction.
1Es 4:36 All God's works quake and **t**,
Man 1: 4 at whom all things shudder, and **t**
2Es 3:18 and caused the depths to **t**, and troubled the times.
6:16 They will **t** and be shaken,
15:29 so that all who hear them will fear and **t**.
16:18 the beginning of calamities, when all shall **t**.

TREMBLED (22) [TREMBLE]

Ge 27:33 Then Isaac **t** violently, and said,
Ex 15:14 The peoples heard, they **t**;
19:16 that all the people who were in the camp **t**.
20:18 they were afraid and **t** and stood at a distance,
Jdg 5: 4 the earth **t**, and the heavens poured,
1Sa 4:13 for his heart **t** for the ark of God.
14:15 the garrison and even the raiders **t**;
28: 5 he was afraid, and his heart **t** greatly.
2Sa 22: 8 the foundations of the heavens **t** and quaked,
Ezr 9: 4 Then all who **t** at the words of the God of Israel,
Est 5: 9 observed that he neither rose nor **t** before him,
Ps 18: 7 foundations also of the mountains **t** and quaked,
77:16 they were afraid; the very deep **t**.
77:18 up the world; the earth **t** and shook.
Da 5:19 nations, and languages **t** and feared before him.

Hab 3: 7 the tent-curtains of the land of Midian **t.**
Jdt 16:10 The Persians **t** at her boldness,
16:11 my weak people cried out, and the enemy **t;**
Sir 48:19 Then their hearts were shaken and their hands **t,**
1Mc 1:28 Even the land **t** for its inhabitants,
6:41 **t,** for the army was very large and strong.
2Es 13: 3 everything under his gaze **t,**

TREMBLES (10) [TREMBLE]

Job 37: 1 "At this also my heart **t,** and leaps out of its place.
Ps 97: 4 up the world; the earth sees and **t.**
104:32 who looks on the earth and it **t,**
119:120 My flesh **t** for fear of you,
Pr 30:21 Under three things the earth **t;**
Isa 10:29 Ramah **t,** Gibeah of Saul has fled.
15: 4 of Moab quiver; his soul **t.**
66: 2 to the humble and contrite in spirit, who **t**
Jer 51:29 The land **t** and writhes, for the LORD's purposes
Na 2: 6 The river gates are opened, the palace **t.**

TREMBLING‡ (43) [TREMBLE]

A. FEAR AND ... TREMBLING (10)

Ge 42:28 At this they lost heart and turned **t** to one another,
Ex 15:15 **t** seized the leaders of Moab;
Dt 28:65 There the LORD will give you a **t** heart,
Jdg 7: 3 'Whoever is fearful and **t,** let him return home.' "
1Sa 13: 7 and all the people followed him **t.**
16: 4 The elders of the city came to meet him **t,**
21: 1 Ahimelech came **t** to meet David, and said to him,
2Sa 22:46 and came **t** out of their strongholds.
1Ki 1:49 of Adonijah got up **t** and went their own ways.
Ezr 10: 9 **t** because of this matter and because of
Job 4:14 and **t,** which made all my bones shake.
Ps 2:11 Serve the LORD with fear, with **t**
18:45 and came **t** out of their strongholds.
48: 6 **t** took hold of them there,
55: 5 Fear and **t** come upon me, A
Isa 21: 4 for has been turned for me into **t.**
33:14 in Zion are afraid; **t** has seized the godless:
Eze 12:18 and drink your water with **t** and with fearfulness;
26:16 They shall clothe themselves with **t,**
Da 10: 7 though a great **t** fell upon them,
10:11 he was speaking this word to me, I stood up **t.**
Hos 11:10 he roars, his children shall come **t** from the west.
11:11 They shall come **t** like birds from Egypt,
13: 1 When Ephraim spoke, there was **t;**
Mic 7:17 they shall come **t** out of their fortresses;
Mk 5:33 came in fear and **t,** fell down before him, A
Lk 8:47 that she could not remain hidden, she came **t;**
Ac 16:29 he fell down **t** before Paul and Silas.
1Co 2: 3 to you in weakness and in fear and in much **t.** A
2Co 7:15 and how you welcomed him with fear and **t.** A
Eph 6: 5 obey your earthly masters with fear and **t,** A
Php 2:12 work out your own salvation with fear and **t;** A
Jdt 15: 2 Overcome with fear and **t,** A
Wis 17:10 they perished in **t,** refusing to look even at
Bar 3:33 he called it, and it obeyed him, **t;**
1Mc 13: 2 and he saw that the people were **t** with fear.
2Mc 3:17 For terror and bodily **t** had come over the man,
15:23 send a good angel to spread terror and **t** before us.
2Es 8:21 before whom the hosts of angels stand **t**
15:33 and fear and **t** shall come upon their army, A
15:37 And there shall be fear and great **t** on the earth; A
15:37 and they shall be seized with **t.**
4Mc 4:10 instilling in them great fear and **t.** A

TREMENDOUS (1)

2Mc 10:24 a **t** force of mercenaries and collected the cavalry

TRENCH (3)

1Ki 18:32 Then he made a **t** around the altar,
18:35 and filled the **t** also with water.
18:38 and even licked up the water that was in the **t.**

TRESPASS (10) [TRESPASSED, TRESPASSES]

Lev 5:15 of you commit a **t** and sins unintentionally in any
6: 2 a **t** against the LORD by deceiving a neighbor in
1Sa 25:28 Please forgive the **t** of your servant;
Ro 5:15 But the free gift is not like the **t.**
5:15 For if the many died through the one man's **t,**
5:16 judgment following one **t** brought condemnation,
5:17 If, because of the one man's **t,**
5:18 just as one man's **t** led to condemnation for all,
5:20 law came in, with the result that the **t** multiplied;
Wis 12: 2 Therefore you correct little by little those who **t,**

TRESPASSED (1) [TRESPASS]

Ezr 10:10 "You have **t** and married foreign women,

TRESPASSES‡ (11) [TRESPASS]

Mt 6:14 For if you forgive others their **t,**
6:15 neither will your Father forgive your **t.**
Mk 11:25 in heaven may also forgive you your **t.**"
Ro 4:25 for our **t** and was raised for our justification.
5:16 the free gift following many **t** brings justification.
2Co 5:19 not counting their **t** against them,
Eph 1: 7 the forgiveness of our **t,** according to the riches
2: 1 You were dead through the **t** and sins
2: 5 even when we were dead through our **t,**
Col 2:13 when you were dead in **t** and the uncircumcision
2:13 when he forgave us all our **t,**

TRESSES (1)

SS 7: 5 a king is held captive in the **t.**

TRIAL (20) [TRIALS]

Nu 35:12 that the slayer may not die until there is a **t** before
Jos 20: 6 that city until there is a **t** before the congregation,
20: 9 until there was a **t** before the congregation.
Jdg 6:39 please, make **t** with the fleece just once more;
Job 9:32 that we should come to **t** together.
Ps 37:33 be condemned when they are brought to **t.**
Isa 43:26 Accuse me, let us go to **t;**
Mt 6:13 And do not bring us to the time of **t,**
26:41 that you may not come into the time of **t;**
Mk 13:11 When they bring you to **t** and hand you over,
14:38 that you may not come into the time of **t;**
Lk 11: 4 And do not bring us to the time of **t.**"
22:40 "Pray that you may not come into the time of **t.**"
22:46 and pray that you may not come into the time of **t.**"
Ac 23: 6 I am on **t** concerning the hope of the resurrection
24:21 about the resurrection of the dead that I am on **t**
26: 6 And now I stand here on **t** on account of my hope
2Pe 2: 9 the Lord knows how to rescue the godly from **t,**
Rev 3:10 I will keep you from the hour of **t** that is coming
Wis 2:19 and make **t** of his forbearance.

TRIALS‡ (11) [TRIAL]

Dt 4:34 by **t,** by signs and wonders, by war,
7:19 the great **t** that your eyes saw,
29: 3 the great **t** that your eyes saw,
Lk 22:28 "You are those who have stood by me in my **t;**
Ac 20:19 enduring the **t** that came to me through the plots
Heb 12: 7 Endure **t** for the sake of discipline.
Jas 1: 2 whenever you face **t** of any kind,
1Pe 1: 6 for a little while you have had to suffer various **t,**
Sir 33: 1 in **t** such a one will be rescued again and again.
1Mc 12:13 many **t** and many wars have encircled us;
2Mc 7:37 to God to show mercy soon to our nation and by **t**

TRIANGLES See Index to Footnotes

TRIBAL (6) [TRIBE]

Jos 11:23 to Israel according to their **t** allotments.
22:14 one from each of the **t** families of Israel,
2Sa 7: 7 did I ever speak a word with any of the **t** leaders
Eze 45: 7 corresponding in length to one of the **t** portions,
48: 8 and in length equal to one of the **t** portions,
48:21 to the west border, parallel to the **t** portions,

TRIBE‡ (246) [HALF-TRIBE, TRIBAL, TRIBES]

A. TRIBE OF JUDAH (25)
B. TRIBE OF BENJAMIN (23)
C. TRIBE OF NAPHTALI (14)
D. TRIBE OF ASHER (11)
E. TRIBE OF LEVI (11)
F. TRIBE OF SIMEON (11)
G. TRIBE OF ZEBULUN (11)
H. TRIBE OF DAN (10)
I. TRIBE OF ISSACHAR (10)
J. TRIBE OF GAD (9)
K. TRIBE OF MANASSEH (9)
L. TRIBE OF REUBEN (7)
M. TRIBE OF EPHRAIM (6)
N. TRIBE OF JOSEPH (6)

Ex 31: 2 Bezalel son of Uri son of Hur, of the **t** of Judah: A
31: 6 Oholiab son of Ahisamach, of the **t** of Dan; H
35:30 Bezalel son of Uri son of Hur, of the **t** of Judah; A
35:34 and Oholiab son of Ahisamach, of the **t** of Dan. H
38:22 Bezalel son of Uri son of Hur, of the **t** of Judah, A
38:23 of the **t** of Dan, engraver, designer, H
Lev 24:11 daughter of Dibri, of the **t** of Dan— H
Nu 1: 4 A man from each **t** shall be with you,
1:21 those enrolled of the **t** of Reuben L
1:23 those enrolled of the **t** of Simeon F
1:25 those enrolled of the **t** of Gad J
1:27 those enrolled of the **t** of Judah A
1:29 those enrolled of the **t** of Issachar I
1:31 those enrolled of the **t** of Zebulun G
1:33 those enrolled of the **t** of Ephraim M
1:35 those enrolled of the **t** of Manasseh K
1:37 those enrolled of the **t** of Benjamin B
1:39 those enrolled of the **t** of Dan H
1:41 those enrolled of the **t** of Asher D
1:43 those enrolled of the **t** of Naphtali C
1:47 were not numbered by their ancestral **t** along
1:49 Only the **t** of Levi you shall not enroll, E
2: 5 to camp next to him shall be the **t** of Issachar. I
2: 7 Then the **t** of Zebulun: The leader of the G
2:12 to camp next to him shall be the **t** of Simeon. F
2:14 Then the **t** of Gad: The leader of the J
2:20 Next to him shall be the **t** of Manasseh. K
2:22 Then the **t** of Benjamin: The leader of the B
2:27 to camp next to him shall be the **t** of Asher. D
2:29 Then the **t** of Naphtali: The leader of the C
3: 6 Bring the **t** of Levi near, E
4:18 the **t** of the clans of the Kohathites be destroyed
7:12 son of Amminadab, of the **t** of Judah; A
10:15 Over the company of the **t** of Issachar was I
10:16 and over the company of the **t** of Zebulun was G
10:19 Over the company of the **t** of Simeon was F
10:20 over the company of the **t** of Gad was Eliasaph J
10:23 Over the company the **t** of Manasseh was K
Nu 10:24 and over the company of the **t** of Benjamin was B
10:26 Over the company of the **t** of Asher was Pagiel D
10:27 over the company of the **t** of Naphtali was C
13: 4 From the **t** of Reuben, Shammua son of Zaccur; L
13: 5 from the **t** of Simeon, Shaphat son of Hori; F
13: 6 from the **t** of Judah, Caleb son of Jephunneh; A
13: 7 from the **t** of Issachar, Igal son of Joseph; I
13: 8 from the **t** of Ephraim, Hoshea son of Nun; M
13: 9 from the **t** of Benjamin, Palti son of Raphu; B
13:10 from the **t** of Zebulun, Gaddiel son of Sodi; G
13:11 from the **t** of Joseph (that is, from the tribe N
13:11 from the **t** of Manasseh), Gaddi son of Susi; K
13:12 from the **t** of Dan, Ammiel son of Gemalli; H
13:13 from the **t** of Asher, Sethur son of Michael; D
13:14 from the **t** of Naphtali, Nahbi son of Vophsi; C
13:15 from the **t** of Gad, Geuel son of Machi. J
18: 2 with you also your brothers of the **t** of Levi, E
18: 2 your ancestral **t,** in order that they may be joined
24: 2 Balaam looked up and saw Israel camping **t** by **t.**
26:54 To a large **t** you shall give a large inheritance, and
to a small **t** you shall give a small inheritance;
every **t** shall be given its inheritance according
31: 5 a thousand from each **t** were conscripted,
31: 6 a thousand from each **t,** along with Phinehas son
34:14 the **t** of the Reubenites by their ancestral houses
and the **t** of the Gadites
34:18 You shall take one leader of every **t** to apportion
34:19 Of the **t** of Judah, Caleb son of Jephunneh. A
34:20 Of the **t** of the Simeonites,
34:21 Of the **t** of Benjamin, Elidad son of Chislon. B
34:22 Of the **t** of the Danites a leader,
34:23 of the **t** of the Manassites a leader,
34:24 and of the **t** of the Ephraimites a leader,
34:25 Of the **t** of the Zebulunites a leader,
34:26 Of the **t** of the Issacharites a leader,
34:27 And of the **t** of the Asherites a leader,
34:28 Of the **t** of the Naphtalites a leader,
36: 3 But if they are married into another Israelite **t,**
36: 3 to the inheritance of the **t** into which they marry;
36: 4 of the **t** into which they have married;
36: 4 be taken from the inheritance of our ancestral **t.**"
36: 5 the **t** of Joseph are right in what they are saying. N
36: 6 into a clan of their father's **t** that they are married,
36: 7 of the Israelites shall be transferred from one **t**
36: 8 in any **t** of the Israelites shall marry one from
36: 8 from the clan of her father's **t,**
36: 9 No inheritance shall be transferred from one **t**
36:12 and their inheritance remained in the **t**
Dt 1:23 and I selected twelve of you, one from each **t.**
10: 8 the LORD set apart the **t** of Levi to carry the ark E
18: 1 The levitical priests, the whole **t** of Levi, E
29:18 a family or **t,** whose heart is already turning away
Jos 3:12 from the tribes of Israel, one from each **t.**
4: 2 from the people, one from each **t,**
4: 4 whom he had appointed, one from each **t.**
7: 1 the **t** of Judah, took some of the devoted things; A
7:14 morning therefore you shall come forward **t** by **t.**
7:14 **t** that the LORD takes shall come near by clans,
7:16 and brought Israel near **t** by **t,**
7:16 and the **t** of Judah was taken. A
7:18 of the **t** of Judah, was taken. A
13:14 the **t** of Levi alone Moses gave no inheritance; E
13:15 to the **t** of the Reubenites according to their clans.
13:24 an inheritance also to the **t** of the Gadites,
13:33 But to the **t** of Levi Moses gave no inheritance; E
15: 1 The lot for the **t** of the people of Judah according
15:20 the inheritance of the **t** of the people of Judah
15:21 the **t** of the people of Judah in the extreme South,
16: 8 Such is the inheritance of the **t** of the Ephraimites
17: 1 Then allotment was made to the **t** of Manasseh, K
17: 2 were made to the rest of the **t** of Manasseh, K
17:14 The **t** of Joseph spoke to Joshua, saying, N
17:16 The **t** of Joseph said, "The hill country is N
18: 4 Provide three men from each **t,**
18:11 the **t** of Benjamin according to its families came B
18:11 allotted to it fell between the **t** of Judah and A
18:11 between the tribe of Judah and the **t** of Joseph. N
18:14 a town belonging to the **t** of Judah. A
18:20 This is the inheritance of the **t** of Benjamin, B
18:21 Now the towns of the **t** of Benjamin according B
18:28 the inheritance of the **t** of Benjamin according B
19: 1 for the **t** of Simeon, according to its families; F
19: 1 lay within the inheritance of the **t** of Judah. A
19: 8 the inheritance of the **t** of Simeon according F
19: 9 The inheritance of the **t** of Simeon formed part F
19: 9 portion of the **t** of Judah was too large for them, A
19: 9 the **t** of Simeon obtained an inheritance F
19:10 The third lot came up for the **t** of Zebulun, G
19:16 This is the inheritance of the **t** of Zebulun, G
19:17 for the **t** of Issachar, according to its families. I
19:23 This is the inheritance of the **t** of Issachar, I
19:24 The fifth lot came out for the **t** of Asher D
19:31 This is the inheritance of the **t** of Asher D
19:32 The sixth lot came out for the **t** of Naphtali, C
19:32 for the **t** of Naphtali, according to its families. C
19:39 of the **t** of Naphtali according to its families— C
19:40 The seventh lot came out for the **t** of Dan, H
19:48 This is the inheritance of the **t** of Dan, H
20: 8 from the **t** of Reuben, and Ramoth in Gilead, L
20: 8 and Ramoth in Gilead, from the **t** of Gad, J
20: 8 and Golan in Bashan, from the **t** of Manasseh. K
21: 5 ten towns from the families of the **t** of Ephraim, M
21: 5 the **t** of Dan, and the half-tribe of Manasseh. H
21: 6 towns from the families of the **t** of Issachar, I
21: 6 from the **t** of Asher, from the tribe of Naphtali, D
21: 6 from the tribe of Asher, from the **t** of Naphtali, C
21: 7 received twelve towns from the **t** of Reuben, L

Nu 21: 7 the t of Gad, and the tribe of Zebulun. J
21: 7 the tribe of Gad, and the t of Zebulun. G
21: 9 the t of Judah and the tribe of Simeon they gave A
21: 9 the tribe of Judah and the t of Simeon they gave F
21:17 Out of the t of Benjamin: B
21:20 allotted to them were out of the t of Ephraim. M
21:23 Out of the t of Dan: H
21:28 Out of the t of Issachar: I
21:30 Out of the t of Asher: D
21:32 Out of the t of Naphtali: C
21:34 were given out of the t of Zebulun: G
21:36 Out of the t of Reuben: L
21:38 Out of the t of Gad: J
22: 7 t of Manasseh Moses had given a possession K
Jdg 4: 6 bringing ten thousand from the t of Naphtali C
4: 6 from the tribe of Naphtali and the t of Zebulun. G
13: 2 of the t of the Danites, whose name was Manoah.
18: 1 in those days the t of the Danites was seeking
18:19 or to be priest to a t and clan in Israel?"
18:30 to the t of the Danites until the time the land went
20:12 of Israel sent men through all the t of Benjamin, B
21: 3 to pass that today there should be one t lacking
21: 6 and said, "One t is cut off from Israel this day.
21:17 that a t may not be blotted out from Israel.
1Sa 9:21 of all the families of the t of Benjamin. B
10:20 and the t of Benjamin was taken by lot. B
10:21 brought the t of Benjamin near by its families, B
2Sa 15: 2 "Your servant is of such and such a t in Israel,"
1Ki 7:14 He was the son of a widow of the t of Naphtali, C
11:13 I will give one t to your son,
11:32 One t will remain his, for the sake
11:36 Yet to his son I will give one t,
12:20 except the t of Judah alone. A
12:21 all the house of Judah and the t of Benjamin, B
2Ki 17:18 none was left but the t of Judah alone. A
1Ch 6:60 From the t of Benjamin, Geba B
6:61 by lot out of the family of the t,
6:66 towns of their territory out of the t of Ephraim. M
6:72 and out of the t of Issachar: I
6:74 out of the t of Asher: D
6:76 and out of the t of Naphtali: C
6:77 the rest of the Merarites out of the t of Zebulun: G
6:78 out of the t of Reuben: L
6:80 and out of the t of Gad: J
23:14 sons were to be reckoned among the t of Levi. E
Ps 74: 2 which you redeemed to be the t of your heritage.
78:67 he did not choose the t of Ephraim; M
78:68 but he chose the t of Judah, A
Jer 10:16 and Israel is the t of his inheritance;
51:19 and Israel is the t of his inheritance;
Eze 47:23 In whatever t aliens reside,
Da 1: 6 Mishael, and Azariah, from the t of Judah. A
Mic 6: 9 Hear, O t and assembly of the city!
Lk 2:36 Anna the daughter of Phanuel, of the t of Asher. D
Ac 13:21 a man of the t of Benjamin, B
Ro 11: 1 a member of the t of Benjamin. B
Php 3: 5 the t of Benjamin, a Hebrew born of Hebrews; B
Heb 7:13 to another t, from which no one has ever served
7:14 and in connection with that t Moses said nothing
Rev 5: 5 the Lion of the t of Judah, the Root of David, A
5: 9 from every t and language and people and nation;
7: 4 sealed out of every t of the people of Israel:
7: 5 From the t of Judah twelve thousand sealed, A
7: 5 from the t of Reuben twelve thousand, L
7: 5 from the t of Gad twelve thousand, J
7: 6 from the t of Asher twelve thousand, D
7: 6 from the t of Naphtali twelve thousand, C
7: 6 from the t of Manasseh twelve thousand, K
7: 7 from the t of Simeon twelve thousand, F
7: 7 from the t of Levi twelve thousand, E
7: 7 from the t of Issachar twelve thousand, I
7: 8 from the t of Zebulun twelve thousand, G
7: 8 from the t of Joseph twelve thousand, N
7: 8 from the t of Benjamin twelve thousand sealed. B
13: 7 over every t and people and language and nation,
14: 6 to every nation and t and language and people.
Tob 1: 1 of the descendants of Asiel, of the t of Naphtali, C
1: 4 the whole t of my ancestor Naphtali deserted
1:16 of charity to my kindred, those of my t.
4:12 who is not of your father's t;
5: 9 about his family and to what t he belongs,
5:11 of what family are you and from what t?
5:12 He replied, "Why do you need to know my t?"
Jdt 6:15 the t of Simeon, and Chabris son of Gothoniel, F
8: 2 who belonged to her t and family,
8:18 has there been any t or family or people or town
9:14 Let your whole nation and every t know
AdE 2: 5 of Shimei son of Kish, of the t of Benjamin; B
11: 2 of the t of Benjamin, had a dream. B
14: 5 Ever since I was born I have heard in the t
Sir 45: 6 Moses who was his brother, of the t of Levi. E
45:25 with David son of Jesse of the t of Judah, A
2Mc 3: 4 But a man named Simon, of the t of Benjamin, B
1Es 5: 5 of the lineage of Phares, of the t of Judah, A
5:66 enemies of the t of Judah and Benjamin heard it, A
9: 5 of the t of Judah and Benjamin assembled A
2Es 1: 3 the t of Levi, who was a captive in the country E
4Mc 2:19 for their irrational slaughter of the entire t of

TRIBES‡ (135) [TRIBE]

A. TRIBES OF ISRAEL (53)
B. ALL THE TRIBES (27)
C. TWELVE TRIBES (11)
D. TRIBES OF THE ISRAELITES (8)

Ge 25:16 twelve princes according to their t.
49:16 judge his people as one of the t of Israel. A
49:28 All these are the twelve t of Israel, AC
Ex 24: 4 corresponding to the twelve t of Israel. AC
28:21 each engraved with its name, for the twelve t. C
39:14 each engraved with its name, for the twelve t. C
Nu 1:16 the leaders of their ancestral t,
7: 2 of their ancestral houses, the leaders of the t,
10: 4 then the leaders, the heads of the t of Israel, A
13: 2 from each of their ancestral t you shall send
26:55 to the names of their ancestral t they shall inherit.
30: 1 Moses said to the heads of the t of the Israelites: D
31: 4 send a thousand from each of the t of Israel A
32:28 the heads of the ancestral houses of the Israelite t.
33:54 according to your ancestral t you shall inherit.
34:13 the LORD has commanded to give to the nine t
34:15 two t and the half-tribe have taken their inheritance
35: 8 from the larger t you shall take many, and from
the smaller t you shall take few;
36: 7 the inheritance of their ancestral t.
36: 9 for each of the t of the Israelites shall retain D
Dt 1:13 for each of your t individuals who are wise,
1:15 So I took the leaders of your t,
1:15 and officials, throughout your t.
5:23 all the heads of your t and your elders;
12: 5 the LORD your God will choose out of all your t
12:14 that the LORD will choose in one of your t—
16:18 and officials throughout your t,
18: 5 of all your t, to stand and minister in the name of
29:10 the leaders of your t, your elders,
29:21 will single them out from all the t of Israel AB
31:28 to me all the elders of your t and your officials,
33: 5 of the people assembled—the united t of Israel. A
Jos 3:12 So now select twelve men from the t of Israel, A
4: 5 one for each of the t of the Israelites, D
4: 8 to the number of the t of the Israelites, D
12: 7 (and Joshua gave their land to the t of Israel A
13: 7 for an inheritance to the nine t and the half-tribe
14: 1 the families of the t of the Israelites distributed D
14: 2 for the nine and one-half t.
14: 3 an inheritance to the two and one-half t beyond
14: 4 For the people of Joseph were two t,
18: 2 the Israelites seven t whose inheritance had not
19:51 the families of the t of the Israelites distributed D
21: 1 heads of the families of the t of the Israelites; D
21: 4 the priest received by lot thirteen towns from the t
21:16 nine towns out of these two t.
23: 4 to you as an inheritance for your t those nations
24: 1 Joshua gathered all the t of Israel to Shechem, AB
Jdg 18: 1 among the t of Israel had been allotted to them. A
20: 2 chiefs of all the people, of all the t of Israel, AB
20:10 of a hundred throughout all the t of Israel, AB
20:12 The t of Israel sent men through all the tribe A
21: 5 "Which of all the t of Israel did not come up AB
21: 8 the t of Israel who did not come up to the LORD A
21:15 the LORD had made a breach in the t of Israel. A
21:24 the Israelites departed from there at that time by t
1Sa 2:28 of all the t of Israel to be my priest, to go up AB
9:21 from the least of the t of Israel, A
10:19 before the LORD by your t and by your clans."
10:20 Then Samuel brought all the t of Israel near, AB
15:17 are you not the head of the t of Israel? A
2Sa 5: 1 all the t of Israel came to David at Hebron, AB
15:10 throughout all the t of Israel, saying, AB
19: 9 were disputing throughout all the t of Israel, AB
20:14 all the t of Israel to Abel of Beth-maacah; AB
24: 2 "Go through all the t of Israel, AB
1Ki 8: 1 the elders of Israel and all the heads of the t,
8:16 not chosen a city from any of the t of Israel A
11:31 the hand of Solomon, and will give you ten t.
11:32 city that I have chosen out of all the t of Israel. AB
11:35 and give it to you—that is, the ten t.
14:21 the LORD had chosen out of all the t of Israel, AB
18:31 the number of the t of the sons of Jacob,
2Ki 21: 7 which I have chosen out of all the t of Israel, AB
1Ch 6:62 the t of Issachar, Asher, Naphtali, and Manasseh
6:63 allotted twelve towns out of the t of Reuben, Gad,
6:65 They also gave them by lot out of the t of Judah,
27:16 Over the t of Israel, for the Reubenites, A
27:22 These were the leaders of the t of Israel. A
28: 1 the officials of the t, the officers of the divisions
29: 6 as did also the leaders of the t,
2Ch 5: 2 the elders of Israel and all the heads of the t,
6: 5 not chosen a city from any of the t of Israel A
11:16 from all the t of Israel to Jerusalem to sacrifice AB
12:13 the LORD had chosen out of all the t of Israel AB
33: 7 which I have chosen out of all the t of Israel, AB
Ezr 6:17 according to the number of the t of Israel. A
Ps 78:55 for a possession and settled the t of Israel A
105:37 there was no one among their t who stumbled.
122: 4 To it the t go up, the t of the LORD,
Isa 19:13 the cornerstones of its t have led Egypt astray.
49: 6 that you should be my servant to raise up the t
63:17 for the sake of the t that are your heritage.
Jer 1:15 calling all the t of the kingdoms of the north, B
25: 9 to send for all the t of the north, says the LORD, B
Eze 20:32 like the t of the countries,
37:19 Ephraim) and the t of Israel associated with it; A
45: 8 of Israel have the land according to their t.
47:13 for inheritance among the twelve t of Israel. AC
47:21 among you according to the t of Israel. A
47:22 be allotted an inheritance among the t of Israel. A
48: 1 These are the names of the t:
48:19 workers of the city, from all the t of Israel, AB
48:23 As for the rest of the t:
48:29 allot as an inheritance among the t of Israel, A
48:31 of the city being named after the t of Israel. A
Hos 5: 9 among the t of Israel I declare what is sure. A
Zec 9: 1 as do all the t of Israel; AB
Mt 19:28 twelve thrones, judging the twelve t of Israel. AC
24:30 and then all the t of the earth will mourn, B
Lk 22:30 on thrones judging the twelve t of Israel. AC
Ac 26: 7 a promise that our twelve t hope to attain, C
Jas 1: 1 To the twelve t in the Dispersion: Greetings. C
Rev 1: 7 on his account all the t of the earth will wail. B
7: 9 from all t and peoples and languages,
11: 9 and a half days members of the peoples and t
21:12 the names of the twelve t of the Israelites; CD
Tob 1: 4 been chosen from among all the t of Israel, AB
1: 4 where all the t of Israel should offer sacrifice AB
Jdt 3: 8 that all their dialects and t should call upon him
Sir 36:13 Gather all the t of Jacob, B
44:23 and distributed them among twelve t. C
45:11 in engraved letters each of the t of Israel; A
48:10 and to restore the t of Jacob.
1Es 2: 8 Then arose the heads of families of the t of Judah
5: 1 up, according to their t, with their wives and sons
5: 4 according to their ancestral houses in the t,
7: 8 number of the twelve leaders of the t of Israel; A
2Es 3: 7 From him there sprang nations and t,
3:32 Or what t have so believed the covenants
3:32 so believed the covenants as these t of Jacob?
4:23 over to godless t, and the law
13:40 these are the nine t that were taken away

TRIBULATION (9)

1Sa 26:24 and may he rescue me from all t."
La 3: 5 and enveloped me with bitterness and t;
AdE 11: 8 of darkness and gloom, of t and distress, affliction
3Mc 2:10 and t should overtake us,
2Es 2:27 for when the day of t and anguish comes,
15:19 of hunger for bread and because of great t.
16:19 t and anguish are sent as scourges for
16:67 and deliver you from all t.
16:74 the days of t are at hand,

TRIBUNAL (6) [TRIBUNE]

Ac 18:12 on Paul and brought him before the t.
18:16 And he dismissed them from the t.
18:17 and beat him in front of the t.
25: 6 on the t and ordered Paul to be brought.
25:10 Paul said, "I am appealing to the emperor's t;
25:17 on the next day took my seat on the t and ordered

TRIBUNE (17) [TRIBUNAL, TRIBUNES]

Ac 21:31 to the t of the cohort that all Jerusalem was in
21:32 When they saw the t and the soldiers,
21:33 Then the t came, arrested him,
21:37 he said to the t, "May I say something to you?"
21:37 The t replied, "Do you know Greek?
22:24 the t directed that he was to be brought into
22:26 he went to the t and said to him,
22:27 The t came and asked Paul, "Tell me,
22:28 The t answered, "It cost me a large sum of money
22:29 and the t also was afraid,
23:10 When the dissension became violent, the t,
23:15 you and the council must notify the t to bring him
23:17 "Take this young man to the t,
23:18 So he took him, brought him to the t, and said,
23:19 The t took him by the hand,
23:22 So the t dismissed the young man, ordering him,
24:22 "When Lysias the t comes down,

TRIBUNES (1) [TRIBUNE]

Ac 25:23 the military t and the prominent men of the city.

TRIBUTARIES, TRIBUTARY (KJV) See also FORCED LABOR, VASSAL

TRIBUTARY (1)

1Mc 1: 4 nations, and princes, and they became t to him.

TRIBUTE (51)

Ge 49:10 until t comes to him; and the obedience of the
Nu 31:28 set aside as t for the LORD,
31:37 and the LORD's t of sheep
31:38 of which the LORD's t was seventy-two.
31:39 of which the LORD's t was sixty-one.
31:40 of which the LORD's t was thirty-two persons.
31:41 Moses gave the t, the offering for the LORD,
Jdg 3:15 Israelites sent t by him to King Eglon of Moab.
3:17 Then he presented the t to King Eglon of Moab.
3:18 When Ehud had finished presenting the t,
3:18 he sent the people who carried the t on their way.
2Sa 8: 2 Moabites became servants to David and brought t.
8: 6 Arameans became servants to David and brought t.
1Ki 4:21 they brought t and served Solomon all the days
2Ki 17: 3 Hoshea became his vassal, and paid him t.
17: 4 and offered no t to the king of Assyria,
23:33 and imposed t on the land of one hundred talents
1Ch 18: 2 Moabites became subject to David and brought t.
18: 6 Arameans became subject to David, and brought t.
2Ch 17: 5 All Judah brought t to Jehoshaphat,
17:11 brought Jehoshaphat presents, and silver for t;
26: 8 The Ammonites paid t to Uzziah,
28:21 and gave t to the king of Assyria;
36: 3 a t of one hundred talents of silver and one talent
Ezr 4:13 they will not pay t, custom, or toll,
4:20 to whom t, custom, and toll were paid.
6: 8 the t of the province Beyond the River.
7:24 that it shall not be lawful to impose t,

Est 10: 1 King Ahasuerus laid **t** on the land and on
Ps 68:30 Trample under foot those who lust after **t;**
72:10 of Tarshish and of the isles render him **t,**
Isa 33:18 Where is the one who weighed the **t?**
Hos 10: 6 The thing itself shall be carried to Assyria as **t** to
Mt 17:25 From whom do kings of the earth take toll or **t?**
1Mc 1:29 to the cities of Judah a chief collector of **t,**
8: 2 they had defeated them and forced them to pay **t,**
8: 4 the rest paid them **t** every year.
8: 7 after him should pay a heavy **t** and give hostages
10:29 from payment of **t** and salt tax and crown levies,
11:28 and the three districts of Samaria from **t,**
13:37 to our officials to grant you release from **t.**
15:30 the cities that you have seized and the **t** money of
15:31 and five hundred talents more for the **t** money of
2Mc 8:10 to make up for the king the **t** due to the Romans,
8:36 to secure **t** for the Romans by the capture of
11: 3 and to levy **t** on the temple as he did on
1Es 2:19 not only refuse to pay **t** but will even resist kings.
2:27 and cruel kings ruled in Jerusalem and exacted **t**
4:50 that they would occupy should be theirs without **t;**
6:29 and that out of the **t** of Coelesyria and Phoenicia
8:22 You are also informed that no **t** or any other tax is

TRICKED (3) [TRICKERY]
Ge 3:13 The woman said, "The serpent **t** me, and I ate."
Mt 2:16 Herod saw that he had been **t** by the wise men,
Jdt 14:18 "The slaves have **t** us! One Hebrew woman has

TRICKERY (5) [TRICKED, TRICKS]
Nu 25:18 the **t** with which they deceived you in the affair
Eph 4:14 about by every wind of doctrine, by people's **t,**
1Th 2: 3 not spring from deceit or impure motives or **t,**
AdE 16: 6 by the false **t** of their evil natures beguile
1Mc 11: 1 to get possession of Alexander's kingdom by **t**

TRICKLETH (KJV) See FLOW

TRICKS (2) [TRICKERY]
Sir 9: 4 or you will be caught by her **t.**
11:29 for many are the **t** of the crafty.

TRIED (59) [TRY]
Ex 4:24 the LORD met him and **t** to kill him.
8:18 magicians **t** to produce gnats by their secret arts,
1Sa 14: 4 by which Jonathan **t** to go over to
17:39 and he **t** in vain to walk,
2Sa 21: 2 Saul had **t** to wipe them out in his zeal
Job 34:36 Would that Job were **t** to the limit,
36:21 because of that you have been **t** by affliction.
Ps 66:10 you have **t** us as silver is **t.**
71:24 for those who **t** to do me harm have been put
109: 7 When he is **t,** let him be found guilty;
119:140 Your promise is well **t,** and your servant loves it.
Jer 51: 9 We **t** to heal Babylon, but she could not
Da 6: 4 So the presidents and the satraps **t** to find grounds
8:15 I, Daniel, had seen the vision, I **t** to understand it.
Hos 12: 3 In the womb he **t** to supplant his brother,
Mk 9:38 and we **t** to stop him,
Lk 9: 9 And he **t** to see him.
9:49 and we **t** to stop him,
Jn 7:30 Then they **t** to arrest him,
10:39 Then they **t** to arrest him again,
19:12 From then on Pilate **t** to release him,
Ac 7:26 as they were quarreling and **t** to reconcile them,
13: 8 opposed them and **t** to turn the proconsul away
16:10 we immediately **t** to cross over to Macedonia,
19:13 Then some itinerant Jewish exorcists **t** to use
19:33 and **t** to make a defense before the people.
24: 6 He even **t** to profane the temple,
25: 9 "Do you wish to go up to Jerusalem and be **t** there
25:10 this is where I should be **t.**
25:20 to go to Jerusalem and be **t** there on these charges.
26:11 By punishing them often in all the synagogues I **t**
26:21 the Jews seized me in the temple and **t** to kill me.
27:30 But when the sailors **t** to escape from the ship
Gal 1:23 now proclaiming the faith he once **t** to destroy."
Tob 6: 3 the water and **t** to swallow the young man's foot,
14:10 because he **t** to kill Ahikar.
Jdt 4: 7 and it would be easy to stop any who **t** to enter,
8:27 For he has not **t** us with fire, as he did them,
AdE 15:16 and all his servants **t** to comfort her.
Wis 3: 6 like gold in the furnace he **t** them,
11: 9 For when they were **t,**
19:17 by yawning darkness, all of them **t** to find the way
Sus 1: 6 and all who had a case to be **t** came to them there.
1Mc 6: 3 So he came and **t** to take the city and plunder it,
9: 9 But they **t** to dissuade him, saying,
9:32 When Bacchides learned of this, he **t** to kill him.
11: 1 and he **t** to get possession of Alexander's kingdom
11:10 for he has **t** to kill me."
12:53 All the nations around them **t** to destroy them,
2Mc 7:19 not think that you will go unpunished for having **t**
13:18 **t** strategy in attacking their positions.
1Es 1:28 but **t** to fight with him,
3Mc 1:25 while the elders near the king **t** in various ways
7: 5 they **t** without any inquiry or examination
2Es 13: 7 And I **t** to see the region or place from which
4Mc 4:26 he himself **t** through torture to compel everyone
12: 2 summoned him to come nearer and **t** to persuade
15:16 **t** now by more bitter pains than even the birth

TRIES (2) [TRY]
Jos 6:26 the LORD be anyone who **t** to build this city—
Lk 16:16 and everyone **t** to enter it by force.

TRIFLE‡ (2) [TRIFLING]
2Ki 3:18 This is only a **t** in the sight of the LORD,
Ps 44:12 You have sold your people for a **t,**

TRIFLING (1) [TRIFLE]
Dt 32:47 This is no **t** matter for you,

TRIGON (4)
Da 3: 5 lyre, **t,** harp, drum, and entire musical ensemble,
3: 7 lyre, **t,** harp, drum, and entire musical ensemble,
3:10 lyre, **t,** harp, drum, and entire musical ensemble,
3:15 when you hear the sound of the horn, pipe, lyre, **t,**

TRIM (2) [TRIMMED]
2Ki 10:32 In those days the LORD began to **t** off parts
Eze 44:20 they shall only **t** the hair of their heads.

TRIMMED (2) [TRIM]
2Sa 19:24 he had not taken care of his feet, or **t** his beard,
Mt 25: 7 all those bridesmaids got up and **t** their lamps.

TRIP (2) [TRIPPED]
Sir 12:17 pretending to help, he will **t** you up.
27:23 and with your own words he will **t** you up.

TRIPOLIS (1)
2Mc 14: 1 of Seleucus had sailed into the harbor of **T** with

TRIPPED (2) [TRIP]
Jer 18:23 Let them be **t** up before you;
Sir 23: 8 by them the reviler and the arrogant are **t** up.

TRIREMES (1)
2Mc 4:20 it was applied to the construction of **t.**

TRIUMPH (17) [TRIUMPHAL, TRIUMPHANT, TRIUMPHED, TRIUMPHING, TRIUMPHS]
Dt 33:29 the shield of your help, and the sword of your **t!**
1Ki 22:12 "Go up to Ramoth-gilead and **t;**
22:15 He answered him, "Go up and **t;**
2Ch 18:11 "Go up to Ramoth-gilead and **t;**
18:14 He answered, "Go up and **t;**
Job 17: 4 therefore you will not let them **t.**
Ps 54: 7 and my eye has looked in **t** on my enemies.
59:10 my God will let me look in **t** on my enemies.
60: 8 over Philistia I shout in **t.**"
108: 9 over Philistia I shout in **t.**"
112: 8 in the end they will look in **t** on their foes.
118: 7 I shall look in **t** on those who hate me.
Pr 28:12 When the righteous **t,** there is great glory,
Isa 45:25 In the LORD all the offspring of Israel shall **t**
Jdt 12: 8 of Israel to direct her way for the **t** of his people.
Wis 4: 2 throughout all time it marches, crowned in **t,**
2Mc 13:16 with terror and confusion and withdrew in **t.**

TRIUMPHAL (1) [TRIUMPH]
2Co 2:14 who in Christ always leads us in **t** procession,

TRIUMPHANT (3) [TRIUMPH]
Dt 32:27 "Our hand is **t;** it was not the LORD who did all
Zec 9: 9 **t** and victorious is he, humble and riding on
1Mc 11:16 to find protection there, and King Ptolemy was **t.**

TRIUMPHED (4) [TRIUMPH]
Ex 15: 1 "I will sing to the LORD, for he has **t** gloriously;
15:21 "Sing to the LORD, for he has **t** gloriously;
Ps 41:11 because my enemy has not **t** over me.
La 1: 9 look at my affliction, for the enemy has **t!**"

TRIUMPHING (1) [TRIUMPH]
Col 2:15 and made a public example of them, **t** over them

TRIUMPHS (4) [TRIUMPH]
Jdg 5:11 there they repeat the **t** of the LORD,
5:11 the **t** of his peasantry in Israel.
Ps 18:50 Great **t** he gives to his king,
Jas 2:13 who has shown no mercy; mercy **t** over judgment.

TRIVIAL (1)
1Co 6: 2 are you incompetent to try **t** cases?

TROAS (6)
Ac 16: 8 so, passing by Mysia, they went down to **T.**
16:11 from **T** and took a straight course to Samothrace,
20: 5 They went ahead and were waiting for us in **T;**
20: 6 and in five days we joined them in **T,**
2Co 2:12 I came to **T** to proclaim the good news of Christ,
2Ti 4:13 bring the cloak that I left with Carpus at **T,**

TROD (5) [TREAD]
Jdg 9:27 the grapes from their vineyards, **t** them,
20:43 and **t** them down as far as a place east of Gibeah.
Job 22:15 to the old way that the wicked have **t?**
Isa 63: 3 I **t** them in my anger and trampled them in my
Hab 3:12 In fury you **t** the earth,

TRODE, TRODDEN (KJV) See also BEATEN DOWN, CONQUERING, TROD, SET FOOT, SPURN[ED], TRAMPLED

TRODDEN (11) [TREAD]
Jos 14: 9 'Surely the land on which your foot has **t** shall be
Job 28: 8 The proud wild animals have not **t** it;
Ps 58: 7 like grass let them be **t** down and wither.
Isa 25:10 be **t** down in their place as straw is **t** down
63: 3 "I have **t** the wine press alone,
Jer 51:33 like a threshing floor at the time when it is **t;**
La 1:15 the Lord has **t** as in a wine press
Eze 34:19 And must my sheep eat what you have **t**
Mic 7:10 she will be **t** down like the mire of the streets.
Rev 14:20 And the wine press was **t** outside the city,

TROGYLLIUM See Index to Footnotes

TROOP‡ (3) [TROOPED, TROOPS]
2Sa 22:30 By you I can crush a **t,**
Ps 18:29 By you I can crush a **t,**
1Mc 10:77 for he had a large **t** of cavalry and put confidence

TROOPED (1) [TROOP]
Jer 5: 7 they committed adultery and **t** to the houses

TROOPS‡ (163) [TROOP]
Nu 31:21 the priest said to the **t** who had gone to battle:
31:32 remaining from the spoil the **t** had taken totaled
31:42 which Moses separated from that of the **t,**
31:53 (The **t** had all taken plunder for themselves.)
Dt 3:18 all your **t** shall cross over armed as the vanguard
20: 2 the priest shall come forward and speak to the **t,**
20: 5 Then the officials shall address the **t,** saying,
20: 8 The officials shall continue to address the **t,**
20: 9 When the officials have finished addressing the **t,**
Jos 8:19 the **t** in ambush rose quickly out of their place
11: 4 They came out, with all their **t,** a great army,
Jdg 4: 7 by the Wadi Kishon with his chariots and his **t;**
4:13 and all the **t** who were with him,
7: 1 the **t** that were with him rose early and encamped
7: 2 "The **t** with you are too many for me to give
7: 3 therefore proclaim this in the hearing of the **t,**
7: 4 LORD said to Gideon, "The **t** are still too many;
7: 5 So he brought the **t** down to the water;
7: 6 but all the rest of the **t** knelt down to drink water.
7: 8 So he took the jars of the **t** from their hands,
8:15 to your **t** who are exhausted?' "
9:32 go by night, you and the **t** that are with you,
9:33 and when he and the **t** that are with him come out
9:34 the **t** with him got up by night and lay in wait
9:35 and the **t** with him rose from the ambush.
9:38 Are not these the **t** you made light of?
9:43 he took his **t** and divided them
9:48 he and all the **t** that were with him.
9:48 Then he said to the **t** with him,
9:49 So every one of the **t** cut down a bundle
20:10 to bring provisions for the **t,**
20:31 As before they began to inflict casualties on the **t,**
20:36 to the **t** in ambush that they had stationed
20:37 The **t** in ambush rushed quickly upon Gibeah.
1Sa 4: 3 When the **t** came to the camp,
4:17 there has also been a great slaughter among the **t;**
13: 5 and **t** like the sand on the seashore in multitude;
13: 6 in distress (for the **t** were hard pressed),
14: 2 **t** that were with him were about six hundred men,
14:17 Then Saul said to the **t** that were with him,
14:23 and the **t** with Saul numbered altogether
14:24 He had laid an oath on the **t,** saying,
14:24 So none of the **t** tasted food.
14:25 All the **t** came upon a honeycomb;
14:26 When the **t** came upon the honeycomb,
14:27 But Jonathan had not heard his father charge the **t**
14:28 "Your father strictly charged the **t** with an oath,
14:28 And so the **t** are faint."
14:30 How much better if today the **t** had eaten freely of
14:31 from Michmash to Aijalon, the **t** were very faint;
14:32 the **t** flew upon the spoil, and took sheep and oxen
14:32 and the **t** ate them with the blood.
14:33 the **t** are sinning against the LORD by eating
14:34 Saul said, "Disperse yourselves among the **t,**
14:34 of the **t** brought their oxen with them that night,
17:52 The **t** of Israel and Judah rose up with a shout
27: 3 David stayed with Achish at Gath, he and his **t,**
2Sa 17: 8 he will not spend the night with the **t.**
17: 9 And when some of our **t** fall at the first attack,
17: 9 a slaughter among the **t** who follow Absalom.'
17:29 "The **t** are hungry and weary and thirsty in
18:16 and the **t** came back from pursuing Israel, for Joab restrained the **t.**
19: 2 that day was turned into mourning for all the **t;**
19: 2 for the **t** heard that day,
19: 3 The **t** stole into the city that day as soldiers steal
19: 8 The **t** were all told, "See,
19: 8 and all the **t** came before the king.
1Ki 12:21 one hundred eighty thousand chosen **t** to fight
16:15 Now the **t** were encamped against Gibbethon,
16:16 and the **t** who were encamped heard it said,
1Ch 12:18 and made them officers of his **t.**
12:23 of the divisions of the armed **t** who came to David
12:24 numbered six thousand eight hundred armed **t.**
12:33 Of Zebulun, fifty thousand seasoned **t,**
12:36 forty thousand seasoned **t** ready for battle.

1Ch 19:11 the rest of his **t** he put in the charge
19:14 So Joab and the **t** who were with him advanced
2Ch 11: 1 assembled one hundred eighty thousand chosen **t**
13:13 thus his **t** were in front of Judah,
14: 8 and two hundred eighty thousand **t**
22: 1 for the **t** who came with the Arabs to
25: 5 that they were three hundred thousand picked **t** fit
Job 10:17 you bring fresh **t** against me.
19:12 His **t** come on together; they have thrown
29:25 and I lived like a king among his **t**,
Ps 76: 5 none of the **t** was able to lift a hand.
Jer 40: 7 in the open country and their **t** heard that the king
40: 8 Jezaniah son of the Maacathite, they and their **t**.
40: 9 of Shaphan swore to them and their **t**,
50:37 and against all the foreign **t** in her midst,
51:14 I will fill you with **t** like a swarm of locusts,
Eze 12:14 his helpers and all his **t**;
17:21 All the pick of his **t** shall fall by the sword,
38: 6 Gomer and all its **t**; Beth-togarmah from the remotest parts of the north with all its **t**—
38: 9 you and all your **t**, and many peoples with you.
38:22 and hailstones, fire and sulfur, upon him and his **t**
39: 4 and all your **t** and the peoples that are with you;
Da 9:26 the **t** of the prince who is to come shall destroy
11:15 of the south shall not stand, not even his picked **t**,
Na 3:13 Look at your **t**: they are women in your midst.
Mt 22: 7 He sent his **t**, destroyed those murderers,
Rev 9:16 of the **t** of cavalry was two hundred million;
Jdt 1:16 he and all his combined forces, a vast body of **t**;
2: 7 the whole face of the earth with the feet of my **t**,
2:15 He mustered the picked **t** by divisions
1Mc 2:31 and to the **t** in Jerusalem the city of David,
4:31 let them be ashamed of their **t** and their cavalry.
4:35 When Lysias saw the rout of his **t** and observed
6:33 and his **t** made ready for battle
6:40 and some **t** were on the plain,
6:57 to the commanders of the forces, and to the **t**,
9:52 and in them he put **t** and stores of food.
10: 6 So Demetrius gave him authority to recruit **t**,
10: 8 that the king had given him authority to recruit **t**.
10:21 and he recruited **t** and equipped them with arms
11:18 and his **t** in the strongholds were killed by
11:38 to him, he dismissed all his **t**, all of them
11:38 the foreign **t** that he had recruited from the islands
11:38 So all the **t** who had served
11:39 that all the **t** were grumbling against Demetrius.
11:40 and told of the hatred that the **t** of Demetrius had
11:41 the **t** of the citadel from Jerusalem, and the **t** in the
11:43 for all my **t** have revolted."
11:55 All the **t** that Demetrius had discharged gathered
12:27 Jonathan commanded his **t** to be alert and
12:28 that Jonathan and his **t** were prepared for battle,
12:29 Jonathan and his **t** did not know it until morning,
12:43 and commanded his Friends and his **t** to obey him
12:45 the other strongholds and the remaining **t** and all
12:46 he sent away the **t**, and they returned to the land
12:49 Then Trypho sent **t** and cavalry into Galilee and
13:43 against Gazara and surrounded it with **t**.
15: 3 of mercenary **t** and have equipped warships,
15:10 All the **t** rallied to him,
15:12 and his **t** had deserted him.
15:26 Simon sent to Antiochus two thousand picked **t**,
15:38 and gave him **t** of infantry and cavalry.
15:41 up Kedron and stationed horsemen and **t** there,
16: 6 when his **t** saw him, they crossed over after him.
16:18 asking him to send **t** to aid him and to turn over
16:19 He sent other **t** to Gazara to do away with John;
16:20 and he sent other **t** to take possession
2Mc 4:29 the commander of the Cyprian **t**.
5: 3 **t** of cavalry drawn up, attacks and counterattacks
5: 5 When the **t** on the wall had been forced back and
5:25 he ordered his **t** to parade under arms.
10:19 and also Zacchaeus and his **t**,
12:37 then he charged against Gorgias's **t**
13:14 of the world and exhorting his **t** to fight bravely to
13:15 He gave his **t** the watchword, "God's victory,"
14:13 with orders to kill Judas and scatter his **t**,
14:18 of the valor of Judas and his **t** and their courage
14:41 When the **t** were about to capture the tower
15: 1 that Judas and his **t** were in the region of Samaria,
15: 8 He exhorted his **t** not to fear the attack of
15:25 Nicanor and his **t** advanced with trumpets
15:26 and his **t** met the enemy in battle with invocations
1Es 2:30 with cavalry and a large number of armed **t**,
3Mc 1: 4 Arsinoë went to the **t** with wailing and tears,
2: 7 he pursued them with chariots and a mass of **t**,

TROPHIES (1)

2Mc 5: 6 but imagining that he was setting up **t** of victory

TROPHIMUS (3)

Ac 20: 4 as well as by Tychicus and **T** from Asia.
21:29 For they had previously seen **T** the Ephesian
2Ti 4:20 **T** I left ill in Miletus.

TROUBLE‡ (126) [TROUBLED, TROUBLER, TROUBLES, TROUBLESOME, TROUBLING]

A. TIME OF TROUBLE (12)
B. DAY OF ... TROUBLE (10)

Ge 34:30 "You have brought **t** on me by making me odious
Ex 5:19 The Israelite supervisors saw that they were in **t**
Nu 23:21 nor has he seen **t** in Israel.
Nu 33:55 they shall **t** you in the land where you are settling.
Dt 31:29 In time to come **t** will befall you,
Jos 6:18 of Israel an object for destruction, bringing **t**
7:25 Joshua said, "Why did you bring **t** on us?
7:25 The LORD is bringing **t** on you today."
Jdg 11: 7 why do you come to me now when you are in **t**?"
11:35 you have become the cause of great **t** to me.
2Sa 11:25 'Do not let this matter **t** you,
12:11 up **t** against you from within your own house;
14: 5 The king asked her, "What is your **t**?"
1Ki 11:25 the days of Solomon, making **t** as Hadad did;
20: 7 See how this man is seeking **t**;
2Ki 4:13 "Say to her, Since you have taken all this **t** for us,
6:33 "This **t** is from the LORD!
14:10 for why should you provoke **t** so that you fall,
2Ch 25:19 why should you provoke **t** so that you fall,
Ne 1: 3 the province who escaped captivity are in great **t**
2:17 Then I said to them, "You see the **t** we are in,
Job 3:10 and hide **t** from my eyes.
3:26 I have no rest; but **t** comes."
4: 8 those who plow iniquity and sow **t** reap the same.
5: 6 nor does **t** sprout from the ground;
5: 7 but human beings are born to **t** just
14: 1 mortal, born of woman, few of days and full of **t**,
27: 9 Will God hear their cry when **t** comes upon them?
38:23 which I have reserved for the time of **t**, A
Ps 9: 9 a stronghold in times of **t**.
10: 1 Why do you hide yourself in times of **t**?
10:14 Indeed you note **t** and grief,
20: 1 The LORD answer you in the day of **t**! B
22:11 for **t** is near and there is no one to help.
25:18 Consider my affliction and my **t**,
27: 5 For he will hide me in his shelter in the day of **t**; B
32: 7 for me; you preserve me from **t**;
34: 6 and was saved from every **t**.
37:39 he is their refuge in the time of **t**. A
41: 1 the LORD delivers them in the day of **t**. B
46: 1 a very present help in **t**.
49: 5 Why should I fear in times of **t**,
50:15 Call on me in the day of **t**; B
54: 7 For he has delivered me from every **t**,
55: 3 For they bring **t** upon me,
55:10 and iniquity and **t** are within it;
66:14 and my mouth promised when I was in **t**.
73: 5 They are not in **t** as others are;
77: 2 In the day of my **t** I seek the Lord; B
86: 7 In the day of my **t** I call on you, B
90:10 even then their span is only toil and **t**;
91:15 I will be with them in **t**,
94:13 giving them respite from days of **t**,
107: 2 those he redeemed from **t**
107: 6 Then they cried to the LORD in their **t**,
107:13 Then they cried to the LORD in their **t**,
107:19 Then they cried to the LORD in their **t**,
107:28 Then they cried to the LORD in their **t**,
107:39 and brought low through oppression, **t**,
119:143 **T** and anguish have come upon me,
138: 7 Though I walk in the midst of **t**,
142: 2 I tell my **t** before him.
143:11 In your righteousness bring me out of **t**.
Pr 10:10 Whoever winks the eye causes **t**,
11: 8 The righteous are delivered from **t**,
11:15 To guarantee loans for a stranger brings **t**,
11:29 Those who **t** their households will inherit wind,
12:13 but the righteous escape from **t**.
12:21 but the wicked are filled with **t**.
13:17 A bad messenger brings **t**, but a faithful envoy,
15: 6 but **t** befalls the income of the wicked.
15:16 the fear of the LORD than great treasure and **t**
15:27 Those who are greedy for unjust gain make **t**
16: 4 even the wicked for the day of **t**. B
17:21 The one who begets a fool gets **t**;
21:23 over mouth and tongue is to keep out of **t**.
25:19 in a faithless person in time of **t**. A
27: 9 but the soul is torn by **t**.
Ecc 12: 1 before the days of **t** come,
Isa 30: 6 Through a land of **t** and distress,
33: 2 our salvation in the time of **t**. A
46: 7 it does not answer or save anyone from **t**.
Jer 2:27 But in the time of their **t** they say,
2:28 if they can save you, in your time of **t**; A
11:12 they will never save them in the time of their **t**.
11:14 when they call to me in the time of their **t**.
14: 8 O hope of Israel, its savior in time of **t**, A
15:11 on you in a time of **t** and in a time of distress. A
16:19 my refuge in the day of **t**, B
51: 2 against her from every side on the day of **t**. B
La 1:21 All my enemies heard of my **t**;
Eze 32: 2 **t** the water with your feet, and foul your streams.
32: 9 I will **t** the hearts of many peoples,
32:13 and no human foot shall **t** them any more,
32:13 nor shall the hoofs of cattle **t** them.
Na 1: 7 The LORD is good, a stronghold in a day of **t**; B
Hab 1: 3 do you make me see wrongdoing and look at **t**?
Mt 6:34 Today's **t** is enough for today.
13:21 **t** or persecution arises on account of the word,
26:10 said to them, "Why do you **t** the woman?
28:14 we will satisfy him and keep you out of **t**."
Mk 4:17 **t** or persecution arises on account of the word,
5:35 Why **t** the teacher any further?"
14: 6 But Jesus said, "Let her alone; why do you **t** her?
Lk 7: 6 do not **t** yourself, for I am not worthy
8:49 do not **t** the teacher any longer."
Ac 15:19 not **t** those Gentiles who are turning to God,
Gal 6:17 From now on, let no one make **t** for me;
Heb 12:15 that no root of bitterness springs up and causes **t**,
AdE 7: 7 for he saw that he was in serious **t**.
Sir 6: 8 but they will not stand by you in time of **t**. A
6:10 but they will not stand by you in time of **t**. A
11:34 into your home and they will stir up **t** for you,
22:13 Stay clear of him, or you may have **t**,
29: 4 and cause **t** to those who help them.
37: 4 but in time of **t** they are against him. A
40: 5 there is anger and envy and **t** and unrest,
40:24 Kindred and helpers are for a time of **t**, A
51:10 do not forsake me in the days of **t**,
51:12 from destruction and rescued me in time of **t**. A
1Mc 12:44 "Why have you put all these people to so much **t**
2Mc 2:30 and to take **t** with details,
4:31 So the king went hurriedly to settle the **t**,
4:47 Menelaus, the cause of all the **t**,
13: 4 that this man was to blame for all the **t**,
3Mc 1:27 in the present **t** and not to overlook this unlawful

TROUBLED (38) [TROUBLE]

Ge 40: 6 he saw that they were **t**.
41: 8 In the morning his spirit was **t**;
1Sa 1:15 "No, my lord, I am a woman deeply **t**;
14:29 Then Jonathan said, "My father has **t** the land;
1Ki 18:18 He answered, "I have not **t** Israel;
2Ch 15: 6 for God **t** them with every sort of distress.
Ps 55: 2 I am **t** in my complaint.
77: 4 I am so **t** that I cannot speak.
Jer 49:23 they are **t** like the sea that cannot be quiet.
Da 2: 1 that his spirit was **t** and his sleep left him.
2: 3 that my spirit is **t** by the desire to understand it."
7:15 As for me, Daniel, my spirit was **t** within me,
9:25 with streets and moat, but in a **t** time.
Lk 6:18 those who were **t** with unclean spirits were cured.
Jn 12:27 "Now my soul is **t**.
13:21 After saying this Jesus was **t** in spirit,
14: 1 "Do not let your hearts be **t**.
14:27 Do not let your hearts be **t**,
AdE 4: 4 and eunuchs came and told her, she was deeply **t**
11: 9 And the whole righteous nation was **t**;
Wis 16: 6 they were **t** for a little while as a warning,
18:17 in dreadful dreams greatly **t** them,
Sir 40: 6 He is **t** by the visions of his mind
1Mc 3: 5 he burned those who **t** his people.
2Mc 8:32 and one who had greatly **t** the Jews.
9:24 the people throughout the realm would not be **t**,
14:28 he was **t** and grieved that he had
2Es 3: 1 I was **t** as I lay on my bed,
3:18 and caused the depths to tremble, and **t** the times.
5: 5 the peoples shall be **t**, and the stars shall fall.
5:14 and my soul was so **t** that it fainted.
6:36 the eighth night my heart was **t** within me again,
8:16 and about the seed of Jacob, for whom I am **t**.
9:27 my heart was **t** again as it was before.
10:31 And why are you **t**?
10:31 and the thoughts of your mind **t**?"
15: 3 not be **t** by the unbelief of those who oppose you.
16:12 and the fish with them shall be **t** at the presence of

TROUBLER (2) [TROUBLE]

1Ki 18:17 Ahab said to him, "Is it you, you **t** of Israel?"
1Ch 2: 7 The sons of Carmi: Achar, the **t** of Israel,

TROUBLES (23) [TROUBLE]

Ge 21:17 and said to her, "What **t** you, Hagar?
Dt 31:17 and many terrible **t** will come upon them.
31:17 not these **t** come upon us because our God is not
31:21 And when many terrible **t** come upon them,
Job 2:11 Now when Job's three friends heard of all these **t**
5:19 He will deliver you from six **t**;
Ps 25:17 Relieve the **t** of my heart,
25:22 Redeem Israel, O God, out of all its **t**.
34:17 and rescues them from all their **t**.
71:20 You who have made me see many **t**
88: 3 For my soul is full of **t**,
Ecc 8: 6 although the **t** of mortals lie heavy upon them.
Isa 65:16 because the former **t** are forgotten and are hidden
Wis 10: 9 Wisdom rescued from **t** those who served her.
Sir 3:27 A stubborn mind will be burdened by **t**,
4: 3 Do not add to the **t** of the desperate,
51: 3 from the many **t** I endured,
1Mc 2:30 because **t** pressed heavily upon them.
2:43 to escape their **t** joined them and reinforced them.
10:15 and of the **t** that they had endured.
15:12 for he knew that **t** had converged on him,
2Es 10:15 and bear bravely the **t** that have come upon you.
10:24 may give you rest, a respite from your **t**."

TROUBLESOME (1) [TROUBLE]

Php 3: 1 To write the same things to you is not **t** to me,

TROUBLING (3) [TROUBLE]

Job 3:17 There the wicked cease from **t**,
1Mc 7:22 and all who were **t** their people joined him.
1Es 2:22 **t** both kings and other cities,

TROUGH (1) [TROUGHS]

Ge 24:20 into the **t** and ran again to the well to draw,

TROUGHS (3) [TROUGH]

Ge 30:38 that he had peeled in front of the flocks in the **t**,
30:41 Jacob laid the rods in the **t** before the eyes of
Ex 2:16 and filled the **t** to water their father's flock.

TROUSERS (1)

Da 3:21 men were bound, still wearing their tunics, their t,

TROWEL (1)

Dt 23:13 With your utensils you shall have a t;

TRUCEBREAKERS (KJV) See IMPLACABLE

TRUE‡ (142) [TRUTH]

Nu 11:23 Now you shall see whether my word will come t
Dt 17: 4 and the charge is proved t that such
18:22 but the thing does not take place or prove t,
22:20 If, however, this charge is t,
Jos 2: 4 Then she said, "T, the men came to me,
7:20 And Achan answered Joshua, "It is t;
Jdg 13:12 Manoah said, "Now when your words come t,
13:17 we may honor you when your words come t?"
Ru 3:12 But now, though it is t that I am a near kinsman,
1Sa 9: 6 Whatever he says always comes t.
2Sa 7:28 you are God, and your words are t,
22:31 the promise of the LORD proves t;
1Ki 10: 6 "The report was t that I heard in my own land
11: 4 and his heart was not t to the LORD his God,
15: 3 his heart was not t to the LORD his God,
15:14 the heart of Asa was t to the LORD all his days.
2Ki 10:15 "Is your heart as t to mine as mine is to yours?"
2Ch 9: 5 "The report was t that I heard in my own land
15: 3 For a long time Israel was without the t God,
15:17 Nevertheless the heart of Asa was t all his days.
16: 9 to strengthen those whose heart is t to him.
25: 2 yet not with a t heart.
Ne 9:13 and gave them right ordinances and t laws,
Job 5:27 See, we have searched this out; it is t.
19: 4 it is t that I have erred, my error remains with me.
Ps 18:30 the promise of the LORD proves t;
19: 9 of the LORD are t and righteous altogether.
78:37 they were not t to his covenant.
119:151 O LORD, and all your commandments are t.
Pr 11:18 but those who sow righteousness get a t reward.
18:24 but a t friend sticks closer than one's nearest kin.
22:21 to show you what is right and t,
22:21 you may give a t answer to those who sent you?
30: 5 Every word of God proves t;
Isa 43: 9 and let them hear and say, "It is t."
Jer 10:10 But the LORD is the t God;
14:13 but I will give you t peace in this place.' "
28: 9 when the word of that prophet comes t,
42: 5 a t and faithful witness against us if we do not act
50: 7 the t pasture, the LORD,
Eze 18: 8 executes t justice between contending parties,
Da 3:14 Nebuchadnezzar said to them, "Is it t,
3:24 They answered the king, "T, O king."
8:26 and the mornings that has been told is t.
10: 1 The word was t, and it concerned a great conflict.
Jnh 2: 8 who worship vain idols forsake their t loyalty.
Zec 7: 9 Render t judgments, show kindness and mercy
8:16 in your gates judgments that are t and make
Mal 2: 6 T instruction was in his mouth,
Lk 16:11 who will entrust to you the t riches?
Jn 1: 9 The t light, which enlightens everyone,
3:21 But those who do what is t come to the light,
3:33 his testimony has certified this, that God is t.
4:18 What you have said is t!"
4:23 the t worshipers will worship the Father in spirit
4:37 For here the saying holds t,
5:31 "If I testify about myself, my testimony is not t.
5:32 and I know that his testimony to me is t.
6:32 but it is my Father who gives you the t bread
6:55 for my flesh is t food and my blood is t drink.
7:18 one who seeks the glory of him who sent him is t,
7:28 one who sent me is t, and you do not know him.
8:26 but the one who sent me is t,
10:41 everything that John said about this man was t."
15: 1 "I am the t vine, and my Father is the vinegrower.
17: 3 that they may know you, the only t God,
19:35 His testimony is t, and he knows that he tells
21:24 and we know that his testimony is t.
Ac 24: 9 in the charge by asserting that all this was t.
Ro 2:28 is t circumcision something external and physical.
3: 4 Although everyone is a liar, let God be proved t,
9: 7 all of Abraham's children are his t descendants;
11:20 That is t. They were broken off
1Co 15:15 whom he did not raise if it is t that the dead are
2Co 6: 8 We are treated as impostors, and yet are t;
7:14 but just as everything we said to you was t,
7:14 so our boasting to Titus has proved t as well.
12:12 of a t apostle were performed among you
Eph 4:24 to the likeness of God in t righteousness
5: 9 in all that is good and right and t.
Php 1:18 whether out of false motives or t;
4: 8 Finally, beloved, whatever is t,
1Th 1: 9 to serve a living and t God,
Tit 1:13 That testimony is t. For this reason rebuke them
Heb 8: 2 a minister in the sanctuary and the t tent that
9:24 a mere copy of the t one,
10: 1 of the good things to come and not the t form
10:22 let us approach with a t heart in full assurance
1Pe 5:12 and to testify that this is the t grace of God.
2Pe 2:22 to them according to the t proverb,
1Jn 1: 6 we lie and do not do what is t;
2: 8 a new commandment that is t in him and in you,
2: 8 and the t light is already shining.
2:27 and is t and is not a lie,
1Jn 5:20 so that we may know him who is t;
5:20 we are in him who is t, in his Son Jesus Christ.
5:20 He is the t God and eternal life.
3Jn 1:12 and you know that our testimony is t.
Rev 3: 7 These are the words of the holy one, the t one,
3:14 words of the Amen, the faithful and t witness,
6:10 "Sovereign Lord, holy and t,
15: 3 Just and t are your ways, King of the nations!
16: 7 the Almighty, your judgments are t and just!"
19: 2 for his judgments are t and just;
19: 9 And he said to me, "These are t words of God."
19:11 Its rider is called Faithful and T,
21: 5 "Write this, for these words are trustworthy and t."
22: 6 "These words are trustworthy and t, for the Lord,
Tob 3: 5 And now your many judgments are t
7:10 let me explain to you the t situation more fully,
13: 6 to do what is t before him,
14: 4 but all will come t at their appointed times.
14: 4 be fulfilled and will come t;
Jdt 6: 9 and none of my words shall fail to come t."
8:28 that you have said was spoken out of a t heart,
10:13 to give him a t report;
11:10 but keep it in your mind, for it is t.
Wis 1: 6 and a t observer of their hearts,
2:17 Let us see if his words are t,
5:21 Shafts of lightning will fly with t aim,
7: 3 my first sound was a cry, as is t of all.
12:27 the t God the one whom they had before refused
15: 1 But you, our God, are kind and t, patient,
Sir 12:18 and whisper much, and show his t face.
28: 6 and be t to the commandments.
32:16 Those who fear the Lord will form t judgments,
34: 4 And from something false what can be t?
41:14 My children, be t to your training and be at peace;
Aza 1: 4 all your works are t and your ways right,
1: 4 and all your judgments are t.
1: 5 You have executed t judgments
1: 5 by a t judgment you have brought all this upon us
1: 8 you have done by a t judgment.
2Mc 1: 1 in Egypt, Greetings and t peace.
4:13 who was ungodly and no t high priest,
3Mc 2:11 And indeed you are faithful and t.
6:18 and t God revealed his holy face and opened
2Es 15: 2 for they are trustworthy and t.
4Mc 6: 5 the courageous and noble man, like a t Eleazar,
15: 4 Especially is this t of mothers,
17: 6 For your children were t descendants

TRULY (137) [TRUTH]

Ge 4:24 t Lamech seventy-sevenfold."
24:49 if you will deal loyally and t with my master,
33:10 t to see your face is like seeing the face of God—
47:29 and promise to deal loyally and t with me.
Ex 4:25 "T you are a bridegroom of blood to me!"
Jos 2:24 "T the LORD has given all the land
1Sa 20: 3 But t, as the LORD lives and
25:34 t by morning there would not have been left
2Ki 19:17 T, O LORD, the kings of Assyria have laid waste
Job 3:25 T the thing that I fear comes upon me,
28:28 And he said to humankind, 'T,
32: 8 But t it is the spirit in a mortal,
36: 4 For t my words are not false;
Ps 33:18 T the eye of the LORD is on those who fear him,
38:14 T, I am like one who does not hear,
49: 7 T, no ransom avails for one's life,
55: 7 t, I would flee far away;
66:19 But t God has listened; he has given heed to the
73: 1 T God is good to the upright,
73:18 T you set them in slippery places;
119:127 T I love your commandments more than gold,
119:128 T I direct my steps by all your precepts;
SS 1:16 Ah, you are beautiful, my beloved, t lovely.
Isa 28:11 T, with stammering lip and
30:19 T, O people in Zion, inhabitants of Jerusalem,
30:33 t it is made ready for the king,
37:18 T, O LORD, the kings of Assyria
45:15 T, you are a God who hides himself,
Jer 1: 6 T I do not know how to speak,
3:23 T the hills are a delusion,
3:23 T in the LORD our God is the salvation of Israel.
7: 5 For if you t amend your ways and your doings,
7: 5 if you t act justly one with another,
10:19 But I said, "T this is my punishment,
14:10 T they have loved to wander,
15:18 T, you are to me like a deceitful brook,
28: 9 be known that the LORD has t sent the prophet."
Da 2:47 The king said to Daniel, "T, your God is God of
Joel 2:11 T the day of the LORD is great;
Zec 2: 8 T, one who touches you touches the apple
Mt 5:18 For t I tell you, until heaven and earth pass away,
5:26 T I tell you, you will never get out
6: 2 T I tell you, they have received their reward.
6: 5 T I tell you, they have received their reward.
6:16 T I tell you, they have received their reward.
8:10 and said to those who followed him, "T I tell you,
10:15 T I tell you, it will be more tolerable for the land
10:23 for t I tell you, you will not have gone through all
10:42 t I tell you, none of these will lose their reward."
11:11 T I tell you, among those born
13:17 T I tell you, many prophets
14:33 saying, "T you are the Son of God."
16:28 T I tell you, there are some standing here who will
17:20 For t I tell you, if you have faith the size of
18: 3 "T I tell you, unless you change and become
18:13 And if he finds it, t I tell you,
18:18 T I tell you, whatever you bind on earth will
Mt 18:19 t I tell you, if two of you agree on earth
19:23 Then Jesus said to his disciples, "T I tell you,
19:28 Jesus said to them, "T I tell you,
21:21 Jesus answered them, "T I tell you,
21:31 Jesus said to them, "T I tell you,
23:36 T I tell you, all this will come
24: 2 T I tell you, not one stone will be left here
24:34 T I tell you, this generation will not pass away
24:47 T I tell you, he will put that one in charge
25:12 But he replied, 'T I tell you, I do not know you.'
25:40 And the king will answer them, 'T I tell you,
25:45 Then he will answer them, 'T I tell you,
26:13 T I tell you, wherever this good news is
26:21 he said, "T I tell you, one of you will betray me."
26:34 Jesus said to him, "T I tell you, this very night,
27:54 "T this man was God's Son!"
Mk 3:28 "T I tell you, people will be forgiven for their sins
8:12 T I tell you, no sign will be given
9: 1 And he said to them, "T I tell you,
9:41 For t I tell you, whoever gives you a cup of water
10:15 T I tell you, whoever does not receive
10:29 "T I tell you, there is no one who has left house
11:23 T I tell you, if you say to this mountain,
11:32 for all regarded John as t a prophet.
12:32 you have t said that 'he is one,
12:43 to them, "T I tell you, this poor widow has put
13:30 T I tell you, this generation will not pass away
14: 9 T I tell you, wherever the good news is
14:18 "T I tell you, one of you will betray me,
14:25 T I tell you, I will never again drink of the fruit of
14:30 Jesus said to him, "T I tell you, this day,
15:39 he said, "T this man was God's Son!"
Lk 4:24 And he said, "T I tell you,
9:27 But t I tell you, there are some standing here who
12:37 t I tell you, he will fasten his belt
12:44 T I tell you, he will put that one in charge
18:17 T I tell you, whoever does not receive
18:29 And he said to them, "T I tell you,
21: 3 "T I tell you, this poor widow has put
21:32 T I tell you, this generation will not pass away
23:43 "T I tell you, today you will be with me
Jn 1:47 toward him, he said of him, "Here is t an Israelite
1:51 And he said to him, "Very t, I tell you,
3: 3 Jesus answered him, "Very t, I tell you,
3: 5 Jesus answered, "Very t, I tell you,
3:11 "Very t, I tell you, we speak of what we know
4:42 we know that this is t the Savior of the world."
5:19 Jesus said to them, "Very t, I tell you,
5:24 Very t, I tell you, anyone who hears my word
5:25 "Very t, I tell you, the hour is coming,
6:26 Jesus answered them, "Very t, I tell you,
6:32 Then Jesus said to them, "Very t, I tell you,
6:47 Very t, I tell you, whoever believes has eternal life.
6:53 So Jesus said to them, "Very t, I tell you,
8:31 in my word, you are t my disciples;
8:34 Jesus answered them, "Very t, I tell you,
8:51 Very t, I tell you, whoever keeps my word will
8:58 Jesus said to them, "Very t, I tell you,
10: 1 "Very t, I tell you, anyone who does not enter
10: 7 So again Jesus said to them, "Very t, I tell you,
12:24 Very t, I tell you, unless a grain of wheat falls
13:16 Very t, I tell you, servants are
13:20 Very t, I tell you, whoever receives one whom
13:21 "Very t, I tell you, one of you will betray me."
13:38 Very t, I tell you, before the cock crows,
14:12 Very t, I tell you, the one who believes in me will
16:20 Very t, I tell you, you will weep and mourn,
16:23 Very t, I tell you, if you ask anything of
21:18 Very t, I tell you, when you were younger,
Ac 10:34 "I t understand that God shows no partiality,
Ro 9: 6 For not all Israelites t belong to Israel,
1Co 2:11 what human being knows what is t human except
2:11 also no one comprehends what is t God's except
Col 1: 6 from the day you heard it and t comprehended
1Jn 1: 3 and t our fellowship is with the Father and
2: 5 t in this person the love of God has reached
Tob 14: 7 in those days and are t mindful of God will
4Mc 5:18 not t divine and we had wrongly held it to
11:23 of tortures and enemy of those who are t devout.
17:11 T the contest in which they were engaged was

TRUMP (KJV) See TRUMPET

TRUMPET (70) [TRUMPETERS, TRUMPETS]

Ex 19:13 When the t sounds a long blast,
19:16 a blast of a t so loud that all the people who were
19:19 As the blast of the t grew louder and louder,
20:18 the sound of the t, and the mountain smoking,
Lev 23:24 a holy convocation commemorated with t blasts.
25: 9 Then you shall have the t sounded loud;
25: 9 the t sounded throughout all your land.
Jos 6: 5 as soon as you hear the sound of the t,
Jdg 3:27 he sounded the t in the hill country of Ephraim;
6:34 the t, and the Abiezrites were called out
7:18 When I blow the t, I and all who are with me,
1Sa 13: 3 And Saul blew the t throughout all the land,
2Sa 2:28 Joab sounded the t and all the people stopped;
6:15 and with the sound of the t.
15:10 saying, "As soon as you hear the sound of the t,
18:16 Then Joab sounded the t,
20: 1 He sounded the t and cried out,
20:22 So he blew the t, and they dispersed from
1Ki 1:34 blow the t, and say, 'Long live King Solomon!'
1:39 Then they blew the t, and all the people said,

1Ki 1:41 When Joab heard the sound of the **t,** he said,
2Ki 9:13 they blew the **t,** and proclaimed, "Jehu is king."
Ne 4:18 The man who sounded the **t** was beside me.
4:20 Rally to us wherever you hear the sound of the **t.**
Job 39:24 it cannot stand still at the sound of the **t.**
39:25 When the **t** sounds, it says 'Aha!'
Ps 47: 5 the LORD with the sound of a **t.**
81: 3 Blow the **t** at the new moon, at the full moon,
150: 3 Praise him with **t** sound; praise him with lute
Isa 18: 3 When a **t** is blown, listen!
27:13 And on that day a great **t** will be blown,
58: 1 Lift up your voice like a **t!**
Jer 4: 5 Blow the **t** through the land;
4:19 for I hear the sound of the **t,** the alarm of war.
4:21 and hear the sound of the **t?**
6: 1 Blow the **t** in Tekoa, and raise a signal on
6:17 "Give heed to the sound of the **t!"**
42:14 or hear the sound of the **t,** or be hungry for bread,
51:27 blow the **t** among the nations;
Eze 33: 3 the sword coming upon the land and blows the **t**
33: 4 then if any who hear the sound of the **t** do
33: 5 the sound of the **t** and did not take warning;
33: 6 the sword coming and does not blow the **t,**
Hos 5: 8 Blow the horn in Gibeah, the **t** in Ramah.
8: 1 Set the **t** to your lips!
Joel 2: 1 Blow the **t** in Zion; sound the alarm on my
2:15 Blow the **t** in Zion; sanctify a fast;
Am 2: 2 amid shouting and the sound of the **t;**
3: 6 Is a **t** blown in a city,
Zep 1:16 of **t** blast and battle cry against the fortified cities
Zec 9:14 the Lord GOD will sound the **t** and march forth
Mt 6: 2 do not sound a **t** before you,
24:31 And he will send out his angels with a loud **t** call,
1Co 15:52 in the twinkling of an eye, at the last **t.**
15:52 For the **t** will sound, and the dead will
1Th 4:16 and with the sound of God's **t,**
Heb 12:19 and the sound of a **t,**
Rev 1:10 and I heard behind me a loud voice like a **t**
4: 1 which I had heard speaking to me like a **t,** said,
8: 7 The first angel blew his **t,**
8: 8 The second angel blew his **t,**
8:10 The third angel blew his **t,**
8:12 The fourth angel blew his **t,**
9: 1 And the fifth angel blew his **t,**
9:13 Then the sixth angel blew his **t,**
9:14 saying to the sixth angel who had the **t,**
10: 7 the days when the seventh angel is to blow his **t,**
11:15 Then the seventh angel blew his **t,**
Sir 26:27 *and garrulous wife is like a **t** sounding the charge,*
2Es 6:23 the **t** shall sound aloud,

TRUMPETERS (6) [TRUMPET]

2Ki 11:14 with the captains and the **t** beside the king,
2Ch 5:12 with one hundred twenty priests who were **t).**
5:13 of the **t** and singers to make themselves heard
23:13 and the captains and the **t** beside the king,
29:28 the singers sang, and the **t** sounded;
Rev 18:22 and of flutists and **t** will be heard in you no more;

TRUMPETS (67) [TRUMPET]

Nu 10: 2 Make two silver **t;** you shall make them of
10: 8 The sons of Aaron, the priests, shall blow the **t;**
10: 9 you shall sound an alarm with the **t,**
10:10 you shall blow the **t** over your burnt offerings and
29: 1 It is a day for you to blow the **t,**
31: 6 the vessels of the sanctuary and the **t** for sounding
Jos 6: 4 with seven priests bearing seven **t** of rams' horns
6: 4 the city seven times, the priests blowing the **t.**
6: 6 and have seven priests carry seven **t**
6: 8 seven priests carrying the seven **t** of rams' horns
before the LORD went forward, blowing the **t,**
6: 9 before the priests who blew the **t;**
6: 9 while the **t** blew continually.
6:13 the seven **t** of rams' horns before the ark of
6:13 blowing the **t** continually.
6:13 while the **t** blew continually.
6:16 when the priests had blown the **t,**
6:20 So the people shouted, and the **t** were blown.
6:20 As soon as the people heard the sound of the **t,**
Jdg 7: 8 of the troops from their hands, and their **t;**
7:16 and put **t** into the hands of all of them,
7:18 then you also blow the **t** around the whole camp,
7:19 and they blew the **t** and smashed the jars
7:20 the three companies blew the **t** and broke the jars,
7:20 and in their right hands the **t** to blow;
7:22 When they blew the three hundred **t,**
2Ki 11:14 all the people of the land rejoicing and blowing **t.**
12:13 bowls, **t,** or any vessels of gold, or of silver,
1Ch 13: 8 and harps and tambourines and cymbals and **t.**
15:24 were to blow the **t** before the ark of God.
15:28 to the sound of the horn, **t,** and cymbals,
16: 6 and Jahaziel were to blow **t** regularly,
16:42 and Jeduthun had with them **t** and cymbals for
2Ch 5:13 and when the song was raised, with **t** and cymbals
7: 6 Opposite them the priests sounded **t;**
13:12 and his priests have their battle **t** to sound the call
13:14 and the priests blew the **t.**
15:14 and with shouting, and with **t,** and with horns.
20:28 with harps and lyres and **t,**
23:13 all the people of the land rejoicing and blowing **t,**
29:26 and the priests with the **t.**
29:27 the song to the LORD began also, and the **t,**
Ezr 3:10 to praise the LORD with **t,** and the Levites,
Ne 12:35 and some of the young priests with **t:**
12:41 Elioenai, Zechariah, and Hananiah, with **t;**
Ps 98: 6 With **t** and the sound of the horn make
Rev 8: 2 and seven **t** were given to them.
8: 6 the seven angels who had the seven **t** made ready
8:13 at the blasts of the other **t** that the three angels are
Sir 50:16 they blew their **t** of hammered metal;
1Mc 3:54 Then they sounded the **t** and gave a loud shout.
4:13 Then the men with Judas blew their **t**
4:40 And when the signal was given with the **t,**
5:31 that the cry of the town went up to Heaven, with **t**
5:33 who sounded their **t** and cried aloud in prayer.
6:33 for battle and sounded their **t.**
7:45 the battle call on the **t.**
9:12 the phalanx advanced to the sound of the **t;**
9:12 and the men with Judas also blew their **t.**
16: 8 the **t,** and Cendebeus and his army were put
2Mc 15:25 and his troops advanced with **t** and battle songs,
1Es 5:59 with musical instruments and **t,** and the Levites,
5:62 And all the people sounded **t** and shouted with
5:64 while many came with **t** and a joyful noise,
5:65 so that the people could not hear the **t** because of
5:65 For the multitude sounded the **t** loudly,
5:66 to find out what the sound of the **t** meant.

TRUNK‡ (2) [TRUNKS]

1Sa 5: 4 only the **t** of Dagon was left to him.
Eze 31:13 On its fallen **t** settle all the birds of the air,

TRUNKS (1) [TRUNK]

Sir 50:12 a young cedar on Lebanon surrounded by the **t**

TRUST‡ (111) [ENTRUST, ENTRUSTED, ENTRUSTING, TRUSTED, TRUSTEES, TRUSTING, TRUSTINGLY, TRUSTS, TRUSTWORTHY]

Ex 19: 9 when I speak with you and so **t** you ever after."
Nu 20:12 "Because you did not **t** in me,
Dt 1:32 you have no **t** in the LORD your God,
Jdg 11:20 Sihon did not **t** Israel to pass through his territory;
1Ch 9:22 Samuel established them in their office of **t.**
Job 4:18 Even in his servants he puts no **t,**
8:14 confidence is gossamer, a spider's house their **t.**
15:15 God puts no **t** even in his holy ones,
15:31 Let them not **t** in emptiness,
31:24 "If I have made gold my **t,**
Ps 4: 5 and put your **t** in the LORD.
9:10 those who know your name put their **t** in you,
25: 2 O my God, in you I **t;**
31: 6 but I **t** in the LORD.
31:14 I **t** in you, O LORD; I say, "You are my God."
32:10 but steadfast love surrounds those who **t** in
33:21 because we **t** in his holy name.
37: 3 **T** in the LORD, and do good;
37: 5 **t** in him, and he will act.
40: 3 and put their **t** in the LORD.
40: 4 Happy are those who make the LORD their **t,**
44: 6 not in my bow do I **t,** nor can my sword save me.
49: 6 those who **t** in their wealth and boast of
52: 8 I **t** in the steadfast love of God forever and ever.
55:23 But I will **t** in you.
56: 3 when I am afraid, I put my **t** in you.
56: 4 In God, whose word I praise, in God I **t;**
56:11 in God I **t;** I am not afraid.
62: 8 **T** in him at all times, O people;
71: 5 For you, O Lord, are my hope, my **t,** O LORD,
78:22 and did not **t** his saving power.
91: 2 my God, in whom I **t."**
115: 8 so are all who **t** in them.
115: 9 O Israel, **t** in the LORD!
115:10 O house of Aaron, **t** in the LORD!
115:11 You who fear the LORD, **t** in the LORD!
119:42 for I **t** in your word.
125: 1 Those who **t** in the LORD are like Mount Zion,
135:18 and all who **t** them shall become like them.
143: 8 for in you I put my **t.**
146: 3 Do not put your **t** in princes, in mortals,
Pr 3: 5 **T** in the LORD with all your heart,
11:28 Those who **t** in their riches will wither,
16:20 and happy are those who **t** in the LORD.
20: 6 but who can find one worthy of **t?**
22:19 So that your **t** may be in the LORD,
25:19 a bad tooth or a lame foot is **t** in a faithless person
28:26 Those who **t** in their own wits are fools;
Isa 12: 2 Surely God is my salvation; I will **t,**
26: 3 in peace because they **t** in you.
26: 4 **T** in the LORD forever,
30:12 and put your **t** in oppression and deceit,
30:15 in quietness and in **t** shall be your strength.
31: 1 who **t** in chariots because they are many and
32:17 of righteousness, quietness and **t** forever.
42:17 those who **t** in carved images,
Jer 2:37 for the LORD has rejected those in whom you **t,**
5:17 the sword your fortified cities in which you **t.**
7: 4 Do not **t** in these deceptive words:
7:14 in which you **t,** and to the place that I gave to you
9: 4 and put no **t** in any of your kin;
17: 5 Cursed are those who **t** in mere mortals
17: 7 Blessed are those who **t** in the LORD,
17: 7 in the LORD, whose **t** is the LORD.
28:15 and you made this people **t** in a lie.
29:31 and has led you to **t** in a lie,
46:25 upon Pharaoh and those who **t** in him.
49:11 and let your widows **t** in me.
Eze 33:13 they **t** in their righteousness and commit iniquity,
Mic 7: 5 Put no **t** in a friend, have no confidence in
Php 2:24 and I **t** in the Lord that I will also come soon.
2Ti 1:12 for I know the one in whom I have put my **t,**
Heb 2:13 And again, "I will put my **t** in him."
1Pe 1:21 Through him you have come to **t** in God,
Tob 1:14 of Media I left bags of silver worth ten talents in **t**
4: 1 the money that he had left in **t** with Gabael
4:20 that I left ten talents of silver in **t** with Gabael son
5: 2 to give him so that he will recognize and **t** me,
5: 3 since I left this money in **t.**
Wis 3: 9 Those who **t** in him will understand truth,
12: 2 be freed from wickedness and put their **t** in you,
13: 7 they keep searching, and they **t** in what they see,
14: 5 therefore people **t** their lives even to
14:29 they **t** in lifeless idols they swear wicked oaths
16:24 and in kindness relaxes on behalf of those who **t**
16:26 but that your word sustains those who **t** in you.
Sir 2: 6 **T** in him, and he will help you;
2: 8 You who fear the Lord, **t** in him,
2:13 Woe to the fainthearted who have no **t!**
6: 7 and do not **t** them hastily.
7:26 but do not **t** yourself to one whom you detest.
11:21 but **t** in the Lord and keep at your job;
12:10 Never **t** your enemy, for like corrosion in copper,
13:11 or **t** his lengthy conversations;
16: 3 Do not **t** in their survival,
22:23 Gain the **t** of your neighbor in his poverty,
33: 3 The sensible person will **t** in the law;
36:31 For who will **t** a nimble robber that skips
36:31 So who will **t** a man that has no nest,
Bar 3:17 which people **t,** and there is no end to their getting;
Aza 1:17 for no shame will come to those who **t** in you.
1Mc 2:61 of those who put their **t** in him will lack strength.
7: 7 Now then send a man whom you **t;**
8:16 They **t** one man each year to rule over them and
10:37 of them be put in positions of **t** in the kingdom.
2Mc 7:40 putting his whole **t** in the Lord.
8:18 "For they **t** to arms and acts of daring," he said,
"but we **t** in the Almighty God,
15: 7 to **t** with all confidence that he would get help
2Es 8:30 but love those who have always put their **t**
4Mc 8: 7 **T** me, then, and you will have positions

TRUSTED (35) [TRUST]

Dt 28:52 in which you **t,** come down throughout your land;
Jdg 20:36 because they **t** to the troops in ambush
1Sa 27:12 Achish **t** David, thinking,
2Ki 18: 5 He **t** in the LORD the God of Israel;
1Ch 5:20 he granted their entreaty because they **t** in him.
Job 12:20 He deprives of speech those who are **t,**
18:14 They are torn from the tent in which they **t,**
Ps 13: 5 But I **t** in your steadfast love;
22: 4 In you our ancestors **t;** they **t,** and you delivered
22: 5 in you they **t,** and were not put to shame.
26: 1 and I have **t** in the LORD without wavering.
41: 9 Even my bosom friend in whom I **t,**
52: 7 **t** in abundant riches, and sought refuge in wealth!"
Pr 21:22 and brought down the stronghold in which they **t.**
Jer 13:25 because you have forgotten me and **t** in lies.
38:22 'Your **t** friends have seduced you
39:18 because you have **t** in me, says the LORD.
48: 7 you **t** in your strongholds and your treasures,
49: 4 You **t** in your treasures, saying,
Eze 16:15 But you **t** in your beauty,
Da 3:28 and delivered his servants who **t** in him.
6:23 because he had **t** in his God.
Hos 10:13 Because you have **t** in your power and in
Zep 3: 2 It has not **t** in the LORD;
Lk 11:22 he takes away his armor in which he **t**
18: 9 also told this parable to some who **t** in themselves
Wis 18: 6 in sure knowledge of the oaths in which they **t.**
Sir 2:10 has anyone **t** in the Lord and been disappointed?
Sus 1:35 for her heart **t** in the Lord.
1Mc 7:16 So they **t** him; but he seized sixty of them
12:46 Jonathan **t** him and did as he said;
2Mc 3:12 be done to those people who had **t** in the holiness
3Mc 2: 4 even giants who **t** in their strength and boldness,
2Es 7:*83* those who have **t** the covenants of the Most High.

TRUSTEES (1) [TRUST]

Gal 4: 2 but they remain under guardians and **t** until

TRUSTING (4) [TRUST]

Dt 9:23 neither **t** him nor obeying him.
Jer 7: 8 Here you are, **t** in deceptive words to no avail.
Jdt 9: 7 and **t** in shield and spear, in bow and sling.
Sir 26:20 *sow it with your own seed, **t** in your fine stock.*

TRUSTINGLY (2) [TRUST]

Pr 3:29 not plan harm against your neighbor who lives **t**
Mic 2: 8 from those who pass by **t** with no thought of war.

TRUSTS‡ (16) [TRUST]

Ps 21: 7 For the king **t** in the LORD,
28: 7 and my shield; in him my heart **t;**
84:12 happy is everyone who **t** in you.
86: 2 save your servant who **t** in you.
Pr 28:25 but whoever **t** in the LORD will be enriched.
29:25 but one who **t** in the LORD is secure.
31:11 The heart of her husband **t** in her,
Isa 28:16 "One who **t** will not panic."
50:10 yet **t** in the name of the LORD and relies
Hab 2:18 For its maker **t** in what has been made,
Mt 27:43 He **t** in God; let God deliver him now,
Ro 4: 5 But to one who without works **t** him who justifies
Sir 4:17 by her discipline until she **t** them,

Sir 19: 4 One who **t** others too quickly has a shallow mind,
32:24 and the one who **t** the Lord will not suffer loss.
4Mc 7:21 by the whole rule of philosophy, and **t** in God,

TRUSTWORTHY‡ (24) [TRUST]

Ex 18:21 men who fear God, are **t**, and hate dishonest gain;
1Sa 3:20 to Beer-sheba knew that Samuel was a **t** prophet
Ps 111: 7 and just; all his precepts are **t**.
Pr 11:13 but one who is **t** in spirit keeps a confidence.
Da 2:45 The dream is certain, and its interpretation **t**."
Mt 25:21 'Well done, good and **t** slave; you have been **t** in a few things,
25:23 'Well done, good and **t** slave; you have been **t** in a few things,
Lk 19:17 Because you have been **t** in a very small thing,
1Co 4: 2 it is required of stewards that they be found **t**.
7:25 as one who by the Lord's mercy is **t**.
Tit 1: 9 the word that is **t** in accordance with the teaching,
Rev 21: 5 "Write this, for these words are **t** and true."
22: 6 And he said to me, "These words are **t** and true,
Tob 5: 3 my son, find yourself a **t** man to go with you,
5: 9 and whether he is **t** enough to go with you."
10: 6 The man who went with him is **t** and is one
Sir 31:23 and their testimony to his generosity is **t**.
36:21 for you and let your prophets be found **t**.
46:15 and by his words he became known as a **t** seer.
48:22 who was great and **t** in his visions.
1Mc 14:41 until a **t** prophet should arise,
2Es 15: 2 for they are **t** and true.

TRUTH‡ (187) [TRUE, TRULY, TRUTHFUL, TRUTHFULNESS]

Ge 42:16 whether there is **t** in you;
1Ki 17:24 that the word of the LORD in your mouth is **t**."
22:16 tell me nothing but the **t** in the name of the LORD?"
2Ch 18:15 tell me nothing but the **t** in the name of the LORD?"
Job 6:13 In **t** I have no help in me,
34:12 Of a **t**, God will not do wickedly,
Ps 5: 9 For there is no **t** in their mouths;
15: 2 and speak the **t** from their heart;
25: 5 Lead me in your **t**, and teach me,
43: 3 O send out your light and your **t**;
45: 4 on victoriously for the cause of **t** and to defend
51: 6 You desire **t** in the inward being;
52: 3 and lying more than speaking the **t**.
86:11 O LORD, that I may walk in your **t**;
96:13 and the peoples with his **t**.
119:43 not take the word of **t** utterly out of my mouth,
119:142 and your law is the **t**.
119:160 The sum of your word is **t**;
145:18 to all who call on him in **t**.
Pr 8: 7 for my mouth will utter **t**;
12:17 Whoever speaks the **t** gives honest evidence,
23:23 Buy **t**, and do not sell it;
Ecc 12:10 and he wrote words of **t** plainly.
Isa 10:20 the Holy One of Israel, in **t**.
45:19 I the LORD speak the **t**, I declare what is right.
48: 1 and invoke the God of Israel, but not in **t** or right.
59:14 for **t** stumbles in the public square,
59:15 **T** is lacking, and whoever turns
Jer 4: 2 in **t**, in justice, and in uprightness,
5: 1 can find one person who acts justly and seeks **t**—
5: 3 O LORD, do your eyes not look for **t**?
7:28 **t** has perished; it is cut off from their lips.
9: 3 in the land for falsehood, and not for **t**;
9: 5 and no one speaks the **t**;
26:15 for in **t** the LORD sent me to you
Eze 13:10 in **t**, because they have misled my people, saying,
Da 4:37 for all his works are **t**, and his ways are justice;
7:16 the attendants to ask him the **t** concerning all this.
7:19 to know the **t** concerning the fourth beast,
8:12 it cast **t** to the ground,
10:21 I am to tell you what is inscribed in the book of **t**.
11: 2 "Now I will announce the **t** to you.
Am 5:10 and they abhor the one who speaks the **t**.
Zec 8:16 Speak the **t** to one another,
8:19 therefore love **t** and peace.
Mt 22:16 and teach the way of God in accordance with **t**,
Mk 5:33 fell down before him, and told him the whole **t**.
12:14 but teach the way of God in accordance with **t**.
Lk 1: 4 so that you may know the **t** concerning the things
4:25 But the **t** is, there were many widows in Israel in
20:21 but teach the way of God in accordance with **t**.
Jn 1:14 as of a father's only son, full of grace and **t**.
1:17 grace and **t** came through Jesus Christ.
4:23 will worship the Father in spirit and **t**,
4:24 who worship him must worship in spirit and **t**."
5:33 and he testified to the **t**.
8:32 and you will know the **t**,
8:32 and the **t** will make you free."
8:40 man who has told you the **t** that I heard from God.
8:44 from the beginning and does not stand in the **t**,
8:44 because there is no **t** in him.
8:45 But because I tell the **t**, you do not believe me.
8:46 If I tell the **t**, why do you not believe me?
14: 6 Jesus said to him, "I am the way, and the **t**,
14:17 This is the Spirit of **t**,
15:26 the Spirit of **t** who comes from the Father,
16: 7 Nevertheless I tell you the **t**:
16:13 When the Spirit of **t** comes,
16:13 he will guide you into all the **t**;
17: 8 and they have received them and know in **t**
17:17 Sanctify them in the **t**; your word is **t**.
17:19 so that they also may be sanctified in **t**.
18:37 for this I came into the world, to testify to the **t**.
Jn 18:37 Everyone who belongs to the **t** listens
18:38 Pilate asked him, "What is **t**?"
19:35 and he knows that he tells the **t**.)
Ac 20:30 from your own group will come distorting the **t**
26:25 but I am speaking the sober **t**.
Ro 1:18 of those who by their wickedness suppress the **t**.
1:25 because they exchanged the **t** about God for a lie
2: 2 those who do such things is in accordance with **t**."
2: 8 and who obey not the **t** but wickedness,
2:20 in the law the embodiment of knowledge and **t**,
9: 1 I am speaking the **t** in Christ—
15: 8 the circumcised on behalf of the **t** of God in order
1Co 5: 8 but with the unleavened bread of sincerity and **t**.
13: 6 not rejoice in wrongdoing, but rejoices in the **t**.
2Co 4: 2 of the **t** we commend ourselves to the conscience
11:10 As the **t** of Christ is in me,
12: 6 I will not be a fool, for I will be speaking the **t**.
13: 8 For we cannot do anything against the **t**, but only for the **t**.
Gal 2: 5 the **t** of the gospel might always remain with you.
2:14 that they were not acting consistently with the **t** of
4:16 now become your enemy by telling you the **t**?
5: 7 who prevented you from obeying the **t**?
Eph 1:13 when you had heard the word of **t**,
4:15 But speaking the **t** in love,
4:21 about him and were taught in him, as **t** is in Jesus.
4:25 let all of us speak the **t** to our neighbors,
6:14 and fasten the belt of **t** around your waist,
Col 1: 5 of this hope before in the word of the **t**,
2Th 2:10 they refused to love the **t** and so be saved.
2:12 the **t** but took pleasure in unrighteousness will
2:13 by the Spirit and through belief in the **t**.
1Ti 2: 4 be saved and to come to the knowledge of the **t**.
2: 7 a herald and an apostle (I am telling the **t**,
2: 7 a teacher of the Gentiles in faith and **t**.
3:15 the pillar and bulwark of the **t**.
4: 3 by those who believe and know the **t**.
6: 5 in mind and bereft of the **t**,
2Ti 2:15 rightly explaining the word of **t**.
2:18 who have swerved from the **t** by claiming that
2:25 that they will repent and come to know the **t**,
3: 7 and can never arrive at a knowledge of the **t**.
3: 8 and counterfeit faith, also oppose the **t**.
4: 4 from listening to the **t** and wander away to myths.
Tit 1: 1 of God's elect and the knowledge of the **t** that is
1:14 or to commandments of those who reject the **t**.
Heb 10:26 after having received the knowledge of the **t**,
Jas 1:18 by the word of **t**, so that we would become a kind
3:14 do not be boastful and false to the **t**.
5:19 from the **t** and is brought back by another,
1Pe 1:22 to the **t** so that you have genuine mutual love,
2Pe 1:12 and are established in the **t** that has come to you.
2: 2 of these teachers the way of **t** will be maligned.
1Jn 1: 8 we deceive ourselves, and the **t** is not in us.
2: 4 is a liar, and in such a person the **t** does not exist;
2:21 I write to you, not because you do not know the **t**,
2:21 and you know that no lie comes from the **t**.
3:18 not in word or speech, but in **t** and action.
3:19 that we are from the **t** and will reassure our hearts
4: 6 From this we know the spirit of **t** and the spirit
5: 6 for the Spirit is the **t**.
2Jn 1: 1 and her children, whom I love in the **t**, and not only I but also all who know the **t**,
1: 2 the **t** that abides in us and will be with us forever:
1: 3 the Father's Son, in **t** and love.
1: 4 to find some of your children walking in the **t**,
3Jn 1: 1 The elder to the beloved Gaius, whom I love in **t**.
1: 3 and testified to your faithfulness to the **t**,
1: 3 namely how you walk in the **t**.
1: 4 to hear that my children are walking in the **t**.
1: 8 so that we may become co-workers with the **t**.
1:12 and so has the **t** itself.
Tob 1: 3 in the ways of **t** and righteousness all the days
3: 2 all your ways are mercy and **t**;
3: 5 not walked in accordance with **t** before you.
4: 6 with **t** will prosper in all their activities.
12:11 the whole **t** to you and will conceal nothing
14: 6 be converted and worship God in **t**.
Jdt 5: 5 and I will tell you the **t** about this people that lives
Wis 3: 9 Those who trust in him will understand **t**,
5: 6 So it was we who strayed from the way of **t**,
6:22 and I will not pass by the **t**;
Sir 4:25 Never speak against the **t**,
4:28 Fight to the death for **t**,
12:12 and at last you will realize the **t** of my words,
37:15 to the Most High that he may direct your way in **t**.
1Mc 7:18 for they said, "There is no **t** or justice in them,
2Mc 7: 6 over us and in **t** has compassion on us,
1Es 3:12 but above all things **t** is victor."
4:13 spoken of women and **t** (and this was Zerubbabel),
4:33 and he began to speak about **t**:
4:35 But **t** is great, and stronger than all things.
4:36 whole earth calls upon **t**, and heaven blesses her.
4:37 There is no **t** in them and
4:38 But **t** endures and is strong forever,
4:40 Blessed be the God of **t**!"
4:41 all the people shouted and said, "Great is **t**,
3Mc 4:16 with a mind alienated from **t** and with
7:12 admitting and approving the **t** of what they said,
2Es 5: 1 and the way of **t** shall be hidden,
6:28 and the **t**, which has been so long without fruit,
7:*34* Only judgment shall remain, **t** shall stand,
7:*104* and displays to all the seal of **t**.
7:*114* [44] has increased and **t** has appeared.
8:23 and whose **t** is established forever—
8:26 but on those who serve you in **t**.
8:35 For in **t** there is no one among those who have
2Es 11:41 You have judged the earth, but not with **t**,
11:42 you have hated those who tell the **t**,
14:18 **T** shall go farther away,
4Mc 5:10 by holding a vain opinion concerning the **t**,
5:11 according to the **t** of what is beneficial,
6:18 if having lived in accordance with **t** up to old age

TRUTHFUL (3) [TRUTH]

Pr 12:19 **T** lips endure forever,
14:25 A **t** witness saves lives, but one who utters lies is
2Co 6: 7 **t** speech, and the power of God;

TRUTHFULNESS (1) [TRUTH]

Ro 3: 7 my falsehood God's **t** abounds to his glory,

TRY (24) [TRIED, TRIES, TRYING]

Jdg 19:13 "Come, let us **t** to reach one of these places,
Ps 17: 3 If you **t** my heart, if you visit me by night,
26: 2 Prove me, O LORD, and **t** me;
139:18 I **t** to count them—they are more than the sand;
Isa 22: 4 do not **t** to comfort me for the destruction of my
Jer 11:20 who **t** the heart and the mind,
Mal 1: 8 **T** presenting that to your governor;
Lk 13:24 I tell you, will **t** to enter and will not be able.
14:19 and I am going to **t** them out;
17:33 Those who **t** to make their life secure will lose it,
Ac 18: 4 in the synagogue and would **t** to convince Jews
1Co 6: 2 are you incompetent to **t** trivial cases?
10:33 just as I **t** to please everyone in everything I do,
2Co 5:11 Therefore, knowing the fear of the Lord, we **t**
Gal 6:12 the flesh that **t** to compel you to be circumcised—
Eph 5:10 **T** to find out what is pleasing to the Lord.
Jdt 8:16 not **t** to bind the purposes of the Lord our God;
8:34 Only, do not **t** to find out what I am doing;
Sir 4:26 and do not **t** to stop the current of a river.
12:12 or else he may **t** to take your own seat,
13:11 Do not **t** to treat him as an equal,
31:25 Do not **t** to prove your strength by wine-drinking,
1Mc 9:71 and he swore to Jonathan that he would not **t**
3Mc 3: 8 They did **t** to console them,

TRYING (25) [TRY]

Dt 13:10 for **t** to turn you away from the LORD your God,
1Sa 19: 2 "My father Saul is **t** to kill you;
20: 1 And what is my sin against your father that he is **t**
2Ki 5: 7 and see how he is **t** to pick a quarrel with me."
Pr 23:30 those who keep **t** mixed wines.
Da 2: 8 "I know with certainty that you are **t** to gain time,
Lk 5:18 They were **t** to bring him in and lay him before
6:19 And all in the crowd were **t** to touch him,
19: 3 He was **t** to see who Jesus was,
Jn 7:20 Who is **t** to kill you?"
7:25 "Is not this the man whom they are **t** to kill?
8:40 but now you are **t** to kill me,
9:34 and are you **t** to teach us?"
11: 8 "Rabbi, the Jews were just now **t** to stone you,
Ac 21:31 While they were **t** to kill him,
25:11 I am not **t** to escape death;
28:23 of God and **t** to convince them about Jesus both
2Co 10: 9 not want to seem as though I am **t** to frighten you
Gal 1:10 Or am I **t** to please people?
1:13 the church of God and was **t** to destroy it.
2Pe 3: 1 in them I am **t** to arouse your sincere intention
Tob 10: 7 Stop **t** to deceive me!
1Mc 6:18 They were **t** in every way to harm them
6:56 that he was **t** to seize control of the government.
4Mc 9: 5 You are **t** to terrify us by threatening us

TRYPHAENA (1)

Ro 16:12 Greet those workers in the Lord, **T** and Tryphosa.

TRYPHO (22)

1Mc 11:39 A certain **T** had formerly been one
11:54 After this **T** returned, and with him
11:56 **T** captured the elephants and gained control
12:39 Then **T** attempted to become king in Asia and put
12:42 When **T** saw that he had come with a large army,
12:49 Then **T** sent troops and cavalry into Galilee and
13: 1 Simon heard that **T** had assembled a large army
13:12 Then **T** left Ptolemais with a large army to invade
13:14 **T** learned that Simon had risen up in place
13:19 **T** broke his word and did not release Jonathan.
13:20 this **T** came to invade the country and destroy it,
13:21 in the citadel kept sending envoys to **T** urging him
13:22 So **T** got all his cavalry ready to go,
13:24 Then **T** turned and went back to his own land.
13:31 **T** dealt treacherously with the young King
13:34 for all that **T** did was to plunder.
14: 1 so that he could make war against **T**.
15:10 so that there were only a few with **T**.
15:11 and **T** came in his flight to Dor,
15:25 he shut **T** up and kept him from going out or in.
15:37 Meanwhile **T** embarked on a ship and escaped
15:39 on the people; but the king pursued **T**.

TRYPHOSA (1)

Ro 16:12 in the Lord, Tryphaena and **T**.

TUBAL (8)

Ge 10: 2 Gomer, Magog, Madai, Javan, **T**, Meshech,
1Ch 1: 5 Gomer, Magog, Madai, Javan, **T**, Meshech,
Isa 66:19 to **T** and Javan, to the coastlands far away
Eze 27:13 Javan, **T**, and Meshech traded with you;

Eze 32:26 Meshech and T are there, and all their multitude,
38: 2 the chief prince of Meshech and T.
38: 3 O Gog, chief prince of Meshech and T;
39: 1 O Gog, chief prince of Meshech and T!

TUBAL-CAIN (2)

Ge 4:22 Zillah bore T, who made all kinds of bronze
4:22 The sister of T was Naamah.

TUBES (1)

Job 40:18 Its bones are t of bronze,

TUMBLE (1) [TUMBLED]

Eze 38:20 and every wall shall t to the ground.

TUMBLED (1) [TUMBLE]

Jdg 7:13 a cake of barley bread t into the camp of Midian,

TUMBLEWEED See Index to Footnotes

TUMORS (7)

1Sa 5: 6 and he terrified and struck them with t,
5: 9 both young and old, so that t broke out on them.
5:12 those who did not die were stricken with t,
6: 4 They answered, "Five gold t and five gold mice,
6: 5 So you must make images of your t and images
6:11 box with the gold mice and the images of their t.
6:17 the gold t, which the Philistines returned as

TUMULT‡ (27) [TUMULTS, TUMULTUOUS]

1Sa 14:19 the t in the camp of the Philistines increased more
2Sa 18:29 I saw a great t, but I do not know what it was."
Job 39: 7 It scorns the t of the city;
Ps 38: 8 I groan because of the t of my heart.
46: 3 though the mountains tremble with its t.
65: 7 the roaring of their waves, the t of the peoples.
83: 2 Even now your enemies are in t;
Isa 13: 4 a t on the mountains as of a great multitude!
22: 5 of t and trampling and confusion in the valley
33: 3 At the sound of t, peoples fled;
Jer 10:13 there is a t of waters in the heavens,
48:45 the scalp of the people of t.
51:16 When he utters his voice there is a t of waters in
Eze 1:24 a sound of t like the sound of an army;
7: 7 of t, not of reveling on the mountains.
22: 5 you infamous one, full of t.
Hos 10:14 the t of war shall rise against your people,
AdE 11: 5 thunders and earthquake, t on the earth!
11: 8 affliction and great t on the earth!
Wis 14:25 theft and deceit, corruption, faithlessness, t,
1Mc 13:44 and a great t arose in the city.
2Mc 15:29 Then there was shouting and t,
3Mc 3: 8 an unexpected t around these people and
5:41 result the city is in a t because of its expectation;
2Es 9: 3 t of peoples, intrigues of nations,
12: 2 and their reign was brief and full of t.
12:30 this was the reign which was brief and full of t,

TUMULTS (1) [TUMULT]

Am 3: 9 and see what great t are within it,

TUMULTUOUS (4) [TUMULT]

Isa 22: 2 that are full of shoutings, t city,
Jer 51:42 she has been covered by its t waves.
1Mc 9:39 a t procession with a great amount of baggage;
3Mc 5:48 and heard the loud and t noise,

TUNES (1)

Sir 44: 5 those who composed musical t, or put verses

TUNIC (12) [TUNICS]

Ex 28: 4 a breastpiece, an ephod, a robe, a checkered t,
28:39 You shall make the checkered t of fine linen,
29: 5 and put on Aaron the t and the robe of the ephod,
Lev 8: 7 He put the t on him,
16: 4 He shall put on the holy linen t,
Job 30:18 he grasps me by the collar of my t.
Lk 9: 3 nor money—not even an extra t.
Jn 19:23 They also took his t; now the t was seamless,
Jude 1:23 hating even the t defiled by their bodies.
2Mc 12:40 Then under the t of each one of
4Mc 9:11 and having torn off his t,

TUNICS (12) [TUNIC]

Ex 28:40 For Aaron's sons you shall make t and sashes
29: 8 Then you shall bring his sons, and put t on them,
39:27 They also made the t, woven of fine linen,
40:14 You shall bring his sons also and put t on them,
Lev 8:13 and clothed them with t, and fastened sashes
10: 5 and carried them by their t out of the camp,
Da 3:21 So the men were bound, still wearing their t,
3:27 the hair of their heads was not singed, their t were
Mt 10:10 or two t, or sandals, or a staff;
Mk 6: 9 but to wear sandals and not to put on two t.
Ac 9:39 weeping and showing t and other clothing
Jdt 14:19 they tore their t and were greatly dismayed,

TUNNELED (1)

Sir 48:17 he t the rock with iron tools,

TURBAN (19) [TURBANS]

Ex 28: 4 a robe, a checkered tunic, a t, and a sash.
28:37 You shall fasten it on the t with a blue cord;
28:37 it shall be on the front of the t.
28:39 and you shall make a t of fine linen,
29: 6 and you shall set the t on his head,
29: 6 and put the holy diadem on the t.
39:28 and the t of fine linen,
39:31 to fasten it on the t above;
Lev 8: 9 And he set the t on his head, and on the t,
16: 4 fasten the linen sash, and wear the linen t;
Job 29:14 my justice was like a robe and a t.
Eze 21:26 Remove the t, take off the crown;
24:17 Bind on your t, and put your sandals on your feet;
Zec 3: 5 And I said, "Let them put a clean t on his head."
3: 5 So they put a clean t on his head and clothed him
AdE 8:15 and wearing a gold crown and a t of purple linen.
Sir 45:12 with a gold crown upon his t,
1Es 3: 6 a t of fine linen, and a necklace around his neck;

TURBANS (5) [TURBAN]

Isa 3:23 the linen garments, the t, and the veils.
Eze 23:15 with flowing t on their heads,
24:23 Your t shall be on your heads and your sandals
44:18 They shall have linen t on their heads,
Jdt 4:15 With ashes on their t, they cried out to the Lord

TURBID (1)

Job 6:16 that run dark with ice, t with melting snow.

TURBULENT (3)

Job 40:23 Even if the river is t, it is not frightened;
Eze 5: 7 Because you are more t than the nations
Wis 13: 2 or the circle of the stars, or t water,

TURMOIL (4)

Job 30:27 My inward parts are in t, and are never still;
Ps 39: 6 Surely for nothing they are in t;
Isa 14: 3 from your pain and t and the hard service
Mt 21:10 he entered Jerusalem, the whole city was in t,

TURN‡ (408) [TURNED, TURNING, TURNS]

Ge 19: 2 t aside to your servant's house and spend
24:49 that I may t either to the right hand or to the left."
37:30 and I, where can I t?"
Ex 3: 3 "I must t aside and look at this great sight,
14: 2 Tell the Israelites to t back and camp in front
23:27 I will make all your enemies t their backs to you.
29:13 and t them into smoke on the altar.
29:18 and t the whole ram into smoke on the altar;
29:25 and t them into smoke on the altar on top of
32: 8 to t aside from the way that I commanded them;
32:12 T from your fierce wrath;
34:22 and the festival of ingathering at the t of the year.
Lev 1: 9 the priest shall t the whole into smoke on the altar
1:13 the priest shall offer the whole and t it into smoke
1:15 and t it into smoke on the altar;
1:17 Then the priest shall t it into smoke on the altar,
2: 2 the priest shall t this token portion into smoke on
2: 9 from the grain offering its token portion and t this
2:11 not t any leaven or honey into smoke as
2:16 priest shall t a token portion of it into smoke—
3: 5 Aaron's sons shall t these into smoke on the altar,
3:11 the priest shall t these into smoke on the altar as
3:16 the priest shall t these into smoke on the altar as
4:10 The priest shall t them into smoke upon the altar
4:19 He shall remove all its fat and t it into smoke on
4:26 All its fat he shall t into smoke on the altar,
4:31 and the priest shall t it into smoke on the altar for
4:35 and the priest shall t it into smoke on the altar,
5:12 and t this into smoke on the altar,
6:12 and t into smoke the fat pieces of the offerings
6:15 and they shall t its memorial portion into smoke
7: 5 The priest shall t them into smoke on the altar as
7:31 The priest shall t the fat into smoke on the altar,
16:25 The fat of the sin offering he shall t into smoke on
17: 6 and t the fat into smoke as a pleasing odor to
19: 4 not t to idols or make cast images for yourselves:
19:31 Do not t to mediums or wizards;
20: 6 If any t to mediums and wizards,
26:16 I in t will do this to you:
26:28 I in t will punish you myself sevenfold
26:41 in t, continued hostile to them and brought them
Nu 5:26 and t it into smoke on the altar,
14:25 t tomorrow and set out for the wilderness by
16:26 "T away from the tents of these wicked men,
18:17 and shall t their fat into smoke as an offering
21:22 we will not t aside into field or vineyard;
22:23 to t it back onto the road.
22:26 where there was no way to t either to the right or
25: 4 that the fierce anger of the LORD may t away
32:15 If you t away from following him,
34: 4 your boundary shall t south of the ascent
34: 5 the boundary shall t from Azmon to the Wadi
Dt 2:27 I will t aside neither to the right nor to the left.
5:32 you shall not t to the right or to the left.
7: 4 would t away your children from following me,
7:15 The LORD will t away from you every illness;
9:12 to t from the way that I commanded them;
9:16 you had been quick to t from the way that
11:28 t from the way that I am commanding you today,
13: 5 to t you from the way in which
13:10 Stone them to death for trying to t you away from
13:17 so that the LORD may t from his fierce anger
Dt 14:25 then you may t it into money.
17:11 not t aside from the decision that they announce
17:17 or else his heart will t away;
23:14 not see anything indecent among you and t away
28:14 and if you do not t aside from any of the words
30:10 because you t to the LORD your God
31:20 they will t to other gods and serve them,
Jos 1: 7 do not t from it to the right hand or to the left,
2:12 to me by the LORD that you in t will deal kindly
7:12 they t their backs to their enemies,
15: 3 up to Addar, makes a t to Karka,
16: 6 the boundary makes a t toward Taanath-shiloh,
19:14 the boundary makes a t to Hannathon, and it ends
22: 4 therefore t and go to your tents in the land
22:18 that you must t away today from following
22:23 an altar to t away from following the LORD;
22:29 and t away this day from following the LORD
23:12 For if you t back, and join the survivors
24:20 then he will t and do you harm, and consume you,
Jdg 4:18 "T aside, my lord, t aside to me; have no fear."
19:11 let us t aside to this city of the Jebusites,
19:12 "We will not t aside into a city of foreigners,
20:39 the main body of Israel should t in battle.
Ru 1:11 But Naomi said, "T back, my daughters,
1:12 T back, my daughters, go your way,
1:16 to leave you or to t back from following you!
1Sa 6: 3 will not his hand then t from you?"
9: 5 "Let us t back, or my father will stop worrying
12:20 yet do not t aside from following the LORD,
12:21 not t aside after useless things that cannot profit
22:17 "T and kill the priests of the LORD,
22:18 "You, Doeg, t and attack the priests."
2Sa 1:22 the bow of Jonathan did not t back,
2:21 Abner said to him, "T to your right or to your left,
2:21 But Asahel would not t away from following him.
2:22 "T away from following me;
2:23 But he refused to t away.
2:26 before you order your people to t from the pursuit
5: 6 even the blind and the lame will t you back"—
14:19 one cannot t right or left from anything
15:31 t the counsel of Ahithophel into foolishness."
18:30 The king said, "T aside, and stand here."
22:23 and from his statutes I did not t aside.
22:38 and did not t back until they were consumed.
22:41 You made my enemies t their backs to me,
1Ki 2: 3 in all that you do and wherever you t.
5:11 Solomon in t gave Hiram twenty thousand cors
8:33 are defeated before an enemy but t again to you,
8:35 and t from their sin, because you punish them,
9: 6 "If you t aside from following me,
12:15 because it was a t of affairs brought about by
12:27 heart of this people will t again to their master,
13:33 this event Jeroboam did not t from his evil way,
15: 5 and did not t aside from anything
17: 3 "Go from here and t eastward,
22:34 so he said to the driver of his chariot, "T around,
22:43 he did not t aside from it,
2Ki 10:29 not t aside from the sins of Jeroboam son
10:31 he did not t from the sins of Jeroboam,
15:24 he did not t away from the sins of Jeroboam son
17:13 and every seer, saying, "T from your evil ways
19:28 I will t you back on the way by which you came.
20: 5 "T back, and say to Hezekiah prince
22: 2 he did not t aside to the right or to the left.
23:26 Still the LORD did not t from the fierceness
1Ch 9:25 in t, to be with them;
12:23 to David in Hebron to t the kingdom of Saul over
13: 3 for we did not t to it in the days of Saul."
2Ch 6:24 are defeated before an enemy but t again to you,
6:26 and t from their sin, because you punish them,
7:14 pray, seek my face, and t from their wicked ways,
7:19 "But if you t aside and forsake my statutes
8:15 not t away from what the king had commanded
10:15 because it was a t of affairs brought about by God
18:33 so he said to the driver of his chariot, "T around,
20:32 in the way of his father Asa and did not t aside
29:10 so that his fierce anger may t away from us.
30: 6 so that he may t again to the remnant
30: 8 so that his fierce anger may t away from you.
30: 9 and will not t away his face from you,
34: 2 he did not t aside to the right or to the left.
34:33 All his days they did not t away from following
35:22 But Josiah would not t away from him,
Ne 4: 4 t their taunt back on their own heads,
9:26 who had warned them in order to t them back
9:29 And you warned them in order to t them back
9:35 and did not t from their wicked works.
Est 2:12 t came for each girl to go in to King Ahasuerus,
2:15 When the t came for Esther daughter of Abihail
Job 1: 4 to go and hold feasts in one another's houses in t;
5: 1 To which of the holy ones will you t?
6:18 The caravans t aside from their course;
6:29 T, I pray, let no wrong be done.
6:29 T now, my vindication is at stake.
9:13 "God will not t back his anger;
10: 8 and now you t and destroy me.
10: 9 and will you t me to dust again?
15:13 so that you t your spirit against God,
23: 9 I t to the right, but I cannot see him.
30:24 "Surely one does not t against the needy,
33:17 that he may t them aside from their deeds,
36:18 do not let the greatness of the ransom t you aside.
36:21 Do not t to iniquity;
37:12 They t round and round by his guidance,
39:22 it does not t back from the sword.
Ps 6: 4 T, O LORD, save my life;
6:10 they shall t back, and in a moment be put

Ps 18:37 and did not **t** back until they were consumed.
18:40 You made my enemies **t** their backs to me,
22:27 of the earth shall remember and **t** to the LORD;
25:16 **T** to me and be gracious to me,
27: 9 Do not **t** your servant away in anger,
39:13 **T** your gaze away from me,
40: 4 who do not **t** to the proud,
44:10 You made us **t** back from the foe,
69:16 according to your abundant mercy, **t** to me.
70: 3 **t** back because of their shame.
73:10 Therefore the people **t** and praise them,
80:14 **T** again, O God of hosts;
80:18 Then we will never **t** back from you;
81:14 and **t** my hand against their foes.
85: 8 to those who **t** to him in their hearts.
86:16 **T** to me and be gracious to me;
90: 3 You **t** us back to dust, and say, "**T** back,
90:13 **T,** O LORD! How long?
106:23 to **t** away his wrath from destroying them.
114: 5 O Jordan, that you **t** back?
119:36 **T** my heart to your decrees,
119:37 **T** my eyes from looking at vanities;
119:39 **T** away the disgrace that I dread,
119:51 but I do not **t** away from your law.
119:59 I think of your ways, I **t** my feet to your decrees;
119:79 Let those who fear you **t** to me,
119:102 I do not **t** away from your ordinances,
119:132 **T** to me and be gracious to me,
125: 5 But those who **t** aside to their own crooked ways
132:10 For your servant David's sake do not **t** away
132:11 a sure oath from which he will not **t** back:
141: 4 Do not **t** my heart to any evil,
Pr 3: 7 fear the LORD, and **t** away from evil.
4: 5 nor **t** away from the words of my mouth.
4:15 **t** away from it and pass on.
4:27 **t** your foot away from evil.
7:25 Do not let your hearts **t** aside to her ways;
9: 4 that are simple, **t** in here!"
9:16 "You who are simple, **t** in here!"
13:19 but to **t** away from evil is an abomination to fools.
14:16 The wise are cautious and **t** away from evil,
17: 8 wherever they **t** they prosper.
24:18 and **t** away his anger from them.
29: 8 but the wise **t** away wrath.
30:30 among wild animals and does not **t** back
Ecc 3:20 all are from the dust, and all **t** to dust again.
SS 2:17 Until the day breathes and the shadows flee, **t,**
6: 5 **T** away your eyes from me,
Isa 1:25 I will **t** my hand against you;
2:22 **T** away from mortals, who have only breath
6:10 and comprehend with their minds, and **t** and
8:21 They will **t** their faces upward,
9:13 The people did not **t** to him who struck them,
10: 2 to **t** aside the needy from justice and to rob
13:14 all will **t** to their own people,
14:27 His hand is stretched out, and who will **t** it back?
28: 6 strength to those who **t** back the battle at the gate.
29:16 You **t** things upside down!
30:11 the way, **t** aside from the path, let us hear no more
30:21 you **t** to the right or when you **t** to the left,
31: 6 **T** back to him whom you have deeply betrayed,
37:29 I will **t** you back on the way by which you came.
38: 8 on the dial of Ahaz **t** back ten steps."
42:15 I will **t** the rivers into islands,
42:16 I will **t** the darkness before them into light,
45:22 **T** to me and be saved, all the ends of the earth!
46: 4 even when you **t** gray I will carry you.
49:11 And I will **t** all my mountains into a road,
50: 5 and I was not rebellious, I did not **t** backward.
59:20 to those in Jacob who **t** from transgression,
63:17 **T** back for the sake of your servants,
Jer 2:21 did you **t** degenerate and become a wild vine?
3:19 My Father, and would not **t** from following me.
4:28 I have not relented nor will I **t** back.
5: 3 they have refused to **t** back.
6: 8 O Jerusalem, or I shall **t** from you in disgust,
8: 4 If they go astray, do they not **t** back?
8: 6 All of them **t** to their own course,
15: 1 yet my heart would not **t** toward this people.
15: 5 Who will **t** aside to ask about your welfare?
15: 7 they did not **t** from their ways.
15:19 Therefore thus says the LORD: If you **t** back,
15:19 they who will **t** to you, not you who will **t** to them.
17: 5 whose hearts **t** away from the LORD.
17:13 those who **t** away from you shall be recorded in
18:11 **T** now, all of you from your evil way,
18:20 to **t** away your wrath from them.
21: 4 I am going to **t** back the weapons of war that are
23:20 not **t** back until he has executed and accomplished
23:26 Will the hearts of the prophets ever **t** back—
25: 5 "**T** now, everyone of you,
26: 3 all of them, and will **t** from their evil way,
30:24 not **t** back until he has executed and accomplished
31:13 I will **t** their mourning into joy,
31:39 straight to the hill Gareb, and shall then **t** to Goah.
32:40 so that they may not **t** from me.
35:15 '**T** now everyone of you from your evil way,
36: 3 all of them may **t** from their evil ways,
36: 7 and that all of them will **t** from their evil ways,
42: 5 They in their **t** said to Jeremiah,
44: 5 to **t** from their wickedness and make no offerings
47: 3 parents do not **t** back for children,
49: 8 Flee, **t** back, get down low, inhabitants of Dedan!
Eze 3:19 and they do not **t** from their wickedness,
3:20 if the righteous **t** from their righteousness
4: 8 I am putting cords on you so that you cannot **t**
7:17 All hands shall grow feeble, all knees **t** to water.
Eze 13:22 to **t** from their wicked way and save their lives;
14: 6 Repent and **t** away from your idols;
14: 6 **t** away your faces from all your abominations.
16:42 and my jealousy shall **t** away from you;
18:21 But if the wicked **t** away from all their sins
18:23 rather that they should **t** from their ways and live?
18:24 the righteous **t** away from their righteousness
18:26 the righteous **t** away from their righteousness
18:27 when the wicked **t** away from
18:30 Repent and **t** from all your transgressions;
18:32 says the Lord GOD. **T,** then,
21: 7 every spirit will faint and all knees will **t** to water.
33: 8 not speak to warn the wicked to **t** from their ways,
33: 9 But if you warn the wicked to **t** from their ways,
33: 9 and they do not **t** from their ways,
33:11 but that the wicked **t** from their ways and live;
33:11 **t** back, **t** back from your evil ways;
33:12 it shall not make them stumble when they **t**
33:14 yet if they **t** from their sin and do what is lawful
33:18 When the righteous **t** from their righteousness,
33:19 And when the wicked **t** from their wickedness,
36: 9 I will **t** to you, and you shall be tilled and sown;
38: 4 I will **t** you around and put hooks into your jaws,
39: 2 I will **t** you around and drive you forward,
Da 2: 9 and misleading words to me until things take a **t.**
9:16 we pray, **t** away from your city Jerusalem,
11:18 Afterward he shall **t** to the coastlands,
11:18 indeed, he shall **t** his insolence back upon him.
11:19 Then he shall **t** back toward the fortresses
11:30 He shall **t** back and pay heed to those who forsake
Hos 2: 3 and **t** her into a parched land,
3: 1 though they **t** to other gods and love raisin cakes."
7:16 They **t** to that which does not profit;
Joel 2:14 Who knows whether he will not **t** and relent,
3: 4 I will **t** your deeds back upon your own heads
3: 7 I will **t** your deeds back upon your own heads.
Am 1: 8 I will **t** my hand against Ekron,
5: 7 Ah, you that **t** justice to wormwood,
8:10 I will **t** your feasts into mourning,
Jnh 3: 8 All shall **t** from their evil ways and from
3: 9 he may **t** from his fierce anger,
Mic 7:17 they shall **t** in dread to the LORD our God,
Zec 13: 7 I will **t** my hand against the little ones.
Mal 4: 6 He will **t** the hearts of parents to their children
Mt 5:39 But if anyone strikes you on the right cheek, **t**
7: 6 or they will trample them under foot and **t**
13:15 and understand with their heart and **t**—
24:18 the one in the field must not **t** back to get a coat.
Mk 4:12 so that they may not **t** again and be forgiven.'"
13:16 the one in the field must not **t** back to get a coat.
Lk 1:16 He will **t** many of the people of Israel to
1:17 to **t** the hearts of parents to their children,
17:31 and likewise anyone in the field must not **t** back.
Jn 12:40 and understand with their heart and **t**—
16:20 you will have pain, but your pain will **t** into joy.
Ac 3:19 and **t** to God so that your sins may be wiped out,
7:45 Our ancestors in **t** brought it in with Joshua
13: 8 and tried to **t** the proconsul away from the faith.
14:15 that you should **t** from these worthless things to
25:11 no one can **t** me over to them.
26:18 so that they may **t** from darkness to light and from
26:20 and **t** to God and do deeds consistent
28:27 and understand with their heart and **t**—
1Co 14:27 and each in **t**; and let one interpret.
15: 1 which you in **t** received, in which also you stand,
15: 3 as of first importance what I in **t** had received:
Gal 4: 9 how can you **t** back again to the weak
Php 1:19 the help of the Spirit of Jesus Christ this will **t** out
2Ti 2:19 the name of the Lord **t** away from wickedness."
4: 4 and will **t** away from listening to the truth
1Pe 3:11 let them **t** away from evil and do good;
2Pe 2:21 to **t** back from the holy commandment
Rev 11: 6 and they have authority over the waters to **t** them
Tob 3: 6 and do not, O Lord, **t** your face away from me.
3:12 And now, Lord, I **t** my face to you,
4: 7 not **t** your face away from anyone who is poor,
13: 6 If you **t** to him with all your heart and
13: 6 he will **t** to you and will no longer hide his face
13: 6 '**T** back, you sinners, and do what is right
Jdt 7:30 by that time the Lord our God will **t** his mercy
8:23 but the Lord our God will **t** it to dishonor.
AdE 2:22 who in **t** revealed the plot to the king.
13:17 **t** our mourning into feasting that we may live
14:11 but **t** their plan against them,
14:13 and **t** his heart to hate the man who is fighting
Wis 2: 3 the body will **t** to ashes,
Sir 4: 4 or **t** your face away from the poor.
5: 7 Do not delay to **t** back to the Lord,
6:12 they **t** against you, and hide themselves from you.
7: 2 and it will **t** away from you.
9: 8 **T** away your eyes from a shapely woman,
9: 9 or your heart may **t** aside to her,
17:25 **T** back to the Lord and forsake your sins;
17:26 to the Most High and **t** away from iniquity,
39:27 but for sinners they **t** into evils.
46:11 not fall into idolatry and who did not **t** away from
48:10 to **t** the hearts of parents to their children,
Bar 2:13 Let your anger **t** away from us, for we are left,
2:29 surely **t** into a small number among the nations,
2:33 **t** from their stubbornness and their wicked deeds;
4: 2 **T,** O Jacob, and take her;
1Mc 2:62 for their splendor will **t** into dung and worms.
9:45 there is no place to **t.**
12:45 and will **t** around and go home.
16:18 asking him to send troops to aid him and to **t** over
2Mc 7: 8 Therefore he in **t** underwent tortures as
7:24 if he would **t** from the ways of his ancestors,
2Mc 10:13 He heard himself called a traitor at every **t,**
10:14 and at every **t** kept attacking the Jews.
1Es 1:28 Josiah, however, did not **t** back to his chariot,
2Es 1:24 I will **t** to other nations
1:31 I will **t** my face from you;
3:34 be found which way the **t** of the scale will incline.
7:*133* [63] to those who **t** in repentance to his law;
8:37 and it will **t** out according to your words.
11: 8 let each sleep in its own place, and watch in its **t;**
15:20 to **t** to me, says God, from the rising sun and from
15:20 to **t** and repay what they have given them.
15:31 and if they combine in great power and **t**
15:32 and silenced by their power, and shall **t** and flee.
16: 3 and who is there to **t** it back?
16: 7 Can one **t** back an arrow shot by a strong archer?
16:20 for all this they will not **t** from their iniquities,
4Mc 1:12 and then I shall **t** to their story,
1:17 This, in **t,** is education in the law,
7: 3 in no way did he **t** the rudder of religion
15:18 firstborn breathed his last, it did not **t** you aside,

TURNED‡ (331) [TURN]

Ge 9:23 their faces were **t** away, and they did
14: 7 then they **t** back and came to En-mishpat (that is,
18:22 So the men **t** from there, and went toward Sodom,
19: 3 so they **t** aside to him and entered his house;
30:30 and the LORD has blessed you wherever I **t.**
41:13 As he interpreted to us, so it **t** out;
42:24 He **t** away from them and wept;
42:28 At this they lost heart and **t** trembling
Ex 3: 4 When the LORD saw that he had **t** aside to see,
5:22 Then Moses **t** again to the LORD and said,
7:15 take in your hand the staff that was **t** into a snake.
7:17 and it shall be **t** to blood.
7:20 and all the water in the river was **t** into blood,
7:23 Pharaoh **t** and went into his house,
8:17 of the earth **t** into gnats throughout the whole land
10: 6 Then he **t** and went out from Pharaoh.
14:21 and **t** the sea into dry land;
14:25 He clogged their chariot wheels so that they **t**
25:20 of the cherubim shall be **t** toward the mercy seat.
32:15 Then Moses **t** and went down from the mountain,
37: 9 of the cherubim were **t** toward the mercy seat.
Lev 6:22 to be **t** entirely into smoke.
8:16 and **t** them into smoke on the altar.
8:20 and Moses **t** into smoke the head and the parts
8:21 Moses **t** into smoke the whole ram on the altar;
8:28 from their hands and **t** them into smoke on
9:10 from the sin offering he **t** into smoke on the altar,
9:13 and the head, which he **t** into smoke on the altar.
9:14 **t** them into smoke on the altar.
9:17 he **t** it into smoke on the altar,
9:20 and the fat was **t** into smoke on the altar;
13: 3 and if the hair in the diseased area has **t** white and
13: 4 and the hair in it has not **t** white,
13:10 if there is a white swelling in the skin that has **t**
13:13 since it has all **t** white, he is clean.
13:17 and if the disease has **t** white,
13:20 the skin and its hair has **t** white,
13:25 in the spot has **t** white and it appears deeper than
26:23 in spite of these punishments you have not **t** back
Nu 5:19 if you have not **t** aside to uncleanness while
12:10 And Aaron **t** towards Miriam and saw
14:43 you have **t** back from following the LORD,
16:42 Moses and Aaron **t** toward the tent of meeting;
20:21 so Israel **t** away from them.
21:33 Then they **t** and went up the road to Bashan;
22:23 the donkey **t** off the road, and went into the field;
22:33 and **t** away from me these three times.
22:33 If it had not **t** away from me,
25:11 has **t** back my wrath from the Israelites
33: 7 and **t** back to Pi-hahiroth,
Dt 9:15 So I **t** and went down from the mountain,
10: 5 So I **t** and came down from the mountain,
23: 5 the LORD your God **t** the curse into a blessing
29:26 They **t** and served other gods, worshiping them,
Jos 7: 5 The hearts of the people melted and **t** to water.
7: 8 now that Israel has **t** their backs to their enemies!
7:26 Then the LORD **t** from his burning anger.
8:20 for the people who fled to the wilderness **t** back
8:21 then they **t** back and struck down the men of Ai.
10:38 with all Israel, **t** back to Debir and assaulted it,
11:10 Joshua **t** back at that time, and took Hazor,
Jdg 2:17 They soon **t** aside from the way
3:19 But he himself **t** back at the sculptured stones
4:18 So he **t** aside to her into the tent,
6:14 Then the LORD **t** to him and said,
7:13 it **t** upside down, and the tent collapsed."
11: 8 "Nevertheless, we have now **t** back to you,
14: 8 and he **t** aside to see the carcass of the lion,
15: 4 and he **t** the foxes tail to tail,
18:15 So they **t** in that direction and came to the house
18:23 who **t** around and said to Micah,
18:26 he **t** and went back to his home.
19:15 They **t** aside there, to go in and spend the night
20:41 Then the main body of Israel **t,**
20:42 Therefore they **t** away from the Israelites in
20:45 When they **t** and fled toward the wilderness to
20:47 But six hundred **t** and fled toward the wilderness
20:48 the Israelites **t** back against the Benjaminites,
21: 8 It **t** out that no one from Jabesh-gilead had come
Ru 1:13 because the hand of the LORD has **t** against me."
3: 8 At midnight the man was startled, and **t** over,
1Sa 6:12 they **t** neither to the right nor to the left,
8: 3 not follow in his ways, but **t** aside after gain;
10: 6 be in a prophetic frenzy along with them and be **t**

1Sa 10: 9 As he t away to leave Samuel,
13:17 one company t toward Ophrah,
13:18 another company t toward Beth-horon,
13:18 and another company t toward the mountain
14:21 into the camp t and joined the Israelites who were
14:47 wherever he t he routed them.
15:11 for he has t back from following me,
15:27 As Samuel t to go away,
15:31 So Samuel t back after Saul;
17:30 He t away from him toward another and spoke in
17:35 and if it t against me, I would catch it by the jaw,
22:18 Doeg the Edomite t and attacked the priests;
25:12 So David's young men t away,
28:15 and God has t away from me
28:16 LORD has t from you and become your enemy?
2Sa 18:30 So he t aside, and stood still.
19: 2 So the victory that day was t into mourning for all
1Ki 2:15 kingdom has t about and become my brother's,
8:14 the king t around and blessed all the assembly
11: 3 and his wives t away his heart.
11: 4 his wives t away his heart after other gods;
11: 9 because his heart had t away from the LORD,
18:37 are God, and that you have t their hearts back."
20:39 then a soldier t and brought a man to me,
21: 4 He lay down on his bed, t away his face,
22:32 So they t to fight against him;
22:33 they t back from pursuing him.
2Ki 2:24 When he t around and saw them,
5:12 He t and went away in a rage.
13:23 he t toward them, because of his covenant
15:20 So the king of Assyria t back,
20: 2 Then Hezekiah t his face to the wall and prayed
23:16 As Josiah t, he saw the tombs there on the mount;
23:16 he t and looked up at the tomb of the man
23:25 who t to the LORD with all his heart,
24: 1 then he t and rebelled against him.
1Ch 10:14 the LORD put him to death and t the kingdom
21:20 Ornan t and saw the angel;
2Ch 6: 3 the king t around and blessed all the assembly
11: 4 and t back from the expedition against Jeroboam.
12:12 the wrath of the LORD t from him,
13:14 When Judah t, the battle was in front of them and
15: 4 but when in their distress they t to the LORD,
18:31 So they t to fight against him;
18:32 they t back from pursuing him.
25:27 that Amaziah t away from the LORD they made
29: 6 and have t away their faces from the dwelling of
29: 6 the dwelling of the LORD, and t their backs.
Ezr 6:22 and had t the heart of the king of Assyria to them,
Ne 2:15 Then I t back and entered by the Valley Gate,
9:28 yet when they t and cried to you,
9:29 They t a stubborn shoulder
13: 2 yet our God t the curse into a blessing.
Est 9:22 the month that had been t for them from sorrow
Job 1: 1 one who feared God and t away from evil.
19:19 and those whom I loved have t against me.
20:14 yet their food is t in their stomachs;
23:11 I have kept his way and have not t aside.
28: 5 but underneath it is t up as by fire.
30:15 Terrors are t upon me; my honor is pursued
30:21 You have t cruel to me;
30:31 My lyre is t to mourning,
31: 7 if my step has t aside from the way,
34:27 because they t aside from following him,
41:28 slingstones, for it, are t to chaff.
Ps 9: 3 When my enemies t back,
30:11 You have t my mourning into dancing;
35: 4 be t back and confounded who devise evil
40:14 let those be t back and brought
44:18 Our heart has not t back,
66: 6 He t the sea into dry land;
70: 2 be t back and brought to dishonor who desire
78: 9 armed with the bow, t back on the day of battle.
78:44 He t their rivers to blood,
78:57 but t away and were faithless like their ancestors;
85: 3 you t from your hot anger.
89:43 Moreover, you have t back the edge of his sword,
105:25 whose hearts he then t to hate his people,
105:29 He t their waters into blood,
114: 3 The sea looked and fled; Jordan t back.
129: 5 be put to shame and t backward.
141: 8 my eyes are t toward you, O GOD, my Lord;
Ecc 2:12 So I t to consider wisdom and madness and folly;
2:20 So I t and gave my heart up to despair
7:25 I t my mind to know and to search out and
SS 5: 6 but my beloved had t and was gone.
6: 1 Which way has your beloved t,
Isa 5:25 For all this his anger has not t away,
9:12 For all this his anger has not t away;
9:17 For all this his anger has not t away,
9:21 For all this his anger has not t away;
10: 4 For all this his anger has not t away;
12: 1 your anger t away, and you comforted me.
21: 4 the twilight I longed for has been t for me
34: 9 And the streams of Edom shall be t into pitch,
38: 2 Then Hezekiah t his face to the wall,
38: 8 So the sun t back on the dial the ten steps
42:17 They shall be t back and utterly put to shame—
43:14 and the shouting of the Chaldeans will be t
53: 6 we have all t to our own way,
56:11 they have all t to their own way,
59:14 Justice is t back, and righteousness stands at
Jer 2:27 they have t their backs to me, and not their faces.
2:35 surely his anger has t from me."
4: 8 "The fierce anger of the LORD has not t away
5:23 they have t aside and gone away.
5:25 Your iniquities have t these away,
Jer 6:12 Their houses shall be t over to others,
8: 5 Why then has this people t away
11:10 They have t back to the iniquities
23:22 and they would have t them from their evil way,
30: 6 Why has every face t pale?
31:19 For after I had t away I repented;
32:33 They have t their backs to me, not their faces;
34:11 But afterward they t around and took back
34:16 but then you t around and profaned my name
36:16 they t to one another in alarm, and said to Baruch,
41:14 from Mizpah t around and came back,
46:21 they too have t and fled together,
48:39 How Moab has t his back in shame!
49:24 Damascus has become feeble, she t to flee,
50: 5 with faces t toward it, and they shall come
La 1:13 for my feet; he t me back;
5: 2 Our inheritance has been t over to strangers,
5:15 our dancing has been t to mourning.
Eze 6: 9 by their wanton heart that t away from me,
6: 9 and their wanton eyes that t after their idols.
17: 6 Its branches t toward him,
18:28 Because they considered and t away from all
23:17 she t from them in disgust.
23:18 I t in disgust from her, as I had t from her sister.
23:22 from whom you t in disgust, and I will bring them
23:28 the hands of those from whom you t in disgust;
28:18 it consumed you, and I t you to ashes on the earth
29:16 when they t to them for aid.
41:19 a human face t toward the palm tree on
41:19 the face of a young lion t toward the palm tree on
42:17 Then he t and measured the north side,
42:18 Then he t and measured the south side,
42:19 Then he t to the west side and measured,
Da 5: 6 king's face t pale, and his thoughts terrified him.
5: 9 became greatly terrified and his face t pale,
7:28 thoughts greatly terrified me, and my face t pale;
9: 3 Then I t to the Lord God,
9:11 "All Israel has transgressed your law and t aside,
10:15 I t my face toward the ground
Hos 7: 8 Ephraim is a cake not t.
14: 4 for my anger has t from them.
Joel 1: 7 their branches have t white.
2:31 The sun shall be t to darkness,
Am 6:12 But you have t justice into poison and the fruit
Jnh 3:10 how they t from their evil ways,
Zep 1: 6 those who have t back from following
3:15 he has t away your enemies.
Zec 7:11 they refused to listen, and t a stubborn shoulder,
14:10 The whole land shall be t into a plain from Geba
Mal 2: 6 and he t many from iniquity.
2: 8 But you have t aside from the way;
3: 7 since the days of your ancestors you have t aside
Mt 9:22 Jesus t, and seeing her he said, "Take heart,
16:23 But he t and said to Peter, "Get behind me, Satan!
Mk 5:30 Jesus t about in the crowd and said,
Lk 9:55 But he t and rebuked them.
14:25 and he t and said to them,
17:15 when he saw that he was healed, t back,
22:32 and you, when once you have t back,
22:61 The Lord t and looked at Peter.
23:28 But Jesus t to them and said,
Jn 1:38 When Jesus t and saw them following,
6:66 of his disciples t back and no longer went about
20:14 she t around and saw Jesus standing there,
20:16 She t and said to him in Hebrew, "Rabbouni!"
21:20 Peter t and saw the disciple whom Jesus loved
Ac 1:25 from which Judas t aside to go to his own place."
2:20 sun shall be t to darkness and the moon to blood,
7:39 and in their hearts they t back to Egypt,
7:42 But God t away from them and handed them over
9:35 the residents of Lydda and Sharon saw him and t
9:40 He t to the body and said, "Tabitha, get up."
11:21 great number became believers and t to the Lord.
16:18 Paul, very much annoyed, t and said to the spirit,
27:15 the ship was caught and could not be t head-on
Ro 3:12 All have t aside, together they have become
1Th 1: 9 and how you t to God from idols,
3: 4 so it t out, as you know.
1Ti 1: 6 Some people have deviated from these and t
1:20 whom I have t over to Satan,
5:15 For some have already t away to follow Satan.
2Ti 1:15 that all who are in Asia have t away from me,
Jas 4: 9 Let your laughter be t into mourning and your joy
Rev 1:12 I t to see whose voice it was that spoke to me,
Tob 2: 6 "Your festivals shall be t into mourning,
4: 7 and the face of God will not be t away from you.
8:16 It has not t out as I expected,
Jdt 1:14 and t its glory into disgrace.
16:11 and the enemy were t back.
AdE 7: 8 Haman, when he heard, t away his face.
15: 7 The queen faltered, and t pale and faint,
Wis 16: 7 For the one who t toward it was saved,
Sir 33:12 and t them out of their place.
39:23 as when he t a watered land into salt.
45:23 and standing firm, when the people t away,
Bar 1:13 the Lord and his wrath have not t away from us.
4:12 because they t away from the law of God.
4:34 and her insolence will be t to grief.
Sus 1: 9 and t away their eyes from looking to Heaven
1:47 All the people t to him and asked,
1Mc 1:18 and Ptolemy t and fled before him,
1:39 her feasts were t into mourning,
1:40 her exaltation was t into mourning.
3: 8 thus he t away wrath from Israel.
3:34 And he t over to Lysias half of his forces and
4:16 Judas and his force t back from pursuing them,
4:27 nor had they t out as the king had ordered.
1Mc 5:28 Then Judas and his army quickly t back by
5:35 Next he t aside to Maapha,
5:68 But Judas t aside to Azotus in the land of
6: 6 but had t and fled before the Jews;
6: 8 things had not t out for him as he had planned.
6:47 and the fierce attack of the forces, they t away
9:16 they t and followed close behind Judas
9:41 So the wedding was t into mourning and the voice
9:72 then he t and went back to his own land,
11:72 Then he t back to the battle against the enemy
12:31 So Jonathan t aside against
12:33 He t aside to Joppa and took it by surprise,
12:51 that they would fight for their lives, they t back.
13:24 Then Trypho t and went back to his own land.
2Mc 5:18 this man would have been flogged and t back
8: 5 for the wrath of the Lord had t to mercy.
10:22 Then he killed these men who had t traitor,
12:42 and they t to supplication,
13:19 was t back, attacked again, and was defeated.
13:26 how the king's attack and withdrawal t out.
15:37 This, then, is how matters t out with Nicanor,
1Es 8:87 but we t back again to transgress your law
3Mc 1: 3 and so it t out that this man incurred
1:27 those who were around him observed this, they t,
6:15 O Lord, and have not t your face from us;
6:21 The animals t back upon the armed forces
6:22 the king's anger was t to pity and tears because of
2Es 7:30 Then the world shall be t back to primeval silence
9:39 with which I had been engaged, and t to her
11:31 and how the head t with those that were with it
13: 3 and wherever he t his face to look,
4Mc 13: 5 in those who were not t back by fiery agonies?

TURNING‡ (45) [TURN]

Ge 3:24 a sword flaming and t to guard the way to the tree
Nu 20:17 we will go along the King's Highway, not t aside
Dt 11:16 Take care, or you will be seduced into t away,
17:20 nor t aside from the commandment,
29:18 whose heart is already t away from
31:18 of all the evil they have done by t to other gods.
31:29 t aside from the way that I have commanded you.
Jos 15: 7 and so northward, t toward Gilgal,
18:14 t on the western side southward from
22:16 the God of Israel in t away today from following
23: 6 t aside from it neither to the right nor to the left,
2Sa 2:19 t neither to the right nor to the left
2Ki 21:13 wiping it and t it upside down.
2Ch 36:13 and hardened his heart against t to the LORD,
Isa 57:17 but they kept t back to their own ways.
59:13 and t away from following our God,
Jer 14: 8 like a traveler t aside for the night?
50: 6 t them away on the mountains;
Eze 1: 9 each of them moved straight ahead, without t
1:12 they went, without t as they went.
Da 9: 5 t aside from your commandments and ordinances.
9:13 t from our iniquities and reflecting on his fidelity.
Hos 11: 7 My people are bent on t away from me.
Mk 8:33 But t and looking at his disciples,
Lk 7: 9 and t to the crowd that followed him, he said,
7:44 Then t toward the woman, he said to Simon,
10:23 Then t to the disciples, Jesus said
Ac 3:26 by t each of you from your wicked ways."
13:46 we are now t to the Gentiles.
15:19 not trouble those Gentiles who are t to God,
17: 6 "These people who have been t the world upside
Gal 1: 6 of Christ and are t to a different gospel—
2Pe 2: 6 and if by t the cities of Sodom and Gomorrah
Rev 1:12 and on t I saw seven golden lampstands,
Sir 8: 5 Do not reproach one who is t away from sin;
11:31 for they lie in wait, t good into evil,
33: 5 and his thoughts like a t axle.
38:29 the potter sitting at his work and t the wheel
Bar 2: 8 not entreated the favor of the Lord by t away,
Aza 1: 6 and broken your law in t away from you;
Sus 1:14 But t back, they met again;
1Mc 2:22 by t aside from our religion to the right hand or to
2Mc 9: 4 the idea of t upon the Jews the injury done
3Mc 1: 4 matters were t out rather in favor of Antiochus,
6: 6 moistening the fiery furnace with dew and t

TURNS‡ (48) [TURN]

Ge 27:44 until your brother's fury t away—
27:45 until your brother's anger against you t away,
Lev 13: 2 it t into a leprous disease on the skin of his body,
13:16 But if the raw flesh again t white,
Dt 30:17 But if your heart t away and you do not hear,
Jos 19:27 then it t eastward, goes to Beth-dagon,
19:29 then the boundary t to Ramah, reaching to
19:29 the boundary t to Hosah, and it ends at the sea;
19:34 then the boundary t westward to Aznoth-tabor,
Ru 3:18 my daughter, until you learn how the matter t out,
Job 1: 8 and upright man who fears God and t away
2: 3 and upright man who fears God and t away
24:18 no treader t toward their vineyards.
30:30 My skin t black and falls from me,
Ps 107:33 He t rivers into a desert,
107:35 He t a desert into pools of water,
114: 8 who t the rock into a pool of water,
Pr 15: 1 A soft answer t away wrath,
21: 1 he t it wherever he will.
26:14 door t on its hinges, so does a lazy person in bed.
28:27 but one who t a blind eye will get many a curse.
Isa 44:25 who t back the wise, and makes their knowledge
59:15 and whoever t from evil is despoiled.
Jer 13:16 he t it into gloom and makes it deep darkness.
18: 8 concerning which I have spoken, t from its evil,

Jer 23:14 so that no one **t** from wickedness;
La 1: 8 she herself groans, and **t** her face away.
3: 3 against me alone he **t** his hand,
Am 5: 8 and **t** deep darkness into the morning,
Na 2: 8 Halt!"—but no one **t** back.
Lk 17: 4 and **t** back to you seven times and says, 'I repent,'
2Co 3:16 but when one **t** to the Lord, the veil is removed.
Heb 3:12 unbelieving heart that **t** away from the living God.
2Pe 2:22 "The dog **t** back to its own vomit," and,
Tob 5:14 It **t** out that you are a kinsman,
Jdt 8:11 to our enemies unless the Lord **t** and helps us
Wis 2: 5 because it is sealed up and no one **t** back.
8: 8 she understands **t** of speech and the solutions
Sir 14: 8 he **t** away and disregards people.
18:13 and **t** them back, as a shepherd his flock.
18:24 of vengeance when he **t** away his face.
26:28 and a man who **t** back from righteousness to sin—
30: 1 so that he may rejoice at the way he **t** out.
30: 8 An unbroken horse **t** out stubborn,
30: 8 and an unchecked son **t** out headstrong.
37: 2 like that for death itself when a dear friend **t** into
1Es 3:20 It **t** every thought to feasting and mirth,
2Es 14:42 and by **t** they wrote what was dictated,

TURQUOISE (4)

Ex 28:18 the second row a **t**, a sapphire and a moonstone;
39:11 a **t**, a sapphire, and a moonstone;
Eze 27:16 they exchanged for your wares **t**, purple,
28:13 beryl, onyx, and jasper, sapphire, **t**, and emerald;

TURTLE[S] (KJV) See DOVE, TURTLEDOVES

TURTLEDOVE (4) [TURTLEDOVES]

Ge 15: 9 a ram three years old, a **t**, and a young pigeon."
Lev 12: 6 and a pigeon or a **t** for a sin offering.
SS 2:12 and the voice of the **t** is heard in our land.
Jer 8: 7 and the **t**, swallow, and crane observe the time

TURTLEDOVES (10) [TURTLEDOVE]

Lev 1:14 you shall choose your offering from **t** or pigeons.
5: 7 that you have committed, two **t** or two pigeons,
5:11 But if you cannot afford two **t** or two pigeons,
12: 8 she shall take two **t** or two pigeons,
14:22 also two **t** or two pigeons,
14:30 of the **t** or pigeons such as he can afford,
15:14 the eighth day he shall take two **t** or two pigeons
15:29 the eighth day she shall take two **t** or two pigeons
Nu 6:10 On the eighth day they shall bring two **t**
Lk 2:24 "a pair of **t** or two young pigeons."

TUSKS (3)

Eze 27:15 they brought you in payment ivory **t** and ebony.
Da 7: 5 had three **t** in its mouth among its teeth
2Es 15:30 and with their **t** they shall devastate a portion of

TUTORS (KJV) See TRUSTEE

TWAIN (KJV) See SECOND, TWO

TWELFTH‡ (33) [TWELVE]

Nu 7:78 On the **t** day Ahira son of Enan,
1Ki 19:19 and he was with the **t**.
2Ki 8:25 In the **t** year of King Joram son of Ahab of Israel,
17: 1 In the **t** year of King Ahaz of Judah,
25:27 in the **t** month, on the twenty-seventh day of
1Ch 24:12 the eleventh to Eliashib, the **t** to Jakim,
25:19 **t** to Hashabiah, his sons and his brothers, twelve;
27:15 **T**, for the **t** month, was Heldai the Netophathite,
2Ch 34: 3 the **t** year he began to purge Judah and Jerusalem
Ezr 8:31 on the **t** day of the first month, to go to Jerusalem;
Est 3: 7 in the **t** year of King Ahasuerus, they cast Pur—
3: 7 the lot fell on the thirteenth day of the **t** month,
3:13 in one day, the thirteenth day of the **t** month,
8:12 on the thirteenth day of the **t** month,
9: 1 Now in the **t** month, which is the month of Adar,
Jer 52:31 in the **t** month, on the twenty-fifth day of
Eze 29: 1 in the tenth month, on the **t** day of the month,
32: 1 In the **t** year, in the **t** month,
32:17 In the **t** year, in the first month,
33:21 In the **t** year of our exile, in the tenth month,
Rev 21:20 the eleventh jacinth, the **t** amethyst.
Jdt 1: 1 It was the **t** year of the reign of Nebuchadnezzar,
AdE 2:16 Esther went in to King Artaxerxes in the **t** month,
3: 7 In the **t** year of King Artaxerxes Haman came to
3:13 the Jewish people on a given day of the **t** month,
8:12 the thirteenth of the **t** month, which is Adar,
9: 1 Now on the thirteenth day of the **t** month,
13: 6 on the fourteenth day of the **t** month, Adar,
16:20 so that on the thirteenth day of the **t** month, Adar,
2Mc 15:36 to celebrate the thirteenth day of the **t** month—
1Es 8:61 the river Theras on the **t** day of the first month;

TWELVE‡ (214) [TWELFTH]

A. TWELVE TRIBES (11)

Ge 5: 8 the days of Seth were nine hundred **t** years;
14: 4 **T** years they had served Chedorlaomer,
17:20 he shall be the father of **t** princes,
25:16 **t** princes according to their tribes.
35:22 Now the sons of Jacob were **t**.
42:13 They said, "We, your servants, are **t** brothers,
42:32 We are **t** brothers, sons of our father;
49:28 All these are the **t** tribes of Israel, A
Ex 15:27 where there were **t** springs of water
24: 4 the mountain, and set up **t** pillars, corresponding
24: 4 corresponding to the **t** tribes of Israel. A
28:21 There shall be **t** stones with names corresponding
28:21 each engraved with its name, for the **t** tribes. A
39:14 There were **t** stones with names corresponding to
39:14 each engraved with its name, for the **t** tribes. A
Lev 24: 5 and bake **t** loaves of it;
Nu 1:44 **t** men, each representing his ancestral house.
7: 3 six covered wagons and **t** oxen,
7:84 **t** silver plates, **t** silver basins, **t** golden dishes,
7:86 the **t** golden dishes, full of incense,
7:87 all the livestock for the burnt offering **t** bulls,
7:87 **t** rams, **t** male lambs a year old, with their grain offering; and **t** male goats for a sin offering;
17: 2 and get **t** staffs from them,
17: 6 **t** staffs; and the staff of Aaron was among theirs.
29:17 On the second day: **t** young bulls, two rams,
31: 5 **t** thousand armed for battle.
33: 9 at Elim there were **t** springs of water
Dt 1:23 plan seemed good to me, and I selected **t** of you,
Jos 3:12 So now select **t** men from the tribes of Israel,
4: 2 "Select **t** men from the people,
4: 3 'Take **t** stones from here out of the middle of
4: 4 Joshua summoned the **t** men from the Israelites,
4: 8 took up **t** stones out of the middle of the Jordan,
4: 9 set up **t** stones in the middle of the Jordan,
4:20 Those **t** stones, which they had taken out of
8:25 both men and women, was **t** thousand—
18:24 **t** towns with their villages:
19:15 **t** towns with their villages.
21: 7 according to their families received **t** towns from
21:40 those allotted to them were **t** in all.
Jdg 19:29 grasping his concubine he cut her into **t** pieces,
21:10 So the congregation sent **t** thousand soldiers there
2Sa 2:15 **t** for Benjamin and Ishbaal son of Saul,
2:15 and **t** of the servants of David.
10: 6 and the men of Tob, **t** thousand men.
17: 1 "Let me choose **t** thousand men,
1Ki 4: 7 Solomon had **t** officials over all Israel,
4:26 and **t** thousand horsemen.
7:15 and a cord of **t** cubits would encircle it;
7:25 It stood on **t** oxen, three facing north,
7:44 the one sea, and the **t** oxen underneath the sea.
10:20 while **t** lions were standing,
10:26 and **t** thousand horses, which he stationed in
11:30 and tore it into **t** pieces.
16:23 he reigned for **t** years, six of them in Tirzah.
18:31 Elijah took **t** stones, according to the number of
19:19 There were **t** yoke of oxen ahead of him,
2Ki 3: 1 in Samaria; he reigned **t** years.
21: 1 Manasseh was **t** years old when he began to reign;
1Ch 6:63 to their families were allotted **t** towns out of
9:22 at the thresholds, were two hundred **t**.
15:10 with one hundred **t** of his kindred.
25: 9 to him and his brothers and his sons, **t**;
25:10 the third to Zaccur, his sons and his brothers, **t**;
25:11 the fourth to Izri, his sons and his brothers, **t**;
25:12 his sons and his brothers, **t**;
25:13 the sixth to Bukkiah, his sons and his brothers, **t**;
25:14 his sons and his brothers, **t**;
25:15 his sons and his brothers, **t**;
25:16 his sons and his brothers, **t**;
25:17 the tenth to Shimei, his sons and his brothers, **t**;
25:18 his sons and his brothers, **t**;
25:19 his sons and his brothers, **t**;
25:20 Shubael, his sons and his brothers, **t**;
25:21 Mattithiah, his sons and his brothers, **t**;
25:22 to Jeremoth, his sons and his brothers, **t**;
25:23 to Hananiah, his sons and his brothers, **t**;
25:24 to Joshbekashah, his sons and his brothers, **t**;
25:25 to Hanani, his sons and his brothers, **t**;
25:26 to Mallothi, his sons and his brothers, **t**;
25:27 to Eliathah, his sons and his brothers, **t**;
25:28 to Hothir, his sons and his brothers, **t**;
25:29 to Giddalti, his sons and his brothers, **t**;
25:30 to Mahazioth, his sons and his brothers, **t**;
25:31 to Romamti-ezer, his sons and his brothers, **t**.
2Ch 1:14 and **t** thousand horses, which he stationed in
4: 4 It stood on **t** oxen, three facing north,
4:15 the one sea, and the **t** oxen underneath it.
9:19 while **t** lions were standing,
9:25 for horses and chariots, and **t** thousand horses,
12: 3 with **t** hundred chariots
33: 1 Manasseh was **t** years old when he began to reign;
Ezr 2: 6 two thousand eight hundred **t**.
2:18 Of Jorah, one hundred **t**.
6:17 and as a sin offering for all Israel, **t** male goats,
8:24 Then I set apart **t** of the leading priests:
8:35 **t** bulls for all Israel, ninety-six rams,
8:35 and as a sin offering **t** male goats;
Ne 5:14 the thirty-second year of King Artaxerxes, **t** years,
7:24 Of Hariph, one hundred **t**.
Est 2:12 after being **t** months under the regulations for
Ps 60: T *Joab on his return killed t thousand Edomites*
Jer 52:20 the **t** bronze bulls that were under the sea,
52:21 its circumference was **t** cubits;
Eze 40:49 vestibule was twenty cubits, and the width **t** cubits;
43:16 **t** cubits long by **t** wide,
47:13 for inheritance among the **t** tribes of Israel. A
Da 4:29 At the end of **t** months he was walking on the roof
Mt 9:20 from hemorrhages for **t** years came up behind him
10: 1 Then Jesus summoned his **t** disciples
10: 2 These are the names of the **t** apostles:
10: 5 These **t** Jesus sent out with
11: 1 Jesus had finished instructing his **t** disciples,
14:20 over of the broken pieces, **t** baskets full.
19:28 also sit on **t** thrones, judging the twelve tribes
19:28 judging the **t** tribes of Israel. A
20:17 he took the **t** disciples aside by themselves,
26:14 Then one of the **t**, who was called Judas Iscariot,
26:20 it was evening, he took his place with the **t**;
26:47 he was still speaking, Judas, one of the **t**, arrived;
26:53 and he will at once send me more than **t** legions
Mk 3:14 And he appointed **t**, whom he
3:16 So he appointed the **t**: Simon (to whom
4:10 along with the **t** asked him about the parables.
5:25 from hemorrhages for **t** years.
5:42 and began to walk about (she was **t** years of age).
6: 7 He called the **t** and began to send them out two
6:43 up **t** baskets full of broken pieces and of the fish.
8:19 They said to him, "**T.**"
9:35 He sat down, called the **t**, and said to them,
10:32 the **t** aside again and began to tell them what was
11:11 he went out to Bethany with the **t**.
14:10 Then Judas Iscariot, who was one of the **t**,
14:17 When it was evening, he came with the **t**.
14:20 He said to them, "It is one of the **t**,
14:43 while he was still speaking, Judas, one of the **t**,
Lk 2:42 And when he was **t** years old,
6:13 he called his disciples and chose **t** of them,
8: 1 of God. The **t** were with him,
8:42 about **t** years old, who was dying.
8:43 from hemorrhages for **t** years;
9: 1 the **t** together and gave them power and authority
9:12 and the **t** came to him and said,
9:17 **t** baskets of broken pieces.
18:31 Then he took the **t** aside and said to them, "See,
22: 3 who was one of the **t**;
22:30 and you will sit on thrones judging the **t** tribes A
22:47 and the one called Judas, one of the **t**,
Jn 6:13 left by those who had eaten, they filled **t** baskets.
6:67 So Jesus asked the **t**, "Do you also wish
6:70 "Did I not choose you, the **t**?
6:71 though one of the **t**, was going to betray him.
11: 9 "Are there not **t** hours of daylight?
20:24 Thomas (who was called the Twin), one of the **t**,
Ac 6: 2 And the **t** called together the whole community of
7: 8 and Jacob of the **t** patriarchs.
19: 7 altogether there were about **t** of them.
24:11 not more than **t** days since I went up to worship
26: 7 a promise that our **t** tribes hope to attain, A
1Co 15: 5 and that he appeared to Cephas, then to the **t**.
Jas 1: 1 To the **t** tribes in the Dispersion: Greetings. A
Rev 7: 5 From the tribe of Judah **t** thousand sealed,
7: 5 from the tribe of Reuben **t** thousand,
7: 5 from the tribe of Gad **t** thousand,
7: 6 from the tribe of Asher **t** thousand,
7: 6 from the tribe of Naphtali **t** thousand,
7: 6 from the tribe of Manasseh **t** thousand,
7: 7 from the tribe of Simeon **t** thousand,
7: 7 from the tribe of Levi **t** thousand,
7: 7 from the tribe of Issachar **t** thousand,
7: 8 from the tribe of Zebulun **t** thousand,
7: 8 from the tribe of Joseph **t** thousand,
7: 8 from the tribe of Benjamin **t** thousand sealed.
12: 1 and on her head a crown of **t** stars.
21:12 high wall with **t** gates, and at the gates **t** angels,
21:12 the gates are inscribed the names of the **t** tribes A
21:14 And the wall of the city has **t** foundations, and on them are the **t** names of the **t** apostles of the Lamb.
21:21 And the **t** gates are **t** pearls,
22: 2 the river is the tree of life with its **t** kinds of fruit,
Tob 14: 2 in peace when he was one hundred **t** years old,
Jdt 2: 5 foot soldiers and **t** thousand cavalry.
2:15 together with **t** thousand archers on horseback,
7: 2 and **t** thousand cavalry, not counting the baggage
AdE 2:12 a girl was to go to the king was **t** months.
Sir 44:23 and distributed them among **t** tribes. A
49:10 the bones of the **T** Prophets send forth new life
Bel 1: 3 for it **t** bushels of choice flour and forty sheep
1Mc 1: 7 And after Alexander had reigned **t** years, he died.
1Es 5:11 two thousand eight hundred **t**.
5:16 The descendants of Arsiphurith, one hundred **t**.
5:41 All those of Israel, **t** or more years of age,
7: 8 and **t** male goats for the sin of all Israel,
7: 8 the number of the **t** leaders of the tribes of Israel;
8:35 and with him two hundred **t** men.
8:54 Then I set apart **t** of the leaders of the priests,
8:57 and **t** bronze vessels of fine bronze that glittered
8:65 the God of Israel, **t** bulls for all Israel,
8:66 and as a thank offering **t** male goats—
2Es 2:18 for you **t** trees loaded with various fruits,
11: 1 from the sea an eagle that had **t** feathered wings
11:22 And after this I looked and saw that the **t** wings
12:14 And **t** kings shall reign in it, one after another.
12:15 for a longer time than any other one of the **t**.
12:16 the interpretation of the **t** wings that you saw.
14:11 For the age is divided into **t** parts,

TWENTIETH (10) [TWENTY]

Nu 10:11 in the second month, on the **t** day of the month,
1Ki 15: 9 In the **t** year of King Jeroboam of Israel,
2Ki 15:30 in the **t** year of Jotham son of Uzziah.
1Ch 24:16 the nineteenth to Pethahiah, the **t** to Jehezkel,
25:27 to the **t**, to Eliathah, his sons
Ezr 10: 9 it was the ninth month, on the **t** day of the month.
Ne 1: 1 In the month of Chislev, in the **t** year,
2: 1 in the **t** year of King Artaxerxes,
5:14 from the **t** year to the thirty-second year
1Es 9: 5 on the **t** day of the month.

TWENTY‡ (175) [TWENTIETH]

Ge 6: 3 their days shall be one hundred t years."
18:31 Suppose t are found there."
18:31 "For the sake of t I will not destroy it."
31:38 These t years I have been with you;
31:41 These t years I have been in your house;
32:14 and t male goats, two hundred ewes and t rams,
32:15 t female donkeys and ten male donkeys.
37:28 sold him to the Ishmaelites for t pieces of silver.
Ex 26:18 t frames for the south side;
26:19 of silver under the t frames, two bases under
26:20 on the north side t frames,
27:10 its t pillars and their t bases shall be of bronze,
27:11 their pillars t and their bases t, of bronze,
27:16 of the court there shall be a screen t cubits long,
30:13 of the sanctuary (the shekel is t gerahs),
30:14 from t years old and upward,
36:23 t frames for the south side;
36:24 he made forty bases of silver under the t frames,
36:25 on the north side, he made t frames
38:10 its t pillars and their t bases were of bronze,
38:11 its t pillars and their t bases were of bronze,
38:18 It was t cubits long and, along the width of it,
38:26 from t years old and upward,
Lev 27: 3 from t to sixty years of age the equivalent shall
27: 5 If the age is from five to t years of age, the
equivalent is t shekels for a male
27:25 t gerahs shall make a shekel.
Nu 1: 3 from t years old and upward,
1:18 to the number of names from t years old
1:20 every male from t years old and upward,
1:22 every male from t years old and upward,
1:24 from t years old and upward,
1:26 from t years old and upward,
1:28 from t years old and upward,
1:30 from t years old and upward,
1:32 from t years old and upward,
1:34 from t years old and upward,
1:36 from t years old and upward,
1:38 from t years old and upward,
1:40 from t years old and upward,
1:42 from t years old and upward,
1:45 from t years old and upward,
3:47 the shekel of the sanctuary, a shekel of t gerahs.
7:86 of the dishes being one hundred t shekels;
11:19 or two days, or five days, or ten days, or t days,
14:29 from t years old and upward,
18:16 to the shekel of the sanctuary (that is, t gerahs).
26: 2 from t years old and upward,
26: 4 from t years old and upward,"
32:11 from t years old and upward,
Dt 31: 2 "I am now one hundred t years old.
34: 7 Moses was one hundred t years old when he died;
Jdg 4: 3 and had oppressed the Israelites cruelly t years.
8:10 hundred t thousand men bearing arms had fallen.
11:33 t towns, and as far as Abel-keramim.
15:20 in the days of the Philistines t years.
16:31 He had judged Israel t years.
1Sa 7: 2 a long time passed, some t years,
14:14 and his armor-bearer killed about t men within
2Sa 3:20 Abner came with t men to David at Hebron,
8: 4 and t thousand foot soldiers.
9:10 Now Ziba had fifteen sons and t servants.
10: 6 the Arameans of Zobah, t thousand foot soldiers,
18: 7 on that day, t thousand men.
19:17 with his fifteen sons and his t servants,
24: 8 to Jerusalem at the end of nine months and t days.
1Ki 4:23 and t pasture-fed cattle, one hundred sheep,
5:11 Solomon in turn gave Hiram t thousand cors
5:11 and t cors of fine oil.
6: 2 t cubits wide, and thirty cubits high.
6: 3 of the nave of the house was t cubits wide,
6:16 He built t cubits of the rear of the house
6:20 interior of the inner sanctuary was t cubits long, t
cubits wide, and t cubits high;
8:63 and one hundred t thousand sheep.
9:10 At the end of t years,
9:11 King Solomon gave to Hiram t cities in the land
9:14 to the king one hundred t talents of gold.
9:28 and imported from there four hundred t talents
10:10 she gave the king one hundred t talents of gold,
2Ki 4:42 t loaves of barley and fresh ears of grain
15:27 in Samaria; he reigned t years.
16: 2 Ahaz was t years old when he began to reign;
1Ch 7: 9 mighty warriors, was t thousand two hundred.
12:30 Of the Ephraimites, t thousand eight hundred,
12:37 one hundred t thousand armed with all
15: 5 Uriel the chief, with one hundred t of his kindred;
15: 6 with two hundred t of his kindred;
18: 4 and t thousand foot soldiers.
23:24 of the names of the individuals from t years old
23:27 of the Levites from t years old and upward—
27:23 David did not count those below t years of age,
2Ch 2:10 t thousand cors of crushed wheat, t thousand cors
of barley, t thousand baths of wine, and t thousand
3: 3 was sixty cubits, and the width t cubits.
3: 4 in front of the nave of the house was t cubits long,
3: 4 and its height was one hundred t cubits.
3: 8 was t cubits, and its width was t cubits;
3:11 wings of the cherubim together extended t cubits:
3:13 The wings of these cherubim extended t cubits;
4: 1 an altar of bronze, t cubits long, t cubits wide,
5:12 with one hundred t priests who were trumpeters).
7: 5 and one hundred t thousand sheep.
8: 1 At the end of t years,
9: 9 she gave the king one hundred t talents of gold,
2Ch 25: 5 He mustered those t years old and upward,
28: 1 Ahaz was t years old when he began to reign;
28: 6 of Remaliah killed one hundred t thousand
31:17 of the Levites from t years old and upwards was
Ezr 2:32 Of Harim, three hundred t.
2:67 and six thousand seven hundred t donkeys.
3: 8 from t years old and upward,
8:19 with his kin and their sons, t;
8:20 besides two hundred t of the temple servants,
8:27 t gold bowls worth a thousand darics,
Ne 7:35 Of Harim, three hundred t.
7:69 and six thousand seven hundred t donkeys.
7:71 into the building fund t thousand darics of gold
7:72 of the people gave was t thousand darics of gold,
Eze 4:10 that you eat shall be t shekels a day by weight;
40:14 He measured also the vestibule, t cubits;
40:49 The depth of the vestibule was t cubits,
41: 2 forty cubits, and its width, t cubits.
41: 4 depth of the room, t cubits, and its width, t cubits,
41:10 of t cubits all around the temple on every side.
42: 3 the t cubits that belonged to the inner court,
45: 1 and t thousand cubits wide;
45:12 The shekel shall be t gerahs.
45:12 T shekels, twenty-five shekels,
48: 9 in length, and t thousand in width.
48:13 and the width t thousand.
Da 6: 1 to set over the kingdom one hundred t satraps,
Jnh 4:11 a hundred and t thousand persons who do
Hag 2:16 When one came to a heap of t measures,
2:16 to draw fifty measures, there were but t.
Zec 5: 2 its length is t cubits, and its width ten cubits."
Lk 14:31 the one who comes against him with t thousand?
Jn 2: 6 each holding t or thirty gallons.
Ac 1:15 the crowd numbered about one hundred t persons)
27:28 So they took soundings and found t fathoms;
Tob 5: 3 now t years have passed since I left this money
Jdt 1:16 and feasted for one hundred t days.
2: 5 one hundred t thousand foot soldiers
2:15 one hundred t thousand of them,
1Mc 6:30 foot soldiers, t thousand horsemen,
8: 6 to fight against them with one hundred t elephants
8:15 every day three hundred t senators constantly
9: 4 and went to Berea with t thousand foot soldiers
11:45 to the number of a hundred and t thousand,
15:13 with him were one hundred t thousand warriors
16: 4 of the country t thousand warriors and cavalry,
2Mc 8: 9 in command of no fewer than t thousand Gentiles
8:20 destroyed one hundred t thousand Galatians
8:30 and Bacchides they killed more than t thousand
10:17 killing no fewer than t thousand.
10:23 he destroyed more than t thousand in
10:31 T thousand five hundred were slaughtered,
10:35 t young men in the army of Maccabeus,
12:20 with him one hundred t thousand infantry
1Es 4:51 that t talents a year should be given for
5:58 the Levites who were t or more years of age
8:48 and their descendants, t men;
8:49 two hundred t temple servants;
8:57 and t golden bowls, and twelve bronze vessels

TWENTY-EIGHT (15)

Ex 26: 2 The length of each curtain shall be t cubits,
36: 9 The length of each curtain was t cubits,
2Ki 10:36 over Israel in Samaria was t years.
1Ch 12:35 t thousand six hundred equipped for battle.
2Ch 11:21 became the father of t sons and sixty daughters).
Ezr 2:23 Of Anathoth, one hundred t.
2:41 singers: the descendants of Asaph, one hundred t.
8:11 Zechariah son of Bebai, and with him t males.
Ne 7:16 Of Bebai, six hundred t.
7:22 Of Hashum, three hundred t.
7:27 Of Anathoth, one hundred t.
11: 8 And his brothers Gabbai, Sallai: nine hundred t.
11:14 valiant warriors, one hundred t;
1Es 5:27 the descendants of Asaph, one hundred t.
8:37 Zechariah son of Bebai, and with him t men.

TWENTY-FIFTH (9) [TWENTY-FIVE]

Ne 6:15 wall was finished on the t day of the month Elul,
Jer 52:31 in the twelfth month, on the t day of the month,
Eze 40: 1 In the t year of our exile,
1Mc 1:59 On the t day of the month they offered sacrifice
4:52 in the morning on the t day of the ninth month,
4:59 beginning with the t day of the month of Chislev.
2Mc 1:18 Since on the t day of Chislev we shall celebrate
10: 5 that is, on the t day of the same month,
3Mc 6:38 So their registration was carried out from the t

TWENTY-FIRST (4) [TWENTY-ONE]

Ex 12:18 the fourteenth day until the evening of the t day,
1Ch 24:17 the t to Jachin, the twenty-second to Gamul,
25:28 the t, to Hothir, his sons and his brothers, twelve;
Hag 2: 1 on the t day of the month,

TWENTY-FIVE‡ (45) [TWENTY-FIFTH]

Nu 8:24 from t years old and upward they shall begin
Jdg 20:35 Israelites destroyed t thousand one hundred men
20:46 of Benjamin were t thousand arms-bearing men,
1Ki 22:42 and he reigned t years in Jerusalem.
2Ki 14: 2 He was t years old when he began to reign,
15:33 He was t years old when he began to reign
18: 2 He was t years old when he began to reign;
23:36 Jehoiakim was t years old when he began
2Ch 20:31 he reigned t years in Jerusalem.
25: 1 Amaziah was t years old when he began to reign,
2Ch 27: 1 Jotham was t years old when he began to reign;
27: 8 He was t years old when he began to reign;
29: 1 Hezekiah began to reign when he was t years old;
36: 5 Jehoiakim was t years old when he began
Ezr 2:33 Of Lod, Hadid, and Ono, seven hundred t.
Eze 8:16 the porch and the altar, were about t men,
11: 1 There, at the entrance of the gateway, were t men;
40:13 a width of t cubits, from wall to wall.
40:21 its depth was fifty cubits, and its width t cubits.
40:25 its depth was fifty cubits, and its width t cubits.
40:29 its depth was fifty cubits, and its width t cubits.
40:30 t cubits deep and five cubits wide.
40:33 its depth was fifty cubits, and its width t cubits.
40:36 Its depth was fifty cubits, and its width t cubits.
45: 1 the land as a holy district, t thousand cubits long
45: 3 a section t thousand cubits long
45: 5 Another section, t thousand cubits long
45: 6 and t thousand cubits long;
45:12 Twenty shekels, t shekels,
48: 8 t thousand cubits in width,
48: 9 the LORD shall be t thousand cubits in length,
48:10 an allotment measuring t thousand cubits on
48:10 and t thousand in length on the southern side,
48:13 an allotment t thousand cubits in length
48:13 The whole length shall be t thousand cubits and
48:15 five thousand cubits in width and t thousand
48:20 be t thousand cubits square,
48:21 from the t thousand cubits of the holy portion to
48:21 from the t thousand cubits to the west border,
2Mc 12:26 and slaughtered t thousand people.
12:28 as many as t thousand of those who were in it.
1Es 1:39 Jehoiakim was t years old when he began to reign
5:19 Those from Kiriatharim, t.
5:22 the other Calamolalus and Ono, seven hundred t.
5:43 and five thousand five hundred t donkeys.

TWENTY-FOUR‡ (27) [TWENTY-FOURTH]

Nu 7:88 for the sacrifice of well-being t bulls,
25: 9 those that died by the plague were t thousand.
2Sa 21:20 and six toes on each foot, t in number;
1Ki 15:33 at Tirzah; he reigned t years.
1Ch 20: 6 and six toes on each foot, t in number;
23: 4 "T thousand of these," David said,
27: 1 each division numbering t thousand:
27: 2 in his division were t thousand.
27: 4 In his division were t thousand.
27: 5 in his division were t thousand.
27: 7 in his division were t thousand.
27: 8 in his division were t thousand.
27: 9 in his division were t thousand.
27:10 in his division were t thousand.
27:11 in his division were t thousand.
27:12 in his division were t thousand.
27:13 in his division were t thousand.
27:14 in his division were t thousand.
27:15 in his division were t thousand.
Ne 7:23 Of Bezai, three hundred t.
Rev 4: 4 Around the throne are t thrones,
4: 4 and seated on the thrones are t elders,
4:10 the t elders fall before the one who is seated on
5: 8 the four living creatures and the t elders fell
11:16 Then the t elders who sit on their thrones
19: 4 the t elders and the four living creatures fell down
2Es 14:45 "Make public the t books that you wrote first,

TWENTY-FOURTH (10) [TWENTY-FOUR]

1Ch 24:18 the twenty-third to Delaiah, the t to Maaziah.
25:31 to the t, to Romamti-ezer, his sons
Ne 9: 1 Now on the t day of this month the people
Da 10: 4 On the t day of the first month,
Hag 1:15 on the t day of the month,
2:10 On the t day of the ninth month,
2:18 from the t day of the ninth month.
2:20 a second time to Haggai on the t day of
Zec 1: 7 On the t day of the eleventh month,
2Mc 11:21 one hundred forty-eighth year, Dioscorinthius t."

TWENTY-NINE (9)

Ge 11:24 When Nahor had lived t years,
Ex 38:24 was t talents and seven hundred thirty shekels,
Jos 15:32 in all, t towns, with their villages.
2Ki 14: 2 and he reigned t years in Jerusalem.
18: 2 he reigned t years in Jerusalem.
2Ch 25: 1 and he reigned t years in Jerusalem.
29: 1 he reigned t years in Jerusalem.
Ezr 1: 9 silver basins, one thousand; knives, t;
1Es 2:13 one thousand silver cups, t silver censers,

TWENTY-ONE (9) [TWENTY-FIRST]

2Ki 24:18 Zedekiah was t years old when he began to reign;
2Ch 36:11 Zedekiah was t years old when he began to reign;
Ezr 2:26 Of Ramah and Geba, six hundred t.
Ne 7:30 Of Ramah and Geba, six hundred t.
7:37 Of Lod, Hadid, and Ono, seven hundred t.
Jer 52: 1 Zedekiah was t years old when he began to reign;
Da 10:13 of the kingdom of Persia opposed me t days.
1Es 1:46 Zedekiah was t years old,
5:20 Those from Kirama and Geba, six hundred t.

TWENTY-SECOND (3) [TWENTY-TWO]

1Ch 24:17 the twenty-first to Jachin, the t to Gamul,
25:29 to the t, to Giddalti, his sons
Jdt 2: 1 on the t day of the first month,

TWENTY-SEVEN‡ (11) [TWENTY-SEVENTH]

Ge 23: 1 Sarah lived one hundred **t** years;
1Ki 20:30 and the wall fell on **t** thousand men that were left.
Est 1: 1 over one hundred **t** provinces from India
8: 9 from India to Ethiopia, one hundred **t** provinces,
9:30 to the one hundred **t** provinces of the kingdom
AdE 1: 1 over one hundred **t** provinces from India
3:12 There were one hundred **t** provinces in all,
8: 9 from Media to Ethiopia, one hundred **t** provinces,
13: 1 of the hundred **t** provinces from India to Ethiopia
16: 1 from India to Ethiopia, one hundred **t** provinces,
1Es 3: 2 in the hundred **t** satrapies from India to Ethiopia.

TWENTY-SEVENTH (6) [TWENTY-SEVEN]

Ge 8:14 In the second month, on the **t** day of the month,
1Ki 16:10 in the **t** year of King Asa of Judah,
16:15 In the **t** year of King Asa of Judah,
2Ki 15: 1 In the **t** year of King Jeroboam
25:27 in the twelfth month, on the **t** day of the month,
Eze 29:17 In the **t** year, in the first month,

TWENTY-SIX (2) [TWENTY-SIXTH]

Jdg 20:15 the Benjaminites mustered **t** thousand armed men
1Ch 7:40 for service in war, was **t** thousand men.

TWENTY-SIXTH (1) [TWENTY-SIX]

1Ki 16: 8 In the **t** year of King Asa of Judah,

TWENTY-THIRD (10) [TWENTY-THREE]

2Ki 12: 6 But by the **t** year of King Jehoash
13: 1 the **t** year of King Joash son of Ahaziah of Judah,
1Ch 24:18 the **t** to Delaiah, the twenty-fourth to Maaziah.
25:30 to the **t**, to Mahazioth, his sons
2Ch 7:10 On the **t** day of the seventh month he sent
Est 8: 9 which is the month of Sivan, on the **t** day;
Jer 52:30 in the **t** year of Nebuchadrezzar, Nebuzaradan
AdE 8: 9 on the **t** day of the first month, that is, Nisan,
1Mc 13:51 On the **t** day of the second month,
1Es 7: 5 the holy house was finished by the **t** day of

TWENTY-THREE (19) [TWENTY-THIRD]

Nu 26:62 The number of those enrolled was **t** thousand,
33:39 Aaron was one hundred **t** years old when he died
Jdg 10: 2 He judged Israel **t** years.
2Ki 23:31 Jehoahaz was **t** years old when he began to reign;
1Ch 2:22 who had **t** towns in the land of Gilead.
2Ch 36: 2 Jehoahaz was **t** years old when he began to reign;
Ezr 2:11 Of Bebai, six hundred **t.**
2:17 Of Bezai, three hundred **t.**
2:19 Of Hashum, two hundred **t.**
2:21 Of Bethlehem, one hundred **t.**
2:28 Of Bethel and Ai, two hundred **t.**
Ne 7:32 Of Bethel and Ai, one hundred **t.**
Jer 25: 3 For **t** years, from the thirteenth year
52:28 in the seventh year, three thousand **t** Judeans;
1Co 10: 8 and **t** thousand fell in a single day.
1Es 1:34 who was **t** years old, and made him king
5:13 The descendants of Bebai, six hundred **t.**
5:16 The descendants of Bezai, three hundred **t.**
5:17 The descendants of Bethlomon, one hundred **t.**

TWENTY-TWO (30) [TWENTY-SECOND]

Nu 3:39 from a month old and upward, was **t** thousand.
3:43 was **t** thousand two hundred seventy-three.
26:14 of the Simeonites, **t** thousand two hundred.
Jos 19:30 **t** towns with their villages.
Jdg 7: 3 **t** thousand returned, and ten thousand remained.
10: 3 who judged Israel **t** years.
20:21 down on that day **t** thousand of the Israelites.
2Sa 8: 5 David killed **t** thousand men of the Arameans.
1Ki 8:63 of well-being to the LORD **t** thousand oxen
14:20 The time that Jeroboam reigned was **t** years;
16:29 of Omri reigned over Israel in Samaria **t** years.
2Ki 8:26 Ahaziah was **t** years old when he began to reign;
21:19 Amon was **t** years old when he began to reign;
1Ch 7: 2 the days of David being **t** thousand six hundred.
7: 7 by genealogies was **t** thousand thirty-four.
12:28 and **t** commanders from his own ancestral house.
18: 5 David killed **t** thousand Arameans.
2Ch 7: 5 as a sacrifice **t** thousand oxen
13:21 became the father of **t** sons and sixteen daughters.
33:21 Amon was **t** years old when he began to reign;
Ezr 2:12 Of Azgad, one thousand two hundred **t.**
2:27 The people of Michmas, one hundred **t.**
Ne 7:17 Of Azgad, two thousand three hundred **t.**
7:31 Of Michmas, one hundred **t.**
11:12 the work of the house, eight hundred **t;**
2Mc 5:24 with an army of **t** thousand,
13: 2 five thousand three hundred cavalry, **t** elephants,
1Es 5:13 one thousand three hundred **t.**
5:20 The Chadiasans and Ammidians, four hundred **t.**
5:21 Those from Macalon, one hundred **t.**

TWICE (30) [TWO]

Ge 43:10 we would now have returned **t.**"
Ex 16: 5 it will be **t** as much as they gather on other days."
16:22 On the sixth day they gathered **t** as much food,
Nu 20:11 up his hand and struck the rock **t** with his staff;
1Sa 18:11 But David eluded him **t.**
26: 8 I will not strike him **t.**"
1Ki 11: 9 the God of Israel, who had appeared to him **t,**
2Ki 6:10 More than once or **t** he warned such a place so
Ne 13:20 the night outside Jerusalem once or **t.**
Job 33:29 "God indeed does all these things, **t,** three times,
40: 5 **t,** but will proceed no further."
42:10 the LORD gave Job **t** as much as he had before.
Ps 62:11 Once God has spoken; **t** have I heard this:
68:17 With mighty chariotry, **t** ten thousand,
Ecc 6: 6 though he should live a thousand years **t** over,
Eze 21:14 Let the sword fall **t,** thrice;
Na 1: 9 He will make an end; no adversary will rise up **t.**
Mt 23:15 and you make the new convert **t** as much a child
Mk 14:30 this day, this very night, before the cock crows **t,**
14:72 "Before the cock crows **t,**
Lk 18:12 I fast **t** a week; I give a tenth of all my income.'
Jude 1:12 autumn trees without fruit, **t** dead, uprooted;
Jdt 13: 8 Then she struck his neck **t** with all her might,
Sir 7: 8 Do not commit a sin **t;**
12: 5 then you will receive **t** as much evil for all
32: 7 if you are obliged to, but no more than **t,**
32:20 and do not stumble at an obstacle **t.**
45:14 be wholly burned **t** every day continually.
48:12 He performed **t** as many signs,
1Mc 10:72 for your ancestors were **t** put to flight

TWIG (1) [TWIGS]

Eze 17: 5 plant by abundant waters, he set it like a willow **t.**

TWIGS (1) [TWIG]

Eze 17:22 a tender one from the topmost of its young **t;**

TWILIGHT (16)

Ex 12: 6 of Israel shall slaughter it at **t.**
16:12 say to them, 'At **t** you shall eat meat,
Lev 23: 5 on the fourteenth day of the month, at **t,**
Nu 9: 3 On the fourteenth day of this month, at **t,**
9: 5 on the fourteenth day of the month, at **t,**
9:11 In the second month on the fourteenth day, at **t,**
28: 4 and the other lamb you shall offer at **t**
28: 8 at **t** with a grain offering and a drink offering like
1Sa 30:17 David attacked them from **t** until the evening of
2Ki 7: 5 So they arose at **t** to go to the Aramean camp;
7: 7 they fled away in the **t** and abandoned their tents,
Job 24:15 The eye of the adulterer also waits for the **t,**
Pr 7: 9 in the **t,** in the evening, at the time of night
Isa 21: 4 the **t** I longed for has been turned for me
59:10 we stumble at noon as in the **t,**
Jer 13:16 before your feet stumble on the mountains at **t;**

TWIN (4) [TWINS]

Jn 11:16 Thomas, who was called the **T,**
20:24 But Thomas (who was called the **T**),
21: 2 the **T,** Nathanael of Cana in Galilee, the sons
Ac 28:11 an Alexandrian ship with the **T** Brothers

TWINE (1)

Job 8:17 Their roots **t** around the stoneheap;

TWINED (KJV) See TWISTED

TWINKLING (1)

1Co 15:52 in the **t** of an eye, at the last trumpet.

TWINS (6) [TWIN]

Ge 25:24 there were **t** in her womb.
38:27 there were **t** in her womb.
SS 4: 2 which bear **t,** and not one among them is bereaved.
4: 5 **t** of a gazelle, that feed among the lilies.
6: 6 them bear **t,** and not one among them is bereaved.
7: 3 like two fawns, **t** of a gazelle.

TWIST (4) [TWISTED, TWISTING]

Isa 24: 1 and he will **t** its surface and scatter its inhabitants
2Pe 3:16 and unstable **t** to their own destruction,
Sir 27:23 but later he will **t** his speech and
4Mc 9:17 Cut my limbs, burn my flesh, and **t** my joints;

TWISTED (29) [TWIST]

Ex 26: 1 with ten curtains of fine **t** linen, and blue, purple,
26:31 purple, and crimson yarns, and of fine **t** linen;
26:36 and of fine **t** linen, embroidered with needlework.
27: 9 of fine **t** linen one hundred cubits long for
27:16 and of fine **t** linen, embroidered with needlework;
27:18 with hangings of fine **t** linen and bases of bronze.
28: 6 purple, and crimson yarns, and of fine **t** linen,
28: 8 purple, and crimson yarns, and of fine **t** linen.
28:14 and two chains of pure gold, **t** like cords;
28:15 and of fine **t** linen you shall make it.
28:22 the breastpiece chains of pure gold, **t** like cords;
36: 8 they were made of fine **t** linen, and blue, purple,
36:35 purple, and crimson yarns, and fine **t** linen,
36:37 and fine **t** linen, embroidered with needlework;
38: 9 the hangings of the court were of fine **t** linen,
38:16 the hangings around the court were of fine **t** linen.
38:18 purple, and crimson yarns and fine **t** linen.
39: 2 purple, and crimson yarns, and of fine **t** linen.
39: 3 and crimson yarns and into the fine **t** linen,
39: 5 purple, and crimson yarns, and of fine **t** linen;
39: 8 purple, and crimson yarns, and of fine **t** linen.
39:15 the breastpiece chains of pure gold, **t** like cords;
39:24 purple, and crimson yarns, and of fine **t** linen.
39:28 and the linen undergarments of fine **t** linen,
39:29 and the sash of fine **t** linen, and of blue, purple,
Ps 78:57 they **t** like a treacherous bow.
Pr 8: 8 there is nothing **t** or crooked in them.
Sir 45:11 with **t** crimson, the work of an artisan;
4Mc 11:10 they **t** his back around the wedge on the wheel,

TWISTING (3) [TWIST]

Isa 27: 1 the **t** serpent, and he will kill the dragon that is in
Mt 27:29 and after **t** some thorns into a crown,
Mk 15:17 **t** some thorns into a crown, they put it on him.

TWO‡ (875) [SECOND, TWICE, TWO-EDGED, TWO-TENTHS, TWO-THIRDS, TWOFOLD]

Ge 1:16 God made the **t** great lights—
4:19 Lamech took **t** wives; the name of the
6:19 you shall bring **t** of every kind into the ark,
6:20 **t** of every kind shall come in to you,
7: 9 **t** and **t,** male and female, went into the ark
7:15 **t** and **t** of all flesh in which there was the breath
9:22 and told his **t** brothers outside.
10:25 To Eber were born **t** sons:
11:10 he became the father of Arpachshad **t** years after
11:19 after the birth of Reu **t** hundred nine years,
11:21 after the birth of Serug **t** hundred seven years,
11:23 after the birth of Nahor **t** hundred years,
11:32 The days of Terah were **t** hundred five years;
15:10 He brought him all these and cut them in **t,**
15:10 but he did not cut the birds in **t.**
19: 1 The **t** angels came to Sodom in the evening,
19: 8 I have **t** daughters who have not known a man;
19:15 take your wife and your **t** daughters who are here,
19:16 and his wife and his **t** daughters by the hand,
19:30 in the hills with his **t** daughters, for he was afraid
19:30 so he lived in a cave with his **t** daughters.
21:27 and the **t** men made a covenant.
22: 3 and took **t** of his young men with him,
22: 6 So the **t** of them walked on together.
22: 8 So the **t** of them walked on together.
24:22 a half shekel, and **t** bracelets
25:23 LORD said to her, "**T** nations are in your womb,
25:23 and **t** peoples born of you shall be divided;
27: 9 Go to the flock, and get me **t** choice kids,
27:36 For he has supplanted me these **t** times.
29:16 Now Laban had **t** daughters;
31:33 and into the tent of the **t** maids,
31:37 so that they may decide between us **t.**
31:41 I served you fourteen years for your **t** daughters,
32: 7 and herds and camels, into **t** companies,
32:10 and now I have become **t** companies.
32:14 **t** hundred female goats and twenty male goats, **t** hundred ewes and twenty rams,
32:22 he got up and took his **t** wives, his **t** maids,
33: 1 among Leah and Rachel and the **t** maids.
34:25 **t** of the sons of Jacob, Simeon and Levi,
40: 2 Pharaoh was angry with his **t** officers,
41: 1 After **t** whole years, Pharaoh dreamed
41:50 the years of famine came, Joseph had **t** sons,
42:37 "You may kill my **t** sons if I do
44:27 'You know that my wife bore me **t** sons;
45: 6 For the famine has been in the land these **t** years;
46:27 who were born to him in Egypt, were **t;**
48: 1 So he took with him his **t** sons,
48: 5 Therefore your **t** sons, who were born to you in
Ex 2:13 he saw **t** Hebrews fighting;
4: 9 not believe even these **t** signs or heed you,
12: 7 on the **t** doorposts and the lintel of the houses
12:22 and the **t** doorposts with the blood in the basin.
12:23 the blood on the lintel and on the **t** doorposts,
16:22 as much food, **t** omers apiece.
16:29 on the sixth day he gives you food for **t** days;
18: 3 along with her **t** sons. The name of the
18: 6 with your wife and her **t** sons."
21:21 slave survives a day or **t,** there is no punishment;
22:11 the **t** of them that the one has not laid hands on
25:10 it shall be **t** and a half cubits long,
25:12 **t** rings on the one side of it, and **t** rings on the
25:17 **t** cubits and a half shall be its length,
25:18 You shall make **t** cherubim of gold;
25:18 at the **t** ends of the mercy seat.
25:19 the cherubim at its **t** ends.
25:22 the **t** cherubim that are on the ark of the covenant,
25:23 **t** cubits long, one cubit wide,
26:17 be **t** pegs in each frame to fit the frames together;
26:19 **t** bases under the first frame for its **t** pegs,
26:19 and **t** bases under the next frame for its **t** pegs;
26:21 **t** bases under the first frame, and **t** bases under the
26:23 You shall make **t** frames for corners of
26:24 they shall form the **t** corners.
26:25 **t** bases under the first frame, and **t** bases under the
27: 7 so that the poles shall be on the **t** sides of the altar
28: 7 shall have **t** shoulder-pieces attached to its **t** edges,
28: 9 You shall take **t** onyx stones,
28:11 so you shall engrave the **t** stones with the names
28:12 the **t** stones on the shoulder-pieces of the ephod,
28:12 the LORD on his **t** shoulders for remembrance.
28:14 and **t** chains of pure gold, twisted like cords;
28:23 you shall make for the breastpiece **t** rings of gold,
28:23 put the **t** rings on the **t** edges of the breastpiece.
28:24 the **t** cords of gold in the **t** rings at the edges of
28:25 the **t** ends of the **t** cords you shall attach to the **t** settings,
28:26 You shall make **t** rings of gold, and put them at the **t** ends of the breastpiece,
28:27 You shall make **t** rings of gold,
28:27 in front to the lower part of the **t** shoulder-pieces

Ex 29: 1 Take one young bull and **t** rams without blemish,
29: 3 and bring the bull and the **t** rams.
29:13 and the **t** kidneys with the fat that is on them,
29:22 the **t** kidneys with the fat that is on them,
29:38 **t** lambs a year old regularly each day.
30: 2 it shall be square, and shall be **t** cubits high;
30: 4 And you shall make **t** golden rings for it;
30: 4 on **t** opposite sides of it you shall make them,
30:23 that is, **t** hundred fifty, and **t** hundred fifty of
31:18 he gave him the **t** tablets of the covenant,
32:15 carrying the **t** tablets of the covenant in his hands,
34: 1 "Cut **t** tablets of stone like the former ones,
34: 4 Moses cut **t** tablets of stone like the former ones;
34: 4 and took in his hand the **t** tablets of stone.
34:29 the mountain with the **t** tablets of the covenant
36:22 Each frame had **t** pegs for fitting together;
36:24 **t** bases under the first frame for its **t** pegs,
36:24 and **t** bases under the next frame for its **t** pegs.
36:26 **t** bases under the first frame and **t** bases under
36:28 He made **t** frames for corners of the tabernacle in
36:29 he made **t** of them in this way, for the **t** corners.
36:30 sixteen bases, under every frame **t** bases.
37: 1 it was **t** and a half cubits long,
37: 3 **t** rings on its one side and **t** rings on its other side.
37: 6 **t** cubits and a half was its length,
37: 7 He made **t** cherubim of hammered gold;
37: 7 at the **t** ends of the mercy seat he made them,
37: 8 the mercy seat he made the cherubim at its **t** ends.
37:10 **t** cubits long, one cubit wide,
37:25 it was square, and was **t** cubits high;
37:27 and made **t** golden rings for it under its molding,
37:27 on **t** opposite sides of it,
38:29 and **t** thousand four hundred shekels;
39: 4 joined to it at its **t** edges.
39:16 and they made **t** settings of gold filigree
39:16 and **t** gold rings, and put the **t** rings on the **t** edges
39:17 and they put the **t** cords of gold in the **t** rings at
39:18 **T** ends of the **t** cords they had attached to the **t** settings
39:19 Then they made **t** rings of gold, and put them at the **t** ends of the breastpiece,
39:20 They made **t** rings of gold,
39:20 in front to the lower part of the **t** shoulder-pieces
Lev 3: 4 **t** kidneys with the fat that is on them at the loins,
3:10 **t** kidneys with the fat that is on them at the loins,
3:15 **t** kidneys with the fat that is on them at the loins,
4: 9 **t** kidneys with the fat that is on them at the loins;
5: 7 **t** turtledoves or **t** pigeons, one for a sin offering
5:11 if you cannot afford **t** turtledoves or **t** pigeons,
7: 4 **t** kidneys with the fat that is on them at the loins,
8: 2 the **t** rams, and the basket of unleavened bread;
8:16 and the **t** kidneys with their fat,
8:25 and the **t** kidneys with their fat—
9:19 the **t** kidneys and the fat on them,
12: 5 she shall be unclean **t** weeks,
12: 8 she shall take **t** turtledoves or **t** pigeons,
14: 4 the priest shall command that **t** living clean birds
14:10 On the eighth day he shall take **t** male lambs
14:22 also **t** turtledoves or **t** pigeons,
14:49 the cleansing of the house he shall take **t** birds,
15:14 eighth day he shall take **t** turtledoves or **t** pigeons
15:29 eighth day she shall take **t** turtledoves or **t** pigeons
16: 1 to Moses after the death of the **t** sons of Aaron,
16: 5 the people of Israel **t** male goats for a sin offering,
16: 7 the **t** goats and set them before the LORD at
16: 8 and Aaron shall cast lots on the **t** goats,
16:12 and **t** handfuls of crushed sweet incense,
19:19 you shall not sow your field with **t** kinds of seed;
19:19 on a garment made of **t** different materials.
23:17 You shall bring from your settlements **t** loaves
23:18 one young bull, and **t** rams;
23:19 and **t** male lambs a year old as a sacrifice
23:20 together with the **t** lambs;
24: 6 You shall place them in **t** rows, six in a row,
Nu 1:35 of Manasseh were thirty-two thousand **t** hundred.
2:21 as enrolled of thirty-two thousand **t** hundred.
3:34 was six thousand **t** hundred.
3:43 was twenty-two thousand **t** hundred seventy-three.
3:46 of the **t** hundred seventy-three of the firstborn of
4:36 by clans was **t** thousand seven hundred fifty.
4:40 ancestral houses was **t** thousand six hundred thirty.
4:44 by their clans was three thousand **t** hundred.
6:10 On the eighth day they shall bring **t** turtledoves
6:10 or **t** young pigeons to the priest at the entrance of
7: 3 a wagon for every **t** of the leaders,
7: 7 **T** wagons and four oxen he gave to the Gershonites
7:17 **t** oxen, five rams, five male goats,
7:23 **t** oxen, five rams, five male goats,
7:29 **t** oxen, five rams, five male goats,
7:35 **t** oxen, five rams, five male goats,
7:41 **t** oxen, five rams, five male goats,
7:47 **t** oxen, five rams, five male goats,
7:53 **t** oxen, five rams, five male goats,
7:59 **t** oxen, five rams, five male goats,
7:65 **t** oxen, five rams, five male goats,
7:71 **t** oxen, five rams, five male goats,
7:77 **t** oxen, five rams, five male goats,
7:83 **t** oxen, five rams, five male goats,
7:85 of the vessels **t** thousand four hundred shekels
7:89 of the covenant from between the **t** cherubim;
9:22 Whether it was **t** days, or a month,
10: 2 Make **t** silver trumpets; you shall make them of
11:19 You shall eat not only one day, or **t** days,
11:26 **T** men remained in the camp, one named Eldad,
11:31 about **t** cubits deep on the ground.
13:23 and they carried it on a pole between **t** of them.
16: 2 **t** hundred fifty Israelite men,
Nu 16:17 before the LORD, **t** hundred fifty censers;
16:35 and consumed the **t** hundred fifty men offering
22:22 and his **t** servants were with him.
25: 8 and pierced the **t** of them,
26:10 when the fire devoured **t** hundred fifty men;
26:14 twenty-two thousand **t** hundred.
28: 3 **t** male lambs a year old without blemish, daily,
28: 9 **t** male lambs a year old without blemish,
28:11 **t** young bulls, one ram, seven male lambs
28:19 **t** young bulls, one ram, and seven male lambs
28:27 **t** young bulls, one ram, seven male lambs
29:13 thirteen young bulls, **t** rams,
29:14 two-tenths for each of the **t** rams,
29:17 On the second day: twelve young bulls, **t** rams,
29:20 On the third day: eleven bulls, **t** rams,
29:23 On the fourth day: ten bulls, **t** rams,
29:26 On the fifth day: nine bulls, **t** rams,
29:29 On the sixth day: eight bulls, **t** rams,
29:32 On the seventh day: seven bulls, **t** rams,
31:27 Divide the booty into **t** parts,
34:15 the **t** tribes and the half-tribe have taken their
35: 5 for the east side **t** thousand cubits, for the south side **t** thousand cubits, for the west side **t** thousand cubits, and for the north side **t** thousand cubits,
Dt 3: 8 from the **t** kings of the Amorites the land beyond
3:21 the LORD your God has done to these **t** kings;
4:13 and he wrote them on **t** stone tablets.
4:42 the **t** not having been at enmity before;
4:47 the **t** kings of the Amorites on the eastern side of
5:22 He wrote them on **t** stone tablets,
9:10 the **t** stone tablets written with the finger of God;
9:11 the LORD gave me the **t** stone tablets,
9:15 **t** tablets of the covenant were in my **t** hands.
9:17 the **t** tablets and flung them from my **t** hands,
10: 1 "Carve out **t** tablets of stone like the former ones,
10: 3 cut **t** tablets of stone like the former ones,
10: 3 up the mountain with the **t** tablets in my hand.
14: 6 that divides the hoof and has the hoof cleft in **t**,
17: 6 of **t** or three witnesses the death sentence shall
18: 3 the **t** jowls, and the stomach.
19: 4 when the **t** had not been at enmity before:
19: 6 since the **t** had not been at enmity before.
19:15 of **t** or three witnesses shall a charge be sustained.
21:15 If a man has **t** wives,
25: 1 Suppose **t** persons have a dispute and enter
25:13 You shall not have in your bag **t** kinds of weights,
25:14 not have in your house **t** kinds of measures,
32:30 and **t** put a myriad to flight,
Jos 2: 1 of Nun sent **t** men secretly from Shittim as spies,
2: 4 But the woman took the **t** men and hid them.
2:10 and what you did to the **t** kings of the Amorites
2:23 the **t** men came down again from the hill country.
3: 4 a distance of about **t** thousand cubits;
6:22 Joshua said to the **t** men who had spied out
7: 3 about **t** or three thousand men should go up
7:21 and **t** hundred shekels of silver,
9:10 to the **t** kings of the Amorites who were beyond
14: 3 an inheritance to the **t** and one-half tribes beyond
14: 4 For the people of Joseph were **t** tribes,
15:60 **t** towns with their villages.
21:16 nine towns out of these **t** tribes.
21:25 with its pasture lands—**t** towns.
21:27 with its pasture lands—**t** towns.
24:12 which drove out before you the **t** kings of
Jdg 3:16 Ehud made for himself a sword with **t** edges,
5:30 A girl or **t** for every man;
5:30 **t** pieces of dyed work embroidered for my neck
7:25 They captured the **t** captains of Midian,
8:12 he pursued them and took the **t** kings of Midian,
9:44 while the **t** companies rushed on all who were in
11:37 Grant me **t** months, so that I may go and wander
11:38 "Go," he said and sent her away for **t** months.
11:39 At the end of **t** months, she returned to her father,
15:13 So they bound him with **t** new ropes,
16: 3 of the doors of the city gate and the **t** posts,
16:28 the Philistines for my **t** eyes."
16:29 the **t** middle pillars on which the house rested,
17: 4 his mother took **t** hundred pieces of silver,
19: 6 So the **t** men sat and ate and drank together;
19: 8 and the **t** of them ate and drank.
20:45 and **t** thousand of them were slain.
Ru 1: 1 he and his wife and **t** sons.
1: 2 the names of his **t** sons were Mahlon and Chilion;
1: 3 died, and she was left with her **t** sons.
1: 5 so that the woman was left without her **t** sons
1: 7 she and her **t** daughters-in-law,
1: 8 But Naomi said to her **t** daughters-in-law,
1:19 **t** of them went on until they came to Bethlehem.
1Sa 1: 2 He had **t** wives; the name of the
1: 3 where the **t** sons of Eli, Hophni and Phinehas,
2:21 and bore three sons and **t** daughters.
2:34 The fate of your **t** sons, Hophni and Phinehas,
4: 4 The **t** sons of Eli, Hophni and Phinehas,
4:11 and the **t** sons of Eli, Hophni and Phinehas, died.
4:17 your **t** sons also, Hophni and Phinehas, are dead,
6: 7 a new cart and **t** milch cows that have never borne
6:10 they took **t** milch cows and yoked them to
10: 2 from me today you will meet **t** men
10: 4 They will greet you and give you **t** loaves
11:11 so that no **t** of them were left together.
13: 1 and he reigned . . . and **t** years over Israel.
13: 2 **t** thousand were with Saul in Michmash and
14:49 and the names of his **t** daughters were these:
15: 4 **t** hundred thousand foot soldiers,
23:18 the **t** of them made a covenant before the LORD;
25:13 while **t** hundred remained with the baggage.
25:18 hurried and took **t** hundred loaves, **t** skins of wine,
1Sa 25:18 and **t** hundred cakes of figs.
27: 3 and David with his **t** wives, Ahinoam of Jezreel,
28: 8 he and **t** men with him.
30: 5 David's **t** wives also had been taken captive,
30:10 **t** hundred stayed behind, too exhausted to cross
30:12 also gave him a piece of fig cake and **t** clusters
30:18 and David rescued his **t** wives.
30:21 to the **t** hundred men who had been too exhausted
2Sa 1: 1 David remained **t** days in Ziklag.
2: 2 So David went up there, along with his **t** wives,
2:10 to reign over Israel, and he reigned **t** years.
4: 2 Saul's son had **t** captains of raiding bands;
8: 2 he measured **t** lengths of cord for those who were
12: 1 "There were **t** men in a certain city,
13:23 After **t** full years Absalom had sheepshearers
14: 6 Your servant had **t** sons, and they fought
14:26 **t** hundred shekels by the king's weight.
14:28 So Absalom lived **t** full years in Jerusalem,
15:11 **T** hundred men from Jerusalem went
15:27 with your **t** sons, Ahimaaz your son,
15:36 Their **t** sons are with them there,
16: 1 carrying **t** hundred loaves of bread,
18:24 Now David was sitting between the **t** gates.
21: 8 king took the **t** sons of Rizpah daughter of Aiah,
23:20 he struck down **t** sons of Ariel of Moab.
1Ki 2: 5 how he dealt with the **t** commanders of the armies
2:32 and killed with the sword **t** men more righteous
2:39 of three years that **t** of Shimei's slaves ran away
3:16 **t** women who were prostitutes came to the king
3:18 only the **t** of us were in the house.
3:25 The king said, "Divide the living boy in **t**;
5:12 and the **t** of them made a treaty.
5:14 be a month in the Lebanon and **t** months at home;
6:23 In the inner sanctuary he made **t** cherubim
6:32 the **t** doors of olivewood with carvings
6:34 and **t** doors of cypress wood; the **t** leaves of the one door were folding, and the **t** leaves of the other
7:15 He cast **t** pillars of bronze.
7:16 He also made **t** capitals of molten bronze,
7:18 the columns with **t** rows around each latticework
7:20 the **t** pillars and also above the rounded projection
7:20 there were **t** hundred pomegranates
7:24 there were **t** rows of panels, cast when it was cast.
7:26 of a lily; it held **t** thousand baths.
7:41 the **t** pillars, the **t** bowls of the capitals
7:41 the **t** latticeworks to cover the **t** bowls
7:42 for the **t** latticeworks, **t** rows of pomegranates
7:42 the **t** bowls of the capitals that were on the pillars;
8: 9 the **t** tablets of stone that Moses had placed there
9:10 in which Solomon had built the **t** houses,
10:16 King Solomon made **t** hundred large shields
10:19 the seat were arm rests and **t** lions standing beside
11:29 The **t** of them were alone in the open country
12:28 the king took counsel, and made **t** calves of gold.
15:25 he reigned over Israel **t** years.
16: 8 in Tirzah; he reigned **t** years.
16:21 the people of Israel were divided into **t** parts;
16:24 of Samaria from Shemer for **t** talents of silver;
18:21 with **t** different opinions?
18:23 Let **t** bulls be given to us;
18:32 large enough to contain **t** measures of seed.
20:15 the district governors, **t** hundred thirty-two;
20:27 like **t** little flocks of goats,
21:10 seat **t** scoundrels opposite him,
21:13 The **t** scoundrels came in and sat opposite him;
22:51 he reigned **t** years over Israel.
2Ki 1:14 from heaven and consumed the **t** former captains
2: 6 So the **t** of them went on.
2: 8 until the **t** of them crossed on dry ground.
2:11 a chariot of fire and horses of fire separated the **t**
2:12 and tore them in **t** pieces.
2:24 Then **t** she-bears came out of the woods
4: 1 but a creditor has come to take my **t** children
4:33 he went in and closed the door on the **t** of them,
5:17 please let **t** mule-loads of earth be given
5:22 '**T** members of a company of prophets
5:22 please give them a talent of silver and **t** changes
5:23 Naaman said, "Please accept **t** talents."
5:23 tied up **t** talents of silver in **t** bags, with **t** changes of clothing, and gave them to **t** of his servants,
7: 1 and **t** measures of barley for a shekel,
7:14 So they took **t** mounted men,
7:16 and **t** measures of barley for a shekel,
7:18 "**T** measures of barley shall be sold for a shekel,
9:32 **T** or three eunuchs looked out at him.
10: 4 "Look, **t** kings could not withstand him;
10: 8 "Lay them in **t** heaps at the entrance of the gate
11: 7 and your **t** divisions that come on duty in force on
15:23 in Samaria; he reigned **t** years.
17:16 and made for themselves cast images of **t** calves;
18:23 I will give you **t** thousand horses,
21: 5 the host of heaven in the **t** courts of the house of
21:19 he reigned **t** years in Jerusalem.
23:12 the altars that Manasseh had made in the **t** courts
25: 4 by the way of the gate between the **t** walls,
25:16 As for the **t** pillars, the one sea, and the stands,
1Ch 1:19 To Eber were born **t** sons:
4: 5 Ashhur father of Tekoa had **t** wives,
5:21 **t** hundred fifty thousand sheep, **t** thousand donkeys
7: 9 mighty warriors, was twenty thousand **t** hundred.
7:11 mighty warriors, seventeen thousand **t** hundred,
9:22 at the thresholds, were **t** hundred twelve.
11:22 he struck down **t** sons of Ariel of Moab.
12:32 to know what Israel ought to do, **t** hundred chiefs,
15: 6 with **t** hundred twenty of his kindred;
15: 8 Shemaiah the chief, with **t** hundred of his kindred;
25: 7 numbered **t** hundred eighty-eight.

1Ch 26:17 as well as **t** and **t** at the storehouse;
26:18 on the west there were four at the road and **t** at
26:32 **t** thousand seven hundred men of ability,
2Ch 3:10 In the most holy place he made **t** carved cherubim
3:15 the house he made **t** pillars thirty-five cubits high,
4: 3 there were **t** rows of panels, cast when it was cast.
4:12 the **t** pillars, the bowls, and the **t** capitals
4:12 and the **t** latticeworks to cover the **t** bowls
4:13 four hundred pomegranates for the **t** latticeworks,
4:13 **t** rows of pomegranates for each latticework,
4:13 the **t** bowls of the capitals that were on the pillars.
5:10 in the ark except the **t** tablets that Moses put there
8:10 **t** hundred fifty of them, who exercised authority
9:15 King Solomon made **t** hundred large shields
9:18 the seat were arm rests and **t** lions standing beside
14: 8 and **t** hundred eighty thousand troops
17:15 with **t** hundred eighty thousand,
17:16 with **t** hundred thousand mighty warriors.
17:17 a mighty warrior, with **t** hundred thousand armed
21:19 In course of time, at the end of **t** years,
24: 3 Jehoiada got **t** wives for him,
26:12 of mighty warriors was **t** thousand six hundred.
28: 8 of Israel took captive **t** hundred thousand
29:32 one hundred rams, and **t** hundred lambs;
33: 5 the host of heaven in the **t** courts of the house of
33:21 he reigned **t** years in Jerusalem.
35: 8 passover offerings **t** thousand six hundred lambs
Ezr 2: 3 **t** thousand one hundred seventy-two.
2: 6 **t** thousand eight hundred twelve.
2: 7 Of Elam, one thousand **t** hundred fifty-four.
2:12 Of Azgad, one thousand **t** hundred twenty-two.
2:14 Of Bigvai, **t** thousand fifty-six.
2:19 Of Hashum, **t** hundred twenty-three.
2:28 Of Bethel and Ai, **t** hundred twenty-three.
2:31 one thousand **t** hundred fifty-four.
2:38 Of Pashhur, one thousand **t** hundred forty-seven.
2:65 and they had **t** hundred male and female singers.
2:66 **t** hundred forty-five mules,
6:17 **t** hundred rams, four hundred lambs,
8: 4 and with him **t** hundred males.
8: 9 and with him **t** hundred eighteen males.
8:20 besides **t** hundred twenty of the temple servants,
8:27 and **t** vessels of fine polished bronze as precious
10:13 Nor is this a task for one day or for **t**,
Ne 7: 8 **t** thousand one hundred seventy-two.
7:11 **t** thousand eight hundred eighteen.
7:12 Of Elam, one thousand **t** hundred fifty-four.
7:17 Of Azgad, **t** thousand three hundred twenty-two.
7:19 Of Bigvai, **t** thousand sixty-seven.
7:34 one thousand **t** hundred fifty-four.
7:41 Of Pashhur, one thousand **t** hundred forty-seven.
7:67 and they had **t** hundred forty-five singers,
7:68 **t** hundred forty-five mules,
7:71 and **t** thousand **t** hundred minas of silver.
7:72 **t** thousand minas of silver,
11:13 heads of ancestral houses, **t** hundred forty-two;
11:18 in the holy city were **t** hundred eighty-four.
12:31 and appointed **t** great companies that gave thanks
Est 2:21 Bigthan and Teresh, **t** of the king's eunuchs,
6: 2 and Teresh, **t** of the king's eunuchs, who guarded
9:27 to observe these **t** days every year,
Job 13:20 Only grant **t** things to me,
16:12 I was at ease, and he broke me in **t**;
33:14 For God speaks in one way, and in **t**,
42: 7 against you and against your **t** friends;
Ps 107:16 and cuts in **t** the bars of iron.
136:13 in **t**, for his steadfast love endures forever;
Pr 30: 7 **T** things I ask of you;
30:15 The leech has **t** daughters; "Give, give," they cry.
Ecc 4: 6 a handful with quiet than **t** handfuls with toil,
4: 9 **T** are better than one, because they have
4:11 Again, if **t** lie together, they keep warm;
4:12 against another, **t** will withstand one.
SS 4: 5 Your **t** breasts are like **t** fawns,
6:13 as upon a dance before **t** armies?
7: 3 Your **t** breasts are like **t** fawns,
8:12 and the keepers of the fruit **t** hundred!
Isa 6: 2 with **t** they covered their faces, and with **t** they
covered their feet, and with **t** they flew,
7: 4 be faint because of these **t** smoldering stumps
7:16 before whose **t** kings you are in dread will
7:21 a young cow and **t** sheep,
17: 6 **t** or three berries in the top of the highest bough,
22:11 between the **t** walls for the water of the old pool.
36: 8 I will give you **t** thousand horses,
51:19 These **t** things have befallen you—who will grieve
Jer 2:13 for my people have committed **t** evils:
3:14 one from a city and **t** from a family,
24: 1 The LORD showed me **t** baskets of figs placed
28: 3 Within **t** years I will bring back to this place all
28:11 from the neck of all the nations within **t** years."
33:24 how these people say, "The **t** families that
34:18 when they cut it in **t** and passed between its parts:
37: 7 This is what the **t** of you shall say to the king
39: 4 through the gate between the **t** walls;
52: 7 by the way of the gate between the **t** walls,
52:20 As for the **t** pillars, the one sea,
Eze 1:11 each creature had **t** wings,
1:11 while **t** covered their bodies.
1:23 of the creatures had **t** wings covering its body.
21:19 mark out **t** roads for the sword of the king
21:21 at the fork in the **t** roads, to use divination;
23: 2 there were **t** women, the daughters of one mother;
35:10 "These **t** nations and these **t** countries shall
37:22 Never again shall they be **t** nations, never again
shall they be divided into **t** kingdoms.
40: 9 eight cubits; and its pilasters, **t** cubits;
Eze 40:39 And in the vestibule of the gate were **t** tables on
40:40 at the entrance of the north gate were **t** tables;
40:40 of the vestibule of the gate were **t** tables.
41: 3 the pilasters of the entrance, **t** cubits;
41:18 Each cherub had **t** faces:
41:22 **t** cubits long, and **t** cubits wide;
41:24 The doors had **t** leaves apiece, **t** swinging leaves
43:14 **t** cubits, with a width of one cubit;
45:15 and one sheep from every flock of **t** hundred,
47:13 Joseph shall have **t** portions.
48:17 on the north **t** hundred fifty cubits, on the south **t**
hundred fifty, on the east **t** hundred fifty, on the
west **t** hundred fifty.
Da 7: 4 from the ground and made to stand on **t** feet like
7:25 be given into his power for a time, **t** times,
8: 3 beside the river. It had **t** horns.
8: 6 the ram with the **t** horns that I had seen standing
8: 7 against it and struck the ram, breaking its **t** horns.
8:14 **t** thousand three hundred evenings and mornings;
8:20 As for the ram that you saw with the **t** horns,
11:27 The **t** kings, their minds bent on evil,
12: 5 Then I, Daniel, looked, and **t** others appeared,
12: 7 for a time, **t** times, and half a time,
12:11 there shall be one thousand **t** hundred ninety days.
Hos 6: 2 After **t** days he will revive us;
Am 1: 1 **t** years before the earthquake.
3: 3 Do **t** walk together unless they have made
3:12 from the mouth of the lion **t** legs,
4: 8 so **t** or three towns wandered to one town
Zec 4: 3 And by it there are **t** olive trees,
4:11 "What are these **t** olive trees on the right and
4:12 "What are these **t** branches of the olive trees,
4:12 the oil through the **t** golden pipes?"
4:14 the **t** anointed ones who stand by the Lord of
5: 9 I looked up and saw **t** women coming forward.
6: 1 from between **t** mountains—
6:13 with peaceful understanding between the **t**
11: 7 to slaughter. I took **t** staffs;
14: 4 the Mount of Olives shall be split in **t** from east
Mt 2:16 around Bethlehem who were **t** years old or under,
4:18 he saw **t** brothers, Simon, who is called Peter,
4:21 As he went from there, he saw **t** other brothers,
6:24 "No one can serve **t** masters;
8:28 **t** demoniacs coming out of the tombs met him.
9:27 **t** blind men followed him, crying loudly,
10:10 or **t** tunics, or sandals, or a staff;
10:29 Are not **t** sparrows sold for a penny?
14:17 "We have nothing here but five loaves and **t** fish."
14:19 Taking the five loaves and the **t** fish,
18: 8 than to have **t** hands or **t** feet and to be thrown into
18: 9 with one eye than to have **t** eyes and to be thrown
18:15 the fault when the **t** of you are alone.
18:16 take one or **t** others along with you,
18:16 by the evidence of **t** or three witnesses.
18:19 if **t** of you agree on earth about anything you ask,
18:20 For where **t** or three are gathered in my name,
19: 5 and the **t** shall become one flesh'?
19: 6 So they are no longer **t**, but one flesh.
20:21 "Declare that these **t** sons of mine will sit,
20:24 ten heard it, they were angry with the **t** brothers.
20:30 There were **t** blind men sitting by the roadside.
21: 1 at the Mount of Olives, Jesus sent **t** disciples,
21:28 "What do you think? A man had **t** sons;
21:31 Which of the **t** did the will of his father?"
22:40 On these **t** commandments hang all the law and
24:40 Then **t** will be in the field;
24:41 **T** women will be grinding meal together;
25:15 to another **t**, to another one,
25:17 one who had the **t** talents made **t** more talents.
25:22 And the one with the **t** talents also came forward,
saying, 'Master, you handed over to me **t** talents;
see, I have made **t** more talents.'
26: 2 that after **t** days the Passover is coming,
26:37 He took with him Peter and the **t** sons of Zebedee,
26:60 witnesses came forward. At last **t** came forward
27:21 of the **t** do you want me to release for you?"
27:38 Then **t** bandits were crucified with him,
27:51 the curtain of the temple was torn in **t**,
Mk 5:13 and the herd, numbering about **t** thousand,
6: 7 the twelve and began to send them out **t** by **t**,
6: 9 but to wear sandals and not to put on **t** tunics.
6:37 to go and buy **t** hundred denarii worth of bread,
6:38 they had found out, they said, "Five, and **t** fish."
6:41 Taking the five loaves and the **t** fish,
6:41 and he divided the **t** fish among them all.
9:43 for you to enter life maimed than to have **t** hands
9:45 for you to enter life lame than to have **t** feet and
9:47 with one eye than to have **t** eyes and to be thrown
10: 8 and the **t** shall become one flesh.'
10: 8 So they are no longer **t**, but one flesh.
11: 1 he sent **t** of his disciples
12:42 poor widow came and put in **t** small copper coins,
14: 1 It was **t** days before the Passover and the festival
14:13 So he sent **t** of his disciples, saying to them,
15:27 And with him they crucified **t** bandits,
15:38 And the curtain of the temple was torn in **t**,
16:12 ⟦this he appeared in another form to **t** of them,⟧
Lk 2:24 "a pair of turtledoves or **t** young pigeons."
3:11 "Whoever has **t** coats must share
5: 2 he saw **t** boats there at the shore of the lake;
7:18 So John summoned **t** of his disciples
7:41 "A certain creditor had **t** debtors;
9:13 "We have no more than five loaves and **t** fish—
9:16 And taking the five loaves and the **t** fish,
9:30 Suddenly they saw **t** men, Moses and Elijah,
9:32 they saw his glory and the **t** men who stood
10:35 The next day he took out **t** denarii,
Lk 12: 6 Are not five sparrows sold for **t** pennies?
12:52 three against **t** and **t** against three;
15:11 Jesus said, "There was a man who had **t** sons.
16:13 No slave can serve **t** masters;
17:34 I tell you, on that night there will be **t** in one bed;
17:35 There will be **t** women grinding meal together;
18:10 "**T** men went up to the temple to pray,
19:29 he sent **t** of the disciples,
21: 2 a poor widow put in **t** small copper coins.
22:38 They said, "Lord, look, here are **t** swords."
23:32 **T** others also, who were criminals,
23:45 and the curtain of the temple was torn in **t**.
24: 4 suddenly **t** men in dazzling clothes stood
24:13 Now on that same day **t** of them were going to
Jn 1:35 The next day John again was standing with **t**
1:37 The **t** disciples heard him say this,
1:40 One of the **t** who heard John speak
4:40 and he stayed there **t** days.
4:43 When the **t** days were over,
6: 9 a boy here who has five barley loaves and **t** fish.
8:17 that the testimony of **t** witnesses is valid.
11: 6 he stayed **t** days longer in the place where he was.
11:18 Bethany was near Jerusalem, some **t** miles away,
19:18 There they crucified him, and with him **t** others,
20: 4 The **t** were running together,
20:12 and she saw **t** angels in white,
21: 2 the sons of Zebedee, and **t** others of his disciples.
Ac 1:10 suddenly **t** men in white robes stood by them.
1:23 So they proposed **t**, Joseph called Barsabbas,
1:24 Show us which one of these **t** you have chosen
7:29 There he became the father of **t** sons.
8:15 The **t** went down and prayed for them
9:38 sent **t** men to him with the request,
10: 7 he called **t** of his slaves and a devout soldier from
12: 6 Peter, bound with **t** chains, was sleeping between **t**
soldiers,
19:10 This continued for **t** years,
19:22 So he sent **t** of his helpers, Timothy and Erastus,
19:34 for about **t** hours all of them shouted in unison,
21:33 and ordered him to be bound with **t** chains;
23:23 Then he summoned **t** of the centurions and said,
23:23 for Caesarea with **t** hundred soldiers, seventy
horsemen, and **t** hundred spearmen.
24:27 After **t** years had passed, Felix was succeeded
27:37 (We were in all **t** hundred seventy-six persons in
28:30 He lived there **t** whole years at his own expense
1Co 6:16 For it is said, "The **t** shall be one flesh."
14:27 let there be only **t** or at most three,
14:29 Let **t** or three prophets speak,
2Co 13: 1 by the evidence of **t** or three witnesses."
Gal 4:22 For it is written that Abraham had **t** sons,
4:24 this is an allegory: these women are **t** covenants.
Eph 2:15 in himself one new humanity in place of the **t**,
5:31 and the **t** will become one flesh."
Php 1:23 I am hard pressed between the **t**:
1Ti 5:19 against an elder except on the evidence of **t**
2Ti 3: 9 because, as in the case of those **t** men,
Heb 6:18 so that through **t** unchangeable things,
10:28 "on the testimony of **t** or three witnesses."
11:37 They were stoned to death, they were sawn in **t**,
Rev 9:12 There are still **t** woes to come.
9:16 of the troops of cavalry was **t** hundred million;
11: 3 And I will grant my **t** witnesses authority
11: 3 for one thousand **t** hundred sixty days,
11: 4 the **t** olive trees and the **t** lampstands that stand
11:10 because these **t** prophets had been a torment to
12: 6 for one thousand **t** hundred sixty days.
12:14 woman was given the **t** wings of the great eagle,
13:11 it had **t** horns like a lamb and it spoke like
14:20 for a distance of about **t** hundred miles.
19:20 These **t** were thrown alive into the lake of fire
Tob 1:21 before **t** of Sennacherib's sons killed him,
2:10 of me for **t** years before he went to Elymais.
5: 3 and I gave him my bond. I divided his in **t**;
5: 6 It is a journey of **t** days from Ecbatana to Rages;
5:14 the **t** sons of Shemeliah, and they used to go
6: 6 The **t** continued on their way together
8: 6 From the **t** of them the human race has sprung.
8:17 because you had compassion on **t** only children.
8:19 and he went out to the herd and brought **t** steers
9: 2 and **t** camels with you and travel to Rages.
9: 5 with the four servants and **t** camels went to Rages
12: 6 Then Raphael called the **t** of them privately
12:16 The **t** of them were shaken;
Jdt 1:12 as far as the coasts of the **t** seas.
4: 7 wide enough for only **t** at a time to pass.
13:10 Then the **t** of them went out together,
AdE 2:23 He investigated the **t** eunuchs and hanged them.
6: 2 about the **t** royal eunuchs who were on guard
10: 7 The **t** dragons are Haman and myself.
10:10 For this purpose he made **t** lots,
10:11 and these **t** lots came to the hour and moment
11: 6 Then **t** great dragons came forward,
12: 1 the **t** eunuchs of the king who kept watch in
12: 3 Then the king examined the **t** eunuchs,
12: 6 and his people because of the **t** eunuchs of
15: 2 she took **t** maids with her;
Wis 14:30 But just penalties will overtake them on **t** counts:
Sir 13: 7 until he has drained you **t** or three times,
23:16 **T** kinds of individuals multiply sins,
26:28 At **t** things my heart is grieved,
38:17 for one day, or **t**, to avoid criticism;
46: 4 and one day become as long as **t**?
46: 8 And these **t** alone were spared out
50:25 **T** nations my soul detests,
Sus 1: 5 That year **t** elders from the people were appointed
1: 8 Every day the **t** elders used to see her,

Sus 1:15 she went in as before with only t maids,
1:16 No one was there except the t elders,
1:19 the t elders got up and ran to her.
1:24 and the t elders shouted against her.
1:28 of her husband Joakim, the t elders came, full
1:34 Then the t elders stood up before the people
1:36 this woman came in with t maids,
1:55 from God and will immediately cut you in t."
1:59 of God is waiting with his sword to split you in t,
1:61 And they took action against the t elders,
Bel 1:32 had been given t human bodies and t sheep;
1Mc 1:29 T years later the king sent to the cities of Judah
5:60 as t thousand of the people of Israel fell that day.
6:38 on the t flanks of the army,
9: 4 thousand foot soldiers and t thousand cavalry.
9:11 The cavalry was divided into t companies,
9:12 Flanked by the t companies,
9:57 and the land of Judah had rest for t years.
10:49 The t kings met in battle,
10:60 with pomp to Ptolemais and met the t kings;
11:13 Thus he put t crowns on his head,
12:47 t thousand of whom he left in Galilee,
13:16 Send now one hundred talents of silver and t
15:26 to Antiochus t thousand picked troops,
16: 2 Simon called in his t eldest sons Judas and John,
16:10 and about t thousand of them fell.
16:16 in the banquet hall and killed him and his t sons,
2Mc 3:11 in all four hundred talents of silver and t hundred
3:26 T young men also appeared to him,
4:28 the t of them were summoned by the king
6:10 t women were brought in
8:10 the tribute due to the Romans, t thousand talents,
10: 3 they offered sacrifices, after a lapse of t years,
10:18 in t very strong towers well equipped to withstand
10:22 and immediately captured the t towers.
10:23 more than twenty thousand in the t strongholds.
10:28 the t armies joined battle,
10:30 T of them took Maccabeus between them,
12: 4 to sea and drowned them, at least t hundred.
12:20 and t thousand five hundred cavalry.
12:43 to the amount of t thousand drachmas of silver,
13:15 at night and killed as many as t thousand men in
1Es 1: 8 for the passover t thousand six hundred sheep
2:13 t thousand four hundred ten silver bowls,
5: 9 t thousand one hundred seventy-two.
5:11 t thousand eight hundred twelve.
5:12 one thousand t hundred fifty-four.
5:14 The descendants of Bigvai, t thousand sixty-six.
5:25 one thousand t hundred forty-seven.
5:42 there were t hundred forty-five musicians
5:43 t hundred forty-five mules,
5:73 They were kept from building for t years,
7: 7 t hundred rams, four hundred lambs,
8:31 and with him t hundred men.
8:32 and with him t hundred fifty men.
8:35 and with him t hundred twelve men.
8:49 t hundred twenty temple servants;
9: 4 if any did not meet there within t or three days,
9:11 This is not a work we can do in one day or t,
3Mc 1: 4 to give them each t minas of gold if they won
3:28 also t thousand drachmas from the royal treasury,
6:18 from which t glorious angels
2Es 1:11 scattered in the east the peoples of t provinces,
6:49 "Then you kept in existence t living creatures;
7:50 the Most High has made not one world but t.
11:22 and the t little wings had disappeared,
11:24 that t little wings separated from the six
11:28 to look the t that remained were planning
11:29 it was greater than the other t heads.
11:30 And I saw how it allied the t heads with itself,
11:31 and devoured the t little wings that were planning
11:34 But the t heads remained,
12: 2 The t wings that had gone over to it rose up
12:21 t of them shall perish when the middle
12:21 but t shall be kept until the end.
12:27 the t who remained, the sword shall devour them.
12:29 As for your seeing t little wings passing over to
14:12 t of its parts remain, besides half of the tenth part.
16:28 For ten shall be left out of a city; and t,
16:38 around her womb for t or three hours beforehand,
4Mc 1:20 The t most comprehensive types of
1:28 and pain are t plants growing from the body and
3:12 t staunch young soldiers,
15: 2 T courses were open to this mother,
15:26 this mother held t ballots,

TWO-EDGED (6) [EDGE, TWO]

Ps 149: 6 be in their throats and t swords in their hands,
Pr 5: 4 as wormwood, sharp as a t sword.
Heb 4:12 sharper than any t sword,
Rev 1:16 and from his mouth came a sharp, t sword,
2:12 the words of him who has the sharp t sword:
Sir 21: 3 All lawlessness is like a t sword;

TWO-TENTHS (11) [TEN, TWO]

Lev 23:13 be t of an ephah of choice flour mixed with oil,
23:17 each made of t of an ephah;
24: 5 t of an ephah shall be in each loaf.
Nu 15: 6 t of an ephah of choice flour mixed with one-third
28: 9 t of an ephah of choice flour for a grain offering,
28:12 and t of choice flour for a grain offering,
28:20 shall you offer for a bull, and t for a ram;
28:28 of an ephah for each bull, t for one ram,
29: 3 three-tenths of one ephah for the bull, t for the ram,
29: 9 of an ephah for the bull, t for the one ram.
29:14 t for each of the two rams,

TWO-THIRDS‡ (2) [THREE, TWO]

1Sa 13:21 The charge was t of a shekel for the plowshares
Zec 13: 8 says the LORD, t shall be cut off and perish,

TWOFOLD (1) [TWO]

Wis 11:12 for a t grief possessed them,

TYCHICUS (5)

Ac 20: 4 as well as by T and Trophimus from Asia.
Eph 6:21 T will tell you everything.
Col 4: 7 T will tell you all the news about me;
2Ti 4:12 I have sent T to Ephesus.
Tit 3:12 When I send Artemas to you, or T,

TYING (3) [TIE]

Lev 8: 7 t the ephod to him with it.
Mt 12:29 without first t up the strong man?
Mk 3:27 and plunder his property without first t up

TYPE (2) [TYPES]

1Ki 22:48 Jehoshaphat made ships of the Tarshish t to go
Ro 5:14 who is a t of the one who was to come.

TYPES (1) [TYPE]

4Mc 1:20 The two most comprehensive t of the emotions

TYRANNICAL (1) [TYRANNY]

4Mc 5:27 be t for you to compel us not only to transgress

TYRANNIZE (1) [TYRANNY]

4Mc 5:38 You may t the ungodly, but you shall not dominate

TYRANNUS (1)

Ac 19: 9 and argued daily in the lecture hall of T.

TYRANNY (5) [TYRANNICAL, TYRANNIZE, TYRANT, TYRANT'S, TYRANTS]

3Mc 3: 8 to help them, for they lived under t.
4Mc 1:11 the cause of the downfall of t over their nation.
8:15 and by their right reasoning nullified his t.
9:30 of your t being defeated by our endurance for
11:24 We six boys have paralyzed your t.

TYRANT (50) [TYRANNY]

Isa 29:20 For the t shall be no more,
49:24 or the captives of a t be rescued?
49:25 and the prey of the t be rescued;
2Mc 4:25 but having the hot temper of a cruel t and the rage
7:27 deriding the cruel t: "My son, have pity on me.
4Mc 1:11 By their endurance they conquered the t,
5: 1 The t Antiochus, sitting in state
5:14 t urged him in this fashion to eat meat unlawfully,
6: 1 to the exhortations of the t,
6:21 the t as unmanly by not contending even to death
6:23 And you, guards of the t, why do you delay?"
7: 2 of the t and overwhelmed by the mighty waves
8: 2 t was conspicuously defeated in his first attempt,
8: 3 the t had given these orders, seven brothers—
8: 4 When the t saw them, grouped about their mother
8:13 and wedges and bellows, the t resumed speaking:
8:15 also opposed the t with their own philosophy,
8:29 that as soon as the t had ceased counseling them
9: 1 "Why do you delay, O t?
9: 3 T and counselor of lawlessness,
9: 7 Therefore, t, put us to the test;
9:10 the t was not only indignant,
9:14 with every member disjointed he denounced the t,
9:15 "Most abominable t, enemy
9:24 and take vengeance on the accursed t."
9:30 To the t he said, "Do you not think, you most savage t,
9:32 You will not escape, you most abominable t,
10:10 most abominable t, are suffering because
10:15 by the eternal destruction of the t,
10:16 t, so that you may learn from them that I am
11: 2 t, to be tortured for the sake of virtue.
11:12 "T, they are splendid favors that you grant us
11:13 When the t inquired whether he was willing to eat
11:21 For religious knowledge, O t, is invincible.
11:27 not the guards of the t but those of the divine law
12: 2 though the t had been vehemently reproached by
12:11 "You profane t, most impious of all the wicked,
15: 1 O reason of the children, t over the emotions!
15: 2 for a time, as the t had promised.
16:14 By steadfastness you have conquered even a t,
17: 2 the violence of the t, frustrated his evil designs,
17: 9 of the t who wished to destroy the way of life of
17:14 The t was the antagonist,
17:17 The t himself and all his council marveled
17:21 the t was punished, and the homeland purified—
17:23 For the t Antiochus, when he saw the courage
18: 5 The t Antiochus was both punished on earth
18:20 that bitter t of the Greeks quenched fire with fire
18:22 and will pursue the accursed t.

TYRANT'S (1) [TYRANNY]

4Mc 5: 4 to many in the t court because of his philosophy.

TYRANTS (5) [TYRANNY]

Isa 13:11 and lay low the insolence of t.
Isa 29: 5 and the multitude of t like flying chaff.
Mt 20:25 and their great ones are t over them.
Mk 10:42 and their great ones are t over them.
3Mc 6:24 "You are committing treason and surpassing t

TYRE‡ (61) [TYRIAN, TYRIANS]

Jos 19:29 reaching to the fortified city of T;
2Sa 5:11 King Hiram of T sent messengers to David,
24: 7 the fortress of T and to all the cities of the Hivites
1Ki 5: 1 King Hiram of T sent his servants to Solomon,
7:13 and received Hiram from T.
7:14 a man of T, had been an artisan in bronze;
9:11 King Hiram of T having supplied Solomon
9:12 But when Hiram came from T to see the cities
1Ch 14: 1 King Hiram of T sent messengers to David,
2Ch 2: 3 Solomon sent word to King Huram of T:
2:11 of T answered in a letter that he sent to Solomon,
Ps 45:12 the people of T will seek your favor with gifts,
83: 7 Philistia with the inhabitants of T;
87: 4 Philistia too, and T, with Ethiopia—
Isa 23: 1 The oracle concerning T.
23: 5 they will be in anguish over the report about T.
23: 8 Who has planned this against T,
23:13 They destined T for wild animals.
23:15 that day T will be forgotten for seventy years,
23:15 to T as in the song about the prostitute:
23:17 the end of seventy years, the LORD will visit T,
Jer 25:22 all the kings of T, all the kings of Sidon,
27: 3 the king of the Ammonites, the king of T,
47: 4 from T and Sidon every helper that remains.
Eze 26: 2 because T said concerning Jerusalem, "Aha,
26: 3 See, I am against you, O T!
26: 4 They shall destroy the walls of T and break
26: 7 against T from the north King Nebuchadrezzar
26:15 Thus says the Lord GOD to T:
27: 2 Now you, mortal, raise a lamentation over T,
27: 3 and say to T, which sits at the entrance to the sea,
27: 3 O T, you have said, "I am perfect in beauty."
27:32 "Who was ever destroyed like T in the midst of
28: 2 say to the prince of T, Thus says the Lord GOD:
28:12 raise a lamentation over the king of T,
29:18 of Babylon made his army labor hard against T;
29:18 from T to pay for the labor that he had expended
Joel 3: 4 What are you to me, O T and Sidon,
Am 1: 9 For three transgressions of T, and for four,
1:10 So I will send a fire on the wall of T,
Zec 9: 2 T and Sidon, though they are very wise.
9: 3 T has built itself a rampart,
Mt 11:21 of power done in you had been done in T
11:22 the day of judgment it will be more tolerable for T
15:21 and went away to the district of T and Sidon.
Mk 3: 8 and the region around T and Sidon.
7:24 and went away to the region of T.
7:31 Then he returned from the region of T,
Lk 6:17 Jerusalem, and the coast of T and Sidon.
10:13 of power done in you had been done in T
10:14 But at the judgment it will be more tolerable for T
Ac 12:20 Herod was angry with the people of T and Sidon.
21: 3 we sailed to Syria and landed at T,
21: 7 When we had finished the voyage from T,
Jdt 2:28 the seacoast, at Sidon and T, and those who lived
1Mc 5:15 that the people of Ptolemais and T and Sidon,
11:59 from the Ladder of T to the borders of Egypt.
2Mc 4:18 When the quadrennial games were being held at T
4:32 he had sold to T and the neighboring cities.
4:44 When the king came to T,
2Es 1:11 T and Sidon; I killed all their enemies.

TYRIAN (1) [TYRE]

2Ch 2:14 of one of the Danite women, his father a T.

TYRIANS (5) [TYRE]

1Ch 22: 4 and T brought great quantities of cedar to David.
Ezr 3: 7 and the T to bring cedar trees from Lebanon to
Ne 13:16 T also, who lived in the city,
2Mc 4:49 Therefore even the T, showing their hatred of
1Es 5:55 and carts to the Sidonians and the T,

TYRUS (KJV) See TYRE, ZEMER

U

UEL (1)

Ezr 10:34 Of the descendants of Bani: Maadai, Amram, U,

UGLY (8)

Ge 41: 3 Then seven other cows, u and thin,
41: 4 The u and thin cows ate up the seven sleek
41:19 other cows came up after them, poor, very u,
41:19 Never had I seen such u ones in all the land
41:20 thin and u cows ate up the first seven fat cows,
41:21 for they were still as u as before.
41:27 The seven lean and u cows that came up
Sir 20:24 A lie is an u blot on a person;

ULAI (2)
Da 8: 2 in the province of Elam, and I was by the river U.
8:16 and I heard a human voice by the U,

ULAM (4)
1Ch 7:16 and his sons were U and Rekem.
7:17 The son of U: Bedan.
8:39 The sons of his brother Eshek: U his firstborn,
8:40 The sons of U were mighty warriors, archers,

ULCERS (1)
Dt 28:27 with the boils of Egypt, with u, scurvy, and itch,

ULLA (1)
1Ch 7:39 The sons of U: Arah, Hanniel, and Rizia.

UMMAH (1)
Jos 19:30 U, Aphek, and Rehob—twenty-two towns with their

UMPIRE (1)
Job 9:33 There is no u between us,

UNABLE‡ (37)
Ge 19:11 so that they were u to find the door.
Ex 7:18 and the Egyptians shall be u to drink water from
22: 1 The thief shall make restitution, but if u to do so,
Dt 1: 9 "I am u by myself to bear you.
14:24 distance is so great that you are u to transport it,
28:29 but you shall be u to find your way;
29:23 nothing sprouting, u to support any vegetation,
Jos 7:12 the Israelites are u to stand before their enemies;
7:13 you will be u to stand before your enemies
1Ki 9:21 the Israelites were u to destroy completely—
Ne 4:10 and there is too much rubbish so that we are u
Ps 36:12 they are thrust down, u to rise.
Eze 3:26 you shall be speechless and u to reprove them;
33:22 and I was no longer u to speak.
Da 4:18 of my kingdom are u to tell me the interpretation.
Mk 9:17 he has a spirit that makes him u to speak;
Lk 1:20 u to speak, until the day these things occur."
1:22 He kept motioning to them and remained u
13:11 She was bent over and was quite u to stand
Ac 13:11 against you, and you will be blind for a while, u
1Co 2:14 and they are u to understand them
Heb 3:19 that they were u to enter because of unbelief.
4:15 not have a high priest who is u to sympathize
Tob 2:10 For four years I remained u to see.
AdE 16:12 But, u to restrain his arrogance,
Wis 12: 9 though you were not u to give the ungodly into
13: 1 and they were u from the good things that are seen
Sir 7: 6 or you may be u to root out injustice;
LtJ 6:14 but is u to destroy anyone who offends it.
6:57 of wood and overlaid with silver and gold are u
1Mc 9:60 but they were u to do it,
2Mc 3:28 and all his bodyguard but was now u
10:13 U to command the respect due his office,
3Mc 2:22 and, besides being paralyzed in his limbs, was u
2Es 10:32 and can still see, I am u to explain."
4Mc 4: 1 of slander he was u to injure Onias in the eyes of
8: 2 being u to compel an aged man

UNADVISEDLY (KJV) See RASH

UNAFRAID (1)
Heb 11:27 By faith he left Egypt, u of the king's anger;

UNANIMOUSLY (1)
Ac 15:25 we have decided u to choose representatives

UNANSWERED (1)
Job 11: 2 "Should a multitude of words go u,

UNAPPROACHABLE (3)
1Ti 6:16 and dwells in u light, whom no one has ever seen
3Mc 2:15 For your dwelling is the heaven of heavens, u
3:29 a Jew is to be made u and burned with fire,

UNAWARE (6) [UNAWARES]
Lev 5: 2 and are u of it, you have become unclean,
5: 3 and are u of it, when you come to know it,
5: 4 whatever people utter in an oath, and are u of it,
1Co 10: 1 I do not want you to be u, brothers and sisters,
2Co 1: 8 We do not want you to be u, brothers and sisters,
Wis 12:10 though you were not u that their origin was evil

UNAWARES (2) [UNAWARE]
Ge 34:25 took their swords and came against the city u,
Ps 35: 8 Let ruin come on them u.

UNAWARES (KJV) See also DECEIVED, SECRETLY, UNEXPECTEDLY, UNINTENTIONALLY, WITHOUT INTENT, WITHOUT KNOWING

UNBEARABLY (1)
2Co 1: 8 u crushed that we despaired of life itself.

UNBECOMING (1)
4Mc 6:17 so basely that out of cowardice we feign a role u

UNBELIEF‡ (10) [UNBELIEVABLE, UNBELIEVER, UNBELIEVER'S, UNBELIEVERS, UNBELIEVING]
Mt 13:58 of power there, because of their u.
Mk 6: 6 And he was amazed at their u.
9:24 of the child cried out, "I believe; help my u!"
Ro 11:20 They were broken off because of their u,
11:23 even those of Israel, if they do not persist in u,
1Ti 1:13 because I had acted ignorantly in u,
Heb 3:19 that they were unable to enter because of u.
2Es 7:*114* [44] to an end, u has been cut off,
15: 3 not be troubled by the u of those who oppose you.
15: 4 For all unbelievers shall die in their u.

UNBELIEVABLE (1) [UNBELIEF]
Jdt 13:13 for it seemed u that she had returned.

UNBELIEVER (6) [UNBELIEF]
1Co 7:12 that if any believer has a wife who is an u,
7:13 And if any woman has a husband who is an u,
10:27 u invites you to a meal and you are disposed to go,
14:24 an u or outsider who enters is reproved by all
2Co 6:15 Or what does a believer share with an u?
1Ti 5: 8 has denied the faith and is worse than an u.

UNBELIEVER'S (1) [UNBELIEF]
1Co 14:25 After the secrets of the u heart are disclosed,

UNBELIEVERS (8) [NON-BELIEVERS, UNBELIEF]
Ro 15:31 that I may be rescued from the u in Judea,
1Co 6: 6 against a believer—and before u at that?
14:22 Tongues, then, are a sign not for believers but for u, while prophecy is not for u but for believers.
14:23 and all speak in tongues, and outsiders or u enter,
2Co 4: 4 of this world has blinded the minds of the u,
6:14 Do not be mismatched with u.
2Es 15: 4 For all u shall die in their unbelief.

UNBELIEVING‡ (7) [UNBELIEF]
Ac 14: 2 But the u Jews stirred up the Gentiles
1Co 7:14 For the u husband is made holy through his wife, and the u wife is made holy through her husband.
7:15 But if the u partner separates, let it be so;
Tit 1:15 but to the corrupt and u nothing is pure.
Heb 3:12 u heart that turns away from the living God.
Wis 10: 7 pillar of salt standing as a monument to an u soul.

UNBIND (1) [UNBOUND]
Jn 11:44 Jesus said to them, "U him, and let him go."

UNBLAMEABLE (KJV) See BLAMELESS

UNBORN (3)
Ps 22:31 and proclaim his deliverance to a people yet u,
78: 6 the children yet u, and rise up and tell them
102:18 so that a people yet u may praise the LORD:

UNBOUND (1) [UNBIND]
Da 3:25 He replied, "But I see four men u,

UNBREAKABLE (1) [UNBROKEN]
3Mc 4: 9 others had their feet secured by u fetters,

UNBROKEN (4) [UNBREAKABLE]
Sir 30: 8 An u horse turns out stubborn,
Bel 1:17 The king said, "Are the seals u, Daniel?"
1:17 He answered, "They are u, O king."
2Mc 3: 1 While the holy city was inhabited in u peace and

UNBURIED (1)
2Mc 5:10 He who had cast out many to lie u had no one

UNCEASING (4) [UNCEASINGLY]
Isa 14: 6 struck down the peoples in wrath with u blows,
Jer 15:18 Why is my pain u, my wound incurable,
Ro 9: 2 I have great sorrow and u anguish in my heart.
4Mc 10:11 will undergo u torments."

UNCEASINGLY (1) [UNCEASING]
3Mc 6:33 to heaven u and lavishly for the unexpected rescue

UNCERTAIN (2) [UNCERTAINTY]
Jn 13:22 u of whom he was speaking.
2Mc 7:34 do not be elated in vain and puffed up by u hopes,

UNCERTAINTY (2) [UNCERTAIN]
1Ti 6:17 or to set their hopes on the u of riches,
3Mc 4: 4 reflected on the u of life and shed tears at

UNCHANGEABLE (2) [UNCHANGING]
Heb 6:17 of the promise the u character of his purpose,
6:18 so that through two u things,

UNCHANGING (1) [UNCHANGEABLE]
AdE 13: 3 for his u goodwill and steadfast fidelity,

UNCHASTE (1) [UNCHASTITY]
Sir 26: 9 The haughty stare betrays an u wife;

UNCHASTITY (2) [UNCHASTE]
Mt 5:32 except on the ground of u,
19: 9 whoever divorces his wife, except for u,

UNCHECKED (1)
Sir 30: 8 and an u son turns out headstrong.

UNCIRCUMCISED‡ (42) [UNCIRCUMCISION]
Ge 17:14 Any u male who is not circumcised in the flesh
34:14 to give our sister to one who is u,
Ex 12:48 But no u person shall eat of it;
Lev 26:41 if then their u heart is humbled
Jos 5: 7 for they were u, because they had
Jdg 14: 3 to take a wife from the u Philistines?"
15:18 and fall into the hands of the u?"
1Sa 14: 6 "Come, let us go over to the garrison of these u;
17:26 For who is this u Philistine that he should defy
17:36 and this u Philistine shall be like one of them,
31: 4 that these u may not come and thrust me through,
2Sa 1:20 the daughters of the u will exult.
1Ch 10: 4 that these u may not come and make sport of me."
Isa 52: 1 for the u and the unclean shall enter you no more.
Jer 9:26 For all these nations are u,
9:26 and all the house of Israel is u in heart.
Eze 28:10 the death of the u by the hand of foreigners;
31:18 you shall lie among the u,
32:19 Be laid to rest with the u!"
32:21 "They have come down, they lie still, the u,
32:24 who went down u into the world below,
32:25 their graves all around it, all of them u,
32:26 their graves all around them, all of them u,
32:28 So you shall be broken and lie among the u,
32:29 they lie with the u, with those who go down to
32:30 they lie u with those who are killed by the sword,
32:32 therefore he shall be laid to rest among the u,
44: 7 u in heart and flesh, to be in my sanctuary,
44: 9 No foreigner, u in heart and flesh,
Ac 7:51 "You stiff-necked people, u in heart and ears,
11: 3 "Why did you go to u men and eat with them?"
Ro 2:26 those who are u keep the requirements of the law,
2:27 Then those who are physically u but keep
3:30 the circumcised on the ground of faith and the u
4: 9 on the circumcised, or also on the u?
4:11 that he had by faith while he was still u.
1Co 7:18 Was anyone at the time of his call u?
Gal 2: 7 that I had been entrusted with the gospel for the u,
Col 3:11 circumcised and u, barbarian, Scythian,
AdE 14:15 of the wicked and abhor the bed of the u and
1Mc 1:48 and to leave their sons u.
2:46 the u boys that they found within the borders

UNCIRCUMCISION‡ (7) [UNCIRCUMCISED]
Ro 2:25 your circumcision has become u.
2:26 will not their u be regarded as circumcision?
1Co 7:19 Circumcision is nothing, and u is nothing;
Gal 5: 6 in Christ Jesus neither circumcision nor u counts
6:15 For neither circumcision nor u is anything;
Eph 2:11 called "the u" by those who are called
Col 2:13 And when you were dead in trespasses and the u

UNCLE (10) [UNCLE'S]
Lev 10: 4 sons of Uzziel the u of Aaron, and said to them,
25:49 or their u or their uncle's son may redeem them,
1Sa 10:14 Saul's u said to him and to the boy,
10:15 Saul's u said, "Tell me what Samuel said to you."
10:16 Saul said to his u, "He told us that
14:50 of his army was Abner son of Ner, Saul's u;
2Ki 24:17 king of Babylon made Mattaniah, Jehoiachin's u,
1Ch 27:32 Jonathan, David's u, was a counselor,
Est 2:15 the turn came for Esther daughter of Abihail the u
Jer 32: 7 Hanamel son of your u Shallum is going to come

UNCLE'S (3) [UNCLE]
Lev 20:20 If a man lies with his u wife,
20:20 he has uncovered his u nakedness;
25:49 or their uncle or their u son may redeem them,

UNCLEAN‡ (215) [UNCLEANNESS, UNCLEANNESSES]
A. UNCLEAN SPIRIT (12)
B. UNCLEAN SPIRITS (10)

Lev 5: 2 when any of you touch any u thing—whether the carcass of an u beast or the carcass of u livestock or the carcass of an u swarming thing—and are unaware of it, you have become u,
5: 3 any uncleanness by which one can become u—
7:19 Flesh that touches any u thing shall not be eaten;
7:21 When any one of you touches any u thing—
7:21 or an u animal or any u creature—
10:10 and between the u and the clean;
11: 4 not have divided hoofs; it is u for you.
11: 5 not have divided hoofs; it is u for you.

Lev 11: 6 not have divided hoofs; it is **u** for you.
11: 7 not chew the cud; it is **u** for you.
11: 8 not touch; they are **u** for you.
11:24 By these you shall become **u**;
11:24 of any of them shall be **u** until the evening,
11:25 of any of them shall wash his clothes and be **u**
11:26 not cleft-footed or does not chew the cud is **u**
11:26 everyone who touches one of them shall be **u**.
11:27 the animals that walk on all fours, are **u** for you;
11:27 of any of them shall be **u** until the evening,
11:28 the carcass shall wash his clothes and be **u** until
11:28 until the evening; they are **u** for you.
11:29 These are **u** for you among the creatures
11:31 These are **u** for you among all that swarm;
11:31 when they are dead shall be **u** until the evening.
11:32 when they are dead shall be **u**, whether an article
11:32 and it shall be **u** until the evening,
11:33 all that is in it shall be **u**,
11:34 be **u** if water from any such vessel comes upon it;
11:34 be drunk shall be **u** if it was in any such vessel.
11:35 on which any part of the carcass falls shall be **u**;
11:35 they are **u**, and shall remain **u** for you.
11:36 while whatever touches the carcass in it shall be **u**.
11:38 and any part of their carcass falls on it, it is **u**
11:39 anyone who touches its carcass shall be **u** until
11:40 of its carcass shall wash their clothes and be **u**
11:40 the carcass shall wash their clothes and be **u** until
11:43 not defile yourselves with them, and so become **u**.
11:47 to make a distinction between the **u** and the clean,
12: 2 she shall be ceremonially **u** seven days;
12: 2 as at the time of her menstruation, she shall be **u**.
12: 5 she bears a female child, she shall be **u** two weeks,
13: 3 he shall pronounce him ceremonially **u**.
13: 8 the priest shall pronounce him **u**;
13:11 The priest shall pronounce him **u**;
13:11 he shall not confine him, for he is **u**.
13:14 if raw flesh ever appears on him, he shall be **u**;
13:15 the raw flesh and pronounce him **u**.
13:15 Raw flesh is **u**, for it is a leprous disease.
13:20 the priest shall pronounce him **u**;
13:22 the priest shall pronounce him **u**; it is diseased.
13:25 and the priest shall pronounce him **u**.
13:27 the priest shall pronounce him **u**.
13:30 the priest shall pronounce him **u**;
13:36 for the yellow hair; he is **u**.
13:44 leprous, he is **u**. The priest shall pronounce him **u**;
13:45 he shall cover his upper lip and cry out, "**U, u**."
13:46 remain **u** as long as he has the disease; he is **u**.
13:51 this is a spreading leprous disease; it is **u**.
13:55 though the disease has not spread, it is **u**;
13:59 to decide whether it is clean or **u**.
14:36 or all that is in the house will become **u**;
14:40 be taken out and thrown into an **u** place outside
14:41 be dumped in an **u** place outside the city.
14:44 a spreading leprous disease in the house; it is **u**.
14:45 and taken outside the city to an **u** place.
14:46 while it is shut up shall be **u** until the evening;
14:57 to determine when it is **u** and when it is clean.
15: 2 his discharge makes him ceremonially **u**.
15: 4 the one with the discharge lies shall be **u**;
15: 4 and everything on which he sits shall be **u**.
15: 5 and bathe in water, and be **u** until the evening.
15: 6 and bathe in water, and be **u** until the evening.
15: 7 and bathe in water, and be **u** until the evening.
15: 8 and bathe in water, and be **u** until the evening.
15: 9 the one with the discharge rides shall be **u**.
15:10 that was under him shall be **u** until the evening,
15:10 and bathe in water, and be **u** until the evening.
15:11 and bathe in water, and be **u** until the evening.
15:16 and be **u** until the evening.
15:17 and be **u** until the evening.
15:18 and be **u** until the evening.
15:19 whoever touches her shall be **u** until the evening.
15:20 during her impurity shall be **u**;
15:20 everything also upon which she sits shall be **u**.
15:21 and bathe in water, and be **u** until the evening.
15:22 and bathe in water, and be **u** until the evening;
15:23 when he touches it he shall be **u** until the evening.
15:24 he shall be **u** seven days;
15:24 and every bed on which he lies shall be **u**.
15:25 as in the days of her impurity, she shall be **u**.
15:26 and everything on which she sits shall be **u**,
15:27 Whoever touches these things shall be **u**,
15:27 and bathe in water, and be **u** until the evening.
15:30 before the LORD for her **u** discharge.
15:32 an emission of semen, becoming **u** thereby,
15:33 and for the man who lies with a woman who is **u**.
17:15 and be **u** until the evening;
20:25 and the **u**, and between the **u** bird and the clean;
20:25 which I have set apart for you to hold **u**.
22: 4 Whoever touches anything made **u** by a corpse or
22: 5 be made **u** or any human being by whom he may be made **u**—
22: 6 the person who touches any such shall be **u**
22: 8 becoming **u** by it: I am the LORD.
27:11 If it concerns any **u** animal that may not
27:27 an **u** animal, it shall be ransomed at its assessment,
Nu 5: 2 everyone who is **u** through contact with a corpse;
9: 6 Now there were certain people who were **u**
9: 7 "Although we are **u** through touching a corpse,
9:10 or your descendants who is **u** through touching
18:15 and the firstborn of **u** animals you shall redeem.
19: 7 but the priest shall remain **u** until evening.
19: 8 he shall remain **u** until evening.
19:10 of the heifer shall wash his clothes and be **u**
19:11 of any human being shall be **u** seven days.
19:13 they remain **u**; their uncleanness is still on them.
Nu 19:14 in the tent, shall be **u** seven days.
19:15 with no cover fastened on it is **u**.
19:16 or a grave, shall be **u** seven days.
19:17 For the **u** they shall take some ashes of
19:19 the **u** ones on the third day and on the seventh day,
19:20 Any who are **u** but do not purify themselves,
19:20 not been dashed on them, they are **u**.
19:21 the water for cleansing shall be **u** until evening.
19:22 Whatever the **u** person touches shall be **u**,
19:22 anyone who touches it shall be **u** until evening.
Dt 12:15 the **u** and the clean may eat of it,
12:22 the **u** and the clean alike may eat it.
14: 7 not divide the hoof; they are **u** for you.
14: 8 the hoof but does not chew the cud, is **u** for you.
14:10 not eat; it is **u** for you.
14:19 And all winged insects are **u** for you;
15:22 the **u** and the clean alike,
23:10 If one of you becomes **u** because of
26:14 I have not removed any of it while I was **u**;
Jos 22:19 But now, if your land is **u**,
Jdg 13: 4 to drink wine or strong drink, or to eat anything **u**,
13: 7 drink no wine or strong drink, and eat nothing **u**,
13:14 to drink wine or strong drink, or eat any **u** thing.
2Ch 23:19 so that no one should enter who was in any way **u**.
29:16 the **u** things that they found in the temple of
Ezr 2:62 so they were excluded from the priesthood as **u**;
9:11 that you are entering to possess is a land **u** with
Ne 7:64 so they were excluded from the priesthood as **u**;
Job 14: 4 Who can bring a clean thing out of an **u**?
Ps 106:39 Thus they became **u** by their acts,
Ecc 9: 2 to the good and the evil, to the clean and the **u**,
Isa 6: 5 I am lost, for I am a man of **u** lips, and I live among a people of **u** lips;
35: 8 the **u** shall not travel on it,
52: 1 uncircumcised and the **u** shall enter you no more.
52:11 from there! Touch no **u** thing;
64: 6 We have all become like one who is **u**,
La 4:15 **U**!" people shouted at them;
Eze 4:13 "Thus shall the people of Israel eat their bread, **u**,
7:19 their gold shall be treated as **u**.
7:20 therefore I will make of it an **u** thing to them.
22:26 the difference between the **u** and the clean,
44:23 and show them how to distinguish between the **u**
Hos 9: 3 and in Assyria they shall eat **u** food.
Am 7:17 you yourself shall die in an **u** land,
Hag 2:13 "If one who is **u** by contact with a dead body touches any of these, does it become **u**?"
2:13 The priests answered, "Yes, it becomes **u**."
2:14 and what they offer there is **u**.
Zec 13: 2 from the land the prophets and the **u** spirit. A
Mt 10: 1 and gave them authority over **u** spirits, B
12:43 "When the **u** spirit has gone out of a person, A
Mk 1:23 in their synagogue a man with an **u** spirit, A
1:26 And the **u** spirit, convulsing him and crying A
1:27 He commands even the **u** spirits, B
3:11 Whenever the **u** spirits saw him, B
3:30 for they had said, "He has an **u** spirit." A
5: 2 a man out of the tombs with an **u** spirit met him. A
5: 8 "Come out of the man, you **u** spirit!" A
5:12 **u** spirits begged him, "Send us into the swine; B
5:13 the **u** spirits came out and entered the swine; B
6: 7 and gave them authority over the **u** spirits. B
7:25 an **u** spirit immediately heard about him, A
9:25 he rebuked the **u** spirit, saying to it, A
Lk 4:33 a man who had the spirit of an **u** demon,
4:36 and power he commands the **u** spirits, B
6:18 who were troubled with **u** spirits were cured. B
8:29 Jesus had commanded the **u** spirit to come out A
9:42 But Jesus rebuked the **u** spirit, healed the boy, A
11:24 "When the **u** spirit has gone out of a person, A
Ac 5:16 the sick and those tormented by **u** spirits, B
8: 7 for **u** spirits, crying with loud shrieks, came out B
10:14 I have never eaten anything that is profane or **u**."
10:28 that I should not call anyone profane or **u**.
11: 8 nothing profane or **u** has ever entered my mouth.'
Ro 14:14 in the Lord Jesus that nothing is **u** in itself; but it is **u** for anyone who thinks it **u**.
1Co 7:14 Otherwise, your children would be **u**, but as it is,
2Co 6:17 and touch nothing **u**; then I will welcome you,
Rev 21:27 But nothing **u** will enter it,
Wis 2:16 and he avoids our ways as **u**;
Sir 34: 4 From an **u** thing what can be clean?
51: 5 from an **u** tongue and lying words—
1Mc 1:47 to sacrifice swine and other **u** animals,
1:48 to make themselves abominable by everything **u**
1:62 and were resolved in their hearts not to eat **u** food.
4:43 and removed the defiled stones to an **u** place.
1Es 1:49 and lawlessness beyond all the **u** deeds of all

UNCLEANNESS (26) [UNCLEAN]

Lev 5: 3 Or when you touch human **u**—any **u** by which one can become unclean—
7:20 while in a state of **u** shall be cut off from their kin.
7:21 human **u** or an unclean animal
14:19 for the one to be cleansed from his **u**.
15: 3 The **u** of his discharge is this:
15: 3 or his member is stopped from discharging, it is **u**
15:25 the days of the discharge she shall continue in **u**;
15:26 as in the **u** of her impurity.
15:31 the people of Israel separate from their **u**,
15:31 not die in their **u** by defiling my tabernacle that is
18:19 while she is in her menstrual **u**.
22: 3 while he is in a state of **u**,
22: 5 be made unclean—whatever his **u** may be—
Nu 5:19 to **u** while under your husband's authority,
19:13 their **u** is still on them.
Ezr 9:11 They have filled it from end to end with their **u**.
La 1: 9 Her **u** was in her skirts;
Eze 36:17 like the **u** of a woman in her menstrual period.
39:24 according to their **u** and their transgressions,
Mic 2:10 of **u** that destroys with a grievous destruction.
1Mc 13:48 He removed all **u** from it,
14: 7 and he removed its **u** from it;
1Es 1:42 and his **u** and impiety, are written in the annals of
8:83 and they have filled it with their **u**.
8:87 by mixing with the **u** of the peoples of the land.

UNCLEANNESSES (5) [UNCLEAN]

Lev 16:16 because of the **u** of the people of Israel,
16:16 which remains with them in the midst of their **u**.
16:19 and hallow it from the **u** of the people of Israel.
Eze 36:25 and you shall be clean from all your **u**,
36:29 I will save you from all your **u**,

UNCLOTHED (1)

2Co 5: 4 we wish not to be **u** but to be further clothed,

UNCOMELY (KJV) See LESS RESPECTABLE, NOT BEHAVING PROPERLY

UNCOMFORTABLE (1)

2Mc 2:27 of many we will gladly endure the **u** toil,

UNCOMPLETED (1)

3Mc 4:15 coming to an end after forty days but still **u**.

UNCONCERNED (1)

Bel 1:13 They were **u**, for beneath the table they had made

UNCONDEMNED (3)

Ac 16:37 Paul replied, "They have beaten us in public, **u**,
22:25 for you to flog a Roman citizen who is **u**?"
2Mc 4:47 who would have been freed **u** if they had pleaded

UNCONQUERED (1)

4Mc 11:27 therefore, **u**, we hold fast to reason."

UNCONTROLLABLE (1)

3Mc 6:17 with them and brought an **u** terror upon the army.

UNCORRUPTIBLE (KJV) See IMMORTAL

UNCOUNTED (2)

Wis 7:11 and in her hands **u** wealth.
3Mc 2:26 He was not content with his **u** licentious deeds,

UNCOVER (26) [UNCOVERED, UNCOVERING, UNCOVERS]

Lev 18: 6 near of kin to **u** nakedness:
18: 7 You shall not **u** the nakedness of your father,
18: 7 she is your mother, you shall not **u** her nakedness.
18: 8 not **u** the nakedness of your father's wife;
18: 9 You shall not **u** the nakedness of your sister,
18:10 not **u** the nakedness of your son's daughter or
18:11 You shall not **u** the nakedness
18:12 not **u** the nakedness of your father's sister;
18:13 not **u** the nakedness of your mother's sister,
18:14 not **u** the nakedness of your father's brother,
18:15 not **u** the nakedness of your daughter-in-law:
18:15 you shall not **u** her nakedness.
18:16 not **u** the nakedness of your brother's wife;
18:17 not **u** the nakedness of a woman and her daughter,
18:17 or her daughter's daughter to **u** her nakedness;
18:19 not approach a woman to **u** her nakedness
20:19 not **u** the nakedness of your mother's sister or
Ru 3: 4 then, go and **u** his feet and lie down;
2Sa 6:20 any vulgar fellow might shamelessly **u** himself!"
Isa 47: 2 remove your veil, strip off your robe, **u** your legs,
La 4:22 he will punish, he will **u** your sins.
Eze 16:37 and will **u** your nakedness to them,
22:10 In you they **u** their fathers' nakedness;
Hos 2:10 Now I will **u** her shame in the sight of her lovers,
Mic 1: 6 into the valley, and **u** her foundations.
1Es 8:79 and to **u** a light for us in the house of

UNCOVERED‡ (22) [UNCOVER]

Ge 9:21 and he lay **u** in his tent.
Lev 20:11 with his father's wife has **u** his father's nakedness;
20:17 he has **u** his sister's nakedness,
20:20 he has **u** his uncle's nakedness;
20:21 he has **u** his brother's nakedness;
Nu 24: 4 who falls down, but with eyes **u**:
24:16 who falls down, but with his eyes **u**:
Ru 3: 7 she came stealthily and **u** his feet, and lay down.
Isa 20: 4 with buttocks **u**, to the shame of Egypt.
22: 6 with chariots and cavalry, and Kir **u** the shield.
47: 3 Your nakedness shall be **u**,
57: 8 for, in deserting me, you have **u** your bed,
Jer 49:10 I have **u** his hiding places,
Eze 16:36 and your nakedness **u** in your whoring
16:57 before your wickedness was **u**?
21:24 in that your transgressions are **u**,
23:10 These **u** her nakedness; they seized her sons
Mt 10:26 for nothing is covered up that will not be **u**,
Lk 12: 2 Nothing is covered up that will not be **u**,

Tob 2: 9 and my face was **u** because of the heat.
Jdt 9: 1 and **u** the sackcloth she was wearing.
LtJ 6:31 their heads and beards shaved, and their heads **u**.

UNCOVERING‡ (2) [UNCOVER]

Lev 18:18 **u** her nakedness while her sister is still alive.
2Sa 6:20 **u** himself today before the eyes

UNCOVERS (2) [UNCOVER]

Lev 20:18 a woman having her sickness and **u** her nakedness,
Job 12:22 He **u** the deeps out of darkness,

UNCTION (KJV) See ANOINTED, ANOINTING

UNDAUNTED (1)

4Mc 13:13 cheerful and **u**, said, "Let us with all our hearts

UNDEFENDED (1)

AdE 16:14 that by these methods he would catch us **u**

UNDEFILED (9)

Heb 7:26 holy, blameless, **u**, separated from sinners,
13: 4 and let the marriage bed be kept **u**;
Jas 1:27 Religion that is pure and **u** before God, the Father,
1Pe 1: 4 **u**, and unfading, kept in heaven for you,
Wis 3:13 For blessed is the barren woman who is **u**,
4: 2 victor in the contest for prizes that are **u**.
8:20 or rather, being good, I entered an **u** body.
2Mc 14:36 keep **u** forever this house that has been
15:34 "Blessed is he who has kept his own place **u**!"

UNDEFILED (KJV) See also BLAMELESS, PERFECT

UNDER‡ (427) [UNDERNEATH, UNDERPARTS]

Ge 1: 7 the waters that were **u** the dome from the waters
1: 9 "Let the waters **u** the sky be gathered together
6:17 to destroy from **u** heaven all flesh in which is
7:19 on the earth that all the high mountains **u**
18: 4 and wash your feet, and rest yourselves **u** the tree.
18: 8 and he stood by them **u** the tree while they ate.
19: 8 for they have come **u** the shelter of my roof."
21:15 she cast the child **u** one of the bushes.
24: 2 "Put your hand **u** my thigh
24: 9 So the servant put his hand **u** the thigh
28:11 he put it **u** his head and lay down in that place.
28:18 that he had put **u** his head and set it up for a pillar
35: 4 Jacob hid them **u** the oak that was near Shechem.
35: 8 died, and she was buried **u** an oak below Bethel.
41:35 up grain **u** the authority of Pharaoh for food in
47:29 put your hand **u** my thigh and promise
48: 6 be recorded **u** the names of their brothers
Ex 2:23 Israelites groaned **u** their slavery, and cried out.
9:19 not brought **u** shelter will die when the hail comes
17:12 they took a stone and put it **u** him, and he sat on it.
17:14 the remembrance of Amalek from **u** heaven."
20: 4 or that is in the water **u** the earth.
23: 5 the donkey of one who hates you lying **u**
24:10 **U** his feet there was something like a pavement
25:35 of one piece with it **u** the first pair of branches,
25:35 of one piece with it **u** the next pair of branches,
25:35 of one piece with it **u** the last pair of branches—
26:19 of silver **u** the twenty frames, two bases under
26:19 two bases **u** the first frame for its two pegs,
26:19 and two bases **u** the next frame for its two pegs;
26:21 two bases **u** the first frame, and two bases **u** the
26:25 two bases **u** the first frame, and two bases **u** the
26:33 You shall hang the curtain **u** the clasps,
27: 5 You shall set it **u** the ledge of the altar so that
30: 4 **u** its molding on two opposite sides
36:24 he made forty bases of silver **u** the twenty frames,
36:24 two bases **u** the first frame for its two pegs,
36:24 and two bases **u** the next frame for its two pegs.
36:26 two bases **u** the first frame and two bases **u** the
36:30 sixteen bases, **u** every frame two bases.
37:21 of one piece with it **u** the first pair of branches,
37:21 of one piece with it **u** the next pair of branches,
37:21 of one piece with it **u** the last pair of branches.
37:27 and made two golden rings for it **u** its molding,
38: 4 **u** its ledge, extending halfway down.
38:21 the Levites being **u** the direction of Ithamar son of
Lev 15:10 that was **u** him shall be unclean until the evening,
25:53 by the year they shall be **u** the alien's authority,
27:32 every tenth one that passes **u** the shepherd's staff,
Nu 2: 2 **u** ensigns by their ancestral houses;
4:28 and their responsibilities are to be **u** the oversight
4:33 **u** the hand of Ithamar son of Aaron the priest.
5:19 to uncleanness while **u** your husband's authority,
5:20 But if you have gone astray while **u**
5:29 when a wife, while **u** her husband's authority,
6:18 and put it on the fire **u** the sacrifice of well-being.
7: 8 **u** the direction of Ithamar son of Aaron the priest.
16:31 the ground **u** them was split apart.
22:27 the angel of the LORD, it lay down **u** Balaam;
31:49 the warriors who are **u** our command,
33: 1 in military formation **u** the leadership of Moses
Dt 2:25 and fear of you upon the peoples everywhere **u**
4:18 likeness of any fish that is in the water **u** the earth.
4:19 to all the peoples everywhere **u** heaven.
4:49 as the Sea of the Arabah, **u** the slopes of Pisgah.
Dt 5: 8 or that is in the water **u** the earth.
7:24 and you shall blot out their name from **u** heaven;
9:14 and blot out their name from **u** heaven;
12: 2 on the hills, and **u** every leafy tree.
20:19 in the field human beings that they should come **u**
21:23 for anyone hung on a tree is **u** God's curse.
25:19 the remembrance of Amalek from **u** heaven;
28:23 and the earth **u** you iron.
29:20 LORD will blot out their names from **u** heaven.
Jos 11: 3 and the Hivites **u** Hermon in the land of Mizpah.
24:26 up there **u** the oak in the sanctuary of the LORD.
Jdg 1: 7 and big toes cut off used to pick up scraps **u**
3:16 and he fastened it on his right thigh **u** his clothes.
3:30 Moab was subdued that day **u** the hand of Israel.
4: 5 to sit **u** the palm of Deborah between Ramah
6:11 of the LORD came and sat **u** the oak at Ophrah,
6:19 in a pot, and brought them to him **u** the oak
9:29 If only this people were **u** my command!
18: 6 mission you are on is **u** the eye of the LORD."
Ru 2:12 **u** whose wings you have come for refuge!"
1Sa 3: 1 boy Samuel was ministering to the LORD **u** Eli.
14: 2 in the outskirts of Gibeah **u** the pomegranate tree
22: 6 **u** the tamarisk tree on the height,
25:20 and came down **u** cover of the mountain, David
25:29 be bound in the bundle of the living **u** the care of
31:13 and buried them **u** the tamarisk tree in Jabesh,
2Sa 18: 2 one third **u** the command of Joab, one third **u** the
18: 2 and one third **u** the command of Ittai the Gittite.
18: 9 the mule went **u** the thick branches of a great oak.
18: 9 while the mule that was **u** him went on.
20: 3 and put them in a house **u** guard,
22:10 thick darkness was **u** his feet.
22:39 not rise; they fell **u** my feet.
22:40 you made my assailants sink **u** me.
22:48 and brought down peoples **u** me,
1Ki 4:25 all of them **u** their vines and fig trees.
5: 3 until the LORD put them **u** the soles of his feet.
7:24 **U** its brim were panels all around it,
13:14 and found him sitting **u** an oak tree.
14:23 on every high hill and **u** every green tree;
19: 4 and came and sat down **u** a solitary broom tree.
19: 5 Then he lay down **u** the broom tree and fell asleep.
2Ki 6: 1 the place where we live **u** your charge is too small
11: 4 and put them **u** oath in the house of the LORD;
14:27 that he would blot out the name of Israel from **u**
16: 4 on the hills, and **u** every green tree.
16:17 the sea from the bronze oxen that were **u** it,
17: 7 the land of Egypt from **u** the hand of Pharaoh king
17:10 on every high hill and **u** every green tree;
1Ch 10:12 Then they buried their bones **u** the oak in Jabesh,
12:32 and all their kindred **u** their command.
17: 1 the ark of the covenant of the LORD is **u** a tent."
24: 4 they organized them **u** sixteen heads
25: 2 sons of Asaph, **u** the direction of Asaph,
25: 2 who prophesied **u** the direction of the king.
25: 3 six, **u** the direction of their father Jeduthun,
25: 6 They were all **u** the direction of their father for
25: 6 Jeduthun, and Heman were **u** the order of the king.
2Ch 4: 3 **U** it were panels all around, each of ten cubits,
14: 5 And the kingdom had rest **u** him.
25: 5 and set them by ancestral houses **u** commanders of
26:11 **u** the direction of Hananiah,
26:13 **U** their command was an army
28: 4 on the hills, and **u** every green tree.
Ezr 5:16 that time until now it has been **u** construction,
Ne 1: 9 though your outcasts are **u** the farthest skies,
3: 7 who were **u** the jurisdiction of the governor of
Est 2: 3 to the harem in the citadel of Susa **u** custody
2:12 after being twelve months **u** the regulations for
Job 20:12 though they hide it **u** their tongues,
28:24 and sees everything **u** the heavens.
30: 7 **u** the nettles they huddle together.
37: 3 **U** the whole heaven he lets it loose,
38:14 It is changed like clay **u** the seal,
40:21 **U** the lotus plants it lies,
41:11 and be safe?—**u** the whole heaven, who?
Ps 8: 6 you have put all things **u** their feet,
10: 7 **u** their tongues are mischief and iniquity
18: 9 thick darkness was **u** his feet.
18:36 You gave me a wide place for my steps **u** me,
18:38 not able to rise; they fell **u** my feet.
18:39 you made my assailants sink **u** me.
18:47 and subdued peoples **u** me;
27: 5 he will conceal me **u** the cover of his tent;
31:20 you hold them safe **u** your shelter
31:21 to me when I was beset as a city **u** siege.
45: 5 of the king's enemies; the peoples fall **u** you.
47: 3 He subdued peoples **u** us, and nations **u** our feet.
61: 4 find refuge **u** the shelter of your wings.
68:30 Trample **u** foot those who lust after tribute;
90: 9 For all our days pass away **u** your wrath;
91: 4 and **u** his wings you will find refuge;
91:13 the young lion and the serpent you will trample **u**
106:42 they were brought into subjection **u** their power.
140: 3 and **u** their lips is the venom of vipers.
144: 2 who subdues the peoples **u** me.
Pr 5:21 For human ways are **u** the eyes of the LORD,
22:27 why should your bed be taken from **u** you?
30:21 **U** three things the earth trembles;
30:21 **u** four it cannot bear up:
Ecc 1: 3 from all the toil at which they toil **u** the sun?
1: 9 there is nothing new **u** the sun.
1:13 to search out by wisdom all that is done **u** heaven;
1:14 I saw all the deeds that are done **u** the sun;
2: 3 to do **u** heaven during the few days of their life.
2:11 and there was nothing to be gained **u** the sun.
2:17 what is done **u** the sun was grievous to me;
Ecc 2:18 I hated all my toil in which I had toiled **u** the sun,
2:19 for which I toiled and used my wisdom **u** the sun.
2:20 concerning all the toil of my labors **u** the sun,
2:22 the toil and strain with which they toil **u** the sun?
3: 1 and a time for every matter **u** heaven:
3:16 I saw **u** the sun that in the place of justice,
4: 1 the oppressions that are practiced **u** the sun.
4: 3 has not seen the evil deeds that are done **u** the sun.
4: 7 Again, I saw vanity **u** the sun:
4:15 I saw all the living who, moving about **u** the sun,
5:13 There is a grievous ill that I have seen **u** the sun:
5:18 with which one toils **u** the sun the few days of
6: 1 There is an evil that I have seen **u** the sun,
6:12 can tell them what will be after them **u** the sun?
7: 6 For like the crackling of thorns **u** a pot,
8: 9 applying my mind to all that is done **u** the sun,
8:15 for there is nothing better for people **u**
8:15 the days of life that God gives them **u** the sun.
8:17 no one can find out what is happening **u** the sun.
9: 3 This is an evil in all that happens **u** the sun,
9: 6 in all that happens **u** the sun.
9: 9 of your vain life that are given you **u** the sun,
9: 9 in life and in your toil at which you toil **u** the sun.
9:11 that **u** the sun the race is not to the swift,
9:13 I have also seen this example of wisdom **u** the sun,
10: 5 There is an evil that I have seen **u** the sun,
SS 2: 6 O that his left hand were **u** my head,
4:11 honey and milk are **u** your tongue;
8: 3 O that his left hand were **u** my head,
8: 5 **U** the apple tree I awakened you.
Isa 3: 6 and this heap of ruins shall be **u** your rule."
10:16 and **u** his glory a burning will be kindled,
14:25 and on my mountains trample him **u** foot;
24: 5 The earth lies polluted **u** its inhabitants;
28: 3 Trampled **u** foot will be the proud garland of
41: 2 and tramples kings **u** foot;
57: 5 with lust among the oaks, **u** every green tree;
57: 5 you that slaughter your children in the valleys, **u**
Jer 2:20 and **u** every green tree you sprawled and played
3: 6 up on every high hill and **u** every green tree,
3:13 and scattered your favors among strangers **u**
10:11 the earth shall perish from the earth and from **u**
10:17 O you who live **u** siege!
15:17 **u** the weight of your hand I sat alone,
27: 8 and put its neck **u** the yoke of the king of Babylon,
27:11 But any nation that will bring its neck **u** the yoke
27:12 Bring your necks **u** the yoke of the king
33:13 flocks shall again pass **u** the hands of
34: 1 and all the peoples **u** his dominion were fighting
51:28 and every land **u** their dominion.
52:20 the twelve bronze bulls that were **u** the sea,
La 3: 1 I am one who has seen affliction **u** the rod
3:34 all the prisoners of the land are crushed **u** foot,
3:66 and destroy them from **u** the LORD's heavens.
4:20 "**U** his shadow we shall live among the nations."
5:13 and boys stagger **u** loads of wood.
Eze 1: 8 **U** their wings on their four sides they had human
1:23 **U** the dome their wings were stretched out straight,
4:17 and waste away **u** their punishment.
6:13 **u** every green tree, and **u** every leafy oak,
10: 8 to have the form of a human hand **u** their wings.
17:13 putting him **u** oath (he had taken away
17:23 **U** it every kind of bird will live;
20:37 I will make you pass **u** the staff,
24: 5 the choicest one of the flock, pile the logs **u** it;
31: 6 **u** its branches all the animals of
32:27 whose swords were laid **u** their heads,
Da 4:12 The animals of the field found shade **u** it,
4:21 **u** which animals of the field lived,
5: 2 **U** the influence of the wine,
7:27 of the kingdoms **u** the whole heaven shall be given
8:25 By his cunning he shall make deceit prosper **u**
9:12 against Jerusalem has never before been done **u**
Hos 4:13 and make offerings upon the hills, **u** oak, poplar,
8:10 They shall soon writhe **u** the burden of kings
Joel 1:17 The seed shrivels **u** the clods,
Jnh 4: 5 He sat **u** it in the shade,
Mic 1: 4 Then the mountains will melt **u** him and
4: 4 shall all sit **u** their own vines and **u** their own fig
7:19 he will tread our iniquities **u** foot.
Hab 3: 7 I saw the tents of Cushan **u** affliction;
Zec 3:10 you shall invite each other to come **u** your vine
Mal 4: 3 for they will be ashes **u** the soles of your feet,
Mt 2:16 around Bethlehem who were two years old or **u**,
5:13 but is thrown out and trampled **u** foot.
5:15 after lighting a lamp puts it **u** the bushel basket,
7: 6 before swine, or they will trample them **u** foot
8: 8 I am not worthy to have you come **u** my roof;
8: 9 I also am a man **u** authority, with soldiers **u** me;
22:44 until I put your enemies **u** your feet" '?
23:37 as a hen gathers her brood **u** her wings,
26:63 "I put you **u** oath before the living God,
Mk 4:21 a lamp brought in to be put **u** the bushel basket, or **u** the bed, and not on the lampstand?
5:26 She had endured much **u** many physicians,
7:28 the dogs **u** the table eat the children's crumbs."
12:36 until I put your enemies **u** your feet." '
14:44 arrest him and lead him away **u** guard."
Lk 2:27 to do for him what was customary **u** the law,
7: 6 for I am not worthy to have you come **u** my roof;
7: 8 I also am a man set **u** authority, with soldiers **u** me;
8:16 "No one after lighting a lamp hides it **u** a jar,
8:16 or puts it **u** a bed, but puts it on a lampstand,
8:29 he was kept **u** guard and bound with chains
12:50 and what stress I am **u** until it is completed!
13:34 as a hen gathers her brood **u** her wings,
23: 7 he learned that he was **u** Herod's jurisdiction,

Lk 23:40 you are **u** the same sentence of condemnation?
Jn 1:48 "I saw you **u** the fig tree before Philip called you."
1:50 because I told you that I saw you **u** the fig tree?
2:20 "This temple has been **u** construction
5:24 and does not come **u** judgment,
Ac 2: 5 Now there were devout Jews from every nation **u**
4:12 for there is no other name **u** heaven given
18:18 for he was **u** a vow.
21:23 We have four men who are **u** a vow.
23:35 that he be kept **u** guard in Herod's headquarters.
27: 4 we sailed **u** the lee of Cyprus,
27: 7 we sailed **u** the lee of Crete off Salmone.
27:16 By running **u** the lee of a small island called Cauda
27:16 scarcely able to get the ship's boat **u** control.
Ro 2:12 and all who have sinned **u** the law will be judged
3: 9 both Jews and Greeks, are **u** the power of sin,
3:13 "The venom of vipers is **u** their lips."
3:19 it speaks to those who are **u** the law,
6:14 since you are not **u** law but **u** grace.
6:15 we sin because we are not **u** law but **u** grace?
7: 6 so that we are slaves not **u** the old written code but
7:14 but I am of the flesh, sold into slavery **u** sin.
16:20 God of peace will shortly crush Satan **u** your feet.
1Co 7:37 being **u** no necessity but having his own desire **u**
9:20 To those **u** the law I became as one **u** the law
(though I myself am not **u** the law) so that I might
win those **u** the law.
9:21 not free from God's law but am **u** Christ's law)
10: 1 that our ancestors were all **u** the cloud,
15:25 until he has put all his enemies **u** his feet.
15:27 "God has put all things in subjection **u** his feet."
15:27 the one who put all things in subjection **u** him.
15:28 to the one who put all things in subjection **u** him,
2Co 5: 4 we are still in this tent, we groan **u** our burden,
9: 7 not reluctantly or **u** compulsion,
11:28 I am **u** daily pressure because of my anxiety for all
11:32 the governor **u** King Aretas guarded the city
Gal 3:10 all who rely on the works of the law are **u** a curse;
3:22 the scripture has imprisoned all things **u** the power
3:23 we were imprisoned and guarded **u** the law
4: 2 but they remain **u** guardians and trustees until
4: 4 born of a woman, born **u** the law,
4: 5 in order to redeem those who were **u** the law,
Eph 1:22 And he has put all things **u** his feet
Php 2:10 in heaven and on earth and **u** the earth,
3: 6 as to righteousness **u** the law, blameless.
Col 1:23 has been proclaimed to every creature **u** heaven.
1Ti 6: 1 Let all who are **u** the yoke of slavery
Heb 2: 8 subjecting all things **u** their feet."
3:16 not all those who left Egypt **u** the leadership
7:11 for the people received the law **u** this priesthood—
9:15 that redeems them from the transgressions **u**
9:22 **u** the law almost everything is purified with blood,
Jas 5:12 so that you may not fall **u** condemnation.
1Pe 5: 2 not **u** compulsion but willingly,
5: 6 Humble yourselves therefore **u** the mighty hand
2Pe 2: 9 to keep the unrighteous **u** punishment until the day
1Jn 5:19 the whole world lies **u** the power of the evil one.
Rev 5: 3 on earth or **u** the earth was able to open the scroll
5:13 in heaven and on earth and **u** the earth and in
6: 9 I saw **u** the altar the souls
12: 1 a woman clothed with the sun, with the moon **u**
Tob 1:22 and in charge of administrations of the accounts **u**
Jdt 8: 9 and how he promised them **u** oath to surrender
10:21 on his bed **u** a canopy that was woven with purple
11: 7 **u** Nebuchadnezzar and all his house.
AdE 2:18 a remission of taxes to those who were **u** his rule.
3: 6 plotted to destroy all the Jews **u** Artaxerxes' rule.
4: 8 being brought up **u** my care—
13: 1 from India to Ethiopia and to the officials **u** them:
13:10 and earth and every wonderful thing **u** heaven.
16:19 and permit the Jews to live **u** their own laws.
Wis 17: 2 of darkness and prisoners of long night, shut in **u**
Sir 6:25 and do not fret **u** her bonds.
14:26 who places his children **u** her shelter, and lodges **u**
her boughs.
20: 4 a girl is the person who does right **u** compulsion.
23:10 for as a servant who is constantly **u** scrutiny will
29:10 and do not let it rust **u** a stone and be lost.
29:22 Better is the life of the poor **u** their own crude roof
51:26 Put your neck **u** her yoke,
Bar 1:12 we shall live **u** the protection
1:12 and **u** the protection of his son Belshazzar,
2: 2 **U** the whole heaven there has not been done the
5: 3 for God will show your splendor everywhere **u**
LtJ 6:18 as though **u** sentence of death,
Sus 1:54 **U** what tree did you see them being intimate
1:54 He answered, **"U** a mastic tree."
1:58 **U** what tree did you catch them being intimate
1:58 He answered, **"U** an evergreen oak."
Bel 1:30 and **u** compulsion he handed Daniel over to them.
1Mc 2:19 "Even if all the nations that live **u** the rule of
6:46 He got **u** the elephant, stabbed it from beneath,
9:38 they went up and hid **u** cover of the mountain.
9:53 and put them **u** guard in the citadel at Jerusalem.
10:38 to be **u** one ruler and obey no other authority than
11:38 So all the troops who had served **u**
13:12 and Jonathan was with him **u** guard.
14: 3 and took him to Arsaces, who put him **u** guard.
14:12 All the people sat **u** their own vines and fig trees,
2Mc 2:18 from everywhere **u** heaven into his holy place,
3: 6 that it was possible for them to fall **u** the control of
3:19 Women, girded with sackcloth **u** their breasts,
4:12 in establishing a gymnasium right **u** the citadel,
4:40 **u** the leadership of a certain Auranus,
5:25 he ordered his troops to parade **u** arms.
6: 7 **u** bitter constraint, to partake of the sacrifices;
2Mc 6:30 When he was about to die **u** the blows,
6:30 I am enduring terrible sufferings in my body **u**
7: 1 **u** torture with whips and thongs,
7:36 a brief suffering have drunk of ever-flowing life, **u**
8:22 putting fifteen hundred men **u** each.
9:11 and to come to his senses **u** the scourge of God,
10:10 we will tell what took place **u** Antiochus Eupator,
12:19 who were captains **u** Maccabeus,
12:40 Then **u** the tunic of each one of
1Es 3: 1 a great banquet for all that were **u** him,
3: 2 the satraps and generals and governors that were **u**
3: 8 and they sealed them and put them **u** the pillow
5:36 **u** the leadership of Cherub, Addan, and Immer,
3Mc 3: 8 not strong enough to help them, for they lived **u**
4: 9 driven **u** the constraint of iron bonds;
4:10 and in addition they were confined **u** a solid deck,
2Es 1:30 I gathered you as a hen gathers her chicks **u**
11: 6 I saw how all things **u** heaven were subjected to it,
11:24 from the six and remained **u** the head that was on
13: 3 everything **u** his gaze trembled,
14: 1 On the third day, while I was sitting **u** an oak,
16:69 and shall be trampled **u** foot.
4Mc 8:14 to you when you transgress **u** compulsion."
8:22 for fearing the king when we are **u** compulsion.
9:19 he was saying these things, they spread fire **u** him,
14:12 for the mother of the seven young men bore up **u**
17:19 "All who are consecrated are **u** your hands."
17:23 of their virtue and their endurance **u** the tortures,

UNDERBRUSH (1)

2Es 16:77 a field choked with **u** and its path overwhelmed

UNDERFOOT (1) [FOOT]

Isa 14:19 to the stones of the Pit, like a corpse trampled **u**.

UNDERGARMENTS (6) [GARMENT]

Ex 28:42 for them linen **u** to cover their naked flesh;
39:28 and the linen **u** of fine twisted linen,
Lev 6:10 after putting on his linen **u** next to his body;
16: 4 and shall have the linen **u** next to his body,
Eze 44:18 and linen **u** on their loins;
Sir 45: 8 the linen **u**, the long robe, and the ephod.

UNDERGIRD (1)

Ac 27:17 hoisting it up they took measures to **u** the ship;

UNDERGIRDING (KJV) See UNDERGIRD

UNDERGO (7) [UNDERGOING, UNDERWENT]

2Ch 32:10 that you **u** the siege of Jerusalem?
Mt 16:21 that he must go to Jerusalem and **u** great suffering
Mk 8:31 that the Son of Man must **u** great suffering,
Lk 9:22 "The Son of Man must **u** great suffering,
3Mc 4:10 they would **u** treatment befitting traitors during
4Mc 9: 9 will deservedly **u** from divine justice eternal
10:11 will **u** unceasing torments."

UNDERGOING (2) [UNDERGO]

1Pe 5: 9 that your brothers and sisters in all the world are **u**
Jude 1: 7 as an example by **u** a punishment of eternal fire.

UNDERGROUND (1) [GROUND]

Dt 8: 7 with springs and **u** waters welling up in valleys

UNDERNEATH‡ (13) [UNDER]

Jos 7:21 in the ground inside my tent, with the silver **u."**
7:22 there it was, hidden in his tent with the silver **u.**
1Ki 7:32 The four wheels were **u** the borders;
7:44 the one sea, and the twelve oxen **u** the sea.
8: 6 **u** the wings of the cherubim.
2Ki 6:30 that he had sackcloth on his body **u**—
2Ch 4:15 the one sea, and the twelve oxen **u** it.
5: 7 **u** the wings of the cherubim.
Job 28: 5 but **u** it is turned up as by fire.
Eze 10: 2 "Go within the wheelwork **u** the cherubim;
10:20 that I saw **u** the God of Israel by the river Chebar;
10:21 and **u** their wings something like human hands.
4Mc 11:18 his back was broken, and he was roasted from **u.**

UNDERPARTS (1) [UNDER]

Job 41:30 Its **u** are like sharp potsherds;

UNDERSETTERS (KJV) See SUPPORTS

UNDERSTAND‡ (154) [UNDERSTANDING, UNDERSTANDS, UNDERSTOOD]

Ge 11: 7 so that they will not **u** one another's speech."
Ex 10: 7 do you not yet **u** that Egypt is ruined?"
Dt 8: 3 in order to make you **u** that one does not live
28:49 a nation whose language you do not **u**,
29: 4 the LORD has not given you a mind to **u**,
32:29 If they were wise, they would **u** this;
2Ki 18:26 in the Aramaic language, for we **u** it;
Ne 8: 3 the men and the women and those who could **u**;
8: 7 the Levites, helped the people to **u** the law,
Job 6:24 make me **u** how I have gone wrong.
15: 9 What do you **u** that is not clear to us?
23: 5 and **u** what he would say to me.
26:14 But the thunder of his power who can **u?"**
Job 32: 9 nor the aged that **u** what is right.
36:29 Can anyone **u** the spreading of the clouds,
42: 3 Therefore I have uttered what I did not **u**,
Ps 73:16 But when I thought how to **u** this,
92: 6 The dullard cannot know, the stupid cannot **u** this:
94: 8 **U**, O dullest of the people;
119:27 Make me **u** the way of your precepts,
119:100 I **u** more than the aged, for I keep your precepts.
Pr 1: 6 to **u** a proverb and a figure,
2: 5 then you will **u** the fear of the LORD and find
2: 9 you will **u** righteousness and justice and equity,
14: 8 It is the wisdom of the clever to **u** where they go,
20:24 how then can we **u** our own ways?
28: 5 The evil do not **u** justice,
28: 5 but those who seek the LORD **u** it completely.
29:19 for though they **u**, they will not give heed.
30:18 too wonderful for me; four I do not **u:**
Isa 1: 3 but Israel does not know, my people do not **u.**
6: 9 keep looking, but do not **u.'**
28:19 and it will be sheer terror to **u** the message.
33:19 stammering in a language that you cannot **u.**
36:11 to your servants in Aramaic, for we **u** it;
41:20 and know, all may consider and **u**, that the hand of
42:25 it set him on fire all around, but he did not **u;**
43:10 you may know and believe me and **u** that I am he.
44:18 and their minds as well, so that they cannot **u.**
Jer 5:15 nor can you **u** what they say.
9:12 Who is wise enough to **u** this?
9:24 that they **u** and know me, that I am the LORD;
17: 9 it is perverse—who can **u** it?
23:20 In the latter days you will **u** it clearly.
30:24 In the latter days you will **u** this.
Eze 3: 6 whose words you cannot **u.**
12: 3 Perhaps they will **u**, though they are
Da 2: 3 that my spirit is troubled by the desire to **u** it."
2:30 and that you may **u** the thoughts of your mind.
8:15 When I, Daniel, had seen the vision, I tried to **u** it.
8:16 calling, "Gabriel, help this man **u** the vision."
8:17 But he said to me, **"U**, O mortal,
8:27 But I was dismayed by the vision and did not **u** it.
9:23 So consider the word and **u** the vision:
9:25 Know therefore and **u:** from the
10:14 to help you **u** what is to happen to your people at
12: 8 I heard but could not **u;**
12:10 None of the wicked shall **u**, but those who are
wise shall **u.**
Hos 14: 9 Those who are wise **u** these things;
Mic 4:12 they do not **u** his plan, that he has gathered them
Mt 13:13 and hearing they do not listen, nor do they **u.'**
13:14 'You will indeed listen, but never **u**,
13:15 and **u** with their heart and turn—
13:19 the kingdom and does not **u** it, the evil one comes
15:10 the crowd to him and said to them, "Listen and **u:**
24:15 of by the prophet Daniel (let the reader **u**),
24:43 But **u** this: if the owner of the
Mk 4:12 but not perceive, and may indeed listen, but not **u;**
4:13 And he said to them, "Do you not **u** this parable?
4:13 Then how will you **u** all the parables?
6:52 for they did not **u** about the loaves,
7:14 "Listen to me, all of you, and **u:**
7:18 He said to them, "Then do you also fail to **u?**
8:17 Do you still not perceive or **u?**
8:21 Then he said to them, "Do you not yet **u?"**
9:32 not **u** what he was saying and were afraid
13:14 be (let the reader **u**), then those in Judea must flee
14:68 "I do not know or **u** what you are talking about."
Lk 2:50 But they did not **u** what he said to them.
8:10 and listening they may not **u.'**
9:45 But they did not **u** this saying;
24:45 Then he opened their minds to **u** the scriptures,
Jn 3:10 and yet you do not **u** these things?
8:27 They did not **u** that he was speaking to them about
8:43 Why do you not **u** what I say?
10: 6 but they did not **u** what he was saying to them.
10:38 that you may know and **u** that the Father is in me
11:50 not **u** that it is better for you to have one man die
12:16 His disciples did not **u** these things at first;
12:40 and **u** with their heart and turn—
13: 7 now what I am doing, but later you will **u."**
20: 9 for as yet they did not **u** the scripture,
Ac 7:25 He supposed that his kinsfolk would **u** that God
7:25 through him was rescuing them, but they did not **u.**
8:30 He asked, "Do you **u** what you are reading?"
10:34 "I truly **u** that God shows no partiality,
13:27 not recognize him or **u** the words of the prophets
28:26 but never **u**, and you will indeed look,
28:27 and **u** with their heart and turn—
Ro 7:15 I do not **u** my own actions.
10:19 Again I ask, did Israel not **u?**
11:25 brothers and sisters, I want you to **u** this mystery:
15:21 and those who have never heard of him shall **u."**
1Co 2:12 so that we may **u** the gifts bestowed on us by God.
2:14 to **u** them because they are spiritually discerned.
11: 3 But I want you to **u** that Christ is the head
12: 3 Therefore I want you to **u** that no one speaking by
13: 2 and **u** all mysteries and all knowledge,
2Co 1:13 nothing other than what you can read and also **u;**
1:13 I hope you will **u** until the end—
10:11 Let such people **u** that what we say by letter
Eph 5:17 but **u** what the will of the Lord is.
2Ti 3: 1 You must **u** this, that in the last days distressing
Heb 11: 3 By faith we **u** that the worlds were prepared by
Jas 1:19 You must **u** this, my beloved:
2Pe 1:20 First of all you must **u** this,
2:12 They slander what they do not **u**,
3: 3 First of all you must **u** this,
3:16 There are some things in them hard to **u**,

Jude 1:10 But these people slander whatever they do not **u**,
Jdt 8:14 the depths of the human heart or **u** the workings of
9:14 Let your whole nation and every tribe know and **u**
AdE 11:12 seeking all day to **u** it in every detail.
13: 5 We **u** that this people, and it alone,
Wis 3: 9 Those who trust in him will **u** truth,
4:15 Yet the peoples saw and did not **u**,
4:17 and will not **u** what the Lord purposed for them,
6: 1 Listen therefore, O kings, and **u**;
Sir Pr: 1 the scriptures must not only themselves **u** them,
3:23 for more than you can **u** has been shown you.
8: 9 to **u** and to give an answer when the need arises.
34:12 and I **u** more than I can express.
38:33 nor do they **u** the decisions of the courts;
LtJ 6:40 as though Bel were able to **u**!
2Mc 9:25 I **u** how the princes along the borders and
2Es 2:34 Therefore I say to you, O nations that hear and **u**,
4:10 to me, "You cannot **u** the things
4:11 by the corrupt world **u** incorruption?"
4:12 and to suffer and not **u** why."
4:21 also those who inhabit the earth can **u** only what is
4:21 above the heavens can **u** what is above the height
5:34 while I strive to **u** the way of the Most High and
5:37 I will explain to you the travail that you ask to **u**."
6:15 the end, and the foundations of the earth will **u**
7:*37* 'Look now, and **u** whom you have denied,
7:*71* But now, **u** from your own words—
7:*95* fourth order, they **u** the rest that they now enjoy,
8:19 Therefore hear my voice and **u** my words,
9:11 and did not **u** but despised it while an opportunity
10:35 and I hear what I do not **u**
13:18 because they **u** the things that are reserved for
13:24 **U** therefore that those who are left are more
16:35 Listen now to these things, and **u** them,

UNDERSTANDING‡ (162) [UNDERSTAND]

Ex 36: 1 the LORD has given skill and **u** to know how
Dt 32:28 there is no **u** in them.
1Ki 3: 9 an **u** mind to govern your people, able to discern
3:11 have asked for yourself **u** to discern what is right,
4:29 breadth of **u** as vast as the sand on the seashore,
1Ch 12:32 Of Issachar, those who had **u** of the times,
22:12 Only, may the LORD grant you discretion and **u**,
27:32 was a counselor, being a man of **u** and a scribe;
2Ch 2:12 endowed with discretion and **u**,
2:13 a skilled artisan, endowed with **u**,
Ne 8: 2 men and women and all who could hear with **u**.
10:28 their daughters, all who have knowledge and **u**,
Job 8:10 and tell you and utter words out of their **u**?
9:10 who does great things beyond **u**,
11:12 But a stupid person will get **u**,
12: 3 I have **u** as well as you; I am not inferior to you.
12:12 Is wisdom with the aged, and **u** in length of days?
12:13 and strength; he has counsel and **u**.
12:24 He strips **u** from the leaders of the earth,
17: 4 Since you have closed their minds to **u**,
20: 3 and a spirit beyond my **u** answers me.
26:12 by his **u** he struck down Rahab.
28:12 And where is the place of **u**?
28:20 And where is the place of **u**?
28:28 and to depart from evil is **u**.' "
32: 8 the breath of the Almighty, that makes for **u**.
34:16 "If you have **u**, hear this; listen to what I say.
36: 5 he is mighty in strength of **u**.
38: 4 Tell me, if you have **u**.
38:36 or given **u** to the mind?
39:17 and given it no share in **u**.
Ps 32: 9 Do not be like a horse or a mule, without **u**,
49: 3 the meditation of my heart shall be **u**.
82: 5 They have neither knowledge nor **u**,
111:10 all those who practice it have a good **u**.
119:32 of your commandments, for you enlarge my **u**.
119:34 Give me **u**, that I may keep your law
119:73 give me **u** that I may learn your commandments.
119:99 I have more **u** than all my teachers,
119:104 Through your precepts I get **u**;
119:125 give me **u**, so that I may know your decrees.
119:130 it imparts **u** to the simple.
119:144 give me **u** that I may live.
119:169 give me **u** according to your word.
136: 5 who by **u** made the heavens,
147: 5 in power; his **u** is beyond measure.
Pr 1: 2 about wisdom and instruction, for **u** words
2: 2 to wisdom and inclining your heart to **u**;
2: 3 and raise your voice for **u**;
2: 6 from his mouth come knowledge and **u**;
2:11 will watch over you; and **u** will guard you.
3:13 those who find wisdom, and those who get **u**,
3:19 by **u** he established the heavens;
5: 1 incline your ear to my **u**,
8: 1 and does not **u** raise her voice?
10:13 On the lips of one who has **u** wisdom is found,
10:23 but wise conduct is pleasure to a person of **u**.
14:29 Whoever is slow to anger has great **u**,
14:33 Wisdom is at home in the mind of one who has **u**,
15:14 The mind of one who has **u** seeks knowledge,
15:21 but a person of **u** walks straight ahead.
15:32 but those who heed admonition gain **u**.
16:16 To get **u** is to be chosen rather than silver.
17:27 one who is cool in spirit has **u**.
18: 2 A fool takes no pleasure in **u**,
19: 8 to keep **u** is to prosper.
21:16 the way of **u** will rest in the assembly of the dead.
21:30 No wisdom, no **u**, no counsel,
23:23 buy wisdom, instruction, and **u**.
24: 3 and by **u** it is established;
Pr 28:16 A ruler who lacks **u** is a cruel oppressor;
29: 7 the wicked have no such **u**.
30: 2 I do not have human **u**.
Isa 10:13 and by my wisdom, for I have **u**;
11: 2 the spirit of wisdom and **u**,
27:11 For this is a people without **u**;
29:16 of the one who formed it, "He has no **u**"?
29:24 And those who err in spirit will come to **u**,
40:14 and showed him the way of **u**?
40:28 or grow weary; his **u** is unsearchable.
56:11 The shepherds also have no **u**;
Jer 3:15 who will feed you with knowledge and **u**.
4:22 they are stupid children, they have no **u**.
10:12 and by his **u** stretched out the heavens.
51:15 and by his **u** stretched out the heavens.
Eze 28: 4 and your **u** you have amassed wealth for yourself,
Da 1:20 and **u** concerning which the king inquired of them,
2:21 to the wise and knowledge to those who have **u**.
5:11 **u**, and wisdom like the wisdom of the gods.
5:12 and **u** to interpret dreams, explain riddles,
5:14 **u**, and excellent wisdom are found in you.
9:22 I have now come out to give you wisdom and **u**.
10: 1 having received **u** in the vision.
10:12 to gain **u** and to humble yourself before your God,
11:33 The wise among the people shall give **u** to many;
Hos 4:11 whoredom. Wine and new wine take away the **u**.
4:14 thus a people without **u** comes to ruin.
13: 2 idols of silver made according to their **u**,
Ob 1: 7 there is no **u** of it.
1: 8 and **u** out of Mount Esau.
Zec 6:13 with peaceful **u** between the two of them.
Mt 15:16 Then he said, "Are you also still without **u**?
Mk 12:33 and with all the **u**, and with all the strength,'
Lk 2:47 And all who heard him were amazed at his **u**
Ro 3:11 there is no one who has **u**,
Eph 3: 4 of which will enable you to perceive my **u** of
4:18 They are darkened in their **u**,
Php 4: 7 And the peace of God, which surpasses all **u**,
Col 1: 9 of God's will in all spiritual wisdom and **u**,
2: 2 so that they may have all the riches of assured **u**
1Ti 1: 7 without **u** either what they are saying or the things
1: 9 This means **u** that the law is laid down not for
6: 4 **u** nothing, and has a morbid craving
2Ti 2: 7 for the Lord will give you **u** in all things.
Heb 5:11 since you have become dull in **u**.
Jas 3:13 Who is wise and **u** among you?
1Jn 5:20 that the Son of God has come and has given us **u**
Rev 13:18 let anyone with **u** calculate the number of
Tob 4:19 For none of the nations has **u**,
Jdt 8:29 of your life all the people have recognized your **u**,
Wis 3:15 and the root of **u** does not fail.
4: 9 but **u** is gray hair for anyone,
4:11 not change their **u** or guile deceive their souls.
6:15 To fix one's thought on her is perfect **u**,
7: 7 Therefore I prayed, and **u** was given me;
7:16 as are all **u** and skill in crafts.
8: 6 if **u** is effective, who more than she is fashioner
8:18 and in the experience of her company, **u**,
9: 5 with little **u** of judgment and laws;
Sir 1: 4 and prudent **u** from eternity.
10: 3 but a city becomes fit to live in through the **u**
16:23 Such are the thoughts of one devoid of **u**;
17: 7 He filled them with knowledge and **u**,
19:24 Better are the God-fearing who lack **u** than
24:26 It runs over, like the Euphrates, with **u**,
25: 5 and **u** and counsel in the venerable!
39: 6 he will be filled with the spirit of **u**;
39: 9 Many will praise his **u**; it will never be blotted
47:14 You overflowed like the Nile with **u**.
50:27 in **u** and knowledge I have written in this book,
51:20 With her I gained **u** from the first;
Bar 3:14 where there is strength, where there is **u**,
3:23 who seek for **u** on the earth,
3:23 the story-tellers and the seekers for **u**,
3:32 he found her by his **u**.
1Es 1:33 and his splendor, and his **u** of the law of the Lord,
8:44 and Meshullam, who were leaders and men of **u**;
2Es 4: 2 "Your **u** has utterly failed regarding this world,
4:22 why have I been endowed with the power of **u**?
5:22 Then my soul recovered the spirit of **u**,
7:72 because though they had **u**,
8: 4 I answered and said, "Then drink your fill of **u**,
8: 6 a seed for our heart and cultivation of our **u** so
8:25 and as long as I have **u** I will answer.
10:30 deprived of my **u**, he grasped my right hand
10:31 And why are your **u** and the thoughts
13:55 and called **u** your mother.
14:25 and I will light in your heart the lamp of **u**,
14:40 and when I had drunk it, my heart poured forth **u**,
14:42 Moreover, the Most High gave **u** to the five men,
14:47 For in them is the spring of **u**,
16:61 and gave each person breath and life and **u**

UNDERSTANDS (11) [UNDERSTAND]

1Ch 28: 9 and **u** every plan and thought.
Job 28:23 "God **u** the way to it, and he knows its place.
Pr 8: 9 They are all straight to one who **u** and right
14: 6 but knowledge is easy for one who **u**.
Isa 57: 1 the devout are taken away, while no one **u**.
Mt 13:23 this is the one who hears the word and **u** it,
1Co 14: 2 to God; for nobody **u** them,
Wis 8: 8 she **u** turns of speech and the solutions of riddles;
9: 9 she **u** what is pleasing in your sight
9:11 For she knows and **u** all things,
Sir 42:18 he **u** their innermost secrets.

UNDERSTOOD‡ (16) [UNDERSTAND]

Ge 42:23 They did not know that Joseph **u** them,
2Sa 3:37 and all Israel **u** that day that the king had no part
1Ch 15:22 was to direct the music, for he **u** it.
Ne 8: 8 so that the people **u** the reading.
8:12 they had **u** the words that were declared to them.
Job 13: 1 my eye has seen all this, my ear has heard and **u** it.
Isa 40:21 Have you not **u** from the foundations of the earth?
Da 10: 1 He **u** the word, having received understanding in
Mt 13:51 "Have you **u** all this?" They answered, "Yes."
16:12 Then they **u** that he had not told them to beware of
17:13 Then the disciples **u** that he was speaking to them
Lk 18:34 But they **u** nothing about all these things;
Ro 1:20 have been **u** and seen through
1Co 2: 8 None of the rulers of this age **u** this;
2Co 1:14 as you have already **u** us in part—
Bar 3:20 nor **u** her paths, nor laid hold of her.

UNDERTAKE (5) [UNDERTAKEN, UNDERTAKES, UNDERTAKING, UNDERTAKINGS, UNDERTOOK]

Dt 14:29 may bless you in all the work that you **u**.
15:10 bless you in all your work and in all that you **u**.
28: 8 and in all that you **u**; he will bless you in the land
AdE 16: 3 even **u** to scheme against their own benefactors.
2Es 4:18 which would you **u** to justify,

UNDERTAKEN (5) [UNDERTAKE]

Lk 1: 1 Since many have **u** to set down an orderly account
1Mc 4:51 Thus they finished all the work they had **u**.
12:10 we have **u** to send to renew our family ties
2Mc 2:26 For us who have **u** the toil of abbreviating,
8:36 So he who had **u** to secure tribute for the Romans

UNDERTAKES (2) [UNDERTAKE]

2Mc 2:29 the one who **u** its painting and decoration has
3Mc 2:14 In our downfall this audacious and profane man **u**

UNDERTAKING (7) [UNDERTAKE]

Jdg 18: 5 the mission we are **u** will succeed."
Ac 5:38 if this plan or this **u** is of human origin, it will fail;
2Co 8: 6 so he should also complete this generous **u**
8: 7 so we want you to excel also in this generous **u**.
8:19 while we are administering this generous **u** for
9: 4 to say nothing of you—in this **u**.
Sir 37:16 and counsel precedes every **u**.

UNDERTAKINGS (9) [UNDERTAKE]

Dt 2: 7 LORD your God has blessed you in all your **u**;
12: 7 rejoicing in all the **u** in which
12:18 the presence of the LORD your God in all your **u**.
16:15 in all your produce and in all your **u**,
23:20 in all your **u** in the land that you are about to enter
24:19 the LORD your God may bless you in all your **u**.
28:12 of your land in its season and to bless all your **u**.
30: 9 in all your **u**, in the fruit of your body, in the fruit
1Sa 18:14 David had success in all his **u**;

UNDERTOOK (6) [UNDERTAKE]

Dt 1: 5 Moses **u** to expound this law as follows:
2Ch 31:21 that he **u** in the service of the house of God,
AdE 16:12 he **u** to deprive us of our kingdom and our life,
2Mc 7:26 she **u** to persuade her son.
10:23 Having success at arms in everything he **u**,
1Es 9:14 of Asahel and Jahzeiah son of Tikvah **u** the matter

UNDERWENT (1) [UNDERGO]

2Mc 7: 8 he in turn **u** tortures as the first brother had done.

UNDERWINGS See Index to Footnotes

UNDERWORLD (1)

Jer 17:13 from you shall be recorded in the **u**,

UNDESERVED (2)

Pr 26: 2 a swallow in its flying, an **u** curse goes nowhere.
Tob 3: 6 because I have had to listen to **u** insults,

UNDETECTED (1)

Nu 5:13 so that she is **u** though she has defiled herself,

UNDID (2) [UNDO]

Jdt 16: 6 with the beauty of her countenance **u** him.
4Mc 3:11 and inflamed him, **u** and consumed him.

UNDISCIPLINED (3)

Sir 6:20 She seems very harsh to the **u**;
10: 3 An **u** king ruins his people,
22: 3 It is a disgrace to be the father of an **u** son,

UNDISTURBED (1)

2Mc 11:23 the kingdom be **u** in caring for their own affairs.

UNDIVIDED (1)

Ps 86:11 give me an **u** heart to revere your name.

UNDO (2) [UNDID, UNDONE]

Ecc 10: 4 for calmness will **u** great offenses.

Isa 58: 6 to **u** the thongs of the yoke,

UNDONE (4) [UNDO]

Nu 21:29 You are **u**, O people of Chemosh!
Jos 11:15 left nothing **u** of all that the LORD had commanded
Isa 15: 1 Because Ar is laid waste in a night, Moab is **u**;
15: 1 because Kir is laid waste in a night, Moab is **u**.

UNDRESSED (KJV) See UNPRUNED

UNDYING (1)

Eph 6:24 Grace be with all who have an **u** love

UNEDUCATED (2)

Ac 4:13 and realized that they were **u** and ordinary men,
Sir 51:23 Draw near to me, you who are **u**,

UNENDING (1)

Eze 25:15 Because with **u** hostilities the Philistines acted

UNENDURABLE (1)

Man 1: 5 and the wrath of your threat to sinners is **u**;

UNEQUALED (1)

Dt 34:11 He was **u** for all the signs and wonders that

UNERRING (1)

Wis 7:17 it is he who gave me **u** knowledge of what exists,

UNEVEN (1)

Isa 40: 4 the **u** ground shall become level,

UNEXPECTED (11) [UNEXPECTEDLY]

Mt 24:44 for the Son of Man is coming at an **u** hour.
Lk 12:40 for the Son of Man is coming at an **u** hour."
Tob 10: 6 Probably something **u** has happened there.
Wis 5: 2 be amazed at the **u** salvation of the righteous.
17:15 for sudden and **u** fear overwhelmed them.
18:17 and **u** fears assailed them;
2Mc 9:24 so that, if anything **u** happened
3Mc 3: 8 an **u** tumult around these people and the crowds
4: 2 the **u** destruction that had suddenly been decreed
5:33 So Hermon suffered an **u** and dangerous threat,
6:33 for the **u** rescue that he had experienced.

UNEXPECTEDLY (2) [UNEXPECTED]

Lk 21:34 and that day catch you **u**,
Wis 11: 7 you gave them abundant water **u**,

UNEXPLORED See Index to Footnotes

UNFADING (2)

1Pe 1: 4 undefiled, and **u**, kept in heaven for you,
Wis 6:12 Wisdom is radiant and **u**, and she is easily

UNFAILING (4)

Lk 12:33 an **u** treasure in heaven, where no thief comes near
Wis 7:14 for it is an **u** treasure for mortals;
8:18 **u** wealth, and in the experience of her company,
2Es 9:19 both with an **u** table and an inexhaustible pasture,

UNFAIR (6) [UNFAIRLY]

Eze 18:25 Yet you say, "The way of the Lord is **u**."
18:25 Hear now, O house of Israel: Is my way **u**?
18:25 Is it not your ways that are **u**?
18:29 house of Israel says, "The way of the Lord is **u**."
18:29 O house of Israel, are my ways **u**?
18:29 Is it not your ways that are **u**?

UNFAIRLY (1) [UNFAIR]

Ex 21: 8 since he has dealt **u** with her.

UNFAITHFUL (10) [UNFAITHFULLY, UNFAITHFULNESS]

Nu 5:12 If any man's wife goes astray and is **u** to him,
5:27 if she has defiled herself and has been **u**
1Ch 10:13 he was **u** to the LORD in that he did not keep
2Ch 12: 2 because they had been **u** to the LORD,
29: 6 For our ancestors have been **u**
36:14 the people also were exceedingly **u**, following all
Ne 1: 8 you are **u**, I will scatter you among the peoples;
Lk 12:46 and will cut him in pieces, and put him with the **u**.
Ro 3: 3 What if some were **u**?
2Es 7:24 they have been **u** to his statutes,

UNFAITHFULLY (1) [UNFAITHFUL]

2Es 7:72 they dealt **u** with what they received.

UNFAITHFULNESS (5) [UNFAITHFUL]

1Ch 9: 1 into exile in Babylon because of their **u**.
10:13 So Saul died for his **u**;
2Ch 21:11 and led the inhabitants of Jerusalem into **u**,
21:13 and the inhabitants of Jerusalem into **u**,
21:13 as the house of Ahab led Israel into **u**,

UNFASTENED (1)

Ac 16:26 and everyone's chains were **u**.

UNFAVORABLE (3)

Nu 13:32 an **u** report of the land that they had spied out,
14:37 an **u** report about the land died by a plague before
2Ti 4: 2 be persistent whether the time is favorable or **u**;

UNFEIGNED (KJV) See GENUINE, SINCERE

UNFIT (3)

1Co 15: 9 **u** to be called an apostle,
Tit 1:16 disobedient, **u** for any good work.
2Mc 6: 4 besides brought in things for sacrifice that were **u**.

UNFOLDING (1)

Ps 119:130 The **u** of your words gives light;

UNFORMED (1)

Ps 139:16 Your eyes beheld my **u** substance.

UNFORTUNATE (2)

Isa 3:11 Woe to the guilty! How **u** they are,
2Mc 4:47 while he sentenced to death those **u** men,

UNFRUITFUL (4)

2Ki 2:19 but the water is bad, and the land is **u**."
Eph 5:11 Take no part in the **u** works of darkness,
2Pe 1: 8 and **u** in the knowledge of our Lord Jesus Christ.
2Es 9:29 into the untrodden and **u** wilderness;

UNGIRDED (KJV) See UNLOADED

UNGODLINESS (12) [UNGODLY]

Isa 32: 6 to practice **u**, to utter error concerning the LORD,
Jer 23:15 the prophets of Jerusalem **u** has spread throughout
Ro 1:18 of God is revealed from heaven against all **u**
11:26 he will banish **u** from Jacob."
Jude 1:15 the deeds of **u** that they have committed in such
Wis 14: 9 to God are the ungodly and their **u**;
2Es 4:12 not to be here than to come here and live in **u**,
4:30 and how much **u** it has produced until now—
4:31 Consider now for yourself how much fruit of **u**
4:38 "But, O sovereign Lord, all of us also are full of **u**.
12:32 He will denounce them for their **u** and
13:37 for their **u** (this was symbolized by the storm),

UNGODLY (71) [UNGODLINESS]

Job 16:11 God gives me up to the **u**,
18:21 Surely such are the dwellings of the **u**,
Ps 43: 1 O God, and defend my cause against an **u** people;
53: 5 For God will scatter the bones of the **u**;
Jer 23:11 Both prophet and priest are **u**;
Ro 4: 5 without works trusts him who justifies the **u**,
5: 6 at the right time Christ died for the **u**.
1Pe 4:18 what will become of the **u** and the sinners?"
2Pe 2: 5 when he brought a flood on a world of the **u**;
2: 6 an example of what is coming to the **u**;
Jude 1: 4 for this condemnation as **u**,
1:15 that they have committed in such an **u** way,
1:15 of all the harsh things that **u** sinners have spoken
1:18 indulging their own **u** lusts."
Wis 1: 9 inquiry will be made into the counsels of the **u**,
1:16 the **u** by their words and deeds summoned death;
3:10 the **u** will be punished as their reasoning deserves,
4: 3 But the prolific brood of the **u** will be of no use,
4:16 the **u** who are living, and youth
5:14 the **u** is like thistledown carried by the wind,
10: 6 a righteous man when the **u** were perishing;
10:20 Therefore the righteous plundered the **u**;
11: 9 how the **u** were tormented when judged in wrath.
11:10 but you examined the **u** as a stern king does
12: 9 though you were not unable to give the **u** into
14: 9 hateful to God are the **u** and their ungodliness;
14:16 Then the **u** custom, grown strong with time,
16:16 for the **u**, refusing to know you, were flogged by
16:18 against the **u**, but that seeing this they might know
19: 1 the **u** were assailed to the end by pitiless anger,
Sir 7:17 for the punishment of the **u** is fire and worms.
9:12 Do not delight in what pleases the **u**;
12: 5 Do good to the humble, but do not give to the **u**;
12: 6 and will inflict punishment on the **u**.
13:24 poverty is evil only in the opinion of the **u**.
16: 1 and do not rejoice in **u** offspring.
16: 3 and to die childless better than to have **u** children.
21:27 **u** person curses an adversary, he curses himself.
22:12 foolish or the **u** it lasts all the days of their lives.
26:26 *she will be known to all as* **u**.
34:23 not pleased with the offerings of the **u**,
39:30 and the sword that punishes the **u** with destruction.
40:15 The children of the **u** put out few branches;
41: 5 and they frequent the haunts of the **u**.
41: 7 Children will blame an **u** father,
41: 8 to you, the **u**, who have forsaken the law of
41:10 so the **u** go from curse to destruction.
42: 2 and of rendering judgment to acquit the **u**;
Bar 2:12 we have been **u**, we have done wrong,
1Mc 3: 8 he destroyed the **u** out of the land;
6:21 the siege and some of the **u** Israelites joined them.
7: 9 He sent him, and with him he sent the **u** Alcimus,
2Mc 4:13 who was **u** and no true high priest,
8:14 by the **u** Nicanor before he ever met them,
9: 9 And so the **u** man's body swarmed with worms,
10:10 who was the son of that **u** man,
2Mc 12: 3 And the people of Joppa did so **u** a deed as this:
15:33 He cut out the tongue of the **u** Nicanor and said
1Es 1:52 because of their **u** acts he gave command to bring
2Es 3: 8 they did **u** things in your sight
3:12 to be more **u** than were their ancestors.
3:29 when I came here I saw **u** deeds without number,
7:17 but that the **u** shall perish.
7:*51* while the **u** abound, hear the explanation for this.
7:*93* the **u** wander and the punishment that awaits them.
7:*102* the righteous will be able to intercede for the **u** or
7:*111* [41] the righteous have prayed for the **u**,
9:13 do not continue to be curious about how the **u** will
14:35 and the deeds of the **u** shall be disclosed.
15: 8 I will be silent no longer concerning their **u** acts
4Mc 5:38 You may tyrannize the **u**,

UNGRACIOUS (1)

Sir 18:18 A fool is **u** and abusive,

UNGRATEFUL (6)

Lk 6:35 for he is kind to the **u** and the wicked.
2Ti 3: 2 arrogant, abusive, disobedient to their parents, **u**,
Wis 16:29 the hope of an **u** person will melt like wintry frost,
Sir 29:17 and the **u** person abandons his rescuer.
2Es 8:60 and have been **u** to him who prepared life
4Mc 9:10 but also infuriated, as at those who are **u**.

UNGRUDGING (1) [UNGRUDGINGLY]

Dt 15:10 Give liberally and be **u** when you do so,

UNGRUDGINGLY (1) [UNGRUDGING]

Jas 1: 5 ask God, who gives to all generously and **u**,

UNHAPPY (4)

Ecc 1:13 an **u** business that God has given to human beings
4: 8 This also is vanity and an **u** business.
2Es 15:59 U above all others, you shall come
4Mc 16: 6 "O how wretched am I and many times **u**!

UNHARMED (8)

Ps 55:18 He will redeem me **u** from the battle that I wage,
Wis 19: 6 so that your children might be kept **u**.
2Mc 12:25 to restore them **u**, they let him go, for the sake
3Mc 6: 6 you rescued **u**, even to a hair,
6: 7 you brought up to the light **u**.
6: 8 watched over and restored **u** to all his family.
6:39 and rescued them all together and **u**.
7:20 they departed **u**, free, and overjoyed,

UNHEALTHY (2)

Mt 6:23 but if your eye is **u**,
Sir 40:15 they are **u** roots on sheer rock.

UNHEARD (1) [UNHEARD-OF]

Wis 1:10 and the sound of grumbling does not go **u**.

UNHEARD-OF (1) [UNHEARD]

Sir 10:13 Therefore the Lord brings upon them **u** calamities,

UNHEWN (3)

Dt 27: 6 the altar of the LORD your God of **u** stones.
Jos 8:31 of **u** stones, on which no iron tool has been used";
1Mc 4:47 Then they took **u** stones, as the law directs,

UNHINDERED (3)

1Co 7:35 to promote good order and **u** devotion to the Lord.
Wis 17:20 and went about its work **u**,
19: 7 an **u** way out of the Red Sea,

UNHOLY (7)

Ex 30: 9 You shall not offer **u** incense on it,
Lev 10: 1 and they offered **u** fire before the LORD,
1Ti 1: 9 for the godless and sinful, for the **u** and profane,
2Ti 3: 2 disobedient to their parents, ungrateful, **u**,
Wis 12: 4 their works of sorcery and **u** rites,
2Mc 7:34 But you, **u** wretch, you most defiled of all mortals,
12:14 and even blaspheming and saying **u** things.

UNICORN[S] (KJV) See WILD OX[EN]

UNIFORM (1)

2Mc 8:35 took off his splendid **u** and made his way alone

UNIFYING (1)

AdE 13: 4 so that the **u** of the kingdom

UNIMPAIRED (1)

Dt 34: 7 his sight was **u** and his vigor had not abated.

UNIMPEDED (1)

3Mc 6:28 until now has granted an **u** and notable stability

UNIMPORTANT See Index to Footnotes

UNINFORMED (2)

1Co 12: 1 brothers and sisters, I do not want you to be **u**.
1Th 4:13 But we do not want you to be **u**,

UNINHABITED (8)
Jer 6: 8 and make you a desolation, an **u** land.
17: 6 of the wilderness, in an **u** salt land.
22: 6 but I swear that I will make you a desert, an **u** city.
Eze 29:11 it shall be **u** forty years.
Zec 9: 5 from Gaza; Ashkelon shall be **u;**
Jdt 5:19 in the hill country, because it was **u.**
Wis 11: 2 They journeyed through an **u** wilderness,
1Mc 3:45 Jerusalem was **u** like a wilderness;

UNINSTRUCTED (1)
Wis 17: 1 therefore **u** souls have gone astray.

UNINTELLIGENT (1)
Sir 22:13 with a senseless person or visit an **u** person.

UNINTENTIONAL (2) [UNINTENTIONALLY]
Nu 15:25 it was **u,** and they have brought their offering,
15:28 when it is **u,** to make atonement for the person,

UNINTENTIONALLY (14) [UNINTENTIONAL]
Lev 4: 2 When anyone sins **u** in any of the LORD's
4:13 of Israel errs **u** and the matter escapes the notice
4:22 doing **u** any one of all the things that
4:27 If anyone of the ordinary people among you sins **u**
5:15 and sins **u** in any of the holy things of the LORD,
5:18 on your behalf for the error that you committed **u,**
22:14 If a man eats of the sacred donation **u,**
Nu 15:22 if you **u** fail to observe all these commandments
15:24 then if it was done **u** without the knowledge of
15:27 An individual who sins **u** shall present
35:23 **u** drops it on another and death ensues,
Dt 4:42 someone who **u** kills another person,
19: 4 someone who has killed another person **u** when
Heb 9: 7 for himself and for the sins committed **u** by

UNION (4) [UNIONS]
Dt 23: 2 an illicit **u** shall not be admitted to the assembly of
Wis 3:13 who has not entered into a sinful **u;**
3:16 and the offspring of an unlawful **u** will perish.
3Mc 1:19 the bridal chambers prepared for wedded **u,**

UNIONS (1) [UNION]
Wis 4: 6 For children born of unlawful **u** are witnesses

UNIQUE (1)
Wis 7:22 There is in her a spirit that is intelligent, holy, **u,**

UNISON (3) [UNITY]
2Ch 5:13 in **u** in praise and thanksgiving to the LORD,
Ac 19:34 for about two hours all of them shouted in **u,**
Jdt 4:12 the altar with sackcloth and cried out in **u,**

UNITED (12) [UNITY]
Dt 33: 5 of the people assembled—the **u** tribes of Israel.
Jdg 20:11 So all the men of Israel gathered against the city, **u**
Ac 18:12 the Jews made a **u** attack on Paul and brought him
Ro 6: 5 For if we have been **u** with him in a death like his,
6: 5 we will certainly be **u** with him in a resurrection
1Co 1:10 you be **u** in the same mind and the same purpose.
6:16 that whoever is **u** to a prostitute becomes one body
6:17 anyone **u** to the Lord becomes one spirit with him.
Col 2: 2 I want their hearts to be encouraged and **u** in love,
Heb 4: 2 they were not **u** by faith with those who listened.
Rev 17:13 These are **u** in yielding their power and authority
1Mc 2:42 Then there **u** with them a company of Hasideans,

UNITS (1)
1Ch 7: 4 were **u** of the fighting force, thirty-six thousand,

UNITY (6) [UNISON, UNITED]
Ps 133: 1 and pleasant it is when kindred live together in **u!**
Zec 11: 7 one I named Favor, the other I named **U,**
11:14 Then I broke my second staff **U,**
Eph 4: 3 making every effort to maintain the **u** of the Spirit
4:13 the **u** of the faith and of the knowledge of the Son
1Pe 3: 8 Finally, all of you, have **u** of spirit, sympathy,

UNIVERSAL (2)
Ac 3:21 of **u** restoration that God announced long ago
4Mc 15:31 carrying the world in the **u** flood,

UNIVERSE‡ (8)
Col 2: 8 according to the elemental spirits of the **u,**
2:20 to the elemental spirits of the **u,**
AdE 13: 9 for the **u** is in your power
Wis 16:17 for the **u** defends the righteous.
Sir 18: 1 He who lives forever created the whole **u;**
23:20 Before the **u** was created, it was known to him,
42:17 so that the **u** may stand firm in his glory.
2Mc 7: 9 of the **u** will raise us up to an everlasting renewal

UNJUST‡ (24) [UNJUSTLY]
Ex 5:16 You are **u** to your own people."
Lev 19:15 You shall not render an **u** judgment;
Ps 43: 1 from those who are deceitful and **u** deliver me!
71: 4 from the grasp of the **u** and cruel.
Pr 15:27 Those who are greedy for **u** gain make trouble
28:16 but one who hates **u** gain will enjoy a long life.
29:27 The **u** are an abomination to the righteous,
Jer 6:13 everyone is greedy for **u** gain;
8:10 to the greatest everyone is greedy for **u** gain;
Zep 3: 5 but the **u** knows no shame.
Lk 18: 6 the Lord said, "Listen to what the **u** judge says.
Ro 3: 5 That God is **u** to inflict wrath on us?
Heb 6:10 For God is not **u;** he will not overlook your work
Sir 1:22 **U** anger cannot be justified,
19:25 There is a cleverness that is exact but **u,**
33:30 be overbearing toward anyone, and do nothing **u.**
40:13 The wealth of the **u** will dry up like a river,
41:18 of **u** dealing, before your partner or your friend;
Aza 1: 9 and to an **u** king, the most wicked in all the world.
Sus 1:53 pronouncing **u** judgments, condemning the
2Mc 4:35 were grieved and displeased at the **u** murder of
4:40 and launched an **u** attack, under the leadership of
4:48 the holy vessels quickly suffered the **u** penalty.
3Mc 6:27 Loose and untie their **u** bonds!

UNJUSTLY (6) [UNJUST]
Ps 82: 2 "How long will you judge **u** and show partiality to
Jer 17:11 so are all who amass wealth **u;**
1Pe 2:19 you endure pain while suffering **u.**
Wis 12:13 that you have not judged **u;**
1Mc 2:37 and earth testify for us that you are killing us **u.**"
15:33 at one time had been **u** taken by our enemies.

UNKNOWINGLY (2) [UNKNOWN]
1Ki 22:34 a certain man drew his bow and **u** struck the king
2Ch 18:33 a certain man drew his bow and **u** struck the king

UNKNOWN (9) [UNKNOWINGLY]
Ac 17:23 an altar with the inscription, 'To an **u** god.'
17:23 What therefore you worship as **u,**
2Co 6: 9 as **u,** and yet are well known;
Gal 1:22 and I was still **u** by sight to the churches of Judea
Wis 11:18 or newly-created **u** beasts full of rage, or such
18: 3 of fire as a guide for your people's **u** journey,
Sir 16:17 Among so many people I am **u,**
2Mc 1:19 that the place was **u** to anyone.
2: 7 "The place shall remain **u** until God gathers his

UNLADE (KJV) See UNLOAD

UNLAWFUL (7) [UNLAWFULLY]
Ac 10:28 that it is **u** for a Jew to associate with or to visit
Wis 3:16 and the offspring of an **u** union will perish.
4: 6 For children born of **u** unions are witnesses of evil
2Mc 4:14 in the **u** proceedings in the wrestling arena after
6:21 Those who were in charge of that **u** sacrifice took
7: 1 to partake of **u** swine's flesh.
3Mc 1:27 in the present trouble and not to overlook this **u**

UNLAWFULLY (1) [UNLAWFUL]
4Mc 5:14 the tyrant urged him in this fashion to eat meat **u,**

UNLEARNED (KJV) See IGNORANT, OUTSIDER[S], STUPID, UNEDUCATED

UNLEAVENED (65)
A. UNLEAVENED BREAD (45)
B. FESTIVAL OF UNLEAVENED BREAD (15)

Ge 19: 3 and he made them a feast, and baked **u** bread, A
Ex 12: 8 shall eat it roasted over the fire with **u** bread A
12:15 Seven days you shall eat **u** bread; A
12:17 You shall observe the festival of **u** bread, AB
12:18 of the twenty-first day, you shall eat **u** bread. A
12:20 in all your settlements you shall eat **u** bread. A
12:39 They baked **u** cakes of the dough
13: 6 Seven days you shall eat **u** bread, A
13: 7 **U** bread shall be eaten for seven days; A
23:15 You shall observe the festival of **u** bread; AB
23:15 as I commanded you, you shall eat **u** bread A
29: 2 and **u** bread, unleavened cakes mixed with oil, A
29: 2 and unleavened bread, **u** cakes mixed with oil,
29: 2 and **u** wafers spread with oil.
29:23 of the basket of **u** bread that is before the LORD; A
34:18 You shall keep the festival of **u** bread. AB
34:18 Seven days you shall eat **u** bread, A
Lev 2: 4 **u** cakes mixed with oil, or **u** wafers spread with oil.
2: 5 it shall be of choice flour mixed with oil, **u;**
6:16 it shall be eaten as **u** cakes in a holy place;
7:12 thank offering **u** cakes mixed with oil, **u** wafers
8: 2 the two rams, and the basket of **u** bread; A
8:26 the basket of **u** bread that was before the LORD, A
8:26 he took one cake of **u** bread, A
10:12 and eat it **u** beside the altar, for it is most holy;
23: 6 of the same month is the festival of **u** bread to AB
23: 6 seven days you shall eat **u** bread. A
Nu 6:15 and a basket of **u** bread, A
6:15 choice flour mixed with oil and **u** wafers spread
6:17 with the basket of **u** bread; A
6:19 and one **u** cake out of the basket, and one **u** wafer,
9:11 they shall eat it with **u** bread and bitter herbs. A
28:17 seven days shall **u** bread be eaten. A
Dt 16: 3 For seven days you shall eat **u** bread with it— A
16: 8 For six days you shall continue to eat **u** bread, A
16:16 festival of **u** bread, at the festival of weeks, AB
Jos 5:11 **u** cakes and parched grain.
Jdg 6:19 and **u** cakes from an ephah of flour;
6:20 "Take the meat and the **u** cakes,
6:21 and touched the meat and the **u** cakes;
6:21 the rock and consumed the meat and the **u** cakes;
1Sa 28:24 and she took flour, kneaded it, and baked **u** cakes.
2Ki 23: 9 but ate **u** bread among their kindred. A
1Ch 23:29 the wafers of **u** bread, the baked offering, A
2Ch 8:13 the festival of **u** bread, the festival of weeks, AB
30:13 in Jerusalem to keep the festival of **u** bread in AB
30:21 the festival of **u** bread seven days with great AB
35:17 and the festival of **u** bread seven days. AB
Ezr 6:22 the festival of **u** bread seven days; AB
Eze 45:21 and for seven days **u** bread shall be eaten. A
Mt 26:17 On the first day of **U** Bread the disciples came A
Mk 14: 1 the Passover and the festival of **U** Bread. AB
14:12 On the first day of **U** Bread, A
Lk 22: 1 Now the festival of **U** Bread, AB
22: 7 Then came the day of **U** Bread, A
Ac 12: 3 (This was during the festival of **U** Bread.) AB
20: 6 sailed from Philippi after the days of **U** Bread, A
1Co 5: 7 that you may be a new batch, as you really are **u.**
5: 8 but with the **u** bread of sincerity and truth. A
1Es 1:10 The priests and the Levites, having the **u** bread, A
1:19 and the festival of **u** bread seven days. AB
7:14 also kept the festival of **u** bread seven days, AB

UNLESS (71)
Ge 32:26 Jacob said, "I will not let you go, **u** you bless me."
42:15 as Pharaoh lives, you shall not leave this place **u**
43: 3 'You shall not see my face **u** your brother is
43: 5 **u** your brother is with you.' "
44:23 '**U** your youngest brother comes down with you,
44:26 the man's face **u** our youngest brother is with us.'
Ex 3:19 the king of Egypt will not let you go **u** compelled
33:16 I and your people, **u** you go with us?
Lev 22: 6 of the sacred donations **u** he has washed his body
Dt 32:30 **u** their Rock had sold them,
Jos 7:12 **u** you destroy the devoted things from among you.
1Sa 25:34 **u** you had hurried and come to meet me,
2Sa 3:13 you shall never appear in my presence **u**
2Ki 4:24 do not hold back for me **u** I tell you."
Est 2:14 **u** the king delighted in her and she was summoned
Ps 127: 1 **U** the LORD builds the house,
127: 1 **U** the LORD guards the city,
Pr 4:16 For they cannot sleep **u** they have done wrong;
4:16 of sleep **u** they have made someone stumble.
La 5:22 **u** you have utterly rejected us,
Da 6: 5 against this Daniel **u** we find it in connection with
Am 3: 3 Do two walk together **u** they have made
3: 6 **u** the LORD has done it?
Mt 5:20 **u** your righteousness exceeds that of the scribes
18: 3 **u** you change and become like children,
26:42 if this cannot pass **u** I drink it, your will be done."
Mk 7: 3 do not eat **u** they thoroughly wash their hands,
7: 4 not eat anything from the market **u** they wash it;
Lk 9:13 **u** we are to go and buy food for all these people."
13: 3 but **u** you repent, you will all perish as they did.
13: 5 **u** you repent, you will all perish just as they did."
Jn 4:48 "**U** you see signs and wonders you will
6:44 to me **u** drawn by the Father who sent me;
6:53 **u** you eat the flesh of the Son of Man
6:65 that no one can come to me **u** it is granted by
8:24 for you will die in your sins **u** you believe
12:24 **u** a grain of wheat falls into the earth and dies,
13: 8 Jesus answered, "**U** I wash you,
15: 4 as the branch cannot bear fruit by itself **u** it abides
15: 4 neither can you **u** you abide in me.
19:11 over me **u** it had been given you from above;
20:25 "**U** I see the mark of the nails in his hands,
Ac 8:31 He replied, "How can I, **u** someone guides me?"
15: 1 "**U** you are circumcised according to the custom
24:21 **u** it was this one sentence that I called out
27:31 "**U** these men stay in the ship,
Ro 10:15 And how are they to proclaim him **u** they are sent?
1Co 14: 5 **u** someone interprets, so that the church may
14: 6 how will I benefit you **u** I speak to you
15: 2 **u** you have come to believe in vain.
15:36 What you sow does not come to life **u** it dies.
2Co 13: 5 **u,** indeed, you fail to meet the test!
2Th 2: 3 that day will not come **u** the rebellion comes first
Rev 2: 5 and remove your lampstand from its place, **u**
2:22 **u** they repent of her doings;
Jdt 8:11 promising to surrender the town to our enemies **u**
11:10 **u** they sin against their God.
AdE 2:14 in to the king again **u** she is summoned by name.
Wis 8:21 But I perceived that I would not possess wisdom **u**
9:17 **u** you have given wisdom and sent your holy spirit
Sir 16: 2 **u** the fear of the Lord is in them.
19: 8 and **u** it would be a sin for you, do not reveal it;
34: 6 **U** they are sent by intervention from
LtJ 6:24 it will not shine **u** someone wipes off the tarnish;
1Mc 6:27 **u** you quickly prevent them,
7:35 "**U** Judas and his army are delivered
2Es 7: 5 how can they come to the broad part **u** they pass
7: 9 the heir receive the inheritance **u** by passing
7:14 Therefore **u** the living pass through the difficult
4Mc 2: 7 **u** reason is clearly lord of the emotions?
9: 2 we are obviously putting our forebears to shame **u**

UNLIKE (2)
Heb 7:27 **U** the other high priests, he has no need to offer
Wis 2:15 because his manner of life is **u** that of others,

UNLIMITED (1)
Ezr 7:22 one hundred baths of oil, and **u** salt.

UNLOAD (1) [UNLOADED]
Ac 21: 3 because the ship was to **u** its cargo there.

UNLOADED (1) [UNLOAD]
Ge 24:32 and Laban **u** the camels, and gave him straw

UNLOOSE (KJV) See UNTIE

UNLOVED (2)
Ge 29:31 When the LORD saw that Leah was **u,**
Pr 30:23 an **u** woman when she gets a husband,

UNMANLY (2)
4Mc 6:21 by the tyrant as **u** by not contending even to death
8:16 if some of them had been cowardly and **u.**

UNMARKED (1)
Lk 11:44 For you are like **u** graves,

UNMARRIED (8)
Eze 44:25 for brother or **u** sister they may defile themselves.
Ac 21: 9 He had four **u** daughters who had the gift
1Co 7: 8 the **u** and the widows I say that it is well for them to remain **u** as I am.
7:11 let her remain **u** or else be reconciled
7:32 The **u** man is anxious about the affairs of the Lord,
7:34 And the **u** woman and the virgin are anxious about
4Mc 16: 9 Alas for my children, some **u,**

UNMERCIFUL (1)
Sir 35:22 not be patient until he crushes the loins of the **u**

UNMINDFUL (3)
Dt 32:18 You were **u** of the Rock that bore you;
Sir 37: 6 not be **u** of him when you distribute your spoils.
2Es 3:33 though they are **u** of your commandments.

UNMIXED (2)
Rev 14:10 poured **u** into the cup of his anger,
3Mc 5: 2 of frankincense and plenty of **u** wine,

UNMOVEABLE (KJV) See IMMOVABLE

UNMOVED (2)
4Mc 6: 5 was **u,** as though being tortured in a dream;
7:12 though being consumed by the fire, remained **u**

UNNATURAL (2)
Ro 1:26 Their women exchanged natural intercourse for **u,**
Jude 1: 7 indulged in sexual immorality and pursued **u** lust,

UNNI (2)
1Ch 15:18 Zechariah, Jaaziel, Shemiramoth, Jehiel, **U,** Eliab,
15:20 Aziel, Shemiramoth, Jehiel, **U,** Eliab, Maaseiah,

UNNO (1)
Ne 12: 9 and **U** their associates stood opposite them in

UNNOTICED (2)
Job 14:21 they are brought low, and it goes **u.**
Wis 10: 8 so that their failures could never go **u.**

UNOBSERVED (2)
Wis 17: 3 For thinking that in their secret sins they were **u**
2Mc 15:36 by public vote never to let this day go **u,** but

UNPERFECT (KJV) See UNFORMED

UNPLEASANT (1)
Ecc 8: 3 do not delay when the matter is **u,**

UNPOLLUTED (1)
Wis 7:22 unique, manifold, subtle, mobile, clear, **u,** distinct,

UNPRODUCTIVE (2)
1Co 14:14 my spirit prays but my mind is **u.**
Tit 3:14 so that they may not be **u.**

UNPROFITABLE‡ (3)
Job 15: 3 Should they argue in **u** talk,
Tit 3: 9 for they are **u** and worthless.
Wis 3:11 Their hope is vain, their labors are **u,**

UNPRUNED (2)
Lev 25: 5 or gather the grapes of your **u** vine:
25:11 or reap the aftergrowth, or harvest the **u** vines.

UNPUNISHED‡ (17)
Pr 6:29 no one who touches her will go **u.**
11:21 Be assured, the wicked will not go **u,**
16: 5 be assured, they will not go **u.**
17: 5 those who are glad at calamity will not go **u.**
19: 5 A false witness will not go **u,**
19: 9 false witness will not go **u,** and the liar will perish.
28:20 but one who is in a hurry to be rich will not go **u.**
Jer 25:29 not go **u,** for I am summoning a sword against all
30:11 and I will by no means leave you **u.**
46:28 and I will by no means leave you **u.**
49:12 shall you be the one to go **u?**
49:12 You shall not go **u;** you must drink it.
Zec 11: 5 Those who buy them kill them and go **u;**
Wis 12:11 not through fear of anyone that you left them **u**
Sir 7: 8 not even for one will you go **u.**
16:11 it would be a wonder if he remained **u.**
2Mc 7:19 But do not think that you will go **u** for having tried

UNQUALIFIED (1)
Ex 30:33 on an **u** person shall be cut off from the people."

UNQUENCHABLE (3)
Mt 3:12 but the chaff he will burn with **u** fire."
Mk 9:43 to have two hands and to go to hell, to the **u** fire.
Lk 3:17 but the chaff he will burn with **u** fire."

UNREAL (1)
Sir 34: 5 Divinations and omens and dreams are **u,**

UNREASONABLE (3) [UNREASONING]
Ac 25:27 to me **u** to send a prisoner without indicating
2Mc 4:36 to him with regard to the **u** murder of Onias,
4Mc 16:23 It is **u** for people who have religious knowledge

UNREASONING (2) [UNREASONABLE]
4Mc 14:14 Even **u** animals, as well as human beings,
14:18 for children by the example of **u** animals,

UNREBUKEABLE (KJV) See BLAME

UNRELENTING (2)
Job 6:10 I would even exult in **u** pain;
Isa 14: 6 that ruled the nations in anger with **u** persecution.

UNREPROVEABLE (KJV) See IRREPROACHABLE

UNRESERVEDLY (5)
Nu 3: 9 they are **u** given to him from among the Israelites.
8:16 they are **u** given to me from among the Israelites;
32:11 because they have not **u** followed me—
32:12 for they have **u** followed the LORD.'
Aza 1:17 and may we **u** follow you,

UNRESPONSIVE (1)
Wis 16:11 not fall into deep forgetfulness and become **u**

UNREST (3)
Jer 50:34 but **u** to the inhabitants of Babylon.
Sir 40: 5 there is anger and envy and trouble and **u,**
2Es 15:16 For there shall be **u** among people;

UNRESTRAINT (1)
2Es 5:10 and unrighteousness and **u** shall increase on earth.

UNRIGHTEOUS (32) [UNRIGHTEOUSLY, UNRIGHTEOUSNESS]
Job 27: 7 and may my opponent be like the **u.**
29:17 I broke the fangs of the **u,**
31: 3 Does not calamity befall the **u,**
Isa 55: 7 wicked forsake their way, and the **u** their thoughts;
Mt 5:45 and sends rain on the righteous and on the **u.**
Ac 24:15 be a resurrection of both the righteous and the **u.**
1Co 6: 1 do you dare to take it to court before the **u,**
1Pe 3:18 the righteous for the **u,** in order to bring you
2Pe 2: 9 the **u** under punishment until the day of judgment
Wis 1: 8 those who utter **u** things will not escape notice,
3:19 For the end of an **u** generation is grievous.
4:16 the prolonged old age of the **u.**
4:18 The **u** will see, and will have contempt for them,
5: 2 When the **u** see them, they will be shaken
10: 3 when an **u** man departed from her in his anger,
12:12 before you to plead as an advocate for the **u?**
14:31 that always pursues the transgression of the **u.**
16:19 to destroy the crops of the **u** land.
16:24 exerts itself to punish the **u,**
Sir 35:23 and breaks the scepters of the **u;**
51: 6 the slander of an **u** tongue to the king.
1Es 4:36 and with him there is nothing **u.**
4:37 Wine is **u,** the king is **u,** women are **u,** all human beings are **u,** all their works are **u,** and all such
4:39 of anything that is **u** or wicked.
4:40 and there is nothing **u** in its judgment.
2Es 2: 8 Assyria, who conceal the **u** within you!
7:35 and **u** deeds shall not sleep.
8:47 But you have often compared yourself to the **u.**

UNRIGHTEOUSLY (3) [UNRIGHTEOUS]
Wis 12:23 Therefore those who lived **u,** in a life of folly,
14:28 or live **u,** or readily commit perjury;
14:30 because in deceit they swore **u** through contempt

UNRIGHTEOUSNESS (14) [UNRIGHTEOUS]
Job 22:23 if you remove **u** from your tents,
Ps 92:15 he is my rock, and there is no **u** in him.
Jer 22:13 Woe to him who builds his house by **u,**
Eze 28:18 in the **u** of your trade,
2Th 2:12 not believed the truth but took pleasure in **u** will
1Jn 1: 9 forgive us our sins and cleanse us from all **u.**
Wis 1: 5 and will be ashamed at the approach of **u.**
Sir 35: 5 and to forsake **u** is an atonement.
1Es 4:37 in them and in their **u** they will perish.
2Es 5: 2 **U** shall be increased beyond what
5:10 and **u** and unrestraint shall increase on earth.
7:105 then all shall bear their own righteousness and **u."**
7:111 [41] corruption has increased and **u** has multiplied,
12:31 to the eagle and reproving him for his **u,**

UNRIPE (1)
Job 15:33 They will shake off their **u** grape, like the vine,

UNROLLED (1)
Lk 4:17 He **u** the scroll and found the place

UNSAFE (1)
Tob 1:15 the highways into Media became **u**

UNSATIABLE (KJV) See INSATIABLE

UNSATISFIED (1)
Isa 32: 6 to leave the craving of the hungry **u,**

UNSAVOURY (KJV) See PERVERSE, TASTELESS

UNSEARCHABLE (7)
Job 5: 9 He does great things and **u,**
36:26 the number of his years is **u.**
Ps 145: 3 be praised; his greatness is **u.**
Pr 25: 3 like the earth for depth, so the mind of kings is **u.**
Isa 40:28 or grow weary; his understanding is **u.**
Ro 11:33 **u** are his judgments and how inscrutable his ways!
Man 1: 6 yet immeasurable and **u** is your promised mercy,

UNSEEMLY (2)
Sir 13:22 he speaks **u** words, but they justify him.
15: 9 Praise is **u** on the lips of a sinner,

UNSEEMLY (KJV) See also RUDE, SHAMELESS

UNSEEN (6)
Ps 77:19 yet your footprints were **u.**
Heb 11: 7 warned by God about events as yet **u,**
Wis 17: 6 that they saw to be worse than that **u** appearance.
17:19 or the **u** running of leaping animals,
Sir 20:30 Hidden wisdom and **u** treasure,
41:14 hidden wisdom and **u** treasure—

UNSETTLE (1) [UNSETTLED]
Gal 5:12 I wish those who **u** you would castrate themselves!

UNSETTLED (1) [UNSETTLE]
Ac 15:24 to disturb you and have **u** your minds,

UNSHAKEN (1)
2Co 1: 7 Our hope for you is **u;**

UNSHEATHE (4)
Lev 26:33 and I will **u** the sword against you;
Eze 5: 2 and I will **u** the sword after them.
5:12 to every wind and will **u** the sword after them.
12:14 and I will **u** the sword behind them.

UNSHOD (1)
Jer 2:25 Keep your feet from going **u** and your throat

UNSHRUNK (2)
Mt 9:16 No one sews a piece of **u** cloth on an old cloak,
Mk 2:21 "No one sews a piece of **u** cloth on an old cloak;

UNSKILFUL (KJV) See UNSKILLED

UNSKILLED (1)
Heb 5:13 is **u** in the word of righteousness.

UNSOLD (1)
Ac 5: 4 While it remained **u,** did it not remain your own?

UNSOUNDLY (1)
Wis 2: 1 For they reasoned **u,** saying to themselves,

UNSOWN (1)
2Es 6:22 Sown places shall suddenly appear **u,**

UNSPEAKABLE (KJV) See INDESCRIBABLE, NOT TO BE TOLD

UNSPIRITUAL (2)
1Co 2:14 Those who are **u** do not receive the gifts
Jas 3:15 but is earthly, **u,** devilish.

UNSPOILED (2)
Jer 48:11 his flavor has remained and his aroma is **u**.
2Es 7:*123* [53] fruit remains **u** and in which are abundance

UNSPOTTED (KJV) See UNSTAINED

UNSTABLE (4)
Ge 49: 4 **U** as water, you shall no longer excel
Job 12: 5 but it is ready for those whose feet are **u**.
Jas 1:7,8 being double-minded and **u** in every way,
2Pe 3:16 the ignorant and **u** twist to their own destruction,

UNSTAINED (1)
Jas 1:27 and to keep oneself **u** by the world.

UNSTEADY (2)
Eze 29: 7 you broke, and made all their legs **u**.
2Pe 2:14 insatiable for sin. They entice **u** souls.

UNSTOPPED (1)
Isa 35: 5 and the ears of the deaf **u**;

UNSUSPECTING (4)
Jdg 18: 7 after the manner of the Sidonians, quiet and **u**,
18:10 When you go, you will come to an **u** people.
18:27 to a people quiet and **u**, put them to the sword,
Eze 30: 9 from me in ships to terrify the **u** Ethiopians;

UNSWERVING (4)
Mic 7:20 You will show faithfulness to Jacob and **u** loyalty
3Mc 3: 3 continued to maintain goodwill and **u** loyalty
4Mc 6: 7 he kept his reason upright and **u**.
17: 3 you held firm and **u** against the earthquake of

UNTAKEN (KJV) See STILL THERE

UNTHANKFUL (KJV) See UNGRATEFUL

UNTIE (9) [UNTIED, UNTYING]
Mt 21: 2 **u** them and bring them to me.
Mk 1: 7 I am not worthy to stoop down and **u** the thong
11: 2 that has never been ridden; **u** it and bring it.
Lk 3:16 I am not worthy to **u** the thong of his sandals.
13:15 of you on the sabbath **u** his ox or his donkey from
19:30 **U** it and bring it here.
Jn 1:27 I am not worthy to **u** the thong of his sandal."
Ac 13:25 I am not worthy to **u** the thong of the sandals
3Mc 6:27 Loose and **u** their unjust bonds!

UNTIED (1) [UNTIE]
Jdt 6:14 they **u** him and brought him into Bethulia

UNTIL‡ (673)
Ge 3:19 of your face you shall eat bread **u** you return to
8: 5 The waters continued to abate **u** the tenth month;
8: 7 and fro **u** the waters were dried up from the earth.
19:22 for I can do nothing **u** you arrive there."
21:26 and I have not heard of it **u** today."
24:19 **u** they have finished drinking."
24:33 he said, "I will not eat **u** I have told my errand."
26:13 and more **u** he became very wealthy.
27:44 **u** your brother's fury turns away—
27:45 **u** your brother's anger against you turns away,
28:15 for I will not leave you **u** I have done
29: 8 "We cannot **u** all the flocks are gathered together,
31:23 and pursued him for seven days **u** he caught up
32: 4 with Laban as an alien, and stayed **u** now;
32:24 and a man wrestled with him **u** daybreak.
33: 3 **u** he came near his brother.
33:14 **u** I come to my lord in Seir."
34: 5 so Jacob held his peace **u** they came.
38:11 "Remain a widow in your father's house **u**
38:17 "Only if you give me a pledge, **u** you send it."
39:16 Then she kept his garment by her **u** his master
46:34 of livestock from our youth even **u** now, both we
49:10 **u** tribute comes to him; and the obedience of the
Ex 7:16 But **u** now you have not listened.'
9:18 in Egypt from the day it was founded **u** now.
10:26 to use to worship the LORD **u** we arrive there."
12: 6 You shall keep it **u** the fourteenth day
12:10 You shall let none of it remain **u** the morning;
12:10 that remains **u** the morning you shall burn.
12:15 the first day **u** the seventh day shall be cut off
12:18 the evening of the fourteenth day **u** the evening of
12:22 of you shall go outside the door of your house **u**
15:16 they became still as a stone **u** your people,
15:16 **u** the people whom you acquired passed by.
16:19 "Let no one leave any of it over **u** morning."
16:20 some left part of it **u** morning,
16:23 that is left over put aside to be kept **u** morning.' "
16:24 So they put it aside **u** morning,
16:35 **u** they came to a habitable land;
16:35 **u** they came to the border of the land of Canaan.
17:12 so his hands were steady **u** the sun set.
18:13 people stood around him from morning **u** evening.
18:14 the people stand around you from morning **u**
23:18 or let the fat of my festival remain **u** the morning.
23:30 **u** you have increased and possess the land.
24:14 "Wait here for us, **u** we come to you again;
29:34 or of the bread, remains **u** the morning,
33: 8 of their tents and watch Moses **u** he had gone into
Ex 33:22 I will cover you with my hand **u** I have passed by;
34:25 of the festival of the passover shall not be left **u**
34:34 he would take the veil off, **u** he came out;
34:35 **u** he went in to speak with him.
40:37 they did not set out **u** the day that it was taken up.
Lev 6: 9 the hearth upon the altar all night **u** the morning,
7:15 you shall not leave any of it **u** morning.
8:33 **u** the day when your period
11:24 of any of them shall be unclean **u** the evening,
11:25 of them shall wash his clothes and be unclean **u**
11:27 of any of them shall be unclean **u** the evening,
11:28 the carcass shall wash his clothes and be unclean **u**
11:31 of them when they are dead shall be unclean **u**
11:32 and it shall be unclean **u** the evening,
11:39 anyone who touches its carcass shall be unclean **u**
11:40 and be unclean **u** the evening;
11:40 and be unclean **u** the evening.
12: 4 **u** the days of her purification are completed.
14:46 while it is shut up shall be unclean **u** the evening;
15: 5 and bathe in water, and be unclean **u** the evening.
15: 6 and bathe in water, and be unclean **u** the evening.
15: 7 and bathe in water, and be unclean **u** the evening.
15: 8 and bathe in water, and be unclean **u** the evening.
15:10 that was under him shall be unclean **u** the evening,
15:10 and bathe in water, and be unclean **u** the evening.
15:11 and bathe in water, and be unclean **u** the evening.
15:16 and be unclean **u** the evening.
15:17 and be unclean **u** the evening.
15:18 and be unclean **u** the evening.
15:19 and whoever touches her shall be unclean **u**
15:21 and bathe in water, and be unclean **u** the evening.
15:22 and bathe in water, and be unclean **u** the evening;
15:23 he touches it he shall be unclean **u** the evening.
15:27 and bathe in water, and be unclean **u** the evening.
16:17 to make atonement in the sanctuary **u**
17:15 and be unclean **u** the evening;
19: 6 over **u** the third day shall be consumed in fire.
19:13 for yourself the wages of a laborer **u** morning.
22: 4 a discharge may eat of the sacred donations **u**
22: 6 be unclean **u** evening and shall not eat of
22:30 you shall not leave any of it **u** morning:
23:14 **u** that very day, **u** you have brought the offering
23:16 You shall count **u** the day after
24:12 **u** the decision of the LORD should be made clear
25:22 **u** the ninth year, when its produce comes in,
25:28 what was sold shall remain with the purchaser **u**
25:29 be redeemed **u** a year has elapsed since its sale;
25:40 They shall serve with you **u** the year of the jubilee.
25:50 the year when they sold themselves to the alien **u**
25:52 and if few years remain **u** the jubilee year,
27:18 the price for it according to the years that remain **u**
Nu 6: 5 **u** the time is completed for which they separate
9:12 They shall leave none of it **u** morning,
9:15 and from evening **u** morning it was over
9:21 the cloud would remain from evening **u** morning;
11:20 **u** it comes out of your nostrils
12:15 on the march **u** Miriam had been brought in again.
14:19 pardoned this people, from Egypt even **u** now."
14:33 **u** the last of your dead bodies lies in
19: 7 but the priest shall remain unclean **u** evening.
19: 8 he shall remain unclean **u** evening.
19:10 the heifer shall wash his clothes and be unclean **u**
19:21 the water for cleansing shall be unclean **u** evening.
19:22 anyone who touches it shall be unclean **u** evening.
20:17 the left **u** we have passed through your territory."
21:22 by the King's Highway **u** we have passed
21:30 and we laid waste **u** fire spread to Medeba."
21:35 and all his people, **u** there was no survivor left;
23:24 down **u** it has eaten the prey and drunk the blood
32:13 **u** all the generation that had done evil in the sight
32:17 **u** we have brought them to their place.
32:18 We will not return to our homes **u** all
32:21 **u** he has driven out his enemies from before him
35:12 that the slayer may not die **u** there is a trial before
35:25 The slayer shall live in it **u** the death of
35:28 in the city of refuge **u** the death of the high priest;
Dt 1:19 **u** we reached Kadesh-barnea.
1:31 the way that you traveled **u** you reached this place.
2:14 of time we had traveled from Kadesh-barnea **u**
2:14 **u** the entire generation of warriors had perished
2:15 against them, to root them out from the camp, **u**
2:29 **u** I cross the Jordan into the land that
3: 3 down **u** not a single survivor was left.
7:20 the pestilence against them, **u** even the survivors
7:23 over to you, and throw them into great panic, **u**
7:24 **u** you have destroyed them.
9: 7 from the day you came out of the land of Egypt **u**
9:21 grinding it thoroughly, **u** it was reduced to dust;
11: 5 **u** you came to this place;
16: 4 on the evening of the first day shall remain **u**
20:20 against the town that makes war with you, **u**
22: 2 and it shall remain with you **u** the owner claims it;
28:20 **u** you are destroyed and perish quickly,
28:21 to you **u** it has consumed you off the land
28:22 they shall pursue you **u** you perish.
28:24 down upon you from the sky **u** you are destroyed.
28:45 pursuing and overtaking you **u** you are destroyed,
28:48 an iron yoke on your neck **u** he has destroyed you.
28:51 and the fruit of your ground **u** you are destroyed,
28:51 **u** it has made you perish.
28:52 It shall besiege you in all your towns **u** your high
28:61 LORD will inflict on you **u** you are destroyed.
Jos 1:15 **u** the LORD gives rest to your kindred as well as
2:16 **u** the pursuers have returned;
2:22 into the hill country and stayed there three days, **u**
3:17 **u** the entire nation finished crossing over
4:10 **u** everything was finished that
Jos 4:23 up the waters of the Jordan for you **u** you crossed
4:23 which he dried up for us **u** we crossed over,
5: 1 of the Jordan for the Israelites **u** they had crossed
5: 6 **u** all the nation, the warriors who came out
5: 8 in their places in the camp **u** they were healed.
6:10 **u** the day I tell you to shout.
7: 6 before the ark of the LORD **u** the evening, he and
7:13 you will be unable to stand before your enemies **u**
8: 6 after us **u** we have drawn them away from
8:22 down **u** no one was left who survived or escaped.
8:26 **u** he had utterly destroyed all the inhabitants
8:29 And he hanged the king of Ai on a tree **u** evening;
10:13 **u** the nation took vengeance on their enemies.
10:20 on them, **u** they were wiped out,
10:26 And they hung on the trees **u** evening.
11: 8 **u** they had left no one remaining.
11:14 **u** they had destroyed them,
20: 6 that city **u** there is a trial before the congregation,
20: 6 **u** the death of the one who is high priest at
20: 9 **u** there was a trial before the congregation.
23:13 a scourge on your sides, and thorns in your eyes, **u**
23:15 **u** he has destroyed you from this good land that
Jdg 3:25 So they waited **u** they were embarrassed.
4:21 **u** it went down into the ground—
4:24 **u** they destroyed King Jabin of Canaan.
6:18 Do not depart from here **u** I come to you,
6:18 And he said, "I will stay **u** you return."
15: 7 I swear I will not stop **u** I have taken revenge
16: 2 thinking, "Let us wait **u** the light of the morning;
16: 3 But Samson lay only **u** midnight.
16:13 "**U** now you have mocked me and told me lies;
18: 1 for **u** then no territory among the tribes
18:30 the Danites **u** the time the land went into captivity.
19: 7 his father-in-law kept urging him **u** he spent
19: 8 So they lingered **u** the day declined,
19: 9 "Look, the day has worn on **u** it is almost evening.
19:25 abused her all through the night **u** the morning.
19:26 of the man's house where her master was, **u**
19:30 the Israelites came up from the land of Egypt **u**
20: 5 and they raped my concubine **u** she died.
20:23 up and wept before the LORD **u** the evening;
20:26 they fasted that day **u** evening.
21: 2 and sat there **u** evening before God,
Ru 1:13 would you then wait **u** they were grown?
1:19 two of them went on **u** they came to Bethlehem.
2: 7 on her feet from early this morning **u** now,
2:14 She ate **u** she was satisfied,
2:17 So she gleaned in the field **u** evening.
2:21 **u** they have finished all my harvest.' "
2:23 gleaning **u** the end of the barley
3: 3 to the man **u** he has finished eating and drinking.
3:13 Lie down **u** the morning."
3:14 So she lay at his feet **u** morning,
3:18 my daughter, **u** you learn how the matter turns out,
1Sa 1:11 before you as a nazirite **u** the day of his death.
1:23 wait **u** you have weaned him;
1:23 So the woman remained and nursed her son, **u**
3:15 Samuel lay there **u** morning;
9:13 For the people will not eat **u** he comes,
10: 8 **u** I come to you and show you what you shall do."
11:11 the camp and cut down the Ammonites **u** the heat
12: 2 I have led you from my youth **u** this day.
14: 9 If they say to us, 'Wait **u** we come to you,'
14:36 after the Philistines by night and despoil them **u**
15:18 and fight against them **u** they are consumed.'
15:35 not see Saul again **u** the day of his death,
16:11 for we will not sit down **u** he comes here."
19:23 **u** he came to Naioth in Ramah.
20: 5 so that I may hide in the field **u** the third evening.
22: 3 **u** I know what God will do for me."
25:36 so she told him nothing at all **u** the morning light.
29: 6 in you from the day of your coming to me **u** today.
29: 8 from the day I entered your service **u** now,
30: 4 **u** they had no more strength to weep.
30:17 David attacked them from twilight **u** the evening
2Sa 1:12 fasted **u** evening for Saul and for his son Jonathan,
2:27 to pursue their kinsmen, not stopping **u** morning."
10: 5 "Remain at Jericho **u** your beards have grown,
13:27 But Absalom pressed him **u** he let Amnon and all
15:24 **u** the people had all passed out of the city.
15:28 at the fords of the wilderness **u** word comes
17:13 **u** not even a pebble is to be found there."
19: 7 that has come upon you from your youth **u** now."
19:24 or washed his clothes, from the day the king left **u**
20: 3 So they were shut up **u** the day of their death,
21:10 from the beginning of harvest **u** rain fell on them
22:38 and did not turn back **u** they were consumed.
23:10 down the Philistines **u** his arm grew weary,
24:15 on Israel from that morning **u** the appointed time;
1Ki 3: 1 **u** he had finished building his own house and
5: 3 **u** the LORD put them under the soles of his feet.
10: 7 The reports **u** I came and my own eyes had seen it.
11:16 **u** he had eliminated every male in Edom);
11:40 and remained in Egypt **u** the death of Solomon.
14:10 just as one burns up dung **u** it is all gone.
15:29 to the house of Jeroboam not one that breathed, **u**
17:14 not fail **u** the day that the LORD sends rain on
18:26 called on the name of Baal from morning **u** noon,
18:28 with swords and lances **u** the blood gushed out
18:29 on **u** the time of the offering of the oblation,
22:11 With these you shall gore the Arameans **u**
22:21 **u** a spirit came forward and stood before
22:27 on reduced rations of bread and water **u** I come
22:35 in his chariot facing the Arameans, **u** at evening
2Ki 2: 8 **u** the two of them crossed on dry ground.
2:17 But when they urged him **u** he was ashamed,
3:20 **u** the country was filled with water.

2Ki 3:25 of land everyone threw a stone, **u** it was covered;
3:25 **u** the slingers surrounded and attacked it.
4:20 the child sat on her lap **u** noon, and he died.
7: 3 "Why should we sit here **u** we die?
7: 9 if we are silent and wait **u** the morning light,
8: 6 of the fields from the day that she left the land **u**
8:11 and stared at him, **u** he was ashamed.
8:15 spread it over the king's face, **u** he died.
10: 8 at the entrance of the gate **u** the morning."
10:11 and priests, **u** he left him no survivor.
10:17 **u** he had wiped them out,
10:21 **u** the temple of Baal was filled from wall to wall.
13:17 the Arameans in Aphek **u** you have made an end
13:19 then you would have struck down Aram **u**
13:23 has he banished them from his presence **u** now.
17:20 **u** he had banished them from his presence.
17:23 **u** the LORD removed Israel out of his sight,
17:23 from their own land to Assyria **u** this day.
18: 4 for **u** those days the people
18:32 **u** I come and take you away to a land
20:17 which your ancestors have stored up **u** this day,
21:16 **u** he had filled Jerusalem from one end to another,
25: 2 So the city was besieged **u** the eleventh year
1Ch 4:31 These were their towns **u** David became king.
5:22 And they lived in their territory **u** the exile.
6:32 **u** Solomon had built the house of the LORD
12:22 **u** there was a great army, like an army of God.
19: 5 "Remain at Jericho **u** your beards have grown,
28:20 **u** all the work for the service of the house of
2Ch 8:16 of the house of the LORD was laid **u** the house of
9: 6 the reports **u** I came and my own eyes saw it.
14:13 and the Ethiopians fell **u** no one remained alive;
15:19 And there was no more war **u** the thirty-fifth year
18:10 With these you shall gore the Arameans **u**
18:20 **u** a spirit came forward and stood before
18:26 on reduced rations of bread and water **u** I return
18:34 up in his chariot facing the Arameans **u** evening;
20:25 for themselves **u** they could carry no more.
21:15 **u** your bowels come out, day after day,
24:10 and dropped it into the chest **u** it was full.
26:15 he was marvelously helped **u** he became strong.
29:28 this continued **u** the burnt offering was finished.
29:34 so, **u** other priests had sanctified themselves,
29:34 helped them **u** the work was finished—
31: 1 **u** they had destroyed them all.
35:14 in offering the burnt offerings and the fat parts **u**
36:16 **u** the wrath of the LORD
36:20 and to his sons **u** the establishment of the kingdom
36:21 **u** the land had made up for its sabbaths.
Ezr 2:63 **u** there should be a priest to consult Urim
4: 5 of Persia and **u** the reign of King Darius of Persia.
4:21 and that this city not be rebuilt, **u** I make a decree.
4:24 in Jerusalem stopped and was discontinued **u**
5: 5 not stop them **u** a report reached Darius and
5:16 that time **u** now it has been under construction,
8:29 Guard them and keep them **u** you weigh them
9: 4 while I sat appalled **u** the evening sacrifice.
9:14 be angry with us **u** you destroy us without remnant
10:14 **u** the fierce wrath of our God
Ne 2: 7 they may grant me passage **u** I arrive in Judah;
4:21 of them held the spears from break of dawn **u**
7: 3 of Jerusalem are not to be opened **u** the sun is hot;
7:65 **u** a priest with Urim and Thummim should come.
8: 3 from early morning **u** midday, in the presence of
9:32 since the time of the kings of Assyria **u** today.
12:22 also the priests **u** the reign of Darius the Persian.
12:23 the Book of the Annals **u** the days of Johanan son
13:19 that they should not be opened **u** after the sabbath.
Job 7: 4 the night is long, and I am full of tossing **u** dawn.
7:19 let me alone **u** I swallow my spittle?
14:12 **u** the heavens are no more,
14:13 that you would conceal me **u** your wrath is past,
14:14 All the days of my service I would wait **u**
27: 5 **u** I die I will not put away my integrity from me.
Ps 10:15 seek out their wickedness **u** you find none.
18:37 and did not turn back **u** they were consumed.
40:12 my iniquities have overtaken me, **u** I cannot see;
57: 1 **u** the destroying storms pass by.
59:13 consume them **u** they are no more.
71:18 **u** I proclaim your might to all the generations to
72: 7 **u** the moon is no more.
73:17 **u** I went into the sanctuary of God;
94:13 **u** a pit is dug for the wicked.
104:23 to their work and to their labor **u** the evening.
105:19 **u** what he had said came to pass,
107: 7 **u** they reached an inhabited town.
110: 1 "Sit at my right hand **u**
123: 2 **u** he has mercy upon us.
132: 5 **u** I find a place for the LORD,
Pr 4:18 which shines brighter and brighter **u** full day.
7:18 Come, let us take our fill of love **u** morning;
7:20 he will not come home **u** full moon."
7:23 **u** an arrow pierces its entrails.
18:17 **u** the other comes and cross-examines.
28:17 let that killer be a fugitive **u** death;
Ecc 2: 3 on folly, **u** I might see what was good for mortals
SS 2: 7 do not stir up or awaken love **u** it is ready!
2:17 **U** the day breathes and the shadows flee, turn,
3: 4 and would not let him go **u** I brought him
3: 5 do not stir up or awaken love **u** it is ready!
4: 6 **U** the day breathes and the shadows flee,
8: 4 do not stir up or awaken love **u** it is ready!
Isa 5: 8 **u** there is room for no one but you,
6:11 "**U** cities lie waste without inhabitant,
6:12 **u** the LORD sends everyone far away,
22:14 this iniquity will not be forgiven you **u** you die,
26:20 for a little while **u** the wrath is past.
Isa 30:17 **u** you are left like a flagstaff on the top of a
32:15 **u** a spirit from on high is poured out on us,
36:17 **u** I come and take you away to a land
38:13 I cry for help **u** morning;
39: 6 which your ancestors have stored up **u** this day,
42: 4 or be crushed **u** he has established justice in
55:10 do not return there **u** they have watered the earth,
62: 1 **u** her vindication shines out like the dawn,
62: 7 and give him no rest **u** he establishes Jerusalem
Jer 1: 3 and **u** the end of the eleventh year
1: 3 **u** the captivity of Jerusalem in the fifth month.
7:25 of the land of Egypt **u** this day,
7:32 they will bury in Topheth **u** there is no more room.
9:16 the sword after them, **u** I have consumed them.
19:11 In Topheth they shall bury **u** there is no more
23:20 of the LORD will not turn back **u** he has executed
24:10 **u** they are utterly destroyed from the land
27: 7 **u** the time of his own land comes;
27: 8 **u** I have completed its destruction by his hand.
27:22 **u** the day when I give attention to them,
30:24 of the LORD will not turn back **u** he has executed
32: 5 and there he shall remain **u** I attend to him,
32:31 from the day it was built **u** this day,
36: 2 from the days of Josiah **u** today.
36:23 **u** the entire scroll was consumed in the fire
37:21 **u** all the bread of the city was gone.
38:28 And Jeremiah remained in the court of the guard **u**
44:27 by the sword and by famine, **u** not one is left.
47: 6 How long **u** you are quiet?
49:37 the sword after them, **u** I have consumed them;
51:39 **u** they become merry and then sleep
52: 5 So the city was besieged **u** the eleventh year
52:11 and put him in prison **u** the day of his death.
La 3:50 **u** the LORD from heaven looks down and sees.
Eze 4: 8 from one side to the other **u** you have completed
4:14 up **u** now I have never eaten what died of itself
21:27 **U** he comes whose right it is; to him I will give it.
24:13 be cleansed **u** I have satisfied my fury upon you.
28:15 **u** iniquity was found in you.
34:21 at all the weak animals with your horns **u**
39:15 **u** the buriers have buried it in the Valley
39:19 You shall eat fat **u** you are filled,
39:19 and drink blood **u** you are drunk,
46: 2 but the gate shall not be closed **u** evening.
Da 1:21 And Daniel continued there **u** the first year
2: 9 and misleading words to me **u** things take a turn.
4:23 **u** seven times pass over him'—
4:25 and seven times shall pass over you, **u** you have
4:32 and seven times shall pass over you, **u** you have
4:33 **u** his hair grew as long as eagles' feathers
5:21 with the dew of heaven, **u** he learned that
6:14 and **u** the sun went down he made every effort
7:22 **u** the Ancient One came;
9:14 So the LORD kept watch over this calamity **u**
9:25 to restore and rebuild Jerusalem **u** the time of
9:27 that desolates, **u** the decreed end is poured out
11:35 purified, and cleansed, **u** the time of the end,
11:35 for there is still an interval **u** the time appointed.
11:36 He shall prosper **u** the period
12: 4 the words secret and the book sealed **u** the time of
12: 6 long shall it be **u** the end of these wonders?"
12: 9 to remain secret and sealed **u** the time of the end.
Hos 5:15 to my place **u** they acknowledge their guilt
7: 4 from the kneading of the dough **u** it is leavened.
9:12 I will bereave them **u** no one is left.
Am 9: 1 Strike the capitals **u** the thresholds shake,
Mic 5: 3 Therefore he shall give them up **u** the time
7: 9 **u** he takes my side and executes judgment for me.
Hab 2:15 pouring out your wrath **u** they are drunk,
Zep 2: 5 and I will destroy you **u** no inhabitant is left.
3: 3 its judges are evening wolves that leave nothing **u**
Zec 10:10 **u** there is no room for them.
Mal 1: 4 **u** they are called the wicked country,
3: 3 **u** they present offerings to the LORD
Mt 1:25 but had no marital relations with her **u**
2: 9 **u** it stopped over the place where the child was.
2:13 and flee to Egypt, and remain there **u** I tell you;
2:15 and remained there **u** the death of Herod.
5:18 For truly I tell you, **u** heaven and earth pass away,
5:18 will pass from the law **u** all is accomplished.
5:26 you will never get out **u** you have paid
10:11 and stay there **u** you leave.
11:12 the days of John the Baptist **u** now the kingdom
11:13 the prophets and the law prophesied **u** John came;
11:23 it would have remained **u** this day.
12:20 a smoldering wick **u** he brings justice to victory.
13:30 Let both of them grow together **u** the harvest;
13:33 and mixed in with three measures of flour **u** all
17: 9 the vision **u** after the Son of Man has been raised
18:30 and threw him into prison **u** he would pay
18:34 over to be tortured **u** he would pay his entire debt.
22:44 **u** I put your enemies under your feet" '?
23:39 I tell you, you will not see me again **u** you say,
24:21 as has not been from the beginning of the world **u**
24:34 not pass away **u** all these things have taken place.
24:38 **u** the day Noah entered the ark,
24:39 and they knew nothing **u** the flood came
26:29 I will never again drink of this fruit of the vine **u**
27:45 darkness came over the whole land **u** three in
27:64 Therefore command the tomb to be made secure **u**
Mk 6:10 stay there **u** you leave the place.
9: 1 not taste death **u** they see that the kingdom
9: 9 **u** after the Son of Man had risen from the dead.
12:36 **u** I put your enemies under your feet." '
13:19 the beginning of the creation that God created **u**
13:30 not pass away **u** all these things have taken place.
14:25 the fruit of the vine **u** that day when I drink it new
Mk 15:33 darkness came over the whole land **u** three in
Lk 1:20 unable to speak, **u** the day these things occur."
1:80 in the wilderness **u** the day he appeared publicly
4:13 he departed from him **u** an opportune time.
9:39 It convulses him **u** he foams at the mouth;
12:50 and what stress I am under **u** it is completed!
12:59 you will never get out **u** you have paid
13: 8 **u** I dig around it and put manure on it.
13:21 and mixed in with three measures of flour **u** all
13:35 not see me **u** the time comes when you say,
15: 4 in the wilderness and go after the one that is lost **u**
15: 8 and search carefully **u** she finds it?
16:16 law and the prophets were in effect **u** John came;
17:27 **u** the day Noah entered the ark,
19:13 'Do business with these **u** I come back.'
20:43 **u** I make your enemies your footstool." '
21:24 **u** the times of the Gentiles are fulfilled.
21:32 not pass away **u** all things have taken place.
22:16 not eat it **u** it is fulfilled in the kingdom of God."
22:18 the fruit of the vine **u** the kingdom of God comes."
22:34 **u** you have denied three times that you know me."
23:44 and darkness came over the whole land **u** three in
24:49 the city **u** you have been clothed with power from
Jn 2:10 But you have kept the good wine **u** now."
9:18 that he had been blind and had received his sight **u**
16:24 **U** now you have not asked for anything
21:22 "If it is my will that he remain **u** I come,
21:23 but, "If it is my will that he remain **u** I come,
Ac 1: 2 **u** the day when he was taken up to heaven,
1:22 of John **u** the day when he was taken up from us—
2:35 **u** I make your enemies your footstool." '
3:21 in heaven **u** the time of universal restoration
4: 3 So they arrested them and put them in custody **u**
7:18 **u** another king who had not known Joseph ruled
7:45 And it was there **u** the time of David,
8:40 he proclaimed the good news to all the towns **u**
13:20 After that he gave them judges **u** the time of
20: 7 he continued speaking **u** midnight.
20:11 he continued to converse with them **u** dawn;
23:12 to eat nor drink **u** they had killed Paul.
23:14 by an oath to taste no food **u** we have killed Paul.
23:21 by an oath neither to eat nor drink **u** they kill him.
25:21 to be held **u** I could send him to the emperor."
28:23 From morning **u** evening he explained the matter
Ro 8:22 creation has been groaning in labor pains **u** now;
11:25 **u** the full number of the Gentiles has come in.
1Co 8: 7 some have become so accustomed to idols **u** now,
11:26 you proclaim the Lord's death **u** he comes.
15:25 For he must reign **u** he has put all his enemies
16: 8 But I will stay in Ephesus **u** Pentecost,
2Co 1:13 I hope you will understand **u** the end—
Gal 2:12 for **u** certain people came from James,
3:19 **u** the offspring would come to whom
3:23 we were imprisoned and guarded under the law **u**
3:24 the law was our disciplinarian **u** Christ came,
4: 2 but they remain under guardians and trustees **u**
4:19 in the pain of childbirth **u** Christ is formed in you,
Eph 4:13 **u** all of us come to the unity of the faith and of
Php 1: 5 of your sharing in the gospel from the first day **u**
1Th 4:15 who are left **u** the coming of the Lord,
2Th 2: 7 only **u** the one who now restrains it is removed.
1Ti 4:13 **U** I arrive, give attention to the public reading
6:14 the commandment without spot or blame **u**
2Ti 1:12 to guard **u** that day what I have entrusted to him.
Heb 1:13 "Sit at my right hand **u** I make your enemies
4:12 piercing **u** it divides soul from spirit,
9:10 regulations for the body imposed **u** the time comes
10:13 since then has been waiting "**u** his enemies would
Jas 5: 7 therefore, beloved, **u** the coming of the Lord.
5: 7 with it **u** it receives the early and the late rains.
2Pe 1:19 **u** the day dawns and the morning star rises
2: 4 of deepest darkness to be kept **u** the judgment;
2: 9 and to keep the unrighteous under punishment **u**
3: 7 being kept **u** the day of judgment and destruction
Rev 2:10 Be faithful **u** death, and I will give you the crown
2:25 only hold fast to what you have **u** I come.
6:11 **u** the number would be complete both
7: 3 **u** we have marked the servants of our God with
15: 8 and no one could enter the temple **u**
16:21 **u** they cursed God for the plague of the hail,
17:17 **u** the words of God will be fulfilled.
20: 3 **u** the thousand years were ended.
20: 5 not come to life **u** the thousand years were ended.)
Tob 1:14 **U** his death I used to go into Media,
2: 2 I will wait for you, **u** you come back."
2: 4 in one of the rooms **u** sunset when I might bury it.
2:10 **u** I became completely blind.
4:14 over **u** the next day the wages of those who work
5: 3 and we will pay him wages **u** you return.
5: 7 young man, **u** I go in and tell my father;
6: 6 on their way together **u** they were near Media.
7:11 "I will neither eat nor drink anything **u** you settle
14: 5 not like the first one **u** the period when the times
Jdt 2:10 and you shall hold them for me **u** the day
6: 5 you shall not see my face again from this day **u**
6: 8 You will not die **u** you perish along with them.
7:20 **u** all the water containers of every inhabitant
8:34 for I will not tell you **u** I have finished what I am
10:10 The men of the town watched her **u** she had gone
10:18 waiting **u** they told him about her.
11:19 **u** you come to Jerusalem;
12: 5 into the tent, and she slept **u** midnight.
12: 9 Then she returned purified and stayed in the tent **u**
12:14 and it will be a joy to me **u** the day of my death."
14: 8 the day she left **u** the moment she began speaking
AdE 14:18 since the day that I was brought here **u** now,
15: 8 and took her in his arms **u** she came to herself.

Wis 10:14 **u** she brought him the scepter of a kingdom
Sir 1:23 Those who are patient stay calm **u**
1:24 They hold back their words **u** the right moment;
4:17 and will torment them by her discipline **u**
11:19 not know how long it will be **u** he leaves them
13: 7 **u** he has drained you two or three times,
18:22 and do not wait **u** death to be released from it.
20: 7 The wise remain silent **u** the right moment,
23:16 a fire will not be quenched **u** it burns itself out;
23:16 of kin will never cease **u** the fire burns him up.
23:17 he will never weary **u** he dies.
29: 5 One kisses another's hands **u** he gets a loan,
35:21 and it will not rest **u** it reaches its goal;
35:21 it will not desist **u** the Most High responds
35:22 a warrior will not be patient **u** he crushes the loins
35:23 **u** he destroys the multitude of the insolent,
35:24 **u** he repays mortals according to their deeds,
35:25 **u** he judges the case of his people
40: 1 from their mother's womb **u** the day they return to
47:24 **u** they were exiled from their land.
47:25 **u** vengeance came upon them.
48:15 **u** they were carried off as plunder from their land,
50:19 **u** the order of worship of the Lord was ended,
51:14 and I will search for her **u** the end.
Bar 1:19 of the land of Egypt **u** today,
1Mc 3:33 to take care of his son Antiochus **u** he returned.
4:41 in the citadel **u** he had cleansed the sanctuary.
4:46 on the temple hill **u** a prophet should come
5:19 but do not engage in battle with the Gentiles **u**
5:53 and encouraging the people all the way **u** he came
8: 4 **u** they crushed them and inflicted great disaster
9: 6 **u** no more than eight hundred of them were left.
9:13 and the battle raged from morning **u** evening.
10:50 He pressed the battle strongly **u** the sun set,
10:80 and shot arrows at his men from early morning **u**
12:29 But Jonathan and his troops did not know it **u**
14:10 **u** his renown spread to the ends of the earth.
14:41 **u** a trustworthy prophet should arise,
16: 2 the wars of Israel from our youth **u** this day,
16: 9 John pursued them **u** Cendebeus reached Kedron,
2Mc 2: 7 "The place shall remain unknown **u**
5:25 to be peaceably disposed and waited **u**
6:14 the Lord waits patiently to punish them **u**
8:35 like a runaway slave across the country **u**
9: 4 without stopping **u** he completed the journey.
1Es 1:14 the priests were offering the fat **u** nightfall;
1:52 **u** in his anger against his people because
1:57 and they were servants to him and to his sons **u**
1:58 "**U** the land has enjoyed its sabbaths,
1:58 it shall keep sabbath all the time of its desolation **u**
2:30 the temple in Jerusalem stopped **u** the second year
4:51 for the building of the temple **u** it was completed,
4:55 for the Levites should be provided **u** the day when
5:40 not to share in the holy things **u**
5:73 from building for two years, **u** the reign of Darius.
6: 6 not prevented from building **u** word could be sent
6:20 in process of construction from that time **u** now,
6:28 **u** the house of the Lord is finished;
8:59 and on guard **u** you deliver them to the leaders of
8:72 and I sat grief-stricken **u** the evening sacrifice.
8:77 to the sword and exile and plundering, in shame **u**
9:13 **u** we are freed from the wrath of the Lord
9:41 before the gate of the temple from early morning **u**
3Mc 4:15 and zealous intensity from the rising of the sun **u**
5:10 the pitiless elephants **u** they had been filled with
6:28 of our ancestors **u** now has granted an unimpeded
6:40 with everything by the king, **u** the fourteenth day,
7: 4 be firmly established **u** this was accomplished,
7:18 to them for their journey **u** all of them arrived
2Es 2:32 Embrace your children **u** I come,
4:30 how much ungodliness it has produced **u** now—
4:30 and will produce **u** the time of threshing comes!
4:37 or arouse them **u** that measure is fulfilled.' "
4:51 "Do you think that I shall live **u** those days?
7:75 of us yields up the soul, we shall be kept in rest **u**
7:77 but it will not be shown to you **u** the last times.
10: 2 I remained quiet **u** the evening of the second day.
10: 4 but will mourn and fast continually **u** I die."
12:21 but two shall be kept **u** the end.
12:32 the Messiah whom the Most High has kept **u**
12:34 and he will make them joyful **u** the end comes,
13:44 the channels of the river **u** they had crossed over.
13:46 "Then they lived there **u** the last times;
14: 9 with my Son and with those who are like you, **u**
14:25 which shall not be put out **u** what you are about
15:21 Just as they have done to my elect **u** this day,
16:14 and shall not return **u** they come over the earth.
16:15 not be put out **u** it consumes the foundations of
4Mc 7: 3 the rudder of religion **u** he sailed into the haven

UNTIMELY‡ (4)

Ps 58: 8 like the **u** birth that never sees the sun.
1Co 15: 8 Last of all, as to one **u** born, he appeared also to
Wis 14:15 a father, consumed with grief at an **u** bereavement,
Sir 20: 1 There is a rebuke that is **u,**

UNTIMELY (KJV) See also LATE, STILLBORN, WINTER

UNTO (1)

4Mc 13: 1 seven brothers despised sufferings even **u** death,

UNTOLD (2)

2Mc 3: 6 that the treasury in Jerusalem was full of **u** sums
2Mc 12:16 and slaughtered **u** numbers,

UNTOWARD (KJV) See CORRUPT

UNTRAINED (2)

Jer 31:18 I was like a calf **u.**
2Co 11: 6 I may be **u** in speech, but not in knowledge;

UNTRODDEN (2)

Wis 11: 2 and pitched their tents in **u** places.
2Es 9:29 from Egypt and when they came into the **u**

UNTROUBLED (2)

Dt 33:28 **u** is Jacob's abode in a land of grain and wine,
AdE 13: 7 government completely secure and **u** hereafter."

UNTRUE (1)

Ps 73:15 I would have been **u** to the circle of your children.

UNTRUSTWORTHY (1)

Sir 42: 6 Where there is an **u** wife, a seal is a good thing;

UNTYING (5) [UNTIE]

Mk 11: 4 outside in the street. As they were **u** it,
11: 5 "What are you doing, **u** the colt?"
Lk 19:31 If anyone asks you, 'Why are you **u** it?'
19:33 As they were **u** the colt, its owners asked them,
19:33 its owners asked them, "Why are you **u** the colt?"

UNUSUAL (5)

Ac 28: 2 The natives showed us **u** kindness.
28: 6 a long time and saw that nothing **u** had happened
Wis 16:16 pursued by **u** rains and hail and relentless storms,
3Mc 4: 4 that at the sight of their **u** punishments,
5:27 and being struck by the **u** invitation to come out—

UNVEILED (5)

1Co 11: 5 with her head **u** disgraces her head—
11:13 for a woman to pray to God with her head **u?**
2Co 3:18 And all of us, with **u** faces,
Sus 1:32 she was veiled, the scoundrels ordered her to be **u,**
3Mc 4: 6 and were carried away **u,** all together raising

UNWALLED (3)

Nu 13:19 and whether the towns that they live in are **u**
1Sa 6:18 both fortified cities and **u** villages.
Eze 38:11 "I will go up against the land of **u** villages;

UNWASHED (1)

Mt 15:20 but to eat with **u** hands does not defile."

UNWEARIED See Index to Footnotes

UNWEIGHED (1)

1Ki 7:47 Solomon left all the vessels **u,**

UNWELCOME (1)

2Mc 9:24 or any **u** news came, the people throughout

UNWILLING (14)

Ex 10:27 and he was **u** to let them go.
Dt 1:26 But you were **u** to go up.
10:10 The LORD was **u** to destroy you.
29:20 the LORD will be **u** to pardon them,
Jos 24:15 Now if you are **u** to serve the LORD,
1Sa 31: 4 But his armor-bearer was **u;** for he was terrified.
2Sa 6:10 So David was **u** to take the ark of the LORD
1Ch 10: 4 But his armor-bearer was **u,** for he was terrified.
Mt 1:19 being a righteous man and **u** to expose her
23: 4 but they themselves are **u** to lift a finger
Ac 7:39 Our ancestors were **u** to obey him;
2Th 3:10 Anyone **u** to work should not eat.
1Mc 12:14 We were **u** to annoy you and our other allies
3Mc 3:19 and are **u** to regard any action as sincere.

UNWISE (2) [UNWISELY]

Hos 13:13 of childbirth come for him, but he is an **u** son;
Eph 5:15 how you live, not as **u** people but as wise,

UNWISELY (1) [UNWISE]

1Mc 5:67 fell in battle, for they went out to battle **u.**

UNWITTING (1)

Tob 3: 3 not punish me for my sins and for my **u** offenses

UNWORTHILY (1) [UNWORTHY]

AdE 16: 7 of those who exercise authority **u** can be seen,

UNWORTHY‡ (7) [UNWORTHILY]

Ac 13:46 Since you reject it and judge yourselves to be **u**
1Co 11:27 of the Lord in an **u** manner will be answerable for
Sir 10:19 Whose offspring are **u** of honor?
10:19 Whose offspring are **u** of honor?
2Mc 14:42 of sinners and suffer outrages **u** of his noble birth.
Man 1:14 for, **u** as I am, you will save me according
2Es 14:45 and let the worthy and the **u** read them;

UP‡ (2367) [UPPER, UPPERMOST, UPWARD, UPWARDS]

Ge 2: 5 and no herb of the field had yet sprung **u—**
2:21 then he took one of his ribs and closed **u** its place
4: 8 Cain rose **u** against his brother Abel,
6:21 of food that is eaten, and store it **u;**
7:17 and the waters increased, and bore **u** the ark,
8: 7 and it went to and fro until the waters were dried **u**
8:13 the waters were dried **u** from the earth;
13: 1 So Abram went **u** from Egypt, he and his wife,
13:17 Rise **u,** walk through the length and the breadth of
17:22 God went **u** from Abraham.
18: 2 He looked **u** and saw three men standing near him.
19:14 who were to marry his daughters, "**U,**
19:15 the angels urged Lot, saying, "Get **u,**
19:28 of the Plain and saw the smoke of the land going **u**
19:30 Now Lot went **u** out of Zoar and settled in the hills
21:16 she lifted **u** her voice and wept.
21:18 lift **u** the boy and hold him fast with your hand,
21:20 God was with the boy, and he grew **u;**
22: 4 On the third day Abraham looked **u** and saw
22:13 And Abraham looked **u** and saw a ram,
22:13 the ram and offered it **u** as a burnt offering instead
23: 3 Abraham rose **u** from beside his dead,
24:16 filled her jar, and came **u.**
24:61 Then Rebekah and her maids rose **u,**
24:63 and looking **u,** he saw camels coming.
24:64 And Rebekah looked **u,** and when she saw Isaac,
25:27 When the boys grew **u,** Esau was a skillful hunter,
26:15 (Now the Philistines had stopped **u** and filled
26:18 the Philistines had stopped them **u** after the death
26:23 From there he went **u** to Beer-sheba.
27:19 now sit **u** and eat of my game,
27:22 So Jacob went **u** to his father Isaac,
27:31 "Let my father sit **u** and eat of his son's game,
27:38 And Esau lifted **u** his voice and wept.
28:12 that there was a ladder set **u** on the earth, the top
28:18 and set it **u** for a pillar and poured oil on the top
28:22 which I have set **u** for a pillar,
29:10 Jacob went **u** and rolled the stone from
31:10 the flock I once had a dream in which I looked **u**
31:12 'Look **u** and see that all the goats that leap on
31:15 and he has been using **u** the money given for us.
31:23 and pursued him for seven days until he caught **u**
31:45 So Jacob took a stone, and set it **u** as a pillar.
31:55 Early in the morning Laban rose **u,**
32:22 The same night he got **u** and took his two wives,
33: 1 Now Jacob looked **u** and saw Esau coming,
33: 5 Esau looked **u** and saw the women and children,
35: 1 God said to Jacob, "Arise, go **u** to Bethel,
35: 3 let us go **u** to Bethel,
35:13 Then God went **u** from him at the place
35:14 Jacob set **u** a pillar in the place
35:20 and Jacob set **u** a pillar at her grave;
37:25 and looking **u** they saw a caravan
37:28 they drew Joseph **u,** lifting him out of the pit,
38: 8 raise **u** offspring for your brother."
38:11 until my son Shelah grows **u"—**
38:12 he went **u** to Timnah to his sheepshearers,
38:13 "Your father-in-law is going **u** to Timnah
38:14 put on a veil, wrapped herself **u,**
38:14 She saw that Shelah was grown **u,**
38:19 Then she got **u** and went away,
40:13 within three days Pharaoh will lift **u** your head
40:19 within three days Pharaoh will lift **u** your head—
40:20 and lifted **u** the head of the chief cupbearer and
41: 2 and there came **u** out of the Nile seven sleek
41: 3 ugly and thin, came **u** out of the Nile after them,
41: 4 and thin cows ate **u** the seven sleek and fat cows.
41: 7 The thin ears swallowed **u** the seven plump
41:18 came **u** out of the Nile and fed in the reed grass.
41:19 Then seven other cows came **u** after them, poor,
41:20 thin and ugly cows ate **u** the first seven fat cows,
41:24 and the thin ears swallowed **u** the seven good ears
41:27 The seven lean and ugly cows that came **u**
41:35 and lay **u** grain under the authority of Pharaoh
41:44 and without your consent no one shall lift **u** hand
41:48 He gathered **u** all the food of the seven years
41:48 and stored **u** food in the cities;
41:48 he stored **u** in every city the food from the fields
41:49 So Joseph stored **u** grain in such abundance—
43: 2 And when they had eaten **u** the grain
43:19 So they went **u** to the steward of Joseph's house
43:29 Then he looked **u** and saw his brother Benjamin,
44:17 but as for you, go **u** in peace to your father."
44:18 Then Judah stepped **u** to him and said,
44:30 then, as his life is bound **u** in the boy's life,
45: 9 Hurry and go **u** to my father and say to him,
45:25 So they went **u** out of Egypt and came
46: 4 and I will also bring you **u** again;
46:29 and went **u** to meet his father Israel in Goshen.
46:31 "I will go **u** and tell Pharaoh, and will say to him,
48: 2 he summoned his strength and sat **u** in bed.
49: 4 you shall no longer excel because you went **u**
49: 4 you went **u** onto my couch!
49: 9 from the prey, my son, you have gone **u.**
49: 9 like a lioness—who dares rouse him **u?**
49:33 he drew **u** his feet into the bed, breathed his last,
50: 5 let me go **u,** so that I may bury my father;
50: 6 Pharaoh answered, "Go **u,** and bury your father,
50: 7 So Joseph went **u** to bury his father.
50: 7 With him went **u** all the servants of Pharaoh,
50: 9 Both chariots and charioteers went **u** with him.
50:14 with his brothers and all who had gone **u** with him
50:24 to you, and bring you **u** out of this land to the land
50:25 you shall carry **u** my bones from here."

Ex 2:10 When the child grew **u**, she brought him
2:11 One day, after Moses had grown **u**,
2:17 Moses got **u** and came to their defense
2:23 Out of the slavery their cry for help rose **u** to God.
3: 3 and see why the bush is not burned **u**."
3: 8 and to bring them **u** out of that land to a good
3:17 that I will bring you **u** out of the misery of Egypt,
7:12 but Aaron's staff swallowed **u** theirs.
7:20 the sight of Pharaoh and of his officials he lifted **u**
8: 3 they shall come **u** into your palace,
8: 4 The frogs shall come **u** on you and on your people
8: 5 and make frogs come **u** on the land of Egypt.' "
8: 6 the frogs came **u** and covered the land of Egypt.
8: 7 and brought frogs **u** on the land of Egypt.
9:13 "Rise **u** early in the morning and present yourself
9:32 for they are late in coming **u**.)
12:31 and said, "Rise **u**, go away from my people,
12:34 with their kneading bowls wrapped **u**
12:38 A mixed crowd also went **u** with them,
13:18 The Israelites went **u** out of the land
14:16 But you lift **u** your staff,
14:20 and it lit **u** the night;
15: 8 At the blast of your nostrils the waters piled **u**,
15: 8 the floods stood **u** in a heap;
16:13 the evening quails came **u** and covered the camp;
17:10 Aaron, and Hur went **u** to the top of the hill.
17:11 Whenever Moses held **u** his hand, Israel prevailed;
17:12 Aaron and Hur held **u** his hands, one on one side,
19: 3 Then Moses went **u** to God;
19:12 not to go **u** the mountain or to touch the edge of it.
19:13 they may go **u** on the mountain."
19:18 the smoke went **u** like the smoke of a kiln,
19:20 to the top of the mountain, and Moses went **u**.
19:23 "The people are not permitted to come **u**
19:24 "Go down, and come **u** bringing Aaron with you;
19:24 the people break through to come **u** to the LORD;
20:26 You shall not go **u** by steps to my altar,
24: 1 Then he said to Moses, "Come **u** to the LORD,
24: 2 and the people shall not come **u** with him."
24: 4 the foot of the mountain, and set **u** twelve pillars,
24: 9 and seventy of the elders of Israel went **u**,
24:12 "Come **u** to me on the mountain, and wait there;
24:13 and Moses went **u** into the mountain of God.
24:15 Then Moses went **u** on the mountain,
24:18 and went **u** on the mountain.
25:37 and the lamps shall be set **u** so as to give light on
26:28 The middle bar, halfway **u** the frames,
27:20 so that a lamp may be set **u** to burn regularly.
30: 8 and when Aaron sets **u** the lamps in the evening,
32: 1 man who brought us **u** out of the land of Egypt,
32: 4 who brought you **u** out of the land of Egypt!"
32: 6 the people sat down to eat and drink, and rose **u**
32: 7 whom you brought **u** out of the land of Egypt,
32: 8 who brought you **u** out of the land of Egypt!' "
32:23 man who brought us **u** out of the land of Egypt,
32:30 But now I will go **u** to the LORD;
33: 1 you and the people whom you have brought **u** out
33: 3 Go **u** to a land flowing with milk and honey;
33: 3 but I will not go **u** among you,
33: 5 if for a single moment I should go **u** among you,
33:12 "See, you have said to me, 'Bring **u** this people';
33:15 do not carry us **u** from here.
34: 2 and come **u** in the morning to Mount Sinai
34: 3 No one shall come **u** with you,
34: 4 and he rose early in the morning and went **u**
34:24 no one shall covet your land when you go **u**
36:33 through from end to end halfway **u** the frames.
38:21 which were drawn **u** at the commandment
40: 2 of the first month you shall set **u** the tabernacle of
40: 4 and you shall bring in the lampstand, and set **u**
40: 5 set **u** the screen for the entrance of the tabernacle.
40: 8 You shall set **u** the court all around,
40: 8 and hang **u** the screen for the gate of the court.
40:17 of the month, the tabernacle was set **u**.
40:18 Moses set **u** the tabernacle;
40:18 he laid its bases, and set **u** its frames,
40:18 and put in its poles, and raised **u** its pillars;
40:21 and set **u** the curtain for screening,
40:25 and set **u** the lamps before the LORD;
40:33 He set **u** the court around the tabernacle and
40:33 and put **u** the screen at the gate of the court.
40:36 the cloud was taken **u** from the tabernacle,
40:37 but if the cloud was not taken **u**,
40:37 not set out until the day that it was taken **u**.
Lev 1: 6 The burnt offering shall be flayed and cut **u**
1:12 It shall be cut **u** into its parts,
5: 1 does not speak **u**, you are subject to punishment.
5:12 and the priest shall scoop **u** a handful of it
6:10 and he shall take **u** the ashes to which
7:17 of the sacrifice shall be burned **u** on the third day.
7:19 be eaten; it shall be burned **u**.
11:45 For I am the LORD who brought you **u** from
14:38 of the house and shut **u** the house seven days.
14:46 the house while it is shut **u** shall be unclean until
24: 3 Aaron shall set it **u** in the tent of meeting,
24: 4 He shall set **u** the lamps on the lampstand
27:23 for it the proportionate assessment **u** to the year
Nu 1:51 to be pitched, the Levites shall set it **u**.
4: 3 from thirty years old **u** to fifty years old,
4:23 from thirty years old **u** to fifty years old
4:30 from thirty years old **u** to fifty years old
4:35 from thirty years old **u** to fifty years old,
4:39 from thirty years old **u** to fifty years old,
4:43 from thirty years old **u** to fifty years old,
4:47 from thirty years old **u** to fifty years old,
6:26 the LORD lift **u** his countenance upon you,
7: 1 when Moses had finished setting **u** the tabernacle,
Nu 8: 2 When you set **u** the lamps,
8: 3 he set **u** its lamps to give light in front of
9:15 On the day the tabernacle was set **u**,
10:21 and the tabernacle was set **u** before their arrival.
11: 6 but now our strength is dried **u**,
13:17 and said to them, "Go **u** there into the Negeb,
13:17 and go **u** into the hill country,
13:21 So they went **u** and spied out the land from
13:22 They went **u** into the Negeb, and came to Hebron;
13:30 and said, "Let us go **u** at once and occupy it,
13:31 Then the men who had gone **u** with him said,
13:31 "We are not able to go **u** against this people,
14:13 for in your might you brought **u** this people from
14:40 They rose early in the morning and went **u** to
14:40 We will go **u** to the place that
14:42 Do not go **u**, for the LORD is not with you;
14:44 But they presumed to go **u** to the heights of
15:14 or who takes **u** permanent residence among you,
16:13 that you have brought us **u** out of a land flowing
16:25 So Moses got **u** and went to Dathan and Abiram;
16:30 the ground opens its mouth and swallows them **u**,
16:32 earth opened its mouth and swallowed them **u**,
19: 9 Then someone who is clean shall gather **u**
20: 5 Why have you brought us **u** out of Egypt,
20:11 Then Moses lifted **u** his hand and struck
20:25 and bring them **u** Mount Hor;
20:27 they went **u** Mount Hor in the sight of
21: 5 "Why have you brought us **u** out of Egypt to die in
21:17 Then Israel sang this song: "Spring **u**, O well!—
21:28 and swallowed **u** the heights of the Arnon.
21:33 Then they turned and went **u** the road to Bashan;
22: 4 "This horde will now lick **u** all that is around us,
as an ox licks **u** the grass of the field."
22:20 get **u** and go with them;
22:21 So Balaam got **u** in the morning,
22:41 and brought him **u** to Bamoth-baal;
23:24 Look, a people rising **u** like a lioness,
24: 2 Balaam looked **u** and saw Israel camping tribe
24: 9 like a lioness; who will rouse him **u**?
24:25 Then Balaam got **u** and went back to his place,
25: 7 saw it, he got **u** and left the congregation.
26:10 the earth opened its mouth and swallowed them **u**
26:62 every male one month old and **u**;
27:12 "Go **u** this mountain of the Abarim range,
32: 9 they went **u** to the Wadi Eshcol and saw the land,
32:11 'Surely none of the people who came **u** out
32:16 Then they came **u** to him and said,
32:17 but we will take **u** arms as a vanguard before
32:20 if you take **u** arms to go before the LORD for
33:38 the priest went **u** Mount Hor at the command of
Dt 1:21 go **u**, take possession, as the LORD,
1:22 to us regarding the route by which we should go **u**
1:24 They set out and went **u** into the hill country,
1:26 But you were unwilling to go **u**.
1:28 the cities are large and fortified **u** to heaven!
1:41 We are ready to go **u** and fight,
1:41 and thought it easy to go **u** into the hill country.
1:42 "Say to them, 'Do not go **u** and do not fight,
1:43 and presumptuously went **u** into the hill country.
3: 1 When we headed **u** the road to Bashan,
3:16 and **u** to the Jabbok, the wadi being boundary of
3:27 Go **u** to the top of Pisgah and look around you to
4:11 of the mountain while the mountain was blazing **u**
4:19 when you look **u** to the heavens and see the sun,
5: 5 because of the fire and did not go **u** the mountain.)
8: 7 with springs and underground waters welling **u**
9: 2 "Who can stand **u** to the Anakim?"
9: 9 I went **u** the mountain to receive the stone tablets,
9:12 Then the LORD said to me, "Get **u**,
9:23 "Go **u** and occupy the land that I have given you,"
10: 1 and come **u** to me on the mountain,
10: 3 and went **u** the mountain with the two tablets
10:11 The LORD said to me, "Get **u**,
11: 6 the earth opened its mouth and swallowed them **u**,
11:17 and he will shut **u** the heavens, so that there will
16:22 nor shall you set **u** a stone pillar—
17: 8 then you shall immediately go **u** to the place that
18:15 The LORD your God will raise **u** for you
18:18 I will raise **u** for them a prophet like you from
19:14 set **u** by former generations,
20: 1 who brought you **u** from the land of Egypt.
22: 4 you shall help to lift it **u**.
22:14 and makes **u** charges against her, slandering her
22:17 now he has made **u** charges against her,
23:13 a hole with it and then cover **u** your excrement.
25: 7 then his brother's widow shall go **u** to the elders at
25: 9 then his brother's wife shall go **u** to him in
25: 9 not build **u** his brother's house."
27: 2 you shall set **u** large stones and cover them
27: 4 you shall set **u** these stones,
27: 6 Then offer **u** burnt offerings on it to
27:15 the work of an artisan, and sets it **u** in secret."
28:33 not know shall eat **u** the fruit of your ground and
29:22 your children who rise **u** after you,
30:12 "Who will go **u** to heaven for us,
32:11 an eagle stirs **u** its nest, and hovers over its young;
32:11 as it spreads its wings, takes them **u**,
32:30 the LORD had given them **u**?
32:34 Is not this laid **u** in store with me, sealed **u** in my
32:38 Let them rise **u** and help you,
32:40 For I lift **u** my hand to heaven, and swear:
34: 1 Then Moses went **u** from the plains of Moab
Jos 2: 6 brought them **u** to the roof and hidden them with
2: 8 she came **u** to them on the roof
2:10 how the LORD dried **u** the water of the Red Sea
3: 6 "Take **u** the ark of the covenant,
3: 6 So they took **u** the ark of the covenant and went
Jos 3:16 rising **u** in a single heap far off at Adam,
4: 5 and each of you take **u** a stone on his shoulder,
4: 8 They took **u** twelve stones out of the middle of
4: 9 (Joshua set **u** twelve stones in the middle of
4:16 to come **u** out of the Jordan."
4:17 "Come **u** out of the Jordan."
4:18 the LORD came **u** from the middle of the Jordan,
4:19 The people came **u** out of the Jordan on
4:20 of the Jordan, Joshua set **u** in Gilgal,
4:23 For the LORD your God dried **u** the waters of
4:23 which he dried **u** for us until we crossed over,
5: 1 the LORD had dried **u** the waters of the Jordan
5: 7 whom he raised **u** in their place,
5:13 he looked **u** and saw a man standing before him
6: 1 Now Jericho was shut **u** inside and out because of
6: 6 "Take **u** the ark of the covenant,
6:12 and the priests took **u** the ark of the LORD.
6:26 at the cost of his youngest he shall set **u** its gates!"
7: 2 and said to them, "Go **u** and spy out the land."
7: 2 And the men went **u** and spied out Ai.
7: 3 "Not all the people need go **u**;
7: 3 or three thousand men should go **u** and attack Ai.
7: 3 do not make the whole people toil **u** there."
7: 4 about three thousand of the people went **u** there;
7:10 The LORD said to Joshua, "Stand **u**!
7:24 and they brought them **u** to the Valley of Achor.
8: 1 take all the fighting men with you, and go **u** now
8: 3 and all the fighting men set out to go **u** against Ai.
8: 7 you shall rise **u** from the ambush and seize
8:10 and went **u**, with the elders of Israel,
8:11 All the fighting men who were with him went **u**,
10: 4 "Come **u** and help me, and let us attack Gibeon;
10: 5 and went **u** with all their armies and camped
10: 6 come **u** to us quickly, and save us, and help us;
10: 7 So Joshua went **u** from Gilgal,
10: 9 having marched **u** all night from Gilgal.
10:33 King Horam of Gezer came **u** to help Lachish;
10:36 Then Joshua went **u** with all Israel from Eglon
14: 8 But my companions who went **u** with me made
15: 3 and goes **u** south of Kadesh-barnea,
15: 3 **u** to Addar, makes a turn to Karka,
15: 6 the boundary goes **u** to Beth-hoglah, and passes
15: 6 and the boundary goes **u** to the Stone of Bohan,
15: 7 and the boundary goes **u** to Debir from the Valley
15: 8 then the boundary goes **u** by the valley of the son
15: 8 the boundary goes **u** to the top of the mountain
15:15 From there he went **u** against the inhabitants
16: 1 going **u** from Jericho into the hill country
17:15 "If you are a numerous people, go **u** to the forest,
18: 1 and set **u** the tent of meeting there.
18:11 of Benjamin according to its families came **u**,
18:12 then the boundary goes **u** to the slope of Jericho
18:12 then **u** through the hill country westward;
19:10 The third lot came **u** for the tribe of Zebulun,
19:11 then its boundary goes **u** westward,
19:12 from there it goes to Daberath, then **u** to Japhia;
19:47 the Danites went **u** and fought against Leshem,
20: 5 they shall not give **u** the slayer,
24:17 and our ancestors **u** from the land of Egypt,
24:26 and set it **u** there under the oak in the sanctuary of
24:32 which the Israelites had brought **u** from Egypt,
Jdg 1: 1 "Who shall go **u** first for us against
1: 2 The LORD said, "Judah shall go **u**.
1: 3 "Come **u** with me into the territory allotted to me,
1: 4 Then Judah went **u** and the LORD gave
1: 7 and big toes cut off used to pick **u** scraps
1:16 went **u** with the people of Judah from the city
1:22 The house of Joseph also went **u** against Bethel;
2: 1 Now the angel of the LORD went **u** from Gilgal
2: 1 and said, "I brought you **u** from Egypt,
2: 4 the people lifted **u** their voices and wept.
2:10 and another generation grew **u** after them,
2:16 Then the LORD raised **u** judges,
2:18 Whenever the LORD raised **u** judges for them,
3: 9 the LORD raised **u** a deliverer for the Israelites,
3:15 the LORD raised **u** for them a deliverer,
4: 5 and the Israelites came **u** to her for judgment.
4: 9 Deborah got **u** and went with Barak to Kedesh.
4:10 and ten thousand warriors went **u** behind him;
4:10 and Deborah went **u** with him.
4:12 of Abinoam had gone **u** to Mount Tabor,
4:14 Then Deborah said to Barak, "**U**!
6: 3 the people of the east would come **u** against them.
6: 5 For they and their livestock would come **u**,
6: 8 I led you **u** from Egypt, and brought you out of
6:13 'Did not the LORD bring us **u** from Egypt?'
6:21 and fire sprang **u** from the rock and consumed
6:35 and Naphtali, and they went **u** to meet them.
7: 9 That same night the LORD said to him, "Get **u**,
7:15 to the camp of Israel, and said, "Get **u**;
8: 8 From there he went **u** to Penuel,
8:11 So Gideon went **u** by the caravan route east
8:28 and they lifted **u** their heads no more.
9:18 but you have risen **u** against my
9:31 and they are stirring **u** the city against you.
9:33 as soon as the sun rises, get **u** and rush on the city;
9:34 the troops with him got **u** by night and lay in wait
9:40 Many fell wounded, **u** to the entrance of the gate.
9:48 So Abimelech went **u** to Mount Zalmon,
9:48 and took it **u** and laid it on his shoulder.
11: 2 and when his wife's sons grew **u**,
11:16 but when they came **u** from Egypt,
11:31 to be offered **u** by me as a burnt offering."
12: 3 Why then have you come **u** to me this day,
13:11 Manoah got **u** and followed his wife,
13:20 the flame went **u** toward heaven from the altar,
14: 2 Then he came **u**, and told his father and mother,

Jdg 15: 5 and burned **u** the shocks and the standing grain,
15: 6 Philistines came **u,** and burned her and her father.
15: 9 the Philistines came **u** and encamped in Judah,
15:10 "Why have you come **u** against us?"
15:10 They said, "We have come **u** to bind Samson,
15:13 and brought him **u** from the rock.
16: 3 Then at midnight he rose **u,** took hold of the doors
16: 3 pulled them **u,** bar and all, put them on his
16:18 saying, "This time come **u,**
16:18 Then the lords of the Philistines came **u** to her,
16:31 and brought him **u** and buried him between Zorah
18: 9 They said, "Come, let us go **u** against them;
18:12 went **u** and encamped at Kiriath-jearim in Judah.
18:30 Then the Danites set **u** the idol for themselves.
19: 5 On the fourth day they got **u** early in the morning,
19: 7 When the man got **u** to go,
19: 8 On the fifth day he got **u** early in the morning
19: 9 with his concubine and his servant got **u** to leave,
19: 9 Tomorrow you can get **u** early in the morning
19:10 he got **u** and departed, and arrived opposite Jebus
19:17 When the old man looked **u** and saw the wayfarer
19:27 In the morning her master got **u,**
19:28 "Get **u,**" he said to her, "we are going."
19:30 that the Israelites came **u** from the land of Egypt
20: 3 that the people of Israel had gone **u** to Mizpah.)
20: 5 The lords of Gibeah rose **u** against me,
20: 8 All the people got **u** as one, saying,
20: 9 we will go **u** against it by lot.
20:18 The Israelites proceeded to go **u** to Bethel,
20:18 "Which of us shall go **u** first to battle against
20:18 the LORD answered, "Judah shall go **u** first."
20:19 Then the Israelites got **u** in the morning,
20:20 the Israelites drew **u** the battle line against them
20:23 The Israelites went **u** and wept before the LORD
20:23 And the LORD said, "Go **u** against them."
20:28 The LORD answered, "Go **u,**
20:30 the Israelites went **u** against the Benjaminites on
20:31 of which goes **u** to Bethel and the other to Gibeah,
20:38 and the men in ambush was that when they sent **u**
20:40 the whole city going **u** in smoke toward the sky!
21: 2 and they lifted **u** their voices and wept bitterly.
21: 4 On the next day, the people got **u** early,
21: 5 "Which of all the tribes of Israel did not come **u** in
21: 5 concerning whoever did not come **u** to the LORD
21: 8 from the tribes of Israel who did not come **u** to
21:19 on the east of the highway that goes **u** from Bethel
Ru 2:14 and he heaped **u** for her some parched grain.
2:15 When she got **u** to glean,
2:18 She picked it **u** and came into the town,
3:14 got **u** before one person could recognize another;
4: 1 No sooner had Boaz gone **u** to the gate and sat
4:11 who together built **u** the house of Israel.
1Sa 1: 3 to go **u** year by year from his town to worship and
1: 7 as often as she went **u** to the house of the LORD,
1:21 The man Elkanah and all his household went **u**
1:22 But Hannah did not go **u,**
1:24 she had weaned him, she took him **u** with her,
2: 6 he brings down to Sheol and raises **u.**
2: 8 He raises **u** the poor from the dust;
2:14 all that the fork brought **u** the priest would take
2:19 when she went **u** with her husband to offer
2:21 boy Samuel grew **u** in the presence of the LORD.
2:28 to go **u** to my altar, to offer incense,
2:35 I will raise **u** for myself a faithful priest,
3: 6 Samuel got **u** and went to Eli, and said,
3: 8 And he got **u** and went to Eli, and said,
3:19 As Samuel grew **u,** the LORD was with him
4: 2 The Philistines drew **u** in line against Israel,
5:12 and the cry of the city went **u** to heaven.
6: 9 And watch; if it goes **u** on the way to its own land,
6:10 and shut **u** their calves at home.
6:13 When they looked **u** and saw the ark,
6:14 so they split **u** the wood of the cart and offered
6:21 Come down and take it **u** to you."
7: 1 And the people of Kiriath-jearim came and took **u**
7: 7 the lords of the Philistines went **u** against Israel.
7:10 As Samuel was offering **u** the burnt offering,
7:12 a stone and set it **u** between Mizpah and Jeshanah,
8: 8 the day I brought them **u** out of Egypt to this day,
9:11 As they went **u** the hill to the town,
9:13 before he goes **u** to the shrine to eat
9:13 Now go **u,** for you will meet him immediately."
9:14 So they went **u** to the town.
9:14 toward them on his way **u** to the shrine.
9:19 go **u** before me to the shrine,
9:24 The cook took **u** the thigh and what went with it
9:26 "Get **u,** so that I may send you on your way."
9:26 Saul got **u,** and both he and Samuel went out into
10: 3 three men going **u** to God
10:18 the God of Israel, 'I brought **u** Israel out of Egypt,
10:25 and he wrote them in a book and laid it **u** before
11: 1 the Ammonite went **u** and besieged Jabesh-gilead;
11: 3 we will give ourselves **u** to you."
11:10 "Tomorrow we will give ourselves **u** to you,
12: 6 and Aaron and brought your ancestors **u** out of
13: 5 they came **u** and encamped at Michmash,
13:15 they went **u** from Gilgal toward Gibeah
14: 9 and we will not go **u** to them.
14:10 if they say, 'Come **u** to us,' then we will go **u;**
14:12 "Come **u** to us, and we will show you something."
14:12 to his armor-bearer, "Come **u** after me;
14:13 Then Jonathan climbed **u** on his hands and feet,
14:21 with the Philistines and had gone **u** with them into
15: 2 in opposing the Israelites when they came **u** out
15: 6 to all the people of Israel when they came **u** out
15:12 where he set **u** a monument for himself,
15:34 and Saul went **u** to his house in Gibeah of Saul.
1Sa 17: 8 "Why have you come out to draw **u** for battle?
17:21 Israel and the Philistines drew **u** for battle,
17:23 came **u** out of the ranks of the Philistines,
17:25 "Have you seen this man who has come **u?**
17:25 Surely he has come **u** to defy Israel.
17:52 The troops of Israel and Judah rose **u** with a shout
19:15 He said, "Bring him **u** to me in the bed,
20:38 So Jonathan's boy gathered **u** the arrows and came
20:42 He got **u** and left; and Jonathan went into the city.
22: 8 for me or discloses to me that my son has stirred **u**
23:13 that David had escaped from Keilah, he gave **u**
23:19 some Ziphites went **u** to Saul at Gibeah and said,
23:29 David then went **u** from there,
24: 7 Saul got **u** and left the cave, and went on his way.
24: 8 also rose **u** and went out of the cave and called
24:16 Saul lifted **u** his voice and wept.
24:22 but David and his men went **u** to the stronghold.
25: 1 Then David got **u** and went down to
25: 5 David said to the young men, "Go **u** to Carmel,
25:13 and about four hundred men went **u** after David,
25:29 If anyone should rise **u** to pursue you and
25:35 he said to her, "Go **u** to your house in peace;
25:42 Abigail got **u** hurriedly and rode away on
26:19 it is the LORD who has stirred you **u** against me,
27: 8 Now David and his men went **u** and made raids on
28: 8 and bring **u** for me the one whom I name to you."
28:11 the woman said, "Whom shall I bring **u** for you?"
28:11 He answered, "Bring **u** Samuel for me."
28:13 "I see a divine being coming **u** out of the ground."
28:14 She said, "An old man is coming **u;**
28:15 "Why have you disturbed me by bringing me **u?"**
28:23 So he got **u** from the ground and sat on the bed.
29: 9 'He shall not go **u** with us to the battle.'
29:11 But the Philistines went **u** to Jezreel.
2Sa 2: 1 "Shall I go **u** into any of the cities of Judah?"
2: 1 The LORD said to him, "Go **u."**
2: 1 David said, "To which shall I go **u?"**
2: 2 So David went **u** there, along with his two wives,
2: 3 David brought **u** the men who were with him,
2:32 They took **u** Asahel and buried him in the tomb
3:10 and set **u** the throne of David over Israel and
3:32 The king lifted **u** his voice and wept at the grave
4: 4 His nurse picked him **u** and fled;
5: 8 let him get **u** the water shaft to attack the lame and
5:17 all the Philistines went **u** in search of David;
5:19 "Shall I go **u** against the Philistines?
5:19 The LORD said to David, "Go **u;**
5:22 Once again the Philistines came **u,**
5:23 he said, "You shall not go **u;**
6: 2 to bring **u** from there the ark of God,
6:12 So David went and brought **u** the ark of God from
6:15 and all the house of Israel brought **u** the ark of
7: 6 in a house since the day I brought **u** the people
7:12 I will raise **u** your offspring after you,
10: 8 and drew **u** in battle array at the entrance of
12: 3 He brought it **u,** and it grew up with him and
12: 3 and it grew **u** with him and with his children;
12:11 I will raise **u** trouble against you from
13:34 When the young man who kept watch looked **u,**
14: 7 They say, 'Give **u** the man who struck his brother,
14:14 which cannot be gathered **u.**
15: 9 So he got **u,** and went to Hebron.
15:14 with him at Jerusalem, "Get **u!**
15:24 Abiathar came **u,** and Zadok also,
15:30 David went **u** the ascent of the Mount of Olives,
15:30 with him covered their heads and went **u,**
17:16 with him will be swallowed **u.' "**
17:21 they had gone, the men came **u** out of the well,
18:18 Now Absalom in his lifetime had taken and set **u**
18:24 sentinel went **u** to the roof of the gate by the wall,
and when he looked **u,**
18:28 be the LORD your God, who has delivered **u**
18:31 delivering you from the power of all who rose **u**
18:32 and all who rise **u** to do you harm,
18:33 and went **u** to the chamber over the gate,
19: 8 Then the king got **u** and took his seat in the gate.
19:34 that I should go **u** with the king to Jerusalem?
20: 3 So they were shut **u** until the day of their death,
20:15 they threw **u** a siege ramp against the city,
20:19 why will you swallow **u** the heritage of
20:20 far be it, that I should swallow **u** or destroy!
20:21 has lifted **u** his hand against King David;
20:21 give him **u** alone, and I will withdraw from
21:12 where the Philistines had hung them **u,**
21:13 He brought **u** from there the bones of Saul and
22: 9 Smoke went **u** from his nostrils,
23: 6 for they cannot be picked **u** with the hand;
24:18 "Go **u** and erect an altar to the LORD on
24:19 Following Gad's instructions, David went **u,**
24:22 the king take and offer **u** what seems good to him;
1Ki 1:35 You shall go **u** following him.
1:40 And all the people went **u** following him,
1:45 and they have gone **u** from there rejoicing,
1:49 Then all the guests of Adonijah got **u** trembling
1:50 got **u** and went to grasp the horns of the altar.
2:34 of Jehoiada went **u** and struck him down
3:15 He offered **u** burnt offerings and offerings
3:20 She got **u** in the middle of the night
5: 9 I will have them broken **u** there for you
6: 8 one went **u** by winding stairs to the middle story,
7:21 He set **u** the pillars at the vestibule of the temple;
7:21 he set **u** the pillar on the south and called it Jachin;
7:21 he set **u** the pillar on the north and called it Boaz.
8: 1 to bring **u** the ark of the covenant of
8: 4 So they brought **u** the ark of the LORD,
8: 4 the priests and the Levites brought them **u.**
8:35 "When heaven is shut **u** and there is no rain
1Ki 9:16 of Egypt had gone **u** and captured Gezer
9:24 But Pharaoh's daughter went **u** from the city
9:25 a year Solomon used to offer **u** burnt offerings
11:14 LORD raised **u** an adversary against Solomon,
11:15 and Joab the commander of the army went **u**
11:23 God raised **u** another adversary against Solomon,
11:27 and closed **u** the gap in the wall of the city
12: 8 with the young men who had grown **u** with him
12:10 The young men who had grown **u** with him said
12:24 not go **u** or fight against your kindred the people
12:27 If this people continues to go **u** to offer sacrifices
12:28 "You have gone **u** to Jerusalem long enough.
12:28 who brought you **u** out of the land of Egypt."
12:33 He went **u** to the altar that he had made in Bethel
12:33 and he went **u** to the altar to offer incense.
13:29 The prophet took **u** the body of the man of God,
14:10 just as one burns **u** dung until it is all gone.
14:14 LORD will raise **u** for himself a king over Israel,
14:15 he will root **u** Israel out of this good land
14:16 He will give Israel **u** because of the sins
14:17 Then Jeroboam's wife got **u** and went away,
14:25 King Shishak of Egypt came **u** against Jerusalem;
15: 4 setting **u** his son after him,
15:17 King Baasha of Israel went **u** against Judah,
16:17 So Omri went **u** from Gibbethon,
16:34 the cost of Abiram his firstborn, and set **u** its gates
17: 7 But after a while the wadi dried **u,**
17:19 carried him **u** into the upper chamber
18:38 and even licked **u** the water that was in the trench.
18:41 Elijah said to Ahab, "Go **u,** eat and drink;
18:42 So Ahab went **u** to eat and to drink.
18:42 Elijah went **u** to the top of Carmel;
18:43 He said to his servant, "Go **u** now,
18:43 He went **u** and looked, and said,
18:46 he girded **u** his loins and ran in front of Ahab to
19: 3 Then he was afraid; he got **u** and fled for his life,
19: 5 an angel touched him and said to him, "Get **u**
19: 7 touched him, and said, "Get **u** and eat,
19: 8 He got **u,** and ate and drank;
20:13 a certain prophet came **u** to King Ahab of Israel
20:22 for in the spring the king of Aram will come **u**
20:26 and went **u** to Aphek to fight against Israel.
20:33 they quickly took it **u** from him and said, "Yes,
20:33 and he had him come **u** into the chariot.
21: 7 Get **u,** eat some food, and be cheerful;
21:19 In the place where dogs licked **u** the blood
21:19 dogs will also lick **u** your blood."
22: 6 or shall I refrain?" They said, "Go **u;**
22:12 "Go **u** to Ramoth-gilead and triumph;
22:15 He answered him, "Go **u** and triumph;
22:20 so that he may go **u** and fall at Ramoth-gilead?'
22:24 Zedekiah son of Chenaanah came **u** to Micaiah,
22:29 of Israel and King Jehoshaphat of Judah went **u**
22:35 and the king was propped **u** in his chariot facing
22:38 the dogs licked **u** his blood,
2Ki 1: 3 the Tishbite, "Get **u,** go to meet the messengers of
1: 9 He went **u** to Elijah, who was sitting on the top of
1:11 He went **u** and said to him, "O man of God,
1:13 So the third captain of fifty went **u,**
2: 1 Now when the LORD was about to take Elijah **u**
2: 8 Then Elijah took his mantle and rolled it **u,**
2:13 He picked **u** the mantle of Elijah that had fallen
2:16 be that the spirit of the LORD has caught him **u**
2:23 He went **u** from there to Bethel;
2:23 and while he was going **u** on the way,
3:19 all springs of water you shall stop **u,**
3:21 that the kings had come **u** to fight against them,
3:21 were called out and were drawn **u** at the frontier.
3:24 the Israelites rose **u** and attacked the Moabites,
3:25 every spring of water they stopped **u,**
4:11 he went **u** to the chamber and lay down there.
4:21 She went **u** and laid him on the bed of the man
4:29 He said to Gehazi, "Gird **u** your loins,
4:30 So he rose **u** and followed her.
4:34 Then he got **u** on the bed and lay upon the child,
4:35 then got **u** again and bent over him;
4:39 and came and cut them **u** into the pot of stew,
5:23 and tied **u** two talents of silver in two bags,
6: 7 He said, "Pick it **u."**
6:28 "This woman said to me, 'Give **u** your son;
6:29 'Give **u** your son and we will eat him.'
7:12 The king got **u** in the night,
8: 1 "Get **u** and go with your household,
8: 2 So the woman got **u** and did according to the word
8:12 and rip **u** their pregnant women."
8:20 and set **u** a king of their own.
9: 1 the company of prophets and said to him, "Gird **u**
9: 6 So Jehu got **u** and went inside;
9:32 He looked **u** to the window and said,
10:15 Jehu took him **u** with him into the chariot.
12:10 the king's secretary and the high priest went **u,**
12:10 and tied it **u** in bags.
12:17 At that time King Hazael of Aram went **u,**
12:17 Hazael set his face to go **u** against Jerusalem,
14:10 and your heart has lifted you **u.**
14:11 So King Jehoash of Israel went **u;**
15:14 of Gadi came **u** from Tirzah and came to Samaria;
16: 5 and King Pekah son of Remaliah of Israel came **u**
16: 7 Come **u,** and rescue me from the hand of the king
16: 9 the king of Assyria marched **u** against Damascus,
16:12 Then the king drew near to the altar, went **u** on it,
17: 3 King Shalmaneser of Assyria came **u** against him;
17: 7 who had brought them **u** out of the land of Egypt
17:10 they set **u** for themselves pillars and sacred poles
18: 9 King Shalmaneser of Assyria came **u**
18:13 King Sennacherib of Assyria came **u** against all
18:17 They went **u** and came to Jerusalem.

2Ki 18:25 that I have come **u** against this place to destroy it?
18:25 The LORD said to me, Go **u** against this land,
19: 4 lift **u** your prayer for the remnant that is left."
19:14 then Hezekiah went **u** to the house of the LORD
19:23 'With my many chariots I have gone **u** the heights
19:24 I dried **u** with the sole of my foot all the streams
19:32 or cast **u** a siege ramp against it.
20: 5 on the third day you shall go **u** to the house of
20: 8 and that I shall go **u** to the house of the LORD on
20:17 which your ancestors have stored **u** until this day,
22: 4 "Go **u** to the high priest Hilkiah,
23: 2 The king went **u** to the house of the LORD,
23: 9 did not come **u** to the altar of the LORD
23:16 he turned and looked **u** at the tomb of the man
23:29 In his days Pharaoh Neco king of Egypt went **u** to
24: 1 King Nebuchadnezzar of Babylon came **u;**
24:10 of King Nebuchadnezzar of Babylon came **u**
24:12 of Judah gave himself **u** to the king of Babylon,
25: 6 the king and brought him **u** to the king of Babylon
1Ch 5:26 So the God of Israel stirred **u** the spirit of King Pul
10:12 the valiant warriors got **u** and took away the body
11: 6 And Joab son of Zeruiah went **u** first,
13: 6 And David and all Israel went **u** to Baalah, that is,
13: 6 to bring **u** from there the ark of God, the LORD,
14: 8 all the Philistines went **u** in search of David;
14:10 "Shall I go **u** against the Philistines?
14:10 The LORD said to him, "Go **u,**
14:11 So he went **u** to Baal-perazim,
14:14 God said to him, "You shall not go **u** after them;
15: 3 David assembled all Israel in Jerusalem to bring **u**
15:12 so that you may bring **u** the ark of the LORD,
15:14 and the Levites sanctified themselves to bring **u**
15:25 to bring **u** the ark of the covenant of the LORD
15:28 So all Israel brought **u** the ark of the covenant of
17:11 I will raise **u** your offspring after you,
18: 3 to set **u** a monument at the river Euphrates.
19: 9 and drew **u** in battle array at the entrance of
19:17 came to them, and drew **u** his forces against them.
21: 1 Satan stood **u** against Israel,
21:16 David looked **u** and saw the angel of
21:18 to tell David that he should go **u** and erect an altar
21:19 So David went **u** following Gad's instructions,
2Ch 1: 4 the ark of God **u** from Kiriath-jearim to the place
1: 6 Solomon went **u** there to the bronze altar before
2:16 you will take it **u** to Jerusalem."
3:17 He set **u** the pillars in front of the temple,
5: 2 to bring **u** the ark of the covenant of
5: 5 So they brought **u** the ark, the tent of meeting,
5: 5 the priests and the Levites brought them **u.**
6:26 "When heaven is shut **u** and there is no rain
6:41 "Now rise **u,** O LORD God,
7:13 When I shut **u** the heavens so that there is no rain,
7:20 then I will pluck you **u** from the land
8:12 Then Solomon offered **u** burnt offerings to
10: 8 and consulted the young men who had grown **u**
10:10 The young men who had grown **u** with him said
11: 4 You shall not go **u** or fight against your kindred.
11: 6 He built **u** Bethlehem, Etam, Tekoa,
12: 2 King Shishak of Egypt came **u** against Jerusalem
12: 9 King Shishak of Egypt came **u** against Jerusalem;
13: 3 and Jeroboam drew **u** his line of battle against him
13: 6 rose **u** and rebelled against his lord;
14:10 and they drew **u** their lines of battle in the valley
16: 1 King Baasha of Israel went **u** against Judah,
16: 6 and with them he built **u** Geba and Mizpah.
18: 2 and induced him to go **u** against Ramoth-gilead.
18: 5 or shall I refrain?" They said, "Go **u;**
18:11 "Go **u** to Ramoth-gilead and triumph;
18:14 He answered, "Go **u** and triumph;
18:19 so that he may go **u** and fall at Ramoth-gilead?'
18:23 Zedekiah son of Chenaanah came **u** to Micaiah,
18:28 of Israel and King Jehoshaphat of Judah went **u**
18:34 of Israel propped himself **u** in his chariot facing
20:16 they will come **u** by the ascent of Ziz;
20:19 stood **u** to praise the LORD, the God of Israel,
21: 8 the rule of Judah and set **u** a king of their own.
21:17 They came **u** against Judah, invaded it,
24:23 the year the army of Aram came **u** against Joash.
25:14 set them **u** as his gods, and worshiped them,
25:19 and your heart has lifted you **u** in boastfulness.
25:21 So King Joash of Israel went **u;**
26:15 In Jerusalem he set **u** machines,
28: 9 in a rage that has reached **u** to heaven.
28:12 stood **u** against those who were coming from
28:15 Then those who were mentioned by name got **u**
28:24 He shut **u** the doors of the house of the LORD
29:20 and went **u** to the house of the LORD.
30:27 and the Levites stood **u** and blessed the people,
31: 7 In the third month they began to pile **u** the heaps,
32: 5 and built **u** the entire wall that was broken down,
33:19 the sites on which he built high places and set **u**
34:30 The king went **u** to the house of the LORD,
35:20 King Neco of Egypt went **u** to fight at Carchemish
36: 6 of Babylon came **u,** and bound him with fetters
36:17 Therefore he brought **u** against them the king of
36:21 until the land had made **u** for its sabbaths.
36:22 the LORD stirred **u** the spirit of King Cyrus
36:23 may the LORD his God be with him! Let him go **u."**
Ezr 1: 1 the LORD stirred **u** the spirit of King Cyrus
1: 3 are now permitted to go **u** to Jerusalem in Judah,
1: 5 to go **u** and rebuild the house of the LORD
1:11 All these Sheshbazzar brought **u,**
1:11 when the exiles were brought **u** from Babylonia
2:59 The following were those who came **u**
3: 3 They set **u** the altar on its foundation,
4:12 be known to the king that the Jews who came **u**
4:15 and that sedition was stirred **u** in it from long ago.
Ezr 7: 6 this Ezra went **u** from Babylonia.
7: 7 and the temple servants also went **u** to Jerusalem,
7: 9 On the first day of the first month the journey **u**
7:22 **u** to one hundred talents of silver,
7:28 and I gathered leaders from Israel to go **u** with me.
8: 1 of those who went **u** with me from Babylonia,
9: 5 At the evening sacrifice I got **u** from my fasting,
9: 6 and our guilt has mounted **u** to the heavens.
9: 9 to give us new life to set **u** the house of our God,
10: 5 Then Ezra stood **u** and made the leading priests,
10:10 Then Ezra the priest stood **u** and said to them,
Ne 2:12 I got **u** during the night, I and a few men with me;
2:15 So I went **u** by way of the valley by night
3: 1 They consecrated it and set **u** its doors;
3: 3 they laid its beams and set **u** its doors, its bolts,
3: 6 they laid its beams and set **u** its doors, its bolts,
3:13 they rebuilt it and set **u** its doors, its bolts,
3:14 he rebuilt it and set **u** its doors, its bolts,
3:15 he rebuilt it and covered it and set **u** its doors,
3:26 on Ophel made repairs **u** to a point opposite
4: 3 any fox going **u** on it would break it down!"
4:12 where they live they will come **u** against us."
4:14 I stood **u** and said to the nobles and the officials
6: 1 (though **u** to that time I had not set **u** the doors in
6: 7 also set **u** prophets to proclaim in Jerusalem
7: 1 the wall had been built and I had set **u** the doors,
7: 6 These are the people of the province who came **u**
7:61 The following were those who came **u**
8: 5 and when he opened it, all the people stood **u.**
8: 6 "Amen, Amen," lifting **u** their hands.
9: 3 They stood **u** in their place and read from the book
9: 5 "Stand **u** and bless the LORD your God
9:18 'This is your God who brought you **u** out
10:38 and the Levites shall bring **u** a tithe of the tithes to
12: 1 and the Levites who came **u** with Zerubbabel son
12:31 I brought the leaders of Judah **u** onto the wall,
12:37 they went straight **u** by the stairs of the city
Est 2: 7 Mordecai had brought **u** Hadassah, that is Esther,
2:20 as when she was brought **u** by him.
4: 2 he went **u** to the entrance of the king's gate,
Job 1: 7 and from walking **u** and down on it."
1:16 of God fell from heaven and burned **u** the sheep
2: 2 and from walking **u** and down on it."
3: 8 those who are skilled to rouse **u** Leviathan.
4:21 Their tent-cord is plucked **u** within them,
5:18 For he wounds, but he binds **u;**
5:26 as a shock of grain comes **u** to the threshing floor
6:18 they go **u** into the waste, and perish.
7: 9 so those who go down to Sheol do not come **u;**
9: 7 not rise; who seals **u** the stars;
10:15 If I am righteous, I cannot lift **u** my head,
11:15 then you will lift **u** your face without blemish;
12:14 if he shuts someone in, no one can open **u.**
12:15 If he withholds the waters, they dry **u;**
14: 2 comes **u** like a flower and withers,
14:11 and a river wastes away and dries **u,**
14:17 my transgression would be sealed **u** in a bag,
15:20 all the years that are laid **u** for the ruthless.
15:30 the flame will dry **u** their shoots,
16: 8 And he has shriveled me **u,**
16: 8 my leanness has risen **u** against me,
16:11 God gives me **u** to the ungodly,
16:12 he set me **u** as his target;
17: 8 the innocent stir themselves **u** against the godless.
18:16 Their roots dry **u** beneath,
19: 8 He has walled **u** my way so that I cannot pass,
19:12 they have thrown **u** siegeworks against me,
20: 6 Even though they mount **u** high as the heavens,
20:15 They swallow down riches and vomit them **u**
20:26 Utter darkness is laid **u** for their treasures;
20:27 and the earth will rise **u** against them.
21:19 'God stores **u** their iniquity for their children.'
22:22 and lay **u** his words in your heart.
22:26 and lift **u** your face to God.
24:16 by day they shut themselves **u;**
24:22 they rise **u** when they despair of life.
26: 8 He binds **u** the waters in his thick clouds,
27: 1 Job again took **u** his discourse and said:
27:16 Though they heap **u** silver like dust,
27:16 and pile **u** clothing like clay—
27:17 they may pile it **u,** but the just will wear it,
27:21 The east wind lifts them **u** and they are gone;
28: 5 but underneath it is turned **u** as by fire.
29: 1 Job again took **u** his discourse and said:
29: 8 and the aged rose **u** and stood;
30:12 On my right hand the rabble rise **u;**
30:13 They break **u** my path, they promote my calamity;
30:22 You lift me **u** on the wind,
30:28 I stand **u** in the assembly and cry for help.
31:14 what then shall I do when God rises **u?**
34: 7 who drinks **u** scoffing like water,
36:27 For he draws **u** the drops of water;
37:19 we cannot draw **u** our case because of darkness.
37:20 Did anyone ever wish to be swallowed **u?**
38: 3 Gird **u** your loins like a man, I will question you,
38:34 "Can you lift **u** your voice to the clouds,
39: 4 they grow **u** in the open;
39:27 the eagle mounts **u** and makes its nest on high?
39:30 Its young ones suck **u** blood;
40: 7 "Gird **u** your loins like a man;
41: 6 Will they divide it **u** among the merchants?
41:10 No one is so fierce as to dare to stir it **u.**
41:15 shut **u** closely as with a seal.
41:25 When it raises itself **u** the gods are afraid;
42: 8 and offer **u** for yourselves a burnt offering;
Ps 3: 3 my glory, and the one who lifts **u** my head.
3: 7 Rise **u,** O LORD! Deliver me,
Ps 7: 6 Rise **u,** O LORD, in your anger;
7: 6 lift yourself **u** against the fury of my enemies;
9:13 the one who lifts me **u** from the gates of death,
9:19 Rise **u,** O LORD! Do not let mortals prevail;
10:12 Rise **u,** O LORD; O God, lift **u** your hand;
12: 5 because the needy groan, I will now rise **u,"**
14: 4 all the evildoers who eat **u** my people
15: 3 nor take **u** a reproach against their neighbors;
16:10 For you do not give me **u** to Sheol,
17:13 Rise **u,** O LORD, confront them,
17:14 be filled with what you have stored **u** for them;
18: 8 Smoke went **u** from his nostrils,
18:28 the LORD, my God, lights **u** my darkness.
20: 5 and in the name of our God set **u** our banners.
21: 9 The LORD will swallow them **u** in his wrath,
22:15 my mouth is dried **u** like a potsherd,
24: 4 who do not lift **u** their souls to what is false,
24: 7 Lift **u** your heads, O gates!
24: 7 and be lifted **u,** O ancient doors!
24: 9 Lift **u** your heads, O gates!
24: 9 and be lifted **u,** O ancient doors!
25: 1 To you, O LORD, I lift **u** my soul.
27: 3 war rise **u** against me, yet I will be confident.
27: 6 Now my head is lifted **u** above my enemies all
27:10 the LORD will take me **u.**
27:12 Do not give me **u** to the will of my adversaries,
28: 2 I lift **u** my hands toward your most holy sanctuary.
28: 5 he will break them down and build them **u**
30: 1 O LORD, for you have drawn me **u,**
30: 3 O LORD, you brought **u** my soul from Sheol,
31:19 that you have laid **u** for those who fear you,
32: 4 my strength was dried **u** as by the heat of summer.
35: 2 and rise **u** to help me!
35:11 Malicious witnesses rise **u;**
35:23 Wake **u!** Bestir yourself
35:25 Do not let them say, "We have swallowed you **u."**
39: 6 they heap **u,** and do not know who will gather.
40: 2 He drew me **u** from the desolate pit,
41: 2 not give them **u** to the will of their enemies.
41:10 you, O LORD, be gracious to me, and raise me **u,**
44:26 Rise **u,** come to our help.
47: 5 God has gone **u** with a shout,
53: 4 who eat **u** my people as they eat bread,
56: 6 They stir **u** strife, they lurk, they watch my steps.
59: 1 protect me from those who rise **u** against me.
59: 3 the mighty stir **u** strife against me.
60: 4 You have set **u** a banner for those who fear you,
60: 6 "With exultation I will divide **u** Shechem,
62: 9 in the balances they go **u;**
63: 4 I will lift **u** my hands and call on your name.
68: 1 Let God rise **u,** let his enemies be scattered;
68: 4 lift **u** a song to him who rides upon the clouds—
68:19 Blessed be the Lord, who daily bears us **u;**
69: 1 O God, for the waters have come **u** to my neck.
69:15 or the deep swallow me **u,**
71:20 the depths of the earth you will bring me **u** again.
74: 4 they set **u** their emblems there.
74:15 you dried **u** ever-flowing streams.
74:22 Rise **u,** O God, plead your cause;
74:23 uproar of your adversaries that goes **u** continually.
75: 4 and to the wicked, "Do not lift **u** your horn;
75: 5 do not lift **u** your horn on high,
75: 6 and not from the wilderness comes lifting **u;**
75: 7 putting down one and lifting **u** another.
76: 9 when God rose **u** to establish judgment,
77: 9 Has he in anger shut **u** his compassion?"
77:18 your lightnings lit **u** the world;
78: 6 and rise **u** and tell them to their children,
78:38 and did not stir **u** all his wrath.
80: 2 Stir **u** your might, and come to save us!
81:10 who brought you **u** out of the land of Egypt.
82: 8 Rise **u,** O God, judge the earth;
85:11 Faithfulness will spring **u** from the ground,
86: 4 for to you, O Lord, I lift **u** my soul.
86:14 O God, the insolent rise **u** against me;
88:10 Do the shades rise **u** to praise you?
88:15 Wretched and close to death from my youth **u,**
91:12 On their hands they will bear you **u,**
93: 3 The floods have lifted **u,** O LORD,
93: 3 O LORD, the floods have lifted **u** their voice;
93: 3 the floods lift **u** their roaring.
94: 2 Rise **u,** O judge of the earth;
94:16 Who rises **u** for me against the wicked?
94:16 Who stands **u** for me against evildoers?
94:18 your steadfast love, O LORD, held me **u.**
97: 4 His lightnings light **u** the world;
102:10 for you have lifted me **u** and thrown me aside.
102:13 You will rise **u** and have compassion on Zion,
102:16 For the LORD will build **u** Zion;
104: 8 They rose **u** to the mountains,
104:28 when you give to them, they gather it **u;**
105:35 and ate **u** the fruit of their ground.
106:17 The earth opened and swallowed **u** Dathan,
106:18 the flame burned **u** the wicked.
106:30 Then Phinehas stood **u** and interceded,
107:25 which lifted **u** the waves of the sea.
107:26 They mounted **u** to heaven,
107:41 but he raises **u** the needy out of distress,
108: 7 "With exultation I will divide **u** Shechem,
110: 7 therefore he will lift **u** his head.
116:13 I will lift **u** the cup of salvation and call on
118:27 **u** to the horns of the altar.
119:117 Hold me **u,** that I may be safe and have regard
121: 1 I lift **u** my eyes to the hills—
122: 4 To it the tribes go **u,** the tribes of the LORD,
122: 5 For there the thrones for judgment were set **u,**
123: 1 To you I lift **u** my eyes,

Ps 124: 3 then they would have swallowed us **u** alive,
127: 2 in vain that you rise **u** early and go late to rest,
129: 6 on the housetops that withers before it grows **u,**
131: 1 not lifted **u,** my eyes are not raised too high;
132: 8 Rise **u,** O LORD, and go to your resting place,
132:17 There I will cause a horn to sprout **u** for David;
134: 2 Lift **u** your hands to the holy place,
137: 2 On the willows there we hung **u** our harps.
139: 2 You know when I sit down and when I rise **u;**
139:20 and lift themselves **u** against you for evil!
139:21 And do I not loathe those who rise **u** against you?
140: 2 who plan evil things in their minds and stir **u**
140: 9 Those who surround me lift **u** their heads;
141: 2 the lifting **u** of my hands as an evening sacrifice.
143: 8 for to you I lift **u** my soul.
145:14 and raises **u** all who are bowed down.
146: 8 The LORD lifts **u** those who are bowed down;
147: 2 The LORD builds **u** Jerusalem;
147: 3 and binds **u** their wounds.
147: 6 The LORD lifts **u** the downtrodden;
148:14 He has raised **u** a horn for his people,
Pr 2: 1 and treasure **u** my commandments within you,
2: 7 he stores **u** sound wisdom for the upright;
7: 1 keep my words and store **u** my commandments
8:23 Ages ago I was set **u,** at the first,
10:12 Hatred stirs **u** strife, but love covers all offenses.
10:14 The wise lay **u** knowledge,
12:25 but a good word cheers it **u.**
13:22 but the sinner's wealth is laid **u** for the righteous.
15: 1 but a harsh word stirs **u** anger.
15:18 Those who are hot-tempered stir **u** strife,
17:22 but a downcast spirit dries **u** the bones.
21:22 One wise person went **u** against a city of warriors
22:15 Folly is bound **u** in the heart of a boy,
22:28 the ancient landmark that your ancestors set **u.**
23: 8 You will vomit **u** the little you have eaten,
25: 7 to be told, "Come **u** here," than to be put lower in
28:25 The greedy person stirs **u** strife,
29:22 One given to anger stirs **u** strife,
30: 4 Who has wrapped **u** the waters in a garment?
30:21 under four it cannot bear **u:**
31:28 Her children rise **u** and call her happy;
Ecc 2:20 and gave my heart **u** to despair concerning all
3: 2 and a time to pluck **u** what is planted;
3: 3 a time to break down, and a time to build **u;**
4:10 For if they fall, one will lift **u** the other;
12: 4 and one rises **u** at the sound of a bird,
SS 2: 7 do not stir **u** or awaken love until it is ready!
3: 5 do not stir **u** or awaken love until it is ready!
3: 6 What is that coming **u** from the wilderness,
4: 2 of shorn ewes that have come **u** from the washing,
6: 6 that have come **u** from the washing;
7:13 new as well as old, which I have laid **u** for you,
8: 4 do not stir **u** or awaken love until it is ready!
8: 5 Who is that coming **u** from the wilderness,
Isa 1: 2 I reared children and brought them **u,**
1: 6 they have not been drained, or bound **u,**
2: 3 "Come, let us go **u** to the mountain of the LORD,
2: 4 nation shall not lift **u** sword against nation,
2:12 against all that is lifted **u** and high;
2:13 the cedars of Lebanon, lofty and lifted **u;**
5:24 and their blossom go **u** like dust;
7: 1 and King Pekah son of Remaliah of Israel went **u**
7: 6 Let us go **u** against Judah and cut off Jerusalem
8: 7 the Lord is bringing **u** against it
8: 8 and, pouring over, it will reach **u** to the neck;
8:16 Bind **u** the testimony, seal the teaching
9:11 and stirred **u** their enemies,
10:15 As if a rod should raise the one who lifts it **u,**
10:24 when they beat you with a rod and lift **u** their staff
10:27 He has gone **u** from Rimmon,
11:16 as there was for Israel when they came **u** from
13:17 See, I am stirring **u** the Medes against them,
14: 4 you will take **u** this taunt against the king
14: 9 Sheol beneath is stirred **u** to meet you
14:22 I will rise **u** against them,
15: 2 Dibon has gone **u** to the temple,
15: 5 For at the ascent of Luhith they go **u** weeping;
15: 7 and what they have laid **u** they carry away over
19: 2 I will stir **u** Egyptians against Egyptians
19: 5 The waters of the Nile will be dried **u,**
19: 6 branches of Egypt's Nile will diminish and dry **u,**
19: 7 and all that is sown by the Nile will dry **u,**
21: 2 Go **u,** O Elam, lay siege, O Media;
21: 5 Rise **u,** commanders, oil the shield!
22: 1 What do you mean that you have gone **u,**
23: 4 I have neither reared young men nor brought **u**
24: 4 The earth dries **u** and withers,
24: 7 The wine dries **u,** the vine languishes,
24:10 every house is shut **u** so that no one can enter.
24:14 They lift **u** their voices, they sing for joy;
24:22 they will be shut **u** in a prison,
25: 7 he will swallow **u** death forever.
26: 1 he sets **u** victory like walls and bulwarks.
26:11 O LORD, your hand is lifted **u,**
27: 4 I will burn it **u.**
28: 4 eats it **u** as soon as it comes to hand.
28:21 For the LORD will rise **u** as on Mount Perazim,
29: 8 a hungry person dreams of eating and wakes **u**
29: 8 or a thirsty person dreams of drinking and wakes **u**
30:18 therefore he will rise **u** to show mercy to you.
30:26 on the day when the LORD binds **u** the injuries
30:28 like an overflowing stream that reaches **u** to
32: 9 Rise **u,** you women who are at ease,
32:13 soil of my people growing **u** in thorns and briers;
33:10 "now I will lift myself **u;** now I will be exalted.
33:20 whose stakes will never be pulled **u,**
Isa 34: 4 and the skies roll **u** like a scroll.
34:10 its smoke shall go **u** forever.
35: 9 nor shall any ravenous beast come **u** on it;
36: 1 King Sennacherib of Assyria came **u** against all
36:10 that I have come **u** against this land to destroy it?
36:10 The LORD said to me, Go **u** against this land,
37: 4 lift **u** your prayer for the remnant that is left."
37:14 then Hezekiah went **u** to the house of the LORD
37:24 'With my many chariots I have gone **u** the heights
37:25 I dried **u** with the sole of my foot all the streams
37:28 I know your rising **u** and your sitting down,
37:33 or cast **u** a siege ramp against it.
38:12 My dwelling is plucked **u** and removed from me
38:12 like a weaver I have rolled **u** my life;
38:22 "What is the sign that I shall go **u** to the house of
39: 6 which your ancestors have stored **u** until this day,
40: 4 Every valley shall be lifted **u,**
40: 9 Get you **u** to a high mountain, O Zion,
40: 9 lift **u** your voice with strength, O Jerusalem,
herald of good tidings, lift it **u,**
40:15 see, he takes **u** the isles like fine dust.
40:20 then seeks out a skilled artisan to set **u** an image
40:26 Lift **u** your eyes on high and see:
40:31 they shall mount **u** with wings like eagles,
41: 2 He delivers **u** nations to him,
41:25 I stirred **u** one from the north, and he has come,
42: 2 He will not cry or lift **u** his voice,
42:11 Let the desert and its towns lift **u** their voice,
42:13 like a warrior he stirs **u** his fury;
42:15 and dry **u** all their herbage;
42:15 I will turn the rivers into islands, and dry **u**
42:18 and you that are blind, look **u** and see!
42:24 Who gave **u** Jacob to the spoiler,
43: 6 "Give them **u,**" and to the south, "Do not withhold;
44: 4 They shall spring **u** like a green tamarisk,
44:11 Let them all assemble, let them stand **u;**
44:13 with human beauty, to be set **u** in a shrine.
44:26 and I will raise **u** their ruins";
44:27 I will dry **u** your rivers";
45: 8 let the earth open, that salvation may spring **u,**
45: 8 and let it cause righteousness to sprout **u** also;
47:13 stand **u** and save you, those who gaze at the stars,
49: 6 that you should be my servant to raise **u** the tribes
49: 7 the slave of rulers, "Kings shall see and stand **u,**
49:11 and my highways shall be raised **u.**
49:18 Lift **u** your eyes all around and see;
49:19 and those who swallowed you **u** will be far away.
49:22 I will soon lift **u** my hand to the nations,
50: 2 By my rebuke I dry **u** the sea,
50: 8 Let us stand **u** together.
50: 9 the moth will eat them **u.**
51: 6 Lift **u** your eyes to the heavens,
51: 8 For the moth will eat them **u** like a garment,
51:10 Was it not you who dried **u** the sea,
51:15 who stirs **u** the sea so that its waves roar—
51:17 Stand **u,** O Jerusalem, you who have drunk at
51:18 the hand among all the children she has brought **u.**
52: 2 Shake yourself from the dust, rise **u,**
52: 8 Your sentinels lift **u** their voices,
52:13 he shall be exalted and lifted **u,**
53: 2 For he grew **u** before him like a young plant,
54:15 If anyone stirs **u** strife, it is not from me;
54:15 whoever stirs **u** strife with you shall fall because
55:13 Instead of the thorn shall come **u** the cypress;
55:13 instead of the brier shall come **u** the myrtle;
57: 7 and there you went **u** to offer sacrifice.
57: 8 Behind the door and the doorpost you have set **u**
57: 8 you have gone **u** to it, you have made it wide;
57:14 It shall be said, "Build **u,** build **u,**
57:20 its waters toss **u** mire and mud.
58: 1 Lift **u** your voice like a trumpet!
58: 8 and your healing shall spring **u** quickly;
58:12 you shall raise **u** the foundations
60: 4 Lift **u** your eyes and look around;
60:10 Foreigners shall build **u** your walls,
61: 1 to bind **u** the brokenhearted,
61: 4 They shall build **u** the ancient ruins,
61: 4 they shall raise **u** the former devastations;
61:11 as a garden causes what is sown in it to spring **u,**
61:11 and praise to spring **u** before all the nations.
62:10 build **u,** build **u** the highway, clear it of stones, lift
u an ensign over the peoples.
63: 9 he lifted them **u** and carried them all the days
63:11 the one who brought them **u** out of the sea with
Jer 1:10 to pluck **u** and to pull down,
1:17 But you, gird **u** your loins; stand **u** and tell them
2: 6 "Where is the LORD who brought us **u** from
2:23 Look **u** to the bare heights, and see!
3: 6 that faithless one, Israel, how she went **u**
4: 3 Break **u** your fallow ground,
4: 7 A lion has gone **u** from its thicket,
4:13 He comes **u** like clouds, his chariots like
5:10 Go **u** through her vine-rows and destroy,
5:17 They shall eat **u** your harvest and your food;
5:17 they shall eat **u** your sons and your daughters;
5:17 they shall eat **u** your flocks and your herds;
5:17 they shall eat **u** your vines and your fig trees;
6: 4 **u,** and let us attack at noon!"
6: 5 **"U,** and let us attack by night,
6: 6 cast **u** a siege ramp against Jerusalem.
6:17 Also I raised **u** sentinels for you:
8: 4 When people fall, do they not get **u** again?
9:10 Take **u** weeping and wailing for the mountains,
9:21 "Death has come **u** into our windows,
10:17 Gather **u** your bundle from the ground,
10:20 to spread my tent again, and to set **u** my curtains.
11: 7 when I brought them **u** out of the land of Egypt,
Jer 11:13 of Jerusalem are the altars you have set **u**
11:14 or lift **u** a cry or prayer on their behalf,
12: 8 she has lifted **u** her voice against me—
12:14 I am about to pluck them **u** from their land, and I
will pluck **u** the house
12:15 And after I have plucked them **u,**
12:16 they shall be built **u** in the midst of my people.
13:19 of the Negeb are shut **u** with no one to open them;
13:20 Lift **u** your eyes and see those who come from
13:22 of your iniquity that your skirts are lifted **u,**
13:26 I myself will lift **u** your skirts over your face,
14: 2 and the cry of Jerusalem goes **u.**
16:14 the people of Israel **u** out of the land of Egypt,"
16:15 the people of Israel **u** out of the land of the north
18: 7 that I will pluck **u** and break down and destroy it,
18:23 Let them be tripped **u** before you;
20: 9 like a burning fire shut **u** in my bones;
22:20 Go **u** to Lebanon, and cry out,
22:20 and cry out, and lift **u** your voice in Bashan;
23: 4 I will raise **u** shepherds over them
23: 5 when I will raise **u** for David a righteous Branch,
23: 7 the people of Israel **u** out of the land of Egypt,"
23:10 and the pastures of the wilderness are dried **u.**
23:39 I will surely lift you **u** and cast you away
24: 6 I will build them **u,** and not tear them down;
24: 6 I will plant them, and not pluck them **u.**
26:10 they came **u** from the king's house to the house of
27:22 I will bring them **u** and restore them to this place.
29:15 "The LORD has raised **u** prophets for us
30: 9 whom I will raise **u** for them.
31: 6 "Come, let us go **u** to Zion,
31:21 Set **u** road markers for yourself,
31:28 as I have watched over them to pluck **u** and break
31:35 who stirs **u** the sea so that its waves roar—
32:24 the siege ramps have been cast **u** against the city
32:34 They set **u** their abominations in the house
32:35 to offer **u** their sons and daughters to Molech,
33:15 a righteous Branch to spring **u** for David;
35:11 when King Nebuchadrezzar of Babylon came **u**
36: 6 the people of Judah who come **u** from their towns.
37:10 they would rise **u** and burn this city with fire.
38:10 and pull the prophet Jeremiah **u** from the cistern
38:13 Then they drew Jeremiah **u** by the ropes
39: 5 and when they had taken him, they brought him **u**
41: 2 with him got **u** and struck down Gedaliah son
42:10 then I will build you **u** and not pull you down;
42:10 I will plant you, and not pluck you **u;**
45: 4 and pluck **u** what I have planted—
46:11 Go **u** to Gilead, and take balm,
48: 5 at the ascent of Luhith they go **u** weeping bitterly;
48:15 The destroyer of Moab and his towns has come **u,**
48:18 the destroyer of Moab has come **u** against you;
49:14 and come against her, and rise **u** for battle!"
49:19 a lion coming **u** from the thickets of the Jordan
49:22 he shall mount **u** and swoop down like an eagle,
49:28 Rise **u,** advance against Kedar!
49:29 and a cry shall go **u:** "Terror is all around!"
49:31 Rise **u,** advance against a nation at ease,
50: 2 set **u** a banner and proclaim, do not conceal it, say:
50: 3 out of the north a nation has come **u** against her;
50: 9 For I am going to stir **u** and bring against Babylon
50:14 Take **u** your positions around Babylon,
50:21 Go **u** to the land of Merathaim; go **u** against her,
50:26 pile her **u** like heaps of grain,
50:32 with no one to raise him **u,**
50:38 that they may be dried **u!**
50:44 a lion coming **u** from the thickets of the Jordan
51: 1 to stir **u** a destructive wind against Babylon and
51: 9 for her judgment has reached **u** to heaven and has
been lifted **u** even to the skies.
51:11 The LORD has stirred **u** the spirit of the kings of
51:27 bring **u** horses like bristling locusts.
51:30 The warriors of Babylon have given **u** fighting,
51:36 I will dry **u** her sea and make her fountain dry;
51:53 Though Babylon should mount **u** to heaven,
52: 9 and brought him **u** to the king of Babylon
52:34 as long as he lived, **u** to the day of his death.
La 3:41 Let us lift **u** our hearts as well as our hands to God
3:58 You have taken **u** my cause, O Lord,
4: 5 those who were brought **u** in purple cling
5:12 Princes are hung **u** by their hands;
Eze 2: 1 He said to me: O mortal, stand **u** on your feet,
3:12 Then the spirit lifted me **u,**
3:14 The spirit lifted me **u** and bore me away;
3:22 and he said to me, Rise **u,** go out into the valley,
3:23 So I rose **u** and went out into the valley;
4: 2 and cast **u** a ramp against it;
4:14 my youth **u** until now I have never eaten what died
5: 4 throw them into the fire and burn them **u;**
8: 3 the spirit lifted me **u** between earth and heaven,
8: 5 lift **u** your eyes now in the direction of the north."
8: 5 So I lifted **u** my eyes toward the north, and there,
9: 3 of the God of Israel had gone **u** from the cherub
10: 4 the glory of the LORD rose **u** from the cherub to
10:15 The cherubim rose **u.** These were the living
10:16 when the cherubim lifted **u** their wings to rise **u**
10:17 and when they rose **u,** the others rose **u** with them;
10:19 The cherubim lifted **u** their wings and rose **u**
11: 1 The spirit lifted me **u** and brought me to
11:22 Then the cherubim lifted **u** their wings,
11:24 The spirit lifted me **u** and brought me in a vision
13: 5 You have not gone **u** into the breaches,
15: 6 so I will give **u** the inhabitants of Jerusalem.
16: 7 and grow **u** like a plant of the field."
16: 7 You grew **u** and became tall and arrived
16:21 You slaughtered my children and delivered them **u**
16:27 and gave you **u** to the will of your enemies,

Eze 16:40 They shall bring **u** a mob against you,
17: 9 Will he not pull **u** its roots,
17:14 the kingdom might be humble and not lift itself **u,**
17:17 when ramps are cast **u** and siege walls built
17:24 I dry **u** the green tree and make the dry tree
18: 6 or lift **u** his eyes to the idols of the house of Israel,
18:12 lifts **u** his eyes to the idols, commits abomination,
18:15 or lift **u** his eyes to the idols of the house of Israel,
19: 1 you, raise **u** a lamentation for the princes of Israel,
19: 3 She raised **u** one of her cubs;
19:12 it was plucked **u** in fury, cast down to the ground;
19:12 the east wind dried it **u;** its fruit was stripped off,
20:26 in their offering **u** all their firstborn,
20:28 there they sent **u** their pleasing odors,
21:22 to cast **u** ramps, to build siege towers.
23: 8 not give **u** her whorings that she had practiced
23:37 and they have even offered **u** to them for food
23:46 Bring **u** an assembly against them,
23:47 and their daughters, and burn **u** their houses.
24:10 Heap **u** the logs, kindle the fire;
26: 8 He shall set **u** a siege wall against you,
26: 8 cast **u** a ramp against you,
26:19 when I bring **u** the deep over you,
29: 4 I will draw you **u** from your channels,
29:21 On that day I will cause a horn to sprout **u** for
30:12 I will dry **u** the channels, and will sell the land
30:21 it has not been bound **u** for healing or wrapped
31:14 that no trees that drink water may reach **u** to them
32: 3 and I will haul you **u** in my dragnet.
32: 6 I will drench the land with your flowing blood **u**
33:25 and lift **u** your eyes to your idols, and shed blood;
34: 4 you have not bound **u** the injured,
34:16 and I will bind **u** the injured,
34:23 I will set **u** over them one shepherd,
37:11 They say, 'Our bones are dried **u,**
37:12 and bring you **u** from your graves, O my people;
37:13 and bring you **u** from your graves, O my people.
38:11 "I will go **u** against the land of unwalled villages;
38:16 you will come **u** against my people Israel,
39: 2 bring you **u** from the remotest parts of the north,
39:15 anyone who sees a human bone shall set **u** a sign
40: 6 going **u** its steps, and measured the threshold of
40:22 Seven steps led **u** to it;
40:26 There were seven steps leading **u** to it;
40:49 ten steps led **u** to it;
41:16 from the floor **u** to the windows
43: 5 the spirit lifted me **u,** and brought me into
43:24 on them and offer them **u** as a burnt offering to
47: 4 and it was **u** to the waist.
Da 2:21 deposes kings and sets **u** kings;
2:44 of heaven will set **u** a kingdom that shall never
3: 1 he set it **u** on the plain of Dura in the province
3: 2 of the statue that King Nebuchadnezzar had set **u.**
3: 3 of the statue that King Nebuchadnezzar had set **u.**
3: 3 before the statue that Nebuchadnezzar had set **u,**
3: 5 that King Nebuchadnezzar has set **u.**
3: 7 that King Nebuchadnezzar had set **u.**
3:12 not worship the golden statue that you have set **u."**
3:14 not worship the golden statue that I have set **u?**
3:18 not worship the golden statue that you have set **u."**
3:19 He ordered the furnace heated **u**
3:24 Nebuchadnezzar was astonished and rose **u**
3:28 and yielded **u** their bodies rather than serve
5:20 But when his heart was lifted **u**
6:19 the king got **u** and hurried to the den of lions.
6:23 and commanded that Daniel be taken **u** out of
6:23 So Daniel was taken **u** out of the den,
7: 2 the four winds of heaven stirring **u** the great sea,
7: 3 and four great beasts came **u** out of the sea,
7: 4 and it was lifted **u** from the ground and made
7: 5 It was raised **u** on one side,
7: 8 a little one coming **u** among them;
7: 8 for it, three of the earlier horns were plucked **u** by
7:20 which came **u** and to make room for which three
8: 3 I looked **u** and saw a ram standing beside
8: 3 and the longer one came **u** second.
8: 8 and in its place there came **u** four prominent horns
8:25 and shall even rise **u** against the Prince of princes.
8:26 As for you, seal **u** the vision,
10: 5 I looked **u** and saw a man clothed in linen,
10:11 while he was speaking this word to me, I stood **u**
11: 1 I stood **u** to support and strengthen him.
11: 2 he shall stir **u** all against the kingdom of Greece.
11: 6 be given **u,** she and her attendants and her child
11: 7 a branch from her roots shall rise **u** in his place.
11:14 among your own people shall lift themselves **u**
11:15 Then the king of the north shall come and throw **u**
11:25 He shall stir **u** his power and determination
11:31 and set **u** the abomination that makes desolate.
12:11 and the abomination that desolates is set **u,**
Hos 2: 6 Therefore I will hedge **u** her way with thorns;
4:15 Do not enter into Gilgal, or go **u** to Beth-aven,
6: 1 he has struck down, and he will bind us **u.**
6: 2 on the third day he will raise us **u,**
8: 4 they set **u** princes, but without my knowledge.
8: 8 Israel is swallowed **u;**
8: 9 For they have gone **u** to Assyria,
8:10 I will now gather them **u.**
9:12 Even if they bring **u** children,
9:16 Ephraim is stricken, their root is dried **u,**
10: 4 so litigation springs **u** like poisonous weeds in
10: 8 Thorn and thistle shall grow **u** on their altars.
10:12 break **u** your fallow ground;
11: 3 I took them **u** in my arms;
11: 7 but he does not raise them **u** at all.
11: 8 How can I give you **u,** Ephraim?
12:13 a prophet the LORD brought Israel **u** from Egypt,
Hos 13:12 Ephraim's iniquity is bound **u;**
13:15 and his fountain shall dry **u,**
Joel 1: 5 Wake **u,** you drunkards, and weep;
1:10 grain is destroyed, the wine dries **u,** the oil fails.
1:12 all the trees of the field are dried **u;**
1:20 to you because the watercourses are dried **u,**
2: 5 like a powerful army drawn **u** for battle.
2: 9 they climb **u** into the houses,
2:20 its stench and foul smell will rise **u.**
3: 9 Prepare war, stir **u** the warriors.
3: 9 Let all the soldiers draw near, let them come **u.**
3:12 and come **u** to the valley of Jehoshaphat;
Am 1: 2 and the top of Carmel dries **u.**
2:10 Also I brought you **u** out of the land of Egypt,
2:11 And I raised **u** some of your children to
3: 1 the whole family that I brought **u** out of the land
3: 5 Does a snare spring **u** from the ground,
3:10 those who store **u** violence and robbery
4:10 the stench of your camp go **u** into your nostrils;
5: 1 that I take **u** over you in lamentation, O house
5: 2 forsaken on her land, with no one to raise her **u.**
5:26 You shall take **u** Sakkuth your king,
6: 8 and I will deliver **u** the city and all that is in it.
6:10 shall take **u** the body to bring it out of the house,
6:14 Indeed, I am raising **u** against you a nation,
7: 4 and it devoured the great deep and was eating **u**
9: 2 though they climb **u** to heaven,
9: 7 Did I not bring Israel **u** from the land of Egypt,
9:11 On that day I will raise **u** the booth of David
9:11 and repair its breaches, and raise **u** its ruins,
9:15 and they shall never again be plucked **u** out of
Ob 1: 1 among the nations: "Rise **u!**
1:21 Those who have been saved shall go **u**
Jnh 1: 2 for their wickedness has come **u** before me."
1: 4 upon the sea that the ship threatened to break **u.**
1: 6 Get **u,** call on your god!
1:12 "Pick me **u** and throw me into the sea;
1:15 they picked Jonah **u** and threw him into the sea;
1:17 LORD provided a large fish to swallow **u** Jonah;
2: 6 yet you brought **u** my life from the Pit,
3: 2 "Get **u,** go to Nineveh, that great city,
4: 6 and made it come **u** over Jonah,
4: 7 But when dawn came **u** the next day,
Mic 2: 4 that day they shall take **u** a taunt song against you,
2: 8 But you rise **u** against my people as an enemy;
2:13 The one who breaks out will go **u** before them;
3: 3 and chop them **u** like meat in a kettle,
4: 1 and shall be raised **u** above the hills.
4: 2 "Come, let us go **u** to the mountain of the LORD,
4: 3 nation shall not lift **u** sword against nation,
5: 3 Therefore he shall give them **u** until the time
5: 9 Your hand shall be lifted **u** over your adversaries,
6: 4 For I brought you **u** from the land of Egypt,
7: 6 the daughter rises **u** against her mother,
Na 1: 4 and he dries **u** all the rivers;
1: 9 no adversary will rise **u** twice.
2: 1 A shatterer has come **u** against you.
2: 5 they hasten to the wall, and the mantelet is set **u.**
3: 5 and will lift **u** your skirts over your face;
Hab 1:10 and heap **u** earth to take it.
1:15 The enemy brings all of them **u** with a hook;
2: 6 "Alas for you who heap **u** what is not your own!"
2: 7 and those who make you tremble wake **u?**
2:19 Alas for you who say to the wood, "Wake **u!"**
Hag 1: 8 Go **u** to the hills and bring wood and build
1:14 the LORD stirred **u** the spirit of Zerubbabel son
Zec 1:18 And I looked **u** and saw four horns.
1:21 the nations that lifted **u** their horns against the land
2: 1 I looked **u** and saw a man with a measuring line
2: 6 **U, u!** Flee from the land of the north,
2: 7 **U!** Escape to Zion, you that live with daughter
5: 1 Again I looked **u** and saw a flying scroll.
5: 5 "Look **u** and see what this is that is coming out."
5: 9 I looked **u** and saw two women coming forward.
5: 9 and they lifted **u** the basket between earth and sky.
6: 1 And again I looked **u** and saw four chariots
9: 3 and heaped **u** silver like dust,
10:11 and all the depths of the Nile dried **u.**
11:16 now raising **u** in the land a shepherd who does
14:16 that have come against Jerusalem shall go **u** year
14:17 the families of the earth do not go **u** to Jerusalem
14:18 of Egypt do not go **u** and present themselves,
14:18 the LORD inflicts on the nations that do not go **u**
14:19 the punishment of all the nations that do not go **u**
Mal 4: 1 the day that comes shall burn them **u,**
Mt 2:13 "Get **u,** take the child and his mother,
2:14 Then Joseph got **u,** took the child and his mother
2:20 "Get **u,** take the child and his mother, and go to
2:21 Then Joseph got **u,** took the child and his mother,
3: 9 from these stones to raise **u** children to Abraham.
3:16 just as he came **u** from the water,
4: 1 Then Jesus was led **u** by the Spirit into
4: 6 and 'On their hands they will bear you **u,**
5: 1 Jesus saw the crowds, he went **u** the mountain;
6: 7 do not heap **u** empty phrases as the Gentiles do;
6:19 "Do not store **u** for yourselves treasures on earth,
6:20 but store **u** for yourselves treasures in heaven,
8:15 and she got **u** and began to serve him.
8:25 And they went and woke him **u,** saying, "Lord,
8:26 Then he got **u** and rebuked the winds and the sea;
9: 5 or to say, 'Stand **u** and walk'?
9: 6 "Stand **u,** take your bed and go to your home."
9: 7 And he stood **u** and went to his home.
9: 9 And he got **u** and followed him.
9:19 Jesus got **u** and followed him, with his disciples.
9:20 for twelve years came **u** behind him and touched
9:25 in and took her by the hand, and the girl got **u.**
Mt 10:26 nothing is covered **u** that will not be uncovered,
10:38 not take **u** the cross and follow me is not worthy
12:29 without first tying **u** the strong man?
12:41 The people of Nineveh will rise **u** at the judgment
12:42 The queen of the South will rise **u** at the judgment
13: 4 and the birds came and ate them **u.**
13: 5 and they sprang **u** quickly,
13: 7 and the thorns grew **u** and choked them.
13:26 So when the plants came **u** and bore grain,
13:40 as the weeds are collected and burned **u** with fire,
14:19 the two fish, he looked **u** to heaven, and blessed
14:20 and they took **u** what was left over of
14:23 he went **u** the mountain by himself to pray.
15:29 and he went **u** the mountain, where he sat down.
15:37 and they took **u** the broken pieces left over,
16:24 let them deny themselves and take **u** their cross
17: 1 and James and his brother John and led them **u**
17: 7 saying, "Get **u** and do not be afraid."
17: 8 And when they looked **u,**
17:17 How much longer must I put **u** with you?
17:27 take the first fish that comes **u;**
20:17 While Jesus was going **u** to Jerusalem,
20:18 we are going **u** to Jerusalem,
21:21 'Be lifted **u** and thrown into the sea,'
22:24 and raise **u** children for his brother.'
23: 4 They tie **u** heavy burdens, hard to bear,
23:32 Fill **u,** then, the measure of your ancestors.
25: 7 Then all those bridesmaids got **u**
26:32 I am raised **u,** I will go ahead of you to Galilee."
26:46 Get **u,** let us be going.
26:49 At once he came **u** to Jesus and said, "Greetings,
26:62 The high priest stood **u** and said,
26:73 After a little while the bystanders came **u** and said
Mk 1:10 And just as he was coming **u** out of the water,
1:31 He came and took her by the hand and lifted her **u.**
1:35 he got **u** and went out to a deserted place,
2: 9 or to say, 'Stand **u** and take your mat and walk'?
2:11 stand **u,** take your mat and go to your home."
2:12 And he stood **u,** and immediately took the mat
2:14 And he got **u** and followed him.
3:13 He went **u** the mountain and called
3:26 if Satan has risen **u** against himself and is divided,
3:27 and plunder his property without first tying **u**
4: 4 and the birds came and ate it **u.**
4: 5 where it did not have much soil, and it sprang **u**
4: 7 and the thorns grew **u** and choked it,
4: 8 growing **u** and increasing and yielding thirty
4:32 yet when it is sown it grows **u** and becomes
4:38 and they woke him **u** and said to him, "Teacher,
4:39 He woke **u** and rebuked the wind,
5:27 and came **u** behind him in the crowd
5:41 "Talitha cum," which means, "Little girl, get **u!"**
5:42 And immediately the girl got **u** and began to walk
6:41 he looked **u** to heaven, and blessed and broke
6:43 and they took **u** twelve baskets full
6:46 he went **u** on the mountain to pray.
7:34 Then looking **u** to heaven,
8: 8 and they took **u** the broken pieces left over,
8:24 And the man looked **u** and said, "I can see people,
8:34 let them deny themselves and take **u** their cross
9: 2 and led them **u** a high mountain apart,
9:19 How much longer must I put **u** with you?
9:27 But Jesus took him by the hand and lifted him **u,**
10:16 And he took them **u** in his arms,
10:17 a man ran **u** and knelt before him, and asked him,
10:32 They were on the road, going **u** to Jerusalem,
10:33 "See, we are going **u** to Jerusalem,
10:49 to him, "Take heart; get **u,**
10:50 he sprang **u** and came to Jesus.
11:23 'Be taken **u** and thrown into the sea,'
12:19 the widow and raise **u** children for his brother.'
13:14 the desolating sacrilege set **u** where it ought not to
14:28 I am raised **u,** I will go before you to Galilee."
14:42 Get **u,** let us be going.
14:45 when he came, he went **u** to him at once and said,
14:57 Some stood **u** and gave false testimony
14:60 high priest stood **u** before them and asked Jesus,
15:11 But the chief priests stirred **u** the crowd
15:41 there were many other women who had come **u**
16: 4 When they looked **u,** they saw that the stone,
16:18 ⟦they will pick **u** snakes in their hands,⟧
16:19 ⟦was taken **u** into heaven and sat down at⟧
Lk 1:52 down the powerful from their thrones, and lifted **u**
1:69 He has raised **u** a mighty savior for us in the house
2:22 they brought him **u** to Jerusalem to present him to
2:42 they went **u** as usual for the festival.
3: 8 from these stones to raise **u** children to Abraham.
3:20 added to them all by shutting **u** John in prison.
4: 5 Then the devil led him **u** and showed him in
4:11 and 'On their hands they will bear you **u,**
4:16 where he had been brought **u,**
4:16 as was his custom. He stood **u** to read,
4:20 And he rolled **u** the scroll,
4:25 the heaven was shut **u** three years and six months,
4:29 They got **u,** drove him out of the town,
4:39 Immediately she got **u** and began to serve them.
5:19 they went **u** on the roof and let him down
5:23 or to say, 'Stand **u** and walk'?
5:24 stand **u** and take your bed and go to your home."
5:25 Immediately he stood **u** before them,
5:28 And he got **u,** left everything, and followed him.
6: 8 He got **u** and stood there.
6:20 Then he looked **u** at his disciples and said:
7:15 The dead man sat **u** and began to speak,
7:40 Jesus spoke **u** and said to him, "Simon,
8: 5 and the birds of the air ate it **u.**
8: 6 and as it grew **u,** it withered for lack of moisture.

Lk 8:24 They went to him and woke him **u**, shouting,
8:24 And he woke **u** and rebuked the wind and
8:44 She came **u** behind him and touched the fringe
8:54 by the hand and called out, "Child, get **u**!"
8:55 Her spirit returned, and she got **u** at once.
9:16 the two fish, he looked **u** to heaven, and blessed
9:17 What was left over was gathered **u**,
9:23 and take **u** their cross daily and follow me.
9:28 and went **u** on the mountain to pray.
9:51 When the days drew near for him to be taken **u**,
10:25 Just then a lawyer stood **u** to test Jesus.
11: 7 I cannot get **u** and give you anything.'
11: 8 though he will not get **u** and give him anything
11: 8 at least because of his persistence he will get **u**
11:32 The people of Nineveh will rise **u** at the judgment
12: 2 Nothing is covered **u** that will not be uncovered,
12:19 you have ample goods laid **u** for many years;
12:21 with those who store **u** treasures for themselves
13:11 She was bent over and was quite unable to stand **u**
13:13 immediately she stood **u** straight
13:25 When once the owner of the house has got **u**
14:10 he may say to you, 'Friend, move **u** higher';
14:33 if you do not give **u** all your possessions.
15:18 I will get **u** and go to my father,
16:23 he looked **u** and saw Abraham far away
17:19 Then he said to him, "Get **u** and go on your way;
17:24 For as the lightning flashes and lights **u** the sky
18:10 "Two men went **u** to the temple to pray,
18:13 standing far off, would not even look **u** to heaven,
18:31 "See, we are going **u** to Jerusalem,
19: 5 he looked **u** and said to him, "Zacchaeus,
19:20 I wrapped it **u** in a piece of cloth,
19:28 he went on ahead, going **u** to Jerusalem.
19:43 when your enemies will set **u** ramparts around you
20:28 the widow and raise **u** children for his brother.
21: 1 He looked **u** and saw rich people putting their gifts
21:14 So make **u** your minds not to prepare your defense
21:28 stand **u** and raise your heads,
21:38 the people would get **u** early in the morning
22:45 When he got **u** from prayer,
22:46 Get **u** and pray that you may not come into
23: 5 "He stirs **u** the people by teaching
23:36 coming **u** and offering him sour wine,
24:12 But Peter got **u** and ran to the tomb;
24:33 same hour they got **u** and returned to Jerusalem;
24:50 and, lifting **u** his hands, he blessed them.
24:51 he withdrew from them and was carried **u**
Jn 2: 7 And they filled them **u** to the brim.
2:13 and Jesus went **u** to Jerusalem.
2:19 and in three days I will raise it **u**."
2:20 and will you raise it **u** in three days?"
3:14 as Moses lifted **u** the serpent in the wilderness,
3:14 so must the Son of Man be lifted **u**,
4:14 a spring of water gushing **u** to eternal life."
5: 1 and Jesus went **u** to Jerusalem.
5: 7 into the pool when the water is stirred **u**;
5: 8 Jesus said to him, "Stand **u**,
5: 9 and he took **u** his mat and began to walk.
5:11 'Take **u** your mat and walk.'"
5:12 the man who said to you, 'Take it **u** and walk'?"
6: 3 Jesus went **u** the mountain and sat down there
6: 5 When he looked **u** and saw a large crowd coming
6:12 "Gather **u** the fragments left over,
6:13 So they gathered them **u**, and from the fragments
6:39 but raise it **u** on the last day.
6:40 and I will raise them **u** on the last day."
6:44 and I will raise that person **u** on the last day.
6:54 and I will raise them **u** on the last day.
7:14 the festival Jesus went **u** into the temple and began
8: 7 ⟦he straightened **u** and said to them,⟧
8:10 ⟦Jesus straightened **u** and said to her, "Woman,⟧
8:28 "When you have lifted **u** the Son of Man,
8:59 So they picked **u** stones to throw at him,
10:17 I lay down my life in order to take it **u** again.
10:18 and I have power to take it **u** again.
10:31 The Jews took **u** stones again to stone him.
11:29 she heard it, she got **u** quickly and went to him.
11:31 consoling her, saw Mary get **u** quickly and go out.
11:55 and many went **u** from the country to Jerusalem
12:20 Now among those who went **u** to worship at
12:32 And I, when I am lifted **u** from the earth,
12:34 that the Son of Man must be lifted **u**?
13: 4 got **u** from the table, took off his outer robe,
17: 1 he looked **u** to heaven and said, "Father,
19: 3 They kept coming **u** to him, saying, "Hail,
19:30 Then he bowed his head and gave **u** his spirit.
20: 7 not lying with the linen wrappings but rolled **u** in
Ac 1: 2 until the day when he was taken **u** to heaven,
1: 9 as they were watching, he was lifted **u**,
1:10 While he was going and they were gazing **u**
1:11 why do you stand looking **u** toward heaven?
1:11 who has been taken **u** from you into heaven,
1:15 In those days Peter stood **u** among
1:22 until the day when he was taken **u** from us—
2:24 But God raised him **u**, having freed him
2:32 This Jesus God raised **u**, and of that all
3: 1 and John were going **u** to the temple at the hour
3: 6 in the name of Jesus Christ of Nazareth, stand **u**
3: 7 he took him by the right hand and raised him **u**;
3: 8 Jumping **u**, he stood and began to walk,
3:22 'The Lord your God will raise **u** for you
3:26 When God raised **u** his servant,
5: 6 The young men came and wrapped **u** his body,
5:30 The God of our ancestors raised **u** Jesus,
5:34 stood **u** and ordered the men to be put outside for
5:36 For some time ago Theudas rose **u**,
5:37 After him Judas the Galilean rose **u** at the time of
Ac 6: 9 stood **u** and argued with Stephen.
6:12 They stirred **u** the people as well as the elders and
6:13 They set **u** false witnesses who said,
7:20 For three months he was brought **u**
7:21 and brought him **u** as her own son.
7:37 'God will raise **u** a prophet for you
7:37 for you from your own people as he raised me **u**.'
8:26 "Get **u** and go toward the south to the road
8:27 So he got **u** and went.
8:30 So Philip ran **u** to it and heard him reading
8:39 When they came **u** out of the water,
9: 6 But get **u** and enter the city,
9: 8 Saul got **u** from the ground,
9:11 "Get **u** and go to the street called Straight,
9:18 Then he got **u** and was baptized,
9:31 Galilee, and Samaria had peace and was built **u**.
9:34 get **u** and make your bed!"
9:34 And immediately he got **u**.
9:39 So Peter got **u** and went with them;
9:40 He turned to the body and said, "Tabitha, get **u**."
9:40 she opened her eyes, and seeing Peter, she sat **u**.
9:41 He gave her his hand and helped her **u**.
10: 9 Peter went **u** on the roof to pray.
10:13 Then he heard a voice saying, "Get **u**, Peter;
10:16 and the thing was suddenly taken **u** to heaven.
10:20 Now get **u**, go down, and go with them
10:23 The next day he got **u** and went with them,
10:26 But Peter made him get **u**, saying, "Stand **u**;
11: 2 So when Peter went **u** to Jerusalem,
11: 7 I also heard a voice saying to me, 'Get **u**, Peter;
11:10 then everything was pulled **u** again to heaven.
11:28 One of them named Agabus stood **u** and predicted
12: 7 the side and woke him, saying, "Get **u** quickly."
13:16 So Paul stood **u** and with a gesture began to speak:
13:18 For about forty years he put **u** with them in
13:31 for many days he appeared to those who came **u**
13:37 he whom God raised **u** experienced no corruption.
13:43 When the meeting of the synagogue broke **u**,
13:50 stirred **u** persecution against Paul and Barnabas,
14: 2 But the unbelieving Jews stirred **u** the Gentiles
14:10 And the man sprang **u** and began to walk.
14:20 he got **u** and went into the city.
15: 2 of the others were appointed to go **u** to Jerusalem
15: 5 to the sect of the Pharisees stood **u** and said
15: 7 Peter stood **u** and said to them, "My brothers,
15:16 from its ruins I will rebuild it, and I will set it **u**,
16:27 jailer woke **u** and saw the prison doors wide open,
16:34 He brought them **u** into the house and set food
17:13 to stir **u** and incite the crowds.
18:22 he went **u** to Jerusalem and greeted the church,
20: 9 to the ground three floors below and was picked **u**
20:32 to build you **u** and to give you the inheritance
21: 4 We looked **u** the disciples and stayed there
21:12 we and the people there urged him not to go **u**
21:15 After these days we got ready and started to go **u**
21:27 stirred **u** the whole crowd.
21:38 not the Egyptian who recently stirred **u** a revolt
22: 3 but brought **u** in this city at the feet of Gamaliel,
22: 4 I persecuted this Way **u** to the point of death
22:10 The Lord said to me, 'Get **u** and go to Damascus;
22:16 now why do you delay? Get **u**, be baptized,
22:22 U to this point they listened to him,
22:25 But when they had tied him **u** with thongs,
23: 1 **u** to this day I have lived my life with
23: 9 and certain scribes of the Pharisees' group stood **u**
23:11 the Lord stood near him and said, "Keep **u**
24:11 it is not more than twelve days since I went **u**
24:12 or stirring **u** a crowd either in the synagogues or
25: 1 he went **u** from Caesarea to Jerusalem
25: 9 to go **u** to Jerusalem and be tried there before me
25:18 When the accusers stood **u**,
26:10 I not only locked **u** many of the saints in prison,
26:16 But get **u** and stand on your feet;
26:30 Then the king got **u**, and with him the governor
27:17 After hoisting it **u** they took measures to undergird
27:21 Paul then stood **u** among them and said, "Men,
27:22 I urge you now to keep **u** your courage,
27:25 So keep **u** your courage, men,
27:41 but the stern was being broken **u** by the force of
28: 6 They were expecting him to swell **u** or drop dead,
28:13 After one day there a south wind sprang **u**,
Ro 1:24 Therefore God gave them **u** in the lusts
1:26 For this reason God gave them **u**
1:27 giving **u** natural intercourse with women,
1:28 God gave them **u** to a debased mind and to things
2: 5 and impenitent heart you are storing **u** wrath
8:32 but gave him **u** for all of us,
9:17 "I have raised you **u** for the very purpose
10: 7 (that is, to bring Christ **u** from the dead).
13: 9 are summed **u** in this word,
15: 1 We who are strong ought to put **u** with the failings
15: 2 for the good purpose of building **u** the neighbor.
1Co 3:15 the work is burned **u**, the builder will suffer loss;
4: 6 that none of you will be puffed **u** in favor of one
8: 1 Knowledge puffs **u**, but love builds **u**.
10: 7 down to eat and drink, and they rose **u** to play."
10:23 "All things are lawful," but not all things build **u**.
14: 4 Those who speak in a tongue build **u** themselves,
but those who prophesy build **u** the church.
14: 5 so that the church may be built **u**.
14:12 strive to excel in them for building **u** the church.
14:17 but the other person is not built **u**.
14:26 Let all things be done for building **u**.
15:54 "Death has been swallowed **u** in victory."
16:17 because they have made **u** for your absence;
2Co 2: 1 So I made **u** my mind not to make you another
4:11 we are always being given **u** to death
2Co 5: 4 so that what is mortal may be swallowed **u** by life.
9: 2 and your zeal has stirred **u** most of them.
9: 7 of you must give as you have made **u** your mind,
10: 5 and every proud obstacle raised **u** against
10: 8 for building you **u** and not for tearing you down,
11:19 For you gladly put **u** with fools,
11:20 For you put **u** with it when someone makes slaves
12: 2 in Christ who fourteen years ago was caught **u** to
12: 4 was caught **u** into Paradise and heard things
12:14 for children ought not to lay **u** for their parents,
12:19 beloved, is for the sake of building you **u**.
13:10 that the Lord has given me for building **u** and not
Gal 1:17 nor did I go **u** to Jerusalem
1:18 Then after three years I did go **u** to Jerusalem
2: 1 after fourteen years I went **u** again to Jerusalem
2: 2 I went **u** in response to a revelation.
2:18 if I build **u** again the very things that I once tore
5:14 whole law is summed **u** in a single commandment,
6: 9 if we do not give **u**.
Eph 1:10 to gather **u** all things in him,
2: 6 and raised us **u** with him and seated us with him in
4:12 for building **u** the body of Christ,
4:15 we must grow **u** in every way into him who is
4:16 promotes the body's growth in building itself **u**
4:28 Thieves must give **u** stealing;
4:29 but only what is useful for building **u**,
5: 2 as Christ loved us and gave himself **u** for us,
5:25 just as Christ loved the church and gave himself **u**
6: 4 but bring them **u** in the discipline and instruction
6:13 Therefore take **u** the whole armor of God,
Php 2:30 risking his life to make **u** for those services
Col 1: 5 because of the hope laid **u** for you in heaven.
2: 7 and built **u** in him and established in the faith,
2:18 puffed **u** without cause by a human way
1Th 2:16 Thus they have constantly been filling **u**
4:17 will be caught **u** in the clouds together with them
5:11 encourage one another and build **u** each other,
1Ti 2: 8 lifting **u** holy hands without anger or argument;
3: 6 or he may be puffed **u** with conceit and fall into
3:16 believed in throughout the world, taken **u** in glory.
5:10 as one who has brought **u** children,
6:19 thus storing **u** for themselves the treasure of
2Ti 4: 3 For the time is coming when people will not put **u**
Heb 1:12 like a cloak you will roll them **u**,
5: 7 Jesus offered **u** prayers and supplications,
6: 6 of God and are holding him **u** to contempt.
6: 7 that drinks **u** the rain falling on it repeatedly,
8: 2 and not any mortal, has set **u**.
11:17 when put to the test, offered **u** Isaac.
11:17 the promises was ready to offer **u** his only son,
11:24 By faith Moses, when he was grown **u**,
12:15 no root of bitterness springs **u** and causes trouble,
Jas 1: 9 the believer who is lowly boast in being raised **u**,
5: 3 You have laid **u** treasure for the last days.
5:15 and the Lord will raise them **u**;
Jude 1:13 casting **u** the foam of their own shame;
1:20 build yourselves **u** on your most holy faith;
Rev 2: 3 that you are enduring patiently and bearing **u** for
3: 2 Wake **u**, and strengthen what remains and is on
3: 3 If you do not wake **u**, I will come like a thief,
4: 1 to me like a trumpet, said, "Come **u** here,
6:14 The sky vanished like a scroll rolling itself **u**,
8: 7 and a third of the earth was burned **u**,
8: 7 and a third of the trees were burned **u**,
8: 7 and all green grass was burned **u**.
9:20 not repent of the works of their hands or give **u**
10: 4 "Seal **u** what the seven thunders have said,
11: 7 the beast that comes **u** from
11:12 from heaven saying to them, "Come **u** here!"
11:12 And they went **u** to heaven in a cloud
14:11 smoke of their torment goes **u** forever and ever.
16:12 and its water was dried **u** in order to prepare
17:16 they will devour her flesh and burn her **u** with fire.
18:21 Then a mighty angel took **u** a stone like
19: 3 The smoke goes **u** from her forever and ever."
20: 9 They marched **u** over the breadth of the earth
20:13 And the sea gave **u** the dead that were in it,
20:13 and Hades gave **u** the dead that were in them,
22:10 not seal **u** the words of the prophecy of this book,
Tob 1: 7 Also for six years I would save **u** a second tenth
2: 4 Then I sprang **u**, left the dinner before
3:10 When she had gone **u** to her father's upper room,
4: 9 be laying **u** a good treasure for yourself against
6: 3 Suddenly a large fish leaped **u** from the water
6: 4 So the young man grasped the fish and drew it **u**
6:18 both of you must first stand **u** and pray,
7: 1 At that Raguel jumped **u** and kissed him and wept.
8: 4 and said to Sarah, "Sister, get **u**, and let us pray
8: 5 So she got **u**, and they began to pray and implore
8:20 and you shall cheer **u** my daughter,
9: 5 So Gabael got **u** and counted out to him
9: 6 In the morning they both got **u** early and went to
9: 6 He sprang **u** and greeted Gabael,
11: 9 Then Anna ran **u** to her son and threw her arms
11:10 Then Tobit got **u** and came stumbling out through
11:10 through the courtyard door. Tobias went **u** to him,
12: 8 It is better to give alms than to lay **u** gold.
12:13 And that time when you did not hesitate to get **u**
12:20 get **u** from the ground, and acknowledge God.
12:21 Then they stood **u**, and could see him no more.
13: 2 and he brings **u** from the great abyss,
Jdt 2:22 and chariots, and went **u** into the hill country.
4: 5 and fortified the villages on them and stored **u**
5: 1 the high hilltops and set **u** barricades in the plains.
5:13 Then God dried **u** the Red Sea before them,
5:15 and took **u** residence in the land of the Amorites,
5:20 then we can go **u** and defeat them.

Jdt 5:24 and your vast army will swallow them **u.**"
6:11 from the plain they went **u** into the hill country
6:12 and all the slingers kept them from coming **u**
7: 1 the passes **u** into the hill country and make war on
7:13 we and our people will go **u** to the tops of
7:18 And the Edomites and Ammonites went **u**
7:32 they went **u** on the walls and towers of their town.
8: 5 at home where she set **u** a tent for herself on
8:12 and to set yourselves **u** in the place of God
9: 3 So you gave **u** their rulers to be killed,
9: 4 You gave **u** their wives for booty
10: 5 then she wrapped **u** all her dishes and gave them
10:23 but his slaves raised her **u.**
12: 4 your servant will not use **u** the supplies I have
12: 5 Toward the morning watch she got **u**
13: 5 the enemies who have risen **u** against us."
13: 6 She went **u** to the bedpost near Holofernes' head,
13:10 and went **u** the mountain to Bethulia,
14: 2 each of you take **u** your weapons,
14: 7 they raised him **u** he threw himself at Judith's feet,
14:13 "Wake **u** our lord, for the slaves have been so bold
14:19 and their loud cries and shouts rose **u** throughout
15:11 She took them and loaded her mules and hitched **u**
16: 2 he sets **u** his camp among his people;
16: 3 their numbers blocked **u** the wadis,
16: 4 He boasted that he would burn **u** my territory,
16:11 they lifted **u** their voices,
16:17 Woe to the nations that rise **u** against my people!
AdE 2: 7 he brought her **u** to womanhood as his own.
4: 8 being brought **u** under my care—
9:13 Also, hang **u** the bodies of Haman's ten sons."
9:14 of the city the bodies of Haman's sons to hang **u.**
Wis 2: 5 because it is sealed **u** and no one turns back.
4:10 and while living among sinners were taken **u.**
4:11 They were caught **u** so that evil might
4:20 with dread when their sins are reckoned **u,**
10:19 and cast them **u** from the depth of the sea.
11: 6 stirred **u** and defiled with blood
12:20 granting them time and opportunity to give **u**
17:12 but a giving **u** of the helps that come from reason;
17:16 thus was kept shut **u** in a prison not made of iron;
19: 4 in order that they might fill **u** the punishment
19:12 to give them relief, quails came **u** from the sea.
Sir 3: 4 like those who lay **u** treasure.
10: 4 over it he will raise **u** the right leader for the time.
10:15 The Lord plucks **u** the roots of the nations,
11:13 raises **u** their heads to the amazement of the many.
11:34 into your home and they will stir **u** trouble
12:17 pretending to help, he will trip you **u.**
14: 2 and who have not given **u** their hope.
16: 6 and in a disobedient nation wrath blazes **u.**
17:23 Afterward he will rise **u** and repay them,
20:28 Those who cultivate the soil heap **u** their harvest,
22: 2 anyone that picks it **u** will shake it off his hand.
23: 8 by them the reviler and the arrogant are tripped **u.**
23:16 of kin will never cease until the fire burns him **u.**
27:23 and with your own words he will trip you **u.**
27:25 a stone straight **u** throws it on his own head,
27:25 and a treacherous blow opens **u** many wounds.
28:24 As you lock **u** your silver and gold,
29:11 Lay **u** your treasure according to
29:12 Store **u** almsgiving in your treasury,
30: 7 Whoever spoils his son will bind **u** his wounds,
31:21 If you are overstuffed with food, get **u** to vomit,
34:20 He lifts **u** the soul and makes the eyes sparkle;
36: 3 Lift **u** your hand against foreign nations
36:27 A woman's beauty lights **u** a man's face,
38:10 Give **u** your faults and direct your hands rightly,
40: 7 At the moment he reaches safety he wakes **u,**
40:13 The wealth of the unjust will dry **u** like a river,
40:16 or river bank are plucked **u** before any grass;
40:26 Riches and strength build **u** confidence,
42: 6 and where there are many hands, lock things **u.**
43:21 the mountains and burns **u** the wilderness,
44:16 Enoch pleased the Lord and was taken **u,**
46: 9 so that he went **u** to the hill country,
46:20 lifted **u** his voice from the ground in prophecy,
47: 1 After him Nathan rose **u** to prophesy in the days
47:12 a wise son rose **u** who because of him lived
47:22 But the Lord will never give **u** his mercy,
48: 3 By the word of the Lord he shut **u** the heavens,
48: 9 You were taken **u** by a whirlwind of fire,
49: 7 to pluck **u** and ruin and destroy,
49:13 set **u** gates and bars, and rebuilt our ruined houses.
49:14 for he was taken **u** from the earth.
50:11 when he went **u** to the holy altar,
51: 9 And I sent **u** my prayer from the earth,
51:12 *He has raised **u** a horn for his people,*
Bar 2: 5 They were brought down and not raised **u,**
3:17 and who hoarded **u** silver and gold
3:29 Who has gone **u** into heaven, and taken her,
4: 8 who brought you **u,** and you grieved Jerusalem,
5: 7 be made low and the valleys filled **u,**
LtJ 6: 3 for a long time, **u** to seven generations;
6:18 so are their gods when they have been set **u** in
6:27 they themselves must pick it **u.**
6:34 They cannot set **u** a king or depose one.
6:53 For they cannot set **u** a king over a country
6:55 but the gods will be burned **u** like timbers.
Aza 1:11 For your name's sake do not give us **u** forever,
Sus 1:19 the two elders got **u** and ran to her.
1:34 Then the two elders stood **u** before the people
1:35 Through her tears she looked **u** toward Heaven,
1:45 God stirred **u** the holy spirit of
Bel 1:39 So Daniel got **u** and ate.
1Mc 1: 3 he was exalted, and his heart was lifted **u.**
1: 6 who had been brought **u** with him from youth,
1Mc 1:20 He went **u** against Israel and came to Jerusalem
1:27 Every bridegroom took **u** the lament;
1:35 they stored **u** arms and food,
1:42 and that all should give **u** their particular customs.
2:36 not answer them or hurl a stone at them or block **u**
2:58 of great zeal for the law, was taken **u** into heaven.
3:15 Once again a strong army of godless men went **u**
3:49 and the first fruits and the tithes, and they stirred **u**
4:12 the foreigners looked **u** and saw them coming
4:21 when they also saw the army of Judas drawn **u** in
4:36 let us go **u** to cleanse the sanctuary
4:37 all the army assembled and went **u** to Mount Zion.
4:38 In the courts they saw bushes sprung **u** as in
4:51 They placed the bread on the table and hung **u**
5: 5 They were shut **u** by him in their towers;
5:26 of them have been shut **u** in Bozrah and Bosor,
5:27 "and some have been shut **u** in the other towns
5:31 and that the cry of the town went **u** to Heaven,
5:33 Then he came **u** behind them in three companies,
5:47 of the town shut them out and blocked **u** the gates
5:54 they went **u** to Mount Zion with joy and gladness,
6:15 and bring him **u** to be king.
6:17 he set **u** Antiochus the king's son to reign.
6:17 Lysias had brought him **u** from boyhood;
6:48 the king's army went **u** to Jerusalem against them,
6:51 He set **u** siege towers, engines of war to throw fire
6:55 while still living had appointed to bring **u**
7:33 After these events Nicanor went **u** to Mount Zion.
7:35 then if I return safely I will burn **u** this house."
8: 5 and the others who rose **u** against them.
9: 8 "Let us get **u** and go against our enemies.
9:38 they went **u** and hid under cover of the mountain.
9:44 "Let us get **u** now and fight for our lives,
10:10 And Jonathan took **u** residence in Jerusalem
10:70 "You are the only one to rise **u** against us,
11:37 to Jonathan and put **u** in a conspicuous place on
11:39 who was bringing **u** Antiochus,
12:26 that the enemy were being drawn **u** in formation
13: 2 So he went **u** to Jerusalem,
13:14 Trypho learned that Simon had risen **u** in place
13:33 But Simon built **u** the strongholds of Judea
13:43 He made a siege engine, brought it **u** to the city,
13:45 went **u** on the wall with their clothes torn,
14:32 then Simon rose **u** and fought for his nation.
14:48 to put them **u** in a conspicuous place in
15:25 and he shut Trypho **u** and kept him from going out
15:39 to build **u** Kedron and fortify its gates,
15:41 He built **u** Kedron and stationed horsemen
16: 1 John went **u** from Gazara and reported
16: 6 Then he and his army lined **u** against them.
16:13 His heart was lifted **u;** he determined to get
16:16 Ptolemy and his men rose **u,** took their weapons,
2Mc 1:22 a great fire blazed **u,** so that all marveled.
1:32 When this was done, a flame blazed **u;**
2: 4 to the mountain where Moses had gone **u**
2: 5 then he sealed **u** the entrance.
2: 6 of those who followed him came **u** intending
3:20 And holding **u** their hands to heaven,
3:27 his men took him **u,** put him on a stretcher,
4:41 some picked **u** stones, some blocks of wood,
5: 3 troops of cavalry drawn **u,**
5: 6 but imagining that he was setting **u** trophies
6:19 went **u** to the rack of his own accord,
6:27 Therefore, by bravely giving **u** my life now,
7: 9 but the King of the universe will raise us **u** to
7:27 and brought you **u** to this point in your life,
7:34 be elated in vain and puffed **u** by uncertain hopes,
7:37 give **u** body and life for the laws of our ancestors,
8:10 Nicanor determined to make **u** for the king
9:18 he gave **u** all hope for himself and wrote to
10:15 and endeavored to keep **u** the war.
10:27 And rising from their prayer they took **u**
10:36 Others who came **u** in the same way wheeled
11: 3 to put **u** the high priesthood for sale every year.
11: 7 Maccabeus himself was the first to take **u** arms,
12:31 Then they went **u** to Jerusalem,
12:39 and his men went to take **u** the bodies of the fallen
12:43 He also took **u** a collection, man by man,
12:45 that is laid **u** for those who fall asleep in godliness,
14: 6 are keeping **u** war and stirring **u** sedition,
14:43 He courageously ran **u** on the wall,
15: 5 to take **u** arms and finish the king's business."
15:20 at hand with their army drawn **u** for battle,
15:33 to the birds and would hang **u** these rewards
1Es 1:40 King Nebuchadnezzar of Babylon came **u**
2: 2 the Lord stirred **u** the spirit of King Cyrus of
2: 5 go **u** to Jerusalem, which is in Judea,
2: 8 and all whose spirit the Lord had stirred to go **u**
2:18 the Jews who came **u** from you to us have gone
2:23 the Jews were rebels and kept setting **u** blockades
3: 3 he went to sleep, but woke **u** again.
4:16 and women brought **u** the very men who plant
4:20 A man leaves his own father, who brought him **u,**
4:47 Then King Darius got **u** and kissed him,
4:47 to him and to all who were going **u** with him
4:49 the Jews who were going **u** from his kingdom
4:50 that the Idumeans should give **u** the villages of
4:58 he lifted **u** his face to heaven toward Jerusalem,
4:63 to go **u** and build Jerusalem and the temple
5: 1 the heads of ancestral houses were chosen to go **u,**
5: 3 And he made them go **u** with them.
5: 4 These are the names of the men who went **u,**
5: 7 the Judeans who came **u** out of their sojourn
5:36 The following are those who came **u**
8: 3 This Ezra came **u** from Babylon as a scribe skilled
8: 5 There came **u** with him to Jerusalem some of
8:20 **u** to a hundred talents of silver,
1Es 8:20 and likewise **u** to a hundred cors of wheat,
8:27 and I gathered men from Israel to go **u** with me."
8:28 who went **u** with me from Babylon,
8:75 and our mistakes have mounted **u** to heaven
8:95 Rise **u** and take action, for it is your task,
8:96 Then Ezra rose **u** and made the leaders of
9: 7 Then Ezra stood **u** and said to them,
9:45 Then Ezra took **u** the book of the law in the sight
9:47 They lifted **u** their hands, and fell to the ground
Man 1: 9 not worthy to look **u** and see the height of heaven
1:10 setting **u** abominations and multiplying offenses.
1:13 be angry with me forever or store **u** evil for me;
3Mc 2: 2 puffed **u** in his audacity and power.
2:27 and he set **u** a stone on the tower in the courtyard
2:31 readily gave themselves **u,**
3:16 and went **u** to honor the temple
6: 5 the spear and was lifted **u** against your holy city,
6: 7 you brought **u** to the light unharmed.
6:32 They stopped their chanting of dirges and took **u**
2Es 2: 3 I brought you **u** with gladness;
2:15 bring them **u** with gladness, as does a dove;
2:16 And I will raise **u** the dead from their places,
3: 1 and my thoughts welled **u** in my heart,
3:23 and you raised **u** for yourself a servant,
4:10 the things with which you have grown **u;**
4:15 let us go **u** and subdue the forest of the plain so
5: 7 and the Dead Sea shall cast **u** fish;
5:14 Then I woke **u,** and my body shuddered violently,
5:36 "Count **u** for me those who have not yet come,
5:37 and bring out for me the winds shut **u** in them,
6: 4 and before the heights of the air were lifted **u,**
6: 5 and before those who stored **u** treasures
6:26 And they shall see those who were taken **u,**
6:42 six parts you dried **u** and kept so that some
6:51 that had been dried **u** on the third day, to live in it,
7:*32* The earth shall give **u** those who are asleep in it,
7:*32* and the chambers shall give **u** the souls
7:*48* For an evil heart has grown **u** in us,
7:*75* as soon as everyone of us yields **u** the soul,
7:*77* a treasure of works stored **u** with the Most High,
7:*83* the reward laid **u** for those who have trusted
7:*84* the torment laid **u** for themselves in the last days.
8: 9 womb gives **u** again what has been created in it,
8:19 the words of Ezra's prayer, before he was taken **u.**
8:23 whose look dries **u** the depths
8:33 righteous, who have many works laid **u** with you,
8:41 all that have been sown will come **u** in due season,
8:43 If the farmer's seed does not come **u,**
8:53 The root of evil is sealed **u** from you,
9:46 And I brought him **u** with much care.
9:47 when he grew **u** and I came to take a wife for him,
10: 3 I got **u** in the night and fled,
10:27 When I looked **u,** the woman was no longer visible
10:33 He said to me, "Stand **u** like a man,
10:47 And as for her telling you that she brought him **u**
11:12 As I watched, one wing on the right side rose **u,**
11:13 Then the next wing rose **u** and reigned,
11:18 Then the third wing raised itself **u,**
11:20 in due time the wings that followed also rose **u** on
11:21 and others of them rose **u,**
11:25 that these little wings planned to set themselves **u**
11:26 As I kept looking, one was set **u,**
11:43 Your insolence has come **u** before the Most High,
12: 2 over to it rose **u** and set themselves **u** to reign,
12: 3 Then I woke **u** in great perplexity of mind
12: 7 if my prayer has indeed come **u** before your face,
12:11 The eagle that you saw coming **u** from the sea is
12:23 In its last days the Most High will raise **u**
12:25 because it is they who shall sum **u** his wickedness
12:31 the lion whom you saw rousing **u** out of the forest
13: 2 wind arose from the sea and stirred **u** all its waves.
13: 3 like the figure of a man come **u** out of the heart of
13: 5 to make war against the man who came **u** out of
13: 6 and flew **u** on to it.
13:11 and burned **u** all of them,
13:13 Then I woke **u** in great terror,
13:25 As for your seeing a man come **u** from the heart of
13:32 whom you saw as a man coming **u** from the sea.
13:51 Why did I see the man coming **u** from the heart of
13:56 for there is a reward laid **u** with the Most High.
13:57 Then I got **u** and walked in the field,
14: 4 and I led him **u** on Mount Sinai,
14: 8 Lay **u** in your heart the signs
14: 9 for you shall be taken **u** from among humankind,
15:15 and nation shall rise **u** to fight against nation,
15:38 heavy storm clouds shall be stirred **u** from
16:12 the sea is churned **u** from the depths,
16:21 and then calamities shall spring **u** on the earth—
16:32 and its fields shall be plowed **u,**
16:78 It is shut off and given **u** to be consumed by fire.
4Mc 1:29 and ties **u** and waters and thoroughly irrigates,
2:14 from marauders and helps raise **u** what has fallen.
4: 4 for his service to the king and went **u** to Seleucus
4:10 and while Apollonius was going **u**
5: 4 When many persons had been rounded **u,**
6: 8 in the side to make him get **u** again after he fell.
6:18 with truth **u** to old age and having maintained
6:26 he lifted **u** his eyes to God and said,
8:19 and give **u** this vain opinion and this arrogance
9:28 flayed all his flesh **u** to his chin,
10: 2 and that I was brought **u** on the same teachings?
11: 1 after being cruelly tortured, the fifth leaped **u,**
12:12 justice has laid **u** for you intense and eternal fire
13:11 "Courage, brother," another said, "Bear **u** nobly,"
13:24 in the same virtues and brought **u** in right living,
14:12 of the seven young men bore **u** under the rackings
18: 9 when these sons had grown **u** their father died.

UPBRAID, UPBRAIDED, UPBRAIDETH (KJV) See also REPROACH, TAUNTED, UNGRUDGINGLY

UPBRAIDED (3) [UPBRAIDS]
Ge 31:36 Then Jacob became angry, and **u** Laban.
Jdg 8: 1 And they **u** him violently.
Mk 16:14 ⟦he **u** them for their lack of faith and⟧

UPBRAIDS (1) [UPBRAIDED]
Sir 20:15 He gives little and **u** much;

UPBRINGING (2)
2Ki 10: 6 who were charged with their **u.**
4Mc 16: 8 and the more grievous anxieties of your **u.**

UPBUILDING (2) [BUILD]
Ro 14:19 for peace and for mutual **u.**
1Co 14: 3 for their **u** and encouragement and consolation.

UPHARSIN (KJV) See PARSIN

UPHAZ (2)
Jer 10: 9 from Tarshish, and gold from **U.**
Da 10: 5 with a belt of gold from **U** around his waist.

UPHELD (5) [UPHOLD]
1Ki 8:20 Now the LORD has **u** the promise that he made;
Ps 41:12 But you have **u** me because of my integrity,
Pr 20:28 and his throne is **u** by righteousness.
Isa 59:16 and his righteousness **u** him.
Ro 14: 4 And they will be **u,** for the Lord is able

UPHOLD‡ (7) [UPHELD, UPHOLDER, UPHOLDS]
Dt 27:26 not **u** the words of this law by observing them."
Ps 119:116 **U** me according to your promise, that I may live,
Isa 9: 7 and **u** it with justice and with righteousness
41:10 I will **u** you with my victorious right hand.
42: 1 Here is my servant, whom I **u,** my chosen,
Jer 30:13 There is no one to **u** your cause,
Ro 3:31 On the contrary, we **u** the law.

UPHOLDER (2) [UPHOLD]
Ps 54: 4 the Lord is the **u** of my life.
Jdt 9:11 **u** of the weak, protector of the forsaken,

UPHOLDS (5) [UPHOLD]
Ps 37:17 but the LORD **u** the righteous.
63: 8 My soul clings to you; your right hand **u** me.
145:14 The LORD **u** all who are falling,
146: 9 he **u** the orphan and the widow,
2Mc 14:15 and always **u** his own heritage

UPLIFTED‡ (3) [LIFT]
Job 38:15 and their **u** arm is broken.
Ac 13:17 and with **u** arm he led them out of it.
2Es 15:11 with a mighty hand and with an **u** arm,

UPON (926) See Index of Articles Etc.

UPPER (49) [UP]
Lev 13:45 and he shall cover his **u** lip and cry out, "Unclean,
Dt 2:37 the whole **u** region of the Wadi Jabbok as well as
24: 6 No one shall take a mill or an **u** millstone
Jos 15:19 So Caleb gave her the **u** springs and
16: 5 the east was Ataroth-addar as far as **U** Beth-horon,
Jdg 1:15 So Caleb gave her **U** Gulloth and Lower Gulloth.
9:53 But a certain woman threw an **u** millstone
2Sa 11:21 not a woman throw an **u** millstone on him from
1Ki 17:19 up into the **u** chamber where he was lodging,
17:23 from the **u** chamber into the house, and gave him
2Ki 1: 2 through the lattice in his **u** chamber in Samaria,
15:35 He built the **u** gate of the house of the LORD.
18:17 they came and stood by the conduit of the **u** pool,
23:12 The altars on the roof of the **u** chamber of Ahaz,
1Ch 7:24 who built both Lower and **U** Beth-horon,
28:11 its treasuries, its **u** rooms, and its inner chambers,
2Ch 3: 9 He overlaid the **u** chambers with gold.
8: 5 also built **U** Beth-horon and Lower Beth-horon,
23:20 marching through the **u** gate to the king's house.
27: 3 He built the **u** gate of the house of the LORD,
32:30 This same Hezekiah closed the **u** outlet of
Ne 3:25 the tower projecting from the **u** house of the king
3:31 and to the **u** room of the corner.
3:32 the **u** room of the corner and the Sheep Gate
Ps 74: 5 At the **u** entrance they hacked the wooden trellis
Isa 7: 3 of the **u** pool on the highway to the Fuller's Field,
36: 2 of the **u** pool on the highway to the Fuller's Field.
Jer 20: 2 in the stocks that were in the **u** Benjamin Gate of
22:13 and his **u** rooms by injustice;
22:14 a spacious house with large **u** rooms,"
36:10 which was in the **u** court,
Eze 9: 2 six men came from the direction of the **u** gate,
24:17 not cover your **u** lip or eat the bread of mourners.
24:22 not cover your **u** lip or eat the bread of mourners.
42: 5 Now the **u** chambers were narrower,
42: 6 for this reason the **u** chambers were set back from
Da 6:10 which had windows in its **u** room open
Am 9: 6 who builds his **u** chambers in the heavens,
Tob 1: 2 to the south of Kedesh Naphtali in **U** Galilee,
3:10 When she had gone up to her father's **u** room,
3:17 of Raguel came down from her **u** room.
Jdt 1: 8 and **U** Galilee and the great plain of Esdraelon,
2:21 near the mountain that is to the north of **U** Cilicia.
1Mc 2:48 and they never let the sinner gain the **u** hand.
3:37 and went through the **u** provinces.
6: 1 the **u** provinces when he heard that Elymais
2Mc 9:23 when he made expeditions into the **u** country,
9:25 of you when I hurried off to the **u** provinces;
2Es 8:20 whose eyes are exalted and whose **u** chambers are

UPPERMOST (2) [UP]
Ge 40:17 in the **u** basket there were all sorts of baked food
Eze 41: 7 One ascended from the bottom story to the **u** story

UPPERMOST (KJV) See also BEST, HIGHEST, HONOR

UPRIGHT‡ (70) [UPRIGHTLY, UPRIGHTNESS]
Ge 37: 7 Suddenly my sheaf rose and stood **u;**
Ex 26:15 You shall make **u** frames of acacia wood for
36:20 the **u** frames for the tabernacle of acacia wood.
Nu 23:10 Let me die the death of the **u,**
Dt 32: 4 A faithful God, without deceit, just and **u** is he;
Job 1: 1 That man was blameless and **u,**
1: 8 and **u** man who fears God and turns away
2: 3 and **u** man who fears God and turns away
4: 7 Or where were the **u** cut off?
8: 6 if you are pure and **u,**
17: 8 The **u** are appalled at this,
23: 7 There an **u** person could reason with him,
33:23 one of a thousand, one who declares a person **u,**
Ps 7:10 God is my shield, who saves the **u** in heart.
11: 2 to shoot in the dark at the **u** in heart.
11: 7 the **u** shall behold his face.
20: 8 but we shall rise and stand **u.**
25: 8 Good and **u** is the LORD;
32:11 O righteous, and shout for joy, all you **u** in heart.
33: 1 Praise befits the **u.**
33: 4 For the word of the LORD is **u,**
36:10 and your salvation to the **u** of heart!
37:37 Mark the blameless, and behold the **u,**
64:10 Let all the **u** in heart glory.
73: 1 Truly God is good to the **u,**
78:72 With **u** heart he tended them,
92:15 showing that the LORD is **u;**
94:15 and all the **u** in heart will follow it.
97:11 and joy for the **u** in heart.
107:42 The **u** see it and are glad;
111: 1 in the company of the **u,** in the congregation.
112: 2 the generation of the **u** will be blessed.
112: 4 They rise in the darkness as a light for the **u;**
119: 7 I will praise you with an **u** heart,
125: 4 and to those who are **u** in their hearts.
140:13 the **u** shall live in your presence.
Pr 2: 7 he stores up sound wisdom for the **u;**
2:21 For the **u** will abide in the land,
3:32 but the **u** are in his confidence.
10:29 The way of the LORD is a stronghold for the **u,**
11: 3 The integrity of the **u** guides them,
11: 6 The righteousness of the **u** saves them,
11:11 By the blessing of the **u** a city is exalted,
12: 6 but the speech of the **u** delivers them.
13: 6 Righteousness guards one whose way is **u,**
14: 9 but the **u** enjoy God's favor.
14:11 but the tent of the **u** flourishes.
15: 8 but the prayer of the **u** is his delight.
15:19 but the path of the **u** is a level highway.
16:17 The highway of the **u** avoids evil;
21:18 and the faithless for the **u.**
21:29 but the **u** give thought to their ways.
28:10 Those who mislead the **u** into evil ways will fall
29:10 and they seek the life of the **u.**
29:27 but the **u** are an abomination to the wicked.
Hos 14: 9 and the **u** walk in them,
Mic 7: 2 and there is no one left who is **u;**
7: 4 the most **u** of them a thorn hedge.
Ac 10:22 a centurion, an **u** and God-fearing man,
14:10 in a loud voice, "Stand **u** on your feet."
1Th 2:10 You are witnesses, and God also, how pure, **u,**
Tit 1: 8 a lover of goodness, prudent, **u,** devout,
2:12 to live lives that are self-controlled, **u,**
Tob 7: 7 "O most miserable of calamities that such an **u**
9: 6 of a father good and noble, **u** and generous!
LtJ 6:27 If anyone sets it **u,** it cannot move itself;
6:73 Better, therefore, is someone **u** who has no idols;
1Es 1:23 the deeds of Josiah were **u** in the sight of the Lord,
3Mc 3: 5 of life with the good deeds of **u** people,
4Mc 6: 7 he kept his reason **u** and unswerving.

UPRIGHTLY (7) [UPRIGHT]
Ps 37:14 to kill those who walk **u;**
84:11 the LORD withhold from those who walk **u.**
Pr 14: 2 Those who walk **u** fear the LORD,
Isa 33:15 Those who walk righteously and speak **u,**
57: 2 those who walk **u** will rest on their couches.
Mic 2: 7 Do not my words do good to one who walks **u?**
Tob 4: 5 Live **u** all the days of your life,

UPRIGHTNESS (16) [UPRIGHT]
Dt 9: 5 It is not because of your righteousness or the **u**
1Ki 3: 6 in righteousness, and in **u** of heart toward you;
9: 4 with integrity of heart and **u,**
1Ch 29:17 that you search the heart, and take pleasure in **u;**
29:17 the **u** of my heart I have freely offered all these
Job 33: 3 My words declare the **u** of my heart,
Ps 25:21 May integrity and **u** preserve me,
111: 8 to be performed with faithfulness and **u.**
Pr 2:13 who forsake the paths of **u** to walk in the ways
4:11 I have led you in the paths of **u.**
Isa 26:10 the land of **u** they deal perversely and do not see
59:14 in the public square, and **u** cannot enter.
Jer 4: 2 in truth, in justice, and in **u,**
Mal 2: 6 He walked with me in integrity and **u,**
Wis 9: 3 and pronounce judgment in **u** of soul,
2Es 6:32 for the Mighty One has seen your **u** and has

UPRISING (1) [UPRISINGS]
2Es 16:70 and in neighboring cities there shall be a great **u**

UPRISINGS (1) [UPRISING]
1Es 5:73 by plots and demagoguery and **u** they prevented

UPROAR (13)
1Sa 4:14 he said, "What is this **u?**"
1Ki 1:41 he said, "Why is the city in an **u?**"
1:45 so that the city is in an **u.**
Ps 46: 6 The nations are in an **u,** the kingdoms totter;
74:23 the **u** of your adversaries that goes up continually.
Isa 13: 4 Listen, an **u** of kingdoms,
66: 6 Listen, an **u** from the city!
Am 2: 2 and Moab shall die amid **u,**
Ac 17: 5 a mob and set the city in an **u.**
20: 1 After the **u** had ceased, Paul sent for the disciples;
21:31 of the cohort that all Jerusalem was in an **u.**
21:34 as he could not learn the facts because of the **u,**
3Mc 1:28 of the crowds resulted in an immense **u;**

UPROOT (5) [UPROOTED, UPROOTS]
Ps 52: 5 he will **u** you from the land of the living.
Jer 12:17 then I will completely **u** it and destroy it,
Mic 5:14 and I will **u** your sacred poles from among you
Mt 13:29 for in gathering the weeds you would **u** the wheat
4Mc 3: 5 not **u** the emotions but is their antagonist.

UPROOTED‡ (9) [UPROOT]
Dt 29:28 The LORD **u** them from their land in anger, fury,
Job 19:10 and I am gone, he has **u** my hope like a tree.
Jer 31:40 It shall never again be **u** or overthrown.
Da 11: 4 be **u** and go to others besides these.
Zep 2: 4 be driven out at noon, and Ekron shall be **u.**
Mt 15:13 that my heavenly Father has not planted will be **u.**
Lk 17: 6 'Be **u** and planted in the sea,'
Jude 1:12 autumn trees without fruit, twice dead, **u;**
Wis 4: 4 and by the violence of the winds they will be **u.**

UPROOTS (1) [UPROOT]
Sir 3: 9 but a mother's curse **u** their foundations.

UPSET‡ (1) [UPSETTING]
Tob 9: 4 if I delay even one day I will **u** him very much.

UPSETTING (2) [UPSET]
2Ti 2:18 They are **u** the faith of some.
Tit 1:11 since they are **u** whole families by teaching

UPSIDE (4)
Jdg 7:13 it turned **u** down, and the tent collapsed."
2Ki 21:13 wiping it and turning it **u** down.
Isa 29:16 You turn things **u** down!
Ac 17: 6 "These people who have been turning the world **u**

UPSTAIRS (7)
Mk 14:15 He will show you a large room **u,**
Lk 22:12 He will show you a large room **u,**
Ac 1:13 they went to the room **u** where they were staying,
9:37 they had washed her, they laid her in a room **u.**
9:39 and when he arrived, they took him to the room **u.**
20: 8 in the room **u** where we were meeting.
20:11 Then Paul went **u,** and after he had broken bread

UPSTREAM (2)
Da 12: 6 in linen, who was **u,** "How long shall it be until
12: 7 The man clothed in linen, who was **u,**

UPWARD‡ (47) [UP]
Ex 30:14 from twenty years old and **u,**
38:26 from twenty years old and **u,**
Nu 1: 3 from twenty years old and **u,**
1:18 the number of names from twenty years old and **u,**
1:20 every male from twenty years old and **u,**
1:22 every male from twenty years old and **u,**
1:24 from twenty years old and **u,**
1:26 from twenty years old and **u,**
1:28 from twenty years old and **u,**
1:30 from twenty years old and **u,**
1:32 from twenty years old and **u,**
1:34 from twenty years old and **u,**
1:36 from twenty years old and **u,**
1:38 from twenty years old and **u,**
1:40 from twenty years old and **u,**
1:42 from twenty years old and **u,**

Nu 1:45 from twenty years old and **u**,
3:15 from a month old and **u**,
3:22 counting all the males from a month old and **u**,
3:28 Counting all the males, from a month old and **u**,
3:34 counting all the males from a month old and **u**,
3:39 all the males from a month old and **u**,
3:40 from a month old and **u**, and count their names.
3:43 all the firstborn males from a month old and **u**,
8:24 and **u** they shall begin to do duty in the service of
14:29 from twenty years old and **u**,
26: 2 from twenty years old and **u**,
26: 4 from twenty years old and **u**,"
32:11 from twenty years old and **u**,
Jdg 1:36 from the ascent of Akrabbim, from Sela and **u**.
2Ki 19:30 shall again take root downward, and bear fruit **u**;
1Ch 23: 3 The Levites, thirty years old and **u**, were counted,
23:24 and **u** who were to do the work for the service of
23:27 of the Levites from twenty years old and **u**—
2Ch 25: 5 He mustered those twenty years old and **u**,
Ezr 3: 8 from twenty years old and **u**,
Job 5: 7 to trouble just as sparks fly **u**.
Pr 15:24 For the wise the path of life leads **u**,
Ecc 3:21 Who knows whether the human spirit goes **u** and
Isa 8:21 They will turn their faces **u**,
9:18 and they swirled **u** in a column of smoke.
37:31 shall again take root downward, and bear fruit **u**;
38:14 My eyes are weary with looking **u**.
Eze 1:27 **U** from what appeared like
43:15 and from the altar hearth projecting **u**, four horns.
Jn 11:41 And Jesus looked **u** and said, "Father,
2Es 6:41 so that one part might move **u** and

UPWARDS (2) [UP]

2Ch 31:16 males from three years old and **u**,
31:17 of the Levites from twenty years old and **u** was

UR (5)

Ge 11:28 in the land of his birth, in **U** of the Chaldeans.
11:31 from **U** of the Chaldeans to go into the land
15: 7 "I am the LORD who brought you from **U** of
1Ch 11:35 of Sachar the Hararite, Eliphal son of **U**,
Ne 9: 7 and brought him out of **U** of the Chaldeans

URBANE (KJV) See URBANUS

URBANUS (1)

Ro 16: 9 Greet **U**, our co-worker in Christ,

URGE (26) [URGED, URGENT, URGENTLY, URGES, URGING]

2Ki 4:24 and said to her servant, "**U** the animal on;
Job 20: 2 My thoughts **u** me to answer,
Ac 27:22 I **u** you now to keep up your courage,
27:34 Therefore I **u** you to take some food,
Ro 16:17 I **u** you, brothers and sisters,
1Co 16:16 I **u** you to put yourselves at the service
2Co 2: 8 So I **u** you to reaffirm your love for him.
6: 1 we **u** you also not to accept the grace of God
8: 6 so that we might **u** Titus that,
9: 5 So I thought it necessary to **u** the brothers to go on
Php 4: 2 I **u** Euodia and I **u** Syntyche to be of the same
1Th 4: 1 we ask and **u** you in the Lord Jesus that,
4:10 But we **u** you, beloved, to do so more and more,
5:14 And we **u** you, beloved, to admonish the idlers,
1Ti 1: 3 I **u** you, as I did when I was on my way
2: 1 First of all, then, I **u** that supplications, prayers,
6: 2 Teach and **u** these duties.
2Ti 4: 1 and his kingdom, I solemnly **u** you:
Tit 2: 6 Likewise, **u** the younger men to be self-controlled.
Heb 13:19 I **u** you all the more to do this,
1Pe 2:11 I **u** you as aliens and exiles to abstain from
Jdt 15: 4 to tell what had taken place and to **u** all to rush out
2Mc 6:12 Now I **u** those who read this book not to
9:26 I therefore **u** and beg you to remember the public
4Mc 2: 4 to rule over the frenzied **u** of sexual desire,

URGED‡ (39) [URGE]

Ge 19: 3 But he **u** them strongly;
19:15 When morning dawned, the angels **u** Lot, saying,
33:11 So he **u** him, and he took it.
Ex 12:33 The Egyptians **u** the people
Jos 15:18 she **u** him to ask her father for a field.
Jdg 1:14 she **u** him to ask her father for a field.
1Sa 24:10 and some **u** me to kill you, but I spared you.
28:23 But his servants, together with the woman, **u** him;
1Ki 21:25 **u** on by his wife Jezebel.
2Ki 2:17 But when they **u** him until he was ashamed,
4: 8 who **u** him to have a meal.
5:16 He **u** him to accept, but he refused.
5:23 He **u** him, and tied up two talents of silver
Est 8:14 hurried out, **u** by the king's command.
Jer 36:25 Even when Elnathan and Delaiah and Gemariah **u**
Mt 15:23 And his disciples came and **u** him, saying,
Lk 24:29 But they **u** him strongly, saying, "Stay with us,
Ac 13:42 the people **u** them to speak
13:43 who spoke to them and **u** them to continue in
16:15 she and her household were baptized, she **u** us,
21:12 the people there **u** him not to go up to Jerusalem.
27:33 Paul **u** all of them to take some food, saying,
1Co 16:12 I strongly **u** him to visit you with
2Co 12:18 I **u** Titus to go, and sent the brother with him.
1Mc 11:40 insistently **u** him to hand Antiochus over to him,
2Mc 4:34 taking Andronicus aside, **u** him to kill Onias.
6:21 and privately **u** him to bring meat
7:25 the mother to him and **u** her to advise the youth
11: 7 and he **u** the others to risk their lives with him
11:15 agreed to all that Lysias **u**.
13: 3 and with utter hypocrisy **u** Antiochus on,
14:25 He **u** him to marry and have children;
3Mc 5:17 When this was done he **u** them to give themselves
5:36 reconvened the party in the same manner and **u**
5:46 and **u** the king on to the matter at hand.
4Mc 5:14 tyrant **u** him in this fashion to eat meat unlawfully,
10: 1 and many repeatedly **u** him to save himself
15:12 and all of them together the mother **u** on to death
16:13 and **u** them on to death for the sake of religion.

URGENT (4) [URGE]

Ex 5:13 The taskmasters were **u**, saying,
Da 2:15 "Why is the decree of the king so **u**?"
3:22 the king's command was **u** and the furnace was
Tit 3:14 to good works in order to meet **u** needs,

URGENTLY (4) [URGE]

Jer 26: 5 my servants the prophets whom I send to you **u**—
Lk 23:23 But they kept **u** demanding with loud shouts
1Mc 6:57 and the affairs of the kingdom press **u** on us.
2Mc 10:19 for places where he was more **u** needed.

URGES (2) [URGE]

Pr 16:26 works for them; their hunger **u** them on.
2Co 5:14 For the love of Christ **u** us on,

URGING (9) [URGE]

Jdg 19: 7 his father-in-law kept **u** him until he spent
2Sa 12:17 **u** him to rise from the ground;
Jn 4:31 Meanwhile the disciples were **u** him, "Rabbi,
Ac 19:31 a message **u** him not to venture into the theater.
1Th 2:12 **u** and encouraging you and pleading that you lead
1Mc 13:21 the citadel kept sending envoys to Trypho **u** him
2Mc 7:26 After much **u** on his part,
1Es 1:27 The Lord is with me, **u** me on!
3Mc 7: 3 frequently **u** us with malicious intent,

URI (8)

Ex 31: 2 by name Bezalel son of **U** son of Hur, of the tribe
35:30 by name Bezalel son of **U** son of Hur, of the tribe
38:22 Bezalel son of **U** son of Hur, of the tribe of Judah,
1Ki 4:19 Geber son of **U**, in the land of Gilead, the country
1Ch 2:20 Hur became the father of **U**, and **U** became the father of Bezalel.
2Ch 1: 5 Moreover the bronze altar that Bezalel son of **U**,
Ezr 10:24 Of the gatekeepers: Shallum, Telem, and **U**.

URIAH (40) [URIAH'S]

2Sa 11: 3 the wife of **U** the Hittite."
11: 6 David sent word to Joab, "Send me **U** the Hittite."
11: 6 And Joab sent **U** to David.
11: 7 When **U** came to him, David asked how Joab and
11: 8 Then David said to **U**, "Go down to your house,
11: 8 **U** went out of the king's house,
11: 9 But **U** slept at the entrance of the king's house
11:10 told David, "**U** did not go down to his house,"
11:10 David said to **U**, "You have just come from
11:11 **U** said to David, "The ark and Israel
11:12 Then David said to **U**, "Remain here today also,
11:12 So **U** remained in Jerusalem that day.
11:14 and sent it by the hand of **U**.
11:15 "Set **U** in the forefront of the hardest fighting,
11:16 he assigned **U** to the place
11:17 **U** the Hittite was killed as well.
11:21 'Your servant **U** the Hittite is dead too.' "
11:24 and your servant **U** the Hittite is dead also."
11:26 the wife of **U** heard that her husband was dead,
12: 9 You have struck down **U** the Hittite with
12:10 and have taken the wife of **U** the Hittite to
23:39 **U** the Hittite—thirty-seven in all.
1Ki 15: 5 except in the matter of **U** the Hittite.
2Ki 16:10 King Ahaz sent to the priest **U** a model of
16:11 The priest **U** built the altar;
16:11 just so did the priest **U** build it,
16:15 King Ahaz commanded the priest **U**, saying,
16:16 The priest **U** did everything
1Ch 11:41 **U** the Hittite, Zabad son of Ahlai,
Ezr 8:33 into the hands of the priest Meremoth son of **U**,
Ne 3: 4 Next to them Meremoth son of **U** son
3:21 of **U** son of Hakkoz repaired another section from
8: 4 beside him stood Mattithiah, Shema, Anaiah, **U**,
Isa 8: 2 the priest **U** and Zechariah son of Jeberechiah.
Jer 26:20 **U** son of Shemaiah from Kiriath-jearim.
26:21 but when **U** heard of it,
26:23 and they took **U** from Egypt and brought him
Mt 1: 6 the father of Solomon by the wife of **U**,
1Es 8:62 of our Lord to the priest Meremoth son of **U**;
9:43 **U**, Hezekiah, and Baalsamus on his right,

URIAH'S (1) [URIAH]

2Sa 12:15 LORD struck the child that **U** wife bore to David,

URIAS, URIJAH (KJV) See URIAH

URIEL (7)

1Ch 6:24 **U** his son, Uzziah his son, and Shaul his son.
15: 5 **U** the chief, with one hundred twenty
15:11 and the Levites **U**, Asaiah, Joel, Shemaiah, Eliel,
2Ch 13: 2 His mother's name was Micaiah daughter of **U**
2Es 4: 1 that had been sent to me, whose name was **U**,
5:20 as the angel **U** had commanded me.
10:28 "Where is the angel **U**, who came to me

URIM (10)

Ex 28:30 In the breastpiece of judgment you shall put the **U**
Lev 8: 8 in the breastpiece he put the **U** and the Thummim.
Nu 27:21 who shall inquire for him by the decision of the **U**
Dt 33: 8 and your **U** to your loyal one,
1Sa 14:41 O LORD God of Israel, give **U**;
28: 6 not by dreams, or by **U**, or by prophets.
Ezr 2:63 until there should be a priest to consult **U**
Ne 7:65 until a priest with **U** and Thummim should come.
Sir 45:10 with the oracle of judgment, **U** and Thummim;
1Es 5:40 until a high priest should appear wearing **U**

URINE (2)

2Ki 18:27 to eat their own dung and to drink their own **u**?"
Isa 36:12 to eat their own dung and drink their own **u**?"

URN (1)

Heb 9: 4 in which there were a golden **u** holding the manna,

US (1926) [WE] See Index of Articles Etc.

USE‡ (78) [USED, USEFUL, USEFULNESS, USELESS, USES, USING]

Ge 25:32 of what **u** is a birthright to me?"
44: 5 Does he not indeed **u** it for divination?
Ex 10:26 to **u** to worship the LORD until we arrive there."
20: 7 You shall not make wrongful **u** of the name of
20:25 for if you **u** a chisel upon it you profane it.
22:27 for it may be your neighbor's only clothing to **u**
27:19 All the utensils of the tabernacle for every **u**,
28: 5 they shall **u** gold, blue, purple, and crimson yarns,
30:38 Whoever makes any like it to **u** as perfume shall
35:24 and everyone who possessed acacia wood of any **u**
35:26 to **u** their skill spun the goats' hair.
Lev 7:24 or was torn by wild animals may be put to any **u**,
13:51 or in the skin, whatever be the **u** of the skin,
Nu 10: 2 you shall **u** them for summoning the congregation,
Dt 5:11 You shall not make wrongful **u** of the name of
20:20 for **u** in building siegeworks against the town
2Sa 7:14 I will punish him with a rod such as mortals **u**,
2Ki 16:18 for **u** on the sabbath that had been built inside
22: 6 and let them **u** it to buy timber and quarried stone
1Ch 28:15 according to the **u** of each in the service,
Job 22: 2 "Can a mortal be of **u** to God?
32:21 not show partiality to any person or **u** flattery
Ps 102: 8 those who deride me **u** my name for a curse.
104:14 and plants for people to **u**,
Pr 18:23 The poor **u** entreaties, but the rich answer roughly.
Ecc 2: 2 "It is mad," and of pleasure, "What **u** is it?"
Isa 22: 3 they were captured without the **u** of a bow.
65:15 to **u** as a curse, and the Lord GOD will put you
Jer 2:22 you wash yourself with lye and **u** much soap,
6:20 Of what **u** to me is frankincense that comes
18:12 But they say, "It is no **u**!
23:31 who **u** their own tongues and say,
31:23 Once more they shall **u** these words in the land
Eze 5: 1 **u** it as a barber's razor and run it over your head
12:23 and they shall **u** it no more as a proverb in Israel."
16:44 everyone who uses proverbs will **u** this proverb
21:21 at the fork in the two roads, to **u** divination;
48:15 shall be for ordinary **u** for the city,
Hab 2:18 What **u** is an idol once its maker has shaped it—
Zec 14:21 that all who sacrifice may come and **u** them to boil
Mk 4:30 or what parable will we **u** for it?
Ac 14: 8 a man sitting who could not **u** his feet
19:13 Then some itinerant Jewish exorcists tried to **u**
Ro 3:13 they **u** their tongues to deceive."
9:21 for special **u** and another for ordinary **u**?
1Co 7:21 make **u** of your present condition
9:12 Nevertheless, we have not made **u** of this right,
9:15 But I have made no **u** of any of these rights,
9:18 so as not to make full **u** of my rights in the gospel.
Gal 5:13 only do not **u** your freedom as an opportunity
Col 2:22 to things that perish with **u**;
2Ti 2:20 some for special **u**, some for ordinary.
1Pe 2:16 yet do not **u** your freedom as a pretext for evil.
2Jn 1:12 I would rather not **u** paper and ink;
Rev 14:15 on the cloud, "**U** your sickle and reap, for the hour
14:18 "**U** your sharp sickle and gather the clusters of
Jdt 11:12 to kill their livestock and have determined to **u** all
12: 4 your servant will not **u** up the supplies I have
12:15 from Bagoas for her daily **u** in reclining.
Wis 2: 6 and make **u** of the creation to the full as in youth.
4: 3 the prolific brood of the ungodly will be of no **u**,
15: 7 the **u** of each of them the worker in clay decides.
15:15 these have neither the **u** of their eyes to see with,
15:15 and their feet are of no **u** for walking.
Sir 13: 4 A rich person will exploit you if you can be of **u**
14: 3 and of what **u** is wealth to a miser?
18: 8 What are human beings, and of what **u** are they?
26:10 when she finds liberty, she will make **u** of it.
30:19 Of what **u** to an idol is a sacrifice?
36: 4 so **u** them to show your glory to us.
LtJ 6:28 the sacrifices that are offered to these gods and **u**
1Mc 11:20 and he built many engines of war to **u** against it.
2Mc 4:19 however, thought best not to **u** it for sacrifice,
6:21 to **u**, and to pretend that he was eating the flesh of
1Es 6:30 daily **u** as the priests in Jerusalem may indicate,
8:17 the Lord that are given you for the **u** of the temple

4Mc 13:13 and let us **u** our bodies as a bulwark for the law.

USED‡ (91) [USE]

Ge 40:13 just as you **u** to do when you were his cupbearer.
Ex 25:27 the poles **u** for carrying the table shall be close to
30:32 not be **u** in any ordinary anointing of the body,
33: 7 Now Moses **u** to take the tent and pitch it outside
33:11 Thus the LORD **u** to speak to Moses face to face,
35:21 and brought the LORD's offering to be **u** for
37:14 the poles **u** for carrying the table were close to
38:24 All the gold that was **u** for the work,
Lev 11:32 any article that is **u** for any purpose;
Nu 4:12 of the service that are **u** in the sanctuary,
4:14 which are **u** for the service there, the firepans,
7: 5 that they may be **u** in doing the service of the tent
11: 5 We remember the fish we **u** to eat in Egypt
Dt 3:13 all that portion of Bashan **u** to be called a land
27: 5 of stones on which you have not **u** an iron tool.
Jos 8:31 on which no iron tool has been **u";**
Jdg 1: 7 with their thumbs and big toes cut off **u** to pick
4: 5 She **u** to sit under the palm of Deborah
16:11 they bind me with new ropes that have not been **u,**
1Sa 1: 3 Now this man **u** to go up year by year
1: 6 Her rival **u** to provoke her severely, to irritate her,
1: 7 to the house of the LORD, she **u** to provoke her.
2:19 His mother **u** to make for him a little robe
17:34 "Your servant **u** to keep sheep for his father;
17:39 for he was not **u** to them.
17:39 for I am not **u** to them."
2Sa 12: 3 it **u** to eat of his meager fare,
14:26 of his head (for at the end of every year he **u** to cut
15: 2 Absalom **u** to rise early and stand beside the road
17:17 a servant-girl **u** to go and tell them,
20:18 Then she said, "They **u** to say in the old days,
1Ki 3: 4 Solomon **u** to offer a thousand burnt offerings on
9:25 a year Solomon **u** to offer up burnt offerings
10:22 of ships of Tarshish **u** to come bringing gold,
2Ki 3: 4 who **u** to deliver to the king
3:11 who **u** to pour water on the hands of Elijah,
13:20 of Moabites **u** to invade the land in the spring of
17:17 they **u** divination and augury;
25:14 and all the bronze vessels **u** in the temple service,
2Ch 4: 6 to rinse what was **u** for the burnt offering.
9:21 the ships of Tarshish **u** to come bringing gold,
24: 7 even **u** all the dedicated things of the house of
Job 1: 4 His sons **u** to go and hold feasts
18:19 and no survivor where they **u** to live.
Ecc 2:19 for which I toiled and **u** my wisdom under the sun.
8:10 they **u** to go in and out of the holy place,
Isa 7:23 On that day every place where there **u** to be
7:25 and as for all the hills that **u** to be hoed with a hoe,
44:15 Then it can be **u** as fuel.
Jer 29:22 And on account of them this curse shall be **u** by all
44:17 **u** to do in the towns of Judah and in the streets
44:17 We **u** to have plenty of food, and prospered,
46:11 In vain you have **u** many medicines;
52:18 all the vessels of bronze **u** in the temple service.
Eze 15: 5 When it was whole it was **u** for nothing;
15: 5 can it ever be **u** for anything!
18: 3 this proverb shall no more be **u** by you in Israel.
19:14 This is a lamentation, and it is **u** as a lamentation.
Hos 2: 8 upon her silver and gold that they **u** for Baal.
Mic 1: 7 as the wages of a prostitute they shall again be **u.**
Mt 22:19 Show me the coin **u** for the tax."
27: 7 they **u** them to buy the potter's field as a place
Mk 15: 6 at the festival he **u** to release a prisoner for them,
15:41 These **u** to follow him and provided for him
Jn 9: 8 "Is this not the man who **u** to sit and beg?"
10: 6 Jesus **u** this figure of speech with them,
12: 6 the common purse and **u** to steal what was put
21:18 you **u** to fasten your own belt and
Ac 3:10 and they recognized him as the one who **u** to sit
7:51 just as your ancestors **u** to do.
24:26 and for that reason he **u** to send for him very often
1Co 6:11 And this is what some of you **u** to be.
Gal 2:12 he **u** to eat with the Gentiles.
Heb 9:21 with the blood both the tent and all the vessels **u**
1Pe 3: 5 in God **u** to adorn themselves by accepting
Tob 1:13 and I **u** to buy everything he needed.
1:14 Until his death I **u** to go into Media,
2:12 She **u** to send what she made to the owners
5:14 and they **u** to go with me to Jerusalem
Jdt 10: 3 and dressed herself in the festive attire that she **u**
AdE 3: 2 all who were at court **u** to do obeisance to Haman,
Sir 36: 4 As you have **u** us to show your holiness to them,
Sus 1: 4 the Jews **u** to come to him because he was
1: 8 Every day the two elders **u** to see her,
Bel 1:13 through which they **u** to go in regularly
1:21 the secret doors through which they **u** to enter
1Mc 3:12 and **u** it in battle the rest of his life.
3:30 before for his expenses and for the gifts that he **u**
14:36 from which they **u** to sally forth and defile
3Mc 4:20 and proved that both the paper and the pens they **u**
4Mc 8:16 what arguments might have been **u** if some

USEFUL (12) [USE]

Eze 15: 4 the middle of it is charred, is it **u** for anything?
Eph 4:29 but only what is **u** for building up, as there is need,
2Ti 2:21 dedicated and **u** to the owner of the house,
3:16 All scripture is inspired by God and is **u**
4:11 for he is **u** in my ministry.
Phm 1:11 but now he is indeed **u** both to you and to me.
Heb 6: 7 a crop **u** to those for whom it is cultivated,
Tob 4:18 and do not despise any **u** counsel.
6: 5 For its gall, heart, and liver are **u** as medicine."
Wis 13:11 then with pleasing workmanship make a **u** vessel
13:13 a cast-off piece from among them, **u** for nothing,
2Mc 12:12 that they might indeed be **u** in many ways, agreed

USEFULNESS (1) [USE]

3Mc 5:32 from our nurture in common and your **u."**

USELESS (14) [USE]

1Sa 12:21 not turn aside after **u** things that cannot profit or save, for they are **u.**
Isa 57:10 but you did not say, "It is **u."**
Hos 8: 8 now they are among the nations as a **u** vessel.
Jn 6:63 It is the spirit that gives life; the flesh is **u.**
Phm 1:11 Formerly he was **u** to you,
Wis 1:11 Beware then of **u** grumbling,
2:11 for what is weak proves itself to be **u.**
3:11 their labors are unprofitable, and their works are **u.**
4: 5 and their fruit will be **u,** not ripe enough to eat,
13:10 or a **u** stone, the work of an ancient hand.
Sir 37:19 and yet be **u** to themselves.
LtJ 6:17 For just as someone's dish is **u** when it is broken,
3Mc 3:29 and shall become **u** for all time

USES (6) [USE]

2Sa 23: 7 to touch them one **u** an iron bar or the shaft of
Eze 16:44 everyone who **u** proverbs will use this proverb
2Th 2: 9 who **u** all power, signs, lying wonders,
1Ti 1: 8 that the law is good, if one **u** it legitimately.
Wis 15: 7 vessels that serve clean **u** and those for contrary **u,**

USHERED (1)

2Mc 4:22 and **u** in with a blaze of torches and with shouts.

USING (8) [USE]

Ge 31:15 and he has been **u** up the money given for us.
1Ki 19:21 **u** the equipment from the oxen,
Mk 16:17 ⟦by **u** my name they will cast out demons;⟧
2Co 13:10 I may not have to be severe in **u** the authority that
Rev 21:17 by human measurement, which the angel was **u.**
Sir 23:15 **u** abusive language will never become disciplined
1Mc 1:58 They kept **u** violence against Israel,
2Es 14:42 **u** characters that they did not know.

USUAL (6) [USUALLY]

Mt 20: 2 agreeing with the laborers for the **u** daily wage,
20: 9 each of them received the **u** daily wage.
20:10 but each of them also received the **u** daily wage.
20:13 did you not agree with me for the **u** daily wage?
Lk 2:42 they went up as **u** for the festival.
Bel 1:15 During the night the priests came as **u,**

USUALLY (2) [USUAL]

Dt 2:11 they are **u** reckoned as Rephaim,
2:20 (It also is **u** reckoned as a land of Rephaim.

USURER (KJV) See CREDITOR

USURP (KJV) See HAVE

UTENSIL (1) [UTENSILS]

LtJ 6:59 or a household **u** that serves its owner's need,

UTENSILS (45) [UTENSIL]

Ex 25:39 and all these **u,** shall be made from a talent
27: 3 you shall make all its **u** of bronze.
27:19 All the **u** of the tabernacle for every use,
30:27 table and all its **u,** and the lampstand and its **u,**
30:28 and the altar of burnt offering with all its **u,** and
31: 8 and its **u,** and the pure lampstand with all its **u,**
31: 9 and the altar of burnt offering with all its **u,**
35:13 the table with its poles and all its **u,** and the bread
35:14 with its **u** and its lamps, and the oil for the light;
35:16 with its grating of bronze, its poles, and all its **u,**
37:24 He made it and all its **u** of a talent of pure gold.
38: 3 He made all the **u** of the altar, the pots,
38: 3 all its **u** he made of bronze.
38:30 the bronze grating for it and all the **u** of the altar,
39:33 the tent and all its **u,** its hooks, its frames, its bars,
39:36 table with all its **u,** and the bread of the Presence;
39:37 with its lamps set on it and all its **u,** and the oil for
39:39 and its grating of bronze, its poles, and all its **u;**
39:40 and all the **u** for the service of the tabernacle,
40:10 also anoint the altar of burnt offering and all its **u,**
Lev 8:11 and anointed the altar and all its **u,**
Nu 4:10 and they shall put it with all its **u** in a covering
4:12 the **u** of the service that are used in the sanctuary,
4:14 on it all the **u** of the altar, which are used for
4:14 the shovels, and the basins, all the **u** of the altar;
4:16 in the sanctuary and in its **u.**
7: 1 and consecrated the altar with all its **u,**
18: 3 not approach either the **u** of the sanctuary or
Dt 23:13 With your **u** you shall have a trowel;
1Ki 15:15 and his own votive gifts—silver, gold, and **u.**
1Ch 9:28 Some of them had charge of the **u** of service,
9:29 and over all the holy **u,** also over the choice flour,
2Ch 15:18 and his own votive gifts—silver, gold, and **u.**
24:14 with it were made **u** for the house of the LORD,
24:14 **u** for the service and for the burnt offerings,
28:24 Ahaz gathered together the **u** of the house of God,
28:24 and cut in pieces the **u** of the house of God.
29:18 the altar of burnt offering and all its **u,**
29:18 and the table for the rows of bread and all its **u.**
29:19 the **u** that King Ahaz repudiated during his reign
2Ti 2:20 In a large house there are **u** not only of gold
2:21 things I have mentioned will become special **u,**
1Mc 1:21 the lampstand for the light, and all its **u.**

UTERUS (3)

Nu 5:21 when the LORD makes your **u** drop,
5:22 and make your womb discharge, your **u** drop!"
5:27 and her womb shall discharge, her **u** drop,

UTHAI (4)

1Ch 9: 4 **U** son of Ammihud, son of Omri, son of Imri, son
Ezr 8:14 Of the descendants of Bigvai, **U** and Zaccur,
1Es 5:30 the descendants of **U,** the descendants of Ketab,
8:40 Of the descendants of Bigvai, **U** son of Istalcurus,

UTMOST (8) [UTTERMOST]

Ac 24: 3 in every way and everywhere with **u** gratitude.
2Co 8: 7 in faith, in speech, in knowledge, in **u** eagerness,
12:12 among you with **u** patience,
1Ti 1:16 Jesus Christ might display the **u** patience,
2Ti 4: 2 and encourage, with the **u** patience in teaching.
Wis 12:27 Therefore the **u** condemnation came upon them.
Sir 7:17 Humble yourself to the **u,**
2Mc 12:23 Judas pressed the pursuit with the **u** vigor,

UTTER‡ (48) [UTTERANCE, UTTERANCES, UTTERED, UTTERING, UTTERLY, UTTERS]

Ex 16: 8 the LORD has heard the complaining that you **u**
Lev 5: 4 Or when any of you **u** aloud a rash oath for a bad
5: 4 whatever people **u** in an oath,
Dt 23:23 Whatever your lips **u** you must diligently perform,
Jos 6:10 or let your voice be heard, nor shall you **u** a word,
Jdg 5:12 Awake, awake, **u** a song!
Ezr 9: 7 to plundering, and to **u** shame, as is now the case.
Job 8:10 not teach you and tell you and **u** words out
20:26 **U** darkness is laid up for their treasures;
27: 4 and my tongue will not **u** deceit.
Ps 12: 2 They **u** lies to each other;
37:30 The mouths of the righteous **u** wisdom,
41: 6 when they come to see me, they **u** empty words,
55:17 and morning and at noon I **u** my complaint
59:12 For the cursing and lies that they **u,**
78: 2 I will **u** dark sayings from of old,
106: 2 Who can **u** the mighty doings of the LORD,
Pr 5:14 I am at the point of **u** ruin in the public assembly."
8: 7 for my mouth will **u** truth;
20:20 your lamp will go out in **u** darkness.
23:33 and your mind **u** perverse things.
Ecc 5: 2 let your heart be quick to **u** a word before God,
Isa 32: 6 to **u** error concerning the LORD,
43:28 I delivered Jacob to **u** destruction,
Jer 1:16 And I will **u** my judgments against them,
15:19 If you **u** what is precious,
25:30 and from his holy habitation **u** his voice;
48:34 as far as Jahaz they **u** their voice,
50:13 but shall be an **u** desolation;
Eze 13: 9 who see false visions and **u** lying divinations;
24: 3 And **u** an allegory to the rebellious house and say
29:10 and I will make the land of Egypt an **u** waste
36: 5 who, with wholehearted joy and **u** contempt,
Hos 10: 4 They **u** mere words; with empty
Zep 3:13 they shall do no wrong and **u** no lies,
Zec 10: 2 the teraphim **u** nonsense, and the diviners see lies;
Mt 5:11 and **u** all kinds of evil against you falsely
12:36 to give an account for every careless word you **u;**
Mk 3:28 for their sins and whatever blasphemies they **u;**
1Co 14: 9 if in a tongue you **u** speech that is not intelligible,
Rev 13: 6 It opened its mouth to **u** blasphemies against God,
Jdt 14:13 against us to give battle, to their **u** destruction."
Wis 1: 8 therefore those who **u** unrighteous things will
Sir 7:13 Refuse to **u** any lie, for it is a habit that results
23: 9 nor habitually **u** the name of the Holy One;
2Mc 13: 3 and with **u** hypocrisy urged Antiochus on,
15: 6 This Nicanor in his **u** boastfulness
2Es 5: 5 and the stone shall **u** its voice;

UTTERANCE (9) [UTTER]

Nu 30: 6 while obligated by her vows or any thoughtless **u**
30: 8 or the thoughtless **u** of her lips,
Job 10: 1 I will give free **u** to my complaint;
Pr 6: 2 you are snared by the **u** of your lips,
Lk 4:36 "What kind of **u** is this?
1Co 12: 8 To one is given through the Spirit the **u**
12: 8 the **u** of knowledge according to the same Spirit,
Sir 21:17 **u** of a sensible person is sought in the assembly,
48:12 and marvels with every **u** of his mouth.

UTTERANCES (1) [UTTER]

2Es 8:22 whose word is sure and whose **u** are certain,

UTTERED (29) [UTTER]

Nu 23: 7 Then Balaam **u** his oracle, saying:
23:18 Then Balaam **u** his oracle, saying:
24: 3 and he **u** his oracle, saying:
24:15 So he **u** his oracle, saying:
24:20 he looked on Amalek, and **u** his oracle, saying:
24:21 he looked on the Kenite, and **u** his oracle, saying:
24:23 Again he **u** his oracle, saying:
Jdg 17: 2 about which you **u** a curse,
2Sa 22:14 the Most High **u** his voice.
2Ki 9:25 how the LORD **u** this oracle against him:
1Ch 16:12 his miracles, and the judgments he **u,**

2Ch 35:25 Jeremiah also **u** a lament for Josiah,
Job 26: 4 With whose help have you **u** words,
42: 3 Therefore I have **u** what I did not understand,
Ps 18:13 and the Most High **u** his voice.
66:14 that my lips **u** and my mouth promised when I was
76: 8 From the heavens you **u** judgment;
105: 5 his miracles, and the judgments he **u**,
Jer 25:13 that land all the words that I have **u** against it,
Eze 13: 7 not seen a false vision or **u** a lying divination,
13: 8 Because you have **u** falsehood and envisioned lies,
35:12 have heard all the abusive speech that you **u**
Sir 15:10 For in wisdom must praise be **u**,
2Mc 6:29 because the words he had **u** were
9:12 he **u** these words, "It is right to be subject to God;
2Es 10:26 she suddenly **u** a loud and fearful cry,
11: 7 and it **u** a cry to its wings, saying,
11:37 and I heard how it **u** a human voice to the eagle,
4Mc 12:19 After he had **u** these imprecations,

UTTERING (7) [UTTER]

Isa 59:13 conceiving lying words and **u** them from the heart.
Mic 2:11 If someone were to go about **u** empty falsehoods,
Rev 13: 5 a mouth **u** haughty and blasphemous words,
2Mc 10:34 kept blaspheming terribly and **u** wicked words.
3Mc 2:24 but went away **u** bitter threats.
4:16 and **u** improper words against the supreme God.
4Mc 4: 8 But, **u** threats, Apollonius went on to the temple.

UTTERLY (107) [UTTER]

Ex 17:14 I will **u** blot out the remembrance of Amalek from
23:24 but you shall **u** demolish them
Lev 26:44 so as to destroy them **u** and break my covenant
Nu 15:31 such a person shall be **u** cut off and bear the guilt.
21: 2 then we will **u** destroy their towns."
21: 3 and they **u** destroyed them and their towns;
Dt 2:34 and in each town we **u** destroyed men, women,
3: 6 And we **u** destroyed them,
3: 6 in each city **u** destroying men, women,
4:26 against you today that you will soon **u** perish from
4:26 not live long on it, but will be **u** destroyed.
7: 2 then you must **u** destroy them.
7:26 You must **u** detest and abhor it,
13:15 **u** destroying it and everything in it—
Jos 2:10 to Sihon and Og, whom you **u** destroyed.
8:26 until he had **u** destroyed all the inhabitants of Ai.
10: 1 how Joshua had taken Ai, and had **u** destroyed it,
10:28 he **u** destroyed every person in it;
10:35 and every person in it he **u** destroyed that day,
10:37 and **u** destroyed it with every person in it.
10:39 and **u** destroyed every person in it;
10:40 but **u** destroyed all that breathed,
11:11 to the sword all who were in it, **u** destroying them;
11:12 with the edge of the sword, **u** destroying them,
11:20 in order that they might be **u** destroyed,
11:21 Joshua **u** destroyed them with their towns.
17:13 but did not **u** drive them out.
1Sa 15: 3 and **u** destroy all that they have;
15: 8 but **u** destroyed all the people with the edge of
15: 9 and would not **u** destroy them;
15: 9 that was despised and worthless they **u** destroyed.
15:15 but the rest we have **u** destroyed."
15:18 'Go, **u** destroy the sinners, the Amalekites,
15:20 and I have **u** destroyed the Amalekites.
27:12 "He has made himself **u** abhorrent
2Sa 12:14 by this deed you have **u** scorned the LORD,
17:10 like the heart of a lion, will **u** melt with fear;
2Ki 10: 4 But they were **u** terrified and said, "Look,
19:11 to all lands, destroying them **u**.
2Ch 20:23 the inhabitants of Mount Seir, destroying them **u**;
32:14 that my ancestors **u** destroyed was able
Ps 38: 6 I am **u** bowed down and prostrate;
38: 8 I am **u** spent and crushed;
73:19 in a moment, swept away **u** by terrors!
74: 8 "We will **u** subdue them";
78:59 he was full of wrath, and he **u** rejected Israel.
119: 8 I will observe your statutes; do not **u** forsake me.
119:43 Do not take the word of truth **u** out of my mouth,
119:51 The arrogant **u** deride me,
SS 8: 7 the wealth of his house, it would be **u** scorned.
Isa 1: 4 the Holy One of Israel, who are **u** estranged!
2:18 The idols shall **u** pass away.
6:11 and the land is **u** desolate;
11:15 the LORD will **u** destroy the tongue of the sea
16: 7 **u** stricken, for the raisin cakes of Kir-hareseth.
19:11 The princes of Zoan are **u** foolish;
24: 3 earth shall be **u** laid waste and **u** despoiled;
24:19 The earth is **u** broken, the earth is torn asunder,
32:19 and the city will be **u** laid low.
37:11 to all lands, destroying them **u**.
42:17 They shall be turned back and **u** put to shame—
60:12 those nations shall be **u** laid waste.
Jer 2:12 O heavens, at this, be shocked, be **u** desolate,
4:10 **u** you have deceived this people and Jerusalem,
5:11 the house of Judah have been **u** faithless to me,
9:19 We are **u** shamed, because we have left the land,
24:10 until they are **u** destroyed from the land that I gave
25: 9 I will **u** destroy them, and make them an object
50:12 your mother shall be **u** shamed,
50:21 and attack the inhabitants of Pekod and **u** destroy
50:26 pile her up like heaps of grain, and destroy her **u**;
51: 3 **u** destroy her entire army.
La 5:22 unless you have **u** rejected us,
Eze 17:10 When the east wind strikes it, will it not **u** wither,
Da 11:22 Armies shall be **u** swept away and broken
Hos 10:15 At dawn the king of Israel shall be **u** cut off.
Am 9: 8 except that I will not **u** destroy the house of Jacob,
Ob 1: 2 among the nations; you shall be **u** despised.
Mic 2: 4 and say, "We are **u** ruined;
Na 1:15 shall the wicked invade you; they are **u** cut off.
3: 1 City of bloodshed, **u** deceitful, full of booty—
Zep 1: 2 I will **u** sweep away everything from the face of
Zec 11:17 be completely withered, his right eye **u** blinded!
Mk 6:51 And they were **u** astounded,
12:17 And they were **u** amazed at him.
Ac 3:11 the portico called Solomon's Portico, **u** astonished.
3:23 to that prophet will be **u** rooted out of the people.'
2Co 1: 8 so **u**, unbearably crushed that we despaired
Jdt 5:18 they were **u** defeated in many battles
6: 4 will survive our attack; they will **u** perish.
7:30 for he will not forsake us **u**.
AdE 13: 6 be **u** destroyed by the swords of their enemies,
14: 2 and she **u** humbled her body;
Wis 4:19 they will be left **u** dry and barren,
13:18 for aid he entreats a thing that is **u** inexperienced;
16:16 and hail and relentless storms, and **u** consumed
Sir 11: 6 Many rulers have been **u** disgraced,
40:14 so lawbreakers will **u** fail.
2Mc 3:12 that it was **u** impossible that wrong should be done
6: 3 Harsh and **u** grievous was the onslaught of evil.
7: 5 When he was **u** helpless, the king ordered them
1Es 1:56 and **u** destroyed all its glorious things.
2Es 4: 2 understanding has **u** failed regarding this world,
7:87 because they shall **u** waste away in confusion and
16:11 and who will not be **u** shattered at his presence?
4Mc 10:17 and **u** abominable Antiochus gave orders

UTTERMOST (1) [UTMOST]

Eze 32:23 Their graves are set in the **u** parts of the Pit.

UTTERMOST (KJV) See also APPROACH, EDGE, ENDS, EXTREME, FAR, FARTHEST, LAST, MOUTH, OUTERMOST, OUTLYING,OUTSKIRTS, SOURCES

UTTERS (11) [UTTER]

Ps 46: 6 he **u** his voice, the earth melts.
101: 7 no one who **u** lies shall continue in my presence.
Pr 10:18 and whoever **u** slander is a fool.
14:25 but one who **u** lies is a betrayer.
Jer 10:13 When he **u** his voice, there is a tumult of waters in
51:16 When he **u** his voice there is a tumult of waters in
Da 3:29 Any people, nation, or language that **u** blasphemy
Joel 2:11 The LORD **u** his voice at the head of his army;
3:16 and **u** his voice from Jerusalem,
Am 1: 2 and **u** his voice from Jerusalem;
Sir 23:10 and **u** the Name will never be cleansed from sin.

UZ (8)

Ge 10:23 descendants of Aram: **U**, Hul, Gether, and Mash.
22:21 **U** the firstborn, Buz his brother, Kemuel the father
36:28 These are the sons of Dishan: **U** and Aran.
1Ch 1:17 Elam, Asshur, Arpachshad, Lud, Aram, **U**, Hul,
1:42 The sons of Dishan: **U** and Aran.
Job 1: 1 a man in the land of **U** whose name was Job.
Jer 25:20 all the kings of the land of **U**;
La 4:21 O daughter Edom, you that live in the land of **U**;

UZAI (1)

Ne 3:25 Palal son of **U** repaired opposite the Angle and

UZAL (3)

Ge 10:27 Hadoram, **U**, Diklah,
1Ch 1:21 Hadoram, **U**, Diklah,
Eze 27:19 Vedan and Javan from **U** entered into trade

UZZA (6)

2Ki 21:18 in the garden of his house, in the garden of **U**.
21:26 He was buried in his tomb in the garden of **U**;
1Ch 8: 7 Heglam, who became the father of **U** and Ahihud.
Ezr 2:49 **U**, Paseah, Besai,
Ne 7:51 of Gazzam, of **U**, of Paseah,
1Es 5:31 the descendants of Gazera, the descendants of **U**,

UZZAH‡ (9) [PEREZ-UZZAH]

2Sa 6: 3 **U** and Ahio, the sons of Abinadab,
6: 6 **U** reached out his hand to the ark of God
6: 7 The anger of the LORD was kindled against **U**;
6: 8 with an outburst upon **U**;
1Ch 6:29 Mahli, Libni his son, Shimei his son, **U** his son,
13: 7 and **U** and Ahio were driving the cart.
13: 9 **U** put out his hand to hold the ark,
13:10 The anger of the LORD was kindled against **U**;
13:11 because the LORD had burst out against **U**;

UZZEN-SHEERAH (1)

1Ch 7:24 both Lower and Upper Beth-horon, and **U**.

UZZI (13)

1Ch 6: 5 Abishua of Bukki, Bukki of **U**,
6: 6 **U** of Zerahiah, Zerahiah of Meraioth,
6:51 Bukki his son, **U** his son, Zerahiah his son,
7: 2 **U**, Rephaiah, Jeriel, Jahmai, Ibsam, and Shemuel,
7: 3 The son of **U**: Izrahiah.
7: 7 The sons of Bela: Ezbon, **U**, Uzziel, Jerimoth,
9: 8 Elah son of **U**, son of Michri,
Ezr 7: 4 son of Zerahiah, son of **U**, son of Bukki,
Ne 11:22 of the Levites in Jerusalem was **U** son of Bani son
Ne 12:19 of Joiarib, Mattenai; of Jedaiah, **U**;
12:42 Shemaiah, Eleazar, **U**, Jehohanan, Malchijah,
1Es 8: 2 of Ahitub son of Amariah son of **U** son
2Es 1: 2 of Arna son of **U** son of Borith son of Abishua son

UZZIA (1)

1Ch 11:44 **U** the Ashterathite, Shama and Jeiel sons

UZZIAH‡ (42) [=AZARIAH]

2Ki 15:13 in the thirty-ninth year of King **U** of Judah;
15:30 in the twentieth year of Jotham son of **U**.
15:32 King Jotham son of **U** of Judah began to reign.
15:34 just as his father **U** had done.
1Ch 6:24 Uriel his son, **U** his son, and Shaul his son.
27:25 and in the towers, was Jonathan son of **U**.
2Ch 26: 1 Then all the people of Judah took **U**,
26: 3 **U** was sixteen years old when he began to reign,
26: 8 The Ammonites paid tribute to **U**,
26: 9 **U** built towers in Jerusalem at the Corner Gate,
26:11 Moreover **U** had an army of soldiers, fit for war,
26:14 **U** provided for all the army the shields, spears,
26:18 they withstood King **U**, and said to him, "It is not
26:18 and said to him, "It is not for you, **U**,
26:19 Then **U** was angry. Now he had a censer in his
26:21 King **U** was leprous to the day of his death,
26:22 Now the rest of the acts of **U**, from first to last,
26:23 **U** slept with his ancestors;
27: 2 of the LORD just as his father **U** had done—
Ezr 10:21 Maaseiah, Elijah, Shemaiah, Jehiel, and **U**.
Ne 11: 4 of **U** son of Zechariah son of Amariah son
Isa 1: 1 concerning Judah and Jerusalem in the days of **U**,
6: 1 In the year that King **U** died,
7: 1 In the days of Ahaz son of Jotham son of **U**,
Hos 1: 1 in the days of Kings **U**, Jotham, Ahaz,
Am 1: 1 concerning Israel in the days of King **U** of Judah
Zec 14: 5 the earthquake in the days of King **U** of Judah.
Mt 1: 8 and Joram the father of **U**,
1: 9 and **U** the father of Jotham,
Jdt 6:15 who in those days were **U** son of Micah,
6:16 and **U** questioned him about what had happened.
6:21 **U** took him from the assembly to his own house
7:23 around **U** and the rulers of the town and cried out
7:30 **U** said to them, "Courage, my brothers and sisters!
8: 9 and when she heard all that **U** said to them,
8:10 to summon **U** and Chabris and Charmis,
8:28 Then **U** said to her, "All
8:35 **U** and the rulers said to her, "Go in peace,
10: 6 and found **U** standing there with the elders of
13:18 Then **U** said to her, "O daughter,
14: 6 So they summoned Achior from the house of **U**.
15: 4 **U** sent men to Betomasthaim and Choba and Kola,

UZZIEL (16) [UZZIELITES]

Ex 6:18 Amram, Izhar, Hebron, and **U**,
6:22 The sons of **U**: Mishael, Elzaphan, and Sithri.
Lev 10: 4 sons of **U** the uncle of Aaron, and said to them,
Nu 3:19 Amram, Izhar, Hebron, and **U**.
3:30 of **U** as head of the ancestral house of the clans of
1Ch 4:42 Neariah, Rephaiah, and **U**, sons of Ishi;
6: 2 sons of Kohath: Amram, Izhar, Hebron, and **U**.
6:18 sons of Kohath: Amram, Izhar, Hebron, and **U**.
7: 7 The sons of Bela: Ezbon, Uzzi, **U**, Jerimoth,
15:10 of the sons of **U**, Amminadab the chief,
23:12 Amram, Izhar, Hebron, and **U**, four.
23:20 sons of **U**: Micah the chief and Isshiah the second.
24:24 sons of **U**, Micah; of the sons of Micah, Shamir.
25: 4 Bukkiah, Mattaniah, **U**, Shebuel, and Jerimoth,
2Ch 29:14 and of the sons of Jeduthun, Shemaiah and **U**.
Ne 3: 8 Next to them **U** son of Harhaiah,

UZZIELITES (2) [UZZIEL]

Nu 3:27 the clan of the Hebronites, and the clan of the **U**;
1Ch 26:23 the Izharites, the Hebronites, and the **U**:

V

VACANT (2)

Eze 42:10 opposite the **v** area and opposite the building,
42:13 and the south chambers opposite the **v** area are

VACILLATING (1)

2Co 1:17 Was I **v** when I wanted to do this?

VAGABOND[S] (KJV) See ITINERANT, WANDER[ER]

VAIL[S] (KJV) See VEIL[S]

VAIN‡ (66) [VAIN-MINDED, VAINGLORY, VAINLY, VANITIES, VANITY]

Lev 26:16 You shall sow your seed in **v**,
1Sa 17:39 and he tried in **v** to walk,

1Sa 25:21 in v that I protected all that this fellow has in
Job 9:29 I shall be condemned; why then do I labor in v?
27:12 why then have you become altogether v?
39:16 though its labor should be in v, yet it has no fear;
Ps 2: 1 and the peoples plot in v?
4: 2 long will you love v words, and seek after lies?
33:17 The war horse is a v hope for victory,
62:10 and set no v hopes on robbery;
73:13 All in v I have kept my heart clean
119:118 for their cunning is in v.
127: 1 those who build it labor in v.
127: 1 the guard keeps watch in v.
127: 2 It is in v that you rise up early and go late to rest,
Pr 1:17 in v is the net baited while the bird is looking on;
14: 6 A scoffer seeks wisdom in v,
31:30 Charm is deceitful, and beauty is v,
Ecc 6:12 while they live the few days of their v life,
7:15 In my v life I have seen everything;
9: 9 all the days of your v life that are given you under
Isa 49: 4 But I said, "I have labored in v,
65:23 They shall not labor in v,
Jer 2:30 In v I have struck down your children;
4:30 In v you beautify yourself.
6:29 in v the refining goes on,
46:11 In v you have used many medicines;
Eze 6:10 not threaten in v to bring this disaster upon them.
24:12 In v I have wearied myself;
Jnh 2: 8 who worship v idols forsake their true loyalty.
Mal 1:10 so that you would not kindle fire on my altar in v!
3:14 You have said, "It is v to serve God.
Mt 15: 9 in v do they worship me,
Mk 7: 7 in v do they worship me,
Ac 4:25 and the peoples imagine v things?
Ro 13: 4 for the authority does not bear the sword in v!
1Co 15: 2 unless you have come to believe in v.
15:10 and his grace toward me has not been in v.
15:14 has been in v and your faith has been in v.
15:58 you know that in the Lord your labor is not in v.
2Co 6: 1 also not to accept the grace of God in v.
Gal 2: 2 that I was not running, or had not run, in v.
Php 2:16 day of Christ that I did not run in v or labor in v.
1Th 2: 1 that our coming to you was not in v,
3: 5 and that our labor had been in v.
Jdt 6: 4 he has spoken; none of his words shall be in v.
AdE 14:10 the mouths of the nations for the praise of v idols,
Wis 3:11 Their hope is v, their labors are unprofitable,
Sir 34: 1 The senseless have v and false hopes,
1Mc 9:68 for his plan and his expedition had been in v.
2Mc 7:18 he said, "Do not deceive yourself in v.
7:34 be elated in v and puffed up by uncertain hopes,
3Mc 6: 6 to the flames so as not to serve v things,
2Es 4:16 But the plan of the forest was in v,
4:17 also the plan of the waves of the sea was in v,
6:34 to think v thoughts concerning the former times;
7:22 they devised for themselves v thoughts,
9:22 let the multitude perish that has been born in v,
16:45 Because of this those who labor, labor in v;
4Mc 5:10 by holding a v opinion concerning the truth,
8:18 in v resolves and venture upon a disobedience
8:19 up this v opinion and this arrogance that threatens
16: 7 O seven childbirths all in v,
16: 8 In v, my sons, I endured many birth pangs

VAIN-MINDED (1) [MIND, VAIN]
3Mc 6:11 not the v praise their vanities at the destruction

VAINGLORY (1) [GLORY, VAIN]
4Mc 2:15 lust for power, v, boasting, arrogance,

VAINLY (1) [VAIN]
La 4:17 Our eyes failed, ever watching v for help;

VAIZATHA (1)
Est 9: 9 Parmashta, Arisai, Aridai, V,

VALE (2) [VALLEY]
Ps 60: 6 and portion out the V of Succoth.
108: 7 and portion out the V of Succoth.

VALE (KJV) See also FOOTHILLS, VALLEY

VALETS (2)
1Ki 10: 5 his v, and his burnt offerings that he offered at
2Ch 9: 4 and their clothing, his v, and their clothing,

VALIANT (19) [VALIANTLY, VALOR]
Jdg 18: 2 So the Danites sent five v men from
1Sa 14:52 and when Saul saw any strong or v warrior,
18:17 only be v for me and fight the LORD's battles."
31:12 all the v men set out,
2Sa 2: 7 Therefore let your hands be strong, and be v;
11:16 to the place where he knew there were v warriors.
13:28 myself commanded you? Be courageous and v."
17:10 even the v warrior, whose heart is like the heart of
17:10 and that those who are with him are v warriors.
23:20 of Jehoiada was a v warrior from Kabzeel, a doer
1Ch 5:18 and the half-tribe of Manasseh had v warriors,
10:12 all the v warriors got up and took away the body
11:22 Benaiah son of Jehoiada was a v man of Kabzeel,
2Ch 13: 3 having an army of v warriors,
28: 6 of them v warriors, because they had abandoned
Ne 11: 6 were four hundred sixty-eight v warriors.
11:14 v warriors, one hundred twenty-eight;

Isa 5:22 heroes in drinking wine and v at mixing drink,
33: 7 the v cry in the streets;

VALIANTLY (7) [VALIANT]
Nu 24:18 a possession of its enemies, while Israel does v.
1Sa 14:48 He did v, and struck down the Amalekites,
Ps 60:12 With God we shall do v;
108:13 With God we shall do v;
118:15 "The right hand of the LORD does v;
118:16 the right hand of the LORD does v."
2Es 2:47 to praise those who had stood v for the name of

VALID (7) [VALIDATED, VALIDATES]
Jn 8:13 on your own behalf; your testimony is not v."
8:14 my testimony is v because I know
8:16 Yet even if I do judge, my judgment is v;
8:17 that the testimony of two witnesses is v.
Heb 2: 2 For if the message declared through angels was v,
1Mc 8:30 or deletion that they may make shall be v.
13:38 All the grants that we have made to you remain v,

VALIDATED (1) [VALID]
Nu 30:14 he has v them, because he said nothing to her at

VALIDATES (1) [VALID]
Nu 30:14 then he v all her vows, or all her pledges,

VALLEY‡ (140) [VALE, VALLEYS]
Ge 14: 3 All these joined forces in the V of Siddim (that is,
14: 8 and they joined battle in the V of Siddim
14:10 Now the V of Siddim was full of bitumen pits;
14:17 at the V of Shaveh (that is, the King's V).
26:17 So Isaac departed from there and camped in the v
26:19 in the v and found there a well of spring water,
37:14 So he sent him from the v of Hebron.
Nu 21:20 from Bamoth to the v lying in the region of Moab
Dt 1:24 they reached the V of Eshcol they spied it out
3:29 So we remained in the v opposite Beth-peor.
4:46 beyond the Jordan in the v opposite Beth-peor,
34: 3 that is, the v of Jericho, the city of palm trees—
34: 6 He was buried in a v in the land of Moab,
Jos 7:24 and they brought them up to the V of Achor.
7:26 that place to this day is called the V of Achor.
8:13 But Joshua spent that night in the v.
10:12 and Moon, in the v of Aijalon."
11: 8 and eastward as far as the v of Mizpeh.
11:17 in the v of Lebanon below Mount Hermon.
12: 2 the middle of the v as far as the river Jabbok,
12: 7 in the v of Lebanon to Mount Halak,
13: 9 and the town that is in the middle of the v,
13:16 and the town that is in the middle of the v,
13:19 and Zereth-shahar on the hill of the v,
13:27 and in the v Beth-haram, Beth-nimrah, Succoth,
15: 7 from the V of Achor, and so northward, turning
15: 7 which is on the south side of the v;
15: 8 the v of the son of Hinnom at the southern slope
15: 8 the top of the mountain that lies over against the v
15: 8 at the northern end of the v of Rephaim;
17:16 and its villages and those in the V of Jezreel."
18:16 the border of the mountain that overlooks the v of
18:16 which is at the north end of the v of Rephaim;
18:16 and it then goes down the v of Hinnom,
19:14 and it ends at the v of Iphtah-el;
19:27 and the v of Iphtah-el northward to Beth-emek
Jdg 5:14 From Ephraim they set out into the v,
5:15 into the v they rushed out at his heels.
6:33 the Jordan they encamped in the V of Jezreel.
7: 1 below the hill of Moreh, in the v.
7: 8 The camp of Midian was below him in the v.
7:12 of the east lay along the v as thick as locusts;
16: 4 After this he fell in love with a woman in the v
18:28 It was in the v that belongs to Beth-rehob.
1Sa 6:13 were reaping their wheat harvest in the v.
13:18 toward the mountain that looks down upon the v
15: 5 the city of the Amalekites and lay in wait in the v.
17: 2 and the Israelites gathered and encamped in the v
17: 3 on the mountain on the other side, with a v
17:19 and all the men of Israel, were in the v of Elah,
21: 9 whom you killed in the v of Elah,
31: 7 of the v and those beyond the Jordan saw that
2Sa 5:18 the Philistines had come and spread out in the v
5:22 and were spread out in the v of Rephaim.
8:13 killed eighteen thousand Edomites in the V of Salt.
17:13 and we shall drag it into the v,
18:18 that is in the King's V, for he said, "I have no son
23:13 while a band of Philistines was encamped in the v
24: 5 and from the city that is in the middle of the v,
2Ki 2:16 down on some mountain or into some v."
14: 7 He killed ten thousand Edomites in the V of Salt
23:10 which is in the v of Ben-hinnom,
1Ch 4:39 to the east side of the v,
10: 7 When all the men of Israel who were in the v saw
11:15 of Philistines was encamped in the v of Rephaim.
14: 9 the Philistines had come and made a raid in the v
14:13 Once again the Philistines made a raid in the v.
18:12 killed eighteen thousand Edomites in the V of Salt.
2Ch 14:10 and they drew up their lines of battle in the v
20:16 you will find them at the end of the v,
20:26 On the fourth day they assembled in the V
20:26 that place has been called the V of Beracah
25:11 he went to the V of Salt,
26: 9 at the V Gate, and at the Angle,
28: 3 he made offerings in the v of the son of Hinnom,
33: 6 He made his son pass through fire in the v of

2Ch 33:14 in the v, reaching the entrance at the Fish Gate;
Ne 2:13 by night by the V Gate past the Dragon's Spring
2:15 by way of the v by night and inspected the wall.
2:15 Then I turned back and entered by the V Gate,
3:13 the inhabitants of Zanoah repaired the V Gate;
11:30 So they camped from Beer-sheba to the v
11:35 Lod, and Ono, the v of artisans.
Job 21:33 The clods of the v are sweet to them;
28: 4 in a v away from human habitation;
Ps 23: 4 I walk through the darkest v, I fear no evil;
60: T *killed twelve thousand Edomites in the V of Salt.*
84: 6 As they go through the v of Baca they make it
Pr 30:17 a mother will be pecked out by the ravens of the v
SS 6:11 to look at the blossoms of the v,
Isa 17: 5 one gleans the ears of grain in the V of Rephaim.
22: 1 The oracle concerning the v of vision.
22: 5 and trampling and confusion in the v of vision,
28:21 he will rage as in the v of Gibeon;
40: 4 Every v shall be lifted up,
57: 6 the smooth stones of the v is your portion;
63:14 Like cattle that go down into the v,
65:10 and the V of Achor a place for herds to lie down,
Jer 2:23 Look at your way in the v;
7:31 which is in the v of the son of Hinnom,
7:32 the v of the son of Hinnom, but the v of Slaughter:
19: 2 to the v of the son of Hinnom at the entry of
19: 6 the v of the son of Hinnom, but the v of Slaughter.
21:13 See, I am against you, O inhabitant of the v,
31:40 The whole v of the dead bodies and the ashes,
32:35 They built the high places of Baal in the v of
48: 8 the v shall perish, and the plain shall be destroyed,
Eze 3:22 and he said to me, Rise up, go out into the v,
3:23 So I rose up and went out into the v;
8: 4 like the vision that I had seen in the v.
37: 1 and set me down in the middle of a v;
37: 2 there were very many lying in the v,
39:11 the V of the Travelers east of the sea;
39:11 it shall be called the V of Hamon-gog.
39:15 the buriers have buried it in the V of Hamon-gog.
Hos 1: 5 On that day I will break the bow of Israel in the v
2:15 and make the V of Achor a door of hope.
Joel 3: 2 and bring them down to the v of Jehoshaphat,
3:12 and come up to the v of Jehoshaphat;
3:14 Multitudes, multitudes, in the v of decision!
3:14 the day of the LORD is near in the v of decision.
Am 1: 5 and cut off the inhabitants from the V of Aven,
Mic 1: 6 I will pour down her stones into the v,
Zec 14: 4 in two from east to west by a very wide v;
14: 5 you shall flee by the v of the LORD's mountain,
14: 5 the v between the mountains shall reach to Azal;
Lk 3: 5 Every v shall be filled, and every mountain
Jn 18: 1 he went out with his disciples across the Kidron v
Jdt 4: 4 and to Choba and Aesora, and the v of Salem.
7: 3 They encamped in the v near Bethulia,
7:17 the v and seized the water supply and the springs
10:10 down the mountain and passed through the v,
10:11 the women were going straight on through the v,
11:17 but every night your servant will go out into the v
12: 7 She went out each night to the v of Bethulia,
13:10 through the camp, circled around the v, and went
1Mc 12:37 part of the wall on the v to the east had fallen,

VALLEYS (25) [VALLEY]
Nu 14:25 the Amalekites and the Canaanites live in the v,
Dt 8: 7 and underground waters welling up in v and hills,
11:11 over to occupy is a land of hills and v,
1Ki 20:28 a god of the hills but he is not a god of the v,'
1Ch 12:15 and put to flight all those in the v,
27:29 Over the herds in the v was Shaphat son of Adlai.
Job 39:10 or will it harrow the v after you?
Ps 65:13 the v deck themselves with grain,
104: 8 ran down to the v to the place that you appointed
104:10 You make springs gush forth in the v;
SS 2: 1 I am a rose of Sharon, a lily of the v.
Isa 22: 7 Your choicest v were full of chariots,
41:18 and fountains in the midst of the v;
57: 5 you that slaughter your children in the v,
Eze 6: 3 to the ravines and the v:
7:16 be found on the mountains like doves of the v,
31:12 and in all the v its branches have fallen,
32: 5 and fill the v with your carcass.
35: 8 in your v and in all your watercourses those killed
36: 4 the watercourses and the v, the desolate wastes
36: 6 to the watercourses and v, Thus say the Lord GOD:
Mic 1: 4 under him and the v will burst open,
Jdt 7: 4 nor the v nor the hills will bear their weight."
Bar 5: 7 the everlasting hills be made low and the v filled
3Mc 6:17 the nearby v resounded with them and brought

VALOR (8) [VALIANT]
1Sa 16:18 a man of v, a warrior, prudent in speech,
2Ki 24:16 to Babylon all the men of v,
2Ch 26:17 of the LORD who were men of v;
Sir 44: 3 and made a name for themselves by their v;
2Mc 8: 7 And talk of his v spread everywhere.
10:28 and victory not only their v but also their reliance
14:18 of the v of Judas and his troops and their courage
15:17 so effective in arousing v and awaking courage in

VALOUR (KJV) See ABILITY, ABLE, ABLE-BODIED, COURAGEOUS FIGHTERS, FAVOR, FIGHTING MEN, SOLDIERS, VALIANT, WARRIOR[S]

VALUABLE (5) [VALUE]
1Sa 15: 9 and the lambs, and all that was v,
2Ch 21: 3 of silver, gold, and v possessions,
Ezr 1: 6 with goods, with animals, and with v gifts,
Mt 12:12 How much more v is a human being than a sheep!
1Ti 4: 8 godliness is v in every way,

VALUE (21) [VALUABLE, VALUED]
Lev 22:14 he shall add one-fifth of its v to it,
27:15 one-fifth shall be added to its assessed v,
27:19 then one-fifth shall be added to its assessed v,
1Ki 21: 2 I will give you its v in money."
Mt 6:26 Are you not of more v than they?
10:31 you are of more v than many sparrows.
13:46 on finding one pearl of great v,
Lk 12: 7 you are of more v than many sparrows.
12:24 Of how much more v are you than the birds!
Ac 19:19 when the v of these books was calculated,
20:24 But I do not count my life of any v to myself,
Ro 2:25 Circumcision indeed is of v if you obey the law;
3: 1 Or what is the v of circumcision?
Php 3: 8 as loss because of the surpassing v
Col 2:23 but they are of no v in checking self-indulgence.
1Ti 4: 8 while physical training is of some v,
Tob 6: 7 what medicinal v is there in the fish's heart
Sir 20:30 and unseen treasure, of what v is either?
26:15 and no scales can weigh the v of her chastity.
41:14 and unseen treasure—of what v is either?
2Mc 4:15 and putting the highest v upon Greek forms

VALUED (5) [VALUE]
Job 28:16 It cannot be v in the gold of Ophir,
28:19 nor can it be v in pure gold.
Zec 11:13 this lordly price at which I was v by them.
Lk 7: 2 A centurion there had a slave whom he v highly,
Wis 18:12 instant their most v children had been destroyed.

VANDAL (1)
Pr 18: 9 One who is slack in work is close kin to a v.

VANGUARD (2)
Nu 32:17 we will take up arms as a v before the Israelites,
Dt 3:18 all your troops shall cross over armed as the v

VANIAH (2)
Ezr 10:36 V, Meremoth, Eliashib,
1Es 9:34 Maerus, Joel, Mamdai and Bedeiah and V,

VANISH (9) [VANISHED, VANISHES, VANISHING]
Job 6:17 when it is hot, they v from their place.
23:17 If only I could v in darkness,
Ps 37:20 they v—like smoke they v away.
58: 7 Let them v like water that runs away;
78:33 So he made their days v like a breath,
Isa 51: 6 for the heavens will v like smoke,
Tob 14: 7 but those who commit sin and injustice will v
Sir 45:26 so that their prosperity may not v,

VANISHED (10) [VANISH]
Jdg 6:21 and the angel of the LORD v from his sight.
Ps 9: 6 The enemies have v in everlasting ruins;
Isa 16: 4 and marauders have v from the land,
Jer 49: 7 perished from the prudent? Has their wisdom v?
Eze 26:17 How you have v from the seas, O city renowned,
Lk 24:31 and he v from their sight.
Rev 6:14 The sky v like a scroll rolling itself up,
Wis 5: 9 "All those things have v like a shadow,
Bar 3:19 They have v and gone down to Hades,
2Mc 3:34 Having said this they v.

VANISHES (2) [VANISH]
Job 7: 9 As the cloud fades and v,
Jas 4:14 a mist that appears for a little while and then v.

VANISHING (1) [VANISH]
2Es 12: 3 When I looked again, they were already v.

VANITIES (6) [VAIN]
Ps 119:37 Turn my eyes from looking at v;
Ecc 1: 2 Vanity of v, says the Teacher, vanity of v!
5: 7 With many dreams come v and a multitude
12: 8 Vanity of v, says the Teacher; all is vanity.
3Mc 6:11 the vain-minded praise their v at the destruction

VANITIES, VANITY (KJV) See also BREATH, CALAMITY, DECEIT, DELUSION, DESTRUCTION, EMPTINESS, EMPTY [WORDS], EVIL, FALSE [IDOLS, VISIONS], FALSEHOOD, FUTILITY, HASTILY, IDOLS, INIQUITY, LIES, NONSENSE, NOTHING, VAIN [WORDS], VAPOR, WORTHLESS [IDOLS, THINGS]

VANITY‡ (35) [VAIN]
Ps 89:47 for what v you have created all mortals!
Ecc 1: 2 V of vanities, says the Teacher, v of vanities! All is v.
1:14 and see, all is v and a chasing after wind.
2: 1 But again, this also was v.
2:11 and again, all was v and a chasing after wind,
2:15 And I said to myself that this also is v.
2:17 for all is v and a chasing after wind.
2:19 used my wisdom under the sun. This also is v.
2:21 This also is v and a great evil.
2:23 at night their minds do not rest. This also is v.
2:26 This also is v and a chasing after wind.
3:19 over the animals; for all is v.
4: 4 This also is v and a chasing after wind.
4: 7 Again, I saw v under the sun:
4: 8 This also is v and an unhappy business.
4:16 Surely this also is v and a chasing after wind.
5:10 of wealth, with gain. This also is v.
6: 2 This is v; it is a grievous ill.
6: 4 For it comes into v and goes into darkness,
6: 9 this also is v and a chasing after wind.
6:11 more words, the more v, so how is one the better?
7: 6 so is the laughter of fools; this also is v.
8:10 where they had done such things. This also is v.
8:14 There is a v that takes place on earth,
8:14 I said that this also is v.
9: 2 is v, since the same fate comes to all,
11: 8 All that comes is v.
11:10 for youth and the dawn of life are v.
12: 8 V of vanities, says the Teacher; all is v.
Isa 49: 4 I have spent my strength for nothing and v;
Hos 5:11 because he was determined to go after v.
Wis 14:14 For through human v they entered the world,

VANQUISH (1)
Job 32:13 God may v him, not a human.'

VAPOR (2) [VAPORS]
Pr 21: 6 a lying tongue is a fleeting v and a snare of death.
Sir 22:24 The v and smoke of the furnace precede the fire;

VAPORS (1) [VAPOR]
Sir 43: 4 it breathes out fiery v, and its bright rays blind the

VAPOUR (KJV) See MIST

VARIABLENESS (KJV) See VARIATION

VARIANCE (1) [VARY]
Wis 18: 2 and they begged their pardon for having been at v

VARIANCE (KJV) See also AGAINST, STRIFE

VARIATION (1) [VARY]
Jas 1:17 with whom there is no v or shadow due to change.

VARIED (6) [VARY]
Wis 15: 4 a figure stained with v colors,
2Mc 15:21 that were in front of him and the v supply of arms
3Mc 2: 6 by inflicting many and v punishments on
2Es 6:44 in endless abundance and of v appeal to the taste,
4Mc 16: 3 as she saw her seven sons tortured in such v ways.
17: 7 of the seven children enduring their v tortures

VARIETIES (4) [VARY]
1Co 12: 4 Now there are v of gifts, but the same Spirit;
12: 5 and there are v of services, but the same Lord;
12: 6 and there are v of activities,
Wis 7:20 the v of plants and the virtues of roots;

VARIETY (2) [VARY]
Eph 3:10 of God in its rich v might now be made known to
Sir 38:27 each is diligent in making a great v;

VARIOUS (31) [VARY]
Lev 6: 3 of the v things that one may do and sin thereby—
2Ch 16:14 on a bier that had been filled with v kinds
Ne 13:24 but spoke the language of v peoples.
Mt 4:24 those who were afflicted with v diseases
24: 7 there will be famines and earthquakes in v places:
Mk 1:34 he cured many who were sick with v diseases,
13: 8 there will be earthquakes in v places;
Lk 4:40 all those who had any who were sick with v kinds
21:11 and in v places famines and plagues;
1Co 12:10 to another v kinds of tongues,
12:28 forms of leadership, v kinds of tongues.
Tit 3: 3 led astray, slaves to v passions and pleasures,
Heb 1: 1 to our ancestors in many and v ways by
2: 4 by signs and wonders and v miracles,
9:10 but deal only with food and drink and v baptisms,
1Pe 1: 6 for a little while you have had to suffer v trials,
Jdt 7:32 Then he dismissed the people to their v posts,
AdE 1: 3 for his Friends and other persons of v nations,
1: 5 for the people of v nations who lived in the city.
1: 6 embroidered in v colors, with roses arranged
1:11 to all the governors and the people of v nations,
2Mc 12: 2 But some of the governors in v places,
3Mc 1:21 V were the supplications of those gathered there
1:25 while the elders near the king tried in v ways
2:26 that he framed evil reports in the v localities;
2Es 2:18 for you twelve trees loaded with v fruits,
4Mc 1: 7 I could prove to you from many and v examples
3:21 and caused many and v disasters.
15:11 of none of them were the v tortures strong enough
15:24 and the ingenious and v rackings,
18:21 and put them to death with v tortures.

VARY (1) [VARIANCE, VARIATION, VARIED, VARIETIES, VARIETY, VARIOUS]
Wis 19:18 as on a harp the notes v the nature of the rhythm,

VASHNI (KJV) See JOEL; See also Index to Footnotes

VASHTI (17)
Est 1: 9 Queen V gave a banquet for the women in
1:11 to bring Queen V before the king, wearing
1:12 But Queen V refused to come at
1:15 what is to be done to Queen V because she has
1:16 "Not only has Queen V done wrong to the king,
1:17 'King Ahasuerus commanded Queen V to
1:19 V is never again to come before King Ahasuerus;
2: 1 he remembered V and what she had done
2: 4 who pleases the king be queen instead of V."
2:17 on her head and made her queen instead of V.
AdE 1: 9 Queen V gave a drinking party for the women in
1:12 But Queen V refused to obey him and would
1:13 "This is how V has answered me.
1:15 be done to Queen V for not obeying the order that
1:16 "Queen V has insulted not only the king but
2: 1 about V or remembered what he had said and
2: 4 who pleases the king shall be queen instead of V.

VASSAL (2)
2Ki 17: 3 Hoshea became his v, and paid him tribute.
La 1: 1 a princess among the provinces has become a v.

VAST (18) [VASTNESS]
1Ki 4:29 of understanding as v as the sand on the seashore,
1Ch 18: 8 David took a v quantity of bronze;
Est 1:20 throughout all his kingdom, v as it is,
Ps 139:17 How v is the sum of them!
Isa 6:12 and v is the emptiness in the midst of the land.
La 2:13 For v as the sea is your ruin; who can heal you?
Eze 37:10 and stood on their feet, a v multitude.
Joel 2:11 how v is his host! Numberless are those who obey
Jdt 1:16 and all his combined forces, a v body of troops;
2:17 He took along a v number of camels and donkeys
5:24 and your v army will swallow them up."
7: 4 When the Israelites saw their v numbers,
7:18 and they formed a v multitude.
15: 7 since there was a v quantity of it.
Wis 19:10 of fish the river spewed out v numbers of frogs.
Bar 3:24 how v the territory that he possesses!
1Es 4:34 The earth is v, and heaven is high,
2Es 7: 3 in a wide expanse so that it is deep and v,

VASTNESS (1) [VAST]
2Es 10:55 in and see the splendor or the v of the building,

VAT (2) [VATS, WINEVAT]
Isa 5: 2 and hewed out a wine v in it;
Hos 9: 2 Threshing floor and wine v shall not feed them,

VATS (3) [VAT]
Pr 3:10 and your v will be bursting with wine.
Joel 2:24 the v shall overflow with wine and oil.
3:13 The v overflow, for their wickedness is great.

VAULT (4)
Am 9: 6 and founds his v upon the earth;
Sir 24: 5 Alone I compassed the v of heaven and traversed
43: 1 The pride of the higher realms is the clear v of
43: 8 shining in the v of the heavens!

VAUNT (1)
Isa 10:15 Shall the ax v itself over the one who wields it,

VAUNT[ETH] (KJV) See also BOASTFUL, TAKE CREDIT

VEDAN (1)
Eze 27:19 V and Javan from Uzal entered into trade

VEER (1) [VEERING]
Eze 10:16 the wheels at their side did not v.

VEERING (3) [VEER]
Eze 1:17 of the four directions without v as they moved.
10:11 of the four directions without v as they moved;
10:11 the others followed without v as they moved.

VEGETABLE (2) [VEGETABLES]
Dt 11:10 and irrigate by foot like a v garden.
1Ki 21: 2 so that I may have it for a v garden,

VEGETABLES (4) [VEGETABLE]
Pr 15:17 Better is a dinner of v where love is than a fatted
Da 1:12 Let us be given v to eat and water to drink.
1:16 and the wine they were to drink, and gave them v.
Ro 14: 2 while the weak eat only v.

VEGETATION (6)
Ge 1:11 Then God said, "Let the earth put forth v:
1:12 The earth brought forth v:
Dt 29:23 nothing sprouting, unable to support any v,
Ps 105:35 they devoured all the v in their land,
Eze 34:29 for them a splendid v so that they shall no more
Zec 10: 1 the v in the field to everyone.

VEHEMENT (1) [VEHEMENTLY]
3Mc 1:28 v, and concerted cry of the crowds resulted in

VEHEMENT (KJV) See also LONGING, RAGING, SULTRY

VEHEMENTLY (4) [VEHEMENT]
Mk 14:31 But he said v, "Even though I must die with you,
Lk 23:10 and the scribes stood by, v accusing him.
4Mc 5:32 and fan the fire more v!
12: 2 the tyrant had been v reproached by the brothers,

VEIL (16) [VEILED, VEILS]
Ge 24:65 So she took her v and covered herself.
38:14 put on a v, wrapped herself up,
38:19 and taking off her v she put on the garments
Ex 34:33 he put a v on his face;
34:34 he would take the v off, until he came out;
34:35 and Moses would put the v on his face again,
SS 4: 1 Your eyes are doves behind your v.
4: 3 like halves of a pomegranate behind your v.
6: 7 like halves of a pomegranate behind your v.
Isa 47: 2 remove your v, strip off your robe,
1Co 11: 6 For if a woman will not v herself,
11: 6 or to be shaved, she should wear a v.
2Co 3:13 a v over his face to keep the people of Israel
3:14 of the old covenant, that same v is still there,
3:15 whenever Moses is read, a v lies over their minds;
3:16 but when one turns to the Lord, the v is removed.

VEILED (5) [VEIL]
SS 1: 7 for why should I be like one who is v beside
1Co 11: 7 For a man ought not to have his head v,
2Co 4: 3 And even if our gospel is v,
4: 3 it is v to those who are perishing.
Sus 1:32 As she was v, the scoundrels ordered her to

VEILS (3) [VEIL]
Isa 3:23 the linen garments, the turbans, and the v.
Eze 13:18 make v for the heads of persons of every height,
13:21 I will tear off your v, and save my people

VEIN (KJV) See MINE

VENERABLE (2)
Sir 25: 5 and understanding and counsel in the v!
4Mc 7:15 O man of blessed age and of v gray hair and

VENGEANCE (68) [AVENGE, AVENGED, AVENGER, AVENGES, AVENGING, REVENGE, REVENGEFULLY, VENGEFUL]
Ge 4:15 Whoever kills Cain will suffer a sevenfold v."
Lev 19:18 You shall not take v or bear a grudge against any
26:25 executing v for the covenant;
Nu 31: 3 to execute the LORD's v on Midian.
Dt 32:35 V is mine, and recompense,
32:41 I will take v on my adversaries,
32:43 and take v on his adversaries;
Jos 10:13 until the nation took v on their enemies.
22:23 may the LORD himself take v.
Jdg 11:36 the LORD has given you v against your enemies,
1Sa 25:26 and from taking v with your own hand,
2Sa 22:48 the God who gave me v and brought
Ps 18:47 the God who gave me v and subdued peoples
58:10 The righteous will rejoice when they see v done;
94: 1 O LORD, you God of v, you God of v,
149: 7 to execute v on the nations and punishment on
Isa 34: 8 For the LORD has a day of v,
35: 4 He will come with v, with terrible recompense.
47: 3 I will take v, and I will spare no one.
59:17 he put on garments of v for clothing,
61: 2 and the day of v of our God;
63: 4 For the day of v was in my heart,
Jer 50:15 For this is the v of the LORD:
50:15 take v on her, do to her as she has done.
50:28 the v of the LORD our God, v for his temple.
51: 6 for this is the time of the LORD's v;
51:11 for that is the v of the LORD, v for his temple.
51:36 I am going to defend your cause and take v
Eze 24: 8 To rouse my wrath, to take v,
25:12 of Judah and has grievously offended in taking v
25:14 I will lay my v upon Edom by the hand of my
25:14 and they shall know my v, says the Lord GOD.
25:15 in v, and with malice of heart took revenge
25:17 I will execute great v on them
25:17 when I lay my v on them.
Mic 5:15 in anger and wrath I will execute v on the nations
Na 1: 2 the LORD takes v on his adversaries and rages
Lk 21:22 for these are days of v,
Ro 12:19 for it is written, "V is mine, I will repay,
2Th 1: 8 inflicting v on those who do not know God and
Heb 10:30 For we know the one who said, "V is mine,
Jdt 8:27 to search their hearts, nor has he taken v on us;
8:35 to take v on our enemies."
16:17 The Lord Almighty will take v on them in the day
Sir 18:24 of the moment of v when he turns away his face.
25:14 And any v, but not the v of enemies!
27:28 but v lies in wait for them like a lion.
28: 1 The vengeful will face the Lord's v,
35:23 and repays v on the nations;
39:28 "There are winds created for v,
39:29 all these have been created for v;
46: 1 to take v on the enemies that rose against them,
47:25 of wickedness, until v came upon them.
48: 7 You heard rebuke at Sinai and judgments of v
1Mc 3:15 to take v on the Israelites.
7: 9 he commanded him to take v on the Israelites.
7:24 taking v on those who had deserted
7:38 Take v on this man and on his army,
9:26 who took v on them and made sport of them.
2Mc 6:15 in order that he may not take v on us afterward
3Mc 1: 3 so it turned out that this man incurred the v meant
5: 8 that he avert with v the evil plot against them and
4Mc 9:24 to our nation and take v on the accursed tyrant."
12:18 on you he will take v both in this present life and

VENGEFUL (1) [VENGEANCE]
Sir 28: 1 The v will face the Lord's vengeance,

VENISON (KJV) See GAME

VENOM (9) [VENOMOUS]
Dt 32:24 with v of things crawling in the dust.
32:33 the poison of serpents, the cruel v of asps.
Job 20:14 it is the v of asps within them.
Ps 58: 4 They have v like the v of a serpent,
140: 3 and under their lips is the v of vipers.
Ro 3:13 "The v of vipers is under their lips."
Sir 25:15 There is no v worse than a snake's v,

VENOMOUS (1) [VENOM]
Wis 16:10 not conquered even by the fangs of v serpents,

VENT (5) [VENTED]
Job 32:19 My heart is indeed like wine that has no v;
Pr 29:11 A fool gives full v to anger,
La 4:11 The LORD gave full v to his wrath;
Eze 5:13 and I will v my fury on them and satisfy myself;
1Mc 2:24 He gave v to righteous anger;

VENTED (1) [VENT]
Ps 78:62 and v his wrath on his heritage.

VENTURE (5) [VENTURED, VENTURES]
Dt 28:56 that she does not v to set the sole of her foot on
Ecc 5:14 and those riches were lost in a bad v;
Ac 19:31 a message urging him not to v into the theater.
Ro 15:18 For I will not v to speak of anything except
4Mc 8:18 why do we take pleasure in vain resolves and v

VENTURED (1) [VENTURE]
3Mc 3:21 and we v to make a change,

VENTURES (1) [VENTURE]
Job 4: 2 "If one v a word with you, will you be offended?

VERDICT (5)
Da 2: 9 there is but one v for you.
Mt 26:66 What is your v?" They answered,
Lk 23:24 So Pilate gave his v that their demand should
Sir 4: 9 and do not be hesitant in giving a v.
19:25 and there are people who abuse favors to gain a v.

VERDURE (1)
Isa 15: 6 the new growth fails, the v is no more.

VERGE (1)
Heb 6: 8 it is worthless and on the v of being cursed;

VERIFIED (1)
Ge 42:20 Thus your words will be v,

VERILY (KJV) See ALL IN VAIN, CERTAINLY, INDEED, SURELY, THOUGH, [VERY] TRULY, WHOLLY, YES

VERITY (KJV) See FAITHFUL, TRUTH

VERMILION (2)
Jer 22:14 paneling it with cedar, and painting it with v.
Eze 23:14 images of the Chaldeans portrayed in v,

VERMIN (3)
Isa 66:17 v, and rodents, shall come to an end together,
Jer 43:12 as a shepherd picks his cloak clean of v;
Sir 10:11 one is dead he inherits maggots and v and worms.

VERSED (2) [WELL-VERSED]
Est 1:13 the king's procedure toward all who were v
Da 1: 4 v in every branch of wisdom,

VERSES (2)
Ps 45: 1 I address my v to the king;
Sir 44: 5 who composed musical tunes, or put v in writing;

VERTEBRAE (1)
4Mc 10: 8 and while his v were being dislocated by this,

VERY‡ (451)
Ge 1:31 and indeed, it was v good.
4: 5 So Cain was v angry, and his countenance fell.
7:13 On the v same day Noah with his sons,
12:14 that the woman was v beautiful.
13: 2 Now Abram was v rich in livestock, in silver,
15: 1 your reward shall be v great."
15: 4 no one but your v own issue shall be your heir."
17:23 the flesh of their foreskins that v day,
17:26 That v day Abraham and his son Ishmael
18:20 and Gomorrah and how v grave their sin!
19:21 "V well, I grant you this favor too,
20: 8 and the men were v much afraid.
21:11 The matter was v distressing to Abraham
24:16 The girl was v fair to look upon, a virgin,
26:13 and more until he became v wealthy.
26:24 that v night the LORD appeared to him and said,
30: 2 Jacob became v angry with Rachel and said,
30:26 you know v well the service I have given you."
34: 7 the men were indignant and v angry,
41:19 other cows came up after them, poor, v ugly,
41:31 for it will be v grievous.
47:13 for the famine was v severe.
50: 9 It was a v great company.
50:10 a v great and sorrowful lamentation;
Ex 1:20 and the people multiplied and became v strong.
8:28 provided you do not go v far away.
10:19 into a v strong west wind, which lifted the locusts
12:17 for on this v day I brought your companies out of
12:41 of four hundred thirty years, on that v day, all
12:51 That v day the LORD brought the Israelites out
14:12 Is this not the v thing we told you in Egypt,
19: 1 of the land of Egypt, on that v day, they came into
24:10 like the v heaven for clearness.
33:17 "I will do the v thing that you have asked;
Lev 19: 9 you shall not reap to the v edges of your field,
23:14 that v day, until you have brought the offering
23:22 you shall not reap to the v edges of your field,
Nu 6: 9 If someone dies v suddenly nearby,
11:10 Then the LORD became v angry,
11:33 LORD struck the people with a v great plague.
12: 3 Now the man Moses was v humble,
13:28 and the towns are fortified and v large;
14:28 "I will do to you the v things I heard you say:
14:29 your dead bodies shall fall in this v wilderness;
16:15 Moses was v angry and said to the LORD,
32: 1 and the Gadites owned a v great number of cattle.
Dt 1:30 just as he did for you in Egypt before your v eyes,
2: 4 be afraid of you, so, be v careful
4:11 the mountain was blazing up to the v heavens,
4:20 to become a people of his v own possession,
4:34 for you in Egypt before your v eyes?
9:26 the people who are your v own possession,
9:29 For they are the people of your v own possession,
20:15 Thus you shall treat all the towns that are v far
24: 8 of a leprous skin disease by being v careful;
26:16 This v day the LORD your God is commanding you
27: 8 on the stones all the words of this law v clearly.
27: 9 This v day you have become the people of
30:14 No, the word is v near to you;
31:22 That v day Moses wrote this song and taught it to
31:24 down in a book the words of this law to the v end,
31:30 to the v end, in the hearing of the whole assembly
32:47 for you, but rather your v life;
32:48 On that v day the LORD addressed Moses
Jos 1: 7 Only be strong and v courageous
5:11 On the day after the passover, on that v day,
8: 4 do not go v far from the city,
8:24 to the v last had fallen by the edge of the sword,
9: 9 "Your servants have come from a v far country,
9:13 of ours are worn out from the v long journey."
9:22 saying, 'We are v far from you,'
10:20 a v great slaughter on them,
10:27 which remain to this v day.
11: 4 with v many horses and chariots.
13: 1 v much of the land still remains to be possessed.
22: 8 and with v much livestock, with silver, gold,
23: 6 be v steadfast to observe and do all that is written
23:11 Be v careful, therefore, to love
Jdg 3:17 Now Eglon was a v fat man.
11: 7 not the v ones who rejected me and drove me out
11:35 You have brought me v low;
15:18 By then he was v thirsty,
18: 9 for we have seen the land, and it is v good.
1Sa 2: 3 Talk no more so v proudly,
2:17 the sin of the young men was v great in the sight
2:22 Now Eli was v old.
4:10 There was a v great slaughter,
5: 9 against the city, causing a v great panic;
5:11 The hand of God was v heavy there;
14:15 and it became a v great panic.
14:20 so that there was v great confusion.
14:24 Now Saul committed a v rash act on that day.
14:31 to Aijalon, the troops were v faint;
15:28 the kingdom of Israel from you this v day,
17:24 fled from him and were v much afraid.
17:46 This v day the LORD will deliver you
17:46 the dead bodies of the Philistine army this v day

1Sa 18: 8 Saul was v angry, for this saying displeased him.
18:30 so that his fame became v great.
21:12 and was v much afraid of King Achish of Gath.
23:22 for I am told that he is v crafty.
24:10 This v day your eyes have seen how
25: 2 The man was v rich;
25:15 Yet the men were v good to us,
25:36 heart was merry within him, for he was v drunk;
28: 2 David said to Achish, "V well,
28: 2 Achish said to David, "V well,
2Sa 2:17 The battle was v fierce that day;
3: 8 The words of Ishbaal made Abner v angry;
11: 2 the woman was v beautiful.
12: 2 The rich man had v many flocks and herds;
12:11 with your wives in the sight of this v sun.
12:15 to David, and it became v ill.
12:30 the spoil of the city, a v great amount.
13: 3 and Jonadab was a v crafty man.
13:15 Amnon was seized with a v great loathing for her;
13:21 of all these things, he became v angry,
13:36 the king and all his servants also wept v bitterly.
14:21 Then the king said to Joab, "V well, I grant this;
18:17 and raised over him a v great heap of stones.
19:32 Barzillai was a v aged man, eighty years old.
19:32 for he was a v wealthy man.
24:10 for I have done v foolishly."
1Ki 1: 4 The girl was v beautiful.
1: 6 He was also a v handsome man,
1:15 in his room. The king was v old;
2:18 Bathsheba said, "V well;
4:29 God gave Solomon v great wisdom, discernment,
10: 2 She came to Jerusalem with a v great retinue, with camels bearing spices, and v much gold,
11:28 The man Jeroboam was v able,
19:10 "I have been v zealous for the LORD,
19:14 "I have been v zealous for the LORD,
2Ki 9:26 I swear I will repay you on this v plot of ground.'
14:26 that the distress of Israel was v bitter;
17:18 Therefore the LORD was v angry with Israel
19:35 That v night the angel of the LORD set out
21:16 Moreover Manasseh shed v much innocent blood,
1Ch 4:40 good pasture, and the land was v broad, quiet,
5:23 they were v numerous from Bashan
17: 5 since the day I brought out Israel to this v day,
20: 2 the booty of the city, a v great amount.
21: 8 for I have done v foolishly."
21:13 the hand of the LORD, for his mercy is v great;
21:17 It is I who have sinned and done v wickedly.
23:17 but the sons of Rehabiah were v numerous.
2Ch 7: 8 and all Israel with him, a v great congregation,
9: 1 having a v great retinue and camels bearing spices and v much gold
9: 9 a v great quantity of spices, and precious stones:
11:12 in all the cities, and made them v strong.
16:14 and they made a v great fire in his honor.
20:19 the God of Israel, with a v loud voice.
24:24 LORD delivered into their hand a v great army,
25:10 But they became v angry with Judah,
26: 8 to the border of Egypt, for he became v strong.
30:13 in the second month, a v large assembly.
32:27 Hezekiah had v great riches and honor;
32:29 for God had given him v great possessions.
33:14 and raised it to a v great height.
Ezr 10: 1 a v great assembly of men, women,
Ne 2: 2 Then I was v much afraid.
4: 7 to be closed, they were v angry,
5: 6 I was v angry when I heard their outcry
5:11 Restore to them, this v day, their fields,
8:17 And there was v great rejoicing.
13: 8 And I was v angry, and I threw all
Est 1:18 This v day the noble ladies of Persia
7: 9 v gallows that Haman has prepared for Mordecai,
9: 1 on the v day when the enemies of the Jews hoped
9:11 That v day the number of those killed in
Job 1: 3 five hundred donkeys, and v many servants;
1:12 The LORD said to Satan, "V well,
2: 6 The LORD said to Satan, "V well,
2:13 for they saw that his suffering was v great.
8: 7 your latter days will be v great.
Ps 9: 6 the v memory of them has perished.
46: 1 a v present help in trouble.
77:16 they were afraid; the v deep trembled.
79: 8 for we are brought v low.
92: 5 Your thoughts are v deep!
93: 5 Your decrees are v sure; holiness befits your house,
104: 1 O LORD my God, you are v great.
105:24 And the LORD made his people v fruitful,
133: 1 How v good and pleasant it is
139:14 Wonderful are your works; that I know v well.
142: 6 Give heed to my cry, for I am brought v low.
146: 4 on that v day their plans perish.
Pr 6:26 but the wife of another stalks a man's v life.
Ecc 2:15 why then have I been so v wise?"
7:24 That which is, is far off, and deep, v deep;
SS 4: 1 How beautiful you are, my love, how v beautiful!
8:12 My vineyard, my v own, is for myself;
Isa 1: 7 in your v presence aliens devour your land;
5: 1 My beloved had a vineyard on a v fertile hill.
10:25 For in a v little while my indignation will come to
10:32 This v day he will halt at Nob,
16:11 and my v soul for Kir-heres.
16:14 and those who survive will be v few and feeble.
21: 7 let him listen diligently, v diligently."
24:16 the treacherous deal v treacherously.
29:17 Shall not Lebanon in a v little while become
31: 1 and in horsemen because they are v strong,
48: 8 For I knew that you would deal v treacherously,
Isa 52:13 be exalted and lifted up, and shall be v high.
Jer 4:18 It has reached your v heart."
6:11 the old folk and the v aged.
14:17 with a v grievous wound.
20:15 a son," making him v glad.
24: 2 One basket had v good figs, like first-ripe figs, but the other basket had v bad figs,
24: 3 "Figs, the good figs v good, and the bad figs v bad,
32:20 a name that continues to this v day.
38:27 in the v words the king had commanded.
42: 4 The prophet Jeremiah said to them, "V well:
48:29 heard of the pride of Moab—he is v proud—
51:24 of Chaldea before your v eyes for all the wrong
La 1:20 because I have been v rebellious.
Eze 2: 3 against me to this v day.
3: 4 the house of Israel and speak my v words to them.
16:47 a v little time you were more corrupt than they
20:26 I defiled them through their v gifts,
24: 2 write down the name of this day, this v day.
24: 2 of Babylon has laid siege to Jerusalem this v day.
26:10 wheels, and chariots your v walls shall shake,
37: 2 v many lying in the valley, and they were v dry.
40: 1 the city was struck down, on that v day, the hand
40: 2 and set me down upon a v high mountain,
47: 9 and there will be v many fish,
Da 5:23 but the God in whose power is your v breath,
5:30 v night Belshazzar, the Chaldean king, was killed.
6:14 king heard the charge, he was v much distressed.
Am 7:10 against you in the v center of the house of Israel;
Jnh 4: 1 But this was v displeasing to Jonah,
4: 6 so Jonah was v happy about the bush.
Hab 2:11 The v stones will cry out from the wall,
Zec 1: 2 The LORD was v angry with your ancestors.
1:14 I am v jealous for Jerusalem and for Zion.
9: 2 Tyre and Sidon, though they are v wise.
14: 4 in two from east to west by a v wide valley;
Mt 4: 8 to a v high mountain and showed him all
21: 8 A v large crowd spread their cloaks on the road,
24:33 you know that he is near, at the v gates.
26: 7 to him with an alabaster jar of v costly ointment,
26:34 Jesus said to him, "Truly I tell you, this v night,
Mk 1:35 In the morning, while it was still v dark,
4: 1 a v large crowd gathered around him that he got
5:15 the v man who had had the legion;
6:35 and the hour is now v late;
13:29 you know that he is near, at the v gates.
14: 3 with an alabaster jar of v costly ointment of nard,
14:30 this v night, before the cock crows twice,
14:40 for their eyes were v heavy;
16: 2 And v early on the first day of the week,
16: 4 which was v large, had already been rolled back.
Lk 1: 3 investigating everything carefully from the v first,
11:53 be v hostile toward him and to cross-examine him
12:12 at that v hour what you ought to say."
12:20 This v night your life is being demanded of you.
12:59 until you have paid the v last penny."
13: 1 that v time there were some present who told him
13:31 that v hour some Pharisees came and said to him,
16:10 "Whoever is faithful in a v little is faithful also
16:10 and whoever is dishonest in a v little is dishonest
18:23 he heard this, he became sad; for he was v rich.
18:30 who will not get back v much more in this age,
19:17 you have been trustworthy in a v small thing,
20:19 they wanted to lay hands on him at that v hour,
23: 8 When Herod saw Jesus, he was v glad,
Jn 1:51 And he said to him, "V truly, I tell you,
3: 3 Jesus answered him, "V truly, I tell you,
3: 5 Jesus answered, "V truly, I tell you,
3:11 "V truly, I tell you, we speak of what we know
5:19 Jesus said to them, "V truly, I tell you,
5:24 V truly, I tell you, anyone who hears my word
5:25 "V truly, I tell you, the hour is coming,
5:36 the v works that I am doing,
6:26 Jesus answered them, "V truly, I tell you,
6:32 Then Jesus said to them, "V truly, I tell you,
6:47 V truly, I tell you, whoever believes has eternal life
6:53 So Jesus said to them, "V truly, I tell you,
8: 4 ⟦caught in the v act of committing adultery.⟧
8:34 Jesus answered them, "V truly, I tell you,
8:51 V truly, I tell you, whoever keeps my word will
8:58 Jesus said to them, "V truly, I tell you,
10: 1 "V truly, I tell you, anyone who does not enter
10: 7 So again Jesus said to them, "V truly, I tell you,
12:24 V truly, I tell you, unless a grain of wheat falls
13:16 V truly, I tell you, servants are
13:20 V truly, I tell you, whoever receives one whom
13:21 "V truly, I tell you, one of you will betray me."
13:38 V truly, I tell you, before the cock crows,
14:12 V truly, I tell you, the one who believes
16:20 V truly, I tell you, you will weep and mourn,
16:23 V truly, I tell you, if you ask anything of
21:18 V truly, I tell you, when you were younger,
Ac 10:30 Cornelius replied, "Four days ago at this v hour,
11:11 At that v moment three men,
12: 6 v night before Herod was going to bring him out,
16:18 But Paul, v much annoyed,
16:18 And it came out that v hour.
17:10 That v night the believers sent Paul and Silas off
17:11 for they welcomed the message v eagerly
22:13 In that v hour I regained my sight and saw him.
24:26 to send for him v often and converse with him.
25:10 to the Jews, as you v well know.
Ro 2: 1 the judge, are doing the v same things.
7:10 the v commandment that promised life proved to
7:15 but I do the v thing I hate.
8:16 it is that v Spirit bearing witness with our spirit
8:26 v Spirit intercedes with sighs too deep for words.
Ro 9:17 up for the v purpose of showing my power in you,
9:26 "And in the v place where it was said to them,
11: 8 and ears that would not hear, down to this v day."
13: 6 are God's servants, busy with this v thing.
16: 6 Greet Mary, who has worked v hard among you.
1Co 4: 3 a v small thing that I should be judged by you or
4:13 the dregs of all things, to this v day.
2Co 3:14 to this v day, when they hear the reading of
3:15 Indeed, to this v day whenever Moses is read,
5: 5 He who has prepared us for this v thing is God,
Gal 2:18 But if I build up again the v things that I once tore
Eph 3: 8 Although I am the v least of all the saints,
6:22 I am sending him to you for this v purpose,
Col 4: 8 I have sent him to you for this v purpose,
1Th 2: 8 because you have become v dear to us.
5: 2 For you yourselves know v well that the day of
5:13 esteem them v highly in love because
1Ti 1:16 But for that v reason I received mercy,
2Ti 1:18 And you know v well how much service
Tit 1:12 It was one of them, their v own prophet,
1:15 Their v minds and consciences are corrupted.
Heb 1: 3 and the exact imprint of God's v being,
6:11 to realize the full assurance of hope to the v end,
10:37 For yet "in a v little while,
13:19 so that I may be restored to you v soon.
Jas 3: 4 yet they are guided by a v small rudder wherever
1Pe 2: 7 that the builders rejected has become the v head
3: 4 which is v precious in God's sight.
4:11 so as one speaking the v words of God;
2Pe 1: 4 his precious and v great promises,
1: 5 For this v reason, you must make every effort
Rev 11:14 The third woe is coming v soon.
21:11 of God and a radiance like a v rare jewel,
Tob 3:16 At that v moment, the prayers of both
6:12 the girl is sensible, brave, and v beautiful,
6:16 I know that this v night she will be given to you
6:18 through his father's lineage, he loved her v much,
7: 9 from the flock and received them v warmly.
9: 4 if I delay even one day I will upset him v much.
9: 6 I see in Tobias the v image of my cousin Tobit."
11:15 on her way there, v near to the gate of Nineveh.
Jdt 1:12 Then Nebuchadnezzar became v angry
5: 9 grew v prosperous in gold and silver and v much livestock.
7: 2 the foot soldiers handling it, a v great multitude.
8: 7 and was v lovely to behold.
9: 1 the v time when the evening incense was being
10: 4 Thus she made herself v beautiful,
10: 7 they were v greatly astounded at her beauty
11:15 on that v day they will be handed over to you to
13:14 by my hand this v night!"
16:16 to you is a v little thing;
AdE 8: 1 that v day King Artaxerxes granted to Esther all
9:11 That v day the number of those killed
16:20 on that v day, they may defend themselves
Wis 2:15 the v sight of him is a burden to us,
11: 5 v things by which their enemies were punished,
11:16 that one is punished by the v things
18: 1 But for your holy ones there was v great light.
Sir 6:20 She seems v harsh to the undisciplined;
13:13 Be on your guard and v careful,
16:19 The v mountains and the foundations of
31:27 Wine is v life to human beings if taken
39:16 "All the works of the Lord are v good,
43:29 Awesome is the Lord and v great,
48:15 The people were left v few in number,
Bar 2: 6 on us and our ancestors this v day.
2:29 this v great multitude will surely turn into
LtJ 6:46 not live v long themselves;
Sus 1: 2 v beautiful woman and one who feared the Lord.
1: 4 Joakim was v rich, and had a fine garden
1:27 the servants felt v much ashamed,
1:55 And Daniel said, "V well!
1:59 Daniel said to him, "V well!
Bel 1:28 they were v indignant and conspired against
1Mc 1: 4 a v strong army and ruled over countries,
1:64 V great wrath came upon Israel.
3:27 the forces of his kingdom, a v strong army.
4:54 At the v season and on the v day that the Gentiles
4:58 There was v great joy among the people,
5: 1 as it was before, they became v angry,
5:38 it is a v large force.
5:45 a v large company, to go to the land of Judah.
5:46 This was a large and v strong town on the road,
6: 2 Its temple was v rich, containing golden shields,
6:41 trembled, for the army was v large and strong.
8: 1 that they were v strong and were well-disposed
8: 2 and that they were v strong.
8: 6 and with cavalry and chariots and a v large army.
8:19 They went to Rome, a v long journey;
9:22 have not been recorded, but they were v many.
9:24 In those days a v great famine occurred,
9:68 They pressed him v hard,
9:69 So he was v angry at the renegades
10: 2 he assembled a v large army and marched out
11:53 but treated him v harshly.
13:22 but that night a v heavy snow fell,
13:49 So they were v hungry, and many
15:36 And the king was v angry.
16: 7 for the cavalry of the enemy were v numerous.
2Mc 3:11 a man of v prominent position,
3:33 "Be v grateful to the high priest Onias,
3:35 to the Lord and made v great vows to the Savior
4:38 and led him around the whole city to that v place
8:30 and they divided a v large amount of plunder,
9: 6 and that v justly, for he had tortured the bowels
10:18 in two v strong towers well equipped to withstand

2Mc 11: 1 V soon after this, Lysias,
12:18 in one place he had left a v strong garrison.
12:43 In doing this he acted v well and honorably,
14:37 and was v well thought of and
1Es 1:30 “Take me away from the battle, for I am v weak.”
2: 9 and with a v great number of votive offerings
4:16 and women brought up the v men who plant
7: 2 supervised the holy work with v great care,
8:53 and we found him v merciful.
8:64 weight of everything was recorded at that v time.
8:91 there gathered around him a v great crowd of men
Man 1: 7 long-suffering, and v merciful,
3Mc 3:16 And when we had granted v great revenues to
5:45 by the v fragrant draughts of wine mixed
5:51 and cried out in a v loud voice,
7: 6 But we v severely threatened them for these acts,
7:16 crowned with all sorts of v fragrant flowers,
2Es 5:21 the thoughts of my heart were v grievous
7:*140* [70] left only v few of the innumerable multitude.”
9: 2 that it is the v time when the Most High is about
12: 5 I am still weary in mind and v weak in my spirit,
13:19 for those also who are left, and for that v reason!
13:50 And then he will show them v many wonders.”
16:52 in a v short time iniquity will be removed from
4Mc 4: 5 the accursed Simon and a v strong military force.
4:20 a gymnasium constructed at the v citadel
5: 8 why should you abhor eating the v excellent meat
6:26 now burned to his v bones and about to expire,
8: 1 For this is why even the v young,
15:23 a man’s courage in the v midst of her emotions,

VESSEL‡ (37) [VESSELS]

Lev 6:28 earthen v in which it was boiled shall be broken;
6:28 but if it is boiled in a bronze v,
11:33 And if any of them falls into any earthen v,
11:33 and you shall break the v.
11:34 be unclean if water from any such v comes
11:34 be drunk shall be unclean if it was in any such v.
14: 5 be slaughtered over fresh water in an earthen v.
14:50 of the birds over fresh water in an earthen v,
15:12 Any earthen v that the one with the discharge
15:12 and every v of wood shall be rinsed in water.
Nu 5:17 the priest shall take holy water in an earthen v,
19:15 And every open v with no cover fastened
19:17 and running water shall be added in a v;
1Ki 17:10 “Bring me a little water in a v,
2Ki 4: 6 she said to her son, “Bring me another v.”
Ps 2: 9 and dash them in pieces like a potter’s v.”
31:12 I have become like a broken v.
Pr 25: 4 and the smith has material for a v;
26:23 the glaze covering an earthen v are smooth lips
Isa 22:24 every small v, from the cups to all the flagons.
30:14 of a potter’s v that is smashed so ruthlessly that
66:20 as the Israelites bring a grain offering in a clean v
Jer 18: 4 The v he was making of clay was spoiled in
18: 4 and he reworked it into another v,
19:11 as one breaks a potter’s v,
22:28 a despised broken pot, a v no one wants?
25:34 and you shall fall like a choice v.
48:11 he has not been emptied from v to v,
48:38 I have broken Moab like a v that no one wants,
51:34 he has made me an empty v,
Eze 4: 9 put them into one v, and make bread for yourself.
Hos 8: 8 now they are among the nations as a useless v.
Wis 13:11 then with pleasing workmanship make a useful v
14: 2 For it was desire for gain that planned that v,
15: 7 and laboriously molds each v for our service,
Sir 50: 9 like a v of hammered gold studded with all kinds

VESSELS (120) [VESSEL]

Ex 7:19 even in v of wood and in v of stone.’ ”
37:16 And he made the v of pure gold that were to be
Nu 3:31 v of the sanctuary with which the priests minister,
4: 9 and all the v for oil with which it is supplied;
7:85 of the v two thousand four hundred shekels
31: 6 with the v of the sanctuary and the trumpets
Jos 6:19 But all silver and gold, and v of bronze and iron,
6:24 and the v of bronze and iron,
Ru 2: 9 go to the v and drink from what
1Sa 21: 5 the v of the young men are holy even when it is
21: 5 how much more today will their v be holy?”
2Sa 17:28 and earthen v, wheat, barley, meal, parched grain,
1Ki 7:45 all these v that Hiram made for King Solomon for
7:47 Solomon left all the v unweighed,
7:48 So Solomon made all the v that were in the house
7:51 the silver, the gold, and the v,
8: 4 and all the holy v that were in the tent;
10:21 All King Solomon’s drinking v were of gold,
10:21 the v of the House of the Forest of Lebanon were
2Ki 4: 3 borrow v from all your neighbors, empty v and
4: 4 and start pouring into all these v;
4: 5 they kept bringing v to her, and she kept pouring.
4: 6 When the v were full, she said to her son,
12:13 bowls, trumpets, or any v of gold, or of silver,
14:14 the v that were found in the house of the LORD
23: 4 the temple of the LORD all the v made for Baal,
24:13 he cut in pieces all the v of gold in the temple of
25:14 and all the bronze v used in the temple service,
25:16 the bronze of all these v was beyond weighing.
1Ch 18: 8 the bronze sea and the pillars and the v of bronze.
22:19 the LORD and the holy v of God may be brought
28:13 the v for the service in the house of the LORD,
28:14 weight of gold for all golden v for each service,
28:14 the weight of silver v for each service,
2Ch 5: 1 and all the v in the treasuries of the house of God.
5: 5 and all the holy v that were in the tent;
9:20 All King Solomon’s drinking v were of gold,
9:20 the v of the House of the Forest of Lebanon were
24:14 and ladles, and v of gold and silver.
25:24 and all the v that were found in the house of God,
36: 7 of the v of the house of the LORD to Babylon
36:10 with the precious v of the house of the LORD,
36:18 All the v of the house of God, large and small,
36:19 and destroyed all its precious v.
Ezr 1: 6 All their neighbors aided them with silver v,
1: 7 King Cyrus himself brought out the v of
1:10 four hundred ten; other v, one thousand;
1:11 and silver v was five thousand four hundred.
5:14 the gold and silver v of the house of God,
5:15 He said to him, “Take these v;
6: 5 let the gold and silver v of the house of God,
7:19 The v that have been given you for the service of
8:25 and the gold and the v, the offering for the house
8:26 and one hundred silver v worth . . . talents,
8:27 two v of fine polished bronze as precious as gold.
8:28 “You are holy to the LORD, and the v are holy;
8:30 the gold, and the v as they were weighed out,
8:33 and the v were weighed into the hands of
Ne 10:39 the storerooms where the v of the sanctuary are,
13: 5 the frankincense, the v, and the tithes of grain,
13: 9 and I brought back the v of the house of God,
Isa 18: 2 sending ambassadors by the Nile in v of papyrus
45: 9 earthen v with the potter!
52:11 you who carry the v of the LORD.
65: 4 with broth of abominable things in their v;
Jer 14: 3 they find no water, they return with their v empty.
27:16 “The v of the LORD’s house will soon
27:18 that the v left in the house of the LORD,
27:19 and the rest of the v that are left in this city,
27:21 concerning the v left in the house of the LORD,
28: 3 to this place all the v of the LORD’s house,
28: 6 to this place from Babylon the v of the house of
40:10 and store them in your v,
48:12 and empty his v, and break his jars in pieces.
52:18 and all the v of bronze used in the temple service.
52:20 the bronze of all these v was beyond weighing.
Eze 27:13 they exchanged human beings and v of bronze
Da 1: 2 as well as some of the v of the house of God.
1: 2 and placed the v in the treasury of his gods.
5: 2 Belshazzar commanded that they bring in the v
5: 3 the v of gold and silver that had been taken out of
5:23 v of his temple have been brought in before you,
11: 8 with their idols and with their precious v of silver
Heb 9:21 with the blood both the tent and all the v used
Jdt 4: 3 and the sacred v and the altar and
Wis 15: 7 of the same clay both the v that serve clean uses
15:13 from earthy matter fragile v and carved images.
Sir 27: 5 The kiln tests the potter’s v;
Bar 1: 8 Baruch took the v of the house of the Lord,
1: 8 the silver v that Zedekiah son of Josiah,
1Mc 1:23 He took the silver and the gold, and the costly v;
2: 9 her glorious v have been carried into exile.
4:49 They made new holy v, and brought
6:12 I seized all its v of silver and gold,
14:15 and added to the v of the sanctuary.
2Mc 4:32 of the gold v of the temple and gave them
4:32 other v, as it happened, he had sold to Tyre and
4:39 many of the gold v had already been stolen.
4:48 and the holy v quickly suffered the unjust penalty.
5:16 He took the holy v with his polluted hands,
9:16 and all the holy v he would give back,
1Es 1:41 Nebuchadnezzar also took some holy v of
1:45 with the holy v of the Lord,
1:54 They took all the holy v of the Lord,
2:10 King Cyrus also brought out the holy v of
2:13 and one thousand other v.
2:14 All the v were handed over, gold and silver,
4:44 and to send back all the v that were taken
4:57 from Babylon all the v that Cyrus had set apart;
6:18 And the holy v of gold and of silver,
6:19 the command that he should take all these v back
6:26 and that the holy v of the house of the Lord,
8:17 deliver the holy v of the Lord that are given you
8:55 the silver and the gold and the holy v of the house
8:56 and silver v worth a hundred talents,
8:57 and twelve bronze v of fine bronze that glittered
8:58 “You are holy to the Lord, and the v are holy,
8:60 and the v that had been in Jerusalem carried them

VESTIBULE (45) [VESTIBULES]

Jdg 3:23 Then Ehud went out into the v,
1Ki 6: 3 The v in front of the nave of the house
7:12 the house of the LORD, and the v of the house.
7:19 the tops of the pillars in the v were of lily-work,
7:21 He set up the pillars at the v of the temple;
1Ch 28:11 the plan of the v of the temple,
2Ch 3: 4 The v in front of the nave of
8:12 of the LORD that he had built in front of the v,
15: 8 the LORD that was in front of the v of the house
29: 7 also shut the doors of the v and put out the lamps,
29:17 on the eighth day of the month they came to the v
Eze 40: 7 and the threshold of the gate by the v of the gate
40: 8 Then he measured the inner v of the gateway,
40: 9 he measured the v of the gateway, eight cubits;
40: 9 and the v of the gate was at the inner end.
40:14 He measured also the v, twenty cubits;
40:15 the end of the inner v of the gate was fifty cubits.
40:21 and its pilasters and its v were of the same size
40:22 its v, and its palm trees were of the same size
40:22 and its v was on the inside.
40:24 and he measured its pilasters and its v;
40:25 There were windows all around in it and in its v,
40:26 its v was on the inside.
40:29 and its v were of the same size as the others;
40:29 there were windows all around in it and in its v;
40:31 Its v faced the outer court,
40:33 its v were of the same dimensions as the others;
40:33 there were windows all around in it and in its v;
40:34 Its v faced the outer court,
40:36 and its v were of the same size as the others;
40:37 Its v faced the outer court,
40:38 There was a chamber with its door in the v of
40:39 in the v of the gate were two tables on either side,
40:40 On the outside of the v at the entrance of
40:40 the other side of the v of the gate were two tables.
40:48 the v of the temple and measured the pilasters of
40:48 and measured the pilasters of the v, five cubits on
40:49 The depth of the v was twenty cubits,
41:15 of the temple and the inner room and the outer v
41:25 a canopy of wood in front of the v outside.
41:26 on the sidewalls of the v.
44: 3 he shall enter by way of the v of the gate,
46: 2 The prince shall enter by the v of the gate
46: 8 he shall come in by the v of the gate,
Joel 2:17 Between the v and the altar let the priests,

VESTIBULES (2) [VESTIBULE]

Eze 40:16 the v also had windows on the inside all around;
40:30 There were v all around, twenty-five cubits deep

VESTMENT (1) [VESTMENTS]

Sir 45:10 with the sacred v, of gold and violet and purple,

VESTMENTS‡ (56) [VESTMENT]

Ex 28: 2 shall make sacred v for the glorious adornment
28: 3 that they make Aaron’s v to consecrate him
28: 4 These are the v that they shall make:
28: 4 When they make these sacred v
29: 5 Then you shall take the v,
29:21 and sprinkle it on Aaron and his v and on his sons
and his sons’ v with him; then he and his v shall
be holy, as well as his sons and his sons’ v.
29:29 The sacred v of Aaron shall be passed on
31:10 and the finely worked v, the holy v for the priest
Aaron and the v of his sons,
35:19 finely worked v for ministering in the holy place,
the holy v for the priest Aaron, and the v of his
35:21 and for all its service, and for the sacred v.
39: 1 and crimson yarns they made finely worked v,
39: 1 they made the sacred v for Aaron;
39:41 finely worked v for ministering in the holy place,
the sacred v for the priest Aaron, and the v of his
40:13 and put on Aaron the sacred v,
Lev 6:10 The priest shall put on his linen v after putting
6:11 he shall take off his v and put on other garments,
8: 2 the v, the anointing oil, the bull of sin offering,
8:30 the altar and sprinkled them on Aaron and his v,
8:30 also on his sons and their v. Thus he consecrated
Aaron and his v, and also his sons and their v.
10: 6 and do not tear your v, or you will die
16: 4 and wear the linen turban; these are the holy v.
16:23 the linen v that he put on when he went into
16:24 in water in a holy place, and put on his v;
16:32 wearing the linen v, the holy v.
21:10 and who has been consecrated to wear the v, shall
not dishevel his hair, nor tear his v.
Nu 20:26 strip Aaron of his v, and put them on his son
20:28 Moses stripped Aaron of his v,
2Ki 10:22 “Bring out the v for all the worshipers of Baal.”
10:22 So he brought out the v for them.
Ezr 3:10 in their v were stationed to praise the LORD
Eze 42:14 of it into the outer court without laying there the v
44:17 of the inner court, they shall wear linen v;
44:19 the v in which they have been ministering,
44:19 to the people with their v.
1Mc 3:49 They also brought the v of the priesthood and
10:21 on the sacred v in the seventh month of
2Mc 3:15 before the altar in their priestly v and called
1Es 1: 2 arrayed in their v, in the temple of the Lord.
4:54 and the priests’ v in which they were to minister.
5:45 and one hundred priests’ v.
5:59 And the priests stood arrayed in their v,
7: 9 in their v, according to kindred, for the services
3Mc 1:16 in all their v prostrated themselves and entreated

VESTRY (KJV) See WARDROBE

VESTURE (KJV) See CLOAK, CLOTHES, CLOTHING, ROBE

VEX, VEXATION, VEXED (KJV) See also ANGUISH, BITTER, CHASING, CONQUER, GREATLY DISTRESSED, GRIEVED, HARM, HARRASS[ED], HOSTILE, OPPRESS[ED], PANIC, PESTERED, RIVAL, ROUTED, SHAKING WITH TERROR, SHEER TERROR, STRAIN, STRUCK WITH TERROR, SUFFER[S], TERRIFY, TORMENT[ED], TREMBLE, TROUBLE[D], TUMULT, VIOLENT, WRONG[ED]

VEXATION (7) [VEXED]

1Sa 1:16 out of my great anxiety and v all this time."
Job 5: 2 v kills the fool, and jealousy slays the simple.
6: 2 "O that my v were weighed,
10:17 and increase your v toward me;
Ecc 1:18 For in much wisdom is much v,
2:23 days are full of pain, and their work is a v;
5:17 in much v and sickness and resentment.

VEXED (1) [VEXATION]

2Mc 11: 1 being v at what had happened,

VIAL (1)

1Sa 10: 1 Samuel took a v of oil and poured it on his head,

VIAL[S] (KJV) See also BOWL[S]

VICES (1)

3Mc 2: 5 who were notorious for their v;

VICINITY‡ (3)

Dt 2:23 who had lived in settlements in the v of Gaza,
Ezr 2:70 some of the people lived in Jerusalem and its v;
1Es 5:46 some of the people settled in Jerusalem and its v;

VICIOUS (1)

Tit 1:12 "Cretans are always liars, v brutes, lazy gluttons."

VICTIM (5) [VICTIM'S, VICTIMS]

Ps 62: 3 will you batter your v, all of you,
Da 11:34 When they fall v, they shall receive a little help,
11:41 and tens of thousands shall fall v,
Sir 28:26 and fall v to one lying in wait.
2Mc 7:10 After him, the third was the v of their sport.

VICTIM'S (2) [VICTIM]

Ex 21:30 for the redemption of the v life.
Pr 29:24 one hears the v curse, but discloses nothing.

VICTIMS (5) [VICTIM]

2Sa 18: 8 the forest claimed more v that day than the sword.
Pr 7:26 those she has laid low, and numerous are her v.
26:28 A lying tongue hates its v,
Jer 14:16 the streets of Jerusalem, v of famine and sword.
Ac 7:42 'Did you offer to me slain v and sacrifices

VICTOR (4) [VICTORY]

Isa 41: 2 Who has roused a v from the east,
Wis 4: 2 v in the contest for prizes that are undefiled.
1Es 3:12 but above all things truth is v."
4Mc 17:15 Reverence for God was v and gave the crown

VICTORIES (3) [VICTORY]

Ps 20: 6 from his holy heaven with mighty v
44: 4 you command v for Jacob.
Isa 26:18 We have won no v on earth,

VICTORIOUS‡ (10) [VICTORY]

Jdg 8: 9 to the people of Penuel, "When I come back v,
11:31 when I return v from the Ammonites,
Isa 41:10 I will uphold you with my v right hand.
Zec 9: 9 and v is he, humble and riding on a donkey,
2Mc 12:11 and his companions, with God's help, were v.
3Mc 3:20 "But we, when we arrived in Egypt v,
2Es 7:*115* [45] or to harm someone who is v."
7:*128* [58] they are v they shall receive what I have said.
4Mc 6:10 while being beaten, was v over his torturers;
18:23 with their v mother are gathered together into

VICTORIOUSLY (1) [VICTORY]

Ps 45: 4 on v for the cause of truth and to defend the right;

VICTORS (1) [VICTORY]

Ex 32:18 But he said, "It is not the sound made by v,

VICTORY (62) [VICTOR, VICTORIES, VICTORIOUS, VICTORIOUSLY, VICTORS]

Dt 20: 4 for you against your enemies, to give you v."
Jdg 15:18 "You have granted this great v by the hand
1Sa 2: 1 because I rejoice in my v.
14:23 So the LORD gave Israel the v that day.
14:45 who has accomplished this great v in Israel?
19: 5 the LORD brought about a great v for all Israel.
2Sa 8: 6 The LORD gave v to David wherever he went.
8:14 the LORD gave v to David wherever he went.
19: 2 So the v that day was turned into mourning for all
23:10 The LORD brought about a great v that day.
23:12 and the LORD brought about a great v.
2Ki 5: 1 because by him the LORD had given v to Aram.
13:17 Then he said, "The LORD's arrow of v,
13:17 the arrow of v over Aram!
1Ch 11:14 and the LORD saved them by a great v.
18: 6 The LORD gave v to David wherever he went.
18:13 the LORD gave v to David wherever he went.
29:11 are the greatness, the power, the glory, the v,
2Ch 20:17 and see the v of the LORD on your behalf,
Job 40:14 to you that your own right hand can give you v.
Ps 20: 5 May we shout for joy over your v,
20: 9 Give v to the king, O LORD;
Ps 33:17 The war horse is a vain hope for v,
44: 3 nor did their own arm give them v;
48:10 Your right hand is filled with v.
60: 5 Give v with your right hand,
98: 1 and his holy arm have gotten him v.
98: 2 The LORD has made known his v;
98: 3 the ends of the earth have seen the v of our God.
108: 6 Give v with your right hand, and answer me,
118:15 There are glad songs of v in the tents of
144:10 the one who gives v to kings,
149: 4 he adorns the humble with v.
Pr 21:31 but the v belongs to the LORD.
24: 6 and in abundance of counselors there is v.
Isa 26: 1 he sets up v like walls and bulwarks.
59:16 so his own arm brought him v,
63: 5 so my own arm brought me v,
Jer 51:14 and they shall raise a shout of v over you.
Hab 3: 8 when you drove your horses, your chariots to v?
Zep 3:17 is in your midst, a warrior who gives v;
Zec 12: 7 the LORD will give v to the tents of Judah first,
Mt 12:20 a smoldering wick until he brings justice to v.
1Co 15:54 "Death has been swallowed up in v."
15:55 "Where, O death, is your v?
15:57 who gives us the v through our Lord Jesus Christ.
1Jn 5: 4 this is the v that conquers the world, our faith.
Wis 10:12 in his arduous contest she gave him the v,
1Mc 3:19 on the size of the army that v in battle depends,
2Mc 5: 6 but imagining that he was setting up trophies of v
8:33 While they were celebrating the v in the city
10:28 as pledge of success and v not only their valor but
10:38 to Israel and gives them the v.
13:15 He gave his troops the watchword, "God's v,"
15: 6 to erect a public monument of v over Judas
15: 8 for the v that the Almighty would give them.
15:21 that he gains the v for those who deserve it.
1Es 3: 5 Darius will give rich gifts and great honors of v.
3: 9 the v shall be given according to what is written."
4: 5 if they win the v, they bring everything to
4:59 "From you comes the v;
4Mc 7: 3 until he sailed into the haven of immortal v.

VICTUAL[S] (KJV) See FOOD, GRAIN, JARS, LIVING, PROVISIONS

VIEW (15) [VIEWED]

Dt 15: 9 therefore v your needy neighbor with hostility
32:49 across from Jericho, and v the land of Canaan,
32:52 Although you may v the land from a distance,
Jos 2: 1 saying, "Go, v the land, especially Jericho."
18: 4 a description of it with a v to their inheritances.
Da 9:16 O Lord, in v of all your righteous acts,
1Co 7:26 I think that, in v of the impending crisis,
2Co 5:16 we regard no one from a human point of v;
5:16 we once knew Christ from a human point of v,
2Ti 4: 1 and in v of his appearing and his kingdom,
Jdt 7: 6 in full v of the Israelites in Bethulia.
1Mc 14:38 "In v of these things King Demetrius confirmed
2Mc 4: 5 not accusing his compatriots but having in v
6:11 in v of their regard for that most holy day.
3Mc 4: 7 and in public v they were violently dragged along

VIEWED (1) [VIEW]

2Ki 16:12 king came from Damascus, the king v the altar.

VIGIL (3) [VIGILANCE, VIGILANT]

Ex 12:42 That was for the LORD a night of v,
12:42 a v to be kept for the LORD by all the Israelites
Sir 33:16 Now I was the last to keep v;

VIGILANCE (1) [VIGIL]

Pr 4:23 Keep your heart with all v,

VIGILANT‡ (1) [VIGIL]

Wis 6:15 and one who is v on her account will soon be free

VIGILANT (KJV) See also ALERT, TEMPERATE

VIGOR (6) [VIGOROUS, VIGOROUSLY]

Ge 49: 3 my might and the first fruits of my v,
Dt 34: 7 his sight was unimpaired and his v had
Job 30: 2 All their v is gone.
33:25 let him return to the days of his youthful v.'
Tob 11:16 along in full v and with no one leading him,
2Mc 12:23 Judas pressed the pursuit with the utmost v,

VIGOROUS (4) [VIGOR]

Ex 1:19 for they are v and give birth before the midwife
Isa 59:10 among the v as though we were dead.
Sir 41: 1 and still is v enough to enjoy food!
2Mc 12:27 before the walls and made a v defense;

VIGOROUSLY‡ (1) [VIGOR]

2Mc 10:17 Attacking them v, they gained possession of

VILE (11) [VILENESS]

Jdg 19:23 Since this man is my guest, do not do this v thing.
19:24 but against this man do not do such a v thing."
20: 6 for they have committed a v outrage in Israel.
2Sa 13:12 do not do anything so v!
Jer 11:15 when she has done v deeds?
Eze 6:11 for all the v abominations of the house of Israel!
8: 9 see the v abominations that they are committing
21:25 As for you, v, wicked prince of Israel,
21:29 they place you over the necks of the v,
2Mc 4:19 the v Jason sent envoys, chosen
15:32 the v Nicanor's head and that profane man's arm,

VILENESS (1) [VILE]

Ps 12: 8 as v is exalted among humankind.

VILLAGE‡ (18) [VILLAGES]

Mt 10:11 Whatever town or v you enter,
21: 2 "Go into the v ahead of you,
Mk 8:23 by the hand and led him out of the v;
8:26 saying, "Do not even go into the v."
11: 2 "Go into the v ahead of you,
Lk 5:17 near by (they had come from every v of Galilee
9:52 On their way they entered a v of the Samaritans
9:56 Then they went on to another v.
10:38 as they went on their way, he entered a certain v,
13:22 Jesus went through one town and v after another,
17:12 As he entered a v, ten lepers approached him.
19:30 "Go into the v ahead of you,
24:13 of them were going to a v called Emmaus,
24:28 they came near the v to which they were going,
Jn 7:42 the v where David lived?"
11: 1 the v of Mary and her sister Martha.
11:30 Now Jesus had not yet come to the v,
2Mc 14:16 and engaged them in battle at a v called Dessau.

VILLAGES‡ (108) [VILLAGE]

Ge 25:16 by their v and by their encampments,
Lev 25:31 in v that have no walls around them shall
Nu 21:25 in Heshbon, and in all its v.
21:32 and they captured its v, and dispossessed
32:41 Jair son of Manasseh went and captured their v,
32:42 And Nobah went and captured Kenath and its v,
Dt 3: 5 double gates, and bars, besides a great many v.
Jos 13:23 according to their families with their towns and v.
13:28 according to their clans, with their towns and v.
15:32 in all, twenty-nine towns, with their v.
15:36 fourteen towns with their v.
15:41 sixteen towns with their v.
15:44 and Mareshah: nine towns with their v.
15:45 Ekron, with its dependencies and its v;
15:46 all that were near Ashdod, with their v.
15:47 its towns and its v; Gaza, its towns and its v;
15:51 eleven towns with their v.
15:54 and Zior: nine towns with their v.
15:57 and Timnah: ten towns with their v.
15:59 and Eltekon: six towns with their v.
15:60 and Rabbah: two towns with their v.
15:62 and En-gedi: six towns with their v.
16: 9 all those towns with their v.
17:11 Manasseh had Beth-shean and its v, Ibleam and its v, the inhabitants of Dor and its v, the inhabitants of En-dor and its v, the inhabitants of Taanach and its v, and the inhabitants of Megiddo and its v
17:16 both those in Beth-shean and its v and those in
18:24 twelve towns with their v:
18:28 fourteen towns with their v.
19: 6 thirteen towns with their v;
19: 7 and Ashan—four towns with their v;
19: 8 together with all the v all around these towns
19:15 twelve towns with their v.
19:16 to its families—these towns with their v.
19:22 sixteen towns with their v.
19:23 to its families—the towns with their v.
19:30 twenty-two towns with their v.
19:31 to its families—these towns with their v.
19:38 nineteen towns with their v.
19:39 to its families—the towns with their v.
19:48 to their families—these towns with their v.
21:12 of the town and its v had been given to Caleb son
Jdg 1:27 and its v, or Taanach and its v, or the inhabitants of Dor and its v, or the inhabitants of Ibleam and its v, or the inhabitants of Megiddo and its v;
11:26 While Israel lived in Heshbon and its v,
11:26 and in Aroer and its v,
1Sa 6:18 both fortified cities and unwalled v.
1Ki 4:13 in Ramoth-gilead (he had the v of Jair son
1Ch 2:23 Kenath and its v, sixty towns.
4:32 And their v were Etam, Ain, Rimmon, Tochen,
4:33 with all their v that were around these towns
6:56 and its v they gave to Caleb son of Jephunneh.
9:16 who lived in the v of the Netophathites.
9:22 They were enrolled by genealogies in their v.
9:25 in their v were obliged to come
18: 1 he took Gath and its v from the Philistines.
27:25 in the cities, in the v and in the towers,
2Ch 13:19 its v and Jeshanah with its v and Ephron with its v.
28:18 its v, Timnah with its v, and Gimzo with its v;
Ne 6: 2 "Come and let us meet together in one of the v in
11:25 And as for the v, with their fields,
11:25 Kiriath-arba and its v, and in Dibon and its v, and in Jekabzeel and its v,
11:27 in Hazar-shual, in Beer-sheba and its v,
11:28 in Ziklag, in Meconah and its v,
11:30 Adullam, and their v, Lachish and its fields, and Azekah and its v.
11:31 at Michmash, Aija, Bethel and its v,
12:28 from the circuit around Jerusalem and from the v
12:29 for the singers had built for themselves v
Est 9:19 Therefore the Jews of the v,
Ps 10: 8 They sit in ambush in the v;

SS 7:11 let us go forth into the fields, and lodge in the v;
Isa 42:11 the v that Kedar inhabits;
Jer 49: 2 and its v shall be burned with fire;
Eze 38:11 "I will go up against the land of unwalled v;
Zec 2: 4 Jerusalem shall be inhabited like v without walls,
Mt 9:35 Then Jesus went about all the cities and v,
14:15 the crowds away so that they may go into the v
Mk 6: 6 Then he went about among the v teaching.
6:36 the surrounding country and v and buy something
6:56 And wherever he went, into v or cities or farms,
8:27 on with his disciples to the v of Caesarea Philippi;
Lk 8: 1 Soon afterwards he went on through cities and v,
9: 6 They departed and went through the v,
9:12 into the surrounding v and countryside, to lodge
Ac 8:25 the good news to many v of the Samaritans.
Jdt 4: 5 the v on them and stored up food in preparation
15: 7 Even the v and towns in the hill country and in
1Mc 5: 8 He also took Jazer and its v;
5:65 and its v and tore down its strongholds
7:46 the surrounding v of Judea, and they outflanked
2Mc 4:48 and the v and the holy vessels quickly suffered
8: 1 and his companions secretly entered the v
8: 6 he would set fire to towns and v.
1Es 4:50 the Idumeans should give up the v of the Jews

VILLAIN (3) [VILLAINIES, VILLAINS, VILLAINY]

Pr 6:12 and a v goes around with crooked speech,
Isa 32: 5 nor a v said to be honorable.
Sir 19:26 There is the v bowed down in mourning,

VILLAINIES (1) [VILLAIN]

Isa 32: 7 The v of villains are evil; they devise wicked

VILLAINS (1) [VILLAIN]

Isa 32: 7 The villainies of v are evil; they devise wicked

VILLAINY (2) [VILLAIN]

Ac 13:10 full of all deceit and v, will you not stop making
18:14 "If it were a matter of crime or serious v,

VINDICATE (7) [VINDICATED, VINDICATES, VINDICATING, VINDICATION, VINDICATOR]

Dt 32:36 Indeed the LORD will v his people,
1Sa 24:15 and plead my cause, and v me against you."
Ps 26: 1 V me, O LORD, for I have walked in my integrity,
35:24 V me, O LORD, my God,
43: 1 V me, O God, and defend my cause against
54: 1 O God, by your name, and v me by your might.
135:14 For the LORD will v his people,

VINDICATED (9) [VINDICATE]

Ge 20:16 before all who are with you; you are completely v.
2Sa 18:31 For the LORD has v you this day,
Job 11: 2 and should one full of talk be v?
13:18 I know that I shall be v.
Mt 11:19 Yet wisdom is v by her deeds."
Lk 7:35 Nevertheless, wisdom is v by all her children."
1Ti 3:16 He was revealed in flesh, v in spirit,
AdE 10:12 God remembered his people and v his inheritance.
4Mc 17:10 They v their nation, looking to God

VINDICATES (1) [VINDICATE]

Isa 50: 8 he who v me is near. Who will contend with me?

VINDICATING (2) [VINDICATE]

1Ki 8:32 and v the righteous by rewarding them according
2Ch 6:23 and v those who are in the right

VINDICATION‡ (16) [VINDICATE]

Job 6:29 Turn now, my v is at stake.
Ps 17: 2 From you let my v come;
24: 5 and v from the God of their salvation.
35:27 Let those who desire my v shout for joy and
37: 6 He will make your v shine like the light,
98: 2 he has revealed his v in the sight of the nations.
103: 6 The LORD works v and justice
Isa 34: 8 a year of v by Zion's cause.
54:17 the servants of the LORD and their v from me,
62: 1 until her v shines out like the dawn,
62: 2 The nations shall see your v,
63: 1 "It is I, announcing v, mighty to save."
Jer 46:10 a day of retribution, to gain v from his foes.
51:10 The LORD has brought forth our v;
Joel 2:23 for he has given the early rain for your v,
Mic 7: 9 He will bring me out to the light; I shall see his v.

VINDICATOR‡ (2) [VINDICATE]

Isa 58: 8 your v shall go before you,
4Mc 15:29 v of the law and champion of religion,

VINE (50) [GRAPEVINE, VINE-ROWS, VINEDRESSERS, VINEGROWER, VINES, VINESTOCK, VINEYARD, VINEYARDS, VINTAGE, VINTAGE-SHOUT]

Ge 40: 9 "In my dream there was a v before me,
40:10 and on the v there were three branches.
49:11 foal to the v and his donkey's colt to the choice v,
Lev 25: 5 or gather the grapes of your unpruned v:
Dt 32:32 Their v comes from the vinestock of Sodom,
Jdg 9:12 trees said to the v, 'You come and reign over us.'
9:13 But the v said to them,
13:14 not eat of anything that comes from the v.
2Ki 4:39 he found a wild v and gathered from it a lapful
18:31 then every one of you will eat from your own v
Job 15:33 They will shake off their unripe grape, like the v,
Ps 80: 8 You brought a v out of Egypt;
80:14 and see; have regard for this v,
128: 3 be like a fruitful v within your house;
SS 7: 8 Oh, may your breasts be like clusters of the v,
Isa 24: 7 The wine dries up, the v languishes,
32:12 for the pleasant fields, for the fruitful v,
34: 4 like a leaf withering on a v,
36:16 then everyone of you will eat from your own v
Jer 2:21 I planted you as a choice v, from the purest stock.
2:21 did you turn degenerate and become a wild v?
6: 9 Glean thoroughly as a v the remnant of Israel;
8:13 says the LORD, there are no grapes on the v,
48:32 for Jazer I weep for you, O v of Sibmah!
Eze 15: 2 does the wood of the v surpass all other wood—
15: 2 the v branch that is among the trees of the forest?
15: 6 the wood of the v among the trees of the forest,
17: 6 It sprouted and became a v spreading out,
17: 6 So it became a v; it brought forth branches,
17: 7 This v stretched out its roots toward him;
17: 8 and bear fruit and become a noble v.
19:10 like a v in a vineyard transplanted by the water,
Hos 10: 1 Israel is a luxuriant v that yields its fruit.
14: 7 they shall blossom like the v,
Joel 1:12 The v withers, the fig tree droops.
2:22 the fig tree and v give their full yield.
Hag 2:19 Do the v, the fig tree, the pomegranate,
Zec 3:10 you shall invite each other to come under your v
8:12 the v shall yield its fruit,
Mal 3:11 and your v in the field shall not be barren,
Mt 26:29 I will never again drink of this fruit of the v until
Mk 14:25 I will never again drink of the fruit of the v until
Lk 22:18 from now on I will not drink of the fruit of the v
Jn 15: 1 "I am the true v, and my Father is the vinegrower.
15: 4 cannot bear fruit by itself unless it abides in the v,
15: 5 I am the v, you are the branches.
Rev 14:18 and gather the clusters of the v of the earth,
Sir 24:17 Like the v I bud forth delights,
2Es 5:23 and from all its trees you have chosen one v,

VINE-ROWS (1) [ROW, VINE]

Jer 5:10 Go up through her v and destroy,

VINEDRESSERS (4) [DRESS, VINE]

2Ki 25:12 the poorest people of the land to be v and tillers
2Ch 26:10 and he had farmers and v in the hills and in
Jer 52:16 the poorest people of the land to be v and tillers
Joel 1:11 Be dismayed, you farmers, wail, you v,

VINEDRESSERS (KJV) See also DRESS YOUR VINES

VINEGAR (5)

Nu 6: 3 they shall drink no wine v or other v,
Ps 69:21 and for my thirst they gave me v to drink.
Pr 10:26 Like v to the teeth, and smoke to the eyes,
25:20 Like v on a wound is one who sings songs to

VINEGROWER (1) [GROW, VINE]

Jn 15: 1 "I am the true vine, and my Father is the v.

VINES (21) [VINE]

Lev 25:11 or harvest the unpruned v.
Nu 20: 5 It is no place for grain, or figs, or v,
Dt 8: 8 of v and fig trees and pomegranates,
1Ki 4:25 all of them under their v and fig trees.
Ps 78:47 He destroyed their v with hail,
105:33 He struck their v and fig trees,
SS 2:13 and the v are in blossom;
6:11 to see whether the v had budded,
7:12 and see whether the v have budded,
Isa 5: 2 and planted it with choice v;
7:23 where there used to be a thousand v,
16: 8 fields of Heshbon languish, and the v of Sibmah,
16: 9 with the weeping of Jazer for the v of Sibmah;
61: 5 foreigners shall till your land and dress your v;
Jer 5:17 they shall eat up your v and your fig trees;
Hos 2:12 I will lay waste her v and her fig trees,
Joel 1: 7 It has laid waste my v,
Mic 4: 4 under their own v and under their own fig trees,
Hab 3:17 and no fruit is on the v;
1Mc 14:12 All the people sat under their own v and fig trees,
2Es 16:43 so also the one who prunes the v,

VINESTOCK (1) [VINE]

Dt 32:32 Their vine comes from the v of Sodom,

VINEYARD (75) [VINE]

Ge 9:20 Noah, a man of the soil, was the first to plant a v.
Ex 22: 5 someone causes a field or v to be grazed over,
22: 5 be made from the best in the owner's field or v.
23:11 You shall do the same with your v,
Lev 19:10 You shall not strip your v bare, or gather the fallen grapes of your v;
25: 3 and six years you shall prune your v,
25: 4 you shall not sow your field or prune your v.
Nu 20:17 We will not pass through field or v,
21:22 we will not turn aside into field or v;
Dt 20: 6 a v but not yet enjoyed its fruit?
22: 9 You shall not sow your v with a second kind
22: 9 that you have sown and the yield of the v itself.
23:24 If you go into your neighbor's v,
24:21 When you gather the grapes of your v,
28:30 You shall plant a v, but not enjoy its fruit.
1Ki 21: 1 Naboth the Jezreelite had a v in Jezreel,
21: 2 And Ahab said to Naboth, "Give me your v,
21: 2 I will give you a better v for it;
21: 6 'Give me your v for money;
21: 6 if you prefer, I will give you another v for it';
21: 6 but he answered, 'I will not give you my v.' "
21: 7 I will give you the v of Naboth the Jezreelite."
21:15 take possession of the v of Naboth the Jezreelite,
21:16 to go down to the v of Naboth the Jezreelite,
21:18 he is now in the v of Naboth,
Job 24: 6 in a field not their own and they glean in the v of
27:18 like booths made by sentinels of the v.
Pr 24:30 by the v of a stupid person;
31:16 with the fruit of her hands she plants a v.
SS 1: 6 but my own v I have not kept!
8:11 Solomon had a v at Baal-hamon; he entrusted the v to keepers;
8:12 My v, my very own, is for myself;
Isa 1: 8 And daughter Zion is left like a booth in a v,
3:14 It is you who have devoured the v;
5: 1 for my beloved my love-song concerning his v:
5: 1 My beloved had a v on a very fertile hill.
5: 3 judge between me and my v.
5: 4 What more was there to do for my v that I have
5: 5 And now I will tell you what I will do to my v.
5: 7 the v of the LORD of hosts is the house of Israel,
5:10 For ten acres of v shall yield but one bath,
27: 2 On that day: A pleasant v, sing about it!
Jer 12:10 Many shepherds have destroyed my v,
35: 7 nor shall you plant a v, or even own one;
35: 9 We have no v or field or seed;
Eze 19:10 Your mother was like a vine in a v transplanted
Mt 20: 1 in the morning to hire laborers for his v.
20: 2 he sent them into his v.
20: 4 'You also go into the v,
20: 7 He said to them, 'You also go into the v.'
20: 8 the owner of the v said to his manager,
21:28 'Son, go and work in the v today.'
21:33 There was a landowner who planted a v,
21:39 So they seized him, threw him out of the v,
21:40 Now when the owner of the v comes,
21:41 and lease the v to other tenants who will give him
Mk 12: 1 "A man planted a v, put a fence around it,
12: 2 from them his share of the produce of the v.
12: 8 killed him, and threw him out of the v.
12: 9 What then will the owner of the v do?
12: 9 and destroy the tenants and give the v to others.
Lk 13: 6 "A man had a fig tree planted in his v;
20: 9 "A man planted a v, and leased it to tenants,
20:10 his share of the produce of the v;
20:13 Then the owner of the v said, 'What shall I do?
20:15 So they threw him out of the v and killed him.
20:15 What then will the owner of the v do to them?
20:16 and destroy those tenants and give the v
1Co 9: 7 Who plants a v and does not eat any of its fruit?
1Mc 3:56 or were about to be married, or were planting a v,
2Es 16:30 or just as when a v is gathered,
16:30 by those who search carefully through the v,
4Mc 2: 9 the harvest nor gathers the last grapes from the v.

VINEYARDS (48) [VINE]

Nu 16:14 or given us an inheritance of fields and v.
22:24 the LORD stood in a narrow path between the v,
Dt 6:11 v and olive groves that you did not plant—
28:39 You shall plant v and dress them,
32:32 the vinestock of Sodom, from the v of Gomorrah;
Jos 24:13 you eat the fruit of v and oliveyards that you did
Jdg 9:27 the field and gathered the grapes from their v,
14: 5 When he came to the v of Timnah,
15: 5 as well as the v and olive groves.
21:20 saying, "Go and lie in wait in the v,
21:21 the v and each of you carry off a wife for himself
1Sa 8:14 the best of your fields and v and olive orchards
8:15 He will take one-tenth of your grain and of your v
22: 7 of Jesse give every one of you fields and v,
2Ki 5:26 olive orchards and v, sheep and oxen,
18:32 a land of grain and wine, a land of bread and v,
19:29 then in the third year sow, reap, plant v,
1Ch 27:27 Over the v was Shimei the Ramathite.
27:27 of the v for the wine cellars was Zabdi
Ne 5: 3 "We are having to pledge our fields, our v,
5: 4 to borrow money on our fields and v to pay
5: 5 and our fields and v now belong to others."
5:11 their v, their olive orchards, and their houses,
9:25 v, olive orchards, and fruit trees in abundance;
Job 24:18 no treader turns toward their v.
Ps 107:37 and plant v, and get a fruitful yield.
Ecc 2: 4 I built houses and planted v for myself;
SS 1: 6 they made me keeper of the v,
1:14 a cluster of henna blossoms in the v of En-gedi.
2:15 foxes, that ruin the v—for our v are in blossom."
7:12 let us go out early to the v,
Isa 16:10 in the v no songs are sung, no shouts are raised;
36:17 a land of grain and wine, a land of bread and v.
37:30 then in the third year sow, reap, plant v,
65:21 they shall plant v and eat their fruit.
Jer 31: 5 Again you shall plant v on the mountains
32:15 and fields and v shall again be bought in this land.

Jer 39:10 and gave them v and fields at the same time.
Eze 28:26 and shall build houses and plant v.
Hos 2:15 From there I will give her her v,
Am 4: 9 I laid waste your gardens and your v;
5:11 you have planted pleasant v,
5:17 in all the v there shall be wailing,
9:14 they shall plant v and drink their wine,
Mic 1: 6 a heap in the open country, a place for planting v.
Zep 1:13 though they plant v, they shall not drink wine from
1Es 4:16 men who plant the v from which comes wine.

VINTAGE (9) [VINE]

Lev 26: 5 Your threshing shall overtake the v, and the v shall overtake the sowing;
Jdg 8: 2 of the grapes of Ephraim better than the v
Isa 32:10 for the v will fail, the fruit harvest will not come.
Jer 48:32 upon your summer fruits and your v
Mic 7: 1 after the v has been gleaned,
Rev 14:19 over the earth and gathered the v of the earth,
Sir 24:27 like the Gihon at the time of v.
2Es 12:42 like a cluster of grapes from the v,

VINTAGE-SHOUT (1) [SHOUT, VINE]

Isa 16:10 treads out wine in the presses; the v is hushed.

VIOL[S] (KJV) See HARP[S]

VIOLATE (9) [VIOLATED, VIOLATING, VIOLATION]

Job 37:23 and abundant righteousness he will not v.
Ps 89:31 if they v my statutes and do not keep my
89:34 I will not v my covenant,
Eze 22:10 in you they v women in their menstrual periods.
Da 11:32 seduce with intrigue those who v the covenant;
Tob 9: 3 and I cannot v his oath."
Sir 20: 4 to v a girl is the person who does right
3Mc 2:14 and profane man undertakes to v the holy place
4Mc 16:24 to die rather than v God's commandment.

VIOLATED (9) [VIOLATE]

Dt 22:24 and the man because he v his neighbor's wife.
22:29 Because he v her he shall not be permitted
27:20 because he has v his father's rights."
Ps 55:20 My companion laid hands on a friend and v
Isa 24: 5 for they have transgressed laws, v the statutes,
Jer 13:22 that your skirts are lifted up, and you are v.
1Ti 5:12 for having v their first pledge.
Heb 10:28 Anyone who has v the law of Moses dies
1Mc 7:18 for they have v the agreement and the oath

VIOLATING (1) [VIOLATE]

Dt 22:30 his father's wife, thereby v his father's rights.

VIOLATION (5) [VIOLATE]

Ecc 5: 8 and the v of justice and right, do not be amazed at
Ac 23: 3 yet in v of the law you order me to be struck?"
Ro 4:15 but where there is no law, neither is there v.
2Mc 15:10 the perfidy of the Gentiles and their v of oaths.
4Mc 4:19 and altered its form of government in complete v

VIOLENCE‡ (73) [VIOLENT, VIOLENTLY]

Ge 6:11 and the earth was filled with v.
6:13 for the earth is filled with v because of them;
49: 5 weapons of v are their swords.
Jdg 9:24 the v done to the seventy sons of Jerubbaal might
2Sa 22: 3 my savior; you save me from v.
Job 16:17 though there is no v in my hands,
19: 7 Even when I cry out, '**V!**'
30:18 With v he seizes my garment;
Ps 7:16 and on their own heads their v descends.
11: 5 and his soul hates the lover of v.
27:12 and they are breathing out v.
55: 9 for I see v and strife in the city.
58: 2 your hands deal out v on earth.
72:14 From oppression and v he redeems their life;
73: 6 v covers them like a garment.
74:20 dark places of the land are full of the haunts of v.
Pr 4:17 the bread of wickedness and drink the wine of v.
10: 6 but the mouth of the wicked conceals v.
10:11 but the mouth of the wicked conceals v.
11:30 a tree of life, but v takes lives away.
19:26 Those who do v to their father
21: 7 The v of the wicked will sweep them away,
24: 2 for their minds devise v, and their lips talk
24:15 do no v to the place where the righteous live;
26: 6 like cutting off one's foot and drinking down v,
Isa 53: 9 although he had done no v,
59: 6 and deeds of v are in their hands.
60:18 V shall no more be heard in your land,
Jer 6: 7 v and destruction are heard within her;
20: 8 I must cry out, I must shout, "**V** and destruction!"
22: 3 And do no wrong or v to the alien, the orphan,
22:17 and for practicing oppression and v.
51:46 rumors of v in the land and of ruler against ruler.
Eze 7:11 V has grown into a rod of wickedness.
7:23 land is full of bloody crimes; the city is full of v.
8:17 Must they fill the land with v,
12:19 on account of the v of all those who live in it.
22:26 Its priests have done v to my teaching
28:16 of your trade you were filled with v,
45: 9 Put away v and oppression,
Hos 12: 1 they multiply falsehood and v;
Joel 3:19 because of the v done to the people of Judah,
Am 3:10 up v and robbery in their strongholds.
6: 3 and bring near a reign of v?
Ob 1:10 the slaughter and v done to your brother Jacob,
Jnh 3: 8 All shall turn from their evil ways and from the v
Mic 6:12 Your wealthy are full of v;
Hab 1: 2 Or cry to you "**V!**" and you will not save?
1: 3 Destruction and v are before me;
1: 9 They all come for v, with faces pressing forward;
2: 8 because of human bloodshed, and v to the earth,
2:17 For the v done to Lebanon will overwhelm you;
2:17 because of human bloodshed and v to the earth,
Zep 1: 9 who fill their master's house with v and fraud.
3: 4 they have done v to the law.
Mal 1:13 You bring what has been taken by v or is lame
2:16 and covering one's garment with v,
Mt 11:12 until now the kingdom of heaven has suffered v,
Ac 5:26 without v, for they were afraid of being stoned by
21:35 the v of the mob was so great that he had to
1Ti 1:13 a persecutor, and a man of v.
Rev 18:21 "With such v Babylon the great city will
AdE 13: 7 and remain so may in a single day go down in v
Wis 4: 4 and by the v of the winds they will be uprooted.
19:13 the sinners without prior signs in the v of thunder,
1Mc 1:58 They kept using v against Israel,
3Mc 1:16 the v of this evil design, and they filled the temple
4: 5 a swift pace by the v with which they were driven
2Es 11:46 freed from your v, may be refreshed and relieved,
4Mc 5:37 as one who does not fear your v even to death.
11:26 and the catapults painless, and your v powerless.
17: 2 with your seven sons nullified the v of the tyrant,
17: 9 the v of the tyrant who wished to destroy the way

VIOLENT (31) [VIOLENCE]

2Sa 3:39 these men, the sons of Zeruiah, are too v for me.
22:49 you delivered me from the v.
Ps 17: 4 of your lips I have avoided the ways of the v.
18:48 you delivered me from the v.
25:19 and with what v hatred they hate me.
140: 1 protect me from those who are v,
140: 4 from the v who have planned my downfall.
140:11 let evil speedily hunt down the v!
Pr 3:31 the v and do not choose any of their ways;
16:29 The v entice their neighbors,
19:19 A v tempered person will pay the penalty;
Eze 7:22 the v shall enter it, they shall profane it.
18:10 If he has a son who is v, a shedder of blood,
28: 8 you shall die a v death in the heart of the seas.
Da 2:12 a v rage and commanded that all the wise men
Mt 11:12 and the v take it by force.
Ac 2: 2 a sound like the rush of a v wind,
12: 1 About that time King Herod laid v hands
16:26 v that the foundations of the prison were shaken;
23:10 When the dissension became v, the tribune,
27:14 But soon a v wind, called the northeaster,
1Ti 3: 3 not v but gentle, not quarrelsome,
Tit 1: 7 or addicted to wine or v or greedy for gain;
Rev 16:18 rumblings, peals of thunder, and a v earthquake,
16:18 so v was that earthquake.
Sir 10:18 or v anger for those born of women.
2Es 4:49 before me and poured down a heavy and v rain,
4:49 and when the v rainstorm had passed,
4Mc 2:15 that reason rules even the more v emotions:
8: 2 then in v rage he commanded that others of
15:32 by the flood of your emotions and the v winds,

VIOLENTLY‡ (14) [VIOLENCE]

Ge 27:33 Then Isaac trembled v, and said,
Ex 19:18 while the whole mountain shook v.
Jdg 8: 1 And they upbraided him v.
Job 39:21 It paws v, exults mightily;
Isa 22:17 LORD is about to hurl you away v, my fellow.
24:19 the earth is torn asunder, the earth is v shaken.
Ac 27:18 We were being pounded by the storm so v that on
Gal 1:13 I was v persecuting the church of God
Wis 17:18 or the rhythm of v rushing water,
3Mc 4: 7 In bonds and in public view they were v dragged
2Es 5:14 Then I woke up, and my body shuddered v,
15:39 the east wind shall be driven v toward the south
15:52 Would I have dealt with you so v, says the Lord,
4Mc 6: 1 the guards who were standing by dragged him v

VIOLET (1)

Sir 45:10 the sacred vestment, of gold and v and purple,

VIPER (5) [VIPERS]

Ge 49:17 a v along the path, that bites the horse's heels so
Job 20:16 the tongue of a v will kill them.
Isa 30: 6 of v and flying serpent, they carry their riches on
59: 5 and the crushed egg hatches out a v.
Ac 28: 3 when a v, driven out by the heat,

VIPERS (7) [VIPER]

Ps 140: 3 and under their lips is the venom of v.
Mt 3: 7 he said to them, "You brood of v!
12:34 You brood of v! How can you speak good things,
23:33 You snakes, you brood of v!
Lk 3: 7 to be baptized by him, "You brood of v!
Ro 3:13 "The venom of v is under their lips."
Sir 39:30 the fangs of wild animals and scorpions and v,

VIRGIN‡ (37) [VIRGIN'S, VIRGINITY, VIRGINS]

Ge 24:16 The girl was very fair to look upon, a v,
Ex 22:16 When a man seduces a v who is not engaged to
Lev 21: 3 likewise, for a v sister, close to him
21:13 He shall marry only a woman who is a v.
21:14 He shall marry a v of his own kin,
Dt 22:19 because he has slandered a v of Israel.
22:23 a v already engaged to be married,
22:28 If a man meets a v who is not engaged,
Jdg 19:24 Here are my v daughter and his concubine;
2Sa 13: 2 for she was a v and it seemed impossible
13:18 how the v daughters of the king were clothed
1Ki 1: 2 "Let a young v be sought for my lord the king,
2Ki 19:21 she scorns you—v daughter Zion;
Job 31: 1 how then could I look upon a v?
Isa 23:12 O oppressed v daughter Sidon;
37:22 she scorns you—v daughter Zion;
47: 1 down and sit in the dust, v daughter Babylon!
Jer 14:17 and let them not cease, for the v daughter—
18:13 The v Israel has done a most horrible thing.
31: 4 and you shall be built, O v Israel!
31:21 Return, O v Israel, return to these your cities.
46:11 and take balm, O v daughter Egypt!
La 1:15 as in a wine press the v daughter Judah.
2:13 that I may comfort you, O v daughter Zion?
Eze 23: 3 and their v bosoms were fondled.
23: 8 and fondled her v bosom and poured out their lust
44:22 but only a v of the stock of the house of Israel,
Joel 1: 8 like a v dressed in sackcloth for the husband
Mt 1:23 the v shall conceive and bear a son,
Lk 1:27 to a v engaged to a man whose name was Joseph,
1:34 "How can this be, since I am a v?"
1Co 7:28 if you marry, you do not sin, and if a v marries,
7:34 the unmarried woman and the v are anxious about
2Co 11: 2 to present you as a chaste v to Christ.
Sir 9: 5 Do not look intently at a v,
42:10 while a v, for fear she may be seduced
4Mc 18: 7 a pure v and did not go outside my father's house;

VIRGIN'S (2) [VIRGIN]

Lk 1:27 The v name was Mary.
Jdt 9: 2 a v clothing to defile her, and exposed her thighs

VIRGINITY (8) [VIRGIN]

Dt 22:14 I lay with her, I did not find evidence of her v."
22:15 then submit the evidence of the young woman's v
22:17 'I did not find evidence of your daughter's v.'
22:17 But here is the evidence of my daughter's v."
22:20 evidence of the young woman's v was not found,
Jdg 11:37 and bewail my v, my companions and I."
11:38 and bewailed her v on the mountains.
4Mc 18: 8 the deceitful serpent, defile the purity of my v.

VIRGINS‡ (15) [VIRGIN]

Ex 22:17 an amount equal to the bride-price for v.
Jdg 21:12 four hundred young v who had never slept with
Est 2: 2 "Let beautiful young v be sought out for the king.
2: 3 of his kingdom to gather all the beautiful young v
2:17 of all the v she won his favor and devotion,
2:19 When the v were being gathered together,
Ps 45:14 behind her the v, her companions, follow.
La 5:11 v in the towns of Judah.
1Co 7:25 concerning v, I have no command of the Lord,
Rev 14: 4 not defiled themselves with women, for they are v;
Jdt 16: 4 and take my v as spoil.
AdE 2: 3 and they shall select beautiful young v to
2:17 and she found favor beyond all the other v,
2Es 10:22 into exile, our v have been defiled,
16:33 V shall mourn because they have no bridegrooms;

VIRILITY (1)

Dt 21:17 since he is the first issue of his v,

VIRTUALLY (1)

3Mc 5:45 animals had been brought v to a state of madness,

VIRTUE‡ (20) [VIRTUES, VIRTUOUS]

Pr 11:16 but she who hates v is covered with shame.
Wis 4: 1 Better than this is childlessness with v,
4: 1 for in the memory of v is immortality,
5:13 ceased to be, and we had no sign of v to show,
3Mc 6: 1 with every v, directed the elders around him
4Mc 1: 2 in addition it includes the praise of the highest v—
1: 8 of those who died for the sake of v,
1:30 over the emotions by v of the restraining power
2:10 so that v is not abandoned for their sakes.
6:30 in the tortures of death he resisted, by v of reason,
7:22 to endure any suffering for the sake of v,
9: 8 shall have the prize of v and shall be with God,
9:18 alone are invincible where v is concerned."
9:31 I lighten my pain by the joys that come from v,
10:10 are suffering because of our godly training and v,
11: 2 tyrant, to be tortured for the sake of v.
11: 4 Hater of v, hater of humankind,
12:14 without cause the contestants for v."
17:12 for on that day v gave the awards and tested them
17:23 of their v and their endurance under the tortures,

VIRTUE (KJV) See also EXCELLENCE, GOODNESS, POWER

VIRTUES (6) [VIRTUE]

Wis 7:20 the varieties of plants and the v of roots;
8: 7 if anyone loves righteousness, her labors are v;
Sir 42:25 Each supplements the v of the other.

4Mc 1:10 for me to praise for their v those who,
1:30 For reason is the guide of the v,
13:24 in the same v and brought up in right living,

VIRTUOUS (6) [VIRTUE]

AdE 2: 2 "Let beautiful and v girls be sought out for
Sir 28:15 Slander has driven v women from their homes,
41:11 but a v name will never be blotted out.
2Es 16:49 as a respectable and v woman abhors a prostitute,
4Mc 11: 5 of all things and live according to his v law?
13:27 and companionship and v habits had augmented

VISAGE (1)

La 4: 8 Now their v is blacker than soot;

VISAGE (KJV) See also APPEARANCE, FACE

VISIBLE (13)

Da 4:11 and it was v to the ends of the whole earth.
4:20 to heaven and was v to the end of the whole earth,
1Co 3:13 the work of each builder will become v,
2Co 4:10 life of Jesus may also be made v in our bodies.
4:11 life of Jesus may be made v in our mortal flesh.
Eph 5:13 but everything exposed by the light becomes v,
5:14 for everything that becomes v is light.
Col 1:16 things v and invisible, whether thrones
Heb 11: 3 what is seen was made from things that are not v.
Wis 14:17 made a v image of the king whom they honored,
3Mc 6:18 of fearful aspect descended, v to all but the Jews.
2Es 10:27 I looked up, the woman was no longer v to me,
11:13 so that even its place was no longer v.

VISION‡ (87) [VISIONS]

Ge 15: 1 a v, "Do not be afraid, Abram, I am your shield;
Nu 24: 4 who sees the v of the Almighty, who falls down,
24:16 who sees the v of the Almighty, who falls down,
1Sa 3:15 Samuel was afraid to tell the v to Eli.
2Sa 7:17 with all these words and with all this v,
1Ch 17:15 In accordance with all these words and all this v,
2Ch 32:32 in the v of the prophet Isaiah son of Amoz in
Job 20: 8 they will be chased away like a v of the night.
33:15 In a dream, in a v of the night,
Ps 89:19 you spoke in a v to your faithful one, and said:
Isa 1: 1 The v of Isaiah son of Amoz,
21: 2 A stern v is told to me;
22: 1 The oracle concerning the valley of v.
22: 5 and trampling and confusion in the valley of v,
28: 7 they err in v, they stumble in giving judgment.
29: 7 shall be like a dream, a v of the night.
29:11 The v of all this has become for you like
Jer 14:14 They are prophesying to you a lying v,
38:22 a v of all the women remaining in the house of
La 2: 9 and her prophets obtain no v from the LORD.
Eze 7:13 For the v concerns all their multitude;
7:26 they shall keep seeking a v from the prophet;
8: 4 like the v that I had seen in the valley.
11:24 The spirit lifted me up and brought me in a v by
11:24 Then the v that I had seen left me.
12:22 and every v comes to nothing"?
12:23 The days are near, and the fulfillment of every v.
12:24 be any false v or flattering divination within
12:27 "The v that he sees is for many years ahead;
13: 7 not seen a false v or uttered a lying divination,
43: 3 The v I saw was like the v that I had seen when
43: 3 and like the v that I had seen by the river Chebar;
Da 2:19 Then the mystery was revealed to Daniel in a v of
7: 2 in my v by night the four winds of heaven stirring
8: 1 the reign of King Belshazzar a v appeared to me,
8: 2 In the v I was looking and saw myself in Susa
8:13 "For how long is this v concerning
8:15 I, Daniel, had seen the v, I tried to understand it.
8:16 calling, "Gabriel, help this man understand the v."
8:17 O mortal, that the v is for the time of the end."
8:26 The v of the evenings and the mornings
8:26 As for you, seal up the v,
8:27 I was dismayed by the v and did not understand
9:21 the man Gabriel, whom I had seen before in a v,
9:23 So consider the word and understand the v:
9:24 to seal both v and prophet,
10: 1 having received understanding in the v.
10: 7 I, Daniel, alone saw the v;
10: 7 the people who were with me did not see the v,
10: 8 So I was left alone to see this great v.
10:14 For there is a further v for those days."
10:16 because of the v such pains have come upon me
11:14 up in order to fulfill the v,
Ob 1: 1 The v of Obadiah. Thus says the Lord GOD
Mic 3: 6 Therefore it shall be night to you, without v,
Na 1: 1 The book of the v of Nahum of Elkosh.
Hab 2: 2 Write the v; make it plain on tablets,
2: 3 For there is still a v for the appointed time;
Mt 17: 9 the v until after the Son of Man has been raised
Lk 1:22 they realized that he had seen a v in the sanctuary.
24:23 that they had indeed seen a v of angels who said
Ac 9:10 The Lord said to him in a v, "Ananias."
9:12 has seen in a v a man named Ananias come in
10: 3 One afternoon at about three o'clock he had a v
10:17 about what to make of the v that he had seen,
10:19 While Peter was still thinking about the v,
11: 5 and in a trance I saw a v.
12: 9 he thought he was seeing a v.
16: 9 During the night Paul had a v:
16:10 When he had seen the v,
Ac 18: 9 One night the Lord said to Paul in a v,
26:19 I was not disobedient to the heavenly v,
Rev 9:17 And this was how I saw the horses in my v:
Tob 2:10 the more my v was obscured by the white films,
12:19 but what you saw was a v.
Sir 49: 8 It was Ezekiel who saw the v of glory,
2Mc 15:11 a sort of v, which was worthy of belief.
2Es 2:21 and let the blind have a v of my splendor.
10:37 an explanation of this bewildering v."
10:40 This therefore is the meaning of the v.
12: 8 the interpretation and meaning of this terrifying v
12:10 the interpretation of this v that you have seen:
12:11 the sea is the fourth kingdom that appeared in a v
13:21 "I will tell you the interpretation of the v,
13:25 "This is the interpretation of the v:
14:18 the eagle that you saw in the v is already hurrying

VISIONS‡ (33) [VISION]

Ge 46: 2 God spoke to Israel in v of the night, and said,
Nu 12: 6 I the LORD make myself known to them in v;
1Sa 3: 1 in those days; v were not widespread.
2Ch 9:29 in the v of the seer Iddo concerning Jeroboam son
Job 4:13 Amid thoughts from v of the night,
7:14 you scare me with dreams and terrify me with v,
Jer 23:16 They speak v of their own minds,
La 2:14 for you false and deceptive v;
Eze 1: 1 the heavens were opened, and I saw v of God.
8: 3 and brought me in v of God to Jerusalem,
13: 9 be against the prophets who see false v
13:16 concerning Jerusalem and saw v of peace for it,
13:23 therefore you shall no longer see false v
21:29 Offering false v for you, divining lies for you,
22:28 seeing false v and divining lies for them, saying,
40: 2 He brought me, in v of God, to the land of Israel,
Da 1:17 Daniel also had insight into all v and dreams.
2:28 the v of your head as you lay in bed were these:
4: 5 in bed and the v of my head terrified me.
4:13 in the v of my head as I lay in bed,
7: 1 Daniel had a dream and v of his head as he lay
7: 7 After this I saw in the v by night a fourth beast,
7:13 As I watched in the night v,
7:15 and the v of my head terrified me.
Hos 12:10 I spoke to the prophets; it was I who multiplied v,
Joel 2:28 and your young men shall see v.
Zec 13: 4 every one, of their v when they prophesy;
Ac 2:17 and your young men shall see v,
2Co 12: 1 but I will go on to v and revelations of the Lord.
Col 2:18 of angels, dwelling on v, puffed up without cause
Sir 40: 6 the v of his mind like one who has escaped from
48:22 who was great and trustworthy in his v.
2Es 10:59 in those dream v what the Most High will do

VISIT (35) [VISITATION, VISITED, VISITING, VISITORS]

Ge 34: 1 went out to v the women of the region.
Jdg 15: 1 Samson went to v his wife, bringing along a kid.
2Ki 9:16 of Judah had come down to v Joram.
10:13 we have come down to v the royal princes and
2Ch 22: 7 about through his going to v Joram.
Job 7:18 v them every morning, test them every moment?
Ps 17: 3 If you try my heart, if you v me by night,
65: 9 You v the earth and water it, you greatly enrich it;
Isa 23:17 the end of seventy years, the LORD will v Tyre,
Jer 15:15 O LORD, you know; remember me and v me,
29:10 Babylon's seventy years are completed will I v
Mt 25:43 sick and in prison and you did not v me.'
Ac 7:12 he sent our ancestors there on their first v.
7:13 On the second v Joseph made himself known
7:23 it came into his heart to v his relatives,
10:28 for a Jew to associate with or to v a Gentile;
15:36 let us return and v the believers in every city
21:18 The next day Paul went with us to v James;
1Co 16: 5 I will v you after passing through Macedonia—
16:12 I strongly urged him to v you with
2Co 1:16 I wanted to v you on my way to Macedonia,
2: 1 up my mind not to make you another painful v.
13: 2 as I did when present on my second v,
Gal 1:18 to v Cephas and stayed with him fifteen days;
Sir 6:36 you see an intelligent person, rise early to v him;
7:35 Do not hesitate to v the sick,
22:13 a senseless person or v an unintelligent person.
29:27 my brother has come for a v,
2Mc 9:17 and would v every inhabited place to proclaim
3Mc 1: 6 to v the neighboring cities and encourage them.
1: 8 the more eager to v them as soon as possible.
2Es 5:56 through whom you will v your creation."
6:18 when I draw near to v the inhabitants of the earth,
9: 2 the very time when the Most High is about to v
4Mc 10:21 God will v you swiftly, for you are cutting out

VISITATION‡ (4) [VISIT]

Lk 19:44 because you did not recognize the time of your v
Wis 3: 7 In the time of their v they will shine forth,
14:11 there will be a v also upon the heathen idols,
Sir 16:18 the abyss and the earth, tremble at his v!

VISITATION (KJV) See also CARE, PUNISH, PUNISHMENT, JUDGE

VISITED (6) [VISIT]

Isa 29: 6 you will be v by the LORD of hosts with thunder
Mt 25:36 I was in prison and you v me.'
25:39 that we saw you sick or in prison and v you?'
Ac 28: 8 Paul v him and cured him by praying
Jdt 7: 7 and v the springs that supplied their water;
2Mc 12: 5 Judas heard of the cruelty v on his compatriots,

VISITING (3) [VISIT]

Ex 34: 7 but v the iniquity of the parents upon the children
Nu 14:18 v the iniquity of the parents upon the children to
1Mc 16:14 Now Simon was v the towns of the country

VISITORS (1) [VISIT]

Ac 2:10 and v from Rome, both Jews and proselytes,

VITALS (1)

La 3:13 He shot into my v the arrows of his quiver;

VOCATION (KJV) See CALLING

VOICE‡ (406) [LOUD-VOICED, VOICES]

A. VOICE OF THE †LORD (38)
B. VOICE OF THE *LORD (6)

Ge 3:17 "Because you have listened to the v of your wife,
4:23 "Adah and Zillah, hear my v;
16: 2 And Abram listened to the v of Sarai.
21:16 she sat opposite him, she lifted up her v and wept.
21:17 And God heard the v of the boy;
21:17 for God has heard the v of the boy where he is.
22:18 because you have obeyed my v."
26: 5 Abraham obeyed my v and kept my charge,
27:22 who felt him and said, "The v is Jacob's v,
27:38 And Esau lifted up his v and wept.
27:43 Now therefore, my son, obey my v;
30: 6 and has also heard my v and given me a son";
39:14 and I cried out with a loud v;
39:15 and when he heard me raise my v and cry out,
39:18 but as soon as I raised my v and cried out,
Ex 3:18 They will listen to your v;
15:26 "If you will listen carefully to the v of the LORD A
19: 5 if you obey my v and keep my covenant,
23:21 Be attentive to him and listen to his v;
23:22 you listen attentively to his v and do all that I say,
24: 3 and all the people answered with one v, and said,
Nu 7:89 the v speaking to him from above the mercy seat
14:22 and have not obeyed my v,
20:16 he heard our v, and sent an angel
21: 3 The LORD listened to the v of Israel,
Dt 1:45 the LORD would neither heed your v
4:12 but saw no form; there was only a v.
4:33 the v of a god speaking out of a fire,
4:36 From heaven he made you hear his v
5:22 a loud v to your whole assembly at the mountain,
5:23 When you heard the v out of the darkness,
5:24 and we have heard his v out of the fire.
5:25 we hear the v of the LORD our God any longer, A
5:26 For who is there of all flesh that has heard the v
8:20 not obey the v of the LORD your God. A
13: 4 his v you shall obey, him you shall serve,
13:18 if you obey the v of the LORD your God A
18:16 "If I hear the v of the LORD my God any more, A
26: 7 the LORD heard our v and saw our affliction,
27:14 Then the Levites shall declare in a loud v to all
Jos 5: 6 not having listened to the v of the LORD. A
6:10 "You shall not shout or let your v be heard,
10:14 when the LORD heeded a human v;
Jdg 2:20 and have not obeyed my v,
6:10 But you have not given heed to my v."
18: 3 they recognized the v of the young Levite;
18:25 "You had better not let your v be heard among us
1Sa 1:13 only her lips moved, but her v was not heard;
2:25 But they would not listen to the v of their father;
7:10 the LORD thundered with a mighty v that day
8: 7 "Listen to the v of the people in all that they say
8: 9 Now then, listen to their v;
8:19 the people refused to listen to the v of Samuel;
8:22 "Listen to their v and set a king over them."
12:14 the LORD and serve him and heed his v
12:15 but if you will not heed the v of the LORD, A
15:19 Why then did you not obey the v of the LORD? A
15:20 "I have obeyed the v of the LORD, A
15:22 as in obeying the v of the LORD? A
15:24 because I feared the people and obeyed their v.
19: 6 Saul heeded the v of Jonathan;
24:16 Saul said, "Is this your v, my son David?"
24:16 Saul lifted up his v and wept.
25:35 see, I have heeded your v,
26:17 Saul recognized David's v, and said, "Is this your v, my son David?"
26:17 David said, "It is my v, my lord, O king."
28:12 woman saw Samuel, she cried out with a loud v;
28:18 Because you did not obey the v of the LORD, A
2Sa 3:32 The king lifted up his v and wept at the grave
19: 4 and the king cried with a loud v,
19:35 to the v of singing men and singing women?
22: 7 From his temple he heard my v,
22:14 the Most High uttered his v.
1Ki 8:55 the assembly of Israel with a loud v:
17:22 The LORD listened to the v of Elijah;
18:26 But there was no v, and no answer.
18:29 but there was no v, no answer, and no response.
19:13 Then there came a v to him that said,
20:25 He heeded their v, and did so.
20:36 you have not obeyed the v of the LORD, A
2Ki 18:12 not obey the v of the LORD their God A
18:28 the Rabshakeh stood and called out in a loud v in
19:22 Against whom have you raised your v

2Ch 15:14 They took an oath to the LORD with a loud v,
20:19 the God of Israel, with a very loud v.
30:27 up and blessed the people, and their v was heard;
32:18 a loud v in the language of Judah to the people
Ezr 3:12 wept with a loud v when they saw this house,
10:12 all the assembly answered with a loud v, "It is so;
Ne 9: 4 of the Levites and cried out with a loud v to
Job 3:18 they do not hear the v of the taskmaster.
4:10 The roar of the lion, the v of the fierce lion,
4:16 there was silence, then I heard a v:
9:16 I do not believe that he would listen to my v.
30:31 and my pipe to the v of those who weep.
37: 2 the thunder of his v and the rumbling that comes
37: 4 his v roars; he thunders with his majestic v and he does not restrain the lightnings when his v is heard.
37: 5 God thunders wondrously with his v;
38:34 "Can you lift up your v to the clouds,
40: 9 and can you thunder with a v like his?
Ps 5: 3 O LORD, in the morning you hear my v;
18: 6 From his temple he heard my v,
18:13 and the Most High uttered his v.
19: 3 nor are there words; their v is not heard;
19: 4 yet their v goes out through all the earth,
28: 2 Hear the v of my supplication,
29: 3 The v of the LORD is over the waters; A
29: 4 The v of the LORD is powerful; A
29: 4 the v of the LORD is full of majesty. A
29: 5 The v of the LORD breaks the cedars; A
29: 7 The v of the LORD flashes forth flames of fire. A
29: 8 The v of the LORD shakes the wilderness; A
29: 9 The v of the LORD causes the oaks to whirl, A
46: 6 he utters his v, the earth melts.
55:17 and he will hear my v.
58: 5 the v of charmers or of the cunning enchanter.
64: 1 Hear my v, O God, in my complaint;
68:33 listen, he sends out his v, his mighty v.
81: 5 I hear a v I had not known:
81:11 "But my people did not listen to my v;
93: 3 O LORD, the floods have lifted up their v;
95: 7 O that today you would listen to his v!
106:25 and did not obey the v of the LORD. A
116: 1 because he has heard my v and my supplications.
119:149 In your steadfast love hear my v;
130: 2 hear my v! Let your ears be attentive to the v of
140: 6 give ear, O LORD, to the v of my supplications."
141: 1 give ear to my v when I call to you.
142: 1 With my v I cry to the LORD; with my v I make
Pr 1:20 in the squares she raises her v.
2: 3 and raise your v for understanding;
5:13 to the v of my teachers or incline my ear
8: 1 and does not understanding raise her v?
27:14 Whoever blesses a neighbor with a loud v,
Ecc 5: 3 and a fool's v with many words.
10:20 for a bird of the air may carry your v,
SS 2: 8 The v of my beloved!
2:12 and the v of the turtledove is heard in our land.
2:14 let me see your face, let me hear your v;
2:14 for your v is sweet, and your face is lovely.
8:13 my companions are listening for your v;
Isa 6: 8 Then I heard the v of the Lord saying, B
28:23 and hear my v; Pay attention,
29: 4 your v shall come from the ground like the v of
30:30 the LORD will cause his majestic v to be heard
30:31 will be terror-stricken at the v of the LORD, A
32: 9 Rise up, you women who are at ease, hear my v;
36:13 the Rabshakeh stood and called out in a loud v in
37:23 Against whom have you raised your v
40: 3 A v cries out: "In the wilderness prepare the way
40: 6 A v says, "Cry out!"
40: 9 lift up your v with strength, O Jerusalem,
42: 2 He will not cry or lift up his v,
42:11 Let the desert and its towns lift up their v,
50:10 among you fears the LORD and obeys the v
51: 3 thanksgiving and the v of song.
58: 1 Lift up your v like a trumpet!
58: 4 as you do today will not make your v heard
66: 6 A v from the temple!
66: 6 The v of the LORD, dealing retribution A
Jer 3:13 and have not obeyed my v, says the LORD.
3:21 A v on the bare heights is heard,
3:25 not obeyed the v of the LORD our God." A
4:15 For a v declares from Dan and proclaims disaster
7:23 But this command I gave them, "Obey my v,
7:28 that did not obey the v of the LORD their God, A
7:34 the v of the bride and bridegroom in the cities
9:13 and have not obeyed my v,
10:13 When he utters his v, there is a tumult of waters
11: 4 Listen to my v, and do all that I command you.
11: 7 even to this day, saying, Obey my v.
12: 8 she has lifted up her v against me—
16: 9 the v of mirth and the v of gladness, the v of the bridegroom and the v of the bride.
18:10 not listening to my v, then I will change my mind
22:20 and cry out, and lift up your v in Bashan;
22:21 for you have not obeyed my v.
25:10 v of the bridegroom and the v of the bride,
25:30 and from his holy habitation utter his v;
26:13 and obey the v of the LORD your God, A
31:15 A v is heard in Ramah, lamentation and bitter
31:16 Keep your v from weeping,
32:23 But they did not obey your v or follow your law;
33:11 the v of mirth and the v of gladness, the v of the bridegroom and the v of the bride,
38:20 Just obey the v of the LORD in what I say A
40: 3 against the LORD and did not obey his v.
42: 6 we will obey the v of the LORD our God A
42: 6 well with us when we obey the v of the LORD A
Jer 42:13 thus disobeying the v of the LORD your God A
42:21 the v of the LORD your God in anything A
43: 4 all the people did not obey the v of the LORD, A
43: 7 for they did not obey the v of the LORD. A
44:23 the LORD and did not obey the v of the LORD A
48:34 as far as Jahaz they utter their v,
51:16 When he utters his v there is a tumult of waters in
Eze 1:25 a v from above the dome over their heads;
1:28 and I heard the v of someone speaking.
8:18 and though they cry in my hearing with a loud v,
9: 1 Then he cried in my hearing with a loud v,
10: 5 like the v of God Almighty when he speaks.
11:13 Then I fell down on my face, cried with a loud v,
19: 9 so that his v should be heard no more on
33:32 a beautiful v and plays well on an instrument;
Da 4:31 the words were still in the king's mouth, a v came
8:16 and I heard a human v by the Ulai,
9:10 and have not obeyed the v of the LORD our God A
9:11 and turned aside, refusing to obey your v.
9:14 for we have disobeyed his v.
Joel 2:11 The LORD utters his v at the head of his army;
3:16 and utters his v from Jerusalem,
Am 1: 2 and utters his v from Jerusalem;
Jnh 2: 2 of the belly of Sheol I cried, and you heard my v.
2: 9 I with the v of thanksgiving will sacrifice to you;
Mic 6: 1 and let the hills hear your v.
6: 9 The v of the LORD cries to A
Na 2:13 the v of your messengers shall be heard no more.
Hab 3:10 torrent of water swept by; the deep gave forth its v.
Zep 3: 2 It has listened to no v;
Hag 1:12 obeyed the v of the LORD their God, A
Zec 6:15 if you diligently obey the v of the LORD A
Mt 2:18 "A v was heard in Ramah, wailing
3: 3 "The v of one crying out in the wilderness:
3:17 And a v from heaven said, "This is my Son,
12:19 nor will anyone hear his v in the streets.
17: 5 and from the cloud a v said, "This is my Son,
27:46 about three o'clock Jesus cried with a loud v,
27:50 Then Jesus cried again with a loud v
Mk 1: 3 the v of one crying out in the wilderness:
1:11 And a v came from heaven, "You are my Son,
1:26 convulsing him and crying with a loud v,
5: 7 and he shouted at the top of his v,
9: 7 and from the cloud there came a v,
15:34 At three o'clock Jesus cried out with a loud v,
Lk 3: 4 "The v of one crying out in the wilderness:
3:22 And a v came from heaven, "You are my Son,
4:33 and he cried out with a loud v,
8:28 down before him and shouted at the top of his v,
9:35 Then from the cloud came a v that said,
9:36 When the v had spoken, Jesus was found alone.
11:27 woman in the crowd raised her v and said to him,
17:15 turned back, praising God with a loud v.
19:37 to praise God joyfully with a loud v for all
23:46 Then Jesus, crying with a loud v, said, "Father,
Jn 1:23 "I am the v of one crying out in the wilderness,
3:29 rejoices greatly at the bridegroom's v.
5:25 when the dead will hear the v of the Son of God,
5:28 when all who are in their graves will hear his v
5:37 You have never heard his v or seen his form,
10: 3 and the sheep hear his v.
10: 4 the sheep follow him because they know his v.
10: 5 because they do not know the v of strangers."
10:16 and they will listen to my v.
10:27 My sheep hear my v.
11:43 When he had said this, he cried with a loud v,
12:28 Then a v came from heaven, "I have glorified it,
12:30 Jesus answered, "This v has come for your sake,
18:37 to the truth listens to my v."
Ac 2:14 raised his v and addressed them,
7:31 there came the v of the Lord: B
7:60 Then he knelt down and cried out in a loud v,
9: 4 He fell to the ground and heard a v saying to him,
9: 7 because they heard the v but saw no one.
10:13 he heard a v saying, "Get up, Peter; kill and eat."
10:15 The v said to him again, a second time,
11: 7 I also heard a v saying to me, 'Get up, Peter;
11: 9 But a second time the v answered from heaven,
12:14 On recognizing Peter's v,
12:22 The people kept shouting, "The v of a god,
14:10 said in a loud v, "Stand upright
16:28 But Paul shouted in a loud v,
22: 7 I fell to the ground and heard a v saying to me,
22: 9 not hear the v of the one who was speaking to me.
22:14 to see the Righteous One and to hear his own v;
26:14 I heard a v saying to me in the Hebrew language,
Ro 10:18 for "Their v has gone out to all the earth,
15: 6 that together you may with one v glorify the God
Heb 3: 7 as the Holy Spirit says, "Today, if you hear his v,
3:15 As it is said, "Today, if you hear his v,
4: 7 if you hear his v, do not harden your hearts."
12:19 and a v whose words made the hearers beg that
12:26 At that time his v shook the earth;
2Pe 1:17 from God the Father when that v was conveyed
1:18 We ourselves heard this v come from heaven,
2:16 a human v and restrained the prophet's madness.
Rev 1:10 and I heard behind me a loud v like a trumpet
1:12 I turned to see whose v it was that spoke to me,
1:15 and his v was like the sound of many waters.
3:20 if you hear my v and open the door,
4: 1 And the first v, which I had heard speaking to me
5: 2 I saw a mighty angel proclaiming with a loud v,
5:11 the v of many angels surrounding the throne and
5:12 singing with full v, "Worthy is the Lamb
6: 1 as with a v of thunder, "Come!"
6: 6 and I heard what seemed to be a v in the midst of
6: 7 I heard the v of the fourth living creature call out,
Rev 6:10 they cried out with a loud v,
7: 2 and he called with a loud v to
7:10 They cried out in a loud v, saying,
8:13 and I heard an eagle crying with a loud v
9:13 a v from the four horns of the golden altar
10: 4 but I heard a v from heaven saying,
10: 8 v that I had heard from heaven spoke to me again,
11:12 they heard a loud v from heaven saying to them,
12:10 Then I heard a loud v in heaven, proclaiming,
14: 2 a v from heaven like the sound of many waters
14: 2 the v I heard was like the sound of harpists
14: 7 in a loud v, "Fear God and give him glory,
14: 9 a third, followed them, crying with a loud v,
14:13 And I heard a v from heaven saying, "Write this:
14:15 with a loud v to the one who sat on the cloud,
14:18 with a loud v to him who had the sharp sickle,
16: 1 a loud v from the temple telling the seven angels,
16:17 and a loud v came out of the temple,
18: 2 He called out with a mighty v, "Fallen,
18: 4 Then I heard another v from heaven saying,
18:23 and the v of bridegroom and bride will be heard
19: 1 After this I heard what seemed to be the loud v of
19: 5 And from the throne came a v saying,
19: 6 Then I heard what seemed to be the v of
19:17 and with a loud v he called to all the birds that fly
21: 3 And I heard a loud v from the throne saying,
Tob 11:15 in rejoicing and praising God at the top of his v.
13: 6 acknowledge him at the top of your v.
Jdt 7:23 the rulers of the town and cried out with a loud v,
7:29 and they cried out to the Lord God with a loud v.
8:17 and he will hear our v, if it pleases him.
9: 1 Judith cried out to the Lord with a loud v,
13:12 When the people of her town heard her v,
13:14 Then she said to them with a loud v, "Praise God,
16:16 with a loud v and wept and groaned and shouted,
16:14 there is none that can resist your v.
AdE 14:19 hear the v of the despairing,
Sir 17:13 and their ears heard the glory of his v.
21:20 A fool raises his v when he laughs,
34:29 to whose v will the Lord listen?
39:35 So now sing praise with all your heart and v,
40:21 but a pleasant v is better than either.
43:17 The v of his thunder rebukes the earth;
45: 5 He allowed him to hear his v,
46:17 and made his v heard with a mighty sound;
46:20 and lifted up his v from the ground in prophecy,
Bar 1:18 and have not heeded the v of the Lord our God, B
1:19 and we have been negligent, in not heeding his v.
1:21 to the v of the Lord our God in all the words of B
2: 5 against the Lord our God, in not heeding his v.
2:10 Yet we have not obeyed his v,
2:22 But if you will not obey the v of the Lord and B
2:23 Jerusalem the v of mirth and the v of gladness, the v of the bridegroom and the v of the bride,
2:24 But we did not obey your v,
2:29 "If you will not obey my v,
3: 4 who did not heed the v of the Lord their God, B
Aza 1:28 with one v praised and glorified and blessed God
Sus 1:24 Then Susanna cried out with a loud v,
1:42 Then Susanna cried out with a loud v, and said,
1:46 and he shouted with a loud v,
Bel 1:18 and shouted in a loud v, "You are great, O Bel,
1:41 The king shouted with a loud v, "You are great,
1Mc 2:19 But Mattathias answered and said in a loud v:
2:27 Mattathias cried out in the town with a loud v,
9:41 the wedding was turned into mourning and the v
13: 8 and they answered in a loud v,
13:45 and they cried out with a loud v,
1Es 9:10 all the multitude shouted and said with a loud v,
3Mc 5: 7 with tears and a v hard to silence they all called
5:51 and cried out in a very loud v,
2Es 5: 5 and the stone shall utter its v;
5: 7 the many do not know shall make his v heard by night, and all shall hear his v.
5:37 or show me the picture of a v;
6:13 and you will hear a full, resounding v.
6:15 while the v is speaking, do not be terrified;
6:17 a v was speaking, and its sound was like
6:32 your v has surely been heard by the Most High;
8:19 Therefore hear my v and understand my words,
9:38 she was mourning and weeping with a loud v,
10:27 I was afraid, and cried with a loud v and said,
11:10 and saw that the v did not come from its heads,
11:15 And a v sounded, saying to it,
11:36 Then I heard a v saying to me,
11:37 and I heard how it uttered a human v to the eagle,
12:17 "As for your hearing a v that spoke,
12:45 And they wept with a loud v.
13: 4 and whenever his v issued from his mouth, all who heard his v melted as wax melts
13:33 "Then, when all the nations hear his v,
14: 1 suddenly a v came out of a bush opposite me
14:38 And on the next day a v called me, saying, "Ezra,
16:27 or even to hear a human v.
4Mc 8:29 all with one v together, as from one mind, said:

VOICES‡ (21) [VOICE]

Jdg 2: 4 the people lifted up their v and wept.
21: 2 and they lifted up their v and wept bitterly.
1Sa 30: 4 and the people who were with him raised their v
2Sa 13:36 and raised their v and wept;
Job 2:12 and they raised their v and wept aloud;
29:10 the v of princes were hushed,
Isa 6: 4 the thresholds shook at the v of those who called,
15: 4 their v are heard as far as Jahaz;
24:14 They lift up their v, they sing for joy;

Isa 52: 8 Your sentinels lift up their v,
Jer 33:11 the v of those who sing,
Lk 23:23 be crucified; and their v prevailed.
Ac 4:24 they raised their v together to God and said,
Rev 11:15 and there were loud v in heaven, saying,
Jdt 16:11 they lifted up their v, and
Wis 18: 1 Their enemies heard their v but did
Sir 47: 9 to make sweet melody with their v.
50:18 Then the singers praised him with their v in sweet
2Es 6:21 Children a year old shall speak with their v,
6:39 the sound of human v was not yet there.
4Mc 15:21 as did the v of the children in torture calling

VOID (10)

Ge 1: 2 the earth was a formless v and darkness covered
Nu 6:12 The former time shall be v,
Dt 32:28 They are a nation v of sense;
Job 26: 7 He stretches out Zaphon over the v,
Jer 4:23 I looked on the earth, and lo, it was waste and v;
19: 7 And in this place I will make v the plans of Judah
Mt 15: 6 you make v the word of God.
Mk 7:13 thus making v the word of God
Ro 4:14 faith is null and the promise is v.
2Es 2: 1 and made my counsels v.

VOID (KJV) See also BROKEN, CLEAR, DESOLATION, EMPTY, LACKS, NULL, NULLIFIED, NULLIFIES, NULLIFY, OVERTHROW, RENOUNCED, THRESHING FLOOR, WITHOUT

VOLUME (KJV) See SCROLL

VOLUMES (1)

2Mc 2:23 set forth by Jason of Cyrene in five v,

VOLUNTARILY (2) [VOLUNTEER]

2Co 8: 3 they v gave according to their means,
3Mc 6: 6 in Babylon who had v surrendered their lives to

VOLUNTARY (3) [VOLUNTEER]

2Ki 12: 4 and the money from the v offerings brought into
2Co 9: 5 it may be ready as a v gift and not as an extortion.
Phm 1:14 in order that your good deed might be v and

VOLUNTEER (2) [VOLUNTARILY, VOLUNTARY]

1Ch 28:21 be every v who has skill for any kind of service;
2Ch 17:16 a v for the service of the LORD,

VOMIT (12) [VOMITED]

Lev 18:28 otherwise the land will v you out for defiling it,
20:22 to settle in may not v you out.
Job 20:15 They swallow down riches and v them up again;
Pr 23: 8 You will v up the little you have eaten,
25:16 or else, having too much, you will v it.
26:11 a dog that returns to its v is a fool who reverts
Isa 19:14 as a drunkard staggers around in v.
28: 8 All tables are covered with filthy v;
Jer 25:27 Drink, get drunk and v, fall and rise no more,
48:26 let Moab wallow in his v;
2Pe 2:22 "The dog turns back to its own v," and,
Sir 31:21 If you are overstuffed with food, get up to v,

VOMITED (2) [VOMIT]

Lev 18:25 and the land v out its inhabitants.
18:28 as it v out the nation that was before you.

VOPHSI (1)

Nu 13:14 from the tribe of Naphtali, Nahbi son of V;

VOTE (4)

Ac 26:10 in prison, but I also cast my v against them
2Mc 10: 8 They decreed by public edict, ratified by v,
12: 4 and this was done by public v of the city.
15:36 by public v never to let this day go unobserved,

VOTIVE (19)

Lev 7:16 a v offering or a freewill offering, it shall be eaten
23:38 and apart from all your v offerings,
Nu 29:39 to your v offerings and your freewill offerings,
Dt 12: 6 your tithes and your donations, your v gifts,
12:11 and your donations, and all your choice v gifts
12:17 any of your v gifts that you vow,
12:26 and your v gifts, you shall bring to the place that
1Ki 15:15 the v gifts of his father and his own v gifts—
2Ki 12:18 of Judah took all the v gifts that Jehoshaphat,
12:18 had dedicated, as well as his own v gifts,
2Ch 15:18 the v gifts of his father and his own v gifts—
Jdt 4:14 offered the daily burnt offerings, the v offerings,
16:19 from his bedchamber she gave as a v offering.
2Mc 2:13 and letters of kings about v offerings.
5:16 the v offerings that other kings had made
1Es 2: 7 besides the other things added as v offerings for
2: 9 and with a very great number of v offerings

VOUCHES (1)

Job 16:19 and he that v for me is on high.

VOW‡ (49) [VOWED, VOWING, VOWS]

Ge 28:20 Then Jacob made a v, saying,
31:13 where you anointed a pillar and made a v to me.
Lev 22:18 of a v or as a freewill offering that is offered to
22:21 in fulfillment of a v or as a freewill offering,
22:23 but it will not be accepted for a v.
27: 2 When a person makes an explicit v to the LORD
27: 8 to what each one making a v can afford.
Nu 6: 2 men or women make a special v, the v of a nazirite,
6: 5 the days of their nazirite v no razor shall come
6:21 This is the law for the nazirites who take a v.
6:21 be in accordance with the nazirite v,
6:21 In accordance with whatever v they take,
15: 3 a sacrifice, to fulfill a v or as a freewill offering or
15: 8 a v or as an offering of well-being to the LORD,
21: 2 Then Israel made a v to the LORD and said,
30: 2 When a man makes a v to the LORD,
30: 3 When a woman makes a v to the LORD,
30: 4 and her father hears of her v or her pledge
30: 5 no v of hers, and no pledge by which she has
30: 8 he shall nullify the v by which she was obligated,
30: 9 (But every v of a widow or of a divorced woman,
30:10 And if she made a v in her husband's house,
30:13 Any v or any binding oath to deny herself,
Dt 12:11 and all your choice votive gifts that you v to
12:17 any of your votive gifts that you v,
23:18 of the LORD your God in payment for any v,
23:21 If you make a v to the LORD your God,
Jdg 11:30 And Jephthah made a v to the LORD, and said,
11:35 and I cannot take back my v."
11:39 who did with her according to the v he had made.
1Sa 1:11 She made this v: "O LORD of hosts,
1:21 the LORD the yearly sacrifice, and to pay his v.
2Sa 15: 7 and pay the v that I have made to the LORD.
15: 8 For your servant made a v while I lived at Geshur
Pr 20:25 and begin to reflect only after making a v.
Ecc 5: 4 you make a v to God, do not delay fulfilling it; for he has no pleasure in fools. Fulfill what you v.
5: 5 not v than that you should v and not fulfill it.
Ac 18:18 he had his hair cut, for he was under a v.
21:23 We have four men who are under a v.
Sir 18:22 Let nothing hinder you from paying a v promptly,
18:23 Before making a v, prepare yourself;
LtJ 6:35 if one makes a v to them and does not keep it,
2Mc 9:13 Then the abominable fellow made a v to the Lord,
1Es 4:43 "Remember the v that you made on the day
4:46 that you fulfill the v whose fulfillment you vowed
5:53 And all who had made any v to God began

VOWED‡ (12) [VOW]

Dt 4:21 and he v that I should not cross the Jordan and
23:23 just as you have freely v to the LORD your God
Ps 132: 2 to the LORD and v to the Mighty One of Jacob,
Jer 44:17 Instead, we will do everything that we have v,
Jnh 2: 9 what I have v I will pay.
1Mc 5: 5 v their complete destruction,
1Es 4:44 and v to send them back there.
4:45 You also v to build the temple,
4:46 that you fulfill the vow whose fulfillment you v to
5:44 v that, to the best of their ability,
8:13 the Lord of Israel that I and my Friends have v,
8:58 and the silver and the gold are v to the Lord,

VOWING (1) [VOW]

Dt 23:22 But if you refrain from v, you will not incur guilt.

VOWS‡ (28) [VOW]

Nu 30: 4 then all her v shall stand,
30: 6 by her v or any thoughtless utterance of her lips
30: 7 at the time that he hears, then her v shall stand,
30:11 then all her v shall stand,
30:12 of her lips concerning her v,
30:14 then he validates all her v, or all her pledges,
Job 22:27 and he will hear you, and you will pay your v.
Ps 22:25 my v I will pay before those who fear him.
50:14 and pay your v to the Most High.
56:12 My v to you I must perform, O God;
61: 5 O God, have heard my v;
61: 8 as I pay my v day after day.
65: 1 and to you shall v be performed,
66:13 I will pay you my v,
76:11 Make v to the LORD your God,
116:14 I will pay my v to the LORD in the presence
116:18 I will pay my v to the LORD in the presence
Pr 7:14 and today I have paid my v;
31: 2 No, son of my v!
Isa 19:21 and burnt offering, and they will make v to
Jer 11:15 Can v and sacrificial flesh avert your doom?
44:25 'We are determined to perform the v
44:25 keep your v and make your libations!
Jnh 1:16 offered a sacrifice to the LORD and made v.
Na 1:15 Celebrate your festivals, O Judah, fulfill your v,
Mal 1:14 in the flock and v to give it, and yet sacrifices to
Mt 5:33 but carry out the v you have made to the Lord.'
2Mc 3:35 to the Lord and made very great v to the Savior

VOYAGE (5)

Ac 21: 7 When we had finished the v from Tyre,
27:10 the v will be with danger and much heavy loss,
Wis 14: 1 about to v over raging waves calls upon a piece
3Mc 4:10 treatment befitting traitors during the whole v.
4:11 and the v was concluded as the king had decreed,

VULGAR (2)

2Sa 6:20 any v fellow might shamelessly uncover himself!"
Eph 5: 4 Entirely out of place is obscene, silly, and v talk;

VULTURE (5) [VULTURES]

Lev 11:13 the eagle, the v, the osprey,
11:18 the water hen, the desert owl, the carrion v,
Dt 14:12 the eagle, the v, the osprey,
14:17 the carrion v and the cormorant,
Hos 8: 1 One like a v is over the house of the LORD,

VULTURES (3) [VULTURE]

Pr 30:17 by the ravens of the valley and eaten by the v.
Mt 24:28 Wherever the corpse is, there the v will gather.
Lk 17:37 "Where the corpse is, there the v will gather."

W

WADI (70) [WADIS]

Nu 13:23 And they came to the W Eshcol,
13:24 That place was called the W Eshcol,
21:12 and camped in the W Zered.
32: 9 they went up to the W Eshcol and saw the land,
34: 5 the boundary shall turn from Azmon to the W
Dt 2:13 "Now then, proceed to cross over the W Zered."
2:13 So we crossed over the W Zered.
2:14 the W Zered was thirty-eight years,
2:24 "Proceed on your journey and cross the W Arnon.
2:36 Aroer on the edge of the W Arnon (including the town that is in the w itself) as far as Gilead,
2:37 the whole upper region of the W Jabbok as well as
3: 8 from the W Arnon to Mount Hermon
3:12 that is on the edge of the W Arnon,
3:16 as far as the W Arnon, with the middle of the w as
3:16 the w being boundary of the Ammonites;
4:48 which is on the edge of the W Arnon,
21: 4 of that town shall bring the heifer down to a w
21: 4 and shall break the heifer's neck there in the w.
21: 6 over the heifer whose neck was broken in the w,
Jos 12: 1 from the W Arnon to Mount Hermon,
12: 2 which is on the edge of the W Arnon,
13: 9 which is on the edge of the W Arnon,
13:16 which is on the edge of the W Arnon,
15: 4 goes out by the W of Egypt,
15:47 to the W of Egypt, and the Great Sea with its coast.
16: 8 the boundary goes westward to the W Kanah,
17: 9 Then the boundary went down to the W Kanah.
17: 9 The towns here, to the south of the w,
17: 9 along the north side of the w and ends at the sea.
19:11 then the w that is east of Jokneam;
Jdg 4: 7 by the W Kishon with his chariots and his troops;
4:13 from Harosheth-ha-goiim to the W Kishon.
1Sa 17:40 and chose five smooth stones from the w,
30: 9 They came to the W Besor,
30:10 too exhausted to cross the W Besor.
30:21 and who had been left at the W Besor.
2Sa 15:23 the king crossed the W Kidron,
1Ki 2:37 on the day you go out, and cross the W Kidron,
8:65 people from Lebo-hamath to the W of Egypt—
15:13 down her image and burned it at the W Kidron.
17: 3 and hide yourself by the W Cherith,
17: 4 You shall drink from the w,
17: 5 he went and lived by the W Cherith,
17: 6 and he drank from the w.
17: 7 w dried up, because there was no rain in the land.
18:40 and Elijah brought them down to the W Kishon,
2Ki 3:16 'I will make this w full of pools.'
3:17 but the w shall be filled with water,
10:33 from Aroer, which is by the W Arnon, that is,
23: 6 to the W Kidron, burned it at the W Kidron,
23:12 and threw the rubble into the W Kidron.
24: 7 that belonged to the king of Egypt from the W
2Ch 7: 8 from Lebo-hamath to the W of Egypt.
15:16 crushed it, and burned it at the W Kidron.
29:16 and carried them out to the W Kidron.
30:14 and threw into the W Kidron.
32: 4 the springs and the w that flowed through the land,
Job 40:22 the willows of the w surround it.
Ps 83: 9 as to Sisera and Jabin at the W Kishon,
Isa 15: 7 up they carry away over the W of the Willows.
27:12 the channel of the Euphrates to the W of Egypt,
Jer 31:40 and all the fields as far as the W Kidron,
Eze 47:19 from there along the W of Egypt to the Great Sea.
48:28 from there along the W of Egypt to the Great Sea.
Joel 3:18 the house of the LORD and water the W Shittim.
Am 6:14 from Lebo-hamath to the W Arabah.
Jdt 7:18 which is near Chusi beside the W Mochmur.

WADIS (6) [WADI]

Nu 21:14 "Waheb in Suphah and the w.
21:15 the slopes of the w that extend to the seat of Ar,
1Ki 18: 5 to all the springs of water and to all the w;
1Ch 11:32 Hurai of the w of Gaash, Abiel the Arbathite,
Job 30: 6 In the gullies of w they must live,

Jdt 16: 3 their numbers blocked up the w,

WAFER (3) [WAFERS]
Ex 29:23 one cake of bread made with oil, and one w,
Lev 8:26 one cake of bread with oil, and one w,
Nu 6:19 and one unleavened w, and shall put them in

WAFERS (6) [WAFER]
Ex 16:31 and the taste of it was like w made with honey.
29: 2 and unleavened w spread with oil.
Lev 2: 4 or unleavened w spread with oil.
7:12 unleavened w spread with oil,
Nu 6:15 with oil and unleavened w spread with oil,
1Ch 23:29 the w of unleavened bread, the baked offering,

WAFTED (1)
SS 4:16 that its fragrance may be w abroad.

WAG (1)
La 2:15 they hiss and w their heads at daughter Jerusalem;

WAGE (19) [WAGED, WAGES]
2Ki 8:28 of Ahab to w war against King Hazael of Aram
16: 5 of Israel came up to w war on Jerusalem;
Ps 55:18 from the battle that I w,
Pr 10:16 The w of the righteous leads to life,
20:18 w war by following wise guidance.
24: 6 for by wise guidance you can w your war,
Da 11:10 "His sons shall w war and assemble a multitude
11:25 of the south shall w war with a much greater
Zec 14:12 the LORD will strike all the peoples that w war
Mt 20: 2 agreeing with the laborers for the usual daily w,
20: 9 each of them received the usual daily w.
20:10 but each of them also received the usual daily w.
20:13 did you not agree with me for the usual daily w?
Lk 14:31 going out to w war against another king,
2Co 10: 3 we do not w war according to human standards;
1Pe 2:11 the desires of the flesh that w war against the soul.
1Mc 12:24 a larger force than before, to w war against him.
2Es 7:*127* [57] contest that all who are born on earth shall w:
13: 8 to w war with him, were filled with fear,

WAGED (5) [WAGE]
1Ki 22:45 and his power that he showed, and how he w war,
1Ch 22: 8 You have shed much blood and have w great wars;
Sir 46: 3 For he w the wars of the Lord.
1Mc 3: 3 he bound on his armor of war and w battles,
12:13 the kings around us have w war against us.

WAGER (2)
2Ki 18:23 make a w with my master the king of Assyria:
Isa 36: 8 make a w with my master the king of Assyria:

WAGES (53) [WAGE]
Ge 29:15 Tell me, what shall your w be?"
30:28 name your w, and I will give it."
30:32 and such shall be my w.
30:33 when you come to look into my w with you.
31: 7 and changed my w ten times,
31: 8 If he said, 'The speckled shall be your w,'
31: 8 and if he said, 'The striped shall be your w,'
31:41 and you have changed my w ten times.
Ex 2: 9 and I will give you your w."
Lev 19:13 for yourself the w of a laborer until morning.
Dt 15:18 given you services worth the w of hired laborers;
23:18 You shall not bring the fee of a prostitute or the w
24:14 not withhold the w of poor and needy laborers,
24:15 You shall pay them their w daily before sunset,
1Ki 5: 6 and I will give you whatever w you set
Job 7: 2 and like laborers who look for their w,
Isa 19:10 and all who work for w will be grieved.
23:18 Her merchandise and her w will be dedicated to
Jer 22:13 and does not give them their w;
Eze 29:19 and it shall be the w for his army.
Mic 1: 7 all her w shall be burned with fire,
1: 7 for as the w of a prostitute she gathered them, and
as the w of a prostitute they shall again be used.
Hag 1: 6 and you that earn w earn w to put them into
Zec 8:10 For before those days there were no w for people
11:12 "If it seems right to you, give me my w;
11:12 they weighed out as my w thirty shekels of silver.
Mal 3: 5 the hired workers in their w,
Lk 3:14 and be satisfied with your w."
Jn 4:36 The reaper is already receiving w
6: 7 "Six months' w would not buy enough bread
Ro 4: 4 w are not reckoned as a gift but as something due.
6:23 For the w of sin is death,
1Co 3: 8 each will receive w according to the labor of each.
Jas 5: 4 The w of the laborers who mowed your fields,
2Pe 2:15 who loved the w of doing wrong,
Tob 2:12 to the owners and they would pay w to her.
2:12 they paid her full w and also gave her a young goat
2:14 "It was given to me as a gift in addition to my w."
4:14 over until the next day the w of those who work
5: 3 and we will pay him w until you return.
5: 7 and I will pay you your w."
5:10 I will pay your w, brother."
5:15 he added, "I will pay you a drachma a day as w,
5:16 and I will add something to your w."
12: 1 see to paying the w of the man who went with you,
12: 5 "Take for your w half of all that you brought back,
Wis 2:22 nor hoped for the w of holiness,
Sir 34:27 to deprive an employee of w is to shed blood.
Sir 40:18 Wealth and w make life sweet,
1Mc 14:32 the soldiers of his nation and paid them w.
1Es 4:56 and w should be provided for all who guarded

WAGGING (KJV) See SHAKING

WAGON (2) [WAGONS]
Nu 7: 3 a w for every two of the leaders,
Ps 65:11 your w tracks overflow with richness.

WAGONS (9) [WAGON]
Ge 45:19 take w from the land of Egypt for your little ones
45:21 Joseph gave them w according to the instruction
45:27 he saw the w that Joseph had sent to carry him,
46: 5 in the w that Pharaoh had sent to carry him.
Nu 7: 3 six covered w and twelve oxen,
7: 6 So Moses took the w and the oxen,
7: 7 Two w and four oxen he gave to the Gershonites,
7: 8 four w and eight oxen he gave to the Merarites,
Eze 23:24 against you from the north with chariots and w and

WAHEB (1)
Nu 21:14 "W in Suphah and the wadis.

WAIL (39) [BEWAIL, BEWAILED, WAILED, WAILING, WAILINGS, WAILS]
Isa 13: 6 W, for the day of the LORD is near;
14:31 W, O gate; cry, O city; melt in fear,
16: 7 Therefore let Moab w, let everyone w for Moab.
23: 1 W, O ships of Tarshish, for your fortress is
23: 6 w, O inhabitants of the coast!
23:14 W, O ships of Tarshish,
65:14 and shall w for anguish of spirit.
Jer 4: 8 Because of this put on sackcloth, lament and w:
25:34 W, you shepherds, and cry out;
25:36 and the w of the lords of the flock!
47: 2 and all the inhabitants of the land shall w.
48:20 for it is broken down; w and cry!
48:31 Therefore I w for Moab; I cry out
48:39 How it is broken! How they w!
49: 3 W, O Heshbon, for Ai is laid waste!
51: 8 and is shattered; w for her!
Eze 21:12 Cry and w, O mortal, for it is against my people;
27:30 and w aloud over you,
30: 2 Thus says the Lord GOD: W, "Alas for the day!"
32:18 w over the hordes of Egypt, and send them down,
Hos 7:14 but they w upon their beds;
10: 5 and its idolatrous priests shall w over it,
Joel 1: 5 and w, all you wine-drinkers, over the sweet wine,
1:11 Be dismayed, you farmers, w, you vinedressers,
1:13 w, you ministers of the altar.
Mic 1: 8 For this I will lament and w;
2: 4 and w with bitter lamentation, and say,
Zep 1:10 a w from the Second Quarter,
1:11 The inhabitants of the Mortar w,
Zec 11: 2 W, O cypress, for the cedar has fallen,
11: 2 W, oaks of Bashan, for the thick forest has been
11: 3 Listen, the w of the shepherds,
Jas 5: 1 and w for the miseries that are coming to you.
Rev 1: 7 and on his account all the tribes of the earth will w.
18: 9 will weep and w over her when they see the smoke
2Es 16: 2 and w for your children, and lament for them;
4Mc 12:14 but you will w bitterly for having killed
16:12 Yet that holy and God-fearing mother did not w

WAILED (4) [WAIL]
Nu 11:18 for you have w in the hearing of the LORD,
11:20 and have w before him, saying,
Mt 11:17 we w, and you did not mourn.'
Lk 7:32 we w, and you did not weep.'

WAILING (19) [WAIL]
Est 4: 1 w with a loud and bitter cry;
Isa 15: 8 w reaches to Eglaim, the w reaches to Beer-elim.
Jer 9:10 Take up weeping and w for the mountains,
9:19 For a sound of w is heard from Zion:
Eze 27:32 In their w they raise a lamentation for you,
Am 5:16 In all the squares there shall be w;
5:16 and those skilled in lamentation, to w;
5:17 in all the vineyards there shall be w,
Mic 1:11 Beth-ezel is w and shall remove its support from
Mt 2:18 w and loud lamentation, Rachel weeping
Mk 5:38 people weeping and w loudly.
Lk 8:52 They were all weeping and w for her;
23:27 who were beating their breasts and w for him.
Sir 38:17 Let your weeping be bitter and your w fervent;
3Mc 1: 4 Arsinoë went to the troops with w and tears,
4: 3 not filled with mourning and w for them?
4: 6 to share married life exchanged joy for w,
6:32 Putting an end to all mourning and w,

WAILINGS (1) [WAIL]
Am 8: 3 songs of the temple shall become w in that day,"

WAILS (2) [WAIL]
Isa 15: 2 over Nebo and over Medeba Moab w.
15: 3 and in the squares everyone w and melts in tears.

WAIST (10) [WAISTCLOTH, WAISTS]
2Sa 20: 8 a belt with a sword in its sheath fastened at his w;
1Ki 2: 5 putting the blood of war on the belt around his w,
2Ki 1: 8 "A hairy man, with a leather belt around his w."
Isa 11: 5 Righteousness shall be the belt around his w,
Eze 47: 4 and it was up to the w.
Da 10: 5 with a belt of gold from Uphaz around his w.
Mt 3: 4 of camel's hair with a leather belt around his w,
Mk 1: 6 with a leather belt around his w,
Eph 6:14 and fasten the belt of truth around your w,
Jdt 8: 5 around her w and dressed in widow's clothing.

WAISTCLOTH (1) [CLOTH, WAIST]
Job 12:18 and binds a w on their loins.

WAISTS (4) [WAIST]
1Ki 20:31 around our w and ropes on our heads, and go out
20:32 So they tied sackcloth around their w,
Eze 23:15 with belts around their w, with flowing turbans
Jdt 4:10 they all put sackcloth around their w.

WAIT‡ (119) [AWAIT, AWAITS, WAITED, WAITING, WAITS]
Ge 49:18 I w for your salvation, O LORD.
Ex 12:39 they were driven out of Egypt and could not w,
24:12 "Come up to me on the mountain, and w there;
24:14 To the elders he had said, "W here for us,
Nu 9: 8 Moses spoke to them, "W,
35:20 or hurls something at another, lying in w,
35:22 or hurls any object without lying in w,
Dt 19:11 with another lies in w and attacks and takes the life
24:11 You shall w outside, while the person
Jdg 9:32 and lie in w in the fields.
9:34 and lay in w against Shechem in four companies.
9:43 and lay in w in the fields.
16: 2 and lay in w for him all night at the city gate.
16: 2 thinking, "Let us w until the light of the morning;
16: 9 While men were lying in w in an inner chamber,
16:12 (The men lying in w were in an inner chamber.)
21:20 saying, "Go and lie in w in the vineyards,
Ru 1:13 would you then w until they were grown?
3:18 She replied, "W, my daughter,
1Sa 1:23 w until you have weaned him;
10: 8 Seven days you shall w, until I come to you
14: 9 If they say to us, 'W until we come to you,'
15: 5 of the Amalekites and lay in w in the valley.
22: 8 to lie in w, as he is doing today."
22:13 so that he has risen against me, to lie in w,
2Sa 15:28 I will w at the fords of the wilderness
1Ki 1: 2 and let her w on the king, and be his attendant;
2Ki 7: 9 if we are silent and w until the morning light,
Job 6:11 What is my strength, that I should w?
14:14 All the days of my service I would w
31: 9 and I have lain in w at my neighbor's door;
32:16 And am I to w, because they do not speak,
38:40 or lie in w in their covert?
Ps 25: 3 Do not let those who w for you be put to shame;
25: 5 for you I w all day long.
25:21 and uprightness preserve me, for I w for you.
27:14 W for the LORD; be strong,
27:14 and let your heart take courage; w for the LORD!
31:24 all you who w for the LORD.
37: 7 before the LORD, and w patiently for him;
37: 9 those who w for the LORD shall inherit the land.
37:34 W for the LORD, and keep to his way,
38:15 But it is for you, O LORD, that I w;
39: 7 "And now, O Lord, what do I w for?
59: 3 Even now they lie in w for my life;
106:13 they did not w for his counsel.
119:95 The wicked lie in w to destroy me,
130: 5 I w for the LORD, my soul waits,
Pr 1:11 they say, "Come with us, let us lie in w for blood;
1:18 yet they lie in w—to kill themselves!
7:12 and at every corner she lies in w.
20:22 w for the LORD, and he will help you.
23:28 in w like a robber and increases the number of
24:15 Do not lie in w like an outlaw against the home of
Isa 8:17 I will w for the LORD,
26: 8 In the path of your judgments, O LORD, we w
30:18 blessed are all those who w for him.
33: 2 O LORD, be gracious to us; we w for you.
40:31 who w for the LORD shall renew their strength,
42: 4 and the coastlands w for his teaching.
49:23 those who w for me shall not be put to shame.
51: 5 the coastlands w for me, and for my arm they hope.
59: 9 not reach us; we w for light,
59:11 We w for justice, but there is none;
60: 9 For the coastlands shall w for me,
64: 4 who works for those who w for him.
La 3:10 He is a bear lying in w for me, a lion in hiding;
3:25 The LORD is good to those who w for him,
3:26 that one should w quietly for the salvation of
4:19 they lay in w for us in the wilderness.
Eze 13: 6 and yet they w for the fulfillment of their word!
Hos 6: 9 As robbers lie in w for someone,
12: 6 and w continually for your God.
Mic 1:12 the inhabitants of Maroth w anxiously for good,
5: 7 not depend upon people or w for any mortal.
7: 2 they all lie in w for blood,
7: 7 I will w for the God of my salvation;
Hab 2: 3 If it seems to tarry, w for it;
3:16 I w quietly for the day of calamity to come upon
Zep 3: 8 Therefore w for me, says the LORD,
Mt 11: 3 or are we to w for another?"
27:49 "W, let us see whether Elijah will come
Mk 15:36 and gave it to him to drink, saying, "W,
Lk 7:19 or are we to w for another?"
7:20 or are we to w for another?' "
11:54 lying in w for him, to catch him

Ac 1: 4 but to **w** there for the promise of the Father.
6: 2 the word of God in order to **w** on tables.
Ro 8:23 groan inwardly while we **w** for adoption,
8:25 we **w** for it with patience.
1Co 1: 7 in any spiritual gift as you **w** for the revealing
11:33 when you come together to eat, **w** for one another.
Gal 5: 5 we eagerly **w** for the hope of righteousness.
1Th 1:10 and to **w** for his Son from heaven, whom he raised
Tit 2:13 while we **w** for the blessed hope and
2Pe 3:13 we **w** for new heavens and a new earth,
Tob 2: 2 I will **w** for you, until you come back."
5: 7 Then Tobias said to him, "**W** for me, young man,
5: 8 He replied, "All right, I will **w**;
Jdt 8:17 Therefore, while we **w** for his deliverance,
13: 3 to stand outside the bedchamber and to **w** for her
15: 2 they did not **w** for one another,
Wis 2:12 "Let us lie in **w** for the righteous man,
8:12 When I am silent they will **w** for me,
10:12 kept him safe from those who lay in **w** for him;
Sir 2: 7 You who fear the Lord, **w** for his mercy;
6:19 and **w** for her good harvest.
11:31 for they lie in **w**, turning good into evil,
11:32 and a sinner lies in **w** to shed blood.
14:22 and lying in **w** on her paths;
18:22 and do not **w** until death to be released from it.
27:10 A lion lies in **w** for prey; so does sin for evildoers.
27:28 but vengeance lies in **w** for them like a lion.
28:26 and fall victim to one lying in **w**.
36:21 Reward those who **w** for you and let your prophets
51: 8 for you rescue those who **w** for you and save them
1Mc 5: 3 because they kept lying in **w** for Israel.
2Es 2:34 that hear and understand, "**W** for your shepherd;
12:39 But as for you, **w** here seven days more,

WAITED (22) [WAIT]

Ge 8:10 He **w** another seven days, and again he sent out
8:12 he **w** another seven days, and sent out the dove;
40: 4 of the guard charged Joseph with them, and he **w**
Jdg 3:25 So they **w** until they were embarrassed.
1Sa 13: 8 He **w** seven days, the time appointed by Samuel;
25: 9 of David; and then they **w**.
1Ki 20:38 and **w** for the king along the road,
Job 29:21 "They listened to me, and **w**,
29:23 They **w** for me as for the rain;
30:26 and when I **w** for light, darkness came.
32: 4 Now Elihu had **w** to speak to Job,
32:11 I **w** for your words, I listened
Ps 40: 1 I **w** patiently for the LORD;
Isa 25: 9 we have **w** for him, so that he might save us.
25: 9 This is the LORD for whom we have **w**;
Mt 4:11 and suddenly angels came and **w** on him.
Mk 1:13 and the angels **w** on him.
Ac 28: 6 but after they had **w** a long time and saw
1Pe 3:20 when God **w** patiently in the days of Noah,
Jdt 6:10 who **w** on him in his tent,
2Mc 5:25 he pretended to be peaceably disposed and **w** until
3Mc 7:17 because of a characteristic of the place, the fleet **w**

WAITING‡ (29) [WAIT]

Ex 5:20 upon Moses and Aaron who were **w** to meet them.
2Sa 17:17 Jonathan and Ahimaaz were **w** at En-rogel;
Job 35:14 that the case is before him, and you are **w** for him!
Ps 69: 3 My eyes grow dim with **w** for my God.
Pr 8:34 watching daily at my gates, **w** beside my doors.
Jer 3: 2 By the waysides you have sat **w** for lovers,
Jnh 4: 5 **w** to see what would become of the city.
Mk 15:43 also himself **w** expectantly for the kingdom
Lk 1:21 Meanwhile the people were **w** for Zechariah,
8:40 for they were all **w** for him.
12:36 be like those who are **w** for their master to return
23:51 and he was **w** expectantly for the kingdom of God.
Ac 17:16 While Paul was **w** for them in Athens,
20: 5 They went ahead and were **w** for us in Troas;
20:23 that imprisonment and persecutions are **w** for me.
23:21 They are ready now and are **w** for your consent."
Heb 9:28 but to save those who are eagerly **w** for him
10:13 then has been **w** "until his enemies would be made
2Pe 3:12 **w** for and hastening the coming of the day of God,
3:14 beloved, while you are **w** for these things,
Jdt 10:18 **w** until they told him about her.
12:16 for he had been **w** for an opportunity to seduce her
Sir 4: 1 and do not keep needy eyes **w**.
29: 8 and do not keep him **w** for your alms.
Sus 1:59 the angel of God is **w** with his sword to split you
2Mc 7:30 the young man said, "What are you **w** for?
9:25 for opportunities and **w** to see what will happen.
3Mc 5:24 and they were eagerly **w** for daybreak.
2Es 7:95 and the glory **w** for them in the last days.

WAITS (11) [WAIT]

Job 24:15 The eye of the adulterer also **w** for the twilight,
Ps 33:20 Our soul **w** for the LORD;
62: 1 For God alone my soul **w** in silence;
62: 5 For God alone my soul **w** in silence,
130: 5 I wait for the LORD, my soul **w**,
130: 6 my soul **w** for the Lord more than those who watch
Isa 30:18 Therefore the LORD **w** to be gracious to you;
Ro 8:19 the creation **w** with eager longing for the revealing
Jas 5: 7 The farmer **w** for the precious crop from the earth,
Sir 21:22 but an experienced person **w** respectfully outside.
2Mc 6:14 the case of the other nations the Lord **w** patiently

WAKE‡ (12) [AWAKE, AWAKEN, AWAKENED, AWAKES, AWAKING, AWOKE, WAKEFUL, WAKEFULNESS, WAKENED, WAKENS, WAKES, WOKE]

Job 41:32 It leaves a shining **w** behind it;
Ps 3: 5 I **w** again, for the LORD sustains me.
35:23 **W** up! Bestir yourself for my defense,
Jer 51:39 and then sleep a perpetual sleep and never **w**,
51:57 they shall sleep a perpetual sleep and never **w**,
Joel 1: 5 **W** up, you drunkards, and weep;
Hab 2: 7 and those who make you tremble **w** up?
2:19 Alas for you who say to the wood, "**W** up!"
Ro 13:11 how it is now the moment for you to **w** from sleep.
Rev 3: 2 **W** up, and strengthen what remains and is on
3: 3 If you do not **w** up, I will come like a thief,
Jdt 14:13 "**W** up our lord, for the slaves have been so bold as

WAKEFUL (1) [WAKE]

Sir 31: 2 **W** anxiety prevents slumber,

WAKEFULNESS (1) [WAKE]

Sir 31: 1 **W** over wealth wastes away one's flesh,

WAKENED (2) [WAKE]

Zec 4: 1 angel who talked with me came again, and **w** me, as one is **w** from sleep.

WAKENS (2) [WAKE]

Isa 50: 4 Morning by morning he **w**—**w** my ear to listen

WAKES (4) [WAKE]

Isa 29: 8 as when a hungry person dreams of eating and **w**
29: 8 a thirsty person dreams of drinking and **w** up faint,
Sir 40: 7 At the moment he reaches safety he **w** up,
1Es 3: 9 "When the king **w**, they will give him the writing;

WALK‡ (173) [WALKED, WALKING, WALKS]

Ge 13:17 **w** through the length and the breadth of the land,
17: 1 **w** before me, and be blameless.
24:40 But he said to me, 'The LORD, before whom I **w**,
24:63 Isaac went out in the evening to **w** in the field;
Lev 11:20 that **w** upon all fours are detestable to you.
11:21 But among the winged insects that **w**
11:27 that **w** on their paws, among the animals that **w** on
26:12 And I will **w** among you, and will be your God,
26:13 the bars of your yoke and made you **w** erect.
Dt 10:12 to **w** in all his ways, to love him,
13: 5 the LORD your God commanded you to **w**.
26:17 and for you to **w** in his ways, to keep his statutes,
28: 9 the commandments of the LORD your God and **w** in
Jos 22: 5 to love the LORD your God, to **w** in all his ways,
Jdg 2:22 or not they would take care to **w** in the way of
5:10 you who sit on rich carpets and you who **w** by
1Sa 17:39 and he tried in vain to **w**,
17:39 Then David said to Saul, "I cannot **w** with these;
1Ki 2: 4 to **w** before me in faithfulness with all their heart
3:14 If you will **w** in my ways,
6:12 if you will **w** in my statutes, obey my ordinances,
8:23 and steadfast love for your servants who **w** before
8:25 to **w** before me as you have walked before me.'
8:36 the good way in which they should **w**;
8:58 to **w** in all his ways,
9: 4 As for you, if you will **w** before me,
11:38 **w** in my ways, and do what is right in my sight
16:31 for him to **w** in the sins of Jeroboam son of Nebat,
2Ki 21:22 and did not **w** in the way of the LORD.
2Ch 6:14 in steadfast love with your servants who **w** before
6:16 to **w** in my law as you have walked before me.'
6:27 the good way in which they should **w**;
6:31 and **w** in your ways all the days that they live in
7:17 As for you, if you **w** before me,
Ne 5: 9 Should you not **w** in the fear of our God,
10:29 enter into a curse and an oath to **w** in God's law,
Est 2:11 Every day Mordecai would **w** around in front of
Job 18: 8 and they **w** into a pitfall.
Ps 15: 2 Those who **w** blamelessly, and do what is right,
23: 4 I **w** through the darkest valley, I fear no evil;
26: 3 and I **w** in faithfulness to you.
26:11 But as for me, I **w** in my integrity;
37:14 to kill those who **w** uprightly;
42: 9 Why must I **w** about mournfully because
43: 2 Why must I **w** about mournfully because of
48:12 **W** about Zion, go all around it, count its towers,
56:13 so that I may **w** before God in the light of life.
68:21 hairy crown of those who **w** in their guilty ways.
78:10 but refused to **w** according to his law.
81:13 that Israel would **w** in my ways!
82: 5 they **w** around in darkness;
84:11 the LORD withhold from those who **w** uprightly.
86:11 O LORD, that I may **w** in your truth;
89:15 who **w**, O LORD, in the light
89:30 If his children forsake my law and do not **w**
101: 2 I will **w** with integrity of heart within my house;
115: 7 but do not **w**; they make no sound in their throats.
116: 9 I **w** before the LORD in the land of the living.
119: 1 who **w** in the law of the LORD.
119: 3 who also do no wrong, but **w** in his ways.
119:45 I shall **w** at liberty, for I have sought your precepts.
138: 7 Though I **w** in the midst of trouble,
142: 3 the path where I **w** they have hidden a trap for me.
Pr 1:15 not **w** in their way, keep your foot from their paths;
2: 7 he is a shield to those who **w** blamelessly,
Pr 2:13 forsake the paths of uprightness to **w** in the ways
2:20 Therefore **w** in the way of the good,
3:23 Then you will **w** on your way securely
4:12 When you **w**, your step will not be hampered;
4:14 and do not **w** in the way of evildoers.
6:22 When you **w**, they will lead you;
6:28 can one **w** on hot coals without scorching the feet?
8:20 I **w** in the way of righteousness,
9: 6 and live, and **w** in the way of insight."
14: 2 Those who **w** uprightly fear the LORD,
20: 7 The righteous **w** in integrity—
28: 6 and **w** in integrity than to be crooked in one's ways
28:26 but those who **w** in wisdom come through safely.
Ecc 2:14 The wise have eyes in their head, but fools **w**
10: 3 Even when fools **w** on the road, they lack sense,
Isa 2: 3 that he may teach us his ways and that we may **w**
2: 5 come, let us **w** in the light of the LORD!
3:16 of Zion are haughty and **w** with outstretched necks,
8:11 and warned me not to **w** in the way of this people,
30:21 "This is the way; **w** in it."
33:15 Those who **w** righteously and speak uprightly,
35: 9 but the redeemed shall **w** there.
40:31 they shall **w** and not faint.
42: 5 the people upon it and spirit to those who **w** in it:
42:24 in whose ways they would not **w**,
43: 2 when you **w** through fire you shall not be burned,
50:11 **W** in the flame of your fire,
51:23 "Bow down, that we may **w** on you";
51:23 the ground and like the street for them to **w** on.
57: 2 those who **w** uprightly will rest on their couches.
59: 9 and for brightness, but we **w** in gloom.
65: 2 who **w** in a way that is not good,
Jer 6:16 and **w** in it, and find rest for your souls.
6:16 But they said, "We will not **w** in it."
6:25 Do not go out into the field, or **w** on the road;
7:23 and **w** only in the way that I command you,
10: 5 they have to be carried, for they cannot **w**.
10:23 that mortals as they **w** cannot direct their steps.
23:14 they commit adultery and **w** in lies;
26: 4 to **w** in my law that I have set before you,
31: 9 I will let them **w** by brooks of water,
44:23 the LORD or **w** in his law and in his statutes and
La 4:18 They dogged our steps so that we could not **w**
Eze 33:15 and **w** in the statutes of life,
Da 4:37 and he is able to bring low those who **w** in pride.
Hos 11: 3 Yet it was I who taught Ephraim to **w**,
14: 9 and the upright **w** in them,
Am 3: 3 Do two **w** together unless they have made
Jnh 3: 3 an exceedingly large city, a three days' **w** across.
3: 4 Jonah began to go into the city, going a day's **w**.
Mic 2: 3 and you shall not **w** haughtily,
4: 2 that he may teach us his ways and that we may **w**
4: 5 For all the peoples **w**, each in the name of its god,
4: 5 but we will **w** in the name of the LORD our God
6: 8 and to **w** humbly with your God?
Zep 1:17 upon people that they shall **w** like the blind;
Zec 3: 7 you will **w** in my ways and keep my requirements,
10:12 and they shall **w** in his name, says the LORD.
Mt 9: 5 or to say, 'Stand up and **w**'?
11: 5 the lame **w**, the lepers are cleansed, the deaf hear,
Mk 2: 9 or to say, 'Stand up and take your mat and **w**'?
5:42 And immediately the girl got up and began to **w**
12:38 who like to **w** around in long robes,
Lk 5:23 or to say, 'Stand up and **w**'?
7:22 the blind receive their sight, the lame **w**,
11:44 and people **w** over them without realizing it."
20:46 who like to **w** around in long robes,
24:17 with each other while you **w** along?"
Jn 1:36 and as he watched Jesus **w** by,
5: 8 said to him, "Stand up, take your mat and **w**."
5: 9 and he took up his mat and began to **w**.
5:11 'Take up your mat and **w**.' "
5:12 the man who said to you, 'Take it up and **w**'?"
8:12 Whoever follows me will never **w** in darkness
11: 9 Those who **w** during the day do not stumble,
11:10 But those who **w** at night stumble,
12:35 **W** while you have the light,
12:35 If you **w** in the darkness,
Ac 3: 6 of Jesus Christ of Nazareth, stand up and **w**."
3: 8 Jumping up, he stood and began to **w**,
3:12 by our own power or piety we had made him **w**?
14:10 And the man sprang up and began to **w**.
Ro 6: 4 so we too might **w** in newness of life.
8: 4 who **w** not according to the flesh but according to
2Co 5: 7 for we **w** by faith, not by sight.
6:16 God said, "I will live in them and **w** among them,
1Jn 1: 7 but if we **w** in the light as he himself is in the light,
2: 6 "I abide in him," ought to **w** just as he walked.
2Jn 1: 6 that we **w** according to his commandments;
1: 6 heard it from the beginning—you must **w** in it.
3Jn 1: 3 namely how you **w** in the truth.
Rev 3: 4 they will **w** with me, dressed in white,
9:20 which cannot see or hear or **w**.
21:24 The nations will **w** by its light,
Tob 4: 5 and do not **w** in the ways of wrongdoing;
Wis 6: 4 or **w** according to the purpose of God,
Sir 4:17 For at first she will **w** with them on tortuous paths;
21: 6 Those who hate reproof **w** in the sinner's steps,
Bar 1:18 to **w** in the statutes of the Lord that he set
2:10 to **w** in the statutes of the Lord that he set
4: 2 **w** toward the shining of her light.
4:13 not **w** in the ways of God's commandments,
5: 7 so that Israel may **w** safely in the glory of God.
Sus 1: 7 Susanna would go into her husband's garden to **w**.
2Mc 5:21 that he could sail on the land and **w** on the sea,
6: 7 to wear wreathes of ivy and to **w** in the procession
2Es 7: 8 so that only one person can **w** on the path.

WALKED (79) [WALK]

Ge 5:22 Enoch w with God after the birth of Methuselah
5:24 Enoch w with God; then he was no more,
6: 9 in his generation; Noah w with God.
9:23 and w backward and covered the nakedness
22: 6 So the two of them w on together.
22: 8 So the two of them w on together.
48:15 before whom my ancestors Abraham and Isaac w,
Ex 2: 5 while her attendants w beside the river.
14:29 But the Israelites w on dry ground through the sea,
15:19 but the Israelites w through the sea on dry ground.
Jdg 2:17 in which their ancestors had w, who had obeyed
2Sa 3:16 as he w behind her all the way to Bahurim.
1Ki 3: 6 because he w before you in faithfulness,
3:14 and my commandments, as your father David w,
8:25 to walk before me as you have w before me.'
9: 4 before me, as David your father w, with integrity
11:33 and has not w in my ways,
16: 2 and you have w in the way of Jeroboam,
16:26 For he w in all the way of Jeroboam son of Nebat,
22:43 He w in all the way of his father Asa;
22:52 and w in the way of his father and mother,
2Ki 4:35 He got down, w once to and fro in the room,
8:18 He w in the way of the kings of Israel,
8:27 He also w in the way of the house of Ahab,
13: 6 which he caused Israel to sin, but w in them;
13:11 which he caused Israel to sin, but he w in them.
16: 3 but he w in the way of the kings of Israel.
17: 8 and w in the customs of the nations whom
17:19 the commandments of the LORD their God but w
20: 3 how I have w before you in faithfulness with
21:21 He w in all the way in which his father w,
22: 2 and w in all the way of his father David;
2Ch 6:16 to walk in my law as you have w before me.'
7:17 if you walk before me, as your father David w,
11:17 for they w for three years in the way of David
17: 3 because he w in the earlier ways of his father;
17: 4 the God of his father and w in his commandments,
20:32 He w in the way of his father Asa and did
21: 6 He w in the way of the kings of Israel,
21:12 not w in the ways of your father Jehoshaphat or in
21:13 but have w in the way of the kings of Israel,
22: 3 He also w in the ways of the house of Ahab,
28: 2 but he w in the ways of the kings of Israel.
34: 2 and w in the ways of his ancestor David;
Job 29: 3 and by his light I w through darkness;
31: 5 "If I have w with falsehood,
38:16 or w in the recesses of the deep?
Ps 26: 1 O LORD, for I have w in my integrity,
55:14 we w in the house of God with the throng.
Isa 9: 2 people who w in darkness have seen a great light;
20: 3 as my servant Isaiah has w naked and barefoot
38: 3 how I have w before you in faithfulness with
Jer 7:24 they w in their own counsels,
9:13 or w in accordance with it,
11: 8 but everyone w in the stubbornness of an evil will.
44:10 nor have they w in my law and my statutes
Eze 28:14 you w among the stones of fire.
Am 2: 4 by the same lies after which their ancestors w.
Mal 2: 6 He w with me in integrity and uprightness,
Mt 4:18 As he w by the Sea of Galilee,
Lk 24:28 he w ahead as if he were going on.
Jn 9: 1 As he w along, he saw a man blind from birth.
11:54 Jesus therefore no longer w about openly among
Ac 12:10 and they went outside and w along a lane,
14: 8 not use his feet and had never w,
1Jn 2: 6 "I abide in him," ought to walk just as he w.
Tob 1: 3 w in the ways of truth and righteousness all
3: 5 not kept your commandments and have not w
AdE 2:11 And every day Mordecai w in the courtyard of
Wis 19:21 to consume the flesh of perishable creatures that w
Sir 45: 9 to send forth a sound as he w,
51:15 my foot w on the straight path;
Bar 3:13 If you had w in the way of God,
Aza 1: 1 They w around in the midst of the flames,
2Es 3: 8 And every nation w after its own will;
7:*122* [52] but we have w in the most wicked ways?
8:50 because they have w in great pride.
13:57 Then I got up and w in the field,

WALKING (53) [WALK]

Ge 3: 8 the sound of the LORD God w in the garden
24:65 w in the field to meet us?"
Dt 8: 6 by w in his ways and by fearing him.
11:22 loving the LORD your God, w in all his ways,
19: 9 the LORD your God and w always in his ways—
30:16 w in his ways, and observing his commandments,
2Sa 11: 2 when David rose from his couch and was w about
15:30 with his head covered and w barefoot;
1Ki 2: 3 w in his ways and keeping his statutes,
3: 3 w in the statutes of his father David;
6:12 and keep all my commandments by w in them,
8:61 w in his statutes and keeping his commandments,
15:26 w in the way of his ancestor and in the sin
15:34 w in the way of Jeroboam and in the sin
16:19 w in the way of Jeroboam,
2Ki 2:11 As they continued w and talking,
6:26 Now as the king of Israel was w on the city wall,
6:30 now since he was w on the city wall,
Job 1: 7 and from w up and down on it."
2: 2 and from w up and down on it."
Pr 12:28 in w its path there is no death.
19: 1 Better the poor w in integrity than one perverse
Ecc 10: 7 and princes w on foot like slaves.
Isa 20: 2 and he had done so, w naked and barefoot.
Da 3:25 w in the middle of the fire, and they are not hurt;
Da 4:29 At the end of twelve months he was w on the roof
Mt 9: 9 As Jesus was w along, he saw
14:25 in the morning he came w toward them on the sea.
14:26 But when the disciples saw him w on the sea,
14:29 So Peter got out of the boat, started w on the water,
15:31 the lame w, and the blind seeing.
Mk 2:14 As he was w along, he saw Levi son of
6:48 in the morning, w on the sea.
6:49 But when they saw him w on the sea,
8:24 "I can see people, but they look like trees, w."
10:32 and Jesus was w ahead of them;
11:27 As he was w in the temple, the chief priests,
16:12 ⟦as they were w into the country.⟧
Jn 6:19 they saw Jesus w on the sea and coming near
10:23 and Jesus was w in the temple,
Ac 3: 8 w and leaping and praising God.
3: 9 All the people saw him w and praising God,
Ro 14:15 you are no longer w in love.
1Jn 1: 6 that we have fellowship with him while we are w
2Jn 1: 4 I was overjoyed to find some of your children w in
3Jn 1: 4 to hear that my children are w in the truth.
Tob 11:16 w along in full vigor and with no one leading him,
Jdt 13:20 w in the straight path before our God."
Wis 15:15 and their feet are of no use for w.
Sir 9:13 and that you are w on the city battlements.
13:13 for you are w about with your own downfall.
Sus 1: 8 to see her, going in and w about, and they began
1:36 elders said, "While we were w in the garden alone,

WALKS (22) [WALK]

Ex 21:19 but recovers and w around outside with the help of
Job 22:14 and he w on the dome of heaven.'
34: 8 in company with evildoers and w with the wicked?
Ps 101: 6 w in the way that is blameless shall minister to
128: 1 the LORD, who w in his ways.
Pr 10: 9 Whoever w in integrity w securely,
13:20 Whoever w with the wise becomes wise,
15:21 but a person of understanding w straight ahead.
28:18 One who w in integrity will be safe,
Isa 50:10 who w in darkness and has no light,
59: 8 no one who w in them knows peace.
Hos 11:12 but Judah still w with God,
Mic 2: 7 Do not my words do good to one who w uprightly?
Zep 3: 6 I have laid waste their streets so that no one w
1Jn 2:11 the darkness, w in the darkness, and does not know
Rev 2: 1 who w among the seven golden lampstands:
Sir 2:12 and to the sinner who w a double path!
12:11 Even if he humbles himself and w bowed down,
19:30 and the way he w, show what he is.
Bar 2:18 the person who is deeply grieved, who w bowed
1Es 4:24 and he w in darkness, and when he steals and robs

WALL‡ (191) [SIDEWALLS, WALLED, WALLS]

Ge 49:22 his branches run over the w.
Ex 14:22 the waters forming a w for them on their right and
14:29 the waters forming a w for them on their right and
Nu 22:24 with a w on either side.
22:25 the w, and scraped Balaam's foot against the w;
35: 4 shall reach from the w of the town outward
Jos 2:15 of the city w and she resided within the w itself.
6: 5 and the w of the city will fall down flat,
6:20 they raised a great shout, and the w fell down flat;
1Sa 18:11 for he thought, "I will pin David to the w."
19:10 Saul sought to pin David to the w with the spear;
19:10 so that he struck the spear into the w.
20:25 as at other times, upon the seat by the w.
25:16 they were a w to us both by night and by day,
31:10 and they fastened his body to the w of Beth-shan.
31:12 the bodies of his sons from the w of Beth-shan.
2Sa 11:20 not know that they would shoot from the w?
11:21 an upper millstone on him from the w,
11:21 Why did you go so near the w?'
11:24 Then the archers shot at your servants from the w;
18:24 sentinel went up to the roof of the gate by the w,
20:15 Joab's forces were battering the w
20:21 "His head shall be thrown over the w to you."
22:30 and by my God I can leap over a w.
1Ki 3: 1 of the LORD and the w around Jerusalem.
4:33 in the Lebanon to the hyssop that grows in the w;
6: 5 He also built a structure against the w of the house,
6: 6 on the w in order that the supporting beams should
6:27 a wing of one was touching the one w, and a wing
of the other cherub was touching the other w;
9:15 the Millo and the w of Jerusalem, Hazor, Megiddo,
11:27 up the gap in the w of the city of his father David.
20:30 and the w fell on twenty-seven thousand men
2Ki 3:27 and offered him as a burnt offering on the w.
6:26 as the king of Israel was walking on the city w,
6:30 now since he was walking on the city w,
9:33 of her blood spattered on the w and on the horses,
10:21 until the temple of Baal was filled from w to w.
14:13 down the w of Jerusalem from the Ephraim Gate to
18:26 within the hearing of the people who are on the w."
18:27 and not to the people sitting on the w,
20: 2 Then Hezekiah turned his face to the w and prayed
25: 4 Then a breach was made in the city w;
2Ch 3:11 touched the w of the house, and its other wing,
3:12 touched the w of the house, and the other wing,
25:23 down the w of Jerusalem from the Ephraim Gate to
26: 6 the w of Gath and the w of Jabneh and the w of
27: 3 and did extensive building on the w of Ophel.
32: 5 and built up the entire w that was broken down,
32: 5 and outside it he built another w;
32:18 to the people of Jerusalem who were on the w,
2Ch 33:14 an outer w for the city of David west of Gihon,
36:19 broke down the w of Jerusalem,
Ezr 9: 9 and to give us a w in Judea and Jerusalem.
Ne 1: 3 the w of Jerusalem is broken down,
2: 8 and for the w of the city,
2:15 by way of the valley by night and inspected the w.
2:17 Come, let us rebuild the w of Jerusalem,
3: 8 and they restored Jerusalem as far as the Broad W.
3:13 and repaired a thousand cubits of the w,
3:15 the w of the Pool of Shelah of the king's garden,
3:27 the great projecting tower as far as the w of Ophel.
4: 1 when Sanballat heard that we were building the w,
4: 3 and he said, "That stone w they are building—
4: 6 rebuilt the w, and all the w was joined together
4:10 so that we are unable to work on the w."
4:13 So in the lowest parts of the space behind the w,
4:15 we all returned to the w, each to his work.
4:17 who were building the w.
4:19 we are separated far from one another on the w.
5:16 Indeed, I devoted myself to the work on this w,
6: 1 to the rest of our enemies that I had built the w and
6: 6 that is why you are building the w;
6:15 So the w was finished on the twenty-fifth day of
7: 1 the w had been built and I had set up the doors,
12:27 of the w of Jerusalem they sought out the Levites
12:30 they purified the people and the gates and the w.
12:31 Then I brought the leaders of Judah up onto the w,
12:31 One went to the right on the w to the Dung Gate;
12:37 at the ascent of the w, above the house of David,
12:38 I followed them with half of the people on the w,
12:38 above the Tower of the Ovens, to the Broad W,
13:21 "Why do you spend the night in front of the w?
Ps 18:29 and by my God I can leap over a w.
62: 3 as you would a leaning w, a tottering fence?
Pr 18:11 in their imagination it is like a high w.
24:31 and its stone w was broken down.
Ecc 10: 8 and whoever breaks through a w will be bitten by
SS 2: 9 Look, there he stands behind our w,
8: 9 a w, we will build upon her a battlement of silver;
8:10 I was a w, and my breasts were like towers;
Isa 2:15 and against every fortified w;
5: 5 I will break down its w, and it shall be trampled
22:10 and you broke down the houses to fortify the w.
30:13 for you like a break in a high w, bulging out,
36:11 within the hearing of the people who are on the w."
36:12 and not to the people sitting on the w,
38: 2 Then Hezekiah turned his face to the w,
54:12 and all your w of precious stones.
59:10 We grope like the blind along a w,
Jer 1:18 and a bronze w, against the whole land—
15:20 And I will make you to this people a fortified w
49:27 And I will kindle a fire at the w of Damascus,
51:44 the w of Babylon has fallen.
51:58 broad w of Babylon shall be leveled to the ground,
52: 7 Then a breach was made in the city w;
La 2: 8 The LORD determined to lay in ruins the w
2: 8 he caused rampart and w to lament;
2:18 O w of daughter Zion!
Eze 4: 2 and build a siege w against it,
4: 3 an iron plate and place it as an iron w between you
8: 7 I looked, and there was a hole in the w.
8: 8 Then he said to me, "Mortal, dig through the w";
8: 8 when I dug through the w, there was an entrance.
8:10 there, portrayed on the w all around,
12: 5 Dig through the w in their sight,
12: 7 and in the evening I dug through the w
12:12 he shall dig through the w and carry it through;
13: 5 or repaired a w for the house of Israel,
13:10 and because, when the people build a w,
13:12 When the w falls, will it not be said to you,
13:14 I will break down the w that you have smeared
13:15 Thus I will spend my wrath upon the w,
13:15 and I will say to you, The w is no more,
22:30 the w and stand in the breach before me on behalf
23:14 she saw male figures carved on the w,
26: 8 He shall set up a siege w against you,
38:20 and every w shall tumble to the ground.
40: 5 a w all around the outside of the temple area.
40: 5 so he measured the thickness of the w, one reed;
40:13 a width of twenty-five cubits, from w to w.
41: 5 he measured the w of the temple, six cubits thick;
41: 6 around the w of the temple to serve as supports for
41: 6 so that they should not be supported by the w of
41: 9 the outer w of the side chambers was five cubits;
41:12 w of the building was five cubits thick all around,
41:20 cherubim and palm trees were carved on the w.
42: 7 There was a w outside parallel to the chambers,
42:10 width of the passage is fixed by the w of the court.
42:12 from the east, along the matching w.
42:20 It had a w around it,
43: 8 with only a w between me and them,
Da 5: 5 and began writing on the plaster of the w of
Hos 2: 6 and I will build a w against her,
Joel 2: 7 like soldiers they scale the w.
Am 1: 7 So I will send a fire on the w of Gaza,
1:10 So I will send a fire on the w of Tyre,
1:14 So I will kindle a fire against the w of Rabbah,
4: 3 Through breaches in the w you shall leave,
5:19 into the house and rested a hand against the w,
7: 7 the Lord was standing beside a w built with
Mic 5: 1 Now you are walled around with a w;
Na 2: 5 they hasten to the w, and the mantelet is set up.
3: 8 her rampart a sea, water her w?
Hab 2:11 The very stones will cry out from the w,
Zec 2: 5 For I will be a w of fire all around it,
Ac 9:25 and let him down through an opening in the w,
23: 3 "God will strike you, you whitewashed w!

2Co 11:33 down in a basket through a window in the **w**,
Eph 2:14 into one and has broken down the dividing **w**,
Rev 21:12 It has a great, high **w** with twelve gates,
21:14 And the **w** of the city has twelve foundations,
21:17 also measured its **w**, one hundred forty-four cubits
21:18 The **w** is built of jasper, while the city is pure gold,
21:19 of the **w** of the city are adorned with every jewel;
Tob 1:17 of my people thrown out behind the **w** of Nineveh,
2: 9 and went into my courtyard and slept by the **w** of
2:10 I did not know that there were sparrows on the **w**;
Jdt 14: 1 and hang it upon the parapet of your **w**.
14:11 the head of Holofernes on the **w**.
Wis 13:15 and sets it in the **w**, and fastens it there with iron.
Sir 22:17 like stucco decoration that makes a **w** smooth.
1Mc 1:33 of David with a great strong **w** and strong towers,
6:62 and gave orders to tear down the **w** all around.
9:54 down the **w** of the inner court of the sanctuary.
12:37 part of the **w** on the valley to the east had fallen,
13:45 went up on the **w** with their clothes torn,
2Mc 1:15 with a few men inside the **w** of the sacred precinct,
5: 5 When the troops on the **w** had been forced back
6:10 and then hurled them down headlong from the **w**.
10:17 and beat off all who fought upon the **w**,
10:35 bravely stormed the **w** and with savage fury cut
14:43 He courageously ran up on the **w**,
3Mc 4:11 with a monstrous perimeter **w** in front of the city,

WALLED (6) [WALL]

Lev 25:29 If anyone sells a dwelling house in a **w** city,
25:30 in a **w** city shall pass in perpetuity to the purchaser,
Job 19: 8 He has **w** up my way so that I cannot pass,
La 3: 7 He has **w** me about so that I cannot escape;
Mic 5: 1 Now you are **w** around with a wall;
1Mc 13:33 up the strongholds of Judea and **w** them all around,

WALLOW (4) [WALLOWING]

Jer 48:26 let Moab **w** in his vomit;
Eze 27:30 They throw dust on their heads and **w** in ashes;
2Pe 2:22 and, "The sow is washed only to **w** in the mud."
Sir 23:12 and they will not **w** in sins.

WALLOWING (1) [WALLOW]

2Sa 20:12 Amasa lay **w** in his blood on the highway,

WALLS‡ (108) [WALL]

Lev 14:37 if the disease is in the **w** of the house with greenish
14:39 if the disease has spread in the **w** of the house,
25:31 in villages that have no **w** around them shall
Dt 3: 5 All these were fortress towns with high **w**,
28:52 and fortified **w**, in which you trusted, come down
1Ki 4:13 sixty great cities with **w** and bronze bars);
6: 5 running around the **w** of the house,
6: 6 not be inserted into the **w** of the house.
6:15 the **w** of the house on the inside with boards
6:29 He carved the **w** of the house all around about
2Ki 3:25 Only at Kir-hareseth did the stone **w** remain,
4:10 Let us make a small roof chamber with **w**,
25: 4 by night by the way of the gate between the two **w**,
25:10 of the guard broke down the **w** around Jerusalem.
1Ch 29: 4 for overlaying the **w** of the house,
2Ch 3: 7 its beams, its thresholds, its **w**, and its doors;
3: 7 and he carved cherubim on the **w**.
8: 5 fortified cities, with **w**, gates, and bars,
14: 7 and surround them with **w** and towers,
Ezr 4:12 they are finishing the **w** and repairing
4:13 if this city is rebuilt and the **w** finished,
4:16 if this city is rebuilt and its **w** finished,
5: 8 and timber is laid in the **w**;
Ne 2:13 the **w** of Jerusalem that had been broken down
4: 7 the Ashdodites heard that the repairing of the **w**
Ps 51:18 rebuild the **w** of Jerusalem,
55:10 Day and night they go around it on its **w**,
80:12 Why then have you broken down its **w**,
89:40 You have broken through all his **w**;
122: 7 Peace be within your **w**, and security
144:14 May there be no breach in the **w**, no exile,
Pr 25:28 Like a city breached, without **w**,
SS 5: 7 took away my mantle, those sentinels of the **w**.
Isa 22: 5 a battering down of **w** and a cry for help to the
22:11 between the two **w** for the water of the old pool.
25:12 high fortifications of his **w** will be brought down,
26: 1 he sets up victory like **w** and bulwarks.
49:16 your **w** are continually before me.
56: 5 in my house and within my **w**,
60:10 Foreigners shall build up your **w**,
60:18 you shall call your **w** Salvation,
62: 6 Upon your **w**, O Jerusalem,
Jer 1:15 of Jerusalem, against all its surrounding **w** and
4:19 Oh, the **w** of my heart!
21: 4 Chaldeans who are besieging you outside the **w**;
39: 4 through the gate between the two **w**;
39: 8 and broke down the **w** of Jerusalem.
50:15 her bulwarks have fallen, her **w** are thrown down."
51:12 Raise a standard against the **w** of Babylon;
52: 7 by night by the way of the gate between the two **w**,
52:14 broke down all the **w** around Jerusalem.
La 2: 7 he has delivered into the hand of the enemy the **w**
Eze 17:17 up and siege **w** built to cut off many lives.
26: 4 They shall destroy the **w** of Tyre and break
26: 9 of his battering rams against your **w** and break
26:10 wheels, and chariots your very **w** shall shake,
26:12 down your **w** and destroy your fine houses.
27:11 of Arvad and Helech were on your **w** all around;
27:11 They hung their quivers all around your **w**;
33:30 your people who talk together about you by the **w**,
Eze 38:11 all of them living without **w**,
41:13 and the yard and the building with its **w**,
41:17 And on all the **w** all around in the inner room and
41:22 its corners, its base, and its **w** were of wood.
41:25 such as were carved on the **w**;
Joel 2: 9 They leap upon the city, they run upon the **w**;
Mic 7:11 A day for the building of your **w**!
Zec 2: 4 be inhabited like villages without **w**,
Heb 11:30 the **w** of Jericho fell after they had been encircled
Rev 21:15 of gold to measure the city and its gates and **w**.
Tob 13:12 down your **w**, all who overthrow your towers
13:16 and all your **w** with precious stones.
Jdt 1: 2 He built **w** around Ecbatana
1: 2 the **w** seventy cubits high and fifty cubits wide.
7:32 they went up on the **w** and towers of their town.
Sir 14:24 near her house and fastens his tent peg to her **w**;
23:18 Darkness surrounds me, the **w** hide me,
49:13 he raised our fallen **w**, and set up gates and bars,
50: 2 He laid the foundations for the high double **w**,
50: 2 the high retaining **w** for the temple enclosure.
1Mc 1:31 and tore down its houses and its surrounding **w**.
4:60 At that time they fortified Mount Zion with high **w**
6: 7 that they had surrounded the sanctuary with high **w**
9:50 and Tephon, with high **w** and gates and bars.
10:11 the work to build the **w** and encircle Mount Zion
10:45 And let the cost of rebuilding the **w** of Jerusalem
10:45 and the cost of rebuilding the **w** in Judea,
12:36 to build the **w** of Jerusalem still higher,
13:10 and hurried to complete the **w** of Jerusalem,
13:33 with high towers and great **w** and gates and bolts,
14:37 and built the **w** of Jerusalem higher.
16:23 and the building of the **w** that he completed,
2Mc 3:19 and some to the **w**, while others peered out of
11: 9 not only humans but the wildest animals or **w**
12:13 that was strongly fortified with earthworks and **w**,
12:14 relying on the strength of the **w** and on their supply
12:15 rushed furiously upon the **w**.
12:27 Stalwart young men took their stand before the **w**
1Es 1:55 broke down the **w** of Jerusalem,
2:18 and **w** and laying the foundations for a temple.
2:19 Now if this city is built and the **w** finished,
2:24 that if this city is built and its **w** finished,
4: 4 they go, and conquer mountains, **w**, and towers.
6: 9 of hewn stone, with costly timber laid in the **w**.
3Mc 1:29 but also the **w** and the whole earth around echoed,
2Es 2:22 Protect the old and the young within your **w**;
11:42 have laid low the **w** of those who did you no harm.
15:42 They shall destroy cities and **w**,

WANDER‡ (23) [WANDERED, WANDERER, WANDERERS, WANDERING, WANDERINGS, WANDERS]

Ge 20:13 when God caused me to **w** from my father's house,
Nu 32:13 he made them **w** in the wilderness for forty years,
Jdg 11:37 so that I may go and **w** on the mountains,
2Sa 15:20 and shall I today make you **w** about with us,
2Ki 21: 8 I will not cause the feet of Israel to **w** any more out
Job 12:24 and makes them **w** in a pathless waste.
15:23 They **w** abroad for bread, saying, 'Where is it?'
38:41 and **w** about for lack of food?
Ps 107:40 on princes and makes them **w** in trackless wastes;
109:10 May his children **w** about and beg;
119:21 accursed ones, who **w** from your commandments;
Pr 5: 6 her ways **w**, and she does not know it.
Isa 47:15 they all **w** about in their own paths;
Jer 14:10 Truly they have loved to **w**,
31:24 and the farmers and those who **w** with their flocks.
49:30 Flee, **w** far away, hide in deep places,
Joel 1:18 of cattle **w** about because there is no pasture
Am 8:12 They shall **w** from sea to sea,
Zec 10: 2 Therefore the people **w** like sheep;
2Ti 4: 4 from listening to the truth and **w** away to myths.
Sir 9: 7 or **w** about in its deserted sections.
2Es 7:*80* but shall immediately **w** about in torments,
7:*93* the perplexity in which the souls of the ungodly **w**

WANDERED (10) [WANDER]

Ge 21:14 and **w** about in the wilderness of Beer-sheba.
1Sa 23:13 they **w** wherever they could go.
1Ki 18:27 either he is meditating, or he has **w** away,
Ps 107: 4 Some **w** in desert wastes, finding no way to
La 4:14 Blindly they **w** through the streets,
Eze 34: 6 they **w** over all the mountains and
Am 4: 8 or three towns **w** to one town to drink water,
1Ti 6:10 in their eagerness to be rich some have **w** away
Heb 11:38 They **w** in deserts and mountains,
Sir 29:18 and they have **w** among foreign nations.

WANDERER (3) [WANDER]

Ge 4:12 you will be a fugitive and a **w** on the earth."
4:14 I shall be a fugitive and a **w** on the earth,
Sir 36:30 a man will become a fugitive and a **w**.

WANDERERS (2) [WANDER]

La 4:15 So they became fugitives and **w**;
Hos 9:17 they shall become **w** among the nations.

WANDERING‡ (13) [WANDER]

Ge 37:15 and a man found him **w** in the fields;
Ex 14: 3 'They are **w** aimlessly in the land;
Dt 26: 5 "A **w** Aramean was my ancestor;
1Ch 16:20 **w** from nation to nation, from one kingdom
Ps 105:13 **w** from nation to nation, from one kingdom
Ecc 6: 9 Better is the sight of the eyes than the **w** of desire;
La 1: 7 in the days of her affliction and **w**,
Hos 8: 9 they have gone up to Assyria, a wild ass **w** alone;
Zec 11:16 or seek the **w**, or heal the maimed,
Jas 5:20 that whoever brings back a sinner from **w** will save
Jude 1:13 **w** stars, for whom the deepest darkness has been
Wis 18: 3 and a harmless sun for their glorious **w**.
2Mc 10: 6 they had been **w** in the mountains and caves

WANDERINGS (1) [WANDER]

Isa 57:10 You grew weary from your many **w**,

WANDERS (4) [WANDER]

Pr 21:16 Whoever **w** from the way of understanding
Mt 12:43 it **w** through waterless regions looking for
Lk 11:24 it **w** through waterless regions looking for
Jas 5:19 among you **w** from the truth and is brought back

WANDS (2)

Jdt 15:12 She took ivy-wreathed **w** in her hands
2Mc 10: 7 carrying ivy-wreathed **w** and beautiful branches

WANES (1)

Sir 43: 7 a light that **w** when it completes its course.

WANT (121) [WANTED, WANTING, WANTS]

Ge 33:11 and because I have everything I **w**."
Ex 5: 5 of the land and yet you **w** them to stop working!"
16:23 bake what you **w** to bake and boil what you **w**
Dt 12:30 I also **w** to do the same."
21:11 a beautiful woman whom you desire and **w**
Jdg 13:16 but if you **w** to prepare a burnt offering,
15: 1 He said, "I **w** to go into my wife's room."
19:24 Ravish them and do whatever you **w** to them;
2Sa 20:16 Tell Joab, 'Come here, I **w** to speak to you.' "
24: 3 But why does my lord the king **w** to do this?"
2Ki 6:22 with your sword and your bow those whom you **w**
Job 24: 8 and cling to the rock for **w** of shelter.
30: 3 Through **w** and hard hunger they gnaw the dry
37:20 Should he be told that I **w** to speak?
Ps 23: 1 The LORD is my shepherd, I shall not **w**.
34: 9 for those who fear him have no **w**.
34:10 The young lions suffer **w** and hunger,
Pr 6:11 and **w**, like an armed warrior.
11:24 others withhold what is due, and only suffer **w**.
21: 5 but everyone who is hasty comes only to **w**.
21:17 Whoever loves pleasure will suffer **w**;
24:34 and **w**, like an armed warrior.
Am 5:18 Why do you **w** the day of the LORD?
Mt 13:28 'Then do you **w** us to go and gather them?'
15:32 and I do not **w** to send them away hungry,
16:24 "If any **w** to become my followers,
16:25 For those who **w** to save their life will lose it,
20:21 And he said to her, "What do you **w**?"
20:32 saying, "What do you **w** me to do for you?"
26:17 "Where do you **w** us to make the preparations
26:39 yet not what I **w** but what you **w**."
27:17 "Whom do you **w** me to release for you,
27:21 of the two do you **w** me to release for you?"
Mk 6:25 "I **w** you to give me at once the head of John
6:26 he did not **w** to refuse her.
7:24 and did not **w** anyone to know he was there.
8:34 "If any **w** to become my followers,
8:35 For those who **w** to save their life will lose it,
9:30 He did not **w** anyone to know it;
10:35 we **w** you to do for us whatever we ask of you."
10:36 "What is it you **w** me to do for you?"
10:51 "What do you **w** me to do for you?"
14:12 "Where do you **w** us to go and make
14:36 yet, not what I **w**, but what you **w**."
15: 9 "Do you **w** me to release for you the King of
Lk 9:23 "If any **w** to become my followers,
9:24 For those who **w** to save their life will lose it,
9:54 do you **w** us to command fire to come down
16:26 so that those who might **w** to pass from here
18:41 "What do you **w** me to do for you?"
19:14 saying, 'We do not **w** this man to rule over us.'
19:27 of mine who did not **w** me to be king over them—
22: 9 "Where do you **w** us to make preparations for it?"
Jn 4:27 but no one said, "What do you **w**?"
5: 6 he said to him, "Do you **w** to be made well?"
9:27 Why do you **w** to hear it again?
9:27 Do you also **w** to become his disciples?"
18:39 Do you **w** me to release for you the King of
19:31 the Jews did not **w** the bodies left on the cross
Ac 7:28 Do you **w** to kill me as you killed
17:18 Some said, "What does this babbler **w** to say?"
19:39 If there is anything further you **w** to know,
23:15 that you **w** to make a more thorough examination
Ro 1:13 I **w** you to know, brothers and sisters,
7:15 I do not do what I **w**, but I do the very thing I hate.
7:16 I do what I do not **w**, I agree that the law is good.
7:19 For I do not do the good I **w**, but the evil I do not
w is what I do.
7:20 Now if I do what I do not **w**,
7:21 to be a law that when I **w** to do what is good,
11:25 I **w** you to understand this mystery:
16:19 I **w** you to be wise in what is good and guileless
1Co 4: 8 Already you have all you **w**!
7:32 I **w** you to be free from anxieties.
10: 1 I do not **w** you to be unaware, brothers and sisters,
10:20 I do not **w** you to be partners with demons.
11: 3 But I **w** you to understand that Christ is the head
12: 1 I do not **w** you to be uninformed.
12: 3 Therefore I **w** you to understand

1Co 16: 7 I do not w to see you now just in passing,
2Co 1: 8 We do not w you to be unaware,
8: 1 We w you to know, brothers and sisters,
8: 7 so we w you to excel also
10: 9 I do not w to seem as though I am trying
11:12 an opportunity to those who w an opportunity to
12:14 because I do not w what is yours but you;
Gal 1: 7 but there are some who are confusing you and w
1:11 For I w you to know, brothers and sisters,
3: 2 The only thing I w to learn from you is this:
4: 9 How can you w to be enslaved to them again?
4:17 w to exclude you, so that you may make much of
5: 4 You who w to be justified by
5:17 to prevent you from doing what you w.
6:12 It is those who w to make a good showing in
6:13 but they w you to be circumcised so
Php 1:12 I w you to know, beloved,
3:10 I w to know Christ and the power
Col 2: 1 For I w you to know how much I am struggling
2: 2 I w their hearts to be encouraged and united
1Th 4:13 But we do not w you to be uninformed,
1Ti 5:11 desires alienate them from Christ, they w to marry,
6: 9 But those who w to be rich fall into temptation
2Ti 3:12 all who w to live a godly life in Christ Jesus will
Heb 6:11 And we w each one of you to show
13:23 I w you to know that our brother Timothy has been
Jas 2:20 Do you w to be shown, you senseless person,
4: 2 You w something and do not have it;
3Jn 1:10 and even prevents those who w to do so
Tob 5:12 But Tobit said, "I w to be sure, brother,
AdE 3:11 and do whatever you w with that nation."
Wis 16: 3 while your people, after suffering w a short time,
16: 4 upon those oppressors inescapable w should come,
Sir 11:11 but are so much the more in w.
26:28 a warrior in w through poverty,
40:26 There is no w in the fear of the Lord,
Sus 1:46 "I w no part in shedding this woman's blood!"
2Es 14:22 those who w to live in the last days may do so."
16:63 Woe to those who sin and w to hide their sins!

WANTED‡ (49) [WANT]

1Ki 13:33 any who w to be priests he consecrated for
Ne 6: 9 —for they all w to frighten us,
6:14 the rest of the prophets who w to make me afraid.
Jer 8:13 When I w to gather them, says the LORD,
49: 9 even they would pillage only what they w.
Da 5:19 He killed those he w to kill, kept alive those he w
to keep alive, honored those he w to honor, and
degraded those he w to degrade.
Ob 1: 5 would they not steal only what they w?
Mt 14: 5 Though Herod w to put him to death,
21:46 They w to arrest him, but they feared the crowds,
27:15 a prisoner for the crowd, anyone whom they w.
Mk 3:13 the mountain and called to him those whom he w,
6:19 And Herodias had a grudge against him, and w
12:12 they w to arrest him, but they feared the crowd.
Lk 1:62 to find out what name he w to give him.
4:42 they w to prevent him from leaving them.
12:47 That slave who knew what his master w, but did
not prepare himself or do what was w,
20:19 they w to lay hands on him at that very hour,
Jn 6:11 so also the fish, as much as they w.
6:21 Then they w to take him into the boat,
7:44 Some of them w to arrest him,
16:19 Jesus knew that they w to ask him,
Ac 5:33 they were enraged and w to kill them.
10:10 He became hungry and w something to eat;
13: 7 who summoned Barnabas and Saul and w to hear
14:13 he and the crowds w to offer sacrifice.
15:37 Barnabas w to take with them John called Mark.
16: 3 Paul w Timothy to accompany him;
22:30 he w to find out what Paul was being accused of
23:28 Since I w to know the charge
24:27 and since he w to grant the Jews a favor,
28:18 the Romans w to release me,
2Co 1:15 Since I was sure of this, I w to come to you first,
1:16 I w to visit you on my way to Macedonia,
1:17 Was I vacillating when I w to do this?
1Th 2:18 For we w to come to you—certainly I, Paul, w to
Phm 1:13 I w to keep him with me,
Heb 12:17 when he w to inherit the blessing, he was rejected,
Tob 5:14 because I w to be sure about your ancestry.
8: 1 When they had finished eating and drinking they w
1Mc 3:34 and gave him orders about all that he w done.
7: 5 they were led by Alcimus, who w to be high priest.
11:48 and they w to kill the king.
2Mc 13:25 so angry that they w to annul its terms.
14:32 not know where the man was whom he w,

WANTING (8) [WANT]

Da 5:27 weighed on the scales and found w;
Mt 12:46 and his brothers were standing outside, w to speak
12:47 and your brothers are standing outside, w to speak
Lk 8:20 and your brothers are standing outside, w to see
10:29 But w to justify himself, he asked Jesus,
23: 8 for he had been w to see him for a long time,
23:20 Pilate, w to release Jesus, addressed them again;
2Pe 3: 9 not w any to perish, but all to come to repentance.

WANTON (4) [WANTONLY]

Ps 106:14 But they had a w craving in the wilderness,
Eze 6: 9 by their w heart that turned away from me,
6: 9 and their w eyes that turned after their idols.
23:44 in to Oholah and to Oholibah, w women.

WANTONLY (5) [WANTON]

Jdg 19:25 They w raped her, and abused her all through
Ps 25: 3 let them be ashamed who are w treacherous.
Pr 1:11 let us w ambush the innocent;
Isa 3:16 glancing w with their eyes,
Sir 27:13 and their laughter is w sinful.

WANTS (12) [WANT]

Ex 12:48 If an alien who resides with you w to celebrate
Jdg 19:20 I will care for all your w;
Jer 22:28 a despised broken pot, a vessel no one w?
48:38 I have broken Moab like a vessel that no one w,
Mt 5:40 and if anyone w to sue you and take your coat,
5:42 do not refuse anyone who w to borrow from you.
27:43 let God deliver him now, if he w to;
Mk 9:35 "Whoever w to be first must be last of all
Lk 13:31 "Get away from here, for Herod w to kill you."
Jn 7: 4 no one who w to be widely known acts in secret.
Rev 11: 5 And if anyone w to harm them,
11: 5 anyone who w to harm them must be killed

WAR‡ (246) [WAR-HORSES, WARFARE, WARRED, WARRING, WARRIOR, WARRIOR'S, WARRIORS, WARS, WARSHIPS]

Ge 14: 2 these kings made w with King Bera of Sodom,
Ex 1:10 or they will increase and, in the event of w,
13:17 for God thought, "If the people face w,
17:16 The LORD will have w with Amalek
32:17 "There is a noise of w in the camp."
Nu 1: 3 everyone in Israel able to go to w.
1:20 everyone able to go to w:
1:22 everyone able to go to w:
1:24 everyone able to go to w:
1:26 everyone able to go to w:
1:28 everyone able to go to w:
1:30 everyone able to go to w:
1:32 everyone able to go to w:
1:34 everyone able to go to w:
1:36 everyone able to go to w:
1:38 everyone able to go to w:
1:40 everyone able to go to w:
1:42 everyone able to go to w:
1:45 everyone able to go to w in Israel—
10: 9 When you go to w in your land against
26: 2 everyone in Israel able to go to w."
31: 3 "Arm some of your number for the w,
31: 4 from each of the tribes of Israel to the w."
31: 6 Moses sent them to the w,
31:14 who had come from service in the w.
31:36 the portion of those who had gone out to w,
32: 6 "Shall your brothers go to w while you sit here?
32:20 up arms to go before the LORD for the w,
32:27 everyone armed for w, to do battle for the LORD,
Dt 4:34 by w, by a mighty hand and an outstretched arm,
20: 1 When you go out to w against your enemies,
20:12 but makes w against you, then you shall besiege it;
20:19 making w against it in order to take it,
20:20 against the town that makes w with you,
21:10 When you go out to w against your enemies,
Jos 4:13 for w crossed over before the LORD to the plains
10: 5 and camped against Gibeon, and made w
11:18 Joshua made w a long time with all those kings.
11:23 And the land had rest from w.
14:11 my strength now is as my strength was then, for w,
14:15 And the land had rest from w.
22:12 of the Israelites gathered at Shiloh, to make w
22:33 and spoke no more of making w against them,
Jdg 3: 1 in Israel who had no experience of any w
3: 2 generations of Israelites might know w,
3:10 he went out to w, and the LORD gave
5: 8 new gods were chosen, then w was in the gates.
11: 4 After a time the Ammonites made w against Israel.
11: 5 And when the Ammonites made w against Israel,
11:25 or did he ever go to w with them?
11:27 the one who does me wrong by making w on me.
18:11 armed with weapons of w,
18:16 armed with their weapons of w,
18:17 the six hundred men armed with weapons of w.
1Sa 4: 1 for w against Israel, and Israel went out to battle
8:12 to make his implements of w and the equipment
17:20 to the battle line, shouting the w cry.
19: 8 Again there was w, and David went out to fight
23: 8 Saul summoned all the people to w,
28: 1 the Philistines gathered their forces for w,
2Sa 1:27 and the weapons of w perished!
3: 1 There was a long w between the house of Saul and
3: 6 While there was w between the house of Saul and
8:10 Now Hadadezer had often been at w with Toi.
11: 7 and how the w was going.
17: 8 Besides, your father is expert in w;
21:15 The Philistines went to w again with Israel,
21:20 There was again w at Gath,
22:35 He trains my hands for w,
1Ki 2: 5 in time of peace for blood that had been shed in w,
2: 5 putting the blood of w on the belt around his waist,
14:30 There was w between Rehoboam
15: 6 The w begun between Rehoboam
15: 7 There was w between Abijam and Jeroboam.
15:16 There was w between Asa and King Baasha
15:32 There was w between Asa and King Baasha
20:18 if they have come out for w, take them alive."
22: 1 three years Aram and Israel continued without w.
22:45 how he waged w, are they not written in the Book
2Ki 6: 8 Once when the king of Aram was at w with Israel,
8:28 of Ahab to wage w against King Hazael of Aram
13:25 that he had taken from his father Jehoahaz in w.
16: 5 of Israel came up to wage w on Jerusalem;
18:20 that mere words are strategy and power for w?
24:16 one thousand, all of them strong and fit for w.
1Ch 5:10 in the days of Saul they made w on the Hagrites,
5:18 and drew the bow, expert in w,
5:19 They made w on the Hagrites, Jetur, Naphish,
5:22 Many fell slain, because the w was of God.
7:11 thousand two hundred, ready for service in w.
7:40 for service in w, was twenty-six thousand men.
12: 1 among the mighty warriors who helped him in w.
12:33 equipped for battle with all the weapons of w,
12:37 with all the weapons of w.
18:10 Now Hadadezer had often been at w with Tou.
20: 4 this, w broke out with the Philistines at Gezer;
20: 5 Again there was w with the Philistines;
20: 6 Again there was w at Gath,
2Ch 13: 2 Now there was w between Abijah and Jeroboam.
14: 6 He had no w in those years,
15:19 And there was no more w until the thirty-fifth year
17:10 and they did not make w against Jehoshaphat.
17:18 with one hundred eighty thousand armed for w.
18: 3 We will be with you in the w."
22: 5 of Israel to make w against King Hazael of Aram
25: 5 picked troops fit for w, able to handle spear
26: 6 He went out and made w against the Philistines,
26:11 Uzziah had an army of soldiers, fit for w,
26:13 who could make w with mighty power,
28:12 up against those who were coming from the w,
35:21 but against the house with which I am at w;
Job 5:20 and in w from the power of the sword.
38:23 for the day of battle and w?
Ps 18:34 He trains my hands for w,
27: 3 w rise up against me, yet I will be confident.
33:17 The w horse is a vain hope for victory,
55:21 but with a heart set on w;
68:30 scatter the peoples who delight in w.
76: 3 the shield, the sword, and the weapons of w.
120: 7 I am for peace; but when I speak, they are for w.
144: 1 my rock, who trains my hands for w,
Pr 20:18 wage w by following wise guidance.
24: 6 for by wise guidance you can wage your w,
25:18 Like a w club, a sword,
Ecc 3: 8 a time for w, and a time for peace.
9:18 Wisdom is better than weapons of w,
SS 3: 8 all equipped with swords and expert in w,
Isa 2: 4 neither shall they learn w any more.
36: 5 that mere words are strategy and power for w?
41:12 those who w against you shall be as nothing at all.
42:25 upon him the heat of his anger and the fury of w;
Jer 4:19 for I hear the sound of the trumpet, the alarm of w.
6: 4 "Prepare w against her; up,
21: 2 for King Nebuchadrezzar of Babylon is making w
21: 4 I am going to turn back the weapons of w that are
21: 9 and shall have their lives as a prize of w.
28: 8 and me from ancient times prophesied w,
38: 2 they shall have their lives as a prize of w, and live.
39:18 but you shall have your life as a prize of w,
42:14 where we shall not see w,
45: 5 a prize of w in every place to which you may go."
51:20 You are my w club, my weapon of battle:
51:27 prepare the nations for w against her,
51:28 Prepare the nations for w against her,
Eze 17:17 and great company will not help him in w,
27:14 for your wares horses, w horses,
32:27 with their weapons of w, whose swords were laid
38: 8 from w, a land where people were gathered
Da 7:21 this horn made w with the holy ones
9:26 and to the end there shall be w.
11: 8 he shall carry off to Egypt as spoils of w.
11:10 "His sons shall wage w and assemble a multitude
11:10 and again shall carry the w as far as his fortress.
11:25 of the south shall wage w with a much greater
Hos 1: 7 I will not save them by bow, or by sword, or by w,
2:18 the sword, and w from the land;
10: 9 Shall not w overtake them in Gibeah?
10:14 the tumult of w shall rise against your people,
Joel 3: 9 Prepare w, stir up the warriors.
Mic 2: 8 by trustingly with no thought of w.
3: 5 but declare w against those who put nothing
4: 3 neither shall they learn w any more;
Zec 9:10 from Ephraim and the w horse from Jerusalem;
10: 3 and will make them like his proud w horse.
14:12 the LORD will strike all the peoples that wage w
Lk 14:31 going out to wage w against another king,
Ro 7:23 but I see in my members another law at w with
2Co 10: 3 we do not wage w according to human standards;
Heb 11:34 became mighty in w, put foreign armies to flight.
Jas 4: 1 Do they not come from your cravings that are at w
1Pe 2:11 to abstain from the desires of the flesh that wage w
Rev 2:16 I will come to you soon and make w against them
11: 7 that comes up from the bottomless pit will make w
12: 7 And w broke out in heaven;
12:17 and went off to make w on the rest of her children,
13: 7 Also it was allowed to make w on the saints and
17:14 they will make w on the Lamb,
19:11 and in righteousness he judges and makes w.
19:19 of the earth with their armies gathered to make w
Jdt 1: 5 Then King Nebuchadnezzar made w
1:11 and refused to join him in the w;
4: 5 on them and stored up food in preparation for w—
5: 1 of Israel had prepared for w and had closed
5:23 a people with no strength or power for making w.
6: 2 as you have done today and tell us not to make w
7: 1 into the hill country and make w on the Israelites.

AdE 11: 7 At their roaring every nation prepared for w,
Wis 8:15 I shall show myself capable, and courageous in w.
Sir 26:27 *every person like this lives in the anarchy of w.*
37:11 a woman about her rival or with a coward about w,
46: 1 Joshua son of Nun was mighty in w,
Bar 3:26 great in stature, expert in w.
LtJ 6:15 but cannot defend itself from w and robbers.
6:48 For when w or calamity comes upon them,
6:49 they cannot save themselves from w or calamity?
1Mc 3: 3 he bound on his armor of w and waged battles,
3:14 I will make w on Judas and his companions,
4: 7 and these men were trained in w.
5: 3 But Judas made w on the descendants of Esau
5:30 carrying ladders and engines of w to capture
5:56 and of the heroic w they had fought.
5:57 let us go and make w on the Gentiles around us."
6:20 and he built siege towers and other engines of w.
6:30 and thirty-two elephants accustomed to w.
6:31 for many days they fought and built engines of w;
6:51 engines of w to throw fire and stones,
6:52 The Jews also made engines of w to match theirs,
8:24 If w comes first to Rome or to any of their allies
8:26 that makes w they shall not give or supply grain,
8:27 if w comes first to the nation of the Jews,
9:64 against it for many days and made machines of w.
9:67 from the town and set fire to the machines of w.
11: 4 of those whom Jonathan had burned in the w,
11:20 and he built many engines of w to use against it.
12:13 the kings around us have waged w against us.
12:24 a larger force than before, to wage w against him.
12:40 but might make w on him,
12:44 to so much trouble when we are not at w?
12:53 Now therefore let us make w on them and blot out
14: 1 so that he could make w against Trypho.
15:19 that they should not seek their harm or make w
15:19 or make alliance with those who w against them.
15:25 against it and making engines of w;
15:31 Otherwise we will come and make w on you."
15:39 and to make w on the people;
2Mc 2:14 the books that had been lost on account of the w
10:15 and endeavored to keep up the w.
12:15 or engines of w overthrew Jericho in the days
12:27 great stores of w engines and missiles were there.
14: 6 are keeping up w and stirring up sedition,
1Es 1:25 went to make w at Carchemish on the Euphrates,
1:27 for my w is at the Euphrates.
2:27 that the people in it were given to rebellion and w,
4: 4 he tells them to make w on one another, they do it;
4: 6 not serve in the army or make w but till the soil;
3Mc 1: 2 to kill him and thereby end the w.
2Es 4:14 'Come, let us go and make w against the sea,
6:24 At that time friends shall make w on friends
13: 5 from the four winds of heaven to make w against
13: 8 to wage w with him, were filled with fear,
13: 9 nor held a spear or any weapon of w;
13:28 not holding a spear or weapon of w, yet destroying
13:31 They shall plan to make w against one another,
16:34 Their bridegrooms shall be killed in w,
4Mc 4:21 and caused Antiochus himself to make w on them.
7: 4 with many ingenious w machines has ever held out

WAR-HORSES (1) [HORSE, WAR]

Joel 2: 4 the appearance of horses, and like w they charge.

WARD (3)

Isa 47:11 which you will not be able to w off;
2Es 2:20 secure justice for the w, give to the needy,
4Mc 14:16 hatch the nestlings and w off the intruder.

WARDROBE (4)

2Ki 10:22 He said to the keeper of the w,
22:14 son of Harhas, keeper of the w;
2Ch 34:22 keeper of the w (who lived in Jerusalem in
Jer 38:11 to a w of the storehouse,

WARES (9)

Eze 27: 9 within you, to barter for your w.
27:12 iron, tin, and lead they exchanged for your w.
27:14 Beth-togarmah exchanged for your w horses,
27:16 they exchanged for your w turquoise, purple,
27:19 from Uzal entered into trade for your w;
27:22 they exchanged for your w the best of all kinds
27:27 Your riches, your w, your merchandise,
27:33 When your w came from the seas,
Rev 18:15 The merchants of these w,

WARFARE (3) [WAR]

1Ki 5: 3 the name of the LORD his God because of the w
2Co 10: 4 for the weapons of our w are not merely human,
2Es 13:33 the nations shall leave their own lands and the w

WARM (11) [LUKEWARM, WARMED, WARMING, WARMLY, WARMS]

Jos 9:12 it was still w when we took it from our houses
1Ki 1: 1 they covered him with clothes, he could not get w.
1: 2 so that my lord the king may be w."
2Ki 4:34 the flesh of the child became w.
Job 30: 4 and to w themselves the roots of broom.
Ecc 4:11 they keep w; but how can one keep w alone?
Isa 44:16 He also warms himself and says, "Ah, I am w,
Hos 11: 8 my compassion grows w and tender.
Hag 1: 6 you clothe yourselves, but no one is w;
Jas 2:16 keep w and eat your fill,"

WARMED (3) [WARM]

Job 31:20 and who was not w with the fleece of my sheep;
39:14 and lets them be w on the ground,
Wis 16:27 not destroyed by fire was melted when simply w

WARMING (6) [WARM]

Isa 47:14 No coal for w oneself is this, no fire to sit before!
Mk 14:54 and he was sitting with the guards, w himself at
14:67 When she saw Peter w himself,
Jn 18:18 they were standing around it and w themselves.
18:18 Peter also was standing with them and w himself.
18:25 Now Simon Peter was standing and w himself.

WARMLY (4) [WARM]

Ac 21:17 the brothers welcomed us w.
1Co 16:19 greet you w in the Lord.
Tob 7: 9 a ram from the flock and received them very w.
2Mc 14:24 he was w attached to the man.

WARMS (2) [WARM]

Isa 44:15 Part of it he takes and w himself;
44:16 He also w himself and says, "Ah, I am warm,

WARN (19) [FOREWARNED, WARNED, WARNING, WARNINGS, WARNS]

Ex 19:21 "Go down and w the people not to break through
Dt 8:19 I solemnly w you today that you shall
1Sa 8: 9 you shall solemnly w them,
Eze 3:18 or speak to w the wicked from their wicked way,
3:19 But if you w the wicked, and they do not turn
3:21 If, however, you w the righteous not to sin,
33: 8 not speak to w the wicked to turn from their ways,
33: 9 But if you w the wicked to turn from their ways,
Lk 12: 5 But I will w you whom to fear:
16:28 that he may w them, so that they will not
Ac 4:17 let us w them to speak no more to anyone
20:31 not cease night or day to w everyone with tears.
2Co 13: 2 and I w them now while absent,
2Th 3:15 not regard them as enemies, but w them
1Ti 5:21 I w you to keep these instructions
2Ti 2:14 and w them before God that they are
Rev 22:18 I w everyone who hears the words of the prophecy
Wis 12: 2 and w them of the things through which they sin,
2Es 14:20 but who will w those who will be born hereafter?

WARNED (30) [WARN]

Ge 26:11 So Abimelech w all the people, saying,
43: 3 But Judah said to him, "The man solemnly w us,
Ex 19:23 for you yourself w us, saying,
21:29 and its owner has been w but has not restrained it,
Jdg 2:15 as the LORD had w them and sworn to them;
2Ki 6:10 More than once or twice he w such a place so
17:13 the LORD w Israel and Judah by every prophet
Ne 9:26 who had w them in order to turn them back to you,
9:29 you w them in order to turn them back to your law.
9:30 and w them by your spirit through your prophets;
13:15 and I w them at that time against selling food.
13:21 But I w them and said to them,
Ps 2:10 O kings, be wise; be w, O rulers of the earth.
19:11 Moreover by them is your servant w;
Isa 8:11 and w me not to walk in the way of this people,
Jer 11: 7 For I solemnly w your ancestors
42:19 Be well aware that I have w you today
Eze 3:20 because you have not w them,
33: 6 so that the people are not w,
Mt 2:12 having been w in a dream not to return to Herod,
2:22 And after being w in a dream,
3: 7 Who w you to flee from the wrath to come?
Lk 3: 7 Who w you to flee from the wrath to come?
2Co 13: 2 I w those who sinned previously and all the others,
Gal 5:21 I am warning you, as I w you before:
1Th 4: 6 already told you beforehand and solemnly w you.
Heb 8: 5 when he was about to erect the tent, was w,
11: 7 w by God about events as yet unseen,
12:25 not escape when they refused the one who w them
AdE 2:22 to Mordecai, and he w Esther, who in turn revealed

WARNING (26) [WARN]

Nu 17:10 to be kept as a w to rebels,
26:10 two hundred fifty men; and they became a w.
Jer 6: 8 Take w, O Jerusalem, or I shall turn from you
6:10 To whom shall I speak and give w,
11: 7 w them persistently, even to this day, saying,
Eze 3:17 you shall give them w from me.
3:18 "You shall surely die," and you give them no w,
3:21 they shall surely live, because they took w;
5:15 a w and a horror, to the nations around you,
23:48 so that all women may take w and
33: 4 the sound of the trumpet do not take w,
33: 5 the sound of the trumpet and did not take w;
33: 5 But if they had taken w,
33: 7 you shall give them w from me.
Da 8:25 Without w he shall destroy many and shall
11:21 he shall come in without w and obtain the kingdom
11:24 Without w he shall come into the richest parts of
Mk 1:43 After sternly w him he sent him away at once,
Gal 5:21 I am w you, as I warned you before:
Col 1:28 w everyone and teaching everyone in all wisdom,
Heb 11: 7 the w and built an ark to save his household;
Wis 11:10 For you tested them as a parent does in w,
12:26 not heeded the w of mild rebukes will experience
16: 6 they were troubled for a little while as a w,
2Mc 8: 6 Coming without w, he would set fire to towns
4Mc 14:17 w them with their own calls.

WARNINGS (3) [WARN]

2Ki 17:15 and the w that he gave them.
Ne 9:34 the commandments and the w that you gave them.
Job 33:16 then he opens their ears, and terrifies them with w,

WARNS (2) [WARN]

Eze 33: 3 the land and blows the trumpet and w the people;
Heb 12:25 if we reject the one who w from heaven!

WARP (9)

Lev 13:48 in w or woof of linen or wool,
13:49 in w or woof or in skin or in anything made
13:51 If the disease has spread in the cloth, in w or woof,
13:52 whether diseased in w or woof, woolen or linen,
13:53 in w or woof or in anything of skin,
13:56 he shall tear the spot out of the cloth, in w or woof,
13:57 If it appears again in the garment, in w or woof,
13:58 But the cloth, w or woof, or anything of skin
13:59 either in w or woof, or in anything of skin,

WARRED (1) [WAR]

1Ki 14:19 acts of Jeroboam, how he w and how he reigned,

WARRING (2) [WAR]

1Sa 28:15 for the Philistines are w against me,
4Mc 4:22 For when he was w against Ptolemy in Egypt,

WARRIOR (45) [WAR]

A. MIGHTY WARRIOR (11)

Ge 10: 8 he was the first on earth to become a mighty w. A
Ex 15: 3 The LORD is a w; the LORD is his name.
Jos 17: 1 and Bashan, because he was a w.
Jdg 6:12 "The LORD is with you, you mighty w." A
11: 1 the son of a prostitute, was a mighty w. A
1Sa 14:52 and when Saul saw any strong or valiant w,
16:18 a man of valor, a w, prudent in speech,
17:33 and he has been a w from his youth."
2Sa 17:10 even the valiant w, whose heart is like the heart of
17:10 for all Israel knows that your father is a w,
23:20 of Jehoiada was a valiant w from Kabzeel, a doer
2Ki 5: 1 man, though a mighty w, suffered from leprosy. A
1Ch 12: 4 a w among the Thirty and a leader over the Thirty;
12:28 a young w, and twenty-two commanders
28: 3 for you are a w and have shed blood.'
2Ch 17:17 Of Benjamin: Eliada, a mighty w, A
28: 7 And Zichri, a mighty w of Ephraim, A
Job 16:14 he rushes at me like a w.
Ps 33:16 a w is not delivered by his great strength.
78:65 like a w shouting because of wine.
127: 4 in the hand of a w are the sons of one's youth.
Pr 6:11 and want, like an armed w.
24:34 and want, like an armed w.
Isa 3: 2 w and soldier, judge and prophet, diviner
42:13 like a w he stirs up his fury;
43:17 who brings out chariot and horse, army and w;
Jer 6:23 they ride on horses, equipped like a w for battle,
14: 9 like a mighty w who cannot give help? A
20:11 But the LORD is with me like a dread w;
46: 6 The swift cannot flee away, nor can the w escape;
46:12 for w has stumbled against w;
50: 9 of a skilled w who does not return empty-handed.
50:42 they ride upon horses, set in array as a w for battle,
Da 11: 3 Then a w king shall arise,
Joel 3:10 let the weakling say, "I am a w."
Zep 1:14 of the LORD is bitter, the w cries aloud there.
3:17 your God, is in your midst, a w who gives victory;
Wis 18:15 the midst of the land that was doomed, a stern w
Sir 26:28 a w in want through poverty,
35:22 a w will not be patient until he crushes the loins of
47: 5 to his right arm to strike down a mighty w, A
1Mc 2:66 Judas Maccabeus has been a mighty w A
4:30 the mighty w by the hand of your servant David, A
10:19 you are a mighty w and worthy to be our friend A

WARRIOR'S (2) [WAR]

Ps 120: 4 A w sharp arrows, with glowing coals of
Zec 9:13 O Greece, and wield you like a w sword.

WARRIORS (121) [WAR]

A. MIGHTY WARRIORS (27)

Ge 6: 4 the heroes that were of old, w of renown.
Nu 31:27 between the w who went out to battle and all
31:28 From the share of the w who went out to battle,
31:49 "Your servants have counted the w who are
Dt 2:14 until the entire generation of w had perished from
2:16 Just as soon as all the w had died off from among
Jos 1:14 But all the w among you shall cross over armed
5: 4 of the people who came out of Egypt, all the w,
5: 6 until all the nation, the w who came out of Egypt,
6: 3 all the w circling the city once.
8: 3 Joshua chose thirty thousand w and sent them out
10: 2 and was larger than Ai, and all its men were w.
10: 7 the fighting force with him, all the mighty w. A
10:24 said to the chiefs of the w who had gone with him,
Jdg 4:10 and ten thousand w went up behind him;
4:14 with ten thousand w following him.
20:17 four hundred thousand armed men, all of them w.
1Sa 10:26 with him went w whose hearts God had touched.
2Sa 10: 7 he sent Joab and all the army with the w.

2Sa 11:16 to the place where he knew there were valiant **w.**
16: 6 now all the people and all the **w** were on his right
17: 8 "You know that your father and his men are **w,**
17:10 and that those who are with him are valiant **w.**
20: 7 the Pelethites, and all the **w;**
23: 8 These are the names of the **w** whom David had:
23: 9 the three **w** was Eleazar son of Dodo son of Ahohi.
23:16 three **w** broke through the camp of the Philistines,
23:17 The three **w** did these things.
23:22 and won a name beside the three **w.**
1Ki 1: 8 and David's own **w** did not side with Adonijah.
1:10 not invite the prophet Nathan or Benaiah or the **w**
2Ki 24:14 all the officials, all the **w,** ten thousand captives,
1Ch 5:18 and the half-tribe of Manasseh had valiant **w,**
5:24 Hodaviah, and Jahdiel, mighty **w,** famous men, A
7: 2 namely of Tola, mighty **w** of their generations, A
7: 5 in all eighty-seven thousand mighty **w,** A
7: 7 Iri, five, heads of ancestral houses, mighty **w;** A
7: 9 mighty **w,** was twenty thousand two hundred. A
7:11 mighty **w,** seventeen thousand two hundred, A
7:40 heads of ancestral houses, select mighty **w,** A
8:40 The sons of Ulam were mighty **w,** archers, A
10:12 all the valiant **w** got up and took away the body
11:10 Now these are the chiefs of David's **w,**
11:11 This is an account of David's mighty **w:** A
11:12 among the three **w** was Eleazar son of Dodo,
11:19 The three **w** did these things.
11:24 and he won a name beside the three **w.**
11:26 The **w** of the armies were Asahel brother of Joab,
12: 1 they were among the mighty **w** who helped him A
12: 8 the wilderness mighty and experienced **w,** expert
12:21 for they were all **w** and commanders in the army.
12:25 Of the Simeonites, mighty **w,** A
12:30 mighty **w,** notables in their ancestral houses. A
12:38 All these, **w** arrayed in battle order,
19: 8 he sent Joab and all the army of the **w.**
28: 1 together with the palace officials, the mighty **w,** A
28: 1 the mighty warriors, and all the **w.**
29:24 All the leaders and the mighty **w,** A
2Ch 13: 3 having an army of valiant **w,**
13: 3 with eight hundred thousand picked mighty **w.** A
14: 8 and drew bows; all these were mighty **w.** A
17:13 He had soldiers, mighty **w,** in Jerusalem. A
17:14 with three hundred thousand mighty **w,** A
17:16 with two hundred thousand mighty **w.** A
25: 6 He also hired one hundred thousand mighty **w** A
26:12 of mighty **w** was two thousand six hundred. A
28: 6 all of them valiant **w,** because they had abandoned
28:14 So the **w** left the captives and the booty before
32: 3 with his officers and his **w** to stop the flow of
32:21 the mighty **w** and commanders and officers in A
Ne 3:16 as far as the artificial pool and the house of the **w.**
11: 6 Jerusalem were four hundred sixty-eight valiant **w.**
11:14 valiant **w,** one hundred twenty-eight;
Pr 21:22 a city of **w** and brought down the stronghold
24: 5 Wise **w** are mightier than strong ones,
SS 4: 4 a thousand bucklers, all of them shields of **w.**
Isa 3:25 Your men shall fall by the sword and your **w**
9: 5 of the tramping **w** and all the garments rolled
10:16 will send wasting sickness among his stout **w,**
13: 3 have summoned my **w,** my proudly exulting ones,
21:17 and the remaining bows of Kedar's **w** will be few;
Jer 5:16 all of them are mighty **w.** A
26:21 King Jehoiakim, with all his **w** and all the officials,
46: 5 their **w** are beaten down, and have fled in haste.
46: 9 Let the **w** go forth: Ethiopia and Put who carry
48:14 can you say, "We are heroes and mighty **w**"? A
48:41 The hearts of the **w** of Moab, on that day,
49:22 the **w** of Edom in that day shall be like the heart of
50:36 A sword against her **w,** so that they may be
51:30 The **w** of Babylon have given up fighting,
51:56 her **w** are taken, their bows are broken;
51:57 also her governors, her deputies, and her **w;**
La 1:15 LORD has rejected all my **w** in the midst of me;
Eze 23: 5 she lusted after her lovers the Assyrians, **w**
23:12 **w** clothed in full armor, mounted horsemen,
23:23 officers and **w,** all of them riding on horses.
27:10 and Put were in your army, your mighty **w;** A
27:27 and all your **w** within you,
32:27 the fallen **w** of long ago who went down to Sheol
32:27 for the terror of the **w** was in the land of the living.
38:13 of Tarshish and all its young **w** will say to you,
39:20 with **w** and all kinds of soldiers,
Hos 10:13 in your power and in the multitude of your **w,**
Joel 2: 7 Like **w** they charge, like soldiers they scale
3: 9 Prepare war, stir up the **w.**
3:11 Bring down your **w,** O LORD.
Ob 1: 9 Your **w** shall be shattered, O Teman,
Na 2: 3 The shields of his **w** are red;
Hab 3:14 with his own arrows the head of his **w,**
Zec 10: 5 Together they shall be like **w** in battle,
10: 7 Then the people of Ephraim shall become like **w,**
Jdt 7: 2 So all their **w** marched off that day;
16: 3 he came with myriads of his **w;**
1Mc 2:42 with them a company of Hasideans, mighty **w** A
4: 3 and his **w** moved out to attack the king's force
9:11 as did all the chief **w.**
12:41 to meet him with forty thousand picked **w,**
13:10 So he assembled all the **w** and hurried to complete
15:13 and with him were one hundred twenty thousand **w**
16: 4 of the country twenty thousand **w** and cavalry,
2Mc 5:26 the city with his armed **w** and killed great numbers

WARS (26) [WAR]

Nu 21:14 Wherefore it is said in the Book of the **W** of
1Ch 22: 8 have shed much blood and have waged great **w;**
2Ch 12:15 There were continual **w** between Rehoboam
16: 9 for from now on you will have **w."**
27: 7 and all his **w** and his ways,
Ps 46: 9 He makes **w** cease to the end of the earth;
140: 2 in their minds and stir up **w** continually.
Mt 24: 6 And you will hear of **w** and rumors of **w;**
Mk 13: 7 When you hear of **w** and rumors of **w,**
Lk 21: 9 "When you hear of **w** and insurrections,
Jdt 9: 7 not know that you are the Lord who crushes **w;**
16: 2 For the Lord is a God who crushes **w;**
Sir 46: 3 For he waged the **w** of the Lord.
1Mc 8: 2 He had been told of their **w** and of the brave deeds
9:22 and his **w** and the brave deeds that he did,
12:13 many trials and many **w** have encircled us;
12:14 and our other allies and friends with these **w,**
13: 3 also the **w** and the difficulties that my brothers
14:29 "Since **w** often occurred in the country, Simon son
16: 2 and my father's house have fought the **w** of Israel
16:23 of John and his **w** and the brave deeds that he did,
2Mc 2:20 and further the **w** against Antiochus Epiphanes
10:10 of the principal calamities of the **w.**
2Es 16:18 beginning of **w,** when the powers shall be terrified;

WARSHIPS (1) [SHIP, WAR]

1Mc 15: 3 a host of mercenary troops and have equipped **w,**

WARY (1)

Sir 37: 8 Be **w** of a counselor, and learn first what is his

WAS (5254) [BE] See Index of Articles Etc.

WASH (77) [WASHBASIN, WASHED, WASHES, WASHING]

Ge 18: 4 Let a little water be brought, and **w** your feet,
19: 2 and spend the night, and **w** your feet;
24:32 for the camels, and water to **w** his feet and the feet
Ex 19:10 Have them **w** their clothes
29: 4 to the entrance of the tent of meeting, and **w** them
29:17 and **w** its entrails and its legs,
30:19 the water Aaron and his sons shall **w** their hands
30:20 they shall **w** with water, so that they may not die.
30:21 They shall **w** their hands and their feet,
40:12 and shall **w** them with water,
Lev 6:27 you shall **w** the bespattered part in a holy place.
11:25 the carcass of any of them shall **w** his clothes and
11:28 the carcass shall **w** his clothes and be unclean until
11:40 of its carcass shall **w** their clothes and be unclean
11:40 the carcass shall **w** their clothes and be unclean
13: 6 and he shall **w** his clothes, and be clean.
13:34 He shall **w** his clothes and be clean.
13:54 the priest shall command them to **w** the article
14: 8 The one who is to be cleansed shall **w** his clothes,
14: 9 Then he shall **w** his clothes,
14:47 all who sleep in the house shall **w** their clothes;
14:47 and all who eat in the house shall **w** their clothes.
15: 5 Anyone who touches his bed shall **w** his clothes,
15: 6 with the discharge has sat shall **w** their clothes,
15: 7 of the one with the discharge shall **w** their clothes,
15: 8 then they shall **w** their clothes, and bathe in water,
15:10 all who carry such a thing shall **w** their clothes,
15:11 in water shall **w** their clothes,
15:13 he shall **w** his clothes and bathe his body
15:21 Whoever touches her bed shall **w** his clothes,
15:22 upon which she sits shall **w** his clothes, and bathe
15:27 and shall **w** his clothes, and bathe in water,
16:26 for Azazel shall **w** his clothes and bathe his body
16:28 The one who burns them shall **w** his clothes
17:15 shall **w** their clothes, and bathe themselves
17:16 if they do not **w** themselves or bathe their body,
Nu 5:23 and **w** them off into the water of bitterness.
8: 7 with a razor and **w** their clothes,
19: 7 the priest shall **w** his clothes and bathe his body
19: 8 The one who burns the heifer shall **w** his clothes
19:10 of the heifer shall **w** his clothes and be unclean
19:19 Then they shall **w** their clothes
19:21 the water for cleansing shall **w** his clothes,
31:24 You must **w** your clothes on the seventh day,
Dt 21: 6 that town nearest the body shall **w** their hands over
23:11 evening comes, he shall **w** himself with water,
Ru 3: 3 Now **w** and anoint yourself,
1Sa 25:41 a slave to **w** the feet of the servants of my lord."
2Sa 11: 8 "Go down to your house, and **w** your feet."
2Ki 5:10 saying, "Go, **w** in the Jordan seven times,
5:12 Could I not **w** in them, and be clean?"
5:13 How much more, when all he said to you was, '**W,**
2Ch 4: 6 He also made ten basins in which to **w,**
4: 6 The sea was for the priests to **w** in.
Job 9:30 If I **w** myself with soap and cleanse my hands
14:19 the torrents **w** away the soil of the earth;
Ps 26: 6 I **w** my hands in innocence,
51: 2 **W** me thoroughly from my iniquity,
51: 7 **w** me, and I shall be whiter than snow.
Isa 1:16 **W** yourselves; make yourselves clean;
Jer 2:22 you **w** yourself with lye and use much soap,
4:14 **w** your heart clean of wickedness so that you may
Mt 6:17 you fast, put oil on your head and **w** your face,
15: 2 For they do not **w** their hands before they eat."
Mk 7: 3 do not eat unless they thoroughly **w** their hands,
7: 4 not eat anything from the market unless they **w** it;
Lk 11:38 to see that he did not first **w** before dinner.
Jn 9: 7 "Go, **w** in the pool of Siloam" (which means Sent).
9:11 and said to me, 'Go to Siloam and **w.'**
13: 5 into a basin and began to **w** the disciples' feet and
13: 6 "Lord, are you going to **w** my feet?"
13: 8 Peter said to him, "You will never **w** my feet."
13: 8 Jesus answered, "Unless I **w** you,
13:10 "One who has bathed does not need to **w,**
13:14 you also ought to **w** one another's feet.
Rev 22:14 Blessed are those who **w** their robes,
Tob 6: 3 Then the young man went down to **w** his feet in

WASHBASIN (2) [BASIN, WASH]

Ps 60: 8 Moab is my **w;** on Edom I hurl my shoe;
108: 9 Moab is my **w;** on Edom I hurl my shoe;

WASHED‡ (46) [WASH]

Ge 43:24 and given them water, and they had **w** their feet,
43:31 Then he **w** his face and came out;
Ex 19:14 the people, and they **w** their clothes.
40:31 and his sons **w** their hands and their feet.
40:32 they **w;** as the LORD had commanded Moses.
Lev 1: 9 but its entrails and its legs shall be **w** with water.
1:13 but the entrails and the legs shall be **w** with water.
8: 6 and his sons forward, and **w** them with water.
8:21 after the entrails and the legs were **w** with water,
9:14 He **w** the entrails and the legs and,
13:55 the diseased article after it has been **w.**
13:56 and the disease has abated after it is **w,**
13:58 the disease disappears when you have **w** it,
13:58 shall then be **w** a second time, and it shall be clean.
15:17 on which the semen falls shall be **w** with water,
22: 6 of the sacred donations unless he has **w** his body
Nu 8:21 from sin and **w** their clothes;
Jdg 19:21 they **w** their feet, and ate and drank.
2Sa 12:20 Then David rose from the ground, **w,**
19:24 or trimmed his beard, or **w** his clothes,
1Ki 22:38 They **w** the chariot by the pool of Samaria;
22:38 and the prostitutes **w** themselves in it,
Job 22:16 their foundation was **w** away by a flood.
29: 6 when my steps were **w** with milk,
Ps 73:13 in vain I have kept my heart clean and **w** my hands
Isa 4: 4 the Lord has **w** away the filth of the daughters
Eze 16: 4 nor were you **w** with water to cleanse you,
16: 9 Then I bathed you with water and **w** off the blood
40:38 where the burnt offering was to be **w.**
Mt 27:24 he took some water and **w** his hands before
Jn 9: 7 Then he went and **w** and came back able to see.
9:11 Then I went and **w** and received my sight."
9:15 Then I **w,** and now I see."
13:12 After he had **w** their feet, had put on his robe,
13:14 So if I, your Lord and Teacher, have **w** your feet,
Ac 9:37 they had **w** her, they laid her in a room upstairs.
16:33 of the night he took them and **w** their wounds;
22:16 Get up, be baptized, and have your sins **w** away,
1Co 6:11 But you were **w,** you were sanctified,
1Ti 5:10 **w** the saints' feet, helped the afflicted,
Heb 10:22 from an evil conscience and our bodies **w**
2Pe 2:22 and, "The sow is **w** only to wallow in the mud."
Rev 7:14 they have **w** their robes and made them white in
Tob 2: 5 I returned, I **w** myself and ate my food in sorrow.
2: 9 That same night I **w** myself and went
7: 9 and **w** themselves and had reclined to dine,

WASHES (2) [WASH]

Ge 49:11 he **w** his garments in wine and his robe in the blood
Sir 34:30 If one **w** after touching a corpse,

WASHING‡ (9) [WASH]

Ex 30:18 a bronze basin with a bronze stand for **w.**
40:30 and put water in it for **w,**
SS 4: 2 of shorn ewes that have come up from the **w,**
6: 6 that have come up from the **w;**
Mk 7: 2 with defiled hands, that is, without **w** them.
7: 4 the **w** of cups, pots, and bronze kettles.)
Lk 5: 2 of them and were **w** their nets.
Eph 5:26 by cleansing her with the **w** of water by the word,
Sir 34:30 and touches it again, what has been gained by **w?**

WASHPOT (KJV) See WASHBASIN

WASPS (1)

Wis 12: 8 and sent **w** as forerunners of your army

WASTE (107) [WASTED, WASTELAND, WASTES, WASTING]

Lev 26:16 that **w** the eyes and cause life to pine away.
26:31 I will lay your cities **w,**
26:33 your land shall be a desolation, and your cities a **w.**
Nu 21:30 and we laid **w** until fire spread to Medeba."
Dt 32:10 in a howling wilderness **w;**
2Sa 18:14 Joab said, "I will not **w** time like this with you."
2Ki 19:17 of Assyria have laid **w** the nations and their lands,
Ezr 4:15 On that account this city was laid **w.**
Ne 2: 3 lies **w,** and its gates have been destroyed by fire?"
Job 6:18 they go up into the **w,** and perish.
12:24 and makes them wander in a pathless **w.**
38:27 to satisfy the **w** and desolate land,
Ps 6: 7 My eyes **w** away because of grief;
31:10 because of my misery, and my bones **w** away.
49:14 and their form shall **w** away;
79: 7 have devoured Jacob and laid **w** his habitation.
102: 6 like a little owl of the **w** places.
107:34 a fruitful land into a salty **w,**
Pr 23: 8 and you will **w** your pleasant words.
Isa 5: 6 I will make it a **w;**
6:11 "Until cities lie **w** without inhabitant,
15: 1 Because Ar is laid **w** in a night, Moab is undone;

Isa 15: 1 because Kir is laid **w** in a night, Moab is undone.
24: 1 about to lay **w** the earth and make it desolate,
24: 3 earth shall be utterly laid **w** and utterly despoiled;
34:10 From generation to generation it shall lie **w**;
37:18 the kings of Assyria have laid **w** all the nations
42:15 I will lay **w** mountains and hills,
49:17 and those who laid you **w** go away from you.
49:19 Surely your **w** and your desolate places
51: 3 he will comfort all her **w** places,
60:12 those nations shall be utterly laid **w**.
Jer 2:15 They have made his land a **w**;
4: 7 to make your land a **w**; your cities will be ruins
4:20 the whole land is laid **w**.
4:23 I looked on the earth, and lo, it was **w** and void;
7:34 for the land shall become a **w**.
9:10 they are laid **w** so that no one passes through,
9:12 the land ruined and laid **w** like a wilderness,
10:25 and have laid **w** his habitation.
25:11 This whole land shall become a ruin and a **w**,
25:12 making the land an everlasting **w**.
25:18 to make them a desolation and a **w**,
25:38 for their land has become a **w** because of
33:10 "It is a **w** without human beings or animals,"
33:12 In this place that is **w**,
44: 6 and they became a **w** and a desolation,
44:22 your land became a desolation and a **w** and a curse,
46:19 For Memphis shall become a **w**, a ruin,
48: 1 Alas for Nebo, it is laid **w**!
48:20 Tell it by the Arnon, that Moab is laid **w**.
49: 3 Wail, O Heshbon, for Ai is laid **w**!
49:13 a **w**, and an object of cursing;
49:33 a lair of jackals, an everlasting **w**;
51:26 but you shall be a perpetual **w**, says the LORD.
51:55 For the LORD is laying Babylon **w**,
La 3: 4 He has made my flesh and my skin **w** away,
Eze 4:17 and **w** away under their punishment.
6: 6 your towns shall be **w** and your high places ruined,
6: 6 so that your altars will be **w** and ruined,
6:14 and make the land desolate and **w**,
12:20 The inhabited cities shall be laid **w**,
19: 7 ravaged their strongholds, and laid **w** their towns;
26:19 When I make you a city laid **w**,
29: 9 the land of Egypt shall be a desolation and a **w**.
29:10 and I will make the land of Egypt an utter **w**
29:12 among cities that are laid **w**.
30: 7 and their cities shall lie among cities laid **w**.
33:10 and we **w** away because of them;
33:24 of these **w** places in the land of Israel keep saying,
33:27 surely those who are in the **w** places shall fall by
33:28 I will make the land a desolation and a **w**,
33:29 when I have made the land a desolation and a **w**
35: 3 against you to make you a desolation and a **w**.
35: 7 I will make Mount Seir a **w** and a desolation;
36:10 towns shall be inhabited and the **w** places rebuilt;
36:33 and the **w** places shall be rebuilt.
36:35 and the **w** and desolate and ruined towns are
38: 8 on the mountains of Israel, which had long lain **w**;
38:12 to assail the **w** places that are now inhabited,
Hos 2:12 I will lay **w** her vines and her fig trees,
Joel 1: 7 It has laid **w** my vines, and splintered my fig trees;
Am 4: 9 I laid **w** your gardens and your vineyards;
7: 9 and the sanctuaries of Israel shall be laid **w**,
Mic 1: 7 and all her idols I will lay **w**;
Zep 1:13 be plundered, and their houses laid **w**.
2: 9 by nettles and salt pits, and a **w** forever.
2:13 and he will make Nineveh a desolation, a dry **w**
3: 6 I have laid **w** their streets so that no one walks in
Mt 12:25 "Every kingdom divided against itself is laid **w**,
26: 8 they were angry and said, "Why this **w**?
Rev 18:17 For in one hour all this wealth has been laid **w**!"
18:19 For in one hour she has been laid **w**.
Jdt 7:14 They and their wives and children will **w** away
Wis 5:23 Lawlessness will lay **w** the whole earth,
16:29 and flow away like **w** water.
Sir 10:16 The Lord lays **w** the lands of the nations,
21: 4 Panic and insolence will **w** away riches;
21: 4 thus the house of the proud will be laid **w**.
1Mc 2:12 our beauty, and our glory have been laid **w**;
1Es 2:23 That is why this city was laid **w**.
4: 8 if he tells them to lay **w**, they lay **w**;
4:45 which the Edomites burned when Judea was laid **w**
2Es 5: 3 land that you now see ruling shall be a trackless **w**,
7:87 because they shall utterly **w** away in confusion and
10:21 For you see how our sanctuary has been laid **w**,

WASTED (8) [WASTE]

Jdg 6: 5 so they **w** the land as they came in.
Job 33:21 Their flesh is so **w** away that it cannot be seen;
Ps 32: 3 While I kept silence, my body **w** away
102: 4 I am too **w** to eat my bread.
Eze 26: 2 I shall be replenished, now that it is **w**."
Mk 14: 4 "Why was the ointment **w** in this way?
Gal 4:11 that my work for you may have been **w**.
Sir 20:13 but the courtesies of fools are **w**.

WASTELAND‡ (5) [LAND, WASTE]

Nu 21:20 of Moab by the top of Pisgah that overlooks the **w**.
23:28 to the top of Peor, which overlooks the **w**.
Dt 8:15 an arid **w** with poisonous snakes and scorpions.
Job 24: 5 scavenging in the **w** food for their young.
Wis 10: 7 a continually smoking **w**, plants bearing fruit

WASTES (11) [WASTE]

Job 13:28 One **w** away like a rotten thing,
14:11 and a river **w** away and dries up,
Ps 31: 9 my eye **w** away from grief, my soul and body also.
91: 6 or the destruction that **w** at noonday.
107: 4 Some wandered in desert **w**,
107:40 on princes and makes them wander in trackless **w**;
Isa 10:18 and it will be as when an invalid **w** away.
Jer 49:13 and all her towns shall be perpetual **w**.
Eze 36: 4 the desolate **w** and the deserted towns,
Sir 29:16 A sinner **w** the property of his guarantor,
31: 1 Wakefulness over wealth **w** away one's flesh,

WASTING (6) [WASTE]

Dt 32:24 **w** hunger, burning consumption,
Ps 106:15 but sent a **w** disease among them.
Isa 10:16 will send **w** sickness among his stout warriors,
Lk 13: 7 Why should it be **w** the soil?'
2Co 4:16 Even though our outer nature is **w** away,
3Mc 6: 8 And Jonah, **w** away in the belly of a huge,

WATCH (73) [WATCHED, WATCHER, WATCHERS, WATCHES, WATCHFUL, WATCHING, WATCHPOST, WATCHTOWER, WATCHWORD]

Ge 31:49 for he said, "The LORD **w** between you and me,
Ex 14:24 At the morning **w** the LORD in the pillar of fire
33: 8 of their tents and **w** Moses until he had gone into
Dt 4: 9 But take care and **w** yourselves closely,
4:15 take care and **w** yourselves closely,
22: 1 not **w** your neighbor's ox or sheep straying away
Jdg 7:19 of the middle **w**, when they had just set the **w**;
21:21 and **w**; when the young women of Shiloh
1Sa 6: 9 And **w**; if it goes up on the way
11:11 At the morning **w** they came into the camp and cut
19:11 Saul sent messengers to David's house to keep **w**
26:15 then have you not kept **w** over your lord the king?
26:16 because you have not kept **w** over your lord,
2Sa 13:28 "**W** when Amnon's heart is merry with wine,
13:34 When the young man who kept **w** looked up,
Ne 7: 3 the inhabitants of Jerusalem, some at their **w** posts,
11:19 who kept **w** at the gates,
Job 10:14 you **w** me, and do not acquit me of my iniquity.
13:27 You put my feet in the stocks, and **w** all my paths;
14:16 you would not keep **w** over my sin;
21:32 a **w** is kept over their tomb.
Ps 5: 3 in the morning I plead my case to you, and **w**.
10: 8 Their eyes stealthily **w** for the helpless;
37:32 wicked **w** for the righteous, and seek to kill them.
56: 6 They stir up strife, they lurk, they **w** my steps.
59: 9 O my strength, I will **w** for you;
61: 7 appoint steadfast love and faithfulness to **w**
66: 7 whose eyes keep **w** on the nations—
71:10 and those who **w** for my life consult together.
90: 4 or like a **w** in the night.
119:148 My eyes are awake before each **w** of the night,
127: 1 LORD guards the city, the guard keeps **w** in vain.
130: 6 my soul waits for the Lord more than those who **w**
130: 6 more than those who **w** for the morning.
141: 3 keep **w** over the door of my lips.
Pr 2:11 prudence will **w** over you;
6:22 when you lie down, they will **w** over you;
15: 3 keeping **w** on the evil and the good.
21:23 To **w** over mouth and tongue is to keep out
22:12 The eyes of the LORD keep **w** over knowledge,
24:12 Does not he who keeps **w** over your soul know it?
Jer 31:28 so I will **w** over them to build and to plant,
44:27 I am going to **w** over them for harm and not
48:19 Stand by the road and **w**, you inhabitant of Aroer!
51:12 of Babylon; make the **w** strong;
Da 9:14 So the LORD kept **w** over this calamity
Na 2: 1 Guard the ramparts; **w** the road;
Hab 2: 1 I will keep **w** to see what he will say to me,
Mt 16: 6 Jesus said to them, "**W** out,
27:36 then they sat down there and kept **w** over him.
27:54 who were keeping **w** over Jesus,
Mk 8:15 And he cautioned them, saying, "**W** out—
13:34 and commands the doorkeeper to be on the **w**.
Lk 2: 8 keeping **w** over their flock by night.
Ac 12: 6 while guards in front of the door were keeping **w**
20:28 Keep **w** over yourselves and over all the flock,
1Co 10:12 **w** out that you do not fall.
Heb 13:17 for they are keeping **w** over your souls
Tob 4:14 "**W** yourself, my son, in everything you do,
10: 7 She would rush out every day and **w**
Jdt 7:13 of the nearby mountains and camp there to keep **w**
12: 5 Toward the morning **w** she got up
AdE 12: 1 the two eunuchs of the king who kept **w** in
Sir 1:29 and keep **w** over your lips.
4:20 **W** for the opportune time, and beware of evil,
26:10 Keep strict **w** over a headstrong daughter, or else,
42:11 Keep strict **w** over a headstrong daughter,
1Es 4:11 but they keep **w** around him,
3Mc 6:12 **w** over us now and have mercy on us who by
2Es 2:13 kingdom is already prepared for you; be on the **w**!
11: 8 "Do not all **w** at the same time;
11: 8 let each sleep in its own place, and **w** in its turn;

WATCHED‡ (28) [WATCH]

Job 29: 2 as in the days when God **w** over me;
Ps 59: T *Saul ordered his house to be w in order to kill him.*
Ecc 5: 8 for the high official is **w** by a higher,
Jer 31:28 as I have **w** over them to pluck up and break down,
Da 7: 4 Then, as I **w**, its wings were plucked off,
7: 6 After this, as I **w**, another appeared, like a leopard.
7: 9 As I **w**, thrones were set in place,
7:11 I **w** then because of the noise of the arrogant words
7:11 And as I **w**, the beast was put to death,
7:13 As I **w** in the night visions,
Mk 3: 2 They **w** him to see whether he would cure him on
12:41 and **w** the crowd putting money into the treasury.
Lk 6: 7 the Pharisees **w** him to see whether he would cure
10:18 "I **w** Satan fall from heaven like a flash
20:20 So they **w** him and sent spies who pretended to
Jn 1:36 and as he **w** Jesus walk by,
Eph 6: 6 while being **w**, and in order to please them,
Col 3:22 only while being **w** and in order to please them,
Rev 11:12 to heaven in a cloud while their enemies **w** them.
Jdt 10:10 The men of the town **w** her until she had gone
Sir 19: 9 for someone may have heard you and **w** you,
46:14 and the Lord **w** over Jacob.
Sus 1:12 Day after day they **w** eagerly to see her.
2Mc 14:29 he **w** for an opportunity to accomplish this by
3Mc 6: 8 **w** over and restored unharmed to all his family.
2Es 11:12 As I **w**, one wing on the right side rose up,
4Mc 15:15 She **w** the flesh of her children being consumed
16:15 you stood and **w** Eleazar being tortured,

WATCHER (4) [WATCH]

Job 7:20 If I sin, what do I do to you, you **w** of humanity?
Isa 21: 8 Then the **w** called out:
Da 4:13 and there was a holy **w**,
4:23 And whereas the king saw a holy **w** coming down

WATCHERS (2) [WATCH]

Jer 4:17 They have closed in around her like **w** of a field,
Da 4:17 The sentence is rendered by decree of the **w**,

WATCHES (13) [WATCH]

Job 33:11 he puts my feet in the stocks, and **w** all my paths.'
36:25 everyone **w** it from far away.
Ps 1: 6 for the LORD **w** over the way of the righteous,
33:14 where he sits enthroned he **w** all the inhabitants of
63: 6 and meditate on you in the **w** of the night;
145:20 The LORD **w** over all who love him,
146: 9 The LORD **w** over the strangers;
La 2:19 cry out in the night, at the beginning of the **w**!
Wis 3: 9 and he **w** over his elect.
4:15 and that he **w** over his holy ones.
Sir 43:10 they never relax in their **w**.
Bar 3:34 the stars shone in their **w**, and were glad;
2Mc 3:39 For he who has his dwelling in heaven **w** over

WATCHFUL (2) [WATCH]

Zec 12: 4 But on the house of Judah I will keep a **w** eye,
1Es 8:59 Be **w** and on guard until you deliver them to

WATCHING (30) [WATCH]

1Sa 4:13 Eli was sitting upon his seat by the road **w**,
14:16 Saul's lookouts in Gibeah of Benjamin were **w** as
1Ki 20:33 Now the men were **w** for an omen;
2Ki 2:12 Elisha kept **w** and crying out, "Father, father!
1Ch 9:27 for on them lay the duty of **w**,
Ps 119:82 My eyes fail with **w** for your promise;
119:123 My eyes fail from **w** for your salvation,
Pr 8:34 **w** daily at my gates, waiting beside my doors.
Jer 1:12 for I am **w** over my word to perform it."
5: 6 A leopard is **w** against their cities;
7:11 You know, I too am **w**, says the LORD.
20:10 All my close friends are **w** for me to stumble.
La 4:17 Our eyes failed, ever **w** vainly for help;
4:17 we were **w** eagerly for a nation that could not save.
Da 5: 5 The king was **w** the hand as it wrote.
8: 5 As I was **w**, a male goat appeared from the west,
Zec 11:11 and the sheep merchants, who were **w** me,
Lk 14: 1 a meal on the sabbath, they were **w** him closely.
23:35 And the people stood by, **w**;
23:49 stood at a distance, **w** these things.
Ac 1: 9 When he had said this, as they were **w**,
9:24 They were **w** the gates day and night so
Tob 12:19 Although you were **w** me,
LtJ 6: 7 my angel is with you, and he is **w** over your lives.
Sus 1:15 Once, while they were **w** for an opportune day,
1:16 who had hidden themselves and were **w** her.
2Mc 7: 6 "The Lord God is **w** over us and
9:25 and the neighbors of my kingdom keep **w**
4Mc 5:13 there is some power **w** over this religion of yours,
13:27 while **w** their brothers being maltreated

WATCHPOST‡ (1) [POST, WATCH]

Hab 2: 1 at my **w**, and station myself on the rampart;

WATCHTOWER (9) [TOWER, WATCH]

2Ki 17: 9 at all their towns, from **w** to fortified city;
18: 8 as Gaza and its territory, from **w** to fortified city.
2Ch 20:24 When Judah came to the **w** of the wilderness,
Isa 5: 2 he built a **w** in the midst of it,
21: 8 Then the watcher called out: "Upon a **w** I stand,
32:14 the hill and the **w** will become dens forever,
Mt 21:33 dug a wine press in it, and built a **w**.
Mk 12: 1 dug a pit for the wine press, and built a **w**;
Sir 37:14 informed than seven sentinels sitting high on a **w**.

WATCHWORD (2) [WATCH, WORD]

2Mc 8:23 and gave the **w**, "The help of God";
13:15 He gave his troops the **w**, "God's victory,"

WATER‡ (539) [WATERCOURSES, WATERED, WATERING, WATERLESS, WATERS, WATERSKINS, WATERY]

A. LIVING WATER (6)

Ge 2: 6 and **w** the whole face of the ground—
2:10 A river flows out of Eden to **w** the garden,
16: 7 of the LORD found her by a spring of **w** in
18: 4 Let a little **w** be brought, and wash your feet,
21:14 and took bread and a skin of **w**,
21:15 When the **w** in the skin was gone,
21:19 God opened her eyes and she saw a well of **w**.
21:19 She went, and filled the skin with **w**,
21:25 a well of **w** that Abimelech's servants had seized,
24:11 down outside the city by the well of **w**;
24:11 the time when women go out to draw **w**.
24:13 I am standing here by the spring of **w**,
24:13 of the townspeople are coming out to draw **w**.
24:14 'Drink, and I will **w** your camels'—
24:15 coming out with her **w** jar on her shoulder.
24:17 "Please let me sip a little **w** from your jar."
24:32 for the camels, and **w** to wash his feet and the feet
24:43 I am standing here by the spring of **w**;
24:43 "Please give me a little **w** from your jar to drink,"
24:45 there was Rebekah coming out with her **w** jar
24:46 and said, 'Drink, and I will also **w** your camels.'
26:18 Isaac dug again the wells of **w** that had been dug in
26:19 in the valley and found there a well of spring **w**,
26:20 with Isaac's herders, saying, "The **w** is ours."
26:32 and said to him, "We have found **w**!"
29: 3 and **w** the sheep, and put the stone back in its place
29: 7 **W** the sheep, and go, pasture them."
29: 8 from the mouth of the well; then we **w** the sheep."
37:24 The pit was empty; there was no **w** in it.
43:24 and given them **w**, and they had washed their feet,
49: 4 as **w**, you shall no longer excel because you went
Ex 2:10 "because," she said, "I drew him out of the **w**."
2:16 They came to draw **w**, and filled the troughs to **w**
2:19 he even drew **w** for us and watered the flock."
4: 9 you shall take some **w** from the Nile and pour it on
4: 9 and the **w** that you shall take from the Nile
7:15 as he is going out to the **w**;
7:17 with the staff that is in my hand I will strike the **w**
7:18 and the Egyptians shall be unable to drink **w** from
7:19 its canals, and its ponds, and all its pools of **w**—
7:20 up the staff and struck the **w** in the river,
7:20 and all the **w** in the river was turned into blood,
7:21 so that the Egyptians could not drink its **w**,
7:24 the Egyptians had to dig along the Nile for **w**
7:24 for they could not drink the **w** of the river.
8:20 as he goes out to the **w**, and say to him,
12: 9 Do not eat any of it raw or boiled in **w**,
14:26 so that the **w** may come back upon the Egyptians,
15:22 in the wilderness and found no **w**.
15:23 not drink the **w** of Marah because it was bitter.
15:25 he threw it into the **w**, and the **w** became sweet.
15:27 where there were twelve springs of **w**
15:27 and they camped there by the **w**.
17: 1 but there was no **w** for the people to drink.
17: 2 and said, "Give us **w** to drink."
17: 3 But the people thirsted there for **w**;
17: 6 Strike the rock, and **w** will come out of it,
20: 4 or that is in the **w** under the earth.
23:25 and I will bless your bread and your **w**;
29: 4 of the tent of meeting, and wash them with **w**.
30:18 and you shall put **w** in it;
30:19 the **w** Aaron and his sons shall wash their hands
30:20 they shall wash with **w**, so that they may not die.
32:20 ground it to powder, scattered it on the **w**,
34:28 he neither ate bread nor drank **w**.
40: 7 the tent of meeting and the altar, and put **w** in it.
40:12 and shall wash them with **w**,
40:30 and put **w** in it for washing,
Lev 1: 9 but its entrails and its legs shall be washed with **w**.
1:13 the entrails and the legs shall be washed with **w**.
6:28 that shall be scoured and rinsed in **w**.
8: 6 and his sons forward, and washed them with **w**.
8:21 after the entrails and the legs were washed with **w**,
11:18 the **w** hen, the desert owl, the carrion vulture,
11:32 it shall be dipped into **w**,
11:34 Any food that could be eaten shall be unclean if **w**
11:36 But a spring or a cistern holding **w** shall be clean,
11:38 but if **w** is put on the seed and any part
14: 5 that one of the birds be slaughtered over fresh **w** in
14: 6 of the bird that was slaughtered over the fresh **w**.
14: 8 and shave off all his hair, and bathe himself in **w**,
14: 9 he shall wash his clothes, and bathe his body in **w**,
14:50 and shall slaughter one of the birds over fresh **w** in
14:51 the blood of the slaughtered bird and the fresh **w**,
14:52 and with the fresh **w**, and with the living bird,
15: 5 and bathe in **w**, and be unclean until the evening.
15: 6 and bathe in **w**, and be unclean until the evening.
15: 7 and bathe in **w**, and be unclean until the evening.
15: 8 then they shall wash their clothes, and bathe in **w**,
15:10 and bathe in **w**, and be unclean until the evening.
15:11 in **w** shall wash their clothes, and bathe in **w**,
15:12 and every vessel of wood shall be rinsed in **w**.
15:13 and bathe his body in fresh **w**,
15:16 he shall bathe his whole body in **w**,
15:17 on which the semen falls shall be washed with **w**,
15:18 both of them shall bathe in **w**,
15:21 and bathe in **w**, and be unclean until the evening.
15:22 and bathe in **w**, and be unclean until the evening;
15:27 and bathe in **w**, and be unclean until the evening.
16: 4 He shall bathe his body in **w**,
Lev 16:24 He shall bathe his body in **w** in a holy place,
16:26 and bathe his body in **w**,
16:28 and bathe his body in **w**,
17:15 and bathe themselves in **w**,
22: 6 unless he has washed his body in **w**.
Nu 5:17 the priest shall take holy **w** in an earthen vessel,
5:17 on the floor of the tabernacle and put it into the **w**.
5:18 the priest shall have the **w** of bitterness that brings
5:19 be immune to this **w** of bitterness that brings
5:22 now may this **w** that brings
5:23 and wash them off into the **w** of bitterness.
5:24 He shall make the woman drink the **w** of bitterness
5:24 and the **w** that brings the curse shall enter her
5:26 and afterward shall make the woman drink the **w**.
5:27 When he has made her drink the **w**, then,
5:27 the **w** that brings the curse shall enter into her
8: 7 sprinkle the **w** of purification on them,
19: 7 in **w**, and afterwards he may come into the camp;
19: 8 wash his clothes in **w** and bathe his body in **w**;
19: 9 for the congregation of the Israelites for the **w**
19:12 with the **w** on the third day and on the seventh day,
19:13 Since **w** for cleansing was not dashed on them,
19:17 and running **w** shall be added in a vessel;
19:18 dip it in the **w**, and sprinkle it on the tent,
19:19 and bathe themselves in **w**,
19:20 the **w** for cleansing has not been dashed on them,
19:21 the **w** for cleansing shall wash his clothes,
19:21 the **w** for cleansing shall be unclean until evening.
20: 2 Now there was no **w** for the congregation;
20: 5 and there is no **w** to drink."
20: 8 command the rock before their eyes to yield its **w**.
20: 8 Thus you shall bring **w** out of the rock for them;
20:10 shall we bring **w** for you out of this rock?"
20:11 **w** came out abundantly, and the congregation
20:17 or drink **w** from any well;
20:19 and if we drink of your **w**, we and our livestock,
21: 5 For there is no food and no **w**,
21:16 the people together, and I will give them **w**."
21:22 we will not drink the **w** of any well;
24: 7 **W** shall flow from his buckets,
24: 7 and his seed shall have abundant **w**,
31:23 it shall also be purified with the **w** for purification;
31:23 shall be passed through the **w**.
33: 9 at Elim there were twelve springs of **w**
33:14 where there was no **w** for the people to drink.
Dt 2: 6 and you shall also buy **w** from them for money,
2:28 and supply me **w** for money, so that I may drink.
4:18 likeness of any fish that is in the **w** under the earth.
5: 8 or that is in the **w** under the earth.
8:15 He made **w** flow for you from flint rock,
9: 9 I neither ate bread nor drank **w**.
9:18 I neither ate bread nor drank **w**,
11: 4 how he made the **w** of the Red Sea flow over them
12:16 you shall pour it out on the ground like **w**.
12:24 you shall pour it out on the ground like **w**.
14: 9 Of all that live in **w** you may eat these:
14:16 the little owl and the great owl, the **w** hen
15:23 you shall pour it out on the ground like **w**.
21: 4 the heifer down to a wadi with running **w**,
23: 4 not meet you with food and **w** on your journey out
23:11 evening comes, he shall wash himself with **w**,
29:11 and those who draw your **w**—
Jos 2:10 For we have heard how the LORD dried up the **w**
3:15 the ark were dipped in the edge of the **w**,
7: 5 The hearts of the people melted and turned to **w**.
9:21 of wood and drawers of **w** for all the congregation,
9:23 hewers of wood and drawers of **w** for the house
9:27 of wood and drawers of **w** for the congregation and
15:19 give me springs of **w** as well."
Jdg 4:19 he said to her, "Please give me a little **w** to drink;
5: 4 the clouds indeed poured **w**.
5:25 He asked **w** and she gave him milk,
6:38 from the fleece to fill a bowl with **w**.
7: 4 take them down to the **w** and I will sift them out
7: 5 So he brought the troops down to the **w**;
7: 5 "All those who lap the **w** with their tongues,
7: 6 but all the rest of the troops knelt down to drink **w**.
15:19 the hollow place that is at Lehi, and **w** came
1Sa 7: 6 and drew **w** and poured it out before the LORD.
9:11 they met some girls coming out to draw **w**,
25:11 Shall I take my bread and my **w** and the meat
26:11 take the spear that is at his head, and the **w** jar,
26:12 the spear that was at Saul's head and the **w** jar,
26:16 or the **w** jar that was at his head?"
30:11 they gave him **w** to drink;
30:12 or drunk **w** for three days and three nights.
2Sa 5: 8 let him get up the **w** shaft to attack the lame and
12:27 moreover, I have taken the **w** city.
14:14 we are like **w** spilled on the ground,
17:20 "They have crossed over the brook of **w**."
17:21 They said to David, "Go and cross the **w** quickly;
22:12 thick clouds, a gathering of **w**.
23:15 "O that someone would give me **w** to drink from
23:16 drew **w** from the well of Bethlehem that was by
1Ki 13: 8 nor will I eat food or drink **w** in this place.
13: 9 You shall not eat food, or drink **w**,
13:16 will I eat food or drink **w** with you in this place;
13:17 You shall not eat food or drink **w** there,
13:18 so that he may eat food and drink **w**."
13:19 and ate food and drank **w** in his house.
13:22 and drunk **w** in the place of which he said to you,
13:22 'Eat no food, and drink no **w**,'
14:15 as a reed is shaken in the **w**;
17:10 "Bring me a little **w** in a vessel,
18: 4 and provided them with bread and **w**.)
18: 5 the land to all the springs of **w** and to all the wadis;
18:13 and provided them with bread and **w**?
1Ki 18:33 with **w** and pour it on the burnt offering and on
18:35 so that the **w** ran all around the altar,
18:35 and filled the trench also with **w**.
18:38 and even licked up the **w** that was in the trench.
19: 6 a cake baked on hot stones, and a jar of **w**.
22:27 and feed him on reduced rations of bread and **w**
2Ki 2: 8 and rolled it up, and struck the **w**;
2: 8 the **w** was parted to the one side and to the other,
2:14 and struck the **w**, saying, "Where is the LORD,
2:14 When he had struck the **w**,
2:14 the **w** was parted to the one side and to the other,
2:19 but the **w** is bad, and the land is unfruitful."
2:21 of **w** and threw the salt into it, and said, "Thus says
2:21 I have made this **w** wholesome;
2:22 So the **w** has been wholesome to this day,
3: 9 a roundabout march of seven days, there was no **w**
3:11 who used to pour **w** on the hands of Elijah,
3:17 but the wadi shall be filled with **w**,
3:19 all springs of **w** you shall stop up,
3:20 suddenly **w** began to flow from the direction
3:20 until the country was filled with **w**.
3:22 and the sun shone upon the **w**,
3:22 Moabites saw the **w** opposite them as red as blood.
3:25 every spring of **w** they stopped up,
6: 5 one was felling a log, his ax head fell into the **w**;
6:22 and **w** before them so that they may eat and drink;
8:15 the bed-cover and dipped it in **w** and spread it over
18:31 and drink **w** from your own cistern,
20:20 the pool and the conduit and brought **w** into
1Ch 11:17 "O that someone would give me **w** to drink from
11:18 and drew **w** from the well of Bethlehem that was
2Ch 18:26 and feed him on reduced rations of bread and **w**
32: 4 "Why should the Assyrian kings come and find **w**
Ezr 10: 6 He did not eat bread or drink **w**,
Ne 3:26 up to a point opposite the **W** Gate on the east and
8: 1 into the square before the **W** Gate.
8: 3 the square before the **W** Gate from early morning
8:16 and in the square at the **W** Gate and in the square
9:15 their thirst you brought **w** for them out of the rock,
9:20 and gave them **w** for their thirst.
12:37 to the **W** Gate on the east.
13: 2 with bread and **w**, but hired Balaam against them
Job 3:24 and my groanings are poured out like **w**.
8:11 Can reeds flourish where there is no **w**?
14: 9 at the scent of **w** it will bud and put forth branches
15:16 one who drinks iniquity like **w**!
22: 7 You have given no **w** to the weary to drink,
22:11 a flood of **w** covers you.
34: 7 who drinks up scoffing like **w**,
36:27 For he draws up the drops of **w**;
Ps 1: 3 They are like trees planted by streams of **w**,
18:11 his canopy thick clouds dark with **w**,
22:14 I am poured out like **w**, and all my bones are out
58: 7 Let them vanish like **w** that runs away;
63: 1 as in a dry and weary land where there is no **w**.
65: 9 You visit the earth and **w** it, you greatly enrich it;
65: 9 the river of God is full of **w**;
65:10 You **w** its furrows abundantly, settling its ridges,
66:12 we went through fire and through **w**;
72: 6 like showers that **w** the earth.
77:17 The clouds poured out **w**;
78:20 though he struck the rock so that **w** gushed out
79: 3 They have poured out their blood like **w** all
104:13 From your lofty abode you **w** the mountains;
105:41 He opened the rock, and **w** gushed out;
107:33 springs of **w** into thirsty ground,
107:35 He turns a desert into pools of **w**,
107:35 a parched land into springs of **w**.
109:18 may it soak into his body like **w**,
114: 8 who turns the rock into a pool of **w**,
114: 8 the flint into a spring of **w**.
Pr 5:15 Drink **w** from your own cistern,
5:15 flowing **w** from your own well.
5:16 streams of **w** in the streets?
8:24 when there were no springs abounding with **w**.
9:17 "Stolen **w** is sweet, and bread eaten
11:25 and one who gives **w** will get **w**.
17:14 The beginning of strife is like letting out **w**;
20: 5 The purposes in the human mind are like deep **w**,
21: 1 The king's heart is a stream of **w** in the hand of
25:21 and if they are thirsty, give them **w** to drink;
25:25 Like cold **w** to a thirsty soul,
27:19 Just as **w** reflects the face,
30:16 the barren womb, the earth ever thirsty for **w**,
Ecc 2: 6 I made myself pools from which to **w** the forest
SS 4:15 a well of living **w**, and flowing streams A
5:12 His eyes are like doves beside springs of **w**,
Isa 1:22 your wine is mixed with **w**.
1:30 and like a garden without **w**.
3: 1 all support of bread, and all support of **w**—
12: 3 With joy you will draw **w** from the wells
14:23 and pools of **w**, and I will sweep it with the broom
19: 8 and those who spread nets on the **w** will languish.
21:14 Bring **w** to the thirsty, meet the fugitive
22:11 between the two walls for the **w** of the old pool.
27: 3 I, the LORD, am its keeper; every moment I **w** it.
30:14 or dipping **w** out of the cistern.
30:20 the bread of adversity and the **w** of affliction,
30:25 high hill there will be brooks running with **w**—
32: 2 like streams of **w** in a dry place,
33:16 their food will be supplied, their **w** assured.
35: 7 and the thirsty ground springs of **w**;
36:16 and drink **w** from your own cistern,
41:17 When the poor and needy seek **w**,
41:18 I will make the wilderness a pool of **w**,
41:18 and the dry land springs of **w**.
43:20 for I give **w** in the wilderness, rivers in the desert,

Isa 44: 3 For I will pour w on the thirsty land,
44:12 he drinks no w and is faint.
48:21 he made w flow for them from the rock;
48:21 he split open the rock and the w gushed out.
49:10 and by springs of w will guide them.
50: 2 their fish stink for lack of w, and die of thirst.
58:11 like a spring of w, whose waters never fail.
64: 2 when fire kindles brushwood and the fire causes w
Jer 2:13 have forsaken me, the fountain of living w, A
2:13 cracked cisterns that can hold no w.
6: 7 As a well keeps its w fresh,
8:14 and has given us poisoned w to drink,
9: 1 O that my head were a spring of w,
9:15 and giving them poisonous w to drink.
9:18 and our eyelids flow with w.
13: 1 and put it on your loins, but do not dip it in w."
14: 3 Her nobles send their servants for w;
14: 3 find no w, they return with their vessels empty.
17: 8 They shall be like a tree planted by w,
17:13 for they have forsaken the fountain of living w, A
23:15 and give them poisoned w to drink;
31: 9 I will let them walk by brooks of w,
38: 6 Now there was no w in the cistern, but only mud,
La 2:19 Pour out your heart like w before the presence of
3:54 w closed over my head; I said, "I am lost."
5: 4 We must pay for the w we drink;
Eze 4:11 you shall drink w by measure, one-sixth of a hin;
4:16 and they shall drink w by measure and in dismay.
4:17 Lacking bread and w, they will look at one another
7:17 All hands shall grow feeble, all knees turn to w.
12:18 drink your w with trembling and with fearfulness;
12:19 and drink their w in dismay,
16: 4 nor were you washed with w to cleanse you,
16: 9 with w and washed off the blood from you,
17: 7 toward him, so that he might w it.
19:10 like a vine in a vineyard transplanted by the w,
19:10 fruitful and full of branches from abundant w.
21: 7 every spirit will faint and all knees will turn to w.
24: 3 Set on the pot, set it on, pour in w also;
26:12 and timber and soil they shall cast into the w.
31: 5 from abundant w in its shoots.
31: 7 for its roots went down to abundant w.
31:14 that no trees that drink w may reach up to them
32: 2 trouble the w with your feet,
34:18 When you drink of clear w,
36:25 I will sprinkle clean w upon you,
47: 1 there, w was flowing from below the threshold of
47: 1 the w was flowing down from below the south end
47: 2 and the w was coming out on the south side.
47: 3 and then led me through the w;
47: 4 and led me through the w; and it was knee-deep.
47: 4 and led me through the w;
47: 5 a river that I could not cross, for the w had risen;
47: 8 "This w flows toward the eastern region and goes
47: 8 of stagnant waters, the w will become fresh.
47:12 because the w for them flows from the sanctuary.
Da 1:12 Let us be given vegetables to eat and w to drink.
Hos 2: 5 they give me my bread and my w,
5:10 on them I will pour out my wrath like w.
6: 3 like the spring rains that w the earth."
Joel 3:18 all the stream beds of Judah shall flow with w;
3:18 the house of the LORD and w the Wadi Shittim.
Am 4: 8 or three towns wandered to one town to drink w,
8:11 not a famine of bread, or a thirst for w,
Jnh 3: 7 They shall not feed, nor shall they drink w.
Na 3: 8 with w around her, her rampart a sea, w her wall?
3:14 Draw w for the siege, strengthen your forts;
Hab 3:10 a torrent of w swept by;
Mt 3:11 "I baptize you with w for repentance,
3:16 just as he came up from the w,
8:32 the steep bank into the sea and perished in the w.
10:42 of cold w to one of these little ones in the name of
14:28 if it is you, command me to come to you on the w.
14:29 Peter got out of the boat, started walking on the w,
17:15 he often falls into the fire and often into the w.
27:24 he took some w and washed his hands before
Mk 1: 8 I have baptized you with w;
1:10 And just as he was coming up out of the w,
9:22 it has often cast him into the fire and into the w,
9:41 a cup of w to drink because you bear the name
14:13 and a man carrying a jar of w will meet you;
Lk 3:16 of them by saying, "I baptize you with w;
5: 4 "Put out into the deep w and let down your nets for
7:44 you gave me no w for my feet,
8:23 and the boat was filling with w,
8:25 that he commands even the winds and the w,
13:15 and lead it away to give it w?
16:24 and send Lazarus to dip the tip of his finger in w
22:10 a man carrying a jar of w will meet you;
Jn 1:26 John answered them, "I baptize with w.
1:31 but I came baptizing with w for this reason,
1:33 the one who sent me to baptize with w said to me,
2: 6 Now standing there were six stone w jars for
2: 7 Jesus said to them, "Fill the jars with w."
2: 9 the steward tasted the w that had become wine,
2: 9 (though the servants who had drawn the w knew),
3: 5 the kingdom of God without being born of w
3:23 near Salim because w was abundant there;
4: 7 A Samaritan woman came to draw w,
4:10 and he would have given you living w." A
4:11 Where do you get that living w? A
4:13 "Everyone who drinks of this w will
4:14 of the w that I will give them will never be thirsty.
4:14 The w that I will give will become in them a spring
4:14 in them a spring of w gushing up to eternal life."
4:15 The woman said to him, "Sir, give me this w,
4:15 be thirsty or have to keep coming here to draw w."
Jn 4:28 the woman left her w jar and went back to the city.
4:46 in Galilee where he had changed the w into wine.
5: 7 to put me into the pool when the w is stirred up;
7:38 believer's heart shall flow rivers of living w.' " A
13: 5 Then he poured w into a basin and began to wash
19:34 and at once blood and w came out.
Ac 1: 5 for John baptized with w, but you will be baptized
8:36 along the road, they came to some w;
8:36 and the eunuch said, "Look, here is w!
8:38 went down into the w, and Philip baptized him.
8:39 When they came up out of the w,
10:47 "Can anyone withhold the w
11:16 how he had said, 'John baptized with w,
Eph 5:26 by cleansing her with the washing of w by
1Ti 5:23 No longer drink only w, but take a little wine for
Tit 3: 5 the w of rebirth and renewal by the Holy Spirit.
Heb 9:19 with w and scarlet wool and hyssop,
10:22 and our bodies washed with pure w.
Jas 3:11 the same opening both fresh and brackish w?
3:12 No more can salt w yield fresh.
1Pe 3:20 that is, eight persons, were saved through w.
2Pe 3: 5 an earth was formed out of w and by means of w,
3: 6 of that time was deluged with w and perished.
1Jn 5: 6 This is the one who came by w and blood,
5: 6 not with the w only but with the w and the blood.
5: 8 the Spirit and the w and the blood,
Rev 7:17 and he will guide them to springs of the w of life,
8:10 on a third of the rivers and on the springs of w.
8:11 and many died from the w,
12:15 the serpent poured w like a river after the woman,
14: 7 the sea and the springs of w."
16: 4 into the rivers and the springs of w,
16:12 and its w was dried up in order to prepare the way
21: 6 To the thirsty I will give w as a gift from the
spring of the w of life.
22: 1 the angel showed me the river of the w of life,
22:17 Let anyone who wishes take the w of life as a gift.
Tob 6: 3 the w and tried to swallow the young man's foot,
Jdt 2: 7 Tell them to prepare earth and w,
7: 7 and visited the springs that supplied their w;
7:12 let your servants take possession of the spring of w
7:13 this is where all the people of Bethulia get their w.
7:17 the valley and seized the w supply and the springs
7:20 until all the w containers of every inhabitant
7:21 and on no day did they have enough w to drink,
7:21 for their drinking w was rationed.
8: 9 because they were faint for lack of w,
10: 3 bathed her body with w, and anointed herself
11:12 and their w has almost given out,
AdE 10: 6 and there was light and sun and abundant w—
11:10 there came a great river, with abundant w;
Wis 5:10 the billowy w, and when it has passed no trace can
5:22 the w of the sea will rage against them,
11: 4 and w was given them out of flinty rock,
11: 7 you gave them abundant w unexpectedly,
13: 2 or the circle of the stars, or turbulent w,
16:17 For—most incredible of all—in w,
16:19 the midst of w it burned more intensely than fire,
16:29 and flow away like waste w.
17:18 or the rhythm of violently rushing w,
19: 7 and dry land emerging where w had stood before,
19:19 land animals were transformed into w creatures,
19:20 Fire even in w retained its normal power,
19:20 and w forgot its fire-quenching nature.
Sir 3:30 As w extinguishes a blazing fire,
15: 3 and give him the w of wisdom to drink.
15:16 He has placed before you fire and w;
18:10 Like a drop of w from the sea and a grain of sand,
24:14 and like a plane tree beside w I grew tall.
24:30 like a w channel into a garden.
24:31 "I will w my garden and drench my flower-beds."
25:25 Allow no outlet to w, and no boldness of speech to
26:12 and drinks from any w near him,
29:21 The necessities of life are w, bread, and clothing,
38: 5 Was not w made sweet with a tree in order
39:13 and blossom like a rose growing by a stream of w.
39:17 and the reservoirs of w at the word of his mouth.
39:26 The basic necessities of human life are w and fire
40:16 The reeds by any w or river bank are plucked up
43:20 cold north wind blows, and ice freezes on the w;
43:20 it settles on every pool of w,
43:20 and the w puts it on like a breastplate.
48:17 and brought w into its midst;
48:17 and built cisterns for the w.
50: 3 In his days a w cistern was dug,
50: 8 like lilies by a spring of w,
1Mc 5:40 Judas and his army drew near to the stream of w,
5:42 When Judas approached the stream of w,
9:33 into the wilderness of Tekoa and camped by the w
9:45 the w of the Jordan is on this side and on that,
2Mc 15:39 or, again, to drink w alone,
15:39 while wine mixed with w is sweet and delicious
1Es 9: 2 and he did not eat bread or drink w,
2Es 1:23 threw a tree into the w and made the stream sweet.
4:49 And after this a cloud full of w passed before me
6:47 where the w had been gathered together,
6:48 The dumb and lifeless w produced living creatures,
6:50 where the w had been gathered together could
7: 7 that there is fire on the right hand and deep w on
7: 8 that is, between the fire and the w,
7:40 and wind or w or air,
8: 8 and w, and for nine months
9:16 as a wave is greater than a drop of w."
14:39 it was full of something like w,
15:41 fire and hail and flying swords and floods of w,
15:58 for bread and drink their own blood in thirst for w.
16:58 by his word he has suspended the earth over the w.
2Es 16:60 he has put springs of w in the desert,
16:60 so as to send rivers from the heights to w the earth.
4Mc 3:11 for the w in the enemy's territory tormented

WATERCOURSES (8) [COURSE, WATER]

Ps 126: 4 O LORD, like the w in the Negeb.
Eze 31:12 and its boughs lie broken in all the w of the land;
32: 6 and the w will be filled with you.
34:13 by the w, and in all the inhabited parts of the land.
35: 8 in all your w those killed with the sword shall fall.
36: 4 the hills, the w and the valleys, the desolate wastes
36: 6 to the w and valleys, Thus says the Lord GOD:
Joel 1:20 to you because the w are dried up,

WATERED (14) [WATER]

Ge 13:10 the plain of the Jordan was well w everywhere like
24:46 So I drank, and she also w the camels.
29: 2 for out of that well the flocks were w.
29:10 and w the flock of his mother's brother Laban.
Ex 2:17 up and came to their defense and w their flock.
2:19 he even drew water for us and w the flock."
Dt 11:11 w by rain from the sky,
Ps 104:16 The trees of the LORD are w abundantly,
Isa 55:10 and do not return there until they have w the earth,
58:11 and you shall be like a w garden,
Jer 31:12 their life shall become like a w garden,
Eze 31:16 and best of Lebanon, all that were well w,
1Co 3: 6 I planted, Apollos w, but God gave the growth.
Sir 39:23 as when he turned a w land into salt.

WATERFLOOD (KJV) See FLOOD

WATERING (2) [WATER]

Ge 30:38 the w places, where the flocks came to drink.
Jdg 5:11 To the sound of musicians at the w places,

WATERLESS (5) [WATER]

Zec 9:11 I will set your prisoners free from the w pit.
Mt 12:43 through w regions looking for a resting place,
Lk 11:24 through w regions looking for a resting place,
2Pe 2:17 These are w springs and mists driven by a storm;
Jude 1:12 They are w clouds carried along by the winds;

WATERPOT[S] (KJV) See [WATER] JARS

WATERS‡ (215) [WATER]

A. MIGHTY WATERS (20)

Ge 1: 2 a wind from God swept over the face of the w.
1: 6 "Let there be a dome in the midst of the w, and let
it separate the w from the w."
1: 7 and separated the w that were under the dome
from the w that were above
1: 9 "Let the w under the sky be gathered together
1:10 the w that were gathered together he called Seas.
1:20 "Let the w bring forth swarms of living creatures,
1:21 of every kind, with which the w swarm,
1:22 "Be fruitful and multiply and fill the w in the seas,
6:17 I am going to bring a flood of w on the earth,
7: 6 when the flood of w came on the earth.
7: 7 into the ark to escape the w of the flood.
7:10 seven days the w of the flood came on the earth.
7:17 and the w increased, and bore up the ark,
7:18 The w swelled and increased greatly on the earth;
7:18 and the ark floated on the face of the w.
7:19 The w swelled so mightily on the earth that all
7:20 the w swelled above the mountains,
7:24 w swelled on the earth for one hundred fifty days.
8: 1 a wind blow over the earth, and the w subsided;
8: 3 and the w gradually receded from the earth.
8: 3 of one hundred fifty days the w had abated;
8: 5 The w continued to abate until the tenth month;
8: 7 to and fro until the w were dried up from the earth.
8: 8 if the w had subsided from the face of the ground;
8: 9 for the w were still on the face of the whole earth.
8:11 Noah knew that the w had subsided from the earth.
8:13 the w were dried up from the earth;
9:11 that never again shall all flesh be cut off by the w
9:15 and the w shall never again become a flood
Ex 7:19 and stretch out your hand over the w of Egypt—
8: 6 Aaron stretched out his hand over the w of Egypt;
14:21 into dry land; and the w were divided.
14:22 the w forming a wall for them on their right and
14:28 The w returned and covered the chariots and
14:29 the w forming a wall for them on their right and
15: 8 At the blast of your nostrils the w piled up,
15:10 they sank like lead in the mighty w. A
15:19 LORD brought back the w of the sea upon them;
Lev 11: 9 These you may eat, of all that are in the w.
11: 9 Everything in the w that has fins and scales,
11:10 of the swarming creatures in the w and among all
11:10 the other living creatures that are in the w—
11:12 Everything in the w that does not have fins
11:46 through the w and every creature that swarms upon
Nu 20:13 These are the w of Meribah,
20:24 against my command at the w of Meribah.
24: 6 like cedar trees beside the w.
27:14 not show my holiness before their eyes at the w."
27:14 the w of Meribath-kadesh in the wilderness
Dt 8: 7 and underground w welling up in valleys and hills,
32:51 the w of Meribath-kadesh in the wilderness of Zin,
33: 8 with whom you contended at the w of Meribah;
Jos 3: 8 you come to the edge of the w of the Jordan,

Jos 3:13 rest in the w of the Jordan,
3:13 the w of the Jordan flowing from above shall
3:16 the w flowing from above stood still,
4: 7 the w of the Jordan were cut off in front of the ark
4: 7 the w of the Jordan were cut off.
4:18 the w of the Jordan returned to their place
4:23 the w of the Jordan for you until you crossed over,
5: 1 that the LORD had dried up the w of the Jordan
11: 5 and came and camped together at the w of Merom,
11: 7 by the w of Merom, and fell upon them.
15: 7 the boundary passes along to the w of En-shemesh,
15: 9 from the top of the mountain to the spring of the W
16: 1 east of the w of Jericho, into the wilderness,
18:15 to the spring of the W of Nephtoah;
Jdg 5:19 by the w of Megiddo; they got no spoils of silver.
7:24 the Midianites and seize the w against them,
7:24 and they seized the w as far as Beth-barah,
2Sa 22:17 he took me, he drew me out of mighty w. A
2Ki 5:12 better than all the w of Israel?
19:24 I dug wells and drank foreign w,
2Ch 32:30 of the w of Gihon and directed them down to
Ne 9:11 like a stone into mighty w. A
Job 5:10 He gives rain on the earth and sends w on
11:16 you will remember it as w that have passed away.
12:15 If he withholds the w, they dry up;
14:11 As w fail from a lake,
14:19 the w wear away the stones;
24:18 "Swift are they on the face of the w;
24:19 Drought and heat snatch away the snow w;
26: 5 shades below tremble, the w and their inhabitants.
26: 8 He binds up the w in his thick clouds,
26:10 He has described a circle on the face of the w,
28:25 and apportioned out the w by measure;
29:19 to the w, with the dew all night on my branches;
37:10 and the broad w are frozen fast.
38:30 The w become hard like stone,
38:34 so that a flood of w may cover you?
Ps 18:16 he drew me out of mighty w. A
23: 2 he leads me beside still w;
29: 3 The voice of the LORD is over the w;
29: 3 thunders, the LORD, over mighty w. A
32: 6 the rush of mighty w shall not reach them. A
33: 7 He gathered the w of the sea as in a bottle;
46: 3 though its w roar and foam,
69: 1 O God, for the w have come up to my neck.
69: 2 I have come into deep w, and the flood sweeps
69:14 from my enemies and from the deep w.
74:13 you broke the heads of the dragons in the w.
77:16 When the w saw you, O God,
77:16 O God, when the w saw you, they were afraid;
77:19 your path, through the mighty w; A
78:13 and made the w stand like a heap.
78:16 and caused w to flow down like rivers.
81: 7 I tested you at the w of Meribah.
93: 4 More majestic than the thunders of mighty w, A
104: 3 you set the beams of your chambers on the w,
104: 6 the w stood above the mountains.
105:29 He turned their w into blood,
106:11 The w covered their adversaries;
106:32 They angered the LORD at the w of Meribah,
107:23 doing business on the mighty w; A
124: 5 then over us would have gone the raging w.
136: 6 on the w, for his steadfast love endures forever;
144: 7 set me free and rescue me from the mighty w, A
147:18 he makes his wind blow, and the w flow.
148: 4 and you w above the heavens!
Pr 8:29 so that the w might not transgress his command,
18: 4 The words of the mouth are deep w;
30: 4 Who has wrapped up the w in a garment?
Ecc 11: 1 Send out your bread upon the w,
SS 8: 7 Many w cannot quench love,
Isa 8: 6 the w of Shiloah that flow gently, and melt in fear
8: 7 against it the mighty flood w of the River, the king
11: 9 of the knowledge of the LORD as the w cover
15: 6 the w of Nimrim are a desolation;
15: 9 For the w of Dibon are full of blood;
17:12 they roar like the roaring of mighty w! A
17:13 The nations roar like the roaring of many w,
18: 2 by the Nile in vessels of papyrus on the w!
19: 5 The w of the Nile will be dried up,
22: 9 and you collected the w of the lower pool.
23: 3 and were on the mighty w; A
28: 2 like a storm of mighty, overflowing w;
28:17 and w will overwhelm the shelter.
35: 6 For w shall break forth in the wilderness,
37:25 I dug wells and drank w,
40:12 Who has measured the w in the hollow of his hand
43: 2 When you pass through the w, I will be with you;
43:16 a path in the mighty w, A
51:10 the w of the great deep;
54: 9 that the w of Noah would never again go over
55: 1 Ho, everyone who thirsts, come to the w;
57:20 its w toss up mire and mud.
58:11 like a spring of water, whose w never fail.
63:12 who divided the w before them to make
Jer 2:18 to drink the w of the Nile?
2:18 to drink the w of the Euphrates?
10:13 there is a tumult of w in the heavens,
15:18 to me like a deceitful brook, like w that fail.
18:14 Do the mountain w run dry,
46: 7 rising like the Nile, like rivers whose w surge?
46: 8 like rivers whose w surge.
47: 2 See, w are rising out of the north and shall become
48:34 For even the w of Nimrim have become desolate.
50:38 drought against her w, that they may be dried up!
51:13 You who live by mighty w, rich in treasures, A
51:16 When he utters his voice there is a tumult of w in
Jer 51:55 Their waves roar like mighty w, A
Eze 1:24 like the sound of mighty w, like the thunder of A
17: 5 A plant by abundant w, he set it like a willow twig.
17: 8 it was transplanted to good soil by abundant w,
26:19 and the great w cover you,
27:34 in the depths of the w;
31: 4 The w nourished it, the deep made it grow tall,
31:14 All this is in order that no trees by the w may grow
31:15 and its mighty w were checked. A
32:13 destroy all its livestock from beside abundant w;
32:14 Then I will make their w clear,
43: 2 the sound was like the sound of mighty w; A
47: 8 and when it enters the sea, the sea of stagnant w,
47: 9 be very many fish, once these w reach there.
47:19 from Tamar as far as the w of Meribath-kadesh,
48:28 the boundary shall run from Tamar to the w
Hos 10: 7 like a chip on the face of the w.
Am 5: 8 who calls for the w of the sea,
5:24 But let justice roll down like w,
9: 6 who calls for the w of the sea,
Jnh 2: 5 The w closed in over me;
Mic 1: 4 like w poured down a steep place.
Na 2: 8 Nineveh is like a pool whose w run away.
Hab 2:14 as the w cover the sea.
3:15 the sea with your horses, churning the mighty w. A
Zec 14: 8 that day living w shall flow out from Jerusalem,
1Co 3: 7 the one who plants nor the one who w is anything,
3: 8 and the one who w have a common purpose,
Rev 1:15 and his voice was like the sound of many w.
8:11 A third of the w became wormwood,
11: 6 and they have authority over the w to turn them
14: 2 a voice from heaven like the sound of many w and
16: 5 And I heard the angel of the w say, "You are just,
17: 1 of the great whore who is seated on many w,
17:15 And he said to me, "The w that you saw,
19: 6 like the sound of many w and like the sound
Jdt 9:12 Lord of heaven and earth, Creator of the w,
16:15 be shaken to their foundations with the w;
Wis 10:18 and led them through deep w;
Sir 39:17 At his word the w stood in a heap,
Aza 1:38 Bless the Lord, all you w above the heavens;
1:57 you whales and all that swim in the w;
1Mc 11:67 and his army encamped by the w of Gennesaret.
2Es 1:20 not split the rock so that w flowed in abundance?
5: 9 Salt w shall be found in the sweet,
6:17 and its sound was like the sound of mighty w. A
6:41 and commanded it to divide and separate the w,
6:42 the w to be gathered together in a seventh part of
15:41 be filled with the abundance of those w.
16:58 he has confined the sea in the midst of the w;
16:59 like a dome and made it secure upon the w;
4Mc 1:29 and ties up and w and thoroughly irrigates,

WATERSKINS (1) [SKIN, WATER]

Job 38:37 Or who can tilt the w of the heavens,

WATERSPOUTS (KJV) See CATARACTS

WATERY (1) [WATER]

2Es 6:52 to Leviathan you gave the seventh part, the w part;

WAVE‡ (7) [WAVES, WAVY]

2Ki 5:11 and would w his hand over the spot,
Ps 72:16 may it w on the tops of the mountains;
Isa 11:15 and will w his hand over the River
13: 2 w the hand for them to enter the gates of
33:15 who w away a bribe instead of accepting it,
Jas 1: 6 for the one who doubts is like a w of the sea,
2Es 9:16 as a w is greater than a drop of water."

WAVER (3) [WAVERED, WAVERING]

Jer 4: 1 from my presence, and do not w,
31:22 How long will you w, O faithless daughter?
Ro 4:20 No distrust made him w concerning the promise

WAVERED (1) [WAVER]

3Mc 5:33 and his eyes w and his face fell.

WAVERING (4) [WAVER]

Ps 26: 1 and I have trusted in the LORD without w.
Heb 10:23 to the confession of our hope without w,
Jude 1:22 And have mercy on some who are w;
2Es 9: 3 w of leaders, confusion of princes,

WAVES (43) [WAVE]

2Sa 22: 5 For the w of death encompassed me,
Job 9: 8 the heavens and trampled the w of the Sea;
38:11 and here shall your proud w be stopped'?
Ps 42: 7 all your w and your billows have gone over me.
65: 7 the roaring of their w, the tumult of the peoples.
88: 7 and you overwhelm me with all your w.
89: 9 when its w rise, you still them.
93: 4 more majestic than the w of the sea,
107:25 which lifted up the w of the sea.
107:29 and the w of the sea were hushed.
Isa 48:18 and your success like the w of the sea;
51:15 who stirs up the sea so that its w roar—
Jer 5:22 though the w toss, they cannot prevail,
31:35 who stirs up the sea so that its w roar—
51:42 she has been covered by its tumultuous w.
51:55 Their w roar like mighty waters,
Eze 26: 3 as the sea hurls its w.
Jnh 2: 3 all your w and your billows passed over me.
Zec 10:11 and the w of the sea shall be struck down,
Mt 8:24 great that the boat was being swamped by the w;
14:24 battered by the w, was far from the land,
Mk 4:37 and the w beat into the boat,
Lk 8:24 up and rebuked the wind and the raging w;
21:25 by the roaring of the sea and the w.
Ac 27:41 stern was being broken up by the force of the w.
Jude 1:13 wild w of the sea, casting up the foam
Wis 5:10 no track of its keel in the w;
14: 1 about to voyage over raging w calls upon a piece
14: 3 and a safe way through the w,
19: 7 and a grassy plain out of the raging w,
Sir 24: 6 Over w of the sea, over all the earth,
29:18 and has tossed them about like w of the sea;
2Mc 9: 8 that he could command the w of the sea,
2Es 4:15 In like manner the w of the sea also made a plan
4:17 likewise also the plan of the w of the sea was
4:19 and the locale of the sea a place to carry its w."
4:21 to the forest and the sea to its w,
13: 2 a wind arose from the sea and stirred up all its w.
16:12 and its w and the fish with them shall be troubled
4Mc 7: 2 of the tyrant and overwhelmed by the mighty w
7: 5 our father Eleazar broke the maddening w of
13: 6 over harbors hold back the threatening w
15:31 in the universal flood, stoutly endured the w,

WAVY (1) [WAVE]

SS 5:11 his locks are w, black as a raven.

WAX (6)

Ps 22:14 my heart is like w; it is melted within my breast;
68: 2 as w melts before the fire,
97: 5 The mountains melt like w before the LORD,
Mic 1: 4 like w near the fire, like waters poured down
Jdt 16:15 before your glance the rocks shall melt like w.
2Es 13: 4 all who heard his voice melted as w melts

WAY‡ (702) [BYWAYS, DOORWAYS, GATEWAY, GATEWAYS, HIGHWAY, HIGHWAYS, WAYFARER, WAYS, WAYSIDE, WAYSIDES, WAYWARD, WAYWARDNESS]

A. IN EVERY WAY (22)
B. WAY OF LIFE (15)
C. WAY OF THE *LORD (10)
D. EVIL WAY (7)
E. WAY OF THE †LORD (7)

Ge 3:24 and a sword flaming and turning to guard the w to
12:20 and they set him on the w,
14:11 and all their provisions, and went their w;
16: 7 the spring on the w to Shur.
18:16 Abraham went with them to set them on their w.
18:19 household after him to keep the w of the LORD E
18:33 And the LORD went his w,
19: 2 then you can rise early and go on your w."
21:16 she went and sat down opposite him a good w off,
24:27 the LORD has led me on the w to the house
24:40 with you and make your w successful.
24:42 you will only make successful the w I am going!
24:48 who had led me by the right w to obtain
24:61 thus the servant took Rebekah, and went his w.
25:22 and she said, "If it is to be this w, why do I live?"
25:34 and he ate and drank, and rose and went his w.
26:31 and Isaac set them on their w,
28:20 and will keep me in this w that I go,
31:35 for the w of women is upon me."
32: 1 on his w and the angels of God met him;
33:12 Then Esau said, "Let us journey on our w,
33:16 So Esau returned that day on his w to Seir.
33:18 on his w from Paddan-aram;
35:19 and she was buried on the w to Ephrath (that is,
37:25 and resin, on their w to carry it down to Egypt.
39:19 saying, "This is the w your servant treated me,"
42:33 for the famine of your households, and go your w.
43: 7 Could we in any w know that he would say,
43: 8 "Send the boy with me, and let us be on our w,
43:13 and be on your w again to the man;
43:15 Then they went on their w down to Egypt,
45:24 Then he sent his brothers on their w,
45:24 "Do not quarrel along the w."
46:28 to Joseph to lead the w before him into Goshen.
48: 7 Rachel, alas, died in the land of Canaan on the w,
48: 7 and I buried her there on the w to Ephrath" (that is,
50:21 In this w he reassured them,
Ex 2:12 He looked this w and that,
4:24 On the w, at a place where they spent the night,
13:17 not lead them by w of the land of the Philistines,
13:18 the people by the roundabout w of the wilderness
13:21 to lead them along the w,
16: 4 In that w I will test them,
18: 8 all the hardship that had beset them on the w,
18:20 to them the w they are to go and the things they are
23:20 to guard you on the w and to bring you to the place
32: 8 to turn aside from the w that I commanded them;
33: 3 or I would consume you on the w,
33:16 In this w, we shall be distinct, I and your people,
36:23 The frames for the tabernacle he made in this w:
36:29 he made two of them in this w,
39:18 in this w they attached it in front to
39:32 In this w all the work of the tabernacle of the tent
Lev 19: 5 in such a w that it is acceptable on your behalf.
26:10 and you shall have to clear out the old to make w
Nu 2:34 and they set out the same w, everyone by clans,

Nu 11:15 If this is the w you are going to treat me,
14:17 of the LORD be great in the w that you promised
14:25 for the wilderness by the w to the Red Sea."
15:13 in this w, in presenting an offering by fire,
21: 1 heard that Israel was coming by the w of Atharim,
21: 4 by the w to the Red Sea, to go around the land
21: 4 but the people became impatient on the w.
22:26 where there was no w to turn either to the right or
22:30 Have I been in the habit of treating you this w?"
22:32 because your w is perverse before me.
24:25 and Balak also went his w.
28:24 In the same w you shall offer daily, for seven days,
Dt 1: 2 (By the w of Mount Seir it takes eleven days
1:19 on the w to the hill country of the Amorites,
1:31 all the w that you traveled
1:33 who goes before you on the w to seek out a place
8: 2 Remember the long w that
9:12 to turn from the w that I commanded them;
9:16 from the w that the LORD had commanded you.
11:28 turn from the w that I am commanding you today,
13: 5 to turn you from the w in which
17:16 "You must never return that w again."
25:18 the w, when you were faint and weary, and struck
28: 7 they shall come out against you one w,
28:25 you shall go out against them one w and flee
28:29 but you shall be unable to find your w;
31:29 from the w that I have commanded you.
Jos 1: 8 For then you shall make your w prosperous,
2: 7 the men pursued them on the w to the Jordan as far
2:16 then afterward you may go your w."
2:22 The pursuers had searched all along the w
3: 4 so that you may know the w you should go,
3: 4 for you have not passed this w before.
5: 7 because they had not been circumcised on the w.
8:20 They had no power to flee this w or that,
10:10 chased them by the w of the ascent of Beth-horon,
18: 8 So the men started on their w;
23:14 "And now I am about to go the w of all the earth,
24:17 He protected us along all the w that we went,
Jdg 1:24 they said to him, "Show us the w into the city,
1:25 So he showed them the w into the city;
2:17 from the w in which their ancestors had walked,
2:22 would take care to walk in the w of the LORD E
3:18 the people who carried the tribute on their w.
5:10 on rich carpets and you who walk by the w.
9:25 They robbed all who passed by them along that w;
18:26 Then the Danites went their w.
19:14 So they passed on and went their w;
19:27 and when he went out to go on his w,
Ru 1: 7 and they went on their w to go back to the land
1:12 Turn back, my daughters, go your w,
1Sa 6: 8 Then send it off, and let it go its w.
6: 9 And watch; if it goes up on the w to its own land,
9: 8 I will give it to the man of God, to tell us our w."
9:14 they saw Samuel coming out toward them on his w
9:21 Why then have you spoken to me in this w?"
9:26 "Get up, so that I may send you on your w."
12:23 and I will instruct you in the good and the right w.
13:15 And Samuel left and went on his w from Gilgal.
17:27 The people answered him in the same w,
17:30 toward another and spoke in the same w;
17:52 on the w from Shaaraim as far as Gath and Ekron.
20:19 you shall go a long w down;
24: 7 Saul got up and left the cave, and went on his w.
26:25 David went his w, and Saul returned to his place.
27: 8 from Telam on the w to Shur and on to the land
28:22 you may have strength when you go on your w."
30: 2 but carried them off, and went their w.
2Sa 2:24 before Giah on the w to the wilderness of Gibeon.
3:16 as he walked behind her all the w to Bahurim.
4: 7 and traveled by w of the Arabah all night long.
5:25 down the Philistines from Geba all the w to Gezer.
13:30 While they were on the w,
18:23 Then Ahimaaz ran by the w of the Plain,
19:36 Your servant will go a little w over the Jordan with
19:40 brought the king on his w.
22:31 This God—his w is perfect;
1Ki 2: 2 "I am about to go the w of all the earth.
2: 4 'If your heirs take heed to their w,
7:37 In this w he made the ten stands;
8:25 if only your children look to their w,
8:36 the good w in which they should walk;
8:44 by whatever w you shall send them,
13: 9 or drink water, or return by the w that you came."
13:10 So he went another w, and did not return by
13:10 did not return by the w that he had come to Bethel.
13:12 Their father said to them, "Which w did he go?"
13:12 And his sons showed him the w that the man
13:17 or return by the w that you came."
13:26 from the w heard of it, he said, "It is the man
13:33 Jeroboam did not turn from his evil w, D
15:26 walking in the w of his ancestor and in the sin
15:34 walking in the w of Jeroboam and in the sin
16: 2 and you have walked in the w of Jeroboam,
16:19 walking in the w of Jeroboam,
16:26 he walked in all the w of Jeroboam son of Nebat,
18: 7 As Obadiah was on the w, Elijah met him;
19:15 return on your w to the wilderness of Damascus;
22:24 "Which w did the spirit of the LORD pass
22:43 He walked in all the w of his father Asa;
22:52 and walked in the w of his father and mother,
22:52 and in the w of Jeroboam son of Nebat,
2Ki 2: 1 Elijah and Elisha were on their w from Gilgal.
2:23 and while he was going up on the w,
3: 8 Then he asked, "By which w shall we march?"
3: 8 "By the w of the wilderness of Edom."
4: 8 So whenever he passed that w,

2Ki 4: 9 that this man who regularly passes our w is
6:19 Elisha said to them, "This is not the w,
6:23 after they ate and drank, he sent them on their w,
7:15 the whole w was littered with garments
8:18 He walked in the w of the kings of Israel,
8:27 He also walked in the w of the house of Ahab,
10:12 On the w, when he was at Beth-eked of
12:20 on the w that goes down to Silla.
16: 3 but he walked in the w of the kings of Israel.
19:28 I will turn you back on the w by which you came.
19:33 By the w that he came, by the same he shall return;
21:21 He walked in all the w in which his father walked,
21:22 and did not walk in the w of the LORD. E
22: 2 and walked in all the w of his father David;
25: 4 the king with all the soldiers fled by night by the w
2Ch 6:16 if only your children keep to their w,
6:27 the good w in which they should walk;
6:34 by whatever w you shall send them,
11:17 for they walked for three years in the w of David
18:23 "Which w did the spirit of the LORD pass
20:32 in the w of his father Asa and did not turn aside
21: 6 He walked in the w of the kings of Israel,
21:13 but have walked in the w of the kings of Israel,
23:19 no one should enter who was in any w unclean.
Ezr 8:22 to protect us against the enemy on our w,
8:31 of the enemy and from ambushes along the w.
9: 2 the officials and leaders have led the w."
Ne 2:15 by w of the valley by night and inspected the wall.
4:17 The burden bearers carried their loads in such a w
6: 4 They sent to me four times in this w,
6: 5 In the same w Sanballat for
6:13 and make me sin by acting in this w,
8:10 Then he said to them, "Go your w,
8:12 And all the people went their w to eat and drink
9:12 on the w in which they should go.
9:19 of cloud that led them in the w did not leave them
9:19 of fire by night that gave them light on the w
13:18 Did not your ancestors act in this w,
Job 3:23 Why is light given to one who cannot see the w,
11:20 all w of escape will be lost to them,
16:22 I shall go the w from which I shall not return.
17: 9 Yet the righteous hold to their w,
19: 8 He has walled up my w so that I cannot pass,
21:31 Who declares their w to their face,
22:15 to the old w that the wicked have trod?
22:21 in this w good will come to you.
23:10 But he knows the w that I take;
23:11 I have kept his w and have not turned aside.
28:13 Mortals do not know the w to it,
28:23 "God understands the w to it,
28:26 and a w for the thunderbolt;
29:25 I chose their w, and sat as chief,
31: 7 from the w, and my heart has followed my eyes,
33:14 For God speaks in one w, and in two,
36:23 Who has prescribed for him his w, or who can say,
38:19 "Where is the w to the dwelling of light,
38:24 the w to the place where the light is distributed,
38:25 and a w for the thunderbolt,
Ps 1: 6 the LORD watches over the w of the righteous,
1: 6 but the w of the wicked will perish.
2:12 or he will be angry, and you will perish in the w;
5: 8 make your w straight before me.
18:30 This God—his w is perfect;
18:32 with strength, and made my w safe.
25: 8 therefore he instructs sinners in the w.
25: 9 and teaches the humble his w.
25:12 He will teach them the w that they should choose.
27:11 Teach me your w, O LORD,
32: 8 and teach you the w you should go;
35: 6 Let their w be dark and slippery,
36: 4 they are set on a w that is not good;
37: 5 Commit your w to the LORD;
37: 7 do not fret over those who prosper in their w,
37:23 when he delights in our w;
37:34 Wait for the LORD, and keep to his w,
44:18 nor have our steps departed from your w,
50:23 the right w I will show the salvation of God."
67: 2 that your w may be known upon earth,
73:15 If I had said, "I will talk on in this w,"
77:13 Your w, O God, is holy.
77:19 Your w was through the sea, your path,
80:12 so that all who pass along the w pluck its fruit?
86:11 Teach me your w, O LORD,
101: 2 I will study the w that is blameless.
101: 6 in the w that is blameless shall minister to me.
107: 4 finding no w to an inhabited town;
107: 7 he led them by a straight w,
119: 1 Happy are those whose w is blameless,
119: 9 How can young people keep their w pure?
119:14 in the w of your decrees as much as in all riches.
119:27 Make me understand the w of your precepts,
119:30 I have chosen the w of faithfulness;
119:32 I run the w of your commandments,
119:33 Teach me, O LORD, the w of your statutes,
119:101 I hold back my feet from every evil w, D
119:104 therefore I hate every false w.
119:128 by all your precepts; I hate every false w.
139:24 See if there is any wicked w in me,
139:24 and lead me in the w everlasting.
142: 3 When my spirit is faint, you know my w.
143: 8 Teach me the w I should go,
146: 9 but the w of the wicked he brings to ruin.
Pr 1:15 in their w, keep your foot from their paths;
1:31 of their w and be sated with their own devices.
2: 8 of justice and preserving the w of his faithful ones.
2:12 It will save you from the w of evil,
2:18 for her w leads down to death, and her paths to

Pr 2:20 Therefore walk in the w of the good,
3:23 on your w securely and your foot will not stumble.
4:11 I have taught you the w of wisdom;
4:14 and do not walk in the w of evildoers.
4:19 The w of the wicked is like deep darkness;
5: 8 Keep your w far from her,
6:23 and the reproofs of discipline are the w of life, B
7:27 Her house is the w to Sheol,
8: 2 On the heights, beside the w,
8:13 and the w of evil and perverted speech I hate.
8:20 I walk in the w of righteousness,
9: 6 and live, and walk in the w of insight."
9:15 who are going straight on their w,
10:29 w of the LORD is a stronghold for the upright, E
12:15 Fools think their own w is right,
12:26 but the w of the wicked leads astray.
13: 6 Righteousness guards one whose w is upright,
13:15 but the w of the faithless is their ruin.
14:12 There is a w that seems right to a person, but its end is the w to death.
15: 9 w of the wicked is an abomination to the LORD,
15:10 for one who forsakes the w,
15:19 The w of the lazy is overgrown with thorns,
16: 9 The human mind plans the w,
16:17 those who guard their w preserve their lives.
16:25 Sometimes there is a w that seems to be right, but in the end it is the w to death.
16:29 and lead them in a w that is not good.
19: 2 and one who moves too hurriedly misses the w.
21: 8 The w of the guilty is crooked,
21:16 the w of understanding will rest in the assembly of
22: 5 Thorns and snares are in the w of the perverse;
22: 6 Train children in the right w, and when old,
23:19 and be wise, and direct your mind in the w.
25:26 or a polluted fountain are the righteous who give w
30:19 the w of an eagle in the sky, the w of a snake on a rock, the w of a ship on the high seas, and the w of a man with a girl.
30:20 This is the w of an adulteress:
Ecc 8: 5 and the wise mind will know the time and w.
8: 6 For every matter has its time and w,
10:15 for they do not even know the w to town.
SS 6: 1 Which w has your beloved turned,
Isa 8:11 and warned me not to walk in the w of this people,
9: 1 but in the latter time he will make glorious the w
11:15 and make a w to cross on foot;
16: 1 by w of the desert, to the mount of daughter Zion.
22:25 that was fastened in a secure place will give w;
26: 7 The w of the righteous is level;
30:11 the w, turn aside from the path, let us hear no more
30:21 saying, "This is the w; walk in it."
35: 8 and it shall be called the Holy W;
37:29 I will turn you back on the w by which you came.
37:34 By the w that he came, by the same he shall return;
40: 3 "In the wilderness prepare the w of the LORD, E
40:14 and showed him the w of understanding?
40:27 O Israel, "My w is hidden from the LORD,
43:16 Thus says the LORD, who makes a w in the sea,
43:19 I will make a w in the wilderness and rivers in
48:15 I have brought him, and he will prosper in his w.
48:17 who leads you in the w you should go.
51:10 of the sea a w for the redeemed to cross over?
53: 6 we have all turned to our own w,
55: 7 let the wicked forsake their w, and
56:11 they have all turned to their own w,
57:14 It shall be said, "Build up, build up, prepare the w,
57:14 remove every obstruction from my people's w."
59: 8 The w of peace they do not know,
62:10 go through the gates, prepare the w for the people;
65: 2 who walk in a w that is not good,
Jer 2:17 while he led you in the w?
2:23 Look at your w in the valley;
3:21 because they have perverted their w,
5: 4 for they do not know the w of the LORD, E
5: 5 surely they know the w of the LORD, E
6:16 for the ancient paths, where the good w lies;
7:23 and walk only in the w that I command you,
10: 2 Do not learn the w of the nations,
10:23 that the w of human beings is not in their control,
12: 1 Why does the w of the guilty prosper?
18:11 Turn now, all of you from your evil w, D
21: 8 I am setting before you the w of life and B
21: 8 before you the way of life and the w of death.
22: 8 the LORD dealt in this w with that great city?"
22:21 This has been your w from your youth,
23:12 Therefore their w shall be to them
23:22 they would have turned them from their evil w, D
25: 5 from your evil w and wicked doings, D
26: 3 all of them, and will turn from their evil w, D
27:12 I spoke to King Zedekiah of Judah in the same w:
28:11 At this, the prophet Jeremiah went his w.
32:39 I will give them one heart and one w,
35:15 'Turn now everyone of you from your evil w, D
39: 4 at night by w of the king's garden through the gate
50: 5 They shall ask the w to Zion,
52: 7 from the city by night by the w of the gate between
La 2:15 All who pass along the w clap their hands at you;
3:11 he led me off my w and tore me to pieces;
Eze 3:18 or speak to warn the wicked from their wicked w,
3:19 or from their wicked w, they shall die
7:27 According to their w I will deal with them;
13:22 to turn from their wicked w and save their lives;
18:25 Yet you say, "The w of the Lord is unfair." C
18:25 Hear now, O house of Israel: Is my w unfair?
18:29 Israel says, "The w of the Lord is unfair." C
21:21 the king of Babylon stands at the parting of the w,
23:13 they both took the same w.

Eze 23:31 You have gone the w of your sister;
24:19 that you are acting this w?"
33:17 your people say, "The w of the Lord is not just," C
33:17 when it is their own w that is not just.
33:20 Yet you say, "The w of the Lord is not just." C
41: 7 from the bottom story to the uppermost story by w
44: 3 he shall enter by w of the vestibule of the gate,
44: 3 and shall go out by the same w.
44: 4 by w of the north gate to the front of the temple;
46: 8 and he shall go out by the same w.
46: 9 not return by w of the gate by which they entered,
47: 2 Then he brought me out by w of the north gate,
47:15 the north side, from the Great Sea by w of Hethlon
Da 3:29 no other god who is able to deliver in this w."
5: 6 His limbs gave w, and his knees knocked together.
12: 9 He said, "Go your w, Daniel,
12:13 But you, go your w, and rest;
Hos 2: 6 Therefore I will hedge up her w with thorns;
13: 7 like a leopard I will lurk beside the w.
Am 2: 7 and push the afflicted out of the w;
8:14 O Dan," and, "As the w of Beer-sheba lives"—
Mic 1:11 Pass on your w, inhabitants of Shaphir,
Na 1: 3 His w is in whirlwind and storm,
Mal 2: 8 But you have turned aside from the w;
3: 1 I am sending my messenger to prepare the w
Mt 1:18 the birth of Jesus the Messiah took place in this w.
3: 3 'Prepare the w of the Lord, C
3:15 for us in this w to fulfill all righteousness."
5:12 the same w they persecuted the prophets who were
5:16 In the same w, let your light shine before others,
5:25 with your accuser while you are on the w to court
6: 9 "Pray then in this w: Our Father in heaven,
7:17 In the same w, every good tree bears good fruit,
8:28 They were so fierce that no one could pass that w.
11:10 who will prepare your w before you.'
15:32 for they might faint on the w."
19:15 And he laid his hands on them and went on his w.
20:17 and said to them on the w,
21:32 For John came to you in the w of righteousness
21:36 and they treated them in the same w.
22:16 and teach the w of God in accordance with truth,
25:17 In the same w, the one who had
26:54 which say it must happen in this w?"
27:41 In the same w the chief priests also,
27:44 with him also taunted him in the same w.
Mk 1: 2 who will prepare your w;
1: 3 'Prepare the w of the Lord, C
2: 7 "Why does this fellow speak in this w?
2:23 and as they made their w his disciples began
7: 9 "You have a fine w of rejecting the commandment
7:31 went by w of Sidon towards the Sea of Galilee,
8: 3 they will faint on the w—
8:27 and on the w he asked his disciples,
9:33 "What were you arguing about on the w?"
9:34 the w they had argued with one another who was
10:52 and followed him on the w.
11:18 they kept looking for a w to kill him;
12:14 but teach the w of God in accordance with truth.
14: 1 and the scribes were looking for a w to arrest Jesus
14: 4 "Why was the ointment wasted in this w?
15:31 In the same w the chief priests,
15:39 saw that in this w he breathed his last, he said,
Lk 1:79 to guide our feet into the w of peace."
3: 4 'Prepare the w of the Lord, make his paths C
4:30 through the midst of them and went on his w.
5: 3 and asked him to put out a little w from the shore.
5:19 finding no w to bring him in because of the crowd,
7:27 who will prepare your w before you.'
8:14 but as they go on their w,
9:52 On their w they entered a village of the Samaritans
10: 3 Go on your w. See, I am sending you out like
10:38 Now as they went on their w,
12:58 on the w make an effort to settle the case,
13: 2 in this w they were worse sinners than all other
13:22 teaching as he made his w to Jerusalem.
13:33 tomorrow, and the next day I must be on my w,
17:11 On the w to Jerusalem Jesus was going through
17:19 Then he said to him, "Get up and go on your w;
19: 4 because he was going to pass that w.
19:47 and the leaders of the people kept looking for a w
20:21 but teach the w of God in accordance with truth.
20:31 and so in the same w all seven died childless.
22: 2 and the scribes were looking for a w to put Jesus
Jn 1:23 'Make straight the w of the Lord,' " C
4:30 They left the city and were on their w to him.
4:50 that Jesus spoke to him and started on his w.
5: 7 and while I am making my w,
8:11 [[Go your w, and from now on do not sin again."]]
10: 1 but climbs in by another w is a thief and a bandit.
14: 4 you know the w to the place where I am going."
14: 5 How can we know the w?"
14: 6 Jesus said to him, "I am the w, and the truth,
14:31 Rise, let us be on our w.
21: 1 and he showed himself in this w.
Ac 1:11 in the same w as you saw him go into heaven."
3:18 In this w God fulfilled what he had foretold
4:21 finding no w to punish them because of the people,
7:40 'Make gods for us who will lead the w for us;
8:39 and went on his w rejoicing.
9: 2 so that if he found any who belonged to the W,
9:17 who appeared to you on your w here,
13:34 he has spoken in this w,
14: 1 into the Jewish synagogue and spoke in such a w
15: 3 So they were sent on their w by the church,
16:17 who proclaim to you a w of salvation."
17:22 see how extremely religious you are in every w. A
18:25 He had been instructed in the W of the Lord; C
Ac 18:26 they took him aside and explained the W of God
19: 9 and spoke evil of the W before the congregation,
19:23 no little disturbance broke out concerning the W.
20:22 a captive to the Spirit, I am on my w to Jerusalem,
21:11 'This is the w the Jews in Jerusalem will bind
22: 4 I persecuted this W up to the point of death
22: 6 "While I was on my w and approaching Damascus,
24: 3 in every w and everywhere with utmost A
24:14 But this I admit to you, that according to the W,
24:22 Felix, who was rather well informed about the W,
25: 3 planning an ambush to kill him along the w.
25: 8 in no w committed an offense against the law of
26: 4 "All the Jews know my w of life from my youth, B
27:15 we gave w to it and were driven.
Ro 1:27 and in the same w also the men,
3: 2 Much, in every w. For in the first place A
3: 5 (I speak in a human w.)
3:17 and the w of peace they have not known."
7: 4 In the same w, my friends,
14:13 a stumbling block or hindrance in the w of another.
15:15 to you rather boldly by w of reminder,
15:28 I will set out by w of you to Spain;
1Co 1: 5 for in every w you have been enriched in him, A
4: 1 Think of us in this w,
7: 6 This I say by w of concession, not of command.
9:12 an obstacle in the w of the gospel of Christ.
9:14 In the same w, the Lord commanded
9:24 Run in such a w that you may win it.
10:13 but with the testing he will also provide the w out
11:25 In the same w he took the cup also, after supper,
12:31 And I will show you a still more excellent w.
13: 5 It does not insist on its own w;
14: 7 It is the same w with lifeless instruments
16: 6 so that you may send me on my w, wherever I go.
16:11 Send him on his w in peace,
2Co 1:16 I wanted to visit you on my w to Macedonia,
4: 8 We are afflicted in every w, but not crushed; A
5:16 we know him no longer in that w.
6: 3 We are putting no obstacle in anyone's w,
6: 4 we have commended ourselves in every w: A
7: 5 but we were afflicted in every w— A
7: 9 so that you were not harmed in any w by us.
9:11 be enriched in every w for your great generosity, A
10:14 we were the first to come all the w to you with
11: 6 in every w and in all things we have made this A
11: 9 to refrain from burdening you in any w.
Gal 6: 2 and in this w you will fulfill the law of Christ.
Eph 2:10 God prepared beforehand to be our w of life. B
4:15 we must grow up in every w into him who is A
4:20 That is not the w you learned Christ!
4:22 were taught to put away your former w of life, B
5:28 In the same w, husbands should love their wives
Php 1: 7 It is right for me to think this w about all of you,
1:18 Just this, that Christ is proclaimed in every w, A
1:20 and hope that I will not be put to shame in any w,
1:28 and are in no w intimidated by your opponents.
2:18 in the same w you also must be glad and rejoice
4: 1 stand firm in the Lord in this w, my beloved.
Col 2:18 puffed up without cause by a human w of thinking,
1Th 2:18 and again—but Satan blocked our w.
3:11 and Father himself and our Lord Jesus direct our w
2Th 2: 3 Let no one deceive you in any w;
3:17 it is the w I write.
1Ti 1: 3 as I did when I was on my w to Macedonia,
3: 4 children submissive and respectful in every w— A
4: 8 godliness is valuable in every w, A
5:10 and devoted herself to doing good in every w. A
2Ti 3: 6 For among them are those who make their w
Tit 3:13 to send Zenas the lawyer and Apollos on their w,
Phm 1:18 If he has wronged you in any w,
Heb 6: 9 Even though we speak in this w, beloved,
6:17 In the same w, when God desired to show
9: 8 the w into the sanctuary has not yet been disclosed
9:21 in the same w he sprinkled with the blood both
10:20 the new and living w that he opened for us through
11:14 for people who speak in this w make it clear
13: 7 consider the outcome of their w of life, B
Jas 1:7,8 being double-minded and unstable in every w, A
1:11 It is the same w with the rich;
1Pe 3: 1 the same w, accept the authority of your husbands,
3: 5 in this w long ago that the holy women who hoped
3: 7 in the same w, show consideration for your wives
5: 5 In the same w, you who are younger must accept
2Pe 1:11 For in this w, entry into the eternal kingdom
2: 2 of these teachers the w of truth will be maligned.
2:21 to have known the w of righteousness than,
3:11 Since all these things are to be dissolved in this w,
1Jn 2:11 and does not know the w to go,
3:10 and the children of the devil are revealed in this w:
4: 9 God's love was revealed among us in this w:
Jude 1: 8 in the same w these dreamers also defile the flesh,
1:11 For they go the w of Cain,
1:15 that they have committed in such an ungodly w,
Rev 16:12 up in order to prepare the w for the kings from
Tob 4:15 or let drunkenness go with you on your w.
5: 4 someone who was acquainted with the w.
5: 5 "Do you know the w to go to Media?"
5:16 to you in good health, because the w is safe."
6: 6 on their w together until they were near Media.
11: 3 prepare the house while they are still on the w."
11:15 on her w there, very near to the gate of Nineveh.
Jdt 5:14 he led them by the w of Sinai and Kadesh-barnea.
5:18 when they departed from the w he had prescribed
7:19 and there was no w of escape from them.
10:13 I am on my w to see Holofernes the commander
10:13 I will show him a w by which he can go
12: 8 she prayed the Lord God of Israel to direct her w
Jdt 13:16 Lord lives, who has protected me in the w I went,
AdE 10: 3 His w of life was such as to make him beloved B
Wis 5: 6 So it was we who strayed from the w of truth,
5: 7 but the w of the Lord we have not known. C
7: 6 for all one entrance into life, and one w out.
10:17 she guided them along a marvelous w,
11:14 they felt thirst in a different w from the righteous.
12:10 and that their w of thinking would never change.
14: 3 and a safe w through the waves,
18:23 and cut off its w to the living.
19: 7 an unhindered w out of the Red Sea,
19:17 to find the w through their own doors.
Sir 19:30 and the w he walks, show what he is.
20:26 A liar's w leads to disgrace,
21:10 The w of sinners is paved with smooth stones,
22:21 do not despair, for there is a w back.
27: 7 for this is the w people are tested.
30: 1 so that he may rejoice at the w he turns out.
33:33 which w will you go to seek him?
37: 9 "Your w is good," and then stand aside
37:15 the Most High that he may direct your w in truth.
40:29 one's w of life cannot be considered a life. B
Bar 3:13 If you had walked in the w of God,
3:20 but they have not learned the w to knowledge,
3:21 Their descendants have strayed far from her w.
3:23 have not learned the w to wisdom,
3:27 or give them the w to knowledge;
3:31 No one knows the w to her,
3:36 He found the whole w to knowledge,
LtJ 6:71 In the same w, their gods of wood,
1Mc 5:29 they went all the w to the stronghold of Dathema.
5:53 and encouraging the people all the w until he came
6:18 They were trying in every w to harm them A
8:27 In the same w, if war comes first to the nation of
13:20 and he circled around by the w to Adora.
13:21 to Trypho urging him to come to them by w of
14: 5 and opened a w to the isles of the sea.
14:35 He sought in every w to exalt his people. A
2Mc 1:17 Blessed in every w be our God, A
2: 6 up intending to mark the w,
2:14 In the same w Judas also collected all the books
4:10 his compatriots over to the Greek w of life. B
4:34 he immediately put him out of the w.
6:14 but he does not deal in this w with us,
6:31 So in this w he died,
7: 7 After the first brother had died in this w,
7:13 and tortured the fourth in the same w.
7:28 in the same w the human race came into being.
8:17 the overthrow of their ancestral w of life. B
8:35 and made his w alone like a runaway slave across
9: 7 Yet he did not in any w stop his insolence,
9:18 But when his sufferings did not in any w abate,
9:21 On my w back from the region of Persia I suffered
10:36 the same w wheeled around against the defenders
11:24 but prefer their own w of living and ask
11:31 and none of them shall be molested in any w
11:36 For we are on our w to Antioch.
12: 8 the same w to wipe out the Jews who were living
14: 3 realized that there was no w for him to be safe or
14:23 on in Jerusalem and did nothing out of the w,
1Es 8:52 and will support them in every w." A
8:61 he delivered us from every enemy on the w,
9:51 "so go your w, eat the fat and drink the sweet,
9:54 Then they all went their w,
3Mc 3: 8 The Greeks in the city, though wronged in no w,
3:23 in accordance with their infamous w of life, B
3:24 that they are ill-disposed toward us in every w, A
4:11 in any w claim to be inside the circuit of the city.
5:20 without delay prepare the elephants in the same w
5:46 of people crowding their w into the hippodrome—
5:49 and giving w to lamentation
7:14 so on their w they punished and put to a public
2Es 3:31 and have not shown to anyone how your w may
3:34 be found which w the turn of the scale will incline.
4: 2 and do you think you can comprehend the w of
4: 4 then I will show you the w you desire to see,
4:11 how then can your mind comprehend the w of
5: 1 and the w of truth shall be hidden,
5:34 the w of the Most High and to search out some part
6:35 and fasted seven days in the same w as before,
7:*79* the w of the Most High, who have despised his law
7:*81* The first w, because they have scorned the law of
7:*82* The second w, because they cannot now make
7:*83* The third w, they shall see the reward laid up
7:*84* The fourth w, they shall consider the torment laid
7:*85* The fifth w, they shall see how the habitations of
7:*86* The sixth w, they shall see how some
7:*87* The seventh w, which is worse than all the ways
7:*129* [59] For this is the w of which Moses,
10:13 with the earth according to the w of the earth—
13:45 Through that region there was a long w to go,
4Mc 1: 4 and those that stand in the w of courage,
1: 6 but so that one may not give w to them.
2: 7 a glutton, or even a drunkard can learn a better w,
2: 8 as soon as one adopts a w of life in accordance B
3: 2 but reason can provide a w for us not to
4:19 the nation's w of life and altered its form B
4:24 in any w to put an end to the people's observance
5:27 but also to eat in such a w that you may deride us
7: 3 in no w did he turn the rudder of religion
8: 3 modest, noble, and accomplished in every w— A
8: 8 your youth by adopting the Greek w of life B
10: 7 they were not able in any w to break his spirit,
10:13 not give w to the same insanity as your brothers,
11: 4 what act of ours are you destroying us in this w?
12:13 and to maltreat and torture them in this w?
17: 5 lighting the w of your star-like seven sons to piety,

4Mc 17: 9 the tyrant who wished to destroy the w of life B
18: 1 obey this law and exercise piety in every w, A
18: 5 Since in no w whatever was he able to compel

WAYFARER (2) [WAY]

Jdg 19:17 and saw the w in the open square of the city,
2Sa 12: 4 or herd to prepare for the w who had come to him,

WAYFARING (KJV) See GUEST, TRAVELER[S], WAYFARER

WAYMARKS (KJV) See ROAD MARKERS

WAYS‡ (257) [WAY]

A. EVIL WAYS (10)

Ge 6:12 for all flesh had corrupted its w upon the earth.
Ex 33:13 I have found favor in your sight, show me your w,
Lev 2: 8 that is prepared in any of these w;
18:24 Do not defile yourselves in any of these w,
25:54 if they have not been redeemed in any of these w,
Dt 8: 6 by walking in his w and by fearing him.
10:12 to walk in all his w, to love him,
11:22 loving the LORD your God, walking in all his w,
12: 4 not worship the LORD your God in such w.
19: 9 the LORD your God and walking always in his w—
26:17 and for you to walk in his w, to keep his statutes,
28: 7 and flee before you seven w.
28: 9 of the LORD your God and walk in his w.
28:25 and flee before them seven w.
29:19 we go our own stubborn w" (thus bringing disaster
30:16 by loving the LORD your God, walking in his w,
32: 4 Rock, his work is perfect, and all his w are just.
Jos 22: 5 to love the LORD your God, to walk in all his w,
Jdg 2:19 not drop any of their practices or their stubborn w.
1Sa 8: 3 Yet his sons did not follow in his w,
8: 5 and your sons do not follow in your w;
8: 9 and show them the w of the king who shall reign
8:11 "These will be the w of the king who will reign
2Sa 22:22 For I have kept the w of the LORD,
1Ki 1:49 up trembling and went their own w.
2: 3 walking in his w and keeping his statutes,
3:14 If you will walk in my w,
8:39 according to all their w, for only you know what is
8:58 to walk in all his w,
11:33 and has not walked in my w,
11:38 walk in my w, and do what is right in my sight
2Ki 17:13 from your evil w and keep my commandments A
2Ch 6:30 according to all their w, for only you know
6:31 and walk in your w all the days that they live in
7:14 pray, seek my face, and turn from their wicked w,
17: 3 because he walked in the earlier w of his father;
17: 4 and not according to the w of Israel.
17: 6 His heart was courageous in the w of the LORD;
21:12 in the w of your father Jehoshaphat or in the w of King Asa
22: 3 He also walked in the w of the house of Ahab,
27: 6 because he ordered his w before
27: 7 and all his wars and his w,
28: 2 but he walked in the w of the kings of Israel.
28:26 Now the rest of his acts and all his w,
34: 2 and walked in the w of his ancestor David;
Job 4: 6 and the integrity of your w your hope?
8:19 See, these are their happy w,
13:15 but I will defend my w to his face.
21:14 We do not desire to know your w.
22: 3 or is it gain to him if you make your w blameless?
22:28 and light will shine on your w.
24:13 who are not acquainted with its w,
24:23 his eyes are upon their w.
26:14 These are indeed but the outskirts of his w;
31: 4 Does he not see my w, and number all my steps?
34:11 according to their w he will make it befall them.
34:21 "For his eyes are upon the w of mortals,
34:27 and had no regard for any of his w,
Ps 10: 5 Their w prosper at all times,
17: 4 by the word of your lips I have avoided the w of
18:21 For I have kept the w of the LORD,
25: 4 Make me to know your w, O LORD;
39: 1 "I will guard my w that I may not sin
51:13 Then I will teach transgressors your w,
68:21 hairy crown of those who walk in their guilty w.
81:13 that Israel would walk in my w!
91:11 concerning you to guard you in all your w.
95:10 and they do not regard my w."
103: 7 He made known his w to Moses,
107:17 Some were sick through their sinful w,
119: 3 who also do no wrong, but walk in his w.
119: 5 O that my w may be steadfast
119:15 and fix my eyes on your w.
119:26 When I told of my w, you answered me;
119:29 Put false w far from me;
119:37 give me life in your w.
119:59 I think of your w, I turn my feet to your decrees;
119:168 for all my w are before you.
125: 5 to their own crooked w the LORD will lead away
128: 1 the LORD, who walks in his w.
138: 5 They shall sing of the w of the LORD,
139: 3 and are acquainted with all my w.
145:17 The LORD is just in all his w,
Pr 2:13 of uprightness to walk in the w of darkness,
2:15 and who are devious in their w.
3: 6 In all your w acknowledge him,
3:17 Her w are w of pleasantness,
Pr 3:31 the violent and do not choose any of their w;
4:26 and all your w will be sure.
5: 6 her w wander, and she does not know it.
5:21 For human w are under the eyes of the LORD,
6: 6 consider its w, and be wise.
7:25 Do not let your hearts turn aside to her w;
8:32 happy are those who keep my w.
10: 9 but whoever follows perverse w will be found out.
11: 5 of the blameless keeps their w straight,
11:20 but those of blameless w are his delight.
14:14 The perverse get what their w deserve,
16: 2 All one's w may be pure in one's own eyes,
16: 7 When the w of people please the LORD,
17:23 a concealed bribe to pervert the w of justice.
19:16 those who are heedless of their w will die.
20:24 how then can we understand our own w?
21:29 but the upright give thought to their w.
22:25 or you may learn their w and entangle yourself in
23:26 and let your eyes observe my w.
28: 6 and walk in integrity than to be crooked in one's w
28:10 who mislead the upright into evil w will fall A
28:18 whoever follows crooked w will fall into the Pit.
31: 3 your w to those who destroy kings.
31:27 She looks well to the w of her household,
Ecc 11: 2 Divide your means seven w, or even eight,
Isa 2: 3 that he may teach us his w and that we may walk
2: 6 For you have forsaken the w of your people,
42:24 in whose w they would not walk,
49: 9 They shall feed along the w,
55: 8 nor are your w my w, says the LORD.
55: 9 so are my w higher than your w
57:17 but they kept turning back to their own w.
57:18 I have seen their w, but I will heal them;
58: 2 and delight to know my w, as if they were a nation
58:13 if you honor it, not going your own w,
63:17 do you make us stray from your w
64: 5 those who remember you in your w.
66: 3 These have chosen their own w,
Jer 2:33 even to wicked women you have taught your w.
2:36 How lightly you gad about, changing your w!
4:18 Your w and your doings have brought this
6:27 so that you may know and test their w.
7: 3 Amend your w and your doings,
7: 5 For if you truly amend your w and your doings,
12: 4 and because people said, "He is blind to our w."
12:16 if they will diligently learn the w of my people,
15: 7 they did not turn from their w.
16:17 For my eyes are on all their w;
17:10 to give to all according to their w,
18:11 and amend your w and your doings.
18:15 they have stumbled in their w, in the ancient roads,
26:13 Now therefore amend your w and your doings,
32:19 whose eyes are open to all the w of mortals,
32:19 to their w and according to the fruit of their doings.
36: 3 all of them may turn from their evil w, A
36: 7 and that all of them will turn from their evil w, A
La 3: 9 he has blocked my w with hewn stones,
3:40 Let us test and examine our w,
Eze 7: 3 I will judge you according to your w,
7: 4 I will punish you for your w,
7: 8 I will judge you according to your w,
7: 9 I will punish you according to your w,
14:22 When you see their w and their deeds,
14:23 when you see their w and their deeds;
16:47 You not only followed their w,
16:47 you were more corrupt than they in all your w.
16:61 Then you will remember your w,
18:23 rather that they should turn from their w and live?
18:25 Is it not your w that are unfair?
18:29 O house of Israel, are my w unfair?
18:29 Is it not your w that are unfair?
18:30 O house of Israel, all of you according to your w,
20:43 There you shall remember your w and all the deeds
20:44 not according to your evil w, or corrupt deeds, A
24:14 to your w and your doings I will judge you,
28:15 in your w from the day that you were created,
33: 8 not speak to warn the wicked to turn from their w,
33: 9 But if you warn the wicked to turn from their w,
33: 9 and they do not turn from their w,
33:11 but that the wicked turn from their w and live;
33:11 turn back, turn back from your evil w; A
33:20 I will judge all of you according to your w!
36:17 they defiled it with their w and their deeds;
36:31 Then you shall remember your evil w, A
36:32 Be ashamed and dismayed for your w,
Da 4:37 for all his works are truth, and his w are justice;
5:23 and to whom belong all your w,
Hos 4: 9 I will punish them for their w,
9: 8 yet a fowler's snare is on all his w,
12: 2 and will punish Jacob according to his w,
14: 9 For the w of the LORD are right,
Jnh 3: 8 from their evil w and from the violence that is A
3:10 how they turned from their evil w, A
Mic 4: 2 that he may teach us his w and that we may walk
Zec 1: 4 from your evil w and from your evil deeds." A
1: 6 of hosts has dealt with us according to our w
3: 7 you will walk in my w and keep my requirements,
Mal 2: 9 not kept my w but have shown partiality
Lk 1:76 for you will go before the Lord to prepare his w,
3: 5 and the rough w made smooth;
Ac 2:28 You have made known to me the w of life;
3:26 by turning each of you from your wicked w."
14:16 the nations to follow their own w;
18:13 to worship God in w that are contrary to the law."
Ro 11:33 and how inscrutable his w!
1Co 4:17 to remind you of my w in Christ Jesus,
13:11 when I became an adult, I put an end to childish w.
Col 3: 7 These are the w you also once followed,
2Th 3:16 at all times in all w.
Heb 1: 1 to our ancestors in many and various w by
3:10 and they have not known my w.'
1Pe 1:18 that you were ransomed from the futile w inherited
2Pe 2: 2 Even so, many will follow their licentious w,
Rev 15: 3 Just and true are your w, King of the nations!
Tob 1: 3 in the w of truth and righteousness all the days
3: 2 all your w are mercy and truth;
4: 5 and do not walk in the w of wrongdoing;
4:19 and ask him that your w may be made straight and
Jdt 5: 8 Since they had abandoned the w of their ancestors,
9: 6 For all your w are prepared in advance,
Wis 2:15 that of others, and his w are strange.
2:16 and he avoids our w as unclean;
Sir 2: 6 make your w straight, and hope in him.
2:15 and those who love him keep his w.
6:26 and keep her w with all your might.
14:21 in his heart on her w and ponders her secrets,
16:20 and who can comprehend his w?
17:15 Their w are always known to him;
17:19 and his eyes are ever upon their w.
33:11 and appointed their different w.
39:24 To the faithful his w are straight,
47:23 into sin and started Ephraim on its sinful w.
48:22 and he kept firmly to the w of his ancestor David,
49: 9 also mentioned Job who held fast to all the w
Bar 2:33 for they will remember the w of their ancestors,
4:13 not walk in the w of God's commandments,
Aza 1: 4 all your works are true and your w right,
2Mc 4:11 the lawful w of living and introduced new customs
4:13 of foreign w because of the surpassing wickedness
4:16 and those whose w of living they admired
7:24 if he would turn from the w of his ancestors,
12:11 and to help his people in all other w.
12:12 in many w, agreed to make peace with them;
12:41 So they all blessed the w of the Lord,
3Mc 1:25 while the elders near the king tried in various w
2Es 4: 3 "I have been sent to show you three w,
4:23 For I did not wish to inquire about the w above,
5:12 they shall labor, but their w shall not prosper.
7:23 not exist, and they ignored his w.
7:*48* has brought us into corruption and the w of death,
7:*80* always grieving and sad, in seven w.
7:*87* the w that have been mentioned,
7:*88* of those who have kept the w of the Most High,
7:*99* and the previously mentioned are the w of torment
7:*122* [52] but we have walked in the most wicked w?
7:*124* [54] because we have lived in perverse w?
8:29 the destruction of those who have the w of cattle,
8:31 and our ancestors have passed our lives in w
8:56 of his law, and abandoned his w.
9: 9 Then those who have now abused my w shall
9:19 have become corrupt in their w.
12: 4 because you search out the w of the Most High.
13:54 because you have forsaken your own w
14:31 the w that the Most High commanded you.
4Mc 2: 8 contrary to natural w and to lend without interest
16: 3 she saw her seven sons tortured in such varied w.

WAYSIDE (1) [WAY]

Ge 38:21 the temple prostitute who was at Enaim by the w?"

WAYSIDE (KJV) See also ALONG THE ROAD, BY THE ROAD

WAYSIDES (1) [WAY]

Jer 3: 2 By the w you have sat waiting for lovers,

WAYWARD (3) [WAY]

Pr 7:11 She is loud and w; her feet do not stay at home;
Hos 10:10 I will come against the w people to punish them;
Heb 5: 2 He is able to deal gently with the ignorant and w,

WAYWARDNESS (1) [WAY]

Pr 1:32 For w kills the simple, and the complacency

WE (2326) [OUR, OURS, OURSELVES, US] See Index of Articles Etc.

WEAK‡ (63) [WEAKEN, WEAKENED, WEAKER, WEAKEST, WEAKLING, WEAKNESS, WEAKNESSES]

Nu 13:18 whether the people who live in it are strong or w,
Jdg 16: 7 then I shall become w, and be like anyone else."
16:11 then I shall become w, and be like anyone else."
16:13 then I shall become w, and be like anyone else."
16:17 I would become w, and be like anyone else."
2Ch 14:11 for you between helping the mighty and the w.
15: 7 Do not let your hands be w,
Job 4: 3 you have strengthened the w hands.
Ps 6: 7 they grow w because of all my foes.
35:10 You deliver the w from those too strong for them,
35:10 the w and needy from those who despoil them."
72:13 He has pity on the w and the needy,
82: 3 Give justice to the w and the orphan;
82: 4 Rescue the w and the needy;
109:24 My knees are w through fasting;
Isa 14:10 "You too have become as w as we!
35: 3 Strengthen the w hands, and make firm
Eze 34: 4 You have not strengthened the w,
34:16 and I will strengthen the w,

Eze 34:21 and butted at all the w animals with your horns
Zep 3:16 do not let your hands grow w.
Mt 26:41 the spirit indeed is willing, but the flesh is w."
Mk 14:38 the spirit indeed is willing, but the flesh is w."
Ac 20:35 that by such work we must support the w,
Ro 5: 6 For while we were still w,
14: 1 Welcome those who are w in faith,
14: 2 while the w eat only vegetables.
15: 1 to put up with the failings of the w,
1Co 1:27 God chose what is w in the world to shame
4:10 We are w, but you are strong.
8: 7 and their conscience, being w, is defiled.
8: 9 not somehow become a stumbling block to the w.
8:10 might they not, since their conscience is w,
8:11 So by your knowledge those w believers
8:12 and wound their conscience when it is w,
9:22 To the w I became w, so that I might win the w.
11:30 For this reason many of you are w and ill,
2Co 10:10 but his bodily presence is w,
11:21 To my shame, I must say, we were too w for that!
11:29 Who is w, and I am not w?
12:10 for whenever I am w, then I am strong.
13: 3 He is not w in dealing with you,
13: 4 For we are w in him,
13: 9 For we rejoice when we are w and you are strong.
Gal 4: 9 to the w and beggarly elemental spirits?
1Th 5:14 encourage the faint hearted, help the w,
Heb 7:18 of an earlier commandment because it was w
12:12 and strengthen your w knees,
Jdt 9:11 upholder of the w, protector of the forsaken,
16:11 my w people cried out, and the enemy trembled;
Wis 2:11 for what is w proves itself to be useless.
9: 5 a man who is w and short-lived,
13:18 For health he appeals to a thing that is w;
Sir 25:23 and w knees come from the wife who does
LtJ 6:36 from death or rescue the w from the strong.
1Es 1:30 "Take me away from the battle, for I am very w."
2Es 2:21 care for the injured and the w,
7:*112* [42] those who were strong prayed for the w.
12: 5 I am still weary in mind and very w in my spirit,
14:14 and divest yourself now of your w nature;

WEAKEN (3) [WEAK]

Jdg 16:19 He began to w, and his strength left him.
Isa 57:10 and so you did not w.
Ro 4:19 not w in faith when he considered his own body,

WEAKENED‡ (2) [WEAK]

Ro 8: 3 For God has done what the law, w by the flesh,
2Es 15:51 be w like a wretched woman who is beaten

WEAKER (7) [WEAK]

2Sa 3: 1 while the house of Saul became w and w.
1Co 12:22 of the body that seem to be w are indispensable,
1Pe 3: 7 paying honor to the woman as the w sex,
1Mc 6:57 men, "Daily we grow w, our food supply is scant,
2Es 14:17 For the w the world becomes through old age,
4Mc 15: 5 that mothers are the w sex and give birth to many,

WEAKEST (1) [WEAK]

Jdg 6:15 My clan is the w in Manasseh,

WEAKLING (1) [WEAK]

Joel 3:10 let the w say, "I am a warrior."

WEAKNESS‡ (13) [WEAK]

Ro 8:26 Likewise the Spirit helps us in our w;
1Co 1:25 and God's w is stronger than human strength.
2: 3 to you in w and in fear and in much trembling.
15:43 It is sown in w, it is raised in power.
2Co 11:30 I will boast of the things that show my w.
12: 9 for power is made perfect in w."
13: 4 For he was crucified in w,
Heb 5: 2 since he himself is subject to w;
7:28 as high priests those who are subject to w,
11:34 won strength out of w, became mighty in war,
Wis 17:13 defeated by this inward w,
Sir 11:30 and like spies they observe your w;
4Mc 7:20 by their emotions because of the w of their reason.

WEAKNESSES (4) [WEAK]

2Co 12: 5 on my own behalf I will not boast, except of my w.
12: 9 So, I will boast all the more gladly of my w,
12:10 Therefore I am content with w, insults, hardships,
Heb 4:15 who is unable to sympathize with our w,

WEAL (1)

Isa 45: 7 I make w and create woe; I the LORD do all these

WEALTH‡ (115) [WEALTHY]

Ge 31: 1 he has gained all this w from what belonged
34:29 All their w, all their little ones and their wives,
Dt 8:17 the might of my own hand have gotten me this w."
8:18 for it is he who gives you power to get w,
Jos 22: 8 "Go back to your tents with much w,
Jdg 18: 7 lacking nothing on earth, and possessing w.
1Sa 9: 1 a Benjaminite, a man of w.
2Ch 1:11 and you have not asked for possessions, w, honor,
Est 1: 4 while he displayed the great w of his kingdom and
Job 5: 5 and the thirsty pant after their w.
6:22 Or, 'From your w offer a bribe for me'?
15:29 and their w will not endure,
Job 20:10 and their hands will give back their w.
27:19 They go to bed with w, but will do so no more;
31:25 if I have rejoiced because my w was great,
Ps 45:13 with all kinds of w. The princess is decked in her
49: 6 those who trust in their w and boast of
49:10 fool and dolt perish together and leave their w
49:16 when the w of their houses increases.
49:17 their w will not go down after them.
52: 7 in abundant riches, and sought refuge in w!"
105:44 and they took possession of the w of the peoples,
112: 3 W and riches are in their houses,
Pr 5:10 of your w, and your labors will go to the house of
8:18 enduring w and prosperity.
8:21 endowing with w those who love me,
10:15 The w of the rich is their fortress;
12:27 but the diligent obtain precious w.
13: 7 others pretend to be poor, yet have great w.
13: 8 W is a ransom for a person's life,
13:11 W hastily gotten will dwindle,
13:22 but the sinner's w is laid up for the righteous.
18:11 The w of the rich is their strong city;
19: 4 W brings many friends,
19:14 House and w are inherited from parents,
28: 8 One who augments w by exorbitant
Ecc 5:10 nor the lover of w, with gain.
5:19 to whom God gives w and possessions
6: 2 those to whom God gives w,
SS 8: 7 If one offered for love all the w of his house,
Isa 8: 4 the w of Damascus and the spoil of Samaria will
10: 3 and where will you leave your w,
10:14 like a nest, the w of the peoples;
45:14 The w of Egypt and the merchandise of Ethiopia,
60: 5 the w of the nations shall come to you.
60:11 so that nations shall bring you their w,
61: 6 you shall enjoy the w of the nations,
66:12 the w of the nations like an overflowing stream;
Jer 9:23 do not let the wealthy boast in their w;
15:13 Your w and your treasures I will give as plunder,
17: 3 Your w and all your treasures I will give for spoil
17:11 so are all who amass w unjustly;
20: 5 I will give all the w of this city, all its gains,
Eze 7:11 not their w; no pre-eminence among them.
27:12 with you out of the abundance of your great w;
27:18 because of your great w of every kind—
27:33 your abundant w and merchandise you enriched
28: 4 and your understanding you have amassed w
28: 5 in trade you have increased your w,
28: 5 and your heart has become proud in your w,
29:19 and he shall carry off its w and despoil it
30: 4 and its w is carried away,
Da 11:24 lavishing plunder, spoil, and w on them.
11:28 He shall return to his land with great w,
Hos 12: 8 "Ah, I am rich, I have gained w for myself;
Ob 1:11 on the day that strangers carried off his w,
Mic 4:13 their w to the Lord of the whole earth.
Hab 2: 5 w is treacherous; the arrogant do not endure.
Zep 1:13 Their w shall be plundered,
Zec 9: 4 of its possessions and hurl its w into the sea,
14:14 And the w of all the surrounding nations shall
Mt 6:24 You cannot serve God and w.
13:22 but the cares of the world and the lure of w choke
Mk 4:19 the lure of w, and the desire for other things come
10:23 "How hard it will be for those who have w to enter
Lk 16: 9 by means of dishonest w so that when it is gone,
16:11 you have not been faithful with the dishonest w,
16:13 You cannot serve God and w."
18:24 "How hard it is for those who have w to enter
Ac 19:25 you know that we get our w from this business.
2Co 8: 2 and their extreme poverty have overflowed in a w
Heb 11:26 for the Christ to be greater w than the treasures
Rev 5:12 and w and wisdom and might and honor and glory
18:15 merchants of these wares, who gained w from her,
18:17 For in one hour all this w has been laid waste!"
18:19 where all who had ships at sea grew rich by her w!
Tob 4:21 You have great w if you fear God and flee
12: 8 A little with righteousness is better than w
AdE 10: 2 and the w and glory of his kingdom,
Wis 5: 8 And what good has our boasted w brought us?
7: 8 I accounted w as nothing in comparison with her.
7:11 and in her hands uncounted w.
7:13 I do not hide her w,
8:18 unfailing w, and in the experience of her company,
Sir 5: 1 Do not rely on your w, or say, "I have enough."
5: 8 Do not depend on dishonest w,
10: 8 on account of injustice and insolence and w.
10:30 while the rich are honored for their w.
10:31 who is honored in poverty, how much more in w!
10:31 one dishonored in w, how much more in poverty!
11:14 life and death, poverty and w, come from the Lord.
14: 3 and of what use is w to a miser?
18:25 in days of w think of poverty and need.
28:10 in proportion to his w he will increase his wrath.
30:16 There is no w better than health of body,
31: 1 Wakefulness over w wastes away one's flesh,
40:13 The w of the unjust will dry up like a river,
40:18 W and wages make life sweet,
44:11 their w will remain with their descendants,
LtJ 6:35 Likewise they are not able to give either w
1Mc 6: 1 that Elymais in Persia was a city famed for its w
2Mc 3: 7 to effect the removal of the reported w.
2Es 3: 2 of Zion and the w of those who lived in Babylon.
3:33 the nations and have seen that they abound in w,
15:63 plunder your w, and mar the glory

WEALTHY (8) [WEALTH]

Ge 24:35 greatly blessed my master, and he has become w;
Ge 26:13 and more until he became very w.
2Sa 19:32 for he was a very w man.
2Ki 4: 8 where a w woman lived, who urged him to have
15:20 the w, fifty shekels of silver from each one, to give
Jer 9:23 do not let the w boast in their wealth;
Da 11:39 who acknowledge him he shall make more w,
Mic 6:12 Your w are full of violence;

WEANED (12)

Ge 21: 8 The child grew, and was w;
21: 8 a great feast on the day that Isaac was w.
1Sa 1:22 "As soon as the child is w, I will bring him,
1:23 wait until you have w him;
1:23 and nursed her son, until she w him.
1:24 When she had w him, she took him up with her,
1Ki 11:20 whom Tahpenes w in Pharaoh's house;
Ps 131: 2 quieted my soul, like a w child with its mother;
131: 2 my soul is like the w child that is with me.
Isa 11: 8 the w child shall put its hand on the adder's den.
28: 9 Those who are w from milk,
Hos 1: 8 When she had w Lo-ruhamah,

WEAPON (12) [WEAPONRY, WEAPONS]

Nu 35:18 with a w of wood in hand that could cause death,
2Ch 23:10 the people as a guard for the king, everyone with w
Ne 4:17 with one hand and with the other held a w.
4:23 each kept his w in his right hand.
Job 20:24 They will flee from an iron w;
Isa 54:16 and produces a w fit for its purpose;
54:17 No w that is fashioned against you shall prosper,
Jer 51:20 You are my war club, my w of battle:
Eze 9: 1 each with his destroying w in his hand."
9: 2 each with his w for slaughter in his hand;
2Es 13: 9 he neither lifted his hand nor held a spear or any w
13:28 not holding a spear or w of war, yet destroying

WEAPONRY (2) [WEAPON]

1Ki 10:25 objects of silver and gold, garments, w, spices,
2Ch 9:24 objects of silver and gold, garments, w, spices,

WEAPONS‡ (45) [WEAPON]

Ge 27: 3 Now then, take your w, your quiver and your bow,
49: 5 w of violence are their swords.
Jdg 18:11 of the Danite clan, armed with w of war, set out
18:16 armed with their w of war,
18:17 of the gate with the six hundred men armed with w
1Sa 20:40 Jonathan gave his w to the boy and said to him,
21: 8 I did not bring my sword or my w with me,
2Sa 1:27 the mighty have fallen, and the w of war perished!
21:16 and who was fitted out with new w,
2Ki 10: 2 and horses, a fortified city, and w,
11: 8 the king, each with w in hand;
11:11 every man with his w in his hand,
1Ch 12:33 equipped for battle with all the w of war,
12:37 one hundred twenty thousand armed with all the w
2Ch 23: 7 each with his w in his hand;
32: 5 and made w and shields in abundance.
Job 39:21 it goes out to meet the w.
Ps 7:13 he has prepared his deadly w,
76: 3 the shield, the sword, and the w of war.
Ecc 9:18 Wisdom is better than w of war,
Isa 13: 5 the LORD and the w of his indignation,
22: 8 On that day you looked to the w of the House of
Jer 21: 4 to turn back the w of war that are in your hands
22: 7 against you, all with their w;
50:25 and brought out the w of his wrath,
Eze 32:27 of long ago who went down to Sheol with their w
39: 9 of Israel will go out and make fires of the w
39:10 for they will make their fires of the w;
Joel 2: 8 they burst through the w and are not halted.
Jn 18: 3 they came there with lanterns and torches and w.
2Co 6: 7 with the w of righteousness for the right hand and
10: 4 for the w of our warfare are not merely human,
Jdt 6:12 they seized their w and ran out of the town to
7: 5 Yet they all seized their w,
14: 2 each of you take up your w,
14:11 Then they all took their w,
1Mc 6: 2 and w left there by Alexander son of Philip,
9:39 with tambourines and musicians and many w.
14:42 over its tasks and over the country and the w and
15: 7 the w that you have prepared and the strongholds
16:16 Ptolemy and his men rose up, took their w,
2Mc 3:25 Its rider was seen to have armor and w of gold.
10:30 and shielding him with their own armor and w,
11: 8 clothed in white and brandishing w of gold.
4Mc 4:10 with lightning flashing from their w appeared

WEAR (47) [WEARING, WEARS, WORE, WORN, WORN-OUT]

Ge 28:20 and will give me bread to eat and clothing to w,
Ex 18:18 You will surely w yourself out,
28:35 Aaron shall w it when he ministers,
28:43 Aaron and his sons shall w them when they go into
29:30 in his place shall w them seven days,
Lev 13:45 the leprous disease shall w torn clothes and let
16: 4 fasten the linen sash, and w the linen turban;
21:10 and who has been consecrated to w the vestments,
Dt 8: 4 on your back did not w out and your feet did
22: 5 A woman shall not w a man's apparel,
22:11 You shall not w clothes made of wool
1Sa 2:28 to offer incense, to w an ephod before me;
1Ki 22:30 and go into battle, but you w your robes."
1Ch 17: 9 and evildoers shall w them down no more,
2Ch 18:29 and go into battle, but you w your robes."

Ne 9:21 their clothes did not w out and their feet did
Job 14:19 the waters w away the stones;
27:17 but the just will w it,
Ps 102:26 they will all w out like a garment.
Pr 23: 4 Do not w yourself out to get rich;
Isa 4: 1 We will eat our own bread and w our own clothes;
50: 9 All of them will w out like a garment;
51: 6 the earth will w out like a garment,
Eze 44:17 they shall w linen vestments;
Da 7:25 shall w out the holy ones of the Most High,
Mt 6:25 or about your body, what you will w.
6:31 or 'What will we w?'
11: 8 Look, those who w soft robes are in royal palaces.
Mk 6: 9 but to w sandals and not to put on two tunics.
Lk 12:22 or about your body, what you will w.
12:33 Make purses for yourselves that do not w out,
18: 5 she may not w me out by continually coming.' "
1Co 11: 6 or to be shaved, she should w a veil.
Heb 1:11 they will all w out like clothing;
Jdt 10: 3 to w while her husband Manasseh was living.
AdE 14:16 and I do not w it on the days when I am at leisure.
Wis 5:18 and w impartial justice as a helmet;
Sir 6:31 You will w her like a glorious robe,
6:36 let your foot w out his doorstep.
27: 8 you will attain it and w it like a glorious robe.
LtJ 6:24 As for the gold that they w for beauty—
6:58 of their gold and silver and of the robes they w,
1Mc 11:58 to drink from gold cups and dress in purple and w
14:43 and that he should be clothed in purple and w gold.
2Mc 4:12 and he induced the noblest of the young men to w
6: 7 to w wreaths of ivy and to walk in the procession
12:40 which the law forbids the Jews to w.

WEARIED (10) [WEARY]

Isa 43:23 or w you with frankincense.
43:24 you have w me with your iniquities.
47:13 You are w with your many consultations;
Jer 12: 5 with foot-runners and they have w you,
Eze 24:12 In vain I have w myself;
Mic 6: 3 In what have I w you?
Mal 2:17 You have w the LORD with your words.
2:17 Yet you say, "How have we w him?"
Sir 22:13 and you will never be w by his lack of sense.
Bar 3: 1 the soul in anguish and the w spirit cry out to you.

WEARIES (1) [WEARY]

Isa 16:12 when he w himself upon the high place,

WEARINESS (3) [WEARY]

Jdg 4:21 he was lying fast asleep from w—and he died.
Ecc 12:12 and much study is a w of the flesh.
Mal 1:13 "What a w this is," you say, and you sniff at me,

WEARING (25) [WEAR]

Lev 16:32 w the linen vestments, the holy vestments.
Ru 3:15 "Bring the cloak you are w and hold it out."
1Sa 2:18 a boy w a linen ephod.
18: 4 of the robe that he was w,
2Sa 13:18 (Now she was w a long robe with sleeves;
13:19 and tore the long robe that she was w;
20: 8 Now Joab was w a soldier's garment and
1Ki 11:30 of the new garment he was w and tore it
Est 1:11 w the royal crown, in order to show the peoples
8:15 w royal robes of blue and white,
Jer 13: 4 "Take the loincloth that you bought and are w,
Da 3:21 So the men were bound, still w their tunics,
Mt 22:11 a man there who was not w a wedding robe,
Mk 14:51 w nothing but a linen cloth.
Jn 19: 5 w the crown of thorns and the purple robe.
Jas 2: 3 and if you take notice of the one w the fine clothes
1Pe 3: 3 and by w gold ornaments or fine clothing;
Rev 11: 3 thousand two hundred sixty days, w sackcloth."
19:14 And the armies of heaven, w fine linen,
Jdt 9: 1 and uncovered the sackcloth she was w.
10: 3 She removed the sackcloth she had been w,
15:13 and w garlands and singing hymns.
AdE 8:15 Mordecai went out dressed in the royal robe and w
Sir 11: 4 Do not boast about w fine clothes,
1Es 5:40 a high priest should appear w Urim and Thummim.

WEARISOME (2) [WEARY]

Ps 73:16 it seemed to me a w task,
Ecc 1: 8 All things are w; more than one can express;

WEARS (4) [WEAR]

Ps 109:19 like a belt that he w every day."
Ecc 10:15 The toil of fools w them out,
1Co 11:14 nature itself teach you that if a man w long hair,
Sir 40: 4 from the one who w purple and a crown to

WEARY‡ (55) [WEARIED, WEARIES, WEARINESS, WEARISOME, WEARYING]

Ge 27:46 "I am w of my life because of the Hittite women.
Ex 17:12 But Moses' hands grew w;
Dt 25:18 when you were faint and w,
2Sa 16:14 and all the people who were with him arrived w at
17: 2 while he is w and discouraged, and throw him into
17:29 "The troops are hungry and w and thirsty in
21:15 against the Philistines, and David grew w.
23:10 down the Philistines until his arm grew w,
Job 3:17 and there the w are at rest.
22: 7 You have given no water to the w to drink,
Ps 6: 6 I am w with my moaning;
63: 1 as in a dry and w land where there is no water.
69: 3 I am w with my crying; my throat is parched.
Pr 3:11 do not despise the LORD's discipline or be w
25:17 the neighbor will become w of you and hate you.
30: 1 I am w, O God, I am w, O God.
Isa 1:14 they have become a burden to me, I am w
5:27 None of them is w, none stumbles,
7:13 Is it too little for you to w mortals, that you w my God also?
28:12 "This is rest; give rest to the w;
32: 2 like the shade of a great rock in a w land.
38:14 My eyes are w with looking upward.
40:28 He does not faint or grow w;
40:30 Even youths will faint and be w,
40:31 they shall run and not be w,
43:22 but you have been w of me, O Israel!
46: 1 you carry are loaded as burdens on w animals.
50: 4 that I may know how to sustain the w with a word.
57:10 You grew w from your many wanderings,
Jer 2:24 None who seek her need w themselves;
6:11 I am w of holding it in.
9: 5 they commit iniquity and are too w to repent.
15: 6 and destroyed you—I am w of relenting.
20: 9 I am w with holding it in, and I cannot.
31:25 I will satisfy the w, and all who are faint I will
45: 3 I am w with my groaning, and I find no rest."
51:58 and the nations w themselves only for fire.
La 5: 5 we are w, we are given no rest.
Hab 2:13 and nations w themselves for nothing?
Mt 11:28 all you that are w and are carrying heavy burdens,
1Co 4:12 and we grow w from the work of our own hands.
Gal 6: 9 So let us not grow w in doing what is right,
2Th 3:13 do not be w in doing what is right.
Heb 12: 3 so that you may not grow w or lose heart.
Rev 2: 3 and that you have not grown w.
Jdt 13: 1 for they all were w because the banquet had lasted
Sir 7:10 Do not grow w when you pray;
16:27 They neither hunger nor grow w,
23:17 he will never w until he dies.
43:30 summon all your strength, and do not grow w,
2Mc 12:36 for a long time and were w,
2Es 2:12 and they shall neither toil nor become w.
12: 5 I am still w in mind and very weak in my spirit,

WEARYING (1) [WEARY]

Ps 77: 2 in the night my hand is stretched out without w;

WEASEL (1)

Lev 11:29 the w, the mouse, the great lizard according

WEATHER (3)

Mt 16: 2 "When it is evening, you say, 'It will be fair w,
Sir 3:15 like frost in fair w, your sins will melt away.
1Es 9: 6 shivering because of the bad w that prevailed.

WEAVE‡ (2) [GOLD-WOVEN, WEAVER, WEAVER'S, WEAVERS, WEAVING, WOVE, WOVEN]

Jdg 16:13 "If you w the seven locks of my head with the web
Isa 59: 5 They hatch adders' eggs, and w the spider's web;

WEAVER (2) [WEAVE]

Ex 35:35 by a w—by any sort of artisan or skilled designer.
Isa 38:12 like a w I have rolled up my life;

WEAVER'S (5) [WEAVE]

1Sa 17: 7 The shaft of his spear was like a w beam,
2Sa 21:19 the shaft of whose spear was like a w beam.
1Ch 11:23 Egyptian had in his hand a spear like a w beam;
20: 5 the shaft of whose spear was like a w beam.
Job 7: 6 My days are swifter than a w shuttle,

WEAVERS (1) [WEAVE]

Isa 19:10 Its w will be dismayed, and all who work

WEAVING (1) [WEAVE]

2Ki 23: 7 where the women did w for Asherah.

WEB‡ (4) [WEBS]

Jdg 16:13 of my head with the w and make it tight with
16:14 of his head and wove them into the w,
16:14 and pulled away the pin, the loom, and the w.
Isa 59: 5 and weave the spider's w;

WEBS (1) [WEB]

Isa 59: 6 Their w cannot serve as clothing;

WEDDED (1) [WEDDING]

3Mc 1:19 the bridal chambers prepared for w union,

WEDDING (30) [WEDDED]

Ps 19: 5 like a bridegroom from his w canopy,
SS 3:11 on the day of his w,
Mt 9:15 "The w guests cannot mourn as long as
22: 2 be compared to a king who gave a w banquet
22: 3 to the w banquet, but they would
22: 4 and everything is ready; come to the w banquet.'
22: 8 Then he said to his slaves, 'The w is ready,
22: 9 and invite everyone you find to the w banquet.'
22:10 so the w hall was filled with guests.
Mt 22:11 a man there who was not wearing a w robe,
22:12 how did you get in here without a w robe?'
25:10 with him into the w banquet;
Mk 2:19 "The w guests cannot fast while the bridegroom is
Lk 5:34 "You cannot make w guests fast while
12:36 for their master to return from the w banquet,
14: 8 "When you are invited by someone to a w banquet,
Jn 2: 1 On the third day there was a w in Cana of Galilee,
2: 2 and his disciples had also been invited to the w.
Tob 9: 2 and then bring him with you to the w celebration.
9: 5 and was inviting him to the w celebration.
9: 6 both got up early and went to the w celebration.
10: 7 the w celebration had ended that Raguel had sworn
11:18 With merriment they celebrated Tobias's w feast
12: 1 When the w celebration was ended,
1Mc 9:37 "The family of Jambri are celebrating a great w,
9:41 So the w was turned into mourning and the voice
10:58 and celebrated her w at Ptolemais with great pomp,
3Mc 4: 6 all together raising a lament instead of a w song,
2Es 10: 1 that when my son entered his w chamber,
10:48 'My son died as he entered his w chamber,'

WEDDINGS See Index to Footnotes

WEDGE (1) [WEDGED, WEDGES]

4Mc 11:10 they twisted his back around the w on the wheel,

WEDGED (1) [WEDGE]

Sir 27: 2 so sin is w in between selling and buying.

WEDGES (1) [WEDGE]

4Mc 8:13 and w and bellows, the tyrant resumed speaking:

[BREAK] WEDLOCK (KJV) See COMMIT ADULTERY

WEEDS (12)

Job 31:40 and foul w instead of barley."
Hos 10: 4 up like poisonous w in the furrows of the field.
Jnh 2: 5 w were wrapped around my head
Mt 13:25 an enemy came and sowed w among the wheat,
13:26 then the w appeared as well.
13:27 Where, then, did these w come from?'
13:29 for in gathering the w you would uproot the wheat
13:30 the w first and bind them in bundles to be burned,
13:36 "Explain to us the parable of the w of the field."
13:38 the w are the children of the evil one,
13:40 Just as the w are collected and burned up with fire,
4Mc 1:29 w and prunes and ties up and waters

WEEK‡ (15) [WEEKS]

Ge 29:27 Complete the w of this one,
29:28 Jacob did so, and completed her w;
Da 9:27 a strong covenant with many for one w, and
9:27 of the w he shall make sacrifice and offering cease;
Mt 28: 1 the sabbath, as the first day of the w was dawning,
Mk 16: 2 And very early on the first day of the w,
16: 9 ⟦Now after he rose early on the first day of the w,⟧
Lk 18:12 I fast twice a w; I give a tenth of all my income.'
24: 1 But on the first day of the w, at early dawn,
Jn 20: 1 Early on the first day of the w,
20:19 it was evening on that day, the first day of the w,
20:26 A w later his disciples were again in the house,
Ac 20: 7 On the first day of the w,
1Co 16: 2 On the first day of every w,
2Es 7:*43* It will last as though for a w of years.

WEEKS (21) [WEEK]

A. FESTIVAL OF WEEKS (7)

Ex 34:22 You shall observe the festival of w, A
Lev 12: 5 she shall be unclean two w, as in her menstruation;
23:15 you shall count off seven w;
25: 8 You shall count off seven w of years,
25: 8 period of seven w of years gives forty-nine years.
Nu 28:26 to the LORD at your festival of w, you shall have A
Dt 16: 9 You shall count seven w;
16: 9 the seven w from the time the sickle is first put to
16:10 the festival of w for the LORD your God, A
16:16 at the festival of w, and at the festival of booths. A
2Ch 8:13 festival of unleavened bread, the festival of w, A
Jer 5:24 and keeps for us the w appointed for the harvest."
Da 9:24 "Seventy w are decreed for your people
9:25 of an anointed prince, there shall be seven w;
9:25 for sixty-two w it shall be built again with streets
9:26 the sixty-two w, an anointed one shall be cut off
10: 2 Daniel, had been mourning for three w.
10: 3 not anointed myself at all, for the full three w.
Tob 2: 1 which is the sacred festival of w, A
2Mc 12:31 as the festival of w was close at hand. A
2Es 6:35 to complete the three w that had been prescribed

WEEP (61) [WEEPING, WEEPS, WEPT]

Ge 23: 2 and Abraham went in to mourn for Sarah and to w
43:30 and he was about to w.
1Sa 1: 8 "Hannah, why do you w?
2:33 be spared to w out his eyes and grieve his heart;
30: 4 until they had no more strength to w.
2Sa 1:24 O daughters of Israel, w over Saul,
2Ki 8:12 Hazael asked, "Why does my lord w?"
Ne 8: 9 to the LORD your God; do not mourn or w."
Job 30:25 Did I not w for those whose day was hard?

Job 30:31 and my pipe to the voice of those who w.
Ecc 3: 4 a time to w, and a time to laugh;
Isa 15: 2 to the high places to w;
16: 9 Therefore I w with the weeping of Jazer for
22: 4 Look away from me, let me w bitter tears;
30:19 inhabitants of Jerusalem, you shall w no more.
33: 7 the envoys of peace w bitterly.
Jer 9: 1 so that I might w day and night for the slain
13:17 my soul will w in secret for your pride;
13:17 my eyes will w bitterly and run down with tears,
22:10 Do not w for him who is dead, nor bemoan him;
22:10 w rather for him who goes away,
48:32 More than for Jazer I w for you, O vine of Sibmah!
La 1:16 For these things I w; my eyes flow with tears;
Eze 24:16 yet you shall not mourn or w,
24:23 you shall not mourn or w,
27:31 and they w over you in bitterness of soul,
Joel 1: 5 Wake up, you drunkards, and w;
2:17 the ministers of the LORD, w.
Mic 1:10 Tell it not in Gath, w not at all;
Zec 12:10 as one mourns for an only child, and w bitterly
Mk 5:39 "Why do you make a commotion and w?
Lk 6:21 "Blessed are you who w now, for you will laugh.
6:25 for you will mourn and w.
7:13 for her and said to her, "Do not w."
7:32 we wailed, and you did not w.'
8:52 "Do not w; for she is not dead but sleeping."
23:28 do not w for me, but w for yourselves and for your
Jn 11:31 that she was going to the tomb to w there.
11:35 Jesus began to w.
16:20 Very truly, I tell you, you will w and mourn,
Ro 12:15 with those who rejoice, w with those who w.
Jas 4: 9 Lament and mourn and w.
5: 1 w and wail for the miseries that are coming to you.
Rev 5: 4 to w bitterly because no one was found worthy
5: 5 Then one of the elders said to me, "Do not w.
18: 9 will w and wail over her when they see the smoke
18:11 the merchants of the earth w and mourn for her,
Tob 5:18 But his mother began to w, and said to Tobit,
10: 4 And she began to w and mourn for her son, saying,
10: 7 in and mourn and w all night long,
Jdt 16:17 they shall w in pain forever.
Sir 7:34 Do not avoid those who w,
22:11 W for the dead, for he has left the light behind;
22:11 w for the fool, for he has left intelligence behind.
22:11 W less bitterly for the dead, for he is at rest;
2Es 2:27 others shall w and be sorrowful,
5:13 and w as you do now, and fast for seven days,
9:41 so that I may w for myself and continue to mourn,
4Mc 15:19 nor did you w when you looked at the eyes

WEEPERS See Index to Footnotes

WEEPING‡ (70) [WEEP]

Ge 50: 4 When the days of w for him were past,
Nu 11:10 the people w throughout their families,
11:13 they come w to me and say, 'Give us meat to eat!'
25: 6 they were w at the entrance of the tent of meeting.
1Sa 11: 5 the matter with the people, that they are w?"
2Sa 3:16 w as he walked behind her all the way to Bahurim.
15:30 w as he went, with his head covered
15:30 covered their heads and went up, w as they went.
19: 1 "The king is w and mourning for Absalom."
Ezr 3:13 the joyful shout from the sound of the people's w,
10: 1 w and throwing himself down before the house
Est 4: 3 with fasting and w and lamenting,
8: 3 w and pleading with him to avert the evil design
Job 16:16 My face is red with w,
Ps 6: 6 I drench my couch with my w.
6: 8 for the LORD has heard the sound of my w.
30: 5 W may linger for the night,
126: 6 Those who go out w, bearing the seed for sowing,
Isa 15: 5 For at the ascent of Luhith they go up w;
16: 9 I weep with the w of Jazer for the vines of Sibmah;
22:12 the Lord GOD of hosts called to w and mourning,
65:19 no more shall the sound of w be heard in it,
Jer 3:21 the plaintive w of Israel's children,
9:10 Take up w and wailing for the mountains,
31: 9 With w they shall come,
31:15 voice is heard in Ramah, lamentation and bitter w.
31:15 Rachel is w for her children;
31:16 Keep your voice from w, and your eyes from tears;
41: 6 from Mizpah to meet them, w as he came.
48: 5 For at the ascent of Luhith they go up w bitterly;
50: 4 they shall come w as they seek
La 2:11 My eyes are spent with w;
Eze 8:14 women were sitting there w for Tammuz.
Joel 2:12 with fasting, with w, and with mourning;
Mal 2:13 the LORD's altar with tears, with w and groaning
Mt 2:18 Rachel w for her children;
8:12 where there will be w and gnashing of teeth."
13:42 where there will be w and gnashing of teeth.
13:50 where there will be w and gnashing of teeth.
22:13 where there will be w and gnashing of teeth.'
24:51 where there will be w and gnashing of teeth.
25:30 where there will be w and gnashing of teeth.'
Mk 5:38 he saw a commotion, people w and wailing loudly.
16:10 ⟦while they were mourning and w.⟧
Lk 7:38 She stood behind him at his feet, w,
8:52 They were all w and wailing for her;
13:28 be w and gnashing of teeth when you see Abraham
Jn 11:33 saw her w, and the Jews who came with her also w,
20:11 But Mary stood w outside the tomb.
20:13 They said to her, "Woman, why are you w?"
20:15 Jesus said to her, "Woman, why are you w?
Ac 9:39 w and showing tunics and other clothing
Ac 20:37 There was much w among them all;
21:13 "What are you doing, w and breaking my heart?
Rev 18:15 in fear of her torment, w and mourning aloud,
Tob 6: 1 So she stopped w. The young man went out
Sir 38:17 Let your w be bitter and your wailing fervent;
Bar 4:11 but I sent them away with w and sorrow.
4:23 For I sent you out with sorrow and w,
Sus 1:33 with her and all who saw her were w.
2Mc 13:12 and had implored the merciful Lord with w
1Es 5:63 the building of this one with outcries and loud w,
5:65 the trumpets because of the w of the people.
8:91 w and lying on the ground before the temple,
8:91 for there was great w among the multitude.
9:50 now they were all w as they heard the law—
2Es 5:20 So I fasted seven days, mourning and w,
9:38 she was mourning and w with a loud voice,
9:40 to her, "Why are you w, and why are you grieved

WEEPS (2) [WEEP]

La 1: 2 She w bitterly in the night,
Zec 12:10 as one w over a firstborn.

WEIGH (12) [OUTWEIGH, OUTWEIGHS, WEIGHED, WEIGHING, WEIGHS, WEIGHT, WEIGHTED, WEIGHTIER, WEIGHTS, WEIGHTY]

Ezr 8:29 Guard them and keep them until you w them
Ps 38: 4 they w like a burden too heavy for me.
Isa 46: 6 and w out silver in the scales—
La 1:14 they w on my neck, sapping my strength;
Eze 33:10 "Our transgressions and our sins w upon us,
Zep 1:11 all who w out silver are cut off.
1Co 14:29 and let the others w what is said.
Sir 26:15 and no scales can w the value of her chastity.
2Mc 9: 8 that he could w the high mountains in a balance,
2Es 3:34 therefore w in a balance our iniquities and those of
4: 5 he said to me, "Go, w for me the weight of fire,
16:76 must not let your sins w you down,

WEIGHED (33) [WEIGH]

Ge 23:16 and Abraham w out for Ephron the silver
1Sa 2: 3 a God of knowledge, and by him actions are w.
17: 7 and his spear's head w six hundred shekels of iron;
2Sa 14:26 he cut it), he w the hair of his head,
21:16 whose spear w three hundred shekels of bronze,
2Ki 12:11 They would give the money that was w out into
1Ch 20: 2 he found that it w a talent of gold,
Ezr 8:25 And I w out to them the silver and the gold and
8:26 I w out into their hand six hundred fifty talents
8:30 the gold, and the vessels as they were w out,
8:33 and the vessels were w into the hands of
8:34 The total was counted and w,
Job 6: 2 "O that my vexation were w,
28:15 and silver cannot be w out as its price.
31: 6 let me be w in a just balance,
Isa 33:18 Where is the one who w the tribute?
40:12 and w the mountains in scales and the hills in
Jer 32: 9 and w out the money to him,
32:10 got witnesses, and w the money on scales.
Da 5:27 you have been w on the scales and found wanting;
Zec 11:12 So they w out as my wages thirty shekels of silver.
Lk 9:32 Peter and his companions were w down with sleep;
21:34 so that your hearts are not w down with dissipation
Ac 27:13 so they w anchor and began to sail past Crete,
28:13 then we w anchor and came to Rhegium.
AdE 9: 3 because fear of Mordecai w upon them.
Sir 21:25 but the words of the prudent are w in the balance.
42: 7 you make a deposit, be sure it is counted and w,
1Es 8:55 and I w out to them the silver and the gold and
8:56 I w and gave to them six hundred fifty talents
8:62 and the gold were w and delivered in the house
8:64 The whole was counted and w,
2Es 4:36 for he has w the age in the balance,

WEIGHING (51) [WEIGH]

Ge 24:22 the man took a gold nose-ring w a half shekel,
24:22 and two bracelets for her arms w ten gold shekels,
Nu 7:13 one silver plate w one hundred thirty shekels,
7:13 one silver basin w seventy shekels,
7:14 one golden dish w ten shekels, full of incense;
7:19 one silver plate w one hundred thirty shekels,
7:19 one silver basin w seventy shekels,
7:20 one golden dish w ten shekels, full of incense;
7:25 one silver plate w one hundred thirty shekels,
7:25 one silver basin w seventy shekels,
7:26 one golden dish w ten shekels, full of incense;
7:31 one silver plate w one hundred thirty shekels,
7:31 one silver basin w seventy shekels,
7:32 one golden dish w ten shekels, full of incense;
7:37 one silver plate w one hundred thirty shekels,
7:37 one silver basin w seventy shekels,
7:38 one golden dish w ten shekels, full of incense;
7:43 one silver plate w one hundred thirty shekels,
7:43 one silver basin w seventy shekels,
7:44 one golden dish w ten shekels, full of incense;
7:49 one silver plate w one hundred thirty shekels,
7:49 one silver basin w seventy shekels,
7:50 one golden dish w ten shekels, full of incense;
7:55 one silver plate w one hundred thirty shekels,
7:55 one silver basin w seventy shekels,
7:56 one golden dish w ten shekels, full of incense;
7:61 one silver plate w one hundred thirty shekels,
7:61 one silver basin w seventy shekels,
7:62 one golden dish w ten shekels, full of incense;
Nu 7:67 one silver plate w one hundred thirty shekels,
7:67 one silver basin w seventy shekels,
7:68 one golden dish w ten shekels, full of incense;
7:73 one silver plate w one hundred thirty shekels,
7:73 one silver basin w seventy shekels,
7:74 one golden dish w ten shekels, full of incense;
7:79 one silver plate w one hundred thirty shekels,
7:79 one silver basin w seventy shekels,
7:80 one golden dish w ten shekels, full of incense;
7:85 each silver plate w one hundred thirty shekels
7:86 w ten shekels apiece according to the shekel of
Jos 7:21 and a bar of gold w fifty shekels,
2Ki 25:16 the bronze of all these vessels was beyond w.
1Ch 22: 3 as well as bronze in quantities beyond w,
22:14 and bronze and iron beyond w,
Ecc 12: 9 w and studying and arranging many proverbs.
Jer 52:20 the bronze of all these vessels was beyond w.
Eze 5: 1 then take balances for w, and divide the hair.
Jn 19:39 w about a hundred pounds.
Rev 16:21 each w about a hundred pounds,
1Mc 14:24 with a large gold shield w one thousand minas,
15:18 have brought a gold shield w one thousand minas.

WEIGHS (6) [WEIGH]

Pr 12:25 Anxiety w down the human heart,
16: 2 but the LORD w the spirit.
21: 2 but the LORD w the heart.
24:12 does not he who w the heart perceive it?
Wis 9:15 for a perishable body w down the soul,
Sir 38:19 but the life of the poor w down the heart.

WEIGHT‡ (41) [WEIGH]

Ge 43:21 in the top of his sack, our money in full w.
Lev 19:35 You shall not cheat in measuring length, w,
26:26 and they shall dole out your bread by w;
Dt 25:15 You shall have only a full and honest w;
Jdg 8:26 The w of the golden earrings
16:29 and he leaned his w against them,
1Sa 17: 5 w of the coat was five thousand shekels of bronze.
2Sa 12:30 the w of it was a talent of gold,
14:26 two hundred shekels by the king's w.
18:12 in my hand the w of a thousand pieces of silver,
1Ki 7:47 the w of the bronze was not determined.
10:14 The w of gold that came to Solomon
1Ch 21:25 of gold by w for the site.
28:14 w of gold for all golden vessels for each service,
28:14 the w of silver vessels for each service,
28:15 the w of the golden lampstands and their lamps,
28:15 the w of gold for each lampstand and its lamps,
28:15 the w of silver for a lampstand and its lamps,
28:16 the w of gold for each table for the rows of bread,
28:17 for the golden bowls and the w of each;
28:17 for the silver bowls and the w of each;
28:18 of incense made of refined gold, and its w;
2Ch 3: 9 The w of the nails was fifty shekels of gold.
4:18 so that the w of the bronze was not determined.
9:13 The w of gold that came to Solomon
Ezr 8:34 and the w of everything was recorded.
Job 28:25 When he gave to the wind its w,
Pr 11: 1 but an accurate w is his delight.
Isa 22:24 on him the whole w of his ancestral house,
Jer 15:17 under the w of your hand I sat alone,
La 4: 2 worth their w in fine gold—
Eze 4:10 that you eat shall be twenty shekels a day by w;
4:16 they shall eat bread by w and with fearfulness;
Zec 5: 8 and pressed the leaden w down on its mouth.
2Co 4:17 for an eternal w of glory beyond all measure,
Heb 12: 1 let us also lay aside every w and the sin that clings
Jdt 7: 4 nor the valleys nor the hills will bear their w."
Wis 11:20 by measure and number and w.
Sir 13: 2 Do not lift a w too heavy for you,
1Es 8:64 the w of everything was recorded at that very time.
2Es 4: 5 he said to me, "Go, weigh for me the w of fire,

WEIGHTED (1) [WEIGH]

Man 1:10 I am w down with many an iron fetter,

WEIGHTIER (1) [WEIGH]

Mt 23:23 and have neglected the w matters of the law:

WEIGHTS (8) [WEIGH]

Ge 23:16 according to the w current among the merchants.
Lev 19:36 You shall have honest balances, honest w,
Dt 25:13 You shall not have in your bag two kinds of w,
Pr 16:11 all the w in the bag are his work.
20:10 Diverse w and diverse measures are both alike
20:23 Differing w are an abomination to the LORD,
Mic 6:11 and a bag of dishonest w?
Sir 42: 4 with scales and w, and of acquiring much or little;

WEIGHTY (4) [WEIGH]

Ps 139:17 How w to me are your thoughts, O God!
Pr 27: 3 A stone is heavy, and sand is w,
2Co 10:10 For they say, "His letters are w and strong,
2Es 13:56 and explain w and wondrous matters to you."

WELCOME (36) [WELCOMED, WELCOMES, WELCOMING]

Mt 10:14 If anyone will not w you or listen to your words,
25:43 I was a stranger and you did not w me,
Mk 6:11 If any place will not w you and they refuse
Lk 9: 5 Wherever they do not w you,
10: 8 Whenever you enter a town and its people w you,

Lk 10:10 whenever you enter a town and they do not w you,
16: 4 people may w me into their homes.'
16: 9 they may w you into the eternal homes.
19: 6 So he hurried down and was happy to w him.
Ac 18:27 and wrote to the disciples to w him.
24: 3 We w this in every way and everywhere
25:13 and Bernice arrived at Caesarea to w Festus.
Ro 14: 1 W those who are weak in faith,
15: 7 W one another, therefore, just
16: 2 so that you may w her in the Lord as is fitting for
2Co 6:17 and touch nothing unclean; then I will w you,
Php 2:29 W him then in the Lord with all joy,
Col 4:10 if he comes to you, w him.
1Th 1: 9 about us what kind of w we had among you,
Phm 1:17 w him as you would w me.
Jas 1:21 and w with meekness the implanted word that has
2Jn 1:10 the house or w anyone who comes to you and does
1:11 for to w is to participate in the evil deeds of such
3Jn 1:10 he refuses to w the friends,
Tob 5:14 Then Tobit said to him, **"W!**
5:14 you come of good stock. Hearty **w!"**
7: 1 brothers; w and good health!"
11:17 "Come in, my daughter, and w.
11:17 Come in now to your home, and w,
Sir 15: 2 and like a young bride she will w him.
35:26 as w in time of distress as clouds of rain in time
40:23 A friend or companion is always w,
41: 2 how w is your sentence to one who is needy
3Mc 1: 8 to bring him gifts of w,
4Mc 13:17 we so die, Abraham and Isaac and Jacob will w us,

WELCOMED (25) [WELCOME]

2Ki 20:13 Hezekiah w them; he showed them all his treasure
Isa 39: 2 Hezekiah w them; he showed them his treasure
Mt 25:35 I was a stranger and you w me,
25:38 when was it that we saw you a stranger and w you,
Lk 8:40 Now when Jesus returned, the crowd w him,
9:11 and he w them, and spoke to them about
10:38 a woman named Martha w him into her home.
Jn 4:45 When he came to Galilee, the Galileans w him,
Ac 2:41 So those who w his message were baptized,
15: 4 they were w by the church and the apostles and
17:11 for they w the message very eagerly and examined
21:17 we arrived in Jerusalem, the brothers w us warmly.
28: 2 they kindled a fire and w all of us around it.
28:30 at his own expense and w all who came to him,
Ro 14: 3 judgment on those who eat; for God has w them.
15: 7 just as Christ has w you, for the glory of God.
2Co 7:15 and how you w him with fear and trembling.
Gal 4:14 but w me as an angel of God, as Christ Jesus.
Jas 2:25 also justified by works when she w the messengers
Jdt 3: 7 in the countryside w him with garlands and dances
13:13 They opened the gate and w them.
1Mc 10: 1 They w him, and there he began to reign.
12: 8 Onias w the envoy with honor,
2Mc 3: 9 and had been kindly w by the high priest of
4:22 He was w magnificently by Jason and the city,

WELCOMES (17) [WELCOME]

Mt 10:40 "Whoever w you w me, and whoever w me w the
one who sent me.
10:41 Whoever w a prophet in the name of a prophet
10:41 and whoever w a righteous person in the name of
18: 5 Whoever w one such child in my name w me.
Mk 9:37 "Whoever w one such child in my name w me,
and whoever w me w not me but the one who sent
Lk 9:48 "Whoever w this child in my name w me, and
whoever w me w the one who sent me;
15: 2 "This fellow w sinners and eats with them."

WELCOMING (1) [WELCOME]

2Mc 6:19 w death with honor rather than life with pollution,

WELFARE (20)

Ge 43:27 He inquired about their w, and said,
Ex 18: 7 each asked after the other's w,
Dt 23: 6 You shall never promote their w or their prosperity
Ne 2:10 that someone had come to seek the w of the people
Est 10: 3 the good of his people and interceded for the w
Ps 35:27 who delights in the w of his servant."
Pr 3: 2 of life and abundant w they will give you.
Isa 38:17 Surely it was for my w that I had great bitterness;
Jer 14:11 Do not pray for the w of this people.
15: 5 Who will turn aside to ask about your w?
29: 7 the w of the city where I have sent you into exile,
29: 7 for in its w you will find your w.
29:11 plans for your w and not for harm,
38: 4 For this man is not seeking the w of this people,
Php 2:20 be genuinely concerned for your w.
1Mc 12:22 please write us concerning your w;
2Mc 4: 5 accusing his compatriots but having in view the w,
11:19 in the future to help promote your w.
13: 3 not for the sake of his country's w,

WELL‡ (348) [WELL'S, WELLED, WELLING, WELLS]

Ge 4: 7 If you do w, will you not be accepted?
4: 7 And if you do not do w, sin is lurking at the door;
12:11 "I know w that you are a woman beautiful
12:13 so that it may go w with me because of you,
12:16 And for her sake he dealt w with Abram;
13:10 the plain of the Jordan was w watered everywhere
16:14 Therefore the w was called Beer-lahai-roi;
19:21 "Very w, I grant you this favor too,
21:19 God opened her eyes and she saw a w of water.
21:25 a w of water that Abimelech's servants had seized,
21:30 you may be a witness for me that I dug this **w."**
24: 1 Now Abraham was old, w advanced in years;
24:11 the camels kneel down outside the city by the w
24:20 into the trough and ran again to the w to draw,
26:19 in the valley and found there a w of spring water,
26:20 So he called the w Esek,
26:21 Then they dug another **w,** and they quarreled over
26:22 He moved from there and dug another **w,**
26:25 And there Isaac's servants dug a **w.**
26:32 and told him about the w that they had dug,
29: 2 he saw a w in the field and three flocks
29: 2 for out of that w the flocks were watered.
29: 3 the stone from the mouth of the **w,**
29: 3 the stone back in its place on the mouth of the **w.**
29: 6 He said to them, "Is it w with him?"
29: 8 and the stone is rolled from the mouth of the **w;**
30:26 you know very w the service I have given you."
37:14 see if it is w with your brothers and with the flock;
40:14 But remember me when it is w with you;
43:15 and they took double the money with them, as w
43:27 and said, "Is your father w,
43:28 They said, "Your servant our father is w;
45:10 as w as your flocks, your herds,
48:10 and he could not see w.
50: 8 as w as all the household of Joseph,
Ex 1:20 So God dealt w with the midwives;
2:15 and sat down by a **w.**
5: 6 of the people, as w as their supervisors,
9:11 for the boils afflicted the magicians as w as all
19:16 as w as a thick cloud on the mountain,
29:21 as w as his sons and his sons' vestments.
Lev 4:11 skin of the bull and all its flesh, as w as its head,
6:21 you shall bring it w soaked,
7:12 and cakes of choice flour w soaked in oil.
10:14 and daughters as w may eat in any clean place;
21:22 of the most holy as w as of the holy.
24:16 Aliens as w as citizens, when they blaspheme
Nu 10:29 come with us, and we will treat you **w;**
13:30 for we are w able to overcome it."
15:26 as w as the aliens residing among them,
16:10 yet you seek the priesthood as **w!**
18:19 the LORD for you and your descendants as **w.**
20:17 or drink water from any **w;**
21:16 that is the w of which the LORD said to Moses,
21:17 Then Israel sang this song: "Spring up, O **w!—**
21:18 the w that the leaders sank,
21:22 we will not drink the water of any **w;**
Dt 1: 7 and go into the hill country of the Amorites as w as
2:35 as w as the plunder of the towns
2:37 the whole upper region of the Wadi Jabbok as w as
3:12 w as half the hill country of Gilead with its towns,
3:21 And I charged Joshua as w at that time, saying:
3:27 Look w, for you shall not cross over this Jordan.
5:14 your male and female slave may rest as w as you.
5:16 so that your days may be long and that it may go w
5:29 so that it might go w with them and
5:33 and that it may go w with you,
6: 3 so that it may go w with you,
6:18 so that it may go w with you,
12:25 all may go w with you and your children after you,
12:28 that it may go w with you and with your children
14:23 as w as the firstlings of your herd and flock,
14:29 as w as the resident aliens, the orphans,
15:16 since he is w off with you,
16:11 as w as the strangers, the orphans,
16:14 your male and female slaves, as w as the Levites,
18: 4 as w as the first of the fleece of your sheep,
19:13 so that it may go w with you.
22: 7 that it may go w with you and you may live long.
22:22 man who lay with the woman as w as the woman.
29:22 as w as the foreigner who comes from
31:12 as w as the aliens residing in your towns—
31:27 For I know w how rebellious and stubborn you are.
Jos 1:15 until the LORD gives rest to your kindred as w as
8:33 All Israel, alien as w as citizen,
15:19 give me springs of water as **w."**
23: 1 and Joshua was old and w advanced in years,
23: 2 "I am now old and w advanced in years;
Jdg 8: 7 **"W** then, when the LORD has given Zebah
9:16 if you have dealt w with Jerubbaal and his house,
15: 5 as w as the vineyards and olive groves.
20:31 as w as in the open country,
Ru 1:17 and more as w, if even death parts me from you!"
3: 1 so that it may be w with you.
1Sa 12:14 the LORD your God, it will be **w;**
16:17 "Provide for me someone who can play w,
18:26 David was w pleased to be the king's son-in-law.
19: 4 Jonathan spoke w of David to his father Saul,
19:22 He came to the great w that is in Secu;
20: 3 "Your father knows w that you like me;
20: 7 it will be w with your servant;
20:12 if he is w disposed toward David,
24:18 Today you have explained how you have dealt w
25:31 And when the LORD has dealt w with my lord,
28: 2 David said to Achish, "Very w,
28: 2 Achish said to David, "Very w,
29:10 for you have done w before me.
2Sa 10: 6 as w as the king of Maacah, one thousand men,
11:17 Uriah the Hittite was killed as **w.**
14: 7 even if we destroy the heir as **w.'**
14:21 Then the king said to Joab, "Very w, I grant this;
17:18 who had a w in his courtyard;
17:21 they had gone, the men came up out of the **w,**
18:28 Then Ahimaaz cried out to the king, "All is **w!"**
18:29 king said, "Is it w with the young man Absalom?"
2Sa 18:32 "Is it w with the young man Absalom?"
20: 9 Joab said to Amasa, "Is it w with you,
23:15 from the w of Bethlehem that is by the gate!"
23:16 drew water from the w of Bethlehem that was by
1Ki 2:18 Bathsheba said, "Very **w;**
2:22 Ask for him the kingdom as **w!**
8:18 'You did w to consider building a house
9:19 as w as all of Solomon's storage cities,
10:13 as w as what he gave her out of Solomon's royal
11:41 all that he did as w as his wisdom,
12:26 the kingdom may w revert to the house of David.
17:15 as w as he and her household ate for many days.
18:24 All the people answered, **"W** spoken!"
20:22 and consider w what you have to do;
2Ki 4:14 Gehazi answered, **"W,** she has no son,
10:30 "Because you have done w
12:12 as w as to buy timber and quarried stone
12:12 as w as for any outlay for repairs of the house.
12:18 had dedicated, as w as his own votive gifts,
13:12 as w as the might with which he fought
14:14 as w as hostages; then he returned to Samaria.
25:13 as w as the stands and the bronze sea that were in
25:15 as w as the firepans and the basins.
25:24 and it shall be w with you."
1Ch 11:17 from the w of Bethlehem that is by the gate!"
11:18 and drew water from the w of Bethlehem that was
22: 3 as w as bronze in quantities beyond weighing,
24:31 the chief as w as the youngest brother.
26:17 as w as two and two at the storehouse;
2Ch 6: 8 'You did w to consider building a house
8: 6 as w as all Solomon's storage towns,
9:12 w beyond what she had brought to the king.
Est 3:11 "The money is given to you, and the people as w,
Job 1:12 The LORD said to Satan, "Very w,
2: 6 The LORD said to Satan, "Very w,
12: 3 But I have understanding as w as you;
13: 9 Will it be w with you when he searches you out?
Ps 48:13 consider w its ramparts; go through its citadels,
49:18 —for you are praised when you do w
75: 8 a cup with foaming wine, w mixed;
78:29 And they ate and were w filled,
112: 5 It is w with those who deal generously and lend,
119:65 You have dealt w with your servant, O LORD,
119:140 Your promise is w tried, and your servant loves it.
128: 2 you shall be happy, and it shall go w with you.
139:14 Wonderful are your works; that I know very **w.**
Pr 5:15 flowing water from your own **w.**
11:10 it goes w with the righteous, the city rejoices;
23:27 prostitute is a deep pit; an adulteress is a narrow **w.**
27: 6 **W** meant are the wounds a friend inflicts,
27:23 Know w the condition of your flocks,
31:27 She looks w to the ways of her household,
Ecc 3:16 wickedness was there as **w.**
7:14 God has made the one as w as the other,
8:12 I know that it will be w with those who fear God,
8:13 but it will not be w with the wicked,
SS 4:15 a w of living water, and flowing streams
7:13 new as w as old, which I have laid up for you,
Isa 7:20 and it will take off the beard as **w.**
28:26 For they are w instructed; their God teaches them.
44:18 so that they cannot see, and their minds as **w,**
65:23 and their descendants as **w.**
Jer 1:12 Then the LORD said to me, "You have seen **w,**
2:33 How w you direct your course to seek lovers!
4:10 saying, 'It shall be w with you,'
6: 7 As a w keeps its water fresh,
6:11 and on the gatherings of young men as **w;**
7:23 so that it may be w with you."
22:15 Then it was w with him.
22:16 of the poor and needy; then it was **w.**
23:17 "It shall be w with you";
31:21 consider w the highway, the road by which you
38:20 and it shall go w with you,
39:12 look after him w and do him no harm,
40: 9 and it shall go w with you.
42: 4 The prophet Jeremiah said to them, "Very **w:**
42: 6 that it may go w with us when we obey the voice
42:19 Be w aware that I have warned you today
42:22 Be w aware, then, that you shall die by the sword,
La 3:41 up our hearts as w as our hands to God in heaven.
Eze 18: 4 of the parent as w as the life of the child is mine:
24:10 Heap up the logs, kindle the fire; boil the meat **w,**
31:16 and best of Lebanon, all that were w watered,
33:32 a beautiful voice and plays w on an instrument;
44: 5 The LORD said to me: Mortal, mark w,
44: 5 and mark w those who may be admitted to
Da 1: 2 as w as some of the vessels of the house of God.
3:15 down and worship the statue that I have made, w
11:22 and the prince of the covenant as **w.**
Am 3:15 down the winter house as w as the summer house;
Na 2: 2 as w as the majesty of Israel,
Mal 2:13 And this you do as **w:**
Mt 3:17 the Beloved, with whom I am w pleased."
5:40 and take your coat, give your cloak as **w;**
6:33 and all these things will be given to you as **w.**
9:12 "Those who are w have no need of a physician,
9:21 "If I only touch his cloak, I will be made **w."**
9:22 your faith has made you **w."**
9:22 And instantly the woman was made **w.**
12:18 my beloved, with whom my soul is w pleased.
13:26 then the weeds appeared as **w.**
17: 5 with him I am w pleased; listen to him!"
25:21 His master said to him, **'W** done,
25:23 His master said to him, **'W** done,
Mk 1:11 with you I am w pleased."
2:17 "Those who are w have no need of a physician,
5:23 so that she may be made **w,** and live."

Mk 5:28 "If I but touch his clothes, I will be made **w**."
5:34 "Daughter, your faith has made you **w**;
7:37 saying, "He has done everything **w**;
10:52 said to him, "Go; your faith has made you **w**."
12:28 and seeing that he answered them **w**,
Lk 3:22 with you I am **w** pleased."
4:22 All spoke **w** of him and were amazed at
5:31 "Those who are **w** have no need of a physician,
6:26 "Woe to you when all speak **w** of you,
6:48 because it had been **w** built.
8: 2 as **w** as some women who had been cured
8:48 your faith has made you **w**; go in peace."
12:31 and these things will be given to you as **w**.
13: 9 If it bears fruit next year, **w** and good;
14: 5 of you has a child or an ox that has fallen into a **w**,
17:19 your faith has made you **w**."
19:17 He said to him, '**W** done, good slave!
20:39 "Teacher, you have spoken **w**."
Jn 4: 6 Jacob's **w** was there, and Jesus,
4: 6 tired out by his journey, was sitting by the **w**.
4:11 "Sir, you have no bucket, and the **w** is deep.
4:12 the **w**, and with his sons and his flocks drank
5: 6 he said to him, "Do you want to be made **w**?"
5: 9 At once the man was made **w**,
5:11 "The man who made me **w** said to me,
5:14 "See, you have been made **w**!
5:15 the Jews that it was Jesus who had made him **w**.
12:10 chief priests planned to put Lazarus to death as **w**,
Ac 1:14 the mother of Jesus, as **w** as his brothers.
6:12 They stirred up the people as **w** as the elders and
7:15 He himself died there as **w** as our ancestors,
10:22 who is **w** spoken of by the whole Jewish nation,
15:29 If you keep yourselves from these, you will do **w**.
16: 2 He was **w** spoken of by the believers in Lystra
17:13 by Paul in Beroea as **w**,
20: 4 as **w** as by Tychicus and Trophimus from Asia.
22:12 a devout man according to the law and **w** spoken
24:22 Felix, who was rather **w** informed about the Way,
25:10 to the Jews, as you very **w** know.
Ro 16: 2 a benefactor of many and of myself as **w**.
1Co 7: 1 "It is **w** for a man not to touch a woman."
7: 8 To the unmarried and the widows I say that it is **w**
7:26 it is **w** for you to remain as you are.
7:37 to keep her as his fiancée, he will do **w**.
7:38 So then, he who marries his fiancée does **w**;
14:17 For you may give thanks **w** enough,
16:18 for they refreshed my spirit as **w** as yours.
2Co 5:11 but we ourselves are **w** known to God,
5:11 that we are also **w** known to your consciences.
6: 9 as unknown, and yet are **w** known;
7:14 so our boasting to Titus has proved true as **w**.
Gal 3: 5 **W** then, does God supply you with the Spirit
5: 7 You were running **w**; who prevented you from
Eph 6: 3 that it may be **w** with you and you may live long
Php 1:29 but of suffering for him as **w**—
Col 4: 3 as **w** that God will open to us a door for the word,
1Th 5: 2 For you yourselves know very **w** that the day of
2Th 1: 7 and to give relief to the afflicted as **w** as to us,
1Ti 3: 4 He must manage his own household **w**,
3: 7 Moreover, he must be **w** thought of by outsiders,
3:12 manage their children and their households **w**;
3:13 for those who serve **w** as deacons gain
5: 7 Give these commands as **w**,
5:10 she must be **w** attested for her good works,
5:17 Let the elders who rule **w** be considered worthy
2Ti 1:18 And you know very **w** how much service
2: 2 who will be able to teach others as **w**.
Heb 5: 3 of this he must offer sacrifice for his own sins as **w**
7:12 there is necessarily a change in the law as **w**.
13: 9 for it is **w** for the heart to be strengthened by grace,
Jas 2: 8 You do **w** if you really fulfill the royal law
2:19 You believe that God is one; you do **w**.
1Pe 5: 1 as **w** as one who shares in the glory to be revealed,
2Pe 1:17 my Beloved, with whom I am **w** pleased."
1:19 You will do **w** to be attentive to this as to
3Jn 1: 2 I pray that all may go **w** with you and that you may
1: 2 just as it is **w** with your soul.
1: 6 You will do **w** to send them on in a manner worthy
Tob 5:15 as **w** as expenses for yourself and my son.
8:21 and we belong to you as **w** as to your wife now
10:10 as **w** as half of all his property:
12: 1 and give him a bonus as **w**."
Jdt 10:16 and he will treat you **w**."
11: 4 Rather, all will treat you **w**,
11:22 "God has done **w** to send you ahead of the people,
15: 8 and to see Judith and to wish her **w**.
15:10 and God is **w** pleased with it.
AdE 2: 9 as **w** as seven maids chosen from the palace;
10: 3 as **w** as honored by the Jews.
16:17 "You will therefore do **w** not to put in execution
Wis 8: 1 and she orders all things **w**.
Sir 10: 1 and the rule of an intelligent person is **w** ordered.
14:11 My child, treat yourself **w**,
17:28 those who are alive and **w** sing the Lord's praises.
31:16 before you like a **w** brought-up person,
38:27 and master artisan who labors by night as **w** as
40:29 but one who is intelligent and **w** instructed guards
Sus 1:55 And Daniel said, "Very **w**!
1:59 Daniel said to him, "Very **w**!
1Mc 8:15 concerning the people, to govern them **w**.
8:23 "May all go **w** with the Romans and with
11:43 you will do **w** to send me men who will help me,
12:45 over to you as **w** as the other strongholds and
16:16 as **w** as some of his servants.
2Mc 9:20 If you and your children are **w** and your affairs are
10:18 in two very strong towers **w** equipped to withstand
10:32 stronghold called Gazara, especially **w** garrisoned,
11:26 You will do **w**, therefore, to send word to them
11:28 If you are **w**, it is as we desire.
12: 2 as **w** as Hieronymus and Demophon,
12:31 and exhorted them to be **w** disposed to their race in
12:43 In doing this he acted very **w** and honorably,
14:37 and was very **w** thought of and
15:38 If it is **w** told and to the point,
3Mc 3:13 "I myself and our government are faring **w**.
3:15 and great benevolence, gladly treating them **w**.
4:11 and that was **w** suited to make them
5:48 as **w** as by the trampling of the crowd,
7: 2 "We ourselves and our children are faring **w**,
2Es 3:35 what nation has kept your commandments so **w**?
7:*111* [41] why will it not be so then as **w**?"
8:58 though they knew **w** that they must die.
9:36 as **w** as our hearts that received it;
14:12 as **w** as half of the tenth part;
4Mc 10: 2 the same father begot me as **w** as those who died,
14:14 Even unreasoning animals, as **w** as human beings,

WELL'S (3) [WELL]

Ge 29: 2 The stone on the **w** mouth was large,
29:10 up and rolled the stone from the **w** mouth,
2Sa 17:19 stretched it over the **w** mouth,

WELL-AGED (2) [AGE]

Isa 25: 6 a feast of **w** wines, of rich food filled with
marrow, of **w** wines strained clear.

WELL-BEING (94) [BE]

Ex 20:24 on it your burnt offerings and your offerings of **w**,
24: 5 and sacrificed oxen as offerings of **w** to
29:28 the Israelites from their sacrifice of offerings of **w**,
32: 6 and brought sacrifices of **w**;
Lev 3: 1 If the offering is a sacrifice of **w**,
3: 3 You shall offer from the sacrifice of **w**,
3: 6 for a sacrifice of **w** to the LORD is from the flock,
3: 9 You shall present its fat from the sacrifice of **w**,
4:10 from the ox of the sacrifice of **w**.
4:26 like the fat of the sacrifice of **w**.
4:31 as the fat is removed from the offering of **w**,
4:35 fat of the sheep is removed from the sacrifice of **w**,
6:12 into smoke the fat pieces of the offerings of **w**.
7:11 the offering of **w** that one may offer to the LORD.
7:13 of **w** you shall bring your offering with cakes
7:14 the blood of the offering of **w**.
7:15 the flesh of your thanksgiving sacrifice of **w** shall
7:18 If any of the flesh of your sacrifice of **w** is eaten on
7:20 of **w** while in a state of uncleanness shall be cut off
7:21 then eats flesh from the LORD's sacrifice of **w**,
7:29 the LORD your sacrifice of **w** must yourself bring
7:29 the LORD your offering from your sacrifice of **w**.
7:32 of **w** you shall give to the priest as an offering;
7:33 of the offering of **w** shall have the right thigh for
7:34 from their sacrifices of **w**,
7:37 the offering of ordination, and the sacrifice of **w**,
9: 4 for an offering of **w** to sacrifice before the LORD;
9:18 and the ram as a sacrifice of **w** for the people.
9:22 the burnt offering, and the offering of **w**.
10:14 the sacrifices of the offerings of **w** of the people
17: 5 and offer them as sacrifices of **w** to the LORD.
19: 5 When you offer a sacrifice of **w** to the LORD,
22:21 anyone offers a sacrifice of **w** to the LORD,
23:19 and two male lambs a year old as a sacrifice of **w**.
Nu 6:14 one ram without blemish as an offering of **w**,
6:17 as a sacrifice of **w** to the LORD, with the basket
6:18 and put it on the fire under the sacrifice of **w**.
7:17 and for the sacrifice of **w**,
7:23 and for the sacrifice of **w**,
7:29 and for the sacrifice of **w**,
7:35 and for the sacrifice of **w**,
7:41 and for the sacrifice of **w**,
7:47 and for the sacrifice of **w**,
7:53 and for the sacrifice of **w**,
7:59 and for the sacrifice of **w**,
7:65 and for the sacrifice of **w**,
7:71 and for the sacrifice of **w**,
7:77 and for the sacrifice of **w**,
7:83 and for the sacrifice of **w**,
7:88 for the sacrifice of **w** twenty-four bulls,
10:10 and over your sacrifices of **w**;
15: 8 a vow or as an offering of **w** to the LORD,
29:39 your drink offerings, and your offerings of **w**.
Dt 4:40 for your own **w** and that of your descendants
10:13 that I am commanding you today, for your own **w**.
27: 7 make sacrifices of **w**, and eat them there, rejoicing
Jos 8:31 and sacrificed offerings of **w**.
22:23 or grain offerings or offerings of **w** on it,
22:27 and sacrifices and offerings of **w**;
Jdg 20:26 and sacrifices of **w** before the LORD.
21: 4 and offered burnt offerings and sacrifices of **w**.
1Sa 10: 8 to present burnt offerings and offer sacrifices of **w**.
11:15 There they sacrificed offerings of **w** before
13: 9 to me, and the offerings of **w**."
2Sa 6:17 and offerings of **w** before the LORD.
6:18 the burnt offerings and the offerings of **w**,
24:25 and offered burnt offerings and offerings of **w**.
1Ki 3:15 He offered up burnt offerings and offerings of **w**,
8:63 of **w** to the LORD twenty-two thousand oxen
8:64 and the fat pieces of the sacrifices of **w**,
8:64 and the fat pieces of the sacrifices of **w**.
9:25 up burnt offerings and sacrifices of **w** on the altar
2Ki 16:13 and dashed the blood of his offerings of **w** against
1Ch 16: 1 and they offered burnt offerings and offerings of **w**
16: 2 and the offerings of **w**, he blessed the people in
21:26 and presented burnt offerings and offerings of **w**.
2Ch 7: 7 the burnt offerings and the fat of the offerings of **w**
29:35 the fat of the offerings of **w**,
30:22 sacrificing offerings of **w** and giving thanks to
31: 2 for burnt offerings and offerings of **w**,
33:16 of the LORD and offered on it sacrifices of **w** and
Ps 119:122 Guarantee your servant's **w**;
Eze 43:27 altar your burnt offerings and your offerings of **w**;
45:15 and offerings of **w**, to make atonement for them,
45:17 the burnt offerings, and the offerings of **w**,
46: 2 and his offerings of **w**, and he shall bow down at
46:12 either a burnt offering or offerings of **w** as
46:12 or his offerings of **w** as he does on the sabbath day.
Am 5:22 and the offerings of **w** of your fatted animals I will
Mal 2: 5 a covenant of life and **w**, which I gave him;
AdE 9:31 pledging their own **w** to the plan.
Sir 35: 2 the commandments makes an offering of **w**.
47: 2 As the fat is set apart from the offering of **w**,
1Mc 4:56 a sacrifice of **w** and a thanksgiving offering.

WELL-DISCIPLINED (1) [DISCIPLINE]

Sir 31:19 How ample a little is for a **w** person!

WELL-DISPOSED (1) [DISPOSED]

1Mc 8: 1 and were **w** toward all who made an alliance

WELL-DRAWN (1) [DRAW]

Wis 5:21 from the clouds to the target, as from a **w** bow,

WELL-FED (2) [FEED]

Jer 5: 8 They were **w** lusty stallions,
Php 4:12 the secret of being **w** and of going hungry,

WELL-FORTIFIED (1) [FORT]

Da 11:15 and throw up siegeworks, and take a **w** city.

WELL-KNOWN (1) [KNOW]

Nu 16: 2 **w** men, and they confronted Moses.

WELL-ORDERED (1) [ORDER]

Sir 26:16 so is the beauty of a good wife in her **w** home.

WELL-PLEASING See Index to Footnotes

WELL-SET (1) [SET]

Isa 3:24 and instead of **w** hair, baldness;

WELL-VERSED (1) [VERSED]

Ac 18:24 He was an eloquent man, **w** in the scriptures.

WELLBELOVED (KJV) See BELOVED

WELLED (1) [WELL]

2Es 3: 1 and my thoughts **w** up in my heart,

WELLING (1) [WELL]

Dt 8: 7 and underground waters **w** up in valleys and hills,

WELLPLEASING (KJV) See PLEASING

WELLS‡ (5) [WELL]

Ge 26:15 the **w** that his father's servants had dug in the days
26:18 Isaac dug again the **w** of water that had been dug
2Ki 19:24 I dug **w** and drank foreign waters,
Isa 12: 3 With joy you will draw water from the **w**
37:25 I dug **w** and drank waters,

WELT (1)

Sir 28:17 The blow of a whip raises a **w**,

WEN (KJV) See DISCHARGE

WENCH (KJV) See SERVANT GIRL

WENT‡ (1428) [GO]

Ge 4:16 Cain **w** away from the presence of the LORD,
6: 4 the sons of God **w** in to the daughters of humans,
7: 7 with his sons and his wife and his sons' wives **w**
7: 9 male and female, **w** into the ark with Noah,
7:15 They **w** into the ark with Noah,
7:16 **w** in as God had commanded him;
8: 7 and it **w** to and fro until the waters were dried up
8:18 So Noah **w** out with his sons and his wife
8:19 **w** out of the ark by families.
9:18 sons of Noah who **w** out of the ark were Shem,
10:11 From that land he **w** into Assyria,
11:31 and they **w** out together from Ur of the Chaldeans
12: 4 So Abram **w**, as the LORD had told him; and Lot **w**
with him.
12:10 Abram **w** down to Egypt to reside there as an alien,
13: 1 So Abram **w** up from Egypt, he and his wife,
13: 5 Now Lot, who **w** with Abram,
14: 8 and the king of Bela (that is, Zoar) **w** out,
14:11 and all their provisions, and **w** their way;
14:14 and **w** in pursuit as far as Dan.
14:17 the king of Sodom **w** out to meet him at the Valley
14:24 and the share of the men who **w** with me—
16: 4 He **w** in to Hagar, and she conceived;

Ge 17:22 when he had finished talking with him, God **w** up
18:16 Abraham **w** with them to set them on their way.
18:22 the men turned from there, and **w** toward Sodom,
18:33 And the LORD **w** his way,
19: 6 Lot **w** out of the door to the men,
19:14 So Lot **w** out and said to his sons-in-law,
19:27 Abraham **w** early in the morning to the place
19:30 Now Lot **w** up out of Zoar and settled in the hills
19:33 and the firstborn **w** in, and lay with her father;
21:16 she **w** and sat down opposite him a good way off,
21:19 She **w**, and filled the skin with water,
22: 3 the burnt offering, and set out and **w** to the place in
22:13 Abraham **w** and took the ram and offered it up as
22:19 and they arose and **w** together to Beer-sheba;
23: 2 and Abraham **w** in to mourn for Sarah and to weep
23:10 of all who **w** in at the gate of his city,
23:18 the presence of all who **w** in at the gate of his city.
24:10 and he set out and **w** to Aram-naharaim,
24:16 She **w** down to the spring, filled her jar,
24:30 "Thus the man spoke to me," he **w** to the man;
24:45 and she **w** down to the spring, and drew.
24:61 thus the servant took Rebekah, and **w** his way.
24:63 Isaac **w** out in the evening to walk in the field;
25:22 So she **w** to inquire of the LORD.
25:34 and he ate and drank, and rose and **w** his way.
26: 1 And Isaac **w** to Gerar, to King Abimelech of
26:23 From there he **w** up to Beer-sheba.
26:26 Then Abimelech **w** to him from Gerar,
27: 5 Esau **w** to the field to hunt for game and bring it,
27:14 he **w** and got them and brought them to his mother;
27:18 So he **w** in to his father, and said, "My father";
27:22 So Jacob **w** up to his father Isaac,
28: 5 and he **w** to Paddan-aram,
28: 9 Esau **w** to Ishmael and took Mahalath daughter
28:10 Jacob left Beer-sheba and **w** toward Haran.
29: 1 Then Jacob **w** on his journey,
29:10 Jacob **w** up and rolled the stone from
29:23 and he **w** in to her.
29:30 So Jacob **w** in to Rachel also,
30: 4 and Jacob **w** in to her.
30:14 of wheat harvest Reuben **w** and found mandrakes
30:16 Leah **w** out to meet him, and said,
31:33 So Laban **w** into Jacob's tent, and into Leah's tent,
31:33 And he **w** out of Leah's tent, and entered Rachel's.
32: 1 Jacob **w** on his way and the angels
33: 3 He himself **w** on ahead of them,
34: 1 **w** out to visit the women of the region.
34: 6 And Hamor the father of Shechem **w** out to Jacob
34:24 And all who **w** out of the city gate heeded Hamor
34:24 all who **w** out of the gate of his city.
34:26 of Shechem's house, and **w** away.
35:13 Then God **w** up from him at the place
35:22 While Israel lived in that land, Reuben **w** and lay
37:12 Now his brothers **w** to pasture their father's flock
37:17 So Joseph **w** after his brothers,
38: 1 at that time that Judah **w** down from his brothers
38: 2 he married her and **w** in to her.
38: 9 the ground whenever he **w** in to his brother's wife,
38:11 So Tamar **w** to live in her father's house.
38:12 he **w** up to Timnah to his sheepshearers,
38:16 He **w** over to her at the road side, and said, "Come,
38:18 So he gave them to her, and **w** in to her,
38:19 Then she got up and **w** away,
39:11 however, when he **w** into the house to do his work,
41:46 And Joseph **w** out from the presence of Pharaoh,
41:46 and **w** through all the land of Egypt.
42: 3 of Joseph's brothers **w** down to buy grain in Egypt.
43:15 Then they **w** on their way down to Egypt,
43:19 So they **w** up to the steward of Joseph's house
43:30 So he **w** into a private room and wept there.
44:24 When we **w** back to your servant my father
45:25 So they **w** up out of Egypt and came
46:29 and **w** up to meet his father Israel in Goshen.
47: 1 So Joseph **w** and told Pharaoh,
47:10 and **w** out from the presence of Pharaoh.
49: 4 because you **w** up onto your father's bed;
49: 4 you **w** up onto my couch!
50: 7 So Joseph **w** up to bury his father.
50: 7 With him **w** up all the servants of Pharaoh,
50: 9 Both chariots and charioteers **w** up with him.
Ex 2: 1 Now a man from the house of Levi **w** and married
2: 8 So the girl **w** and called the child's mother.
2:11 he **w** out to his people and saw their forced labor.
2:13 When he **w** out the next day,
4:18 Moses **w** back to his father-in-law Jethro and said
4:20 on a donkey and **w** back to the land of Egypt;
4:27 So he **w**; and he met him at the mountain of God
4:29 and Aaron **w** and assembled all the elders of
5: 1 Afterward Moses and Aaron **w** to Pharaoh
5:10 and the supervisors of the people **w** out and said to
7:10 So Moses and Aaron **w** to Pharaoh and did as
7:23 Pharaoh turned and **w** into his house,
8:12 Then Moses and Aaron **w** out from Pharaoh;
8:30 So Moses **w** out from Pharaoh and prayed to
9:33 So Moses left Pharaoh, **w** out of the city,
10: 3 So Moses and Aaron **w** to Pharaoh,
10: 6 Then he turned and **w** out from Pharaoh.
10:18 he **w** out from Pharaoh and prayed to the LORD.
12:28 The Israelites **w** and did just as
12:38 A mixed crowd also **w** up with them,
12:41 the companies of the LORD **w** out from the land
13:18 The Israelites **w** up out of the land
13:21 The LORD **w** in front of them in a pillar of cloud
14:19 the Israelite army moved and **w** behind them;
14:22 The Israelites **w** into the sea on dry ground,
14:23 Egyptians pursued, and **w** into the sea after them,
15: 5 they **w** down into the depths like a stone.
Ex 15:19 with his chariots and his chariot drivers **w** into
15:20 the women **w** out after her with tambourines and
15:22 and they **w** into the wilderness of Shur.
15:22 They **w** three days in the wilderness
16:27 On the seventh day some of the people **w** out
17:10 Aaron, and Hur **w** up to the top of the hill.
18: 7 Moses **w** out to meet his father-in-law;
18: 7 after the other's welfare, and they **w** into the tent.
18:27 and he **w** off to his own country.
19: 3 Then Moses **w** up to God;
19:14 Moses **w** down from the mountain to the people.
19:18 the smoke **w** up like the smoke of a kiln,
19:20 to the top of the mountain, and Moses **w** up.
19:25 So Moses **w** down to the people and told them.
24: 9 and seventy of the elders of Israel **w** up,
24:13 and Moses **w** up into the mountain of God.
24:15 Then Moses **w** up on the mountain,
24:18 and **w** up on the mountain.
32:15 Moses turned and **w** down from the mountain,
33: 8 Whenever Moses **w** out to the tent,
34: 4 and he rose early in the morning and **w** up
34:34 but whenever Moses **w** in before the LORD
34:35 until he **w** in to speak with him.
40:32 When they **w** into the tent of meeting,
Lev 16:23 the linen vestments that he put on when he **w** into
Nu 7:89 When Moses **w** into the tent of meeting to speak
8:22 Thereafter the Levites **w** in to do their service in
11: 8 The people **w** around and gathered it,
11:24 So Moses **w** out and told the people the words of
11:31 Then a wind **w** out from the LORD,
12:10 When the cloud **w** away from over the tent,
13:21 So they **w** up and spied out the land from
13:22 They **w** up into the Negeb, and came to Hebron;
14: 7 "The land that we **w** through as spies is
14:24 I will bring into the land into which he **w**,
14:38 of those men who **w** to spy out the land.
14:40 They rose early in the morning and **w** up to
16:25 So Moses got up and **w** to Dathan and Abiram;
16:33 that belonged to them **w** down alive into Sheol;
17: 8 When Moses **w** into the tent of the covenant on
20: 6 Then Moses and Aaron **w** away from the assembly
20:15 how our ancestors **w** down to Egypt, and we lived
20:27 they **w** up Mount Hor in the sight of
21:23 and **w** out against Israel to the wilderness;
21:33 Then they turned and **w** up the road to Bashan;
22:14 So the officials of Moab rose and **w** to Balak,
22:21 and **w** with the officials of Moab.
22:23 donkey turned off the road, and **w** into the field;
22:26 Then the angel of the LORD **w** ahead,
22:35 So Balaam **w** on with the officials of Balak.
22:36 he **w** out to meet him at Ir-moab,
22:39 Then Balaam **w** with Balak,
23: 3 And he **w** to a bare height.
24:25 and **w** back to his place, and Balak also **w** his way.
25: 8 he **w** after the Israelite man into the tent,
31:13 the congregation **w** to meet them outside the camp.
31:27 between the warriors who **w** out to battle and all
31:28 From the share of the warriors who **w** out to battle,
32: 9 they **w** up to the Wadi Eshcol and saw the land,
32:39 The descendants of Machir son of Manasseh **w**
32:41 Jair son of Manasseh **w** and captured their villages,
32:42 Nobah **w** and captured Kenath and its villages,
33: 1 the stages by which the Israelites **w** out of the land
33: 3 the passover the Israelites **w** out boldly in the sight
33: 8 **w** a three days' journey in the wilderness
33:38 Aaron the priest **w** up Mount Hor at the command
Dt 1:19 and **w** through all that great and terrible wilderness
1:24 They set out and **w** up into the hill country,
1:43 and presumptuously **w** up into the hill country.
9: 9 I **w** up the mountain to receive the stone tablets,
9:15 So I turned and **w** down from the mountain,
10: 3 and **w** up the mountain with the two tablets
10:22 Your ancestors **w** down to Egypt seventy persons;
26: 5 he **w** down into Egypt and lived there as an alien,
31:14 and Joshua **w** and presented themselves in the tent
34: 1 Then Moses **w** up from the plains of Moab
Jos 2: 1 So they **w**, and entered the house of
2: 5 to close the gate at dark, the men **w** out.
2: 5 Where the men **w** I do not know.
2: 8 Before they **w** to sleep, she came up to them on
2:22 They departed and **w** into the hill country
3: 2 At the end of three days the officers **w** through
3: 6 So they took up the ark of the covenant and **w**
5:13 Joshua **w** to him and said to him,
6: 1 no one came out and no one **w** in.
6: 8 of rams' horns before the LORD **w** forward,
6: 9 And the armed men **w** before the priests who blew
6:11 So the ark of the LORD **w** around the city,
6:13 The armed men **w** before them,
6:23 So the young men who had been spies **w** in
7: 2 And the men **w** up and spied out Ai.
7: 4 So about three thousand of the people **w** up there;
8: 9 and they **w** to the place of ambush,
8:10 and **w** up, with the elders of Israel,
8:11 All the fighting men who were with him **w** up,
9: 4 they **w** and prepared provisions,
9: 6 They **w** to Joshua in the camp at Gilgal,
10: 5 and **w** up with all their armies and camped
10: 7 So Joshua **w** up from Gilgal,
10:36 Joshua **w** up with all Israel from Eglon to Hebron;
14: 8 But my companions who **w** up with me made
15:15 From there he **w** up against the inhabitants
16: 1 The allotment of the Josephites **w** from the Jordan
17: 9 Then the boundary **w** down to the Wadi Kanah.
18: 8 and Joshua charged those who **w** to write
18: 9 So the men **w** and traversed the land and set down
19:47 the Danites **w** up and fought against Leshem,
Jos 21:10 which **w** to the descendants of Aaron,
22: 6 and they **w** to their tents.
24: 4 but Jacob and his children **w** down to Egypt.
24:11 When you **w** over the Jordan and came to Jericho,
24:17 He protected us along all the way that we **w**,
Jdg 1: 3 So Simeon **w** with him.
1: 4 Then Judah **w** up and the LORD gave
1: 9 Afterward the people of Judah **w** down to fight
1:10 Judah **w** against the Canaanites who lived
1:11 From there they **w** against the inhabitants of Debir
1:16 **w** up with the people of Judah from the city
1:16 Then they **w** and settled with the Amalekites.
1:17 Judah **w** with his brother Simeon,
1:22 The house of Joseph also **w** up against Bethel;
1:26 man **w** to the land of the Hittites and built a city,
2: 1 angel of the LORD **w** up from Gilgal to Bochim,
2: 6 the Israelites all **w** to their own inheritances
3:10 he **w** out to war,
3:13 with the Ammonites and the Amalekites, he **w**
3:19 and all his attendants **w** out from his presence.
3:22 the hilt also **w** in after the blade, and the fat closed
3:23 Then Ehud **w** out into the vestibule,
3:27 Israelites **w** down with him from the hill country,
3:28 So they **w** down after him,
4: 9 Then Deborah got up and **w** with Barak to Kedesh.
4:10 and ten thousand warriors **w** up behind him;
4:10 and Deborah **w** up with him.
4:14 So Barak **w** down from Mount Tabor
4:21 **w** softly to him and drove the peg into his temple,
4:21 until it **w** down into the ground—
4:22 Jael **w** out to meet him, and said to him, "Come,
4:22 So he **w** into her tent;
5: 4 "LORD, when you **w** out from Seir,
6:19 So Gideon **w** into his house and prepared a kid,
6:35 and Naphtali, and they **w** up to meet them.
7:11 Then he **w** down with his servant Purah to
8: 1 when you **w** to fight against the Midianites?"
8: 8 From there he **w** up to Penuel,
8:11 So Gideon **w** up by the caravan route east
8:29 Jerubbaal son of Joash **w** to live in his own house.
9: 1 Now Abimelech son of Jerubbaal **w** to Shechem
9: 5 He **w** to his father's house at Ophrah,
9: 6 and they **w** and made Abimelech king,
9: 7 he **w** and stood on the top of Mount Gerizim,
9: 8 trees once **w** out to anoint a king over themselves.
9:27 They **w** out into the field and gathered the grapes
9:27 Then they **w** into the temple of their god,
9:35 of Ebed **w** out and stood in the entrance of the gate
9:39 So Gaal **w** out at the head of the lords of Shechem,
9:42 the following day the people **w** out into the fields.
9:48 So Abimelech **w** up to Mount Zalmon,
9:50 Then Abimelech **w** to Thebez,
9:51 and they **w** to the roof of the tower.
9:55 that Abimelech was dead, they all **w** home.
11: 3 Outlaws collected around Jephthah and **w** raiding
11: 5 the elders of Gilead **w** to bring Jephthah from
11:11 So Jephthah **w** with the elders of Gilead,
11:16 Israel **w** through the wilderness to the Red Sea
11:18 **w** around the land of Edom and the land of Moab,
13:20 the flame **w** up toward heaven from the altar,
14: 1 Once Samson **w** down to Timnah,
14: 5 Then Samson **w** down with his father and mother
14: 7 Then he **w** down and talked with the woman,
14: 9 and **w** on, eating as he **w**.
14:10 His father **w** down to the woman,
14:18 to him on the seventh day before the sun **w** down,
14:19 and he **w** down to Ashkelon.
14:19 In hot anger he **w** back to his father's house.
15: 1 Samson **w** to visit his wife, bringing along a kid.
15: 4 So Samson **w** and caught three hundred foxes,
15: 8 and he **w** down and stayed in the cleft of the rock
15:11 of Judah **w** down to the cleft of the rock of Etam,
16: 1 Once Samson **w** to Gaza, where he saw a
prostitute and **w** in to her.
18: 3 so they **w** over and asked him,
18: 7 The five men **w** on, and when they came to Laish,
18:12 and **w** up and encamped at Kiriath-jearim in Judah.
18:18 the men **w** into Micah's house and took the idol
18:20 and the idol, and **w** along with the people.
18:26 Then the Danites **w** their way.
18:26 he turned and **w** back to his home.
18:30 the Danites until the time the land **w** into captivity.
19: 2 and she **w** away from him to her father's house
19:14 So they passed on and **w** their way;
19:14 and the sun **w** down on them near Gibeah,
19:15 He **w** in and sat down in the open square of
19:18 I **w** to Bethlehem in Judah;
19:23 **w** out to them and said to them, "No, my brothers,
19:27 and when he **w** out to go on his way,
20:20 The Israelites **w** out to battle against Benjamin;
20:23 The Israelites **w** up and wept before the LORD
20:26 the whole army, **w** back to Bethel and wept,
20:30 Then the Israelites **w** up against the Benjaminites
20:31 When the Benjaminites **w** out against the army,
21:23 Then they **w** and returned to their territory,
21:24 and they **w** out from there to their own territories.
Ru 1: 1 and a certain man of Bethlehem in Judah **w** to live
1: 2 They **w** into the country of Moab
1: 7 and they **w** on their way to go back to the land
1:19 two of them **w** on until they came to Bethlehem.
1:21 I **w** away full, but the LORD has brought me back
2: 3 So she **w**. She came and gleaned in the
3: 6 So she **w** down to the threshing floor and did just
3: 7 he **w** to lie down at the end of the heap of grain.
3:15 then he **w** into the city.
4: 1 And he **w** over and sat down.
1Sa 1: 7 So it **w** on year by year;

1Sa 1: 7 as often as she w up to the house of the LORD,
1: 18 Then the woman w to her quarters,
1: 19 then they w back to their house at Ramah.
1: 21 and all his household w up to offer to the LORD
2: 11 Then Elkanah w home to Ramah,
2: 19 when she w up with her husband to offer
3: 5 So he w and lay down.
3: 6 Samuel got up and w to Eli, and said, "Here I am,
3: 8 And he got up and w to Eli, and said, "Here I am,
3: 9 So Samuel w and lay down in his place.
4: 1 and Israel w out to battle against them;
5: 12 and the cry of the city w up to heaven.
6: 12 The cows w straight in the direction
6: 12 along one highway, lowing as they w;
6: 12 and the lords of the Philistines w after them as far
6: 13 they w with rejoicing to meet it.
7: 7 the lords of the Philistines w up against Israel.
7: 11 the men of Israel w out of Mizpah and pursued
7: 16 He w on a circuit year by year to Bethel, Gilgal,
9: 9 anyone who w to inquire of God would say,
9: 10 So they w to the town where the man of God was.
9: 11 As they w up the hill to the town,
9: 14 So they w up to the town.
9: 24 The cook took up the thigh and what w with it
9: 26 and both he and Samuel w out into the street.
10: 2 'The donkeys that you w to seek are found,
10: 13 When his prophetic frenzy had ended, he w home.
10: 14 and when we saw they were not to be found, we w
10: 26 Saul also w to his home at Gibeah, and with him w
warriors whose hearts God had touched.
11: 1 the Ammonite w up and besieged Jabesh-gilead;
11: 15 So all the people w to Gilgal,
12: 8 When Jacob w into Egypt and
13: 10 and Saul w out to meet him and salute him.
13: 15 And Samuel left and w on his way from Gilgal.
13: 15 they w up from Gilgal toward Gibeah of Benjamin.
13: 20 so all the Israelites w down to the Philistines
14: 18 at that time the ark of God w with the Israelites.
14: 20 the people who were with him rallied and w into
14: 46 and the Philistines w to their own place.
15: 12 and Samuel was told, "Saul w to Carmel,
15: 34 Then Samuel w to Ramah;
15: 34 and Saul w up to his house in Gibeah of Saul.
16: 13 Samuel then set out and w to Ramah.
17: 7 and his shield-bearer w before him.
17: 13 of his three sons who w to the battle were Eliab
17: 15 but David w back and forth from Saul
17: 20 and w as Jesse had commanded him.
17: 22 ran to the ranks, and w and greeted his brothers.
17: 35 I w after it and struck it down, rescuing the lamb
18: 5 David w out and was successful wherever
18: 27 and w, along with his men, and killed one hundred
19: 8 and David w out to fight the Philistines.
19: 18 He and Samuel w and settled at Naioth.
19: 22 Then he himself w to Ramah.
19: 23 He w there, toward Naioth in Ramah;
20: 11 So they both w out into the field.
20: 35 In the morning Jonathan w out into the field to
20: 42 He got up and left; and Jonathan w into the city.
21: 10 he w to King Achish of Gath.
22: 1 they w down there to him.
22: 3 David w from there to Mizpeh of Moab.
22: 5 So David left, and w into the forest of Hereth.
23: 5 So David and his men w to Keilah,
23: 18 David remained at Horesh, and Jonathan w home.
23: 19 some Ziphites w up to Saul at Gibeah and said,
23: 24 So they set out and w to Ziph ahead of Saul.
23: 25 Saul and his men w to search for him.
23: 25 he w down to the rock and stayed in the wilderness
23: 26 Saul w on one side of the mountain,
23: 28 and w against the Philistines;
23: 29 David then w up from there,
24: 2 and w to look for David and his men in
24: 3 and Saul w in to relieve himself.
24: 4 Then David w and stealthily cut off a corner
24: 7 Saul got up and left the cave, and w on his way.
24: 8 up and w out of the cave and called after Saul,
24: 22 Then Saul w home; but David and his men w up to
25: 1 Then David got up and w down to the wilderness
25: 13 and about four hundred men w up after David,
25: 42 She w after the messengers of David
26: 2 Saul rose and w down to the Wilderness of Ziph,
26: 7 So David and Abishai w to the army by night;
26: 12 at Saul's head and the water jar, and they w away.
26: 13 Then David w over to the other side,
26: 25 David w his way, and Saul returned to his place.
27: 2 So David set out and w over,
27: 8 Now David and his men w up and made raids on
28: 8 and put on other clothes and w there,
28: 25 Then they rose and w away that night.
29: 11 But the Philistines w up to Jezreel.
30: 2 but carried them off, and w their way.
30: 10 But David w on with the pursuit,
30: 21 They w out to meet David and to meet
2Sa 2: 2 So David w up there, along with his two wives,
2: 12 w out from Mahanaim to Gibeon.
2: 13 w out and met them at the pool of Gibeon.
3: 16 But her husband w with her,
3: 16 "Go back home!" So he w back.
3: 19 then Abner w to tell David at Hebron all that Israel
3: 21 David dismissed Abner, and he w away in peace.
3: 24 Joab w to the king and said, "What have you done?
5: 17 all the Philistines w up in search of David; but
David heard about it and w down to the stronghold.
6: 2 David and all the people with him set out and w
6: 4 and Ahio w in front of the ark.
6: 12 So David w and brought up the ark of God from
6: 19 Then all the people w back to their homes.
7: 9 and I have been with you wherever you w,
7: 18 Then King David w in and sat before the LORD,
7: 23 on earth whose God w to redeem it as a people,
8: 3 as he w to restore his monument at
8: 6 The LORD gave victory to David wherever he w.
8: 14 the LORD gave victory to David wherever he w.
11: 8 Uriah w out of the king's house,
11: 13 in the evening he w out to lie on his couch with
11: 22 So the messenger w, and came and told David all
12: 15 Then Nathan w to his house.
12: 16 and w in and lay all night on the ground.
12: 20 He w into the house of the LORD, and worshiped;
12: 20 he then w to his own house;
12: 24 David consoled his wife Bathsheba, and w to her,
12: 29 So David gathered all the people together and w
13: 8 So Tamar w to her brother Amnon's house,
13: 9 So everyone w out from him.
13: 19 she put her hand on her head, and w away,
13: 19 and went away, crying aloud as she w.
13: 37 Absalom fled, and w to Talmai son of Ammihud,
13: 39 the heart of the king w out, yearning for Absalom;
14: 23 So Joab set off, w to Geshur,
14: 24 So Absalom w to his own house,
14: 31 Then Joab rose and w to Absalom at his house,
14: 33 Then Joab w to the king and told him;
15: 9 So he got up, and w to Hebron.
15: 11 Two hundred men from Jerusalem w
15: 11 and they w in their innocence,
15: 30 But David w up the ascent of the Mount of Olives,
weeping as he w, with his head covered
15: 30 covered their heads and w up, weeping as they w.
16: 13 So David and his men w on the road,
16: 13 while Shimei w along on the hillside opposite him
and cursed as he w,
16: 22 and Absalom w in to his father's concubines in
17: 18 so both of them w away quickly,
17: 18 and they w down into it.
17: 21 and w and told King David.
17: 23 he saddled his donkey and w off home
18: 6 So the army w out into the field against Israel;
18: 9 the mule w under the thick branches of a great oak.
18: 9 while the mule that was under him w on.
18: 24 sentinel w up to the roof of the gate by the wall,
18: 33 and w up to the chamber over the gate, and wept;
18: 33 and as he w, he said, "O my son Absalom, my son,
19: 31 he w on with the king to the Jordan,
19: 40 The king w on to Gilgal, and Chimham w on with
20: 5 So Amasa w to summon Judah;
20: 7 Joab's men w out after him,
20: 7 they w out from Jerusalem to pursue Sheba son
20: 8 as he w forward it fell out.
20: 13 all the people w on after Joab to pursue Sheba son
20: 22 the woman w to all the people with her wise plan.
20: 22 and all w to their homes,
21: 12 David w and took the bones of Saul and the bones
21: 15 The Philistines w to war again with Israel,
21: 15 and David w down together with his servants.
22: 9 Smoke w up from his nostrils,
23: 13 the beginning of harvest three of the thirty chiefs w
23: 17 Can I drink the blood of the men who w at the risk
23: 20 He also w down and killed a lion in a pit on a day
23: 21 but Benaiah w against him with a staff,
24: 4 of the army w out from the presence of the king
24: 6 and from Dan they w around to Sidon,
24: 7 they w out to the Negeb of Judah at Beer-sheba.
24: 19 Following Gad's instructions, David w up,
24: 20 and Araunah w out and prostrated himself before
1Ki 1: 15 So Bathsheba w to the king in his room.
1: 38 w down and had Solomon ride
1: 40 And all the people w up following him,
1: 48 and w on to pray thus,
1: 49 up trembling and w their own ways.
1: 50 got up and w to grasp the horns of the altar.
2: 8 a terrible curse on the day when I w to Mahanaim;
2: 19 So Bathsheba w to King Solomon,
2: 34 Then Benaiah son of Jehoiada w up and struck him
2: 40 and w to Achish in Gath, to search for his slaves;
2: 40 Shimei w and brought his slaves from Gath.
2: 46 and he w out and struck him down, and he died.
3: 4 The king w to Gibeon to sacrifice there,
6: 8 one w up by winding stairs to the middle story,
8: 66 and they blessed the king, and w to their tents,
9: 24 But Pharaoh's daughter w up from the city
9: 28 They w to Ophir, and imported
10: 16 of gold w into each large shield.
10: 17 three minas of gold w into each shield;
11: 15 the commander of the army w up to bury the dead,
11: 24 they w to Damascus, settled there,
12: 1 Rehoboam w to Shechem,
12: 5 So the people w away.
12: 16 So Israel w away to their tents.
12: 24 the word of the LORD and w home again,
12: 25 he w out from there and built Penuel.
12: 30 the people w to worship before the one at Bethel
12: 33 He w up to the altar that he had made in Bethel on
12: 33 and he w up to the altar to offer incense.
13: 10 So he w another way, and did not return by
13: 14 He w after the man of God,
13: 19 Then the man of God w back with him,
13: 24 Then as he w away, a lion met him on the road
13: 28 and he w and found the body thrown in the road,
14: 4 she set out and w to Shiloh,
14: 17 Then Jeroboam's wife got up and w away,
14: 28 often as the king w into the house of the LORD,
15: 17 King Baasha of Israel w up against Judah,
16: 17 So Omri w up from Gibbethon,
1Ki 16: 18 he w into the citadel of the king's house;
16: 31 and w and served Baal, and worshiped him.
17: 5 he w and did according to the word of the LORD;
17: 5 he w and lived by the Wadi Cherith,
17: 10 So he set out and w to Zarephath.
17: 15 She w and did as Elijah said,
18: 2 So Elijah w to present himself to Ahab.
18: 6 Ahab w in one direction by himself,
18: 6 and Obadiah w in another direction by himself.
18: 16 So Obadiah w to meet Ahab, and told him;
18: 16 and Ahab w to meet Elijah.
18: 42 So Ahab w up to eat and to drink.
18: 42 Elijah w up to the top of Carmel;
18: 43 He w up and looked, and said, "There is nothing."
18: 45 Ahab rode off and w to Jezreel.
19: 4 he himself w a day's journey into the wilderness,
19: 8 then he w in the strength of that food forty days
19: 13 in his mantle and w out and stood at the entrance
20: 16 They w out at noon,
20: 17 the district governors w out first.
20: 21 The king of Israel w out,
20: 26 and w up to Aphek to fight against Israel.
20: 27 they w out to engage them;
20: 32 put ropes on their heads, w to the king of Israel,
20: 39 "Your servant w out into the thick of the battle;
21: 4 Ahab w home resentful and sullen because
21: 27 lay in the sackcloth, and w about dejectedly.
22: 29 the king of Israel and King Jehoshaphat of Judah w
22: 30 king of Israel disguised himself and w into battle.
22: 36 Then about sunset a shout w through the army,
2Ki 1: 4 you shall surely die.' " So Elijah w.
1: 9 He w up to Elijah, who was sitting on the top of
1: 11 He w up and said to him, "O man of God,
1: 13 So the third captain of fifty w up,
1: 15 So he set out and w down with him to the king,
2: 2 So they w down to Bethel.
2: 6 So the two of them w on.
2: 7 Fifty men of the company of prophets also w,
2: 13 and w back and stood on the bank of the Jordan.
2: 14 to the one side and to the other, and Elisha w over.
2: 21 Then he w to the spring of water and threw the salt
2: 23 He w up from there to Bethel;
2: 25 From there he w on to Mount Carmel,
3: 7 he w he sent word to King Jehoshaphat of Judah,
3: 12 of Israel and Jehoshaphat and the king of Edom w
4: 11 he w up to the chamber and lay down there.
4: 18 he w out one day to his father among the reapers.
4: 21 She w up and laid him on the bed of the man
4: 31 Gehazi w on ahead and laid the staff on the face of
4: 33 So he w in and closed the door on the two of them,
4: 39 One of them w out into the field to gather herbs;
5: 4 So Naaman w in and told his lord just what the girl
5: 5 He w, taking with him ten talents of silver,
5: 11 But Naaman became angry and w away, saying,
5: 12 He turned and w away in a rage.
5: 14 So he w down and immersed himself seven times
5: 21 So Gehazi w after Naaman.
5: 25 He w in and stood before his master;
6: 4 So he w with them.
6: 15 of God rose early in the morning and w out,
6: 23 and they w to their master.
7: 8 they w into a tent, ate and drank, carried off silver,
gold, and clothing, and w and hid them.
7: 8 carried off things from it, and w and hid them.
7: 10 and told them, "We w to the Aramean camp,
7: 15 So they w after them as far as the Jordan;
7: 16 Then the people w out, and plundered the camp of
8: 2 she w with her household and settled in the land of
8: 7 Elisha w to Damascus while King Ben-hadad
8: 9 So Hazael w to meet him,
8: 14 he left Elisha, and w to his master Ben-hadad,
8: 28 He w with Joram son of Ahab to wage war
8: 29 King Ahaziah son of Jehoram of Judah w down
9: 4 the young prophet, w to Ramoth-gilead.
9: 6 So Jehu got up and w inside;
9: 16 Then Jehu mounted his chariot and w to Jezreel,
9: 18 So the horseman w to meet him;
9: 21 each in his chariot, and w to meet Jehu;
9: 34 Then he w in and ate and drank;
9: 35 But when they w to bury her,
10: 9 Then in the morning when he w out,
10: 12 Then he set out and w to Samaria.
10: 25 and then w into the citadel of the temple of Baal.
11: 13 she w into the house of the LORD to the people;
11: 16 she w through the horses' entrance to
11: 18 all the people of the land w to the house of Baal,
12: 10 the king's secretary and the high priest w up,
12: 17 At that time King Hazael of Aram w up,
13: 14 King Joash of Israel w down to him,
14: 11 So King Jehoash of Israel w up;
16: 10 When King Ahaz w to Damascus
16: 12 Then the king drew near to the altar, w up on it,
17: 15 They w after false idols and became false;
18: 7 wherever he w, he prospered.
18: 17 They w up and came to Jerusalem.
19: 1 and w into the house of the LORD.
19: 14 then Hezekiah w up to the house of the LORD
19: 36 Then King Sennacherib of Assyria left, w home,
22: 14 and Asaiah w to the prophetess Huldah the wife
23: 2 The king w up to the house of the LORD,
23: 2 and with him w all the people of Judah,
23: 29 In his days Pharaoh Neco king of Egypt w up to
23: 29 King Josiah w to meet him;
25: 4 They w in the direction of the Arabah.
25: 21 So Judah w into exile out of its land.
25: 26 the captains of the forces set out and w to Egypt;
1Ch 2: 21 Afterward Hezron w in to the daughter

1Ch 4:42 **w** to Mount Seir, having as their leaders Pelatiah,
6:15 and Jehozadak **w** into exile when
7:23 Ephraim **w** in to his wife, and she conceived
11: 6 Joab son of Zeruiah **w** up first, so he became chief.
11:15 of the thirty chiefs **w** down to the rock to David at
11:22 He also **w** down and killed a lion in a pit on a day
11:23 but Benaiah **w** against him with a staff,
12: 8 the Gadites there **w** over to David at the stronghold
12:17 David **w** out to meet them and said to them,
12:20 he **w** to Ziklag these Manassites deserted to him:
13: 6 And David and all Israel **w** up to Baalah, that is,
14: 8 all the Philistines **w** up in search of David; and
David heard of it and **w** out against them.
14:11 So he **w** up to Baal-perazim,
14:17 The fame of David **w** out into all lands,
15:25 **w** to bring up the ark of the covenant of
16:43 and David **w** home to bless his household.
17: 8 and I have been with you wherever you **w**,
17:16 Then King David **w** in and sat before the LORD,
17:21 the earth whom God **w** to redeem to be his people,
18: 3 he **w** to set up a monument at the river Euphrates.
18: 6 The LORD gave victory to David wherever he **w**.
18:13 the LORD gave victory to David wherever he **w**.
21: 4 So Joab departed and **w** throughout all Israel,
21:19 So David **w** up following Gad's instructions,
21:21 he **w** out from the threshing floor,
27: 1 the divisions that came and **w**, month after month
2Ch 1: 3 **w** to the high place that was at Gibeon;
1: 6 Solomon **w** up there to the bronze altar before
8: 3 Solomon **w** to Hamath-zobah, and captured it.
8:17 Then Solomon **w** to Ezion-geber and Eloth on
8:18 They **w** to Ophir, together with the servants
9:15 of beaten gold **w** into each large shield.
9:16 three hundred shekels of gold **w** into each shield;
9:21 the king's ships **w** to Tarshish with the servants
10: 1 Rehoboam **w** to Shechem,
10: 5 So the people **w** away.
12:11 the king **w** into the house of the LORD,
14:10 Asa **w** out to meet him,
15: 2 He **w** out to meet Asa and said to him, "Hear me,
16: 1 King Baasha of Israel **w** up against Judah,
17: 9 they **w** around through all the cities of Judah
18: 2 After some years he **w** down to Ahab in Samaria.
18:28 the king of Israel and King Jehoshaphat of Judah **w**
18:29 So the king of Israel disguised himself, and they **w**
19: 2 Jehu son of Hanani the seer **w** out to meet him
19: 4 then he **w** out again among the people,
20:20 They rose early in the morning and **w** out into
20:20 and as they **w** out, Jehoshaphat stood and said,
20:21 as they **w** before the army, saying,
22: 5 and **w** with Jehoram son of King Ahab of Israel
22: 6 And Ahaziah son of King Jehoram of Judah **w**
22: 7 For when he came there he **w** out with Jehoram
23: 2 They **w** around through Judah and gathered
23:12 she **w** into the house of the LORD to the people;
23:15 she **w** into the entrance of the Horse Gate of
23:17 Then all the people **w** to the house of Baal,
24:13 and the repairing **w** forward at their hands,
25:11 he **w** to the Valley of Salt,
25:21 So King Joash of Israel **w** up;
26: 6 He **w** out and made war against the Philistines,
26:17 But the priest Azariah **w** in after him,
28: 9 he **w** out to meet the army that came to Samaria,
29:15 and **w** in as the king had commanded,
29:16 The priests **w** into the inner part of the house of
29:18 Then they **w** inside to King Hezekiah and said,
29:20 and **w** up to the house of the LORD.
30: 6 So couriers **w** throughout all Israel and Judah
30:10 the couriers **w** from city to city through the country
31: 1 all Israel who were present **w** out to the cities
34:22 So Hilkiah and those whom the king had sent **w** to
34:30 The king **w** up to the house of the LORD,
35:20 King Neco of Egypt **w** up to fight at Carchemish
35:20 and Josiah **w** out against him.
Ezr 5: 8 be known to the king that we **w** to the province
7: 6 this Ezra **w** up from Babylonia.
7: 7 and the temple servants also **w** up to Jerusalem,
8: 1 of those who **w** up with me from Babylonia,
10: 6 **w** to the chamber of Jehohanan son of Eliashib,
Ne 2:13 I **w** out by night by the Valley Gate past
2:14 I **w** on to the Fountain Gate and to the King's Pool;
2:15 So I **w** up by way of the valley by night
6:10 One day when I **w** into the house of Shemaiah son
8:12 And all the people **w** their way to eat and drink and
8:16 So the people **w** out and brought them,
9:24 So the descendants **w** in and possessed the land,
12:31 that gave thanks and **w** in procession.
12:31 One **w** to the right on the wall to the Dung Gate;
12:32 them **w** Hoshaiah and half the officials of Judah,
12:36 and the scribe Ezra **w** in front of them.
12:37 they **w** straight up by the stairs of the city
12:38 The other company of those who gave thanks **w** to
13: 6 of King Artaxerxes of Babylon I **w** to the king.
Est 2:13 When the girl **w** in to the king
2:14 In the evening she **w** in;
3:15 The couriers **w** quickly by order of the king,
4: 1 and **w** through the city, wailing with a loud
4: 2 he **w** up to the entrance of the king's gate,
4: 6 Hathach **w** out to Mordecai in the open square of
4: 9 Hathach **w** and told Esther what Mordecai had
4:17 Mordecai then **w** away and did everything
5: 9 Haman **w** out that day happy and in good spirits.
5:10 Haman restrained himself and **w** home.
7: 1 king and Haman **w** in to feast with Queen Esther.
7: 7 The king rose from the feast in wrath and **w** into
8:15 Mordecai **w** out from the presence of the king,
Job 1:12 So Satan **w** out from the presence of the LORD.
Job 2: 7 So Satan **w** out from the presence of the LORD,
21:33 and those who **w** before are innumerable.
29: 7 When I **w** out to the gate of the city,
42: 9 and Zophar the Naamathite **w** and did what
Ps 18: 8 Smoke **w** up from his nostrils,
34: T *so that he drove him out, and he* **w** *away.*
35:14 I **w** about as one who laments for a mother,
42: 4 how I **w** with the throng, and led them in
54: T *of David, when the Ziphites* **w** *and told Saul,*
66:12 we **w** through fire and through water;
68: 7 O God, when you **w** out before your people,
73:17 until I **w** into the sanctuary of God;
81: 5 when he **w** out over the land of Egypt.
89:34 or alter the word that **w** forth from my lips.
106:32 and it **w** ill with Moses on their account;
107:23 Some **w** down to the sea in ships,
107:26 they **w** down to the depths;
114: 1 When Israel **w** out from Egypt,
119:67 Before I was humbled I **w** astray,
Pr 21:22 One wise person **w** up against a city of warriors
SS 3: 3 sentinels found me, as they **w** about in the city.
6:11 I **w** down to the nut orchard,
Isa 7: 1 and King Pekah son of Remaliah of Israel **w** up
8: 3 And I **w** to the prophetess,
37: 1 and **w** into the house of the LORD.
37:14 then Hezekiah **w** up to the house of the LORD
37:37 Then King Sennacherib of Assyria left, **w** home,
48: 3 they **w** out from my mouth
52: 4 my people **w** down into Egypt to reside there
57: 7 and there you **w** up to offer sacrifice.
Jer 2: 5 they **w** far from me, and **w** after worthless things,
2: 8 and **w** after things that do not profit.
3: 6 that faithless one, Israel, how she **w** up
3: 8 but she too **w** and played the whore.
13: 5 So I **w**, and hid it by the Euphrates,
13: 7 Then I **w** to the Euphrates, and dug,
15: 9 her sun **w** down while it was yet day;
18: 3 So I **w** down to the potter's house,
22:11 and who **w** away from this place:
28: 4 and all the exiles from Judah who **w** to Babylon,
28:11 At this, the prophet Jeremiah **w** his way.
31:21 the highway, the road by which you **w**.
36:12 he **w** down to the king's house,
36:20 they **w** to the court of the king;
38:11 the men with him and **w** to the house of the king,
39: 4 and they **w** toward the Arabah.
40: 6 Jeremiah **w** to Gedaliah son of Ahikam at Mizpah,
40: 8 they **w** to Gedaliah at Mizpah—
41:12 and **w** to fight against Ishmael son of Nethaniah.
41:14 and **w** to Johanan son of Kareah.
41:15 with eight men, and **w** to the Ammonites.
44: 3 that they **w** to make offerings and serve other gods
51: 7 and so the nations **w** mad.
51:59 he **w** with King Zedekiah of Judah to Babylon,
52: 7 the soldiers fled and **w** out from the city by night
52: 7 They **w** in the direction of the Arabah.
52:27 So Judah **w** into exile out of its land.
La 1:13 From on high he sent fire; it **w** deep into my bones;
Eze 1:12 they **w**, without turning as they **w**.
1:20 Wherever the spirit would go, they **w**,
3:14 I **w** in bitterness in the heat of my spirit,
3:23 So I rose up and **w** out into the valley;
8:10 So I **w** in and looked;
9: 2 They **w** in and stood beside the bronze altar.
9: 7 So they **w** out and killed in the city.
10: 2 He **w** in as I looked on.
10: 3 on the south side of the house when the man **w** in;
10: 6 he **w** in and stood beside a wheel.
10: 7 who took it and **w** out.
10:18 the LORD **w** out from the threshold of the house
10:19 the earth in my sight as they **w** out with the wheels
20:16 for their heart **w** after their idols.
23:44 Thus they **w** in to Oholah and to Oholibah,
25: 3 and over the house of Judah when it **w** into exile;
31: 7 for its roots **w** down to abundant water.
31:12 the peoples of the earth **w** away from its shade
31:15 On the day it **w** down to Sheol I closed the deep
31:17 They also **w** down to Sheol with it,
32:24 who **w** down uncircumcised into the world below,
32:27 not lie with the fallen warriors of long ago who **w**
39:23 the nations shall know that the house of Israel **w**
40: 6 Then he **w** into the gateway facing east,
41: 3 Then he **w** into the inner room and measured
44:10 But the Levites who **w** far from me, going away
from me after their idols when Israel **w** astray,
44:15 of my sanctuary when the people of Israel **w** astray
48:11 not go astray when the people of Israel **w** astray,
Da 2:16 So Daniel **w** in and requested that
2:17 Then Daniel **w** to his home
2:24 Therefore Daniel **w** to Arioch,
6:14 and until the sun **w** down he made every effort
6:18 king **w** to his palace and spent the night fasting;
8:27 then I arose and **w** about the king's business.
9:23 the beginning of your supplications a word **w** out,
9:25 the word **w** out to restore and rebuild Jerusalem
Hos 1: 3 So he **w** and took Gomer daughter of Diblaim,
2:13 and **w** after her lovers, and forgot me,
5:13 and Judah his wound, then Ephraim **w** to Assyria,
11: 2 The more I called them, the more they **w** from me;
Am 5:19 or **w** into the house and rested a hand against
Jnh 1: 3 He **w** down to Joppa and found a ship going
1: 3 so he paid his fare and **w** on board,
2: 6 I **w** down to the land whose bars closed upon me
3: 3 So Jonah set out and **w** to Nineveh,
4: 5 Then Jonah **w** out of the city and sat down east of
Na 3:10 Yet she became an exile, she **w** into captivity;
Hab 3: 5 Before him **w** pestilence,
Zec 7:14 so that no one **w** to and fro,
8:10 from the foe for those who **w** out or came in,
Mt 2: 9 **w** the star that they had seen at its rising,
2:14 the child and his mother by night, and **w** to Egypt,
2:21 and **w** to the land of Israel.
2:22 he **w** away to the district of Galilee.
4:21 As he **w** from there, he saw two other brothers,
4:23 Jesus **w** throughout Galilee,
5: 1 Jesus saw the crowds, he **w** up the mountain;
8:25 they **w** and woke him up, saying, "Lord, save us!
9: 7 And he stood up and **w** to his home.
9:25 he **w** in and took her by the hand,
9:27 As Jesus **w** on from there,
9:31 But they **w** away and spread the news about him
9:35 Then Jesus **w** about all the cities and villages,
11: 1 he **w** on from there to teach
11: 7 As they **w** away, Jesus began to speak to
12: 1 At that time Jesus **w** through the grainfields on
12:14 But the Pharisees **w** out and conspired against him,
13: 1 That same day Jesus **w** out of the house and sat
13: 3 A sower **w** out to sow.
13:25 among the wheat, and then **w** away.
13:36 Then he left the crowds and **w** into the house.
13:46 he **w** and sold all that he had and bought it.
14:12 then they **w** and told Jesus.
14:14 When he **w** ashore, he saw a great crowd;
14:23 he **w** up the mountain by himself to pray.
15:21 Jesus left that place and **w** away to the district
15:29 and he **w** up the mountain, where he sat down.
15:39 into the boat and **w** to the region of Magadan.
16: 4 Then he left them and **w** away.
18:12 and go in search of the one that **w** astray?
18:13 over the ninety-nine that never **w** astray.
18:28 But that same slave, as he **w** out,
18:30 then he **w** and threw him into prison
18:31 and they **w** and reported to their lord all
19: 1 he left Galilee and **w** to the region of Judea beyond
19:15 And he laid his hands on them and **w** on his way.
19:22 young man heard this word, he **w** away grieving,
20: 1 like a landowner who **w** out early in the morning
20: 3 When he **w** out about nine o'clock,
20: 4 and I will pay you whatever is right.' So they **w**.
20: 5 he **w** out again about noon and about three o'clock,
20: 6 And about five o'clock he **w** out
21: 6 disciples **w** and did as Jesus had directed them;
21: 9 The crowds that **w** ahead of him and
21:17 He left them, **w** out of the city to Bethany,
21:19 he **w** to it and found nothing at all on it but leaves.
21:28 A man had two sons; he **w** to the first and said,
21:29 but later he changed his mind and **w**.
21:30 The father **w** to the second and said the same;
21:33 he leased it to tenants and **w** to another country.
22: 5 But they made light of it and **w** away,
22:10 Those slaves **w** out into the streets
22:15 Then the Pharisees **w** and plotted to entrap him
22:22 and they left him and **w** away.
25: 1 Ten bridesmaids took their lamps and **w** to meet
25:10 And while they **w** to buy it, the bridegroom came,
25:10 and those who were ready **w** with him into
25:15 to his ability. Then he **w** away.
25:16 the five talents **w** off at once and traded with them,
25:18 But the one who had received the one talent **w** off
25:25 and I **w** and hid your talent in the ground.
26:14 was called Judas Iscariot, **w** to the chief priests
26:30 they **w** out to the Mount of Olives.
26:36 Jesus **w** with them to a place called Gethsemane;
26:42 Again he **w** away for the second time and prayed,
26:44 he **w** away and prayed for the third time,
26:71 When he **w** out to the porch,
26:75 And he **w** out and wept bitterly.
27: 5 and he **w** and hanged himself.
27:32 As they **w** out, they came upon a man
27:58 He **w** to Pilate and asked for the body of Jesus;
27:60 a great stone to the door of the tomb and **w** away.
27:66 So they **w** with the guard and made
28: 1 Mary Magdalene and the other Mary **w** to see
28:11 some of the guard **w** into the city and told
28:16 Now the eleven disciples **w** to Galilee,
Mk 1:19 As he **w** a little farther,
1:21 They **w** to Capernaum;
1:35 he got up and **w** out to a deserted place,
1:39 And he **w** throughout Galilee,
1:45 But he **w** out and began to proclaim it freely,
2:12 and immediately took the mat and **w** out before all
2:13 Jesus **w** out again beside the sea;
3: 6 The Pharisees **w** out and immediately conspired
3:13 He **w** up the mountain and called
3:19 who betrayed him. Then he **w** home;
3:21 his family heard it, they **w** out to restrain him,
4: 3 "Listen! A sower **w** out to sow.
5:20 And he **w** away and began to proclaim in
5:24 So he **w** with him.
5:40 and **w** in where the child was.
6: 6 Then he **w** about among the villages teaching.
6:12 they **w** out and proclaimed that all should repent.
6:24 She **w** out and said to her mother,
6:27 He **w** and beheaded him in the prison,
6:32 And they **w** away in the boat to a deserted place
6:34 As he **w** ashore, he saw a great crowd;
6:46 he **w** up on the mountain to pray.
6:56 And wherever he **w**, into villages or cities
7:24 From there he set out and **w** away to the region
7:30 So she **w** home, found the child lying on the bed,
7:31 and **w** by way of Sidon towards the Sea of Galilee,
8:10 into the boat with his disciples and **w** to the district
8:13 he **w** across to the other side.
8:27 Jesus **w** on with his disciples to the villages

Mk 9:30 They **w** on from there and passed through Galilee.
10: 1 that place and **w** to the region of Judea and beyond
10:22 he was shocked and **w** away grieving,
11: 4 They **w** away and found a colt tied near a door,
11: 9 Then those who **w** ahead
11:11 Then he entered Jerusalem and **w** into the temple;
11:11 he **w** out to Bethany with the twelve.
11:13 in the distance a fig tree in leaf, he **w**
11:19 Jesus and his disciples **w** out of the city.
12: 1 he leased it to tenants and **w** to another country.
12:12 So they left him and **w** away.
14:10 **w** to the chief priests in order to betray him
14:16 So the disciples set out and **w** to the city,
14:26 they **w** out to the Mount of Olives.
14:32 They **w** to a place called Gethsemane;
14:39 And again he **w** away and prayed,
14:45 So when he came, he **w** up to him at once and said,
14:68 And he **w** out into the forecourt.
15:43 **w** boldly to Pilate and asked for the body of Jesus.
16: 2 when the sun had risen, they **w** to the tomb.
16: 8 So they **w** out and fled from the tomb,
16:10 ⟦She **w** out and told those who had been with him⟧
16:13 ⟦And they **w** back and told the rest,⟧
16:20 ⟦And they **w** out and proclaimed⟧
Lk 1:23 his time of service was ended, he **w** to his home.
1:39 In those days Mary set out and **w** with haste to
2: 1 a decree **w** out from Emperor Augustus that all
2: 3 All **w** to their own towns to be registered.
2: 4 also **w** from the town of Nazareth in Galilee
2: 5 He **w** to be registered with Mary,
2:16 So they **w** with haste and found Mary and Joseph,
2:41 Now every year his parents **w** to Jerusalem for
2:42 they **w** up as usual for the festival.
2:44 in the group of travelers, they **w** a day's journey.
2:51 Then he **w** down with them and came to Nazareth,
3: 3 He **w** into all the region around the Jordan,
4:16 he **w** to the synagogue on the sabbath day,
4:30 But he passed through the midst of them and **w**
4:31 He **w** down to Capernaum, a city in Galilee,
4:42 At daybreak he departed and **w** into
5:19 they **w** up on the roof and let him down
5:25 and **w** to his home, glorifying God.
5:27 this he **w** out and saw a tax collector named Levi,
6:12 Now during those days he **w** out to the mountain
7: 6 And Jesus **w** with them, but when he was not far
7:11 Soon afterwards he **w** to a town called Nain,
7:11 and his disciples and a large crowd **w** with him.
7:36 and he **w** into the Pharisee's house
8: 1 Soon afterwards he **w** on through cities
8: 5 "A sower **w** out to sow his seed;
8:24 They **w** to him and woke him up, shouting,
8:39 So he **w** away, proclaiming throughout the city
8:42 As he **w**, the crowds pressed in on him.
9: 6 They departed and **w** through the villages,
9:28 and **w** up on the mountain to pray.
9:56 Then they **w** on to another village.
10:30 beat him, and **w** away, leaving him half dead.
10:34 He **w** to him and bandaged his wounds,
10:38 Now as they **w** on their way,
11:37 so he **w** in and took his place at the table.
11:53 When he **w** outside, the scribes and
13:22 Jesus **w** through one town and village
15:15 So he **w** and hired himself out to one of
15:20 So he set off and **w** to his father.
17:14 And as they **w**, they were made clean.
18:10 "Two men **w** up to the temple to pray,
18:14 this man **w** down to his home justified rather than
19:11 he **w** on to tell a parable,
19:12 "A nobleman **w** to a distant country
19:28 After he had said this, he **w** on ahead,
20: 9 and **w** to another country for a long time.
22: 4 he **w** away and conferred with the chief priests
22:13 they **w** and found everything as he had told them;
22:39 He came out and **w**, as was his custom,
22:62 And he **w** out and wept bitterly.
23:52 This man **w** to Pilate and asked for the body
24: 3 but when they **w** in, they did not find the body.
24:12 then he **w** home, amazed at what had happened.
24:15 Jesus himself came near and **w** with them,
24:24 Some of those who were with us **w** to the tomb
24:29 So he **w** in to stay with them.
Jn 2:12 this he **w** down to Capernaum with his mother,
2:13 and Jesus **w** up to Jerusalem.
3:22 and his disciples **w** into the Judean countryside,
4:28 woman left her water jar and **w** back to the city.
4:43 he **w** from that place to Galilee
4:47 he **w** and begged him to come down
5: 1 and Jesus **w** up to Jerusalem.
5:15 The man **w** away and told the Jews
6: 1 this Jesus **w** to the other side of the Sea of Galilee,
6: 3 Jesus **w** up the mountain and sat down there
6:16 evening came, his disciples **w** down to the sea,
6:24 the boats and **w** to Capernaum looking for Jesus.
6:66 of his disciples turned back and no longer **w** about
7: 1 After this Jesus **w** about in Galilee.
7:10 to the festival, then he also **w**, not publicly but
7:14 the festival Jesus **w** up into the temple and began
7:45 Then the temple police **w** back to the chief priests
7:53 ⟦Then each of them **w** home,⟧
8: 1 ⟦while Jesus **w** to the Mount of Olives.⟧
8: 9 ⟦When they heard it, they **w** away, one by one,⟧
8:59 but Jesus hid himself and **w** out of the temple.
9: 7 Then he **w** and washed and came back able to see.
9:11 Then I **w** and washed and received my sight."
10:40 He **w** away again across the Jordan to the place
11:20 she **w** and met him, while Mary stayed at home.
11:28 she **w** back and called her sister Mary,
Jn 11:29 she heard it, she got up quickly and **w** to him.
11:46 But some of them **w** to the Pharisees
11:54 but **w** from there to a town called Ephraim in
11:55 and many **w** up from the country to Jerusalem
12:13 So they took branches of palm trees and **w** out
12:18 that he had performed this sign that the crowd **w**
12:20 Now among those who **w** up to worship at
12:22 Philip **w** and told Andrew; then Andrew and Philip
w and told Jesus.
13:30 the piece of bread, he immediately **w** out.
18: 1 he **w** out with his disciples across
18:15 he **w** with Jesus into the courtyard of
18:16 **w** out, spoke to the woman who guarded the gate,
18:29 So Pilate **w** out to them and said,
18:38 he **w** out to the Jews again and told them,
19: 4 Pilate **w** out again and said to them, "Look,
19:17 he **w** out to what is called The Place of the Skull,
20: 2 and **w** to Simon Peter and the other disciple,
20: 3 the other disciple set out and **w** toward the tomb.
20: 6 following him, and **w** into the tomb.
20: 8 who reached the tomb first, also **w** in,
20:18 Mary Magdalene **w** and announced to
21: 3 They **w** out and got into the boat,
21:11 Simon Peter **w** aboard and hauled the net ashore,
Ac 1:13 they **w** to the room upstairs
1:21 during all the time that the Lord Jesus **w** in and out
4:23 they **w** to their friends and reported what
5:21 they entered the temple at daybreak and **w** on
5:22 But when the temple police **w** there,
5:26 Then the captain **w** with the temple police
7:15 so Jacob **w** down to Egypt.
8: 4 those who were scattered **w** from place to place,
8: 5 Philip **w** down to the city of Samaria
8:15 The two **w** down and prayed for them
8:27 So he got up and **w**.
8:38 **w** down into the water, and Philip baptized him.
8:39 and **w** on his way rejoicing.
9: 1 and murder against the disciples of the Lord, **w** to
9:17 So Ananias **w** and entered the house.
9:28 So he **w** in and out among them in Jerusalem,
9:32 as Peter **w** here and there among all the believers,
9:39 So Peter got up and **w** with them;
10: 9 Peter **w** up on the roof to pray.
10:21 So Peter **w** down to the men and said,
10:23 The next day he got up and **w** with them,
10:27 he **w** in and found that many had assembled;
10:38 how he **w** about doing good
11: 2 So when Peter **w** up to Jerusalem,
11:25 Then Barnabas **w** to Tarsus to look for Saul,
12: 9 Peter **w** out and followed him;
12:10 and they **w** outside and walked along a lane,
12:12 soon as he realized this, he **w** to the house of Mary,
12:17 Then he left and **w** to another place.
12:19 Then Peter **w** down from Judea to Caesarea
13: 4 So, being sent out by the Holy Spirit, they **w** down
13:11 and he **w** about groping for someone to lead him
13:14 but they **w** on from Perga and came to Antioch
13:14 And on the sabbath day they **w** into the synagogue
13:51 in protest against them, and **w** to Iconium.
14: 1 and Barnabas **w** into the Jewish synagogue
14:20 he got up and **w** into the city.
14:20 The next day he **w** on with Barnabas to Derbe.
14:25 When they had spoken the word in Perga, they **w**
15:30 So they were sent off and **w** down to Antioch.
15:41 He **w** through Syria and Cilicia,
16: 1 Paul **w** on also to Derbe and to Lystra,
16: 4 As they **w** from town to town,
16: 6 They **w** through the region of Phrygia and Galatia,
16: 8 so, passing by Mysia, they **w** down to Troas.
16:13 the sabbath day we **w** outside the gate by the river,
16:40 After leaving the prison they **w** to Lydia's home;
17: 2 And Paul **w** in, as was his custom,
17:10 they arrived, they **w** to the Jewish synagogue.
17:23 For as I **w** through the city and looked carefully at
18: 1 After this Paul left Athens and **w** to Corinth.
18: 2 to leave Rome. Paul **w** to see them,
18: 7 and **w** to the house of a man named Titius Justus,
18:19 but first he himself **w** into the synagogue and had
18:22 he **w** up to Jerusalem and greeted the church,
18:22 and then **w** down to Antioch.
18:23 After spending some time there he departed and **w**
20: 5 They **w** ahead and were waiting for us in Troas;
20:10 But Paul **w** down, and bending over him took him
20:11 Then Paul **w** upstairs,
20:13 We **w** ahead to the ship and set sail for Assos,
20:14 we took him on board and **w** to Mitylene.
21: 2 we **w** on board and set sail.
21: 6 we **w** on board the ship, and they returned home.
21: 8 and we **w** into the house of Philip the evangelist,
21:18 The next day Paul **w** with us to visit James;
22: 5 and I **w** there in order to bind those who were there
22:26 he **w** to the tribune and said to him,
23:14 They **w** to the chief priests and elders and said,
23:16 so he **w** and gained entrance to the barracks
24:11 not more than twelve days since I **w** up to worship
25: 1 he **w** up from Caesarea to Jerusalem
25: 6 among them not more than eight or ten days, he **w**
2Co 2:13 So I said farewell to them and **w** on to Macedonia.
Gal 1:17 but I **w** away at once into Arabia,
1:21 Then I **w** into the regions of Syria and Cilicia,
2: 1 after fourteen years I **w** up again to Jerusalem
2: 2 I **w** up in response to a revelation.
Heb 11:37 they **w** about in skins of sheep and goats, destitute,
1Pe 3:19 also he **w** and made a proclamation to the spirits
1Jn 2:19 They **w** out from us, but they did not belong to us;
Rev 5: 7 He **w** and took the scroll from the right hand of
10: 9 So I **w** to the angel and told him to give me
Rev 11:12 And they **w** up to heaven in a cloud
12:17 and **w** off to make war on the rest of her children,
16: 2 the first angel **w** and poured his bowl on the earth,
Tob 1: 6 But I alone **w** often to Jerusalem for the festivals,
1:19 Then one of the Ninevites **w** and informed the king
2: 3 So Tobias **w** to look for some poor person
2: 3 Then he **w** on to say, "Look, father,
2: 7 sun had set, I **w** and dug a grave and buried him.
2: 9 and **w** into my courtyard and slept by the wall of
2:10 I **w** to physicians to be healed,
2:10 of me for two years before he **w** to Elymais.
5: 4 So Tobias **w** out to look for a man to go with him
5: 4 He **w** out and found the angel Raphael standing
5: 9 Tobias **w** in to tell his father Tobit and said to him,
5:10 Then Tobias **w** out and called him, and said,
5:10 So he **w** in to him, and Tobit greeted him first.
5:17 Before he **w** out to start his journey,
6: 1 young man **w** out and the angel **w** with him;
6: 2 the dog came out with him and **w** along with them.
6: 3 Then the young man **w** down to wash his feet in
6:14 On the night when they **w** in to her,
7:11 and all died on the night when they **w** in to her.
7:16 So she **w** and made the bed in the room
7:16 Take courage, my daughter." Then she **w** out.
8: 9 Then they **w** to sleep for the night.
8: 9 and they **w** and dug a grave,
8:11 Raguel **w** into his house and called his wife,
8:13 she **w** in and found them sound asleep together.
8:19 and he **w** out to the herd and brought two steers
9: 5 with the four servants and two camels **w** to Rages
9: 6 In the morning they both got up early and **w** to
10: 6 The man who **w** with him is trustworthy and is one
11: 4 As they **w** on together Raphael said to him,
11: 4 And the dog **w** along behind them.
11: 6 and the man who **w** with him!"
11:10 through the courtyard door. Tobias **w** up to him,
11:15 So Tobit **w** in rejoicing and praising God at the top
11:16 **w** out to meet his daughter-in-law at the gate
12: 1 to paying the wages of the man who **w** with you,
14:10 but Nadab **w** into the eternal darkness,
Jdt 2:20 Along with them **w** a mixed crowd like a swarm
2:22 and chariots, and **w** up into the hill country.
2:27 Then he **w** down into the plain of Damascus during
3: 6 Then he **w** down to the seacoast with his army
5:10 of Canaan they **w** down to Egypt and lived there
6:11 the plain they **w** up into the hill country and came
7:18 the Edomites and Ammonites **w** up and encamped
7:32 they **w** up on the walls and towers of their town.
8:36 So they returned from the tent and **w** to their posts.
9: 5 "For you have done these things and those that **w**
10: 2 She called her maid and **w** down into the house
10: 6 Then they **w** out to the town gate of Bethulia
10:10 When they had done this, Judith **w** out,
12: 7 She **w** out each night to the valley of Bethulia,
12:15 Her maid **w** ahead and spread for her on
13: 1 They **w** to bed, for they all were weary because
13: 4 So everyone **w** out, and no one,
13: 6 She **w** up to the bedpost near Holofernes' head,
13: 9 afterward she **w** out and gave Holofernes' head to
13:10 Then the two of them **w** out together,
13:10 and **w** up the mountain to Bethulia,
13:16 Lord lives, who has protected me in the way I **w**,
14:11 they **w** out in companies to the mountain passes.
14:12 who then **w** to the generals and the captains and
14:14 Bagoas **w** in and knocked at the entry of the tent,
14:15 he opened it and **w** into the bedchamber
14:17 Then he **w** to the tent where Judith had stayed,
15:13 She **w** before all the people in the dance,
16:21 Judith **w** to Bethulia, and remained on her estate.
AdE 2:16 So Esther **w** in to King Artaxerxes in
4: 9 Hachratheus **w** in and told Esther all these things.
4:17 So Mordecai **w** away and did what Esther had told
5: 9 So Haman **w** out from the king joyful and glad
5:10 he **w** home and summoned his friends
7: 1 the king and Haman **w** in to drink with the queen.
7: 7 king rose from the banquet and **w** into the garden,
8:15 Mordecai **w** out dressed in the royal robe
9:25 he **w** in to the king, telling him to hang Mordecai;
15: 7 on the head of the maid who **w** in front of her.
Wis 8:18 I **w** about seeking how to get her for myself.
12:24 For they **w** far astray on the paths of error,
17:20 and **w** about its work unhindered,
Sir 41: 3 remember those who **w** before you
46: 9 so that he **w** up to the hill country,
48:23 In Isaiah's days the sun **w** backward,
50:11 when he **w** up to the holy altar,
51:13 before I **w** on my travels,
Bar 5: 6 For they **w** out from you on foot,
Sus 1:15 she **w** in as before with only two maids,
1:18 the doors of the garden and **w** out by the side doors
Bel 1: 4 The king revered it and **w** every day to worship it.
1:10 So the king **w** with Daniel into the temple of Bel.
1:14 Then they **w** out, shut the door and sealed it with
1Mc 1:13 and some of the people eagerly **w** to the king,
1:20 He **w** up against Israel and came to Jerusalem with
1:24 Taking them all, he **w** into his own land.
2:29 and justice **w** down to the wilderness to live there,
2:45 and his friends **w** around and tore down the altars;
3: 8 He **w** through the cities of Judah;
3:11 When Judas learned of it, he **w** out to meet him,
3:13 of faithful soldiers who stayed with him and **w** out
3:15 Once again a strong army of godless men **w** up
3:16 Judas **w** out to meet him with a small company.
3:37 He crossed the Euphrates river and **w** through
3:41 and **w** to the camp to get the Israelites for slaves.
3:45 not one of her children **w** in or out.
3:46 Then they gathered together and **w** to Mizpah,

1Mc 4:13 they **w** out from their camp to battle
4:26 of the foreigners who escaped **w** and reported
4:37 all the army assembled and **w** up to Mount Zion.
5:21 So Simon **w** to Galilee and fought many battles
5:29 they **w** all the way to the stronghold of Dathema.
5:31 the battle had begun and that the cry of the town **w**
5:39 And Judas **w** to meet them.
5:54 So they **w** up to Mount Zion with joy and gladness,
5:65 and his brothers **w** out and fought the descendants
5:67 fell in battle, for they **w** out to battle unwisely.
6:22 They **w** to the king and said,
6:36 wherever it **w**, they **w** with it,
6:48 of the king's army **w** up to Jerusalem against them,
7:20 then Bacchides **w** back to the king.
7:24 Judas **w** out into all the surrounding parts of Judea,
7:31 he **w** out to meet Judas in battle
7:33 After these events Nicanor **w** up to Mount Zion.
7:35 And he **w** out in great anger.
7:36 At this the priests **w** in and stood before the altar
7:39 Now Nicanor **w** out from Jerusalem and encamped
7:41 your angel **w** out and struck
8: 6 who **w** to fight against them
8:19 They **w** to Rome, a very long journey;
9: 2 They **w** by the road that leads to Gilgal
9: 4 and **w** to Berea with twenty thousand foot soldiers
9:11 the slingers and the archers **w** ahead of the army,
9:14 then all the stouthearted men **w** with him,
9:24 and the country **w** over to their side.
9:38 they **w** up and hid under cover of the mountain.
9:47 but he eluded him and **w** to the rear.
9:59 And they **w** and consulted with him.
9:65 while he **w** out into the country;
9:65 and he **w** with only a few men.
9:67 to attack and **w** into battle with his forces;
9:72 then he turned and **w** back to his own land,
10:13 all of them left their places and **w** back
10:60 So he **w** with pomp to Ptolemais and met
10:77 and **w** to Azotus as though he were going farther.
11: 2 of the towns opened their gates to him and **w**
11: 7 And Jonathan **w** with the king as far as
11:21 But certain renegades who hated their nation **w** to
11:24 for he **w** to the king at Ptolemais,
11:39 So he **w** to Imalkue the Arab,
11:61 From there he **w** to Gaza,
11:64 He **w** to meet them, but left his brother Simon in
12: 3 So they **w** to Rome and entered the senate chamber
12:32 Then he broke camp and **w** to Damascus,
12:33 Simon also **w** out and marched through the country
12:41 Jonathan **w** out to meet him
13: 2 So he **w** up to Jerusalem,
13:20 along opposite him to every place he **w**.
13:22 He marched off and **w** into the land of Gilead.
13:24 Then Trypho turned and **w** back to his own land.
13:45 **w** up on the wall with their clothes torn,
14: 3 general **w** and defeated the army of Demetrius,
16: 1 John **w** up from Gazara and reported
16:14 and he **w** down to Jericho with his sons Mattathias
2Mc 1:32 when the light from the altar shone back, it **w** out.
2: 4 and that he **w** out to the mountain
3: 5 he **w** to Apollonius of Tarsus,
3:14 So he set a day and **w** in to direct the inspection
3:23 Heliodorus **w** on with what had been decided.
4:11 who **w** on the mission to establish friendship
4:31 So the king **w** hurriedly to settle the trouble,
5:12 and to kill those who **w** into their houses.
6:19 **w** up to the rack of his own accord,
6:28 When he had said this, he **w** at once to the rack.
12: 1 and the Jews **w** about their farming.
12:12 receiving his pledges they **w** back to their tents.
12:31 Then they **w** up to Jerusalem,
12:38 Then Judas assembled his army and **w** to the city
12:39 and his men **w** to take up the bodies of the fallen
13:25 and **w** to Ptolemais. The people of Ptolemais
14: 4 and **w** to King Demetrius in about
14:26 he took the covenant that had been made and **w**
14:30 and **w** into hiding from Nicanor.
14:31 he **w** to the great and holy temple while
14:34 Having said this, he **w** away.
1Es 1:25 **w** to make war at Carchemish on the Euphrates,
1:25 and Josiah **w** out against him.
2:30 the scribe Shimshai and their associates **w** quickly
3: 3 and when they were satisfied they **w** away,
3: 3 and King Darius **w** to his bedroom;
3: 3 he **w** to sleep, but woke up again.
4:58 When the young man **w** out,
4:61 and **w** to Babylon and told this to all his kindred.
5: 4 These are the names of the men who **w** up,
6: 8 when we **w** to the country of Judea and entered
8:28 who **w** up with me from Babylon,
9: 1 and **w** from the court of the temple to the chamber
9:54 Then they all **w** their way,
Pm 151: 6 I **w** out to meet the Philistine,
3Mc 1: 4 Arsinoë **w** to the troops with wailing and tears,
2:24 but **w** away uttering bitter threats.
3:16 **w** up to honor the temple of those wicked people,
4:12 from the city frequently **w** out in secret
5: 5 the Jews **w** out in the evening and bound the hands
5:21 and all **w** to their own homes.
2Es 4: 8 'I never **w** down into the deep,
4:13 "I **w** into a forest of trees of the plain,
6:43 your word **w** forth, and at once the work was done.
9:26 So I **w**, as he directed me,
10:32 I did as you directed, and **w** out into the field,
11:19 And so it **w** with all the wings;
12:50 So the people **w** into the city, as I told them to do.
13:43 And they **w** in by the narrow passages of
14:27 Then I **w** as he commanded me,
2Es 15:23 And a fire **w** forth from his wrath,
4Mc 3:13 they **w** searching throughout the enemy camp
4: 4 he praised Simon for his service to the king and **w**
4: 8 uttering threats, Apollonius **w** on to the temple.
4:14 **w** away to report to the king what had happened

WEPT‡ (83) [WEEP]

Ge 21:16 she sat opposite him, she lifted up her voice and **w**.
27:38 And Esau lifted up his voice and **w**.
29:11 Then Jacob kissed Rachel, and **w** aloud.
33: 4 and fell on his neck and kissed him, and they **w**.
42:24 He turned away from them and **w**;
43:30 So he went into a private room and **w** there.
45: 2 And he **w** so loudly that the Egyptians heard it,
45:14 he fell upon his brother Benjamin's neck and **w**,
while Benjamin **w** upon his neck.
45:15 And he kissed all his brothers and **w** upon them;
46:29 fell on his neck, and **w** on his neck a good while.
50: 1 on his father's face and **w** over him
50: 3 And the Egyptians **w** for him seventy days.
50:17 Joseph **w** when they spoke to him.
50:18 Then his brothers also **w**, fell down before him,
Nu 11: 4 and the Israelites also **w** again, and said,
14: 1 and the people **w** that night.
Dt 1:45 When you returned and **w** before the LORD,
34: 8 The Israelites **w** for Moses in the plains
Jdg 2: 4 the people lifted up their voices and **w**.
14:16 So Samson's wife **w** before him, saying,
14:17 She **w** before him the seven days
20:23 The Israelites went up and **w** before the LORD
20:26 the whole army, went back to Bethel and **w**,
21: 2 and they lifted up their voices and **w** bitterly.
Ru 1: 9 Then she kissed them, and they **w** aloud.
1:14 Then they **w** aloud again.
1Sa 1: 7 Therefore Hannah **w** and would not eat.
1:10 and prayed to the LORD, and **w** bitterly.
11: 4 and all the people **w** aloud.
20:41 and **w** with each other; David **w** the more.
24:16 Saul lifted up his voice and **w**.
30: 4 with him raised their voices and **w**,
2Sa 1:12 They mourned and **w**, and fasted until evening
3:32 and **w** at the grave of Abner, and all the people **w**.
3:34 And all the people **w** over him again.
12:21 You fasted and **w** for the child while it was alive;
12:22 "While the child was still alive, I fasted and **w**;
13:36 and raised their voices and **w**;
13:36 the king and all his servants also **w** very bitterly.
15:23 whole country **w** aloud as all the people passed by;
18:33 and went up to the chamber over the gate, and **w**;
2Ki 8:11 Then the man of God **w**.
13:14 and **w** before him, crying, "My father, my father!
20: 3 in your sight." Hezekiah **w** bitterly.
22:19 you have torn your clothes and **w** before me,
2Ch 34:27 and have torn your clothes and **w** before me,
Ezr 3:12 **w** with a loud voice when they saw this house,
10: 1 of Israel; the people also **w** bitterly.
Ne 1: 4 When I heard these words I sat down and **w**,
8: 9 For all the people **w** when they heard the words of
Job 2:12 and they raised their voices and **w** aloud;
31:38 and its furrows have **w** together;
Ps 137: 1 down and there we **w** when we remembered Zion.
Isa 38: 3 in your sight." And Hezekiah **w** bitterly.
Hos 12: 4 he **w** and sought his favor;
Mt 26:75 And he went out and **w** bitterly.
Mk 14:72 And he broke down and **w**.
Lk 19:41 As he came near and saw the city, he **w** over it,
22:62 And he went out and **w** bitterly.
Jn 20:11 As she **w**, she bent over to look into the tomb;
Rev 18:19 as they **w** and mourned, crying out, "Alas, alas,
Tob 2: 6 into lamentation." And I **w**.
3: 1 Then with much grief and anguish of heart I **w**,
3:10 On that day she was grieved in spirit and **w**.
7: 6 At that Raguel jumped up and kissed him and **w**.
7: 7 He then embraced his kinsman Tobias and **w**.
7: 8 His wife Edna also **w** for him,
7: 8 and their daughter Sarah likewise **w**.
7:16 She **w** for her daughter.
9: 6 who **w** and blessed him with the words,
11: 9 I am ready to die." And she **w**.
11:14 and he **w** and said to him,
Jdt 14:16 with a loud voice and **w** and groaned and shouted,
Bar 1: 5 they **w**, and fasted, and prayed before the Lord;
1Mc 7:36 and the temple; they **w** and said,
9:20 and **w** for him. All Israel made great lamentation
2Mc 4:37 and **w** because of the moderation
3Mc 6:23 he **w** and angrily threatened his Friends, saying,
2Es 6:35 Now after this I **w** again and fasted seven days in
12:45 And they **w** with a loud voice.

WERE (3182) [BE] See Index of Articles Etc.

WEST (95) [NORTHWEST, SOUTHWEST, WESTERN, WESTWARD]

Ge 12: 8 with Bethel on the **w** and Ai on the east;
28:14 to the **w** and to the east and to the north and to
Ex 10:19 into a very strong **w** wind, which lifted the locusts
27:12 of the court on the **w** side there shall be fifty cubits
38:12 the **w** side there were hangings fifty cubits long,
Nu 2:18 On the **w** side shall be the regimental encampment
3:23 to camp behind the tabernacle on the **w**,
35: 5 for the **w** side two thousand cubits,
Dt 3:27 to the top of Pisgah and look around you to the **w**,
11:30 to the **w**, in the land of the Canaanites who live in
33:23 possess the **w** and the south.
Jos 1: 4 to the Great Sea in the **w** shall be your territory.
5: 1 of the Amorites beyond the Jordan to the **w**,
8: 9 and lay between Bethel and Ai, to the **w** of Ai;
8:12 to the **w** of the city.
8:13 that was north of the city and its rear guard **w** of
11: 2 and in the lowland, and in Naphoth-dor on the **w**,
11: 3 to the Canaanites in the east and the **w**,
12: 7 the Israelites defeated on the **w** side of the Jordan,
15: 8 over against the valley of Hinnom, on the **w**, at
15:10 the boundary circles **w** of Baalah to Mount Seir,
15:12 **w** boundary was the Mediterranean with its coast.
19:26 on the **w** it touches Carmel and Shihor-libnath,
19:34 at the south, and Asher on the **w**, and Judah on
22: 7 beside their fellow Israelites in the land **w** of
23: 4 from the Jordan to the Great Sea in the **w**.
Jdg 18:12 to this day; it is **w** of Kiriath-jearim.
20:33 in ambush rushed out of their place **w** of Geba.
1Ki 4:24 For he had dominion over all the region **w** of
4:24 over all the kings **w** of the Euphrates;
7:25 three facing **w**, three facing south,
1Ch 9:24 The gatekeepers were on the four sides, east, **w**,
12:15 to the east and to the **w**.
26:16 For Shuppim and Hosah it came out for the **w**,
26:18 the colonnade on the **w** there were four at the road
26:30 had the oversight of Israel **w** of the Jordan for all
2Ch 4: 4 three facing **w**, three facing south,
32:30 of Gihon and directed them down to the **w** side of
33:14 an outer wall for the city of David **w** of Gihon,
Job 18:20 They of the **w** are appalled at their fate,
Ps 75: 6 For not from the east or from the **w** and not from
103:12 as far as the east is from the **w**,
107: 3 from the east and from the **w**,
Isa 9:12 Arameans on the east and the Philistines on the **w**,
11:14 down on the backs of the Philistines in the **w**,
24:14 from the **w** over the majesty of the LORD.
43: 5 and from the **w** I will gather you;
45: 6 from the rising of the sun and from the **w**,
49:12 and lo, these from the north and from the **w**,
59:19 those in the **w** shall fear the name of the LORD,
Eze 41:12 on the **w** side was seventy cubits wide;
41:15 the depth of the building facing the yard at the **w**,
42:19 Then he turned to the **w** side and measured,
45: 7 on the **w** and on the east,
47:20 On the **w** side, the Great Sea shall be the boundary
47:20 This shall be the **w** side.
48: 1 and extending from the east side to the **w**, Dan,
48: 2 from the east side to the **w**, Asher, one portion.
48: 3 from the east side to the **w**, Naphtali, one portion.
48: 4 from the east side to the **w**, Manasseh, one portion.
48: 5 from the east side to the **w**, Ephraim, one portion.
48: 6 from the east side to the **w**, Reuben, one portion.
48: 7 from the east side to the **w**, Judah, one portion.
48: 8 from the east side to the **w**,
48: 8 from the east side to the **w**,
48:16 and the **w** side four thousand and five hundred.
48:17 on the **w** two hundred fifty.
48:18 and ten thousand to the **w**,
48:21 the twenty-five thousand cubits to the **w** border,
48:23 from the east side to the **w**, Benjamin, one portion.
48:24 from the east side to the **w**, Simeon, one portion.
48:25 from the east side to the **w**, Issachar, one portion.
48:26 from the east side to the **w**, Zebulun, one portion.
48:27 from the east side to the **w**, Gad, one portion.
48:34 On the **w** side, which is to be four thousand
Da 8: 5 I was watching, a male goat appeared from the **w**,
Hos 11:10 his children shall come trembling from the **w**.
Zec 6: 6 the white ones go toward the **w** country,
8: 7 from the east country and from the **w** country;
14: 4 of Olives shall be split in two from east to **w** by
Mt 8:11 many will come from east and **w** and will eat
24:27 from the east and flashes as far as the **w**,
Mk 16: S ⟦to **w**, the sacred and imperishable proclamation⟧
Lk 12:54 "When you see a cloud rising in the **w**,
13:29 Then people will come from east and **w**,
Rev 21:13 on the south three gates, and on the **w** three gates.
Tob 1: 2 above Asher toward the **w**, and north of Phogor.
Jdt 1: 7 in Persia and to all who lived in the **w**,
2: 6 March out against all the land to the **w**,
2:19 of the earth to the **w** with their chariots and cavalry
5: 4 And why have they alone, of all who live in the **w**,
Bar 4:37 they are coming, gathered from east and **w**,
5: 5 and see your children gathered from **w** and east at
2Es 15:38 and from the north, and another part from the **w**.
15:39 be driven violently toward the south and **w**.

WESTERN (11) [WEST]

Nu 34: 6 For the **w** boundary, you shall have the Great Sea
34: 6 this shall be your **w** boundary.
Dt 11:24 the river Euphrates, to the **W** Sea.
34: 2 all the land of Judah as far as the **W** Sea,
Jos 18:14 the **w** side southward from the mountain that lies
18:14 This forms the **w** side.
Eze 45: 7 and extending from the **w** to the eastern boundary
46:19 there I saw a place at the extreme **w** end of them.
48:10 ten thousand cubits in width on the **w** side,
Joel 2:20 and its rear into the **w** sea;
Zec 14: 8 to the eastern sea and half of them to the **w** sea;

WESTWARD‡ (13) [WEST]

Ge 13:14 northward and southward and eastward and **w**;
Ex 26:22 rear of the tabernacle **w** you shall make six frames.
26:27 of the side of the tabernacle at the rear **w**.
36:27 the rear of the tabernacle **w** he made six frames.
36:32 for the frames of the tabernacle at the rear **w**.
Jos 16: 3 it goes down **w** to the territory of the Japhletites,
16: 8 the boundary goes **w** to the Wadi Kanah,
18:12 then up through the hill country **w**;

Jos 19:11 up w, and on to Maralah, and touches Dabbesheth,
19:34 then the boundary turns w to Aznoth-tabor,
1Ch 7:28 and w Gezer and its towns, Shechem and its towns,
Eze 48:21 and w from the twenty-five thousand cubits to
Da 8: 4 the ram charging w and northward and southward.

WET (2)

Job 24: 8 They are w with the rain of the mountains,
SS 5: 2 for my head is w with dew,

WHALE, WHALE'S, WHALES (KJV) See also DRAGON, SEA MONSTER

WHALES (1)

Aza 1:57 you w and all that swim in the waters;

WHAT (2117) [WHATEVER] See Index of Articles Etc.

WHATEVER‡ (205) [WHAT]

Ge 2:19 and w the man called every living creature,
21:12 w Sarah says to you, do as she tells you,
31:16 now then, do w God has said to you."
34:11 and w you say to me I will give.
34:12 and I will give w you ask me;
34:28 and w was in the city and in the field.
39:22 and w was done there, he was the one who did it.
39:23 and w he did, the LORD made it prosper.
Ex 13: 2 w is the first to open the womb among
21:30 then the owner shall pay w is imposed for
29:37 w touches the altar shall become holy.
30:29 w touches them will become holy.
Lev 5: 4 w people utter in an oath, and are unaware of it,
6:27 W touches its flesh shall become holy;
7:26 You must not eat any blood w,
11:36 while w touches the carcass in it shall be unclean.
11:42 W moves on its belly, and w moves on all fours,
11:42 or w has many feet, all the creatures that swarm
13:51 or in the skin, w be the use of the skin,
22: 5 w his uncleanness may be—
Nu 3:38 w had to be done for the Israelites;
5:10 w anyone gives to the priest shall be his.
6:21 In accordance with w vow they take,
10:32 if you go with us, w good the LORD does for us,
18:11 a perpetual due, w is set aside from the gifts of all
19:22 W the unclean person touches shall be unclean,
22:17 and w you say to me I will do;
23: 3 W he shows me I will tell you."
23:26 'W the LORD says, that is what I must do'?"
30:12 w proceeds out of her lips concerning her vows,
31:23 and w cannot withstand fire,
Dt 14: 9 w has fins and scales you may eat.
14:10 w does not have fins and scales you shall not eat;
14:26 spend the money for w you wish—
14:26 oxen, sheep, wine, strong drink, or w you desire.
15: 3 but you must remit your claim on w any member
15: 8 to meet the need, w it may be.
23:23 W your lips utter you must diligently perform,
24: 8 you shall carefully observe w
Jos 1:18 w you command, shall be put to death.
Jdg 10:15 do to us w seems good to you;
19:24 Ravish them and do w you want to them;
1Sa 2:16 and then take w you wish," he would say, "No,
9: 6 W he says always comes true.
10: 7 when these signs meet you, do w you see fit to do,
11:10 and you may do to us w seems good to you."
14:36 They said, "Do w seems good to you."
20: 4 Then Jonathan said to David, "W you say,
21: 3 Give me five loaves of bread, or w is here."
25: 8 Please give w you have at hand to your servants
2Sa 15:15 "Your servants are ready to do w our lord
15:35 So w you hear from the king's house,
17:12 in w place he may be found, and we shall light
18: 4 king said to them, "W seems best to you I will do."
19:37 and do for him w seems good to you."
19:38 and I will do for him w seems good to you;
1Ki 2:36 and do not go out from there to any place w.
2:42 that on the day you go out and go to any place w,
5: 6 I will give you w wages you set for your servants;
8:37 w plague, w sickness there is;
8:38 w prayer, w plea there is from any individual or
8:44 by w way you shall send them,
9:19 and w Solomon desired to build, in Jerusalem,
20: 6 and lay hands on w pleases them,
22:14 "As the LORD lives, w the LORD says to me,
2Ki 10: 5 not make anyone king; do w you think right."
18:14 w you impose on me I will bear."
1Ch 26:31 of David's reign search was made, of w genealogy
2Ch 2:16 We will cut w timber you need from Lebanon,
6:28 w suffering, w sickness there is;
6:29 w prayer, w plea from any individual or
6:33 and do w the foreigners ask of you,
6:34 by w way you shall send them,
8: 6 and w Solomon desired to build, in Jerusalem,
18:13 "As the LORD lives, w my God says,
Ezr 1: 4 in w place they reside, be assisted by the people
6: 9 W is needed—young bulls,
7:18 W seems good to you and your colleagues to do
7:20 And w else is required for the house of your God,
7:21 W the priest Ezra, the scribe of the law of the God
7:23 W is commanded by the God of heaven,
Est 2:13 to the king she was given w she asked for to take
Ps 8: 8 w passes along the paths of the seas.
115: 3 Our God is in the heavens; he does w he pleases.
Ps 135: 6 W the LORD pleases he does,
Pr 4: 7 Get wisdom, and w else you get, get insight.
Ecc 2:10 W my eyes desired I did not keep from them;
3:14 I know that w God does endures forever;
6:10 W has come to be has already been named,
8: 3 the matter is unpleasant, for he does w he pleases.
9:10 W your hand finds to do, do with your might;
Jer 1: 7 and you shall speak w I command you,
42: 4 and w the LORD answers you I will tell you;
42:20 and w the LORD our God says,
Eze 10:11 but in w direction the front wheel faced,
47:23 In w tribe aliens reside, there you shall assign them
Zec 14:15 and w animals may be in those camps.
Mt 10:11 W town or village you enter,
14: 7 on oath to grant her w she might ask.
15: 5 'W support you might have had from me is given
15:17 Do you not see that w goes into the mouth enters
16:19 w you bind on earth will be bound in heaven, and
w you loose on earth will be loosed in heaven."
17:12 but they did to him w they pleased.
18:18 w you bind on earth will be bound in heaven, and
w you loose on earth will be loosed in heaven.
20: 4 and I will pay you w is right.'
21:22 W you ask for in prayer with faith,
23: 3 do w they teach you and follow it;
Mk 3:28 for their sins and w blasphemies they utter;
6:22 the king said to the girl, "Ask me for w you wish,
6:23 And he solemnly swore to her, "W you ask me,
7:11 'W support you might have had
7:18 Do you not see that w goes into a person
9:13 and they did to him w they pleased,
10:35 we want you to do for us w we ask of you."
11:24 So I tell you, w you ask for in prayer,
13:11 but say w is given you at that time,
Lk 9: 4 W house you enter, stay there,
10: 5 W house you enter, first say, 'Peace to this house!'
10: 7 eating and drinking w they provide,
10:35 I come back, I will repay you w more you spend.'
11: 8 up and give him w he needs.
12: 3 Therefore w you have said in the dark will
Jn 2: 5 to the servants, "Do w he tells you."
5:19 for w the Father does, the Son does likewise.
11:22 I know that God will give you w you ask of him."
14:13 I will do w you ask in my name,
15: 7 and my words abide in you, ask for w you wish,
15:16 Father will give you w you ask him in my name.
16:13 but will speak w he hears,
Ac 3:22 You must listen to w he tells you.
4:28 to do w your hand and your plan had predestined
15:20 from fornication and from w has been strangled
Ro 3:19 Now we know that w the law says,
14:23 for w does not proceed from faith is sin.
15: 4 For w was written in former days was written
16: 2 and help her in w she may require from you,
1Co 7:24 In w condition you were called,
10:25 Eat w is sold in the meat market
10:27 eat w is set before you
10:31 So, whether you eat or drink, or w you do,
16: 2 of you is to put aside and save w extra you earn,
2Co 11:21 But w anyone dares to boast of—
Gal 6: 7 God is not mocked, for you reap w you sow.
Eph 6: 8 knowing that w good we do,
6:15 on w will make you ready to proclaim the gospel
Php 3: 7 Yet w gains I had, these I have come to regard
4: 8 Finally, beloved, w is true, w is honorable, w is
just, w is pure, w is pleasing, w is commendable,
4:11 for I have learned to be content with w I have.
Col 3: 5 Put to death, therefore, w in you is earthly:
3:17 And w you do, in word or deed,
3:23 W your task, put yourselves into it,
3:25 be paid back for w wrong has been done,
1Th 3:10 to face and restore w is lacking in your faith.
1Ti 1:10 and w else is contrary to the sound teaching
1Pe 4:10 with w gift each of you has received.
2Pe 2:19 for people are slaves to w masters them.
1Jn 3:22 and we receive from him w we ask,
5: 4 for w is born of God conquers the world.
5:15 And if we know that he hears us in w we ask,
3Jn 1: 5 you do faithfully w you do for the friends,
Jude 1:10 But these people slander w they do not understand,
Tob 2: 2 and bring w poor person you may find
4: 3 Do w pleases her, and do not grieve her
14: 4 For I know and believe that w God has said will
14:10 On w day you bury your mother beside me,
Jdt 3: 2 Do with us w you will.
12:14 W pleases him I will do at once,
AdE 1:20 Let w law the king enacts be proclaimed
2: 3 let ointments and w else they need be given them.
3:11 and do w you want with that nation."
8: 8 for w is written at the king's command and sealed
9:12 W more you ask will be done for you."
Sir 2: 4 Accept w befalls you, and in times of humiliation
33:13 to be given w he decides.
39:16 and w he commands will be done at
41:10 W comes from earth returns to earth;
LtJ 6:44 W is done for these idols is false.
6:69 So we have no evidence w that they are gods;
1Mc 13:39 and w other tax has been collected
14:34 and provided in those towns w was necessary
2Mc 11: 4 He took no account w of the power of God,
13:20 Judas sent in to the garrison w was necessary.
1Es 4: 3 and w he says to them they obey.
4: 5 w spoil they take and everything else.
8:16 W you and your kindred are minded to do with
8:18 And w else occurs to you as necessary for
8:19 and Phoenicia that w Ezra the priest and reader of
3Mc 6:10 and destroy us, Lord, by w fate you choose.
3Mc 7: 7 of every charge of w kind.
2Es 12:39 that you may be shown w it pleases the Most High
13:58 because he governs the times and w things come
4Mc 8:14 w justice you revere will be merciful to you
18: 5 in no way w was he able to compel the Israelites

WHEAT (52)

Ge 30:14 of w harvest Reuben went and found mandrakes in
Ex 9:32 But the w and the spelt were not ruined,
29: 2 You shall make them of choice w flour.
34:22 the first fruits of w harvest,
Dt 8: 8 a land of w and barley,
32:14 together with the choicest w—
Jdg 6:11 as his son Gideon was beating out w in
15: 1 After a while, at the time of the w harvest,
Ru 2:23 gleaning until the end of the barley and w harvests;
1Sa 6:13 of Beth-shemesh were reaping their w harvest in
12:17 Is it not the w harvest today?
2Sa 4: 6 They came inside the house as though to take w,
17:28 w, barley, meal, parched grain, beans and lentils,
1Ki 5:11 in turn gave Hiram twenty thousand cors of w
1Ch 21:20 Ornan continued to thresh w.
21:23 and the w for a grain offering.
2Ch 2:10 twenty thousand cors of crushed w,
2:15 Now, as for the w, barley, oil, and wine,
27: 5 ten thousand cors of w and ten thousand of barley.
Ezr 6: 9 to the God of heaven, w, salt, wine, or oil,
7:22 one hundred cors of w, one hundred baths of wine,
Job 31:40 let thorns grow instead of w,
Ps 81:16 I would feed you with the finest of the w,
147:14 he fills you with the finest of w.
SS 7: 2 Your belly is a heap of w, encircled with lilies.
Isa 28:25 and plant w in rows and barley in its proper place,
Jer 12:13 They have sown w and have reaped thorns,
23:28 What has straw in common with w?
41: 8 "Do not kill us, for we have stores of w, barley,
Eze 4: 9 And you, take w and barley, beans and lentils,
27:17 they exchanged for your merchandise w
45:13 one-sixth of an ephah from each homer of w,
Joel 1:11 wail, you vinedressers, over the w and the barley;
Am 8: 5 and the sabbath, so that we may offer w for sale?
8: 6 and selling the sweepings of the w."
Mt 3:12 and will gather his w into the granary;
13:25 an enemy came and sowed weeds among the w,
13:29 for in gathering the weeds you would uproot the w
13:30 but gather the w into my barn.' "
Lk 3:17 to clear his threshing floor and to gather the w
16: 7 He replied, 'A hundred containers of w.'
22:31 Satan has demanded to sift all of you like w,
Jn 12:24 unless a grain of w falls into the earth and dies,
Ac 27:38 they lightened the ship by throwing the w into
1Co 15:37 perhaps of w or of some other grain.
Rev 6: 6 "A quart of w for a day's pay,
18:13 frankincense, wine, olive oil, choice flour and w,
Jdt 2:27 into the plain of Damascus during the w harvest,
3: 3 and all our land and all our w fields and our flocks
Sir 39:26 and iron and salt and w flour and milk and honey,
1Es 6:30 and likewise w and salt and wine and oil,
8:20 and likewise up to a hundred cors of w,

WHEEL‡ (27) [WHEELED, WHEELS, WHEELWORK]

1Ki 7:32 and the height of a w was a cubit and a half.
7:33 The wheels were made like a chariot w;
Pr 20:26 and drives the w over them.
Ecc 12: 6 and the w broken at the cistern,
Isa 28:27 nor is a cart w rolled over cummin;
28:28 one drives the cart w and horses over it,
Jer 18: 3 and there he was working at his w.
Eze 1:15 I saw a w on the earth beside the living creatures,
1:16 something like a w within a w.
10: 6 he went in and stood beside a w.
10:10 something like a w within a w.
10:11 but in whatever direction the front w faced,
Na 3: 2 The crack of whip and rumble of w,
Sir 33: 5 The heart of a fool is like a cart w,
38:29 the potter sitting at his work and turning the w
4Mc 5: 3 they were to be broken on the w and killed.
9:12 they placed him upon the w.
9:17 your w is not so powerful as to strangle my reason.
9:19 fanning the flames they tightened the w further.
9:20 The w was completely smeared with blood,
10: 8 They immediately brought him to the w,
11:10 they twisted his back around the wedge on the w,
11:17 When he had said this, they led him to the w.
12:11 and torture on the w those who practice religion?
15:22 then suffered as her sons were tortured on the w

WHEELED (1) [WHEEL]

2Mc 10:36 up in the same way w around against the defenders

WHEELS (28) [WHEEL]

Ex 14:25 He clogged their chariot w so that they turned
1Ki 7:30 Each stand had four bronze w and axles of bronze;
7:32 The four w were underneath the borders;
7:32 the axles of the w were in the stands;
7:33 The w were made like a chariot wheel;
Isa 5:28 and their w like the whirlwind.
Jer 47: 3 at the rumbling of their w,
Eze 1:16 for the appearance of the w and their construction:
1:19 living creatures moved, the w moved beside them;
1:19 the living creatures rose from the earth, the w rose.
1:20 they went, and the w rose along with them;
1:20 for the spirit of the living creatures was in the w.

Eze 1:21 the w rose along with them;
1:21 for the spirit of the living creatures was in the w.
3:13 and the sound of the w beside them,
10: 9 and there were four w beside the cherubim,
10: 9 the appearance of the w was like gleaming beryl.
10:12 their rims, their spokes, their wings, and the w—
10:12 the w of the four of them—
10:13 As for the w, they were called in my hearing
10:16 the cherubim moved, the w moved beside them;
10:16 the w at their side did not veer.
10:19 the earth in my sight as they went out with the w
11:22 the cherubim lifted up their wings, with the w
26:10 At the noise of cavalry, w,
Da 7: 9 and its w were burning fire.
4Mc 5:32 Therefore get your torture w ready and fan
8:13 When the guards had placed before them w

WHEELWORK (3) [WHEEL]

Eze 10: 2 "Go within the w underneath the cherubim;
10: 6 "Take fire from within the w,
10:13 they were called in my hearing "the w."

WHELP (2) [WHELPS]

Ge 49: 9 Judah is a lion's w; from the prey, my son,
Dt 33:22 Dan is a lion's w that leaps forth from Bashan.

WHELP[S] (KJV) See also CUBS

WHELPS‡ (3) [WHELP]

Job 4:11 and the w of the lioness are scattered.
Jer 51:38 they shall growl like lions' w.
Na 2:12 for his w and strangled prey for his lionesses;

WHEN (3693) [WHENEVER] See Index of Articles Etc.

WHENCE (1)

4Mc 13:12 "Remember w you came, and the father

WHENCE (KJV) See also HOW, THERE, WHERE, WHICH, WHY

WHENEVER (61) [WHEN]

Ge 30:41 W the stronger of the flock were breeding,
38: 9 on the ground w he went in to his brother's wife,
Ex 17:11 W Moses held up his hand, Israel prevailed; and w he lowered his hand, Amalek prevailed.
33: 8 W Moses went out to the tent,
34:34 but w Moses went in before the LORD to speak
40:36 W the cloud was taken up from the tabernacle,
Nu 9:17 W the cloud lifted from over the tent,
10: 6 An alarm is to be blown w they are to set out.
10:35 W the ark set out, Moses would say, "Arise,
10:36 And w it came to rest, he would say, "Return,
15:19 w you eat of the bread of the land,
21: 9 and w a serpent bit someone,
Dt 4: 7 to it as the LORD our God is w we call to him?
12:15 Yet w you desire you may slaughter and eat meat
12:20 you may eat meat w you have the desire.
12:21 then you may eat within your towns w you desire.
18: 6 (and he may come w he wishes),
Jdg 2:15 W they marched out, the hand of the LORD was
2:18 W the LORD raised up judges for them,
2:19 But w the judge died, they would relapse
6: 3 For w the Israelites put in seed,
12: 5 W one of the fugitives of Ephraim said,
1Sa 16:23 And w the evil spirit from God came upon Saul,
17:34 and w a lion or a bear came,
23:20 Now, O king, w you wish to come down, do so;
2Sa 15: 5 W people came near to do obeisance to him,
1Ki 8:52 listening to them w they call to you.
2Ki 4: 8 So w he passed that way,
4:10 so that he can stay there w he comes to us."
12:10 W they saw that there was a great deal of money in
1Ch 23:31 and w burnt offerings are offered to the LORD
2Ch 7: 6 w David offered praises by their ministry.
12:11 W the king went into the house of the LORD,
19:10 w a case comes to you from your kindred who live
24:11 W the chest was brought to the king's officers by
Jer 20: 8 For w I speak, I must cry out, I must shout,
48:27 but w you spoke of him you shook your head!
Eze 3:17 w you hear a word from my mouth,
33: 7 w you hear a word from my mouth,
Mt 6: 2 "So w you give alms, do not sound a trumpet
6: 5 "And w you pray, do not be like the hypocrites;
6: 6 But w you pray, go into your room and shut
6:16 "And w you fast, do not look dismal,
Mk 3:11 W the unclean spirits saw him,
9:18 and w it seizes him, it dashes him down;
11:25 "W you stand praying, forgive,
14: 7 and you can show kindness to them w you wish;
Lk 10: 8 W you enter a town and its people welcome you,
10:10 w you enter a town and they do not welcome you,
2Co 3:15 Indeed, to this very day w Moses is read,
12:10 for w I am weak, then I am strong.
Gal 6:10 So then, w we have an opportunity,
Jas 1: 2 w you face trials of any kind,
1Jn 3:20 w our hearts condemn us;
Rev 4: 9 And w the living creatures give glory and honor
Tob 12:12 and likewise w you would bury the dead.
Wis 12:18 for you have power to act w you choose.
1Es 1:51 and w the Lord spoke, they scoffed at his prophets,
1Es 4: 6 w they sow and reap, and bring some to the king;
2Es 13: 4 and w his voice issued from his mouth,

WHERE‡ (625) [ANYWHERE, ELSEWHERE, EVERYWHERE, NOWHERE, SOMEWHERE, WHEREVER]

Ge 2:11 around the whole land of Havilah, w there is gold;
3: 9 and said to him, "W are you?"
4: 9 LORD said to Cain, "W is your brother Abel?"
13: 3 to the place w his tent had been at the beginning,
13: 4 to the place w he had made an altar at the first;
13:14 and look from the place w you are,
16: 8 w have you come from and w are you going?"
17: 8 the land w you are now an alien,
18: 9 They said to him, "W is your wife Sarah?"
19: 5 "W are the men who came to you tonight?
19:27 Abraham went early in the morning to the place w
20:15 before you; settle w it pleases you."
21:17 for God has heard the voice of the boy w he is.
21:23 and with the land w you have resided as an alien."
22: 7 but w is the lamb for a burnt offering?"
28: 4 so that you may take possession of the land w you
29: 4 "My brothers, w do you come from?"
30:38 the watering places, w the flocks came to drink.
31: 4 and called Rachel and Leah into the field w
31:13 w you anointed a pillar and made a vow to me.
32:17 'To whom do you belong? W are you going?
35:13 from him at the place w he had spoken with him.
35:14 up a pillar in the place w he had spoken with him,
35:15 the place w God had spoken with him Bethel.
35:27 w Abraham and Isaac had resided as aliens.
36: 7 the land w they were staying could
37: 1 Jacob settled in the land w his father had lived as
37:16 "tell me, please, w they are pasturing the flock."
37:30 and I, w can I turn?"
38:21 "W is the temple prostitute who was at Enaim by
39:20 the place w the king's prisoners were confined;
40: 3 in the prison w Joseph was confined.
42: 7 "W do you come from?"
42:19 of your brothers stay here w you are imprisoned.
Ex 2:20 He said to his daughters, "W is he?
4:24 On the way, at a place w they spent the night,
8:21 so also the land w they live.
8:22 w my people live, so that no swarms of flies shall
9:26 Only in the land of Goshen, w the Israelites were,
10:23 three days they could not move from w they were;
10:23 but all the Israelites had light w they lived.
12:13 The blood shall be a sign for you on the houses w
15:27 w there were twelve springs of water
16:29 each of you stay w you are;
18: 5 came into the wilderness w Moses was encamped
20:21 Moses drew near to the thick darkness w God was.
20:24 in every place w I cause my name to
29:42 w I will meet with you, to speak to you there.
30: 6 w I will meet with you.
30:36 the covenant in the tent of meeting w I shall meet
33:21 a place by me w you shall stand on the rock;
Lev 4:24 the spot w the burnt offering is slaughtered before
4:33 at the spot w the burnt offering is slaughtered.
6:25 be slaughtered before the LORD at the spot w
7: 2 at the spot w the burnt offering is slaughtered,
14:13 the lamb in the place w the sin offering and
14:28 w the blood of the guilt offering was placed.
18: 3 not do as they do in the land of Egypt, w you lived,
21:11 He shall not go w there is a dead body;
Nu 5: 3 not defile their camp, w I dwell among them.
9:17 and in the place w the cloud settled down,
10:31 for you know w we should camp in the wilderness,
11:13 W am I to get meat to give to all this people?
16:47 w the plague had already begun among the people.
17: 4 of meeting before the covenant, w I meet with you.
20:13 w the people of Israel quarreled with the LORD,
22:26 w there was no way to turn either to the right or to
31:10 All their towns w they had settled,
33:14 w there was no water for the people to drink.
33:55 they shall trouble you in the land w
35: 6 w you shall permit a slayer to flee,
Dt 1:28 W are we headed? Our kindred have made our
1:31 w you saw how the LORD your God carried you,
4:27 only a few of you will be left among the nations w
8: 9 a land w you may eat bread without scarcity, w you
11:10 w you sow your seed and irrigate by foot like
12: 2 You must demolish completely all the places w
12:21 If the place w the LORD your God will choose
14:24 the place w the LORD your God will choose
17: 9 w you shall consult with the levitical priests and
28:36 w you shall serve other gods, of wood and stone.
28:37 among all the peoples w the LORD will lead you.
30: 1 if you call them to mind among all the nations w
32:37 Then he will say: W are their gods,
33:28 w the heavens drop down dew.
Jos 2: 4 but I did not know w they came from.
2: 5 W the men went I do not know.
4: 3 from the place w the priests' feet stood,
4: 3 lay them down in the place w you camp tonight.' "
4: 8 over with them to the place w they camped,
4: 9 the place w the feet of the priests bearing the ark of
5:15 for the place w you stand is holy."
8:24 of Ai in the open wilderness w they pursued them,
9: 8 And w do you come from?"
10:27 from the trees and threw them into the cave w
22: 4 therefore turn and go to your tents in the land w
22:19 into the LORD's land w the LORD's tabernacle
22:33 against them, to destroy the land w the Reubenites
Jdg 5:27 w he sank, there he fell dead.
Jdg 6:13 And w are all his wonderful deeds
9:21 w he remained for fear of his brother Abimelech.
9:38 Then Zebul said to him, "W is your boast now,
13: 6 I did not ask him w he came from,
16: 1 w he saw a prostitute and went in to her.
17: 9 Micah said to him, "From w do you come?"
18:10 a place w there is no lack of anything on earth."
19:17 "W are you going and w do you come from?"
19:26 at the door of the man's house w her master was,
20:18 w they inquired of God, "Which of us shall go
20:22 in the same place w they had formed it on
Ru 1: 7 she set out from the place w she had been living,
1:16 W you go, I will go; W you lodge, I will lodge;
1:17 W you die, I will die—there will I be buried.
2:19 to her, "W did you glean today?
2:19 And w have you worked?
3: 4 When he lies down, observe the place w he lies;
1Sa 1: 3 w the two sons of Eli, Hophni and Phinehas,
3: 3 w the ark of God was.
9:10 So they went to the town w the man of God was.
9:18 "Tell me, please, w is the house of the seer?"
10: 5 at the place w the Philistine garrison is;
10:14 to him and to the boy, "W did you go?"
14:11 of the holes w they have hidden themselves."
15:12 w he set up a monument for himself,
19: 3 in the field w you are, and I will speak to my father
19:22 he asked, "W are Samuel and David?"
20:19 go to the place w you hid yourself earlier,
20:37 to the place w Jonathan's arrow had fallen,
23:22 find out exactly w he is,
23:23 around and learn all the hiding places w he lurks,
24: 3 the sheepfolds beside the road, w there was a cave;
25:11 give it to men who come from I do not know w?"
26: 5 and came to the place w Saul had encamped;
26: 5 and David saw the place w Saul lay,
26:16 See now, w is the king's spear,
30: 9 w those stayed who were left behind.
30:13 "To whom do you belong? W are you from?"
30:31 all the places w David and his men had roamed.
2Sa 1: 3 David said to him, "W have you come from?"
1:13 to the young man who had reported to him, "W
2:23 He fell there, and died w he lay.
2:23 to the place w Asahel had fallen and died,
9: 4 The king said to him, "W is he?"
11:16 to the place w he knew there were valiant warriors.
13: 8 So Tamar went to her brother Amnon's house, w
13:13 As for me, w could I carry my shame?
15:25 and let me see both it and the place w it stays.
15:32 David came to the summit, w God was worshiped,
16: 3 The king said, "And w is your master's son?"
17:20 they said, "W are Ahimaaz and Jonathan?"
21:12 w the Philistines had hung them up,
21:20 w there was a man of great size,
23:11 w there was a plot of ground full of lentils;
1Ki 3:15 He came to Jerusalem w he stood before the ark of
7: 7 of the Throne w he was to pronounce judgment,
7: 8 His own house w he would reside,
7:36 w each had space, with wreaths all around.
8: 9 w the LORD made a covenant with the Israelites,
8:54 w he had knelt with hands outstretched
11:36 the city w I have chosen to put my name.
12: 2 w he had fled from King Solomon),
13:25 and told it in the town w the old prophet lived.
17:19 up into the upper chamber w he was lodging,
18:12 spirit of the LORD will carry you I know not w;
21:18 w he has gone to take possession.
21:19 In the place w dogs licked up the blood of Naboth,
2Ki 2:14 and struck the water, saying, "W is the LORD,
4: 8 w a wealthy woman lived,
5:25 Elisha said to him, "W have you been, Gehazi?"
6: 1 the place w we live under your charge is too small
6: 6 Then the man of God said, "W did it fall?"
6:13 He said, "Go and find w he is;
8:28 w the Arameans wounded Joram.
9:16 and went to Jezreel, w Joram was lying ill.
14: 6 w the LORD commanded,
16: 6 Edomites came to Elath, w they live to this day.
18:34 W are the gods of Hamath and Arpad?
18:34 W are the gods of Sepharvaim, Hena, and Ivvah?
19:13 W is the king of Hamath, the king of Arpad,
20:14 From w did they come to you?"
22:14 she resided in Jerusalem in the Second Quarter, w
23: 7 w the women did weaving for Asherah.
23: 8 the high places w the priests had made offerings,
1Ch 3: 4 w he reigned for seven years and six months.
4:40 w they found rich, good pasture,
11: 4 w the Jebusites were, the inhabitants of the land.
20: 6 w there was a man of great size,
2Ch 3: 1 w the LORD had appeared to his father David,
5:10 w the LORD made a covenant with the people
6:20 the place w you promised to set your name,
10: 2 w he had fled from King Solomon),
25: 4 in the book of Moses, w the LORD commanded,
Ezr 6: 1 the archives w the documents were stored
6: 3 at Jerusalem, let the house be rebuilt, the place w
10: 6 of Jehohanan son of Eliashib, w he spent the night.
Ne 2:16 not know w I had gone or what I was doing;
4:12 "From all the places w they live they will come up
10:39 the storerooms w the vessels of the sanctuary are,
10:39 and w the priests that minister,
13: 5 for Tobiah a large room w they had previously put
Est 7: 5 and w is he, who has presumed to do this?"
7: 8 Haman had thrown himself on the couch w
Job 1: 7 LORD said to Satan, "W have you come from?"
2: 2 LORD said to Satan, "W have you come from?"
4: 7 Or w were the upright cut off?
8:11 "Can papyrus grow w there is no marsh?

Job 8:11 Can reeds flourish **w** there is no water?
10:22 of gloom and chaos, **w** light is like darkness."
14:10 humans expire, and **w** are they?
15:23 They wander abroad for bread, saying, '**W** is it?'
17:15 **w** then is my hope? Who will see my hope?
18:19 and no survivor **w** they used to live.
20: 7 those who have seen them will say, '**W** are they?'
21:28 For you say, '**W** is the house of the prince?
21:28 **W** is the tent in which the wicked lived?'
23: 3 Oh, that I knew **w** I might find him,
28:12 "But **w** shall wisdom be found?
28:12 And **w** is the place of understanding?
28:20 "**W** then does wisdom come from?
28:20 And **w** is the place of understanding?
34:22 or deep darkness **w** evildoers may hide themselves.
35:10 But no one says, '**W** is God my Maker,
36:16 into a broad place **w** there was no constraint,
38: 4 "**W** were you when I laid the foundation of
38:19 "**W** is the way to the dwelling of light,
38:19 and **w** is the place of darkness,
38:24 the way to the place **w** the light is distributed,
38:24 or **w** the east wind is scattered upon the earth?
38:26 to bring rain on a land **w** no one lives,
39:30 and **w** the slain are, there it is."
40:12 tread down the wicked **w** they stand.
40:20 For the mountains yield food for it **w** all
Ps 26: 8 and the place **w** your glory abides.
33:14 From **w** he sits enthroned he watches all
41: 8 that I will not rise again from **w** I lie.
42: 3 people say to me continually, "**W** is your God?"
42:10 they say to me continually, "**W** is your God?"
63: 1 as in a dry and weary land **w** there is no water.
68:16 **w** the LORD will reside forever?
69: 2 I sink in deep mire, **w** there is no foothold;
74: 2 Remember Mount Zion, **w** you came to dwell.
78:60 the tent **w** he dwelt among mortals,
79:10 Why should the nations say, "**W** is their God?"
84: 3 **w** she may lay her young, at your altars,
89:49 **w** is your steadfast love of old,
115: 2 Why should the nations say, "**W** is their God?"
121: 1 from **w** will my help come?
139: 7 **W** can I go from your spirit?
139: 7 Or **w** can I flee from your presence?
142: 3 In the path **w** I walk they have hidden a trap for
Pr 11:14 **W** there is no guidance, a nation falls,
14: 4 **W** there are no oxen, there is no grain;
14: 8 the wisdom of the clever to understand **w** they go,
15:17 of vegetables **w** love is than a fatted ox and hatred
24:15 do no violence to the place **w** the righteous live;
26:20 and **w** there is no whisperer, quarreling ceases.
29:18 **W** there is no prophecy, the people cast off
Ecc 1: 5 and hurries to the place **w** it rises.
1: 7 to the place **w** the streams flow,
8:10 of the holy place, and were praised in the city **w**
11: 3 in the place **w** the tree falls, there it will lie.
SS 1: 7 **w** you pasture your flock, **w** you make it lie down
6: 1 **W** has your beloved gone,
Isa 7:23 On that day every place **w** there used to be
7:25 a place **w** cattle are let loose and **w** sheep tread.
10: 3 and **w** will you leave your wealth,
19:12 **W** now are your sages?
29: 1 Ah, Ariel, Ariel, the city **w** David encamped!
33:18 "**W** is the one who counted?
33:18 **W** is the one who weighed the tribute?
33:18 **W** is the one who counted the towers?"
33:21 **w** no galley with oars can go,
36:19 **W** are the gods of Hamath and Arpad?
36:19 **W** are the gods of Sepharvaim?
37:13 **W** is the king of Hamath, the king of Arpad,
39: 3 From **w** did they come to you?"
49:21 **w** then have these come from?"
50: 1 **W** is your mother's bill of divorce
51:13 But **w** is the fury of the oppressor?
60:13 and I will glorify **w** my feet rest.
63:11 **W** is the one who brought them up out of the sea
63:11 **W** is the one who put within them his holy spirit,
63:15 **W** are your zeal and your might?
64:11 **w** our ancestors praised you,
Jer 2: 6 "**W** is the LORD who brought us up from the land
2: 6 a land that no one passes through, **w** no one lives?"
2: 8 The priests did not say, "**W** is the LORD?"
2:28 But **w** are your gods that you made for yourself?
3: 2 **W** have you not been lain with?
6:16 and ask for the ancient paths, **w** the good way lies;
7:12 **w** I made my name dwell at first,
8: 3 that remains of this evil family in all the places **w**
13: 7 the loincloth from the place **w** I had hidden it.
13:20 **W** is the flock that was given you,
15: 2 And when they say to you, "**W** shall we go?"
16:15 of the land of the north and out of all the lands **w**
17:15 "**W** is the word of the LORD?
19:14 **w** the LORD had sent him to prophesy,
22:12 but in the place **w** they have carried him captive
22:26 **w** you were not born, and there you shall die.
23: 3 the remnant of my flock out of all the lands **w**
23: 8 of the land of the north and out of all the lands **w**
24: 9 and a curse in all the places **w** I shall drive them.
29: 7 the welfare of the city **w** I have sent you into exile,
29:14 the nations and all the places **w** I have driven you,
29:18 among all the nations **w** I have driven them,
32: 3 **w** King Zedekiah of Judah had confined him.
35: 7 you may live many days in the land **w** you reside.'
36:19 and let no one know **w** you are."
37:19 **W** are your prophets who prophesied to you,
42: 3 Let the LORD your God show us **w** we should go
42:14 **w** we shall not see war,
42:22 and by pestilence in the place **w** you desire to go
Jer 44: 8 in the land of Egypt **w** you have come to settle?
La 2:12 They cry to their mothers, "**W** is bread and wine?"
Eze 6: 9 among the nations **w** they are carried captive,
11:16 for a little while in the countries **w** they have gone.
11:17 of the countries **w** you have been scattered,
12:16 of all their abominations among the nations **w**
13:12 "**W** is the whitewash you smeared on it?"
17: 6 its roots remained **w** it stood.
17: 7 From the bed **w** it was planted
17:10 wither on the bed **w** it grew?
17:16 the place **w** the king resides who made him king,
20:34 the peoples and gather you out of the countries **w**
20:38 I will bring them out of the land **w** they reside
20:41 of the countries **w** you have been scattered;
21:30 In the place **w** you were created,
38: 8 a land **w** people were gathered from many nations
40:38 **w** the burnt offering was to be washed.
42:13 **w** the priests who approach the LORD shall eat
43: 7 **w** I will reside among the people of Israel forever.
46:20 the place **w** the priests shall boil the guilt offering
46:20 and **w** they shall bake the grain offering,
46:24 "These are the kitchens **w** those who serve at
47: 9 and everything will live **w** the river goes.
Da 6:20 When he came near the den **w** Daniel was,
8:17 So he came near **w** I stood;
Hos 1:10 and in the place **w** it was said to them,
13:10 **W** now is your king, that he may save you?
13:10 **W** in all your cities are your rulers,
13:14 O Death, **w** are your plagues?
13:14 O Sheol, **w** is your destruction?
Joel 2:17 be said among the peoples, '**W** is their God?' "
Jnh 1: 8 **W** do you come from?
Mic 7:10 "**W** is the LORD your God?"
Na 2:11 **w** the lion goes, and the lion's cubs,
3: 7 **W** shall I seek comforters for you?
3:17 no one knows **w** they have gone.
Hab 3: 4 from his hand, **w** his power lay hidden.
Zec 1: 5 Your ancestors, **w** are they?
2: 2 Then I asked, "**W** are you going?"
5:10 "**W** are they taking the basket?"
Mal 1: 6 If then I am a father, **w** is the honor due me?
1: 6 And if I am a master, **w** is the respect due me?
2:17 Or by asking, "**W** is the God of justice?"
Mt 2: 2 "**W** is the child who has been born king of
2: 4 he inquired of them **w** the Messiah was to be born.
2: 9 until it stopped over the place **w** the child was.
6:19 **w** moth and rust consume and **w** thieves break in
6:20 **w** neither moth nor rust consumes and **w** thieves
6:21 **w** your treasure is, there your heart will be also.
8:12 **w** there will be weeping and gnashing of teeth."
13: 5 **w** they did not have much soil,
13:27 **W**, then, did these weeds come from?'
13:42 **w** there will be weeping and gnashing of teeth.
13:50 **w** there will be weeping and gnashing of teeth.
13:54 "**W** did this man get this wisdom and these deeds
13:56 **W** then did this man get all this?"
15:29 and he went up the mountain, **w** he sat down.
15:33 "**W** are we to get enough bread in the desert
18:20 For **w** two or three are gathered in my name,
22:13 **w** there will be weeping and gnashing of teeth.'
24:51 **w** there will be weeping and gnashing of teeth.
25:24 reaping **w** you did not sow, and gathering **w** you
25:26 that I reap **w** I did not sow, and gather **w** I did not
25:30 **w** there will be weeping and gnashing of teeth.'
26:17 "**W** do you want us to make the preparations
28: 6 Come, see the place **w** he lay.
Mk 4: 5 **w** it did not have much soil,
4:15 These are the ones on the path **w** the word is sown:
5:40 and went in **w** the child was.
6: 2 They said, "**W** did this man get all this?
9:48 **w** their worm never dies,
13:14 up **w** it ought not to be (let the reader understand),
14:12 "**W** do you want us to go and make
14:14 **W** is my guest room **w** I may eat the Passover
15:47 the mother of Joses saw **w** the body was laid.
Lk 1:40 **w** she entered the house of Zechariah
4: 2 **w** for forty days he was tempted by the devil.
4:16 he came to Nazareth, **w** he had been brought up,
4:17 the scroll and found the place **w** it was written:
8:25 He said to them, "**W** is your faith?"
10: 1 on ahead of him in pairs to every town and place **w**
10:38 **w** a woman named Martha welcomed him
12:33 **w** no thief comes near and no moth destroys.
12:34 **w** your treasure is, there your heart will be also.
13:25 'I do not know **w** you come from.'
13:27 But he will say, 'I do not know **w** you come from;
16:23 In Hades, **w** he was being tormented,
17:17 But the other nine, **w** are they?
17:37 Then they asked him, "**W**, Lord?"
17:37 He said to them, "**W** the corpse is,
20: 7 So they answered that they did not know **w**
20:37 **w** he speaks of the Lord as the God of Abraham,
22: 9 "**W** do you want us to make preparations for it?"
22:11 "**W** is the guest room, **w** I may eat the Passover
23: 5 from Galilee **w** he began even to this place."
23:53 in a rock-hewn tomb **w** no one had ever been laid.
Jn 1:28 This took place in Bethany across the Jordan **w**
1:38 translated means Teacher), "**w** are you staying?"
1:39 They came and saw **w** he was staying,
1:48 "**W** did you get to know me?"
2: 9 and did not know **w** it came from (though
3: 8 The wind blows **w** it chooses,
3: 8 you do not know **w** it comes from or **w** it goes.
4:11 **W** do you get that living water?
4:20 the place **w** people must worship is in Jerusalem."
4:46 in Galilee **w** he had changed the water into wine.
6: 5 "**W** are we to buy bread for these people to eat?"
Jn 6:23 near the place **w** they had eaten the bread after
6:62 if you were to see the Son of Man ascending to **w**
7:11 for him at the festival and saying, "**W** is he?"
7:27 Yet we know **w** this man is from;
7:27 Messiah comes, no one will know **w** he is from."
7:28 "You know me, and you know **w** I am from.
7:34 and **w** I am, you cannot come."
7:35 "**W** does this man intend to go that we will
7:36 for me and you will not find me' and '**W** I am,
7:42 the village **w** David lived?"
8:10 ⟦and said to her, "Woman, **w** are they?⟧
8:14 I know **w** I have come from and **w** I am going.
8:14 not know **w** I come from or **w** I am going.
8:19 Then they said to him, "**W** is your Father?"
8:21 **W** I am going, you cannot come."
8:22 Is that what he means by saying, '**W** I am going,
9:12 They said to him, "**W** is he?"
9:29 we do not know **w** he comes from."
9:30 You do not know **w** he comes from,
10:40 to the place **w** John had been baptizing earlier,
11: 6 he stayed two days longer in the place **w** he was.
11:30 but was still at the place **w** Martha had met him.
11:32 When Mary came **w** Jesus was and saw him,
11:34 He said, "**W** have you laid him?"
11:57 orders that anyone who knew **w** Jesus was
12:26 Whoever serves me must follow me, and **w** I am,
12:35 you do not know **w** you are going.
13:33 '**W** I am going, you cannot come.'
13:36 Simon Peter said to him, "Lord, **w** are you going?"
13:36 Jesus answered, "**W** I am going,
14: 3 so that **w** I am, there you may be also.
14: 4 And you know the way to the place **w** I am going."
14: 5 "Lord, we do not know **w** you are going.
16: 5 yet none of you asks me, '**W** are you going?'
17:24 whom you have given me, may be with me **w** I am,
18: 1 the Kidron valley to a place **w** there was a garden,
18:20 **w** all the Jews come together.
19: 9 and asked Jesus, "**W** are you from?"
19:20 the place **w** Jesus was crucified was near the city;
19:41 there was a garden in the place **w** he was crucified,
20: 2 and we do not know **w** they have laid him."
20:12 sitting **w** the body of Jesus had been lying,
20:13 and I do not know **w** they have laid him."
20:15 tell me **w** you have laid him,
20:19 of the house **w** the disciples had met were locked
21:18 around you and take you **w** you do not wish to go."
Ac 1:13 to the room upstairs **w** they were staying,
2: 2 and it filled the entire house **w** they were sitting.
7:33 for the place **w** you are standing is holy ground.
11:11 arrived at the house **w** we were.
12:12 **w** many had gathered and were praying.
14: 1 **w** Paul and Barnabas went into the Jewish
14:26 **w** they had been commended to the grace of God
15:36 let us return and visit the believers in every city **w**
16: 1 **w** there was a disciple named Timothy,
16:13 **w** we supposed there was a place of prayer;
17: 1 **w** there was a synagogue of the Jews.
17:26 the boundaries of the places **w** they would live,
19: 1 **w** he found some disciples.
20: 3 **w** he stayed for three months.
20: 6 **w** we stayed for seven days.
20: 8 There were many lamps in the room upstairs **w**
25: 2 **w** the chief priests and the leaders of
25:10 this is **w** I should be tried.
27:12 **w** they could spend the winter.
Ro 4:15 but **w** there is no law, neither is there violation.
5:20 but **w** sin increased, grace abounded all the more,
9:26 "And in the very place **w** it was said to them,
15:20 not **w** Christ has already been named,
1Co 1:20 **W** is the one who is wise? **W** is the scribe? **W** is
the debater of this age?
12:17 whole body were an eye, **w** would the hearing be?
12:17 were hearing, **w** would the sense of smell be?
12:19 If all were a single member, **w** would the body be?
15:55 "**W**, O death, is your victory?
15:55 **W**, O death, is your sting?"
2Co 3:17 Lord is the Spirit, and **w** the Spirit of the Lord is,
Col 3: 1 **w** Christ is, seated at the right hand of God.
Heb 3: 9 **w** your ancestors put me to the test,
6:20 **w** Jesus, a forerunner on our
9:16 **W** a will is involved, the death of
10:18 **W** there is forgiveness of these,
11: 8 and he set out, not knowing **w** he was going.
Jas 3:16 For **w** there is envy and selfish ambition,
4: 1 and disputes among you, **w** do they come from?
2Pe 3: 4 "**W** is the promise of his coming?
3:13 **w** righteousness is at home.
Rev 2:13 "I know **w** you are living, **w** Satan's throne is.
2:13 who was killed among you, **w** Satan lives.
7:13 robed in white, and **w** have they come from?"
11: 8 **w** also their Lord was crucified.
12: 6 **w** she has a place prepared by God,
12:14 to her place **w** she is nourished for a time,
17:15 "The waters that you saw, **w** the whore is seated,
18:19 **w** all who had ships at sea grew rich by her wealth!
20:10 **w** the beast and the false prophet were,
Tob 1: 4 **w** all the tribes of Israel should offer sacrifice and
w the temple,
2:13 So I called her and said, "**W** did you get this goat?
2:14 she replied to me, "**W** are your acts of charity?
2:14 **W** are your righteous deeds?
5: 5 Tobias said to him, "**W** do you come from,
6: 9 a person's eyes **w** white films have appeared
7: 1 **w** they found him sitting beside the courtyard door.
7: 3 Edna questioned them, saying, "**W** are you from,
8: 2 the bag **w** he had them and put them on the embers
Jdt 5: 9 the place **w** they were living and go to the land

Jdt 5:19 and have come back from the places w
5:19 and have occupied Jerusalem, w their sanctuary is,
7:10 but on the height of the mountains w they live,
7:13 this is w all the people of Bethulia get their water.
7:14 be strewn about in the streets w they live.
8: 5 at home w she set up a tent for herself on the roof
9: 8 the tabernacle w your glorious name resides,
10: 2 she rose from w she lay prostrate.
10: 2 down into the house w she lived on sabbaths and
10:10 w they lost sight of her.
10:12 and w are you coming from, and w are you going?"
12: 1 to bring her in w his silver dinnerware was kept,
12: 3 w can we get you more of the same?
14:17 Then he went to the tent w Judith had stayed,
AdE 1: 9 the women in the palace w King Artaxerxes was.
2:14 w Gai the king's eunuch is in charge of
4: 3 And in every province w the king's proclamation
Wis 19: 7 and dry land emerging w water had stood before,
19: 8 w those protected by your hand passed through
Sir Pr: 2 and to be indulgent in cases w,
8:16 and w no help is at hand,
23:21 and w he least suspects it, he will be seized.
27:27 and he will not know w it came from.
32: 4 W there is entertainment, do not pour out talk;
36:30 W there is no fence, the property will
36:30 and w there is no wife,
41:19 in the place w you live.
42: 6 W there is an untrustworthy wife,
42: 6 and w there are many hands, lock things up.
43:28 W can we find the strength to praise him?
46:12 May their bones send forth new life from w
49:10 of the Twelve Prophets send forth new life from w
Bar 2: 4 w the Lord has scattered them.
2:13 among the nations w you have scattered us.
2:29 into a small number among the nations, w
3: 8 we are today in our exile w you have scattered us,
3:14 Learn w there is wisdom, w there is strength, w
there is understanding, so that you may at the
same time discern w there is length of days, and
life, w there is light for the eyes, and peace.
3:16 W are the rulers of the nations,
LtJ 6:48 as to w they can hide themselves and their gods.
1Mc 3:50 W shall we take them?
5: 6 w he found a strong band and many people,
5:49 to be made to the army that all should encamp w
10:73 w there is no stone or pebble, or place to flee."
14:33 w formerly the arms of the enemy had been stored,
14:34 w the enemy formerly lived.
16: 5 w a large force of infantry and cavalry was coming
2Mc 1:19 w they took such precautions that
1:33 the place w the exiled priests had hidden the fire,
2: 4 the mountain w Moses had gone up and had seen
4:38 to that very place w he had committed the outrage
10:19 for places w he was more urgently needed.
10:32 w Chaereas was commander.
12:27 a fortified town w Lysias lived with multitudes
14:32 not know w the man was whom he wanted,
1Es 6:24 w they sacrifice with perpetual fire;
6:26 to be placed w they had been."
3Mc 1: 1 w the army of Antiochus was encamped.
4: 1 In every place, then, w this decree arrived,
2Es 1:13 made safe highways for you w there was no road;
1:17 W are the benefits that I bestowed on you?
4:29 and if the place w the evil has been sown does
4:29 the field w the good has been sown will not come.
5:16 came to me and said, "W have you been?
6:14 if the place w you are standing is greatly shaken
6:29 by little the place w I was standing began to rock
6:47 w the water had been gathered together,
6:50 from the other, for the seventh part w
6:51 to live in it, w there are a thousand mountains;
9:24 into a field of flowers w no house has been built,
10:28 "W is the angel Uriel, who came to me
10:51 to remain in the field w no house had been built,
10:53 to go into the field w there was no foundation
10:54 of human construction could endure in a place w
13:41 w no human beings had ever lived,
14: 4 w I kept him with me many days.
4Mc 9:18 that children of the Hebrews alone are invincible w

WHEREAS (9)

1Sa 24:17 w I have repaid you evil.
1Ki 12:11 Now, w my father laid on you a heavy yoke,
2Ch 10:11 Now, w my father laid on you a heavy yoke,
Isa 60:15 W you have been forsaken and hated,
Da 4:23 And w the king saw a holy watcher coming down
1Co 12:24 w our more respectable members do not need this.
2Pe 2:11 w angels, though greater in might and power, do
Wis 16:23 w the fire, in order that the righteous might be fed,
1Mc 15: 3 W certain scoundrels have gained control of

WHEREFORE (1)

Nu 21:14 W it is said in the Book of the Wars of the LORD,

WHEREVER (71) [WHERE]

Ge 28:15 that I am with you and will keep you w you go,
30:30 and the LORD has blessed you w I turned.
35: 3 and has been with me w I have gone."
Ex 5:11 Go and get straw yourselves, w you can find it;
Nu 35:29 for you throughout your generations w you live.
Dt 18: 6 from w he has been residing in Israel,
23:16 w they please; you shall not oppress them.
Jos 1: 7 so that you may be successful w you go.
1: 9 for the LORD your God is with you w you go."
1:16 and w you send us we will go.
Jdg 17: 8 to live w he could find a place.
17: 9 and I am going to live w I can find a place."
1Sa 14:47 w he turned he routed them.
18: 5 and was successful w Saul sent him;
23:13 they wandered w they could go.
2Sa 7: 7 W I have moved about among all the people
7: 9 and I have been with you w you went,
8: 6 The LORD gave victory to David w he went.
8:14 And the LORD gave victory to David w he went.
15:20 while I go w I can?
15:21 w my lord the king may be,
1Ki 2: 3 you may prosper in all that you do and w you turn.
2Ki 8: 1 and go with your household, and settle w you can;
12: 5 the house w any need of repairs is discovered."
18: 7 LORD was with him; w he went, he prospered.
1Ch 17: 6 W I have moved about among all Israel,
17: 8 and I have been with you w you went,
18: 6 The LORD gave victory to David w he went.
18:13 And the LORD gave victory to David w he went.
Ne 4:20 Rally to us w you hear the sound of the trumpet.
Est 4: 3 w the king's command and his decree came,
8:17 w the king's command and his edict came,
Ps 119:54 statutes have been my songs w I make my home.
Pr 17: 8 of those who give it; w they turn they prosper.
21: 1 he turns it w he will.
Jer 40: 4 go w you think it good and right to go.
40: 5 or go w you think it right to go."
Eze 1:12 Each moved straight ahead; w the spirit would go,
1:20 W the spirit would go, they went,
6: 6 W you live, your towns shall be waste
6:13 w they offered pleasing odor to all their idols.
20:28 then w they saw any high hill or any leafy tree,
21:16 W your edge is directed.
36:20 But when they came to the nations, w they came,
47: 9 W the river goes, every living creature
Da 2:38 w they live, the wild animals of the field,
Mt 8:19 "Teacher, I will follow you w you go."
24:28 W the corpse is, there the vultures will gather.
26:13 w this good news is proclaimed in
Mk 6:10 He said to them, "W you enter a house,
6:55 to bring the sick on mats to w they heard he was.
6:56 And w he went, into villages or cities or farms,
14: 9 w the good news is proclaimed in the whole world,
14:14 and w he enters, say to the owner of the house,
Lk 9: 5 W they do not welcome you,
9:57 "I will follow you w you go."
Jn 21:18 to fasten your own belt and to go w you wished.
1Co 16: 6 so that you may send me on my way, w I go.
Jas 3: 4 a very small rudder w the will of the pilot directs.
Rev 14: 4 these follow the Lamb w he goes.
Jdt 8:22 on our heads among the Gentiles, w we serve
11:16 the whole world w people shall hear about them.
AdE 8:17 and province w the decree was published;
8:17 w the proclamation was made,
Sir 36:31 but lodges w night overtakes him?
38:32 and w they live, they will not go hungry.
1Mc 5:63 among all the Gentiles, w their name was heard.
6:36 These took their position beforehand w
6:36 w it went, they went with it, and they never left it.
1Es 2: 6 and let each of you, w you may live, be helped by
2Es 13: 3 and w he turned his face to look,

WHET (5)

Dt 32:41 when I w my flashing sword,
Ps 7:12 If one does not repent, God will w his sword;
64: 3 who w their tongues like swords,
Ecc 10:10 If the iron is blunt, and one does not w the edge,
Jer 46: 4 w your lances, put on your coats of mail!

WHETHER (162)

Ge 18:21 and see w they have done altogether according to
24:21 The man gazed at her in silence to learn w or not
27:21 to know w you are really my son Esau or not."
31:39 w stolen by day or stolen by night.
37:32 see now w it is your son's robe or not."
42:16 w there is truth in you;
Ex 4:18 in Egypt and see w they are still living."
12:19 w an alien or a native of the land,
16: 4 w they will follow my instruction or not.
19:13 w animal or human being, they shall not live.'
20: 4 w in the form of anything that is in heaven above,
21:16 w that person has been sold or is still held
22: 4 When the animal, w ox or donkey or sheep,
22: 8 to determine w or not the owner had laid hands on
Lev 3: 1 of the herd, w male or female, you shall offer one
5: 2 w the carcass of an unclean beast or the carcass
11: 9 w in the seas or in the streams—such you may eat.
11:32 w an article of wood or cloth or skin or sacking,
11:35 w an oven or stove, it shall be broken in pieces;
12: 6 w for a son or for a daughter,
13:49 w in warp or woof or in skin or in anything made
13:52 w diseased in warp or woof, woolen or linen,
13:55 you shall burn it in fire, w the leprous spot is on
13:59 to decide w it is clean or unclean.
15: 3 w his member flows with his discharge,
15:23 w it is the bed or anything upon which she sits,
18: 9 w born at home or born abroad.
22:18 the aliens residing in Israel presents an offering, w
27:12 The priest shall assess it: w good or bad,
27:14 w good or bad, as the priest assesses it,
27:26 w ox or sheep, it is the LORD's.
27:30 w the seed from the ground or the fruit from
27:33 Let no one inquire w it is good or bad,
Nu 9:22 W it was two days, or a month, or a longer time,
11:23 Now you shall see w my word will come true
13:18 and w the people who live in it are strong or weak,
13:18 w they are few or many,
13:19 and w the land they live in is good or bad,
13:19 and w the towns that they live in are unwalled
13:20 and w the land is rich or poor,
13:20 and w there are trees in it or not.
15: 3 w a burnt offering or a sacrifice,
15:30 w a native or an alien, affronts the LORD,
18: 9 w grain offering, sin offering, or guilt offering,
31:28 one item out of every five hundred, w persons,
31:30 w persons, oxen, donkeys, sheep, or goats—
Dt 1:16 w citizen or resident alien.
5: 8 w in the form of anything that is in heaven above,
8: 2 w or not you would keep his commandments.
13: 3 to know w you indeed love the LORD your God
13: 7 w near you or far away from you,
15:12 w a Hebrew man or a Hebrew woman,
17: 3 w the sun or the moon or any of the host
18: 3 from those offering a sacrifice, w an ox or a sheep:
24:14 w other Israelites or aliens who reside in your land
27:22 w the daughter of his father or the daughter
Jos 24:15 w the gods your ancestors served in the region
Jdg 2:22 w or not they would take care to walk in the way
3: 4 to know w Israel would obey the commandments
6:36 to see w you will deliver Israel by my hand,
18: 5 "Inquire of God that we may know w
Ru 3:10 you have not gone after young men, w poor
1Sa 30:19 Nothing was missing, w small or great,
2Sa 15:21 w for death or for life,
2Ki 1: 2 w I shall recover from this injury."
8: 8 w I shall recover from this illness."
2Ch 15:13 should be put to death, w young or old,
Ezr 2:59 w they belonged to Israel:
5:17 to see w a decree was issued by King Cyrus for
7:26 w for death or for banishment or for confiscation
Ne 7:61 w they belonged to Israel:
Est 3: 4 in order to see w Mordecai's words would avail;
Job 34:29 w it be a nation or an individual?—
37:13 W for correction, or for his land, or for love,
Ps 58: 9 w green or ablaze, may he sweep them away!
Pr 20:11 by w what they do is pure and right.
Ecc 2:19 —and who knows w they will be wise or foolish?
3:21 Who knows w the human spirit goes upward and
5:12 w they eat little or much;
9: 1 w it is love or hate one does not know.
11: 3 w a tree falls to the south or to the north,
11: 6 this or that, or w both alike will be good.
12:14 including every secret thing, w good or evil.
SS 6:11 to see w the vines had budded,
6:11 w the pomegranates were in bloom.
7:12 and see w the vines have budded,
7:12 w the grape blossoms have opened and
Jer 42: 6 W it is good or bad,
La 3:63 W they sit or rise—see, I am the object of their
Eze 2: 5 W they hear or refuse to hear (for they are
2: 7 w they hear or refuse to hear;
3:11 w they hear or refuse to hear.
44:31 priests shall not eat of anything, w bird or animal,
Joel 2:14 Who knows w he will not turn and relent,
Mt 27:49 "Wait, let us see w Elijah will come to save him."
Mk 3: 2 They watched him to see w he would cure him on
11:13 he went to see w perhaps he would find anything
15:36 let us see w Elijah will come to take him down."
15:44 he asked him w he had been dead for some time.
Lk 3:15 w he might be the Messiah,
6: 7 the Pharisees watched him to see w he would cure
11:35 consider w the light in you is not darkness.
14:28 to see w he has enough to complete it?
14:31 will not sit down first and consider w he is able
23: 6 he asked w the man was a Galilean.
Jn 7:17 to do the will of God will know w the teaching is
7:17 the teaching is from God or w I am speaking
9:25 He answered, "I do not know w he is a sinner.
Ac 4:19 "W it is right in God's sight to listen
5: 8 "Tell me w you and your husband sold the land
10:18 They called out to ask w Simon,
17:11 to see w these things were so.
25:20 I asked w he wished to go to Jerusalem and
26:29 Paul replied, "W quickly or not,
Ro 14: 8 w we live or w we die, we are the Lord's.
1Co 1:16 I do not know w I baptized anyone else.)
3:22 w Paul or Apollos or Cephas or the world or life
10:31 So, w you eat or drink, or whatever you do,
15:11 W then it was I or they,
2Co 2: 9 and to know w you are obedient in everything.
5: 9 So w we are at home or away,
5:10 for what has been done in the body, w good
12: 2 w in the body or out of the body I do not know;
12: 3 w in the body or out of the body I do not know;
13: 5 Examine yourselves to see w you are living in
Eph 6: 8 w we are slaves or free.
Php 1:18 w out of false motives or true; and in that I rejoice.
1:20 w by life or by death.
1:27 w I come and see you or am absent and hear
Col 1:16 w thrones or dominions or rulers or powers—
1:20 w on earth or in heaven,
1Th 2: 6 w from you or from others,
5:10 w we are awake or asleep we may live with him.
2Ti 4: 2 be persistent w the time is favorable
1Pe 2:13 w of the emperor as supreme,
1Jn 4: 1 but test the spirits to see w they are from God;
Tob 5: 9 and w he is trustworthy enough to go with you."
AdE 4:14 who knows w it was not for such a time as this
Wis 11:11 W absent or present, they were equally distressed,
14:23 For w they kill children in their initiations,
17:17 for w they were farmers or shepherds
17:18 W there came a whistling wind,
Sir 26: 4 W rich or poor, his heart is content,

Sir 41: 4 **W** life lasts for ten years or a hundred or
LtJ 6:34 **W** one does evil to them or good,
1Mc 4:10 to see **w** he will favor us
2Mc 3: 9 and he inquired **w** this really was the situation.
6:26 yet **w** I live or die I shall not escape the hands of
1Es 8:24 **w** by death or some other punishment,
3Mc 1:15 **w** they wish it or not?"
3:27 **w** old people or children or even infants,
2Es 4:40 "Go and ask a pregnant woman **w**,
4:45 **w** more time is to come than has passed,
4:45 or **w** for us the greater part has gone by.
7:*75* **w** after death, as soon as everyone of us yields up
7:*75* or **w** we shall be tormented at once?"
7:*102* **w** on the day of judgment the righteous will
4Mc 1: 1 **w** devout reason is sovereign over the emotions.
1:13 is **w** reason is sovereign over the emotions.
1:14 and **w** reason rules over all these.
11:13 When the tyrant inquired **w** he was willing to eat

WHICH (1284) [WHICHEVER] See Index of Articles Etc.

WHICHEVER (3) [WHICH]

Lev 5:13 for **w** of these sins you have committed,
Sir 15:16 stretch out your hand for **w** you choose.
15:17 and **w** one chooses will be given.

WHILE (602)

Ge 1: 2 **w** a wind from God swept over the face of
13:12 **w** Lot settled among the cities of the Plain
18: 8 and he stood by them under the tree **w** they ate.
18:22 **w** Abraham remained standing before the LORD.
20: 1 **W** residing in Gerar as an alien,
24:55 "Let the girl remain with us a **w**, at least ten days;
25: 6 the sons of his concubines Abraham gave gifts, **w**
25:27 a man of the field, **w** Jacob was a quiet man,
27:44 a **w**, until your brother's fury turns away—
29: 9 **W** he was still speaking with them,
30:36 **w** Jacob was pasturing the rest of Laban's flock.
35:22 **W** Israel lived in that land,
38:28 **W** she was in labor, one put out a hand;
39:11 and **w** no one else was in the house,
42:16 **w** the rest of you remain in prison,
44:14 Judah and his brothers came to Joseph's house **w**
45:14 **w** Benjamin wept upon his neck.
46:29 fell on his neck, and wept on his neck a good **w**.
48: 7 **w** there was still some distance to go to Ephrath;
Ex 2: 5 **w** her attendants walked beside the river.
17:10 and fought with Amalek, **w** Moses, Aaron,
18:13 **w** the people stood around him from morning
18:14 **w** all the people stand around you from morning
19:18 **w** the whole mountain shook violently.
20:21 **w** Moses drew near to the thick darkness
33:22 and **w** my glory passes by I will put you in a cleft
Lev 5: 9 **w** the rest of the blood shall be drained out at
6: 9 **w** the fire on the altar shall be kept burning.
7:20 the LORD's sacrifice of well-being **w** in a state
11:36 **w** whatever touches the carcass in it shall
14:46 the house **w** it is shut up shall be unclean until
18:18 uncovering her nakedness **w** her sister is still alive.
18:19 not approach a woman to uncover her nakedness **w**
22: 3 **w** he is in a state of uncleanness,
26:34 **w** you are in the land of your enemies;
26:43 **w** they shall make amends for their iniquity,
Nu 5:19 to uncleanness **w** under your husband's authority,
5:20 But if you have gone astray **w**
5:29 when a wife, **w** under her husband's authority,
11:33 But **w** the meat was still between their teeth,
12: 1 **W** they were at Hazeroth, Miriam and Aaron spoke
18: 1 **w** you and your sons alone shall bear responsibility
18: 2 and serve you **w** you and your sons with you are
23: 3 "Stay here beside your burnt offerings **w**
23:15 **w** I meet the LORD over there.
24:18 Seir a possession of its enemies, **w** Israel does
25: 1 **W** Israel was staying at Shittim,
25: 6 **w** they were weeping at the entrance of the tent
30: 3 **w** within her father's house, in her youth,
30: 6 If she marries, **w** obligated by her vows
30:16 and a father and his daughter **w** she is still young
32: 6 "Shall your brothers go to war **w** you sit here?
33: 4 **w** the Egyptians were burying all their firstborn,
35:23 **w** handling any stone that could cause death,
Dt 3: 9 **w** the Amorites call it Senir),
4: 4 **w** those of you who held fast to
4:11 of the mountain **w** the mountain was blazing up to
4:36 **w** you heard his words coming out of the fire.
5:23 **w** the mountain was burning with fire,
9:15 **w** the mountain was ablaze;
24:11 **w** the person to whom you are making
25: 4 You shall not muzzle an ox **w** it is treading out
26:14 I have not eaten of it **w** in mourning;
26:14 I have not removed any of it **w** I was unclean;
28:32 and daughters shall be given to another people, **w**
28:43 **w** you shall descend lower and lower.
31:27 so rebellious toward the LORD **w** I am still alive
Jos 3:16 **w** those flowing toward the sea of the Arabah,
3:17 **W** all Israel were crossing over on dry ground,
5:10 **W** the Israelites were camped in Gilgal they kept
6: 9 **w** the trumpets blew continually.
6:13 **w** the trumpets blew continually.
8: 6 as before.' **W** we flee from them,
9:22 **w** in fact you are living among us?
10:11 **w** they were going down the slope of Beth-horon,
14:10 **w** Israel was journeying through the wilderness;
Jdg 3:20 **w** he was sitting alone in his cool roof chamber,
3:26 Ehud escaped **w** they delayed,
4:16 **w** Barak pursued the chariots and the army
9:44 **w** the two companies rushed on all who were in
11:26 **W** Israel lived in Heshbon and its villages,
13:20 of the LORD ascended in the flame of the altar **w**
14: 8 After a **w** he returned to marry her,
15: 1 After a **w**, at the time of the wheat harvest,
16: 9 **W** men were lying in wait in an inner chamber,
16:14 So **w** he slept, Delilah took the seven locks
16:27 who looked on **w** Samson performed.
18: 3 **W** they were at Micah's house,
18:16 **W** the six hundred men of the Danites,
19:22 **W** they were enjoying themselves,
20:33 **w** those Israelites who were in ambush rushed out
1Sa 2:11 **w** the boy remained to minister to the LORD,
2:13 **w** the meat was boiling, with a three-pronged fork
9:27 stop here yourself for a **w**,
14:19 **W** Saul was talking to the priest,
18:10 **w** David was playing the lyre,
19: 9 **w** David was playing music.
20:25 Jonathan stood, **w** Abner sat by Saul's side;
23:26 **w** Saul and his men were closing in on David
25:13 **w** two hundred remained with the baggage.
25:16 all the **w** we were with them keeping the sheep.
26: 5 **w** the army was encamped around him.
29: 1 **w** the Israelites were encamped by the fountain
2Sa 1: 6 **w** the chariots and the horsemen drew close
2:13 **w** the other sat on the other side of the pool.
3: 1 **w** the house of Saul became weaker and weaker.
3: 6 **W** there was war between the house of Saul and
3:35 to persuade David to eat something **w**
4: 5 **w** he was taking his noonday rest.
4: 7 Now they had come into the house **w** he was lying
5: 2 For some time, **w** Saul was king over us,
7:19 also of your servant's house for a great **w** to come.
12:18 for they said, "**W** the child was still alive,
12:21 You fasted and wept for the child **w** it was alive;
12:22 He said, "**W** the child was still alive,
13:30 **W** they were on the way,
15: 8 For your servant made a vow **w** I lived at Geshur
15:12 **W** Absalom was offering the sacrifices,
15:20 **w** I go wherever I can?
16: 7 Shimei shouted **w** he cursed, "Out!
16:13 **w** Shimei went along on the hillside opposite him
17: 2 upon him **w** he is weary and discouraged,
17:24 **w** Absalom crossed the Jordan with all the men
18: 4 **w** all the army marched out by hundreds and
18: 9 **w** the mule that was under him went on.
18:14 **w** he was still alive in the oak.
19:18 **w** the crossing was taking place,
19:32 He had provided the king with food **w** he stayed
20:22 **w** Joab returned to Jerusalem to the king.
23:13 **w** a band of Philistines was encamped in the valley
24: 3 **w** the eyes of my lord the king can still see it!
24:13 Or will you flee three months before your foes **w**
1Ki 1:14 Then **w** you are still there speaking with the king,
1:22 **W** she was still speaking with the king,
1:42 **W** he was still speaking, Jonathan son of
3:17 and I gave birth **w** she was in the house.
3:20 of the night and took my son from beside me **w**
3:23 and your son is dead'; **w** the other says,
6: 7 nor any tool of iron was heard in the temple **w**
8:14 **w** all the assembly of Israel stood.
10:20 **w** twelve lions were standing,
12: 6 older men who had attended his father Solomon **w**
13: 1 **W** Jeroboam was standing by the altar
17: 7 But after a **w** the wadi dried up,
18:45 In a little **w** the heavens grew black with clouds
20:16 **w** Ben-hadad was drinking himself drunk in
20:27 **w** the Arameans filled the country.
20:40 **W** your servant was busy here and there,
2Ki 2:23 and **w** he was going up on the way,
3:15 And then, **w** the musician was playing,
4:34 and **w** he lay bent over him,
4:40 But **w** they were eating the stew, they cried out,
6:33 **W** he was still speaking with them,
8: 5 **W** he was telling the king how Elisha had restored
8: 7 to Damascus **w** King Ben-hadad of Aram was ill.
9: 5 He arrived **w** the commanders of the army were
11: 3 **w** Athaliah reigned over the land.
19:26 **w** their inhabitants, shorn of strength, are dismayed
24:11 **w** his servants were besieging it;
1Ch 11: 2 For some time now, even **w** Saul was king,
11:15 **w** the army of Philistines was encamped in
12: 1 **w** he could not move about freely because
16:38 **w** Obed-edom son of Jeduthun and Hosah were to
17:17 also spoken of your servant's house for a great **w**
21:12 **w** the sword of your enemies overtakes you;
21:20 and **w** his four sons who were
2Ch 6: 3 **w** all the assembly of Israel stood.
9:19 **w** twelve lions were standing,
10: 6 older men who had attended his father Solomon **w**
14: 6 He built fortified cities in Judah **w**
15: 2 The LORD is with you, **w** you are with him.
22: 9 who was captured **w** hiding in Samaria
22:12 **w** Athaliah reigned over the land.
31:13 **w** Jehiel, Azaziah, Nahath,
32: 9 **w** King Sennacherib of Assyria was at Lachish
33:12 **W** he was in distress he entreated the favor of
34: 3 in the eighth year of his reign, **w** he was still a boy,
34:14 **W** they were bringing out the money
35:11 **w** the Levites did the skinning.
Ezr 9: 4 gathered around me **w** I sat appalled until
10: 1 **W** Ezra prayed and made confession,
Ne 1: 1 in the twentieth year, **w** I was in Susa the capital,
4:18 of the builders had his sword strapped at his side **w**
6: 3 the work stop **w** I leave it to come down to you?"
Ne 7: 3 **w** the gatekeepers are still standing guard,
8: 7 **w** the people remained in their places.
11: 1 **w** nine-tenths remained in the other towns.
13: 6 **W** this was taking place I was not in Jerusalem,
Est 1: 4 **w** he displayed the great wealth of his kingdom
2:21 **w** Mordecai was sitting at the king's gate,
5: 6 **W** they were drinking wine,
6:14 **W** they were still talking with him,
8:15 **w** the city of Susa shouted and rejoiced.
Job 1:16 **W** he was still speaking, another came and said,
1:17 **W** he was still speaking, another came and said,
1:18 **W** he was still speaking, another came and said,
7: 8 **w** your eyes are upon me, I shall be gone.
7:19 Will you not look away from me for a **w**,
8:12 **W** yet in flower and not cut down,
24:24 They are exalted a little **w**, and then are gone;
32:11 **w** you searched out what to say.
33:15 **w** they slumber on their beds,
34:26 He strikes them for their wickedness **w** others look
Ps 6: 3 My soul also is struck with terror, **w** you,
28: 3 **w** mischief is in their hearts.
32: 3 **W** I kept silence, my body wasted away
36: 4 They plot mischief **w** on their beds;
37:10 Yet a little **w**, and the wicked will be no more;
39: 3 **W** I mused, the fire burned;
41: 6 **w** their hearts gather mischief;
42: 3 **w** people say to me continually,
42:10 **w** they say to me continually,
72: 5 May he live **w** the sun endures,
78:30 **w** the food was still in their mouths,
81: 8 O my people, **w** I admonish you;
104:33 I will sing praise to my God **w** I have being.
109: 4 even **w** I make prayer for them.
129: 8 **w** those who pass by do not say,
141:10 wicked fall into their own nets, **w** I alone escape.
Pr 1:17 in vain is the net baited **w** the bird is looking on;
12:24 **w** the lazy will be put to forced labor.
13: 4 **w** the appetite of the diligent is richly supplied.
19:18 Discipline your children **w** there is hope;
26:24 in speaking **w** harboring deceit within;
31:15 She rises **w** it is still night and provides food
Ecc 6:12 For who knows what is good for mortals **w**
8: 9 **w** one person exercises authority over another to
9: 3 madness is in their hearts **w** they live,
11: 9 Rejoice, young man, **w** you are young,
SS 1:12 **W** the king was on his couch,
Isa 8:11 to me **w** his hand was strong upon me,
10:25 a very little **w** my indignation will come to an end,
26:20 hide yourselves for a little **w** until the wrath is past.
29:13 **w** their hearts are far from me,
29:17 Shall not Lebanon in a very little **w** become
37:27 **w** their inhabitants, shorn of strength, are dismayed
49: 1 **w** I was in my mother's womb he named me.
55: 6 Seek the LORD **w** he may be found,
55: 6 call upon him **w** he is near;
57: 1 the devout are taken away, **w** no one understands.
63:18 Your holy people took possession for a little **w**;
65:24 **w** they are yet speaking I will hear.
Jer 2:17 **w** he led you in the way?
4:10 even **w** the sword is at the throat!"
13:16 **w** you look for light, he turns it into gloom
15: 9 her sun went down **w** it was yet day;
17: 2 **w** their children remember their altars
18:23 deal with them **w** you are angry.
20: 4 and they shall fall by the sword of their enemies **w**
33: 1 **w** he was still confined in the court of the guard:
39:15 the LORD came to Jeremiah **w** he was confined
51:33 yet a little **w** and the time of her harvest will come.
La 1:19 **w** seeking food to revive their strength.
Eze 1:11 **w** two covered their bodies.
7: 4 **w** your abominations are among you.
7: 9 **w** your abominations are among you.
9: 8 **W** they were killing, and I was left alone,
11:13 **w** I was prophesying, Pelatiah son of Benaiah died.
11:16 yet I have been a sanctuary to them for a little **w** in
16:13 **w** your clothing was of fine linen, rich fabric,
16:34 **w** no payment was given to you;
23: 5 Oholah played the whore **w** she was mine;
42: 8 on the outer court were fifty cubits long, **w**
43: 6 **W** the man was standing beside me,
44:17 **w** they minister at the gates of the inner court,
Da 4:19 was severely distressed for a **w**.
4:31 **W** the words were still in the king's mouth,
9:20 **W** I was speaking, and was praying
9:21 **w** I was speaking in prayer,
10:11 So **w** he was speaking this word to me,
10:15 **W** he was speaking these words to me,
11: 4 And **w** still rising in power,
Hos 1: 4 for in a little **w** I will punish the house of Jehu for
Jnh 4: 2 Is not this what I said **w** I was still
Hag 1: 4 **w** this house lies in ruins?
1: 9 **w** all of you hurry off to your own houses.
2: 6 in a little **w**, I will shake the heavens and the earth
Zec 1:15 for **w** I was only a little angry,
12: 6 **w** Jerusalem shall again be inhabited in its place,
14:12 their flesh shall rot **w** they are still on their feet;
Mt 5:25 to terms quickly with your accuser **w** you are on
7: 4 **w** the log is in your own eye?
8:12 **w** the heirs of the kingdom will be thrown into
9:18 **W** he was saying these things to them,
12:46 **W** he was still speaking to the crowds,
13: 2 **w** the whole crowd stood on the beach.
13:21 but endures only for a **w**,
13:25 but **w** everybody was asleep,
14:22 **w** he dismissed the crowds.
17: 5 **W** he was still speaking, suddenly
20:17 **W** Jesus was going up to Jerusalem,

Mt 22: 6 w the rest seized his slaves,
22:41 Now w the Pharisees were gathered together,
25:10 And w they went to buy it, the bridegroom came,
26: 6 Now w Jesus was at Bethany in the house
26:21 and w they were eating, he said,
26:26 W they were eating, Jesus took a loaf of bread,
26:36 "Sit here w I go over there and pray."
26:47 W he was still speaking, Judas, one of the twelve,
26:73 a little w the bystanders came up and said to Peter,
27:19 W he was sitting on the judgment seat,
27:63 we remember what that impostor said w
28:11 W they were going, some of the guard went into
28:13 'His disciples came by night and stole him away w
Mk 1:35 In the morning, w it was still very dark,
2:19 "The wedding guests cannot fast w
4: 1 w the whole crowd was beside the sea on the land.
4:17 But they have no root, and endure only for a w;
5:35 W he was still speaking, some people came from
6:31 to a deserted place all by yourselves and rest a w."
6:45 to Bethsaida, w he dismissed the crowd.
12:35 W Jesus was teaching in the temple, he said,
14: 3 W he was at Bethany in the house of Simon
14:22 W they were eating, he took a loaf of bread,
14:32 and he said to his disciples, "Sit here w I pray."
14:43 Immediately, w he was still speaking, Judas,
14:66 W Peter was below in the courtyard,
14:70 after a little w the bystanders again said to Peter,
16:10 ⟦w they were mourning and weeping.⟧
16:20 ⟦w the Lord worked with them and confirmed⟧
Lk 2: 2 and was taken w Quirinius was governor of Syria.
2: 6 W they were there, the time came for her
5: 1 Once w Jesus was standing beside the lake
5:17 One day, w he was teaching,
5:34 "You cannot make wedding guests fast w
6: 1 One sabbath w Jesus was going through
8:13 for a w and in a time of testing fall away.
8:23 and w they were sailing he fell asleep.
8:49 W he was still speaking, someone came from
9:29 And w he was praying, the appearance
9:34 W he was saying this, a cloud came
9:42 W he was coming, the demon dashed him to
9:43 W everyone was amazed at all that he was doing,
10:33 But a Samaritan w traveling came near him;
11:27 W he was saying this, a woman in
11:37 W he was speaking, a Pharisee invited him to dine
14:32 If he cannot, then, w the other is still far away,
15:20 But w he was still far off,
17: 8 put on your apron and serve me w I eat and drink;
18: 4 For a w he refused; but later he said to himself,
22:47 W he was still speaking, suddenly a crowd came,
22:60 At that moment, w he was still speaking,
23:45 w the sun's light failed;
24: 4 W they were perplexed about this,
24: 6 w he was still in Galilee,
24:15 W they were talking and discussing,
24:17 "What are you discussing with each other w
24:32 not our hearts burning within us w he was talking
24:32 w he was opening the scriptures to us?"
24:36 W they were talking about this,
24:41 W in their joy they were disbelieving
24:44 that I spoke to you w I was still with you—
24:51 W he was blessing them, he withdrew from them
Jn 5: 7 and w I am making my way,
5:35 and you were willing to rejoice for a w in his light.
6:59 He said these things w he was teaching in
7:12 W some were saying, "He is a good man,"
7:33 "I will be with you a little w longer,
7:37 the great day, w Jesus was standing there,
8: 1 ⟦w Jesus went to the Mount of Olives.⟧
8:20 He spoke these words w he was teaching in
9: 4 We must work the works of him who sent me w
11:20 she went and met him, w Mary stayed at home.
12:35 Walk w you have the light,
12:36 W you have the light, believe in the light,
13:25 So w reclining next to Jesus, he asked him, "Lord,
14:19 In a little w the world will no longer see me,
14:25 "I have said these things to you w I am still
16:16 "A little w, and you will no longer see me, and again a little w,
16:17 "What does he mean by saying to us, 'A little w, and you will no longer see me, and again a little w,
16:18 "What does he mean by this 'a little w'?
16:19 'A little w, and you will no longer see me, and again a little w,
17:12 W I was with them, I protected them in your name
20: 1 on the first day of the week, w it was still dark,
Ac 1: 4 W staying with them, he ordered them not
1:10 W he was going and they were gazing up
3:11 W he clung to Peter and John,
4: 1 W Peter and John were speaking to the people,
4:15 to leave the council w they discussed the matter
4:30 w you stretch out your hand to heal,
5: 4 W it remained unsold, did it not remain your own?
6: 4 w we, for our part, will devote ourselves to prayer
7:59 W they were stoning Stephen, he prayed,
9:39 that Dorcas had made w she was with them.
10:10 and w it was being prepared, he fell into a trance.
10:17 Now w Peter was greatly puzzled about what
10:19 W Peter was still thinking about the vision,
10:44 W Peter was still speaking,
12: 5 W Peter was kept in prison,
12: 6 w guards in front of the door were keeping watch
13: 2 W they were worshiping the Lord and fasting,
13:11 and you will be blind for a w,
16:17 W she followed Paul and us, she would cry out,
17: 5 W they were searching for Paul and Silas
17:16 W Paul was waiting for them in Athens,
Ac 17:30 W God has overlooked the times
19: 1 W Apollos was in Corinth,
19:22 w he himself stayed for some time longer in Asia.
20: 9 into a deep sleep w Paul talked still longer.
21:10 W we were staying there for several days,
21:31 W they were trying to kill him,
22: 6 "W I was on my way and approaching Damascus,
22:17 to Jerusalem and w I was praying in the temple,
22:20 w the blood of your witness Stephen was shed,
22:23 And w they were shouting,
23: 1 W Paul was looking intently at the council he said,
23:32 w they returned to the barracks.
24:18 W I was doing this, they found me in the temple,
24:21 unless it was this one sentence that I called out w
26:24 W he was making this defense, Festus exclaimed,
28:24 w others refused to believe.
Ro 2: 8 w for those who are self-seeking and who obey not
2:21 W you preach against stealing, do you steal?
4:11 as a seal of the righteousness that he had by faith w
5: 6 For w we were still weak,
5: 8 in that w we still were sinners Christ died for us.
5:10 For if w we were enemies,
7: 3 an adulteress if she lives with another man w
7: 5 W we were living in the flesh, our sinful passions,
8:23 groan inwardly w we wait for adoption,
14: 2 w the weak eat only vegetables.
14: 5 w others judge all days to be alike.
14: 6 w those who abstain, abstain in honor of the Lord
15:24 once I have enjoyed your company for a little w.
16:19 For w your obedience is known to all,
1Co 9: 9 "You shall not muzzle an ox w it is treading out
14:22 w prophecy is not for unbelievers but for believers.
2Co 4:11 For w we live, we are always being given up
5: 4 For w we are still in this tent,
5: 6 even though we know that w we are at home in
8:19 by the churches to travel with us w
9:14 w they long for you and pray for you because of
13: 2 and I warn them now w absent,
13:10 So I write these things w I am away from you,
Gal 4: 3 So with us; w we were minors,
Eph 6: 6 not only w being watched,
Col 1:11 be prepared to endure everything with patience, w
3:22 only w being watched and in order to please them,
1Th 2: 9 and day, so that we might not burden any of you w
1Ti 4: 8 w physical training is of some value,
5: 6 the widow who lives for pleasure is dead even w
5:18 "You shall not muzzle an ox w it is treading out
5:24 w the sins of others follow them there.
Tit 2:13 w we wait for the blessed hope and
Phm 1:15 the reason he was separated from you for a w,
Heb 2: 4 w God added his testimony by signs and wonders
2: 7 You have made them for a little w lower than
2: 9 who for a little w was made lower than the angels,
4: 1 w the promise of entering his rest is still open,
10:37 For yet "in a very little w,
Jas 2: 3 w to the one who is poor you say, "Stand there,"
4:14 a mist that appears for a little w and then vanishes.
1Pe 1: 6 for a little w you have had to suffer various trials,
2:19 you endure pain w suffering unjustly.
4:19 to a faithful Creator, w continuing to do good.
5:10 And after you have suffered for a little w,
2Pe 1:18 w we were with him on the holy mountain.
2:13 reveling in their dissipation w they feast with you.
3:14 beloved, w you are waiting for these things,
1Jn 1: 6 with him w we are walking in darkness, we lie
2: 9 w hating a brother or sister, is still in the darkness.
Jude 1: 3 w eagerly preparing to write to you about
1:12 w they feast with you without fear,
Rev 11:12 in a cloud w their enemies watched them.
17:10 when he comes, he must remain only a little w.
20: 3 After that he must be let out for a little w.
21:18 The wall is built of jasper, w the city is pure gold,
Tob 1: 4 in the land of Israel, w I was still a young man,
1:14 W in the country of Media I left bags
4: 4 because she faced many dangers for you w
5: 6 w Ecbatana is in the middle of the plain."
11: 3 and prepare the house w they are still on the way."
14: 4 and it will be desolate for a w.
14:10 w the people are without shame.
14:10 w still alive, brought down into the earth?
Jdt 8:17 Therefore, w we wait for his deliverance,
8:26 w he was tending the sheep of Laban,
10: 3 to wear w her husband Manasseh was living.
15:13 w all the men of Israel followed,
AdE 2:12 six months w they are anointing themselves
3:15 And w the king and Haman caroused together,
5: 6 W they were drinking wine,
6: 4 W the king was inquiring about
6:14 W they were still talking, the eunuchs arrived
9:19 w those who live in the large cities keep
15: 4 w the other followed, carrying her train.
15:15 And w she was speaking, she fainted and fell.
Wis 4: 4 For even if they put forth boughs for a w,
4:10 and w living among sinners were taken up.
7:27 and w remaining in herself, she renews all things;
12:22 So w chastening us you scourge our enemies ten
13: 1 nor did they recognize the artisan w paying heed
13: 6 for perhaps they go astray w seeking God
13: 7 For w they live among his works,
15: 8 of earth a short time before and after a little w go
16: 3 w your people, after suffering want a short time,
16: 4 w to these others it was merely shown
16: 6 they were troubled for a little w as a warning,
17:21 w over those people alone heavy night was spread,
18:14 For w gentle silence enveloped all things,
18:16 and touched heaven w standing on the earth.
19: 3 For w they were still engaged in mourning,
Wis 19:15 but, w punishment of some sort will come upon
19:18 w each note remains the same.
Sir 10:30 w the rich are honored for their wealth.
12:15 He stands by you for a w, but if you falter,
13:11 and w he smiles he will be examining you.
20: 5 w others are detested for being talkative.
20: 6 w others keep silent because they know when
30:12 and beat his sides w he is young,
33:21 W you are still alive and have breath in you,
37:27 My child, test yourself w you live;
42:10 w a virgin, for fear she may be seduced
47:10 w they praised God's holy name,
51:13 W I was still young, before I went
Sus 1:15 Once, w they were watching for an opportune day,
1:36 "W we were walking in the garden alone,
1Mc 1: 6 and divided his kingdom among them w
4: 4 w the division was still absent from the camp.
5:14 W the letter was still being read, other messengers,
5:55 Now w Judas and Jonathan were in Gilead
6:38 to harass the enemy w being themselves protected
6:55 whom King Antiochus w still living had appointed
9:65 w he went out into the country;
12:47 w one thousand accompanied him.
2Mc 1:23 And w the sacrifice was being consumed,
2:22 w the Lord with great kindness became gracious
2:28 w devoting our effort to arriving at the outlines of
2:29 w the one who undertakes its painting
2:32 be foolish to lengthen the preface w cutting short
3: 1 W the holy city was inhabited in unbroken peace
3:19 w others peered out of the windows.
3:22 W they were calling upon the Almighty Lord
3:29 W he lay prostrate, speechless because of
3:30 a little w before was full of fear and disturbance,
3:33 W the high priest was making an atonement,
4:29 in the high priesthood, w Sostratus left Crates,
4:30 W such was the state of affairs,
4:47 w he sentenced to death those unfortunate men,
5:17 for a little w because of the sins of those who lived
6:25 w I defile and disgrace my old age.
7: 4 w the rest of the brothers and
7:30 W she was still speaking, the young man said,
7:33 And if our living Lord is angry for a little w,
8:33 W they were celebrating the victory in the city
9: 3 W he was in Ecbatana, news came to him
9: 8 Thus he who only a little w before had thought
9: 9 and w he was still living in anguish and pain,
9:10 to carry the man who a little w before had thought
10:28 w the other made rage their leader in the fight.
11: 8 And there, w they were still near Jerusalem,
14:31 and holy temple w the priests were offering
15:39 w wine mixed with water is sweet and delicious
1Es 5:64 w many came with trumpets and a joyful noise,
7: 3 w the prophets Haggai and Zechariah prophesied;
8:91 W Ezra was praying and making his confession,
3Mc 1:25 w the elders near the king tried in various ways
2:24 After a w he recovered,
3: 2 W these matters were being arranged,
5:19 the corroboration of his Friends, pointed out that w
5:26 and w the king was receiving his Friends,
2Es 5:34 w I strive to understand the way of the Most High
6:15 w the voice is speaking, do not be terrified;
6:29 W he spoke to me, little by little the place
7:18 can endure difficult circumstances w hoping
7:*51* not many but few, w the ungodly abound, hear
7:*87* of the Most High in whose presence they sinned w
7:*126* [56] For w we lived and committed iniquity we did
7:*129* [59] the way of which Moses, w he was alive,
9:11 many as scorned my law w they still had freedom,
9:11 not understand but despised it w an opportunity
9:27 After seven days, w I lay on the grass,
10:25 W I was talking to her, her face suddenly began
10:25 W I was wondering what this meant,
10:29 W I was speaking these words,
10:41 The woman who appeared to you a little w ago,
11:14 W it was reigning its end came also,
11:28 W I continued to look the two
11:29 and w they were planning, one of the heads
11:33 And w I looked, I saw the head on
12: 1 W the lion was saying these words to the eagle,
14: 1 On the third day, w I was sitting under an oak,
4Mc 4: 9 W the priests together with women
4:10 and w Apollonius was going up
6: 4 w a herald who faced him cried out,
6: 6 yet w the old man's eyes were raised to heaven,
6:10 Like a noble athlete the old man, w being beaten,
6:20 be shameful if we should survive for a little w and
9: 6 of their religion lived piously w enduring torture,
9:19 W he was saying these things,
9:19 and w fanning the flames they tightened
9:26 W all were marveling at his courageous spirit,
10: 8 and w his vertebrae were being dislocated by this,
11: 9 W he was saying these things,
11:20 W being tortured he said, "O contest befitting
13:11 W one said, "Courage, brother," another said,
13:27 w watching their brothers being maltreated
16:17 w an aged man endures such agonies for the sake
18:10 W he was still with you,

WHIM (1)

Ge 49: 6 and at their w they hamstrung oxen.

WHIP (6) [WHIPPED, WHIPS]

Pr 26: 3 A w for the horse, a bridle for the donkey,
Isa 10:26 The LORD of hosts will wield a w against them,
Na 3: 2 The crack of w and rumble of wheel,
Jn 2:15 Making a w of cords, he drove all of them out of

Sir 28:17 The blow of a w raises a welt,
30: 1 He who loves his son will w him often,

WHIPPED (1) [WHIP]

Job 30: 8 they have been w out of the land.

WHIPS (7) [WHIP]

1Ki 12:11 My father disciplined you with w,
12:14 my father disciplined you with w,
2Ch 10:11 My father disciplined you with w,
10:14 my father disciplined you with w,
Jer 49: 3 lament, and slash yourselves with w!
Sir 23: 2 Who will set w over my thoughts,
2Mc 7: 1 under torture with w and thongs,

WHIRL (2) [WHIRLED, WHIRLING, WHIRLWIND, WHIRLWINDS]

Ps 29: 9 The voice of the LORD causes the oaks to w,
Isa 22:18 w you round and round, and throw you like a ball

WHIRLED (1) [WHIRL]

Sir 47: 4 when he w the stone in the sling and struck down

WHIRLING (4) [WHIRL]

Ps 83:13 O my God, make them like w dust,
Isa 17:13 the mountains before the wind and w dust before
Jer 23:19 a w tempest; it will burst upon the head of the
30:23 a w tempest; it will burst upon the head of the

WHIRLWIND (21) [WHIRL, WIND]

2Ki 2: 1 about to take Elijah up to heaven by a w,
2:11 and Elijah ascended in a w into heaven.
Job 27:20 in the night a w carries them off.
37: 9 From its chamber comes the w,
38: 1 Then the LORD answered Job out of the w:
40: 6 Then the LORD answered Job out of the w:
Ps 77:18 The crash of your thunder was in the w;
Pr 1:27 and your calamity comes like a w,
Isa 5:28 and their wheels like the w.
29: 6 and great noise, with w and tempest, and the flame
66:15 and his chariots like the w,
Jer 4:13 He comes up like clouds, his chariots like the w;
Da 11:40 the king of the north shall rush upon him like a w,
Hos 8: 7 For they sow the wind, and they shall reap the w.
Am 1:14 with a storm on the day of the w;
Na 1: 3 His way is in w and storm,
Hab 3:14 who came like a w to scatter us,
Zec 7:14 a w among all the nations that they had not known.
Sir 43:17 so do the storm from the north and the w.
48: 9 You were taken up by a w of fire,
48:12 When Elijah was enveloped in the w,

WHIRLWINDS (2) [WHIRL, WIND]

Isa 21: 1 As w in the Negeb sweep on,
Zec 9:14 the trumpet and march forth in the w of the south.

WHIRRING (1)

Isa 18: 1 Ah, land of w wings beyond the rivers of Ethiopia,

WHISPER (5) [WHISPERED, WHISPERER, WHISPERING, WHISPERS]

Job 4:12 my ear received the w of it.
26:14 and how small a w do we hear of him!
Ps 41: 7 All who hate me w together about me;
Isa 29: 4 and your speech shall w out of the dust.
Sir 12:18 and w much, and show his true face.

WHISPERED (2) [WHISPER]

Mt 10:27 what you hear w, proclaim from the housetops.
Lk 12: 3 and what you have w behind closed doors will

WHISPERER (5) [WHISPER]

Pr 16:28 and a w separates close friends.
18: 8 The words of a w are like delicious morsels;
26:20 and where there is no w, quarreling ceases.
26:22 The words of a w are like delicious morsels;
Sir 21:28 A w degrades himself and is hated

WHISPERING (3) [WHISPER]

2Sa 12:19 when David saw that his servants were w together,
Ps 31:13 For I hear the w of many—
Jer 20:10 For I hear many w: "Terror is all around!

WHISPERS (1) [WHISPER]

La 3:62 The w and murmurs of my assailants are against

WHISTLE (2) [WHISTLING]

Isa 5:26 and w for a people at the ends of the earth;
7:18 On that day the LORD will w for the fly that is at

WHISTLING (2) [WHISTLE]

Wis 17:18 Whether there came a w wind,
Aza 1:27 of the furnace as though a moist wind were w

WHIT (KJV) See ALL, ENTIRELY, EVERYTHING, IN THE LEAST, WHOLE

WHITE‡ (69) [REDDISH-WHITE, WHITE-HAIRED, WHITENESS, WHITER, WHITEWASH, WHITEWASHED]

Ge 30:35 every one that had w on it,
30:37 and peeled w streaks in them, exposing the w of
Ex 4: 6 he took it out, his hand was leprous, as w as snow.
16:31 it was like coriander seed, w,
Lev 13: 3 and if the hair in the diseased area has turned w
13: 4 But if the spot is w in the skin of his body,
13: 4 and the hair in it has not turned w,
13:10 a w swelling in the skin that has turned the hair w,
13:13 since it has all turned w, he is clean.
13:16 But if the raw flesh again turns w,
13:17 and if the disease has turned w,
13:19 the place of the boil there appears a w swelling or
13:20 the skin and its hair has turned w,
13:21 if the priest examines it and the hair on it is not w,
13:24 of the burn becomes a spot, reddish-white or w,
13:25 in the spot has turned w and it appears deeper than
13:26 priest examines it and the hair in the spot is not w,
13:38 on the skin of the body, w spots,
13:39 if the spots on the skin of the body are of a dull w,
Nu 12:10 Miriam had become leprous, as w as snow.
Jdg 5:10 "Tell of it, you who ride on w donkeys,
2Ki 5:27 So he left his presence leprous, as w as snow.
Est 1: 6 There were w cotton curtains
8:15 wearing royal robes of blue and w,
Ecc 9: 8 Let your garments always be w;
Eze 27:18 wine of Helbon, and w wool.
Da 7: 9 his clothing was w as snow,
Joel 1: 7 their branches have turned w.
Zec 1: 8 and behind him were red, sorrel, and w horses.
6: 3 the third chariot w horses,
6: 6 the w ones go toward the west country,
Mt 5:36 for you cannot make one hair w or black.
17: 2 and his clothes became dazzling w.
28: 3 and his clothing w as snow.
Mk 9: 3 and his clothes became dazzling w,
16: 5 dressed in a w robe, sitting on the right side;
Lk 9:29 and his clothes became dazzling w.
Jn 20:12 and she saw two angels in w,
Ac 1:10 suddenly two men in w robes stood by them.
Rev 1:14 head and his hair were w as w wool, w as snow;
2:17 I will give a w stone, and on the w stone is written
3: 4 they will walk with me, dressed in w,
3: 5 you will be clothed like them in w robes,
3:18 and w robes to clothe you and to keep the shame
4: 4 dressed in w robes, with golden crowns
6: 2 I looked, and there was a w horse!
6:11 They were each given a w robe and told to rest
7: 9 robed in w, with palm branches in their hands.
7:13 robed in w, and where have they come from?"
7:14 they have washed their robes and made them w in
14:14 Then I looked, and there was a w cloud,
19:11 I saw heaven opened, and there was a w horse!
19:14 linen, w and pure, were following him on w horses.
20:11 I saw a great w throne and the one who sat on it;
Tob 2:10 into my eyes and produced w films.
2:10 the more my vision was obscured by the w films,
3:17 Tobit, by removing the w films from his eyes,
6: 9 a person's eyes where w films have appeared
6: 9 blow upon them, upon the w films,
11: 8 the w films shrink and peel off from his eyes,
11:13 with both his hands he peeled off the w films from
2Mc 11: 8 clothed in w and brandishing weapons of gold.
2Es 2:40 close the list of your people who are clothed in w,

WHITE-HAIRED (1) [HAIR, WHITE]

Job 41:32 one would think the deep to be w.

WHITENESS (1) [WHITE]

Sir 43:18 The eye is dazzled by the beauty of its w,

WHITER (3) [WHITE]

Ge 49:12 and his teeth w than milk.
Ps 51: 7 wash me, and I shall be w than snow.
La 4: 7 Her princes were purer than snow, w than milk;

WHITEWASH (7) [WHITE]

Job 13: 4 As for you, you w with lies;
Eze 13:10 people build a wall, these prophets smear w on it.
13:11 Say to those who smear w on it that it shall fall.
13:12 "Where is the w you smeared on it?"
13:14 down the wall that you have smeared with w,
13:15 and upon those who have smeared it with w;
22:28 Its prophets have smeared w on their behalf,

WHITEWASHED (2) [WHITE]

Mt 23:27 For you are like w tombs,
Ac 23: 3 "God will strike you, you w wall!

WHITHER (KJV) See TO WHOM, THAT, WHERE, WHEREVER, WHICH

WHITHERSOEVER (KJV) See EVERYWHERE, WHATEVER, WHEREVER

WHO (6635) [WHOEVER, WHOM, WHOMEVER, WHOSE] See Index of Articles Etc.

WHOEVER‡ (292) [WHO]

Ge 4:15 W kills Cain will suffer a sevenfold vengeance."
9: 6 W sheds the blood of a human,
26:11 "W touches this man or his wife shall be put
Ex 12:15 from your houses, for w eats leavened bread from
12:19 for w eats what is leavened shall be cut off from
21:12 W strikes a person mortally shall be put to death.
21:15 W strikes father or mother shall be put to death.
21:16 W kidnaps a person, whether
21:17 W curses father or mother shall be put to death.
22:19 W lies with an animal shall be put to death.
22:20 W sacrifices to any god, other than
24:14 w has a dispute may go to them."
30:33 W compounds any like it or w puts any of it
30:38 W makes any like it to use as perfume shall
31:14 w does any work on it shall be cut off from among
31:15 w does any work on the sabbath day shall be put
32:24 So I said to them, 'W has gold, take it off';
32:33 "W has sinned against me I will blot out
35: 2 w does any work on it shall be put to death.
35: 5 let w is of a generous heart bring
Lev 11:24 w touches the carcass of any of them shall
11:25 and w carries any part of the carcass of any
11:27 w touches the carcass of any of them shall
11:31 w touches one of them when they are dead shall
15:19 w touches her shall be unclean until the evening.
15:21 W touches her bed shall wash his clothes,
15:22 W touches anything upon which
15:27 W touches these things shall be unclean,
17:14 w eats it shall be cut off.
18:29 For w commits any of these abominations shall
22: 4 W touches anything made unclean by a corpse or
22: 5 and w touches any swarming thing
Nu 15: 4 then w presents such an offering to
15:30 But w acts high-handedly,
19:16 W in the open field touches one who has been
19:18 and on w touched the bone, the slain, the corpse,
19:21 and w touches the water for cleansing shall
31:19 w of you has killed any person or touched
Dt 18:12 w does these things is abhorrent to the LORD;
22: 5 for w does such things is abhorrent to
Jos 1:18 W rebels against your orders
15:16 Caleb said, "W attacks Kiriath-sepher and takes it,
Jdg 1:12 Caleb said, "W attacks Kiriath-sepher and takes it,
6:31 W contends for him shall be put to death
7: 3 'W is fearful and trembling,
11:31 w comes out of the doors of my house to meet me,
21: 5 a solemn oath had been taken concerning w did
1Sa 11: 7 "W does not come out after Saul and Samuel,
2Sa 5: 8 "W would strike down the Jebusites,
17: 9 the first attack, w hears it will say, 'There has been
20:11 "W favors Joab, and w is for David,
1Ki 19:17 W escapes from the sword of Hazael,
19:17 w escapes from the sword of Jehu, Elisha shall kill.
2Ki 10:19 w is missing shall not live."
10:24 "W allows any of those to escape whom I deliver
11: 8 and w approaches the ranks is to be killed.
1Ch 11: 6 "W attacks the Jebusites first shall be chief
29: 8 W had precious stones gave them to the treasury of
2Ch 13: 9 W comes to be consecrated with a young bull
15:13 W would not seek the LORD, the God of Israel,
23: 7 and w enters the house shall be killed.
36:23 W is among you of all his people,
Ps 101: 6 w walks in the way that is blameless shall minister
Pr 8:35 For w finds me finds life and obtains favor from
9: 7 W corrects a scoffer wins abuse;
9: 7 w rebukes the wicked gets hurt.
10: 9 W walks in integrity walks securely,
10: 9 but w follows perverse ways will be found out.
10:10 W winks the eye causes trouble,
10:17 W heeds instruction is on the path to life,
10:18 and w utters slander is a fool.
11:12 W belittles another lacks sense,
11:19 W is steadfast in righteousness will live,
11:19 but w pursues evil will die.
11:27 W diligently seeks good seeks favor,
12: 1 W loves discipline loves knowledge,
12:17 W speaks the truth gives honest evidence,
13:20 W walks with the wise becomes wise,
14:29 W is slow to anger has great understanding,
16:14 and w is wise will appease it.
19:17 W is kind to the poor lends to the LORD,
20: 1 and w is led astray by it is not wise.
21:16 W wanders from the way of understanding
21:17 W loves pleasure will suffer want;
21:17 w loves wine and oil will not be rich.
21:21 W pursues righteousness
22: 8 W sows injustice will reap calamity,
24: 8 W plans to do evil will be called a mischief-maker.
24:24 W says to the wicked, "You are innocent,"
26:27 W digs a pit will fall into it,
27:11 so that I may answer w reproaches me.
27:14 W blesses a neighbor with a loud voice,
28:18 but w follows crooked ways will fall into the Pit.
28:23 W rebukes a person will afterward find more favor
28:25 but w trusts in the LORD will be enriched.
28:27 W gives to the poor will lack nothing,
29: 5 W flatters a neighbor is spreading a net for
Ecc 8: 5 W obeys a command will meet no harm,
9: 4 But w is joined with all the living has hope,
10: 8 W digs a pit will fall into it;
10: 8 w breaks through a wall will be bitten by a snake.
10: 9 W quarries stones will be hurt by them;
10: 9 and w splits logs will be endangered by them.
11: 4 W observes the wind will not sow;
11: 4 and w regards the clouds will not reap.

Isa 4: 3 **W** is left in Zion and remains in Jerusalem will
13:15 **W** is found will be thrust through,
13:15 and **w** is caught will fall by the sword.
24:18 **W** flees at the sound of the terror shall fall into
24:18 **w** climbs out of the pit shall be caught in the snare.
28: 4 **w** sees it, eats it up as soon as it comes to hand.
41:24 **w** chooses you is an abomination.
54:15 **w** stirs up strife with you shall fall because of you.
57:13 But **w** takes refuge in me shall possess the land
59: 5 **w** eats their eggs dies, and the crushed egg hatches
59:15 and **w** turns from evil is despoiled.
65:16 Then **w** invokes a blessing in the land shall bless
65:16 and **w** takes an oath in the land shall swear by
66: 3 **W** slaughters an ox is like one who kills a human
66: 3 **w** sacrifices a lamb, like one who breaks a dog's
66: 3 **w** presents a grain offering,
66: 3 **w** makes a memorial offering of frankincense,
Eze 46: 9 **w** enters by the north gate to worship shall go out
46: 9 and **w** enters by the south gate shall go out by
Da 3: 6 **W** does not fall down and worship shall
3:11 and **w** does not fall down and worship shall
5: 7 the wise men of Babylon, "**W** can read this writing
6: 7 that **w** prays to anyone, divine or human,
Zec 4:10 For **w** has despised the day
Mt 5:19 **w** breaks one of the least of these commandments,
5:19 but **w** does them and teaches them will
5:21 and '**w** murders shall be liable to judgment.'
5:31 "It was also said, '**W** divorces his wife,
5:32 **w** marries a divorced woman commits adultery.
10:33 but **w** denies me before others,
10:37 **W** loves father or mother more than me is
10:37 and **w** loves son or daughter more than me is
10:38 and **w** does not take up the cross and follow me is
10:40 "**W** welcomes you welcomes me, and **w** welcomes
10:41 **W** welcomes a prophet in the name of a prophet
10:41 and **w** welcomes a righteous person in the name of
10:42 and **w** gives even a cup of cold water to one
12:30 **W** is not with me is against me, and **w** does not
12:32 **W** speaks a word against the Son of Man will
12:32 but **w** speaks against the Holy Spirit will not
12:50 For **w** does the will of my Father
15: 4 '**W** speaks evil of father or mother must
15: 5 But you say that **w** tells father or mother,
18: 4 **W** becomes humble like this child is the greatest in
18: 5 **W** welcomes one such child
19: 9 And I say to you, **w** divorces his wife,
20:26 but **w** wishes to be great among you must
20:27 and **w** wishes to be first among you must
23:16 '**W** swears by the sanctuary is bound by nothing,
but **w** swears by the gold of the sanctuary is bound
23:18 '**W** swears by the altar is bound by nothing, but **w**
swears by the gift that is on the altar
23:20 So **w** swears by the altar, swears by it and
23:21 and **w** swears by the sanctuary, swears by it and by
23:22 and **w** swears by heaven, swears by the throne
Mk 3:29 but **w** blasphemes against the Holy Spirit can never
3:35 **W** does the will of God is my brother and sister
7:10 and, '**W** speaks evil of father or mother must
9:35 "**W** wants to be first must be last of all and servant
9:37 "**W** welcomes one such child in my name
9:37 and **w** welcomes me welcomes not me but
9:40 **W** is not against us is for us.
9:41 **w** gives you a cup of water to drink
10:11 to them, "**W** divorces his wife
10:15 **w** does not receive the kingdom of God as
10:43 but **w** wishes to become great among you must
10:44 and **w** wishes to be first among you must be slave
Lk 3:11 "**W** has two coats must share with anyone
3:11 and **w** has food must do likewise."
9:48 "**W** welcomes this child in my name welcomes
me, and **w** welcomes me welcomes the one who
9:50 for **w** is not against you is for you."
10:16 "**W** listens to you listens to me, and **w** rejects you
rejects me, and **w** rejects me rejects the one who
11:23 **W** is not with me is against me,
11:23 and **w** does not gather with me scatters.
12: 9 but **w** denies me before others will be denied
12:10 but **w** blasphemes against the Holy Spirit will not
14:26 "**W** comes to me and does not hate father
14:27 **W** does not carry the cross and follow me cannot
16:10 "**W** is faithful in a very little is faithful also
16:10 and **w** is dishonest in a very little is dishonest also
16:18 and **w** marries a woman divorced
18:17 **w** does not receive the kingdom of God as
Jn 3:15 that **w** believes in him may have eternal life.
3:33 **W** has accepted his testimony has certified this,
3:36 **W** believes in the Son has eternal life; **w** disobeys
the Son will not see life,
6:35 **W** comes to me will never be hungry, and **w**
believes in me will never be thirsty.
6:47 Very truly, I tell you, **w** believes has eternal life.
6:51 **W** eats of this bread will live forever;
6:57 so **w** eats me will live because of me.
8:12 **W** follows me will never walk in darkness
8:47 **W** is from God hears the words of God.
8:51 I tell you, **w** keeps my word will never see death."
8:52 '**W** keeps my word will never taste death.'
10: 9 **W** enters by me will be saved,
12:26 **W** serves me must follow me, and where I am,
12:26 **W** serves me, the Father will honor.
12:44 "**W** believes in me believes not in me but
12:45 And **w** sees me sees him who sent me.
13:20 **w** receives one whom I send receives me;
13:20 and **w** receives me receives him who sent me."
14: 9 **W** has seen me has seen the Father.
14:24 **W** does not love me does not keep my words;
15: 6 **W** does not abide in me is thrown away like

Jn 15:23 **W** hates me hates my Father also.
Ro 2: 1 Therefore you have no excuse, **w** you are,
2: 3 Do you imagine, **w** you are,
6: 7 For **w** has died is freed from sin.
9:33 and **w** believes in him will not be put to shame."
13: 2 **w** resists authority resists what God has appointed,
1Co 6:16 that **w** is united to a prostitute becomes one body
7:22 For **w** was called in the Lord as a slave is a freed
7:22 just as **w** was free when called is a slave of Christ.
9:10 for **w** plows should plow in hope and **w** threshes
11:27 **W**, therefore, eats the bread or drinks the cup of
Gal 3:12 "**W** does the works of the law will live by them."
5:10 **w** it is that is confusing you will pay the penalty.
1Th 4: 8 **w** rejects this rejects not human authority but God,
1Ti 3: 1 **w** aspires to the office of bishop desires
5: 8 And **w** does not provide for relatives,
6: 3 **W** teaches otherwise and does not agree with
Heb 11: 6 for **w** would approach him must believe
Jas 2:10 For **w** keeps the whole law but fails
4: 4 Therefore **w** wishes to be a friend of
4:11 **W** speaks evil against another or judges another,
5:20 you should know that **w** brings back a sinner
1Pe 2: 6 and **w** believes in him will not be put to shame."
4: 1 also with the same intention (for **w** has suffered in
4:11 **W** speaks must do so as one speaking
4:11 **w** serves must do so with the strength
1Jn 2: 4 **W** says, "I have come to know him,"
2: 5 but **w** obeys his word, truly in this person the love
2: 6 **w** says, "I abide in him," ought to walk just
2: 9 **W** says, "I am in the light,"
2:10 **W** loves a brother or sister lives in the light,
2:11 But **w** hates another believer is in the darkness,
3:14 **W** does not love abides in death.
4: 6 **W** knows God listens to us, and **w** is not from God
4: 8 **W** does not love does not know God,
4:18 and **w** fears has not reached perfection in love.
5:12 **W** has the Son has life;
5:12 **w** does not have the Son of God does not have life.
2Jn 1: 9 **w** abides in the teaching has both the Father and
3Jn 1:11 **W** does good is from God;
1:11 **w** does evil has not seen God.
Rev 2:11 **W** conquers will not be harmed by
Jdt 16:16 but **w** fears the Lord is great forever.
Wis 17:16 And **w** was there fell down,
Sir 3:16 **W** forsakes a father is like a blasphemer,
3:16 and **w** angers a mother is cursed by the Lord.
3:26 and **w** loves danger will perish in it.
4:12 **W** loves her loves life, and those who seek her
4:13 **W** holds her fast inherits glory,
6:14 **w** finds one has found a treasure.
13: 1 **W** touches pitch gets dirty,
13: 1 and **w** associates with a proud person becomes
15: 1 **W** fears the Lord will do this,
15: 1 and **w** holds to the law will obtain wisdom.
20: 8 **W** talks too much is detested,
20: 8 and **w** pretends to authority is hated.
21: 8 **W** builds his house with other people's money is
21:11 **W** keeps the law controls his thoughts,
22: 9 **W** teaches a fool is like one
22:10 **W** tells a story to a fool tells it to a drowsy man;
22:26 **w** hears of it will beware of him.
24:22 **W** obeys me will not be put to shame,
27:16 **W** betrays secrets destroys confidence,
27:21 but **w** has betrayed secrets is without hope.
27:22 **W** winks the eye plots mischief,
27:25 **W** throws a stone straight up throws it
27:26 **W** digs a pit will fall into it,
27:26 and **w** sets a snare will be caught in it.
30: 7 **W** spoils his son will bind up his wounds,
34:25 **w** deprives them of it is a murderer.
1Mc 1:50 "And **w** does not obey the command of
14:45 **W** acts contrary to these decisions or rejects any
2Es 6:25 be that **w** remains after all that I have foretold

WHOLE‡ (458) [WHOLEHEARTED, WHOLEHEARTEDLY, WHOLESOME, WHOLLY]

A. WHOLE EARTH (42)
B. WHOLE CONGREGATION (41)
C. WHOLE LAND (38)
D. WHOLE WORLD (31)
E. WHOLE ASSEMBLY (22)
F. WHOLE BODY (18)
G. WHOLE HEART (17)
H. WHOLE HOUSE (17)
I. WHOLE ARMY (12)
J. WHOLE KINGDOM (10)
K. WHOLE NATION (10)

Ge 2: 6 and water the **w** face of the ground—
2:11 the **w** land of Havilah, where there is gold; C
2:13 the one that flows around the **w** land of Cush. C
7:19 under the **w** heaven were covered;
8: 9 the waters were still on the face of the **w** earth. A
9:19 and from these the **w** earth was peopled. A
11: 1 **w** earth had one language and the same words. A
11: 4 scattered abroad upon the face of the **w** earth." A
13: 9 Is not the **w** land before you? C
18:26 I will forgive the **w** place for their sake."
18:28 Will you destroy the **w** city for lack of five?"
23:17 that were in the field, throughout its **w** area,
41: 1 After two **w** years, Pharaoh dreamed
Ex 1: 6 and all his brothers, and that **w** generation.
7:19 and there shall be blood throughout the **w** land C
7:21 there was blood throughout the **w** land of Egypt. C

Ex 8: 2 I will plague your **w** country with frogs.
8:16 that it may become gnats throughout the **w** land C
8:17 the earth turned into gnats throughout the **w** land C
9: 9 on humans and animals throughout the **w** land C
9:22 so that hail may fall on the **w** land C
10:14 of Egypt and settled on the **w** country of Egypt,
10:15 They covered the surface of the **w** land, C
11: 6 be a loud cry throughout the **w** land of Egypt, C
12: 3 Tell the **w** congregation of Israel that on the B
12: 4 If a household is too small for a **w** lamb,
12: 6 then the **w** assembled congregation
12:47 The **w** congregation of Israel shall celebrate it. B
16: 1 **w** congregation of the Israelites set out from B
16: 2 The **w** congregation of the Israelites complained B
16: 3 into this wilderness to kill this **w** assembly E
16: 9 "Say to the **w** congregation of the Israelites, B
16:10 And as Aaron spoke to the **w** congregation of B
17: 1 From the wilderness of Sin the **w** congregation B
19: 5 Indeed, the **w** earth is mine, A
19:18 while the **w** mountain shook violently.
25:36 the **w** of it one hammered piece of pure gold.
26: 6 so that the tabernacle may be one **w**.
26:11 and join the tent together, so that it may be one **w**.
29:18 and turn the **w** ram into smoke on the altar;
36:13 so the tabernacle was one **w**.
36:18 to join the tent together so that it might be one **w**.
37:22 the **w** of it one hammered piece of pure gold.
Lev 1: 9 the priest shall turn the **w** into smoke on the altar
1:13 the priest shall offer the **w** and turn it into smoke
3: 9 the **w** broad tail, which shall be removed close to
4:13 the **w** congregation of Israel errs unintentionally B
8: 3 and assemble the **w** congregation at the entrance B
8:21 Moses turned into smoke the **w** ram on the altar;
9: 5 and the **w** congregation drew near and stood B
10: 6 but your kindred, the **w** house of Israel, H
15:16 he shall bathe his **w** body in water, F
24:14 and let the **w** congregation stone him. B
24:16 the **w** congregation shall stone the blasphemer. B
Nu 1: 2 a census of the **w** congregation of Israelites, B
1:18 the **w** congregation together. B
1:45 So the **w** number of the Israelites,
1:46 their **w** number was six hundred three thousand
3: 7 **w** congregation in front of the tent of meeting, B
4:31 as the **w** of their service in the tent of meeting:
4:33 **w** of their service relating to the tent of meeting,
8: 7 on them, have them shave their **w** body with F
8: 9 assemble the **w** congregation of the Israelites. B
8:20 and the **w** congregation of the Israelites did B
10: 3 the **w** congregation shall assemble before you B
10:14 the **w** company was Nahshon son of Amminadab.
10:18 over the **w** company was Elizur son of Shedeur.
10:22 the **w** company was Elishama son of Ammihud.
10:25 the **w** company was Ahiezer son of Ammishaddai.
11:20 for a **w** month—until it comes out of your
11:21 that they may eat for a **w** month'!
14: 2 the **w** congregation said to them, B
14:10 the **w** congregation threatened to stone them. B
15:24 the **w** congregation shall offer one young bull B
15:26 because the **w** people was involved in the error.
15:33 Aaron, and to the **w** congregation. B
15:36 **w** congregation brought him outside the camp B
16:19 the **w** congregation against them at the entrance B
16:19 of the LORD appeared to the **w** congregation. B
16:22 you become angry with the **w** congregation?" B
16:41 the **w** congregation of the Israelites rebelled B
18: 3 for you and for the **w** tent.
20: 1 The Israelites, the **w** congregation, B
20:22 the **w** congregation, came to Mount Hor. B
20:27 Mount Hor in the sight of the **w** congregation. B
25: 6 of Moses and in the sight of the **w** congregation B
26: 2 a census of the **w** congregation of the Israelites, B
27:21 the Israelites with him, the **w** congregation." B
27:22 before Eleazar the priest and the **w** congregation; B
Dt 2:37 the **w** upper region of the Wadi Jabbok as well as
3: 4 sixty towns, the **w** region of Argob,
3:10 the **w** of Gilead, and all of Bashan,
3:13 Og's kingdom. (The **w** region of Argob:
3:14 Jair the Manassite acquired the **w** region of Argob
5:22 loud voice to your **w** assembly at the mountain, E
13:16 as a **w** burnt offering to the LORD your God.
18: 1 The levitical priests, the **w** tribe of Levi,
22: 9 or the **w** yield will have to be forfeited,
31:30 in the hearing of the **w** assembly of Israel: E
33:10 and **w** burnt offerings on your altar.
34: 1 and the LORD showed him the **w** land: C
Jos 2: 3 they have come only to search out the **w** land." C
7: 3 do not make the **w** people toil up there."
10:13 and did not hurry to set for about a **w** day.
10:40 So Joshua defeated the **w** land, C
11:23 So Joshua took the **w** land, C
13:30 the **w** kingdom of King Og of Bashan, J
18: 1 the **w** congregation of the Israelites assembled B
22:12 **w** assembly of the Israelites gathered at Shiloh, E
22:16 "Thus says the **w** congregation of the LORD, B
22:18 with the **w** congregation of Israel tomorrow. B
Jdg 2:10 that **w** generation was gathered to their ancestors,
7:18 you also blow the trumpets around the **w** camp,
9: 1 to them and to the **w** clan of his mother's family,
16:17 So he told her his **w** secret, and said to her,
16:18 Delilah realized that he had told her his **w** secret,
16:18 for he has told his **w** secret to me."
18: 2 from the **w** number of their clan, from Zorah and
20: 6 throughout the **w** extent of Israel's territory;
20:26 Then all the Israelites, the **w** army, I
20:37 Then they put the **w** city to the sword.
20:40 and there was the **w** city going up in smoke
21:13 Then the **w** congregation sent word to B

Ru 1:19 the w town was stirred because of them;
1Sa 5:11 there was a deathly panic throughout the w city.
7: 9 a sucking lamb and offered it as a w burnt offering
2Sa 2:29 marching the w forenoon, they came to Mahanaim.
3:19 and the w house of Benjamin were ready to do. H
6:19 the w multitude of Israel, both men and women,
8: 9 David had defeated the w army of Hadadezer, I
14: 7 Now the w family has risen against your servant.
15:23 w country wept aloud as all the people passed by;
1Ki 6:10 He built the structure against the w house, H
6:22 Next he overlaid the w house with gold, H
6:22 in order that the w house might be perfect; H
6:22 even the w altar that belonged to
10:24 The w earth sought the presence of Solomon A
11:34 Nevertheless I will not take the w kingdom away J
2Ki 7:13 the fate of the w multitude of Israel
7:15 the w way was littered with garments
9: 8 For the w house of Ahab shall perish; H
20: 3 before you in faithfulness with a w heart, G
1Ch 13: 2 David said to the w assembly of Israel, E
13: 4 The w assembly agreed to do so, E
18: 9 the w army of King Hadadezer of Zobah, I
29: 1 King David said to the w assembly, E
29:20 Then David said to the w assembly, E
2Ch 1: 3 Then Solomon, and the w assembly with him, E
6:12 of the LORD in the presence of the w assembly E
6:13 on his knees in the presence of the w assembly E
15:15 and had sought him with their w desire,
19: 9 in faithfulness, and with your w heart; G
23: 3 the w assembly made a covenant with the king E
26:12 The w number of the heads of ancestral houses
29:28 The w assembly worshiped, the singers sang, E
30:23 w assembly agreed together to keep the festival E
30:25 The w assembly of Judah, E
30:25 and the w assembly that came out of Israel, E
31:18 their sons, and their daughters, the w multitude;
Ezr 2:64 w assembly together was forty-two thousand E
4:20 over the w province Beyond the River,
7:16 that you shall find in the w province of Babylonia,
10:14 Let our officials represent the w assembly, E
Ne 4:16 leaders posted themselves behind the w house H
7:66 w assembly together was forty-two thousand E
Est 3: 6 throughout the w kingdom of Ahasuerus. J
Job 34:13 the earth and who laid on him the w world? D
37: 3 Under the w heaven he lets it loose,
41:11 —under the w heaven, who?
Ps 9: 1 I will give thanks to the LORD with my w heart; G
23: 6 in the house of the LORD my w life long.
51:19 in burnt offerings and w burnt offerings;
72:19 may his glory fill the w earth. A
86:12 O Lord my God, with my w heart, G
111: 1 I will give thanks to the LORD with my w heart, G
119: 2 who seek him with their w heart, G
119:10 With my w heart I seek you; G
119:34 and observe it with my w heart. G
119:69 but with my w heart I keep your precepts. G
119:145 With my w heart I cry; answer me, O LORD. G
138: 1 O LORD, with my w heart; G
Pr 1:12 like Sheol let us swallow them alive and w,
Ecc 12:13 for that is the w duty of everyone.
Isa 1: 5 The w head is sick, and the whole heart faint.
1: 5 The whole head is sick, and the w heart faint. G
4: 5 over the w site of Mount Zion and over its places
6: 3 the w earth is full of his glory." A
13: 5 of his indignation, to destroy the w earth. A
14: 7 The w earth is at rest and quiet; A
14:26 the plan that is planned concerning the w earth; A
22:24 on him the w weight of his ancestral house,
27: 6 and fill the w world with fruit. D
28:22 from the Lord GOD of hosts upon the w land. C
38: 3 before you in faithfulness with a w heart, G
39: 2 his w armory, all that was found in his storehouses.
53: 5 upon him was the punishment that made us w,
54: 5 the God of the w earth he is called. A
61:10 my w being shall exult in my God;
Jer 1:18 and a bronze wall, against the w land— C
3:10 not return to me with her w heart, G
4:20 the w land is laid waste. C
4:27 The w land shall be a desolation; C
8:16 the neighing of their stallions the w land quakes. C
12:11 w land is made desolate, but no one lays it to C
13:11 the w house of Israel and the whole house H
13:11 of Israel and the w house of Judah cling to me, H
15:10 a man of strife and contention to the w land! C
19:13 to the w host of heaven,
24: 7 for they shall return to me with their w heart. G
25:11 This w land shall become a ruin and a waste, C
31:40 The w valley of the dead bodies and the ashes,
35: 3 and the w house of the Rechabites. H
37:10 the w army of Chaldeans who are fighting I
40: 4 See, the w land is before you; C
45: 4 what I have planted—that is, the w land. C
50:23 hammer of the w earth is cut down and broken! A
51:25 says the LORD, that destroys the w earth; A
51:41 the pride of the w earth seized! A
51:47 her w land shall be put to shame, C
Eze 11:15 your fellow exiles, the w house of Israel, H
15: 5 When it was w it was used for nothing;
32: 4 wild animals of the w earth gorge themselves A
35:14 the w earth rejoices, I will make you desolate. A
36:10 the w house of Israel, all of it; H
37:11 "Mortal, these bones are the w house of Israel. H
39:25 and have mercy on the w house of Israel; H
41:19 They were carved on the w temple all around;
43:11 its exits and its entrances, and its w form—
43:12 the w territory on the top of the mountain all
45: 6 it shall belong to the w house of Israel. H
Eze 48:13 The w length shall be twenty-five thousand cubits
48:20 The w portion that you shall set apart shall
Da 1:20 the magicians and enchanters in his w kingdom. J
2:35 a great mountain and filled the w earth. A
2:39 which shall rule over the w earth. A
2:48 over the w province of Babylon and chief prefect
4:11 and it was visible to the ends of the w earth. A
4:20 and was visible to the end of the w earth, A
6: 1 stationed throughout the w kingdom, J
6: 3 king planned to appoint him over the w kingdom. J
6:25 of every language throughout the w world: D
7:23 it shall devour the w earth, and trample it down, A
7:27 the kingdoms under the w heaven shall be given
8: 5 across the face of the w earth without touching A
9:12 before been done under the w heaven.
11:17 to come with the strength of his w kingdom, J
Am 3: 1 the w family that I brought up out of the land
Mic 4:13 their wealth to the Lord of the w earth. A
Zep 1:18 of his passion the w earth shall be consumed; A
Zec 1:11 and lo, the w earth remains at peace." A
4:10 which range through the w earth." A
4:14 by the Lord of the w earth." A
5: 3 curse that goes out over the face of the w land; C
13: 8 In the w land, says the LORD, C
14:10 The w land shall be turned into a plain from C
Mal 3: 9 for you are robbing me—the w nation of you! K
Mt 5:29 lose one of your members than for your w body F
5:30 lose one of your members than for your w body F
6:22 your w body will be full of light; F
6:23 your w body will be full of darkness. F
8:32 the w herd rushed down the steep bank into the sea
8:33 they told the w story about what had happened to
8:34 Then the w town came out to meet Jesus;
13: 2 while the w crowd stood on the beach.
15:31 the maimed w, the lame walking,
16:26 if they gain the w world but forfeit their life? D
21:10 he entered Jerusalem, the w city was in turmoil,
26:13 in the w world, what she has done will be told D
26:59 and the w council were looking for false testimony
27:25 Then the people as a w answered,
27:27 and they gathered the w cohort around him.
27:45 darkness came over the w land until three in C
Mk 1: 5 And people from the w Judean countryside and all
1:33 And the w city was gathered around the door.
2:13 w crowd gathered around him, and he taught them.
4: 1 while the w crowd was beside the sea on the land.
5:33 fell down before him, and told him the w truth.
6:55 and rushed about that w region and began to bring
8:36 For what will it profit them to gain the w world D
9:15 When the w crowd saw him,
11:18 the w crowd was spellbound by his teaching.
12:33 much more important than all w burnt offerings
14: 9 the good news is proclaimed in the w world, D
14:55 the chief priests and the w council were looking
15: 1 with the elders and scribes and the w council.
15:16 and they called together the w cohort.
15:33 darkness came over the w land until three in C
16:15 ⟦and proclaim the good news to the w creation.⟧
Lk 1:10 the w assembly of the people was praying E
9:25 does it profit them if they gain the w world, D
11:34 your eye is healthy, your w body is full of light; F
11:36 If then your w body is full of light, F
19:37 the w multitude of the disciples began
21:35 upon all who live on the face of the w earth. A
23:44 and darkness came over the w land until three C
Jn 4:53 he himself believed, along with his w household.
7:23 because I healed a man's w body on the sabbath? F
11:50 the people than to have the w nation destroyed." K
Ac 4:32 Now the w group of those who believed were
5:11 the w church and all who heard of these things.
5:20 and tell the people the w message about this life."
5:21 they called together the council and the w body F
6: 2 And the twelve called together the w community
6: 5 What they said pleased the w community,
10:22 who is well spoken of by the w Jewish nation,
13: 6 When they had gone through the w island as far
13:44 the w city gathered to hear the word of the Lord.
15:12 The w assembly kept silence, E
15:22 with the consent of the w church,
17:26 to inhabit the w earth, and he allotted the times A
19:26 but in almost the w of Asia this Paul has persuaded
20:27 not shrink from declaring to you the w purpose
21:27 in the temple, stirred up the w crowd.
22: 5 and the w council of elders can testify about me.
25:24 the w Jewish community petitioned me,
28:30 He lived there two w years at his own expense
Ro 3:19 the w world may be held accountable to God. D
8:22 We know that the w creation has been groaning
11:16 then the w batch is holy;
16:23 Gaius, who is host to me and to the w church,
1Co 5: 6 that a little yeast leavens the w batch of dough?
12:17 w body were an eye, where would the hearing F
12:17 If the w body were hearing, F
14:23 w church comes together and all speak in tongues,
Gal 5: 9 A little yeast leavens the w batch of dough.
5:14 the w law is summed up in a single commandment,
Eph 2:21 In him the w structure is joined together and grows
4:16 from whom the w body, joined and knit together F
6:11 Put on the w armor of God,
6:13 Therefore take up the w armor of God,
6:23 Peace be to the w community, and love with faith,
Php 1:13 the w imperial guard and to everyone else
Col 1: 6 as it is bearing fruit and growing in the w world, D
2: 9 For in him the w fullness of deity dwells bodily,
2:19 to the head, from whom the w body, nourished F
Tit 1:11 since they are upsetting w families by teaching
Jas 2:10 For whoever keeps the w law but fails
Jas 3: 2 able to keep the w body in check with a bridle. F
3: 3 to make them obey us, we guide their w bodies.
3: 6 the w body, sets on fire the cycle of nature, F
1Jn 2: 2 but also for the sins of the w world. D
5:19 the w world lies under the power of the evil one. D
Rev 3:10 the w world to test the inhabitants of the earth. D
12: 9 the deceiver of the w world— D
13: 3 In amazement the w earth followed the beast. A
16:14 who go abroad to the kings of the w world, D
Tob 1: 4 the w tribe of my ancestor Naphtali deserted
8: 5 the heavens and the w creation bless you forever.
12:11 the w truth to you and will conceal nothing
14: 4 and the w land of Israel will be desolate, C
14: 6 w world will all be converted and worship God D
Jdt 1: 9 and Tahpanhes and Raamses and the w land C
1:11 But all who lived in the w region disregarded
1:12 with this w region, and swore by his throne
1:12 the w territory of Cilicia and Damascus and Syria,
1:13 the w army of Arphaxad and all his cavalry I
2: 1 about carrying out his revenge on the w region,
2: 5 the lord of the w earth: A
2: 7 and will cover the w face of the earth with the feet
2: 9 to the ends of the w earth. A
2:11 to slaughter and plunder throughout your w region.
2:19 Then he set out with his w army, I
2:19 of King Nebuchadnezzar and to cover the w face
2:22 From there Holofernes took his w army, I
3:10 and remained for a w month in order to collect all
4: 8 and the senate of the w people of Israel,
4:15 to look with favor on the w house of Israel. H
5:12 the w land of Egypt with incurable plagues. C
5:21 the laughingstock of the w world." D
6: 4 says King Nebuchadnezzar, lord of the w earth. A
7: 1 The next day Holofernes ordered his w army, I
7: 4 "They will now strip clean the w land; C
7:18 and covered the w face of the land.
7:20 The w Assyrian army, their infantry, chariots,
7:26 the w town as booty to the army of Holofernes and
9:14 Let your w nation and every tribe know K
10:18 There was great excitement in the w camp,
10:19 be able to beguile the w world!" D
11: 7 the life of Nebuchadnezzar, king of the w earth, A
11: 8 the w world that you alone are the best D
11: 8 that you alone are the best in the w kingdom, J
11:16 the w world wherever people shall hear D
11:18 so that you may go out with your w army, I
11:23 and be renowned throughout the w world." D
12:18 because today is the greatest day in my w life."
16:16 of all w burnt offerings to you is a very little thing;
16:21 throughout the w country.
AdE 3: 7 on one day to destroy the w race of Mordecai.
9:22 The w month (namely, Adar),
10: 3 as to make him beloved to his w nation. K
11: 9 And the w righteous nation was troubled;
13: 2 of the w world (not elated with presumption D
16:13 together with their w nation. K
Wis 5:17 The Lord will take his zeal as his w armor,
5:23 Lawlessness will lay waste the w earth, A
8:21 and with my w heart I said: G
11:22 Because the w world before you is like a speck D
17:20 the w world was illumined with brilliant light, D
18:24 For on his long robe the w world was depicted, D
19: 6 the w creation in its nature was fashioned anew,
Sir 1:17 she fills their w house with desirable goods, H
1:30 and overthrow you before the w congregation, B
18: 1 He who lives forever created the w universe;
19:20 The w of wisdom is fear of the Lord,
26:20 *Seek a fertile field within the w plain,*
50:13 their hands before the w congregation of Israel. B
50:20 and raised his hands over the w congregation B
Bar 2: 2 Under the w heaven there has not been done the
2:23 w land will be a desolation without inhabitants. C
3:36 He found the w way to knowledge,
LtJ 6:62 commands the clouds to go over the w world, D
Aza 1:22 glorious over the w world." D
Sus 1:60 Then the w assembly raised a great shout and E
Bel 1:14 and they scattered them throughout the w temple
1Mc 1:41 to his w kingdom that all should be one people, J
1:51 In such words he wrote to his w kingdom. J
5:43 and the w army followed him. I
8: 4 and how they had gained control of the w region
2Mc 2:10 down and consumed the w burnt offerings.
2:21 though few in number they seized the w land C
2:29 be concerned with the w construction,
3:12 temple that is honored throughout the w world. D
3:14 There was no little distress throughout the w city.
3:21 the prostration of the w populace and the anxiety
4:38 and led him around the w city to that very place
7:38 that has justly fallen on our w nation." K
7:40 putting his w trust in the Lord.
8: 9 to wipe out the w race of Judea.
8:18 and even, if necessary, the w world." D
9: 9 because of the stench the w army felt revulsion I
10: 8 public edict, ratified by vote, that the w nation K
12: 7 to come again and root out the w community
14: 8 our w nation is now in no small misfortune. K
15:12 with outstretched hands for the w body of F
1Es 1:32 be done throughout the w nation of Israel. K
4:36 w earth calls upon truth, and heaven blesses her. A
8:64 The w was counted and weighed,
9:38 the w multitude gathered with one accord in
3Mc 1:29 also the walls and the w earth around echoed, A
2: 7 the Ruler over the w creation.
4:10 treatment befitting traitors during the w voyage.
5: 5 w nation would experience its final destruction. K
5:30 of God his w mind had been deranged
6: 5 who had already gained control of the w world D

3Mc 6:14 The w throng of infants
6:36 a public rite for these things in their w community
7:13 and the w multitude shouted the Hallelujah
2Es 10: 8 but we, the w world, for our mother. D
11: 2 I saw it spread its wings over the w earth, A
11:32 this head gained control of the w earth, A
11:45 your most evil talons, and your w worthless body,
11:46 so that the w earth, freed from your violence, A
12: 3 The w body of the eagle was burned, F
15:27 Already calamities have come upon the w earth, A
4Mc 3: 8 the w army of our ancestors had encamped. I
7:18 But as many as attend to religion with a w heart, G
7:21 as a philosopher by the w rule of philosophy,
16:13 and giving rebirth for immortality to the w number

WHOLEHEARTED (1) [HEART, WHOLE]

Eze 36: 5 who, with w joy and utter contempt,

WHOLEHEARTEDLY (7) [HEART, WHOLE]

Nu 14:24 he has a different spirit and has followed me w,
Jos 14: 8 yet I w followed the LORD my God.
14: 9 you have w followed the LORD my God.'
14:14 because he w followed the LORD,
Col 3:22 and in order to please them, but w, fearing
Tob 2: 2 who is w mindful of God,
1Mc 8:25 the nation of the Jews shall act as their allies w,

WHOLESOME (4) [WHOLE]

2Ki 2:21 "Thus says the LORD, I have made this water w;
2:22 So the water has been w to this day,
Pr 15:31 The ear that heeds w admonition will lodge among
Wis 1:14 the generative forces of the world are w,

WHOLLY (9) [WHOLE]

Lev 6:23 Every grain offering of a priest shall be w burned;
Jos 3:16 the Dead Sea, were w cut off.
1Ch 28:21 and all the people will be w at your command."
Job 19:13 and my acquaintances are w estranged from me.
21:23 being w at ease and secure,
Jer 13:19 all Judah is taken into exile, w taken into exile.
Sir 45:14 be w burned twice every day continually.
2Mc 8:29 and implored the merciful Lord to be w reconciled
12:42 that had been committed might be w blotted out.

WHOM (822) [WHO] See Index of Articles Etc.

WHOMEVER (10) [WHO]

Nu 22: 6 for I know that w you bless is blessed,
22: 6 and w you curse is cursed."
Jer 27: 5 and I give it to w I please.
49:19 and I will appoint over it w I choose.
50:44 and I will appoint over her w I choose.
Da 5:21 and sets over it w he will.
Jn 5:21 so also the Son gives life to w he wishes.
Ro 9:18 So then he has mercy on w he chooses,
9:18 and he hardens the heart of w he chooses.
3Mc 5:11 is bestowed by him who grants it to w he wishes.

WHOMSOEVER (KJV) See ANY, ANYONE, ONE[S], WHOEVER, WHOM

WHORE (39) [WHOREDOM, WHOREDOMS, WHORES, WHORING, WHORINGS]

Ge 34:31 they said, "Should our sister be treated like a w?"
38:24 "Your daughter-in-law Tamar has played the w;
Isa 1:21 How the faithful city has become a w!
57: 3 you offspring of an adulterer and a w.
Jer 2:20 every green tree you sprawled and played the w.
3: 1 You have played the w with many lovers;
3: 3 yet you have the forehead of a w,
3: 6 under every green tree, and played the w there?
3: 8 but she too went and played the w.
Eze 16:15 and played the w because of your fame,
16:16 and on them played the w;
16:17 and with them played the w;
16:26 You played the w with the Egyptians,
16:28 You played the w with the Assyrians,
16:28 you played the w with them,
16:30 the deeds of a brazen w;
16:31 Yet you were not like a w,
16:34 no one solicited you to play the w;
16:35 Therefore, O w, hear the word of the LORD:
16:41 I will stop you from playing the w,
23: 3 they played the w in Egypt;
23: 3 they played the w in their youth;
23: 5 Oholah played the w while she was mine;
23:19 when she played the w in the land of Egypt
23:30 because you played the w with the nations,
23:44 For they have gone in to her, as one goes in to a w.
Hos 2: 5 For their mother has played the w;
3: 3 you shall not play the w,
4:10 they shall play the w, but not multiply;
4:12 and they have played the w, forsaking their God.
4:13 Therefore your daughters play the w,
4:14 when they play the w, nor your daughters-in-law
4:15 Though you play the w, O Israel,
5: 3 for now, O Ephraim, you have played the w;
9: 1 you have played the w, departing from your God.
Rev 17: 1 of the great w who is seated on many waters,
17:15 "The waters that you saw, where the w is seated,
17:16 they and the beast will hate the w;
19: 2 he has judged the great w who corrupted the earth with her fornication,

WHORE, WHORE'S, WHORES (KJV) See also CONCUBINE, PROSTITUTE, PROSTITUTING, PROSTITUTION, WHORINGS

WHOREDOM (10) [WHORE]

Ge 38:24 moreover she is pregnant as a result of w."
Jer 3: 9 Because she took her w so lightly,
Hos 1: 2 for yourself a wife of w and have children of w,
1: 2 land commits great w by forsaking the LORD."
2: 4 because they are children of w.
4:11 w. Wine and new wine take away the understanding.
4:12 For a spirit of w has led them astray,
5: 4 For the spirit of w is within them,
6:10 Ephraim's w is there, Israel is defiled.

WHOREDOM (KJV) See also ADULTERIES, DEFILE, IDOLATRY, LUST, PROSTITUTED, PROSTITUTING, SEXUAL ORGIES, SEXUAL RELATIONS, WHORE, WHOREMONGER, WHORINGS

WHOREDOMS (1) [WHORE]

2Ki 9:22 so long as the many w and sorceries

WHORES (3) [WHORE]

Eze 16:33 Gifts are given to all w;
Hos 4:14 for the men themselves go aside with w,
Rev 17: 5 mother of w and of earth's abominations."

WHORING (8) [WHORE]

Jer 3: 2 You have polluted the land with your w
Eze 16:25 to every passer-by, and multiplying your w.
16:26 multiplying your w, to provoke me to anger.
16:29 You multiplied your w with Chaldea,
16:36 and your nakedness uncovered in your w
23:27 to your lewdness and your w brought from the land
43: 7 neither they nor their kings, by their w,
Hos 2: 2 that she put away her w from her face,

WHORINGS (13) [WHORE]

Eze 16:15 and lavished your w on any passer-by.
16:20 As if your w were not enough!
16:22 And in all your abominations and your w you did
16:33 to come to you from all around for your w.
16:34 you were different from other women in your w:
23: 8 She did not give up her w that she had practiced
23:11 in her lusting and in her w,
23:14 But she carried her w further;
23:18 on her w so openly and flaunted her nakedness,
23:19 Yet she increased her w, remembering the days
23:29 and the nakedness of your w shall be exposed.
23:29 Your lewdness and your w
23:35 bear the consequences of your lewdness and w.

WHOREMONGERS (KJV) See FORNICATOR[S]

WHOSE (347) [WHO] See Index of Articles Etc.

WHOSO[EVER] (KJV) See ANYONE, IF YOU, ONE, THOSE, WHO, WHOEVER

WHY‡ (533)

Ge 4: 6 The LORD said to Cain, "W are you angry,
4: 6 and w has your countenance fallen?
12:18 W did you not tell me that she was your wife?
12:19 W did you say, 'She is my sister,'
18:13 The LORD said to Abraham, "W did Sarah laugh,
24:31 W do you stand outside when I have prepared
25:22 and she said, "If it is to be this way, w do I live?"
26: 9 W then did you say, 'She is my sister'?"
26:27 Isaac said to them, "W have you come to me,
27:45 W should I lose both of you in one day?"
29:25 W then have you deceived me?"
31:27 W did you flee secretly and deceive me and
31:28 And w did you not permit me to kiss my sons
31:30 w did you steal my gods?"
32:29 But he said, "W is it that you ask my name?"
33:15 But he said, "W should my lord be so kind to me?"
40: 7 "W are your faces downcast today?"
42: 1 "W do you keep looking at one another?
42:21 That is w this anguish has come upon us."
43: 6 "W did you treat me so badly as to tell the man
44: 4 say to them, 'W have you returned evil for good?
44: 4 W have you stolen my silver cup?
44: 7 "W does my lord speak such words as these?
44: 8 w then would we steal silver or gold
Ge 47:15 W should we die before your eyes?
Ex 1:18 "W have you done this, and allowed the boys
Ex 2:13 "W do you strike your fellow Hebrew?"
2:20 W did you leave the man?
3: 3 and see w the bush is not burned up."
5: 4 w are you taking the people away from their work?
5: 8 that is w they cry, 'Let us go and offer sacrifice
5:14 "W did you not finish the required quantity
5:15 "W do you treat your servants like this?
5:17 He said, "You are lazy, lazy; that is w you say,
5:22 "O LORD, w have you mistreated this people?
5:22 W did you ever send me?
6:30 w would Pharaoh listen to me?"
9:16 But this is w I have let you live:
14:15 LORD said to Moses, "W do you cry out to me?
15:23 That is w it was called Marah.
17: 2 Moses said to them, "W do you quarrel with me?
17: 2 W do you test the LORD?"
17: 3 "W did you bring us out of Egypt,
18:14 W do you sit alone, while all the people stand
32:11 w does your wrath burn hot against your people,
32:12 W should the Egyptians say,
Lev 10:17 "W did you not eat the sin offering in
Nu 9: 7 w must we be kept from presenting
11:11 "W have you treated your servant so badly?
11:11 W have I not found favor in your sight,
11:20 saying, 'W did we ever leave Egypt?' "
12: 8 W then were you not afraid to speak
14: 3 W is the LORD bringing us into this land to fall
14:41 "W do you continue to transgress the command of
16: 3 So w then do you exalt yourselves above
20: 4 W have you brought the assembly of the LORD
20: 5 W have you brought us up out of Egypt,
21: 5 "W have you brought us up out of Egypt to die in
22:32 "W have you struck your donkey these three
22:37 W did you not come to me?
27: 4 W should the name of our father be taken away
32: 7 W will you discourage the hearts of the Israelites
Dt 5:25 So now w should we die?
29:24 "W has the LORD done thus to this land?
Jos 5: 4 This is the reason w Joshua circumcised them:
7: 7 W have you brought this people across the Jordan
7:10 W have you fallen upon your face?
7:25 Joshua said, "W did you bring trouble on us?
9:22 and said to them, "W did you deceive us, saying,
17:14 "W have you given me but one lot and one portion
Jdg 5:16 W did you tarry among the sheepfolds,
5:17 and Dan, w did he abide with the ships?
5:28 'W is his chariot so long in coming?
5:28 W tarry the hoofbeats of his chariots?'
6:13 w then has all this happened to us?
9:28 W then should we serve him?
11: 7 So w do you come to me now when you are
11:26 w did you not recover them within that time?
12: 1 "W did you cross over to fight against
12: 3 W then have you come up to me this day,
13:18 "W do you ask my name?
14:16 W should I tell you?"
15: 2 W not take her instead?"
15:10 "W have you come up against us?"
19: 6 "W not spend the night and enjoy yourself?"
21: 3 w has it come to pass that today there should
Ru 1:11 "Turn back, my daughters, w will you go with me?
1:21 w call me Naomi when the LORD has dealt harshly
2:10 "W have I found favor in your sight,
1Sa 1: 8 "Hannah, w do you weep? W do you not eat? W is your heart sad?
2:23 He said to them, "W do you do such things?
2:29 W then look with greedy eye at my sacrifices
4: 3 "W has the LORD put us to rout today before
5: 5 This is w the priests of Dagon and all who enter
5:10 "W have they brought around to us the ark of
6: 6 W should you harden your hearts as the Egyptians
9:21 W then have you spoken to me in this way?"
14:41 w have you not answered your servant today?
15:19 W then did you not obey the voice of the LORD?
15:19 W did you swoop down on the spoil,
17: 8 "W have you come out to draw up for battle?
17:28 He said, "W have you come down?
19: 5 w then will you sin against an innocent person
19:17 "W have you deceived me like this,
19:17 'Let me go; w should I kill you?' "
20: 2 and w should my father hide this from me?
20: 8 w should you bring me to your father?"
20:27 "W has the son of Jesse not come to the feast,
20:32 "W should he be put to death?
21: 1 "W are you alone, and no one with you?"
21:14 w then have you brought him to me?
22: 8 Is that w all of you have conspired against me?
22:13 "W have you conspired against me,
24: 9 "W do you listen to the words of those who say,
26:15 W then have you not kept watch over your lord
26:18 he added, "W does my lord pursue his servant?
27: 5 for w should your servant live in the royal city
28: 9 W then are you laying a snare for my life to bring
28:12 woman said to Saul, "W have you deceived me?
28:15 "W have you disturbed me by bringing me up?"
28:16 Samuel said, "W then do you ask me,
2Sa 2:22 w should I strike you to the ground?
3: 7 "W have you gone in to my father's concubine?"
3:24 w did you dismiss him, so that he got away?
7: 7 "W have you not built me a house of cedar?"
11:10 W did you not go down to your house?"
11:20 'W did you go so near the city to fight?
11:21 W did you go so near the wall?'
12: 9 W have you despised the word of the LORD,
12:23 But now he is dead; w should I fast?
13: 4 w are you so haggard morning after morning?
13:26 The king said to him, "W should he go with you?"

2Sa 14:13 “**W** then have you planned such a thing against
14:31 “**W** have your servants set my field on fire?”
14:32 ‘**W** have I come from Geshur?
15:19 “**W** are you also coming with us?
16: 2 king said to Ziba, “**W** have you brought these?”
16: 9 “**W** should this dead dog curse my lord the king?
16:10 who then shall say, ‘**W** have you done so?’ ”
16:17 **W** did you not go with your friend?”
18:11 **W** then did you not strike him there to the ground?
18:22 And Joab said, “**W** will you run, my son,
19:10 therefore **w** do you say nothing about bringing
19:11 ‘**W** should you be the last to bring the king back
19:12 **w** then should you be the last to bring back
19:25 the king said to him, “**W** did you not go with me,
19:29 “**W** speak any more of your affairs?
19:35 **W** then should your servant be an added burden
19:36 **W** should the king recompense me with such
19:41 “**W** have our kindred the people
19:42 **W** then are you angry over this matter?
19:43 **W** then did you despise us?
20:19 **w** will you swallow up the heritage of
24: 3 But **w** does my lord the king want to do this?”
24:21 “**W** has my lord the king come to his servant?”
1Ki 1: 6 “**W** have you done thus and so?”
1:13 **W** then is Adonijah king?’
1:41 he said, “**W** is the city in an uproar?”
2:22 “And **w** do you ask Abishag the Shunammite
2:43 **W** then have you not kept your oath to the LORD
9: 8 ‘**W** has the LORD done such a thing to this land
14: 6 **w** do you pretend to be another?
21: 5 “**W** are you so depressed that you will not eat?”
2Ki 1: 5 who said to them, “**W** have you returned?”
4:23 He said, “**W** go to him today?
5: 8 “**W** have you torn your clothes?
6:33 **W** should I hope in the LORD any longer?”
7: 3 “**W** should we sit here until we die?
8:12 Hazael asked, “**W** does my lord weep?”
9:11 **W** did that madman come to you?”
12: 7 “**W** are you not repairing the house?
14:10 for **w** should you provoke trouble so that you fall,
20:19 For he thought, “**W** not, if there will be peace
1Ch 17: 6 saying, **W** have you not built me a house of cedar?
21: 3 **W** then should my lord require this?
21: 3 **W** should he bring guilt on Israel?”
2Ch 7:21 ‘**W** has the LORD done such a thing to this land
24: 6 “**W** have you not required the Levites to bring in
24:20 **W** do you transgress the commandments of
25:15 a prophet, who said to him, “**W** have you resorted
25:16 **W** should you be put to death?”
25:19 **w** should you provoke trouble so that you fall,
32: 4 “**W** should the Assyrian kings come and find water
Ezr 4:22 **w** should damage grow to the hurt of the king?”
Ne 2: 2 So the king said to me, “**W** is your face sad,
2: 3 **W** should my face not be sad, when the city,
6: 3 **W** should the work stop while I leave it to come
6: 6 that is **w** you are building the wall;
13:11 “**W** is the house of God forsaken?”
13:21 “**W** do you spend the night in front of the wall?
Est 3: 3 “**W** do you disobey the king’s command?”
4: 5 to Mordecai to learn what was happening and **w**.
Job 3:11 “**W** did I not die at birth,
3:12 **W** were there knees to receive me,
3:16 Or **w** was I not buried like a stillborn child,
3:20 “**W** is light given to one in misery,
3:23 **W** is light given to one who cannot see the way,
7:20 **W** have you made me your target?
7:20 **W** have I become a burden to you?
7:21 **W** do you not pardon my transgression
9:29 I shall be condemned; **w** then do I labor in vain?
10: 2 let me know **w** you contend against me.
10:18 “**W** did you bring me forth from the womb?
13:24 **W** do you hide your face,
15:12 **W** does your heart carry you away,
15:12 and **w** do your eyes flash,
18: 3 **W** are we counted as cattle?
18: 3 **W** are we stupid in your sight?
19:22 **W** do you, like God, pursue me,
21: 4 **W** should I not be impatient?
21: 7 **W** do the wicked live on, reach old age,
24: 1 “**W** are times not kept by the Almighty,
24: 1 and **w** do those who know him never see his days?
27:12 **w** then have you become altogether vain?
33:13 **W** do you contend against him, saying,
Ps 2: 1 **W** do the nations conspire,
10: 1 **W**, O LORD, do you stand far off?
10: 1 **W** do you hide yourself in times of trouble?
10:13 **W** do the wicked renounce God,
22: 1 my God, **w** have you forsaken me?
22: 1 **W** are you so far from helping me,
42: 5 **W** are you cast down, O my soul,
42: 5 O my soul, and **w** are you disquieted within me?
42: 9 I say to God, my rock, “**W** have you forgotten me?
42: 9 **W** must I walk about mournfully because
42:11 **W** are you cast down, O my soul,
42:11 O my soul, and **w** are you disquieted within me?
43: 2 **w** have you cast me off?
43: 2 **W** must I walk about mournfully because of
43: 5 **W** are you cast down, O my soul,
43: 5 O my soul, and **w** are you disquieted within me?
44:23 **W** do you sleep, O Lord?
44:24 **W** do you hide your face?
44:24 **W** do you forget our affliction and oppression?
49: 5 **W** should I fear in times of trouble,
52: 1 **W** do you boast, O mighty one, of mischief done
68:16 **W** do you look with envy,
74: 1 **w** do you cast us off forever?
74: 1 **W** does your anger smoke against the sheep

Ps 74:11 **W** do you hold back your hand;
74:11 **w** do you keep your hand in your bosom?
79:10 **W** should the nations say, “Where is their God?”
80:12 **W** then have you broken down its walls,
88:14 O LORD, **w** do you cast me off?
88:14 **W** do you hide your face from me?
114: 5 **W** is it, O sea, that you flee?
115: 2 **W** should the nations say, “Where is their God?”
Pr 5:20 **W** should you be intoxicated, my son,
17:16 **W** should fools have a price in hand
22:27 **w** should your bed be taken from under you?
Ecc 2:15 **w** then have I been so very wise?”
5: 6 **w** should God be angry at your words,
7:10 “**W** were the former days better than these?”
7:16 **w** should you destroy yourself?
7:17 **w** should you die before your time?
SS 1: 7 for **w** should I be like one who is veiled beside
6:13 **W** should you look upon the Shulammite,
Isa 1: 5 **W** do you seek further beatings?
1: 5 **W** do you continue to rebel?
5: 4 **w** did it yield wild grapes?
9:17 That is **w** the Lord did not have pity
40:27 **W** do you say, O Jacob, and speak, O Israel,
48:11 I do it, for **w** should my name be profaned?
50: 2 **W** was no one there when I came?
50: 2 **W** did no one answer when I called?
51:12 **w** then are you afraid of
55: 2 **W** do you spend your money for that which is
58: 3 “**W** do we fast, but you do not see?
58: 3 **W** humble ourselves, but you do not notice?”
63: 2 “**W** are your robes red, and your garments
63:17 **W**, O LORD, do you make us stray
Jer 2:14 **W** then has he become plunder?
2:29 **W** do you complain against me?
2:31 **W** then do my people say, “We are free,
5:19 “**W** has the LORD our God done all these things
8: 5 **W** then has this people turned away
8:14 **W** do we sit still?
8:19 (“**W** have they provoked me to anger
8:22 **W** then has the health of my poor people
9:12 **W** is the land ruined and laid waste like
12: 1 **W** does the way of the guilty prosper?
12: 1 **W** do all who are treacherous thrive?
13:22 “**W** have these things come upon me?”
14: 8 **w** should you be like a stranger in the land,
14: 9 **W** should you be like someone confused,
14:19 **W** have you struck us down so
15:18 **W** is my pain unceasing, my wound incurable,
16:10 “**W** has the LORD pronounced all this great evil
20:18 **W** did I come forth from the womb to see toil
22: 8 “**W** has the LORD dealt in this way with
22:28 **W** are he and his offspring hurled out
26: 9 **W** have you prophesied in the name of the LORD,
27:13 **W** should you and your people die by the sword,
27:17 **W** should this city become a desolation?
29:27 So now **w** have you not rebuked Jeremiah
30: 6 **W** then do I see every man with his hands
30: 6 **W** has every face turned pale?
30:15 **W** do you cry out over your hurt?
32: 3 Zedekiah had said, “**W** do you prophesy and say:
35:11 That is **w** we are living in Jerusalem.”
36:29 to burn this scroll, saying, **W** have you written in it
40:15 **W** should he take your life,
44: 7 **W** are you doing such great harm to yourselves,
44: 8 **W** do you provoke me to anger with the works
46: 5 **W** do I see them terrified?
46:15 **W** has Apis fled? **W** did your bull not stand?
49: 1 **W** then has Milcom dispossessed Gad,
49: 4 **W** do you boast in your strength?
La 3:39 **W** should any who draw breath complain about
5:20 **W** have you forgotten us completely?
5:20 **W** have you forsaken us these many days?
Eze 18:19 “**W** should not the son suffer for the iniquity of
18:31 **W** will you die, O house of Israel?
20: 3 Thus says the Lord GOD: **W** are you coming?
21: 7 And when they say to you, “**W** do you moan?”
33:11 for **w** will you die, O house of Israel?
Da 2:15 “**W** is the decree of the king so urgent?”
10:20 he said, “Do you know **w** I have come to you?
Joel 2:17 **W** should it be said among the peoples,
Am 5:18 **W** do you want the day of the LORD?
Jnh 1: 8 “Tell us **w** this calamity has come upon us.
4: 2 That is **w** I fled to Tarshish at the beginning;
Mic 4: 9 Now **w** do you cry aloud?
Na 1: 9 **W** do you plot against the LORD?
Hab 1: 3 **W** do you make me see wrongdoing and look
1:13 **w** do you look on the treacherous,
Hag 1: 9 when you brought it home, I blew it away. **W?**
Mal 2:10 **W** then are we faithless to one another,
2:14 You ask, “**W** does he not?”
Mt 6:28 And **w** do you worry about clothing?
7: 3 **W** do you see the speck in your neighbor’s eye,
8:26 And he said to them, “**W** are you afraid,
9: 4 said, “**W** do you think evil in your hearts?
9:11 “**W** does your teacher eat with tax collectors
9:14 saying, “**W** do we and the Pharisees fast often,
13:10 “**W** do you speak to them in parables?”
14:31 “You of little faith, **w** did you doubt?”
15: 2 “**W** do your disciples break the tradition of
15: 3 “And **w** do you break the commandment of God
16: 8 **w** are you talking about having no bread?
17:10 And the disciples asked him, “**W**, then,
17:19 “**W** could we not cast it out?”
19: 7 “**W** then did Moses command us to give
19:17 “**W** do you ask me about what is good?
20: 6 ‘**W** are you standing here idle all day?’
21:25 ‘**W** then did you not believe him?’

Mt 22:18 “**W** are you putting me to the test, you hypocrites?
26: 8 they were angry and said, “**W** this waste?
26:10 said to them, “**W** do you trouble the woman?
26:65 **W** do we still need witnesses?
27:23 Then he asked, “**W**, what evil has he done?”
27:46 is, “My God, my God, **w** have you forsaken me?”
Mk 2: 7 “**W** does this fellow speak in this way?
2: 8 “**W** do you raise such questions in your hearts?
2:16 “**W** does he eat with tax collectors and sinners?”
2:18 to him, “**W** do John’s disciples and the disciples of
2:24 **w** are they doing what is not lawful on
4:40 He said to them, “**W** are you afraid?
5:35 **W** trouble the teacher any further?”
5:39 “**W** do you make a commotion and weep?
7: 5 “**W** do your disciples not live according to
8:12 “**W** does this generation ask for a sign?
8:17 “**W** are you talking about having no bread?
9:11 “**W** do the scribes say that Elijah must come first?”
9:28 “**W** could we not cast it out?”
10:18 Jesus said to him, “**W** do you call me good?
11: 3 If anyone says to you, ‘**W** are you doing this?’
11:31 he will say, ‘**W** then did you not believe him?’
12:15 he said to them, “**W** are you putting me to the test?
14: 4 “**W** was the ointment wasted in this way?
14: 6 Jesus said, “Let her alone; **w** do you trouble her?
14:63 “**W** do we still need witnesses?
15:14 Pilate asked them, “**W**, what evil has he done?”
15:34 “My God, my God, **w** have you forsaken me?”
Lk 1:43 And **w** has this happened to me,
2:48 “Child, **w** have you treated us like this?
2:49 He said to them, “**W** were you searching for me?
5:22 “**W** do you raise such questions in your hearts?
5:30 “**W** do you eat and drink with tax collectors
6: 2 “**W** are you doing what is not lawful on
6:41 **W** do you see the speck in your neighbor’s eye,
6:46 “**W** do you call me ‘Lord, Lord,’
8:47 of all the people **w** she had touched him,
12:26 **w** do you worry about the rest?
12:56 but **w** do you not know how to interpret
12:57 **w** do you not judge for yourselves what is right?
13: 7 **W** should it be wasting the soil?’
18:19 Jesus said to him, “**W** do you call me good?
19:23 **W** then did you not put my money into the bank?
19:31 If anyone asks you, ‘**W** are you untying it?’
19:33 “**W** are you untying the colt?”
20: 5 he will say, ‘**W** did you not believe him?’
22:46 and he said to them, “**W** are you sleeping?
23:22 A third time he said to them, “**W**,
24: 5 “**W** do you look for the living among the dead?
24:38 He said to them, “**W** are you frightened,
24:38 and **w** do doubts arise in your hearts?
Jn 1:25 “**W** then are you baptizing if you are neither
4:27 or, “**W** are you speaking with her?”
7:19 **W** are you looking for an opportunity to kill me?”
7:45 who asked them, “**W** did you not arrest him?”
8:25 Jesus said to them, “**W** do I speak to you at all?
8:43 **W** do you not understand what I say?
8:46 If I tell the truth, **w** do you not believe me?
9:27 **W** do you want to hear it again?
10:20 of his mind. **W** listen to him?”
12: 5 “**W** was this perfume not sold
13:28 no one at the table knew **w** he said this to him.
13:37 “Lord, **w** can I not follow you now?
18:21 **W** do you ask me?
18:23 But if I have spoken rightly, **w** do you strike me?”
20:13 They said to her, “Woman, **w** are you weeping?”
20:15 Jesus said to her, “Woman, **w** are you weeping?
Ac 1:11 **w** do you stand looking up toward heaven?
3:12 **w** do you wonder at this, or **w** do you stare at us,
4:25 ‘**W** did the Gentiles rage, and the peoples imagine
5: 3 “**w** has Satan filled your heart to lie to
7:26 **w** do you wrong each other?’
9: 4 “Saul, Saul, **w** do you persecute me?”
10:29 Now may I ask **w** you sent for me?”
11: 3 “**W** did you go to uncircumcised men and eat
14:15 **w** are you doing this? We are mortals just like you,
15:10 Now therefore **w** are you putting God to the test
19:32 of them did not know **w** they had come together.
22: 7 ‘Saul, Saul, **w** are you persecuting me?’
22:16 And now **w** do you delay?
26: 8 **W** is it thought incredible by any of you
26:14 ‘Saul, Saul, **w** are you persecuting me?
Ro 3: 7 **w** am I still being condemned as a sinner?
3: 8 And **w** not say (as some people slander us
9:19 “**W** then does he still find fault?
9:20 “**W** have you made me like this?”
9:32 **W** not? Because they did
14:10 **W** do you pass judgment on your brother or sister?
14:10 Or you, **w** do you despise your brother or sister?
1Co 4: 7 **w** do you boast as if it were not a gift?
6: 7 **W** not rather be wronged? **W** not rather be
10:29 For **w** should my liberty be subject to the judgment
10:30 **w** should I be denounced because of that
15:29 **w** are people baptized on their behalf?
15:30 **w** are we putting ourselves in danger every hour?
2Co 11:11 And **w**? Because I do not love you?
Gal 3:19 **W** then the law? It was added
5:11 **w** am I still being persecuted
Col 2:20 **w** do you live as if you still belonged to the world?
2:20 **W** do you submit to regulations,
1Jn 3:12 And **w** did he murder him?
Rev 17: 7 But the angel said to me, “**W** are you so amazed?
Tob 3: 9 **W** do you beat us?
3:15 **W** should I still live?
4: 2 **W** do I not call my son Tobias and explain to him
5:12 He replied, “**W** do you need to know my tribe?”
5:18 “**W** is it that you have sent my child away?

Jdt 5: 4 And **w** have they alone, of all who live in the west,
8: 19 That was **w** our ancestors were handed over to
11: 3 But now tell me **w** you have fled from them
AdE 3: 3 **w** do you disobey the king's command?"
Wis 5: 5 **W** have they been numbered among the children
5: 5 And **w** is their lot among the saints?
18: 18 made known **w** they were dying;
18: 19 not perish without knowing **w** they suffered.
Sir 18: 11 That is **w** the Lord is patient with them
23: 18 and no one sees me. **W** should I worry?
33: 7 **W** is one day more important than another,
37: 3 **w** were you formed to cover the land with deceit?
39: 17 'What is this?' or '**W** is that?'—
39: 21 'What is this?' or '**W** is that?'—
41: 4 **w** then should you reject the will of
51: 24 **W** do you say you are lacking in these things,
51: 24 and **w** do you endure such great thirst?
Bar 3: 10 **W** is it, O Israel, why is it that you are in the land
3: 10 **w** is it that you are in the land of your enemies,
LtJ 6: 40 **W** then must anyone think that they are gods,
6: 44 **W** then must anyone think that they are gods,
6: 56 **W** then must anyone admit or think
Sus 1: 21 and this was **w** you sent your maids away."
Bel 1: 4 the king said to him, "**W** do you not worship Bel?"
1Mc 2: 7 **W** was I born to see this, the ruin of my people,
2: 13 **W** should we live any longer?"
8: 31 '**W** have you made your yoke heavy on our friends
10: 70 **W** do you assume authority against us in
12: 44 "**W** have you put all these people to
12: 45 For that is **w** I am here."
2Mc 3: 9 that had been made and stated **w** he had come,
1Es 2: 23 That is **w** this city was laid waste.
4: 12 Gentlemen, **w** is not the king the strongest,
4: 32 Gentlemen, **w** are not women strong,
3Mc 1: 13 he inquired **w**, when he entered every other temple,
1: 15 the king said, "**w** should not I at least enter,
5: 18 and with sharp threats demanded to know **w**
2Es 1: 18 '**W** have you led us into this wilderness to kill us?
3: 28 Is that **w** it has gained dominion over Zion?
4: 4 and will teach you **w** the heart is evil."
4: 12 and to suffer and not understand **w**."
4: 20 but **w** have you not judged so in your own case?
4: 22 **w** have I been endowed with the power
4: 23 **w** Israel has been given over to the Gentiles
4: 23 **w** the people whom you loved has been given over
4: 33 **W** are our years few and evil?"
5: 16 And **w** is your face sad?
5: 28 **w** have you handed the one over to the many,
5: 35 And I said, "**W** not, my lord?
5: 35 **W** then was I born?
5: 35 **w** did not my mother's womb become my grave,
5: 46 'If you bear ten children, **w** one after another?'
5: 52 '**W** are those whom you have borne recently not
6: 59 **w** do we not possess our world as an inheritance?
7: 15 **w** are you disturbed, seeing that you are to perish?
7: 15 **W** are you moved, seeing that you are mortal?
7: 16 **W** have you not considered in your mind what is
7: *111* [41] **w** will it not be so then as well?"
9: 40 "**W** are you weeping, and why are you grieved
9: 40 and **w** are you grieved at heart?"
10: 31 And **w** are you troubled?
10: 31 And **w** are your understanding and the thoughts
13: 51 **W** did I see the man coming up from the heart of
4Mc 1: 5 **w** is it not sovereign over forgetfulness
2: 1 And **w** is it amazing that the desires of the mind
2: 19 **W** else did Jacob, our most wise father,
5: 8 **w** should you abhor eating the very excellent meat
6: 14 **w** are you so irrationally destroying yourself
6: 23 And you, guards of the tyrant, **w** do you delay?"
8: 1 For this is **w** even the very young,
8: 18 **w** do we take pleasure in vain resolves and venture
8: 23 **W** do we banish ourselves
8: 26 **W** does such contentiousness excite us and such
9: 1 "**W** do you delay, O tyrant?
14: 18 And **w** is it necessary to demonstrate sympathy

WICK (3)

Isa 42: 3 and a dimly burning **w** he will not quench;
43: 17 they are extinguished, quenched like a **w**:
Mt 12: 20 not break a bruised reed or quench a smoldering **w**

WICKED‡ (349) [WICKEDLY, WICKEDNESS]

Ge 13: 13 Now the people of Sodom were **w**,
18: 23 the righteous with the **w**?
18: 25 to slay the righteous with the **w**, so that the righteous fare as the **w**!
38: 7 was **w** in the sight of the LORD,
Ex 23: 1 You shall not join hands with the **w** to act as
Nu 14: 27 How long shall this **w** congregation complain
14: 35 to all this **w** congregation gathered together
16: 26 "Turn away from the tents of these **w** men,
1Sa 2: 9 but the **w** shall be cut off in darkness;
24: 13 'Out of the **w** comes forth wickedness';
2Sa 3: 34 as one falls before the **w** you have fallen."
4: 11 when **w** men have killed a righteous man
2Ki 17: 11 They did **w** things, provoking the LORD to anger;
21: 11 has done things more **w** than all that
1Ch 2: 3 was **w** in the sight of the LORD,
2Ch 7: 14 pray, seek my face, and turn from their **w** ways,
19: 2 "Should you help the **w** and love those who hate
24: 7 For the children of Athaliah, that **w** woman,
Ezr 4: 12 They are rebuilding that rebellious and **w** city;
Ne 9: 35 not serve you and did not turn from their **w** works.
Est 7: 6 Esther said, "A foe and enemy, this **w** Haman!"
Est 9: 25 in writing that the **w** plot that he had devised
Job 3: 17 There the **w** cease from troubling,
8: 16 The **w** thrive before the sun,
8: 22 and the tent of the **w** will be no more."
9: 22 I say, he destroys both the blameless and the **w**.
9: 24 The earth is given into the hand of the **w**;
10: 3 of your hands and favor the schemes of the **w**?
10: 15 If I am **w**, woe to me!
11: 20 But the eyes of the **w** will fail;
15: 20 The **w** writhe in pain all their days,
16: 11 and casts me into the hands of the **w**.
18: 5 "Surely the light of the **w** is put out,
20: 5 that the exulting of the **w** is short,
20: 29 This is the portion of the **w** from God,
21: 7 Why do the **w** live on, reach old age,
21: 16 The plans of the **w** are repugnant to me.
21: 17 "How often is the lamp of the **w** put out?
21: 28 Where is the tent in which the **w** lived?'
21: 30 that the **w** are spared in the day of calamity,
22: 15 Will you keep to the old way that the **w** have trod?
22: 18 but the plans of the **w** are repugnant to me.
24: 2 The **w** remove landmarks;
24: 6 and they glean in the vineyard of the **w**.
27: 7 "May my enemy be like the **w**,
27: 13 "This is the portion of the **w** with God,
34: 8 in company with evildoers and walks with the **w**?
34: 18 and to princes, 'You **w** men!';
34: 36 because his answers are those of the **w**.
36: 6 He does not keep the **w** alive,
36: 17 "But you are obsessed with the case of the **w**;
38: 13 and the **w** be shaken out of it?
38: 15 Light is withheld from the **w**,
40: 12 tread down the **w** where they stand.
Ps 1: 1 of the **w**, or take the path that sinners tread, or sit
1: 4 The **w** are not so, but are like chaff that
1: 5 Therefore the **w** will not stand in the judgment,
1: 6 but the way of the **w** will perish.
3: 7 you break the teeth of the **w**.
7: 9 O let the evil of the **w** come to an end,
9: 5 you have destroyed the **w**;
9: 16 the **w** are snared in the work of their own hands.
9: 17 The **w** shall depart to Sheol,
10: 2 In arrogance the **w** persecute the poor—
10: 3 For the **w** boast of the desires of their heart,
10: 4 In the pride of their countenance the **w** say,
10: 13 Why do the **w** renounce God,
10: 15 Break the arm of the **w** and evildoers;
11: 2 the **w** bend the bow, they have fitted their arrow to
11: 5 The LORD tests the righteous and the **w**,
11: 6 On the **w** he will rain coals of fire and sulfur;
12: 8 On every side the **w** prowl,
15: 4 the **w** are despised, but who honor those who fear
17: 9 from the **w** who despoil me,
17: 13 By your sword deliver my life from the **w**,
26: 5 and will not sit with the **w**.
28: 3 Do not drag me away with the **w**,
31: 17 let the **w** be put to shame; let them go
32: 10 Many are the torments of the **w**,
34: 21 Evil brings death to the **w**,
36: 1 Transgression speaks to the **w** deep in their hearts;
36: 11 or the hand of the **w** drive me away.
37: 1 Do not fret because of the **w**;
37: 9 For the **w** shall be cut off,
37: 10 Yet a little while, and the **w** will be no more;
37: 12 The **w** plot against the righteous,
37: 13 but the LORD laughs at the **w**,
37: 14 The **w** draw the sword and bend their bows
37: 16 the abundance of many **w**.
37: 17 For the arms of the **w** shall be broken,
37: 20 the **w** perish, and the enemies of the LORD are
37: 21 The **w** borrow, and do not pay back,
37: 28 but the children of the **w** shall be cut off.
37: 32 **w** watch for the righteous, and seek to kill them.
37: 34 you will look on the destruction of the **w**.
37: 35 I have seen the **w** oppressing,
37: 38 the posterity of the **w** shall be cut off.
37: 40 he rescues them from the **w**, and saves them,
39: 1 on my mouth as long as the **w** are in my presence."
50: 16 But to the **w** God says:
55: 3 because of the clamor of the **w**.
58: 3 The **w** go astray from the womb;
58: 10 they will bathe their feet in the blood of the **w**.
64: 2 Hide me from the secret plots of the **w**,
68: 2 let the **w** perish before God.
71: 4 Rescue me, O my God, from the hand of the **w**,
73: 3 I saw the prosperity of the **w**.
73: 12 Such are the **w**; always at ease,
75: 4 and to the **w**, "Do not lift up your horn;
75: 8 the **w** of the earth shall drain it down to the dregs.
75: 10 All the horns of the **w** I will cut off,
82: 2 and show partiality to the **w**?
82: 4 deliver them from the hand of the **w**."
89: 22 the **w** shall not humble him.
91: 8 with your eyes and see the punishment of the **w**.
92: 7 the **w** sprout like grass and all evildoers flourish,
94: 3 how long shall the **w**, how long shall the **w** exult?
94: 13 until a pit is dug for the **w**.
94: 16 Who rises up for me against the **w**?
94: 20 Can **w** rulers be allied with you,
97: 10 he rescues them from the hand of the **w**.
101: 8 Morning by morning I will destroy all the **w** in
104: 35 and let the **w** be no more.
106: 18 the flame burned up the **w**.
109: 2 For **w** and deceitful mouths are opened against me,
109: 6 They say, "Appoint a **w** man against him;
112: 10 The **w** see it and are angry;
112: 10 the desire of the **w** comes to nothing.
Ps 119: 53 Hot indignation seizes me because of the **w**,
119: 61 Though the cords of the **w** ensnare me,
119: 95 The **w** lie in wait to destroy me,
119: 110 The **w** have laid a snare for me,
119: 119 All the **w** of the earth you count as dross;
119: 155 Salvation is far from the **w**,
129: 4 LORD is righteous; he has cut the cords of the **w**.
139: 19 O that you would kill the **w**, O God,
139: 24 See if there is any **w** way in me,
140: 4 O LORD, from the hands of the **w**;
140: 8 Do not grant, O LORD, the desires of the **w**;
141: 4 to busy myself with **w** deeds in company
141: 5 Never let the oil of the **w** anoint my head,
141: 5 for my prayer is continually against their **w** deeds.
141: 10 Let the **w** fall into their own nets,
145: 20 but all the **w** he will destroy.
146: 9 but the way of the **w** he brings to ruin.
147: 6 he casts the **w** to the ground.
Pr 2: 22 but the **w** will be cut off from the land,
3: 25 or of the storm that strikes the **w**;
3: 33 The LORD's curse is on the house of the **w**,
4: 14 Do not enter the path of the **w**,
4: 19 The way of the **w** is like deep darkness;
5: 22 The iniquities of the **w** ensnare them,
6: 18 a heart that devises **w** plans,
9: 7 whoever rebukes the **w** gets hurt.
10: 3 but he thwarts the craving of the **w**.
10: 6 but the mouth of the **w** conceals violence.
10: 7 but the name of the **w** will rot.
10: 11 but the mouth of the **w** conceals violence.
10: 16 the gain of the **w** to sin.
10: 20 the mind of the **w** is of little worth.
10: 24 What the **w** dread will come upon them,
10: 25 When the tempest passes, the **w** are no more,
10: 27 but the years of the **w** will be short.
10: 28 but the expectation of the **w** comes to nothing.
10: 30 but the **w** will not remain in the land.
10: 32 but the mouth of the **w** what is perverse.
11: 5 but the **w** fall by their own wickedness.
11: 7 When the **w** die, their hope perishes,
11: 8 and the **w** get into it instead.
11: 10 and when the **w** perish, there is jubilation.
11: 11 but it is overthrown by the mouth of the **w**.
11: 18 The **w** earn no real gain,
11: 21 Be assured, the **w** will not go unpunished,
11: 23 the expectation of the **w** in wrath.
11: 31 how much more the **w** and the sinner!
12: 5 the advice of the **w** is treacherous.
12: 6 The words of the **w** are a deadly ambush,
12: 7 The **w** are overthrown and are no more,
12: 10 but the mercy of the **w** is cruel.
12: 12 The **w** covet the proceeds of wickedness,
12: 21 but the **w** are filled with trouble.
12: 26 but the way of the **w** leads astray.
13: 5 but the **w** act shamefully and disgracefully.
13: 6 whose way is upright, but sin overthrows the **w**.
13: 9 but the lamp of the **w** goes out.
13: 25 but the belly of the **w** is empty.
14: 11 The house of the **w** is destroyed,
14: 19 the **w** at the gates of the righteous.
14: 32 The **w** are overthrown by their evildoing,
15: 6 but trouble befalls the income of the **w**.
15: 8 sacrifice of the **w** is an abomination to the LORD,
15: 9 The way of the **w** is an abomination to the LORD,
15: 28 but the mouth of the **w** pours out evil.
15: 29 The LORD is far from the **w**,
16: 4 even the **w** for the day of trouble.
17: 4 An evildoer listens to **w** lips;
17: 15 One who justifies the **w** and one who condemns
17: 23 The **w** accept a concealed bribe to pervert the ways
19: 28 and the mouth of the **w** devours iniquity.
20: 26 A wise king winnows the **w**,
21: 4 the lamp of the **w**—are sin.
21: 7 The violence of the **w** will sweep them away,
21: 10 The souls of the **w** desire evil;
21: 12 The Righteous One observes the house of the **w**;
21: 12 he casts the **w** down to ruin.
21: 18 The **w** is a ransom for the righteous,
21: 26 All day long the **w** covet,
21: 27 The sacrifice of the **w** is an abomination;
21: 29 The **w** put on a bold face,
24: 1 Do not envy the **w**, nor desire to be with them;
24: 16 but the **w** are overthrown by calamity.
24: 19 of evildoers. Do not envy the **w**;
24: 20 the lamp of the **w** will go out.
24: 24 Whoever says to the **w**, "You are innocent,"
24: 25 but those who rebuke the **w** will have delight,
25: 5 take away the **w** from the presence of the king,
25: 26 the righteous who give way before the **w**.
28: 1 The **w** flee when no one pursues,
28: 4 Those who forsake the law praise the **w**,
28: 12 but when the **w** prevail, people go into hiding.
28: 15 or a charging bear is a **w** ruler over a poor people.
28: 28 When the **w** prevail, people go into hiding;
29: 2 but when the **w** rule, the people groan.
29: 7 the **w** have no such understanding.
29: 12 all his officials will be **w**.
29: 16 When the **w** are in authority,
29: 27 but the upright are an abomination to the **w**.
Ecc 3: 17 God will judge the righteous and the **w**,
7: 15 and there are **w** people who prolong their life
7: 17 Do not be too **w**, and do not be a fool;
8: 10 Then I saw the **w** buried;
8: 13 but it will not be well with the **w**,
8: 14 according to the conduct of the **w**,
8: 14 and there are **w** people who are treated according
9: 2 to the righteous and the **w**,

Ecc 10:13 and their talk ends in w madness;
Isa 11: 4 and with the breath of his lips he shall kill the w.
13:11 and the w for their iniquity;
14: 5 The LORD has broken the staff of the w,
26:10 If favor is shown to the w,
32: 7 they devise w devices to ruin the poor
48:22 "There is no peace," says the LORD, "for the w."
53: 9 They made his grave with the w and his tomb with
55: 7 let the w forsake their way,
57:17 Because of their w covetousness I was angry;
57:20 the w are like the tossing sea that cannot keep still;
57:21 There is no peace, says my God, for the w.
58: 4 to quarrel and to fight and to strike with a w fist.
Jer 2:33 that even to w women you have taught your ways.
6:29 for the w are not removed.
15:21 I will deliver you out of the hand of the w,
23:19 it will burst upon the head of the w.
25: 5 everyone of you, from your evil way and w doings,
30:23 it will burst upon the head of the w.
Eze 3:18 If I say to the w, "You shall surely die,"
3:18 or speak to warn the w from their w way,
3:18 those w persons shall die for their iniquity;
3:19 the w, and they do not turn from their wickedness,
3:19 from their w way, they shall die for their iniquity;
5: 6 becoming more w than the nations and
7:21 to the w of the earth as plunder;
11: 2 and who give w counsel in this city;
13:22 encouraged the w not to turn from their w way
18:20 and the wickedness of the w shall be his own.
18:21 But if the w turn away from all their sins
18:23 Have I any pleasure in the death of the w,
18:24 and do the same abominable things that the w do,
18:27 when the w turn away from
21: 3 and will cut off from you both righteous and w.
21: 4 I will cut off from you both righteous and w,
21:25 As for you, vile, w prince of Israel,
21:29 they place you over the necks of the vile, w ones—
33: 8 If I say to the w, "O w ones,
33: 8 not speak to warn the w to turn from their ways,
33: 8 the w shall die in their iniquity,
33: 9 But if you warn the w to turn from their ways,
33: 9 the w shall die in their iniquity,
33:11 I have no pleasure in the death of the w, but that
the w turn from their ways and live;
33:12 and as for the wickedness of the w,
33:14 Again, though I say to the w,
33:15 if the w restore the pledge,
33:19 And when the w turn from their wickedness,
Da 12:10 but the w shall continue to act wickedly.
12:10 None of the w shall understand,
Hos 7: 1 and the w deeds of Samaria;
Mic 6:10 the treasures of wickedness in the house of the w,
6:11 Can I tolerate w scales and a bag
Na 1:15 for never again shall the w invade you;
Hab 1: 4 The w surround the righteous—
1:13 the w swallow those more righteous than they?
3:13 You crushed the head of the w house,
Zep 1: 3 I will make the w stumble.
Mal 1: 4 until they are called the w country,
3:18 the difference between the righteous and the w,
4: 3 And you shall tread down the w,
Mt 18:32 and said to him, 'You w slave!
24:48 But if that w slave says to himself,
25:26 But his master replied, 'You w and lazy slave!
Lk 6:35 for he is kind to the ungrateful and the w.
19:22 'I will judge you by your own words, you w slave!
Ac 3:26 by turning each of you from your w ways."
1Co 5:13 "Drive out the w person from among you."
2Th 2:10 of w deception for those who are perishing,
3: 2 that we may be rescued from w and evil people;
2Ti 3:13 w people and impostors will go from bad to worse,
Tob 3: 8 the w demon Asmodeus had killed each of them
3:17 by setting her free from the w demon Asmodeus.
AdE 9:25 but the w plot he had devised against
14:15 that I hate the splendor of the w and abhor the bed
Wis 3:14 and who has not devised w things against the Lord;
10: 5 nations in w agreement had been put to confusion,
11:15 In return for their foolish and w thoughts,
14:29 in lifeless idols they swear w oaths and expect
19:13 for they justly suffered because of their w acts;
Sir 15:20 He has not commanded anyone to be w,
20:18 the downfall of the w will occur just as speedily.
21: 9 An assembly of the w is like a bundle of tow,
33:27 and for a w slave there are racks and tortures.
39:24 but full of pitfalls for the w.
40:10 All these were created for the w,
42: 5 and of drawing blood from the back of a w slave.
46: 7 and stilled their w grumbling.
49: 2 and removing the w abominations.
Bar 1:22 of us followed the intent of our own w hearts
2: 8 each of us, from the thoughts of our w hearts.
2:33 turn from their stubbornness and their w deeds;
Aza 1: 9 and to an unjust king, the most w in all the world.
Sus 1:28 full of their w plot to have Susanna put to death.
1:43 the w things that they have charged against me!"
1:52 "You old relic of w days,
1Mc 11: 8 and he kept devising w designs against Alexander.
13:46 not treat us according to our w acts but according
2Mc 8:32 a most w man, and one who had greatly troubled
10:34 kept blaspheming terribly and uttering w words.
1Es 2:18 and are building that rebellious and w city,
2:29 and that such w proceedings go no further to
4:39 of anything that is unrighteous or w.
3Mc 3:16 and went up to honor the temple of those w people,
2Es 2: 8 O w nation, remember what I did to Sodom
7:23 and proposed to themselves w frauds;
7:*122* [52] but we have walked in the most w ways?
15: 8 neither will I tolerate their w practices.
4Mc 12:11 "You profane tyrant, most impious of all the w,

WICKEDLY (32) [WICKED]

Ge 19: 7 and said, "I beg you, my brothers, do not act so w.
Jdg 19:23 "No, my brothers, do not act so w.
1Sa 12:25 But if you still do w, you shall be swept away,
2Sa 3:39 The LORD pay back the one who does w
22:22 and have not w departed from my God.
24:17 "I alone have sinned, and I alone have done w;
1Ki 8:47 and have done wrong; we have acted w';
1Ch 21:17 It is I who have sinned and done very w.
2Ch 6:37 and have done wrong; we have acted w';
20:35 with King Ahaziah of Israel, who did w.
22: 3 for his mother was his counselor in doing w.
Ne 9:33 for you have dealt faithfully and we have acted w;
Job 34:12 Of a truth, God will not do w,
Ps 18:21 and have not w departed from my God.
106: 6 we have committed iniquity, have done w.
Jer 38: 9 these men have acted w in all they did to
Da 9: 5 and done wrong, acted w and rebelled,
9:15 we have sinned, we have done w.
12:10 and refined, but the wicked shall continue to act w.
Mic 3: 4 because they have acted w.
AdE 16: 7 "What has been w accomplished through
Sus 1:61 as they had w planned to do to their neighbor.
1Mc 7:42 let the rest learn that Nicanor has spoken w against
2Mc 8:16 of Gentiles who were w coming against them,
1Es 1:24 concerning those who sinned and acted w toward
2Es 3:30 and have spared those who act w,
7:18 but those who have done w have suffered
7:*121* [51] for us, but we have lived w?
8:27 not take note of the endeavors of those who act w,
8:28 not think of those who have lived w in your sight,
8:35 those who have been born who has not acted w;
4Mc 2:13 so that one rebukes friends when they act w.

WICKEDNESS (129) [WICKED]

Ge 6: 5 that the w of humankind was great in the earth,
39: 9 then could I do this great w, and sin against God?"
Dt 9: 4 it is rather because of the w of these nations that
9: 5 but because of the w of these nations
9:27 to the stubbornness of this people, their w
13:11 and never again do any such w.
Jdg 9:57 and God also made all the w of the people
1Sa 12:17 and see that the w that you have done in the sight
24:13 'Out of the wicked comes forth w';
2Sa 3:39 one who does wickedly in accordance with his w!"
1Ki 1:52 but if w is found in him, he shall die."
Job 11:14 and do not let w reside in your tents.
20:12 "Though w is sweet in their mouth,
22: 5 Is not your w great?
24:20 so w is broken like a tree.
34:10 far be it from God that he should do w,
34:26 He strikes them for their w while others look on,
35: 8 Your w affects others like you,
Ps 5: 4 For you are not a God who delights in w;
10:15 seek out their w until you find none.
17: 3 if you test me, you will find no w in me;
45: 7 you love righteousness and hate w.
84:10 in the house of my God than live in the tents of w.
94:23 for their iniquity and wipe them out for their w;
107:34 because of the w of its inhabitants.
107:42 and all w stops its mouth.
125: 3 the scepter of w shall not rest on the land allotted
Pr 4:17 For they eat the bread of w and drink the wine
8: 7 w is an abomination to my lips.
10: 2 Treasures gained by w do not profit,
11: 5 but the wicked fall by their own w.
12: 3 No one finds security by w,
12:12 The wicked covet the proceeds of w,
18: 3 When w comes, contempt comes also;
26:26 the enemy's w will be exposed in the assembly.
Ecc 3:16 w was there, and in the place of righteousness, w
was there as well.
7:25 that w is folly and that foolishness is madness.
8: 8 nor does w deliver those who practice it.
Isa 9:18 w burned like a fire, consuming briers and thorns;
47:10 You felt secure in your w;
59: 3 your lips have spoken lies, your tongue mutters w.
Jer 1:16 for all their w in forsaking me;
2:19 Your w will punish you,
3: 2 the land with your whoring and w.
4:14 wash your heart clean of w so that you may
5:28 They know no limits in deeds of w;
6: 7 so she keeps fresh her w;
7:12 see what I did to it for the w of my people Israel.
8: 6 no one repents of w, saying, "What have I done!"
12: 4 For the w of those who live in it the animals and
14:16 For I will pour out their w upon them.
14:20 We acknowledge our w, O LORD,
22:22 be ashamed and dismayed because of all your w.
23:11 even in my house I have found their w,
23:14 so that no one turns from w;
33: 5 from this city because of all their w.
44: 3 because of the w that they committed,
44: 5 from their w and make no offerings to other gods.
Eze 3:19 and they do not turn from their w,
7:11 Violence has grown into a rod of w.
16:23 After all your w (woe, woe to you!
16:57 before your w was uncovered?
18:20 and the w of the wicked shall be his own.
18:27 the w they have committed and do what is lawful
31:11 he has dealt with it as its w deserves.
33:12 and as for the w of the wicked,
33:12 when they turn from their w;
33:19 And when the wicked turn from their w,
Da 8:12 of w, the host was given over to it together with
Hos 7: 2 they do not consider that I remember all their w.
7: 3 By their w they make the king glad,
9:15 of the w of their deeds I will drive them out
10:13 You have plowed w, you have reaped injustice,
10:15 O Bethel, because of your great w.
Joel 3:13 The vats overflow, for their w is great.
Jnh 1: 2 for their w has come up before me."
Mic 2: 1 Alas for those who devise w and evil deeds
6:10 Can I forget the treasures of w in the house of
Na 1:11 against the LORD, who counsels w.
Zec 5: 8 And he said, "This is W."
Mk 7:22 avarice, w, deceit, licentiousness, envy, slander,
Lk 11:39 but inside you are full of greed and w.
Ac 1:18 this man acquired a field with the reward of his w;
8:22 Repent therefore of this w of yours,
8:23 in the gall of bitterness and the chains of w."
Ro 1:18 and w of those who by their w suppress the truth.
1:29 They were filled with every kind of w, evil,
2: 8 and who obey not the truth but w,
6:13 to sin as instruments of w,
2Ti 2:19 on the name of the Lord turn away from w."
Heb 1: 9 You have loved righteousness and hated w;
Jas 1:21 of all sordidness and rank growth of w,
3:16 there will also be disorder and w of every kind.
Tob 14:10 For I see that there is much w within it,
Jdt 2: 2 with his own lips, all the w of the region.
Wis 2:21 but they were led astray, for their w blinded them,
4:12 For the fascination of w obscures what is good,
4:14 he took them quickly from the midst of w.
5:13 but were consumed in our w."
10: 7 Evidence of their w still remains:
12: 2 that they may be freed from w and put their trust
12:10 that their origin was evil and their w inborn,
12:20 and opportunity to give up their w,
16:14 A person in w kills another,
17:11 For w is a cowardly thing,
Sir 12:10 for like corrosion in copper, so is his w.
19: 5 One who rejoices in w will be condemned,
19:22 The knowledge of w is not wisdom,
25:13 Any w, but not the w of a woman!
25:17 A woman's w changes her appearance,
35: 5 To keep from w is pleasing to the Lord,
42:13 and from a woman comes woman's w.
42:14 the w of a man than a woman who does good;
46:20 to blot out the w of the people.
47:25 For they sought out every kind of w,
Bar 2:26 of the w of the house of Israel and the house
Sus 1: 5 "W came forth from Babylon,
1:38 and when we saw this w we ran to them.
1:57 but a daughter of Judah would not tolerate your w.
1Mc 5: 4 He also remembered the w of the sons of Baean,
7:42 and judge him according to this w."
2Mc 3: 1 of the high priest Onias and his hatred of w,
4:13 of foreign ways because of the surpassing w
4:50 remained in office, growing in w,
2Es 12:25 because it is they who shall sum up his w
12:32 for their ungodliness and for their w,

WIDE‡ (73) [WIDE-SPREADING, WIDELY, WIDENED, WIDER, WIDESPREAD, WIDTH]

Ex 25:10 a cubit and a half w, and a cubit and a half high.
25:23 one cubit w, and a cubit and a half high.
25:25 You shall make around it a rim a handbreadth w,
27: 1 five cubits long and five cubits w;
30: 2 It shall be one cubit long, and one cubit w;
37: 1 a cubit and a half w, and a cubit and a half high.
37:10 one cubit w, and a cubit and a half high.
37:12 He made around it a rim a handbreadth w,
37:25 one cubit long, and one cubit w;
38: 1 it was five cubits long, and five cubits w;
Nu 16:37 then scatter the fire far and w.
Dt 3:11 it is nine cubits long and four cubits w.)
2Sa 22:33 with strength has opened w my path.
1Ki 6: 2 twenty cubits w, and thirty cubits high.
6: 3 of the nave of the house was twenty cubits w,
6: 6 The lowest story was five cubits w, the middle one
was six cubits w, and the third was seven cubits w;
6:20 twenty cubits w, and twenty cubits high;
7: 2 fifty cubits w, and thirty cubits high,
7: 6 of Pillars fifty cubits long and thirty cubits w.
7:27 each stand was four cubits long, four cubits w,
7:31 it was a cubit and a half w.
2Ch 4: 1 twenty cubits w, and ten cubits high.
6:13 five cubits w, and three cubits high,
Ne 7: 4 The city was w and large,
Job 30:14 a w breach they come; amid the crash they roll on.
Ps 18:36 You gave me a w place for my steps under me,
22:13 they open w their mouths at me,
35:21 They open w their mouths against me;
81:10 Open your mouth w and I will fill it.
104:25 Yonder is the sea, great and w,
110: 6 he will shatter heads over the w earth.
Pr 13: 3 those who open w their lips come to ruin.
Isa 22:18 and throw you like a ball into a w land;
30:33 its pyre made deep and w,
57: 4 Against whom do you open your mouth w
57: 8 you have gone up to it, you have made it w;
Jer 8:19 cry of my poor people from far and w in the land:
Eze 23:32 You shall drink your sister's cup, deep and w;
34:21 until you scattered them far and w,
40: 7 and each recess was one reed w and one reed deep;
40:30 twenty-five cubits deep and five cubits w.

Eze 40:42 a cubit and a half long, and one cubit and a half w,
40:47 and one hundred cubits w, a square;
41:12 on the west side was seventy cubits w;
41:22 two cubits long, and two cubits w;
42: 4 ten cubits w and one hundred cubits deep,
42:20 and five hundred cubits w,
43:13 its base shall be one cubit high, and one cubit w,
43:16 twelve cubits long by twelve w.
43:17 fourteen cubits long by fourteen w,
43:17 with a rim around it half a cubit w,
45: 1 and twenty thousand cubits w;
45: 3 and ten thousand w, in which shall be
45: 5 and ten thousand cubits w,
45: 6 for the city an area five thousand cubits w,
46:22 forty cubits long and thirty w,
Na 3:13 The gates of your land are w open to your foes;
Hab 2: 5 They open their throats w as Sheol;
Zec 14: 4 in two from east to west by a very w valley;
Mt 7:13 for the gate is w and the road is easy that leads
Ac 16:27 jailer woke up and saw the prison doors w open,
1Co 16: 9 for a w door for effective work has opened to me,
2Co 6:11 our heart is w open to you.
6:13 to children—open w your hearts also.
Jdt 1: 2 the walls seventy cubits high and fifty cubits w.
1: 3 and sixty cubits w at the foundations.
1: 4 and forty cubits w to allow his armies to march out
4: 7 w enough for only two at a time to pass.
Wis 8: 8 And if anyone longs for w experience,
2Mc 12:16 so that the adjoining lake, a quarter of a mile w,
2Es 7: 3 "There is a sea set in a w expanse so that it is deep

WIDE-SPREADING (1) [SPREAD, WIDE]

Wis 17:18 or a melodious sound of birds in w branches,

WIDELY (6) [WIDE]

Ne 4:19 "The work is great and w spread out,
Jn 7: 4 for no one who wants to be w known acts in secret.
Sir 21: 7 The mighty in speech are w known;
LtJ 6:61 So also the lightning, when it flashes, is w seen;
2Mc 7: 5 The smoke from the pan spread w,
2Es 3:33 For I have traveled w among the nations

WIDENED (1) [WIDE]

Eze 41: 7 The passageway of the side chambers w from story

WIDENESS (KJV) See WIDTH

WIDER (1) [WIDE]

Eze 41: 7 For this reason the structure became w from story

WIDESPREAD (1) [SPREAD, WIDE]

1Sa 3: 1 in those days; visions were not w.

WIDOW (69) [WIDOW'S, WIDOWED, WIDOWHOOD, WIDOWS, WIDOWS']

Ge 38:11 "Remain a w in your father's house
Ex 22:22 You shall not abuse any w or orphan.
Lev 21:14 A w, or a divorced woman,
Nu 30: 9 (But every vow of a w or of a divorced woman,
Dt 10:18 who executes justice for the orphan and the w,
24:19 it shall be left for the alien, the orphan, and the w,
24:20 it shall be for the alien, the orphan, and the w.
24:21 it shall be for the alien, the orphan, and the w.
25: 7 if the man has no desire to marry his brother's w,
25: 7 then his brother's w shall go up to the elders at
27:19 deprives the alien, the orphan, and the w of justice.
Ru 4: 5 the w of the dead man,
1Sa 27: 3 and Abigail of Carmel, Nabal's w.
30: 5 and Abigail the w of Nabal of Carmel.
2Sa 2: 2 and Abigail the w of Nabal of Carmel.
3: 3 Chileab, of Abigail the w of Nabal of Carmel;
14: 5 She answered, "Alas, I am a w;
1Ki 7:14 He was the son of a w of the tribe of Naphtali,
11:26 whose mother's name was Zeruah, a w,
17: 9 for I have commanded a w there to feed you."
17:10 a w was there gathering sticks;
17:20 have you brought calamity even upon the w
Job 24:21 and do no good to the w.
31:16 or have caused the eyes of the w to fail,
31:18 and from my mother's womb I guided the w—
Ps 94: 6 They kill the w and the stranger,
109: 9 May his children be orphans, and his wife a w.
146: 9 he upholds the orphan and the w,
Isa 1:17 defend the orphan, plead for the w.
47: 8 I shall not sit as a w or know the loss of children"
Jer 7: 6 and the w, or shed innocent blood in this place,
22: 3 and the w, or shed innocent blood in this place.
La 1: 1 How like a w she has become,
Eze 22: 7 the orphan and the w are wronged in you.
44:22 They shall not marry a w, or a divorced woman,
44:22 or a w who is the w of a priest.
Zec 7:10 do not oppress the w, the orphan, the alien,
Mal 3: 5 the hired workers in their wages, the w and
Mt 22:24 his brother shall marry the w,
22:25 and died childless, leaving the w to his brother.
Mk 12:19 the man shall marry the w and raise up children
12:42 A poor w came and put in two small copper coins,
12:43 to them, "Truly I tell you, this poor w has put
Lk 2:37 then as a w to the age of eighty-four.
4:26 yet Elijah was sent to none of them except to a w
7:12 He was his mother's only son, and she was a w;
18: 3 In that city there was a w who kept coming to him
18: 5 yet because this w keeps bothering me,
Lk 20:28 the man shall marry the w and raise up children
21: 2 also saw a poor w put in two small copper coins.
21: 3 this poor w has put in more than all of them;
1Ti 5: 4 If a w has children or grandchildren,
5: 5 The real w, left alone, has set her hope on God
5: 6 but the w who lives for pleasure is dead even
5: 9 Let a w be put on the list if she is
Rev 18: 7 I am no w, and I will never see grief,'
Jdt 8: 4 as a w for three years and four months
9: 4 my God, hear me also—a w.
9: 9 Give to me, a w, the strong hand to do what I plan.
Wis 2:10 let us not spare the w or regard the gray hairs of
Sir 35:17 or the w when she pours out her complaint.
35:18 Do not the tears of the w run down her cheek
Bar 4:12 a w and bereaved of many;
LtJ 6:38 They cannot take pity on a w or do good to
2Es 2: 2 'Go, my children, because I am a w and forsaken.
2: 4 For I am a w and forsaken.
2:20 "Guard the rights of the w,
4Mc 16:10 so many and beautiful children am a w and alone,

WIDOW'S (10) [WIDOW]

Ge 38:14 she put off her w garments,
Dt 24:17 you shall not take a w garment in pledge.
Job 24: 3 they take the w ox for a pledge.
29:13 and I caused the w heart to sing for joy.
Pr 15:25 but maintains the w boundaries.
Isa 1:23 and the w cause does not come before them.
Jdt 8: 5 around her waist and dressed in w clothing.
10: 3 took off her w garments, bathed her body
16: 7 For she put away her w clothing to exalt
Bar 4:16 They led away the w beloved sons,

WIDOWED (3) [WIDOW]

Lev 22:13 but if a priest's daughter is w or divorced,
Jer 18:21 let their wives become childless and w.
2Es 16:44 and those who do not marry, like those who are w.

WIDOWHOOD (6) [WIDOW]

Ge 38:19 on the garments of her w.
2Sa 20: 3 up until the day of their death, living as if in w.
Isa 47: 9 the loss of children and w shall come upon you in
54: 4 disgrace of your w you will remember no more.
Jdt 8: 6 She fasted all the days of her w,
2Es 15:49 w, poverty, famine, sword, and pestilence,

WIDOWS‡ (32) [WIDOW]

Ex 22:24 and your wives shall become w
Dt 14:29 the orphans, and the w in your towns,
16:11 the orphans, and the w who are among you—
16:14 the orphans, and the w resident in your towns.
26:12 the aliens, the orphans, and the w,
26:13 the resident aliens, the orphans, and the w,
Job 22: 9 You have sent w away empty-handed,
27:15 and their w make no lamentation.
Ps 68: 5 and protector of w is God in his holy habitation.
78:64 and their w made no lamentation.
Isa 9:17 or compassion on their orphans and w;
10: 2 that w may be your spoil, and that you may make
Jer 15: 8 Their w became more numerous than the sand of
49:11 and let your w trust in me.
La 5: 3 fatherless; our mothers are like w.
Eze 22:25 they have made many w within it.
Lk 4:25 there were many w in Israel in the time of Elijah,
Ac 6: 1 the Hebrews because their w were being neglected
9:39 All the w stood beside him,
9:41 calling the saints and w, he showed her to be alive.
1Co 7: 8 To the unmarried and the w I say that it is well
1Ti 5: 3 Honor w who are really w.
5:11 But refuse to put younger w on the list;
5:14 So I would have younger w marry, bear children,
5:16 believing woman has relatives who are really w,
5:16 so that it can assist those who are real w.
Jas 1:27 to care for orphans and w in their distress,
Tob 1: 8 A third tenth I would give to the orphans and w
2Mc 3:10 that there were some deposits belonging to w
8:28 to those who had been tortured and to the w
8:30 and to the orphans and w,

WIDOWS' (2) [WIDOW]

Mk 12:40 They devour w houses and for the sake
Lk 20:47 They devour w houses and for the sake

WIDTH‡ (59) [WIDE]

Ge 6:15 its w fifty cubits, and its height thirty cubits.
Ex 25:17 and a cubit and a half its w.
26: 2 and the w of each curtain four cubits;
26: 8 and the w of each curtain four cubits;
26:16 and a cubit and a half the w of each frame.
27:12 For the w of the court on the west side there shall
27:13 The w of the court on the front to the east shall
27:18 the w fifty, and the height five cubits,
28:16 a span in length and a span in w.
36: 9 and the w of each curtain four cubits;
36:15 and the w of each curtain four cubits;
36:21 and a cubit and a half the w of each frame.
37: 6 and a cubit and a half its w.
38:18 It was twenty cubits long and, along the w of it,
39: 9 a span in length and a span in w when doubled.
1Ki 6: 3 across the w of the house.
2Ch 3: 3 was sixty cubits, and the w twenty cubits.
3: 4 across the w of the house;
3: 8 its length, corresponding to the w of the house, was twenty cubits, and its w was twenty cubits;
Ezr 6: 3 be sixty cubits and its w sixty cubits,
Eze 40:11 he measured the w of the opening of the gateway,
40:11 and the w of the gateway, thirteen cubits.
40:13 a w of twenty-five cubits, from wall to wall.
40:20 that faced north—its depth and w.
40:21 and its w twenty-five cubits.
40:25 and its w twenty-five cubits.
40:29 and its w twenty-five cubits.
40:33 and its w twenty-five cubits.
40:36 and its w twenty-five cubits.
40:48 and the w of the gate was fourteen cubits;
40:49 was twenty cubits, and the w twelve cubits;
41: 1 on each side six cubits was the w of the pilasters.
41: 2 The w of the entrance was ten cubits;
41: 2 forty cubits, and its w, twenty cubits.
41: 3 and the w of the entrance, six cubits;
41: 4 and its w, twenty cubits, beyond the nave.
41: 5 and the w of the side chambers, four cubits,
41:10 of the court was a w of twenty cubits all around
41:11 and the w of the part
41:14 the w of the east front of the temple and the yard,
42: 2 side was one hundred cubits, and the w fifty cubits.
42:10 w of the passage is fixed by the wall of the court.
42:11 on the north, of the same length and w,
43:14 two cubits, with a w of one cubit;
43:14 four cubits, with a w of one cubit;
48: 8 twenty-five thousand cubits in w,
48: 9 and twenty thousand in w.
48:10 ten thousand cubits in w on the western side,
48:10 ten thousand in w on the eastern side,
48:13 in length and ten thousand in w.
48:13 and the w twenty thousand.
48:15 five thousand cubits in w and twenty-five thousand
Da 3: 1 and whose w was six cubits;
Zec 2: 2 to see what is its w and what is its length."
5: 2 its length is twenty cubits, and its w ten cubits."
Rev 21:16 city lies foursquare, its length the same as its w;
21:16 its length and w and height are equal.
1Es 6:25 its height to be sixty cubits and its w sixty cubits,

WIELD (4) [WIELDED, WIELDER, WIELDING, WIELDS]

Isa 10:26 The LORD of hosts will w a whip against them,
Jer 50:42 They w bow and spear, they are cruel
Eze 30:21 so that it may become strong to w the sword.
Zec 9:13 O Greece, and w you like a warrior's sword.

WIELDED (3) [WIELD]

2Sa 23: 8 w his spear against eight hundred whom he killed
1Ch 11:11 w his spear against three hundred whom he killed
2Es 11:19 they w power one after another and

WIELDER (1) [WIELD]

Jer 50:16 and the w of the sickle in time of harvest;

WIELDING (3) [WIELD]

Dt 20:19 not destroy its trees by w an ax against them.
Eze 38: 4 all of them with shield and buckler, w swords.
4Mc 16:20 and when Isaac saw his father's hand w a knife

WIELDS (1) [WIELD]

Isa 10:15 Shall the ax vaunt itself over the one who w it,

WIFE‡ (427) [WIFE'S, WIVES, WIVES']

Ge 2:24 and his mother and clings to his w,
2:25 And the man and his w were both naked,
3: 8 and his w hid themselves from the presence of
3:17 "Because you have listened to the voice of your w,
3:20 The man named his w Eve,
3:21 of skins for the man and for his w,
4: 1 Now the man knew his w Eve,
4:17 Cain knew his w, and she conceived
4:25 Adam knew his w again, and she bore a son
6:18 your sons, your w, and your sons' wives with you.
7: 7 with his sons and his w and his sons' wives went
7:13 and Noah's w and the three wives
8:16 and your w, and your sons and your sons' wives
8:18 with his sons and his w and his sons' wives.
11:29 the name of Abram's w was Sarai,
11:29 and the name of Nahor's w was Milcah.
11:31 and his daughter-in-law Sarai, his son Abram's w,
12: 5 Abram took his w Sarai and his brother's son Lot,
12:11 he was about to enter Egypt, he said to his w Sarai,
12:12 they will say, 'This is his w';
12:17 with great plagues because of Sarai, Abram's w.
12:18 Why did you not tell me that she was your w?
12:19 'She is my sister,' so that I took her for my w?
12:19 Now then, here is your w, take her, and be gone."
12:20 with his w and all that he had.
13: 1 So Abram went up from Egypt, he and his w,
16: 1 Now Sarai, Abram's w, bore him no children.
16: 3 Sarai, Abram's w, took Hagar the Egyptian,
16: 3 and gave her to her husband Abram as a w.
17:15 God said to Abraham, "As for Sarai your w,
17:19 "No, but your w Sarah shall bear you a son,
18: 9 They said to him, "Where is your w Sarah?"
18:10 and your w Sarah shall have a son."
19:15 take your w and your two daughters who are here,
19:16 and his w and his two daughters by the hand,
19:26 But Lot's w, behind him, looked back,
20: 2 Abraham said of his w Sarah,
20: 7 Now then, return the man's w;
20:11 and they will kill me because of my w.

Ge 20:12 daughter of my mother; and she became my **w**.
20:14 and restored his **w** Sarah to him.
20:17 and God healed Abimelech, and also healed his **w**
20:18 of Abimelech because of Sarah, Abraham's **w**.
21:21 his mother got a **w** for him from the land of Egypt.
23:19 Abraham buried Sarah his **w** in the cave of
24: 3 not get a **w** for my son from the daughters of
24: 4 and to my kindred and get a **w** for my son Isaac."
24: 7 and you shall take a **w** for my son from there.
24:15 the **w** of Nahor, Abraham's brother,
24:36 And Sarah my master's **w** bore a son to my master
24:37 not take a **w** for my son from the daughters of
24:38 to my kindred, and get a **w** for my son.'
24:40 You shall get a **w** for my son from my kindred,
24:51 and let her be the **w** of your master's son,
24:67 He took Rebekah, and she became his **w**;
25: 1 Abraham took another **w**, whose name was
25:10 There Abraham was buried, with his **w** Sarah.
25:21 Isaac prayed to the LORD for his **w**,
25:21 and his **w** Rebekah conceived.
26: 7 When the men of the place asked him about his **w**,
26: 7 for he was afraid to say, "My **w**," thinking,
26: 8 of a window and saw him fondling his **w** Rebekah.
26: 9 and said, "So she is your **w**!
26:10 of the people might easily have lain with your **w**,
26:11 "Whoever touches this man or his **w** shall be put
28: 2 as **w** from there one of the daughters of Laban,
28: 6 and sent him away to Paddan-aram to take a **w**
28: 9 to be his **w** in addition to the wives he had.
29:21 "Give me my **w** that I may go in to her,
29:28 then Laban gave him his daughter Rachel as a **w**.
30: 4 So she gave him her maid Bilhah as a **w**;
30: 9 and gave her to Jacob as a **w**.
34: 4 saying, "Get me this girl to be my **w**."
34:12 only give me the girl to be my **w**."
36:10 Eliphaz son of Adah the **w** of Esau;
36:10 Reuel, the son of Esau's **w** Basemath.
36:12 These were the sons of Adah, Esau's **w**.
36:13 These were the sons of Esau's **w**, Basemath.
36:14 These were the sons of Esau's **w** Oholibamah,
36:17 they are the sons of Esau's **w** Basemath.
36:18 These are the sons of Esau's **w** Oholibamah:
36:18 these are the clans born of Esau's **w** Oholibamah,
38: 6 Judah took a **w** for Er his firstborn;
38: 8 "Go in to your brother's **w** and perform the duty of
38: 9 the ground whenever he went in to his brother's **w**,
38:12 In course of time the **w** of Judah, Shua's daughter,
39: 7 after a time his master's **w** cast her eyes on Joseph
39: 8 But he refused and said to his master's **w**, "Look,
39: 9 from me except yourself, because you are his **w**.
39:19 his master heard the words that his **w** spoke to him,
41:45 of Potiphera, priest of On, as his **w**.
44:27 'You know that my **w** bore me two sons;
46:19 The children of Jacob's **w** Rachel:
49:31 There Abraham and his **w** Sarah were buried;
49:31 there Isaac and his **w** Rebekah were buried;
Ex 4:20 So Moses took his **w** and his sons,
18: 2 After Moses had sent away his **w** Zipporah,
18: 5 bringing Moses' sons and **w** to him.
18: 6 am coming to you, with your **w** and her two sons."
20:17 you shall not covet your neighbor's **w**,
21: 3 then his **w** shall go out with him.
21: 4 If his master gives him a **w** and she bears him sons
21: 4 the **w** and her children shall be her master's
21: 5 But if the slave declares, "I love my master, my **w**,
21:10 If he takes another **w** to himself,
21:10 clothing, or marital rights of the first **w**.
22:16 the bride-price for her and make her his **w**.
Lev 18: 8 not uncover the nakedness of your father's **w**;
18:14 you shall not approach his **w**; she is your aunt.
18:15 of your daughter-in-law: she is your son's **w**;
18:16 not uncover the nakedness of your brother's **w**;
18:20 not have sexual relations with your kinsman's **w**,
20:10 man commits adultery with the **w** of his neighbor,
20:11 The man who lies with his father's **w** has
20:14 man takes a **w** and her mother also, it is depravity;
20:20 If a man lies with his uncle's **w**,
20:21 If a man takes his brother's **w**, it is impurity;
Nu 5:12 any man's **w** goes astray and is unfaithful to him,
5:14 and he is jealous of his **w** who has defiled herself;
5:14 and he is jealous of his **w**,
5:15 then the man shall bring his **w** to the priest.
5:29 This is the law in cases of jealousy, when a **w**,
5:30 on a man and he is jealous of his **w**;
26:59 The name of Amram's **w** was Jochebed daughter
30:16 concerning a husband and his **w**,
Dt 5:21 Neither shall you covet your neighbor's **w**.
13: 6 the **w** you embrace, or your most intimate friend—
21:13 to her and be her husband, and she shall be your **w**.
22:19 She shall remain his **w**;
22:22 If a man is caught lying with the **w** of another man,
22:24 and the man because he violated his neighbor's **w**.
22:29 and she shall become his **w**.
22:30 A man shall not marry his father's **w**,
24: 2 and goes off to become another man's **w**.
24: 4 is not permitted to take her again to be his **w**
24: 5 to be happy with the **w** whom he has married.
25: 5 the **w** of the deceased shall not be married outside
25: 9 then his brother's **w** shall go up to him in
25:11 the **w** of one intervenes to rescue her husband from
27:20 "Cursed be anyone who lies with his father's **w**,
28:54 to the **w** whom he embraces,
Jos 15:16 to him I will give my daughter Achsah as **w**."
15:17 and he gave him his daughter Achsah as **w**.
Jdg 1:12 I will give him my daughter Achsah as **w**."
1:13 and he gave him his daughter Achsah as **w**.
4: 4 a prophetess, **w** of Lappidoth, was judging Israel.
Jdg 4:17 on foot to the tent of Jael **w** of Heber the Kenite;
4:21 But Jael **w** of Heber took a tent peg,
5:24 the **w** of Heber the Kenite,
11: 2 Gilead's **w** also bore him sons;
13: 2 His **w** was barren, having borne no children.
13:11 Manoah got up and followed his **w**,
13:20 of the altar while Manoah and his **w** looked on;
13:21 not appear again to Manoah and his **w**.
13:22 And Manoah said to his **w**, "We shall surely die,
13:23 But his **w** said to him,
14: 2 now get her for me as my **w**."
14: 3 to take a **w** from the uncircumcised Philistines?"
14:15 On the fourth day they said to Samson's **w**,
14:16 So Samson's **w** wept before him, saying,
14:20 And Samson's **w** was given to his companion,
15: 1 Samson went to visit his **w**, bringing along a kid.
15: 6 because he has taken Samson's **w** and given her
21:18 "Cursed be anyone who gives a **w** to Benjamin."
21:21 a **w** for himself from the young women of Shiloh,
21:22 we did not capture in battle a **w** for each man.
Ru 1: 1 he and his **w** and two sons.
1: 2 and the name of his **w** Naomi, and the names
4:10 the **w** of Mahlon, to be my **w**,
4:13 So Boaz took Ruth and she became his **w**.
1Sa 1: 4 he would give portions to his **w** Peninnah and
1:19 Elkanah knew his **w** Hannah,
2:20 Then Eli would bless Elkanah and his **w**, and say,
4:19 Now his daughter-in-law, the **w** of Phinehas,
14:50 of Saul's **w** was Ahinoam daughter of Ahimaaz.
18:17 I will give her to you as a **w**;
18:19 she was given to Adriel the Meholathite as a **w**.
18:27 Saul gave him his daughter Michal as a **w**.
19:11 David's **w** Michal told him,
25: 3 and the name of his **w** Abigail.
25:14 But one of the young men told Abigail, Nabal's **w**,
25:37 his **w** told him these things,
25:39 David sent and wooed Abigail, to make her his **w**.
25:40 to you to take you to him as his **w**."
25:42 after the messengers of David and became his **w**.
25:44 Saul had given his daughter Michal, David's **w**,
30:22 except that each man may take his **w** and children,
2Sa 3: 5 Ithream, of David's **w** Eglah.
3:14 saying, "Give me my **w** Michal,
11: 3 the **w** of Uriah the Hittite."
11:11 to eat and to drink, and to lie with my **w**?
11:26 the **w** of Uriah heard that her husband was dead,
11:27 and she became his **w**, and bore him a son.
12: 9 and have taken his **w** to be your **w**,
12:10 have taken the **w** of Uriah the Hittite to be your **w**.
12:15 The LORD struck the child that Uriah's **w** bore
12:24 Then David consoled his **w** Bathsheba,
17:19 The man's **w** took a covering,
1Ki 2:17 to give me Abishag the Shunammite as my **w**."
2:21 be given to your brother Adonijah as his **w**."
4:11 Solomon's daughter, as his **w**);
4:15 Solomon's daughter, as his **w**);
9:16 as dowry to his daughter, Solomon's **w**;
11:19 so that he gave him his sister-in-law for a **w**,
14: 2 Jeroboam said to his **w**, "Go, disguise yourself,
14: 2 that you are the **w** of Jeroboam, and go to Shiloh;
14: 4 Jeroboam's **w** did so; she set out
14: 5 "The **w** of Jeroboam is coming to inquire of you
14: 6 **w** of Jeroboam; why do you pretend to be another?
14:17 Then Jeroboam's **w** got up and went away,
16:31 he took as his **w** Jezebel daughter of King Ethbaal
21: 5 His **w** Jezebel came to him and said,
21: 7 His **w** Jezebel said to him,
21:25 urged on by his **w** Jezebel.
2Ki 4: 1 Now the **w** of a member of the company
5: 2 and she served Naaman's **w**.
8:18 for the daughter of Ahab was his **w**.
14: 9 saying, 'Give your daughter to my son for a **w**';
22:14 and Asaiah went to the prophetess Huldah the **w**
1Ch 2:18 of Hezron had children by his **w** Azubah,
2:24 Abijah **w** of Hezron bore him Ashhur,
2:26 Jerahmeel also had another **w**,
2:29 The name of Abishur's **w** was Abihail,
3: 3 the sixth Ithream, by his **w** Eglah;
4:18 And his Judean **w** bore Jered father of Gedor,
4:19 The sons of the **w** of Hodiah, the sister of Naham,
7:15 Machir took a **w** for Huppim and for Shuppim.
7:16 Maacah the **w** of Machir bore a son,
7:23 Ephraim went in to his **w**,
8: 9 He had sons by his **w** Hodesh:
8:29 and the name of his **w** was Maacah.
9:35 Jeiel, and the name of his **w** was Maacah.
2Ch 8:11 "My **w** shall not live in the house of King David
11:18 Rehoboam took as his **w** Mahalath daughter
21: 6 for the daughter of Ahab was his **w**.
22:11 of King Jehoram and **w** of the priest Jehoiada—
25:18 saying, 'Give your daughter to my son for a **w**';
34:22 the **w** of Shallum son of Tokhath son of Hasrah,
Est 5:10 he sent and called for his friends and his **w** Zeresh,
5:14 Then his **w** Zeresh and all his friends said to him,
6:13 When Haman told his **w** Zeresh
6:13 his advisers and his **w** Zeresh said to him,
Job 2: 9 Then his **w** said to him,
19:17 My breath is repulsive to my **w**;
31:10 then let my **w** grind for another,
Ps 109: 9 May his children be orphans, and his **w** a widow.
128: 3 Your **w** will be like a fruitful vine
Pr 5:18 and rejoice in the **w** of your youth,
6:24 to preserve you from the **w** of another,
6:26 but the **w** of another stalks a man's very life.
6:29 So is he who sleeps with his neighbor's **w**;
12: 4 A good **w** is the crown of her husband,
18:22 He who finds a **w** finds a good thing,
Pr 19:14 but a prudent **w** is from the LORD.
21: 9 in a house shared with a contentious **w**.
21:19 a desert land than with a contentious and fretful **w**.
25:24 in a house shared with a contentious **w**.
27:15 on a rainy day and a contentious **w** are alike;
31:10 A capable **w** who can find?
Ecc 9: 9 Enjoy life with the **w** whom you love,
Isa 54: 6 For the LORD has called you like a **w** forsaken
54: 6 like the **w** of a man's youth when she is cast off,
Jer 3: 1 If a man divorces his **w** and she goes from him
and becomes another man's **w**,
3:20 Instead, as a faithless **w** leaves her husband,
5: 8 each neighing for his neighbor's **w**.
6:11 both husband and **w** shall be taken,
16: 2 You shall not take a **w**,
Eze 16:32 Adulterous **w**, who receives strangers instead
18: 6 not defile his neighbor's **w** or approach a woman
18:11 upon the mountains, defiles his neighbor's **w**,
18:15 does not defile his neighbor's **w**,
22:11 One commits abomination with his neighbor's **w**;
24:18 and at evening my **w** died.
33:26 and each of you defiles his neighbor's **w**;
Hos 1: 2 a **w** of whoredom and have children of whoredom,
2: 2 for she is not my **w**, and I am not her husband—
2:19 And I will take you for my **w** forever;
2:19 I will take you for my **w** in righteousness and
2:20 I will take you for my **w** in faithfulness;
12:12 Israel served for a **w**, and for a **w** he guarded sheep.
Am 7:17 'Your **w** shall become a prostitute in the city,
Mal 2:14 the LORD was a witness between you and the **w**
2:14 she is your companion and your **w** by covenant.
2:15 do not let anyone be faithless to the **w** of his youth.
Mt 1: 6 And David was the father of Solomon by the **w**
1:20 do not be afraid to take Mary as your **w**,
1:24 he took her as his **w**,
5:31 "It was also said, 'Whoever divorces his **w**,
5:32 But I say to you that anyone who divorces his **w**,
14: 3 on account of Herodias, his brother Philip's **w**,
18:25 with his **w** and children and all his possessions,
19: 3 for a man to divorce his **w** for any cause?"
19: 5 and mother and be joined to his **w**,
19: 9 And I say to you, whoever divorces his **w**,
19:10 "If such is the case of a man with his **w**,
22:28 then, whose **w** of the seven will she be?
27:19 his **w** sent word to him,
Mk 6:17 on account of Herodias, his brother Philip's **w**,
6:18 "It is not lawful for you to have your brother's **w**."
10: 2 "Is it lawful for a man to divorce his **w**?"
10: 7 and mother and be joined to his **w**,
10:11 to them, "Whoever divorces his **w**
12:19 leaving a **w** but no child,
12:23 In the resurrection whose **w** will she be?
Lk 1: 5 His **w** was a descendant of Aaron,
1:13 Your **w** Elizabeth will bear you a son,
1:18 I am an old man, and my **w** is getting on in years."
1:24 After those days his **w** Elizabeth conceived,
3:19 because of Herodias, his brother's **w**, and because
8: 3 the **w** of Herod's steward Chuza, and Susanna,
14:26 **w** and children, brothers and sisters, yes,
16:18 "Anyone who divorces his **w**
17:32 Remember Lot's **w**.
18:29 there is no one who has left house or **w** or brothers
20:28 leaving a **w** but no children,
20:33 therefore, whose **w** will the woman be?
Jn 19:25 and his mother's sister, Mary the **w** of Clopas,
Ac 5: 1 with the consent of his **w** Sapphira,
5: 7 an interval of about three hours his **w** came in,
18: 2 from Italy with his **w** Priscilla,
24:24 when Felix came with his **w** Drusilla,
1Co 5: 1 for a man is living with his father's **w**.
7: 2 each man should have his own **w**
7: 3 husband should give to his **w** her conjugal rights,
and likewise the **w** to her husband.
7: 4 the **w** does not have authority over her own body,
7: 4 have authority over his own body, but the **w** does.
7:10 that the **w** should not separate from her husband
7:11 and that the husband should not divorce his **w**.
7:12 that if any believer has a **w** who is an unbeliever,
7:14 unbelieving husband is made holy through his **w**,
7:14 unbelieving **w** is made holy through her husband.
7:16 **W**, for all you know, you might save your husband
7:16 Husband, for all you know, you might save your **w**.
7:27 Are you bound to a **w**?
7:27 Are you free from a **w**? Do not seek a **w**.
7:33 about the affairs of the world, how to please his **w**,
7:39 A **w** is bound as long as her husband lives.
9: 5 the right to be accompanied by a believing **w**,
11: 3 and the husband is the head of his **w**,
Eph 5:23 the husband is the head of the **w** just as Christ is
5:28 He who loves his **w** loves himself.
5:31 and mother and be joined to his **w**,
5:33 however, should love his **w** as himself, and a **w**
should respect her husband.
Rev 21: 9 I will show you the bride, the **w** of the Lamb."
Tob 1:20 not taken into the royal treasury except my **w** Anna
2: 1 and my **w** Anna and my son Tobias were restored
2:11 also, my **w** Anna earned money at women's work.
3:15 for whom I should keep myself as **w**.
4:13 to take a **w** for yourself from among them.
6:16 to take a **w** from your father's house?
7: 2 He said to his **w** Edna,
7: 8 His **w** Edna also wept for him,
7:12 "Take her to be your **w** in accordance with the law
7:13 to the effect that he gave her to him as **w** according
7:15 Raguel called his **w** Edna and said to her, "Sister,
8: 6 him you made his **w** Eve as a helper and support.
8:11 Raguel went into his house and called his **w**,

Tob 8:19 this he asked his **w** to bake many loaves of bread;
8:21 the other half will be yours when my **w** and I die.
8:21 and we belong to you as well as to your **w** now
9: 6 the blessing of heaven to you and your **w**,
10: 4 His **w** Anna said, "My child has perished
10:10 So Raguel promptly gave Tobias his **w** Sarah,
10:11 The Lord of heaven prosper you and your **w** Sarah,
10:12 on I am your mother and Sarah is your beloved **w**.
10:13 Finally, he blessed Raguel and his **w** Edna,
11: 3 Let us run ahead of your **w** and prepare the house
11:17 When Tobit met Sarah the **w** of his son Tobias,
12: 3 he has led me back to you safely, he cured my **w**,
14:12 Then he and his **w** and children returned to Media
AdE 5:10 and summoned his friends and his **w** Zosara.
5:14 His **w** Zosara and his friends said to him,
6:13 Haman told his **w** Zosara
6:13 His friends and his **w** said to him,
7: 8 even assault my **w** in my own house?"
Sir 7:19 Do not dismiss a wise and good **w**,
7:26 Do you have a **w** who pleases you?
9: 1 Do not be jealous of the **w** of your bosom,
9: 9 Never dine with another man's **w**,
25: 1 and a **w** and a husband who live in harmony.
25: 8 Happy the man who lives with a sensible **w**,
25:20 such is a garrulous **w** to a quiet husband.
25:22 and great disgrace when a **w** supports her husband.
25:23 and wounded heart come from an evil **w**.
25:23 from the **w** who does not make her husband happy.
25:25 and no boldness of speech to an evil **w**.
26: 1 Happy is the husband of a good **w**;
26: 2 A loyal **w** brings joy to her husband,
26: 3 A good **w** is a great blessing;
26: 6 But it is heartache and sorrow when a **w** is jealous
26: 7 A bad **w** is a chafing yoke;
26: 8 A drunken **w** arouses great anger;
26: 9 The haughty stare betrays an unchaste **w**;
26:14 A silent **w** is a gift from the Lord,
26:15 A modest **w** adds charm to charm,
26:16 the beauty of a good **w** in her well-ordered home.
26:23 *A godless **w** is given as a portion to a lawless man,*
26:23 *a pious **w** is given to the man who fears the Lord.*
26:25 *A headstrong **w** is regarded as a dog,*
26:26 *A **w** honoring her husband will seem wise to all,*
26:26 *Happy is the husband of a good **w**;*
26:27 *garrulous **w** is like a trumpet sounding the charge,*
33:20 To son or **w**, to brother or friend,
36:29 He who acquires a **w** gets his best possession,
36:30 and where there is no **w**,
40:19 but a blameless **w** is accounted better than either.
40:23 but a sensible **w** is better than either.
41:21 and of gazing at another man's **w**;
42: 6 there is an untrustworthy **w**, a seal is a good thing;
Sus 1:29 for Susanna daughter of Hilkiah, the **w** of Joakim."
1:63 and his **w** praised God for their daughter Susanna,
1Mc 10:54 give me now your daughter as my **w**,
11: 9 in marriage my daughter who was Alexander's **w**,
1Es 4:20 and his own country, and clings to his **w**.
4:21 With his **w** he ends his days,
4:25 A man loves his **w** more than his father
2Es 9:47 when he grew up and I came to take a **w** for him,
4Mc 2: 5 not covet your neighbor's **w** or anything
2:11 It is superior to love for one's **w**,

WIFE'S (9) [WIFE]

Ge 36:39 his **w** name was Mehetabel,
Lev 18:11 the nakedness of your father's **w** daughter,
Jdg 11: 2 and when his **w** sons grew up,
15: 1 He said, "I want to go into my **w** room."
1Ch 1:50 and his **w** name Mehetabel daughter of Matred,
Pr 19:13 and a **w** quarreling is a continual dripping of rain.
Ac 5: 2 with his **w** knowledge, he kept back some of
Tob 9: 6 and to your **w** father and mother.
Sir 26:13 A **w** charm delights her husband,

WILD‡ (135) [WILDEST, WILDLY, WILDS]

Ge 1:24 and creeping things and **w** animals of the earth
1:25 the **w** animals of the earth of every kind,
1:26 and over all the **w** animals of the earth,
3: 1 serpent was more crafty than any other **w** animal
3:14 among all animals and among all **w** creatures;
7:14 they and every **w** animal of every kind,
7:21 birds, domestic animals, **w** animals,
8: 1 and all the **w** animals and all the domestic animals
16:12 He shall be a **w** ass of a man,
31:39 which was torn by **w** beasts I did not bring to you;
37:20 we shall say that a **w** animal has devoured him,
37:33 A **w** animal has devoured him;
Ex 23:11 and what they leave the **w** animals may eat.
23:29 and the **w** animals would multiply against you.
32:25 When Moses saw that the people were running **w**
32:25 (for Aaron had let them run **w**,
Lev 7:24 an animal that died or was torn by **w** animals may
17:15 of itself or what has been torn by **w** animals,
22: 8 That which died or was torn by **w** animals he shall
25: 7 for the **w** animals in your land all its yield shall be
26:22 I will let loose **w** animals against you,
Nu 23:22 is like the horns of a **w** ox for them.
24: 8 is like the horns of a **w** ox for him;
Dt 7:22 the **w** animals would become too numerous
14: 5 the roebuck, the **w** goat, the ibex, the antelope,
33:17 His horns are the horns of a **w** ox;
1Sa 17:44 to the birds of the air and to the **w** animals of
17:46 to the birds of the air and to the **w** animals of
24: 2 in the direction of the Rocks of the **W** Goats.
2Sa 2:18 Now Asahel was as swift of foot as a **w** gazelle.
21:10 or the **w** animals by night.
2Ki 4:39 he found a **w** vine and gathered from it a lapful of **w** gourds,
14: 9 but a **w** animal of Lebanon passed by and trampled
2Ch 25:18 but a **w** animal of Lebanon passed by and trampled
Ne 8:15 and bring branches of olive, **w** olive, myrtle, palm,
Job 5:22 and shall not fear the **w** animals of the earth.
5:23 and the **w** animals shall be at peace with you.
6: 5 Does the **w** ass bray over its grass,
11:12 when a **w** ass is born human.
24: 5 Like **w** asses in the desert they go out to their toil,
28: 8 The proud **w** animals have not trodden it;
39: 5 "Who has let the **w** ass go free?
39: 9 "Is the **w** ox willing to serve you?
39:15 and that a **w** animal may trample them.
40:20 for it where all the **w** animals play.
Ps 22:21 the horns of the **w** oxen you have rescued me.
29: 6 and Sirion like a young **w** ox.
50:10 For every **w** animal of the forest is mine,
68:30 Rebuke the **w** animals that live among the reeds,
74:19 not deliver the soul of your dove to the **w** animals;
79: 2 flesh of your faithful to the **w** animals of the earth.
92:10 you have exalted my horn like that of the **w** ox;
104:11 giving drink to every **w** animal; the **w** asses quench their thirst.
104:18 The high mountains are for the **w** goats;
148:10 **W** animals and all cattle, creeping things
Pr 30:30 which is mightiest among **w** animals and does
SS 2: 7 by the gazelles or the **w** does:
3: 5 by the gazelles or the **w** does:
Isa 5: 2 to yield grapes, but it yielded **w** grapes.
5: 4 why did it yield **w** grapes?
13:21 But **w** animals will lie down there,
23:13 They destined Tyre for **w** animals.
32:14 the joy of **w** asses, a pasture for flocks;
34: 7 **W** oxen shall fall with them,
43:20 The **w** animals will honor me,
56: 9 All you **w** animals, all you **w** animals in the forest,
Jer 2:21 did you turn degenerate and become a **w** vine?
2:24 a **w** ass at home in the wilderness,
12: 9 Go, assemble all the **w** animals;
14: 6 The **w** asses stand on the bare heights,
15: 3 of the air and the **w** animals of the earth to devour
16: 4 for the birds of the air and for the **w** animals of
19: 7 for food to the birds of the air and to the **w** animals
27: 6 even the **w** animals of the field to serve him.
28:14 I have even given him the **w** animals.
34:20 the birds of the air and the **w** animals of the earth.
48: 6 Be like a **w** ass in the desert!
50:39 **w** animals shall live with hyenas in Babylon,
Eze 5:17 I will send famine and **w** animals against you,
14:15 If I send **w** animals through the land to ravage it,
14:21 sword, famine, **w** animals, and pestilence,
31:13 and among its boughs lodge all the **w** animals.
32: 4 the **w** animals of the whole earth gorge themselves
33:27 in the open field I will give to the **w** animals to
34: 5 scattered, they became food for all the **w** animals.
34: 8 my sheep have become food for all the **w** animals,
34:25 a covenant of peace and banish **w** animals from
34:25 so that they may live in the **w** and sleep in
39: 4 of every kind and to the **w** animals to be devoured.
39:17 to the birds of every kind and to all the **w** animals:
Da 2:38 the **w** animals of the field, and the birds of the air,
4:25 and your dwelling shall be with the **w** animals.
5:21 His dwelling was with the **w** asses,
Hos 2:12 and the **w** animals shall devour them.
2:18 on that day with the **w** animals, the birds of the air,
4: 3 together with the **w** animals and the birds of
8: 9 up to Assyria, a **w** ass wandering alone;
13: 8 as a **w** animal would mangle them.
Joel 1:20 Even the **w** animals cry to you because
Zep 2:14 Herds shall lie down in it, every **w** animal;
2:15 a desolation it has become, a lair for **w** animals!
Mt 3: 4 and his food was locusts and **w** honey.
Mk 1: 6 and he ate locusts and **w** honey.
1:13 and he was with the **w** beasts;
Ro 11:17 a **w** olive shoot, were grafted in their place to share
11:24 from what is by nature a **w** olive tree and grafted,
1Co 15:32 with merely human hopes I fought with **w** animals
Jude 1:13 **w** waves of the sea, casting up the foam
Rev 6: 8 and pestilence, and by the **w** animals of the earth.
AdE 16:24 most hateful to **w** animals and birds for all time.
Wis 7:20 the tempers of **w** animals, the powers of spirits and
12: 9 or to destroy them at one blow by dread **w** animals
16: 5 For when the terrible rage of **w** animals came
17: 9 scared by the passing of **w** animals and the hissing
Sir 12:13 or all those who go near **w** animals?
13:19 **W** asses in the wilderness are the prey of lions;
39:30 the fangs of **w** animals and scorpions and vipers,
LtJ 6:68 The **w** animals are better than they are,
Aza 1:59 Bless the Lord, all **w** animals and cattle;
2Mc 4:25 of a cruel tyrant and the rage of a savage **w** beast.
4:41 and threw them in **w** confusion at Lysimachus
5:27 in the mountains as **w** animals do;
5:27 they continued to live on what grew **w**,
9:15 to throw out with their children for the **w** animals
10: 6 in the mountains and caves like **w** animals.
3Mc 4: 9 They were brought on board like **w** animals,
6: 7 into the ground to lions as food for **w** animals,
2Es 5: 8 the **w** animals shall roam beyond their haunts,
6:53 **w** animals, and creeping things;
7:65 but let the **w** animals of the field be glad;
8:30 with those who are deemed worse than **w** animals,
15:30 shall go forth like **w** boars from the forest,

WILDCATS (1)

Isa 34:14 **W** shall meet with hyenas,

WILDERNESS‡ (298)

Ge 14: 6 of Seir as far as El-paran on the edge of the **w**;
16: 7 by a spring of water in the **w**,
21:14 and wandered about in the **w** of Beer-sheba.
21:20 he lived in the **w**, and became an expert with
21:21 He lived in the **w** of Paran;
36:24 he is the Anah who found the springs in the **w**,
37:22 throw him into this pit here in the **w**,
Ex 3: 1 he led his flock beyond the **w**, and came to Horeb,
3:18 let us now go a three days' journey into the **w**,
4:27 "Go into the **w** to meet Moses."
5: 1 that they may celebrate a festival to me in the **w**.' "
5: 3 a three days' journey into the **w** to sacrifice to
7:16 so that they may worship me in the **w**."
8:27 a three days' journey into the **w** and sacrifice to
8:28 to sacrifice to the LORD your God in the **w**,
13:18 the people by the roundabout way of the **w** toward
13:20 and camped at Etham, on the edge of the **w**.
14: 3 the **w** has closed in on them.'
14:11 that you have taken us away to die in the **w**?
14:12 for us to serve the Egyptians than to die in the **w**."
15:22 and they went into the **w** of Shur.
15:22 They went three days in the **w** and found no water.
16: 1 and Israel came to the **w** of Sin,
16: 2 against Moses and Aaron in the **w**.
16: 3 for you have brought us out into this **w**
16:10 they looked toward the **w**,
16:14 on the surface of the **w** was a fine flaky substance,
16:32 the food with which I fed you in the **w**,
17: 1 From the **w** of Sin the whole congregation of
18: 5 the **w** where Moses was encamped at the mountain
19: 1 on that very day, they came into the **w** of Sinai.
19: 2 the **w** of Sinai, and camped in the **w**;
23:31 and from the **w** to the Euphrates;
Lev 7:38 to bring their offerings to the LORD, in the **w**
16:10 that it may be sent away into the **w** to Azazel.
16:21 into the **w** by means of someone designated for
16:22 and the goat shall be set free in the **w**.
Nu 1: 1 The LORD spoke to Moses in the **w** of Sinai,
1:19 So he enrolled them in the **w** of Sinai.
3: 4 before the LORD in the **w** of Sinai,
3:14 LORD spoke to Moses in the **w** of Sinai, saying:
9: 1 The LORD spoke to Moses in the **w** of Sinai,
9: 5 at twilight, in the **w** of Sinai.
10:12 the Israelites set out by stages from the **w** of Sinai,
10:12 and the cloud settled down in the **w** of Paran.
10:31 for you know where we should camp in the **w**,
12:16 and camped in the **w** of Paran.
13: 3 So Moses sent them from the **w** of Paran,
13:21 and spied out the land from the **w** of Zin to Rehob,
13:26 the congregation of the Israelites in the **w** of Paran,
14: 2 Or would that we had died in this **w**!
14:16 that he has slaughtered them in the **w**.'
14:22 and the signs that I did in Egypt and in the **w**,
14:25 turn tomorrow and set out for the **w** by the way to
14:29 your dead bodies shall fall in this very **w**;
14:32 as for you, your dead bodies shall fall in this **w**.
14:33 And your children shall be shepherds in the **w**
14:33 until the last of your dead bodies lies in the **w**.
14:35 in this **w** they shall come to a full end,
15:32 When the Israelites were in the **w**,
16:13 with milk and honey to kill us in the **w**,
20: 1 came into the **w** of Zin in the first month,
20: 4 of the LORD into this **w** for us and our livestock
21: 5 up out of Egypt to die in the **w**?
21:11 in the **w** bordering Moab toward the sunrise.
21:13 in the **w** that extends from the boundary of
21:18 with the staff." From the **w** to Mattanah,
21:23 and went out against Israel to the **w**;
24: 1 to look for omens, but set his face toward the **w**.
26:64 who had enrolled the Israelites in the **w** of Sinai.
26:65 LORD had said of them, "They shall die in the **w**."
27: 3 "Our father died in the **w**;
27:14 in the **w** of Zin when the congregation quarreled
27:14 (These are the waters of Meribath-kadesh in the **w**
32:13 and he made them wander in the **w** for forty years,
32:15 he will again abandon them in the **w**;
33: 6 which is on the edge of the **w**.
33: 8 passed through the sea into the **w**,
33: 8 went a three days' journey in the **w** of Etham,
33:11 from the Red Sea and camped in the **w** of Sin.
33:12 They set out from the **w** of Sin and camped
33:15 They set out from Rephidim and camped in the **w**
33:16 the **w** of Sinai and camped at Kibroth-hattaavah.
33:36 from Ezion-geber and camped in the **w** of Zin
34: 3 your south sector shall extend from the **w** of Zin
Dt 1: 1 in the **w**, on the plain opposite Suph,
1:19 through all that great and terrible **w** that you saw,
1:31 and in the **w**, where you saw how
1:40 But as for you, journey back into the **w**,
2: 1 we journeyed back into the **w**,
2: 7 he knows your going through this great **w**.
2: 8 When we had headed out along the route of the **w**
2:26 the **w** of Kedemoth to King Sihon of Heshbon with
4:43 the **w** on the tableland belonging to the Reubenites,
8: 2 in the **w**, in order to humble you, testing you
8:15 who led you through the great and terrible **w**,
8:16 in the **w** with manna that your ancestors did
9: 7 the LORD your God to wrath in the **w**;
9:28 he has brought them out to let them die in the **w**.'
11: 5 to you in the **w**, until you came to this place;
11:24 from the **w** to the Lebanon and from the River,
29: 5 I have led you forty years in the **w**.
32:10 in a desert land, in a howling **w** waste;
32:51 at the waters of Meribath-kadesh in the **w** of Zin,
Jos 1: 4 the **w** and the Lebanon as far as the great river,

Jos 5: 4 the journey through the w after they had come out
5: 5 the journey through the w after they had come out
5: 6 For the Israelites traveled forty years in the w,
8: 15 and fled in the direction of the w.
8: 20 the people who fled to the w turned back against
8: 24 of Ai in the open w where they pursued them,
12: 8 in the w, and in the Negeb, the land of the Hittites,
14: 10 while Israel was journeying through the w;
15: 1 to the w of Zin at the farthest south.
15: 61 In the w, Beth-arabah, Middin, Secacah,
16: 1 east of the waters of Jericho, into the w,
18: 12 and it ends at the w of Beth-aven.
20: 8 they appointed Bezer in the w on the tableland,
24: 7 Afterwards you lived in the w a long time.
Jdg 1: 16 from the city of palms into the w of Judah,
8: 7 I will trample your flesh on the thorns of the w and
8: 16 the city and he took thorns of the w and briers and
11: 16 Israel went through the w to the Red Sea and came
11: 18 Then they journeyed through the w,
11: 22 from the Arnon to the Jabbok and from the w to
20: 42 from the Israelites in the direction of the w;
20: 45 and fled toward the w to the rock of Rimmon,
20: 47 But six hundred turned and fled toward the w to
1Sa 4: 8 the Egyptians with every sort of plague in the w.
13: 18 down upon the valley of Zeboim toward the w.
17: 28 whom have you left those few sheep in the w?
23: 14 David remained in the strongholds in the w,
23: 14 in the hill country of the W of Ziph.
23: 15 in the W of Ziph at Horesh when he learned
23: 24 David and his men were in the w of Maon,
23: 25 down to the rock and stayed in the w of Maon.
23: 25 he pursued David into the w of Maon.
24: 1 he was told, "David is in the w of En-gedi."
25: 1 David got up and went down to the w of Paran.
25: 4 in the w that Nabal was shearing his sheep.
25: 14 "David sent messengers out of the w
25: 21 that I protected all that this fellow has in the w, so
26: 2 So Saul rose and went down to the W of Ziph,
26: 2 to seek David in the W of Ziph.
26: 3 But David remained in the w.
26: 3 he learned that Saul came after him into the w,
2Sa 2: 24 before Giah on the way to the w of Gibeon.
15: 23 and all the people moved on toward the w.
15: 28 I will wait at the fords of the w until word comes
16: 2 the wine is for those to drink who faint in the w."
17: 16 'Do not lodge tonight at the fords of the w,
17: 29 troops are hungry and weary and thirsty in the w."
1Ki 2: 34 and he was buried at his own house near the w.
9: 18 Baalath, Tamar in the w, within the land,
19: 4 But he himself went a day's journey into the w,
19: 15 "Go, return on your way to the w of Damascus;
2Ki 3: 8 "By the way of the w of Edom."
1Ch 12: 8 in the w mighty and experienced warriors, expert
21: 29 which Moses had made in the w,
2Ch 1: 3 the servant of the LORD had made in the w,
8: 4 He built Tadmor in the w and all the storage towns
20: 16 at the end of the valley, before the w of Jeruel.
20: 20 in the morning and went out into the w of Tekoa;
20: 24 When Judah came to the watchtower of the w,
24: 9 the servant of God laid on Israel in the w.
26: 10 in the w and hewed out many cisterns,
Ne 9: 19 not forsake them in the w;
9: 21 Forty years you sustained them in the w so
Ps 29: 8 The voice of the LORD shakes the w;
29: 8 the LORD shakes the w of Kadesh.
55: 7 I would lodge in the w;
63: T *A Psalm of David, when he was in the W of Judah.*
65: 12 The pastures of the w overflow,
68: 7 when you marched through the w,
74: 14 you gave him as food for the creatures of the w.
75: 6 from the west and not from the w comes lifting up;
78: 15 He split rocks open in the w,
78: 19 saying, "Can God spread a table in the w?
78: 40 against him in the w and grieved him in the desert!
78: 52 and guided them in the w like a flock.
95: 8 as at Meribah, as on the day at Massah in the w,
102: 6 I am like an owl of the w,
106: 14 But they had a wanton craving in the w,
106: 26 to them that he would make them fall in the w,
136: 16 the w, for his steadfast love endures forever;
SS 3: 6 What is that coming up from the w,
8: 5 Who is that coming up from the w,
Isa 21: 1 The oracle concerning the w of the sea.
27: 10 a habitation deserted and forsaken, like the w;
32: 15 and the w becomes a fruitful field,
32: 16 Then justice will dwell in the w,
35: 1 The w and the dry land shall be glad,
35: 6 For waters shall break forth in the w,
40: 3 "In the w prepare the way of the LORD,
41: 18 I will make the w a pool of water,
41: 19 I will put in the w the cedar, the acacia, the myrtle,
43: 19 I will make a way in the w and rivers in the desert.
43: 20 for I give water in the w, rivers in the desert,
51: 3 and will make her w like Eden,
64: 10 Your holy cities have become a w,
64: 10 Zion has become a w, Jerusalem a desolation.
Jer 2: 2 how you followed me in the w, in a land not sown.
2: 6 who led us in the w, in a land of deserts and pits,
2: 24 a wild ass at home in the w,
2: 31 Have I been a w to Israel, or a land of thick
3: 2 like a nomad in the w.
9: 10 and a lamentation for the pastures of the w,
9: 12 Why is the land ruined and laid waste like a w,
12: 10 they have made my pleasant portion a desolate w.
17: 6 They shall live in the parched places of the w,
23: 10 and the pastures of the w are dried up.
31: 2 the sword found grace in the w;
Jer 50: 12 Lo, she shall be the last of the nations, a w,
La 4: 3 like the ostriches in the w.
4: 19 they lay in wait for us in the w.
5: 9 because of the sword in the w.
Eze 6: 14 throughout all their settlements, from the w
19: 13 Now it is transplanted into the w,
20: 10 of the land of Egypt and brought them into the w.
20: 13 the house of Israel rebelled against me in the w;
20: 13 upon them in the w, to make an end
20: 15 in the w that I would not bring them into the land
20: 17 not destroy them or make an end of them in the w.
20: 18 I said to their children in the w,
20: 21 and spend my anger against them in the w.
20: 23 the w that I would scatter them among the nations
20: 35 and I will bring you into the w of the peoples,
20: 36 with your ancestors in the w of the land of Egypt,
23: 42 of the rabble brought in drunken from the w;
29: 5 I will fling you into the w,
Hos 2: 3 make her like a w, and turn her into a parched land,
2: 14 I will now allure her, and bring her into the w,
9: 10 Like grapes in the w, I found Israel.
13: 5 It was I who fed you in the w,
13: 15 a blast from the LORD, rising from the w;
Joel 1: 19 For fire has devoured the pastures of the w,
1: 20 and fire has devoured the pastures of the w.
2: 3 but after them a desolate w,
2: 22 for the pastures of the w are green;
3: 19 a desolation and Edom a desolate w,
Am 2: 10 and led you forty years in the w,
5: 25 and offerings the forty years in the w,
Mt 3: 1 In those days John the Baptist appeared in the w
3: 3 "The voice of one crying out in the w:
4: 1 by the Spirit into the w to be tempted by the devil.
11: 7 "What did you go out into the w to look at?
24: 26 He is in the w,' do not go out.
Mk 1: 3 the voice of one crying out in the w:
1: 4 John the baptizer appeared in the w,
1: 12 the Spirit immediately drove him out into the w.
1: 13 He was in the w forty days, tempted by Satan;
Lk 1: 80 the w until the day he appeared publicly to Israel.
3: 2 of God came to John son of Zechariah in the w.
3: 4 "The voice of one crying out in the w:
4: 1 from the Jordan and was led by the Spirit in the w,
7: 24 "What did you go out into the w to look at?
15: 4 does not leave the ninety-nine in the w and go after
Jn 1: 23 "I am the voice of one crying out in the w,
3: 14 And just as Moses lifted up the serpent in the w,
6: 31 Our ancestors ate the manna in the w;
6: 49 Your ancestors ate the manna in the w,
11: 54 to a town called Ephraim in the region near the w;
Ac 7: 30 an angel appeared to him in the w of Mount Sinai,
7: 36 at the Red Sea, and in the w for forty years.
7: 38 He is the one who was in the congregation in the w
7: 42 and sacrifices forty years in the w,
7: 44 "Our ancestors had the tent of testimony in the w,
8: 26 (This is a w road.)
13: 18 For about forty years he put up with them in the w.
21: 38 the four thousand assassins out into the w?"
1Co 10: 5 and they were struck down in the w.
2Co 11: 26 danger in the city, danger in the w, danger at sea,
Heb 3: 8 as on the day of testing in the w,
3: 17 whose bodies fell in the w?
Rev 12: 6 and the woman fled into the w,
12: 14 so that she could fly from the serpent into the w,
17: 3 So he carried me away in the spirit into a w,
Wis 11: 2 They journeyed through an uninhabited w,
17: 17 or workers who toiled in the w, they were seized,
Sir 13: 19 Wild asses in the w are the prey of lions;
43: 21 He consumes the mountains and burns up the w,
45: 18 and envied him in the w,
1Mc 2: 29 and justice went down to the w to live there,
2: 31 down to the hiding places in the w.
3: 45 Jerusalem was uninhabited like a w;
5: 24 and made three days' journey into the w.
5: 28 and his army quickly turned back by the w road
9: 33 and they fled into the w of Tekoa and camped by
9: 62 and Simon, withdrew to Bethbasi in the w;
13: 21 to them by way of the w and to send them food.
2Mc 5: 27 with about nine others, got away to the w,
2Es 1: 17 When you were hungry and thirsty in the w,
1: 18 'Why have you led us into this w to kill us?
1: 18 for us to serve the Egyptians than to die in this w.'
1: 22 When you were in the w, at the bitter stream,
9: 29 to our ancestors in the w when they came out
9: 29 into the untrodden and unfruitful w;

WILDEST (1) [WILD]

2Mc 11: 9 ready to assail not only humans but the w animals

WILDLY (2) [WILD]

Job 39: 13 "The ostrich's wings flap w,
Jer 4: 19 My heart is beating w; I cannot keep silent;

WILDS (1) [WILD]

Lk 8: 29 the bonds and be driven by the demon into the w.)

WILES (1) [WILY]

Eph 6: 11 so that you may be able to stand against the w of

WILILY (KJV) See CUNNING

WILL‡ (114 of 7473) [FREEWILL, GOODWILL, ILL-WILL, WILLED, WILLFUL, WILLFULLY, WILLING, WILLINGLY, WILLS] See Index of Articles Etc. for an Exhaustive Listing (See Introduction, page xi)

A. WILL OF ... *GOD (21)
B. GOD'S WILL (7)

Nu 24: 13 to do either good or bad of my own w;
1Sa 2: 25 for it was the w of the LORD to kill them.
1Ch 13: 2 and if it is the w of the LORD our God,
Ezr 7: 18 you may do, according to the w of your God. A
10: 11 the LORD the God of your ancestors, and do his w;
Ps 27: 12 Do not give me up to the w of my adversaries,
40: 8 I delight to do your w, O my God;
41: 2 You do not give them up to the w of their enemies.
103: 21 all his hosts, his ministers that do his w.
143: 10 Teach me to do your w,
Isa 30: 1 who make an alliance, but against my w,
53: 10 it was the w of the LORD to crush him with pain.
53: 10 through him the w of the LORD shall prosper.
Jer 3: 17 no longer stubbornly follow their own evil w.
7: 24 in the stubbornness of their evil w, they walked
11: 8 everyone walked in the stubbornness of an evil w.
13: 10 who stubbornly follow their own w
16: 12 following your stubborn evil w, refusing to listen
18: 12 act according to the stubbornness of our evil w."
Eze 16: 27 and gave you up to the w of your enemies,
Dan 11: 28 He shall work his w, and return to his own land.
Mt 6: 10 Your w be done, on earth as it is in heaven.
7: 21 the one who does the w of my Father in heaven.
11: 26 yes, Father, for such was your gracious w.
12: 50 For whoever does the w of my Father in heaven
18: 14 So it is not the w of your Father in heaven
21: 31 Which of the two did the w of his father?"
26: 42 this cannot pass unless I drink it, your w be done."
Mk 3: 35 Whoever does the w of God is my brother and A
Lk 10: 21 yes, Father, for such was your gracious w.
22: 42 remove this cup from me; yet, not my w but yours
Jn 1: 13 who were born, not of blood or of the w of the flesh or of the w of man, but of God.
4: 34 "My food is to do the w of him who sent me
5: 30 not my own w but the w of him who sent me.
6: 38 not to do my own w, but the w of him who sent me
6: 39 And this is the w of him who sent me,
6: 40 This is indeed the w of my Father,
7: 17 Anyone who resolves to do the w of God A
9: 31 listen to one who worships him and obeys his w.
21: 22 "If it is my w that he remain until I come,
21: 23 "If it is my w that he remain until I come,
Ac 21: 14 except to say, "The Lord's w be done."
22: 14 God of our ancestors has chosen you to know his w
Ro 1: 10 by God's w I may somehow at last succeed B
2: 18 and know his w and determine what is best
8: 20 not of its own w but by the w of the one who subjected it,
8: 27 the Spirit intercedes for the saints according to the w of God. A
9: 16 So it depends not on human w or exertion,
9: 19 For who can resist his w?"
12: 2 the w of God—what is good and acceptable A
15: 32 so that by God's w I may come to you with joy B
1Co 1: 1 an apostle of Christ Jesus by the w of God, A
9: 17 For if I do this of my own w, I have a reward;
9: 17 but if not of my own w, I am entrusted
2Co 1: 1 Paul, an apostle of Christ Jesus by the w of God, A
8: 5 first to the Lord and, by the w of God, to us, A
Gal 1: 4 according to the w of our God and Father, A
3: 15 once a person's w has been ratified, no one adds
Eph 1: 1 Paul, an apostle of Christ Jesus by the w of God, A
1: 5 according to the good pleasure of his w,
1: 9 he has made known to us the mystery of his w,
1: 11 all things according to his counsel and w.
5: 17 but understand what the w of the Lord is.
6: 6 doing the w of God from the heart. A
Php 2: 13 both to w and to work for his good pleasure.
Col 1: 1 Paul, an apostle of Christ Jesus by the w of God, A
1: 9 may be filled with the knowledge of God's w B
1Th 4: 3 For this is the w of God, your sanctification: A
5: 18 give thanks in all circumstances; for this is the w of God A
2Ti 1: 1 Paul, an apostle of Christ Jesus by the w of God, A
2: 26 having been held captive by him to do his w.
Heb 2: 4 gifts of the Holy Spirit, distributed according to his w.
9: 16 Where a w is involved, the death of the one
9: 17 For a w takes effect only at death,
10: 7 'See, God, I have come to do your w, O God'
10: 9 then he added, "See, I have come to do your w."
10: 10 it is by God's w that we have been sanctified B
10: 36 when you have done the w of God, A
13: 21 so that you may do his w,
Jas 3: 4 wherever the w of the pilot directs.
1Pe 2: 15 God's w that by doing right you should silence B
3: 17 for doing good, if suffering should be God's w, B
4: 2 no longer by human desires but by the w of God. A
4: 19 let those suffering in accordance with God's w B
2Pe 1: 21 because no prophecy ever came by human w,
1Jo 2: 17 but those who do the w of God live forever. A
5: 14 if we ask anything according to his w, he hears us.
Rev 4: 11 and by your w they existed and were created."
Tob 12: 18 not acting on my own w, but by the w of God. A
AdE 13: 9 who can oppose you when it is your w to save
Wis 14: 5 It is your w that works of your wisdom should not

Sir 41: 4 then should you reject the **w** of the Most High?
42:15 and all his creatures do his **w.**
43:16 At his **w** the south wind blows;
1Mc 3:60 But as his **w** in heaven may be, so shall he do."
2Mc 1: 3 give you all a heart to worship him and to do his **w**
6:29 toward him with goodwill now changed to ill **w,**
12: 3 as though there were no ill **w** to the Jews;
12:16 They took the town by the **w** of God, A
1Es 7:15 he had changed the **w** of the king of the Assyrians
8:16 in accordance with the **w** of your God; A
9: 9 do his **w;** separate yourselves from the peoples
3Mc 2:26 themselves also followed his **w.**
2Es 3: 8 And every nation walked after its own **w;**
8: 5 not of your own **w** did you come into the world,
8: 5 and against your **w** you depart,
8:29 not **w** the destruction of those who have the ways
4Mc 11:12 splendid favors that you grant us against your **w,**
18:16 'There is a tree of life for those who do his **w.**'

WILLED (2) [WILL]

Wis 11:25 would anything have endured if you had not **w** it?
12: 6 you **w** to destroy by the hands of our ancestors,

WILLFUL (1) [WILL]

2Pe 2:10 Bold and **w,** they are not afraid to slander

WILLFULLY (4) [WILL]

Ex 21:14 someone **w** attacks and kills another by treachery,
Heb 10:26 For if we **w** persist in sin after having received
2Mc 14: 3 but had **w** defiled himself in the times
3Mc 7:10 the Jewish nation who had **w** transgressed against

WILLING (37) [WILL]

Ge 23: 8 "If you are **w** that I should bury my dead out
24: 5 the woman may not be **w** to follow me to this land;
24: 8 But if the woman is not **w** to follow you,
Ex 35:21 and everyone whose spirit was **w,**
35:22 all who were of a **w** heart brought brooches
35:29 and women whose hearts made them **w**
Dt 2:30 of Heshbon was not **w** to let us pass through,
Ru 3:13 If he is not **w** to act as next-of-kin for you, then,
1Ki 22:49 but Jehoshaphat was not **w.**
2Ki 24: 4 and the LORD was not **w** to pardon.
1Ch 19:19 not **w** to help the Ammonites any more.
28: 9 and serve him with single mind and **w** heart;
2Ch 29:31 all who were of a **w** heart brought burnt offerings.
Job 39: 9 "Is the wild ox **w** to serve you?
Ps 51:12 and sustain in me a **w** spirit.
Pr 31:13 She seeks wool and flax, and works with **w** hands.
Isa 1:19 If you are **w** and obedient,
Eze 3: 7 for they are not **w** to listen to me;
Mt 11:14 and if you are **w** to accept it,
23:37 under her wings, and you were not **w!**
26:41 the spirit indeed is **w,** but the flesh is weak."
Mk 14:38 the spirit indeed is **w,** but the flesh is weak."
Lk 13:34 under her wings, and you were not **w!**
22:42 if you are **w,** remove this cup from me;
Jn 5:35 and you were **w** to rejoice for a while in his light.
Ac 26: 5 if they are **w** to testify,
1Co 16:12 but he was not at all **w** to come now.
Heb 12: 9 even more **w** to be subject to the Father of spirits
Jas 3:17 gentle, **w** to yield, full of mercy and good fruits,
AdE 13:13 for I would have been **w** to kiss the soles
Sir 6:32 If you are **w,** my child, you can be disciplined,
39: 6 the great Lord is **w,** he will be filled with the spirit
2Mc 1: 3 to do his will with a strong heart and a **w** spirit.
3Mc 3:28 Any who are **w** to give information will receive
4Mc 5: 3 If any were not **w** to eat defiling food,
9:27 torturing him, they inquired if he were **w** to eat,
11:13 When the tyrant inquired whether he was **w** to eat

WILLINGLY (18) [WILL]

Dt 15: 8 **w** lending enough to meet the need,
Jdg 5: 2 when the people offer themselves **w**—
5: 9 of Israel who offered themselves **w** among
8:25 "We will **w** give them," they answered.
1Ch 29: 5 then will offer **w,** consecrating themselves today
29: 9 the people rejoiced because these had given **w,**
2Ch 35: 8 His officials contributed **w** to the people,
Ezr 7:16 given **w** for the house of their God in Jerusalem.
Ne 11: 2 the people blessed all those who **w** offered to live
Ps 110: 3 Your people will offer themselves **w** on
La 3:33 for he does not **w** afflict or grieve anyone.
1Pe 5: 2 not under compulsion but **w,**
1Mc 2:42 all who offered themselves **w** for the law.
8:27 the Romans shall **w** act as their allies,
2Mc 6:28 to die a good death **w** and nobly for the revered
3Mc 6:26 toward us and often have accepted **w** the worst
2Es 8:28 but remember those who have **w** acknowledged
4Mc 5:23 so that we endure any suffering **w;**

WILLOW (1) [WILLOWS]

Eze 17: 5 A plant by abundant waters, he set it like a **w** twig.

WILLOWS (5) [WILLOW]

Lev 23:40 boughs of leafy trees, and **w** of the brook;
Job 40:22 the **w** of the wadi surround it.
Ps 137: 2 On the **w** there we hung up our harps.
Isa 15: 7 up they carry away over the Wadi of the **W.**
44: 4 like **w** by flowing streams.

WILLS (6) [WILL]

Dt 21:16 on the day when he **w** his possessions to his sons,
Da 4:35 and he does what he **w** with the host of heaven and
Ac 18:21 he said, "I will return to you, if God **w.**"
1Co 4:19 But I will come to you soon, if the Lord **w,**
Col 4:12 and fully assured in everything that God **w.**
Wis 9:13 Or who can discern what the Lord **w?**

WILY (2) [WILES]

Job 5:13 the schemes of the **w** are brought to a quick end.
Pr 7:10 decked out like a prostitute, **w** of heart.

WIN (16) [WINNING, WINS, WON]

2Ch 32: 1 thinking to **w** them for himself.
Ps 44: 3 for not by their own sword did they **w** the land,
Ac 7:10 and enabled him to **w** favor and to show wisdom
Ro 15:18 through me to **w** obedience from the Gentiles,
1Co 9:19 so that I might **w** more of them.
9:20 To the Jews I became as a Jew, in order to **w** Jews.
9:20 not under the law) so that I might **w** those under
9:21 under Christ's law) so that I might **w** those outside
9:22 so that I might **w** the weak.
9:24 Run in such a way that you may **w** it.
1Pe 5: 4 you will **w** the crown of glory
1Mc 3:14 a name for myself and **w** honor in the kingdom.
6:44 So he gave his life to save his people and to **w**
14:35 the glory that he had resolved to **w** for his nation,
2Mc 4:45 to Ptolemy son of Dorymenes to **w** over the king.
1Es 4: 5 if they **w** the victory, they bring everything to

WIND‡ (167) [WHIRLWIND, WHIRLWINDS, WINDBLOWN, WINDFALL, WINDING, WINDS, WINDSTORM, WINDY]

A. EAST WIND (19)

Ge 1: 2 a **w** from God swept over the face of the waters.
8: 1 And God made a **w** blow over the earth,
41: 6 seven ears, thin and blighted by the east **w,** A
41:23 and blighted by the east **w,** sprouting after them; A
41:27 are the seven empty ears blighted by the east **w.** A
Ex 10:13 the LORD brought an east **w** upon the land A
10:13 the east **w** had brought the locusts. A
10:19 changed the **w** into a very strong west **w,** which lifted the locusts
14:21 by a strong east **w** all night, and turned the sea A
15:10 You blew with your **w,** the sea covered them;
Nu 11:31 Then a **w** went out from the LORD,
2Sa 22:11 he was seen upon the wings of the **w.**
1Ki 18:45 while the heavens grew black with clouds and **w;**
19:11 a great **w,** so strong that it was splitting mountains
19:11 but the LORD was not in the **w;**
19:11 and after the **w** an earthquake,
2Ki 3:17 'You shall see neither **w** nor rain,
Job 1:19 and suddenly a great **w** came across the desert,
6:26 as if the speech of the desperate were **w?**
8: 2 and the words of your mouth be a great **w?**
15: 2 and fill themselves with the east **w?** A
15:30 and their blossom will be swept away by the **w.**
21:18 How often are they like straw before the **w,**
26:13 By his **w** the heavens were made fair;
27:21 The east **w** lifts them up and they are gone; A
28:25 When he gave to the **w** its weight,
30:15 my honor is pursued as by the **w,**
30:22 You lift me up on the **w,** you make me ride on it,
37:17 when the earth is still because of the south **w?**
37:21 when the **w** has passed and cleared them.
38:24 or where the east **w** is scattered upon the earth? A
Ps 1: 4 but are like chaff that the **w** drives away.
11: 6 a scorching **w** shall be the portion of their cup.
18:10 he came swiftly upon the wings of the **w.**
18:42 I beat them fine, like dust before the **w;**
35: 5 Let them be like chaff before the **w,**
48: 7 as when an east **w** shatters the ships of Tarshish. A
55: 8 to find a shelter for myself from the raging **w**
78:26 He caused the east **w** to blow in the heavens, A
78:26 and by his power he led out the south **w;**
78:39 a **w** that passes and does not come again
83:13 like whirling dust, like chaff before the **w.**
103:16 for the **w** passes over it,
104: 3 you ride on the wings of the **w,**
107:25 For he commanded and raised the stormy **w,**
135: 7 the rain and brings out the **w** from his storehouses.
147:18 he makes his **w** blow, and the waters flow.
148: 8 snow and frost, stormy **w** fulfilling his command!
Pr 11:29 Those who trouble their households will inherit **w,**
25:14 Like clouds and **w** without rain is one who boasts
25:23 The north **w** produces rain,
27:16 to restrain her is to restrain the **w** or to grasp oil in
30: 4 Who has gathered the **w** in the hollow of the hand?
Ecc 1: 6 **w** blows to the south, and goes around to the north;
1: 6 round goes the **w,** and on its circuits the **w** returns.
1:14 and see, all is vanity and a chasing after **w.**
1:17 I perceived that this also is but a chasing after **w.**
2:11 and again, all was vanity and a chasing after **w,**
2:17 for all is vanity and a chasing after **w.**
2:26 This also is vanity and a chasing after **w.**
4: 4 This also is vanity and a chasing after **w.**
4: 6 with toil, and a chasing after **w.**
4:16 Surely this also is vanity and a chasing after **w.**
5:16 what gain do they have from toiling for the **w?**
6: 9 this also is vanity and a chasing after **w.**
8: 8 No one has power over the **w** to restrain the **w,**
11: 4 Whoever observes the **w** will not sow;
SS 4:16 Awake, O north **w,** and come, O south **w!**
Isa 7: 2 as the trees of the forest shake before the **w.**
11:15 over the River with his scorching **w;**
17:13 on the mountains before the **w** and whirling dust
26:18 we writhed, but we gave birth only to **w.**
27: 8 in the day of the east **w.** A
32: 2 Each will be like a hiding place from the **w,**
41:16 and the **w** shall carry them away,
41:29 their images are empty **w.**
49:10 neither scorching **w** nor sun shall strike them
57:13 The **w** will carry them off,
59:19 for he will come like a pent-up stream that the **w** of
64: 6 and our iniquities, like the **w,** take us away.
Jer 2:24 in her heat sniffing the **w!**
4:11 A hot **w** comes from me out of the bare heights in
4:12 a **w** too strong for that.
5:13 The prophets are nothing but **w,**
10:13 and he brings out the **w** from his storehouses.
13:24 I will scatter you like chaff driven by the **w** from
18:17 Like the **w** from the east,
22:22 The **w** shall shepherd all your shepherds,
49:32 scatter to every **w** those who have shaven temples,
51: 1 up a destructive **w** against Babylon and against
51:16 and he brings out the **w** from his storehouses.
Eze 1: 4 As I looked, a stormy **w** came out of the north:
5: 2 and one third you shall scatter to the **w,**
5:10 any of you who survive I will scatter to every **w.**
5:12 to every **w** and will unsheathe the sword
12:14 I will scatter to every **w** all who are around him,
13:11 and a stormy **w** will break out.
13:13 In my wrath I will make a stormy **w** break out,
17:10 When the east **w** strikes it, A
17:21 and the survivors shall be scattered to every **w;**
19:12 the east **w** dried it up; its fruit was stripped off, A
27:26 east **w** has wrecked you in the heart of the seas. A
Da 2:35 and the **w** carried them away,
Hos 4:19 A **w** has wrapped them in its wings,
8: 7 they sow the **w,** and they shall reap the whirlwind.
12: 1 Ephraim herds the **w,** and pursues the east wind
12: 1 and pursues the east **w** all day long; A
13:15 the east **w** shall come, a blast from the LORD, A
Am 4:13 the one who forms the mountains, creates the **w,**
Jnh 1: 4 But the LORD hurled a great **w** upon the sea,
4: 8 the sun rose, God prepared a sultry east **w,** A
Hab 1:11 Then they sweep by like the **w;**
Zec 5: 9 The **w** was in their wings;
Mt 11: 7 A reed shaken by the **w?**
14:24 was far from the land, for the **w** was against them.
14:30 But when he noticed the strong **w,**
14:32 When they got into the boat, the **w** ceased.
Mk 4:39 He woke up and rebuked the **w,**
4:39 Then the **w** ceased, and there was a dead calm.
4:41 that even the **w** and the sea obey him?"
6:48 at the oars against an adverse **w,**
6:51 he got into the boat with them and the **w** ceased.
Lk 7:24 A reed shaken by the **w?**
8:24 up and rebuked the **w** and the raging waves;
12:55 And when you see the south **w** blowing, you say,
Jn 3: 8 The **w** blows where it chooses,
6:18 because a strong **w** was blowing.
Ac 2: 2 a sound like the rush of a violent **w,**
27: 7 and as the **w** was against us,
27:13 When a moderate south **w** began to blow,
27:14 But soon a violent **w,** called the northeaster,
27:15 and could not be turned head-on into the **w,**
27:40 then hoisting the foresail to the **w,**
28:13 After one day there a south **w** sprang up,
Eph 4:14 to and fro and blown about by every **w** of doctrine,
Jas 1: 6 driven and tossed by the **w;**
Rev 7: 1 the earth so that no **w** could blow on earth or sea or
Wis 4: 4 standing insecurely they will be shaken by the **w,**
5:14 of the ungodly is like thistledown carried by the **w,**
5:14 it is dispersed like smoke before the **w,**
5:23 a mighty **w** will rise against them,
13: 2 but they supposed that either fire or **w** or swift air,
17:18 Whether there came a whistling **w,**
Sir 5: 9 Do not winnow in every **w,** or follow every path.
22:18 on a high place will not stand firm against the **w;**
34: 2 one who catches at a shadow and pursues the **w,**
34:19 from scorching **w** and a shade from noonday sun,
43:16 At his will the south **w** blows;
43:20 cold north **w** blows, and ice freezes on the water;
LtJ 6:61 and the **w** likewise blows in every land.
Aza 1:27 of the furnace as though a moist **w** were whistling
Bel 1:36 the speed of the **w** he set him down in Babylon,
3Mc 2:22 on this side and that as a reed is shaken by the **w,**
2Es 1:33 I will drive you out as the **w** drives straw;
3:19 through the four gates of fire and earthquake and **w**
4: 5 or measure for me a blast of **w,**
4: 9 But now I have asked you only about fire and **w**
7:40 or **w** or water or air,
8:22 at whose command they are changed to **w** and fire,
13: 2 a **w** arose from the sea and stirred up all its waves.
13: 3 As I kept looking the **w** made something like
13:27 for your seeing **w** and fire and a storm coming out
15:39 that was to cause destruction by the east **w** shall A

WINDBLOWN (1) [WIND]

Job 13:25 Will you frighten a **w** leaf and pursue dry chaff?

WINDFALL (3) [WIND]

Sir 20: 9 and a **w** may result in a loss.
29: 4 Many regard a loan as a **w,**
29: 6 and will regard that as a **w.**

WINDING (1) [WIND]

1Ki 6: 8 one went up by **w** stairs to the middle story,

WINDOW‡ (19) [WINDOWS]

Ge 8: 6 the end of forty days Noah opened the **w** of the ark
26: 8 of a **w** and saw him fondling his wife Rebekah.
Jos 2:15 Then she let them down by a rope through the **w**,
2:18 and you do not tie this crimson cord in the **w**
2:21 Then she tied the crimson cord in the **w**.
Jdg 5:28 of the **w** she peered, the mother of Sisera gazed
1Sa 19:12 So Michal let David down through the **w**;
2Sa 6:16 Michal daughter of Saul looked out of the **w**,
1Ki 7: 4 There were **w** frames in the three rows,
2Ki 9:30 and adorned her head, and looked out of the **w**.
9:32 He looked up to the **w** and said,
13:17 he said, "Open the **w** eastward"; and he opened it.
1Ch 15:29 Michal daughter of Saul looked out of the **w**,
Pr 7: 6 the **w** of my house I looked out through my lattice,
Hos 13: 3 from the threshing floor or like smoke from a **w**.
Zep 2:14 the owl shall hoot at the **w**,
Ac 20: 9 who was sitting in the **w**,
2Co 11:33 I was let down in a basket through a **w** in the wall,
Tob 3:11 with hands outstretched toward the **w**,

WINDOWS (28) [WINDOW]

Ge 7:11 and the **w** of the heavens were opened.
8: 2 of the deep and the **w** of the heavens were closed,
1Ki 6: 4 For the house he made **w** with recessed frames.
2Ki 7: 2 "Even if the LORD were to make **w** in the sky,
7:19 "Even if the LORD were to make **w** in the sky,
Ecc 12: 3 and those who look through the **w** see dimly;
SS 2: 9 gazing in at the **w**, looking through the lattice.
Isa 24:18 For the **w** of heaven are opened,
60: 8 and like doves to their **w**?
Jer 9:21 "Death has come up into our **w**,
22:14 and who cuts out **w** for it, paneling it with cedar,
Eze 40:16 The recesses and their pilasters had **w**,
40:16 the vestibules also had **w** on the inside all around;
40:22 Its **w**, its vestibule, and its palm trees were of
40:25 There were **w** all around in it and in its vestibule,
40:25 like the **w** of the others;
40:29 there were **w** all around in it and in its vestibule;
40:33 there were **w** all around in it and in its vestibule;
40:36 and it had **w** all around.
41:16 all around, all three had **w** with recessed frames.
41:16 up to the **w** (now the **w** were covered),
41:26 And there were recessed **w** and palm trees on
Da 6:10 which had **w** in its upper room open
Joel 2: 9 they enter through the **w** like a thief.
Mal 3:10 if I will not open the **w** of heaven for you and pour
Sir 14:23 who peers through her **w** and listens at her doors;
2Mc 3:19 while others peered out of the **w**.

WINDS‡ (31) [WIND]

Job 37: 9 and cold from the scattering **w**.
Ps 104: 4 you make the **w** your messengers,
Jer 49:36 upon Elam the four **w** from the four quarters
49:36 and I will scatter them to all these **w**,
Eze 37: 9 Come from the four **w**, O breath,
Da 7: 2 in my vision by night the four **w** of heaven stirring
8: 8 up four prominent horns toward the four **w**
11: 4 the four **w** of heaven, but not to his posterity,
Zec 2: 6 for I have spread you abroad like the four **w**
6: 5 "These are the four **w** of heaven going out,
Mt 7:25 and the **w** blew and beat on that house,
7:27 and the **w** blew and beat against that house,
8:26 Then he got up and rebuked the **w** and the sea;
8:27 that even the **w** and the sea obey him?"
24:31 and they will gather his elect from the four **w**,
Mk 13:27 and gather his elect from the four **w**,
Lk 8:25 that he commands even the **w** and the water,
Ac 27: 4 because the **w** were against us.
Heb 1: 7 "He makes his angels **w**, and his servants flames
Jas 3: 4 though they are so large that it takes strong **w**
Jude 1:12 They are waterless clouds carried along by the **w**;
Rev 7: 1 the four **w** of the earth so that no wind could blow
Wis 4: 4 and by the violence of the **w** they will be uprooted.
Sir 39:28 "There are **w** created for vengeance,
Aza 1:43 Bless the Lord, all you **w**;
2Es 5:37 and bring out for me the **w** shut up in them,
6: 1 and before the assembled **w** blew,
11: 2 and all the **w** of heaven blew upon it,
13: 5 of people were gathered together from the four **w**
15:39 But the **w** from the east shall prevail over the cloud
4Mc 15:32 by the flood of your emotions and the violent **w**,

WINDSTORM (3) [STORM, WIND]

Mt 8:24 A **w** arose on the sea, so great that
Mk 4:37 A great **w** arose, and the waves beat into the boat,
Lk 8:23 A **w** swept down on the lake,

WINDY (2) [WIND]

Job 15: 2 "Should the wise answer with **w** knowledge,
16: 3 Have **w** words no limit?

WINDY (KJV) See also TEMPEST

WINE‡ (297) [WINE-CUP, WINE-DRINKERS, WINE-DRINKING, WINE-JAR, WINEBIBBERS, WINES, WINESKIN, WINESKINS, WINEVAT]

A. NEW WINE (14)

Ge 9:21 He drank some of the **w** and became drunk,
9:24 When Noah awoke from his **w**
14:18 of Salem brought out bread and **w**;
19:32 Come, let us make our father drink **w**,
19:33 So they made their father drink **w** that night;
19:34 let us make him drink **w** tonight also;
19:35 So they made their father drink **w** that night also;
27:25 and he brought him **w**, and he drank.
27:28 and plenty of grain and **w**.
27:37 and with grain and **w** I have sustained him.
49:11 he washes his garments in **w** and his robe in
49:12 his eyes are darker than **w**,
Ex 29:40 and one-fourth of a hin of **w** for a drink offering.
Lev 10: 9 Drink no **w** or strong drink, neither you
23:13 and the drink offering with it shall be of **w**,
Nu 6: 3 they shall separate themselves from **w**
6: 3 they shall drink no **w** vinegar or other vinegar,
6:20 After that the nazirites may drink **w**.
15: 5 of **w** as a drink offering with the burnt offering or
15: 7 of a hin of **w**, a pleasing odor to the LORD.
15:10 as a drink offering half a hin of **w**,
18:12 of the oil and all the best of the **w** and of the grain,
18:27 the threshing floor and the fullness of the **w** press.
18:30 and as produce of the **w** press.
28:14 Their drink offerings shall be half a hin of **w** for
Dt 7:13 your grain and your **w** and your oil,
11:14 and you will gather in your grain, your **w**,
12:17 your **w**, and your oil, the firstlings of your herds
14:23 you shall eat the tithe of your grain, your **w**,
14:26 oxen, sheep, **w**, strong drink,
15:14 your threshing floor, and your **w** press,
16:13 from your threshing floor and your **w** press.
18: 4 The first fruits of your grain, your **w**, and your oil,
28:39 you shall neither drink the **w** nor gather the grapes,
28:51 leaving you neither grain, **w**, and oil,
29: 6 and you have not drunk **w** or strong drink—
32:14 you drank fine **w** from the blood of grapes.
32:33 their **w** is the poison of serpents,
32:38 and drank the **w** of their libations?
33:28 of grain and **w**, where the heavens drop down dew.
Jdg 6:11 in the **w** press, to hide it from
7:25 and Zeeb they killed at the **w** press of Zeeb,
9:13 'Shall I stop producing my **w** that cheers gods
13: 4 Now be careful not to drink **w** or strong drink,
13: 7 So then drink no **w** or strong drink,
13:14 She is not to drink **w** or strong drink,
19:19 and **w** for me and the woman and the young man
Ru 2:14 and dip your morsel in the sour **w**."
1Sa 1:11 He shall drink neither **w** nor intoxicants,
1:14 of yourself? Put away your **w**."
1:15 I have drunk neither **w** nor strong drink,
1:24 an ephah of flour, and a skin of **w**.
10: 3 and another carrying a skin of **w**.
16:20 a skin of **w**, and a kid,
25:18 two skins of **w**, five sheep ready dressed,
25:37 In the morning, when the **w** had gone out of Nabal,
2Sa 13:28 "Watch when Amnon's heart is merry with **w**,
16: 1 one hundred of summer fruits, and one skin of **w**.
16: 2 and the **w** is for those to drink who faint in
2Ki 6:27 From the threshing floor or from the **w** press?"
18:32 a land of grain and **w**,
1Ch 9:29 the **w**, the oil, the incense, and the spices.
12:40 **w**, oil, oxen, and sheep, for there was joy in Israel.
27:27 of the vineyards for the **w** cellars was Zabdi
2Ch 2:10 twenty thousand baths of **w**,
2:15 Now, as for the wheat, barley, oil, and **w**,
11:11 and stores of food, oil, and **w**.
31: 5 **w**, oil, honey, and of all the produce of the field;
32:28 also for the yield of grain, **w**, and oil;
Ezr 6: 9 salt, **w**, or oil, as the priests in Jerusalem require—
7:22 one hundred baths of **w**, one hundred baths of oil,
Ne 2: 1 of King Artaxerxes, when **w** was served him,
2: 1 I carried the **w** and gave it to the king.
5:11 and the interest on money, grain, **w**,
5:15 and took food and **w** from them,
5:18 and every ten days skins of **w** in abundance;
8:10 eat the fat and drink sweet **w** and send portions
10:37 the fruit of every tree, the **w** and the oil,
10:39 **w**, and oil to the storerooms where the vessels of
13: 5 the vessels, and the tithes of grain, **w**, and oil,
13:12 Then all Judah brought the tithe of the grain, **w**,
13:15 in Judah people treading **w** presses on the sabbath,
13:15 and also **w**, grapes, figs, and all kinds of burdens,
Est 1: 7 the royal **w** was lavished according to the bounty
1:10 when the king was merry with **w**,
5: 6 While they were drinking **w**,
7: 2 On the second day, as they were drinking **w**,
Job 1:13 and drinking **w** in the eldest brother's house,
1:18 and drinking **w** in their eldest brother's house,
24:11 they tread the **w** presses, but suffer thirst.
32:19 My heart is indeed like **w** that has no vent;
Ps 4: 7 when their grain and **w** abound.
60: 3 you have given us **w** to drink that made us reel.
75: 8 of the LORD there is a cup with foaming **w**,
78:65 like a warrior shouting because of **w**.
104:15 and **w** to gladden the human heart,
Pr 3:10 and your vats will be bursting with **w**.
4:17 of wickedness and drink the **w** of violence.
9: 2 she has mixed her **w**, she has also set her table.
9: 5 eat of my bread and drink of the **w** I have mixed.
20: 1 **W** is a mocker, strong drink a brawler,
21:17 whoever loves **w** and oil will not be rich.
23:30 Those who linger late over **w**,
23:31 Do not look at **w** when it is red,
31: 4 O Lemuel, it is not for kings to drink **w**,
31: 6 and **w** to those in bitter distress;
Ecc 2: 3 with my mind how to cheer my body with **w**—
9: 7 and drink your **w** with a merry heart;
10:19 **w** gladdens life, and money meets every need.
SS 1: 2 For your love is better than **w**,
1: 4 we will extol your love more than **w**;
4:10 how much better is your love than **w**,
5: 1 I drink my **w** with my milk.
7: 2 a rounded bowl that never lacks mixed **w**.
7: 9 like the best **w** that goes down smoothly,
8: 2 I would give you spiced **w** to drink,
Isa 1:22 your **w** is mixed with water.
5: 2 and hewed out a **w** vat in it;
5:11 who linger in the evening to be inflamed by **w**,
5:12 tambourine and flute and **w**,
5:22 you who are heroes in drinking **w** and valiant
16:10 no treader treads out **w** in the presses;
22:13 eating meat and drinking **w**.
24: 7 The **w** dries up, the vine languishes,
24: 9 No longer do they drink **w** with singing;
24:11 There is an outcry in the streets for lack of **w**;
28: 1 of those overcome with **w**!
28: 7 also reel with **w** and stagger with strong drink;
28: 7 they are confused with **w**,
29: 9 Be drunk, but not from **w**;
36:17 a land of grain and **w**,
49:26 be drunk with their own blood as with **w**.
51:21 who are drunk, but not with **w**:
55: 1 Come, buy **w** and milk without money and
56:12 "Come," they say, "let us get **w**;
62: 8 not drink the **w** for which you have labored;
63: 2 your garments like theirs who tread the **w** press?"
63: 3 "I have trodden the **w** press alone,
65: 8 As the **w** is found in the cluster, and they say,
65:11 for Fortune and fill cups of mixed **w** for Destiny;
Jer 13:12 Every wine-jar should be filled with **w**.
13:12 that every wine-jar should be filled with **w**?"
23: 9 like a drunkard, like one overcome by **w**,
25:15 Take from my hand this cup of the **w** of wrath,
31:12 over the grain, the **w**, and the oil,
35: 2 then offer them **w** to drink.
35: 5 Then I set before the Rechabites pitchers full of **w**,
35: 5 and I said to them, "Have some **w**."
35: 6 But they answered, "We will drink no **w**,
35: 6 'You shall never drink **w**, neither you
35: 8 to drink no **w** all our days, ourselves, our wives,
35:14 of Rechab gave to his descendants to drink no **w**;
40:10 but as for you, gather **w** and summer fruits and oil,
40:12 and they gathered **w** and summer fruits
48:11 settled like **w** on its dregs;
48:33 I have stopped the **w** from the **w** presses;
51: 7 the nations drank of her **w**,
La 1:15 as in a **w** press the virgin daughter Judah.
2:12 to their mothers, "Where is bread and **w**?"
Eze 27:18 **w** of Helbon, and white wool.
44:21 No priest shall drink **w** when he enters
Da 1: 5 a daily portion of the royal rations of food and **w**.
1: 8 with the royal rations of food and **w**;
1:16 to withdraw their royal rations and the **w** they were
5: 1 he was drinking **w** in the presence of the thousand.
5: 2 Under the influence of the **w**,
5: 4 They drank the **w** and praised the gods of gold
5:23 and your concubines have been drinking **w**
10: 3 no meat or **w** had entered my mouth,
Hos 2: 8 that it was I who gave her the grain, the **w**, and
2: 9 and my **w** in its season;
2:22 the **w**, and the oil, and they shall answer Jezreel;
3: 2 and a homer of barley and a measure of **w**.
4:11 **W** and new wine take away the understanding.
4:11 Wine and new **w** take away the understanding. A
7: 5 the officials became sick with the heat of **w**;
7:14 they gash themselves for grain and **w**;
9: 2 Threshing floor and **w** vat shall not feed them,
9: 2 and the new **w** shall fail them. A
9: 4 not pour drink offerings of **w** to the LORD,
14: 7 their fragrance shall be like the **w** of Lebanon.
Joel 1: 5 over the sweet **w**, for it is cut off from your mouth.
1:10 the grain is destroyed, the **w** dries up, the oil fails.
2:19 I am sending you grain, **w**, and oil,
2:24 the vats shall overflow with **w** and oil.
3: 3 and sold girls for **w**, and drunk it down.
3:13 Go in, tread, for the **w** press is full.
3:18 In that day the mountains shall drip sweet **w**,
Am 2: 8 and in the house of their God they drink **w** bought
2:12 But you made the nazirites drink **w**,
5:11 but you shall not drink their **w**.
6: 6 who drink **w** from bowls, and anoint themselves
9:13 the mountains shall drip sweet **w**,
9:14 they shall plant vineyards and drink their **w**,
Mic 2:11 "I will preach to you of **w** and strong drink,"
6:15 you shall tread grapes, but not drink **w**.
Zep 1:13 they shall not drink **w** from them.
Hag 1:11 the new **w**, the oil, on what the soil produces, A
2:12 and with the fold touches bread, or stew, or **w**,
Zec 9:15 they shall drink their blood like **w**,
9:17 and new **w** the young women. A
10: 7 and their hearts shall be glad as with **w**.
14:10 the Tower of Hananel to the king's **w** presses.
Mt 9:17 Neither is new **w** put into old wineskins; A
9:17 otherwise, the skins burst, and the **w** is spilled,
9:17 but new **w** is put into fresh wineskins, A
21:33 dug a **w** press in it, and built a watchtower.
27:34 they offered him **w** to drink, mixed with gall;
27:48 filled it with sour **w**, put it on a stick,
Mk 2:22 And no one puts new **w** into old wineskins; A
2:22 otherwise, the **w** will burst the skins,
2:22 the wine will burst the skins, and the **w** is lost,
2:22 but one puts new **w** into fresh wineskins." A
12: 1 dug a pit for the **w** press, and built a watchtower;
15:23 And they offered him **w** mixed with myrrh;
15:36 And someone ran, filled a sponge with sour **w**,

Lk 1:15 He must never drink w or strong drink;
5:37 And no one puts new w into old wineskins; A
5:37 new w will burst the skins and will be spilled, A
5:38 But new w must be put into fresh wineskins. A
5:39 And no one after drinking old w desires new wine,
5:39 no one after drinking old wine desires new w, A
7:33 and drinking no w, and you say, 'He has a demon';
10:34 having poured oil and w on them.
23:36 coming up and offering him sour w,
Jn 2:3 When the w gave out, the mother of Jesus said
2:3 the mother of Jesus said to him, "They have no w."
2:9 the steward tasted the water that had become w,
2:10 "Everyone serves the good w first,
2:10 the inferior w after the guests have become drunk.
2:10 But you have kept the good w until now."
4:46 in Galilee where he had changed the water into w.
19:29 A jar full of sour w was standing there.
19:29 So they put a sponge full of the w on a branch
19:30 Jesus had received the w, he said, "It is finished."
Ac 2:13 "They are filled with new w." A
Ro 14:21 it is good not to eat meat or drink w or do anything
Eph 5:18 Do not get drunk with w, for that is debauchery;
1Ti 3:8 not indulging in much w, not greedy for money;
5:23 but take a little w for the sake of your stomach
Tit 1:7 not be arrogant or quick-tempered or addicted to w
Rev 6:6 but do not damage the olive oil and the w!"
14:8 She has made all nations drink of the w of
14:10 they will also drink the w of God's wrath,
14:19 and he threw it into the great w press of the wrath
14:20 And the w press was trodden outside the city,
14:20 and blood flowed from the w press,
17:2 with the w of whose fornication the inhabitants of
18:3 the nations have drunk of the w of the wrath
18:13 frankincense, w, olive oil, choice flour and wheat,
19:15 he will tread the w press of the fury of the wrath
Tob 1:7 likewise the tenth of the grain, w, olive oil,
4:15 Do not drink w to excess or let drunkenness go
Jdt 10:5 She gave her maid a skin of w and a flask of oil,
11:13 the first fruits of the grain and the tithes of the w
12:1 and with some of his own w to drink.
12:13 and to enjoy drinking w with us,
12:20 and drank a great quantity of w,
AdE 1:7 There was abundant sweet w,
5:6 While they were drinking w,
7:2 And the second day, as they were drinking w,
14:17 not honored the king's feast or drunk the w
Wis 2:7 Let us take our fill of costly w and perfumes,
Sir 9:9 or revel with her at w;
9:10 A new friend is like new w; A
19:2 W and women lead intelligent men astray,
31:25 for w has destroyed many.
31:26 so w tests hearts when the insolent quarrel.
31:27 W is very life to human beings if taken
31:27 What is life to one who is without w?
31:28 W drunk at the proper time and
31:29 W drunk to excess leads to bitterness of spirit,
31:31 Do not reprove your neighbor at a banquet of w,
32:5 of gold is a concert of music at a banquet of w.
32:6 of gold is the melody of music with good w.
33:17 and like a grape-picker I filled my w press.
40:20 W and music gladden the heart,
49:1 and like music at a banquet of w.
Bel 1:3 and forty sheep and six measures of w.
1:11 O king, set out the food and prepare the w,
2Mc 15:39 For just as it is harmful to drink w alone, or, again,
15:39 while w mixed with water is sweet and delicious
1Es 3:10 The first wrote, "W is strongest."
3:17 the first, who had spoken of the strength of w,
3:18 how is w the strongest? It leads astray the minds
3:23 And when they recover from the w,
3:24 Gentlemen, is not w the strongest,
4:14 and are not men many, and is not w strong?
4:16 the vineyards from which comes w.
4:37 W is unrighteous, the king is unrighteous,
6:30 and likewise wheat and salt and w and oil,
8:20 a hundred baths of w, and salt in abundance.
3Mc 5:2 of frankincense and plenty of unmixed w,
5:10 with a great abundance of w and satiated
5:45 by the very fragrant draughts of w mixed
2Es 9:24 and taste no meat and drink no w,

WINE-CUP (1) [CUP, WINE]

Rev 16:19 and gave her the w of the fury of his wrath.

WINE-DRINKERS (1) [DRINK, WINE]

Joel 1:5 and wail, all you w, over the sweet wine,

WINE-DRINKING (1) [DRINK, WINE]

Sir 31:25 Do not try to prove your strength by w,

WINE-JAR (2) [JAR, WINE]

Jer 13:12 Every w should be filled with wine.
13:12 not know that every w should be filled with wine?"

WINEBIBBER[S] (KJV) See also DRUNKARD

WINEBIBBERS (1) [WINE]

Pr 23:20 be among w, or among gluttonous eaters of meat;

WINEFAT (KJV) See WINE PRESS

WINES (4) [WINE]

Pr 23:30 those who keep trying mixed w.
Isa 25:6 of well-aged w, of rich food filled with marrow,
25:6 of well-aged w strained clear.
3Mc 6:30 to the Jews both w and everything else needed for

WINESKIN (1) [SKIN, WINE]

Ps 119:83 For I have become like a w in the smoke,

WINESKINS‡ (9) [SKIN, WINE]

Jos 9:4 and took worn-out sacks for their donkeys, and w,
9:13 these w were new when we filled them,
Job 32:19 like new w, it is ready to burst.
Mt 9:17 Neither is new wine put into old w;
9:17 but new wine is put into fresh w,
Mk 2:22 And no one puts new wine into old w;
2:22 but one puts new wine into fresh w."
Lk 5:37 And no one puts new wine into old w;
5:38 But new wine must be put into fresh w.

WINEVAT (1) [VAT, WINE]

Hag 2:16 when one came to the w to draw fifty measures,

WING (23) [WINGED, WINGS]

1Ki 6:24 Five cubits was the length of one w of the cherub,
6:24 five cubits the length of the other w of the cherub;
6:24 it was ten cubits from the tip of one w to the tip of
6:27 a w of one was touching the one wall, and a w of
6:27 the center of the house were touching w to w.
2Ch 3:11 one w of the one, five cubits long, touched the wall of the house, and its other w, five cubits long, touched the w of the other cherub;
3:12 of this cherub, one w, five cubits long, touched the wall of the house, and the other w, also five cubits long was joined to the w of the first cherub.
Isa 10:14 and there was none that moved a w,
Eze 1:11 each of which touched the w of another,
1Mc 9:1 and with them the right w of the army.
9:12 Bacchides was on the right w.
9:15 and they crushed the right w,
9:16 on the left w saw that the right w was crushed,
2Es 11:12 As I watched, one w on the right side rose up,
11:13 Then the next w rose up and reigned,
11:18 Then the third w raised itself up,

WINGED (11) [WING]

Ge 1:21 and every w bird of every kind.
7:14 every bird, every w creature.
Lev 11:20 All w insects that walk upon all fours
11:21 But among the w insects that walk on all fours
11:23 But all other w insects that have four feet
Dt 4:17 the likeness of any w bird that flies in the air,
14:19 And all w insects are unclean for you;
14:20 You may eat any clean w creature.
Ps 78:27 w birds like the sand of the seas;
Ecc 10:20 or some w creature tell the matter.
Eze 17:23 of its branches will nest w creatures of every kind.

WINGS (101) [WING]

Ex 19:4 I bore you on eagles' w and brought you to myself.
25:20 The cherubim shall spread out their w above,
25:20 overshadowing the mercy seat with their w.
37:9 The cherubim spread out their w above, overshadowing the mercy seat with their w.
Lev 1:17 He shall tear it open by its w without severing it.
Dt 32:11 as it spreads its w, takes them up,
Ru 2:12 under whose w you have come for refuge!"
2Sa 22:11 he was seen upon the w of the wind.
1Ki 6:27 the w of the cherubim were spread out so that
6:27 their other w toward the center of
8:6 underneath the w of the cherubim.
8:7 For the cherubim spread out their w over the place
1Ch 28:18 of the cherubim that spread their w and covered
2Ch 3:11 The w of the cherubim together extended twenty
3:13 The w of these cherubim extended twenty cubits;
5:7 underneath the w of the cherubim.
5:8 For the cherubim spread out their w over the place
Job 39:13 "The ostrich's w flap wildly,
39:26 and spreads its w toward the south?
Ps 17:8 hide me in the shadow of your w,
18:10 he came swiftly upon the w of the wind.
36:7 in the shadow of your w.
55:6 And I say, "O that I had w like a dove!
57:1 in the shadow of your w I will take refuge,
61:4 find refuge under the shelter of your w.
63:7 and in the shadow of your w I sing for joy.
68:13 the w of a dove covered with silver,
91:4 and under his w you will find refuge;
104:3 you ride on the w of the wind,
139:9 If I take the w of the morning and settle at
Pr 23:5 for suddenly it takes w to itself,
Isa 6:2 above him; each had six w:
8:8 its outspread w will fill the breadth of your land,
18:1 land of whirring w beyond the rivers of Ethiopia,
40:31 they shall mount up with w like eagles,
Jer 48:40 and spread his w against Moab;
49:22 and spread his w against Bozrah,
Eze 1:6 Each had four faces, and each of them had four w.
1:8 Under their w on their four sides they had human
1:8 And the four had their faces and their w thus:
1:9 their w touched one another;
1:11 Their w were spread out above;
1:11 each creature had two w, each of which touched
1:23 the dome their w were stretched out straight, one
1:23 each of the creatures had two w covering its body.
1:24 of their w like the sound of mighty waters,
1:24 when they stopped, they let down their w.
1:25 when they stopped, they let down their w.
3:13 the sound of the w of the living creatures brushing
10:5 The sound of the w of the cherubim was heard
10:8 to have the form of a human hand under their w.
10:12 Their entire body, their rims, their spokes, their w,
10:16 when the cherubim lifted up their w to rise up from
10:19 up their w and rose up from the earth in my sight
10:21 Each had four faces, each four w,
10:21 underneath their w something like human hands.
11:22 Then the cherubim lifted up their w,
17:3 A great eagle, with great w and long pinions,
17:7 with great w and much plumage.
Da 7:4 The first was like a lion and had eagles' w.
7:4 Then, as I watched, its w were plucked off,
7:6 The beast had four w of a bird on its back
Hos 4:19 A wind has wrapped them in its w,
Zec 5:9 The wind was in their w; they had w like the w of a stork,
Mal 4:2 of righteousness shall rise, with healing in its w.
Mt 23:37 as a hen gathers her brood under her w,
Lk 13:34 as a hen gathers her brood under her w,
Rev 4:8 the four living creatures, each of them with six w,
9:9 of their w was like the noise of many chariots
12:14 the woman was given the two w of the great eagle,
Wis 5:11 is traversed by the movement of its w,
Sir 34:1 and dreams give w to fools.
2Es 1:30 as a hen gathers her chicks under her w.
11:1 from the sea an eagle that had twelve feathered w
11:2 I saw it spread its w over the whole earth,
11:3 I saw that out of its w there grew opposing w;
11:3 but they became little, puny w.
11:5 Then I saw that the eagle flew with its w,
11:7 and it uttered a cry to its w, saying,
11:11 I counted its rival w, and there were eight of them.
11:19 And so it went with all the w;
11:20 and in due time the w that followed also rose up on
11:22 And after this I looked and saw that the twelve w
11:22 and the two little w had disappeared,
11:23 the three heads that were at rest and six little w.
11:24 As I kept looking I saw that two little w separated
11:25 that these little w planned to set themselves up
11:31 and devoured the two little w that were planning
11:32 over the world than all the w that had gone before.
11:33 just as the w had done.
11:45 will surely disappear, you and your terrifying w,
11:45 your most evil little w, your malicious heads,
12:2 The two w that had gone over to it rose up
12:16 the interpretation of the twelve w that you saw.
12:19 for your seeing eight little w clinging to its w,
12:29 As for your seeing two little w passing over to

WINK (1) [WINKING, WINKS]

Ps 35:19 or those who hate me without cause w the eye.

WINKING (1) [WINK]

Pr 6:13 w the eyes, shuffling the feet, pointing the fingers,

WINKS (3) [WINK]

Pr 10:10 Whoever w the eye causes trouble,
16:30 One who w the eyes plans perverse things;
Sir 27:22 Whoever w the eye plots mischief,

WINNING (1) [WIN]

Ac 12:20 and after w over Blastus, the king's chamberlain,

WINNOW (5) [WINNOWED, WINNOWERS, WINNOWING, WINNOWS]

Isa 41:16 You shall w them and the wind shall carry them
Jer 4:11 toward my poor people, not to w or cleanse—
51:2 to Babylon, and they shall w her.
Wis 5:23 and like a tempest it will w them away.
Sir 5:9 Do not w in every wind, or follow every path.

WINNOWED (3) [WINNOW]

Isa 21:10 O my threshed and w one,
30:24 which has been w with shovel and fork.
Jer 15:7 I have w them with a winnowing fork in the gates

WINNOWERS (1) [WINNOW]

Jer 51:2 and I will send w to Babylon,

WINNOWING (4) [WINNOW]

Ru 3:2 See, he is w barley tonight at the threshing floor.
Jer 15:7 I have winnowed them with a w fork in the gates
Mt 3:12 His w fork is in his hand,
Lk 3:17 His w fork is in his hand,

WINNOWS (2) [WINNOW]

Pr 20:8 on the throne of judgment w all evil with his eyes.
20:26 A wise king w the wicked,

WINS (2) [WIN]

Pr 9:7 Whoever corrects a scoffer w abuse;
13:15 Good sense w favor, but the way of

WINTER‡ (20) [WINTERED, WINTRY]

Ge 8:22 summer and w, day and night, shall not cease."

Ps 74:17 of the earth; you made summer and **w**.
SS 2:11 for now the **w** is past, the rain is over and gone.
Isa 18: 6 and all the animals of the earth will **w** on them.
25: 4 the blast of the ruthless was like a **w** rainstorm,
Jer 36:22 the king was sitting in his **w** apartment (it was
Am 3:15 down the **w** house as well as the summer house;
Zec 14: 8 it shall continue in summer as in **w**.
Mt 24:20 that your flight may not be in **w** or on a sabbath.
Mk 13:18 Pray that it may not be in **w**.
Jn 10:22 the Dedication took place in Jerusalem. It was **w**,
Ac 27:12 the harbor was not suitable for spending the **w**,
27:12 where they could spend the **w**.
1Co 16: 6 perhaps I will stay with you or even spend the **w**,
2Ti 4:21 Do your best to come before **w**.
Tit 3:12 for I have decided to spend the **w** there.
Rev 6:13 the fig tree drops its **w** fruit when shaken by a gale.
Aza 1:45 Bless the Lord, **w** cold and summer heat;
1Es 9:11 But the multitude is great and it is **w**,
2Es 7:*41* or summer or spring or heat or **w** or frost or cold,

WINTERED (1) [WINTER]

Ac 28:11 Three months later we set sail on a ship that had **w**

WINTRY (2) [WINTER]

Wis 16:29 hope of an ungrateful person will melt like **w** frost,
4Mc 15:32 and withstood the **w** storms that assail religion.

WIPE (17) [WIPED, WIPES, WIPING]

1Sa 24:21 not **w** out my name from my father's house."
2Sa 21: 2 to **w** them out in his zeal for the people of Israel
2Ki 21:13 I will **w** Jerusalem as one wipes a dish,
Ne 13:14 and do not **w** out my good deeds that I have done
Ps 83: 4 They say, "Come, let us **w** them out as a nation;
94:23 and **w** them out for their wickedness;
94:23 the LORD our God will **w** them out.
Isa 25: 8 Lord GOD will **w** away the tears from all faces,
Lk 10:11 we **w** off in protest against you.
Jn 13: 5 to **w** them with the towel that was tied around him.
Rev 7:17 and God will **w** away every tear from their eyes."
21: 4 he will **w** every tear from their eyes.
Sir 36: 9 destroy the adversary and **w** out the enemy.
1Mc 3:35 to send a force against them to **w** out and destroy
2Mc 8: 9 to **w** out the whole race of Judea.
12: 8 in the same way to **w** out the Jews who were living
3Mc 2:19 **W** away our sins and disperse our errors,

WIPED (14) [WIPE]

Jos 10:20 on them, until they were **w** out,
11:21 that time Joshua came and **w** out the Anakim from
2Ki 10:17 until he had **w** them out,
10:28 Thus Jehu **w** out Baal from Israel.
Pr 6:33 and his disgrace will not be **w** away.
Isa 26:14 and **w** out all memory of them.
Eze 6: 6 down, and your works **w** out.
Jn 11: 2 the Lord with perfume and **w** his feet with her hair;
12: 3 anointed Jesus' feet, and **w** them with her hair.
Ac 3:19 and turn to God so that your sins may be **w** out,
Sir 47: 7 For he **w** out his enemies on every side,
48:21 and his angel **w** them out.
LtJ 6:13 their faces are **w** because of the dust from
2Es 15:57 your cities shall be **w** out,

WIPES (3) [WIPE]

2Ki 21:13 I will wipe Jerusalem as one **w** a dish,
Pr 30:20 she eats, and **w** her mouth, and says,
LtJ 6:24 it will not shine unless someone **w** off the tarnish;

WIPING (2) [WIPE]

2Ki 21:13 **w** it and turning it upside down.
Tob 7:16 Then, **w** away the tears, she said to her,

WIRES (KJV) See THREADS

WISDOM‡ (346) [WISE]

Dt 4: 6 for this will show your **w** and discernment to
34: 9 Joshua son of Nun was full of the spirit of **w**,
2Sa 14:20 But my lord has **w** like the **w** of the angel of God
1Ki 2: 6 Act therefore according to your **w**,
3:28 they perceived that the **w** of God was in him,
4:29 God gave Solomon very great **w**, discernment,
4:30 so that Solomon's **w** surpassed the **w** of all the
people of the east, and all the **w** of Egypt.
4:34 People came from all the nations to hear the **w**
4:34 the kings of the earth who had heard of his **w**.
5:12 the LORD gave Solomon **w**, as he promised him.
10: 4 When the queen of Sheba had observed all the **w**
10: 6 of your accomplishments and of your **w**,
10: 7 your **w** and prosperity far surpass the report
10: 8 who continually attend you and hear your **w**!
10:23 the kings of the earth in riches and in **w**.
10:24 the presence of Solomon to hear his **w**,
11:41 all that he did as well as his **w**,
2Ch 1:10 now **w** and knowledge to go out and come in
1:11 but have asked for **w** and knowledge for yourself
1:12 **w** and knowledge are granted to you.
9: 3 queen of Sheba had observed the **w** of Solomon,
9: 5 of your accomplishments and of your **w**,
9: 6 even half of the greatness of your **w** had been told
9: 7 who continually attend you and hear your **w**!
9:22 the kings of the earth in riches and in **w**.
9:23 the presence of Solomon to hear his **w**,
Ezr 7:25 Ezra, according to the God-given **w** you possess,
Job 4:21 and they die devoid of **w**.'
Job 11: 6 tell you the secrets of **w**! For **w** is many-sided.
12: 2 and **w** will die with you.
12:12 Is **w** with the aged, and understanding in length
12:13 "With God are **w** and strength;
12:16 With him are strength and **w**;
13: 5 you would only keep silent, that would be your **w**!
15: 8 And do you limit **w** to yourself?
26: 3 How you have counseled one who has no **w**,
28:12 "But where shall **w** be found?
28:18 the price of **w** is above pearls.
28:20 "Where then does **w** come from?
28:28 'Truly, the fear of the Lord, that is **w**;
32: 7 I said, 'Let days speak, and many years teach **w**.'
32:13 Yet do not say, 'We have found **w**;
33:33 not, listen to me; be silent, and I will teach you **w**."
38:36 Who has put **w** in the inward parts,
38:37 Who has the **w** to number the clouds?
39:17 because God has made it forget **w**,
39:26 "Is it by your **w** that the hawk soars,
Ps 37:30 The mouths of the righteous utter **w**,
49: 3 My mouth shall speak **w**;
51: 6 therefore teach me **w** in my secret heart.
104:24 In **w** you have made them all;
105:22 and to teach his elders **w**.
111:10 The fear of the LORD is the beginning of **w**;
Pr 1: 2 For learning about **w** and instruction,
1: 7 fools despise **w** and instruction.
1:20 **W** cries out in the street;
2: 2 to **w** and inclining your heart to understanding;
2: 6 For the LORD gives **w**; from his
2: 7 he stores up sound **w** for the upright;
2:10 for **w** will come into your heart,
3:13 Happy are those who find **w**,
3:19 The LORD by **w** founded the earth;
3:21 keep sound **w** and prudence,
4: 5 Get **w**; get insight:
4: 7 The beginning of **w** is this: Get **w**,
4:11 I have taught you the way of **w**;
5: 1 My child, be attentive to my **w**;
7: 4 Say to **w**, "You are my sister,"
8: 1 Does not **w** call, and does not understanding raise
8:11 for **w** is better than jewels,
8:12 I, **w**, live with prudence, and I attain knowledge
8:14 I have good advice and sound **w**;
9: 1 **W** has built her house, she has hewn her seven
9:10 The fear of the LORD is the beginning of **w**,
10:13 the lips of one who has understanding **w** is found,
10:31 The mouth of the righteous brings forth **w**,
11: 2 but **w** is with the humble.
13:10 but **w** is with those who take advice.
14: 6 A scoffer seeks **w** in vain,
14: 8 the **w** of the clever to understand where they go,
14:24 The crown of the wise is their **w**,
14:33 **W** is at home in the mind of the one who has
15:33 The fear of the LORD is instruction in **w**,
16:16 How much better to get **w** than gold!
16:22 **W** is a fountain of life to one who has it,
17:16 Why should fools have a price in hand to buy **w**,
17:24 The discerning person looks to **w**,
18: 4 the fountain of **w** is a gushing stream.
19: 8 To get **w** is to love oneself;
19:20 that you may gain **w** for the future.
21:30 No **w**, no understanding, no counsel,
23: 9 who will only despise the **w** of your words.
23:23 buy **w**, instruction, and understanding.
24: 3 By **w** a house is built,
24: 7 **W** is too high for fools;
24:14 Know that **w** is such to your soul;
28:26 but those who walk in **w** come through safely.
29: 3 A child who loves **w** makes a parent glad,
29:15 The rod and reproof give **w**,
30: 3 I have not learned **w**, nor have I knowledge of
31:26 She opens her mouth with **w**,
Ecc 1:13 applied my mind to seek and to search out by **w** all
1:16 I said to myself, "I have acquired great **w**,
1:16 and my mind has had great experience of **w**
1:17 to know **w** and to know madness and folly.
1:18 For in much **w** is much vexation,
2: 3 my mind still guiding me with **w**—
2: 9 also my **w** remained with me.
2:12 So I turned to consider **w** and madness and folly;
2:13 I saw that **w** excels folly as light excels darkness.
2:19 be master of all for which I toiled and used my **w**
2:21 with **w** and knowledge and skill must leave all to
2:26 For to the one who pleases him God gives **w**
7:10 For it is not from **w** that you ask this.
7:11 **W** is as good as an inheritance,
7:12 the protection of **w** is like the protection of money,
7:12 and the advantage of knowledge is that **w** gives life
7:19 **W** gives strength to the wise more than ten rulers
7:23 All this I have tested by **w**;
7:25 to search out and to seek **w** and the sum of things,
8: 1 **W** makes one's face shine,
8:16 When I applied my mind to know **w**,
9:10 for there is no work or thought or knowledge or **w**
9:13 I have also seen this example of **w** under the sun,
9:15 and he by his **w** delivered the city.
9:16 So I said, "**W** is better than might;
9:16 yet the poor man's **w** is despised,
9:18 **W** is better than weapons of war,
10: 1 so a little folly outweighs **w** and honor.
10:10 but **w** helps one to succeed.
Isa 10:13 and by my **w**, for I have understanding;
11: 2 the spirit of **w** and understanding,
28:29 he is wonderful in counsel, and excellent in **w**.
29:14 The **w** of their wise shall perish,
33: 6 abundance of salvation, **w**, and knowledge;
Isa 47:10 Your **w** and your knowledge led you astray,
Jer 8: 9 the word of the LORD, what **w** is in them?
9:23 Do not let the wise boast in their **w**,
10:12 who established the world by his **w**,
49: 7 Is there no longer **w** in Teman?
49: 7 perished from the prudent? Has their **w** vanished?
51:15 who established the world by his **w**,
Eze 28: 4 by your **w** and your understanding you have
28: 5 By your great **w** in trade you have increased your
28: 7 the beauty of your **w** and defile your splendor.
28:12 You were the signet of perfection, full of **w**
28:17 you corrupted your **w** for the sake
Da 1: 4 versed in every branch of **w**,
1:17 and skill in every aspect of literature and **w**;
1:20 of **w** and understanding concerning which
2:20 of God from age to age, for **w** and power are his.
2:21 he gives **w** to the wise and knowledge to those who
2:23 for you have given me **w** and power,
2:30 not been revealed to me because of any **w**
5:11 understanding, and **w** like the **w** of the gods.
5:14 understanding, and excellent **w** are found in you.
9:22 now come out to give you **w** and understanding.
Mic 6: 9 of the LORD cries to the city (it is sound **w**
Mt 11:19 Yet **w** is vindicated by her deeds."
12:42 the ends of the earth to listen to the **w** of Solomon,
13:54 did this man get this **w** and these deeds of power?
Mk 6: 2 What is this **w** that has been given to him?
Lk 1:17 and the disobedient to the **w** of the righteous,
2:40 The child grew and became strong, filled with **w**;
2:52 And Jesus increased in **w** and in years,
7:35 Nevertheless, **w** is vindicated by all her children."
11:31 the ends of the earth to listen to the **w** of Solomon,
11:49 Therefore also the **W** of God said,
21:15 and a **w** that none of your opponents will be able
Ac 6: 3 full of the Spirit and of **w**,
6:10 But they could not withstand the **w** and the Spirit
7:10 and to show **w** when he stood before Pharaoh,
7:22 in all the **w** of the Egyptians and was powerful
Ro 11:33 O the depth of the riches and **w** and knowledge
1Co 1:17 with eloquent **w**, so that the cross of Christ might
1:19 For it is written, "I will destroy the **w** of the wise,
1:20 Has not God made foolish the **w** of the world?
1:21 For since, in the **w** of God, the world did not know
God through **w**,
1:22 For Jews demand signs and Greeks desire **w**,
1:24 Christ the power of God and the **w** of God.
1:25 For God's foolishness is wiser than human **w**,
1:30 who became for us **w** from God,
2: 1 the mystery of God to you in lofty words or **w**.
2: 4 not with plausible words of **w**,
2: 5 that your faith might rest not on human **w** but on
2: 6 Yet among the mature we do speak **w**, though it is
not a **w** of this age or of the rulers of this age,
2: 7 But we speak God's **w**, secret and hidden,
2:13 of these things in words not taught by human **w**
3:19 For the **w** of this world is foolishness with God.
12: 8 through the Spirit the utterance of **w**,
2Co 1:12 not by earthly **w** but by the grace of God—
Eph 1: 8 that he lavished on us. With all **w** and insight
1:17 of **w** and revelation as you come to know him,
3:10 the church the **w** of God in its rich variety might
Col 1: 9 with the knowledge of God's will in all spiritual **w**
1:28 warning everyone and teaching everyone in all **w**,
2: 3 in whom are hidden all the treasures of **w**
2:23 These have indeed an appearance of **w**
3:16 teach and admonish one another in all **w**;
Jas 1: 5 If any of you is lacking in **w**, ask God,
3:13 with gentleness born of **w**.
3:15 Such **w** does not come down from above,
3:17 But the **w** from above is first pure, then peaceable,
2Pe 3:15 to you according to the **w** given him,
Rev 5:12 and wealth and **w** and might and honor and glory
7:12 and **w** and thanksgiving and honor and power
13:18 This calls for **w**: let anyone with understanding
17: 9 "This calls for a mind that has **w**:
Jdt 8:29 Today is not the first time your **w** has been shown,
11: 8 For we have heard of your **w** and skill,
11:20 They marveled at her **w** and said,
Wis 1: 4 because **w** will not enter a deceitful soul,
1: 6 For **w** is a kindly spirit, but will
3:11 those who despise **w** and instruction are miserable.
6: 9 so that you may learn **w** and not transgress.
6:12 **W** is radiant and unfading,
6:17 of **w** is the most sincere desire for instruction,
6:20 so the desire for **w** leads to a kingdom.
6:21 honor **w**, so that you may reign forever.
6:22 I will tell you what **w** is and how she came to be,
6:23 for envy does not associate with **w**.
7: 7 I called on God, and the spirit of **w** came to me.
7:12 I rejoiced in them all, because **w** leads them;
7:15 the guide even of **w** and the corrector of the wise.
7:22 for **w**, the fashioner of all things,
7:24 For **w** is more mobile than any motion;
7:28 so much as the person who lives with **w**.
7:30 but against **w** evil does not prevail.
8: 5 in life, what is richer than **w**, the active cause
8:17 that in kinship with **w** there is immortality,
8:21 that I would not possess **w** unless God gave her
9: 2 and by your **w** have formed humankind
9: 4 give me the **w** that sits by your throne,
9: 6 be regarded as nothing without the **w** that comes
9: 9 With you is **w**, she who knows your works
9:17 unless you have given **w** and sent your holy spirit
9:18 taught what pleases you, and were saved by **w**."
10: 1 **W** protected the first-formed father of the world,
10: 4 **w** again saved it, steering the righteous man by
10: 5 **W** also, when the nations in wicked

Wis 10: 6 **W** rescued a righteous man when
10: 8 For because they passed **w** by,
10: 9 **W** rescued from troubles those who served her.
10:13 a righteous man was sold, **w** did not desert him,
10:15 A holy people and blameless race **w** delivered
10:21 for **w** opened the mouths of those who were mute,
11: 1 **W** prospered their works by the hand of
14: 2 and **w** was the artisan who built it;
14: 5 that works of your **w** should not be without effect;
17: 7 and their boasted **w** was scornfully rebuked.
Sir Pr: 1 these we should praise Israel for instruction and **w**.
Pr: 1 to write something pertaining to instruction and **w**,
1: 1 All **w** is from the Lord,
1: 3 the abyss, and **w**—who can search them out?
1: 4 **W** was created before all other things,
1: 6 The root of **w**—to whom has it been revealed?
1:14 To fear the Lord is the beginning of **w**;
1:16 To fear the Lord is fullness of **w**;
1:18 The fear of the Lord is the crown of **w**,
1:20 To fear the Lord is the root of **w**,
1:25 In the treasuries of **w** are wise sayings,
1:26 If you desire **w**, keep the commandments,
1:27 For the fear of the Lord is **w** and discipline,
3:25 without knowledge there is no **w**.
4:11 **W** teaches her children and gives help
4:23 and do not hide your **w**.
4:24 For **w** becomes known through speech,
6:18 and when you have gray hair you will still find **w**.
6:22 For **w** is like her name;
6:37 and your desire for **w** will be granted.
7: 5 or display your **w** before the king.
10:26 a display of your **w** when you do your work,
11: 1 The **w** of the humble lifts their heads high,
14:20 Happy is the person who meditates on **w**
15: 1 and whoever holds to the law will obtain **w**.
15: 3 and give him the water of **w** to drink.
15:10 For in **w** must praise be uttered,
15:18 For great is the **w** of the Lord;
18:28 Every intelligent person knows **w**,
19:20 The whole of **w** is fear of the Lord,
19:20 and in all **w** there is the fulfillment of the law.
19:22 The knowledge of wickedness is not **w**,
19:23 and there is a fool who merely lacks **w**.
20:30 Hidden **w** and unseen treasure,
20:31 who hide their folly than those who hide their **w**.
21:11 and the fulfillment of the fear of the Lord is **w**.
21:18 Like a house in ruins is **w** to a fool,
22: 6 but a thrashing and discipline are at all times **w**.
23: 2 and the discipline of **w** over my mind,
24: 1 THE PRAISE OF W **W** praises herself,
24:25 It overflows, like the Pishon, with **w**,
24:28 The first man did not know **w** fully,
24:34 but for all who seek **w**.
25: 5 How attractive is **w** in the aged,
25:10 How great is the one who finds **w**!
33: 8 By the Lord's **w** they were distinguished,
34: 8 and **w** is complete in the mouth of the faithful.
37:21 since he is lacking in all **w**.
38:24 The **w** of the scribe depends on the opportunity
39: 1 He seeks out the **w** of all the ancients,
39: 6 of **w** of his own and give thanks to the Lord
39: 8 He will show the **w** of what he has learned,
39:10 Nations will speak of his **w**,
40:19 but better than either is the one who finds **w**.
41:14 hidden **w** and unseen treasure—
41:15 who hide their folly than those who hide their **w**.
42:21 He has set in order the splendors of his **w**;
43:33 and to the godly he has given **w**.
44:15 The assembly declares their **w**,
45:26 the Lord grant you **w** of mind to judge his people
50:27 whose mind poured forth **w**.
51:13 I sought **w** openly in my prayer.
51:17 to him who gives **w** I will give glory.
51:18 For I resolved to live according to **w**,
51:19 My soul grappled with **w**,
51:25 Acquire **w** for yourselves without money.
Bar 3: 9 O Israel; give ear, and learn **w**!
3:12 You have forsaken the fountain of **w**,
3:14 Learn where there is **w**, where there is strength,
3:23 have not learned the way to **w**,
3:28 so they perished because they had no **w**,
2Mc 2: 9 of **w** Solomon offered sacrifice for the dedication
1Es 3: 7 and because of his **w** he shall sit next to Darius
4:59 from you comes **w**, and yours is the glory.
4:60 Blessed are you, who have given me **w**;
8:23 "And you, Ezra, according to the **w** of God,
2Es 5: 9 and **w** shall withdraw into its chamber,
5:39 As for me, I am without **w**,
8: 4 O my soul, and drink **w**, O my heart.
8:12 and reproved it in your **w**.
8:52 and **w** perfected beforehand.
13:55 for you have devoted your life to **w**,
14:40 and **w** increased in my breast,
14:47 the fountain of **w**, and the river of knowledge."
4Mc 1:15 that with sound logic prefers the life of **w**.
1:16 **W**, next, is the knowledge of divine
1:18 Now the kinds of **w** are rational judgment, justice,

WISE‡ (232) [ALL-WISE, WISDOM, WISELY, WISER, WISEST]

A. WISE MEN (20)

Ge 3: 6 and that the tree was to be desired to make one **w**,
41: 8 for all the magicians of Egypt and all its **w** men. A
41:33 let Pharaoh select a man who is discerning and **w**,
41:39 there is no one so discerning and **w** as you.
Ex 7:11 Pharaoh summoned the **w** men and the sorcerers; A
Dt 1:13 for each of your tribes individuals who are **w**,
1:15 **w** and reputable individuals,
4: 6 this great nation is a **w** and discerning people!"
16:19 of the **w** and subverts the cause of those who are in
32:29 If they were **w**, they would understand this;
2Sa 14: 2 to Tekoa and brought from there a **w** woman.
20:16 Then a **w** woman called from the city, "Listen!
20:22 the woman went to all the people with her **w** plan.
1Ki 2: 9 do not hold him guiltless, for you are a **w** man;
3:12 Indeed I give you a **w** and discerning mind;
5: 7 to David a **w** son to be over this great people."
2Ch 2:12 who has given King David a **w** son,
Ezr 8:16 and for Joiarib and Elnathan, who were **w**,
Job 5:13 He takes the **w** in their own craftiness;
9: 4 He is **w** in heart, and mighty
15: 2 "Should the **w** answer with windy knowledge,
32: 9 It is not the old that are **w**,
32:11 I listened for your **w** sayings,
34: 2 you **w** men, and give ear to me, you who know; A
34:34 and the **w** who hear me will say,
37:24 not regard any who are **w** in their own conceit."
Ps 2:10 O kings, be **w**; be warned, O rulers of the earth.
14: 2 on humankind to see if there are any who are **w**,
19: 7 the decrees of the LORD are sure, making **w**
49:10 When we look at the **w**, they die;
53: 2 on humankind to see if there are any who are **w**,
90:12 to count our days that we may gain a **w** heart.
94: 8 fools, when will you be **w**?
107:43 Let those who are **w** give heed to these things,
Pr 1: 3 in **w** dealing, righteousness, justice, and equity;
1: 5 Let the **w** also hear and gain in learning,
1: 6 the words of the **w** and their riddles.
3: 7 Do not be **w** in your own eyes;
3:35 **w** will inherit honor, but stubborn fools, disgrace.
6: 6 consider its ways, and be **w**.
8:33 Hear instruction and be **w**, and do not neglect it.
9: 8 the **w**, when rebuked, will love you.
9: 9 to the **w**, and they will become wiser still;
9:12 If you are **w**, you are **w** for yourself;
10: 1 A **w** child makes a glad father,
10: 8 The **w** of heart will heed commandments,
10:14 The **w** lay up knowledge, but the babbling of
10:23 **w** conduct is pleasure to a person of understanding.
11:29 and the fool will be servant to the **w**.
12:15 but the **w** listen to advice.
12:18 but the tongue of the **w** brings healing.
13: 1 A **w** child loves discipline,
13:14 The teaching of the **w** is a fountain of life,
13:20 Whoever walks with the **w** becomes **w**,
14: 1 The **w** woman builds her house,
14: 3 but the lips of the **w** preserve them.
14:16 The **w** are cautious and turn away from evil,
14:24 The crown of the **w** is their wisdom,
15: 2 The tongue of the **w** dispenses knowledge,
15: 7 The lips of the **w** spread knowledge;
15:12 they will not go to the **w**.
15:20 A **w** child makes a glad father,
15:24 For the **w** the path of life leads upward,
15:31 wholesome admonition will lodge among the **w**.
16:14 and whoever is **w** will appease it.
16:21 The **w** of heart is called perceptive,
16:23 The mind of the **w** makes their speech judicious,
17:28 Even fools who keep silent are considered **w**;
18:15 and the ear of the **w** seeks knowledge.
20: 1 and whoever is led astray by it is not **w**.
20:18 wage war by following **w** guidance.
20:26 A **w** king winnows the wicked,
21:11 the **w** are instructed, they increase in knowledge.
21:20 Precious treasure remains in the house of the **w**,
21:22 One **w** person went up against a city of warriors
22:17 The words of the **w**: Incline your ear
23: 4 to get rich; be **w** enough to desist.
23:15 My child, if your heart is **w**,
23:19 Hear, my child, and be **w**,
23:24 he who begets a **w** son will be glad in him.
24: 5 **W** warriors are mightier than strong ones,
24: 6 for by **w** guidance you can wage your war,
24:23 These also are sayings of the **w**:
25:12 a gold ring or an ornament of gold is a **w** rebuke to
26: 5 or they will be **w** in their own eyes.
26:12 Do you see persons **w** in their own eyes?
27:11 Be **w**, my child, and make my heart glad,
28: 7 Those who keep the law are **w** children,
28:11 The rich is **w** in self-esteem,
29: 8 but the **w** turn away wrath.
29: 9 If the **w** go to law with fools,
29:11 but the **w** quietly holds it back.
30:24 yet they are exceedingly **w**:
Ecc 2:14 The **w** have eyes in their head,
2:15 why then have I been so very **w**?"
2:16 For there is no enduring remembrance of the **w** or
2:16 How can the **w** die just like fools?
2:19 who knows whether they will be **w** or foolish?
4:13 a poor but **w** youth than an old but foolish king,
6: 8 For what advantage have the **w** over fools?
7: 4 The heart of the **w** is in the house of mourning;
7: 5 It is better to hear the rebuke of the **w** than to hear
7: 7 Surely oppression makes the **w** foolish,
7:16 Do not be too righteous, and do not act too **w**;
7:19 to the **w** more than ten rulers that are in a city.
7:23 I said, "I will be **w**," but it was far from me.
8: 1 Who is like the **w** man?
8: 5 and the **w** mind will know the time and way.
8:17 even though those who are **w** claim to know,
9: 1 how the righteous and the **w** and their deeds are in
9:11 nor bread to the **w**, nor riches to the intelligent,
Ecc 9:15 Now there was found in it a poor **w** man,
9:17 the **w** are more to be heeded than the shouting of
10: 2 The heart of the **w** inclines to the right,
10:12 Words spoken by the **w** bring them favor,
12: 9 Besides being **w**, the Teacher also taught
12:11 The sayings of the **w** are like goads,
Isa 5:21 Ah, you who are **w** in your own eyes,
19:11 the **w** counselors of Pharaoh give stupid counsel.
29:14 The wisdom of their **w** shall perish,
31: 2 Yet he too is **w** and brings disaster;
44:25 who turns back the **w**, and makes their knowledge
Jer 8: 8 How can you say, "We are **w**,
8: 9 The **w** shall be put to shame,
9:12 Who is **w** enough to understand this?
9:23 Do not let the **w** boast in their wisdom,
10: 7 among all the **w** ones of the nations and
18:18 not perish from the priest, nor counsel from the **w**,
Da 2:12 violent rage and commanded that all the **w** men A
2:13 and the **w** men were about to be executed; A
2:14 who had gone out to execute the **w** men A
2:18 rest of the **w** men of Babylon might not perish. A
2:21 he gives wisdom to the **w** and knowledge to
2:24 the king had appointed to destroy the **w** men A
2:24 "Do not destroy the **w** men of Babylon; A
2:27 Daniel answered the king, "No **w** men, A
2:48 and chief prefect over all the **w** men of Babylon. A
4: 6 all the **w** men of Babylon should be brought A
4:18 the **w** men of my kingdom are unable to tell me A
5: 7 and the king said to the **w** men of Babylon, A
5: 8 Then all the king's **w** men came in, A
5:15 Now the **w** men, the enchanters, A
11:33 The **w** among the people shall give understanding
11:35 Some of the **w** shall fall,
12: 3 Those who are **w** shall shine like the brightness of
12:10 but those who are **w** shall understand.
Hos 14: 9 Those who are **w** understand these things;
Ob 1: 8 says the LORD, I will destroy the **w** out of Edom,
Zec 9: 2 Tyre and Sidon, though they are very **w**.
Mt 2: 1 **w** men from the East came to Jerusalem, A
2: 7 the **w** men and learned from them the exact time A
2:16 saw that he had been tricked by the **w** men, A
2:16 to the time that he had learned from the **w** men. A
7:24 on them will be like a **w** man who built his house
10:16 so be **w** as serpents and innocent as doves.
11:25 because you have hidden these things from the **w**
24:45 "Who then is the faithful and **w** slave,
25: 2 Five of them were foolish, and five were **w**.
25: 4 but the **w** took flasks of oil with their lamps.
25: 8 The foolish said to the **w**,
25: 9 But the **w** replied, 'No!
Lk 10:21 because you have hidden these things from the **w**
Ro 1:14 both to the **w** and to the foolish
1:22 Claiming to be **w**, they became fools;
16:19 be **w** in what is good and guileless in what is evil.
16:27 the only **w** God, through Jesus Christ, to whom be
1Co 1:19 it is written, "I will destroy the wisdom of the **w**,
1:20 Where is the one who is **w**?
1:26 not many of you were **w** by human standards,
1:27 in the world to shame the **w**;
3:18 If you think that you are **w** in this age,
3:18 so that you may become **w**.
3:19 it is written, "He catches the **w** in their craftiness,"
3:20 "The Lord knows the thoughts of the **w**,
4:10 but you are **w** in Christ.
6: 5 that there is no one among you **w** enough to decide
2Co 11:19 you gladly put up with fools, being **w** yourselves!
Eph 5:15 not as unwise people but as **w**,
Jas 3:13 Who is **w** and understanding among you?
Tob 4:18 Seek advice from every **w** person and do
Jdt 10:19 It is not **w** to leave one of their men alive,
11:23 not only beautiful in appearance, but **w** in speech.
Wis 4:17 For they will see the end of the **w**,
6:24 multitude of the **w** is the salvation of the world,
7:15 even of wisdom and the corrector of the **w**.
Sir 1: 8 There is but one who is **w**, greatly to be feared,
1:25 In the treasuries of wisdom are **w** sayings,
3:29 and an attentive ear is the desire of the **w**.
6:33 and if you pay attention you will become **w**.
6:34 in the company of the elders. Who is **w**?
6:35 and let no **w** proverbs escape you.
7:19 Do not dismiss a **w** and good wife,
9:14 to know your neighbors, and consult with the **w**.
9:17 so a people's leader is proved **w** by his words.
10: 1 A **w** magistrate educates his people,
10:25 Free citizens will serve a **w** servant,
18:27 One who is **w** is cautious in everything;
18:29 in words become **w** themselves,
20: 1 there is the person who is **w** enough to keep silent.
20: 5 Some people keep silent and are thought to be **w**,
20: 7 The **w** remain silent until the right moment,
20:13 **w** make themselves beloved by only few words,
20:27 The **w** person advances himself by his words,
20:29 Favors and gifts blind the eyes of the **w**;
21:13 The knowledge of the **w** will increase like a flood,
21:15 When an intelligent person hears a **w** saying,
21:20 when he laughs, but the **w** smile quietly.
21:26 but the mouth of the **w** is in their mind.
26:26 *A wife honoring her husband will seem w to all,*
27:11 The conversation of the godly is always **w**,
33: 2 The **w** will not hate the law,
37:22 If a person is **w** to his own advantage,
37:23 A **w** person instructs his own people,
37:24 A **w** person will have praise heaped upon him,
37:26 One who is **w** among his people will inherit honor,
38:24 only the one who has little business can become **w**.
38:25 How can one become **w** who handles the plow,
44: 4 they were **w** in their words of instruction;

Sir 47:12 a w son rose up who because of him lived
47:14 How w you were when you were young!
50:28 and those who lay them to heart will become w.
1Mc 2:65 your brother Simeon who, I know, is w in counsel;
1Es 5:6 who spoke w words before King Darius of
6:21 Now therefore, O king, if it seems w to do so,
2Es 12:38 you shall teach them to the w among your people,
14:13 and instruct those that are w.
14:26 and some you shall deliver in secret to the w;
14:46 in order to give them to the w among your people.
4Mc 2:19 Why else did Jacob, our most w father,
7:23 For only the w and courageous are masters

WISELY‡ (9) [WISE]

2Ch 11:23 He dealt w, and distributed some of his sons
Ps 36:3 they have ceased to act w and do good.
Pr 14:35 A servant who deals w has the king's favor,
17:2 A slave who deals w will rule over
Jer 23:5 and he shall reign as king and deal w,
Mk 12:34 When Jesus saw that he answered w,
Col 4:5 Conduct yourselves w toward outsiders,
Jdt 11:21 to the other looks so beautiful or speaks so w!"
Wis 9:11 and she will guide me w in my actions

WISER (12) [WISE]

1Ki 4:31 He was w than anyone else,
4:31 w than Ethan the Ezrahite, and Heman, Calcol,
Job 35:11 and makes us w than the birds of the air?'
Ps 119:98 Your commandment makes me w than my enemies
Pr 9:9 and they will become w still;
21:11 When a scoffer is punished, the simple become w;
26:16 The lazy person is w in self-esteem
Eze 28:3 You are indeed w than Daniel;
Ro 11:25 So that you may not claim to be w than you are,
12:16 do not claim to be w than you are.
1Co 1:25 For God's foolishness is w than human wisdom,
2Es 7:19 or w than the Most High!

WISEST (5) [WISE]

Jdg 5:29 Her w ladies make answer, indeed,
Job 22:2 Can even the w be of service to him?
1Es 3:5 and to the one whose statement seems w,
3:9 of Persia judge to be w the victory shall be given
4:42 for you have been found to be the w.

WISH‡ (63) [WISHED, WISHES, WISHING]

Lev 27:31 If persons w to redeem any of their tithes,
Nu 22:29 I w I had a sword in my hand!
Dt 12:20 because you w to eat meat,
14:26 spend the money for whatever you w—
23:24 you may eat your fill of grapes, as many as you w,
Jos 15:18 Caleb said to her, "What do you w?"
Jdg 1:14 Caleb said to her, "What do you w?"
1Sa 2:16 burn the fat first, and then take whatever you w,"
23:20 O king, whenever you w to come down, do so;
1Ki 1:16 and the king said, "What do you w?"
2Ki 9:15 So Jehu said, "If this is your w,
Ne 6:6 to this report you w to become their king.
Est 6:6 the king w to honor more than me?"
Job 37:20 Did anyone ever w to be swallowed up?
Jer 40:4 If you w to come with me to Babylon, come,
40:4 but if you do not w to come with me to Babylon,
Mt 12:38 "Teacher, we w to see a sign from you."
15:28 Let it be done for you as you w."
17:4 if you w, I will make three dwellings here,
19:17 you w to enter into life, keep the commandments."
19:21 Jesus said to him, "If you w to be perfect, go,
Mk 6:22 king said to the girl, "Ask me for whatever you w,
14:7 you can show kindness to them whenever you w;
15:12 "Then what do you w me to do with the man
Lk 12:49 and how I w it were already kindled!
Jn 6:67 "Do you also w to go away?"
7:1 He did not w to go about in Judea because
12:21 and said to him, "Sir, we w to see Jesus."
15:7 in you, ask for whatever you w, and it will be done
21:18 a belt around you and take you where you do not w
Ac 18:15 I do not w to be a judge of these matters."
25:9 "Do you w to go up to Jerusalem and be tried there
Ro 9:3 For I could w that I myself were accursed
13:3 Do you w to have no fear of the authority?
1Co 4:8 Indeed, I w that you had become kings,
7:7 I w that all were as I myself am.
2Co 5:4 we w not to be unclothed but to be further clothed,
11:1 I w you would bear with me in a little foolishness.
12:6 But if I w to boast, I will not be a fool,
12:20 I fear that when I come, I may find you not as I w,
12:20 and that you may find me not as you w;
Gal 4:20 I w I were present with you now
5:12 I w those who unsettle you would castrate
Rev 3:15 I w that you were either cold or hot.
Jdt 5:7 because they did not w to follow the gods
15:8 and to see Judith and to w her well.
AdE 5:3 The king said to her, "What do you w, Esther?
6:6 What shall I do for the person whom I w to honor?
6:6 the king w to honor more than me?"
Sir 23:14 then you will w that you had never been born,
LtJ 6:45 they can be nothing but what the artisans w them
1Mc 8:13 Those whom they w to help and to make kings,
8:13 and those whom they w they depose;
2Mc 2:24 and the difficulty there is for those who w to enter
2:25 we have aimed to please those who w to read,
9:20 and your affairs are as you w,
11:29 Menelaus has informed us that you w
1Es 4:42 Then the king said to him, "Ask what you w,
3Mc 1:15 whether they w it or not?"
2Es 4:23 For I did not w to inquire about the ways above,
6:52 to be eaten by whom you w, and when you w.
7:5 If there are those who w to reach the sea,

WISHED (15) [WISH]

Job 9:3 If one w to contend with him,
Mt 18:23 to a king who w to settle accounts with his slaves.
Lk 23:25 and he handed Jesus over as they w.
Jn 21:18 to fasten your own belt and to go wherever you w.
Ac 18:27 And when he w to cross over to Achaia,
19:30 Paul w to go into the crowd,
25:20 I asked whether he w to go to Jerusalem and
AdE 1:8 but the king w to have it so,
8:11 as they w against their opponents and enemies
Sir Pr:3 for those living abroad who w to gain learning
Sus 1:15 and w to bathe in the garden, for it was a hot day.
1Mc 5:67 who w to do a brave deed, fell in battle,
2Mc 4:16 and w to imitate completely became their enemies
12:4 they w to live peaceably and suspected nothing,
4Mc 17:9 of the tyrant who w to destroy the way of life of

WISHES (29) [WISH]

Lev 27:15 the one who consecrates the house w to redeem it,
27:19 if the one who consecrates the field w to redeem it,
Nu 9:14 Any alien residing among you who w to keep
15:14 and w to offer an offering by fire,
Dt 18:6 (and he may come whenever he w),
Est 6:6 "What shall be done for the man whom the king w
6:7 "For the man whom the king w to honor,
6:9 let him robe the man whom the king w to honor,
6:9 be done for the man whom the king w to honor.' "
6:11 be done for the man whom the king w to honor."
Eze 46:5 with the lambs shall be as much as he w to give,
46:7 and with the lambs as much as he w,
46:11 and with the lambs as much as one w to give,
Mt 20:26 but whoever w to be great among you must
20:27 and whoever w to be first among you must
Mk 10:43 but whoever w to become great among you must
10:44 and whoever w to be first among you must
Jn 5:21 so also the Son gives life to whomever he w.
Ac 13:22 who will carry out all my w.'
1Co 7:36 and so it has to be, let him marry as he w;
7:39 husband dies, she is free to marry anyone she w,
Jas 4:4 Therefore whoever w to be a friend of
4:15 Instead you ought to say, "If the Lord w,
Rev 22:17 Let anyone who w take the water of life as a gift.
Tob 5:10 "My son Tobias w to go to Media.
AdE 6:7 "For a person whom the king w to honor,
6:11 be done to everyone whom the king w to honor."
2Mc 9:19 and general sends hearty greetings and good w
3Mc 5:11 by him who grants it to whomever he w.

WISHING (9) [WISH]

Est 9:30 Letters were sent w peace and security to all
Mk 15:15 So Pilate, w to satisfy the crowd,
Ac 25:9 But Festus, w to do the Jews a favor, asked Paul,
27:43 but the centurion, w to save Paul, kept them
Wis 14:19 For he, perhaps w to please his ruler,
2Mc 12:35 w to take the accursed man alive,
14:39 w to exhibit the enmity that he had for the Jews,
3Mc 5:47 the animals, w to witness, with invulnerable heart
2Es 13:34 as you saw, w to come and conquer him.

WIST (KJV) See KNOW, KNOWING, REALIZE, UNINTENTIONALLY

WIT (KJV) See KNOW, LEARN, NAMELY, SEE, THAT IS

WITCH (KJV) See [FEMALE] SORCERER

WITCHCRAFT (1)

Lev 19:26 You shall not practice augury or w.

WITH (7619) See Index of Articles Etc.

WITHDRAW‡ (21) [WITHDRAWAL, WITHDRAWN, WITHDRAWS, WITHDREW]

Lev 26:25 and if you w within your cities,
1Sa 14:19 and Saul said to the priest, "W your hand."
15:6 W from among the Amalekites,
2Sa 20:21 give him up alone, and I will w from the city."
1Ki 15:19 so that he may w from me."
2Ki 18:14 "I have done wrong; w from me;
2Ch 16:3 so that he may w from me."
Job 13:21 w your hand far from me,
36:7 He does not w his eyes from the righteous,
Ps 104:22 the sun rises, they w and lie down in their dens.
Isa 60:20 down, or your moon w itself;
Jer 21:2 and will make him w from us."
Da 1:16 So the guard continued to w their royal rations and
11:30 and he shall lose heart and w.
Joel 2:10 and the stars w their shining.
3:15 and the stars w their shining.
Zec 14:4 so that one half of the Mount shall w northward,
Lk 5:16 But he would w to deserted places and pray.
Aza 1:12 Do not w your mercy from us,
1Mc 6:57 So he quickly gave orders to w,
2Es 5:9 and wisdom shall w into its chamber,

WITHDRAWAL (1) [WITHDRAW]

2Mc 13:26 This is how the king's attack and w turned out.

WITHDRAWN (10) [WITHDRAW]

2Ch 24:25 When they had w, leaving him severely wounded,
Jer 34:21 to the army of the king of Babylon, which has w
37:11 when the Chaldean army had w from Jerusalem at
La 2:3 he has w his right hand from them in the face of
Hos 5:6 not find him; he has w from them.
Jdt 13:14 who has not w his mercy from the house of Israel,
Sir 10:12 the heart has w from its Maker.
2Mc 4:33 having first w to a place of sanctuary at Daphne
2Es 7:*33* shall pass away, and patience shall be w.
12:48 I have neither forsaken you nor w from you;

WITHDRAWS (2) [WITHDRAW]

2Sa 17:13 If he w into a city,
2Mc 6:16 Therefore he never w his mercy from us.

WITHDREW‡ (26) [WITHDRAW]

Ex 35:20 Then all the congregation of the Israelites w from
1Sa 14:46 Then Saul w from pursuing the Philistines;
15:6 So the Kenites w from the Amalekites.
2Sa 20:2 of Israel w from David and followed Sheba son
23:9 gathered there for battle. The Israelites w,
2Ki 3:27 so they w from him and returned to their own land.
12:18 Then Hazael w from Jerusalem.
Ezr 10:6 Then Ezra w from before the house of God,
Job 29:8 the young men saw me and w, and the aged rose
Ps 85:3 You w all your wrath; you turned from your
Jer 37:5 of them, they w from Jerusalem.
Mt 4:12 that John had been arrested, he w to Galilee.
14:13 he w from there in a boat to a deserted place
Lk 9:10 He took them with him and w privately to
22:41 Then he w from them about a stone's throw,
24:51 he w from them and was carried up into heaven.
Jn 6:15 he w again to the mountain by himself.
Jdt 13:1 When evening came, his slaves quickly w.
1Mc 4:35 he w to Antioch and enlisted mercenaries in order
7:19 Then Bacchides w from Jerusalem and encamped
9:62 and Simon, w to Bethbasi in the wilderness;
12:28 so they kindled fires in their camp and w.
2Mc 9:29 he w to Ptolemy Philometor in Egypt.
12:7 Then, because the city's gates were closed, he w,
13:16 with terror and confusion and w in triumph.
13:22 received theirs, w, attacked Judas and his men,

WITHER (23) [WITHERED, WITHERING, WITHERS]

Job 8:12 they w before any other plant.
18:16 and their branches w above.
24:24 they w and fade like the mallow;
Ps 1:3 and their leaves do not w.
37:2 and w like the green herb.
58:7 like grass let them be trodden down and w.
102:11 like an evening shadow; I w away like grass.
137:5 If I forget you, O Jerusalem, let my right hand w!
Pr 11:28 Those who trust in their riches will w,
Isa 34:4 their host shall w like a leaf withering on a vine,
40:24 when he blows upon them, and they w,
Jer 12:4 and the grass of every field w?
Eze 17:9 cause its fruit to rot and w,
17:10 When the east wind strikes it, will it not utterly w,
17:10 w on the bed where it grew?
47:12 Their leaves will not w nor their fruit fail,
Am 1:2 the pastures of the shepherds w,
Na 1:4 Bashan and Carmel w, and the bloom of Lebanon
Mt 21:20 saying, "How did the fig tree w at once?"
Jas 1:11 in the midst of a busy life, they will w away.
Wis 2:8 with rosebuds before they w.
2Es 7:*87* and shall w with fear at seeing the glory of
15:50 the glory of your strength shall w like a flower

WITHERED (23) [WITHER]

Ge 41:23 w, thin, and blighted by the east wind,
1Ki 13:4 that he stretched out against him w so that he could
Ps 102:4 My heart is stricken and w like grass;
Isa 15:6 the grass is w, the new growth fails,
Jer 8:13 the leaves are w, and what I gave them has passed
Eze 19:12 its strong stem was w; the fire consumed it.
Am 4:7 and the field on which it did not rain w;
Jnh 4:7 a worm that attacked the bush, so that it w.
Zec 9:5 Ekron also, because its hopes are w.
11:17 Let his arm be completely w,
Mt 12:10 a man was there with a w hand,
13:6 and since they had no root, they w away.
21:19 And the fig tree w at once.
Mk 3:1 and a man was there who had a w hand.
3:3 And he said to the man who had the w hand,
4:6 and since it had no root, it w away.
11:20 they saw the fig tree w away to its roots.
11:21 The fig tree that you cursed has w."
Lk 6:6 there was a man there whose right hand was w.
6:8 he said to the man who had the w hand,
8:6 and as it grew up, it w for lack of moisture.
Sir 6:3 and you will be left like a w tree.
2Es 5:36 and make the w flowers bloom again for me;

WITHERING (2) [WITHER]

Isa 34:4 All their host shall wither like a leaf w on a vine, or fruit w on a fig tree.

WITHERS (16) [WITHER]
Job 14: 2 comes up like a flower and **w**,
Ps 90: 6 in the evening it fades and **w**.
129: 6 Let them be like the grass on the housetops that **w**
Isa 1:30 For you shall be like an oak whose leaf **w**,
24: 4 The earth dries up and **w**, the world languishes
24: 4 the world languishes and **w**;
33: 9 Lebanon is confounded and **w** away;
40: 7 The grass **w**, the flower fades,
40: 8 The grass **w**, the flower fades;
Joel 1:12 The vine **w**, the fig tree droops.
1:12 surely, joy **w** away among the people.
Jn 15: 6 in me is thrown away like a branch and **w**;
Jas 1:11 sun rises with its scorching heat and **w** the field;
1Pe 1:24 The grass **w**, and the flower falls,
Sir 14: 9 greedy injustice **w** the soul.
43:21 and **w** the tender grass like fire.

WITHHELD (15) [WITHHOLD]
Ge 22:12 since you have not **w** your son, your only son,
22:16 you have done this, and have not **w** your son,
30: 2 who has **w** from you the fruit of the womb?"
Job 22: 7 and you have **w** bread from the hungry.
31:16 "If I have **w** anything that the poor desired,
38:15 Light is **w** from the wicked,
Ps 21: 2 and have not **w** the request of his lips.
Isa 63:15 They are **w** from me.
Jer 3: 3 Therefore the showers have been **w**,
Eze 20:22 But I **w** my hand, and acted for the sake
Joel 1:13 Grain offering and drink offering are **w** from
Am 4: 7 And I also **w** the rain from you
Hag 1:10 Therefore the heavens above you have **w** the dew,
1:10 and the earth has **w** its produce.
Sir 37:21 for the Lord has **w** the gift of charm,

WITHHOLD (20) [WITHHELD, WITHHOLDS]
Ge 23: 6 none of us will **w** from you any burial ground
Dt 22: 3 You may not **w** your help.
24:14 not **w** the wages of poor and needy laborers,
2Sa 13:13 for he will not **w** me from you."
14:18 "Do not **w** from me anything I ask you."
Ne 9:20 and did not **w** your manna from their mouths,
Job 6:14 "Those who **w** kindness from a friend forsake
Ps 40:11 Do not, O LORD, **w** your mercy from me;
84:11 the LORD **w** from those who walk uprightly.
Pr 3:27 Do not **w** good from those to whom it is due,
11:24 others **w** what is due, and only suffer want.
23:13 Do not **w** discipline from your children;
Isa 43: 6 "Give them up," and to the south, "Do not **w**;
La 2: 8 he did not **w** his hand from destroying;
Zec 1:12 how long will you **w** mercy from Jerusalem and
Lk 6:29 from anyone who takes away your coat do not **w**
Ac 10:47 "Can anyone **w** the water
Ro 8:32 He who did not **w** his own Son,
Sir 7:21 do not **w** from them their freedom.
7:33 do not **w** kindness even from the dead.

WITHHOLDS (3) [WITHHOLD]
Job 12:15 If he **w** the waters, they dry up;
Eze 18: 8 not take advance or accrued interest, **w** his hand
18:17 **w** his hand from iniquity, takes no advance

WITHIN‡ (217) [IN]
Ge 18:24 Suppose there are fifty righteous **w** the city;
25:22 The children struggled together **w** her;
40:13 **w** three days Pharaoh will lift up your head
40:19 **w** three days Pharaoh will lift up your head—
Ex 8:25 and said, "Go, sacrifice to your God **w** the land."
26:33 the ark of the covenant in there, **w** the curtain;
Lev 22:24 such you shall not do **w** your land,
24:14 and let all who were **w** hearing lay their hands
26:25 and if you withdraw **w** your cities,
Nu 3:38 having charge of the rites **w** the sanctuary,
30: 3 while **w** her father's house, in her youth,
Dt 12:15 and eat meat **w** any of your towns,
12:17 may you eat **w** your towns the tithe of your grain,
12:21 you may eat **w** your towns whenever you desire.
14:28 and store it **w** your towns;
15: 7 of your community in any of your towns **w**
15:22 **w** your towns you may eat it,
16: 5 to offer the passover sacrifice **w** any of your towns
18: 1 shall have no allotment or inheritance **w** Israel.
23:10 he must not come **w** the camp.
26:12 so that they may eat their fill **w** your towns,
Jos 2:15 on the outer side of the city wall and she resided **w**
13:13 but Geshur and Maacath live **w** Israel to this day.
16: 9 the towns that were set apart for the Ephraimites **w**
16:10 so the Canaanites have lived **w** Ephraim to this day
17:11 **W** Issachar and Asher, Manasseh had Beth-shean
19: 1 its inheritance lay **w** the inheritance of the tribe
19: 9 the tribe of Simeon obtained an inheritance **w**
21:41 of the Levites **w** the holdings of the Israelites were
Jdg 2: 9 So they buried him **w** the bounds of his inheritance
9:51 But there was a strong tower **w** the city,
11:26 why did you not recover them **w** that time?
14:12 If you can explain it to me **w** the seven days of
1Sa 13:11 and that you did not come **w** the days appointed,
14:14 and his armor-bearer killed about twenty men **w**
18:10 and he raved **w** his house,
25:36 Nabal's heart was merry **w** him,
25:37 and his heart died **w** him; he became like a stone.
26: 5 Saul was lying **w** the encampment,
26: 7 there Saul lay sleeping **w** the encampment,
1Sa 27: 1 then Saul will despair of seeking me any longer **w**
2Sa 12:11 up trouble against you from **w** your own house;
20: 4 the men of Judah together to me **w** three days,
1Ki 3:26 because compassion for her son burned **w** her—
6:16 and he built this **w** as an inner sanctuary,
6:18 The cedar **w** the house had carvings of gourds
7:28 the borders were **w** the frames;
7:31 Its opening was **w** the crown whose height was
9:18 Baalath, Tamar in the wilderness, **w** the land,
21:23 dogs shall eat Jezebel **w** the bounds of Jezreel.'
2Ki 18:26 of Judah **w** the hearing of the people who are on
1Ch 6:54 according to their settlements **w** their borders:
Ezr 8:29 **w** the chambers of the house of the LORD."
8:33 On the fourth day, **w** the house of our God,
10: 8 and that if any did not come **w** three days,
10: 9 of Judah and Benjamin assembled at Jerusalem **w**
Ne 6:10 **w** the temple, and let us close the doors of
7: 4 people **w** it were few and no houses had been built.
Est 1:12 and his anger burned **w** him.
Job 4:21 Their tent-cord is plucked up **w** them,
19:27 My heart faints **w** me!
20: 2 because of the agitation **w** me.
20:14 it is the venom of asps **w** them.
30:16 "And now my soul is poured out **w** me;
32:18 I am full of words; the spirit **w** me constrains me.
Ps 22:14 it is melted **w** my breast;
39: 3 my heart became hot **w** me.
40: 8 your law is **w** my heart."
40:10 I have not hidden your saving help **w** my heart,
42: 5 O my soul, and why are you disquieted **w** me?
42: 6 My soul is cast down **w** me;
42:11 O my soul, and why are you disquieted **w** me?
43: 5 O my soul, and why are you disquieted **w** me?
48: 3 **W** its citadels God has shown himself
51:10 O God, and put a new and right spirit **w** me.
55: 4 My heart is in anguish **w** me,
55:10 and iniquity and trouble are **w** it;
74: 4 Your foes have roared **w** your holy place;
78:28 he let them fall **w** their camp,
101: 2 I will walk with integrity of heart **w** my house;
103: 1 and all that is **w** me, bless his holy name.
107: 5 hungry and thirsty, their soul fainted **w** them.
109:22 and my heart is pierced **w** me.
122: 2 Our feet are standing **w** your gates, O Jerusalem.
122: 7 Peace be **w** your walls, and security **w** your towers.
122: 8 relatives and friends I will say, "Peace be **w** you."
128: 3 Your wife will be like a fruitful vine **w** your house;
143: 4 my spirit faints **w** me; my heart **w** me is appalled.
147:13 he blesses your children **w** you.
147:14 He grants peace **w** your borders;
Pr 2: 1 and treasure up my commandments **w** you,
4:21 from your sight; keep them **w** your heart.
22:18 for it will be pleasant if you keep them **w** you,
26:24 in speaking while harboring deceit **w**;
26:25 for there are seven abominations concealed **w**;
Isa 7: 8 (**W** sixty-five years Ephraim will be shattered,
19: 1 and the heart of the Egyptians will melt **w** them.
19: 3 of the Egyptians **w** them will be emptied out,
21:16 **W** a year, according to the years of a hired worker,
26: 9 my spirit **w** me earnestly seeks you.
36:11 of Judah **w** the hearing of the people who are on
56: 5 in my house and **w** my walls,
60:18 devastation or destruction **w** your borders;
63:11 Where is the one who put **w** them his holy spirit,
Jer 4:14 How long shall your evil schemes lodge **w** you?
6: 6 there is nothing but oppression **w** her.
6: 7 violence and destruction are heard **w** her;
20: 9 then **w** me there is something like
23: 9 My heart is crushed **w** me, all my bones shake;
28: 3 **W** two years I will bring back to this place all
28:11 from the neck of all the nations **w** two years."
28:16 **W** this year you will be dead,
31:33 I will put my law **w** them,
La 1:20 my heart is wrung **w** me, because I have been very
3:20 of it and is bowed down **w** me.
Eze 1:16 being something like a wheel **w** a wheel.
10: 2 "Go **w** the wheelwork underneath the cherubim;
10: 6 "Take fire from **w** the wheelwork,
10:10 something like a wheel **w** a wheel.
11: 7 The slain whom you have placed **w** it are the meat,
11:19 and put a new spirit **w** them;
12:24 or flattering divination **w** the house of Israel.
13:14 when it falls, you shall perish **w** it;
16:47 **w** a very little time you were more corrupt than
20:37 and will bring you **w** the bond of the covenant.
22: 3 A city! Shedding blood **w** itself;
22: 7 the alien residing **w** you suffers extortion;
22:13 and at the blood that has been shed **w** you.
22:21 and you shall be melted **w** it.
22:25 Its princes **w** it are like a roaring lion tearing
22:25 they have made many widows **w** it.
22:27 Its officials **w** it are like wolves tearing the prey,
25: 6 with all the malice **w** you against the land of Israel,
26:15 when slaughter goes on **w** you?
27: 8 skilled men of Zemer were **w** you,
27: 9 The elders of Gebal and its artisans were **w** you,
27: 9 all the ships of the sea with their mariners were **w**
27:27 and all your warriors **w** you,
28:18 So I brought out fire from **w** you;
30: 6 from Migdol to Syene they shall fall **w** it by
36:26 and a new spirit I will put **w** you;
36:27 I will put my spirit **w** you,
37:14 I will put my spirit **w** you, and you shall live,
44:17 at the gates of the inner court, and **w**.
Da 6:12 divine or human, **w** thirty days except to you,
7:15 As for me, Daniel, my spirit was troubled **w** me,
11:20 but **w** a few days he shall be broken,
Hos 5: 4 For the spirit of whoredom is **w** them,
7: 6 like an oven, their heart burns **w** them;
11: 8 My heart recoils **w** me; my compassion grows
Am 3: 9 and see what great tumults are **w** it,
Mic 5: 6 the Assyrians if they come into our land or tread **w**
6:14 and there shall be a gnawing hunger **w** you;
Hab 3:16 and I tremble **w**; my lips quiver at the sound.
Zep 3: 3 The officials **w** it are roaring lions;
3: 5 The LORD **w** it is righteous; he does no wrong.
Zec 2: 5 says the LORD, and I will be the glory **w** it."
12: 1 the earth and formed the human spirit **w**:
Mk 7:21 For it is from **w**, from the human heart,
7:23 All these evil things come from **w**,
Lk 11: 7 And he answers from **w**, 'Do not bother me;
11:41 So give for alms those things that are **w**;
19:44 you and your children **w** you,
19:44 they will not leave **w** you one stone upon another;
24:32 not our hearts burning **w** us while he was talking
Ro 7:17 but sin that dwells **w** me.
7:18 For I know that nothing good dwells **w** me, that is,
7:20 it is no longer I that do it, but sin that dwells **w** me.
8:29 that he might be the firstborn **w** a large family.
1Co 2:11 the human spirit that is **w**?
6:19 that your body is a temple of the Holy Spirit **w**
12:25 that there may be no dissension **w** the body,
2Co 7: 5 disputes without and fears **w**.
10:13 will keep **w** the field that God has assigned to us,
Eph 3:20 Now to him who by the power at work **w** us is able
Col 1:29 with all the energy that he powerfully inspires **w**
2Ti 1: 6 the gift of God that is **w** you through the laying on
Jas 4: 1 not come from your cravings that are at war **w**
1Pe 1:11 about the person or time that the Spirit of Christ **w**
Rev 7:15 and worship him day and night **w** his temple,
11:19 and the ark of his covenant was seen **w** his temple;
Tob 3: 6 and great is the sorrow **w** me.
13:10 May he cheer all those **w** you who are captives,
13:10 and love all those **w** you who are distressed,
14:10 do not stay overnight **w** the confines of the city.
14:10 For I see that there is much wickedness **w** it,
14:10 and that much deceit is practiced **w** it,
Jdt 8:11 unless the Lord turns and helps us **w** so many days.
8:15 if he does not choose to help us **w** these five days,
8:15 he has power to protect us **w** any time he pleases,
8:33 and **w** the days after which you have promised
14: 4 Then you and all who live **w** the borders
Wis 7: 2 **w** the period of ten months,
Sir 17:30 For not everything is **w** human capability,
26:20 *Seek a fertile field **w** the whole plain,*
1Mc 2:46 the uncircumcised boys that they found **w**
5:30 the stronghold, and attacking the Jews **w**.
11:45 Then the people of the city assembled **w** the city,
2Mc 5:14 **W** the total of three days eighty thousand were
6: 4 with prostitutes and had intercourse with women **w**
7:20 she saw her seven sons perish **w** a single day,
7:22 nor I who set in order the elements **w** each of you.
10:34 The men **w**, relying on the strength of the place,
12:14 Those who were **w**, relying on the strength of
1Es 9: 4 that if any did not meet there **w** two or three days,
9: 5 of Judah and Benjamin assembled at Jerusalem **w**
3Mc 5:42 of the changes of mind that had come about **w** him
2Es 2: 8 Assyria, who conceal the unrighteous **w** you!
2:22 Protect the old and the young **w** your walls;
4:40 her womb can keep the fetus **w** her any longer."
6:36 Then on the eighth night my heart was troubled **w**
7:59 "Consider **w** yourself what you have thought,
9: 8 and will see my salvation in my land and **w**
13:48 who are found **w** my holy borders, shall be saved.
4Mc 18: 2 not only of sufferings from **w**,

WITHOUT‡ (433) [OUT]
Ge 37:33 Joseph is **w** doubt torn to pieces."
41:44 and **w** your consent no one shall lift up hand
Ex 12: 5 Your lamb shall be **w** blemish, a year-old male;
12:30 for there was not a house **w** someone dead.
21: 2 in the seventh he shall go out a free person, **w** debt.
21:11 she shall go out **w** debt, **w** payment of money.
22:10 or is injured or is carried off, **w** anyone seeing it,
29: 1 Take one young bull and two rams **w** blemish,
Lev 1: 3 you shall offer a male **w** blemish;
1:10 your offering shall be a male **w** blemish.
1:17 He shall tear it open by its wings **w** severing it.
3: 1 you shall offer one **w** blemish before the LORD.
3: 6 male or female, you shall offer one **w** blemish.
4: 3 the herd **w** blemish as a sin offering to the LORD.
4:23 shall bring as his offering a male goat **w** blemish.
4:28 a female goat **w** blemish as your offering,
4:32 you shall bring a female **w** blemish.
5: 8 wringing its head at the nape **w** severing it.
5:15 a ram **w** blemish from the flock,
5:17 If any of you sin **w** knowing it,
5:18 You shall bring to the priest a ram **w** blemish from
6: 6 a ram **w** blemish from the flock, or its equivalent,
9: 2 **w** blemish, and offer them before the LORD.
9: 3 a calf and a lamb, yearlings **w** blemish,
14:10 On the eighth day he shall take two male lambs **w**
14:10 and one ewe lamb in its first year **w** blemish,
15:11 the one with the discharge touches **w**
22:13 **w** offspring, and returns to her father's house,
22:19 to be acceptable in your behalf it shall be a male **w**
23:12 **w** blemish, as a burnt offering to the LORD.
23:18 with the bread seven lambs a year old **w** blemish,
26:43 enjoy its sabbath years by lying desolate **w** them,
Nu 6:14 male lamb a year old **w** blemish as a burnt offering,
6:14 ewe lamb a year old **w** blemish as a sin offering,
6:14 one ram **w** blemish as an offering of well-being,
15:24 if it was done unintentionally **w** the knowledge of

Nu 19: 2 the Israelites to bring you a red heifer **w** defect,
27:17 the LORD may not be like sheep **w** a shepherd."
28: 3 two male lambs a year old **w** blemish, daily,
28: 9 two male lambs a year old **w** blemish,
28:11 one ram, seven male lambs a year old **w** blemish;
28:19 see that they are **w** blemish.
28:31 They shall be **w** blemish.
29: 2 one ram, seven male lambs a year old **w** blemish.
29: 8 They shall be **w** blemish.
29:13 They shall be **w** blemish.
29:17 fourteen male lambs a year old **w** blemish,
29:20 fourteen male lambs a year old **w** blemish,
29:23 fourteen male lambs a year old **w** blemish,
29:26 fourteen male lambs a year old **w** blemish,
29:29 fourteen male lambs a year old **w** blemish,
29:32 fourteen male lambs a year old **w** blemish,
29:36 one ram, seven male lambs a year old **w** blemish,
35:11 a slayer who kills a person **w** intent may flee there.
35:15 anyone who kills a person **w** intent may flee there.
35:22 But if someone pushes another suddenly **w** enmity,
35:22 or hurls any object **w** lying in wait,
Dt 4:22 For I am going to die in this land **w** crossing over
8: 9 a land where you may eat bread **w** scarcity,
28:29 and you shall be continually abused and robbed, **w**
28:31 be given to your enemies, **w** anyone to help you.
32: 4 A faithful God, **w** deceit, just and upright is he;
Jos 3:10 the living God who **w** fail will drive out from
20: 3 a person **w** intent or by mistake may flee there;
20: 9 that anyone who killed a person **w**
Jdg 7:12 and their camels were **w** number,
15: 3 when I do mischief to the Philistines, I will be **w**
Ru 1: 5 woman was left **w** her two sons and her husband.
2: 7 **w** resting even for a moment."
4: 6 for myself **w** damaging my own inheritance.
4:14 who has not left you this day **w** next-of-kin;
1Sa 19: 5 an innocent person by killing David **w** cause?"
20: 2 My father does nothing either great or small **w**
25:31 for having shed blood **w** cause or
2Sa 3:29 and may the house of Joab never be **w** one who has
14:28 **w** coming into the king's presence.
1Ki 2:31 the guilt for the blood that Joab shed **w** cause.
2:32 because, **w** the knowledge of my father David,
22: 1 For three years Aram and Israel continued **w** war.
2Ki 4:30 and as you yourself live, I will not leave **w** you."
18:25 is it **w** the LORD that I have come up
1Ch 22: 4 and cedar logs **w** number—
22:15 carpenters, and all kinds of artisans **w** number,
2Ch 5:11 **w** regard to their divisions,
15: 3 For a long time Israel was **w** the true God, and **w** a teaching priest, and **w** law;
18:16 on the mountains, like sheep **w** a shepherd;
28:19 for he had behaved **w** restraint in Judah
Ezr 6: 8 in full and **w** delay, from the royal revenue,
6: 9 let that be given to them day by day **w** fail,
9:14 be angry with us until you destroy us **w** remnant
Est 1: 8 Drinking was by flagons, **w** restraint;
4:11 or woman goes to the king inside the inner court **w**
9:27 that **w** fail they would continue
Job 4:20 they perish forever **w** any regarding it.
5: 9 marvelous things **w** number.
6: 6 Can that which is tasteless be eaten **w** salt,
7: 6 and come to their end **w** hope.
9:10 and marvelous things **w** number.
9:17 and multiplies my wounds **w** cause;
9:35 then I would speak **w** fear of him,
11:15 Surely then you will lift up your face **w** blemish;
12:25 They grope in the dark **w** light;
21:10 Their bull breeds **w** fail; their cow calves
24: 7 They lie all night naked, **w** clothing,
24:10 They go about naked, **w** clothing;
27:22 It hurls at them **w** pity;
31:19 or a poor person **w** covering,
31:39 if I have eaten its yield **w** payment, and caused
33: 9 You say, 'I am clean, **w** transgression;
34: 6 though I am **w** transgression.'
34:24 He shatters the mighty **w** investigation,
34:35 'Job speaks **w** knowledge,
34:35 without knowledge, his words are **w** insight.'
35:16 he multiplies words **w** knowledge."
36:12 by the sword, and die **w** knowledge.
38: 2 "Who is this that darkens counsel by words **w**
41:33 On earth it has no equal, a creature **w** fear.
42: 3 'Who is this that hides counsel **w** knowledge?'
Ps 7: 4 with harm or plundered my foe **w** cause,
26: 1 and I have trusted in the LORD **w** wavering.
32: 9 Do not be like a horse or a mule, **w** understanding,
35: 7 For **w** cause they hid their net for me;
35: 7 **w** cause they dug a pit for my life.
35:15 ruffians whom I did not know tore at me **w**
35:19 or those who hate me **w** cause wink the eye.
38:19 Those who are my foes **w** cause are mighty,
40:12 For evils have encompassed me **w** number;
64: 4 they shoot suddenly and **w** fear.
69: 4 the hairs of my head are those who hate me **w**
77: 2 in the night my hand is stretched out **w** wearying;
105:34 and young locusts **w** number;
109: 3 with words of hate, and attack me **w** cause.
119:86 I am persecuted **w** cause; help me!
119:161 Princes persecute me **w** cause,
Pr 1:33 to me will be secure and will live at ease, **w** dread
3:30 Do not quarrel with anyone **w** cause,
6: 7 **W** having any chief or officer or ruler,
6:27 be carried in the bosom **w** burning one's clothes?
6:28 Or can one walk on hot coals **w** scorching the feet?
7: 7 among the youths, a young man **w** sense,
9: 4 To those **w** sense she says,
9:16 And to those **w** sense she says,
Pr 11:22 a gold ring in a pig's snout is a beautiful woman **w**
14:28 **w** people a prince is ruined.
15:22 **W** counsel, plans go wrong,
19: 2 Desire **w** knowledge is not good,
23:29 Who has wounds **w** cause?
24:28 not be a witness against your neighbor **w** cause,
25:14 Like clouds and wind **w** rain is one who boasts of
25:28 Like a city breached, **w** walls,
28:14 Happy is the one who is never **w** fear,
29: 9 there is ranting and ridicule **w** relief.
30:25 a people **w** strength, yet they provide their food in
30:26 a people **w** power, yet they make their homes in
Ecc 4: 8 the case of solitary individuals, **w** sons or brothers;
7:18 **w** letting go of the other;
7:20 on earth so righteous as to do good **w** ever sinning.
SS 6: 8 and eighty concubines, and maidens **w** number.
Isa 1:30 and like a garden **w** water.
5: 9 large and beautiful houses, **w** inhabitant.
5:13 Therefore my people go into exile **w** knowledge;
6:11 And he said: "Until cities lie waste **w** inhabitant,
6:11 houses **w** people, and the land is utterly desolate;
22: 3 they were captured **w** the use of a bow.
27:11 For this is a people **w** understanding;
29:21 and **w** grounds deny justice to the one in the right.
30: 2 to Egypt **w** asking for my counsel, to take refuge in
34:16 none shall be **w** its mate.
36:10 is it **w** the LORD that I have come up
47: 1 Sit on the ground **w** a throne, daughter Chaldea!
52: 3 and you shall be redeemed **w** money.
52: 4 the Assyrian, too, has oppressed them **w** cause.
52: 5 seeing that my people are taken away **w** cause?
55: 1 buy wine and milk **w** money and **w** price.
56:10 sentinels are blind, they are all **w** knowledge;
Jer 2:15 his cities are in ruins, **w** inhabitant.
2:32 Yet my people have forgotten me, days **w** number.
4: 7 your cities will be ruins **w** inhabitant.
9:11 and I will make the towns of Judah a desolation, **w**
10:14 Everyone is stupid and **w** knowledge;
15:13 and your treasures I will give as plunder, **w** price,
20:16 be like the cities that the LORD overthrew **w** pity;
26: 9 and this city shall be desolate, **w** inhabitant'?"
32:43 It is a desolation, **w** human beings or animals;
33:10 "It is a waste **w** human beings or animals,"
33:10 **w** inhabitants, human or animal,
33:12 **w** human beings or animals,
34:22 of Judah I will make a desolation **w** inhabitant.
44: 2 today they are a desolation, **w** an inhabitant
44: 7 leaving yourselves **w** a remnant?
44:19 with her image, and poured out libations to her **w**
44:22 **w** inhabitant, as it is to this day.
46:19 For Memphis shall become a waste, a ruin, **w**
46:23 more numerous than locusts; they are **w** number.
51:17 Everyone is stupid and **w** knowledge;
51:29 the land of Babylon a desolation, **w** inhabitant.
51:37 an object of horror and of hissing, **w** inhabitant.
La 1: 6 they fled **w** strength before the pursuer.
2: 2 The Lord has destroyed **w** mercy all the dwellings
2:17 as he ordained long ago, he has demolished **w** pity;
2:21 of your anger you have killed them, slaughtering **w**
3: 2 he has driven and brought me into darkness **w**
3:43 with anger and pursued us, killing **w** pity;
3:49 My eyes will flow **w** ceasing, **w** respite,
3:52 Those who were my enemies **w** cause
Eze 1: 9 each of them moved straight ahead, **w** turning
1:12 they went, **w** turning as they went.
1:17 they moved in any of the four directions **w** veering
10:11 they moved in any of the four directions **w** veering
10:11 the others followed **w** veering as they moved.
14:23 not **w** cause that I did all that I have done in it,
22:29 and have extorted from the alien **w** redress.
38:11 all of them living **w** walls,
42:14 not go out of it into the outer court **w** laying there
43:22 On the second day you shall offer a male goat **w**
43:23 bull **w** blemish and a ram from the flock **w** blemish
43:25 also a bull and a ram from the flock, **w** blemish,
45:18 you shall take a young bull **w** blemish,
45:23 to the LORD seven young bulls and seven rams **w**
46: 4 six lambs **w** blemish and a ram **w** blemish;
46: 6 he shall offer a young bull **w** blemish,
46: 6 which shall be **w** blemish;
46:13 He shall provide a lamb, a yearling, **w** blemish,
Da 1: 4 young men **w** physical defect and handsome,
8: 5 the face of the whole earth **w** touching the ground.
8:25 **W** warning he shall destroy many and shall
11:21 he shall come in **w** warning and obtain
11:24 **W** warning he shall come into the richest parts of
Hos 3: 4 Israelites shall remain many days **w** king or prince, **w** sacrifice or pillar, **w** ephod or teraphim.
4:14 thus a people **w** understanding comes to ruin.
7:11 like a dove, silly and **w** sense;
8: 4 they set up princes, but **w** my knowledge.
Am 3: 7 **w** revealing his secret to his servants the prophets.
Mic 3: 6 Therefore it shall be night to you, **w** vision, and darkness to you, **w** revelation.
Na 3: 3 dead bodies **w** end—they stumble over the bodies!
3: 9 Egypt too, and that **w** limit;
Hab 1:17 and destroying nations **w** mercy?
Zep 3: 5 each dawn **w** fail; but the unjust knows no shame.
3: 6 have been made desolate, **w** people, **w** inhabitants.
Zec 2: 4 Jerusalem shall be inhabited like villages **w** walls,
Mt 9:36 and helpless, like sheep **w** a shepherd.
10: 8 You received **w** payment; give **w** payment.
12:29 **w** first tying up the strong man?
13:34 **w** a parable he told them nothing.
13:57 not **w** honor except in their own country and
15:16 Then he said, "Are you also still **w** understanding?
22:12 how did you get in here **w** a wedding robe?'
Mt 23:23 to have practiced **w** neglecting the others.
Mk 3:27 a strong man's house and plunder his property **w**
6: 4 Jesus said to them, "Prophets are not **w** honor,
6:34 because they were like sheep **w** a shepherd;
7: 2 with defiled hands, that is, **w** washing them.
8: 1 when there was again a great crowd **w** anything
Lk 1:74 from the hands of our enemies, might serve him **w**
4:35 he came out of him **w** having done him any harm.
6:49 like a man who built a house on the ground **w**
11:42 to have practiced, **w** neglecting the others.
11:44 and people walk over them **w** realizing it."
22:35 He said to them, "When I sent you out **w** a purse,
Jn 1: 3 and **w** him not one thing came into being.
3: 3 no one can see the kingdom of God **w** being born
3: 5 no one can enter the kingdom of God **w** being born
3:34 for he gives the Spirit **w** measure.
7:51 not judge people **w** first giving them a hearing
8: 7 [["Let anyone among you who is **w** sin be the first]]
15:25 'They hated me **w** a cause.'
Ac 5:26 with the temple police and brought them, but **w**
9: 9 For three days he was **w** sight,
9:38 "Please come to us **w** delay."
10:20 get up, go down, and go with them **w** hesitation;
10:29 So when I was sent for, I came **w** objection.
14:17 not left himself **w** a witness in doing good—
16:33 he and his entire family were baptized **w** delay.
24:18 **w** any crowd or disturbance.
25:27 to me unreasonable to send a prisoner **w** indicating
27:21 Since they had been **w** food for a long time,
27:33 that you have been in suspense and remaining **w**
28:31 the Lord Jesus Christ with all boldness and **w**
Ro 1: 9 that **w** ceasing I remember you always
1:20 the things he has made. So they are **w** excuse;
4: 5 But to one who **w** works trusts him who justifies
4:11 to make him the ancestor of all who believe **w**
10:14 how are they to hear **w** someone to proclaim him?
1Co 10:25 in the meat market **w** raising any question on
10:27 before you **w** raising any question on the ground
11:29 For all who eat and drink **w** discerning the body,
14:10 of sounds in the world, and nothing is **w** sound.
2Co 7: 5 in every way—disputes **w** and fears within.
10:16 **w** boasting of work already done
11:27 hungry and thirsty, often **w** food, cold and naked.
Eph 2:12 remember that you were at that time **w** Christ,
2:12 having no hope and **w** God in the world.
5:27 **w** a spot or wrinkle or anything of the kind—
5:27 yes, so that she may be holy and **w** blemish.
Php 1:14 dare to speak the word with greater boldness and **w**
2:14 Do all things **w** murmuring and arguing,
2:15 of God **w** blemish in the midst of a crooked
Col 1:23 **w** shifting from the hope promised by the gospel
2:18 puffed up **w** cause by a human way of thinking,
1Th 5:17 pray **w** ceasing,
2Th 3: 8 and we did not eat anyone's bread **w** paying for it;
1Ti 1: 7 **w** understanding either what they are saying or
2: 8 lifting up holy hands **w** anger or argument;
3:16 **W** any doubt, the mystery of our religion is great:
5:21 I warn you to keep these instructions **w** prejudice,
6:14 to keep the commandment **w** spot or blame until
2Ti 2: 5 no one is crowned **w** competing according to
Phm 1:14 but I preferred to do nothing **w** your consent,
Heb 4:15 in every respect has been tested as we are, yet **w**
7: 3 **W** father, **w** mother, **w** genealogy,
7:20 for others who became priests took their office **w**
9: 7 not **w** taking the blood that he offers for himself
9:14 who through the eternal Spirit offered himself **w**
9:18 even the first covenant was inaugurated **w** blood.
9:22 **w** the shedding of blood there is no forgiveness
10:23 Let us hold fast to the confession of our hope **w**
10:28 Anyone who has violated the law of Moses dies **w**
11: 6 And **w** faith it is impossible to please God,
11:13 All of these died in faith **w** having received
12:14 and the holiness **w** which no one will see the Lord.
13: 2 for by doing that some have entertained angels **w**
Jas 2:13 be **w** mercy to anyone who has shown no mercy;
2:26 For just as the body **w** the spirit is dead,
2:26 so faith **w** works is also dead.
3:17 **w** a trace of partiality or hypocrisy.
1Pe 1:19 like that of a lamb **w** defect or blemish.
3: 1 be won over **w** a word by their wives' conduct,
4: 9 Be hospitable to one another **w** complaining.
2Pe 3:14 to be found by him at peace, **w** spot or blemish;
Jude 1:12 while they feast with you **w** fear,
1:12 autumn trees **w** fruit, twice dead, uprooted;
1:24 and to make you stand **w** blemish in the presence
Rev 4: 8 Day and night **w** ceasing they sing, "Holy, holy,
Tob 5:10 I am a man **w** eyesight;
6:13 to another man **w** incurring the penalty of death
8:12 he is dead, let us bury him **w** anyone knowing it."
14:10 while the people are **w** shame.
Jdt 2:13 as I have ordered you; do it **w** delay."
9:11 protector of the forsaken, savior of those **w** hope.
10:13 and capture all the hill country **w** losing one
12:12 if we let such a woman go **w** having intercourse
AdE 4:11 or woman goes to the king inside the inner court **w**
4:16 and my maids and I will also go **w** food.
9:27 upon all who would join them, to observe it **w** fail.
13: 6 by the swords of their enemies, **w** pity or restraint,
16:24 "Every city and country, **w** exception,
Wis 1:11 because no secret word is **w** result,
3:17 and finally their old age will be **w** honor.
5: 4 and that their end was **w** honor.
7:13 I learned **w** guile and I impart **w** grudging;
9: 6 be regarded as nothing **w** the wisdom that comes
14: 5 that works of your wisdom should not be **w** effect;
16:20 and **w** their toil you supplied them from heaven
16:22 Snow and ice withstood fire **w** melting,

Wis 18:19 not perish w knowing why they suffered.
19:13 The punishments did not come upon the sinners w
Sir 3:25 W eyes there is no light; w knowledge there is no wisdom.
13: 5 he will drain your resources w a qualm.
19:16 A person may make a slip w intending it.
27:21 but whoever has betrayed secrets is w hope.
29:25 the host and provide drink w being thanked,
30: 5 in his life he looked upon with joy and at death, w
31:27 What is life to one who is w wine?
32:19 Do nothing w deliberation,
34: 8 W such deceptions the law will be fulfilled,
37:25 but the days of Israel are w number.
37:29 and do not eat w restraint;
38:32 W them no city can be inhabited,
51:25 Acquire wisdom for yourselves w money.
Bar 2:23 the whole land will be a desolation w inhabitants.
LtJ 6:25 They are bought w regard to cost,
Sus 1:48 as to condemn a daughter of Israel w examination and w learning the facts?
Bel 1:26 and I will kill the dragon w sword or club."
1Mc 2: 8 Her temple has become like a person w honor;
6:12 to destroy the inhabitants of Judah w good reason.
8:26 and they shall keep their obligations w
8:28 and they shall keep these obligations and do so w
10:33 into any part of my kingdom, I set free w payment;
14:44 an assembly in the country w his permission,
2Mc 2:32 w adding any more to what has already been said;
4: 6 that w the king's attention public affairs could
8: 6 Coming w warning, he would set fire to towns
9: 4 to drive w stopping until he completed the journey.
11:13 As he was not w intelligence,
12:15 who w battering-rams or engines of war
12:18 by then left there w accomplishing anything,
13: 7 w even burial in the earth.
13:12 and fasting and lying prostrate for three days w
14:27 to send Maccabeus to Antioch as a prisoner w
1Es 4:17 men cannot exist w women.
4:50 that they would occupy should be theirs w tribute;
6:30 regularly every year, w quibbling,
8:88 not angry enough with us to destroy us w leaving
3Mc 1:20 and w a backward look they crowded together at
5: 6 the Gentiles it appeared that the Jews were left w
5:20 "tomorrow w delay prepare the elephants in
5:42 that he would send them to death w delay,
7: 5 they tried w any inquiry or examination
7:12 and w royal authority or supervision,
2Es 1:35 who w having heard me will believe.
3: 4 when you planted the earth—and that w help—
3: 7 peoples and clans w number.
3:29 when I came here I saw ungodly deeds w number,
4:32 When heads of grain w number are sown,
5:39 As for me, I am w wisdom,
6:28 which has been so long w fruit, shall be revealed."
7:*98* and shall be confident w confusion,
7:*98* and shall be glad w fear,
13:36 as you saw the mountain carved out w hands.
13:38 and will destroy them w effort by means of
14:20 and its inhabitants are w light.
4Mc 2: 8 to natural ways and to lend w interest to the needy
9:12 w accomplishing anything,
12:14 but you will wail bitterly for having killed w cause
16: 9 some unmarried, others married and w offspring.
18: 2 but also of those from w.

WITHS (KJV) See BOWSTRINGS

WITHSTAND (27) [WITHSTOOD]

Nu 31:23 everything that can w fire, shall be passed through
31:23 and whatever cannot w fire, shall be passed
Jos 23: 9 for you, no one has been able to w you to this day.
Jdg 2:14 so that they could no longer w their enemies.
2Ki 10: 4 "Look, two kings could not w him;
2Ch 13: 7 and irresolute and could not w them.
13: 8 "And now you think that you can w the kingdom
20: 6 so that no one is able to w you.
Est 9: 2 and no one could w them,
Ecc 4:12 one might prevail against another, two will w one.
La 1:14 Lord handed me over to those whom I cannot w.
Da 8: 4 All beasts were powerless to w it,
8: 7 The ram did not have power to w it;
11:16 and no one shall w him.
Lk 21:15 of your opponents will be able to w or contradict.
Ac 6:10 But they could not w the wisdom and the Spirit
Eph 6:13 so that you may be able to w on that evil day,
Jdt 11:18 and not one of them will be able to w you.
Wis 11:21 and who can w the might of your arm?
Sir 43: 3 and who can w its burning heat?
1Mc 3:53 will we be able to w them, if you do not help us?"
6:49 the town because they had no provisions there to w
7:25 and realized that he could not w them,
10:73 now you will not be able to w my cavalry and such
2Mc 8: 5 the Gentiles could not w him,
10:18 in two very strong towers well equipped to w
4Mc 16:23 who have religious knowledge not to w pain."

WITHSTANDS See Index to Footnotes

WITHSTOOD (9) [WITHSTAND]

Jos 21:44 not one of all their enemies had w them,
2Ch 26:18 they w King Uzziah, and said to him, "It is not
Wis 10:16 and w dread kings with wonders and signs.
11: 3 They w their enemies and fought off their foes.
16:22 Snow and ice w fire without melting,
18:21 he w the anger and put an end to the disaster,
1Mc 6: 4 and they w him in battle.
2Es 7:*89* and w danger every hour so that they might keep
4Mc 15:32 and w the wintry storms that assail religion.

WITNESS‡ (105) [EYEWITNESSES, WITNESSED, WITNESSES]

A. FALSE WITNESS (16)

Ge 21:30 that you may be a w for me that I dug this well."
31:44 and let it be a w between you and me."
31:48 "This heap is a w between you and me today."
31:50 remember that God is w between you and me."
31:52 This heap is a w, and the pillar is a w,
Ex 20:16 shall not bear false w against your neighbor. A
23: 1 with the wicked to act as a malicious w.
23: 2 when you bear w in a lawsuit,
Nu 5:13 and there is no w against her since she was
35:30 be put to death on the testimony of a single w.
Dt 4:26 I call heaven and earth to w against you today
5:20 Neither shall you bear false w against your A
17: 6 not be put to death on the evidence of only one w.
19:15 A single w shall not suffice to convict a person
19:16 If a malicious w comes forward to accuse someone
19:18 If the w is a false witness,
19:18 If the witness is a false w, A
19:19 you shall do to the false w just as the false A
19:19 false witness just as the false w had meant to do A
30:19 and earth to w against you today that I have set
31:19 in their mouths, in order that this song may be a w
31:21 this song will confront them as a w,
31:26 let it remain there as a w against you.
31:28 in their hearing and call heaven and earth to w
32:46 the words that I am giving in w against you today;
Jos 22:27 but to be a w between us and you,
22:28 but to be a w between us and you.'
22:34 Reubenites and the Gadites called the altar W;
22:34 "it is a w between us that the LORD is God."
24:27 "See, this stone shall be a w against us;
24:27 therefore it shall be a w against you,
Jdg 11:10 "The LORD will be w between us;
1Sa 6:18 is a w to this day in the field of Joshua
12: 5 He said to them, "The LORD is w against you, and his anointed is w this day,
12: 5 And they said, "He is w."
12: 6 Samuel said to the people, "The LORD is w,
20:23 the LORD is w between you and me forever."
1Ki 1:48 to sit on my throne and permitted me to w it.'"
Ezr 4:14 the salt of the palace and it is not fitting for us to w
Job 16: 8 he has shriveled me up, which is a w against me;
16:19 Even now, in fact, my w is in heaven,
Ps 89:37 an enduring w in the skies."
Pr 6:19 a lying w who testifies falsely,
12:17 but a false w speaks deceitfully. A
14: 5 A faithful w does not lie,
14: 5 but a false w breathes out lies. A
14:25 A truthful w saves lives, but one who utters lies
19: 5 A false w will not go unpunished, A
19: 9 A false w will not go unpunished, A
19:28 A worthless w mocks at justice,
21:28 A false w will perish, but a good listener A
24:28 not be a w against your neighbor without cause,
25:18 a sharp arrow is one who bears false w against A
Isa 3: 9 The look on their faces bears w against them;
19:20 It will be a sign and a w to the LORD of hosts in
30: 8 that it may be for the time to come as a w forever.
55: 4 See, I made him a w to the peoples,
Jer 29:23 I am the one who knows and bears w,
42: 5 and faithful w against us if we do not act according
Mic 1: 2 and let the Lord GOD be a w against you,
Zep 3: 8 says the LORD, for the day when I arise as a w.
Mal 2:12 any to w or answer, or to bring an offering to
2:14 Because the LORD was a w between you and
3: 5 I will be swift to bear w against the sorcerers,
Mt 15:19 adultery, fornication, theft, false w, slander. A
19:18 You shall not bear false w; A
Mk 10:19 You shall not bear false w; A
Lk 18:20 You shall not bear false w; A
Jn 1: 7 He came as a w to testify to the light,
Ac 1:22 one of these must become a w with us
14:17 not left himself without a w in doing good—
22:15 be his w to all the world of what you have seen
22:20 And while the blood of your w Stephen was shed,
23:11 so you must bear w also in Rome."
Ro 1: 9 by announcing the gospel of his Son, is my w that
2:15 to which their own conscience also bears w;
8:16 it is that very Spirit bearing w with our spirit
2Co 1:23 But I call on God as w against me:
Php 1: 8 For God is my w, how I long for all of you with
1Th 2: 5 As you know and as God is our w,
1Pe 5: 1 an elder myself and a w of the sufferings of Christ,
Rev 1: 5 the faithful w, the firstborn of the dead,
2:13 in me even in the days of Antipas my w,
3:14 The words of the Amen, the faithful and true w,
15: 5 the temple of the tent of w in heaven was opened,
Tob 9: 3 You are w to the oath Raguel has sworn,
13:14 with you and w all your glory forever.
Jdt 7:27 not w our little ones dying before our eyes,
7:28 to w against you heaven and earth and our God,
15: 8 of the Israelites who lived in Jerusalem came to w
Wis 1: 6 because God is w of their inmost feelings,
Sir 36:20 Bear w to those whom you created in
46:19 Samuel bore w before the Lord and his anointed:
Sus 1:61 Daniel had convicted them of bearing false w; A
2Mc 7: 6 as Moses declared in his song that bore w against
12:30 the Jews who lived there bore w to the goodwill
3Mc 5:47 the animals, wishing to w, with invulnerable heart
2Es 1:37 to w the gratitude of the people that is to come,
2: 5 as a w in addition to the mother of the children,
2:14 Call, O call heaven and earth to w:
2:36 I publicly call on my savior to w.
7:*94* they see the w that he who formed them bears
4Mc 16:16 the contest to which you are called to bear w for

WITNESSED (3) [WITNESS]

Ex 20:18 When all the people w the thunder and lightning,
Jer 32:44 and deeds shall be signed and sealed and w,
4Mc 15:24 Although she w the destruction of seven children

WITNESSES (49) [WITNESS]

Nu 35:30 be put to death on the evidence of w;
Dt 17: 6 or three w the death sentence shall be executed;
17: 7 The hands of the w shall be the first raised against
19:15 on the evidence of two or three w shall a charge
21: 7 "Our hands did not shed this blood, nor were we w
Jos 24:22 "You are w against yourselves
24:22 And they said, "We are w."
Ru 4: 9 "Today you are w that I have acquired from
4:10 gate of his native place; today you are w."
4:11 along with the elders, said, "We are w.
Job 10:17 You renew your w against me,
Ps 27:12 for false w have risen against me,
35:11 Malicious w rise up; they ask me about things
Isa 8: 2 and have it attested for me by reliable w,
43: 9 Let them bring their w to justify them,
43:10 You are my w, says the LORD,
43:12 and you are my w, says the LORD.
44: 8 and declared it? You are my w!
44: 9 their w neither see nor know.
Jer 32:10 I signed the deed, sealed it, got w,
32:12 in the presence of the w who signed the deed
32:25 "Buy the field for money and get w"—
Mt 18:16 be confirmed by the evidence of two or three w.
26:60 though many false w came forward.
26:65 Why do we still need w?
Mk 14:63 "Why do we still need w?
Lk 11:48 So you are w and approve of the deeds
24:48 You are w of these things.
Jn 3:28 You yourselves are my w that I said,
8:17 that the testimony of two w is valid.
Ac 1: 8 and you will be my w in Jerusalem,
2:32 and of that all of us are w.
3:15 To this we are w.
5:32 And we are w to these things,
6:13 They set up false w who said,
7:58 the w laid their coats at the feet of a young man
10:39 We are w to all that he did both in Judea and
10:41 but to us who were chosen by God as w,
13:31 and they are now his w to the people.
2Co 13: 1 be sustained by the evidence of two or three w."
1Th 2:10 You are w, and God also, how pure, upright,
1Ti 5:19 an elder except on the evidence of two or three w.
6:12 the good confession in the presence of many w.
2Ti 2: 2 through many w entrust to faithful people who will
Heb 10:28 "on the testimony of two or three w."
12: 1 since we are surrounded by so great a cloud of w,
Rev 11: 3 And I will grant my two w authority to prophesy
17: 6 with the blood of the saints and the blood of the w
Wis 4: 6 For children born of unlawful unions are w of evil

WITS (2) [WITS']

Pr 27:17 and one person sharpens the w of another.
28:26 Those who trust in their own w are fools;

WITS' (1) [WITS]

Ps 107:27 and were at their w end.

WITTY (KJV) See DISCRETION

WIVES‡ (153) [WIFE]

Ge 4:19 Lamech took two w; the name of the one
4:23 Lamech said to his w: "Adah and Zillah,
4:23 you w of Lamech, listen to what I say:
6: 2 they took w for themselves of all that they chose.
6:18 your sons, your wife, and your sons' w with you.
7: 7 with his sons and his wife and his sons' w went
7:13 and the three w of his sons entered the ark,
8:16 and your sons and your sons' w with you.
8:18 with his sons and his wife and his sons' w.
11:29 Abram and Nahor took w;
28: 9 to be his wife in addition to the w he had.
30:26 Give me my w and my children
31:17 and set his children and his w on camels;
31:50 or if you take w in addition to my daughters,
32:22 The same night he got up and took his two w,
34:29 All their wealth, all their little ones and their w,
36: 2 Esau took his w from the Canaanites:
36: 6 Then Esau took his w, his sons, his daughters,
37: 2 to the sons of Bilhah and Zilpah, his father's w;
45:19 of Egypt for your little ones and for your w,
46: 5 their little ones, and their w,
46:26 not including the w of his sons,
Ex 22:24 and your w shall become widows
32: 2 the gold rings that are on the ears of your w,
34:16 And you will take w from among their daughters
Nu 14: 3 Our w and our little ones will become booty;
16:27 together with their w, their children,
32:26 Our little ones, our w, our flocks,
Dt 3:19 Only your w, your children, and your livestock—
17:17 And he must not acquire many w for himself,
21:15 If a man has two w,

Jos 1:14 Your **w**, your little ones,
Jdg 3:6 and they took their daughters as **w** for themselves,
8:30 his own offspring, for he had many **w**.
21:7 What shall we do for **w** for those who are left,
21:7 not give them any of our daughters as **w**?"
21:16 "What shall we do for **w** for those who are left,
21:18 we cannot give any of our daughters to them as **w**."
21:23 they took **w** for each of them from
Ru 1:4 These took Moabite **w**; the name of the
1Sa 1:2 He had two **w**; the name of the
25:43 both of them became his **w**.
27:3 and David with his two **w**, Ahinoam of Jezreel,
30:3 and their **w** and sons and daughters taken captive.
30:5 David's two **w** also had been taken captive,
30:18 and David rescued his two **w**.
2Sa 2:2 So David went up there, along with his two **w**,
5:13 David took more concubines and **w**;
12:8 and your master's **w** into your bosom,
12:11 and I will take your **w** before your eyes,
12:11 to your neighbor, and he shall lie with your **w** in
19:5 and the lives of your **w** and your concubines,
1Ki 10:8 Happy are your **w**! Happy are these your servants,
11:3 Among his **w** were seven hundred princesses
11:3 and his **w** turned away his heart.
11:4 his **w** turned away his heart after other gods;
11:8 He did the same for all his foreign **w**,
20:3 your fairest **w** and children also are mine."
20:5 to me your silver and gold, your **w** and children';
20:7 for he sent to me for my **w**, my children, my silver,
2Ki 24:15 the king's mother, the king's **w**, his officials,
1Ch 4:5 Ashhur father of Tekoa had two **w**,
7:4 thirty-six thousand, for they had many **w** and sons.
8:8 after he had sent away his **w** Hushim and Baara.
14:3 David took more **w** in Jerusalem,
2Ch 11:21 all his other **w** and concubines (he took eighteen **w**
11:23 and found many **w** for them.
13:21 He took fourteen **w**, and became the father
20:13 with their little ones, their **w**, and their children.
21:14 your children, your **w**, and all your possessions,
21:17 along with his sons and his **w**,
24:3 Jehoiada got two **w** for him,
29:9 and our sons and our daughters and our **w** are
31:18 their **w**, their sons, and their daughters,
Ezr 9:2 For they have taken some of their daughters as **w**
10:3 a covenant with our God to send away all these **w**
10:11 the peoples of the land and from the foreign **w**."
10:14 in our towns who have taken foreign **w** come
10:19 They pledged themselves to send away their **w**,
Ne 4:14 your daughters, your **w**, and your homes."
5:1 the people and of their **w** against their Jewish kin.
10:28 their **w**, their sons, their daughters,
Isa 13:16 be plundered, and their **w** ravished.
Jer 6:12 their fields and **w** together;
8:10 Therefore I will give their **w** to others
14:16 themselves, their **w**, their sons,
18:21 let their **w** become childless and widowed.
29:6 Take **w** and have sons and daughters;
29:6 take **w** for your sons, and give your daughters
29:23 with their neighbors' **w**, and have spoken
35:8 to drink no wine all our days, ourselves, our **w**,
38:23 All your **w** and your children shall be led out to
44:9 of the kings of Judah, of their **w**,
44:9 your own crimes and those of your **w**,
44:15 that their **w** had been making offerings
44:25 You and your **w** have accomplished
Da 5:2 his **w**, and his concubines might drink from them.
5:3 his **w**, and his concubines drank from them.
5:23 in before you, and you and your lords, your **w**
6:24 they, their children, and their **w**.
Zec 12:12 and their **w** by themselves;
12:12 and their **w** by themselves;
12:13 and their **w** by themselves;
12:13 and their **w** by themselves;
12:14 each by itself, and their **w** by themselves.
Mt 19:8 that Moses allowed you to divorce your **w**,
Ac 21:5 and all of them, with **w** and children,
1Co 7:29 from now on, let even those who have **w** be as
Eph 5:22 **W**, be subject to your husbands as you are to
5:24 so also **w** ought to be, in everything,
5:25 love your **w**, just as Christ loved the church
5:28 husbands should love their **w**
Col 3:18 **W**, be subject to your husbands,
3:19 love your **w** and never treat them harshly.
1Pe 3:1 **W**, in the same way, accept the authority
3:7 consideration for your **w** in your life together,
Tob 3:8 with her as is customary for **w**.
4:12 all took **w** from among their kindred.
Jdt 4:10 They and their **w** and their children and their cattle
4:12 to allow their infants to be carried off and their **w**
7:14 They and their **w** and children will waste away
7:27 and our **w** and children drawing their last breath.
9:4 You gave up their **w** for booty and their daughters
AdE 1:18 so now the other ladies who are **w** of the Persian
13:6 **w** and children included—
Wis 3:12 Their **w** are foolish, and their children evil;
LtJ 6:28 Likewise their **w** preserve some of the meat
6:33 of the clothing of their gods to clothe their **w**
Bel 1:10 besides their **w** and children.
1:15 as usual, with their **w** and children, and they ate
1:21 he arrested the priests and their **w** and children.
1Mc 2:30 their sons, their **w**, and their livestock,
2:38 with their **w** and children and livestock,
3:20 and our **w** and our children, and to despoil us;
5:13 the enemy have captured their **w** and children
5:23 with their **w** and children, and all they possessed,
5:45 with their **w** and children and goods,
8:10 and the Romans took captive their **w** and children;
1Mc 13:6 and the sanctuary and your **w** and children,
13:45 The men in the city, with their **w** and children,
2Mc 12:3 among them to embark, with their **w** and children,
15:18 Their concern for **w** and children,
1Es 5:1 with their **w** and sons and daughters,
8:93 that we will put away all our foreign **w**,
9:9 the peoples of the land and from your foreign **w**."
9:12 in our settlements who have foreign **w** come at
9:17 the men who had foreign **w** were brought to an end
9:18 in and found to have foreign **w** were:
9:20 They pledged themselves to put away their **w**,
3Mc 1:4 and their children and **w** bravely,
3:25 together with their **w** and children,
2Es 10:22 and our **w** have been ravished;

WIVES' (2) [WIFE]

1Ti 4:7 nothing to do with profane myths and old **w** tales.
1Pe 3:1 be won over without a word by their **w** conduct,

WIZARD (1) [WIZARDS]

Lev 20:27 A man or a woman who is a medium or a **w** shall

WIZARDS (7) [WIZARD]

Lev 19:31 Do not turn to mediums or **w**;
20:6 If any turn to mediums and **w**,
1Sa 28:3 Saul had expelled the mediums and the **w** from
28:9 how he has cut off the mediums and the **w** from
2Ki 21:6 and dealt with mediums and with **w**.
23:24 Moreover Josiah put away the mediums, **w**,
2Ch 33:6 and dealt with mediums and with **w**.

WOE‡ (85) [WOES]

Nu 21:29 **W** to you, O Moab!
1Sa 4:7 They also said, "**W** to us!
4:8 **W** to us! Who can deliver us from the
Job 10:15 If I am wicked, **w** to me!
Ps 120:5 **W** is me, that I am an alien in Meshech,
Pr 23:29 Who has **w**? Who has sorrow?
Ecc 4:10 but **w** to one who is alone and falls and does
Isa 3:9 **W** to them! For they have brought evil on
3:11 **W** to the guilty! How unfortunate they are,
6:5 And I said: "**W** is me!
24:16 I pine away, I pine away. **W** is me!
45:7 I make weal and create **w**;
45:9 **W** to you who strive with your Maker,
45:10 **W** to anyone who says to a father,
Jer 4:13 **w** to us, for we are ruined!
4:31 stretching out her hands, "**W** is me!
6:4 "**W** to us, for the day declines,
10:19 **W** is me because of my hurt!
13:27 **W** to you, O Jerusalem! How long will it be
15:10 **W** is me, my mother, that you ever bore me,
22:13 **W** to him who builds his house
23:1 **W** to the shepherds who destroy and scatter
45:3 You said, "**W** is me! The LORD has added sorrow
48:46 **W** to you, O Moab!
La 5:16 **w** to us, for we have sinned!
Eze 2:10 of lamentation and mourning and **w**.
13:18 **W** to the women who sew bands on all wrists,
16:23 After all your wickedness (**w**, **w** to you!
24:6 **W** to the bloody city, the pot whose rust is in it,
24:9 **W** to the bloody city! I will even make the pile
Hos 7:13 **W** to them, for they have strayed from me!
9:12 **W** to them indeed when I depart from them!
Mic 7:1 **W** is me! For I have become like one
Mt 11:21 "**W** to you, Chorazin! **W** to you,
18:7 **W** to the world because of stumbling blocks!
18:7 **w** to the one by whom the stumbling block comes!
23:13 "But **w** to you, scribes and Pharisees, hypocrites!
23:15 **W** to you, scribes and Pharisees, hypocrites!
23:16 "**W** to you, blind guides, who say,
23:23 "**W** to you, scribes and Pharisees, hypocrites!
23:25 "**W** to you, scribes and Pharisees, hypocrites!
23:27 "**W** to you, scribes and Pharisees, hypocrites!
23:29 "**W** to you, scribes and Pharisees, hypocrites!
24:19 **W** to those who are pregnant and
26:24 but **w** to that one by whom the Son
Mk 13:17 **W** to those who are pregnant and
14:21 but **w** to that one by whom the Son
Lk 6:24 "But **w** to you who are rich,
6:25 "**W** to you who are full now,
6:25 "**W** to you who are laughing now,
6:26 "**W** to you when all speak well of you,
10:13 "**W** to you, Chorazin! **W** to you,
11:42 "But **w** to you Pharisees!
11:43 **W** to you Pharisees! For you love to have
11:44 **W** to you! For you are like unmarked
11:46 And he said, "**W** also to you lawyers!
11:47 **W** to you! For you build the tombs of the
11:52 **W** to you lawyers! For you have taken away the
17:1 but **w** to anyone by whom they come!
21:23 **W** to those who are pregnant and
22:22 but **w** to that one by whom he is betrayed!"
1Co 9:16 and **w** to me if I do not proclaim the gospel!
Jude 1:11 **W** to them! For they go the way of Cain,
Rev 8:13 "**W**, **w**, **w** to the inhabitants of the earth,
9:12 The first **w** has passed.
11:14 The second **w** has passed.
11:14 The third **w** is coming very soon.
12:12 But **w** to the earth and the sea,
Tob 10:5 "**W** to me, my child, the light of my eyes,
Jdt 16:17 **W** to the nations that rise up against my people!
Sir 2:12 **W** to timid hearts and to slack hands,
2:13 **W** to the fainthearted who have no trust!
2:14 **W** to you who have lost your nerve!
Sir 41:8 **W** to you, the ungodly, who have forsaken the law
2Es 2:8 "**W** to you, Assyria, who conceal the unrighteous
15:47 **w** to you, miserable wretch!
16:1 **W** to you, Babylon and Asia!
16:1 **W** to you, Egypt and Syria!
16:63 **W** to those who sin and want to hide their sins!
16:77 **W** to those who are choked by their sins

WOES (1) [WOE]

Rev 9:12 There are still two **w** to come.

WOKE (12) [WAKE]

Ge 28:16 Then Jacob **w** from his sleep and said,
Mt 8:25 they went and **w** him up, saying, "Lord, save us!
Mk 4:38 and they **w** him up and said to him, "Teacher,
4:39 He **w** up and rebuked the wind, and said to the sea,
Lk 8:24 They went to him and **w** him up, shouting,
8:24 And he **w** up and rebuked the wind and
Ac 12:7 He tapped Peter on the side and **w** him, saying,
16:27 jailer **w** up and saw the prison doors wide open,
1Es 3:3 he went to sleep, but **w** up again.
2Es 5:14 Then I **w** up, and my body shuddered violently,
12:3 I **w** up in great perplexity of mind and great fear,
13:13 Then I **w** up in great terror,

WOLF (7) [WOLVES]

Ge 49:27 Benjamin is a ravenous **w**,
Isa 11:6 The **w** shall live with the lamb,
65:25 The **w** and the lamb shall feed together,
Jer 5:6 a **w** from the desert shall destroy them.
Jn 10:12 sees the **w** coming and leaves the sheep
10:12 and the **w** snatches them and scatters them.
Sir 13:17 What does a **w** have in common with a lamb?

WOLVES (8) [WOLF]

Eze 22:27 Its officials within it are like **w** tearing the prey,
Hab 1:8 more menacing than **w** at dusk;
Zep 3:3 its judges are evening **w** that leave nothing until
Mt 7:15 in sheep's clothing but inwardly are ravenous **w**.
10:16 like sheep into the midst of **w**;
Lk 10:3 like lambs into the midst of **w**.
Ac 20:29 savage **w** will come in among you,
2Es 5:18 the flock in the power of savage **w**."

WOMAN‡ (443) [KINSWOMAN, WOMAN'S, WOMANHOOD, WOMEN, WOMEN'S]

A. WOMAN IN LABOR (17)
B. YOUNG WOMAN (14)

Ge 2:22 from the man he made into a **w** and brought her to
2:23 this one shall be called **W**,
3:1 He said to the **w**, "Did God say,
3:2 The **w** said to the serpent, "We may eat of the fruit
3:4 But the serpent said to the **w**, "You will not die;
3:6 So when the **w** saw that the tree was good for food,
3:12 man said, "The **w** whom you gave to be with me,
3:13 Then the LORD God said to the **w**,
3:13 The **w** said, "The serpent tricked me, and I ate."
3:15 I will put enmity between you and the **w**,
3:16 the **w** he said, "I will greatly increase your pangs
12:11 that you are a **w** beautiful in appearance;
12:14 the Egyptians saw that the **w** was very beautiful.
12:15 And the **w** was taken into Pharaoh's house.
20:3 to die because of the **w** whom you have taken;
20:3 for she is a married **w**."
21:10 "Cast out this slave **w** with her son;
21:10 for the son of this slave **w** shall not inherit along
21:12 because of the boy and because of your slave **w**;
21:13 As for the son of the slave **w**,
24:5 the **w** may not be willing to follow me to this land;
24:8 But if the **w** is not willing to follow you,
24:39 'Perhaps the **w** will not follow me.'
24:43 let the young **w** who comes out to draw, B
24:44 let her be the **w** whom the LORD has appointed
38:20 to recover the pledge from the **w**,
46:10 Zohar, and Shaul, the son of a Canaanite **w**.
Ex 2:1 the house of Levi went and married a Levite **w**.
2:2 The **w** conceived and bore a son;
2:9 So the **w** took the child and nursed it.
3:22 each **w** shall ask her neighbor and any **w** living in
6:15 Zohar, and Shaul, the son of a Canaanite **w**;
11:2 and every **w** is to ask her neighbor for objects
19:15 do not go near a **w**."
21:22 When people who are fighting injure a pregnant **w**
21:28 When an ox gores a man or a **w** to death,
21:29 and it kills a man or a **w**, the ox shall be stoned,
36:6 or **w** is to make anything else as an offering for
Lev 12:2 If a **w** conceives and bears a male child,
13:29 man or **w** has a disease on the head or in the beard,
13:38 a man or a **w** has spots on the skin of the body,
15:18 a man lies with a **w** and has an emission of semen,
15:19 When a **w** has a discharge of blood
15:25 If a **w** has a discharge of blood for many days,
15:33 and for the man who lies with a **w** who is unclean.
18:17 You shall not uncover the nakedness of a **w**
18:18 And you shall not take a **w** as a rival to her sister,
18:19 not approach a **w** to uncover her nakedness
18:22 You shall not lie with a male as with a **w**;
18:23 nor shall any **w** give herself to an animal
19:20 a man has sexual relations with a **w** who is a slave,
20:13 If a man lies with a male as with a **w**,
20:16 If a **w** approaches any animal and has sexual
20:16 you shall kill the **w** and the animal;
20:18 If a man lies with a **w** having her sickness

Lev 20:27 A man or a **w** who is a medium or a wizard shall
21: 7 not marry a prostitute or a **w** who has been defiled;
21: 7 neither shall they marry a **w** divorced
21:13 He shall marry only a **w** who is a virgin.
21:14 or a divorced **w**, or a **w** who has been defiled,
Nu 5: 6 When a man or a **w** wrongs another,
5:18 The priest shall set the **w** before the LORD,
5:21 the **w** take the oath of the curse and say to the **w**—
5:22 And the **w** shall say, "Amen.
5:24 He shall make the **w** drink the water of bitterness
5:26 and afterward shall make the **w** drink the water.
5:27 **w** shall become an execration among her people.
5:28 But if the **w** has not defiled herself and is clean,
5:30 then he shall set the **w** before the LORD,
5:31 but the **w** shall bear her iniquity.
12: 1 because of the Cushite **w** whom he had married
(for he had indeed married a Cushite **w**);
25: 6 of the Israelites came and brought a Midianite **w**
25: 8 the Israelite and the **w**, through the belly.
25:14 who was killed with the Midianite **w**,
25:15 Midianite **w** who was killed was Cozbi daughter
30: 3 When a **w** makes a vow to the LORD,
30: 9 (But every vow of a widow or of a divorced **w**,
31:17 and kill every **w** who has known a man by sleeping
Dt 15:12 whether a Hebrew man or a Hebrew **w**,
17: 2 a man or **w** who does what is evil in the sight of
17: 5 that man or that **w** who has committed this crime
17: 5 and you shall stone the man or **w** to death.
20: 7 Has anyone become engaged to a **w** but not
21:11 among the captives a beautiful **w** whom you desire
22: 5 A **w** shall not wear a man's apparel,
22:13 Suppose a man marries a **w**,
22:14 slandering her by saying, "I married this **w**;
22:15 of the young **w** and her mother shall then submit B
22:16 father of the young **w** shall say to the elders: B
22:21 then they shall bring the young **w** out to B
22:22 the man who lay with the **w** as well as the **w**.
22:23 If there is a young **w**, a virgin already engaged B
22:24 the young **w** because she did not cry for help in B
22:25 the man meets the engaged **w** in the open country,
22:26 You shall do nothing to the young **w**; B
22:26 the young **w** has not committed an offense B
22:27 the engaged **w** may have cried for help,
24: 1 Suppose a man enters into marriage with a **w**,
28:30 You shall become engaged to a **w**,
29:18 It may be that there is among you a man or **w**,
32:25 for young man and **w** alike,
Jos 2: 4 But the **w** took the two men and hid them.
6:22 and bring the **w** out of it and all who belong to her,
Jdg 4: 9 the LORD will sell Sisera into the hand of a **w**."
9:18 and have made Abimelech, the son of his slave **w**,
9:53 But a certain **w** threw an upper millstone
9:54 not say about me, 'A **w** killed him.' "
11: 2 for you are the son of another **w**."
13: 3 the angel of the LORD appeared to the **w** and said
13: 6 Then the **w** came and told her husband,
13: 9 the angel of God came again to the **w** as she sat in
13:10 So the **w** ran quickly and told her husband,
13:11 "Are you the man who spoke to this **w**?"
13:13 "Let the **w** give heed to all that I said to her.
13:24 The **w** bore a son, and named him Samson.
14: 1 and at Timnah he saw a Philistine **w**.
14: 2 "I saw a Philistine **w** at Timnah;
14: 3 "Is there not a **w** among your kin,
14: 7 Then he went down and talked with the **w**,
14:10 His father went down to the **w**,
16: 4 this he fell in love with a **w** in the valley of Sorek,
19:19 and wine for me and the **w** and the young man
19:26 the **w** came and fell down at the door of
20: 4 Levite, the husband of the **w** who was murdered,
21:11 every male and every **w** that has lain with
Ru 1: 5 **w** was left without her two sons and her husband.
2: 5 "To whom does this young **w** belong?" B
3: 8 and there, lying at his feet, was a **w**!
3:11 of my people know that you are a worthy **w**.
3:14 for he said, "It must not be known that the **w** came
4:11 the **w** who is coming into your house like Rachel
4:12 that the LORD will give you by this young **w**, B
1Sa 1:15 "No, my lord, I am a **w** deeply troubled;
1:16 Do not regard your servant as a worthless **w**,
1:18 Then the **w** went to her quarters,
1:23 So the **w** remained and nursed her son,
1:26 the **w** who was standing here in your presence,
2:20 with children by this **w** for the gift that she made to
15: 3 do not spare them, but kill both man and **w**,
20:30 "You son of a perverse, rebellious **w**!
25: 3 The **w** was clever and beautiful,
27: 9 leaving neither man nor **w** alive,
27:11 nor **w** alive to be brought back to Gath,
28: 7 "Seek out for me a **w** who is a medium,
28: 8 They came to the **w** by night.
28: 9 The **w** said to him,
28:11 Then the **w** said, "Whom shall I bring up for you?"
28:12 the **w** saw Samuel, she cried out with a loud voice;
28:12 the **w** said to Saul, "Why have you deceived me?
28:13 The **w** said to Saul, "I see a divine being coming
28:21 The **w** came to Saul, and when she saw
28:23 But his servants, together with the **w**, urged him;
28:24 Now the **w** had a fatted calf in the house.
2Sa 3: 8 now with a crime concerning this **w**.
11: 2 the roof a **w** bathing; the **w** was very beautiful.
11: 3 David sent someone to inquire about the **w**.
11: 5 The **w** conceived; and she sent and told David,
11:21 Did not a **w** throw an upper millstone on him from
13:17 "Put this **w** out of my presence,
13:20 So Tamar remained, a desolate **w**,
14: 2 to Tekoa and brought from there a wise **w**.
2Sa 14: 2 like a **w** who has been mourning many days for
14: 4 When the **w** of Tekoa came to the king,
14: 8 Then the king said to the **w**, "Go to your house,
14: 9 The **w** of Tekoa said to the king,
14:12 the **w** said, "Please let your servant speak a word
14:13 The **w** said, "Why then have you planned such
14:18 Then the king answered the **w**,
14:18 The **w** said, "Let my lord the king speak."
14:19 The **w** answered and said, "As surely as you live,
14:27 whose name was Tamar; she was a beautiful **w**.
17:20 Absalom's servants came to the **w** at the house,
17:20 The **w** said to them, "They have crossed over
20:16 Then a wise **w** called from the city, "Listen!
20:17 He came near her; and the **w** said, "Are you Joab?"
20:21 The **w** said to Joab, "His head shall be thrown over
20:22 the **w** went to all the people with her wise plan.
1Ki 3:17 The one **w** said, "Please, my lord,
3:17 my lord, this **w** and I live in the same house;
3:18 Then on the third day after I gave birth, this **w**
3:22 But the other **w** said, "No, the living son is mine,
3:26 But the **w** whose son was alive said to the king—
3:27 "Give the first **w** the living boy; do not kill him.
14: 5 When she came, she pretended to be another **w**.
17:17 After this the son of the **w**,
17:24 So the **w** said to Elijah,
2Ki 4: 8 where a wealthy **w** lived, who urged him to have
4:12 to his servant Gehazi, "Call the Shunammite **w**."
4:17 The **w** conceived and bore a son at that season,
4:25 "Look, there is the Shunammite **w**;
4:36 and said, "Call the Shunammite **w**."
6:26 a **w** cried out to him, "Help, my lord king!"
6:28 She answered, "This **w** said to me,
6:30 king heard the words of the **w** he tore his clothes—
8: 1 to the **w** whose son he had restored to life, "Get up
8: 2 So the **w** got up and did according to the word of
8: 3 the **w** returned from the land of the Philistines,
8: 5 the **w** whose son he had restored to life appealed to
8: 5 Gehazi said, "My lord king, here is the **w**,
8: 6 When the king questioned the **w**, she told him.
9:34 he said, "See to that cursed **w** and bury her;
1Ch 2: 3 these three the Canaanite **w** Bath-shua bore to him.
16: 3 in Israel—man and **w** alike—
2Ch 15:13 whether young or old, man or **w**.
24: 7 For the children of Athaliah, that wicked **w**,
36:17 had no compassion on young man or young **w**, B
Est 4:11 that if any man or **w** goes to the king inside
Job 2:10 "You speak as any foolish **w** would speak.
14: 1 born of **w**, few of days and full of trouble,
15:14 Or those born of **w**, that they can be righteous?
24:21 "They harm the childless **w**,
25: 4 How can one born of **w** be pure?
31: 9 "If my heart has been enticed by a **w**,
Ps 48: 6 pains as of a **w** in labor, A
113: 9 He gives the barren **w** a home,
Pr 2:16 You will be saved from the loose **w**,
5: 3 For the lips of a loose **w** drip honey,
5:20 by another **w** and embrace the bosom of
7: 5 that they may keep you from the loose **w**,
7:10 Then a **w** comes toward him,
9:13 The foolish **w** is loud; she is ignorant
11:16 A gracious **w** gets honor,
11:22 a pig's snout is a beautiful **w** without good sense.
14: 1 The wise **w** builds her house,
22:14 The mouth of a loose **w** is a deep pit;
30:23 an unloved **w** when she gets a husband,
31:30 but a **w** who fears the LORD is to be praised.
Ecc 7:26 I found more bitter than death the **w** who is a trap,
7:28 but a **w** among all these I have not found.
Isa 7:14 the young **w** is with child and shall bear a son, B
13: 8 they will be in anguish like a **w** in labor. A
21: 3 like the pangs of a **w** in labor; A
26:17 Like a **w** with child, who writhes and cries out
42:14 now I will cry out like a **w** in labor, A
45:10 or to a **w**, "With what are you in labor?"
49:15 Can a **w** forget her nursing child,
54: 1 of the desolate **w** will be more than the children
62: 5 For as a young man marries a young **w**, B
Jer 4:31 For I heard a cry as of a **w** in labor, A
6:24 pain as of a **w** in labor. A
13:21 like those of a **w** in labor? A
22:23 pain as of a **w** in labor! A
30: 6 with his hands on his loins like a **w** in labor? A
31:22 on the earth: a **w** encompasses a man.
44: 7 to cut off man and **w**, child and infant,
48:19 Ask the man fleeing and the **w** escaping;
48:41 that day, shall be like the heart of a **w** in labor. A
49:22 that day shall be like the heart of a **w** in labor. A
49:24 have taken hold of her, as of a **w** in labor. A
50:43 seized him, pain like that of a **w** in labor. A
51:22 with you I smash man and **w**;
Eze 18: 6 does not defile his neighbor's wife or approach a **w**
36:17 the uncleanness of a **w** in her menstrual period.
44:22 They shall not marry a widow, or a divorced **w**,
Da 11:17 he shall give him a **w** in marriage;
Hos 3: 1 "Go, love a **w** who has a lover and is an adulteress,
Mic 4: 9 that pangs have seized you like a **w** in labor? A
4:10 O daughter Zion, like a **w** in labor; A
Zec 5: 7 and there was a **w** sitting in the basket!
Mt 5:28 But I say to you that everyone who looks at a **w**
5:32 whoever marries a divorced **w** commits adultery.
9:20 a **w** who had been suffering from hemorrhages
9:22 And instantly the **w** was made well.
13:33 a **w** took and mixed in with three measures of flour
15:22 Just then a Canaanite **w** from that region came out
15:28 Then Jesus answered her, "**W**, great is your faith!
22:27 Last of all, the **w** herself died.
26: 7 a **w** came to him with an alabaster jar
Mt 26:10 said to them, "Why do you trouble the **w**?
Mk 5:25 a **w** who had been suffering from hemorrhages
5:33 But the **w**, knowing what had happened to her,
7:25 but a **w** whose little daughter had
7:26 the **w** was a Gentile, of Syrophoenician origin.
12:22 Last of all the **w** herself died.
14: 3 a **w** came with an alabaster jar
Lk 7:37 And a **w** in the city, who was a sinner,
7:39 and what kind of **w** this is who is touching him—
7:44 Then turning toward the **w**, he said to Simon, "Do
you see this **w**?
7:50 And he said to the **w**, "Your faith has saved you;
8:43 a **w** who had been suffering from hemorrhages
8:47 When the **w** saw that she could not remain hidden,
10:38 a **w** named Martha welcomed him into her home.
11:27 a **w** in the crowd raised her voice and said to him,
13:11 And just then there appeared a **w** with a spirit
13:12 Jesus saw her, he called her over and said, "**W**,
13:16 And ought not this **w**, a daughter
13:21 a **w** took and mixed in with three measures of flour
15: 8 "Or what **w** having ten silver coins,
16:18 a **w** divorced from her husband commits adultery.
20:32 Finally the **w** also died.
20:33 therefore, whose wife will the **w** be?
22:57 But he denied it, saying, "**W**, I do not know him."
Jn 2: 4 And Jesus said to her, "**W**,
4: 7 A Samaritan **w** came to draw water,
4: 9 The Samaritan **w** said to him, "How is it that you,
a Jew, ask a drink of me, a **w** of Samaria?"
4:11 The **w** said to him, "Sir, you have no bucket,
4:15 The **w** said to him, "Sir, give me this water,
4:17 The **w** answered him, "I have no husband."
4:19 **w** said to him, "Sir, I see that you are a prophet.
4:21 Jesus said to her, "**W**, believe me,
4:25 The **w** said to him, "I know
4:27 that he was speaking with a **w**,
4:28 the **w** left her water jar and went back to the city.
4:42 to the **w**, "It is no longer because of what you said
8: 3 ⟦the Pharisees brought a **w** who had been caught⟧
8: 4 ⟦this **w** was caught in the very act of committing⟧
8: 9 ⟦and Jesus was left alone with the **w** standing⟧
8:10 ⟦Jesus straightened up and said to her, "**W**,⟧
16:21 When a **w** is in labor, she has pain,
18:16 went out, spoke to the **w** who guarded the gate,
18:17 The **w** said to Peter, "You are not also one
19:26 he said to his mother, "**W**, here is your son."
20:13 They said to her, "**W**, why are you weeping?"
20:15 Jesus said to her, "**W**, why are you weeping?
Ac 16: 1 the son of a Jewish **w** who was a believer;
16:14 A certain **w** named Lydia, a worshiper of God,
17:34 the Areopagite and a **w** named Damaris,
Ro 7: 2 a married **w** is bound by the law to her husband
1Co 7: 1 "It is well for a man not to touch a **w**."
7: 2 and each **w** her own husband.
7:13 And if any **w** has a husband who is an unbeliever,
7:34 the unmarried **w** and the virgin are anxious about
7:34 married **w** is anxious about the affairs of the world,
11: 5 but any **w** who prays or prophesies
11: 6 For if a **w** will not veil herself,
11: 6 if it is disgraceful for a **w** to have her hair cut off
11: 7 but **w** is the reflection of man.
11: 8 man was not made from **w**, but **w** from man.
11: 9 Neither was man created for the sake of **w**, but **w**
for the sake of man.
11:10 For this reason a **w** ought to have a symbol
11:11 in the Lord **w** is not independent of man or man
independent of **w**.
11:12 as **w** came from man, so man comes through **w**;
11:13 for a **w** to pray to God with her head unveiled?
11:15 but if a **w** has long hair,
14:35 For it is shameful for a **w** to speak in church.
Gal 4: 4 God sent his Son, born of a **w**, born under the law,
4:22 one by a slave **w** and the other by a free **w**.
4:23 the other, the child of the free **w**,
4:24 One **w**, in fact, is Hagar, from Mount Sinai,
4:26 the other **w** corresponds to the Jerusalem above;
4:27 of the desolate **w** are more numerous than
4:30 the inheritance with the child of the free **w**."
4:31 we are children, not of the slave but of the free **w**.
1Th 5: 3 as labor pains come upon a pregnant **w**,
1Ti 2:11 Let a **w** learn in silence with full submission.
2:12 I permit no **w** to teach or to have authority over
2:14 but the **w** was deceived and became a transgressor.
5:16 believing **w** has relatives who are really widows,
1Pe 3: 7 paying honor to the **w** as the weaker sex,
Rev 2:20 you tolerate that **w** Jezebel,
12: 1 a **w** clothed with the sun,
12: 4 Then the dragon stood before the **w** who was about
12: 6 and the **w** fled into the wilderness,
12:13 the **w** who had given birth to the male child.
12:14 the **w** was given the two wings of the great eagle,
12:15 the serpent poured water like a river after the **w**,
12:16 But the earth came to the help of the **w**;
12:17 Then the dragon was angry with the **w**,
17: 3 a **w** sitting on a scarlet beast that was full
17: 4 The **w** was clothed in purple and scarlet,
17: 6 And I saw that the **w** was drunk with the blood of
17: 7 I will tell you the mystery of the **w**,
17: 9 on which the **w** is seated;
17:18 The **w** you saw is the great city that rules over
Tob 1: 9 When I became a man I married a **w**,
4:12 marry a **w** from among the descendants
4:12 a foreign **w**, who is not of your father's tribe;
6: 8 in the presence of a man or **w** afflicted by a demon
Jdt 8:31 Now since you are a God-fearing **w**, pray for us,
9:10 crush their arrogance by the hand of a **w**.
11: 1 Then Holofernes said to her, "Take courage, **w**,

Jdt 11:21 "No other w from one end of the earth to
12:11 the Hebrew w who is in your care to join us and
12:12 if we let such a w go without having intercourse
13:15 The Lord has struck him down by the hand of a w.
14:18 One Hebrew w has brought disgrace on the house
16: 5 Lord Almighty has foiled them by the hand of a w.
AdE 1:11 for she was indeed a beautiful w.
1:19 the king give her royal rank to a w better than she.
2: 4 the w who pleases the king shall be queen instead
4:11 of the empire know that if any man or w goes to
Wis 3:13 For blessed is the barren w who is undefiled,
Sir 9: 2 Do not give yourself to a w and let her trample
9: 3 Do not go near a loose w,
9: 8 Turn away your eyes from a shapely w,
19:11 the fool suffers birth pangs like a w in labor A
23:22 a w who leaves her husband and presents him with
25:13 Any wickedness, but not the wickedness of a w!
25:16 with a lion and a dragon than live with an evil w.
25:21 and do not desire a w for her possessions.
25:24 From a w sin had its beginning,
26:22 *and a married w as a tower of death to her lovers.*
26:24 *A shameless w constantly acts disgracefully,*
34: 5 and like a w in labor, the mind has fantasies. A
36:26 A w will accept any man as a husband,
37:11 a w about her rival or with a coward about war,
42:13 and from a w comes woman's wickedness.
42:14 the wickedness of a man than a w who does good;
42:14 it is w who brings shame and disgrace.
Bar 4:16 and bereaved the lonely w of her daughters.
LtJ 6:43 she derides the w next to her,
Sus 1: 2 a very beautiful w and one who feared the Lord.
1:31 Now Susanna was a w of great refinement
1:36 this w came in with two maids,
1:40 seize this w and asked who the young man was,
1:54 Now then, if you really saw this w, tell me this:
1Es 1:53 and did not spare young man or young w, B
4:18 and then see a w lovely in appearance and beauty,
4:24 he brings it back to the w he loves.
2Es 4:40 "Go and ask a pregnant w whether,
4:42 as a w who is in labor makes haste to escape
5:49 and a w who has become old does
5:51 He replied to me, "Ask a w who bears children,
9:38 I looked around, and on my right I saw a w;
10:27 I looked up, the w was no longer visible to me,
10:41 The w who appeared to you a little while ago,
10:42 (you do not now see the form of a w,
10:44 The w whom you saw is Zion,
10:46 then it was that the barren w bore a son.
15:51 like a wretched w who is beaten and wounded,
16:38 as a pregnant w, in the ninth month when the time
16:49 as a respectable and virtuous w abhors a prostitute,
4Mc 14:11 the mind of w despised even more diverse agonies,
15:17 O w, who alone gave birth
16: 1 a w, advanced in years and mother of seven sons,
16: 2 but also that a w has despised the fiercest tortures.
16: 5 If this w, though a mother, had been fainthearted,
16:14 of God in the cause of religion, elder and w!
17: 9 "Here lie buried an aged priest and an aged w
18: 7 but I guarded the rib from which w was made.

WOMAN'S (23) [WOMAN]

Ex 21:22 be fined what the w husband demands,
Lev 24:10 and the Israelite w son and
24:11 Israelite w son blasphemed the Name in a curse.
Nu 5:18 the woman before the LORD, dishevel the w hair,
5:25 of the w hand, and shall elevate the grain offering
Dt 22: 5 nor shall a man put on a w garment;
22:15 of the young w virginity to the elders of the city at
22:19 to the young w father) because he has slandered
22:20 evidence of the young w virginity was not found,
22:29 give fifty shekels of silver to the young w father,
1Ki 3:19 Then this w son died in the night,
Jn 4:39 in him because of the w testimony,
Jdt 12:15 she proceeded to dress herself in all her w finery.
Sir 9: 8 many have been seduced by a w beauty,
25:15 and no anger worse than a w wrath.
25:17 A w wickedness changes her appearance,
25:19 Any iniquity is small compared to a w iniquity;
25:21 Do not be ensnared by a w beauty,
36:27 A w beauty lights up a man's face,
42:13 and from a woman comes w wickedness.
Sus 1:46 "I want no part in shedding this w blood!"
2Mc 7:21 she reinforced her w reasoning with
2Es 5:46 He said to me, "Ask a w womb, and say to it,

WOMANHOOD (2) [WOMAN]

Eze 16: 7 grew up and became tall and arrived at full w;
AdE 2: 7 he brought her up to w as his own.

WOMB‡ (94) [WOMBS]

Ge 25:23 LORD said to her, "Two nations are in your w,
25:24 there were twins in her w.
29:31 he opened her w; but Rachel was barren.
30: 2 who has withheld from you the fruit of the w?"
30:22 and God heeded her and opened her w.
38:27 there were twins in her w.
49:25 blessings of the breasts and of the w.
Ex 13: 2 the first to open the w among the Israelites,
13:12 to the LORD all that first opens the w.
13:15 to the LORD every male that first opens the w,
34:19 All that first opens the w is mine,
Nu 3:12 the firstborn that open the w among the Israelites.
5:21 LORD makes your uterus drop, your w discharge;
5:22 and make your w discharge,
5:27 and her w shall discharge, her uterus drop,
Nu 8:16 in place of all that open the w,
12:12 when it comes out of its mother's w."
18:15 The first issue of the w of all creatures,
Dt 7:13 the fruit of your w and the fruit of your ground,
28: 4 Blessed shall be the fruit of your w,
28:11 in the fruit of your w, in the fruit of your livestock,
28:18 Cursed shall be the fruit of your w,
28:53 you will eat the fruit of your w,
Jdg 16:17 I have been a nazirite to God from my mother's w.
Ru 1:11 in my w that they may become your husbands?
1Sa 1: 5 though the LORD had closed her w.
1: 6 because the LORD had closed her w.
Job 1:21 He said, "Naked I came from my mother's w,
3:10 it did not shut the doors of my mother's w,
3:11 come forth from the w and expire?
10:18 "Why did you bring me forth from the w?
10:19 carried from the w to the grave.
24:20 The w forgets them; the worm finds them sweet;
31:15 Did not he who made me in the w make them?
31:15 And did not one fashion us in the w?
31:18 and from my mother's w I guided the widow—
38: 8 the sea with doors when it burst out from the w?—
38:29 From whose w did the ice come forth,
Ps 22: 9 Yet it was you who took me from the w;
58: 3 The wicked go astray from the w;
71: 6 it was you who took me from my mother's w.
110: 3 From the w of the morning, like dew,
127: 3 the fruit of the w a reward.
139:13 you knit me together in my mother's w.
Pr 30:16 the barren w, the earth ever thirsty for water,
31: 2 No, son of my w!
Ecc 5:15 As they came from their mother's w,
11: 5 the breath comes to the bones in the mother's w,
Isa 13:18 they will have no mercy on the fruit of the w;
44: 2 who formed you in the w and will help you:
44:24 your Redeemer, who formed you in the w:
46: 3 by me from your birth, carried from the w;
49: 1 while I was in my mother's w he named me.
49: 5 who formed me in the w to be his servant,
49:15 or show no compassion for the child of her w?
66: 9 Shall I open the w and not deliver?
66: 9 shall I, the one who delivers, shut the w?
Jer 1: 5 "Before I formed you in the w I knew you,
20:17 because he did not kill me in the w;
20:17 have been my grave, and her w forever great.
20:18 Why did I come forth from the w to see toil
Hos 9:14 Give them a miscarrying w and dry breasts.
9:16 I will kill the cherished offspring of their w.
12: 3 In the w he tried to supplant his brother,
13:13 not present himself at the mouth of the w.
Lk 1:31 now, you will conceive in your w and bear a son,
1:41 the child leaped in her w.
1:42 and blessed is the fruit of your w.
1:44 the child in my w leaped for joy.
2:21 by the angel before he was conceived in the w.
11:27 "Blessed is the w that bore you and the breasts
Jn 3: 4 a second time into the mother's w and be born?"
Ro 4:19 when he considered the barrenness of Sarah's w.
Tob 4: 4 for you while you were in her w.
Jdt 9: 2 and polluted her w to disgrace her;
Wis 7: 1 and in the w of a mother I was molded into flesh,
Sir 1:14 she is created with the faithful in the w.
40: 1 from their mother's w until the day they return to
49: 7 who even in the w had been consecrated a prophet,
2Mc 7:22 "I do not know how you came into being in my w.
7:27 I carried you nine months in my w,
2Es 4:40 her w can keep the fetus within her any longer."
4:41 "In Hades the chambers of the souls are like the w.
5:35 Or why did not my mother's w become my grave,
5:46 He said to me, "Ask a woman's w, and say to it,
5:48 so I have given the w of the earth to those who
5:53 during the time of old age, when the w is failing.'
8: 8 to the body that is now fashioned in the w,
8: 8 the w endures your creature that has been created
8: 9 the w gives up again what has been created in it,
10:12 for I have lost the fruit of my w,
16:38 around her w for two or three hours beforehand,
16:38 but when the child comes forth from the w,
4Mc 13:19 and which was implanted in the mother's w.

WOMBS (2) [WOMB]

Ge 20:18 the w of the house of Abimelech because of Sarah,
Lk 23:29 'Blessed are the barren, and the w that never bore,

WOMEN‡ (294) [WOMAN]

A. MEN AND WOMEN (29)
B. YOUNG WOMEN (21)
C. FOREIGN WOMEN (11)
D. WOMEN AND CHILDREN (10)

Ge 14:16 and the w and the people.
18:11 ceased to be with Sarah after the manner of w.
24:11 the time when w go out to draw water.
27:46 "I am weary of my life because of the Hittite w.
27:46 If Jacob marries one of the Hittite w such as these,
27:46 one of the w of the land,
28: 1 "You shall not marry one of the Canaanite w.
28: 6 "You shall not marry one of the Canaanite w,"
28: 8 the Canaanite w did not please his father Isaac,
30:13 w will call me happy"; so she named him Asher.
31:35 for the way of w is upon me."
33: 5 Esau looked up and saw the w and children, D
34: 1 went out to visit the w of the region.
Ex 1:16 to the Hebrew w, and see them on the birthstool,
1:19 the Hebrew w are not like the Egyptian w;
2: 7 "Shall I go and get you a nurse from the Hebrew w
Ex 15:20 and all the w went out after her with tambourines
35:22 So they came, both men and w; A
35:25 All the skillful w spun with their hands,
35:26 all the w whose hearts moved them
35:29 men and w whose hearts made them willing A
38: 8 the mirrors of the w who served at the entrance to
Lev 26:26 ten w shall bake your bread in a single oven,
Nu 6: 2 When either men or w make a special vow,
25: 1 to have sexual relations with the w of Moab.
31: 9 the w of Midian and their little ones captive;
31:15 "Have you allowed all the w to live?
31:16 These w here, on Balaam's advice,
31:35 w who had not known a man by sleeping with him.
Dt 2:34 and in each town we utterly destroyed men, w,
3: 6 in each city utterly destroying men, w,
20:14 You may, however, take as your booty the w,
29:11 your w, and the aliens who are in your camp,
31:12 Assemble the people—men, w, and children,
Jos 6:21 both men and w, young and old, oxen, sheep, A
8:25 total of those who fell that day, both men and w, A
8:35 and the w, and the little ones,
23:12 so that you marry their w and they yours,
Jdg 5:24 "Most blessed of w be Jael,
5:24 of tent-dwelling w most blessed.
9:49 about a thousand men and w. A
9:51 the men and w and all the lords of the city fled A
12: 9 in thirty young w from outside for his sons. B
16:27 Now the house was full of men and w; A
16:27 about three thousand men and w, A
21:10 including the w and the little ones.
21:14 the w whom they had saved alive of the w
21:16 since there are no w left in Benjamin?"
21:21 when the young w of Shiloh come out to dance B
21:21 a wife for himself from the young w of Shiloh, B
Ru 1:19 and the w said, "Is this Naomi?"
2: 8 but keep close to my young w. B
2:22 my daughter, that you go out with his young w, B
2:23 So she stayed close to the young w of Boaz, B
3: 2 with whose young w you have been working. B
4:14 Then the w said to Naomi,
4:17 The w of the neighborhood gave him a name,
1Sa 2:22 with the w who served at the entrance to the tent
4:20 the w attending her said to her, "Do not be afraid,
15:33 "As your sword has made w childless, so your
mother shall be childless among w."
18: 6 the w came out of all the towns of Israel,
18: 7 the w sang to one another as they made merry,
21: 4 that the young men have kept themselves from w."
21: 5 "Indeed w have been kept from us as always
22:19 men and w, children and infants, oxen, donkeys, A
30: 2 the w and all who were in it, both small and great;
2Sa 1:26 to me was wonderful, passing the love of w.
6:19 the whole multitude of Israel, both men and w, A
19:35 to the voice of singing men and singing w?
1Ki 3:16 two w who were prostitutes came to the king
11: 1 King Solomon loved many foreign w along with C
11: 1 Ammonite, Edomite, Sidonian, and Hittite w,
2Ki 8:12 and rip up their pregnant w."
15:16 He ripped open all the pregnant w in it.
23: 7 where the w did weaving for Asherah.
2Ch 2:14 the son of one of the Danite w,
28: 8 of their kin, w, sons, and daughters;
35:25 and all the singing men and singing w have spoken
Ezr 10: 1 w, and children gathered to him out of Israel;
10: 2 and have married foreign w from the peoples of C
10:10 "You have trespassed and married foreign w, C
10:17 end of all the men who had married foreign w. C
10:18 of the priests who had married foreign w, C
10:44 All these had married foreign w, C
Ne 8: 2 both men and w and all who could hear with A
8: 3 and the w and those who could understand;
12:43 the w and children also rejoiced. D
13:23 In those days also I saw Jews who had married w
13:26 of Israel sin on account of such w?
13:26 nevertheless, foreign w made even him to sin. C
13:27 against our God by marrying foreign w?" C
Est 1: 9 for the w in the palace of King Ahasuerus.
1:17 of the queen will be made known to all w,
1:20 all w will give honor to their husbands,
2: 3 the king's eunuch, who is in charge of the w;
2: 8 many young w were gathered in the citadel B
2: 8 who had charge of the w.
2:12 under the regulations for the w,
2:12 with perfumes and cosmetics for w.
2:15 who had charge of the w, advised.
2:17 the king loved Esther more than all the other w;
3:13 young and old, w and children, in one day, D
7: 4 we had been sold merely as slaves, men and w, A
8:11 with their children and w,
Job 42:15 In all the land there were no w so beautiful
Ps 68:12 The w at home divide the spoil,
148:12 Young men and w alike, old and young together! A
Pr 31: 3 Do not give your strength to w,
31:29 "Many w have done excellently,
Ecc 2: 8 I got singers, both men and w, A
12: 3 w who grind cease working because they are few,
SS 1: 8 If you do not know, O fairest among w,
5: 9 more than another beloved, O fairest among w?
6: 1 has your beloved gone, O fairest among w?
Isa 3:12 children are their oppressors, and w rule over them.
4: 1 Seven w shall take hold of one man in that day,
19:16 On that day the Egyptians will be like w,
23: 4 reared young men nor brought up young w." B
27:11 w come and make a fire of them.
32: 9 Rise up, you w who are at ease, hear my voice;
32:11 Tremble, you w who are at ease, shudder,
Jer 2:33 that even to wicked w you have taught your ways.

Jer 7:18 the fathers kindle fire, and the **w** knead dough,
9:17 Consider, and call for the mourning **w** to come;
9:17 send for the skilled **w** to come;
9:20 Hear, O **w**, the word of the LORD,
31:13 Then shall the young **w** rejoice in the dance, B
38:22 of all the **w** remaining in the house of the king
40: 7 and had committed to him men, **w**, and children,
41:16 soldiers, **w**, children, and eunuchs,
43: 6 the **w**, the children, the princesses,
44:15 and all the **w** who stood by, a great assembly,
44:19 And the **w** said, "Indeed we will go
44:20 Jeremiah said to all the people, men and **w**, A
44:24 Jeremiah said to all the people and all the **w**,
50:37 so that they may become **w**!
51:30 their strength has failed, they have become **w**;
La 1:18 my young **w** and young men have gone B
2:20 Should **w** eat their offspring,
2:21 my young **w** and my young men have fallen by B
3:51 at the fate of all the young **w** in my city. B
4:10 compassionate **w** have boiled their own children;
5:11 **W** are raped in Zion, virgins in the towns of Judah.
Eze 8:14 **w** were sitting there weeping for Tammuz.
9: 6 Cut down old men, young men and young **w**, B
9: 6 little children and **w**, but touch no one who has
13:18 Woe to the **w** who sew bands on all wrists,
16:34 you were different from other **w** in your whorings:
16:38 I will judge you as **w** who commit adultery
16:41 on you in the sight of many **w**;
22:10 in you they violate **w** in their menstrual periods.
23: 2 there were two **w**, the daughters of one mother;
23:10 and she became a byword among **w**.
23:42 and they put bracelets on the arms of the **w**,
23:44 in to Oholah and to Oholibah, wanton **w**.
23:48 so that all **w** may take warning and
32:16 The **w** of the nations shall chant it.
Da 11:37 or to the one beloved by **w**;
Hos 13:16 and their pregnant **w** ripped open.
Am 1:13 because they have ripped open pregnant **w**
8:13 In that day the beautiful young **w** and B
Mic 2: 9 The **w** of my people you drive out
Na 2: 7 be exiled, its slave **w** led away, moaning like doves
3:13 Look at your troops: they are **w** in your midst.
Zec 5: 9 Then I looked up and saw two **w** coming forward.
8: 4 Old men and old **w** shall again sit in the streets
9:17 and new wine the young **w**. B
14: 2 be taken and the houses looted and the **w** raped;
Mt 11:11 of **w** no one has arisen greater than John
14:21 five thousand men, besides **w** and children. D
15:38 four thousand men, besides **w** and children. D
24:41 Two **w** will be grinding meal together;
27:55 Many **w** were also there, looking on from
28: 5 But the angel said to the **w**, "Do not be afraid;
Mk 15:40 There were also **w** looking on from a distance;
15:41 and there were many other **w** who had come up
Lk 1:42 "Blessed are you among **w**,
7:28 among those born of **w** no one is greater than John;
8: 2 as some **w** who had been cured of evil spirits
12:45 men and **w**, and to eat and drink and get drunk, A
17:35 There will be two **w** grinding meal together;
23:27 among them were **w** who were beating their breasts
23:49 the **w** who had followed him from Galilee,
23:55 **w** who had come with him from Galilee followed,
24: 5 The **w** were terrified and bowed their faces to
24:10 the other **w** with them who told this to the apostles.
24:22 Moreover, some **w** of our group astounded us.
24:24 to the tomb and found it just as the **w** had said;
Jn 8: 5 ⟦in the law Moses commanded us to stone such **w**⟧
Ac 1:14 to prayer, together with certain **w**, including Mary
2:18 Even upon my slaves, both men and **w**, A
5:14 great numbers of both men and **w**, A
8: 3 dragging off both men and **w**, A
8:12 they were baptized, both men and **w**. A
9: 2 to the Way, men or **w**, he might bring them bound
13:50 But the Jews incited the devout **w** of high standing
16:13 down and spoke to the **w** who had gathered there.
17: 4 the devout Greeks and not a few of the leading **w**.
17:12 not a few Greek **w** and men of high standing.
22: 4 the point of death by binding both men and **w** A
Ro 1:26 Their **w** exchanged natural intercourse
1:27 giving up natural intercourse with **w**,
1Co 14:34 **w** should be silent in the churches.
Gal 4:24 this is an allegory: these **w** are two covenants.
Eph 6: 7 as to the Lord and not to men and **w**, A
Php 4: 3 my loyal companion, help these **w**,
1Ti 2: 9 also that the **w** should dress themselves modestly
2:10 as is proper for **w** who profess reverence for God.
3:11 **W** likewise must be serious, not slanderers,
5: 2 to older **w** as mothers, to younger **w** as sisters—
2Ti 3: 6 into households and captivate silly **w**,
Tit 2: 3 tell the older **w** to be reverent in behavior,
2: 4 so that they may encourage the young **w** B
Heb 11:35 **W** received their dead by resurrection.
1Pe 3: 5 in this way long ago that the holy **w** who hoped
2Pe 1:21 men and **w** moved by the Holy Spirit spoke A
Rev 14: 4 these who have not defiled themselves with **w**,
Jdt 4:11 And all the Israelite men, **w**,
6:16 all their young men and **w** ran to the assembly. A
7:22 and the **w** and young men fainted from thirst
7:23 Then all the people, the young men, the **w**,
7:32 The **w** and children he sent home. D
8: 7 men and **w** slaves, livestock, and fields; A
10:11 the **w** were going straight on through the valley,
10:19 who have **w** like this among them?
12:13 like one of the Assyrian **w** who serve in the palace
13:18 by the Most High God above all other **w** on earth;
15:12 All the **w** of Israel gathered to see her,
15:12 and distributed them to the **w** who were with her;
Jdt 15:13 the people in the dance, leading all the **w**, while all
AdE 1: 9 Queen Vashti gave a drinking party for the **w** in
1:20 and thus all **w** will give honor to their husbands,
2: 3 to the king's eunuch who is in charge of the **w**,
2: 8 who had custody of the **w**.
2:12 and six months with spices and ointments for **w**.
2:14 where Gai the king's eunuch is in charge of the **w**;
2:15 the eunuch in charge of the **w**, had commanded.
Sir 10:18 or violent anger for those born of **w**.
19: 2 Wine and **w** lead intelligent men astray,
28:15 Slander has driven virtuous **w** from their homes,
42:12 or spend her time among married **w**;
47:19 But you brought in **w** to lie at your side,
48:19 and they were in anguish, like **w** in labor.
LtJ 6:29 to them may even be touched by **w** in their periods
6:30 **W** serve meals for gods of silver and gold
6:42 And the **w**, with cords around them,
Bel 1:20 see the footprints of men and **w** and children." AD
1Mc 1:26 young **w** and young men became faint, B
1:26 the beauty of the **w** faded.
1:32 They took captive the **w** and children, D
1:60 to death the **w** who had their children circumcised,
2Mc 3:19 **W**, girded with sackcloth under their breasts,
3:19 young **w** who were kept indoors ran together B
5:13 destruction of boys, **w**, and children, D
5:24 kill all the grown men and to sell the **w** and boys
6: 4 with prostitutes and had intercourse with **w** within
6:10 For example, two **w** were brought in
12:21 the **w** and the children and also the baggage to
1Es 1:32 and the principal men, with the **w**,
3:12 The third wrote, "**W** are strongest,
4:13 spoken of **w** and truth (and this was Zerubbabel),
4:14 or has the mastery over them? Is it not **w**?
4:15 **W** gave birth to the king and to every people
4:16 From **w** they came; and **w** brought up the very men
4:17 **W** make men's clothes; they bring men glory;
4:17 men cannot exist without **w**.
4:22 Therefore you must realize that **w** rule over you!
4:22 and bring everything and give it to **w**?
4:26 Many men have lost their minds because of **w**,
4:27 or stumbled, or sinned because of **w**.
4:32 Gentlemen, why are not **w** strong,
4:34 are not **w** strong? The earth is vast,
4:37 the king is unrighteous, **w** are unrighteous,
8:91 around him a very great crowd of men and **w** A
8:92 and have married foreign **w** from the peoples of C
9: 7 You have broken the law and married foreign **w**, C
9:36 All these had married foreign **w**, C
9:40 men and **w**, and all the priests to hear the law, A
9:41 in the presence of both men and **w**; A
3Mc 1:18 Young **w** who had been secluded B
1:19 Those **w** who had recently been arrayed
4: 6 And young **w** who had just entered B
2Es 5: 8 and menstruous **w** shall bring forth monsters.
6:21 and pregnant **w** shall give birth
10: 6 most foolish of **w**, do you not see our mourning,
10:16 and will be praised among **w**.
16:33 **w** shall mourn because they have no husbands;
4Mc 4: 9 with **w** and children were imploring God in D
4:25 —even to the extent that **w**, because they had

WOMEN'S (2) [WOMAN]

Rev 9: 8 like **w** hair, and their teeth like lions' teeth;
Tob 2:11 also, my wife Anna earned money at **w** work.

WOMENSERVANTS (KJV) See MAIDS, FEMALE SLAVES

WON (22) [WIN]

2Sa 8:13 David **w** a name for himself.
23:18 and **w** a name beside the Three.
23:22 and **w** a name beside the three warriors.
1Ch 11:20 and **w** a name beside the Three.
11:24 and he **w** a name beside the three warriors.
26:27 From booty **w** in battles they dedicated gifts for
Est 2: 9 The girl pleased him and **w** his favor,
2:17 of all the virgins she **w** his favor and devotion,
5: 2 she **w** his favor and he held out to her
5: 8 If I have **w** the king's favor,
7: 3 Queen Esther answered, "If I have **w** your favor,
8: 5 "If it pleases the king, and if I have **w** his favor,
Ps 78:54 to the mountain that his right hand had **w**.
Isa 26:18 We have **w** no victories on earth,
Ac 14:19 from Antioch and Iconium and **w** over the crowds.
Heb 11:34 **w** strength out of weakness,
1Pe 3: 1 be **w** over without a word by their wives' conduct,
Jdt 8:16 or like a mere mortal, to be **w** over by pleading.
AdE 2: 9 The girl pleased him and **w** his favor,
1Mc 11:24 And he **w** his favor.
2Mc 15: 9 reminding them also of the struggles they had **w**,
3Mc 1: 4 to give them each two minas of gold if they **w**

WONDER (8) [WONDERED, WONDERFUL, WONDERFULLY, WONDERING, WONDERS, WONDROUS, WONDROUSLY]

Ex 7: 9 'Perform a **w**,' then you shall say to Aaron,
Dt 29:24 they and indeed all the nations will **w**,
Ps 41: 5 My enemies **w** in malice when I will die,
Ac 3:10 with **w** and amazement at what had happened
3:12 why do you **w** at this, or why do you stare at us,
2Co 11:14 And no **w**! Even Satan disguises himself
Sir 11:21 Do not **w** at the works of a sinner,
Sir 16:11 it would be a **w** if he remained unpunished.

WONDER-WORKING See Index to Footnotes

WONDERED (2) [WONDER]

Mk 15:44 Then Pilate **w** if he were already dead;
Lk 1:21 and **w** at his delay in the sanctuary.

WONDERFUL (30) [WONDER]

Ge 18:14 Is anything too **w** for the LORD?
Jdg 6:13 And where are all his **w** deeds
13:18 "Why do you ask my name? It is too **w**."
2Sa 1:26 your love to me was **w**,
1Ch 16: 9 sing praises to him, tell of all his **w** works.
16:12 Remember the **w** works he has done, his miracles,
2Ch 2: 9 the house I am about to build will be great and **w**.
Job 42: 3 things too **w** for me, which I did not know.
Ps 9: 1 I will tell of all your **w** deeds.
105: 2 tell of all his **w** works.
105: 5 Remember the **w** works he has done, his miracles,
106: 7 did not consider your **w** works;
107: 8 for his **w** works to humankind.
107:15 for his **w** works to humankind.
107:21 for his **w** works to humankind.
107:31 for his **w** works to humankind.
111: 4 He has gained renown by his **w** deeds;
119:129 Your decrees are **w**;
139: 6 Such knowledge is too **w** for me;
139:14 **W** are your works; that I know very well.
Pr 30:18 Three things are too **w** for me;
Isa 9: 6 and he is named **W** Counselor, Mighty God,
25: 1 for you have done **w** things, plans formed of old,
28:29 he is **w** in counsel, and excellent in wisdom.
Jer 21: 2 perhaps the LORD will perform a **w** deed for us,
Lk 13:17 the entire crowd was rejoicing at all the **w** things
Jdt 16:13 O Lord, you are great and glorious, **w** in strength,
AdE 13:10 and earth and every **w** thing under heaven.
15:14 For you are **w**, my lord,
Sir 11: 4 for the works of the Lord are **w**,

WONDERFULLY (1) [WONDER]

Ps 139:14 I praise you, for I am fearfully and **w** made.

WONDERING (4) [WONDER]

Lk 24:41 in their joy they were disbelieving and still **w**,
Ac 5:24 **w** what might be going on.
3Mc 5:39 **w** at his instability of mind,
2Es 10:25 While I was **w** what this meant,

WONDERS (65) [WONDER]

Ex 3:20 and strike Egypt with all my **w** that I will perform
4:21 see that you perform before Pharaoh all the **w**
7: 3 and I will multiply my signs and **w** in the land
11: 9 that my **w** may be multiplied in the land of Egypt."
11:10 and Aaron performed all these **w** before Pharaoh;
15:11 awesome in splendor, doing **w**?
Dt 4:34 by trials, by signs and **w**, by war,
6:22 before our eyes great and awesome signs and **w**
7:19 the great trials that your eyes saw, the signs and **w**,
26: 8 display of power, and with signs and **w**;
29: 3 the signs, and those great **w**.
34:11 for all the signs and **w** that the LORD sent him
Jos 3: 5 for tomorrow the LORD will do **w** among you."
Jdg 13:19 on the rock to the LORD, to him who works **w**.
Ne 9:10 and **w** against Pharaoh and all his servants and all
9:17 and were not mindful of the **w** that you performed
Ps 77:11 I will remember your **w** of old.
77:14 You are the God who works **w**;
78: 4 and his might, and the **w** that he has done.
78:32 they did not believe in his **w**.
88:10 Do you work **w** for the dead?
88:12 Are your **w** known in the darkness,
89: 5 Let the heavens praise your **w**,
135: 9 he sent signs and **w** into your midst,
136: 4 who alone does great **w**,
Jer 32:20 You showed signs and **w** in the land of Egypt,
32:21 and **w**, with a strong hand and outstretched arm,
Da 4: 2 and **w** that the Most High God has worked
4: 3 How great are his signs, how mighty his **w**!
6:27 he works signs and **w** in heaven and on earth;
12: 6 "How long shall it be until the end of these **w**?"
Jn 4:48 "Unless you see signs and **w** you will not believe."
Ac 2:22 **w**, and signs that God did through him among you,
2:43 many **w** and signs were being done by the apostles.
4:30 and signs and **w** are performed through the name
5:12 and **w** were done among the people through
6: 8 did great **w** and signs among the people.
7:36 having performed **w** and signs in Egypt,
14: 3 to the word of his grace by granting signs and **w** to
15:12 the signs and **w** that God had done through them
Ro 15:19 by the power of signs and **w**,
2Co 12:12 signs and **w** and mighty works.
2Th 2: 9 who uses all power, signs, lying **w**,
Heb 2: 4 while God added his testimony by signs and **w**
AdE 10: 9 God has done great signs and **w**,
10: 9 **w** that have never happened among the nations.
Wis 8: 8 and **w** and of the outcome of seasons and times.
10:16 and withstood dread kings with **w** and signs.
19: 8 after gazing on marvelous **w**.
Sir 18: 6 nor is it possible to fathom the **w** of the Lord.
31: 9 For he has done **w** among his people.
36: 6 Give new signs, and work other **w**;

Sir 45:19 he performed w against them to consume them
48:14 In his life he did w,
50:22 who everywhere works great w,
Bar 2:11 of Egypt with a mighty hand and with signs and w
2Mc 15:21 and called upon the Lord who works w;
3Mc 6:32 praising God, their Savior and worker of w.
2Es 1:14 and did great w among you.
2:48 tell my people how great and how many are the w
7:27 from the evils that I have foretold shall see my w.
9:6 beginnings are manifest in w and mighty works,
13:14 beginning you have shown your servant these w,
13:50 And then he will show them very many w."
13:57 and praise to the Most High for the w that he does

WONDROUS‡ (18) [WONDER]

Job 37:14 stop and consider the w works of God.
37:16 w works of the one whose knowledge is perfect,
Ps 26:7 and telling all your w deeds.
40:5 your w deeds and your thoughts toward us;
71:17 and I still proclaim your w deeds.
72:18 the God of Israel, who alone does w things.
75:1 People tell of your w deeds.
86:10 you are great and do w things; you alone are God.
106:22 w works in the land of Ham,
107:24 his w works in the deep.
119:18 so that I may behold w things out of your law.
119:27 and I will meditate on your w works.
145:5 and on your w works, I will meditate.
Sir 48:4 How glorious you were, Elijah, in your w deeds!
2Es 6:48 therefore the nations might declare your w works.
13:56 and explain weighty and w matters to you."
14:5 I told him many w things,
4Mc 15:4 upon the character of a small child a w likeness

WONDROUSLY (4) [WONDER]

Job 37:5 God thunders w with his voice;
Ps 17:7 W show your steadfast love,
31:21 for he has w shown his steadfast love to me
Joel 2:26 who has dealt w with you.

WONT (KJV) See ACCUSTOMED, CUSTOM, CUSTOMARY, HABIT, SUPPOSED, USED

WOOD‡ (136) [BRUSHWOOD, CEDARWOOD, OLIVEWOOD, WOODCUTTER, WOODED, WOODEN, WOODS, WOODWORK]

Ge 6:14 Make yourself an ark of cypress w;
22:3 he cut the w for the burnt offering,
22:6 Abraham took the w of the burnt offering
22:7 He said, "The fire and the w are here,
22:9 Abraham built an altar there and laid the w
22:9 and laid him on the altar, on top of the w.
Ex 7:19 even in vessels of w and in vessels of stone.' "
15:25 and the LORD showed him a piece of w;
25:5 tanned rams' skins, fine leather, acacia w,
25:10 They shall make an ark of acacia w;
25:13 You shall make poles of acacia w,
25:23 You shall make a table of acacia w,
25:28 You shall make the poles of acacia w,
26:15 You shall make upright frames of acacia w for
26:26 You shall make bars of acacia w,
27:1 You shall make the altar of acacia w,
27:6 poles of acacia w, and overlay them with bronze;
30:1 you shall make it of acacia w.
30:5 You shall make the poles of acacia w,
31:5 and in carving w, in every kind of craft.
35:7 tanned rams' skins, and fine leather; acacia w,
35:24 and everyone who possessed acacia w of any use
35:33 and in carving w, in every kind of craft.
36:20 the upright frames for the tabernacle of acacia w.
36:31 He made bars of acacia w,
37:1 Bezalel made the ark of acacia w;
37:4 He made poles of acacia w,
37:10 He also made the table of acacia w,
37:15 He made the poles of acacia w to carry the table,
37:25 He made the altar of incense of acacia w,
37:28 And he made the poles of acacia w,
38:1 the altar of burnt offering also of acacia w;
38:6 he made the poles of acacia w,
Lev 1:7 on the altar and arrange w on the fire.
1:8 on the w that is on the fire on the altar;
1:12 and the priest shall arrange them on the w that is
1:17 on the w that is on the fire;
3:5 with the burnt offering that is on the w on the fire,
4:12 to the ash heap, and shall burn it on a w fire;
6:12 Every morning the priest shall add w to it,
11:32 whether an article of w or cloth or skin or sacking,
15:12 and every vessel of w shall be rinsed in water.
Nu 31:20 of goats' hair, and every article of w."
35:18 with a weapon of w in hand that could cause death,
Dt 4:28 objects of w and stone that neither see, nor hear,
10:1 and make an ark of w.
10:3 So I made an ark of acacia w,
19:5 into the forest with another to cut w, and when one
28:36 where you shall serve other gods, of w and stone.
28:64 there you shall serve other gods, of w and stone,
29:11 both those who cut your w
29:17 the filthy idols of w and stone, of silver and gold,
Jos 9:21 of w and drawers of water for all the congregation,
9:23 hewers of w and drawers of water for the house
9:27 of w and drawers of water for the congregation and
Jdg 6:26 the w of the sacred pole that you shall cut down."
1Sa 6:14 so they split up the w of the cart and offered
2Sa 24:22 and the yokes of the oxen for the w.
1Ki 6:15 he covered them on the inside with w;
6:34 and two doors of cypress w;
10:11 a great quantity of almug w and precious stones.
10:12 the almug w the king made supports for the house
10:12 no such almug w has come or been seen
18:23 and lay it on the w, but put no fire to it;
18:23 I will prepare the other bull and lay it on the w,
18:33 Next he put the w in order, cut the bull in pieces, and laid it on the w.
18:33 and pour it on the burnt offering and on the w."
18:38 the burnt offering, the w, the stones, and the dust,
2Ki 19:18 w and stone—and so they were destroyed.
1Ch 21:23 and the threshing sledges for the w,
29:2 and w for the things of w,
2Ch 2:14 silver, bronze, iron, stone, and w, and in purple,
9:10 from Ophir brought algum w and precious stones.
9:11 the algum w, the king made steps for the house of
Ne 10:34 the Levites, and the people, for the w offering,
13:31 and I provided for the w offering,
Job 41:27 It counts iron as straw, and bronze as rotten w.
Pr 25:20 Like a moth in clothing or a worm in w,
26:20 For lack of w the fire goes out,
26:21 As charcoal is to hot embers and w to fire,
SS 2:3 As an apple tree among the trees of the w,
3:9 a palanquin from the w of Lebanon.
Isa 10:15 or as if a staff should lift the one who is not w!
30:33 with fire and w in abundance;
37:19 w and stone—and so they were destroyed.
40:20 As a gift one chooses mulberry w—w that will not
44:19 Shall I fall down before a block of w?"
60:17 instead of w, bronze, instead of stones, iron.
Jer 5:14 and this people w, and the fire shall devour them.
7:18 The children gather w, the fathers kindle fire,
10:8 the instruction given by idols is no better than w!
La 4:8 it has become as dry as w.
5:4 the w we get must be bought.
5:13 and boys stagger under loads of w.
Eze 15:2 how does the w of the vine surpass all other w—
15:3 Is w taken from it to make anything?
15:6 the w of the vine among the trees of the forest,
20:32 and worship w and stone."
39:10 They will not need to take w out of the field or cut
41:16 the threshold the temple was paneled with w all
41:22 an altar of w, three cubits high, two cubits long,
41:22 its corners, its base, and its walls were of w.
41:25 a canopy of w in front of the vestibule outside.
Da 5:4 bronze, iron, w, and stone.
5:23 w, and stone, which do not see or hear or know;
Hos 4:12 My people consult a piece of w,
Hab 2:19 Alas for you who say to the w, "Wake up!"
Hag 1:8 Go up to the hills and bring w and build the house,
Zec 12:6 the clans of Judah like a blazing pot on a pile of w,
Lk 23:31 For if they do this when the w is green,
1Co 3:12 silver, precious stones, w, hay, straw—
2Ti 2:20 not only of gold and silver but also of w and clay,
Rev 9:20 of gold and silver and bronze and stone and w,
18:12 purple, silk and scarlet, all kinds of scented w,
18:12 all articles of ivory, all articles of costly w, bronze,
Wis 10:4 steering the righteous man by a paltry piece of w.
14:1 of w more fragile than the ship that carries him.
14:5 even to the smallest piece of w,
14:7 blessed is the w by which righteousness comes.
14:21 on objects of stone or w the name that ought not to
Sir 8:3 and do not heap w on their fire.
LtJ 6:4 of silver and gold and w,
6:11 these gods of silver and gold and w
6:30 for gods of silver and gold and w;
6:39 These things that are made of w and overlaid
6:50 Since they are made of w and overlaid with gold
6:57 of w and overlaid with silver and gold are unable
6:70 which guards nothing, so are their gods of w,
6:71 In the same way, their gods of w,
2Mc 1:21 the liquid on the w and on the things laid upon it.
4:41 some picked up stones, some blocks of w,
2Es 5:5 from w, and the stone shall utter its voice;

WOODCUTTER (1) [CUT, WOOD]

Wis 13:11 A skilled w may saw down a tree easy to handle

WOODED (3) [WOOD]

2Ch 27:4 and forts and towers on the w hills.
Jer 26:18 and the mountain of the house a w height.'
Mic 3:12 and the mountain of the house a w height.

WOODEN (9) [WOOD]

Ne 8:4 a w platform that had been made for the purpose;
Ps 74:5 At the upper entrance they hacked the w trellis
Isa 45:20 those who carry about their w idols,
Jer 28:13 You have broken w bars only to forge iron bars
Sir 22:16 A w beam firmly bonded into a building is
LtJ 6:55 in a temple of w gods overlaid with gold or silver,
6:59 better also a w pillar in a palace,
1Mc 6:37 On the elephants were w towers,
1Es 9:42 and reader of the law stood on the w platform

WOODS (4) [WOOD]

2Ki 2:24 out of the w and mauled forty-two of the boys.
Eze 34:25 in the wild and sleep in the w securely.
Bar 5:8 The w and every fragrant tree have shaded Israel
LtJ 6:63 and w does what it is ordered.

WOODWORK (1) [WOOD]

Hab 2:11 and the plaster will respond from the w.

WOOED (1)

1Sa 25:39 David sent and w Abigail, to make her his wife.

WOOF (9)

Lev 13:48 in warp or w of linen or wool,
13:49 in warp or w or in skin or in anything made
13:51 If the disease has spread in the cloth, in warp or w,
13:52 whether diseased in warp or w, woolen or linen,
13:53 in warp or w or in anything of skin,
13:56 he shall tear the spot out of the cloth, in warp or w,
13:57 If it appears again in the garment, in warp or w,
13:58 But the cloth, warp or w, or anything of skin
13:59 either in warp or w, or in anything of skin,

WOOL (17) [WOOLEN]

Lev 13:48 in warp or woof of linen or w,
13:59 the ritual for a leprous disease in a cloth of w
Dt 22:11 You shall not wear clothes made of w
Jdg 6:37 to lay a fleece of w on the threshing floor;
2Ki 3:4 and the w of one hundred thousand rams.
Ps 147:16 He gives snow like w; he scatters frost like ashes.
Pr 31:13 She seeks w and flax, and works
Isa 1:18 like crimson, they shall become like w.
51:8 and the worm will eat them like w;
Eze 27:18 wine of Helbon, and white w.
34:3 You eat the fat, you clothe yourselves with the w,
44:17 they shall have nothing of w on them,
Da 7:9 and the hair of his head like pure w;
Hos 2:5 my w and my flax, my oil and my drink."
2:9 and I will take away my w and my flax,
Heb 9:19 with water and scarlet w and hyssop,
Rev 1:14 His head and his hair were white as white w,

WOOLEN (2) [WOOL]

Lev 13:47 a leprous disease appears in it, in w or linen cloth,
13:52 whether diseased in warp or woof, w or linen,

WORD‡ (712) [BYWORD, WATCHWORD, WORDS]

A. WORD OF THE †LORD (237)
B. WORD OF *GOD (42)
C. WORD OF THE *LORD (25)

Ge 15:1 the w of the LORD came to Abram in a vision, A
15:4 But the w of the LORD came to him, A
27:8 therefore, my son, obey my w as I command you.
27:13 only obey my w, and go, get them for me."
31:24 "Take heed that you say not a w to Jacob,
37:14 and bring w back to me."
38:25 she sent w to her father-in-law,
44:18 let your servant please speak a w in my lord's ears,
Ex 9:20 of Pharaoh who feared the w of the LORD A
9:21 the w of the LORD left their slaves and livestock A
18:6 He sent w to Moses, "I, your father-in-law Jethro,
36:6 and w was proclaimed throughout the camp:
Nu 3:16 enrolled them according to the w of the LORD, A
3:51 according to the w of the LORD, A
11:23 Now you shall see whether my w will come true
13:26 they brought back w to them and to all
15:31 Because of having despised the w of the LORD A
22:8 "Stay here tonight, and I will bring back w to you,
22:38 w God puts in my mouth, that is what I must say."
23:5 The LORD put a w in Balaam's mouth, and said,
23:16 The LORD met Balaam, put a w into his mouth,
24:13 not be able to go beyond the w of the LORD, A
27:14 against my w in the wilderness of Zin when
27:21 at his w they shall go out, and at his w they shall come in,
30:2 he shall not break his w;
36:5 the Israelites according to the w of the LORD, A
Dt 8:3 every w that comes from the mouth of the LORD.
18:20 in my name a w that I have not commanded
18:21 "How can we recognize a w that the LORD has
18:22 it is a w that the LORD has not spoken.
30:14 No, the w is very near to you;
33:9 For they observed your w, and kept your covenant.
Jos 1:13 "Remember the w that Moses the servant of
6:10 or let your voice be heard, nor shall you utter a w,
8:27 the w of the LORD that he had issued to Joshua. A
8:35 a w of all that Moses commanded that Joshua did
14:10 the time that the LORD spoke this w to Moses,
22:32 to the Israelites, and brought back w to them.
Jdg 21:13 Then the whole congregation sent w to
1Sa 1:23 may the LORD establish his w."
3:1 The w of the LORD was rare in those days; A
3:7 w of the LORD had not yet been revealed to him. A
3:21 to Samuel at Shiloh by the w of the LORD. A
4:1 And the w of Samuel came to all Israel.
9:27 that I may make known to you the w of God." B
15:10 The w of the LORD came to Samuel: A
15:23 Because you have rejected the w of the LORD, A
15:26 for you have rejected the w of the LORD, A
2Sa 3:11 And Ishbaal could not answer Abner another w,
3:17 Abner sent w to the elders of Israel, saying,
7:4 same night the w of the LORD came to Nathan: A
7:7 did I ever speak a w with any of the tribal leaders
7:25 as for the w that you have spoken
11:6 David sent w to Joab, "Send me Uriah the Hittite."
12:9 Why have you despised the w of the LORD, A
14:12 "Please let your servant speak a w to my lord

2Sa 14:17 'The **w** of my lord the king will set me at rest';
14:32 Absalom answered Joab, "Look, I sent **w** to you:
15:28 the fords of the wilderness until **w** comes from you
19:14 and they sent **w** to the king, "Return,
23: 2 his **w** is upon my tongue.
24: 4 But the king's **w** prevailed against Joab and
24:11 the **w** of the LORD came to the prophet Gad, A
1Ki 2: 4 Then the LORD will establish his **w** that he spoke
2:14 Then he said, "May I have a **w** with you?"
2:27 **w** of the LORD that he had spoken concerning A
2:30 Then Benaiah brought the king **w** again, saying,
3:12 I now do according to your **w**.
5: 2 Solomon sent **w** to Hiram, saying,
5: 8 Hiram sent **w** to Solomon,
6:11 Now the **w** of the LORD came to Solomon, A
8:26 O God of Israel, let your **w** be confirmed,
8:56 not one **w** has failed of all his good promise,
12:15 about by the LORD that he might fulfill his **w**,
12:22 **w** of God came to Shemaiah the man of God: B
12:24 heeded the **w** of the LORD and went home again, A
12:24 according to the **w** of the LORD. A
13: 1 of God came out of Judah by the **w** of the LORD A
13: 2 against the altar by the **w** of the LORD, A
13: 5 the man of God had given by the **w** of the LORD. A
13: 9 thus I was commanded by the **w** of the LORD: A
13:17 for it was said to me by the **w** of the LORD: A
13:18 and an angel spoke to me by the **w** of the LORD: A
13:20 the **w** of the LORD came to the prophet A
13:21 Because you have disobeyed the **w** of the LORD, A
13:26 man of God who disobeyed the **w** of the LORD; A
13:26 according to the **w** that the LORD spoke to him." A
13:32 that he proclaimed by the **w** of the LORD against A
14:18 according to the **w** of the LORD, A
15:29 according to the **w** of the LORD that he spoke A
16: 1 The **w** of the LORD came to Jehu son of Hanani A
16: 7 the **w** of the LORD came by the prophet Jehu son A
16:12 according to the **w** of the LORD, A
16:34 according to the **w** of the LORD, A
17: 1 nor rain these years, except by my **w**."
17: 2 The **w** of the LORD came to him, saying, A
17: 5 he went and did according to the **w** of the LORD; A
17: 8 Then the **w** of the LORD came to him, saying, A
17:16 according to the **w** of the LORD that he spoke A
17:24 that the **w** of the LORD in your mouth is truth." A
18: 1 many days the **w** of the LORD came to Elijah, A
18:21 The people did not answer him a **w**.
18:31 to whom the **w** of the LORD came, saying, A
19: 9 Then the **w** of the LORD came to him, saying, A
20: 9 The messengers left and brought him **w** again.
21:11 did as Jezebel had sent **w** to them.
21:17 the **w** of the LORD came to Elijah the Tishbite, A
21:28 the **w** of the LORD came to Elijah the Tishbite: A
22: 5 "Inquire first for the **w** of the LORD." A
22:13 let your **w** be like the **w** of one of them,
22:19 "Therefore hear the **w** of the LORD: A
22:38 to the **w** of the LORD that he had spoken. A
2Ki 1:16 in Israel to inquire of his **w**?—
1:17 to the **w** of the LORD that Elijah had spoken. A
2:22 according to the **w** that Elisha spoke.
3: 7 he went he sent **w** to King Jehoshaphat of Judah,
3:12 "The **w** of the LORD is with him." A
4:13 Would you have a **w** spoken on your behalf to
4:44 according to the **w** of the LORD. A
5: 7 that this man sends **w** to me to cure a man
5:14 according to the **w** of the man of God;
6: 9 But the man of God sent **w** to the king of Israel,
6:10 The king of Israel sent **w** to the place of which
7: 1 But Elisha said, "Hear the **w** of the LORD: A
7:16 according to the **w** of the LORD. A
8: 2 the woman got up and did according to the **w** of
9:26 in accordance with the **w** of the LORD." A
9:36 he said, "This is the **w** of the LORD, A
10: 5 with the elders and the guardians, sent **w** to Jehu:
10:10 to the earth nothing of the **w** of the LORD, which A
10:17 according to the **w** of the LORD that he spoke A
10:21 Jehu sent **w** throughout all Israel;
14: 9 King Jehoash of Israel sent **w** to King Amaziah
14:25 according to the **w** of the LORD, A
18:28 "Hear the **w** of the great king, the king of Assyria!
18:36 the people were silent and answered him not a **w**,
19:21 the **w** that the LORD has spoken concerning him:
20: 4 the **w** of the LORD came to him: A
20:16 "Hear the **w** of the LORD: A
20:19 **w** of the LORD that you have spoken is good." A
23:16 and defiled it, according to the **w** of the LORD A
24: 2 the **w** of the LORD that he spoke by his servants A
1Ch 11: 3 according to the **w** of the LORD by Samuel. A
11:10 to the **w** of the LORD concerning Israel. A
12:23 according to the **w** of the LORD. A
15:15 had commanded according to the **w** of the LORD. A
16:15 the **w** that he commanded,
17: 3 same night the **w** of the LORD came to Nathan, A
17: 6 did I ever speak a **w** with any of the judges
17:23 as for the **w** that you have spoken
21: 4 But the king's **w** prevailed against Joab.
22: 8 But the **w** of the LORD came to me, saying, A
2Ch 2: 3 Solomon sent **w** to King Huram of Tyre:
6:17 O LORD, God of Israel, let your **w** be confirmed,
10:15 by God so that the LORD might fulfill his **w**,
11: 2 the **w** of the LORD came to Shemaiah the man A
11: 4 the **w** of the LORD and turned back from A
12: 7 the **w** of the LORD came to Shemaiah, saying: A
18: 4 "Inquire first for the **w** of the LORD." A
18:12 let your **w** be like the **w** of one of them,
18:18 "Therefore hear the **w** of the LORD: A
25:18 King Joash of Israel sent **w** to King Amaziah
30: 1 Hezekiah sent **w** to all Israel and Judah,
2Ch 30:12 the officials commanded by the **w** of the LORD. A
31: 5 As soon as the **w** spread, the people of Israel gave
34:21 our ancestors did not keep the **w** of the LORD, A
34:29 the king sent **w** and gathered together all the elders
35: 6 according to the **w** of the LORD by Moses." A
36:21 the **w** of the LORD by the mouth of Jeremiah, A
36:22 in fulfillment of the **w** of the LORD spoken A
Ezr 1: 1 in order that the **w** of the LORD by the mouth A
6:13 Then, according to the **w** sent by King Darius,
Ne 1: 8 the **w** that you commanded your servant Moses,
5: 8 They were silent, and could not find a **w** to say.
Est 7: 9 whose **w** saved the king, stands at Haman's house,
9:26 these days are called Purim, from the **w** Pur.
Job 2:13 and no one spoke a **w** to him,
4: 2 "If one ventures a **w** with you,
4:12 "Now a **w** came stealing to me,
15:11 or the **w** that deals gently with you?
29:22 and my **w** dropped upon them like dew.
32:15 they have not a **w** to say.
Ps 17: 4 by the **w** of your lips I have avoided the ways of
33: 4 For the **w** of the LORD is upright, A
33: 6 By the **w** of the LORD the heavens were made, A
56: 4 In God, whose **w** I praise, in God I trust;
56:10 In God, whose **w** I praise, in the LORD,
56:10 in the LORD, whose **w** I praise,
89:34 or alter the **w** that went forth from my lips.
103:20 who do his bidding, obedient to his spoken **w**.
105: 8 of the **w** that he commanded,
105:19 the **w** of the LORD kept testing him. A
107:20 he sent out his **w** and healed them,
119: 9 By guarding it according to your **w**.
119:11 I treasure your **w** in my heart,
119:16 I will not forget your **w**.
119:17 so that I may live and observe your **w**.
119:25 revive me according to your **w**.
119:28 strengthen me according to your **w**.
119:42 for I trust in your **w**.
119:43 Do not take the **w** of truth utterly out of my mouth,
119:49 Remember your **w** to your servant,
119:65 O LORD, according to your **w**.
119:67 but now I keep your **w**.
119:74 because I have hoped in your **w**.
119:81 for your salvation; I hope in your **w**.
119:89 your **w** is firmly fixed in heaven.
119:101 in order to keep your **w**.
119:105 Your **w** is a lamp to my feet and a light to my path.
119:107 give me life, O LORD, according to your **w**.
119:114 and my shield; I hope in your **w**.
119:160 The sum of your **w** is truth;
119:162 I rejoice at your **w** like one who finds great spoil.
119:169 give me understanding according to your **w**.
130: 5 my soul waits, and in his **w** I hope;
138: 2 for you have exalted your name and your **w**
139: 4 Even before a **w** is on my tongue, O LORD,
147:15 to the earth; his **w** runs swiftly.
147:18 He sends out his **w**, and melts them;
147:19 He declares his **w** to Jacob,
Pr 12:25 but a good **w** cheers it up.
13:13 Those who despise the **w** bring destruction
15: 1 but a harsh **w** stirs up anger.
15:23 and a **w** in season, how good it is!
25:11 A **w** fitly spoken is like apples of gold in a setting
30: 5 Every **w** of God proves true; B
Ecc 5: 2 nor let your heart be quick to utter a **w** before God,
8: 4 For the **w** of the king is powerful,
Isa 1:10 Hear the **w** of the LORD, you rulers of Sodom! A
2: 1 The **w** that Isaiah son of Amoz saw
2: 3 and the **w** of the LORD from Jerusalem. A
5:24 and have despised the **w** of the Holy One of Israel.
8:10 speak a **w**, but it will not stand, for God is with us.
9: 8 Lord sent a **w** against Jacob, and it fell on Israel;
16:13 the **w** that the LORD spoke concerning Moab in
24: 3 for the LORD has spoken this **w**.
28:13 Therefore the **w** of the LORD will be to them, A
28:14 Therefore hear the **w** of the LORD, A
30:12 Because you reject this **w**,
30:21 your ears shall hear a **w** behind you, saying,
36:21 But they were silent and answered him not a **w**,
37:22 the **w** that the LORD has spoken concerning him:
38: 4 Then the **w** of the LORD came to Isaiah: A
39: 5 "Hear the **w** of the LORD of hosts: A
39: 8 **w** of the LORD that you have spoken is good." A
40: 8 but the **w** of our God will stand forever.
44:26 who confirms the **w** of his servant, and fulfills
45:23 in righteousness a **w** that shall not return:
50: 4 I may know how to sustain the weary with a **w**.
55:11 so shall my **w** be that goes out from my mouth;
66: 2 and contrite in spirit, who trembles at my **w**.
66: 5 Hear the **w** of the LORD, A
66: 5 you who tremble at his **w**:
Jer 1: 2 to whom the **w** of the LORD came in the days A
1: 4 Now the **w** of the LORD came to me saying, A
1:11 The **w** of the LORD came to me, saying, A
1:12 for I am watching over my **w** to perform it."
1:13 The **w** of the LORD came to me a second time, A
2: 1 The **w** of the LORD came to me, saying: A
2: 4 Hear the **w** of the LORD, O house of Jacob, A
2:31 you, O generation, behold the **w** of the LORD! A
5:13 for the **w** is not in them.
5:14 Because they have spoken this **w**,
6:10 The **w** of the LORD is to them an object of scorn; A
7: 1 The **w** that came to Jeremiah from the LORD:
7: 2 and proclaim there this **w**, and say,
7: 2 Hear the **w** of the LORD, all you people of Judah, A
8: 9 since they have rejected the **w** of the LORD, A
9:20 Hear, O women, the **w** of the LORD, A
9:20 and let your ears receive the **w** of his mouth;
Jer 10: 1 Hear the **w** that the LORD speaks to you,
11: 1 The **w** that came to Jeremiah from the LORD:
13: 2 a loincloth according to the **w** of the LORD, A
13: 3 the **w** of the LORD came to me a second time, A
13: 8 Then the **w** of the LORD came to me: A
13:12 You shall speak to them this **w**:
14: 1 The **w** of the LORD that came to Jeremiah A
14:17 You shall say to them this **w**:
16: 1 The **w** of the LORD came to me: A
17:15 "Where is the **w** of the LORD? A
17:20 Hear the **w** of the LORD, you kings of Judah, A
18: 1 The **w** that came to Jeremiah from the LORD:
18: 5 Then the **w** of the LORD came to me: A
18:18 nor the **w** from the prophet.
19: 3 You shall say: Hear the **w** of the LORD, A
20: 8 **w** of the LORD has become for me a reproach A
21: 1 the **w** that came to Jeremiah from the LORD,
21:11 Hear the **w** of the LORD, A
22: 1 of the king of Judah, and speak there this **w**,
22: 2 Hear the **w** of the LORD, A
22: 4 For if you will indeed obey this **w**,
22:29 O land, land, land, hear the **w** of the LORD! A
23:17 to those who despise the **w** of the LORD, A
23:18 of the LORD so as to see and to hear his **w**?
23:18 Who has given heed to his **w** so as to proclaim it?
23:28 the one who has my **w** speak my **w** faithfully.
23:29 Is not my **w** like fire, says the LORD,
23:36 for the burden is everyone's own **w**,
24: 4 Then the **w** of the LORD came to me: A
25: 1 The **w** that came to Jeremiah concerning all
25: 3 to this day, the **w** of the LORD has come to me, A
26: 1 this **w** came from the LORD:
26: 2 do not hold back a **w**.
27: 1 this **w** came to Jeremiah from the LORD.
27: 3 Send **w** to the king of Edom, the king of Moab,
27:18 and if the **w** of the LORD is with them, A
28: 7 now to this **w** that I speak in your hearing and in
28: 9 when the **w** of that prophet comes true,
28:12 the **w** of the LORD came to Jeremiah: A
29:20 hear the **w** of the LORD: A
29:30 Then the **w** of the LORD came to Jeremiah: A
30: 1 The **w** that came to Jeremiah from the LORD:
31:10 Hear the **w** of the LORD, O nations, A
32: 1 The **w** that came to Jeremiah from the LORD in
32: 6 Jeremiah said, The **w** of the LORD came to me: A
32: 8 in accordance with the **w** of the LORD, A
32: 8 Then I knew that this was the **w** of the LORD. A
32:26 The **w** of the LORD came to Jeremiah: A
33: 1 **w** of the LORD came to Jeremiah a second time, A
33:19 The **w** of the LORD came to Jeremiah: A
33:23 The **w** of the LORD came to Jeremiah: A
34: 1 The **w** that came to Jeremiah from the LORD,
34: 4 Yet hear the **w** of the LORD, A
34: 5 For I have spoken the **w**, says the LORD.
34: 8 The **w** that came to Jeremiah from the LORD,
34:12 The **w** of the LORD came to Jeremiah from A
35: 1 The **w** that came to Jeremiah from the LORD in
35:12 Then the **w** of the LORD came to Jeremiah: A
36: 1 this **w** came to Jeremiah from the LORD:
36:27 the **w** of the LORD came to Jeremiah: A
37: 6 **w** of the LORD came to the prophet Jeremiah: A
37:17 and said, "Is there any **w** from the LORD?"
39:15 The **w** of the LORD came to Jeremiah A
40: 1 The **w** that came to Jeremiah from the LORD
42: 7 of ten days the **w** of the LORD came to Jeremiah. A
42:15 then hear the **w** of the LORD, A
43: 8 **w** of the LORD came to Jeremiah in Tahpanhes: A
44: 1 The **w** that came to Jeremiah for all the Judeans
44:16 for the **w** that you have spoken to us in the name
44:24 "Hear the **w** of the LORD, A
44:26 Therefore hear the **w** of the LORD, A
45: 1 The **w** that the prophet Jeremiah spoke
46: 1 The **w** of the LORD that came to the prophet A
46:13 The **w** that the LORD spoke to the prophet
47: 1 The **w** of the LORD that came to the prophet A
49:34 The **w** of the LORD that came to the prophet A
50: 1 The **w** that the LORD spoke concerning Babylon,
51:59 The **w** that the prophet Jeremiah commanded
La 1:18 for I have rebelled against his **w**;
Eze 1: 3 the **w** of the LORD came to the priest Ezekiel A
3:16 the **w** of the LORD came to me: A
3:17 whenever you hear a **w** from my mouth,
6: 1 The **w** of the LORD came to me: A
6: 3 hear the **w** of the Lord GOD! C
7: 1 The **w** of the LORD came to me: A
9:11 with the writing case at his side, brought back **w**,
11:14 Then the **w** of the LORD came to me: A
12: 1 The **w** of the LORD came to me: A
12: 8 In the morning the **w** of the LORD came to me: A
12:17 The **w** of the LORD came to me: A
12:21 The **w** of the LORD came to me: A
12:25 But I the LORD will speak the **w** that I speak,
12:25 O rebellious house, I will speak the **w** and fulfill it,
12:26 The **w** of the LORD came to me: A
12:28 but the **w** that I speak will be fulfilled,
13: 1 The **w** of the LORD came to me: A
13: 2 "Hear the **w** of the LORD!" A
13: 6 and yet they wait for the fulfillment of their **w**!
14: 2 And the **w** of the LORD came to me: A
14: 9 If a prophet is deceived and speaks a **w**,
14:12 The **w** of the LORD came to me: A
15: 1 The **w** of the LORD came to me: A
16: 1 The **w** of the LORD came to me: A
16:35 Therefore, O whore, hear the **w** of the LORD: A
17: 1 The **w** of the LORD came to me: A
17:11 Then the **w** of the LORD came to me: A
18: 1 The **w** of the LORD came to me: A

Eze 20: 2 And the w of the LORD came to me: A
20:45 The w of the LORD came to me: A
20:47 Hear the w of the LORD: A
21: 1 The w of the LORD came to me: A
21: 8 And the w of the LORD came to me: A
21:18 The w of the LORD came to me: A
22: 1 The w of the LORD came to me: A
22:17 The w of the LORD came to me: A
22:23 The w of the LORD came to me: A
23: 1 The w of the LORD came to me: A
24: 1 the w of the LORD came to me: A
24:15 The w of the LORD came to me: A
24:20 The w of the LORD came to me: A
25: 1 The w of the LORD came to me: A
25: 3 Hear the w of the Lord GOD: C
26: 1 the w of the LORD came to me: A
27: 1 The w of the LORD came to me: A
28: 1 The w of the LORD came to me: A
28:11 Moreover the w of the LORD came to me: A
28:20 The w of the LORD came to me: A
29: 1 the w of the LORD came to me: A
29:17 the w of the LORD came to me: A
30: 1 The w of the LORD came to me: A
30:20 the w of the LORD came to me: A
31: 1 the w of the LORD came to me: A
32: 1 the w of the LORD came to me: A
32:17 the w of the LORD came to me: A
33: 1 The w of the LORD came to me: A
33: 7 whenever you hear a w from my mouth,
33:23 The w of the LORD came to me: A
33:30 "Come and hear what the w is that comes from
34: 1 The w of the LORD came to me: A
34: 7 you shepherds, hear the w of the LORD: A
34: 9 you shepherds, hear the w of the LORD: A
35: 1 The w of the LORD came to me: A
36: 1 O mountains of Israel, hear the w of the LORD. A
36: 4 hear the w of the Lord GOD: C
36:16 The w of the LORD came to me: A
37: 4 O dry bones, hear the w of the LORD. A
37:15 The w of the LORD came to me: A
38: 1 The w of the LORD came to me: A
Da 9: 2 to the w of the LORD to the prophet Jeremiah, A
9:23 the beginning of your supplications a w went out,
9:23 So consider the w and understand the vision:
9:25 the w went out to restore and rebuild Jerusalem
10: 1 Cyrus of Persia a w was revealed to Daniel,
10: 1 The w was true, and it concerned a great conflict.
10: 1 the w, having received understanding in
10:11 So while he was speaking this w to me,
Hos 1: 1 w of the LORD that came to Hosea son of Beeri, A
4: 1 Hear the w of the LORD, O people of Israel; A
Joel 1: 1 w of the LORD that came to Joel son of Pethuel: A
Am 3: 1 Hear this w that the LORD has spoken
4: 1 Hear this w, you cows of Bashan who are
5: 1 Hear this w that I take up over you in lamentation,
7:16 "Now therefore hear the w of the LORD. A
8:12 seeking the w of the LORD, A
Jnh 1: 1 the w of the LORD came to Jonah son of Amittai, A
3: 1 The w of the LORD came to Jonah a second time, A
3: 3 according to the w of the LORD. A
Mic 1: 1 The w of the LORD that came to Micah A
4: 2 and the w of the LORD from Jerusalem. A
Zep 1: 1 The w of the LORD that came to Zephaniah A
2: 5 The w of the LORD is against you, O Canaan, A
Hag 1: 1 the w of the LORD came by the prophet Haggai A
1: 3 the w of the LORD came by the prophet Haggai, A
2: 1 the w of the LORD came by the prophet Haggai, A
2:10 the w of the LORD came by the prophet Haggai, A
2:20 The w of the LORD came a second time A
Zec 1: 1 the w of the LORD came to A
1: 7 the w of the LORD came to A
4: 6 "This is the w of the LORD to Zerubbabel: A
4: 8 Moreover the w of the LORD came to me, A
6: 9 The w of the LORD came to me: A
7: 1 the w of the LORD came to Zechariah on A
7: 4 Then the w of the LORD of hosts came to me: A
7: 8 The w of the LORD came to Zechariah, saying: A
8: 1 The w of the LORD of hosts came to me, saying: A
8:18 The w of the LORD of hosts came to me, saying: A
9: 1 The w of the LORD is against the land A
11:11 knew that it was the w of the LORD. A
12: 1 The w of the LORD concerning Israel: A
Mal 1: 1 The w of the LORD to Israel by Malachi. A
Mt 2: 8 and when you have found him, bring me w so
4: 4 by every w that comes from the mouth of God.' "
5:37 Let your w be 'Yes, Yes' or 'No, No';
8: 8 only speak the w, and my servant will be healed.
8:16 and he cast out the spirits with a w,
11: 2 he sent w by his disciples
12:32 Whoever speaks a w against the Son of Man will
12:36 to give an account for every careless w you utter;
13:19 When anyone hears the w of the kingdom and does
13:20 the w and immediately receives it with joy;
13:21 trouble or persecution arises on account of the w,
13:22 this is the one who hears the w,
13:22 of the world and the lure of wealth choke the w,
13:23 this is the one who hears the w and understands it,
14:35 they sent w throughout the region
15: 6 your tradition, you make void the w of God. B
18:16 so that every w may be confirmed by the evidence
19:22 When the young man heard this w,
27:19 his wife sent w to him,
Mk 1:45 to spread the w, so that Jesus could no longer go
2: 2 and he was speaking the w to them.
4:14 The sower sows the w.
4:15 the ones on the path where the w is sown:
4:15 Satan immediately comes and takes away the w
Mk 4:16 when they hear the w, they immediately receive it
4:17 trouble or persecution arises on account of the w,
4:18 these are the ones who hear the w,
4:19 desire for other things come in and choke the w,
4:20 they hear the w and accept it and bear fruit,
4:33 With many such parables he spoke the w to them,
7:13 void the w of God through your tradition B
Lk 1: 2 were eyewitnesses and servants of the w,
1:38 let it be with me according to your w."
2:29 in peace, according to your w;
3: 2 the w of God came to John son of Zechariah B
5: 1 was pressing in on him to hear the w of God, B
5:15 more than ever the w about Jesus spread abroad;
7: 7 only speak the w, and let my servant be healed.
7:17 This w about him spread throughout Judea and all
8:11 the parable is this: The seed is the w of God. B
8:12 then the devil comes and takes away the w
8:13 when they hear the w, receive it with joy.
8:15 these are the ones who, when they hear the w,
8:21 my brothers are those who hear the w of God B
11:28 Blessed rather are those who hear the w of God B
12:10 And everyone who speaks a w against the Son
22:61 Then Peter remembered the w of the Lord, C
24:19 a prophet mighty in deed and w before God
Jn 1: 1 In the beginning was the W, and the W was with
God, and the W was God.
1:14 And the W became flesh and lived among us,
2:22 the scripture and the w that Jesus had spoken.
4:41 And many more believed because of his w.
4:50 The man believed the w that Jesus spoke to him
5:24 I tell you, anyone who hears my w
5:38 and you do not have his w abiding in you,
8:31 "If you continue in my w,
8:37 because there is no place in you for my w.
8:43 It is because you cannot accept my w.
8:51 whoever keeps my w will never see death."
8:52 'Whoever keeps my w will never taste death.'
8:55 But I do know him and I keep his w.
10:35 to whom the w of God came were called 'gods' B
12:38 to fulfill the w spoken by the prophet Isaiah:
12:48 and does not receive my w has a judge;
12:48 on the last day the w that I have spoken will serve
14:23 "Those who love me will keep my w,
14:24 and the w that you hear is not mine,
15: 3 You have already been cleansed by the w
15:20 Remember the w that I said to you,
15:20 if they kept my w, they will keep yours also.
15:25 It was to fulfill the w that is written in their law,
17: 6 and they have kept your w.
17:14 I have given them your w,
17:17 Sanctify them in the truth; your w is truth.
17:20 of those who will believe in me through their w,
18: 9 This was to fulfill the w that he had spoken,
Ac 4: 4 But many of those who heard the w believed;
4:29 to your servants to speak your w with all boldness,
4:31 with the Holy Spirit and spoke the w of God B
6: 2 not right that we should neglect the w of God B
6: 4 to prayer and to serving the w."
6: 7 The w of God continued to spread; B
8: 4 from place to place, proclaiming the w.
8:14 that Samaria had accepted the w of God, B
8:25 had testified and spoken the w of the Lord, C
10:44 the Holy Spirit fell upon all who heard the w.
11: 1 that the Gentiles had also accepted the w of God. B
11:16 And I remembered the w of the Lord, C
11:19 and they spoke the w to no one except Jews.
12:24 the w of God continued to advance and gain B
13: 5 they proclaimed the w of God in the synagogues B
13: 7 and Saul and wanted to hear the w of God. B
13:15 if you have any w of exhortation for the people,
13:44 whole city gathered to hear the w of the Lord. C
13:46 that the w of God should be spoken first to you. B
13:48 they were glad and praised the w of the Lord; C
13:49 the w of the Lord spread throughout the region. C
14: 3 the w of his grace by granting signs and wonders
14:25 When they had spoken the w in Perga,
15:27 who themselves will tell you the same things by w
15:35 they taught and proclaimed the w of the Lord. C
15:36 where we proclaimed the w of the Lord and see C
16: 6 by the Holy Spirit to speak the w in Asia.
16:32 the w of the Lord to him and to all who were C
16:36 saying, "The magistrates sent w to let you go;
17:13 Jews of Thessalonica learned that the w of God B
18: 5 Paul was occupied with proclaiming the w,
18:11 teaching the w of God among them. B
19:10 both Jews and Greeks, heard the w of the Lord. C
19:20 the w of the Lord grew mightily and prevailed. C
21:31 w came to the tribune of the cohort
Ro 9: 6 It is not as though the w of God had failed. B
10: 8 "The w is near you, on your lips and in your heart"
10: 8 the w of faith that we proclaim);
10:17 and what is heard comes through the w of Christ.
13: 9 are summed up in this w, "Love your neighbor
15:18 to win obedience from the Gentiles, by w
1Co 14:36 Or did the w of God originate with you? B
2Co 1:18 our w to you has not been "Yes and No."
2:17 For we are not peddlers of God's w like so many;
4: 2 to practice cunning or to falsify God's w;
Gal 6: 6 Those who are taught the w must share
Eph 1:13 when you had heard the w of truth,
5:26 with the washing of water by the w,
6:17 the sword of the Spirit, which is the w of God. B
Php 1:14 dare to speak the w with greater boldness and
2:16 to the w of life that I can boast on the day of Christ
Col 1: 5 You have heard of this hope before in the w of
1:25 to make the w of God fully known, B
3:16 Let the w of Christ dwell in you richly;
Col 3:17 And whatever you do, in w or deed,
4: 3 as well that God will open to us a door for the w,
1Th 1: 5 in w only, but also in power and in the Holy Spirit
1: 6 for in spite of persecution you received the w
1: 8 the w of the Lord has sounded forth from you C
2:13 received the w of God that you heard from us, B
2:13 not as a human w but as what it really is,
2:13 God's w, which is also at work in you believers.
4:15 For this we declare to you by the w of the Lord, C
2Th 2: 2 either by spirit or by w or by letter,
2:15 either by w of mouth or by our letter.
2:17 and strengthen them in every good work and w.
3: 1 so that the w of the Lord may spread rapidly C
1Ti 4: 5 for it is sanctified by God's w and by prayer.
2Ti 2: 9 But the w of God is not chained. B
2:15 rightly explaining the w of truth.
Tit 1: 3 in due time he revealed his w through
1: 9 of the w that is trustworthy in accordance with
2: 5 so that the w of God may not be discredited. B
Heb 1: 3 and he sustains all things by his powerful w.
4:12 Indeed, the w of God is living and active, B
5:13 is unskilled in the w of righteousness.
6: 5 the w of God and the powers of the age to come, B
7:28 but the w of the oath, which came later
11: 3 that the worlds were prepared by the w of God, B
12:19 the hearers beg that not another w be spoken
12:24 to the sprinkled blood that speaks a better w than
13: 7 those who spoke the w of God to you; B
13:22 bear with my w of exhortation,
Jas 1:18 of his own purpose he gave us birth by the w
1:21 with meekness the implanted w that has the power
1:22 But be doers of the w,
1:23 For if any are hearers of the w and not doers,
1Pe 1:23 through the living and enduring w of God. B
1:25 but the w of the Lord endures forever." C
1:25 w is the good news that was announced to you.
2: 8 They stumble because they disobey the w,
3: 1 so that, even if some of them do not obey the w,
3: 1 be won over without a w by their wives' conduct,
2Pe 3: 5 that by the w of God heavens existed long ago B
3: 7 But by the same w the present heavens
1Jn 1: 1 concerning the w of life—
1:10 we make him a liar, and his w is not in us.
2: 5 but whoever obeys his w, truly in this person
2: 7 old commandment is the w that you have heard.
2:14 you are strong and the w of God abides in you, B
3:18 Little children, let us love, not in w or speech,
Rev 1: 2 testified to the w of God and to the testimony B
1: 9 island called Patmos because of the w of God B
3: 8 and yet you have kept my w and have
3:10 Because you have kept my w of patient endurance,
6: 9 the w of God and for the testimony they had B
12:11 of the Lamb and by the w of their testimony,
19:13 and his name is called The W of God. B
20: 4 their testimony to Jesus and for the w of God. B
Tob 13:12 Cursed are all who speak a harsh w against you;
14: 4 the w of God that Nahum spoke about Nineveh, B
14: 4 not a single w of the prophecies will fail.
Jdt 4: 4 So they sent w to every district of Samaria,
14:12 When the Assyrians saw them they sent w
AdE 9:26 in their language this is the w that means "lots").
Wis 1:11 because no secret w is without result,
9: 1 who have made all things by your w,
12: 9 at one blow by dread wild animals or your stern w.
16:12 but it was your w, O Lord, that heals all people.
16:26 but that your w sustains those who trust in you.
18:15 your all-powerful w leaped from heaven,
18:22 but by his w he subdued the avenger,
Sir Pr: 1 be able through the spoken and written w to help
3: 8 Honor your father by w and deed,
16:28 and they never disobey his w.
18:16 So a w is better than a gift.
18:17 Indeed, does not a w surpass a good gift?
31:31 speak no w of reproach to him,
39:17 At his w the waters stood in a heap,
39:17 and the reservoirs of water at the w of his mouth.
42:15 By the w of the Lord his works are made; C
43:26 and by his w all things hold together.
43:27 let the final w be: "He is the all."
48: 1 a prophet like fire, and his w burned like a torch.
48: 3 By the w of the Lord he shut up the heavens, C
48: 5 by the w of the Most High.
Bar 4:37 w of the Holy One, rejoicing in the glory of God.
5: 5 from west and east at the w of the Holy One,
1Mc 7:16 in accordance with the w that was written,
9:55 that he could no longer say a w or give commands
11:53 But he broke his w about all that he had promised;
13:19 Trypho broke his w and did not release Jonathan.
15:35 Athenobius did not answer him a w,
2Mc 8:12 W came to Judas concerning Nicanor's invasion;
10:21 w of what had happened came to Maccabeus,
11: 6 and his men got w that Lysias was besieging
11:26 to send w to them and give them pledges
13: 1 the one hundred forty-ninth year w came to Judas
13:23 he got w that Philip, who had been left in charge of
14: 1 w came to Judas and his men that Demetrius son
1Es 1:26 And the king of Egypt sent w to him saying,
1:57 in fulfillment of the w of the Lord by the mouth C
2: 1 the w of the Lord by the mouth of Jeremiah C
6: 6 not prevented from building until w could be sent
8:43 I sent w to Eliezar, Iduel, Maasmas,
8:72 all who were ever moved at the w of the Lord C
Man 1: 3 by your w of command, who confined the deep
3Mc 3:17 They accepted our presence by w,
2Es 1: 4 The w of the Lord came to me, saying, C
6:15 because the w concerns the end,
6:38 and your w accomplished the work.

2Es 6:43 your **w** went forth, and at once the work was done.
7:*139* [69] his **w** and blot out the multitude of their sins,
8:22 whose **w** is sure and whose utterances are certain,
16:36 This is **w** of the Lord; receive it C
16:56 At his **w** the stars were fixed in their places,
16:58 by his **w** he has suspended the earth over the water.
4Mc 5:14 Eleazar asked to have a **w**.
14: 9 not only heard the direct **w** of threat,
16:14 and in **w** and deed you have proved more powerful

WORDS‡ (656) [WORD]

A. ALL THE WORDS (39)
B. WORDS OF THE/THIS LAW (14)
C. WORDS OF *GOD (8)

Ge 11: 1 the whole earth had one language and the same **w**.
24:30 and when he heard the **w** of his sister Rebekah,
24:52 When Abraham's servant heard their **w**,
27:34 When Esau heard his father's **w**,
27:42 the **w** of her elder son Esau were told to Rebekah;
34:18 Their **w** pleased Hamor and Hamor's son
37: 8 even more because of his dreams and his **w**.
39:19 his master heard the **w** that his wife spoke to him,
42:16 in order that your **w** may be tested,
42:20 Thus your **w** will be verified,
44: 6 he overtook them, he repeated these **w** to them.
44: 7 "Why does my lord speak such **w** as these?
44:10 in accordance with your **w**, let it be:
44:24 to your servant my father we told him the **w**
45:27 But when they told him all the **w** of Joseph A
Ex 4:15 You shall speak to him and put the **w** in his mouth;
4:28 all the **w** of the LORD with which he had sent A
4:30 Aaron spoke all the **w** that the LORD had spoken A
5: 9 at it and pay no attention to deceptive **w**."
19: 6 the **w** that you shall speak to the Israelites."
19: 7 and set before them all these **w** that
19: 8 Moses reported the **w** of the people to the LORD.
19: 9 Moses had told the **w** of the people to the LORD,
20: 1 Then God spoke all these **w**:
24: 3 and told the people all the **w** of the LORD and A
24: 3 "All the **w** that the LORD has spoken we will do. A
24: 4 And Moses wrote down all the **w** of the LORD. A
24: 8 with you in accordance with all these **w**."
33: 4 When the people heard these harsh **w**,
34: 1 on the tablets the **w** that were on the former tablets,
34:27 The LORD said to Moses: Write these **w**;
34:27 in accordance with these **w** I have made a covenant
34:28 And he wrote on the tablets the **w** of the covenant,
Nu 11:24 So Moses went out and told the people the **w** of
12: 6 And he said, "Hear my **w**:
14:39 When Moses told these **w** to all the Israelites,
16:31 As soon as he finished speaking all these **w**,
24: 4 the oracle of one who hears the **w** of God, C
24:16 the oracle of one who hears the **w** of God, C
Dt 1: 1 These are the **w** that Moses spoke to all Israel
1:34 LORD heard your **w**, he was wrathful and swore:
4:10 and I will let them hear my **w**,
4:12 You heard the sound of **w** but saw no form;
4:36 while you heard his **w** coming out of the fire.
5: 5 and you to declare to you the **w** of the LORD;
5:22 These **w** the LORD spoke with a loud voice
5:28 The LORD heard your **w** when you spoke to me,
5:28 "I have heard the **w** of this people,
6: 6 Keep these **w** that I am commanding you today
9:10 were all the **w** that the LORD had spoken A
10: 2 on the tablets the **w** that were on the former tablets,
10: 4 Then he wrote on the tablets the same **w** as before,
11:18 You shall put these **w** of mine in your heart
12:28 to obey all these **w** that I command you today,
13: 3 the **w** of those prophets or those who divine
17:19 diligently observing all the **w** of this law AB
18:18 I will put my **w** in the mouth of the prophet,
18:19 the **w** that the prophet shall speak in my name,
27: 3 shall write on them all the **w** of this law AB
27: 8 on the stones all the **w** of this law very clearly. AB
27:26 not uphold the **w** of this law by observing them." B
28:14 and if you do not turn aside from any of the **w**
28:58 all the **w** of this law that are written in this AB
29: 1 These are the **w** of the covenant that
29: 9 diligently observe the **w** of this covenant,
29:19 the **w** of this oath and bless themselves, thinking
29:29 to observe all the **w** of this law. AB
31: 1 When Moses had finished speaking all these **w**
31:12 and to observe diligently all the **w** of this law, AB
31:24 in a book the **w** of this law to the very end, B
31:28 so that I may recite these **w** in their hearing
31:30 Then Moses recited the **w** of this song,
32: 1 let the earth hear the **w** of my mouth.
32:44 and recited all the **w** of this song in the hearing A
32:45 When Moses had finished reciting all these **w**
32:46 "Take to heart all the **w** that I am giving A
32:46 may diligently observe all the **w** of this law. AB
Jos 1:18 against your orders and disobeys your **w**,
2:21 She said, "According to your **w**, so be it."
3: 9 near and hear the **w** of the LORD your God."
8:34 And afterward he read all the **w** of the law, AB
22:30 heard the **w** that the Reubenites and the Gadites
24:26 Joshua wrote these **w** in the book of the law
24:27 heard all the **w** of the LORD that he spoke to us; A
Jdg 2: 4 When the angel of the LORD spoke these **w** to all
9: 3 So his mother's kinsfolk spoke all these **w**
9:30 When Zebul the ruler of the city heard the **w**
11:11 and Jephthah spoke all his **w** before the LORD
13:12 Then Manoah said, "Now when your **w** come true,
13:17 that we may honor you when your **w** come true?"
16:16 after she had nagged him with her **w** day after day,
1Sa 3:19 the LORD was with him and let none of his **w** fall
8:10 So Samuel reported all the **w** of the LORD to A
8:21 When Samuel had heard all the **w** of the people, A
11: 6 upon Saul in power when he heard these **w**,
15: 1 now therefore listen to the **w** of the LORD.
15:24 the commandment of the LORD and your **w**,
17:11 Saul and all Israel heard these **w** of the Philistine,
17:23 and spoke the same **w** as before.
17:31 When the **w** that David spoke were heard,
18:23 So Saul's servants reported these **w** to David
18:26 When his servants told David these **w**,
21:12 David took these **w** to heart
24: 9 "Why do you listen to the **w** of those who say,
24:16 David had finished speaking these **w** to Saul,
25:24 and hear the **w** of your servant.
26:19 let my lord the king hear the **w** of his servant.
28:20 filled with fear because of the **w** of Samuel;
28:23 and he listened to their **w**.
2Sa 3: 8 The **w** of Ishbaal made Abner very angry;
7:17 with all these **w** and with all this vision,
7:28 O Lord GOD, you are God, and your **w** are true,
14: 3 And Joab put the **w** into her mouth.
14:19 it was he who put all these **w** into the mouth
19:43 But the **w** of the people of Judah were fiercer than the **w** of the people of Israel.
20:17 she said to him, "Listen to the **w** of your servant."
22: 1 to the LORD the **w** of this song on the day when
23: 1 Now these are the last **w** of David:
1Ki 1:14 I will come in after you and confirm your **w**."
5: 7 When Hiram heard the **w** of Solomon,
8:59 Let these **w** of mine, with which I pleaded before
12: 7 and speak good **w** to them when you answer them,
13:11 the **w** also that he had spoken to the king,
21:27 When Ahab heard those **w**,
22:13 to summon Micaiah said to him, "Look, the **w** of
2Ki 6:12 who tells the king of Israel the **w** that you speak
6:30 the **w** of the woman he tore his clothes—
18:20 Do you think that mere **w** are strategy and power
18:27 to speak these **w** to your master and to you,
18:37 with their clothes torn and told him the **w** of
19: 4 your God heard all the **w** of the Rabshakeh, A
19: 4 the **w** that the LORD your God has heard;
19: 6 not be afraid because of the **w** that you have heard,
19:16 hear the **w** of Sennacherib,
22:11 When the king heard the **w** of the book of the law,
22:13 concerning the **w** of this book that has been found;
22:13 our ancestors did not obey the **w** of this book,
22:16 all the **w** of the book that the king of Judah A
22:18 Regarding the **w** that you have heard,
23: 2 he read in their hearing all the **w** of the book of A
23: 3 to perform the **w** of this covenant that were written
23:24 the **w** of the law that were written in the book B
1Ch 17:15 In accordance with all these **w** and all this vision,
23:27 to the last **w** of David these were the number of
2Ch 10: 7 and speak good **w** to them,
15: 8 When Asa heard these **w**, the prophecy
18:12 to summon Micaiah said to him, "Look, the **w** of
29:15 by the **w** of the LORD,
29:30 to sing praises to the LORD with the **w** of David
32: 8 The people were encouraged by the **w**
33:18 the **w** of the seers who spoke to him in the name of
34:19 king heard the **w** of the law he tore his clothes. B
34:21 concerning the **w** of the book that has been found;
34:26 Regarding the **w** that you have heard,
34:27 when you heard his **w** against this place
34:30 he read in their hearing all the **w** of the book of A
34:31 to perform the **w** of the covenant that were written
35:22 not listen to the **w** of Neco from the mouth of God,
36:16 despising his **w**, and scoffing at his prophets,
Ezr 9: 4 all who trembled at the **w** of the God of Israel,
Ne 1: 1 The **w** of Nehemiah son of Hacaliah.
1: 4 When I heard these **w** I sat down and wept,
2:18 and also the **w** that the king had spoken to me.
6: 7 it will be reported to the king according to these **w**.
6:19 and reported my **w** to him.
8: 9 people wept when they heard the **w** of the law. B
8:12 because they had understood the **w**
8:13 scribe Ezra in order to study the **w** of the law. B
Est 3: 4 in order to see whether Mordecai's **w** would avail;
7: 8 As the **w** left the mouth of the king,
Job 4: 4 Your **w** have supported those who were stumbling,
6: 3 therefore my **w** have been rash.
6:10 for I have not denied the **w** of the Holy One.
6:25 How forceful are honest **w**!
6:26 Do you think that you can reprove **w**,
8: 2 and the **w** of your mouth be a great wind?
8:10 and tell you and utter **w** out of their understanding?
9:14 then can I answer him, choosing my **w** with him?
11: 2 "Should a multitude of **w** go unanswered,
12:11 Does not the ear test **w** as the palate tastes food?
13:17 Listen carefully to my **w**, and let my declaration be
15: 3 or in **w** with which they can do no good?
15:13 and let such **w** go out of your mouth?
16: 3 Have windy **w** no limit?
16: 4 I could join **w** together against you,
18: 2 "How long will you hunt for **w**?
19: 2 and break me in pieces with **w**?
19:23 "O that my **w** were written down!
21: 2 "Listen carefully to my **w**,
22:22 and lay up his **w** in your heart.
23:12 I have treasured in my bosom the **w** of his mouth.
26: 4 With whose help have you uttered **w**,
31:40 The **w** of Job are ended.
32:11 "See, I waited for your **w**,
32:12 no one among you that answered his **w**.
32:14 He has not directed his **w** against me,
32:18 I am full of **w**; the spirit within me constrains me.
Job 33: 1 hear my speech, O Job, and listen to all my **w**.
33: 3 My **w** declare the uprightness of my heart,
33: 5 set your **w** in order before me; take your stand.
33: 8 and I have heard the sound of your **w**.
33:13 saying, 'He will answer none of my **w**'?
34: 2 "Hear my **w**, you wise men, and give ear
34: 3 for the ear tests **w** as the palate tastes food.
34:35 his **w** are without insight.'
34:37 and multiplies his **w** against God."
35:16 he multiplies **w** without knowledge."
36: 4 For truly my **w** are not false;
38: 2 that darkens counsel by **w** without knowledge?
41: 3 Will it speak soft **w** to you?
42: 7 After the LORD had spoken these **w** to Job,
Ps 4: 2 long will you love vain **w**, and seek after lies?
5: 1 Give ear to my **w**, O LORD;
17: 6 incline your ear to me, hear my **w**.
18: T *who addressed the* **w** *of this song to the LORD*
19: 3 There is no speech, nor are there **w**;
19: 4 and their **w** to the end of the world.
19:14 the **w** of my mouth and the meditation of my heart
22: 1 from the **w** of my groaning?
35:20 but they conceive deceitful **w**
36: 3 The **w** of their mouths are mischief and deceit;
41: 6 when they come to see me, they utter empty **w**,
44:16 at the **w** of the taunters and revilers,
50:17 you hate discipline, and you cast my **w** behind you.
52: 4 You love all **w** that devour, O deceitful tongue.
54: 2 give ear to the **w** of my mouth.
55:21 with **w** that were softer than oil,
59: 7 with sharp **w** on their lips—
59:12 For the sin of their mouths, the **w** of their lips,
64: 3 who aim bitter **w** like arrows,
66:19 he has given heed to the **w** of my prayer.
78: 1 incline your ears to the **w** of my mouth.
94: 4 They pour out their arrogant **w**;
105:28 they rebelled against his **w**.
106:12 Then they believed his **w**; they sang his praise.
106:33 and he spoke **w** that were rash.
107:11 for they had rebelled against the **w** of God, C
109: 3 They beset me with **w** of hate,
119:57 LORD is my portion; I promise to keep your **w**.
119:103 How sweet are your **w** to my taste,
119:130 The unfolding of your **w** gives light;
119:139 because my foes forget your **w**.
119:147 I put my hope in your **w**.
119:161 but my heart stands in awe of your **w**.
138: 4 for they have heard the **w** of your mouth.
141: 6 then they shall learn that my **w** were pleasant.
145:13 The LORD is faithful in all his **w**,
Pr 1: 2 for understanding **w** of insight,
1: 6 the **w** of the wise and their riddles.
1:23 I will make my **w** known to you.
2: 1 if you accept my **w** and treasure
2:16 from the adulteress with her smooth **w**,
4: 4 and said to me, "Let your heart hold fast my **w**;
4: 5 nor turn away from the **w** of my mouth.
4:10 Hear, my child, and accept my **w**,
4:20 My child, be attentive to my **w**;
5: 7 and do not depart from the **w** of my mouth.
6: 2 caught by the **w** of your mouth.
7: 1 keep my **w** and store up my commandments
7: 5 from the adulteress with her smooth **w**.
7:24 and be attentive to the **w** of my mouth.
8: 8 All the **w** of my mouth are righteous; A
10:19 When **w** are many, transgression is not lacking,
12: 6 The **w** of the wicked are a deadly ambush,
12:18 Rash **w** are like sword thrusts,
13: 2 the fruit of their **w** good persons eat good things,
14: 7 for there you do not find **w** of knowledge.
15:26 to the LORD, but gracious **w** are pure.
16:24 Pleasant **w** are like a honeycomb,
17:27 One who spares **w** is knowledgeable;
18: 4 The **w** of the mouth are deep waters;
18: 8 The **w** of a whisperer are like delicious morsels;
19:27 my child, from the **w** of knowledge,
22:12 but he overthrows the **w** of the faithless.
22:17 The **w** of the wise: Incline your ear and hear my **w**,
23: 8 and you will waste your pleasant **w**.
23: 9 who will only despise the wisdom of your **w**.
23:12 Apply your mind to instruction and your ear to **w**
26:22 The **w** of a whisperer are like delicious morsels;
29:19 By mere **w** servants are not disciplined,
30: 1 The **w** of Agur son of Jakeh.
30: 6 Do not add to his **w**, or else he will rebuke you,
31: 1 The **w** of King Lemuel.
Ecc 1: 1 The **w** of the Teacher, the son of David,
5: 2 therefore let your **w** be few.
5: 3 and a fool's voice with many **w**.
5: 6 why should God be angry at your **w**,
5: 7 many dreams come vanities and a multitude of **w**;
6:11 more **w**, the more vanity, so how is one the better?
9:16 and his **w** are not heeded."
9:17 The quiet **w** of the wise are more to be heeded than
10:12 **W** spoken by the wise bring them favor,
10:13 The **w** of their mouths begin in foolishness,
12:10 The Teacher sought to find pleasing **w**,
12:10 and he wrote **w** of truth plainly.
Isa 29: 4 from low in the dust your **w** shall come;
29:11 of all this has become for you like the **w** of
29:18 On that day the deaf shall hear the **w** of a scroll,
31: 2 he does not call back his **w**,
32: 7 to ruin the poor with lying **w**,
36: 5 Do you think that mere **w** are strategy and power
36:12 to speak these **w** to your master and to you,
36:13 "Hear the **w** of the great king, the king of Assyria!
36:22 and told him the **w** of the Rabshakeh.

Isa 37: 4 It may be that the LORD your God heard the w of
37: 4 the w that the LORD your God has heard;
37: 6 not be afraid because of the w that you have heard,
37:17 hear all the w of Sennacherib, A
41:26 none who proclaimed, none who heard your w.
51:16 I have put my w in your mouth,
59:13 conceiving lying w and uttering them from
59:21 and my w that I have put in your mouth,
Jer 1: 1 The w of Jeremiah son of Hilkiah,
1: 9 "Now I have put my w in your mouth.
3:12 Go, and proclaim these w toward the north,
5:14 I am now making my w in your mouth a fire,
6:19 because they have not given heed to my w;
7: 4 Do not trust in these deceptive w:
7: 8 Here you are, trusting in deceptive w to no avail.
7:27 So you shall speak all these w to them,
9: 8 They all speak friendly w to their neighbors,
11: 2 Hear the w of this covenant,
11: 3 Cursed be anyone who does not heed the w
11: 6 Proclaim all these w in the cities of Judah,
11: 6 Hear the w of this covenant and do them.
11: 8 I brought upon them all the w of this covenant, A
11:10 who refused to heed my w;
12: 6 though they speak friendly w to you.
13:10 This evil people, who refuse to hear my w,
15:16 Your w were found, and I ate them,
15:16 and your w became to me a joy and the delight
16:10 And when you tell this people all these w,
18: 2 and there I will let you hear my w."
18:18 and let us not heed any of his w."
19: 2 and proclaim there the w that I tell you.
19:15 stiffened their necks, refusing to hear my w.
22: 5 But if you will not heed these w,
23: 9 because of the LORD and because of his holy w.
23:16 not listen to the w of the prophets who prophesy
23:22 they would have proclaimed my w to my people,
23:30 who steal my w from one another.
23:36 and so you pervert the w of the living God,
23:38 Because you have said these w,
25: 8 Because you have not obeyed my w,
25:13 that land all the w that I have uttered against it, A
25:30 therefore, shall prophesy against them all these w,
26: 2 speak to them all the w that I command you; A
26: 5 the w of my servants the prophets whom I send
26: 7 all the people heard Jeremiah speaking these w
26:12 and this city all the w you have heard. A
26:15 the LORD sent me to you to speak all these w
26:20 against this city and against this land in w exactly
26:21 heard his w, the king sought to put him to death;
27:14 to the w of the prophets who are telling you not
27:16 to the w of your prophets who are prophesying
28: 6 the LORD fulfill the w that you have prophesied,
29: 1 the w of the letter that the prophet Jeremiah sent
29:19 because they did not heed my w,
29:23 in my name lying w that I did not command them;
30: 2 Write in a book all the w that I have spoken A
30: 4 the w that the LORD spoke concerning Israel
31:23 Once more they shall use these w in the land
34: 6 Then the prophet Jeremiah spoke all these w
35:13 Can you not learn a lesson and obey my w?
36: 2 and write on it all the w that I have spoken A
36: 4 all the w of the LORD that he had spoken to him. A
36: 6 in the LORD's house you shall read the w of
36: 8 about reading from the scroll the w of the LORD
36:10 Baruch read the w of Jeremiah from the scroll,
36:11 of Shaphan heard all the w of the LORD from A
36:13 Micaiah told them all the w that he had heard, A
36:16 When they heard all the w, A
36:16 "We certainly must report all these w to the king."
36:17 "Tell us now, how did you write all these w?
36:18 "He dictated all these w to me,
36:20 and they reported all the w to the king. A
36:24 nor any of his servants who heard all these w,
36:27 the w that Baruch wrote at Jeremiah's dictation,
36:28 another scroll and write on it all the former w
36:32 wrote on it at Jeremiah's dictation all the w of A
36:32 and many similar w were added to them.
37: 2 nor the people of the land listened to the w of
38: 1 of Malchiah heard the w that Jeremiah was saying
38: 4 and all the people, by speaking such w to them.
38:27 in the very w the king had commanded.
39:16 I am going to fulfill my w against this city for evil
43: 1 the people all these w of the LORD their God,
44:25 in deeds what you declared in w,
44:28 shall know whose w will stand, mine or theirs!
44:29 that my w against you will surely be carried out:
45: 1 when he wrote these w in a scroll at the dictation
51:60 all these w that are written concerning Babylon.
51:61 see that you read all these w,
51:64 Thus far are the w of Jeremiah.
Eze 2: 6 and do not be afraid of their w,
2: 6 do not be afraid of their w,
2: 7 You shall speak my w to them,
2:10 the front and on the back, and written on it were w
3: 4 the house of Israel and speak my very w to them.
3: 6 whose w you cannot understand.
3:10 Mortal, all my w that I shall speak to you receive
12:28 None of my w will be delayed any longer,
33:31 and they hear your w, but they will not obey them.
35:13 and multiplied your w against me; I heard it.
Da 2: 9 You have agreed to speak lying and misleading w
4:31 While the w were still in the king's mouth,
7:11 then because of the noise of the arrogant w that
7:25 He shall speak w against the Most High,
9:12 He has confirmed his w, which he spoke against us
10: 6 and the sound of his w like the roar of a multitude.
10: 9 Then I heard the sound of his w;
Da 10: 9 and when I heard the sound of his w,
10:11 pay attention to the w that I am going to speak
10:12 your w have been heard, and I have come because
10:12 and I have come because of your w.
10:15 While he was speaking these w to me,
12: 4 the w secret and the book sealed until the time of
12: 9 the w are to remain secret and sealed until the time
Hos 6: 5 I have killed them by the w of my mouth,
10: 4 They utter mere w; with empty
14: 2 Take w with you and return to the LORD;
Am 1: 1 The w of Amos, who was among the shepherds
7:10 the land is not able to bear all his w.
8:11 but of hearing the w of the LORD.
Mic 2: 7 Do not my w do good to one who walks uprightly?
Hag 1:12 and the w of the prophet Haggai,
Zec 1: 6 But my w and my statutes,
1:13 and comforting w to the angel who talked with me.
7: 7 Were not these the w that the LORD proclaimed
7:12 not to hear the law and the w that the LORD
8: 9 you that have recently been hearing these w from
Mal 2:17 You have wearied the LORD with your w.
3:13 You have spoken harsh w against me,
Mt 6: 7 that they will be heard because of their many w.
7:24 "Everyone then who hears these w of mine
7:26 And everyone who hears these w of mine and does
10:14 anyone will not welcome you or listen to your w,
12:37 for by your w you will be justified, and by your w
you will be condemned."
24:35 but my w will not pass away.
26:44 and prayed for the third time, saying the same w.
Mk 8:38 of my w in this adulterous and sinful generation,
10:24 And the disciples were perplexed at these w.
13:31 but my w will not pass away.
14:39 and prayed, saying the same w.
Lk 1:20 But now, because you did not believe my w,
1:29 But she was much perplexed by his w
2:19 But Mary treasured all these w and pondered them
3: 4 the book of the w of the prophet Isaiah,
4:22 and were amazed at the gracious w that came
6:47 hears my w, and acts on them.
9:26 Those who are ashamed of me and of my w,
9:44 "Let these w sink into your ears:
19:22 He said to him, 'I will judge you by your own w,
21:15 for I will give you w and a wisdom that none
21:33 but my w will not pass away.
24: 8 Then they remembered his w,
24:11 But these w seemed to them an idle tale,
24:44 "These are my w that I spoke to you
Jn 3:34 He whom God has sent speaks the w of God, C
6:63 The w that I have spoken to you are spirit and life.
6:68 You have the w of eternal life.
7:40 When they heard these w, some in the crowd said,
8:20 He spoke these w while he was teaching in
8:47 Whoever is from God hears the w of God. C
10:19 Again the Jews were divided because of these w.
10:21 "These are not the w of one who has a demon.
12:47 I do not judge anyone who hears my w and does
14:10 The w that I say to you I do not speak on my own;
14:24 Whoever does not love me does not keep my w;
15: 7 If you abide in me, and my w abide in you,
17: 1 After Jesus had spoken these w,
17: 8 for the w that you gave to me I have given to them,
18: 1 After Jesus had spoken these w,
19:13 When Pilate heard these w,
Ac 5: 5 Ananias heard these w, he fell down and died.
5:24 of the temple and the chief priests heard these w,
6:11 "We have heard him speak blasphemous w
7:22 of the Egyptians and was powerful in his w
13:27 the w of the prophets that are read every sabbath,
13:27 they fulfilled those w by condemning him.
14:18 with these w, they scarcely restrained the crowds
15:15 This agrees with the w of the prophets,
16:38 The police reported these w to the magistrates,
18:15 of questions about w and names and your own law,
20:35 remembering the w of the Lord Jesus,
Ro 3: 4 "So that you may be justified in your w,
4:23 Now the w, "it was reckoned to him,"
8:26 very Spirit intercedes with sighs too deep for w.
10:18 and their w to the ends of the world."
1Co 2: 1 the mystery of God to you in lofty w or wisdom.
2: 4 and my proclamation were not with plausible w
2:13 of these things in w not taught by human wisdom
14:19 in church I would rather speak five w with my
mind, than ten thousand w in a tongue.
Eph 3: 3 as I wrote above in a few w,
4:29 so that your w may give grace to those who hear.
5: 6 Let no one deceive you with empty w,
1Th 2: 5 we never came with w of flattery or with a pretext
4:18 Therefore encourage one another with these w.
5:20 Do not despise the w of prophets,
1Ti 4: 6 on the w of the faith and of the sound teaching
6: 3 with the sound w of our Lord Jesus Christ and
6: 4 for controversy and for disputes about w.
2Ti 2:14 that they are to avoid wrangling over w,
Heb 4: 7 in the w already quoted, "Today,
12:19 and a voice whose w made the hearers beg that
1Pe 4:11 so as one speaking the very w of God; C
2Pe 2: 3 their greed they will exploit you with deceptive w.
3: 2 that you should remember the w spoken in the past
Rev 1: 3 the one who reads aloud the w of the prophecy,
2: 1 These are the w of him who holds the seven stars
2: 8 These are the w of the first and the last,
2:12 the w of him who has the sharp two-edged sword:
2:18 These are the w of the Son of God,
3: 1 the w of him who has the seven spirits of God and
3: 7 These are the w of the holy one, the true one,
3:14 The w of the Amen, the faithful and true witness,
Rev 13: 5 a mouth uttering haughty and blasphemous w,
17:17 until the w of God will be fulfilled. C
19: 9 And he said to me, "These are true w of God." C
21: 5 "Write this, for these w are trustworthy and true."
22: 6 he said to me, "These w are trustworthy and true,
22: 7 the one who keeps the w of the prophecy
22: 9 and with those who keep the w of this book.
22:10 "Do not seal up the w of the prophecy of this book,
22:18 I warn everyone who hears the w of the prophecy
22:19 if anyone takes away from the w of the book
Tob 6:18 When Tobias heard the w of Raphael and learned
8: 2 Then Tobias remembered the w of Raphael,
8:20 for Tobias and swore on oath to him in these w:
9: 6 who wept and blessed him with the w,
14: 1 So ended Tobit's w of praise.
14: 4 None of all their w will fail,
Jdt 3: 1 to him to sue for peace in these w:
6: 4 For he has spoken; none of his w shall be in vain.
6: 5 you have said these w in a moment of perversity;
6: 9 and none of my w shall fail to come true."
7:16 These w pleased Holofernes and all his attendants,
8: 9 the harsh w spoken by the people against the ruler,
8:28 and there is no one who can deny your w.
9:13 Make my deceitful w bring wound and bruise
10: 1 and had ended all these w,
10:14 the men heard her w, and observed her face—
11: 5 Judith answered him, "Accept the w of your slave,
11: 6 If you follow out the w of your servant,
11: 9 in your council, we have heard his w, for
11:20 Her w pleased Holofernes and all his servants.
AdE 6: 2 He found the w written about Mordecai,
15: 8 He comforted her with soothing w, and said to her,
Wis 1: 6 not free blasphemers from the guilt of their w;
1: 9 and a report of their w will come to the Lord,
1:16 ungodly by their w and deeds summoned death;
2:17 Let us see if his w are true,
6: 9 To you then, O monarchs, my w are directed,
6:11 Therefore set your desire on my w;
6:25 be instructed by my w, and you will profit.
7:16 For both we and our w are in his hand,
8:18 understanding, and renown in sharing her w,
Sir 1:24 They hold back their w until the right moment;
2:15 Those who fear the Lord do not disobey his w,
4:24 and education through the w of the tongue.
8:11 or they may lie in ambush against your w.
9:17 so a people's leader is proved wise by his w.
12:12 and at last you will realize the truth of my w,
13:22 he speaks unseemly w, but they justify him.
16:24 and pay close attention to my w.
18:15 or spoil your gift by harsh w.
18:29 in w become wise themselves,
20:13 The wise make themselves beloved by only few w,
20:27 The wise person advances himself by his w,
21:17 and they ponder his w in their minds.
21:25 the w of the prudent are weighed in the balance.
27:23 his mouth is all sweetness, and he admires your w;
27:23 and with your own w he will trip you up.
28:25 so make balances and scales for your w.
29:25 and besides this you will hear rude w like these:
31:22 and in the end you will appreciate my w.
32: 8 Be brief; say much in few w;
36:24 so an intelligent mind detects false w.
39: 6 he will pour forth w of wisdom of his own
41:16 Therefore show respect for my w;
41:22 of abusive w, before friends—
44: 4 they were wise in their w of instruction;
45: 3 By his w he performed swift miracles;
46:15 by his w he became known as a trustworthy seer.
51: 5 from an unclean tongue and lying w—
Bar 1: 1 the w of the book that Baruch son of Neriah son
1: 3 the w of this book to Jeconiah son of Jehoiakim,
1:21 in all the w of the prophets whom he sent to us, A
1Mc 1:30 Deceitfully he spoke peaceable w to them,
1:51 In such w he wrote to his whole kingdom.
2:22 the king's w by turning aside from our religion to
2:23 When he had finished speaking these w,
2:62 Do not fear the w of sinners,
7:10 and his brothers with peaceable but treacherous w.
7:11 But they paid no attention to their w,
7:15 Alcimus spoke peaceable w to them
10: 3 Demetrius sent Jonathan a letter in peaceable w
10:17 a letter and sent it to him, in the following w:
10:24 I also will write them w of encouragement
10:25 So he sent a message to them in the following w:
10:46 When Jonathan and the people heard these w,
10:47 he had been the first to speak peaceable w to them,
10:74 When Jonathan heard the w of Apollonius,
11: 2 He set out for Syria with peaceable w,
13: 7 the people was rekindled when they heard these w,
14:23 and to put a copy of their w in the public archives,
15:36 in wrath to the king and reported to him these w,
2Mc 2: 3 And with other similar w he exhorted them that
6:29 because the w he had uttered were
7:24 Antiochus not only appealed to him in w,
8:21 With these w he filled them with courage
9:12 he uttered these w, "It is right to be subject to God;
10:34 kept blaspheming terribly and uttering wicked w.
12:25 with many w he had confirmed his solemn promise
14:34 the constant Defender of our nation, in these w:
15:11 and spears as with the inspiration of brave w,
15:17 Encouraged by the w of Judas,
15:22 He called upon him in these w:
15:24 With these w he ended his prayer.
1Es 1:24 so that the w of the Lord fell upon Israel.
1:28 the w of the prophet Jeremiah from the mouth of
1:47 the w that were spoken by the prophet Jeremiah
5: 6 who spoke wise w before King Darius of

1Es 9:55 by the **w** which they had been taught.
3Mc 4:16 and uttering improper **w** against the supreme God.
5:30 But at these **w** he was filled with
6: 5 speaking grievous **w** with boasting and insolence,
7:16 in **w** of praise and all kinds of melodious songs.
2Es 3: 3 and I began to speak anxious **w** to the Most High,
5:22 and I began once more to speak **w** in the presence
5:31 When I had spoken these **w**,
7: 1 When I had finished speaking these **w**,
7: 2 listen to the **w** that I have come to speak to you."
7:*71* But now, understand from your own **w**—
8:19 Therefore hear my voice and understand my **w**,
8:19 The beginning of the **w** of Ezra's prayer,
8:24 of your creature; attend to my **w**.
8:37 and it will turn out according to your **w**.
9:30 and give heed to my **w**, O descendants of Jacob.
10:29 While I was speaking these **w**,
12: 1 While the lion was saying these **w** to the eagle,
12:31 and as for all his **w** that you have heard,
14: 6 'These **w** you shall publish openly,
14:28 "Hear these **w**, O Israel.
15: 1 of my people the **w** of the prophecy that I will put
16:40 Hear my **w**, O my people;
4Mc 4: 7 The people indignantly protested his **w**,
4:13 Moved by these **w**, the high priest Onias,
5:38 either by **w** or through deeds."
7: 9 but by your deeds you made your **w**
16:24 By these **w** the mother of the seven encouraged
17: 8 to inscribe on their tomb these **w** as a reminder to

WORE‡ (6) [WEAR]

Ge 37:23 the long robe with sleeves that he **w**;
1Sa 22:18 on that day he killed eighty-five who **w**
1Ch 15:27 and David **w** a linen ephod.
Ps 35:13 But as for me, when they were sick, I **w** sackcloth;
Mt 3: 4 Now John **w** clothing of camel's hair with
Rev 9:17 the riders **w** breastplates the color of fire and

WORK‡ (414) [CO-WORKER, CO-WORKERS, REWORKED, WORKED, WORKER, WORKERS, WORKING, WORKINGS, WORKMAN, WORKMANSHIP, WORKMEN'S, WORKS]

Ge 2: 2 And on the seventh day God finished the **w**
2: 2 on the seventh day from all the **w** that he had done.
2: 3 on it God rested from all the **w** that he had done
5:29 from our **w** and from the toil of our hands."
39:11 however, when he went into the house to do his **w**,
Ex 5: 4 the people away from their **w**?
5: 9 Let heavier **w** be laid on them;
5:11 but your **w** will not be lessened in the least.' "
5:13 saying, "Complete your **w**,
5:18 Go now, and **w**; for no straw shall be given
12:16 no **w** shall be done on those days;
14:31 Israel saw the great **w** that the LORD did against
20: 9 Six days you shall labor and do all your **w**.
20:10 you shall not do any **w**—
23:12 Six days you shall do your **w**,
25:18 you shall make them of hammered **w**,
25:31 of the lampstand shall be made of hammered **w**;
28:15 a breastpiece of judgment, in skilled **w**;
31: 4 to **w** in gold, silver, and bronze,
31:14 whoever does any **w** on it shall be cut off from
31:15 Six days shall **w** be done, but the seventh day is
31:15 whoever does any **w** on the sabbath day shall
32:16 The tablets were the **w** of God,
34:10 the people among whom you live shall see the **w**
34:21 Six days you shall **w**, but on the seventh day
35: 2 Six days shall **w** be done,
35: 2 whoever does any **w** on it shall be put to death.
35:24 of any use in the **w**,
35:29 the **w** that the LORD had commanded by Moses
35:32 to **w** in gold, silver, and bronze,
35:35 with skill to do every kind of **w** done by an artisan
36: 1 to know how to do any **w** in the construction of
36: 1 of the sanctuary shall **w** in accordance with all that
36: 2 to come to do the **w**;
36: 3 that the Israelites had brought for doing the **w** on
36: 5 the **w** that the LORD has commanded us to do."
36: 7 brought was more than enough to do all the **w**.
37:17 of the lampstand were made of hammered **w**;
38:21 the **w** of the Levites being under the direction
38:24 All the gold that was used for the **w**,
39: 3 and cut into threads to **w** into the blue,
39: 8 He made the breastpiece, in skilled **w**, like the **w** of the ephod, of gold,
39:32 In this way all the **w** of the tabernacle of the tent
39:42 the **w** just as the LORD had commanded Moses.
39:43 When Moses saw that they had done all the **w** just
40:33 So Moses finished the **w**.
Lev 16:29 you shall deny yourselves, and shall do no **w**,
23: 3 Six days shall **w** be done;
23: 3 a holy convocation; you shall do no **w**:
23: 7 you shall not **w** at your occupations.
23: 8 you shall not **w** at your occupations.
23:21 you shall not **w** at your occupations.
23:25 You shall not **w** at your occupations;
23:28 and you shall do no **w** during that entire day;
23:30 anyone who does any **w** during that entire day,
23:31 You shall do no **w**: it is a statute forever
23:35 you shall not **w** at your occupations.
23:36 you shall not **w** at your occupations.
Nu 4: 3 all who qualify to do **w** relating to the tent
4:23 all who qualify to do **w** in the tent of meeting.
Nu 4:30 everyone who qualifies to do the **w** of the tent
4:35 everyone who qualified for **w** relating to the tent
4:39 everyone who qualified for **w** relating to the tent
4:43 everyone who qualified for **w** relating to the tent
4:47 to do the **w** of service and the **w** of bearing burdens
8: 4 out of hammered **w** of gold.
8: 4 From its base to its flowers, it was hammered **w**;
10: 2 you shall make them of hammered **w**;
28:18 You shall not **w** at your occupations.
28:25 you shall not **w** at your occupations.
28:26 you shall not **w** at your occupations.
29: 1 you shall not **w** at your occupations.
29: 7 and deny yourselves; you shall do no **w**.
29:12 you shall not **w** at your occupations.
29:35 you shall not **w** at your occupations.
Dt 5:13 Six days you shall labor and do all your **w**.
5:14 you shall not do any **w**—
14:29 the LORD your God may bless you in all the **w**
15:10 the LORD your God will bless you in all your **w**
15:19 you shall not do **w** with your firstling ox nor shear
16: 8 when you shall do no **w**.
27:15 the **w** of an artisan, and sets it up in secret."
31:29 to anger through the **w** of your hands."
32: 4 Rock, his **w** is perfect, and all his ways are just.
33:11 his substance, and accept the **w** of his hands;
Jos 24:31 and had known all the **w** that the LORD did
Jdg 2: 7 the great **w** that the LORD had done for Israel.
2:10 the LORD or the **w** that he had done for Israel.
5:30 two pieces of dyed **w** embroidered for my neck
17: 8 in the hill country of Ephraim to carry on his **w**.
19:16 an old man coming from his **w** in the field.
1Sa 8:16 and put them to his **w**.
2Sa 12:31 to **w** with saws and iron picks and iron axes,
1Ki 5:16 over the **w**, having charge of the people who did the **w**.
6:35 with gold evenly applied upon the carved **w**.
7:14 He came to King Solomon, and did all his **w**.
7:17 checker **w** with wreaths of chain **w** for the capitals
7:22 Thus the **w** of the pillars was finished.
7:29 there were wreaths of beveled **w**.
7:40 the **w** that he did for King Solomon on the house
7:51 Thus all the **w** that King Solomon did on the house
9:23 the chief officers who were over Solomon's **w**:
9:23 of the people who carried on the **w**.
16: 7 provoking him to anger with the **w** of his hands,
2Ki 19:18 they were no gods but the **w** of human hands—
22:17 that they have provoked me to anger with all the **w**
1Ch 6:49 doing all the **w** of the most holy place,
9:13 qualified for the **w** of the service of the house
9:19 were in charge of the **w** of the service,
20: 3 set them to **w** with saws and iron picks and axes.
22:16 Now begin the **w**, and the LORD be with you."
23: 4 "shall have charge of the **w** in the house of
23:24 and upward who were to do the **w** for the service
23:28 and any **w** for the service of the house of God;
25: 1 list of those who did the **w** and of their duties was:
26:30 for all the **w** of the LORD and for the service of
27:26 Over those who did the **w** of the field,
28:13 all the **w** of the service in the house of the LORD;
28:20 until all the **w** for the service of the house of
28:21 in all the **w** will be every volunteer who has skill
29: 1 is young and inexperienced, and the **w** is great;
29: 5 and for all the **w** to be done by artisans,
29: 6 and the officers over the king's **w**.
2Ch 2: 7 So now send me an artisan skilled to **w** in gold,
2: 8 My servants will **w** with your servants
2:14 He is trained to **w** in gold, silver, bronze, iron,
2:18 as overseers to make the people **w**.
4:11 the **w** that he did for King Solomon on the house
5: 1 Thus all the **w** that Solomon did for the house of
8: 9 of Israel Solomon made no slaves for his **w**;
8:16 Thus all the **w** of Solomon was accomplished from
15: 7 for your **w** shall be rewarded."
16: 5 he stopped building Ramah, and let his **w** cease.
24:12 to those who had charge of the **w** of the house of
24:13 So those who were engaged in the **w** labored,
29:34 helped them until the **w** was finished—
30:14 They set to **w** and removed the altars that were
31:21 And every **w** that he undertook in the service of
32: 5 to **w** resolutely and built up the entire wall
32:19 which are the **w** of human hands.
34:12 The people did the **w** faithfully.
34:13 over the burden bearers and directed all who did **w**
Ezr 3: 8 the oversight of the **w** on the house of the LORD.
4:24 the **w** on the house of God in Jerusalem stopped
5: 8 this **w** is being done diligently and prospers
6: 7 let the **w** on this house of God alone;
6:22 that he aided them in the **w** on the house of God,
Ne 2:16 the officials, and the rest that were to do the **w**.
3: 1 to **w** with his fellow priests and rebuilt
3: 5 not put their shoulders to the **w** of their Lord.
4: 6 for the people had a mind to **w**.
4:10 so that we are unable to **w** on the wall."
4:11 upon them and kill them and stop the **w**."
4:15 we all returned to the wall, each to his **w**.
4:17 that each labored on the **w** with one hand and with
4:19 "The **w** is great and widely spread out,
4:21 So we labored at the **w**,
5:16 Indeed, I devoted myself to the **w** on this wall,
5:16 and all my servants were gathered there for the **w**.
6: 3 "I am doing a great **w** and I cannot come down.
6: 3 the **w** stop while I leave it to come down to you?"
6: 9 thinking, "Their hands will drop from the **w**,
6:16 that this **w** had been accomplished with the help
7:70 the heads of ancestral houses contributed to the **w**.
10:33 and for all the **w** of the house of our God.
11:12 and their associates who did the **w** of the house,
Ne 11:16 who were over the outside **w** of the house of God;
11:22 the singers, in charge of the **w** of the house of God.
13:30 the duties of the priests and Levites, each in his **w**;
Job 1:10 You have blessed the **w** of his hands,
10: 3 the **w** of your hands and favor the schemes of
14:15 you would long for the **w** of your hands.
34:19 for they are all the **w** of his hands?
36: 9 to them their **w** and their transgressions,
36:24 "Remember to extol his **w**,
Ps 8: 3 I look at your heavens, the **w** of your fingers,
9:16 the wicked are snared in the **w** of their own hands.
28: 4 Repay them according to their **w**,
28: 4 repay them according to the **w** of their hands;
28: 5 or the **w** of his hands,
33: 4 and all his **w** is done in faithfulness.
59: 2 Deliver me from those who **w** evil;
62:12 For you repay to all according to their **w**.
74: 6 they smashed all its carved **w**.
77:12 I will meditate on all your **w**,
88:10 Do you **w** wonders for the dead?
90:16 Let your **w** be manifest to your servants,
90:17 and prosper for us the **w** of our hands—O prosper the **w** of our hands!
92: 4 you, O LORD, have made me glad by your **w**;
95: 9 though they had seen my **w**.
101: 3 I hate the **w** of those who fall away;
102:25 and the heavens are the **w** of your hands.
104:13 the earth is satisfied with the fruit of your **w**.
104:23 People go out to their **w** and to their labor until
111: 3 Full of honor and majesty is his **w**,
115: 4 and gold, the **w** of human hands.
135:15 The idols of the nations are silver and gold, the **w**
138: 8 Do not forsake the **w** of your hands.
141: 4 in company with those who **w** iniquity;
Pr 8:22 The LORD created me at the beginning of his **w**,
16: 3 Commit your **w** to the LORD,
16:11 all the weights in the bag are his **w**.
18: 9 One who is slack in **w** is close kin to a vandal.
22:29 Do you see those who are skillful in their **w**?
24:27 Prepare your **w** outside, get everything ready
Ecc 2:23 and their **w** is a vexation;
2:26 the sinner he gives the **w** of gathering and heaping,
3:17 a time for every matter, and for every **w**.
3:22 that all should enjoy their **w**, for that is their lot;
4: 4 and all skill in **w** come from one person's envy
5: 6 and destroy the **w** of your hands?
7:13 Consider the **w** of God; who can make straight
8:17 then I saw all the **w** of God,
9:10 for there is no **w** or thought or knowledge
11: 5 so you do not know the **w** of God,
SS 5:14 His body is ivory **w**, encrusted with sapphires.
7: 1 the **w** of a master hand.
Isa 1:31 and their **w** like a spark;
1:31 they and their **w** shall burn together,
2: 8 they bow down to the **w** of their hands,
5:12 or see the **w** of his hands!
5:19 let him speed his **w** that we may see it;
10:12 the Lord has finished all his **w** on Mount Zion and
17: 8 not have regard for the altars, the **w** of their hands,
19:10 and all who **w** for wages will be grieved.
19:25 and Assyria the **w** of my hands,
28:21 and to **w** his **w**—alien is his **w**!
29:23 For when he sees his children, the **w** of my hands,
31: 2 and against the helpers of those who **w** iniquity.
37:19 but the **w** of human hands—
41:24 indeed, are nothing and your **w** is nothing at all;
43:13 I **w** and who can hinder it?
45: 9 or "Your **w** has no handles"?
45:11 or command me concerning the **w** of my hands?
60:21 the **w** of my hands, so that I might be glorified.
63: 4 and the year for my redeeming **w** had come.
64: 8 we are all the **w** of your hand.
65:22 my chosen shall long enjoy the **w** of their hands.
Jer 10: 9 They are the **w** of the artisan and of the hands of
10:15 They are worthless, a **w** of delusion;
17:22 of your houses on the sabbath or do any **w**,
17:24 but keep the sabbath day holy and do no **w** on it,
22:13 who makes his neighbors **w** for nothing,
25: 6 not provoke me to anger with the **w** of your hands.
25: 7 and so you have provoked me to anger with the **w**
25:14 according to their deeds and the **w** of their hands.
31:16 for there is a reward for your **w**, says the LORD:
32:30 but provoke me to anger by the **w** of their hands,
48:10 the one who is slack in doing the **w** of the LORD;
51:10 in Zion the **w** of the LORD our God.
51:18 They are worthless, a **w** of delusion;
La 3:64 O LORD, according to the **w** of their hands!
4: 2 how they are reckoned as earthen pots, the **w** of
Eze 27:16 embroidered **w**, fine linen, coral, and rubies.
27:24 in clothes of blue and embroidered **w**,
Da 11:28 He shall **w** his will, and return to his own land.
Hos 13: 2 all of them the **w** of artisans.
14: 3 'Our God,' to the **w** of our hands.
Mic 5:13 and you shall bow down no more to the **w**
Hab 1: 5 For a **w** is being done in your days that you would
3: 2 and I stand in awe, O LORD, of your **w**.
Zep 2:14 for its cedar **w** will be laid bare.
Hag 2: 4 **w**, for I am with you, says the LORD of hosts,
2:14 and so with every **w** of their hands;
Mt 14: 2 and for this reason these powers are at **w** in him."
21:28 'Son, go and **w** in the vineyard today.'
24:46 that slave whom his master will find at **w**
Mk 6:14 and for this reason these powers are at **w** in him."
13:34 with his **w**, and commands the doorkeeper to be on
Lk 3:23 about thirty years old when he began his **w**.
10:40 not care that my sister has left me to do all the **w**
12:43 that slave whom his master will find at **w**

Lk 13:14 "There are six days on which **w** ought to be done;
13:32 and on the third day I finish my **w**.
Jn 4:34 the will of him who sent me and to complete his **w**.
6:27 Do not **w** for the food that perishes,
6:29 Jesus answered them, "This is the **w** of God,
6:30 What **w** are you performing?
7:21 Jesus answered them, "I performed one **w**,
9: 4 We must **w** the works of him who sent me
9: 4 night is coming when no one can **w**.
10:33 not for a good **w** that we are going to stone you,
17: 4 on earth by finishing the **w** that you gave me to do.
Ac 13: 2 and Saul for the **w** to which I have called them."
13:25 And as John was finishing his **w**, he said,
13:41 I am doing a **w**, a **w** that you will never believe,
14:26 of God for the **w** that they had completed.
15:38 and had not accompanied them in the **w**.
20:35 an example that by such **w** we must support
Ro 7: 5 were at **w** in our members to bear fruit for death.
8:28 We know that all things **w** together for good
14:20 Do not, for the sake of food, destroy the **w** of God.
15:17 then, I have reason to boast of my **w** for God.
16: 3 who **w** with me in Christ Jesus,
1Co 3:13 the **w** of each builder will become visible,
3:13 and the fire will test what sort of **w** each has done.
3:15 If the **w** is burned up, the builder will suffer loss;
4:12 and we grow weary from the **w** of our own hands.
9: 1 Are you not my **w** in the Lord?
12:29 Are all teachers? Do all **w** miracles?
15:58 immovable, always excelling in the **w** of the Lord,
16: 9 for a wide door for effective **w** has opened to me,
16:10 for he is doing the **w** of the Lord just as I am;
2Co 4:12 So death is at **w** in us, but life in you.
6: 1 As we **w** together with him,
9: 8 you may share abundantly in every good **w**.
10:16 of **w** already done in someone else's sphere
Gal 3: 5 with the Spirit and **w** miracles among you
4:11 that my **w** for you may have been wasted.
6: 4 All must test their own **w**; then that **w**, rather than
their neighbor's **w**,
6:10 let us **w** for the good of all,
Eph 1:20 to **w** in Christ when he raised him from the dead
2: 2 that is now at **w** among those who are disobedient.
3:20 to him who by the power at **w** within us is able
4:12 to equip the saints for the **w** of ministry,
4:28 and **w** honestly with their own hands,
Php 1: 6 a good **w** among you will bring it to completion by
2:12 **w** out your own salvation with fear and trembling;
2:13 for it is God who is at **w** in you, enabling you both
to will and to **w** for his good pleasure.
2:22 a son with a father he has served with me in the **w**
2:30 because he came close to death for the **w** of Christ,
4: 3 for they have struggled beside me in the **w** of
Col 1:10 in every good **w** and as you grow in the knowledge
1Th 1: 3 remembering before our God and Father your **w**
2:13 God's word, which is also at **w** in you believers.
4:11 and to **w** with your hands, as we directed you,
5:13 in love because of their **w**.
2Th 1:11 by his power every good resolve and **w** of faith,
2: 7 For the mystery of lawlessness is already at **w**,
2:17 and strengthen them in every good **w** and word.
3:10 Anyone unwilling to **w** should not eat.
3:11 mere busybodies, not doing any **w**.
3:12 to do their **w** quietly and to earn their own living.
2Ti 2: 6 It is the farmer who does the **w** who ought to have
2:21 to the owner of the house, ready for every good **w**.
3:17 equipped for every good **w**.
4: 5 endure suffering, do the **w** of an evangelist,
Tit 1:16 disobedient, unfit for any good **w**.
3: 1 to be obedient, to be ready for every good **w**,
Heb 1:10 and the heavens are the **w** of your hands;
6:10 not overlook your **w** and the love that you showed
Rev 22:12 to repay according to everyone's **w**.
Tob 2:11 also, my wife Anna earned money at women's **w**.
4:14 over until the next day the wages of those who **w**
5: 5 he replied, "and I have come here to **w**."
Jdt 13: 4 in this hour on the **w** of my hands for the exaltation
Wis 13:10 or a useless stone, the **w** of an ancient hand.
13:12 the cast-off pieces of his **w** to prepare his food,
13:19 and **w** and success with his hands he asks strength
14:20 attracted by the charm of his **w**,
17:20 and went about its **w** unhindered,
Sir 7:15 Do not hate hard labor or farm **w**,
7:20 Do not abuse slaves who **w** faithfully,
9:17 A **w** is praised for the skill of the artisan;
10:26 a display of your wisdom when you do your **w**,
11:11 There are those who **w** and struggle and hurry,
11:20 and grow old in your **w**.
14:19 Every **w** decays and ceases to exist,
24:22 and those who **w** with me will not sin."
31:26 As the furnace tests the **w** of the smith,
33:25 bread and discipline and **w** for a slave.
33:26 Set your slave to **w**, and you will find rest;
33:28 Put him to **w**, in order that he may not be idle,
33:30 Set him to **w**, as is fitting for him,
34:28 what do they gain but hard **w**?
36: 6 Give new signs, and **w** other wonders;
37:11 with an idler about any **w** or with a seasonal
37:11 or with a seasonal laborer about completing his **w**,
37:16 Discussion is the beginning of every **w**,
38:25 who drives oxen and is occupied with their **w**,
38:27 and they are careful to finish their **w**.
38:29 the potter sitting at his **w** and turning the wheel
38:31 and all are skillful in their own **w**.
40: 1 Hard **w** was created for everyone,
42:16 and the **w** of the Lord is full of his glory.
43: 2 the **w** of the Most High.
45:10 and violet and purple, the **w** of an embroiderer;
Sir 45:11 with twisted crimson, the **w** of an artisan;
45:11 in a setting of gold, the **w** of a jeweler,
45:12 a distinction to be prized, the **w** of an expert,
51:30 Do your **w** in good time,
LtJ 6:51 that they are not gods but the **w** of human hands,
6:51 and that there is no **w** of God in them.
1Mc 2:47 and the **w** prospered in their hands.
4:51 Thus they finished all the **w** they had undertaken.
9:54 He tore down the **w** of the prophets!
9:55 Alcimus was stricken and his **w** was hindered;
10:11 the **w** to build the walls and encircle Mount Zion
2Mc 5:25 then, finding the Jews not at **w**,
15:39 the story delights the ears of those who read the **w**.
1Es 5:45 to the sacred treasury for the **w** a thousand minas
5:58 or more years of age to have charge of the **w** of
5:58 the **w** on the house of God with a single purpose.
6:10 and the **w** is prospering in their hands
7: 2 supervised the holy **w** with very great care,
7: 3 The holy **w** prospered, while the prophets Haggai
9:11 This is not a **w** we can do in one day or two,
2Es 6:38 and your word accomplished the **w**.
6:43 your word went forth, and at once the **w** was done.
8: 7 For you alone exist, and we are a **w** of your hands,
8:13 and make it live as your **w**.
9:17 and as is the **w**, so is the product;
10:54 because no **w** of human construction could endure

WORKED (38) [WORK]

Ex 26: 1 you shall make them with cherubim skillfully **w**
26:31 it shall be made with cherubim skillfully **w** into it.
28: 6 and of fine twisted linen, skillfully **w**.
31:10 and the finely **w** vestments,
35:19 the finely **w** vestments for ministering in
36: 8 with cherubim skillfully **w** into them.
36:35 with cherubim skillfully **w** into it.
39: 1 and crimson yarns they made finely **w** vestments,
39:41 the finely **w** vestments for ministering in
Nu 11:32 So the people **w** all that day and night and all
Dt 21: 3 the body shall take a heifer that has never been **w**,
Ru 2:19 And where have you **w**?
2:19 she told her mother-in-law with whom she had **w**,
2:19 name of the man with whom I **w** today is Boaz."
1Sa 14:45 for he has **w** with God today."
2Ki 12:11 the carpenters and the builders who **w** on the house
2Ch 3:14 and fine linen, and **w** cherubim into it.
Ne 4:16 half of my servants **w** on construction,
Ps 78:12 In the sight of their ancestors he **w** marvels in
Jer 10: 3 and **w** with an ax by the hands of an artisan;
Eze 28:13 **w** in gold were your settings and your engravings.
29:20 because they **w** for me, says the Lord GOD.
Da 4: 2 that the Most High God has **w** for me I am pleased
Hag 1:14 and they came and **w** on the house of the LORD
Mt 20:12 'These last **w** only one hour,
Mk 16:20 ⟦Lord **w** with them and confirmed the message⟧
Lk 5: 5 we have **w** all night long but have caught nothing.
Ac 18: 3 he stayed with them, and they **w** together—
20:34 that I **w** with my own hands to support myself
Ro 16: 6 Greet Mary, who has **w** very hard among you.
16:12 who has **w** hard in the Lord.
1Co 15:10 On the contrary, I **w** harder than any of them—
Gal 2: 8 (for he who **w** through Peter making him
2: 8 also **w** through me in sending me to the Gentiles),
Col 4:13 For I testify for him that he has **w** hard for you and
1Th 2: 9 we **w** night and day, so that we might
2Th 3: 8 but with toil and labor we **w** night and day,
2Jn 1: 8 so that you do not lose what we have **w** for,

WORKER[‡] (8) [WORK]

Ps 52: 2 like a sharp razor, you **w** of treachery.
Pr 8:30 then I was beside him, like a master **w**;
Isa 16:14 In three years, like the years of a hired **w**,
21:16 Within a year, according to the years of a hired **w**,
2Ti 2:15 a **w** who has no need to be ashamed,
Wis 15: 7 be the use of each of them the **w** in clay decides.
Sir 10:27 Better is the **w** who has goods in plenty than
3Mc 6:32 praising God, their Savior and **w** of wonders.

WORKERS (38) [WORK]

Ex 36: 8 the **w** made the tabernacle with ten curtains;
2Ki 12:11 into the hands of the **w** who had the oversight of
12:14 the **w** who were repairing the house of the LORD
12:15 the money to pay out to the **w**,
22: 5 into the hand of the **w** who have the oversight of
22: 5 let them give it to the **w** who are at the house of
22: 9 the hand of the **w** who have oversight of the house
1Ch 4:21 the families of the guild of linen **w** at Beth-ashbea;
22:15 You have an abundance of **w**:
2Ch 2: 7 to join the skilled **w** who are with me in Judah
24:12 and also **w** in iron and bronze to repair the house
26:15 up machines, invented by skilled **w**, on the towers
34:10 They delivered it to the **w** who had the oversight of
34:10 and the **w** who were working in the house of
34:17 into the hand of the overseers and the **w**."
Ezr 3: 9 together took charge of the **w** in the house of God.
Job 31: 3 and disaster the **w** of iniquity?
Ps 6: 8 Depart from me, all you **w** of evil,
28: 3 with those who are **w** of evil,
Pr 16:26 The appetite of **w** works for them;
Ecc 3: 9 What gain have the **w** from their toil?
Isa 19: 9 The **w** in flax will be in despair,
58: 3 on your fast day, and oppress all your **w**.
Jer 10: 9 they are all the product of skilled **w**.
Eze 48:18 Its produce shall be food for the **w** of the city.
48:19 The **w** of the city, from all the tribes of Israel,
Mal 3: 5 against those who oppress the hired **w**
Ac 19:25 with the **w** of the same trade, and said, "Men,
Ro 16:12 Greet those **w** in the Lord,
2Co 1:24 rather, we are **w** with you for your joy,
11:13 For such boasters are false apostles, deceitful **w**,
Php 3: 2 Beware of the dogs, beware of the evil **w**,
Phm 1:24 Aristarchus, Demas, and Luke, my fellow **w**.
Wis 15: 8 these **w** form a futile god from the same clay—
15: 9 the **w** are not concerned that mortals are destined
15: 9 with **w** in gold and silver, and imitate **w** in copper;
17:17 or shepherds or **w** who toiled in the wilderness,

WORKING[‡] (24) [WORK]

Ex 5: 5 of the land and yet you want them to stop **w**!"
Ru 3: 2 with whose young women you have been **w**.
1Ki 7:14 intelligence, and knowledge in **w** bronze.
1Ch 22:15 of artisans without number, skilled in **w**
2Ch 34:10 and the workers who were **w** in the house of
Ps 74:12 Yet God my King is from of old, **w** salvation in
Ecc 12: 3 women who grind cease **w** because they are few,
Jer 18: 3 and there he was **w** at his wheel.
Eze 46: 1 shall remain closed on the six **w** days;
Lk 15:29 all these years I have been **w** like a slave for you,
Jn 5:17 "My Father is still **w**, and I also am **w**."
Ro 7:13 It was sin, **w** death in me through what is good,
1Co 3: 9 For we are God's servants, **w** together;
9: 6 and I who have no right to refrain from **w** for
12:10 to another the **w** of miracles,
Gal 5: 6 the only thing that counts is faith **w** through love.
Eph 1:19 according to the **w** of his great power.
3: 7 the gift of God's grace that was given me by the **w**
4:16 as each part is **w** properly,
2Th 2: 9 The coming of the lawless one is apparent in the **w**
Heb 13:21 **w** among us that which is pleasing in his sight,
Wis 7:26 a spotless mirror of the **w** of God,
13: 4 And if people were amazed at their power and **w**,

WORKINGS (1) [WORK]

Jdt 8:14 the depths of the human heart or understand the **w**

WORKMAN (1) [MAN, WORK]

Isa 40:19 An idol?—A **w** casts it, and a goldsmith overlays it

WORKMANSHIP (3) [WORK]

Ex 28: 8 The decorated band on it shall be of the same **w**
39: 5 and **w**, of gold, of blue, purple, and crimson yarns,
Wis 13:11 and then with pleasing **w** make a useful vessel

WORKMEN'S (1) [MAN, WORK]

Jdg 5:26 to the tent peg and her right hand to the **w** mallet;

WORKS[‡] (218) [WORK]

A. GOOD WORKS (12)
B. WONDERFUL WORKS (9)
C. WORKS OF THE LAW (7)

Nu 16:28 that the LORD has sent me to do all these **w**;
Dt 15:12 is sold to you and **w** for you six years,
Jdg 13:19 on the rock to the LORD, to him who **w** wonders.
1Ch 16: 9 sing praises to him, tell of all his wonderful **w**. B
16:12 Remember the wonderful **w** he has done, B
16:24 his marvelous **w** among all the peoples.
28:19 he made clear to me—the plan of all the **w**."
2Ch 17:13 He carried out great **w** in the cities of Judah.
32:30 Hezekiah prospered in all his **w**.
34:25 that they have provoked me to anger with all the **w**
Ne 9:35 and did not turn from their wicked **w**.
Job 34:25 knowing their **w**, he overturns them in the night,
37:14 stop and consider the wondrous **w** of God.
37:16 the balancings of the clouds, the wondrous **w** of
Ps 8: 6 You have given them dominion over the **w**
28: 5 Because they do not regard the **w** of the LORD,
46: 8 behold the **w** of the LORD;
73:28 the Lord GOD my refuge, to tell of all your **w**.
77:14 You are the God who **w** wonders;
78: 7 and not forget the **w** of God,
86: 8 O Lord, nor are there any **w** like yours.
92: 4 at the **w** of your hands I sing for joy.
92: 5 How great are your **w**, O LORD!
96: 3 his marvelous **w** among all the peoples.
103: 6 The LORD **w** vindication and justice
103:22 Bless the LORD, all his **w**,
104:24 O LORD, how manifold are your **w**!
104:31 may the LORD rejoice in his **w**—
105: 2 tell of all his wonderful **w**. B
105: 5 Remember the wonderful **w** he has done, B
106: 7 did not consider your wonderful **w**; B
106:13 But they soon forgot his **w**;
106:22 wondrous **w** in the land of Ham,
107: 8 for his wonderful **w** to humankind. B
107:15 for his wonderful **w** to humankind. B
107:21 for his wonderful **w** to humankind. B
107:24 his wondrous **w** in the deep.
107:31 for his wonderful **w** to humankind. B
111: 2 Great are the **w** of the LORD,
111: 6 He has shown his people the power of his **w**,
111: 7 The **w** of his hands are faithful and just;
119:27 and I will meditate on your wondrous **w**.
139:14 Wonderful are your **w**; that I know very well.
143: 5 I meditate on the **w** of your hands.
145: 4 One generation shall laud your **w** to another,
145: 5 and on your wondrous **w**, I will meditate.
145:10 All your **w** shall give thanks to you, O LORD,
Pr 16:26 The appetite of workers **w** for them;
26:28 and a flattering mouth **w** ruin.

Pr 31:13 She seeks wool and flax, and w with willing hands.
31:31 and let her w praise her in the city gates.
Ecc 2: 4 I made great w; I built houses
Isa 41:29 their w are nothing; their images are empty wind.
44:12 The ironsmith fashions it and w it over the coals,
57:12 I will concede your righteousness and your w,
59: 6 Their w are w of iniquity,
64: 4 who w for those who wait for him.
66:18 For I know their w and their thoughts,
Jer 1:16 and worshiped the w of their own hands.
44: 8 Why do you provoke me to anger with the w
Eze 6: 6 down, and your w wiped out.
Da 4:37 for all his w are truth, and his ways are justice;
6:27 he w signs and wonders in heaven and on earth;
Mic 6:16 the statutes of Omri and all the w of the house
Mt 5:16 that they may see your good w and give glory A
Jn 5:20 and he will show him greater w than these,
5:36 The w that the Father has given me to complete,
5:36 the very w that I am doing,
6:28 "What must we do to perform the w of God?"
7: 3 also may see the w you are doing;
7: 7 because I testify against it that its w are evil.
9: 3 so that God's w might be revealed in him.
9: 4 the w of him who sent me while it is day;
10:25 The w that I do in my Father's name testify to me;
10:32 have shown you many good w from the Father. A
10:37 If I am not doing the w of my Father,
10:38 even though you do not believe me, believe the w,
14:10 but the Father who dwells in me does his w.
14:11 then believe me because of the w themselves.
14:12 the one who believes in me will also do the w
14:12 in fact, will do greater w than these,
15:24 not done among them the w that no one else did,
Ac 7:41 and reveled in the w of their hands.
9:36 She was devoted to good w and acts of charity. A
Ro 3:27 By what law? By that of w?
3:28 by faith apart from w prescribed by the law.
4: 2 For if Abraham was justified by w,
4: 4 to one who w, wages are not reckoned as a gift but
4: 5 But to one who without w trusts him who justifies
4: 6 to whom God reckons righteousness apart from w:
9:12 not by w but by his call) she was told,
9:32 but as if it were based on w.
11: 6 if it is by grace, it is no longer on the basis of w,
13:12 Let us then lay aside the w of darkness and put on
1Co 16:16 and of everyone who w and toils with them.
2Co 12:12 signs and wonders and mighty w.
Gal 2:16 that a person is justified not by the w of the law C
2:16 and not by doing the w of the law, C
2:16 no one will be justified by the w of the law. C
3: 2 the w of the law or by believing what you heard? C
3: 5 among you by your doing the w of the law, C
3:10 who rely on the w of the law are under a curse; C
3:12 "Whoever does the w of the law will live by C
5:19 Now the w of the flesh are obvious:
Eph 2: 9 not the result of w, so that no one may boast.
2:10 created in Christ Jesus for good w, A
5:11 Take no part in the unfruitful w of darkness,
1Ti 2:10 but with good w, as is proper A
5:10 she must be well attested for her good w, A
5:25 So also good w are conspicuous; A
6:18 They are to do good, to be rich in good w, A
2Ti 1: 9 to our w but according to his own purpose
Tit 2: 7 Show yourself in all respects a model of good w, A
3: 5 of any w of righteousness that we had done,
3: 8 be careful to devote themselves to good w; A
3:14 to good w in order to meet urgent needs, A
Heb 3: 9 though they had seen my w
4: 3 his w were finished at the foundation of the world.
4: 4 God rested on the seventh day from all his w."
6: 1 repentance from dead w and faith toward God,
9:14 purify our conscience from dead w to worship
Jas 2:14 if you say you have faith but do not have w?
2:17 So faith by itself, if it has no w, is dead.
2:18 someone will say, "You have faith and I have w."
2:18 Show me your faith apart from your w, and I by
my w will show you my faith.
2:20 that faith apart from w is barren?
2:21 by w when he offered his son Isaac on the altar?
2:22 You see that faith was active along with his w, and
faith was brought to completion by the w.
2:24 a person is justified by w and not by faith alone.
2:25 was not Rahab the prostitute also justified by w
2:26 so faith without w is also dead.
3:13 Show by your good life that your w are done
1Jn 3: 8 to destroy the w of the devil.
Rev 2: 2 "I know your w, your toil
2: 5 repent, and do the w you did at first.
2: 6 you hate the w of the Nicolaitans,
2:19 "I know your w—your love,
2:19 I know that your last w are greater than the first.
2:23 and I will give to each of you as your w deserve.
2:26 to do my w to the end, I will give authority over
3: 1 and the seven stars: "I know your w;
3: 2 not found your w perfect in the sight of my God.
3: 8 "I know your w. Look, I have set
3:15 "I know your w; you are neither cold
9:20 the w of their hands or give up worshiping demons
20:12 And the dead were judged according to their w,
Tob 3:11 let all your w praise you forever.
12: 7 but to acknowledge and reveal the w of God,
12:11 but to reveal with due honor the w of God.'
AdE 13: 8 calling to remembrance all the w of the Lord.
Wis 1:12 or bring on destruction by the w of your hands;
2: 4 and no one will remember our w;
3:11 labors are unprofitable, and their w are useless.
6: 3 he will search out your w and inquire
Wis 8: 4 and an associate in his w.
9: 9 she who knows your w and was present
9:12 Then my w will be acceptable,
11: 1 Wisdom prospered their w by the hand of
12: 4 their w of sorcery and unholy rites,
12:19 Through such w you have taught your people that
13: 1 the artisan while paying heed to his w;
13: 7 For while they live among his w,
13:10 are those who give the name "gods" to the w
14: 5 It is your will that w of your wisdom should not be
Sir 1: 9 he poured her out upon all his w,
2:17 and equal to his name are his w.
11: 4 for the w of the Lord are wonderful,
11: 4 and his w are concealed from humankind.
11:21 Do not wonder at the w of a sinner,
16:21 so most of his w are concealed.
16:26 When the Lord created his w from the beginning,
16:27 he arranged his w in an eternal order,
17: 8 into their hearts to show them the majesty of his w.
17: 9 to proclaim the grandeur of his w.
17:19 All their w are as clear as the sun before him,
18: 4 To none has he given power to proclaim his w;
33:15 Look at all the w of the Most High;
35:24 and the w of all according to their thoughts;
38: 6 that he might be glorified in his marvelous w.
38: 8 God's w will never be finished;
39:14 bless the Lord for all his w.
39:16 "All the w of the Lord are very good,
39:19 The w of all are before him,
39:33 All the w of the Lord are good,
42:15 I will now call to mind the w of the Lord,
42:15 By the word of the Lord his w are made;
42:17 even his holy ones to recount all his marvelous w,
42:22 How desirable are all his w,
43: 4 A man tending a furnace w in burning heat,
43:28 For he is greater than all his w.
43:32 for I have seen but few of his w.
47:22 or cause any of his w to perish;
50:22 who everywhere w great wonders,
Bar 2: 9 in all the w that he has commanded us to do.
3:18 and were anxious, but there is no trace of their w?
Aza 1: 4 all your w are true and your ways right,
1:20 Deliver us in accordance with your marvelous w,
1:35 "Bless the Lord, all you w of the Lord;
2Mc 15:21 and called upon the Lord who w wonders;
1Es 4:36 All God's w quake and tremble,
4:37 all their w are unrighteous, and all such things.
3Mc 2: 8 And when they had seen w of your hands,
2Es 6:40 so that your w could be seen.
6:48 the nations might declare your wondrous w.
6:54 as ruler over all the w that you had made;
7:24 and have not performed his w.
7:77 a treasure of w stored up with the Most High,
8:32 who have no w of righteousness,
8:33 the righteous, who have many w laid up with you,
8:36 to those who have no store of good w." A
9: 6 beginnings are manifest in wonders and mighty w,
9: 7 and will be able to escape on account of their w,
13:23 who have w and faith toward the Almighty.
16:51 Therefore do not be like her or her w.
16:64 The Lord will strictly examine all their w,

WORLD‡ (356) [WORLD'S, WORLDLY, WORLDS]

A. WHOLE WORLD (31)
B. ALL THE WORLD (10)

Ge 19:31 to come in to us after the manner of all the w. B
41:57 all the w came to Joseph in Egypt to buy grain, B
41:57 the famine became severe throughout the w.
Dt 30: 4 Even if you are exiled to the ends of the w,
1Sa 2: 8 and on them he has set the w.
2Sa 22:16 the w were laid bare at the rebuke of the LORD,
1Ch 16:30 w is firmly established; it shall never be moved.
Job 18:18 and driven out of the w.
34:13 and who laid on him the whole w? A
37:12 on the face of the habitable w.
40:13 bind their faces in the w below.
Ps 9: 8 He judges the w with righteousness;
17:14 from mortals whose portion in life is in this w.
18:15 foundations of the w were laid bare at your rebuke,
19: 4 and their words to the end of the w.
24: 1 the w, and those who live in it;
33: 8 let all the inhabitants of the w stand in awe of him.
49: 1 give ear, all inhabitants of the w,
50:12 for the w and all that is in it is mine.
77:18 your lightnings lit up the w;
89:11 the w and all that is in it—
90: 2 or ever you had formed the earth and the w,
93: 1 He has established the w;
96:10 w is firmly established; it shall never be moved.
96:13 He will judge the w with righteousness,
97: 4 His lightnings light up the w;
98: 7 the w and those who live in it.
98: 9 He will judge the w with righteousness,
Pr 8:31 rejoicing in his inhabited w and delighting in
Isa 13:11 I will punish the w for its evil,
14:17 the w like a desert and overthrew its cities,
14:21 the earth or cover the face of the w with cities.
18: 3 All you inhabitants of the w,
23:17 the kingdoms of the w on the face of the earth.
24: 4 the w languishes and withers;
26: 9 the inhabitants of the w learn righteousness.
26:18 and no one is born to inhabit the w.
27: 6 and fill the whole w with fruit. A
34: 1 the w, and all that comes from it.
Isa 38:11 among the inhabitants of the w.
Jer 10:12 who established the w by his wisdom,
25:26 and all the kingdoms of the w that are on the face
51:15 who established the w by his wisdom,
La 4:12 nor did any of the inhabitants of the w,
Eze 26:20 and I will make you live in the w below,
31:14 of them are handed over to death, to the w below;
31:16 were consoled in the w below.
31:18 down with the trees of Eden to the w below;
32:18 to the w below, with those who go down to the Pit.
32:24 who went down uncircumcised into the w below,
Da 6:25 of every language throughout the whole w: A
Na 1: 5 the w and all who live in it.
Mt 4: 8 and showed him all the kingdoms of the w
5:14 "You are the light of the w.
13:22 but the cares of the w and the lure of wealth choke
13:35 from the foundation of the w."
13:38 the w, and the good seed are the children of
16:26 if they gain the whole w but forfeit their life? A
18: 7 Woe to the w because of stumbling blocks!
24:14 throughout the w, as a testimony to all the nations;
24:21 as has not been from the beginning of the w until
25:34 for you from the foundation of the w;
26:13 in the whole w, what she has done will be told A
Mk 4:19 but the cares of the w, and the lure of wealth,
8:36 For what will it profit them to gain the whole w A
14: 9 the good news is proclaimed in the whole w, A
16:15 ⟦"Go into all the w and proclaim the good news⟧ B
Lk 2: 1 that all the w should be registered. B
4: 5 in an instant all the kingdoms of the w.
9:25 does it profit them if they gain the whole w, A
11:50 the prophets shed since the foundation of the w,
12:30 of the w that strive after all these things,
21:26 and foreboding of what is coming upon the w,
Jn 1: 9 which enlightens everyone, was coming into the w.
1:10 He was in the w, and the w came into being
through him; yet the w did not know him.
1:29 the Lamb of God who takes away the sin of the w!
3:16 "For God so loved the w that he gave his only Son,
3:17 not send the Son into the w to condemn the w,
3:17 in order that the w might be saved through him.
3:19 that the light has come into the w,
4:42 and we know that this is truly the Savior of the w."
6:14 the prophet who is to come into the w."
6:33 down from heaven and gives life to the w."
6:51 that I will give for the life of the w is my flesh."
7: 4 If you do these things, show yourself to the w."
7: 7 The w cannot hate you, but it hates me
8:12 saying, "I am the light of the w.
8:23 you are of this w, I am not of this w.
8:26 I declare to the w what I have heard from him."
9: 5 As long as I am in the w, I am the light of the w."
9:32 the w began has it been heard that anyone opened
9:39 into this w for judgment so that those who do
10:36 and sent into the w is blaspheming because I said,
11: 9 because they see the light of this w.
11:27 the Son of God, the one coming into the w."
12:19 Look, the w has gone after him!"
12:25 and those who hate their life in this w will keep it
12:31 Now is the judgment of this w; now the ruler of
this w will be driven out.
12:46 I have come as light into the w,
12:47 for I came not to judge the w, but to save the w.
13: 1 that his hour had come to depart from this w
13: 1 Having loved his own who were in the w,
14:17 whom the w cannot receive,
14:19 In a little while the w will no longer see me,
14:22 to us, and not to the w?"
14:27 I do not give to you as the w gives.
14:30 for the ruler of this w is coming.
14:31 so that the w may know that I love the Father.
15:18 "If the w hates you, be aware that it hated me
15:19 If you belonged to the w, the w would love you as
15:19 you do not belong to the w, but I have chosen you
out of the w—therefore the w hates you.
16: 8 the w wrong about sin and righteousness
16:11 because the ruler of this w has been condemned.
16:20 you will weep and mourn, but the w will rejoice;
16:21 of having brought a human being into the w.
16:28 I came from the Father and have come into the w;
16:28 I am leaving the w and am going to the Father."
16:33 In the w you face persecution.
16:33 But take courage; I have conquered the w!"
17: 5 that I had in your presence before the w existed.
17: 6 to those whom you gave me from the w.
17: 9 I am not asking on behalf of the w,
17:11 I am no longer in the w, but they are in the w,
17:13 and I speak these things in the w so
17:14 the w has hated them because they do not belong
to the w, just as I do not belong to the w.
17:15 I am not asking you to take them out of the w,
17:16 They do not belong to the w, just as I do not
belong to the w.
17:18 As you have sent me into the w, so I have sent
them into the w.
17:21 so that the w may believe that you have sent me.
17:23 so that the w may know that you have sent me
17:24 before the foundation of the w.
17:25 "Righteous Father, the w does not know you,
18:20 Jesus answered, "I have spoken openly to the w;
18:36 Jesus answered, "My kingdom is not from this w.
18:36 If my kingdom were from this w,
18:37 For this I was born, and for this I came into the w,
21:25 the w itself could not contain the books that would
Ac 11:28 there would be a severe famine over all the w; B
17: 6 "These people who have been turning the w upside
17:24 The God who made the w and everything in it,

Ac 17:31 a day on which he will have the **w** judged
19:27 that brought all Asia and the **w** to worship her."
22:15 be his witness to all the **w** of what you have seen B
24: 5 an agitator among all the Jews throughout the **w**,
Ro 1: 8 because your faith is proclaimed throughout the **w**.
1:20 Ever since the creation of the **w** his eternal power
3: 6 For then how could God judge the **w**?
3:19 the whole **w** may be held accountable to God. A
4:13 For the promise that he would inherit the **w** did
5:12 just as sin came into the **w** through one man,
5:13 sin was indeed in the **w** before the law,
10:18 and their words to the ends of the **w**."
11:12 Now if their stumbling means riches for the **w**,
11:15 For if their rejection is the reconciliation of the **w**,
12: 2 Do not be conformed to this **w**,
1Co 1:20 Has not God made foolish the wisdom of the **w**?
1:21 the **w** did not know God through wisdom,
1:27 But God chose what is foolish in the **w** to shame
1:27 God chose what is weak in the **w** to shame
1:28 God chose what is low and despised in the **w**,
2:12 Now we have received not the spirit of the **w**,
3:19 For the wisdom of this **w** is foolishness with God.
3:22 or Cephas or the **w** or life or death or the present or
4: 9 because we have become a spectacle to the **w**,
4:13 We have become like the rubbish of the **w**,
5:10 not at all meaning the immoral of this **w**,
5:10 since you would then need to go out of the **w**.
6: 2 Do you not know that the saints will judge the **w**?
6: 2 And if the **w** is to be judged by you,
7:31 with the **w** as though they had no dealings with it.
7:31 For the present form of this **w** is passing away.
7:33 married man is anxious about the affairs of the **w**,
7:34 woman is anxious about the affairs of the **w**,
8: 4 we know that "no idol in the **w** really exists,"
11:32 that we may not be condemned along with the **w**.
14:10 of sounds in the **w**, and nothing is
2Co 1:12 in the **w** with frankness and godly sincerity,
4: 4 of this **w** has blinded the minds of the unbelievers,
5:19 in Christ God was reconciling the **w** to himself,
Gal 4: 3 we were enslaved to the elemental spirits of the **w**.
6:14 the **w** has been crucified to me, and I to the **w**.
Eph 1: 4 the **w** to be holy and blameless before him in love.
2: 2 following the course of this **w**,
2:12 having no hope and without God in the **w**.
Php 2:15 in which you shine like stars in the **w**.
Col 1: 6 as it is bearing fruit and growing in the whole **w**, A
2:20 why do you live as if you still belonged to the **w**?
1Ti 1:15 that Christ Jesus came into the **w** to save sinners—
3:16 believed in throughout the **w**, taken up in glory.
6: 7 into the **w**, so that we can take nothing out of it;
2Ti 4:10 in love with this present **w**,
Heb 1: 6 And again, when he brings the firstborn into the **w**,
2: 5 Now God did not subject the coming **w**,
4: 3 his works were finished at the foundation of the **w**.
9:26 and again since the foundation of the **w**.
10: 5 Consequently, when Christ came into the **w**,
11: 7 by this he condemned the **w** and became an heir to
11:38 of whom the **w** was not worthy.
Jas 1:27 and to keep oneself unstained by the **w**.
2: 5 not God chosen the poor in the **w** to be rich in faith
3: 6 The tongue is placed among our members as a **w**
4: 4 that friendship with the **w** is enmity with God?
4: 4 to be a friend of the **w** becomes an enemy of God.
1Pe 1:20 He was destined before the foundation of the **w**,
5: 9 in all the **w** are undergoing the same kinds B
2Pe 1: 4 from the corruption that is in the **w** because of lust,
2: 5 the ancient **w**, even though he saved Noah,
2: 5 when he brought a flood on a **w** of the ungodly;
2:20 after they have escaped the defilements of the **w**
3: 6 through which the **w** of that time was deluged
1Jn 2: 2 but also for the sins of the whole **w**. A
2:15 Do not love the **w** or the things in the **w**.
2:15 love of the Father is not in those who love the **w**;
2:16 for all that is in the **w**—
2:16 comes not from the Father but from the **w**.
2:17 And the **w** and its desire are passing away,
3: 1 the **w** does not know us is that it did not know him.
3:13 brothers and sisters, that the **w** hates you.
4: 1 for many false prophets have gone out into the **w**.
4: 3 and now it is already in the **w**.
4: 4 in you is greater than the one who is in the **w**.
4: 5 They are from the **w**; therefore what they say is
from the **w**, and the **w** listens to them.
4: 9 into the **w** so that we might live through him.
4:14 the Father has sent his Son as the Savior of the **w**.
4:17 because as he is, so are we in this **w**.
5: 4 for whatever is born of God conquers the **w**.
5: 4 this is the victory that conquers the **w**, our faith.
5: 5 that conquers the **w** but the one who believes
5:19 whole **w** lies under the power of the evil one. A
2Jn 1: 7 Many deceivers have gone out into the **w**,
Rev 3:10 the whole **w** to test the inhabitants of the earth. A
11:15 of the **w** has become the kingdom of our Lord
12: 9 the deceiver of the whole **w**— A
13: 8 from the foundation of the **w** in the book of life
16:14 who go abroad to the kings of the whole **w**, A
17: 8 in the book of life from the foundation of the **w**,
Tob 3: 2 your ways are mercy and truth; you judge the **w**.
6:18 she was set apart for you before the **w** was made.
14: 6 the whole **w** will all be converted and worship A
Jdt 5:21 become the laughingstock of the whole **w**." A
10:19 be able to beguile the whole **w**!" A
11: 8 the whole **w** that you alone are the best A
11:16 the whole **w** wherever people shall hear A
11:23 and be renowned throughout the whole **w**." A
AdE 13: 2 of the whole **w** (not elated with presumption A
13: 4 in the **w** there is scattered a certain hostile people,
Wis 1: 7 Because the spirit of the Lord has filled the **w**,
1:14 the generative forces of the **w** are wholesome,
2:24 but through the devil's envy death entered the **w**,
6:24 The multitude of the wise is the salvation of the **w**,
7:17 to know the structure of the **w** and the activity of
9: 3 and rule the **w** in holiness and righteousness,
9: 9 and was present when you made the **w**;
10: 1 Wisdom protected the first-formed father of the **w**,
11:17 which created the **w** out of formless matter,
11:22 Because the whole **w** before you is like a speck A
13: 2 luminaries of heaven were the gods that rule the **w**.
13: 9 to know so much that they could investigate the **w**,
14: 6 the hope of the **w** took refuge on a raft,
14: 6 and guided by your hand left to the **w** the seed of
14:14 For through human vanity they entered the **w**,
17:20 the whole **w** was illumined with brilliant light, A
18: 4 of the law was to be given to the **w**.
18:24 For on his long robe the whole **w** was depicted, A
Sir 38:34 But they maintain the fabric of the **w**,
LtJ 6:62 commands the clouds to go over the whole **w**, A
Aza 1: 9 to an unjust king, the most wicked in all the **w**. B
1:14 and are brought low this day in all the **w** because B
1:22 glorious over the whole **w**." A
2Mc 2:22 the temple famous throughout the **w**, and liberated
3:12 temple that is honored throughout the whole **w**. A
5:15 to enter the most holy temple in all the **w**, B
7:23 Therefore the Creator of the **w**,
8:18 and even, if necessary, the whole **w**." A
12:15 calling against the great Sovereign of the **w**,
13:14 of the **w** and exhorting his troops to fight bravely
1Es 2: 3 the Lord Most High, has made me king of the **w**,
3Mc 6: 5 who had already gained control of the whole **w** A
2Es 2:47 whom they confessed in the **w**."
3: 9 upon the inhabitants of the **w** and destroyed them.
3:18 the heavens and shook the earth, and moved the **w**,
3:34 and those of the inhabitants of the **w**;
4: 2 understanding has utterly failed regarding this **w**,
4:11 by the corrupt **w** understand incorruption?"
4:24 We pass from the **w** like locusts,
5:24 of the **w** you have chosen for yourself one region,
5:24 and from all the flowers of the **w** you have chosen
5:44 the Creator, nor can the **w** hold
5:49 I have made the same rule for the **w** that I created."
6: 1 before the portals of the **w** were in place,
6:25 and shall see my salvation and the end of my **w**.
6:55 that it was for us that you created this **w**.
6:59 If the **w** has indeed been created for us,
6:59 why do we not possess our **w** as an inheritance?
7:11 For I made the **w** for their sake,
7:12 And so the entrances of this **w** were made narrow
7:13 the entrances of the greater **w** are broad and safe,
7:21 into the **w**, when they came, what they should do
7:30 the **w** shall be turned back to primeval silence
7:31 After seven days the **w** that is not yet awake shall
7:*47* I see that the **w** to come will bring delight to few,
7:*50* For this reason the Most High has made not one **w**
7:*70* the **w** and Adam and all who have come from him,
7:*74* with those who inhabit the **w**!—
7:*112* [42] "This present **w** is not the end;
7:*132* [62] on those who have not yet come into the **w**;
7:*137* [67] **w** with those who inhabit it would not have
8: 1 "The Most High made this **w** for the sake of many,
8: 1 but the **w** to come for the sake of only a few.
8: 2 so is the course of the present **w**.
8: 5 For not of your own will did you come into the **w**,
8:41 so also those who have been sown in the **w** will
8:50 the **w** in the last times,
9: 2 when the Most High is about to visit the **w**
9: 3 So when there shall appear in the **w** earthquakes,
9: 5 just as with everything that has occurred in the **w**,
9:18 before the **w** was made for them to live in,
9:19 but now those who have been created in this **w**,
9:20 So I considered my **w**, and saw that it was lost.
10: 8 but we, the whole **w**, for our mother. A
10:45 in the **w** before any offering was offered in it.
11:32 over the **w** than all the wings that had gone before.
11:39 the four beasts that I had made to reign in my **w**,
11:40 you have held sway over the **w** with great terror,
13:20 than to pass from the **w** like a cloud,
14:17 For the weaker the **w** becomes through old age,
14:20 For the **w** lies in darkness,
14:22 that has happened in the **w** from the beginning,
15: 5 says the Lord, I am bringing evils upon the **w**,
15:14 Alas for the **w** and for those who live in it!
16:13 and when they are shot to the ends of the **w** will
16:39 in coming upon the earth, and the **w** will groan,
4Mc 5:25 of the **w** in giving us the law has shown sympathy
8:23 and deprive ourselves of this delightful **w**?
15:31 carrying the **w** in the universal flood,
16:18 through God that you have had a share in the **w**
17:14 and the **w** and the human race were the spectators.

WORLD'S (2) [WORLD]

Pr 8:26 or the **w** first bits of soil.
1Jn 3:17 in anyone who has the **w** goods and sees a brother

WORLDLY (3) [WORLD]

2Co 7:10 but **w** grief produces death.
Tit 2:12 training us to renounce impiety and **w** passions,
Jude 1:19 It is these **w** people, devoid of the Spirit,

WORLDS (2) [WORLD]

Heb 1: 2 through whom he also created the **w**.
11: 3 By faith we understand that the **w** were prepared

WORM (11) [WORMS]

Dt 28:39 for the **w** shall eat them.
Job 17:14 'You are my father,' and to the **w**, 'My mother,'
24:20 The womb forgets them; the **w** finds them sweet;
25: 6 who is a maggot, and a human being, who is a **w**!"
Ps 22: 6 But I am a **w**, and not human;
Pr 25:20 Like a moth in clothing or a **w** in wood,
Isa 41:14 Do not fear, you **w** Jacob, you insect Israel!
51: 8 and the **w** will eat them like wool;
66:24 for their **w** shall not die,
Jnh 4: 7 God appointed a **w** that attacked the bush,
Mk 9:48 where their **w** never dies,

WORMS (12) [WORM]

Ex 16:20 and it bred **w** and became foul.
16:24 it did not become foul, and there were no **w** in it.
Job 7: 5 My flesh is clothed with **w** and dirt;
21:26 down alike in the dust, and the **w** cover them.
Isa 14:11 the bed beneath you, and **w** are your covering.
Ac 12:23 and he was eaten by **w** and died.
Jdt 16:17 he will send fire and **w** into their flesh;
Sir 7:17 for the punishment of the ungodly is fire and **w**.
10:11 one is dead he inherits maggots and vermin and **w**.
19: 3 Decay and **w** will take possession of him,
1Mc 2:62 for their splendor will turn into dung and **w**.
2Mc 9: 9 And so the ungodly man's body swarmed with **w**,

WORMWOOD (9)

Pr 5: 4 but in the end she is bitter as **w**,
Jer 9:15 I am feeding this people with **w**,
23:15 "I am going to make them eat **w**,
La 3:15 he has sated me with **w**.
3:19 of my affliction and my homelessness is **w**
Am 5: 7 Ah, you that turn justice to **w**,
6:12 into poison and the fruit of righteousness into **w**—
Rev 8:11 The name of the star is **W**.
8:11 A third of the waters became **w**,

WORN (16) [WEAR]

Dt 29: 5 The clothes on your back have not **w** out,
29: 5 and the sandals on your feet have not **w** out;
Jos 9:13 and these garments and sandals of ours are **w** out
Jdg 8:26 and the purple garments **w** by the kings of Midian,
19: 9 "Look, the day has **w** on until it is almost evening.
Est 6: 8 be brought, which the king has **w**, and a horse that
Job 16: 7 Surely now God has **w** me out;
Ps 39:10 I am **w** down by the blows of your hand.
Eze 23:43 Then I said, Ah, she is **w** out with adulteries,
Lk 8:27 For a long time he had **w** no clothes,
AdE 6: 8 the fine linen robe that the king has **w**,
Sir 11: 5 but one who was never thought of has **w** a crown.
41: 2 **w** down by age and anxious about everything;
1Mc 8:14 not one of them has put on a crown or **w** purple as
2Es 4:11 And how can one who is already **w** out by
4Mc 9:12 When they had **w** themselves out beating him

WORN-OUT (5) [WEAR]

Jos 9: 4 and took **w** sacks for their donkeys, and wineskins,
w and torn and mended,
9: 5 with **w**, patched sandals on their feet, and **w** clothes
Jer 38:11 and took from there old rags and **w** clothes,

WORRIED (1) [WORRY]

Lk 10:41 Martha, you are **w** and distracted by many things;

WORRIES (2) [WORRY]

Mt 6:34 for tomorrow will bring **w** of its own.
Lk 21:34 down with dissipation and drunkenness and the **w**

WORRY (18) [WORRIED, WORRIES, WORRYING]

1Sa 9: 5 about the donkeys and **w** about us."
Mt 6:25 "Therefore I tell you, do not **w** about your life,
6:28 And why do you **w** about clothing?
6:31 Therefore do not **w**, saying, 'What will we eat?'
6:34 "So do not **w** about tomorrow,
10:19 not **w** about how you are to speak or what you are
Mk 13:11 do not **w** beforehand about what you are to say;
Lk 12:11 do not **w** about how you are to defend yourselves
12:22 "Therefore I tell you, do not **w** about your life,
12:26 why do you **w** about the rest?
Php 4: 6 not **w** about anything, but in everything by prayer
Tob 5:21 Tobit said to her, "Do not **w**;
10: 3 And he began to **w**.
Sir 22:22 do not **w**, for reconciliation is possible.
23:18 and no one sees me. Why should I **w**?
41: 1 who has nothing to **w** about and is prosperous
42: 9 and **w** over her robs him of sleep;
1Mc 6:10 from my eyes and I am downhearted with **w**.

WORRYING (7) [WORRY]

1Sa 9: 5 or my father will stop **w** about the donkeys
10: 2 and now your father has stopped **w** about them
10: 2 about them and is **w** about you, saying:
Mt 6:27 of you by **w** add a single hour to your span of life?
Lk 12:25 of you by **w** add a single hour to your span of life?
12:29 and what you are to drink, and do not keep **w**.
Tob 10: 6 But Tobit kept saying to her, "Be quiet and stop **w**,

WORSE (38) [BAD]

Ge 19: 9 Now we will deal **w** with you than with them."
Jdg 2:19 and behave **w** than their ancestors,

2Sa 19: 7 be **w** for you than any disaster that has come
Ps 39: 2 to no avail; my distress grew **w**,
Jer 7:26 They did **w** than their ancestors did.
16:12 because you have behaved **w** than your ancestors,
Eze 23:11 which were **w** than those of her sister.
Zec 1:15 I was only a little angry, they made the disaster **w**.
Mt 9:16 and a **w** tear is made.
12:45 and the last state of that person is **w** than the first.
27:64 and the last deception would be **w** than the first."
Mk 2:21 the new from the old, and a **w** tear is made.
5:26 and she was no better, but rather grew **w**.
Lk 11:26 and the last state of that person is **w** than the first."
13: 2 they were **w** sinners than all other Galileans?
13: 4 do you think that they were **w** offenders than all
Jn 5:14 so that nothing **w** happens to you."
1Co 8: 8 We are no **w** off if we do not eat,
11:17 not for the better but for the **w**.
2Co 12:13 How have you been **w** off than the other churches,
1Ti 5: 8 has denied the faith and is **w** than an unbeliever.
2Ti 3:13 and impostors will go from bad to **w**,
Heb 10:29 How much **w** punishment do you think will
2Pe 2:20 the last state has become **w** for them than the first.
Wis 15:18 which are **w** than all others when judged
17: 6 that they saw to be **w** than that unseen appearance.
Sir 14: 6 No one is **w** than one who is grudging to himself;
22:11 but the life of the fool is **w** than death.
25:15 There is no venom **w** than a snake's venom,
25:15 and no anger **w** than a woman's wrath.
26: 5 all these are **w** than death.
2Mc 5:23 over his compatriots **w** than the others did.
7:39 and handled him **w** than the others,
13: 9 to show the Jews things far **w** than those
3Mc 5:20 possessed by a savagery **w** than that of Phalaris,
2Es 7:87 which is **w** than all the ways
8:30 with those who are deemed **w** than wild animals,
14:16 For evils **w** than those that you have

WORSHIP (175) [WORSHIPED, WORSHIPER, WORSHIPERS, WORSHIPING, WORSHIPS]

Ge 22: 5 we will **w**, and then we will come back to you."
Ex 3:12 you shall **w** God on this mountain."
4:23 I said to you, "Let my son go that he may **w** me."
7:16 so that they may **w** me in the wilderness."
8: 1 Let my people go, so that they may **w** me.
8:20 Let my people go, so that they may **w** me.
9: 1 Let my people go, so that they may **w** me.
9:13 Let my people go, so that they may **w** me.
10: 3 Let my people go, so that they may **w** me.
10: 7 so that they may **w** the LORD their God;
10: 8 and he said to them, "Go, **w** the LORD your God!
10:11 Your men may go and **w** the LORD,
10:24 and said, "Go, **w** the LORD.
10:26 for we must choose some of them for the **w** of
10:26 and we will not know what to use to **w** the LORD
12:31 Go, **w** the LORD, as you said.
20: 5 You shall not bow down to them or **w** them;
23:24 or **w** them, or follow their practices,
23:25 You shall **w** the LORD your God,
23:33 if you **w** their gods, it will surely be a snare to you.
24: 1 and seventy of the elders of Israel, and **w** at
34:14 (for you shall **w** no other god,
Lev 26: 1 to **w** at them; for I am the LORD your God.
Dt 5: 9 You shall not bow down to them or **w** them;
8:19 and follow other gods to serve and **w** them,
10:20 fear the LORD your God; him alone you shall **w**;
12: 4 not **w** the LORD your God in such ways.
12:30 saying, "How did these nations **w** their gods?
13: 6 saying, "Let us go **w** other gods,"
13:13 saying, "Let us go and **w** other gods,"
32:43 Praise, O heavens, his people, **w** him, all you gods!
Jos 22:25 might make our children cease to **w** the LORD.
Jdg 10: 6 the LORD, and did not **w** him.
1Sa 1: 3 up year by year from his town to **w** and to sacrifice
15:25 and return with me, so that I may **w** the LORD."
15:30 so that I may **w** the LORD your God."
2Sa 15: 8 then I will **w** the LORD in Hebron."
1Ki 1:47 The king bowed in **w** on the bed
9: 6 but go and serve other gods and **w** them,
12:30 the people went to **w** before the one at Bethel and
2Ki 5:18 into the house of Rimmon to **w** there,
17:25 they first settled there, they did not **w** the LORD;
17:28 he taught them how they should **w** the LORD.
17:34 They do not **w** the LORD and they do not follow
17:35 "You shall not **w** other gods or bow yourselves
17:36 but you shall **w** the LORD, who brought you out
17:37 You shall not **w** other gods;
17:38 You shall not **w** other gods,
17:39 but you shall **w** the LORD your God;
18:22 'You shall **w** before this altar in Jerusalem'?
1Ch 16:29 **W** the LORD in holy splendor;
2Ch 7:19 and go and serve other gods and **w** them,
32:12 saying, 'Before one altar you shall **w**,
33:14 and **w** the LORD and his will shall **w**,
33:14 and made all who were in Israel **w**
Ezr 4: 2 for we **w** your God as you do,
6:21 from the pollutions of the nations of the land to **w**
Ps 22:27 all the families of the nations shall **w** before him.
29: 2 **w** the LORD in holy splendor.
95: 6 O come, let us **w** and bow down,
96: 9 **W** the LORD in holy splendor;
99: 5 Extol the LORD our God; **w** at his footstool.
99: 9 and **w** at his holy mountain;
100: 2 **W** the LORD with gladness;
102:22 and kingdoms, to **w** the LORD.
132: 7 let us **w** at his footstool."

Isa 2:20 which they made for themselves to **w**,
19:21 and will **w** with sacrifice and burnt offering,
19:23 and the Egyptians will **w** with the Assyrians.
27:13 the land of Egypt will come and **w** the LORD on
29:13 while their hearts are far from me, and their **w**
36: 7 'You shall **w** before this altar'?
46: 6 then they fall down and **w**!
66:23 all flesh shall come to **w** before me,
Jer 7: 2 you that enter these gates to **w** the LORD.
13:10 after other gods to serve them and **w** them,
25: 6 do not go after other gods to serve and **w** them,
26: 2 and speak to all the cities of Judah that come to **w**
Eze 20:32 the tribes of the countries, and **w** wood and stone."
46: 9 whoever enters by the north gate to **w** shall go out
Da 3: 5 you are to fall down and **w** the golden statue
3: 6 and **w** shall immediately be thrown into a furnace
3:10 shall fall down and **w** the golden statue,
3:11 not fall down and **w** shall be thrown into a furnace
3:12 They do not serve your gods and they do not **w**
3:14 that you do not serve my gods and you do not **w**
3:15 and entire musical ensemble to fall down and **w**
3:15 But if you do not **w**, you shall immediately be
3:18 that we will not serve your gods and we will not **w**
3:28 and **w** any god except their own God.
Jnh 1: 9 "I **w** the LORD, the God of heaven,
2: 8 Those who **w** vain idols forsake their true loyalty.
Zec 14:16 against Jerusalem shall go up year after year to **w**
14:17 the earth do not go up to Jerusalem to **w** the King,
Mt 4: 9 if you will fall down and **w** me."
4:10 '**W** the Lord your God, and serve only him.' "
15: 9 in vain do they **w** me,
Mk 7: 7 in vain do they **w** me,
Lk 4: 7 If you, then, will **w** me, it will all be yours."
4: 8 '**W** the Lord your God, and serve only him.' "
Jn 4:20 but you say that the place where people must **w** is
4:21 the hour is coming when you will **w**
4:22 You **w** what you do not know; we **w** what we know, for salvation is from the Jews.
4:23 when the true worshipers will **w** the Father in spirit
4:23 for the Father seeks such as these to **w** him.
4:24 those who **w** him must **w** in spirit and truth."
12:20 up to **w** at the festival were some Greeks.
16: 2 that by doing so they are offering **w** to God.
Ac 7: 7 that they shall come out and **w** me in this place.'
7:42 to **w** the host of heaven, as it is written in the book
7:43 the images that you made to **w**;
8:27 He had come to Jerusalem to **w**
17:23 and looked carefully at the objects of your **w**,
17:23 What therefore you **w** as unknown,
18:13 "This man is persuading people to **w** God in ways
19:27 that brought all Asia and the world to **w** her."
24:11 not more than twelve days since I went up to **w**
24:14 I **w** the God of our ancestors,
26: 7 as they earnestly **w** day and night.
27:23 of the God to whom I belong and whom I **w**,
Ro 9: 4 the giving of the law, the **w**, and the promises;
12: 1 and acceptable to God, which is your spiritual **w**.
1Co 10:14 my dear friends, flee from the **w** of idols.
14:25 that person will bow down before God and **w** him,
Php 3: 3 who **w** in the Spirit of God and boast
Col 2:18 insisting on self-abasement and **w** of angels,
2Th 2: 4 above every so-called god or object of **w**,
2Ti 1: 3 whom I **w** with a clear conscience,
Heb 1: 6 he says, "Let all God's angels **w** him."
8: 5 They offer **w** in a sanctuary that is a sketch
9: 1 Now even the first covenant had regulations for **w**
9:14 purify our conscience from dead works to **w**
9:21 both the tent and all the vessels used in **w**.
11:21 "bowing in **w** over the top of his staff."
12:28 to God an acceptable **w** with reverence and awe;
Rev 4:10 before the one who is seated on the throne and **w**
7:15 and **w** him day and night within his temple,
11: 1 of God and the altar and those who **w** there,
13: 8 and all the inhabitants of the earth will **w** it,
13:12 the earth and its inhabitants **w** the first beast,
13:15 and cause those who would not **w** the image of
14: 7 and **w** him who made heaven and earth,
14: 9 "Those who **w** the beast and its image,
14:11 or night for those who **w** the beast and its image
15: 4 All nations will come and **w** before you,
19:10 Then I fell down at his feet to **w** him,
19:10 who hold the testimony of Jesus. **W** God!
22: 3 and his servants will **w** him;
22: 8 to **w** at the feet of the angel who showed them
22: 9 who keep the words of this book. **W** God!"
Tob 14: 6 the whole world will all be converted and **w** God
Jdt 3: 8 so that all nations should **w** Nebuchadnezzar alone,
Wis 11:15 to **w** irrational serpents and worthless animals,
14:18 not know the king to intensify their **w**.
14:20 as an object of **w** the one whom shortly
14:27 For the **w** of idols not to be named is the beginning
15: 6 either make or desire or **w** them.
15:17 for they are better than the objects they **w**,
15:18 Moreover, they **w** even the most hateful animals,
Sir 35:10 Be generous when you **w** the Lord,
50:17 to **w** their Lord, the Almighty, God Most High.
50:19 until the order of **w** of the Lord was ended,
50:21 and they bowed down in **w** a second time,
LtJ 6: 6 "It is you, O Lord, whom we must **w**."
Aza 1:10 we, your servants who **w** you,
1:68 All who **w** the Lord, bless the God of gods,
Bel 1: 4 The king revered it and went every day to **w** it.
1: 4 So the king said to him, "Why do you not **w** Bel?"
1:24 that this is a living god; so **w** him."
1:25 Daniel said, "I **w** the Lord my God,
2Mc 1: 3 to **w** him and to do his will with a strong heart and
1Es 1: 4 **w** the Lord your God and serve his people Israel;

3Mc 3: 7 instead they gossiped about the differences in **w**
4Mc 5:24 with proper reverence who **w** the only living God.

WORSHIPED‡ (75) [WORSHIP]

Ge 24:26 The man bowed his head and **w** the LORD
24:48 Then I bowed my head and **w** the LORD,
Ex 4:31 he had seen their misery, they bowed down and **w**.
12:27 And the people bowed down and **w**.
32: 8 and have **w** it and sacrificed to it, and said,
34: 8 quickly bowed his head toward the earth, and **w**.
Jos 5:14 And Joshua fell on his face to the earth and **w**,
Jdg 2: 7 The people **w** the LORD all the days of Joshua,
2:11 in the sight of the LORD and **w** the Baals;
2:13 and **w** Baal and the Astartes.
3: 6 to their sons; and they **w** their gods.
7:15 telling of the dream and its interpretation, he **w**;
10:10 because we have abandoned our God and have **w**
10:13 Yet you have abandoned me and **w** other gods;
10:16 the foreign gods from among them and **w**
1Sa 1:19 They rose early in the morning and **w** before
15:31 after Saul; and Saul **w** the LORD.
2Sa 12:20 He went into the house of the LORD, and **w**;
15:32 David came to the summit, where God was **w**,
1Ki 11:33 he has forsaken me, **w** Astarte the goddess of the
16:31 and went and served Baal, and **w** him.
22:53 He served Baal and **w** him;
2Ki 17: 7 They had **w** other gods
17:16 they made a sacred pole, **w** all the host of heaven,
17:32 They also **w** the LORD and appointed from
17:33 they **w** the LORD but also served their own gods,
17:41 So these nations **w** the LORD,
21: 3 **w** all the host of heaven, and served them.
21:21 served the idols that his father served, and **w** them;
2Ch 7: 3 and **w** and gave thanks to the LORD, saying,
7:22 and **w** them and served them;
25:14 and **w** them, making offerings to them.
29:28 The whole assembly **w**, the singers sang,
29:29 with him bowed down and **w**.
29:30 and they bowed down and **w**.
33: 3 made sacred poles, **w** all the host of heaven,
Ne 8: 6 and **w** the LORD with their faces to the ground.
9: 3 and for another fourth they made confession and **w**
Job 1:20 shaved his head, and fell on the ground and **w**.
Ps 106:19 They made a calf at Horeb and **w** a cast image.
Jer 1:16 and **w** the works of their own hands.
8: 2 and which they have inquired of and **w**;
16:11 after other gods and have served and **w** them,
22: 9 and **w** other gods and served them."
Da 2:46 King Nebuchadnezzar fell on his face, **w** Daniel,
3: 7 and languages fell down and **w** the golden statue
Mt 14:33 And those in the boat **w** him, saying,
28: 9 they came to him, took hold of his feet, and **w** him.
28:17 they saw him, they **w** him; but some doubted.
Lk 2:37 but **w** there with fasting and prayer night and day.
24:52 And they **w** him, and returned to Jerusalem
Jn 4:20 Our ancestors **w** on this mountain,
9:38 He said, "Lord, I believe." And he **w** him.
Ac 10:25 and falling at his feet, **w** him.
Ro 1:25 for a lie and **w** and served the creature rather than
Rev 5:14 And the elders fell down and **w**.
7:11 on their faces before the throne and **w** God,
11:16 before God fell on their faces and **w** God,
13: 4 They **w** the dragon, for he had given his authority
13: 4 and they **w** the beast, saying,
16: 2 the mark of the beast and who **w** its image.
19: 4 down and **w** God who is seated on the throne,
19:20 the mark of the beast and those who **w** its image.
20: 4 They had not **w** the beast or its image and had not
Tob 5:14 to go with me to Jerusalem and **w** with me there,
Jdt 5: 8 and **w** the God of heaven,
6:18 the people fell down and **w** God, and cried out:
13:17 They bowed down and **w** God,
16:18 When they arrived at Jerusalem, they **w** God.
AdE 15: 1 she took off the garments in which she had **w**,
Wis 14:16 the command of monarchs carved images were **w**.
Bel 1: 4 But Daniel **w** his own God.
1Mc 4:55 on their faces and **w** and blessed Heaven,
1Es 9:47 and fell to the ground and **w** the Lord.
3Mc 3: 4 they **w** God and conducted themselves by his law,

WORSHIPER (5) [WORSHIP]

Lev 2: 1 the **w** shall pour oil on it,
2Ki 10:23 that there is no **w** of the LORD here among you,
Ac 16:14 A certain woman named Lydia, a **w** of God,
18: 7 of a man named Titius Justus, a **w** of God;
Heb 9: 9 that cannot perfect the conscience of the **w**,

WORSHIPERS (10) [WORSHIP]

2Ki 10:19 summon to me all the prophets of Baal, all his **w**,
10:19 with cunning in order to destroy the **w** of Baal.
10:21 all the **w** of Baal came,
10:22 "Bring out the vestments for all the **w** of Baal."
10:23 he said to the **w** of Baal,
10:23 the LORD here among you, but only **w** of Baal."
Ps 97: 7 All **w** of images are put to shame,
Jn 4:23 true **w** will worship the Father in spirit and truth,
Heb 10: 2 since the **w**, cleansed once for all,
Wis 14:28 For their **w** either rave in exultation,

WORSHIPING (14) [WORSHIP]

Dt 11:16 serving other gods and **w** them,
17: 3 by going to serve other gods and **w** them—
29:26 They turned and served other gods, **w** them,
Jdg 2:19 **w** them and bowing down to them.
3: 7 and **w** the Baals and the Asherahs.

Jdg 10: 6 w the Baals and the Astartes, the gods of Aram,
1Ki 9: 9 w them and serving them;
2Ki 19:37 As he was w in the house of his god Nisroch,
2Ch 20:18 fell down before the LORD, w the LORD.
Isa 37:38 As he was w in the house of his god Nisroch,
Ac 13: 2 While they were w the Lord and fasting,
Rev 9:20 or give up w demons and idols of gold and silver
LtJ 6: 6 the multitude before and behind them w them.
Bel 1:27 Then Daniel said, "See what you have been w!"

WORSHIPS (6) [WORSHIP]

Ne 9: 6 and the host of heaven w you.
Ps 66: 4 All the earth w you; they sing praises to you,
Isa 44:15 Then he makes a god and w it,
44:17 his idol, bows down to it and w it;
Jn 9:31 to one who w him and obeys his will.
Jdt 8:18 or town of ours that w gods made with hands,

WORST‡ (5) [BAD]

Ps 41: 7 they imagine the w for me.
Eze 7:24 I will bring the w of the nations to take possession
Tob 12:10 and do wrong are their own w enemies.
3Mc 6:26 toward us and often have accepted willingly the w
2Es 10:23 And, w of all, the seal of Zion has been deprived

WORTH (20) [WORTHLESS, WORTHLESSNESS, WORTHY]

Ge 23:15 a piece of land w four hundred shekels of silver—
Dt 15:18 for six years they have given you services w
2Sa 18: 3 But you are w ten thousand of us;
Ezr 8:26 and one hundred silver vessels w . . . talents,
8:27 twenty gold bowls w a thousand darics,
Pr 10:20 the mind of the wicked is of little w.
Isa 7:23 w a thousand shekels of silver,
La 4: 2 w their weight in fine gold—
Mk 6:37 to go and buy two hundred denarii w of bread,
12:42 in two small copper coins, which are w a penny.
Ro 8:18 of this present time are not w comparing with
Php 2:22 But Timothy's w you know,
Tob 1:14 of Media I left bags of silver w ten talents in trust
AdE 1: 7 made of ruby, w thirty thousand talents.
Wis 15:10 and their lives are of less w than clay,
Sir 6:15 no amount can balance their w.
7:19 for her charm is w more than gold.
2Mc 9:15 not considered w burying but had planned
1Es 8:56 and silver vessels w a hundred talents,
2Es 7:*58* "O sovereign Lord, what is plentiful is of less w,

WORTHIES (KJV) See OFFICERS

WORTHILY (KJV) See PRODUCE CHILDREN; See also Index to Footnotes

WORTHLESS (40) [WORTH]

Jdg 9: 4 with which Abimelech hired w and reckless
1Sa 1:16 Do not regard your servant as a w woman,
10:27 some w fellows said, "How can this man save us?"
15: 9 all that was despised and w they utterly destroyed.
30:22 and w fellows among the men who had gone
2Ch 13: 7 and certain w scoundrels gathered around him
Job 11:11 For he knows those who are w;
13: 4 all of you are w physicians.
Ps 26: 4 I do not sit with the w,
31: 6 You hate those who pay regard to w idols,
60:11 against the foe, for human help is w.
97: 7 those who make their boast in w idols;
108:12 against the foe, for human help is w.
Pr 12:11 but those who follow w pursuits have no sense.
19:28 A w witness mocks at justice,
28:19 but one who follows w pursuits will have plenty
Isa 30: 7 For Egypt's help is w and empty,
Jer 2: 5 from me, and went after w things,
2: 5 and became w themselves?
10:15 They are w, a work of delusion;
14:14 w divination, and the deceit of their own minds.
15:19 If you utter what is precious, and not what is w,
16:19 w things in which there is no profit.
51:18 They are w, a work of delusion;
La 1:11 Look, O LORD, and see how w I have become.
Na 1:14 I will make your grave, for you are w."
Zec 11:15 Take once more the implements of a w shepherd.
11:17 Oh, my w shepherd, who deserts the flock!
Mt 25:30 for this w slave, throw him into the outer darkness,
Lk 17:10 that you were ordered to do, say, 'We are w slaves;
Ac 14:15 that you should turn from these w things to
Ro 3:12 together they have become w;
Tit 3: 9 for they are unprofitable and w.
Heb 6: 8 it is w and on the verge of being cursed;
Jas 1:26 but deceive their hearts, their religion is w.
Wis 9:14 For the reasoning of mortals is w,
11:15 to worship irrational serpents and w animals,
13:14 like some w animal, giving it a coat of red paint
Sir 16: 1 Do not desire a multitude of w children,
2Es 11:45 your most evil talons, and your whole w body,

WORTHLESSNESS‡ (1) [WORTH]

LtJ 6:26 revealing to humankind their w.

WORTHY‡ (81) [WORTH]

Ge 32:10 not w of the least of all the steadfast love and all
Ru 3:11 of my people know that you are a w woman.
2Sa 22: 4 I call upon the LORD, who is w to be praised,
1Ki 1:42 you are a w man and surely you bring good news."
1:52 Solomon responded, "If he proves to be a w man,
Ps 18: 3 I call upon the LORD, who is w to be praised,
Pr 20: 6 but who can find one w of trust?
Mt 3: 8 Bear fruit w of repentance.
3:11 I am not w to carry his sandals.
8: 8 I am not w to have you come under my roof;
10:11 find out who in it is w,
10:13 If the house is w, let your peace come upon it;
10:13 but if it is not w, let your peace return to you.
10:37 or mother more than me is not w of me;
10:37 or daughter more than me is not w of me;
10:38 not take up the cross and follow me is not w of me.
22: 8 but those invited were not w.
Mk 1: 7 I am not w to stoop down and untie the thong
Lk 3: 8 Bear fruits w of repentance.
3:16 I am not w to untie the thong of his sandals.
7: 4 saying, "He is w of having you do this for him,
7: 6 for I am not w to have you come under my roof;
15:19 I am no longer w to be called your son;
15:21 I am no longer w to be called your son.'
20:35 but those who are considered w of a place in
Jn 1:27 I am not w to untie the thong of his sandal."
Ac 5:41 that they were considered w to suffer dishonor for
13:25 not w to untie the thong of the sandals on his feet.'
Eph 4: 1 beg you to lead a life w of the calling
Php 1:27 live your life in a manner w of the gospel
4: 8 if there is any excellence and if there is anything w
Col 1:10 so that you may lead lives w of the Lord,
1Th 2:12 and pleading that you lead a life w of God,
2Th 1: 5 is intended to make you w of the kingdom of God,
1:11 asking that our God will make you w of his call
1Ti 1:15 The saying is sure and w of full acceptance,
4: 9 The saying is sure and w of full acceptance.
5:17 Let the elders who rule well be considered w
6: 1 under the yoke of slavery regard their masters as w
Heb 3: 3 Yet Jesus is w of more glory than Moses,
11:38 of whom the world was not w.
3Jn 1: 6 You will do well to send them on in a manner w
Rev 3: 4 dressed in white, for they are w.
4:11 "You are w, our Lord and God, to receive glory
5: 2 "Who is w to open the scroll and break its seals?"
5: 4 because no one was found w to open the scroll or
5: 9 "You are w to take the scroll and to open its seals,
5:12 "W is the Lamb that was slaughtered
Wis 3: 5 God tested them and found them w of himself;
6:16 because she goes about seeking those w of her,
7:15 and to have thoughts w of what I have received;
9:12 and shall be w of the throne of my father.
12: 7 to you might receive a w colony of the servants
Sir 10:19 Whose offspring are w of honor?
10:19 Whose offspring are w of honor?
10:20 Among family members their leader is w of honor,
10:20 those who fear the Lord are w of honor in his eyes.
11:31 and to w actions they attach blame.
14:11 and present w offerings to the Lord.
38:17 make your mourning w of the departed,
Aza 1: 3 and w of praise; and glorious is your name forever!
1Mc 10:19 you are a mighty warrior and w to be our friend.
2Mc 6:23 w of his years and the dignity of his old age and
6:24 "Such pretense is not w of our time of life,"
6:27 I will show myself w of my old age
7:20 The mother was especially admirable and w
7:29 but prove w of your brothers.
9:19 "To his w Jewish citizens,
15:11 a sort of vision, which was w of belief.
Man 1: 9 I am not w to look up and see the height of heaven
3Mc 3:21 both to deem them w of Alexandrian citizenship
2Es 4:24 and we are not w to obtain mercy.
4:44 and if it is possible, and if I am w,
12: 9 For you have judged me w to be shown the end of
12:36 And you alone were w to learn this secret of
13:14 and have deemed me w to have my prayer heard
14:45 and let the w and the unworthy read them;
4Mc 7: 6 O priest, w of the priesthood,
9:21 the courageous youth, w of Abraham,
10:12 he too had died in a manner w of his brothers,
18: 3 were deemed w to share in a divine inheritance.

WOT[TETH] (KJV) See CONCERN, KNOW

WOULD (884) See Index of Articles Etc.

WOUND (29) [WOUNDED, WOUNDING, WOUNDS]

Ex 21:25 burn for burn, w for w, stripe for stripe.
Dt 32:39 I kill and I make alive; I w and I heal;
1Ki 22:35 the blood from the w had flowed into the bottom
Job 34: 6 my w is incurable, though I am
Ps 42:10 As with a deadly w in my body,
Pr 20:30 Blows that w cleanse away evil;
25:20 on a w is one who sings songs to a heavy heart.
Jer 6:14 They have treated the w of my people carelessly,
8:11 They have treated the w of my people carelessly,
10:19 Woe is me because of my hurt! My w is severe.
14:17 with a crushing blow, with a very grievous w.
15:18 Why is my pain unceasing, my w incurable,
30:12 Your hurt is incurable, your w is grievous.
30:13 no medicine for your w, no healing for you.
51: 8 Bring balm for her w; perhaps she may be healed.
Eze 28: 9 and no god, in the hands of those who w you?
Hos 5:13 When Ephraim saw his sickness, and Judah his w,
5:13 But he is not able to cure you or heal your w.
Mic 1: 9 For her w is incurable.
Na 3:19 There is no assuaging your hurt, your w is mortal.
1Co 8:12 and w their conscience when it is weak,
Rev 13: 3 but its mortal w had been healed.
13:12 whose mortal w had been healed.
Jdt 9:13 Make my deceitful words bring w and bruise
Sir 21: 3 there is no healing for the w it inflicts.
25:13 Any w, but not a w of the heart!
27:21 For a w may be bandaged,

WOUNDED (44) [WOUND]

Jdg 9:40 Many fell w, up to the entrance of the gate.
1Sa 17:52 the w Philistines fell on the way from Shaaraim
31: 3 archers found him, and he was badly w by them.
2Sa 10:18 and w Shobach the commander of their army,
1Ki 22:34 and carry me out of the battle, for I am w."
2Ki 8:28 where the Arameans w Joram.
8:29 of Ahab in Jezreel, because he was w.
1Ch 10: 3 archers found him, and he was w by the archers.
2Ch 18:33 and carry me out of the battle, for I am w."
22: 5 at Ramoth-gilead. The Arameans w Joram,
24:25 they had withdrawn, leaving him severely w,
35:23 "Take me away, for I am badly w."
Job 24:12 and the throat of the w cries for help;
Ps 64: 7 at them; they will be w suddenly.
69:26 and those whom you have w,
SS 5: 7 beat me, they w me, they took away my mantle,
Isa 51:21 Therefore hear this, you who are w,
53: 5 But he was w for our transgressions,
Jer 37:10 there remained of them only w men in their tents,
51: 4 in the land of the Chaldeans, and w in her streets.
51:52 and through all her land the w shall groan.
La 2:12 as they faint like the w in the streets of the city,
Eze 26:15 at the sound of your fall, when the w groan,
30:24 before him with the groans of one mortally w.
Lk 20:12 this one also they w and threw out.
Ac 19:16 that they fled out of the house naked and w.
Rev 13:14 to make an image for the beast that had been w by
Jdt 2: 8 Their w shall fill their ravines and gullies,
6: 6 and you shall fall among their w.
16:12 through and w them like the children of fugitives;
Sir 25:23 gloomy face, and w heart come from an evil wife.
1Mc 1:18 and many were w and fell.
3:11 Many were w and fell, and the rest fled.
8:10 Many of them were w and fell,
9:17 and many on both sides were w and fell.
9:40 Many were w and fell, and the rest fled to
16: 8 of them fell w and the rest fled into the stronghold.
16: 9 At that time Judas the brother of John was w,
2Mc 3:16 the appearance of the high priest was to be w
4:42 As a result, they w many of them, and killed some,
8:24 and w and disabled most of Nicanor's army,
10:30 they kept him from being w.
11:12 Most of them got away stripped and w,
2Es 15:51 like a wretched woman who is beaten and w,

WOUNDING (2) [WOUND]

Ge 4:23 I have killed a man for w me,
1Ki 20:37 So the man hit him, striking and w him.

WOUNDS‡ (25) [WOUND]

2Ki 8:29 in Jezreel of the w that the Arameans had inflicted
9:15 in Jezreel of the w that the Arameans had inflicted
2Ch 22: 6 in Jezreel of the w that he had received at Ramah,
Job 5:18 For he w, but he binds up;
9:17 and multiplies my w without cause;
Ps 38: 5 My w grow foul and fester because
147: 3 He heals the brokenhearted, and binds up their w.
Pr 6:33 He will get w and dishonor,
23:29 Who has w without cause?
26:10 Like an archer who w everybody is one who hires
27: 6 Well meant are the w a friend inflicts,
Isa 1: 6 but bruises and sores and bleeding w;
30:26 and heals the w inflicted by his blow.
Jer 6: 7 sickness and w are ever before me.
30:17 I will restore health to you, and your w I will heal,
50:13 be appalled and hiss because of all her w.
Zec 13: 6 "What are these w on your chest?"
13: 6 the answer will be "The w I received in the house
Lk 10:34 He went to him and bandaged his w,
Ac 16:33 of the night he took them and washed their w;
1Pe 2:24 by his w you have been healed.
Sir 27:25 and a treacherous blow opens up many w.
30: 7 Whoever spoils his son will bind up his w,
31:30 reducing his strength and adding w.
2Mc 14:45 and his w were severe he ran through the crowd;

WOVE (2) [WEAVE]

Jdg 16:14 the seven locks of his head and w them into
Jn 19: 2 soldiers w a crown of thorns and put it on his head,

WOVEN (8) [WEAVE]

Ex 28:32 with a w binding around the opening,
39:22 also made the robe of the ephod w all of blue yarn;
39:27 They also made the tunics, w of fine linen,
Dt 22:11 of wool and linen w together.
Ps 139:15 intricately w in the depths of the earth.
Jn 19:23 tunic was seamless, w in one piece from the top.
Tob 2:12 when she cut off a piece she had w and sent it to
Jdt 10:21 on his bed under a canopy that was w with purple

WRANGLE (1) [WRANGLING]

Mt 12:19 He will not w or cry alound,

WRANGLING (3) [WRANGLE]

Eph 4:31 from you all bitterness and wrath and anger and **w**
1Ti 6: 5 and **w** among those who are depraved in mind
2Ti 2:14 and warn them before God that they are to avoid **w**

WRAP (2) [ENWRAP, WRAPPED, WRAPPINGS, WRAPS]

Isa 28:20 and the covering too narrow to **w** oneself in it.
Ac 12: 8 "**W** your cloak around you and follow me."

WRAPPED‡ (28) [WRAP]

Ge 38:14 put on a veil, **w** herself up,
Ex 12:34 with their kneading bowls **w** up in their cloaks
19:18 Now Mount Sinai was **w** in smoke,
1Sa 21: 9 is here **w** in a cloth behind the ephod;
28:14 "An old man is coming up; he is **w** in a robe."
1Ki 19:13 he **w** his face in his mantle and went out and stood
Ps 104: 2 **w** in light as with a garment.
109:29 may they be **w** in their own shame as in a mantle.
Pr 30: 4 Who has **w** up the waters in a garment?
Isa 59:17 and **w** himself in fury as in a mantle.
La 3:43 You have **w** yourself with anger and pursued us,
3:44 you have **w** yourself with a cloud so
Eze 7:27 king shall mourn, the prince shall be **w** in despair,
16: 4 nor rubbed with salt, nor **w** in cloths.
30:21 it has not been bound up for healing or **w** with
Hos 4:19 A wind has **w** them in its wings,
Jnh 2: 5 weeds were **w** around my head
Mt 27:59 Joseph took the body and **w** it in a clean linen cloth
Mk 15:46 and taking down the body, **w** it in the linen cloth,
Lk 2: 7 And she gave birth to her firstborn son and **w** him
2:12 a child **w** in bands of cloth and lying in a manger."
19:20 I **w** it up in a piece of cloth,
23:53 Then he took it down, **w** it in a linen cloth,
Jn 11:44 and his face **w** in a cloth.
19:40 They took the body of Jesus and **w** it with the spices in linen cloths,
Ac 5: 6 The young men came and **w** up his body,
Rev 10: 1 **w** in a cloud, with a rainbow over his head;
Jdt 10: 5 then she **w** up all her dishes and gave them to her

WRAPPINGS (3) [WRAP]

Jn 20: 5 down to look in and saw the linen **w** lying there,
20: 6 He saw the linen **w** lying there,
20: 7 not lying with the linen **w** but rolled up in a place

WRAPS (1) [WRAP]

Ps 109:19 May it be like a garment that he **w** around himself,

WRATH (267) [WRATHFUL]

Ge 49: 7 Cursed be their anger, for it is fierce, and their **w**,
Ex 22:24 my **w** will burn, and I will kill you with the sword,
32:10 so that my **w** may burn hot against them
32:11 why does your **w** burn hot against your people,
32:12 Turn from your fierce **w**;
Lev 10: 6 you will die and **w** will strike all the congregation;
Nu 1:53 that there may be no **w** on the congregation of
16:46 For **w** has gone out from the LORD;
18: 5 that **w** may never again come upon the Israelites.
25:11 has turned back my **w** from the Israelites
Dt 9: 7 how you provoked the LORD your God to **w** in
9: 8 Even at Horeb you provoked the LORD to **w**,
9:22 you provoked the LORD to **w**.
29:28 fury, and great **w**, and cast them into another land,
Jos 9:20 so that **w** may not come upon us,
22:20 and **w** fell upon all the congregation of Israel?
1Sa 28:18 and did not carry out his fierce **w** against Amalek,
2Ki 3:27 And great **w** came upon Israel,
22:13 for great is the **w** of the LORD that is kindled
22:17 therefore my **w** will be kindled against this place,
23:26 not turn from the fierceness of his great **w**,
1Ch 27:24 yet **w** came upon Israel for this,
2Ch 12: 7 and my **w** shall not be poured out on Jerusalem by
12:12 the **w** of the LORD turned from him,
19: 2 **w** has gone out against you from the LORD.
19:10 before the LORD and **w** may not come on you
24:18 And **w** came upon Judah and Jerusalem
28:11 for the fierce **w** of the LORD is upon you."
28:13 and there is fierce **w** against Israel."
29: 8 **w** of the LORD came upon Judah and Jerusalem,
32:25 **w** came upon him and upon Judah and Jerusalem.
32:26 that the **w** of the LORD did not come upon them
34:21 **w** of the LORD that is poured out on us is great,
34:25 my **w** will be poured out on this place and will not
36:16 the **w** of the LORD against his people became
Ezr 7:23 or **w** will come upon the realm of the king
8:22 and his **w** are against all who forsake him.
10:14 the fierce **w** of our God on this account is averted
Ne 13:18 Yet you bring more **w** on Israel by profaning
Est 1:18 and there will be no end of contempt and **w**!
7: 7 The king rose from the feast in **w** and went into
Job 14:13 that you would conceal me until your **w** is past,
16: 9 He has torn me in his **w**, and hated me;
19:11 He has kindled his **w** against me,
19:29 for **w** brings the punishment of the sword,
20:28 dragged off in the day of God's **w**.
21:20 and let them drink of the **w** of the Almighty.
21:30 and are rescued in the day of **w**?
36:18 Beware that **w** does not entice you into scoffing,
42: 7 "My **w** is kindled against you and
Ps 2: 5 Then he will speak to them in his **w**,
2:12 for his **w** is quickly kindled.
6: 1 or discipline me in your **w**.
21: 9 The LORD will swallow them up in his **w**,
37: 8 Refrain from anger, and forsake **w**.
38: 1 or discipline me in your **w**.
56: 7 in **w** cast down the peoples, O God!
59:13 consume them in **w**; consume them until they
76:10 Human **w** serves only to praise you,
76:10 when you bind the last bit of your **w** around you.
78:38 and did not stir up all his **w**.
78:49 He let loose on them his fierce anger, **w**,
78:59 When God heard, he was full of **w**,
78:62 and vented his **w** on his heritage.
79: 5 Will your jealous **w** burn like fire?
85: 3 You withdrew all your **w**;
88: 7 Your **w** lies heavy upon me,
88:16 Your **w** has swept over me;
89:38 you are full of **w** against your anointed.
89:46 How long will your **w** burn like fire?
90: 7 by your **w** we are overwhelmed.
90: 9 For all our days pass away under your **w**;
90:11 Your **w** is as great as the fear that is due you.
106:23 to turn away his **w** from destroying them.
110: 5 he will shatter kings on the day of his **w**.
138: 7 you preserve me against the **w** of my enemies;
Pr 11: 4 Riches do not profit in the day of **w**,
11:23 the expectation of the wicked in **w**.
14:35 but his **w** falls on one who acts shamefully.
15: 1 A soft answer turns away **w**,
16:14 A king's **w** is a messenger of death,
21:14 and a concealed bribe in the bosom, strong **w**.
27: 4 **W** is cruel, anger is overwhelming,
29: 8 but the wise turn away **w**.
Isa 1:24 Ah, I will pour out my **w** on my enemies,
9:19 the **w** of the LORD of hosts the land was burned,
10: 6 and against the people of my **w** I command him,
13: 9 cruel, with **w** and fierce anger,
13:13 at the **w** of the LORD of hosts in the day
14: 6 down the peoples in **w** with unceasing blows,
26:20 hide yourselves for a little while until the **w** is past.
27: 4 I have no **w**. If it gives me thorns
51:17 at the hand of the LORD the cup of his **w**,
51:20 they are full of the **w** of the LORD,
51:22 you shall drink no more from the bowl of my **w**.
54: 8 In overflowing **w** for a moment I hid my face
59:18 **w** to his adversaries, requital to his enemies;
60:10 for in my **w** I struck you down,
63: 3 in my anger and trampled them in my **w**;
63: 5 arm brought me victory, and my **w** sustained me.
63: 6 I crushed them in my **w**,
Jer 4: 4 or else my **w** will go forth like fire,
6:11 But I am full of the **w** of the LORD;
7:20 and my **w** shall be poured out on this place,
7:29 and forsaken the generation that provoked his **w**.
10:10 At his **w** the earth quakes,
10:25 Pour out your **w** on the nations that do
18:20 to turn away your **w** from them.
21: 5 in anger, in fury, and in great **w**.
21:12 or else my **w** will go forth like fire, and burn,
23:19 **W** has gone forth, a whirling tempest;
25:15 Take from my hand this cup of the wine of **w**,
30:23 **W** has gone forth, a whirling tempest;
32:31 This city has aroused my anger and **w**,
32:37 to which I drove them in my anger and my **w** and
33: 5 shall strike down in my anger and my **w**,
36: 7 the anger and **w** that the LORD has pronounced
42:18 Just as my anger and my **w** were poured out on
42:18 of Jerusalem, so my **w** will be poured out on you
44: 6 So my **w** and my anger were poured out
50:13 of the **w** of the LORD she shall not be inhabited,
50:25 and brought out the weapons of his **w**,
La 2: 2 in his **w** he has broken down the strongholds
3: 1 under the rod of God's **w**;
4:11 The LORD gave full vent to his **w**;
Eze 7: 8 Soon now I will pour out my **w** upon you;
7:12 for **w** is upon all their multitude.
7:14 for my **w** is upon all their multitude.
7:19 and gold cannot save them on the day of the **w** of
8:18 Therefore I will act in **w**;
9: 8 of Israel as you pour out your **w** upon Jerusalem?"
13:13 In my **w** I will make a stormy wind break out,
13:13 and hailstones in **w** to destroy it.
13:15 Thus I will spend my **w** upon the wall,
14:19 and pour out my **w** upon it with blood,
16:38 and bring blood upon you in **w** and jealousy.
20: 8 Then I thought I would pour out my **w** upon them
20:13 Then I thought I would pour out my **w** upon them
20:21 Then I thought I would pour out my **w** upon them
20:33 and with **w** poured out, I will be king over you.
20:34 and an outstretched arm, and with **w** poured out;
21:31 with the fire of my **w** I will blow upon you.
22:20 so I will gather you in my anger and in my **w**,
22:21 and blow upon you with the fire of my **w**,
22:22 that I the LORD have poured out my **w** upon you.
22:31 I have consumed them with the fire of my **w**;
24: 8 To rouse my **w**, to take vengeance,
25:14 according to my anger and according to my **w**;
30:15 I will pour my **w** upon Pelusium,
36: 6 I am speaking in my jealous **w**,
36:18 So I poured out my **w** upon them for the blood
38:18 says the Lord GOD, my **w** shall be aroused.
38:19 For in my jealousy and in my blazing **w** I declare:
Da 8:19 what will take place later in the period of **w**;
9:16 let your anger and **w**, we pray,
11:36 until the period of **w** is completed,
Hos 5:10 on them I will pour out my **w** like water.
11: 9 and I will not come in **w**.
13:11 and I took him away in my **w**.
Am 1:11 his anger perpetually, and kept his **w** forever.
Mic 5:15 And in anger and **w** I will execute vengeance on
Na 1: 6 His **w** is poured out like fire,
Hab 2:15 pouring out your **w** until they are drunk,
3: 2 in **w** may you remember mercy.
3: 8 Was your **w** against the rivers, O LORD?
Zep 1:15 That day will be a day of **w**,
1:18 to save them on the day of the LORD's **w**;
2: 2 there comes upon you the day of the LORD's **w**.
2: 3 be hidden on the day of the LORD's **w**.
Zec 7:12 Therefore great **w** came from the LORD of hosts.
8: 2 and I am jealous for her with great **w**.
8:14 when your ancestors provoked me to **w**,
Mt 3: 7 Who warned you to flee from the **w** to come?
Lk 3: 7 Who warned you to flee from the **w** to come?
21:23 For there will be great distress on the earth and **w**
Jn 3:36 but must endure God's **w**.
Ro 1:18 For the **w** of God is revealed from heaven
2: 5 and impenitent heart you are storing up **w**
2: 5 up wrath for yourself on the day of **w**,
2: 8 there will be **w** and fury.
3: 5 That God is unjust to inflict **w** on us?
4:15 For the law brings **w**; but where there is no law,
5: 9 will we be saved through him from the **w** of God.
9:22 to show his **w** and to make known his power,
9:22 with much patience the objects of **w** that are made
12:19 but leave room for the **w** of God;
13: 4 the servant of God to execute **w** on the wrongdoer.
13: 5 only because of **w** but also because of conscience.
Eph 2: 3 and we were by nature children of **w**,
4:31 Put away from you all bitterness and **w** and anger
5: 6 the **w** of God comes on those who are disobedient.
Col 3: 6 On account of these the **w** of God is coming
3: 8 anger, **w**, malice, slander, and abusive language
1Th 1:10 Jesus, who rescues us from the **w** that is coming.
2:16 but God's **w** has overtaken them at last.
5: 9 For God has destined us not for **w** but
Rev 6:16 of the one seated on the throne and from the **w** of
6:17 for the great day of their **w** has come,
11:18 The nations raged, but your **w** has come,
12:12 great **w**, because he knows that his time is short!"
14: 8 She has made all nations drink of the wine of the **w**
14:10 they will also drink the wine of God's **w**,
14:19 and he threw it into the great wine press of the **w**
15: 1 for with them the **w** of God is ended.
15: 7 the seven angels seven golden bowls full of the **w**
16: 1 and pour out on the earth the seven bowls of the **w**
16:19 and gave her the wine-cup of the fury of his **w**.
18: 3 For all the nations have drunk of the wine of the **w**
19:15 he will tread the wine press of the fury of the **w**
Jdt 9: 9 and send your **w** upon their heads.
AdE 16:24 accordingly shall be destroyed in **w** with spear
Wis 5:20 and sharpen stern **w** for a sword,
5:22 and hailstones full of **w** will be hurled as from
10:10 When a righteous man fled from his brother's **w**,
11: 9 the ungodly were tormented when judged in **w**.
16: 5 your **w** did not continue to the end;
18:20 but the **w** did not long continue.
18:22 He conquered the **w** not by strength of body,
18:23 he intervened and held back the **w**,
18:25 for merely to test the **w** was enough.
Sir 5: 6 for both mercy and **w** are with him,
5: 7 suddenly the **w** of the Lord will come upon you,
16: 6 and in a disobedient nation **w** blazes up.
16:11 For mercy and **w** are with the Lord;
16:11 but he also pours out **w**.
18:24 Think of his **w** on the day of death,
23:16 of individuals multiply sins, and a third incurs **w**.
25:15 and no anger worse than a woman's **w**.
25:22 There is **w** and impudence and great disgrace when
27:30 Anger and **w**, these also are abominations,
28: 5 If a mere mortal harbors **w**,
28:10 in proportion to his wealth he will increase his **w**.
36: 8 Rouse your anger and pour out your **w**;
36:11 Let survivors be consumed in the fiery **w**,
39:23 But his **w** drives out the nations,
44:17 in the time of **w** he kept the race alive;
45:18 and the company of Korah, in **w** and anger.
47:20 so that you brought **w** upon your children,
48:10 to calm the **w** of God before it breaks out in fury,
Bar 1:13 the Lord and his **w** have not turned away from us.
2:20 For you have sent your anger and your **w** upon us,
4: 9 For she saw the **w** that came upon you from God,
4:25 endure with patience the **w** that has come upon you
1Mc 1:64 Very great **w** came upon Israel.
2:44 in their anger and renegades in their **w**;
3: 8 thus he turned away **w** from Israel.
15:36 in **w** to the king and reported to him these words,
2Mc 5:20 in the **w** of the Almighty was restored again
7:38 an end the **w** of the Almighty that has justly fallen
8: 5 for the **w** of the Lord had turned to mercy.
1Es 8:21 that **w** may not come upon the kingdom of the king
9:13 until we are freed from the **w** of the Lord
Man 1: 5 and the **w** of your threat to sinners is unendurable;
1:10 for I have provoked your **w**
3Mc 2:17 the transgressors will boast in their **w** and exult in
5: 1 was filled with overpowering anger and **w**;
5:30 an overpowering **w**, because by the providence
2Es 15:23 And a fire went forth from his **w**,
15:30 Also the Carmonians, raging in **w**,
15:34 exceedingly threatening, full of **w** and storm.
15:37 those who see that **w** shall be horror-stricken,
15:39 the cloud that was raised in **w**, and shall dispel it;
15:40 Great and mighty clouds, full of **w** and tempest,
16: 9 Fire will go forth from his **w**,
16:68 burning **w** of a great multitude is kindled over you;
4Mc 4:11 for him and propitiate the **w** of the heavenly army.
9:32 the judgments of the divine **w**."

WRATHFUL (3) [WRATH]
Dt 1:34 LORD heard your words, he was w and swore:
Eze 25:17 great vengeance on them with w punishments.
Na 1: 2 the LORD is avenging and w;

WREATH (2) [IVY-WREATHED, WREATHES, WREATHS]
1Co 9:25 they do it to receive a perishable w,
Sir 32: 2 and receive a w for your excellent leadership.

WREATHES (1) [WREATH]
2Mc 6: 7 they were compelled to wear w of ivy and to walk

WREATHS (5) [WREATH]
1Ki 7:17 with w of chain work for the capitals on the tops of
7:29 there were w of beveled work.
7:30 The supports were cast with w at the side of each.
7:36 where each had space, with w all around.
Jdt 15:13 with her crowned themselves with olive w.

WRECKED (4) [SHIPWRECK, SHIPWRECKED]
1Ki 22:48 for the ships were w at Ezion-geber.
2Ch 20:37 ships were w and were not able to go to Tarshish.
Eze 27:26 The east wind has w you in the heart of the seas.
27:34 you are w by the seas, in the depths of the waters;

WRENCHED (1)
Mk 5: 4 the chains he w apart, and the shackles he broke

WREST (KJV) See DISTORT, INJURE, PERVERT, TWIST

WRESTLED (3) [WRESTLING, WRESTLINGS]
Ge 30: 8 "With mighty wrestlings I have w with my sister,
32:24 and a man w with him until daybreak.
32:25 Jacob's hip was put out of joint as he w with him.

WRESTLING (2) [WRESTLED]
Col 4:12 He is always w in his prayers on your behalf,
2Mc 4:14 in the unlawful proceedings in the w arena after

WRESTLINGS (1) [WRESTLED]
Ge 30: 8 "With mighty w I have wrestled with my sister,

WRETCH (5) [WRETCHED, WRETCHES]
2Mc 7: 9 he said, "You accursed w,
7:34 unholy w, you most defiled of all mortals,
15: 3 the thrice-accursed w asked if there were
3Mc 5:37 "How many times, you poor w,
2Es 15:47 woe to you, miserable w!

WRETCHED (12) [WRETCH]
Nu 20: 5 to bring us to this w place?
Job 29:13 The blessing of the w came upon me,
Ps 88:15 W and close to death from my youth up,
Ro 7:24 W man that I am! Who will rescue me
Rev 3:17 You do not realize that you are w, pitiable, poor,
Bar 4:31 W will be those who mistreated you
4:32 W will be the cities that your children served
4:32 w will be the city that received your offspring.
3Mc 5: 5 and bound the hands of the w people and arranged
2Es 15:51 like a w woman who is beaten and wounded,
4Mc 16: 6 "O how w am I and many times unhappy!
16: 7 fruitless nurturings and w nursings!

WRETCHES (2) [WRETCH]
Mt 21:41 "He will put those w to a miserable death,
4Mc 8:17 "O w that we are and so senseless!

WRING (1) [WRINGING, WRUNG]
Lev 1:15 priest shall bring it to the altar and w off its head,

WRINGING (1) [WRING]
Lev 5: 8 w its head at the nape without severing it.

WRINKLE (1)
Eph 5:27 without a spot or w or anything of the kind—

WRISTS (2)
Eze 13:18 Woe to the women who sew bands on all w,
Ac 12: 7 And the chains fell off his w.

WRIT (1) [WRITE]
Est 8:13 A copy of the w was to be issued as a decree

WRITE (94) [WRIT, WRITER, WRITES, WRITING, WRITINGS, WRITTEN, WROTE]
Ex 17:14 "W this as a reminder in a book and recite it in
34: 1 and I will w on the tablets the words that were on
34:27 The LORD said to Moses: W these words;
Nu 17: 2 W each man's name on his staff,
17: 3 and w Aaron's name on the staff of Levi.
Dt 6: 9 and w them on the doorposts of your house and
10: 2 I will w on the tablets the words that were on
Dt 11:20 W them on the doorposts of your house and
27: 3 You shall w on them all the words of this law
27: 8 You shall w on the stones all the words
31:19 therefore w this song, and teach it to the Israelites;
Jos 18: 8 to w the description of the land, saying, "Go
18: 8 "Go throughout the land and w a description of it,
Ezr 5:10 so that we might w down the names of the men
Est 8: 8 You may w as you please with regard to the Jews,
Job 13:26 For you w bitter things against me,
Pr 3: 3 w them on the tablet of your heart.
7: 3 w them on the tablet of your heart.
Isa 8: 1 a large tablet and w on it in common characters,
10: 1 who w oppressive statutes,
10:19 be so few that a child can w them down.
30: 8 Go now, w it before them on a tablet,
44: 5 yet another will w on the hand, "The LORD's,"
Jer 30: 2 W in a book all the words that I have spoken
31:33 and I will w it on their hearts;
36: 2 and w on it all the words that I have spoken to you
36:17 "Tell us now, how did you w all these words?
36:28 and w on it all the former words that were in
Eze 24: 2 w down the name of this day, this very day.
37:16 take a stick and w on it, "For Judah,
37:16 then take another stick and w on it,
37:20 on which you w are in your hand before their eyes,
43:11 and w it down in their sight,
Hos 8:12 I w for him the multitude of my instructions,
Hab 2: 2 W the vision; make it plain on tablets,
Mk 10: 4 to w a certificate of dismissal and to divorce her."
Lk 1: 3 to w an orderly account for you,
Jn 19:21 chief priests of the Jews said to Pilate, "Do not w,
Ac 15:20 but we should w to them to abstain only
25:26 But I have nothing definite to w to our sovereign
25:26 I may have something to w—
1Co 16:21 I, Paul, w this greeting with my own hand.
2Co 1:13 we w you nothing other than what you can read
9: 1 not necessary for me to w you about the ministry
13:10 So I w these things while I am away from you,
Php 3: 1 To w the same things to you is not troublesome
Col 4:18 I, Paul, w this greeting with my own hand.
1Th 4: 9 you do not need to have anyone w to you,
2Th 3:17 I, Paul, w this greeting with my own hand.
3:17 mark in every letter of mine; it is the way I w.
Heb 8:10 and w them on their hearts, and I will be their God,
10:16 and I will w them on their minds,"
1Jn 2:14 I w to you, children, because you know the Father.
2:14 I w to you, fathers, because you know him who is
2:14 I w to you, young people, because you are strong
2:21 I w to you, not because you do not know the truth,
2:26 I w these things to you concerning those who
5:13 I w these things to you who believe in the name of
2Jn 1:12 Although I have much to w to you,
3Jn 1:13 I have much to w to you, but I would rather not w with pen and ink;
Jude 1: 3 while eagerly preparing to w to you about
1: 3 to w and appeal to you to contend for the faith
Rev 1:11 "W in a book what you see and send it to
1:19 Now w what you have seen, what is,
2: 1 "To the angel of the church in Ephesus w:
2: 8 "And to the angel of the church in Smyrna w:
2:12 "And to the angel of the church in Pergamum w:
2:18 "And to the angel of the church in Thyatira w:
3: 1 "And to the angel of the church in Sardis w:
3: 7 "And to the angel of the church in Philadelphia w:
3:12 I will w on you the name of my God,
3:14 "And to the angel of the church in Laodicea w:
10: 4 the seven thunders had sounded, I was about to w,
10: 4 and do not w it down."
14:13 And I heard a voice from heaven saying, "W this:
19: 9 And the angel said to me, "W this:
21: 5 "W this, for these words are trustworthy and true."
Tob 12:20 W down all these things that have happened
AdE 8: 8 W in my name what you think best and seal it
Sir Pr: 1 also led to w something pertaining to instruction
Bar 2:28 the day when you commanded him to w your law
1Mc 10:24 I also will w them words of encouragement
12:22 please w us concerning your welfare;
12:23 we on our part w to you that your livestock
13:37 a general peace with you and to w to our officials
13:42 and the people began to w in their documents
15:19 to w to the kings and countries that they should
2Mc 2:16 about to celebrate the purification, we w to you.
2Es 12:37 w all these things that you have seen in a book,
14:22 and I will w everything that has happened in
14:24 these five, who are trained to w rapidly;
14:25 until what you are about to w is finished.
14:26 tomorrow at this hour you shall begin to w."

WRITER (1) [WRITE]
Ro 16:22 I Tertius, the w of this letter, greet you in the Lord.

WRITES (4) [WRITE]
Dt 24: 1 and so he w her a certificate of divorce,
24: 3 w her a bill of divorce, puts it in her hand,
Ro 10: 5 Moses w concerning the righteousness that comes
AdE 13: 1 "The Great King, Artaxerxes, w the following to

WRITHE (5) [WRITHED, WRITHES, WRITHING]
Job 15:20 The wicked w in pain all their days,
Jer 4:19 My anguish, my anguish! I w in pain!
Hos 8:10 They shall soon w under the burden of kings and
Mic 4:10 W and groan, O daughter Zion,
Zec 9: 5 Gaza too, and shall w in anguish;

WRITHED (2) [WRITHE]
Isa 26:18 we w, but we gave birth only to wind.
Hab 3:10 The mountains saw you, and w;

WRITHES (2) [WRITHE]
Isa 26:17 who w and cries out in her pangs when she is
Jer 51:29 and w, for the LORD's purposes

WRITHING (1) [WRITHE]
Wis 16: 5 of w serpents, your wrath did not continue to

WRITING‡ (58) [WRITE]
Ex 32:16 and the w was the w of God,
Nu 5:23 Then the priest shall put these curses in w,
Dt 31:24 When Moses had finished w down in a book
Jos 18: 4 w a description of it with a view
1Ch 28:19 "All this, in w at the LORD's direction,
Ne 9:38 of all this we make a firm agreement in w,
Est 9:25 in w that the wicked plot that he had devised
9:32 and it was recorded in w.
Isa 38: 9 A w of King Hezekiah of Judah,
Eze 2:10 it had w on the front and on the back,
9: 2 with a w case at his side.
9: 3 who had the w case at his side;
9:11 man clothed in linen, with the w case at his side,
Da 5: 5 a human hand appeared and began w on the plaster
5: 7 "Whoever can read this w and tell me its
5: 8 not read the w or tell the king the interpretation.
5:15 have been brought in before me to read this w
5:16 to read the w and tell me its interpretation,
5:17 Nevertheless I will read the w to the king
5:24 the hand was sent and this w was inscribed.
5:25 And this is the w that was inscribed:
Zec 5: 3 be cut off according to the w on one side,
5: 3 be cut off according to the w on the other side.
Lk 1:63 He asked for a w tablet and wrote,
1Co 4:14 I am not w this to make you ashamed,
5:11 But now I am w to you not to associate
9:15 am I w this so that they may be applied in my case.
14:37 that what I am w to you is a command of the Lord.
Gal 1:20 In what I am w to you, before God, I do not lie!
6:11 See what large letters I make when I am w
1Ti 3:14 but I am w these instructions to you so that,
Phm 1:19 I, Paul, am w this with my own hand:
1:21 Confident of your obedience, I am w to you,
2Pe 3: 1 beloved, the second letter I am w to you;
1Jn 1: 4 We are w these things so that our joy may
2: 1 I am w these things to you so that you may not sin.
2: 7 Beloved, I am w you no new commandment,
2: 8 Yet I am w you a new commandment that is true
2:12 I am w to you, little children,
2:13 I am w to you, fathers,
2:13 I am w to you, young people,
2Jn 1: 5 not as though I were w you a new commandment,
Tob 7:13 and told her to bring w material;
AdE 8: 9 to the Jews was given in w to the administrators
Sir 39:32 of all this and have thought it out and left it in w:
42: 7 and when you give or receive, put it all in w.
44: 5 who composed musical tunes, or put verses in w;
1Mc 12:21 It has been found in w concerning the Spartans and
2Mc 11:15 which Maccabeus delivered to Lysias in w.
1Es 2: 2 throughout all his kingdom and also put it in w:
3: 9 "When the king wakes, they will give him the w;
3:13 the king awoke, they took the w and gave it to him,
3:15 and the w was read in their presence.
5:55 the decree that they had in w from King Cyrus of
6:12 that we might inform you in w who the leaders are,
3Mc 4:20 the pens they used for w had already given out.
2Es 14:24 But prepare for yourself many w tablets,

WRITINGS (3) [WRITE]
Ro 16:26 the prophetic w is made known to all the Gentiles,
2Ti 3:15 how from childhood you have known the sacred w
2Mc 2:13 the books about the kings and prophets, and the w

WRITTEN‡ (281) [WRITE]
A. WRITTEN IN ... LAW (18)

Ex 24:12 which I have w for their instruction."
31:18 tablets of stone, w with the finger of God.
32:15 tablets that were w on both sides, w on the front and on the back.
32:32 if not, blot me out of the book that you have w."
Dt 9:10 the LORD gave me the two stone tablets w with
17:18 a copy of this law w for him in the presence of
28:58 the words of this law that are w in this book,
29:20 All the curses w in this book will descend on them,
29:21 in accordance with all the curses of the covenant w
29:27 bringing on it every curse w in this book.
30:10 and decrees that are w in this book of the law,
Jos 1: 8 be careful to act in accordance with all that is w
8:31 as it is w in the book of the law of Moses,
8:32 a copy of the law of Moses, which he had w.
8:34 according to all that is w in the book of the law.
10:13 Is this not w in the Book of Jashar?
23: 6 be very steadfast to observe and do all that is w in
2Sa 1:18 it is w in the Book of Jashar.)
1Ki 2: 3 his testimonies, as it is w in the law of Moses, A
11:41 not w in the Book of the Acts of Solomon?
14:19 are w in the Book of the Annals of the Kings
14:29 not w in the Book of the Annals of the Kings
15: 7 not w in the Book of the Annals of the Kings
15:23 not w in the Book of the Annals of the Kings
15:31 not w in the Book of the Annals of the Kings

1Ki 16: 5 not w in the Book of the Annals of the Kings
16:14 not w in the Book of the Annals of the Kings
16:20 not w in the Book of the Annals of the Kings
16:27 not w in the Book of the Annals of the Kings
21:11 as it was w in the letters that she had sent to them,
22:39 not w in the Book of the Annals of the Kings
22:45 not w in the Book of the Annals of the Kings
2Ki 1:18 not w in the Book of the Annals of the Kings
8:23 not w in the Book of the Annals of the Kings
10:34 not w in the Book of the Annals of the Kings
12:19 not w in the Book of the Annals of the Kings
13: 8 not w in the Book of the Annals of the Kings
13:12 not w in the Book of the Annals of the Kings
14: 6 to what is w in the book of the law of Moses,
14:15 not w in the Book of the Annals of the Kings
14:18 not w in the Book of the Annals of the Kings
14:28 not w in the Book of the Annals of the Kings
15: 6 not w in the Book of the Annals of the Kings
15:11 are w in the Book of the Annals of the Kings
15:15 are w in the Book of the Annals of the Kings
15:21 not w in the Book of the Annals of the Kings
15:26 are w in the Book of the Annals of the Kings
15:31 are w in the Book of the Annals of the Kings
15:36 not w in the Book of the Annals of the Kings
16:19 not w in the Book of the Annals of the Kings
20:20 not w in the Book of the Annals of the Kings
21:17 not w in the Book of the Annals of the Kings
21:25 not w in the Book of the Annals of the Kings
22:13 to do according to all that is w concerning us."
23: 3 to perform the words of this covenant that were w
23:24 the words of the law that were w in the book that
23:28 not w in the Book of the Annals of the Kings
24: 5 not w in the Book of the Annals of the Kings
1Ch 9: 1 and these are w in the Book of the Kings of Israel.
16:40 according to all that is w in the law of the LORD A
29:29 are w in the records of the seer Samuel,
2Ch 9:29 are they not w in the history of the prophet Nathan,
12:15 not w in the records of the prophet Shemaiah and
13:22 are w in the story of the prophet Iddo.
16:11 are w in the Book of the Kings of Judah and Israel.
20:34 are w in the Annals of Jehu son of Hanani,
23:18 as it is w in the law of Moses, A
24:27 and of the rebuilding of the house of God are w in
25: 4 according to what is w in the law, A
25:26 are they not w in the Book of the Kings of Judah
27: 7 are w in the Book of the Kings of Israel and Judah.
28:26 are w in the Book of the Kings of Judah and Israel.
31: 3 as it is w in the law of the LORD. A
32:32 are w in the vision of the prophet Isaiah son
33:19 these are w in the records of the seers.
34:21 the LORD, to act in accordance with all that is w
34:24 that are w in the book that was read before the king
34:31 the words of the covenant that were w in this book.
35: 4 following the w directions of King David of Israel
35: 4 of Israel and the w directions of his son Solomon.
35:12 as it is w in the book of Moses.
35:26 in accordance with what is w in the law of the A
35:27 are w in the Book of the Kings of Israel and Judah.
36: 8 are w in the Book of the Kings of Israel and Judah;
36:22 and also declared in a w edict:
Ezr 1: 1 and also in a w edict declared:
4: 7 the letter was w in Aramaic and translated.
5: 7 in which was w as follows:
6: 2 that a scroll was found on which this was w:
6:18 as it is w in the book of Moses.
Ne 6: 6 In it was w, "It is reported among the nations—
7: 5 and I found the following w in it:
8:14 And they found it w in the law, A
8:15 and other leafy trees to make booths, as it is w."
10:34 as it is w in the law. A
10:36 as it is w in the law, A
13: 1 and in it was found w that no Ammonite
Est 1:19 and let it be w among the laws of the Persians and
3:12 was w to the king's satraps and to the governors
3:12 it was w in the name of King Ahasuerus and sealed
4: 8 of the w decree issued in Susa for their destruction,
6: 2 It was found w how Mordecai had told
8: 5 be w to revoke the letters devised by Haman son
8: 8 an edict w in the name of the king and sealed with
8: 9 and an edict was w, according to all that Mordecai
9:23 as Mordecai had w to them.
9:26 Thus because of all that was w in this letter,
9:27 as it was w and at the time appointed.
9:29 gave full w authority, confirming this second letter
10: 2 are they not w in the annals of the kings of Media
Job 19:23 "O that my words were w down!
31:35 Oh, that I had the indictment w by my adversary!
Ps 40: 7 in the scroll of the book it is w of me.
139:16 In your book were w all the days that were formed
Pr 22:20 Have I not w for you thirty sayings of admonition
Isa 65: 6 See, it is w before me: I will not keep silent,
Jer 17: 1 The sin of Judah is w with an iron pen;
25:13 everything w in this book,
36: 6 from the scroll that you have w at my dictation.
36:29 to burn this scroll, saying, Why have you w in it
51:60 all these words that are w concerning Babylon.
Eze 2: 9 and a w scroll was in it.
2:10 and w on it were words of lamentation
Da 9:11 So the curse and the oath w in the law of Moses, A
9:13 Just as it is w in the law of Moses, A
12: 1 everyone who is found w in the book.
Mal 3:16 and a book of remembrance was w before him
Mt 2: 5 for so it has been w by the prophet:
4: 4 But he answered, "It is w, 'One does not live by
4: 6 for it is w, 'He will command his angels
4: 7 Jesus said to him, "Again it is w, 'Do not put
4:10 for it is w, 'Worship the Lord your God,
Mt 11:10 This is the one about whom it is w, 'See,
21:13 He said to them, "It is w, 'My house shall be
26:24 The Son of Man goes as it is w of him,
26:31 for it is w, 'I will strike the shepherd,
Mk 1: 2 As it is w in the prophet Isaiah, "See,
7: 6 as it is w, 'This people honors me with their lips,
9:12 How then is it w about the Son of Man,
9:13 whatever they pleased, as it is w about him."
11:17 He was teaching and saying, "Is it not w,
14:21 For the Son of Man goes as it is w of him,
14:27 for it is w, 'I will strike the shepherd,
Lk 2:23 (as it is w in the law of the Lord, A
3: 4 as it is w in the book of the words of
4: 4 Jesus answered him, "It is w, 'One does not live by
4: 8 Jesus answered him, "It is w, ''Worship the Lord
4:10 for it is w, 'He will command his angels
4:17 the scroll and found the place where it was w:
7:27 This is the one about whom it is w, 'See,
10:20 but rejoice that your names are w in heaven."
10:26 He said to him, "What is w in the law? A
18:31 that is w about the Son of Man by the prophets will
19:46 "It is w, 'My house shall be a house of prayer';
21:22 as a fulfillment of all that is w.
22:37 and indeed what is w about me is being fulfilled."
24:44 that everything w about me in the law of Moses,
24:46 to them, "Thus it is w, that the Messiah is to suffer
Jn 2:17 His disciples remembered that it was w,
6:31 it is w, 'He gave them bread from heaven to eat.' "
6:45 It is w in the prophets, 'And they shall be taught
8:17 In your law it is w that the testimony
10:34 Jesus answered, "Is it not w in your law, A
12:14 and sat on it; as it is w:
12:16 then they remembered that these things had been w
15:25 It was to fulfill the word that is w in their law, A
19:19 also had an inscription w and put on the cross.
19:20 and it was w in Hebrew, in Latin, and in Greek.
19:22 Pilate answered, "What I have w I have w."
20:30 which are not w in this book.
20:31 But these are w so that you may come to believe
21:24 to these things and has w them,
21:25 if every one of them were w down,
21:25 could not contain the books that would be w.
Ac 1:20 "For it is w in the book of Psalms,
7:42 as it is w in the book of the prophets:
13:29 When they had carried out everything that was w
13:33 also it is w in the second psalm, 'You are my Son;
15:15 with the words of the prophets, as it is w,
23: 5 for it is w, 'You shall not speak evil of a leader
24:14 down according to the law or w in the prophets.
Ro 1:17 as it is w, "The one who is righteous will live
2:15 that what the law requires is w on their hearts,
2:24 as it is w, "The name of God is blasphemed among
2:27 that have the w code and circumcision but break
3: 4 let God be proved true, as it is w,
3:10 as it is w: "There is no one who is righteous,
4:17 as it is w, "I have made you the father
4:23 were w not for his sake alone,
7: 6 so that we are slaves not under the old w code but
8:36 As it is w, "For your sake we are being killed all
9:13 As it is w, "I have loved Jacob,
9:33 as it is w, "See, I am laying in Zion a stone
10:15 As it is w, "How beautiful are the feet
11: 8 as it is w, "God gave them a sluggish spirit, eyes
11:26 as it is w, "Out of Zion will come the Deliverer;
12:19 for it is w, "Vengeance is mine, I will repay,
14:11 For it is w, "As I live, says the Lord,
15: 3 For Christ did not please himself; but, as it is w,
15: 4 For whatever was w in former days was w for our
15: 9 As it is w, "Therefore I will confess you among
15:15 on some points I have w to you rather boldly
15:21 but as it is w, "Those who have never been told
1Co 1:19 For it is w, "I will destroy the wisdom of the wise,
1:31 as it is w, "Let the one who boasts,
2: 9 But, as it is w, "What no eye has seen,
3:19 For it is w, "He catches the wise
4: 6 "Nothing beyond what is w,"
9: 9 For it is w in the law of Moses, A
9:10 It was indeed w for our sake,
10: 7 as it is w, "The people sat down to eat and drink,
10:11 and they were w down to instruct us,
14:21 the law it is w, "By people of strange tongues and
15:45 Thus it is w, "The first man, Adam,
15:54 then the saying that is w will be fulfilled:
2Co 3: 2 You yourselves are our letter, w on our hearts,
3: 3 w not with ink but with the Spirit of
8:15 As it is w, "The one who had much did
9: 9 it is w, "He scatters abroad, he gives to the poor;
Gal 3:10 for it is w, "Cursed is everyone who does
3:10 and obey all the things w in the book of the law."
3:13 for it is w, "Cursed is everyone who hangs on
4:22 For it is w that Abraham had two sons,
4:27 For it is w, "Rejoice, you childless one,
1Th 5: 1 you do not need to have anything w to you.
Heb 10: 7 O God' (in the scroll of the book it is w of me)."
13:22 for I have w to you briefly.
1Pe 1:16 for it is w, "You shall be holy, for I am holy."
5:12 I have w this short letter to encourage you and
3Jn 1: 9 I have w something to the church;
Rev 1: 3 and who keep what is w in it;
2:17 and on the white stone is w a new name
5: 1 the throne a scroll w on the inside and on the back,
13: 8 not been w from the foundation of the world in
14: 1 and his Father's name w on their foreheads.
17: 5 and on her forehead was w a name, a mystery:
17: 8 not been w in the book of life from the foundation
20:15 not found w in the book of life was thrown into
21:27 only those who are w in the Lamb's book of life.
Tob 7:12 with the law and decree w in the book of Moses
AdE 3:10 the decree that was to be w against the Jews.
6: 2 He found the words w about Mordecai,
8: 8 for whatever is w at the king's command
8:10 The edict was w with the king's authority
9: 1 which is Adar, the decree w by the king arrived.
9:23 the Jews accepted what Mordecai had w to them
9:26 And so, because of what was w in this letter,
9:32 and it was w for a memorial.
13: 6 the letters w by Haman, who is in charge of affairs
Sir Pr: 1 of learning be able through the spoken and w word
48:10 At the appointed time, it is w,
50:27 in understanding and knowledge I have w
Bar 2: 2 with the threats that were w in the law of Moses. A
1Mc 7:16 in accordance with the word that was w,
8:31 we have w to him as follows,
11:31 to our kinsman Lasthenes we have w to you also,
14:43 and that all contracts in the country should be w
15:15 in which the following was w:
16:24 are w in the annals of his high priesthood,
2Mc 9:25 and I have w to him what is written here.
9:25 and I have written to him what is w here.
11:16 letter w to the Jews by Lysias was to this effect:
1Es 1:11 the offering to the Lord as it is w in the book
1:33 These things are w in the book of the histories of
1:42 are w in the annals of the kings.
2:22 You will find in the annals what has been w
3: 9 the victory shall be given according to what is w."
3:17 "Explain to us what you have w."
4:42 even beyond what is w, and we will give it to you,
6:32 or nullify any of the things herein w,
7: 6 did according to what was w in the book of Moses.
8: 8 a copy of the w commission from King Artaxerxes
3Mc 3:30 The letter was w in the above form.
2Es 4:23 to destruction and the w covenants no longer exist.
14:22 the things that were w in your law, A
14:44 during the forty days, ninety-four books were w.
14:46 but keep the seventy that were w last,
15: 2 and cause them to be w on paper;

WRONG (106) [WRONGDOER, WRONGDOERS, WRONGDOING, WRONGDOINGS, WRONGED, WRONGFUL, WRONGFULLY, WRONGING, WRONGLY, WRONGS]

Ge 16: 5 "May the w done to me be on you!
42:22 "Did I not tell you not to w the boy?
44: 5 You have done w in doing this.' "
50:15 and pays us back in full for all the w that we did
50:17 the crime of your brothers and the w they did
Ex 2:13 and he said to the one who was in the w,
9:27 and I and my people are in the w.
22:21 You shall not w or oppress a resident alien,
Nu 5: 7 The person shall make full restitution for the w,
5: 8 of kin to whom restitution may be made for the w,
5: 8 the restitution for w shall go to the LORD for
Dt 1:39 who today do not yet know right from w,
17: 1 or a sheep that has a defect, anything seriously w;
25: 1 be in the right and the other to be in the w.
25: 2 If the one in the w deserves to be flogged,
Jdg 11:27 but you are the one who does me w by making war
1Sa 24:11 you may know for certain that there is no w
26:21 Then Saul said, "I have done w;
29: 6 for I have found nothing w in you from the day
2Sa 13:16 for this w in sending me away is greater than
19:19 how your servant did w on the day my lord
1Ki 8:47 saying, 'We have sinned, and have done w;
2Ki 7: 9 they said to one another, "What we are doing is w.
18:14 of Assyria at Lachish, saying, "I have done w;
1Ch 12:17 though my hands have done no w,
2Ch 6:37 saying, 'We have sinned, and have done w;
26:18 Go out of the sanctuary; for you have done w,
Ne 13: 7 the w that Eliashib had done on behalf of Tobiah,
Est 1:16 "Not only has Queen Vashti done w to the king,
Job 6:24 make me understand how I have gone w.
6:29 Turn, I pray, let no w be done.
6:30 Is there any w on my tongue?
19: 3 are you not ashamed to w me?
19: 6 know then that God has put me in the w,
21:27 I know your thoughts, and your schemes to w me.
32: 3 though they had declared Job to be in the w.
34:10 and from the Almighty that he should do w.
36:23 or who can say, 'You have done w'?
40: 8 Will you even put me in the w?
Ps 7: 3 if I have done this, if there is w in my hands,
119: 3 who also do no w, but walk in his ways.
125: 3 righteous might not stretch out their hands to do w.
Pr 4:16 For they cannot sleep unless they have done w;
10:23 Doing w is like sport to a fool,
15:22 Without counsel, plans go w,
28:21 yet for a piece of bread a person may do w.
30:20 wipes her mouth, and says, "I have done no w."
Jer 2: 5 What w did your ancestors find in me
22: 3 And do no w or violence to the alien, the orphan,
37:18 "What w have I done to you or your servants
51:24 of Chaldea before your very eyes for all the w
La 3:59 You have seen the w done to me, O LORD;
Eze 18:16 does not w anyone, exacts no pledge,
Da 6:22 and also before you, O king, I have done no w."
9: 5 we have sinned and done w,
Mic 3:10 who build Zion with blood and Jerusalem with w!
Zep 3: 5 The LORD within it is righteous; he does no w.
3:13 they shall do no w and utter no lies,
Mal 1: 8 you offer blind animals in sacrifice, is that not w?
1: 8 that are lame or sick, is that not w?

Mal 2: 6 and no w was found on his lips.
Mt 20:13 'Friend, I am doing you no w;
22:29 Jesus answered them, "You are w,
Mk 12:24 "Is not this the reason you are w,
12:27 but of the living; you are quite w."
Lk 23:41 but this man has done nothing w."
Jn 16: 8 the world w about sin and righteousness
18:23 "If I have spoken wrongly, testify to the w.
Ac 7:26 why do you w each other?'
23: 9 "We find nothing w with this man.
25: 5 and if there is anything w about the man,
25:10 I have done no w to the Jews,
25:11 if I am in the w and have committed something
Ro 13: 4 But if you do what is w, you should be afraid,
13:10 Love does no w to a neighbor;
14:20 it is w for you to make others fall by what you eat;
1Co 6: 8 But you yourselves w and defraud—
2Co 7:12 it was not on account of the one who did the w,
12:13 I myself did not burden you? Forgive me this w!
13: 7 we pray to God that you may not do anything w—
Gal 4:12 You have done me no w.
Col 3:25 be paid back for whatever w has been done,
1Th 4: 6 that no one w or exploit a brother or sister
1Pe 2:14 as sent by him to punish those who do w and
2:20 If you endure when you are beaten for doing w,
2Pe 2:13 suffering the penalty for doing w.
2:15 who loved the wages of doing w,
Tob 8:14 that he was alive and that nothing was w.
12:10 and do w are their own worst enemies.
Jdt 11:11 to anger when they do what is w.
Sir 3:24 and w opinion has impaired their judgment.
7: 2 Stay away from w, and it will turn away from you.
13: 3 A rich person does w, and even adds insults;
13: 3 a poor person suffers w, and must add apologies.
19: 4 and one who sins does w to oneself.
28: 2 Forgive your neighbor the w he has done,
32: 4 do not display your cleverness at the w time.
Bar 2:12 we have been ungodly, we have done w,
1Mc 2:67 and avenge the w done to your people.
6:12 But now I remember the w I did in Jerusalem.
2Mc 3:12 that it was utterly impossible that w should
10:12 to the Jews because of the w that had been done
14:28 when the man had done no w.
3Mc 1:14 And someone answered thoughtlessly that it was w
2Es 8:35 have existed there is no one who has not done w.
4Mc 5: 9 and w to spurn the gifts of nature.

WRONGDOER (2) [DO, WRONG]

Ro 13: 4 It is the servant of God to execute wrath on the w.
Col 3:25 For the w will be paid back

WRONGDOERS (3) [DO, WRONG]

Ps 37: 1 do not be envious of w,
1Co 6: 9 not know that w will not inherit the kingdom
1Mc 9:23 in all parts of Israel; all the w reappeared.

WRONGDOING (14) [DO, WRONG]

Ex 23: 2 You shall not follow a majority in w;
Dt 19:15 of any crime or w in connection with any offense
19:16 witness comes forward to accuse someone of w,
Job 1:22 In all this Job did not sin or charge God with w.
Pr 13: 2 but the desire of the treacherous is for w.
Isa 61: 8 I the LORD love justice, I hate robbery and w;
Hab 1: 3 Why do you make me see w and look at trouble?
1:13 and you cannot look on w;
1Co 13: 6 it does not rejoice in w, but rejoices in the truth.
1Jn 5:17 All w is sin, but there is sin that is not mortal.
Tob 4: 5 and do not walk in the ways of w;
12: 8 with righteousness is better than wealth with w.
Sir 18:27 when sin is all around, one guards against w.
26:29 A merchant can hardly keep from w,

WRONGDOINGS (1) [DO, WRONG]

Ps 99: 8 a forgiving God to them, but an avenger of their w.

WRONGED (11) [WRONG]

Nu 5: 7 and giving it to the one who was w.
Eze 22: 7 the orphan and the widow are w in you.
Ac 7:24 When he saw one of them being w,
1Co 6: 7 Why not rather be w?
2Co 7: 2 we have w no one, we have corrupted no one,
7:12 nor on account of the one who was w,
Phm 1:18 If he has w you in any way, or owes you anything,
Wis 18: 2 though previously w, were doing them no injury;
Sir 35:16 but he will listen to the prayer of one who is w.
LtJ 6:54 or deliver one who is w, for they have no power;
3Mc 3: 8 The Greeks in the city, though w in no way,

WRONGFUL (2) [WRONG]

Ex 20: 7 shall not make w use of the name of the LORD
Dt 5:11 shall not make w use of the name of the LORD

WRONGFULLY (1) [WRONG]

Ps 38:19 and many are those who hate me w.

WRONGING (1) [WRONG]

Ac 7:27 man who was w his neighbor pushed Moses aside,

WRONGLY (4) [WRONG]

Jn 18:23 Jesus answered, "If I have spoken w,
Jas 4: 3 You ask and do not receive, because you ask w,
Wis 14:30 because they thought w about God
4Mc 5:18 our law were not truly divine and we had w held it

WRONGS (7) [WRONG]

Nu 5: 6 When a man or a woman w another,
Ps 58: 2 No, in your hearts you devise w;
69: 5 the w I have done are not hidden from you.
1Mc 7:23 the w that Alcimus and those with him had done
8:31 "Concerning the w that King Demetrius is doing
10: 5 for he will remember all the w that we did to him
10:46 the great w that Demetrius had done in Israel and

WROTE (104) [WRITE]

Ex 24: 4 And Moses w down all the words of the LORD.
34:28 And he w on the tablets the words of the covenant,
39:30 and w on it an inscription,
Nu 33: 2 Moses w down their starting points, stage by stage,
Dt 4:13 and he w them on two stone tablets.
5:22 He w them on two stone tablets,
10: 4 Then he w on the tablets the same words as before,
31: 9 Then Moses w down this law,
31:22 That very day Moses w this song and taught it to
Jos 8:32 Joshua w on the stones a copy of the law of Moses,
24:26 Joshua w these words in the book of the law
1Sa 10:25 and he w them in a book and laid it up before
2Sa 11:14 In the morning David w a letter to Joab,
11:15 In the letter he w, "Set Uriah in the forefront of
1Ki 21: 8 So she w letters in Ahab's name and sealed them
21: 9 She w in the letters, "Proclaim a fast,
2Ki 10: 1 So Jehu w letters and sent them to Samaria,
10: 6 Then he w them a second letter, saying,
17:37 the law and the commandment that he w for you,
2Ch 26:22 the prophet Isaiah son of Amoz w.
30: 1 and w letters also to Ephraim and Manasseh,
32:17 He also w letters to throw contempt on the LORD
Ezr 4: 6 they w an accusation against the inhabitants
4: 7 of their associates w to King Artaxerxes of Persia;
4: 8 Rehum the royal deputy and Shimshai the scribe w
4:10 in the rest of the province Beyond the River w—
Est 8: 5 which he w giving orders to destroy
8:10 He w letters in the name of King Ahasuerus,
Ecc 12:10 and he w words of truth plainly.
Jer 36: 4 and Baruch w on a scroll at Jeremiah's dictation all
36:18 and I w them with ink on the scroll."
36:27 that Baruch w at Jeremiah's dictation, the word of
36:32 who w on it at Jeremiah's dictation all the words
45: 1 when he w these words in a scroll at the dictation
51:60 Jeremiah w in a scroll all the disasters
Da 5: 5 The king was watching the hand as it w.
6:25 Then King Darius w to all peoples and nations
7: 1 Then he w down the dream:
Mk 10: 5 of your hardness of heart he w this commandment
12:19 Moses w for us that 'if a man's brother dies,
Lk 1:63 He asked for a writing tablet and w,
20:28 Moses w for us that if a man's brother dies,
Jn 1:45 in the law and also the prophets w,
5:46 you would believe me, for he w about me.
5:47 But if you do not believe what he w,
8: 6 ⟦bent down and w with his finger on the ground.⟧
8: 8 ⟦once again he bent down and w on the ground.⟧
Ac 1: 1 I w about all that Jesus did and taught from
18:27 and w to the disciples to welcome him.
23:25 He w a letter to this effect:
1Co 5: 9 I w to you in my letter not to associate
7: 1 Now concerning the matters about which you w:
2Co 2: 3 And I w as I did, so that when I came,
2: 4 For I w you out of much distress and anguish
2: 9 I w for this reason: to test you and to know
7:12 So although I w to you,
Eph 3: 3 as I w above in a few words,
2Pe 3:15 also our beloved brother Paul w to you according
Tob 7:13 and he w out a copy of a marriage contract,
Jdt 4: 6 w to the people of Bethulia and Betomesthaim,
AdE 3:12 in accordance with Haman's instructions they w in
8: 5 the letters that Haman w and sent to destroy
9:29 of Aminadab along with Mordecai the Jew w
12: 4 and Mordecai w an account of them.
Bar 1: 1 of Zedekiah son of Hasadiah son of Hilkiah w
1Mc 1:41 the king w to his whole kingdom that all should
1:51 In such words he w to his whole kingdom.
8:22 of the letter that they w in reply, on bronze tablets,
10:17 And he w a letter and sent it to him,
10:56 And now I will do for you as you w,
10:59 Then King Alexander w to Jonathan to come
11:22 and he w Jonathan not to continue the siege,
11:29 and w a letter to Jonathan about all these things;
11:31 This copy of the letter that we w concerning you
11:57 Then the young Antiochus w to Jonathan, saying,
12: 5 a copy of the letter that Jonathan w to the Spartans:
13:35 and w him a letter as follows,
14:18 they w to him on bronze tablets to renew with him
14:27 This is a copy of what they w:
15:22 The consul w the same thing to King Demetrius
16:18 Then Ptolemy w a report about these things
2Mc 1: 7 we Jews w to you, in the critical distress that came
8: 8 with more frequent successes, he w to Ptolemy,
9:18 for himself and w to the Jews the following letter,
14:27 w to Nicanor, stating that he was displeased with
1Es 2:16 w him the following letter,
2:25 in Samaria and Syria and Phoenicia, w as follows:
3: 8 Then each w his own statement,
3:10 The first w, "Wine is strongest."
3:11 The second w, "The king is strongest."
3:12 The third w, "Women are strongest,
4:47 and w letters for him to all the treasurers
4:48 And he w letters to all the governors in Coelesyria
4:49 He w in behalf of all the Jews who were going up
1Es 4:54 He w also concerning their support and
4:55 He w that the support for the Levites should
4:56 He w that land and wages should be provided
6: 7 the local rulers in Syria and Phoenicia, w and sent
6:17 King Cyrus w that this house should be rebuilt.
3Mc 3:11 in his same purpose, w this letter against them:
6:41 and w the following letter for them to the generals
2Es 14:42 and by turns they w what was dictated,
14:42 They sat forty days; they w during the daytime,
14:45 the twenty-four books that you w first,

WROUGHT (2)

2Sa 7:21 you have w all this greatness,
Eze 27:19 w iron, cassia, and sweet cane were bartered

WRUNG (2) [WRING]

Jdg 6:38 he w enough dew from the fleece to fill a bowl
La 1:20 my heart is w within me, because I have been very

XANTHICUS (3)

2Mc 11:30 by the thirtieth of X will have our pledge
11:33 The one hundred forty-eighth year, X fifteenth."
11:38 The one hundred forty-eighth year, X fifteenth."

YAH, YAMIN, YAPHT See Index to Footnotes

YAHWEH See †LORD, †LORD'S

YARD (5) [COURTYARD, COURTYARDS]

Eze 41:12 The building that was facing the temple y on
41:13 and the y and the building with its walls,
41:14 the width of the east front of the temple and the y,
41:15 the depth of the building facing the y at the west,
42: 1 to the chambers that were opposite the temple y

YARDS (1)

Jn 21: 8 not far from the land, only about a hundred y off.

YARN (7) [YARNS]

Ex 35:23 or purple or crimson y or fine linen or goats' hair
39:22 the robe of the ephod woven all of blue y;
Lev 14: 4 and cedarwood and crimson y and hyssop
14: 6 the cedarwood and the crimson y and the hyssop,
14:49 with cedarwood and crimson y and hyssop,
14:51 the cedarwood and the hyssop and the crimson y,
14:52 with the cedarwood and hyssop and crimson y;

YARNS (25) [YARN]

Ex 25: 4 purple, and crimson y and fine linen, goats' hair,
26: 1 and blue, purple, and crimson y;
26:31 purple, and crimson y, and of fine twisted linen;
26:36 purple, and crimson y, and of fine twisted linen,
27:16 purple, and crimson y, and of fine twisted linen,
28: 5 blue, purple, and crimson y, and fine linen.
28: 6 purple, and crimson y, and of fine twisted linen,
28: 8 purple, and crimson y, and of fine twisted linen.
28:15 of gold, of blue and purple and crimson y,
28:33 purple, and crimson y, all around the lower hem,
35: 6 purple, and crimson y, and fine linen;
35:25 in blue and purple and crimson y and fine linen;
35:35 and crimson y, and in fine linen, or by a weaver—
36: 8 and blue, purple, and crimson y,
36:35 purple, and crimson y, and fine twisted linen,
36:37 purple, and crimson y, and fine twisted linen,
38:18 purple, and crimson y and fine twisted linen.
38:23 and embroiderer in blue, purple, and crimson y,
39: 1 crimson y they made finely worked vestments,
39: 2 purple, and crimson y, and of fine twisted linen.
39: 3 and crimson y and into the fine twisted linen,
39: 5 purple, and crimson y, and of fine twisted linen;
39: 8 purple, and crimson y, and of fine twisted linen.
39:24 purple, and crimson y, and of fine twisted linen.
39:29 and crimson y, embroidered with needlework;

YAWNING (1)

Wis 19:17 when, surrounded by y darkness,

YEA (KJV) See YES, INDEED

YEAR‡ (451) [THREE-YEAR-OLD, YEAR'S, YEAR-OLD, YEARLING, YEARLINGS, YEARLY, YEARS]

A. SEVENTH YEAR (23)
B. FIRST YEAR (17)
C. EVERY YEAR (11)

Ge 7:11 In the six hundredth **y** of Noah's life,
8:13 In the six hundred first **y**, in the first month,
14: 4 but in the thirteenth **y** they rebelled.
14: 5 In the fourteenth **y** Chedorlaomer and
17:21 to you at this season next **y**."
26:12 and in the same **y** reaped a hundredfold.
47:17 That **y** he supplied them with food in exchange
47:18 When that **y** was ended, they came to him the following **y**,
Ex 12: 2 it shall be the first month of the **y** for you.
13:10 at its proper time from **y** to **y**.
23:11 the seventh **y** you shall let it rest and lie fallow, A
23:14 Three times in the **y** you shall hold a festival
23:16 the festival of ingathering at the end of the **y**,
23:17 Three times in the **y** all your males shall appear
23:29 I will not drive them out from before you in one **y**,
29:38 two lambs a **y** old regularly each day.
30:10 a **y** Aaron shall perform the rite of atonement
30:10 the atonement for it once a **y** with the blood of
34:22 and the festival of ingathering at the turn of the **y**.
34:23 Three times in the **y** all your males shall appear
34:24 before the LORD your God three times in the **y**.
40:17 In the first month in the second **y**,
Lev 12: 6 a lamb in its first **y** for a burnt offering, B
14:10 and one ewe lamb in its first **y** without blemish, B
16:34 the people of Israel once in the **y** for all their sins.
19:24 In the fourth **y** all their fruit shall be set apart
19:25 But in the fifth **y** you may eat of their fruit,
23:12 you shall offer a lamb a **y** old, without blemish,
23:18 the bread seven lambs a **y** old without blemish,
23:19 and two male lambs a **y** old as a sacrifice
23:41 as a festival to the LORD seven days in the **y**;
25: 4 but in the seventh **y** there shall be a sabbath A
25: 5 it shall be a **y** of complete rest for the land.
25:10 the fiftieth **y** and you shall proclaim liberty
25:11 That fiftieth **y** shall be a jubilee for you:
25:13 In this **y** of jubilee you shall return,
25:20 What shall we eat in the seventh **y**, A
25:21 I will order my blessing for you in the sixth **y**,
25:22 When you sow in the eighth **y**,
25:22 until the ninth **y**, when its produce comes in,
25:28 with the purchaser until the **y** of jubilee;
25:29 be redeemed until a **y** has elapsed since its sale;
25:29 the right of redemption shall be one **y**.
25:30 If it is not redeemed before a full **y** has elapsed,
25:40 They shall serve with you until the **y** of the jubilee.
25:50 from the **y** when they sold themselves to the alien until the jubilee **y**;
25:52 until the jubilee **y**, they shall compute thus:
25:53 by the **y** they shall be under the alien's authority,
25:54 with them shall go free in the jubilee **y**.
27:17 person consecrates the field as of the **y** of jubilee,
27:18 for it according to the years that remain until the **y**
27:23 the proportionate assessment up to the **y** of jubilee,
27:24 In the **y** of jubilee the field shall return to the one
Nu 1: 1 in the second **y** after they had come out of the land
6:12 and bring a male lamb a **y** old as a guilt offering.
6:14 a **y** old without blemish as a burnt offering,
6:14 a **y** old without blemish as a sin offering,
7:15 one male lamb a **y** old, for a burnt offering;
7:17 five male goats, and five male lambs a **y** old.
7:21 one male lamb a **y** old, as a burnt offering;
7:23 five male goats, and five male lambs a **y** old.
7:27 one male lamb a **y** old, for a burnt offering;
7:29 five male goats, and five male lambs a **y** old.
7:33 one male lamb a **y** old, for a burnt offering;
7:35 five male goats, and five male lambs a **y** old.
7:39 one male lamb a **y** old, for a burnt offering;
7:41 five male goats, and five male lambs a **y** old
7:45 one male lamb a **y** old, for a burnt offering;
7:47 five male goats, and five male lambs a **y** old.
7:51 one male lamb a **y** old, for a burnt offering;
7:53 five male goats, and five male lambs a **y** old.
7:57 one male lamb a **y** old, for a burnt offering;
7:59 five male goats, and five male lambs a **y** old.
7:63 one male lamb a **y** old, for a burnt offering;
7:65 five male goats, and five male lambs a **y** old.
7:69 one male lamb a **y** old, for a burnt offering;
7:71 five male goats, and five male lambs a **y** old.
7:75 one male lamb a **y** old, for a burnt offering;
7:77 five male goats, and five male lambs a **y** old.
7:81 one male lamb a **y** old, for a burnt offering;
7:83 five male goats, and five male lambs a **y** old.
7:87 twelve rams, twelve male lambs a **y** old,
7:88 the male goats sixty, the male lambs a **y** old sixty.
9: 1 of the second **y** after they had come out of the land
10:11 In the second **y**, in the second month,
14:34 for every day a **y**, you shall bear your iniquity,
15:27 a female goat a **y** old for a sin offering.
28: 3 two male lambs a **y** old without blemish, daily,
28: 9 two male lambs a **y** old without blemish,
28:11 seven male lambs a **y** old without blemish;
28:14 of every month throughout the months of the **y**.
28:19 one ram, and seven male lambs a **y** old;
28:27 one ram, seven male lambs a **y** old.
29: 2 seven male lambs a **y** old without blemish.
Nu 29: 8 one ram, seven male lambs a **y** old
29:13 two rams, fourteen male lambs a **y** old.
29:17 fourteen male lambs a **y** old without blemish,
29:20 fourteen male lambs a **y** old without blemish,
29:23 fourteen male lambs a **y** old without blemish,
29:26 fourteen male lambs a **y** old without blemish,
29:29 fourteen male lambs a **y** old without blemish,
29:32 fourteen male lambs a **y** old without blemish,
29:36 seven male lambs a **y** old without blemish,
33:38 in the fortieth **y** after the Israelites had come out of
Dt 1: 3 In the fortieth **y**, on the first day of
11:12 from the beginning of the **y** to the end of the **y**.
14:28 Every third **y** you shall bring out the full tithe of produce for that **y**, and store it within your towns;
15: 1 Every seventh **y** you shall grant a remission A
15: 9 thinking, "The seventh **y**, the **y** of remission, A
15: 9 thinking, "The seventh year, the **y** of remission,
15:12 in the seventh **y** you shall set that person free. A
15:20 presence of the LORD your God **y** by **y** at the place
16:16 Three times a **y** all your males shall appear before
24: 5 He shall be free at home one **y**,
26:12 of your produce in the third **y** (which is the **y** of
31:10 Moses commanded them: "Every seventh **y**, A
31:10 in the scheduled **y** of remission,
Jos 5:12 they ate the crops of the land of Canaan that **y**.
Jdg 10: 8 they crushed and oppressed the Israelites that **y**.
11:40 for four days every **y** the daughters C
17:10 and I will give you ten pieces of silver a **y**,
1Sa 1: 3 to go up **y** by **y** from his town to worship and
1: 7 So it went on **y** by **y**;
2:19 for him a little robe and take it to him each **y**,
7:16 He went on a circuit **y** by **y** to Bethel, Gilgal,
27: 7 of the Philistines was one **y** and four months.
2Sa 11: 1 In the spring of the **y**, the time when kings go out
14:26 of his head (for at the end of every **y** he used C
21: 1 **y** after **y**; and David inquired of the LORD.
1Ki 4: 7 to make provision for one month in the **y**.
5:11 Solomon gave this to Hiram **y** by **y**.
6: 1 In the four hundred eightieth **y** after the Israelites
6: 1 in the fourth **y** of Solomon's reign over Israel,
6:37 In the fourth **y** the foundation of the house of
6:38 In the eleventh **y**, in the month of Bul,
9:25 a **y** Solomon used to offer up burnt offerings
10:14 in one **y** was six hundred sixty-six talents of gold,
10:25 spices, horses, and mules, so much **y** by **y**.
14:25 In the fifth **y** of King Rehoboam,
15: 1 the eighteenth **y** of King Jeroboam son of Nebat,
15: 9 In the twentieth **y** of King Jeroboam of Israel,
15:25 over Israel in the second **y** of King Asa of Judah;
15:28 So Baasha killed Nadab in the third **y** of King Asa
15:33 In the third **y** of King Asa of Judah,
16: 8 In the twenty-sixth **y** of King Asa of Judah,
16:10 in the twenty-seventh **y** of King Asa of Judah,
16:15 In the twenty-seventh **y** of King Asa of Judah,
16:23 In the thirty-first **y** of King Asa of Judah,
16:29 In the thirty-eighth **y** of King Asa of Judah,
18: 1 in the third **y** of the drought, saying, "Go,
22: 2 But in the third **y** King Jehoshaphat of Judah came
22:41 over Judah in the fourth **y** of King Ahab of Israel.
22:51 to reign over Israel in Samaria in the seventeenth **y**
2Ki 1:17 the second **y** of King Jehoram son of Jehoshaphat
3: 1 In the eighteenth **y** of King Jehoshaphat of Judah,
8:16 In the fifth **y** of King Joram son of Ahab of Israel,
8:25 the twelfth **y** of King Joram son of Ahab of Israel,
8:26 he reigned one **y** in Jerusalem.
9:29 In the eleventh **y** of Joram son of Ahab,
11: 4 the seventh **y** Jehoiada summoned the captains A
12: 1 In the seventh **y** of Jehu, Jehoash began to reign; A
12: 6 But by the twenty-third **y** of King Jehoash
13: 1 In the twenty-third **y** of King Joash son of Ahaziah
13:10 In the thirty-seventh **y** of King Joash of Judah,
13:20 to invade the land in the spring of the **y**.
14: 1 the second **y** of King Joash son of Joahaz of Israel,
14:23 In the fifteenth **y** of King Amaziah son of Joash
15: 1 In the twenty-seventh **y** of King Jeroboam
15: 8 In the thirty-eighth **y** of King Azariah of Judah,
15:13 in the thirty-ninth **y** of King Uzziah of Judah;
15:17 In the thirty-ninth **y** of King Azariah of Judah,
15:23 In the fiftieth **y** of King Azariah of Judah,
15:27 In the fifty-second **y** of King Azariah of Judah,
15:30 in the twentieth **y** of Jotham son of Uzziah.
15:32 In the second **y** of King Pekah son of Remaliah
16: 1 In the seventeenth **y** of Pekah son of Remaliah,
17: 1 In the twelfth **y** of King Ahaz of Judah,
17: 4 as he had done **y** by **y**;
17: 6 In the ninth **y** of Hoshea the king
18: 1 the third **y** of King Hoshea son of Elah of Israel,
18: 9 In the fourth **y** of King Hezekiah,
18: 9 which was the seventh **y** of King Hoshea A
18:10 In the sixth **y** of Hezekiah,
18:10 which was the ninth **y** of King Hoshea of Israel,
18:13 In the fourteenth **y** of King Hezekiah,
19:29 This **y** you shall eat what grows of itself,
19:29 and in the second **y** what springs from that;
19:29 then in the third **y** sow, reap, plant vineyards,
22: 3 In the eighteenth **y** of King Josiah,
23:23 but in the eighteenth **y** of King
24:12 of Babylon took him prisoner in the eighth **y**
25: 1 And in the ninth **y** of his reign, in the tenth month,
25: 2 So the city was besieged until the eleventh **y**
25: 8 the nineteenth **y** of King Nebuchadnezzar, king
25:27 In the thirty-seventh **y** of the exile
25:27 in the **y** that he began to reign,
1Ch 20: 1 In the spring of the **y**,
26:31 the fortieth **y** of David's reign search was made,
27: 1 month after month throughout the **y**,
2Ch 3: 2 the second day of the second month of the fourth **y**
2Ch 9:13 in one **y** was six hundred sixty-six talents of gold,
9:24 spices, horses, and mules, so much **y** by **y**.
12: 2 In the fifth **y** of King Rehoboam,
13: 1 In the eighteenth **y** of King Jeroboam,
15:10 at Jerusalem in the third month of the fifteenth **y**
15:19 And there was no more war until the thirty-fifth **y**
16: 1 In the thirty-sixth **y** of the reign of Asa,
16:12 In the thirty-ninth **y** of his reign Asa was diseased
16:13 dying in the forty-first **y** of his reign.
17: 7 In the third **y** of his reign he sent his officials,
22: 2 he reigned one **y** in Jerusalem.
23: 1 But in the seventh **y** Jehoiada took courage, A
24: 5 **y** by **y**; and see that you act quickly."
24:23 of the **y** the army of Aram came up against Joash.
27: 5 that **y** one hundred talents of silver,
29: 3 In the first **y** of his reign, in the first month, B
34: 3 For in the eighth **y** of his reign,
34: 3 and in the twelfth **y** he began to purge Judah
34: 8 In the eighteenth **y** of his reign,
35:19 In the eighteenth **y** of the reign
36:10 the **y** King Nebuchadnezzar sent and brought him
36:22 In the first **y** of King Cyrus of Persia, B
Ezr 1: 1 In the first **y** of King Cyrus of Persia, B
3: 8 the second **y** after their arrival at the house of God
4: 6 In the reign of Ahasuerus, in his accession **y**,
4:24 the second **y** of the reign of King Darius of Persia.
5:13 Cyrus of Babylon, in the first **y** of his reign, B
6: 3 In the first **y** of his reign, B
6:15 in the sixth **y** of the reign of King Darius.
7: 7 in the seventh **y** of King Artaxerxes. A
7: 8 which was in the seventh **y** of the king. A
Ne 1: 1 In the month of Chislev, in the twentieth **y**,
2: 1 in the twentieth **y** of King Artaxerxes,
5:14 from the twentieth **y** to the thirty-second **y**
10:31 and we will forego the crops of the seventh **y** A
10:34 by ancestral houses, at appointed times, **y** by **y**,
10:35 **y** by **y**, to the house of the LORD;
13: 6 for in the thirty-second **y** of King Artaxerxes
Est 1: 3 in the third **y** of his reign,
2:16 in the seventh **y** of his reign, A
3: 7 in the twelfth **y** of King Ahasuerus,
9:21 also the fifteenth day of the same month, **y** by **y**,
9:27 to observe these two days every **y**, C
Job 3: 6 let it not rejoice among the days of the **y**;
Ps 65:11 You crown the **y** with your bounty;
Isa 6: 1 In the **y** that King Uzziah died,
14:28 In the **y** that King Ahaz died this oracle came:
20: 1 In the **y** that the commander-in-chief,
21:16 For thus the Lord said to me: Within a **y**,
29: 1 Add **y** to **y**; let the festivals run their round.
32:10 In little more than a **y** you will shudder,
34: 8 a **y** of vindication by Zion's cause.
36: 1 In the fourteenth **y** of King Hezekiah,
37:30 This **y** eat what grows of itself,
37:30 and in the second **y** what springs from that;
37:30 then in the third **y** sow, reap, plant vineyards,
61: 2 to proclaim the **y** of the LORD's favor,
63: 4 and the **y** for my redeeming work had come.
Jer 1: 2 in the thirteenth **y** of his reign.
1: 3 of the eleventh **y** of King Zedekiah son of Josiah
11:23 the **y** of their punishment.
17: 8 in the **y** of drought it is not anxious,
23:12 for I will bring disaster upon them in the **y**
25: 1 in the fourth **y** of King Jehoiakim son of Josiah
25: 1 the first **y** of King Nebuchadrezzar of Babylon), B
25: 3 from the thirteenth **y** of King Josiah son of Amon
28: 1 In that same **y**, at the beginning of the reign
28: 1 in the fifth month of the fourth **y**,
28:16 Within this **y** you will be dead,
28:17 In that same **y**, in the seventh month,
32: 1 from the LORD in the tenth **y** of King Zedekiah
32: 1 which was the eighteenth **y** of Nebuchadrezzar.
34:14 "Every seventh **y** each of you A
36: 1 In the fourth **y** of King Jehoiakim son of Josiah
36: 9 In the fifth **y** of King Jehoiakim son of Josiah
39: 1 In the ninth **y** of King Zedekiah of Judah,
39: 2 in the eleventh **y** of Zedekiah,
45: 1 in the fourth **y** of King Jehoiakim son of Josiah
46: 2 in the fourth **y** of King Jehoiakim son of Josiah
48:44 For I will bring these things upon Moab in the **y**
51:46 one **y** one rumor comes, the next **y** another,
51:59 in the fourth **y** of his reign.
52: 4 And in the ninth **y** of his reign, in the tenth month,
52: 5 So the city was besieged until the eleventh **y**
52:12 the nineteenth **y** of King Nebuchadrezzar, king
52:28 into exile: in the seventh **y**, A
52:29 in the eighteenth **y** of Nebuchadrezzar he took
52:30 in the twenty-third **y** of Nebuchadrezzar,
52:31 In the thirty-seventh **y** of the exile
52:31 in the **y** he began to reign,
Eze 1: 1 In the thirtieth **y**, in the fourth month,
1: 2 On the fifth day of the month (it was the fifth **y** of
4: 6 forty days I assign you, one day for each **y**.
8: 1 In the sixth **y**, in the sixth month,
20: 1 In the seventh **y**, in the fifth month, A
24: 1 In the ninth **y**, in the tenth month,
26: 1 In the eleventh **y**, on the first day of the month,
29: 1 In the tenth **y**, in the tenth month,
29:17 In the twenty-seventh **y**, in the first month,
30:20 In the eleventh **y**, in the first month,
31: 1 In the eleventh **y**, in the third month,
32: 1 In the twelfth **y**, in the twelfth month,
32:17 In the twelfth **y**, in the first month,
33:21 In the twelfth **y** of our exile, in the tenth month,
40: 1 In the twenty-fifth **y** of our exile,
40: 1 at the beginning of the **y**,
40: 1 in the fourteenth **y** after the city was struck down,

Eze 46:17 it shall be his to the y of liberty;
Da 1: 1 In the third y of the reign of King Jehoiakim
1:21 And Daniel continued there until the first y B
2: 1 In the second y of Nebuchadnezzar's reign,
7: 1 In the first y of King Belshazzar of Babylon, B
8: 1 In the third y of the reign of King Belshazzar
9: 1 In the first y of Darius son of Ahasuerus, B
9: 2 in the first y of his reign, B
10: 1 In the third y of King Cyrus of Persia
11: 1 As for me, in the first y of Darius the Mede, B
Mic 6: 6 with burnt offerings, with calves a y old?
Hag 1: 1 In the second y of King Darius, in the sixth month,
1:15 In the second y of King Darius,
2:10 in the second y of Darius,
Zec 1: 1 In the eighth month, in the second y of Darius,
1: 7 the month of Shebat, in the second y of Darius,
7: 1 In the fourth y of King Darius,
14:16 that have come against Jerusalem shall go up y
14:16 against Jerusalem shall go up year after y
Lk 2:41 Now every y his parents went to Jerusalem for C
3: 1 In the fifteenth y of the reign of Emperor Tiberius,
4:19 to proclaim the y of the Lord's favor."
13: 8 He replied, 'Sir, let it alone for one more y,
13: 9 If it bears fruit next y, well and good;
Jn 11:49 one of them, Caiaphas, who was high priest that y,
11:51 that y he prophesied that Jesus was about to die
18:13 of Caiaphas, the high priest that y.
Ac 11:26 for an entire y they met with the church and taught
18:11 He stayed there a y and six months,
2Co 8:10 for you who began last y not only to do something
9: 2 saying that Achaia has been ready since last y;
Heb 9: 7 priest goes into the second, and he but once a y,
9:25 the high priest enters the Holy Place y after y
10: 1 sacrifices that are continually offered y after y,
10: 3 these sacrifices there is a reminder of sin y after y.
Jas 4:13 to such and such a town and spend a y there,
Rev 9:15 the month, and the y, to kill a third of humankind.
Tob 1: 8 I would bring it and give it to them in the third y,
Jdt 1: 1 the twelfth y of the reign of Nebuchadnezzar,
1:13 In the seventeenth y he led his forces
2: 1 In the eighteenth y, on the twenty-second day of
AdE 1: 3 in the third y of his reign,
2:16 which is Adar, in the seventh y of his reign. A
3: 7 In the twelfth y of King Artaxerxes Haman came
8: 9 that is, Nisan, in the same y;
11: 1 the fourth y of the reign of Ptolemy and Cleopatra,
11: 2 the second y of the reign of Artaxerxes the Great,
13: 6 of the twelfth month, Adar, of this present y,
Wis 7:19 cycles of the y and the constellations of the stars,
Sir Pr: 3 When I came to Egypt in the thirty-eighth y of
33: 7 when all the daylight in the y is from the sun?
47:10 and arranged their times throughout the y,
Bar 1: 2 in the fifth y, on the seventh day of the month,
Sus 1: 5 That y two elders from the people were appointed
1Mc 1:10 the one hundred thirty-seventh y of the kingdom
1:20 in the one hundred forty-third y.
1:54 in the one hundred forty-fifth y,
2:70 in the one hundred forty-sixth y and was buried in
3:37 in the one hundred and forty-seventh y.
4:28 next y he mustered sixty thousand picked infantry
4:52 in the one hundred forty-eighth y,
4:59 the assembly of Israel determined that every y at C
6:16 in the one hundred forty-ninth y.
6:20 the citadel in the one hundred fiftieth y;
6:49 since it was a sabbatical y for the land.
6:53 because it was the seventh y; A
7: 1 In the one hundred fifty-first y Demetrius son
7:49 be celebrated each y on the thirteenth day of Adar.
8: 4 the rest paid them tribute every y. C
8:16 They trust one man each y to rule over them and
9: 3 of the one hundred fifty-second y they encamped
9:54 In the one hundred and fifty-third y,
10: 1 the one hundred sixtieth y Alexander Epiphanes,
10:21 the seventh month of the one hundred sixtieth y,
10:42 of silver that my officials have received every y C
10:57 to Ptolemais in the one hundred sixty-second y.
10:67 In the one hundred sixty-fifth y Demetrius son
11:19 in the one hundred sixty-seventh y.
11:34 that the king formerly received from them each y,
13:41 In the one hundred seventieth y the yoke of
13:42 "In the first y of Simon the great high priest B
13:51 in the one hundred seventy-first y,
13:52 that every y they should celebrate this day C
14: 1 one hundred seventy-second y King Demetrius
14:27 in the one hundred seventy-second y,
14:27 which is the third y of the great high priest Simon,
15:10 one hundred seventy-fourth y Antiochus set out
16:14 in the one hundred seventy-seventh y,
2Mc 1: 7 in the one hundred sixty-ninth y,
1: 9 in the one hundred eighty-eighth y.
6:24 that Eleazar in his ninetieth y had gone over to
10: 8 of the Jews should observe these days every y. C
11: 3 to put up the high priesthood for sale every y. C
11:21 The one hundred forty-eighth y,
11:33 one hundred forty-eighth y, Xanthicus fifteenth."
11:38 one hundred forty-eighth y, Xanthicus fifteenth."
13: 1 the one hundred forty-ninth y word came to Judas
14: 4 in about the one hundred fifty-first y,
1Es 1:22 In the eighteenth y of the reign
1:45 A y later Nebuchadnezzar sent and removed him
2: 1 In the first y of Cyrus as king of the Persians, B
2:30 the temple in Jerusalem stopped until the second y
4:51 a y should be given for the building of the temple
4:52 and an additional ten talents a y for burnt offerings
5: 6 in the second y of his reign, in the month of Nisan,
5:56 In the second y after their coming to the temple
5:57 the new moon of the second month in the second y
1Es 6: 1 Now in the second y of the reign of Darius,
6:17 the first y that Cyrus reigned over the country B
6:24 the first y of the reign of King Cyrus, he ordered B
6:30 regularly every y, without quibbling, C
7: 5 in the sixth y of King Darius.
8: 6 in the seventh y of the reign of Artaxerxes, A
8: 6 the fifth month (this was the king's seventh y); A
3Mc 1:11 and he only once a y—
2Es 3: 1 In the thirtieth y after the destruction of the city,
6:21 Children a y old shall speak with their voices,
13:45 a journey of a y and a half;
4Mc 2: 8 to cancel the debt when the seventh y arrives. A

YEAR'S (1) [YEAR]

1Mc 3:28 He opened his coffers and gave a y pay

YEAR-OLD (1) [OLD, YEAR]

Ex 12: 5 Your lamb shall be without blemish, a y male;

YEARLING (1) [YEAR]

Eze 46:13 He shall provide a lamb, a y, without blemish,

YEARLINGS (1) [YEAR]

Lev 9: 3 a calf and a lamb, y without blemish,

YEARLY (7) [YEAR]

Dt 14:22 of all the yield of your seed that is brought in y
Jdg 21:19 y festival of the LORD is taking place at Shiloh,
1Sa 1:21 up to offer to the LORD the y sacrifice,
2:19 up with her husband to offer the y sacrifice.
20: 6 for there is a y sacrifice there for all the family.'
Ne 10:32 the obligation to charge ourselves y one-third of
1Mc 10:40 I also grant fifteen thousand shekels of silver y

YEARNED (1) [YEARNING]

SS 5: 4 and my inmost being y for him.

YEARNING (4) [YEARNED, YEARNS]

2Sa 13:39 And the heart of the king went out, y for Absalom;
Isa 63:15 The y of your heart and your compassion?
Wis 15: 5 whose appearance arouses y in fools,
4Mc 15:13 y of parents toward offspring,

YEARNS (2) [YEARNING]

Isa 26: 9 My soul y for you in the night,
Jas 4: 5 "God y jealously for the spirit that he has made

YEARS‡ (583) [YEAR]

A. FORTY YEARS (41)
B. THREE YEARS (34)
C. SEVEN YEARS (32)

Ge 1:14 be for signs and for seasons and for days and y,
5: 3 When Adam had lived one hundred thirty y,
5: 4 the father of Seth were eight hundred y;
5: 5 that Adam lived were nine hundred thirty y;
5: 6 When Seth had lived one hundred five y,
5: 7 after the birth of Enosh eight hundred seven y,
5: 8 the days of Seth were nine hundred twelve y;
5: 9 When Enosh had lived ninety y,
5:10 after the birth of Kenan eight hundred fifteen y,
5:11 the days of Enosh were nine hundred five y;
5:12 When Kenan had lived seventy y,
5:13 the birth of Mahalalel eight hundred and forty y,
5:14 the days of Kenan were nine hundred and ten y;
5:15 When Mahalalel had lived sixty-five y,
5:16 after the birth of Jared eight hundred thirty y,
5:17 of Mahalalel were eight hundred ninety-five y;
5:18 Jared had lived one hundred sixty-two y
5:19 after the birth of Enoch eight hundred y,
5:20 the days of Jared were nine hundred sixty-two y;
5:21 When Enoch had lived sixty-five y,
5:22 after the birth of Methuselah three hundred y,
5:23 the days of Enoch were three hundred sixty-five y.
5:25 Methuselah had lived one hundred eighty-seven y,
5:26 the birth of Lamech seven hundred eighty-two y,
5:27 of Methuselah were nine hundred sixty-nine y;
5:28 Lamech had lived one hundred eighty-two y,
5:30 after the birth of Noah five hundred ninety-five y,
5:31 of Lamech were seven hundred seventy-seven y;
5:32 After Noah was five hundred y old,
6: 3 their days shall be one hundred twenty y."
7: 6 Noah was six hundred y old when the flood
9:28 After the flood Noah lived three hundred fifty y.
9:29 All the days of Noah were nine hundred fifty y;
11:10 When Shem was one hundred y old,
11:10 he became the father of Arpachshad two y after
11:11 after the birth of Arpachshad five hundred y,
11:12 When Arpachshad had lived thirty-five y,
11:13 after the birth of Shelah four hundred three y,
11:14 When Shelah had lived thirty y,
11:15 after the birth of Eber four hundred three y,
11:16 When Eber had lived thirty-four y,
11:17 after the birth of Peleg four hundred thirty y,
11:18 When Peleg had lived thirty y,
11:19 after the birth of Reu two hundred nine y,
11:20 When Reu had lived thirty-two y,
11:21 after the birth of Serug two hundred seven y,
11:22 When Serug had lived thirty y,
11:23 after the birth of Nahor two hundred y,
11:24 When Nahor had lived twenty-nine y,
11:25 after the birth of Terah one hundred nineteen y,
Ge 11:26 When Terah had lived seventy y,
11:32 The days of Terah were two hundred five y;
12: 4 Abram was seventy-five y old when he departed
14: 4 Twelve y they had served Chedorlaomer,
15: 9 He said to him, "Bring me a heifer three y old, B
15: 9 a female goat three y old, a ram three years old, B
15: 9 a female goat three years old, a ram three y old, B
15:13 and they shall be oppressed for four hundred y;
16: 3 after Abram had lived ten y in the land of Canaan,
16:16 Abram was eighty-six y old when Hagar bore
17: 1 When Abram was ninety-nine y old,
17:17 a child be born to a man who is a hundred y old?
17:17 Can Sarah, who is ninety y old, bear a child?"
17:24 Abraham was ninety-nine y old when he was
17:25 And his son Ishmael was thirteen y old
21: 5 a hundred y old when his son Isaac was born
23: 1 Sarah lived one hundred twenty-seven y;
24: 1 Now Abraham was old, well advanced in y;
25: 7 Abraham's life, one hundred seventy-five y.
25: 8 died in a good old age, an old man and full of y,
25:17 one hundred thirty-seven y;
25:20 Isaac was forty y old when he married Rebekah, A
25:26 Isaac was sixty y old when she bore them.
26:34 When Esau was forty y old, A
29:18 so he said, "I will serve you seven y C
29:20 So Jacob served seven y for Rachel, C
29:27 also in return for serving me another seven y." C
29:30 He served Laban for another seven y. C
31:38 These twenty y I have been with you;
31:41 These twenty y I have been in your house;
31:41 I served you fourteen y for your two daughters,
31:41 for your two daughters, and six y for your flock,
35:28 Now the days of Isaac were one hundred eighty y.
37: 2 Joseph, being seventeen y old,
41: 1 After two whole y, Pharaoh dreamed
41:26 The seven good cows are seven y, C
41:26 and the seven good ears are seven y; C
41:27 that came up after them are seven y, C
41:27 They are seven y of famine. C
41:29 There will come seven y of great plenty C
41:30 After them there will arise seven y of famine, C
41:34 of the land of Egypt during the seven plenteous y.
41:35 Let them gather all the food of these good y
41:36 for the land against the seven y of famine that C
41:46 Joseph was thirty y old when he entered
41:47 During the seven plenteous y
41:48 the food of the seven y when there was plenty C
41:50 Before the y of famine came, Joseph had two sons,
41:53 The seven y of plenty that prevailed in the land C
41:54 and the seven y of famine began to come, C
45: 6 For the famine has been in the land these two y;
45: 6 and there are five more y in which there will
45:11 since there are five more y of famine to come—
47: 8 "How many are the y of your life?"
47: 9 y of my earthly sojourn are one hundred thirty;
47: 9 few and hard have been the y of my life.
47: 9 not compare with the y of the life of my ancestors
47:28 Jacob lived in the land of Egypt seventeen y;
47:28 so the days of Jacob, the y of his life, were one hundred forty-seven y.
50:22 and Joseph lived one hundred ten y.
50:26 And Joseph died, being one hundred ten y old;
Ex 6:16 of Levi's life was one hundred thirty-seven y.
6:18 of Kohath's life was one hundred thirty-three y.
6:20 of Amram's life was one hundred thirty-seven y.
7: 7 Moses was eighty y old and Aaron eighty-three
12:40 in Egypt was four hundred thirty y.
12:41 At the end of four hundred thirty y,
16:35 The Israelites ate manna forty y, A
21: 2 a male Hebrew slave, he shall serve six y, but in
23:10 For six y you shall sow your land and gather
30:14 from twenty y old and upward,
38:26 from twenty y old and upward,
Lev 19:23 three y it shall be forbidden to you, B
25: 3 Six y you shall sow your field,
25: 3 and six y you shall prune your vineyard,
25: 8 You shall count off seven weeks of y,
25: 8 of years, seven times seven y, so that the period C
25: 8 period of seven weeks of y gives forty-nine y.
25:15 you shall pay only for the number of y since
25:15 shall charge you only for the remaining crop y.
25:16 If the y are more, you shall increase the price, and if the y are fewer, you shall diminish the price;
25:21 so that it will yield a crop for three y. B
25:27 the y since its sale shall be computed and
25:50 of the sale shall be applied to the number of y:
25:51 If many y remain, they shall pay for their
25:52 and if few y remain until the jubilee year,
25:52 to the y involved they shall make payment
26:34 Then the land shall enjoy its sabbath y as long
26:34 then the land shall rest, and enjoy its sabbath y.
26:43 enjoy its sabbath y by lying desolate without them,
27: 3 from twenty to sixty y of age the equivalent shall
27: 5 If the age is from five to twenty y of age,
27: 6 If the age is from one month to five y,
27: 7 And if the person is sixty y old or over,
27:18 the price for it according to the y that remain until
Nu 1: 3 from twenty y old and upward,
1:18 to the number of names from twenty y old
1:20 every male from twenty y old and upward,
1:22 every male from twenty y old and upward,
1:24 from twenty y old and upward,
1:26 from twenty y old and upward,
1:28 from twenty y old and upward,
1:30 from twenty y old and upward,
1:32 from twenty y old and upward,
1:34 from twenty y old and upward,

Nu 1:36 from twenty y old and upward,
1:38 from twenty y old and upward,
1:40 from twenty y old and upward,
1:42 from twenty y old and upward,
1:45 from twenty y old and upward,
4: 3 from thirty y old up to fifty y old,
4:23 from thirty y old up to fifty y old you shall enroll
4:30 from thirty y old up to fifty y old you shall enroll
4:35 from thirty y old up to fifty y old,
4:39 from thirty y old up to fifty y old,
4:43 from thirty y old up to fifty y old,
4:47 from thirty y old up to fifty y old,
8:24 twenty-five y old and upward they shall begin to
8:25 the age of fifty y they shall retire from the duty of
13:22 Hebron was built seven y before Zoan in Egypt.) C
14:29 from twenty y old and upward,
14:33 be shepherds in the wilderness for forty y, A
14:34 forty y, and you shall know my displeasure." A
26: 2 from twenty y old and upward,
26: 4 from twenty y old and upward,"
32:11 from twenty y old and upward,
32:13 in the wilderness for forty y, A
33:39 Aaron was one hundred twenty-three y old
Dt 2: 7 These forty y the LORD your God has been A
2:14 the Wadi Zered was thirty-eight y.
8: 2 the LORD your God has led you these forty y in A
8: 4 and your feet did not swell these forty y. A
15:12 is sold to you and works for you six y,
15:18 for six y they have given you services worth
29: 5 I have led you forty y in the wilderness. A
31: 2 "I am now one hundred twenty y old.
32: 7 the days of old, consider the y long past;
34: 7 Moses was one hundred twenty y old
Jos 5: 6 the Israelites traveled forty y in the wilderness, A
13: 1 Now Joshua was old and advanced in y;
13: 1 "You are old and advanced in y,
14: 7 I was forty y old when Moses the servant of A
14:10 these forty-five y since the time that
14:10 and here I am today, eighty-five y old.
23: 1 and Joshua was old and well advanced in y,
23: 2 "I am now old and well advanced in y;
24:29 died, being one hundred ten y old.
Jdg 2: 8 died at the age of one hundred ten y.
3: 8 the Israelites served Cushan-rishathaim eight y.
3:11 So the land had rest forty y. A
3:14 Israelites served King Eglon of Moab eighteen y.
3:30 And the land had rest eighty y.
4: 3 and had oppressed the Israelites cruelly twenty y.
5:31 And the land had rest forty y. A
6: 1 into the hand of Midian seven y. C
6:25 the second bull seven y old, C
8:28 the land had rest forty y in the days of Gideon. A
9:22 Abimelech ruled over Israel three y. B
10: 2 He judged Israel twenty-three y.
10: 3 who judged Israel twenty-two y.
10: 8 For eighteen y they oppressed all the Israelites
11:26 three hundred y, why did you not recover them
12: 7 Jephthah judged Israel six y.
12: 9 He judged Israel seven y. C
12:11 and he judged Israel ten y.
12:14 on seventy donkeys; he judged Israel eight y.
13: 1 into the hand of the Philistines forty y. A
15:20 in the days of the Philistines twenty y.
16:31 He had judged Israel twenty y.
Ru 1: 4 When they had lived there about ten y,
1Sa 4:15 Eli was ninety-eight y old and his eyes were set,
4:18 He had judged Israel forty y. A
7: 2 a long time passed, some twenty y,
13: 1 Saul was . . . y old when he began to reign; and he
reigned . . . and two y over Israel.
17:12 the man was already old and advanced in y.
29: 3 who has been with me now for days and y?
2Sa 2:10 Saul's son, was forty y old when he began A
2:10 to reign over Israel, and he reigned two y.
2:11 the house of Judah was seven y and six months. C
4: 4 He was five y old when the news about Saul
5: 4 David was thirty y old when he began to reign,
5: 4 when he began to reign, and he reigned forty y. A
5: 5 At Hebron he reigned over Judah seven y C
5: 5 over all Israel and Judah thirty-three y.
13:23 After two full y Absalom had sheepshearers
13:38 having fled to Geshur, stayed there three y. B
14:28 So Absalom lived two full y in Jerusalem,
15: 7 At the end of four y Absalom said to the king,
19:32 Barzillai was a very aged man, eighty y old.
19:34 "How many y have I still to live,
19:35 Today I am eighty y old;
21: 1 in the days of David for three y, year after year; B
24:13 he asked him, "Shall three y of famine come B
1Ki 1: 1 King David was old and advanced in y;
2:11 time that David reigned over Israel was forty y; A
2:11 he reigned seven y in Hebron, C
2:11 and thirty-three y in Jerusalem.
2:39 of three y that two of Shimei's slaves ran away B
6:38 He was seven y in building it. C
7: 1 Solomon was building his own house thirteen y,
9:10 At the end of twenty y,
10:22 Once every three y the fleet of ships B
11:42 in Jerusalem over all Israel was forty y. A
14:20 time that Jeroboam reigned was twenty-two y;
14:21 Rehoboam was forty-one y old when he began to
reign, and he reigned seventeen y in Jerusalem,
15: 2 He reigned for three y in Jerusalem. B
15:10 he reigned forty-one y in Jerusalem.
15:25 he reigned over Israel two y.
15:33 at Tirzah; he reigned twenty-four y.
16: 8 in Tirzah; he reigned two y.
1Ki 16:23 he reigned for twelve y, six of them in Tirzah.
16:29 over Israel in Samaria twenty-two y.
17: 1 there shall be neither dew nor rain these y,
22: 1 three y Aram and Israel continued without war. B
22:42 Jehoshaphat was thirty-five y old when he began
to reign, and he reigned twenty-five y in Jerusalem.
22:51 he reigned two y over Israel.
2Ki 3: 1 in Samaria; he reigned twelve y.
8: 1 and it will come on the land for seven y." C
8: 2 and settled in the land of the Philistines seven y. C
8: 3 At the end of the seven y, C
8:17 He was thirty-two y old when he became king, and
he reigned eight y in Jerusalem.
8:26 Ahaziah was twenty-two y old when he began
10:36 over Israel in Samaria was twenty-eight y.
11: 3 he remained with her six y,
11:21 Jehoash was seven y old when he began to reign. C
12: 1 he reigned forty y in Jerusalem. A
13: 1 in Samaria; he reigned seventeen y.
13:10 in Samaria; he reigned sixteen y.
14: 2 He was twenty-five y old when he began to reign,
and he reigned twenty-nine y in Jerusalem.
14:17 of Joash of Judah lived fifteen y after the death
14:21 of Judah took Azariah, who was sixteen y old,
14:23 in Samaria; he reigned forty-one y.
15: 2 He was sixteen y old when he began to reign, and
he reigned fifty-two y in Jerusalem.
15:17 he reigned ten y in Samaria.
15:23 in Samaria; he reigned two y.
15:27 in Samaria; he reigned twenty y.
15:33 He was twenty-five y old when he began to reign
and reigned sixteen y
16: 2 Ahaz was twenty y old when he began to reign; he
reigned sixteen y in Jerusalem.
17: 1 to reign in Samaria over Israel; he reigned nine y.
17: 5 for three y he besieged it. B
18: 2 He was twenty-five y old when he began to reign;
he reigned twenty-nine y in Jerusalem.
18:10 and at the end of three y, B
20: 6 I will add fifteen y to your life.
21: 1 Manasseh was twelve y old when he began to
reign; he reigned fifty-five y in Jerusalem.
21:19 Amon was twenty-two y old when he began to
reign; he reigned two y in Jerusalem.
22: 1 Josiah was eight y old when he began to reign; he
reigned thirty-one y in Jerusalem.
23:31 Jehoahaz was twenty-three y old when he began
23:36 Jehoiakim was twenty-five y old when he began to
reign; he reigned eleven y in Jerusalem.
24: 1 Jehoiakim became his servant for three y; B
24: 8 Jehoiachin was eighteen y old when he began
24:18 Zedekiah was twenty-one y old when he began
24:18 he reigned eleven y in Jerusalem.
1Ch 2:21 whom he married when he was sixty y old;
3: 4 where he reigned for seven y and six months. C
3: 4 And he reigned thirty-three y in Jerusalem.
21:12 either three y of famine; B
23: 3 The Levites, thirty y old and upward,
23:24 of the names of the individuals from twenty y old
23:27 of the Levites from twenty y old and upward—
27:23 David did not count those below twenty y of age,
29:27 period that he reigned over Israel was forty y; A
29:27 he reigned seven y in Hebron, C
29:27 and thirty-three y in Jerusalem.
2Ch 8: 1 At the end of twenty y,
9:21 once every three y the ships of Tarshish used B
9:30 in Jerusalem over all Israel forty y. A
11:17 and for three y they made Rehoboam son B
11:17 for they walked for three y in the way of David B
12:13 Rehoboam was forty-one y old when he began to
reign; he reigned seventeen y in Jerusalem,
13: 2 He reigned for three y in Jerusalem. B
14: 1 In his days the land had rest for ten y.
14: 6 He had no war in those y,
18: 2 After some y he went down to Ahab in Samaria.
20:31 He was thirty-five y old when he began to reign;
he reigned twenty-five y in Jerusalem.
21: 5 Jehoram was thirty-two y old when he began to
reign; he reigned eight y in Jerusalem.
21:19 In course of time, at the end of two y,
21:20 He was thirty-two y old when he began to reign;
he reigned eight y in Jerusalem.
22: 2 Ahaziah was forty-two y old when he began
22:12 he remained with them six y,
24: 1 Joash was seven y old when he began to reign; C
24: 1 he reigned forty y in Jerusalem; A
24:15 he was one hundred thirty y old at his death.
25: 1 Amaziah was twenty-five y old when he began to
reign, and he reigned twenty-nine y in Jerusalem.
25: 5 He mustered those twenty y old and upward,
25:25 lived fifteen y after the death of King Joash son
26: 1 of Judah took Uzziah, who was sixteen y old,
26: 3 Uzziah was sixteen y old when he began to reign,
and he reigned fifty-two y in Jerusalem.
27: 1 Jotham was twenty-five y old when he began to
reign; he reigned sixteen y in Jerusalem.
27: 5 the same amount in the second and the third y.
27: 8 He was twenty-five y old when he began to reign;
he reigned sixteen y in Jerusalem.
28: 1 Ahaz was twenty y old when he began to reign; he
reigned sixteen y in Jerusalem.
29: 1 Hezekiah began to reign when he was twenty-five
y old; he reigned twenty-nine y in Jerusalem.
31:16 males from three y old and upwards, B
31:17 of the Levites from twenty y old and upwards was
33: 1 Manasseh was twelve y old when he began to
reign; he reigned fifty-five y in Jerusalem.
2Ch 33:21 Amon was twenty-two y old when he began to
reign; he reigned two y in Jerusalem.
34: 1 Josiah was eight y old when he began to reign; he
reigned thirty-one y in Jerusalem.
36: 2 Jehoahaz was twenty-three y old when he began
36: 5 Jehoiakim was twenty-five y old when he began
36: 5 he reigned eleven y in Jerusalem.
36: 9 Jehoiachin was eight y old when he began
36:11 Zedekiah was twenty-one y old when he began to
reign; he reigned eleven y in Jerusalem.
36:21 it lay desolate it kept sabbath, to fulfill seventy y.
Ezr 3: 8 from twenty y old and upward,
5:11 the house that was built many y ago,
Ne 5:14 twelve y, neither I nor my brothers ate the food
9:21 Forty y you sustained them in the wilderness so A
9:30 Many y you were patient with them,
Job 10: 5 or your y like human y,
15:20 through all the y that are laid up for the ruthless.
16:22 For when a few y have come,
32: 6 "I am young in y, and you are aged;
32: 7 'Let days speak, and many y teach wisdom.'
36:11 and their y in pleasantness.
36:26 the number of his y is unsearchable.
42:16 After this Job lived one hundred and forty y,
Ps 31:10 For my life is spent with sorrow, and my y
61: 6 may his y endure to all generations!
77: 5 and remember the y of long ago.
78:33 like a breath, and their y in terror.
90: 4 For a thousand y in your sight are like yesterday
90: 9 our y come to an end like a sigh.
90:10 The days of our life are seventy y,
90:15 and as many y as we have seen evil.
95:10 For forty y I loathed that generation and said, A
102:24 you whose y endure throughout all generations."
102:27 but you are the same, and your y have no end.
Pr 3: 2 for length of days and y of life
4:10 that the y of your life may be many.
5: 9 and your y to the merciless,
9:11 and y will be added to your life.
10:27 but the y of the wicked will be short.
Ecc 6: 3 a hundred children, and live many y;
6: 3 but however many are the days of his y,
6: 6 though he should live a thousand y twice over,
11: 8 those who live many y should rejoice in them all;
12: 1 and the y draw near when you will say,
Isa 7: 8 (Within sixty-five y Ephraim will be shattered,
16:14 But now the LORD says, In three y, B
16:14 In three years, like the y of a hired worker,
20: 3 for three y as a sign and a portent against Egypt B
21:16 according to the y of a hired worker,
23:15 that day Tyre will be forgotten for seventy y,
23:15 of seventy y, it will happen to Tyre as in the song
23:17 At the end of seventy y,
38: 5 I will add fifteen y to your life.
38:10 to the gates of Sheol for the rest of my y.
65:20 for one who dies at a hundred y will be considered
Jer 25: 3 For twenty-three y, from the thirteenth year
25:11 the king of Babylon seventy y.
25:12 Then after seventy y are completed,
28: 3 Within two y I will bring back to this place all
28:11 from the neck of all the nations within two y."
29:10 Babylon's seventy y are completed will I visit you,
34:14 to you and have served you six y;
52: 1 Zedekiah was twenty-one y old when he began to
reign; he reigned eleven y in Jerusalem.
Eze 4: 5 equal to the number of the y of their punishment;
12:27 "The vision that he sees is for many y ahead;
22: 4 the appointed time of your y has come.
29:11 it shall be uninhabited forty y. A
29:12 and her cities shall be a desolation forty y A
29:13 the end of forty y I will gather the Egyptians A
38: 8 in the latter y you shall go against a land restored
38:17 of Israel, who in those days prophesied for y
39: 9 and they will make fires of them for seven y. C
Da 1: 5 They were to be educated for three y, B
5:31 being about sixty-two y old.
9: 2 perceived in the books the number of y that,
9: 2 the devastation of Jerusalem, namely, seventy y.
11: 6 After some y they shall make an alliance,
11: 8 For some y he shall refrain from attacking the king
11:13 after some y he shall advance with a great army
Joel 2:25 for the y that the swarming locust has eaten,
Am 1: 1 two y before the earthquake.
2:10 and led you forty y in the wilderness, A
5:25 to me sacrifices and offerings the forty y in A
Zec 1:12 with which you have been angry these seventy y?"
7: 3 as I have done for so many y?"
7: 5 for these seventy y, was it for me that you fasted?
Mal 3: 4 as in the days of old and as in former y.
Mt 2:16 around Bethlehem who were two y old or under,
9:20 for twelve y came up behind him and touched
Mk 5:25 from hemorrhages for twelve y.
5:42 up and began to walk about (she was twelve y
Lk 1: 7 and both were getting on in y.
1:18 I am an old man, and my wife is getting on in y."
2:36 with her husband seven y after her marriage, C
2:42 And when he was twelve y old,
2:52 And Jesus increased in wisdom and in y,
3:23 about thirty y old when he began his work.
4:25 the heaven was shut up three y and six months, B
8:42 about twelve y old, who was dying.
8:43 from hemorrhages for twelve y;
12:19 'Soul, you have ample goods laid up for many y;
13: 7 For three y I have come looking for fruit B
13:11 with a spirit that had crippled her for eighteen y.
13:16 for eighteen long y, be set free from this bondage
15:29 For all these y I have been working like a slave

Jn 2:20 temple has been under construction for forty-six y,
5: 5 man was there who had been ill for thirty-eight y.
8:57 the Jews said to him, "You are not yet fifty y old,
Ac 4:22 had been performed was more than forty y old. A
7: 6 and mistreat them during four hundred y.
7:23 "When he was forty y old, A
7:30 "Now when forty y had passed, A
7:36 at the Red Sea, and in the wilderness for forty y. A
7:42 to me slain victims and sacrifices forty y in A
9:33 who had been bedridden for eight y,
13:18 For about forty y he put up with them in A
13:20 for about four hundred fifty y.
13:21 the tribe of Benjamin, who reigned for forty y. A
19:10 This continued for two y,
20:31 remembering that for three y I did not cease B
24:10 for many y you have been a judge over this nation.
24:17 after some y I came to bring alms to my nation
24:27 After two y had passed, Felix was succeeded
28:30 He lived there two whole y at his own expense
Ro 4:19 good as dead (for he was about a hundred y old),
15:23 I desire, as I have for many y,
2Co 12: 2 a person in Christ who fourteen y ago was caught
Gal 1:18 Then after three y I did go up to Jerusalem B
2: 1 Then after fourteen y I went up again to Jerusalem
3:17 the law, which came four hundred thirty y later,
4:10 and months, and seasons, and y.
1Ti 5: 9 be put on the list if she is not less than sixty y old
Heb 1:12 But you are the same, and your y will never end."
3:10 for forty y. Therefore I was angry with that A
3:17 But with whom was he angry forty y? A
Jas 5:17 and for three y and six months it did not rain B
2Pe 3: 8 that with the Lord one day is like a thousand y,
and a thousand y are like one day.
Rev 20: 2 and bound him for a thousand y,
20: 3 until the thousand y were ended.
20: 4 to life and reigned with Christ a thousand y.
20: 5 not come to life until the thousand y were ended.)
20: 6 and they will reign with him a thousand y.
20: 7 When the thousand y are ended,
Tob 1: 7 for six y I would save up a second tenth in money
2:10 For four y I remained unable to see.
2:10 of me for two y before he went to Elymais.
5: 3 now twenty y have passed since I left this money
14: 2 in peace when he was one hundred twelve y old,
14: 2 He was sixty-two y old when he lost his eyesight,
14:14 at the age of one hundred seventeen y.
Jdt 8: 4 as a widow for three y and four months B
Wis 4: 8 or measured by number of y;
4:13 in a short time, they fulfilled long y;
Sir 18: 9 in their life is great if they reach one hundred y.
18:10 so are a few y among the days of eternity.
26: 2 and he will complete his y in peace.
26:26 *for the number of his y will be doubled.*
41: 4 Whether life lasts for ten y or a hundred or
LtJ 6: 3 to Babylon you will remain there for many y, for
1Mc 1: 7 after Alexander had reigned twelve y, he died.
1: 9 so did their descendants after them for many y;
1:29 Two y later the king sent to the cities of Judah
9:57 and the land of Judah had rest for two y.
10:41 not paid as they did in the first y,
16: 3 and you by Heaven's mercy are mature in y.
2Mc 1: 7 in the critical distress that came upon us in those y
1:20 But after many y had passed, when it pleased God,
4:23 After a period of three y Jason sent Menelaus, B
4:40 a man advanced in y and no less advanced in folly.
6:23 worthy of his y and the dignity of his old age and
7:27 and nursed you for three y, B
10: 3 they offered sacrifices, after a lapse of two y,
14: 1 Three y later, word came to Judas and his men B
1Es 1:34 who was twenty-three y old,
1:39 Jehoiakim was twenty-five y old when he began
1:43 when he was made king he was eighteen y old,
1:46 Zedekiah was twenty-one y old, and he reigned
eleven y.
1:58 of its desolation until the completion of seventy y."
5:41 All those of Israel, twelve or more y of age,
5:58 or more y of age to have charge of the work of
5:73 They were kept from building for two y,
6:14 The house was built many y ago by a king
2Es 3:23 So the times passed and the y were completed,
3:25 This was done for many y;
3:29 soul has seen many sinners during these thirty y.
4:33 Why are our y few and evil?"
6: 5 and before the present y were reckoned and before
7:28 those who remain shall rejoice four hundred y.
7:29 After those y my son the Messiah shall die,
7:43 It will last as though for a week of y.
9:43 though I lived with my husband for thirty y.
9:44 during those thirty y I prayed to the Most High,
9:45 And after thirty y God heard your servant,
10:45 for her telling you that she was barren for thirty y,
10:45 the reason is that there were three thousand y in
10:46 And after three thousand y Solomon built the city,
12:20 whose times shall be short and their y swift;
4Mc 5:11 adopt a mind appropriate to your y,
16: 1 a woman, advanced in y and mother of seven sons,

YEAST (13)

Mt 13:33 of heaven is like y that a woman took and mixed
16: 6 beware of the y of the Pharisees and Sadducees."
16:11 Beware of the y of the Pharisees and Sadducees!"
16:12 that he had not told them to beware of the y
Mk 8:15 of the y of the Pharisees and the y of Herod."
Lk 12: 1 "Beware of the y of the Pharisees, that is,
13:21 It is like y that a woman took and mixed in with
1Co 5: 6 that a little y leavens the whole batch of dough?
1Co 5: 7 the old y so that you may be a new batch,
5: 8 not with the old y, the y of malice and evil,
Gal 5: 9 A little y leavens the whole batch of dough.

YELLOW (3)

Lev 13:30 the skin and the hair in it is y and thin,
13:32 the itch has not spread, and there is no y hair in it,
13:36 the priest need not seek for the y hair;

YES‡ (62)

Ge 18:15 He said, "Oh y, you did laugh."
20: 6 Then God said to him in the dream, "Y,
27:33 y, and blessed he shall be!"
29: 6 "Y," they replied, "and here is his daughter
Ex 2: 8 Pharaoh's daughter said to her, "Y."
1Sa 9:12 They answered, "Y, there he is just ahead of you.
23: 4 LORD answered him, "Y, go down to Keilah;
2Sa 2:20 He answered, "Y, it is."
1Ki 20:33 they quickly took it up from him and said, "Y,
2Ki 2: 3 And he said, "Y, I know; keep silent."
2: 5 And he answered, "Y, I know; be silent."
5:22 He replied, "Y, but my master has sent me to say,
Job 3: 7 Y, let that night be barren;
Pr 22:19 I have made them known to you today—y,
Isa 32:13 y, for all the joyous houses in the jubilant city.
41:11 Y, all who are incensed against you shall
Eze 16:59 Y, thus says the Lord GOD:
Jnh 4: 9 And he said, "Y, angry enough to die."
Hag 2:13 The priests answered, "Y, it becomes unclean."
Mt 5:37 Let your word be 'Y, Y' or 'No, No';
9:28 They said to him, "Y, Lord."
11: 9 Y, I tell you, and more than a prophet.
11:26 y, Father, for such was your gracious will.
13:51 you understood all this?" They answered, "Y."
15:27 "Y, Lord, yet even the dogs eat the crumbs
17:25 He said, "Y, he does."
21:16 what these are saying?" Jesus said to them, "Y;
Lk 7:26 Y, I tell you, and more than a prophet.
10:21 y, Father, for such was your gracious will.
11:51 Y, I tell you, it will be charged
12: 5 Y, I tell you, fear him!
14:26 y, and even life itself, cannot be my disciple.
24:21 Y, and besides all this, it is now the third day
Jn 11:27 She said to him, "Y, Lord,
16:29 "Y, now you are speaking plainly,
21:15 He said to him, "Y, Lord;
21:16 He said to him, "Y, Lord;
Ac 5: 8 And she said, "Y, that was the price."
22:27 are you a Roman citizen?" And he said, "Y."
Ro 3:29 the God of Gentiles also? Y, of Gentiles also,
8:34 It is Christ Jesus, who died, y, who was raised,
2Co 1:17 ready to say "Y, y" and "No, no" at the same time?
1:18 our word to you has not been "Y and No."
1:19 was not "Y and No"; but in him it is always "Y."
1:20 For in him every one of God's promises is a "Y."
4:15 Y, everything is for your sake, so that grace,
5: 8 Y, we do have confidence,
Eph 5:27 y, so that she may be holy and without blemish.
Php 1:18 Y, and I will continue to rejoice,
4: 3 Y, and I ask you also, my loyal companion,
1Th 2:20 Y, you are our glory and joy!
Phm 1:20 Y, brother, let me have this benefit from you in
Jas 5:12 but let your "Y" be y and your "No" be no,
Rev 14:13 "Y," says the Spirit, "they will rest
16: 7 And I heard the altar respond, "Y, O Lord God,
Tob 5: 6 "Y," he replied, "I have been there many times;
7: 4 And they replied, "Y, we know him."
2Es 4: 3 Then I said, "Y, my lord."

YESTERDAY‡ (10)

Ex 5:14 the required quantity of bricks y and today,
1Sa 20:27 of Jesse not come to the feast, either y or today?"
2Sa 15:20 You came only y, and shall I today make you
2Ki 9:26 and for the blood of his children that I saw y,
Job 8: 9 for we are but of y,
Ps 90: 4 a thousand years in your sight are like y when it is
Jn 4:52 "Y at one in the afternoon the fever left him."
Ac 7:28 to kill me as you killed the Egyptian y?'
Heb 13: 8 Jesus Christ is the same y and today and forever.
Sir 38:22 y it was his, and today it is yours.

YESTERNIGHT (KJV) See LAST NIGHT

YET‡ (478)

Ge 2: 5 no plant of the field was y in the earth and no herb
of the field had y sprung up—
3:16 y your desire shall be for your husband,
15:16 for the iniquity of the Amorites is not y complete."
21: 7 Y I have borne him a son in his old age."
31: 7 y your father has cheated me
32:12 Y you have said, 'I will surely do you good,
32:30 and y my life is preserved."
38: 5 Y again she bore a son,
38:14 y she had not been given to him in marriage.
40:23 Y the chief cupbearer did not remember Joseph,
49:24 Y his bow remained taut,
Ex 3: 2 and the bush was blazing, y it was not consumed.
5: 5 of the land and y you want them to stop working!"
5:16 y they say to us, 'Make bricks!'
9:30 I know that you do not y fear the LORD God."
10: 7 do you not y understand that Egypt is ruined?"
21:22 and y no further harm follows,
33:12 Y you have said, 'I know you by name,
34: 7 y by no means clearing the guilty,
Lev 10:19 and y such things as these have befallen me!
26:44 Y for all that, when they are in the land
Nu 9:13 and y refrains from keeping the passover,
13:28 Y the people who live in the land are strong,
14:22 and y have tested me these ten times and have
16:10 y you seek the priesthood as well!
24:22 y Kain is destined for burning.
Dt 1:39 who today do not y know right from wrong,
10:15 y the LORD set his heart in love
12: 9 not y come into the rest and the possession that
12:15 Y whenever you desire you may slaughter
14: 7 Y of those that chew the cud or have
20: 6 Has anyone planted a vineyard but not y
20: 7 Has anyone become engaged to a woman but not y
23: 5 (Y the LORD your God refused to heed Balaam;
32: 5 y his degenerate children have dealt falsely
Jos 3: 4 Y there shall be a space between you and it,
5: 5 y all the people born on the journey through
13:13 Y the Israelites did not drive out the Geshurites or
14: 8 y I wholeheartedly followed the LORD my God.
17:12 Y the Manassites could not take possession
17:16 y all the Canaanites who live in
18: 2 whose inheritance had not y been apportioned.
22:17 of the sin at Peor from which even y we have
Jdg 2:17 Y they did not listen even to their judges;
10:13 Y you have abandoned me
21:18 Y we cannot give any of our daughters to them
1Sa 3: 3 the lamp of God had not y gone out,
3: 7 Now Samuel did not y know the LORD,
3: 7 the word of the LORD had not y been revealed
8: 3 Y his sons did not follow in his ways,
12:20 y do not turn aside from following the LORD,
15:30 y honor me now before the elders of my people
16:11 And he said, "There remains y the youngest,
25:15 Y the men were very good to us,
2Sa 1: 9 and y my life still lingers.'
3: 8 and y you charge me now with a crime
6:22 I will make myself y more contemptible than this,
7:19 And y this was a small thing in your eyes,
1Ki 3: 2 because no house had y been built for the name of
8:47 y if they come to their senses in the land
11:12 Y for the sake of your father David I will not do it
11:36 Y to his son I will give one tribe,
14: 8 y you have not been like my servant David,
18:14 Y now you say, 'Go, tell your lord
19:18 Y I will leave seven thousand in Israel,
22: 3 y we are doing nothing to take it out of the hand of
22:43 y the high places were not taken away,
2Ki 2:10 He responded, "You have asked a hard thing; y,
8:19 Y the LORD would not destroy Judah,
14: 3 y not like his ancestor David;
17: 2 y not like the kings of Israel who were before him.
17:13 Y the LORD warned Israel and Judah
1Ch 5: 2 y the birthright belonged to Joseph.)
12:19 (Y he did not help them,
27:24 y wrath came upon Israel for this,
28: 4 Y the LORD God of Israel chose me
2Ch 13: 6 Y Jeroboam son of Nebat,
16: 8 Y because you relied on the LORD,
16:12 y even in his disease he did not seek the LORD,
20:33 Y the high places were not removed;
20:33 the people had not y set their hearts upon the God
21: 7 Y the LORD would not destroy the house
24:19 Y he sent prophets among them
25: 2 y not with a true heart.
28:22 the time of his distress he became y more faithless
30:18 y they ate the passover otherwise than
Ezr 3: 6 of the temple of the LORD was not y laid.
5:16 now it has been under construction, and it is not y
9: 9 y our God has not forsaken us in our slavery,
Ne 2:16 I had not y told the Jews, the priests, the nobles,
5: 5 and y we are forcing our sons and daughters to
5:18 y with all this I did not demand
9:28 y when they turned and cried to you,
9:29 Y they acted presumptuously and did
9:30 through your prophets; y they would not listen.
13: 2 y our God turned the curse into a blessing.
13:18 Y you bring more wrath on Israel by profaning
Est 5:13 Y all this does me no good so long as I see
Job 8:12 While y in flower and not cut down,
8:21 He will y fill your mouth with laughter,
9:31 y you will plunge me into filth,
10:13 Y these things you hid in your heart;
14: 9 y at the scent of water it will bud
17: 9 Y the righteous hold to their way,
20:14 y their food is turned in their stomachs;
22:18 Y he filled their houses with good things—
24:12 y God pays no attention to their prayer.
24:22 Y God prolongs the life of the mighty
32:13 Y do not say, 'We have found wisdom;
36: 2 for I have y something to say on God's behalf.
39:16 though its labor should be in vain, y it has no fear;
Ps 8: 5 Y you have made them a little lower than God,
19: 4 y their voice goes out through all the earth,
22: 3 Y you are holy, enthroned on the praises of Israel.
22: 9 Y it was you who took me from the womb;
22:31 and proclaim his deliverance to a people y unborn,
27: 3 war rise up against me, y I will be confident.
37:10 Y a little while, and the wicked will be no more;
37:25 y I have not seen the righteous forsaken
44: 9 Y you have rejected us and abased us,
44:17 y we have not forgotten you,
44:19 y you have broken us in the haunt of jackals,
66:12 y you have brought us out to a spacious place.
71:14 and will praise you y more and more.
74:12 Y God my King is from of old,
77:19 y your footprints were unseen.

Ps 78: 6 the children **y** unborn, and rise up and tell them
78:17 **Y** they sinned still more against him,
78:23 **Y** he commanded the skies above,
78:38 **Y** he, being compassionate, forgave their iniquity,
78:56 **Y** they tested the Most High God,
102:18 so that a people **y** unborn may praise the LORD:
106: 8 **Y** he saved them for his name's sake,
119:83 **y** I have not forgotten your statutes.
119:141 **y** I do not forget your precepts.
119:151 **Y** you are near, O LORD,
119:157 **y** I do not swerve from your decrees.
129: 2 **y** they have not prevailed against me.
139:16 when none of them as **y** existed.
Pr 1:18 **y** they lie in wait—to kill themselves!
6:31 **Y** if they are caught, they will pay sevenfold;
8:26 when he had not **y** made earth and fields,
11:24 Some give freely, **y** grow all the richer;
13: 7 Some pretend to be rich, **y** have nothing;
13: 7 others pretend to be poor, **y** have great wealth.
19: 3 **y** the heart rages against the LORD.
28:21 **y** for a piece of bread a person may do wrong.
29: 1 One who is often reproved, **y** remains stubborn,
30:12 There are those who are pure in their own eyes **y**
30:24 **y** they are exceedingly wise:
30:25 **y** they provide their food in the summer;
30:26 **y** they make their homes in the rocks;
30:27 **y** all of them march in rank;
30:28 **y** it is found in kings' palaces.
Ecc 1:11 of people **y** to come by those who come after them.
2:14 **Y** I perceived that the same fate befalls all
2:19 **Y** they will be master of all for which I toiled
3:11 **y** they cannot find out what God has done from
4: 3 but better than both is the one who has not **y** been,
4: 8 **y** there is no end to all their toil,
4:16 **Y** those who come later will not rejoice in him.
5: 8 and there are **y** higher ones over them.
6: 2 **y** God does not enable them to enjoy these things,
6: 5 **y** it finds rest rather than he.
6: 6 **y** enjoy no good—do not all go to one place?
6: 7 **y** the appetite is not satisfied.
8:12 **y** I know that it will be well
9:15 **Y** no one remembered that poor man.
9:16 **y** the poor man's wisdom is despised,
10:14 **y** fools talk on and on.
11: 8 **y** let them remember that the days of darkness will
Isa 6: 5 **y** my eyes have seen the King,
11:11 the Lord will extend his hand **y** a second time
15: 9 **y** I will bring upon Dibon even more—
17:11 **y** the harvest will flee away in a day of grief
28:12 and this is repose"; **y** they would not hear.
29: 2 **Y** I will distress Ariel, and there shall be moaning
30:20 **y** your Teacher will not hide himself any more,
31: 2 **Y** he too is wise and brings disaster;
43: 8 Bring forth the people who are blind, **y** have eyes, who are deaf, **y** have ears!
43:22 **Y** you did not call upon me, O Jacob;
44: 5 **y** another will write on the hand, "The LORD's,"
44: 7 Let them tell us what is **y** to be.
46:10 the beginning and from ancient times things not **y**
49: 4 **y** surely my cause is with the LORD,
49:15 Even these may forget, **y** I will not forget you.
49:20 of your bereavement will **y** say in your hearing:
50:10 **y** trusts in the name of the LORD and relies
53: 4 **y** we accounted him stricken, struck down by God,
53: 7 and he was afflicted, **y** he did not open his mouth;
53:10 **Y** it was the will of the LORD to crush him
53:12 **y** he bore the sin of many,
58: 2 **Y** day after day they seek me and delight
64: 8 **Y**, O LORD, you are our Father;
65:24 while they are **y** speaking I will hear.
66: 8 **Y** as soon as Zion was in labor
Jer 2:21 **Y** I planted you as a choice vine,
2:32 **Y** my people have forgotten me,
2:34 **Y** in spite of all these things
3: 3 **y** you have the forehead of a whore,
3: 8 **y** her false sister Judah did not fear,
3:10 **Y** for all this her false sister Judah did not return
4:27 **y** I will not make a full end.
5: 2 "As the LORD lives," **y** they swear falsely.
6:15 **y** they were not ashamed, they did not know how
7:24 **Y** they did not obey or incline their ear, but,
7:26 **y** they did not listen to me,
8:12 **y** they were not at all ashamed,
11: 8 **Y** they did not obey or incline their ear,
12: 2 near in their mouths **y** far from their hearts.
14: 9 **Y** you, O LORD, are in the midst of us,
15: 1 **y** my heart would not turn toward this people.
15: 9 her sun went down while it was **y** day;
15:10 nor have I borrowed, **y** all of them curse me.
17:23 **Y** they did not listen or incline their ear;
18:20 **Y** they have dug a pit for my life.
18:23 **Y** you, O LORD, know all their plotting
23:21 I did not send the prophets, **y** they ran;
23:21 I did not speak to them, **y** they prophesied.
25: 7 **Y** you did not listen to me, says the LORD,
30: 7 **y** he shall be rescued from it.
32:25 **Y** you, O Lord GOD, have said to me,
34: 4 **Y** hear the word of the LORD,
36:24 **Y** neither the king, nor any of his servants
37: 4 for he had not **y** been put in prison.
44: 4 **Y** I persistently sent to you all my servants
48:47 **Y** I will restore the fortunes of Moab in
51:33 **y** a little while and the time of her harvest will
La 3:29 to put one's mouth to the dust (there may **y**
Eze 5: 9 I will do to you what I have never **y** done,
8: 6 **Y** you will see still greater abominations."
11:16 **y** I have been a sanctuary to them for a little while
12:13 the land of the Chaldeans, **y** he shall not see it;
13: 6 and **y** they wait for the fulfillment of their word!
14: 4 and **y** come to the prophet—
14: 7 and **y** come to a prophet to inquire of me by him,
14:22 **Y**, survivors shall be left in it,
16: 7 **y** you were naked and bare.
16:31 **Y** you were not like a whore,
16:60 **y** I will remember my covenant with you in
17:15 Can he break the covenant and **y** escape?
17:18 he gave his hand and **y** did all these things,
18:19 **Y** you say, "Why should not the son suffer for
18:25 **Y** you say, "The way of the Lord is unfair."
18:29 **Y** the house of Israel says,
23:11 **y** she was more corrupt than she in her lusting and
23:19 **Y** she increased her whorings,
24:13 **Y**, when I cleansed you in your filthy lewdness,
24:16 **y** you shall not mourn or weep,
28: 2 in the heart of the seas," **y** you are but a mortal,
29:18 **y** neither he nor his army got anything from Tyre
33:13 **y** if they trust in their righteousness
33:14 **y** if they turn from their sin and do what is lawful
33:17 **Y** your people say, "The way of the Lord is
33:20 **Y** you say, "The way of the Lord is not just."
33:24 **y** he got possession of the land;
36:20 and **y** they had to go out of his land."
44:14 **Y** I will appoint them to keep charge of
Da 2:39 and **y** a third kingdom of bronze,
11:45 **Y** he shall come to his end,
Hos 1:10 **Y** the number of the people of Israel shall be like
4: 4 **Y** let no one contend, and let none accuse,
7:10 **y** they do not return to the LORD their God,
7:15 **y** they plot evil against me.
9: 8 **y** a fowler's snare is on all his ways,
11: 3 **Y** it was I who taught Ephraim to walk,
13: 4 **Y** I have been the LORD your God ever since
Joel 2:12 **Y** even now, says the LORD,
Am 2: 9 **Y** I destroyed the Amorite before them,
4: 6 **y** you did not return to me, says the LORD.
4: 8 **y** you did not return to me, says the LORD.
4: 9 **y** you did not return to me, says the LORD.
4:10 **y** you did not return to me, says the LORD.
4:11 **y** you did not return to me, says the LORD.
Jnh 2: 6 **y** you brought up my life from the Pit,
Mic 1:12 **y** disaster has come down from the LORD to
3:11 **y** they lean upon the LORD and say,
Na 3:10 **Y** she became an exile, she went into captivity;
Hab 3:18 **y** I will rejoice in the LORD;
Hag 1: 2 not **y** come to rebuild the LORD's house.
2: 4 **Y** now take courage, O Zerubbabel,
2:17 **y** you did not return to me, says the LORD.
Zec 8:20 Peoples shall **y** come, the inhabitants
10: 9 **y** in far countries they shall remember me,
Mal 1: 2 **Y** I have loved Jacob
1:14 and **y** sacrifices to the Lord what is blemished;
2:17 **Y** you say, "How have we wearied him?"
3: 8 **Y** you are robbing me!
3:13 **Y** you say, "How have we spoken against you?"
Mt 6:26 and **y** your heavenly Father feeds them.
6:29 **y** I tell you, even Solomon in all his glory was
10:29 **Y** not one of them will fall to the ground apart
11:11 **y** the least in the kingdom
11:19 **Y** wisdom is vindicated by her deeds."
12: 5 the temple break the sabbath and **y** are guiltless?
13:21 **y** such a person has no root,
14: 9 **y** out of regard for his oaths and for the guests,
15:27 **y** even the dogs eat the crumbs that fall
24: 6 for this must take place, but the end is not **y**.
26:39 **y** not what I want but what you want."
Mk 4:32 **y** when it is sown it grows up and becomes
6:20 and **y** he liked to listen to him.
6:26 **y** out of regard for his oaths and for the guests,
7:24 **Y** he could not escape notice,
8:21 Then he said to them, "Do you not **y** understand?"
14:36 **y**, not what I want, but what you want."
Lk 4:26 **y** Elijah was sent to none of them except to
5: 5 **Y** if you say so, I will let down the nets."
7:28 **y** the least in the kingdom
10:11 **Y** know this: the kingdom of God has come near.'
12: 6 **Y** not one of them is forgotten in God's sight.
12:24 nor barn, and **y** God feeds them.
12:27 **y** I tell you, even Solomon in all his glory was
13:33 **Y** today, tomorrow, and the next day I must be
15:29 **y** you have never given me even a young goat so
18: 5 **y** because this widow keeps bothering me,
18: 8 And **y**, when the Son of Man comes,
22:42 **y**, not my will but yours be done."
Jn 1:10 **y** the world did not know him.
2: 4 My hour has not **y** come."
3:10 and **y** you do not understand these things?
3:11 **y** you do not receive our testimony.
3:24 of course, had not **y** been thrown into prison.
3:32 **y** no one accepts his testimony.
5:40 **Y** you refuse to come to me to have life.
6:17 and Jesus had not **y** come to them.
6:36 to you that you have seen me and **y** do not believe.
6:70 **Y** one of you is a devil."
7: 6 Jesus said to them, "My time has not **y** come,
7: 8 for my time has not **y** fully come."
7:13 **Y** no one would speak openly about him for fear
7:19 **Y** none of you keeps the law.
7:27 **Y** we know where this man is from;
7:30 because his hour had not **y** come.
7:31 **Y** many in the crowd believed in him
7:39 for as **y** there was no Spirit,
7:39 because Jesus was not **y** glorified.
8:16 **Y** even if I do judge, my judgment is valid;
8:20 because his hour had not **y** come.
8:37 **y** you look for an opportunity to kill me,
8:50 **Y** I do not seek my own glory;
8:52 Abraham died, and so did the prophets; **y** you say,
8:57 Jews said to him, "You are not **y** fifty years old,
9:30 and **y** he opened my eyes.
11:30 Now Jesus had not **y** come to the village,
16: 5 **y** none of you asks me, 'Where are you going?'
16:32 **Y** I am not alone because the Father is with me.
20: 9 for as **y** they did not understand the scripture,
20:17 because I have not **y** ascended to the Father.
20:29 Blessed are those who have not seen and **y**
21:23 **Y** Jesus did not say to him that he would not die,
Ac 5:14 **Y** more than ever believers were added to
5:28 **y** here you have filled Jerusalem
7:48 **Y** the Most High does not dwell in houses made
7:53 and **y** you have not kept it."
8:16 as **y** the Spirit had not come upon any of them;
14:17 **y** he has not left himself without a witness
23: 3 and **y** in violation of the law you order me to
28:17 **y** I was arrested in Jerusalem and handed over to
Ro 1:32 **y** they not only do them but
2: 3 when you judge those who do such things and **y**
5:14 **Y** death exercised dominion from Adam to Moses,
7: 7 **Y**, if it had not been for the law,
1Co 2: 6 **Y** among the mature we do speak wisdom,
7:28 **Y** those who marry will experience distress
8: 2 Anyone who claims to know something does not **y**
8: 6 **y** for us there is one God,
12:20 As it is, there are many members, **y** one body.
14:21 **y** even then they will not listen to me,"
2Co 6: 8 We are treated as impostors, and **y** are true;
6: 9 **y** are well known; as punished, and **y** not killed;
6:10 **y** always rejoicing; as poor, **y** making many rich;
6:10 as having nothing, and **y** possessing everything.
8: 9 **y** for your sakes he became poor,
Gal 2:16 **y** we know that a person is justified not by
Php 3: 7 **Y** whatever gains I had, these I have come
Col 2: 5 **y** I am absent in body, **y** I am with you in spirit,
1Ti 2:15 **Y** she will be saved through childbearing,
2Ti 3:11 **Y** the Lord rescued me from all of them.
Phm 1: 9 **y** I would rather appeal to you on the basis
Heb 2: 8 we do not **y** see everything in subjection to them,
3: 3 **Y** Jesus is worthy of more glory than Moses,
3:16 who were they who heard and **y** were rebellious?
4:15 in every respect has been tested as we are, **y**
9: 8 into the sanctuary has not **y** been disclosed as long
10:37 For **y** "in a very little while,
11: 7 warned by God about events as **y** unseen,
11:39 **Y** all these, though they were commended
12: 4 In your struggle against sin you have not **y** resisted
12:26 now he has promised, "**Y** once more I will shake
12:27 This phrase, "**Y** once more,"
Jas 2:16 and **y** you do not supply their bodily needs,
3: 4 **y** they are guided by a very small rudder wherever
3: 5 **y** it boasts of great exploits.
4:14 **Y** you do not even know what tomorrow will
1Pe 2: 4 though rejected by mortals **y** chosen and precious
2:16 **y** do not use your freedom as a pretext for evil.
3:16 **y** do it with gentleness and reverence.
4:16 **Y** if any of you suffers as a Christian,
1Jn 2: 8 **Y** I am writing you a new commandment
3: 2 what we will be has not **y** been revealed.
3:17 a brother or sister in need and **y** refuses help?
Jude 1: 8 **Y** in the same way these dreamers also defile
Rev 2: 6 **Y** this is to your credit:
2:13 **Y** you are holding fast to my name,
3: 4 **Y** you have still a few persons in Sardis who have
3: 8 and **y** you have kept my word and have
13:14 that had been wounded by the sword and **y** lived;
17:10 one is living, and the other has not **y** come;
17:12 that you saw are ten kings who have not **y**
Tob 2: 8 **y** here he is again burying the dead!"
Jdt 3: 8 **Y** he demolished all their shrines and cut
7: 5 **Y** they all seized their weapons,
9: 2 'It shall not be done'—**y** they did it.
AdE 4:14 **Y**, who knows whether it was not for such a time
Wis 4:15 **Y** the peoples saw and did not understand,
13: 6 **Y** these people are little to be blamed,
13: 8 **Y** again, not even they are to be excused;
17: 9 For even if nothing disturbing frightened them, **y**,
18:13 **y**, when their firstborn were destroyed,
Sir 5: 4 "I sinned, **y** what has happened to me?"
17:24 **Y** to those who repent he grants a return,
17:31 **Y** it can be eclipsed.
27:30 **y** a sinner holds on to them.
28:12 **y** both come out of your mouth.
36:23 **y** one food is better than another.
37: 5 **y** in battle they will carry his shield.
37:19 and **y** be useless to themselves.
38:32 **Y** they are not sought out for the council of
Bar 2: 8 **Y** we have not entreated the favor of the Lord
2:10 **Y** we have not obeyed his voice,
2:27 **Y** you have dealt with us, O Lord our God,
LtJ 6:41 **Y** they themselves cannot perceive this
Aza 1:16 **Y** with a contrite heart and a humble spirit may we
1Mc 8:14 **Y** for all this not one of them has put on a crown
2Mc 6:26 **y** whether I live or die I shall not escape the hands
7:35 not **y** escaped the judgment of the almighty,
8:20 **y** when the Macedonians were hard pressed,
9: 7 **Y** he did not in any way stop his insolence,
1Es 4: 7 And **y** he is only one man!
4:29 **Y** I have seen him with Apame,
5:53 though the temple of God was not **y** built.
6: 5 **Y** the elders of the Jews were dealt with kindly,
6:20 it has not **y** reached completion.'
Man 1: 6 **y** immeasurable and unsearchable is your promised
3Mc 5:26 The rays of the sun were not **y** shed abroad,

2Es 1:14 **Y** you have forgotten me, says the Lord.
1:36 y will recall their former state.
1:37 with bodily eyes, y with the spirit they will believe
3: 5 **Y** he was the creation of your hands,
3:20 **"Y** you did not take away their evil heart
3:33 **Y** their reward has not appeared
4: 8 to me, 'I never went down into the deep, nor as y
4:28 but the harvest of it has not y come.
5:13 you shall hear y greater things than these."
5:36 "Count up for me those who have not y come,
5:41 **"Y,** O Lord, you have charge
6:39 the sound of human voices was not y there.
7:31 the world that is not y awake shall be roused,
7:*132* [62] because he has mercy on those who have not y
7:*136* [66] those who are gone and to those y to come—
8:41 and y not all that have been sown will come up
9:32 y the fruit of the law did not perish—
9:33 **Y** those who received it perished,
9:35 y with us it has not been so.
11:20 of them that ruled, y disappeared suddenly;
13: 8 were filled with fear, and y they dared to fight.
13:20 **Y** it is better to come into these things,
13:28 y destroying the onrushing multitude that came
16:20 **Y** for all this they will not turn
4Mc 6: 6 y while the old man's eyes were raised to heaven,
15: 8 y because of the fear of God she disdained
16:12 **Y** that holy and God-fearing mother did not wail
18:20 O bitter was that day—and y not bitter—

YHWH See Index to Footnotes

YIELD (51) [YIELDED, YIELDING, YIELDS]

Ge 4:12 it will no longer y to you its strength;
Ex 23:10 you shall sow your land and gather in its **y;**
Lev 19:25 that their y may be increased for you:
25: 3 shall prune your vineyard, and gather in their **y;**
25: 7 and for the wild animals in your land all its y shall
25:19 The land will y its fruit,
25:21 so that it will y a crop for three years.
26: 4 and the land shall y its produce,
26: 4 and the trees of the field shall y their fruit.
26:20 your land shall not y its produce,
26:20 and the trees of the land shall not y their fruit.
Nu 20: 8 command the rock before their eyes to y its water.
Dt 11:17 there will be no rain and the land will y no fruit;
13: 8 you must not y to or heed any such persons.
14:22 of all the y of your seed that is brought in yearly
22: 9 or the whole y will have to be forfeited,
22: 9 both the crop that you have sown and the y of
33:14 and the rich y of the months;
2Ch 30: 8 but y yourselves to the LORD and come
32:28 storehouses also for the y of grain, wine, and oil;
Ne 9:37 Its rich y goes to the kings whom you have set
Job 31:39 if I have eaten its y without payment, and caused
40:20 For the mountains y food for it where all
Ps 1: 3 which y their fruit in its season,
72: 3 May the mountains y prosperity for the people,
85:12 and our land will y its increase.
107:37 and plant vineyards, and get a fruitful **y.**
Pr 8:19 even fine gold, and my y than choice silver.
13:23 The field of the poor may y much food,
18:20 the y of the lips brings satisfaction.
Isa 5: 2 he expected it to y grapes,
5: 4 When I expected it to y grapes,
5: 4 why did it y wild grapes?
5:10 For ten acres of vineyard shall y but one bath,
5:10 and a homer of seed shall y a mere ephah.
Eze 34:27 The trees of the field shall y their fruit,
34:27 and the earth shall y its increase.
36: 8 and y your fruit to my people Israel;
Hos 8: 7 standing grain has no heads, it shall y no meal;
8: 7 if it were to y, foreigners would devour it.
Joel 2:22 the fig tree and vine give their full **y.**
Hab 3:17 produce of the olive fails and the fields y no food;
Hag 2:19 the pomegranate, and the olive tree still y nothing?
Zec 8:12 the vine shall y its fruit,
Jas 3:12 Can a fig tree, my brothers and sisters, y olives,
3:12 No more can salt water y fresh.
3:17 gentle, willing to y, full of mercy and good fruits,
Jdt 2:10 They must y themselves to you,
2Es 7:13 and y the fruit of immortality.
4Mc 8: 5 to y to me and enjoy my friendship.
12: 5 if you y to persuasion you will be my friend and

YIELDED (7) [YIELD]

Ps 67: 6 The earth has y its increase;
Isa 5: 2 he expected it to yield grapes, but it y wild grapes.
Da 3:28 They disobeyed the king's command and y
Mk 4: 7 thorns grew up and choked it, and it y no grain.
Jas 5:18 the heaven gave rain and the earth y its harvest.
Wis 18:25 To these the destroyer y, these he feared;
2Mc 13:23 y and swore to observe all their rights,

YIELDING (6) [YIELD]

Ge 1:11 plants y seed, and fruit trees of every kind on earth
1:12 plants y seed of every kind,
1:29 I have given you every plant y seed that is upon
SS 5:13 His cheeks are like beds of spices, y fragrance.
Mk 4: 8 growing up and increasing and y thirty and sixty
Rev 17:13 These are united in y their power and authority to

YIELDS (8) [YIELD]

Lev 25: 6 You may eat what the land y during its sabbath—
Hos 10: 1 Israel is a luxuriant vine that y its fruit.
Mt 13:22 lure of wealth choke the word, and it y nothing.
13:23 who indeed bears fruit and y,
Mk 4:19 come in and choke the word, and it y nothing.
Heb 12:11 but later it y the peaceful fruit of righteousness
2Es 7:*75* as soon as everyone of us y up the soul,
4Mc 6:35 it masters pleasures and in no respect y to them.

YOKE[‡] (70) [YOKED, YOKES]

Ge 27:40 you shall break his y from your neck."
Lev 26:13 the bars of your y and made you walk erect.
Nu 19: 2 and on which no y has been laid.
Dt 21: 3 one that has not pulled in the **y;**
28:48 an iron y on your neck until he has destroyed you.
1Sa 6: 7 never borne a y, and y the cows to the cart,
11: 7 He took a y of oxen,
1Ki 12: 4 "Your father made our y heavy.
12: 4 the hard service of your father and his heavy y
12: 9 'Lighten the y that your father put on us'?"
12:10 'Your father made our y heavy,
12:11 father laid on you a heavy y, I will add to your **y.**
12:14 father made your y heavy, but I will add to your **y;**
19:19 There were twelve y of oxen ahead of him,
19:21 took the y of oxen, and slaughtered them;
2Ch 10: 4 "Your father made our y heavy.
10: 4 the hard service of your father and his heavy y
10: 9 'Lighten the y that your father put on us'?"
10:10 'Your father made our y heavy,
10:11 father laid on you a heavy y, I will add to your **y.**
10:14 "My father made your y heavy, but I will add to it;
Job 1: 3 three thousand camels, five hundred y of oxen,
42:12 a thousand y of oxen, and a thousand donkeys.
Isa 9: 4 For the y of their burden,
10:27 and his y will be destroyed from your neck.
14:25 his y shall be removed from them,
47: 6 on the aged you made your y exceedingly heavy.
58: 6 to undo the thongs of the y,
58: 6 the oppressed go free, and to break every **y?**
58: 9 If you remove the y from among you,
Jer 2:20 long ago you broke your y and burst your bonds,
5: 5 But they all alike had broken the y,
27: 2 Make yourself a y of straps and bars,
27: 8 put its neck under the y of the king of Babylon,
27:11 under the y of the king of Babylon and serve him,
27:12 Bring your necks under the y of the king
28: 2 I have broken the y of the king of Babylon.
28: 4 for I will break the y of the king of Babylon."
28:10 the prophet Hananiah took the y from the neck of
28:11 the y of King Nebuchadnezzar of Babylon from
28:12 after the prophet Hananiah had broken the y from
28:14 an iron y on the neck of all these nations so
30: 8 I will break the y from off his neck,
La 1:14 My transgressions were bound into a **y;**
3:27 It is good for one to bear the y in youth,
5: 5 With a y on our necks we are hard driven;
Eze 34:27 when I break the bars of their y,
Na 1:13 And now I will break off his y from you and snap
Mt 11:29 Take my y upon you, and learn from me;
11:30 For my y is easy, and my burden is light."
Lk 14:19 Another said, 'I have bought five y of oxen,
Ac 15:10 the test by placing on the neck of the disciples a y
Gal 5: 1 and do not submit again to a y of slavery.
1Ti 6: 1 the y of slavery regard their masters as worthy
Sir 6:30 Her y is a golden ornament,
26: 7 A bad wife is a chafing **y;**
28:19 who has not borne its y, and has not been bound
28:20 For its y is y of iron,
30:13 Discipline your son and make his y heavy,
33:27 **Y** and thong will bow the neck,
40: 1 and a heavy y is laid on the children of Adam,
51:26 Put your neck under her y,
1Mc 8:18 and to free themselves from the **y;**
8:31 'Why have you made your y heavy on our friends
13:41 the y of the Gentiles was removed from Israel,

YOKED (4) [YOKE]

Nu 25: 3 Thus Israel y itself to the Baal of Peor,
25: 5 of your people who have y themselves to the Baal
Dt 22:10 not plow with an ox and a donkey y together.
1Sa 6:10 they took two milch cows and y them to the cart,

YOKES (1) [YOKE]

2Sa 24:22 and the threshing sledges and the y of the oxen for

YONDER (1)

Ps 104:25 **Y** is the sea, great and wide,

YONDER (KJV) See also BEYOND, FAR AND WIDE, THERE

YOU (16651) [YOUR, YOURS, YOURSELF, YOURSELVES] See Index of Articles Etc.

YOUNG[‡] (391) [YOUNGER, YOUNGEST, YOUTH, YOUTHFUL, YOUTHS]

A. YOUNG MEN (108)
B. YOUNG MAN (71)
C. YOUNG WOMEN (21)
D. YOUNG WOMAN (14)

Ge 4:23 man for wounding me, a y man for striking me. B
14:24 take nothing but what the y men have eaten, A
15: 9 a turtledove, and a y pigeon."
19: 4 both y and old, all the people to the last man,
22: 3 and took two of his y men with him, A
22: 5 Then Abraham said to his y men, A
22:19 So Abraham returned to his y men, A
24:43 let the y woman who comes out to draw, D
30:39 and so the flocks produced y that were striped,
34:19 And the y man did not delay to do the thing, B
41:12 A y Hebrew was there with us,
44:20 'We have a father, an old man, and a y brother,
Ex 10: 9 Moses said, "We will go with our y and our old;
24: 5 He sent y men of the people of Israel, A
29: 1 Take one y bull and two rams without blemish,
33:11 but his y assistant, Joshua son of Nun,
Lev 16: 3 with a y bull for a sin offering and a ram for
22:28 an animal with its y on the same day.
23:18 one y bull, and two rams;
Nu 6:10 or two y pigeons to the priest at the entrance of
7:15 one y bull, one ram, one male lamb a year old,
7:21 one y bull, one ram, one male lamb a year old,
7:27 one y bull, one ram, one male lamb a year old,
7:33 one y bull, one ram, one male lamb a year old,
7:39 one y bull, one ram, one male lamb a year old,
7:45 one y bull, one ram, one male lamb a year old,
7:51 one y bull, one ram, one male lamb a year old,
7:57 one y bull, one ram, one male lamb a year old,
7:63 one y bull, one ram, one male lamb a year old,
7:69 one y bull, one ram, one male lamb a year old,
7:75 one y bull, one ram, one male lamb a year old,
7:81 one y bull, one ram, one male lamb a year old,
8: 8 Then let them take a y bull and its grain offering
8: 8 and you shall take another y bull for a sin offering.
11:27 And a y man ran and told Moses, B
15:24 the whole congregation shall offer one y bull for
28:11 two y bulls, one ram, seven male lambs a year old
28:19 two y bulls, one ram, and seven male lambs
28:27 two y bulls, one ram, seven male lambs a year old.
29: 2 one y bull, one ram, seven male lambs a year old
29: 8 one y bull, one ram, seven male lambs a year old.
29:13 thirteen y bulls, two rams,
29:17 On the second day: twelve y bulls, two rams,
30:16 and a father and his daughter while she is still y
31:18 the y girls who have not known a man by sleeping
Dt 22: 6 you shall not take the mother with the **y.**
22: 7 Let the mother go, taking only the y for yourself,
22:15 the y woman and her mother shall then submit D
22:15 the y woman's virginity to the elders of the city
22:16 father of the y woman shall say to the elders: D
22:19 to the y woman's father) because he has slandered
22:20 that evidence of the y woman's virginity was
22:21 then they shall bring the y woman out to D
22:23 If there is a y woman, D
22:24 the y woman because she did not cry for help in D
22:26 You shall do nothing to the y woman; D
22:26 the y woman has not committed D
22:29 of silver to the y woman's father,
28:50 to the old or favor to the **y.**
32:11 As an eagle stirs up its nest, and hovers over its **y;**
32:25 for y man and woman alike, B
Jos 6:21 both men and women, y and old, oxen, sheep,
6:23 So the y men who had been spies went in A
Jdg 8:14 he caught a y man, one of the people of Succoth, B
9:54 the y man who carried his armor and said to him, B
9:54 So the y man thrust him through, and he died. B
12: 9 in thirty y women from outside for his sons. C
14: 5 suddenly a y lion roared at him.
14:10 feast there as the y men were accustomed to do. A
17: 7 Now there was a y man of Bethlehem in Judah, B
17:11 the y man became to him like one of his sons. B
17:12 and the y man became his priest, B
18: 3 they recognized the voice of the y Levite;
18:15 and came to the house of the y Levite,
19:19 and wine for me and the woman and the y man B
21:12 four hundred y virgins who had never slept with
21:21 when the y women of Shiloh come out to dance C
21:21 a wife for himself from the y women of Shiloh, C
Ru 2: 5 "To whom does this y woman belong?" D
2: 8 but keep close to my y women. C
2: 9 I have ordered the y men not to bother you. A
2: 9 and drink from what the y men have drawn." A
2:15 she got up to glean, Boaz instructed his y men, A
2:22 my daughter, that you go out with his y women, C
2:23 So she stayed close to the y women of Boaz, C
3: 2 with whose y women you have been working. C
3:10 you have not gone after y men, A
4:12 that the LORD will give you by this y woman, D
1Sa 1:24 at Shiloh; and the child was **y.**
2:17 the sin of the y men was very great in the sight A
5: 9 both y and old, so that tumors broke out on them.
9: 2 a son whose name was Saul, a handsome y man. B
14: 1 of Saul said to the y man who carried his armor, B
14: 6 said to the y man who carried his armor, B
16:18 One of the y men answered, A
17:55 "Abner, whose son is this y man?" B
17:58 Saul said to him, "Whose son are you, y man?" B
20:22 But if I say to the y man, 'Look, B
21: 2 appointment with the y men for such and such A
21: 4 the y men have kept themselves from women." A
21: 5 the vessels of the y men are holy even when A
25: 5 So David sent ten y men; A
25: 5 and David said to the y men, "Go up to Carmel, A
25: 8 Ask your y men, and they will tell you. A
25: 8 Therefore let my y men find favor in your sight; A
25: 9 When David's y men came, A
25:12 So David's y men turned away, A
25:14 But one of the y men told Abigail, Nabal's wife, A
25:19 and said to her y men, "Go on ahead of me; A
25:25 your servant, did not see the y men of my lord, A

1Sa 25:27 be given to the y men who follow my lord. A
26:22 Let one of the y men come over and get it. A
30:13 He said, "I am a y man of Egypt, B
30:17 of them escaped, except four hundred y men, A
2Sa 1: 5 David asked the y man who was reporting to B
1: 6 The y man reporting to him said, B
1:13 David said to the y man who had reported to B
1:15 Then David called one of the y men and said, A
2:14 "Let the y men come forward and have a contest A
2:21 and seize one of the y men, and take his spoil." A
4:12 So David commanded the y men, A
9:12 Mephibosheth had a y son whose name was Mica.
13:17 He called the y man who served him and said, B
13:32 they have killed all the y men the king's sons; A
13:34 When the y man who kept watch looked up, B
14:21 go, bring back the y man Absalom." B
16: 2 the bread and summer fruit for the y men to eat, A
18: 5 for my sake with the y man Absalom." B
18:12 For my sake protect the y man Absalom! B
18:15 And ten y men, Joab's armor-bearers, A
18:29 king said, "Is it well with the y man Absalom?" B
18:32 "Is it well with the y man Absalom?" B
18:32 up to do you harm, be like that y man." B
1Ki 1: 2 "Let a y virgin be sought for my lord the king,
11:17 He was a y boy at that time.
11:28 the y man was industrious he gave him charge B
12: 8 consulted with the y men who had grown up A
12:10 y men who had grown up with him said to him, A
12:14 of the y men, "My father made your yoke heavy, A
20:14 By the y men who serve the district governors." A
20:15 the y men who serve the district governors, A
20:17 The y men who serve the district governors A
20:19 the y men who serve the district governors, A
2Ki 5: 2 on one of their raids had taken a y girl captive
5:14 his flesh was restored like the flesh of a y boy,
8:12 you will kill their y men with the sword, A
9: 4 y man, the young prophet, went to B
9: 4 young man, the y prophet, went to Ramoth-gilead.
9: 6 the y man poured the oil on his head, B
1Ch 12:28 a y warrior, and twenty-two commanders
22: 5 "My son Solomon is y and inexperienced,
29: 1 is y and inexperienced, and the work is great;
2Ch 10: 8 and consulted the y men who had grown up A
10:10 y men who had grown up with him said to him, A
10:14 the y men, "My father made your yoke heavy, A
13: 7 when Rehoboam was y and irresolute and could
13: 9 Whoever comes to be consecrated with a y bull
15:13 should be put to death, whether y or old,
31:15 old and y alike, by divisions,
36:17 had no compassion on y man or young woman, B
36:17 had no compassion on young man or y woman, D
Ezr 6: 9 Whatever is needed—y bulls, rams,
Ne 12:35 and some of the y priests with trumpets:
Est 2: 2 "Let beautiful y virgins be sought out for the king.
2: 3 of his kingdom to gather all the beautiful y virgins
2: 8 many y women were gathered in the citadel C
3:13 to kill, and to annihilate all Jews, y and old,
Job 1:19 and it fell on the y people, and they are dead;
4:10 and the teeth of the y lions are broken.
14: 9 and put forth branches like a y plant.
19:18 Even y children despise me;
24: 5 scavenging in the wasteland food for their y.
29: 8 the y men saw me and withdrew, A
32: 6 "I am y in years, and you are aged;
38:39 or satisfy the appetite of the y lions,
38:41 when its y ones cry to God,
39: 3 and are delivered of their y?
39: 4 Their y ones become strong,
39:16 It deals cruelly with its y,
39:30 Its y ones suck up blood;
Ps 17:12 like a y lion lurking in ambush.
29: 6 and Sirion like a y wild ox.
34:10 The y lions suffer want and hunger,
37:25 I have been y, and now am old,
58: 6 tear out the fangs of the y lions, O LORD!
78:63 Fire devoured their y men, A
84: 3 where she may lay her y, at your altars,
91:13 y lion and the serpent you will trample under foot.
104:21 The y lions roar for their prey,
105:34 and y locusts without number;
119: 9 How can y people keep their way pure?
144:14 and may our cattle be heavy with y.
147: 9 and to the y ravens when they cry.
148:12 Y men and women alike, old and young A
148:12 Young men and women alike, old and y together!
Pr 1: 4 knowledge and prudence to the y—
7: 7 among the youths, a y man without sense, B
Ecc 11: 9 Rejoice, y man, while you are young, B
11: 9 Rejoice, young man, while you are y,
SS 2: 3 so is my beloved among y men. A
2: 9 My beloved is like a gazelle or a y stag.
2:17 be like a gazelle or a y stag on the cleft mountains.
8:14 or a y stag upon the mountains of spices!
Isa 5:29 Their roaring is like a lion, like y lions they roar;
7:14 the y woman is with child and shall bear a son, D
7:21 On that day one will keep alive a y cow
9:17 on their y people, or compassion on their orphans
11: 7 their y shall lie down together;
13:18 Their bows will slaughter the y men; A
20: 4 both the y and the old, naked and barefoot,
23: 4 nor given birth, I have neither reared y men A
23: 4 nor brought up y women." C
31: 4 As a lion or a y lion growls over its prey, and—
31: 8 and his y men shall be put to forced labor. A
34: 7 and y steers with the mighty bulls.
40:30 and the y will fall exhausted;
53: 2 For he grew up before him like a y plant,
Isa 60: 6 the y camels of Midian and Ephah;
62: 5 For as a y man marries a young woman, B
62: 5 For as a young man marries a y woman, D
Jer 2:23 a restive y camel interlacing her tracks,
6:11 and on the gatherings of y men as well; A
9:21 the streets and the y men from the squares." A
11:22 the y men shall die by the sword; A
31:12 and over the y of the flock and the herd;
31:13 Then shall the y women rejoice in the dance, C
31:13 and the y men and the old shall be merry. A
48:15 and the choicest of his y men have gone down A
49:26 Therefore her y men shall fall in her squares, A
50:30 Therefore her y men shall fall in her squares, A
51: 3 Do not spare her y men; utterly destroy her A
51:22 with you I smash the y man and the girl; B
La 1: 4 her y girls grieve, and her lot is bitter.
1:15 a time against me to crush my y men; A
1:18 my y women and young men have gone C
1:18 my young women and y men have gone A
2:10 the y girls of Jerusalem have bowed their heads
2:21 y and the old are lying on the ground in the streets;
2:21 my y women and my young men have fallen by C
2:21 my young women and my y men have fallen by A
3:51 at the fate of all the y women in my city. C
4: 3 Even the jackals offer the breast and nurse their y,
5:13 Y men are compelled to grind, A
5:14 the city gate, the y men their music. A
Eze 9: 6 Cut down old men, y men and young women, A
9: 6 Cut down old men, young men and y women, C
17:22 a tender one from the topmost of its y twigs;
19: 2 She lay down among y lions, rearing her cubs.
19: 3 he became a y lion, and he learned to catch prey;
19: 5 took another of her cubs and made him a y lion.
19: 6 he became a y lion, and he learned to catch prey;
23: 6 of them handsome y men, mounted horsemen. A
23:12 horsemen, all of them handsome y men. A
23:21 and caressed your y breasts.
23:23 all the Assyrians with them, handsome y men, A
30:17 The y men of On and of Pi-beseth shall fall by A
31: 6 the animals of the field gave birth to their y;
38:13 of Tarshish and all its y warriors will say to you,
41:19 the face of a y lion turned toward the palm tree on
45:18 you shall take a y bull without blemish,
45:22 for himself and all the people of the land a y bull
45:23 as a burnt offering to the LORD seven y bulls
46: 6 On the day of the new moon he shall offer a y bull
46:11 the grain offering with a y bull shall be an ephah,
Da 1: 4 y men without physical defect and handsome, A
1:10 in poorer condition than the other y men A
1:13 with the appearance of the y men who eat A
1:15 fatter than all the y men who had been eating A
1:17 To these four y men God gave knowledge A
Hos 5:14 and like a y lion to the house of Judah.
9:13 Once I saw Ephraim as a y palm planted in
Joel 2:28 and your y men shall see visions. A
Am 3: 4 Does a y lion cry out from its den,
4:10 I killed your y men with the sword; A
8:13 In that day the beautiful y women and C
8:13 and the y men shall faint for thirst. A
Mic 2: 9 from their y children you take away my glory
5: 8 like a y lion among the flocks of sheep, which,
Na 2:11 the cave of the y lions, where the lion goes,
2:13 and the sword shall devour your y lions;
Zec 2: 4 and said to him, "Run, say to that y man: B
9:17 Grain shall make the y men flourish, A
9:17 and new wine the y women. C
Mt 19:20 The y man said to him, "I have kept all these; B
19:22 When the y man heard this word, B
Mk 14:51 A certain y man was following him, B
16: 5 As they entered the tomb, they saw a y man, B
Lk 2:24 "a pair of turtledoves or two y pigeons."
7:14 And he said, "Y man, I say to you, rise!" B
15:29 a y goat so that I might celebrate with my friends.
Jn 12:14 Jesus found a y donkey and sat on it;
Ac 2:17 and your y men shall see visions, A
5: 6 The y men came and wrapped up his body, A
5:10 When the y men came in they found her dead, A
7:58 at the feet of a y man named Saul. B
20: 9 A y man named Eutychus, B
23:17 "Take this y man to the tribune, B
23:18 and asked me to bring this y man to you; B
23:22 So the tribune dismissed the y man, ordering B
Tit 2: 4 so that they may encourage the y women C
1Jn 2:13 I am writing to you, y people,
2:14 I write to you, y people, because you are strong
Tob 1: 4 in the land of Israel, while I was still a y man, B
2:12 paid her full wages and also gave her a y goat
5: 5 "Where do you come from, y man?" B
5: 7 Then Tobias said to him, "Wait for me, y man, B
5:10 went out and called him, and said, "Y man, B
5:10 But the y man said, "Take courage; B
6: 1 The y man went out and the angel went with B
6: 3 Then the y man went down to wash his feet in B
6: 3 the water and tried to swallow the y man's foot,
6: 4 But the angel said to the y man, B
6: 4 y man grasped the fish and drew it up on the B
6: 6 the y man gathered together the gall, heart, B
6: 7 the y man questioned the angel and said to him, B
6:11 Raphael said to the y man, B
7: 2 much the y man resembles my kinsman Tobit!" B
8: 1 the y man and brought him into the bedroom. B
Jdt 2:27 and ravaged their lands and put all their y men A
6:16 all their y men and women ran to the assembly. A
7:22 y men fainted from thirst and were collapsing A
7:23 Then all the people, the y men, the women, A
10: 9 they ordered the y men to open the gate for her, A
16: 4 and kill my y men with the sword, A
Jdt 16: 6 not fall by the hands of the y men, nor did A
AdE 2: 3 and they shall select beautiful y virgins to
Wis 3:18 If they die y, they will have no hope
8:10 in the presence of the elders, though I am y.
Sir 15: 2 and like a y bride she will welcome him.
30:12 and beat his sides while he is y,
32: 7 Speak, you who are y, if you are obliged to,
42: 9 when she is y, for fear she may not marry,
47: 3 He played with lions as though they were y goats,
47:14 How wise you were when you were y!
50:12 he was like a y cedar on Lebanon surrounded by
51:13 While I was still y, before I went
Sus 1:21 we will testify against you that a y man was B
1:37 Then a y man, who was hiding there, B
1:40 seize this woman and asked who the y man was, B
1:45 stirred up the holy spirit of a y lad named Daniel,
1Mc 1:26 y women and young men became faint, C
1:26 young women and y men became faint, A
11:39 up Antiochus, the y son of Alexander,
11:54 with him the y boy Antiochus who began to reign
11:57 Then the y Antiochus wrote to Jonathan, saying,
13:31 with the y King Antiochus;
2Mc 3:19 y women who were kept indoors ran together C
3:26 Two y men also appeared to him, A
3:33 the same y men appeared again A
4:12 and he induced the noblest of the y men to wear A
5:13 Then there was massacre of y and old,
5:13 and children, and slaughter of y girls and infants.
6:24 "for many of the y might suppose that Eleazar
6:28 and leave to the y a noble example of how to die
6:31 only to the y but to the great body of his nation.
7:12 with him were astonished at the y man's spirit,
7:25 Since the y man would not listen to him at all, B
7:30 While she was still speaking, the y man said, B
10:35 twenty y men in the army of Maccabeus, A
12:27 Stalwart y men took their stand before the walls A
13:15 and with a picked force of the bravest y men, A
15:17 and awaking courage in the souls of the y,
1Es 1:53 These killed their y men with the sword A
1:53 and did not spare y man or young woman, B
1:53 and did not spare young man or y woman, D
3: 4 Then the three y men of the bodyguard, A
3:16 He said, "Call the y men, A
4:58 When the y man went out, B
8:50 There I proclaimed a fast for the y men A
3Mc 1:18 Y women who had been secluded C
4: 6 And y women who had just entered C
2Es 2:22 Protect the old and the y within your walls;
2:43 In their midst was a y man of great stature, B
2:46 "Who is that y man who is placing crowns B
5:50 Is our mother, of whom you have told me, still y?
10:22 our y men have been enslaved A
4Mc 2: 3 when he was y and in his prime for intercourse,
3:12 of the king's craving, two staunch y soldiers,
5:31 not so old and cowardly as not to be y in reason
6:19 and ourselves become a pattern of impiety to the y
7:13 his sinews feeble, he became y again
8: 1 For this is why even the very y,
8: 5 "Y men, with favorable feelings I admire each A
8:14 "Be afraid, y fellows; whatever justice you revere
9: 6 we y men should die despising your coercive A
14: 9 as we hear of the suffering of these y men; A
14:12 for the mother of the seven y men bore up under A
14:15 the ones that are tame protect their y by building
14:17 to help their y by flying in circles around them in
14:20 not sway the mother of the y men; A
16:17 you y men were to be terrified by tortures. A

YOUNGER (31) [YOUNG]

Ge 19:31 And the firstborn said to the y, "Our father is old,
19:34 On the next day, the firstborn said to the y, "Look,
19:35 and the y rose, and lay with him;
19:38 The y also bore a son and named him Ben-ammi;
25:23 the elder shall serve the y."
27:15 and put them on her y son Jacob;
27:42 so she sent and called her y son Jacob and said
29:16 and the name of the y was Rachel.
29:18 for your y daughter Rachel."
29:26 giving the y before the firstborn.
48:14 and laid it on the head of Ephraim, who was the y,
48:19 Nevertheless his y brother shall be greater than he,
Jdg 1:13 Othniel son of Kenaz, Caleb's y brother, took it;
3: 9 Othniel son of Kenaz, Caleb's y brother.
15: 2 Is not her y sister prettier than she?
1Sa 14:49 and the name of the y, Michal.
Job 30: 1 they make sport of me, those who are y than I,
Eze 16:46 and your y sister, who lived to the south of you,
16:61 both your elder and your y,
Mk 15:40 and Mary the mother of James the y and of Joses,
Lk 15:12 The y of them said to his father, 'Father,
15:13 A few days later the y son gathered all he had
Jn 21:18 Very truly, I tell you, when you were y,
Ro 9:12 "The elder shall serve the y."
1Ti 5: 1 to him as to a father, to y men as brothers,
5: 2 to y women as sisters—with absolute purity.
5:11 But refuse to put y widows on the list;
5:14 So I would have y widows marry, bear children,
Tit 2: 6 Likewise, urge the y men to be self-controlled.
1Pe 5: 5 you who are y must accept the authority of
4Mc 11:14 "I am y in age than my brothers,

YOUNGEST (26) [YOUNG]

Ge 9:24 from his wine and knew what his y son had done
42:13 the y, however, is now with our father,
42:15 unless your y brother comes here!
42:20 and bring your y brother to me.

Ge 42:32 y is now with our father in the land of Canaan.'
42:34 Bring your y brother to me,
43:29 "Is this your y brother, of whom you spoke to me?
43:33 to his birthright and the y according to his youth,
44: 2 the silver cup, in the top of the sack of the y,
44:12 beginning with the eldest and ending with the y;
44:23 'Unless your y brother comes down with you,
44:26 Only if our y brother goes with us,
44:26 the man's face unless our y brother is with us.'
Jos 6:26 and at the cost of his y he shall set up its gates!"
Jdg 9: 5 but Jotham, the y son of Jerubbaal, survived,
1Sa 16:11 And he said, "There remains yet the y,
17:14 David was the y; the three eldest followed Saul,
1Ki 16:34 and set up its gates at the cost of his y son Segub,
2Ki 3:21 from the y to the oldest,
1Ch 24:31 the chief as well as the y brother.
2Ch 21:17 to him except Jehoahaz, his y son.
22: 1 of Jerusalem made his y son Ahaziah king
Lk 22:26 the greatest among you must become like the y,
2Mc 7:24 The y brother being still alive,
Pm 151: 1 and the y in my father's house;
4Mc 12: 1 the seventh and y of all came forward.

YOUR (8109) [YOU] See Index of Articles Etc.

YOURS (103) [YOU] See Index of Articles Etc.

YOURSELF (323) [SELF, YOU] See Index of Articles Etc.

YOURSELVES (245) [SELF, YOU] See Index of Articles Etc.

YOUTH‡ (92) [YOUNG]

Ge 8:21 the inclination of the human heart is evil from y;
43:33 and the youngest according to his y,
46:34 of livestock from our y even until now, both we
Lev 22:13 and returns to her father's house, as in her y,
Nu 30: 3 while within her father's house, in her y,
1Sa 12: 2 I have led you from my y until this day.
17:33 and he has been a warrior from his y."
17:42 he disdained him, for he was only a y,
2Sa 19: 7 that has come upon you from your y until now."
1Ki 18:12 I your servant have revered the LORD from my y.
Job 13:26 and make me reap the iniquities of my y.
20:11 Their bodies, once full of y,
31:18 from my y I reared the orphan like a father,
33:25 let his flesh become fresh with y;
36:14 They die in their y, and their life ends in shame.
Ps 25: 7 the sins of my y or my transgressions;
71: 5 are my hope, my trust, O LORD, from my y.
71:17 O God, from my y you have taught me,
88:15 Wretched and close to death from my y up,
89:45 You have cut short the days of his y;
103: 5 as long as you live so that your y is renewed like
110: 3 like dew, your y will come to you.
127: 4 in the hand of a warrior are the sons of one's y.
129: 1 from my y"—let Israel now say—
129: 2 "often have they attacked me from my y,
144:12 May our sons in their y be like plants full grown,
Pr 2:17 of her y and forgets her sacred covenant;
5:18 and rejoice in the wife of your y,
Ecc 4:13 a poor but wise y than an old but foolish king,
4:15 follow that y who replaced the king;
11: 9 and let your heart cheer you in the days of your y.
11:10 for y and the dawn of life are vanity.
12: 1 Remember your creator in the days of your y,
Isa 3: 5 the y will be insolent to the elder,
47:12 with which you have labored from your y;
47:15 who have trafficked with you from your y;
54: 4 for you will forget the shame of your y,
54: 6 like the wife of a man's y when she is cast off,
65:20 at a hundred years will be considered a y,
Jer 2: 2 I remember the devotion of your y,
3: 4 "My Father, you are the friend of my y—
3:24 from our y the shameful thing has devoured all
3:25 we and our ancestors, from our y even to this day;
22:21 This has been your way from your y,
31:19 because I bore the disgrace of my y."
32:30 but evil in my sight from their y;
48:11 Moab has been at ease from his y,
La 3:27 It is good for one to bear the yoke in y,
Eze 4:14 my y up until now I have never eaten what died of
16:22 not remember the days of your y,
16:43 you have not remembered the days of your y,
16:60 with you in the days of your y,
23: 3 they played the whore in their y;
23: 8 for in her y men had lain with her
23:19 remembering the days of her y,
23:21 Thus you longed for the lewdness of your y,
Hos 2:15 There she shall respond as in the days of her y,
Joel 1: 8 in sackcloth for the husband of her y.
Zec 13: 5 for the land has been my possession since my y."
Mal 2:14 a witness between you and the wife of your y,
2:15 do not let anyone be faithless to the wife of his y.
Mk 10:20 "Teacher, I have kept all these since my y."
Lk 18:21 He replied, "I have kept all these since my y."
Ac 26: 4 "All the Jews know my way of life from my y,
1Ti 4:12 Let no one despise your y,
Wis 2: 6 and make use of the creation to the full as in y.
4:16 and y that is quickly perfected will condemn
8: 2 I loved her and sought her from my y;
Sir 6:18 My child, from your y choose discipline,
7:23 and make them obedient from their y.
25: 3 If you gathered nothing in your y,
26:19 *My child, keep sound the bloom of your y,*
30:11 Give him no freedom in his y,
30:12 Bow down his neck in his y,
47: 4 In his y did he not kill a giant,
51:15 from my y I followed her steps.
1Mc 1: 6 who had been brought up with him from y,
2:66 a mighty warrior from his y;
16: 2 the wars of Israel from our y until this day,
2Mc 4: 9 by his authority a gymnasium and a body of y
7:25 the mother to him and urged her to advise the y
3Mc 4: 8 Their husbands, in the prime of y,
2Es 5:53 of y are different from those born during the time
5:55 that already is aging and passing the strength of y."
6:32 the purity that you have maintained from your y.
14:10 age has lost its y, and the times begin to grow old.
4Mc 8: 8 Enjoy your y by adopting the Greek way of life
8:10 for your y and handsome appearance.
8:20 Let us take pity on our y and have compassion
9:13 When the noble y was stretched out around this,
9:21 the courageous y, worthy of Abraham,
9:25 the saintly y broke the thread of life.

YOUTHFUL (4) [YOUNG]

Job 33:25 let him return to the days of his y vigor.'
2Ti 2:22 Shun y passions and pursue righteousness, faith,
2Mc 15:30 the man who maintained his y goodwill
3Mc 4: 8 lamentations instead of good cheer and y revelry,

YOUTHS (16) [YOUNG]

2Ch 36:17 who killed their y with the sword in the house
Pr 7: 7 among the simple ones, I observed among the y,
20:29 The glory of y is their strength,
Isa 40:30 Even y will faint and be weary,
Jer 15: 8 I have brought against the mothers of y a destroyer
18:21 their y be slain by the sword in battle.
Am 2:11 of your children to be prophets and some of your y
1Mc 2: 9 her y by the sword of the foe.
14: 9 and the y put on splendid military attire.
1Es 8:91 a very great crowd of men and women and y
4Mc 8:27 But the y, though about to be tortured,
13: 7 so the seven-towered right reason of the y,
13: 9 let us imitate the three y in Assyria who despised
14: 4 the seven y proved coward or shrank from death,
14: 6 with the guidance of the mind, so those holy y,
14: 8 so these y, forming a chorus, encircled

Z

ZAANAIM (KJV) See ELON-BEZAANANNIM

ZAANAN (1)

Mic 1:11 the inhabitants of Z do not come forth;

ZAANANNIM (1)

Jos 19:33 its boundary ran from Heleph, from the oak in Z,

ZAAVAN (2)

Ge 36:27 These are the sons of Ezer: Bilhan, Z, and Akan.
1Ch 1:42 The sons of Ezer: Bilhan, Z, and Jaakan.

ZABAD (11) [=JOZACAR]

1Ch 2:36 the father of Nathan, and Nathan of Z.
2:37 Z became the father of Ephlal, and Ephlal of Obed.
7:21 Z his son, Shuthelah his son, and Ezer
11:41 Uriah the Hittite, Z son of Ahlai,
2Ch 24:26 Those who conspired against him were Z son
Ezr 10:27 Elioenai, Eliashib, Mattaniah, Jeremoth, Z,
10:33 Mattenai, Mattattah, Z, Eliphelet, Jeremai,
10:43 Of the descendants of Nebo: Jeiel, Mattithiah, Z,
1Es 9:28 Eliashib, Othoniah, Jeremoth, and Z and Zerdaiah.
9:33 and Mattattah and Z and Eliphelet and Manasseh
9:35 Mazitias, Z, Iddo, Joel, Benaiah.

ZABADEANS (1)

1Mc 12:31 against the Arabs who are called Z,

ZABAL See Index to Footnotes

ZABBAI (3)

Ezr 10:28 Jehohanan, Hananiah, Z, and Athlai.
Ne 3:20 After him Baruch son of Z repaired another section
1Es 9:29 Jehohanan and Hananiah and Z and Emathis.

ZABBUD (KJV) See ZACCUR

ZABDI (6)

Jos 7: 1 Achan son of Carmi son of Z son of Zerah,
7:17 family by family, and Z was taken.
Jos 7:18 and Achan son of Carmi son of Z son of Zerah,
1Ch 8:19 Jakim, Zichri, Z,
27:27 of the vineyards for the wine cellars was Z
Ne 11:17 of Mica son of Z son of Asaph, who was the leader

ZABDIEL (3)

1Ch 27: 2 of Z was in charge of the first division in
Ne 11:14 their overseer was Z son of Haggedolim.
1Mc 11:17 Z the Arab cut off the head of Alexander

ZABUD (1)

1Ki 4: 5 Z son of Nathan was priest and king's friend;

ZABULON (KJV) See ZEBULUN

ZABUTHEUS (1)

AdE 9: 9 Marmasima, Aruphaeus, Arsaeus, Z,

ZACCAI (2)

Ezr 2: 9 Of Z, seven hundred sixty.
Ne 7:14 Of Z, seven hundred sixty.

ZACCHAEUS (4)

Lk 19: 2 A man was there named Z;
19: 5 he looked up and said to him, "Z, hurry and come
19: 8 Z stood there and said to the Lord, "Look,
2Mc 10:19 Z and his troops, a force sufficient to besiege them;

ZACCUR (11)

Nu 13: 4 From the tribe of Reuben, Shammua son of Z;
1Ch 4:26 Hammuel his son, Z his son, Shimei his son.
24:27 of Jaaziah, Beno, Shoham, Z, and Ibri.
25: 2 Z, Joseph, Nethaniah, and Asarelah,
25:10 the third to Z, his sons and his brothers, twelve;
Ezr 8:14 Of the descendants of Bigvai, Uthai and Z,
Ne 3: 2 And next to them Z son of Imri built.
10:12 Z, Sherebiah, Shebaniah,
12:35 of Mattaniah son of Micaiah son of Z son
13:13 as their assistant Hanan son of Z son of Mattaniah,
1Es 9:24 Of the temple singers: Eliashib and Z.

ZACHARIAH, ZACHARIAS (KJV) See ZECHARIAH

ZACHER (KJV) See ZECHER

ZADOK (57) [ZADOK'S]

2Sa 8:17 Z son of Ahitub and Ahimelech son
15:24 Abiathar came up, and Z also, with all the Levites,
15:25 Then the king said to Z,
15:27 The king also said to the priest Z, "Look,
15:29 So Z and Abiathar carried the ark of God back
15:35 The priests Z and Abiathar will be with you there.
15:35 tell it to the priests Z and Abiathar.
17:15 Then Hushai said to the priests Z and Abiathar,
18:19 Then Ahimaaz son of Z said, "Let me run,
18:22 Then Ahimaaz son of Z said again to Joab,
18:27 like the running of Ahimaaz son of Z."
19:11 King David sent this message to the priests Z
20:25 Sheva was secretary; Z and Abiathar were priests;
1Ki 1: 8 But the priest Z, and Benaiah son of Jehoiada,
1:26 he did not invite me, your servant, and the priest Z,
1:32 King David said, "Summon to me the priest Z,
1:34 There let the priest Z and the prophet Nathan
1:38 So the priest Z, the prophet Nathan,
1:39 There the priest Z took the horn of oil from the tent
1:44 the priest Z, the prophet Nathan, and Benaiah
1:45 the priest Z and the prophet Nathan have anointed
2:35 the king put the priest Z in the place of Abiathar.
4: 2 Azariah son of Z was the priest;
4: 4 Z and Abiathar were priests;
2Ki 15:33 His mother's name was Jerusha daughter of Z.
1Ch 6: 8 Ahitub of Z, Z of Ahimaaz,
6:12 Ahitub of Z, Z of Shallum,
6:53 Z his son, Ahimaaz his son.
9:11 son of Meshullam, son of Z, son of Meraioth,
12:28 Z, a young warrior, and twenty-two commanders
15:11 David summoned the priests Z and Abiathar,
16:39 And he left the priest Z and his kindred the priests
18:16 Z son of Ahitub and Ahimelech son
24: 3 Along with Z of the sons of Eleazar,
24: 6 and Z the priest, and Ahimelech son of Abiathar,
24:31 in the presence of King David, Z, Ahimelech,
27:17 for Levi, Hashabiah son of Kemuel; for Aaron, Z;
29:22 they anointed him as the LORD's prince, and Z
2Ch 27: 1 His mother's name was Jerushah daughter of Z.
31:10 chief priest Azariah, who was of the house of Z,
Ezr 7: 2 son of Shallum, son of Z, son of Ahitub,
Ne 3: 4 Next to them Z son of Baana made repairs.
3:29 After them Z son of Immer
10:21 Meshezabel, Z, Jaddua,
11:11 of Meshullam son of Z son of Meraioth son
13:13 the scribe Z, and Pedaiah of the Levites,
Eze 40:46 these are the descendants of Z,
43:19 to the levitical priests of the family of Z,
44:15 But the levitical priests, the descendants of Z,
48:11 the descendants of Z, who kept my charge,
Mt 1:14 Azor the father of Z, and Z the father of Achim,
Sir 51:12 *to him who has chosen the sons of Z to be priests,*
1Es 8: 2 of Z son of Ahitub son of Amariah son of Uzzi son
2Es 1: 1 of Hilkiah son of Shallum son of Z son of Ahitub

ZADOK'S (1) [ZADOK]
2Sa 15:36 **Z** son Ahimaaz and Abiathar's son Jonathan;

ZAHAM (1)
2Ch 11:19 She bore him sons: Jeush, Shemariah, and **Z.**

ZAIR (1)
2Ki 8:21 Then Joram crossed over to **Z** with all his chariots.

ZALAPH (1)
Ne 3:30 and Hanun sixth son of **Z** repaired another section.

ZALMON (3)
Jdg 9:48 So Abimelech went up to Mount **Z,**
2Sa 23:28 **Z** the Ahohite; Maharai of Netophah;
Ps 68:14 the Almighty scattered kings there, snow fell on **Z.**

ZALMONAH (2)
Nu 33:41 They set out from Mount Hor and camped at **Z.**
33:42 They set out from **Z** and camped at Punon.

ZALMUNNA (12)
Jdg 8: 5 and I am pursuing Zebah and **Z,**
8: 6 in your possession the hands of Zebah and **Z,**
8: 7 the LORD has given Zebah and **Z** into my hand,
8:10 Now Zebah and **Z** were in Karkor with their army,
8:12 Zebah and **Z** fled; and he pursued them
8:12 Zebah and **Z,** and threw all the army into a panic.
8:15 and said, "Here are Zebah and **Z,**
8:15 in your possession the hands of Zebah and **Z,**
8:18 Then he said to Zebah and **Z,**
8:21 Then Zebah and **Z** said, "You come and kill us;
8:21 So Gideon proceeded to kill Zebah and **Z;**
Ps 83:11 all their princes like Zebah and **Z,**

ZAMBRIS (1)
1Es 9:34 Shashai, Azarel, Azael, Samatus, **Z,** Joseph.

ZAMOTH (1)
1Es 9:28 Of the descendants of **Z:** Eliadas,

ZAMZUMMIM (1) [=REPHAIM]
Dt 2:20 though the Ammonites call them **Z,**

ZANOAH (5)
Jos 15:34 **Z,** En-gannim, Tappuah, Enam,
15:56 Jezreel, Jokdeam, **Z,**
1Ch 4:18 Heber father of Soco, and Jekuthiel father of **Z.**
Ne 3:13 and the inhabitants of **Z** repaired the Valley Gate;
11:30 **Z,** Adullam, and their villages, Lachish

ZAPHENATH-PANEAH (1) [=JOSEPH]
Ge 41:45 Pharaoh gave Joseph the name **Z;**

ZAPHON‡ (4)
Jos 13:27 Beth-nimrah, Succoth, and **Z,**
Jdg 12: 1 and they crossed to **Z** and said to Jephthah,
Job 26: 7 He stretches out **Z** over the void,
Isa 14:13 on the mount of assembly on the heights of **Z;**

ZARA, ZARAH (KJV) See ZERAH

ZAREAH (KJV) See ZORAH

ZAREATHITES (KJV) See ZORATHITES

ZARED (KJV) See ZERED

ZAREPHATH (4)
1Ki 17: 9 now to **Z,** which belongs to Sidon, and live there;
17:10 So he set out and went to **Z.**
Ob 1:20 in Halah shall possess Phoenicia as far as **Z;**
Lk 4:26 to none of them except to a widow at **Z** in Sidon.

ZARETHAN (3)
Jos 3:16 the city that is beside **Z,**
1Ki 4:12 which is beside **Z** below Jezreel,
7:46 in the clay ground between Succoth and **Z.**

ZARETHSHAHAR (KJV) See ZERETH SHAHAR

ZARIUS (1)
1Es 1:38 and seized his brother **Z** and brought him back

ZARTANAH, ZARTHAN (KJV) See ZARETHAN

ZATHOLTHA (1)
AdE 1:10 he told Haman, Bazan, Tharra, Boraze, **Z,** Abataza,

ZATTU‡ (7)
Ezr 2: 8 Of **Z,** nine hundred forty-five.
8: 5 the descendants of **Z,** Shecaniah son of Jahaziel,
10:27 Of the descendants of **Z:** Elioenai,
Ne 7:13 Of **Z,** eight hundred forty-five.
10:14 Parosh, Pahath-moab, Elam, **Z,** Bani,
1Es 5:12 The descendants of **Z,** nine hundred forty-five.
8:32 the descendants of **Z,** Shecaniah son of Jahaziel,

ZAVAN (KJV) See ZAAVAN

ZAZA (1)
1Ch 2:33 The sons of Jonathan: Peleth and **Z.**

ZEAL (30) [ZEALOT, ZEALOUS, ZEALOUSLY]
Nu 25:11 by manifesting such **z** among them on my behalf
2Sa 21: 2 to wipe them out in his **z** for the people of Israel
2Ki 10:16 "Come with me, and see my **z** for the LORD."
19:31 The **z** of the LORD of hosts will do this.
Ezr 7:23 be done with **z** for the house of the God of heaven,
Ps 69: 9 It is **z** for your house that has consumed me;
119:139 My **z** consumes me because my foes forget your
Isa 9: 7 The **z** of the LORD of hosts will do this.
26:11 Let them see your **z** for your people,
37:32 The **z** of the LORD of hosts will do this.
63:15 Where are your **z** and your might?
Jn 2:17 "**Z** for your house will consume me."
Ro 10: 2 I can testify that they have a **z** for God,
12:11 Do not lag in **z,** be ardent in spirit, serve the Lord.
2Co 7: 7 your **z** for me, so that I rejoiced still more.
7:11 what longing, what **z,** what punishment!
7:12 in order that your **z** for us might be made known
9: 2 and your **z** has stirred up most of them.
Php 3: 6 as to **z,** a persecutor of the church;
Jdt 9: 4 among your beloved children who burned with **z**
Wis 5:17 The Lord will take his **z** as his whole armor,
14:17 so that by their **z** they might flatter the absent one
Sir 48: 2 and by his **z** he made them few in number.
Bar 4:28 return with tenfold **z** to seek him.
1Mc 2:24 he burned with **z** and his heart was stirred.
2:26 Thus he burned with **z** for the law,
2:50 Now, my children, show **z** for the law,
2:58 Elijah, because of great **z** for the law,
4Mc 13:25 common **z** for nobility strengthened their goodwill
18:12 He told you of the **z** of Phinehas,

ZEALOT (3) [ZEAL]
Lk 6:15 and Simon, who was called the **Z,**
Ac 1:13 and Simon the **Z,** and Judas son of James.
2Mc 4: 2 and a **z** for the laws.

ZEALOUS‡ (14) [ZEAL]
Nu 25:13 because he was **z** for his God,
1Ki 19:10 He answered, "I have been very **z** for the LORD,
19:14 He answered, "I have been very **z** for the LORD,
Ac 21:20 and they are all **z** for the law.
22: 3 being **z** for God, just as all of you are today.
Gal 1:14 I was far more **z** for the traditions of my ancestors.
Tit 2:14 a people of his own who are **z** for good deeds.
Sir 45:23 son of Eleazar ranks third in glory for being **z**
51:18 and I was **z** for the good,
1Mc 2:27 "Let every one who is **z** for the law and supports
2:54 Phinehas our ancestor, because he was deeply **z,**
3Mc 4:15 with bitter haste and **z** intensity from the rising of
2Es 6:58 only begotten, **z** for you, and most dear,
4Mc 16:20 For his sake also our father Abraham was **z**

ZEALOUSLY (4) [ZEAL]
Mk 7:36 the more **z** they proclaimed it.
2Mc 14:38 he had most **z** risked body and life for Judaism.
3Mc 5:27 for which this had been so **z** completed for him.
4Mc 16:16 Fight **z** for our ancestral law.

ZEBADIAH (10)
1Ch 8:15 **Z,** Arad, Eder,
8:17 **Z,** Meshullam, Hizki, Heber,
12: 7 and Joelah and **Z,** sons of Jeroham of Gedor.
26: 2 Jediael the second, **Z** the third, Jathniel the fourth,
27: 7 for the fourth month, and his son **Z** after him;
2Ch 17: 8 Nethaniah, **Z,** Asahel, Shemiramoth, Jehonathan,
19:11 and **Z** son of Ishmael, the governor of the house
Ezr 8: 8 **Z** son of Michael, and with him eighty males.
10:20 Of the descendants of Immer: Hanani and **Z.**
1Es 9:21 and **Z** and Maaseiah and Shemaiah and Jehiel

ZEBAH (12)
Jdg 8: 5 and I am pursuing **Z** and Zalmunna,
8: 6 in your possession the hands of **Z** and Zalmunna,
8: 7 LORD has given **Z** and Zalmunna into my hand,
8:10 **Z** and Zalmunna were in Karkor with their army,
8:12 **Z** and Zalmunna fled; and he pursued them
8:12 the two kings of Midian, **Z** and Zalmunna,
8:15 and said, "Here are **Z** and Zalmunna,
8:15 in your possession the hands of **Z** and Zalmunna,
8:18 Then he said to **Z** and Zalmunna,
8:21 Then **Z** and Zalmunna said, "You come and kill us;
8:21 So Gideon proceeded to kill **Z** and Zalmunna;
Ps 83:11 all their princes like **Z** and Zalmunna,

ZEBAIM (KJV) See POCHERETH HAZZEBAIM

ZEBEDEE (12)
Mt 4:21 James son of **Z** and his brother John,
4:21 in the boat with their father **Z,** mending their nets,
10: 2 James son of **Z,** and his brother John;
20:20 mother of the sons of **Z** came to him with her sons,
26:37 He took with him Peter and the two sons of **Z,**
27:56 and the mother of the sons of **Z.**
Mk 1:19 he saw James son of **Z** and his brother John,
1:20 and they left their father **Z** in the boat with
3:17 James son of **Z** and John the brother of James
10:35 James and John, the sons of **Z,**
Lk 5:10 sons of **Z,** who were partners with Simon.
Jn 21: 2 the sons of **Z,** and two others of his disciples.

ZEBIDAH (1)
2Ki 23:36 His mother's name was **Z** daughter of Pedaiah

ZEBINA (1)
Ezr 10:43 Jeiel, Mattithiah, Zabad, **Z,** Jaddai, Joel,

ZEBOIIM (5)
Ge 10:19 Gomorrah, Admah, and **Z,** as far as Lasha.
14: 2 King Shemeber of **Z,** and the king of Bela (that is,
14: 8 the king of **Z,** and the king of Bela (that is,
Dt 29:23 Admah and **Z,** which the LORD destroyed
Hos 11: 8 How can I treat you like **Z?**

ZEBOIM (2)
1Sa 13:18 the mountain that looks down upon the valley of **Z**
Ne 11:34 Hadid, **Z,** Neballat,

ZEBUDAH (KJV) See ZEBIDAH

ZEBUL (6)
Jdg 9:28 Did not the son of Jerubbaal and **Z** his officer serve
9:30 When **Z** the ruler of the city heard the words
9:36 And when Gaal saw them, he said to **Z,** "Look,
9:36 And **Z** said to him, "The shadows on the
9:38 Then **Z** said to him, "Where is your boast now,
9:41 and **Z** drove out Gaal and his kinsfolk,

ZEBULONITE (KJV) See ZEBULUNITE

ZEBULUN (45) [ZEBULUNITE, ZEBULUNITES]
Ge 30:20 I have borne him six sons"; so she named him **Z.**
35:23 Simeon, Levi, Judah, Issachar, and **Z.**
46:14 The children of **Z:** Sered, Elon, and Jahleel
49:13 **Z** shall settle at the shore of the sea;
Ex 1: 3 Issachar, **Z,** and Benjamin,
Nu 1: 9 From **Z,** Eliab son of Helon.
1:30 The descendants of **Z,** their lineage, in their clans,
1:31 of **Z** were fifty-seven thousand four hundred.
2: 7 Then the tribe of **Z:** The leader of the
10:16 over the company of the tribe of **Z** was Eliab son
13:10 from the tribe of **Z,** Gaddiel son of Sodi;
26:26 The descendants of **Z** by their clans:
Dt 27:13 Reuben, Gad, Asher, **Z,** Dan, and Naphtali.
33:18 And of **Z** he said: Rejoice, **Z,** in your going out;
Jos 19:10 The third lot came up for the tribe of **Z,**
19:16 This is the inheritance of the tribe of **Z,**
19:27 and touches **Z** and the valley
19:34 touching **Z** at the south, and Asher on the west,
21: 7 the tribe of Gad, and the tribe of **Z.**
21:34 were given out of the tribe of **Z:**
Jdg 1:30 **Z** did not drive out the inhabitants of Kitron,
4: 6 from the tribe of Naphtali and the tribe of **Z.**
4:10 Barak summoned **Z** and Naphtali to Kedesh;
5:14 and from **Z** those who bear the marshal's staff;
5:18 **Z** is a people that scorned death;
6:35 He also sent messengers to Asher, **Z,** and Naphtali,
12:12 and was buried at Aijalon in the land of **Z.**
1Ch 2: 1 Reuben, Simeon, Levi, Judah, Issachar, **Z,**
6:63 of the tribes of Reuben, Gad, and **Z.**
6:77 To the rest of the Merarites out of the tribe of **Z:**
12:33 Of **Z,** fifty thousand seasoned troops,
12:40 from as far away as Issachar and **Z** and Naphtali,
27:19 for **Z,** Ishmaiah son of Obadiah;
2Ch 30:10 of Ephraim and Manasseh, and as far as **Z;**
30:11 and **Z** humbled themselves and came to Jerusalem.
30:18 Issachar, and **Z,** had not cleansed themselves,
Ps 68:27 the princes of Judah in a body, the princes of **Z,**
Isa 9: 1 into contempt the land of **Z** and the land
Eze 48:26 from the east side to the west, **Z,** one portion.
48:27 Adjoining the territory of **Z,**
48:33 the gate of Issachar, and the gate of **Z.**
Mt 4:13 in the territory of **Z** and Naphtali,
4:15 Land of **Z,** land of Naphtali, on the road by the sea,
Rev 7: 8 from the tribe of **Z** twelve thousand,

ZEBULUNITE (2) [ZEBULUN]
Jdg 12:11 After him Elon the **Z** judged Israel;
12:12 Then Elon the **Z** died, and was buried at Aijalon in

ZEBULUNITES (4) [ZEBULUN]
Nu 2: 7 The leader of the **Z** shall be Eliab son of Helon,
7:24 of Helon, the leader of the **Z:**
26:27 These are the clans of the **Z;**
34:25 Of the tribe of the **Z** a leader,

ZECHARIAH‡ (67) [BETH-ZECHARIAH, ZECHARIAH'S]
2Ki 14:29 the kings of Israel; his son **Z** succeeded him.

2Ki 15: 8 Z son of Jeroboam reigned over Israel
15:11 the rest of the deeds of Z are written in the Book of
18: 2 His mother's name was Abi daughter of Z.
1Ch 5: 7 generations was reckoned: the chief, Jeiel, and Z,
9:21 Z son of Meshelemiah was gatekeeper at
9:37 Gedor, Ahio, Z, and Mikloth;
15:18 Z, Jaaziel, Shemiramoth, Jehiel, Unni, Eliab,
15:20 Z, Aziel, Shemiramoth, Jehiel,
15:24 Shebaniah, Joshaphat, Nethanel, Amasai, Z,
16: 5 Asaph was the chief, and second to him Z, Jeiel,
24:25 brother of Micah, Isshiah; of the sons of Isshiah, Z.
26: 2 Meshelemiah had sons: Z the firstborn,
26:11 Tebaliah the third, Z the fourth:
26:14 They cast lots also for his son Z,
27:21 of Manasseh in Gilead, Iddo son of Z;
2Ch 17: 7 Ben-hail, Obadiah, Z, Nethanel, and Micaiah,
20:14 spirit of the LORD came upon Jahaziel son of Z,
21: 2 Azariah, Jehiel, Z, Azariah, Michael,
24:20 Then the spirit of God took possession of Z son of
26: 5 He set himself to seek God in the days of Z,
29: 1 His mother's name was Abijah daughter of Z.
29:13 and of the sons of Asaph, Z and Mattaniah;
34:12 along with Z and Meshullam,
35: 8 Z, and Jehiel, the chief officers of the house
Ezr 5: 1 Now the prophets, Haggai and Z son of Iddo,
6:14 the prophesying of the prophet Haggai and Z son
8: 3 Of Parosh, Z, with whom were registered
8:11 Of the descendants of Bebai, Z son of Bebai,
8:16 Shemaiah, Elnathan, Jarib, Elnathan, Nathan, Z,
10:26 Mattaniah, Z, Jehiel, Abdi, Jeremoth, and Elijah.
Ne 8: 4 Mishael, Malchijah, Hashum, Hash-baddanah, Z,
11: 4 of Z son of Amariah son of Shephatiah son
11: 5 son of Adaiah son of Joiarib son of Z son of
11:12 of Amzi son of Z son of Pashhur son of Malchijah,
12:16 of Iddo, Z; of Ginnethon, Meshullam;
12:35 Z son of Jonathan son of Shemaiah son
12:41 Miniamin, Micaiah, Elioenai, Z, and Hananiah,
Isa 8: 2 the priest Uriah and Z son of Jeberechiah.
Zec 1: 1 the word of the LORD came to the prophet Z son of
1: 7 the word of the LORD came to the prophet Z son of
Berechiah son of Iddo; and Z said,
7: 1 word of the LORD came to Z on the fourth day of
7: 8 The word of the LORD came to Z, saying:
Mt 23:35 the blood of righteous Abel to the blood of Z son
Lk 1: 5 there was a priest named Z,
1:12 When Z saw him, he was terrified;
1:13 But the angel said to him, "Do not be afraid, Z,
1:18 Z said to the angel, "How will I know
1:21 Meanwhile the people were waiting for Z,
1:40 she entered the house of Z and greeted Elizabeth.
1:59 and they were going to name him Z after his father.
1:67 Then his father Z was filled with the Holy Spirit
3: 2 of God came to John son of Z in the wilderness.
11:51 from the blood of Abel to the blood of Z,
1Mc 5:18 But he left Joseph, son of Z, and Azariah,
5:56 Joseph son of Z, and Azariah, the commanders of
1Es 1: 8 Z, and Jehiel, the chief officers of the temple,
1:15 Z, and Eddinus, who represented the king.
6: 1 the prophets Haggai and Z son of Iddo prophesied
7: 3 while the prophets Haggai and Z prophesied;
8:30 Of the descendants of Parosh, Z,
8:37 Of the descendants of Bebai, Z son of Bebai,
8:44 Jarib, Nathan, Elnathan, Z, and Meshullam,
9:27 Of the descendants of Elam: Mattaniah and Z,
9:44 Mishael, Malchijah, Lothasubus, Nabariah, and Z.
2Es 1:40 Zephaniah, Haggai, Z and Malachi,

ZECHARIAH'S (1) [ZECHARIAH]
2Ch 24:22 Z father, had shown him, but killed his son.

ZECHER (1)
1Ch 8:31 Gedor, Ahio, Z,

ZEDAD (2)
Nu 34: 8 and the outer limit of the boundary shall be at Z;
Eze 47:15 by way of Hethlon to Lebo-hamath, and on to Z,

ZEDEKIAH (69) [=MATTANIAH]
1Ki 22:11 Z son of Chenaanah made for himself horns
22:24 Then Z son of Chenaanah came up to Micaiah,
2Ki 24:17 king in his place, and changed his name to Z.
24:18 Z was twenty-one years old when he began
24:20 Z rebelled against the king of Babylon.
25: 2 until the eleventh year of King Z.
25: 7 They slaughtered the sons of Z before his eyes,
25: 7 then put out the eyes of Z,
1Ch 3:15 the second Jehoiakim, the third Z,
3:16 Jeconiah his son, Z his son;
2Ch 18:10 Z son of Chenaanah made for himself horns
18:23 Then Z son of Chenaanah came up to Micaiah,
36:10 made his brother Z king over Judah and Jerusalem.
36:11 Z was twenty-one years old when he began
Ne 10: 1 the governor, son of Hacaliah, and Z;
Jer 1: 3 the eleventh year of King Z son of Josiah of Judah,
21: 1 when King Z sent to him Pashhur son of Malchiah
21: 4 Thus you shall say to Z:
21: 7 says the LORD, I will give King Z of Judah,
24: 8 so will I treat King Z of Judah, his officials,
27: 1 the beginning of the reign of King Z son of Josiah
27: 3 the envoys who have come to Jerusalem to King Z
27:12 I spoke to King Z of Judah in the same way:
28: 1 at the beginning of the reign of King Z of Judah,
29: 3 whom King Z of Judah sent to Babylon
29:21 and Z son of Maaseiah, who are prophesying a lie
29:22 "The LORD make you like Z and Ahab,
Jer 32: 1 the LORD in the tenth year of King Z of Judah,
32: 3 where King Z of Judah had confined him.
32: 3 Z had said, "Why do you prophesy and say:
32: 4 King Z of Judah shall not escape out of the hands
32: 5 and he shall take Z to Babylon,
34: 2 Go and speak to King Z of Judah and say to him:
34: 4 hear the word of the LORD, O King Z of Judah!
34: 6 the prophet Jeremiah spoke all these words to Z
34: 8 after King Z had made a covenant with all
34:21 And as for King Z of Judah and his officials,
36:12 Gemariah son of Shaphan, Z son of Hananiah,
37: 1 Z son of Josiah, whom King Nebuchadrezzar
37: 3 King Z sent Jehucal son of Shelemiah and
37:17 Then King Z sent for him, and received him.
37:18 Jeremiah also said to King Z,
37:21 So King Z gave orders,
38: 5 King Z said, "Here he is;
38:14 King Z sent for the prophet Jeremiah
38:15 Jeremiah said to Z, "If I tell you,
38:16 So King Z swore an oath in secret to Jeremiah,
38:17 Then Jeremiah said to Z, "Thus says the LORD,
38:19 King Z said to Jeremiah, "I am afraid of
38:24 Then Z said to Jeremiah, "Do not let anyone else
39: 1 In the ninth year of King Z of Judah,
39: 2 in the eleventh year of Z,
39: 4 King Z of Judah and all the soldiers saw them,
39: 5 and overtook Z in the plains of Jericho;
39: 6 of Babylon slaughtered the sons of Z at Riblah
39: 7 He put out the eyes of Z,
44:30 just as I gave King Z of Judah into the hand
49:34 at the beginning of the reign of King Z of Judah.
51:59 when he went with King Z of Judah to Babylon,
52: 1 Z was twenty-one years old when he began
52: 3 Z rebelled against the king of Babylon.
52: 5 until the eleventh year of King Z.
52: 8 and overtook Z in the plains of Jericho;
52:10 of Babylon killed the sons of Z before his eyes,
52:11 He put out the eyes of Z, and bound him in fetters,
Bar 1: 1 of Mahseiah son of Z son of Hasadiah son
1: 8 the silver vessels that Z son of Josiah,
1Es 1:46 and made Z king of Judea and Jerusalem.
1:46 Z was twenty-one years old,

ZEEB (6)
Jdg 7:25 the two captains of Midian, Oreb and Z;
7:25 and Z they killed at the wine press of Z,
7:25 They brought the heads of Oreb and Z to Gideon
8: 3 the captains of Midian, Oreb and Z;
Ps 83:11 Make their nobles like Oreb and Z,

ZELA (2)
Jos 18:28 Z, Haeleph, Jebus (that is, Jerusalem), Gibeah
2Sa 21:14 of his son Jonathan in the land of Benjamin in Z,

ZELEK (2)
2Sa 23:37 Z the Ammonite; Naharai of Beeroth,
1Ch 11:39 Z the Ammonite, Naharai of Beeroth,

ZELOPHEHAD (12)
Nu 26:33 Now Z son of Hepher had no sons, but daughters:
26:33 and the names of the daughters of Z were Mahlah,
27: 1 Then the daughters of Z came forward.
27: 1 Z was son of Hepher son of Gilead son
27: 7 daughters of Z are right in what they are saying;
36: 2 the LORD to give the inheritance of our brother Z
36: 6 of Z, 'Let them marry whom they think best;
36:10 of Z did as the LORD had commanded Moses.
36:11 Hoglah, Milcah, and Noah, the daughters of Z,
Jos 17: 3 Now Z son of Hepher son of Gilead son
1Ch 7:15 name of the second was Z; and Z had daughters.

ZELOTES (KJV) See ZEALOT

ZELZAH (1)
1Sa 10: 2 in the territory of Benjamin at Z;

ZEMARAIM (2)
Jos 18:22 Beth-arabah, Z, Bethel,
2Ch 13: 4 Then Abijah stood on the slope of Mount Z that is

ZEMARITES (2)
Ge 10:18 the Z, and the Hamathites.
1Ch 1:16 the Arvadites, the Z, and the Hamathites.

ZEMER (1)
Eze 27: 8 skilled men of Z were within you,

ZEMIRAH (1)
1Ch 7: 8 The sons of Becher: Z, Joash, Eliezer, Elioenai,

ZENAN (1)
Jos 15:37 Z, Hadashah, Migdal-gad,

ZENAS (1)
Tit 3:13 to send Z the lawyer and Apollos on their way,

ZEPHANIAH (11)
2Ki 25:18 the second priest Z, and the three guardians of
1Ch 6:36 son of Joel, son of Azariah, son of Z,
Jer 21: 1 of Malchiah and the priest Z son of Maaseiah,
29:25 and to the priest Z son of Maaseiah,
Jer 29:29 The priest Z read this letter in the hearing of
37: 3 of Shelemiah and the priest Z son of Maaseiah to
52:24 the second priest Z, and the three guardians of
Zep 1: 1 that came to Z son of Cushi son of Gedaliah son
Zec 6:10 go the same day to the house of Josiah son of Z.
6:14 Tobijah, Jedaiah, and Josiah son of Z,
2Es 1:40 Z, Haggai, Zechariah and Malachi,

ZEPHATH (1)
Jdg 1:17 and they defeated the Canaanites who inhabited Z,

ZEPHATHAH (1)
2Ch 14:10 up their lines of battle in the valley of Z

ZEPHI (1) [=ZEPHO]
1Ch 1:36 The sons of Eliphaz: Teman, Omar, Z, Gatam,

ZEPHO (2) [=ZEPHI]
Ge 36:11 The sons of Eliphaz were Teman, Omar, Z, Gatam,
36:15 the clans Teman, Omar, Z, Kenaz,

ZEPHON (1) [=ZIPHION, ZEPHONITES]
Nu 26:15 of Z, the clan of the Zephonites;

ZEPHONITES (1) [ZEPHON]
Nu 26:15 of Zephon, the clan of the Z;

ZER (1)
Jos 19:35 The fortified towns are Ziddim, Z, Hammath,

ZERAH (22)
Ge 36:13 Nahath, Z, Shammah, and Mizzah.
36:17 the clans Nahath, Z, Shammah, and Mizzah;
36:33 Jobab son of Z of Bozrah succeeded him as king.
38:30 on his hand; and he was named Z.
46:12 Z (but Er and Onan died in the land of Canaan);
Nu 26:13 of Z, the clan of the Zerahites;
26:20 of Z, the clan of the Zerahites.
Jos 7: 1 Achan son of Carmi son of Zabdi son of Z,
7:18 and Achan son of Carmi son of Zabdi son of Z,
7:24 and all Israel with him took Achan son of Z, with
22:20 of Z break faith in the matter of the devoted things,
1Ch 1:37 sons of Reuel: Nahath, Z, Shammah, and Mizzah.
1:44 Jobab son of Z of Bozrah succeeded him.
2: 4 also bore him Perez and Z.
2: 6 The sons of Z: Zimri, Ethan,
4:24 Nemuel, Jamin, Jarib, Z, Shaul;
6:21 Iddo his son, Z his son, Jeatherai his son.
6:41 son of Ethni, son of Z, son of Adaiah,
9: 6 Of the sons of Z: Jeuel
2Ch 14: 9 Z the Ethiopian came out against them with
Ne 11:24 of the descendants of Z son of Judah,
Mt 1: 3 and Judah the father of Perez and Z by Tamar,

ZERAHIAH (6)
1Ch 6: 6 Uzzi of Z, Z of Meraioth,
6:51 Bukki his son, Uzzi his son, Z his son,
Ezr 7: 4 son of Z, son of Uzzi, son of Bukki,
8: 4 of Pahath-moab, Eliehoenai son of Z, and
1Es 8:31 of Pahath-moab, Eliehoenai son of Z, and

ZERAHITES (6)
Nu 26:13 of Zerah, the clan of the Z;
26:20 of Zerah, the clan of the Z.
Jos 7:17 and the clan of the Z was taken; and he brought
near the clan of the Z,
1Ch 27:11 was Sibbecai the Hushathite, of the Z;
27:13 was Maharai of Netophah, of the Z;

ZERAIAH (1)
1Es 8:34 Z son of Michael, and with him seventy men.

ZERDAIAH (1)
1Es 9:28 Eliashib, Othoniah, Jeremoth, and Zabad and Z.

ZERED (4)
Nu 21:12 and camped in the Wadi Z.
Dt 2:13 "Now then, proceed to cross over the Wadi Z."
2:13 So we crossed over the Wadi Z.
2:14 until we crossed the Wadi Z was thirty-eight years,

ZEREDAH‡ (2)
1Ki 11:26 Jeroboam son of Nebat, an Ephraimite of Z,
2Ch 4:17 in the clay ground between Succoth and Z.

ZEREDATHAH (KJV) See ZEREDAH

ZERERAH (1)
Jdg 7:22 and the army fled as far as Beth-shittah toward Z,

ZERESH (4)
Est 5:10 he sent and called for his friends and his wife Z,
5:14 Then his wife Z and all his friends said to him,
6:13 When Haman told his wife Z
6:13 his advisers and his wife Z said to him,

ZERETH (1)
1Ch 4: 7 The sons of Helah: Z, Izhar, and Ethnan.

ZERETH-SHAHAR (1)
Jos 13:19 and Sibmah, and **Z** on the hill of the valley,

ZERI (1)
1Ch 25: 3 Of Jeduthun, the sons of Jeduthun: Gedaliah, **Z**,

ZEROR (1)
1Sa 9: 1 of Abiel son of **Z** son of Becorath son of Aphiah,

ZERUAH (1)
1Ki 11:26 whose mother's name was **Z**, a widow,

ZERUBBABEL (37)
1Ch 3:19 sons of Pedaiah: **Z** and Shimei; and the sons of **Z**:
Ezr 2: 2 They came with **Z**, Jeshua, Nehemiah, Seraiah,
3: 2 and **Z** son of Shealtiel with his kin set out to build
3: 8 **Z** son of Shealtiel and Jeshua son of Jozadak made
4: 2 they approached **Z** and the heads of families
4: 3 But **Z**, Jeshua, and the rest of the heads of families
5: 2 Then **Z** son of Shealtiel and Jeshua son
Ne 7: 7 They came with **Z**, Jeshua, Nehemiah, Azariah,
12: 1 the priests and the Levites who came up with **Z**
12:47 of **Z** and in the days of Nehemiah all Israel gave
Hag 1: 1 the prophet Haggai to **Z** son of Shealtiel, governor
1:12 Then **Z** son of Shealtiel, and Joshua son
1:14 LORD stirred up the spirit of **Z** son of Shealtiel,
2: 2 Speak now to **Z** son of Shealtiel,
2: 4 Yet now take courage, O **Z**, says the LORD;
2:21 Speak to **Z**, governor of Judah, saying, I am about
2:23 O **Z** my servant, son of Shealtiel, says the LORD,
Zec 4: 6 "This is the word of the LORD to **Z**:
4: 7 Before **Z** you shall become a plain;
4: 9 hands of **Z** have laid the foundation of this house;
4:10 and shall see the plummet in the hand of **Z**.
Mt 1:12 and Salathiel the father of **Z**,
1:13 and **Z** the father of Abiud,
Lk 3:27 son of Rhesa, son of **Z**, son of Shealtiel,
Sir 49:11 How shall we magnify **Z**?
1Es 4:13 spoken of women and truth (and this was **Z**),
5: 5 of Jozadak son of Seraiah and Joakim son of **Z**
5: 8 They came with **Z** and Jeshua, Nehemiah, Seraiah,
5:48 with his fellow priests, and **Z** son of Shealtiel,
5:56 **Z** son of Shealtiel and Jeshua son of Jozadak made
5:68 So they approached **Z** and Jeshua and the heads of
5:70 But **Z** and Jeshua and the heads of
6: 2 Then **Z** son of Shealtiel and Jeshua son
6:18 and they were delivered to **Z** and Sheshbazzar
6:27 to keep away from the place, and to permit **Z**,
6:29 that is, to **Z** the governor, for sacrifices to the Lord,

ZERUIAH (26)
1Sa 26: 6 and to Joab's brother Abishai son of **Z**,
2Sa 2:13 Joab son of **Z**, and the servants of David,
2:18 The three sons of **Z** were there, Joab, Abishai,
3:39 these men, the sons of **Z**, are too violent for me.
8:16 Joab son of **Z** was over the army;
14: 1 Joab son of **Z** perceived that the king's mind was
16: 9 Then Abishai son of **Z** said to the king,
16:10 "What have I to do with you, you sons of **Z**?
17:25 sister of **Z**, Joab's mother.
18: 2 one third under the command of Abishai son of **Z**,
19:21 Abishai son of **Z** answered,
19:22 "What have I to do with you, you sons of **Z**,
21:17 But Abishai son of **Z** came to his aid,
23:18 Now Abishai son of **Z**, the brother of Joab,
23:37 the armor-bearer of Joab son of **Z**;
1Ki 1: 7 with Joab son of **Z** and with the priest Abiathar,
2: 5 you know also what Joab son of **Z** did to me,
2:22 also for the priest Abiathar and for Joab son of **Z**!"
1Ch 2:16 and their sisters were **Z** and Abigail.
2:16 The sons of **Z**: Abishai, Joab, and Asahel, three.
11: 6 Joab son of **Z** went up first, so he became chief.
11:39 the armor-bearer of Joab son of **Z**,
18:12 of **Z** killed eighteen thousand Edomites in
18:15 Joab son of **Z** was over the army;
26:28 and Joab son of **Z** had dedicated—
27:24 Joab son of **Z** began to count them,

ZETHAM (2)
1Ch 23: 8 sons of Ladan: Jehiel the chief, **Z**, and Joel, three.
26:22 The sons of Jehieli, **Z** and his brother Joel,

ZETHAN (1)
1Ch 7:10 Jeush, Benjamin, Ehud, Chenaanah, **Z**, Tarshish,

ZETHAR (1)
Est 1:10 Harbona, Bigtha and Abagtha, **Z** and Carkas,

ZEUS (3) [ZEUS-THE-FRIEND-OF-STRANGERS]
Ac 14:12 Barnabas they called **Z**, and Paul they called
14:13 The priest of **Z**, whose temple was just outside
2Mc 6: 2 and to call it the temple of Olympian **Z**,

ZEUS-OUTSIDE-THE-CITY See Index to Footnotes

ZEUS-THE-FRIEND-OF-STRANGERS (1) [ZEUS]
2Mc 6: 2 and to call the one in Gerizim the temple of **Z**,

ZIA (1)
1Ch 5:13 Michael, Meshullam, Sheba, Jorai, Jacan, **Z**,

ZIBA (15) [ZIBA'S]
2Sa 9: 2 a servant of the house of Saul whose name was **Z**,
9: 2 The king said to him, "Are you **Z**?"
9: 3 **Z** said to the king, "There remains a son
9: 4 **Z** said to the king, "He is in the house
9: 9 Then the king summoned Saul's servant **Z**,
9:10 Now **Z** had fifteen sons and twenty servants.
9:11 Then **Z** said to the king,
16: 1 **Z** the servant of Mephibosheth met him,
16: 2 king said to **Z**, "Why have you brought these?"
16: 2 **Z** answered, "The donkeys are for the king's
16: 3 **Z** said to the king, "He remains in Jerusalem;
16: 4 Then the king said to **Z**, "All that belonged
16: 4 now yours." **Z** said, "I do obeisance;
19:17 And **Z**, the servant of the house of Saul,
19:29 I have decided: you and **Z** shall divide the land."

ZIBA'S (1) [ZIBA]
2Sa 9:12 in **Z** house became Mephibosheth's servants.

ZIBEON (8)
Ge 36: 2 Oholibamah daughter of Anah son of **Z** the Hivite,
36:14 daughter of Anah son of **Z**:
36:20 of the land: Lotan, Shobal, **Z**,
36:24 These are the sons of **Z**:
36:24 as he pastured the donkeys of his father **Z**.
36:29 the clans Lotan, Shobal, **Z**, Anah,
1Ch 1:38 Lotan, Shobal, **Z**, Anah, Dishon, Ezer, and Dishan.
1:40 The sons of **Z**: Aiah and Anah.

ZIBIA (1)
1Ch 8: 9 He had sons by his wife Hodesh: Jobab, **Z**, Mesha,

ZIBIAH (2)
2Ki 12: 1 His mother's name was **Z** of Beer-sheba.
2Ch 24: 1 his mother's name was **Z** of Beer-sheba.

ZICHRI (12)
Ex 6:21 The sons of Izhar: Korah, Nepheg, and **Z**.
1Ch 8:19 Jakim, **Z**, Zabdi,
8:23 Abdon, **Z**, Hanan,
8:27 Jaareshiah, Elijah, and **Z** were the sons of Jeroham.
9:15 Galal, and Mattaniah son of Mica, son of **Z**,
26:25 his son Joram, his son **Z**, and his son Shelomoth.
27:16 Eliezer son of **Z** was chief officer;
2Ch 17:16 and next to him Amasiah son of **Z**,
23: 1 Maaseiah son of Adaiah, and Elishaphat son of **Z**.
28: 7 And **Z**, a mighty warrior of Ephraim,
Ne 11: 9 Joel son of **Z** was their overseer;
12:17 of Abijah, **Z**; of Miniamin, of Moadiah, Piltai;

ZIDDIM (1)
Jos 19:35 The fortified towns are **Z**, Zer, Hammath, Rakkath,

ZIDKIJAH (KJV) See ZEDEKIAH

ZIDON, ZIDONIANS (KJV) See SIDONIANS

ZIF (KJV) See ZIV

ZIHA (3)
Ezr 2:43 The temple servants: the descendants of **Z**,
Ne 7:46 the descendants of **Z**, of Hasupha, of Tabbaoth,
11:21 and **Z** and Gishpa were over the temple servants.

ZIKLAG (15)
Jos 15:31 **Z**, Madmannah, Sansannah,
19: 5 **Z**, Beth-marcaboth, Hazar-susah,
1Sa 27: 6 So that day Achish gave him **Z**;
27: 6 **Z** has belonged to the kings of Judah to this day.
30: 1 David and his men came to **Z** on the third day,
30: 1 a raid on the Negeb and on **Z**.
30: 1 They had attacked **Z**, burned it down,
30:14 on the Negeb of Caleb; and we burned **Z** down."
30:26 When David came to **Z**, he sent part of the spoil
2Sa 1: 1 David remained two days in **Z**.
4:10 I seized him and killed him at **Z**—
1Ch 4:30 Bethuel, Hormah, **Z**,
12: 1 The following are those who came to David at **Z**,
12:20 As he went to **Z** these Manassites deserted to him:
Ne 11:28 in **Z**, in Meconah and its villages,

ZILLAH (3)
Ge 4:19 and the name of the other **Z**.
4:22 **Z** bore Tubal-cain, who made all kinds of bronze
4:23 "Adah and **Z**, hear my voice;

ZILLETHAI (2)
1Ch 8:20 Elienai, **Z**, Eliel,
12:20 Elihu, and **Z**, chiefs of the thousands in Manasseh.

ZILPAH (7)
Ge 29:24 (Laban gave his maid **Z** to his daughter Leah to
30: 9 she took her maid **Z** and gave her to Jacob as
30:10 Then Leah's maid **Z** bore Jacob a son.
30:12 Leah's maid **Z** bore Jacob a second son.
35:26 The sons of **Z**, Leah's maid: Gad and Asher.
37: 2 he was a helper to the sons of Bilhah and **Z**,
46:18 (these are the children of **Z**, whom Laban gave

ZILTHAI (KJV) See ZILLETHAI

ZIMMAH (3)
1Ch 6:20 Libni his son, Jahath his son, **Z** his son,
6:42 son of Ethan, son of **Z**, son of Shimei,
2Ch 29:12 and of the Gershonites, Joah son of **Z**,

ZIMRAN (2)
Ge 25: 2 She bore him **Z**, Jokshan, Medan, Midian, Ishbak,
1Ch 1:32 she bore **Z**, Jokshan, Medan, Midian, Ishbak,

ZIMRI (16)
Nu 25:14 the Midianite woman, was **Z** son of Salu, head of
1Ki 16: 9 But his servant **Z**, commander of half his chariots,
16:10 **Z** came in and struck him down and killed him,
16:12 Thus **Z** destroyed all the house of Baasha,
16:15 **Z** reigned seven days in Tirzah.
16:16 "**Z** has conspired, and he has killed the king";
16:18 When **Z** saw that the city was taken,
16:20 Now the rest of the acts of **Z**,
2Ki 9:31 As Jehu entered the gate, she said, "Is it peace, **Z**,
1Ch 2: 6 **Z**, Ethan, Heman, Calcol, and Dara, five in all.
8:36 and **Z**; **Z** became the father of Moza.
9:42 and **Z**; and **Z** became the father of Moza.
Jer 25:25 all the kings of **Z**, all the kings of Elam, and all
1Mc 2:26 just as Phinehas did against **Z** son of Salu.

ZIN (10)
Nu 13:21 and spied out the land from the wilderness of **Z**
20: 1 came into the wilderness of **Z** in the first month,
27:14 of **Z** when the congregation quarreled with me.
27:14 of Meribath-kadesh in the wilderness of **Z**.)
33:36 and camped in the wilderness of **Z** (that is,
34: 3 from the wilderness of **Z** along the side of Edom.
34: 4 and cross to **Z**, and its outer limit shall be south
Dt 32:51 of Meribath-kadesh in the wilderness of **Z**,
Jos 15: 1 to the wilderness of **Z** at the farthest south.
15: 3 of Akrabbim, passes along to **Z**, and goes up south

ZINA (1) [=ZIZAH]
1Ch 23:10 the sons of Shimei: Jahath, **Z**, Jeush, and Beriah.

ZION‡ (196) [ZION'S]
A. MOUNT ZION (32)
B. DAUGHTER ZION (26)
C. DAUGHTERS OF ZION (4)

2Sa 5: 7 Nevertheless David took the stronghold of **Z**,
1Ki 8: 1 of the LORD out of the city of David, which is **Z**.
2Ki 19:21 she scorns you—virgin daughter **Z**; B
19:31 and from Mount **Z** a band of survivors. A
1Ch 11: 5 Nevertheless David took the stronghold of **Z**,
2Ch 5: 2 of the LORD out of the city of David, which is **Z**.
Ps 2: 6 "I have set my king on **Z**, my holy hill."
9:11 Sing praises to the LORD, who dwells in **Z**.
9:14 and, in the gates of daughter **Z**, B
14: 7 O that deliverance for Israel would come from **Z**!
20: 2 and give you support from **Z**.
48: 2 Mount **Z**, in the far north, the city of the great A
48:11 Let Mount **Z** be glad, let the towns of Judah A
48:12 Walk about **Z**, go all around it, count its towers,
50: 2 Out of **Z**, the perfection of beauty,
51:18 Do good to **Z** in your good pleasure;
53: 6 O that deliverance for Israel would come from **Z**!
65: 1 Praise is due to you, O God, in **Z**;
69:35 God will save **Z** and rebuild the cities of Judah;
74: 2 Remember Mount **Z**, where you came to dwell. A
76: 2 in Salem, his dwelling place in **Z**.
78:68 but he chose the tribe of Judah, Mount **Z**, A
84: 5 in whose heart are the highways to **Z**.
84: 7 the God of gods will be seen in **Z**.
87: 2 the gates of **Z** more than all the dwellings of Jacob.
87: 5 And of **Z** it shall be said,
97: 8 **Z** hears and is glad, and the towns of Judah rejoice,
99: 2 The LORD is great in **Z**;
102:13 You will rise up and have compassion on **Z**,
102:16 For the LORD will build up **Z**;
102:21 that the name of the LORD may be declared in **Z**,
110: 2 The LORD sends out from **Z** your mighty scepter.
125: 1 Those who trust in the LORD are like Mount **Z**, A
126: 1 When the LORD restored the fortunes of **Z**,
128: 5 The LORD bless you from **Z**.
129: 5 May all who hate **Z** be put to shame
132:13 For the LORD has chosen **Z**;
133: 3 which falls on the mountains of **Z**.
134: 3 maker of heaven and earth, bless you from **Z**.
135:21 Blessed be the LORD from **Z**,
137: 1 down and there we wept when we remembered **Z**.
137: 3 saying, "Sing us one of the songs of **Z**!"
146:10 The LORD will reign forever, your God, O **Z**,
147:12 Praise your God, O **Z**!
149: 2 let the children of **Z** rejoice in their King.
SS 3:11 Look, O daughters of **Z**, at King Solomon, C
Isa 1: 8 daughter **Z** is left like a booth in a vineyard, B
1:27 **Z** shall be redeemed by justice,
2: 3 For out of **Z** shall go forth instruction,
3:16 the daughters of **Z** are haughty and walk with C
3:17 with scabs the heads of the daughters of **Z**, C

Isa 4: 3 Whoever is left in Z and remains in Jerusalem
4: 4 has washed away the filth of the daughters of Z C
4: 5 will create over the whole site of Mount Z A
8: 18 the LORD of hosts, who dwells on Mount Z. A
10: 12 the Lord has finished all his work on Mount Z A
10: 24 O my people, who live in Z,
10: 32 he will shake his fist at the mount of daughter Z, B
12: 6 Shout aloud and sing for joy, O royal Z,
14: 32 "The LORD has founded Z,
16: 1 way of the desert, to the mount of daughter Z. B
18: 7 whose land the rivers divide, to Mount Z, A
24: 23 for the LORD of hosts will reign on Mount Z A
28: 16 I am laying in Z a foundation stone, a tested stone,
29: 8 of all the nations be that fight against Mount Z. A
30: 19 Truly, O people in Z, inhabitants of Jerusalem,
31: 4 of hosts will come down to fight upon Mount Z A
31: 9 says the LORD, whose fire is in Z,
33: 5 he filled Z with justice and righteousness;
33: 14 The sinners in Z are afraid;
33: 20 Look on Z, the city of our appointed festivals!
35: 10 and come to Z with singing;
37: 22 she scorns you—virgin daughter Z; B
37: 32 and from Mount Z a band of survivors. A
40: 9 Get you up to a high mountain, O Z,
41: 27 I first have declared it to Z,
46: 13 I will put salvation in Z, for Israel my glory.
49: 14 But Z said, "The LORD has forsaken me,
51: 3 For the LORD will comfort Z;
51: 11 and come to Z with singing;
51: 16 and saying to Z, "You are my people."
52: 1 Awake, awake, put on your strength, O Z!
52: 2 the bonds from your neck, O captive daughter Z! B
52: 7 who announces salvation, who says to Z,
52: 8 the return of the LORD to Z.
59: 20 And he will come to Z as Redeemer,
60: 14 the Z of the Holy One of Israel.
61: 3 to provide for those who mourn in Z—
62: 11 Say to daughter Z, "See, your salvation comes; B
64: 10 Z has become a wilderness, Jerusalem a desolation.
66: 8 soon as Z was in labor she delivered her children.
Jer 3: 14 and I will bring you to Z.
4: 6 Raise a standard toward Z, flee for safety,
4: 31 the cry of daughter Z gasping for breath, B
6: 2 have likened daughter Z to the loveliest pasture. B
6: 23 for battle, against you, O daughter Z! B
8: 19 "Is the LORD not in Z? Is her King not in her?"
9: 19 For a sound of wailing is heard from Z:
14: 19 Does your heart loathe Z?
26: 18 Z shall be plowed as a field;
30: 17 "It is Z; no one cares for her!"
31: 6 "Come, let us go up to Z, to the LORD our God."
31: 12 They shall come and sing aloud on the height of Z,
50: 5 They shall ask the way to Z,
50: 28 the land of Babylon are coming to declare in Z
51: 10 in Z the work of the LORD our God.
51: 24 for all the wrong that they have done in Z,
51: 35 the inhabitants of Z shall say.
La 1: 4 to Z mourn, for no one comes to the festivals;
1: 6 From daughter Z has departed all her majesty. B
1: 17 Z stretches out her hands, but there is no one
2: 1 the Lord in his anger has humiliated daughter Z! B
2: 4 in whom we took pride in the tent of daughter Z; B
2: 6 the LORD has abolished in Z festival and sabbath,
2: 8 to lay in ruins the wall of daughter Z; B
2: 10 elders of daughter Z sit on the ground in silence; B
2: 13 that I may comfort you, O virgin daughter Z? B
2: 18 O wall of daughter Z! B
4: 2 The precious children of Z,
4: 11 kindled a fire in Z that consumed its foundations.
4: 22 The punishment of your iniquity, O daughter Z, B
5: 11 Women are raped in Z, virgins in the towns
5: 18 because of Mount Z, which lies desolate; A
Joel 2: 1 Blow the trumpet in Z; sound the alarm on my
2: 15 Blow the trumpet in Z; sanctify a fast;
2: 23 of Z, be glad and rejoice in the LORD your God;
2: 32 for in Mount Z and in Jerusalem there shall A
3: 16 The LORD roars from Z,
3: 17 the LORD your God, dwell in Z,
3: 21 for the LORD dwells in Z.
Am 1: 2 And he said: The LORD roars from Z,
6: 1 Alas for those who are at ease in Z,
Ob 1: 17 But on Mount Z there shall be those that escape, A
1: 21 up to Mount Z to rule Mount Esau; A
Mic 1: 13 it was the beginning of sin to daughter Z, B
3: 10 who build Z with blood and Jerusalem with wrong!
3: 12 because of you Z shall be plowed as a field;
4: 2 For out of Z shall go forth instruction,
4: 7 the LORD will reign over them in Mount Z now A
4: 8 you, O tower of the flock, hill of daughter Z, B
4: 10 Writhe and groan, O daughter Z, B
4: 11 her be profaned, and let our eyes gaze upon Z."
4: 13 Arise and thresh, O daughter Z, B
Zep 3: 14 Sing aloud, O daughter Z; shout, O Israel! B
3: 16 Do not fear, O Z; do not let your hands grow weak.
Zec 1: 14 I am very jealous for Jerusalem and for Z.
1: 17 the LORD will again comfort Z
2: 7 Escape to Z, you that live with daughter Babylon.
2: 10 Sing and rejoice, O daughter Z! B
8: 2 I am jealous for Z with great jealousy,
8: 3 Thus says the LORD: I will return to Z,
9: 9 Rejoice greatly, O daughter Z! B
9: 13 I will arouse your sons, O Z, against your sons,
Mt 21: 5 "Tell the daughter of Z, Look, your king is coming
Jn 12: 15 not be afraid, daughter of Z.
Ro 9: 33 laying in Z a stone that will make people stumble,
11: 26 as it is written, "Out of Z will come the Deliverer;
Heb 12: 22 But you have come to Mount Z and to the city A
1Pe 2: 6 "See, I am laying in Z a stone,
Rev 14: 1 and there was the Lamb, standing on Mount Z! A
Jdt 9: 13 against your sacred house, and against Mount Z, A
Sir 24: 10 and so I was established in Z.
36: 19 Fill Z with your majesty, and your temple
48: 18 he shook his fist against Z,
48: 24 and comforted the mourners in Z.
51: 12 *Give thanks to him who has chosen Z,*
Bar 4: 9 Listen, you neighbors of Z,
4: 14 Let the neighbors of Z come;
4: 24 as the neighbors of Z have now seen your capture,
1Mc 4: 37 all the army assembled and went up to Mount Z. A
4: 60 that time they fortified Mount Z with high walls A
5: 54 So they went up to Mount Z with joy and A
6: 48 the king encamped in Judea and at Mount Z. A
6: 62 But when the king entered Mount Z and saw A
7: 33 After these events Nicanor went up to Mount Z. A
10: 11 work to build the walls and encircle Mount Z A
14: 27 bronze tablets and put it on pillars on Mount Z. A
1Es 8: 81 and raised Z from desolation,
2Es 2: 40 Take again your full number, O Z,
2: 42 saw on Mount Z a great multitude that I could A
3: 2 of Z and the wealth of those who lived in Babylon.
3: 28 Is that why it has gained dominion over Z?
3: 31 Are the deeds of Babylon better than those of Z?
5: 25 that have been built you have consecrated Z
6: 4 and before the footstool of Z was established,
6: 19 and when the humiliation of Z is complete.
10: 7 For Z, the mother of us all,
10: 20 for how many are the adversities of Z?—
10: 23 the seal of Z has been deprived of its glory,
10: 39 for your people and mourned greatly over Z.
10: 44 The woman whom you saw is Z,
12: 44 if we also had been consumed in the burning of Z.
12: 48 to pray on account of the desolation of Z,
13: 35 But he shall stand on the top of Mount Z. A
13: 36 Z shall come and be made manifest to all people,
14: 31 to you for a possession in the land of Z;

ZION'S (3) [ZION]

Isa 33: 6 the fear of the LORD is Z treasure.
34: 8 a year of vindication by Z cause.
62: 1 For Z sake I will not keep silent,

ZIOR (1)

Jos 15: 54 Hebron), and Z: nine towns with their villages.

ZIPH (10) [ZIPHITES]

Jos 15: 24 Z, Telem, Bealoth,
15: 55 Maon, Carmel, Z, Juttah,
1Sa 23: 14 in the hill country of the Wilderness of Z.
23: 15 in the Wilderness of Z at Horesh when he learned
23: 24 So they set out and went to Z ahead of Saul.
26: 2 Saul rose and went down to the Wilderness of Z,
26: 2 to seek David in the Wilderness of Z.
1Ch 2: 42 Mesha his firstborn, who was father of Z.
4: 16 sons of Jehallelel: Z, Ziphah, Tiria, and Asarel.
2Ch 11: 8 Gath, Mareshah, Z,

ZIPHAH (1)

1Ch 4: 16 The sons of Jehallelel: Ziph, Z, Tiria, and Asarel.

ZIPHION (1) [=ZEPHON]

Ge 46: 16 Z, Haggi, Shuni, Ezbon, Eri, Arodi, and Areli.

ZIPHITES (3) [ZIPH]

1Sa 23: 19 Then some Z went up to Saul at Gibeah and said,
26: 1 Then the Z came to Saul at Gibeah, saying,
Ps 54: T *when the Z went and told Saul, "David is in hiding*

ZIPHRON (1)

Nu 34: 9 the boundary shall extend to Z, and its end shall be

ZIPPOR (7)

Nu 22: 2 Now Balak son of Z saw all that Israel had done to
22: 4 Balak son of Z was king of Moab at that time.
22: 10 "King Balak son of Z of Moab,
22: 16 "Thus says Balak son of Z:
23: 18 listen to me, O son of Z:
Jos 24: 9 Then King Balak son of Z of Moab,
Jdg 11: 25 Now are you any better than King Balak son of Z

ZIPPORAH (3)

Ex 2: 21 and he gave Moses his daughter Z in marriage.
4: 25 But Z took a flint and cut off her son's foreskin,
18: 2 After Moses had sent away his wife Z,

ZITHRI (KJV) See SITHRI

ZIV (2)

1Ki 6: 1 in the month of Z, which is the second month,
6: 37 of the LORD was laid, in the month of Z.

ZIZ (1)

2Ch 20: 16 they will come up by the ascent of Z;

ZIZA (2)

1Ch 4: 37 Z son of Shiphi son of Allon son of Jedaiah son
2Ch 11: 20 who bore him Abijah, Attai, Z, and Shelomith.

ZIZAH (1) [=ZINA]

1Ch 23: 11 Jahath was the chief, and Z the second;

ZOAN (7)

Nu 13: 22 (Hebron was built seven years before Z in Egypt.)
Ps 78: 12 in the land of Egypt, in the fields of Z.
78: 43 and his miracles in the fields of Z.
Isa 19: 11 The princes of Z are utterly foolish;
19: 13 The princes of Z have become fools,
30: 4 his officials are at Z and his envoys reach Hanes,
Eze 30: 14 and will set fire to Z,

ZOAR (10)

Ge 13: 10 like the land of Egypt, in the direction of Z;
14: 2 and the king of Bela (that is, Z).
14: 8 and the king of Bela (that is, Z) went out,
19: 22 Therefore the city was called Z.
19: 23 sun had risen on the earth when Lot came to Z.
19: 30 of Z and settled in the hills with his two daughters,
19: 30 for he was afraid to stay in Z;
Dt 34: 3 of Jericho, the city of palm trees—as far as Z.
Isa 15: 5 his fugitives flee to Z, to Eglath-shelishiyah.
Jer 48: 34 from Z to Horonaim and Eglath shelishiyah.

ZOBAH (12) [HAMATH-ZOBAH]

1Sa 14: 47 against the kings of Z, and against the Philistines;
2Sa 8: 3 down King Hadadezer son of Rehob of Z,
8: 5 of Damascus came to help King Hadadezer of Z,
8: 12 the spoil of King Hadadezer son of Rehob of Z.
10: 6 of Beth-rehob and the Arameans of Z,
10: 8 but the Arameans of Z and of Rehob,
23: 36 Igal son of Nathan of Z; Bani the Gadite;
1Ki 11: 23 from his master, King Hadadezer of Z.
1Ch 18: 3 David also struck down King Hadadezer of Z,
18: 5 of Damascus came to help King Hadadezer of Z,
18: 9 the whole army of King Hadadezer of Z,
19: 6 from Aram-maacah and from Z.

ZOBEBAH (1)

1Ch 4: 8 Koz became the father of Anub, Z,

ZOHAR‡ (4)

Ge 23: 8 hear me, and entreat for me Ephron son of Z,
25: 9 in the field of Ephron son of Z the Hittite,
46: 10 Jemuel, Jamin, Ohad, Jachin, Z, and Shaul,
Ex 6: 15 Jemuel, Jamin, Ohad, Jachin, Z, and Shaul,

ZOHELETH (1)

1Ki 1: 9 oxen, and fatted cattle by the stone Z,

ZOHETH (1)

1Ch 4: 20 The sons of Ishi: Z and Ben-zoheth.

ZOPHAH (2)

1Ch 7: 35 Z, Imna, Shelesh, and Amal.
7: 36 The sons of Z: Suah, Harnepher,

ZOPHAI (1)

1Ch 6: 26 Elkanah his son, Z his son, Nahath his son,

ZOPHAR (4)

Job 2: 11 Bildad the Shuhite, and Z the Naamathite.
11: 1 Then Z the Naamathite answered:
20: 1 Then Z the Naamathite answered:
42: 9 and Bildad the Shuhite and Z the Naamathite went

ZOPHIM (1)

Nu 23: 14 he took him to the field of Z, to the top of Pisgah.

ZORAH (10) [ZORATHITES]

Jos 15: 33 And in the Lowland, Eshtaol, Z, Ashnah,
19: 41 The territory of its inheritance included Z, Eshtaol,
Jdg 13: 2 There was a certain man of Z,
13: 25 in Mahaneh-dan, between Z and Eshtaol.
16: 31 and buried him between Z and Eshtaol in the tomb
18: 2 from Z and from Eshtaol, to spy out the land and
18: 8 When they came to their kinsfolk at Z and Eshtaol,
18: 11 set out from Z and Eshtaol,
2Ch 11: 10 Z, Aijalon, and Hebron, fortified cities that are
Ne 11: 29 in En-rimmon, in Z, in Jarmuth,

ZORATHITES (2) [ZORAH]

1Ch 2: 53 from these came the Z and the Eshtaolites.
4: 2 These were the families of the Z.

ZORITES (1)

1Ch 2: 54 and half of the Manahathites, the Z.

ZOROBABEL (KJV) See ZERUBBABEL

ZOSARA (3)

AdE 5: 10 and summoned his friends and his wife Z.
5: 14 His wife Z and his friends said to him,
6: 13 Haman told his wife Z

ZUAR (5)

Nu 1: 8 From Issachar, Nethanel son of Z.
2: 5 of the Issacharites shall be Nethanel son of Z,

Nu 7:18 On the second day Nethanel son of **Z**,
7:23 This was the offering of Nethanel son of **Z**.
10:15 of the tribe of Issachar was Nethanel son of **Z**;

ZUPH (3) [ZUPHITE]

1Sa 1: 1 of Jeroham son of Elihu son of Tohu son of **Z**,
9: 5 When they came to the land of **Z**,
1Ch 6:35 son of **Z**, son of Elkanah, son of Mahath, son

ZUPHITE (1) [ZUPH]

1Sa 1: 1 a **Z** from the hill country of Ephraim,

ZUR (5)

Nu 25:15 Cozbi daughter of **Z**, who was the head of a clan,
31: 8 They killed the kings of Midian: Evi, Rekem, **Z**,
Jos 13:21 Evi and Rekem and **Z** and Hur and Reba,
1Ch 8:30 His firstborn son: Abdon, then **Z**, Kish, Baal,
9:36 His firstborn son was Abdon, then **Z**, Kish, Baal,

ZURIEL (1)

Nu 3:35 of the clans of Merari was **Z** son of Abihail;

ZURISHADDAI (5)

Nu 1: 6 From Simeon, Shelumiel son of **Z**.
2:12 of the Simeonites shall be Shelumiel son of **Z**,
7:36 On the fifth day Shelumiel son of **Z**,
7:41 This was the offering of Shelumiel son of **Z**.
10:19 of the tribe of Simeon was Shelumiel son of **Z**,

ZUZIM (1)

Ge 14: 5 the **Z** in Ham, the Emim in Shaveh-kiriathaim,

INDEX OF ARTICLES, CONJUNCTIONS, PARTICLES, PREPOSITIONS, AND PRONOUNS

A (10838)

Ge 1:2[2], 6; **2:**6, 7, 8, 10, 18, 20, 21, 22, 24; **3:**6, 24; **4:**1, 2[2], 12[2], 14[2], 15[2], 17, 23[2], 25, 26; **5:**3, 28; **6:**9, 16[2], 17; **7:**2; **8:**1, 11; **9:**5[2], 6[2], 11[2], 13, 15, 20[2], 23; **10:**8, 9[2]; **11:**2, 4[3]; **12:**2[2], 10, 11; **14:**23[2]; **15:**1, 3, 9[5], 12[2] 13, 15, 17[2], 18; **16:**3, 7, 11, 12[2], 15; **17:**4, 5, 8, 11, 16, 17[4], 19, 20, 27; **18:**4, 5, 7, 10, 13, 14, 18, 25; **19:**3, 8, 20[2], 26, 28, 30, 31, 37, 38; **20:**3[2], 7, 16; **21:**2, 5, 7, 8, 13, 14, 16[2], 18, 19[2], 21, 25, 27, 30, 32, 33; **22:**2, 7, 8, 13[3], 15; **23:**4[2], 6, 9[2], 15, 18, 20; **24:**3, 4, 7, 16, 17, 18, 19, 22[2], 25, 29, 31, 36, 37, 38, 40, 43, 55; **25:**8, 25, 27[3], 29, 32; **26:**1, 8[2], 12, 14, 19, 25, 28, 30; **27:**11[2], 12[2], 27, 36, 44; **28:**3, 6, 11, 12, 18, 20, 22; **29:**2, 14, 20, 22, 28, 32, 33, 34, 35; **30:**4, 5, 6, 7, 9, 10, 12, 15, 17, 19, 20, 21, 23, 36; **31:**10, 13[2], 24[2], 44[2], 45[2], 46, 48, 52[2], 54; **32:**13, 16, 18, 24; **33:**13, 17; **34:**7, 14, 31; **35:**5, 11[2], 14[3], 20; **36:**6, 12; **37:**2[2], 3, 5, 15, 18, 20, 24, 25, 31, 33; **38:**1, 2, 3, 4, 5, 6, 8, 11, 14, 15, 17[2], 24, 28[2], 29; **39:**2, 7, 14[2]; **40:**9, 16, 19, 20; **41:**5, 7, 11, 12[2], 15[2], 16, 22, 33, 36, 42; **42:**13, 22; **43:**2, 11[3], 30; **44:**4, 7, 18, 19[2], 20[2], 25, 33; **45:**7, 8, 22; **46:**3, 10, 29; **47:**11, 22, 26; **48:**4[2], 16, 19[2]; **49:**9[3], 13, 14, 15[2], 17[2], 21, 22[3], 27, 28, 30; **50:**9, 10[2], 11, 13, 15, 20, 26; **Ex 1:**8, 16[2]; **2:**1[2], 2[2], 3, 4, 7, 11, 14, 15, 22[2], 23; **3:**2[2], 8[2], 17, 18, 19; **4:**2, 3, 4, 16, 20, 24, 25[2], 26; **5:**1, 3, 21; **6:**1[2], 8, 15, 30; **7:**9[2], 10, 15; **8:**15, 23, 27; **9:**3, 4, 5, 19, 20, 24; **10:**7, 14, 19[2], 21, 26; **11:**3, 6, 7[2]; **12:**3[2], 4[2], 5, 13, 14[3], 16[2], 17, 19, 22, 24, 30[2], 32, 38, 42[2], 48; **13:**5, 6, 9[3], 13, 16, 19, 21[2]; **14:**21, 22, 29; **15:**3, 5, 8, 16, 20, 25[2]; **16:**13, 14, 16, 23[2], 25, 26, 33, 35, 36; **17:**12, 14[2], 16; **18:**3, 12, 16; **19:**6[2], 9, 13, 15, 16[3], 18; **20:**5, 10, 18, 21, 25; **21:**2[2], 4, 5, 7[2], 8, 9, 12, 13, 16, 18, 19, 20[3], 21, 22[2], 26[3], 27[3], 28[2], 29[2], 30, 31[2], 32, 33[3]; **22:**1[4], 2, 3, 7, 10, 16[7], 18, 21, 25, 28; **23:**1[2] 2[2], 3, 7, 8, 9, 14, 19, 22, 33; **24:**1, 10, 14, 17; **25:**8, 10[5], 11, 17[4], 23[3], 24, 25[3], 31, 35[3], 39; **26:**7, 14, 16[3], 31, 36; **27:**4[2], 16, 20, 21; **28:**4[5], 11, 15, 16[2], 17, 18[3], 19, 20[2], 28, 29, 32[2], 34[2], 36[2], 37, 39[2], 43; **29:**9, 14, 18[2], 22, 28, 31, 36[3], 38, 40[4], 41[2], 42; **30:**3, 8, 9[3], 10[2], 12[2], 13[2], 16, 18[2], 21, 24, 25[2]; **31:**13, 15, 16, 17; **32:**4[2], 5, 8, 10, 11, 17, 21, 29[3], 30, 31, 35; **33:**3[2], 5[2], 11, 21, 22; **34:**6, 9, 10, 12[2], 14, 15, 20[2], 26, 27, 33; **35:**2, 5, 22, 29, 35[2]; **36:**14, 19, 21[3], 37; **37:**1[5], 2, 6[4], 10[2], 11, 12[3], 21[3], 24, 26; **38:**4[2], 26[3], 27[2]; **39:**6, 9[2], 10, 11[3], 12, 13[2], 21, 23[2], 26[4], 30, 31; **40:**15; **Lev 1:**3[2], 9, 10[2], 13, 14, 17; **2:**1, 2, 3, 4, 5, 6, 7, 10, 12, 14, 15, 16; **3:**1, 6, 7, 11, 12, 16[2], 17; **4:**3[2], 12[2], 14[2], 22, 23, 24, 28, 31, 32[3], 33; **5:**1, 4[3], 6[4], 7[3], 9, 10, 11[2], 12[2], 15[3], 18[2], 19; **6:**2[6], 6[2], 11, 13, 15[2], 16, 20, 21[3], 22[2], 23, 26[2], 27[2], 28; **7:**5, 6, 9[2], 14, 16[2], 20, 33, 34, 36; **8:**21[2], 28; **9:**2[4], 3[5], 4[2], 15, 17, 18; **10:**4, 9, 13; **11:**36[2], 47; **12:**2[2], 5, 6[7], 7, 8[3]; **13:**2[4], 3, 8, 9[2], 10, 11, 15, 18, 19[2], 20, 24[2], 25[2], 27, 28, 29[2], 30, 38[2], 39[2], 42[2], 43, 47, 48, 49, 51, 52, 58, 59[2]; **14:**10, 12, 21[3], 22[2], 31[3], 32, 34[3], 44, 56[2]; **15:**2, 10, 13, 15[2], 16, 18[2], 19[2], 25[3], 30[2], 32, 33[2]; **16:**3[4], 5[2], 6, 9, 11[2], 12, 22, 24, 29, 31[2]; **17:**3[2], 6, 7, 8; **18:**17, 18[2], 19, 22[2]; **19:**5[2], 13, 14, 16, 18, 19[2], 20[3], 21[2], 29; **20:**10, 12, 13[3], 14[2], 15, 16, 17[4], 18[2], 20, 21, 24, 25, 27[4]; **21:**1, 3, 4, 7[3], 9, 11, 13[2], 14[5], 17, 18[3], 19[2], 20[4], 21[2], 23; **22:**3, 4[4], 11, 12[2], 13, 14, 16, 18[3], 19, 20, 21[3], 22, 23[4], 25[2], 27[2], 29; **23:**3[3], 5, 7, 8, 12[3], 13, 14, 18[2], 19[3], 21[2], 24[2], 27, 28, 30, 31, 32, 35, 36[2], 39[2], 41[2]; **24:**2, 3, 6, 7, 8[2], 9[2], 10[2], 11, 17, 21; **25:**2, 4[2], 5, 10, 11, 12, 14, 16, 21, 25, 29[3], 30[3], 33, 36, 37, 46, 47, 50, 53; **26:**8[2], 26, 33[2], 36, 37; **27:**2[2], 3, 4, 5[2], 6[2], 7[2], 8, 14[2], 16[2], 21, 22[2], 23, 25, 26[2], 28; **Nu 1:**2, 4, 49; **2:**4, 6, 8, 11, 13, 15, 19, 21, 23, 26, 28, 30; **3:**10, 15, 22, 28, 34, 39, 40, 43, 47; **4:**2, 6[2], 7, 8[2], 9, 10, 11[2], 12[2], 13, 14, 19, 20, 22; **5:**2[2], 6[2], 13, 14[2], 15[2], 26, 29, 30[2]; **6:**2[2], 6, 11[2], 12[3], 14[4], 15, 17, 20, 21; **7:**3, 13, 15[2], 16, 17, 19, 21[2], 22, 23, 25, 27[2], 28, 29, 31, 33[2], 34, 35, 37, 39[2], 40, 41, 43, 45[2], 46, 47, 49, 51[2], 52, 53, 55, 57[2], 58, 59, 61, 63[2], 64, 65, 67, 69[2], 70, 71, 73, 75[2], 76, 77, 79, 81[2], 82, 83, 87[2], 88; **8:**7, 8[2], 12[2], 19; **9:**6, 7, 10[2], 12, 13[2], 20, 21[2], 22[2]; **10:**6, 8, 10, 33; **11:**4, 12[2], 20, 21, 27, 31[3], 33; **12:**1, 5, 11; **13:**2[2], 23[3], 32; **14:**1, 4, 8, 12, 14[2], 24, 34, 35, 36, 37; **15:**3[5], 4[2], 5[2], 6[3], 7[3], 8[4], 9[2], 10[3], 13, 14, 15[2], 19, 20[3], 21, 24[3], 27[3], 30, 31, 32, 38; **16:**13, 14, 21, 29[2], 38[2], 39, 40, 45; **17:**5, 10; **18:**6, 7, 8, 9, 10, 11, 17[4], 19[2], 21, 23, 26; **19:**2[2], 9[2], 10, 13[2], 14, 16[3], 17, 18, 21; **20:**15, 16, 19, 20; **21:**2, 8[2], 9[3]; **22:**5, 11, 23, 24[2], 26, 29[2]; **23:**2[2], 3, 4[2], 5, 9, 14[2], 16, 19[2], 20, 21, 22, 24[3], 30[2]; **24:**6, 8, 9[2], 17[2], 18[2]; **25:**6, 7, 13, 15, 18; **26:**2, 4, 10, 54[4]; **27:**1, 4, 8, 11, 17, 18; **28:**3[2], 5[2], 6[2], 7[2], 8[3], 9[2], 11[2], 12[2], 13[2], 14[6], 15, 16, 17, 18, 19[2], 20[2], 22, 24, 25, 26[2], 27[3]; **29:**1[2], 2[3], 5, 6, 7, 8[3], 11, 12[2], 13[3], 16, 17, 19, 20, 22, 23, 25, 26, 28, 29, 31, 32, 34, 35, 36[3], 38; **30:**2[3], 3[3], 9[2], 10[2], 16[2]; **31:**4, 5, 6, 17, 18, 19, 35, 54; **32:**1[2], 4, 5, 14, 17, 29; **33:**8, 54[4]; **34:**22, 23, 24, 25, 26, 27, 28; **35:**4, 6, 11[2], 12[2], 15, 16, 17[2], 18[2], 21, 29, 30, 31[2], 32; **36:**6; **Dt 1:**11, 14, 16, 22, 25[2], 31, 33; **2:**5[2], 9[2], 10, 12, 19, 20, 21, 34; **3:**3, 5, 13, 16; **4:**6, 7, 12, 20, 24[2], 27, 31, 33[2], 34[2], 38, 42; **5:**2, 9, 14, 15[2], 22, 29; **6:**3, 8, 10, 15, 21; **7:**6, 8, 9, 16, 21, 22; **8:**5[2], 7[2], 8[2], 9[2]; **9:**2, 3, 6, 13, 14, 16, 26; **10:**7; **11:**9, 10, 11, 12, 18, 26[2]; **12:**11; **13:**14, 16[2]; **14:**2, 21[3], 22, 23; **15:**1, 2[3], 3, 4, 7, 9, 12[3], 13[4], 13, 18, 22, **16:**2, 6, 8, 10, 11, 12, 16, 19, 21, 22; **17:**1[2], 2, 4, 6, 8, 14, 15[2], 18; **18:**3[2], 6, 10[3], 15[2], 18, 20, 21, 22[2]; **19:**3, 4, 5, 6, 15[3], 16, 18[2], 20; **20:**5, 6, 7, 10, 19[2]; **21:**1, 3, 4, 11, 13, 14, 15, 17, 18, 20[2], 22[2], 23; **22:**3[2], 5[4], 6, 8[2], 9, 10, 13[2], 19, 21, 22, 23[3], 26, 28[2], 30; **23:**5, 10, 12, 13[2], 17[2], 18[2], 20, 21, 24, 25; **24:**1[3], 3, 4, 5, 6[2], 8, 10, 17[2], 18, 19, 22; **25:**1, 5[2], 7, 11, 15[2]; **26:**2[2], 5[2], 8[2], 9, 15, 19; **27:**3, 14, 17, 18, 24, 25; **28:**30[3], 33, 36, 37[2], 46[2], 49[2], 50, 65[2], 68; **29:**4, 18[3], 22; **31:**15, 19, 21, 24, 26; **32:**4, 5, 10[2], 20, 21, 22, 28, 30[2], 46, 49, 52; **33:**2, 4, 5, 7, 17[2], 20, 21, 22, 28, 29; **34:**6, 10; **Jos 1:**13; **2:**1, 12, 15, 19; **3:**4[2], 13, 16; **4:**5, 6, 7; **5:**2, 6, 13[2]; **6:**5[2], 10, 20; **7:**12, 21[2], 26; **8:**11, 15, 17, 28, 29[2], 32, 35; **9:**6[2], 7, 9[2], 11, 15, 16, 24; **10:**2, 3, 10[2], 13, 14, 20; **11:**4, 18, 19; **12:**6, 7; **15:**3, 13, 18, 19; **16:**6; **17:**1, 14, 15, 17, 18; **18:**4[2], 8, 9[2], 10, 14, 17; **19:**14; **20:**3[2], 4, 6, 9[2]; **22:**7[2], 8, 14, 17, 19, 25, 27, 28, 34; **23:**1, 10, 13[3]; **24:**7, 13, 19[2], 25, 26, 27[2]; **Jdg 1:**14, 15, 24, 26; **2:**2, 3; **3:**9, 15[2], 16[2], 17, 19, 20; **4:**4, 9, 15, 18, 19[3], 21[2]; **5:**7, 12, 18, 25, 26, 30; **6:**8, 17, 19[3], 26, 31, 37, 38; **7:**5, 13[4], 14, 20; **8:**12, 14, 18, 20, 24, 25, 27, 31, 32; **9:**8, 48, 49[2], 51, 53, 54; **10:**1; **11:**1[2], 4, 30, 31, 33, 39; **13:**2, 3, 5[2], 6, 7[2], 15, 16, 23[2], 24; **14:**1, 2, 3[2], 4, 5, 6, 8[2], 10, 12, 16, 18; **15:**1[2], 4, 9, 15[3], 16[3]; **16:**1, 4, 9, 12, 17[2], 19, 23; **17:**1, 2, 5, 7[2], 8, 9[2], 10[4]; **18:**1, 10, 19[3], 23, 27; **19:**1[2], 3, 5, 9, 10, 12, 22, 24, 29, 30; **20:**6, 10[4], 16[2], 38, 40, 43; **21:**5, 11, 12, 15, 17, 18, 21, 22; **Ru 1:**1[2], 12[2]; **2:**1[2], 7, 10, 11, 12, 20; **3:**7, 8, 11, 12; **4:**7[2], 11, 13, 15[2], 17[2]; **1Sa 1:**1[2], 5, 11[2], 14, 15, 16, 20, 22, 24[2]; **2:**3, 8, 13, 18[2], 19, 24, 27, 31, 35[2], 36[3]; **3:**8, 20; **4:**5, 10, 12, 17, 20; **5:**9, 11; **6:**3, 7[2], 8[2], 14[2], 17, 18, 19; **7:**2, 9[2], 10, 12, 16; **8:**5, 6, 10, 19, 22; **9:**1[3], 2[3], 6[2], 8, 9[2], 12, 16, 21, 22, 25, 27; **10:**1, 3, 5[2], 6[2], 10[2], 12[2], 19, 25, 27; **11:**1[2], 2, 7; **12:**1, 3, 12, 13, 17, 19, 22; **13:**2, 14, 21[2], 23; **14:**4[2], 14, 15[2], 24, 25, 29, 33, 43; **15:**12, 18, 23, 28, 29; **16:**1, 2, 18[4], 20[3]; **17:**3, 4[2], 5[2], 6, 7, 8[2], 10, 20, 29, 33[2], 34[3], 38[2], 42, 43, 46, 49, 50[2], 52; **18:**3, 5, 13[2], 17[2], 19, 21[2], 23[2], 25, 27; **19:**2, 5, 8, 13, 20[2], 21[2], 23, 24; **20:**3, 6, 8, 16, 19, 20, 29, 30, 35; **21:**2[2], 5, 7, 9; **22:**8, 13; **23:**5, 7, 18, 27[2]; **24:**3, 4, 5, 14[2]; **25:**2[2], 3, 8, 16, 28, 29, 36[2], 37, 41, 42; **26:**12, 13[2], 15, 20[2], 21[2]; **27:**5, 10; **28:**7[3], 8, 9, 12, 13, 14, 22, 24; **30:**1, 12, 13, 14, 25, 26; **2Sa 1:**2, 13; **2:**14, 18, 25[2]; **3:**1, 7, 8[2], 13, 20, 21, 22, 29[2], 33, 38[2]; **4:**2, 4, 11; **5:**3, 11, 20; **6:**3, 13, 14, 19[3]; **7:**2[2], 5, 6[3], 7[2], 9, 10, 11, 13, 14[3], 19[2], 23[2], 27; **8:**2, 4, 8, 13; **9:**2, 3, 8, 12; **11:**2, 8, 10, 11, 14, 21, 27; **12:**1, 3, 4, 24, 25, 30[3]; **13:**1, 2, 3[2], 6, 12, 15, 18, 20, 27[2]; **14:**2[3], 5, 12, 13, 14, 27, 29; **15:**1, 2[2], 4, 8, 13, 19, 33; **16:**1[2], 5, 8, 22; **17:**2, 3, 8, 9, 10[2], 13[2], 17, 18[3], 19, 25; **18:**9, 10, 11, 12, 17[2], 18, 21, 24, 27, 29; **19:**4, 7, 17, 26, 32[2], 36[2]; **20:**1[2], 3, 8[3], 10, 12[2], 15, 16, 18, 19[2], 21; **21:**1, 4, 10, 18, 19, 20; **22:**11, 12[2], 20, 28, 30[2], 31, 32, 35, 51; **23:**4, 7, 8, 10, 11, 12, 13, 18, 20[5], 21[3], 22; **24:**2, 3, 4, 15, 24; **1Ki 1:**2, 3, 6, 42, 52; **2:**4, 8, 9, 14, 19, 24, 36, 40; **3:**1, 4, 5, 6, 7, 8, 12, 15[2], 24[2]; **4:**32; **5:**1, 3, 5, 7, 12, 14[2]; **6:**5, 27[2]; **7:**6[2], 8, 14[2], 15, 23, 26[3], 30, 31[3], 32[3], 33, 35[2], 38; **8:**7, 9, 10, 13, 16[2], 17, 18, 21, 25, 31, 41[2], 42, 55, 65; **9:**2, 5, 7[2], 8[2], 25, 26; **10:**2, 10, 11, 18, 20, 22, 25, 28, 29[2]; **11:**7, 17, 18, 19, 24, 26[2], 29, 36; **12:**7, 11, 15, 30, 32, 33; **13:**1, 2, 3, 7, 13[2], 18, 23, 24, 27; **14:**3, 14, 15; **15:**4, 19, 22; **16:**11, 31, 33; **17:**7, 9, 10[3], 11, 12[5], 13, 24; **18:**4[2], 13[2], 21, 22, 27[2], 32, 34[4], 41, 44[2], 45[2]; **19:**2, 4[4], 6[4], 7, 9, 11, 12[2], 13; **20:**10, 13, 20, 21, 28[3], 34, 35[2], 36[2], 38, 39[3]; **21:**1, 2[2], 9, 10, 12, 13; **22:**8, 21, 22, 23, 34, 36, 47; **2Ki 1:**6, 8[2], 9[2], 10, 12, 13; **2:**1, 9, 10, 11[2], 15, 20; **3:**4, 9, 14[2], 15, 18, 25, 27; **4:**1[2], 2, 3, 8[3], 9, 10[5], 13, 16, 17, 28, 38, 39[2], 42, 43; **5:**1[2], 2, 5, 7[2], 8[2], 10, 12, 14, 15, 19, 22[2], 26; **6:**2, 5, 6, 8, 10, 14, 23, 25[2], 26, 32; **7:**1[3], 2, 6, 8, 9, 16[3], 18[3], 19; **8:**1, 5, 8, 9, 13, 19, 20, 26; **9:**1, 5, 17[2], 19, 20, 28, 34; **10:**2, 6, 19, 20, 27; **11:**2, 4, 6, 17; **12:**9[2], 10, 20; **13:**5, 15[2], 21[2]; **14:**9[4], 13, 19; **15:**5, 19, 30; **16:**8, 10, 17; **17:**16, 35; **18:**17, 21, 23, 24, 28, 32[4], 36; **19:**3, 7[2], 31[2], 32[2]; **20:**3, 7, 12, 14; **21:**3, 13, 14[2]; **22:**10, 19[2]; **23:**3, 10[2], 30, 33; **25:**4, 8, 17, 28, 30[2]; **1Ch 1:**10; **4:**33; **5:**2, 6; **7:**15, 16, 23; **10:**13; **11:**3, 13, 14, 20, 22[5], 23[4], 24, 42; **12:**4[2], 14[2], 22, 28, 34, 38; **13:**7; **14:**1, 9, 11, 13; **15:**1[2], 27[2]; **16:**3[3], 15, 17; **17:**1[2], 4, 5[3], 6[2], 8, 9, 10, 12, 13[2], 17[2], 21, 25; **18:**3, 8; **19:**6; **20:**2[3], 5, 6; **21:**2, 3, 14, 16, 23; **22:**6, 7, 8, 9[2], 10[3], 19; **23:**11; **24:**6; **26:**14; **27:**3, 6, 12, 32[3]; **28:**2, 3[2], 6[2], 10, 15; **29:**3, 15, 16, 21[3], 22, 28; **2Ch 1:**4, 6, 9, 17[2]; **2:**1[2], 3, 4, 6[3], 11, 12[3], 13, 14, 17; **3:**15; **4:**2, 5[3]; **5:**8, 10, 13; **6:**2, 5[2], 7, 8, 13, 16, 32, 36; **7:**5, 8, 9, 12, 18, 20[2], 21; **9:**1, 9, 17, 18, 19, 24; **10:**11, 15; **12:**3; **13:**5, 6, 8, 9[2]; **14:**9, 13; **15:**3[2], 12, 14; **16:**8, 10, 14[2]; **17:**16, 17; **18:**1, 7, 16, 20, 21, 22, 33; **19:**10; **20:**2, 3, 8, 14, 19; **21:**7, 8, 12, 14, 15[2]; **22:**2, 11[2]; **23:**1, 3, 10, 16; **24:**8, 9, 11, 24; **25:**2, 7, 15[2], 16, 18[4], 23, 27; **26:**19[2], 21; **28:**5, 7, 9[2]; **29:**10, 21, 24, 31, 32; **30:**5, 7, 11, 13, 18, 24[2]; **32:**4, 18, 24; **33:**14; **34:**3, 18, 31; **35:**1, 18, 25[2]; **36:**3, 22[2], 23; **Ezr 1:**1[2], 2; **2:**63; **3:**5, 8, 11, 12; **4:**1, 3, 8, 11, 15[2], 19, 21; **5:**3, 5, 7, 9, 11, 13, 14, 17[2]; **6:**1, 2[2], 3, 8, 11[2], 12[2], 17; **7:**6, 11[2], 27; **8:**18, 21[2], 22, 27, 28, 35[2]; **9:**8[4], 9, 11, 13, 15; **10:**1, 3, 7, 12, 13[2], 19; **Ne 2:**6, 8, 12; **3:**13, 16, 26; **4:**2, 4, 6, 9[2], 17[2], 22; **5:**1, 7, 8; **6:**3, 7, 11[2], 13; **7:**2, 65; **8:**4, 18; **9:**3, 4, 8, 10, 11, 12[2], 14, 17, 18, 25, 29[2], 31, 38; **10:**29, 31, 32, 38; **11:**23[2]; **12:**39, 46; **13:**2, 5, 7; **Est 1:**3, 5, 6, 9, 19; **2:**5[2], 18[2]; **3:**4, 8, 9, 14[2]; **4:**1, 8, 10, 14[2], 16; **5:**4, 14; **6:**8[2]; **7:**6; **8:**12, 13[2], 15[2], 17[2]; **9:**1, 14, 17, 18, 19[2], 22, 23, 27; **Job 1:**1, 8, 10, 14, 17, 19; **2:**3, 8, 12, 13; **3:**3, 16; **4:**2, 12, 15, 16[2], 19; **5:**13, 26; **6:**14, 15, 22[2]; **7:**1[2], 2, 6, 7, 12, 16, 19, 20; **8:**2, 9, 14, 20; **9:**2, 3, 17, 19[2], 25, 32; **10:**16, 20; **11:**2, 12[2]; **12:**4[3], 18, 24, 25; **13:**25, 27, 28[2]; **14:**1, 2[2], 3, 4, 7, 9, 11[2], 13, 17; **15:**23, 24, 26; **16:**8, 14, 21[2], 22; **17:**3, 6, 7, 10; **18:**8[2], 9[2], 10[2]; **19:**10, 15, 23, 24, 29; **20:**3, 5, 8[2], 16, 19, 24, 26; **21:**11, 32; **22:**2, 11, 16, 28; **24:**3, 6, 9, 14, 20, 24, 25; **25:**4, 6[4]; **26:**10, 14; **27:**20[2]; **28:**1[2], 4, 22, 26[2]; **29:**14[2], 16, 25; **30:**5, 8, 9, 14, 15, 29[2]; **31:**1[2], 6, 9, 11[2], 12, 13, 18, 19, 30, 36, 37; **32:**8, 13, 15; **33:**6, 15[2], 23[3], 24; **34:**6, 12, 18, 20, 23, 29; **36:**2, 16, 22; **37:**7, 18; **38:**3, 14, 25[2], 26, 28, 34, 38; **39:**15[2], 25; **40:**2, 7, 9, 17, 24; **41:**1[2], 2[2], 4, 5, 15, 20, 21, 30, 31[2], 32, 33; **42:**8, 11[2], 12[2]; **Ps 2:**9[2]; **3:**T, 3; **4:**T; **5:**T, 4, 12; **6:**T, 10; **7:**T[2], 2, 6, 11[2], 15; **8:**T, 2, 5; **9:**T, 9[2]; **10:**9; **11:**1, 6; **12:**T, 2, 6; **13:**T; **15:**T, 3, 5; **16:**T, 6; **17:**T, 1, 12[2]; **18:**T, 10, 19, 27, 29[2], 30, 31, 33, 34, 36; **19:**T, 4, 5[2]; **20:**T; **21:**T, 3, 9; **22:**T, 6, 13, 15, 16, 31; **23:**T, 5; **24:**T; **26:**7; **27:**5, 11; **29:**T, 6[2]; **30:**T[2], 5[2], 7; **31:**T, 2[2], 8, 11, 12, 21; **32:**T, 6, 7, 9[2]; **33:**3, 7, 16[2], 17; **35:**7, 14[3]; **36:**4; **37:**10, 16, 26, 35; **38:**T, 4; **39:**T, 1, 5[2], 6, 11[2]; **40:**T, 2, 3[2]; **41:**T, 8; **42:**T, 1, 4, 8, 10; **44:**T, 12, 14[2], 20; **45:**T[2], 1[2], 6; **46:**T, 1, 4; **47:**T, 2, 5[2], 7; **48:**T[2], 3, 6; **49:**T, 4; **50:**T, 3[2], 5, 9, 10, 14, 18; **51:**T, 5, 10[2], 12, 16, 17[2]; **52:**1, 2, 8; **53:**T; **54:**T, 6; **55:**T, 6, 8, 20[2], 21; **56:**T, 11; **57:**T, 6[2]; **58:**T, 4, 11[2]; **59:**T, 16[2]; **60:**T, 4; **61:**3; **62:**T, 3[3], 4, 8, 9[3]; **63:**T, 1, 5; **64:**T, 6; **65:**T[2]; **66:**T[2], 1, 12; **67:**T[2]; **68:**T[2], 4, 6[2], 10, 13, 20, 27; **69:**8, 11, 22[2], 25, 30, 31; **71:**3[2], 7; **72:**1; **73:**T, 6, 16, 19, 20, 22; **74:**T; **75:**T[2], 8[2]; **76:**T[2], 5; **77:**T, 20; **78:**T, 2, 5[2], 8[2], 13, 14[2], 19, 21, 33, 39, 49, 50, 52, 55, 57, 65; **79:**T, 4; **80:**T[2], 1, 8; **81:**2, 4, 5[2], 9; **82:**T; **83:**T[2], 4, 5; **84:**T, 3[2], 6, 10[3], 11; **85:**T, 13; **86:**T, 14, 15, 17; **87:**T[2]; **88:**T[3], 8, 17; **89:**T, 3, 7, 10, 13, 19; **90:**T, 4[2], 5, 9, 12; **91:**4, 7, 12; **92:**T[2], 12; **94:**13; **95:**1, 2, 3[2], 10; **96:**1; **98:**T, 1, 4, 6; **99:**8; **100:**T, 1; **101:**T, 5[2]; **102:**T, 3, 6, 7, 8, 18[2], 26; **103:**13, 15; **104:**2[2], 6, 9, 18; **105:**8, 10, 17[2], 18, 39[2], 41; **106:**9, 14, 15, 19[2], 29, 36; **107:**7, 33, 34[2], 35[2], 36, 37; **108:**T[2]; **109:**T, 6, 9, 12, 19[2], 23[2], 29; **110:**T, 4; **111:**10; **112:**4; **113:**9; **114:**1, 8[2]; **116:**11, 17; **118:**5, 12; **119:**63, 83, 96, 105[2], 110, 164, 176; **120:**T, 2, 4; **121:**T; **122:**T, 3; **123:**T, 2; **124:**T, 7; **125:**T; **126:**T; **127:**T, 3[2], 4; **128:**T, 3; **129:**T; **130:**T; **131:**T, 2; **132:**T, 5[2], 11, 17[2]; **133:**T; **134:**T; **135:**12[2]; **136:**12, 21, 22; **137:**4; **139:**T, 4; **140:**T, 3, 5[2]; **141:**T, 3, 7; **142:**T[2], 3; **143:**T, 6, 10; **144:**4[2], 9[2], 12; **147:**1, 10; **148:**14; **149:**1;

13[2], 15, 18, 19[2], 24, 30, 31, 32, 34[3], 40, 42, 47, 48, 49[2]; **5:**3, 16, 18, 31, 37, 42, 46, 49, 51, 55; **6:**10[2], 12[2], 13, 17, 21, 26, 40, 42, 51, 56[2]; **7:**3[2], 4[2], 6[2], 7, 19, 39, 43, 48, 52, 61[2], 66, 77, 78, 82, 104[4], 105, 122, 123; **8:**1, 2[3], 3, 5, 6[2], 7, 11, 34, 41, 52, 62, 63; **9:**16[2], 18, 21[2], 24, 34, 38[2], 45, 47[2]; **10:**10, 11, 24, 26, 27[3], 28, 30, 33, 41, 42[2], 44, 46, 54; **11:**1, 6, 7, 13[2], 15, 27, 36, 37[2]; **12:**5, 11, 13, 15, 17, 37[2], 42[6], 45; **13:**1, 2, 3, 6, 9, 10[3], 20, 25, 27, 28, 32, 41, 45[4], 56; **14:**1[2], 3, 31, 32, 38, 39; **15:**10, 11, 13, 17[2], 23, 28, 30, 35[2], 36[2], 40, 50, 51, 55, 60[2]; **16:**4, 6[2], 7, 16, 27[2], 28, 30, 38[2], 42[2], 49[2], 52, 59, 61, 64, 68, 70, 77; **4Mc 1:**24, 25; **2:**7[4], 8[2], 22, 23; **3:**2, 11, 12, 14, 19, 20, 21; **4:**1[2], 5, 12, 20, 22, 23; **5:**1, 4, 7[2], 10, 11, 14, 19, 27; **6:**4, 5[2], 10, 17, 18, 19, 20[2]; **7:**1, 5, 18, 21; **8:**1, 4, 6, 18, 26; **9:**5, 15; **10:**1, 7, 12, 14, 16, 21; **11:**10, 13, 23; **12:**1, 5, 7, 13; **13:**8, 13, 25; **14:**8, 13, 14; **15:**2, 4[3], 9, 23, 27; **16:**1, 2, 5, 10, 12, 13, 14[2], 18, 20; **17:**3, 8, 21; **18:**3, 7, 8, 9, 11, 16

ALSO (1224)

Ge 2:9; **3:**6, 22; **4:**26; **6:**4, 21; **7:**3; **9:**26; **10:**21; **13:**5, 16; **14:**7, 12, 16; **16:**10; **19:**34, 35, 38; **20:**17; **21:**13; **22:**20; **24:**19, 44, 46[2], 53; **26:**21; **27:**31, 34, 38; **29:**27, 30, 33; **30:**6, 15, 30; **34:**11; **38:**10; **40:**15, 16; **42:**9; **43:**8, 13; **44:**16, 29; **46:**4, 6; **48:**11, 19[2]; **50:**18, 23; **Ex 3:**9, 15; **6:**2, 4, 5; **7:**11; **8:**21, 32; **9:**25; **10:**25, 26; **12:**38; **18:**21; **21:**29, 35; **24:**11; **26:**7; **27:**4; **29:**22, 36[2], 44; **33:**12; **34:**16; **35:**14; **36:**14, 37; **37:**10, 17, 29; **38:**1, 17; **39:**22, 25, 27; **40:**10, 11, 14, 28; **Lev 8:**30[2]; **14:**22; **15:**20; **20:**14; **23:**19; **25:**7, 45; **26:**39, 42[2]; **Nu 3:**37; **4:**7, 22; **6:**17; **7:**10; **10:**10; **11:**4; **12:**2; **13:**23; **15:**4; **16:**13, 17; **18:**2, 11, 28, 30; **24:**24, 25; **27:**8, 13; **28:**5, 12, 22; **29:**16, 19, 22, 25, 28, 31, 34, 38; **31:**8, 23; **34:**14; **35:**2, 34; **Dt 1:**37; **2:**6, 20; **3:**3, 17; **9:**19, 20, 22; **10:**19; **12:**30; **17:**17; **29:**15; **31:**3; **Jos 10:**30; **13:**22, 24; **19:**22; **24:**11, 18; **Jdg 1:**15, 22; **3:**22; **6:**35; **7:**18, 24[2]; **8:**17, 22, 31; **9:**2, 19, 49, 57; **10:**9, 12; **11:**2, 17; **20:**48; **Ru 1:**5; **2:**16, 20; **4:**5, 10; **1Sa 2:**7; **3:**17; **4:**7, 17[2]; **6:**18; **7:**14; **8:**8, 20; **10:**11, 12, 26; **13:**4; **14:**44; **15:**23; **17:**18; **19:**20, 21[2], 24; **20:**3, 13; **22:**17; **23:**17; **24:**8; **25:**13, 22, 43; **28:**19, 22; **30:**5, 12, 20; **31:**5; **2Sa 1:**4[2]; **3:**19; **7:**19; **8:**2, 3, 11; **11:**12, 24; **12:**30; **13:**36; **15:**19[2], 21, 24, 27; **17:**5; **18:**2, 22, 26; **19:**40, 43; **20:**26; **23:**20; **1Ki 1:**6; **2:**5, 8, 22, 23, 44; **3:**13, 18; **4:**26, 28; **5:**15; **6:**5, 20, 25, 28, 33; **7:**8, 16, 20, 27, 40; **10:**12, 18; **12:**31; **13:**5, 11, 18, 24; **14:**23, 24, 26; **15:**13; **16:**7, 33; **18:**35; **19:**2, 16; **20:**3, 10, 24, 30; **21:**19[2], 23; **22:**5, 44; **2Ki 2:**7; **3:**18; **7:**4; **8:**22, 27; **9:**27; **11:**17; **13:**6, 11; **16:**8; **17:**19, 32, 33, 41; **21:**11; **22:**19; **23:**5, 15, 27; **24:**4; **1Ch 2:**4, 26, 46, 49, 55; **5:**9; **6:**65; **7:**29; **8:**11, 32; **9:**29, 32, 38; **10:**5; **11:**22; **12:**3, 40; **15:**16, 24, 27; **16:**35, 38; **17:**17; **18:**3, 11; **19:**18; **20:**2, 6; **22:**3, 17; **23:**29; **24:**31; **25:**1; **26:**6, 14, 28; **28:**18, 21; **29:**6, 9, 24; **2Ch 1:**12; **2:**7, 8, 12; **3:**12; **4:**6, 8; **7:**6; **8:**5; **9:**11, 17; **11:**12; **12:**9; **14:**5, 15; **17:**11; **18:**4; **21:**4, 10, 13; **22:**3; **24:**12, 20; **25:**6, 24[2]; **28:**5, 8; **29:**7, 22, 27; **30:**1, 12; **31:**6; **32:**5, 17, 28, 31; **33:**14, 16; **34:**5, 27; **35:**9, 25; **36:**7, 13, 14, 22; **Ezr 1:**1; **2:**61; **5:**4, 10; **6:**21; **7:**7, 15, 24; **8:**19, 36; **10:**1; **Ne 2:**6, 18; **4:**22; **5:**3, 13, 18; **6:**6, 7, 14, 19; **7:**63; **8:**7; **9:**13, 37; **10:**32, 34, 36; **11:**31; **12:**22, 29, 43; **13:**10, 15, 16, 22, 23; **Est 1:**16; **2:**8, 18; **4:**8, 16; **5:**12; **8:**9; **9:**12, 13, 15, 16, 21; **Job 1:**6; **2:**1; **13:**2; **16:**4; **23:**2; **24:**15; **31:**28; **32:**3, 10, 17[2]; **33:**19; **36:**16; **37:**1; **40:**14; **42:**13; **Ps 6:**3; **8:**7; **16:**7, 9; **18:**7, 13; **19:**10, 13; **31:**9; **38:**10; **71:**22, 23; **74:**16; **78:**20; **83:**8; **84:**6; **89:**11, 21; **95:**4; **99:**6; **106:**18; **119:**3, 46; **132:**12; **145:**19; **Pr 1:**5, 26; **9:**2; **18:**3; **24:**23; **Ecc 1:**17; **2:**1, 7, 8, 9, 15[2], 19, 21, 23, 24, 26; **4:**4, 8, 16; **5:**10, 16; **6:**9; **7:**6; **8:**10, 14; **9:**13; **12:**9; **SS 6:**9; **Isa 5:**6; **7:**13; **21:**12; **28:**7, 29; **38:**22; **43:**13; **44:**16, 19; **45:**8; **54:**16; **56:**11; **57:**15; **66:**4, 21; **Jer 1:**3; **2:**34, 37; **6:**17; **13:**23; **25:**14; **28:**4; **31:**36; **36:**6; **37:**18; **39:**6; **41:**3; **43:**6; **48:**2, 7; **51:**57; **52:**10, 19; **La 4:**21; **Eze 4:**2; **8:**13; **16:**17, 19, 41, 52[2]; **21:**9; **23:**26; **24:**3, 5, 25; **31:**17; **36:**37; **39:**16; **40:**14, 16, 42; **41:**8, 14; **42:**10; **43:**17, 21, 25; **44:**30; **Da 1:**17; **6:**22; **Hos 2:**4; **4:**5, 6; **5:**5; **6:**11; **Am 2:**10; **4:**7; **7:**6; **Jnh 4:**11; **Na 3:**11; **Zep 1:**5; **2:**12; **Zec 4:**9; **8:**6; **9:**2, 5, 11; **11:**8; **12:**2; **13:**2; **Mt 2:**8; **5:**31, 39, 41; **6:**12, 14, 21; **8:**9; **10:**2, 32, 33; **12:**45; **15:**16; **17:**12; **18:**35; **19:**19, 28; **20:**4, 7, 10; **21:**24[2]; **22:**26; **23:**26, 28; **24:**33, 44; **25:**11, 22, 24, 44; **26:**69, 73; **27:**41, 44, 52, 55, 57; **Mk 1:**38; **2:**15; **3:**14; **4:**26, 30; **7:**4, 18; **8:**7, 38; **11:**25; **13:**29; **14:**65, 67; **15:**31, 32, 40, 43; **Lk 1:**36; **2:**4, 36; **3:**14, 21; **4:**23, 27, 41, 43; **5:**10, 36; **6:**13, 29, 39; **7:**8; **11:**18, 40, 46, 49; **12:**8, 34, 40, 54; **14:**12; **16:**10[2], 22, 28; **17:**10; **18:**9; **20:**3, 11, 12, 32; **21:**2, 31; **22:**24, 56, 58, 59, 64; **23:**32, 36, 38; **Jn 1:**45; **2:**2, 15; **3:**23; **5:**17, 18, 21, 26; **6:**1, 11, 22, 67; **7:**3, 10, 52; **8:**19, 53; **9:**15, 27; **10:**16; **11:**16, 33; **12:**9, 18, 26, 39; **13:**9, 14, 15, 32, 34; **14:**1, 3, 7, 12, 19; **15:**20, 23, 27; **17:**19, 20, 21, 24; **18:**2, 17, 18, 25; **19:**19, 23, 35, 39; **20:**8; **21:**25; **Ac 1:**23; **3:**17, 24; **5:**16, 37; **8:**19; **9:**32; **11:**1, 7, 12, 20; **12:**3; **13:**5, 9, 33, 35; **16:**1; **17:**6, 17, 18; **19:**18, 21, 26, 27; **21:**16; **22:**5, 29; **23:**11, 24, 30, 33; **24:**9, 15; **26:**10, 20, 29; **27:**10; **28:**9; **Ro 1:**15, 16, 27; **2:**9, 10, 12, 15; **3:**29[2]; **4:**6, 9, 12, 16, 24; **5:**3, 21; **6:**8, 11; **8:**11, 17, 29, 30[3], 32; **9:**24; **11:**16, 22; **13:**5, 6; **14:**6; **15:**27; **16:**4, 5, 13; **1Co 1:**8, 16; **2:**11; **6:**14; **9:**8; **10:**13; **11:**23, 25; **14:**15[2], 19, 34; **15:**1, 2, 8, 18, 21, 28, 44, 49; **16:**4; **2Co 1:**5, 6, 7, 11, 13; **2:**10; **4:**10, 13, 14; **5:**11; **6:**1, 13; **7:**7; **8:**6, 7, 19, 21; **9:**6[2], 12; **10:**7, 11; **11:**12, 15, 18, 21; **Gal 2:**8; **4:**7, 12, 29; **5:**25; **Eph 1:**11, 13, 21; **2:**19, 22; **4:**9; **5:**24; **6:**19, 21; **Php 2:**9, 18, 24, 27; **3:**21; **4:**3; **Col 2:**11, 12; **3:**4, 7, 13; **4:**1, 16[2]; **1Th 1:**5; **2:**8, 10, 13[2]; **3:**6; **4:**8; **2Th 1:**5; **1Ti 2:**5, 9; **5:**13, 20, 25; **2Ti 2:**10, 11, 12[2], 20; **3:**8; **4:**8, 13, 15; **Tit 1:**10; **Phm 1:**9; **Heb 1:**2; **3:**2; **4:**10; **5:**5, 6; **7:**2, 5, 22; **8:**3; **10:**15, 17; **12:**1, 26; **13:**12; **Jas 2:**2, 11, 25, 26; **3:**5, 16; **5:**8; **1Pe 2:**18, 21; **3:**7, 18, 19; **4:**1, 13; **2Pe 2:**1, 12; **3:**15; **1Jn 1:**3; **2:**2, 23; **4:**11, 21; **2Jn 1:**1; **3Jn 1:**12; **Jude 1:**8, 14; **Rev 2:**3, 6, 15, 28[2]; **11:**8; **13:**7, 16; **14:**10; **17:**9; **20:**4, 12; **21:**5, 17; **Tob 1:**7, 18; **2:**11, 12; **3:**7; **5:**2; **6:**12; **7:**7, 8; **11:**18; **13:**14; **14:**8; **Jdt 1:**12; **2:**18, 25; **3:**4; **9:**4; **11:**7; **15:**3, 5; **16:**19; **AdE 1:**16; **2:**8; **3:**15; **4:**8, 16; **8:**14; **9:**13, 18, 19; **16:**24; **Wis 3:**14; **5:**13; **7:**1; **10:**5, 8; **14:**11; **16:**8, 25; **18:**20; **19:**11, 17; **Sir Pr:**T[3]; **4:**16; **6:**17; **8:**6; **12:**6; **16:**11, 12; **23:**10; **27:**30; **29:**21; **44:**10, 12, 22; **46:**11; **48:**3, 11; **49:**9, 13; **Bar 1:**13; **LtJ 6:**59, 61; **Sus 1:**59; **1Mc 1:**22, 23, 54; **3:**33, 42, 49; **4:**21, 38, 48, 61; **5:**4, 8, 39, 57; **6:**7, 25, 29, 37, 52; **7:**42; **8:**4, 6, 20; **9:**12, 18, 52; **10:**20, 24, 32, 33, 40, 45, 63, 89; **11:**5, 31, 40, 58; **12:**2, 17, 33, 38; **13:**3, 28, 34, 48; **14:**34, 36; **15:**24, 36; **16:**10, 21; **2Mc 1:**18; **2:**4, 9, 10, 12, 13, 14; **3:**11, 18, 26; **4:**35; **6:**2; **7:**1, 16; **8:**1, 4, 22, 30; **9:**17; **10:**2, 7, 19, 28; **11:**25, 28, 32, 34, 35; **12:**13, 21, 27, 31, 43; **13:**3; **14:**8; **15:**5, 9, 18, 39; **1Es 1:**15, 41, 47; **2:**2, 10; **4:**45, 54, 57; **7:**14; **8:**22, 48; **3Mc 1:**5, 29; **2:**26, 29[2]; **3:**16, 23, 28; **5:**35, 41, 43; **6:**33, 40; **7:**5, 8, 21; **2Es 1:**25, 40; **3:**1, 21, 26; **4:**15[2], 17, 21, 38, 42, 45; **5:**8, 54; **6:**32; **7:**10, 55, 60, 75, 76, 104, 118; **8:**18, 39, 41, 44; **9:**6; **10:**14; **11:**14, 18, 20, 27, 34; **12:**28, 44; **13:**15, 19, 21; **14:**30; **15:**30; **16:**43; **4Mc 1:**4, 10; **2:**4; **4:**20; **5:**23, 27; **6:**35; **8:**5, 15, 22; **9:**6, 10; **10:**18; **11:**22; **12:**11; **14:**1, 9; **15:**9; **16:**2, 5, 20, 25; **17:**1, 20; **18:**2, 3, 6

AM (1265)

See also the selected listing for "I AM" in the Main Concordance.

Ge 4:9; **6:**7, 13, 17; **9:**9; **15:**1, 7, 8; **16:**8; **17:**1; **18:**13, 17, 27; **22:**1, 7, 11; **23:**4; **24:**13, 24, 34, 42, 43; **25:**30, 32; **26:**24[2]; **27:**1, 2, 11, 18, 19, 24, 32, 46; **28:**13, 15; **29:**33; **30:**2, 13; **31:**11, 13; **32:**10, 11; **35:**11; **37:**13, 16; **39:**9; **41:**44; **42:**36; **43:**14[2]; **45:**3, 4, 13; **46:**2, 3; **48:**4, 21; **49:**20; **50:**5, 19, 24; **Ex 3:**4, 6, 11, 14[3]; **4:**10; **6:**2, 6, 7, 8, 12, 29[2], 30; **7:**5, 17; **8:**9, 22; **10:**2; **12:**12; **14:**4, 18; **15:**26; **16:**4, 12; **18:**6; **19:**9; **20:**2, 5; **22:**27; **23:**20; **29:**46[2]; **Lev 8:**35; **10:**13; **11:**44[2], 45[2]; **18:**2, 3, 4, 5, 6, 21, 24, 30; **19:**2, 3, 4, 10, 12, 14, 16, 18, 25, 28, 30, 31, 32, 34, 36, 37; **20:**7, 8, 23, 24, 26; **21:**8, 12, 15, 23; **22:**2, 3, 8, 9, 16, 30, 31, 32, 33; **23:**10, 22, 43; **24:**22; **25:**2, 17, 38, 55; **26:**1, 2, 13, 44, 45; **Nu 3:**13, 41, 45; **10:**10; **11:**13, 14, 21; **13:**2; **15:**2, 18, 41[2]; **18:**20; **22:**30, 37; **24:**14; **Dt 1:**9, 42; **4:**1, 2, 8, 22, 40; **5:**1, 6, 9, 31; **6:**2, 6; **7:**11; **8:**11; **10:**13; **11:**8, 13, 22, 26, 27, 28, 32; **12:**20; **13:**18; **24:**22; **27:**1, 4, 10; **28:**1, 13, 14, 15; **29:**6, 14; **30:**2, 8, 11, 16; **31:**2[2], 27; **32:**39, 46, 49, 52; **Jos 1:**2; **7:**20; **14:**10, 11; **23:**2, 14; **Jdg 4:**19; **6:**10, 15, 37; **8:**5; **9:**2; **13:**11; **15:**18; **17:**9[2]; **19:**18; **Ru 1:**12; **2:**10, 13; **3:**9, 12; **1Sa 1:**8, 15, 26; **3:**4, 5, 6, 8, 11, 13, 16; **9:**19, 21; **12:**2, 3; **14:**7, 43; **17:**8, 39, 43, 58; **18:**18, 23; **20:**14; **22:**12, 22; **23:**22; **25:**19; **28:**15; **30:**13; **2Sa 1:**8, 13, 26; **3:**8, 39; **7:**2, 18; **9:**6; **11:**5; **14:**5; **15:**26; **19:**22, 35; **20:**17[2], 19; **22:**4; **24:**14; **1Ki 2:**2; **3:**7; **11:**31; **13:**14, 18; **14:**6; **15:**19; **17:**12, 20; **18:**22, 36; **19:**4, 10, 14; **20:**4, 13, 28; **22:**4, 34; **2Ki 1:**10, 12; **2:**9, 10; **3:**7; **4:**9; **5:**7; **16:**7; **21:**12; **1Ch 17:**1, 16; **21:**13; **29:**14; **2Ch 2:**4, 5, 6, 9; **16:**3; **18:**3, 33; **35:**21[2], 23; **Ezr 9:**6; **Ne 6:**3; **Est 5:**12; **Job 3:**26[2]; **7:**3, 4, 12; **9:**15, 20[2], 21, 32, 35[2]; **10:**7, 15[3]; **11:**4; **12:**3, 4[2]; **13:**2; **17:**6; **19:**7, 10, 17; **21:**6; **23:**15[2]; **30:**9, 29; **32:**6, 16, 18; **33:**6, 9[2]; **34:**5, 6[2]; **35:**2, 3; **40:**4; **Ps 3:**6; **6:**2, 6; **13:**4; **22:**6, 14; **25:**16; **28:**7; **31:**9, 11, 22; **35:**3; **37:**25; **38:**6, 8, 13, 14, 17, 18; **39:**9, 10, 12, 13; **40:**7, 17; **46:**10[3]; **50:**7; **52:**8; **55:**2[2]; **56:**3, 4, 11; **69:**3, 12, 17, 20, 29; **70:**5; **73:**14, 23; **77:**4; **81:**10; **86:**1, 2; **88:**4[2], 8, 15; **102:**4, 6, 7; **109:**22, 23[2], 25; **116:**10, 16[2]; **119:**63, 86, 94, 107, 120, 125, 141; **120:**5, 7; **139:**14, 18; **142:**6; **143:**12; **Pr 5:**14; **20:**9; **26:**19; **30:**1[2], 2; **Ecc 4:**8; **SS 1:**5, 6; **2:**1, 5, 16; **5:**8; **6:**3; **7:**10; **Isa 1:**14; **6:**5[2], 8; **13:**17; **19:**11; **21:**3[2], 8; **27:**3; **28:**16; **33:**24; **38:**10, 14; **41:**4, 10[2], **42:**6, 8; **43:**3, 5, 10, 11, 13[2], 15, 19, 25; **44:**5, 6[2], 16, 24; **45:**5, 6, 18, 22; **46:**4, 9[2]; **47:**8, 10; **48:**12[3], 17; **49:**5, 23, 26; **51:**12, 15; **52:**5, 6; **54:**11; **56:**3; **58:**9; **60:**16, 22; **65:**1[2], 5, 17, 18[2]; **66:**18; **Jer 1:**6, 7, 8, 12, 15, 19; **2:**23, 35[2]; **3:**12, 14; **4:**6, 31; **5:**14, 15; **6:**11[2], 19, 21; **7:**11; **8:**17, 21; **9:**15, 24; **10:**18; **11:**11, 22; **12:**14; **13:**13; **15:**6, 16, 20; **16:**9, 16, 21[2]; **18:**11; **19:**3, 15; **20:**4, 9; **21:**4, 8, 13; **23:**15, 23, 30, 31, 32; **24:**7; **25:**9, 16, 27, 29[2]; **26:**14; **28:**16; **29:**17, 21, 23, 32[2]; **30:**10, 11, 18; **31:**8, 20; **32:**3, 27, 28, 37; **33:**6; **34:**2, 17, 22; **35:**17; **36:**5; **37:**14; **38:**19; **39:**16; **40:**10; **42:**4, 10, 11, 17; **43:**10; **44:**11, 27, 29, 30; **45:**3, 4, 5; **46:**25, 27, 28; **49:**5, 35; **50:**9, 18, 31; **51:**1, 25, 36, 64; **La 1:**20, 21; **3:**1, 54, 63; **Eze 2:**3, 4; **4:**8, 16; **5:**8; **6:**7, 10, 13, 14; **7:**4, 27; **11:**10, 12; **12:**11, 15, 16, 20; **13:**8, 9, 14, 20, 21, 23; **14:**8; **15:**7; **16:**62; **17:**24; **20:**5, 7, 19, 20, 26, 38, 42, 44; **21:**3; **22:**16, 26; **23:**49; **24:**16, 24, 27; **25:**4, 5, 7, 11, 17; **26:**3, 6; **27:**3; **28:**2, 9, 22[2], 23, 24, 26; **29:**3, 6, 9, 10, 16, 21; **30:**8, 19, 22, 25, 26; **32:**15; **33:**29; **34:**10, 27, 30, 31; **35:**3, 4, 9, 15; **36:**5, 6, 9, 11, 22, 23, 38; **37:**6, 12, 13, 19; **38:**3, 23; **39:**1, 6, 7, 17, 19, 22, 28; **44:**28[2]; **Da 1:**10; **4:**2; **10:**11, 17, 20, 21; **Hos 1:**9; **2:**2; **5:**12; **11:**9; **12:**8, 9; **14:**8; **Joel 2:**19, 27[2]; **3:**10; **Am 6:**14; **7:**8, 14[2]; **Jnh 1:**9; **2:**4; **Mic 2:**3; **3:**8; **Na 2:**13; **3:**5; **Hab 1:**6; **Zep 2:**15; **Hag 1:**13; **2:**4, 21, 22; **Zec 1:**14, 15; **2:**9; **3:**8; **8:**2[2], 21; **10:**6; **11:**16; **12:**2; **13:**5[2]; **Mal 1:**6[2], 14; **3:**1; **Mt 3:**11, 17; **8:**8, 9; **9:**28; **10:**16; **11:**10, 29; **16:**15; **17:**5; **18:**20; **20:**13, 15[2], 22; **21:**27; **22:**32; **24:**5; **26:**32, 38, 61; **27:**24, 43; **28:**20; **Mk 1:**2, 7, 11; **8:**27, 29; **10:**38, 39; **11:**33; **12:**26; **13:**6; **14:**28, 34, 62; **Lk 1:**18, 19, 34, 38; **2:**10; **3:**16, 22; **5:**8; **7:**6, 8, 27; **9:**18, 20; **10:**3; **12:**50; **13:**32; **14:**19; **15:**17, 19, 21; **16:**3[2], 4, 24; **18:**11; **20:**8; **21:**8; **22:**27, 33, 58, 70; **24:**49; **Jn 1:**20, 21, 23, 27; **3:**28; **4:**26; **5:**7, 17, 36; **6:**35, 41, 48, 51; **7:**8, 17, 28, 29, 33, 34, 36; **8:**12, 14[2], 21[2], 22, 23[2], 24, 28, 42, 58; **9:**5[2], 9; **10:**7, 9, 11, 14, 36, 37, 38; **11:**11, 15, 25; **12:**26, 32; **13:**7, 13, 18, 19, 33[2], 36; **14:**3, 4, 6, 10, 11, 12, 18, 20, 25, 28[3]; **15:**1, 5, 17; **16:**5, 10, 17, 28[2], 32; **17:**9[2], 11[2], 13, 15, 21, 24; **18:**5, 6, 8, 11, 17, 25, 35[2], 37; **19:**4, 21, 28; **20:**17; **21:**3; **Ac 7:**32; **9:**5, 10; **10:**21, 26; **12:**11; **13:**25[3], 41; **17:**3; **18:**6, 10; **20:**22, 26; **21:**13, 39; **22:**3, 8, 10; **23:**6[2]; **24:**21; **25:**10, 11[2]; **26:**2, 7, 15, 17, 25[2], 26, 29; **28:**20; **Ro 1:**11, 14, 16; **3:**7; **6:**19; **7:**1, 14, 24, 25[2]; **8:**38; **9:**1[2], 33; **11:**1, 3, 13[2]; **14:**14; **15:**25; **1Co 4:**4[2], 14, 18, 21; **5:**3, 11; **7:**7, 8; **9:**1[2], 2[2], 15, 17, 19, 20, 21[2]; **11:**1; **12:**15, 16; **13:**1, 2; **14:**37; **15:**9, 10[2], 50; **16:**10, 11; **2Co 2:**3; **7:**4[2]; **8:**8, 10; **9:**3; **10:**1[2], 2, 9; **11:**3, 5, 16, 17[2], 21, 22[3], 23[2], 28, 29[2]; **12:**10[3], 11[2], 14, 15; **13:**1, 10; **Gal 1:**6, 10[2], 20; **2:**18; **4:**11, 12, 18, 19, 20; **5:**2, 10, 11[2], 21; **6:**11; **Eph 3:**1, 8; **5:**32; **6:**20, 21[2], 22; **Php 1:**6, 22, 23, 25, 27; **2:**17[2], 28; **4:**11, 18; **Col 1:**24[2]; **2:**1, 4, 5[2]; **4:**3; **1Ti 1:**12, 13, 10, **2:**7[2]; **3:**14, 15; **2Ti 1:**3, 5[2], 12[2]; **4:**6; **Phm 1:**8, 10, 12, 19, 21, 22; **Heb 2:**13; **Jas 1:**13; **1Pe 1:**16; **2:**6; **2Pe 1:**13, 17; **3:**1[2]; **1Jn 2:**1, 7, 8, 9, 12, 13[2]; **Rev 1:**8, 17, 18; **2:**22[2], 23; **3:**11, 16, 17, 20; **16:**15; **18:**7; **19:**10; **21:**5, 6; **22:**7, 8, 9, 12, 13, 16, 20; **Tob 2:**3; **3:**14, 15; **5:**2, 6, 10[3], 13; **6:**11, 15[2]; **7:**10; **8:**7, 21; **10:**12; **11:**9; **12:**15, 20; **Jdt 2:**7; **8:**32, 34[2]; **10:**12[2], 13; **12:**14; **AdE 5:**12; **14:**3, 14, 16; **15:**9; **Wis 7:**1; **8:**10, 12; **9:**5; **Sir 16:**17[3]; **22:**25; **26:**5; **37:**1; **39:**12; **Bar 2:**31; **Sus 1:**22, 43; **1Mc 6:**10, 11, 13; **10:**72; **12:**45; **13:**4, 5; **2Mc 6:**30[2]; **9:**20, 27; **14:**8; **15:**5; **1Es 1:**30; **4:**59; **8:**74; **Man 1:**8, 9, 10[2], 14; **2Es 2:**4, 14, 31; **3:**1; **4:**44; **5:**13, 39; **8:**15, 16[2]; **9:**41; **10:**32; **12:**5; **14:**2; **15:**5, 20; **4Mc 1:**1; **4:**3; **5:**31; **6:**27; **8:**6; **9:**15; **10:**16; **11:**14[2]; **16:**6[2], 10

AN (1495)

Ge 4:3; **6:**13, 14; **8:**20; **12:**7, 8, 10; **13:**4, 18; **16:**1; **17:**7, 8, 13, 19; **19:**9; **20:**1, 4; **21:**20, 23, 31, 34; **22:**9; **23:**4; **25:**8; **26:**3, 25, 28; **27:**34; **28:**4; **32:**4; **33:**20; **34:**7; **35:**1, 3, 7, 8; **37:**1; **39:**1[2]; **41:**12, 53; **42:**23; **43:**12, 16, 18, 32; **44:**20; **50:**5; **Ex 2:**11, 19, 22; **6:**6; **10:**13; **12:**19, 48; **13:**16; **15:**25; **16:**16, 18, 32, 33, 36[2]; **17:**15; **18:**3; **20:**4, 24, 25; **21:**6, 13, 28, 33; **22:**1[2], 11, 14, 17, 19; **23:**9, 20, 22; **24:**4; **25:**2, 10; **26:**14; **28:**4, 19[2], 20, 32; **29:**18, 24, 25, 26, 27[2], 28[2], 41; **30:**1, 13, 20, 33, 34, 35; **32:**4, 5, 8; **33:**2; **34:**10; **35:**5, 22, 24, 35[2]; **36:**6, 19; **39:**12[2], 13, 30; **Lev 1:**2, 9, 13, 17; **2:**2, 9, 11, 12, 16; **3:**1, 3, 5, 9, 14; **5:**2[2], 4, 11; **6:**20, 28; **7:**5, 18, 21, 24, 25[2], 30, 32; **8:**21, 27, 28[2], 29; **9:**4[2], 21; **10:**15; **11:**13, 32, 35, 39; **13:**2, 6, 8, 10, 13, 20, 30, 39, 53, 56; **14:**3, 5, 10, 12, 21, 24, 39, 40, 41, 45, 48, 50, 54, 56; **15:**16, 18, 32; **16:**34; **17:**3, 4, 13; **18:**22, 23; **19:**7, 15, 20, 33, 36[2]; **20:**13, 15; **21:**20; **22:**4, 18, 22, 23, 27, 28; **23:**13[2], 16, 17[2], 18, 20; **24:**5, 7, 10[2], 18, 21; **25:**47; **27:**2, 9[2], 11, 27; **Nu 5:**15, 17, 19, 21[2], 27; **6:**14, 20; **7:**3, 18; **8:**11, 13, 15, 21; **10:**5, 6, 7, 9; **13:**32; **14:**7, 37; **15:**3, 4[2], 6, 8, 9, 10, 13, 14[2], 25, 27, 28, 30; **16:**14; **17:**10; **18:**17, 24, 26, 28; **20:**16; **21:**29; **22:**4, 32; **25:**14, 15; **27:**7; **28:**5, 6, 8, 9, 12, 13, 19, 20, 24, 28; **29:**6, 9, 13, 14, 36; **30:**2, 10; **31:**26, 29; **34:**2; **35:**16; **36:**8; **Dt 3:**11; **4:**16, 23, 25, 34; **5:**8, 15; **6:**8; **7:**26; **8:**15; **9:**12, 16; **10:**1, 3; **11:**18; **13:**14; **15:**17; **17:**1, 4; **18:**3, 10; **19:**10[2]; **20:**1, 16, 19; **22:**10, 26; **23:**2, 7; **24:**6, 8, 17; **25:**4, 19; **26:**1, 5, 8; **27:**5[3], 15[3]; **28:**25, 37, 48, 49; **29:**8, 12, 14; **32:**11; **Jos 6:**18; **7:**15; **8:**2, 14, 30, 31; **9:**15; **11:**23; **13:**6, 7, 15, 24, 29; **14:**3, 7, 9, 13; **15:**11; **17:**4[2], 6, 14; **19:**9, 49; **22:**10[2], 11, 16, 19, 23, 26, 29; **23:**4; **24:**32; **Jdg 3:**31; **6:**19, 24, 26; **8:**24, 25, 27; **9:**23, 48, 53; **11:**39; **12:**5; **13:**6; **16:**9, 12; **17:**3, 4, 5; **18:**10, 14[2]; **19:**16; **21:**4; **Ru 2:**17; **1Sa 1:**1, 24; **2:**28; **4:**18; **7:**17; **14:**3, 14[2], 24, 28, 35; **16:**14, 15; **17:**12, 17; **18:**10; **19:**5, 9, 13; **20:**36; **21:**2, 5; **23:**6; **24:**19; **26:**19; **28:**14; **29:**4, 9; **30:**11, 13, 25; **2Sa 1:**8, 13; **6:**8, 13; **11:**21, 23; **14:**14; **15:**19; **18:**10; **19:**22, 35; **23:**5, 7, 21; **24:**18, 21, 25; **1Ki 1:**41, 45; **3:**9; **6:**16; **7:**14; **8:**13, 31, 33, 36, 46; **11:**14, 18, 25, 26, 38; **13:**11, 14, 18; **15:**13, 19; **16:**32; **18:**10, 32; **19:**5, 11; **20:**25, 33; **22:**9, 25; **2Ki 6:**15[2]; **8:**6; **9:**2; **12:**15; **13:**7, 17, 19; **17:**36; **19:**32; **23:**10; **25:**19; **1Ch 2:**34; **11:**11, 23; **12:**22; **16:**17, 18, 29; **21:**15, 18, 22, 26; **22:**15; **28:**8; **2Ch 2:**7; **4:**1; **6:**2, 22, 24, 27, 36; **13:**3, 13; **14:**8, 9; **15:**14, 16; **16:**3; **18:**2, 8, 24; **20:**22, 23; **21:**18; **26:**11, 13; **29:**8; **32:**8, 21; **33:**14; **35:**5; **Ezr 4:**6, 17, 21; **9:**12; **Ne 5:**12; **6:**5; **9:**18, 31; **10:**29; **13:**25; **Est 3:**12; **8:**5, 8, 9; **Job 3:**16; **6:**23; **9:**26; **14:**4; **19:**5, 15, 24; **20:**24; **23:**7; **28:**3; **31:**28, 37; **32:**22; **33:**23; **34:**29; **35:**13; **40:**9, 15; **42:**15; **Ps 7:**9; **27:**3; **31:**11; **39:**12; **40:**6; **43:**1; **46:**6; **48:**7; **54:**5; **66:**15; **69:**8, 13, 31; **73:**27; **74:**18; **77:**8; **81:**4; **86:**11; **89:**37; **90:**9; **94:**11; **96:**8; **99:**8; **101:**5; **102:**6, 11; **105:**10, 11, 23; **106:**20; **107:**4, 7; **109:**6, 25; **119:**7, 19, 42, 87, 106, 142; **120:**5; **136:**12; **141:**2; **145:**13; **Pr 1:**18; **3:**32; **5:**10, 20; **6:**11, 16; **7:**22, 23; **8:**7; **11:**1[2], 12, 14, 20; **12:**16, 22; **13:**19, 22; **15:**8, 9, 23, 26; **16:**5, 12; **17:**4, 9, 15; **18:**15, 18, 19; **19:**11, 15; **20:**10, 21, 23; **21:**27; **23:**5, 10, 27, 32; **24:**9, 15, 26, 34; **25:**12; **26:**2, 10, 23[2], 24, 25; **27:**6; **28:**2, 9, 11; **29:**27[2]; **30:**1, 19, 20, 23; **31:**1; **Ecc 1:**13; **4:**8, 13; **5:**9; **6:**1; **7:**11[2]; **8:**11; **9:**2, 3; **10:**5[2]; **SS 2:**3; **4:**13; **6:**4, 10; **7:**4; **Isa 1:**13, 30; **6:**13; **7:**1; **9:**17; **10:**18, 25, 34; **13:**4[2], 11; **14:**29; **15:**1; **17:**1, 6, 10; **19:**1, 19; **21:**2, 16; **24:**11, 13; **26:**4; **28:**15; **29:**2, 5; **30:**1, 6, 13, 28; **33:**19, 20; **34:**13; **37:**33; **38:**12, 13; **40:**19, 20; **41:**24, 28; **44:**10, 14, 19; **48:**4; **49:**18; **51:**20; **53:**10; **55:**3, 13; **56:**5; **57:**3; **61:**8; **62:**10; **63:**12; **65:**16, 20[2]; **66:**3[2], 6, 12, 17, 20, 24; **Jer 1:**11, 18; **2:**7; **5:**15[2], 16, 30; **6:**8, 10, 26; **7:**34; **9:**8; **10:**3[2]; **11:**8; **17:**1, 6; **20:**16; **22:**6; **24:**9; **25:**9[2], 12, 18, 31; **28:**14; **29:**18; **30:**11[2], 14, 17; **31:**3; **32:**14, 40; **38:**16; **40:**5; **42:**18; **44:**2, 8, 11, 12; **46:**28[2]; **47:**2, 7; **48:**35, 40; **49:**13[4], 17, 22, 33; **50:**5, 13; **51:**34, 37, 41, 43; **52:**25; **La 2:**4, 5; **3:**22; **5:**10; **Eze 1:**10[2], 24; **4:**3[2]; **5:**14; **7:**2, 6, 20, 24; **8:**8; **10:**14; **12:**3[2], 23; **16:**3, 21, 45, 60; **17:**2; **19:**4; **20:**13, 17, 33, 34; **23:**27, 46[2], 48; **24:**3; **28:**14; **29:**10; **30:**10, 13, 18; **32:**3; **33:**28, 32; **35:**5; **36:**3, 4; **37:**26; **38:**10; **41:**22; **44:**6; **45:**1, 2, 6, 10[2], 13[2], 24[2]; **46:**5, 7[2], 11[3], 14; **47:**22[2]; **48:**10, 13, 29; **Da 2:**44; **4:**3, 16, 34; **5:**12, 21, 26; **6:**3, 7[2], 12; **7:**9, 14, 27; **9:**3, 24, 25, 26, 27; **11:**6, 18, 20, 23, 27, 35; **12:**7; **Hos 1:**4; **2:**11; **3:**1; **4:**1; **7:**6, 7; **8:**6; **12:**2; **13:**13; **14:**8; **Am 3:**3, 11, 12, 15; **5:**13, 24; **7:**17; **8:**10; **Jnh 3:**3; **Mic 2:**3[2], 8; **6:**16; **Na 1:**1, 9; **2:**9; **3:**10; **Hab 1:**8; **2:**18[2]; **Zec 3:**8; **9:**1, 6; **12:**1, 10; **Mal 1:**1, 10; **2:**12; **3:**10; **4:**1; **Mt 1:**1, 20; **2:**13, 19; **5:**38[2], 39; **9:**16; **12:**35, 36, 39; **13:**12, 25, 28; **16:**4; **17:**15; **22:**46; **24:**44, 50; **25:**29; **26:**7, 16, 72, 74; **28:**2; **Mk 1:**23; **2:**21; **3:**29, 30; **5:**2; **6:**21, 48; **7:**11, 25, 32; **14:**3, 11, 71; **Lk 1:**1, 3, 11, 18; **2:**9; **4:**5, 13, 33; **5:**14, 36; **6:**7; **7:**37; **8:**15, 42; **9:**3, 46; **10:**34; **11:**12, 29; **12:**33, 40, 46, 58; **14:**5; **16:**2, 15; **21:**13; **22:**6, 43, 59; **23:**4, 11, 19, 38; **24:**11; **Jn 1:**22, 47; **7:**1, 19; **8:**37; **9:**30; **12:**29; **13:**15; **16:**2; **19:**19; **Ac 2:**30; **5:**7, 19; **6:**15; **7:**30; **8:**26, 27; **9:**15, 25; **10:**3, 22; **11:**26; **12:**7, 21, 23; **13:**7, 19; **14:**5; **16:**26;

17:5, 23[2], 29; **18:**24; **20:**35; **21:**16, 31, 39; **23:**9, 12, 14, 21; **24:**1, 5, 19, 25; **25:**3, 8, 16; **27:**6, 23; **28:**11; **Ro 1:**1; **7:**3[2], 8, 11; **11:**1, 13; **16:**17; **1Co 1:**1; **5:**11; **7:**12, 13; **8:**7, 10; **9:**1, 2, 9, 12, 16, 25; **10:**11, 19, 27; **11:**27; **12:**16, 17; **13:**8[2], 10, 11[2]; **14:**8, 16, 24, 26; **15:**9, 52; **2Co 1:**1; **4:**17; **5:**12; **6:**2, 15; **9:**5; **11:**12[2], 14; **Gal 1:**1, 8; **2:**8; **3:**15; **4:**7, 14, 24; **5:**13; **6:**10; **Eph 1:**1, 11; **5:**5; **6:**20, 24; **Col 1:**1; **2:**23; **1Th 1:**7; **4:**6; **2Th 3:**9; **1Ti 1:**1, 16; **2:**7; **3:**2; **4:**12; **5:**1, 8, 18, 19; **2Ti 1:**1, 11; **2:**5, 24; **4:**5; **Tit 1:**1; **2:**10; **Phm 1:**9; **Heb 3:**12; **4:**13; **5:**13; **6:**16[2], 17; **7:**16, 18, 20[2], 21; **9:**1; **10:**22; **11:**7[2], 8; **12:**16, 20, 28; **13:**10, 17; **Jas 4:**4; **5:**10; **1Pe 1:**1, 4, 8; **2:**21; **3:**15, 21; **4:**5; **5:**1; **2Pe 2:**6; **3:**5; **1Jn 2:**1, 7; **Jude 1:**7, 15; **Rev 2:**7, 11, 17, 27, 29; **3:**6, 8, 13, 22; **4:**3, 7; **8:**1, 5, 13; **11:**19; **13:**9, 14; **14:**6; **17:**11; **18:**22; **19:**17; **20:**1; **Tob 1:**6, 8; **2:**2; **3:**4; **4:**11; **5:**4; **6:**17; **7:**7; **8:**10; **12:**22; **14:**11; **Jdt 8:**22, 24, 30; **10:**11; **12:**2, 16; **AdE 4:**1, 8; **6:**10; **8:**5; **10:**13; **12:**4; **14:**5, 11, 13; **15:**13; **16:**10; **Wis 3:**16, 19; **4:**18; **5:**12, 19; **7:**14, 26; **8:**4[2], 13, 20; **9:**8; **10:**3, 7; **11:**2, 6; **12:**10, 11, 12; **13:**10, 16; **14:**11, 15[2], 20; **15:**12, 14; **16:**29; **17:**19, 21; **18:**21; **19:**5, 7; **Sir 1:**15, 25; **3:**28, 29; **6:**1, 36; **7:**9; **8:**9; **9:**1; **10:**1, 3, 25; **11:**21, 27; **12:**8, 16[3]; **13:**9, 11, 20[2]; **14:**8, 25; **15:**6; **16:**6, 27; **17:**12; **19:**12; **20:**19, 23, 24; **21:**9, 15, 22, 27[2]; **22:**3, 5, 13, 16, 17, 27; **23:**22, 23, 26; **24:**12, 23; **25:**2, 8, 16, 23, 25; **26:**9; **28:**5, 21; **29:**6, 27; **30:**6, 8[2], 19; **32:**18, 20; **34:**4, 9, 10, 27; **35:**2, 5; **36:**24; **37:**2, 11; **41:**7, 19; **42:**6; **44:**16, 21[2]; **45:**7, 10, 11, 12, 15; **46:**9; **47:**13; **49:**4; **50:**10; **51:**5, 6; **Bar 2:**4, 35; **4:**3; **LtJ 6:**15, 38; **Aza 1:**9, 15; **Sus 1:**15, 50, 53, 58; **Bel 1:**3; **1Mc 1:**36[2]; **2:**44, 51, 56; **4:**35, 43; **6:**44, 60; **8:**1; **10:**73, 80; **11:**42, 68; **13:**29, 47; **14:**44; **16:**17; **2Mc 2:**4; **3:**11, 33; **4:**8, 13, 24, 40; **5:**5, 24; **6:**1, 24, 31; **7:**9, 38; **9:**5, 21; **10:**26[2]; **14:**5, 29, 40; **1Es 4:**52; **8:**51, 85, 93; **9:**17; **Man 1:**10; **3Mc 1:**28; **2:**2, 5, 30, 31; **3:**8; **4:**11, 15, 21; **5:**15, 30, 31, 32, 33, 42; **6:**17, 28, 32; **7:**9; **2Es 2:**44; **3:**15, 21; **5:**49; **6:**59; **7:**4, 9, 48, 114, 119, 120; **9:**11, 19[2]; **10:**37; **11:**1, 13; **13:**5, 34; **14:**1; **15:**11, 19, 33; **16:**7, 16, 29; **4Mc 1:**12, 24; **3:**15, 16; **4:**15, 24; **6:**19; **7:**13, 16; **8:**2; **11:**12, 20; **13:**21; **14:**6, 13, 19; **16:**17; **17:**4, 7, 9[2], 22, 23

AND (41295)

Ge 1:1, 2, 3, 4[2], 5[3], 6[2], 7[2], 8[2], 9[3], 10[2], 11[2], 12[2], 13[2], 14[5], 15[2], 16[2], 18[3], 19[2], 20[2], 21[3], 22[3], 23[2], 24[4], 25[3], 26[5], 27, 28[7], 29, 30[4], 31[3]; **2:**1[2], 2[2], 3, 4[2], 5[2], 6, 7[2], 8[2], 9[3], 10[2], 12[2], 14, 15[2], 16, 17, 19[3], 20[2], 21[2], 22[2], 23, 24[3], 25[3]; **3:**5[2], 6[5], 7[3], 8[2], 9, 10[2], 12, 13, 14[2], 15[4], 16, 17[2], 18[2], 19, 21[3], 22[5], 24[3]; **4:**1[2], 2, 4[3], 5[2], 6, 7, 8[2], 10, 11, 12, 14[3], 15, 16, 17[4], 18[3], 19, 20, 21, 22, 23, 25[2], 26; **5:**2[3], 3, 4[2], 5, 7[2], 8, 10[2], 11, 13[3], 14[2], 16[2], 17, 19[2], 20, 22[2], 26[2], 27, 29, 30[2], 31, 32; **6:**1, 2, 4, 5, 6[2], 7[2], 10[2], 11, 12, 13, 14[2], 15, 16[3], 18[2], 19[2], 20, 21[3]; **7:**1, 2[3], 3[2], 4[2], 5, 7[3], 8[3], 9[2], 10, 11, 12, 13[4], 14[4], 15, 16[3], 17[3], 18[2], 21[2], 23[4], 24; **8:**1[4], 2, 3, 4, 7[3], 9[3], 10, 11[2], 12[2], 13[3], 16[3], 17[4], 18[2], 19[2], 20[3], 21, 22[4]; **9:**1[4], 2[3], 3, 5, 7[3], 8, 9, 10[2], 11, 12[2], 13[2], 14, 15[3], 16[2], 17, 18, 19, 21[2], 22[2], 23[4], 24, 26, 27[2], 29; **10:**1, 2, 3, 4, 6, 7[2], 10, 11[2], 12, 14, 15, 16, 18, 19[3], 20, 22, 23, 24, 25, 29, 31, 32; **11:**1, 2[2], 3[4], 4[2], 5, 6[3], 7, 8, 9, 11[3], 13[3], 15[3], 17[3], 19[3], 21[3], 23[3], 25[3], 26, 27[2], 29[3], 31[3], 32; **12:**1[2], 2[2], 3[2], 4, 5[4], 7, 8[4], 9, 12, 13, 15, 16[4], 17, 18, 19, 20[3]; **13:**1[3], 2, 3, 4, 5[2], 7[3], 8[3], 10[2], 11, 12, 14[4], 15, 17, 18[3]; **14:**1, 2, 5[2], 6, 7[3], 8[2], 9, 10[3], 11[3], 12[2], 13[2], 14, 15[3], 16[3], 17, 18[2], 19[2], 20[2], 22, 24[2]; **15:**2, 3[2], 5[2], 6[2], 9, 10, 11, 12[2], 13[2], 14, 16, 17[2], 21; **16:**2[2], 3, 4[2], 5[2], 6, 8[2], 9, 11[2], 12[2], 13, 14, 15; **17:**1[2], 2[3], 3, 6[2], 7[3], 8[3], 9, 10[2], 11[2], 12, 13, 16[2], 17[2], 18, 19, 20[3], 22, 23[2], 25, 26, 27[2]; **18:**2[2], 4[2], 5, 6[3], 7[3], 8[4], 9, 10[2], 11, 12, 13, 14, 16[2], 18[2], 19[2], 20[2], 21[2], 22, 23, 24, 26, 27, 28, 33[2]; **19:**1[2], 2[3], 3[4], 4, 5, 7, 8, 9[3], 10[2], 11[2], 13, 14, 15, 16[4], 18, 19[2], 20[2], 21, 24[2], 25[4], 26, 28[4], 29, 30, 31[2], 32, 33[2], 34, 35[3], 37, 38; **20:**1[2], 2[2], 3, 5[2], 7[3], 8[3], 9[2], 10, 11, 12, 13, 14[5], 17[3]; **21:**1, 2, 4, 7, 8[2], 12, 14[6], 16[3], 17[3], 18, 19[3], 20[2], 21, 23, 24, 26, 27[3], 29, 32, 33, 34; **22:**1, 2[2], 3[4], 4, 5[2], 6[3], 7[2], 9[2], 10, 11[2], 13[4], 16[2], 17[3], 18, 19[3], 22, 24; **23:**2[3], 3, 4, 7, 8, 10, 11, 15, 16, 17, 20; **24:**1, 3[2], 4[2], 7[4], 9, 10[3], 12[2], 13, 14[2], 16, 17, 18[2], 20[2], 22, 23, 25[2], 26, 27[2], 28, 29, 30[3], 31, 32[5], 35[5], 36[2], 38, 40, 42, 44[2], 45[2], 46[3], 47, 48[2], 49[2], 50, 51[2], 53[5], 54[3], 55, 57, 58[2], 59[2], 60[2], 61[3], 62, 63, 64[2], 65[2], 66, 67[2]; **25:**2, 3[2], 4, 6, 8[3], 9, 11, 13, 15, 16[2], 17[2], 20, 21[2], 22, 23[2], 29, 33, 34[5]; **26:**1, 2, 3[4], 4[2], 5[2], 8, 9, 10, 12, 13[2], 14[2], 15, 16, 17[2], 18, 19, 21, 22[3], 24[4], 25[2], 26, 27, 28[2], 29[2], 30[2], 31[3], 32[2], 34, 35[2]; **27:**1[3], 3[3], 4, 5, 7, 9, 10, 11, 12[3], 13, 14[3], 15, 16[2], 17, 18[2], 19, 22, 25[4], 26, 27[4], 28[3], 29[3], 31[3], 33[5], 34[2], 35, 36, 37[3], 38[2], 39, 40, 41, 42[2], 44, 45[2]; **28:**1[2], 2, 3[2], 4, 5[2], 6[2], 7[3], 9[2], 10, 11[2], 12[3], 13[4], 14[7], 15[2], 16[2], 17[3], 18[3], 20[3], 22[2]; **29:**1, 2, 3[3], 6, 7, 8, 10[3], 11, 12[4], 13[2], 14[3], 16, 17[2], 20, 22, 23[2], 25, 27, 28, 30, 32[2], 33[3], 34[2], 35[2]; **30:**1, 2, 3, 4, 5[2], 6[2], 7, 8, 9, 11, 13, 14[2], 16, 17[3], 19[2], 21, 22[2], 23[2], 24, 25, 26[2], 28, 29, 30[2], 31, 32[5], 33[2], 35[5], 36[2], 37[3], 38, 39[2], 40[4], 42, 43[5]; **31:**2, 3[2], 4[2], 5, 7, 8, 9, 10[2], 11, 12[3], 13[2], 14, 15, 16, 17[2], 18, 19, 20, 21, 23, 24, 25, 26, 27[4], 28[2], 32, 33[4], 34[2], 35, 36, 37, 38[2], 40[2], 41[2], 42[3], 43[2], 44[3], 45, 46[4], 48, 49[2], 50, 51[2], 52[3], 53, 54[4], 55[4]; **32:**1, 2, 4, 5[3], 6[2], 7[5], 8, 9[4], 10[2], 11, 12, 13, 14[2], 15[3], 16[3], 17[2], 18, 19[2], 20[2], 21, 22[3], 23[2], 24, 25, 27, 28[2], 29, 30; **33:**1[4], 2[2], 4[4], 5[2], 6[2], 7[5], 11[2], 12, 13[3], 14[2], 17[2], 18, 19, 20; **34:**2, 3[2], 6, 7, 9, 10[3], 11[2], 12[2], 13, 15, 16[3], 17[2], 18, 19, 20[2], 21[2], 23[2], 24[3], 25[3], 26[3], 27[2], 28[3], 29[2], 30[5]; **35:**1, 2[3], 3, 4[2], 6, 7[2], 8[2], 9, 11[3], 12[2], 14[2], 16[2], 19, 20, 21, 22[2], 23, 24, 25, 26, 27, 29[5]; **36:**3, 5[2], 6[3], 11, 13, 14, 16, 17, 18, 19, 21, 22[2], 23, 24, 25, 26, 27, 28, 30, 33, 34, 35, 36, 37, 38, 39, 40, 43; **37:**2[2], 3, 4, 5, 7[2], 8, 9[2], 10[5], 13, 14[2], 15, 17, 18, 20[2], 22, 24[2], 25[2], 26, 27[2], 28[2], 29, 30[2], 31, 32, 33, 34[2], 35[2]; **38:**1, 2, 3[2], 4, 5, 7, 8, 10, 12, 14, 16, 17, 18[4], 19[2], 22, 23, 24[2], 25[3], 26[2], 28[2], 29[2], 30; **39:**1, 2, 3, 4[2], 5[2], 6[2], 7[2], 8[2], 9, 10, 11, 12[2], 13, 14[2], 15[3], 17, 18[2], 20[2], 21, 22, 23; **40:**1, 2, 3, 4[2], 5[2], 8[2], 9, 10[2], 11[3], 13[2], 14, 15, 17, 18, 19[2], 20[2], 21; **41:**2[3], 3[2], 4[3], 5[2], 6, 7[2], 8[2], 10[2], 11, 13, 14[2], 15[2], 18[3], 19, 20, 22[2], 23[2], 24, 25, 26, 27, 30, 32[2], 33[2], 34, 35[2], 37, 39, 40, 41, 42, 43, 44, 45, 46[2], 48, 51, 54, 56[2]; **42:**2[2], 6[2], 7, 13, 16, 17, 18, 19, 20[3], 24[4], 25, 26, 28, 30, 32, 33, 34[2], 35, 36[3], 37, 38; **43:**2, 4, 7, 8[4], 9, 11[3], 13, 14, 15[2], 16[2], 17, 18[2], 19, 21[2], 23, 24[3], 26, 27, 28[2], 29[2], 30[2], 31[2], 32[2], 33, 34; **44:**1, 2, 4, 11, 12[2], 13, 14[2], 16[2], 18[2], 20[3], 25, 28[2], 29, 30, 31, 33; **45:**1, 2[2], 4, 5, 6, 7, 8[2], 9[2], 10[4], 11[2], 12[2], 13[2], 14, 15[3], 16, 17, 18[3], 19[3], 21, 22, 23[2], 24, 25, 26, 27, 28; **46:**1, 2[2], 4[2], 5[2], 6[3], 7[2], 8, 9[2], 10, 11, 12[4], 13, 14, 15, 16, 17[2], 18, 19, 20, 21, 24, 25, 29[2], 31[4], 32[3], 33, 34; **47:**1[4], 2, 3, 5, 6[2], 7[2], 9, 10, 11[2], 12[2], 13, 14[2], 15[2], 16[2], 17[2], 18[3], 19[4], 20, 22, 23, 24[5], 26, 27[3], 29[3], 30, 31[2]; **48:**1, 2, 3[2], 4[3], 5[2], 7, 9, 10[3], 11, 12, 13[2], 14[2], 15[2], 16[4], 19[3], 20, 21, 22; **49:**1, 2, 3[2], 5, 6, 7[2], 10, 11[2], 12, 13, 15[2], 20, 23, 24, 25, 27, 28, 31[3], 32, 33; **50:**1[2], 3, 6, 7, 8[2], 9, 10[2], 13, 14, 15, 17, 18, 21, 22[2], 24[2], 26[2]; **Ex 1:**2, 3, 4[2], 6[2], 7[2], 9, 10[3], 11, 12, 14[3], 15, 16, 18[2], 19, 20[2], 21; **2:**1, 2[2], 3[3], 5, 6, 7, 8, 9[3], 10, 11, 12[3], 13, 14[2], 15, 16, 17[3], 19, 21, 22, 23, 24[2], 25; **3:**1, 2, 3[2], 4, 6[2], 8[5], 11, 12, 13[2], 15[2], 16[4], 17[2], 18[3], 20, 22[6]; **4:**3[3], 4[3], 5, 6, 7, 9[2], 10, 12[2], 14[2], 15[4], 16, 18[3], 20[3], 21, 24, 25[3], 27[2], 28, 29[2], 30, 31[3]; **5:**1[2], 2[2], 4, 5, 7, 8, 9, 10[2], 11, 14[3], 15, 17, 18, 20, 21[3], 22, 23; **6:**2, 3, 5, 6[3], 7, 8, 9, 11, 13[3], 14, 15, 16[2], 17, 18[2], 19, 20[3], 21, 22, 23[3], 24, 25, 26, 27; **7:**1, 2, 3[2], 4, 5, 6, 7, 8, 9[2], 10[4], 11[2], 12, 13, 15, 17, 18, 19[5], 20[4], 21[2], 22, 23[2], 24; **8:**1, 3[5], 4[2], 5[3], 6[2], 7, 8[4], 9[4], 10, 11[3], 12[2], 13[2], 14[2], 15, 16, 17[4], 18, 19[2], 20[2], 21[3], 23, 24[2], 25[2], 27, 29, 30, 31[2], 32; **9:**1, 2, 3, 4, 6, 7[2], 8[2], 9[2], 10[4], 12, 13[2], 14[2], 15[3], 16, 17, 19[3], 20, 21, 22[2], 23[4], 25[2], 27[4], 28, 29, 30, 31[2], 32, 33[3], 34[4], 35; **10:**1, 2[3], 3[2], 5, 6[3], 8[2], 9[4], 11[2], 12, 13[2], 14, 15[2], 16[3], 17, 18, 19, 20, 22, 23, 24[2], 25, 26, 27; **11:**1, 2[2], 3, 5, 7, 8[3], 10[2]; **12:**1, 7[2], 8, 9, 11[2], 12[2], 13, 16, 21[2], 22[2], 23[2], 24, 26, 27[2], 28[2], 29, 30[3], 31[3], 32[3], 35[2], 36[2], 38[2], 39, 43, 46, 49, 50; **13:**2, 5[2], 6, 7, 9, 11[2], 16, 17, 19[2], 20, 21[2]; **14:**2[2], 4[4], 5[2], 6, 7, 8, 9[2], 10, 12, 13, 14, 16[2], 17[3], 18[2], 19[3], 20[3], 21[2], 22, 23[2], 24[2], 26, 27, 28[2], 29, 30, 31[2]; **15:**1[2], 2[4], 4, 16, 17, 18, 19, 20[2], 21[2], 22[2], 24, 25[4], 26[3], 27[2]; **16:**1[2], 2, 3, 4[2], 6, 7, 8[2], 10[2], 11, 12, 13[2], 18, 19, 20[3], 22, 23[2], 24[2], 27, 28, 31, 33[3]; **17:**2, 3[4], 5[2], 6, 7[2], 8, 9, 10[2], 11, 12[4], 13[2], 14, 15[2]; **18:**1, 4[2], 5, 6, 7[2], 8[2], 10, 12[3], 16[4], 18, 19[2], 20[3], 21[2], 22, 23[2], 24, 25[2], 26, 27; **19:**2, 3, 4[2], 5, 6, 7, 9, 10[2], 11, 14, 15, 16[2], 19[2], 20, 21, 23, 24, 25; **20:**5, 6, 8, 9, 11[3], 12, 18[4], 19[2], 20, 24[4]; **21:**4[3], 5, 6[2], 11, 14, 18, 19[2], 20, 22, 28, 29[3], 32, 33[2], 35[2], 36; **22:**1[2], 2, 6, 7, 10, 11, 14, 16[2], 24[3], 27, 29, 30; **23:**5, 7[2], 8, 10, 11[3], 12[3], 20, 21, 22[2], 23[3], 24, 25[3], 27[2], 28[2], 29, 30, 31[2], 32; **24:**1[4], 2, 3[4], 4[3], 5, 6[2], 7[3], 8[2], 9[3], 10, 11[2], 12[3], 13, 14, 15, 16, 18[2]; **25:**3, 4[2], 6, 7[2], 8, 9, 10[4], 11[2], 12[2], 13, 14, 17[3], 19, 21, 22, 23[2], 24, 25, 26, 28[2], 29[3], 30, 31[2], 32[2], 33[3], 34, 35, 36, 37, 38, 39, 40; **26:**1[2], 2, 3, 4, 5, 6, 8, 9[2], 10, 11[2], 13[2], 14, 16[2], 19[2], 20, 21[2], 22, 25[2], 27[2], 29[2], 31[2], 32, 33[2], 35[2], 36[2], 37[2]; **27:**1[2], 2, 3[4], 4, 6, 10[2], 11[2], 12, 14, 15, 16[3], 17, 18[2], 19[2], 21; **28:**1[4], 3, 4[2], 5[2], 6[2], 8[3], 9, 10, 12, 14[2], 15[3], 16[2], 17, 18[2], 19[2], 20[2], 23[2], 25, 26, 27, 28, 30[2], 33, 34, 35[2], 36, 38, 39[2], 40[2], 41[4], 43[3]; **29:**1, 2[2], 3[3], 4[2], 5[5], 6[2], 7[2], 8, 9[4], 10, 11, 12[3], 13[3], 14[2], 15[2], 16[3], 17[4], 18, 19[2], 20[7], 21[7], 22, 23[2], 24[3], 25, 26[2], 27[2], 28[2], 29, 31, 32[3], 33, 35, 36, 37[2], 39, 40[2], 41[3], 43, 44[2], 45, 46; **30:**2[2], 3[3], 4[2], 5, 8, 9, 14, 15, 16, 18[2], 19[2], 21[2], 23[2], 24[2], 25, 26, 27[5], 28[2], 30[2], 32[2], 34[2], 35[2], 36[2]; **31:**3[2], 4, 5, 6, 7[3], 8[3], 9[2], 10[2], 11[2], 13, 17[4]; **32:**1, 2[2], 3, 4[2], 5[2], 6[5], 8[3], 10[2], 11[2], 12[2], 13[3], 14, 15[2], 16, 19[4], 20, 22, 24[2], 26[2], 27[3], 28, 29, 31; **33:**1[3], 2[2], 3, 4, 5, 7[2], 8[2], 9[2], 10, 12, 13, 14, 15, 16[2], 17, 19[4], 20, 21, 22[2], 23; **34:**1, 2[2], 3[2], 4[3], 5[2], 6[4], 7[4], 8[2], 9[2], 10, 11, 13, 15[2], 16[2], 19, 21, 22, 24, 25, 27, 28[2], 30[2], 31[3], 32, 34[2], 35; **35:**1, 5, 6[2], 7, 8, 9[3], 10, 11[3], 12, 13[2], 14[2], 15[4], 16, 17[2], 18[2], 19, 21[5], 22[4], 23, 24, 25[4], 27[3], 28[4], 29, 31, 32, 33, 34[2], 35[2]; **36:**1[3], 2[2], 3, 5, 6, 8[2], 9, 10, 12, 13[2], 15, 16, 17, 19[2], 21[2], 24[2], 26[2], 32[2], 34[3], 35[2], 36[2], 37[2], 38[2]; **37:**1[4], 2[2], 3, 4, 5, 6[3], 8, 10[2], 11, 12, 13, 15, 16[4], 17[2], 18, 19[3], 20, 21, 22, 23[2], 24, 25[2], 26[3], 27, 28[2], 29; **38:**1[2], 2, 3, 6, 7, 10[2], 11[2], 12[2], 13, 14, 15[2], 17[2], 18[3], 19[2], 20, 23[4], 24, 25, 26, 27, 28[2], 29, 30[2], 31[2]; **39:**1, 2[2], 3[3], 5[3], 6, 8[2], 9, 10, 11[2], 12[2], 13[2], 16[3], 17, 19, 20, 21, 23, 24[2], 25, 26[2], 27, 28[3], 29[3], 30, 33[2], 34[2], 35, 36, 37[2], 38[2], 39[2], 40[4], 41; **40:**3, 4[3], 5, 7[3], 8, 9[4], 10[2], 11, 12[2], 13[3], 14, 15[2], 18[3], 19[2], 20[3], 21[3], 23, 25, 27, 29[2], 30[2], 31[3], 32, 33[2], 34, 35, 38; **Lev 1:**1, 2, 4, 5, 6, 7, 8, 9, 11, 12[2], 13[2], 15[3], 16; **2:**1, 2[2], 3[2], 6, 8, 9, 10[2], 15, 16[2]; **3:**2[2], 3, 4, 8[2], 9, 10, 13[2], 14, 15; **4:**2, 4, 5, 6, 7, 8, 9, 11[2], 12, 13[3], 14, 15, 17[2], 18, 19, 20, 21, 22, 25[2], 26, 27, 29, 30[2], 31[2], 33, 34[2], 35[2]; **5:**1, 2[2], 3, 4, 6[2], 7, 10[2], 12[2], 13, 15, 16[4], 17, 18[2]; **6:**2, 3[2], 4[2], 5, 6, 7[2], 9, 10[2], 11[2], 12, 15[2], 16, 17, 20[2], 21, 22, 25, 27, 28; **7:**2, 4, 9[2], 12, 15, 16, 18, 21, 31, 32, 33, 34[3], 35, 37; **8:**2[2], 3, 4, 6[2], 7, 8[2], 9[2], 10[3], 11[4], 12, 13[4], 14[2], 15[2], 16[3], 17[2], 18, 19, 20[3], 21[2], 22, 23[4], 24[3], 25[2], 26[3], 27[2], 28, 29, 30[8], 31[4], 32[2], 35, 36; **9:**1[2], 2[2], 3[2], 4[3], 5[2], 6, 7[6], 8, 9[3], 10, 11[2], 12, 13[2], 14[2], 15[2], 16, 17, 18, 19[4], 20, 21[2], 22[3], 23[4], 24[4]; **10:**1[3], 2[3], 3[2], 4[3], 5, 6[5], 7, 8, 10[3], 11, 12[3], 13, 14[4], 15[2], 16[3], 17, 19[3], 20; **11:**1, 3[2], 7, 8, 9, 10[2], 11[2], 12, 19, 22, 25[2], 28[2], 30, 32[3], 33[2], 34, 35, 38, 40[3], 42, 43, 44, 46[3], 47[3]; **12:**2, 6, 7, 8[3]; **13:**1, 2, 3[2], 4[2], 5[2], 6[4], 8, 10[2], 13, 15, 17, 19, 20[2], 21, 23, 24, 25[2], 26[2], 28[2], 30[2], 31[2], 32[2], 34[2], 37[2], 39, 41, 45[3], 49, 50, 53, 54, 56, 58; **14:**3, 4[3], 6[4], 7, 8[3], 9[2], 10[3], 12[2], 13, 14[3], 15, 16[2], 17[2], 20[3], 21[3], 22, 24[3], 25[4], 27, 28[2], 30, 31[2], 33, 34, 35, 36, 37, 38, 39, 40, 41, 42[3], 43[2], 44, 45[3], 47[2], 48[2], 49[2], 50, 51[6], 52[5], 53[2], 55, 56, 57; **15:**1, 2, 4, 5[2], 6[2], 7[2], 8[2], 10[3], 11[2], 12, 13[2], 14[2], 15[2], 16, 17, 18[2], 19, 21[2], 22[2], 24[2], 26, 27[3], 28, 29, 30[2], 33; **16:**1, 3, 4[3], 5, 6[2], 7, 8[2], 9, 11[2], 12[2], 13, 14[2], 15[3], 16[2], 17[3], 18[4], 19[2], 20[2], 21[3], 22, 23[2], 24[4], 26[2], 27[3], 28[2], 29, 31, 32, 33[4], 34; **17:**2[3], 4[2], 5, 6, 8, 9, 10, 11, 13[2], 15[2]; **18:**2, 3, 4, 5, 17[2], 18, 20, 21, 23, 25[2], 26[2], 27, 30; **19:**2, 3[2], 6, 8, 10, 11, 12, 13, 16, 22[2], 23, 29, 30, 32[2], 36, 37[2]; **20:**3[2], 4[2], 5[3], 6[2], 7, 8, 10, 14[2], 15, 16[2], 17[3], 18[2], 22[2], 24[2], 25[3], 26; **21:**1, 4, 6, 8, 10, 12, 17, 24[2]; **22:**2, 5, 6, 7, 9, 11, 13, 14, 18[3], 27, 31; **23:**2, 6, 10[2], 13[2], 15, 18[2], 19, 22, 25, 27, 28, 30, 32, 34, 36, 37[2], 38[3], 39, 40[2]; **24:**5, 9, 10[3], 11, 12, 14[2], 15, 22, 23[2]; **25:**2, 3[2], 6[2], 7, 10[3], 16, 18, 19[2], 23, 25[2], 26, 27[2], 28, 31, 35, 41[2], 44[2], 45[2], 47[2], 52, 54[2]; **26:**1[2], 2, 3[2], 4[2], 5[2], 6[4], 7, 8, 9[3], 10, 11, 12[3], 13, 14, 15[2], 16[2], 17[2], 18, 19[2], 20, 21, 22[3], 25[2], 26[2], 27, 29, 30, 31, 33[3], 34, 36[3], 37, 38, 39, 40[2], 41[2], 42[2], 43[2], 44, 46[3]; **27:**2, 5, 6, 7[2], 8, 10[2], 15[2], 18, 19[2], 23, 32, 33[2]; **Nu 1:**3[2], 17, 18[2], 20, 22, 24, 26, 28, 30, 32, 34, 36, 38, 40, 42, 44, 45, 49, 50[5], 51[2], 53; **2:**1, 12, 34; **3:**1, 2[2], 4[3], 6, 7, 8, 9, 10[2], 13, 15[2], 17, 18, 19, 20, 21, 22, 26[2], 27, 28, 31, 32, 33, 34, 36, 37[2], 38[3], 39[2], 40[2], 41, 43, 45[2], 46, 48, 49, 51[2]; **4:**1, 2, 5[3], 6[2], 7[2], 8[2], 9[2], 10[2], 11[2], 12[4], 13, 14[4], 15[2], 16[3], 17, 19[3], 22, 24, 25[3], 26[6], 27[3], 28, 29, 31, 32[4], 34[3], 36, 37, 38, 40, 41, 42, 45, 46[3], 47; **5:**2, 3, 7[2], 12[2], 13, 14[2], 15[2], 16, 17[2], 18, 20, 21[2], 22[2], 23, 24[2], 25[2], 26[3], 27[4], 28[2], 29, 30[2]; **6:**2, 3[2], 11[3], 12[2], 14, 15[3], 16[2], 17[2], 18[2], 19[3], 20, 23, 24, 25, 26, 27; **7:**1[4], 3[2], 5, 6[2], 7, 8[2], 17[2], 23[2], 29[2], 35[2], 41[2], 47[2], 53[2], 59[2], 65[2], 71[2], 77[2], 83[2], 85, 87, 88; **8:**2, 6, 7[2], 8[2], 9, 11, 12[2], 13[2], 14, 15, 17, 19[2], 20[2], 21[2], 22, 24, 25[2]; **9:**3, 6, 7, 11, 13[2], 14[2], 15, 16, 17, 18, 19, 20, 21[2], 22, 23; **10:**2[2], 9, 10[2], 12, 14, 16, 17[2], 18, 20, 21, 22, 24, 25, 27, 29, 30, 31, 35, 36; **11:**1[2], 2[2], 4[2], 5, 6, 7, 8[3], 10, 13, 15, 16[2], 17[4], 18[3], 20[2], 21, 22, 24[3], 25[4], 26[3], 27[3], 28, 29, 30[2], 31[3], 32[3], 33; **12:**1, 2[2], 4, 5[4], 6, 8, 9[2], 10[2], 13, 14, 15, 16; **13:**16, 17[2], 18[2], 19[2], 20[3], 21, 22[3], 23[4], 26[5], 27[3], 28[3], 29[3], 30[2], 32, 33[2]; **14:**1, 2[2], 3, 4, 5, 6[2], 7, 8[2], 9[2], 11[2], 12[3], 14[4], 17, 18[3], 21, 22[4], 24[2], 25[2], 26[2], 29[2], 30, 31, 33[2], 34, 35, 36[2], 38, 40, 43[2], 44, 45[2]; **15:**2, 3, 7, 10, 12, 14, 15[2], 16[2], 18, 23, 24[2], 25[3], 28, 29, 30, 31[2], 33, 36, 38[2], 39[3], 40[2]; **16:**1[2], 2, 3[3], 5[3], 6, 7[3], 9[2], 10, 11, 12, 13, 14[2], 15[2], 16[4], 17[4], 18[4], 19, 20, 22[2], 23, 24, 25[2], 26, 27[5], 28, 30[3], 32[2], 33, 35[2], 37, 38, 39, 40, 41, 42[3], 43, 44, 45, 46[3], 47[2], 48[2]; **17:**2, 3, 5, 6[2], 8, 9[2], 10; **18:**1[3], 2[2], 3[2], 5, 7[2], 8, 9, 11, 12[2], 15[2], 17, 18, 19[2], 20, 22, 23, 27, 28, 30, 31; **19:**1, 2, 3[2], 4, 5, 6[2], 7[2], 8, 9[2], 10[2], 12[3], 13, 14, 15, 17, 18[2], 19[3], 21, 22; **20:**1[2], 2, 3, 4, 5, 6[2], 8[4], 10[2], 11[3], 12, 13, 15[3], 16[4], 19[2], 20, 22, 23, 25[2], 26[2], 28[3]; **21:**1, 2, 3[3], 5[3], 6, 7[2], 8[4], 9[3], 10, 11, 12, 13[2], 14, 15[2], 16, 20, 23[2], 24, 25[2], 26, 28, 29, 30, 32[2], 33[3], 34, 35[2]; **22:**1, 4, 5, 6[2], 7[3], 8, 9, 11[2], 13, 14[2], 15, 16, 17, 18, 20[2], 21, 22[2], 23[2], 25, 26, 27[2], 28, 30, 31[2], 33[2], 39, 40[3], 41[2]; **23:**1[2], 2[3], 3, 4[3], 5[2], 9, 10, 13, 14[2], 16[2], 18, 19[2], 20, 23, 24[2], 25, 29[2], 30[2]; **24:**2, 3, 7[2], 8, 9[2], 10, 12, 13, 16, 17[2], 19, 20, 21[2], 24[3], 25[2]; **25:**2[2], 3, 4, 5, 6[2], 7, 8[2], 13[2], 17, 18; **26:**1, 2, 3, 4, 8, 9[3], 10[3], 19[2], 28, 29, 31[2], 32[2], 33[2], 36, 40[2], 46, 51, 54, 56, 59[2], 60, 61, 62, 63, 64, 65; **27:**1, 2[2], 3, 6, 7, 8, 11[3], 12, 17[2], 18, 19[2], 21[2], 22[2], 23; **28:**2, 3, 4, 8, 9[2], 10, 12, 13, 14, 15[2], 17, 19, 20, 24, 25, 31; **29:**2, 4, 6[4], 7, 11[3], 15, 16, 18[2], 19[2], 21[2], 22[2], 24[2], 25, 27[2], 28[2], 30[2], 31, 33[2], 34, 37[3], 38[2], 39[2]; **30:**4[3], 5[2], 7[3], 8, 10, 11[4], 12, 16[4]; **31:**6, 7, 8[2], 9[3], 10, 11[2], 12[3], 13, 14, 17, 19[2], 20, 22, 23[2], 24, 26[3], 27, 29, 30, 31, 35, 36, 37[2], 43, 46, 47[2], 48, 49[2], 50[3], 51, 52[2], 54[3]; **32:**1[2], 2[3], 3, 4, 6, 9, 10, 11[2], 12, 13[2], 14, 15, 16[2], 19, 21, 22[4], 23, 24, 25, 26, 28, 29[3], 31, 33[4], 34, 36[2], 37, 38[3], 39, 40, 41[2], 42[4]; **33:**1, 2, 5, 6, 7[2], 8, 9[3], 10, 11, 12, 13, 14, 15, 16, 17, 18, 19, 20, 21, 22, 23, 24, 25, 26, 27, 28, 29, 30, 31, 32, 33, 34, 35, 36, 37, 38, 41, 42, 43, 44, 45, 46, 47, 48, 51, 52, 53, 54, 55, 56; **34:**2, 4[3], 5, 6, 8, 9, 11[3], 12[2], 13, 14[2], 15, 17, 24, 27; **35:**3[2], 5, 6, 8[2], 10, 14, 16, 17, 18, 20, 21, 23[2], 24, 25, 27[2], 29, 33; **36:**1[2], 2, 3, 4[2], 11, 12, 13; **Dt 1:**1[2], 4[2], 7[3], 8[3], 11, 13, 15[3], 16[2], 17[2], 19[2], 22[3], 23, 24[2], 25[2], 27, 28[2], 31, 33, 34, 36[2], 39[2], 41[2], 42, 43, 44, 45; **2:**1, 4, 6, 8[2], 10, 12, 14, 21[2], 22, 23, 24[2], 25[2], 28, 29, 30, 31, 32, 33[2], 34[2]; **3:**1, 2, 3, 5, 6[2], 7, 10[2], 11, 12, 13[2], 14[2], 16[3], 17, 19, 20, 21, 24[2], 25, 26, 27[2], 28[3]; **4:**1[2], 5[2], 6[2], 8[2], 9[2], 10[2], 11, 13, 14[3], 15, 19[5], 20, 21[2], 23, 25[3], 26, 28, 29[2], 30, 33, 34[4], 37, 38, 39[2], 40[2], 42, 43, 45[2], 46, 47; **5:**1[3], 5[3], 9, 10, 12, 13, 14, 15[2], 16[2], 22[3], 23, 24[4], 26, 27[3], 28, 29[2], 31[2], 33[2]; **6:**1[2], 2[4], 3[3], 5[2], 7[3], 9[2], 10, 11[2], 13, 15, 17[2], 18[3], 20[2], 22[3]; **7:**1[4], 2[3], 4, 5, 7, 8[2], 9, 10, 11, 13[5], 18, 19[2], 20, 21, 23, 24, 25, 26; **8:**1[3], 4, 6, 7[2], 8[4], 9, 10, 11, 12[2], 13[5], 15[2], 16[3], 17, 19[2]; **9:**1[2], 2, 3[2], 5, 7, 8, 9, 10, 11, 14[3], 15, 17, 18, 21[3], 22[2], 23[2], 25, 26, 27[2], 28, 29; **10:**1[2], 2, 3, 4, 5[3], 6, 7, 8, 10[2], 11, 12, 13[2], 14, 15, 16, 17[3], 18[3], 20, 21, 22; **11:**1[2], 2, 3[2], 4, 6[4], 8, 9[3], 10, 11, 13[2], 14[3], 15[2], 16, 17[2], 18[3], 19[2], 20, 21, 22, 23[2], 24, 25, 26, 28, 29, 31[2], 32; **12:**1, 2, 3[2], 6[4], 7[2], 9, 10[2], 11[3], 12[4], 14, 15[2], 17[2], 18[3], 20, 21, 22, 23, 25, 26, 27, 28[2], 29, 31; **13:**1, 2[3], 3, 4, 5, 8, 9, 11[2], 13[2], 14, 15, 16, 17[2]; **14:**5, 6[2], 7, 8[2], 9, 10[2], 16, 17[2], 18, 19, 23[2], 26[2], 28, 29[2]; **15:**2, 9[3], 10[2], 11, 12, 13, 14, 15, 16, 17[2], 18, 19, 22; **16:**2, 4, 7, 8, 11[4], 12, 13, 14[4], 15[2], 16, 18[2], 19[2], 20[2]; **17:**2, 3, 4[3], 5, 7, 8[3], 9, 13[2], 14[3], 17[2], 19[2], 20; **18:**3, 4, 5[2], 6[2], 14; **19:**1[3], 3, 4, 5[3], 6[2], 8, 9, 11[3], 12, 17, 18, 20[2]; **20:**1[2], 2, 3, 5, 6, 7, 11, 13, 14, 17[3], 18; **21:**1, 2, 4, 5[3], 7, 10[2], 11, 12, 13[4], 14, 15[3], 18[2], 19[2], 20[2], 21[2], 22[2]; **22:**1, 2, 3[2], 4, 7, 9, 10, 11, 14, 15, 18, 21, 23[2], 24[2], 25[2], 26, 28[3], 29; **23:**4[2], 11, 13, 14[2], 20, 21; **24:**1[2], 2, 3, 4, 13[2], 14, 15[2], 18, 19[2], 20, 21; **25:**1[3], 2, 5[3], 6, 7, 8, 9, 11[2], 13, 14, 15[2], 18[2]; **26:**1[2], 2[2], 3, 4, 5[3], 6, 7[2], 8[3], 9[3], 10, 11[2], 12, 13[2], 14, 15[3], 16[2], 17[3], 18, 19[3]; **27:**1, 2, 3, 4, 5, 7, 9[2], 10, 12, 13[2], 15, 19; **28:**2, 3, 4[2], 5, 6, 7, 8, 9, 10, 11, 12, 13[2], 14, 15[2], 16, 17, 18, 19, 20[2], 22[3], 23, 24, 25, 26[2], 27, 28, 29[2], 31, 32, 33[2], 34, 35, 36[2], 37, 39, 41, 42, 43[2], 44, 45[2], 46[2], 47, 48[2], 51[3], 52, 53, 54[2], 56[3], 57, 58, 59[4], 60, 61, 63[3], 64[2], 65, 66, 67[2], 68[2]; **29:**2[3], 3, 5, 6, 7, 8[2], 10, 11[2], 13[3], 16, 17[2], 18, 19[2], 20[2], 22, 23[3], 24, 26[2], 28[2], 29; **30:**1, 2[4], 3, 4, 5[2], 6[2], 7, 9[2], 10[2], 12[2], 13[2], 14, 15[2], 16[4], 17[2], 18, 19[4], 20[3]; **31:**2, 3, 4[2], 5, 6, 7[3], 9[2], 12[3], 13[2], 14[3], 15, 17[2], 19, 20[5], 21, 22, 23[2], 26, 27, 28[3]; **32:**1, 4[2], 5, 6[2], 7[2], 11[2], 13, 14[3], 15[3], 19[2], 22[3], 25[3], 26, 27, 30, 35, 38[2], 39[3], 40, 41[2], 42[2], 43[2], 44[2], 49, 50[2]; **33:**2, 6, 7[3], 8[2], 9[3], 10[2], 11, 13[2], 14, 15, 16[2], 18[2], 19, 20[2], 21, 22, 23[2], 24[2], 25[2], 27, 28, 29[2]; **34:**1, 2, 3, 4, 7, 9, 11[3], 12[2]; **Jos 1:**2, 4, 6, 7, 8[2], 9, 11, 12, 13, 14[2], 15[2], 16, 18[2]; **2:**1[2], 4, 5, 6, 9[3], 10[2], 11[2], 13[4], 14, 15, 18[4], 19, 21, 22[3], 23; **3:**1[2], 3, 4, 6[2], 9, 10, 15; **4:**3[2], 5, 8, 9, 11, 12, 14, 18[2], 19, 24; **5:**1[2], 2, 3, 6, 9, 11, 12, 13[2], 14[3], 15; **6:**1[2], 2, 5[2], 6[2], 7, 9, 11[2], 12, 13, 14, 15, 16, 17[2], 18[2], 19[3], 20[3], 21[3], 22[2], 23[3], 24[4], 25, 26, 27; **7:**1, 2[4], 3[2], 4, 5[2], 6[3], 9[3], 11, 13, 14, 15[2], 16[2], 17[3], 18[2], 19, 20, 21[3], 22[2], 23[3], 24[7], 25, 26; **8:**1[2], 2[3], 3[2], 5, 7, 8, 9[3], 10[2], 11[3], 12, 13, 14, 15[3], 16, 17, 18, 19[2], 21[3], 22[3], 23, 24[2], 25, 27, 28, 29[4], 31[2], 32, 33[3], 34[2], 35[3]; **9:**1[2], 2, 3, 4[5], 5[3], 6[2], 8[2], 10[2], 11[2], 12, 13[3], 14, 15[2], 16, 17[2], 19, 21, 22, 23[2], 24[2], 25[2], 26, 27[2]; **10:**1[5], 2[2], 3, 4[3], 5[4], 6[3], 7, 10[3], 11, 12[2], 13[3], 15, 16, 17, 18, 19, 20[2], 22, 23[2], 24[2], 25[2], 26[3], 27[2], 28[3], 29[2], 30[4], 31[3], 32[3], 33[2], 34[2], 35[3], 37[6], 38, 39[6], 40[4], 41[2], 42, 43; **11:**2[4], 3[3], 4, 5[2], 6[2], 7, 8[4], 9[2], 10[2], 11[2], 12[3], 14[2], 15, 16[6], 17, 20, 21[3], 22, 23[2]; **12:**2[2], 3[2], 4[2], 5[5], 6[4], 7[2], 8[2]; **13:**1[4], 2, 3[2], 4, 5[2], 7, 8, 9[2], 10, 11[5], 12[2], 13, 16[2], 17[3], 18[3], 19[3], 20[3], 21[5], 23[3], 25[2], 26[3], 27[3], 28, 30, 31[3]; **14:**1[2], 2, 3, 4[3], 6[2], 7, 9[2], 10[2], 11[2], 12, 13, 15; **15:**2, 3, 4, 5[2], 6[3], 7[4], 8, 9, 10[3], 11[2], 12, 14[2], 16[2], 17, 19, 32, 33, 41, 44, 45, 47[3], 48, 51, 54, 57, 59, 60, 62; **16:**3, 4, 6[2], 7[2], 8; **17:**1, 2[2], 3[2], 4[3], 5, 9, 10[2], 11[8], 14, 15[3], 16[2], 17[2], 18[2]; **18:**1, 3, 4, 5, 6[2], 7[3], 8[4], 9[2], 10[2], 11[2], 12, 14, 15, 16[2], 17, 18, 19, 24, 28; **19:**6, 7, 11[2], 13, 14, 15[2], 22[2], 26[2], 27[3], 29, 30, 33[4], 34[3], 38, 46, 47[4], 50, 51[2]; **20:**4[4], 5, 7[2], 8[3], 9; **21:**1[2], 3, 4, 5, 6, 7, 8, 9, 12, 16, 18, 22, 25, 27, 31, 32, 37, 43, 44; **22:**1, 2[2], 4[2], 5[4], 6[2], 7[2], 8[3], 9[2], 10[2], 11[2], 12, 13[2], 14, 15[2], 17, 19, 20[2], 21, 22, 25[2], 27[4], 28[2], 29, 30[3], 31[2], 32[3], 33[3], 34; **23:**1[2], 2[4], 3, 5[2], 6, 9[2], 12[3], 13[2], 14[3], 16[4]; **24:**1[3], 2[4], 3[2], 4[3], 5[3], 6[2], 7[4], 8[3], 9, 11[4], 13[3], 14[4], 15, 17[3], 18, 20[3], 21, 22, 23, 24, 25[2], 26[2], 31[2], 33; **Jdg 1:**4[3], 5[3], 6[3], 7[2], 8[2], 9, 10[3], 12, 13[2], 15, 16, 17[2], 18, 19, 20, 22, 24, 25[2], 26[2], 27[5], 29,

12, 13^4, 14^3, 16, 17^2, 18, 19^3, 20^4, 21, 22, 23^2, 24, 25, 26^3, 27^3, 28^2, 29, 30^3, 31^2, 32^2; **3:**1^2, 2^3, 3^4, 4^3, 5^2, 6, 7, 8^2, 10, 12, 15^2, 16^3, 17^2, 18^2, 19, 20, 21; **Am 1:**1, 2^3, 3, 4, 5^3, 6, 8^2, 9^2, 11^3, 12, 13, 15; **2:**1, 2^3, 3, 4^2, 5, 6^2, 7^2, 8, 9^2, 10, 11^2, 12, 14, 15, 16; **3:**6, 9^4, 10, 11^2, 12, 13, 14^2, 15^2; **4:**3, 4^2, 5, 6, 7^3, 8, 9^3, 10, 11^2, 13; **5:**3, 4, 5^2, 6^2, 7, 8^4, 10, 11, 12^2, 14^2, 15^2, 16^2, 19^3, 20, 21, 22^2, 24, 25, 26; **6:**1, 2, 3, 4^3, 5, 6, 7, 8^3, 10^2, 11^2, 12, 14; **7:**4^2, 8^2, 9^2, 11, 12^2, 13, 14, 15^2, 16, 17^4; **8:**2, 4, 5^3, 6^2, 8^4, 9, 10^3, 12^2, 13, 14^3; **9:**1^3, 3^3, 4^4, 5^4, 6^2, 7^2, 8, 9, 11^3, 12, 13^2, 14^5, 15; **Ob 1:**1, 8, 10^2, 11^2, 16^2, 17^2, 18^3, 19^3, 20, 21; **Jnh 1:**2, 3^2, 4, 5^3, 6, 7, 8, 9, 10, 11, 12, 13, 15^2, 16^2, 17^2; **2:**2^2, 3^2, 7, 10; **3:**2, 3, 4^2, 5^3, 6, 7, 8^3, 9, 10; **4:**1, 2^4, 3, 4, 5^2, 6, 8^2, 9, 10^2, 11^3; **Mic 1:**1^2, 2^2, 3^2, 4, 5^2, 6, 7^2, 8^3, 11^2, 16; **2:**1, 2^4, 3, 4^2, 10, 11, 13; **3:**1^2, 2^2, 3, 6^2, 7, 8^3, 9^2, 10, 11, 12; **4:**1, 2^4, 3^2, 4^2, 5, 6^2, 7^3, 8, 10^2, 11, 13^3; **5:**4^3, 5^3, 6, 8^2, 9, 10, 11^2, 12^2, 13^3, 14^2, 15^2; **6:**1, 2^2, 4^3, 5, 6, 8^3, 9, 10, 11, 14^2, 16^3; **7:**2^2, 3^2, 9, 10, 12^2, 14, 16, 17, 18, 20; **Na 1:**2^3, 3^3, 4^4, 5^2, 6, 8, 12^2, 13^2, 14; **2:**2, 4, 5, 7, 10^2, 11, 12^2, 13^3; **3:**2^2, 3, 4, 5^3, 6^2, 7, 9^2, 16; **Hab 1:**2^2, 3^3, 4, 5, 6, 7^2, 10^2, 11, 12, 13^2, 15, 16^2, 17; **2:**1^2, 2, 3, 5, 6, 7, 8^2, 11, 12, 13, 16^2, 17^2, 19^2; **3:**2, 3, 5, 6^2, 10, 16^2, 17^3, 19; **Zep 1:**3^2, 4^3, 5, 8^3, 9, 12, 13, 14, 15^4, 16^2, 17; **2:**4^2, 5, 6^2, 7^2, 8^2, 9^4, 10, 11^2, 13^3, 14, 15^2; **3:**9, 11, 12, 13^3, 14, 19^4, 20; **Hag 1:**1, 6^2, 8^3, 9^2, 10, 11^4, 12^3, 14^5; **2:**2^3, 6^3, 7^2, 8, 9, 12, 14^3, 17^3, 19, 21, 22^5, 23; **Zec 1:**3, 4, 5, 6^3, 7, 8^2, 11, 12, 13, 14, 15, 16, 17, 18^2, 19^2, 21; **2:**1, 2, 3, 4^2, 5, 9, 10^2, 11^3, 12; **3:**1, 2, 4^2, 5^3, 7^3, 8, 9, 10; **4:**1, 2, 3^2, 7, 10, 11, 12; **5:**1, 2^2, 3, 4^5, 5^2, 6, 7, 8^2, 9^3, 11; **6:**1^2, 3, 6, 7^2, 10^3, 11^3, 12, 13^2, 14^2, 15^2; **7:**2^2, 3^3, 5^3, 6^3, 7^3, 9, 10, 11^2, 12, 14^3; **8:**2, 3^2, 4, 5^2, 7, 8^3, 10, 12^2, 13^2, 14, 15, 16, 17, 19^6, 21, 22^2, 23; **9:**1, 2, 3^2, 4^2, 5^2, 6, 7^2, 8, 9^2, 10^4, 13, 14^2, 15^3, 17^2; **10:**2^2, 3^2, 5, 6^3, 7^2, 8^2, 9^2, 10^2, 11^3, 12; **11:**5^3, 6^3, 7, 8, 9, 10, 11, 13, 14, 17; **12:**1^2, 3, 4, 6^2, 7^2, 8, 9, 10^4, 12^2, 13^2, 14^2; **13:**1^2, 2^2, 3^4, 6, 8^2, 9^4; **14:**2^3, 3, 4^2, 5^3, 7^2, 8, 9^2, 10, 11, 12, 13, 14^2, 15^2, 16, 18^2, 19, 20, 21^4; **Mal 1:**3, 5, 6^2, 7, 8, 9, 10, 11^2, 12, 13^2, 14^3; **2:**1, 2, 3^2, 5^3, 6^3, 7, 9^2, 11^3, 13^2, 14^2, 15^3, 16^2, 17; **3:**1, 2^2, 3^4, 4^2, 5^2, 7^2, 8, 10^2, 11, 16^3, 17, 18^2; **4:**1, 3, 4, 5, 6^2; **Mt 1:**2^3, 3^4, 4^3, 5^3, 6^2, 7^3, 8^3, 9^3, 10^3, 11^2, 12^2, 13^3, 14^3, 15^3, 16, 17^2, 19, 20, 21, 23^2, 25; **2:**2, 3, 4^2, 6, 7, 8^3, 9, 11^3, 12, 13^4, 14^2, 15, 16^3, 18, 19, 20^2, 21^2, 22; **3:**4^2, 5^2, 6, 7, 10, 11, 12^2, 14, 16^3, 17; **4:**2^2, 3, 5, 6, 8^2, 9^2, 10, 11^2, 13^2, 16^2, 18, 19^2, 20, 21^2, 22^2, 23^3, 24^4, 25^2; **5:**1, 2, 6, 11^2, 12, 13, 15, 16, 18, 19^2, 20, 21, 22^2, 24^3, 25^2, 29, 30^2, 32, 36, 38, 40^2, 41, 42, 43, 44, 45^3, 47^2; **6:**2, 4, 5^3, 6^3, 12, 13, 16, 17, 18, 19^3, 20^2, 24^3, 25, 26, 27, 28, 30, 32, 33^2; **7:**2, 5, 6^3, 7^3, 8^2, 12, 13^2, 14^2, 19, 22^2, 24, 25^2, 26^2, 27^5, 29; **8:**2^2, 3, 4, 6, 7^2, 8, 9^6, 10, 11^4, 12, 13^2, 15^3, 16^2, 17, 19, 20^2, 21, 22, 23, 25^2, 26^4, 27, 32^4, 33, 34; **9:**1^2, 2, 5, 6, 7^2, 8, 9^3, 10^4, 11, 13, 14, 15^2, 16, 17^3, 18^3, 19^2, 20, 22^2, 23^2, 24, 25^2, 26, 28, 29, 30, 31, 33^3, 35^4, 36; **10:**1^3, 2^2, 3^3, 4, 5, 11, 15, 16, 17, 18^3, 21^3, 22, 25, 26, 27, 28, 30, 35^2, 36, 37, 38^2, 39, 40, 41, 42; **11:**1, 3, 4^2, 5, 6, 9, 12, 13, 14, 16, 17^2, 18, 19^4, 21^2, 22, 23, 25^3, 27^3, 28^2, 29^3, 30; **12:**1^2, 3, 4, 5, 7, 9, 10, 11^2, 13, 14, 15, 16, 18, 21, 22^3, 23, 25^2, 29, 30, 31, 33^2, 35, 37, 38, 39, 40^2, 41^2, 42^2, 44, 45^4, 46, 47, 48, 49^2, 50^2; **13:**1, 2, 3, 4^3, 5, 6, 7^2, 8, 10, 12, 13, 14, 15^6, 16, 17^2, 19^2, 20, 21, 22^2, 23^3, 25^2, 26, 27^2, 28, 30^2, 31, 32^2, 33, 36^2, 38, 39^2, 40, 41^2, 42^2, 44^3, 46^2, 47, 48, 49, 50^2, 52^2, 54^3, 55^4, 56, 57^2, 58; **14:**2^2, 3, 6, 9, 10, 11, 12^3, 14^2, 15^3, 17, 18, 19^5, 20^3, 21^2, 22, 23, 25, 26, 27, 29, 30, 31, 33, 35, 36^2; **15:**1^2, 3, 4^2, 10^2, 12, 14, 17, 18, 21^2, 22, 23^2, 25, 26, 28, 29, 30^2, 31^2, 32^3, 34, 36^4, 37^3, 38, 39; **16:**1^2, 3^2, 4^2, 6^2, 8, 9, 10, 11, 12, 14^2, 17^2, 18^3, 19^2, 21^5, 22^2, 23, 24^2, 25, 27; **17:**1^3, 2^3, 3, 4, 5, 6, 7^2, 8, 10, 11, 12, 15^3, 16, 17, 18^3, 19, 20^2, 23^3, 24, 25, 27^4; **18:**1, 3^2, 6, 8^2, 9^3, 12^2, 13, 15, 17^2, 18, 21, 25^4, 26, 27^2, 28, 29^2, 30, 31^2, 32, 34; **19:**1, 2, 3, 4, 5^4, 7, 9^2, 12^2, 13, 14, 15^2, 16, 17, 18, 19, 21^2, 25, 26, 27, 29^2, 30; **20:**4^2, 5, 6^3, 8^2, 11, 12^2, 14, 16, 17, 18^3, 19^3, 20, 21^2, 23, 25^2, 27, 28, 32, 34; **21:**1, 2^3, 3, 5^2, 6, 7^3, 8^2, 9, 12^4, 14^2, 15^2, 16^2, 17, 19^3, 21^2, 23^3, 25, 27, 28^2, 29, 30^2, 31, 32^4, 33^2, 35^2, 36, 38, 39, 41, 42, 43, 44, 45; **22:**4^2, 5, 6, 7, 9, 10^2, 12^2, 13^3, 15, 16^2, 19, 20, 21, 22^2, 23, 24, 25, 31, 32, 33, 35, 37^2, 38, 39, 40; **23:**1, 2, 3, 4, 5, 6, 7^2, 8, 9, 12, 13^2, 15^3, 18, 20, 21^2, 22^2, 23^5, 25^3, 27^2, 28, 29^2, 30, 34^4, 35, 37^2; **24:**1, 3^2, 5, 6^2, 7^3, 9^2, 10^2, 11^2, 12, 14^2, 19, 21, 22, 24^3, 27, 29^2, 30^3, 31^2, 32, 35, 36, 38^2, 39^2, 40, 41, 43, 45, 49^3, 50, 51^2; **25:**1, 2, 5, 7, 9^2, 10^3, 14, 16^2, 18^2, 19, 21, 22, 23, 24, 25^2, 26^2, 27, 28, 29, 30, 31, 32, 33^2, 35^3, 36^3, 37^2, 38^3, 39^2, 40, 41, 42^2, 43^4, 44, 46; **26:**2, 3, 4^2, 7, 8, 9, 15, 16, 18, 19, 21, 22^2, 26^2, 27, 31, 35, 36^2, 37^3, 38, 39^2, 40^2, 41, 42, 43, 44, 45^3, 47^2, 49^2, 50^2, 51, 53, 55^2, 56, 57, 58, 59, 61^2, 62, 64, 65, 67^2, 69, 71, 73, 74, 75^2; **27:**1, 2, 3^2, 5^2, 9, 10, 11, 12, 20^2, 21, 24, 25, 26, 27, 28, 29^3, 30^2, 31, 33, 35, 36, 38, 40^2, 41, 42, 46, 48^2, 50, 51, 52, 53^2, 54^3, 55, 56^3, 58, 59, 60^2, 61, 62, 63, 64^3, 66; **28:**1, 2^3, 3, 4, 7^2, 8^2, 9^3, 10, 11, 13, 14, 15^2, 18^3, 19^3, 20^2; **Mk 1:**5^3, 6^2, 7, 9, 10^2, 11, 12, 13^2, 15^3, 16, 17^2, 18^2, 19, 20^2, 21^2, 22, 24, 25, 26^2, 27^2, 29^2, 30, 31^3, 33, 34^3, 35^2, 36^2, 39^2, 40, 41^2, 42, 44, 45^3; **2:**2, 4^2, 8, 9^2, 11, 12^4, 13, 14^3, 15^3, 16^2, 18^4, 20, 21, 22^3, 23, 25^3, 26^2, 27; **3:**1, 3, 5^2, 6, 7, 8^2, 11, 13^2, 14^2, 15, 17, 18^8, 19, 20, 22^2, 23^2, 25, 26^2, 27, 28, 31^3, 32^3, 33^2, 34^2, 35^2; **4:**1, 2, 4^3, 5, 6^2, 7^3, 8^5, 9, 11, 12^2, 13, 15, 16, 17, 18, 19^4, 20^5, 21, 24^2, 25, 27^5, 32^2, 36, 37, 38^2, 39^3, 41^3; **5:**2, 3, 4^3, 5^3, 6, 7, 12, 13^4, 14^2, 15^3, 16, 19^3, 20^3, 21, 22, 23^3, 24^2, 26^2, 27^2, 29, 30, 31, 33^2, 34, 37, 38, 39, 40^5, 41, 42^2, 43; **6:**1^2, 2, 3^6, 4^2, 5^2, 6, 7^2, 9, 11, 12, 13^2, 14, 15, 17, 19^2, 20^3, 21^2, 22^4, 23, 24, 25, 26, 27, 28, 29^2, 30^2, 31^3, 32, 33^3, 34^2, 35^2, 36^2, 37^2, 38^3, 40, 41^5, 42^2, 43^2, 45, 47, 49, 50^2, 51^2, 53, 55^2, 56^3; **7:**1, 3, 4^3, 5, 8, 10^2, 13, 14^2, 17, 19, 20, 23, 24^2, 25^2, 27, 30, 31, 32, 33^3, 34, 35^2, 37; **8:**1, 2, 3, 6^4, 7, 8^2, 9, 10^2, 11, 12^2, 13^2, 14, 15^2, 17, 18^3, 20^2, 22, 23^3, 24^2, 25^3, 27, 28^3, 30, 31^4, 32^2, 33^2, 34^3, 35^2, 36, 38^2; **9:**1, 2^4, 3, 4, 5, 7, 12, 13, 14, 15, 18^5, 20^3, 21, 22^2, 25^2, 26^2, 27^2, 30, 31^2, 32, 33, 35^2, 36^2, 37, 38, 42, 43, 45^2, 47^2, 48, 50; **10:**1^4, 2, 4, 6, 7^2, 8, 11, 12^2, 13, 14, 16^2, 17^2, 19, 21^3, 22, 23, 24, 26, 27, 28, 29, 30^4, 31, 32^3, 33^3, 34^4, 35^2, 36, 37^2, 39, 41, 42^2, 44, 45, 46^2, 47, 49^2, 50, 52; **11:**1, 2^3, 3, 4, 6, 7^2, 8, 9, 11^2, 14, 15^5, 16, 17, 18^2, 19^2, 21, 23^2, 24, 27, 28, 29, 33; **12:**1^2, 3^2, 4^2, 5^3, 7, 8, 9^2, 11, 12, 13, 14^3, 15, 16^2, 17^2, 18, 19, 20, 21^3, 26^2, 28^2, 30^3, 32, 33^5, 37, 38, 39^2, 40, 41, 42, 43; **13:**1, 3, 4, 6^2, 7, 8, 9^3, 10, 11, 12^3, 13, 17, 19, 20, 21, 22^3, 24, 25^2, 26, 27, 28, 31, 34^2, 37; **14:**1^3, 3^2, 5^2, 7, 11, 12, 13, 14, 15, 16^3, 18^2, 19, 22^2, 23^2, 27^2, 31, 32, 33^4, 34^2, 35^2, 37^2, 38, 39^2, 40^3, 41^2, 43^3, 44, 45^2, 46, 47, 48, 49, 50, 52, 53^2, 54, 55, 56, 57, 58, 60, 61, 62^2, 63, 65^2, 67, 68, 69, 71, 72^2; **15:**1^3, 8, 15, 16, 17^2, 18, 19, 20, 21, 23, 24^2, 27^2, 29^2, 30, 31, 32, 36^2, 37, 38, 40^3, 41^2, 42, 43, 44, 46^2, 47; **16:**1^3, 2, 5, 7, 8^3, 10^2, 11, 13^2, 14^2, 15^2, 16, 17, 18^2, 19, 20^3, 99^3; **Lk 1:**2, 5, 6, 7, 8, 9, 12, 13, 14^2, 17^2, 18, 19^2, 21, 22^2, 24, 25, 28^2, 29, 31^3, 32^2, 33, 35, 36^2, 39, 40, 41, 42^2, 43, 45, 46, 47, 49, 52, 53, 55, 56^2, 57, 58^2, 59, 63^2, 64^2, 65, 66, 67, 68, 71, 72, 75, 76, 79, 80^2; **2:**2, 4, 5, 7^3, 9^2, 12, 13^2, 14, 15^2, 16^3, 18, 19, 20^2, 21, 24, 25^2, 27, 28, 32, 33^2, 34^3, 35, 37^2, 38^2, 40^2, 42, 43, 44, 46, 47^2, 48^2, 51^2, 52^4; **3:**1^4, 2, 5^4, 6, 9, 10, 11, 12, 14^2, 15, 16, 17, 19, 21^2, 22^2; **4:**1, 2, 5, 6^3, 8, 9, 11, 14, 15, 17^2, 18, 20^2, 22, 23, 24, 25^2, 27, 29, 30, 31, 33, 35, 36^3, 37, 38, 39^3, 40^2, 41, 42^3; **5:**1, 2, 3^2, 4, 7^3, 9, 10^2, 11, 12, 13, 14^3, 15, 16, 17^4, 18, 19, 21, 23, 24^2, 25, 26^2, 27^2, 28^2, 29^2, 30^3, 33^2, 35, 36^2, 37^3, 39; **6:**1, 3, 4^3, 6^2, 7, 8^2, 10, 11, 12, 13^2, 14^5, 15^4, 16^2, 17^4, 18^2, 19^2, 20, 22^2, 23, 25, 29, 30, 35^3, 37^3, 38, 42, 45, 46, 47, 48, 49^2; **7:**2^2, 3, 5, 6, 7, 8^6, 9, 11^2, 12^2, 13, 14^3, 15^2, 16^2, 17, 19, 21^2, 22^3, 23, 25, 26, 29, 30, 31, 32^3, 33^2, 34^4, 36^2, 37, 38^3, 39, 40, 41, 43, 44, 50; **8:**1^2, 2, 3^3, 4, 5^3, 6, 7^2, 8, 10, 12^2, 13, 14^3, 15^2, 17, 18, 19, 20^2, 21^2, 22, 23^3, 24^5, 25^4, 27, 28, 29^3, 32, 33^3, 34^2, 35^3, 37, 39, 41, 43, 44^2, 45, 47^2, 50, 51^3, 52, 53, 54, 55; **9:**1^3, 2^2, 4, 6^2, 7, 8, 9, 10, 11^3, 12^4, 13^2, 14, 15, 16^5, 17^2, 19, 21, 22^4, 23^2, 24, 26^3, 28^3, 29^2, 30, 31, 32^2, 33, 34^2, 36^2, 39^2, 41^2, 42, 43, 45, 47, 48^2, 49, 52, 54^2, 55, 58^2, 59, 60, 62; **10:**1^2, 4, 6, 7, 8, 9, 10^2, 13^2, 14, 15, 16^2, 19^3, 21^4, 22^2, 24^2, 27^4, 28^2, 29, 30^2, 31, 32, 33, 34^3, 35^2, 37, 39, 40, 41; **11:**1, 4^2, 5^3, 6, 7^3, 8^2, 9^3, 10^2, 14, 17^2, 22^2, 23, 25, 26^4, 27^2, 28, 31^2, 32^2, 37, 39^2, 41, 42^4, 43, 44, 46^2, 48^2, 49^2, 51, 52, 53^2; **12:**2, 3, 4, 0, 10, 11, 15, 17, 18^3, 19, 20, 23, 24, 25, 28, 29^3, 30, 31, 33^2, 35, 36, 37^3, 38, 42^2, 45^2, 46^3, 48^2, 49, 50, 52, 53^3, 54, 55^2, 56, 57, 58^2; **13:**6^2, 7, 8, 9, 11^2, 12, 13, 14^2, 15^2, 16, 17, 18, 19^3, 20, 21, 22, 24, 25^3, 26^2, 28^5, 29^3, 30, 31, 32^4, 33, 34^2, 35; **14:**3^2, 4^2, 6, 9^3, 10, 11, 12, 13, 14, 16, 18^2, 19, 20, 21^5, 22^2, 23^2, 25^2, 26^5, 27, 28, 29, 30, 31, 32; **15:**1, 2^4, 4^2, 5, 6^2, 8, 9, 13^2, 14, 15, 16, 17, 18^3, 20^4, 21, 22^2, 23^4, 24^3, 25^3, 26, 27^2, 28^2, 29, 31, 32^3; **16:**1, 2, 3, 6, 7^2, 8, 9, 10, 12, 13^3, 14, 16^2, 17, 18^2, 19^2, 20, 21, 22^2, 23, 24^2, 25^2, 26^2, 29, 31; **17:**2, 3, 4^3, 6^2, 7, 8^3, 11, 14^2, 16^2, 18, 19, 20, 22, 24, 25, 27^5, 28^3, 29^2, 31, 34, 35; **18:**1, 3, 4, 6, 7^2, 8, 9, 10, 13, 15, 16^2, 20, 22^2, 24, 28, 29, 30, 31^2, 32^3, 33, 34, 40^2, 43^2; **19:**1, 2, 4, 5^2, 6, 7, 8^2, 10, 11, 12, 13^2, 14, 16, 19, 21, 22, 24, 25, 27, 29, 30^2, 32, 35, 38, 41, 43^2, 44^2, 45, 46, 47; **20:**1^2, 2, 3, 9^2, 10, 11^2, 12^2, 14, 15, 16^2, 17, 18, 19, 20^2, 21^2, 23, 24, 25, 26^2, 28^2, 29, 31^2, 34, 35, 36, 37^2, 46^3, 47; **21:**1, 5, 7, 8^3, 9, 10, 11^4, 12^4, 15, 16^3, 21^2, 23^2, 24^2, 25^3, 26, 27, 28, 29, 30, 33, 34^3, 36, 37^2, 38; **22:**2, 4^2, 5, 6, 8^2, 11, 13^2, 14, 17^2, 19^2, 20, 21, 25, 26, 29, 30^2, 32, 33^2, 36^3, 37^2, 39^2, 41, 43, 44, 45, 46^2, 47, 50, 51^2, 52^2, 53, 54, 55, 56, 61, 62^2, 63, 64, 66^2, 68; **23:**1, 2, 4, 5, 7, 8, 10, 11^2, 12, 13, 14^3, 16, 19, 22, 23, 25^2, 26^2, 27^2, 28^2, 29^2, 30, 33, 34, 35, 36, 37, 39^2, 41, 44, 45, 47, 48, 50, 51^2, 52, 53, 54, 55^2, 56; **24:**5, 7^2, 9^2, 10, 11, 12^2, 14, 15^2, 17, 19^2, 20^3, 21, 23^2, 24, 25, 26, 27, 29, 30^2, 31^2, 33^3, 34, 35, 36, 37^2, 38, 39^3, 40^2, 41, 43^2, 44, 46^2, 47^2, 49, 50, 51, 52^2, 53; **Jn 1:**1^2, 3, 4, 5, 10, 11, 14^4, 15, 17, 19, 20, 21, 29, 32^2, 33, 34^2, 36, 37, 38, 39^3, 40, 41, 42, 43, 44, 45^2, 46, 51^3; **2:**1, 2, 4^2, 7, 8, 9, 10^2, 11^2, 12^2, 13, 14^2, 15^2, 19, 20, 22^2, 25; **3:**2, 4, 5, 6, 8, 10, 11, 12, 14, 19^2, 20, 22^3, 23^2, 25, 26^2, 29, 31, 32, 35; **4:**1, 3, 6, 7, 10^2, 11, 12^2, 16, 18, 23^2, 24^2, 28, 29, 30, 34, 35, 36^2, 37, 38, 40, 41, 42, 47^2, 48, 50, 51, 52; **5:**1, 3, 6, 7, 8, 9^2, 11, 12, 14, 15, 17, 20^2, 21, 24^2, 25^2, 27, 29^2, 30, 32, 33, 35^2, 37, 38, 39, 43, 44; **6:**3, 5, 9, 11, 13, 15, 17^2, 19^2, 21, 24, 30, 33, 35, 36, 37, 39, 40^2, 42, 44, 45^2, 49, 50, 51, 53, 54^2, 55, 56^2, 57, 58, 63, 64, 65, 66, 69; **7:**3, 11, 12, 14, 18, 21, 22, 26, 28^2, 29, 31, 32^2, 33, 34, 35, 36^2, 38, 42, 45, 50, 52; **8:**2^2, 3^2, 6, 7, 8^2, 9, 10, 11^2, 14, 16, 18, 21, 26^2, 28, 29, 32^2, 33, 42, 44^3, 48, 49, 50, 52, 55, 56, 57, 59; **9:**6^2, 7^2, 8^2, 11^4, 14, 15, 16, 18, 19, 20, 24, 27, 30, 31, 34^2, 35, 36, 37, 38, 39, 40; **10:**1, 3^2, 4, 8, 9^3, 10^3, 12^5, 14, 15^2, 16, 18, 20, 23, 24, 25, 27, 28, 29, 30, 35, 36, 38^2, 40, 41, 42; **11:**1, 2, 5^2, 8, 19^2, 20, 25, 26^2, 28^3, 29^2, 31, 32^2, 33^2, 34, 38, 41^2, 44^3, 45, 46, 47^2, 48^3, 52, 54, 55, 56, 57; **12:**2, 3, 5, 6, 11, 13, 14, 16, 17, 21, 22^3, 24, 25, 26, 27, 28, 29, 32, 36, 38, 39, 40^4, 41, 45, 47, 48, 49, 50; **13:**1, 2, 3^2, 4, 5^2, 9, 10, 12, 13^2, 14, 20, 21, 30, 31, 32, 33; **14:**3^3, 4, 6^2, 7, 8, 9, 10, 11, 12, 16^2, 17, 20^2, 21^4, 22, 23^3, 24, 26, 27, 28, 29; **15:**1, 5, 6^2, 7^2, 8, 10, 11, 16^2, 22, 24^2; **16:**3, 8^3, 10, 13, 14, 15, 16^3, 17^4, 19^3, 20, 22^2, 24, 27, 28^2, 30, 32; **17:**1, 3^2, 6^2, 8^3, 10^2, 11^2, 12, 13, 14, 19, 21, 23^2, 25, 26^2; **18:**1, 3^4, 4, 6, 7, 10, 12^2, 15, 16, 18^4, 19, 20, 25^2, 27, 28, 29, 31, 33, 35, 37, 38; **19:**1, 2^3, 3, 4, 5, 6^2, 7, 9, 10, 13, 14, 17, 18, 19, 20^2, 23, 24, 25^3, 26, 27, 29, 30, 31, 32^2, 33, 34^2, 35, 37, 38, 39, 40, 41, 42^2; **20:**1, 2^4, 3^2, 4, 5, 6, 7, 8^2, 12^2, 13, 14, 15, 16, 17^3, 18^2, 19^3, 20, 22, 25^2, 26^3, 27^2, 28, 29, 31; **21:**1, 2, 3, 6^2, 7, 9, 11^2, 12, 13^3, 17, 18^3, 20^2, 24^2; **Ac 1:**1, 3, 8^3, 9, 10, 13^7, 15, 17, 18^2, 20^2, 21, 23, 24, 25, 26^3; **2:**2^2, 3, 4, 6^2, 7, 8, 9^3, 10^4, 11, 12, 13, 14^3, 17^4, 18^2, 19^4, 20^2, 22, 23^2, 26, 29^2, 32, 33^2, 36, 37^2, 38^2, 39, 40^2, 41, 42^2, 43, 44, 45^2, 46^2, 47^2; **3:**1, 2, 3, 4, 5, 6, 7^4, 8^4, 9, 10^4, 11, 13^2, 14^2, 15, 16^3, 17, 19, 20, 23, 24^2, 25^2; **4:**1^2, 2, 3, 4, 5, 6^2, 8, 9, 10, 13^4, 18, 19, 20, 23^2, 24^3, 25, 26^2, 27^2, 28, 29^2, 30^2, 31^2, 32^2, 33, 34, 35, 37; **5:**2^2, 3, 4, 5^2, 6^2, 8^3, 9, 10^2, 11^2, 12^2, 14, 15^2, 16^2, 17, 18, 19, 20, 21^4, 22, 23, 24, 25^2, 26, 28, 29, 31^2, 32^2, 33, 34, 36^3, 37^2, 38, 40^2, 42^3; **6:**2^2, 3, 4, 5^3, 6, 7, 8^2, 9^3, 10, 11, 12^2, 13, 14, 15^2; **7:**2^2, 3^3, 4, 5, 6^2, 7^2, 8^4, 10^4, 11^3, 13, 14^2, 16^2, 17, 19, 20, 21^2, 22^2, 24, 26, 27, 29, 31, 32^2, 34^2, 35^3, 36^2, 38^2, 39, 41, 42^2, 43, 45, 46, 49, 51, 52^2, 53, 54, 55^2, 56, 57, 58^2, 60; **8:**1^3, 2, 3, 5, 6, 7, 9, 11, 12^2, 13^2, 14, 15, 17^2, 22, 23, 25^2, 26, 27, 28, 29, 30, 31^2, 32, 35, 36, 38^3, 39, 40; **9:**1, 2, 3, 4, 6^2, 8^2, 9, 11^2, 12^2, 14, 15^2, 17^3, 18^3, 19, 20, 21^2, 22, 24, 25, 26, 27^2, 28, 29, 30, 31^3, 32, 34^2, 35^3, 36, 37, 39^4, 40^4, 41^2, 42; **10:**2, 3, 4^2, 7, 8, 9, 10^2, 11, 12^2, 13, 16, 17, 20, 21, 22^2, 23^3, 24^2, 25, 27^2, 28, 31, 32, 33, 35, 38^2, 39, 40, 41^2, 42^2, 46; **11:**1, 3, 5^2, 6, 7, 12^3, 13^2, 14, 15, 16, 18, 19^2, 20, 21^2, 22, 23^2, 24^2, 26^3, 28^2, 30; **12:**4, 7^3, 8^2, 9, 10^3, 11^3, 12, 14, 16^2, 17^4, 19^3, 20^2, 21, 22, 23^3, 24, 25^2; **13:**1^2, 2^2, 3^2, 4, 5, 7^2, 8, 10^2, 11^4, 13^3, 14^3, 15, 16^2, 17^2, 21, 25, 26, 27, 29, 31^2, 32, 36, 41, 42, 43^3, 45, 46^2, 48^2, 50^4, 51, 52^2; **14:**1^3, 2, 3, 4, 5^3, 6^3, 7, 8, 9^2, 10^2, 12, 13^2, 14^2, 15^4, 17^3, 19^3, 20, 21^2, 22, 23^2, 24, 27^2, 28; **15:**1, 2^6, 3^3, 4^3, 5^2, 6, 7^2, 8, 9^2, 12^3, 16^2, 20^3, 22^4, 23^3, 24, 25^2, 27, 28, 29^3, 30, 32^2, 35^3, 36^2, 38, 39, 40, 41; **16:**1, 2, 3^2, 4, 5, 6, 9^2, 11, 12^2, 13^2, 14, 15^3, 16, 17, 18^2, 19^2, 21, 22^2, 23, 24, 25^3, 26^2, 27^2, 29^2, 30, 31^2, 32, 33^2, 34^3, 36^2, 37^3, 38, 39^3, 40^3; **17:**1^2, 2^2, 3^3, 4^3, 5^3, 6, 7, 8, 9^2, 10^2, 11, 12, 13, 14, 15^2, 17^2, 18^2, 19^2, 21, 22, 23, 24^2, 25^2, 26^2, 27^2, 28^2, 29, 31, 34^3; **18:**1, 3^2, 4^2, 5, 6^2, 7, 8^2, 9, 10, 11, 12, 15^2, 16, 17, 18^2, 19, 22^2, 23^2, 25^2, 26^2, 27^2; **19:**1, 6^2, 8^2, 9^2, 10, 12, 15, 16^2, 17^2, 18, 19, 20, 21^2, 22, 25, 26^2, 27^3, 28, 29^2, 32, 33^2, 35, 36, 38^2; **20:**1^2, 2, 3, 4^3, 5, 6, 9, 10^2, 11^2, 12, 13, 14, 15^2, 19, 20^2, 21^2, 22, 23, 24, 25, 28, 32^3, 34, 36, 37; **21:**1^3, 2, 3^2, 4, 5^4, 6^2, 7^2, 8^3, 11^4, 12, 13, 15, 16, 18, 20, 21, 24^2, 25^3, 26, 28^2, 29, 30^3, 32^3, 33^2, 34, 38, 40^2; **22:**1, 4^2, 5^3, 6, 7, 10, 11, 12, 13^2, 14, 15, 16^2, 17, 18^2, 19^2, 20^2, 23^2, 24, 26, 27^2, 29^2, 30^3; **23:**3, 5, 6, 7^2, 9^2, 10, 11, 12, 14^2, 15^2, 16^2, 17, 18^2, 19, 21, 23^2, 24, 27^2, 31, 33, 34; **24:**1^2, 2, 3, 5, 6, 15, 16, 17, 23, 24, 25^3, 26^2, 27; **25:**2, 3, 4, 5, 6, 9, 11, 13, 15^2, 16, 17, 19, 20, 23^4, 24^3, 25, 26; **26:**1, 3, 4, 5, 6, 7, 10, 11, 12, 13, 16^3, 17, 18^2, 20^4, 21, 22^3, 23^2, 26, 30^3, 31; **27:**1, 3^2, 5, 6, 7^2, 9, 10^2, 11, 12, 13, 15^2, 17, 19, 20, 21^4, 23, 24^2, 28^2, 29, 30, 31, 32, 33, 35^2, 36, 40, 41, 42, 43, 44^3; **28:**2^2, 3, 5, 6^2, 7, 8^3, 9, 10, 12, 13^2, 14^2, 15^2, 17, 20, 21, 23^2, 25, 26^2, 27^6, 30, 31^2; **Ro 1:**4, 5, 7^2, 12, 13, 14^2, 16, 18, 20^2, 21, 23, 25^2, 27^2, 28^2; **2:**3, 4^2, 5, 7^2, 8^2, 9^2, 10^3, 12, 15, 17^2, 18^2, 19, 20, 27, 28, 29^2; **3:**4, 8, 9, 14, 16, 17, 19, 21^2, 23, 26, 30^2; **4:**3, 7, 11, 12, 14, 16, 17, 25; **5:**2, 3, 4^2, 5, 12^2, 15, 16, 17, 18; **6:**6, 11, 13, 18, 19^2, 22; **7:**1, 3, 10^2, 11, 12^3, 13; **8:**2, 3, 6, 8, 12, 17^2, 21, 23, 27, 30^3; **9:**2, 3, 4^2, 5, 7, 9, 15, 18, 21, 22, 23, 25, 26, 27, 28, 29^2, 33; **10:**1^2, 3, 8, 9, 10^3, 12^2, 14^2, 15, 17, 18, 21; **11:**3, 8, 9^3, 10, 12, 14, 16, 17, 22, 23, 24, 25, 26, 27, 29, 33^3, 36^2; **12:**1^2, 2^2, 4, 5, 14; **13:**1, 2, 3, 9, 12, 13^3, 14; **14:**3, 4, 6, 7, 8, 9^2, 11, 14, 17^3, 18, 19; **15:**1, 4, 5, 6, 9^2, 10, 11^2, 12, 13, 14^2, 18, 19^2, 21, 24, 26, 27, 28, 29, 30^2, 31, 32; **16:**2^2, 3, 4, 7^2, 9, 12, 13, 14^2, 15^3, 17^2, 18^2, 19, 21^2, 23^2, 25, 26; **1Co 1:**1, 2, 3^2, 5, 10^3, 11, 14, 17, 19, 22, 23, 24^2, 25, 26, 28, 30^3; **2:**1, 2, 3^3, 4^2, 7, 13, 14, 15; **3:**1^2, 3^2, 4, 8^2, 10, 13, 16, 17, 20, 23^2; **4:**1, 5, 6^2, 7, 9, 11^3, 12, 17, 19; **5:**1, 2, 3, 4, 8^2, 10; **6:**2, 5, 6, 8^2, 11^2, 13^4, 14^2, 15, 19; **7:**2, 3, 5, 7, 8, 11, 12^2, 13^2, 14, 19, 24, 28^2, 29, 30^3, 31, 34^4, 35, 36, 37, 38, 40; **8:**4, 5, 6^3, 7, 8, 12; **9:**4, 5^2, 6, 7^2, 10, 13, 16, 27; **10:**1^2, 2^2, 3, 4^2, 5, 7^2, 8, 9, 10^2, 11, 13, 20, 21^2, 26, 27, 28; **11:**2, 3^2, 5, 7, 18, 21^2, 22^2, 24^2, 26, 27, 28^2, 29^2, 30^2, 33; **12:**1, 2, 3, 5, 6, 8, 11, 12^2, 13, 16, 23^2, 27, 28, 31; **13:**1, 2^4, 3, 9, 13^3; **14:**1^2, 3^2, 6, 8, 10, 11, 20, 21, 23^2, 24, 25, 27^2, 28^2, 29, 31, 32, 39, 40; **15:**1, 4^2, 5, 6, 10, 11, 14^2, 17, 24^2, 30, 31, 32, 34^2, 37, 38, 39, 40^2, 41^2, 46, 48, 50^2, 52^2, 53, 54, 56; **16:**2, 3, 6, 9, 15^2, 16^2, 17^2, 19, 20; **2Co 1:**1, 2^2, 3^2, 6, 8, 12^2, 13, 16^2, 17, 18, 19^3, 21, 22; **2:**3, 4^2, 7, 9, 11, 13, 14, 15, 17; **3:**2, 3, 17, 18; **4:**3, 5, 7, 13^2, 14, 15; **5:**8^2, 11, 12, 15^2, 18, 19; **6:**2, 7^2, 8^3, 9^3, 10, 14^2, 16^3, 17^2, 18^3; **7:**1, 3, 5, 7, 10, 15^3; **8:**1, 2, 3, 5^2, 7, 10, 13, 14, 15, 19^2, 22^2, 23, 24; **9:**2, 4, 5^2, 6, 8, 10^3, 13^2, 14; **10:**1, 5^2, 8, 10^2, 12; **11:**3, 4, 6, 9^3, 11, 12, 14, 23, 25, 26, 27^3, 28, 29^2, 31, 33; **12:**1, 3, 4, 10, 12^2, 14, 15, 18, 20^2, 21^3; **13:**2^2, 9, 10, 11^3, 13; **Gal 1:**1, 2, 3^2, 4, 5, 6, 7, 11, 13, 15, 17, 18, 21, 22, 24; **2:**6, 9^5, 12, 13, 14, 15, 16^2, 20^3; **3:**5, 6, 8, 10, 15, 16^3, 19, 23, 28, 29; **4:**2, 6, 7, 9, 10^3, 15, 18, 20, 22, 25, 26, 27, 30; **5:**1, 13, 15, 16, 17, 21, 23, 24^2; **6:**2, 10, 14, 16^2, 18; **Eph 1:**1, 2^2, 3, 4, 8, 10, 11, 13, 15^2, 17, 19, 20, 21^4, 22^2; **2:**1, 3^2, 6^2, 8, 12^2, 14, 15, 16, 17^2, 19^2, 20, 21; **3:**3, 5, 6, 9, 10, 12, 15, 17^2, 18^3, 19, 21^2; **4:**2, 4, 6^3, 11, 13, 14^2, 16, 17, 18, 19, 21, 22, 23, 24^2, 27, 28, 30, 31^4, 32; **5:**2^3, 3, 4, 5, 9^2, 14, 19^3, 20, 25, 27, 29, 31^3, 32^2, 33; **6:**2, 3, 4^2, 5, 6, 7^2, 9^2, 10, 12, 13, 14^2, 17, 18^2, 21^2, 22, 23^2; **Php 1:**1^2, 2^2, 7^2, 9^3, 10, 11, 13, 14^3, 15, 18^2, 19, 20, 21, 22, 23, 25^2, 27^2, 28^2, 30; **2:**1, 2, 7, 8, 9, 10^2, 11, 12, 13, 14, 15^2, 17^2, 18^2, 24, 25^3, 26, 27, 28, 29; **3:**1^2, 3^2, 8, 9, 10^2, 13, 15, 17^2, 18, 19, 20; **4:**1^3, 2, 3^2, 6, 7^2, 8, 9^4, 12^4, 15, 18^2, 19, 20^2; **Col 1:**1, 2^3, 4, 6^2, 8, 9^2, 10, 11, 13, 16^3, 17, 20, 21^2, 22^2, 23, 24, 26, 28, 29; **2:**1^2, 2^2, 3, 5^2, 7^2, 8^2, 10^2, 13^2, 15^2, 16, 18, 19^3, 22, 23; **3:**3, 5, 8, 10, 11^4, 12^2, 13, 15^2, 16^3, 17, 19, 22, 23, 25; **4:**1, 7, 8, 9, 11^2, 12, 13^2, 14, 15^3, 16^2, 17; **1Th 1:**1^3, 2, 3^3, 4, 5^2, 6^2, 7, 8, 9^2, 10; **2:**1, 2, 5, 9^3, 10^2, 12^3, 14, 15^3, 17, 18, 20; **3:**2^3, 5, 6^3, 7^2, 10^2, 11^2, 12^3, 13^2; **4:**1^4, 4, 6, 9, 10^3, 11, 12, 13, 14, 16^2, 17; **5:**1^2, 3^2, 5, 6, 7, 8^3, 11, 12^3, 14, 15, 23^4, 24, 26; **2Th 1:**1^2, 2^2, 3^2, 4^2, 5, 7, 8, 9, 10, 11^2, 12^2; **2:**1^2, 3, 4, 6, 8, 10^2, 13^2, 15^2, 16^3, 17^2; **3:**1^2, 2^2, 3, 4^2, 5, 6, 8^3, 12^2, 13; **1Ti 1:**1, 2^2, 4^2, 5, 6, 9^3, 10, 12, 13, 14^2, 15, 17^2, 19, 20; **2:**1, 2^3, 3, 4, 5, 7^2, 9, 14^2, 15^2; **3:**3, 4, 6, 7, 10, 12^2, 13, 15; **4:**1, 3^2, 4, 5, 6^2, 7, 8, 9, 10, 11, 12, 16^2; **5:**4, 5^3, 8^3, 9, 10, 12, 13^2, 14, 17, 18, 21^2, 22, 23, 24, 25; **6:**1, 2^2, 3^2, 4^2, 5^2, 8, 9^3, 10^2, 12, 13, 15^2, 16^2, 18, 20; **2Ti 1:**2^2, 3, 5^2, 7^2, 9^2, 10^2, 11^2, 12^2, 13, 15, 16, 17, 18; **2:**2, 5, 14, 16, 17^2, 19, 20^2, 21, 22^2, 23, 24, 25, 26; **3:**6^2, 7, 8^2, 11^2, 13^2, 14, 15, 16^2; **4:**1^4, 2, 4^2, 6, 8, 10, 11, 13, 17^2, 18^2, 19^2, 21^4; **Tit 1:**1^2, 4^2, 5, 6, 8, 9, 10, 15^2; **2:**2^2, 7, 8, 9, 10, 12^3, 13^2, 14, 15; **3:**1, 2, 3^2, 4, 5, 8, 9^2, 10, 11, 13^2, 14; **Phm 1:**1^2, 2, 3^2, 5, 7, 9^2, 11, 14, 16, 24^2; **Heb 1:**1, 3^2, 5, 6, 7, 8^2, 9, 10^2, 12^2; **2:**2, 3, 4^3, 7, 9, 10, 11^2, 12, 13^3, 14, 15, 17^2; **3:**1^2, 6^2, 10^2, 12, 16, 18; **4:**4, 5, 6, 12^2, 13^2, 16; **5:**1, 2, 3, 4, 7^3, 9; **6:**1^2, 2, 3, 4^2, 5^2, 6^2, 7, 8^2, 10, 11, 12, 14, 15, 16, 19; **7:**1, 2, 5, 6, 14, 18, 21, 26, 27; **8:**2^2, 3, 5, 6, 8, 9, 10^3, 11, 12, 13^2; **9:**1, 2, 4^3, 7^3, 9, 10^2, 11, 12, 13, 19^5, 21^2, 22, 25, 26, 27^2; **10:**1, 4, 5, 6, 8^3, 10, 11^2, 13, 15, 16, 17, 20, 21, 22, 24^2, 25, 27, 29, 30, 33^2, 34^2, 37, 39^2; **11:**5, 6^2, 7^2, 8, 9, 10, 11, 12^2, 13^2, 19, 20, 22, 23, 28, 32^3, 36^3, 37, 38^3; **12:**1^2, 2^2, 5, 6, 8, 9^2, 12, 13, 14, 15^2, 16, 18^3, 19^2, 22^2, 23^3, 24^2, 28; **13:**4^2, 5, 7, 8^2, 13, 16, 17^3, 21, 22, 23, 24; **Jas 1:**1, 2, 4^2, 5^2, 6, 7, 10, 11^2, 12, 13, 14, 15, 21^2, 22, 23, 24, 25, 26, 27^3; **2:**1, 2^2, 3^2, 4, 5^2, 9, 12, 14, 15, 16^3, 18^2, 19, 22, 23^2, 24, 25; **3:**1, 6^2, 7^3, 9^2, 10^2, 11, 12, 13, 14^2, 16^2, 17, 18; **4:**1, 2^4, 3, 7, 8^2, 9^3, 10, 11^2, 12^2, 13^3, 14, 15, 17; **5:**1, 2, 3^3, 4, 5, 6, 7, 10, 11^2, 12, 14, 15^2, 16^2, 17^3, 18^2, 19^2, 20; **1Pe 1:**1, 2^4, 3, 4^2, 7^2, 8^3, 10, 11, 21^2, 23, 24^2; **2:**1^2, 4^2, 6^2, 8^2, 11, 12, 14, 18, 20, 22, 25; **3:**2, 3, 4, 6^2, 8, 10^2, 11^2, 12, 14, 16, 19, 21, 22^2; **4:**3, 4, 5, 7, 11^2, 13, 18^2; **5:**1, 4, 5, 9, 10^2, 11, 12, 13; **2Pe 1:**1^2, 2^2, 3^2, 4^2, 5, 6^3, 7^2, 8^2, 9^2, 10^2, 11, 12, 15, 16, 17, 19, 21; **2:**2, 3^2, 4, 5, 6^3, 7, 8, 9, 10^2, 11, 12^2, 13, 15, 16, 17, 18, 20^2, 22; **3:**2^2, 3, 4, 5^2, 6, 7^2, 8, 10^4, 11, 12^3, 13, 15, 16, 17, 18^3; **1Jn 1:**1, 2^4, 3^3, 5^2, 6, 7, 8, 9^2, 10; **2:**2^2, 4, 8^2, 10, 11, 14^2, 17^2, 20, 21, 22,

24, 25, 27^4, 28^2; **3:**1, 3, 5, 10^2, 12^3, 13, 15, 16, 17^2, 18, 19^2, 20, 22^2, 23^2, 24^2; **4:**3^3, 4, 5, 6^2, 7, 10, 12, 13, 14^2, 15, 16^3, 18, 20, 21; **5:**1, 2, 3, 4, 6^3, 8^3, 11^2, 14, 15, 16, 18, 19, 20^4; **2Jn 1:**1^2, 2, 3^3, 6, 7, 9, 10, 12^2; **3Jn 1:**2, 3, 10^3, 12^2, 13, 14; **Jude 1:**1^2, 2, 3, 4^2, 6, 7^3, 8, 9, 10, 11^2, 15^2, 16, 22, 23, 24, 25^3; **Rev 1:**2, 3^2, 4^4, 5^3, 6^4, 7, 8^3, 9^3, 10, 11^2, 12, 13^2, 14, 15, 16^2, 17, 18^5, 19, 20^2; **2:**2^2, 3^2, 5^2, 8^3, 9^2, 10^2, 12, 13, 14, 16, 17^2, 18^2, 19, 20^3, 22, 23^4, 26; **3:**1^2, 2^2, 3^3, 5^2, 7^3, 8^2, 9^3, 12^2, 14^2, 16, 17^2, 18^3, 19^2, 20^3, 21; **4:**1^3, 2, 3^3, 4, 5^3, 6^3, 7, 8^5, 9^4, 10^2, 11^5; **5:**1, 2^2, 3, 4, 5, 6^3, 7, 8^2, 9^5, 10^2, 11^4, 12^6, 13^9, 14^3; **6:**1, 2^3, 4^2, 5, 6^3, 8^4, 9, 10^2, 11^3, 12, 13, 14^2, 15^7, 16^3, 17; **7:**2^2, 4, 9^4, 10, 11^5, 12^7, 13, 14, 15^3, 16, 17^2; **8:**2^2, 3, 4, 5^4, 7^6, 8, 9, 10^3, 11, 12^4, 13; **9:**1^3, 2^3, 3, 5, 6, 8, 9, 10, 11, 13, 15, 17^6, 18^2, 19^2, 20^5, 21; **10:**1^2, 2, 3, 4^2, 5, 6^6, 8, 9^3, 10, 11^3; **11:**1^4, 2, 3, 4, 5^2, 6^2, 7^2, 8^2, 9^5, 10^3, 11^3, 12, 13^3, 15^4, 16, 17^2, 18^5, 19^3; **12:**1, 2, 3^2, 4, 5^3, 6, 7^3, 8, 9^2, 10^4, 11, 12^2, 14^2, 16, 17^2; **13:**1^4, 2^5, 4^2, 5^2, 6, 7^4, 8, 10, 11, 12^2, 14^2, 15^2, 16^3; **14:**1^3, 2^2, 3^3, 4, 5, 6^3, 7^4, 9^2, 10^3, 11^4, 12, 13, 14^3, 15, 16, 17, 18^2, 19^2, 20^2; **15:**1, 2^4, 3^4, 4^2, 5, 6, 7, 8^3; **16:**1, 2^4, 3^2, 4^2, 5^2, 6, 7^2, 8, 9^2, 10, 11^3, 12, 13^2, 15^2, 16, 17, 18^2, 19^2, 20^2, 21; **17:**1, 2, 3^3, 4^5, 5^2, 6^2, 7^2, 8^6, 10^2, 11^2, 12, 13, 14^5, 15^4, 16^4; **18:**1, 2^2, 3^2, 4, 5, 6, 7^3, 8^3, 9^3, 10, 11^2, 12^3, 13^4, 14^2, 15, 16^2, 17^3, 18, 19^2, 20^2, 21^2, 22^6, 23^4, 24^3; **19:**1^2, 2^2, 3, 4^3, 5^3, 6, 7^3, 8, 9^2, 10, 11^4, 12^2, 13, 14^2, 15, 16^2, 17, 18^3, 19^2, 20^3, 21^2; **20:**1, 2^2, 3^3, 4^4, 6^3, 8^2, 9^4, 10^6, 11^3, 12^4, 13^3, 14, 15; **21:**1^3, 2, 3^2, 4^2, 5^2, 6^2, 7^2, 8^2, 9, 10^2, 11, 12^2, 13, 14^2, 15^2, 16^3, 21^2, 22, 23^2, 24, 25, 26; **22:**1, 2, 3^2, 4, 5^3, 6^2, 8^3, 9^2, 10, 11^3, 13^3, 14, 15^6, 16, 17^3, 19; **Tob 1:**2, 3^2, 4^3, 5^2, 6^2, 7^3, 8^6, 9, 10^2, 13^2, 14, 15^2, 17^2, 18, 19^3, 20, 21^3, 22^3; **2:**1^3, 2^3, 3^3, 4^2, 5, 6^2, 7^2, 8^3, 9^3, 10^2, 12^3, 13, 14; **3:**1^2, 2^2, 3^4, 4^3, 5^2, 6^4, 8^2, 10^4, 11, 12^2, 13, 15^2, 17^2; **4:**2^2, 3^3, 4, 5^2, 7^2, 10, 12^2, 13^5, 14, 15, 16^2, 18, 19^4, 20, 21^2; **5:**2^3, 3^4, 4, 5, 6^2, 7^2, 9^3, 10^8, 11, 12, 14^6, 15, 16^2, 17^5, 18^2, 21, 22; **6:**1, 2^3, 3^2, 4^2, 5^3, 6^3, 7^3, 8^3, 9^2, 10, 11, 12^4, 13^4, 14, 15^3, 16, 17^2, 18^8; **7:**1^2, 4, 5^2, 6^2, 7^3, 8, 9^3, 10^3, 11^9, 12^4, 13^2, 14, 15^2, 16^2; **8:**1^2, 2^3, 3^2, 4^5, 5^4, 6^2, 7^2, 8, 9^3, 10^2, 11, 12, 13^3, 14^2, 15, 17^2, 19^4, 20^3, 21^5; **9:**1, 2^3, 3, 4, 5^5, 6^9; **10:**1^3, 2, 3, 4^3, 6^2, 7^6, 8, 10^4, 11^3, 12^9, 13^4; **11:**3, 4, 6, 8^3, 9^2, 10, 11, 12, 13, 14^4, 15^2, 16^2, 17^6, 18^2; **12:**1^2, 3, 5^2, 6^3, 7^3, 9, 10, 11, 12^3, 13^3, 14^2, 15, 18, 20^2, 21, 22^2; **13:**2^3, 4^2, 6^7, 7, 8, 10^2, 12^2, 13^2, 14^2, 16^5, 17^3; **14:**2^4, 3^2, 4^{11}, 5^4, 6, 7^5, 8^5, 10^2, 11^3, 12^3, 13^2, 15^4; **Jdt 1:**2^2, 3, 4^2, 6^3, 7^4, 8^4, 9^{10}, 10^2, 11^2, 12^7, 13^3, 14^2, 15^2, 16^4; **2:**2^3, 4, 5^2, 7^2, 8^2, 10^2, 11, 12, 13, 14^2, 16, 17^5, 18^2, 19^3, 21, 22^2, 23^3, 24^2, 25, 26^2, 27^6, 28^6; **3:**3^5, 4^2, 5, 6^2, 7^3, 8^3, 10^2; **4:**1^2, 2, 3^4, 4^5, 5^2, 6, 7, 8, 9^2, 10^6, 11^4, 12^5, 13^2, 14^3; **5:**1^3, 2^2, 3^4, 4^2, 5, 8^2, 9^4, 10, 11, 12, 14^2, 15^3, 16^2, 18^2, 19^3, 20^4, 21^2, 22^2, 24; **6:**2^3, 4, 6^2, 7, 9, 10^2, 11^3, 12^2, 13^2, 14^3, 15^2, 16^3, 17^3, 18^2, 19^2, 20, 21^2; **7:**1^4, 2^2, 3^2, 4, 5, 7^3, 8^3, 9, 11, 12, 13^3, 14^3, 15, 16^2, 17^3, 18^8, 19, 20, 21, 22^4, 23^4, 24, 25, 26^2, 27^3, 28^3, 29^2, 30, 31, 32^3; **8:**2, 3^3, 4, 5, 6^4, 7^5, 9^2, 10^2, 11^4, 12, 14, 17, 19^2, 20, 21^2, 22^4, 24^2, 26^2, 28, 30, 33, 35^2, 36; **9:**1^2, 2^2, 3^3, 4^4, 5^3, 6^2, 7^4, 8^3, 9, 10, 12, 13^4, 14^4; **10:**1, 2^2, 3^2, 4^2, 5^4, 6^2, 7^2, 8^2, 9, 10, 12^3, 13, 14, 15, 16, 17^2, 18, 19, 20^2, 21^2, 23^2; **11:**1, 3^2, 5, 6, 7^4, 8^3, 9, 10, 11, 12^2, 13^3, 15, 17^3, 18^2, 19^2, 20^2, 22, 23^2; **12:**1^2, 5, 6^2, 7, 9, 10, 11^3, 13^4, 14, 15, 16^2, 17, 19^2, 20; **13:**1, 3, 4, 5, 6, 7, 8, 9^2, 10^2, 11, 12, 13^3, 15^3, 16^2, 17^2, 18^2, 20^3; **14:**1, 2^2, 3^4, 4^2, 5^2, 6, 7^2, 9, 10, 11, 12^2, 13, 14, 15^2, 16^4, 17^2, 18, 19^3; **15:**2^3, 4^4, 5^4, 6, 7^3, 8^3, 9, 10^2, 11^5, 12^3, 13^4, 14; **16:**1^2, 3, 4^4, 8, 9, 11^2, 12, 13, 14^2, 16, 17, 18, 19, 20, 21, 22, 23^3, 24^2; **AdE 1:**3^3, 4, 6^5, 7^2, 8^2, 10, 11^3, 12^2, 13, 14^3, 15, 16^2, 17^2, 18, 19, 20^2, 21^2; **2:**1^2, 2, 3^3, 4^2, 7^2, 8, 9^4, 11, 12^2, 13, 14^2, 17^2, 18^2, 20, 21, 22, 23; **3:**1, 6, 7, 8, 9, 10, 11, 12^3, 13, 14, 15^2; **4:**1, 2^2, 3^4, 4^3, 5, 7, 8^4, 9, 10^2, 11, 13, 14^2, 16^5, 17; **5:**4^2, 7, 8^2, 9, 10^2, 11^3, 12^2, 14^3; **6:**1, 2, 5, 6, 8, 9^4, 10, 11^2, 12^2, 13^3, 14; **7:**1, 2^2, 3^2, 4^4, 6, 7^2; **8:**2^2, 3, 4^2, 5^2, 7, 8^2, 9^2, 10^2, 11^2, 13, 14, 15^2, 16^2, 17^5; **9:**3, 10, 13, 14, 15, 16, 17^2, 18, 19, 20^2, 21, 22^4, 24, 25^3, 26^3, 27^4, 28, 29, 31^2, 32; **10:**1, 2^5, 3, 4, 5, 6^4, 7, 9^3, 10, 11^4, 12^2, 13^3; **11:**1^4, 4, 5^2, 6, 8^3, 9^2, 10, 11^3, 12; **12:**1, 2^3, 3, 4, 5^2, 6; **13:**1, 2^4, 3^3, 4, 5^3, 6^2, 7^3, 9, 10^2, 11, 12, 14^2, 15^3, 17^2, 18; **14:**2^5, 3^2, 5^2, 6^2, 8, 9^3, 10, 11^2, 12^2, 13^2, 14^2, 15^3, 16, 17^2, 19^2; **15:**1, 2, 5, 6, 7^3, 8^3, 11, 12, 13, 14, 15^2, 16; **16:**1, 3, 5^2, 8, 9, 10, 11, 12, 13^4, 14, 16^2, 19, 20, 23^2, 24^3; **Wis 1:**1, 2, 3, 5^3, 6^2, 7, 8, 9, 10, 11^2, 13, 14^2, 16^2; **2:**1^3, 2^2, 3, 4^3, 5^2, 6, 7^2, 9, 12^2, 13, 15, 16^2, 17, 18, 19^2, 22, 23, 24; **3:**1, 2, 3, 5, 6, 7, 8^2, 9^3, 10, 11^2, 12, 14^2, 15, 16, 17, 18; **4:**1, 2, 3, 4, 5^2, 9, 10^2, 12, 15^3, 16, 17^2, 18^2, 19^4, 20; **5:**1, 2, 3^2, 4^2, 5, 6^2, 7^2, 8, 9, 10, 11^2, 13, 14^2, 15, 16^2, 17, 18, 20^2, 21, 22^2, 23^2; **6:**1, 2, 3^2, 5, 7^2, 9, 10, 11, 12^3, 15, 16^2, 17, 18^2, 19, 21, 22^4, 24, 25; **7:**1, 2, 3^2, 6, 7^2, 8^2, 9, 10^2, 11, 13, 15^2, 16^2, 17, 18^3, 19, 20^3, 21, 23^2, 24, 25, 26, 27^3, 29; **8:**1, 2^2, 3, 4, 6, 7^3, 8^6, 9^2, 10, 11, 12, 13, 14, 15, 16^2, 17, 18^4, 19, 21^3; **9:**1, 2, 3^3, 4, 5^2, 7^2, 8, 9^2, 10^2, 11^3, 12^2, 14, 15, 16, 17, 18^3; **10:**2, 5^2, 7, 10^2, 11,

12, 14^3, 15, 16^2, 17^2, 18, 19, 20, 21; **11:**2, 3, 4^2, 6, 12, 14, 15^2, 20^3, 21, 22, 23, 24; **12:**2^3, 4, 5^2, 8, 10^2, 11, 15, 16, 17, 18, 19, 20^3, 21, 22, 27; **13:**1, 4^2, 5, 6, 7, 10^2, 11^2, 12^2, 13^3, 14^2, 15^2, 16, 17^2, 19^2; **14:**1, 2, 3, 5, 6, 8^2, 9, 11, 12, 14, 15^2, 16, 17, 20, 21, 25^3, 26, 27^2, 29, 30; **15:**1^2, 3, 6, 7^2, 8, 9^3, 10, 11^2, 12, 13, 14, 15, 16, 17, 19^2; **16:**1, 2, 5, 6, 8, 9^2, 10, 11^2, 13^2, 16^3, 19, 20^2, 21, 22^2, 24, 28, 29; **17:**1, 2, 3, 4, 5, 6, 7, 8, 9, 13, 14, 15^3, 16^2, 17, 20; **18:**1, 2^2, 3, 4, 5^3, 7, 8, 9^3, 10, 11, 12, 14, 16^3, 17, 18^2, 20, 21^2, 22, 23^2, 24^2; **19:**2^2, 3^3, 4, 5, 7^2, 9, 10, 15, 19, 20, 22^3; **Sir Pr:**T^{17}; **1:**1, 2, 3, 4, 9, 11^3, 12^3, 15, 17, 18, 19^2, 20, 23, 26, 27^2, 29, 30^3; **2:**2^2, 3, 4, 5, 6^2, 8, 9, 10^4, 11^2, 12^2, 15, 16, 17^2; **3:**2, 4, 5, 6, 8, 11, 12, 14, 16, 24, 26, 27, 29; **4:**1, 5, 8, 9, 10^2, 11, 12, 13, 15, 17^3, 18^2, 19, 20^2, 21^2, 23, 24, 26, 28, 29, 31; **5:**2, 6^2, 7^2, 10, 13^2, 14^2, 15; **6:**1^2, 3^2, 4, 5, 7, 9^2, 10, 11, 12, 13, 16, 18, 19^3, 21, 23, 24, 25^2, 26, 27^3, 28, 29, 30, 31, 32, 33, 35, 37^2; **7:**1, 2, 3, 6, 7, 9, 11, 14, 17, 19, 23, 24, 25, 27, 29, 30, 31^3, 36; **8:**2, 3, 8, 9, 15, 16^2; **9:**2, 5, 8^2, 9, 13^2, 14, 15, 16, 18; **10:**1, 4, 5, 6, 7^2, 8^2, 9, 11^2, 13^2, 14, 15, 16, 17^2, 22^2, 23, 24^2, 25, 26, 28, 29, 31; **11:**1, 4^2, 6, 7, 8, 9, 10, 11^2, 12^2, 13, 14^3, 17, 18^2, 19^2, 20^2, 21, 22, 23, 24, 25, 27, 30, 31, 32, 33, 34^2; **12:**1, 2, 5, 6, 11, 12^3, 14, 18^3; **13:**1, 2^2, 3^2, 6^3, 7^2, 8, 9, 11, 13, 15, 16, 18^3, 23^3; **14:**1, 2, 3, 4, 7, 8, 10, 11, 12, 13^2, 15, 16^2, 18^3, 19^2, 20, 21, 22, 23, 24, 25, 26, 27; **15:**1, 2, 3, 4^3, 5, 6^2, 7, 8, 10, 14, 15, 16, 17^2, 18, 19, 20; **16:**1, 3, 5, 6, 11, 13, 17, 18^2, 19^2, 20, 23, 24^2, 25, 26, 27^2, 28, 29, 30; **17:**1, 3, 4^2, 6^3, 7^3, 10, 11, 12, 13, 14, 19, 20, 22, 23^2, 24, 25^2, 26^2, 28, 29, 31, 32; **18:**4, 5, 7, 8^2, 10, 11, 12, 13^3, 14, 18^2, 19, 20, 21, 22, 24, 25, 28, 29; **19:**2^2, 3^2, 4, 7, 8, 9^2, 17, 20, 23, 25, 27, 29, 30^2; **20:**1, 3, 5, 8, 9, 10, 11, 15^3, 16, 17, 23, 26, 27, 28, 29, 30; **21:**2, 4, 5, 9, 11, 13, 15^2, 17, 18, 19, 21, 28; **22:**1, 3, 5^2, 6, 10, 11, 13^3, 14, 15, 19, 20, 24, 25, 27^2; **23:**1^2, 2^2, 3^3, 4, 5, 6, 8, 10, 11^2, 12, 14^3, 16, 18, 19^2, 20, 21, 22, 23^2, 24, 25, 26, 27; **24:**1, 2, 3, 4, 5, 6^2, 8^2, 9, 10, 11, 13, 14^2, 15^4, 16^2, 17^2, 19, 20, 21, 22, 25, 26, 29, 31^3, 32, 33; **25:**1^5, 2^2, 4, 5^2, 6, 7, 8^3, 9, 14, 15, 16, 17, 18, 21, 22^2, 23^2, 24, 25; **26:**2, 4, 5^2, 6^2, 11, 12^2, 13, 14, 15, 18, 19, 20, 21, 22, 27^2, 28^2; **27:**1, 2, 8, 13, 14^2, 15, 16, 17, 19^2, 20, 21, 22, 23^2, 25, 26, 27, 28, 29, 30; **28:**2, 3, 6^3, 7^2, 8, 9^2, 10^2, 11, 13, 14^2, 15, 19, 20, 21, 23, 24, 25^2, 26; **29:**3^2, 4, 5^3, 6^4, 8, 9, 10^2, 11, 12, 13, 17, 18^2, 21^2, 23, 25^2, 27, 28; **30:**2, 3, 5, 6, 7, 8, 9^2, 10, 11, 12^3, 13, 14^2, 15^2, 16, 17, 20, 21, 22, 23^3, 24^2, 25; **31:**1, 2, 3, 4, 6, 7, 8, 10^4, 11, 12, 14, 15, 16, 17, 20^3, 21, 22^3, 23, 24, 28^2, 29, 30, 31^2; **32:**1, 2, 3, 7, 8, 9, 10, 11^2, 14, 16, 17, 18, 20, 22, 24; **33:**1, 4^2, 5, 8^2, 9^2, 10, 11, 12^5, 14, 17, 19, 20^2, 21, 25^4, 26^2, 27^3, 30^2, 32^2; **34:**1^2, 2, 4, 5^3, 7, 8, 9, 12, 18, 19^3, 20^3, 28, 29, 30, 31^3; **35:**4, 5, 8, 9, 10, 11, 12, 13, 15^2, 20, 21, 22^3, 23^2, 24, 25; **36:**2, 3, 6, 7, 8, 9, 10^2, 11, 16, 19, 20, 21, 22, 27, 28, 29, 30^2; **37:**6, 8, 9^2, 12, 13, 16, 18^3, 19, 23, 24, 26, 27, 28, 29, 30; **38:**2, 3, 4, 6, 7, 8, 9, 10^2, 11^2, 14, 16^2, 17, 18, 20, 21, 22, 23, 25^3, 26, 27^2, 28^3, 29^2, 30^2, 31, 32, 33, 34; **39:**1, 2, 3, 4^3, 5^2, 6, 7, 8, 9, 10, 11, 13, 14^2, 15^2, 16, 17, 18, 19, 20, 22, 25, 26^8, 28^2, 29^3, 30^3, 31, 32^2, 33, 35^2; **40:**1, 2^2, 3, 4, 5^7, 8, 9^6, 10, 11, 12, 13, 17, 18, 19^2, 20, 21, 22, 24, 25, 26^2, 27, 29; **41:**1^2, 2^3, 3, 5, 6, 9, 14^2, 17, 18^2, 19^2, 20, 21^2, 22^2; **42:**1^3, 2^2, 3, 4^2, 5^2, 6, 7^2, 8, 9, 10, 11^2, 13, 14, 15^2, 16, 18, 19^2, 20, 21^2, 22, 23, 24; **43:**3, 4, 11, 13, 14, 15, 17^2, 18, 19, 20^2, 21^2, 23, 24, 25^2, 26, 29^2, 30^2, 31, 33; **44:**3, 4, 7, 9, 11, 13, 15, 16, 17, 19, 20^2, 21^3, 22, 23^2; **45:**1^2, 2, 3, 4, 5^4, 7^2, 8^2, 9, 10^3, 13, 15^4, 16, 17^3, 18^5, 19^2, 20^2, 21, 22^2, 23^2, 24^2, 26^2; **46:**1, 2, 4, 5, 6, 7^3, 8^2, 9, 11, 12, 13, 14, 15, 16, 17, 18, 19^2, 20^2; **47:**3, 4^2, 5^2, 6, 7, 8, 10^2, 11^2, 13, 15, 16, 17^2, 18, 19, 20^2, 21, 22, 23^3, 24; **48:**1, 2, 3, 5, 6, 7, 8, 10, 11, 12, 13, 14, 15, 16, 17^2, 18^2, 19^2, 20, 21, 22^2, 23, 24, 25; **49:**1, 2, 4^2, 5, 6, 7^4, 10, 12^2, 13^3, 16^2; **50:**1^2, 4, 9, 10, 11, 14, 15, 18, 19^2, 20^2, 21, 22^2, 23, 24, 25, 26^2, 27, 28; **51:**1^2, 2^3, 3^2, 4, 5, 6, 7^2, 8^2, 9^2, 11, 12^4, 14, 16^2, 18^2, 19^2, 20, 22, 23, 24, 25, 26, 27, 28^2, 29, 30; **Bar 1:**2, 3, 4^5, 5^2, 7^3, 9^5, 10^4, 11^2, 12^4, 13^2, 14^2, 15, 16^2, 18, 19, 20^2, 22; **2:**1^4, 3, 4, 5, 6, 9^2, 11^6, 14^3, 15, 16^2, 17, 18^3, 20, 21^2, 22, 23^4, 24^2, 25^4, 26^2, 27, 31^2, 32, 33^2, 34^4, 35^2; **3:**1, 2, 3, 5, 6, 7, 8^2, 9, 14^2, 15, 16, 17^3, 18, 19^2, 20, 23^2, 25^2, 29^2, 30^2, 33^2, 34^2, 36^2, 37; **4:**1, 2, 7, 8, 9, 10, 11, 12, 14, 15^2, 16, 20, 21^2, 22, 23^2, 24, 25, 27, 31, 33, 34, 35, 36, 37; **5:**1^2, 5^2, 7^2, 8, 9; **LtJ 6:**4^3, 6, 7, 8^3, 9, 10^3, 11^2, 12, 15^2, 18^3, 20, 22^3, 26, 27, 28, 30^2, 31^3, 32, 33, 35, 39^3, 40, 41, 42, 43^2, 45, 47, 48, 50^2, 51^2, 55^2, 57^2, 58^4, 60^3, 61, 63^2, 68, 70, 71, 72^3; **Aza 1:**1, 2, 3^2, 4^2, 5, 6, 8, 9^2, 10^2, 11, 12^2, 13, 14, 15, 16, 17^2, 18^2, 19, 20, 21^2, 23, 24, 25^2, 26^2, 27^2, 28^2, 29^2, 30^3, 31^2, 32^2, 33^2, 34^2, 35, 36, 37, 38, 39, 40^2, 41, 42^2, 43, 44^2, 45^2, 46^2, 47^2, 48^2, 49^2, 50^2, 51^2, 52, 53^2, 54, 55^2, 56, 57^2, 58, 59^2, 60, 61, 62, 63, 64^2, 65^2, 66^4, 68; **Sus 1:**2, 3, 4, 6, 8^2, 9, 13, 14, 15, 16, 17^2, 18, 19,

20^2, 21, 22, 24, 25^2, 27, 30^2, 31, 33, 34, 36, 37, 38, 39^2, 40, 41^2, 42^2, 43, 46, 47, 48, 50^2, 51, 52, 53^2, 55^2, 56^3, 57, 60, 61, 63^3, 64; **Bel 1:**2, 3^3, 4, 5^2, 6, 7^4, 8^2, 10, 11^3, 13, 14^3, 15^3, 16^2, 18^2, 19^2, 20^2, 21^3, 22^2, 26, 27^4, 28^3, 29, 30, 31, 32^2, 33^2, 35, 36, 38, 39^2, 40, 41, 42^2; **1Mc 1:**1, 2, 3^2, 4^3, 5, 6, 7, 9^2, 11^2, 13, 15^3, 17^3, 18^4, 19, 20, 21^2, 22, 23^2, 24, 26^2, 28, 29, 30^2, 31^2, 32^2, 33^2, 35^3, 38, 42, 43, 44^2, 45^3, 46, 47^3, 48^2, 49, 50, 51, 52, 55^2, 56, 61^3, 62, 63; **2:**1, 5, 6, 7^2, 10, 12^2, 14^2, 16^2, 17^3, 18^8, 19^2, 20^2, 21, 24^2, 25, 27, 28^2, 29, 30, 31^2, 32^2, 33^2, 34, 37, 38^3, 39, 40^3, 43^2, 44^2, 45^3, 47, 48^2, 49^3, 50, 51^2, 52, 53, 59^2, 61, 62, 63, 64, 66, 67, 68, 69, 70^2; **3:**2, 3, 5, 6, 7, 10, 11^4, 12^2, 13, 14^2, 17^2, 20^4, 21, 23^2, 24, 25^2, 26, 27^2, 28^2, 29^2, 30, 31^2, 34^4, 35^2, 36, 37^3, 38^2, 39^3, 40, 41^5, 42^2, 43^2, 44^3, 45^2, 46, 47^2, 48, 49^3, 50, 51^2, 54, 55^3, 57, 58^3, 59; **4:**1^2, 2, 3^2, 6, 7^3, 10^3, 11, 12, 14^2, 15^5, 16, 17, 18^3, 20, 21, 23^5, 24, 26, 27, 28, 29^2, 30^2, 31^2, 33, 34, 35^3, 36^2, 37, 38, 39, 40^2, 43^2, 45, 46, 47, 48^2, 49^2, 50^2, 51, 53, 54^4, 55^2, 56^2, 57^3, 58, 59^3, 60^2; **5:**1, 2^2, 3^2, 4^2, 5^3, 6, 7, 8, 9, 10^2, 11^2, 12, 13^4, 14, 15^3, 16^2, 17^3, 18, 19, 20, 21^2, 22, 23^4, 24^2, 25, 26^4, 27^3, 28^4, 29, 30^3, 31^2, 32, 33, 34^2, 35^4, 36^3, 37, 38, 39^3, 40, 41^2, 42, 43^3, 44, 45^3, 46^2, 47, 50^3, 51^2, 53, 54^2, 55^2, 56^2, 57, 58, 59, 60^2, 61, 63^2, 64, 65^3, 66, 68^2; **6:**1, 2, 3^2, 4^2, 5, 6^2, 7^2, 8^2, 9, 10^2, 11^2, 12^2, 14, 15^3, 18, 19, 20^3, 21, 22^2, 23, 24^2, 26^2, 27, 28, 29, 30, 31^5, 32, 33^3, 34, 35^2, 36, 37^3, 39^2, 40^3, 41^2, 42^2, 43, 44, 45^2, 46^2, 47, 48^2, 49, 50, 51^2, 52, 56^2, 57^3, 58^2, 59, 60^3, 61, 62^2, 63^2; **7:**1, 2, 4, 5, 6^2, 7^4, 8, 9^2, 10^3, 12, 14, 15, 16, 17^2, 18^2, 19^6, 20, 22^2, 23^2, 24, 25^3, 26^2, 27^2, 28, 29, 30^2, 32, 33^2, 34^3, 35^3, 36^3, 37^2, 38^3, 39^2, 40, 41, 42, 43, 44, 45, 46^2, 47^4, 48; **8:**1, 2^3, 3^2, 4^3, 5^3, 6^3, 7^4, 8^2, 9, 10^6, 11^2, 12^3, 13^3, 15, 16^2, 17^3, 18, 19^2, 20^4, 22^3, 23^4, 26, 28^3, 30, 31, 32^2; **9:**1^3, 2^3, 4^2, 5, 6, 7, 8, 9^2, 10, 11^3, 12, 13, 14, 15^2, 16^2, 17^2, 18, 19^2, 20^2, 22^3, 24, 25, 26^3, 28, 29^2, 30, 33^4, 34, 35, 36^3, 37^2, 38, 39^5, 40^4, 41, 44^2, 45^3, 47^2, 48^3, 49, 50^9, 51, 52^4, 53^2, 54, 55^2, 56, 57, 58^4, 59^2, 60^2, 61^2, 62^2, 63, 64^2, 65, 66^2, 67^4, 68^2, 69, 70, 71^2, 72^2, 73^2; **10:**1^2, 2, 5^2, 6^2, 7^2, 9, 10^3, 11^2, 13, 14, 15^3, 16, 17^2, 19, 20^4, 21^2, 22, 24^2, 26^3, 27, 28, 29^3, 30^5, 31^3, 32, 33^2, 34^6, 36, 37^3, 38, 39, 41, 43^2, 44, 45^3, 46^2, 47, 48, 49^3, 50, 52^3, 53^3, 54^3, 55^2, 56^2, 57^2, 58^2, 59, 60^5, 62^2, 63^3, 64, 65^3, 66^2, 68, 69^3, 70^2, 71, 72^2, 73^2, 74^2, 76^3, 77^3, 78, 80, 81, 82^2, 83^2, 84^4, 86^2, 87, 89^2; **11:**1^3, 2^2, 4^4, 6^2, 7, 8, 9^2, 12^2, 13^2, 15^2, 16, 17, 18, 20, 21, 22^3, 23^2, 24^4, 27^2, 28^2, 29, 30, 33, 34^4, 35^4, 36, 37^2, 38, 40^3, 41, 42^3, 44, 45^2, 46, 47^3, 48^2, 49, 50^2, 51^4, 52, 53, 54^2, 55^2, 56, 57^2, 58^4, 60^4, 61^2, 62^4, 65^2, 66^2, 67, 68, 69, 70, 71, 72^2, 73^2, 74; **12:**1^2, 2, 3^4, 4, 6, 8^2, 10, 11^3, 12, 13, 14^2, 15^2, 16^3, 17^2, 18, 21^2, 22, 23^2, 25, 26^2, 27^2, 28^3, 29, 31^2, 32^2, 33^3, 34, 35, 36^2, 37, 38, 39^2, 40^3, 41, 43^4, 45^6, 46^2, 48^2, 49^2, 50^3, 52^4, 53; **13:**1, 2^2, 3^5, 4, 5, 6^3, 8^2, 9, 10^2, 11^2, 12, 14^2, 16^2, 17, 18, 19^2, 20^3, 21, 22^2, 23, 24, 25^2, 26, 27^3, 28^2, 29^2, 32^2, 33^5, 34, 35, 36^3, 37^3, 38, 39^3, 40^2, 42^4, 43^3, 44, 45^2, 47^4, 48^2, 49^3, 50^2, 51^7, 52^2, 53^2; **14:**1, 2, 3^3, 5, 6, 7^4, 8, 9, 10, 11, 12^2, 13, 14^2, 15, 16^2, 17^2, 18^2, 19, 20^4, 21^2, 22, 23^2, 25, 26^4, 27, 28^3, 29^4, 30, 31, 32^2, 33^2, 34^2, 35^5, 36, 37^3, 39, 40^3, 41^2, 42^7, 43^4, 47^4, 48, 49^2; **15:**1^2, 2^2, 3^3, 4^2, 5, 7^4, 8^2, 9^2, 10, 11, 12, 13^2, 14^3, 15^2, 17^3, 18, 19^3, 20, 22^3, 23^{20}, 25^3, 26^4, 27^2, 28^2, 29, 30, 31^2, 32^4, 35^2, 36^4, 37, 38^2, 39^2, 40^4, 41^3; **16:**1, 2^6, 3^5, 4^3, 5^3, 6^2, 7, 8^3, 10^2, 11, 13^2, 14^3, 15, 16^4, 17, 18^3, 19^2, 20^2, 21^3, 22, 23^4; **2Mc 1:**1^2, 2^3, 3^2, 4^2, 5^2, 7^2, 8^7, 9, 10^5, 15, 16^4, 18^2, 19, 20^2, 21, 22^2, 23^3, 24^4, 25^3, 26^2, 27^2, 28, 33^2, 34^2, 35, 36; **2:**2^3, 3, 4^3, 5^4, 7^2, 8^3, 9, 10^4, 11, 13^6, 14, 17^4, 18^2, 19^3, 20^2, 21^2, 22^3, 24, 25, 26, 27, 29, 30, 31; **3:**1^2, 2, 5, 6^2, 7, 8, 9^3, 10, 11^3, 12^3, 14, 15, 16, 17, 19, 20, 21, 22, 24^3, 25^2, 26^2, 27, 28^2, 29, 30^3, 33^2, 34, 35^2, 39^3, 40; **4:**1, 2, 4^3, 5, 6, 7, 8, 9^2, 10, 11^3, 12, 13^2, 14, 15, 16^3, 18, 21, 22^3, 23, 24, 25, 30, 32^2, 34^2, 35, 36, 37^3, 38^2, 39, 40^3, 41^3, 42^2, 48^3; **5:**2^2, 3^3, 5^2, 6, 7, 8^2, 10, 11, 12, 13^4, 14, 15, 16^2, 17^2, 18, 20^2, 21^2, 22, 23^2, 24^3, 25, 26, 27^2; **6:**1, 2^2, 3, 4^3, 7^2, 8, 9, 10, 11, 18, 21^2, 22, 23^4, 25^2, 28^3, 30, 31; **7:**1^3, 2, 3^2, 4^5, 5^2, 6^2, 7, 8, 9, 10, 11^3, 12, 13, 14, 15, 16, 17^2, 18, 20, 21, 22, 23^2, 24^4, 25, 27^4, 28^4, 33^2, 34, 37^3, 38^2, 39, 42; **8:**1^4, 2, 3, 4^2, 6^2, 7, 8^2, 9^2, 11, 12, 13^2, 14, 15^2, 16^2, 17^2, 18^2, 20^2, 21^2, 22^2, 23, 24^3, 26, 27^3, 28^4, 29, 30^6, 31, 32, 33, 35, 36; **9:**2^5, 3, 5^2, 6^2, 7^3, 8^2, 9^4, 11, 12, 14, 15^2, 16^3, 17^2, 18, 19^3, 20^2, 21^2, 25^4, 26^4, 27^2, 28, 29; **10:**1^2, 2, 3^4, 4^3, 6, 7^2, 10, 11^2, 12, 13^2, 14, 15, 16^2, 17^2, 19^4, 20, 21, 22, 24, 25^2, 26^2, 27^3, 28, 29, 30^5, 33^2, 34, 35, 36^4, 37^2, 38^2; **11:**1, 2^2, 3^2, 4^2, 5, 6^3, 7, 8^2, 9^2, 11^3, 12^2, 13, 14, 17^2, 18, 20^3, 24, 25, 26^3, 27, 29, 30, 31^2, 32, 34, 37; **12:**1, 2^4, 3^2, 4^3, 6^2, 7, 9^2, 11^2, 12, 13^2, 14^4, 15, 16, 19^2, 20^2, 21^3, 22^2, 23, 24^3, 25, 26^2, 27^4, 28^2, 30, 31, 33, 35^4, 36^3, 37, 38^2, 39^2, 40, 42, 43^2, 44, 45; **13:**1, 2^2, 3, 4^2, 5, 8^2, 10^3, 11, 12^4, 13^2, 14^2, 15^3, 16^2, 19, 21, 22, 23^3, 25, 26^2; **14:**1^2, 2^2, 4^3, 5^2, 6^2, 7, 8, 9, 12, 13^2, 14^2, 15^3, 16, 18^2, 19^2, 20^2, 23, 24, 25^2, 26, 27^2, 28, 30^2, 31^2, 33^3, 34, 37^2, 38^2, 41^2, 42, 43^2, 44, 45^4, 46^2; **15:**1, 2^2, 5^2, 6^2, 8, 9^2, 10,

11^2, 12^3, 13^3, 14^3, 15^2, 17^5, 18^5, 19, 20^2, 21^3, 22, 23, 25^2, 26^2, 27^2, 28, 29^2, 30^3, 31^2, 32, 33^2, 34, 35, 36, 37, 38^2, 39^3; **1Es 1:**3, 4^3, 5, 6^3, 7^4, 8^2, 9^7, 10, 11, 12^2, 13^2, 14, 15^2, 18, 19^2, 21^4, 23, 24^2, 25, 26, 27^2, 28, 29, 30, 31^2, 32, 33^6, 34, 35, 36^2, 37, 38^2, 39, 40, 41^2, 42^2, 44^2, 45, 46^3, 47, 48^3, 49^3, 50, 51, 53, 54^3, 56, 57^2; **2:**2^2, 4, 5, 6^2, 7^2, 8^4, 9^3, 10, 12, 13, 14, 15, 16^3, 17^4, 18^4, 19, 22^2, 23^2, 24^3, 25^4, 26, 27^5, 28, 29, 30^5; **3:**1^2, 2^3, 3^3, 5^2, 6^5, 7^2, 8^2, 9^3, 13^2, 14^6, 15^2, 16^2, 17, 19^3, 20^3, 21^2, 22^2, 23; **4:**2^2, 3^2, 4^3, 5^3, 6^3, 7, 10^3, 11, 12, 13^2, 14^2, 15^2, 16, 18^3, 19^3, 20^2, 22^3, 23^5, 24^4, 26, 28, 30^3, 33^2, 34^3, 35, 36^3, 37^2, 38^4, 40^4, 41^2, 42^2, 44^2, 46^3, 47^6, 48^4, 52, 53^3, 54, 55, 56, 57^2, 58, 59, 61^2, 62^2, 63^4; **5:**1^5, 2^2, 3, 5, 8^4, 9, 11, 15, 19, 20^2, 22, 24, 26^3, 35, 36^2, 37, 38^2, 39, 40^3, 41, 42^2, 43^2, 45^2, 46^4, 47, 48^2, 50^6, 51, 52^4, 53, 54^3, 55^3, 56^3, 57^2, 58^7, 59^3, 60, 61, 62^2, 63^2, 64, 66^2, 68^3, 69, 70^2, 72, 73^3; **6:**1^2, 2, 3^4, 4^3, 6, 7^5, 8, 10^3, 11, 12, 13, 14^2, 15, 16^3, 18^5, 19^2, 22, 23, 25^2, 26^3, 27^8, 28^2, 29^4, 30^4, 31^2, 32, 33; **7:**1^3, 2, 3, 4^3, 6^2, 8, 9^3, 10, 12^3, 13; **8:**4, 5^5, 6, 7, 8, 9, 10^3, 11, 12, 13^4, 14^4, 16^2, 18, 19^2, 20^2, 21, 22, 23^4, 26^4, 27, 28, 30, 31, 32^2, 33, 34, 35, 36, 37, 38, 39^2, 40, 41^2, 44^2, 46^3, 47^2, 48^3, 49^2, 50^2, 51^2, 52, 53^2, 54^2, 55^6, 56^3, 57^2, 58^4, 59^3, 60^3, 61^2, 62^2, 63^2, 64^2, 65, 66, 67^4, 68, 69^5, 70^4, 71^5, 72^2, 73^3, 74, 75, 76, 77^5, 78^2, 79^2, 81^3, 82, 83, 84, 85^2, 86^2, 87, 91^4, 92^2, 94, 95^2, 96^3; **9:**1, 2^2, 3^2, 4^2, 5, 7^3, 8, 9^2, 10, 11^2, 12, 13, 14^4, 15, 16, 17, 18, 19^2, 20, 21^5, 22^3, 23^6, 24, 25, 26^3, 27^4, 28^2, 29^3, 30^2, 31^6, 32^4, 33^5, 34^4, 36, 37^3, 39, 40^2, 41^2, 42, 43^2, 44^2, 46, 47^3, 48^4, 49^3, 51^2, 52, 54^4, 55; **Man 1:**1^3, 2, 3^2, 4, 5, 6, 7^4, 8^2, 9, 10^3, 11, 12, 14, 15^2; **Pm 151:**1, 3, 4^2, 5, 6, 7; **3Mc 1:**1^2, 2^2, 3^3, 4^5, 5^2, 6, 7, 8^2, 9^4, 10, 11, 13, 14, 16^4, 17, 18^2, 19, 20^4, 23^4, 26, 27^2, 28, 29; **2:**1, 2^3, 3^3, 4, 5^2, 6, 7^2, 8, 9^4, 10^3, 11^2, 12^2, 13^2, 14, 17, 19^2, 20^3, 21, 22^2, 23^2, 24, 25, 26, 27, 28^3, 29, 32^2, 33^3; **3:**1^2, 3, 4, 7^2, 8^2, 10^5, 11, 12^3, 13, 15^3, 16^2, 17^2, 18, 19^2, 20, 21^3, 22, 23, 24, 25^4, 26, 28^2, 29^2; **4:**1^2, 2^2, 3, 4^2, 5, 6^2, 7, 8, 10, 11^3, 12, 14, 15, 16^3, 18, 20^2; **5:**1, 2^3, 3, 4, 5^2, 7^3, 8, 10, 11, 12^3, 13, 14, 15^2, 16, 17, 18, 21^2, 24, 25^2, 26^2, 27, 29^2, 30, 31^2, 32, 33^3, 34, 36, 40, 41, 42^3, 43^4, 44^2, 45, 46, 47^2, 48^3, 49^6, 51^2; **6:**1^2, 4, 5^2, 6, 8^2, 9^3, 10, 12^2, 13, 14, 15, 16, 17^2, 18^2, 19^2, 20, 21^2, 22, 23^2, 24^3, 25, 26, 27, 28^2, 29^2, 30^2, 31^4, 32^3, 33, 34^3, 35^2, 36^3, 38, 39^2, 41; **7:**1^2, 2, 3, 5, 6, 7^3, 9, 10, 12^2, 13^2, 14^3, 15, 16^3, 19, 20^4, 21^2; **2Es 1:**5, 6, 7, 8, 10, 11^2, 12, 13^2, 14, 15, 17, 19, 21, 22, 23, 24, 26, 29^3, 31^2, 32^2, 34^2, 38^2, 39^7, 40^3; **2:**1^2, 2, 3^2, 4^2, 6, 8, 9, 11, 12, 13, 14^2, 16^2, 18^2, 19^4, 21^2, 22, 23^2, 24, 27^3, 31, 32^2, 33, 34, 37, 38, 40, 42, 43^2, 45^4, 46, 47, 48; **3:**1, 2, 3^2, 4^2, 5^3, 6, 7^5, 8^3, 9, 10, 11, 12^3, 13, 14, 15^4, 16, 17, 18^4, 19^4, 21, 22, 23^2, 24, 26, 29^2, 30^3, 31, 33^2, 34^2; **4:**2^2, 3^2, 4, 5, 6, 7, 9^4, 11, 12^4, 13^2, 14^3, 15^2, 16, 17, 18, 19^2, 20, 21^2, 22, 23^2, 24^2, 26^2, 27, 29, 30^2, 33^2, 34, 35, 36^2, 37^3, 38, 40^2, 41, 44^3, 47^2, 48^4, 49^4, 50^2, 51, 52; **5:**1^2, 2, 3^2, 4^2, 5^2, 6^2, 7^3, 8, 9^2, 10^3, 11, 13^3, 14^2, 15^3, 16^2, 18^2, 19^2, 20, 22, 23, 24^2, 25^2, 26^2, 27^2, 28^3, 29, 32^2, 33, 34, 35^2, 36^2, 37^2, 39, 43^3, 44, 45, 46, 49, 50, 51, 53, 54, 55^2; **6:**1, 2^3, 3^3, 4^3, 5^3, 6^3, 7^2, 8, 9, 10^2, 11, 13^2, 14, 15, 16, 17^2, 19^2, 20, 21^4, 22, 23, 24^2, 25^2, 26^3, 27, 28^2, 29, 30, 31, 32, 33^2, 35, 36, 37, 38^3, 39^2, 41^3, 42^3, 43, 44^3, 45, 46, 47^2, 48, 49, 50, 51, 52^2, 53, 54^2, 56^2, 57^2, 58; **7:**2, 3^2, 6^2, 7^2, 8, 11, 12^5, 13^2, 14, 17, 18, 21, 22, 23^2, 24^2, 25, 26, 28, 29, 31, 32^2, 33^2, 34, 35^2, 36^3, 37, 38^4, 44^2, 45^3, 47, 48^5, 49^3, 52, 54^3, 55^5, 56^4, 57, 59, 60, 61^4, 62, 64^2, 65, 66, 68^2, 69, 70^4, 72^2, 74, 75, 76, 79^2, 80, 87^3, 89, 93, 95^2, 96^5, 97, 98^3, 99, 100, 101, 102, 104^2, 105, 106^2, 107, 108^3, 109^2, 110^2, 111, 112, 113, 114^2, 116^2, 117, 120, 121, 123^2, 126, 127, 132, 133, 134, 135, 136^4, 138, 139^2; **8:**1, 4^2, 5, 6^2, 7, 8^4, 9^2, 11, 12^2, 13, 14, 15, 16^3, 17, 18, 19^2, 20, 21, 22^4, 23^2, 24, 25, 31, 36, 37^2, 39^2, 41^3, 42, 44^2, 45, 46^2, 49, 51, 52, 53^2, 54, 56^2, 58, 59, 60, 62^2; **9:**1^2, 5, 6^3, 7, 8^2, 9, 11^2, 13, 14, 15^2, 17^4, 18, 19, 20, 21^4, 22, 24^3, 25^2, 26^2, 28^2, 29^2, 30^2, 31^2, 32, 34, 36, 38^4, 39, 40^2, 41^2, 43^2, 44^2, 45^7, 46, 47; **10:**1, 2, 3^2, 4^2, 5^2, 6, 7, 8, 9, 10^3, 12, 15, 16, 19, 20, 22^4, 23^2, 24^2, 25, 26, 27^3, 28, 29, 30^3, 31^3, 32^3, 33, 35, 36, 38^3, 39^2, 41, 43, 45, 46^2, 47, 48^2, 49, 50^2, 55^2, 56, 57, 59^2; **11:**1, 2^2, 5^2, 6^2, 7, 8, 10, 11, 12, 13^4, 15, 18^2, 19^2, 20, 21, 22^3, 23^2, 24, 25, 27, 29, 30, 31^2, 32, 33, 34, 35, 36, 37^2, 38, 40^3, 42^3, 43, 44, 45^2, 46^3; **12:**2^4, 3^3, 5^2, 7^2, 8^2, 9, 13, 14, 18, 20, 21, 23^2, 24, 25, 30, 31^5, 32^4, 33, 34, 35, 36, 38^2, 40^3, 41^2, 42^2, 45^2, 46, 47, 48, 49, 51^2; **13:**2^2, 3^2, 4, 5, 6^3, 7, 8^2, 10^2, 11^5, 12, 13^4, 14, 16, 19^2, 20^2, 21, 22, 23, 26, 27^3, 28, 30, 31, 32, 33, 34^2, 36^3, 38^3, 39, 40, 41, 43, 44, 45^2, 46, 50, 53, 54^2, 55, 56^2, 57^2, 58^3; **14:**1, 2^2, 3, 4^3, 5^2, 6, 7, 8, 9^2, 10, 11, 13^3, 14^2, 15, 18, 19, 20^2, 21, 22^2, 23^3, 24^2, 25^2, 26^2, 27^2, 29, 30, 31^2, 32, 33^2, 34^2, 35^2, 36, 37^2, 38^2, 39, 40^3, 41^2, 42^2, 43, 45^3, 47, 48; **15:**2^2, 3, 5^2, 6, 8^2, 9, 11^3, 12^2, 13^3, 14, 15^2, 17, 18, 19^2, 20^3, 21, 22, 23^3, 24, 26, 27, 29^2, 30^3, 31^3, 32^3, 33^5, 34^2, 35^3, 36^2, 37^3, 38^2, 39^3, 40^6, 41^4, 42^4, 43, 44^4, 45, 46^2, 47, 48, 49^2, 50, 51, 53^2, 56, 57^2,

58[3], 59, 60[2], 61, 62[3], 63; **16:**1[2], 2[3], 3, 4, 5, 8, 9, 10[2], 11, 12[4], 13[2], 14, 15, 19[2], 21[2], 22, 23[3], 28[2], 32[3], 34, 35, 36, 37, 39[2], 40, 42, 44, 46[3], 47[2], 49, 50, 52, 53, 54[2], 55[3], 56, 57[2], 58, 59, 60, 61[4], 62[2], 63[2], 64, 65, 66, 67[2], 68, 69[3], 70, 71, 72[3], 76, 77[2], 78; **4Mc 1:**2, 3, 4[2], 5, 6[2], 7, 8[2], 10, 11[3], 12, 14[2], 16[2], 17, 18, 20[3], 21, 22, 23, 24, 26, 27, 28[2], 29[6], 32, 34[3], 35; **2:**1, 3, 8[2], 14, 15, 17, 18, 19, 21, 23[2], 24; **3:**7, 8, 10, 11[2], 12, 14[2], 17, 18, 20[2], 21[2]; **4:**1, 2[2], 4, 5, 7, 9, 10[2], 11[2], 12, 13, 15, 16, 18, 19, 21, 22, 23, 24, 26; **5:**1, 2[3], 3, 4, 7, 9, 12, 18, 23[2], 24, 30, 31, 32, 35; **6:**5, 6, 7, 8, 9[2], 11, 13, 18, 19, 20, 21, 23, 24, 25, 26[2], 28, 29, 35; **7:**2[2], 4, 6, 7, 8, 9, 11, 13, 14, 15[2], 19[2], 21, 22, 23; **8:**2, 3, 4[4], 5[4], 7, 8, 9, 10, 13[8], 15[2], 16, 17[2], 18, 19[4], 20, 21, 23, 26, 28; **9:**2, 3, 6, 7, 8[2], 11[2], 14, 16, 17, 19, 20[2], 24[2], 26[2], 27, 28[2]; **10:**1, 2[2], 5, 6[4], 7, 8[2], 10, 11, 13, 15, 17; **11:**5, 9, 10[2], 11, 13, 15, 18, 19, 20, 23[2], 26[2]; **12:**1, 2, 4, 5, 6[2], 8, 11[2], 12[3], 13[3], 17, 18, 19; **13:**2, 4, 6, 8, 12[2], 13[3], 15, 17[3], 19[2], 20[3], 22[4], 23, 24[2], 25, 27[3]; **14:**2, 3, 6, 8, 9, 10[2], 14, 16[4], 18, 19[2]; **15:**2, 4, 5, 7, 9, 10[5], 12, 13[2], 14, 15[2], 19, 20[2], 22[2], 24[2], 25, 26, 29, 30, 32[2]; **16:**1, 4, 5, 6, 7, 8, 9, 10[2], 11, 12, 13[2], 14[3], 15[3], 18, 19, 20[2], 21[3], 22, 24, 25[3]; **17:**1, 2, 3, 5, 9[2], 10, 12, 13, 14[2], 15, 17, 18, 21, 22[2], 23, 24[5]; **18:**1, 4, 5[3], 7, 9[2], 10, 11[2], 12[2], 13, 19[2], 20[3], 21[2], 22, 23[2], 24

ARE (4738)

Ge 2:4, 12; **3:**9, 14, 19; **4:**6, 11; **6:**3, 9, 15; **7:**1, 2, 8; **9:**2; **10:**1, 5, 20, 31, 32; **11:**6, 10, 27; **12:**11, 13; **13:**8, 14, 18; **15:**5; **16:**8, 13; **17:**8; **18:**24[2], 28, 29, 30, 31, 32; **19:**5, 13, 15; **20:**3, 7, 16[2]; **22:**7; **23:**6, 8; **24:**13, 23, 47; **25:**12, 13, 16[2], 19, 23; **26:**29; **27:**18, 21, 22, 24, 32, 41; **29:**4, 8, 14, 15; **31:**12, 15, 43[3], 49; **32:**6, 17[2], 18; **33:**5, 13[4], 14, 15; **34:**15, 21, 22, 30; **35:**2; **36:**1, 5, 9, 10, 15, 16[2], 17[3], 18[2], 19[2], 20, 21, 23, 24, 25, 26, 27, 28, 29, 30, 31, 40, 43; **37:**8[2], 13, 15, 16; **38:**25; **39:**9; **40:**7, 12, 18; **41:**25, 26[3], 27[3], 35, 36; **42:**9, 11[2], 13, 14, 16, 19[2], 21, 31[2], 32, 33, 34, 38; **43:**16; **44:**16, 18; **45:**6, 11, 19; **46:**8, 15, 18, 22, 25, 30, 32, 34; **47:**1, 3, 6, 8, 9, 18; **48:**5[2], 8, 9; **49:**3, 5[2], 12, 26, 28; **50:**18; **Ex 1:**1, 9, 19[2]; **3:**5, 7; **4:**12, 18, 19, 25; **5:**4, 5, 8, 16[2], 17; **6:**5, 14[2], 15, 16, 19, 24, 25; **8:**26[2]; **9:**17, 27, 32; **10:**8, 11; **12:**3; **13:**4, 12; **14:**3; **16:**7, 8, 29; **17:**4; **18:**14, 17, 20[2], 21; **19:**6, 23; **21:**1, 22; **22:**7; **23:**8; **24:**14; **25:**22; **28:**4; **29:**33; **31:**13; **32:**2, 4, 8, 9, 22; **33:**3, 5; **34:**12; **35:**1, 10; **36:**5; **38:**21; **Lev 4:**10; **5:**1, 2[2], 3, 4, 17; **7:**19; **10:**3, 10, 11, 15; **11:**2, 8, 9, 10[2], 13, 20, 23, 27, 28, 29, 31[2], 32, 35, 41, 42; **12:**4, 6; **13:**39; **14:**13; **15:**8; **16:**4; **18:**17; **21:**7; **22:**7, 11, 25; **23:**2, 4, 37, 42; **24:**9; **25:**16[3], 23, 33, 39, 42[2], 45, 55[2]; **26:**34, 44, 46; **27:**30[2], 34; **Nu 1:**5, 44, 50; **3:**2, 3, 9, 13, 18, 20, 27, 33; **4:**12, 14, 15[2], 27[2], 28, 31, 32; **5:**10; **6:**8, 20; **8:**16, 17; **9:**7; **10:**3, 6, 29; **11:**14, 15, 22[2], 27, 29; **12:**6; **13:**18[2], 19, 20, 28[2], 30, 31[2], 32; **14:**9, 14[2], 40; **15:**2; **16:**3; **17:**12[3], 13; **18:**2, 4, 6, 17, 18; **19:**20[2]; **20:**13, 16; **21:**29; **22:**6, 9, 12; **24:**5, 8; **26:**7, 9, 14, 18, 22, 25, 27, 30, 34, 35, 36, 37[2], 41, 42[2], 47, 50, 58; **27:**7[2], 14; **28:**19; **29:**6; **30:**16; **31:**49; **33:**1, 2, 55; **34:**17, 19; **36:**3, 5[2], 6, 13; **Dt 1:**1, 10, 13, 28[3], 41; **2:**4, 11, 18; **3:**21; **4:**4, 5, 14, 20, 22, 26, 45; **5:**3, 28, 33; **6:**1, 7[2], 14; **7:**1, 6, 17, 19, 20, 23; **8:**9; **9:**1, 5, 6, 26, 29; **10:**5; **11:**8, 10, 11, 12, 19[2], 21, 29, 30; **12:**1, 2, 8, 26, 29, 30; **13:**7; **14:**1, 2, 4, 7, 12, 19, 21, 24; **16:**5, 11, 17, 19; **17:**14, 15; **18:**1, 14, 17; **19:**17; **20:**3, 15[2], 19; **21:**2, 14; **22:**28; **23:**1, 7, 8, 9, 18, 20; **24:**11, 15; **25:**3, 16; **28:**10, 20, 21, 24, 45, 51, 58, 61, 63; **29:**1, 11, 15, 19; **30:**4, 10, 16, 17, 18; **31:**7, 13, 16, 21, 27; **32:**4, 20, 28, 31, 32[2], 37, 47; **33:**6, 17[2], 25, 29; **Jos 1:**11; **2:**19; **3:**8; **4:**9; **5:**13; **6:**17, 19; **7:**3, 12, 13; **8:**5, 6; **9:**8[2], 11, 13[2], 22[2], 23, 25; **10:**6; **12:**1, 7; **13:**1, 3, 14, 17, 30, 32; **14:**1; **17:**3, 14, 15, 17, 18; **19:**35, 51; **24:**15[2], 22[2], 23; **Jdg 3:**1; **4:**9, 22; **5:**2, 30; **6:**13; **7:**2, 4, 18; **8:**5, 15[2], 18; **9:**9, 15, 28, 31, 32, 33, 36, 37, 38; **10:**4[2]; **11:**2, 7[2], 25, 26, 27; **12:**4, 5; **13:**3, 8, 11; **15:**11; **16:**7, 9, 12, 14, 20; **18:**3, 5, 6, 14, 18; **19:**17, 18, 24, 28; **20:**10, 32, 39; **21:**7, 16[2]; **Ru 3:**9[2], 11, 15; **4:**5, 9, 10, 11, 18; **1Sa 2:**3, 4, 5, 8; **4:**8, 17; **6:**8, 17; **7:**3; **8:**5, 8, 19; **9:**13; **10:**2; **11:**5; **12:**2, 21; **14:**11, 28, 33; **15:**17[2], 18; **16:**11; **17:**8, 33[2], 58; **18:**18; **19:**3, 22[2]; **20:**21[2], 22; **21:**1, 5; **23:**1[2], 3; **24:**11, 17; **25:**10[2]; **26:**14, 15; **28:**1, 9, 12, 15; **29:**3, 9; **30:**13; **2Sa 1:**8; **3:**25, 28, 39; **4:**3; **5:**1, 14; **7:**5, 12, 22, 28[2]; **9:**2; **10:**11[2]; **11:**11, 24; **12:**7; **13:**4; **14:**14, 20; **15:**2, 3, 15, 19[2], 36; **16:**2, 8, 21; **17:**2, 8[2], 10[2], 16, 20, 29; **18:**3, 20, 25; **19:**3, 6, 12[2], 13[2], 42; **20:**17, 19; **22:**28, 29; **23:**1, 6[2], 7, 8; **24:**2, 22; **1Ki 1:**14, 20, 25, 42; **2:**9, 39; **4:**13; **6:**12; **8:**8, 33, 46[2], 51; **9:**13[2], 21; **10:**8[2]; **11:**41; **12:**28; **13:**3, 14, 18, 32; **14:**2, 19, 29; **15:**7, 23, 31; **16:**5, 14, 20, 27; **17:**24; **18:**25, 36, 37; **19:**9, 10, 13, 14; **20:**3[2], 23, 31; **21:**5; **22:**3, 4[3], 11, 13, 22, 39, 45; **2Ki 1:**3, 6, 18; **3:**7[2]; **4:**6, 26; **5:**12; **6:**9, 16[2], 32; **7:**9[2], 12; **8:**13, 23; **10:**2, 5, 6[2], 9, 13[2], 34; **11:**5; **12:**7, 19; **13:**8, 12; **14:**15, 18, 28; **15:**6, 11, 15, 21, 26, 31, 36; **16:**7, 19; **17:**26; **18:**20, 21, 23, 26, 27, 34[2]; **19:**15[2], 19, 26; **20:**17, 18, 20; **21:**17, 25; **22:**5; **23:**28; **24:**5; **1Ch 1:**29, 31, 43, 54; **2:**1, 55; **3:**1; **4:**12, 17, 22; **6:**17, 19, 31, 33, 50, 54, 65; **7:**33; **8:**6, 38; **9:**1, 33, 44; **11:**1, 10; **12:**1, 15, 18, 23; **14:**4; **15:**12; **16:**14, 26, 27[2]; **17:**11, 26, 27; **19:**12[2]; **21:**3; **22:**13; **23:**31; **28:**3, 21; **29:**10, 11[2], 12, 15[2], 17, 29; **2Ch 1:**12; **2:**7, 8; **3:**3; **5:**9; **6:**23, 24, 32, 36[2]; **7:**14; **8:**11; **9:**7[2], 29; **11:**10; **12:**15; **13:**8, 9, 10, 22; **14:**11; **15:**2; **16:**11; **18:**3, 10, 12, 21; **19:**6; **20:**2, 6[2], 12[2], 34[2]; **21:**16; **23:**4, 6; **24:**27; **25:**26; **26:**18; **27:**7; **28:**26; **29:**9, 19; **32:**10, 19, 32; **33:**18, 19; **34:**16, 21, 24; **35:**25, 27; **36:**8; **Ezr 1:**3[2]; **4:**12[2]; **5:**4[2], 11[2]; **6:**3[2]; **7:**14, 20; **8:**1, 22, 28[3]; **9:**9, 11, 15[2]; **10:**4, 13; **Ne 1:**3, 8, 9, 10; **2:**2, 17, 19[2], 20; **4:**2, 3, 4, 10, 19; **5:**2, 3, 4, 5[3], 7, 8, 9, 10; **6:**6, 8, 10[2]; **7:**3[2], 6; **9:**6, 7, 8, 17, 31, 36, 37, 38; **10:**1, 8, 39[2]; **11:**3, 7; **12:**1; **13:**17; **Est 1:**16; **3:**8; **4:**11; **8:**5; **9:**13, 26; **10:**2; **Job 1:**19; **3:**8, 17, 18, 19[2], 22, 24; **4:**5[2], 9, 10, 11, 19, 20; **5:**4[2], 7, 11[2], 13; **6:**4[2], 7, 15, 20[2], 21, 25; **7:**1, 3, 6, 8, 16, 17; **8:**6, 9[2], 13, 18, 19; **9:**12, 25; **10:**5, 20; **11:**11; **12:**2, 5, 6[2], 13, 16[2], 20; **13:**4, 12[2], 23; **14:**5, 10[2], 12, 21; **15:**4, 7, 10, 11, 14, 15, 20, 21, 22; **16:**2; **17:**1, 2, 7, 8, 11[2], 14; **18:**3[2], 7, 8, 14[2], 18, 20, 21; **19:**3, 13; **20:**7, 13; **21:**8, 9, 16, 18, 22, 30[2], 32, 33[2]; **22:**3, 10, 12, 18, 19, 20, 29, 30; **23:**14; **24:**1, 8, 9, 13[2], 17, 18, 20, 23[2], 24[3]; **25:**2, 5; **26:**11, 14; **27:**5, 14, 21; **28:**4, 6; **30:**1, 5, 15, 27[2]; **31:**40; **32:**6, 9, 15; **33:**6, 12, 19; **34:**19, 20[2], 21, 25, 35, 36; **35:**5, 6, 7, 14; **36:**4, 7, 8, 9, 17, 20; **37:**10, 17, 24; **38:**35; **39:**3, 30; **40:**11, 12, 17, 18; **41:**17, 18, 25[2], 28, 29, 30, 34; **Ps 1:**1, 3, 4[2]; **2:**7, 12; **3:**1[2], 2, 3; **4:**4, 6; **5:**4, 9[2]; **6:**2; **7:**14; **8:**4[2]; **9:**13, 16, 20; **10:**4, 5, 7[2]; **11:**3; **12:**4, 5, 6[2]; **14:**1, 2[2], 3; **15:**4; **16:**2, 3, 11; **17:**12; **19:**1, 3, 7, 8, 9, 10; **22:**1, 3, 14, 16; **23:**4; **25:**3, 5, 10, 12, 15, 19; **26:**10[2]; **27:**12; **28:**1, 3; **31:**3, 4, 14, 15; **32:**1, 2, 6, 7, 10; **34:**8, 15[2], 19; **35:**20; **36:**3, 4, 6, 12; **37:**19, 20, 21, 23, 26, 33; **38:**7, 19[3], 20; **39:**1, 6; **40:**4, 12, 17; **41:**1, 2, 11; **42:**5[2], 11[2]; **43:**1, 2, 5[2]; **44:**4, 22; **45:**2, 5, 8, 9, 15; **46:**6; **49:**11, 12, 13, 14, 18, 20; **50:**8; **51:**4; **52:**2; **53:**1, 2[2], 3; **55:**10, 18; **56:**5, 8; **57:**4; **59:**5, 7, 9, 13, 17; **61:**3; **62:**9[3]; **63:**1; **64:**6; **65:**4, 5, 6, 8; **66:**3; **68:**24, 26; **69:**4[2], 5, 19, 33; **70:**5; **71:**3, 5, 7; **72:**20; **73:**1, 4, 5[3], 12, 19, 20, 27[2]; **74:**20; **76:**4, 7, 11; **77:**8, 14; **79:**8; **80:**1; **82:**5, 6; **83:**2, 8, 18; **84:**4, 5[2]; **86:**2, 5, 8, 10[2], 15; **87:**3, 7; **88:**5, 12, 18; **89:**7, 11, 14, 15, 17, 26, 38; **90:**2, 4, 5, 7[2], 10[3]; **92:**5[2], 7, 8, 13, 14; **93:**2, 5; **94:**11, 12, 19; **95:**4[2], 7, 10; **96:**5, 6[2]; **97:**2[2], 7, 9[2]; **100:**3[2]; **102:**11, 12, 25, 27; **103:**6, 11, 14, 15; **104:**1[2], 16, 18[2], 24, 25, 28, 29, 30; **105:**7; **106:**3; **107:**39, 42, 43; **109:**2, 24; **110:**4; **111:**2, 7[2], 8; **112:**1, 3, 4, 7[2], 8, 10; **115:**4, 8[2], 16; **118:**15, 28[2]; **119:**1, 2, 12, 24[2], 39, 68, 70, 75, 86, 91, 99, 103, 111[2], 114, 129, 137[2], 143, 144, 148, 150, 151[2], 157, 168, 172; **120:**7; **122:**2; **123:**1, 4; **125:**1, 4[2]; **127:**3, 4; **131:**1; **135:**15; **139:**3, 8[2], 14, 17, 18; **140:**1, 6; **141:**6, 8; **142:**5, 6; **143:**10; **144:**3, 4[2], 8, 11, 15[2]; **145:**14[2]; **146:**5, 8; **148:**14; **Pr 1:**9, 19; **2:**15[2]; **3:**13, 16, 17[2], 18, 32[2]; **4:**16, 22; **5:**11, 21, 22, 23; **6:**2, 16[2], 23, 30[2], 31; **7:**4, 26[2]; **8:**8, 9, 18, 32; **9:**4, 12[2], 15, 16, 18[2]; **10:**6, 19[2], 25[2], 20; **11:**6, 8, 9, 17, 20[2], 21, 31; **12:**1, 5, 6, 7[2], 13, 18, 21, 22[2]; **13:**18, 24; **14:**4, 16, 18[2], 20, 21[3], 31, 32; **15:**3, 15, 18[2], 26[2], 27; **16:**5[2], 10, 11[2], 13, 20[2], 24; **17:**5, 6, 15, 17, 25, 28[2]; **18:**4, 7, 8, 10, 21; **19:**4, 7[3], 11, 14, 16, 26; **20:**5, 7, 10, 15, 18, 23[2], 24; **21:**2, 4, 11; **22:**5, 9[2], 11, 18, 22, 29; **23:**3, 7; **24:**4, 5, 13, 16, 23, 24; **25:**1, 13, 21[2], 26; **26:**22, 23, 25; **27:**6[2], 10, 15, 20[2]; **28:**1, 7, 9, 26; **29:**2, 16, 18, 19, 27[2]; **30:**11, 12[3], 13[2], 14[3], 15, 18, 24[2], 25, 26, 29[2]; **31:**21, 25; **Ecc 1:**8, 11, 14; **2:**23; **3:**18, 20; **4:**1, 2, 3, 8, 9; **5:**8, 14; **6:**3, 10[3]; **7:**8, 15[2], 19, 26; **8:**4, 14[4], 17; **9:**1, 2[3], 3, 9, 10, 12, 16, 17; **10:**3, 17, 19; **11:**3, 9, 10; **12:**2, 3[2], 4[2], 5, 11[3]; **SS 1:**3, 10, 15[3], 16, 17[2]; **2:**13, 15; **3:**7; **4:**1[2], 2, 3[2], 5, 7, 11; **5:**11, 12, 13[2], 14, 15; **6:**4, 6, 7, 8; **7:**1[2], 3, 4, 5, 6, 7[2], 12, 13; **8:**6, 13; **Isa 1:**4, 7, 15, 18[2], 19, 23; **2:**6, 9, 22; **3:**8, 10, 11, 12, 16; **5:**7, 8, 13, 15[2], 21, 22, 28; **7:**16, 25; **8:**18, 21; **9:**15[2]; **10:**8; **14:**11[2], 12[2], 15, 19; **15:**4, 6, 9; **16:**2, 6, 10[3]; **17:**14; **19:**11, 12, 13[2]; **21:**3; **22:**2[3], 16; **24:**6, 12, 17, 18; **25:**1; **26:**8, 9, 15; **27:**11[2]; **28:**7, 8, 9, 26; **29:**13, 15; **30:**4, 9, 17, 18, 27; **31:**1[2], 3[2]; **32:**7, 8, 9, 11; **33:**8[2], 12, 13[2], 14; **35:**4; **36:**5, 6, 8, 11, 12, 19[2]; **37:**16[2], 20, 27; **38:**14; **39:**6, 7; **40:**6, 7, 15[2], 16, 17[2], 22, 24; **41:**5, 9, 11, 22, 23, 24, 29[3]; **42:**7, 16, 17, 18[2], 20, 22; **43:**1, 4, 8[2], 10, 12, 17; **44:**8, 9, 11, 17, 18, 21[2]; **45:**9, 10[2], 15, 16, 24; **46:**1[2], 12; **47:**13, 14, 15; **48:**1, 4, 7; **49:**3, 9, 16; **50:**4, 8, 11; **51:**12, 16, 20, 21[2]; **52:**5, 7; **53:**5; **55:**8[2], 9[2]; **56:**10[3]; **57:**1[2], 4[2], 6, 15, 20; **59:**3, 6[2], 7[2], 12[2]; **60:**8, 21; **61:**9; **63:**2, 8, 15[2], 16[2], 17; **64:**6, 8[4], 9; **65:**5, 16[2], 24; **66:**2; **Jer 2:**11, 15, 27, 28, 31; **3:**4, 22, 23; **4:**13[2], 16, 20, 22[3], 29; **5:**4, 6[2], 7, 10, 13, 16, 26, 27; **6:**7[2], 10, 20[2], 23, 28[2], 29, 30; **7:**8, 10, 17, 32; **8:**8, 13[2], 20; **9:**2, 4, 5, 8, 10[2], 19[2], 25[2], 26; **10:**2, 3, 5, 6, 8, 9[2], 14[2], 15, 20[2], 21; **11:**13; **12:**1, 2, 4, 6, 9; **13:**4, 19, 22[2], 23, 27; **14:**3, 4, 7, 9[2], 13, 14[2]; **15:**6, 18; **16:**3, 12, 14, 17[2], 20; **17:**5, 7, 11, 14, 17; **18:**6, 16, 23; **19:**6; **20:**10; **21:**4[3], 9; **22:**6, 15, 17, 20, 25, 28; **23:**5, 7, 10, 11, 16, 33; **24:**8, 10; **25:**12, 18, 26, 37; **26:**19; **27:**5, 9, 10, 14[2], 15[2], 16[2], 18, 19; **29:**1, 8, 9, 10, 17, 21, 25; **30:**3, 4, 14, 15; **31:**15, 18, 25, 27, 29, 31, 38; **32:**19, 24, 29, 43; **33:**5, 10, 14; **35:**11; **36:**19; **37:**10, 13, 19; **38:**4, 21, 22; **40:**14, 15, 16; **42:**2, 6, 15; **43:**2, 11[3]; **44:**2, 6, 7, 12, 16, 24, 25, 27; **46:**5, 21, 23[2]; **47:**2, 3, 6; **48:**14, 30[2], 37, 43; **49:**10, 23[2]; **50:**2[2], 7, 9, 15, 28, 33[2], 41, 42; **51:**17[2], 18, 20, 30[2], 32, 39, 47, 51, 56[2], 60, 64; **La 1:**4, 16, 21, 22; **2:**9, 11, 14, 21; **3:**23, 34, 35, 62; **4:**2, 8; **5:**3, 5[3], 7, 11, 12, 13, 17, 22; **Eze 2:**4, 5, 6, 7; **3:**5, 7, 9, 26, 27; **5:**2, 7[3]; **6:**9, 12[2]; **7:**4, 9, 15; **8:**6[2], 9, 12, 13, 17; **9:**4; **11:**2, 3, 7, 12, 15; **12:**2, 3[2], 9, 14, 22, 23; **13:**2; **14:**5; **16:**33, 38, 45[2], 52, 57; **17:**17; **18:**2, 4, 24, 25, 29[2]; **20:**3, 34, 49; **21:**12, 24, 26; **22:**5[2], 7[2], 9, 24, 25, 27; **23:**45; **24:**19; **26:**18, 19; **27:**4, 34, 35[3]; **28:**2, 3, 9, 19, 25; **29:**12; **30:**4, 8; **31:**2, 14, 18; **32:**2, 20, 23, 25, 26, 27, 28, 29[2], 30[2], 32; **33:**6[2], 24, 27[3], 32; **34:**12, 30, 31; **35:**12[2]; **36:**7, 20, 35, 36; **37:**11[3], 20; **38:**5, 6, 7, 8, 12[2], 14, 17, 20, 22; **39:**4, 19[2]; **40:**46; **42:**13, 14; **43:**11, 13, 18, 27; **44:**5, 9, 13; **46:**24; **47:**11, 13; **48:**1, 29; **Da 2:**8, 20, 26, 38; **3:**4, 5, 12, 15, 25; **4:**3, 9, 18[3], 35[2], 37[2]; **5:**13, 14, 16; **6:**7; **8:**20; **9:**7[2], 23, 24, 26; **10:**19; **11:**32; **12:**3, 9, 10, 12; **Hos 1:**9, 10; **2:**4, 12, 23[2]; **4:**3, 6, 8; **6:**9; **7:**2, 4[2], 6, 7, 9; **8:**8, 12; **9:**15; **10:**10; **11:**7; **12:**7; **13:**2, 10, 14; **14:**9[3]; **Joel 1:**6, 9, 10, 11, 12, 13, 17[2], 18, 20; **2:**6, 8, 10, 11, 22; **3:**4[3], 15; **Am 2:**15, 16; **3:**6, 9[2]; **4:**1; **5:**12[2]; **6:**1, 2, 6; **9:**1, 7, 8, 12; **Ob 1:**20[2]; **Jnh 1:**6, 8; **4:**2, 10, 11; **Mic 2:**4, 7; **4:**11; **5:**1, 2; **6:**12; **7:**3, 6; **Na 1:**3, 6, 10[3], 12, 14, 15; **2:**3[2], 6; **3:**8, 12, 13[2], 17, 18[2]; **Hab 1:**3, 7, 8, 12, 13[2]; **2:**15; **Zep 1:**11; **2:**2; **3:**3[2], 4, 6; **Zec 1:**5, 9[2], 10, 15, 19[2], 21[2]; **2:**2; **3:**7, 8; **4:**2[2], 3, 4, 5, 7, 10, 11, 12, 13, 14; **5:**10; **6:**4, 5, 15; **8:**16[2], 17; **9:**2, 5, 16, 17; **11:**2, 3, 9; **12:**14; **13:**6, 9; **14:**12; **Mal 1:**4[2], 8; **2:**10, 15, 17; **3:**8[2], 9[2]; **Mt 1:**17, 21; **2:**6, 18, 20; **4:**3, 6; **5:**3, 4, 5, 6, 7, 8, 9, 10[2], 11, 13, 14, 22, 23, 25, 47; **6:**7, 16, 26; **7:**11, 13, 14, 15, 16; **8:**25, 26; **9:**2, 5, 12[2], 17[2], 37; **10:**2, 19[3], 29, 30, 31; **11:**3[2], 5[2], 8, 14, 28[2]; **12:**2, 5, 34, 47, 48, 49; **13:**15, 16, 38[2], 39, 40, 55, 56, 57; **14:**2, 33; **15:**8, 14, 16, 20, 33; **16:**8, 16, 17, 18, 23[2], 28; **17:**26; **18:**7, 15, 16, 20; **19:**6, 12[3], 26, 30; **20:**6, 15, 18, 22[3], 25; **21:**13, 16, 23, 26, 31; **22:**14[2], 16, 18, 21[2], 29, 30[2]; **23:**4, 8[2], 10, 13, 19, 25, 27[2], 28, 31, 37; **24:**6, 19[2]; **25:**8, 34, 40, 41; **26:**45, 50, 63, 70, 73; **27:**6, 11, 40; **28:**5; **Mk 1:**11, 24; **2:**5, 9, 17[2], 22, 24; **3:**11, 32, 33, 34; **4:**15, 16, 18[2], 20, 38, 40; **5:**9; **6:**2, 3, 4, 14, 37; **7:**4, 6, 15; **8:**17[2], 29, 33, 38; **9:**1, 16, 22, 23; **10:**8, 27, 31, 33, 38[2], 39, 42; **11:**3, 5, 28; **12:**14, 15, 17[2], 24, 25[2], 27, 32, 34, 42, 43; **13:**4, 11, 17[2]; **14:**36, 37, 41, 61, 68, 70[2], 71; **15:**2; **16:**6; **Lk 1:**42; **2:**29; **3:**22; **4:**3, 9, 34, 41; **5:**20, 23, 31[2]; **6:**2, 20[2], 21[3], 22, 24, 25[2], 44[2]; **7:**19[2], 20[2], 22[2], 25, 31, 32, 48; **8:**12, 13, 14[2], 15, 20, 21, 24; **9:**5, 12, 13, 26, 27; **10:**2, 9, 20, 23, 41; **11:**7, 13, 28, 39, 41, 44, 48; **12:**6, 7[2], 11[2], 21, 24, 26, 29[2], 36, 37, 38, 41; **13:**12, 14, 30[2], 34; **14:**8, 10; **15:**31; **16:**8[2], 15, 25; **17:**1, 10, 17, 22; **18:**31; **19:**21, 31, 33, 42; **20:**2, 6, 21, 25[2], 34, 35[2], 36[2], 37, 38; **21:**8, 22, 23[3], 24, 34; **22:**25, 28, 38, 42, 46, 48, 58, 60, 67, 70; **23:**3, 29[2], 34, 37, 39, 40, 41; **24:**17, 18, 25, 38, 44, 48; **Jn 1:**19, 21[2], 22, 25[2], 38[2], 42[2], 49[2]; **3:**2, 10, 18[2], 26, 28; **4:**12, 17, 19, 27, 35; **5:**28; **6:**5, 9, 26, 30[2], 63, 64, 69; **7:**3, 7, 19, 21, 23, 25, 49, 51, 52[2]; **8:**10, 13, 23[2], 25, 31, 33, 37, 40, 41[2], 44, 47, 48[2], 53, 57; **9:**28[2], 34, 40[2]; **10:**8, 21, 24, 30, 32, 33[2], 34; **11:**8, 9, 27, 47; **12:**35; **13:**6, 10, 11, 13, 16[2], 17, 27, 35, 36; **14:**2, 5, 21; **15:**5, 6, 14, 20, 27; **16:**2, 5, 13, 19, 29; **17:**9, 10[2], 11[2], 21, 22; **18:**4, 7, 8, 17[2], 25[2], 31, 33, 37; **19:**9, 12; **20:**13, 15[2], 23[2], 29, 30, 31; **21:**12, 25; **Ac 2:**7[2], 13, 15, 22, 32, 39; **3:**15, 25; **4:**9[2], 30; **5:**9, 25, 28, 32; **7:**1, 4, 26, 33, 34, 51, 53; **8:**23, 30; **9:**5[2], 6; **10:**19, 21, 33, 39; **12:**15; **13:**27, 31, 33, 46; **14:**15[2]; **15:**1, 10, 19, 36; **16:**17, 20[2], 21[2], 28, 37[2]; **17:**7, 19, 22, 28, 29; **18:**10[2], 13; **19:**15, 26, 37, 38[2], 40; **20:**23, 32; **21:**13, 20[2], 23, 38; **22:**3, 7, 8[2], 26, 27; **23:**3, 15, 21[3]; **26:**3, 5, 14, 15[2], 18, 24, 28, 29; **27:**24; **28:**27; **Ro 1:**6, 7, 15, 20[2], 29; **2:**1[2], 3, 5, 8, 13, 14, 18, 19[3], 26, 27; **3:**9[2], 13, 14, 15, 16, 19, 24; **4:**1, 4, 7[3], 12, 14; **5:**1; **6:**1, 14, 15, 16, 21; **7:**6[2]; **8:**1, 8, 9[2], 12, 14[2], 16, 18, 28, 31, 36[2], 37; **9:**4, 7, 8[2], 14, 20, 22, 26, 30; **10:**14[3], 15[3], 19; **11:**3, 16, 25, 28[2], 29, 33, 36; **12:**5[3], 16, 20[2]; **13:**3, 6, 7, 9; **14:**1, 4, 8, 15, 22, 23; **15:**1, 14; **16:**7, 14, 15; **1Co 1:**2, 7, 11, 18[2], 24, 28[2]; **2:**6, 13, 14[4], 15[2]; **3:**2, 3[2], 4, 9[2], 16, 17, 18, 20, 21; **4:**10[5], 11[2]; **5:**2, 4, 5, 7, 12[2]; **6:**2, 3, 12[3], 15, 19; **7:**9, 14, 26, 27[2], 34[2], 36; **8:**5, 6[2], 8, 11; **9:**1, 2, 13; **10:**12, 17[2], 18, 22[2], 23[3], 26, 27; **11:**18, 19, 30, 32[2], 34; **12:**4, 5, 6, 11, 12, 20, 22, 23, 27, 29[3]; **14:**2, 10, 12, 16, 22, 23, 25, 32, 34, 36; **15:**2, 6, 15[2], 16, 17, 19, 27, 28, 29[2], 30, 32, 35, 40, 48[4]; **16:**9; **2Co 1:**4[2], 5, 6[3], 14[2], 24; **2:**9, 11, 15[3], 17; **3:**1, 2, 3, 5, 18; **4:**1, 3, 8, 11; **5:**4, 6[3], 9, 11[2], 12, 13[2], 14, 20; **6:**3, 8[2], 9[2], 16; **7:**3; **8:**18, 19, 20, 22, 23; **9:**4; **10:**2, 4, 6, 7, 10, 18; **11:**13, 22[3], 23; **12:**4, 19; **13:**4, 5, 9[2]; **Gal 1:**2, 6[2], 7[2], 22; **2:**15; **3:**3[2], 7, 9, 10, 25, 26, 28, 29; **4:**1[3], 6, 7, 8, 10, 12, 24, 27, 28, 31; **5:**15, 17, 18[2], 19; **6:**1, 3[2], 6; **Eph 1:**1[2], 18; **2:**2, 10, 11, 19[2], 22; **3:**13, 17; **4:**18, 25; **5:**6, 8, 16, 22, 30; **6:**8, 22; **Php 1:**1, 27, 28, 30; **2:**21; **3:**3, 15, 19, 20; **4:**3, 21; **Col 1:**27; **2:**3, 17, 22, 23; **3:**1, 2[2], 6, 7; **4:**8, 11; **1Th 2:**8, 10, 14, 20; **3:**3; **4:**1, 15[2], 17[2]; **5:**4, 5[2], 7, 10, 11; **2Th 1:**4, 5; **2:**10; **3:**4, 6, 11; **1Ti 1:**7, 14, 20; **2:**2; **4:**2, 11; **5:**3, 13, 16[2], 24, 25[2]; **6:**1, 2[2], 5, 9, 17, 18; **2Ti 1:**13, 15[2]; **2:**13, 14[2], 17, 18, 19, 20; **3:**6, 7, 15; **Tit 1:**6, 10, 11, 12, 15[2], 16; **2:**3, 9, 12, 14; **3:**8, 9, 15; **Heb 1:**5, 10, 12, 14[2]; **2:**5, 6[2], 11, 18; **3:**6; **4:**13, 15; **5:**5, 6; **6:**6[2], 9; **7:**5, 8[2], 13, 17, 21, 28; **8:**1, 4, 8; **9:**9, 15, 28; **10:**1, 8, 14, 39[3]; **11:**3, 14; **12:**1, 5, 8, 23, 28; **13:**3[2], 11, 14, 16, 17, 18; **Jas 1:**23[2], 26; **2:**9, 12; **3:**4[2], 9, 13; **4:**1, 11, 12, 14; **5:**1, 2, 13[2], 14; **1Pe 1:**5, 9, 21; **2:**9, 10, 18[2], 20; **3:**7, 12[2], 13, 14, 16; **4:**4, 13, 14[2]; **5:**5, 9, 14; **2Pe 1:**8[2], 12; **2:**10, 12[2], 13, 17, 19[2], 20; **3:**8, 11, 14, 16, 17[2]; **1Jn 1:**4, 6; **2:**5, 12, 14, 17; **3:**1, 2, 10[3], 15, 19; **4:**1, 4, 5, 6, 17, 20; **5:**3, 7, 18, 19, 20; **3Jn 1:**4, 5; **Jude 1:**1[2], 5, 10, 12[2], 16[2], 19, 22; **Rev 1:**3, 4[2], 20[2]; **2:**1, 2, 3, 8, 9[4], 10, 12, 13[2], 18[2], 19, 27; **3:**1[2], 4, 7, 9[3], 15, 16, 17; **4:**4[2], 5[2], 6, 8, 11; **5:**6, 8, 9; **7:**13, 14[2], 15; **8:**13; **9:**12, 14, 19; **11:**4, 17; **13:**10; **14:**4, 5, 13, 18; **15:**1, 3[2], 4; **16:**5[2], 7, 14; **17:**7, 9[2], 12[2], 13, 14, 15; **18:**5, 14; **19:**2, 9[3], 12[2]; **20:**6, 7, 8; **21:**5, 12, 14, 16, 19, 21, 27; **22:**2, 6, 14, 15, 19; **Tob 2:**14[3]; **3:**2[3], 5, 8, 9, 11; **4:**12; **5:**11, 12, 14[2]; **6:**5, 13, 18; **7:**3[2], 10, 11; **8:**5, 15, 16, 17; **9:**3; **10:**12; **11:**2, 3; **12:**10; **13:**10[2], 12[2], 14[3]; **14:**7[2], 8, 10; **Jdt 3:**4; **5:**6, 21, 23[2]; **6:**2, 7, 19; **8:**12, 13, 21, 27, 31; **9:**5[2], 6[2], 7[2], 11, 14; **10:**12[3]; **11:**8, 11, 23; **12:**3; **13:**17, 18; **14:**7; **15:**9[3]; **16:**13; **AdE 1:**18; **2:**12[2]; **3:**8, 9; **4:**16; **9:**19; **10:**7, 8; **13:**11, 14, 15; **14:**3, 7, 8[2]; **15:**14; **16:**1, 2, 5, 15[2], 16; **Wis 1:**14, 16; **2:**15, 16, 17; **3:**1, 3, 9, 11[3], 12, 13; **4:**2, 6, 15, 16, 20; **5:**4; **6:**9; **7:**16[2], 23; **8:**5, 7; **9:**14; **11:**23, 26; **12:**15, 18, 22; **13:**1, 6, 7[2], 8, 10; **14:**9; **15:**1, 2, 6, 8, 9[2], 10, 14, 15, 16, 17[2], 18, 19; **17:**1; **Sir Pr:**T[2]; **1:**20, 23, 25, 27; **2:**16, 17; **3:**4, 18, 23; **4:**12; **5:**6; **6:**6, 8[2], 9, 10, 11, 12, 14, 15, 16, 17[2], 32; **7:**22; **8:**6; **9:**13[2], 18; **10:**2[2], 19[4], 20, 24, 26, 30[2]; **11:**4[3], 11[2], 12[2], 27, 29, 32; **12:**9; **13:**4, 8, 12, 13, 19[2], 20, 23, 24[2]; **14:**1, 2, 3, 18; **15:**13, 17, 19; **16:**11, 21, 23; **17:**15, 19[2], 20[2], 24, 28, 30, 32; **18:**7[2], 8[2], 10, 14, 17, 29; **19:**24, 25; **20:**5[2], 11[2], 13, 16, 31; **21:**2, 7, 25; **22:**6, 15; **23:**8[2], 15, 19; **24:**16, 29; **25:**1; **26:**5, 18, 28; **27:**7, 30; **28:**9, 20; **29:**21; **30:**15, 18, 25; **31:**7, 12, 18, 20, 21; **32:**3, 7[2]; **33:**13, 19, 21, 27; **34:**5, 6, 19, 22; **36:**22[2]; **37:**1, 4, 10, 25[2]; **38:**2, 3, 9, 27, 28, 31, 32, 33; **39:**16, 19, 24, 26, 27, 28, 33; **40:**2, 15, 16, 24; **41:**4, 5, 13, 15; **42:**6, 8, 15, 18, 22[2]; **43:**14, 15, 25; **44:**14; **48:**10, 11; **50:**28; **51:**10, 23, 24; **Bar 1:**1, 14; **2:**13, 15[2], 17, 30; **3:**3[2], 6, 8, 10[3], 11, 16, 34; **4:**4, 37[2]; **LtJ 6:**8[3], 13, 16, 18[3], 20[2], 23, 25, 26[2], 27, 28, 29, 35, 39[2], 40, 44, 45, 47, 49, 50[2], 51, 52, 55, 56, 57, 60[2], 63, 64[2], 65, 68[2], 69, 70, 71, 72; **Aza 1:**3, 4[3], 14, 22, 29, 31, 32, 33, 34, 65; **Sus 1:**20[2], 42, 47, 48; **Bel 1:**11, 17[2], 18, 19, 41; **1Mc 2:**17, 18, 37; **3:**17[2], 52; **4:**5, 18, 30, 36; **5:**11, 27, 39; **6:**57; **7:**35; **8:**30; **9:**9, 37[2], 44, 58; **10:**19, 20[2], 34, 43, 70, 72[2]; **11:**33; **12:**7, 9, 21[2], 31, 44; **13:**8, 15, 37, 40; **15:**28, 34; **16:**3, 24; **2Mc 1:**6, 24[3], 25[2], 27[3], 28; **2:**13, 14, 16, 25; **7:**2, 16, 18, 30, 32; **8:**18; **9:**12, 20[2]; **11:**28[2], 36[2]; **12:**17, 41; **14:**6[2], 9; **1Es 1:**33[3], 42[2]; **2:**5, 18; **3:**12; **4:**2, 5, 14, 32, 34, 37[3], 60; **5:**4, 7, 36, 61; **6:**4[3], 10, 11, 12[2], 13, 21; **8:**11[2], 16, 17, 22, 28, 58[3], 76, 83, 89[2], 90, 95; **9:**11, 13; **Man 1:**7, 9[3], 13; **3Mc 1:**12; **2:**2, 3, 11, 13, 18, 20, 28, 29[2]; **3:**13, 19, 23, 24, 25, 26, 28; **4:**16; **5:**40; **6:**3, 9, 12, 15, 24[2]; **7:**2; **2Es 1:**8, 17, 26; **2:**23, 40, 44, 45[2], 48; **3:**28, 31, 33; **4:**7[5], 24, 26, 32, 33, 34, 35, 38, 41; **5:**1, 13, 33, 41, 42[2], 43, 48, 52, 53, 54; **6:**14, 18, 51, 56[2], 57; **7:**5, 12, 13, 15[4], 19, 20, 25[2], 28, 32, 38[2], 45[2], 51, 57[3], 61[4], 64, 68[2], 76, 85, 87, 96, 97, 98, 99, 103, 118, 123, 127, 128[2], 134, 136; **8:**7, 20[2], 22[2], 28, 30, 31, 34[3], 36, 44[2], 46[4], 51, 59; **9:**6[2], 15, 17[2], 35, 40[2]; **10:**8[3], 11, 20, 22, 31[2], 50, 57; **11:**39; **12:**13, 24, 38, 42, 43, 45; **13:**16, 17, 18, 19, 24[2], 26, 29[2], 38, 40, 46, 48[2], 49, 52; **14:**9[2], 13, 15, 20[2], 24, 25, 33[2]; **15:**2, 10, 44, 57, 58; **16:**13[2], 14, 16, 19, 35, 37, 44, 74, 77[2]; **4Mc 1:**6, 10, 14, 18, 20, 28[2], 32[2], 33, 34, 35[2]; **2:**1, 14; **3:**4, 18; **4:**3[2]; **5:**7, 9, 27; **6:**14; **7:**8, 18, 23; **8:**17, 21, 22; **9:**1, 2, 5, 10[2], 15, 18, 30; **10:**10, 18, 21; **11:**4, 12, 23, 27; **12:**8, 13, 18; **13:**19, 21; **14:**6, 15, 17; **15:**5[2];

AS (4664)

AT (2631)

BE (6394)

27; **23:**4, 15, 18, 19, 20, 24, 25, 34; **24:**1, 8, 14, 17, 18, 24, 28; **25:**5, 7^{2}, 15, 17; **26:**4, 5, 26; **27:**11, 14, 18, 22, 27; **28:**6^{2}, 17, 18, 20, 25; **29:**1, 12, 14, 24; **30:**2, 6, 9^{2}, 10, 17, 28; **31:**30; **Ecc 1:**9^{2}, 11, 13, 15^{2}; **2:**11, 19^{2}, 21; **3:**2, 10, 12, 14, 15, 22; **5:**2^{3}, 6, 8, 10, 18; **6:**10, 12; **7:**9, 14, 16, 17^{2}, 23; **8:**3, 7^{2}, 12, 13; **9:**8^{2}, 17; **10:**8, 9^{2}, 10; **11:**6^{2}, 8; **SS 1:**7; **2:**17; **4:**16; **5:**1; **7:**8; **8:**7, 14; **Isa 1:**18, 20, 26, 27, 28^{2}, 29, 30; **2:**2^{2}, 11^{3}, 17^{3}; **3:**5^{2}, 6^{2}, 7, 11, 24; **4:**1, 2^{2}, 3, 5; **5:**5^{2}, 6^{2}, 9, 11; **6:**10, 13; **7:**4^{2}, 8, 11, 16, 23, 24, 25; **8:**4, 9^{3}, 10, 12, 13^{2}, 15^{2}, 21, 22; **9:**1, 5, 7; **10:**2, 16, 18, 19, 24, 25, 26, 27^{2}, 33^{2}; **11:**3, 5, 9, 10, 13^{3}, 16; **12:**2, 5; **13:**7, 8^{3}, 10, 13, 15, 16^{2}, 19, 20, 21, 22; **14:**20^{2}, 24, 25, 29; **16:**4, 5, 14^{2}; **17:**1, 2^{2}, 3, 4, 5, 6, 9^{2}; **18:**6, 7; **19:**3, 5^{2}, 7^{3}, 9, 10^{2}, 15, 16, 18^{2}, 19, 20, 23, 24, 25; **20:**5; **21:**17; **22:**14, 19, 21, 25; **23:**2, 4, 5, 15, 16, 18^{2}; **24:**2, 3, 13, 18, 22^{3}, 23; **25:**2, 9^{2}, 10, 11, 12; **26:**1, 11; **27:**9^{2}, 12, 13; **28:**3, 4, 5, 13^{2}, 18^{2}, 19, 22; **29:**2^{2}, 5, 6, 7, 8, 9^{3}, 14, 16, 17, 20^{3}, 22; **30:**8, 15^{2}, 16, 18, 19, 23, 25, 26^{2}, 30^{2}, 31, 32; **31:**8; **32:**2, 3, 5^{2}, 14, 17, 19, 20; **33:**1^{2}, 2^{2}, 6, 10, 12, 16^{2}, 20^{2}, 21, 23, 24; **34:**3, 7, 9, 10, 12, 13, 16^{2}; **35:**1, 2, 4, 5, 8^{3}, 9^{2}, 10; **36:**14, 15; **37:**4, 6, 10, 11, 30; **38:**14; **39:**6^{2}, 7^{2}, 8; **40:**4^{2}, 5, 30, 31; **41:**4, 7, 10, 11^{2}, 12, 23; **42:**4, 17; **43:**2^{2}, 10, 14, 26; **44:**5, 7, 8, 9, 11^{3}, 13, 15, 21, 23, 26^{2}, 27, 28^{2}; **45:**1, 14, 17, 18, 22, 24^{2}; **47:**1, 3^{2}, 5, 7, 11, 12; **48:**11, 14, 16, 19; **49:**3, 5^{2}, 6, 9, 11, 19^{2}, 22, 23^{2}, 24^{2}, 25^{2}, 26; **50:**7; **51:**3, 6^{2}, 7, 8, 11, 14; **52:**3, 12, 13^{2}; **54:**1, 2, 4^{2}, 9, 10^{2}, 13^{2}, 14^{2}; **55:**6, 11, 12, 13^{2}; **56:**1, 5, 6, 7^{2}, 12; **57:**6, 14, 16; **58:**8, 10, 11, 12^{2}; **60:**4, 5^{2}, 7^{2}, 11^{2}, 12, 18, 19^{3}, 20^{2}, 21^{2}; **61:**3, 6^{2}, 7, 9; **62:**2, 3, 4^{4}, 6, 8, 12^{2}; **64:**9; **65:**1^{2}, 13^{3}, 17, 18, 19, 20^{3}, 22, 23, 25; **66:**5^{2}, 8^{2}, 10, 11, 12, 13, 14, 16, 24^{2}; **Jer 1:**8; **2:**12^{3}, 26, 36; **3:**1, 3, 5^{2}, 12, 16^{2}, 17; **4:**2, 7, 9, 10, 11, 14, 27; **5:**6, 13; **6:**6, 11, 12, 15; **7:**20^{2}, 23^{3}, 32, 33; **8:**1, 2^{3}, 3, 9^{2}, 12, 17; **10:**2, 5^{2}; **11:**3, 4^{2}, 5, 16, 19, 23; **12:**1, 12, 13, 16; **13:**10, 11, 12^{2}, 15, 21, 26, 27; **14:**8, 9, 15, 16^{2}; **15:**18; **16:**4^{2}, 6^{2}, 14; **17:**6, 8, 11, 13^{2}, 14^{2}, 18^{4}, 25, 27; **18:**16, 21, 22, 23; **19:**6, 8^{2}, 11, 13; **20:**6, 10, 11^{2}, 14^{2}, 15, 16; **21:**10; **22:**19, 22; **23:**3, 4^{2}, 6^{2}, 7, 12^{2}, 17, 40; **24:**2, 3, 7^{2}, 8; **25:**33, 35; **26:**3, 9^{2}, 15, 18, 24; **27:**10, 16, 22; **28:**9, 16; **29:**17, 18, 22, 26, 28; **30:**7, 10, 16^{2}, 18, 19^{2}, 20^{2}, 21, 22^{2}; **31:**1^{2}, 4, 6, 12, 13, 14, 15, 30, 32, 33^{2}, 36, 37^{2}, 38, 40^{2}; **32:**4, 15, 38^{2}, 43, 44^{2}; **33:**9, 10, 12, 16^{2}, 21, 22^{2}; **34:**3, 10, 16, 20; **36:**3, 7, 30; **37:**17, 20; **38:**3^{2}, 4, 7, 17^{2}, 18, 19, 20, 23^{3}; **39:**14, 16, 17; **40:**9, 15; **41:**3; **42:**2, 5, 11^{2}, 14, 18, 19, 22; **44:**8, 26, 29^{2}; **46:**10, 14, 24^{2}, 26, 27; **47:**6, 7; **48:**2, 6, 7, 8, 13, 28, 41^{2}, 42, 44; **49:**2, 5, 12, 13, 17, 20^{2}, 21, 22, 23, 26, 36; **50:**5, 8, 9, 10^{2}, 12^{3}, 13^{3}, 19, 20^{3}, 26, 30, 36, 37, 38, 39, 45^{2}, 46; **51:**8, 9, 26^{2}, 35^{2}, 46, 47, 58^{2}, 62; **52:**16; **La 1:**21; **2:**20; **3:**29, 30, 65; **4:**21; **5:**4, 21; **Eze 2:**6^{4}, 8; **3:**9, 20, 25^{2}, 26; **4:**3, 10; **5:**12, 15; **6:**4, 6^{2}, 8, 9; **7:**13, 16, 18, 19, 24, 25, 27; **8:**2; **11:**7, 11^{2}, 20^{2}; **12:**11, 13, 19, 20, 24, 25^{2}, 28^{2}; **13:**9^{3}, 11, 12, 13, 14, 21; **14:**3, 10, 11^{2}, 16^{2}, 18, 22^{3}; **15:**5; **16:**13, 16, 20, 42^{2}, 52, 54, 61, 63; **17:**9, 14, 20, 21; **18:**3, 13, 20^{2}, 22, 24, 30; **19:**9; **20:**3, 9, 14, 19, 20, 22, 31^{2}, 32, 33, 47^{2}, 48; **21:**5, 7^{2}, 11^{3}, 24, 32^{2}; **22:**16, 21, 22; **23:**25, 29, 32, 33; **24:**8, 10, 11, 13, 23, 24, 27^{3}; **25:**10; **26:**2, 6, 10, 13, 14^{2}, 16, 20, 21^{2}; **27:**36; **28:**19; **29:**5, 9, 11, 12, 14, 15, 16, 19; **30:**3, 4, 7, 11, 13, 16^{2}, 18^{2}; **31:**18; **32:**6, 16, 19, 28, 31, 32; **33:**4, 5, 12, 13, 16, 27, 28; **34:**10, 14, 15, 22, 23, 24^{2}, 26, 27, 28, 29; **35:**9, 10, 15; **36:**9, 10, 11^{2}, 12, 25, 27, 28^{2}, 32^{2}, 33^{2}, 34, 38; **37:**19, 22^{3}, 23^{2}, 24^{2}, 25, 26, 27^{3}; **38:**7, 8, 9, 18, 19, 20, 21; **39:**4, 7, 11^{2}, 20, 25; **40:**38, 39, 41, 42, 43; **41:**6; **43:**10, 12, 13^{2}, 16, 17, 21, 22, 25; **44:**2, 5^{2}, 6, 7, 11, 14, 28, 29; **45:**1, 2, 3, 4^{3}, 5, 8, 11^{2}, 12, 17, 21; **46:**1^{2}, 2, 4, 5^{2}, 6, 11, 12^{2}, 15, 17, 18; **47:**5, 9, 10^{2}, 11, 12, 15, 17, 18, 19, 20^{2}, 22^{2}; **48:**8, 9, 10, 11, 13, 15^{2}, 16, 18^{3}, 20, 22, 30^{2}, 32, 33, 34, 35^{2}; **Da 1:**4, 5^{2}, 12, 18; **2:**2, 5^{2}, 12, 13, 20, 29^{2}, 30, 35, 40, 41^{2}, 42, 44^{2}, 45, 46; **3:**6, 11, 13, 15, 18, 28, 29; **4:**6, 15^{2}, 16^{2}, 19, 23^{2}, 25^{4}, 26, 27^{2}, 32^{3}; **5:**7, 12, 16, 17; **6:**4, 7, 8^{2}, 12^{2}, 15, 17, 23, 26; **7:**11, 14, 23^{2}, 24, 25, 26^{2}, 27^{2}; **8:**13, 14, 25^{2}; **9:**2, 25^{2}, 26^{2}, 27; **10:**19; **11:**2, 4^{2}, 6, 11, 12, 15, 16, 17, 19, 20, 22, 25, 26, 28, 29, 30, 35, 36; **12:**1^{2}, 4, 6, 7^{2}, 8, 10, 11; **Hos 1:**10^{3}, 11^{2}; **2:**17; **4:**9, 10, 19; **5:**14; **8:**5, 6; **9:**4^{3}, 6; **10:**6^{3}, 8, 10, 14, 15^{2}; **11:**5; **12:**8, 11; **13:**3, 15, 16; **14:**5, 6, 7; **Joel 1:**11; **2:**2, 17, 19, 21, 23, 24, 26^{2}, 27, 31, 32^{3}; **3:**17, 20; **Am 2:**11^{2}; **3:**11, 12, 14; **4:**3, 7; **5:**14, 15^{2}, 16, 17; **6:**7, 11; **7:**3, 6, 9^{2}, 17; **8:**3^{2}, 5, 8; **9:**15; **Ob 1:**2, 9^{2}, 10, 15, 16, 17^{2}, 18^{2}, 21; **Jnh 3:**4, 8; **4:**4, 9, 11; **Mic 1:**2, 7^{3}, 14; **2:**3, 7, 11; **3:**6^{2}, 7, 12; **4:**1^{2}, 10, 11; **5:**4, 5, 7, 8, 9^{2}; **6:**7, 14^{2}; **7:**8, 10, 11, 13, 16^{2}; **Na 1:**12, 14; **2:**7, 13; **3:**11; **Hab 1:**5^{2}; **2:**7, 9, 14, 16; **Zep 1:**7, 10, 13, 15, 17, 18^{2}; **2:**3, 4^{3}, 6, 7, 10, 11, 12, 14; **3:**8, 11^{2}, 13, 16; **Hag 1:**8; **2:**9; **Zec 1:**4, 16^{2}, 21; **2:**4, 5^{2}, 11, 13; **5:**3^{2}; **6:**13, 14; **8:**3^{2}, 5, 8^{2}, 9, 12, 13^{3}, 15, 19; **9:**4, 5^{2}, 7^{3}, 10^{2}, 15; **10:**5, 6, 7, 8, 11^{2}; **11:**4, 5, 9^{3}, 17; **12:**2, 6, 7, 8^{2}, 11; **13:**1, 2, 4, 6, 7, 8^{2}; **14:**1, 2^{2}, 4, 6, 7^{2}, 9, 10, 11^{2}, 12, 13, 14, 15, 17, 19, 20^{2}, 21^{2}; **Mal 1:**7, 8, 9, 12, 14; **2:**15, 16; **3:**4, 5, 10, 11, 12, 17; **4:**1, 3; **Mt 1:**18, 20; **2:**4, 18, 23^{2}; **3:**13, 14, 15; **4:**1, 14; **5:**4, 6, 9, 12, 13, 14, 19^{2}, 21, 22^{3}, 24, 25, 29, 37, 45, 48; **6:**1, 2, 4, 5^{2}, 7, 8, 9, 10, 18, 21, 22, 23, 24, 33; **7:**1, 2^{2}, 7^{2}, 8, 24, 26; **8:**3, 8, 12^{2}, 13; **9:**21, 29; **10:**15, 16, 18, 19, 22^{2}, 25, 26, 31, 36; **11:**22, 23^{2}, 24; **12:**23, 27, 29, 31^{2}, 32^{2}, 37^{2}, 39, 40, 45; **13:**12^{2}, 24, 30, 40, 42, 49, 50; **14:**9, 27; **15:**13, 28; **16:**2, 3, 4, 19^{2}, 21^{2}; **17:**4, 7, 17, 20, 22, 23; **18:**6, 8, 9, 14, 16, 17, 18^{2}, 19, 23, 25^{2}, 34; **19:**5, 21, 23, 25, 30^{2}; **20:**16^{2}, 18, 19^{2}, 26^{3}, 27^{2}, 28, 31, 33; **21:**13, 21^{2}, 43, 44; **22:**2, 13, 28, 45; **23:**5, 7, 8, 10, 11, 12^{2}; **24:**2^{2}, 3^{2}, 7, 9^{2}, 13, 14, 20, 21^{2}, 22^{2}, 27, 29^{2}, 37, 39, 40^{3}, 41^{3}, 43, 44, 51; **25:**1, 9, 29^{2}, 30, 32; **26:**2^{2}, 5, 13, 31, 37, 42, 46, 54, 56; **27:**22, 23, 25, 26, 58, 64^{2}; **28:**5, 10; **Mk 1:**25, 41; **3:**14^{2}, 25, 27, 28; **4:**12, 21, 22, 24^{2}, 25^{2}, 39; **5:**18, 23, 28, 34; **6:**50; **7:**27, 34; **8:**7, 12, 31^{2}, 38; **9:**5, 12, 19, 23, 31, 35^{2}, 39, 42, 45, 47, 49, 50; **10:**7, 23, 26, 31^{2}, 33, 38, 39, 41, 43, 44^{2}, 45, 48; **11:**17, 23^{2}, 24; **12:**7, 23, 37, 38; **13:**2^{2}, 4^{3}, 7, 8^{2}, 9, 10, 13^{2}, 14, 18, 19^{2}, 20, 23, 24, 25^{2}, 34; **14:**2, 9, 19, 27, 33, 42, 49; **15:**15; **16:**6, 16^{2}; **Lk 1:**13, 15^{2}, 20, 29, 30, 32^{2}, 33, 34, 35^{3}, 36, 37, 38, 45, 60, 68, 71, 76; **2:**1, 3, 5, 10, 12, 23, 34^{2}, 35, 49; **3:**5^{3}, 7, 12, 14, 15; **4:**7, 35; **5:**10^{2}, 13, 15, 35, 36, 37^{2}, 38; **6:**18, 21, 25, 35^{2}, 36, 37^{3}, 38^{3}, 40; **7:**7, 30; **8:**12, 17, 18^{2}, 29, 38, 50; **9:**11, 22^{3}, 26, 33, 41, 44, 51; **10:**7, 12, 14, 15^{2}, 42; **11:**2, 9^{2}, 10, 19, 29, 30, 36, 41, 43, 50, 51, 53; **12:**2, 3^{2}, 7, 9, 10^{2}, 14, 15, 19, 20, 31, 32, 34, 35, 36, 39, 40, 48^{2}, 50, 52, 53, 55, 58; **13:**7, 14^{2}, 16, 23, 24, 28, 30^{2}, 33^{2}; **14:**10, 11^{2}, 12, 14^{2}, 23, 26, 27, 34; **15:**7, 14, 19, 21; **16:**2, 13, 17, 22, 31; **17:**2, 3, 6, 20, 24, 25, 26, 30, 34^{2}, 35^{2}; **18:**13, 14^{2}, 26, 31, 32^{2}, 39, 40; **19:**7, 15, 26^{2}, 27, 46; **20:**14, 18, 20, 33, 44, 46; **21:**6^{2}, 7^{2}, 9, 11^{2}, 12, 15, 16, 17, 23, 24^{2}, 25, 26, 34, 36; **22:**7, 23, 24, 37, 42, 69; **23:**23, 24, 32, 43; **24:**7^{2}, 20, 36, 44, 47; **Jn 1:**31, 42; **3:**4^{2}, 7^{2}, 9, 14, 17, 20, 21; **4:**13, 14, 15, 29; **5:**6, 20, 28, 34; **6:**12, 20, 35^{2}, 45; **7:**4, 23, 26, 33; **8:**7, 33, 36, 39, 53, 55; **9:**3, 22^{2}; **10:**9, 16, 35; **11:**4, 12; **12:**15, 23, 26, 31, 34, 42; **14:**1, 3, 8, 13, 16, 17, 21, 27^{2}, 31; **15:**7, 11^{2}, 18; **16:**24, 32; **17:**11, 12^{2}, 19, 21^{2}, 22, 24, 26; **18:**28, 36; **19:**7, 12, 16, 36^{2}; **20:**15, 19, 21, 26; **21:**25; **Ac 1:**5, 8, 16, 20; **2:**14, 17, 20, 21, 24, 25, 38^{2}; **3:**19, 23^{2}, 25; **4:**10, 12; **5:**24, 34, 36, 39^{2}; **7:**6; **8:**22; **9:**6, 17, 41; **10:**48; **11:**14, 16, 28; **12:**17, 19; **13:**11, 22, 38, 39, 41, 46^{2}, 47; **14:**3, 9; **15:**1, 5, 7, 11; **16:**15, 22, 30, 31; **17:**17, 18; **18:**6, 9^{2}, 14, 15; **19:**27^{2}, 36^{2}, 39; **20:**10, 16, 31; **21:**13, 14^{2}, 22, 26, 33, 34, 35, 37; **22:**10, 15, 16, 22, 24^{2}; **23:**3, 21, 27, 30, 35; **24:**8, 15, 19, 26; **25:**6, 9, 10, 17, 19, 20, 21^{2}; **27:**3, 10, 15, 22, 24, 25, 31; **28:**4, 28; **Ro 1:**1, 4, 7, 12, 19, 22, 28; **2:**5, 8, 9, 12, 13, 26; **3:**4^{2}, 19^{2}, 20; **4:**14, 16, 18, 24; **5:**9, 10, 19; **6:**5, 6^{2}, 17; **7:**3, 10, 13^{2}, 21, 25; **8:**4, 17, 18, 21, 29^{2}, 36, 39; **9:**7, 17, 26, 27, 33; **10:**1, 4, 9, 11, 13; **11:**6, 10, 15, 19, 22, 23, 24, 25, 26, 32, 36; **12:**2^{2}, 9, 11, 12, 16^{2}, 21; **13:**1, 4, 5; **14:**4, 5^{3}, 9, 12, 16; **15:**16^{2}, 24, 27, 31^{2}, 32, 33; **16:**19, 20, 27; **1Co 1:**1, 2, 8, 10^{3}, 17; **3:**13, 15; **4:**2, 3, 6, 8, 16; **5:**5, 7; **6:**2, 5, 7^{2}, 9, 11, 12, 16; **7:**9, 11, 14, 15, 17, 21, 27, 29, 32, 34, 36; **8:**5, 10; **9:**5, 15, 27; **10:**1, 13^{2}, 20, 29, 30, 33; **11:**1, 6, 16, 19, 27, 31, 32, 34; **12:**1, 3, 17^{2}, 19, 22, 25; **14:**5, 9, 11, 20^{3}, 26^{2}, 27, 28, 30, 31, 34^{2}, 37, 38, 39, 40; **15:**9, 15, 19, 22, 26, 28^{2}, 33, 37, 51, 52^{2}, 54, 57, 58; **16:**2, 13^{2}, 14, 22, 23, 24; **2Co 1:**3, 4, 8; **2:**3, 7, 11, 14; **3:**2, 6; **4:**7, 10, 11, 18^{4}; **5:**2, 3, 4^{3}, 8, 12, 20, 21; **6:**3, 14, 16^{2}, 17, 18^{2}; **7:**12; **8:**11, 13, 14^{2}, 16; **9:**3^{2}, 4, 5, 11, 15; **10:**8, 15; **11:**3, 6, 7, 10, 12, 31; **12:**1, 4, 6^{2}, 14, 15^{2}, 16, 20; **13:**1, 2, 10, 11, 13; **Gal 1:**5, 8, 9, 10; **2:**3, 6, 16^{2}, 17^{2}; **3:**8, 22, 23, 24; **4:**9^{2}, 18, 21; **5:**2^{2}, 3, 4, 25; **6:**7, 12^{2}, 13, 16, 18; **Eph 1:**3, 4; **2:**10; **3:**10, 16, 19, 21; **4:**11, 14, 23, 26, 32; **5:**1, 3, 4, 5, 7, 15, 17, 18, 21, 22, 24, 27, 31; **6:**3, 10, 11, 13, 16, 19, 23, 24; **Php 1:**10, 20^{2}, 23; **2:**2, 5, 6, 15, 18, 19, 20, 28; **3:**4, 9, 15, 21; **4:**2, 5, 6, 9, 11, 20, 23; **Col 1:**9, 11^{2}; **2:**2; **3:**4, 15, 18, 25; **4:**6, 18; **1Th 1:**5; **2:**4, 16; **3:**1, 3, 13; **4:**12, 13, 17^{2}; **5:**3, 6, 8, 13, 14, 23, 27, 28; **2Th 1:**10^{2}, 12; **2:**2, 4, 6, 8, 10, 12; **3:**1, 2, 13, 14, 16, 18; **1Ti 1:**7, 17; **2:**1, 4, 15; **3:**2, 6^{2}, 7, 8, 10, 11, 12; **4:**3, 4, 6; **5:**7, 9, 10, 13, 16, 17, 18; **6:**1, 2, 8, 9, 10, 16, 17, 18, 21; **2Ti 1:**4, 8; **2:**1, 2, 15, 24; **3:**2, 12, 17; **4:**2, 5, 16, 17, 18, 22^{2}; **Tit 1:**5, 7^{2}, 8, 9, 11; **2:**2, 3^{2}, 5^{2}, 6, 8^{2}, 9, 10; **3:**1^{3}, 2, 8, 14, 15; **Phm 1:**13, 14, 22, 25; **Heb 1:**5^{2}, 12; **2:**17; **3:**5, 13; **5:**12; **6:**8, 18; **8:**4, 10^{2}, 12; **9:**16, 23; **10:**13, 29; **11:**16, 18, 24, 26, 40; **12:**9^{2}, 13^{2}, 18, 19, 20, 27, 28; **13:**4^{2}, 5, 6, 9^{2}, 17, 19, 21, 23, 25; **Jas 1:**4, 5, 13, 16, 19, 22, 25; **2:**5^{2}, 12, 13, 20; **3:**1, 7, 10, 14, 16; **4:**4, 9; **5:**3, 7, 8, 9, 12^{2}, 15, 16; **1Pe 1:**2^{3}, 3, 5, 7, 10, 14, 15, 16; **2:**5^{2}, 6; **3:**1, 4, 14, 15, 16, 17; **4:**7, 9, 11, 12, 13, 17, 18; **5:**1, 3, 11; **2Pe 1:**2, 10, 11, 15, 19; **2:**1, 2, 4, 12^{2}; **3:**10^{2}, 11^{2}, 12, 14, 18; **1Jn 1:**4; **2:**3, 5, 28, 29; **3:**1, 2^{2}, 12, 13; **4:**10; **2Jn 1:**2, 3, 8, 12; **3Jn 1:**2; **Jude 1:**2, 18, 25; **Rev 1:**6^{2}, 7, 17; **2:**2^{2}, 10^{2}, 11; **3:**5, 18, 19; **5:**10, 13; **6:**6, 10, 11^{2}; **7:**12, 17; **10:**6, 7, 9; **11:**5, 9; **12:**6; **13:**10^{2}, 15, 16; **14:**10; **15:**2; **16:**20; **17:**8, 17; **18:**8, 14, 21^{2}, 22^{3}, 23; **19:**1, 6, 8; **20:**3, 6, 7, 10; **21:**3^{2}, 4^{2}, 7^{2}, 8, 25^{2}; **22:**3^{2}, 4, 5^{2}, 11^{2}, 21; **Tob 1:**19; **2:**6, 8, 10; **3:**6^{3}, 13, 15; **4:**7, 8, 9, 19^{2}, 21; **5:**12, 14, 17, 19, 22; **6:**6, 9, 13, 16, 17, 18^{4}; **7:**10, 11, 12; **8:**5, 6, 17, 19, 21; **9:**4, 6; **10:**6^{2}, 7; **11:**7, 14^{4}, 17^{4}; **12:**6, 17^{2}; **13:**1, 10, 12, 13, 16^{5}, 17; **14:**4^{7}, 5, 6, 7^{2}, 8^{2}; **Jdt 2:**3, 7, 8, 20; **4:**7^{2}, 12^{4}; **5:**10, 22; **6:**4^{3}, 9; **7:**14, 25, 27^{3}; **8:**16^{2}, 21^{2}, 22; **9:**2, 3, 4; **10:**8, 9, 12^{2}, 19; **11:**1, 10, 11, 15^{2}, 18, 23^{2}; **12:**2, 12, 13, 14, 17; **13:**3, 18, 20; **14:**7; **16:**15; **AdE 1:**15, 19, 20, 22; **2:**2, 3^{3}, 4, 23; **3:**2, 9^{2}, 10, 14; **5:**3, 6, 11, 14; **6:**9^{3}, 10, 11, 13^{2}; **7:**2, 3, 4, 9; **8:**5, 6, 8, 13^{2}; **9:**4, 12, 13, 14, 22, 27, 28; **10:**5; **13:**3, 4, 6; **14:**13; **16:**7, 21, 23, 24^{2}; **Wis 1:**5, 9; **2:**2, 4^{2}, 11^{2}, 20; **3:**2, 3, 10, 14, 17^{2}; **4:**3, 4^{2}, 5^{2}, 7, 19; **5:**2^{2}, 10, 13, 22; **6:**6^{2}, 10, 11, 14, 15, 22, 25; **7:**9, 29; **8:**11^{2}, 14, 15; **9:**6, 7^{2}, 12^{2}; **10:**14; **12:**2, 15, 19, 27; **13:**3, 6, 8; **14:**5, 10, 11, 21, 27; **15:**7; **16:**9, 23; **17:**6, 10; **18:**4^{2}, 13; **19:**6, 18; **Sir Pr:**T^{7}; **1:**8, 13, 22, 29; **2:**2^{2}, 3, 4, 8; **3:**1, 5, 13, 14^{2}, 15, 17, 27; **4:**9, 10^{3}, 20^{2}, 25, 26, 29, 30, 31; **5:**5, 10, 11, 13, 14; **6:**2, 3^{2}, 6^{2}, 13, 21, 28, 32, 35, 37; **7:**6^{2}, 24, 32, 35; **8:**4, 10, 13, 15, 18; **9:**1, 4, 9, 11, 12, 13, 15^{2}, 16^{2}; **10:**9; **11:**10, 19, 23; **12:**1, 2, 11^{3}, 12, 15; **13:**2, 4, 8, 9, 10^{3}, 11, 13; **14:**5, 15; **15:**4, 10, 17, 20; **16:**3, 4, 11, 13; **17:**15, 31; **18:**17, 22, 23; **19:**3, 5, 8, 10; **20:**3, 5, 9, 10, 20, 21; **21:**4, 12, 24; **22:**3, 13^{2}, 16; **23:**3, 7, 10, 11^{2}, 12^{2}, 16, 21^{2}, 24, 26; **24:**9, 22; **25:**21; **26:**1, 3, 11^{2}, 24, 26^{2}; **27:**3, 21, 26, 29; **28:**2, 6, 7, 8, 10, 12, 22, 23^{2}; **29:**3, 8, 10, 14, 20, 23, 27; **30:**4, 13; **31:**5^{2}, 7, 10, 11, 12, 15, 17^{2}, 22; **32:**1, 2, 8^{2}, 11, 15, 18, 21; **33:**1, 4, 13^{2}, 28, 30; **34:**4^{2}, 8, 16; **35:**9, 10, 20, 22; **36:**11, 21, 30; **37:**6, 8, 12, 19^{2}, 20^{2}, 22, 29; **38:**5, 6, 8, 15, 17^{2}, 23, 32; **39:**6, 9, 16, 17, 19; **40:**12, 29; **41:**6, 9, 11, 14^{2}, 16, 17, 19, 22; **42:**1^{2}, 2, 7, 8^{2}, 9, 10^{2}, 18, 19, 21^{2}; **43:**27; **44:**13, 18, 21; **45:**12, 14, 24; **46:**11, 15; **50:**23, 29; **51:**12, 18, 20, 26, 29; **Bar 1:**11; **2:**4, 23, 24, 34, 35^{2}; **3:**8, 13, 35; **4:**27, 31, 32^{2}, 33, 34, 35; **5:**7; **LtJ 6:**1, 2, 18, 29, 30, 34, 39, 45^{2}, 47, 50, 51, 55, 58, 59^{2}, 63, 72^{2}, 73; **Aza 1:**16, 17, 21^{3}, 26, 29, 30, 31, 32, 33, 34; **Sus 1:**6, 32, 42; **Bel 1:**7, 9; **1Mc 1:**41, 63; **2:**18^{3}, 21, 63^{2}, 64, 65; **3:**18, 22, 25, 28, 44, 53, 56, 58^{2}, 60; **4:**8, 17, 31, 45, 59; **5:**30, 40, 49; **6:**15, 27, 55; **7:**5, 28, 37^{2}, 49; **8:**20, 23, 28, 30; **9:**10, 46; **10:**6, 19, 20^{2}, 31, 34, 36^{2}, 37^{3}, 38^{3}, 43, 44, 45, 73; **11:**27, 36, 37; **12:**27^{2}; **13:**5, 27, 29, 38, 39, 40^{3}; **14:**29, 41, 42, 43^{3}, 44^{2}, 45, 47^{3}; **15:**8; **16:**3; **2Mc 1:**5, 17, 31; **2:**2, 8, 22, 29, 31, 32; **3:**6, 12, 13, 16, 18, 33, 37; **5:**25; **6:**6, 12, 22^{2}, 25; **7:**4, 14, 33, 34, 42; **8:**3, 16, 29; **9:**12, 14, 24, 25; **10:**4^{2}, 11, 26^{2}; **11:**14, 18, 23, 24, 25^{2}, 26, 31, 36; **12:**12, 16, 24, 31, 42, 45; **13:**3; **14:**3, 26, 35, 41; **15:**24, 39; **1Es 1:**32; **2:**1, 5, 6, 18, 21, 26, 28; **3:**6, 7, 9^{2}, 22; **4:**12, 31, 40, 42^{2}, 50, 51, 52, 55^{2}, 56, 57^{3}; **6:**6, 8, 17, 19, 21, 23, 25^{2}, 26^{2}, 28^{2}, 29, 31^{2}, 32^{2}, 34; **8:**13, 21, 22, 24, 25, 52, 59, 85; **9:**4, 52, 53; **Man 1:**5, 7, 13; **3Mc 1:**12; **2:**28^{2}, 29^{2}, 30, 31, 33; **3:**1, 9, 26, 27, 28, 29; **4:**11^{2}, 13, 14^{3}; **5:**22, 31, 40, 51; **6:**15, 34; **7:**4, 11, 23; **2Es 1:**29^{4}; **2:**7^{2}, 13^{3}, 24, 27^{2}, 28, 35, 37, 41; **3:**12, 31, 34; **4:**9, 12, 27, 33, 34, 43, 51; **5:**1^{3}, 2, 3, 5, 8, 9, 10^{2}, 30, 43, 45, 55; **6:**7^{2}, 15, 16^{2}, 20, 22^{2}, 23, 24, 25^{2}, 26, 27^{2}, 28^{2}, 33, 34, 38, 40^{2}, 42^{3}, 46, 52, 57, 59; **7:**20, 26, 28, 30^{2}, 31, 33^{2}, 35, 36^{2}, 53, 60^{2}, 65, 67, 72, 75^{2}, 77, 87^{2}, 88, 97, 98^{2}, 100, 101, 102, 104^{2}, 111, 113, 115, 123, 125, 131, 138, 140; **8:**3, 6^{2}, 9, 10, 11, 28, 30, 32, 36, 40, 41, 48, 49, 59; **9:**7^{3}, 9, 13^{3}, 15, 22, 31; **10:**3, 8, 16^{2}, 20^{2}, 24, 54, 55^{2}, 57; **11:**9, 37, 46; **12:**9, 13, 18, 20, 21^{2}, 39, 46; **13:**16, 17, 32, 34, 36, 38, 47, 48, 56; **14:**9, 17, 20, 21, 22, 25, 34, 35; **15:**2, 3, 8, 13, 16, 17, 18^{3}, 32, 35, 37^{3}, 38, 39, 41, 51, 57, 61^{2}; **16:**10^{2}, 11, 12, 15, 18^{2}, 20, 21, 23^{4}, 24, 26, 28, 29, 30, 31, 32^{2}, 34, 38, 40, 41^{2}, 42^{2}, 43, 48, 51, 52, 55^{2}, 65, 69^{2}, 70, 71, 73, 78; **4Mc 1:**33; **2:**7, 19; **3:**2, 6; **4:**7; **5:**3, 18^{2}, 19, 26^{2}, 27, 31; **6:**18, 20^{2}, 21, 28, 34; **7:**8, 20, 22; **8:**2^{3}, 6, 12, 14^{2}, 27; **9:**4, 6, 8, 16; **10:**20; **11:**2, 13; **12:**4, 5, 17; **13:**4, 10; **14:**10; **16:**1, 17^{2}, 22; **17:**1, 8; **18:**24

BEEN (1259)

Ge 13:3; **14:**14; **26:**8, 18, 28; **31:**5, 15, 38, 41, 42; **34:**27; **35:**3; **38:**14, 21, 22; **42:**11, 28; **43:**18; **44:**16, 28; **45:**6; **46:**32, 34; **47:**9; **48:**15; **Ex 2:**22; **3:**16; **4:**10; **9:**15; **10:**14; **11:**6; **12:**44^{2}; **14:**12; **18:**3; **21:**16, 29^{2}; **32:**8; **34:**10, 29, 34; **Lev 7:**35; **8:**34; **10:**14, 16, 19; **13:**55; **17:**15; **19:**20; **21:**7, 10^{2}, 14; **25:**45, 54; **27:**20, 22, 28, 29; **Nu 1:**17; **5:**7, 27; **6:**13; **12:**15; **16:**28, 39; **19:**2, 16, 20; **22:**30; **Dt 2:**3, 7; **4:**32, 42; **9:**7, 12, 16, 24; **12:**30; **13:**14; **15:**2; **18:**6; **19:**4, 6; **21:**3; **24:**4; **31:**27; **Jos 5:**5^{2}, 7; **6:**23; **7:**7; **8:**31; **10:**14, 17; **16:**10; **18:**2; **20:**5; **21:**12; **22:**3; **23:**9, 15; **24:**33; **Jdg 6:**28, 31; **8:**3; **14:**20; **16:**11, 17, 22; **18:**1; **20:**12; **21:**5; **Ru 1:**7, 13; **2:**7, 11, 18; **3:**2; **4:**17; **1Sa 1:**15, 16; **3:**7; **4:**9, 17^{2}, 21, 22; **9:**20, 22; **10:**16, 27; **14:**21, 24, 30; **17:**33; **18:**19; **19:**4; **20:**7, 13; **21:**5; **22:**6; **25:**7, 17, 34; **26:**21; **29:**3, 6; **30:**5, 19, 21^{2}; **2Sa 3:**17; **5:**17; **7:**6, 9; **8:**10; **10:**15, 19; **12:**8; **13:**20, 32; **14:**2; **15:**34; **17:**9; **18:**11; **20:**5; **21:**13; **24:**9; **1Ki 1:**27, 37; **2:**5; **3:**2, 12, 15; **5:**1; **7:**14; **8:**43, 47; **10:**7, 12; **11:**11; **12:**19; **14:**8; **15:**22; **16:**31; **18:**13, 30; **19:**10, 14; **20:**12, 27; **21:**14, 15; **2Ki 2:**22; **5:**25; **8:**22; **9:**14; **11:**10, 20; **16:**18; **17:**14, 33; **20:**12; **22:**4, 13; **23:**2, 22; **25:**19; **1Ch 9:**19; **14:**8; **17:**8; **18:**10; **19:**16, 19; **29:**25; **2Ch 6:**33, 37; **9:**6; **10:**19; **12:**2; **16:**6, 14; **20:**26; **21:**10; **23:**9, 21; **28:**19; **29:**6; **30:**26; **31:**6; **32:**15, 31^{2}; **34:**9, 14, 21, 30; **35:**10, 18; **Ezr 4:**2, 18, 19; **5:**16; **7:**19; **9:**1, 7^{2}, 8; **10:**5; **Ne 1:**3; **2:**1, 3, 13^{2}, 18; **5:**5, 8, 11; **6:**8, 16; **7:**1^{2}, 4; **8:**4; **9:**33; **13:**10; **Est 2:**1, 6; **3:**6; **4:**1, 5, 11; **6:**3^{2}; **7:**4^{2}; **9:**1, 22; **Job 6:**3; **10:**19; **19:**26; **30:**8; **31:**9, 27, 28; **36:**21; **38:**17; **Ps 9:**15; **10:**14; **22:**10; **25:**6; **27:**9; **37:**25; **42:**3; **44:**17; **50:**21; **53:**5; **59:**16; **60:**1; **63:**7; **71:**7, 24; **73:**14, 15; **76:**2; **90:**1; **94:**17; **106:**31; **115:**12; **119:**54, 92, 126; **124:**1, 2; **Pr 3:**30; **8:**25; **30:**32^{2}; **31:**5; **Ecc 1:**9^{2}, 10; **2:**7, 12, 15, 16; **3:**15; **4:**3; **6:**10; **12:**13; **Isa 1:**6, 9; **4:**3; **6:**6; **9:**6, 10; **10:**14; **21:**4; **25:**4; **27:**7; **30:**24, 33; **33:**1; **38:**9; **39:**1; **40:**21; **43:**22; **46:**3; **48:**8, 16, 18, 19; **50:**7; **52:**15; **53:**1; **54:**1; **59:**2; **60:**15; **63:**19; **64:**11; **Jer 2:**10, 31; **3:**2, 3, 20; **5:**11; **8:**22; **13:**17; **14:**4; **15:**9; **19:**13^{2}; **20:**17; **21:**12; **22:**3, 21; **23:**10; **32:**24^{2}, 25, 29^{2}, 43; **33:**24; **34:**14; **35:**14; **37:**4, 15; **38:**27; **40:**7, 12; **42:**11; **43:**5; **44:**15; **48:**11^{2}, 33, 46; **49:**14; **50:**6; **51:**5, 9, 32^{2}, 42; **52:**25; **La 1:**20; **4:**6; **5:**2, 15; **Eze 2:**5; **7:**13; **11:**16, 17; **13:**4; **16:**16; **18:**19; **20:**41; **22:**6, 13; **30:**21; **32:**20; **33:**22, 33; **34:**2, 12; **36:**23; **37:**7; **44:**19; **Da 1:**15; **2:**30, 47; **5:**3, 15, 23^{2}, 27; **6:**10, 20; **8:**26; **9:**11, 12^{2}; **10:**2, 11, 12; **11:**12, 21; **Hos 5:**1; **12:**8; **13:**4; **Joel 2:**2; **Am 2:**4; **Ob 1:**1, 5, 6, 16, 21; **Mic 4:**6; **7:**1^{2}; **Hab 2:**18; **Zep 3:**6; **Zec 1:**12; **8:**9, 13; **11:**2; **13:**5; **Mal 1:**13; **2:**11^{2}, 14; **Mt 1:**18, 22; **2:**2, 5, 12, 15, 16, 17, 23; **3:**16; **4:**12, 14; **7:**25; **8:**17; **9:**20, 25, 33^{3}; **11:**20, 21, 23, 27; **12:**17, 22; **13:**11^{2}, 35^{2}, 52; **14:**2, 4; **15:**32; **16:**27; **17:**9; **19:**12^{2}; **20:**23; **21:**4, 21; **22:**3, 4^{2}; **24:**21, 22; **25:**21, 23; **26:**9, 24^{2}; **27:**8, 9^{2}, 64; **28:**6, 7, 18; **Mk 4:**11; **5:**4, 18, 25; **6:**2, 14, 16, 18; **8:**2; **9:**21; **10:**40; **11:**2; **13:**19; **14:**5, 21^{2}; **15:**44, 46; **16:**3, 4, 6, 10, 11, 99; **Lk 1:**1, 4, 13, 19; **2:**17, 20, 26, 48; **3:**19, 21; **4:**6, 16, 21; **5:**25; **6:**48; **7:**10, 29, 47; **8:**2, 10, 36^{2}, 43, 47; **9:**7; **10:**13, 22; **11:**7, 14; **12:**48^{2}; **14:**8, 17, 20, 22; **15:**29, 32; **16:**11, 12, 26; **19:**17, 30; **22:**22; **23:**8, 12, 19, 25, 41, 53; **24:**35, 49; **Jn 1:**24; **2:**2, 20; **3:**21, 24, 27, 28, 29; **5:**5, 6, 10, 13, 14; **6:**22; **7:**15, 47; **8:**3, 33; **9:**13, 18, 24, 32; **10:**40; **11:**13, 17, 21, 32, 39; **12:**16^{2}, 17, 38; **13:**31^{2}, 32; **14:**9; **15:**3, 27; **16:**11; **17:**10; **19:**11, 32, 41; **20:**1, 7, 12; **Ac 1:**11; **4:**9, 14, 16, 22; **8:**16; **9:**33; **10:**31^{2}, 33, 45; **13:**26, 48; **14:**8, 26; **15:**7, 10, 17^{2}, 20, 21, 29, 33; **16:**4, 6; **17:**6, 13; **18:**25; **19:**21; **21:**21, 24, 25; **22:**10; **24:**2^{2}, 10; **25:**16; **26:**30, 32; **27:**9, 21, 25, 33; **28:**28; **Ro 1:**13, 20; **3:**21; **4:**10; **5:**5^{2}, 9, 10; **6:**3, 4, 5, 13, 17, 18, 22; **7:**4, 7; **8:**22; **9:**11, 29; **10:**20; **11:**24, 31, 34; **13:**1; **15:**20, 21, 22, 26, 28; **16:**2; **1Co 1:**4, 5, 6, 11, 13; **3:**11, 14; **5:**2, 7; **10:**28; **13:**12; **15:**10, 13, 14^{3}, 16, 17, 20, 54; **2Co 1:**18; **2:**10; **5:**10; **7:**13, 14; **8:**1, 19; **9:**2, 3; **12:**11^{2}, 13, 19^{2}; **Gal 2:**7^{2}, 9, 17, 19; **3:**15, 19, 21; **4:**11, 15; **5:**11; **6:**14; **Eph 1:**11; **2:**5, 8, 13; **3:**5; **4:**1; **Php 1:**14, 16; **2:**26^{2}; **4:**18; **Col 1:**6, 16, 23, 26^{2}; **3:**1, 25; **4:**11, 16; **1Th 2:**2, 4, 16; **3:**5, 7; **4:**9; **1Ti 5:**9; **6:**20; **2Ti 1:**10; **2:**26; **Tit 1:**3; **3:**7; **Phm 1:**7; **Heb 4:**15; **5:**9, 10, 14; **6:**4; **7:**11^{2}, 28; **8:**6, 7^{2}; **9:**6, 8, 13, 19, 28; **10:**10, 13, 32; **11:**9, 15, 18, 30; **12:**11; **13:**23; **Jas 3:**7; **1Pe 1:**2, 12, 23; **2:**21, 24; **4:**6; **2Pe 1:**16; **2:**3, 17, 21; **3:**7; **1Jn 2:**20, 29; **3:**2, 8, 9^{2}; **4:**17; **5:**1; **2Jn 1:**4; **Jude 1:**13; **Rev 5:**6; **6:**9, 11; **7:**2; **9:**15; **11:**10; **12:**10, 13; **13:**3, 8, 12, 14; **14:**3, 4; **15:**4; **17:**8; **18:**17, 19, 24; **19:**8; **20:**4; **Tob 1:**4^{2}; **2:**3, 8; **3:**8^{3}; **5:**6; **6:**14; **7:**11; **8:**20; **10:**2, 13; **11:**15, 17; **13:**5; **Jdt 3:**8; **4:**3, 5, 8; **8:**18, 29; **10:**3; **11:**14; **12:**16; **14:**13; **AdE 2:**6; **4:**1, 3, 8; **7:**4; **8:**2^{2}; **9:**22; **11:**1; **13:**7, 13, 15; **16:**5^{3}, 7, 18; **Wis 2:**1, 2; **3:**5; **5:**5; **6:**10; **10:**1, 5; **11:**14, 25; **14:**14, 15; **18:**2, 5, 12; **Sir Pr:**T; **1:**6; **2:**10^{3}; **3:**22, 23; **7:**31; **9:**8; **11:**6^{2}; **14:**12; **15:**9; **23:**14; **28:**19^{2}; **31:**10^{2}, 13, 27; **34:**13, 30; **39:**21, 29, 32; **42:**19; **44:**9, 10, 19; **46:**12; **49:**7, 14; **51:**2^{2}; **Bar 1:**8, 19^{2}; **2:**2, 12, 17, 25; **3:**22; **4:**19; **LtJ 6:**12, 18, 21; **Sus 1:**18, 27, 57; **Bel 1:**27, 32; **1Mc 1:**6, 10; **2:**9^{2}, 11, 12, 66; **4:**20, 44; **5:**1, 13, 26, 27; **6:**5; **7:**31; **8:**2, 13; **9:**22, 27, 29, 38, 62, 68; **10:**38, 47; **11:**39; **12:**21, 50; **13:**39, 51; **14:**33; **15:**17,

33; 16:11; 2Mc 1:11, 20, 22[2], 31; 2:1, 11, 14, 23, 32; 3:4, 7, 9[2], 22, 23, 24, 32, 34; 4:1, 30, 39[2], 47; 5:4, 5, 18[2]; 6:21, 30; 8:2, 14, 28, 30, 35; 10:2, 5, 6, 12, 24; 11:31; 12:1, 36, 42, 44; 13:9, 23; 14:3, 12, 17, 20, 26, 30, 31, 36, 38; 15:12[2], 32, 37; 1Es 1:20, 24; 2:22, 26; 4:42; 5:69; 6:8, 20, 26; 8:60, 62, 68, 70[2]; 9:39, 42, 55; 3Mc 1:1, 2, 12, 18, 19; 2:24, 30; 3:26; 4:1, 2, 11[2], 14, 19; 5:10, 18[2], 24, 27[2], 30, 32, 45[2]; 6:1, 31; 7:20; 2Es 1:18; 2:38, 41; 4:1, 3, 6, 12, 19, 21, 22, 23[3], 27, 28, 29[3], 40; 5:16, 17, 25, 26[2], 43, 44; 6:28, 32, 35, 47, 50, 51, 58, 59; 7:1, 11, 14, 24, 27, 32, 37, 42, 48, 60, 63[3], 65, 68, 69, 74, 87, 96, 98, 100, 101, 114, 115, 116, 119, 120, 121; 8:3, 5, 8, 9, 11, 35, 41[2], 43, 44, 53, 60; 9:8, 19, 22, 24, 33, 35, 39; 10:10, 21, 22[13], 23, 51, 57[2]; 12:5, 7, 13, 34, 44[2]; 13:26, 53; 14:21[2]; 16:3, 4, 5; 4Mc 3:7; 4:13, 14, 24; 5:4, 16; 6:24; 8:5, 16[3]; 10:16, 21; 11:19, 20[2], 25; 12:2, 6; 13:2[2], 23, 24; 16:5; 17:20, 22

BUT (5047)

Ge 2:6, 17, 20; 3:3, 4, 9; 4:5, 7; 6:8, 18; 8:1, 9; 11:31; 12:12, 17; 14:4, 21, 22, 24; 15:2, 4[2], 8, 10, 14; 16:6; 17:5, 15, 19, 21; 18:15, 27; 19:3, 4, 9, 10, 14, 16, 19, 26; 20:3, 7, 12; 21:9, 12, 23; 22:7, 11; 24:4, 8, 33, 38, 40, 56; 25:6, 28; 26:19, 29; 27:11, 20, 22, 35, 40, 42; 28:19; 29:8, 20, 23, 31; 30:15, 27, 30, 35, 42; 31:5, 7, 24, 29, 32, 33, 34, 35, 43, 47; 32:26, 28, 29; 33:4, 9, 13, 15, 17; 34:5, 8, 17, 31; 35:10, 18; 37:4, 10, 11, 21, 22, 35; 38:7, 9, 21, 29; 39:6, 8, 12, 18, 21; 40:14, 17, 22, 23; 41:8, 21, 24, 54; 42:4, 7, 12, 14, 21, 22, 31, 34, 38; 43:3, 5, 34; 44:10, 17[2]; 45:3, 8, 22, 27; 46:12; 47:18; 48:14, 19, 21; 49:19; 50:19, 24; Ex 1:7, 12, 16, 17[2], 22; 2:15, 17; 3:11, 13; 4:1[2], 10[2], 13, 21, 23, 25; 5:2, 4, 8, 11, 18; 6:3, 9, 12, 30; 7:3, 12, 16, 22; 8:7, 15, 18, 19, 22, 26, 32; 9:4, 6, 7, 12, 16, 30, 32, 34; 10:8, 20, 23, 25, 27; 11:7, 10; 12:9, 27, 44, 48; 13:13, 15; 14:13, 16, 29; 15:19; 16:8, 18, 20, 21, 26; 17:1, 3, 12; 18:22, 26; 19:6, 13, 24; 20:6, 10, 11, 19, 25; 21:2, 5, 13, 14, 19, 21, 28, 29, 34, 36[2]; 22:1, 3, 12, 17; 23:11, 12, 22, 24; 24:2; 26:24; 27:10, 11; 29:14, 33; 31:15; 32:11, 18, 30, 32[2], 33, 34; 33:3, 11, 12, 20, 23; 34:7, 21, 31, 34; 35:2; 36:29, 38; 38:10, 11, 17; 40:37; Lev 1:9, 13; 2:12; 4:11; 5:7, 11; 6:28, 30; 7:10, 16, 17, 20, 24, 31; 8:17; 9:10; 10:6, 14; 11:4, 10, 21, 23, 26, 36, 38; 13:4, 7, 12, 14, 16, 21[2], 23, 26[2], 28[2], 33, 35, 37, 40, 41, 42, 58; 14:8, 21; 16:10; 17:16; 18:26; 19:18, 20, 21, 25; 20:24; 21:4, 23; 22:11, 13, 23, 28; 23:3; 24:21; 25:4, 17, 23, 26, 28, 31, 34, 36, 43, 46; 26:14, 23, 27, 40, 45; 27:13, 18, 20, 21; Nu 1:53; 3:10, 41; 4:15, 20; 5:13, 20, 28, 31; 7:9; 8:18, 26; 9:13, 22; 10:4, 7[2], 30[2]; 11:2, 6[2], 20, 21, 25, 26, 29, 33; 12:14[2]; 13:30; 14:10, 13, 18, 24, 31, 32, 38, 41, 44; 15:22, 30; 16:12, 30; 18:3, 7, 15, 17, 18, 23[2], 32; 19:7, 12, 20; 20:12, 18, 20, 26; 21:4, 23, 34; 22:18, 20, 30, 35, 38; 23:11[2], 26; 24:1, 4, 10, 11, 16, 17[2], 20, 24; 26:33, 55, 61; 27:3, 21; 30:5, 8, 9, 12, 14, 15; 31:11, 18, 30; 32:6, 17, 23, 24, 27, 30, 32; 33:55; 35:16, 22, 26, 28, 30; 36:3; Dt 1:12, 26, 32, 40; 2:12, 21, 30; 3:7, 26, 28; 4:2, 9, 12, 20, 22, 26; 5:3, 10, 14, 31; 6:21; 7:5, 10, 13, 23; 8:3, 10; 9:5, 19, 20; 11:2, 11, 28; 12:5, 14, 26, 27; 13:5, 9; 14:7, 8, 12, 24; 15:3, 6[2], 16, 21; 16:6; 18:2, 20, 22; 19:6, 11; 20:5, 6, 7, 12, 16; 21:14; 22:13, 14, 16, 17, 25, 27; 23:20, 22, 24, 25; 24:1; 25:3, 7; 28:12, 15, 29, 30[3], 31, 32, 38, 39, 40, 41, 44, 68; 29:4, 7, 15, 29; 30:17[2]; 32:27, 47; 34:4, 6; Jos 1:14; 2:4[2], 19, 20; 5:14; 6:19, 25; 7:1; 8:4, 9, 13, 14, 23; 9:3, 7, 12, 16, 18, 19, 27; 10:19, 40; 11:13, 14, 20; 13:13, 33; 14:3, 4, 8; 15:63; 16:10; 17:3, 8, 12, 13[2], 14, 18; 21:12; 22:3, 7, 19, 27, 28; 23:8, 13, 15; 24:4, 10, 15, 19; Jdg 1:6, 19, 21, 25, 27, 28, 29, 30, 32, 33, 35; 2:2, 3, 19; 3:9, 15, 19; 4:8, 21; 5:31; 6:10, 13[2], 15, 16, 23, 27, 31, 34; 7:6, 8, 10; 8:6, 20; 9:5, 11, 13, 15, 18, 20, 23, 51, 53; 10:15; 11:7, 16, 17[2], 20, 27, 28; 12:2; 13:7, 9, 16, 18, 23; 14:3[2], 6, 9, 13, 14, 16; 15:1; 16:3, 9, 12, 14, 20, 22; 17:2; 18:9, 29; 19:2, 5, 10, 12[2], 15, 24, 25, 28; 20:9, 13, 32, 34, 39, 40, 42, 47; 21:6, 14, 22; Ru 1:3, 8, 11, 14, 16, 21; 2:8, 11; 3:3, 12, 14, 18; 4:4; 1Sa 1:2, 5, 11, 13, 15[2], 22; 2:4, 5[2], 9, 15, 25[2], 30; 3:5, 6, 16; 4:20; 5:4, 9, 10; 6:3, 7, 9; 7:10; 8:3, 6, 7, 18, 19[2]; 9:4[3], 6, 7; 10:16, 19[2], 21, 27[3]; 11:2, 13; 12:2, 9, 10, 12[2], 15[2], 20, 25; 13:8, 14, 16, 22; 14:1, 10, 26, 27, 36, 37, 39, 41[2]; 15:3, 8, 14, 15, 21, 33, 35; 16:7[2], 11; 17:9, 15, 34, 45[2], 54; 18:8, 11, 12, 16, 19, 28; 19:1, 10; 20:3[3], 5, 7, 8, 13, 14, 22, 25, 27, 33, 39; 22:17, 20; 23:3, 14; 24:10, 12, 13, 22; 25:3, 10, 14, 19, 21, 25, 29; 26:3, 9, 11, 19, 23; 27:9; 28:10, 23; 29:4, 8, 11; 30:2, 6, 10, 23; 31:4, 11; 2Sa 1:4; 2:8, 10, 21, 23, 24, 31; 3:13, 16, 22, 26, 35; 4:12; 5:17; 6:20, 22; 7:2, 4, 6, 15; 8:4; 9:10; 10:8, 11, 15; 11:1, 9, 13, 23, 27; 12:3[2], 4, 12, 17, 19, 21, 23[2]; 13:3, 9, 11, 14, 16[2], 19, 21, 22, 25[3], 27, 32, 34, 37; 14:2, 14, 20, 29[2]; 15:3, 10, 21, 26, 30, 34; 16:10, 18; 17:11, 16, 18; 18:3[2], 12, 20, 29; 19:10, 22, 27, 28, 34, 37, 43[2]; 20:2, 3, 5, 10, 21; 21:2, 7, 17; 22:19, 28, 32, 42[2]; 23:6, 10[2], 12, 16, 19, 21, 23; 24:3[2], 4, 10[2], 14, 16, 17, 24[2]; 1Ki 1:4, 8, 10, 18, 19, 20, 26, 52; 2:6, 8, 22, 26, 30, 33, 39, 45; 3:11, 21, 22, 26; 5:4; 8:8, 16, 18, 19, 27, 33, 58; 9:6, 12, 14, 22, 24; 10:7; 11:10, 17, 22, 34, 35, 39, 40; 12:8, 10, 11, 14[2], 17, 22; 13:4, 8, 16, 18, 22, 33; 14:5, 6, 9; 15:14, 23; 16:9, 22; 17:7, 12, 13, 19; 18:11, 18, 21, 22, 23[2], 25, 26, 29, 46; 19:4, 11[2], 12; 20:9, 19, 20, 23, 28, 35; 21:3, 6, 15, 29; 22:2, 5, 7, 8[2], 14, 16[2], 18, 30, 31, 34, 48, 49; 2Ki 1:3, 4, 6, 10, 12, 14, 16; 2:2, 4, 6, 12, 17[2], 19; 3:5, 11, 13, 15, 17, 24, 26; 4:1, 6, 27, 31, 40, 43; 5:8, 11, 13, 16[2], 18, 19, 22, 26; 6:5, 9, 28, 29; 7:1, 2[2], 4[2], 5, 10[2], 19; 8:10, 15, 21; 9:15, 18, 20, 35; 10:4, 9, 18, 19, 23, 29, 31; 11:2, 4; 12:6, 7, 13, 17; 13:4, 6, 11, 19, 23; 14:4, 6[2], 9, 11, 19, 27; 16:3, 5, 15; 17:4, 14, 18, 19, 29, 33, 36, 39, 40, 41; 18:6, 12, 22, 27, 36; 19:18, 27; 21:9, 24; 22:7, 18; 23:9, 23, 29, 34, 35; 25:5, 12, 25; 1Ch 2:23, 34; 4:22, 27; 5:1, 25; 6:49, 56; 10:4, 11; 11:14, 18, 21, 23, 25; 12:17; 15:2, 21; 16:26; 17:1, 3, 5, 14; 18:4; 19:12, 16; 20:1; 21:3, 4, 6, 7, 8, 13, 15, 17[2], 24, 30; 22:8; 23:11, 14, 17, 22, 28; 24:2; 27:24; 28:3, 9; 29:1, 14; 2Ch 1:4, 11; 2:6; 5:9; 6:6, 8, 9, 18, 24; 7:19; 8:9; 9:6; 10:8, 10, 11, 14[2], 17; 11:2; 12:7, 10; 13:10, 11, 21; 15:2, 4, 7, 17; 16:12; 17:4; 18:4, 6, 7[2], 13, 15[2], 17, 29, 30, 33; 19:6; 20:12, 15; 21:3, 13, 20; 22:7, 11; 23:1, 6; 24:5, 15, 19, 21, 22, 25; 25:4[2], 7, 9, 10, 13, 16[2], 18, 20, 27; 26:16, 17, 18; 27:2; 28:2, 9[2], 10, 21, 23, 27; 29:34; 30:8, 10, 18; 32:8, 25; 33:10, 17, 23, 25; 34:26; 35:21[2], 22[3]; 36:4, 16; Ezr 2:62; 3:6, 12; 4:3[2]; 5:5, 12; 6:2; 8:22; 9:8, 9, 15; 10:2, 13; Ne 1:9; 2:14, 19, 20; 3:5; 4:7, 10; 5:8, 15; 6:2, 9, 11, 12; 7:4, 61, 64; 9:11, 16, 17[2], 28, 29; 11:3, 21; 13:2, 21, 24; Est 1:12, 16; 2:22; 3:2, 6, 15; 4:4, 11, 14; 5:9, 12; 6:12, 13; 7:4, 7; 9:1, 10, 15, 16, 18, 25; Job 1:11; 2:5, 10; 3:9, 21, 26; 4:2, 5, 16; 5:3, 7, 15, 18[2]; 6:25, 28; 7:4, 21; 8:9[2]; 9:2, 11, 18; 11:5, 12, 20; 12:3, 5, 7; 13:3, 15; 14:10, 18; 15:4; 17:10; 19:7, 16; 20:5; 21:34; 22:18; 23:6, 9, 10, 13; 24:11; 26:14[2]; 27:17, 19; 28:5, 12; 30:1, 26; 32:5, 8, 12; 33:1, 12; 35:10, 12; 36:6, 7, 12, 17; 40:5; 42:5; Ps 1:2, 4, 6; 3:3; 4:3; 5:7, 11; 7:9; 9:7; 10:14; 13:5; 14:6; 15:4; 18:18, 27, 41[2]; 19:12; 20:7, 8; 22:2[2], 6, 19, 24; 26:11; 30:5[2]; 31:6, 14, 22, 23; 32:10; 34:10, 19; 35:13, 15, 20; 37:9, 11, 13, 17, 20, 21, 22, 28, 38; 38:13, 15; 40:6, 16, 17; 41:10, 12; 44:2[2], 3, 7; 49:15; 50:16, 21; 52:5, 7, 8; 54:4; 55:13, 16, 21[2], 23[2]; 57:6; 59:8, 16; 62:4, 9; 63:9, 11; 64:7; 66:19; 68:3, 6, 21; 69:13, 20[2], 29; 70:5; 71:7, 14; 73:2, 16, 25, 26, 28; 75:7, 9, 10; 76:7; 78:7, 10, 30, 36, 39, 50, 53, 57, 68; 80:17; 81:8, 11; 86:15; 88:13; 89:33, 38; 91:7; 92:8, 10; 94:11, 22; 96:5; 99:8; 102:12, 26, 27; 103:17; 106:7, 13, 14, 15, 35, 43; 107:41; 109:16, 21, 28; 115:1, 5[2], 6[2], 7[2], 16, 18; 118:13, 17, 18; 119:3, 51, 67, 69, 70, 87, 95, 96, 109, 110, 113, 143, 161, 163; 120:7; 125:1, 5; 130:4; 131:2; 132:18; 135:16[2], 17; 136:15; 138:6; 141:8; 145:20; 146:9; 147:11; Pr 1:28[2], 33; 2:22; 3:1, 32, 33, 34, 35; 4:18; 5:4; 6:26, 32; 8:36; 9:18; 10:1, 2, 3, 4, 5, 6, 7, 8, 9, 10, 11, 12, 13, 14, 17, 19, 21, 23, 24, 25, 27, 28, 29, 30, 31, 32; 11:1, 2, 3, 4, 5, 6, 9, 11, 12, 13, 14, 15, 16[2], 17, 18, 19, 20, 21, 26, 27, 28, 30; 12:1, 2, 3, 4, 6, 7, 8, 10, 11, 12, 13, 15, 16, 17, 18, 19, 20, 21, 22, 23, 25, 26, 27; 13:1, 2, 5, 6, 8, 9, 10, 11, 12, 13, 15, 16, 17, 18, 19, 20, 21, 22, 23, 24, 25; 14:1, 2, 3, 5, 6, 8, 9, 11, 12, 15, 16, 18, 20, 21, 23, 24, 25, 29, 30, 31, 32, 33, 34, 35; 15:1, 2, 4, 5, 6, 8, 9, 10, 13, 14, 15, 18, 19, 20, 21, 22, 25, 26, 27, 28, 29, 32; 16:1, 2, 9, 22, 25, 33; 17:3, 9, 11, 22, 24; 18:2, 12, 14, 23, 24; 19:4, 12, 14, 21; 20:3, 5, 6, 15, 17, 29; 21:2, 5, 8, 15, 20, 26, 28, 29, 31; 22:3, 12, 15; 23:7, 17, 35[2]; 24:16, 25; 25:2; 27:3, 4, 6, 7, 9, 12, 22; 28:1, 2, 4, 5, 7, 10, 11, 12, 13, 14, 16, 18, 19, 20, 25, 26, 27, 28; 29:2, 3, 4, 6, 8, 11, 15, 16, 18, 23, 24, 25, 26, 27; 31:29, 30; Ecc 1:4, 7, 17; 2:1, 14, 26; 3:18; 4:3, 10, 11, 13[2]; 5:7, 9, 11, 12; 6:2, 3; 7:4, 23, 26, 28[2], 29; 8:13; 9:4, 5, 11, 18; 10:2, 10, 12; 11:9; SS 1:6; 3:1[2], 2; 5:2, 6[3]; 8:9; Isa 1:2, 3, 6, 20, 21, 28; 3:7; 5:2, 7[2], 8, 10, 12, 16; 6:9[2]; 7:1, 12, 25; 8:10[2], 13, 22; 9:1[2], 9, 10[2], 20[2]; 10:7[2], 20; 11:4, 14; 13:21; 14:1, 15, 19, 30; 16:14; 17:13; 22:11, 13; 23:18; 24:16; 26:11, 13, 15, 18; 28:27, 28[2]; 29:5, 9[2]; 30:1[2], 5, 15, 20; 31:1, 2; 32:8; 33:21; 34:11; 35:8, 9; 36:7, 12, 21; 37:19; 38:15, 17; 40:8, 31; 41:8, 12, 28; 42:19, 20[2], 22, 25[2]; 43:1, 22, 24; 44:1; 45:17; 46:2; 47:11; 48:1, 10; 49:4, 14, 25; 50:11; 51:2[2], 6, 8, 13, 21; 53:5; 54:7, 8, 10; 55:11; 57:3, 10, 12, 13, 17, 18, 20; 58:3[2]; 59:9, 11[2]; 60:2, 10, 19; 61:6; 62:4, 9; 63:5[2], 9, 10, 18; 64:5; 65:6, 11, 12, 13[3], 14, 15, 18, 20, 25; 66:2, 4, 5; Jer 1:7, 17, 19; 2:7, 11, 25, 27, 28; 3:5, 7, 8, 10, 24; 4:22; 5:3[2], 5, 10, 13, 18, 21[2], 23, 31; 6:6, 11, 16, 17; 7:23, 24, 26, 27[2], 32; 8:6, 7, 15[2]; 9:8, 14, 24; 10:10, 19, 24; 11:8[2], 12, 16, 19, 20; 12:1, 3, 11, 13, 17; 13:1, 7, 11, 17; 14:12, 13, 19[2]; 15:20; 16:15, 19; 17:16, 18[2], 22, 24[2], 27; 18:8, 10, 12, 15; 19:6; 20:3, 11; 21:9; 22:5, 6, 12, 17, 21, 27; 23:8, 14, 22, 28, 36, 38; 24:2, 8; 25:3; 26:14, 19, 21, 24; 27:8, 11, 15; 28:7; 29:7, 19, 20; 30:9, 10, 11; 31:30, 33; 32:4, 18, 23, 30[2]; 34:3, 11, 14, 16; 35:6, 7, 10, 11, 14, 15, 16, 18; 36:26, 31; 37:2, 14; 38:2, 4, 6, 18, 21, 23; 39:5, 12, 17, 18; 40:4, 10, 14, 16; 41:8, 11, 15; 42:13, 21; 43:3, 5; 44:5, 18; 45:5; 46:27, 28; 48:27, 38; 49:6, 10, 39; 50:13, 24, 34; 51:9, 26; 52:8, 16; La 1:17, 18, 19; 2:14; 3:21, 56; 4:3, 4, 21, 22; 5:19; Eze 2:8; 3:5, 7, 18, 19[2], 20, 27; 4:6; 5:6, 7; 6:8; 7:14, 25; 9:6, 10; 10:11; 11:7, 12, 21; 12:2[2], 16, 23, 25[2], 28; 14:16, 18; 16:5, 15, 33, 43, 49, 61; 17:6, 15; 18:7, 14, 16, 21, 24; 19:12; 20:8, 9, 13[2], 14, 21, 22, 24, 38, 39; 21:23[2]; 22:30; 23:14, 43, 45; 24:17, 23; 28:2, 9; 30:24, 25; 32:2; 33:5, 6[2], 8, 9[2], 11, 13, 22, 24, 31[2], 32; 34:3, 4, 8, 16, 18; 36:8, 20, 21, 22; 37:8; 44:8, 10, 13, 15, 22; 45:8, 17; 46:1, 2, 9, 17; 47:11, 12; Da 1:8; 2:6, 9, 28, 30[2], 35, 41, 43, 49; 3:15, 18, 23, 25; 4:7, 15, 23; 5:8, 15, 16, 20, 23; 6:4, 13; 7:12, 18, 28; 8:3, 8, 17, 22, 25, 27; 9:7, 18, 25; 10:10, 13, 21; 11:4, 5, 6, 9, 12, 14, 16, 17, 18, 19, 20, 24, 25, 27, 28, 29, 32, 40, 41, 44; 12:1, 4, 8, 10[2], 13; Hos 1:7; 2:7[2]; 4:10[2]; 5:2, 6, 13; 6:7; 7:2, 9[2], 13, 14; 8:4[2], 14; 9:3, 10, 13; 10:11; 11:3, 7, 12; 12:6; 13:1, 4, 13; 14:9; Joel 2:3; 3:7, 16, 20; Am 2:4, 12; 3:8; 5:5, 11[2], 24; 6:6, 12; 7:13, 14; 8:11, 12; 9:9; Ob 1:12, 17; Jnh 1:3, 4, 13, 17; 2:9; 4:1, 7, 9; Mic 2:8; 3:4, 5, 8; 4:4, 5, 12; 5:2; 6:8, 14[2], 15[3]; 7:7, 13; Na 1:3; 2:8; Hab 2:4, 14, 20; Zep 1:5; 3:5, 7; Hag 1:6[3]; 2:15, 16[2]; Zec 1:4, 6, 21; 4:6; 7:11; 8:11, 13; 9:4; 11:12, 16; 12:4; 13:5; 14:2, 10; Mal 1:2, 3, 4[2], 12; 2:8, 9; 3:2, 7, 8, 15; 4:2; Mt 1:18, 20, 25; 2:22; 3:7, 11, 12, 15; 4:4[2]; 5:13[2], 15, 17, 19, 22, 28, 32, 33, 34, 39[2], 44; 6:3, 6, 13, 15, 17, 18, 20, 23, 30, 33; 7:3, 15, 17, 21, 25; 8:4, 8, 20, 22, 24; 9:4, 6, 12[2], 13, 14, 17, 18, 24, 25, 31, 34, 37; 10:6, 13, 20, 22, 28, 33, 34; 11:16, 22, 24; 12:4, 7, 14, 24, 28, 31, 32, 39[2], 43, 48; 13:6, 11, 12, 14[2], 16, 17[2], 21, 22, 23, 25, 29, 30, 32, 48, 57; 14:6, 13, 17, 24, 26, 27, 30; 15:5, 8, 11, 15, 18, 20, 23, 25; 16:3, 4, 12, 14, 15, 17, 23[2], 26; 17:7, 12[2], 16; 18:7, 16, 22, 28, 30; 19:6, 8, 11[2], 14, 26[2], 30; 20:10, 13, 22, 23[2], 25, 26, 28, 31; 21:13, 15, 19, 21, 26, 29, 30, 32, 35, 38, 46; 22:3, 5, 8, 11, 14, 18, 30, 32; 23:3, 4, 8, 13, 16, 18, 24, 25, 27, 28; 24:6, 8, 13, 22, 35, 36[2], 43, 48; 25:4, 6, 9, 12, 18, 26, 29, 46; 26:5, 8, 10, 11, 24, 32, 39, 41, 54, 56, 58, 60, 63, 64, 70; 27:4, 6, 12, 14, 23, 24, 34, 49; 28:5, 17; Mk 1:8, 25, 44, 45[2]; 2:7, 10, 17[2], 18, 22, 26; 3:4, 12, 26, 27, 29[2]; 4:11, 12[2], 17, 19, 29, 34, 38; 5:4, 19, 26, 28, 33, 36, 39; 6:9, 15, 16, 19, 21, 37, 49, 50, 52; 7:5, 6, 11, 15, 19, 25, 28, 36; 8:24, 29, 33[2]; 9:8, 13, 18, 22, 27, 32, 34, 37, 39, 50; 10:5, 6, 8, 14, 18, 24, 27, 31, 38, 40[2], 43[2], 45, 48; 11:13, 17, 23, 32; 12:3, 7, 12, 14, 15, 19, 25, 27, 44; 13:7, 8, 11[2], 13, 14, 20, 23, 24, 31, 32[2]; 14:4, 6, 7, 21, 28, 31, 36, 38, 47, 49, 51, 52, 55, 59, 61, 68, 70, 71; 15:5, 11, 14, 23; 16:6, 7, 11, 13, 16; Lk 1:7, 13, 20, 29, 60; 2:10, 19, 37, 43, 50; 3:16, 17, 19; 4:25, 30, 35, 41, 43; 5:5, 8, 15, 16, 19, 21, 24, 31, 32, 33, 38, 39; 6:2, 4, 11, 24, 27, 35, 40, 41, 48, 49; 7:6, 7, 30, 44, 45, 46, 47, 49; 8:10, 13, 14, 15, 16, 19, 21, 27, 29, 38, 46, 52[2], 54, 56; 9:9, 13, 19, 20, 25, 27, 32, 40, 42, 45, 47, 50, 53, 55, 58, 59, 60[2], 61; 10:2, 6, 10, 14, 20, 24[2], 29, 33, 40, 41; 11:15, 17, 20, 22, 24, 28, 29, 33, 34, 39, 42; 12:5, 7, 9, 10, 14, 20, 21, 28, 39, 45, 47, 48, 51, 56; 13:3, 5, 9, 14, 15, 27; 14:4, 10, 13, 18, 34; 15:17[2], 20, 22, 29, 30, 32; 16:15, 17, 25[2], 30; 17:1, 17, 25, 29, 33; 18:4, 13[2], 14, 16, 19, 23, 34, 39; 19:3, 14, 26, 27, 42, 46, 48; 20:6, 10, 14, 17, 19, 21, 23, 28, 35, 38; 21:4, 9, 12, 18, 33; 22:21, 22, 25, 26, 27, 32, 36, 42, 48, 51, 53, 54, 57, 58, 60, 69; 23:5, 9, 21, 23, 28[2], 35, 40, 41, 49; 24:1, 3, 5[2], 11, 12, 16, 21, 24, 29; Jn 1:8, 12, 13, 20, 31, 33; 2:10, 21, 24; 3:8, 16, 17, 18, 21, 28, 30, 36; 4:2, 4, 14, 20, 23, 27, 32, 35; 5:11, 17, 18, 19, 22, 24, 30, 34, 36, 42, 47; 6:9, 20, 22, 26, 27, 32, 36, 38, 39, 58, 61, 64; 7:6, 7, 10[2], 16, 18, 22, 24, 26, 27, 28, 30, 34, 41, 44, 49; 8:12, 14, 16, 20, 21, 26, 28, 40, 42, 45, 49, 55[2], 59; 9:9, 10, 16, 21, 28, 29, 31, 41; 10:1, 5, 6, 8, 18, 26, 33, 38, 39, 41; 11:4, 10, 11, 13, 15, 22, 30, 37, 42, 46, 49, 51, 52, 54; 12:4, 6, 8, 9, 16, 24, 42, 44, 47, 49; 13:7, 9, 10, 18, 36; 14:10, 11, 19, 24, 26, 31; 15:15, 16, 19, 21, 22, 24; 16:4, 5, 6, 7, 12, 13, 20[2], 21, 22, 25, 33; 17:9, 11, 13, 15, 20, 25; 18:16, 23, 36, 39, 40; 19:9, 12, 15, 21, 24, 33; 20:4, 5, 7, 11, 14, 17, 24, 25, 27, 31; 21:3, 4, 8, 18, 23, 25; Ac 1:4, 5, 8; 2:13, 14, 24, 34; 3:6[2], 14; 4:4, 17, 19, 32; 5:1, 4, 13, 19, 22, 23, 26, 29, 34, 36, 39; 6:10; 7:5, 7, 9, 12, 17, 25, 27, 42, 47, 55, 57; 8:3, 12, 20, 40; 9:6, 7, 13, 15, 24, 25, 27, 29; 10:14, 26, 28, 35, 40, 41; 11:8, 9, 16, 20; 12:15, 24; 13:8, 9, 14, 25, 30, 37, 45, 50; 14:2, 4, 19, 20; 15:5, 20, 35, 38, 40; 16:1, 7, 18, 19, 28, 37; 17:5, 13, 14, 21, 32, 34; 18:9, 12, 15, 17, 19, 21, 26; 19:15[2], 26, 27, 30, 34, 35; 20:6, 10, 24; 21:13, 24, 25; 22:3, 9, 22, 25, 28; 23:8, 21, 27, 29; 24:4, 14, 19, 22, 23; 25:9, 11, 17, 19, 21, 25, 26; 26:10, 16, 20, 22, 25[2], 29; 27:10, 11, 14, 22, 26, 30, 39, 41[2], 43; 28:6, 19, 22, 26[2]; Ro 1:13, 21, 32; 2:5, 8, 10, 13, 17, 25, 27[2], 29; 3:5, 7, 21, 27; 4:2, 4, 5, 10, 12, 13, 15, 16, 20, 24; 5:3, 8, 11, 13, 15, 16, 20[2]; 6:8, 10, 13, 14, 15, 17, 22, 23; 7:2, 3, 6[2], 8, 9, 14, 15, 17[2], 18, 19, 20, 23, 25; 8:4, 5, 6, 9, 10, 13, 15, 20, 23, 25, 26, 32; 9:7, 8, 12, 13, 16, 20, 24, 31, 32; 10:2, 6, 8, 14, 16, 18, 21; 11:4, 6, 7, 11, 15, 17, 18, 20[2], 22, 28, 30; 12:2, 3, 16, 17, 19, 21; 13:3, 4, 5; 14:1, 13, 14, 17, 20, 23; 15:3, 21, 23; 16:4, 18, 26; 1Co 1:10, 17, 18, 23, 24, 27; 2:4, 5, 7, 9, 12, 13, 16; 3:1, 6, 7, 15; 4:3, 4, 10[3], 14, 18, 19[2], 20; 5:8, 11; 6:6, 8, 11, 12[2], 13, 17, 18; 7:2, 4[2], 7, 9, 10, 11, 14, 15, 19, 25, 28, 33, 34, 35, 37[2], 39, 40; 8:1, 3, 4, 9, 12; 9:12, 15, 17, 21, 24, 25, 27; 10:13, 23[2], 24, 28, 33; 11:3, 5, 6, 7, 8, 9, 12, 15, 16, 17, 31, 32; 12:4, 5, 6, 14, 18, 24, 25, 31; 13:1, 2, 3, 6, 8, 10, 12; 14:2, 4, 5, 14, 15[2], 17, 20, 22[2], 24, 28, 33, 34, 40; 15:10[2], 20, 23, 27, 35, 37, 38, 39, 40, 46[2], 51, 57; 16:8, 12; 2Co 1:9, 12, 19, 21, 23; 2:2, 4, 5[2], 13, 14, 17; 3:3[2], 6[2], 14, 16; 4:2, 7, 8[2], 9[2], 12, 13, 18[2]; 5:4, 11, 12, 15; 6:4, 12; 7:5, 6, 7, 9, 10, 12, 14; 8:8, 10, 13, 16, 17, 19, 21, 22; 9:3, 12; 10:1, 3, 4, 10, 12, 13, 15, 18; 11:3, 6, 16, 17, 21, 33; 12:1, 5, 6[2], 9, 14[2]; 13:3, 4[2], 7[2], 8; Gal 1:1, 7, 8, 12, 15, 17, 19; 2:3, 4, 11, 12, 14, 16, 17, 18, 20; 3:12, 16, 18, 20, 22, 25; 4:2, 4, 7, 14, 17, 26, 29, 30, 31; 5:10, 11, 13, 18; 6:8, 13, 15; Eph 1:21; 2:4, 13, 19; 4:7, 9, 15, 26, 29; 5:3, 4, 8, 11, 13, 15, 17, 18, 29; 6:4, 6, 12; Php 1:15, 17, 20, 24, 28, 29; 2:3, 4, 7, 12, 17, 22, 27[2]; 3:9, 12, 13, 20; 4:6, 10, 17; Col 1:26; 2:17, 23; 3:8, 11, 22; 1Th 1:5, 8; 2:2, 4[2], 7, 8, 13, 16, 18; 3:6; 4:7, 8, 10, 13; 5:4, 6, 8, 9, 12, 15, 21; 2Th 2:7, 12, 13; 3:3, 8, 9, 15; 1Ti 1:5, 9, 13, 16; 2:10, 14; 3:3, 11, 14; 4:12; 5:1, 6, 11, 13, 23; 6:8, 9, 11, 17; 2Ti 1:7, 8, 9, 10, 12; 2:9, 14, 19, 20, 24; 3:5, 9, 13, 14; 4:3, 8, 16, 17; Tit 1:8, 15, 16; 2:1, 10; 3:4, 5, 9; Phm 1:11, 14, 16[2]; Heb 1:2, 8, 11, 12, 13; 2:6, 9, 16; 3:4, 13, 17; 4:2, 13, 15; 5:4, 5, 14; 6:8, 12; 7:3, 6, 16, 21, 24, 28; 8:6; 9:7[2], 10, 11, 12, 23, 24, 26, 28; 10:3, 5, 12, 25, 27, 32, 38, 39[2]; 11:4, 13, 16, 29; 12:10, 11, 13, 22, 26[2]; 13:14; Jas 1:2, 6, 14, 22, 25[2], 26; 2:6, 9, 10, 11, 14, 18; 3:8, 14, 15, 17; 4:6[2], 11[2]; 5:12; 1Pe 1:12, 19, 20, 23, 25; 2:7, 9, 10[2], 18, 20, 23, 25; 3:9, 12, 14, 15, 18, 21; 4:2, 5, 13, 15, 16; 5:2[2], 3, 5; 2Pe 1:16, 21; 2:1, 4, 16, 19; 3:7, 8, 9[2], 10, 13, 18; 1Jn 1:7; 2:1, 2, 4, 5, 7, 11, 16, 17, 19[2], 20, 21, 22, 27; 3:18; 4:1, 10, 18; 5:5, 6, 17, 18; 2Jn 1:1, 5[2], 8, 9; 3Jn 1:9, 11, 13; Jude 1:6, 9[2], 10, 17, 20; Rev 1:17; 2:2, 4, 9, 14, 20, 21, 24; 3:1, 8, 9; 6:6; 9:4, 5, 6[2]; 10:4, 7, 9, 10; 11:2, 11, 18; 12:5, 8, 11, 12, 14, 16; 13:3; 16:9; 17:7, 11, 12; 19:10, 12; 20:6; 21:8, 27[2]; 22:3, 9; Tob 1:6, 11, 15, 18, 19, 21; 2:10, 14[2]; 3:10[3], 15; 4:14, 17, 19[2]; 5:2, 3, 4, 8, 10[4], 12, 18, 19; 6:4, 5, 15, 16; 7:10[2], 11[2]; 8:3, 7, 9, 12, 16, 20; 10:6, 8, 9; 12:7, 8, 10, 11, 17, 18, 19; 13:5, 9, 12; 14:4, 5[2], 7, 10[2], 11; Jdt 1:11[2]; 2:11[2], 13; 5:18, 19, 21; 7:10, 27, 30, 31; 8:13, 20[2], 23, 27, 29, 30; 9:11, 14; 10:12, 16, 23; 11:3, 7, 10, 11, 17, 23; 12:2[2]; 13:2, 14; 14:5, 15; 15:2; 16:5, 6, 15, 16, 22; AdE 1:8, 12, 16, 19; 2:20; 3:4; 4:4, 14; 5:9, 13; 9:15, 16, 18, 25; 12:6; 13:2, 14[2]; 14:3, 8, 11, 14[2]; 15:5; 16:3, 4, 12, 15[2], 23, 24; Wis 1:6, 16; 2:11, 21, 24; 3:1, 3, 10, 16; 4:3, 7, 9, 18; 5:7, 13, 14, 15; 6:6, 8, 22; 7:9, 12, 27, 30; 8:16, 21; 9:16; 10:3, 8, 13, 19; 11:10, 19, 20, 23; 12:8[2], 10, 26; 13:2, 10, 13; 14:3, 8, 22, 24, 30, 31; 15:1, 2, 7, 9[2], 12, 14, 17, 19; 16:7, 10, 12, 14, 18, 26; 17:4, 12, 14, 21; 18:1[2], 10, 20, 22; 19:1, 5, 14, 15; Sir Pr:T[2]; 1:8, 25; 2:17; 3:9, 20; 4:25; 5:11, 12; 6:6, 8, 10, 12, 19; 7:25, 26, 34; 8:8, 12, 13; 9:13; 10:3, 20, 23, 24; 11:3, 5, 11, 12, 21; 12:4, 5, 7, 9, 15, 16[2]; 13:4, 21, 22[2], 26; 16:4, 11, 20; 17:2, 17, 32; 18:13, 30; 19:6, 25, 26, 27; 20:7, 12, 13, 25; 21:1, 6, 10, 12, 16, 20, 22, 23, 25, 26; 22:4, 6, 11, 12, 22, 26; 24:34; 25:10, 13[2], 14[2]; 26:6, 23, 24, 25, 26; 27:11, 12, 17, 21, 23, 24, 28; 28:17, 18; 29:5, 7, 14, 20; 32:3, 7, 12, 13, 15, 19; 33:1, 2, 12, 18, 31[2]; 34:3, 11, 13, 28; 35:16; 36:5, 12, 25, 26, 31; 37:1, 4, 7, 12, 15, 25, 31; 38:9, 19, 34; 39:23, 24, 25, 27;

40:8, 12, 17, 18, 19[2], 20, 21, 22, 23, 24, 25, 26, 29, 30; 41:11, 13; 43:4, 27, 32; 44:9, 10, 14; 45:13, 22; 47:19, 22; 48:15, 16, 20; 49:16; 51:27, 28; Bar 1:15, 22; 2:6, 18, 22, 24, 30; 3:5, 18, 20, 32; 4:6, 11, 17, 23, 25; 5:6; LtJ 6:6, 8, 14, 15, 20, 25, 28, 45, 51, 55, 63; Aza 1:19, 26; Sus 1:10, 14, 41, 57; Bel 1:4, 5, 9, 19, 26, 32, 34; 1Mc 1:30, 62; 2:19, 34, 36, 63; 3:7, 17, 19, 21, 43, 60; 4:3, 6, 8, 18, 28; 5:3, 9, 18, 19, 41, 42, 44, 47, 48, 62, 68; 6:3, 6, 12, 21, 31, 42, 46, 53, 62, 63; 7:3, 10, 11, 16, 29, 34; 8:10, 12, 15; 9:8, 9, 10, 22, 33, 36, 47, 55, 60, 65; 10:9, 56, 61, 75, 81, 84; 11:3, 5, 18, 21, 22, 42, 46, 53[2], 61, 64, 68; 12:13, 29, 30, 40, 48, 50; 13:6, 17, 19, 20, 22, 33, 46, 47, 50; 15:27, 33, 36, 39; 16:3, 9, 21; 2Mc 1:20[2], 32, 36; 2:6, 26, 31; 3:4, 6, 8, 13, 24, 28; 4:5, 19, 20, 24, 25, 32, 35, 41, 45, 50; 5:6[2], 18, 19[2], 27; 6:12[2], 13, 14, 19, 23, 30, 31; 7:5, 9, 14[2], 16[2], 19, 24, 27, 29, 30, 31, 34, 36; 8:16[2], 18; 9:4, 5, 7, 15, 18, 23; 10:4, 16, 20, 28, 35; 11:4, 9, 24, 36; 12:2, 8, 15, 20, 22, 28, 30, 35, 45; 13:3, 4, 10, 21; 14:3, 5, 17, 23, 26, 30, 43, 44; 15:2, 5, 7, 8, 17, 21, 26, 36; 1Es 1:28, 42, 51; 2:19, 21; 3:3, 12; 4:3, 6, 11, 35, 38, 39; 5:38, 70, 72; 6:15, 17; 7:11; 8:7, 80, 87, 92; 9:11; Man 1:8; Pm 151:5, 7; 3Mc 1:2, 3, 11, 15, 26, 29; 2:7, 16, 24, 26, 30, 32; 3:1, 4, 5, 7, 11, 15, 17, 18, 20, 22, 23, 27; 4:2, 14, 15, 17, 21; 5:7, 11, 14, 19, 20, 22, 25, 27, 30, 39, 50; 6:12, 15, 18, 36; 7:6, 9, 10, 16; 2Es 1:7, 12, 16, 23, 30, 32; 2:1, 3, 4, 27, 28, 43; 3:7, 9, 11, 16, 22, 25, 36; 4:9, 16, 20, 23, 25, 28, 34, 38, 46, 50, 52; 5:4, 10, 12[2], 15, 34, 41, 47, 52; 6:52, 58; 7:4, 7, 13, 17, 18, 42, 46, 47, 48, 50, 51, 54, 56, 64, 65[2], 67, 71, 74, 76, 77, 80, 113, 118, 119, 120, 121, 122, 123, 125, 128, 130; 8:1, 2[2], 3, 9, 15, 26, 27, 28, 29, 30, 31, 34, 39, 44, 45, 47, 48, 51, 60, 62, 63; 9:11, 13, 19, 22, 24[2], 32, 35, 37; 10:1, 3, 4[2], 8, 12, 13, 18, 20, 27, 42, 55, 58; 11:3, 4[2], 9, 10, 21, 24, 26, 34, 41; 12:12, 15, 17, 18, 21, 26, 27, 28, 34, 39, 48, 51; 13:7, 10, 11, 18, 19, 35, 41, 48; 14:20, 24, 31, 36, 39, 43, 46; 15:11, 19, 39; 16:25, 26, 38, 71, 74; 4Mc 1:6[2], 8, 10, 12, 30; 2:4, 14, 17, 22; 3:1[2], 2, 3, 4, 5, 10, 11, 15; 4:3, 8, 20, 24; 5:23, 26, 27, 28, 38; 6:5, 9, 16, 33, 35; 7:9, 18, 19; 8:2, 5, 9, 11, 15[2], 27; 9:9, 10, 15, 22, 28, 32; 10:2, 11, 13, 14, 18; 11:6, 14, 27; 12:5, 7, 14, 18; 13:3, 27; 14:1, 5, 9, 20; 15:9, 12, 23, 28; 16:2, 4; 17:20; 18:2, 3, 7, 23

BY (3455)

Ge 3:19; 8:19; 9:6, 11, 26; 10:5, 20, 31; 12:9; 13:3, 18; 14:13, 15, 19; 16:2, 7; 17:16; 18:1, 3, 8, 19; 19:16, 36; 20:3; 21:23; 22:13, 16, 18; 24:3, 11, 13, 14, 30, 43, 48; 25:16[2]; 27:40, 42; 30:27; 31:15, 24, 31, 39[3], 40[2], 46, 53; 32:16; 33:8; 34:2, 7, 30; 36:30, 40; 37:28; 38:18, 20, 21; 39:16; 41:1, 3, 6, 23, 27, 32; 42:33; 43:32[3]; 45:1; 48:20; 49:17, 19, 22, 24[2], 25[2]; Ex 2:15; 3:19; 4:4, 26; 6:1[2], 3, 17, 25, 26; 7:4[2], 11, 15, 17, 22; 8:7, 18, 29; 9:15; 12:16, 26, 42, 51; 13:3, 14, 16, 17, 18, 21[4], 22[2]; 14:2, 9[2], 21; 15:13, 16[3], 27; 16:3[2], 21; 17:1; 20:26; 21:13, 14; 22:13, 31; 23:30; 25:14; 26:9[2]; 27:21; 28:28; 29:9, 18, 25, 28, 33, 41, 43; 30:20, 24, 25, 35, 37; 31:2; 32:13, 18[2]; 33:12, 17, 21, 22[2]; 34:7; 35:29, 30, 35[5]; 36:16[2]; 37:29; 38:24, 25, 26; 39:21; 40:38[2]; Lev 1:9, 13, 17[2]; 2:2, 3, 9, 10, 11, 16; 3:3, 5, 9, 11, 14, 16; 4:13, 22, 27, 35; 5:3, 12, 15, 17; 6:2[2], 4[2], 17, 18; 7:5, 24, 25, 30, 35; 8:21, 28; 9:13; 10:5, 12, 13, 15; 11:24; 15:31; 16:21; 17:15; 18:5, 11, 24, 30; 19:12, 16, 29, 31; 20:25[3]; 21:6, 21; 22:4, 5[2], 8[2], 11, 16, 22, 27; 23:8, 13, 18, 25, 27, 36[2], 37; 24:7, 9; 25:53; 26:7, 8, 17, 26, 43[2]; 27:3, 25, 26; Nu 1:2, 3, 17, 18, 20, 22, 24, 26, 28, 30, 32, 34, 36, 38, 40, 42, 45, 47, 52; 2:2, 3, 9, 10, 16, 17, 18, 24, 25, 31, 32[2], 34[2]; 3:15[2], 17, 18, 19, 20[2], 39, 47, 48, 49, 50; 4:2, 22[2], 29, 32, 34, 36, 37, 38, 40, 42, 44, 45, 46, 49; 6:4, 11; 9:16[2], 23; 10:12, 13, 14, 18, 22, 25, 28, 34; 11:17; 13:29; 14:3, 14[2], 18, 25, 36, 37, 43; 15:3, 10, 13, 14, 23, 25; 16:39, 49; 18:17, 32; 19:16; 20:13; 21:1, 4, 7, 20, 22; 22:36; 24:2; 25:9, 11, 18; 26:2, 3, 12, 15, 20, 23, 26, 28, 37, 38, 41, 42[2], 44, 48, 50, 55, 57, 63[2], 64; 27:21; 28:2, 3, 6, 8, 13, 19, 24; 29:6, 13, 36; 30:2, 3, 4[2], 5, 6[2], 7, 8[2], 9, 10, 11, 14; 31:8, 12, 17, 18, 35; 33:1, 2[2], 10, 48, 49, 50, 54; 34:2, 13, 14[2]; 35:1, 27[2], 33; 36:2[2], 13; Dt 1:2, 9, 12, 17, 22, 28, 33[2], 42; 2:8, 22, 24; 3:11; 4:16, 25, 28, 34[5], 37; 5:31; 6:13; 7:12, 19, 22, 25; 8:3[4], 6[2], 11; 9:16, 18, 29[2]; 10:20; 11:10, 11; 13:1, 2, 3, 5, 18; 15:5, 20; 16:1[2]; 17:3; 18:22; 19:9, 14; 20:19; 21:5, 22; 22:14, 21, 26; 24:8, 13; 25:11; 26:6; 27:26; 28:1, 10, 13, 15, 34, 45, 68; 29:12, 14, 23; 30:10, 16; 31:18; 32:22, 27, 51; 33:13, 29; Jos 2:12, 15; 3:3, 10; 5:1, 13; 6:21; 7:14[4], 16, 17, 18; 8:3, 22, 24; 9:15, 18, 19; 10:10, 18; 11:7; 13:14, 16; 14:2; 15:3, 4, 8, 10; 16:1, 5, 8; 17:2[2]; 18:9, 20; 19:50, 51; 20:3, 5, 9; 21:3, 4, 5, 6, 8, 9; 22:9, 10, 16, 19, 29; 23:7; 24:12[2]; Jdg 2:18; 3:4, 15; 4:7, 16; 5:10, 17, 19; 6:27[2], 31, 36, 37; 7:22; 8:11, 13, 26; 9:6, 9, 25, 32, 34; 11:27, 31; 15:18[2]; 16:26; 17:2; 18:16, 17; 19:29; 20:9; 21:7, 22, 24; Ru 2:20, 21; 3:10; 4:1, 12; 1Sa 1:3, 7; 2:3, 9, 16, 20, 28, 29, 33; 3:14, 21; 4:2, 13, 18; 6:3, 9; 7:16; 10:2, 19[2], 20, 21[4]; 11:7, 9; 12:23; 13:8; 14:4, 6[2], 33, 34, 36, 41; 15:13; 16:9, 20; 17:23, 26, 35, 43, 47; 18:10, 25; 19:5; 20:7, 9, 12, 17, 25[2]; 21:6; 22:13[2], 15; 23:7, 21; 24:11, 21; 25:16[2], 22, 33, 34; 26:7; 27:1; 28:6[3], 8, 10, 15[3], 17; 29:1, 2[2]; 30:15, 24; 31:3; 2Sa 1:12; 2:5, 15, 16, 17; 3:29; 4:7; 6:2, 22[2]; 7:14, 23; 8:7; 10:8, 15, 19; 11:14; 12:14, 25, 28; 13:31, 32, 34; 14:26; 15:3, 16, 17, 18, 23, 36; 16:23[2]; 17:11, 16, 22; 18:4[2], 7, 18, 23, 24; 19:7; 20:9, 11, 12; 21:10[2], 22; 22:30[2]; 23:15, 16; 24:16; 1Ki 1:6, 9, 17, 27, 30; 2:8, 23, 42; 3:5; 4:20; 5:9[2], 11; 6:8, 12; 8:32[2], 44; 9:8; 10:25; 11:20, 24, 38; 12:15[2]; 13:1[2], 2[2], 5, 9[2], 10, 17[2], 18, 25[2], 32; 14:18; 15:29; 16:7, 12, 26, 34; 17:1, 3, 5, 16, 20; 18:6[2], 24; 19:2, 11, 19; 20:14[2], 39; 21:25; 22:8, 28, 38; 2Ki 2:1, 7; 3:8[2]; 5:1, 20; 6:14; 8:21; 9:25, 27, 36; 10:33; 11:14; 12:6; 14:7, 9, 12, 25, 27; 16:15; 17:4, 13[2]; 18:17, 30, 32; 19:7, 10, 23, 28, 33[2]; 20:11; 21:10; 23:3, 11, 15, 16, 26; 24:2; 25:4[3], 30; 1Ch 2:18[2]; 3:1[2], 3[2], 5; 4:38, 41; 5:7, 10, 17; 6:15, 61, 65[2]; 7:4, 5, 7, 9, 40; 8:9, 11; 9:1, 22; 10:3; 11:3, 14, 17, 18; 13:6; 14:11; 16:7; 18:7; 19:9, 16, 19; 20:8; 21:12, 15, 25; 23:24; 24:5, 19; 26:13; 28:9; 29:5; 2Ch 2:16; 6:23[2], 34; 7:6, 14, 21; 9:24; 10:15[2]; 12:7, 15; 13:5; 15:2, 4, 15; 16:14; 17:14; 18:7, 27; 19:5; 20:11, 16; 21:9; 22:7; 23:13; 24:5, 6, 11, 21; 25:5, 8, 18, 22; 26:11, 15, 19; 28:15; 29:9, 15, 27; 30:12, 21[2]; 31:2, 13, 15, 16[2], 17, 19[2]; 32:8, 11[2]; 35:4[2], 6, 18[4]; 36:13, 15, 21, 22; Ezr 1:1, 4; 2:61; 3:4; 4:23; 5:5, 17; 6:9, 13, 14[2], 21[2]; 7:14, 23; 8:15, 20; 9:8, 11; 10:8, 16, 17; Ne 1:3, 10; 2:3, 13[3], 15[3]; 3:7; 4:22[2]; 5:8; 6:13, 18; 7:5, 63; 8:14, 18; 9:12[2], 19[3], 29, 30; 10:29, 34[2], 35; 12:37, 39[2], 44; 13:5, 18, 26, 27; Est 1:8, 12, 15, 20; 2:14, 15, 20; 3:13, 14, 15; 5:12; 8:5, 10, 11, 14; 9:21; Job 4:9[2]; 9:11, 26; 15:30; 16:12; 18:8, 9, 12, 13; 19:20; 20:26, 29; 22:16; 23:7; 24:1, 16, 22; 26:8, 12[2], 13; 27:18; 28:4, 5, 9, 25; 29:3; 30:15, 18; 31:9, 28, 30, 33, 35; 33:26; 34:20; 36:12, 15[2], 21, 31; 37:10, 12; 38:2; 39:26; 42:5; Ps 1:3; 5:10; 10:10; 15:4; 17:3, 4, 13, 14; 18:29[2]; 19:11; 20:6; 22:2[2], 6[2]; 30:7; 32:4; 33:6[2], 16[2], 17; 34:6; 37:22[2], 23, 24, 36; 39:10; 41:11; 42:8; 44:3; 50:5; 54:1[2]; 55:3; 57:1; 59:11; 63:11; 65:5, 6, 8; 66:7; 73:19; 74:13; 77:20; 78:18, 26, 64; 79:4; 89:17, 35, 41, 49; 90:7[2]; 91:5; 92:2, 4; 94:20; 101:8; 104:12; 105:39; 106:22, 39, 46; 107:7, 38; 110:7; 111:2, 4; 115:15; 119:9, 91, 93, 128; 121:6[2]; 129:8; 134:1; 136:5; 137:1; 144:13[2]; Pr 3:19[2], 20; 5:19, 20; 6:2[2]; 8:15, 16; 9:11, 15; 10:2; 11:5, 6, 9, 11[2]; 12:3, 13; 13:10, 11; 14:4, 20, 32; 15:13; 16:6[2], 12; 19:7[2]; 20:1, 11[2], 15, 17, 18[2], 24, 28; 21:6; 24:3[2], 4, 6, 16, 24[2], 30[2]; 26:6, 9, 17; 27:9, 21; 28:8; 29:4, 15, 19; 30:17[2]; Ecc 1:11, 13; 2:21; 3:15; 5:1, 8, 13; 7:3, 23, 26; 9:15; 10:8, 9[2], 12; 12:11; SS 2:7; 3:5, 8; 7:4; Isa 1:7, 20, 27[2]; 3:5[2], 15[2], 25; 4:1, 4[2], 5[2], 6; 5:11, 16[2]; 7:15; 8:2, 4; 9:16; 10:13[2]; 11:3[2]; 13:15; 14:19; 16:1; 18:2; 19:7[2]; 20:1; 21:8; 22:2; 27:8[2], 9, 12; 28:18, 19[3]; 29:6, 13; 30:26; 31:4, 8; 32:8; 34:8; 36:2, 15, 18; 37:7, 10, 24, 29, 34[2]; 38:8[2], 16; 40:17, 26, 27; 41:25; 42:6, 16[2]; 43:1, 7; 44:4, 5, 21, 24; 45:3, 4, 17, 23; 46:3; 48:1[2]; 49:7, 10; 50:2, 4; 51:18; 53:3, 4, 5, 8; 54:13; 60:19[2]; 62:2, 8[2]; 63:19; 64:11; 65:1[2], 16[2], 23; 66:16[3]; Jer 2:8, 17, 18[2], 36[2]; 3:2; 4:2[2]; 5:7; 6:5, 29; 7:10, 11, 14, 30; 8:3; 10:3, 8, 12[3], 14; 11:17, 21, 22[2]; 12:16[2]; 13:5, 24; 14:9, 12[3], 15, 18; 15:16; 16:4[2]; 17:4, 8[2], 19[2], 20, 21, 24, 25; 18:16, 21[2]; 19:4, 7[2], 8; 20:4; 21:9[3]; 22:5, 8, 13[2]; 23:6, 9, 13, 23, 27, 32; 25:29, 33; 27:3, 5, 8, 13[3]; 29:3, 22; 30:11; 31:9, 21, 32, 35[2]; 32:7, 17[2], 30, 36[3]; 33:16, 24; 34:4, 15[2], 17; 36:30[2]; 38:2[3], 4, 6, 9, 11, 13, 23; 39:4, 18; 42:17[3], 22[3]; 44:12[4], 15, 18[2], 25, 26, 27[2]; 46:2, 6, 10, 18, 28; 48:19, 20; 49:9, 13, 15, 17; 50:1, 5, 13, 17; 51:5, 13, 14, 15[3], 17, 42; 52:7[3], 34; La 1:12, 14; 2:21; 4:9[2]; 5:12; Eze 1:1, 3; 3:15, 23; 4:10, 11, 14, 16[2]; 5:12[2], 14; 6:9, 11[3], 12; 7:15; 8:3; 10:15, 20, 22; 11:10, 24; 12:3, 4, 7; 13:19; 14:3, 7, 13, 14, 20; 16:6, 8, 51; 17:5, 8, 14, 15, 21; 18:2, 3; 19:10; 20:3, 11, 13, 21, 25, 27, 31[2], 43, 47; 22:4[2], 12; 23:25[2]; 24:6, 21; 25:13, 14; 26:6, 18; 27:34; 28:4, 5, 10, 18, 23; 30:5, 6, 10, 12, 16, 17, 18; 31:14, 17, 18; 32:12, 20, 21, 22, 23, 24, 25, 26, 28, 29, 30[2], 31, 32; 33:12, 15, 19, 22, 27[2], 30; 34:13; 36:34; 37:1, 18; 38:17; 39:15, 23; 40:7, 28; 41:6, 7; 42:3, 10, 15, 16, 17, 18, 19; 43:3, 4, 7[2], 8[2], 13, 16, 17; 44:2[2], 3[2], 4, 25, 31; 45:2; 46:2[2], 8[2], 9[6], 13, 14, 15, 16; 47:2, 13, 15; 48:30, 33; Da 2:3, 34, 45; 4:17[2], 30; 7:2, 7, 8; 8:2, 16, 25[2], 27; 9:1, 3, 10[2], 12; 11:11, 26, 31, 33, 37, 39; 12:7; Hos 1:2, 7[6]; 2:17; 4:5[2]; 6:5[2]; 7:3[2], 16; 12:13[2]; 13:16; Am 2:4; 4:2; 5:19[2]; 6:8, 13; 7:8, 11, 17[2]; 8:2, 7, 14; 9:10, 12; Ob 1:5; Jnh 3:7; Mic 2:5, 8, 13; 5:7, 8; Na 1:3, 6; 3:8; Hab 1:11, 16; 2:4, 10, 12; 3:10, 11; Zep 1:5; 2:9, 12, 15; 3:11; Hag 1:1, 3; 2:1, 10, 13, 22; Zec 3:5; 4:3, 6[3], 14; 5:4; 6:13; 7:7, 12; 9:4; 11:13; 12:12[5], 13[4], 14[2]; 14:4, 5; Mal 1:1, 7[2], 13; 2:8, 14, 17[2]; 3:14[2]; Mt 1:3, 5[2], 6, 22; 2:5, 6, 12, 14, 15, 16; 3:6, 13, 14; 4:1[2], 4[2], 13, 15, 18; 5:34, 35[2], 36; 6:1, 2, 5, 18[2], 27; 7:16, 20; 8:24; 9:25, 34; 10:22; 11:2, 7, 12, 19, 27; 12:24, 27[2], 28, 33, 37[2]; 14:8, 13, 23, 24[2]; 15:22; 17:1, 6; 18:7, 16, 19, 28; 19:12; 20:17, 23, 30[2]; 21:19, 23, 24, 27; 22:31, 43; 23:5, 16[4], 18[4], 20[3], 21[3], 22[3]; 24:9, 15; 25:34; 26:4, 12, 24, 52; 27:4, 12, 35, 39, 66; 28:13; Mk 1:5, 9, 13, 31; 2:3; 3:22; 5:7, 18, 21, 41; 6:2, 7, 31, 32, 48; 7:15, 31; 8:23, 31; 9:2, 27, 41; 10:46; 11:18, 20, 28, 29, 33; 12:36; 13:13; 14:1, 21, 66; 15:29; 16:11, 17, 20; Lk 1:2, 9, 26, 29, 45, 77, 78; 2:8, 21, 26, 27, 39; 3:7, 14, 16, 19, 20; 4:1, 2, 4, 15; 5:17; 6:44; 7:24, 30[2], 35; 8:14, 29, 36, 54; 9:7, 8[2], 22, 47; 10:22, 31[2], 32, 40[2], 41; 11:15, 18, 19[2], 20; 12:1, 25; 14:8[2]; 16:5, 9, 15, 16, 22, 23; 17:1, 20, 25; 18:5, 11, 31, 35, 36, 37; 19:15, 22, 48; 20:2, 8, 20, 26[2]; 21:16[2], 17, 19, 20, 24[2], 25; 22:22, 28; 23:5, 10, 35; 24:12; Jn 1:19, 36; 3:2; 4:6[2]; 5:2; 6:13, 15[2], 44, 45, 65; 7:24, 36; 8:9, 15, 22, 33; 10:1[2], 2, 3, 9; 12:38; 13:35; 14:21; 15:3, 4, 8; 16:2, 17, 18, 30; 17:4; 19:17, 39; 20:7; 21:1, 19; Ac 1:3, 7, 10; 2:22, 23, 43, 46, 47; 3:7, 12, 16, 26; 4:7[2], 10, 11, 12, 25; 5:15, 16, 26, 30, 34, 39; 7:24, 53; 8:3, 6; 9:8, 22, 25; 10:6, 11, 14, 17[2], 22[2], 32, 36, 38, 39, 41, 42; 11:4, 5, 8, 14, 28, 30; 12:23; 13:4, 11, 27, 33, 39[2], 45; 14:3, 5; 15:3, 4, 8, 9, 10, 20, 27, 33; 16:2, 4, 6, 8, 13, 14, 16; 17:13, 24, 25, 29, 31[2]; 18:3, 18, 28; 19:13, 26; 20:3, 4[5], 9, 13, 35; 21:1, 19, 35; 22:4, 12, 20, 24, 25, 30; 23:10, 12, 14, 19, 21[2], 23, 27[2]; 24:8, 9, 26, 27; 25:14; 26:6, 7, 8, 11, 18, 23; 27:2, 9, 16, 18, 23, 38, 41; 28:3, 8, 16, 24; Ro 1:4, 9, 10, 12, 17, 18; 2:5, 7, 12, 23; 3:4, 6, 8, 20[2], 21, 24, 25, 27[3], 28[2], 31[2]; 4:1, 2, 11; 5:1, 9, 10, 19[2]; 6:2, 4[2], 15; 7:2, 5, 7, 13; 8:3[2], 13, 14, 20; 9:1, 10, 12[2], 14; 10:5, 20; 11:1, 5, 6, 11, 24, 31; 12:1, 2, 3, 20, 21; 13:1; 14:15, 20; 15:4[2], 13, 15[2], 16, 18, 19[2], 24, 28, 30[2], 32; 16:18; 1Co 1:1, 9, 10, 11, 26; 2:12, 13[2]; 4:3[2]; 6:2, 12, 14; 7:5, 6, 25; 8:3, 11; 9:5, 14, 22; 10:9, 10; 11:32; 12:3[2], 9[2], 11; 14:21[2], 24[2], 31; 15:10, 32; 2Co 1:1, 4, 11, 12[2], 22; 2:6, 7, 11; 3:2, 3; 4:1, 2, 16; 5:4, 7[2]; 6:6; 7:6, 7[2], 9, 13; 8:5, 9, 11, 19; 9:8, 13[2]; 10:1, 2, 11, 12; 11:3, 7, 8, 9; 12:1, 16; 13:1, 4[2]; Gal 1:1, 11, 22; 2:13, 15, 16[4], 20; 3:2[2], 5[2], 8, 11[2], 12, 13, 17, 19, 24; 4:2, 8, 9, 16, 22[2]; 5:4, 5, 15, 16, 18, 22, 25[2]; 6:14; Eph 1:1; 2:3, 5, 8, 11[3], 13; 3:3, 5, 7, 20; 4:14[3], 16, 22; 5:13, 26[2]; Php 1:6, 14, 20[3], 27, 28; 2:16, 19; 3:10, 21; 4:6; Col 1:1, 20, 23; 2:11, 18, 19; 1Th 1:4, 6; 2:4, 16, 17; 3:3; 4:9, 15[2]; 5:27; 2Th 1:10, 11; 2:2[3], 8, 13[2], 15[3]; 1Ti 1:1, 4, 18, 19; 3:7, 16; 4:1, 3, 4, 5[2], 14; 6:2, 9, 21; 2Ti 1:1; 2:15, 18, 26; 3:6[2], 16; 4:17; Tit 1:3, 11, 16; 3:5, 7; Heb 1:1, 2, 3; 2:3, 4[2], 9, 15, 18; 3:4, 13; 4:2; 5:4, 5, 10, 12, 14; 6:13[2], 16, 17; 7:7, 8[2], 23; 8:9; 9:7, 8, 19, 24, 26; 10:1, 10, 14, 19, 20, 29[2], 38; 11:2, 3[2], 4, 5, 7[3], 8, 9, 11, 12, 17, 20, 21, 22, 23[2], 24, 27, 28, 29, 30, 31, 35, 37; 12:1, 5, 11, 28; 13:2, 4, 9[3], 11, 12, 20; Jas 1:6, 13[2], 14[2], 18, 27; 2:9, 12, 17, 18, 21, 22, 24[2], 25[2]; 3:4, 5, 6, 7, 13; 5:4, 12[3], 19; 1Pe 1:2[2], 3, 5, 7, 12, 22; 2:2, 4, 14, 15, 24; 3:1, 3[2], 5; 4:2[2]; 2Pe 1:3, 17, 21[2]; 2:6, 7, 8, 17; 3:1, 2, 5[2], 7, 14; 1Jn 2:3, 5, 19, 20; 3:16, 19, 24[2]; 4:2, 13; 5:2, 6, 10; 2Jn 1:4; 3Jn 1:15; Jude 1:7, 10[2], 12, 23[2]; Rev 1:1, 5; 2:11; 3:18; 4:11; 5:9; 6:8, 13; 9:18[2], 20; 10:6; 12:6, 11[2]; 13:14[2]; 16:9; 17:17; 18:19, 23; 19:20, 21; 21:17, 24, 25; 22:14; Tob 1:6, 9; 2:9, 10; 3:7, 17[3]; 4:13; 5:20; 6:2, 8, 13, 18; 7:12; 8:5; 10:1, 13; 11:5; 12:18; 14:4; Jdt 1:12; 2:12[2], 15; 4:7, 8; 5:14, 15, 18, 21; 6:1, 12; 7:27, 30, 31; 8:3, 9, 16, 18, 33; 9:8, 10[2]; 10:10, 13, 15, 19; 11:7[2], 11, 12; 12:4; 13:14, 15, 18; 15:2; 16:5, 6; AdE 1:6, 15; 2:14, 23; 3:7[2], 13; 4:4; 6:4; 8:1, 10; 9:1, 32; 10:1, 3; 11:1; 13:2, 6[2]; 14:14; 16:4, 5, 6, 9, 11, 14, 15[2], 17; Wis 1:2, 8, 12[2], 16; 2:2[2], 4[2], 7, 16; 4:1[2], 4[2], 8, 10; 5:9, 11[3], 14[2]; 6:12[2], 22, 25; 7:30; 8:3; 9:1, 2, 4, 18; 10:4, 8, 11, 17; 11:1, 5, 8, 16[2], 19, 20[3], 25; 12:2, 6, 8, 9, 10, 27; 13:1; 14:6, 7, 17, 20, 24, 31; 15:12, 18; 16:1, 5, 7[2], 8, 9[2], 10, 16[3], 18, 22, 27[2]; 17:3, 9, 11[2], 13, 15[2]; 18:5, 7, 8[2], 12, 21, 22[3]; 19:1, 8, 17; Sir Pr:T; 3:8, 10, 16, 17, 20, 27; 4:17; 6:2, 8, 10, 22; 7:15; 9:4, 8[2], 13, 17; 11:10, 20, 28; 12:2[2], 5, 12, 15; 13:7, 11, 21[2]; 14:7, 14, 15[2], 27; 15:13; 18:15, 32, 33; 19:1, 29; 20:13, 21, 27; 21:24; 22:5, 13, 16, 23; 23:8, 22, 23; 25:21; 28:18; 29:1; 30:2, 13, 19; 31:5, 7, 10, 15, 25, 31; 32:18; 33:8, 17; 34:6, 30, 31; 36:17; 38:2, 7, 27[2], 28; 39:13; 40:6[2], 16; 41:2; 42:8, 15; 43:13, 18, 23, 26; 44:3, 4[2], 12, 18; 45:1, 3; 46:13, 14, 15[2]; 47:6; 48:2, 3, 5, 9, 22, 24; 49:1, 2; 50:5, 8, 12[2]; 51:2, 26; Bar 1:4, 22; 2:8, 15, 20, 24, 25, 26, 28; 3:32; 4:7, 24, 26, 27, 35; 5:6; LtJ 6:1, 2, 8, 18[2], 21, 29[2], 43[2], 45, 47; Aza 1:5, 8; Sus 1:18; Bel 1:36[2]; 1Mc 1:44, 48, 51, 57, 63; 2:9, 17, 20, 22, 64; 3:3, 6, 7, 18[3], 29, 36; 4:1, 5, 15, 30, 31, 58; 5:5, 16, 28[2], 48, 51; 6:2, 23, 33, 37, 38, 41[2], 59, 63; 7:1, 5, 37, 38, 46; 8:4, 6; 9:2, 12, 13, 33, 68; 10:37, 53, 82, 85; 11:1[2], 8, 18, 67; 12:26, 33; 13:4, 20, 21, 29; 14:34, 40, 43; 15:11, 17[2], 33; 16:3; 2Mc 1:11, 13[2], 20, 36; 2:23; 3:9, 24, 32, 34; 4:3, 7, 9, 15, 20[2], 22, 24, 26, 28, 39, 42, 44; 5:8, 11, 15, 22; 6:1, 4, 5, 12, 21, 22, 27; 7:1, 7, 14, 34, 36, 37; 8:2[2], 8, 10, 14, 15, 16, 20, 35, 36[2]; 9:2, 4, 28; 10:2, 4, 5, 8[2], 13, 20, 21, 24[2]; 11:12, 16, 17, 30; 12:4, 6, 9, 13, 16, 18, 22[2], 35, 43; 13:4, 7, 13; 14:5, 15, 17, 18, 21, 27, 29, 31, 40; 15:11, 13, 17[2], 21, 24, 27, 36; 1Es 1:4, 15, 21, 27, 47, 48, 57; 2:1, 6, 12, 15; 4:45, 63; 5:37, 38, 73; 6:4, 14, 22; 7:4, 5; 8:3, 6, 14, 24, 27, 47, 61, 80, 82, 87; 9:16, 17, 39, 55; Man 1:3; Pm 151:6; 3Mc 1:1, 2, 3, 7[2], 9, 11, 23; 2:4, 6, 9, 13, 15, 17, 22[2], 24, 25, 28, 29, 31, 32; 3:1, 2[2], 4, 14, 15, 17[2], 18, 19, 21, 23[2], 24; 4:4, 5, 6, 9[2]; 5:2, 11, 12[2], 15, 17, 20[2], 27[2], 30, 34, 42, 43, 45, 48[3]; 6:4, 5, 9, 10, 12, 24, 34, 40; 7:20, 21; 2Es 2:19; 3:14; 4:11, 37[2], 45, 46, 48[2]; 5:7, 10, 27; 6:29, 32, 52; 7:9, 42, 85, 95, 139; 8:6, 9, 14, 43, 44; 9:7; 10:22; 12:28; 13:14, 37, 38[3], 43; 14:21, 42; 15:3, 13[2], 32, 39, 57[2], 60, 61; 16:7, 16, 22[2], 30, 31, 58, 73, 77[2], 78; 4Mc 1:9, 11, 12, 17, 19, 20, 24, 30, 34[2], 35[2]; 2:2, 3, 9, 17; 3:2, 4, 6, 18[2]; 4:5, 13[3], 21, 24, 26; 5:4, 6, 10, 12, 16, 22, 25, 33, 38; 6:1, 6, 11, 15, 16, 19, 21[2], 24, 30; 7:2[2], 4, 6, 9, 12, 14, 20, 21; 8:1, 4, 8[2], 9, 15; 9:5[2], 7, 9, 20, 22, 30, 31, 32; 10:1, 5[2], 8, 15[3]; 11:3; 12:2, 9, 14; 13:2, 3, 5, 7, 12, 24; 14:5, 6, 15, 16, 17, 18; 15:13, 14, 15, 16, 32; 16:4, 14, 17, 24; 17:20; 18:3, 4, 11

COULD (305)

Ge 13:6[2]; 27:1; 36:7; 37:4; 38:20, 23; 39:9; 41:8, 24; 43:7, 32; 45:1, 3, 26; 48:10; Ex 2:3; 7:21, 24; 8:18; 9:11, 15; 10:23[2]; 12:39; 15:23; 35:24; Lev 11:34[2]; Nu 9:6; 22:18, 41; 35:17, 18, 23; Dt 2:21, 22; 4:42[2]; 7:25; 32:30; Jos 15:63; 17:12; 20:9; 22:28; Jdg 1:19; 2:14; 6:5; 9:41; 10:16; 12:6; 14:14; 16:6[2], 10, 13; 17:8; 20:16; Ru 3:14; 1Sa 3:2; 4:15; 10:21; 23:13; 29:4; 2Sa 1:10; 2:22; 3:11; 13:13; 17:17, 20; 1Ki 1:1; 5:3; 8:5, 8, 11; 10:3, 29; 13:4; 14:4; 2Ki 2:12; 3:26; 4:40; 5:12; 6:30; 7:2, 19; 10:4; 16:5; 1Ch 12:1, 2; 21:30; 2Ch 5:6, 9, 14; 7:2, 7; 9:2; 13:7; 20:25; 25:15; 26:13; 29:34; 30:3; Ezr 2:59; 3:13; Ne 5:8; 6:13; 7:61; 8:2, 3; 13:24; Est 6:1; 9:2; Job 4:16; 9:3; 16:4[2], 5; 23:7, 17; 30:2; 31:1, 23; Ps 37:36; 55:12[2]; 78:44; 130:3; 137:4; SS 5:3[2]; Isa 7:1; 48:7; 53:8; Jer 3:5; 24:2; 33:20, 21; 44:22; 51:9; La 4:12, 17, 18; Eze 20:25; 31:8; 47:5[2]; Da 1:5; 2:35; 4:7; 5:8; 6:4[2]; 8:4, 7; 12:8; Hos 10:3; Jnh 1:13; Zec 1:21; Mt 8:28; 12:22; 16:11; 17:16, 19; 18:25; 26:9, 40; 27:24; Mk 1:45; 2:4; 3:20; 5:3; 6:5, 19; 7:24; 9:3, 10, 18, 28; 14:5, 8, 37; Lk 1:22; 6:48; 7:42; 8:19, 43, 47; 9:40, 45; 14:6; 17:6; 19:3, 23, 48; 22:23; Jn 9:33; 11:37; 12:39; 21:25; Ac 3:2; 6:10; 7:11; 8:20; 9:8; 11:17; 12:19; 13:39; 14:8; 17:6; 21:34; 22:11; 25:7, 21; 26:32; 27:12[2], 13, 15, 39, 43; Ro 3:6; 8:3; 9:3; 1Co 3:1; 12:2; 2Co 2:13; 3:7; Gal 3:21; 4:20; Php 2:30; 1Th 3:1, 5; Heb 12:20; Rev 7:1, 9; 12:14; 13:15; 14:3; 15:8; Tob 1:15, 18; 12:21; Jdt 2:20; 4:7; 5:10; Wis 10:8; 11:19[2], 20; 13:9; 14:17; 17:10; Sir 42:25; 43:27[2]; 48:12; Bar 1:6; Sus 1:14, 39; 1Mc 5:30, 44, 46; 6:3; 7:25; 9:55; 12:36; 13:29; 14:1; 2Mc 2:6; 3:5, 6; 4:6; 5:21; 6:6, 9; 8:5; 9:8[2], 10, 12; 13:13; 15:38; 1Es 5:37, 65; 6:6; 3Mc 4:11; 2Es 2:42; 5:43; 6:40, 50; 7:53, 138; 9:32; 10:54; 13:7; 4Mc 1:7; 2:6, 7, 20; 3:10; 4:7; 6:7; 13:26; 14:10

EVEN (612)

Ge 24:41; 31:30; 37:5, 8; 44:10; 45:26; 46:34; 50:20; Ex 2:19; 4:9, 10, 14; 7:19, 23; 10:24; 19:22; 34:21; Lev 11:4, 5, 6, 7; 21:11; Nu 4:20; 6:4, 7; 9:19; 14:19, 44; 33:4; Dt 1:37; 2:5, 22; 7:20; 9:8; 12:31; 13:6, 15; 17:16; 18:8; 23:2, 3; 28:54, 57, 61; 29:19; 30:4; 31:21; 32:39; 33:6; Jos 13:6; 22:17; Jdg 2:17; 6:5; 17:2; Ru 1:12[2], 17; 2:7, 13, 15, 21; 1Sa 14:15, 39; 18:4, 5; 20:15; 21:5; 2Sa 3:39; 5:6; 13:15; 14:7; 17:9, 10, 13;

18:12; **1Ki 4:**21, 25; **6:**22; **8:**27; **10:**7; **13:**33; **14:**14; **17:**20; **18:**22, 38; **2Ki 7:**2, 19; **16:**3; **21:**15; **1Ch 11:**2; **17:**17; **2Ch 1:**11; **2:**6; **6:**18; **9:**6; **15:**16; **16:**12; **22:**5; **24:**7; **26:**8; **28:**2; **30:**19; **Ezr 10:**2; **Ne 5:**15; **9:**18, 35; **13:**26; **Est 5:**3, 6, 12; **7:**2, 8; **Job 4:**18; **5:**5; **6:**10, 27; **15:**15; **16:**19; **19:**4, 7, 18; **20:**6; **22:**2, 30; **23:**3; **25:**5; **40:**8, 23; **41:**9; **Ps 15:**4; **19:**10; **23:**4; **33:**22; **41:**9; **59:**3; **68:**18; **71:**18; **78:**20; **83:**2; **84:**3; **90:**10; **105:**30; **109:**4; **116:**10; **119:**23; **139:**4, 10, 12; **Pr 8:**19; **14:**13, 20; **16:**4, 7; **17:**28; **19:**7, 24; **20:**11; **27:**7; **28:**6, 9; **Ecc 2:**23; **4:**14; **6:**6; **8:**17; **9:**5; **10:**3, 15, 20^2; **11:**2, 8; **Isa 1:**6, 15; **3:**6; **6:**13; **15:**9; **23:**12; **25:**12; **32:**7; **33:**23; **35:**8; **40:**15, 30; **46:**4^2; **48:**15; **49:**15, 25; **57:**9, 16; **Jer 2:**11, 33; **3:**25; **4:**10; **5:**18; **8:**7, 13; **11:**7, 23; **12:**6^2; **14:**5; **22:**24^2, 25; **23:**11; **25:**9; **27:**6; **28:**14; **35:**7; **36:**25; **37:**10; **46:**21; **48:**34; **49:**9; **51:**9; **La 1:**10; **4:**3; **Eze 13:**7; **14:**14, 16, 20; **16:**29; **23:**37, 40; **24:**9; **25:**13; **41:**17; **Da 3:**27; **5:**22; **8:**11, 25; **9:**15; **11:**8, 15; **Hos 4:**3; **9:**6, 12, 16; **Joel 1:**18, 20; **2:**12, 16, 29; **Am 4:**2; **5:**22; **Jnh 1:**10, 16; **Na 1:**8; **3:**10; **Zec 8:**6; **11:**16; **14:**14; **Mt 3:**10; **5:**46, 47; **6:**29; **8:**27; **10:**30, 42; **13:**12; **14:**36; **15:**27; **18:**17; **20:**31; **21:**21, 32; **24:**24; **25:**29; **26:**35, 38; **27:**14; **Mk 1:**27; **2:**2, 28; **3:**20; **4:**25, 41; **5:**3; **6:**23, 31, 56; **7:**28, 37; **8:**26; **10:**48; **14:**29, 31, 34, 59; **Lk 1:**15; **3:**9, 12; **6:**8, 29, 32, 33, 34; **7:**9, 49; **8:**18, 25; **9:**3; **10:**11, 17; **11:**8; **12:**7, 27, 48; **14:**26; **15:**29; **16:**21, 31; **18:**11, 13, 15, 39; **19:**26, 42; **21:**16; **23:**5, 11; **Jn 7:**5; **8:**14, 16; **10:**38; **11:**22, 25; **12:**42; **17:**23; **Ac 2:**18; **5:**15, 39; **7:**5^2; **8:**13; **10:**45; **11:**18; **13:**28, 41; **14:**18; **15:**17; **17:**28; **19:**2, 31; **20:**30; **21:**13; **22:**2; **24:**6; **26:**11; **27:**9; **28:**19; **Ro 1:**32; **3:**10, 12; **5:**11, 14; **9:**11; **11:**23; **1Co 2:**10; **3:**2; **4:**3; **5:**1, 11; **7:**21, 29; **8:**5; **13:**12; **14:**5, 21; **15:**15; **16:**6; **2Co 1:**14; **4:**3, 16; **5:**6, 16; **7:**5, 8; **8:**3, 10; **10:**8, 13; **11:**14; **12:**7, 11; **Gal 1:**8; **2:**3, 5, 13; **6:**13; **Eph 2:**5; **5:**3, 12; **Php 2:**8, 17; **3:**4, 18; **4:**16; **1Th 2:**4; **4:**14; **2Th 3:**10; **1Ti 1:**13; **5:**6, 25; **2Ti 2:**9; **Phm 1:**19, 21; **Heb 6:**9, 17; **7:**4, 9, 15; **9:**1, 18; **11:**11, 19, 36; **12:**9, 17, 20; **Jas 2:**19; **4:**14; **1Pe 1:**6, 8; **3:**1, 14; **4:**6, 15; **2Pe 2:**1, 2, 5; **3Jn 1:**5, 10; **Jude 1:**23; **Rev 1:**2, 7; **2:**9, 13, 28; **12:**11; **13:**13, 15; **Tob 2:**4; **9:**4; **13:**4; **14:**4; **Jdt 1:**10; **4:**12; **6:**4; **8:**11, 15; **11:**2, 13, 14; **15:**5, 7; **AdE 4:**16; **5:**3; **7:**2, 8, 9; **16:**3, 4; **Wis 3:**17; **4:**4; **7:**15; **9:**6; **11:**20; **12:**8, 24; **13:**8; **14:**4, 5, 6, 18; **15:**2, 12, 18, 19; **16:**10, 19, 23; **17:**4, 9, 10; **18:**12; **19:**1, 20; **Sir Pr:**T^2; **3:**13; **7:**8, 33; **10:**9; **12:**9, 11; **13:**3, 21, 22, 23; **16:**11; **19:**28; **22:**21; **26:**24; **27:**24; **42:**17; **43:**30; **46:**20; **49:**7, 15; **50:**25; **LtJ 6:**11, 24, 29, 40, 59; **1Mc 1:**28, 37, 43; **2:**19; **4:**35; **7:**46; **8:**4; **2Mc 3:**3; **4:**3, 47, 49; **6:**20, 23, 26; **8:**18; **9:**7^2; **12:**14; **13:**7; **1Es 1:**49; **2:**19; **4:**42; **8:**80, 92; **3Mc 1:**11^2, 12^2, 20; **2:**4, 22, 26; **3:**27; **4:**4, 16; **6:**6, 10, 11, 15, 17, 20, 24; **7:**16; **2Es 5:**45, 48; **7:**23, 130; **8:**48, 57; **11:**13, 17; **12:**5; **16:**27; **4Mc 1:**11, 25; **2:**7, 8, 10, 14, 15, 16; **3:**18, 20; **4:**25; **5:**10, 18^2, 30, 37; **6:**11, 21, 30, 34; **7:**8, 16; **8:**1, 2, 10, 25, 27; **9:**6; **10:**18; **11:**3; **12:**2; **13:**1; **14:**9, 11, 14, 19^2; **15:**10, 16; **16:**14; **17:**10; **18:**14

FOR (11031)

Ge 1:14^3, 29, 30; **2:**5, 9, 17, 20, 23; **3:**5, 6, 7, 16, 18, 19, 21^2; **4:**4^2, 5, 7, 23^2, 25^2; **6:**2, 3, 7, 12, 13, 16, 17, 21^2; **7:**1, 1^2, 21; **8:**9, 21; **9:**3, 5^3, 6, 9, 12, 27; **10:**25; **11:**3^2, 4, 6; **12:**10, 16, 19; **13:**6, 8, 11, 15, 17; **14:**21; **15:**2, 13^2, 15, 16; **16:**10, 11, 13; **17:**4, 5, 7, 8, 9, 15, 19, 20; **18:**14, 15, 19^2, 24, 26, 28, 29, 31, 32; **19:**8, 13, 14, 17, 19, 22, 30; **20:**3, 7^2, 18; **21:**1, 6, 10, 12^2, 13, 16, 17, 18, 21, 30; **22:**3, 7, 8, 12, 18; **23:**2^2, 4, 6, 8, 9^2, 16; **24:**3, 4, 7, 14, 19, 20, 22, 23, 27, 31, 32, 37, 38, 40, 44^2, 48; **25:**21, 30; **26:**3, 4, 7^2, 9, 16, 18, 22, 24^2, 35; **27:**3, 4, 5, 7, 9, 13, 36^2, 37, 41; **28:**11, 15, 18, 22; **29:**2, 7, 9, 15, 18, 20^2, 21, 25, 27, 30, 32; **30:**13, 15, 16, 26^2, 30^2, 31, 33, 42; **31:**12, 15^2, 23, 30, 31, 35, 41^2, 49, 52; **32:**10, 11, 13, 20, 26, 28, 30; **33:**9, 10, 13, 17, 19; **34:**7, 8, 9, 14, 16, 21^2; **35:**17, 18; **36:**7^2; **37:**17, 27, 28, 34; **38:**6, 8, 11, 15, 16, 29; **39:**5, 6; **40:**4, 15, 17, 20; **41:**8, 14, 21, 31, 35, 36, 51, 52, 55, 56; **42:**2, 4, 5, 17, 18, 19, 21, 22, 25^2, 33, 38; **43:**5, 9^2, 14, 16, 23, 25^2, 30, 32; **44:**2, 4, 5, 17, 18, 22, 26, 32^2, 34; **45:**5, 6, 7^2, 11, 19^2, 20, 21, 23; **46:**3, 30, 32; **47:**4^2, 13, 14, 15, 16, 17^2, 19, 20, 21, 22, 23^2, 24^3; **48:**4, 6, 7, 14; **49:**6, 7^2, 13, 18; **50:**3^3, 4, 5, 10, 12, 15, 20, 21; **Ex 1:**11, 19; **2:**3, 7, 9, 19, 22, 23; **3:**5, 6, 12, 15, 22; **4:**16^3, 19; **5:**7, 8, 12, 18; **6:**8; **7:**24^2; **8:**9^3, 21, 26, 28; **9:**2, 11, 14, 15, 30, 31, 32; **10:**1, 4, 11, 22, 23, 26^2, 28; **11:**2; **12:**2^2, 3^2, 4, 12, 13, 14, 15, 17, 19^2, 21, 23, 24, 27, 30, 33, 35^2, 39, 42^2, 43, 49^2; **13:**7, 8, 9^2, 17, 18; **14:**4, 12^2, 13^2, 14, 17, 18, 22, 25^2, 29; **15:**1, 21, 25, 26; **16:**3, 4^2, 7, 9, 15, 16, 25, 29, 34; **17:**1, 3, 9; **18:**1^2, 3, 4, 8, 9, 13, 14^2, 18^2, 21, 22^2; **19:**6, 11, 12, 15, 23; **20:**4, 5^2, 7, 11, 20, 22, 23, 24, 25^2; **21:**6, 8, 9, 11, 13, 14, 19^2, 21, 23, 24^4, 25^3, 26, 27, 30, 36; **22:**1^3, 7, 10, 13, 16, 17, 21, 27^2; **23:**7, 8, 9, 10, 14, 15^2, 21^2, 31, 33; **24:**10, 12, 14^2, 16, 18; **25:**2^2, 6^3, 7, 12, 22, 26, 27, 29, 33, 35, 37, 40; **26:**7, 14, 15, 17, 18^2, 19^2, 20, 22, 23, 26, 27^2, 30, 33, 36, 37^2; **27:**2, 3, 4, 6, 9, 11, 12, 16, 19, 20; **28:**2, 3, 4, 12^2, 21, 22, 23, 29, 32, 40^2, 42, 43^2; **29:**22, 28^2, 34, 36^3, 37, 40, 41; **30:**3, 4, 10, 12^2, 15, 16^2, 18, 21^3, 36, 37; **31:**5, 10^2, 11, 13, 14; **32:**1^2, 8, 23, 25, 29, 30, 31, 34^2; **33:**3, 5^2, 16, 17, 20; **34:**7, 9, 10, 14, 15, 16, 18, 24; **35:**8^3, 12, 14^2, 15, 17, 19^3, 21^3, 28^3, 29, 33; **36:**3, 5, 6, 7, 14, 19, 20, 22^2, 23^2, 24^2, 25, 27, 28, 29, 31, 32^2, 34, 36^2, 37; **37:**3^2, 13, 14, 16, 19, 26, 27; **38:**2, 4, 9, 11, 12, 13, 14, 15, 17, 18, 20^2, 24, 26^2, 27^3, 28^2, 30^2; **39:**1^2, 4, 7, 14, 26, 27, 34, 37, 38, 40^3, 41^2; **40:**5^2, 8, 21, 28, 30, 38; **Lev 1:**3, 4, 10, 16; **2:**3, 10, 11, 12; **3:**6, 16; **4:**3, 14, 20, 21, 26, 28, 31, 35; **5:**4, 6^2, 7^3, 8, 10^2, 11^3, 13^2, 16, 18; **6:**6, 7, 30; **7:**7, 12, 19, 33, 34; **8:**15, 21, 28, 33^2, 34, 35^2; **9:**2^2, 3^2, 4^2, 7^3, 8, 15, 18; **10:**7, 12, 13, 14, 15, 17; **11:**4^2, 5^2, 6^2, 7^2, 8, 26, 27, 28, 29, 31, 32, 35, 37, 38, 42, 44^2, 45^2; **12:**6^4, 7, 8^2; **13:**4, 7, 11, 15, 28, 31, 33, 36, 50, 52, 59; **14:**2, 4, 13, 19, 21^2, 22^2, 23, 31^2, 32^2, 34, 49, 53, 54^2, 55, 56, 57; **15:**3, 13, 15^3, 19, 25, 30^3, 32^2, 33^3; **16:**2, 3^2, 5^2, 6^3, 8^2, 9, 10, 11^4, 15, 16^2, 17^3, 20, 21, 24^2, 26, 30^2, 33^5, 34^3; **17:**7, 11^4, 14^2; **18:**10, 13, 24, 25, 27, 28, 29; **19:**2, 4, 10, 13, 20, 21, 22^2, 23, 24, 25, 28, 34; **20:**7, 19, 25, 26; **21:**1, 2, 3^2, 6, 7, 8, 11, 12, 15, 18, 23; **22:**7, 9, 16, 20, 23^2; **23:**4, 8, 19, 20, 22^2, 27, 28, 29, 37, 40, 42; **24:**2, 7, 9^3, 18^2, 20^3, 21, 22^3; **25:**2, 4^2, 5, 7^3, 10, 11, 12, 15^2, 16, 17, 21^2, 23, 24, 32, 34^2, 42, 44, 46^3, 51, 52, 55; **26:**1^2, 10, 16, 18, 21, 24, 25, 28, 36, 41, 43^2, 44^2; **27:**2, 3, 5^2, 6^2, 7^2, 10^4, 18, 23, 28, 33^2, 34; **Nu 3:**7^2, 8, 12, 13^2, 25, 26, 38, 41^3, 45^2; **4:**7^2, 9^2, 14, 16, 20, 25, 26^2, 29, 35, 39, 43; **5:**7, 8^4, 15^2; **6:**5, 11, 12, 13, 20, 21^2; **7:**3^2, 10, 11, 13, 15, 16, 17, 19^2, 23, 25, 27, 28, 29, 31, 33, 34, 35, 37, 39, 40, 41, 43, 45, 46, 47, 49, 51, 52, 53, 55, 57, 58, 59, 61, 63, 64, 65, 67, 69, 70, 71, 73, 75, 76, 77, 79, 81, 82, 83, 84, 87^2, 88^2; **8:**8, 12^3, 16^2, 17^2, 19^3, 21; **9:**12, 13^2, 14, 21; **10:**2^2, 8, 13, 29^2, 31^2, 32^2, 33; **11:**5, 13, 14^2, 16, 18^3, 20, 21, 22^2, 23, 29, 32; **12:**1, 11, 14^2, 15; **13:**30, 31; **14:**3, 9^2, 13, 14, 25, 32, 33^2, 34, 40, 42, 43; **15:**3, 5, 6, 11^2, 15^2, 24^2, 25^2, 27, 28^2, 29^2; **16:**9, 12, 16, 26, 34, 38^3, 39, 46^2, 47; **17:**2, 3^2, 6, 8; **18:**1^2, 3^2, 4, 17, 19, 21^2, 23, 26, 31^2; **19:**9^3, 10^2, 13, 17, 20^2, 21^3; **20:**2, 4, 5, 8^2, 10, 19, 24, 29; **21:**5, 7, 13, 24, 26, 28, 34; **22:**6^2, 7, 11, 12, 13, 17^2, 34; **23:**1, 7, 9, 13, 22, 27, 29; **24:**1, 8, 22; **25:**13^4, 18; **26:**53, 62, 65; **27:**3, 11, 21; **28:**2, 5, 6, 7, 9, 10, 12^4, 13, 14^3, 15, 20^2, 21, 22^2, 24, 28^2, 29, 30; **29:**1, 3^2, 4, 5^2, 6, 9^2, 10, 11, 14^2, 15, 16, 18^3, 19, 21^3, 22, 24^3, 25, 27^3, 28, 30^3, 31, 33^3, 34, 37^3, 38; **31:**3, 5, 6, 18, 23, 28, 41, 42, 50, 53, 54; **32:**1, 4, 5, 12, 13, 16^2, 20, 24^2, 27^2, 29^2, 36; **33:**14, 53; **34:**2, 6, 14, 17, 18, 29; **35:**2, 3^3, 5^5, 8, 11, 12, 13, 15^2, 28, 29, 31, 32, 33^3, 34; **36:**2, 7, 9; **Dt 1:**13, 17^2, 22, 30^2, 33, 38, 39, 40, 42; **2:**1, 5, 6^2, 9, 19, 22, 23, 28^2, 29, 30, 32, 35, 36; **3:**1, 2, 7, 12, 22^2, 27; **4:**3, 5, 6, 7, 10, 14, 16, 21, 22, 23, 24, 32, 34^2, 38, 40^2; **5:**5, 8, 9^2, 11, 25, 26; **6:**24; **7:**3, 4, 6, 7, 16, 21, 22, 25^2, 26^3; **8:**7, 10, 15, 18; **9:**6, 12^2, 16, 19, 29; **10:**13, 17, 18, 19, 21; **11:**7, 10, 14, 15, 17; **12:**9, 11, 23, 31^2; **13:**3, 5, 10; **14:**1, 2, 7, 8, 10, 19, 21^2, 23, 26, 27, 28; **15:**10, 12, 15, 18; **16:**1^2, 2^2, 3, 4, 6, 8^2, 10, 11, 13, 13^2, 18, 19, 21; **17:**1, 8, 11, 12, 16, 17^2, 18; **18:**5^2, 12, 14, 15, 18; **19:**21^5; **20:**1, 4^2, 16, 18, 19, 20; **21:**5, 13, 14, 23^2; **22:**5, 7, 8, 24, 27; **23:**5, 7, 18^2, 21; **24:**4, 6, 16^3, 19, 20, 21; **25:**16; **26:**2, 17, 19^2; **27:**12, 13; **28:**12, 26, 32, 38, 39, 40, 41, 47, 57, 65, 68; **29:**7, 20, 21; **30:**9, 11, 12^2, 13^2, 14, 20; **31:**7, 19, 20, 21, 23, 27, 29; **32:**3, 10, 20, 22, 25, 27, 35, 40, 43^2, 47, 49; **33:**4, 7, 9, 19, 21^3; **34:**8^2, 11, 12; **Jos 1:**6, 8, 9, 11; **2:**3, 5, 10, 14, 15, 19^2; **3:**4, 5; **4:**5, 13^2, 23^3; **5:**1, 6, 7, 15; **6:**3, 14, 16, 17, 18^2, 25; **7:**9, 12, 13^2, 15^2; **8:**2, 6, 7, 18, 20, 26; **9:**4, 9, 11, 12, 21, 23, 24^2, 26, 27^2; **10:**4, 6, 8, 13, 14^2, 19, 25, 42; **11:**6, 14, 20, 23; **12:**6; **13:**6, 7, 31; **14:**2, 3, 4^2, 9, 11^2, 12, 13; **15:**1, 18; **16:**9; **17:**1, 15^2, 16, 18^2; **18:**6, 7, 8, 10; **19:**1^2, 2, 9, 10, 17^2, 24, 32^2, 40, 50; **20:**3, 9^2; **21:**2, 4, 13, 21, 27, 32, 38, 40, 44; **22:**17, 19, 20, 23, 25, 26^2, 28^2, 29, 34; **23:**3^3, 4, 9^2, 10, 12, 13, 14, 15; **24:**15, 17, 18, 19, 25, 27, 31, 32; **Jdg 1:**1, 14, 32, 33; **2:**2, 7, 10, 17, 18^2; **3:**4, 6, 9, 15, 16, 19, 20, 22, 28; **4:**3^2, 5, 9, 14, 17, 19; **5:**13, 16, 30^3; **6:**2, 3, 5, 6, 22, 30, 31^3; **7:**2, 4, 9, 15, 18^2, 20^2; **8:**5, 10, 11, 14, 20, 21, 22, 24, 30, 35; **9:**2, 3, 5, 17^2, 21, 56; **10:**8; **11:**2, 18, 23, 24, 27^2, 35, 37, 38, 40; **12:**6, 9; **13:**5^2, 7, 15, 16, 22; **14:**2, 3, 4, 14; **16:**2, 17, 18, 23, 24, 25, 28; **17:**3; **18:**1^2, 4, 9, 19, 26, 30; **19:**9, 19^2, 20, 28; **20:**6, 10^2, 27, 28, 41, 47; **21:**5, 6, 7^2, 9, 14, 16^2, 17, 18, 21, 22, 23; **Ru 1:**6, 12^2, 13^2, 20; **2:**7, 11, 12^2, 13, 14, 16^2; **3:**1, 9, 11^2, 13^3, 14, 16, 17, 18; **4:**4, 6^2, 8, 15; **1Sa 1:**16, 20, 22^2, 27, 28; **2:**3, 5, 8, 9, 12, 13, 14, 15^2, 17, 19, 20, 23, 25^2, 30, 35, 36; **3:**5, 6, 8, 9, 10, 13^2, 21; **4:**1, 7^2, 10, 13^2, 18, 19, 20, 22; **5:**7, 11; **6:**2, 4, 17^5; **7:**5, 8, 9, 12, 17; **8:**5, 7, 10, 12, 18; **9:**3, 7, 9, 13^2, 16, 19, 20^2, 24, 25, 27; **10:**7; **11:**13; **12:**7^2, 13, 17, 19^3, 21, 22^3, 23^2, 24^2; **13:**6, 19^2, 21^4; **14:**6^2, 10^2, 12, 18, 26, 30, 39, 45; **15:**2, 6, 11, 12, 15, 23, 24, 26, 29; **16:**1^2, 3, 7, 11, 12, 16, 17, 22; **17:**1, 8^2, 16, 17, 21, 26^2, 27, 28, 31, 33, 34, 39^2, 42, 47; **18:**8, 11, 14, 16, 17^2, 21; **19:**5^2, 15; **20:**4, 6^2, 8, 17^2, 21^2, 22, 23, 26, 29^2, 31^2, 34^2; **21:**2, 6, 9; **22:**3, 8, 10, 11^2, 13, 15^2, 22, 23; **23:**4, 7, 17, 21, 22, 25, 27; **24:**2, 6, 10, 11^2, 17, 19^2; **25:**1, 8, 11, 17, 21, 25, 28, 31^2, 34, 36; **26:**9, 12, 15, 18, 19, 20, 21, 23^2; **27:**1, 4, 5, 8; **28:**1, 2, 3, 7, 8^2, 9, 10, 11^2, 15, 17, 20; **29:**3, 4, 6, 10^3; **30:**6^2, 8, 12^2, 24, 25, 26, 27; **31:**4; **2Sa 1:**9, 10, 12^4, 16, 21, 26; **2:**7, 15; **3:**8, 9^2, 17, 18, 20, 22, 27, 28, 33, 39; **4:**2, 10; **5:**2, 10, 12, 19, 24; **6:**6, 17; **7:**3, 9, 10, 13, 19^2, 20, 22, 23^2, 24, 25, 27, 29; **8:**2^2, 4, 13; **9:**1, 7^2, 10, 13; **10:**5, 11^2, 12^2; **11:**25, 26; **12:**4^2, 10, 12, 16, 18, 21, 22; **13:**2, 7, 12, 13^3, 15^2, 16, 18, 20, 21, 22, 33, 37, 39^2; **14:**2, 7, 13, 16, 17, 19, 25, 26, 29, 32; **15:**2, 6, 8, 12, 14, 19, 21^2, 34; **16:**2^3, 3, 8, 11, 12, 22; **17:**10, 11, 14, 17, 21, 29^2; **18:**3, 5, 12^2, 16, 18^2, 22, 31^2; **19:**1, 2^3, 6^3, 7^2, 20, 21, 22, 26^3, 28, 32, 33, 37, 38^2; **20:**3, 6, 11; **21:**1, 2, 3, 4^2, 10, 14; **22:**5, 18^2, 22, 23, 31, 32, 35, 40^2, 50, 51; **23:**5, 6, 9, 17; **24:**10, 14, 22^2, 24^2, 25; **1Ki 1:**2, 3, 5, 25, 35, 42, 43; **2:**5, 7, 9, 15, 19, 20, 22^6, 23, 26, 28, 31, 37^2, 40, 42; **3:**2, 4, 6, 9, 11^3, 15, 26; **4:**7^2, 22, 24, 26, 27^2, 28; **5:**1, 3, 5^2, 6^3, 9^2, 10, 11; **6:**2, 4, 6, 8, 31, 33; **7:**8, 17^3, 30, 38, 40, 42^2, 45^2, 48, 50^3; **8:**7, 11, 13, 17, 18, 19, 20^2, 21, 23, 24, 25, 39, 42, 44, 46, 48, 51, 53, 64; **9:**3, 4, 7, 19^2, 21, 24, 25; **10:**12^3, 22, 29^2; **11:**2, 4, 5, 7^2, 8, 12, 13^2, 15, 16, 19, 31^2, 32^2, 34, 38, 39; **12:**1, 2, 5, 10, 24, 30, 33; **13:**6, 9, 13^2, 17, 23, 27, 32, 33^2; **14:**2, 4, 5, 6^2, 9, 11, 13^2, 14, 18, 23^2; **15:**2, 4, 13, 27; **16:**19, 23, 24, 26, 31, 32; **17:**9, 12, 13, 14, 15; **18:**19, 23, 25^2, 41; **19:**3, 4, 7, 10^2, 11, 14^2, 20; **20:**7^2, 10, 18^2, 22, 25^2, 33, 34, 38, 39, 42^2; **21:**2^2, 4, 6^2, 15^2; **22:**1, 5, 6, 8, 11, 23, 34, 48^2; **2Ki 2:**2, 4, 6, 9, 17; **3:**2, 9^2, 14, 17, 18; **4:**2, 8, 10, 13^2, 14, 24, 27, 28, 38, 40, 43; **5:**11, 17; **6:**1, 2^2, 16, 23, 25^2; **7:**1^2, 6, 7, 16^2, 18^3; **8:**1^3, 3, 5, 6, 18, 19, 27; **9:**2, 5^3, 8, 13, 20, 25, 26^2, 34; **10:**3, 10, 16, 19, 20, 22^2; **11:**15; **12:**4, 7, 12^3, 13, 14, 15; **13:**4, 7, 17; **14:**6^3, 9, 10, 26, 28; **16:**6, 15, 18^2; **17:**4, 5, 9, 10, 16, 32, 37; **18:**4, 6, 18, 20, 24^2, 26, 29, 31, 36; **19:**4, 8, 29, 31, 34^3; **20:**1, 6^2, 10, 12, 19; **21:**3^2, 5, 13^2; **22:**7^2, 13^4; **23:**4^3, 7, 13^3, 35; **24:**1, 3^2, 4^2, 7, 16; **25:**3, 14, 15^2, 16^2, 26, 30; **1Ch 1:**19; **3:**4; **4:**39, 40, 41; **5:**18, 20; **6:**48, 49, 54, 70; **7:**4, 11, 15^2, 40; **9:**13, 26, 27, 28, 32, 33; **10:**4, 13; **11:**2, 9, 13, 19; **12:**18, 19^2, 21, 33, 35, 36, 39^3, 40; **13:**3, 4, 9; **14:**1, 2, 15; **15:**1^3, 2, 3, 12, 22, 23, 24; **16:**1, 15, 18, 25, 26, 33^2, 34^2, 41, 42^2; **17:**2, 5, 8, 9, 12, 17, 18, 19, 21^2, 23, 25^2, 27; **19:**2, 5, 12^2, 13^2, 14; **21:**6, 8, 13, 23^3, 24^2, 25, 29, 30; **22:**1, 2, 3^3, 4, 5^3, 6^2, 9, 10, 13, 14^2, 18, 19; **23:**5, 14, 24, 25, 26, 27, 28^2, 29, 32; **24:**5, 6^2, 19; **25:**1, 5, 6^2, 8, 9; **26:**1, 5, 6, 8, 10, 13, 14^3, 15, 16^2, 18, 27, 29, 30^2, 32^2; **27:**3, 5, 7, 8, 9, 10, 11, 12, 13, 14, 15, 16^2, 17^2, 18^2, 19^2, 20^2, 21^2, 22, 23, 24, 27; **28:**2^3, 3^2, 4, 5, 6, 8, 9, 10, 11, 12^2, 13^3, 14^3, 15^2, 16^3, 17^3, 18^2, 20^2, 21^2; **29:**1^3, 2^7, 3, 4, 5^3, 7, 9, 11, 14, 15, 16^2, 19, 21; **2Ch 1:**3, 4^3, 9, 10, 11^4, 17^2; **2:**1^2, 4^5, 5, 6, 8, 9^2, 10, 12^2, 15; **3:**3; **4:**6^2, 9, 11, 13^2, 16^3, 19, 22; **5:**1, 8, 11, 13^2, 14; **6:**2, 7, 8, 9, 10^3, 13, 16, 30, 31, 36, 38, 42; **7:**3^2, 6^3, 7, 8, 9, 12, 16^2, 17, 20; **8:**6^2, 8, 9, 11^3, 13, 14^4; **9:**8, 11^3, 21, 25, 28; **10:**1, 2, 10; **11:**4, 5, 15^3, 17^3, 22, 23; **12:**14; **13:**2, 8, 9, 10^2, 11^2, 12; **14:**1, 6, 11^2, 13, 14^2; **15:**3, 5^2, 6, 7, 9, 15, 16; **16:**9^2, 10, 14; **17:**11, 16, 18; **18:**2^2, 4, 5, 7, 10, 22, 32, 33; **19:**3, 6, 7, 8; **20:**1, 8, 9, 12, 15, 17, 21, 23, 25, 26, 27, 30; **21:**6, 19; **22:**1, 3, 4, 7, 9^2; **23:**6, 8, 10, 14; **24:**3, 6, 7^2, 9, 14^3, 16, 18; **25:**4^3, 5^2, 6, 7, 8, 18; **26:**8, 10^2, 11, 14^2, 15^2, 16, 18^3, 21, 23; **28:**2, 11, 13^2, 16, 17, 19^2, 21, 23; **29:**6, 9, 11, 17, 18, 21^4, 23, 24^3, 25, 32, 34, 35, 36^2; **30:**2, 3, 5, 9^2, 14, 17^2, 18^2, 21, 22, 23^2, 24^2, 26; **31:**2, 3^2, 10, 14, 16, 18, 19; **32:**1, 7, 15, 25, 26, 27^7, 28^2, 29^2; **33:**3, 5, 8, 14; **34:**3, 10, 11^2, 21^3; **35:**5, 7, 8, 9, 10, 14^4, 15^2, 23, 24, 25; **36:**21; **Ezr 1:**4; **2:**62, 68; **3:**4, 11^2, 12, 13; **4:**2, 14; **5:**10, 17; **6:**8^2, 9, 10, 17, 18, 20^4, 22; **7:**6, 9, 10, 11, 14, 16, 19, 20^2, 23, 26^4, 28; **8:**16^2, 17, 21, 22^2, 23, 25, 35; **9:**2^3, 6, 7, 8, 9, 10, 12^2, 13^2; **10:**2, 4, 6, 13^3, 19; **Ne 1:**4, 6; **2:**8^4, 11, 12, 14; **3:**17; **4:**4, 5, 6, 14, 20, 22; **5:**2, 16, 18^2, 19^2; **6:**5, 9, 10, 13, 16, 18; **7:**2; **8:**4, 5, 9, 10^3, 11, 16, 17; **9:**3^2, 8, 10^2, 15^3, 18, 20, 31, 33; **10:**30, 32, 33^3, 34, 37, 39; **11:**23^2, 25; **12:**22, 29^2, 43, 44^4, 46, 47^3; **13:**5^2, 6, 7, 13, 14^2, 25^2, 31^3; **Est 1:**3, 4, 5^2, 8, 9, 11, 13, 17; **2:**2, 7, 10, 12^3, 13, 15^2, 20; **3:**2, 4, 7^2, 8, 9, 14; **4:**2, 5, 7, 8^2, 10, 11, 14^3, 16; **5:**4, 8, 10; **6:**3^2, 4, 6, 7, 9, 11; **7:**4^2, 7, 9, 10; **8:**1, 6, 8, 16; **9:**4, 19, 22^2, 27, 31^2; **10:**3^3; **Job 1:**5, 9; **2:**3, 4, 13; **3:**9, 12, 14, 21^3, 24; **4:**11; **5:**6, 8, 18, 23, 27; **6:**3, 4, 10, 22, 28; **7:**2^2, 16, 19, 21; **8:**6, 8, 9^2; **9:**15, 17, 28, 32, 35; **10:**6, 15; **11:**4, 6, 10, 11; **12:**5^2; **13:**4, 7^2, 8, 19, 26; **14:**7^2, 15, 16, 22; **15:**5, 11, 20, 22, 23, 24, 31, 34; **16:**19, 21, 22; **17:**1, 3^2, 5, 13; **18:**2, 8, 10^2, 12; **19:**21, 25, 29; **20:**5, 19, 26, 29; **21:**4, 19, 21^2, 28, 31; **22:**4, 6^2, 28, 29; **23:**14^2; **24:**3, 5, 8, 12, 15, 17^2; **27:**6, 8, 14; **28:**1^2, 5, 15, 17, 24, 26^2; **29:**6, 13, 21, 23^3; **30:**12, 23, 24, 25^2, 26^2, 28; **31:**8, 10, 11, 12, 18, 19, 23, 28, 30; **32:**8, 11^2, 18, 22; **33:**14, 23, 26, 32; **34:**3, 5, 9, 11, 19, 21, 23^2, 26, 27, 31, 33, 37; **35:**9, 14; **36:**2, 4, 13, 20, 23, 27, 31; **37:**6, 13^3; **38:**7, 10, 21, 23^2, 25^2, 39, 41^2; **39:**6^2, 14; **40:**20^2, 22; **41:**5, 28; **42:**3, 7, 8^4, 10, 11; **Ps 1:**6; **2:**12; **3:**2, 5, 7; **4:**3, 8; **5:**T, 2, 4, 9, 10, 11, 12; **6:**2^2, 4, 5, 8; **8:**4; **9:**4, 7, 9, 10, 12, 18; **10:**3^2, 5, 8, 18; **11:**2, 7; **12:**1, 5; **14:**5, 7; **16:**1, 3, 6, 10; **17:**4, 6, 14, 15; **18:**6, 17^2, 21, 22, 27, 30, 31, 34, 36, 39^2, 41, 49; **19:**4; **20:**5; **21:**3, 4, 7, 12; **22:**11, 16, 18, 24, 28, 29; **23:**3, 4; **24:**2; **25:**3, 5^2, 6, 7, 10, 11^2, 14, 15, 16, 20, 21^2; **26:**1, 3, 11; **27:**5, 12, 14^2; **28:**1, 2, 6; **30:**1, 2, 5^4, 6; **31:**2, 3, 4^2, 9, 10, 13, 17, 19^2, 21, 22, 24; **32:**4, 7, 11; **33:**4, 9, 17, 20; **34:**9, 17; **35:**7^3, 10, 12, 13, 14^2, 20, 23^2, 27; **36:**2, 9; **37:**2, 7, 9^2, 10, 13, 17, 22, 24, 28, 32, 34, 37^2; **38:**T, 2, 4^2, 7, 10, 15, 16, 17, 18, 20; **39:**6, 7, 9, 11, 12; **40:**1, 12, 17^2; **41:**4^2, 7; **42:**1^2, 2^2, 5, 11; **43:**2, 5; **44:**3^2, 4, 6, 11, 12^2, 21, 22, 25, 26; **45:**4; **47:**2, 4, 7, 9; **49:**7^2, 8, 14, 15, 17, 18^2; **50:**6, 8, 10, 12, 17, 19; **51:**3, 16; **52:**9; **53:**5^2, 6; **54:**3, 5, 6, 7; **55:**3, 8, 9, 15, 18; **56:**1, 2, 5, 7, 9, 13; **57:**1, 2, 6, 10; **58:**11; **59:**3^2, 4, 7, 9^2, 12^2, 15, 16^2, 17; **60:**T, 2, 4, 11; **61:**3, 5; **62:**1, 5^2, 8, 12; **63:**1^2, 7^2, 10, 11; **64:**6; **65:**8, 9, 13; **66:**10, 16; **67:**4^2; **68:**10, 16, 28; **69:**1, 3, 7, 9, 10, 12, 13, 16, 17, 20^2, 21^2, 22^2, 26, 33, 35; **70:**T; **71:**3, 5, 10^2, 11, 22, 23, 24; **72:**3, 12, 15^2; **73:**2, 3, 4, 14, 28; **74:**14, 15, 20^2; **75:**6, 8; **77:**8; **78:**20, 29, 34, 50, 55, 58; **79:**2, 7, 8, 9^2; **80:**9, 14, 17; **81:**1, 4^2; **82:**8; **83:**10, 12; **84:**2^2, 3, 10, 11; **85:**8, 9, 13; **86:**1, 2, 3, 4, 5, 7, 10, 13; **87:**5; **88:**3, 5, 10; **89:**4, 6, 17, 18, 28, 35, 47; **90:**4, 7, 9, 17; **91:**3, 11; **92:**T, 4^2, 9^2; **94:**13, 14, 15, 16^2, 23^2; **95:**3, 5, 7, 10; **96:**4, 5, 12, 13^2; **97:**9, 11^2; **98:**1, 8, 9; **99:**9; **100:**5; **102:**3, 8, 9, 10, 13, 14, 16, 18; **103:**6, 11, 13^2, 14, 15, 16; **104:**8, 14^2, 18^2, 19, 21, 34; **105:**8, 11, 32, 38, 39, 42; **106:**1^2, 8, 13, 20, 33, 45; **107:**1^2, 8^2, 9, 11, 15^2, 16, 21^2, 25, 31^2; **108:**4, 12; **109:**2, 4^2, 5^2, 16, 21, 22, 31; **111:**5; **112:**4, 6; **115:**1; **116:**7, 8, 12; **117:**2; **118:**1, 29^2; **119:**20, 22, 28, 32, 35, 38, 39, 40, 42^2, 43, 45, 56, 66, 71, 77, 78, 81, 82, 83, 85, 91, 93, 94, 98, 99, 100, 102, 110, 117, 118, 120, 123^2, 126^2, 131, 147, 153, 155, 164, 166, 168, 172, 173, 174, 176; **120:**7^2; **122:**4, 5^2, 6, 8, 9; **123:**3; **125:**3; **126:**2, 3, 6; **127:**2; **130:**5, 6^3, 7; **131:**1; **132:**5^2, 9, 10, 13^2, 14, 16, 17^2; **133:**3; **135:**3^2, 4^2, 5, 7, 14; **136:**1^2, 2, 3, 4, 5, 6, 7, 8, 9, 10, 11, 12, 13, 14, 15, 16, 17, 18, 19, 20, 21, 22, 23, 24, 25, 26; **137:**3^3; **138:**2^2, 4, 5, 6, 8; **139:**6, 12, 13, 14, 16, 20; **140:**5^2, 12; **141:**5, 9; **142:**3, 4, 6^3, 7; **143:**2, 3, 6, 8^2, 9, 10, 11, 12; **144:**1^2, 12; **146:**7, 10; **147:**1, 8, 13; **148:**5, 13, 14^3; **149:**4, 5, 9; **150:**2; **Pr 1:**2^2, 3, 9^3, 11, 16, 17, 18, 19, 32; **2:**3^2, 4^2, 6, 7, 10, 18, 21; **3:**2, 8^2, 12, 14, 22^2, 26, 32; **4:**2, 13, 16, 17, 22, 23; **5:**3, 17^2, 21, 23; **6:**3, 23, 26, 34; **7:**6, 19, 26; **8:**6, 7, 11, 35; **9:**11, 12; **10:**13, 21, 29^2; **11:**15, 27; **12:**8; **13:**2, 8, 18, 22; **14:**3, 6, 7; **15:**10, 24, 27^2; **16:**4^2, 6, 12, 26; **17:**3^2, 13, 18, 26; **18:**1; **19:**10^2, 20, 29^2; **20:**16^2, 22, 25; **21:**18^2, 25, 31; **22:**3, 4, 9, 18, 20, 23, 26; **23:**3, 5, 7, 11, 21, 27; **24:**2, 6, 7, 13, 16, 20, 22, 27, 29; **25:**3^2, 4, 7, 8, 16, 22; **26:**1, 3^3, 12^2, 20, 21, 25; **27:**1, 12, 13^2, 21^2, 24^2, 27^3; **28:**8, 21; **29:**5, 19, 20^2; **30:**16, 18, 33; **31:**4^3, 8^2, 15^2, 21^2; **Ecc 1:**18; **2:**3, 4, 8, 10^2, 12, 16, 17, 19, 21, 23, 24, 25, 26; **3:**1^2, 8^2, 11, 12, 17^3, 19^2, 22; **4:**8, 9, 10; **5:**1, 2, 3, 4, 8, 9^2, 15, 16, 18, 20; **6:**4, 7, 8, 12^3; **7:**2, 3, 6, 9, 10, 12, 18; **8:**3, 4, 6, 7, 15^3; **9:**4, 7, 10, 12; **10:**4, 15, 16, 17^2, 19, 20; **11:**1, 2, 6, 7, 9, 10; **12:**13, 14; **SS 1:**2, 7; **2:**5, 11, 14, 15; **5:**2, 4; **6:**5; **7:**10, 13; **8:**6, 7, 8^2, 11, 12, 13; **Isa 1:**2, 17, 20, 29^2, 30; **2:**3, 4, 6, 12, 20, 22; **3:**1, 8, 9, 10, 11; **4:**3; **5:**1, 4, 7, 8, 10, 20^4, 23, 24, 25, 26^2; **6:**5, 8; **7:**6, 8, 13, 16, 18^2, 22, 24, 25^2; **8:**2, 4, 10, 11, 14^2, 17, 20^2; **9:**1, 4, 5^2, 6^2, 7, 12, 16, 17^2, 18, 19, 21; **10:**3, 4, 8, 13^2, 22, 23, 25, 29, 31; **11:**4, 9, 12, 16^2; **12:**1, 2, 5, 6^2; **13:**2, 4, 6, 10, 11^2, 17, 20; **14:**21, 27, 29, 31; **15:**5^2, 8, 9^3; **16:**7^2, 8, 9^2, 11^2; **17:**2, 8, 10; **18:**4, 5; **19:**10, 15; **20:**3, 6; **21:**4^2, 6, 15, 16, 17; **22:**4, 5^2, 11^2, 13, 16^2, 25; **23:**1, 4, 13, 14, 15, 18; **24:**3, 5, 6, 11, 13, 14, 16, 18, 23; **25:**1, 2, 4, 6, 8, 9^2, 10; **26:**4, 5, 8, 9^2, 11^2, 12^3, 19^2, 20, 21^2; **27:**5, 10, 11; **28:**10, 15, 19, 20, 21, 22, 24, 26, 28; **29:**10, 11^2, 15, 20, 21, 23; **30:**2, 4, 7, 8, 9, 13, 14, 15, 18^2, 23, 33^2; **31:**1^2, 4, 7^2; **32:**6, 10, 12^2, 13^2, 14^2; **33:**2, 21, 22;

28, 37, 39, 41, 44^2, 55, 56^2, 57; **14:**9, 11, 16, 17, 18, 20^2, 21, 23, 24, 31, 35, 36, 40, 43, 47; **15:**2, 4, 14^2, 15, 16^2, 17, 19^2, 24, 26, 44, 47^2, 58^2; **16:**2^3, 13, 17^2, 19, 20, 21, 22, 23, 26, 28, 38, 40, 46^2, 48, 52, 53, 70, 72, 75; **4Mc 1:**1, 2, 6^2, 8, 10^4, 26, 30, 33, 35; **2:**1, 2, 3^2, 10^3, 11, 12^2, 15, 16^2, 18, 19, 20; **3:**1, 2, 5, 11, 17, 20; **4:**1, 4, 11, 12, 13, 22; **5:**7^2, 13, 18^2, 21, 25, 26, 27^2; **6:**11, 12, 13, 18, 20^2, 21, 22, 27, 28, 29, 30, 32, 34; **7:**1, 5, 6, 11, 22, 23; **8:**1, 2, 10, 11, 22, 25, 28; **9:**1, 3, 4, 8, 24, 29, 30; **10:**13, 19, 20, 21; **11:**2, 3, 4, 11, 12, 15, 16, 20, 21, 27; **12:**2, 3, 6, 12, 14^2; **13:**2, 4, 6^2, 8, 9, 12, 13, 15, 17, 25, 27; **14:**6, 7, 10, 12, 13, 14, 15, 18, 19, 20; **15:**2, 3, 7, 10, 11, 12, 16, 23, 25, 26, 27; **16:**8, 9, 12, 13^2, 15, 16^2, 17^2, 19, 20, 21, 23, 25; **17:**6, 7^2, 12^2, 15, 19, 20, 21, 23^2, 24; **18:**3, 16, 18, 22

FROM (5841)

Ge 1:2, 4, 6, 7, 14, 18; **2:**2, 3, 6, 7, 10, 22; **3:**1, 8, 11, 12, 22, 23^2; **4:**10, 11^2, 14^2, 16; **5:**29^2; **6:**7, 17; **7:**4, 23; **8:**2, 3, 7, 8^2, 10, 11, 13, 21; **9:**5^2, 19, 24; **10:**5, 11, 14, 19, 30, 32; **11:**2, 8, 9, 31; **12:**1, 4, 8; **13:**1, 3, 9, 11, 14^2; **14:**17; **15:**7, 18; **16:**2, 6, 8^2; **17:**6, 12, 14, 16, 22, 27; **18:**2, 16, 17, 22, 25^2; **19:**24; **20:**1, 6, 13; **21:**17, 21, 30; **22:**11, 12, 15; **23:**3, 6, 13, 20; **24:**3, 5, 7^3, 8, 10, 17, 37, 40^2, 41^2, 43, 46, 50, 62, 64; **25:**6, 10, 18, 29; **26:**16, 17, 22, 23, 26, 27, 31; **27:**9, 30^2, 39^2, 40, 45; **28:**2, 6, 16; **29:**3, 4^2, 8, 10; **30:**2, 16, 32; **31:**1, 16, 31, 40, 49; **32:**11^2, 13; **33:**10, 18, 19; **34:**7; **35:**1, 5, 7, 9, 11^2, 13, 16^2; **36:**2, 6; **37:**14, 18, 25; **38:**1, 17, 20; **39:**1, 5, 9; **40:**19^2; **41:**42, 46, 48; **42:**7^2, 24; **43:**2, 34; **44:**4, 5, 7, 8^2, 17, 29; **45:**1, 19; **46:**5, 34; **47:**1, 2, 10, 15^2, 18, 21, 22; **48:**7, 12, 16, 17, 22; **49:**9, 10^2, 26, 30, 32; **50:**13, 25; **Ex 1:**10; **2:**1, 7, 15; **3:**5, 8; **4:**3, 9^2; **5:**4; **6:**6^2, 7, 13; **7:**5, 18; **8:**8, 9, 12, 29^3, 30, 31^3; **9:**8, 10, 15, 18; **10:**6^2, 11, 17, 18, 23, 28; **11:**1, 5; **12:**5^2, 15^3, 18, 19, 29, 31, 33, 37, 41; **13:**3, 10, 14, 15, 19, 20; **14:**19, 25, 30; **15:**22; **16:**1^2, 4; **17:**1, 14, 16; **18:**4, 9, 10^2, 11, 13, 14, 25; **19:**2, 3, 14; **20:**22; **21:**14; **22:**5, 7, 14, 25, 29^2; **23:**5, 7, 16, 25, 28, 29, 30, 31^2; **25:**2, 3, 15, 22^2, 39; **26:**28, 33; **27:**21; **28:**1, 28, 42; **29:**25, 27^2, 28^2; **30:**14, 16, 33, 38; **31:**14; **32:**1, 3, 4, 8, 12^2, 15, 19, 27; **33:**6, 7, 15, 16; **34:**16, 18, 29^2; **35:**5, 20; **36:**3, 4, 6, 33; **38:**8, 24, 25, 26; **39:**21; **40:**36; **Lev 1:**1, 2^2, 3, 10^2, 14; **2:**2, 9, 13, 14; **3:**3, 6, 9, 14; **4:**8, 10, 31, 35; **5:**6, 15, 18; **6:**6, 15, 18, 22, 30; **7:**14^2, 20^2, 21^2, 25^2, 27, 29, 32, 34^3, 35, 36; **8:**26, 28; **9:**10, 24; **10:**2, 4, 12, 13, 14; **11:**2, 34, 45; **12:**7; **13:**12, 28, 40, 41, 58; **14:**19; **15:**2, 3, 19, 31; **16:**5, 12, 17, 19, 30; **17:**4, 9, 10; **18:**29; **19:**8; **20:**3, 5, 6, 18, 24, 26; **21:**7; **22:**3, 21^2, 25, 27, 28; **23:**15^2, 17, 29, 30, 32, 38^4; **24:**3, 9; **25:**14, 15, 22, 33, 36, 41, 44, 45^2, 50, 55; **26:**6, 36; **27:**3, 5, 6, 24, 30^3; **Nu 1:**3, 4, 5, 6, 7, 8, 9, 10^3, 11, 12, 13, 14, 15, 16, 18, 20, 22, 24, 26, 28, 30, 32, 34, 36, 38, 40, 42, 45; **3:**9, 12, 15, 22, 28, 34, 39, 40, 43, 49, 50; **4:**2, 3, 13, 18, 23, 30, 35, 39, 43, 47; **5:**13, 31; **6:**3, 18, 21; **7:**5, 84, 89^2; **8:**4, 6, 11, 14, 16, 19, 21, 24, 25^2; **9:**7, 13^2, 15, 17, 21; **10:**9, 11, 12, 33, 34; **11:**31^2, 35; **12:**10, 16; **13:**2, 3, 4, 5, 6, 7, 8, 9, 10, 11^2, 12, 13, 14, 15, 21, 23, 24, 25, 33; **14:**9, 13, 19, 29, 43; **15:**3^2, 20^2, 21, 23, 30; **16:**2, 9, 15, 21, 24, 26, 27, 33, 35, 45, 46^2; **17:**2^2, 9; **18:**6, 9^2, 11, 16, 22, 20^2, 28^2; **19:**13, 20; **20:**6, 9, 14, 17, 21, 22, 28; **21:**4, 7, 11, 12, 13^2, 16, 18, 19^2, 20, 24, 28^2, 30; **22:**1, 6, 16, 33^2, 41; **23:**7^2, 9^2, 13^2, 27; **24:**7, 24; **25:**4, 11, 18; **26:**2, 4, 9; **27:**4; **30:**14; **31:**4, 5, 6, 14, 28, 29, 30, 32, 42, 47, 51, 52, 54; **32:**7, 8, 9, 11, 15, 21; **33:**3, 5, 6, 7, 8, 9, 10, 11, 12, 13, 14, 15, 16, 17, 18, 19, 20, 21, 22, 23, 24, 25, 26, 27, 28, 29, 30, 31, 32, 33, 34, 35, 36, 37, 41, 42, 43, 44, 45, 46, 47, 48, 49, 52, 55; **34:**3^2, 5, 7, 8, 10, 11; **35:**2, 4, 8^3, 12, 20, 25; **36:**3^2, 4, 7, 8, 9; **Dt 1:**2, 19, 23, 39; **2:**6^2, 14^2, 15, 16, 21, 23, 26, 36; **3:**4, 8^2, 16, 17, 26; **4:**2, 3, 9, 26, 29, 32, 34, 36, 48; **5:**15; **6:**15, 19, 23; **7:**4, 8^2, 15, 24; **8:**3, 9, 15; **9:**7, 12^3, 14, 15, 16, 17, 23, 28; **10:**5, 6, 7^2; **11:**10, 11, 12, 24^2, 28; **12:**3, 10, 21, 26, 32; **13:**5^3, 7^2, 10, 13, 17; **14:**22, 24; **15:**13, 16, 18; **16:**2, 3, 6, 9, 10, 13; **17:**7, 10, 11, 12, 20; **18:**3^2, 6, 8, 11, 15, 18; **19:**5, 12, 13, 19; **20:**1, 15, 19^2; **21:**9, 21; **22:**8, 21, 22, 24; **23:**4, 14, 15, 22; **24:**7, 18; **25:**11, 19^2; **26:**2, 4, 13, 15^2; **28:**14, 24, 35, 49^2, 57, 64; **29:**18, 20, 21, 22, 28; **30:**3, 4^2; **31:**17, 21, 29; **32:**13^2, 14^3, 20, 26, 32^2, 39, 42, 49, 52; **33:**2^3, 3, 22; **34:**1; **Jos 1:**4, 7; **2:**1, 4, 13, 17, 20, 23; **3:**1, 3, 10, 12^2, 13, 14, 16; **4:**2^2, 3^2, 4^2, 18; **5:**9, 15; **6:**18; **7:**2, 5, 9, 12, 13, 19, 21, 26; **8:**4, 5, 6^3, 7, 16, 22, 29; **9:**6, 8, 9, 12, 13, 14, 22, 26; **10:**7, 9, 11, 19, 22, 23, 27, 29, 31, 34, 36, 41; **11:**17, 21^6, 23; **12:**1, 2^2, 7; **13:**3, 5, 6^2, 9^2, 16, 26^2, 30; **14:**7, 15; **15:**2^2, 5, 7, 9^2, 14, 15, 18, 46; **16:**1^2, 2, 6, 7, 8; **17:**7; **18:**4, 13, 14, 15, 17; **19:**12^2, 13, 33^2, 34; **20:**3, 8^3; **21:**4, 5^2, 6^4, 7; **22:**9, 14, 16, 17, 18, 23, 24, 29^2, 31, 32; **23:**1, 4, 6, 13, 15, 16; **24:**3, 16, 17, 32^2; **Jdg 1:**11, 14, 16, 20, 36^2; **2:**1^2, 12, 17, 18; **3:**3, 19, 20^2, 21, 27; **4:**6^2, 11, 13, 14, 15, 21; **5:**4^2, 14^3, 20^2; **6:**8, 9^2, 11, 13, 14, 18, 19, 21^2, 38; **7:**2, 8, 23^3; **8:**8, 13, 26, 34; **9:**17, 20^3, 27, 35, 36, 37^2; **10:**11^4, 16; **11:**3, 5, 13^2, 16, 22^2, 29, 31, 33; **12:**2, 4, 9; **13:**5^2, 6, 7, 14, 20; **14:**3, 4, 9; **15:**13, 19; **16:**14, 17, 20; **17:**2, 3, 9; **18:**2^3, 7, 11, 13, 22, 28; **19:**1, 2, 16^2, 17, 18^2, 30; **20:**1, 13, 15, 17, 25, 31, 32, 42, 43; **21:**6, 8^2, 17, 19, 21, 23, 24^2; **Ru 1:**2, 6, 7, 13, 16, 17, 22; **2:**4, 6, 7, 9, 12, 16; **4:**3, 5, 9, 10^2; **1Sa 1:**1, 3; **2:**3, 8^2, 15, 23, 28, 30, 33; **3:**12, 17^2, 18, 20; **4:**3^2, 4, 8, 12, 16^2, 18, 21, 22; **5:**1; **6:**3, 7; **7:**2, 3, 8, 14^3; **8:**7, 8; **9:**16^2, 21, 25; **10:**1, 2, 3, 4, 5, 10, 18^2, 19, 23, 27; **11:**5^2, 8^2; **12:**2, 3, 4, 20, 23; **13:**8, 11, 15^2; **14:**6, 17, 30, 31, 45, 46; **15:**6^2, 7, 11, 15, 21, 23, 26, 28; **16:**1, 13, 14^2, 15, 16, 23^2; **17:**4, 15, 18, 24, 26, 30, 33, 34, 35, 37^3, 40, 52, 53, 57; **18:**6, 9, 10, 12, 13, 29; **19:**9; **20:**1, 2^2, 9, 15^2, 34, 41; **21:**4, 5, 6, 10; **22:**3; **23:**13, 26, 29; **24:**1, 21; **25:**10, 11, 23, 26^2, 29, 33^2, 34, 35, 39, 44; **26:**12, 19, 20, 24; **27:**8; **28:**3, 9, 15, 16, 23; **29:**6, 8; **30:**13, 16^2, 17, 25, 26; **31:**12; **2Sa 1:**1, 2, 3^2, 4, 13, 22^2; **2:**12, 21, 22, 26, 30; **3:**10^2, 15, 18^2, 22, 26^2; **4:**2, 4, 11; **5:**9, 13, 25; **6:**2^2, 12; **7:**1, 6, 8^2, 9, 11^2, 12, 15^3; **8:**4, 8^2, 11, 12^2; **9:**5; **10:**14; **11:**2^2, 8, 10, 15, 20, 21, 24; **12:**3, 7, 10, 11, 17, 20, 30; **13:**5, 6, 9^2, 10, 13, 32, 34; **14:**2, 14, 16^2, 18, 19, 25, 32; **15:**2, 11, 12, 14, 18, 19, 28, 35; **17:**11, 27^3, 29; **18:**3, 13, 16, 19, 31; **19:**7, 9^2, 13, 16, 17, 24, 25, 31; **20:**2^2, 6, 7, 12, 13, 16, 20, 21, 22; **21:**10^2, 12^2, 13, 20, 22; **22:**1^2, 3, 4, 7, 9^3, 14, 17, 18^2, 22, 23, 24, 44, 49^2; **23:**4, 11, 15, 16, 20; **24:**2, 4, 5^2, 6, 15^2, 21^2, 24, 25; **1Ki 1:**29, 39, 45, 53; **2:**7, 8, 15, 27, 31^2, 33, 36, 40, 41; **3:**20; **4:**12, 21, 24, 25, 33, 34^2; **5:**6, 9; **6:**8, 15, 16, 24; **7:**7, 9^2, 13, 23; **8:**8^2, 16, 35, 38^2, 41, 51, 53, 54, 65; **9:**6, 7, 12, 24, 28; **10:**3, 11^2, 12, 15^3, 28^2, 29; **11:**2, 9, 11, 18^2, 23, 31, 34, 35; **12:**2^2, 24, 25, 31; **13:**4, 5, 12, 14, 21, 26, 33^2, 34; **14:**7, 8, 10; **15:**5, 13, 17, 19; **16:**17, 24; **17:**3, 4, 6, 19, 23; **18:**12^2, 26; **19:**17^2, 19, 21^2; **20:**17, 24, 33, 34, 41; **21:**21; **22:**24, 33, 35, 43; **2Ki 1:**2, 10^2, 12^2, 14; **2:**1, 3, 5, 7, 9, 10, 13, 14, 21^2, 23, 25; **3:**3, 20, 21, 27; **4:**3, 27, 39, 42^2; **5:**1, 2, 4, 15, 19, 20, 21, 22, 24; **6:**27^2, 32, 33; **7:**2, 8, 19; **8:**3, 6, 8, 9; **9:**8; **10:**21, 28, 29, 31, 33^2; **11:**2^2, 11, 19; **12:**4^2, 5, 7, 8, 13, 15, 16^2, 18; **13:**2, 5, 6, 11, 23, 25^2; **14:**13, 24, 25^2, 27; **15:**9, 14, 16, 18, 20^3, 24, 28; **16:**6, 7^2, 11^2, 12, 14^2, 17^2, 18; **17:**7, 9, 13, 20, 21^2, 22, 23, 24, 27, 28, 32, 33; **18:**6, 8, 14, 16^2, 17, 31^2; **19:**14, 19, 25, 29, 31^2; **20:**9, 14^3; **21:**16; **22:**4, 7; **23:**6, 8, 12, 17, 26, 30, 35^2; **24:**7, 15, 20; **25:**19, 27; **1Ch 1:**12; **2:**23, 53, 55; **4:**10; **5:**2, 23; **6:**60, 78; **9:**4, 33; **10:**14; **11:**8, 13, 17, 18; **12:**8, 22, 28, 37, 40; **13:**5^2, 6, 7; **14:**16; **15:**25; **16:**20^2, 23, 35, 36; **17:**7^2, 10, 13^2, 21; **18:**1, 4, 8^2, 11^2; **19:**6^3, 7; **20:**2, 6, 8; **21:**2, 21, 22, 26; **22:**9; **23:**24, 27; **26:**25, 27; **28:**4; **29:**12, 14, 16, 29; **2Ch 1:**4, 13^2, 16^2, 17; **2:**8, 16; **3:**6; **4:**2; **5:**9^2; **6:**5, 21, 23, 25, 26, 29^2, 30, 32, 33, 35, 39, 40; **7:**1, 8, 14^2, 20; **8:**8, 11, 15, 16, 18; **9:**2, 10, 11, 26, 28^2, 29; **10:**2^2; **11:**4^2, 13, 14, 16; **12:**3, 12, 15; **13:**13, 19; **14:**5, 8^2; **15:**8^2, 9^2, 11, 16; **16:**1, 2, 3, 9, 11, 12; **17:**6; **18:**23, 31, 32; **19:**2, 4, 10; **20:**2^2, 4^2, 10, 25, 32, 34; **21:**12; **22:**11^2; **23:**2, 10, 20; **24:**5, 6, 23; **25:**6, 10, 12, 13, 14, 15, 23, 26, 27^2; **26:**18, 21, 22; **28:**8, 11, 12, 26; **29:**5, 6, 10, 25; **30:**5, 6^2, 8, 9, 10, 11, 16, 18; **31:**3, 16, 17; **32:**11, 14^2, 15^2, 17^2, 22^2, 23; **33:**8, 15; **34:**9^4, 33^2; **35:**7^2, 11, 22^2; **36:**12, 20; **Ezr 1:**7, 11; **2:**1, 59, 62; **3:**6, 7^2, 8^2, 13; **4:**12, 15, 19; **5:**16; **6:**4, 8, 21^2; **7:**6, 9, 28; **8:**1, 21, 31^2, 35; **9:**1^2, 3, 5, 7, 11; **10:**2, 6, 8, 11^2, 14; **Ne 1:**2, 9; **3:**15, 16, 20, 21, 24, 25; **4:**5, 12, 16, 19, 21; **5:**7, 11, 12, 13^2, 14^2, 15, 17; **6:**9; **7:**3, 61, 64; **8:**3^2, 8^2, 17^2, 18^2; **9:**2, 3, 5, 13, 15, 20, 27^2, 28, 35; **10:**28, 31, 37; **11:**23, 30, 31; **12:**28^2, 29^2, 44; **13:**1, 3, 19, 21, 28, 30; **Est 1:**1, 19; **2:**6, 9, 13; **3:**8, 10; **4:**14; **7:**7^2, 8; **8:**2, 9, 10, 15; **9:**16, 22^3, 26; **Job 1:**1, 7^3, 8, 12, 16, 21; **2:**2^3, 3, 7^2, 11, 12; **3:**10, 11, 17, 19; **4:**2, 13; **5:**4, 6^2, 15^2, 19, 20^2, 21; **6:**13, 14, 17, 18, 22, 23^2; **7:**19; **8:**18; **9:**34; **10:**18, 19; **12:**24; **13:**20, 21; **14:**6, 11, 18; **15:**22, 30; **16:**22; **17:**7; **18:**14, 17, 18; **19:**9^2, 13^2; **20:**4, 18, 24, 29; **21:**9; **22:**6, 7, 22, 23; **23:**12; **24:**9, 12; **26:**4; **27:**5^2, 13, 22, 23; **28:**2, 4^2, 20, 21^2, 28; **29:**9, 17; **30:**2, 5, 10, 30; **31:**2^2, 7, 17, 18^2, 22^2, 23; **33:**6, 17^2, 18^2, 24, 28, 30; **34:**10^2, 27; **35:**7; **36:**3, 7, 10, 19, 25; **37:**2, 9^2; **38:**8, 15, 29; **39:**22, 25, 29^2; **41:**19, 20; **Ps 2:**3; **3:**T, 4; **6:**8; **7:**1; **9:**13^2; **10:**16, 18; **12:**1, 7; **13:**1; **14:**2, 7; **15:**2; **16:**2; **17:**1, 2, 7, 9, 13, 14^2; **18:**T^2, 3, 6, 8^3, 16, 17^2, 21, 22, 23, 43, 48^2; **19:**5, 6^2, 12, 13; **20:**2^2, 6; **21:**10^2; **22:**1^2, 9, 10, 11, 20^2, 21^2, 24, 25; **24:**5^2; **25:**6; **27:**9; **30:**3^2; **31:**9, 11, 15, 20^2, 22; **32:**7; **33:**13, 14, 19; **34:**4, 6, 13^2, 14, 16, 17, 19; **35:**10^2, 17^2, 22; **36:**8; **37:**8, 27, 39, 40; **38:**9, 10, 11, 21; **39:**8, 10, 13; **40:**2, 10, 11; **41:**8, 13; **42:**6^2; **43:**1; **44:**7, 10, 18; **45:**8; **49:**15; **50:**1, 9^2; **51:**2^2, 9, 11^2, 14; **52:**5^2; **53:**2, 6; **54:**7; **55:**1, 8, 11, 12, 18, 19; **56:**13^2; **57:**T, 3; **58:**3^2; **59:**1^2, 2^2; **61:**2; **62:**1, 5; **64:**1, 2^2, 4; **66:**20; **68:**17, 18^2, 20, 22^2, 23, 31; **69:**5, 14^3, 17, 27; **71:**4^2, 5, 6^2, 12, 17, 20; **72:**8^2, 14; **73:**27; **74:**12; **75:**6^3, 8; **76:**8; **77:**4; **78:**2, 4, 15, 42, 50, 65, 70, 71; **79:**13; **80:**13, 14, 18; **81:**6, 16; **82:**4; **84:**7, 11; **85:**3, 11^2; **86:**13; **88:**5, 14, 15, 17; **89:**19, 33, 34, 44; **90:**2; **91:**3^2; **93:**2^2; **94:**13; **96:**2; **97:**10; **101:**4, 8; **102:**2, 19^2; **103:**4, 12^2, 17; **104:**13, 14, 21, 35; **105:**13^2, 40; **106:**10^2, 23, 31, 47, 48; **107:**2, 3^5, 6, 13, 19, 20, 28; **109:**15, 17, 20, 31; **110:**2, 3, 7; **113:**2, 3, 7^2; **114:**1^2; **115:**18; **116:**8^3; **118:**26; **119:**10, 19, 21, 22, 29, 37, 51, 52, 101, 102, 110, 115, 118, 123, 134, 150, 152, 155, 157; **120:**2^2; **121:**1, 2, 7, 8; **124:**7; **125:**2; **127:**3; **128:**5; **129:**1, 2; **130:**8; **131:**3; **132:**11; **134:**3; **135:**7, 21; **136:**11, 24; **138:**6; **139:**2, 7^2, 15, 19; **140:**1^2, 4^2; **141:**9^2; **142:**6; **143:**7, 9; **144:**7^3, 11^2; **148:**1, 7; **Pr 1:**15; **2:**6, 12^2, 16^2, 22; **3:**7, 21, 26, 27; **4:**5, 15, 21, 23, 24^2, 27; **5:**7, 8, 15^2; **6:**5^2, 9, 24^2; **7:**5^2; **8:**6, 35; **9:**3; **10:**2; **11:**4, 8; **12:**2, 13, 14; **13:**2, 19; **14:**16; **15:**29; **16:**1; **17:**13; **18:**20, 22; **19:**14^2, 27; **20:**3, 9; **21:**16; **22:**5, 27; **23:**13, 14; **24:**11, 18, 22; **25:**4, 5, 25; **27:**8^2; **29:**21, 26; **30:**8, 14^2; **31:**14; **Ecc 1:**3; **2:**6, 10^2, 22, 24, 25; **3:**5, 9, 11, 14, 20; **4:**4; **5:**1, 15, 16; **7:**10, 23; **8:**3, 8; **10:**5; **11:**10^2; **SS 3:**6, 9; **4:**2, 8^6, 15; **6:**5, 6; **8:**5; **Isa 1:**6, 12, 15, 16; **2:**3, 6, 10^2, 19^2, 21^2, 22; **3:**1^2; **4:**4, 6^2; **6:**6; **7:**17; **8:**17, 18; **9:**7, 14; **10:**2, 3, 27^3; **11:**1, 11^8, 12, 16^2; **12:**3; **13:**5^2, 6, 9; **14:**3, 9, 12, 19, 22, 25^2, 29; **16:**1, 4^2, 10; **17:**3^2; **18:**4, 7^2; **19:**23; **20:**2, 6; **21:**1^2, 10, 11, 15^4; **22:**4, 19^2, 24; **23:**1, 7, 15; **24:**14, 16; **25:**4^2, 8^2; **26:**21; **27:**12; **28:**9^2, 22, 29; **29:**4^3, 9^2, 13; **30:**11, 14, 27; **31:**8; **32:**2^2, 15; **33:**15^2; **34:**1, 10, 16, 17; **36:**2, 16^2; **37:**14, 20, 26, 30, 32^2; **38:**7, 9, 12^3, 13, 17; **39:**3^3; **40:**2, 15, 21^2, 27; **41:**2, 4, 9^2, 25^2, 26; **42:**5, 7^2, 10, 11; **43:**5^2, 6^2, 13; **44:**7, 8; **45:**6^2, 8, 23; **46:**3^2, 6, 7^2, 10^2, 11^2, 12; **47:**12, 14, 15; **48:**1, 3, 5, 6, 8^2, 16^2, 19, 20^2, 21; **49:**1, 12^4, 17, 21, 24; **50:**6, 11; **51:**1^2, 4, 22^2; **52:**2^2, 11^2; **53:**3, 8; **54:**8, 10, 14^2, 15, 17; **55:**10, 11; **56:**2, 3; **57:**1, 10, 14; **58:**7, 9, 13^2; **59:**2, 9, 11, 13^2, 15, 20, 21; **60:**4, 6, 9, 15; **63:**1^2, 3, 15^3, 16, 17; **64:**4, 7; **65:**9^2, 16; **66:**6^2, 11^2, 19, 20, 23^2; **Jer 1:**13; **2:**5, 6, 21, 25^2, 35, 37; **3:**1, 14^2, 18, 19, 24, 25; **4:**1, 6, 7^2, 8, 11, 15^2, 16; **5:**6^2, 15; **6:**1, 8, 13^2, 20^2, 22^2; **7:**1, 25, 28; **8:**10^2, 13, 16, 19; **9:**2, 3, 19, 21^2; **10:**3, 9^2, 11^2, 13^2, 17, 20, 22; **11:**1, 4, 19; **12:**2, 12, 14^2; **13:**6, 7, 18, 20, 24; **15:**7, 12, 21; **16:**5, 9, 16, 17^2, 19; **17:**5, 12, 13, 16^2, 26^5; **18:**1, 8, 11, 17, 18^3, 20, 22, 23; **19:**14; **20:**3, 13, 18; **21:**1, 2, 12; **22:**3, 11, 20, 21, 24; **23:**14, 15, 16, 22^2, 30, 39; **24:**1, 5^2, 10; **25:**3, 5^2, 10, 15, 17, 28, 30^2, 32^2, 33; **26:**1, 3, 10, 20, 23; **27:**1, 10, 16, 20; **28:**1, 3, 4, 6, 8, 10, 11, 12; **29:**1^2, 2, 4, 14^2, 20, 22; **30:**1, 7, 8, 10^2, 21; **31:**3, 8^2, 11, 16^3, 34, 36, 38; **32:**1, 9, 30, 31^2, 37, 40^2; **33:**5, 8; **34:**1, 3, 8, 12, 14, 21; **35:**1, 15; **36:**1, 2^2, 3, 5, 6^2, 7, 8, 9, 10, 11, 21, 29; **37:**5, 9, 11, 12, 17, 21; **38:**10^2, 11, 14, 18, 23, 25; **39:**14; **40:**1^2, 4, 12; **41:**5, 6, 14, 15, 16^2; **42:**1, 4, 8, 11, 17; **43:**5, 12; **44:**5, 7, 12, 18, 28; **46:**10, 20, 24, 27^2; **47:**4; **48:**2, 3, 10, 11^2, 18, 33^2, 34, 44, 45^2; **49:**5, 7, 14, 16, 19^2, 32, 36^2; **50:**6, 8, 9^2, 15, 16, 26, 28, 41^2, 44^2; **51:**2, 6, 16^2, 25, 26, 31, 45, 53, 54^2; **52:**3, 7, 25, 29; **La 1:**6, 13, 16; **2:**1, 3, 8, 9, 22; **3:**18, 38, 50, 55, 66; **5:**8, 10, 16; **Eze 1:**13, 19, 21, 25, 27^2; **3:**12, 17^2, 18, 19^2, 20; **4:**8, 14; **5:**3, 4^2; **6:**9, 14; **7:**20, 22, 26^3; **8:**6; **9:**2, 3; **10:**2, 4, 6^2, 7, 10, 18, 19; **11:**15, 17, 18, 19, 23; **12:**3, 16^2; **13:**20, 21, 22, 23; **14:**5, 6^2, 7, 8, 9, 11, 13, 17, 19, 21; **15:**3^2, 7; **16:**9, 33, 34, 37, 41, 42; **17:**5, 7, 9, 22^2; **18:**8, 17, 21, 23, 24, 26, 27, 28, 30, 31; **19:**8, 10, 14; **20:**34, 41, 47; **21:**3, 4^2, 19; **22:**5, 29; **23:**17, 18^2, 22^2, 24, 27, 28, 40, 42; **24:**13, 16, 25; **25:**7, 9, 13^2; **26:**4, 7, 16, 17; **27:**5^2, 6^2, 7^2, 17, 19, 29, 33; **28:**3, 15, 16^2, 18, 25; **29:**4, 8, 10, 13, 18; **30:**6, 9, 22; **31:**5, 12^2; **32:**13; **33:**7^2, 8, 9^2, 11^2, 12, 14, 18, 19, 21, 30; **34:**10, 12, 13^2, 25, 27; **35:**7; **36:**3, 24^2, 25^2, 26, 29, 33; **37:**9, 12, 13, 21^2, 23; **38:**6, 8^3, 12, 15; **39:**2, 3, 17, 22, 23, 24, 27^2, 29; **40:**13^2, 15, 19, 23, 27; **41:**7^3, 16, 20; **42:**5^2, 6, 9^2, 12; **43:**2, 9, 14^2, 15, 23, 25, 27; **44:**5, 10^2, 15, 30; **45:**7, 13^2, 14, 15^2; **46:**2, 17; **47:**1^2, 10, 12, 15, 17, 19^2; **48:**1^2, 2, 3, 4, 5, 6, 7, 8^2, 12, 19, 21^2, 23, 24, 25, 26, 27, 28^2, 35; **Da 1:**6, 9; **2:**5, 6, 18, 20, 25, 45; **3:**17, 26, 27, 29; **4:**3, 12, 13, 14^2, 16, 23, 25, 26, 31^2, 32, 33, 34; **5:**2, 3, 13, 20^2, 21, 23, 24; **6:**13, 18, 20, 27; **7:**3, 4, 7, 10, 19, 23, 24; **8:**4, 5, 7, 11, 22, 26; **9:**5, 13, 16, 25; **10:**5, 12; **11:**7, 8, 41, 44; **12:**11; **Hos 2:**2^2, 15, 17, 18; **4:**6; **5:**3, 6; **7:**4, 13, 14; **8:**6; **9:**1, 12; **10:**5; **11:**2, 7, 10, 11^2; **12:**9, 13; **13:**3^2, 14^3, 15^2; **14:**4, 8; **Joel 1:**5, 9, 13, 15, 16; **2:**2, 7, 13, 20; **3:**6, 16^2, 18; **Am 1:**2^2, 5^2, 8^2; **2:**3, 14; **3:**4, 5, 12; **4:**7, 11; **5:**11, 19, 23; **6:**2, 4^2, 6, 14; **7:**11, 15, 17; **8:**12^2; **9:**2^2, 3^2, 7^3, 8; **Ob 1:**1, 4, 9; **Jnh 1:**3^2, 8, 10, 15; **2:**1, 4, 6; **3:**6, 8^2, 9, 10; **4:**2, 3, 6, 11; **Mic 1:**2, 11, 12, 16; **2:**3, 4, 8^2, 9^2; **3:**4, 7; **4:**2, 10^2; **5:**2^3, 6, 7, 10, 12, 13, 14; **6:**4^2, 5; **7:**2, 5, 12^4, 20; **Na 1:**11, 13, 14; **2:**13; **3:**7, 11; **Hab 1:**7, 8, 12; **2:**9, 11^2, 13; **3:**3^2, 4, 13, 17; **Zep 1:**2, 3, 4, 6, 10^3, 13; **3:**10, 11, 18; **Hag 2:**15, 18^2, 19; **Zec 1:**4^2, 12; **2:**6, 13; **3:**2, 4; **4:**1; **6:**1, 10^3; **7:**12; **8:**7^2, 9, 10, 23; **9:**5, 7^2, 10^4, 11; **10:**1^2, 10^2; **11:**6; **13:**1, 2^2; **14:**1, 2, 4, 5, 8, 10^3, 13; **Mal 1:**10, 11, 13; **2:**6, 7, 8, 12; **3:**7; **4:**2; **Mt 1:**17^3, 18, 20, 21, 24; **2:**1, 6, 7, 16; **3:**7, 9, 13, 16, 17; **4:**4, 17, 21, 25^2; **5:**18, 37, 42^2; **6:**1, 13; **7:**16^2, 23; **8:**1, 11, 30; **9:**15, 16, 20, 27; **10:**14, 27, 29; **11:**1, 12, 25, 29; **12:**38, 42, 44; **13:**12, 27, 35, 49; **14:**2, 13^2, 24; **15:**1, 5, 8, 18, 22, 27; **16:**1, 21; **17:**5, 9, 20, 25^3, 26; **18:**35; **19:**8, 12; **21:**8, 11, 19, 25^2, 43; **22:**46; **23:**34, 35; **24:**21, 27, 29, 31^2, 32; **25:**28, 29, 32^2, 34, 41; **26:**16, 27, 39, 47, 64; **27:**32, 40, 42, 45, 51, 55^2, 57, 64; **28:**2, 7; **Mk 1:**5, 9, 11, 45; **2:**20, 21^2; **3:**7, 8, 22; **4:**25; **5:**6, 25, 30, 35; **6:**14, 33; **7:**1, 4, 6, 11, 18, 21^2, 23, 24, 31, 33; **8:**3, 11; **9:**7, 9, 10, 17, 21, 25, 30; **10:**6; **11:**12, 14, 30, 31; **12:**2, 25, 34; **13:**19, 25, 27^2, 28; **14:**23, 35, 36, 43, 67; **15:**21, 30, 32, 38, 40, 45; **16:**3, 8, 9, 99; **Lk 1:**2, 3, 38, 48, 50, 52, 70, 71^2, 74, 78; **2:**1, 4^2; **3:**7, 8, 14, 22; **4:**1, 9, 13, 22, 38, 42; **5:**3^2, 8, 10, 17^2, 35, 36^2; **6:**17, 19, 29, 30, 34, 44^2; **7:**6, 12, 45; **8:**2, 4, 12, 18, 35, 38, 43, 46, 49; **9:**4, 7, 35, 37, 38, 45, 54; **10:**7, 18, 21, 30, 42; **11:**7, 16^2, 24, 31, 51; **12:**3, 36, 48^2, 52; **13:**12, 15, 16, 25, 27^2, 29^2, 31; **16:**3, 18, 21, 26^2, 30, 31; **17:**7, 24, 29; **18:**34; **19:**24, 26, 37, 42, 44; **20:**4, 5, 7, 35; **21:**11, 26; **22:**18, 41, 42, 43, 45, 69, 71; **23:**5, 26, 49, 51, 55; **24:**2, 9, 13, 16, 31, 46, 47, 49, 51; **Jn 1:**6, 16, 19, 24, 32, 44, 45; **2:**9, 22; **3:**2^2, 3, 7, 8, 13, 27, 31^2; **4:**12, 22, 39, 43, 47, 54; **5:**24, 41, 44^2; **6:**13, 23, 31, 32^2, 33, 38, 41, 42, 45, 46, 50, 51, 58, 64; **7:**17, 22^2, 27^2, 28, 29, 41, 42^2, 52^2; **8:**11, 14^2, 23^2, 26, 38, 40, 42, 44^2, 47^2; **9:**1, 16, 29, 30, 33; **10:**5, 18^2, 32, 39; **11:**37, 53, 54, 55; **12:**1, 9, 17, 21, 27, 28, 32, 34, 36, 43; **13:**1, 3, 4; **14:**7, 24; **15:**5, 15, 26^2, 27; **16:**1, 4, 22, 27, 28, 30; **17:**6, 7, 8, 15; **18:**3, 28, 36^4; **19:**9, 11, 12, 23, 27; **20:**1, 9; **21:**8, 14; **Ac 1:**1, 4, 5, 11, 12, 22^2, 25; **2:**2, 5, 10, 24, 33, 40; **3:**2^2, 5, 15, 20, 22, 24, 26; **4:**10, 17, 20; **5:**16, 38; **6:**3, 9; **7:**4, 10, 16, 33, 37, 40, 42; **8:**4, 10, 26, 33, 36; **9:**3, 8, 13, 14, 18; **10:**7, 23, 41; **11:**5, 9, 11, 27; **12:**11^2, 19; **13:**4, 8, 13, 14, 29, 30, 31, 34, 39^2; **14:**8, 15, 17, 18, 19, 26; **15:**1, 14, 16, 18, 20^4, 22, 24^2, 29^5; **16:**4, 11, 12, 14; **17:**2, 3, 9, 26, 27, 31; **18:**2, 5, 6^2, 16, 21, 23; **19:**25, 35; **20:**4^4, 6, 15, 17, 18, 20^2, 24, 27, 30; **21:**1^2, 7, 10, 16, 25^4, 27, 39; **22:**5, 6, 22, 29; **23:**34; **24:**8, 19, 23; **25:**1, 7; **26:**4^2, 10, 13, 17^2, 18^2, 22, 23; **27:**2, 4, 12, 14, 21, 29, 30^2, 34, 43; **28:**4^2, 15, 21, 22, 23^3; **Ro 1:**3, 4, 7, 18; **2:**12^2, 29^2; **3:**21, 28; **4:**6, 24; **5:**9, 14; **6:**4, 7, 9, 13, 17, 18, 21, 22; **7:**2, 3, 4, 6, 8, 9, 24; **8:**2, 11^2, 21, 35, 39; **9:**3, 5, 24^2; **10:**3, 5, 6, 7, 9, 17; **11:**15, 24, 26, 36; **13:**1, 11; **14:**23^2; **15:**18, 19, 22, 31; **16:**2; **1Co 1:**3, 30; **2:**12; **4:**5, 8, 12; **5:**2, 13; **6:**19; **7:**7, 10, 27, 29, 32, 38; **8:**6; **9:**6, 13, 21; **10:**4, 14; **11:**8^2, 12^2, 23; **15:**12, 20, 41, 47^2; **2Co 1:**2, 10, 16; **2:**3, 14, 16^2, 17; **3:**1, 5^2, 13, 18^2; **4:**4, 7; **5:**1, 6, 8, 16^3, 18; **6:**17^2; **7:**1; **11:**3, 4^2, 8, 9^2, 24, 26^5, 33; **12:**6^2, 7^2; **13:**10; **Gal 1:**1^2, 3, 4, 8, 12; **2:**6, 12; **3:**2, 13, 15, 18^2; **4:**24; **5:**4^2, 7, 8, 17; **6:**8^2, 17; **Eph 1:**2, 20; **2:**12; **3:**15; **4:**16, 18, 31; **5:**14; **6:**6, 8, 23; **Php 1:**2, 5, 15^2; **2:**1, 3; **3:**9^2, 11, 20; **4:**18; **Col 1:**2, 6, 7, 11, 13, 18, 23; **2:**12, 19^2; **3:**8, 24; **4:**16; **1Th 1:**8, 9, 10^3; **2:**3, 6^3, 13, 14^2, 16, 17; **3:**6; **4:**1, 3, 16; **5:**22; **2Th 1:**2, 7, 9^2; **2:**2; **3:**2, 3, 6^2; **1Ti 1:**2, 5, 6; **4:**3; **5:**11, 13; **6:**4, 10; **2Ti 1:**2, 13, 15, 16; **2:**2, 8, 18, 19, 22, 26; **3:**11, 13, 14, 15; **4:**4, 8, 17, 18; **Tit 1:**4; **2:**14; **Phm 1:**3, 7, 15, 20; **Heb 2:**1; **3:**12; **4:**4, 10^2, 12^2; **5:**1, 7, 14; **6:**1, 7; **7:**1, 5^3, 6, 13, 14, 23, 26; **8:**11; **9:**14, 15; **10:**22; **11:**3, 12, 13, 19, 40; **12:**3, 25; **13:**5, 10, 20, 24; **Jas 1:**7, 17^2; **2:**18, 20; **3:**10, 11, 15, 17; **4:**1^2, 7; **5:**7, 19, 20^2; **1Pe 1:**3, 12, 18^2, 21, 22; **2:**11, 24; **3:**10^2, 11, 15, 21; **2Pe 1:**4, 8, 17, 18, 21; **2:**9, 11, 18, 21; **3:**4; **1Jn 1:**1, 5, 7, 9; **2:**7, 13, 14, 16^2, 18, 19, 21, 24^2, 27; **3:**8, 10, 11, 12, 14, 19, 22; **4:**1, 2, 3, 4, 5^2, 6^3, 7, 21; **5:**21; **2Jn 1:**3^2, 5, 6; **3Jn 1:**7, 10, 11; **Jude 1:**14, 24; **Rev 1:**4^2, 5^2, 16; **2:**5^2, 7, 28; **3:**10, 12, 18^2; **4:**5; **5:**7, 9; **6:**4, 14, 16^2; **7:**2, 5^3, 6^3, 7^3, 8^3, 9^2, 13, 17; **8:**4, 5, 10, 11, 12; **9:**1, 2^2, 3, 6, 13; **10:**1, 4, 8, 10; **11:**5, 7, 11, 12; **12:**14, 15, 16; **13:**8, 13; **14:**2, 3, 4, 13^3, 18, 20; **15:**8^2; **16:**1, 12, 13^3, 17, 21; **17:**8^2; **18:**1, 3, 4, 14, 15; **19:**3, 5, 15, 21; **20:**1, 7, 9, 11; **21:**2, 3, 4, 6, 10; **22:**1, 19; **Tob 1:**2, 4, 11, 18; **2:**4; **3:**5, 6^4, 13, 17^4; **4:**7^3, 8, 10^2, 12^2, 13, 18, 19, 21; **5:**2, 3, 5^2, 6, 11; **6:**3, 13^3, 16; **7:**3, 9, 11^3; **8:**6; **10:**12^2, 13; **11:**8, 13; **12:**9, 11, 20; **13:**2, 5, 6, 11; **14:**4, 5, 7; **Jdt 2:**18, 21, 22; **3:**6; **4:**3; **5:**5^2, 6, 8, 18, 19; **6:**2, 5, 11, 12, 14, 21; **7:**3, 12, 19, 22; **8:**29, 31, 36; **10:**2, 12^2, 17, 18; **11:**3, 14, 16, 21; **12:**15, 16; **13:**1^2, 9, 11, 14, 19; **14:**6, 8; **15:**7; **16:**2, 3, 19; **AdE 1:**1; **2:**6, 9, 13; **3:**8, 12; **4:**5, 8, 14; **5:**9; **6:**1, 10; **7:**7^2, 8; **8:**2, 9;

9:16, 22^3, 27; 10:4, 9, 13; 11:4, 10; 13:1, 15; 14:5, 19^2; 15:8; 16:1, 4, 7^2; Wis 1:3, 5, 6, 11; 2:1, 5, 18; 3:3; 4:14, 19; 5:6, 16, 21^2, 22; 6:3^2, 15, 22^2; 7:2, 14, 23; 8:1, 2; 9:4, 6, 8, 10^2, 17; 10:1, 3, 8, 9, 10, 12^2, 13, 15, 19; 11:4, 14, 18, 20; 12:2, 5, 11; 13:1, 4, 5, 13; 14:4, 13, 15; 15:8^2, 13; 16:8, 15, 20; 17:2, 4, 12, 14, 19; 18:15^2; 19:12, 18; Sir 1:1, 4; 4:4, 5, 9, 12, 23; 5:7, 13; 6:12, 13, 18; 7:2^2, 4^2, 21, 23, 33; 8:5, 8, 9^2; 9:8, 13; 10:8, 12, 17; 11:4, 14, 32; 13:24; 14:17, 27; 15:8, 9; 16:17^2, 26; 17:15, 20, 26, 28^2; 18:10, 16, 22^2, 26; 19:28; 20:3, 11, 20, 21; 21:2^2, 5, 23; 22:9, 25; 23:5, 10, 12; 24:3, 30, 32; 25:14, 23^2, 24, 26; 26:12, 14, 28, 29; 27:19, 20, 27, 28; 28:3, 8, 14, 15, 19; 29:7, 12, 24; 30:12, 23^2, 25; 33:7, 10, 22; 34:4^2, 6, 19^2, 24; 35:5; 36:31; 37:10; 38:2, 8^2, 10; 39:19, 20, 25, 32; 40:1^2, 3, 4, 6, 11; 41:10^2; 42:5^2, 13^2, 18, 20, 21; 43:7, 17, 22; 44:2, 21^2, 23; 45:25; 46:7, 11, 12, 17, 19, 20; 47:2^2, 10, 22, 24; 48:5^2, 6, 15^2, 20; 49:10, 14; 50:4, 12, 21, 22; 51:2^3, 3^3, 4^2, 5^2, 8^2, 9^2, 12, 15^2, 20; Bar 1:8, 9, 13, 19; 2:8, 13, 16, 17, 23^2, 33, 35; 3:7, 21, 29; 4:9, 12, 18, 21, 22^2, 25, 28, 35, 36, 37; 5:1, 2, 5, 6, 9; LtJ 6:3, 10, 12, 13, 15, 16, 20, 23, 36^2, 39, 49, 57, 63, 72; Aza 1:6, 12, 32, 66^4; Sus 1:5^3, 9, 13, 51, 52, 55, 64; Bel 1:19; 1Mc 1:1, 6, 10, 11^2, 43, 61; 2:1, 16, 21, 22, 40, 59, 60, 61, 66; 3:8, 10, 19, 29^2, 31, 32, 35, 41, 45; 4:2, 4, 5, 13, 16, 60; 5:12, 14, 36; 6:6^2, 8, 10, 17, 21, 29^2, 32, 37, 46, 53, 56; 7:1, 13, 19, 24, 33, 39, 41, 45; 8:4^2, 8, 18, 23; 9:6, 10^2, 11, 13, 36, 37, 40, 46, 67, 72, 73; 10:29, 30^5, 31, 33, 35, 38, 40, 41, 42, 44, 45, 57, 61, 67, 74, 80; 11:12^2, 28, 34^4, 35, 36, 38, 41, 53, 58, 59, 61, 63, 66, 69; 12:7, 10, 15^2, 17, 25, 36, 53; 13:5, 37, 41, 47, 48, 49^2, 50^2, 51; 14:7, 36; 15:1, 5^2, 8, 14^2, 15, 20, 21, 25, 27; 16:1, 2, 3, 24; 2Mc 1:7, 25, 32; 2:3, 10, 18^2, 21, 30; 3:3, 13; 4:8, 19, 34, 36, 38; 5:7, 8, 9, 18, 21; 6:10, 11, 16, 22, 23, 30; 7:2, 5, 9, 11^2, 24; 8:11, 20, 23; 9:1, 16, 21, 22; 10:15, 24, 27^2, 29, 30; 11:5, 25; 12:10, 17, 29^2, 42, 45; 13:21, 24; 14:4, 16, 18, 21, 30^2, 46; 15:7, 8, 9, 12, 16, 35, 37; 1Es 1:7, 28, 30, 35, 38, 47; 2:9, 10, 15, 18, 23, 26, 27, 28, 30; 3:2, 6, 23; 4:16^2, 30, 44, 48, 49, 53, 57, 59^2; 5:18^3, 19^2, 20, 21^2, 36, 39, 50, 53, 55^2, 56, 67, 73; 6:6, 18, 20, 25, 27, 28; 7:6, 10, 13^2; 8:3, 7, 8, 27, 28, 50, 51, 61, 65, 69, 70, 71, 73, 76, 78, 81, 91, 92; 9:1, 3, 4^2, 9^2, 13, 15, 41; Pm 151:4, 7; 3Mc 1:1, 3, 25; 2:2, 12, 32, 33; 3:2, 16, 18, 21, 28; 4:11, 12, 15, 16, 21; 5:8, 11, 32, 50^2; 6:10, 15, 18, 25, 26^2, 28, 38; 7:16; 2Es 1:14, 30, 31, 38; 2:4, 7, 16^2, 26, 33, 36, 39^2, 41; 3:7, 11, 20, 21, 24; 4:9, 24, 30, 42; 5:5, 19, 23^2, 24^2, 25^2, 26^2, 27, 48, 53; 6:8^3, 19, 26, 32, 40, 50, 54, 56^2; 7:27, 37, 48^2, 63, 70, 71, 78, 88, 92, 96, 97, 98, 100, 116; 8:2^2, 10^2, 53^2; 9:4^2, 8, 29; 10:10, 14, 24; 11:1, 10^2, 24, 37, 46; 12:11, 17^2, 32, 40, 42^2, 48; 13:2, 4, 5, 7, 10^3, 12, 14, 20, 25, 32, 40, 51, 57; 14:9, 14^2, 15, 22, 29, 32; 15:9, 20^4, 22, 23, 28, 29, 30, 33, 34^2, 35, 38^3, 39, 60; 16:9, 12, 20, 38, 52, 60, 67^2, 74; 4Mc 1:4, 7, 8, 28, 33^2; 2:6, 9, 14; 3:3, 10, 14; 4:10^2, 16, 25; 5:11, 13; 6:13; 8:23, 29; 9:5, 9, 16, 31, 32; 10:5, 8, 16; 11:3, 18; 12:11; 13:20, 21^2, 22^2; 14:4; 15:32; 16:12; 18:2^2, 7, 23

HAD (3470)

See also the selected listing for "HAD" in the Main Concordance.

Ge 1:31; 2:2^2, 3, 5^2, 8, 22; 3:1; 4:4, 5; 5:3, 4, 6, 7, 9, 10, 12, 13, 15, 16, 18, 19, 21, 22, 25, 26, 28, 30; 6:6, 10, 12; 7:5, 9, 16; 8:3, 6, 8, 11; 9:24; 11:1, 3, 5, 11, 12, 13, 14, 15, 16, 17, 18, 19, 20, 21, 22, 23, 24, 25, 26, 30; 12:4, 5^3, 7, 16, 20; 13:1, 3, 4, 5, 10, 14; 14:4, 13, 14; 15:17; 16:1, 3, 4, 5; 17:22, 23; 18:8, 11, 33; 19:17, 23, 27, 29; 20:4, 18; 21:1^2, 2, 4, 9, 25, 32; 22:3, 9; 23:16; 24:1, 2^2, 15, 16, 19, 21, 22, 29, 30, 45, 48, 62, 66; 25:5; 26:1, 8, 14, 15^2, 18^3, 32; 27:17, 30^2, 41; 28:6, 7, 9, 11, 18; 29:16, 20; 30:9, 25, 30, 35, 38, 43; 31:10, 18^2, 19, 21, 22, 25, 30, 32, 34, 42; 32:13, 23; 33:19; 34:1, 5, 7, 13, 27; 35:4, 7, 13, 14, 15, 16, 27; 36:6; 37:1, 3, 5, 9^2, 10, 32, 36; 38:14, 15; 39:1, 4, 5^2, 6^2, 13^2; 40:8, 16, 22; 41:14, 15, 19, 21^2, 43, 50, 54, 56; 42:5, 8, 9, 24, 29; 43:2^2, 6, 10, 24^3, 25, 26; 44:4; 45:27^2; 46:1, 5, 6; 47:11, 22; 50:12, 14^2; Ex 2:11, 16; 3:4; 4:28^2, 30, 31^2; 5:14; 7:10, 13, 22, 24, 25; 8:12, 15, 19; 9:12, 24, 34, 35; 10:13, 14, 15, 23; 12:28, 35^2, 36, 39^2, 40, 50; 13:19; 14:5, 6, 28; 16:1, 3, 18^2; 18:1^2, 2, 8^3, 9, 24; 19:1, 2, 7, 9, 18; 22:8; 24:14; 32:20, 25; 33:5, 8; 34:4, 29, 32, 33, 34; 35:25, 29; 36:2, 3, 7, 22; 39:1, 5, 7, 18, 21, 26, 29, 31, 32^2, 42^2, 43^2; 40:16, 19, 21, 23, 25, 27, 29, 32; Lev 9:21; 10:1, 5, 7, 16, 19; 16:34; 21:3; 22:4; 24:23; Nu 1:1, 17, 48; 2:33, 34; 3:4, 32, 38, 51; 5:4, 13, 20; 7:1^3, 9; 8:3, 4, 20, 22; 9:1, 5; 11:4^2, 18, 26, 34; 12:1^2, 10, 14, 15; 13:31, 32; 14:2^2, 6, 44; 15:36; 16:39, 40, 42^2, 47^2; 17:8; 20:3, 9, 27, 29; 21:26; 22:2, 29, 33, 36; 23:2, 30; 26:33, 64, 65; 27:3, 4, 22, 23; 29:40; 30:5; 31:7, 10, 14, 21, 31, 32, 35, 36, 41, 47^2, 53; 32:9, 13^2; 33:4, 38; 36:10; Dt 1:3, 4, 19, 46; 2:1, 8, 10, 12, 14^3, 15, 16, 23, 30, 35, 37; 3:6; 4:25, 45; 5:29; 9:10, 16^3, 18, 21; 10:4, 5, 10; 19:4, 6, 19; 29:1, 26^2; 31:1, 24; 32:17^2, 30^2, 45; 34:7, 9^2; Jos 2:6^2, 7, 22, 23; 3:15; 4:1, 4, 9, 10, 11, 12, 14, 20; 5:1^2, 4^2, 5^3, 6, 7, 12; 6:8, 16, 22, 23; 7:7, 24; 8:20, 21, 24^2, 26, 27, 31, 32, 33; 9:3, 16^2, 18, 21, 24; 10:1^4, 20^2, 24, 27, 28, 30, 32, 35, 37, 39^2; 11:8, 12, 14, 15^2, 20, 23^2; 13:12; 14:2, 3, 15; 17:3, 11; 18:2; 19:2, 49; 21:8, 12, 42, 44^3, 45^2; 22:7^2, 9, 11, 17; 23:1; 24:13^2, 31, 32^2, 33; Jdg 1:19, 20; 2:1, 7^2, 10, 12, 15, 17^2, 23^2; 3:1, 2, 11, 12, 18, 24, 30; 4:3^2, 11^2, 12, 17; 5:31; 6:27, 28; 7:13, 19; 8:8, 10, 19, 24, 25, 28, 30^2, 34, 35; 10:4^2; 11:34, 39^2; 12:9, 14; 13:23; 14:4, 6, 9, 18, 19, 20; 15:2, 5, 17; 16:8, 16, 18, 19, 20, 22, 30, 31; 17:5; 18:1, 7, 14, 17, 25, 27, 28, 31; 19:3, 10, 29; 20:3, 22, 36, 39; 21:1, 5, 6, 8, 12, 14, 15^2, 18; Ru 1:4, 6^2, 7; 2:1, 14, 17, 18^2, 19; 3:6, 7, 16; 4:1^2; 1Sa 1:2^3, 5, 6, 9, 24; 2:12; 3:2, 3, 7; 4:6, 18, 21; 5:4, 9; 6:6, 19; 7:7, 14; 8:21; 9:2, 3, 15, 22; 10:13, 16^2, 26, 27^4; 11:9; 13:4^2, 10, 22, 23; 14:3, 17, 21^2, 22, 24, 27, 30, 31, 47; 15:35; 16:12; 17:5, 6, 12, 13, 20; 18:1, 10, 12, 14, 15, 26, 30; 19:18; 20:34, 37, 41; 22:6, 21; 23:7, 13, 15; 24:5, 16; 25:2, 21, 34, 35, 37, 44; 26:4, 5, 12; 27:4; 28:3^3, 20, 24; 30:1^2, 4, 5, 12^2, 14, 16^2, 18, 19, 21^2, 22, 31; 31:7, 11; 2Sa 1:1, 10, 12, 13; 2:8, 23, 27, 30, 31; 3:7, 22^2, 30, 37; 4:1, 2, 3, 4, 7; 5:8, 12^2, 17, 18, 25; 6:8, 13, 17, 18, 23; 7:1; 8:9, 10^2; 9:10, 12; 10:6, 15, 19; 11:22, 27; 12:2, 3^2, 4^2, 6, 8; 13:1, 3, 10, 15, 22, 23, 29, 30, 36; 14:6; 15:4, 18, 24; 16:1; 17:14, 18, 20, 21, 22, 25^2; 18:13, 18, 33; 19:8, 24, 31, 32; 20:3, 5; 21:2^2, 11, 12^2, 13, 20; 22:44; 23:8, 20, 21; 24:8, 9, 10, 19; 1Ki 1:6, 38, 44; 2:5, 19, 27, 28^2, 41; 3:1, 2, 10, 15, 21, 28; 4:7^2, 11, 13^2, 15, 24^2, 26, 34; 5:1^2, 15; 6:18, 25; 7:5, 8, 12^2, 14, 28, 30, 36, 51; 8:5, 9, 17, 54, 66; 9:1, 2, 10, 12, 14, 16^3, 23, 24; 10:4^2, 7^3, 19, 22, 24, 26; 11:2, 6, 9^2, 10, 16, 23, 29; 12:1, 2, 6, 8, 10, 12, 13, 15, 20, 32^2, 33^2; 13:5, 10, 11^2, 12, 20, 23^3, 26, 28, 31; 14:21, 22, 26; 15:11, 12, 13, 22, 29; 16:11, 31, 33; 18:10, 26, 30; 19:1^2; 20:12, 17, 19, 27, 33, 36, 42; 21:1, 4^2, 11^2, 15, 26; 22:13, 15, 31, 35, 38, 53; 2Ki 1:2, 17^2; 2:9, 13, 14^2, 18; 3:2, 9, 21; 4:12, 15, 17, 44; 5:1, 2, 4, 8, 13, 19; 6:18, 30; 7:6, 8, 15, 17^2, 18, 19^2; 8:1^2, 5^2, 18, 19, 21, 27, 29; 9:14, 15^2, 16; 10:1, 16, 17, 24, 25; 11:4, 10, 20; 12:6, 11, 18; 13:7, 14, 19, 23, 25; 14:3, 5, 27, 28; 15:3, 9, 34; 16:2, 11, 18; 17:4^2, 7^3, 8, 12, 14, 15, 19, 20, 21, 23, 28, 29, 33, 35; 18:3, 4^2, 12, 16; 19:8^2; 20:4, 11, 12^2; 21:3^2, 4, 7, 9, 16, 20, 24; 23:2, 5, 8, 11, 12^2, 13, 16, 19^2, 22, 24, 26, 32, 37; 24:3, 4, 7, 9, 13^2, 19; 25:11, 16, 17, 19, 22, 23; 1Ch 2:4, 18, 22, 26, 34^2, 52; 4:5, 27, 43; 5:9, 18, 25; 6:32, 49, 66; 7:4, 15, 23; 8:3, 8^2, 9, 11, 38; 9:19, 27, 28, 32, 44; 10:7, 11, 13; 11:6, 13, 22, 23; 12:29, 32, 39; 13:11, 14; 14:2, 4, 8, 9, 16; 15:2, 3, 15; 16:1, 2, 42; 18:9, 10^2, 11; 19:6, 9, 16, 19; 20:6; 21:19, 28, 29; 22:7; 23:17; 24:2, 19^2, 28; 25:5; 26:2, 4, 9, 10, 12, 20, 26, 28, 30; 27:23; 28:2, 12; 29:8, 9^2, 25; 2Ch 1:3, 4^3, 5, 12, 14; 2:17; 3:1^2; 5:1, 6, 11; 6:7, 13^2; 7:1, 6, 7, 9, 10, 11; 8:1, 2, 8, 11, 12, 14, 15; 9:3^2, 6^2, 12, 18, 23, 25; 10:1, 2, 6, 8, 10, 12, 15; 11:14^3, 15^2, 16; 12:2, 5, 9, 13; 13:13; 14:1, 5, 6^2, 8, 15; 15:8, 9, 11, 15^2, 16; 16:6, 14^2; 17:2, 5, 13, 19; 18:1, 12, 14, 30; 19:8; 20:21, 22, 23, 24, 27, 29, 33; 21:2, 4, 6, 7^2, 9, 10; 22:1, 4, 6, 7, 9; 23:9, 18, 21; 24:7^2, 12, 14, 16, 22, 24^2, 25; 25:3, 10, 20; 26:4, 10^2, 11, 16, 19, 20; 27:2; 28:1, 6, 17, 18^2, 19^2, 23; 29:2, 15, 34, 36^2; 30:2, 3^2, 5, 6, 17^2, 18, 26; 31:1, 6, 10; 32:2, 27, 29, 31^2; 33:3, 4, 7, 9, 15, 22^2, 23, 25; 34:4, 8, 9^2, 10, 11, 14, 22, 30; 35:10, 18^2, 20; 36:13, 14, 15, 17, 20, 21; Ezr 1:5, 7, 8; 2:1, 61, 65, 66; 3:7, 8, 12; 4:20; 5:12, 14^3; 6:13, 20, 21^2, 22^2; 7:6, 10; 8:20, 22, 25, 35; 9:1; 10:5, 17^2, 18, 44; Ne 1:2; 2:1, 9, 10, 12, 13^2, 16^2, 18^2; 4:6, 15, 18; 5:8, 12, 13; 6:1^2, 12^3, 16, 18; 7:1^3, 4, 6, 63, 67, 68; 8:1, 4, 12, 14, 17^2; 9:18^2, 23, 26, 28^2; 12:29, 43; 13:5, 7, 10^3, 23; Est 1:8, 14; 2:1^3, 6^2, 7^2, 8, 10, 15^2, 20^2; 3:2, 4; 4:1, 5, 7^2, 9, 12, 17; 5:5, 11^2, 14; 6:2^2, 4^2, 13, 14; 7:4, 7, 8, 10; 8:1, 2, 3, 17; 9:1, 2^2, 3, 22, 23^2, 24^2, 25, 26^2, 31; Job 1:3, 5; 2:11; 10:18^2, 19; 20:21; 29:12, 24; 31:21, 25, 35^2; 32:3^2, 4; 34:27; 35:3; 42:5, 7, 9, 10^2, 11^2, 12, 13; Ps 18:43; 30:7; 31:22; 44:20; 51:T; 55:6; 66:18; 73:2^2, 15; 78:11^2, 22, 30, 54, 63; 81:5; 90:2; 94:17; 95:9; 105:17, 19, 26, 38; 106:14, 21, 23; 107:11, 30; 119:92; 120:6; 123:3, 4; 124:1, 2; Pr 7:14; 8:25, 26; Ecc 1:16; 2:7^3, 11^2, 18; 8:10; SS 3:4; 5:3^2, 6; 6:11; 8:11; Isa 1:9, 11; 5:1; 6:2, 6; 7:2; 20:2^2; 22:3; 37:8^2; 38:8, 9^2, 17, 21, 22; 39:1^2; 48:18; 52:15^2; 53:2, 9; 60:10; 63:4; Jer 3:8, 24; 4:23, 25; 5:5^2; 9:2; 13:7; 15:17; 16:15; 18:10; 19:14; 23:8, 22; 24:1^2, 2^2; 26:8^2, 19; 28:12; 29:1, 2; 31:19; 32:3^2, 16; 33:25; 34:8, 10, 11, 16; 36:4, 13, 27, 32; 37:4, 5, 11, 15; 38:7, 27^2; 39:5, 9; 40:1, 7^3, 11^2, 12; 41:2, 9^4, 10, 11, 14, 16^2, 18^2; 43:1, 5^2, 6; 44:3, 15; 52:2, 15, 20, 22, 25; La 3:18; 4:18; Eze 1:6^2, 8^2, 10, 11, 16, 23; 2:10; 3:23; 8:4, 11; 9:3^2; 10:14, 21, 22; 11:24, 25; 16:7, 13, 14, 17, 20, 49; 17:13; 18:28; 20:6, 14, 15, 22, 24^2, 28; 23:8^2, 18, 37, 39, 41; 29:18; 33:5, 21, 22^2; 36:18^2, 20, 21^2; 37:7, 8^2; 38:8; 40:16^2, 24, 26, 31, 34^2, 35, 36, 37^2; 41:8, 16, 18, 23, 24; 42:6, 15, 20; 43:3^2; 47:5; Da 1:11, 15, 17, 18; 2:3, 14, 24; 3:2, 3^2, 7, 27^2; 4:21; 5:2, 3; 6:10^3, 23, 24; 7:1, 4, 5, 6, 7^2, 20; 8:1, 3, 5, 6, 15; 9:21; 10:2, 3^3; 11:21, 24; Hos 1:8; Joel 2:18; Am 7:2; Ob 1:16; Jnh 1:5^2, 10; 3:7, 10; Hag 1:12; Zec 5:9; 6:2; 7:2, 12, 14; 10:6; 11:8, 10; Mt 1:18, 20, 22, 25^2; 2:7, 9^2, 10, 13, 15, 16^2, 17, 23; 3:16; 4:12, 14; 7:25, 28; 8:1, 17, 33; 9:8, 20, 25, 32, 33^2, 36; 11:1, 20, 21, 23; 12:7, 17, 22, 48; 13:5, 6, 35, 46, 53; 14:3, 4, 10, 14, 23, 34; 15:5, 29, 38; 16:5, 12; 18:31^2, 33^2; 19:1, 22; 21:1^2, 4, 6, 28, 34; 22:3, 28, 34; 23:30; 24:22, 43; 25:9, 16, 17, 18, 20, 24; 26:1, 19, 30, 48, 57^2, 75; 27:9^3, 16, 17, 18, 35, 52, 55^2, 60; 28:11, 12, 16; Mk 3:1, 3, 10^2, 30; 4:5, 6, 35; 5:2, 4^2, 8, 14, 15^2, 16^2, 18, 20, 21, 25, 26^3, 27, 30, 32, 33, 39; 6:14, 17^2, 18, 19, 30, 31, 34, 38, 44, 53; 7:1, 11, 17, 25, 32; 8:7, 14^2, 23; 9:9^2, 28, 34; 10:22; 11:6, 8, 11; 12:6, 12, 23, 44^2; 13:20; 14:16, 18, 26, 44, 54, 72; 15:7, 10, 41, 42, 44, 46; 16:2, 3, 4, 8, 9, 10, 11, 14^2, 19, 99; Lk 1:7, 22, 58; 2:15, 17, 20^2, 21, 26^2, 39; 3:19^2, 21; 4:13, 16, 33, 35, 40; 5:2, 4, 6, 9, 11, 17, 25; 6:8, 18, 48; 7:1, 2, 10, 12, 13, 20, 21^2, 24, 29, 39, 41; 8:2^2, 27^2, 29^2, 30, 34, 35^2, 36^3, 38, 39, 42, 43^3, 46, 47^2, 56; 9:7^2, 8^2, 10, 32, 36^2, 37; 10:13, 39; 11:1, 14^2; 12:39; 13:1, 6, 11, 14; 14:2, 12, 17; 15:9, 11, 13, 14, 32; 16:1, 8; 17:6; 18:2; 19:15^2, 28, 29, 32, 37, 42; 20:19, 33; 21:4; 22:7, 13, 19, 52, 55, 61; 23:8^2, 12, 19^2, 25, 47, 48^2, 49, 51, 53, 55; 24:1, 12, 14, 21, 23, 24, 35^2, 40; Jn 1:24; 2:2, 9^2, 22^2; 3:24; 4:1, 4, 5, 8, 18, 44, 45^3, 46, 47, 53; 5:5, 6, 10, 13^2, 15; 6:11, 13, 14, 17, 19, 22^4, 23^2; 7:10, 30, 50; 8:3, 20, 31; 9:6, 8, 13, 15, 18^3, 22, 24, 35; 10:40; 11:13, 17, 19, 21, 28, 30^2, 32, 43, 45^2, 46, 57; 12:1, 9, 12, 16^2, 17, 18, 36, 37; 13:1, 2, 3^2, 12^3, 26, 29, 31; 15:22, 24; 17:1, 5; 18:1, 9, 10, 14, 18, 22, 26, 32, 38; 19:1, 11, 19, 23, 30, 32, 39, 41; 20:1, 7, 12, 14, 18, 19, 22; 21:9, 15, 20^2; Ac 1:2, 6, 9, 13, 16; 2:1, 30, 44, 45; 3:10, 12, 13, 18; 4:7, 14^2, 21, 22, 23, 28, 31, 35; 5:7, 27^2, 30, 40^2; 6:6; 7:4, 5, 16, 17, 18, 30, 44^2, 60; 8:9, 11, 14, 16^2, 25, 27; 9:23, 26, 27^3, 31, 33, 37, 39; 10:3, 7, 17, 24, 27, 45^2; 11:1, 13, 15, 16, 26; 12:2, 4, 10, 12, 17, 18, 19, 23; 13:5, 6, 12, 19, 22, 24, 29, 36, 48; 14:8^2, 9, 11, 21^2, 23^2, 25, 26^2, 27^2; 15:2, 4, 7, 12, 21, 33^2, 38^2; 16:3, 4, 7, 9, 10^2, 13, 16, 20, 22, 23, 27, 34, 40; 17:1, 9, 13; 18:2^2, 18, 19, 22, 25, 27; 19:6, 12, 13, 21, 32, 33, 35, 41; 20:1, 2^2, 11, 12, 13, 16, 36, 38; 21:1, 7, 9^2, 19, 27, 29^2, 33, 35, 40; 22:17, 25, 29, 30; 23:12, 27, 28; 24:2, 20, 27; 25:1, 6, 7, 12, 13, 16^2, 19^2, 21, 25; 26:14, 22, 30, 32; 27:5, 9^2, 21, 27, 30, 35, 38; 28:1, 2, 3, 6^2, 9, 11, 17^2, 18, 19, 23, 24; Ro 3:25; 4:10, 11, 12, 21; 7:7^2; 9:6, 10, 11^2, 29; 1Co 2:8; 4:8; 7:29, 30, 31; 11:24; 15:3; 2Co 1:9; 3:10; 7:5; 8:6, 15^2; Gal 1:15; 2:2, 7^2, 9; 3:19, 21; 4:4, 15, 22; Eph 1:13^2; 4:9; Php 1:30; 2:27; 3:7; 4:10; 1Th 1:9; 2:2^2; 3:5^2; 1Ti 1:13; Tit 3:5; Heb 1:3; 2:17; 3:9; 4:8; 6:13; 7:6, 11; 8:7, 9; 9:1, 19, 26; 10:12, 32, 34; 11:5^2, 9, 11, 15^3, 17, 18, 30, 31, 40; 12:9; 1Pe 1:6, 14; 2:10; 4:6; 2Pe 1:16; 1Jn 2:7, 19; 2Jn 1:5; Rev 2:4; 4:1; 5:6, 8; 6:2, 9^2, 11; 7:2; 8:6; 9:1, 9, 14, 15; 10:4, 8, 10; 11:10; 12:13^2, 16; 13:3, 4, 11, 12, 14; 14:1, 17, 18; 15:2; 16:2, 9, 18; 17:1, 3; 18:19; 19:20^2; 20:4^3, 10, 13; 21:1, 9, 15; Tob 1:3, 4^2, 5, 8^2, 21; 2:3, 7, 12; 3:6, 8^3, 10^2, 17; 4:1; 7:9^2, 16; 8:1, 2, 4, 11, 17; 9:5; 10:1, 7^4, 13; 11:7, 15^4, 17^2; 12:22; 14:10^2, 15^2; Jdt 2:1, 3, 4, 15; 3:8; 4:1^2, 3^3, 5, 8, 12, 13; 5:1^2, 8^2, 10, 18, 22; 6:1, 16, 17^3; 7:1, 5, 16, 19, 22; 8:2, 7; 9:2, 3, 5; 10:1^2, 3, 10^2; 11:2, 9, 13; 12:11, 15, 16, 19, 20; 13:1, 3^2, 13; 14:8, 9, 10, 17; 15:1, 3, 4, 5, 8; 16:19^2; AdE 1:4, 15, 17^3, 21; 2:1^2, 6^2, 7, 8, 10^2, 15, 20^2; 3:2, 4; 4:1, 3, 4, 7^2, 8, 17; 5:5, 11^2; 6:2, 4^2, 13, 14; 7:8, 10; 8:1, 2^2, 3, 14, 16, 17; 9:22, 23, 25, 26^2, 29; 10:5; 11:1, 2, 4, 12^2; 12:3; 14:18; 15:1, 6; Wis 2:2; 5:13; 7:5; 10:1, 5; 11:12, 13, 14^2, 24, 25; 12:27^2; 13:9; 14:15, 20; 15:17; 16:17, 25; 18:4, 5^2, 12^2, 13, 23; 19:2, 3, 4, 7, 14, 16; Sir Pr:T^2; 11:5; 23:14; 25:24; 31:10; 44:9^2; 46:20; 49:6, 7^2; 51:4; Bar 1:8^2, 9; 3:13, 28; 4:13, 15; LtJ 6:1; Sus 1:3, 4, 5, 6, 16, 18, 19, 26, 27, 61^2, 64; Bel 1:3, 13, 14, 32, 33^2, 42; 1Mc 1:1^2, 6, 7, 10, 53, 60; 2:2, 23, 28, 31^2; 3:2, 13, 29^2, 30, 39, 42^2, 46, 49; 4:20^2, 25, 26, 27^4, 41, 44, 45, 51, 53, 54, 55, 60; 5:1, 15, 25, 31, 46, 54^2, 56; 6:3, 5^2, 6^5, 7^3, 8^2, 17, 49, 53^3, 55, 56^2, 62; 7:11, 19, 23^2, 24, 25, 30, 31, 44, 47, 50; 8:2^2, 3, 4, 5, 6; 9:1, 7^2, 27, 35, 36, 38, 42, 57, 62, 68, 69, 72; 10:8, 12, 14, 15^4, 46^2, 47, 75, 77, 79, 81, 84; 11:2, 4^2, 5, 26, 27^2, 38^2, 39, 40^2, 49, 53^2, 55, 63, 68; 12:24, 27, 30, 34^2, 37, 42, 48, 50^2; 13:1, 14, 51, 53; 14:2, 4, 16, 17, 18, 33, 35^3, 36, 40^2; 15:12^2, 17, 27, 33, 36, 41; 16:1, 9, 11^2, 15, 21, 22; 2Mc 1:15^2, 20^3, 22^3, 31, 33^3; 2:4^2, 11, 14^2; 3:4^2, 7, 9^4, 11, 12, 13, 15^2, 17, 22^2, 23, 24, 28, 30^2, 32, 36; 4:1^3, 21, 30, 32^2, 38, 39^3, 47, 48; 5:5, 9, 10^3, 11, 15, 16, 18^2; 6:4, 9, 11, 21, 23, 24, 28, 29^2; 7:7, 8, 13; 8:1, 2, 5, 14, 15, 17, 25, 27^2, 28, 29, 30, 32, 33^2, 34, 36^2; 9:1, 2, 3, 4, 6, 8^2, 10, 15^2, 16, 18, 28; 10:2, 4, 5, 6, 7, 12, 13^3, 15, 21, 22, 24, 38; 11:1, 10, 13; 12:1, 3, 6, 10, 17, 18^2, 19, 20, 25, 30, 36, 39, 40, 42^4, 44; 13:2^2, 8, 9, 11, 12^2, 18, 23^2; 14:1, 2, 3^2, 11, 12, 14, 17^2, 20^3, 23, 26^2, 28^2, 30, 31, 38^2, 39; 15:3, 6, 8, 9, 10, 12^2, 19, 31, 32, 34; 1Es 1:3, 17, 20, 21, 33, 48, 49; 2:8, 10; 3:17, 24; 4:1, 13, 57^7, 62; 5:7, 38^2, 53, 55, 56, 63, 67; 6:8, 18, 26; 7:13^2, 15; 8:49, 52, 55, 60, 62, 65, 68; 9:3, 4, 15, 17, 36, 39, 42, 45, 54, 55; Pm 151:T; 3Mc 1:1^2, 2^2, 3, 6, 8^2, 9, 12, 13, 18, 19, 25; 2:6, 7, 8, 9^2, 21, 23, 24; 3:9, 10, 16; 4:1, 2, 6, 9, 11^3, 12, 14, 19^2, 20; 5:3, 10^2, 13, 15, 18^2, 19, 21, 23, 24, 25, 27^2, 28^2, 30, 35^2, 42, 45^2, 47, 50; 6:1^2, 5, 6, 22, 29, 30^2, 31, 33, 34^2, 36^2; 7:4, 7, 10, 11, 12, 13, 14, 15, 16^2, 17, 18, 19, 20; 2Es 1:27; 2:11, 47; 3:6, 26^2; 4:1, 7, 48, 49; 5:15, 20, 31^2; 6:35, 47, 50, 51, 54; 7:1^2, 11, 63, 72, 116^3; 8:56; 9:11, 20, 33, 39, 43; 10:3, 29, 48, 49, 51, 59; 11:1^2, 18, 22, 32^2, 33, 39; 12:2^2, 40, 44, 51; 13:8, 41, 42, 44; 14:32, 40; 15:53; 4Mc 1:33; 3:7^2, 8, 20; 4:6, 7, 12, 13^2, 14, 22^2, 23, 24, 25^2; 5:4, 7, 15, 18; 6:1, 3, 24, 32; 7:6; 8:3, 12, 13, 15, 16, 29; 9:10, 12, 25; 10:1, 12; 11:13, 17, 19; 12:1, 2, 6^2, 7, 19; 13:2^3, 23, 24, 27; 14:11; 15:2, 6, 7; 16:5, 10, 18; 17:22; 18:9

HAS (2937)

See also the selected listing for "HAS" in the Main Concordance.

Ge 1:30; 3:22; 4:6, 11, 25; 5:29; 14:20; 16:2, 11; 17:14; 18:19, 21; 19:13^2, 19; 21:6, 17, 26; 22:20; 24:27^2, 35^3, 36^2, 44, 51, 56; 26:22, 28; 27:27, 35, 36^2; 29:32, 33^2; 30:2, 6^2, 18, 20, 23, 27, 30^2; 31:1^2, 5, 7, 9, 15^2, 16^2; 33:5, 11; 35:3; 37:20, 33; 38:21, 22, 24; 39:8^3, 9, 14; 41:25, 28, 39, 51, 52; 42:21, 28^2, 36; 44:16^2, 28; 45:6, 8, 9; 48:2, 9, 11, 15, 16; Ex 3:9, 13, 14, 15, 16^2, 18; 4:5; 5:3, 23; 6:7; 9:18; 10:12; 11:6; 12:25, 44^2; 13:11^2; 14:3; 15:1^2, 2, 21^2; 16:7, 8, 9, 15, 16, 23, 29, 32; 18:10; 19:8; 20:20; 21:8, 16, 29^3, 36; 22:11; 24:3, 7, 8, 14; 32:1, 23, 24, 31, 33; 35:1, 4, 10, 30, 31, 34, 35; 36:1^2, 5; Lev 4:3, 23; 5:1; 6:10; 7:8; 8:5, 34^2; 9:7; 10:6, 11, 15, 17; 11:3, 7, 9, 26, 42; 13:2, 3^2, 4, 5, 6^2, 7, 8, 10, 13^2, 17, 18, 20, 21, 24, 25^2, 26, 28, 29, 32, 34, 36, 37, 38, 39, 41, 45, 46, 51, 53, 55^3, 56; 14:32, 39, 43, 44, 48; 15:2, 6, 16, 18, 19, 25^2, 32, 33; 16:17, 20; 17:2, 4, 15; 19:20^2; 20:11, 15, 16, 17, 18^2, 20, 21; 21:3, 7, 10^2, 14, 17, 18^2, 19, 21^2, 23; 22:4^2, 6, 20, 23, 24; 25:25, 26, 29, 30; 27:20, 22, 28; Nu 5:2, 7, 8, 13^2, 14^2, 19, 20, 27^3, 28; 6:13; 10:29; 12:2^2; 14:16, 24^2, 40; 15:22, 23; 16:9, 10, 28^2, 29, 46^2; 19:2^2, 13, 16^2, 20; 20:14; 21:29; 22:5, 10, 11^2, 13; 23:7, 8^2, 17, 19^2, 20, 21^2, 23, 24; 24:6, 11; 25:11; 27:8, 9, 10, 11; 30:1, 4^2, 5, 6, 7, 9, 12, 14, 15; 31:17, 19, 21; 32:7, 19, 21, 31; 34:13; 35:32; Dt 1:10, 11, 21^2, 27; 2:7^2, 12, 30; 3:18, 21; 4:5, 7, 8, 19, 20, 23, 32^2, 33, 34; 5:24, 26, 32, 33; 6:3, 10, 17, 19, 20, 25; 7:6, 8; 8:2, 10; 9:3, 4, 24, 28; 10:9, 21, 22; 11:4, 29; 12:1, 7, 15, 20, 21, 29; 13:14; 14:2, 6, 9, 24; 15:2, 6, 14, 21; 16:17; 17:1, 4, 5, 16, 18; 18:5, 6, 21, 22^2; 19:1, 4; 20:5, 6, 7, 14, 17; 21:3^2, 5, 15, 17, 18; 22:17, 19, 26; 23:11; 24:4, 5; 25:5, 7, 19; 26:11, 18, 19; 27:20; 28:9, 21, 48, 51, 52, 53; 29:4, 22, 24; 30:1, 3; 31:2, 7; 34:10; Jos 2:9^2, 24; 6:16, 25; 7:8, 11, 15; 8:8, 31; 10:4, 14, 19; 14:9, 10; 17:14; 18:3; 22:4, 25; 23:3^2, 9^2, 13, 14^2, 15^2, 16; 24:27; Jdg 1:7; 3:28; 4:14; 6:13^2, 29, 30, 31; 7:2, 14, 15; 8:3, 7, 24; 11:23, 24, 36^2; 13:10; 15:6^2, 14; 16:2, 17, 18, 23, 24^2; 17:13; 18:10; 19:9^2, 18, 30; 20:12; 21:3, 11; Ru 1:13^2, 15, 20, 21^3; 2:7, 11, 20; 3:3; 4:3, 14, 15, 17; 1Sa 1:27; 2:5^2, 8, 27; 4:3, 7, 17^3, 21, 22^2; 6:9; 7:12; 9:12, 16, 27; 10:1^2, 2, 11, 22, 24; 11:13; 12:13, 22, 24;

13:14[2]; 14:10, 12, 17, 29, 30, 38, 45[2]; 15:11[2], 22, 23, 26, 28[2], 33; 16:8, 9, 10, 22; 17:25[2], 33, 36[2]; 18:7; 19:4, 17; 20:7, 13, 22, 26, 27, 29[2], 32; 21:2, 11; 22:8, 13, 15; 23:7[3], 10, 11, 22; 24:14, 19; 25:17, 21[2], 26, 27, 30[3], 31, 34, 39[3], 40; 26:8, 19, 20; 27:6, 11, 12; 28:9[2], 15, 16, 17[2], 18, 21; 29:3, 5; 30:23[2]; 2Sa 1:16; 2:7; 3:9, 18, 23[2], 29, 38; 4:8, 9; 5:20, 24; 6:12; 7:27; 10:3[2]; 12:5, 13; 13:20, 24, 32, 35; 14:2, 7, 19, 20, 22, 30; 15:10; 16:8[3], 10, 11, 21; 17:5, 6, 7, 9[2], 21; 18:19, 28, 31; 19:7, 9, 11, 27, 30, 42; 20:21; 22:25, 33[2], 36; 23:3[2], 5; 24:21; 1Ki 1:11, 18, 19[3], 25[3], 27, 29, 37, 43, 44, 48, 51; 2:15, 23, 24[2], 29, 31, 38; 3:12; 5:4, 7; 8:12, 15, 20, 43, 56[2]; 9:8, 9; 10:9[2], 12; 11:11, 33[2]; 12:19; 13:3, 26[2]; 14:11; 16:16[2]; 18:10, 13, 27; 19:18; 21:14, 18, 29[2]; 22:23[2], 28; 2Ki 2:2, 4, 6, 16, 22; 3:7, 10, 13; 4:1, 2, 14, 27[2], 31; 5:20, 22, 25; 6:29, 32; 7:6; 8:1, 4, 7, 9, 10, 13, 22; 10:10; 13:23; 14:10; 17:26; 18:22, 27, 33; 19:4[2], 9, 16, 21, 28; 20:9[2]; 21:11[3]; 22:4, 10, 13, 16; 1Ch 14:11, 15; 16:12; 17:25; 19:3; 22:11, 18[2]; 23:25; 28:5[2], 10, 21; 29:1; 2Ch 2:11, 12, 15; 6:1, 4, 10, 33; 7:21, 22; 8:11; 9:8[2]; 10:19; 14:7; 16:7; 18:22[2], 27; 19:2; 20:26; 21:10; 24:20; 25:8, 16, 19; 28:9; 29:8, 11; 30:8; 31:10; 32:15; 34:18, 21; 35:21; 36:23[2]; Ezr 1:2[2]; 4:3, 18, 19, 20; 5:16; 6:12; 9:2, 6, 8[2], 9[2], 13; Ne 2:5; 9:32, 33; Est 1:15, 16; 5:8; 6:3[2], 8[2], 13; 7:5, 9; Job 1:10, 11, 12, 21; 3:23; 4:5; 9:4; 10:12; 12:9, 13; 13:1[2]; 16:7[2], 8[2], 9[2]; 17:6, 7; 19:6, 8[2], 9, 10, 11, 13, 21, 26; 22:20; 23:10, 11, 16[2]; 26:2[2], 3, 4, 6, 10; 27:2[2]; 28:7, 8; 30:11, 15, 19; 31:5, 7[3], 9, 17, 27[2], 32, 38; 32:14, 19; 33:4, 28; 34:5[2], 9, 23, 31; 36:23; 37:7, 21; 38:25, 28[2], 29, 36, 37; 39:5[2], 16, 17; 41:33; 42:7, 8; Ps 2:4; 4:3; 6:8, 9; 7:11, 12, 13; 9:6, 7, 15, 16[2]; 10:11[2]; 13:6; 18:24, 35[2]; 19:4; 22:31; 24:2; 28:6; 31:21; 33:12; 37:16; 38:2, 10; 41:8, 9, 11; 44:15, 17, 18; 45:2, 7; 46:8; 47:5; 48:3; 52:T; 53:5[2]; 54:7[2]; 60:6; 62:11; 64:9[2]; 66:5, 9[2], 16, 19[2], 20; 67:6[2]; 69:7, 9; 71:11; 72:13; 74:3; 76:2; 77:8, 9[2], 10; 78:4, 69; 82:1; 83:8; 88:16; 89:41; 93:1; 94:22; 98:1, 2[2], 3; 102:13, 23[2]; 103:13[2], 19; 104:17; 105:5; 106:31; 108:7; 109:11, 24; 110:4; 111:4, 6, 9; 115:12, 16; 116:1, 7; 118:14, 18, 22, 24, 27; 119:56, 126; 123:2, 4; 124:6; 126:2, 3; 127:5; 129:4; 132:13[2]; 135:4; 143:3; 145:9; 147:20; 148:14; Pr 3:30; 6:32; 7:19, 26; 9:1[2], 2[3], 3; 10:13; 12:14; 14:26, 29[2], 33, 35; 15:14, 15, 21; 16:4, 22; 17:21, 27; 20:12, 16; 23:29[6]; 25:4; 27:13; 28:2; 30:4[4], 15; 31:5; Ecc 1:9[2], 10, 13, 16; 2:12, 21; 3:10, 11[3], 14, 15[2], 17; 4:3[2]; 5:4, 11; 6:3, 5, 10[2]; 7:13, 14, 28; 8:6, 8; 9:4, 7; 12:13; SS 1:4, 6; 2:12; 6:1[2], 2; 8:8; Isa 1:2, 20, 21, 22; 2:12; 3:8[2]; 4:3, 4; 5:9, 14, 25; 6:7[2]; 7:5; 8:6, 18; 9:2, 6, 12, 17, 21; 10:4, 10, 12, 14, 27, 28[2], 29; 12:2, 5; 14:3, 4[2], 5, 24, 27, 32; 15:2, 8; 16:4, 9; 19:12, 14, 25; 20:3, 6; 21:2, 4[2], 17; 22:5, 8, 14, 25; 23:4, 8, 9, 11[3]; 24:3, 8, 11; 25:8; 26:5; 27:7; 28:2, 12; 29:10[2], 11, 16; 30:24, 33; 33:1, 14; 34:2[2], 5, 6[2], 8, 16[2], 17[2]; 36:7, 12, 18; 37:4[2], 9, 17, 22, 29; 38:7, 15[3]; 40:2[2], 5, 12, 13[2], 21, 24; 41:2, 4, 20[2], 25; 42:4; 44:7, 20, 23[2]; 45:9, 23; 48:8, 14, 16, 20; 49:5, 7, 10, 13, 14[2], 21[2]; 50:4, 5, 10; 51:5, 18[2]; 52:4, 9[2], 10; 53:1[2], 4, 6; 54:6, 10; 55:5; 58:14; 60:1[2], 9; 61:1[2], 9, 10[2]; 62:8, 11; 63:7[2]; 64:4[3], 10, 11; 66:2, 8[2]; Jer 2:10, 11, 14, 35, 37; 3:3, 7, 11, 24; 4:7[3], 8, 17, 18; 5:19, 23, 30; 6:24, 25, 30; 7:11, 28, 29; 8:5, 8, 13, 14[2], 21, 22; 9:12, 21[2]; 11:15[3], 17; 12:8[2]; 13:15, 17, 18; 14:4; 15:9[3]; 16:10; 18:6, 13[2]; 20:3, 8, 13; 21:2, 12; 22:3, 8, 21; 23:10, 15, 18[2], 19, 20, 28[3], 35[2], 37[2]; 25:3, 5, 31, 38[2]; 26:11, 13, 16; 27:13; 28:9, 15; 29:15, 26, 28, 31[2], 32; 30:6, 23, 24; 31:11[2], 22; 32:24[2], 25, 31, 43; 34:21; 35:14, 16; 36:7, 28; 38:21; 40:3[3], 14; 42:19; 44:23; 45:3; 46:12, 15, 21; 47:5, 7[2]; 48:8, 11[4], 15, 18[2], 19, 21, 32, 39[2], 45[2]; 49:1[3], 7[2], 14, 20[2], 24, 30, 31; 50:3, 14, 15[2], 17, 23, 25[2], 27, 29[2], 31, 45[2]; 51:8, 9[2], 10, 11, 12, 13, 14, 30, 34[6], 41, 42[2], 44[2], 51, 56; La 1:1[2], 2, 3, 5, 6, 8, 9, 10, 13, 15[2], 16, 17[2]; 2:1[3], 2[3], 3[3], 4[3], 5[3], 6[4], 7[2], 9, 17[4], 22; 3:1, 2, 4, 5, 6, 7[2], 9[2], 11, 15[2], 16, 28, 37; 4:1, 3, 6, 8[2], 16; 5:1, 2, 15[2], 16; Eze 2:5; 4:14; 5:6; 7:2, 6[3], 7[2], 10[3], 11, 12, 13; 8:12; 9:6, 9; 12:9; 13:6; 15:4, 5; 16:16, 51; 17:20; 18:10, 13, 14[2], 19[2]; 19:14[2]; 21:7, 25, 27, 29; 22:3, 4, 13, 18, 28; 24:2, 6, 24, 26, 27; 25:12; 26:2; 27:26; 28:5; 30:21; 31:11; 32:20; 33:21, 32, 33; 36:23, 35; 39:8[2]; 44:2, 26; 45:20; 46:12; Da 1:10; 2:10, 28, 30, 37, 38[2], 45; 3:5, 25, 28; 4:2, 22, 24, 25, 31, 32; 5:21, 26; 6:20, 26, 27; 8:26; 9:11, 12[3], 13, 14; 11:2, 12; 12:1; Hos 2:5[2]; 3:1; 4:1, 12, 19; 5:6; 6:1[2]; 7:11; 8:3, 7, 9, 14[2]; 10:5; 11:12; 12:2, 8[2], 14; 13:16; 14:4; Joel 1:2, 4[3], 6[2], 7[2], 17, 19, 20; 2:2, 20, 21, 23[2], 25, 26, 32; 3:8; Am 3:1, 4[2], 5, 6, 8[2]; 4:2; 6:8; 7:10, 11; 8:2, 7; Ob 1:1, 3, 6, 18; Jnh 1:2, 7, 8, 12; Mic 1:9[2], 12; 4:4, 9, 12; 5:3; 6:2, 8; 7:1[2], 4; Na 1:11, 14; 2:1, 12[2]; 3:13, 19; Hab 2:18[2]; Zep 1:7[2]; 2:15; 3:2[4], 15[2]; Hag 1:2, 10; Zec 1:6, 10; 2:9, 11, 13; 3:2; 4:9, 10; 6:15; 9:3; 11:2[2]; 13:5; Mal 1:13, 14; 2:10, 11[4]; Mt 2:2, 5; 3:2; 4:16, 17; 5:13, 23, 28; 8:20; 9:6, 18, 22, 33; 10:7; 11:11, 12, 18; 12:11, 28, 43; 13:11[2], 15, 21, 28, 32, 35, 44, 52; 14:2; 15:13; 16:17, 27; 17:9, 12; 18:12[2]; 19:6, 29; 20:7, 23; 21:21, 42; 23:17; 24:21, 45; 26:10, 12, 13, 23, 56, 65; 27:8, 23, 64; 28:6, 7, 18; Mk 1:15; 2:10; 3:21, 22, 26[2], 30; 4:11, 29; 5:19[2], 34; 6:2, 14, 16; 7:29, 37; 9:1, 13, 17, 21, 22, 50; 10:9, 29, 40, 52; 11:2, 21; 12:10, 43, 44; 13:19, 20; 14:6, 8[2], 9, 41; 15:14; 16:6; Lk 1:13, 25, 36, 43, 48, 49, 51[2], 52, 53, 54, 61, 68, 69, 72[2]; 2:15[2]; 3:11[3]; 4:6, 18[2], 21; 5:24; 7:16[2], 20, 33[2], 34, 44, 45, 46, 47, 50; 8:10, 39, 48; 9:19, 58; 10:9, 11, 40, 42; 11:5, 6, 7, 20, 24; 12:5[2], 48[2]; 13:25; 14:5[2], 8, 22, 28, 29, 34; 15:5, 9, 27[3], 30, 32[2]; 16:26; 17:7, 19, 31; 18:29, 42; 19:7, 9, 16, 18, 24, 25, 30; 20:17; 21:3, 4, 20; 22:22, 29, 31, 36[2]; 23:15[2], 22, 41; 24:5, 34[2]; Jn 1:3, 18[2]; 2:4, 20; 3:2, 13, 19, 27, 29[2], 32, 33[2], 34, 35, 36; 4:33, 44; 5:2, 22, 24[2], 26[2], 27, 36[2], 37, 38; 6:9, 27, 29, 39, 45, 46[2], 47; 7:6, 8, 15, 31, 38, 42, 46, 48; 8:10, 29, 35, 40; 9:29, 32; 10:4, 20, 21, 29, 36; 11:11, 12, 39; 12:19, 23, 29, 30, 38[2], 40, 48, 49, 50; 13:10, 18, 31[2], 32; 14:9[2], 30, 31; 15:9, 13; 16:6, 11, 15, 21[2], 32; 17:1, 14; 18:11; 19:7, 35; 20:21; 21:24; Ac 1:7, 8, 11; 2:33, 36; 3:13, 16[2]; 4:9, 11, 16; 5:3, 32; 7:40; 9:12, 13, 14, 17, 21; 10:15, 28, 31, 33; 11:8, 9, 18; 12:11; 13:23, 26, 33, 34, 35, 47; 14:17; 15:9, 14, 16, 17[2], 20, 21[2], 28, 29; 17:7, 30, 31[3]; 19:26; 20:28; 21:25, 28[2]; 22:10, 14; 23:9, 17, 18; 26:26; 27:24; 28:4[2], 21, 27, 28; Ro 1:16, 19, 20; 2:25; 3:1, 11, 21, 26; 4:2; 5:5[2]; 6:7, 9; 7:4; 8:2, 3, 22; 9:18, 21, 22, 23[2], 24; 10:16, 18; 11:1, 2, 11, 23, 25[2], 32, 34[2], 35; 12:3; 13:2, 8; 14:3, 18; 15:7, 8, 18, 20, 28; 16:2, 6, 12; 1Co 1:4, 6, 11, 13, 20; 2:9[2], 10, 16; 3:11, 13, 14; 4:9; 5:2, 4, 7; 6:1; 7:7, 12, 13, 15, 17, 29, 36, 37; 8:7; 10:13, 28; 11:15; 12:12, 24, 28; 14:26, 36; 15:10, 13, 14[3], 16, 17, 20, 21, 24, 25, 27, 38, 54; 16:9, 10, 12, 22; 2Co 1:18, 21; 2:5[2], 10; 3:6, 10, 11; 4:4, 6; 5:5[2], 10, 14, 17[2], 18; 6:16; 7:11, 13, 14; 8:1, 12, 19; 9:2[2], 14; 10:13; 13:10; Gal 3:1, 15, 22, 25; 4:6, 15; 5:1, 11; 6:14; Eph 1:3, 9, 18, 22[2]; 2:10, 14[2], 15; 3:5, 11; 4:32; 5:5; Php 1:12[2], 13, 29; 2:22, 26[2]; 3:4, 12; Col 1:6[2], 8, 12, 13, 22, 23, 26[2]; 3:13[2], 25; 4:13, 16; 1Th 1:4, 8[2]; 2:16; 3:6[3]; 5:9; 1Ti 1:12; 5:4, 5, 8, 9, 10, 16; 6:4, 16[2], 20; 2Ti 1:10; 2:15, 18; 4:6, 10[2]; Tit 2:11; Phm 1:18; Heb 1:2, 4, 9, 13; 2:6, 13, 14; 3:3; 4:3, 14, 15; 6:20; 7:13, 16, 21, 22, 27, 28; 8:2, 6[2], 13; 9:8, 15, 20, 26; 10:1, 13, 14, 23, 28; 11:10, 16; 12:2, 26; 13:5, 23; Jas 1:12[2], 15, 21; 2:5[2], 10, 13, 17; 3:7; 4:5; 5:15; 1Pe 1:3; 2:7; 3:22; 4:1[2], 10, 17; 5:10; 2Pe 1:3, 4, 12, 14; 2:3, 17, 20, 22; 1Jn 2:5, 11, 23[2], 25, 27, 29; 3:1, 2, 6, 8, 17, 23, 24; 4:2, 12, 13, 14, 16, 17, 18[2]; 5:1, 9, 10, 12[2], 20[2]; 2Jn 1:7, 9; 3Jn 1:11, 12[2]; Jude 1:6, 13; Rev 2:7, 11, 12, 17, 18, 29; 3:1, 6, 7, 13, 22; 5:5; 6:17; 9:12; 11:14, 15, 18; 12:6, 10, 12; 13:8, 9; 14:7, 8, 15, 18; 17:9, 10, 17; 18:2, 5, 6, 10, 14, 17, 19, 20; 19:2[2], 7[2], 8, 12, 16; 20:6; 21:11, 12, 14, 23; 22:6; Tob 2:3, 8; 3:15[2]; 4:19; 6:11, 12, 14, 15; 7:7, 10, 11; 8:6, 16, 20; 9:3; 10:2[2], 4, 6, 7; 11:15, 17; 12:3, 6; 13:3, 4, 6; 14:4; Jdt 6:4; 7:25; 8:15, 18, 27[2], 29; 9:5; 11:7, 11, 12[2], 16, 22; 12:4; 13:11, 14[2], 15, 16, 18; 14:18; 16:5; AdE 1:13, 16, 18; 4:8; 6:8; 7:4, 9; 10:5, 9[3]; 13:3, 15; 14:9, 11, 17, 18; 16:7, 16, 18[2], 21; Wis 1:7; 2:1; 3:13, 14; 4:2; 5:8[2], 10; 7:3; 8:8, 16[2]; 9:16, 17; 13:16; 14:14; 15:4; 17:11; Sir 1:6; 2:10[3]; 3:23, 24[2], 28; 5:4; 6:14; 8:2[2]; 9:10; 10:12, 27; 11:5; 13:7, 17; 14:12; 15:9, 12, 16, 20[2]; 16:5[2], 17; 17:28; 18:4, 14; 19:4, 6, 16; 21:18; 22:11[2]; 23:23[3]; 25:8, 11; 26:25; 27:20, 21; 28:2, 4, 14[2], 15, 19[3], 22; 29:6[2], 14, 15, 18[3], 27; 30:4, 6, 23; 31:6, 9, 10[2], 13, 25, 27; 34:5, 11, 30, 31; 35:12; 36:31; 37:21; 38:23, 24; 39:8, 21; 40:6, 14; 41:1, 2; 42:17[2], 19, 21, 24; 43:31, 33[2]; 44:19; 45:22[2], 26; 51:12[3]; Bar 2:2[2], 4, 9[3], 17; 3:15[2], 22, 25, 29, 30; 4:9, 22, 25[2]; 5:5, 7; LtJ 6:15, 18, 73; Aza 1:66[2]; Sus 1:50, 55[2], 56[2], 59; Bel 1:5, 9, 12, 28[2], 37; 1Mc 2:8, 10[2], 11[2], 66; 6:10; 7:7, 14, 42; 8:14, 26, 28; 9:10, 29; 10:23, 37; 11:10; 12:10, 21; 13:39; 14:23; 15:20; 16:21; 2Mc 1:17; 2:1, 17[2], 18[2], 23, 29, 32; 3:33, 39; 7:6, 16, 38; 11:18, 23, 29, 35; 13:5; 14:36; 15:2, 34, 37; 1Es 1:58; 2:3, 4, 22, 26[2]; 4:14; 5:71; 6:20[2]; 8:22, 70, 78, 86[2]; 3Mc 1:15, 27; 4:14; 6:11, 25, 26, 28; 2Es 2:37[2]; 3:28, 29, 32, 33[2], 35; 4:2, 19, 21, 23[3], 28[2], 29[3], 30, 31, 36, 45[2], 46; 5:11, 17, 49; 6:28, 32[3], 59; 7:4, 27, 39, 42, 46[2], 48[4], 50, 59[2], 60, 74[2], 78, 111[2], 113, 114[4], 115, 119, 120, 132; 8:8, 9, 11, 35[2], 43[2], 53[2]; 9:2, 5, 22, 24, 34, 35, 42; 10:6, 14, 21, 22[6], 23, 28, 38, 39, 50; 11:40, 43, 44; 12:7, 30, 32, 33, 47[2]; 13:26; 14:10, 21, 22; 15:6; 16:3, 4, 6, 38, 57, 58[2], 59, 60; 4Mc 2:6, 14; 5:8, 25, 26[2]; 6:33, 35; 7:4, 15; 8:5, 17; 10:21; 12:12; 13:19; 16:2

HAVE (5723)

See also the selected listing for "HAVE" in the Main Concordance.

Ge 1:26, 28, 29[2], 30; 3:11, 13, 14, 17[2]; 4:1, 10, 14, 20, 23; 6:7[2], 13; 7:1, 4; 8:21; 9:13, 17; 11:6; 12:18; 14:22, 23, 24; 15:3; 16:8, 11, 13; 17:5, 20; 18:5[2], 10, 12[2], 14, 19, 21; 19:8[3], 12[2], 19, 21; 20:3, 9[4], 16; 21:7[2], 23[2], 26, 29; 22:12, 16[3], 18; 24:14[2], 19, 25, 31, 33; 26:10[3], 16, 27[2], 29[3], 32; 27:19, 20, 33, 36, 37[3], 38, 45; 28:15[2], 22; 29:25[2], 34; 30:3, 8[2], 15, 16, 20, 26[2], 27, 29[2], 34; 31:6, 12, 26[2], 27, 28, 32, 36, 37[2], 38[3], 41[2], 42, 43, 51; 32:4, 5[2], 10[2], 12, 28[2], 30; 33:9[2], 10, 11; 34:30; 35:3, 17; 37:8, 9, 10, 17, 32; 38:22, 29; 39:17; 40:8, 15[2]; 41:15[2], 21, 41; 42:2, 9, 10, 11, 12, 14, 36; 43:7, 10, 18[2], 21, 22, 23; 44:4[2], 5, 15, 19, 20, 28; 45:10, 11, 13, 16; 46:31, 32[3], 34; 47:1, 4, 5, 9, 23, 25, 26, 29, 30; 49:9; 50:4, 21; Ex 1:18; 2:18, 22; 3:7[2], 8, 9, 12, 16; 4:10[2], 21; 5:8, 21[2], 22, 23; 6:5[2], 12; 7:1, 16; 9:15[2], 16, 19[2], 27, 29; 10:1, 2[2], 6, 9, 10, 16, 25; 12:36; 14:5, 11[2], 12, 14, 18; 15:9, 17; 16:3, 12[2]; 17:16; 18:3, 16; 19:4, 10; 20:3, 22; 21:8; 23:12, 13, 20, 30; 24:12; 25:8; 26:32; 27:9, 16; 28:3[2], 7, 32; 29:35; 31:2, 3, 6[3], 11; 32:7, 8[3], 9, 13, 21, 29[2], 30, 31, 32, 34; 33:1, 12[4], 13, 16, 17[2], 22; 34:9, 10, 27; 35:2; Lev 4:14, 28[2], 35; 5:1, 2, 5, 6, 7, 10, 11, 13, 17, 19; 6:2, 3, 4, 5, 17; 7:7, 33, 34[2], 35; 10:14, 18, 19[2]; 11:4[2], 5, 6, 10, 12, 21, 23; 13:58; 14:41, 45; 15:32; 16:4; 17:11, 12, 14; 18:20, 23[2], 24; 19:8, 36; 20:3, 12, 13, 24[2], 25, 26; 23:7, 14, 39; 24:22; 25:9[2], 31, 32, 44, 45, 48[2], 54; 26:10, 13, 23, 35[2], 37; 27:29; Nu 3:32; 4:15, 16, 27; 5:18, 19, 20[2]; 6:19; 8:7, 13, 15, 16, 18, 19; 9:14; 11:11[2], 15, 16, 18, 20[2]; 12:11; 13:32; 14:11, 14, 15, 19, 20, 22[3], 27, 29, 31, 35, 40, 43; 15:16, 25, 29, 39; 16:3, 7, 11, 13, 14, 15[2], 30, 38, 41; 18:8[2], 11, 12, 19, 20[2], 21, 23, 24[3], 26, 30, 32; 19:20; 20:4, 5, 12, 17, 24; 21:5, 7, 22, 34; 22:5[2], 20, 28[2], 29, 30[2], 32[2], 33, 34, 38[2]; 23:4[2], 11[2]; 24:7, 10; 25:1, 5, 18; 27:12, 13, 19; 28:25, 26; 29:1, 7, 12, 35; 31:15, 18, 30, 49, 50; 32:4, 5, 11, 12, 14, 17, 18, 23, 24, 30; 33:53; 34:6, 14, 15; 36:4; Dt 1:6, 8, 14, 20, 28, 29, 32, 41; 2:3, 5, 7, 9, 19, 24, 29, 31; 3:2, 19[2], 20[2], 21, 24; 4:3, 9, 25, 30, 33; 5:7, 24[2], 26, 28[3]; 6:11; 7:21, 24; 8:12[2], 13[2], 17; 9:2, 7, 12[4], 13, 23, 24, 28; 10:21; 11:2, 7, 8, 10, 28; 12:9, 12, 20, 21, 29, 30, 31; 13:2, 6, 13[2]; 14:7, 10, 27, 29; 15:18; 16:10, 13; 17:3, 14[2], 18; 18:1, 2, 8[2], 17, 20; 19:1, 12; 20:9; 21:14, 15; 22:8, 9[2], 27; 23:12, 13, 15, 23; 24:8; 25:1, 8, 13, 14, 15[2]; 26:1, 3, 10, 12, 13[3], 14[4], 15, 17; 27:3, 4, 5, 9, 12; 28:20, 36, 40, 41, 64; 29:2, 5[3], 6[2], 17; 30:1[2], 3, 15, 19; 31:5, 6, 13, 16, 17, 18, 20[2], 21, 27, 29; 32:5, 30, 36; 34:4; Jos 1:3, 16; 2:2, 3[2], 10, 12, 16, 17; 3:4; 5:9, 14; 6:2, 6, 7; 7:7, 10, 11[5], 12, 19; 8:1, 6, 8[2]; 9:6, 9[2], 19; 10:8, 17; 13:6; 14:9; 15:19; 16:10[2]; 17:14, 16, 17[2], 18; 18:7[2]; 22:2[3], 3[2], 16, 17[2], 24, 25, 27, 31[2]; 23:3, 4[2], 8, 14, 15; 24:22; Jdg 1:7, 15, 21; 2:2[2], 20[2]; 3:19, 20; 4:18; 6:10, 17, 22, 36, 37; 7:9; 8:1, 2, 3, 6, 15, 22; 9:16[2], 18[3], 19, 31, 48[2]; 10:10[3], 13, 14, 15; 11:8, 12, 27, 35[3], 36; 12:3; 13:22, 23; 14:15, 16[3], 18; 15:7, 10[2], 11[2], 12, 16, 18; 16:10, 11, 13, 15[2], 17; 18:4, 9, 24; 19:19, 22; 20:6, 10; 21:7, 22; Ru 1:8, 11, 12[2]; 2:9[2], 10, 11, 12[2], 13, 19, 21; 3:2, 10; 4:9, 10; 1Sa 1:15[2], 16, 17, 20, 23, 28; 2:5; 3:12, 13; 4:7, 9, 16, 20; 5:10; 6:7, 21; 7:1, 6; 8:7[2], 8, 18, 19; 9:6, 7, 8, 12, 16, 20, 21; 10:19[2]; 11:9; 12:1[3], 2, 3[5], 4, 5, 10[3], 13[2], 17, 19, 20; 13:11, 12, 13[3], 14; 14:11, 24, 29, 33, 41, 43; 15:3, 13, 15[2], 20[4], 23, 24[2], 26, 30; 16:1[2], 2, 5, 7, 18; 17:8, 25, 28[3], 29, 45; 18:8[3], 19; 19:4, 17; 20:1, 8, 12, 23, 29, 30, 42; 21:2[2], 3, 4[2], 5, 14, 15; 22:8, 13, 15; 23:27; 24:10, 11, 17[2], 18[2], 19; 25:6, 7[2], 8[2], 11, 31, 33, 34, 35[2]; 26:15, 16[2], 18, 19, 21[3]; 27:5, 10; 28:12, 13, 15[2], 21[3], 22; 29:3, 4, 6[2], 8[2], 9, 10[2]; 30:22; 2Sa 1:3[2], 9, 10, 16, 19, 25, 27; 2:6, 14, 27; 3:7, 8, 17, 24, 34; 4:11; 6:21, 22; 7:3, 6[2], 7[2], 9[2], 18, 19, 21, 22, 25[2], 27, 28, 29; 9:9, 10; 10:5; 11:10, 19; 12:8, 9[4], 10[2], 13, 14, 21, 27[2]; 13:28, 32, 35; 14:13, 15[2], 22, 31, 32; 15:7, 13, 34; 16:2, 8, 10[2], 18, 19, 21; 17:15, 20; 18:11, 13, 18, 21, 22; 19:5[2], 6, 20[2], 22, 28, 29, 34, 41, 42, 43[2]; 20:1; 21:5; 22:22[2], 36, 37; 24:10[3], 17[3]; 1Ki 1:6, 11, 24, 27, 33, 35, 45[2], 53; 2:14, 16, 20, 43; 3:6[3], 7, 8, 11[3], 13; 5:8[2], 9; 8:13, 16, 20[2], 21, 24, 25, 27, 35, 36, 43, 44[2], 47[4], 48[2], 50[3], 53; 9:3[3], 4, 6, 7[2], 9, 13; 11:11[2], 13, 32, 36[2]; 12:9, 16[2], 28; 13:21[2], 22[2]; 14:8, 9[3], 15; 16:2[2]; 17:4, 9, 12, 13, 18[2], 20; 18:9, 12[2], 18[3], 19, 36, 37; 19:10[2], 14[2], 18, 20; 20:4, 13, 17, 18[2], 22, 25, 28, 31, 36[2], 40, 42; 21:2, 10[2], 19, 20[3], 22[2], 29; 22:17[2]; 2Ki 1:4, 5, 6, 16[2]; 2:10, 16, 21; 3:13, 14, 23; 4:2, 8, 13[2], 43; 5:6, 8, 13, 22, 25; 7:12[2], 13, 17; 9:5, 18, 19; 10:2, 8, 13, 19, 30[2]; 13:17, 19[2]; 14:10; 17:26, 38; 18:14, 20, 25, 34, 35; 19:3, 6[2], 11[2], 12, 15, 17, 18, 20, 22[2], 23[3], 25, 26, 28; 20:3[2], 5[2], 14, 15[2], 17, 19; 21:7, 8, 15[2]; 22:4[2], 5, 8, 9[3], 17[3], 18, 19[2]; 23:17, 27[2]; 1Ch 4:27, 43; 12:17[3]; 13:2; 15:12; 17:2, 5[2], 6[2], 8[2], 16, 17, 19, 20, 23[2], 25, 26, 27; 19:3, 5; 21:8[3], 17[2]; 22:8[3], 14[2], 15; 23:4, 5, 11; 26:32; 28:3, 6; 29:2, 3[2], 14, 16, 17[2], 19; 2Ch 1:8[2], 9, 11[4], 12; 2:13; 6:2, 5, 6[2], 10[2], 11, 15[2], 16, 18, 26, 27, 33, 34[2], 37[4], 38[2], 39; 7:12[2], 16, 17, 19, 20[2]; 10:9, 16[2]; 12:5, 7; 13:8, 9, 10[2], 11, 12; 14:7[2], 11; 16:9[2]; 18:16; 19:3; 20:8[2], 11, 37[2]; 21:12, 13[3], 15; 24:6, 20; 25:9, 15, 16[3], 19; 26:18; 28:9, 10, 11; 29:6[4], 7, 9, 18, 19, 31; 30:6; 31:10[3]; 32:13; 33:7, 8; 34:12, 15, 17[2], 25[3], 26, 27[3]; 35:21, 25; Ezr 3:8; 4:2, 3, 12, 16, 19; 5:17; 7:15, 19; 9:1, 2[2], 6, 7[2], 10, 11, 13[2], 15; 10:2[2], 10, 12, 13, 14; Ne 1:3, 6[2], 7, 9; 2:3, 20; 4:5; 5:5, 8, 11, 19; 6:7, 8; 9:6, 8, 33[3], 34, 37[2]; 10:28[2], 34; 13:14, 29; Est 1:18; 3:9; 4:11, 14; 5:4, 8, 14; 6:10[2]; 7:3, 4[2]; 8:5[2], 7[2]; 9:12[2]; Job 1:5, 7, 8, 10[3], 15, 16, 17, 19; 2:2, 3, 4; 3:9, 15, 26; 4:3[2], 4[2], 8; 5:3, 16, 27; 6:3, 8, 10, 13, 21, 22, 24; 7:1, 20[2]; 8:8, 18; 10:4, 12; 11:16, 18; 12:3, 5; 13:13, 15, 18; 14:5; 15:8, 17, 18[2], 27; 16:2, 3, 10[2], 15[2], 22; 17:4, 9; 18:17, 19; 19:3, 4, 12, 14, 15[2], 19, 20, 21[2]; 20:7, 19[2]; 21:3, 29, 31; 22:6, 7[2], 9[2], 15; 23:11[2], 12[2]; 24:7, 19; 26:2[2], 3, 4; 27:12[2], 14; 28:8, 22; 30:1, 8, 11, 16, 19, 21; 31:1, 5, 9, 13, 16[2], 17, 19, 20, 21, 23, 24, 25, 26, 28, 29, 30, 32, 33, 38, 39; 32:13, 15; 33:8[2], 24, 32; 34:10, 16, 31, 32, 34; 35:3, 6; 36:2, 21, 23, 24, 25; 38:4, 12, 16, 17[2], 18, 22[2], 23; 39:6, 12; 40:5, 9; 42:3, 7, 8; Ps 2:6, 7; 3:6; 4:7; 5:10; 7:3, 4, 6, 15; 8:1, 2, 3, 5, 6[2]; 9:4[2], 5[3], 6[2], 10, 15; 10:2, 14; 11:2; 12:1; 13:2, 4; 14:3, 4; 16:2, 6[2]; 17:4, 5[2], 14[2]; 18:21[2], 35; 19:13; 21:2[2]; 22:1, 10, 16, 21; 24:4; 25:6; 26:1[2]; 27:9, 12; 30:1, 2, 11[2]; 31:5, 7[2], 8[2], 12[2], 19; 34:9; 35:21, 22, 25[2]; 36:3; 37:19, 25[2], 35; 38:2, 4; 39:5, 9; 40:5, 6[2], 9[2], 10[3], 12[2]; 41:4, 12; 42:3, 7, 9; 43:2; 44:1[2], 7[2], 8, 9[2], 10, 11[2], 12, 13, 14, 17, 18, 19; 45:16; 48:8[2]; 50:16, 21[2]; 51:1, 4, 8, 16; 52:9; 53:3, 4; 54:3; 55:4; 56:6, 8, 13; 57:6; 58:4; 59:16; 60:1[2], 2[2], 3[2], 4, 10; 61:5[2]; 62:11; 63:2, 7; 64:6; 65:9; 66:10[2], 12, 18; 68:23, 28; 69:1, 2, 5, 7, 8, 9, 20, 26[2], 27; 71:6, 7, 17, 19, 20, 23, 24; 72:8, 12; 73:4, 13, 14, 15, 25, 28; 74:4, 17, 20; 77:14; 78:3[2]; 79:1[3], 2, 3, 4, 7; 80:5, 12, 14, 16[2]; 82:5; 83:2; 86:9, 13, 17; 88:4, 6, 8[2], 18; 89:3[2], 11, 13, 19[2], 20[2], 35, 38, 39[2], 40[2], 42[2], 43[2], 44, 45[2], 47; 90:1, 8, 13, 15[2]; 91:9; 92:4, 10[2], 11[2]; 93:3[2]; 94:17; 95:5; 98:1, 3; 99:4[2]; 102:10, 13, 14, 27; 104:12, 19, 24, 33; 106:6[3]; 108:11; 109:27; 111:10; 112:9[2]; 115:5, 6, 7; 116:8, 16; 118:21[2]; 119:4, 22, 30, 40, 42, 45, 49, 54, 56, 65, 73, 74, 75, 78, 83[2], 85, 87[2], 90, 92, 93, 94, 96, 99, 102, 106, 110, 117, 121, 133, 138, 143, 152, 165, 173, 176; 120:6; 123:3[3]; 124:3, 4[2], 5, 7[2]; 129:1, 2[2]; 131:2; 132:14, 17; 135:14, 16[2], 17; 137:8; 138:2, 4; 139:1; 140:4, 5[3], 7; 141:9; 142:3; 143:9; Pr 1:14, 24[2], 25[2], 30; 3:28; 4:11[2], 16[2]; 6:1[2], 3; 7:14, 15[2], 16, 17; 8:14[3]; 9:5; 12:9, 11[2], 20; 13:7[2], 25; 14:20, 26; 17:16[2]; 18:1; 19:19; 20:9, 13; 22:2, 11, 19, 20, 27; 23:2, 8; 24:5[2], 20, 25, 29[2]; 25:7, 10, 16; 28:10, 19[2]; 29:7, 13; 30:2, 3[2], 20, 27, 32[2]; 31:11, 29; Ecc 1:16; 2:14, 15, 16, 25; 3:9, 10, 19[2]; 4:2, 9, 10; 5:13, 14, 16, 18; 6:1, 8[2]; 7:15, 22, 23, 28[2], 29; 9:5, 6[2], 13; 10:5, 7; 12:1; SS 1:6; 3:3; 4:2, 9[2]; 6:6; 7:12[2], 13; 8:8, 12; Isa 1:2, 4[2], 6, 9, 11, 14, 29; 2:6, 8, 22; 3:6, 9, 11, 14; 5:4, 24[2]; 6:5; 7:17; 8:2, 20; 9:2, 3[2], 4, 10[2], 17; 10:7, 11, 13[5], 14[2], 29; 13:3[2], 17, 18; 14:1, 10[2], 20[2], 24[2]; 15:7[2]; 16:1, 6; 17:8[2], 10[2]; 19:13[2], 14; 21:3, 10, 15; 22:1, 3, 11, 16[2]; 23:4[2], 12; 24:5; 25:1, 2, 4, 9[2]; 26:1, 4, 12[2], 13, 14, 15[3], 18; 27:4, 7, 11; 28:15[5], 22, 25; 30:7, 29; 31:6, 7; 32:3[2], 4; 33:1[3], 8, 13; 34:5; 36:5, 10, 19, 20; 37:3, 6[2], 11[2], 12, 16, 18, 19, 21, 23[2], 24[3], 26, 27, 29; 38:3[2], 5[2], 12, 17[2]; 39:3, 4[2], 6, 8; 40:21[3], 28[2]; 41:5[2], 8, 9, 27; 42:1, 6[3], 9, 14[2], 16, 22, 24; 43:1[2], 8[2], 10, 22, 23[2], 24[3]; 44:1, 2, 8, 19, 22[2]; 45:1, 8, 13, 20, 23; 46:3, 4, 11[2]; 47:12, 15[2]; 48:6[2], 7, 8[2], 10[2], 15[2], 16[2], 18, 19; 49:4[2], 8[3], 13, 16, 21; 50:1, 2, 7[2], 11[2]; 51:7, 13, 16, 17[2], 19, 20, 22, 23[2]; 53:1, 6[2], 8; 54:1, 8, 9, 16[2]; 55:1, 7, 10; 56:11[4]; 57:6[2], 7, 8[7], 11, 16, 18; 59:2[2], 3, 8, 10, 21; 60:10, 15; 62:6, 8; 63:3, 18, 19; 64:6, 7[2], 10, 11; 65:10; 66:3, 5, 19, 24; Jer 1:9, 12, 16, 18; 2:11, 13[2], 15[3], 16, 17, 23[2], 25, 27, 28[2], 29, 30, 31, 32, 33, 35; 3:1, 2[3], 3[2], 4, 5[2], 6, 13[2], 16, 20, 21[2], 25[2]; 4:10, 17, 18, 22, 28[3]; 5:3[4], 4, 7[2], 11, 12[2], 14, 19, 21[2], 23, 25[2], 27, 28, 31; 6:2, 14, 19[2], 23, 24, 27; 7:9, 13, 25, 30[2]; 8:2[3], 3, 5[2], 6[2], 9, 11, 14, 19; 9:3, 5, 10, 13[2], 14[2], 16[2], 19[2]; 10:5, 20, 21, 25[3]; 11:10[3], 13[2], 17, 20; 12:5[2], 6, 7[3], 10[3], 11, 12, 13[3], 14, 15[2]; 13:10, 14, 21, 22, 25[2], 27; 14:7, 10[2], 13, 18, 19[2], 20; 15:5, 6[2], 7[3], 8[2], 10[2], 11[2]; 16:2, 5, 10, 11[5], 12, 13, 18[2], 19; 17:13, 16[2]; 18:8, 15[3], 20, 22; 19:4[4], 13[2], 15[2]; 20:6, 7[4], 12, 17; 21:7, 9, 10; 22:12, 21; 23:2[3], 3, 9, 11, 14[2], 22[2], 25[4], 38; 24:5; 25:3[2], 4, 7, 8, 13, 23, 34; 26:4, 5, 9, 11, 12; 27:3, 5, 6[2], 8, 15; 28:2,

6, 13, 14[2], 16; **29:**4, 6, 7, 11, 14, 15, 18, 23[3], 27, 32; **30:**2, 5, 10[2], 14[2], 15, 17, 18; **31:**3[2], 9, 20, 28, 29, 37; **32:**20, 23, 24, 25, 29[2], 30[2], 33[2], 42; **33:**3, 5, 21, 24[2], 26; **34:**5, 14[2], 17; **35:**5, 8, 9, 10[2], 14[3], 15, 16, 17[5], 18; **36:**2, 6, 29[2], 30, 31; **37:**18[2]; **38:**2, 9, 14, 19, 22[2], 25; **39:**18[2]; **40:**4, 10; **41:**8; **42:**10, 11, 12, 17[2], 19, 20, 21[2]; **43:**10; **44:**2[2], 8, 9, 10[2], 13, 14, 16, 17[2], 18[2], 25[2], 28; **45:**4[2]; **46:**5[2], 6, 11, 12[2], 21, 27[2], 28[2]; **48:**5, 15, 29, 33[2], 34, 36, 38, 46[2]; **49:**10[2], 12, 13, 14, 16, 23, 24, 32, 37; **50:**6[4], 7[3], 15, 20, 21, 33, 42; **51:**5, 24, 30[2], 32[2], 43, 49, 51[2]; **La 1:**2[2], 3, 5[2], 6, 8, 10, 11, 18[2], 20, 21[2], 22; **2:**9, 10[2], 14[3], 16[2], 20[2], 21[2]; **3:**14, 17, 21, 32, 37, 42[2], 43, 44, 45, 46, 47, 52, 58[2], 59, 60, 61; **4:**10; **5:**3, 6, 14, 16, 17, 20[2], 22; **Eze 2:**3[2]; **3:**7, 8, 9, 17, 19, 20[2], 21; **4:**6, 8, 14[2], 15; **5:**5, 7[2], 9, 11[2], 13, 15, 17; **6:**9; **7:**4, 9, 14; **8:**12, 15, 17, 18; **9:**10, 11; **10:**8; **11:**6[2], 7, 8, 12[3], 15[2], 16[2], 17; **12:**2[2], 6, 11; **13:**3, 4, 5, 6, 7[2], 8, 10, 14, 15, 19, 22[3]; **14:**3, 9, 22[2], 23; **15:**6, 8; **16:**43[4], 48[2], 51[3], 52[2], 54, 59[2], 63; **17:**21, 24; **18:**2, 21, 22[2], 23, 24[2], 26, 27, 31, 32; **20:**41, 43[2], 48; **21:**5, 10, 15, 17, 23, 24[2], 32; **22:**4[5], 6, 8, 12, 13, 14, 18, 19, 22, 25[3], 26[5], 28, 29[3], 31[3]; **23:**30, 31, 34, 35, 37[3], 38[2], 44, 48; **24:**8, 12, 13, 14, 22; **25:**6, 7; **26:**5, 14, 17, 20; **27:**3, 26, 34, 36; **28:**2, 4[2], 5, 10, 19, 24, 26; **29:**5, 20; **30:**8, 12, 21; **31:**11, 12[2]; **32:**9, 21, 25, 30; **33:**5, 7, 9, 10, 11, 13, 15, 16[2], 29[2]; **34:**2, 4[6], 8[5], 12, 19[2], 24; **35:**12; **36:**2, 4, 6, 22, 23, 36[2]; **37:**14, 21, 23, 24; **38:**13[2]; **39:**5, 8, 15, 21[2], 25, 26, 27[2]; **40:**45, 46; **43:**8, 11, 23; **44:**7, 8[2], 12, 13, 17, 18, 19; **45:**8, 10; **47:**6, 13, 22; **48:**10, 13, 17; **Da 2:**3, 8, 9, 21, 23[3], 25, 26, 30, 47; **3:**10, 12[2], 14, 15, 16, 18; **4:**1, 22, 25, 30, 32; **5:**7, 11, 14, 15, 16[2], 22, 23[5], 27; **6:**13, 22, 25; **8:**7, 23; **9:**5, 6, 7[2], 8, 9, 10, 11[2], 14, 15[2], 16, 22, 23, 26; **10:**11, 12[2], 14, 16, 19, 20; **Hos 1:**2, 6, 7; **2:**4, 12, 23; **3:**3; **4:**6[2], 10, 12; **5:**1, 3, 7[2], 10; **6:**5[2], 10; **7:**7, 13[2], 16; **8:**1, 9; **9:**1[2], 7[2], 9, 17; **10:**3, 9[2], 13[4]; **11:**5; **12:**8; **13:**4; **14:**1, 8; **Joel 1:**7, 19; **2:**4; **3:**2[2], 5[2], 6, 7, 19; **Am 1:**3, 13; **2:**4[3]; **3:**2, 3; **5:**3[2], 11[2], 14; **6:**12, 13; **9:**15; **Ob 1:**1, 5, 7[4], 12[3], 13[3], 14[2], 15, 16, 21; **Jnh 1:**10, 14; **2:**9; **Mic 1:**16; **2:**5; **3:**4, 5; **4:**6[2], 9; **5:**12; **6:**3[2], 13, 16[2]; **7:**1, 2, 5, 9, 19, 20; **Na 1:**12; **2:**2; **3:**17; **Hab 1:**12[2], 14[2]; **2:**5, 8, 10[2]; **3:**2; **Zep 1:**6[2], 11, 17; **2:**8[2]; **3:**4[2], 6[3], 7, 11; **Hag 1:**5, 6[3], 7, 9, 10, 11; **2:**23; **Zec 1:**11, 12, 16, 19, 21; **2:**6; **3:**4, 7, 9; **4:**9; **5:**4; **6:**8, 10; **7:**3; **8:**9, 13, 15, 23; **9:**8, 13[2]; **10:**6, 8; **11:**5[2], 6; **12:**5, 10; **14:**16; **Mal 1:**2[3], 3[2], 6, 7, 10; **2:**2, 4, 8[3], 9[2], 10, 14, 17[2]; **3:**6, 7[2], 13[2], 14; **Mt 2:**2, 8, 15; **3:**9, 14; **4:**16; **5:**17[2], 21, 26, 27, 33[2], 38, 43, 46; **6:**1, 2, 5, 12, 16; **7:**12; **8:**8, 10, 20[2], 29[2]; **9:**12, 13, 27; **10:**21, 23, 25, 26, 34[2], 35; **11:**5, 21, 23, 25[2], 27; **12:**3, 5, 7, 18, 36; **13:**5, 12[4], 15, 51; **14:**4, 17; **15:**5, 22, 32[3], 34; **16:**7; **17:**15, 20; **18:**8, 9, 15, 26, 29, 33; **19:**4, 12[3], 16, 20, 21, 27[2], 28; **20:**12[2], 30, 31; **21:**16[2], 21, 42; **22:**4[3], 31; **23:**6, 7, 8, 9, 10, 23[2], 30, 37; **24:**25, 34, 43[2]; **25:**20, 21, 22, 23, 25, 27[2], 29[4]; **26:**9, 11[2], 24[2], 25, 55, 62, 64, 65; **27:**4, 19[2], 20, 46, 65; **28:**20; **Mk 1:**8, 24[2]; **2:**12, 17[2], 19, 25; **3:**9, 15, 29; **4:**5, 17, 25[3], 40; **5:**7; **6:**18, 38; **7:**9, 11, 13; **8:**2[3], 3, 5, 16, 18[2]; **9:**22, 43, 45, 47, 50; **10:**20, 21, 23, 28, 47, 48; **11:**17, 22, 24, 25; **12:**10, 26, 32, 39, 44; **13:**12, 23, 30; **14:**5, 7[2], 21[2], 48, 60, 64; **15:**4, 11, 34; **Lk 1:**1[2], 4, 14, 19, 25, 30; **2:**30, 31, 48[2]; **3:**8; **4:**23, 34[2]; **5:**5[2], 26, 31, 32; **6:**3, 24, 31; **7:**6, 9, 22[2], 39, 40, 43, 47; **8:**12, 13, 18[3], 28; **9:**13, 58[2]; **10:**13, 19, 21[2], 22, 28; **11:**6, 42, 43, 52; **12:**3[2], 17, 19, 20, 24, 35, 37, 39, 50, 51, 59; **13:**7, 34; **14:**18, 19, 20; **15:**6, 9, 16, 17, 18, 21, 29[3]; **16:**4, 11, 12, 24, 28, 29; **17:**10[3], 13; **18:**4, 21, 22, 24, 28, 33, 38, 39; **19:**8, 17, 23, 26[3], 46; **20:**39, 46; **21:**4, 32, 36; **22:**10, 15, 28, 32[2], 34, 52, 71; **23:**14[2], 16, 22[2], 41; **24:**18, 25, 39[2], 41, 49; **Jn 1:**14, 16, 22, 34[2], 41, 45; **2:**3, 10[2]; **3:**11, 12, 15, 16, 18, 21, 28; **4:**10[2], 11, 15, 17[2], 18[3], 29, 32, 38[2], 39, 42; **5:**7, 14, 26, 29[2], 36, 37, 38, 39, 40, 42, 43, 45; **6:**36, 38, 40, 42, 53, 54, 63, 65, 68, 69; **7:**15, 20, 28, 47[2]; **8:**6, 12, 14, 26[2], 28, 33, 35, 38[2], 41, 48, 49, 52, 57; **9:**27, 37, 41; **10:**10[2], 16, 18[3], 25, 32; **11:**21, 32, 34, 37, 42, 50[2]; **12:**8[2], 27, 28, 34, 35, 36, 46, 48, 49; **13:**8, 12, 14, 15[2], 18, 26, 34, 35, 38; **14:**2, 7, 9, 21, 25, 26, 29; **15:**3[2], 9, 10, 11, 12, 15[3], 19, 22[2], 24[2], 27; **16:**1, 3, 4, 6, 12, 20, 22, 24, 25, 27[2], 28, 30, 33[3]; **17:**2[2], 3, 6[2], 7, 8[3], 10, 11, 12, 13, 14, 18[2], 21, 22[2], 23[3], 24[2], 25, 26; **18:**14, 20[3], 23[2], 30, 35[2], 39; **19:**7, 10, 11, 15, 22[2], 31, 37; **20:**2[2], 13[2], 15[2], 17, 18, 25, 29[4], 31; **21:**5[2], 10, 12; **Ac 1:**4, 21, 24; **2:**22, 28; **3:**6[2], 14, 24; **4:**20, 26; **5:**4, 9[2], 21, 28; **6:**11, 14; **7:**34[3], 52, 53; **8:**21, 24; **9:**13, 15; **10:**4, 14, 20, 22, 31, 33, 47[2]; **13:**2, 15, 22, 28, 33, 47; **14:**11; **15:**10, 19, 24[4], 25, 26, 27; **16:**15, 37[2]; **17:**6[2], 15, 28[2], 31; **19:**2, 21, 37, 38; **20:**16, 25, 29, 35; **21:**21, 22, 23, 24, 25[2]; **22:**15, 16; **23:**1, 11, 14[2], 19, 20, 21, 22, 30; **24:**2[2], 5, 10, 15, 16, 19, 23, 25; **25:**3, 5, 8, 10, 11, 12, 26[4]; **26:**1, 5[2], 16[2], 22, 32; **27:**21[2], 25[2], 26, 33; **28:**20, 21, 27; **Ro 1:**5, 13[3], 20; **2:**1, 12[2], 27; **3:**9, 12[2], 17, 23; **4:**11, 17; **5:**1, 2, 9, 11, 12, 15; **6:**3, 4, 5, 8, 13, 14, 17, 18, 22; **7:**4, 7[2]; **8:**9, 15, 23; **9:**2, 9, 13[2], 15[4], 17, 20, 29, 30, 32; **10:**2, 3, 14[2], 16, 18[2], 20[2], 21; **11:**3[2], 4[2], 11, 22, 24, 30, 31; **12:**4[2], 6; **13:**1, 3; **14:**22[3], 23; **15:**3, 4, 15, 17, 19, 21[2], 22, 23, 24, 26, 27, 28[2]; **16:**17; **1Co 1:**5; **2:**8, 12, 16; **3:**8; **4:**6, 7, 8[3], 9, 13, 15[2], 18; **5:**2[2], 3, 12; **6:**4[2], 7, 19; **7:**2, 4[2], 25, 29, 40; **8:**2, 7; **9:**1, 4, 5, 6, 11, 12, 15, 17, 19, 22; **10:**11; **11:**6, 7, 10, 16, 19, 22[2], 30; **12:**21[2], 25; **13:**1, 2[3], 3, 12; **14:**37; **15:**2, 6, 11, 18[2], 19, 20, 32, 34, 49; **16:**15, 17; **2Co 1:**10, 12, 14, 15, 16; **2:**2, 3, 4, 10[2]; **3:**4, 12; **4:**2, 7, 13; **5:**1, 3, 8, 14; **6:**2[2], 4, 11, 15; **7:**1, 2[3], 4, 11, 14, 16; **8:**2, 12, 15[2], 16, 22; **9:**3, 5, 7; **10:**4; **11:**6, 24; **12:**11[2], 13, 19[2], 21[3]; **13:**6, 7[2], 10; **Gal 1:**9, 13; **2:**4, 16, 17, 19; **3:**27; **4:**9, 11, 12[2], 15, 16; **5:**4[2], 24; **6:**1, 10; **Eph 1:**7, 11, 15; **2:**5, 8, 13, 18; **3:**2, 6, 7, 12, 18; **4:**1, 19[2], 21, 28; **6:**9, 24; **Php 1:**16, 30; **2:**12, 20, 27; **3:**3, 4[2], 7, 8, 12[2], 13, 16, 17, 18; **4:**3, 9, 10, 11[2], 12[3], 18[3]; **Col 1:**4[2], 5, 9, 14, 16, 18; **2:**1, 2[2], 6, 10, 23; **3:**1, 3, 9, 10; **4:**1, 8, 10, 11, 16, 17; **1Th 1:**8; **2:**4, 7, 8, 16; **3:**7; **4:**6, 9[2], 13[2], 14, 15; **5:**1, 12; **2Th 1:**10; **2:**12; **3:**2, 4, 9, 14; **1Ti 1:**6, 19, 20; **2:**12; **4:**6, 7, 10; **5:**14, 15; **6:**2, 8, 10, 21; **2Ti 1:**12[2], 13, 15; **2:**2, 6, 11, 18, 21, 23; **3:**10, 14, 15; **4:**7[3], 8, 12; **Tit 1:**3, 9; **3:**8, 10, 12; **Phm 1:**7[2], 10, 15, 20; **Heb 1:**5, 9; **2:**1, 7[2], 11; **3:**10, 12, 14; **4:**1, 3, 14, 15[2]; **5:**5, 11[2], 14; **6:**4[3], 5, 6, 18, 19; **7:**5, 11, 26; **8:**1, 3, 7; **9:**11, 13, 26; **10:**2[2], 5[2], 6, 7, 8, 9, 10, 19, 21, 29, 36, 39; **11:**15; **12:**4, 5, 8, 11, 18, 22; **13:**2, 5, 9, 10[2], 14, 16, 18, 22; **Jas 1:**4; **2:**3, 4, 6, 11, 14[2], 18[2]; **3:**14; **4:**2[2]; **5:**2, 3[2], 4, 5[2], 6, 11[2], 14; **1Pe 1:**2, 6, 8, 12, 21, 22[2], 23; **2:**3, 10, 20, 21, 24, 25; **3:**6, 8; **4:**3, 5; **5:**2, 10, 12; **2Pe 1:**1, 19; **2:**14[2], 15[2], 18, 20, 21[2]; **3:**7; **1Jn 1:**1[3], 2, 3[2], 5, 6, 7, 8, 10; **2:**1, 4, 7[2], 13, 14, 18[2], 19, 20[2], 28; **3:**3, 9[2], 11, 14, 15, 21; **4:**1, 3, 4, 14, 16, 17, 20[2], 21; **5:**10[2], 12[2], 13, 14, 15; **2Jn 1:**4, 5, 6, 7, 8, 9, 12; **3Jn 1:**4, 6, 9, 13; **Jude 1:**4, 15[2], 22, 23; **Rev 1:**18, 19; **2:**2[2], 3, 4[2], 5, 10, 14[2], 15, 20, 24, 25; **3:**1, 2, 4[2], 8[4], 9, 10, 11, 17; **5:**10; **7:**3, 13, 14[2]; **9:**4, 10, 11; **10:**4; **11:**6[2], 7, 17; **12:**10, 11; **13:**3, 17; **14:**3, 4[2]; **15:**4; **16:**5, 6; **17:**2[2], 8, 10, 12; **18:**3[3], 24; **21:**4; **22:**14; **Tob 2:**13; **3:**4, 5[2], 6, 8[2], 15[2], 17; **4:**2, 8[2], 21[2]; **5:**1, 3, 5, 6[2], 9, 10[2], 17, 18; **6:**9, 12, 13, 14[2], 15, 18; **7:**11; **8:**12, 16[2]; **10:**7, 11, 13; **11:**4, 9; **12:**11, 20; **13:**5, 9; **14:**5[2], 6; **Jdt 2:**12, 13; **5:**4, 19[4]; **6:**2, 5, 9, 19; **7:**9, 21, 24, 25, 28; **8:**11[2], 28, 29, 30, 33, 34; **9:**5[2], 13; **10:**9, 15, 16[2], 19; **11:**1, 2[2], 3[3], 8, 9, 12[2], 13, 14[2], 17, 19, 22, 23; **12:**2, 4, 17; **13:**5, 17; **14:**8, 13, 18; **15:**10[2]; **AdE 1:**8, 11; **5:**8[2], 14; **6:**3, 10[3], 13; **7:**3, 4; **8:**5, 7[2]; **9:**12[2]; **10:**4, 9; **13:**2, 4, 6, 7, 10, 13, 17; **14:**3, 5, 6[2], 8, 14, 15, 17; **16:**5[3], 11; **Wis 2:**13; **3:**2, 13, 14, 18; **4:**16, 18; **5:**1, 5, 7, 9; **6:**10, 14; **7:**10, 15[2]; **8:**10, 13; **9:**1, 2[3], 7, 8, 17; **11:**20, 24[2], 25[2]; **12:**12, 13, 14, 18, 19[2], 21, 26; **13:**19; **14:**3; **15:**15, 17, 19; **16:**13; **17:**1; **19:**22[2]; **Sir Pr:**T[4]; **1:**13; **2:**13[2], 14; **3:**5, 6, 13, 22; **5:**1, 3; **6:**4, 18; **7:**22, 23, 24, 26, 28, 31; **9:**8, 13; **11:**5, 6[2], 19, 24; **12:**5, 12, 16[2]; **13:**17; **14:**2; **16:**3; **18:**7, 21, 33; **19:**9, 10; **20:**6, 11, 16; **21:**1; **22:**13; **24:**6, 34; **27:**1, 18, 19, 24; **28:**18[2]; **29:**18, 26; **30:**10, 12; **31:**6, 21; **32:**2, 19; **33:**18, 21, 31[3]; **34:**1, 7[2], 12, 13[2]; **36:**1, 4, 5, 17[2], 18; **37:**24, 31; **39:**12, 29, 32[2]; **41:**8, 9, 12; **42:**15; **43:**12, 32; **44:**8, 9[2], 10; **45:**24; **46:**12, 19; **49:**14; **50:**27; **51:**2[3], 21, 27; **Bar 1:**13[2], 17, 18[2], 19[2], 20; **2:**7, 8, 10, 12[3], 13, 14, 20, 24, 25, 26, 27, 35; **3:**2[2], 4, 7[2], 8, 12, 19[2], 20[3], 21, 23; **4:**10, 19, 20, 22, 24, 26; **5:**8; **LtJ 6:**2, 3, 12, 18, 21, 41, 47, 54, 69; **Aza 1:**4, 5[3], 6[2], 7[3], 8[3], 9, 10, 14, 15; **Sus 1:**28, 43[3], 49, 52[2], 57; **Bel 1:**9, 27, 34, 35, 38[2]; **1Mc 1:**11; **2:**9[2], 12[2], 18, 19, 40, 49, 63[2]; **3:**17, 30, 58; **4:**6, 61; **5:**10, 11, 12, 13[3], 26, 27, 38, 39; **6:**11, 13, 24[3], 25[2], 26[2]; **7:**6[2], 18; **8:**12[4], 13, 15, 20, 31[2]; **9:**8, 9, 22, 30; **10:**19, 20, 23, 24, 26[4], 35, 38, 39, 41, 42, 52[2], 53, 56, 70, 71[2]; **11:**31, 33, 34[2], 43; **12:**3, 9[2], 10, 13[2], 15, 16[2], 17, 22, 44, 53; **13:**3[2], 4, 6, 37, 38[2]; **14:**21, 22[2], 23[2], 26[2], 41, 49; **15:**3[3], 4[2], 5[2], 7[2], 17, 18, 19, 21, 29[3], 30[2], 31, 33, 34; **16:**2[3], 3; **2Mc 1:**17; **2:**15, 18[2], 25, 26; **3:**25, 34, 38; **4:**47; **5:**4, 18; **6:**14, 15, 17, 20, 30; **7:**3, 6, 7, 9, 16, 18, 27[3], 31, 35, 36; **8:**2, 3; **9:**13, 21, 22, 25[3]; **10:**11; **11:**17[2], 18, 20, 24, 30, 31, 32, 36, 37; **12:**44; **14:**3, 7[2], 8[2], 25, 35; **1Es 1:**24, 26, 32, 50; **2:**18, 24, 26, 28; **3:**6, 17, 23; **4:**26[2], 27, 29, 42, 53, 60; **5:**58, 69, 70; **6:**28, 34; **8:**10, 11, 13, 19, 69, 70[2], 75[2], 80, 82[2], 83, 85, 92[2]; **9:**7[2], 10, 11, 12, 18, 51; **Man 1:**7[3], 8[2], 9, 10[3], 12[2]; **3Mc 2:**3, 9, 10, 18, 30[2]; **3:**18, 24[2], 25, 26; **5:**31[2], 32; **6:**10, 12[2], 13, 15[2], 26, 35; **7:**6[2], 7[2], 8[2], 9; **2Es 1:**5, 6[3], 7, 8, 9, 10, 14, 16, 18[2], 25, 26, 27, 28, 31, 32, 34[3], 35[2], 36, 37; **2:**3[3], 6, 7, 9, 15, 17, 18, 21, 26, 27, 38, 39[2], 40, 41, 45[3], 48; **3:**11, 30[3], 31, 32, 33[2], 35, 36; **4:**3, 6, 8, 9[3], 10, 12, 20[2], 22, 25, 27, 40, 44; **5:**16, 23, 24[2], 25[3], 26[4], 27[3], 28, 29, 34, 36, 39, 40, 41, 43[2], 44, 45, 48, 49, 50[2], 52, 56; **6:**11, 25, 26, 30, 32, 52, 54[2], 55[2], 56[3], 58[2]; **7:**2, 14, 16, 17, 18[2], 24[2], 26, 27, 32, 37[4], 44, 48, 51, 52, 59, 60[2], 62, 63[2], 65, 68, 69, 70, 71, 73, 75, 76, 77, 79[3], 81, 83, 87, 88, 91, 92, 96[2], 98, 100[2], 101[2], 102, 104, 111, 115, 116, 118, 119, 120, 121[2], 122[2], 124, 128[2], 130, 132, 134, 137, 138[2]; **8:**3, 5, 7, 8, 10, 12, 18, 25, 27, 28[2], 29[2], 30, 31, 32[3], 33, 35[2], 36, 37, 38, 40, 41[2], 42, 44[3], 45[2], 47, 49[2], 50, 54, 57, 59, 60[2], 62, 63[2]; **9:**1, 7, 8[2], 9[2], 19[2], 22, 36; **10:**9, 10, 12, 15, 22[9], 32, 35, 39, 57[2]; **11:**16, 17, 40[4], 41, 42[5], 44[2]; **12:**4, 5, 7[2], 9, 10, 12, 13, 30, 31, 34, 37, 41[3], 43, 44, 48[2]; **13:**14[3], 21, 23, 24, 33, 53, 54[3], 55, 56; **14:**8[3], 11, 16, 20, 21, 22, 26, 30; **15:**6, 16, 19, 20, 21, 27[2], 45, 47[3], 48, 52; **16:**5, 28, 33[3], 44, 47, 53[2]; **4Mc 1:**12, 21; **2:**18, 20; **4:**3; **5:**7, 12, 14, 16, 28; **6:**27, 32, 35; **7:**17[2]; **8:**1, 7, 10, 16[2], 20; **9:**8; **10:**14, 16; **11:**3, 20[2], 24, 25; **12:**11, 13; **13:**12, 18; **14:**14; **15:**4; **16:**2[2], 5, 9, 11, 14[2], 18[2], 22, 23; **17:**7, 20; **18:**9, 23

HAVING (172)

See also the selected listing for "HAVING" in the Main Concordance.

Ge 41:11; **46:**30; **Lev 15:**11; **20:**9, 18; **22:**9, 22; **Nu 3:**38; **9:**15; **15:**31; **Dt 4:**42; **13:**5; **19:**18; **Jos 5:**6; **7:**15[3]; **10:**9; **20:**5; **21:**43; **24:**20; **Jdg 3:**27; **13:**2, 3; **18:**27; **1Sa 25:**31[2]; **2Sa 13:**38; **1Ki 5:**16; **8:**33; **9:**11; **1Ch 4:**42; **8:**40; **23:**22, 28; **2Ch 6:**24; **9:**1; **13:**3; **17:**9; **Ne 5:**3, 4; **Est 3:**6; **6:**4; **Job 21:**25; **Ps 106:**24; **119:**6; **Pr 6:**7; **25:**16; **Isa 41:**15; **Eze 38:**11; **44:**11; **Da 8:**15; **10:**1; **Mt 2:**12; **7:**29; **16:**8; **Mk 1:**22; **2:**4; **8:**17; **Lk 2:**36; **4:**35; **7:**4, 37; **10:**34; **15:**4, 8; **19:**15; **23:**46; **Jn 3:**4; **11:**6, 41; **13:**1; **16:**21; **Ac 2:**24, 33, 47; **7:**36; **16:**6; **21:**26; **27:**33; **Ro 2:**14, 20; **5:**10; **6:**17, 18; **1Co 7:**7, 37; **11:**5; **2Co 6:**10; **9:**8; **Gal 3:**3; **Eph 1:**11; **2:**12; **6:**13; **Php 1:**11, 14, 30; **2:**2; **3:**9; **4:**12; **1Ti 1:**19; **5:**12; **2Ti 2:**26; **4:**3; **Tit 2:**8; **3:**7; **Heb 1:**4; **5:**9, 10; **6:**15, 20; **7:**3; **9:**6, 28; **10:**26; **11:**13; **Rev 5:**6; **7:**2; **9:**19; **13:**1; **18:**1; **Jdt 6:**13; **12:**12; **AdE 13:**2; **16:**10; **Wis 3:**5; **14:**8; **18:**1, 2; **19:**15, 16; **Sir 19:**11; **26:**21; **42:**10; **47:**15; **LtJ 6:**26; **2Mc 1:**11, 20; **2:**4; **3:**34, 35; **4:**5, 25, 33, 50; **5:**9; **6:**10; **7:**19; **8:**35[2]; **9:**28; **10:**21, 23, 28; **11:**10, 15; **13:**18; **14:**2, 34; **1Es 1:**2, 10; **3Mc 2:**21; **5:**23; **2Es 1:**35; **4Mc 4:**14; **6:**18[2]; **9:**11, 26; **12:**14; **16:**13; **17:**21

HE (10591)

Ge 1:5, 10, 27[2], 31; **2:**2[3], 3, 8[2], 19, 21[2], 22; **3:**1, 6, 10, 11, 15, 16[2], 17, 22, 23, 24[2]; **4:**5, 9, 17, 20, 21, 26; **5:**1, 2[2], 3, 4[2], 5, 6, 8, 9, 11, 12, 14, 15, 17, 18, 20, 21, 24, 25, 27, 28, 29, 31; **6:**6, 22; **7:**23; **8:**6, 8, 9, 10[2], 12; **9:**21[2], 25[2], 26, 29; **10:**8, 9, 11; **11:**10, 12, 14, 16, 18, 20, 22, 24, 26; **12:**4, 7, 8[2], 11[2], 16[2], 20; **13:**1[2], 3, 4, 18; **14:**14, 15[2], 16, 18, 19; **15:**5[2], 6, 7, 8, 9, 10[2]; **16:**4, 8, 12[2]; **17:**12, 14, 20, 22, 23, 24, 25; **18:**1, 2[3], 3, 8[3], 9, 15, 19[2], 28, 29[2], 30[2], 31[2], 32[2], 33; **19:**1, 2, 3[2], 9, 14, 16, 21, 25, 27, 28, 29, 30[2], 33, 35, 37, 38; **20:**4, 5[2], 7[2], 13, 16; **21:**1[2], 4, 13, 17, 20[2], 21, 30; **22:**1[2], 2, 3, 6, 7[2], 9, 11, 12; **23:**8, 9[2], 13, 16; **24:**2, 7, 10, 11, 12, 15, 30[4], 31, 33[2], 34, 35[2], 36[2], 40, 52, 53, 54[2], 56, 63, 66, 67[2]; **25:**5, 6[2], 17, 18, 20, 26, 28, 29, 30, 33, 34; **26:**7[2], 13[2], 14, 18, 20, 21, 22[2], 23, 25, 30, 33, 34; **27:**1[3], 2, 9, 10[2], 14, 18[2], 20, 23[2], 24[2], 25[5], 27[2], 31[2], 32, 33, 34, 35[2], 36[5], 45; **28:**4, 5, 6[2], 9, 11[2], 12, 17, 18[2], 19; **29:**2[2], 5, 6, 7, 9, 12[2], 13[2], 14, 18, 20, 23[2], 30[2], 31, 33, 34; **30:**15, 16, 31, 36, 38[2], 40, 42; **31:**1, 2, 5, 8[2], 12, 15[2], 18[3], 20[2], 21[3], 23[2], 33[2], 35, 48, 49, 55; **32:**2[2], 6, 7, 11, 13[3], 16, 17, 18, 19, 20[2], 21, 22, 23[2], 25[3], 26, 27[2], 29[2], 31, 32; **33:**1, 2, 3[2], 5, 11[2], 15, 18, 19[2], 20; **34:**2, 3, 7, 13, 19[2]; **35:**6, 7[2], 9[2], 10, 13, 14[2], 29; **36:**6[2], 24[2]; **37:**2, 3[2], 5, 6, 9, 10, 13, 14[3], 16, 18, 21, 22, 23, 27, 29, 30, 33, 35; **38:**2, 3, 9[3], 10[2], 11[2], 12[2], 15, 16[2], 17, 18[2], 20, 21, 22, 26, 29[2], 30; **39:**2[2], 3, 4[2], 5[3], 6[4], 8[3], 9[2], 10, 11, 12, 13, 14, 15[2], 18, 19, 20, 21, 22, 23; **40:**3, 4, 6, 7, 16, 20, 21[2], 22; **41:**1, 5, 8, 11, 12, 13, 14[3], 25, 28, 42, 43[2], 45, 46, 48[2], 49, 51, 52, 55; **42:**1, 2, 4, 6, 7[3], 9[2], 12, 17, 21, 23, 24[3], 27, 28, 38[2]; **43:**7, 14, 16, 18, 23[2], 24, 27[2], 28, 29, 30[3], 31[2]; **44:**1, 2, 5, 6[2], 10[2], 12, 14, 17, 20, 22, 28, 31[2]; **45:**1, 2, 4, 8, 14, 15, 21, 22[2], 23, 24[2], 26[3], 27[2]; **46:**1[2], 2, 3, 7, 29; **47:**2, 17, 21, 22, 29, 30, 31[2]; **48:**1, 2, 3, 8, 9, 10[2], 12, 15, 17, 19[3], 20[2]; **49:**9[2], 11, 13, 15[2], 19, 20, 28, 29, 33; **50:**5, 6, 10, 12, 14, 16, 20, 21, 22, 24, 26; **Ex 1:**9, 21; **2:**2, 6, 11[2], 12[2], 13[3], 14, 15[2], 18, 19, 20[2], 21, 22[2]; **3:**1, 2, 4[2], 5, 6[2], 12, 14, 20; **4:**2, 3[2], 4, 6[2], 7[2], 13, 14[4], 16[2], 21, 23, 26, 27[2], 28[2], 31; **5:**3, 17, 23; **6:**1[2], 29; **7:**13, 14, 15, 20, 22, 23; **8:**10, 12, 15, 19, 20, 27, 31; **9:**7, 12, 34[2], 35; **10:**6, 8, 10, 17, 18, 20, 27; **11:**1[3], 8, 10; **12:**23, 25, 27[2], 30, 31, 44, 48[2]; **13:**5, 11; **14:**4, 6, 7, 8, 25; **15:**1[2], 2, 4, 21[2], 25[3], 26; **16:**7, 9, 23, 29; **17:**7, 11, 12, 16; **18:**3, 4, 6, 7, 11, 14[2], 24, 27; **19:**14, 15, 24; **21:**2[2], 3[3], 4, 6[2], 8[3], 9[2], 10[2], 11; **22:**16, 17; **23:**21; **24:**1, 4, 5, 6, 7, 14, 16; **28:**29, 30, 35[4]; **29:**21, 30; **30:**7[2], 8, 10; **31:**17, 18; **32:**4, 5, 12, 14, 17, 18, 19[2], 20, 27; **33:**7, 8, 11, 14, 15, 19, 20; **34:**4, 9, 10, 28[3], 29[2], 32, 33, 34[4], 35; **35:**31, 34, 35; **36:**10[2], 11[2], 12[2], 13, 14[2], 16, 17, 18, 19, 20, 22, 23, 24, 25, 27, 28, 29, 31, 33, 34, 35, 36[2], 37, 38; **37:**2, 3, 4, 6, 7[2], 8, 10, 11, 12, 13, 15, 16, 17, 23, 24, 25, 26[2], 28, 29; **38:**1, 2[2], 3[2], 4, 5, 6, 7[2], 8, 9, 28, 30; **39:**2, 7, 8, 22, 43; **40:**13, 18, 19, 20, 21, 22, 24, 26, 28, 29, 30, 33; **Lev 1:**16, 17; **2:**8; **3:**4; **4:**3[2], 4, 7, 8, 9, 12, 18[2], 19, 20[2], 21[2], 23[2], 24, 26[2], 30, 31; **5:**9, 10; **6:**10, 11, 20; **7:**8, 36, 38; **8:**7[2], 8[2], 9[2], 11, 12, 14, 15[2], 17, 18, 22, 25, 26, 27, 30; **9:**2, 9[2], 10, 11, 12[2], 13, 14, 15[2], 16, 17[2], 18[2], 22; **10:**1, 3, 16, 20; **12:**7; **13:**2, 3, 5, 6, 7[2], 9, 11[2], 13[2], 14, 16, 17, 33[2], 34, 35, 36, 37, 39, 40[2], 41[3], 44[2], 45, 46[4], 51, 52, 54, 56; **14:**2, 6, 7[3], 8[2], 9[4], 10, 13, 18, 19, 20, 21[2], 22, 23, 29, 30[2], 37, 41, 43, 45, 49, 52, 53[2]; **15:**4, 13[3], 14, 16, 23[2], 24[2]; **16:**2, 4[2], 5, 7, 11, 12[2], 13, 14[2], 15[2], 16[2], 17[2], 18, 19, 20[2], 23[2], 24[2], 25, 33[3]; **17:**4[3]; **19:**21, 22[2]; **20:**14, 15, 17[2], 18, 20, 21; **21:**3, 4, 11[2], 12, 13, 14[2], 15, 21[2], 22, 23[3]; **22:**3, 4, 5[2], 6, 7[2], 8, 14; **23:**11; **24:**4; **Nu 1:**19; **3:**3, 16, 50; **5:**14[2], 15[2], 24, 27, 30[2]; **7:**7, 8, 9, 19, 89; **8:**3, 4, 12; **10:**30, 31, 36; **11:**24; **12:**1[2], 2, 6, 7, 8, 9; **14:**8, 16[2], 24[2]; **16:**4, 5[3], 10, 26, 31, 47, 48; **17:**11; **19:**7, 8; **20:**9, 10, 13, 16, 20, 24; **21:**1, 23, 29, 33; **22:**5, 8, 22[2], 25, 27, 30, 31[2], 36, 41; **23:**3[2], 6, 12, 14[2], 17[2], 19[6], 20, 21[2]; **24:**1, 3, 8[2], 9[2], 10, 15, 20, 21, 23, 24; **25:**7, 8, 13; **27:**3[2], 4, 9, 10, 11, 21[2], 22, 23; **30:**2[2], 5, 7, 8[2], 12, 14[4], 15[3]; **32:**10, 13, 15, 21, 40; **33:**39; **Dt 1:**4, 11, 27, 30, 34, 36[2], 38; **2:**7, 22, 30, 32; **3:**1, 14, 28; **4:**13[3], 21, 31[3], 36[2], 37[3]; **5:**5, 22[2]; **6:**10, 15, 17, 23[2], 25; **7:**1, 4, 8, 10, 12, 13[3], 15[2], 24; **8:**3, 10, 15, 18[4]; **9:**3, 8, 19, 20, 24, 28[3]; **10:**4, 6, 21[2]; **11:**3, 4[2], 5, 6, 14, 15, 17, 25; **12:**10, 20; **13:**17; **14:**23; **15:**6, 16[3], 17; **16:**16, 17; **17:**16, 17[2], 18[2], 19[2], 20; **18:**2, 6[3], 7; **19:**8[3]; **20:**5[2], 6[2], 7[2], 8[2]; **21:**16[2], 17[3], 20[2]; **22:**13, 16, 17, 19[3], 24, 27, 29[3]; **23:**10[2], 11[2], 14; **24:**1[2], 5[3]; **25:**7, 8, 18[2]; **26:**5[2], 9, 18, 19[2]; **27:**20; **28:**8, 9, 45, 48[2], 54, 55, 60; **29:**1, 13[4], 25[2], 26; **30:**4, 5, 9; **31:**2, 3, 4[2], 6, 8[2], 11; **32:**4, 6, 7, 8[2], 10[2], 13[2], 15, 19, 20, 36, 37, 39, 43[2], 44, 46; **33:**2[2], 7, 8, 9, 12, 13, 17, 18, 20[2], 21[3], 22, 23, 24[3], 27[2]; **34:**6, 7, 11; **Jos 1:**17; **4:**4, 23; **5:**6[2], 7, 13, 14[2]; **6:**7, 26[2]; **7:**6, 15, 17[2], 18, 24; **8:**12, 14[2], 19, 26[2], 27, 29, 32, 34; **9:**9, 10, 26[2], 27; **10:**1, 2, 7, 12, 26, 28[4], 30[4], 32[2], 35[2], 37[2], 39[5], 40; **11:**1, 9, 11, 15, 17; **13:**12, 14, 33; **14:**3, 10, 14; **15:**13, 15, 17; **17:**1[2], 4; **19:**50[2]; **21:**43[2], 44; **22:**4, 8, 18, 20, 22; **23:**10, 15, 16[2]; **24:**7, 9, 10, 17, 18, 19[3], 20, 23, 26, 27; **Jdg 1:**7, 13, 19, 20, 25; **2:**10, 14[2], 18, 20, 21; **3:**4, 8, 10[2], 13, 16, 17, 18, 19, 20[2], 22, 24[2], 25, 27[2], 28, 31; **4:**3, 18, 19, 20, 21[2], 22; **5:**17, 25, 27[7]; **6:**8, 15, 17, 18, 19[2], 20, 27[2], 30[2], 31, 32, 34, 35[2], 38[2]; **7:**4[2], 5, 8[2], 11, 13, 15[2], 16, 17; **8:**2, 3, 4, 5, 8, 9, 12, 14[2], 15, 16[3], 17, 18, 19, 20[3], 21, 24, 25, 26, 30, 31, 35; **9:**3, 5[2], 7, 18, 21, 31, 33, 36, 40, 43[3], 45[2], 48[2], 54[2], 56; **10:**2[2], 4, 7, 16, 18; **11:**17, 25[2], 29[3], 33, 34, 35[2], 38, 39; **12:**5, 6[2], 9[3], 11, 14[2]; **13:**5, 6[2], 7, 11, 12, 16, 23; **14:**1, 2, 4, 5, 6[3], 7, 8[2], 9[6], 14, 16, 17, 18, 19[3]; **15:**1, 4, 5[2], 6, 8[2], 10, 11, 14, 15[2], 17[2], 18[2], 19[2], 20; **16:**1, 3, 4, 9, 11, 12, 13, 14[2], 16, 17, 18[2], 19, 20[3], 21, 25, 29, 30[3], 31; **17:**2, 3, 4, 5, 7, 8[2], 9; **18:**4[2], 20, 24, 26, 31; **19:**3[2], 4[2], 5, 7, 8, 10[2], 13, 15, 16, 17, 18, 21, 27, 28[2], 29[3], 30[2]; **Ru 1:**1; **2:**4, 14, 20, 21; **3:**2, 3, 4[3], 7[2], 9, 10, 13[2], 14, 15[3], 17[2]; **4:**1, 3, 4, 8, 15, 17; **1Sa 1:**2, 4, 5[2], 11, 22, 28[2]; **2:**6, 7[2], 8[3], 9, 10, 14, 15, 16, 22, 23, 35; **3:**2, 4, 5[2], 6, 8, 9, 13[2], 15, 16, 17[2], 18; **4:**3, 13, 14, 15, 16, 18[4]; **5:**6, 9; **6:**5, 6, 9, 19, 20; **7:**3, 8, 12, 16[2], 17[2]; **8:**1, 11[2], 12, 13, 14, 15, 16, 17, 21; **9:**2[3], 4[2], 6[4], 12[2], 13[3], 16, 17, 25, 26, 27; **10:**1, 9, 10, 11, 13, 14, 16[2], 21[3], 22, 23[2], 25, 27[2]; **11:**6, 7, 8; **12:**5[2], 7, 9, 17, 24; **13:**1[2], 2, 8, 9, 10, 13; **14:**1, 24, 27, 33, 35, 37, 39, 40, 45[2], 47[3], 48, 52; **15:**8, 11[2], 12[2], 16, 23, 29[2], 35; **16:**2, 5[2], 6, 8, 9, 11[3], 12[2], 16, 21, 22; **17:**5[2], 6, 8, 9, 20, 23, 25, 26, 28, 30, 31, 33, 36, 38, 39[2], 40[2], 42[2], 47, 49, 51[2], 54, 55; **18:**3, 4, 8[2], 10[2], 11, 15[2], 16, 25, 27; **19:**4, 5[2], 6, 7, 8, 9, 10[2], 12, 14, 15, 17[2], 18[2], 21, 22[3], 23[4], 24[3]; **20:**1[2], 2, 3[2], 7[2], 12, 13, 17[2], 26[3], 29[2], 30, 31, 32[2], 34, 36[2], 41, 42; **21:**10, 13[3]; **22:**2, 3, 4, 7, 8, 10, 12, 13[2], 14, 17, 18, 19[2], 22; **23:**6, 7, 9, 11, 13, 15, 16, 17, 22[2], 23[2], 25[2]; **24:**1, 3, 5, 6[2], 10, 15, 17; **25:**2[2], 3, 14, 17, 21, 25, 29, 30, 35, 36[2], 37, 38, 39; **26:**3, 10, 18, 19, 24; **27:**2, 3, 4, 11, 12[2]; **28:**5, 8[2], 9, 11, 14[3], 17, 20, 21, 23[3]; **29:**3, 4[3], 9; **30:**8, 9, 10, 11, 12[2], 13, 15, 16, 21, 23, 25, 26; **31:**3, 4, 5; **2Sa 1:**2[2], 3, 4, 7[2], 8, 9, 10[2], 13, 15[2], 18[2]; **2:**1, 9, 10[2], 19, 20, 23[3], 30; **3:**8, 9, 11, 13, 16[2], 21, 22, 23[2], 24, 26, 27[2], 28, 30; **4:**4[2], 5, 7, 10; **5:**4[2], 5[2], 12, 13, 20, 23, 25; **6:**7[2], 9, 13, 18; **7:**13, 14[2]; **8:**2[2], 3, 6, 10, 11[2], 13[2], 14[3]; **9:**2[2], 3, 4[2], 6, 8, 13[2]; **10:**3, 5, 7, 9, 10[2], 11, 17, 18;

32[2]; **8:3**[2], 9, 15[3], 17, 20, 21, 22, 25, 26[3], 27[3]; **10:**13, 16, 22; **11:9**[2], 10, 17; **12:**1, 4, 11, 16[2], 20[2]; **13:**2, 11, 15, 16, 20; **14:5**, 6[2], 7, 10[2], 14[2], 15, 16, 17[3]; **16:2**[2], 3, 4[2], 17; **AdE 1:3**, 4, 8, 10, 12, 13, 17; **2:1**[3], 4, 6, 7[2], 9[2], 17, 18, 22, 23; **3:4**[2], 5; **4:1**[2], 2[2], 4, 8[3]; **5:9**[2], 10, 11[2]; **6:1**, 2[2], 4, 7, 11; **7:7**[2], 8[2], 10; **8:1**, 7, 9, 11; **9:14**, 24, 25[3]; **10:10**; **11:1**, 3, 4, 12[2]; **12:2**[2]; **13:9**; **15:6**[2], 7, 8[2], 11, 12; **16:11**, 12, 14[2], 18[2]; **Wis 1:2**, 13, 14; **2:12**[2], 13, 14, 16[2], 18, 19, 20[2]; **3:6**[2], 9; **4:14**, 15, 17, 19; **5:16**[2], 18, 19; **6:3**, 5, 7[2]; **7:15**, 17; **10:1**, 3[2], 6, 12, 14; **13:13**[2], 15, 16[2], 17[2], 18[3], 19; **14:8**, 15, 19; **18:21**[3], 22[2], 23, 25; **Sir 1:9**[3], 10; **2:6**, 11; **3:2**, 12, 20; **4:10**; **5:6**; **6:37**; **7:9**[2]; **10:4**, 5, 11, 17; **11:12**, 19[3], 28; **12:11**, 12[2], 13, 15[2], 16[3], 17, 18; **13:4**, 5[2], 6[3], 7[5], 9, 11[3], 21[2], 22[2], 23[2]; **14:4**[2], 5[2], 7[2], 8; **15:4**[2], 6, 11[2], 12[2], 14[2], 16, 18, 19, 20[2]; **16:7**, 8[2], 9, 11[3], 12, 14, 19, 27, 30; **17:2**, 3, 4, 6, 7, 8, 11, 12, 14[2], 17, 22, 23[2], 24[2], 26, 32; **18:1**, 4, 12[2], 13, 14, 24; **19:13**[3], 14[3], 26, 27[2], 28[2], 30[2]; **20:14**, 15[4], 20, 21[2]; **21:15**[2], 20, 27; **22:10**, 11[3], 13; **23:11**[5], 17[2], 19, 21[2]; **24:8**, 9, 11; **25:18**; **26:2**; **27:4**, 7, 20, 23[3], 27; **28:1**, 2, 4, 10; **29:5**[2], 6[4], 15; **30:1**[3], 2, 3, 4[2], 5, 6, 9[2], 12[2], 20; **31:3**[2], 4[2], 9[2], 19, 20; **33:8**, 9[2], 12[3], 13[2], 26, 28, 30, 32; **34:9**, 11, 16, 18, 20[2], 23, 31; **35:12**, 13, 14, 16[2], 17, 22, 23, 24, 25; **36:27**, 29; **37:8**[2], 15, 20, 21; **38:6**[2], 9, 14, 15, 26[2], 28[3], 29[2], 30[3]; **39:1**, 2, 3, 4[2], 5[2], 6[2], 7, 8[2], 11[3], 16, 18, 20, 23, 33; **40:6**[4], 7[2]; **42:18**[3], 19[2], 21[3], 24; **43:13**, 15, 16, 17, 19, 21, 23, 27, 28, 30, 31, 33; **44:17**, 20[4], 21, 22, 23[3]; **45:2**, 3[2], 4, 5[2], 6, 7[2], 8, 9[2], 16, 17, 19, 20[2], 21, 22[2], 23, 24[2]; **46:1**[2], 2[2], 3, 5, 6[4], 7[2], 9, 13, 14, 15[2], 16[2], 18, 20[2]; **47:3**, 4[2], 5[2], 6, 7[2], 8[4], 9, 10, 11, 13, 22[2]; **48:2**[2], 3, 12[2], 13, 14, 17, 18[2], 22[2], 23, 24, 25; **49:2**, 3[2], 11, 13, 14; **50:2**, 4, 5[2], 11[3], 12[3], 15[2], 23, 24[2]; **51:12**[2]; **Bar 1:18**, 20, 21; **2:1**, 2, 4, 9, 10; **3:24**, 32, 33, 34, 36[2]; **4:15**, 18, 21; **LtJ 6:7**; **Aza 1:66**[2], 67; **Sus 1:2**, 4, 39[2], 46, 48, 52, 54, 56[2], 58; **Bel 1:5**, 6, 9, 17, 19, 21, 25, 27, 28, 30, 31, 33, 36, 40[2], 42; **1Mc 1:1**[2], 2, 3[2], 4, 5[2], 6[2], 7, 10[2], 16[2], 17, 18, 19, 20, 21, 22[2], 23[3], 24[2], 29, 30[2], 31, 44, 50, 51[2]; **2:2**, 6, 23, 24[3], 25[2], 26, 28, 49, 54, 55, 56, 57, 65, 66, 69, 70; **3:3**[3], 4, 5[2], 7[2], 8[3], 9[2], 11[2], 14, 16, 22, 23[2], 27[2], 28, 29[2], 30[4], 31[2], 32, 33, 34[2], 35, 37, 56, 60; **4:3**, 5[3], 10, 17, 24, 27[3], 28, 30[2], 35, 41, 42, 61; **5:3**, 4, 5, 6[2], 7[2], 8[2], 18, 19, 22[2], 23, 28[2], 29, 32, 33, 34, 35[2], 36, 40[2], 41, 42, 43, 44, 50, 51[2], 53, 65, 66, 68[3]; **6:1**, 3[2], 4, 7, 8[3], 9[3], 10, 14, 15[2], 17[2], 20, 23, 28[2], 43, 44, 45[2], 46[2], 49, 51[2], 56, 57, 60, 62[2], 63[2]; **7:2**, 3, 8, 9[4], 10, 14, 16, 19, 20, 25[2], 26, 29, 30, 31, 34, 35[2], 43, 47; **8:2**, 6, 7; **9:1**, 7[2], 8[2], 15, 22, 32, 34, 36, 43, 47, 51, 52[2], 53, 54, 55[3], 57, 58, 60, 62, 63, 64[2], 65[2], 66, 67, 68, 69[3], 70, 71[5], 72[3], 73; **10:1**, 2, 4[2], 5, 6, 9, 11, 15, 16, 17, 20, 21, 22, 25, 32, 46, 47, 50, 53, 57, 60[2], 63, 68, 69[2], 74, 75, 77[4], 84, 87, 88, 89[2]; **11:1**, 2[2], 3, 4, 7, 8, 9, 10, 11[2], 12[2], 13, 15, 20, 22[5], 23[2], 24[2], 26, 27[2], 38[2], 39[2], 40[2], 41, 53[3], 55, 58, 59, 60, 61[2], 62[2], 64, 66[2], 72; **12:1**, 2, 25[2], 26, 27, 30, 31, 32, 33, 34[2], 35, 37, 38, 40[3], 41, 42[2], 43[2], 44, 46[2], 47[2]; **13:2**[2], 3, 10[2], 11[2], 14[2], 15, 16, 17[2], 19, 20[2], 22[2], 23[3], 27, 28, 29[3], 30, 31, 32, 33, 43, 47, 48[2], 50[2], 52[2], 53[2]; **14:1**, 2, 4, 5, 6, 7[3], 10, 11, 14[2], 15, 17, 26, 32[3], 33[2], 34[2], 35[4], 37, 40, 42[3], 43[2], 44; **15:12**, 14[2], 21, 25, 27[2], 28, 32[3], 36, 39, 41; **16:6**[3], 7, 9, 10, 11, 12, 13, 14, 15[2], 17, 19[3], 20, 21, 22[4], 23[2], 24; **2Mc 1:2**, 3, 4[2], 5[2], 12, 15, 20, 35; **2:3**, 4, 5[2], 7, 13, 18[3]; **3:5**[2], 7[2], 9[4], 12, 13, 14, 15, 22, 24, 27, 29, 35, 36[2], 37, 38, 39[2]; **4:1**, 2, 5, 6, 9, 10, 11[2], 12[2], 21[2], 22[2], 24, 25, 27, 32[2], 33, 34[2], 38[4], 47[2], **5:6**, 7[2], 8[2], 9, 10[2], 11[2], 12, 16, 17, 18, 21, 22, 25[2], 26; **6:14**, 15, 16[3], 19, 21, 22, 23[2], 24, 28[2], 29, 30[2], 31; **7:4**, 5, 6[2], 8[2], 9[2], 10, 12, 13, 14[2], 16, 18[2], 24[5], 33, 37, 40; **8:6**[2], 7, 8[2], 9, 11, 12, 14, 15, 18, 19, 21[2], 22, 23[2], 35[2], 36; **9:2**, 3, 4[2], 5[2], 6, 7[2], 8[3], 9, 10, 11[2], 12[2], 14[2], 15[2], 16[4], 17, 18, 23, 27, 28, 29; **10:11**, 13[4], 14, 19[2], 21, 22, 23[2], 24, 25; **11:2**, 3, 4, 5, 7, 13[3], 14, 18, 36; **12:5**, 6, 7, 9, 13, 18[2], 21, 24[2], 25, 27, 37[2], 43[2], 44, 45[2]; **13:3**[2], 4, 8[2], 10, 13, 14, 15[3], 19, 21, 23[2], 24; **14:4**, 5[3], 11, 12, 19, 24[2], 25, 26[3], 27, 28[2], 29, 30, 31[2], 32, 33, 34, 38[2], 39, 40[2], 43[2], 44, 45[2], 46; **15:1**, 2, 5[2], 7, 8, 9, 10[2], 11[2], 12, 15[2], 21[2], 22[2], 24, 31[2], 32, 33[2], 34; **1Es 1:1**, 3, 4, 7, 29, 31[3], 33, 35, 39[2], 40, 43[2]; 44[2], 46, 47, 48[2], 50, 52, 53, 56; **2:2**, 4, 5, 11; **3:3**, 6, 7, 13, 14, 15, 16, 24[2]; **4:3**[2], 4[2], 7[3], 8[3], 9[2], 10[2], 12[2], 21, 24[3], 31[2], 33, 41, 43, 44, 48, 49, 54, 55, 56, 57[2], 58, 61, 62; **5:3**; **6:15**, 19, 24, 32; **7:15**; **8:4**, 7, 61, 80; **9:2**[2], 41, 45, 46; **Pm 151:T**, 3, 4, 6; **3Mc 1:1**[2], 2, 6, 7, 8, 9[2], 10, 11, 12[2], 13[2], 25, 26; **2:7**, 22[3], 23, 24[3], 25[2], 26[2], 27[2], 30[2]; **3:1**[3], 11; **4:11**, 14, 19[2]; **5:1**, 3[2], 8, 10, 11, 12[2], 15[3], 17, 19[2], 20, 27[2], 28[2], 30[2], 37, 42[2], 47[2]; **6:1**, 20, 22, 23[2], 29, 30, 33; **2Es 2:34**[2], 43[2], 45, 47[2]; **3:5**[2], 7; **4:3**, 5, 7, 10, 13, 20, 21, 25, 26, 34, 36, 37, 40, 41, 47, 50, 52; **5:19**, 32, 33, 35, 36, 38, 40, 42, 44, 46, 48, 51; **6:1**, 8, 13, 29, 30, 33; **7:2**, 3, 10, 19, 38, 49, 54, 59, 70[2], 74, 76, 94, 101, 104, 109, 112, 127, 129, 132, 133, 134, 135, 136, 137, 138[2], 139; **8:1**, 19[2], 37, 46; **9:1**, 2, 17, 26, 47; **10:1**, 28, 29, 30, 33, 38, 39, 48, 59; **12:6**, 10, 28, 32, 33[3], 34[2], 39; **13:3**, 6, 9[2], 10[2], 20, 26[2], 35, 37, 40, 49[2], 50, 52, 57, 58; **14:3**, 23, 27, 32[3], 37; **15:26**; **16:10**[2], 13, 50, 54, 55, 56, 57[2], 58[2], 59, 60, 61, 63; **4Mc 2:2**, 3[2], 17, 20, 21, 22, 23; **3:8**, 10, 15, 16; **4:1**[2], 2, 4, 5, 6[2], 12[4], 13, 17, 22[3], 23[2], 24, 26; **5:4**, 5, 15[2], 26[2]; **6:2**, 7[2], 8, 9, 11, 24[2], 26[2], 30[2]; **7:3**[2], 4, 13[2], 14; **8:2**, 4[2], 12[2]; **9:14**, 17, 19, 22, 23, 25, 27, 28, 30; **10:1**, 2, 8, 9[2], 12, 14, 17, 18; **11:1**, 9, 10, 12, 13[3], 17, 18[2], 20; **12:1**, 2[4], 6[2], 8, 11, 15[2], 18, 19[2]; **13:14**; **16:20**; **17:23**, 24; **18:5**[2], 9, 10[2], 11, 12[2], 13, 14, 15, 16, 17, 18

HER (2182)

Ge 2:22; **3:6**[2]; **12:15**[2], 16, 19[2]; **16:2**, 3[3], 4, 6[3], 7, 9[2], 10, 11, 13; **17:15**[2], 16[4]; **19:33**; **20:4**, 6, 7, 13; **21:9**, 10, 14[2], 16, 17, 19; **23:2**; **24:14**, 15[2], 16, 17, 18[2], 20, 21, 22, 28, 41, 44, 45[3], 46[2], 47[3], 51[2], 53[2], 55[2], 57, 58, 59, 60, 61, 65, 67[2]; **25:22**, 23, 24[2]; **26:9**; **27:6**, 15[3], 17, 42[2]; **29:9**, 12[2], 19[2], 20, 21, 23[2], 24, 28, 29, 31; **30:1**, 3[2], 4[2], 9[2], 15, 16, 21, 22[2]; **31:19**, 35; **33:2**, 7; **34:2**[3], 3, 8, 11[2]; **35:17**[2], 18, 20; **38:2**[2], 6, 8, 11, 14, 15[3], 16, 18[3], 19[2], 20, 22, 23[3], 24[2], 25, 26[2], 27[2]; **39:7**, 10[2], 12, 13, 14, 16; **48:7**; **Ex 2:5**[2], 8, 9, 10; **3:22**; **4:25**; **11:2**; **15:20**[2]; **18:2**, 3, 6; **21:4**[2], 8[3], 9[2], 11; **22:16**[3], 17[2]; **Lev 12:2**, 4[2], 5[2], 6, 7[3], 8; **15:19**[4], 20, 21, 24[2], 25[3], 26[3], 28, 30[2], 33[2]; **18:7**, 15, 17[4], 18[3], 19[2], 20; **19:20**, 29; **20:14**, 17, 18[4]; **21:3**, 7, 9; **22:13**[3]; **Nu 5:13**[3], 15, 16[2], 18, 19, 24, 27[6], 29, 30, 31; **12:12**, 13, 14[4]; **30:3**[2], 4[5], 5[5], 6[2], 7[4], 8[4], 9, 10, 11[4], 12[6], 13[2], 14[5], 15, 16; **36:8**; **Dt 20:7**[2]; **21:12**[3], 13[4], 14[5]; **22:13**[2], 14[4], 15, 16, 17, 19, 21[4], 23[2], 25[3], 27[3], 28[2], 29[3]; **24:1**[4], 3[3], 4[3]; **25:5**[4], 8, 11, 12; **28:30**, 56[3], 57; **Jos 2:14**, 15, 17; **6:17**[2], 22[2], 23[5], 25[3]; **15:18**[3], 19; **Jdg 1:14**[3], 15; **4:5**, 8, 18, 19, 20, 21, 22; **5:26**[3], 27[2], 29; **11:34**, 35, 37, 38[3], 39[2]; **13:6**, 9, 10, 13, 14; **14:2**, 3, 8, 16, 17[2]; **15:1**, 2[5], 6[3]; **16:1**, 5[2], 7, 8, 11, 13, 16, 17[2], 18[2], 19; **19:2**, 3[5], 25[4], 26, 27[2], 28[2], 29[2]; **20:6**[2]; **Ru 1:3**, 5[2], 6, 7, 8, 10, 14[2], 15[2], 18[2], 22[2]; **2:1**, 2, 7, 10, 11, 14[2], 15[2], 16[3], 18[2], 19[3], 20[2], 22, 23; **3:1**[2], 5, 6[2], 15, 16[3]; **4:13**, 16; **1Sa 1:4**, 5[2], 6[4], 7, 8[2], 12, 13[2], 14, 18[3], 19, 22, 23[3], 24; **2:19**; **4:19**[4], 20[2], 21[2]; **18:17**, 21; **25:19**[2], 20, 23, 35[2], 39, 40, 41, 42[2]; **28:7**[2], 10, 13, 14; **2Sa 3:15**[2], 16[3]; **4:4**; **6:16**, 23; **11:4**[4], 26, 27; **12:24**[2]; **13:1**, 2, 5, 6, 8, 10, 11[2], 14[3], 15[3], 16, 17, 18[2], 19[3], 20[3]; **14:2**, 3, 4, 5; **17:3**, 8; **20:17**, 22; **1Ki 1:2**[2], 3, 4, 31; **2:19**[2], 20; **3:1**, 20[2], 26[3]; **9:24**[2]; **10:2**, 3[2], 5, 13[3]; **14:5**[2], 6; **15:13**; **17:10**, 11, 13, 15, 19[2], 20; **21:6**; **2Ki 4:2**, 5[3], 6[2], 9, 12, 13, 14[2], 15[2], 17, 20, 22, 24, 25, 26[2], 27[2], 30, 36, 37; **5:3**; **6:28**, 29[2]; **8:2**, 3[2], 5[3], 6; **9:10**, 30[2], 33[4], 34, 35[3]; **11:1**, 3, 14, 15[3], 16; **19:21**; **22:14**; **1Ch 2:18**; **15:29**; **2Ch 8:11**; **9:1**, 2[2], 4, 12[2]; **11:20**; **15:16**; **22:10**; **23:13**, 14[3], 15[2]; **34:22**; **Est 1:11**, 19; **2:1**, 7[3], 9[5], 10[2], 13, 14, 15[2], 17[2], 20[3]; **4:4**[2], 5, 8[3]; **5:1**, 2, 3, 12; **8:1**; **Job 2:10**; **31:10**; **Ps 45:13**, 14[2]; **84:3**; **113:9**; **123:2**; **Pr 1:20**; **2:16**, 17[2], 18[2], 19; **3:14**[2], 15, 16[2], 17[2], 18[2]; **4:6**[2], 8[2], 13; **5:3**, 5[2], 6, 8[2], 19[2]; **6:25**[3], 29; **7:5**, 8[2], 11, 21, 22, 25[2], 26, 27; **8:1**, 2, 11; **9:1**[2], 3, 14, 18; **12:4**; **14:1**[2]; **17:25**; **23:25**; **27:16**; **30:20**, 23; **31:11**[2], 12, 14, 15[2], 16, 17, 18[2], 19[2], 20[2], 21[2], 22, 23, 25, 26[2], 27, 28[4], 31[4]; **Ecc 7:26**[2]; **SS 3:4**; **6:9**[6]; **8:5**, 9[2]; **Isa 1:21**, 27; **3:26**; **5:14**[3]; **10:11**[2], 30; **14:32**; **17:2**; **21:9**; **23:7**, 13[2], 17, 18[4]; **24:2**; **26:17**[2]; **29:7**[3]; **30:7**; **34:9**[2]; **37:22**; **40:2**[4]; **49:15**[2]; **50:1**; **51:3**[4], 18[2]; **54:1**; **61:10**; **62:1**[2], 4; **66:7**[2], 8, 10[4], 11[2], 12[3], 13; **Jer 2:23**, 24[5], 32[2]; **3:1**, 7, 8[2], 9, 10[2], 20; **4:17**, 31[2]; **5:10**[2]; **6:3**[2], 4, 5, 6[2], 7[2]; **8:19**[2]; **9:20**; **12:7**, 8[2], 9[2]; **14:2**, 3, 5; **15:8**, 9; **20:17**; **30:17**; **31:15**[2]; **44:17**, 18, 19[4], 25; **46:20**, 21[2], 22[2], 23, 25[2]; **48:2**[2], 4, 9; **49:13**, 14, 24[2], 26[3]; **50:2**[2], 3[2], 9, 10, 13, 14, 15[5], 21, 26[5], 27, 29[4], 30[3], 35[2], 36, 37[4], 38, 39, 40, 44[2], 46; **51:2**[3], 3[2], 4, 6[2], 7, 8[2], 9[2], 27, 28, 30[2], 33, 36[2], 43, 45, 47[3], 52[2], 53[2], 55, 56[2], 57[5], 58, 64; **La 1:2**[8], 3[3], 4[5], 5[5], 6[2], 7[4], 8[4], 9[5], 10[2], 11, 17[2]; **2:7**, 9[4], 16; **4:7**, 13[2]; **Eze 5:5**[2], 6; **16:2**, 32, 45[2], 46[2], 48, 49, 53[2], 55[2], 57; **18:6**; **19:2**, 3, 5[2]; **23:4**, 5, 7, 8[5], 9[2], 10[5], 11[4], 14, 17[2], 18[4], 19[2], 20, 31, 42, 43, 44; **29:12**; **36:17**, 38; **Da 11:6**[4], 7; **Hos 1:6**; **2:2**[5], 3[5], 4, 6[3], 7, 8[2], 9, 10[3], 11[5], 12[2], 13[3], 14[3], 15[3], 17; **3:2**, 3; **10:11**; **13:8**, 16[2]; **Joel 1:8**; **2:16**; **Am 5:2**[2]; **Mic 1:6**[2], 7[3], 9; **4:11**; **7:5**, 6[2], 10[2]; **Na 3:4**[2], 7, 8[3], 9[2], 10[3]; **Zec 5:8**; **8:2**; **Mal 2:15**; **Mt 1:19**[3], 20, 24, 25; **2:18**; **5:28**, 31, 32; **8:15**[2]; **9:18**, 22, 25; **10:35**[2]; **11:19**; **14:4**, 7, 8, 11; **15:23**[2], 28[2]; **19:7**; **20:20**, 21; **21:2**; **22:28**; **23:37**[2]; **26:13**; **Mk 1:30**, 31[3]; **5:23**, 29[3], 33, 34, 41[2], 43; **6:17**, 23, 24, 26, 28; **7:26**, 27, 29; **10:4**, 11, 12; **12:21**, 23, 44; **14:5**, 6[2], 9; **16:11**; **Lk 1:5**, 28, 30, 35, 36[2], 38, 41, 45, 56[2], 58[3], 61; **2:6**[2], 7, 19, 36[2], 51; **4:38**, 39[2]; **7:12**, 13[3], 35, 38[2], 44[2], 47, 48; **8:43**, 44, 48, 52, 54, 55[2], 56; **10:38**, 40[2], 41, 42; **11:27**; **12:53**; **13:11**, 12[2], 13, 34[2]; **15:9**; **16:18**; **18:5**; **20:31**, 33; **21:4**; **Jn 2:4**; **4:7**, 10, 13, 16, 17, 21, 26, 27, 28; **8:3**, 7, 10; **11:1**, 2[2], 5, 23, 25, 28[2], 31[3], 33[2], 40, 41[3]; **12:3**, 7; **16:21**[2]; **19:26**, 27; **20:13**, 15, 16, 17, 18; **Ac 5:8**, 9, 10[4]; **7:21**; **8:27**; **9:37**[2], 40, 41[3]; **12:15**; **16:14**, 15, 16, 18, 19; **19:27**[2]; **Ro 7:2**[2], 3[2]; **9:25**; **16:2**[2]; **1Co 6:16**; **7:2**, 3[2], 4, 10, 11[2], 12, 13, 14, 34, 37, 39; **11:5**[3], 6[2], 10, 13, 15[3]; **Gal 4:25**, 30; **Eph 5:25**, 26[2], 33; **Col 4:15**; **1Th 2:7**; **1Ti 5:5**, 10, 16; **1Pe 3:6**; **2Jn 1:1**; **Rev 2:21**[2], 22[3], 23; **12:1**[2], 4, 5, 14, 15, 17; **14:8**; **16:19**; **17:4**[2], 5, 6, 7, 16[3]; **18:3**[3], 4[3], 5[2], 6[4], 7[2], 8[2], 9[3], 10, 11, 15[2], 18, 19, 20[2]; **19:2**[3], 3, 8; **21:2**; **Tob 1:9**; **2:12**[3], 13, 14[3]; **3:7**, 8[2], 10[2], 17[5]; **4:3**[4], 4[3]; **5:21**; **6:12**[4], 13[9], 14, 15[2], 16, 18[6]; **7:10**, 11[3], 12[5], 13[3], 15[2], 16[3]; **8:12**; **10:4**, 6, 7, 12[2]; **11:5**, 9[2], 15, 17; **13:17**; **14:12**; **Jdt 8:2**[2], 5[2], 6, 7[2], 8, 10[2], 11, 28, 35; **9:1**, 2[5]; **10:2**[2], 3[4], 4[4], 5[3], 7[3], 9, 10[3], 11, 12[2], 14[3], 17[2], 18[3], 19[2], 20, 22, 23[2]; **11:1**, 20[2], 22; **12:1**[2], 3, 5, 7, 8, 9, 12[2], 13, 15[4], 16[3], 17, 19, 20; **13:3**[3], 4, 8, 9, 10, 12[2], 18; **14:7**, 17; **15:8**, 9[3], 11[2], 12[3], 13; **16:6**, 7[2], 8, 9[2], 10[2], 19, 21[2], 22[3], 23[4], 24[4], 25; **AdE 1:11**[4], 15, 19; **2:1**, 7[3], 9[4], 10[2], 15, 17, 20[2]; **4:4**, 5[2], 8, 12, 13; **5:3**; **8:1**; **14:2**[4]; **15:1**, 2, 4, 5, 7[2], 8[3], 11, 12, 16; **Wis 6:12**[2], 13, 14, 15[2], 16, 17, 18[3], 22[2]; **7:8**[2], 9[3], 10[3], 11[2], 13, 22, 24, 25; **8:2**[4], 3[2], 7, 9, 10, 13, 16[3], 18[5], 21; **9:10**[2], 11; **10:3**, 9; **Sir 1:6**, 9[4], 10, 16, 17, 19, 20, 26; **3:2**; **4:11**[2], 12[2], 13, 14[2], 15[2], 16[2], 17[2], 18; **6:19**[4], 20, 21, 22, 24[2], 25[2], 26[2], 27[2], 29[2], 30[2], 31[2]; **7:19**, 25, 26; **9:1**, 2, 3, 4, 5, 9[2]; **14:21**[2], 22[2], 23[2], 24[2], 25, 26[2], 27[2]; **15:4**[2], 7[2], 8; **18:28**; **22:4**[2]; **23:22**, 23[2], 24[2], 25[2], 26, 27; **24:1**[2], 2[2], 28, 29[2]; **25:17**[2], 18, 19, 21, 22, 23, 24, 26; **26:2**, 7, 8, 9[2], 11, 12, 13[2], 14, 15, 16, 22, 24, 26[2]; **35:17**, 18; **36:28**[2]; **37:11**; **41:22**; **42:9**[2], 10, 11, 12[3]; **51:14**[2], 15[2], 16, 17, 19, 20[3], 21, 26; **Bar 3:15**[2], 20[2], 21, 23, 29[2], 30[2], 31[2], 32[2], 36; **4:1**[2], 2[2], 16, 33, 34[3], 35; **LtJ 6:43**[2]; **Sus 1:3**, 7, 8[2], 10, 11, 12, 14, 16, 17, 19, 26, 28, 30[4], 32[2], 33[2], 34, 35[2], 37[2], 41, 44, 49, 63[2]; **1Mc 1:38**[3], 39[4], 40[3]; **2:8**, 9[4], 10[2], 11; **3:45**; **10:54**, 58; **11:12**; **2Mc 1:14**; **7:20**[2], 21, 24, 25, 26, 41; **1Es 4:19**[3], 30[2], 31[3], 36; **2Es 1:28**[2], 30[2]; **4:40**[3]; **5:52**; **7:54**, 55; **9:38**[2], 39, 40, 42; **10:5**, 9, 10, 14[2], 19, 25[4], 43, 45, 47, 48[2], 49[3], 50[3]; **15:46**, 47, 48; **16:38**[2], 50[2], 51[2]; **4Mc 2:11**; **12:6**[2]; **14:12**, 13[2], 20; **15:1**, 2, 6, 8, 9, 10, 11[2], 14, 15, 22, 23[4], 25[2], 26; **16:1**, 3[2], 13, 24; **17:1**; **18:6**

HERSELF (72)

Ge 18:12; **20:5**; **24:65**; **38:14**; **Lev 18:23**; **21:9**; **Nu 5:13**, 14[2], 27, 28, 29; **30:3**, 4[2], 5, 6, 7, 8, 9, 10, 11, 12, 13; **Dt 22:21**; **Jdg 5:29**; **Ru 2:18**; **1Sa 1:9**; **2Sa 11:4**; **21:10**; **Ps 84:3**; **Pr 31:17**, 22; **Isa 23:17**; **61:10**; **Jer 3:11**; **La 1:8**; **Eze 23:7**, 17; **Hos 2:13**; **Mt 9:21**; **22:27**; **Mk 12:22**; **1Co 11:6**; **1Ti 5:10**; **Heb 11:11**; **Rev 2:20**; **18:6**, 7; **19:7**; **Tob 3:10**[2]; **Jdt 8:5**; **9:1**; **10:3**[2], 4, 23; **12:15**; **16:19**, 22; **AdE 15:1**, 8; **Wis 6:13**; **7:27**; **Sir 23:24**; **24:1**; **LtJ 6:43**; **2Es 5:53**; **16:50**; **4Mc 15:6**; **17:1**

HIM (6317)

Ge 2:15, 18; **3:9**, 23; **4:8**, 15[3], 25[2], 26; **5:3**, 24, 29; **6:6**, 22; **7:5**, 16[2], 23; **8:1**, 8, 9[2], 11, 12; **9:8**, 24, 27; **12:4**[2], 7, 20[2]; **13:1**, 10, 14; **14:5**, 17[2], 19, 20; **15:4**, 5[2], 6, 7, 9, 10, 12; **16:1**, 11, 12, 13, 16; **17:1**, 3, 19[3], 20[3], 22, 23, 27; **18:2**, 9, 10, 18, 19[3], 29; **19:3**, 6, 16[4], 21, 26, 32, 34[3], 35, 37, 38; **20:3**, 6, 9, 14; **21:2**, 3, 4, 5, 7, 13, 16[2], 18[2], 21; **22:1**, 2, 3[2], 9[2], 11, 12; **23:9**; **24:5**, 6, 9, 18, 19, 24, 32[2], 33, 35, 36, 47, 54; **25:2**, 9, 25, 33; **26:7**, 8, 9, 12, 14, 20, 24, 26, 31, 32[2]; **27:1**, 12, 13, 22, 23[2], 25[2], 26, 27[2], 32, 33, 37[3], 39, 41, 42, 44, 45; **28:1**[2], 6[3], 13; **29:6**, 13[4], 14[2], 20, 28, 32, 33, 34, 35; **30:4**, 6, 8, 11, 13, 16, 18, 20[2], 24, 27, 29; **31:2**, 7, 14, 15, 20, 23[3], 24; **32:1**, 3, 6, 7, 11, 13, 19, 20, 21, 24, 25[2], 27, 29[2], 31; **33:1**, 4[3], 11, 13; **34:6**, 8; **35:2**, 6, 7, 9, 10, 11, 13[2], 14, 15, 18[2], 26, 29; **36:5**, 33, 34, 35, 36, 37, 38, 39; **37:3**, 4[3], 5, 8[2], 10[2], 11, 14[2], 15[2], 18[2], 20[3], 21, 22[4], 23, 24[2], 27[2], 28[2], 33, 35[2], 36; **38:3**, 5[2], 7, 10, 14, 18; **39:1**[3], 3, 4[3], 5, 6, 17, 19, 20[2], 21[3], 23; **40:7**, 8, 9, 12, 23; **41:12**, 33, 42, 43[3], 45, 50; **42:4**, 6, 8, 10, 24, 29, 31, 37[3], 38; **43:3**, 5, 7, 9[4], 19, 26[2], 32[3], 33, 34; **44:2**, 7, 9, 14, 18, 20, 21[2], 24, 28, 29, 32; **45:1**[2], 3, 9, 15, 26, 27[2], 28; **46:5**, 6, 7[3], 20, 27, 28, 29, 31; **47:7**, 18[2], 29, 31; **48:1**, 10, 13, 17; **49:9**, 10, 23[3], 26; **50:1**[2], 3, 4, 7, 9, 12, 13[2], 14, 15, 17, 18; **Ex 1:16**; **2:2**, 3[2], 4, 6, 10[4], 12, 20, 22; **3:2**, 4, 18; **4:2**, 6, 11, 15, 16, 18, 23, 24[2], 26, 27[2], 28[2]; **5:2**; **6:2**, 20, 23, 25, 29; **7:15**, 16; **8:1**, 20; **9:1**, 13, 29; **10:3**, 7, 28; **13:19**; **14:6**; **15:2**[2], 25; **16:8**; **17:10**, 12; **18:5**, 7, 13, 17; **19:3**, 7, 19, 24; **20:20**; **21:3**, 4[2], 6[2]; **22:17**; **23:21**[3]; **24:2**; **28:1**, 3, 41, 43[2]; **29:5**, 7, 21, 29; **30:21**; **31:3**, 6, 18; **32:1**[2], 23, 26; **33:15**; **34:4**, 5, 6, 30, 31, 32, 34, 35; **35:31**, 34[2]; **36:3**; **38:23**; **40:13**[2], 16; **Lev 1:1**; **4:23**; **8:2**, 4, 7[6], 8, 12[2]; **9:9**, 12, 13, 18; **13:3**[2], 5[2], 6[2], 8, 11[2], 13, 14, 15, 17, 20, 21, 22, 23, 25, 26, 27[2], 28, 30, 34, 36, 37, 43, 44; **14:7**; **15:2**, 3, 10, 24, 32; **16:34**; **19:22**[2]; **21:3**, 12, 15; **24:9**, 11, 12, 14, 23; **Nu 2:5**, 12, 20, 27; **3:6**, 7, 9, 42; **4:49**; **5:12**, 14[2]; **7:89**[2]; **8:2**; **9:7**; **10:30**; **11:20**, 25[2], 29; **12:8**; **13:27**, 31; **14:36**; **15:33**[2], 34[2], 35, 36[2]; **16:5**[2], 9, 10, 11, 25, 40; **17:6**, 11; **20:9**, 18, 19; **21:24**, 34[3], 35; **22:5**, 7, 16, 20, 22, 32, 36, 40, 41; **23:4**, 9[2], 13, 14, 17[2]; **24:2**, 8[2], 9, 17[2]; **25:12**, 13[2]; **27:18**, 19[2], 20, 21[2], 22[2], 23[2]; **31:17**, 18, 35; **32:15**, 16, 21; **Dt 1:3**, 36, 38; **2:24**, 30, 33[2]; **3:2**[3], 3, 28; **4:7**, 25, 29[2], 30, 35; **6:13**, 16; **7:9**, 10[2]; **8:6**; **9:20**, 23[2]; **10:6**, 8, 9, 12, 20[2]; **11:13**, 22; **13:4**[3]; **15:13**, 14; **17:18**, 19; **18:4**, 5; **21:5**, 15, 17, 18, 19[2], 21, 22, 23; **22:18**, 19; **24:1**; **25:8**[2], 9, 10; **26:3**, 17, 19; **28:55**; **30:2**, 20[2]; **31:7**, 14, 29; **32:5**, 10[4], 12[2], 13[3], 15, 16[2], 43[2]; **33:2**, 7[2], 11, 12; **34:1**, 4, 9[2], 11; **Jos 2:23**; **4:14**; **5:13**[3]; **7:3**, 19, 24, 25, 26; **8:11**, 14; **9:6**, 9[2]; **10:7**, 15, 23, 24, 29, 31, 33[2], 43; **11:9**; **13:1**; **14:6**, 7, 13; **15:16**, 17, 18[2], 19; **19:50**; **22:5**[2], 14, 30; **24:3**[2], 14, 22, 24, 30, 33[2]; **Jdg 1:3**, 5, 6[2], 7, 12, 13, 14[2], 15, 24; **2:9**; **3:10**, 15, 20, 23, 27[2], 28, 31; **4:6**, 7, 10[2], 13, 14, 18[2], 19[2], 21, 22[2]; **5:13**, 25[2]; **6:12**[2], 13, 14, 16, 17, 19, 20, 23, 25, 27, 31[3], 32, 34, 35; **7:1**, 3, 8, 9, 19; **8:1**[2], 3, 4, 8, 14[2], 31[2]; **9:4**[2], 16, 19, 25, 26, 28[2], 29, 33, 34, 35, 36, 38[2], 40[2], 44, 48[2], 54[3]; **10:3**, 6; **11:2**[2], 3, 11, 15, 19, 28, 34, 36; **12:5**, 6[3], 8, 11, 13; **13:6**, 11, 18, 19, 23, 24[2], 25; **14:3**, 5, 6, 11[2], 13, 16, 17[2], 18, 19; **15:1**, 10, 12, 13[3], 14[2]; **16:2**[2], 5[4], 8, 9, 12[2], 14, 15, 16[2], 19[3], 20, 21[3], 24, 25[2], 26, 31[3]; **17:9**, 10, 11; **18:3**, 5, 15, 19, 25, 26, 27; **19:2**[2], 3[3], 4[2], 7, 9, 10[2], 12, 18, 21, 22, 25; **Ru 2:10**; **3:13**; **4:15**, 16, 17[2]; **1Sa 1:11**, 17, 20[2], 22[2], 23[2], 24[3], 27, 28[2]; **2:3**, 16, 19[2], 27, 28, 35, 36; **3:7**, 13, 18[4], 19; **5:3**, 4; **6:3**, 4, 8, 20; **7:3**, 9; **8:5**, 10; **9:5**, 6, 13[2], 16, 17; **10:1**, 9, 10[2], 11, 14, 16, 21, 23, 24, 26, 27[2]; **11:3**, 5; **12:14**, 24; **13:7**, 10[2], 14, 15; **14:2**, 7, 13[2], 17, 20, 37, 39, 43, 52; **15:13**, 28, 32; **16:1**, 4, 7, 8, 11, 12[2], 13, 14, 15, 17, 18, 21, 23; **17:7**, 8, 9[2], 13, 20, 23, 24, 25[2], 26, 27[2], 28, 30[2], 31, 32, 33, 38, 41, 42, 50, 51, 57[2], 58; **18:1**, 2[3], 3, 5[2], 8, 11, 12, 13[2], 14, 15, 17[2], 20, 21[3], 24, 27, 28; **19:4**, 7, 8, 11[3], 15[2], 18[2], 23; **20:2**, 7, 17[2], 18, 26, 30, 31, 33[2], 34, 35, 36, 40; **21:1**, 6, 11[2], 14; **22:1**, 2[2], 4, 6[2], 7, 10[3], 13[3], 15, 17; **23:3**, 4, 7, 9, 14[2], 17, 20, 22, 23, 25; **24:4**[2], 6, 8; **25:1**[2], 5, 6, 12, 17, 21, 22, 25, 35, 36[2], 37[2], 40; **26:3**, 5, 7, 8[2], 9, 10; **27:2**, 4, 6; **28:3**[2], 6, 7, 8, 9, 20, 21, 23; **29:3**, 4[3], 6; **30:4**, 6, 8, 9, 11[3], 12, 13, 15, 16, 21; **31:3**, 5; **2Sa 1:3**[2], 4, 5, 6[2], 7, 8, 10[2], 11, 13, 14, 15[2], 16; **2:1**, 3, 5, 8, 9, 19, 21[2], 23, 32; **3:9**, 11, 16, 20, 22, 23[2], 24, 26, 27[3], 31, 34; **4:4**, 6, 7[3], 10[3]; **5:8**, 10, 12, 14, 25; **6:2**, 7, 12, 16; **7:1**[2], 14[2], 15; **8:4**, 10[4]; **9:2**, 4, 5, 7, 9, 10; **10:1**, 2, 9, 12, 13[2], 17; **11:1**, 4, 7, 8, 13[2], 15, 21, 22, 25, 26, 27; **12:1**[2], 3[2], 4[2], 9, 17[2], 18[3], 20, 21, 23[2], 24[2], 25; **13:4**[2], 5[2], 6, 7, 9[2], 11, 12, 16, 17, 21, 25[2], 26, 27[2], 28; **14:3**, 6, 7, 10, 24, 25, 26, 29[2], 31, 32, 33; **15:1**, 5, 9, 14, 18[2], 22, 26[2], 30, 32, 33; **16:1**, 10, 11[3], 13[2], 14, 15, 18; **17:2**[3], 6, 10, 12[3], 16, 22, 29; **18:1**, 9, 11[3], 15[2], 17[2], 19, 20, 23; **19:15**, 17, 23, 25, 26, 29, 30, 31, 37[2], 38, 39, 40, 41[2]; **20:5**, 6, 7, 9, 10, 11, 12[2], 14, 15, 17, 21; **21:4**, 17[2], 21; **22:1**, 9, 12, 13, 24, 31; **23:9**, 10, 11, 21[2], 23; **24:2**, 13[2], 18, 20, 22; **1Ki 1:1**, 2, 4, 5, 6, 13, 17, 20, 25, 27, 33, 34, 35[3], 38, 40, 41, 44[2], 45, 52, 53[2]; **2:8**, 9[2], 16, 19, 22[2], 25, 29, 30, 31[3], 34[2], 36, 42, 46; **3:6**[2], 11, 16, 19, 20, 21, 26, 27, 28; **4:10**; **5:1**, 3, 12; **8:5**[2], 24, 25, 58, 62, 65; **9:2**, 3, 12[2]; **10:1**, 2; **11:9**, 10, 18[3], 19, 20, 22, 24[2], 28, 29, 34[2], 43; **12:1**, 3, 7, 8[3], 10[2], 13, 18, 20[2]; **13:4**[2], 6, 11, 12, 13, 14[2], 15, 18[3], 19, 20, 23[2], 24[2], 26[3], 29, 30, 31; **14:3**, 13[3], 18[2], 20, 22, 31; **15:3**, 4[2], 5, 8[2], 24, 27[2], 28; **16:6**, 7, 9, 10[3], 11, 17, 21, 25, 28, 30, 31[2], 33; **17:2**, 6, 8, 17, 19[3], 21, 22, 23[2]; **18:7**[2], 8, 15, 16, 17, 21[3], 30; **19:5**[2], 7, 9, 13, 15, 18, 19[3], 20, 21; **20:1**, 2, 7, 8, 9, 10, 11, 16, 17, 22, 23, 31, 33[4], 34[3], 35, 36[4], 37[2], 40, 41, 42; **21:4**, 5, 6, 7, 10[4], 13[3], 19[2]; **22:8**, 13, 15[2], 16, 19[2], 21, 22[2], 24, 26, 27, 32, 33, 40, 50, 53; **2Ki 1:6**[2], 8, 9[2], 10, 11[2], 12, 13, 15[3], 16, 17; **2:3**, 4, 5, 6, 12, 13, 14, 15[3], 16[3], 17[2], 18, 20, 23; **3:12**[2], 13, 15, 26[2], 27[3]; **4:5**, 8, 10, 12, 13, 19, 20[2], 21[2], 23, 31[2], 34, 35, 36, 38; **5:1**, 3, 5, 6, 8, 10, 13, 15, 16, 19[2], 20[3], 21[2], 23, 25, 26; **6:6**, 13, 18, 26, 28, 29[2], 32[3], 33; **7:17**[2], 20[2]; **8:6**, 7, 8, 9[3], 10[2], 11, 14, 15, 19, 21, 24, 29; **9:1**, 2[2], 6, 11, 13, 15, 17[2], 18, 21, 25[3], 26[2], 27[3], 28[2], 32, 36; **10:3**, 4, 7, 8, 9, 11, 15[6], 16, 35[2]; **11:2**[3], 4, 12[4]; **12:2**, 21[2]; **13:4**, 9[2], 14[2], 15, 19, 20, 24, 25; **14:16**, 19[3], 20, 21, 29; **15:7**[2], 10[4], 14[2], 16, 19, 22, 25[4], 30[3], 38; **16:5**, 9, 20; **17:2**, 3[2], 4[2], 17, 27, 36[2]; **18:5**[3], 6, 7[2], 15, 21, 36[2], 37; **19:3**, 7[2], 21, 37[2]; **20:1**[2], 4, 14, 21; **21:6**, 11, 18, 23, 24, 26; **22:4**, 18; **23:1**, 2, 17, 18, 25[4], 26, 29[3], 30[5], 33; **24:1**, 2, 6, 12; **25:5**[2],

HIMSELF (447)

HIS (7714)

67, 68; **Sus 1:**4, 48, 59, 63; **Bel 1:**1[2], 2, 4, 14, 36[2], 39, 42[2]; **1Mc 1:**3, 6[2], 8[2], 9, 16, 24, 41, 43, 51; **2:**14, 16, 19, 24, 28, 39, 45, 49, 53, 60, 66, 69, 70; **3:**1[2], 2[2], 3[4], 4, 5, 6, 7[2], 12, 14, 23, 25, 26, 27, 28[2], 30, 33, 34, 37[2], 42, 60; **4:**2, 3, 9, 10, 16, 18, 24, 30, 35, 36, 59; **5:**10, 17, 24, 28, 32, 40[2], 50, 59, 61, 63, 65; **6:**3, 7, 8, 10, 14[2], 15[2], 23, 28[2], 30, 33[2], 42, 44[2], 55; **7:**2, 4[2], 6, 10, 21, 26, 27, 31, 35, 38, 44; **8:**20; **9:**1, 7, 14, 16, 22[2], 30, 31, 33, 34, 35[2], 37, 39[2], 47, 55[3], 58, 60[2], 62, 63, 65, 66, 67[2], 68[2], 69, 72; **10:**5[2], 6, 15, 18, 32, 47[2], 53[2], 57, 58, 63[2], 64, 65, 67, 74[2], 80[2], 81, 82, 89; **11:**1, 4, 11, 12, 13, 18, 24, 25, 26[2], 27, 30, 32, 38[2], 40, 47, 51, 52, 53, 64, 67, 71[2], 73; **12:**25, 27, 28, 29, 39, 42, 43[3], 50, 52; **13:**14, 16, 19, 20, 22, 24, 25[2], 27[2], 28, 32, 52, 53; **14:**1, 2[2], 4[3], 5, 6, 10, 14, 17[2], 18, 25, 26[2], 29, 30, 32[3], 35[3], 36[2], 39, 43, 44, 49; **15:**10, 11, 12, 15, 25, 28, 32; **16:**1, 2, 6[2], 8, 13[2], 14, 16[4], 21, 23[2], 24[2]; **2Mc 1:**2[2], 3, 4[2], 7, 14, 16, 33, 36; **2:**7[2], 17, 18, 19, 20; **3:**1, 3, 7, 8, 16[3], 17, 21, 24, 27, 28, 30, 31, 33, 35[2], 36, 39; **4:**1, 2, 3, 5, 6, 9, 10, 21[2], 22, 26, 28, 29, 31, 34, 38, 41, 46, 50; **5:**1, 6, 7, 8[2], 10, 12, 15, 16, 18, 21[2], 23[2], 25, 26, 27; **6:**16[2], 18, 19, 21, 22, 23[3], 24, 30, 31[2]; **7:**4, 6[2], 7, 8, 9[2], 10[2], 11, 12, 17, 23[2], 24[2], 26, 33, 39, 40[2]; **8:**1, 4[2], 5, 7, 12, 15, 16, 21, 22, 29, 35[3]; **9:**2, 4[2], 5, 7[4], 8, 9[2], 10, 11[2], 12, 16, 18, 19, 23, 28, 29[2]; **10:**1, 7, 13[2], 16, 19, 25, 33, 37; **11:**2, 4[3], 6, 22; **12:**5[2], 6, 11[2], 12, 14, 15, 20, 25, 28, 35[2], 36, 38, 39; **13:**1, 2, 3, 8, 9, 14[2], 15, 22; **14:**1, 2, 5, 13, 15[2], 18, 24, 26, 30[3], 33, 37[2], 41, 42, 45[2], 46[3]; **15:**1, 5, 6[2], 8, 10, 13, 15, 21, 24, 25, 26, 30[3], 31, 33, 34; **1Es 1:**1, 4, 5, 9, 16, 23, 24, 28, 30[2], 31[2], 33[2], 34, 37, 38, 41, 42, 43[2], 48[3], 50[2], 51[2], 52[2], 57; **2:**2, 5, 10, 11; **3:**1, 3, 6, 7, 8, 15; **4:**10[2], 11, 20[3], 21[5], 23, 25[3], 28, 49, 58, 61, 63; **5:**6, 8, 38, 48[2], 58[2], 61[2]; **6:**18, 31; **8:**4, 21, 25, 26[2], 46, 47, 48, 55, 91; **9:**9, 19, 43, 44; **Pm 151:**T, 4[2], 6, 7; **3Mc 1:**1[2], 3, 7, 22[2], 25, 26; **2:**1[2], 2, 22, 23, 25, 26[3]; **3:**4, 7[2], 11[2], 12; **4:**13, 16; **5:**3[2], 12[2], 13, 16, 19, 26, 30, 33[2], 35, 39, 47[2]; **6:**1, 4[2], 5, 8, 16[2], 18, 20, 23, 39, 41; **7:**1, 6, 12; **2Es 1:**10[2], 28; **3:**7, 11, 15, 17, 26; **4:**25; **5:**7[2], 33, 34; **7:**23, 24[4], 79, 104[5], 133, 134, 136, 138, 139; **8:**56[2], 57; **10:**1, 48; **11:**44[2]; **12:**25[2], 26, 31[2], 33; **13:**3[2], 4[3], 9, 10[3], 26, 27, 28, 33, 52; **15:**23; **16:**9, 11, 12, 13[2], 53, 56, 58, 66; **4Mc 2:**3[2], 17; **3:**7, 10, 12, 15; **4:**4, 7, 10, 11, 15, 22, 24[2], 26; **5:**1[2], 4; **6:**2, 3, 6[3], 7[2], 10, 11[3], 12, 13, 25, 26[2], 30; **7:**4[2], 5, 12, 13[3]; **8:**2, 15; **9:**11[3], 13, 21, 26, 27, 28[4]; **10:**5[2], 6, 7, 8[3], 12, 17; **11:**5, 10[3], 18, 19[3]; **12:**7, 8, 11, 19; **15:**18, 19, 28; **16:**20[3]; **17:**2, 17, 23, 24; **18:**5, 9, 16, 20[2]

I (9803)

See also the selected listing for "I AM" in the Main Concordance.

Ge 1:29, 30; **2:**18; **3:**10[4], 11, 12, 13, 15, 16, 17; **4:**1, 9[2], 13, 14[2], 23[2]; **6:**7[4], 13[2], 17, 18; **7:**1, 4[3]; **8:**21[3]; **9:**3[2], 5[3], 9, 11, 12, 13, 14, 15, 16, 17; **12:**1, 2[2], 3[2], 7, 11, 19; **13:**9[2], 15, 16, 17; **14:**22, 23[2], 24; **15:**1, 2, 7, 8[2], 14, 18; **16:**2, 5, 8, 10, 13; **17:**1, 2, 5, 6[2], 7, 8[2], 16[3], 19, 20[3], 21; **18:**3, 10, 12[2], 13[2], 14, 15, 17[2], 19, 21[2], 26[2], 27, 28[2], 29, 30[3], 31, 32[2]; **19:**7, 8, 19[2], 21, 22, 34; **20:**5, 6[3], 9, 11[2], 13, 16; **21:**7, 13, 18, 23, 24, 26[2], 30; **22:**1, 2, 5, 7, 11, 12, 16, 17[2]; **23:**4[2], 8, 11[3], 13[2]; **24:**3[2], 5, 7, 13, 14[4], 19, 24, 31, 33[2], 34, 37, 39, 40, 42[2], 43[2], 44, 45[2], 46[2], 47[2], 48, 49, 56, 58; **25:**22, 30, 32; **26:**2, 3[4], 4, 9[2], 24[2]; **27:**1, 2[2], 4[3], 6, 7[2], 8, 9, 11, 12, 18, 19[2], 21, 24, 25, 32, 33[2], 37[4], 41, 45[2], 46; **28:**13[2], 15[4], 16, 20, 21, 22[2]; **29:**18, 19[2], 21, 25, 33, 34, 35; **30:**1, 2, 3, 8, 13, 16, 18, 20, 25, 26[2], 27, 28, 29, 30[3], 31[2]; **31:**3, 5, 6, 10[2], 11[2], 12, 13, 27, 31[2], 32, 35, 38[2], 39[2], 41[2], 43, 44, 51, 52; **32:**4, 5[3], 9, 10[3], 11, 12, 20[2], 26, 30; **33:**8, 9, 10, 11[2], 12, 14[2]; **34:**11, 12, 30[2]; **35:**3[2], 11, 12[3]; **37:**6, 9, 10, 13[2], 16, 17, 30[2], 35; **38:**17, 18, 22, 23, 26[2]; **39:**9[2], 14, 18; **40:**11, 15[2], 16; **41:**9, 11, 13, 15[2], 16, 17, 19, 21, 22[2], 24, 28, 40, 41, 44; **42:**2, 14, 18, 22, 33, 34[2], 36, 37[2]; **43:**9[2], 14[2], 23; **44:**15, 17, 21, 28[2], 30, 32[2], 34[2]; **45:**3, 4, 11, 13, 18, 28[2]; **46:**2, 3[2], 4[2], 30, 31; **47:**16, 23, 29, 30[2]; **48:**4[2], 5, 7[2], 9, 11, 19[2], 21, 22[2]; **49:**1, 6[2], 7, 18, 29, 31; **50:**4, 5[4], 17, 19, 21, 24; **Ex 2:**7, 9, 10, 22; **3:**3, 4, 6, 7[3], 8, 9, 10, 11[2], 12[2], 13[2], 14[3], 16, 17[2], 19, 20[2], 21; **4:**10[2], 11, 12, 14, 15, 21[2], 23[2]; **5:**2[3], 10, 23; **6:**1, 2, 3[2], 4, 5[2], 6[3], 7[3], 8[4], 12, 29[2], 30; **7:**1, 2, 3[2], 4, 5[2], 17[2]; **8:**2, 8, 9, 21, 22[2], 23, 28, 29[2]; **9:**14, 15, 16, 18, 27[2], 28, 29[2], 30; **10:**1[2], 2[3], 4, 10, 16, 29; **11:**1, 4, 8; **12:**12[4], 13[3], 17; **13:**8, 15[2]; **14:**4[3], 17[2], 18[2]; **15:**1, 2[2], 9[4], 26[3]; **16:**4[2], 12[2], 32[2]; **17:**4, 6, 9, 14; **18:**3, 6, 11, 16[2], 19; **19:**4[2], 9[2]; **20:**2, 5, 22, 24[2]; **21:**5[2], 13; **22:**23, 24, 27[2]; **23:**7, 13, 15, 20[2], 22[2], 23, 25[2], 26, 27[2], 28, 29, 30, 31[2]; **24:**12[2]; **25:**8, 9, 16, 21, 22[2]; **28:**3; **29:**35, 42, 43, 44[2], 45[2], 46[3]; **30:**6, 36; **31:**2, 3, 6[3], 11, 13; **32:**8, 9, 10[2], 13[3], 18, 24[2], 30[2], 33, 34[2]; **33:**1[2], 2[2], 3[2], 5[3], 12, 13[2], 14, 16[3], 17[2], 18, 19[4], 22[3], 23; **34:**1, 9[2], 10[3], 11[2], 18, 24, 27; **Lev 6:**17; **7:**34; **8:**31, 35; **10:**3[2], 13, 18, 19; **11:**44[2], 45[2]; **14:**34[2]; **16:**2; **17:**10, 11, 12, 14; **18:**2, 3, 4, 5, 6, 21, 24, 25, 30; **19:**2, 3, 4, 10, 12, 14, 16, 18, 25, 28, 30, 31, 32, 34, 36, 37; **20:**3, 5, 6, 7, 8[2], 22, 23[2], 24[4], 25, 26[2]; **21:**8[2], 12, 15[2], 23[2]; **22:**2, 3, 8, 9[2], 16[2], 30, 31, 32[3], 33[2]; **23:**10, 22, 30, 43[3]; **24:**22; **25:**2, 17, 21, 38, 42, 55[2]; **26:**1, 2, 4, 6[2], 9[2], 11[2], 12, 13[2], 16[2], 17, 18, 19[2], 21, 22, 24[2], 25[2], 26, 28[2], 30[3], 31[2], 32, 33[2], 36, 41, 42[3], 44[2], 45[3]; **Nu 3:**12, 13[3], 41, 45; **5:**3; **6:**27; **8:**16, 17[2], 18, 19; **9:**8; **10:**10, 29, 30[2]; **11:**11, 12[2], 13, 14, 15, 17[2], 21[2]; **12:**6[2], 8; **13:**2; **14:**11, 12[2], 20, 21, 22, 23, 24, 27, 28[3], 30, 31, 35[2]; **15:**2, 18, 41[2]; **16:**15[2], 21, 45; **17:**4, 5[2]; **18:**6, 7, 8[2], 11, 12, 19, 20, 21, 24[2], 26; **20:**12, 24; **21:**16, 34; **22:**6[3], 8, 11, 17[2], 18, 19, 20, 28, 29[3], 30[2], 32, 33, 34[3], 35, 37[2], 38[3]; **23:**3[2], 4, 8[2], 9[2], 11, 12, 15, 20[2], 26[2], 27; **24:**10, 11[2], 12, 13[2], 14, 17[2]; **25:**11, 12; **27:**12; **32:**8, 11; **33:**53, 56[2]; **35:**34[2]; **Dt 1:**8[2], 9[2], 12, 15, 16, 17, 18, 20, 23, 29, 35, 36, 39, 42, 43; **2:**5[2], 9[2], 19[2], 24, 25, 26, 27[2], 28[2], 29, 31; **3:**2, 12, 13, 15, 16, 18, 19[2], 20, 21, 23; **4:**1, 2[2], 5, 8, 10, 21[2], 22, 26, 40; **5:**1, 5, 6, 9, 28, 31[2]; **6:**2, 6; **7:**11, 17[2]; **8:**1, 11, 19; **9:**9[3], 12, 13, 14[2], 15, 16, 17, 18[2], 19, 20, 21[2], 23, 25, 26; **10:**2, 3, 5[2], 10[2], 11, 13; **11:**8, 13, 22, 26, 27, 28, 32; **12:**11, 14, 20, 21, 28, 30, 32; **13:**18; **15:**5, 11, 15, 16; **17:**3, 14; **18:**16[2], 18[3], 19, 20; **19:**7, 9; **22:**14[3], 16, 17; **24:**8, 18, 22; **25:**8; **26:**3[2], 10, 13[3], 14[5]; **27:**1, 4, 10; **28:**1, 13, 14, 15, 68; **29:**5, 6, 14; **30:**1, 2, 8, 11, 15, 16, 18, 19[2]; **31:**2[2], 5, 14, 16, 17, 18, 20[2], 21[3], 23[2], 27[2], 28, 29[2]; **32:**1, 3, 20[2], 21, 23, 24, 26, 27, 39[6], 40[2], 41[2], 42, 46, 49, 52; **33:**9; **34:**4[3]; **Jos 1:**2, 3[2], 5[3], 6, 9; **2:**4, 5, 9, 12; **3:**7[3]; **5:**9, 14; **6:**2, 10; **7:**8, 11, 12, 20[2], 21[2]; **8:**1, 5, 8, 18; **10:**8; **11:**6; **13:**6[2]; **14:**7[2], 8, 10, 11[2], 12; **15:**16; **18:**4, 6, 8; **20:**2; **22:**2; **23:**2, 4[2], 14; **24:**3[2], 4[2], 5[4], 6, 7, 8[3], 10[2], 11, 12, 13; **Jdg 1:**2, 3, 7, 12; **2:**1[4], 3[2], 20, 21; **3:**19, 20; **4:**7[2], 8[2], 9, 19, 22; **5:**3[2]; **6:**8, 9, 10[2], 14, 15[2], 16, 17, 18[2], 22, 37[2]; **7:**4[3], 7, 9, 13, 17[2], 18[2]; **8:**2, 3, 5, 7, 9[2], 19, 23; **9:**2, 9, 11, 13, 19, 29[2], 48; **10:**11, 12, 13; **11:**9, 27, 31, 35[2], 37[2]; **12:**2[2], 3[2]; **13:**6, 8, 11, 13, 14, 16; **14:**2, 12, 16[2]; **15:**1, 2[2], 3[2], 7[3], 11, 16, 18; **16:**7, 11, 13, 15, 17[2], 20, 26, 28; **17:**2[2], 3, 9[3], 10, 13; **18:**4, 24[2]; **19:**18[3], 20; **20:**4[2], 6, 28; **Ru 1:**11, 12[3], 16[2], 17[2], 21; **2:**2, 9, 10[2], 13[2], 19; **3:**1, 5, 9, 11, 12[2], 13; **4:**4[5], 6[2], 9, 10; **1Sa 1:**8, 11, 15[3], 16, 20, 22[2], 26, 27[2], 28; **2:**1, 16, 23, 24, 27, 28[2], 29, 30[2], 31, 33, 35[2], 36; **3:**4, 5[2], 6[2], 8, 11, 12[2], 13[2], 14, 16; **4:**16[2]; **7:**5; **8:**8; **9:**8[2], 16[2], 17, 19[2], 21, 23[2], 26, 27; **10:**2, 8[2], 18[2]; **11:**2[2]; **12:**1, 2[2], 3[7], 7[2], 17, 23[2]; **13:**11, 12[3]; **14:**7, 24, 29, 37, 40, 43[3]; **15:**2, 6, 11[2], 13, 14, 16, 20[4], 24[3], 25[2], 26, 30[2]; **16:**1[3], 2[2], 3[2], 5, 7, 18; **17:**8, 9, 10, 28, 29, 35[2], 39[2], 43, 44, 45, 46[2], 55, 58; **18:**11, 17[2], 18[2], 23; **19:**3[4], 15, 17; **20:**1, 4, 5[2], 9[2], 12[2], 13, 14[2], 20[2], 21[2], 22, 23, 29, 30, 36; **21:**2[3], 4, 5, 8, 15; **22:**3, 9, 12, 15, 22[2]; **23:**2, 4, 11, 17, 22, 23[2]; **24:**4, 6, 10[3], 11[2], 17[2], 20; **25:**7, 11[3], 19, 21, 22, 25, 35[2]; **26:**6, 8, 11, 18, 21[3], 23; **27:**1[2], 5[2]; **28:**2, 7, 8, 11, 13, 15[3], 21, 23; **29:**3, 6, 8[3], 9, 10; **30:**8[2], 13[2], 15; **2Sa 1:**3, 6, 7, 8[2], 10[4], 13, 16, 26; **2:**1[2], 6, 22[2]; **3:**8[2], 9, 12, 13[2], 14, 18, 28, 35, 39; **4:**10[2], 11; **5:**19[2]; **6:**21, 22[3]; **7:**2, 6[3], 7[3], 8, 9[2], 10, 11[2], 12[2], 13, 14[2], 15[3], 18, 27; **9:**1, 3, 6, 7[2], 8, 9; **10:**2, 11; **11:**5, 11[2], 12; **12:**7[2], 8[2], 11[2], 12, 13, 22[2], 23[3], 27[2], 28; **13:**4, 5, 6, 10, 13[2], 28[2]; **14:**5, 8, 15[2], 18, 21, 22, 32[3]; **15:**4[2], 7, 8[2], 20[3], 25, 26[2], 28, 31, 34[3]; **16:**4, 10, 18[2], 19[3]; **17:**1, 2[2], 3, 15; **18:**2, 4, 10, 11, 12[2], 13, 14, 18, 23, 27, 29[2], 33; **19:**6, 7, 20[2], 22[3], 26, 28, 29, 33, 34[2], 35[3], 37, 38[2]; **20:**16, 17[2], 19, 20, 21; **21:**3[2], 4, 6; **22:**3, 4[2], 7[2], 22, 23, 24[4], 30[4], 38, 39[2], 41, 43[2], 44, 50; **23:**17[2]; **24:**2, 10[4], 12[2], 13, 14, 17[3], 24[2]; **1Ki 1:**5, 14, 21, 30[2], 35; **2:**2, 7, 8[3], 14, 16, 18, 20[2], 26, 30, 42[2], 43; **3:**5, 7[2], 12[2], 13, 14, 17[2], 18, 21[4]; **5:**5[2], 6, 8[2], 9[2]; **6:**12[2], 13; **8:**13, 16[3], 20[2], 21, 27, 43, 44, 48, 59; **9:**3[2], 4, 5[2], 6, 7[4]; **10:**6, 7[3]; **11:**11[2], 12[2], 13[3], 21, 31, 32, 34[2], 35, 36[2], 37, 38[4], 39; **12:**11[2], 14[2]; **13:**7, 8[2], 9, 14, 16[2], 18, 31; **14:**2, 6, 7, 10[2]; **15:**19; **16:**2, 3[2]; **17:**1, 4, 9, 10, 12[3], 20, 24; **18:**1, 8, 9, 12[4], 13[2], 15[2], 18, 22[2], 23, 24, 36[2]; **19:**2, 4, 10[2], 14[2], 18, 20[2]; **20:**4[2], 5, 6, 7, 9[2], 13[2], 28[2], 34[2], 42; **21:**2[3], 3, 4, 6[3], 7, 20, 21[2], 22, 29[2]; **22:**4, 6[2], 8, 14, 16, 17, 18, 19, 21, 22, 27, 30, 34; **2Ki 1:**2, 10, 12; **2:**2, 3, 4, 5, 6, 9[2], 10, 18, 21; **3:**7[2], 13, 14[3], 16; **4:**2, 9, 13, 22, 24, 28[2], 30, 43; **5:**5, 6, 7, 11, 12, 15, 16[2], 18[2], 20, 26; **6:**3, 13, 19, 21[2], 27, 29, 33; **7:**12; **8:**8, 9, 12; **9:**3, 5, 6, 7, 8, 9, 12, 17, 25, 26[3]; **10:**9, 19, 24, 30; **16:**7; **17:**13[2], 38; **18:**14[2], 23, 25, 32; **19:**7[2], 19, 20, 23[3], 24[2], 25[3], 27, 28[2], 34; **20:**3[2], 5[3], 6[3], 8, 15; **21:**4, 7[2], 8[3], 12, 13[2], 14; **22:**8, 16, 19[2], 20[2]; **23:**17, 27[5]; **1Ch 4:**9; **11:**19[2]; **13:**12; **14:**10[2]; **15:**12; **16:**18; **17:**1, 5[3], 6[3], 7, 8[2], 9, 10[3], 11[2], 12, 13[3], 14, 16; **19:**2, 12; **21:**2, 8[4], 10[2], 12, 13, 17[3], 22, 23[2], 24[2]; **22:**5, 7, 9[2], 10[2], 14[2]; **23:**5; **28:**2[2], 6[2], 7; **29:**2[2], 3[3], 14, 17[3], 19; **2Ch 1:**7, 11, 12; **2:**4, 5, 6, 8, 9, 10, 13; **6:**2, 5[3], 6[2], 10, 11, 18, 33, 34, 38; **7:**12, 13, 14, 16, 17, 18[2], 19, 20[4]; **9:**5, 6[3]; **10:**11[2], 14[2]; **12:**5, 7[2]; **16:**3; **18:**3, 5, 7, 13, 14, 15, 16, 17, 18, 20, 21, 26, 29, 33; **25:**9, 16, 19; **28:**23; **32:**13; **33:**7[2], 8[3]; **34:**15, 24, 27, 28[2]; **35:**21[3], 23; **Ezr 4:**19, 21; **6:**8, 11, 12; **7:**13, 21, 28[2]; **8:**15[3], 16, 21, 22, 24, 25, 26, 28; **9:**3[2], 4, 5, 6; **Ne 1:**1, 2, 4[2], 5, 6[2], 8, 9[2], 11; **2:**1[2], 2, 3, 4, 5[3], 6, 7[2], 8[2], 9, 11, 12[5], 13[2], 14[2], 15[2], 16[3], 17, 18, 20; **4:**13, 14[2], 19, 22, 23; **5:**6[2], 7[3], 9, 10, 12, 13, 14[2], 15, 16, 18, 19; **6:**1[2], 3[4], 4, 8, 10, 11[2], 12; **7:**1, 2, 3, 5[2]; **12:**31, 38, 40; **13:**6[3], 7, 8[2], 9[2], 10, 11[2], 13, 14, 15[2], 17, 19[2], 21[2], 22, 23, 25[2], 28, 30[2], 31; **Est 3:**9; **4:**11, 16[4]; **5:**4, 8[3], 12, 13; **7:**3, 4[2]; **8:**5[2], 6[2], 7; **Job 1:**15, 16, 17, 19, 21[2]; **3:**3, 11, 13[3], 16, 25[2], 26[3]; **4:**8, 16[2]; **5:**3[2], 8[2]; **6:**8, 10[2], 11[2], 13, 22, 24[2], 28, 29; **7:**3, 4[4], 8, 11[3], 12, 13, 15, 16[2], 19, 20[3], 21[2]; **8:**18; **9:**2, 11[2], 14, 15[3], 16[2], 20[2], 21[3], 22, 27[3], 28[2], 29[2], 30, 32[2], 35[4]; **10:**1[3], 2, 7, 13, 14, 15[4], 18, 19, 20, 21; **11:**4; **12:**3[2], 4[3]; **13:**2[2], 3[2], 13, 14, 15[2], 18[3], 19, 20, 22; **14:**14, 15; **15:**6, 17[3]; **16:**2, 4[2], 5, 6[2], 12, 15, 22[2]; **17:**6, 10, 13[2], 14; **19:**4, 7[3], 8, 10, 15, 16[2], 17, 18, 19, 20, 25, 26, 27; **20:**3; **21:**3[2], 4, 6[2], 27; **23:**3[3], 4, 5, 7, 8[2], 9[3], 10[2], 11, 12[2], 15[3], 17; **24:**25; **27:**5[2], 6, 11[2]; **29:**2, 3, 4, 7[2], 12, 13, 14, 15, 16[2], 17, 18[3], 22, 24, 25[2]; **30:**1[2], 2, 9, 19, 20[2], 23, 25, 26[2], 28[2], 29; **31:**1[2], 5, 9, 13, 14[2], 16, 18[2], 19, 21[3], 23[2], 24, 25, 26, 28, 29, 30, 32, 33, 34[2], 35[2], 36[2], 37[2], 39; **32:**6[2], 7, 10, 11[2], 12, 14, 16, 17[2], 18, 20[3], 21, 22; **33:**2, 6[2], 8, 9[2], 12, 24, 27, 31, 32, 33; **34:**5, 6[2], 16, 31[2], 32[3], 33; **35:**2, 3[3], 4; **36:**2[2], 3; **37:**20; **38:**3, 4, 9, 23; **39:**6; **40:**4[3], 5[2], 7, 14, 15[2]; **41:**12; **42:**2, 3[3], 4[2], 5, 6, 8; **Ps 2:**6, 7[2], 8; **3:**4, 5[2], 6; **4:**1[2], 3, 8; **5:**2, 3, 7[2]; **6:**2, 6[3]; **7:**1, 3, 4, 17; **8:**3; **9:**1[2], 2[2], 13, 14; **11:**1; **12:**5[2]; **13:**2, 3, 4[2], 5, 6; **16:**1, 2[2], 4, 6, 7, 8[2]; **17:**4, 6, 15[3]; **18:**1, 2, 3[2], 6[2], 21, 22, 23[2], 29[2], 37, 38, 40, 42[2], 43, 49; **19:**13; **20:**6; **22:**2, 6, 10, 14, 17, 22[2], 24, 25, 29; **23:**1, 4[2], 6; **25:**1, 2, 5, 16, 20, 21; **26:**1[2], 3, 4[2], 5, 6, 8, 11, 12; **27:**1[2], 3, 4[2], 6[2], 7, 8, 13[2]; **28:**1[2], 2[2], 7[2]; **30:**1, 2, 6[2], 7, 8[2], 9, 12; **31:**1, 5, 6, 7, 9, 11, 12[2], 13, 14[2], 17, 21, 22[3]; **32:**3, 5[4], 8[2]; **34:**1, 4, 11; **35:**3, 11, 13[3], 14[2], 15, 18[2]; **37:**25[2], 35, 36[2]; **38:**6[2], 8[2], 13[2], 14, 15, 16, 17, 18[2], 20; **39:**1[4], 2[2], 3[2], 7, 9[2], 10, 12, 13[2]; **40:**1, 5, 7[2], 8, 9[2], 10[3], 12, 17; **41:**4[2], 5, 8[2], 9, 10, 11; **42:**2, 4[3], 5, 6, 9[2], 11; **43:**2[2], 4[2], 5; **44:**6; **45:**1, 17; **46:**10[3]; **49:**4[2], 5; **50:**7[3], 8, 9, 11, 12[2], 13, 15, 21[3], 22, 23; **51:**3, 4, 5, 7[2], 13, 16; **52:**8[2], 9[2]; **54:**6[2]; **55:**2[2], 6[3], 7[2], 8, 9, 12[2], 14, 16, 17, 18, 23; **56:**3[2], 4[3], 9[2], 10[2], 11[2], 12[2], 13; **57:**1, 2, 4, 7, 8, 9[2]; **59:**9, 16[2], 17; **60:**6, 8[2]; **61:**2[2], 8[2]; **62:**2, 6, 11; **63:**1, 2, 4[3], 6, 7; **66:**13[2], 14, 15[2], 16, 17, 18; **68:**22[2]; **69:**2[2], 3, 4[2], 5, 7, 8, 10, 11[2], 12, 17, 19, 20[3], 29, 30[2]; **70:**5; **71:**1, 6, 7, 14, 16[2], 17, 18, 22[2], 23; **73:**3[2], 13, 14, 15[3], 16, 17[2], 21, 22[2], 23, 25[2], 28; **75:**2[2], 3, 4, 9[2], 10; **77:**1, 2, 3[3], 4[2], 5, 6[2], 10, 11[2], 12; **78:**2[2]; **81:**5[2], 6, 7[3], 8, 10[2], 12, 14, 16[2]; **82:**6; **84:**10; **86:**1, 2, 3, 4, 7, 11, 12[2]; **87:**4; **88:**1, 4[2], 8[2], 9[2], 13, 15[2]; **89:**1[2], 2, 3[2], 4, 19[2], 20[2], 23, 25, 27, 28, 29, 32, 33, 34, 35[2], 50; **91:**2, 14[2], 15[3], 16; **92:**4; **94:**18; **95:**10, 11; **101:**1[2], 2[3], 3[2], 4, 5[2], 6, 8; **102:**2, 4, 6, 7[2], 9, 11, 24; **104:**33[4], 34; **105:**11; **106:**5[3]; **108:**1, 2, 3[2], 7, 9[2]; **109:**4, 22, 23[2], 25, 30[2]; **110:**1; **111:**1; **116:**1, 2[2], 3, 4[2], 6, 9, 10[3], 11, 12, 13, 14, 16[2], 17, 18; **118:**5, 6, 7, 10, 11, 12, 13[2], 17[2], 19, 21, 28[2]; **119:**6, 7[2], 8, 10, 11[2], 13, 14, 15, 16[2], 17, 18, 19, 22, 26, 27, 30[2], 31, 32, 33, 34, 35, 39, 40, 42[2], 44, 45[2], 46, 47[2], 48[3], 51, 52[2], 54, 55, 56, 57, 58, 59[2], 60, 61, 62, 63, 66, 67[3], 69, 70, 71[2], 73, 74, 75, 77, 78, 80, 81, 82, 83[2], 86, 87, 88, 92, 93, 94[2], 95, 96, 97, 99, 100[2], 101, 102, 104[2], 106, 107, 109[2], 110, 112, 113[2], 114, 115, 116, 117, 119, 120, 121, 125[2], 127, 128[2], 131[2], 134, 141[2], 144, 145[2], 146[2], 147[2], 148, 152, 153, 157, 158, 159, 162, 163[2], 164, 166[2], 167, 168, 173, 174, 175, 176[2]; **120:**1, 5[2], 6, 7[2]; **121:**1; **122:**1, 8, 9; **123:**1; **130:**1, 5[2]; **131:**1, 2; **132:**3, 4, 5, 11, 12, 14[2], 15[2], 16, 17[2], 18; **135:**5; **137:**5, 6[2]; **138:**1[2], 2, 3, 7; **139:**2[2], 6, 7[2], 8[2], 9, 11, 14[3], 15, 18[3], 21[2], 22[2]; **140:**6, 12; **141:**1[2], 8, 10; **142:**1[2], 2[2], 3, 5[2], 6, 7; **143:**5[3], 6, 7, 8[3], 9, 12; **144:**2, 9[2]; **145:**1, 2, 5, 6; **146:**2[3]; **Pr 1:**23[2], 24, 26[2], 28; **3:**28; **4:**2, 3, 11[2]; **5:**12, 13, 14; **7:**6, 7[2], 14[2], 15[2], 16, 17; **8:**4, 6, 12[2], 13, 14[3], 17, 20, 23, 24, 25, 27, 30[2]; **9:**5; **20:**9[2], 22; **22:**13, 19, 20; **23:**35[4]; **24:**29[2], 30, 32[2]; **26:**19; **27:**11; **30:**1[3], 2[2], 3[2], 7[2], 8, 9[2], 18, 20; **Ecc 1:**12, 14, 16[2], 17[2]; **2:**1[2], 2, 3[2], 4[2], 5, 6, 7[2], 8[2], 9, 10[2], 11[2], 12, 13, 14, 15[3], 17, 18[3], 19, 20, 24; **3:**10, 12, 14, 16, 17, 18, 22; **4:**1, 2, 4, 7, 8, 15; **5:**13, 18; **6:**1, 3; **7:**15, 23[3], 25, 26, 27, 28[3], 29; **8:**9, 10, 12, 14, 15, 16, 17; **9:**1, 11, 13, 16; **10:**5, 7; **12:**1; **SS 1:**5, 6[2], 7, 9; **2:**1, 3, 5, 7, 16; **3:**1[3], 2[3], 4[4], 5; **4:**6; **5:**1[4], 2, 3[4], 5, 6[3], 8[2]; **6:**3, 11, 12; **7:**8[2], 10, 12, 13; **8:**1[2], 2[2], 4, 5, 10[2]; **Isa 1:**2, 11[2], 13, 14, 15[2], 24, 25[2], 26; **3:**4, 7; **5:**4[2], 5[4], 6[2]; **6:**1, 5[4], 8[4], 11; **7:**12[2]; **8:**3, 17[2], 18; **10:**6[2], 11[2], 13[4], 14; **12:**1, 2; **13:**3, 11[2], 12, 13, 17; **14:**13[3], 14[2], 22, 23[2], 24[2], 25, 30[2]; **15:**9; **16:**9[2]; **18:**4; **19:**2, 3, 4, 11; **21:**2, 3[4], 4, 8[2], 10[2]; **22:**4, 19, 20, 21, 22, 23; **23:**4[2]; **24:**16[3]; **25:**1[2]; **27:**3[3], 4[3]; **28:**16, 17, 22; **29:**2, 3[2], 14; **30:**7; **33:**10[3], 13, 24; **34:**5; **36:**8, 10, 17; **37:**7[2], 24[3], 25[4], 26[2], 28, 29[3], 33; **38:**6[2], 5[3], 6, 8, 10[3], 11[3], 12, 13, 14[3], 15, 17, 19, 22; **39:**4; **40:**6[2]; **41:**4, 8, 9[2], 10[5], 13[3], 14, 15, 17[2], 18[2], 19[2], 25, 27[2], 28[2]; **42:**1[2], 6[4], 8[2], 9[2], 14[4], 15[2], 16[5], 19; **43:**1[2], 2, 3[2], 4[2], 5[3], 6, 7[2], 10[2], 11[2], 12, 13[3], 14, 15, 19[2], 20, 21, 23, 25[3], 28[2]; **44:**1, 2, 3[2], 5, 6[2], 8[2], 16[2], 19[5], 21, 22[2], 24, 26, 27; **45:**1, 2[2], 3[2], 4[2], 5[2], 6, 7[3], 8, 12[2], 13[2], 18, 19[4], 21, 22, 23; **46:**4[5], 9[2], 10, 11[4], 13[2]; **47:**3[2], 6[3], 7, 8[2], 10; **48:**3[3], 4, 5[2], 6, 7, 8, 9[3], 10[2], 11[2], 12[4], 13, 15[3], 16[2], 17; **49:**1[2], 3, 4[3], 5, 6, 8[3], 11, 15, 16, 18, 21[2], 22, 23, 25[2], 26[2]; **50:**1[2], 2[5], 3, 4, 5[2], 6[2], 7[4]; **51:**2[2], 5, 12[2], 15, 16, 22, 23; **52:**5, 6[2]; **53:**12; **54:**7[2], 8[2], 9[3], 11, 12, 16[2]; **55:**3, 4, 11[2]; **56:**3, 5[2], 7, 8; **57:**6, 11, 12, 15, 16[3], 17[3], 18[3], 19; **58:**5, 6, 9, 14[2]; **59:**21; **60:**7, 10[2], 13, 15, 16, 17[3], 21[2], 22[2]; **61:**8[4], 10; **62:**1[2], 6, 8; **63:**1, 3[2], 5[2], 6[3], 7; **65:**1[4], 2, 5, 6[3], 7, 8, 9, 12[4], 17, 18[2], 19, 24[2]; **66:**2, 4[3], 9[2], 12, 13, 18[2], 19[2], 21, 22; **Jer 1:**5[4], 6[3], 7[3], 8, 9, 10, 11[2], 12, 13[2], 15, 16, 17[2], 18, 19; **2:**2, 7, 9[2], 20, 21, 23[2], 25[2], 30, 31, 35[3]; **3:**7, 8, 12[3], 14[3], 15, 18, 19[3], 22; **4:**6, 10, 12, 19[3], 21, 23, 24, 25, 26, 27, 28[4], 31[2]; **5:**1, 4, 7[2], 9[2], 14, 15, 18, 22, 29[2]; **6:**2, 8, 10, 11[2], 12, 15, 17, 19, 21, 27; **7:**7[2], 11, 12[2], 13[2], 14[3], 15[2], 16, 19, 22[2], 23[3], 25, 31, 34; **8:**3, 6[2], 10, 12, 13[2], 17, 21[2]; **9:**1, 2[2], 7[2], 9[2], 11[2], 13, 15, 16[3], 24[3], 25; **10:**18[2], 19[2], 23; **11:**4[4], 5[3], 7[2], 8[2], 10, 11[2], 14, 18, 19[2], 20, 22, 23; **12:**1, 7[3], 8, 14[3], 15[3], 17; **13:**2, 5, 6, 7[3], 9, 11, 13, 14[3], 24, 25, 26, 27; **14:**12[3], 13[2], 14[2], 15, 16, 18[2]; **15:**3, 4, 6[2], 7[3], 8[2], 9, 10[2], 11[2], 13, 14, 15, 16[2], 17[3], 19, 20[2], 21; **16:**5, 9, 13[2], 15[2], 16[2], 18, 21[2]; **17:**3, 4[2], 10, 14[2], 16[2], 22, 27; **18:**2, 3, 6, 7[2], 8[3], 9[2], 10[2], 11, 17[2], 20; **19:**2, 3, 5, 7[2], 8, 9, 11, 12, 15[2]; **20:**4[2], 5, 7[2], 8[3], 9[4], 10, 12, 14, 18; **21:**4[2], 5, 6, 7, 8, 10, 13, 14[2]; **22:**5, 6[2], 7, 14, 21[2], 24[2], 26; **23:**2, 3[3], 4, 5, 9, 11, 12, 13, 14, 15, 21[2], 23, 24[2], 25[3], 30, 31, 32[2], 33, 34, 38, 39[2], 40; **24:**3, 5[2], 6[4], 7[3], 8, 9[2], 10[2]; **25:**3, 6, 9[3], 10, 12, 13[2], 14, 15, 16, 17, 27, 29[2]; **26:**2, 3[2], 4, 5, 6[2], 14; **27:**5[3], 6[2], 8[2], 10, 11, 12, 15[2], 16, 22[2]; **28:**2, 3, 4[2], 7, 11, 14[2], 16; **29:**4, 7, 9, 10[2], 11[2], 12, 14[5], 17[2], 18[2], 19, 20, 21, 23[2], 31, 32[2]; **30:**2, 3[3], 6, 8[2], 9, 10, 11[6], 14, 15, 16, 17[2], 18, 19[2], 20, 21, 22; **31:**1, 3[2], 4, 8, 9[3], 13[2], 14, 18[3], 19[7], 20[5], 23, 25[2], 26, 27, 28[2], 31, 32[3], 33[4], 34, 37; **32:**3, 5, 8, 9, 10, 11, 12, 13, 16[2], 27, 28, 31, 33, 35, 37[4], 38, 39, 40[2], 41[2], 42[3], 44; **33:**3, 5[2], 6[2], 7, 8[2], 9[2], 11, 14[2], 15, 22, 25, 26[2]; **34:**2, 5, 13[2], 17[2], 18, 21, 22[2]; **35:**3, 4, 5[2], 14, 15[2], 17[4]; **36:**2[2], 3[2], 5, 18, 31[3]; **37:**14, 18; **38:**14, 15[2], 16, 19[2], 20, 25, 26; **39:**16, 17, 18; **40:**4[2], 10; **42:**4[3], 10[4], 11, 12, 17, 19, 21; **43:**10[2]; **44:**2, 4[3], 10, 11, 12, 13[2], 26, 27, 29, 30[2]; **45:**3[2], 4[3], 5[2]; **46:**5, 18, 25, 26, 27, 28[6]; **48:**12, 30, 31[3], 32, 33, 35, 38, 44, 47; **49:**2, 5, 6, 8[2], 10[2], 11, 13, 14, 15, 16, 19[3], 27, 32[2], 35, 36[2], 37[4], 38, 39; **50:**9, 18[2], 19, 20[2], 21, 31[2], 32, 44[3]; **51:**1, 2, 14, 20[2], 21[2], 22[3], 23[3], 24, 25[2], 36[2], 39, 40, 44, 47, 52, 57, 64; **La 1:**11, 14, 16, 18, 19, 20[2], 21[2]; **2:**13[3], 22; **3:**1, 7, 8, 14, 17, 18[2], 21[2], 24, 54[2], 55, 57, 63; **Eze 1:**1[2], 4, 15[2], 24, 27[2], 28[3]; **2:**1, 2, 3, 4, 8[2], 9; **3:**2, 3[2], 6, 8, 9, 10, 12, 14, 15[2], 17, 18[2], 20[2], 22, 23[3], 26, 27[2]; **4:**5, 6, 8, 13, 14[3], 15, 16; **5:**2, 5, 8[3], 9[3], 10[2], 11[3], 12, 13[3], 14, 15[2], 16[3], 17[3]; **6:**3[3], 4, 5[2], 7, 8, 9, 10[2], 12, 13, 14[2]; **7:**3[3], 4[3], 8[3], 9[3], 20, 21, 22, 24[2], 27[3]; **8:**1, 2, 4, 5, 7, 8, 10, 18[3]; **9:**8[2], 10[2], 11; **10:**1, 2, 9, 15, 20[2], 22; **11:**1, 5, 8, 9, 10[2], 11, 12, 13[2], 16[3], 17[2], 19[2], 20, 21, 24, 25; **12:**6, 7[5], 11[2], 13[2], 14[2], 15[2], 16[2], 20, 23, 25[3], 28; **13:**7, 8, 9, 13, 14[2], 15[2], 20[2], 21[2], 22, 23[2]; **14:**3, 4, 5, 7, 8[3], 9[2], 11, 13, 15, 16, 17[2], 18, 19, 20, 21, 22[2], 23[2]; **15:**6[2], 7[3], 8; **16:**6[2], 8[3], 9, 10[2], 11[2], 14, 17, 19[2], 27, 37[2], 38, 39, 41, 42[2], 43, 48, 50[2], 53[2], 59, 60[2], 61, 62[2], 63; **17:**16, 19[2], 20[2], 21, 22[4], 23, 24[6]; **18:**3, 23, 30, 32; **20:**3[2], 5[4], 6[3], 7[2], 8[2], 9[2], 10, 11, 12[2], 13[2], 14[2], 15[3], 17, 18, 19, 20, 21[2], 22[2], 23[2], 25, 26[3], 28[2], 29, 31[3], 33[2], 34, 35[2], 36[2], 37, 38[3], 40[2], 41[3], 42[3], 44[2], 47, 48, 49; **21:**3, 4, 5, 15, 17[3], 27[3], 30, 31[3], 32; **22:**4, 13, 14[3], 15[2], 16[2], 19, 20[2], 21, 22, 26, 30[3], 31[3]; **23:**9, 13, 18[2], 22[2], 24, 25, 27, 28, 31, 34, 43, 48, 49; **24:**8, 9, 12, 13[2], 14[6], 16, 18[3], 20, 21, 22, 24, 25, 27; **25:**4, 5[2], 7[4], 9, 10, 11[2], 13[2], 14, 16, 17[3]; **26:**2, 3[2], 4, 5, 6, 7, 13, 14[2], 19[2], 20[2], 21; **27:**3; **28:**2[2], 7, 9, 10, 14, 16, 17[2], 18[2], 22[4], 23[2], 24, 25[2], 26[2]; **29:**3[2], 4[2], 5[2], 6, 8, 9[2], 10[2], 12[2], 13, 14, 15, 16, 19, 20, 21[3]; **30:**8[2], 10, 12[3], 13[2], 14, 15, 16, 18, 19[2], 21, 22[2], 23, 24[2], 25[3], 26[2]; **31:**9, 11[2], 15[3], 16[2]; **32:**3[2], 4[3], 5, 6, 7[3], 8, 9[2], 10[2], 12, 13, 14, 15[3]; **33:**2, 6, 7, 8[2], 11[2], 13, 14, 20, 22, 27[2], 28, 29[2]; **34:**8, 10[3], 11, 12[2], 13[2], 14, 15[2], 16[6], 17, 20, 22[2], 23, 24[2], 25, 26[2], 27[2], 29, 30, 31; **35:**3[2], 4[2], 6[2], 7[2], 8, 9[2], 11[4], 12, 13, 14, 15[2]; **36:**5, 6, 7, 9[2], 10, 11[3], 12, 15, 18, 19[2], 21, 22, 23[3], 24, 25[2], 26[3], 27, 28[2], 29[2], 30, 32, 33[2], 36[3], 37, 38; **37:**3, 5, 6[2], 7[3], 8, 10, 12[2], 13[2], 14[3], 19[2], 21, 22, 23[2], 25, 26[2], 27, 28; **38:**3, 4[2], 11[2], 16[2], 17[2], 19, 21, 22[2], 23[2]; **39:**1, 2, 3, 4, 5, 6[2], 7[3], 8, 11, 13, 17, 19, 21[3], 22, 23, 24, 25[2], 27, 28[3], 29[2]; **40:**4[2]; **41:**8; **43:**3[4], 6, 7, 8, 9, 27; **44:**4[2], 5, 12, 14, 28[2]; **46:**19; **47:**5, 7[2], 14; **Da 1:**10; **2:**3, 8[2], 9, 23, 24, 25, 26, 30; **3:**14, 15, 25, 29; **4:**2, 4, 5, 6, 7, 8, 9[2], 10, 13[2], 18, 30, 34[2], 36, 37; **5:**14, 16, 17; **6:**22[2], 26; **7:**2, 4,

IN (14450)

INTO (1736)

17:46, 47, 49; 19:10, 20, 21^2, 23, 24; 20:8, 11^2, 35, 42; 21:15; 22:5^2; 23:4, 7, 12, 14, 20, 25; 24:4, 10, 18; 26:3, 6, 8, 10, 23; 28:19^2; 30:24; 2Sa 2:1; 3:8; 4:7; 5:8, 19^2; 6:9, 10, 16; 10:2, 13; 12:8, 20; 13:10^2; 14:3, 19, 24^2, 28, 32; 15:2, 25, 31, 37; 16:8; 17:2, 13^2, 18; 18:2, 6, 14, 17; 19:2, 3, 5; 20:12; 21:9; 22:20; 24:14^2; 1Ki 1:28; 3:1; 5:9; 6:6; 10:16, 17, 24; 11:2, 30; 13:18; 14:28; 15:15, 18; 16:18, 21; 17:19, 21, 22, 23; 19:4; 20:2, 13, 28, 30, 33, 39; 22:6, 12, 15, 30^2, 35; 2Ki 2:11, 16, 21; 4:4, 32, 39^2, 41; 5:18; 6:5, 23; 7:8, 12; 9:2; 10:15, 24, 25; 11:13; 12:4^2, 9, 11, 13, 15, 16; 13:3^2, 21; 17:20; 18:30; 19:1, 10, 18, 25, 32, 33, 37; 20:20; 21:14; 22:4, 5, 7, 9; 23:12; 24:15; 25:11, 21; 1Ch 4:22; 5:6, 20; 6:15^2; 8:6; 9:1; 13:12, 13^2; 14:10^2, 17; 21:13^2, 27; 22:18, 19; 27:24; 29:8; 2Ch 3:14; 9:15, 16, 23; 12:11; 13:16; 15:12, 18; 16:1, 8; 18:5, 11, 14, 29^2; 20:20; 21:11, 13^2; 23:1, 12, 15; 24:7, 10, 24; 28:5^2, 9, 27; 29:16^2; 30:14, 15; 31:10; 32:21; 34:7, 9, 14, 17; 36:17, 20; Ezr 1:8; 5:12, 14; 7:27; 8:26, 33; Ne 2:12; 6:10, 11; 7:5, 6, 71; 8:1; 9:11^2, 23, 24, 27; 10:29, 34; 12:44; 13:2, 12, 15; Est 2:8; 3:9^2, 15; 4:7; 7:7; 9:22^2, 28; Job 3:6; 6:18; 8:4; 9:24, 31; 14:3; 16:11; 17:12, 16; 18:8^2, 18; 20:23; 22:4; 30:19; 33:24, 26; 36:16, 18; 37:8; 38:16, 38; Ps 7:15; 10:14; 18:19; 30:11; 31:5, 8; 38:2; 55:23; 57:6; 58:8; 63:9; 66:6, 11, 13; 68:17, 24; 69:2; 73:17; 76:5; 79:1, 12; 95:2; 96:8; 98:4; 100:2; 105:29; 106:41, 42; 107:33^2, 34, 35^2; 109:18^2; 114:8^2; 115:17; 132:3; 135:9; 140:10; 141:10; 143:2; Pr 2:10; 6:3; 7:23, 25; 11:8; 16:33; 17:10^2, 20; 18:8, 10; 22:14; 25:8; 26:22, 27; 28:10^2, 12, 14, 18, 28; Ecc 3:11; 5:6; 6:4^2; 10:8; 11:9; 12:14; SS 1:4; 3:4^2; 5:4; 7:11; 8:2^2; Isa 2:4^2, 10; 3:14; 5:13; 8:8, 22; 9:1; 11:15; 14:7; 16:14; 19:4, 14, 23^2; 21:4; 22:18; 24:12, 18; 34:9^2; 36:15; 37:1, 10, 19, 26, 33, 34, 38; 42:15, 16^2; 44:17, 23; 46:2, 6; 47:5, 6; 49:11, 13; 51:23; 52:4, 9; 54:1; 55:12; 57:2; 58:7; 63:14; 64:7; 65:6, 7; 66:17; Jer 2:7; 4:5; 6:25; 7:31; 8:6, 8, 14; 9:21; 12:7; 13:16, 19^2; 14:16, 18; 16:8, 13; 18:4, 15; 20:4, 5, 6; 21:4, 7^3, 10; 22:7, 22, 25^4, 26; 23:12; 24:1; 25:31; 26:23, 24; 27:6, 20; 29:1, 4, 7, 14, 16, 21; 30:16; 31:13; 32:3, 4, 18, 24, 25, 28^2, 36, 43; 34:2, 10, 11, 16; 35:2, 4; 36:12, 23; 38:6, 7, 9; 40:7; 41:7, 9; 42:16; 43:3, 7; 44:21, 30^2; 47:6; 48:7, 11, 44, 46; 49:3; 51:50, 51, 63; 52:15, 27, 28, 29, 30; La 1:3, 7, 13, 14, 18; 2:7, 9; 3:2, 13, 53; Eze 2:2; 3:22, 23, 24; 4:9, 14; 5:4; 7:11, 19; 8:16; 10:7; 11:5, 24; 12:3, 4, 11^2; 13:5; 14:3, 4, 7, 19; 16:8, 39; 17:20; 19:9, 13^2; 20:6, 10, 15, 28, 35^2, 36^2, 42; 21:22, 31; 22:19, 20; 23:9^2, 17, 28^2, 31, 39; 25:3; 26:12, 20; 27:19, 26, 27; 28:4, 23^2; 29:5; 30:12, 17, 18, 25; 31:11; 32:9, 24; 34:13; 36:24; 37:10, 17, 22, 23; 38:4, 10, 22; 39:23^2, 28^2; 40:6, 17; 41:3; 42:1, 14; 43:5; 44:12, 19, 27^2; 46:20; 47:8; Da 1:2, 17, 18; 2:12, 38; 3:6, 11, 15, 20, 21, 23, 24; 5:10; 6:7, 12, 16, 24; 7:25; 8:18; 10:9; 11:24, 29, 41; 12:1; Hos 2:3, 14; 4:7, 15; Joel 2:9, 20^3; 3:2, 5, 8, 10^2; Am 1:5, 6, 15; 2:7; 3:5; 4:3, 10; 5:5^2, 8^2, 19, 27; 6:7, 12^2; 7:11, 17; 8:10^2; 9:2, 4; Jnh 1:5^2, 12, 15; 2:3^2, 7; 3:4; 4:10; Mic 1:6, 16; 3:5; 4:3^2; 5:5, 6; 7:19; Na 1:8; 3:10, 11, 12; Hab 3:16; Zep 3:19; Hag 1:6; Zec 5:8; 9:4; 11:6^2, 13^2; 13:9; 14:2, 10; Mal 3:10; Mt 3:10, 12; 4:1, 18; 5:25, 29, 30; 6:6, 26, 30; 7:19; 8:12, 23, 31, 32, 33; 9:1, 17^2, 38; 10:16; 11:7; 12:11; 13:2, 30, 36, 42, 47, 48, 50; 14:15, 22, 32; 15:11, 14, 17^2, 39; 16:13; 17:15^2, 22; 18:8, 9, 30; 19:17; 20:2, 4, 7; 21:2, 21, 31; 22:9, 10, 13; 24:43; 25:10, 21, 23, 30, 41, 46^2; 26:18, 23, 41, 45, 52; 27:6, 27, 29; 28:11; Mk 1:12, 16, 45; 2:22^2; 4:1, 8, 37; 5:12, 13, 18; 6:36, 45, 51, 56; 7:18, 19, 33; 8:10, 13, 26; 9:22^2, 31, 42, 45, 47; 11:2, 11, 23; 12:41; 14:13, 20, 38, 41, 54, 68; 15:16, 17; 16:12, 15, 19; Lk 1:79; 2:15, 27; 3:3, 9, 17; 4:42; 5:3, 4, 19, 37, 38; 6:38, 39; 7:24, 36; 8:8, 22, 29, 31, 33, 37; 9:12, 44^2; 10:2, 3, 10, 30, 36, 38; 12:5, 28, 39; 14:5, 21, 23; 16:4, 9, 28; 17:2; 19:23, 30; 21:1; 22:3, 10, 40, 46, 54; 23:42, 46; 24:26, 51; Jn 1:3^3, 9, 10; 3:4, 13, 17, 19, 22, 24; 4:38, 46; 5:7; 6:14, 17, 21, 22, 24; 7:14; 9:39; 10:36; 11:27, 52; 12:6, 24, 46; 13:2, 3, 5, 27; 15:6; 16:13, 20, 21, 28; 17:18^2; 18:11, 15, 37; 19:23, 27; 20:6, 11; 21:3, 7; Ac 1:11^2; 2:34; 3:3; 5:15; 7:9, 23, 55; 8:38; 9:8; 10:10; 12:10; 13:14; 14:1, 14, 20; 16:7, 19, 23, 34, 37; 18:19; 19:3^2, 27, 30, 31; 20:9; 21:8, 28, 29, 34, 37, 38; 22:17, 23, 24; 23:10, 20; 27:15, 30, 38; 28:5, 16; Ro 4:17; 5:5, 12; 6:3^2, 4; 7:14; 8:15; 10:6, 7; 11:24^2; 1Co 1:9; 10:2; 12:13; 14:9; 2Co 3:18; 4:14; 7:5; 12:4; Gal 1:17, 21; 3:27; 4:6, 27; Eph 2:14, 21, 22; 4:9, 15^2; Col 1:13; 3:23; 1Th 2:12; 1Ti 1:15; 3:6, 7; 4:15; 6:7, 9^2; 2Ti 2:16; 3:6; Heb 1:6; 9:6, 7, 8, 12, 24; 10:5, 31; 13:11; Jas 1:25; 2:2, 6; 3:3; 4:9^2; 1Pe 1:3, 4, 12; 2:2, 5, 9; 3:22; 2Pe 1:11; 2:4; 1Jn 4:1, 9; 2Jn 1:7, 10; Jude 1:4; Rev 2:10, 22; 5:3, 4, 6; 8:8; 9:9; 11:6; 12:6, 14; 13:10; 14:10, 19; 16:3, 4, 10, 17, 19; 17:3, 17; 18:21; 19:20; 20:3, 10, 14, 15; 21:24, 26; Tob 1:2, 14, 15, 20; 2:3, 6^2, 9, 10; 3:17; 4:10; 7:1; 8:1, 11; 9:6; 11:11; 14:5, 6, 10^4, 15; Jdt 1:14; 2:22, 27; 6:7, 11^2, 14; 7:1, 25; 8:23; 10:2, 12, 20, 23; 11:17; 12:5; 14:3^2, 15; 16:17; AdE 1:19, 22; 3:9, 15; 4:7; 7:7; 9:22; 12:2; 13:17; Wis 1:9; 3:13; 6:3; 7:1, 6, 25, 27; 10:13; 12:9; 15:11; 16:11, 25; 18:15; 19:19; Sir Pr:T; 2:17^2; 6:2, 9, 24^2, 28; 8:1; 9:3, 9; 11:29, 31, 34; 12:16; 16:30; 17:8; 21:22, 23; 22:16; 23:19; 24:30; 27:2, 26; 28:23; 29:18; 37:2; 39:23, 27; 44:20; 45:5; 46:8, 11; 47:19, 23; 48:17; 50:29; Bar 2:14, 29, 34; 3:29; Aza 1:26, 32; Sus 1:7, 23; Bel 1:10, 31, 33^2, 42; 1Mc 1:24, 39^3, 40, 53; 2:9, 58, 62; 3:24, 39, 48; 4:14, 22, 29, 30, 49; 5:24, 43, 50, 52, 66; 6:5, 11, 45; 7:10, 19, 24^2, 32, 35; 9:1, 11, 33, 41^2, 48, 65, 67, 69, 72; 10:33, 63, 70, 77; 11:16, 46; 12:49; 13:22, 44; 14:1; 16:5, 8, 10; 2Mc 2:18, 23; 3:18; 4:22, 26, 46; 5:7, 9, 12, 14, 26; 7:3, 22, 28, 39; 8:10, 21, 33; 9:23; 10:4, 30; 12:24, 28; 13:5, 11; 14:1, 30, 42, 43; 1Es 1:31, 53; 6:15; 8:12, 25, 80; 3Mc 2:30; 3:1; 4:11^2; 5:46^2, 49; 6:7; 7:7; 2Es 1:18, 23; 3:5, 6; 4:8^3, 13; 5:4, 9; 6:45, 58; 7:21, 48, 69, 80, 86, 92, 95, 132; 8:5; 9:20, 24, 26, 29; 10:9, 17, 18, 22, 23, 28, 32, 53; 12:50; 13:20, 23, 40^2; 14:11, 22; 15:17, 21; 4Mc 6:25; 7:3; 9:22; 12:1, 19; 13:6; 16:21; 17:1; 18:23

IS (8219)

Ge 1:29; 2:9, 11^3, 12, 13^2, 14^2, 18, 23; 3:3, 13, 17; 4:7^2, 9, 10, 13, 24; 5:1; 6:13, 15, 17^2, 21; 8:17, 21; 9:4, 10, 12^2, 14, 15, 16^2, 17^2; 10:9, 12; 11:6; 12:12, 18, 19^2; 13:9; 14:2, 3, 7, 8, 17, 23; 15:2, 3, 13, 16; 16:6; 17:4, 10, 12^2, 14, 17^2; 18:9, 12, 14, 20, 25; 19:14, 20^3, 31^2, 37, 38; 20:2, 3, 5^2, 7, 11, 12, 13^2, 15, 16; 21:12, 13, 17, 22, 29; 22:7, 14, 17; 23:2, 9, 11, 15, 19, 20; 24:8, 23, 51, 65^2; 25:7, 17, 18, 22, 32; 26:7^2, 9^2, 10, 20, 33; 27:11, 20, 22, 27, 36, 42; 28:16, 17^3; 29:6^2, 7^2, 8, 19, 21, 25, 26; 30:3, 15, 33, 38; 31:12, 14, 28, 29, 32, 35, 36^2, 43, 48, 50^2, 52^2; 32:2, 6, 8, 18, 20, 26, 27, 29, 30, 32; 33:10, 11, 17, 18; 34:14, 21; 35:6^2, 10, 19, 20^2, 27; 36:1, 8, 19, 24, 43; 37:2, 10, 14, 26, 27, 30, 32, 33^2; 38:13, 14, 18, 21, 24, 26; 39:9, 19; 40:8, 12, 14, 18; 41:15, 16, 25, 28^2, 32, 33, 38, 39; 42:2, 13^2, 14, 15, 16, 21, 28^2, 32^2, 36^2, 38^2; 43:3, 5, 7, 18, 27^2, 28^2, 29, 32; 44:5, 10, 15, 20^2, 26, 30^2, 31, 34; 45:3, 12, 20, 26^2, 28; 46:33; 47:3, 4^2, 6, 15, 16, 18^2, 23; 48:1, 7, 18; 49:7^2, 9, 10, 14, 21, 22, 27, 28, 32; 50:3, 10, 11^2, 20; Ex 1:16^2, 22; 2:14, 18, 20; 3:3, 5, 12, 13, 15; 4:2, 11, 14, 22; 5:2, 8, 16, 17; 7:14, 15, 17^2; 8:10, 19; 9:14, 16, 19^2, 27, 29; 10:7, 11; 11:2^2, 5; 12:4, 11^2, 19, 22, 27, 42, 43; 13:2^2, 8; 14:12, 25; 15:2^2, 3^2, 11^2, 23, 26; 16:1, 8, 15^2, 16, 23^3, 25, 26, 32, 36; 17:7, 15; 18:11, 14, 17, 18; 19:5; 20:4^3, 10, 11, 12; 21:16, 18, 21^2, 22, 30^2; 22:2^3, 3, 4, 6, 8, 9, 10^2, 14, 15, 16, 31; 23:21; 25:3, 40; 26:5, 10^2; 27:7, 21; 29:1, 13, 14, 18^2, 21, 22^2, 23, 25, 28, 30, 32, 33, 34, 38; 30:6^2, 10, 13^3, 14, 23, 32; 31:7, 13, 14, 15, 17; 32:17, 18^2, 26; 33:13, 21; 34:9, 10, 14^2, 19; 35:4, 5; 36:6; 38:26; 40:9; Lev 1:3, 5, 8, 10, 12, 13, 14, 17^2; 2:3, 5, 6, 7, 8^2, 10^2, 15, 16; 3:1, 3, 4, 5, 6, 9, 10, 12, 14, 15, 16; 4:3, 7^2, 8, 9, 18^2, 20, 21, 23, 24^2, 28, 31, 32, 33, 35; 5:9, 11, 12, 15, 19; 6:9, 14, 15, 16, 17, 20^2, 22, 25^3, 27, 28, 29, 30; 7:1^2, 2, 4, 5, 6, 7^2, 9, 11, 15, 16^2, 17, 18, 34, 35, 37; 8:5, 31, 33; 9:6; 10:3, 7, 9, 12^2, 13, 14^2, 15^2, 17; 11:3, 4, 5, 6, 7^2, 12, 26^2, 32, 33, 37, 38^2, 46; 12:7; 13:3, 4, 5, 6, 8, 10^2, 11^2, 13, 15^2, 17, 18, 20, 21^2, 22, 23, 25^2, 26^2, 27^2, 28^2, 30^2, 31, 32, 36, 37^3, 39^2, 40^2, 41, 42^2, 43, 44^3, 46, 49, 51^2, 52, 55^2, 56, 57, 59^2; 14:3, 4, 7, 8, 13, 16, 18, 21, 27, 28, 29, 32, 36, 37, 41, 44^2, 46, 48, 54, 57^3; 15:3^3, 13, 19, 23, 28, 31, 32, 33^2; 16:2, 13, 15, 18, 31^2, 32; 17:2, 5, 11^2, 14^2; 18:7^2, 8, 10, 11, 12, 13, 14^2, 15, 16, 17, 18, 19, 22, 23; 19:5, 7^2, 8, 20; 20:9, 11, 12, 13, 14, 16, 17, 19, 21, 27^2; 21:10, 11, 12, 13, 18; 22:3, 4, 13, 18, 27; 23:3^2, 6, 14, 21, 27, 28, 31, 36; 24:20; 25:12, 16, 23, 28, 30^2, 34, 44, 49; 26:41; 27:4^2, 5^2, 6^3, 7^2, 10, 13, 18, 20, 21, 22, 24, 26, 27^2, 28, 33; Nu 1:51^2; 2:9, 16, 24, 31; 3:1, 10, 26, 48; 4:5, 9, 16, 19, 24, 25, 26, 28, 31, 33, 45; 5:2^2, 8, 12, 13^3, 14^2, 15, 17, 18, 28, 29, 30; 6:4, 5, 7, 13, 19, 20^2, 21; 9:10^2, 13^2; 10:4, 6, 7; 11:6^2, 15, 17, 20, 23; 12:7, 12; 13:11, 18, 19, 20, 27, 32; 14:3, 7, 8, 9^2, 16, 18, 42; 15:28; 16:3, 5^2, 9, 11, 13, 14, 28, 40; 18:6, 11^3, 13^2, 15, 16, 18, 19, 29, 31; 19:2^2, 6, 9^2, 13, 14^2, 15; 20:5^2, 19; 21:5, 8, 13, 14, 16; 22:4, 5, 6^2, 32, 34, 38; 23:5, 9, 16, 19, 21, 22, 23, 26; 24:3, 8, 9^2, 13, 15, 20, 21^2, 22; 26:57; 27:18; 28:3, 6, 10, 14, 17; 29:1; 30:1, 14, 16; 31:21, 49; 32:4, 22; 33:6, 36; 34:2, 13; 35:12, 16, 17, 18, 19, 21, 27^2, 31, 33; 36:6; Dt 1:14, 17^2, 20, 25^2, 27, 30, 38; 2:20, 29, 36; 3:11, 12, 14^2, 20, 22, 28; 4:1, 6, 7, 13, 17, 18, 21, 24, 25, 31, 35^2, 38, 39^2, 40, 44, 48^2; 5:8^3, 14, 16, 26; 6:1, 4, 15^2, 18, 20, 24; 7:5, 9, 16, 21^2, 25^2, 26; 8:7, 13^2, 18^2, 20; 9:3, 4^3, 5^2, 6, 13; 10:9, 14, 15, 17^2, 21^2; 11:2, 7, 10, 11, 17, 31; 12:9, 10, 21, 22, 23, 25, 28; 13:3, 6, 12, 14, 18; 14:2, 8, 10, 22, 24^2; 15:2^3, 4^2, 7^2, 9, 12, 16; 16:5, 9, 18, 20; 17:1, 2^3, 4^2, 8, 9, 14, 15; 18:2, 9, 10, 12^3, 16, 22; 19:1, 2, 4^2, 6, 10, 14, 18; 20:1, 4, 8, 16; 21:1^3, 4, 9, 15, 16^2, 17^3, 20^2, 22^2, 23^2; 22:2, 5, 17, 20, 22, 23, 26, 28; 23:1, 19; 24:4^2, 5, 7, 12, 20, 21; 25:4, 9^2, 15, 19; 26:1, 2, 3, 12, 16; 27:2, 3; 28:8, 55, 56, 57; 29:12, 18^3, 25, 28; 30:11^2, 12, 13, 14^2; 31:6, 8, 14, 17, 29; 32:4^2, 6, 20, 21^2, 22, 27, 28, 31, 33, 34, 35^2, 36, 39, 47, 49; 33:1, 17, 22, 25, 26, 28, 29; 34:1, 3, 4; Jos 1:2, 8, 9, 13, 15; 2:11, 19; 3:10, 11, 16; 4:24; 5:4, 9, 15; 6:17; 7:2, 15, 20^2, 25, 26; 8:18, 28, 31, 34; 9:12^2, 20, 26; 10:13; 12:2^2, 9; 13:2, 3^2, 9^2, 16^2, 21, 25, 28, 33; 14:11; 15:5, 7^2, 8, 9, 10, 12, 13, 20, 25, 49, 54, 60; 16:6, 8; 17:5, 7, 10^3, 11, 15, 16, 18; 18:7, 13, 14, 16, 17, 19, 20, 28^2; 19:11, 16, 23, 31, 39, 48; 20:5, 6^2, 7; 21:11, 40; 22:9, 16, 19, 31, 34^2; 23:3, 6, 10; 24:17, 18, 19^2, 30; Jdg 1:26; 4:11^2, 14^2, 20; 5:18, 28; 6:12, 13, 15, 17, 24, 25, 31, 32, 37^2; 7:1, 3, 14; 8:2, 21^2, 35; 9:2, 3, 18, 28, 37, 38^2; 10:8; 11:12, 27^2; 13:5^2, 12^2, 14^2, 17, 18; 14:3, 18^2; 15:2, 7, 19^2; 16:3, 15; 17:2; 18:3, 6, 9, 10^2, 12^2, 14, 19, 23, 24; 19:9, 10, 23; 20:9, 12; 21:6, 8, 11, 12, 19^2; Ru 1:19; 2:6, 9, 19, 20, 22; 3:2^2, 10, 12^2, 13; 4:3, 4, 11, 15; 1Sa 1:8, 22, 28; 2:1, 2^2, 3, 5, 14, 24, 31, 35, 36; 3:9, 10, 18; 4:4, 14; 5:5, 7; 6:4, 9^2, 18, 20; 9:6^2, 7^2, 9, 11, 12, 17^2, 18, 19, 20, 21, 24^2; 10:2, 5, 7, 11, 12^2, 24; 11:3, 5, 9, 12; 12:2, 5^3, 6, 13, 17^2; 14:2, 7^2, 24, 39, 41^2; 15:7, 14, 22, 23^2, 28, 29, 32; 16:6, 11, 12, 15, 16^2, 18^2, 19; 17:9, 26, 46, 47, 55, 56; 18:17, 22, 24; 19:2, 14, 19, 22, 24^2; 20:1^3, 3, 5, 6, 7, 8, 12, 18, 21^2, 23, 26^2, 29, 37; 21:3, 5, 6^2, 8, 9^3, 11, 14; 22:8^3, 13, 14^4, 15, 17; 23:17, 19^2, 22^2, 23; 24:1, 4, 6, 10, 11, 16; 25:10^2, 17, 25^4, 28, 41; 26:1^2, 3, 11, 15, 16^2, 17^2, 18, 19^2, 22; 27:1; 28:7^2, 14^3; 29:1, 3, 5; 30:20, 26; 2Sa 1:18; 2:7, 16, 20^2, 26; 3:29; 4:2, 8, 10; 5:2, 7, 8, 20; 6:2^2, 8; 7:3, 18, 22^2, 23^2, 26; 9:1, 3^2, 4^2, 8; 10:3; 11:3, 21, 24; 12:9, 14, 18, 19^2, 21, 23; 13:12, 16, 18, 20, 23, 28, 32, 33; 14:5^2, 17, 19, 24, 30, 32; 15:2, 3; 16:2, 3, 4, 10, 17; 17:2, 6, 7, 8, 10^2, 11, 13, 14; 18:3, 13, 18^2, 20, 25, 26, 27^2, 28, 29, 32; 19:1, 2, 8, 10, 26, 27, 35^2, 37, 42; 20:8, 9, 11, 19, 21; 21:1, 4^2; 22:2, 4, 31^2, 32^2, 51; 23:2, 4, 5, 15; 24:5, 14, 16; 1Ki 1:9, 13, 23, 41, 45^2, 51, 52; 2:3, 8, 22, 29, 38, 42; 3:8, 11, 22^4, 23^5, 27; 4:12, 13, 33; 5:4, 6; 6:1, 17, 38; 7:31; 8:1, 2, 21, 23, 31, 35^2, 37^3, 38, 39, 41, 46, 60^2; 9:15, 26; 11:33^2, 35, 38; 12:10, 24; 13:3, 26, 31; 14:2, 5^2, 10, 13, 15; 17:3, 5, 23, 24; 18:7, 8^2, 10^2, 11, 14, 17, 21, 24, 27^4, 39^2, 41, 43, 44; 19:4, 11; 20:7, 28^2, 32^2, 33, 39; 21:2, 14, 15, 18, 20; 22:7, 8, 32; 2Ki 1:3^2, 6^2, 8, 11, 16^2; 2:14, 19^3; 3:11^2, 12, 13, 18, 23; 4:1, 4, 9, 14, 23, 25, 26^3, 27, 40; 5:3, 7, 8, 15, 21, 26; 6:1, 12, 13^2, 19^2, 28, 32, 33; 7:4, 9^2; 8:5^2, 13^2; 9:11, 12, 13, 15, 17, 18^2, 19, 20, 22, 27, 31, 32, 34, 36, 37; 10:3, 15^4, 19, 23, 33^2; 11:5, 8; 12:4^2, 5; 14:6, 7; 15:20; 18:17, 21, 22, 25; 19:3^2, 4, 13, 21, 26; 20:3, 9, 10, 15^2, 17, 19; 21:15; 22:6, 7, 13^3; 23:10, 17^2; 1Ch 1:27; 5:1; 8:7; 9:23; 11:2, 4, 11, 17; 12:18; 13:2, 6^3, 11; 14:11; 16:14, 25^2, 30, 31, 34, 40; 17:1, 2, 16, 20^2, 21, 24; 19:3; 21:13, 17, 24; 22:5^3, 14, 18^2; 23:28; 27:1, 6; 28:6, 7, 20^2; 29:1^2, 11^3, 12, 14, 15, 16; 2Ch 2:5, 6, 14; 5:2, 3, 13; 6:11, 14, 22, 26^2, 28^3, 36; 7:3, 13, 15; 8:8; 10:10; 11:4; 12:6; 13:4, 10, 12; 14:7, 11; 15:2; 16:9; 18:6, 7, 31; 19:3, 6, 7, 9, 11; 20:2^2, 6, 9, 12, 15, 17; 22:9; 23:3, 4, 14, 18; 25:4, 7, 9; 26:18, 23; 28:11, 13^2; 29:10; 30:9; 31:3; 32:7^2, 8^2, 11; 34:21^3; 35:12, 21, 26; 36:23^2; Ezr 1:3^2; 3:11; 4:9, 11, 13, 14, 15, 16; 5:8^3, 16; 6:8, 9, 18; 7:11, 14, 15, 20, 23; 8:1, 22; 9:7, 11, 15; 10:2, 4, 12, 13^2, 14, 23; Ne 1:3; 2:2, 19, 20; 4:10^2, 14, 19; 5:5, 9; 6:6^2, 7; 7:3; 8:9, 10^3, 11, 15; 9:5, 6^2, 18; 10:34, 36, 37; 13:11, 17; Est 1:15, 19^2, 20^2; 2:3, 7, 16; 3:7^2, 8^2, 11, 13; 4:11, 16; 5:3^2, 6^2, 7; 6:4, 5, 13; 7:2^2, 3^2, 5^2; 8:6, 9, 12; 9:1, 12^2, 24; Job 1:5, 8, 12; 2:3, 6; 3:3, 20, 23; 4:6, 19, 21; 5:1, 4, 17, 24, 27; 6:6^2, 7, 11^2, 12^2, 13, 17, 29, 30; 7:4, 5, 7; 8:11^2, 14; 9:2, 4, 19^3, 22, 24^3, 32, 33; 10:7, 22; 11:4, 6, 8, 9, 12, 14, 18, 20; 12:5, 10, 12; 13:19, 28; 14:5, 7^2, 13, 18; 15:9, 16, 23^2, 34; 16:6, 8, 16^2, 17^2, 19^2; 17:1^2, 3, 12, 15; 18:5, 6^2, 10, 12^2, 13, 15, 21; 19:4, 7, 17, 28, 29; 20:5^2, 12, 14^2, 25, 26^2, 29; 21:4, 9, 15, 16, 17, 21, 28^2, 32, 34; 22:3^2, 4, 5^2, 12, 25, 29; 23:2^2, 8; 24:14, 17, 18, 20, 25^2; 25:3, 5, 6^2; 26:6, 8; 27:3^2, 8, 11, 13, 14, 19; 28:1, 2^2, 5, 12, 13, 14^2, 18, 20, 21, 28^2; 30:2, 15, 16, 31; 31:35; 32:8, 9^2, 19^2; 33:9, 12, 21, 24, 26; 34:4^2, 6, 7, 17, 22, 29; 35:10, 14; 36:4^2, 5^2, 22^2, 26^2, 33; 37:4, 10, 16, 17, 21, 22, 23; 38:2, 14^2, 15^2, 19^2, 21, 24^3, 26, 30; 39:9, 11, 20, 22, 26, 27, 30; 40:16, 19, 23^3; 41:10, 14, 15, 16, 23, 24, 34^2; 42:3, 7^2, 8; Ps 1:2; 2:12; 3:2; 5:9; 6:3, 5; 7:3, 8, 10, 11; 8:1, 9; 9:9, 12; 10:4, 16; 11:4^2, 7; 12:1^2, 4, 8; 14:1^2, 3, 5, 6; 15:2; 16:3, 5, 8, 9, 11; 17:14; 18:2, 3, 28, 30^2, 31^2; 19:3^2, 6^2, 7, 8, 9, 11^2; 20:7; 21:5; 22:11^2, 14^2, 15; 23:1; 24:1^2, 4, 6, 8, 10^2; 25:8, 9, 11, 14; 26:3; 27:1^2, 6; 28:3, 7, 8^2; 29:3, 4^2; 30:5^2, 9; 31:4, 10, 12, 19; 32:1^2, 2; 33:4^2, 5, 12^2, 16^2, 17, 18, 20, 21; 34:8, 16, 18; 35:10, 12, 27; 36:1, 4, 6, 7, 9; 37:13, 16, 31, 37, 39^2; 38:3^2, 7, 9^2, 14, 15^2, 17; 39:4^2, 5, 7, 9, 11^2; 40:7, 8, 16; 42:3, 6, 8, 10; 44:15; 45:1, 2, 6, 11, 13, 14; 46:1, 4, 5, 7^2, 11^2; 47:2, 7, 8, 9; 48:1, 2, 10, 14; 49:7, 8, 13; 50:3, 6, 10, 11, 12^2; 51:3, 4, 17; 52:2, 9; 53:1^2, 3; 54:T, 4^2, 6; 55:4, 11, 12^2, 13, 15, 19; 56:9; 57:7^2, 10; 58:1, 11^2; 60:2, 7^4, 8, 11, 12; 61:2^2; 62:2, 4, 5, 6, 7, 8; 63:1, 3, 5; 65:1, 9; 66:5, 10; 68:2, 4, 5, 11, 19, 20, 27, 34^2, 35; 69:2, 3, 7, 9, 13, 16; 70:4; 71:6, 8, 9, 11, 15, 19; 72:7, 14; 73:1, 6, 11, 25, 26, 28; 74:9^2, 10^2, 12, 16; 75:1, 3, 7, 8; 76:1^2, 7, 11; 77:2, 10, 13^2; 79:10; 81:4; 83:18; 84:1, 5, 10, 11, 12; 85:9, 12; 86:8, 13; 88:3, 11; 89:2^2, 6, 8, 11^2, 13, 17, 19, 47, 49, 50; 90:4, 5, 6, 10, 11^2; 91:4; 92:1, 15^3; 93:1^4, 2, 4; 94:13, 18; 95:3, 5, 7; 96:4^2, 10^2, 13^2; 97:1, 8; 98:9; 99:1, 2^2, 3, 5, 9; 100:3^2, 5; 101:2, 3, 6; 102:4, 13; 103:1, 5, 8, 11, 12, 16, 17; 104:13, 20, 24, 25; 105:7, 8; 106:1; 107:1; 108:1^2, 4, 8^4, 9, 12, 13; 109:7, 21, 22, 27; 110:5; 111:3, 4, 5, 9, 10; 112:5, 9; 113:3, 4, 5^2; 114:5; 115:2, 3, 9, 10, 11; 116:5^2, 11, 15; 117:2; 118:1, 7, 8, 9, 14, 16, 20, 23^2, 24, 26, 27, 29; 119:1, 20, 38, 43, 50, 57, 64, 71, 72, 77, 89, 96, 97, 98, 105, 118, 121, 126, 132, 136, 140, 142^2, 155, 156, 160, 174; 120:5; 121:5^2; 122:3; 124:7, 8; 127:2, 5; 128:1; 129:4; 130:4, 7^2, 8; 131:1, 2^2; 132:14; 133:1, 2, 3; 135:3^2, 5^2, 7, 17; 136:1, 23; 138:5, 6; 139:4, 6^2, 12^3, 17, 24; 140:3; 141:5; 142:3, 4; 143:2, 4; 144:15; 145:3^2, 8, 9^2, 13^2, 17, 18; 146:3, 5^2, 6; 147:1^3, 5^2, 10; 148:13^2; 149:9; Pr 1:7, 17^2, 19; 2:7; 3:14, 15, 16, 18, 27^2, 33, 34; 4:7, 13, 18, 19; 5:3, 4; 6:23, 26, 29; 7:11, 19, 23, 27; 8:4, 6, 7, 8, 11, 13, 15, 19, 34; 9:8, 10^2, 13^2, 17^2; 10:1, 5, 7, 11, 13^2, 15^2, 17, 18, 19, 20^2, 23^2, 29, 32^2; 11:1^2, 2, 10, 11^2, 13, 14^2, 15, 16, 19, 22, 24, 26, 30; 12:4^2, 5, 8^2, 10, 14, 15, 20, 23, 28^2; 13:2, 4, 6, 8, 10, 12, 14, 15, 18, 19^2, 22, 23, 25; 14:2, 3, 4, 6, 8, 11, 12^2, 13^2, 16, 17^2, 23, 24^2, 25, 27, 28^2, 29, 33^2, 34; 15:4, 5, 6, 8^2, 9, 10, 13, 16, 17^2, 19^2, 21, 23^2, 29, 33; 16:1, 6, 8, 12^2, 13, 14^2, 15^2, 16, 19, 21, 22^2, 25^2, 27, 29, 31^2, 32^3, 33^2; 17:1, 3^2, 6, 7^2, 8, 14, 18, 22, 26, 27^2; 18:1, 4, 5, 9^2, 10, 11^2, 12, 13, 19^2, 20; 19:1, 2, 6, 8^2, 10, 11, 12^2, 13^2, 14, 17, 18, 21, 22^3, 23, 29; 20:1^3, 2, 3^2, 4, 11, 15, 17, 25^2, 27, 28, 29^2; 21:1, 3, 5, 6, 7, 8^2, 9, 11, 15^2, 18, 19, 23, 25, 27, 31; 22:1^2, 2, 4, 7, 13, 14^2, 15, 21; 23:1, 5, 11, 15, 16, 18, 22, 27^2, 31; 24:3^2, 6, 7, 9^2, 13, 14, 23; 25:2^2, 3, 7, 11, 12, 14, 18, 19, 20, 24, 25, 27, 28; 26:1, 6, 8, 9, 10, 11, 12, 13^2, 15, 16, 17, 19, 20, 21^2, 26; 27:3^3, 4^3, 5, 7, 8, 9, 10^2, 16, 21^3, 25^2; 28:2, 3, 8, 11, 12, 14^3, 15, 16, 17, 20, 21, 22^2, 24^2; 29:1, 3, 5, 6, 9, 15, 18, 20^2, 23, 24, 25, 26; 30:4^2, 5, 9, 20, 28, 30; 31:4^2, 6, 10, 14, 15, 18, 21, 22, 23, 26, 30^3; Ecc 1:2, 7, 8, 9^3, 10^3, 13^2, 14, 15^2, 17, 18; 2:2^2, 15, 16, 17^2, 19, 21, 23^2, 24^2, 26; 3:1, 2, 12, 13, 15^3, 18, 19^2, 22^2; 4:3, 4, 6, 8^2, 10, 12, 13, 16; 5:1, 2, 5, 8, 9, 10, 12, 13, 16, 18^3, 19; 6:1, 2^2, 3, 4, 7^2, 9^2, 10, 11, 12; 7:1, 2^2, 3^2, 4^2, 5, 6^2, 8, 10, 11, 12^2, 18, 20, 24^2, 25^2, 26^3, 27; 8:1^2, 3, 4, 7, 8, 9, 10, 11^2, 14^2, 15, 16, 17; 9:1, 2, 3^2, 4^2, 5, 9, 10, 11, 16^2, 18; 10:5, 6, 10, 11^2, 14, 16, 17; 11:7^2, 8; 12:4, 5, 6^3, 8, 12^2, 13; SS 1:1, 2, 3, 7, 13, 14, 16; 2:2, 3, 7, 9, 11^2, 12, 14^2, 16; 3:5, 6, 7; 4:1, 2, 3, 4, 7, 10^2, 11, 12, 13; 5:2^2, 9^2, 10, 11, 14, 15, 16^4; 6:3, 5, 6, 9, 10; 7:2^2, 4^2, 5, 10; 8:4, 5, 6, 8, 9^2, 12; Isa 1:5, 6, 7, 8, 11, 13^2, 22; 2:7^4, 8, 9, 12^2; 3:1, 7, 14^2; 4:3; 5:7, 8, 13, 15, 16, 25, 27^2, 29; 6:3^2, 5, 7, 11, 12, 13^2; 7:8^2, 9^2, 13, 14, 18^2, 22; 8:7, 10, 17; 9:6, 12, 17^2, 21; 10:4, 5, 7^2, 9^3, 15, 22, 31; 11:11, 16; 12:2^2, 4, 6; 13:4, 6, 15^2, 22; 14:7, 9, 11, 16, 26^4, 27, 29, 31; 15:1^4, 2^2, 6^2; 16:4, 5^2, 6, 10; 17:6, 14; 18:3^2, 5; 19:1, 7, 17^2; 20:6; 21:2, 9, 11; 22:15, 17; 23:1, 7^2, 10, 13, 14; 24:1, 8^2, 9, 10^2, 11^2, 12, 13^2, 16, 19^3; 25:2, 7^2, 9^2, 10; 26:7, 10, 11, 17, 18, 19, 20; 27:1, 10, 11; 28:1, 2, 4, 8, 10, 12^2, 20, 21^2, 27^3, 28, 29; 29:11^2, 12, 13; 30:7, 10, 14^3, 18, 21, 27, 28, 29, 33; 31:2, 4^2, 9^2; 32:7, 15^2; 33:5, 6, 8^2, 9^2, 11, 18^3, 22^3; 34:2, 6^2; 35:4; 36:6, 7, 10; 37:3^2, 4, 13, 22, 27; 38:3, 7, 12, 16, 22; 39:4^2, 6, 8; 40:2, 6, 9, 10, 22, 25, 26^2, 27^2, 28^2; 41:7, 13, 14, 17^2, 22, 23, 24^2, 26, 28^2; 42:1, 8, 19^2, 22; 43:7, 9, 11, 13; 44:6, 7^2, 8^2, 12, 16, 19, 20, 28; 45:3, 5^2, 6^2, 14^3, 17, 18^2, 19, 21^2, 22; 46:9^2, 13; 47:4^2, 8, 10, 14, 15; 48:2, 4, 22; 49:4, 6, 7, 20; 50:1^2, 2, 8, 9, 11; 51:13^2, 15, 18^2; 52:5, 6; 53:7^2; 54:1, 5^4, 6, 9, 15, 16, 17^2; 55:2^2, 6; 56:1, 2; 57:6, 10, 15, 21; 58:5^2, 6, 7;

59:1, 8, 9^2, 11^2, 14, 15^2, 21^2; **61:**1, 11; **62:**4, 11; **63:**1^3, 11^2, 16; **64:**6, 7; **65:**2, 6, 8^2; **66:**1^4, 2, 3, 5, 14^2; **Jer 2:**6, 8, 14^2, 19^2, 22, 25, 26, 34; **3:**5, 21, 23; **4:**10, 12, 18^2, 19, 20, 31; **5:**6, 13, 15^2, 16, 19; **6:**6^2, 10, 13, 14, 20, 22^2, 23, 25, 29; **7:**4, 10, 11, 14, 19^2, 28^2, 30, 31, 32; **8:**8, 9, 10, 11, 15, 16, 18^3, 19^2, 20^2, 22^2; **9:**8, 10, 12^2, 19, 26; **10:**3, 5, 6^2, 7^2, 8, 9^2, 10^2, 12, 13, 14^2, 16^4, 19^3, 20^2, 21, 22, 23; **12:**3, 4, 9, 11; **13:**10, 19, 20, 22, 25; **14:**4, 5, 6, 17, 19^2, 22^2; **15:**10, 14, 18, 19^3; **16:**10^2, 11, 17, 19, 21; **17:**1^2, 4, 7, 8, 9^2, 15; **18:**12, 20; **19:**11; **20:**9, 10, 11, 15; **21:**1, 2, 14; **22:**10, 16, 28; **23:**2, 6^2, 9, 10^2, 29, 33, 36; **25:**29, 31, 32^2, 36; **26:**12; **27:**4, 5, 18; **28:**11; **29:**9; **30:**7^3, 12^2, 13, 14, 15^2, 17; **31:**9, 15^2, 16, 17, 20^2, 33, 35; **32:**7^3, 8^2, 17^2, 18, 27, 36, 43; **33:**2, 10, 11, 12, 16^2; **34:**15; **35:**11; **36:**7; **37:**7^2, 14, 17^2; **38:**4^2, 5^3, 9, 21; **40:**4; **41:**12; **42:**6; **43:**3, 9, 13; **44:**22, 23^2, 27; **45:**3, 4; **46:**5, 7, 10, 11, 12, 18^2, 20, 23; **47:**4^2, 5; **48:**1^4, 2, 4, 10^3, 11, 12, 15, 16, 17, 20^3, 25^2, 29, 33, 37, 38, 39, 47; **49:**2, 3, 4, 7, 10^2, 19^2, 25, 29; **50:**2^3, 15, 17, 22, 23, 34^2, 38, 41, 42, 44^2; **51:**5, 6^3, 8, 11^2, 13, 15, 16, 17^2, 19^4, 31, 33^2, 41, 48, 52, 55, 56, 57; **52:**28; **La 1:**4, 12^2, 16, 17, 18, 20^2, 22; **2:**9, 11, 12^2, 13, 15, 16; **3:**10, 17^2, 18, 19, 20, 23, 24, 25, 26, 27, 36, 38; **4:**1, 8, 22; **5:**8, 10, 12; **Eze 3:**1; **4:**3; **5:**5; **7:**3, 7, 9, 12, 14, 15, 23^2; **8:**17; **9:**9^2; **11:**3^2, 5, 7, 15; **12:**12, 22, 27^2; **13:**10, 12, 15; **14:**9, 15; **15:**2, 3, 4^3, 5; **16:**30, 46^2; **17:**10; **18:**4^2, 5^2, 9^2, 10, 18, 19, 21, 25^3, 27, 29^2; **19:**13, 14^2; **20:**29^2, 32, 49; **21:**9^2, 10, 11^3, 12^2, 14, 15^2, 16, 26^2, 27; **22:**22, 24; **23:**4^2, 33, 37, 39, 43, 45; **24:**6, 7, 14; **25:**8; **26:**2^2; **27:**27; **28:**2, 3, 23; **29:**3, 9; **30:**3^2, 4, 9; **31:**14, 18; **32:**15, 16, 22, 23, 24, 29; **33:**14, 16, 17^3, 19, 20, 24, 30, 31^2; **34:**18; **36:**22, 32; **37:**11, 19, 28; **39:**8, 16; **40:**45, 46; **41:**4, 22; **42:**10, 13; **43:**7, 12^2, 18; **44:**3, 14, 16^2, 22; **45:**8, 9, 13, 15; **46:**14, 16, 20; **47:**16, 17; **48:**1, 14, 20, 29, 30, 32, 33, 34, 35; **Da 2:**3, 5, 9, 10, 11^3, 15, 22, 27, 28, 29, 45, 47; **3:**14, 15, 17, 29^2; **4:**3^2, 8, 9, 10, 17^3, 18, 22, 24^2, 26, 30, 31, 34, 35, 37; **5:**11^2, 14, 23, 25, 26, 28; **6:**13, 15, 26; **7:**14^2, 23; **8:**13, 17, 21^2, 26; **9:**7, 13, 14, 26, 27; **10:**4, 14^2, 17, 21^2; **11:**23, 35, 36^2; **12:**1, 11^2; **Hos 2:**2; **3:**1; **4:**1, 4, 13, 16, 17, 18; **5:**3^2, 4, 9, 11, 13; **6:**1, 3, 4, 8, 10^2, 11; **7:**1, 4, 8; **8:**1, 5, 6^2, 8; **9:**7^3, 8^2, 12, 16^2; **10:**1, 2, 12; **11:**12; **12:**1, 5, 11; **13:**4, 10, 12^2, 13, 14^2; **14:**2, 8; **Joel 1:**5, 10, 15, 16, 18; **2:**1^2, 3, 11^2, 13, 17, 27; **3:**13^3, 14, 16; **Am 2:**7, 11, 13; **3:**5, 6; **4:**2, 13; **5:**2, 8, 13, 18, 20, 27; **6:**2, 8, 10; **7:**1, 2, 4, 5, 7, 10, 13^2; **8:**1, 11; **9:**6, 11, 13; **Ob 1:**3, 4, 7, 15; **Jnh 1:**8^2, 10, 12; **3:**8; **4:**2^2, 3, 4, 8, 9; **Mic 1:**2, 3, 5^5, 9, 11; **2:**1, 7, 10; **3:**7, 11; **4:**9; **5:**1, 2^2, 3; **6:**8, 9, 10; **7:**1^2, 2^2, 4^2, 10, 18; **Na 1:**2^2, 3^2, 6, 7; **2:**2, 4, 5, 7, 8, 9; **3:**7, 19^2; **Hab 1:**5, 11, 16^2, 17; **2:**3, 4, 5, 6, 13, 18^2, 19^2, 20; **3:**17^3, 19; **Zep 1:**7, 14^2; **2:**5^2, 15^2; **3:**4, 5, 8, 15, 17; **Hag 1:**4, 6; **2:**3^2, 8^2, 13, 14^2, 19; **Zec 2:**2^2; **3:**2; **4:**1, 6; **5:**2, 3, 5^2, 6^3, 8, 11; **6:**12^2, 13; **7:**1; **8:**23; **9:**1, 9; **10:**3, 5, 10; **11:**3, 9^2; **13:**7, 9^2; **14:**1, 7; **Mal 1:**2, 4, 5, 6^2, 8^2, 9, 11^3, 12, 13^2, 14^2; **2:**1, 7, 14, 17; **3:**1, 2, 14; **4:**1; **Mt 1:**16, 20, 23; **2:**2, 6, 13; **3:**3, 9, 10^2, 11^2, 12, 15, 17; **4:**4, 6, 7, 10, 18; **5:**3, 10, 12, 13^2, 18, 29, 30, 34, 35^2, 48; **6:**3, 6, 10, 18, 21, 22^2, 23^3, 25, 30^2, 32, 34; **7:**4, 6, 9, 12, 13^2, 14^2, 19; **8:**6, 27; **9:**3, 5, 15^2, 16, 17^3, 24, 37; **10:**11, 13^2, 20, 24, 25, 26, 37^2, 38; **11:**3, 6, 10^2, 11, 14^2, 16, 19, 30^2; **12:**2, 6, 8, 10, 12^2, 18^2, 24, 25, 26, 28, 30^2, 33, 41, 42, 45, 48, 50; **13:**13, 14, 19^2, 20, 22, 23, 31, 32^2, 33, 37, 38, 39^2, 44, 45, 47, 52^3, 55^2; **14:**2, 4, 15^2, 26, 27, 28; **15:**5, 11^2, 18, 22, 26, 28; **16:**2^2, 3, 7, 13, 27; **17:**4, 5, 11, 12, 15, 22; **18:**1, 4, 8, 9, 14; **19:**3, 10^2, 11, 14, 17^3, 24^2, 26, 28; **20:**1, 4, 23^2; **21:**5, 9, 10, 11, 13, 38, 42; **22:**4, 8, 17, 20, 23, 32, 36, 38, 39, 42, 43; **23:**16^2, 17, 18^3, 19, 22, 23, 38, 39; **24:**6, 8, 17, 23^2, 26^2, 28, 32, 33, 42, 44, 45, 46, 48; **25:**6, 14, 25; **26:**2, 13, 18, 24^2, 26, 28^2, 31, 39, 41^2, 45^2, 46, 48, 62, 66, 68; **27:**4, 6, 17, 22, 37, 42, 46, 47, 62; **28:**6, 7^2, 15; **Mk 1:**2, 7^2, 15, 27, 37, 38; **2:**7, 9, 19, 20, 21, 22, 24, 26, 28; **3:**4, 17, 24, 25, 26, 29, 35; **4:**15^2, 21, 22^2, 26, 29, 31^2, 32, 41; **5:**9^2, 23, 35, 39; **6:**2, 3, 11, 15^2, 18, 35^2, 50; **7:**2, 6, 11^2, 15, 20, 21, 27, 34; **8:**16; **9:**5, 7, 12^3, 13, 26, 31, 40^2, 43, 45, 47, 48, 50; **10:**2, 14, 18, 24, 25^2, 27, 29, 36, 40^2, 43, 49; **11:**9, 10, 17; **12:**7, 11, 14, 16, 18, 24, 27, 28, 29^2, 31^2, 32^2, 33, 35; **13:**7, 8, 11^2, 21^2, 28, 29, 34; **14:**9, 12, 14, 18, 20^2, 21^2, 22, 24^2, 27, 38^2, 41, 42, 44, 58, 60, 64, 69; **15:**16, 35, 42; **16:**6^2, 7, 16; **Lk 1:**18^2, 25, 28, 36, 42, 45, 49, 50, 60, 63; **2:**11^2, 23, 24, 34; **3:**4, 8, 9^2, 16^2, 17; **4:**4, 8, 10, 12, 18, 22, 24, 25, 36; **5:**21^2, 23, 34, 39; **6:**2, 4, 5, 9, 20, 23^2, 26, 32, 33, 34, 35, 36, 40^2, 44, 45, 47, 48, 49; **7:**4, 5, 19, 20, 23, 27^2, 28^2, 35, 39^3, 47, 49; **8:**11^2, 17^2, 25^2, 26, 30, 49, 52; **9:**9, 33, 35, 38, 44, 48, 50^2, 62; **10:**2, 6, 8, 22^2, 26, 29, 42; **11:**8, 11, 18, 20, 21, 23^2, 26, 27, 29, 31, 32, 34^5, 35, 36, 42; **12:**1, 2, 6, 20, 21, 23, 28^2, 30, 32, 34, 40, 42, 43, 45, 50, 54, 57; **13:**18, 19, 21, 33, 35^2; **14:**3, 15, 17, 22, 29, 31, 32, 34, 35; **15:**4, 10, 24^2, 31^2; **16:**2, 3, 9, 10^4, 12, 15^2, 16, 17, 25; **17:**3, 20, 21^3, 30, 37; **18:**16, 19, 22, 24, 25^2, 27^2, 29, 31, 37; **19:**7, 9, 20, 38, 46; **20:**2, 14, 22, 27, 38, 41; **21:**7, 8, 22, 26, 28, 30, 31; **22:**1, 11, 16, 19^2, 20^2, 21^2, 22^2, 27^3, 37^2, 38, 48, 53, 59, 64; **23:**2, 31^2, 33, 35, 38; **24:**5, 21, 29^2, 39, 46^2, 47; **Jn 1:**18^2, 19, 27, 29, 30, 33, 34, 36, 41, 42, 47^2; **2:**4; **3:**6^4, 8^2, 19, 21, 26, 29, 31^3, 33; **4:**1, 9, 10^2, 11, 18^2, 20, 21, 22, 23^2, 24, 25^2, 26, 34, 36^2, 42^2; **5:**2, 7, 10^2, 12, 17, 20, 25^2, 27, 28, 30, 31, 32^2, 39, 44, 45; **6:**9, 14^2, 20, 27, 29, 31, 32, 33, 39, 40, 42, 45, 46, 50, 51, 55^2, 58, 60, 63^2, 65, 70; **7:**6, 11, 12^2, 16, 17, 18^2, 20, 22, 25, 26^2, 27^2, 28, 37, 40, 41, 42, 52; **8:**7, 13, 14, 16^2, 17^2, 19, 22^2, 26, 29^2, 34, 37, 39, 40, 43, 44^2, 47^2, 50^2, 54^3; **9:**4^2, 8, 9^2, 12, 16^2, 17, 19, 20, 21^2, 23, 24, 25, 30, 36, 37; **10:**1, 2, 12, 20, 29, 33, 34, 36, 38; **11:**3, 4, 10, 14, 28^2, 39, 47, 50; **12:**13, 14, 15, 27^2, 31, 34, 35, 50; **13:**10, 13, 18, 25, 26; **14:**10, 11, 17, 22, 24^2, 28, 30; **15:**1, 6, 8, 12, 15, 25; **16:**2, 7, 14, 15^2, 18, 21^2, 25, 32^2; **17:**3, 7, 17; **18:**22, 36^3, 38; **19:**5, 11, 14, 17^2, 25, 26, 27, 30, 35; **20:**31; **21:**7, 20^2, 22^2, 23^2, 24^3; **Ac 1:**4, 6, 7, 12, 19, 20; **2:**8, 15, 16, 25, 29, 39; **3:**16, 20; **4:**2, 10, 11, 12^2, 16, 19, 25; **5:**4, 9, 17, 32, 38, 39; **6:**2; **7:**33, 37, 38, 42, 49^3; **8:**10^2, 21, 26, 33, 36^2; **9:**11, 15, 20, 21, 36; **10:**4, 5, 6^2, 14, 21, 22, 28, 32^2, 35^2, 36, 42; **11:**13; **12:**15; **13:**8, 11, 25, 33, 38, 39; **14:**15, 22; **15:**5, 15, 29; **16:**12; **17:**3, 7, 19, 24, 25, 27, 29; **18:**13, 15, 28; **19:**2, 4, 27, 28, 34, 35^2, 39, 40; **20:**10, 32, 35; **21:**11, 22, 24, 25, 28^2; **22:**25^2, 26; **23:**5, 8, 19; **24:**11, 21; **25:**5, 10, 11, 14; **26:**2, 7, 8, 10, 24, 31; **27:**5, 33; **28:**20, 22; **Ro 1:**8, 9, 16, 17^3, 18, 19, 25; **2:**2, 4, 13, 15, 18, 24^2, 25, 28^3, 29^4; **3:**1, 4^2, 5, 8, 10^3, 11^2, 12^2, 13, 18, 21, 22, 24, 26, 27, 28, 29^2, 30; **4:**5, 8, 9, 14^3, 15^2, 16, 17; **5:**13^2, 14, 15, 16; **6:**7, 21, 22^2, 23^2; **7:**1, 2^2, 3^3, 7^2, 12^2, 13^2, 14, 16, 17, 18^2, 19, 20, 21; **8:**1, 6^2, 7^2, 10^3, 16, 24^3, 27, 31^2, 33, 34^3, 36; **9:**5, 6, 7, 8, 9, 10, 13, 14, 20, 30, 31, 33; **10:**1, 2, 4, 6, 7, 8^2, 9, 10^2, 12^3, 15, 17^2, 20; **11:**4, 5, 6^2, 8, 15, 16^3, 18, 20, 24, 26, 27; **12:**1, 2^2, 9^2, 17, 18, 19^2; **13:**1, 3, 4^3, 7^4, 10, 11^3, 12^2; **14:**4^2, 11, 14^2, 15, 17, 18, 20^2, 21, 23; **15:**3, 9, 21, 22; **16:**2, 10, 19^3, 23, 25, 26^2; **1Co 1:**2, 9, 12, 18^2, 19, 20^4, 25^2, 27^2, 28, 30, 31; **2:**6, 9, 11^3, 12; **3:**3, 5^2, 7, 10, 11, 15, 17, 19^2; **4:**2, 3, 4, 6, 17; **5:**1^4, 4, 6, 11^2, 12; **6:**2, 5, 7, 11, 13^2, 16^2, 18, 19; **7:**1, 8, 9, 12, 13, 14^3, 15^2, 17, 19^3, 22^2, 25, 26, 31, 32, 33, 34, 36^2, 39^2, 40^2; **8:**3, 4, 6, 7^2, 10, 12, 13; **9:**3, 6, 9^4, 11, 13, 16, 18; **10:**7, 13^2, 16^2, 17, 19^2, 25, 27; **11:**3^3, 5, 6, 7^2, 11, 13, 14, 15^2, 16, 17, 20, 24^2, 25; **12:**3, 6, 7, 8, 12^2, 18, 20, 26; **13:**4^3, 5, 13; **14:**5, 7^2, 9^2, 10, 14, 17, 21, 22, 24, 25, 28, 29, 30, 33, 35^2, 37, 38; **15:**10, 12^2, 13, 15, 17, 26, 27, 31, 37, 39^2, 40^2, 41, 42^5, 43^4, 44^4, 45, 46^2, 47, 48, 50, 54, 55^2, 56^2, 58; **16:**2, 10; **2Co 1:**1, 5, 6^2, 7, 12, 18, 19, 20^2, 21; **2:**2, 6, 16; **3:**4, 5, 14^2, 15, 16, 17^3; **4:**1, 3^2, 4, 6, 12, 13, 15, 16^2, 17, 18^2; **5:**1, 4, 5, 13^2, 17^2, 18, 19, 20; **6:**2^2, 11, 12, 14^2; **8:**10, 12^2, 13, 15, 17^2, 18, 21, 22, 23; **9:**1, 2, 6, 8, 9; **10:**6, 7, 10, 15^2, 18; **11:**10, 15, 29^2; **12:**1^2, 4, 6, 9^2, 14, 19; **13:**1, 3^3, 5, 7, 9; **Gal 1:**7, 11, 23; **2:**16, 17, 20^2; **3:**2, 10^2, 11^3, 13^2, 16^2, 17, 20, 21, 28^3; **4:**1, 18, 19, 22, 24^2, 25^2, 26^2, 27^2, 29; **5:**3, 6, 10^2, 14, 17^2, 22, 23; **6:**1, 7, 9, 12, 15^2; **Eph 1:**14, 18, 19, 21, 23; **2:**2, 4, 8^2, 14^2, 21; **3:**1, 6, 9, 18, 20; **4:**4, 6, 8, 10, 15, 16^2, 20, 21, 29^2; **5:**3, 4, 5^2, 9^2, 10, 12, 14, 17, 18, 23^3, 24, 32; **6:**1, 2, 9, 12, 17, 21; **Php 1:**7, 8, 9, 10, 13, 18, 20, 21^2, 23^2, 24, 28^2; **2:**1, 9, 11, 13^2, 16; **3:**1^2, 3, 19^3, 20^2; **4:**5, 8^8, 12^2; **Col 1:**6, 7, 15, 17, 18^2, 24^2, 27, 28; **2:**2, 10, 17, 19; **3:**1, 3, 4^2, 5^2, 6, 10, 11^2, 18, 20, 25; **4:**7, 9^2, 11, 12^2; **1Th 1:**10; **2:**5, 13^2, 19^2; **3:**3, 10; **4:**3, 6; **5:**3, 18, 21, 24; **2Th 1:**3^3, 5^2, 6, 7; **2:**2, 3, 6, 7^2, 9, 11; **3:**1, 3, 13, 17^2; **1Ti 1:**4, 5, 8, 9, 10, 15; **2:**3^2, 5^2, 10, 12; **3:**1, 13, 15, 16; **4:**4^3, 5, 8^2, 9, 10, 14; **5:**4, 6, 8, 9, 18; **6:**3, 4, 5, 6, 10, 15, 16, 19, 20; **2Ti 1:**1, 6, 12; **2:**1, 4, 5, 6, 8, 9, 10, 11; **3:**16^2; **4:**1, 2, 3, 8, 11^2; **Tit 1:**1, 6, 9, 11, 13, 15; **2:**1, 3, 14; **3:**8, 11; **Phm 1:**11, 12, 15; **Heb 1:**3, 4, 8^2; **2:**8, 11, 14, 16, 18; **3:**3, 4^2, 13, 15; **4:**1, 12^2, 13, 15; **5:**1, 2^2, 11, 13, 14; **6:**4, 7, 8^2, 10, 18; **7:**2^2, 4, 5, 7^2, 8, 12^2, 14, 15, 17, 18, 19, 25; **8:**1^2, 3^2, 5, 6, 10, 13; **9:**2, 8, 9, 11, 13, 15, 16, 17^2, 20, 22^2, 25, 26, 27; **10:**3, 4, 7, 10, 16, 18^2, 20, 23, 25, 30, 31, 37; **11:**1, 3, 6, 7, 10, 16^3, 18, 19, 27; **12:**1, 7^2, 13, 25, 27^2, 29; **13:**6, 8, 9, 11, 14, 15, 21; **Jas 1:**5, 6, 9, 11, 12, 14, 15, 17^2, 26, 27^2; **2:**3, 6^2, 7, 14, 15, 16, 17, 19, 20, 24, 26^2; **3:**2, 5^2, 6^3, 13, 15, 16, 17, 18; **4:**4, 5, 12^2, 14, 16^2; **5:**8, 9, 11, 16, 19; **1Pe 1:**4, 7^2, 13, 15, 16, 24, 25; **2:**3, 7, 15, 19, 20; **3:**4, 6, 9, 12, 13, 14, 15, 17, 20, 22; **4:**6^2, 7, 12, 13, 14^2, 18; **5:**2, 12; **2Pe 1:**4, 9^2, 17, 20; **2:**3, 6, 22; **3:**1, 4, 8, 9^2, 10, 13; **1Jn 1:**3, 5^3, 6, 7, 8, 9, 10; **2:**2, 4, 7, 8^3, 9, 10, 11, 13, 14, 15, 16, 18^3, 22^3, 25, 27^2, 28, 29; **3:**1^2, 2^3, 3, 4^2, 5, 7^3, 8, 10, 11, 20, 23; **4:**2, 3^4, 4^3, 5, 6, 7^2, 8, 10, 12, 15, 16, 17, 18, 21; **5:**1, 3, 4^2, 5^2, 6^3, 9^2, 11^2, 14, 16^4, 17^3, 20^3; **2Jn 1:**6^2, 7, 11; **3Jn 1:**2, 10, 11^3, 12; **Jude 1:**14, 19, 24; **Rev 1:**3^3, 4^2, 7^2, 8^2, 19^2; **2:**6, 7^2, 10, 11, 13, 17^2, 20, 29; **3:**2, 6, 8, 10, 13, 22; **4:**3, 6, 8^2, 9, 10; **5:**2, 12, 13; **6:**17; **7:**10, 15; **8:**3, 11; **9:**10, 11^2, 19; **10:**6^3, 7, 8^2; **11:**2, 8, 14; **12:**5, 9, 12, 14; **13:**4, 6, 10, 14, 17, 18^2; **14:**4, 8, 11, 12, 15; **15:**1; **16:**6, 15^2, 16, 17; **17:**1, 8^4, 9, 10, 11^2, 14, 15, 18; **18:**2, 8, 17; **19:**4, 8, 10, 11, 13^2; **20:**2, 5, 14; **21:**3, 6, 8, 18^2, 21^2, 22, 23^2; **22:**2, 7, 10, 12, 16, 17; **Tob 1:**2, 6; **2:**1, 2, 8^2, 13^2; **3:**6^3, 8, 10, 11, 15; **4:**7, 11, 12, 13^3, 21; **5:**6^2, 9^2, 10^3, 12, 16, 18^2, 20^2; **6:**7, 11, 12^3; **7:**4, 5^2, 11^3; **8:**5, 6, 10, 12^2, 21; **10:**2^2, 4, 6^3, 12; **11:**1, 6; **12:**7, 8^4, 11; **13:**2, 4^4, 6^2, 10; **14:**8^2, 10^2; **Jdt 1:**5; **2:**16, 21; **5:**3^2, 17, 19, 20; **6:**2; **7:**10, 13, 18; **8:**11, 16, 25, 28, 29^2; **9:**6, 7, 14; **10:**19; **11:**8, 10, 11, 12, 13, 17; **12:**11, 18; **13:**5, 11, 15; **14:**18^2; **15:**10; **16:**2, 14, 16^3; **AdE 1:**13; **2:**3, 13, 14^2, 16; **3:**8^2, 13; **4:**1, 11^3; **5:**3, 4, 6, 7; **6:**4, 5, 10, 13^2; **7:**2^3, 5, 6, 9; **8:**6, 8, 9, 12; **9:**1, 26; **10:**6, 9; **13:**1, 3, 4, 5, 6^2, 9^3, 11; **14:**4, 13, 16, 19; **15:**9, 14; **16:**1; **Wis 1:**2, 3, 6^2, 7, 11, 14^2, 15; **2:**1^2, 2^2, 3, 4, 5^3, 9, 11, 12, 15^2, 16, 18, 19; **3:**4, 11, 13^2, 14, 15, 19; **4:**1^3, 2, 8, 9^2, 12, 16; **5:**5, 11^3, 12, 14^2, 15; **6:**8, 12^3, 15^2, 17^2, 18^2, 22, 24^2; **7:**3, 6, 9, 14, 15, 17, 21^2, 22^2, 24, 25, 26, 27, 29^2, 30; **8:**4, 5, 6^2, 7, 17; **9:**5, 6, 9^3, 10, 14, 16^3; **10:**12; **11:**16, 21, 22; **12:**1, 13^2, 16; **13:**3, 4, 16, 17, 18^3; **14:**3, 5, 7, 8^2, 25, 26, 27, 31; **15:**3^2, 9, 10^2, 16, 17; **16:**8, 15, 26; **17:**11, 12; **Sir 1:**1, 8^2, 9, 11, 14^2, 16, 18, 20, 25, 27; **2:**5, 11, 17; **3:**10, 11^2, 16^2, 20^2, 21^2, 22^2, 25^2, 28, 29; **4:**21^3, 31; **5:**4, 6; **6:**1, 22^2, 30, 34, 37; **7:**11^2, 13, 17, 19; **8:**4, 5, 6, 12, 16, 18; **9:**8, 10, 17^2, 18^2; **10:**1, 2^2, 4, 5^2, 7^2, 11, 12, 13, 20, 22, 23^4, 24, 27, 31; **11:**3^2, 8, 18, 21, 22, 25^2, 26, 30; **12:**7, 8^2, 10, 13; **13:**18, 20, 21^2, 22, 23, 24, 26; **14:**3, 5, 6^3, 7, 8, 9, 10, 17, 18, 20, 27; **15:**8, 9, 15, 18^2; **16:**2, 6, 11, 12, 22^2; **17:**17, 22, 29, 30, 31; **18:**2, 6^2, 8^2, 9, 11^2, 12, 13^2, 16, 18, 27^3; **19:**2, 12, 15, 20^2, 22^2, 23^3, 25^2, 26^2, 29^2, 30; **20:**1^4, 2, 4, 8^2, 10, 15, 18, 19, 24^2, 25^2, 26, 27, 30; **21:**3^2, 8, 9^2, 10^2, 11, 12^2, 14, 16^2, 17, 18^2, 19, 21, 24, 25, 26^2, 28; **22:**1, 2, 3^2, 4, 5, 6, 9, 10, 11^2, 14^2, 16, 17, 21, 22; **23:**10, 11, 12, 17, 19, 20, 22, 27; **24:**20, 23; **25:**4, 5, 6^2, 8, 9, 10^2, 15, 19, 20, 22; **26:**1, 3, 4^2, 5, 6^2, 7^2, 14^2, 16, 17, 22, 23^2, 25, 26, 27, 28, 29; **27:**2^2, 3, 4, 5, 7, 11, 13^2, 15, 20, 21^2, 23; **28:**19^2, 20, 21^2; **29:**5, 22, 24, 27, 28; **30:**12, 16, 17, 18, 19^2, 22; **31:**7, 8^2, 9, 12, 13, 16, 19, 23^2, 24^2, 27^3, 28; **32:**3, 4, 5, 6, 9, 10, 23; **33:**2^2, 3, 5, 6^2, 7^2, 14^2, 22, 30; **34:**2, 3^2, 8, 9, 15, 16, 17, 18, 21, 23, 24, 25^2, 26, 27; **35:**5^2, 7, 9, 13, 15^2, 16, 20, 26; **36:**5, 12, 23, 26, 27, 28, 30^2; **37:**2, 8, 9, 12, 13^2, 16, 17, 18, 21, 22, 26, 27, 28; **38:**19^2, 21, 22^2, 23, 25^2, 26, 27^2, 28^2, 29^2, 34; **39:**1, 3, 4, 6, 11, 15, 17^2, 18, 20, 21^2, 34; **40:**1, 4, 5, 6, 11^2, 17, 18, 19^2, 20, 21, 23^2, 25, 26^3, 27, 28, 29, 30; **41:**1^3, 2^3, 4, 9^2, 11, 14, 16^2; **42:**6^2, 7, 9^2, 11, 14^2, 16, 19, 20, 21, 23; **43:**1, 2, 4, 5, 6, 8, 9, 11, 17, 18^2, 27, 28, 29^2, 31; **44:**9; **45:**1, 22, 25; **46:**10; **47:**2, 18; **48:**4, 10, 20; **49:**1^2, 13; **50:**25, 29; **51:**10, 12, 26; **Bar 1:**15^2, 22; **2:**6^2, 9, 18, 19, 26^2; **3:**6, 10^2, 14^5, 17, 18, 24, 25^2, 31, 35; **4:**1, 4, 36; **LtJ 6:**6, 7^2, 13, 14, 16, 17^2, 20, 25, 27, 37, 43^2, 44^2, 51, 54, 59, 61, 63, 73; **Aza 1:**3, 30, 67; **Sus 1:**13, 42, 47, 57, 59; **Bel 1:**6, 7, 8, 9, 12, 18, 24, 25, 41; **1Mc 2:**27, 49, 65^2; **3:**7, 18^2, 19, 51, 59; **4:**11, 17, 24, 52; **5:**11, 38; **6:**13, 25, 57^2; **7:**18; **8:**16, 20, 22, 31; **9:**21, 45^3; **10:**23, 36, 42, 63, 73, 89; **12:**5, 11, 19, 45; **13:**15, 30; **14:**20, 27^2, 34^2; **15:**11; **16:**14; **2Mc 1:**10, 36; **2:**17, 24, 26, 27, 29^2, 30; **3:**12, 38; **4:**17; **5:**6; **6:**13, 20, 24, 30; **7:**6, 28, 33, 37; **8:**18; **9:**12, 20, 25; **10:**5; **11:**25, 28; **12:**29, 45; **13:**4, 5, 26; **14:**6, 8, 10; **15:**4, 14, 21, 34, 36, 37, 38^3, 39^2; **1Es 1:**10, 11, 27^3; **2:**4, 5^2, 7, 19, 20, 23, 24; **3:**5, 9, 10, 11, 12, 18, 24; **4:**2, 3^2, 7, 12^2, 14^4, 28, 34^3, 35^2, 36, 37^3, 38, 39^3, 40, 41, 42, 46, 59, 63; **5:**44, 51; **6:**2, 10, 15, 20, 22^2, 23, 28, 29, 33; **8:**8, 12, 14^2, 15, 17, 22, 25, 83, 92, 95; **9:**11^3, 50, 52, 53; **Man 1:**5, 6, 10, 15; **Pm 151:**T^2, 3; **3Mc 2:**15, 22; **3:**22, 29; **5:**11, 13, 41^2; **6:**26; **2Es 1:**27, 33, 34, 37, 40; **2:**3, 9, 13, 34, 41, 46^2, 47; **3:**24, 28; **4:**4, 5, 11, 21^3, 24, 25^2, 26, 27, 29, 34, 36, 37, 39^2, 42, 44, 45, 46, 50^2; **5:**16, 27, 38^2, 42^2, 50^2, 53, 55; **6:**9^2, 10^2, 14, 15, 19, 20^2; **7:**3^2, 4, 6^2, 7^2, 8^2, 9, 10^2, 16^2, 20, 25, 26^2, 31^2, 44, 46^2, 56, 58^4, 59^2, 60, 61, 62, 66, 78, 79, 87, 88, 90, 96^2, 97^2, 98, 99^2, 104, 112, 115, 116, 117, 119, 120, 127, 129, 131, 132, 133, 138; **8:**2^2, 8^2, 9, 10, 18, 21^2, 22^3, 23, 31, 34, 35^2, 49, 52^8, 53^3, 54, 58, 61; **9:**2^2, 5, 16, 17^6, 19, 26, 34^2; **10:**7, 8, 9, 12, 13^2, 14, 28, 31, 36, 40, 43, 44, 45, 55; **12:**5, 10, 11, 15, 16, 17, 19, 22, 25, 30^2, 32, 35^2; **13:**20, 22, 25, 26, 28, 45, 52, 53, 56; **14:**11, 13, 18, 25, 32, 47; **15:**34, 50, 51, 55; **16:**2, 3, 4, 5, 9, 12, 13, 15, 21, 30, 36, 67, 68, 73, 75, 78; **4Mc 1:**1^4, 2^2, 3, 4, 5^2, 6, 7, 10, 12, 13^2, 14^2, 15, 16, 17, 19, 20, 24, 25, 26, 30^3, 31, 33^3; **2:**1, 2^2, 4, 5, 6^2, 7^2, 8, 9^2, 10, 11, 13, 15, 16, 18, 23, 24^2; **3:**1^2, 5; **5:**9, 11, 13, 16, 20, 21; **6:**31, 34; **7:**16, 22; **8:**1; **9:**17, 18, 29; **10:**19; **11:**5, 21, 25, 26, 27; **13:**1, 3, 14, 15, 16; **14:**10, 13, 18; **15:**4; **16:**1, 16, 18, 23; **18:**2, 5, 16, 19

IT (6836)

Ge 1:6, 7, 9, 10, 11^2, 12^2, 15, 18, 21, 24, 25, 28, 30, 31; **2:**3^2, 5, 10, 11, 13, 15^2, 17, 18; **3:**3, 5, 6, 17^2, 18, 19; **4:**7, 12, 17; **6:**6, 14, 15, 16^2, 21^2; **7:**17; **8:**7, 9^3, 12; **9:**5, 7, 13, 16, 23; **10:**9; **11:**9; **12:**13; **13:**17; **15:**6, 8, 17; **16:**2, 14; **17:**11; **18:**6, 7^2, 8, 11, 24^2, 25, 27, 28, 29, 30, 31^2, 32; **19:**9, 13, 20^2, 29; **20:**6, 11, 15, 16; **21:**12, 14^2, 24, 26; **22:**6, 13, 14^2, 20; **23:**9^2, 11^2, 13, 17, 20; **24:**6, 11, 65; **25:**22; **26:**21, 22^2, 33; **27:**4, 5, 10, 20^2, 25^2, 31, 33^3; **28:**11, 12^2, 16, 18^2; **29:**2, 6, 7^2, 19, 25; **30:**15, 28, 30, 31, 32, 34, 35; **31:**29, 32, 37, 39^2, 40, 44, 45, 47^2, 48; **32:**8, 29; **33:**11, 20; **34:**7, 10^2, 21; **35:**7, 8, 14^2, 20, 22; **37:**5, 7, 9, 10, 14, 21, 24, 25, 26, 32, 33^2; **38:**1, 17, 25; **39:**22, 23; **40:**10, 14, 17; **41:**7, 13, 15^3, 16, 24^2, 28, 31, 32, 35, 42, 48, 49^2; **42:**6, 14, 28; **43:**11, 12, 18, 21; **44:**5^2, 7, 9, 10^2, 17; **45:**2^2, 8, 12; **47:**25, 26^2, 27; **48:**14, 17^2; **49:**4, 7^2, 32; **50:**9, 11, 20; **Ex 1:**16^2; **2:**3^3, 5, 6, 9^2, 15, 18; **3:**2, 12, 20; **4:**3^3, 4^3, 6, 7^2, 9, 11, 25, 26; **5:**8, 9, 11; **6:**8, 26, 27; **7:**9^2, 10, 17; **8:**16, 26; **9:**8, 9, 10^2, 18, 24^2; **10:**12; **12:**2, 4^2, 5, 6^2, 7^2, 8, 9, 10, 11^3, 14^2, 22, 27, 34, 39, 43, 44, 45, 46, 47, 48^2; **13:**8, 9, 11, 13, 16; **14:**2, 11, 12, 16, 20^2, 27; **15:**7, 23^2, 25; **16:**5, 6, 15^4, 16, 18, 19, 20^2, 21^2, 24^3, 25^2, 26, 31^3, 32, 33^2, 34; **17:**6, 12^2, 14, 15; **18:**18, 22; **19:**12, 18, 23; **20:**8, 11, 24, 25^3, 26; **21:**13, 26, 29^2, 31, 33^2, 35^2, 36^2; **22:**1^2, 3, 10^2, 12, 13^2, 14, 15, 26, 27, 30^2, 31; **23:**4, 5^2, 11, 15, 33; **24:**6, 7, 8, 16; **25:**9, 10, 11^3, 12^2, 15, 24^2, 25, 26, 31, 32^2, 35^3, 36^2, 37^2, 39; **26:**11, 13, 24, 30, 31^2, 32; **27:**1, 2^3, 3, 4, 5, 7, 8, 16, 21^2; **28:**7^2, 8, 15^2, 16, 17, 25, 28, 32^3, 35, 36, 37^2, 38^2; **29:**7, 12, 14, 16, 18^2, 20, 21, 22, 25, 26^2, 28, 34^2, 36^3, 37, 41, 42, 43; **30:**1, 2^3, 3^2, 4^3, 6, 7^2, 8, 9^2, 10^2, 16^2, 18^2, 21, 25, 26, 32^4, 33^2, 36^3, 37^2, 38; **31:**7, 14^3, 17; **32:**4, 5, 8^2, 12, 13, 18^2, 20^4, 24^3; **33:**1, 7^2, 16; **34:**10, 12, 20; **35:**2, 24^2, 29; **36:**18, 35, 36; **37:**1, 2^2, 3, 11^2, 12, 13, 17, 18^2, 21^3, 22^2, 24, 25^2, 26^2, 27^3; **38:**1^2, 2^3, 7^2, 18^2, 30^2; **39:**4, 5, 9, 10, 18, 21, 23^2, 30, 31^2, 37; **40:**3, 7, 9^3, 11, 19, 20, 23, 27, 29, 30, 35, 37; **Lev 1:**3, 4, 11, 12, 13^2, 15^2, 16, 17^4; **2:**1^2, 2^2, 4, 5, 6^3, 7, 8^2, 10, 15^3, 16^2; **3:**2, 7, 8, 12, 13, 14, 17; **4:**3, 5, 12^2, 14, 17, 19, 21^2, 24^2, 25, 30, 31, 33, 34, 35; **5:**2, 3^2, 4^2, 8, 9, 11^3, 12^3, 15, 16^2, 17, 19; **6:**3, 5^2, 12^3, 13, 14, 15, 16^3, 17^3, 18, 20, 21^3, 22^2, 23, 25, 26^3, 28^2, 29^2, 30; **7:**1, 5, 6^3, 7^2, 9, 12, 14, 15^2, 16^2, 18^5, 19, 24, 25; **8:**7, 10, 11, 15^3, 19, 21, 23^2, 29^2, 31^2, 33; **9:**9, 12, 15^2, 16, 17^2, 24; **10:**1^2, 9, 12^2, 13^2, 16, 17^2, 18, 19; **11:**4^3, 5^3, 6^3, 7^3, 32^3, 33, 34^2, 35, 36, 37, 38^2; **12:**7; **13:**2, 3, 4, 6, 8, 11, 12, 13, 15, 19, 20, 21^3, 22^2, 23, 25^4, 26^2, 27, 28^2, 30^3, 31^2, 32, 34, 37, 39, 42, 47, 49, 51, 52^2, 54, 55^3, 56, 57^2, 58^2, 59; **14:**7, 12, 13, 14, 15, 25, 37, 43, 44^2, 46, 53, 57^2; **15:**3, 23^2; **16:**9, 10^2, 12, 14, 15, 18, 19^3, 21^2, 31^2; **17:**3, 4^2, 9^2, 11^2, 13, 14; **18:**8, 16, 17, 22, 23^3, 25, 28^2; **19:**5^2, 6^2, 7^3, 8, 23^2; **20:**14, 16, 17, 21, 24; **22:**8, 9, 13, 14, 19, 20, 21^2, 23, 27^2, 29^2, 30^2; **23:**3, 11, 13^2, 14, 27, 28, 31, 32, 36, 41^2; **24:**3^2, 5, 18, 21; **25:**5, 10, 12^2, 16, 19, 21, 26, 27, 28^2, 29, 30^2, 44; **26:**16, 32^2, 34, 35^4; **27:**9, 10, 11, 12^2, 13, 14^3, 15^2, 18, 19^2, 20^2, 21^2, 23, 24, 26, 27^4, 28, 33^4; **Nu 1:**50^2, 51^2; **3:**10; **4:**5, 6, 7^2, 8, 9, 10^2, 11, 13, 14^2, 16, 25; **5:**7^2, 13, 15^3, 17, 25, 26; **6:**9, 18, 19; **7:**1, 10, 84, 88, 89; **8:**4; **9:**3^2, 11^2, 12^3, 15, 16^2, 21, 22^3; **10:**29, 36; **11:**1, 8^6, 9, 17^2, 18, 20, 25, 31, 33; **12:**2, 12; **13:**18, 20^2, 23, 27, 30^2, 32; **14:**3, 8, 13, 16, 23, 24; **15:**11, 20, 24, 25, 28, 34, 39; **16:**4, 9, 13^2, 14, 17, 28, 42, 46^3, 47; **17:**8; **18:**6, 10^3, 13, 19, 23, 26, 27, 30, 31^2, 32^2; **19:**3^2, 4, 9, 15, 18^2, 21, 22; **20:**5, 19^2; **21:**8^2, 9, 14, 17, 27, 28; **22:**23, 25^2, 27, 28, 33^2, 34; **23:**19^2, 20, 23, 24^2, 27; **24:**1, 17; **25:**7, 13; **27:**11^2, 13; **28:**6, 8, 15, 24; **29:**1; **30:**5, 7, 8, 11; **31:**23^2, 29^2, 54; **32:**39, 42; **33:**53; **34:**4, 8; **35:**8, 23, 25, 33^2; **36:**3, 6; **Dt 1:**2, 17, 24, 25, 27, 36, 38, 39^2, 41; **2:**10, 19, 20^2; **3:**9, 11, 14, 22, 28; **4:**2, 7, 26, 35, 38; **5:**12, 16, 27, 29, 33; **6:**3, 18; **7:**7, 8, 25^3, 26^3; **8:**18; **9:**2, 4^2, 5, 21^5; **10:**14, 15; **11:**2^2, 7, 12, 31^2; **12:**15, 16, 22^2, 24^2, 25, 28, 32^2; **13:**6, 12, 15^2, 16; **14:**2, 8, 10, 21^2, 24, 25, 28; **15:**2, 3, 8, 17, 18, 20, 21^2, 22, 23; **16:**3^2, 7^2; **17:**4^2, 14^2, 19^2; **18:**12, 22^3; **19:**13; **20:**4, 5^2, 10^2, 11^2, 12^2, 13, 19^2, 20; **21:**1, 7; **22:**2^4, 4^2, 7, 8; **23:**13, 21^2; **24:**1, 3, 13, 19^2, 20, 21; **25:**4; **26:**1^2, 2, 4, 10, 12, 13, 14^3; **27:**6, 15; **28:**21, 30, 31, 38, 51^2, 52^2, 67^2; **29:**8, 18^2, 22, 25, 27; **30:**5, 11, 12^4, 13^4, 14; **31:**6, 7, 8, 9, 13, 19^2, 21, 22, 26^2; **32:**11, 19, 22, 27, 47, 52; **34:**4^2; **Jos 1:**7, 8^2, 15; **2:**5, 11, 21; **3:**3, 4^2; **4:**7; **5:**7; **6:**11, 15, 17, 18, 20, 22, 24; **7:**9, 19, 20, 22; **8:**2, 4, 7, 18, 19, 24, 28^2, 29^2, 31^2; **9:**12^3, 24, 25; **10:**1, 4, 5,

ITS (1757)

26, 30[2], 31, 34, 35; 5:8, 12; 6:5, 6, 15, 27[2]; 7:2, 3; 8:11[2], 17[2], 20, 23; 10:18; 11:22[4], 29, 39, 40, 42; 12:6; 13:20; 14:10, 45; 16:15[2], 18; 17:13, 14[3]; 18:25[2]; 19:26; 22:14, 24, 27, 28; 23:10, 37; 25:6, 7, 10, 19, 22, 27, 29; 26:4, 20, 34[2], 43; 27:10, 15, 16[2], 19, 27[2]; Nu 1:50[2]; 3:25, 26; 4:6, 8, 9[3], 10, 11, 14, 16, 25, 31; 5:26; 7:1[2]; 8:3, 4[2], 8; 9:2, 3[3], 7, 13, 14; 11:7; 12:12; 13:27, 32; 15:24[2]; 16:30, 32; 19:4, 5[4]; 20:8; 21:25, 32; 24:18, 20; 26:10, 54[2]; 28:2, 7, 9, 10, 15, 24, 31; 29:6[2], 11, 16[2], 19, 22[2], 25[2], 28[2], 31[2], 34[2], 38[2]; 32:33, 42; 34:2, 4, 5, 6, 9, 12[2]; 35:8; 36:9; Dt 2:9; 3:12, 17; 4:32; 11:6, 14; 13:15, 16[3]; 14:21; 15:23; 20:6[2], 13, 14, 19; 28:12, 30; 29:23; 32:11[4], 22; 33:16; Jos 3:15; 4:18; 6:2, 26[2]; 8:2[4], 13; 10:1[2], 2, 28, 30[2], 37[2], 39[4]; 11:10, 16; 13:17, 23, 27; 15:4, 12, 45[2], 47[5]; 17:10, 11[6], 16, 18; 18:5, 11, 20[2], 28; 19:1[2], 2, 8, 10[2], 11, 16, 17, 18, 22, 23, 24, 25, 31, 32, 33, 39, 40, 41; 21:12, 13[2], 14[2], 15[2], 16[3], 17[2], 18[2], 21[2], 22[2], 23[2], 24[2], 25[2], 27[2], 28[2], 29[2], 30[2], 31[2], 32[3], 34[2], 35[2], 36[2], 37[2], 38[2], 39[2], 42; 24:5; Jdg 1:18[3], 26, 27[5]; 5:23, 31; 7:15; 8:11; 11:26[2]; 20:33; 1Sa 5:6, 11; 6:2, 8[2], 9; 10:21; 17:35, 51; 19:13, 16; 2Sa 6:17; 20:8; 1Ki 6:3, 38[2]; 7:24, 26[2], 31[4], 35[2], 36[2]; 8:6, 7; 15:22; 16:34[2]; 21:2; 2Ki 2:12; 12:9; 13:14; 14:7; 15:16; 16:9, 10[2]; 17:24, 29; 18:8, 33; 19:23[4]; 22:16, 19; 25:21; 1Ch 2:23; 5:16; 6:55, 56, 57[2], 58[2], 59[2], 60[3], 67[2], 68[2], 69[2], 70[2], 71[2], 72[2], 73[2], 74[2], 75[2], 76[3], 77[2], 78[2], 79[2], 80[2], 81[2]; 7:28[4], 29[4]; 8:12; 12:15; 15:3; 18:1; 21:22, 27; 23:26; 28:11[4], 15[2], 18; 2Ch 3:4, 7[4], 8[2], 11; 4:5[2]; 5:7, 8; 13:11, 19[3]; 16:6; 20:25; 24:11, 13; 28:18[3]; 29:18[2]; 30:3; 34:24, 27, 28; 36:19[2], 21; Ezr 2:68, 70; 3:3, 12; 4:16; 5:15; 6:3[2], 5, 7; 9:9; Ne 1:3; 2:3, 13, 17; 3:1, 3[4], 6[4], 13[3], 14[3], 15[3]; 4:6; 9:36[2], 37; 11:25[3], 27, 28, 30[2], 31; Est 1:22[2]; 3:12[2]; 6:8; 8:9[2]; Job 3:9; 4:16; 5:16, 26; 6:5[2]; 8:15; 9:6[2], 24; 11:9, 17; 14:7, 8[2], 18; 18:4; 24:13[2]; 27:22, 23[2]; 28:6[2], 15, 23, 25; 31:22, 38, 39[2]; 36:33; 37:1, 9; 38:5, 6[2], 9[2], 12, 20[2], 32, 41[2]; 39:6[2], 8, 11, 13, 14, 16[3], 18[2], 19[2], 20, 26, 27, 28, 29, 30; 40:16[4], 17[2], 18[2], 19, 23, 24; 41:1, 2[2], 7[2], 12[3], 13[2], 14[2], 15, 18[2], 19, 20, 21[2], 22, 23, 24, 30; Ps 1:3; 10:9; 19:5, 6[3]; 25:22; 33:17; 34:2; 46:3[2]; 48:3, 12, 13[2]; 50:1; 55:10, 11[2]; 58:4; 65:10[3]; 67:6; 68:13, 31; 69:15; 72:16; 74:6; 75:3[2]; 80:10[2], 11[2], 12[2]; 85:12; 89:9; 102:14[2]; 103:16; 104:5, 17, 19; 107:34, 42; 113:3; 123:4; 130:8; 131:2; 132:15[2], 16[2]; 137:7; 149:2; Pr 1:19; 6:6, 8[2]; 7:23; 8:29; 12:14, 28; 14:10[2], 12; 16:4; 17:12; 18:21; 24:31; 26:2[2], 11, 14, 28; 27:8, 18; Ecc 1:6; 3:11; 6:4; 7:8; 8:6; SS 1:12; 2:13; 3:10[4]; 4:16[2]; 7:7, 8; 8:6, 11; Isa 1:3[2]; 4:4, 5; 5:5[2], 14[2]; 6:13; 8:7[2], 8; 9:3; 10:14, 34; 11:8; 13:9, 10[2], 11, 13, 21, 22[3]; 14:17, 29, 31; 16:14; 19:6, 10, 13, 14, 19; 23:11; 24:1[2], 5, 6, 11, 20; 26:21; 27:3, 10, 11; 28:1, 4, 25[2]; 29:16; 30:14[2], 33; 31:4[2]; 33:8[2], 23; 34:5, 10, 11, 12, 13[2], 15[2], 16; 37:24[4]; 40:16, 22; 41:9; 42:11; 44:11, 19; 45:11; 46:7[2]; 48:19; 51:15; 53:7; 54:16; 57:20; 60:22; 61:11; 65:18, 25; Jer 1:15, 18[2]; 2:7[2], 11; 4:7, 26; 5:1, 24; 6:7, 9; 8:1, 7; 11:16, 19; 14:8; 17:8[2], 27; 18:8; 19:8, 12, 15; 20:5[2]; 21:14; 23:14; 25:9, 18; 26:15; 27:8[2], 11[2]; 29:7[2]; 30:18[2]; 31:23, 24, 35; 33:12; 34:1, 18; 37:7; 46:10; 48:11; 49:1, 2, 17; 50:17, 19[2]; 51:21, 42; 52:21[2], 27; La 2:2, 5[2]; 4:4, 11; Eze 1:23; 3:12; 8:2; 11:6, 18[2]; 13:14; 14:13; 17:4, 6[2], 7[2], 9[4], 12[2], 22, 23; 19:11[3], 12[2], 14[2]; 21:3, 4, 5, 30; 22:2, 3[2], 25, 26, 27, 28; 23:34; 24:5[2], 11[3], 12[2]; 25:9; 26:3, 4[2], 6; 27:9; 28:23[2]; 29:3, 19; 30:4[2], 6, 18[2]; 31:3, 4[2], 5[3], 6[3], 7[3], 8[2], 9, 10[3], 11, 12[3], 13[2], 15[2], 16, 17[2]; 32:7, 12, 13, 16, 20, 22, 23[2], 24[2], 25, 29[2]; 33:28; 34:27; 35:8; 36:5; 37:7; 38:6[2], 8, 13; 40:6, 9, 20, 21[5], 22[4], 24[2], 25[3], 26[2], 29[6], 31[3], 33[6], 34[3], 36[5], 37[3], 38; 41:2, 4, 12, 13, 15, 22[3]; 42:4; 43:11[8], 13[2], 17[2], 20; 44:5, 14; 45:1; 47:10, 11; 48:16, 18; Da 2:5, 6[2], 7, 9, 26, 31[2], 32[2], 33[2], 34, 36, 45; 4:7, 9, 10, 11, 12[3], 14[4], 15, 19, 20, 21, 23; 5:7, 15, 16; 6:10; 7:4, 5[2], 6, 7, 9, 11, 19[2], 20; 8:4, 5, 7[2], 8[2], 14, 21; 9:26; Hos 2:9[2]; 4:19; 9:10; 10:1, 5[3]; Joel 1:6; 2:7, 8, 20[3], 22; Am 1:7, 10, 14; 2:3[2]; 3:4, 9, 14; 7:17; 9:11[2]; Jnh 1:15; Mic 1:11; 2:12; 3:11[3]; 4:5; 7:13; Na 2:7; 3:16; Hab 2:18[2]; 3:10[2], 11; Zep 2:11, 14[2]; 3:2, 3, 4[2]; Hag 1:10; 2:3; Zec 1:21; 2:2[2]; 3:9; 4:3; 5:2[2], 8, 11; 8:5, 12[2]; 9:4[2], 5, 7[4], 13; 12:4, 6; 14:10; Mal 1:11; 4:2; Mt 2:2, 9; 5:13[2]; 6:34; 7:27; 12:33[3]; 13:32; 17:27; 24:29, 32[3]; 26:52; Mk 4:32; 9:50; 11:20; 13:24, 28[3]; 14:8; Lk 6:44; 9:45; 10:8, 10; 11:36; 13:19; 14:34[2]; 19:33; 21:20; Jn 7:7; 15:19; 18:11; Ac 2:24; 8:32; 10:11; 11:5; 12:10; 15:16, 31; 21:3; 28:11; Ro 8:20, 21; 13:3, 14; 1Co 1:17; 9:7[2], 23; 10:26; 13:5; 15:38; 2Co 3:10; 11:3; Gal 5:24; Eph 2:15; 3:10, 15; 4:22; Col 1:25; 2:14, 19; 3:9, 10; 2Ti 3:5; Heb 6:8; 12:2; Jas 1:4, 11[3]; 5:18; 1Pe 1:24; 2Pe 2:22; 1Jn 2:17; Rev 2:5; 5:2, 5, 9; 6:2, 4, 5, 8, 13, 14; 12:16; 13:1[2], 2[2], 3[2], 6, 12[2], 17, 18; 14:9, 11[2], 18; 15:2[2]; 16:2, 10, 12; 19:11, 20[2]; 20:4[2]; 21:15, 16[3], 17, 22, 23[2], 24, 25; 22:2[2]; Tob 5:10[3]; 6:5[2]; 14:15; Jdt 1:3, 4, 9, 14[3]; 8:21; 13:10; 15:5; AdE 1:22; 8:9; 13:2; Wis 2:1, 4; 5:10, 11[5], 12; 13:11, 14; 14:3; 16:23; 17:11, 20; 18:14, 23; 19:6, 20[2]; Sir 9:7; 10:2, 3, 12; 13:15; 16:30; 18:32; 19:17; 21:2, 10; 22:14, 19; 23:20; 25:24; 27:6; 28:19[3], 20[2], 21, 22, 23; 35:8, 21; 38:5, 28; 39:21, 33, 34; 42:16; 43:3, 4, 5, 7, 8, 11, 12, 17, 18, 24; 46:1; 47:23; 48:17; 49:6; LtJ 6:15, 59[2]; Bel 1:22; 1Mc 1:21, 28, 31[2]; 5:8, 28, 65[3]; 6:1, 2, 12, 37; 9:11; 10:31[3], 43, 75, 89; 11:4, 29, 61; 12:36; 13:11, 48, 50; 14:7, 8, 26, 36, 42; 15:2, 32, 39; 2Mc 1:14; 2:29[2]; 3:25[2]; 4:20; 5:20[2]; 9:18; 12:13; 13:15, 25; 1Es 1:56, 58[2]; 2:18, 24; 4:34[2], 39, 40; 5:44, 46, 50; 6:19, 25[2], 27; 3Mc 1:9[2]; 3:9, 12; 4:15; 5:5, 41; 6:31; 2Es 3:8, 9; 4:19, 21, 26; 5:5, 9, 11, 23, 47; 6:17; 7:44; 9:37; 10:23; 11:2, 3, 4, 5, 7[2], 8[2], 10[2], 11, 13[2], 14, 32, 34; 12:17, 18, 19, 21[2], 23, 24, 35; 13:2; 14:10, 11, 12, 17, 20, 39, 40; 15:11, 12, 40, 44; 16:12[2], 23, 32[3], 57[2], 77; 4Mc 1:6; 3:1; 4:19; 14:6; 17:15

ITSELF (96)

Ge 32:16; Ex 7:18; 25:34; 37:20; Lev 6:9; 8:17; 16:22; 17:15; 25:12; Nu 23:9, 24; 25:3; Dt 2:36; 14:21; 22:9; Jos 2:15; 22:22; Jdg 18:1; 2Ki 19:29; Ezr 9:2; Job 41:25, 30; Pr 20:2; 23:5; Ecc 12:5; Isa 7:2; 10:15[2]; 37:30; 60:20; Eze 4:14; 5:13; 17:14; 22:3[2]; 29:15; 44:31; Hos 10:6; Zep 2:15; Zec 9:3; 12:12[3], 13[2], 14; Mt 12:25[2], 45; Mk 3:24, 25; 4:28; Lk 11:17, 26; 14:26; Jn 15:4; 20:7; 21:25; Ac 3:16; 28:3; Ro 8:21; 14:14; 1Co 6:18; 11:14; 2Co 1:8; Eph 4:8, 16; Heb 3:3; 9:19, 24; Jas 2:17; 3:6; 3Jn 1:12; Rev 6:14; Jdt 8:6; Wis 2:11; 13:16; 16:24; Sir Pr:T; 23:16; 30:22; 34:3; 37:2; 43:8; LtJ 6:15, 27[2]; 2Mc 2:32; 5:20; 2Es 5:9; 7:63; 10:27; 11:18, 30; 4Mc 8:25; 9:4

MAY (1702)

Ge 2:16; 3:2; 4:14; 8:17; 9:27; 12:13[2]; 16:2, 5[2]; 18:5[2], 19[2]; 19:5, 32, 34; 21:30; 23:4, 9, 13; 24:5, 14, 49, 55, 56, 60[2]; 27:4, 7, 9, 10, 19, 21, 25, 28, 29, 31; 28:3[2], 4[2]; 29:21; 30:3[2], 15, 24, 25; 31:37, 53; 32:5, 11, 20; 35:3; 38:16; 41:36; 42:2, 16, 34, 37; 43:8, 14[2], 18; 44:21; 45:18[2]; 46:34; 47:19[2], 25; 48:9; 49:1, 6[2], 26; 50:5; Ex 3:18; 4:5, 8, 23; 5:1; 7:16, 19; 8:1, 9, 10, 16, 20, 22, 29; 9:1, 13, 14, 22, 29; 10:1, 2[2], 3, 7, 11, 12, 21, 24; 11:7, 9; 12:5, 16, 44, 45, 48; 13:9, 17; 14:16, 26; 16:32; 17:6; 19:9, 13; 20:12, 26; 21:13; 22:27; 23:11[2], 12[2]; 24:14; 25:8; 26:6, 11; 27:20; 28:7, 28, 32, 35, 38, 41; 29:1; 30:12, 20, 21, 29, 30; 31:6, 13; 32:10[2]; 33:13; 40:13, 15; Lev 2:12; 6:3, 7; 7:11, 19, 24, 25, 30; 9:6; 10:6, 9, 14, 17; 11:2, 3, 9[2], 21, 22, 39, 47[2]; 16:10, 13, 26, 28; 17:5[2], 7, 13; 19:25[2]; 20:14, 22; 21:3, 15, 17, 22, 23; 22:2, 4, 5[3], 7, 9, 11[2], 13, 23, 29, 32; 23:11, 43; 24:2; 25:6, 18, 20, 29, 31, 33, 34, 44[2], 45[2], 46[2], 48, 49[3]; 27:9[2], 11, 28; Nu 1:53; 3:6; 4:19; 5:8, 22; 6:7, 20; 7:5; 8:11, 15, 19, 26; 9:8; 10:9; 11:21; 12:14; 16:21, 45; 17:10; 18:2, 5, 10, 11, 13, 31; 19:7; 22:19[2]; 23:13, 27; 25:4; 27:17, 20; 30:13[2]; 31:3, 24; 32:22; 35:11, 12, 15, 28; 36:8; Dt 1:11; 2:6[2], 28[2]; 3:20; 4:1, 10[2], 40; 5:14, 16[2], 24[2], 31, 33[3]; 6:2[2], 3[2], 18[2]; 8:1, 9[2], 18; 9:3, 14; 10:11; 11:8, 9, 21; 12:15[2], 17, 20, 21, 22[2], 25, 27, 28; 13:17; 14:4, 6, 9[2], 11, 20, 21[2], 23, 25, 29[2]; 15:3, 8, 22; 16:3, 7, 20; 17:15[2], 19, 20; 18:1, 6, 7, 21; 19:5, 10, 13, 15; 20:14[2], 18, 19, 20[2]; 21:13; 22:3, 7[2], 27; 23:8, 11, 14, 20[3], 24, 25; 24:13, 16, 19; 25:3, 6, 15; 26:12; 29:6, 9, 13[2], 18[2]; 30:6, 12, 13, 19, 20; 31:12, 13, 14, 19, 28; 32:2, 46, 47, 52; 33:6, 24[2]; Jos 1:7, 8, 17; 2:16[2]; 3:4, 7; 4:6, 24[2]; 8:2; 9:20; 14:12; 18:4; 20:3, 6; 22:23, 27; 23:7; Jdg 1:3; 5:31; 6:30; 9:7, 33; 11:6, 8, 37; 13:14, 17; 15:12; 16:5[2], 26, 28; 17:2; 18:5; 19:5, 22; 20:13; 21:17; Ru 1:8, 9, 11, 17; 2:2, 12[2], 13; 3:1, 10; 4:4, 10, 11[2], 12, 14; 1Sa 1:22, 23; 2:20, 36; 3:17; 4:3; 5:11; 6:20; 7:8; 8:20[2]; 9:26, 27; 11:3, 10, 12; 12:7, 17, 19; 14:6; 15:13, 25, 30; 17:10, 37, 46, 47; 18:21[2], 25; 19:15; 20:5, 13[2], 16; 23:21; 24:11, 12[2], 15[2], 19; 26:19[2], 24[2]; 27:5; 28:7, 22; 29:4[2]; 30:22; 31:4; 2Sa 2:5, 6; 3:9[2], 21[2], 29[2], 35; 7:10, 19, 21, 29[2]; 9:1, 3, 10; 10:12; 11:15; 12:18, 22[2]; 13:5, 6, 10; 14:7, 11[2], 15, 32; 15:20, 21; 16:11, 12; 17:12; 18:20, 22, 23, 32; 19:13, 19[2], 26, 37; 21:3; 24:2, 3, 21, 23; 1Ki 1:2, 12, 31, 36, 37, 47; 2:3, 14, 23; 8:29[2], 40, 43[2], 50, 57, 59, 60; 11:21, 36; 12:26; 13:6, 18; 15:19; 17:10, 12[2]; 18:5, 37; 19:2; 20:34; 21:2; 22:7, 8, 20; 2Ki 2:9, 16; 3:11; 4:13, 14, 22; 5:6, 8, 18[2]; 6:17, 20, 22, 31; 9:7; 18:32; 19:4, 19; 20:7; 1Ch 10:4; 12:17; 13:2; 15:12; 16:35; 17:9, 27[2]; 19:13; 21:2, 3, 10, 22[2]; 22:11, 12[2], 19; 28:8; 29:19[2]; 2Ch 1:11; 2:14; 6:6, 20[2], 21, 23, 25, 27, 30, 31, 33[3]; 7:16; 9:8; 12:8; 13:11; 16:3; 18:6, 7, 19; 19:10[2], 11; 23:6; 24:22; 28:23; 29:10; 30:6, 8; 36:23; Ezr 1:3; 4:12, 13, 15; 5:8; 6:10, 12; 7:13, 18, 20, 25; 9:8, 12; Ne 2:3, 5, 7, 17; 4:22[2]; 5:2, 13[2]; Est 1:19; 3:9; 4:11; 5:5; 8:8; Job 1:5; 3:4, 9; 10:20; 13:13; 14:6; 19:29; 21:19; 27:7[2], 17; 32:13, 20; 33:17, 30; 34:22; 37:7; 38:20[2], 34, 35; 39:15[2]; 40:8; Ps 3:8; 5:11; 9:14; 10:9, 14, 18; 12:3; 15:1[2]; 17:14[3]; 20:2, 3, 4, 5[2]; 22:26; 24:7, 9; 25:21; 29:11[2]; 30:5, 12; 36:7; 39:1, 13; 40:16[2]; 41:10; 48:13; 50:4; 56:13; 58:9; 59:11; 60:5; 61:6, 7; 67:1, 2, 7; 68:23[2]; 69:25, 27; 72:2, 3, 4, 5, 6, 7, 8, 9, 10[2], 11, 15[3], 16[4], 17[3], 19; 73:26; 77:1; 80:3, 7, 16, 19; 83:16; 84:3; 85:6, 9; 86:11, 17; 90:12, 14; 91:7; 101:6; 102:18, 21; 104:9, 31[2], 34; 106:5[3], 47; 108:6; 109:8[2], 9, 10[2], 11[2], 12, 13[2], 14, 15, 17, 18, 19, 20, 28, 29[2]; 115:14, 15; 118:19; 119:5, 11, 17, 18, 34, 73, 77, 79, 80[2], 88, 115, 116, 117, 125, 134, 144, 146, 148, 175; 120:1; 122:6; 126:5; 128:5, 6; 129:5; 130:4; 134:3; 142:7; 144:12, 13[2], 14[2]; Pr 4:1, 10; 5:2[2], 19[2]; 7:5; 8:11; 13:14, 23; 14:27; 16:2; 19:20, 21, 27; 22:19, 21, 25; 25:15; 27:1, 11; 28:21; Ecc 5:15; 6:3; 7:14, 21; 8:17; 10:20; 11:2; SS 4:16; 6:1, 13; 7:8; 8:12; Isa 2:3[2]; 5:19[2]; 6:10; 10:2[2]; 14:20; 23:16; 26:2; 28:13; 30:8, 20; 37:4, 20; 38:21; 41:20[2], 22[2], 23[2]; 43:10, 26; 45:3, 6, 8; 47:12[2]; 48:9; 49:6, 15; 50:4; 51:23; 54:10; 55:3, 6, 7; 66:5, 11[2]; Jer 4:14; 5:1; 6:10, 27; 7:23; 9:12, 18; 11:5; 18:7, 9, 21, 22; 26:3[2]; 27:18; 28:6[2], 14; 29:6, 26; 32:14, 39, 40; 35:7; 36:3[3], 7; 39:12; 42:5, 6; 43:3; 44:29; 45:5; 50:34, 36[2], 37[2], 38; 51:8, 35[2]; La 2:13; 3:29; 5:21; Eze 4:15; 7:22; 11:20; 12:6, 12, 16; 14:5, 11, 15; 16:37, 54, 63; 17:23; 20:20[2]; 23:25, 48; 24:8, 11; 30:21; 31:14[2]; 34:10, 25; 36:30; 37:9, 17, 19; 38:16; 40:46; 43:11; 44:3, 5, 19, 25, 30; 46:17; Da 2:30[2]; 4:1, 17, 19, 27[2]; 6:16, 25; 11:35; Hos 6:2; 10:12; 13:10, 15; Am 5:14, 15; 8:5[2]; 9:12; Jnh 1:7, 11; 3:9[2]; Mic 4:2[2]; 6:5; Hab 2:2; 3:2; Zep 2:3; 3:9; Hag 1:8; Zec 11:1, 17; 12:7; 13:7; 14:15, 21; Mal 1:4, 7, 9, 12; 2:4, 12; 3:10; Mt 2:8; 5:16, 25, 45; 6:2, 4, 5, 18; 7:1; 9:6; 13:24; 14:15; 18:16, 23; 21:19; 22:2; 23:26, 35; 24:20; 26:5, 41, 56; 27:64; Mk 1:38; 2:10; 4:12[3]; 5:23; 6:36; 7:29; 11:14, 25; 13:18, 36; 14:2, 14, 38; 15:32; Lk 1:4; 5:24; 8:10[2], 12, 16; 9:12; 11:33, 50; 12:36, 58; 14:9, 10, 12, 23; 16:4, 9, 28; 17:8; 18:5; 20:14; 21:36; 22:8, 11, 30, 32, 40, 46; Jn 3:15, 16[2], 20, 21; 4:15, 36; 5:23, 34; 6:12, 30, 40, 50; 7:3, 23; 9:36, 39[2]; 10:10, 38; 11:4, 15, 16, 42; 12:35, 36; 13:19; 14:3, 13, 29, 31; 15:11[2], 17; 16:4, 24, 33; 17:1, 3, 11, 13, 19, 21[3], 22, 23[2], 24, 26; 19:35; 20:31[2]; Ac 2:29, 38; 3:19, 20[2]; 5:39; 6:3; 8:19, 20, 22, 24, 34; 9:17; 10:29; 13:47; 15:17; 17:19; 19:27; 20:24; 21:37; 25:26; 26:18[2]; Ro 1:10, 11, 12, 13; 3:4, 8, 19[2]; 4:16; 6:1; 7:4[2]; 8:17; 9:17; 10:1, 4; 11:25, 31, 32; 12:2; 15:5, 6, 13[2], 16, 31[2], 32; 16:2[2]; 1Co 1:8; 2:12; 3:18; 4:6; 5:5, 7; 7:5, 17, 34; 8:5, 13; 9:15, 18, 23, 24; 10:13, 33; 11:32; 12:25[2]; 13:3; 14:1, 5, 17, 31; 15:28; 16:6, 11; 2Co 1:4; 2:7, 11; 4:7, 10, 11, 15; 5:4, 10, 12; 6:3; 8:11, 14[2]; 9:3[2], 5, 8; 10:15, 16; 11:6, 16; 12:6, 9, 20[3], 21[2]; 13:7[4], 9, 10; Gal 4:11, 17; 6:12, 13, 14, 18; Eph 1:17, 18; 2:9; 3:13, 16[2], 17, 18, 19; 4:29; 5:27; 6:3[2], 11, 13, 19, 20, 21; Php 1:9, 10, 26; 2:15, 19, 28[2]; 3:8, 11, 21; Col 1:9, 10, 11[2], 28; 2:2, 4; 3:21; 4:3, 4, 6, 8[2], 12; 1Th 2:16; 3:10, 11, 12, 13[2]; 4:12, 13; 5:10, 23[2]; 2Th 1:12; 2:6, 14, 16; 3:1, 2, 5, 14, 16; 1Ti 1:3, 18, 20; 2:2; 3:6, 7, 15; 4:15; 5:7, 20; 6:1, 19; 2Ti 1:4, 16, 18; 2:10, 25, 26; 3:17; 4:16; Tit 1:9, 13; 2:4, 5, 10; 3:8, 14; Phm 1:6[2]; Heb 3:12, 13; 4:11, 16; 6:12; 9:15; 10:36; 12:3, 10, 13, 27; 13:19, 20, 21; Jas 1:4; 5:9, 12, 16; 1Pe 1:2, 7; 2:2, 9, 12; 3:1, 7, 16; 4:11, 13; 5:6; 2Pe 1:2, 4[2], 15; 1Jn 1:3, 4; 2:1, 3, 5, 28, 29; 4:17; 5:13, 20; 2Jn 1:8, 12; 3Jn 1:2[2], 8; Jude 1:2; Rev 2:10; 3:11, 18[2]; 11:6; 22:14; Tob 2:2; 3:6, 9, 10; 4:19[2]; 5:9, 17[2]; 6:13, 15, 18; 7:11, 12; 8:7[2]; 9:6; 10:7, 11, 12[3]; 11:14; 13:6, 10[2]; Jdt 5:5; 8:31, 33, 35; 10:8[3], 9; 11:11, 18; 13:20[2]; 14:5; 15:10; AdE 1:19[2]; 5:5; 13:5, 7, 17; 14:13; 16:20, 23[2]; Wis 2:19; 6:6, 9, 21; 7:15; 9:10[2]; 11:23; 12:2, 22[2]; 13:11, 16; 14:4; 19:18; Sir Pr:T; 1:30; 2:3, 7; 3:1, 8; 5:13; 6:2; 7:6[2], 32; 8:1, 4, 10, 11, 19; 9:5, 6, 9[2], 13; 11:33; 12:12[2], 16; 13:10; 18:32; 19:9, 13, 14, 16; 20:9[2], 21, 22; 22:13, 23[2], 27[2]; 23:3[4], 12, 14; 25:19; 27:21; 30:1, 13; 31:9; 32:2; 33:28; 36:11; 37:8, 15, 19, 20; 38:13, 18; 42:9[2], 10[3], 11, 17, 18; 45:26[3]; 46:11, 12[2]; 49:10; 50:23[2], 24[2]; 51:29[2]; Bar 1:11; 2:15; 3:14; 5:7; LtJ 6:18, 29, 40; Aza 1:16, 17[2]; 1Mc 3:60; 8:20, 23[2], 25, 27, 30; 9:8, 46; 10:24, 32, 38, 56; 11:31; 12:10; 14:23; 15:3, 4, 21; 16:3; 2Mc 1:2[2], 3, 4[2], 5[2], 18; 6:15; 7:29; 11:26, 31, 36, 37; 14:9; 15:24; 1Es 2:5, 6, 21; 4:11, 31; 6:30, 31, 33; 8:10, 13, 18, 21, 85; Man 1:7; 3Mc 3:23; 2Es 1:5, 24; 2:6[2], 13[2], 29, 41; 3:31, 36; 4:14[2], 15; 5:19; 7:82, 101, 129; 8:6[3], 11; 9:41; 10:24[2], 34; 11:46[2]; 12:6, 8, 39; 13:47; 14:22[2]; 16:29, 30; 4Mc 1:6; 5:27, 38; 6:17; 9:16, 24; 10:16

ME (4470)

Ge 3:12[2], 13; 4:10, 14[3], 23[2], 25; 7:1; 9:9, 12, 13, 15, 17; 12:12, 13, 18[2]; 13:8, 9; 14:21, 24; 15:2, 3, 9; 16:2, 5[3]; 17:1, 2, 4, 7, 10, 11; 18:5, 21, 27, 31; 19:8, 19[2], 20; 20:5, 6, 9[2], 11, 13[3]; 21:6[2], 16, 23[3], 26, 30; 22:12; 23:4, 8[2], 9[2], 11, 13[2], 15[2]; 24:5, 7[3], 12, 17, 23, 27[2], 30, 37, 39, 40, 43, 44, 45, 48, 49[2], 54, 56[2]; 25:30, 31, 32, 33; 26:7, 27[3]; 27:3, 4[2], 7[2], 9, 12, 13[2], 19[2], 20, 25, 26, 31, 33, 34[2], 36[2], 38[2], 46; 28:20[3], 22; 29:15[2], 19, 21, 25[2], 27, 32, 33, 34; 30:1, 6[2], 13, 14, 16, 18, 20[2], 24, 25, 26[2], 27[2], 29, 31[2], 32, 33[2]; 31:5[2], 7[2], 9, 11, 13, 26, 27[2], 28, 29, 31, 35, 36, 40[2], 42, 44, 48, 49, 50, 51, 52; 32:9, 11, 16, 20[2], 26[2], 29; 33:10, 11, 13, 14, 15[3]; 34:4, 11[2], 12[2], 30[4]; 35:3[2]; 37:9, 14, 16; 38:16[3], 17, 25; 39:7, 8, 9, 12, 14[2], 15[2], 17[2], 18, 19; 40:8, 9, 14[4], 15; 41:10, 24, 51, 52; 42:20, 33, 34, 36; 43:6, 8, 9[2], 14, 16, 29; 44:17, 21, 27, 28, 29, 34; 45:1, 4, 5[2], 7, 8[2], 9[2], 10, 18; 46:31; 47:16, 29[2], 30[2], 31; 48:3[2], 4, 9[2], 11, 16; 49:29; 50:5[3], 20; Ex 2:9, 14; 3:9, 13[2], 14, 15, 16; 4:1[2], 18, 23, 25; 5:1, 22; 6:12[2], 30; 7:16[2]; 8:1, 8, 9, 20, 28; 9:1, 13, 14; 10:3[2], 17, 28; 11:8[2]; 12:32; 13:2, 8; 14:15; 17:2, 4; 18:4, 15, 16, 19; 19:6; 20:3, 5, 6, 23, 24, 25; 22:23, 27, 29, 30, 31; 23:14, 15, 33; 24:12; 25:2[2], 8, 30; 28:1, 4, 41; 29:1, 44; 30:30; 31:13, 17; 32:2, 10, 23, 24, 26, 32, 33; 33:12[3], 13, 18, 20, 21; 34:2, 20; 40:13, 15; Lev 10:3, 19; 14:35; 20:26; 22:2; 25:23, 55; 26:14, 18, 21[2], 23[2], 27[2], 40[2]; Nu 3:41; 8:16; 11:11, 12, 13, 14, 15[3], 16; 14:11[2], 22, 23, 24, 27[2], 29, 35; 16:28, 29; 17:10; 18:8, 9; 20:12; 21:22; 22:5, 6, 8, 10, 11, 13, 16, 17[2], 18, 19, 28, 29, 32, 33[3], 34, 37; 23:1[2], 3[2], 7[2], 10, 11, 13[2], 18, 27, 29[2]; 24:12, 13, 14; 27:14; 28:2; 32:11; Dt 1:14, 17, 22, 23, 37, 41, 42; 2:1, 2, 9, 17, 27, 28[3], 29, 31; 3:2, 25, 26[4]; 4:5, 10[3], 14, 21; 5:7, 9, 10, 22, 23, 28[2], 29, 31; 6:1; 7:4; 8:17; 9:4, 10, 11, 12, 13, 14, 19; 10:1[2], 4, 5, 10, 11; 17:14[2]; 18:15, 17; 25:7; 26:10, 13, 14; 28:20; 31:2, 16, 19, 20, 28; 32:21[2], 34, 39, 41, 51; Jos 2:4, 12[2]; 7:19[2]; 8:5; 10:4, 22; 14:6, 7, 8, 10, 11, 12[2]; 15:19[3]; 17:14; 18:4, 6, 8; 22:2; 24:15; Jdg 1:3[2], 7, 15[3]; 3:28; 4:8[2], 18, 19; 6:17[2], 22, 39[3]; 7:2[3], 17, 18; 8:15, 24[2]; 9:7, 15, 48, 54[2]; 10:12, 13; 11:7[3], 9[2], 12[2], 27[2], 31[2], 35[2], 36, 37[2]; 12:2, 3[3], 5; 13:6[2], 7, 10[2], 16; 14:2, 3[2], 12[2], 13[2], 16[3]; 15:11, 12[2]; 16:6, 7, 10[3], 11, 13[3], 15[3], 17, 18, 26, 28[2], 30; 17:10[2], 13; 18:4[2], 24; 19:18, 19, 24; 20:5[2]; Ru 1:8, 11, 12, 13[2], 16, 17[2], 20[3], 21[4]; 2:2, 7, 10, 11, 13, 21; 3:5, 17; 4:4; 1Sa 1:11, 27; 2:28, 29, 30[4], 36; 3:5, 6, 8, 17[2]; 8:7, 8[2]; 9:8, 16, 18, 19[2], 21; 10:2, 8, 15; 12:1, 3[2], 12, 23[2]; 13:9, 11, 12; 14:12, 33, 41, 42, 43, 44; 15:1, 11, 16, 20, 25, 30[2], 32; 16:2, 3, 5, 17[2], 19; 17:8, 9[2], 10, 35, 37[2], 43, 44, 45; 18:8, 17, 21; 19:15, 17[3]; 20:2[2], 3[2], 5, 6[2], 8[3], 10, 14, 23, 28, 29[3], 31, 42; 21:2[2], 3, 8, 9, 14; 22:3, 8[5], 13[2], 17, 23[2]; 23:12, 21, 23; 24:10, 11, 12[2], 15[2], 17, 18[3], 19, 21[2]; 25:19, 21, 24, 32, 33, 34[2], 39; 26:6, 8, 19[2], 24; 27:1[2], 5; 28:1, 7, 8[2], 11, 12, 15[6], 16, 17, 19, 21, 22; 29:3[2], 6[3], 10; 30:7, 13, 15[4]; 31:4[3]; 2Sa 1:4, 7[2], 8, 9[4], 26[2]; 2:7, 22; 3:8, 12, 13, 14, 21, 35, 39; 4:10; 5:20; 6:21[2]; 7:5, 7, 14, 16, 18; 10:2, 11[2]; 11:6; 12:10, 22, 23; 13:4, 5, 9, 11, 12, 13[2], 16[2]; 14:9, 10, 15, 16, 17, 18, 19, 32[4]; 15:4, 7, 8, 25[2], 26, 28, 33[2], 34, 36; 16:3, 4, 9, 12[2]; 17:1; 18:19, 22; 19:13, 19, 22, 25, 26[2], 33, 36, 38[2]; 20:4, 20; 22:3, 5[2], 6[2], 17[2], 18[3], 19, 20[3], 21[2], 23, 25, 33, 34, 36[2], 37, 40[2], 41[2], 44[3], 45[3], 48[2], 49[3]; 23:2, 3, 5, 15; 24:13, 14, 17, 24; 1Ki 1:12, 13, 17, 24, 26, 28, 30, 32, 48, 51; 2:4[2], 5, 7, 8[2], 15, 16, 17, 20, 23, 24[3], 30, 31, 42; 3:20, 24; 5:4, 6, 8; 8:25[3]; 9:3, 4, 6, 13; 10:7; 11:21, 22[2], 33, 36; 12:5, 6, 9, 12, 24, 27; 13:6[2], 7, 8, 13, 15, 17, 18, 27, 31; 14:2, 8, 9[2]; 15:19[2]; 16:2; 17:10, 11, 13[2], 18[2], 19; 18:9, 12, 14, 19, 30, 37[2]; 19:2, 20; 20:5, 7, 10[2], 32, 35, 36, 37, 39; 21:2, 6, 20, 22, 29[2]; 22:4, 8, 14, 16, 18, 24, 28, 34; 2Ki 2:2, 4, 6, 9[2], 10, 20; 3:7[2], 15; 4:2, 6, 22, 24, 27[2], 28; 5:7[2], 8, 11, 22[2]; 6:11, 19, 28, 31; 8:4, 9, 10, 13, 14; 9:12, 18, 19; 10:6[2], 15, 16, 19; 16:7[2], 15; 18:14[2], 20, 22, 25, 27, 31[2]; 19:6, 20, 27, 28; 20:8; 21:15; 22:10, 13, 15, 17[2], 19; 1Ch 4:10[3]; 10:4[2]; 11:17; 12:17[3]; 17:4, 6, 12, 13, 16, 17; 19:2, 12[2]; 21:2, 12, 13[2], 17, 22[2], 24; 22:8, 10; 28:2, 3, 4[2], 5, 6[2], 19; 2Ch 1:8, 9, 10; 2:7[2], 8, 9; 6:16[2]; 7:17; 9:6; 10:5, 6, 9, 12; 11:4; 12:5, 8; 13:4; 15:2; 16:3[2]; 18:3, 7, 15, 17, 23, 27, 33; 20:20; 28:11, 23; 29:5; 34:18, 21, 23, 25[2], 27[2]; 35:21[2], 23; 36:23[2]; Ezr 1:2[2]; 4:18; 7:28[3]; 8:1;

9:1, 4; **Ne 1:**9; **2:**2, 4, 5, 6[2], 7[2], 8[3], 9, 12, 18[2]; **4:**18, 23; **5:**15, 18; **6:**2[2], 4, 5, 11[2], 12, 13[4], 14, 19; **12:**40; **13:**14, 22, 28, 31; **Est 5:**13; **6:**6; **7:**3; **Job 2:**3; **3:**12[2], 25[2]; **4:**12, 14; **5:**8; **6:**4[2], 7, 9[2], 13[2], 21, 22[2], 23[2], 24[2], 28; **7:**3, 8[3], 12, 13, 14[2], 16, 19[2], 20, 21; **9:**11, 16, 17, 18[2], 20[2], 28, 31[2], 34[2]; **10:**2[3], 8[2], 9[2], 10[2], 11[2], 12, 14[2], 15, 16[2], 17[3], 18[2], 20; **12:**4; **13:**13[2], 15, 19, 20, 21[2], 22[2], 23, 24, 26[2]; **14:**3, 13[4]; **15:**17; **16:**6, 7, 8[3], 9[4], 10[3], 11[2], 12[4], 13, 14[2], 19, 20; **17:**1, 2, 3[2], 6; **19:**2[2], 3[2], 4, 5[2], 6[2], 9, 10, 11[2], 12, 13[2], 14, 15[2], 16, 18[2], 19[2], 21[3], 22, 27; **20:**2[2], 3[2]; **21:**3, 4, 5, 16, 27, 34; **22:**18; **23:**5[2], 6[2], 10, 14, 16; **24:**15, 25; **27:**3, 5[2], 6; **28:**14[2]; **29:**2, 5[2], 6, 8, 11, 13, 14, 20, 21, 23; **30:**1, 9, 10[3], 11, 12, 15, 16[2], 17, 18, 19, 20[2], 21[2], 22[3], 23, 27, 30; **31:**6, 8[2], 13, 15, 20, 29, 34, 35[2], 36, 38; **32:**10[2], 14, 18[2], 22; **33:**4[2], 5[2], 7, 9, 10[2], 27, 31, 32, 33; **34:**2, 10, 32, 34[2]; **36:**2; **38:**3, 4; **40:**7, 8[2]; **42:**3, 4, 7, 8; **Ps 2:**7, 8; **3:**1, 2, 3, 4, 5, 6, 7; **4:**1[3], 8; **5:**8[2]; **6:**1[2], 2[2], 4, 8; **7:**1[2], 2[2], 5, 8[2]; **9:**13[3]; **11:**1; **13:**1[2], 2, 3, 6; **16:**1, 6, 7[2], 8, 10, 11; **17:**3[3], 6[2], 8[2], 9[2], 11[3], 15; **18:**4[2], 5[2], 16[2], 17[3], 18, 19[3], 20[2], 22[2], 24, 32, 33, 35[3], 36[2], 39[2], 40[2], 43[3], 44[3], 47[2], 48[3]; **19:**12, 13; **22:**1[2], 7[3], 9[2], 10, 11, 12[2], 13, 15, 16[2], 17, 21[2], 24; **23:**2[2], 3, 4[2], 5, 6; **25:**2[2], 4[2], 5[2], 7, 16[2], 17, 19, 20[2], 21; **26:**1, 2[2], 9, 11[3]; **27:**2, 3[2], 5[3], 6, 7[2], 9[3], 10[2], 11[2], 12[2]; **28:**1[2], 3; **30:**1[2], 2, 3, 6, 7, 10, 11; **31:**1[2], 2[4], 3[2], 4[2], 5, 8, 9, 11[2], 13, 15, 16, 17, 21; **32:**4, 7[3]; **34:**3, 4[2], 11; **35:**1[2], 2, 4, 7, 11, 12, 13, 15[2], 16, 17, 19[2], 21, 22, 24[2], 26; **36:**11[2]; **38:**1[2], 2[2], 4, 10[2], 12, 16[2], 17, 19, 20, 21[2], 22; **39:**3, 4[2], 8[2], 10, 13; **40:**1, 2, 6, 7, 11[2], 12[3], 13[2], 15, 17[2]; **41:**4[3], 6, 7[3], 8, 9, 10[2], 11[2], 12[2]; **42:**3, 5, 6, 7, 8, 9[2], 10[2], 11; **43:**1[2], 2, 3[2], 5; **44:**6, 15; **49:**5, 15; **50:**5[2], 8, 15[2], 23; **51:**1, 2[2], 3, 5, 6, 7[2], 8, 10[2], 11[2], 12[2], 14; **54:**1[2], 3, 7; **55:**2[2], 3[2], 4[2], 5[2], 12[2], 16, 18[2], 20; **56:**1[3], 2[2], 4, 5, 9, 11; **57:**1[2], 2, 3[2]; **59:**1[3], 2[2], 3, 10[2], 16, 17; **60:**9[2]; **61:**2, 4, 5; **63:**8; **64:**2; **66:**16, 20; **69:**1, 2, 4[3], 6[2], 9[2], 10, 12, 13[2], 14[2], 15[3], 16[2], 17, 18[3], 21[2], 29; **70:**1[2], 2, 5; **71:**1, 2[4], 3[2], 4, 6, 9[2], 10, 12[2], 13, 17, 18, 20[3], 21, 24; **73:**2, 16, 24[2], 28; **77:**1; **81:**8, 11, 13; **85:**8; **86:**1, 3, 7, 11[2], 13, 14, 16[2], 17[4]; **87:**4; **88:**6, 7[2], 8[2], 14[2], 16[2], 17[2], 18; **89:**26, 36; **91:**14, 15; **92:**4, 10; **94:**16[2], 18; **95:**9[2]; **101:**3, 4, 6[2]; **102:**2[3], 8[2], 10[2], 24; **103:**1; **106:**4[2]; **108:**6, 10[2]; **109:**2[2], 3[2], 4, 5, 21, 22, 25, 26[2]; **116:**2, 3[2], 6, 12; **118:**5[2], 6, 7[2], 10, 11[2], 12, 13, 18[2], 19, 21; **119:**8, 10, 12, 19, 22, 23, 25, 26[2], 27, 28, 29[2], 30, 31, 33, 34, 35, 37, 40, 41, 42, 49, 50, 51, 53, 56, 58, 61, 64, 66, 68, 69, 71, 72, 73[2], 74, 75, 77, 78[2], 79, 82, 84, 85, 86, 87, 93, 94, 95, 98[2], 102, 107, 108, 110, 115, 116[2], 117, 121, 122, 124, 125, 132[2], 133, 134, 135, 139, 143, 144, 145, 146, 150, 153, 154[2], 156, 161, 169, 170, 171, 173, 175[2]; **120:**1, 2, 5; **122:**1; **129:**1, 2[2]; **131:**1, 2; **138:**3, 7[2], 8; **139:**1[2], 5[2], 6, 10[2], 11[2], 13, 16, 17, 19, 23[2], 24[2]; **140:**1[2], 4[2], 5[2], 9; **141:**1, 4, 5[2], 8, 9[2]; **142:**3, 4[3], 6[2], 7[3]; **143:**1, 3[2], 4[2], 7[2], 8[2], 9, 10[2], 11; **144:**2, 7[2], 11[2]; **Pr 1:**28[3], 33; **4:**4[2]; **5:**7; **7:**24; **8:**15, 16, 17[3], 18, 21, 22, 32, 34, 35, 36[2]; **9:**11; **23:**26, 35[2]; **24:**29; **27:**11; **30:**7, 8[3], 18; **Ecc 1:**16; **2:**3, 7, 9[2], 15, 17, 18; **7:**23; **9:**13; **SS 1:**2, 4[2], 6[4], 7, 13, 14; **2:**4[2], 5[2], 6, 10, 14[2]; **3:**3, 4; **4:**8[2]; **5:**2, 6, 7[3]; **6:**5[2], 12; **7:**10; **8:**1[2], 2, 3, 6, 13; **Isa 1:**2, 11, 12, 13, 14; **3:**7; **5:**1, 3; **6:**5, 6, 8; **8:**1, 2, 3, 5, 11[3], 18; **12:**1[2]; **18:**4; **21:**2, 3, 4[2], 6, 11, 16; **22:**4[3]; **24:**16; **26:**9; **27:**4, 5[3]; **29:**2, 13[3], 16; **31:**4; **36:**5, 7, 10, 12, 16[2]; **37:**6, 21, 28, 29; **38:**12[3], 13, 15, 16[2], 20; **39:**3; **40:**25; **41:**1; **43:**10[3], 11, 20, 22[2], 23[2], 24[4], 26, 27; **44:**6, 7[2], 8, 17, 21, 22; **45:**4, 5[2], 6, 11[2], 19, 21[2], 22, 23, 24; **46:**3[2], 5[3], 9, 12; **47:**8, 10[2]; **48:**12, 16[2], 19; **49:**1[3], 2[3], 3, 5, 14[2], 16, 20[2], 21, 23; **50:**4, 6, 7, 8[3], 9[2]; **51:**1, 4[3], 5, 7; **54:**9, 15, 17; **55:**2, 3, 11; **56:**3, 4; **57:**8, 11[3], 13, 16; **58:**2[2]; **59:**21; **60:**9; **61:**1[3], 10[2]; **63:**3, 5[3], 15; **65:**1, 3, 5, 6, 7, 10; **66:**1, 4, 22, 23, 24; **Jer 1:**4, 7, 9, 11, 12, 13, 14, 16; **2:**1, 2, 5[2], 8[2], 13, 19, 22, 27[2], 29[2], 32, 35; **3:**1, 4, 6, 7, 10, 11, 19[2], 20; **4:**1, 11, 17, 22, 31; **5:**5, 7, 11, 19, 22[2]; **6:**7, 20[2]; **7:**3, 10, 16, 18, 26; **8:**18, 19, 21; **9:**3, 6, 24; **10:**19, 20, 24[2]; **11:**6, 9, 11, 14, 17, 18[2], 19, 20; **12:**1, 3[3], 8[2], 11; **13:**1, 3, 5, 6, 8, 11[2], 22, 25; **14:**11, 14; **15:**1[2], 6, 10[3], 15[4], 16, 17, 18, 19; **16:**1, 11[2], 12; **17:**14[2], 15, 17, 18[2], 19, 24, 27; **18:**5, 15, 19, 22, 23; **19:**4; **20:**7[3], 8, 9, 10, 11, 12, 14, 17; **22:**6, 16; **23:**9, 14; **24:**1, 3, 4, 7; **25:**3, 6, 7[2], 15, 17; **26:**4, 12, 14[2], 15[2]; **27:**2; **28:**1, 8; **29:**12[2], 13[3], 14; **30:**20, 21[2]; **31:**18[3], 26, 34, 36; **32:**6, 8[2], 25, 27, 29, 30, 32, 33, 39, 40[2]; **33:**3, 8[2], 9, 22; **34:**14[2], 15, 17, 18; **35:**14, 15, 16, 19; **36:**18; **37:**7[2], 18, 20[2]; **38:**14, 15[2], 19, 21, 26; **39:**18; **40:**4[2], 10, 15; **42:**9, 20, 21; **44:**3, 8; **45:**3; **46:**8[3]; **49:**4, 10, 11, 19[3]; **50:**44[3]; **51:**34[5], 53; **La 1:**12, 13[2], 14, 15[2], 16, 19, 20, 21, 22; **3:**2, 3, 5, 6, 7[2], 10, 11[3], 12, 15[2], 16, 20, 51, 52, 53[2], 56, 59, 60, 61, 62; **Eze 2:**1, 2[4], 3[3], 9, 10; **3:**1, 2, 3, 4, 7, 10, 12[2], 14[3], 16, 17, 22[2], 24[4]; **4:**15, 16; **6:**1, 9[2]; **7:**1; **8:**1[2], 3[3], 5, 6[2], 7, 8, 9, 12, 13, 14, 15, 16, 17; **9:**9, 10, 11; **11:**1[2], 2, 5[2], 14, 24[3], 25; **12:**1, 8, 17, 21, 26; **13:**1, 19; **14:**1[2], 2, 5, 7[2], 11, 12, 13; **15:**1; **16:**1, 20, 26, 43, 50; **17:**1, 11, 20; **18:**1, 31; **20:**1, 2, 3, 8[2], 12, 13, 20, 21, 27[2], 38, 39, 40, 45, 49; **21:**1, 8, 18; **22:**1, 12, 17, 18, 23, 30; **23:**1, 35[2], 36, 37, 38; **24:**1, 15, 19, 20; **25:**1; **26:**1, 2; **27:**1; **28:**1, 11, 20; **29:**1, 17, 20; **30:**1, 9, 20; **31:**1; **32:**1, 17; **33:**1, 7, 21, 22[2], 23; **34:**1; **35:**1, 13[2]; **36:**16, 37; **37:**1[3], 2, 3, 4, 9, 10, 11, 15; **38:**1, 16; **39:**23, 26; **40:**1[2], 2[2], 3, 4, 17, 24, 28, 32, 35, 45, 48; **41:**1, 4, 22; **42:**1[2], 13, 15; **43:**1, 5[2], 6[2], 7, 8, 9, 18, 19[2]; **44:**1, 2, 4, 5, 7, 10[2], 13[2], 15[5], 16; **46:**19, 20, 21[2], 24; **47:**1, 2[2], 3, 4[2], 6[2], 8; **Da 2:**5, 6[3], 9[4], 23[2], 24, 26, 30[2]; **4:**2, 5[2], 6[2], 7, 8, 9, 18, 34, 36[4]; **5:**7, 15[2], 16; **6:**22; **7:**15[3], 16, 28[2]; **8:**1[2], 15, 17, 18[3]; **9:**21, 22; **10:**7, 8, 10[2], 11[2], 12, 13[2], 15, 16[2], 17[2], 18[2], 19[2], 21; **11:**1; **Hos 2:**5, 7, 12, 13, 16[2]; **3:**1; **4:**6, 7; **5:**3; **6:**7; **7:**7, 13[3], 14[2], 15; **8:**2, 4; **11:**2, 5, 7, 8, 12; **12:**8; **13:**4[2], 6, 10; **14:**8; **Joel 2:**12; **3:**4[3]; **Am 4:**6, 8, 9, 10, 11; **5:**4, 22, 23, 25; **7:**1, 4, 7, 8, 15[2]; **8:**1, 2; **9:**7; **Ob 1:**3; **Jnh 1:**2, 12[3]; **2:**2, 3[3], 5[2], 6; **4:**3[2], 8; **Mic 2:**4; **3:**8; **5:**2; **6:**3; **7:**1, 7[2], 8[2], 9[2], 10; **Hab 1:**3[2]; **2:**1, 2; **3:**16, 19; **Zep 3:**7, 8, 11; **Hag 2:**14, 17; **Zec 1:**3, 4, 9[2], 13, 14[2], 19[2], 20; **2:**2, 3, 8, 9, 11; **3:**1; **4:**1[2], 2, 4, 5[2], 6, 8, 9, 13; **5:**2, 3, 5[2], 10, 11; **6:**4, 5, 8, 9, 15; **7:**4, 5; **8:**1, 6, 14, 18; **10:**9; **11:**8, 11, 12, 13, 15; **Mal 1:**6[2], 13; **2:**5, 6; **3:**1, 5, 7, 8, 9, 10, 13; **Mt 2:**8; **3:**11, 14; **4:**9, 19; **7:**4, 21, 22, 23; **8:**2, 9, 21, 22; **9:**9; **10:**18, 32, 33, 37[4], 38[2], 40[3]; **11:**6, 27, 28, 29; **12:**30[3]; **14:**8, 18, 28, 30; **15:**5, 8[2], 9, 22, 25, 32; **16:**23[2], 24; **17:**17, 27; **18:**5, 6, 21, 26, 29, 32; **19:**14, 17, 21, 28; **20:**13, 15, 32; **21:**2, 24; **22:**18, 19; **23:**39; **25:**20, 22, 35[3], 36[3], 40, 41, 42[2], 43[3], 45; **26:**10, 11, 12, 15, 21, 23[2], 31, 34, 38, 39, 40, 53, 55[2], 75; **27:**10, 17, 21, 46; **28:**10, 18; **Mk 1:**7, 17, 40; **2:**14; **5:**7[2], 31; **6:**22, 23, 25; **7:**6[2], 7, 11, 14; **8:**2, 33, 34, 38; **9:**19, 37[4], 39, 42; **10:**14, 18, 21, 36, 47, 48, 51[2]; **11:**29, 30; **12:**15[3]; **13:**9; **14:**6, 7, 18[2], 20, 30, 36, 48, 49, 72; **15:**9, 12, 34; **Lk 1:**25[2], 38, 43[2], 48, 49; **2:**49; **4:**6, 7, 18[3], 23; **5:**8, 12, 27; **6:**42, 46, 47; **7:**8, 23, 44, 45; **8:**28[2], 45, 46[2]; **9:**23, 26, 48[3], 59[2], 61; **10:**16[4], 22, 40[2]; **11:**5, 7[2], 23[3]; **12:**8, 9, 13, 14; **13:**27, 32, 35; **14:**26, 27; **15:**6, 9, 12[2], 19, 29, 31; **16:**2, 3, 4, 24; **17:**8[2]; **18:**3, 5[2], 13, 16, 19, 22, 38, 39, 41[2]; **19:**27; **20:**3, 24; **22:**19, 21[2], 28, 29, 34, 37[2], 42, 53, 61; **23:**14, 28, 42, 43; **24:**39, 44; **Jn 1:**15[3], 27, 30[3], 33[2], 43, 48; **2:**4, 17; **4:**7, 9, 10, 15, 21, 29, 34, 39; **5:**7[2], 11[2], 24, 30, 32, 36[2], 37, 40, 43, 46[2]; **6:**26, 35[2], 36, 37[3], 38, 39[2], 44[2], 45, 56, 57[3], 65; **7:**7, 16, 19, 23, 28[2], 29, 33, 34[2], 36[2], 37, 38; **8:**12, 16, 18, 19[2], 21, 26, 28, 29[3], 37, 40, 42[2], 45, 46[2], 49, 54; **9:**4, 11, 36; **10:**8, 9, 14, 15, 17, 18, 25, 27, 29, 32, 37, 38[2]; **11:**25, 26, 41, 42[2]; **12:**8, 26[3], 27, 44[3], 45[2], 46, 48, 49[2], 50; **13:**8, 13, 18, 20[3], 21, 33, 36, 38[2]; **14:**1, 6, 7, 9[2], 10[2], 11[3], 12, 14, 15, 19[2], 20, 21[2], 23, 24[2], 28[2], 30, 31; **15:**2, 4[2], 5[2], 6, 7, 9, 16, 18, 20, 21, 23, 24, 25, 27; **16:**3, 5[2], 9, 10, 14, 16[2], 17[2], 19[2], 23, 27, 32[2], 33; **17:**4, 5, 6[2], 7, 8[2], 9, 11, 12, 18, 20, 21[2], 22, 23[3], 24[4], 25, 26; **18:**8, 9, 11, 21, 23, 34, 35, 36, 39; **19:**10, 11[2]; **20:**15, 17, 21, 29; **21:**15, 16, 17[2], 19, 22; **Ac 1:**4; **2:**25, 28[2]; **3:**22; **5:**8; **7:**2, 7, 28, 37, 42, 49; **8:**19, 24[2], 31, 36; **9:**4, 17; **10:**28, 29, 30; **11:**5, 7, 11, 12[2]; **12:**8, 11; **13:**2, 25; **15:**13; **16:**15; **20:**19, 22, 23[2]; **21:**39; **22:**5, 6, 7[2], 8, 9[2], 10, 11[2], 13[2], 18[2], 21, 27, 28; **23:**3[2], 11, 18[2], 19, 22; **24:**12, 13, 18, 19; **25:**5, 9, 11[2], 15, 24, 27; **26:**3, 13, 14[2], 16, 18, 21[2], 28, 29; **27:**21, 23; **28:**18[2]; **Ro 7:**8, 10, 11[2], 13[2], 17, 18, 20, 23, 24; **9:**19, 20; **10:**20[2]; **12:**3; **14:**11; **15:**3, 15, 18, 23, 30; **16:**3, 7, 13, 23; **1Co 1:**11, 17; **3:**10; **4:**3, 4, 16; **6:**12[2]; **9:**3, 15, 16[3]; **11:**1, 2, 24, 25; **14:**11, 21; **15:**8, 10[2]; **16:**4, 6, 9, 11; **2Co 1:**16, 23; **2:**2, 3, 5, 12; **7:**7; **9:**1, 4; **11:**1[2], 10, 16, 32; **12:**6[3], 7[4], 8, 9[2], 11[2], 13, 20, 21; **13:**3, 10; **Gal 1:**2, 11, 15[2], 16, 17, 24; **2:**1, 3, 6[2], 8[2], 9[2], 20[3]; **4:**12, 14[2], 15, 21; **6:**14, 17; **Eph 3:**2, 3, 7, 8; **6:**19[2]; **Php 1:**7[3], 12, 21, 22; **2:**12, 18, 22, 23, 27, 30; **3:**1, 12, 17; **4:**3, 9, 10[2], 13, 15, 16, 21; **Col 1:**25, 29; **2:**1; **4:**7, 11; **1Ti 1:**11, 12[3], 14, 16[2]; **2Ti 1:**8[2], 13, 15, 16, 17[2]; **2:**2; **3:**11[2]; **4:**6, 8[3], 9, 10, 11, 14, 16, 17[3], 18[2]; **Tit 3:**12, 15; **Phm 1:**11, 13[2], 16, 17[2], 19, 20, 22; **Heb 2:**13; **3:**9; **8:**11; **10:**5, 7; **11:**32; **13:**6, 23; **Jas 2:**18; **2Pe 1:**14; **Rev 1:**10, 12, 17; **2:**13; **3:**4, 18, 20, 21; **4:**1; **5:**5; **7:**13, 14; **10:**8, 9[2], 11; **17:**1, 3, 7, 15; **19:**9[2], 10; **21:**6, 9, 10[2], 15; **22:**1, 6, 8, 9, 10, 12; **Tob 1:**3, 8, 13, 19[2], 20, 22; **2:**1[2], 2[3], 10[3], 13, 14[3]; **3:**3[3], 5, 6[7], 10, 15; **4:**3, 4, 20; **5:**1, 2[3], 3, 7[2], 10, 11, 14[3], 17; **6:**13[2], 15, 16; **7:**1, 9, 10, 11; **8:**16, 20; **10:**5, 7[4], 8, 9; **11:**15[2]; **12:**2, 3[2], 14, 18, 19, 20; **13:**7; **14:**10, 11; **Jdt 2:**10[2]; **5:**3, 4; **8:**11, 32; **9:**4, 9; **10:**9[2]; **11:**2, 3, 16, 17, 19[3]; **12:**2, 4, 14; **13:**7, 16[3]; **14:**1, 5, 8; **16:**2; **AdE 1:**13; **5:**4, 12, 13; **6:**6; **7:**3; **14:**3, 12, 14, 19; **15:**12; **Wis 7:**7[2], 11, 15, 17, 22; **8:**9[2], 12, 13, 14, 15[2], 21; **9:**4[2], 7, 11[2]; **Sir 3:**1; **5:**3, 4; **11:**24; **15:**12; **16:**17, 24; **22:**26, 27; **23:**1[2], 2, 3, 4, 5, 6[2], 18[4]; **24:**8, 9, 11, 19[2], 20[2], 21[2], 22[2], 30; **26:**28; **29:**26; **31:**22[2]; **33:**19; **39:**13; **51:**2, 3[2], 7[2], 10, 12[2], 22, 23, 28; **Bar 2:**30, 32; **4:**9, 12, 22, 23; **Sus 1:**17, 22, 43[2], 54, 58; **Bel 1:**8, 26, 38; **1Mc 2:**27; **6:**13; **7:**3, 28; **10:**54, 56, 71, **11:**10, 12[2]; **12:**15; **13:**5; **15:**5, 31; **2Mc 6:**25; **7:**27, 38; **9:**26; **14:**33; **1Es 1:**27[3], 30; **2:**3, 4, 26; **4:**28, 42, 60; **8:**26, 27, 28, 68, 72; **Man 1:**8, 13[6], 14[2]; **Pm 151:**4[2], 6; **3Mc 5:**31; **6:**24; **2Es 1:**4, 5, 6, 7, 14, 17, 24, 25[2], 26, 27, 31, 35, 37; **2:**9, 33, 45, 47, 48; **3:**29; **4:**1, 2, 3, 4, 5[4], 6, 7, 8, 9, 10, 13, 20, 26, 28, 34, 40, 41, 45, 47, 48, 49, 50, 52[2]; **5:**15[4], 16, 19[4], 20, 21, 31[2], 32[3], 33, 35, 36[4], 37[3], 39[2], 40, 41, 42, 44, 46, 48, 50[3], 51; **6:**1, 6[2], 8, 12, 13, 29, 30, 33, 35, 36; **7:**1[2], 2, 3, 10, 19, 49[2], 54, 59, 70, 76, 100, 101, 102, 104, 112; **8:**1, 37, 42, 46, 63[2]; **9:**1, 10, 17, 18, 26[2], 30, 41[2], 42, 43, 45; **10:**2, 3[2], 12, 18, 27, 28[2], 29[3], 30[3], 32, 33, 34, 38[2], 59; **11:**16, 36; **12:**4, 5, 6, 8[2], 9, 10, 39, 40[2], 48, 51; **13:**14, 15, 20, 51, 52; **14:**1, 3, 4, 19, 20, 22, 23, 27, 36[2], 37, 38, 39, 43, 45; **15:**8, 20; **16:**17[3]; **4Mc 1:**1, 10; **5:**7, 10[2], 28, 34, 37; **8:**5, 6, 7, 9; **9:**15, 23; **10:**2[2], 3, 14; **11:**3, 16; **12:**8[2]; **16:**11; **18:**8

MINE (85)

See also the selected listing for "MINE" in the Main Concordance.

Ge 24:8; **31:**43[2]; **48:**5[2]; **Ex 10:**1; **13:**2; **19:**5; **22:**9; **34:**19; **Lev 20:**26; **25:**23; **Nu 3:**12, 13[2], 45; **8:**14, 17; **Dt 8:**9; **11:**18; **32:**35; **1Sa 14:**7; **2Sa 14:**30; **1Ki 2:**15; **3:**22[2], 26; **8:**59; **20:**3[2]; **2Ki 10:**15[2]; **Job 28:**1; **Ps 50:**10, 11, 12; **59:**3, 4; **60:**7[2]; **108:**8[2]; **SS 2:**16; **6:**3; **Isa 30:**1; **43:**1; **66:**2; **Jer 44:**28; **Eze 16:**8; **18:**4[2]; **23:**4, 5; **29:**9; **35:**10; **Hos 3:**3; **Hag 2:**8[2]; **Mal 3:**17; **Mt 7:**24, 26; **20:**21, 23; **Mk 10:**40; **Lk 11:**6; **15:**24, 31; **19:**27; **Jn 7:**16; **12:**30; **14:**24; **16:**14, 15[2]; **17:**10[2]; **Ro 1:**12; **12:**19; **2Co 11:**10; **2Th 3:**17; **Heb 10:**30; **Tob 3:**15; **8:**7; **Sir 11:**23; **2Es 13:**54

MY (5481)

Ge 2:23[2]; **4:**9, 13, 23; **6:**3, 17, 18; **9:**9, 11, 13, 15, 26; **12:**13[2], 19[2]; **13:**8; **15:**2, 3[2]; **16:**2, 5, 8; **17:**2, 4, 7, 9, 10, 13, 14, 19, 21; **18:**3, 12; **19:**2, 7, 8, 18, 19, 20, 34; **20:**2, 5[4], 9, 11, 12[4], 13[2], 15; **21:**10, 23[2], 30; **22:**7, 8, 18; **23:**4[2], 6, 8[2], 11[2], 13, 15; **24:**2, 3, 4[3], 6, 7[3], 8, 12[2], 14, 18, 27[3], 33, 35, 36[2], 37[2], 38[3], 39, 40[3], 41[3], 42, 44, 45, 48[3], 49, 54, 56[2], 65; **26:**5[5], 7[2], 9, 24; **27:**1, 2, 8[2], 11, 12, 13[2], 18[2], 19, 20, 21[2], 24, 25, 26, 27, 31, 36[2], 37, 41[2], 43[3], 46[2]; **28:**21[2]; **29:**4, 14[2], 15, 21[2], 32[2], 34; **30:**3[2], 6, 8, 15[2], 16, 18[3], 20, 23, 25, 26[2], 30, 32, 33[2]; **31:**5, 6, 7, 26, 28[2], 29, 30, 35, 36[2], 37[2], 39, 40[2], 41, 42[4], 43[3], 50[2]; **32:**4, 5, 9[2], 10, 11, 17, 18, 29, 30; **33:**8, 9, 10[2], 11, 13, 14[2], 15; **34:**4, 8, 12, 30[2]; **35:**3; **37:**7[2], 16, 33, 35; **38:**11, 26; **39:**8[2], 14, 15, 18; **40:**9, 11, 16, 17; **41:**9, 13, 17, 22, 40[2], 51[2], 52; **42:**10, 28[2], 37[2], 38[2]; **43:**3, 5, 14, 20, 29; **44:**2, 4, 5, 7, 9, 10, 16[2], 17, 18[2], 19, 20, 21, 22, 23, 24[2], 27[2], 29, 30, 32[3], 33, 34[2]; **45:**3, 9, 12[2], 13[2], 28; **46:**31[2]; **47:**1[2], 6, 9[3], 18[3], 25, 29, 30; **48:**9, 15[3], 16[2], 18, 19, 22[2]; **49:**3[3], 4, 9, 29[2]; **50:**5[2], 25; **Ex 3:**7, 10, 15[2], 20[2]; **4:**10, 13, 18, 22, 23; **5:**1; **6:**3, 4, 5, 7; **7:**3, 4[2], 5, 16, 17; **8:**1, 8, 20, 21, 22, 23; **9:**1, 13, 14, 15, 16[2], 17, 27, 29; **10:**3, 4, 17, 28[2]; **11:**9; **12:**31; **13:**15, 19; **15:**2[5], 9[3]; **16:**4, 28; **17:**9, 15; **18:**4[2]; **19:**5[3]; **20:**6, 24, 26; **21:**5[3], 14; **22:**24, 25; **23:**18[2], 21, 23, 27; **25:**22; **28:**3; **29:**43; **30:**31; **31:**13; **32:**10, 22, 33, 34; **33:**12, 14, 17, 19, 20, 22[2], 23[3]; **34:**25; **Lev 6:**17; **14:**35; **15:**31; **17:**10; **18:**4[2], 5[2], 26[2], 30; **19:**3, 12, 19, 30[2], 37[2]; **20:**3[3], 5, 6, 8, 22[2]; **21:**23; **22:**2, 3, 9, 31, 32; **23:**2; **25:**18[2], 21, 42, 55; **26:**2[2], 3[2], 9, 11, 12, 15[4], 17, 42[3], 43[2], 44; **Nu 3:**13; **6:**27; **10:**30[2]; **11:**15, 23, 28, 29; **12:**6, 7[2], 8, 11; **14:**22[2], 24, 34; **15:**40; **16:**28; **20:**12, 24; **22:**18, 29, 38; **23:**10, 11, 12; **24:**10, 13, 14; **25:**11[3], 12; **27:**14[2]; **28:**2[3]; **32:**25, 27; **36:**2[2]; **Dt 4:**5, 10; **5:**10, 29; **8:**17[2]; **9:**4, 15, 17; **10:**3; **18:**16, 18, 19, 20; **22:**16, 17; **25:**7; **26:**5, 14; **31:**16, 17[2], 18, 20, 27, 29; **32:**1, 2[2], 20, 22, 23, 34, 39, 40, 41[3], 42[2], 51; **Jos 1:**2, 7; **2:**12, 13[2]; **5:**14; **7:**11, 19, 21; **9:**23; **14:**8[2], 9, 11[2]; **15:**16; **24:**15; **Jdg 1:**7, 12; **2:**1, 2, 20[2]; **4:**18; **5:**9, 21, 30; **6:**10, 15[2], 18, 36, 37; **7:**2; **8:**5, 7, 19[2], 23; **9:**9, 11[2], 13, 15, 17, 18, 29; **11:**7, 12, 13, 30, 31, 35[3], 36, 37[2]; **12:**2, 3[3]; **13:**18; **14:**2, 16[3], 18[2]; **15:**1; **16:**13, 17[4], 28; **17:**2[3], 3[2], 13; **18:**24; **19:**18, 23[2], 24; **20:**4, 5, 6; **Ru 1:**11[2], 12, 13, 16[2]; **2:**2, 8[2], 13, 21[2], 22; **3:**1, 10, 11[2], 16, 18; **4:**4, 6[2], 10; **1Sa 1:**15[2], 16, 26[2]; **2:**1[6], 24, 28[3], 29[3], 33, 35[3]; **3:**6, 16; **4:**16; **9:**5, 16[3], 17, 21; **10:**2; **12:**2[2], 3, 5; **14:**24, 29[2], 39, 40, 41, 42, 43; **15:**11, 14, 25, 30; **16:**22[2]; **17:**46; **18:**17, 18[2], 21; **19:**2, 3[2], 17; **20:**1[3], 2[2], 9, 12, 13[2], 15, 29[2], 42; **21:**8[2], 15[2]; **22:**3, 8[3], 12, 15, 23; **23:**7, 10, 12, 17[2]; **24:**6[2], 8, 10[3], 11[4], 12, 13, 15, 16, 21[3]; **25:**5, 8, 11[3], 24, 25[2], 26[2], 27[2], 28[2], 29, 30, 31[2], 33, 41; **26:**11, 17[3], 18[2], 19[2], 20, 21[4], 23[3], 24[0], 25; **27:**12; **28:**2, 9[2], 21[2]; **29:**8, 9; **30:**13, 15, 23; **2Sa 1:**9, 10, 26; **2:**22; **3:**7, 12, 13, 14, 18[2], 21, 28; **4:**8, 9; **5:**2, 19, 20; **6:**9, 22; **7:**5, 7, 8[2], 10, 11, 13, 15, 18; **9:**7, 10, 11; **11:**11[4]; **12:**28; **13:**4, 5[2], 6[2], 11, 12, 13, 16, 17, 20, 25, 26, 32, 33; **14:**5, 7[2], 9[2], 11, 12, 15, 16, 17[2], 18, 19[2], 20, 22, 24, 31; **15:**21[2]; **16:**3, 4, 9, 11[2], 12; **17:**11; **18:**5, 12[3], 18, 22, 28, 31, 32, 33[5]; **19:**4[3], 12[3], 13[3], 19[2], 20, 26[2], 27[2], 28[2], 30, 33, 35, 37[4]; **20:**9; **22:**2[3], 3[7], 4, 7[4], 18, 19[2], 21[2], 22, 25[2], 29[2], 30, 33, 34, 35[2], 37, 38, 39, 40, 41, 47[3], 49[2]; **23:**2, 5[3]; **24:**3[2], 17, 21, 22, 24; **1Ki 1:**2[2], 13[2], 17[2], 18, 20[2], 21[2], 24[2], 27[2], 29, 30[2], 31, 33[2], 35[2], 36, 37[2], 48[2]; **2:**15, 17, 20, 22, 24, 26[2], 31, 32, 38, 44; **3:**6, 7[2], 14[3], 17, 20[2], 21, 23[2], 26; **5:**3, 4, 5[3], 6, 9[3]; **6:**12[4], 13; **8:**15, 16[3], 17, 18[2], 19, 20, 24, 25, 26, 28, 29; **9:**3[3], 4[2], 6[2], 7[2], 13; **10:**6, 7; **11:**11[2], 13, 21, 32, 33[4], 34[3], 36[2], 38[5]; **12:**10[2], 11[2], 14[2]; **13:**6, 30, 31; **14:**7, 8[3]; **15:**19; **16:**2[2]; **17:**1, 12, 18[2], 20, 21; **18:**7, 10, 12, 13; **19:**4[2], 10, 14, 20[2]; **20:**4, 6, 7[4], 9, 32, 34[2]; **21:**2, 3, 4, 6, 20; **22:**4[2], 49; **2Ki 1:**13, 14; **2:**19; **3:**7[2]; **4:**1[2], 13, 16, 19[2], 28, 29[2]; **5:**3, 6, 18[2], 20, 22; **6:**8, 12, 26, 28, 29, 32; **8:**5, 12; **9:**7, 32; **10:**6, 9, 16, 30; **13:**14[2]; **14:**9; **17:**13[3]; **18:**23, 24, 27, 29, 34, 35[2]; **19:**12, 23, 24, 28[3], 34[2]; **20:**5, 6[2], 15[2], 19; **21:**4, 7, 8, 14, 15; **22:**17; **23:**27[2]; **1Ch 4:**10; **11:**2[2], 19; **12:**17[3]; **13:**12; **14:**10, 11[2]; **16:**22[2]; **17:**4, 6, 7[2], 9, 10, 13, 14[2], 16, 25; **21:**3[3], 17[2], 23; **22:**5, 7[2], 8[2], 10, 11, 18; **28:**2[2], 3, 4[3], 5[2], 6[2], 7[2], 9, 20; **29:**1, 2, 3[4], 14, 17[2], 19; **2Ch 1:**8, 9, 11; **2:**3, 4, 7, 8, 14, 15; **6:**4, 5[3], 6[2], 7, 8[2], 9, 10, 15, 16[2], 19, 40; **7:**13, 14[3], 15[2], 16[3], 17[2], 19[2], 20[2]; **8:**11; **9:**5, 6; **10:**10[2], 11[2], 14[2]; **12:**7; **16:**3; **18:**3, 13; **25:**16, 18; **29:**10, 11; **32:**13[2], 14[3], 15[3], 17[2]; **33:**4, 7; **34:**25; **Ezr 7:**13, 28; **9:**3[3], 5[6], 6[3]; **10:**3; **Ne 1:**2, 6, 9[2]; **2:**3[2], 5, 8, 12[2], 18; **4:**16, 23[2]; **5:**10[2], 13, 14, 16, 17, 19[2]; **6:**9, 14, 19[2]; **7:**2, 5[2]; **13:**14[3], 19, 22[2], 29, 31; **Est 4:**16[2]; **5:**3, 6, 7, 8[2]; **7:**2, 3[4], 4[2], 8[2]; **8:**6[2]; **Job 1:**5, 8, 21; **2:**3; **3:**10[2], 24[3]; **4:**12, 14, 15[2], 16; **5:**8; **6:**2[2], 3, 4, 7, 8[2], 10, 11[2], 12[2], 15, 21, 29, 30[2]; **7:**5[2], 6, 7[2], 11[3], 13[3], 16[2], 19, 21[2]; **9:**14, 15, 16, 17, 18, 20, 21, 25, 27[2], 28, 30, 31; **10:**1[3], 6[2], 12, 14, 15[2], 20; **11:**4; **12:**4; **13:**1[2], 3, 6[2], 14[4], 15, 16, 17[2], 18, 23[4], 26, 27[3]; **14:**14[2], 16[2], 17[2]; **16:**4[2], 5[2], 6, 7, 8[2], 9, 13[2], 15[2], 16[2], 17[2], 18[2], 19, 20[2]; **17:**1[2], 2, 7[2], 11[3], 13[2], 14[3], 15[2]; **19:**4, 5, 8[2], 9[2], 10, 12, 13[2], 14[2], 15[2], 16, 17[3], 19, 20[4], 21, 22, 23, 25, 26[2], 27[3]; **20:**2, 3; **21:**2, 4, 6; **23:**2[2], 4[2], 7, 11, 12, 16, 17; **27:**2[2], 3[2], 4[2], 5, 6[3], 7[2]; **29:**3, 4[2], 5, 6, 7, 14, 18[2], 19[2], 20[3], 21, 22, 24; **30:**1, 11[2], 12[2], 13[2], 15[2], 16, 17, 18[2], 25, 27, 30[2], 31[2]; **31:**1, 2[2], 4[2], 5, 6, 7[4], 9[2], 10, 12, 13, 17, 18[2], 20, 21, 22[3], 24[2], 25[2], 27[3], 30, 31, 32, 33[3], 35[2], 36, 37, 38; **32:**6, 10, 12, 17[2], 19, 20, 22; **33:**1[2], 2[2], 3[3], 7, 8, 11[2], 13, 28[2]; **34:**2, 5, 6; **35:**10; **36:**3[2], 4; **37:**1; **40:**4[2]; **42:**5, 7[2], 8[3]; **Ps 2:**6[2], 7; **3:**1, 3[2], 7[2]; **4:**1[2], 2, 7; **5:**1[2], 2[3], 3[2], 8; **6:**2, 3, 4, 6[4], 7[2], 8, 9[2], 10; **7:**1[2], 3[2], 4[2], 5[2], 6[2], 8, 10; **9:**1, 3, 4; **13:**2[3], 3[2], 4[2], 5; **14:**4; **16:**2, 3, 4, 5[3], 7, 8, 9[3]; **17:**1[2], 2, 3[2], 5[2], 6, 9, 13; **18:**1, 2[8], 3, 6[4], 17, 18[2], 20[2], 21, 24[2], 28[3], 29, 32, 33, 34[2], 36[2], 37, 38, 39, 40, 46[2], 48[2]; **19:**14[4]; **22:**1[3], 2, 9, 10[3], 14[3], 15[3], 16, 17, 18[2], 19[2], 20[2], 22, 25[2]; **23:**1, 3, 5[3], 6[2]; **25:**1, 2[2], 5, 7[2], 11, 15[2], 17[2], 18[3], 19, 20; **26:**1, 2, 3, 6, 9, 11, 12; **27:**1[3], 2[2], 3, 4, 6[2], 8, 9[2], 10, 11, 12; **28:**1, 2[2], 6, 7[5]; **30:**1, 2, 3, 6, 9, 10, 11[2], 12[2]; **31:**3[2], 4, 5, 7[2], 8, 9[2], 10[5], 11[3], 13, 14, 15[2], 22[2]; **32:**3[2], 4, 5[4], 8; **34:**1, 2, 4; **35:**3[2], 4, 7, 9, 10, 12, 13, 15, 17, 19, 23[4], 24, 26, 27, 28; **38:**3[3], 4[2], 5[2], 7[2], 8, 9[2], 10[3], 11[3], 12, 15, 16, 17, 18[2], 19, 20, 21, 22; **39:**1[4], 2[2], 3[2], 4[3], 5[2], 7, 8, 9, 12[4]; **40:**1, 2[2], 3, 5, 8[2], 9, 10, 12[3], 14[2], 17[3]; **41:**5[2], 9[2], 11, 12; **42:**1, 2, 3[2], 4, 5[2], 6[2], 8, 9, 10[2], 11[3]; **43:**1, 4[2], 5[3]; **44:**4[2], 6[2], 15[2]; **45:**1[3]; **49:**3[2], 4[2], 5, 15; **50:**5, 7, 16[2], 17; **51:**1, 2[2], 3[2], 5, 6, 9[2], 14[2], 15[2]; **53:**4; **54:**2[2], 3, 4[2], 5, 7[2]; **55:**1[2], 2, 4, 13[3], 17[2], 20; **56:**2, 3, 5, 6[2], 8[2], 9, 12, 13[3]; **57:**1, 6[3], 7[2], 8; **59:**1[2], 3, 4, 9[2], 10[3], 11, 16, 17[2]; **60:**7[2], 8[2]; **61:**1[2], 2, 3, 5, 8; **62:**1[2], 2[3], 5[2], 6[3], 7[4]; **63:**1[3], 3, 4, 5[2], 6, 7, 8, 9; **64:**1[3]; **66:**13, 14[2], 17, 18, 19, 20; **68:**24[2]; **69:**1, 3[4], 4[2], 5, 7, 8[2], 10, 11, 13, 14, 18, 19[2], 20, 21; **70:**2, 5[2]; **71:**3[2], 4, 5[3], 6[3], 7, 8, 9, 10[2], 12, 13, 15[2], 17, 21, 22, 23[2], 24; **73:**2[2], 13[2], 21, 23, 26[4], 28; **74:**12; **77:**2[3], 3, 4, 6[2], 10; **78:**1[3], 2; **81:**8, 11[2], 13[2], 14; **83:**13; **84:**2[3], 3[2], 8, 10; **86:**2[2], 4, 6[2], 7, 12[2], 13, 14; **87:**7; **88:**1, 2[2], 3[2], 8, 9[2], 13, 15, 18; **89:**1, 3[2], 20[2], 21[2], 24[2], 26[3], 28[2], 30[2], 31[2], 33[2], 34[2], 35, 47, 50; **91:**2[3], 14, 16; **92:**10, 11[4], 15; **94:**17[2], 18, 19[2], 22[3]; **95:**9, 10, 11[2]; **101:**2, 3, 7[2]; **102:**1[2], 2, 3[2], 4[2], 5[3], 8[2], 9, 11, 23[2], 24[2]; **103:**1, 2, 22; **104:**1[2], 33, 34, 35; **105:**15[2]; **108:**1[3], 8[2], 9[2]; **109:**1, 4, 5, 20[2], 21[2], 22, 24[2], 25, 26, 28, 29, 30; **110:**1[2]; **111:**1; **116:**1[2], 4, 7, 8[3], 10, 11, 14, 16, 18; **118:**5, 6, 7, 14[3], 21, 28[2]; **119:**5, 6, 10, 11, 13, 15, 18, 20, 24[2], 25, 26, 28, 32, 34, 36, 37, 43[2], 47, 50[2], 54[2], 57, 58, 59, 69, 76, 77, 80, 81, 82, 88, 92[2], 97, 98, 99[2], 101, 103[2], 105[2], 108, 109[2], 111[2], 112, 114[2], 115, 116, 120, 121, 123, 128, 129, 133, 136, 139[2], 143, 145, 147, 148, 149[2], 153, 154, 157[2], 159, 161, 167, 168, 169, 170, 171, 172,

MYSELF (180)

NO (2336)

NOR (418)

NOT (7614)

O (1304)

OF (35325)

OH (25)

ON (5394)

For "ON" as a proper name see the Main Concordance.

4, 16; 5:11, 14; 6:2[2], 3, 4, 8, 9, 10, 11; 7:4, 8, 9, 10; 8:1, 6, 7, 9, 12, 13, 14, 15; 9:1, 2, 15, 17, 18, 19, 22, 31; 10:3, 13; 11:2, 5, 8, 12; 12:2; 13:6; 14:2, 16[2]; 15:1, 3, 6, 7; 16:7, 18, 20[2]; Wis 1:12, 14; 3:18; 5:6, 18; 6:5, 11, 15[2]; 7:7; 8:12; 9:8, 16, 17, 18; 10:6, 10; 11:22; 12:5, 24; 13:10; 14:5, 6, 15, 21, 30; 16:24; 18:16, 23, 24[3]; 19:4, 8, 18, 21; Sir 1:13; 4:17; 5:1, 6, 8[2]; 6:13, 31, 37[2]; 8:3; 9:13; 10:8; 11:5, 19, 26; 12:6, 11; 13:13; 14:4, 18, 20, 21, 22; 15:4[2], 9, 19; 16:3, 8, 9[2], 10, 17; 17:2, 23; 18:14, 24; 20:18, 19, 24[2], 29; 21:16, 19[2], 21; 22:17, 18; 23:11; 24:13; 26:11, 13, 17[2], 18; 27:12, 14, 25, 30; 28:12[2]; 29:3; 30:24; 31:20; 32:20, 21; 34:19; 35:15, 23; 36:17[2], 18, 22; 37:14; 38:11, 24, 26, 27, 28[3], 31; 39:7, 12, 15, 28, 31; 40:1, 3, 10, 15; 41:6, 19; 42:16; 43:5, 8, 10, 20[3]; 44:14, 17, 23; 45:7, 13; 46:1, 5, 6, 16; 47:5, 7, 23; 49:3, 11, 14; 50:7, 8[2], 11, 12, 17; 51:4, 6, 7, 13, 15; Bar 1:2, 8, 10, 11, 14, 15[3], 16; 2:6, 28; 3:16, 23, 37; 4:20; 5:1, 2[2], 6[2]; LtJ 6:4, 10, 11, 18, 22, 26, 38, 71; Aza 1:13, 32, 33, 60; Sus 1:32, 34; Bel 1:21, 40; 1Mc 1:9[2], 22, 37, 54[2], 59[3]; 2:14, 23, 24, 32, 38, 41; 3:3[2], 14, 15, 19, 25, 47[2]; 4:24, 38, 40, 46, 50[2], 51, 52, 53, 54, 55; 5:3, 4, 36, 37, 41, 46, 48, 57, 65, 67; 6:7, 25, 35, 37[3], 38[2], 39, 40[2], 43, 45, 57, 59, 61; 7:4, 7[2], 9, 18, 24, 38[2], 43, 45, 49; 8:4, 12, 14, 22, 23, 29, 31, 32[2]; 9:12, 14, 16, 17, 26, 34, 40, 43, 45[2]; 10:21, 33, 41, 50, 52, 53, 55[2]; 11:5, 11, 13[2], 36, 37, 42, 47, 48, 52, 54, 71; 12:11[2], 23, 37, 39, 40, 53; 13:10, 29, 32[2], 45, 51; 14:9, 18, 27[4], 31, 33, 34, 44, 48; 15:9, 12, 31, 37, 39; 2Mc 1:14, 17, 18, 21[2], 26, 27, 31; 2:2, 14, 18; 3:8, 23, 26[2], 27, 37; 4:11, 28; 5:3[2], 5[2], 21[2], 27; 6:7, 15, 17, 22; 7:4, 6[2], 17, 18, 26, 27, 38; 8:2, 3, 11; 9:13, 21, 23, 28; 10:1, 5[3], 16, 20, 24, 25, 28, 29, 30, 34; 11:3[2], 10, 13, 14, 23, 26, 36; 12:3, 5, 10, 14[2], 35[2], 38, 39; 13:3, 5, 10; 14:15, 21, 22, 23, 32, 43; 15:1, 5, 17, 20; 1Es 1:1, 4, 18, 25, 27; 2:20; 3:6; 4:4, 30, 43, 52; 5:44, 52, 57, 58; 6:10, 19, 27; 7:10; 8:6[2], 15, 22[2], 59, 61[2], 91; 9:5, 14, 16, 37, 40, 42, 43, 44; 3Mc 1:8; 2:4, 6, 14, 16, 22[2], 27[2], 29; 3:16; 4:4, 9; 5:2, 7, 18, 27, 35, 46, 50; 6:4, 12, 39, 40; 7:10, 14, 20; 2Es 1:9, 17, 23; 2:6, 13, 19, 33, 35, 36, 42, 43, 45, 46; 3:1, 12; 4:11, 21, 34, 39[2]; 5:10, 15, 16, 29, 31; 6:12, 24, 36, 38, 41, 42, 44, 45, 47, 51, 53; 7:1, 6, 7[2], 8, 33, 38[3], 61, 72, 97, 102, 105[2], 115, 127, 132; 8:26[2], 32, 45[2], 57; 9:7[2], 27, 38[2]; 10:30; 11:1, 6, 12, 20, 23, 24, 35[2], 40; 12:13, 29, 48[2]; 13:6, 11, 29, 35, 52; 14:1, 4, 38; 15:2, 22, 35, 37, 43, 44; 16:2, 21, 22, 29, 39, 40, 50, 53, 60, 65; 4Mc 1:10, 24; 4:5, 8, 10, 17, 21; 5:1, 3, 12, 31; 6:3; 8:10, 11, 16, 20[2]; 9:8, 11, 24; 10:2; 11:10[3], 16; 12:6, 11, 17, 18; 13:16; 14:3, 15; 15:12, 15, 20, 22; 16:13[2]; 17:3, 8, 12; 18:5, 8

OR (2379)

Ge 3:3; 13:9; 14:23[2]; 17:23; 19:12, 15, 17[2], 33, 35; 21:23[2]; 22:12; 24:21, 49, 50; 26:7, 11; 27:21; 30:1; 31:14, 24, 39, 43, 50; 35:27; 37:32; 39:10; 41:44; 42:16; 44:8, 19; 45:5; Ex 1:10; 4:1, 8, 9, 11[2]; 5:3[2]; 9:19; 11:6; 12:5, 9, 19, 45; 16:4; 17:7; 19:12, 13[2], 22, 24; 20:4[2], 5, 10[3], 17[5], 19; 21:4, 6, 10, 15, 16, 17, 18, 20, 21, 26, 27, 28, 29, 31, 32, 33[2]; 22:1[2], 4[2], 5[3], 6[2], 7, 8, 9, 10[3], 14, 21, 22, 28; 23:4, 18, 24[2], 26, 29, 33; 28:43[2]; 29:34; 30:9[2], 20, 33; 32:18, 29; 33:3; 34:3, 10, 12, 20; 35:23[6], 24, 35[4]; 36:6; Lev 1:2, 10, 14; 2:4, 11; 3:1, 6, 17; 5:1, 2[3], 3, 4[2], 6, 7, 11[2], 18; 6:2[3], 3, 4[3], 5, 6; 7:9, 10, 16, 21[2], 23[2], 24, 26; 10:6, 7, 9; 11:4, 9, 10, 26, 32[3], 35, 36, 42; 12:4, 6[2], 7, 8; 13:2[3], 19, 24[2], 29[2], 30, 38, 42[2], 43, 47, 48[4], 49[4], 51[2], 52[3], 53[2], 55, 56[2], 57[2], 58[2], 59[4]; 14:22, 30, 36, 37, 56[2]; 15:3, 14, 17, 23, 25, 29, 33; 16:2, 13; 17:3[3], 8[2], 10, 13[2], 15[2], 16; 18:9[2], 10, 17, 26; 19:4, 6, 9, 10, 14, 15, 17, 18, 20, 26, 27, 28, 31, 35; 20:2, 9[2], 17, 19, 25[2], 27[2]; 21:5[2], 7, 11, 14[2], 18[3], 19[2], 20[6], 23; 22:4[2], 5, 8, 10, 13, 18[2], 19[2], 21[2], 22[6], 23[2], 24[3], 27[2], 28; 23:14[2], 22; 25:4, 5, 11[2], 14, 20, 36, 37, 40, 47, 49[4]; 26:1, 44; 27:7, 10[2], 12, 14, 20, 26, 28[3], 30, 33[2]; Nu 4:15, 19, 49; 5:2, 6, 14, 30; 6:2, 3[3], 4, 7[2], 10; 9:10[2], 21, 22[2]; 11:8, 19[4], 23; 13:18[2], 19[2], 20[2]; 14:2; 15:3[4], 5, 8[2], 11[3], 14, 30; 16:14, 26, 29; 17:10; 18:3, 9, 17[2], 22; 19:16[3], 18; 20:5[3], 17[3], 18; 21:22; 22:18, 26; 23:10, 19; 24:13; 30:2, 3, 4, 6, 8, 9, 10, 12, 13[2], 14; 31:19, 28, 30; 35:15, 17, 18, 20, 21, 22, 23; Dt 1:16, 21, 29; 2:9, 19; 3:24; 4:16, 32, 34; 5:8[2], 9, 14[8], 21[6], 32; 7:3, 14, 25, 26; 8:2; 9:5; 10:9; 11:2, 16; 12:12, 15, 17, 21, 22, 32; 13:1[2], 2, 3, 5, 6[5], 7, 8[2]; 14:1, 7, 21, 26, 27, 29; 15:7, 12, 21, 22; 17:1, 2, 3[2], 4, 5[2], 6, 8, 11[2], 12, 16, 17, 20; 18:1, 3, 10[5], 11[4], 16, 20, 22; 19:15[2]; 20:3[3], 5, 6, 7, 8[2]; 22:1, 2, 4, 6[3], 9; 23:1, 3, 6, 18; 24:3, 5, 6, 7, 14, 17; 27:15, 16, 22; 28:14, 50; 29:4[2], 6, 18[3]; 31:6[2], 8[2]; Jos 1:5, 7, 9; 5:13; 6:10; 7:3; 8:1, 17, 20, 22; 10:14, 25; 13:13; 20:3; 22:19, 22, 23[3], 28, 29; 23:7[4]; 24:12, 15, 19; Jdg 1:27[4], 30, 31[6], 33; 2:10, 19, 22; 5:8, 30; 6:4[2], 31; 9:2; 11:15, 25, 27, 34; 13:4[2], 7, 14[2], 23[2]; 14:3, 6, 15, 16; 18:19, 25; 19:13; 20:28; 21:22; Ru 1:16; 2:8, 20; 3:10; 1Sa 2:13, 14[3], 36; 3:14; 4:20; 9:5; 12:3[3], 4[2], 21; 13:19, 20; 14:6, 34, 41, 52; 15:6, 29; 16:7; 17:34; 20:2, 3, 12, 27; 21:3, 8[2]; 22:8, 15[2]; 24:11; 25:31[2]; 26:10[2], 12, 16; 27:10[2]; 28:6[2], 15; 29:4; 30:12, 15, 19[3]; 2Sa 1:20, 21; 2:21, 28; 3:29[4], 35; 12:4, 28, 31; 13:25; 14:19; 15:4, 14[2], 21; 17:9; 19:19, 24[2], 35, 42; 20:6, 20; 21:4[2], 10; 23:7; 24:13[2]; 1Ki 1:10[3]; 3:7, 8, 11[2]; 8:5, 23, 37, 38, 46, 57; 9:6; 10:12; 12:24; 13:8, 9[2], 16[2], 17[2], 28; 15:17; 16:11; 18:10[2], 27[3]; 20:8, 39; 21:2, 6, 21; 22:6, 15, 31; 2Ki 2:16; 3:9, 13; 4:13, 31; 5:7, 17; 6:10, 27; 7:10; 9:8, 32; 12:13[2]; 13:19; 14:6, 26; 17:34[3], 35[3]; 18:5; 19:13, 32; 20:13; 22:2; 23:10, 22[2]; 1Ch 12:2; 21:12[2]; 22:13; 23:26, 29; 26:31; 28:20[2]; 2Ch 1:11; 5:6; 6:14, 28, 29, 36; 7:13[2]; 8:15; 11:4; 13:9; 15:5, 13[2]; 16:1; 18:5, 14, 30; 19:7[2], 10[2]; 20:9[2], 15, 17; 21:12; 25:4, 8[2]; 29:7; 32:7, 15[3]; 34:2; 36:17[2]; Ezr 2:59; 4:13; 6:9[2], 12[2]; 7:13[2], 23, 24[2], 26[3]; 9:12, 14; 10:6, 13; Ne 2:16, 20[2]; 4:11; 7:61; 8:9; 9:31, 34; 10:30, 31[2]; 13:1, 20, 25[2]; Est 2:10, 20; 3:2, 5; 4:11, 16; 6:3; 8:6, 11; Job 1:22; 3:4, 12, 15, 16; 4:7; 6:5, 6, 12, 22, 23[2]; 7:12; 8:3; 10:5; 13:9, 22; 14:12; 15:3, 11, 14; 16:3; 17:14; 18:4, 19; 22:3, 11; 23:8; 28:16, 18; 31:13, 16, 17, 19, 24, 25, 26, 29; 32:21, 22; 34:22, 29, 30; 35:7; 36:19, 23; 37:13[2]; 38:5, 6, 8, 16, 17, 22, 24, 28, 31, 32, 36, 37, 39, 40; 39:10; 40:24; 41:1, 2, 5, 7, 12[2], 26; Ps 1:1[2]; 2:12; 6:1; 7:2, 4; 13:3; 16:4, 10; 22:24; 25:7; 28:5; 32:9; 35:14, 19; 36:11; 37:25, 33; 38:1; 44:17, 20; 50:9, 13, 16, 22; 58:5, 9; 59:3, 11; 66:20; 69:15[2], 31; 75:5, 6; 78:20, 42; 83:1; 88:11, 12; 89:33, 34; 90:2, 4, 10; 91:5, 6[2]; 106:2; 129:7; 132:3, 4; 139:7; 143:7; 144:3; Pr 3:11, 25; 4:27; 5:9, 13; 6:7[2], 28; 7:22; 8:8, 26; 17:26; 18:5; 20:13, 20; 22:1, 22, 25; 23:10, 20; 24:18; 25:6, 10, 12, 16, 18, 19, 20, 26, 27; 26:1, 4, 5, 10; 27:10, 16; 28:15, 24; 30:6, 9[2], 10, 32; 31:4, 5; Ecc 1:8; 2:16, 19, 25; 4:8; 5:12; 6:3, 5; 7:21; 8:8; 9:1, 10[3]; 10:20[2]; 11:2, 3, 6[2]; 12:14; SS 2:7[2], 9, 17; 3:5[2]; 8:4, 14; Isa 1:6[2], 11[2]; 5:6, 12, 27; 6:13; 7:11; 8:4, 12, 22; 9:13, 17; 10:4, 14[2], 15[2]; 11:3, 9; 13:14, 20; 14:21; 17:6[2], 8; 19:15; 22:11; 23:18; 27:5, 7, 9; 28:22; 29:8, 16; 30:14, 21; 31:1, 4[2]; 33:23; 34:4; 37:13, 33; 38:14; 39:2; 40:13, 18, 25, 28; 41:22, 23; 42:2[2], 4, 19[2]; 43:18, 23[2], 24; 44:8, 10, 14[2], 19, 20; 45:9, 10, 11, 13, 17; 46:7; 47:7, 8; 48:1, 19; 49:10, 15, 24; 50:1, 2; 53:2; 57:11; 58:13; 59:21[2]; 60:18, 20; 63:9; 64:7; 65:17, 19, 20, 23, 25; 66:19; Jer 1:17; 2:18, 31, 32; 3:16[2]; 4:4, 11; 5:12; 6:8, 20, 25; 7:6, 16, 22, 24, 26, 32; 8:2; 9:13; 10:2, 24; 11:8, 14[2], 21; 13:14[2], 23; 14:14, 22; 15:5; 16:2, 5[2], 7; 17:21, 22, 23[2]; 18:7, 9; 19:5, 6; 20:9; 21:7[2], 12, 13; 22:3[2], 18[2]; 23:4, 32, 33[2], 34, 35, 37; 25:33[2]; 27:8, 9; 31:34, 40; 32:23, 43; 33:10[2], 12; 34:10, 14; 35:7[2], 8, 9[2], 15; 36:23; 37:18[2]; 38:16, 24, 25; 40:5; 42:6, 14[2], 17; 43:3; 44:5, 10, 14[2], 23, 28; 49:31; 50:39; 51:46; La 2:22; 3:33, 63; 4:12; Eze 2:5, 7; 3:9, 11, 18, 19; 4:14; 5:7, 12; 7:19; 12:24; 13:5, 7, 23; 14:7, 17, 19; 16:16; 17:9; 18:6[2], 8, 13, 15, 17; 20:17, 28, 44; 21:20; 22:14; 23:27; 24:16, 17, 22, 23; 26:20; 28:24; 30:21; 31:14; 34:6; 37:23; 38:11; 39:10; 44:20, 22[2], 25[3], 31[2]; 45:20; 46:12[2]; 48:14; Da 2:10[2], 27; 3:29; 4:19, 35; 5:8, 10, 17, 23[2]; 6:4[2], 7, 12, 13, 15; 10:3; 11:17, 20, 37; Hos 1:6, 7[4]; 2:3; 3:4[3]; 4:1, 15; 5:13; 7:10; 13:3[2]; Joel 1:2; Am 3:12; 4:8; 5:5, 6, 19; 6:2; 8:11; 9:10; Jnh 3:7[2]; Mic 5:6, 7; Hab 1:2; 3:8[2]; Zep 1:6; Hag 2:12[4]; Zec 1:4; 7:10; 8:10[2]; 11:16[3]; 14:6; Mal 1:8[2], 13[2]; 2:12[2], 13, 17; 3:14; Mt 2:16; 5:17, 22[2], 23, 24, 25, 35[2], 36, 37; 6:24, 25[2], 31[2]; 7:4, 6, 10, 16; 9:5; 10:9[2], 10[3], 11, 14[2], 19, 37[2]; 11:3; 12:4, 5, 19, 20, 25, 29, 32, 33; 13:21; 15:4, 5; 16:10, 14, 26; 17:25[2]; 18:8[3], 16[2], 20, 35; 19:29[6]; 20:15; 21:25; 22:17; 23:17, 19; 24:20, 23; 25:37, 38, 39, 44[5]; 26:5; 27:17; Mk 1:32; 2:9; 3:4[2]; 4:17, 21, 30; 6:56[2]; 7:10, 11, 12; 8:17; 10:29[6], 38, 40; 11:30; 12:14, 15; 13:15, 21, 32, 35[3], 36; 14:2, 68; Lk 1:15; 2:24; 3:14; 5:23; 6:9[2], 42; 7:19, 20; 8:16; 9:25; 10:22; 11:12; 12:11, 14, 22, 38, 41, 47, 58; 13:4, 15; 14:3, 5, 12[4], 31; 15:8; 16:13; 17:7, 21, 23; 18:11, 29[4]; 20:4, 22; 21:15; 22:27, 35; Jn 1:13[2]; 2:6; 3:8; 4:15, 27; 5:37; 6:19; 7:17, 48; 8:14; 9:2; 13:29; 16:3; 18:34; 19:13; Ac 1:7; 2:27; 3:6, 12[2]; 4:7, 18, 34; 5:38; 7:49; 8:7, 21, 34; 9:2; 10:14, 28[2]; 11:8; 13:27; 16:21; 17:21, 29[2]; 18:14; 19:12; 20:31, 33[2]; 21:21; 23:8[2], 9, 29; 24:12[2], 14, 18, 20; 25:6, 8[2]; 26:29, 31; 28:6, 17, 21; Ro 1:12, 21, 23[3]; 2:4, 15; 3:1, 29; 4:9, 10, 13, 19; 6:16; 8:35[6]; 9:11[2], 16; 10:7; 11:34, 35; 14:4, 8, 10[3], 13, 15, 21[3]; 1Co 1:12[3], 13; 2:1, 6; 3:22[7]; 4:3, 21; 5:10[2], 11[4]; 6:19; 7:11, 15; 8:5; 9:6, 7, 10; 10:19, 22, 31[2], 32[2]; 11:4, 5, 6, 11, 22, 27; 12:13[2]; 13:1, 4[2], 5[2]; 14:6[3], 7, 23, 24, 26, 27, 29, 36[2], 37; 15:11, 37; 16:6; 2Co 3:1; 4:2; 5:9, 10; 6:14, 15; 9:7; 10:12; 11:4[2], 20[4]; 12:2, 3, 6; 13:1; Gal 1:8, 10[2]; 2:2; 3:2, 5, 15, 28[2]; 4:9, 14; Eph 3:20; 5:3, 5[2], 27[2]; 6:8; Php 1:18, 20, 27; 2:3, 16; 3:12; Col 1:16[3], 20; 2:16[2]; 3:17, 21; 1Th 2:3[2], 5, 6, 19[2]; 4:6[2]; 5:5, 10; 2Th 2:2[3], 4, 15; 1Ti 1:7, 9; 2:8, 9[2], 12; 3:6; 5:4, 19; 6:14, 16, 17; 2Ti 1:8; 4:2; Tit 1:7[4], 14; 2:3; 3:12; Phm 1:18; Heb 1:5; 2:2, 6; 8:11; 10:28; 12:3, 5; 13:5; Jas 1:17; 2:3, 15; 3:4, 12, 17; 4:5, 11, 13, 15; 5:12[2]; 1Pe 1:11, 18, 19; 2:14; 3:3, 9; 4:15; 2Pe 3:14; 1Jn 2:9, 10, 15; 3:6, 15, 17, 18; 4:20[2]; 5:16; 2Jn 1:10; Rev 3:15; 5:3[3], 4; 7:1[2], 3[2]; 9:4[2], 20[3], 21[3]; 13:16, 17[2]; 14:9, 11; 20:4[2]; 21:23, 27; 22:5; Tob 3:9, 15[2]; 4:5, 15; 5:2; 6:8[2], 13; 10:2; 12:19; Jdt 5:23; 8:14[2], 15, 16, 18[3], 20; 10:13; 11:21; 12:2; 13:4; 16:25; AdE 2:1, 10; 4:11, 16; 6:3; 13:6, 12[2]; 14:17; Wis 1:4, 12; 2:10; 4:3, 8, 11, 15; 5:11, 12; 6:4[2], 7; 8:20; 9:13; 11:11, 17, 18[4], 25; 12:9[2], 12[2], 14; 13:2[5], 10, 14; 14:21[2], 23[2], 24[2], 28[3]; 15:6[2], 9; 16:14; 17:17[2], 18[2], 19[4]; Sir 1:30; 2:7, 10[2]; 4:2, 3, 4, 22, 27, 29, 30; 5:1, 9; 6:2; 7:4, 5, 6, 12, 15, 18, 20; 8:1, 4, 10, 11, 15, 19; 9:1, 3, 4, 5, 6, 7, 9[2], 13; 10:18; 11:2; 12:3, 12[2], 13; 13:2, 7, 10[2], 11, 12, 25; 16:3, 10, 22; 18:6, 15, 32; 19:8, 13, 14; 20:22; 22:9, 12, 13[2], 22; 23:14; 26:4, 10; 29:10, 23; 30:10, 12; 31:16, 17; 33:20[2]; 34:16; 35:17; 37:11[4]; 38:17, 33; 39:17, 21; 40:6, 16, 23; 41:4[2], 17[2], 18[2], 19[2], 21; 42:3, 4, 7, 8[2], 9, 10[2], 11, 12, 21; 43:31; 44:5; 47:22[2]; Bar 2:17, 19; 3:22, 23, 27, 31; 4:3, 13; LtJ 6:5, 11, 28, 29, 34[2], 35, 36, 38, 40, 44, 48, 49, 53, 54, 55, 56[2], 57, 59, 63, 64, 67[2], 71; Aza 1:7, 15[5], 17, 27; Sus 1:9; Bel 1:7, 26, 29; 1Mc 1:57, 63; 2:22, 36[2]; 3:18, 45, 56[3]; 4:8, 35, 38; 5:46; 7:15, 18; 8:14, 16, 24, 26[2], 28, 30[2]; 9:55; 10:30, 35, 43[2], 46, 73[2]; 12:53; 14:44[5], 45; 15:14, 19[2], 25, 31; 2Mc 2:2; 3:38; 6:26; 9:24; 11:9; 12:15; 13:6; 14:3; 15:39; 1Es 1:24, 53[2]; 4:6, 14, 18, 19[2], 21[2], 25, 27[2], 39[2], 49[3]; 5:37, 41, 58; 6:32, 33; 8:7, 22[6], 24[3], 42, 88[2]; 9:2, 4, 11; Man 1:13; 3Mc 1:15, 22; 2:17; 3:27[2]; 4:3[3], 16; 5:31; 6:31; 7:5[2], 8, 9, 12; 2Es 1:28[2]; 3:32[2], 35; 4:5[2], 7[4], 37, 45, 51; 5:11, 17, 33, 35, 37, 40, 41[2], 50; 6:7; 7:5, 19, 39[2], 40[9], 41[9], 42[6], 46, 57, 66, 73, 75, 76, 102, 103[2], 104[6], 115, 116, 121, 122, 123, 125, 130[2]; 8:34, 38[2], 43; 9:7, 34[5]; 10:11, 36, 55; 12:12; 13:7, 9, 28, 52[2]; 14:21; 15:16; 16:6, 20, 24, 27, 29, 30, 31, 38, 51, 66, 75, 76; 4Mc 2:5, 7; 5:20, 38; 8:24; 9:15, 23; 11:25; 13:18; 14:4; 16:9

OUR (1674)

Ge 1:26[2]; 5:29[2]; 19:31, 32[2], 34; 23:6; 24:60; 29:26; 31:1[2], 14, 16[2], 32; 33:12; 34:9, 14, 16, 17, 21, 31; 37:26, 27[3]; 41:12; 42:13, 21, 32[2]; 43:4, 7, 8[2], 18[2], 21[2], 22[2], 28; 44:8, 25, 26[2], 31; 46:34[2]; 47:3, 15, 18[3], 19[3], 25; Ex 1:10; 3:18; 5:3, 8; 8:10, 26, 27; 10:9[4], 25, 26[2]; 12:27; 14:5; 16:3; 17:3; 34:9[2]; Lev 25:20; Nu 11:6; 14:3[2]; 20:3, 4, 15[2], 16, 19; 21:2; 27:3, 4[2]; 31:49; 32:16[2], 17, 18, 19, 26[4], 32; 36:2, 3[2], 4; Dt 1:6, 19, 20, 25, 28[2], 41; 2:8, 29, 33, 36, 37; 3:3; 4:7; 5:2, 3, 24, 25, 27[2]; 6:4, 20, 22, 23, 24[2], 25; 12:8; 21:7; 26:3, 7[5], 15; 29:14, 18, 19, 29[2]; 31:17[2]; 32:3, 27, 31[2]; Jos 2:11, 13, 14, 24; 5:13; 7:9; 9:11[2], 12[3], 24; 17:4; 18:6; 21:2; 22:19, 24, 25, 27[2], 28[2], 29; 24:17[3], 18, 24; Jdg 6:13; 9:3; 10:10; 11:2, 6, 19, 24[2]; 13:23; 14:3; 16:23[3], 24[4]; 19:19; 20:8[2], 23, 28; 21:7, 18; Ru 2:20; 3:2; 4:3; 1Sa 2:2; 4:3; 5:7, 10, 11; 7:8; 8:20[2]; 9:7, 8; 12:10, 19; 14:9, 10; 16:16; 17:9, 47; 20:29; 23:20; 25:14, 17; 2Sa 7:22; 10:12[2]; 15:15; 17:9; 18:12; 19:9, 41, 43; 22:32; 1Ki 1:11, 43, 47; 8:21, 40, 53, 57[2], 58[2], 59, 61, 65; 12:4, 10; 20:31[2]; 2Ki 4:9; 7:4; 18:22; 19:19; 22:13; 1Ch 12:17, 19; 13:2[2], 3; 15:13; 16:14, 35; 17:20; 19:13[2]; 28:2, 8; 29:10, 13, 15[2], 16, 18; 2Ch 2:4, 5; 6:31; 10:4, 10; 13:10, 11, 12; 14:7, 11[2]; 19:7; 20:6, 7, 9, 12[2]; 28:13[2]; 29:6[2], 9[4]; 32:8[2], 11; 34:21; Ezr 4:3; 5:12; 7:27; 8:17, 18, 21[3], 22[2], 23[2], 25, 30, 31, 33; 9:6[3], 7[4], 8[3], 9[3], 10, 13[4], 15; 10:2, 3[2], 14[3]; Ne 4:4, 9, 11, 15, 20, 23; 5:2[2], 3[3], 4, 5[6], 8, 9[2]; 6:1, 16[2]; 8:10; 9:9, 10, 16, 32[6], 34[4], 36, 37[3], 38[3]; 10:29, 30[2], 32, 33, 34[2], 35, 36[6], 37[5], 38, 39; 13:2, 4, 18, 27; Job 8:9; 15:10; 22:20; 28:22; 37:19; Ps 8:1, 9; 12:4[4]; 18:31; 20:5[2], 7[2]; 22:4; 33:20[2], 21; 35:21, 25; 37:23[2]; 40:3; 44:1[2], 5[2], 7, 9, 10, 13, 18[2], 20[2], 24, 25, 26; 46:1, 7, 11; 47:3, 4, 6; 48:1, 8, 14[2]; 50:3; 59:11; 60:1, 10, 12; 64:6; 65:3, 5; 66:8, 9, 11, 12; 67:6; 68:19, 20; 74:9; 77:13; 78:3, 5; 79:4, 8, 9[2], 10, 12; 80:6[2]; 81:1, 3; 83:12; 84:9; 85:4, 9, 12; 89:17, 18[2]; 90:1, 8[2], 9[2], 10, 12, 14, 17[3]; 92:13; 94:11, 23; 95:1, 6, 7; 98:3; 99:5, 8, 9[2]; 103:10[2], 12; 105:7; 106:6, 7, 47; 108:11, 13; 113:5; 115:3; 116:5; 118:23; 122:2, 9; 123:2[2], 4; 124:1, 2[2], 8; 126:2[2], 4; 135:2, 5; 136:23, 24; 137:2, 3[2]; 144:12[2], 13[3], 14[2]; 147:1, 5, 7; Pr 1:13; 7:18; 20:24[2]; Ecc 5:18; SS 1:16, 17[2]; 2:9, 12, 15; 7:13; 8:8; Isa 1:10; 3:6; 4:1[3]; 25:9; 26:13; 28:15; 33:2[2], 20, 22[3]; 35:2; 36:7; 37:20; 38:20; 40:3, 8; 42:17; 47:4; 52:10; 53:4[2], 5[2], 6; 55:7; 59:12[4], 13; 61:2, 6; 63:16[3], 17, 18; 64:6[2], 7, 8[2], 11[3]; Jer 3:22, 23, 24[2], 25[6]; 5:19, 24; 6:24; 8:14; 9:18[2], 19, 21[2]; 11:21; 12:4; 14:7[2], 20[2], 22[2]; 16:10[2], 19; 17:12; 18:12[2]; 20:10; 21:2, 13; 23:6, 36; 26:16; 31:6; 33:16; 35:6, 8[5], 10; 37:3; 38:16; 42:2, 6[2], 20[2]; 43:2; 44:17[3], 19; 46:16[2]; 50:28; 51:9, 10[2], 51; La 3:40, 41[2], 46; 4:17, 18[5], 19, 20; 5:1, 2[2], 3, 5, 7, 9[2], 10, 15[2], 16, 17[2], 21; Eze 33:10[2], 21; 36:2; 37:11[2]; 40:1; Da 1:13; 3:17; 9:6[3], 8[3], 9, 10, 12, 13[2], 14, 15, 16[3], 17, 18[3]; Hos 7:5; 14:2, 3[2]; Joel 1:16[2]; Am 6:13; Mic 2:4[2]; 4:5, 11; 5:5[2], 6[2]; 7:17, 19[2], 20; Hab 3:2[2]; Zec 1:6; 9:7; 13:9; Mal 2:10; Mt 3:9; 6:9, 11, 12[2]; 8:17[2]; 20:33; 21:42; 23:30; 25:8; 27:25; Mk 11:10; 12:11, 29; Lk 1:55, 71, 72, 73, 74, 75, 78, 79; 3:8; 7:5[2]; 10:11; 11:3, 4; 13:26; 17:5; 18:28; 23:2, 41; 24:20, 22, 32; Jn 3:11; 4:12, 20; 6:31; 7:51; 8:39, 53, 54; 9:20; 11:11, 48[2]; 12:38; 14:23, 31; Ac 2:8, 11, 29, 39; 3:12, 13; 4:25; 5:30; 6:4; 7:2, 11, 12, 15, 17, 19[2], 38, 39, 44, 45[2]; 13:17, 32; 15:10, 25, 26; 16:20; 17:28; 19:25, 37; 20:21; 21:3, 5[2], 25, 28[2]; 22:3, 14; 24:14; 25:26; 26:5, 6, 7, 23; 27:10, 20; 28:17[2]; Ro 1:4, 7; 3:5; 4:1, 12, 24, 25[2]; 5:1, 2, 3, 5, 11, 21; 6:6, 23; 7:5[2], 25; 8:16, 23, 26, 39; 9:10; 10:16; 15:2, 4, 6, 30; 16:1, 9, 18, 20, 23; 1Co 1:1, 2, 3, 7, 8, 9, 10, 21; 2:7; 4:12; 5:4, 7; 6:11; 9:1, 4, 10[2]; 10:1; 12:23, 24; 15:3, 14, 31, 57; 16:12, 22; 2Co 1:1, 2, 3, 4, 5, 7[3], 10, 11, 12[2], 14, 18, 22; 3:2[2], 5; 4:3, 6, 10, 11, 16[2]; 5:2, 4, 9, 13, 21; 6:3, 11, 12; 7:3, 4, 5, 13, 14; 8:7, 9, 17, 19, 22, 23, 24; 9:3; 10:4, 8, 14, 15[2]; 11:12; Gal 1:3, 4[2]; 2:17; 3:24; 4:6, 26; 6:14, 18; Eph 1:2, 3, 7, 12, 14, 17; 2:3, 5, 10, 14; 3:11; 4:25; 5:20; 6:12, 24; Php 1:2; 3:20, 21; 4:20; Col 1:1, 2, 3[2], 7; 2:13; 1Th 1:2, 3[2], 5; 2:1, 2, 3, 4, 5, 8, 9, 10, 18, 19[2], 20; 3:2, 5, 7, 9, 11[3], 13[2]; 5:9, 23, 28; 2Th 1:1, 2, 8, 10, 11, 12[2]; 2:1[2], 14[2], 15, 16[2]; 3:6, 18; 1Ti 1:1[2], 2, 12, 14; 2:3; 3:16; 4:10; 6:3, 14, 17; 2Ti 1:2, 8, 9, 10; 4:15; Tit 1:3, 4; 2:10, 13; 3:3, 4, 6; Phm 1:1[2], 2[2], 3; Heb 1:1; 3:1, 14; 4:14, 15; 6:20; 7:14; 9:14, 24; 10:22[2], 23; 11:2; 12:2, 10, 29; 13:20, 23; Jas 2:1, 21; 3:6; 1Pe 1:3; 2:24; 2Pe 1:1, 2, 8, 11, 14, 16; 2:20; 3:4, 15[2], 18; 1Jn 1:1[2], 3, 4, 9[2]; 2:2; 3:16, 19, 20[2], 21; 4:10; 5:4; 2Jn 1:12; 3Jn 1:9, 12; Jude 1:4[2], 17, 21, 25[2]; Rev 1:5; 4:11; 5:10; 6:10; 7:3, 10, 12; 11:15; 12:10[3]; 19:1, 5, 6; Tob 1:5, 9; 2:1, 2, 3[2]; 4:12; 5:6, 9, 18, 19, 21; 7:1, 4, 11; 8:4, 5; 10:6, 12; 13:4[3]; 14:4; Jdt 3:3[5], 4; 6:3, 4, 19; 7:13, 27[4], 28[4], 30; 8:11, 14, 15, 16, 17, 18, 19[2], 20, 21[2], 22[3], 23[2], 24, 25[2], 31, 32, 33, 35; 10:8, 15; 11:10, 13, 22; 13:11[2], 14, 17, 18, 20[3]; 14:13; 15:9; AdE 4:8[2]; 7:4[2], 6; 13:5[2], 6, 7, 15, 17; 14:3, 5, 6, 11, 12; 15:10[2]; 16:1, 3, 8, 9[2], 10[2], 11, 12[2], 13[2], 16; Wis 2:1, 2[2], 4[3], 5[2], 7, 9[3], 11[2], 12[2], 14, 16; 5:7, 8[2], 13; 7:16; 9:14; 12:6, 22; 15:1, 7, 12; 16:8; 18:6, 8, 22; Sir Pr:T[2]; 37:14; 44:1[2]; 47:7; 49:13[2]; 50:22, 23, 24; Bar 1:10, 12, 13[2], 15, 16[5], 18, 19[2], 20, 21, 22[2]; 2:1[3], 5[2], 6[2], 8, 12, 14[2], 15, 19[4], 24[2], 27; 3:5, 6, 7[4], 8[3], 35; Aza 1:3, 5[2], 7, 9, 10, 14, 15, 17, 18, 29; 1Mc 2:12[3], 20, 22, 37, 40[3], 41, 50, 54; 3:20[2], 21[2], 43[2], 58, 59; 4:9, 10, 18, 36; 5:13, 48; 6:22, 24[2], 57; 7:6; 8:31; 9:8, 9[2], 10[3], 29[2], 30[2], 44, 46; 10:16, 19, 20, 26, 52, 53; 11:31, 33, 50; 12:7, 9, 10, 11[2], 14, 15[3], 16, 17, 23[2]; 13:8, 9, 37, 40, 46; 14:20, 21, 22, 23; 15:3, 4, 9, 17[2], 33[2], 34, 35; 16:2[2], 3; 2Mc 1:11, 17, 19, 27[2]; 2:14, 28, 32; 6:12, 15, 24; 7:2, 16, 18[3], 30, 32, 33, 36, 37[2], 38; 11:23, 24, 25, 26, 30, 36; 14:8, 9[2], 34; 1Es 2:17, 18, 21; 4:60; 5:70; 6:8, 15, 21, 22; 8:10, 46, 47, 50[2], 51, 52, 53, 55, 58, 59, 61, 62, 75[3], 76, 77[5], 79[2], 80[2], 81, 86[3], 90, 93; 9:8, 12; Man 1:1; 3Mc 1:27; 2:10, 12, 13[2], 14, 19[2]; 3:13, 14, 17, 18, 21[2], 23, 24; 5:32; 6:10[2], 25, 28[2]; 7:2[3], 3, 4, 7; 2Es 3:34; 4:23, 24, 33, 35; 5:50; 6:59; 7:106, 125; 8:6[2], 31[2]; 9:29, 32, 36; 10:2, 6, 8, 21[3], 22[15]; 12:48; 14:29; 4Mc 1:13, 17; 2:19; 3:4, 8, 20; 4:5, 20; 5:16[2], 18[2], 22, 24, 26; 6:18, 20, 21, 28; 7:1, 5, 9, 11, 19; 8:20[2]; 9:1, 2[2], 4, 6, 7[2], 23, 24[2], 29, 30; 10:10, 15, 19, 20; 11:12, 25; 12:17[2]; 13:10, 13[3], 22; 16:16, 20[2]; 17:8, 20[2], 21

OURS (19)

Ge 26:20; 34:23; Dt 21:20; Jos 2:14, 20; 9:13; Ru 2:20; 2Ch 14:7; Mk 12:7; Lk 20:14; Ac 19:27; Ro 4:24; 1Co 1:2; 2Pe 1:1; 1Jn 2:2; Jdt 8:18; 1Mc 12:23; 2Es 7:118; 4Mc 11:4

OURSELVES (76)

OUT (3056)

SHALL (6472)

19, 23, 25, 26, 27[2], 29, 30, 32; **5:**3, 7[2], 8, 9, 10, 15[3], 16, 17, 18[2], 19, 22, 23, 24[2], 25[2], 26[2], 27[3], 28, 30[2], 31[2]; **6:**3[3], 4, 5[3], 6, 9[2], 10, 11[2], 12, 13, 14, 16, 17[2], 18[2], 19[2], 20, 21, 23[2], 27; **7:**11; **8:**2, 7, 8, 9, 10, 11, 12[2], 13[2], 14[2], 24, 25, 26[2]; **9:**3[2], 10, 11[2], 12[2], 13[2], 14[2]; **10:**2[2], 3, 4, 5, 6, 7[2], 8[2], 9, 10[2]; **11:**17, 18[2], 19, 23; **13:**2; **14:**21, 23[2], 24, 27, 29, 30, 31, 32, 33[2], 34[2], 35[2], 43; **15:**4, 5, 6, 7, 9, 10, 11, 12, 13, 14, 15[2], 16, 19, 20[2], 21, 24, 25[2], 26, 27, 28[2], 29, 30, 31, 35[2], 40[2]; **16:**7, 22, 28, 30, 38, 40; **17:**3, 5; **18:**1[2], 3, 4, 5, 7[2], 9[2], 10[2], 13, 14, 15[3], 16, 17[3], 18, 20[2], 22, 23[4], 24, 26[2], 27, 28[2], 29, 30, 32[2]; **19:**3[2], 4, 5[2], 6, 7[2], 8[2], 9[2], 10[2], 11, 12, 13, 14, 16, 17[2], 18, 19[3], 20, 21[3], 22[2]; **20:**8[2], 10, 12, 18, 20, 24, 26[2]; **21:**8, 34; **22:**6, 11, 12[2]; **23:**13[2], 16, 23; **24:**7[4], 8[2], 17[3], 19, 22, 23, 24[3]; **25:**5, 13; **26:**53, 54[3], 55[2], 56, 65; **27:**7, 8[2], 9, 10, 11[3], 13, 17[2], 20, 21[4]; **28:**2, 3[2], 4[2], 7[2], 8[2], 11, 14, 15[2], 16, 17, 18[2], 19, 20[2], 21, 23, 24[2], 25[2], 26[2], 27, 28, 31[2]; **29:**1[2], 2, 3, 7[2], 8[2], 9, 12[3], 13[2], 14, 35[2], 36, 39; **30:**2[2], 4[2], 5, 7[2], 8, 9, 11[2], 12, 15; **31:**2, 4, 20, 23[4], 24, 30; **32:**6, 11, 22, 26, 29[2], 30, 32; **33:**52, 53, 54[5], 55[2]; **34:**2, 3[2], 4[3], 5[2], 6[2], 7[2], 8[2], 9[3], 10, 11[2], 12[3], 13, 17, 18; **35:**2, 3[2], 4[2], 5[2], 6[3], 7, 8[4], 11, 12, 13, 14, 15, 16, 17, 18, 19[2], 21[2], 24, 25[3], 26, 27, 29, 30[2], 31, 32, 33, 34; **36:**7[2], 8, 9[2]; **Dt 1:**17, 35, 36, 37, 38, 39[2]; **2:**6[2], 28; **3:**18, 19, 27, 28[2]; **5:**1, 7, 8, 9, 11, 13, 14, 17, 18, 19, 20, 21[2], 25, 31, 32; **6:**5, 13[3], 21; **7:**14, 16[2], 24, 25; **8:**10, 19, 20; **10:**2, 19, 20[4]; **11:**1, 18[2], 24[2], 29; **12:**4, 5[2], 7, 8, 11, 12, 14[2], 16, 18, 23, 24, 26, 27[2]; **13:**4[6], 5[2], 9[2], 11, 14, 15, 16[2]; **14:**3, 7, 8[2], 10, 12, 19, 21[2], 23, 26, 28; **15:**1, 2, 12, 13, 17[3], 19[2], 20, 21, 23; **16:**2, 3, 4[2], 6, 7, 8[3], 9, 10, 13, 15[2], 16[2], 17, 18[2], 20, 21, 22; **17:**5[2], 6, 7[2], 8, 9[2], 12[2], 18, 19[2]; **18:**1, 2, 3[2], 4, 8, 10, 15, 18, 19, 20; **19:**2, 3, 7, 9, 12, 13, 15[2], 17, 18, 19[2], 20[2]; **20:**1, 2, 3, 5, 8, 9, 11, 12, 13, 15, 17; **21:**2, 3, 4[2], 5[2], 6, 7, 9, 12, 13[2], 14, 19, 20, 21[2], 23; **22:**1[2], 2[3], 3[3], 4[2], 5[2], 6, 8, 9, 10, 11, 12, 15, 16, 17, 18, 19[4], 21[3], 22[2], 24[2], 25, 26, 29[3], 30; **23:**1, 2[2], 3[2], 6, 7[2], 9, 10, 11, 12[2], 13[2], 15, 16[2], 17[2], 18, 19, 24, 25; **24:**4, 5[2], 6, 7[2], 8, 10, 11, 12, 13, 14, 15, 16[2], 17[2], 19[2], 20, 21; **25:**2, 4, 5[2], 6, 7, 8, 9, 10, 12, 13, 14, 15[2], 19; **26:**2[2], 3, 5, 10, 11, 13; **27:**2, 3, 4[2], 5, 8, 12, 13, 14, 15, 16, 17, 18, 19, 20, 21, 22, 23, 24, 25, 26; **28:**2, 3[2], 4, 5, 6[2], 7, 10[2], 13, 15, 16[2], 17, 18, 19[2], 22, 23, 24, 25[2], 26[2], 29[3], 30[4], 31[5], 32, 33[2], 34, 36, 37, 38[3], 39[3], 40[3], 41[3], 42, 43[2], 44[4], 45, 46, 48, 51, 52[2], 60, 62, 63, 64, 65, 66[2], 67[4], 68; **30:**8, 16, 18[2]; **31:**2, 3, 5, 11, 23; **32:**25, 35, 42, 50[2], 52; **33:**29[2]; **34:**4; **Jos 1:**4, 5, 6, 8[4], 14[3], 15, 18; **2:**19[3], 20; **3:**3, 4, 8[2], 10, 13[2]; **4:**7[2], 22; **6:**3[2], 4, 5[2], 10[3], 17[2], 19, 26[2]; **7:**14[4], 15; **8:**2, 4, 5, 7, 8; **9:**23; **10:**8; **11:**6; **14:**9, 12; **15:**4; **17:**17, 18[3]; **18:**5, 6; **20:**3, 4[4], 5, 6; **23:**5, 13, 16; **24:**27[2]; **Jdg 1:**1, 2; **2:**3[2]; **6:**10, 16, 23, 26, 31, 37; **7:**4[4], 5[2], 11[2]; **9:**9, 11, 13; **10:**18; **11:**2, 31; **13:**3, 5[3], 7[2], 22; **14:**13; **16:**7, 11, 13; **19:**30; **20:**18[2], 23, 28[2]; **21:**1, 5, 7, 11[2], 16; **Ru 1:**16; **4:**15; **1Sa 1:**11[2]; **2:**9, 10, 30, 32[2], 33[3], 34[2], 35[2], 36[2]; **3:**9, 14; **5:**8; **6:**2, 4, 9, 20; **8:**9[2], 17; **9:**16[2], 17, 19; **10:**1[2], 2, 3, 4, 5, 8[3]; **11:**7, 9[2], 12, 13; **12:**12, 17, 25; **14:**37, 39, 40, 44, 45[2]; **15:**33; **16:**3[2]; **17:**9, 26, 27, 36; **18:**21, 25; **19:**6; **20:**2, 12, 19, 31[2], 42; **21:**15; **22:**16; **23:**2, 17[3]; **24:**4, 12, 13, 20[2]; **25:**6, 11, 28, 29[2], 31; **27:**1[2], 12; **28:**2, 10, 11, 19; **29:**4, 9; **30:**8[4], 23, 24[2]; **2Sa 2:**1[2]; **3:**13; **4:**11; **5:**2[2], 8, 19, 23; **6:**22; **7:**8, 10, 12, 13, 14, 16[2], 29; **9:**7, 10[3]; **10:**11; **11:**11, 21, 25; **12:**6, 10, 11, 13, 14, 23; **14:**10, 11; **15:**20, 36; **16:**10, 20; **17:**6, 12[2], 13; **18:**3, 20; **19:**21, 22, 23, 29, 38; **20:**21; **21:**3[2], 17; **24:**13[3]; **1Ki 1:**13[2], 17[2], 20, 24[2], 30[2], 35[2], 52[2]; **2:**4, 24, 33[2], 37[2], 42, 45[2]; **3:**12, 13, 26; **5:**5, 9[2]; **8:**19[3], 25, 29, 42, 44; **9:**5; **11:**2[2], 37[2]; **12:**24; **13:**2[3], 3[2], 9, 17, 22, 32; **14:**3, 5, 11[2], 12, 13[2], 14; **16:**4[2]; **17:**1, 4; **18:**31; **19:**15, 16[2], 17[2]; **20:**6, 13, 14, 23, 25, 28, 39[2], 40, 42; **21:**19[2], 23, 24[2]; **22:**6[2], 11, 15[2], 22; **2Ki 1:**2, 4[2], 6[2], 16[2]; **2:**21; **3:**8, 17[3], 19[4]; **4:**2, 16, 43; **5:**10[2], 27; **6:**8, 15, 21[2]; **7:**1, 2[2], 4[4], 12, 18, 19[2]; **8:**8, 9, 10[2]; **9:**7, 8, 10[2], 36, 37; **10:**10, 19, 24, 30; **11:**6, 8; **13:**17; **14:**6[2]; **15:**12; **16:**15; **17:**12, 35, 36[3], 37[2], 38[2], 39; **18:**22; **19:**7, 10, 11, 29[2], 30, 31, 32, 33[2]; **20:**1[2], 5, 8[2], 9, 17[2], 18[2]; **21:**14; **22:**7, 18, 20[2]; **23:**27; **25:**24; **1Ch 11:**2[2], 6; **14:**10, 14; **16:**30, 33; **17:**4, 7, 9, 12, 13, 14; **19:**12; **21:**12; **22:**1, 8, 9[3], 10[2]; **23:**4[2], 5, 28, 30, 32[2]; **28:**3, 6; **2Ch 1:**12; **6:**9[3], 16, 34; **7:**18; **8:**11; **11:**4; **12:**7, 8; **15:**7; **18:**5[2], 10, 14[2], 21; **19:**9, 10; **23:**4, 5[2], 6, 7[2]; **25:**4[2], 9; **28:**13; **32:**12[2]; **33:**4; **34:**26, 28[2]; **Ezr 4:**3; **6:**3, 5, 8, 11[3], 12; **7:**16, 17[2], 19, 24, 25; **9:**10, 14; **Ne 2:**8; **9:**29; **10:**38[2], 39; **13:**25, 27; **Est 5:**3, 6[2]; **6:**6, 9, 11; **7:**2[2]; **9:**12[2]; **Job 1:**21; **2:**10; **5:**19, 21[2], 22[2], 23[2], 24[2], 25, 26; **7:**4, 8, 21[2]; **8:**13; **9:**29; **11:**3; **13:**16, 18; **16:**22[2]; **17:**10, 16; **18:**2, 4; **19:**26, 27[2]; **23:**10; **28:**12, 18; **29:**18[2]; **31:**14[2]; **33:**28; **34:**17; **36:**12; **37:**19; **38:**3, 11[2]; **40:**2, 4; **42:**8; **Ps 2:**9; **4:**2; **6:**10[2]; **9:**17, 18; **10:**6[2], 16; **11:**6, 7; **13:**2, 5; **14:**5; **15:**5; **16:**8; **17:**15[2]; **18:**3; **19:**13; **20:**8; **21:**7; **22:**26[2], 27[2], 29[3]; **23:**1, 6[2]; **24:**3[2]; **25:**13; **27:**1[2], 2, 3, 13; **28:**1; **30:**6; **32:**6; **34:**1, 5; **35:**9, 10, 28; **37:**9[2], 11, 15[2], 17, 22[2], 24, 27, 28[2], 29, 38[2]; **42:**2, 5, 11; **43:**5; **45:**16; **46:**5; **49:**3[2], 14[3]; **50:**15; **51:**7[2]; **53:**5; **55:**23; **60:**12; **62:**2, 6; **63:**9, 10[2], 11[2]; **65:**1, 2, 4; **69:**35, 36[2]; **75:**8, 10; **81:**9[2]; **82:**7; **86:**9[2]; **87:**5; **89:**21[2], 22[2], 24[2], 26, 36, 37; **91:**10; **92:**9[2]; **93:**1; **94:**3[2]; **95:**11; **96:**10, 12; **101:**2, 3, 4, 6, 7[2]; **102:**28[2]; **104:**5; **108:**13; **116:**12; **118:**7, 17[2], 20; **119:**6, 42, 45, 46, 74; **120:**3[2]; **121:**6; **125:**3; **126:**6; **127:**5; **128:**2[3], 4; **132:**12[2]; **135:**18; **137:**8, 9; **138:**4, 5; **139:**10[2], 11; **140:**13[2]; **141:**6[2], 7; **143:**7; **145:**4[2], 6, 7[2], 10[2], 11; **Pr 1:**13[2], 31; **22:**13; **23:**35; **30:**9[2]; **Ecc 5:**15[2], 16; **7:**18; **SS 8:**8; **Isa 1:**18[2], 19, 20, 26, 27, 28[2], 29[2], 30, 31[2]; **2:**2[3], 3[2], 4[5], 11[2], 17[2], 18; **3:**4, 6[2], 7, 10, 11, 25, 26[2]; **4:**1, 2[2]; **5:**5[2], 6[2], 9, 10[2], 17[2]; **6:**8; **7:**7[2], 9, 14[2], 15, 22; **8:**10, 13, 15[3]; **9:**5, 7[2]; **10:**11, 15; **11:**1[2], 2, 3[2], 4[3], 5, 6[3], 7[3], 8[2], 10[3], 13[4], 14[4], 16; **14:**24[2], 25; **16:**5[2]; **17:**5; **18:**6; **20:**4, 5, 6; **22:**18[2], 21, 22[4]; **24:**2, 3, 13, 18[2]; **25:**10; **26:**19[2]; **27:**6[2]; **29:**2[2], 4[4], 5, 7, 8, 14[2], 16[2], 17, 18[2], 19[2], 20[3], 22[2]; **30:**3, 13, 15[2], 16[2], 17[2], 19, 20, 21, 29; **31:**7, 8[4], 9; **34:**3[3], 4[2], 7[2], 9[2], 10[4], 11[3], 12[2], 13[2], 14[3], 15[2], 16[2], 17[2]; **35:**1[2], 2[3], 5, 6[2], 7[3], 8[5], 9[4], 10[4]; **36:**7; **37:**7, 10, 11, 30, 31, 32, 33, 34[2]; **38:**1[2], 11[2], 22; **39:**6[2], 7[2]; **40:**4[2], 5[2], 6, 31[4]; **41:**11[3], 12[3], 15[2], 16[5], 25; **42:**17; **43:**2[3], 10; **44:**4, 11[3], 19[2], 26[2], 28[3]; **45:**1, 13, 14[3], 17, 23[3], 24[2], 25; **46:**10; **47:**1, 3[2], 5, 7, 8, 9[2], 11[3], 13; **48:**14[2]; **49:**7[2], 9[2], 10[2], 11, 12, 18[2], 22[2], 23[3], 25, 26[2]; **50:**7, 11[2]; **51:**11[4], 14[3], 22; **52:**1, 3, 6[2], 10, 12[2], 13[3], 15[4]; **53:**10[3], 11[4], 12; **54:**10[2], 13[2], 14[4], 15, 17[3]; **55:**5[2], 11[3], 12[3], 13[4]; **56:**5, 7; **57:**6, 13, 14; **58:**8[4], 9[2], 10, 11, 12[3], 14; **59:**19, 21; **60:**2, 3, 4[2], 5[4], 6[4], 7[3], 9, 10[2], 11[3], 12[2], 13, 14[3], 16[3], 18[2], 19[2], 20[2], 21[2], 22; **61:**4[3], 5[2], 6[4], 7[2], 9[2], 10; **62:**2[2], 3, 4[4], 5[2], 6, 8, 9[2], 12[2]; **65:**9[2], 10, 12, 13[6], 14[3], 15, 16[2], 17, 19, 20, 21[2], 22[4], 23[2], 25[4]; **66:**5, 8[2], 9[2], 12, 13, 14[4], 16, 17, 18[2], 19, 20, 22[2], 23, 24[4]; **Jer 1:**7[2], 14, 15[2], 19; **2:**26, 36; **3:**16[3], 17[3], 18[2]; **4:**2[2], 9[2], 10, 14, 27, 28; **5:**6[3], 9[2], 12, 13, 14, 17[5], 19[2], 29[2]; **6:**3[3], 8, 10, 11, 12, 15[2], 21[2]; **7:**20, 23, 27[2], 28, 34; **8:**1, 2[3], 3, 4, 9[2], 12[2], 17; **9:**9[2], 22[2]; **10:**11[2], 15, 18; **11:**3, 4, 21, 22[2], 23; **12:**12, 13, 16; **13:**10, 12, 13; **14:**13[2], 15[2], 16[2], 17; **15:**2[2], 14, 19[2], 20; **16:**2[2], 4[6], 6[4], 7[2], 8, 11, 13, 14, 16[2], 19, 21; **17:**4[2], 6[3], 8[3], 13[2], 14[2], 25[2], 26, 27[2]; **18:**18; **19:**3, 6, 9, 10, 11[2], 13; **20:**4[3], 5, 6[4]; **21:**4, 6, 7[2], 8, 9[3], 10[2], 14; **22:**4, 5, 7, 10, 11, 12[2], 18[2], 19, 22[2], 26, 27, 30[2]; **23:**3, 4[2], 5[2], 7, 8, 12[2], 17[2], 33, 35, 36, 37, 38, 40; **24:**7[2], 9; **25:**11[2], 14, 16, 26, 27, 28, 29, 30, 33[3], 34, 35[2]; **26:**4, 8, 9[2], 18[2]; **27:**4, 7[2], 9, 22[2]; **28:**14; **29:**21, 22, 24, 32; **30:**3, 7, 8, 9, 10[2], 16[3], 18, 19[3], 20[2], 21[3], 22; **31:**1, 4[2], 5[3], 6, 8, 9[2], 12[4], 13[2], 14, 16, 17, 23, 24, 29, 30[2], 33, 34[2], 38, 39[2], 40[2]; **32:**3, 4[3], 5[3], 15, 28, 29, 38, 43, 44[2]; **33:**5, 9[3], 10, 12, 13, 15, 17, 18; **34:**2, 3[4], 4, 5[2], 20[2]; **35:**6, 7[3], 15, 19; **36:**6[2], 29, 30[2]; **37:**7, 8[2], 17; **38:**2[3], 3, 17[3], 18[3], 20[2], 23[4], 26; **39:**16, 17, 18[2]; **40:**9; **42:**14, 16[3], 17[2], 18[2], 22; **43:**11, 12[4], 13[2]; **44:**12[5], 14[2], 26, 27, 28[2], 29; **45:**4; **46:**10, 14, 19, 23, 24[2], 26, 27[2]; **47:**2[4]; **48:**2[2], 7[2], 8[4], 9, 12, 13, 26, 40, 41[2], 42, 44[2]; **49:**2[3], 3, 12[2], 13[2], 17, 18[2], 20[2], 21[2], 22[2], 26[2], 27, 29, 32, 33[3], 36[2]; **50:**3[3], 4[2], 5[2], 9[2], 10[2], 12[3], 13[3], 16[2], 19[2], 20[3], 30[2], 32, 39[3], 40[2], 45[2], 46[2]; **51:**2[2], 4, 14, 18, 26[2], 35[2], 37, 38[2], 44, 47[2], 48[2], 52, 57, 58[2], 62[2], 64; **La 4:**15, 20, 21[2]; **Eze 2:**4, 5, 7; **3:**10, 17, 18[2], 19, 20[3], 21, 25[2], 26, 27; **4:**4, 5, 6, 7[2], 9, 10[2], 11[2], 12, 13, 16[2]; **5:**2[3], 3, 4, 10[2], 12[2], 13[2], 15, 17; **6:**4[2], 6, 7[2], 8, 9, 10, 11, 12[3], 13, 14; **7:**4, 9, 11, 13[2], 16, 17, 18[3], 19[3], 21, 22[2], 24, 25, 26[2], 27[4]; **9:**5[2]; **11:**7, 10[2], 11[2], 12, 20; **12:**3, 4[2], 6[2], 11[2], 12[4], 13[3], 15, 16, 19[2], 20[3], 23, 24; **13:**9[3], 11, 13, 14[2], 21[2], 23; **14:**3, 8, 10[2], 11, 22, 23[2]; **15:**7[2]; **16:**16, 39[2], 40[2], 41[2], 42, 55[3], 62; **17:**16, 18, 20, 21[3], 24; **18:**3, 4, 9, 13[4], 17[2], 19, 20[4], 21[2], 22[2], 24[3], 26[2], 27, 28[2]; **20:**11, 13, 21, 31, 32, 38[2], 39, 40, 42, 43[2], 44, 47[3], 48[2]; **21:**4, 5[2], 7, 19, 24, 26, 32[3]; **22:**3, 14, 16[2], 21, 22[2]; **23:**24[3], 25[4], 26, 27, 29[2], 32[2], 33, 34, 45, 47[3], 49[3]; **24:**13, 16[2], 21, 22[2], 23[3], 24[3], 27[4]; **25:**4[3], 5, 7, 10, 11, 13, 14[2], 17; **26:**2, 4, 5[2], 6[2], 8[2], 9, 10[3], 11[3], 12[2], 13, 14[2], 15, 16[5], 17, 21; **27:**36; **28:**7, 8[2], 10, 19, 22, 23[2], 24[2], 25, 26[4]; **29:**5, 6, 9[2], 11[3], 12, 14, 15, 16[2], 19[2], 21; **30:**4[2], 5, 6[3], 7[2], 8, 9[2], 11[2], 13, 16[2], 17[2], 18[4], 19, 25[3], 26; **31:**18[2]; **32:**7, 10[2], 11, 12[2], 13[2], 15, 16[3], 20, 21, 28, 32; **33:**4, 5, 7, 8[2], 9, 12[3], 13[3], 14, 15[2], 16[2], 18, 19, 25, 26, 27[2], 28[2], 29, 33; **34:**10, 14[3], 17, 22, 23[2], 24, 26, 27[4], 28[4], 29, 30; **35:**4[2], 6[2], 8, 9[2], 10, 12, 15[2]; **36:**7, 8[2], 9, 10, 11[2], 12[3], 14, 15[2], 23, 25, 28[2], 31[2], 33, 34, 36, 38[2]; **37:**5, 6[2], 13, 14[2], 22[3], 23[2], 24[3], 25[3], 26, 27[2], 28; **38:**8[2], 9[2], 18, 19, 20[4], 23; **39:**4, 5, 6, 7, 11[2], 12, 13, 14, 15, 16, 17, 18, 19, 20, 21, 22, 23, 26, 28; **40:**4; **42:**13[2], 14[2]; **43:**7, 12, 13[2], 16, 17[2], 19, 20[2], 21[2], 22[2], 23, 24[2], 25[2], 26, 27; **44:**2[4], 3[2], 5, 9, 10, 11[3], 12, 13[2], 15[2], 16[3], 17[2], 18[2], 19[2], 20[2], 21, 22, 23, 24[4], 25, 26, 27, 28[2], 29[2], 30[2], 31; **45:**1[2], 2, 3[2], 4[3], 5, 6[2], 7, 8[2], 10, 11[2], 12[2], 13, 16, 17[2], 18, 19, 20[2], 21[2], 22, 23, 24, 25; **46:**1[3], 2[6], 3, 4, 5[2], 6[2], 7, 8[2], 9[4], 10[2], 11, 12[4], 13[2], 14, 15, 16, 17[2], 18[3], 20[2], 24; **47:**13[2], 14[2], 15, 17[2], 18, 19[2], 20[2], 21, 22[3], 23; **48:**8[2], 9[2], 10[2], 11, 12, 13[2], 14[2], 15[2], 16, 17, 18[3], 19, 20[2], 21[2], 22[2], 28, 29, 30, 35[2]; **Da 2:**5[2], 6, 9, 39[2], 40[2], 41[2], 42, 44[4], 45; **3:**6, 10, 11, 15, 29; **4:**25[5], 26, 32[4]; **5:**7, 16; **6:**5, 7, 12, 26; **7:**14[2], 17, 18, 23[3], 24[4], 25[4], 26[2], 27[3]; **8:**14, 22, 23, 24[4], 25[5]; **9:**25[2], 26[5], 27[3]; **11:**2[3], 3[2], 4[2], 5[3], 6[5], 7[3], 8[2], 9, 10[3], 11[3], 12[3], 13[2], 14[3], 15[3], 16[4], 17[4], 18[4], 19[3], 20[3], 21[2], 22, 23, 24[2], 25[4], 26[3], 27[2], 28[3], 29[2], 30[4], 31[2], 32[2], 33[2], 34[2], 35, 36[5], 37[3], 38[2], 39[4], 40[3], 41[3], 42[2], 43[2], 44[2], 45[2]; **12:**1[3], 2, 3, 4[2], 6, 8, 10[4], 11, 13; **Hos 1:**10[2], 11[4]; **2:**7[4], 10, 12, 15, 17, 20, 21, 22[2], 23; **3:**3[2], 4, 5[2]; **4:**5[2], 9, 10[2], 19; **5:**6, 7, 9, 14; **6:**4[2]; **7:**16; **8:**3, 6, 7[2], 10, 13, 14; **9:**2[2], 3[3], 4[6], 6[4], 11, 16, 17; **10:**5[2], 6[3], 7, 8[3], 9, 10, 14[2], 15[2]; **11:**5[2], 10[2], 11; **12:**11[2]; **13:**3, 14[2], 15[4], 16[3]; **14:**3, 5[2], 6[2], 7[4]; **Joel 2:**24[2], 26[2], 27[2], 28[3], 31, 32[3]; **3:**17[3], 18[4], 19, 20; **Am 1:**4, 5, 7, 8, 10, 12, 14, 15; **2:**2[2], 5, 12, 14[3], 15[3], 16; **3:**11[2], 12, 14, 15[2]; **4:**2, 3[2]; **5:**3[2], 5[2], 11[2], 16[3], 17, 26; **6:**7[2], 9, 10[3], 11, 14; **7:**3, 6, 9[2], 11, 17[5]; **8:**3[2], 8, 12[3], 13, 14; **9:**1[2], 2, 3, 4, 9, 10[2], 13[3], 14[3], 15; **Ob 1:**2, 9, 10[2], 15[2], 16[3], 17[3], 18[3], 19[3], 20[2], 21[2]; **Jnh 1:**11; **2:**4; **3:**4, 7[3], 8[3]; **Mic 1:**7[3], 11, 14[2], 15; **2:**3, 4; **3:**6[3], 7[2], 11, 12[2]; **4:**1[3], 2[2], 3[5], 4[2], 8[2], 10[3], 13[2]; **5:**2, 3[2], 4[3], 5, 6[2], 7, 8, 9[2], 12, 13; **6:**6[2], 7, 14[3], 15[3], 16; **7:**8, 9, 11, 16[3], 17[4]; **Na 1:**14, 15; **2:**13[2]; **3:**7; **Hab 1:**2, 12; **2:**6, 8; **Zep 1:**13[3], 17[2], 18; **2:**4[4], 6, 7[3], 9[3], 10, 11, 12, 14[3]; **3:**8, 10, 11[2], 12, 13[3], 15, 16; **Hag 2:**7, 9, 22; **Zec 1:**16[2], 17; **2:**4, 9, 11[3]; **3:**7, 10; **4:**7[2], 9, 10[2]; **5:**3[2], 4[2]; **6:**12[2], 13[4], 14, 15[2]; **8:**3[2], 4, 5, 8, 12[4], 13, 16, 19, 20, 21, 22, 23; **9:**4, 5[4], 6, 7[3], 8[2], 10[3], 15[2], 16, 17; **10:**4, 5[3], 6, 7[4], 8, 9[2], 11[4], 12; **11:**6; **12:**3[2], 5, 6[2], 8[2], 10, 12; **13:**1, 2, 3[2], 8[2]; **14:**2[3], 4[3], 5[3], 6, 7[2], 8[2], 10[2], 11[3], 12[4], 13, 14, 15, 16, 18, 19, 20[2], 21[2]; **Mal 1:**5[2], 13; **3:**7, 11, 17, 18; **4:**1, 2[2], 3; **Mt 1:**23[2]; **2:**6; **5:**21[2], 27, 33, 43; **19:**5[2], 18[4], 19; **21:**13; **22:**24, 37, 39; **Mk 10:**7, 8, 19[5]; **11:**17, 32; **12:**19, 30, 31; **Lk 2:**23; **3:**5[3], 6; **10:**27; **18:**20[4]; **19:**46; **20:**13, 28; **Jn 6:**45; **7:**38; **19:**15, 36; **Ac 2:**17[3], 18, 20, 21; **3:**25; **7:**7; **23:**5; **Ro 4:**18; **7:**7; **9:**7, 9, 12, 26; **10:**13; **13:**9[4]; **14:**11[2]; **15:**12[2], 21[2]; **1Co 6:**16; **9:**9; **2Co 6:**16, 18; **Gal 3:**8; **5:**14; **1Ti 5:**18; **Heb 4:**3, 5; **8:**10, 11[2]; **11:**18; **12:**20; **Jas 2:**8, 11[2]; **1Pe 1:**16; **Tob 2:**2, 6; **3:**10[2]; **5:**16; **6:**13; **8:**20[3]; **12:**2, 3; **14:**5; **Jdt 2:**8[2], 10[2]; **5:**5, 21; **6:**4, 5, 6[2], 9; **7:**27[2]; **8:**22; **9:**2; **11:**16, 23[2]; **16:**15[2], 17; **AdE 2:**3[2], 4; **5:**3, 4, 6, 8; **6:**6, 9, 11; **7:**2; **13:**6; **15:**10; **16:**22, 24[2]; **Wis 2:**2; **8:**10, 11[2], 13, 14, 15, 16; **9:**12[2]; **15:**7; **Sir 11:**19; **24:**9; **39:**15; **45:**14; **48:**11; **49:**11; **51:**18; **Bar 1:**12[2], 14, 15; **2:**35; **Sus 1:**53; **Bel 1:**8, 9; **1Mc 1:**50; **2:**65, 66, 67; **3:**50[2], 60; **7:**28; **8:**25, 26[2], 27, 28[2], 30[3]; **10:**16, 31, 35, 41; **11:**9, 35, 36; **13:**39; **14:**25, 44, 45; **15:**7, 8; **2Mc 1:**18; **2:**7, 23; **6:**26; **11:**25, 31; **1Es 1:**58; **3:**6, 7[2], 9, 16; **4:**42; **6:**32, 33; **8:**19, 23, 24, 82; **3Mc 2:**28[2], 29, 30; **3:**24, 29; **7:**9; **2Es 1:**9, 24, 30; **2:**12[2], 27[2], 28[2]; **4:**51; **5:**1[3], 2, 3[2], 4[2], 5[4], 6[2], 7[3], 8[4], 9[4], 10[3], 11, 12[3], 13, 42; **6:**6, 20[2], 21[3], 22[2], 23[2], 24[4], 25[3], 26[2], 27[2], 28[3]; **7:**17[2], 26[2], 27, 28[2], 29, 30[2], 31[2], 32[2], 33[3], 34[3], 35[4], 36[3], 42, 60, 67, 72, 75[2], 78, 80[2], 83, 84, 85, 86, 87[2], 88, 91[2], 96, 98[3], 99, 101[2], 105[3], 123[2], 125[2], 127, 128[2], 131; **8:**3, 9, 33, 40; **9:**3, 7, 9[2], 31[2]; **10:**58; **11:**17; **12:**13[2], 14, 15, 18[4], 20[2], 21[3], 23[2], 25, 26, 27, 28[2], 38; **13:**19, 30, 31, 33, 34, 35, 36, 48; **14:**6[2], 9[2], 16, 17, 18[2], 25[2], 26[3], 34[2], 35[3]; **15:**4, 13[2], 15, 16[2], 17, 18[3], 19[2], 27, 29[2], 30[3], 31, 32[2], 33[2], 35[3], 37[3], 38, 39[3], 40[2], 41, 42, 43, 44[4], 45, 50[2], 51, 55, 57[4], 58[2], 59, 60[2], 61[2], 62[2], 63; **16:**12, 14, 15, 16, 18[5], 21, 22[2], 23[4], 24, 25, 26[2], 28, 31, 32[3], 33[3], 34[2], 46, 50[2], 65[2], 68, 69[2], 70, 71, 72, 73; **4Mc 1:**12[3], 14; **2:**5; **5:**28, 36, 38; **9:**8[2]; **12:**7; **16:**9, 11; **18:**14, 17

SHE (1296)

Ge 3:6[2], 12, 20; **4:**1, 2, 17, 25[2]; **11:**29, 30; **12:**18, 19; **16:**1, 4[4], 5[3], 6, 8, 13[2]; **17:**16; **18:**15; **19:**26, 33[2], 35[2]; **20:**2, 3, 5[2], 12[2]; **21:**7, 9, 10, 12, 14, 15, 16[4], 19[2]; **24:**16, 18, 19[2], 20[2], 24[2], 25, 36, 45, 46[2], 47, 55, 58, 64[2], 65, 67; **25:**2, 21, 22[2], 26; **26:**7[2], 9[2]; **27:**16, 17[2], 42; **29:**9, 12, 32[2], 33[2], 34, 35[3]; **30:**1[3], 3[2], 4, 6, 8, 9[2], 11, 13, 15, 17, 18, 19, 20, 21, 23, 24; **31:**35; **34:**1; **35:**8, 16, 17, 18[2], 19; **36:**12, 14; **38:**3, 4[2], 5[4], 14[3], 15, 16[2], 17, 18[2], 19[2], 24, 25[3], 26, 28, 29; **39:**10, 12, 13, 14, 16, 17; **46:**15, 18, 25; **Ex 1:**16; **2:**2[2], 3[3], 5, 6[4], 10[4], 22; **4:**26; **6:**20, 23, 25; **21:**4, 7, 8, 11; **Lev 12:**2[2], 4, 5[2], 6, 7, 8[3]; **15:**19, 20[2], 22, 23, 25[3], 26[2], 28[3], 29; **18:**7, 11, 12, 13, 14, 15, 19; **19:**20; **20:**17, 18; **21:**3, 9[2]; **22:**12, 13; **Nu 5:**13[3], 14, 27, 28; **12:**10, 14[2]; **25:**18; **26:**59; **30:**4[2], 5, 6[2], 7, 8[2], 9, 10, 11, 14, 16; **Dt 21:**12, 13; **22:**19, 21, 24, 29; **24:**1[2], 4; **25:**6; **28:**56[3], 57[2]; **Jos 2:**4, 6[2], 8, 15[2], 16, 21[3]; **6:**17, 25; **15:**18[3], 19; **Jdg 1:**14[3], 15; **4:**5, 6, 9, 18, 19; **5:**25[2], 26[4], 28, 29; **11:**34, 36, 37, 38[2], 39[2]; **13:**9, 14[3]; **14:**3, 7, 17[3]; **15:**2; **16:**8, 9, 14, 15, 16, 18, 19[2], 20; **19:**2; **20:**5; **Ru 1:**3, 6[2], 7[3], 9, 15, 18[2], 20; **2:**2, 3[3], 6, 7[3], 10, 13, 14[4], 15, 17[3], 18[4], 19[2], 23[2]; **3:**5, 6, 7, 9, 14, 15, 16[2], 18; **4:**13[2]; **1Sa 1:**7[2], 10, 11, 12, 13, 18, 20[2], 22, 23, 24[3], 26, 28; **2:**5, 19, 20, 21; **4:**19[2], 20[2], 21, 22; **18:**19, 21; **19:**13, 14; **25:**18, 19, 20[2], 23, 24, 35, 36, 41, 42; **28:**12, 14, 21[2], 24[2], 25; **2Sa 6:**16; **11:**4[3], 5, 26, 27; **12:**24; **13:**2, 8, 9, 10, 11, 12, 14, 16, 18, 19[3]; **14:**4, 5, 11, 27; **20:**17, 18; **21:**8[2], 10; **1Ki 1:**4, 17, 22, 28; **2:**13, 14, 16, 19, 20, 21; **3:**17, 19, 20[2], 27; **10:**1, 2[3], 6, 10, 13[2]; **14:**4, 5[2], 6, 17[2]; **15:**13; **17:**11, 12, 15[2], 18; **21:**8[2], 9, 11; **2Ki 4:**2, 5[2], 6, 7, 9, 12, 13, 14, 15, 16, 21, 22, 23, 24, 25, 26, 27[3], 28, 36, 37[2]; **5:**2, 3; **6:**28, 29; **8:**2, 3, 6[2]; **9:**30, 31, 34; **11:**1, 2[2], 13, 14, 16[2]; **19:**21[3]; **22:**14, 15; **1Ch 1:**32; **2:**21, 26, 29, 35, 49; **4:**17; **7:**14, 16, 23; **15:**29; **2Ch 9:**1[3], 5, 9, 12[3]; **11:**19; **15:**16; **22:**10, 11[3]; **23:**12, 13, 15; **34:**23; **Est 1:**11, 15, 17, 19; **2:**1, 7, 11, 13[2], 14[4], 15, 17, 20; **4:**4; **5:**2, 12; **8:**3, 5; **Ps 45:**14; **84:**3; **Pr 1:**20, 21[2]; **3:**15, 18; **4:**6[2], 8[2], 9[2], 13; **5:**4, 6[2]; **7:**11, 12, 13[2], 21[2], 26; **8:**2, 3; **9:**1, 2[3], 3[2], 4, 13, 14, 16; **11:**16; **12:**4; **23:**22, 28; **30:**20, 23[2]; **31:**10, 12, 13, 14[2], 15, 16[2], 17, 18, 19, 20, 21, 22, 24[2], 25, 26, 27; **SS 8:**5, 8[2], 9[2]; **Isa 1:**21; **3:**26; **8:**3; **21:**2; **23:**17; **26:**17; **37:**22[3]; **40:**2[2]; **51:**18[2]; **54:**6; **66:**7[3], 8; **Jer 3:**1, 6[2], 7[3], 8[2], 9[2]; **4:**17; **6:**7; **11:**15; **12:**8; **15:**9[3]; **31:**15; **46:**22, 24; **48:**9; **49:**24; **50:**9, 12[2], 13, 14, 15[2], 29[2], 39; **51:**8, 9, 42, 53; **La 1:**1[3], 2[2], 3, 8[2], 9, 10; **Eze 5:**6; **16:**49; **19:**2, 3, 5[3]; **23:**5[2], 7[3], 8[2], 9, 10, 11[2], 12, 13, 14[2], 16[2], 17[2], 18, 19[2], 43; **24:**7[3], 8; **Da 5:**10; **11:**6[3]; **Hos 1:**3, 6, 8[2]; **2:**2[2], 3, 5[2], 6, 7[3], 8, 12, 13, 15[2]; **13:**16; **Mic 1:**7; **5:**3; **7:**10; **Na 3:**10[2]; **Mal 2:**14; **Mt 1:**18, 21, 25; **2:**18; **8:**15; **9:**18, 21; **12:**42; **14:**6, 7, 8; **15:**23, 25, 27; **20:**20, 21; **22:**28; **26:**7, 10, 12, 13, 71; **Mk 1:**31; **5:**23, 26[3], 27, 28, 29[2], 42; **6:**19, 22, 24[2], 25; **7:**25, 26, 28, 30; **10:**12[2]; **12:**23, 44[3]; **14:**3, 6, 8[3], 9, 67[2]; **16:**10; **Lk 1:**24[2], 29, 40, 45, 57; **2:**7, 36, 37, 38; **4:**39; **7:**12, 38[2], 39, 44, 45, 46, 47; **8:**43[2], 44, 47[5], 50, 52, 53, 55; **10:**39, 40; **11:**31; **13:**11, 13; **15:**8[2], 9[2]; **18:**5; **21:**4[2]; **Jn 4:**28; **8:**11; **11:**20, 27, 28[2], 29[2], 31, 32; **12:**7[2]; **16:**21[2]; **20:**2, 11[2], 12, 13, 14[3], 15, 16, 18; **Ac 5:**8, 10; **9:**36, 37, 39, 40[2]; **12:**14[2], 15; **16:**14, 15[3], 17[2], 18; **19:**27; **Ro 7:**2, 3[5]; **9:**10, 12; **16:**2[2]; **1Co 7:**11, 12, 13, 28, 39[2], 40[3]; **11:**6[2]; **Gal 4:**25, 26[2]; **Eph 5:**27; **1Ti 2:**12, 15; **5:**6, 9, 10; **Heb 11:**31; **Jas 2:**25; **Rev 2:**21; **12:**2, 5, 6[2], 14[2]; **14:**8; **18:**6[2], 7[2], 8, 19; **Tob 2:**12[4], 13, 14[2]; **3:**8, 10[5], 11; **4:**4[2]; **6:**1, 14, 16, 18[3]; **7:**4[2], 11[4], 12, 16[4]; **8:**5, 7, 13; **10:**4, 7[3], 12; **11:**6[2], 9, 15; **Jdt 8:**1, 5[2], 6, 7[2], 8, 9, 10[2], 11; **9:**1; **10:**2[4], 3[4], 4[2], 5[2], 8, 9[2], 10, 12, 14, 18, 23; **12:**5[2], 7[2], 8, 9[2], 12, 15[2], 19; **13:**3[4], 6, 7, 8, 9[2], 13, 14, 15; **14:**8[3], 9; **15:**11, 12, 13[2]; **16:**7[2], 8, 19[2], 21, 22, 23[3], 24[2]; **AdE 1:**11, 17[2], 18, 19; **2:**13[2], 14[4], 15, 17, 20[3]; **4:**4[2], 10; **5:**7; **7:**3; **8:**3[2], 4; **14:**2[5], 3; **15:**1[3], 2, 3, 5[2], 6[2], 8, 13, 15[2]; **Wis 3:**13; **6:**12, 13, 14, 16[2], 22; **7:**12, 24, 25, 26, 27[4], 29[2]; **8:**1[2], 3, 4, 6, 7, 8[3], 9, 21; **9:**9[2], 10, 11[2]; **10:**1, 10[3], 11, 12[2], 13, 14[4], 16, 17[2], 18, 19; **Sir 1:**14, 15[2], 16, 17, 19[2]; **4:**13, 17[4], 18, 19; **6:**20, 21, 22, 27, 28[2]; **15:**2[2], 3, 5, 8; **23:**23[3], 24, 26; **24:**2[2]; **25:**26; **26:**3, 8, 10[2], 11, 12, 26[2]; **35:**17, 19; **42:**9[3], 10[3], 11; **Bar 3:**22, 37; **4:**1, 9[2], 33[2], 35; **LtJ 6:**43[2]; **Sus 1:**15, 17, 18, 30, 32, 35, 41, 45, 63; **1Mc 1:**27, 38[2]; **2:**11; **2Mc 7:**20[2], 21[2], 26, 27, 30; **1Es 4:**29, 31[3]; **2Es 5:**50, 51, 53; **7:**54[2]; **9:**38, 41, 43; **10:**9[2], 11, 18, 26, 45, 47, 49; **16:**50; **4Mc 2:**11; **14:**20; **15:**3, 6, 7[2], 8, 9, 15, 24, 25, 27, 28; **16:**3, 5, 12[2], 13; **17:**1[2]

SHOULD (534)

Ge 2:18; **23:**8; **27:**45; **29:**15, 19; **33:**15; **34:**31; **40:**15; **42:**38; **44:**7, 9, 17, 22; **47:**15, 26; **Ex 3:**11; **5:**2; **18:**19[2], 21; **32:**12; **33:**5; **39:**21[2]; **Lev 10:**18; **20:**4; **24:**12; **25:**20; **Nu 6:**7; **9:**4; **10:**31; **11:**12; **15:**34; **23:**19[2]; **24:**13; **27:**4; **Dt 1:**18, 22, 33; **4:**21[2]; **5:**25; **15:**8; **20:**5, 6, 7, 8, 19; **22:**8; **30:**12, 13; **Jos 3:**4; **7:**3; **8:**33; **9:**27; **22:**28, 29; **24:**16; **Jdg 8:**6, 15; **9:**28[2], 38; **11:**24[2]; **14:**16; **20:**39; **21:**3; **Ru 1:**12; **2:**10; **1Sa 2:**30; **6:**2, 6; **12:**23; **15:**29; **17:**26; **18:**18, 19; **19:**4, 17; **20:**2, 5, 8, 9, 32; **24:**6; **25:**17, 29; **26:**11; **27:**5; **28:**15; **29:**6, 8; **2Sa 2:**22; **3:**33; **9:**8; **12:**23; **13:**26; **16:**9, 19[2]; **19:**11, 12, 22, 34, 35, 36; **20:**20; **21:**4, 5; **23:**17; **1Ki 1:**27; **3:**5; **6:**6; **8:**36; **11:**10; **12:**10[2]; **14:**2; **20:**11; **21:**3; **2Ki 6:**33; **7:**3; **8:**13; **11:**17; **13:**19; **14:**10; **17:**15, 28; **18:**35; **19:**25; **22:**19; **23:**1; **1Ch 11:**19; **21:**3[2], 18; **23:**13; **25:**1; **29:**14; **2Ch 1:**7; **6:**27; **10:**10; **15:**13; **19:**2; **22:**7; **23:**16, 19; **25:**16, 19; **29:**24; **30:**1, 5; **32:**4, 14; **Ezr 2:**63; **4:**22; **5:**13; **10:**7, 8; **Ne 2:**3; **5:**9; **6:**3, 11; **7:**65; **8:**14, 15; **9:**12, 19; **13:**1, 19[2], 22; **Est 1:**22; **9:**21, 22, 25[2], 28[3], 31; **Job 6:**11[2]; **9:**32; **11:**2[2], 3; **14:**14; **15:**2, 3, 28; **21:**4, 15; **23:**7; **31:**28; **33:**23; **34:**10[2], 14, 30; **37:**20; **39:**16; **Ps 25:**12; **32:**8; **46:**2; **49:**5, 9; **78:**7, 8; **79:**10; **115:**2; **130:**3; **143:**8; **Pr 5:**16, 20; **17:**16; **22:**27; **Ecc 3:**13, 14, 22; **5:**5[2], 6; **6:**6; **7:**16, 17, 18; **11:**8;

SS 1:7; 6:13; Isa 8:19; 10:15[2]; 36:20; 37:26; 48:11, 17; 49:6; 53:2[2]; Jer 13:12[2]; 14:8, 9; 27:13, 17; 32:35; 34:9[2]; 38:25[2]; 40:15; 42:3[2]; 51:53[2]; La 1:17; 2:20[2]; 3:26, 39; Eze 13:19[2]; 18:19, 23; 19:9; 20:9, 14, 22; 34:2; 41:6; Da 1:10; 4:6; 5:29; 6:7, 26; 7:14; Joel 2:17; Ob 1:12[3], 13[3], 14[2]; Jnh 4:11; Mic 2:6, 7; 3:1; Zec 7:3; 8:6; Mal 2:7[2]; Mt 18:14, 21, 33; 27:22; Mk 5:43; 6:12, 24; 8:7; 12:15[2]; 15:24; Lk 2:1; 3:10, 12, 14; 12:17; 13:7, 18, 20; 16:29; 22:49; 23:23, 24; 24:26; Jn 6:39; 8:38; 11:57; 12:27, 46; 13:15, 29, 34; Ac 2:37; 6:2; 10:28; 13:46; 14:15; 15:7, 19, 20; 21:25; 22:22; 25:10; 26:20; 27:21; Ro 1:28; 3:5; 6:1, 15; 7:7; 13:4; 1Co 3:18; 4:3; 5:2; 6:15; 7:2, 3, 9, 10, 11, 12, 13; 9:10[2], 14, 27; 10:29, 30; 11:6[2], 22[2]; 14:13, 15, 26, 34[2], 40; 16:1, 4; 2Co 2:3, 7; 8:6, 13, 20; 12:11; Gal 1:8; 2:9; 6:1; Eph 5:28, 33[2]; Php 2:10, 11; Col 4:4; 1Th 4:1; 2Th 3:10; 1Ti 2:8, 9; 5:4, 13; Tit 1:5[2]; Heb 2:10; 4:1; 7:26; 11:32; 12:9; Jas 1:13; 3:1; 5:13[2], 14, 20; 1Pe 2:15, 21; 3:17; 2Pe 3:2; 1Jn 3:1, 11, 23; 5:16; Tob 1:4; 3:15[2]; 8:6; 13:16; Jdt 2:3; 3:8[2]; 5:22; AdE 9:21, 27; Wis 12:13; 14:5; 16:4; Sir Pr:T[2]; 4:6; 13:7, 23; 22:26; 23:18; 24:7; 29:24; 33:22[2]; 41:4; 44:18; 45:24[2]; 1Mc 1:41, 42; 2:13; 4:46, 59; 5:16, 49; 7:49; 8:7; 10:6, 30; 13:52; 14:41[2], 42[3], 43[3]; 15:19; 2Mc 1:31; 2:3, 4, 8, 31; 3:12, 15; 6:8, 9; 9:12; 10:4, 8; 11:25; 14:35; 1Es 1:3, 32; 4:47, 49, 50[2], 51, 53, 55, 56; 5:40; 6:17, 19[2], 26, 32[2]; 9:3; 3Mc 1:3, 15; 2:5, 10[2]; 3:1, 15[2]; 4:11; 6:30; 7:9, 10; 2Es 1:29[4]; 4:6; 5:30, 54; 7:21[2], 126; 8:10, 59; 4Mc 4:7, 23; 5:8, 17; 6:18, 20; 7:8; 8:19; 9:2, 6

SO (3960)

For "SO" as a proper name see the Main Concordance.

Ge 1:7[2], 9, 11, 15, 21, 24, 27, 30; 2:3, 19, 21; 3:6; 4:5, 15[2]; 6:7; 7:19; 8:9, 11, 17, 18; 11:7, 8; 12:2, 4, 7, 10, 13, 18, 19; 13:1, 6[2], 11, 16, 18; 14:11, 23; 15:3, 5; 16:3, 10, 13; 17:13; 18:5, 12, 19, 22, 25; 19:3, 5, 7, 11, 14, 16, 29, 30, 32, 33, 34, 35; 20:4, 8, 17; 21:10, 14, 27; 22:3, 6, 8, 14, 19; 23:4, 9, 13, 17; 24:9, 20, 32, 34, 46, 47, 49, 59, 65, 67; 25:22, 25, 26, 33; 26:6, 9[2], 11, 14, 17, 20, 21, 22, 25, 28, 29, 30; 27:1, 4, 5, 9, 10, 14, 18, 19, 20, 22, 23, 25, 27, 31, 42; 28:4, 8, 18, 21; 29:18, 20, 22, 28, 30; 30:4, 8, 11, 13, 16, 18, 20, 27, 33, 39, 42; 31:4, 17, 21, 23, 33, 35, 37, 45, 53; 32:2, 13, 21, 27, 30; 33:1, 11, 15[2], 16; 34:4, 5, 20; 35:2, 4, 5, 8, 10, 15, 19; 36:8; 37:8, 11, 14[2], 17, 23; 38:9, 11, 18, 22; 39:4, 6; 40:7, 9, 14; 41:8, 13, 21, 36, 39[2], 49; 42:3, 20, 22; 43:6, 8, 11, 14, 15, 18, 19, 21, 30, 34; 44:10, 17, 21; 45:1, 2, 3, 8, 11, 18, 21, 25; 47:1, 17, 19, 20, 26, 28; 48:1, 10, 17, 18, 20[2]; 49:15, 17; 50:2, 5, 7, 16, 21, 22, 25; Ex 1:7, 12, 18, 20; 2:8, 9, 18; 3:10, 18, 20, 22; 4:3, 4, 5, 7, 20, 21, 26, 27; 5:1, 10, 12; 7:6, 10, 16, 19, 21, 22; 8:1, 6, 10, 16, 17, 20, 21, 22, 24, 26, 28, 30; 9:1, 4, 6, 10, 13, 14, 22, 29, 33, 35; 10:2, 3[2], 5, 7, 8, 12, 13, 15, 18, 21, 22; 11:7; 12:34, 36[2]; 13:9, 18, 21; 14:4[2], 6, 17[2], 20, 25, 26, 27, 31; 16:6, 17, 24, 30, 34; 17:4, 6[2], 10, 12[2]; 18:22, 23, 24; 19:7, 9, 14, 16, 25; 20:12, 20, 26; 21:18, 22, 35; 22:1, 6; 23:2, 11, 12; 24:13; 25:8, 9, 33, 35, 37; 26:6, 11, 25; 27:5, 7, 20; 28:7, 11, 25, 28[2], 29, 32, 35, 41; 29:1; 30:12, 20, 21, 29; 31:6; 32:3, 10, 21, 24[2], 29, 31; 33:5, 13; 34:4; 35:22; 36:4, 6[2], 13, 18; 37:19; 38:15; 39:21, 23; 40:9, 10, 13, 33; Lev 6:22; 7:8, 30; 8:35[2]; 9:6; 10:13; 11:43; 13:12[2]; 14:21, 53; 15:31; 16:16; 17:7; 18:5, 21, 30; 20:22; 21:4; 22:2, 9, 29; 23:43; 25:8, 18, 21, 26, 39; 26:15, 32, 41, 44; 27:12, 14; Nu 1:19, 45, 54; 3:6, 16, 42, 49; 4:34; 5:4[2], 13; 6:21, 27; 7:6; 8:3, 4, 7, 22; 9:4, 5, 6, 8, 14, 16; 10:9, 33; 11:3, 11[2], 16, 17, 24, 25, 26, 32, 34; 12:3, 4, 7, 11, 15; 13:3, 21, 32, 33; 14:4; 15:12, 39, 40; 16:3, 18, 21, 25, 27, 33, 39, 40, 45, 47; 17:7, 10, 11[2]; 18:2, 5; 19:12; 20:2, 9, 21; 21:3, 6, 7, 9, 30, 35; 22:3, 7, 8, 13, 14, 19, 21, 23, 25, 35; 23:6, 13, 14, 27, 28, 30; 24:1, 14, 15; 25:8; 27:17, 18, 20, 22; 29:40; 31:3[2], 5, 16, 54; 32:20, 28, 31, 40; 33:5; 35:11, 12, 15; 36:3, 7, 8; Dt 1:10, 15, 18, 41; 2:4, 5, 6[2], 8, 13, 21, 22, 26, 28[2], 32; 3:3, 8, 21, 29; 4:1[2], 7, 9, 10[2], 16, 23, 32, 35, 39, 40; 5:14, 16, 25, 29, 31, 33; 6:2[2], 3[2], 18[2], 24; 8:1, 5, 18, 20; 9:3, 8, 15, 17, 19, 20; 10:3, 5, 12; 11:4, 8, 9, 17, 21; 12:10, 22, 25, 28; 13:5, 17; 14:23, 24, 29; 15:10; 16:3, 20; 17:7, 12, 16, 19, 20; 18:14; 19:3, 10, 13, 19; 20:18; 21:9, 12, 21; 22:21, 22, 24; 23:14, 20; 24:1, 7, 13, 19; 25:6, 15; 26:10, 12, 16; 27:4; 28:56, 63; 29:6, 27; 30:6, 12, 13, 19, 20; 31:12, 13, 14[2], 27, 28; 32:21, 46; 33:11, 25, 28; Jos 1:5, 7, 8, 17; 2:1, 7, 16, 21; 3:4, 6, 7, 12, 15; 4:6, 7, 24[2]; 5:3, 7, 9, 15; 6:6, 11, 18, 20[2], 23, 27; 7:3, 4, 7, 16, 22; 8:3, 9, 13, 16, 20, 22, 28; 9:6, 11, 14, 17, 20, 21, 24; 10:3, 7, 9, 23, 39, 40; 11:7, 15[2], 16, 20, 23; 14:12, 14; 15:7, 19, 63; 16:10; 17:4; 18:3, 8, 9; 19:51; 20:3, 7, 9; 21:3, 4, 42; 22:6, 9, 23, 25, 27; 23:7, 12, 15; 24:10, 25, 28; Jdg 1:3, 7, 15, 17, 21, 25, 26; 2:3, 5, 9, 14[2], 20; 3:5, 11, 14, 19, 20, 25, 28, 30; 4:2, 14, 18, 19, 22, 23; 5:28, 31; 6:5, 19, 20, 27, 29, 30, 38, 40; 7:5, 8, 13, 19, 20, 24; 8:2, 5, 9, 11, 16, 18, 20, 21[2], 25, 28[2]; 9:3, 7, 8, 14, 24, 25, 34, 39, 41[2], 48, 49[2], 54[2]; 10:7, 9, 10, 16; 11:6, 7, 8, 11, 17, 20, 21, 23, 32, 33, 37, 38, 39; 13:7, 10, 17, 19; 14:13, 16; 15:2, 4, 6, 11, 12, 13, 19; 16:2, 5[2], 6[3], 9, 12, 14, 15, 17, 21, 25, 26, 28, 30; 17:4, 12; 18:2, 3, 15, 21, 31; 19:4, 6, 8, 14, 21, 22, 23, 25; 20:7, 11, 13, 24, 29, 39, 46; 21:10, 16, 19, 23, 24; Ru 1:5, 7, 15, 17, 19, 22; 2:3, 7, 14, 17, 19, 23; 3:1, 6, 14, 15; 4:1, 2, 4[3], 8, 13; 1Sa 1:7, 14, 23; 2:3, 31; 3:2, 5, 9, 17, 18; 4:3, 4, 5, 10, 15; 5:3, 8[2], 9, 10; 6:5, 10, 14, 20, 21; 7:4, 6, 9, 13; 8:8, 10, 20; 9:3, 10, 14, 24[2], 26; 10:22; 11:5, 7, 10, 11, 12, 15; 12:7, 18, 19; 13:9, 12, 20, 22; 14:7, 11, 20, 23, 24, 27, 28, 32, 34, 37, 44, 45; 15:4, 6, 25, 30, 31, 33; 16:17, 19; 17:27, 37, 39, 46, 50, 52; 18:9, 13, 23, 29, 30; 19:7, 8, 10, 12, 17; 20:5, 11, 13[2], 24, 29, 33, 38; 21:6, 13; 22:5, 13, 14; 23:5, 17, 20, 24, 28; 24:7, 19, 22; 25:5, 12, 17, 21, 22[2], 25, 28, 34, 36; 26:2, 7, 12, 24, 25; 27:2, 5, 6, 11[2]; 28:7, 8, 14, 15, 23; 29:4, 7, 11; 30:7, 9, 23; 31:4[2], 6; 2Sa 1:10, 15; 2:2, 15, 16, 23[2]; 3:9[2], 16, 21, 24, 27, 30, 35, 37; 4:12; 5:3, 20; 6:8, 10, 12, 15; 7:10, 21, 29; 8:15; 9:10, 11; 10:2, 4, 13, 18, 19; 11:4, 6, 12, 15, 20, 21[2], 22; 12:25, 29; 13:2, 4, 5, 6[2], 8, 9, 10[2], 12, 18, 20, 29, 35; 14:7, 11, 14, 23, 24, 25, 28, 30, 33; 15:6, 9, 16, 22, 29, 34, 35, 37; 16:10, 13, 19, 22, 23; 17:12, 14, 15[2], 18, 21, 22; 18:4, 6, 20, 23, 30; 19:2, 7, 13, 15, 26, 37; 20:2, 3, 5, 10, 18, 22; 21:2, 5, 17; 22:35, 39; 24:2[2], 4, 8, 13, 15, 21, 24, 25; 1Ki 1:2[2], 3, 6, 12, 15, 28, 30, 36, 37, 38, 40, 45, 52; 2:3, 12, 19, 23, 25, 27, 30, 33, 38[2], 44, 46; 3:8, 22, 23, 24; 4:30; 5:5, 10, 12, 18; 6:7, 9, 14, 26, 27, 33; 7:12, 20, 40, 47, 48; 8:4, 5, 7, 8, 11, 38, 40, 43[2], 46, 50, 60, 63, 65; 9:13, 17, 21, 25; 10:6, 25, 29; 11:6, 19, 36; 12:5, 12, 15, 16, 19, 24, 28, 32; 13:4, 6[2], 10, 13, 18, 27, 34; 14:2, 4, 27; 15:19, 28; 16:17, 22; 17:5, 10[2], 12, 15, 17, 24; 18:2, 6, 12, 16, 20, 26, 35, 37, 42; 19:2, 11, 19; 20:9, 10, 23, 25, 32, 33, 34, 37, 40; 21:2, 5, 8, 13; 22:20, 23, 29, 30, 32, 34, 37, 40; 2Ki 1:2, 4, 13, 15, 17; 2:2, 4, 6, 17, 20, 22; 3:6, 9, 12, 17, 27; 4:5, 8, 10, 22, 25, 30, 33, 36, 43; 5:4, 9, 14, 21, 27; 6:2, 4, 7, 10, 14, 17, 18, 20, 22, 23, 25, 29, 31, 32; 7:5, 6, 7, 10, 12, 14, 15[2], 16; 8:2, 6, 9, 22, 24; 9:4, 6, 7, 12, 15, 18, 22, 24, 33, 37; 10:1, 5, 11, 15, 16, 20, 21, 22, 25, 35; 11:2, 16, 20; 12:8, 21; 13:3, 5, 7, 9, 13, 15, 20; 14:10, 11, 27; 15:5, 12, 19, 20; 16:11; 17:4, 23, 26, 28, 33, 41; 18:5; 19:7, 18, 19[2]; 20:7; 21:16; 22:14, 17; 23:10, 18, 24, 33; 24:6, 20; 25:2, 3, 21, 25, 29; 1Ch 2:35; 5:1, 26; 6:64; 9:1, 23; 10:4[2], 13; 11:3, 6; 13:4, 5, 11, 13; 14:11; 15:12, 14, 17, 25, 28; 17:9; 18:14; 19:2, 4, 14, 19; 21:2[2], 4, 10, 11, 14, 19, 22, 25; 22:5, 8, 11, 12, 14, 19; 23:11, 13, 26; 24:2; 29:2[2]; 2Ch 1:13, 17; 2:7; 3:7; 4:18, 19; 5:5, 6, 8, 9, 14; 6:5, 29, 36; 7:5, 13, 16; 8:14; 9:5, 24; 10:5, 12, 15[2], 16, 19; 11:4, 12; 12:5, 8, 9, 12, 13; 13:11; 14:1, 7, 12; 16:3; 18:19, 22, 28, 29, 31, 33; 19:10[2]; 20:6, 22, 31; 21:10, 17; 22:1, 11; 23:15, 19, 21; 24:6, 8, 11, 13, 20, 25; 25:12, 16, 19, 21; 27:6; 28:14, 20, 23; 29:10, 22, 34; 30:5, 6[2], 7, 8, 10, 22, 23; 31:4, 10; 32:17, 21, 22, 23, 26, 31; 33:9, 20; 34:22, 25; 35:12, 14, 16, 21, 24; 36:16, 22; Ezr 1:1; 2:62; 3:7, 13[2]; 4:15, 19; 5:10; 6:10, 14, 20, 22; 8:23, 30; 9:12; 10:3, 5, 10, 12, 16; Ne 2:2, 4, 5, 6, 11, 15[2], 17, 18; 4:6, 9, 10, 13, 21, 22, 23; 5:2, 9, 13, 15; 6:3, 7, 13, 15; 7:64, 73; 8:8[2], 11, 16, 17; 9:11, 21, 22, 24, 25, 28; 11:30; 12:40; 13:10, 11, 21; Est 1:19, 20; 2:4, 8, 17, 23; 3:2, 6, 8, 9, 10; 4:4; 5:5[2], 13; 6:5, 6, 7, 10, 11; 7:1, 10; 8:2, 14; 9:5, 14, 23; Job 1:3, 12; 2:7; 5:12, 16; 7:3, 9, 15, 17; 9:2; 14:12, 19; 15:13; 19:8, 29; 21:19; 22:11, 14; 24:19, 20, 25; 27:19; 31:34; 32:1, 20; 33:20, 21, 30; 34:28, 30; 37:7; 38:13, 34, 35; 41:10, 16; 42:9, 15; Ps 1:4; 5:11; 9:14; 10:18; 18:3, 34, 38; 22:1; 28:7; 30:12; 34:T, 5; 37:3, 27; 42:1; 48:8; 51:4; 56:7, 13; 58:5; 60:5; 61:8; 63:2, 4; 65:9; 68:2, 23[2]; 69:10, 20, 23; 71:18; 77:4, 13; 78:7, 20, 33, 44, 53; 80:12; 81:12; 83:15, 16; 85:6; 86:17; 88:8; 90:12, 14; 91:12; 101:6; 102:18, 21; 103:5, 11, 12, 13; 104:5, 9; 105:43; 106:8, 10, 41; 107:2; 108:6; 109:5; 115:8; 118:13; 119:11, 17, 18, 71, 79, 80, 88, 125; 123:2; 125:2, 3; 130:4; 139:6; 141:7; 142:7; 144:5; Pr 3:4; 5:2; 6:3, 29; 7:15; 8:29; 10:26; 11:15; 13:14; 14:27; 15:7; 17:14; 22:19, 21; 23:7; 25:3, 25; 26:1, 7, 14, 19, 21; 27:11, 19, 21; 30:33; Ecc 2:9, 12, 15, 17, 20; 3:14, 19, 22; 5:15, 16; 6:2, 11; 7:6, 14, 20; 8:15; 9:2, 12, 16; 10:1; 11:5; SS 2:2, 3; Isa 2:9; 5:24; 6:10; 9:11, 14; 10:4, 14, 19; 11:16; 14:24[2]; 16:2; 20:2, 4; 21:3[2]; 24:2[6], 10; 25:9; 26:2, 17; 27:3; 29:8, 14; 30:8, 14; 31:4, 5; 37:7, 19, 20[2]; 38:8, 21; 41:7, 20, 22, 26[2]; 42:25; 43:10, 21, 26; 44:9, 18[2]; 45:3, 6; 47:7; 48:5, 7, 9; 49:21; 51:11, 15; 52:14, 15; 53:7; 54:9; 55:3, 9, 11; 57:10, 11[2]; 59:2, 16, 18, 19; 60:11, 21; 61:11; 62:5[2]; 63:1, 5, 17; 64:1, 2, 12; 65:8; 66:2, 5, 13, 22; Jer 2:26, 33; 3:9, 20; 4:14; 5:1, 19, 31; 6:7, 27; 7:23, 27; 9:1, 10, 12[2], 18; 10:4, 18; 11:4, 5, 8, 19; 13:2, 5, 9, 11; 14:19; 15:6; 17:11; 18:3, 6; 19:11[2]; 20:17; 23:2, 14, 18[2], 24, 32, 36; 24:2, 3, 5, 8[2]; 25:7, 17; 26:24; 28:6, 14; 29:17, 26, 27; 30:7, 14, 15; 31:28, 35; 32:31, 40, 42; 33:20, 21, 22; 34:5, 9, 10; 35:3; 36:3, 6, 14, 15; 37:21[2]; 38:6, 8, 11, 12, 16, 27; 39:13, 14; 40:5, 15; 41:8, 14; 42:18, 21; 43:4; 44:6, 14; 47:3; 48:39; 50:33, 36[2], 37, 40; 51:7, 62; 52:3, 5, 6, 27, 33; La 1:8; 3:7, 18, 44; 4:14, 15, 18; Eze 3:2, 23, 25, 26; 4:5, 8; 6:6; 7:22; 8:5, 10; 9:6, 7; 11:20; 12:6, 11, 12, 16; 13:5, 14; 14:11, 15; 15:6; 16:19, 34, 37, 42, 52; 17:6, 7, 8, 14; 19:9, 14; 20:10, 12, 14, 20, 22, 26, 29, 36; 21:24; 22:20, 22, 26, 30; 23:18, 27, 32, 48; 24:8, 11, 18, 27; 26:10, 20; 27:25; 28:16, 18; 29:15; 30:13, 21; 31:5; 32:28; 33:6, 7, 22, 28; 34:5, 10, 12, 25, 29; 35:15; 36:3, 18, 30, 38; 37:7, 17; 38:16, 23; 39:14, 23; 40:5; 41:6; 42:12; 43:11, 26; 44:19; 45:20; 46:18, 20; 47:17, 21; Da 1:5, 8, 14, 16; 2:2, 15, 16, 18, 35, 42, 43; 3:3, 13, 19, 21, 22, 26; 4:6, 20, 27; 5:2, 3, 13, 20, 24; 6:2, 4, 6, 8, 17, 22, 23, 28; 7:16; 8:17, 27; 9:11, 12, 14, 23; 10:8, 11, 13; 11:35; 12:8; Hos 1:3; 2:6; 3:2; 6:9; 7:16; 10:4; 12:11, 14; 13:7; Joel 3:17; Am 1:4, 7, 10, 12, 14; 2:2, 5, 7, 11, 13; 3:12; 4:5, 8; 5:9, 14; 7:2, 5; 8:5[2]; Ob 1:9; Jnh 1:3, 6, 7[2], 10, 15; 3:3, 9; 4:6, 7, 8; Mic 6:16; Hab 1:4, 15; 2:2; Zep 3:6, 18; Hag 1:8; 2:7, 14[2]; Zec 1:6, 10, 14, 21; 3:5; 5:8; 6:7; 7:3, 13, 14; 8:13, 15; 9:8; 11:1, 7, 9, 11, 12, 13; 12:8, 10; 13:2; 14:4, 13, 21; Mal 1:10; 2:9, 15, 16; 3:10, 11; 4:1, 6; Mt 1:17; 2:5, 8, 23; 3:15; 4:6, 14, 24; 5:16, 23, 45; 6:2[2], 4, 5, 16, 18, 22, 30, 34; 7:1; 8:24, 28, 32; 9:6, 17; 10:16, 26, 31; 12:10, 12, 22, 40, 45; 13:15, 26, 32, 40, 49, 54; 14:7, 15, 29; 15:6, 31, 33; 17:12, 27; 18:14, 16, 26, 35; 19:6, 8[2], 12; 20:4, 16, 26; 21:27, 39; 22:10, 16, 26; 23:20, 26, 28, 35; 24:15, 26, 27, 33, 37, 39; 25:25, 28; 26:19, 25, 35, 40, 44, 56, 59, 64; 27:11, 14, 17, 24, 26, 59, 66; 28:8, 15; Mk 1:38, 45; 2:2, 10, 12, 22, 28; 3:2, 9, 10, 16, 20; 4:12, 32, 37; 5:13, 23, 24; 6:12, 36, 40; 7:5, 30; 9:10, 18, 26; 10:8, 42, 43, 50; 11:24, 25, 33; 12:5, 8, 12, 37; 13:29; 14:11, 13, 16, 45; 15:2, 5, 8, 15, 32; 16:1, 8, 19; Lk 1:4, 18; 2:16, 35; 3:18; 4:11, 29, 44; 5:5, 6, 7[2], 10, 24; 6:7, 10; 7:18; 8:10, 12, 16, 22, 32, 37, 39; 9:12, 15, 45; 10:32, 40; 11:9, 30, 33, 37, 41, 48, 50; 12:1, 21, 26, 28, 36, 38, 54; 13:7; 14:4, 10, 21, 23, 33; 15:3, 7, 10, 12, 15, 20, 29; 16:2, 4, 5, 9, 15, 26[2], 28; 17:10, 24, 26; 18:5; 19:4, 6, 12, 15, 32; 20:7, 14, 15, 20[2], 21, 31, 44; 21:14, 31, 34; 22:6, 8, 13, 26, 30; 23:3, 24; 24:29, 49; Jn 1:7; 2:8; 3:8, 14, 16[2], 20, 21; 4:5, 15, 33, 36, 40, 52, 53; 5:10, 14, 20, 21, 23, 26, 34; 6:9, 10, 11, 12, 13, 24, 30[2], 50, 53, 57, 67; 7:3[2], 43; 8:6, 28, 36, 52, 59; 9:3, 17, 24, 36, 39; 10:7, 16, 24, 38; 11:3, 4, 15, 36, 41, 42, 47, 53, 57; 12:7, 10, 13, 17, 35, 36, 37, 39, 40, 46; 13:14, 19, 25, 26, 30, 33; 14:2, 3, 13, 29, 31; 15:9, 11, 16, 17; 16:2, 4, 19, 22, 24, 33; 17:1, 5, 11, 12, 13, 18, 19, 21, 22, 23, 26; 18:3, 8, 12, 16, 28, 29, 37; 19:5, 10, 24, 29, 31, 35, 36, 38, 42; 20:2, 21, 25, 31; 21:6[2], 11[2], 23; Ac 1:6, 19, 21, 23; 2:25, 38, 41; 3:2, 19, 20; 4:3, 15, 18; 5:10, 15, 22, 32, 38; 7:1, 8, 15, 19, 22, 43; 8:8, 19, 27, 30, 32; 9:2, 8, 12, 17[2], 24, 28, 39; 10:21, 23, 29, 33, 48; 11:2, 26; 12:8, 14, 15, 20; 13:4, 16, 47[2], 51; 14:3; 15:3, 17, 30, 39; 16:5, 8, 26, 39; 17:11, 17, 19, 20, 27; 19:10, 12, 16, 20, 22; 20:3, 16; 21:23, 35; 23:11, 16, 18, 22, 31; 24:6; 25:5, 17, 23, 26; 26:11, 18[2], 22, 28; 27:13, 17, 18, 25, 28, 40, 42, 44; 28:8, 14, 25, 27; Ro 1:11, 12, 20; 2:26; 3:4, 8, 19; 4:6, 18; 5:12, 18, 19, 21[2]; 6:4[2], 6, 11, 19, 21; 7:4, 6, 12, 21, 25; 8:4, 12, 17; 9:11, 16, 17, 18, 23; 10:4, 10[2], 17, 20; 11:5, 10, 11[3], 19, 20, 25, 26, 31, 32; 12:2, 5, 18; 14:8, 9, 12, 16; 15:4, 6, 13, 16, 19, 20, 22, 28, 32; 16:2, 19, 21; 1Co 1:7, 8, 15, 17, 29; 2:5, 11, 12, 16; 3:1, 7, 18, 21; 4:6[2], 8; 5:2, 5, 7; 7:5, 15, 34, 36, 38; 8:7, 11, 13; 9:15, 18, 19, 20, 21, 22, 23, 26, 27; 10:6, 12, 13, 31, 33; 11:12, 19, 32, 33, 34; 12:12, 24; 13:2, 3; 14:5, 9, 12, 31, 39; 15:11[2], 22, 28, 42, 48[2]; 16:2, 6, 11, 18; 2Co 1:4, 5, 7, 8, 9, 10, 11, 15; 2:1, 3, 7[2], 8, 11, 13, 17; 3:7; 4:7, 10, 11, 12, 13[2], 15, 16; 5:4, 6, 9, 10, 12, 15, 17, 20, 21; 6:3; 7:7, 9, 12, 14; 8:6[2], 7, 9, 11, 14; 9:3, 5[2], 8; 10:7, 16; 11:7, 9, 15, 16, 22[3]; 12:6, 9[2]; 13:10[2]; Gal 1:6, 9, 16; 2:4, 5, 13, 16, 19; 3:3, 4, 7, 14, 17, 22, 24; 4:3, 5, 7, 17, 29, 31; 6:9, 10, 13; Eph 1:12, 18; 2:7, 9, 11, 17, 19; 3:10, 19; 4:10, 25, 28, 29; 5:17, 24, 27[2]; 6:3, 11, 13, 19, 21; Php 1:10, 13, 26, 27; 2:10, 15, 19, 27[2]; Col 1:6, 10, 18, 22, 28; 2:2, 4; 3:1, 13; 4:4, 6, 8, 12; 1Th 1:7, 8; 2:4, 8, 9, 16; 3:3, 4, 13; 4:1, 10, 12, 13, 14, 17; 5:6, 10; 2Th 1:12; 2:4, 6, 10, 12, 14, 15; 3:1, 8, 14; 1Ti 1:3, 16, 18, 20; 2:2; 3:7, 14; 4:15; 5:7, 12, 14[2], 16, 20, 25; 6:1, 7, 19; 2Ti 1:4; 2:10; 3:8, 17; 4:17[2]; Tit 1:5, 9, 13; 2:4, 5, 10; 3:7, 8, 14; Phm 1:13, 15, 17, 24; Heb 2:1, 3, 9, 14, 17; 3:13, 19; 4:9, 11, 16; 5:5; 6:11, 12, 18; 8:9; 9:13, 15, 28; 10:33, 36, 39[2]; 11:3, 5, 28, 29, 40; 12:1[2], 3, 13, 21, 27; 13:6, 19, 21; Jas 1:4, 18; 2:12[2], 17, 26; 3:4, 5, 10; 4:2[2], 12; 5:9, 12, 16; 1Pe 1:7, 21, 22; 2:2, 12, 21, 24; 3:1, 7, 16; 4:2, 4, 6, 11[3], 13; 5:6, 13; 2Pe 1:4, 15, 19; 2:2; 3:15; 1Jn 1:3, 4; 2:1, 18, 27, 28; 4:9, 11, 16, 17; 5:13, 20; 2Jn 1:8, 12; 3Jn 1:8, 10[2], 12; Rev 1:7; 2:10, 14, 15; 3:11, 16, 18[2]; 5:5; 6:4; 7:1; 8:12; 9:15; 10:9, 10; 11:6; 12:4, 6, 13, 14; 13:15, 17; 14:16, 19; 16:2, 18, 21; 17:3, 7; 18:4[2], 7; 20:3; 22:14; Tob 1:18, 19, 22[2]; 2:3, 13; 3:4, 6[3], 8, 17[2]; 4:9, 13, 19; 5:2, 3, 4, 9[2], 10, 15, 16, 17; 6:1, 2, 4, 6, 13[3], 15; 7:1, 11[2], 16; 8:1, 3, 5, 13, 15, 19; 9:5[2]; 10:7[2], 10; 11:15, 17; 12:5, 12, 20; 13:6, 10; 14:1, 4, 8[2], 11; Jdt 1:11; 2:14, 28; 3:8; 4:4, 8; 5:8, 10, 11, 12, 20; 6:4, 11, 13; 7:2, 13, 17; 8:3, 11, 19, 20, 30, 31, 33, 36; 9:3; 10:8, 9[2]; 11:16, 17, 18, 19, 21[2]; 12:7, 13, 15, 17; 13:1, 4; 14:5, 6, 8, 10[2], 13, 14; AdE 1:8, 18, 19, 22; 2:4, 8, 16, 17, 20; 3:2[2], 5, 10, 12; 4:7, 17; 5:5[2], 9, 14; 6:1, 7, 11; 7:1, 9, 10; 8:14; 9:14, 23, 26; 10:13; 13:4, 5, 7[2], 14; 14:13; 16:7, 11, 20, 23; Wis 1:14; 2:19; 4:11; 5:6, 12, 13; 6:9, 20, 21; 7:28; 8:21; 10:8, 12; 11:16, 23; 12:2, 7, 22[2]; 13:9, 16; 14:4, 8, 17; 15:5, 19; 16:11, 18, 22, 26; 18:6, 9, 19; 19:6, 15; Sir Pr:T[2]; 2:3; 3:18, 30; 5:5; 6:1, 17; 7:6, 32; 9:17; 10:2[2]; 11:11, 30; 12:10, 14; 14:18, 25; 16:12, 17, 21; 17:31; 18:10, 16; 19:12, 13, 14, 15; 20:21, 23; 21:1; 22:16, 18, 23[2], 24, 27; 23:2, 10, 20, 22; 24:10; 26:12, 14, 16, 17, 18, 21; 27:2, 4, 5, 6, 9, 10, 18, 19; 28:10[2], 25[2]; 30:1, 13, 19; 31:26; 32:2; 33:13, 14; 34:2, 31; 36:4, 24, 31; 38:27, 28, 29; 39:32, 35; 40:14; 41:10; 42:17; 43:17; 44:8; 45:5, 25, 26; 46:1, 3, 6, 9, 10, 19; 47:2, 6, 13, 20, 22; 49:12; Bar 1:10, 11, 20; 2:1, 15; 3:4, 7, 14, 28; 4:24, 33; 5:7; LtJ 6:5, 16, 18[2], 22, 23, 59, 61, 69, 70; Aza 1:8; Sus 1:13, 17, 20, 30, 32, 50, 59, 63; Bel 1:4, 10, 24, 32, 39; 1Mc 1:6, 9, 14, 17, 49; 2:34, 38, 41, 61; 3:17[2], 40, 44, 60; 4:5, 37, 45[2], 56, 61; 5:2, 21, 31, 46, 50, 54, 57, 58; 6:3, 4, 10, 15, 44, 50, 57, 61; 7:4, 8, 10, 16, 24, 27, 29, 42, 43, 46, 47, 50; 8:17, 20, 28, 30; 9:27, 31, 35, 41, 47, 55, 58, 69; 10:6, 11, 16, 20, 21, 24, 25, 32, 38, 56, 57, 60, 62, 76; 11:8, 12, 16, 19, 31, 38, 39, 44, 47, 51, 52, 61, 66; 12:3, 10, 15, 25, 27[2], 28, 31, 36, 37, 40[2], 43, 44, 52; 13:2, 10, 14, 16, 17, 19, 22, 27, 29, 47, 49, 50, 53; 14:1, 23, 27, 36, 47, 49; 15:3, 4, 9, 10, 13, 21, 32, 40, 41; 16:2, 4, 6, 17, 19; 2Mc 1:22; 2:10, 15, 21; 3:6, 14, 24[2], 32; 4:5, 20, 26, 31, 48; 5:11, 21, 27; 6:6, 22, 31; 7:29, 40; 8:1, 11, 33, 36; 9:4, 7[2], 9, 24, 25, 28; 10:30; 11:13, 26, 36, 37; 12:3, 9, 16, 22, 35, 41, 45; 13:14, 25; 14:22, 25, 30, 36[2]; 15:2, 8, 11, 17[2], 23, 27, 37, 39; 1Es 1:14, 17, 24; 2:1, 26; 3:16; 4:31, 61; 5:58, 65[2], 68; 6:21, 27; 7:4; 8:7, 10, 11, 15, 21, 60, 61, 80, 85; 9:7, 12, 40, 51; Man 1:7, 10; 3Mc 1:3, 5; 2:22; 3:1, 7, 24; 4:10, 11; 5:1, 2, 9, 12, 22, 27, 33, 45, 47; 6:6, 15, 17, 26, 38; 7:12, 14, 22[2]; 2Es 1:5, 20, 24, 29; 2:6[2], 29, 47; 3:10, 20, 23, 27, 32, 35; 4:14[2], 15, 20, 21, 42, 48, 50; 5:14, 20, 35, 40, 42, 43, 48, 49; 6:24, 28, 40, 41, 42, 47, 48, 59; 7:3, 4, 7, 8, 10, 12, 30, 60, 63, 82, 89, 92, 101, 105, 111[2], 129, 131, 138; 8:2, 6, 11, 14, 34, 40, 41, 47, 59; 9:3, 6, 17[4], 20, 22, 26, 35, 41, 47; 10:2, 9, 11, 14, 18, 19, 24, 25, 26, 34, 49, 59; 11:13, 14, 19, 39, 40, 46; 12:8, 39, 50; 13:11, 42, 47, 52; 14:12, 21, 22[2], 37, 39, 44, 48; 15:17, 21, 29, 41, 51, 52, 56; 16:16, 21, 31, 39, 43, 47, 50, 60, 67, 77; 4Mc 1:1, 6, 28, 29, 33; 2:6, 9, 10, 11, 12, 13; 3:4, 20; 4:2, 9, 13[2], 14, 18, 20; 5:7, 18, 23[2], 24[2], 31, 33; 6:14, 17, 24; 7:12; 8:6, 12, 17, 29; 9:16, 17; 10:16; 11:3, 10, 16, 19, 20; 12:6, 19; 13:3, 7, 17, 23; 14:1, 6, 8; 15:9, 10, 11, 32; 16:3[2], 4, 10; 17:1, 5

THAT (9652)

Ge 1:4, 7[2], 10[2], 11, 12, 18, 21[2], 25[2], 26, 28, 29, 30[2], 31; 2:2[2], 3, 4, 9, 11, 12, 13, 17, 18, 19, 22; 3:1, 3, 5, 6[3], 7, 11, 13; 4:15, 26; 5:5, 29; 6:2[2], 4, 5[2], 6, 7, 12, 17, 21, 22; 7:1, 2, 4, 5, 8[2], 11, 14, 16, 19, 21[2], 23[2]; 8:1, 6, 11, 13, 17[3], 19; 9:2, 3, 4, 6, 10, 11, 12[2], 15, 16, 17[2]; 10:11, 12; 11:6, 7; 12:1, 2, 5, 6, 11, 13[2], 14,

THE (70933)

8[3], 9[2], 11, 12[2], 13[2], 14[2], 15, 16, 17, 18, 19[2], 24[5], 25, 26[3], 27, 29[8], 30, 31, 32[3], 34[2], 35[4], 37[5], 38[2], 39[2], 40, 41[6], 42[3], 43[2], 44, 45[5], 48[4], 49[5], 52, 54, 55, 56, 57[2], 58, 59[2]; **4:**2[3], 3, 4[2], 5[2], 6, 7[2], 9, 11, 12, 13, 14[2], 15[3], 17, 18[2], 19, 20[3], 21[2], 22[2], 23, 26, 27, 28, 30[7], 31, 32, 33, 34, 35[2], 36, 37, 38[7], 40[3], 41[2], 42, 43[2], 44, 45[2], 46[2], 47[2], 48[4], 49[4], 50[4], 51[4], 52[5], 53[2], 54[3], 55, 56[2], 57[5], 58[3], 59[5], 60, 61; **5:**1[3], 2[2], 3, 4[4], 6, 9[3], 10, 11, 13[2], 14, 15[2], 16, 18[3], 19, 21[2], 22[2], 23, 24[2], 25, 27[3], 28[4], 29[3], 30[2], 31[3], 32, 34, 36, 37[2], 38[2], 39, 40[2], 41[2], 42[5], 43[3], 44[2], 45[4], 46[3], 47[3], 49, 50[5], 51[6], 52[2], 53[4], 56[3], 57, 58[2], 59, 60[2], 61, 62, 63[2], 65[3], 66[2], 68[5]; **6:**1, 2[2], 3[2], 5[2], 6[4], 7[3], 8, 12[2], 15[2], 16, 17[2], 18[4], 19, 20[2], 21[3], 22, 24[2], 25, 26[2], 28[2], 29, 30, 31, 32[3], 33[3], 34[2], 35[2], 36, 37, 38[6], 39[3], 40[3], 41[5], 42[2], 43[3], 45[2], 46[2], 47[4], 48[3], 49[3], 50, 51, 52, 53[4], 54[3], 56[3], 57[7], 60[4], 61[4], 62[4], 63[2]; **7:**1[2], 2[2], 4[2], 5, 6[2], 7[3], 8[6], 9[2], 10, 13[2], 14[2], 16, 17, 18[4], 19[2], 20[2], 22, 23[3], 24[3], 25, 26[2], 29, 32[3], 33[6], 36[3], 38, 39, 41[3], 42[2], 43[6], 45[3], 46[3], 47[4], 48, 49, 50; **8:**1[2], 2[2], 3[2], 4[6], 5[2], 6, 8, 9, 10[3], 11, 15, 16, 18[3], 19, 20[2], 21, 22, 23[3], 25[3], 26, 27[5], 29[2], 31[2]; **9:**1[3], 2, 3[2], 6[3], 7, 8, 9, 11[8], 12[6], 13[4], 14[3], 15, 16[2], 17, 18, 19, 21[2], 22[3], 23[3], 24, 25[2], 26, 27, 28, 29, 31, 33[3], 34[2], 35[3], 36, 37[3], 38, 39, 40[4], 41[2], 42[3], 43[3], 45[3], 46, 47[2], 48[5], 50, 52[2], 53[4], 54[7], 57[2], 58, 61[2], 62[2], 63, 65[2], 66, 67[2], 69[2], 70, 72[2], 73[3]; **10:**1, 5, 6[2], 7[4], 8, 9[2], 10, 11[2], 12[2], 14[2], 15[4], 17, 20[2], 21[4], 23, 25[3], 29, 30[7], 32[2], 33[3], 34[4], 36[5], 37[5], 38[3], 39[4], 40, 41[5], 42[5], 43[2], 44[5], 45[6], 46[2], 47, 49[2], 50[2], 51, 52, 53, 55[4], 57, 60, 61, 62, 63[3], 64[2], 65[2], 67[2], 69[3], 70[2], 71[3], 72, 73, 74, 75[2], 76[3], 77[2], 78, 81, 82[2], 83[3], 84[2], 85[2], 86[2], 89[2]; **11:**1[3], 2[2], 3, 4[4], 5[2], 6[2], 7[2], 8[2], 13[2], 14, 17[2], 18[3], 19, 20[2], 21[2], 22, 23[3], 24, 26[2], 27, 28[2], 29, 30[2], 31, 33[3], 34[10], 35[5], 37, 38[5], 39[3], 40[2], 41[5], 44[2], 45[5], 46[6], 47[3], 48[2], 49[5], 50, 51[4], 52[2], 53, 54[2], 55, 56, 57[4], 58, 59[2], 60[5], 61, 62[3], 63, 64, 66, 67[3], 68[4], 69, 70[3], 72[2], 73, 74; **12:**1[2], 2[2], 3[4], 4[4], 5[2], 6[7], 7[2], 8[2], 9, 11, 13, 15, 17, 19, 20[2], 21[3], 24, 25, 26[2], 27[2], 28, 29, 30, 31, 33[2], 34, 35[2], 36[4], 37[5], 38, 39, 45[3], 46[2], 48[3], 49, 52, 53[2]; **13:**1, 2[2], 3[5], 4, 6[2], 7[2], 10[2], 12, 13, 15[3], 17[3], 18[2], 19[2], 20[2], 21[3], 22[2], 25[2], 27[2], 29[4], 30, 31, 32[2], 33[2], 34, 36[3], 37[2], 38[2], 39, 41[3], 42[4], 43, 44[4], 45[3], 47[3], 48, 49[2], 50, 51[4], 52[3], 53; **14:**1, 3[2], 4[4], 5[2], 6[2], 7, 8[3], 9[2], 10[4], 11, 12, 13[2], 14[3], 15[3], 17[2], 18, 19, 20[10], 21, 22, 23[4], 24[2], 25, 26, 27[4], 28[8], 29[4], 30, 32, 33[4], 34[3], 35[3], 36[5], 37[4], 38, 40[4], 41, 42[5], 43, 44[2], 46[2], 47, 48[2], 49; **15:**1[5], 2[3], 3[2], 4, 5[3], 7[3], 8, 9[2], 10[3], 11, 14[4], 15[2], 16, 17[4], 19, 20, 21, 22[2], 23[2], 24, 25, 27, 28, 29, 30[4], 31[3], 32[4], 33, 34[2], 35, 36[3], 38[2], 39[2], 40[2], 41[2]; **16:**2, 3, 4[2], 5[2], 6[2], 7[6], 8[3], 9, 10[2], 11, 12, 13, 14[5], 15[2], 16, 18[3], 19, 20, 22, 23[5], 24[2]; **2Mc 1:**1[2], 7[5], 8[4], 9[3], 10[5], 11, 12, 13[4], 14[2], 15[6], 16[3], 18[8], 19[5], 20[4], 21[6], 22, 23[4], 24, 25, 27[2], 30[2], 31[3], 32[2], 33[8], 34[3], 35; **2:**1[3], 2[5], 3, 4[6], 5[4], 6, 7, 8[6], 9[2], 10[4], 11, 12, 13[6], 14[3], 16[2], 17[4], 18[2], 19[5], 20, 21[3], 22[5], 24[4], 26, 27[3], 28[4], 29[4], 30[3], 31[2], 32[2]; **3:**1[4], 2[4], 3[4], 4[5], 6[7], 7[5], 8[2], 9[4], 10, 11[2], 12[5], 13[3], 14[2], 15[3], 16[4], 17[2], 18, 19[5], 21[4], 22, 24[3], 27, 28[2], 29, 30[3], 31, 32[5], 33[5], 34, 35[3], 36[2], 37, 38, 40[4]; **4:**1[4], 2[6], 4[2], 5[3], 6, 7[3], 8, 9, 10[2], 11[7], 12[4], 13[2], 14[8], 15[2], 17, 18[2], 19[3], 20[4], 21, 22, 23[5], 24[2], 25[4], 26, 27[3], 28[6], 29[3], 30[3], 31[2], 32[3], 34[2], 35[2], 36[7], 37[2], 38[6], 39[4], 40[2], 41[2], 42[3], 44[3], 45, 46[2], 47[3], 48[4], 49[2], 50[2]; **5:**2[2], 3, 4, 5[5], 6[2], 7[4], 8[4], 9, 10, 11[2], 14, 15[3], 16[4], 17[5], 18, 19[7], 20[6], 21[3], 22[2], 23[2], 24[4], 25[2], 26[2], 27[3]; **6:**1[4], 2[5], 3, 4[3], 5[2], 6[2], 7[5], 8[6], 9, 10[2], 11[2], 13, 14[4], 17, 18, 19[2], 20[2], 21[4], 23[3], 24, 25, 26[4], 28[3], 29, 30[2], 31[2]; **7:**1, 2, 3, 4[4], 5[5], 6[2], 7[4], 8[2], 9[2], 10[2], 12[2], 13[2], 14[2], 15, 16, 18, 20[2], 21, 22, 23[5], 24[2], 25[4], 27, 28[4], 30[4], 31[2], 34, 35[2], 36, 37, 38[2], 39[2], 40, 41, 42[2]; **8:**1[2], 2[4], 3[3], 4[3], 5[3], 6, 7, 8[4], 9[2], 10[4], 11[4], 12[2], 14[3], 15[2], 16[3], 17[6], 18[2], 19[2], 20[6], 23[4], 24[2], 25[2], 26[2], 27[5], 28[4], 29, 30[3], 31[4], 32[2], 33[4], 34[3], 35[5], 36[6]; **9:**1, 2[7], 3, 4[3], 5[2], 6, 7[2], 8[4], 9[3], 10[2], 11, 13[2], 14[2], 15[3], 16[5], 17, 18[4], 21[2], 23[2], 24[3], 25[4], 26, 28[4], 29; **10:**1[3], 2[4], 3[3], 4, 5[7], 6[4], 7, 8[2], 9, 10[3], 11[2], 12[3], 13[2], 14[2], 15[3], 16[2], 17[2], 20, 21[2], 22, 23, 24[2], 26[3], 27[2], 28[5], 29[3], 30, 33, 34[3], 35[4], 36[8], 38[2]; **11:**1[2], 2[2], 3[4], 4, 6[3], 7[2], 9[2], 10, 11[2], 13[3], 14, 15[3], 16[4], 17, 18, 19[2], 21, 22, 23[3], 24, 25, 26, 27[5], 30, 31, 33, 34[4], 35[2], 36[2], 38; **12:**1[2], 2[2], 3[3], 4[2], 5, 6[4], 7[2], 8[3], 9[5], 11, 14[2], 15[4], 16[3], 17, 19, 20, 21[6], 22[3], 23[4], 24[3], 25, 26, 27[2], 28[4], 30[3], 31[2], 32[2], 34, 35[2], 36[2], 37[2], 38[4], 39[4], 40[6], 41[4], 42[5], 43[2], 44, 45[2]; **13:**1, 2, 3, 4[5], 5, 7[2], 8, 9[2], 10[5], 11[3], 12[2], 13[5], 14[5], 15[5], 16[2], 17, 18[3], 19, 20, 21[3], 22[2], 23[4], 25[2], 26[3]; **14:**1, 2, 3[2], 4[3], 5[3], 6[2], 7, 8[3], 9[2], 10, 11[2], 12, 13, 14[3], 15[3], 16[2], 17[3], 18[2], 20[4], 21, 22[3], 23[2], 24, 25, 26[3], 27[3], 28, 29, 30, 31[6], 32, 33[3], 34[2], 37[2], 38, 39[2], 41[5], 42, 43[6], 44[2], 45, 46[3]; **15:**1[2], 2[2], 3[3], 4[3], 5, 7, 8[5], 9[4], 10[3], 11, 12[2], 13, 14[4], 17[7], 18, 19[3], 20[5], 21[7], 22[2], 23, 24, 26, 28, 29[2], 30[3], 31[3], 32[3], 33[4], 34, 35[3], 36[4], 37[3], 38[2], 39[5]; **1Es 1:**1[4], 2[3], 3[6], 4, 5[6], 6[5], 7[4], 8[4], 9[2], 10[3], 11[7], 12[2], 13[4], 14[5], 15[4], 16[3], 17[4], 18[4], 19[3], 20[2], 21[3], 22[2], 23[3], 24[5], 25, 26, 27[5], 28[4], 29[2], 30[3], 31, 32[4], 33[9], 34[2], 35, 36, 37, 38, 39[2], 41, 42[3], 44[2], 45[2], 47[6], 48[5], 49[8], 50, 51, 52[2], 53, 54[5], 55[3], 56[2], 57[4], 58[3]; **2:**1[5], 2[3], 3[4], 5[3], 6, 7[3], 8[7], 10[2], 11, 12, 13, 14, 15, 16[5], 17[4], 18[3], 19, 20[2], 21[2], 22, 23, 25[4], 26, 27, 28, 29, 30[8]; **3:**1, 2[2], 4[4], 5, 8, 9[6], 10, 11[2], 12, 13[2], 14[2], 15[2], 16, 17[2], 18[2], 19[7], 23, 24; **4:**1[3], 3, 4, 5[3], 6[4], 12[2], 13, 14[2], 15, 16[2], 23, 24, 28, 29[4], 30[3], 31, 33[2], 34[4], 35, 36, 37, 40[6], 41, 42[2], 43[3], 44, 45[3], 46[3], 47, 48[2], 49[2], 50[4], 51[2], 52[2], 53[2], 54, 55[4], 56, 57, 58[2], 59[2], 61, 62, 63; **5:**1, 2, 4[3], 5[5], 6[4], 7, 8, 9[4], 10, 11[2], 12[4], 13[2], 14[3], 15[3], 16[4], 17[2], 20, 21, 22[3], 23, 24[4], 25[2], 26[2], 27[2], 28[7], 29[9], 30[8], 31[17], 32[8], 33[7], 34[11], 35[2], 36[2], 37[2], 38[7], 39[2], 40, 44[4], 45[2], 46[5], 47[5], 48[2], 49[3], 50[7], 51[3], 52[2], 53[3], 54[2], 55[5], 56[4], 57[5], 58[11], 59[3], 60[2], 61, 62[5], 63[3], 65[7], 66[4], 67[2], 68[2], 69[2], 70[4], 71[3], 72[2], 73[3]; **6:**1[6], 2[5], 3[2], 4[2], 5[5], 7[3], 8[5], 9[3], 10, 11, 12[2], 13[4], 14, 15[3], 16[2], 17[2], 18[4], 19[3], 20[3], 21[2], 22[5], 23[3], 24[5], 25[2], 26[5], 27[7], 28[3], 29[3], 30, 31[2], 32[4], 33[2]; **7:**1[2], 2[5], 3[2], 4[4], 5[4], 6[5], 7[3], 8[4], 9[6], 10[6], 11[2], 12[3], 13[5], 14[2], 15[5]; **8:**1[3], 2, 3[2], 4[2], 5[2], 6[10], 7[4], 8[5], 9[3], 10[2], 11, 12[2], 13[5], 14[2], 15, 16[2], 17[4], 18[2], 19[4], 21[4], 22, 23[2], 24[3], 25[4], 26[2], 27[2], 28[2], 29[3], 30, 31, 32[2], 33, 34, 35, 36, 37, 38, 39[2], 40, 41, 42[3], 45[3], 46[2], 47[2], 48, 49[5], 50[2], 51, 52[2], 54[2], 55[6], 58[6], 59[7], 60[7], 61[5], 62[4], 63, 64[2], 65[2], 66, 67[6], 68, 69[13], 70[7], 72[3], 73, 76, 77[4], 79[3], 80[2], 81, 82, 83[4], 85[2], 86, 87[3], 91[3], 92[4], 93, 94[2], 96[2]; **9:**1[3], 2[3], 4[5], 5[5], 6[4], 7[2], 8[2], 9[2], 10, 11[2], 12[3], 13[3], 14, 16[5], 17[4], 18, 19, 21, 22, 23, 24, 25, 26, 27, 28, 29, 30, 31, 32, 33, 34[2], 35, 37[7], 38[4], 39[3], 40[7], 41[6], 42[3], 45[6], 46[4], 47[3], 48[4], 49[3], 50[2], 51[2], 52[3], 53[2], 55; **Man 1:**3[2], 5, 7[2], 8[2], 9[5], 11, 13[3], 15[3]; **Pm 151:**T, 1, 3, 5, 6, 7; **3Mc 1:**1[3], 2[5], 3[6], 4[2], 5[2], 6[2], 7, 8[2], 9[3], 10[3], 11[3], 12, 15, 16[5], 17, 18, 19[2], 20[2], 21[2], 22[4], 23[6], 24, 25[3], 26, 27, 28[2], 29[5]; **2:**1[2], 2[3], 3[2], 4, 5, 6, 7[4], 8, 9[2], 10, 14, 15, 17[3], 18[4], 20, 21[3], 22[2], 23, 25, 26[2], 27[3], 28, 29, 30[2], 31[3], 32[2], 33; **3:**1[3], 2[2], 3[2], 5, 7[2], 8[4], 11[3], 14, 15[3], 16[3], 18[2], 19, 21[2], 23, 25, 26[3], 27[2], 28[3], 30[2]; **4:**1[2], 2[2], 4[6], 5, 6[3], 7, 8[2], 9[4], 10, 11[11], 12[4], 13[2], 14[5], 15[3], 16[2], 17[5], 18[4], 19, 20[2], 21[2]; **5:**1[2], 2[4], 3[2], 4[2], 5[7], 6[2], 7, 8[2], 10[4], 11[3], 12[2], 13[4], 14[6], 15[3], 16[2], 17[3], 18[4], 19[2], 20[6], 21, 22[2], 23[4], 24[2], 25[3], 26[4], 27[3], 28[3], 29[3], 30, 31[2], 34[2], 35[3], 36[4], 38[3], 39, 40[2], 41, 42[6], 43[3], 44[4], 45[3], 46[5], 47[3], 48[8], 49, 50[3], 51[2]; **6:**1[4], 3[3], 4[4], 5[3], 6[4], 7[2], 8, 9[2], 10[2], 11[2], 12[3], 13[2], 14, 15[2], 16[4], 17[3], 18[3], 19[2], 20, 21[2], 22[2], 23, 24, 26[2], 28[3], 29[2], 30[5], 31, 32, 33[2], 34, 35[4], 36[3], 37, 38[5], 39, 40[3], 41[4]; **7:**1, 2, 3[2], 4, 6[3], 7, 8, 9[2], 10[6], 11[3], 12[3], 13[2], 15[2], 16[4], 17[3], 18, 19, 20[3], 22[2], 23; **2Es 1:**1[2], 3[5], 4[2], 5, 6, 7[2], 8, 11[2], 12, 13, 14, 15[2], 16, 17[2], 18, 19, 20[3], 21[4], 22[3], 23[2], 27, 28, 31, 32[2], 33[2], 37[4], 38[2], 40[2]; **2:**1[2], 2, 3, 4, 5[2], 7[2], 8, 9, 10[2], 11, 12, 13[2], 14[2], 15, 16, 17, 19, 20[6], 21[5], 22[2], 23[2], 26, 27, 28[2], 30, 31[3], 33[2], 34[2], 35[2], 36[2], 37[2], 38[3], 39[2], 40[3], 41[3], 42, 43[2], 45[2], 46, 47[4], 48[3]; **3:**1[3], 2[2], 3, 4[3], 5[2], 6[2], 9[3], 10[2], 11, 14[2], 18[5], 19[4], 21, 22[6], 23[2], 25[2], 26, 28, 31, 32, 33, 34[4], 35[2]; **4:**1, 2[2], 4[2], 5[2], 7[7], 8, 9, 10, 11[3], 13, 14, 15[4], 16[3], 17[4], 19[4], 21[8], 22, 23[5], 24, 26, 27[2], 28[2], 29[4], 30[2], 34[2], 35[3], 36[4], 37[2], 39[4], 40, 41[3], 42[2], 43, 45, 47, 48[2], 49[2], 50[5], 52; **5:**1[5], 3, 4[5], 5[3], 6[2], 7[2], 8, 9, 13, 15, 16[2], 17, 18[2], 20, 21, 22[3], 23, 24[4], 25[3], 26[2], 27[2], 28[5], 31, 34[2], 35[3], 36[2], 37[4], 39, 40[3], 41, 43, 44[3], 45, 48[2], 49[2], 50, 53[3], 55; **6:**1[6], 2[3], 3[3], 4[5], 5[2], 6, 7[6], 8, 9[3], 10[6], 12, 14, 15[5], 16, 17, 18[3], 19[3], 20[5], 23, 24[3], 25, 26[2], 28, 29, 32[3], 34[2], 35[2], 36[3], 38[3], 39[2], 41[5], 42[3], 43, 44[2], 45[7], 47[3], 48[2], 49[3], 50[3], 51[2], 52[2], 53[2], 54[2], 56, 59; **7:**1[2], 2, 5[3], 7[3], 8[3], 9[4], 11, 12, 13[3], 14[2], 17[2], 18[3], 19[2], 20, 21[2], 23, 25[3], 26[4], 27, 28, 29, 30[2], 31, 32[4], 33[2], 35, 36[4], 37[3], 38, 42[3], 46, 47, 48[2], 50, 51[3], 54, 59[2], 60[2], 61, 62[3], 63[2], 64, 65[5], 70[5], 71, 72[2], 73[2], 74[3], 75[2], 77[2], 78[7], 79[2], 81[3], 82, 83[4], 84[3], 85[3], 86, 87[5], 88[3], 89[4], 90, 91, 92[2], 93[5], 94[3], 95[4], 96[3], 97[4], 98[2], 99[5], 100[2], 101, 102[4], 104[2], 106[2], 107, 108[3], 109[2], 110[2], 111[2], 112[3], 113[4], 115, 116, 118, 122[3], 125[2], 127[2], 129[2], 130, 132[2], 137, 138, 139[2], 140; **8:**1[4], 2[3], 5, 6, 8[3], 9, 10[4], 16, 17[2], 18[2], 19[2], 20, 21, 23[2], 24[2], 26, 27[2], 29[2], 33, 38, 39[2], 41[3], 43, 44, 47, 48, 49[2], 50[2], 51, 52[2], 53, 54[2], 55, 56, 59[3], 60, 63[2]; **9:**1, 2[3], 3, 4[4], 5[3], 6[5], 7, 8[5], 13[3], 17[8], 18, 20, 22, 24[7], 25, 26[5], 27, 28, 29[2], 32[4], 34[3], 35, 36, 37, 39, 44, 45, 47; **10:**2[2], 3, 4, 5, 7, 8, 9, 10, 11, 12[2], 13[4], 14[2], 15, 16, 17, 18, 20[2], 22[3], 23[2], 24[2], 26[2], 27, 28, 29, 31[2], 32, 38[2], 40[2], 41, 42, 43[2], 44, 45[2], 46[2], 47, 48, 50[3], 51, 52, 53, 54[2], 55[3], 57, 59[5]; **11:**1[2], 2[3], 4[2], 5[2], 6, 7, 8, 9[2], 10[2], 12[2], 13, 14, 16, 18[3], 19, 20[2], 21, 22[2], 23[2], 24[3], 25, 27, 28, 29[4], 30, 31[2], 32[3], 33[3], 34[2], 35[4], 37[2], 38, 39[3], 40[5], 41, 42[5], 43[2], 44, 46[2]; **12:**1[2], 2[2], 3[3], 4[2], 5, 6[2], 8, 9[4], 10, 11[3], 13[2], 15[2], 16[2], 17[3], 18[2], 19, 21[3], 22, 23[2], 24[2], 26[2], 27[2], 28[3], 29[2], 30[4], 31[3], 32[4], 34[4], 35, 36, 38, 39, 40[5], 42[2], 43, 44, 47[2], 48[2], 50[2], 51[4]; **13:**1, 2, 3[5], 4, 5[3], 7[2], 9[2], 11[7], 12[2], 13, 14, 15, 18[2], 20[2], 21[3], 22, 23[3], 25[4], 26, 28[2], 29[3], 30, 32[2], 33[3], 35, 36, 37[2], 38[4], 40[4], 41[2], 43[2], 44[3], 46, 47[4], 49[3], 51[3], 52[3], 53[2], 56, 57[3], 58; **14:**1, 5[4], 8[3], 9, 10[2], 11, 12[2], 13[2], 14, 15, 17[3], 18[2], 20[2], 21, 22[6], 23, 25, 26, 27, 30, 31[3], 33, 35[5], 37[2], 38, 42[3], 43, 44, 45[5], 46[2], 47[3]; **15:**1[4], 3[2], 5[3], 7, 8[2], 9[2], 10[2], 12[2], 13[2], 14, 15, 16, 18[2], 19, 20[5], 21, 22, 23[3], 24, 27, 28, 29[4], 30[4], 31, 33[2], 34[4], 35[2], 37, 38[3], 39[6], 40, 41[3], 42[2], 44[3], 46[2], 50[2], 52, 55, 56, 57[3], 58, 60, 63; **16:**3, 6[2], 8, 11, 12[7], 13[3], 14, 15[3], 16[2], 18[6], 19, 20, 21[2], 22[3], 23[2], 24, 25, 26, 28[2], 30, 31, 32, 35, 36[2], 37, 38[4], 39[3], 40[3], 41[2], 42[2], 43[4], 47, 48[2], 50, 52, 53, 54, 55[2], 56[3], 57[2], 58[5], 59[2], 60[5], 61, 62, 64, 66, 67, 68, 70, 71, 73, 74[2], 76; **4Mc 1:**1[2], 2[3], 4[2], 5, 6, 7, 8[3], 9, 10[2], 11[3], 12, 13, 15[2], 16[2], 17, 18, 19, 20[2], 21, 25[2], 26, 27, 28[2], 29[2], 30[5], 31, 33, 34, 35[5]; **2:**1[3], 2, 3[2], 4, 5, 6[3], 7, 8[4], 9[5], 10, 11, 13, 14[4], 15, 16, 18[3], 19[3], 22[3], 23[2], 24; **3:**1, 3, 5, 6, 7[2], 8[2], 9, 10, 11[2], 12[3], 13[3], 14[2], 16, 17[4], 18, 19, 20[2], 21; **4:**1[6], 3[4], 4[3], 5, 6[3], 7[2], 8, 9[3], 10, 11[4], 12[2], 13, 14, 15, 16, 17[2], 18[2], 19[2], 20[2], 21, 22, 23, 24[2], 25, 26[2]; **5:**1, 2, 3, 4[4], 7[2], 8, 9, 10, 11, 14, 15, 16[2], 20, 21, 24, 25[5], 27, 29[3], 32, 33, 35, 36, 38; **6:**1[4], 2[2], 4, 5, 6, 7[2], 8[2], 9[3], 10, 13, 17, 18, 19[2], 21, 23, 24[4], 27[2], 30[4], 31, 32, 33[2], 34; **7:**1[4], 2[3], 3[2], 4[2], 5[2], 6, 7, 8, 9[2], 10, 11[4], 12[2], 14, 15, 16, 18[2], 20, 21, 22[2], 23; **8:**1[2], 2[2], 3, 4, 5[4], 7, 8, 11, 12[2], 13[2], 15[3], 16[2], 17, 19[2], 22, 24, 25[2], 26, 27, 28, 29; **9:**2, 4, 6[2], 7, 8, 9, 10, 11[2], 12, 13, 14, 15, 16[2], 18, 19[2], 20[5], 21[2], 22, 24[3], 25[2], 26[3], 28, 29, 30[3], 31, 32[3]; **10:**1[2], 2[3], 3, 5, 7, 8, 12, 13[2], 14, 15[5], 17, 20; **11:**1, 2, 3, 5, 9[2], 10[2], 12, 13[2], 15, 17, 19, 26, 27[3]; **12:**1[2], 2[2], 3, 5[2], 6[2], 7, 8, 9, 10[2], 11[2], 13[2], 14, 16, 17, 19; **13:**1[2], 4[3], 5, 6[2], 7[5], 9[5], 10, 12[2], 13, 15[4], 16, 17, 18[2], 19[4], 20[6], 21, 22, 23[2], 24[3], 26, 27[2]; **14:**1[2], 2, 3, 4, 5, 6[3], 7, 8, 9[3], 10, 11, 12[3], 15[2], 16[3], 17[2], 18, 19[2], 20[3]; **15:**1[3], 2, 3, 4[3], 5, 6[2], 7, 8[2], 9[2], 10, 11[3], 12, 15[5], 16, 18[3], 19[4], 20[4], 21[5], 22[3], 23[2], 24[2], 25[2], 26, 27[2], 28, 29[4], 31[3], 32[5]; **16:**1, 2[2], 3[2], 4, 6, 8, 9, 13[3], 14, 15, 16[2], 17, 18, 19, 20, 21[4], 22, 24[2], 25[2]; **17:**1[2], 2[3], 3[3], 5[3], 7[4], 8, 9[4], 11, 12[2], 13[5], 14[5], 15, 16[2], 17, 18[2], 20[2], 21[3], 22, 23[3]; **18:**1, 3, 4[4], 5[3], 6, 7, 8[3], 9[2], 10[2], 12[2], 13[2], 14[3], 15[3], 17, 18, 19, 20[3], 21, 22, 23[3]

THEIR (5689)

Ge 2:1; **4:**4; **6:**3, 5, 20[2]; **7:**3; **9:**23[4]; **10:**5[4], 20[4], 31[4], 32[2]; **11:**7; **13:**6; **14:**11[2], 24; **17:**7, 8, 9, 23; **18:**16, 20, 26; **19:**10, 33, 35, 36; **22:**17; **24:**52, 59, 60; **25:**13, 16[4]; **26:**31; **31:**43, 53; **32:**12, 15; **33:**2, 6; **34:**13, 18, 20[2], 21, 23[3], 25, 27, 28[3], 29[4]; **35:**4; **36:**7[2], 19, 40[3], 43; **37:**2, 4, 12, 21, 22, 25[2], 32; **40:**1; **42:**6, 24, 25[2], 26[2], 29, 35[3], 36; **43:**2, 11, 15, 24[2], 27, 28; **44:**3, 13; **45:**24, 25, 27; **46:**5[3], 6, 17, 32[2]; **47:**1, 9, 12, 17[2], 20, 22, 30; **48:**6[2]; **49:**5, 6[4], 7[2], 19, 28; **50:**8[3], 15; **Ex 1:**14; **2:**11, 16, 17[2], 18, 23[2], 24; **3:**7[3]; **4:**5, 31; **5:**4, 6, 21; **6:**9[2], 14, 16, 17, 19, 25; **7:**11, 22; **8:**7, 18; **9:**20, 21; **10:**7; **12:**33, 34[4], 42; **13:**17; **14:**22[2], 25, 26, 29[2]; **16:**16; **18:**19, 23; **19:**10, 14, 17; **22:**23; **23:**6, 24[3], 27, 32, 33; **24:**12; **25:**20[2], 36[2]; **26:**21, 25, 29, 37; **27:**10[2], 11[3], 17[2], 21; **28:**10[2], 12, 38, 40, 42; **29:**10, 15, 19, 20[2], 25, 28[2], 45, 46[2]; **30:**12, 19[2], 21[3]; **31:**10, 16; **32:**3, 25, 32, 34; **33:**6, 8, 10; **34:**13[3], 15[2], 16[4]; **35:**18, 19, 25, 26; **36:**26, 30, 36, 38[4]; **37:**9[2], 22[2]; **38:**10[2], 11[2], 12, 17[2], 19[4], 28; **40:**15[2], 31[2], 36, 38; **Lev 4:**15; **6:**17, 18; **7:**20, 34, 36, 38; **8:**14, 16, 18, 22, 24[3], 25, 28, 30[2]; **9:**24; **10:**5, 17, 19[2]; **11:**8[2], 11[2], 21, 27, 37, 38, 40[2]; **14:**47[2]; **15:**6, 7, 8, 10, 11, 31[3]; **16:**16[3], 21[2], 22, 27[3], 34; **17:**5, 7[2], 15, 16[2]; **18:**3, 10, 29; **19:**23, 24, 25[2]; **20:**2, 3, 4[2], 5[2], 9, 11, 12, 13, 16, 17, 18, 24, 27; **21:**5[3], 6[3], 7, 17; **22:**16; **23:**18[2]; **24:**14; **25:**3, 33, 34[2], 41[3], 45, 48, 49[4], 51, 52, 54; **26:**4[2], 13, 20, 36[2], 39[2], 40[2], 41[3], 43, 44[2], 45[3]; **27:**31; **Nu 1:**2, 16, 18[2], 20[3], 22[3], 24[3], 26[3], 28[3], 30[3], 32[3], 34[3], 36[3], 38[3], 40[3], 42[3], 45, 46, 47, 52; **2:**2[2], 17, 32[2]; **3:**4, 17, 18, 19, 20[2], 22, 31, 34, 36, 37, 39, 40, 45; **4:**2[2], 22[2], 26[2], 27, 28, 29[2], 31, 32[3], 33, 34[2], 36, 38[2], 40[3], 42[2], 44[2], 46[2], 48, 49; **5:**3, 10; **6:**4, 5, 7[2], 8, 9, 12, 13, 14, 15[2], 16, 21[2]; **7:**2, 3, 7, 8, 10, 11, 87; **8:**7[2], 10, 12, 21, 22, 26[3]; **10:**21; **11:**1, 10[2], 12, 16, 33; **13:**2, 4; **14:**5, 6, 9, 23; **15:**25[3], 38[2]; **16:**15, 22, 26, 27[4], 32[2], 34, 38, 45; **17:**2, 6[2], 10; **18:**13, 16, 17[2], 18, 20, 23, 24; **19:**13, 19; **20:**6, 8[2], 11, 21; **21:**2, 3, 30; **22:**7; **23:**21; **24:**8; **25:**2[2], 18; **26:**2, 12, 15, 20, 23, 26, 28, 35, 37, 38, 41, 42[2], 44, 48, 50, 55, 56, 57, 59; **27:**5, 7[2], 14, 19; **28:**14, 20, 28, 31; **29:**3, 6, 9, 11, 14, 18, 19, 21, 24, 27, 30, 33, 37; **31:**9[4], 10[2], 29; **32:**17, 18, 41; **33:**2[3], 4[2], 52[3]; **34:**14[3], 15; **35:**3[4], 5, 7; **36:**3, 4[2], 6, 7, 8, 11, 12[2]; **Dt 1:**8; **2:**5, 12, 21, 22, 23; **3:**28; **4:**10, 37, 38; **5:**29; **7:**3[2], 5[4], 10[2], 16, 24[2], 25; **9:**5, 14, 27[2]; **10:**11, 15; **11:**4, 6[3], 9; **12:**2, 3[6], 29, 30[2], 31[4]; **14:**8[2], 29; **18:**2, 18; **19:**1[2]; **20:**18; **21:**5, 6; **22:**1; **23:**2, 3, 6[2], 7, 15; **24:**15[2], 16[3]; **26:**12; **29:**8, 17, 19, 20, 25, 28; **31:**4, 7, 11, 13, 16, 19, 20[2], 21, 28; **32:**20, 21, 27, 30, 31, 32[3], 33, 35[3], 36, 37, 38[2]; **33:**29; **Jos 1:**6; **2:**19[2]; **3:**14; **4:**18, 21; **5:**1, 6, 7[2], 8; **7:**6, 8[2], 11, 12[3]; **8:**19, 27, 33[2]; **9:**4[2], 5[2], 14, 15, 16, 17[2]; **10:**5[2], 13, 19, 24[2], 40, 42; **11:**4, 5, 6[2], 9[2], 12, 14, 17, 20, 21, 23; **12:**6, 7[2]; **13:**8, 14, 15, 16, 23[2], 24, 25, 28[2], 29, 30, 31, 33; **14:**2, 4[2]; **15:**1, 2, 12, 20, 32, 36, 41, 44, 46, 51, 54, 57, 59, 60, 62; **16:**4, 5[2], 8, 9; **17:**2[2], 4; **18:**4, 5, 7[2], 8, 12, 21, 24, 28; **19:**6, 7, 9, 15, 16, 22, 23, 30, 31, 38, 39, 47, 48[2]; **21:**2, 3, 7, 8, 19, 26, 33, 41, 43, 44[4]; **22:**6, 7[2], 9; **23:**1, 2[2], 5, 7, 12; **24:**8, 28; **Jdg 1:**4, 7; **2:**2, 3, 4, 6, 10, 12, 14[2], 17[3], 18[2], 19[3], 20, 22; **3:**4, 6[4], 7, 18, 25, 27; **5:**20; **6:**5[3], 9; **7:**2, 5[3], 7, 8[3], 12, 19, 20[2]; **8:**3, 10, 21, 26, 28, 33, 34[2]; **9:**3, 24[2], 27[2], 57; **10:**12; **11:**23; **12:**2; **13:**20; **14:**17, 19; **15:**13; **16:**18, 23, 24, 25; **17:**6; **18:**2, 8, 14, 16, 21, 26, 29, 31; **19:**14, 21; **20:**13, 15, 33; **21:**2, 6, 22[2], 23, 24, 25; **Ru 1:**7; **1Sa 1:**19; **2:**20, 25; **6:**6, 7, 10, 11, 13; **7:**14; **8:**9, 22; **9:**16; **10:**1, 12, 25; **12:**9; **13:**2, 20; **14:**26[2], 30, 34[3], 46; **15:**24; **17:**1, 18, 51, 53; **18:**27; **21:**5, 13; **22:**17[2]; **23:**5; **25:**10; **28:**1, 23; **29:**1; **30:**2, 3, 4, 6; **31:**7, 9, 13; **2Sa 2:**25, 26, 27; **3:**18, 30; **4:**12[2]; **5:**21, 23; **6:**5, 19; **7:**10, 23, 24; **10:**3, 4[2], 16, 18; **13:**31, 36; **15:**11, 30, 36; **18:**17, 28; **19:**8; **20:**2, 3, 22; **22:**41, 46; **23:**17, 19; **1Ki 1:**40, 49; **2:**4[3], 33; **4:**8, 25; **6:**27; **7:**33[4]; **8:**7, 23, 25, 32[3], 34, 35, 37[2], 38[2], 39, 44, 45[3], 47[2], 48[4], 49[3], 50[2], 66; **9:**9[2], 21; **10:**5; **11:**2, 8; **12:**16, 27; **13:**11, 12; **14:**15[2], 22[2]; **15:**16, 32; **16:**2, 13, 26; **18:**28, 37, 39; **19:**21; **20:**12, 23, 25, 32[2]; **22:**10[2]; **2Ki 1:**14; **2:**1; **3:**27; **5:**2; **6:**20, 22, 23[2]; **7:**7[4], 15; **8:**12[4], 20, 21; **9:**13; **10:**6, 7; **11:**12; **13:**5; **14:**6; **16:**15[2]; **17:**7, 9[2], 14[2], 15, 16, 17[2], 19, 23, 31, 33, 34, 40, 41[4]; **18:**12, 27[2], 35, 37; **19:**17, 18, 26, 29; **21:**8, 14[2], 15; **22:**7, 17; **23:**2, 4, 9, 35; **25:**23[2], 24; **1Ch 1:**29; **2:**16; **3:**9, 19; **4:**3, 27, 31, 32, 33[2], 38[2], 39, 41[3], 42; **5:**7[2], 9, 10[2], 13[2], 15, 16, 20[2], 21[2], 22, 24[2], 25; **6:**19, 32, 33, 44, 48, 54[3], 60[2], 62, 63, 64, 66; **7:**2[3], 4[2], 5, 7, 9[3], 11, 21, 22, 28, 30, 32, 40; **8:**28, 32[2], 38; **9:**1, 2[2], 6, 9[3], 13[2], 17, 19, 22[2], 23, 25[2], 32, 34, 38[2], 44; **10:**7, 9, 10, 12; **11:**14, 19, 21; **12:**29, 30, 32[2], 39, 40; **13:**8; **14:**12; **15:**15, 16, 17, 18; **16:**21, 43; **17:**9, 22; **19:**4[2], 7, 16, 18; **21:**2, 16; **23:**22, 24, 28, 32; **24:**2, 3, 19[3], 30, 31; **25:**1, 3, 6, 7, 8; **26:**6, 8, 12[2], 13; **27:**1; **28:**15, 18; **29:**6, 18, 20[2], 21, 24; **2Ch 3:**13; **4:**9, 20; **5:**8, 11, 12; **6:**14, 16, 23[3], 25, 26, 28, 29[3], 30, 34, 35[3], 37[2], 38[4], 39[3]; **7:**3, 6[2], 10, 14[3], 22; **8:**8, 14[3]; **9:**4[2]; **10:**16; **11:**13, 14[2], 16[2]; **13:**10, 12, 16, 18; **14:**4, 10; **15:**4, 12[3], 15[2]; **18:**9[2]; **19:**4, 8, 10; **20:**13[3], 27[2], 33[2]; **21:**3, 8; **22:**5; **23:**13; **24:**10, 13, 18, 24[2]; **25:**4[2], 15; **26:**13; **28:**6, 8, 15; **29:**6[2], 15, 22[2], 23, 24, 34; **30:**7, 9, 16, 19[2], 22, 27[2]; **31:**1[2], 6, 15, 16[3], 17[3], 18[4], 19; **32:**13, 17; **33:**17; **34:**5, 6, 25, 30, 32, 33[2]; **35:**2, 10[2], 15[3], 25; **36:**15, 17[2]; **Ezr 1:**3, 4, 6; **2:**1, 59[2], 61, 62, 65, 69, 70[2]; **3:**8[2], 9, 10; **4:**5, 7, 9, 17, 23; **5:**3, 5, 8, 10[2], 11; **6:**6, 13, 14, 18[2], 20; **7:**13, 16, 17[2], 26; **8:**1, 13, 19, 24, 26; **9:**1, 2[2], 11[2], 12[3]; **10:**3, 8, 16, 19[3], 44; **Ne 3:**5[3], 18, 23; **4:**4[2], 5[2], 13[4], 15, 17; **5:**1[2], 5, 6, 11[4], 14, 15; **6:**6, 9, 16; **7:**3[2], 61[2], 63, 64, 67, 73[2]; **8:**6[3], 7, 12, 15, 16[2]; **9:**1, 2[2], 3[3], 4, 6, 9, 11, 15[2], 16, 17[2], 20[2], 21[2], 23[2], 24[2], 26, 27[3], 28, 29, 35[2], 37; **10:**10, 28[3], 29[2], 30; **11:**3[2], 9, 12, 14[2], 19, 20, 25, 30; **12:**7, 9, 24, 27, 42, 45; **13:**10, 11, 13[3], 24, 25[3]; **Est 1:**17, 20; **2:**3, 12; **3:**8, 9, 13; **4:**8; **8:**9[2], 11[3], 13, 14; **9:**1, 2[2], 5, 16[2], 22, 27, 28, 31[4]; **Job 1:**4, 5[2], 18; **2:**4, 12[3]; **3:**15, 19; **4:**17, 21; **5:**3, 4, 5[2], 12, 13, 15; **6:**4, 17, 18; **7:**1, 2, 6, 10[2]; **8:**4, 8, 10, 14[2], 16, 17, 18, 19; **11:**20[2]; **12:**6[2], 18; **14:**5[2], 6, 12, 20, 21, 22; **15:**18, 20, 21, 25, 27[3], 29, 30[2], 31, 32[2], 33[2], 35; **16:**10; **17:**2, 4, 5, 9; **18:**5, 6, 7[2], 8, 11, 12[2], 13[2], 15[2], 16[2], 17, 19, 20; **19:**15; **20:**6, 7, 9, 10[3], 11, 12[2], 13, 14[2], 15, 18[2], 20[2], 21, 23[2], 25[2], 26[2], 27, 28; **21:**8[4], 9, 10[2], 11[2], 13, 16[2], 19[2], 20[2], 21[2], 29, 31[2], 32; **22:**6, 16[2], 18; **24:**5[2], 6, 11, 12, 18[2], 23; **26:**5; **27:**8, 9, 14[2], 15, 18, 19, 21; **28:**9, 10; **29:**9[2], 10[2], 17[2], 23, 25; **30:**2[2]; **31:**30; **33:**15, 16, 17, 18[2], 19[2], 20[2], 21[2], 22[2], 30; **34:**11[2], 21, 24, 25, 26; **36:**6, 9[2], 10, 11[2], 14[2], 15[2], 20; **37:**8[2], 24; **38:**15, 32, 33, 40[2]; **39:**3[2], 4; **40:**13; **42:**15[2]; **Ps 1:**2, 3[2]; **2:**3[2]; **4:**7; **5:**9[4], 10[3]; **7:**16[4]; **8:**6; **9:**5, 6, 10, 15, 16; **10:**3, 4[2], 5[3], 6, 7[2], 8, 9, 10, 11, 13, 15, 17; **11:**2, 6; **14:**1, 6; **15:**2, 3[3], 4[2]; **16:**4[3]; **17:**7, 10[2], 11, 14[3]; **18:**40, 45; **19:**3, 4[2], 12; **21:**10[2], 12; **22:**7, 13; **24:**4, 5; **25:**13; **28:**3[2], 4[4], 9; **33:**6, 15, 19; **34:**15, 17, 20; **35:**6, 7, 8, 16, 17, 21; **36:**1[2], 2[2], 3, 4; **37:**7, 10, 12, 13, 14, 15[3], 18, 25, 26, 30, 31[3], 33, 39; **38:**12; **40:**3, 4, 15; **41:**2, 3[3], 6; **44:**1, 3[2]; **49:**6[2], 10, 11[4], 12, 13, 14[3], 16, 17, 18, 19, 20; **50:**23; **53:**1; **54:**5; **55:**9, 15[2], 23; **56:**5, 7; **57:**4[2]; **58:**3, 6, 10; **59:**7[2], 12[3], 15; **62:**4[2], 12; **64:**3, 5, 8; **65:**7; **68:**21, 23; **69:**22[2], 23[2], 25[2], 27; **70:**3; **71:**15; **72:**14[2]; **73:**4, 6, 7[2], 9[2], 17, 20; **74:**4; **76:**5; **78:**4, 5, 6, 7, 8, 12, 18, 28[2], 30[2], 33[2], 35[2], 36[2], 37, 38, 44[2], 46[2], 47[2], 48[2], 50, 51, 53, 55, 57, 58[2], 63[2], 64[2]; **79:**3, 10; **81:**12[2], 14[2], 15; **83:**2, 11[2], 16; **85:**2, 8; **89:**17, 32[2]; **90:**10, 16; **91:**12; **93:**3[2]; **94:**4, 23[2]; **97:**7; **98:**8; **99:**8; **102:**17, 28; **103:**15; **104:**11, 12, 17, 21[2], 22, 23[2], 27, 29[2]; **105:**14, 24, 29[2], 30[2], 31, 32, 33[2], 35[2], 36[2], 37; **106:**11, 18, 21, 25, 27, 29, 32, 36, 37[2], 38, 39[2], 42[2], 43[2], 44[2], 45; **107:**5, 6[2], 12, 13[2], 14, 17[2], 19[2], 26[2], 27, 28[2], 30, 38, 41; **109:**16, 25, 29; **112:**2, 3[2], 5, 7, 8[2], 9[2], 10; **115:**2, 4, 7, 9[2], 10[2], 11[2]; **119:**2, 9, 22, 70, 118; **123:**2; **124:**3, 6; **125:**3, 4, 5; **126:**6; **129:**3, 7[2]; **132:**12; **135:**12, 17; **136:**10, 21; **140:**2, 3[2], 8, 9[2]; **141:**4, 5, 7, 10; **144:**4, 12; **145:**15, 19; **146:**4[2], 5; **147:**3, 4, 9; **148:**6; **149:**2, 5, 6[2], 8[2]; **Pr 1:**6, 15[2], 16, 18, 22, 31[2]; **2:**15; **3:**31; **4:**22; **5:**10, 21, 22, 23; **6:**30, 31; **8:**21; **9:**15; **10:**15[2], 26; **11:**5[2], 6, 7, 9[2], 28, 29; **12:**10, 11, 13, 15, 16, 27; **13:**2, 3[3], 15, 22, 24, 25; **14:**3, 14[2], 15, 20, 21, 24, 31, 32[2]; **15:**20,

27; **16:**7, 17[2], 23[2], 26, 27, 29; **17:**5, 6, 25, 26, 28; **18:**7[2], 11[2]; **19:**7[2], 11, 16, 18, 26[2]; **20:**11, 29[2]; **21:**10[2], 29; **22:**9, 23, 25, 29; **23:**6, 11[2], 14; **24:**2[2], 7, 12; **25:**13, 22; **26:**4, 5[2], 12; **28:**7, 10, 26; **29:**16; **30:**11[2], 12[2], 13[2], 25, 26, 29[2]; **31:**7[2]; **Ecc 2:**3, 14, 23[3], 24; **3:**9, 11, 13, 22[2]; **4:**1, 5[2], 8[2], 9; **5:**11, 13[2], 14, 15[3], 17, 19[2], 20[2]; **6:**12; **7:**15[3]; **8:**12, 13, 15; **9:**1, 3, 6[3]; **10:**13[2]; **12:**5; **SS 5:**7; **Isa 1:**31[2]; **2:**4[2], 7[4], 8[3], 20[2], 22; **3:**4, 8[2], 9[2], 10, 11, 12, 16[2], 17; **5:**13[2], 17, 23, 24[2], 25, 28[4], 29[2]; **6:**2[2], 10[5]; **8:**19, 21[3]; **9:**4[3], 10, 11, 17[2], 20; **10:**2, 5, 13, 24, 25; **11:**7, 14; **13:**8, 10[2], 11, 14[2], 16[4], 18[2], 20[2]; **14:**1, 2[2], 9, 21, 25; **15:**4; **16:**8; **17:**5, 7[2], 8[2], 9; **19:**3, 22; **20:**5[2]; **22:**7; **23:**13; **24:**6, 14; **25:**4, 10, 11[4]; **26:**19, 21; **27:**7; **28:**24, 26; **29:**1, 13[4], 14, 18; **30:**6[2]; **31:**3, 4[2]; **32:**6; **33:**9, 15[2], 16[3], 24; **34:**2, 3[3], 4, 7[2]; **35:**10; **36:**12[2], 18, 20, 22; **37:**18, 19, 27, 30; **40:**6, 24, 26, 31; **41:**1, 17, 22, 29[2]; **42:**10, 11, 15; **43:**9; **44:**9, 18[2], 25, 26; **45:**1, 12, 20; **46:**1, 7; **47:**7, 15; **48:**19; **49:**9, 22[2], 23[2], 26[2]; **50:**2, 3; **51:**11; **52:**5, 8, 15; **53:**3, 11; **54:**17; **55:**7[2], 12; **56:**7[2], 11[2]; **57:**2, 8[2], 17[2], 18[2]; **58:**1[2], 2; **59:**5, 6[3], 7[3], 8[2], 18; **60:**4, 8, 9, 10, 11[2]; **61:**6, 7[2], 8, 9[2]; **63:**3, 6, 8, 9, 10; **65:**2, 4, 6, 7[4], 21, 22, 23; **66:**3[2], 18[2], 24[2]; **Jer 1:**15, 16[2]; **2:**11, 26[4], 27[3]; **3:**17, 21[2], 24[4]; **5:**3, 4, 5, 6[3], 16, 24, 27; **6:**3[3], 10, 12[2], 19, 23, 27; **7:**16, 19, 24[3], 26[2], 28[2], 30, 31[2]; **8:**1, 6, 7, 10[2], 16[2], 19[2]; **9:**3, 5[2], 8[2], 14[2], 16, 23[3]; **10:**5, 7, 9, 14[2], 15, 21, 23[2]; **11:**8, 10[2], 12, 14[2], 18, 22[2], 23; **12:**2[2], 13, 14, 15[2]; **13:**10, 23[2]; **14:**3[3], 4, 6, 10[3], 12, 14, 16[4], 18; **15:**7, 8, 9; **16:**4, 7[2], 15[2], 17[2], 18[4]; **17:**1[2], 2[3], 5, 10[2], 11, 23[2], 25; **18:**15, 16[2], 17, 21[4], 22, 23[3]; **19:**4, 5, 7[3], 9[5], 15; **20:**4, 5, 11; **21:**7[2], 9; **22:**4[2], 7, 9, 13; **23:**3, 8, 10[2], 11, 12[2], 16, 17, 22[2], 26, 27[2], 31, 32[2], 34; **24:**7[2], 10; **25:**12, 14[2], 16, 36, 38; **26:**3[2], 10; **27:**4, 7; **29:**23; **30:**3, 9[2], 10, 20[2], 21[4]; **31:**12, 13, 14, 17, 23, 24, 30, 32[2], 33[2], 34[2]; **32:**13, 18, 19[2], 22, 30[2], 32[4], 33[2], 34, 35, 38, 39[2], 40, 44; **33:**5, 8[2], 12, 20, 26; **34:**9, 10, 14, 16, 20[3], 21[2]; **35:**14, 16; **36:**3[3], 6, 7[2], 24, 31; **37:**10; **38:**2, 4, 18, 23; **40:**7, 8, 9; **41:**5[3], 8, 12; **42:**5; **43:**1[2]; **44:**5[2], 9, 15; **46:**5, 8, 10, 21[2], 26, 27; **47:**3[2], 5; **48:**13, 34, 35, 44; **49:**7, 18, 20[2], 21[2], 29[5], 32[2], 35, 37[2], 38; **50:**4, 6[2], 7[2], 9, 16[2], 27[2], 33, 34[2], 40, 45[2]; **51:**5[2], 17[2], 18, 23[2], 28[2], 30[2], 39, 55[2], 56; **La 1:**10, 11[2], 19, 22; **2:**10[2], 12[3], 15[2], 16[2], 20; **3:**14, 39, 46, 60[2], 61[2], 63, 64[2]; **4:**2, 3, 7[2], 8[3], 10[2], 14, 20; **5:**7, 8, 12, 14; **Eze 1:**5, 7[2], 8[4], 9, 10, 11[3], 16[3], 18, 22, 23, 24[2], 25[2], 26; **2:**3, 6[3]; **3:**8[2], 9, 18[4], 19[3], 20[4]; **4:**4, 5, 12, 13, 17; **5:**10[2]; **6:**5, 9[5], 13[4], 14; **7:**11[2], 12, 13[3], 14, 16, 18, 19[6], 20[3], 24[2], 27[2]; **8:**16[2], 17; **9:**10[2]; **10:**8, 10, 12[4], 16[2], 19, 21, 22; **11:**19, 20, 21[4], 22; **12:**3[2], 4[2], 5, 6, 7, 16, 19[3]; **13:**2, 3, 6, 17, 22[2]; **14:**3[3], 4[4], 5, 7[3], 10, 11[2], 14[2], 20[2], 22[2], 23[2]; **16:**39, 40, 45[2], 47[2], 53, 55[2]; **18:**21, 23, 24, 26, 27; **19:**4, 7[2], 8[2]; **20:**4, 8, 16[2], 18[3], 24[2], 26[3], 28[4], 30; **21:**6, 15, 23[2], 28; **22:**10[2], 28, 31[2]; **23:**3[3], 4, 8, 15[2], 17, 24, 30, 36, 37[2], 39[2], 42, 43, 45, 47[4]; **24:**25[6]; **25:**4[2]; **26:**10, 16[3]; **27:**9, 11, 29, 30, 32, 35[2]; **28:**7, 17, 24, 25, 26[2]; **29:**7[2], 14, 16; **30:**7, 11; **31:**6[2], 14; **32:**7, 10[2], 14[2], 21, 22, 23, 24, 25[2], 26[2], 27[3], 29, 30[2]; **33:**2[2], 4[2], 5[2], 6[2], 8[3], 9[3], 11, 12[2], 13[2], 14, 17, 18, 19, 29, 31[3]; **34:**10[3], 12[2], 13, 14, 23, 24, 26, 27[3], 30; **35:**5[2]; **36:**5, 12, 17[4], 19[2], 23, 37; **37:**10, 20, 21, 23[4], 25[3], 27; **38:**16, 21; **39:**10, 14, 22, 23[2], 24[2], 26[2], 27, 28[2]; **40:**16; **43:**7[4], 8[3], 9[2], 10, 11; **44:**10[2], 12[2], 13, 18[2], 19, 20[3], 28[3]; **45:**4, 5, 8; **46:**16, 18[3]; **47:**12[4], 23; **48:**29; **Da 1:**16; **3:**21[4], 27[2], 28[2], 29; **6:**24[3]; **7:**12[2], 27; **8:**23[2]; **9:**27; **11:**8[3], 27, 32; **Hos 1:**7; **2:**5; **3:**5[2]; **4:**7, 8, 9[2], 12[2], 13, 18[2], 19; **5:**4[2], 6, 7, 15[2]; **7:**2[2], 3[2], 6[2], 7[2], 10, 12, 14, 15, 16[3]; **8:**4[2], 13[2]; **9:**4[3], 6[2], 9[2], 15[2], 16[2]; **10:**2[4], 8, 10, 14; **11:**4, 5, 6[3], 11; **12:**11; **13:**2, 6, 8, 16[2]; **14:**4, 7; **Joel 1:**3[2], 7[2]; **2:**2, 7, 10, 17, 22; **3:**6, 13, 15, 21; **Am 1:**13, 15; **2:**4, 8, 14[2], 15; **3:**10; **4:**1; **5:**11; **6:**2, 4; **8:**7; **9:**4, 14[2], 15; **Ob 1:**12, 13; **Jnh 1:**2; **2:**8; **3:**8[2], 10; **4:**11[2]; **Mic 2:**1[2], 2, 9[2], 13[2]; **3:**2, 3[2], 5, 7; **4:**3[2], 4[2], 13[2]; **6:**12, 16; **7:**3, 4[3], 13, 16[4], 17; **Na 2:**2, 4, 7; **3:**19; **Hab 1:**6, 7, 8[3], 11[2]; **2:**4[2], 5[2], 15; **Zep 1:**9, 12[2], 13[2], 17[2], 18[2]; **2:**7[2], 8, 10[2]; **3:**6[3], 7, 13, 19; **Hag 1:**11, 12[2], 14; **2:**14, 22[2]; **Zec 1:**21; **2:**9; **5:**6, 9; **7:**2, 11, 12; **8:**4, 8, 12; **9:**15, 16; **10:**6, 7[3], 9; **11:**3, 5, 6, 16; **12:**5, 8, 12[2], 13[2], 14; **13:**3[3], 4; **14:**12[6]; **Mal 1:**6; **3:**5, 17; **4:**6[2]; **Mt 1:**21; **2:**11, 12; **3:**6; **4:**6, 8, 20, 21[2], 22, 23; **6:**2, 5, 7, 14, 16[2]; **7:**16, 20, 29; **8:**22, 34; **9:**2, 4, 29, 30, 35; **10:**10, 17, 39[2], 42; **11:**1, 5; **12:**9; **13:**15[5], 43, 54, 57[2], 58; **14:**14; **15:**2, 8[2], 27; **16:**24, 25[2], 26[2]; **17:**12, 25; **18:**10, 31; **20:**8, 25, 34[2]; **21:**7, 8; **22:**7, 16, 18; **23:**5[3]; **24:**45; **25:**1, 3, 4, 7; **26:**43; **27:**39; **Mk 1:**5, 18, 19, 20, 23, 39; **2:**5, 6, 23; **3:**5, 28; **5:**17; **6:**4[3], 6, 8[2], 52; **7:**3, 6[2]; **8:**3, 34, 35[2], 36, 37; **9:**48; **10:**42[2]; **11:**7, 8; **12:**15, 44; **14:**18, 40, 56, 59; **15:**29; **16:**14, 18[2]; **Lk 1:**16, 17, 20, 51, 52, 65, 77; **2:**3, 8, 22, 39, 44; **3:**15; **4:**6, 11, 15, 29; **5:**2, 6, 7, 11, 15, 20, 22, 30; **6:**1, 18, 23, 26; **7:**22; **8:**3, 12, 14[2]; **9:**10, 23, 24[2], 47, 52, 60; **10:**38; **11:**48; **12:**1, 36, 42; **13:**1; **16:**4, 8; **17:**12, 33[2]; **18:**1; **19:**35, 36; **20:**23; **21:**1, 4; **22:**66; **23:**23, 24, 27, 48, 51; **24:**5, 16, 31[2], 33, 41, 43, 45; **Jn 2:**14, 15; **3:**19, 20, 21; **4:**30, 38; **5:**28; **7:**18[2]; **10:**39; **11:**19; **12:**25[2], 37, 40[4]; **13:**12, 16; **15:**20, 22, 25; **16:**4; **17:**9, 19, 20; **18:**12; **20:**10; **Ac 1:**9, 19; **2:**45, 46, 47; **4:**5, 7, 23, 24, 26, 29, 33; **5:**21; **6:**1, 6; **7:**12, 16, 19, 34, 39, 41, 54, 57, 58; **8:**1, 17; **9:**24; **10:**9; **11:**29; **12:**20, 25; **13:**3, 17, 19, 22, 27, 33, 50, 51; **14:**2, 5, 14, 16; **15:**3, 9, 22, 26; **16:**19, 22, 24, 33; **17:**21, 26; **19:**12, 18, 19; **21:**21, 24; **22:**23; **23:**21, 28, 29, 31; **24:**1; **25:**11, 19; **26:**18; **27:**13, 19, 38, 43; **28:**6, 27[5]; **Ro 1:**18, 21[2], 24[2], 26, 27[2]; **2:**15[3], 26; **3:**3, 8, 13[3], 14, 15, 16, 18; **6:**12; **8:**5[2]; **10:**3, 18[2]; **11:**9, 10[2], 11, 12[3], 15[2], 17, 20, 24, 27, 28, 30; **12:**20; **14:**4, 5; **15:**26, 27; **16:**4, 5, 18; **1Co 1:**2; **3:**19; **4:**19; **8:**7, 10, 12, 13; **9:**13, 14; **14:**3, 35; **15:**29; **16:**19; **2Co 3:**14, 15; **4:**4; **5:**19; **6:**16; **8:**2[3], 3[2], 14[2]; **11:**15[2]; **12:**14[2]; **Gal 2:**13; **6:**4[2], 5, 6; **Eph 4:**14, 17, 18[2], 28; **5:**24, 28[2]; **Php 1:**28; **2:**21; **3:**19[5]; **Col 2:**2; **1Th 2:**16; **5:**13; **2Th 3:**12[2]; **1Ti 1:**9; **2:**9; **3:**12[2]; **5:**4[3], 11, 12, 14; **6:**1, 2, 10, 17; **2Ti 2:**17; **3:**2, 6[2], 9; **4:**3; **Tit 1:**12, 15, 16; **2:**4[2], 5, 9; **3:**13; **Heb 2:**8[2], 10, 15; **3:**10; **4:**10; **5:**1; **6:**6; **7:**5, 6, 20; **8:**9, 10[3], 12[2]; **9:**6, 13; **10:**16[2], 17[2]; **11:**16, 35, 39; **13:**7[2]; **Jas 1:**25, 26[3], 27; **2:**16; **3:**3; **5:**3; **1Pe 1:**17; **3:**1, 5, 10[2], 12; **2Pe 2:**2, 3[3], 8, 10, 13; **3:**3, 16; **1Jn 3:**10; **4:**20, 21; **5:**10; **2Jn 1:**13; **3Jn 1:**7, 15; **Jude 1:**6[2], 13, 16[2], 18, 23; **Rev 3:**4; **4:**4, 10; **6:**11[2], 17; **7:**3, 9, 11, 14, 17[2]; **8:**12; **9:**4, 5, 7[2], 8[2], 9, 10[2], 16, 17, 18, 19[3], 20, 21[4]; **11:**5[2], 6, 7, 8[2], 9, 11, 12, 16[2]; **12:**11; **14:**1, 2, 5, 9[2], 11, 13[2]; **15:**2, 6; **16:**10, 11[2]; **17:**13, 17[2]; **18:**11, 19; **19:**18, 19, 21; **20:**4[3], 12; **21:**3, 4, 7, 8, 24; **22:**4, 5, 14; **Tob 2:**10; **4:**6, 12[3]; **6:**6, 15; **7:**8; **8:**17; **9:**5; **12:**10; **13:**11, 16; **14:**4[2], 5, 6[2], 8, 13; **Jdt 1:**4; **2:**5, 8[3], 10[2], 19, 26[2], 27[5]; **3:**4, 8[3]; **4:**1, 2, 3, 5, 10[4], 11[2], 12[2], 13[2], 14, 15[2]; **5:**3[3], 7, 8[3], 9, 10, 12[2], 15, 17, 18[3], 19[2], 20[2], 21; **6:**2[2], 4[5], 6, 12, 13, 14[2], 16[2], 19[2]; **7:**2[2], 4[2], 5[2], 7[2], 10[2], 13[2], 14, 18[2], 19[3], 20, 21[2], 22, 25, 27, 32[2]; **8:**24, 27, 36; **9:**3[3], 4[4], 7[2], 8[2], 9[2], 10; **10:**14, 17, 19; **11:**10, 11, 12[3], 13, 17; **14:**3, 4, 9, 11, 12[2], 13, 19[2]; **15:**13; **16:**3[2], 6, 11, 15, 17, 18[3], 21; **AdE 1:**18, 20; **3:**8, 13; **4:**8; **8:**11[2], 13; **9:**16, 19, 22[3], 26, 27, 28, 31[2]; **11:**7, 10; **12:**2[2]; **13:**6, 18[2]; **14:**5, 7, 8, 11; **16:**2, 3[2], 6[2], 13, 19; **Wis 1:**6[4], 9[2], 16; **2:**21; **3:**2, 3[2], 4, 7, 10, 11[3], 12[2], 13, 17; **4:**3, 5, 6, 11[2], 14, 20[3]; **5:**1, 4[2], 5, 15; **6:**16; **7:**12; **8:**12[2]; **10:**7, 8[2], 17, 19; **11:**1, 2, 3[2], 4, 5[2], 8[2], 13, 15, 18; **12:**2, 4[2], 5[2], 10[3], 11, 20, 23, 24, 27; **13:**3, 4, 5, 10; **14:**5, 9, 14, 17[3], 18, 23, 24[2], 28; **15:**9, 10[3], 15[3], 18; **16:**4, 10, 20, 22; **17:**2[2], 3, 7[2], 15; **18:**1[3], 2, 3, 4, 5, 7, 10[3], 12, 13[2], 21; **19:**1, 2, 3, 4, 10, 13, 14, 17; **Sir 1:**13, 15, 17[2], 24[2]; **2:**17; **3:**3, 4, 5[2], 6[2], 7[2], 9, 11, 24[2]; **4:**1, 6[2], 8, 10, 16, 19; **5:**13; **6:**4, 15, 17[2]; **7:**20, 21, 23, 24; **8:**1, 2, 3, 8, 9, 10, 15; **9:**11, 12, 18; **10:**14, 15, 20, 22, 30[2]; **11:**1, 2, 12, 13, 26; **12:**5; **13:**16; **14:**1, 2; **15:**14; **16:**3[2], 7, 8, 9, 10, 26, 27[2]; **17:**8, 13[2], 15, 19[2], 20[2], 23[2]; **18:**9, 12, 13; **20:**11, 28, 31[2]; **21:**5, 6, 9, 13, 17, 25, 26[2]; **22:**12; **23:**1, 8, 14; **25:**2, 6; **26:**21; **27:**1, 9, 13, 14[3], 15, 22, 29; **28:**1, 15[2]; **29:**1, 9, 22; **30:**25; **31:**6, 23, 24; **32:**1, 9; **33:**11, 12, 13; **34:**7, 15, 16; **35:**24[2]; **36:**16; **37:**5, 7; **38:**1, 2, 25, 27[2], 31[2], 34[2]; **39:**28[3], 31; **40:**1, 2, 10; **41:**6, 15[2]; **42:**18; **43:**6, 10[2], 15; **44:**1, 3[2], 4[3], 6, 7[2], 8, 9, 11[4], 12[3], 13[2], 14[2], 15[2]; **45:**9, 18, 26[3]; **46:**7, 8, 11[2], 12[2]; **47:**7, 9, 10, 24[2]; **48:**6, 10, 15[2], 19[2], 20; **49:**5[2], 12; **50:**13[2], 16, 17[2], 18, 19, 29; **51:**8; **Bar 1:**11, 12; **2:**3[2], 17, 24, 30, 31, 32, 33[3], 34, 35; **3:**4, 17, 18, 19, 21, 28, 34; **4:**25[2]; **5:**6; **LtJ 6:**4, 8, 9, 10[2], 11, 13, 18[3], 19, 20[2], 21, 22, 26, 28, 29, 31[4], 32, 33[2], 48, 54, 55, 58, 70, 71; **Aza 1:**13, 21; **Sus 1:**3, 9[3], 10, 11, 14, 27, 28, 32, 34, 61[2], 63; **Bel 1:**10, 15, 21; **1Mc 1:**9, 33, 34, 42, 48, 60, 61[2], 62; **2:**14, 19, 30[3], 36, 38, 40, 41, 43, 44[2], 47, 51, 61, 62, 63; **3:**12, 36[2], 40, 42[2], 47[2], 48, 49; **4:**8, 13[2], 20, 24, 30, 31[2], 32[2], 39, 55; **5:**5[3], 6, 9, 11, 12, 13, 14, 16, 23, 25, 33, 43, 45, 55, 56, 63, 68[2]; **6:**25[2], 33, 35, 36, 41[2], 54, 58, 59[2], 61; **7:**3, 11, 17, 22, 38, 44, 46; **8:**2, 4, 7, 10[2], 12[2], 16, 24[2], 25, 26, 27, 28, 30, 32; **9:**12, 19[2], 24, 38, 40, 41, 42, 60, 66, 72; **10:**9, 13[2], 24, 33, 37[3], 43, 55, 60, 72, 83; **11:**2, 12, 21, 33, 34, 38, 44, 49, 51, 62, 69, 73; **12:**6, 26, 27, 28, 45, 51[2]; **13:**42, 45[2]; **14:**8[2], 12, 21, 22, 23, 29[3], 30, 31[3], 34, 35, 41[2]; **15:**19[3], 21[2], 29; **16:**14, 16; **2Mc 1:**1, 16; **2:**2[2], 3; **3:**15, 18, 19, 20; **4:**14, 15, 16, 30, 36, 49[2]; **5:**9[2], 12; **6:**1, 6, 10[3], 11[2], 14, 15, 21, 29; **7:**1, 2, 4, 5, 6, 7, 10, 21, 27; **8:**1, 14, 15[2], 17[2], 19, 21[2], 24, 26, 27, 28, 30, 33[2]; **9:**15, 19[2]; **10:**16, 21[2], 25[2], 26[2], 27[2], 28[3], 30; **11:**7[2], 8, 10, 13, 14, 20, 23, 24[2], 25[2], 26, 31; **12:**1, 3, 10, 12, 14, 22[3], 24, 25, 27, 28, 30, 31, 36, 37, 39[2], 42, 45; **13:**10, 18, 23, 26; **14:**15, 18[2], 26, 28, 34; **15:**10[2], 18[2], 20, 27[2], 29; **1Es 1:**2[2], 13, 14, 15, 16, 50, 52, 53[3], 55; **2:**9, 16, 17, 30; **3:**15, 16, 22; **4:**3, 26, 37[2], 49[2], 53[2], 54, 62; **5:**1[4], 3, 4[2], 7, 8, 9, 37, 42, 44, 46, 47, 48, 56[2], 58, 59, 72[2]; **6:**3, 7, 10, 12, 27, 31, 33; **7:**1, 9, 12, 15; **8:**14, 15, 28[2], 39, 48, 49, 54, 69, 70, 83, 84[2], 93; **9:**4, 16[2], 20[2], 36, 37, 47, 54; **Man 1:**1, 2; **3Mc 1:**4, 7, 8, 11, 16, 18[3], 23; **2:**4, 5, 7, 12, 17[2], 23, 28, 29[2], 31[3], 32; **3:**2, 4, 5, 6[2], 10[2], 16, 17, 18, 19[3], 20, 21[2], 22, 23, 25, 27, 28; **4:**1, 2, 4[3], 6, 8[3], 9, 10, 12, 13, 17, 18; **5:**2, 5, 7[2], 9, 13, 21[2], 25[2], 34, 36, 46, 49[4], 50; **6:**6[2], 11[2], 14, 15, 25, 26, 27[2], 29, 30[2], 31, 32[3], 34, 36[2], 37, 38[2], 40, 41; **7:**6[2], 8, 10[2], 13, 14[2], 16[2], 18[3], 19, 20, 21[2], 22[2]; **2Es 1:**5[3], 6, 10, 11, 32[2], 36; **2:**6, 7, 11, 15, 16[2], 18, 25, 43, 46; **3:**12, 20, 33[2]; **4:**27, 35; **5:**8, 12, 17; **6:**16, 19, 21, 26, 56, 58; **7:**11, 74, 88, 94, 95, 97, 98, 101, 103, 105, 131, 139; **8:**30, 33[2], 38[3], 39[4], 58; **9:**7, 10, 19; **11:**24; **12:**2, 20, 32[3]; **13:**33, 37, 38[2], 40, 42[2], 58; **14:**42; **15:**4, 6[2], 8[2], 13[2], 15, 16[3], 18, 19[3], 21, 29, 30[2], 31, 32, 33[2], 34, 35, 42, 53, 58[2]; **16:**20, 31, 33, 34[2], 46[5], 47[3], 48, 54[3], 56, 63, 64, 72, 77[2]; **4Mc 1:**5, 8, 10[2], 11[5], 12; **2:**10, 19[2]; **3:**5, 20[2]; **4:**10, 25[2]; **6:**13, 24, 29, 32; **7:**8, 17, 20[2], 23; **8:**3, 4[2], 15[2]; **9:**6; **10:**5[2], 7; **11:**14; **12:**3, 14; **13:**2, 3, 19, 25[2], 26[2], 27; **14:**1, 10, 11, 14, 15, 17[2], 19; **15:**4[3], 5, 9, 10[2], 15, 19, 21[2]; **17:**7, 8, 10, 12, 17, 22, 23[3]; **18:**3, 5, 9, 21[2], 23

THEIRS (25)

Ge 15:13; **43:**34; **Ex 7:**12; **29:**9; **Nu 16:**26; **17:**6; **18:**9; **35:**3; **2Ch 24:**18; **Isa 61:**7; **63:**2; **Jer 44:**28; **Eze 16:**53; **44:**29; **Hos 9:**15; **Mt 5:**3, 10; **Heb 1:**4; **4:**11; **Sir 40:**2; **41:**9; **1Mc 6:**52; **2Mc 13:**22; **1Es 4:**50; **4Mc 6:**29

THEM (7051)

Ge 1:14, 15, 17, 22, 26, 27[2], 28[2], 29; **2:**19[2]; **3:**21; **5:**1, 2[3]; **6:**1, 4, 7, 13[2], 19, 20, 21; **7:**20; **9:**1; **10:**1, 10; **11:**3, 6, 8, 9; **13:**6; **14:**10, 14, 15[3], 24; **15:**5, 10, 11; **18:**2[2], 8[2], 16[2]; **19:**1[2], 3[2], 5[2], 8[2], 9, 10, 12, 17, 18; **20:**8, 14; **21:**27, 31; **22:**6, 8; **23:**8; **24:**53, 56; **25:**6, 26; **26:**18[3], 27, 30, 31; **27:**9, 13, 14[2], 15; **29:**4, 5, 6, 7, 9[2]; **30:**14, 35, 37, 40, 42; **31:**5, 9, 33, 34[3], 55; **32:**2, 4, 23[2]; **33:**3; **34:**8, 14, 21[3], 23; **35:**4, 5[2]; **36:**7[2]; **37:**2, 6, 13, 17[2], 18, 22; **38:**18, 26; **39:**14; **40:**3, 4[2], 6, 8[3], 11, 22; **41:**3, 6, 8[2], 19, 21, 23, 27, 30, 35[2]; **42:**7[3], 9[2], 12, 14, 17, 18, 22, 23[2], 24[2], 25[2], 27, 29, 36; **43:**2, 11[2], 15, 16, 23, 24, 32, 34; **44:**4[2], 6[2], 15; **45:**15, 21[2], 22, 24, 26, 27; **47:**2, 6[3], 11, 17[2], 20, 21, 22; **48:**6, 9[2], 10[3], 12, 13[2], 16[2], 20; **49:**7[2], 28[3], 29[2]; **50:**12, 19, 21[2]; **Ex 1:**7, 10, 11[2], 14, 16, 17, 18, 19, 21; **2:**17, 25; **3:**8[2], 9, 13[2], 16, 22; **4:**11, 20; **5:**4, 5, 7, 8, 9, 14, 20, 21; **6:**1[2], 3, 4[2], 6, 13[2]; **7:**5, 6, 13, 22; **8:**2, 14, 15, 19, 26; **9:**2[2], 12, 17, 19, 27; **10:**1, 2, 8, 10, 19, 26, 27; **12:**21, 35, 36, 38, 42; **13:**17, 21[3]; **14:**3, 4, 7, 9[2], 10, 17, 19[3], 22, 23, 25, 28[2], 29; **15:**5, 7, 9[2], 10, 12, 13, 16, 17[2], 19, 21, 25[2]; **16:**3, 4, 12, 15, 18, 19, 20, 23, 24; **17:**2; **18:**8[2], 9, 11, 16, 20[2], 21, 22[2], 25; **19:**7, 10[2], 13, 21, 22, 24, 25; **20:**5[2], 11; **21:**1; **22:**11, 23, 25[2]; **23:**13, 23, 24[2], 29, 30, 31, 32; **24:**14; **25:**2, 3, 8[2], 12, 13, 18, 28, 29, 40[2]; **26:**1[2], 24, 37[2]; **27:**6, 16; **28:**9, 11, 26, 27, 33, 40, 41[4], 42, 43; **29:**1[2], 2, 3[2], 4, 8, 9[2], 13[2], 17, 22, 24, 25[2], 29[2], 30, 33[2], 35, 46[2]; **30:**4, 5, 12[3], 21, 29[2], 30; **32:**2[2], 3, 4, 8, 10[2], 12[3], 13[2], 19, 21, 24, 25, 27, 34; **33:**8, 10; **34:**15, 31[2], 32, 33; **35:**1, 23, 26, 29, 35; **36:**8, 11, 29, 34, 36[2]; **37:**4, 7, 15, 28; **38:**6, 7, 28; **39:**7, 19, 20, 43; **40:**12, 14, 15[2]; **Lev 1:**2, 12; **2:**12; **3:**4, 10, 15; **4:**2, 9, 10, 20; **5:**8; **6:**10, 18; **7:**4, 5, 7, 34, 36[2]; **8:**6, 10, 11, 13[3], 16, 26, 27, 28[2], 30; **9:**2, 7, 14, 19, 22; **10:**1, 2, 4, 5, 11; **11:**1, 22, 24, 25, 26, 27, 31, 32, 33, 43; **13:**54; **14:**6, 12, 23, 24, 42, 51; **15:**2, 14, 15, 18, 29; **16:**4, 7, 16, 21, 23, 28; **17:**2, 5[2], 7, 8[2], 10, 13; **18:**2, 4, 21, 30; **19:**2, 10, 31[2], 37; **20:**2, 3[2], 4[2], 5[4], 6[3], 8, 9, 11[2], 12[2], 13[2], 16, 18, 22, 23, 27; **21:**1, 8, 23; **22:**3, 9, 11, 16[2], 18, 22, 25, 31; **23:**2, 4, 10, 20, 22, 43; **24:**6, 8, 9, 12; **25:**2, 31, 32, 33, 35, 36[2], 37[2], 39, 41, 43, 45, 46[2], 47, 48, 49[2], 53, 54; **26:**1, 3, 36, 41[2], 43[2], 44[4]; **27:**2, 8[2], 31; **Nu 1:**3, 19, 22, 47, 49; **3:**6, 16, 48; **4:**8, 12[3], 19, 23, 26, 29, 30; **5:**3[2], 4, 12, 23; **6:**2, 11, 16, 19, 20, 23, 27; **7:**3, 5[2], 6, 13, 19, 25, 31, 37, 43, 49, 55, 61, 67, 73, 79; **8:**6, 7[4], 8, 13, 15[2], 16, 17, 20, 21[3], 22; **9:**8; **10:**2[2], 33[2], 34; **11:**1, 3, 4, 12[2], 16[3], 17, 21, 22[2], 24, 25, 26, 28, 29, 31, 32; **12:**4, 6[2], 9; **13:**2, 3[2], 17[2], 23, 26[2], 33; **14:**2, 9[2], 10, 11, 12[2], 13, 14[2], 16[2], 28, 45[2]; **15:**2, 18, 26, 29, 38, 39; **16:**3[3], 7[2], 9, 15[2], 18, 19, 21, 29, 30[2], 31, 32, 33[2], 34, 38[2], 42, 45, 46; **17:**2, 4; **18:**8, 11, 20, 24, 26, 28, 29, 30; **19:**6, 9, 10, 13[2], 19, 20, 21; **20:**6, 8, 10, 12, 20, 21, 25, 26, 28; **21:**1, 3, 16, 33; **22:**6[2], 8, 11[3], 12, 20, 40; **23:**11, 13[4], 21[2], 22[2], 25[2], 27; **24:**10; **25:**4, 8, 11, 17; **26:**3, 10, 62, 65[2]; **27:**7[2], 17[4]; **28:**2, 3, 31; **29:**6; **30:**12[3], 14[2], 15[2]; **31:**6, 8, 13, 15, 30, 47, 51; **32:**7, 8, 9, 13, 15, 17, 19, 20, 28, 29[2], 33, 41; **33:**4, 51, 56; **34:**2; **35:**5, 6, 10, 15; **36:**6; **Dt 1:**3, 8[2], 15, 29, 39, 42; **2:**5, 6[2], 9, 11, 12[3], 14, 15[2], 19[2], 20, 21[2], 22[2], 23; **3:**4, 6, 14, 20, 22; **4:**6, 9[2], 10, 13, 19[2], 31, 37; **5:**1[3], 9[2], 22[2], 29, 30, 31[3]; **6:**3, 7[2], 8[2], 9; **7:**2[5], 3, 5, 12, 15, 16, 17, 18, 20, 21, 22, 23[2], 24, 25; **8:**12, 19; **9:**2, 3[3], 4[2], 5, 10, 12, 14, 17[2], 28[5]; **10:**2, 4, 11, 15, 18; **11:**4[2], 6, 9, 16, 18[2], 19[2], 20, 21; **12:**29[2], 30; **13:**2[2], 8[2], 9[3], 10; **14:**21, 27; **15:**18; **17:**3; **18:**2, 12, 18[2]; **19:**1, 3, 5; **20:**1, 3[2], 9, 17, 19[3], 20; **21:**5, 10[2], 15, 18; **22:**1[2], 22, 24[2]; **23:**8, 15, 16; **24:**8, 15[2]; **25:**1, 5; **26:**16; **27:**2, 3, 4, 7, 26; **28:**13, 14, 25[2], 26, 32, 39[2], 44, 55, 57; **29:**1, 2, 7, 17, 20[3], 21, 25[2], 26[2], 28[2]; **30:**1, 17; **31:**2, 3, 4[2], 5[2], 6, 7[2], 10, 16, 17[4], 20[2], 21[4], 23, 28; **32:**11[2], 20, 21[2], 23[2], 24, 26[2], 28, 30[2], 38[2], 46[2]; **33:**9, 17[2]; **Jos 1:**2, 6, 14, 15; **2:**4, 5[2], 6[2], 7, 8, 13, 15, 16, 21, 23; **4:**3[3], 5, 7, 8[3], 12; **5:**1, 4, 6[2]; **6:**6, 8, 13, 23; **7:**2, 5[3], 11[2], 21[2], 23[3], 24, 25[2]; **8:**3, 5, 6[2], 9, 11, 12, 15, 16, 22[2], 24[2], 33[2], 35; **9:**8, 11[2], 13, 15[2], 16[2], 18[2], 19[2], 20[3], 21[3], 22[2], 26[3], 27; **10:**1, 8[3], 9, 10[4], 11, 18, 19[3], 20, 25, 26[3], 27[2], 39, 41; **11:**6[2], 7[2], 8[4], 9, 11, 12[2], 14, 17[2], 21; **12:**6; **13:**6, 8[2], 14, 33; **14:**1, 3, 12; **17:**4, 13, 15; **18:**1, 4, 7, 10; **19:**9, 47, 49; **20:**4, 5, 9; **21:**2, 10, 11, 20, 21, 40, 43, 44[2]; **22:**2, 4, 6[2], 7[2], 8, 12, 14, 15, 32, 33; **23:**2, 5[2], 7[3], 12, 14, 16; **24:**7[2], 8[2], 11, 13, 25; **Jdg 1:**1, 4, 22, 25, 28, 29, 30, 32, 33, 34, 35; **2:**3, 10, 12[3], 14[3], 15[3], 16[2], 17, 18[3], 19[2], 21, 23[2]; **3:**8, 9, 15, 23, 25, 28; **4:**2; **5:**21; **6:**1, 3, 4, 8, 9, 16, 19[2], 20, 35; **7:**1, 3, 4[2], 16, 17, 24; **8:**2, 8, 12, 16, 18, 19, 20, 23, 24, 25, 34; **9:**1, 7, 9, 11, 13, 24, 25, 27, 33, 36, 38, 43[3], 44, 49, 57; **10:**7, 14, 16; **11:**9, 11, 21, 25, 26, 32[2], 33; **12:**2, 3; **13:**1; **14:**9[2], 12, 14, 18; **15:**3, 7, 8, 11, 12; **16:**3[3], 8, 12, 14[2], 25, 26, 29; **18:**1, 2, 4, 8, 9, 18, 21, 27; **19:**8, 14, 15, 23[2], 24[3], 25; **20:**13, 17, 20, 23, 25[2], 28, 32, 34, 35, 39, 40, 41, 42[2], 43[2], 44, 45[2], 46, 48; **21:**7, 10, 12, 13, 14[2], 18, 22[3], 23[2]; **Ru 1:**6, 9, 19[2], 20; **2:**9, 16; **1Sa 2:**8[2], 16, 23, 25, 34; **3:**13; **4:**1; **5:**6, 9; **6:**6, 7, 10, 12, 15, 19; **7:**10, 11; **8:**7, 8, 9[3], 11, 14, 16, 21, 22; **9:**4[2], 11, 14, 20, 22[2], 24; **10:**1, 2, 4, 5, 6, 10, 18, 23, 25, 27; **11:**2, 7[2], 8, 11, 12[2]; **12:**5, 8[2], 9[2]; **13:**16, 22; **14:**8, 9, 10, 11, 12, 13, 21, 22, 32[2], 34[4], 36[2], 37, 47, 48; **15:**3, 4, 6, 9, 15, 18; **16:**5, 20; **17:**3, 17, 18, 23, 31, 36, 39[3], 40; **18:**16; **19:**8, 20; **20:**21, 40; **21:**13; **22:**2, 4, 11; **23:**5, 18, 26; **24:**7; **25:**7, 13, 14, 15, 16, 18, 20, 43; **26:**12, 13, 25; **28:**25; **30:**2[2], 8, 15, 17[2], 21, 22; **31:**3, 7, 12, 13; **2Sa 1:**10, 11; **2:**5, 7, 13, 14, 32; **3:**22, 36; **4:**12; **5:**3, 19, 20, 21, 23; **6:**22; **7:**10[2], 23; **8:**1, 2[2], 7; **10:**4, 5, 9, 10, 19; **11:**23; **12:**11, 17, 31[2]; **13:**9, 10, 11, 30; **14:**6; **15:**4, 5[2], 36[2]; **17:**17, 18[2], 20[2]; **18:**1, 4, 14; **20:**3[3], 8, 18; **21:**2[3], 6[2], 7, 9[3], 10, 12[2]; **22:**15[2], 28, 38, 39[2], 41, 42[2], 43[3]; **23:**7, 18; **24:**1, 12, 24; **1Ki 1:**20, 33; **2:**7; **4:**25; **5:**3, 9, 12, 14; **6:**12, 15, 32, 35; **7:**6, 25, 37, 46, 47, 51; **8:**4, 21, 32, 34, 35, 36, 37, 44, 46[2], 48, 50[2], 52, 53; **9:**6, 7, 9[3]; **10:**17, 25, 28; **11:**2, 18, 29; **12:**5, 7[3], 9, 10, 14, 16; **13:**12; **14:**15, 27, 28[2]; **15:**18[2], 22; **16:**23; **18:**4[2], 6, 13, 23, 26, 27, 28, 40[5]; **19:**2, 21; **20:**6, 15, 18[2], 19, 20, 23, 24, 25, 27[2]; **21:**8, 10, 11[2]; **22:**6[2], 10, 13; **2Ki 1:**2, 3, 5, 7, 12; **2:**6, 7, 8, 11, 12, 16[2], 17, 18, 24[2]; **3:**9, 21, 22, 24; **4:**33, 39[2], 41, 42, 43, 44; **5:**12, 22, 23[2], 24[2]; **6:**3, 4, 11, 16, 18, 19[2], 21[3], 22[2], 23[2], 33; **7:**8[2], 10, 12, 14, 15; **8:**24; **9:**11, 13, 17, 18, 19, 20; **10:**1, 6, 7[3], 8, 14[4], 17, 18, 22, 25[3], 32; **11:**4[4], 5; **12:**5, 7; **13:**2, 3, 4, 6, 7[2], 11, 17, 18[2], 23[5]; **14:**27; **16:**17; **17:**6, 7, 11, 12, 15[3], 18, 20[3], 21, 22, 24, 25[2], 26[2], 27, 28, 29, 32, 35[5]; **18:**11, 13, 18, 19, 23, 27; **19:**3, 6, 11, 12; **20:**7, 13[3], 15; **21:**3, 8[2], 9, 14, 21; **22:**5, 6, 7, 15; **23:**4, 16, 19, 20; **24:**2, 3, 16, 20; **25:**20[2], 21[2], 24; **1Ch 2:**23; **4:**41, 42; **5:**11, 20[2], 25, 26[2]; **6:**54, 55, 65; **7:**3, 4, 21; **9:**20, 22, 25, 27, 28[2], 29, 32; **10:**7, 12; **11:**3, 14, 20; **12:**17[2], 18[2], 19, 39; **14:**8, 10[2], 11, 14[2]; **15:**2, 12, 18; **16:**21, 31, 41, 42; **17:**9[2]; **18:**1, 4, 7; **19:**4[2], 5, 10, 17[2]; **20:**3; **21:**3, 10, 24; **23:**6, 22, 31; **24:**3, 4, 5, 6, 19; **26:**31; **27:**24; **29:**8, 19; **2Ch 1:**16, 17; **2:**2, 11, 15, 18; **3:**10, 16[2]; **4:**4, 7, 8, 17; **5:**5; **6:**23, 25[2], 26, 27, 28, 34, 36[2]; **7:**6, 19, 22[4]; **8:**2, 10; **9:**8[2], 11, 16, 24; **10:**5, 7[2], 9, 10, 13, 14, 16; **11:**11, 12, 14, 16, 23[2]; **12:**5, 7[2], 10[2], 11[2], 12; **13:**7, 13[2], 14[2], 16, 17; **14:**7, 9, 13, 14[2]; **15:**4, 6, 9, 15[2]; **16:**2, 6, 8; **17:**8, 9, 14; **18:**5[2], 9, 12, 31; **19:**4, 9, 10; **20:**1, 12, 16[2], 17, 23, 25, 27; **21:**3; **22:**8, 12; **23:**3, 14; **24:**5, 17, 19[3], 20, 23; **25:**5, 10, 12[3], 13[2], 14[3], 20, 24; **26:**9; **27:**5; **28:**5, 6, 8, 9[3], 13, 15[7], 23[2]; **29:**3, 4, 5, 8, 16[2], 21, 23, 24, 34; **30:**7, 10[2], 12, 18[2]; **31:**1, 6, 7, 11[2], 12; **32:**1, 6[2], 18, 22, 26, 30; **33:**3, 8, 11, 15, 22; **34:**4[3], 12, 23; **35:**2, 11, 12, 13, 15; **36:**7, 15, 17[2]; **Ezr 1:**3, 6, 8[2]; **2:**63; **4:**2, 3, 4, 23; **5:**1, 2[2], 3[2], 4, 5, 9, 10, 12, 15; **6:**5, 9, 20, 21, 22[3]; **7:**17, 25, 26; **8:**13, 14, 15, 17[2], 24, 25, 28, 29[3], 30, 33; **10:**10, 14, 15, 16, 44; **Ne 1:**2, 9[3]; **2:**9, 10, 17, 18, 20; **3:**2, 4[3], 5, 7, 8, 9, 10, 23[2], 29; **4:**4, 9, 11[2], 12, 14, 21; **5:**7[2], 8, 10, 11[2], 12[2], 15; **6:**3, 4, 8, 17; **7:**3[2], 65; **8:**10[2], 12, 16, 17; **9:**6[2], 11, 12[2], 13[2], 14[2], 15[4], 17[2], 19[4], 20[2], 21, 22[2], 23, 24[3], 26[2], 27[5], 28[3], 29[2], 30[3], 31[2], 34, 35[2]; **10:**31; **11:**20, 23; **12:**9, 24, 27, 32, 36, 37, 38, 43, 44; **13:**2[2], 10, 11[2], 15[2], 16, 17, 21[2], 25[4], 29,

30; **Est 1:**17; **2:**3; **3:**4[2], 8, 11; **4:**3, 4, 13; **5:**8, 11; **8:**10[2], 11, 17; **9:**1, 2[2], 3, 5[2], 16, 21, 22[2], 23, 24[2], 26, 27; **Job 1:**4, 5[2], 6, 14, 15[2], 16, 17; **2:**1, 11; **4:**21; **5:**4; **6:**7; **7:**10, 17[2], 18[2]; **8:**4, 18; **9:**5; **11:**20; **12:**15, 23[2], 24, 25; **14:**6, 20[2]; **15:**19, 21, 24[2], 31; **17:**4; **18:**6, 7, 9[2], 10[2], 11[2]; **20:**7, 9[3], 11, 14, 15[2], 16, 22, 23[2], 24, 25, 26, 27, 29; **21:**9, 17, 19, 20, 21, 26, 31, 33; **22:**19; **24:**2, 17, 20[2], 23; **26:**8; **27:**8, 9, 15, 20[2], 21[2], 22, 23[2]; **29:**17, 22, 24; **30:**5, 9, 13; **31:**15, 29; **33:**16, 17[2], 23; **34:**11[2], 25, 26; **36:**7, 9, 13; **37:**12, 15, 21; **39:**4, 14, 15[2]; **40:**11, 12, 13; **41:**16; **42:**9, 11, 15; **Ps 2:**4, 5[2], 9[2]; **5:**10[3], 11[2], 12; **8:**4[2], 5[2], 6; **9:**6, 12, 20; **10:**2, 5, 9; **12:**5; **17:**13[2], 14; **18:**14[2], 37, 38, 41[2], 42[2]; **19:**6, 11[2], 13; **21:**9[3], 12; **22:**4; **25:**3, 12, 14; **28:**4[3], 5[2], 9; **31:**17, 20[2]; **32:**6; **33:**15, 19; **34:**7, 16, 17, 19[2], 20; **35:**4[2], 5[2], 6, 8[3], 10[2], 24, 25[2]; **36:**8; **37:**12, 32, 33[2], 36, 40[4]; **38:**16; **39:**11; **40:**5; **41:**1, 2[3], 3, 10; **42:**4; **43:**3[2]; **44:**2[2], 3[2], 12; **45:**16; **48:**6; **49:**17; **53:**5; **54:**3, 5; **55:**12, 15[2], 19, 23; **56:**7; **58:**7[2], 8, 9; **59:**8, 11[3], 12, 13[2]; **62:**10; **64:**7, 8[2]; **68:**2, 3[2], 22[2], 25, 27; **69:**11, 22, 24[2], 28[2], 34; **73:**6, 10[2], 18[2]; **74:**8; **76:**11; **78:**4, 6[2], 11, 13, 14, 15, 24[2], 25, 27, 28, 29, 31[2], 34, 38, 42, 45[3], 49, 50, 52, 53, 54, 55[2], 66, 72[2]; **79:**3; **80:**5[2]; **81:**12; **82:**4; **83:**4, 8, 9, 13, 15[2], 17[2], 18; **86:**14; **88:**8; **89:**9, 11, 12; **90:**5; **91:**15[4], 16[2]; **94:**13, 23[3]; **97:**10; **99:**3, 6, 7[2], 8[2]; **102:**26; **104:**8, 17, 24, 27, 28; **105:**14, 17, 24, 27, 32, 38, 40, 44; **106:**4, 8, 9, 10[2], 11, 15[2], 23[2], 26[2], 27, 29, 34, 36, 41[3], 42, 43, 46[2]; **107:**5, 6, 7, 8, 13, 14, 15, 19, 20[2], 21, 22, 28, 30, 31, 32, 40; **109:**4, 15, 27, 28, 31[2]; **110:**6; **111:**2, 6; **113:**8; **115:**8[3]; **118:**10, 11, 12, 19; **119:**47, 93, 129, 152, 165, 167; **126:**2; **127:**5; **129:**6; **132:**12; **135:**18[3]; **136:**11; **137:**9; **139:**16, 17, 18, 22[2]; **140:**9, 10[2]; **141:**6; **144:**3[2], 6[2]; **145:**15, 19; **146:**6; **147:**4, 18; **148:**5, 6, 13; **149:**3, 5, 9; **Pr 1:**12, 32; **3:**3[2]; **4:**21[2], 22; **5:**17, 22; **6:**21[2]; **7:**3[2]; **8:**8; **10:**24; **11:**3[2], 6; **12:**6; **13:**24[2]; **14:**3; **16:**7, 26[2], 29; **17:**11, 25; **19:**7; **20:**5, 7, 12, 26; **21:**7; **22:**2, 5, 18[2], 19, 23; **23:**13, 14, 21; **24:**1, 18, 21, 22, 25, 29; **25:**13, 21[2]; **26:**12; **28:**4, 13; **30:**7, 27; **31:**7, 24, 29; **Ecc 1:**11; **2:**5, 10, 14; **3:**12, 18, 22[2]; **4:**1[2]; **5:**8, 11[2], 12, 19, 20; **6:**2[2], 12[2]; **7:**14; **8:**6, 7, 15[2]; **9:**1, 5, 11, 12; **10:**9[2], 12[2], 15; **11:**8[2]; **12:**1; **SS 3:**4; **4:**2, 4; **5:**3; **6:**6[2]; **Isa 1:**2, 14, 23, 31; **2:**9; **3:**4, 9[2], 11, 12; **5:**25[2], 27; **8:**15; **9:**2, 11, 13, 16[2]; **10:**6, 19, 20, 22, 26; **11:**6, 14; **13:**2[2], 8, 14, 17, 19; **14:**1[2], 2[3], 10, 20, 21, 22, 25; **16:**4; **17:**2, 11[3], 13; **18:**6[2]; **19:**1, 3, 4, 12, 14, 16, 17, 20[2], 21, 22; **26:**11[2], 14[2], 16; **27:**7[2], 8[2], 11[5]; **28:**2, 13, 26; **30:**5, 6, 8, 12, 22[2], 28; **34:**2[2], 7, 16, 17[2]; **36:**1, 4, 8; **37:**3, 6, 11, 12; **38:**21; **39:**2[3], 4; **40:**11, 22, 24[2], 26[2]; **41:**1[2], 2, 3, 12, 15, 16[3], 17[2], 22[3]; **42:**5, 9, 11, 12, 16[3], 20, 22; **43:**6, 9[4]; **44:**7[3], 11[2]; **45:**16, 21; **47:**6[2], 14; **48:**3[2], 5[4], 7[2], 13, 14, 21[2]; **49:**10[4], 18[2]; **50:**8, 9[2]; **51:**8[2], 23; **52:**4, 15; **55:**7[2]; **56:**5, 7, 8; **57:**6, 8, 13[2], 17, 18[3], 19; **58:**7; **59:**8, 13, 21; **60:**9, 22; **61:**3, 8[2], 9; **63:**3[2], 6, 7, 9[4], 10, 11[2], 12, 13, 14; **65:**8, 21; **66:**4[2], 19[2], 21; **Jer 1:**8, 15, 16, 17[3]; **2:**3, 25, 28, 34, 37; **4:**12, 29; **5:**3[2], 5, 6[3], 7, 9, 13[2], 14, 16, 19, 29; **6:**10, 13, 15, 18, 24, 28, 30; **7:**22[2], 23, 25, 27[2], 28, 33; **8:**3, 4, 6, 9, 12, 13[3]; **9:**2, 7, 9, 13, 14, 15, 16[3], 18, 22; **10:**2, 5[2], 11, 14, 18; **11:**3, 4, 5, 6, 7[2], 8[2], 10, 11[2], 12, 20, 22, 23; **12:**2, 3[2], 6, 9, 14[2], 15[4]; **13:**10[2], 12, 13, 14[2], 19; **14:**10, 12[2], 13, 14[3], 15, 16[2], 17[2]; **15:**1[2], 2, 3, 4, 7[2], 9, 10, 16, 19; **16:**3[2], 5, 6[2], 7, 8, 11[2], 15[2], 16[2], 21[2]; **17:**11, 18[3], 20; **18:**17[2], 20[2], 21, 22, 23[2]; **19:**7, 9[2], 11; **20:**4[2], 5[3], 12; **21:**3, 4, 7[3]; **22:**7, 8, 9, 13; **23:**2[2], 3[2], 4[2], 8, 12[2], 14, 15[2], 21, 22, 24, 32[3], 33, 34; **24:**1, 6[6], 7, 9[2], 10[2]; **25:**6, 9[3], 10, 14[2], 16, 18, 26, 27, 28, 30[2]; **26:**2, 3[2], 4, 19; **27:**2, 4, 15, 17, 18[2], 22[3]; **28:**13; **29:**5, 9, 17[2], 18[3], 21[2], 22, 23, 28; **30:**3, 9, 16, 19[3], 20; **31:**8[3], 9[2], 13[2], 28[2], 32[2], 33, 34; **32:**14, 18, 22[2], 23[2], 33, 35, 37[4], 39[2], 40[2], 41[2], 42[2]; **33:**5, 6[2], 7, 8, 9, 13, 24, 26; **34:**8, 10, 11, 13, 14, 16, 21, 22; **35:**2[3], 4, 5, 15[2], 16, 17[3]; **36:**3[2], 6, 7, 13, 14, 15, 18[2], 23[2], 25, 26, 31[2], 32; **37:**5, 10; **38:**4, 19, 26, 27; **39:**4, 5, 10; **40:**9, 10, 11, 14; **41:**6[3], 7[2], 8[2], 10, 18; **42:**4, 9, 17; **43:**1, 9, 10[2], 12[2]; **44:**2[2], 21, 27; **45:**5; **46:**5, 21, 26; **48:**9, 33; **49:**11, 32, 36, 37[3]; **50:**6[2], 7[2], 16[2], 21, 27[2], 33[2], 42, 43, 44; **51:**17, 39, 40, 48[2]; **52:**3, 26[2], 27[2]; **La 1:**17, 21, 22; **2:**3, 21; **3:**64, 65[2], 66[2]; **4:**4, 15, 16[2]; **Eze 1:**6, 9, 15, 19, 20, 21; **2:**4[2], 5, 6, 7; **3:**4, 6, 9, 11[2], 13, 15, 17, 18, 20[2], 25, 26, 27; **4:**9, 13; **5:**2, 3, 4[2], 12, 13[2]; **6:**2, 10, 12, 14; **7:**11[2], 15, 16, 18, 19, 20, 22, 27[2]; **8:**11[2], 18; **9:**2, 7; **10:**1, 2, 12, 16, 17[2], 19[2]; **11:**1, 4, 15, 16[3], 19[3], 20, 22[2]; **12:**10, 11, 12, 14, 15[2], 16, 23[2], 28; **13:**6, 17, 20, 22; **14:**3[2], 4[3], 7[2], 8[3]; **15:**7[3]; **16:**16, 17, 18[2], 19, 20, 21[2], 28, 33, 36, 37[2], 50, 54, 61; **17:**12[2]; **18:**11, 22; **20:**3, 4[3], 5[3], 6[3], 7, 8[3], 9[2], 10[2], 11[2], 12[3], 13[2], 14, 15[3], 17[3], 21[2], 22, 23[3], 25, 26[2], 27, 28[2], 29, 38, 40[2]; **21:**14, 19, 23; **22:**18, 20[2], 26, 28, 30, 31[2]; **23:**6, 7[2], 12, 15, 16[3], 17[2], 22, 23[3], 24, 27, 36, 37, 40, 45, 46[2], 47[2]; **24:**3, 20, 25, 27; **25:**2, 12, 17[2]; **28:**24, 25, 26; **29:**12, 14, 15, 16, 21; **30:**5, 9, 23, 26; **31:**14[2]; **32:**10[2], 12, 13[2], 18, 21, 22, 23, 24, 25[2], 26[2], 30, 31; **33:**2, 4, 6, 7, 10, 11, 12[2], 16, 25, 27, 31, 32, 33; **34:**2, 4, 6, 10, 11, 12, 13[4], 14, 15, 16, 20, 21, 23[3], 24, 25, 26, 27[2], 28[2], 29, 30; **35:**10, 11; **36:**12, 18, 19[2], 20, 23, 37; **37:**2, 4, 8[4], 10, 12, 17, 19[2], 21[3], 22[2], 23[2], 24, 26[5], 27, 28; **38:**4[2], 5[2], 7, 8, 11, 15, 17; **39:**9[2], 10[2], 12, 13[2], 18, 21, 23[2], 24[2], 26, 27[3], 28[3], 29; **42:**5, 9, 11; **43:**8[2], 9[2], 10[2], 11, 24[3]; **44:**11[2], 12[2], 14, 17, 19, 23, 28; **45:**15; **46:**10, 18, 19, 20; **47:**12, 23; **48:**12; **Da 1:**5, 6, 7, 14, 16, 18[2], 19[2], 20[2]; **2:**3, 13, 18, 34, 35[2], 38, 44; **3:**14, 20, 27; **4:**7; **5:**2, 3, 23; **6:**2, 24; **7:**8, 20, 21, 24, 27; **8:**9, 10; **9:**7; **10:**7; **11:**2, 7, 17, 24, 34, 39; **12:**6; **Hos 1:**6, 7[2], 10[2]; **2:**5, 7[3], 12[2], 13; **4:**9[2], 12[2], 16, 19; **5:**2, 4[2], 5, 6, 7, 10; **6:**5[2]; **7:**2, 6, 7[2], 12[3], 13[3]; **8:**5, 10, 13; **9:**2[2], 6[2], 12[3], 14[2], 15[3], 17; **10:**9, 10[2]; **11:**2, 3[2], 4[4], 7, 11; **13:**2, 6, 7, 8[3], 14[2]; **14:**4[2], 9[3]; **Joel 1:**18; **2:**2, 3[5], 6, 10, 17; **3:**2[3], 6, 7[2], 8, 9; **Am 1:**6; **2:**9; **4:**5; **5:**8, 11[2], 22; **7:**8; **8:**2; **9:**1[3], 2[2], 3[2], 4[2], 6, 14, 15[2]; **Ob 1:**11, 17, 18[2]; **Jnh 1:**3, 5, 10, 12, 13; **3:**10; **Mic 1:**7; **2:**2[2], 12, 13[2]; **3:**3[2], 4[2], 6; **4:**4, 7, 12; **5:**3, 5; **7:**4[2], 14; **Na 2:**2, 3, 11; **3:**18; **Hab 1:**12[2], 15[3], 16; **2:**4, 6, 7, 8, 17; **Zep 1:**13[2], 18; **2:**7, 9[2], 11; **3:**6, 8, 9, 13; **Hag 1:**6; **Zec 1:**3, 21; **2:**9; **3:**5; **6:**13; **7:**14; **8:**8, 10; **9:**8, 14, 15, 16; **10:**3, 4[4], 5, 6[4], 8[3], 9, 10[4], 12; **11:**5[4], 6, 8, 12[2], 13[2]; **12:**8; **13:**1, 3[4], 5, 6, 9[3]; **14:**8[2], 13, 17, 18, 21; **Mal 2:**2, 17; **3:**3, 7, 17[2]; **4:**1[2]; **Mt 2:**4, 7, 8, 9; **3:**7; **4:**19, 21, 24; **5:**2, 19[2]; **6:**1, 8, 26; **7:**6, 12, 16, 20, 23, 24, 26, 29; **8:**4, 26, 30, 32; **9:**15[3], 18, 28, 30, 36; **10:**1[2], 17, 18, 21, 26, 29; **11:**4, 5, 25; **12:**3, 11, 15, 16, 25, 27, 39; **13:**3, 4, 7, 10, 11, 13, 14, 15, 24, 28, 29, 30[2], 31, 33, 34, 39, 42, 50, 52, 57; **14:**14, 16[2], 18, 19[2], 24, 25, 27; **15:**3, 10, 14, 30[3], 32, 34, 36[3], 37; **16:**1, 2, 4, 6, 12, 15, 24, 26; **17:**1, 2, 3, 5, 7, 9, 13, 20, 22, 27[2]; **18:**2, 12, 17, 20; **19:**2, 4[2], 8, 11, 13[2], 14, 15, 26, 28; **20:**2, 4, 6, 7, 8, 9, 10, 12, 13, 17, 23, 25[3], 31, 32; **21:**2[3], 3[2], 6, 7[2], 8, 13, 14, 16, 17, 21, 24, 27, 31, 36, 37, 42, 45; **22:**1, 6[2], 20, 21, 28, 29, 35, 41, 43; **23:**4[2], 7, 13, 30; **24:**2, 4, 39; **25:**2, 3, 5, 14, 16, 19, 40, 45; **26:**10, 19, 27, 31, 36, 38, 40, 43, 44, 45, 48, 70, 73; **27:**6, 7, 10, 17, 21, 22[2], 26, 48, 56, 65; **28:**9, 10, 13, 16, 18, 19, 20; **Mk 1:**17, 20, 22, 31, 44; **2:**2[2], 3, 8, 12, 13, 17, 19[3], 20, 25, 27; **3:**4, 5, 12, 23[2]; **4:**2[2], 11, 13, 15, 21, 24, 33, 34, 35, 36, 40; **5:**10, 12, 13, 19, 39, 40, 43[2]; **6:**4, 5, 7[2], 8, 10, 11, 13, 31, 33[3], 34[2], 36, 37[3], 38, 39, 41[2], 46, 48[2], 50, 51; **7:**2, 6, 9, 14, 18, 36[2]; **8:**1, 3[2], 5, 6[3], 7, 9, 13, 14, 15, 17, 21, 29, 30, 31, 34[2], 36, 38; **9:**1, 2[2], 3, 4, 7, 8, 9, 12, 14[2], 16[2], 19, 26, 29, 31, 33, 35, 36[2]; **10:**1, 3, 5, 6, 11, 13[2], 14[2], 16[3], 24, 27, 32[2], 36, 38, 39, 42[4]; **11:**2, 5, 6[2], 22, 28, 29, 33; **12:**1, 2, 4, 6, 12, 15[2], 16, 17, 24, 28[2], 43, 44; **13:**5, 9, 12; **14:**7, 10, 13, 16, 20, 22, 23[2], 24, 27, 31, 34, 37, 40, 41, 44, 48, 50, 60, 64, 69, 70; **15:**6, 8, 9, 11, 12, 14, 15, 24, 40; **16:**6, 8, 12, 13, 14, 15, 18, 19, 20, 99[2]; **Lk 1:**6, 22[2], 63, 66[2], 68; **2:**7, 9[2], 10, 15, 17, 18, 19, 20, 34, 46[2], 49, 50, 51[2]; **3:**11, 13, 14, 16, 20; **4:**21, 23, 26, 27, 30, 31, 35, 39, 40[3], 41[2], 42, 43; **5:**2, 7, 14, 22, 25, 26, 29, 34[2], 35, 36; **6:**1[2], 5, 9, 10, 13, 17, 19, 30, 31, 32, 39, 47; **7:**6, 16, 19, 22[2], 38[2], 42[2], 44; **8:**3, 21, 22, 25, 31, 32[2], 36, 37, 55, 56; **9:**1, 2, 3, 5, 10, 11[2], 13[2], 14, 15, 16[2], 18, 20, 21, 23[2], 25, 26, 34, 45, 46[2], 48, 54, 55; **10:**1, 2, 9, 18, 21, 23, 34, 35; **11:**2, 5, 15, 17, 19, 31, 44, 46, 48, 49; **12:**6, 15, 16, 24, 30, 37[2], 38, 42; **13:**2, 4, 23, 32; **14:**5, 7, 19, 25; **15:**2, 3, 4, 6, 8, 12[2]; **16:**15, 28, 29, 30; **17:**14[2], 15, 18, 27, 29, 31, 37; **18:**1, 7, 8, 15[2], 16[2], 29, 31, 34; **19:**13[2], 27[3], 32, 33; **20:**3, 8, 15, 17, 19, 23, 25, 34, 38, 41; **21:**3, 4, 8, 10, 29; **22:**4, 6, 10, 13, 15, 19, 23, 24[2], 25[3], 35, 36, 40, 41, 45, 46, 47, 50, 55, 58, 70[2]; **23:**14, 20, 22, 27, 28, 34; **24:**4, 5, 10, 11[2], 13, 15, 17, 18, 19, 25, 27, 29, 30[2], 35, 36[2], 38, 40, 41, 44, 46, 50[2], 51[2]; **Jn 1:**26, 38[2], 39; **2:**7[2], 8, 15, 19, 24; **3:**22; **4:**14[2], 32, 34, 40, 52; **5:**11, 17, 19, 21, 39; **6:**7, 11, 13, 17, 20, 26, 29, 31, 32, 35, 40, 43, 53, 54, 56, 61, 70; **7:**6, 16, 21, 44, 45, 50, 51, 53; **8:**2, 3, 7, 12, 21, 23, 25, 27, 34, 39, 42, 47, 58; **9:**15, 19, 27, 41; **10:**3, 4, 6[2], 7, 8, 12[2], 16, 20, 27, 28[2], 38; **11:**10, 11, 14, 19, 37, 44, 46[2], 49[2], 57; **12:**3, 23, 35, 36, 40, 47; **13:**1, 5, 12, 16, 17; **14:**21[3], 23[3], 27; **15:**5, 22, 24; **16:**4, 12, 19, 31; **17:**6, 8[2], 10, 11, 12[4], 14[2], 15[2], 17, 18, 22, 23[2], 26[3]; **18:**4, 5, 6, 7, 18, 21, 29, 31, 38; **19:**4, 5, 6, 15, 16, 18, 23; **20:**2, 13, 17, 18, 19, 20, 21, 22[2], 23, 24, 25, 26[2]; **21:**3, 5, 6, 10, 11, 12, 13, 20, 24, 25; **Ac 1:**3[2], 4[2], 10, 26; **2:**3[2], 4[2], 6, 11, 14, 38, 40; **3:**3, 5[2], 8, 11; **4:**1, 3[2], 8, 13, 14, 15, 16[2], 17, 18[2], 19, 21[4], 23, 24, 33, 34[2]; **5:**13[2], 15[2], 18, 19, 21, 22, 23, 24, 26, 27[3], 33, 35, 38, 39, 40[3]; **6:**6; **7:**6[2], 24, 25, 26[2], 34, 36, 42[2], 60; **8:**3, 5, 10, 11, 14, 15, 16, 17, 18, 38; **9:**2, 21, 27, 28, 39[2], 40; **10:**8[2], 20[2], 23[3], 24, 28, 34, 46, 48; **11:**3, 4, 12[2], 15, 17, 20, 21, 23, 28; **12:**10, 17[2], 19, 21, 25; **13:**2, 3[2], 5, 8, 13, 15, 17, 18, 19, 20, 21, 42, 43[2], 50, 51; **14:**3, 5[2], 15, 18, 22, 23[2], 27; **15:**2, 4, 5, 7, 8[2], 9, 12, 14, 20, 22, 25, 33, 37, 38[3]; **16:**4, 7, 10, 19, 20, 22[3], 23[3], 24, 25, 30, 33, 34[2], 37, 39[3]; **17:**2, 4, 5, 6, 7, 9, 12, 16, 23, 33, 34[2]; **18:**2, 3, 6, 11, 16, 17, 19, 21; **19:**2, 6[2], 7, 9, 12[2], 15, 16[3], 19, 29, 32, 34, 38; **20:**1, 6, 7, 11, 18, 30, 36, 37; **21:**1, 5, 7, 19, 21, 24, 26[2], 32, 40; **22:**2, 4, 5[2], 30; **23:**21, 27; **24:**21; **25:**3, 5, 6, 11, 16; **26:**10, 11[4], 30; **27:**9, 21, 33, 36, 40, 43; **28:**14, 15, 17, 23[2], 27; **Ro 1:**19[2], 24, 26, 28, 32[2]; **2:**3, 15; **4:**11; **9:**4, 5[2], 26, 27, 33; **10:**1, 5; **11:**8, 9, 14, 23, 27; **12:**14, 20[2]; **13:**7; **14:**3, 4; **15:**27[2], 28; **16:**14, 15, 17; **1Co 2:**14[2]; **4:**17; **6:**15; **7:**8, 36; **8:**13; **9:**19; **10:**4, 5, 7, 8, 9, 10, 11; **11:**2; **12:**6, 18; **14:**2, 12, 28, 35; **15:**10; **16:**16; **2Co 2:**13; **4:**4; **5:**15, 19; **6:**16[2], 17[2]; **8:**22, 24; **9:**2, 13; **11:**8; **13:**2; **Gal 2:**2, 5, 14; **3:**12; **4:**9, 15, 17; **6:**16; **Eph 2:**3; **4:**28; **5:**7, 11; **6:**4, 6, 9[2]; **Php 1:**28; **2:**21; **3:**8, 18; **Col 1:**27; **2:**15[2]; **3:**19, 22; **1Th 2:**16; **4:**17; **5:**3, 13, 14, 27; **2Th 2:**11[2], 17; **3:**14, 15[2]; **1Ti 1:**18, 20; **3:**10[2], 12; **4:**15; **5:**11, 16, 20, 24[2]; **6:**2[2], 17; **2Ti 2:**14[2], 17; **3:**5, 6, 11; **4:**16; **Tit 1:**12, 13; **3:**1; **Heb 1:**12; **2:**6[2], 7[2], 8[2], 11; **4:**2[2], 8; **7:**25; **8:**8, 9[3], 10, 11; **9:**15; **10:**16[2]; **11:**13, 16; **12:**9, 10, 19, 25; **13:**3, 9, 17[2]; **Jas 2:**16, 25; **3:**3, 4; **5:**14[3], 15; **1Pe 1:**11, 12; **2:**8[2]; **3:**1, 10, 11[2]; **4:**4; **2Pe 1:**4, 12; **2:**1, 3, 4[2], 6[2], 8, 11, 17, 19[2], 20[2], 21[2], 22; **3:**1, 16; **1Jn 2:**19; **3:**9, 15, 24; **4:**4, 5, 16; **5:**18[2]; **3Jn 1:**6, 10; **Jude 1:**11, 23; **Rev 2:**2, 16, 27; **3:**5, 9; **4:**8; **5:**10, 13; **7:**14, 15, 16, 17; **8:**2, 6; **9:**5[2], 6, 11, 19; **11:**5[2], 6, 7[3], 9, 10, 11[2], 12[2]; **12:**4, 8, 10, 12; **13:**7, 14; **14:**9, 13; **15:**1; **16:**6, 8, 14, 16; **17:**14; **19:**15; **20:**4, 8, 9, 10, 11, 13; **21:**3[2], 14; **22:**8[2], 18; **Tob 1:**8, 18[3], 19; **3:**8[2], 9, 16, 17; **4:**8, 13, 14, 19[2]; **5:**10, 21; **6:**2[2], 5, 8, 9[2], 14, 15, 17; **7:**1, 3, 4[2], 9; **8:**2[2], 6, 13, 14, 15, 17[2], 19; **9:**5; **10:**11, 12[4]; **11:**4, 12, 17; **12:**6[2], 16, 17, 22; **13:**3; **14:**5[2], 6, 7, 13; **Jdt 2:**2, 7[3], 9, 10, 11, 13, 15, 16, 20; **3:**3, 4, 6; **4:**5, 7[2]; **5:**3[2], 8, 9, 11[3], 12, 13, 14, 16, 17, 18, 20, 21[2], 24; **6:**2[3], 3, 4, 8, 12[3], 17; **7:**7[2], 11, 13, 14, 15, 19[2], 20, 25, 26, 27, 30; **8:**9[2], 11, 27[2], 30, 32; **10:**5, 9, 12, 17, 19[3]; **11:**2, 3, 9, 10, 11[2], 12, 15, 16[2], 18, 19; **12:**1[2], 2; **13:**10, 13[2], 14, 15; **14:**1, 2, 3, 4[2], 8, 12; **15:**3, 4, 5[2], 11[2], 12[2]; **16:**5, 12[2], 14, 17, 20; **AdE 1:**4, 6, 17; **2:**3[2], 23; **3:**4[2], 8; **5:**8, 11; **9:**2, 3, 16, 21, 23, 24[2], 26, 27, 28; **10:**5; **11:**9; **12:**2, 4; **13:**1; **14:**5, 11[2]; **16:**20[2], 21; **Wis 1:**8, 9, 14; **2:**21; **3:**1, 5[2], 6[2], 8; **4:**6, 14, 17[2], 18[2], 19[3], 20; **5:**1, 2, 15, 16[2], 22[2], 23[2]; **6:**10, 11, 16[2]; **7:**12[2], 27; **10:**17[2], 18[2], 19; **11:**4, 7, 10, 12, 15[3], 17, 19; **12:**2, 8, 9, 10[2], 11, 20, 25, 27[2]; **13:**3[3], 4[3], 13; **14:**12, 22, 30; **15:**6, 7, 11[3], 16[2], 19; **16:**3, 6, 9, 10, 11, 12, 20; **17:**4[3], 6, 9, 14, 15, 19, 21; **18:**1, 2[2], 5, 12, 17[2], 19[2]; **19:**2[2], 4[2], 9, 11, 12, 14, 16, 17, 21, 22; **Sir Pr:**T[3]; **1:**2, 3, 6, 23; **4:**17[5], 18[3], 19[2]; **6:**4, 7[2], 8, 16, 21; **7:**21, 22[2], 23[2], 24; **8:**8, 9, 15, 16[2]; **9:**10, 13; **10:**13[2], 16, 17[3], 24; **11:**1, 12[2], 19; **12:**2, 5[2]; **14:**2, 13; **15:**14; **16:**2[2], 19, 22, 26; **17:**1, 2[2], 3[2], 4[2], 6, 7[2], 8, 11[2], 12[2], 14[2], 23; **18:**6, 8, 11[2], 12, 13[2]; **22:**20, 27; **23:**1, 8; **27:**28, 29, 30; **28:**14, 15, 23[3]; **29:**4, 9, 18; **31:**6; **32:**1[2], 2; **33:**11, 12; **34:**6, 7, 15, 25; **35:**19, 25; **36:**3, 4[2], 16; **37:**18; **38:**1, 3, 4, 7, 8, 14, 29, 32; **41:**9; **44:**2, 8, 9, 21, 23; **45:**13, 19[2]; **46:**1; **47:**25; **48:**2[2], 16, 20[2], 21; **49:**4, 10; **50:**28, 29; **51:**8; **Bar 1:**8, 9, 10, 12; **2:**4[2], 9, 29, 31, 34[2], 35[2]; **3:**27[2], 34[2]; **4:**10, 11[2], 13, 14, 15; **5:**5, 6; **LtJ 6:**1, 6[2], 13, 14, 16, 19[2], 20, 23, 25, 26, 27, 29[2], 34, 35, 39, 40[2], 41, 42, 43, 44, 45, 46, 47, 48, 51, 58, 63, 64, 65, 69, 72; **Aza 1:**7, 21, 22, 23, 27[2]; **Sus 1:**4, 5, 6, 18, 25, 38, 39, 41, 48, 51[3], 52, 54, 56, 58, 61[2], 62; **Bel 1:**8, 9, 14, 22, 27[2], 30; **1Mc 1:**6, 9, 10, 11, 12, 13, 24, 30, 35, 38, 44, 52, 61; **2:**12, 15, 16, 19, 25, 30, 32[4], 33, 35, 36[2], 38, 39, 42, 43[2], 69; **3:**17, 22[2], 24[2], 25, 28, 35[2], 39, 41[2], 50, 53; **4:**2, 5, 9, 12[2], 15[2], 16, 18, 28, 29, 31, 32[2], 33, 45, 46, 55, 57, 60; **5:**2, 3[3], 4, 5[2], 7[2], 9, 15, 19, 22[2], 23, 25[2], 26, 33, 34[2], 39[2], 42[2], 43, 44, 47, 48, 54, 58, 59, 64[2]; **6:**10, 18, 19[2], 21, 27[2], 34, 39, 48, 54, 58, 59, 61; **7:**2, 4, 7[2], 13, 15[2], 16[2], 17, 18[2], 19[2], 25[2], 34[3], 38[2], 45, 46[2], 47[2]; **8:**1[2], 2[2], 4[5], 5, 6[2], 9, 10[5], 11, 12[2], 14, 15, 16[2], 17, 21, 22, 23, 25, 27, 31; **9:**1, 6, 7, 8, 9, 10, 15, 25, 26[3], 27, 35, 39, 40[2], 48, 51, 52, 53, 58, 60, 61, 68, 69; **10:**6, 9, 13, 21, 24[2], 25, 30[2], 34, 35[2], 36, 37[3], 38, 43, 46[2], 47, 49, 60[2], 61, 79, 84; **11:**2, 4, 34[2], 35, 38, 61, 62[2], 64, 66[2], 70, 72; **12:**1[2], 3, 4[2], 16[2], 17, 25[2], 30[2], 31[2], 35, 45, 53[4]; **13:**3[2], 21[2], 29, 33, 34, 40, 45, 47[3], 49, 50[2]; **14:**4, 10, 12, 13, 23, 32, 42, 45, 47, 48, 49[2]; **15:**19[2], 20, 21[2], 27, 35, 40; **16:**2, 5[2], 6, 8, 9, 10, 13, 15[2], 19[2], 22; **2Mc 1:**16[2], 20, 25; **2:**2, 3, 7, 15[2], 22; **3:**6, 15[2], 25; **4:**16[2], 28, 32, 33, 39, 41[2], 42; **5:**26; **6:**8, 9, 10[2], 11, 13, 14, 22, 23; **7:**2, 5, 8, 11[2], 21[2], 28[2]; **8:**11, 14, 15, 16[2], 19, 20, 21[2], 24, 25[2], 27[3], 30, 31; **9:**15; **10:**1, 12[2], 17, 19, 20, 21, 26, 30[2], 38; **11:**10, 11, 12, 13, 14, 24, 25, 26[2], 31, 34, 36; **12:**2, 3, 4[2], 8, 10, 11, 12, 14, 22, 24[2], 25, 30[2], 31[2], 37, 39; **13:**2, 3, 4, 12[2], 23, 26[2]; **14:**16, 31, 40, 46[3]; **15:**1, 8[2], 9[3], 11[2], 18, 30[2], 32; **1Es 1:**13, 16, 41[2], 50[2], 52, 53, 54; **2:**9, 11, 22, 25; **3:**8[2], 17; **4:**2, 3, 4[2], 7[2], 8[3], 9[2], 14[2], 26, 37, 44, 62; **5:**2[2], 3[2], 40, 50[2], 55, 68, 70; **6:**1, 2, 3, 6, 12[2], 15, 19; **7:**6, 15; **8:**6, 14, 22, 39, 41[2], 45, 46, 52, 54, 55, 56, 58, 59, 60, 63, 85; **9:**7, 14, 16, 36; **Pm 151:**5; **3Mc 1:**4[2], 6, 8, 27; **2:**4, 5, 7, 12[2], 30, 33[3]; **3:**2, 7, 8[2], 10[2], 11, 15[2], 21[3], 23; **4:**2, 3, 8, 11, 18, 19; **5:**2, 8[3], 17, 23, 25, 31, 42, 51; **6:**4, 11, 15, 17, 19[2], 21[2], 23, 25, 27, 34, 36, 39, 41; **7:**3, 5[2], 6, 7, 8[2], 9[2], 12, 17, 18[2], 20[2], 22; **2Es 1:**6, 7, 8, 9, 11, 12, 15, 24, 32, 39; **2:**1[2], 2[2], 6, 7, 10, 12, 15, 16[2], 23, 26, 31[2], 32, 33, 43, 46; **3:**8, 9, 10[2], 11, 13, 17, 20[2]; **4:**4, 9, 18, 37, 42; **5:**37, 45[2]; **6:**16, 42, 46, 50, 52; **7:**8, 14, 20, 32, 38, 52, 60, 66[2], 72, 86, 90, 91, 92[2], 93, 94[2], 95, 97, 102, 130, 137, 138; **8:**17, 34, 44, 59, 60[2], 63; **9:**9, 11, 18, 22, 23, 33, 35; **10:**3, 10; **11:**4, 11, 20, 21, 39; **12:**21, 24, 27, 32[3], 33[3], 34, 38, 45, 50; **13:**11, 13, 18, 38[2], 40, 44, 50; **14:**13, 23, 30, 45, 46, 47; **15:**2, 9[2], 10, 11, 15, 20, 25, 26, 27, 29, 30, 31, 33[2], 61; **16:**2, 5, 8, 12, 21, 23, 26, 32, 35, 48, 67, 72, 74; **4Mc 1:**6[2], 10, 11, 33; **2:**12, 17, 21, 22; **3:**7, 10, 20; **4:**7, 10, 21, 22, 23[2]; **5:**2, 7; **6:**19, 28, 35; **8:**4[4], 12, 13, 16, 27, 29; **10:**14, 16; **11:**10; **12:**13; **13:**12, 13[2]; **14:**1, 5, 17[2]; **15:**3, 6, 7[2], 9, 11[2], 12, 14, 16; **16:**5, 12[2], 13[2]; **17:**5, 12, 20, 23, 24; **18:**4, 21

THEMSELVES (457)

Ge 3:7, 8; **6:**2; **22:**18; **26:**4; **34:**30; **41:**40; **42:**6; **43:**32[2]; **Ex 5:**7; **12:**39; **18:**22, 26; **19:**22; **26:**9[2]; **28:**43; **29:**33; **32:**8, 31; **33:**6; **34:**15, 16[2]; **36:**16[2]; **Lev 17:**7, 15, 16; **18:**24; **20:**5, 6; **25:**39, 47, 48, 49, 50; **Nu 1:**18; **6:**2, 3, 5, 6, 7, 12; **8:**7, 21; **11:**32; **19:**12[2], 13, 19, 20; **25:**5; **27:**3; **31:**53; **Dt 9:**12; **29:**19; **31:**14, 16; **Jos 7:**12; **10:**16, 27; **24:**1; **Jdg 3:**6; **5:**2, 9; **6:**2; **8:**27, 33; **9:**8, 51; **18:**30; **19:**22; **20:**2, 30; **1Sa 2:**5; **13:**6, 19; **14:**11[2]; **19:**15; **21:**4; **2Sa 10:**8, 15, 17; **1Ki 14:**23; **18:**23, 28; **22:**38; **2Ki 7:**12; **17:**9, 10, 16, 17, 32; **1Ch 5:**25; **15:**14; **19:**6, 9; **21:**20; **29:**5, 20; **2Ch 5:**11, 13; **7:**14; **11:**13; **12:**6, 7[2]; **20:**25; **29:**15, 34[2]; **30:**3, 11, 15, 17, 18, 24; **31:**4, 18; **34:**32; **35:**14[2]; **Ezr 6:**20[2], 21; **9:**1, 2; **10:**8, 19; **Ne 2:**18; **4:**16; **8:**16; **9:**2, 18, 25; **10:**28; **12:**29, 30; **13:**22; **Est 9:**27, 31; **Job 1:**6; **2:**1; **3:**14; **14:**22; **15:**2, 31; **16:**10; **17:**8; **24:**4, 16; **30:**4; **34:**22; **41:**25; **Ps 2:**2; **3:**6; **10:**14; **22:**18; **35:**25, 26; **36:**2; **37:**11; **49:**18; **57:**6; **65:**12, 13[2]; **66:**7; **74:**8; **80:**6; **106:**28, 39; **110:**3; **139:**20; **Pr 1:**18; **8:**36; **11:**17[2]; **13:**13; **15:**32; **18:**7; **20:**6, 11; **Ecc 3:**12; **6:**8; **8:**15; **Isa 2:**20; **3:**9; **14:**1; **46:**2; **47:**14; **48:**2; **49:**7; **56:**6; **59:**6; **66:**17; **Jer 2:**5, 13, 24; **7:**19; **12:**13; **14:**16; **16:**20; **50:**5, 9; **51:**58[2]; **Eze 8:**16; **14:**7, 11; **23:**24; **26:**16; **27:**31; **30:**17; **32:**4; **33:**5; **34:**8, 10; **36:**7; **37:**23; **44:**18, 25[2]; **Da 10:**7; **11:**14; **Hos 1:**11; **4:**10, 14; **7:**14; **9:**9, 10; **13:**2; **Joel 3:**12; **Am 2:**8, 15; **6:**6; **9:**3; **Hab 1:**7; **2:**5, 13; **Zep 1:**8; **Zec 2:**11; **6:**5; **12:**3, 5, 12[2], 13[2], 14; **14:**18; **Mt 9:**3; **14:**15; **16:**24; **17:**1; **19:**12; **20:**17; **21:**38; **23:**4, 12[2]; **27:**35; **Mk 2:**8; **6:**32, 36; **8:**34; **9:**2, 10; **15:**31; **16:**14; **Lk 7:**30, 49; **9:**23, 25; **12:**21; **14:**11[2]; **18:**9, 14[2]; **20:**14; **24:**12; **Jn 6:**24, 52; **11:**55; **14:**11; **17:**13; **18:**18, 28; **19:**24; **Ac 1:**14; **2:**42; **15:**27, 32; **16:**37; **22:**19; **23:**12, 21; **24:**15; **27:**36; **Ro 1:**24; **2:**14; **14:**22; **1Co 2:**15; **11:**29; **14:**4, 28; **16:**15; **2Co 5:**15; **8:**5; **10:**12[3], 18; **11:**13, 15; **Gal 5:**12; **6:**3, 13; **Eph 4:**19; **1Ti 1:**4; **2:**9; **3:**10, 13; **6:**10, 19; **2Ti 2:**21; **3:**2; **4:**3; **Tit 3:**8, 14; **Heb 6:**16; **9:**23; **Jas 1:**22, 23, 24; **1Pe 1:**12; **3:**5; **4:**19; **2Pe 2:**1, 19; **1Jn 3:**3; **Jude 1:**11, 12; **Rev 6:**11; **14:**4; **Tob 1:**8; **7:**9; **Jdt 2:**10; **4:**9, 11; **9:**6, 7; **11:**2; **15:**13; **AdE 2:**12; **8:**11; **9:**10, 16, 27; **16:**20; **Wis 2:**1; **11:**5; **14:**30; **15:**16; **17:**2, 8, 21; **19:**2, 5; **Sir Pr:**T; **2:**17; **6:**12; **7:**20; **8:**9; **10:**29[2]; **13:**16; **18:**29; **20:**13; **37:**19; **44:**3; **50:**28; **Bar 2:**30; **LtJ 6:**8, 10, 12, 19, 27, 28, 40, 41, 46, 48, 49, 57, 58, 68, 72; **Sus 1:**16; **1Mc 1:**15, 48; **2:**42; **4:**39; **6:**38; **8:**15, 18; **11:**68; **14:**29, 36; **2Mc 3:**2, 15; **6:**6, 11; **8:**28; **11:**11; **12:**38, 42; **14:**14, 21; **1Es 1:**3, 13, 14; **7:**12, 13; **8:**69; **9:**4, 20, 54; **3Mc 1:**4, 16; **2:**26, 31, 32, 33; **3:**4; **5:**17, 50; **6:**34; **7:**5; **2Es 7:**22, 23, 84; **8:**10, 60; **11:**25, 28; **12:**2; **13:**41; **16:**28; **4Mc 3:**12; **9:**12, 26; **14:**19

THEN (3602)

Ge 1:3, 11, 26; **2:**7, 18, 21, 23; **3:**7, 13, 22; **4:**9, 15, 16; **5:**24; **6:**3; **7:**1; **8:**8, 12, 15, 20; **9:**8, 23; **11:**4; **12:**7, 12, 19; **13:**8, 9[2]; **14:**7, 8, 13, 16, 21; **15:**5, 7, 13; **16:**5, 6; **17:**3, 17, 23; **18:**8, 10, 16, 20, 23, 24, 30, 32; **19:**2, 9, 12, 24, 34; **20:**6, 7, 9, 14, 17; **21:**16, 19; **22:**5[2], 10; **23:**12; **24:**5, 8, 10, 17, 28, 33, 41, 47, 48, 49, 50, 54, 61, 67; **25:**34; **26:**9, 21, 26; **27:**3, 4, 15, 17, 21, 25, 26, 33[2], 36, 37, 39, 41, 45, 46; **28:**1, 16, 20, 21; **29:**1, 8, 11, 15, 21, 25, 28, 35; **30:**3, 6, 8, 10, 14, 15, 20, 22, 37; **31:**3, 8[2], 11, 14, 16, 36, 43, 51, 55; **32:**7, 8, 18, 26, 28, 29; **33:**2, 6, 10, 12; **34:**16, 17, 30;

THERE (2448)

THESE (1438)

THEY (8792)

22, 24^{3}, 25^{2}, 26^{2}, 27, 31^{2}, 34, 35^{2}, 36^{2}, 37, 40, 45, 47, 49^{2}, 53, 59^{2}, 60; **7:**5, 6, 10, 11^{3}, 14, 16, 17, 18^{3}, 22, 29, 36, 44, 45^{2}, 46^{2}, 47, 49; **8:**1^{2}, 2^{3}, 3, 4^{3}, 5, 6, 7, 8, 10^{2}, 11, 12^{2}, 13^{5}, 15, 16^{2}, 18, 19^{2}, 22, 26^{2}, 28, 30^{2}, 32; **9:**2^{2}, 3, 4, 6^{2}, 9, 15, 16, 20, 22, 26, 33, 35, 38, 39, 40, 42^{2}, 44, 59, 60, 62, 68^{2}; **10:**1, 8^{2}, 11, 15^{2}, 38, 41^{2}, 43, 46^{2}, 47^{2}, 62, 64, 76, 80, 82, 83; **11:**4^{2}, 5, 6, 33, 41, 44, 45, 47^{2}, 48, 49^{2}, 51^{2}, 55, 66, 67, 68^{2}, 72, 73^{2}; **12:**3, 19, 21, 26, 28^{2}, 29, 30, 34, 37, 43, 46, 48, 50^{2}, 51^{2}, 52^{2}, 53^{2}; **13:**7, 8, 17, 29, 45, 46, 49, 50, 52; **14:**8, 9, 16, 17, 18^{2}, 22, 23, 25, 26, 27^{2}, 29, 35, 36, 48; **15:**5, 17, 19, 24, 28, 35, 41; **16:**4, 5, 6, 8, 10, 22; **2Mc 1:**13, 15, 16^{2}, 19, 20^{2}; **2:**8, 11, 14, 21; **3:**6, 20, 22, 28, 30, 33, 34; **4:**14, 16, 42^{2}, 47; **5:**12, 18, 27^{2}; **6:**7, 8, 10, 14, 25; **7:**4, 7^{2}, 13, 15, 18; **8:**1, 2, 18, 24, 25^{2}, 26, 27^{2}, 28, 29^{2}, 30^{2}, 31^{2}, 32, 33^{2}, 36; **9:**12, 24; **10:**2, 3^{3}, 4^{5}, 6^{2}, 7, 8, 15, 17^{2}, 26, 27^{3}, 29, 30^{3}, 33, 35, 36^{2}, 37, 38^{2}; **11:**6, 7, 8, 9, 10, 11, 25, 26; **12:**3^{2}, 4^{2}, 10, 12^{2}, 16, 17^{2}, 18, 22^{2}, 25, 28, 29, 31^{2}, 32, 34, 37, 38, 40, 41, 42^{2}, 45; **13:**6, 12, 16, 25^{2}; **14:**15, 16, 20^{2}, 22, 32^{2}, 41, 44; **15:**4, 9, 17, 27, 28^{2}, 29, 34, 36; **1Es 1:**3, 11, 12^{2}, 13, 24, 32, 51^{2}, 54, 55, 57; **2:**12, 15, 19; **3:**3^{3}, 8, 9, 13, 16^{2}, 17, 22^{2}, 23^{3}; **4:**3, 4^{2}, 5^{4}, 6^{2}, 7^{2}, 8^{3}, 9^{2}, 11^{2}, 16, 17, 19, 32, 37, 47, 50^{2}, 53, 54, 62, 63; **5:**8, 37^{2}, 39, 44^{2}, 45, 47, 50^{3}, 51, 54, 55, 57^{2}, 58, 61, 66, 67, 68, 73^{2}; **6:**1, 6, 13, 16, 18, 24, 26; **7:**4, 7, 12, 14; **8:**6, 19, 47, 67, 70, 80, 83, 96^{2}; **9:**3, 16, 20, 36, 39, 46, 47, 50^{2}, 54, 55^{3}; **Man 1:**7, 9; **3Mc 1:**4, 11, 15, 16, 20, 23^{2}, 27; **2:**8^{2}, 29, 30, 31, 32, 33^{2}; **3:**2, 4^{3}, 5^{2}, 7^{2}, 8^{3}, 17, 18^{2}, 19, 22^{2}, 23^{3}, 24; **4:**2, 4, 5, 6, 7, 9, 10^{2}, 11^{2}, 17, 19, 20^{2}; **5:**7^{2}, 10, 13, 22^{2}, 24, 35, 40, 44, 49^{2}, 50^{3}, 51; **6:**15, 17, 19, 29, 30^{2}, 31, 32^{2}, 34, 36^{2}, 37, 40^{2}; **7:**4, 5^{2}, 7, 10^{2}, 11, 12^{2}, 13, 14^{2}, 15^{3}, 17, 18, 19^{2}, 20^{2}, 21^{2}, 22; **2Es 1:**5^{2}, 6, 7, 8^{2}, 24, 34, 36, 37^{2}; **2:**1, 5, 6, 7, 12, 13, 28, 33, 42, 43, 45^{2}, 47; **3:**8, 12^{2}, 13, 26, 33^{2}; **4:**13, 32; **5:**12, 30; **6:**6, 16^{2}, 23, 24, 26, 56^{2}; **7:**5^{2}, 12, 14, 21^{3}, 22^{2}, 23^{2}, 24^{2}, 60, 61^{2}, 66^{2}, 72^{7}, 73^{2}, 81, 82^{2}, 83, 84, 85, 86, 87^{4}, 88, 89^{3}, 91^{2}, 92, 93, 94^{3}, 95^{2}, 96^{5}, 97, 98^{4}, 100, 101^{3}, 117, 128^{4}, 130, 134; **8:**22, 44, 50, 56^{2}, 57, 58^{2}; **9:**7, 10, 11, 26, 29^{2}, 32, 33, 35; **11:**3, 19, 29, 44; **12:**3, 23, 24, 25, 40, 45; **13:**8, 18, 19, 31, 33, 38, 40, 41^{2}, 42^{2}, 43, 44, 46^{2}, 47; **14:**29, 30, 42^{4}; **15:**2, 8, 16, 20, 21, 29, 30^{2}, 31, 35, 37, 42, 43, 44^{2}, 58, 60^{3}, 61, 62^{2}, 63; **16:**13, 14, 18, 20, 33^{3}, 46, 47, 53, 68, 71, 72, 77; **4Mc 1:**10, 11^{2}; **2:**13; **3:**13, 18; **4:**7, 23, 25^{3}; **5:**3; **6:**2, 3^{2}, 24, 25; **7:**19^{2}; **8:**2, 15^{3}, 16, 28; **9:**10, 11, 12^{2}, 19^{2}, 26, 27^{2}; **10:**5, 7^{2}, 8, 12; **11:**10^{2}, 12, 17, 19; **12:**3, 9, 14; **13:**2^{2}, 3, 8, 20, 21^{2}, 22, 24^{2}, 26; **14:**1^{2}, 9, 17^{3}; **15:**5, 10^{2}; **16:**12, 25; **17:**7, 10, 11, 18, 21; **18:**4

THIS (3373)

Ge 2:23^{3}; **3:**13, 14; **5:**1, 29; **6:**15, 22; **7:**1; **9:**12, 17; **11:**6; **12:**7, 12, 18; **13:**10; **15:**4, 7, 13, 18; **17:**4, 10, 21; **19:**9, 13, 14, 21, 37, 38; **20:**5, 6, 10, 11, 13; **21:**10^{2}, 26, 30; **22:**14, 16; **23:**1, 19; **24:**5, 7, 8, 9, 14, 58; **25:**7, 17, 22; **26:**3, 10, 11, 33; **28:**15, 16, 17^{3}, 20, 22; **29:**25, 26, 27, 33, 34, 35; **30:**31; **31:**1, 13, 40, 48, 51, 52^{4}; **32:**2, 10, 32; **33:**8; **34:**4, 14, 15, 22; **35:**20; **37:**2, 6, 10, 19, 22, 32; **38:**23, 28; **39:**9^{2}, 19; **40:**1, 12, 14, 18; **41:**38, 39; **42:**15, 18, 21, 25, 28^{2}, 33, 36; **43:**11, 29; **44:**5^{2}, 13, 15, 29; **45:**17, 19; **47:**23, 26; **48:**1, 4, 15, 18; **49:**28; **50:**3, 11, 16, 21, 24; **Ex 1:**18; **2:**6, 9, 12; **3:**3, 12^{2}, 15^{2}, 21; **4:**17; **5:**15, 22, 23; **6:**9, 26; **7:**17, 23; **8:**19, 22, 23, 32; **9:**5, 14, 16, 18, 27; **10:**6, 7, 17^{2}; **12:**2, 3, 6, 11, 14, 17^{2}, 24, 25, 26, 43; **13:**3, 5^{2}, 10, 14; **14:**12; **15:**1, 2; **16:**3^{2}, 16, 23, 32; **17:**4, 14; **18:**14, 23; **21:**31; **22:**9; **25:**3; **26:**13; **28:**43; **29:**1, 28, 38; **30:**13, 15, 31, 37; **31:**13; **32:**1, 5, 9, 13, 21, 23, 24, 29, 31; **33:**1, 12, 13, 16; **34:**9; **35:**4; **36:**22, 23, 29; **39:**18, 32; **Lev 2:**2, 9; **4:**20; **5:**12; **6:**9, 14, 20, 25; **7:**1, 11, 14, 35, 37; **8:**5, 28; **9:**6; **10:**3; **11:**46; **12:**7; **13:**20, 25, 27, 51, 59; **14:**2, 32, 54, 57; **15:**3, 32; **16:**29, 30, 34; **17:**2, 5, 7; **23:**21, 27, 34; **25:**13; **26:**16, 18, 27; **Nu 2:**32; **3:**1; **4:**19, 24, 28, 31, 33, 37, 41, 45; **5:**19, 22, 29, 30; **6:**13, 21; **7:**17, 23, 29, 35, 41, 47, 53, 59, 65, 71, 77, 83, 84, 88; **8:**4, 24; **9:**3; **10:**8, 28; **11:**6, 11, 12, 13, 14, 15, 31; **13:**27, 31; **14:**2, 3, 8, 11, 13, 14^{2}, 15, 16, 19^{2}, 27, 29, 32, 35^{2}; **15:**13; **16:**6, 21, 28, 45; **18:**9, 11; **19:**2, 10, 14; **20:**4, 5, 10, 12; **21:**2, 5, 17; **22:**4, 6, 10, 17, 30^{2}; **23:**5, 16; **24:**14, 23; **26:**51, 57; **27:**12; **28:**3, 10, 14, 17; **29:**7; **30:**1; **31:**21; **32:**5, 8, 15, 19, 20, 22, 23, 32; **34:**2, 6, 7, 9, 12, 13; **35:**5; **36:**6; **Dt 1:**4, 5, 6, 31, 32, 35; **2:**3, 7, 22, 25; **3:**14, 18, 26, 27, 28; **4:**6^{2}, 8, 22, 32, 44; **5:**3, 25, 28, 29; **6:**1, 25; **7:**5; **8:**1, 17; **9:**4, 6, 7, 13, 27; **10:**8; **11:**4, 5, 8, 22; **15:**2, 5, 10, 15^{2}; **17:**5, 18, 19; **18:**3, 16^{2}; **19:**4, 9, 20; **21:**7, 20; **22:**14, 16, 20, 26; **24:**18, 22; **25:**9; **26:**5, 9^{2}, 16; **27:**3, 8, 9, 26; **28:**58^{3}, 61; **29:**4, 7, 9, 14, 19, 20, 21, 24^{2}, 27, 29; **30:**10, 11; **31:**2, 7, 9, 11, 12, 16, 19^{2}, 21, 22, 24, 26, 30; **32:**27, 29, 34, 44, 46, 47, 49; **33:**1, 7; **34:**4, 6; **Jos 1:**2, 6, 8, 13; **2:**14, 17, 18, 20^{2}; **3:**4, 7, 10; **4:**6, 9; **5:**4, 9; **6:**10, 14, 26^{3}; **7:**7, 20, 26^{2}; **8:**14, 20, 28, 29; **9:**1, 20, 24, 26, 27; **10:**13, 27; **11:**1, 6; **13:**2, 7, 13, 23, 28; **14:**10, 12, 14, 15; **15:**4, 12, 20, 63; **16:**10; **18:**14, 19, 20, 28; **19:**8, 16, 23, 31, 39, 48; **22:**3, 16, 28^{2}, 29, 31; **23:**8, 9, 13, 15; **24:**15, 27; **Jdg 1:**21, 26; **2:**2, 20; **4:**14; **6:**13, 14, 20, 24, 29; **7:**3, 4^{2}, 14; **8:**3, 9; **9:**18, 19, 24, 29; **10:**4, 15; **11:**37; **12:**3; **13:**11; **14:**4; **15:**3, 6, 7, 18, 19; **16:**4, 18, 28^{2}; **17:**5, 8; **18:**3, 12^{2}; **19:**11, 23^{2}, 24, 30; **20:**3, 9, 12, 16; **21:**6, 11; **Ru 1:**19; **2:**5, 7, 8, 14; **3:**10, 13; **4:**6, 7^{2}, 12, 14; **1Sa 1:**3, 11, 16, 27; **2:**14, 20; **4:**6, 7, 14; **5:**5^{2}; **6:**9, 18, 20; **8:**8; **9:**6, 16, 21; **10:**1, 27; **11:**2, 13; **12:**2, 5, 8, 16, 20; **14:**28, 29, 38, 41^{2}, 45; **15:**14, 28, 32; **16:**8, 9, 12; **17:**17, 25, 26^{2}, 32, 33, 36, 37, 46^{2}, 47, 55; **18:**8, 24; **19:**17; **20:**2, 3, 12, 21, 29; **21:**11, 15^{2}; **22:**15; **23:**17; **24:**6, 10, 16, 19, 22; **25:**9, 12, 17, 21, 25, 27; **26:**16, 17; **27:**6; **28:**10, 18; **29:**3^{2}, 4, 5; **30:**8, 15, 20, 24; **2Sa 1:**17; **2:**1, 5, 6; **3:**8, 38; **4:**3, 8, 10; **6:**8, 22; **7:**6, 17, 19^{2}, 21, 27^{2}, 28; **11:**3, 25; **12:**5, 6, 11, 12, 14, 21; **13:**16, 17, 18, 20, 32; **14:**13, 15, 19, 20, 21; **15:**1; **16:**9, 11, 12, 17, 18; **17:**6, 7; **18:**14, 18, 31; **19:**7^{2}, 11, 20, 21, 22^{2}, 42; **21:**18; **22:**1, 31, 50; **23:**5, 17; **24:**3, 23; **1Ki 1:**27, 30, 45; **2:**23, 26; **3:**6, 9, 10, 11, 17, 18, 19, 23; **5:**7, 11; **6:**12, 16; **7:**8, 28, 37; **8:**8, 24, 27, 29^{2}, 30, 31, 33, 35, 38, 42, 43, 54^{2}, 61; **9:**3, 8^{3}, 9, 13, 15, 21; **10:**12; **11:**10, 11, 33, 39; **12:**6, 7, 9, 10, 19, 24, 27^{2}, 30; **13:**3, 8, 16, 33, 34; **14:**2, 15; **17:**17, 21; **18:**36, 37; **19:**2; **20:**6, 7, 9, 12, 13, 24, 28, 39; **22:**27; **2Ki 1:**2, 11; **2:**19, 21, 22; **3:**16, 18, 23; **4:**9, 13, 16, 43; **5:**6, 7, 18, 26; **6:**9, 11, 18, 19^{2}, 28, 32, 33; **7:**1, 9, 18; **8:**8, 9, 13, 22; **9:**1, 12, 15, 25, 26, 27, 36, 37; **10:**6, 27; **11:**5; **14:**7; **15:**12; **16:**6, 18; **17:**7, 12, 23, 34, 41; **18:**19, 22, 25^{2}, 30; **19:**3, 21, 29^{2}, 31, 32, 33, 34; **20:**6^{2}, 9, 17; **21:**7, 15; **22:**13^{2}, 16, 17, 19, 20; **23:**3^{2}, 21, 23, 27; **24:**3, 13; **1Ch 4:**41, 43; **5:**9, 26; **11:**11, 19; **13:**11; **17:**5, 15, 17, 26; **20:**4; **21:**3, 7, 8; **26:**26; **27:**1, 6, 24; **28:**8, 19; **29:**14, 16; **2Ch 1:**10^{2}, 11; **3:**12; **5:**9; **6:**15, 18, 20^{2}, 21, 22, 24, 26, 29, 32, 33, 34, 40; **7:**12, 15, 16, 20, 21^{3}, 22; **10:**6, 7, 9, 19; **11:**4; **14:**11; **16:**9, 10; **17:**14; **18:**26; **19:**2, 9; **20:**1, 7, 9^{2}, 12, 15, 17, 26, 35; **21:**10, 18; **23:**4; **24:**18; **25:**9, 16; **28:**22; **29:**9, 28; **30:**9, 26; **31:**1, 10, 20; **32:**9, 12, 15, 20, 30; **33:**7, 23; **34:**21, 24, 25, 27, 28, 31; **35:**19, 20, 25; **Ezr 1:**9; **3:**12; **4:**11, 13, 15^{2}, 16, 19, 21, 22; **5:**3^{2}, 4^{2}, 8, 9^{2}, 11, 12, 13, 16, 17^{2}; **6:**2, 7^{2}, 8, 11, 12^{2}, 15, 16, 17; **7:**1, 6, 11, 17, 24, 27; **8:**1, 23, 35; **9:**2, 3, 7, 10, 13, 15; **10:**2, 9, 13^{2}, 14, 15; **Ne 1:**11; **2:**2, 10, 19; **5:**10, 11, 13, 16, 18, 19; **6:**4, 6, 13^{2}, 16; **8:**2, 9, 10, 11; **9:**1, 10, 18, 36, 38; **13:**4, 6, 14, 17, 18^{3}, 22, 27; **Est 1:**1, 12, 13, 17, 18, 21; **2:**4, 12; **4:**14^{2}; **5:**7, 13, 14; **6:**3; **7:**4, 5, 6; **9:**13, 14, 17, 26^{2}, 29; **Job 1:**3, 5, 22; **2:**10; **3:**1; **5:**27; **6:**10; **7:**15; **9:**2; **10:**13; **12:**9; **13:**1, 16; **17:**8; **20:**4, 29; **21:**2; **22:**21; **27:**13; **31:**28; **33:**12; **34:**16; **35:**2; **37:**1, 14; **38:**2, 18; **42:**3, 16; **Ps 7:**3; **12:**7; **17:**14; **18:**T, 30, 49; **24:**10; **34:**6; **41:**11; **44:**17, 21; **48:**14; **49:**1; **50:**22; **56:**9; **62:**11; **69:**31; **73:**15, 16; **74:**18; **78:**32; **80:**14; **87:**4, 5, 6; **92:**6; **102:**18; **109:**27; **113:**2; **115:**18; **118:**20, 23, 24; **119:**50, 56; **121:**8; **125:**2; **131:**3; **132:**14; **149:**9; **Pr 4:**7; **6:**3; **22:**2; **24:**12; **29:**13; **30:**20; **Ecc 1:**10, 17; **2:**1, 10, 15, 19, 21, 23, 24, 26; **3:**14; **4:**4, 8, 16; **5:**9, 10, 16, 18^{2}, 19; **6:**2, 9; **7:**2, 6, 10, 23, 27, 29; **8:**9, 10, 14, 15; **9:**1, 3, 13; **11:**6; **SS 5:**8, 16^{2}; **6:**10; **Isa 1:**12; **3:**6; **5:**25; **6:**7, 9, 10; **8:**6, 11, 12, 20; **9:**7^{2}, 12, 16, 17, 21; **10:**4, 7^{2}, 32; **12:**5; **14:**4, 16, 26^{2}, 28; **16:**13; **17:**14; **20:**6^{2}; **22:**14, 15; **23:**7, 8, 10, 13; **24:**3; **25:**6, 7, 9^{2}, 10; **26:**1; **27:**9^{2}, 11; **28:**11, 12^{2}, 14, 29; **29:**11^{2}, 12, 14; **30:**12, 13, 21; **36:**4, 7, 10^{2}, 15; **37:**3, 22, 30^{2}, 32, 33, 34, 35; **38:**6^{2}, 7^{2}, 19; **39:**6; **41:**4, 20; **42:**22, 23; **43:**9; **44:**5, 16, 20; **45:**21; **46:**8; **47:**8, 14; **48:**1, 6^{2}, 16, 20; **50:**11; **51:**21; **54:**9, 17; **56:**2; **58:**5, 6; **59:**21; **63:**1^{2}; **64:**12; **66:**2; **Jer 2:**12, 17; **3:**5, 7, 10, 25; **4:**8, 10, 11, 18^{2}, 28; **5:**9, 14^{2}, 20, 21, 23, 29; **6:**6, 19, 21; **7:**2, 3, 4, 6, 7, 10, 11, 16, 20, 23, 25, 28, 33; **8:**3, 5; **9:**9, 12, 15, 24; **10:**18, 19; **11:**2, 3, 5, 6, 7, 8, 14; **13:**10^{2}, 12, 13, 25; **14:**10, 11, 13, 15, 17, 22; **15:**1, 20; **16:**2, 3^{2}, 5, 6, 9, 10^{2}, 13, 21; **17:**24, 25^{2}; **18:**6, 13; **19:**3, 4^{2}, 6, 7, 8, 11^{2}, 12^{2}, 15; **20:**5; **21:**1, 4, 6, 7, 8, 9, 10; **22:**1, 3, 4^{2}, 5, 8^{2}, 11, 12, 16, 21, 28, 30; **23:**6, 32, 33; **24:**1, 5, 6, 8; **25:**3, 9, 11, 13, 15; **26:**1, 6^{2}, 9^{2}, 11^{2}, 12^{2}, 15, 16, 20^{2}; **27:**1, 4^{2}, 8, 16, 17, 19, 22; **28:**3^{2}, 4, 6, 7, 11^{2}, 15, 16; **29:**2, 10, 16, 22, 29, 32; **30:**24; **31:**33, 36; **32:**3, 8, 14^{2}, 15, 20^{2}, 22, 28, 29, 31^{2}, 35, 36, 37, 41, 42^{2}, 43; **33:**4, 5, 9, 10, 12, 16; **34:**2, 22; **35:**14, 16; **36:**1, 7, 29^{2}; **37:**7, 8, 10, 18, 19; **38:**2, 3, 4^{4}, 17, 18, 21, 23, 24; **39:**16; **40:**2^{2}, 3; **42:**2, 10, 13, 18; **44:**4, 10, 20, 22, 23, 29^{2}; **46:**7; **50:**15; **51:**6, 62, 63; **52:**28; **La 2:**15, 16, 20; **3:**21; **5:**17; **Eze 1:**5, 28; **2:**3; **3:**1, 3; **4:**3; **5:**5; **6:**10; **8:**5, 15, 17; **11:**2, 3, 5, 6, 7, 11, 15; **12:**10, 22, 23; **16:**16, 29, 44, 49; **17:**7; **18:**2, 3, 14; **19:**14; **20:**27, 29, 31; **23:**11, 30, 38, 39; **24:**2^{3}, 19, 24; **31:**14, 18; **32:**16; **33:**27, 33; **36:**35, 37; **39:**8; **40:**18, 45; **41:**4, 7, 22; **42:**6; **43:**7, 12^{2}, 13; **44:**2, 28; **45:**2, 13, 15, 16, 17; **46:**14, 20; **47:**6, 8, 14, 15, 17, 18, 19, 20, 21; **48:**11, 14, 29; **Da 1:**14; **2:**5, 12, 18, 30, 31, 36, 44, 47; **3:**8, 16, 29; **4:**10, 18, 24, 28, 30; **5:**7, 12, 15, 22, 24, 25, 26; **6:**5, 28; **7:**6, 7, 8, 16, 21, 23, 24^{2}; **8:**13, 16; **9:**7, 13, 14, 15; **10:**8, 11; **11:**29; **12:**5; **Hos 5:**1; **7:**10; **Joel 1:**2; **3:**9; **Am 3:**1; **4:**1, 12; **5:**1; **7:**1, 3, 4, 6^{2}, 7; **8:**1, 4, 8; **9:**12; **Jnh 1:**7, 8, 10, 12, 14; **4:**1, 2; **Mic 1:**5, 8; **2:**3, 7, 10, 11; **3:**9; **Zep 1:**4; **2:**10, 15; **Hag 1:**4; **2:**3, 7, 9^{2}, 14^{2}, 15, 18, 19; **Zec 1:**14; **3:**2, 9; **4:**6, 9; **5:**3, 5, 6^{2}, 8, 11; **6:**15; **8:**6, 11, 12; **11:**13; **13:**9; **14:**12, 15; **Mal 1:**5, 13^{2}; **2:**1, 4, 5, 12, 13; **Mt 1:**18, 20, 22; **2:**3, 15; **3:**3, 15, 17; **5:**37; **6:**9, 11; **7:**12; **8:**9, 17, 27; **9:**3, 11, 12, 13, 26, 28, 30, 33; **11:**10, 16, 23; **12:**7, 15, 17, 23, 24, 32, 41, 42, 45, 48; **13:**15, 19, 20, 22, 23, 28, 35, 51, 54^{2}, 55, 56^{2}; **14:**2^{2}, 13, 15, 24; **15:**8, 15, 18; **16:**17, 18, 22; **17:**5, 6, 20; **18:**4, 23; **19:**5, 11, 12, 22, 25; **20:**14, 23; **21:**3, 4, 10, 11, 21, 23, 38, 42, 44; **22:**20, 22, 38, 41; **23:**36^{2}; **24:**3, 6, 8, 14, 34, 43; **25:**1, 30; **26:**8, 9, 10, 12, 13, 26, 28, 29, 31, 34, 39, 42, 54, 56, 58, 61, 71; **27:**8^{2}, 24, 32, 37, 47, 54; **28:**7, 14, 15^{2}; **Mk 1:**27; **2:**7^{2}, 12, 17; **4:**13, 41; **5:**42, 43; **6:**2^{3}, 3, 14, 35; **7:**6, 13; **8:**12^{2}, 32, 38; **9:**7, 10, 21, 25, 29; **10:**5, 7, 10, 14, 22, 30, 41; **11:**3^{2}, 23, 28; **12:**4, 7, 10, 11, 12, 16, 24, 31, 33, 43; **13:**4, 7, 8, 30; **14:**4, 5, 22, 24, 30^{2}, 36, 58, 59, 69, 71; **15:**39^{2}; **16:**12; **Lk 1:**18, 19, 25, 29, 34, 36, 43, 61, 66, 67; **2:**2, 11, 12, 15, 17^{2}, 25, 34, 48; **4:**3, 6, 21, 22, 23, 28, 36, 43; **5:**6, 21, 27; **7:**4, 8, 9, 17, 27, 29, 31, 39^{2}, 44, 49; **8:**8, 9, 11, 25, 50; **9:**9, 34, 35, 45^{2}, 48; **10:**1, 5, 11, 20, 28; **11:**27, 29, 30, 31, 32, 50, 51; **12:**18, 20, 39, 41; **13:**2, 6, 7, 16^{2}, 17; **14:**6, 9, 15, 21, 30; **15:**2, 3, 24, 30, 32; **16:**1, 2, 8, 14, 26, 28; **17:**6, 18, 25; **18:**5, 9, 11, 14, 22, 23, 30; **19:**9, 11, 14, 28, 31, 42; **20:**2, 9, 12, 14, 16, 17, 19, 34; **21:**3, 7^{2}, 12, 13, 23, 32, 34; **22:**15, 17, 19^{2}, 20, 23, 34, 37, 42, 51, 53, 56, 59; **23:**2, 4, 5, 6, 12, 14^{2}, 18, 19, 31, 38, 41, 46, 47, 48, 52; **24:**4, 9, 10, 21, 22, 36, 40; **Jn 1:**15, 19, 28, 30, 31, 34, 37; **2:**11, 12, 18, 19, 20, 22; **3:**19, 22, 29, 33; **4:**13, 15, 20, 21, 42, 53, 54; **5:**1, 18, 28; **6:**1, 6, 14, 29, 34, 39, 40, 42, 50, 51, 52, 58^{2}, 60, 61, 65, 66; **7:**1, 8, 9, 15, 25, 26, 27, 31, 35, 39, 40, 41, 46, 49; **8:**4, 6, 23^{2}, 40; **9:**2, 3, 6, 8, 16, 19, 20, 22, 24, 29, 33, 39, 40; **10:**6, 16, 17, 18, 41; **11:**4, 7, 9, 11, 26, 28, 37, 42, 43, 47, 48, 51; **12:**5, 6, 18, 25, 27^{3}, 30, 31^{2}, 33, 34, 36, 38, 41; **13:**1, 11, 19, 21, 26, 28, 35; **14:**9, 17, 29, 30; **15:**8, 12, 13; **16:**3, 11, 15, 18, 30, 33; **17:**3; **18:**9, 17, 22, 29, 30, 32, 34, 36^{2}, 37^{2}, 38, 40; **19:**8, 12, 20, 21, 24, 28, 35; **20:**14, 20, 22, 30; **21:**1, 14, 19^{2}, 23, 24; **Ac 1:**4, 6, 9, 11, 17, 18, 19, 25; **2:**6, 12, 14, 16, 23, 29, 31, 32, 33, 36, 37, 40; **3:**12, 15, 16^{2}, 18; **4:**7, 9, 10, 11, 17, 22, 27; **5:**4, 20, 21, 28^{2}, 33, 38^{2}; **6:**3, 13^{2}, 14^{2}; **7:**4, 7, 20, 29, 35, 37, 40, 60^{2}; **8:**10, 19, 21, 22, 26, 29, 32, 34, 35; **9:**11, 13, 21^{2}, 42; **10:**16, 30; **11:**10, 18, 22, 28, 30; **12:**3, 12, 17; **13:**17, 23, 26, 34, 38, 39, 48; **14:**15; **15:**2, 6, 15, 16; **16:**12, 18; **17:**3, 8, 18^{2}, 19, 23, 31, 32; **18:**1, 10, 13; **19:**5, 10, 14, 17, 25, 26, 27, 28, 40, 41; **20:**13, 26, 35; **21:**11^{2}, 12, 28^{3}; **22:**3, 4, 22, 24, 26; **23:**1, 3, 7, 9, 13, 17, 18, 22, 25, 27; **24:**2, 3, 5, 9, 10, 14, 18, 21; **25:**10, 24; **26:**7, 12, 16, 21, 22, 24, 26, 31, 32; **27:**21, 35; **28:**4, 9, 20^{2}, 22, 26, 27, 28; **Ro 1:**26; **3:**23, 31; **4:**9, 16; **5:**2; **7:**24; **8:**7, 18; **9:**8, 9^{2}, 20; **11:**8, 25, 27; **12:**2, 20; **13:**6, 9, 11; **14:**9; **15:**22, 27, 28; **16:**22; **1Co 1:**20; **2:**6^{2}, 8^{2}; **3:**18, 19; **4:**1, 6, 13, 14, 17; **5:**2, 5, 10; **6:**5, 11; **7:**6, 10, 17, 28, 31, 35; **8:**7, 9; **9:**3, 8, 12^{2}, 15, 16, 17, 18; **10:**28; **11:**10, 22, 24^{2}, 25^{2}, 26, 30; **12:**24; **14:**21, 38; **15:**19, 27, 34, 50, 53^{2}, 54^{2}; **16:**21; **2Co 1:**12, 15, 17, 20; **2:**6, 9, 11; **3:**14, 15, 18; **4:**1, 4, 7^{2}, 17; **5:**2, 4, 5, 18; **7:**3, 11, 13; **8:**4, 5, 6, 7, 8, 10, 19, 20; **9:**3, 4, 5, 6, 12, 13; **10:**7; **11:**6, 10, 17; **12:**8, 13, 14; **13:**1, 9; **Gal 2:**13; **3:**2, 9, 17; **4:**1, 24; **6:**2, 16; **Eph 1:**14, 15, 20, 21; **2:**2, 8; **3:**1, 5, 7, 8, 11, 14; **4:**17; **5:**5, 31, 32; **6:**1, 2, 12, 22; **Php 1:**6, 7, 9, 18, 19, 25, 28^{2}; **3:**12, 13, 15; **4:**1; **Col 1:**5, 7, 9, 23, 27, 29; **2:**4, 14; **3:**20; **4:**8, 16, 18; **1Th 2:**13; **3:**3, 5, 7; **4:**3, 6, 8, 15; **5:**18, 24, 27; **2Th 1:**5, 11; **2:**11, 14; **3:**9, 10, 14, 17^{2}; **1Ti 1:**9; **2:**3, 6, 7; **4:**10, 16; **5:**4; **6:**11; **2Ti 1:**6, 9, 11, 12; **2:**14, 19; **3:**1; **4:**10; **Tit 1:**5, 13; **3:**6; **Phm 1:**8, 9, 15, 19, 20; **Heb 2:**11; **4:**5; **5:**3, 4, 11, 12; **6:**3, 9, 19; **7:**1, 6, 11, 20, 21, 27; **8:**1, 3, 10; **9:**2, 8, 9, 11, 15, 20; **10:**16; **11:**4, 7, 12, 14; **12:**27; **13:**17, 19; **Jas 1:**19, 27; **3:**10; **4:**15; **1Pe 1:**6, 10; **2:**21; **3:**5, 9, 21; **4:**6, 16; **5:**12^{2}; **2Pe 1:**5, 10, 11, 13, 17, 18, 19, 20; **3:**1, 3, 5, 8, 11, 16; **1Jn 1:**2, 5; **2:**3, 5^{2}, 18, 22, 25; **3:**2, 3, 8, 10, 11, 16, 19, 23, 24; **4:**2, 3, 6, 9, 10, 13, 17^{2}, 21; **5:**2, 3, 4, 6, 9, 11^{2}, 14; **2Jn 1:**6^{2}, 10; **3Jn 1:**4; **Jude 1:**4; **Rev 1:**19; **2:**4, 6, 20, 24; **4:**1^{2}; **7:**1, 9, 15; **9:**17; **11:**5; **13:**18; **14:**13; **15:**5; **17:**9; **18:**1, 17; **19:**1, 9; **20:**5, 14; **21:**5; **22:**7, 9, 10, 16, 18^{2}, 19^{2}; **Tob 1:**1, 4; **2:**8, 13, 14; **3:**6; **5:**3; **6:**11, 16^{2}; **7:**11; **8:**7, 19; **11:**11; **14:**3, 5, 10; **Jdt 1:**12; **3:**5; **5:**3, 5, 20; **6:**5^{2}; **7:**10, 13; **8:**7, 11, 22; **10:**10, 19; **11:**2, 5, 14, 16, 19; **12:**6, 13; **13:**4, 14, 17, 20; **14:**1, 5, 10, 19; **15:**10, 14^{2}; **16:**21; **AdE 1:**1, 4, 5, 12, 13^{2}, 21; **2:**4, 12; **4:**14^{2}, 15; **5:**14; **7:**4, 5, 6^{2}; **9:**14, 19, 26^{4}, 31; **10:**9, 10; **11:**4, 12; **13:**1, 3, 5, 6; **13:**12^{2}, 14; **14:**11, 12; **16:**1, 15, 19, 21, 22; **Wis 2:**9^{2}; **4:**1, 18; **9:**15; **14:**21; **16:**2, 8, 18; **17:**13; **18:**19; **19:**4, 18; **Sir Pr:**T^{2}; **11:**18; **13:**23; **14:**6; **15:**1; **16:**20; **19:**1; **23:**21; **24:**23; **26:**27; **27:**7; **29:**25; **32:**23; **39:**15, 17, 21, 32, 34; **41:**4; **43:**8; **48:**15; **50:**27; **51:**12; **Bar 1:**3, 13, 14, 20; **2:**6, 11, 29; **3:**5, 35; **4:**27; **LtJ 6:**16, 23, 41, 58; **Aza 1:**5, 14; **Sus 1:**21, 22, 27, 36, 38, 40, 46, 47, 54^{2}, 55, 57, 59; **Bel 1:**7, 24; **1Mc 1:**5, 12; **2:**7, 17, 33, 41; **3:**55; **4:**1, 10, 19, 21, 31; **5:**19^{2}, 42, 46, 48; **6:**8, 13, 24, 28; **7:**3, 6, 15, 27, 35^{3}, 36, 37, 38, 42^{2}, 49; **8:**10^{2}, 14, 22; **9:**32, 34, 43, 45, 61, 63, 70; **10:**23, 30^{2}, 42; **11:**22, 23, 31, 36, 37, 42, 49, 54, 73; **12:**5, 17, 18, 19, 22; **13:**4, 20, 30^{2}, 35, 39, 52; **14:**20, 23, 24, 27, 48; **16:**2, 22; **2Mc 1:**22, 24, 26, 32, 33, 36; **2:**23, 32; **3:**9, 13, 28, 34, 40; **4:**9, 16, 20, 28, 35, 43; **5:**1, 3, 15, 17, 18, 25; **6:**1, 12, 14, 22, 28, 30, 31; **7:**7, 9, 27, 29, 42; **8:**29; **9:**17, 18; **10:**4, 11, 15; **11:**1, 16, 25; **12:**1, 3, 4, 40, 43; **13:**4, 8, 10, 17, 26; **14:**9, 11, 28, 29, 30, 33^{2}, 34, 36, 46; **15:**6, 12, 14, 16, 36, 37; **1Es 1:**10, 11, 22, 32^{2}; **2:**19, 22, 23, 24, 26; **3:**24; **4:**12, 13, 31, 46^{2}, 61; **5:**1, 63; **6:**4^{2}, 11^{2}, 17, 19, 20, 23, 27; **8:**3, 6, 22, 25, 70^{2}, 72, 76, 77, 87, 89, 93, 96; **9:**5, 11, 13, 15, 50, 53; **Pm 151:**T; **3Mc 1:**3, 7, 11, 12, 15, 16, 27^{2}; **2:**9^{2}, 10, 14, 16, 17, 19, 22, 27, 28; **3:**1, 4, 11, 22, 25; **4:**1, 12, 21; **5:**16, 17, 24, 27, 28, 35, 42, 49, 50; **6:**4, 17; **7:**4, 10; **2Es 1:**16, 18^{2}; **2:**1, 36, 39; **3:**25; **4:**2, 11, 27, 45, 49; **5:**27; **6:**9, 17, 30, 35, 55^{2}, 59; **7:**12, 38, 44, 50, 51, 72, 75, 88, 90, 99, 104, 112, 113, 116, 127, 129; **8:**1, 36, 48, 62; **9:**18, 19, 34; **10:**3, 25, 28, 37, 40, 43, 48; **11:**16^{2}, 22, 27, 32, 33; **12:**4, 8, 10^{2}, 16, 17, 19, 22, 30^{2}, 32, 35^{2}, 36, 41, 48; **13:**3, 5, 8, 12, 15, 22, 25, 26, 28, 37, 41, 51, 53^{2}; **14:**26; **15:**21; **16:**20, 36, 45; **4Mc 1:**10, 12, 17, 24; **2:**2, 16, 23; **3:**1, 6; **4:**5, 25; **5:**8, 13^{2}, 14, 26; **6:**1, 16, 30; **8:**1, 11, 19^{2}, 23^{2}; **9:**4, 8, 13, 15, 25, 28; **10:**8, 17, 19; **11:**4, 11, 15, 17, 25; **12:**2, 12, 13, 18; **13:**22; **14:**10; **15:**2, 4, 14, 24, 26; **16:**5^{2}; **17:**20, 24; **18:**1, 19

THOSE (2220)

Ge 4:20, 21; **6:**4; **7:**16, 23; **12:**3; **17:**27; **19:**25; **45:**1; **Ex 4:**19; **9:**20, 21; **12:**16; **16:**16, 18^{2}; **20:**5, 6; **23:**7, 8; **36:**8; **38:**25; **Lev 7:**20; **10:**3; **11:**4, 21, 40^{2}; **14:**42; **15:**11, 32; **22:**11; **26:**36, 39; **Nu 1:**21, 22, 23, 25, 27, 29, 31, 33, 35, 37, 39, 41, 43, 44; **2:**3, 5, 12, 27; **3:**32, 38, 49^{2}; **4:**46; **7:**2; **11:**26; **14:**6, 23, 38; **15:**33; **16:**39, 49^{2}; **19:**11, 20; **23:**8; **25:**9; **26:**7, 18, 22, 27, 34, 37, 41, 47, 50, 62, 63, 64; **27:**3; **31:**36; **32:**21; **33:**55; **Dt 4:**4; **5:**9, 10; **7:**9, 10^{2}; **13:**1, 3^{2}, 5^{2}; **14:**7; **16:**19; **17:**9; **18:**3, 9; **19:**17; **23:**2; **28:**65; **29:**3, 11^{2}, 15, 18; **32:**41, 43; **33:**11; **Jos 3:**15, 16; **4:**6, 20; **8:**25; **10:**22; **11:**10, 12, 18; **13:**2, 3^{2}, 22; **16:**9; **17:**12, 16^{2}; **18:**8; **21:**4, 40; **23:**4; **24:**17; **Jdg 2:**16, 18, 23; **3:**1, 2; **5:**14; **7:**5^{2}, 6; **14:**19; **16:**20^{2}; **17:**6; **18:**1^{2}; **19:**1; **20:**13, 27, 28, 33, 42; **21:**7, 16, 25; **Ru 4:**4; **1Sa 2:**5^{2}, 30^{2}; **3:**1; **4:**1; **5:**12; **9:**13, 22; **11:**8^{2}, 11; **14:**8, 48; **17:**28; **22:**2, 6; **24:**9; **25:**26; **28:**1; **30:**9, 27; **31:**7; **2Sa 2:**23; **5:**8, 14; **6:**13; **8:**2^{2}; **16:**2, 23; **17:**10, 12; **19:**6^{2}, 28; **20:**19; **21:**13; **22:**18, 41; **24:**9^{2}; **1Ki 2:**7; **4:**27; **14:**9; **20:**34; **21:**27; **2Ki 6:**22; **7:**13; **10:**24, 32; **11:**5, 9; **12:**15; **15:**37; **18:**4, 5; **20:**1; **21:**24; **23:**5; **1Ch 12:**1, 15, 32; **16:**10, 41; **25:**1; **27:**23, 26; **2Ch 1:**11; **2:**10; **6:**23; **9:**9; **11:**16; **14:**6, 15; **15:**5, 9; **16:**9; **17:**19; **19:**2; **20:**21; **23:**8; **24:**12, 13, 26; **25:**5; **28:**12, 15; **31:**16; **32:**13, 14, 24; **33:**25; **34:**4, 21, 22; **36:**20; **Ezr 1:**3; **2:**1, 59; **5:**9; **7:**25; **8:**1, 13, 35; **10:**3; **Ne 1:**2, 5; **5:**2, 3, 4, 17; **6:**17; **7:**5, 6, 61, 64; **8:**3, 10, 17; **9:**2; **11:**2; **12:**38, 40; **13:**3, 15, 23; **Est 1:**2, 14; **2:**21; **3:**8, 9; **9:**2, 5, 11, 16; **Job 3:**8^{2}; **4:**4, 8, 19; **5:**11^{2}; **6:**14; **7:**9; **8:**22; **11:**11; **12:**5^{2}, 6, 20; **15:**10, 14; **17:**5; **18:**20, 21; **19:**19; **20:**7; **21:**22, 29, 33; **22:**30; **24:**1, 9, 13, 19; **27:**15; **30:**1, 25, 31; **31:**29, 31; **33:**22; **34:**30, 34, 36; **Ps 1:**1; **5:**6, 11; **9:**10^{2}, 13; **10:**3, 18; **12:**4; **15:**2, 4, 5; **16:**4; **17:**7; **18:**17, 40; **21:**8; **22:**25, 26; **24:**1, 4, 6; **25:**3, 10, 14; **26:**10; **28:**1, 3; **30:**3; **31:**6, 11, 19^{2}; **32:**1, 2, 10; **33:**18^{2}; **34:**7, 8, 9, 10, 21, 22; **35:**1^{2}, 10^{2}, 19, 20, 26^{2}, 27; **36:**10; **37:**7^{2}, 9, 14, 22^{2}; **38:**12^{2}, 16, 19^{2}, 20; **40:**4^{2}, 14^{2}, 15, 16; **41:**1; **43:**1; **44:**7, 13; **49:**6, 13; **50:**23^{2}; **53:**4; **57:**3; **59:**1, 2, 5; **60:**4, 5;

61:5; 62:9[2]; 63:9; 65:4, 8; 66:14; 68:1, 11, 18, 21, 30; 69:4[2], 6[2], 9, 12, 26[2], 36; 70:2[2], 3, 4; 71:10, 13, 24; 72:12; 73:1, 27[2]; 79:4, 11; 81:15; 83:2, 3; 84:4, 5, 11; 85:8, 9; 86:17; 87:4; 88:4[2], 5[2]; 89:23; 91:14[2]; 94:12, 20; 97:7, 10; 98:7; 99:6; 101:3; 102:8, 20; 103:11, 13, 17, 18; 105:3; 106:3, 41; 107:2, 43; 108:6; 109:20, 31; 111:5, 10; 112:1, 5; 115:8, 13; 118:4, 7; 119:1, 2, 38, 42, 53, 63, 74, 79, 84, 132, 150, 165; 120:6; 123:4; 125:1, 4[2], 5; 126:1, 5, 6; 127:1; 129:8; 130:6[2]; 135:18; 139:20, 21[2]; 140:1, 9; 141:4, 6; 143:3, 7; 146:5, 8; 147:11[2]; Pr 1:12, 33; 2:7, 12, 15, 19; 3:13[2], 18[2], 27; 4:22; 7:26; 8:9, 17[2], 21, 32, 36; 9:4, 15, 16; 11:17, 18, 20, 21, 26[2], 28, 29; 12:1, 2, 11[2], 20[2], 22; 13:3[2], 10, 11, 13[2], 24[2]; 14:2, 21[2], 22, 31[2]; 15:18[2], 27[2], 32[2]; 16:5, 13, 17, 20[2]; 17:5[2], 8; 18:21; 19:11, 16[2], 26; 22:9, 11, 21, 23, 24, 26, 29; 23:30[2]; 24:5[2], 11[2], 25; 25:13; 28:4[2], 5, 7, 10, 26[2]; 29:18; 30:5, 11, 12, 13, 14; 31:3, 6, 8; Ecc 1:11, 18; 2:18; 4:16[2]; 5:11, 14; 6:2, 10; 7:11; 8:8, 12, 17; 9:2[4]; 11:8; 12:3; SS 5:7; Isa 1:27, 28; 6:4; 8:20; 9:1, 2, 16[2]; 10:10, 13; 14:2[2], 16, 19; 15:9; 16:14; 17:14[2]; 19:8[2], 9, 13; 20:6; 23:18; 24:9; 26:3, 19; 27:7, 13[2]; 28:1[2], 4, 6, 9[2], 24; 29:11, 12, 20, 21, 24[2]; 30:18; 31:1, 2; 32:3[2], 8; 33:15; 35:4; 38:1, 18; 40:31; 41:11, 12[2]; 42:5, 7, 17; 45:20; 46:6; 47:13[2], 15; 49:9, 17, 19, 23, 25; 50:4, 6[2]; 51:6; 56:8; 57:2, 15; 59:10, 19[2], 20; 60:6, 12, 14; 61:3; 62:9[2]; 63:19[2]; 64:4, 5[2]; 65:1[2]; 66:16, 17; Jer 2:8, 37; 3:16, 18; 5:7, 18; 6:15; 8:12, 16; 9:24, 25, 26; 12:4; 13:20, 21[2]; 14:15, 18[2]; 15:2[4]; 17:5, 7, 13; 19:7, 9, 10; 21:7[2], 9[2]; 22:25[2]; 23:17, 26, 32; 24:8; 25:30, 33; 26:20; 30:16; 31:8[2], 24, 29, 33; 33:5, 11, 15, 16; 34:18, 20, 21; 38:2[2]; 39:9, 17; 40:7; 41:9; 43:11[3]; 44:9, 13, 28, 30; 46:14, 22, 25, 26; 47:2; 48:35; 49:2, 12, 32, 37; 50:4, 20; 52:19[2]; La 1:10, 14; 2:22; 3:25, 52; 4:5[2], 9[2]; Eze 3:18, 27[2]; 6:9, 12[2]; 7:15[2]; 9:4; 11:15, 21; 12:4, 19; 13:2, 11, 15[2]; 14:4[2], 7; 16:37[2], 57; 20:38; 21:29, 31; 22:5[2], 9[2]; 23:11, 20, 28[2]; 26:10, 20[2]; 28:9[2]; 30:6; 31:14, 16, 17[2], 18; 32:18, 20, 24, 25, 28, 29[2], 30[2], 32; 33:27[3]; 34:27; 35:8; 38:17; 39:6, 9, 10[2]; 40:21, 22; 42:8; 44:5[2]; 46:24; Da 2:21, 44; 3:13, 27; 4:19, 37; 5:19[4]; 6:24; 9:4, 7[2]; 10:14; 11:6, 14, 26, 30, 32, 39; 12:2, 3[2], 10, 12; Hos 5:10; 11:4; 14:9[2]; Joel 2:11, 29, 32[2]; 3:1; Am 2:15[3], 16; 3:10; 5:16; 6:1[2], 4; 8:14; 9:1; Ob 1:7, 17[2], 19[2], 21; Jnh 2:8; Mic 2:1, 8; 3:5; 4:6[2], 7; Na 1:7; Hab 1:13; 2:7; Zep 1:5[2], 6, 12; Zec 1:10; 3:4, 7; 6:8, 15; 8:10[2], 23; 11:5[2], 9; 14:3, 15; Mal 1:8; 3:5[3], 16[2]; Mt 2:20; 3:1; 4:16, 24; 5:4, 6, 10, 21, 33, 44, 46; 7:11; 8:10; 9:12[2]; 10:25, 28, 39[2]; 11:8, 11; 13:12[2]; 14:21, 33; 15:38; 16:25[2]; 19:11, 13; 20:9, 23; 21:12, 40, 41; 22:3, 4, 7, 8, 10; 23:31, 37; 24:16, 19[3], 22[2], 29, 38; 25:7, 10, 19, 29[2], 34, 41; 26:51, 57; 27:39, 54; Mk 1:9; 2:17[2]; 3:13, 34; 4:10, 11, 18, 25[2]; 5:16, 40; 6:44; 8:1, 35[2], 38; 10:23, 32, 40, 42; 11:9[2], 15[3]; 12:7, 43; 13:14, 17[3], 19, 20[2], 24; 14:47; 15:29, 32; 16:10, 14, 17, 99; Lk 1:2, 24, 39, 50, 79; 2:1, 14; 4:2, 40; 5:31[2], 35; 6:12, 18, 27, 28[2], 32[2], 33, 34; 7:10, 25, 28, 49; 8:12, 13, 16, 18[2], 21, 36; 9:11, 24[2], 26, 36, 61; 11:13, 28, 33, 41, 52; 12:4, 21, 36, 37, 38; 13:4, 14, 34; 14:11, 17, 24; 16:15, 26; 17:33[2]; 18:24, 26, 39; 19:26[2], 32, 45; 20:16, 27, 34, 35; 21:21[3], 23[3]; 22:25, 28, 49; 24:24; Jn 1:22; 2:16; 3:18[2], 21; 4:14, 24; 5:25, 29[2]; 6:11, 13, 54, 56; 7:18; 9:8, 39[2]; 10:35; 11:9, 10, 25; 12:2, 20, 25[2]; 14:21[2], 23; 15:5; 16:2; 17:6, 9, 20, 24; 18:9, 21; 20:29; Ac 1:15, 16; 2:18, 23, 41, 47; 3:2, 24; 4:4, 32; 5:9, 16, 21, 32; 6:1, 9[2]; 7:52; 8:4; 9:21; 10:7; 11:19; 13:27, 31, 39; 15:19, 21, 33; 16:3, 35; 17:11, 15, 17; 18:27; 19:13, 18, 19; 20:2; 22:5, 9, 11, 19, 20, 29; 23:2, 4; 25:5; 26:16, 18, 20, 30; 27:24, 43; Ro 1:18, 32; 2:2, 3, 7, 8, 19, 26, 27; 3:19; 4:6, 7, 16; 5:14, 17; 6:13, 21; 7:1; 8:1, 5[2], 8, 28, 29, 30[3]; 9:25; 10:15, 19, 20[2]; 11:22, 23; 12:14, 15[2]; 13:1, 2; 14:1, 3[4], 6[3], 22, 23; 15:3, 21[2]; 16:10, 11, 12, 17; 1Co 1:2[2], 18, 21, 24; 2:9, 13, 14, 15; 5:12[2], 13; 6:4; 7:28, 29, 30[3], 31; 8:11; 9:3, 13[2], 14, 20[2], 21[2]; 10:18; 11:22; 12:23; 14:2, 3, 4[2]; 15:18, 20, 23, 29, 48[2]; 2Co 1:4; 2:3, 15[2]; 4:3; 5:12, 15; 10:2, 12, 18[2]; 11:12; 12:17; 13:2; Gal 1:17; 2:6[2]; 3:7, 9, 22; 4:5; 5:12, 21, 24; 6:3, 6, 10, 12, 16; Eph 2:2, 11, 17; 4:29; 5:6; Php 2:21, 30; 3:2, 15, 17; 4:22; Col 2:1; 3:6; 4:13; 1Th 1:9; 4:13, 14, 15; 5:7[2], 12; 2Th 1:6, 8[2]; 2:10; 3:14; 1Ti 1:9, 16; 3:13; 4:3, 10; 5:16, 17, 20; 6:2[2], 5, 9, 17; 2Ti 2:14, 19, 22; 3:6, 9; Tit 1:9, 10, 14; 3:8, 15; Heb 1:14; 2:3, 11, 15, 18; 3:16, 17, 18; 4:2, 6, 10; 5:3, 14; 6:4, 7, 12; 7:5, 8, 25, 27, 28; 8:10; 9:13, 15, 28; 10:1, 14, 16, 29, 32, 33, 34, 39[2]; 11:6, 31; 12:6, 11; 13:3[2], 7, 9, 10, 11, 24; Jas 1:12, 23, 25; 2:5, 12; 3:9, 18; 4:1; 5:11; 1Pe 1:12; 2:7, 14[2], 18[2]; 3:10, 12, 16; 4:17, 19; 5:3; 2Pe 1:1; 2:10, 12, 18; 1Jn 2:15, 17, 26; 3:9, 10; 4:15, 16, 20[2], 21; 5:10[2], 16, 18; 2Jn 1:7[2]; 3Jn 1:10[2]; Jude 1:5, 10; Rev 1:3, 7; 2:2, 9, 22; 3:9, 19; 6:9; 7:4; 9:4, 6; 11:1, 11, 18; 12:12, 17; 13:6, 15; 14:6, 9, 11, 12; 15:2; 16:2; 17:14; 19:9, 20[2]; 20:4[2], 6; 21:7, 27; 22:9, 14; Tob 1:16, 18; 3:3; 4:6[2], 14; 10:12; 12:9, 10; 13:10[2], 14[2]; 14:7[3], 15; Jdt 1:1, 6, 7, 8; 2:11, 28[2]; 6:15, 19; 8:1, 3, 22, 27; 9:2, 5[3], 11, 13; 11:22; 13:19; 14:7; 15:3, 5, 13; 16:15, 24; AdE 1:2; 2:6, 18; 3:8; 9:11, 19; 10:8; 11:11; 13:4, 6, 7, 17; 14:9, 13; 16:1, 4, 5, 7, 20, 23; Wis 1:2[2], 8; 2:24; 3:9, 10, 11; 5:1[2], 9; 6:5, 10, 12[2], 13, 16; 7:14; 8:13; 9:18; 10:9, 12, 14, 21; 12:2, 3, 14, 17, 20, 23, 24, 26, 27; 13:10; 14:18, 31; 15:6, 7; 16:1, 3, 4, 24, 25, 26; 17:8, 21; 18:4; 19:3, 8, 16, 17; Sir Pr:T[3]; 1:10, 13, 19, 23; 2:5, 15[2], 16[2], 17; 3:3, 4[2], 5, 6[2], 17, 31; 4:11, 12, 14[2], 15; 6:4, 6, 16, 17; 7:34[2]; 9:13; 10:18, 19[2], 20, 29[2]; 11:11; 12:13; 13:12, 16; 14:1, 2; 15:13, 19; 16:9; 17:24[2], 28, 29; 18:14, 29; 20:16, 28[2], 31[2]; 21:6[2]; 23:15, 27; 24:21[2], 22; 25:14; 27:1, 9, 22, 29; 28:9, 16, 23; 29:4; 30:25; 31:7; 32:14, 16; 34:7, 14, 16, 19; 36:11, 20, 21; 37:10; 38:27; 41:3[2], 15[2], 20; 43:24; 44:3[3], 4, 5; 46:12; 48:11; 50:26, 28[2]; 51:3, 8; Bar 2:7, 14; 3:4, 11, 16, 17, 18; 4:1, 31; LtJ 6:1, 18, 26, 39, 46, 47; Aza 1:17, 25; Sus 1:33, 60; Bel 1:38, 42; 1Mc 1:11, 58, 61; 2:1, 18, 31, 61; 3:5[2], 9, 31, 48, 56; 4:8, 15, 26, 33, 35, 41; 5:62; 6:28, 53; 7:23, 24[2], 25; 8:1, 7, 12, 13[2]; 9:8, 16, 24, 29, 44; 10:7, 9, 11, 84, 85[2], 87; 11:4, 20, 34; 12:34; 13:43, 48, 49; 14:13, 34, 36; 15:4[2], 19; 2Mc 1:1, 7, 12, 17, 27[2], 28, 35; 2:1, 2, 6, 21, 24, 25[2]; 3:12, 15, 17, 22, 39; 4:16, 19, 47, 48, 50; 5:12, 17, 26; 6:9, 12, 21, 29; 7:12; 8:1, 13, 14, 18, 25, 28, 30, 33; 9:4; 10:15, 17, 20[2]; 11:30; 12:6, 14, 19, 28, 42, 44, 45; 13:9, 10; 14:6, 8; 15:19, 21, 31, 39; 1Es 1:24; 2:16; 4:6, 19, 48; 5:9, 18[3], 19[2], 20, 21[2], 36, 41, 67, 72; 6:12, 27, 28; 7:6, 13; 8:10[2], 23[2], 52, 65; 9:4, 12, 15, 18, 51, 54; Man 1:7, 13; 3Mc 1:1, 12, 17, 19, 21, 27; 2:3, 4, 5, 7, 20, 28[2], 29, 30, 33; 3:1[2], 6, 16, 23, 25, 27, 28; 4:11; 5:3, 16, 21, 22, 23, 24, 25, 26, 31, 34; 7:10, 11, 12, 16, 22; 2Es 1:35; 2:9, 38, 39, 47; 3:2, 12, 28, 30[2], 31, 34; 4:6, 21, 23, 36, 39, 42, 51[2]; 5:1, 6, 29[2], 36, 41[3], 42[2], 43[3], 44, 48, 52[2], 53[2], 54, 55; 6:5[2], 24, 26; 7:5, 14, 18, 21, 28[2], 29, 32[2], 45, 46, 57[2], 61, 72, 74, 75, 76[2], 79[2], 83, 88, 99, 103, 108, 109, 112, 122, 125, 131, 132, 133, 134, 136[3], 137, 138, 139; 8:26, 27[2], 28[2], 29[2], 30[2], 35[2], 36, 38, 41, 46[2], 50, 51, 55, 60; 9:9[2], 13, 15, 18, 19, 20, 33, 44; 10:23, 59[2]; 11:5, 31, 42[3]; 12:34, 45, 51; 13:16[3], 17, 19, 22[2], 23, 24[2], 26, 29, 30, 48, 52; 14:9, 13, 16, 20, 22; 15:3, 14, 22, 24, 37, 41, 45[2], 58; 16:17, 22[2], 28, 30, 31[2], 44[4], 45, 47, 63, 69, 70, 71, 77; 4Mc 1:3, 4, 6, 8, 10; 3:1; 4:7; 7:8; 8:6[2]; 9:10[2]; 10:2, 16, 18; 11:23, 27; 12:11; 13:5, 6, 15, 18, 27; 14:6, 19; 16:25; 17:7, 22; 18:2, 3, 16, 20

TO (25824)

Ge 1:14, 15, 16[2], 17, 18[2], 26, 28, 30[3]; 2:5[2], 9[2], 10, 15, 19[2], 20[3], 21, 22, 24; 3:1, 2, 4, 6[4], 9[2], 11, 12, 13, 14, 16, 17[2], 19[2], 23, 24[2]; 4:3, 6, 8[2], 9, 10, 11, 12, 13, 15, 18, 23[2], 26[2]; 5:3; 6:1[2], 4[2], 6, 13[3], 15, 16, 17[2], 19, 20[5]; 7:1, 3, 7; 8:4, 5, 7, 8, 9[3], 11, 12, 15, 20; 9:1, 8[2], 11, 15, 17, 20, 24, 25; 10:1, 8, 21, 25, 32; 11:3, 5, 6, 31[2]; 12:1[2], 5[3], 6[2], 7[4], 8[2], 10[2], 11[2], 15, 18; 13:3, 4, 8, 9[2], 14, 15[2], 17, 18; 14:7, 10, 15, 17, 21, 22[2]; 15:1, 3, 4, 5[2], 6, 7[3], 8, 9, 13, 15, 18[2]; 16:2[3], 3, 4, 5[3], 6[2], 7, 9[3], 10, 11[2], 13; 17:1[2], 3, 7[3], 8[2], 9, 15, 16, 17[2], 18, 21, 23; 18:1, 2[2], 5, 6, 7[3], 9, 10, 11, 12, 13, 14, 16, 17, 19, 21[2], 25[2], 27[2], 29, 31[2], 33[2]; 19:1[3], 2, 3, 4, 5[3], 6, 8[3], 9, 11, 12, 13[2], 14[3], 16, 17, 18, 19, 20[2], 21, 23, 27, 30, 31[3], 34, 37, 38; 20:3[3], 5, 6, 9[4], 10, 13[3], 14[2], 16, 17; 21:2, 3, 5, 7, 9, 10, 11, 12[2], 14, 17[2], 22, 23, 25, 27, 29, 32; 22:1, 2, 3, 5[2], 7, 9, 10, 11, 12, 14, 15, 19[2], 20, 23; 23:2[3], 3, 7, 8, 9, 11, 13[2], 15, 16, 17, 18, 28; 24:2, 4[2], 5[4], 6[2], 7[3], 8, 9, 10[2], 11, 12, 13, 14[2], 15, 16[2], 17, 20[2], 21, 23, 24[2], 25, 27, 29[2], 30[2], 32, 33, 36, 38[2], 39, 40, 41[2], 42, 43[3], 44, 45[2], 47, 48, 49[2], 50, 52, 53[3], 54, 56[2], 58, 60, 63, 65[2]; 25:5, 6[2], 8, 12, 16, 17, 18, 21, 22[2], 23, 24, 30, 32[3], 33[2]; 26:1[2], 2[2], 3[3], 4, 7, 9, 10, 11, 16, 23, 24, 26, 27[2], 29, 32, 33; 27:1, 3, 4[2], 5[3], 6[2], 7, 9, 10[2], 11, 12, 13, 14, 17, 18, 19, 20, 21[2], 22, 25[2], 26, 29[2], 31[2], 32, 33, 34, 38, 41, 42[3], 43, 45, 46[2]; 28:2[2], 4[2], 5[2], 6[2], 7, 9[3], 11, 12, 13[2], 14[4], 15, 20[2], 21, 22; 29:1, 4, 5, 6, 7, 13[2], 14, 15, 19[2], 20, 21[2], 23[2], 24[2], 25[2], 29[2], 30, 34; 30:1, 3, 4, 9, 14[2], 15, 16[2], 18, 24, 25[2], 27[2], 29, 33, 38[2]; 31:1, 3[3], 5, 7, 9, 11, 12, 13[2], 14, 16[3], 18[2], 19, 20, 24[3], 26, 28, 29[3], 30, 35, 36, 39, 43, 46, 50, 51, 52[2], 54; 32:3, 4, 5, 6[3], 8, 9[3], 10, 16, 17, 18[2], 19, 27, 30, 32; 33:3, 4, 8, 10, 11, 13[2], 14[3], 15, 16, 17, 18; 34:1[2], 3[2], 4[2], 6[2], 7, 8, 9, 10, 11[3], 12, 14[4], 15, 16, 17, 19, 20[2], 22[3], 30[2]; 35:1[4], 2[2], 3[3], 4, 6, 7, 9, 10, 11, 12[3], 17, 19, 20, 26, 27, 29; 36:4, 5, 6, 7, 12, 14, 40, 43; 37:2[2], 4, 5, 6[2], 7, 8[3], 9[2], 10[4], 12, 13[2], 14[3], 17, 18[2], 19, 22[2], 23, 25[3], 26, 27, 28[2], 29, 30, 32, 33, 35[4], 36; 38:2, 7, 8[3], 9[2], 10, 11[2], 12[2], 13[2], 14[3], 15, 16[3], 18[2], 20, 22, 25, 26; 39:1, 3, 8, 10[3], 11, 14[3], 17[2], 19, 22, 23; 40:6, 8[3], 9[2], 12, 13[2], 14[2], 16, 21, 22; 41:8, 9, 12[3], 13[2], 15, 17, 24[2], 25[3], 28[2], 34, 36, 38, 39, 40, 41, 44, 50, 53, 54, 55[4], 56, 57[2]; 42:1, 3, 4, 5, 6[2], 7[2], 9[2], 10[2], 12[2], 14[2], 18, 20[2], 21[2], 22, 24, 25[4], 27, 28[3], 29[2], 30, 31, 33, 34[2], 36[2], 37[3], 38[3]; 43:2, 3, 5, 6, 7, 8, 9, 11[2], 13, 15, 16[2], 17, 18[3], 19[2], 20, 21, 22, 23, 26, 29[2], 30, 32, 33[2], 34; 44:4[2], 6, 7, 8, 11, 13, 14[2], 15, 16, 17, 18, 20, 21[2], 22, 23, 24, 27, 28, 29[2], 30, 31, 32[2], 33, 34[2]; 45:1, 3, 4[2], 5, 7[2], 8, 9[3], 11[2], 12, 17[3], 18, 19, 20, 21, 22[2], 23, 24, 25, 27[2]; 46:1[2], 2, 3[2], 4, 5, 8, 15, 18[2], 20[2], 22, 25[2], 26, 27, 28[3], 29[2], 30, 31[4], 34; 47:2, 3[2], 4[2], 5[2], 8, 9, 12, 14, 15, 17, 18[2], 19, 21, 23, 24, 25, 26, 29[2], 31[2]; 48:2, 3[2], 4[3], 5[2], 6[2], 7[3], 9[2], 11[2], 12, 15, 17[2], 18, 21[3], 22[2]; 49:1[2], 2, 6, 10, 11[2], 15, 28, 29[3], 33[2]; 50:2, 4, 5, 6, 7, 10, 13, 14[2], 15, 17[2], 19, 20[3], 21, 24[2], 25; Ex 1:1, 5, 9, 11, 12, 15, 16, 18[2], 19[2], 22; 2:4[2], 5[2], 7[2], 8, 9, 10, 11, 13, 14, 15, 16[2], 17, 18, 20[2], 21, 23; 3:1, 2, 4[2], 6, 8[4], 9, 10[2], 11[2], 13[3], 14[3], 15[3], 16[3], 17, 18[4]; 4:1[2], 2, 4, 5, 6, 10[2], 11[2], 12, 14, 15, 16, 18[4], 19[2], 20, 21[2], 22, 23[2], 24, 25, 27[2], 30, 31; 5:1[2], 3[3], 4[2], 5, 7, 8, 9, 10, 12, 15, 16[3], 17, 20, 21[2], 22, 23[3]; 6:1[2], 2[2], 3[2], 4, 6[2], 8[3], 9[2], 10, 11, 12[3], 13[2], 16, 19, 26, 27[2], 28, 29[2], 30; 7:1[2], 2, 4, 7, 8, 9[2], 10, 13, 14[2], 15[3], 16[3], 17, 18, 19[2], 22, 23, 24[2]; 8:1[3], 2, 5[2], 8[4], 9[2], 12, 15, 16[2], 18, 19[2], 20[3], 25, 26[4], 27, 28[2], 29[3], 30; 9:1[3], 2, 3[4], 4, 5, 6, 7[2], 8[3], 9, 10, 12, 17, 18, 21, 25[2], 26[2], 27, 28; 11:1, 2[2], 5, 8[2], 9[2]; 12:1, 3, 4, 14, 21, 23[3], 25, 27, 29, 33, 37, 42[2], 43, 48[3]; 13:1, 2[2], 3, 5[2], 6, 10, 11[2], 12, 15[3], 17, 21[2]; 14:1, 2, 10, 11[3], 12[2], 13, 14, 15[3], 26, 27; 15:1[2], 13, 21[2], 22, 23, 25[2], 26[2], 27; 16:1, 3[2], 4[2], 6, 8, 9[3], 10, 11, 12, 15[3], 16[2], 19, 20, 23[5], 25, 27, 28[2], 33[2], 35[2]; 17:1, 2[2], 3, 4[2], 5, 9, 10, 14, 16; 18:5, 6[2], 7, 8[2], 9, 12[2], 15[3], 16[2], 17, 19, 20[3], 22, 23[2], 24, 26, 27; 19:3[3], 4[2], 6, 8, 9[4], 10[2], 12[3], 14, 15, 17, 20[2], 21[4], 23[3], 24[3], 25; 20:5[2], 6, 10, 17, 19[3], 20[3], 21, 22[2], 24[2], 26; 21:6, 8[2], 10, 12, 13, 15, 16, 17, 18, 19[2], 26, 27, 28, 29[2], 31, 32, 34, 36; 22:1, 2, 5[2], 7, 8, 9, 10, 12, 16, 17[3], 18, 19, 20[2], 23, 25[2], 27[2], 29[2], 30, 31[2]; 23:1, 2, 3, 5, 6, 13[2], 20[4], 21[2], 22[3], 23, 24, 27, 31[3], 33; 24:1[2], 4, 5, 12[2], 14[3], 16; 25:1, 2, 7, 14, 20, 22, 26, 27, 29, 37, 40; 26:3[2], 6, 13, 17, 28, 29, 30; 27:3, 13, 20[2], 21[2]; 28:1[2], 3[2], 4, 7, 14, 21, 25[2], 26, 27, 28, 36, 42[2], 43; 29:1[2], 4, 18[2], 25, 27, 28, 29, 30, 33, 35[2], 36, 41, 42[2], 44; 30:1, 4, 10, 11, 12[3], 13[2], 15[2], 16, 17, 20[3], 22, 31, 32, 34, 37[2], 38; 31:1, 4[2], 6, 12, 13[2], 14, 15[2]; 32:1[2], 2[2], 3, 5, 6[2], 7, 8[2], 9, 12[2], 13[3], 14, 17, 20, 21[2], 23, 24[2], 25, 26, 27[2], 30[2], 31, 33, 34[2]; 33:1[4], 3, 5[4], 7[2], 8, 11[5], 12[2], 15, 17, 19; 34:1, 2[2], 6, 7, 12[2], 15[2], 16[2], 24, 26, 27, 30, 31[2], 34, 35; 35:1[2], 2[2], 4, 5, 9, 21, 22, 26, 27, 29[3], 30, 32[2], 34, 35; 36:1[3], 2[3], 5[2], 6, 7, 10[2], 13, 18, 33[2], 34, 37; 37:5, 13, 14, 15, 16[2], 27[2]; 38:5, 7, 8, 13, 18[2]; 39:3, 4, 6, 7, 14, 18[2], 19, 20, 21, 30, 31[2], 33, 41; 40:1, 12, 15[2], 35; Lev 1:1, 2[3], 3, 9, 13, 14, 15, 17; 2:1, 2[2], 3, 8[3], 9, 10, 11[2], 12, 14, 15, 16; 3:5, 6, 9[2], 11, 14; 4:1, 2[2], 3, 4, 12[2], 13, 22, 23, 27, 28, 31, 35; 5:1[3], 3, 4, 6, 7, 8, 10, 12[2], 14, 15, 16[2], 17[2], 18; 6:1, 4, 5[2], 6[2], 8, 10[2], 11, 12, 15, 19, 20, 21, 22, 24, 25; 7:5, 9, 10, 11, 14[2], 18, 22, 23, 24, 25, 28, 29[3], 31, 32, 34[2], 35[4], 36, 38[2]; 8:1, 5[2], 7, 11, 12, 15, 21, 28, 31, 33, 34[2]; 9:2, 3, 4[2], 5, 6[2], 7[2], 8, 9, 16, 17, 23; 10:3, 4[2], 6[2], 8, 10, 11[2], 12[2], 13, 14, 15[2], 17[2], 19[2]; 11:1[2], 2, 10, 12, 20, 21, 22[4], 23, 29, 45, 46, 47; 12:1, 2, 6; 13:1, 2[3], 3, 7, 9, 12, 16, 19, 32, 34, 49, 54, 59; 14:1, 2, 4, 7, 8, 11, 13, 14, 17, 18, 19[2], 21[2], 23[2], 25, 28, 29[2], 33, 35[2], 36[2], 37, 38, 45, 57; 15:1, 2[2], 14[2], 29[2]; 16:1, 2[2], 4, 10[2], 17, 18, 22, 27, 29, 30, 31, 34; 17:1, 2[3], 4[3], 5[3], 6, 7[2], 8, 9[3], 11, 12, 14; 18:1, 2[2], 3, 6, 17, 18, 19, 21[2], 23[2], 30[2]; 19:1, 2[2], 4, 5, 8[2], 9, 11, 15[2], 20, 21, 23, 31[2], 32, 34; 20:1, 2[4], 3, 4[3], 5, 6[2], 9, 10, 11, 12, 13, 14, 15, 16, 17, 19[2], 20, 22[2], 24[3], 25, 26[2], 27[2]; 21:1[3], 3, 6, 7, 8, 9, 10, 16, 17[2], 21[2], 24[3]; 22:1, 2[2], 3[2], 13, 14[2], 15, 16, 17, 18[3], 19, 21[2], 22[2], 24, 25[2], 26, 29, 33; 23:1, 2[2], 3, 5, 6, 9, 10[3], 12, 13, 16, 17, 18[2], 20, 22, 23, 24, 26, 28, 32[2], 33, 34[2], 37, 38, 41, 44; 24:1, 2, 3[2], 7[2], 9, 11, 12, 13, 15, 16[2], 17, 20, 21, 23[2]; 25:1, 2[2], 10[3], 12, 13, 14, 16, 26[2], 27[2], 28, 30, 32, 33, 38[2], 39, 41[2], 46, 47[2], 50[2], 51, 52, 55; 26:1, 5, 7, 8[2], 10[2], 13, 16[2], 18, 20, 21[2], 23[2], 24, 27, 28, 32, 36, 37[2], 40, 41, 43, 44, 45; 27:1, 2[3], 3, 5, 6, 8, 9[2], 11, 12, 13[2], 14, 15[3], 16[2], 18, 19[3], 20, 21, 22, 23[2], 24, 26, 28[2], 29[2], 30, 31[2], 32, 34; Nu 1:1, 2, 3[2], 18, 20[3], 22[3], 24[3], 26[3], 28[3], 30[3], 32[3], 34[3], 36[3], 38[3], 40[3], 42[3], 45[2], 48, 50[2], 51[3]; 2:1, 3, 5[2], 12[2], 20, 27[2], 34; 3:3, 5, 8, 9[2], 10[2], 11, 14, 16, 21, 23, 25, 26, 27, 28, 29, 31[2], 32[2], 33, 35, 36[3], 38[4], 40, 44, 48, 51[2]; 4:1, 3[3], 4, 5, 15[2], 17, 19[2], 20, 21, 23[2], 26[2], 27[4], 28[2], 30[2], 31, 32, 33, 35[2], 37, 39[2], 41, 43[2], 45, 47[3], 49[2]; 5:1, 2, 4, 5, 6, 7[2], 8[3], 9, 10, 11, 12[3], 15[2], 19[2], 21, 25, 27, 28, 30; 6:1, 2[4], 5, 6, 7, 8, 10, 12, 13, 14, 17, 21, 22, 23[2], 25[2]; 7:4, 5[3], 6, 7[2], 8[2], 9[2], 11, 13, 19, 25, 31, 37, 43, 49, 55, 61, 67, 73, 79, 85, 86, 89[3]; 8:1, 2[2], 3, 4[2], 5, 7[2], 12[2], 13, 15, 16, 19[4], 21, 22, 23, 24[2]; 9:1, 3, 7, 8, 9, 10[2], 12, 14[4], 20[2]; 10:1, 6[2], 7, 9, 29[3], 30[3], 33, 36; 11:2[2], 4, 5, 6, 11, 12[4], 13[3], 14, 15[2], 16[3], 18[2], 20, 22[2], 23, 25, 26, 29, 30, 35; 12:4[2], 6[2], 8[2], 11, 13, 14; 13:1, 2[2], 3, 16[2], 17[2], 21, 22, 23, 26[4], 27[2], 30, 32, 33[2]; 14:2, 3[3], 4[2], 7, 8, 10[2], 11[2], 13, 14, 16[2], 18[2], 19, 23[2], 25, 26[2], 28[2], 30, 34, 35[2], 36, 38, 39, 40[2], 41, 44[2]; 15:1, 2[3], 3[3], 4, 7, 8[2], 10, 12, 13, 14[2], 17, 18[3], 19, 21, 22[2], 24[2], 25, 28, 33[2], 34, 35[2], 36, 37, 38[3], 40, 41; 16:3, 5[3], 8, 9[4], 10, 13, 15[2], 16, 19, 20[2], 23, 24, 25, 26, 28, 30, 32, 33, 36, 37, 38, 40[4], 43, 44, 46[2], 50; 17:1, 2, 5, 6[2], 9, 10[3], 12, 13; 18:1, 2, 4[2], 6[2], 7, 8[3], 9[2], 10, 11, 12[3], 13, 15, 16, 17, 19[2], 20, 21, 24[2], 25, 26[2], 27, 28[2], 29[3], 30[2]; 19:1, 2, 3; 20:4, 5[3], 6[2], 7, 8, 10, 12[2], 14, 15, 16, 17[2], 18, 19, 21, 22, 23, 24[2], 26; 21:2, 3, 4[2], 5, 7[3], 8, 15, 16[2], 17, 18, 19[2], 20, 21, 23[2], 24[3], 27, 29[2], 30[2], 32, 33[2], 34[3]; 22:2, 4, 5[2], 6, 7, 8[3], 9, 10, 11, 12, 13[3], 14[2], 16[3], 17, 18[3], 19, 20[4], 23, 26[3], 28[2], 29, 30[2], 32, 34[3], 35[2], 36, 37[4], 38[3], 39, 40[2], 41; 23:1, 3[3], 4, 5, 6, 11[3], 12, 13[2], 14[2], 15, 16, 17[2], 18, 20, 25, 27[3], 28, 29; 24:1[2], 10[2], 12[2], 13[3], 20, 25; 25:1, 2[2], 3, 4, 5[2], 10, 14, 16; 26:1[2], 2[2], 35, 52, 53[2], 54[3], 55, 56, 59[2], 60, 62; 27:4, 6, 7, 8[2], 9, 10, 11, 12[2], 13, 15, 18; 28:1, 2[3], 3[2], 6, 7, 8, 10, 11, 13, 15[2], 16, 19, 22, 23[2], 24[2], 26, 27, 30, 31; 29:1, 2, 5, 6[3], 8, 11, 12, 13, 16, 19, 22, 25, 28, 31, 36, 38, 39[2]; 30:1, 2[3], 3, 4, 5[2], 7, 8, 11[2], 13[2], 14[3]; 31:1, 2, 3[2], 4, 6, 8, 12[3], 13, 15[2], 21[2], 25, 27, 28, 29[2], 30, 36, 41, 47, 49, 50, 52; 32:2[3], 5, 6[3], 8, 9, 11[4], 14, 16, 17, 18, 19[2], 20[2], 22[2], 25, 27, 28[3], 29, 31, 33[4], 38, 39, 40; 33:2, 7, 9, 14, 50, 51[2], 53, 54[5], 56[3]; 34:1, 2[2], 4[3], 5, 7, 8, 9, 10, 11, 12, 13[3], 16, 17, 18, 29; 35:1, 2[3], 3, 4, 5, 6[3], 7, 8[2], 9, 10[2], 11, 14, 16, 17, 18, 19, 21[2], 25, 30[2], 31[2], 32[3]; 36:2[4], 3, 4, 5, 7, 8, 9, 13; Dt 1:1, 2, 3[2], 5, 6, 8[7], 9[2], 13, 17, 19, 20, 21, 22[4], 23, 25[2], 26, 27[3], 28, 29, 33[3], 35[2], 36[3], 39, 41[2], 42[2]; 2:2, 4, 5[2], 9[2], 13, 15, 19[2], 22, 24[2], 25, 26, 27[2], 28, 30[3], 31[4], 33, 36; 3:1, 2[4], 3, 6, 8, 12, 13[2], 14, 15, 16[2], 17, 18, 19, 20[4], 21[3], 24, 25, 26[2], 27[2]; 4:1[3], 2, 3, 4, 5[2], 6, 7[2], 9[3], 10[2], 11, 12, 13[2], 14[3], 15, 19[3], 20, 22[3], 23[2], 25, 26[2], 30[3], 31, 32, 34, 35, 36, 38, 39, 42[2], 43[3], 45; 5:1[2], 4, 5[2], 9[2], 10, 14, 15, 21, 22[2], 24, 28[3], 29[2], 30[2], 31, 32[3], 33; 6:1[3], 7, 10[5], 16, 18[2], 20, 21, 23[3], 24[3]; 7:1, 2, 3, 4, 6[2], 8, 9, 12, 13[2], 16[2], 17, 18[2], 19, 22, 23, 24[2], 25; 8:1, 2[2], 3, 11, 16[3], 17, 18, 19, 20, 21, 22; 9:1[3], 2, 4[2], 5[6], 6, 7[2], 8[2], 9, 10, 12[2], 13, 16, 19, 20, 21, 22, 25, 26, 27, 28[2]; 10:1[2], 4[2], 6, 7[2], 8[6], 10[2], 11[3], 12[4], 13, 14, 20, 22; 11:3[2], 4[3], 5[2], 6, 8[2], 9[3], 10[2], 11, 12, 19, 21[2], 22, 24[2], 25, 28, 29, 30, 31[2]; 12:1, 2, 5, 8, 10, 11, 13, 15, 20[2], 21, 26, 28, 29[2], 30, 31, 32; 13:3, 4, 5[3], 7, 8, 9, 10[2], 12, 15[2], 16[2], 17[3]; 14:2[2], 21[4], 23, 24[2], 25; 15:4[2], 6, 8, 9, 11[2], 12, 14, 16, 17, 19, 21; 16:5, 7, 8, 9[2], 10, 17; 17:1[2], 3, 4, 5[2], 6, 7, 8[2], 9, 10, 11[4], 12[3], 15, 16[3], 19, 20[2]; 18:3, 5, 6, 7, 8, 9, 12, 13, 14[3], 17, 18, 20[2], 21; 19:2, 3, 5[3], 6, 8[2], 9, 12[4], 14[2], 15, 16, 17, 19[3]; 20:1, 2, 3[2], 4[2], 5, 6[2], 7[2], 8[3], 10[2], 11, 12, 13, 18, 19; 21:1, 2[2], 4, 5[3], 7, 10[2], 11, 12, 13, 16[3], 19, 20, 21; 22:1, 2, 4, 5, 9, 13, 15, 16[2], 19[2], 21[2], 23, 24[2], 26, 27, 29[2]; 23:1, 2[3], 3[3], 4, 5, 6, 7, 8, 12, 14[3], 15[2], 18, 19, 20[3], 21, 23, 25; 24:2, 4[3], 5, 9, 10, 11[2], 13, 15, 16[3], 18, 19, 22; 25:1[3], 2[2], 5[3], 6, 7[4], 8[2], 9[2], 11, 16, 17, 19; 26:1, 2, 3[2], 7, 11[2], 12, 13, 14, 15, 16, 17[4], 18[2], 19[3]; 27:3, 5, 6, 9, 14, 15, 25; 28:7, 9, 11[2], 12[3], 14[3], 20, 21[2], 25[2], 26, 29[2], 30, 31[3], 32[2], 35, 36, 44[2], 49, 50[2], 53, 54[2], 55[3], 56[4], 57, 60, 63[2], 64, 68[2]; 29:1[2], 2[4], 4[4], 7, 8, 12, 13[4], 18, 20, 23, 24, 26, 29[4]; 30:1[2], 2, 4, 10, 12, 13, 14[2], 16, 17[2], 18[2], 19, 20[3]; 31:1, 2[2], 4[3], 5[2], 7[3], 9[2], 11, 12[2], 13[2], 14[2], 15, 16[3], 18, 19, 20[2], 21, 22, 24, 28[2], 29[2], 30; 32:3, 8, 17[3], 22, 26, 30, 40, 45, 46[3], 47, 49, 50[2], 51, 52; 33:7[2], 8[2], 17, 19, 26, 29; 34:1[2], 4[3], 6, 10, 11; Jos 1:1, 2[3], 3[2], 4, 5, 6[2], 7[3], 8, 11[4], 12, 15[4], 18; 2:2, 3[3], 4, 5, 6, 7, 8[2], 9, 10[2], 12, 13, 14, 16, 17[2], 20, 21, 23[2], 24; 3:1, 4, 5, 6, 7[2], 8, 9, 11, 14, 15; 4:1, 5, 6[2], 7, 8[2], 9, 10[2], 13, 15, 16, 18, 21[2], 23; 5:1, 2, 6[4], 9[2], 13[2], 14[2], 15; 6:2[2], 6, 7, 10[2], 14, 16, 17, 18[2], 19, 21, 22[3], 23, 25[2], 26; 7:1, 2[2], 3[2], 5, 6, 7[4], 8, 10, 12[2], 13[2], 19[3], 22, 23, 24, 25, 26[2]; 8:1[3], 2[2], 3, 9[2], 10, 12, 14[2], 16, 18, 20[3], 23, 24[2], 27[2], 28, 29, 30, 31, 34; 9:2, 3[2], 6[3], 7, 8[2], 9, 10, 11[3], 12[2], 15, 18, 19[2], 20[2], 21, 22, 24[3], 25[2], 27[2]; 10:1[2], 3[4], 6[2], 8[2], 12[3], 13, 15, 18, 21[2], 22, 23, 24[2], 25[2], 26, 27, 28[2], 29, 30[2], 31[2], 32, 33, 34[2], 35, 36, 37, 38, 39[3], 41, 43; 11:1[3], 2, 3, 5, 6[2], 8, 9, 11, 17, 20, 23[4]; 12:1, 3[2], 5[2], 6, 7[3], 9; 13:1[2], 3, 4[3], 5, 6[2], 7, 11, 13, 14[3], 15[2], 22[2], 23, 24[2], 25, 26[2], 28, 29[3], 31[2], 33[2]; 14:1, 3[2], 4[2], 6[3], 7, 10, 13, 14; 15:1[3], 3[3], 4[2], 5, 6[2], 7[2], 8, 9[3], 10[3], 11[5], 12, 13[3], 16, 18[3], 19, 20, 21, 46, 47, 63; 16:1, 2[2], 3[2], 6[2], 7[3], 8, 10[2]; 17:1[2], 2, 4[2], 5, 6, 7[2], 8[2], 9[3], 10[2], 12, 13, 14, 15[2], 17[2], 18; 18:3, 4[3], 6, 8[2], 9, 10[2], 11[2], 12, 13, 14[2], 15[2], 16[2], 17[3], 18[2], 19, 20, 21, 28; 19:1, 8, 10, 11, 12[3], 13[3], 14, 16, 17, 23, 24, 27[3], 29[3], 31, 32, 34[2], 39, 40, 47[2], 48, 49; 20:1, 2[2], 4[2], 6, 9; 21:1[3], 2[2], 3, 7, 8, 10[3], 12, 13, 20[3], 21, 27, 34, 40, 43[2], 44, 45[2]; 22:2, 3[2], 4[2], 5[7], 6, 7[3], 8[2], 9[2], 10, 11, 12, 13, 15[2], 21, 23[2], 24[3], 25, 27[3], 28[4],

TOO (192)

UPON (926)

19:7; 22:4, 7, 11, 19, 28; 23:2; 1Ki 6:35; 9:9; 14:10; 17:20, 21; 18:42; 2Ki 3:22, 27; 4:34^{4}; 13:13; 16:15; 21:12; 23:6; 24:3; 1Ch 12:18; 21:26; 27:24; 28:5; 29:25; 2Ch 6:27; 7:22; 15:1; 19:7; 20:9, 12, 14, 33; 24:18; 28:11; 29:8; 32:12, 25^{2}, 26; 34:24^{2}; Ezr 3:3; 5:5; 7:6, 9, 23, 28; 8:18, 31; 9:13; Ne 2:8, 18; 4:11; 9:13, 32^{2}, 33; 10:1; Est 8:17; 9:2, 3, 25; Job 2:11, 12; 3:5, 25; 4:14; 7:8; 10:15; 12:4; 13:11; 15:21, 27; 16:14, 15; 18:15; 19:3, 8, 25; 20:22, 23, 25; 21:5, 9, 17; 24:23; 25:3; 26:7; 27:9, 10; 29:4, 13, 22; 30:15; 31:1; 33:19; 34:21; 36:28; 37:15; 38:5, 24; 39:23; 42:11; Ps 7:16; 14:4; 16:4; 17:6; 18:3, 6, 10; 31:16; 32:4, 8; 33:22; 40:2; 44:17; 45:2; 53:4; 55:3, 4, 5, 15, 16; 63:2; 67:1, 2, 4; 68:4, 17; 69:24; 71:6; 78:27; 80:1, 17; 88:7; 90:17; 99:1; 105:38; 119:135, 143; 123:2, 3^{2}; 125:5; 128:6; 129:8; 133:2; 139:5; 141:1; 144:9; Pr 1:27, 28; 6:11, 21; 10:24; 23:5; 24:25, 34; 25:10; 29:16; Ecc 5:2; 6:1; 8:6; 9:12; 11:1; SS 2:8; 3:1; 4:16; 5:5, 15; 6:13^{3}; 8:5, 6^{2}, 9, 14; Isa 3:26; 5:6; 8:11; 9:6; 15:9; 16:12; 21:8; 24:17, 20; 28:10^{4}, 13^{4}, 22; 29:10; 30:16^{2}, 32; 31:4^{2}; 33:4; 34:5^{2}; 35:10; 38:11; 40:7, 24; 42:1, 5, 25; 43:22; 44:3; 45:12; 47:9^{2}, 11^{2}; 50:10; 51:11; 52:7; 53:5; 55:6; 57:7; 58:14; 59:21; 60:1, 2; 61:1; 62:6; 66:4, 7; Jer 2:3, 17; 4:18; 5:12, 15; 6:26; 8:18; 9:6^{2}, 22; 11:8, 11, 20, 23; 12:12; 13:22; 14:16; 15:8; 18:22; 19:3, 13, 15^{2}; 20:12; 22:23; 23:12, 17, 19, 40; 24:6, 10; 25:5, 13; 26:15^{2}; 29:12; 30:18, 23; 32:23, 42^{2}; 33:26; 36:30; 40:3; 41:12; 42:10, 17; 45:5; 46:20, 21, 25^{2}; 47:5; 48:8, 21^{2}, 32, 44; 49:5, 8, 36, 37; 50:42; 51:53; 52:22; La 1:12; 3:47; Eze 3:14, 22; 4:4; 5:16, 17; 6:3, 10, 12; 7:2, 3^{2}, 8, 12, 14, 26; 8:1; 9:8, 10; 11:5, 8, 9, 21; 13:15^{2}; 14:13, 17, 19, 21, 22^{2}; 16:12, 38, 43; 17:19; 18:6, 11, 13, 15; 19:8; 20:8, 13, 21; 21:31^{2}; 22:9, 20, 21, 22, 24, 31^{2}; 23:7, 8, 10, 30, 42; 24:11, 13; 25:11, 12, 14; 28:26; 29:8; 30:4, 9, 12, 15; 32:27; 33:2, 3, 4, 5, 10, 22; 36:11, 12, 18^{2}, 25, 29; 37:1, 6, 8, 9, 19; 38:11, 22; 39:4, 29; 40:1, 2, 4; 43:3, 18, 20, 27; 44:4; Da 4:10, 24, 28; 8:7; 9:11, 12, 13, 14, 17, 27; 10:7, 16; 11:18, 40; Hos 2:4, 8; 4:13; 5:1; 7:7, 9, 11, 14; 8:14; 10:12; 13:8; 14:3; Joel 2:2, 9^{2}; 3:4, 7; Am 4:2, 7; 5:9, 22; 8:2; 9:6^{2}, 8, 15; Jnh 1:4^{2}, 7, 8, 12; 2:4, 6, 10; 3:10; Mic 1:3, 15; 3:6, 11^{2}; 4:11; 5:1, 5, 7; 7:19; Hab 2:16; 3:16, 19; Zep 1:17; 2:2^{2}; 3:7, 8; Hag 2:15; Zec 8:14; 9:1; 14:17; Mt 10:13; 11:29; 12:18; 18:28; 23:22, 35, 36; 24:2; 27:32; Mk 3:10; 4:31; 10:34; 13:2; 15:19; Lk 1:35, 78; 2:40; 3:22; 4:18; 18:32; 19:43, 44; 21:6, 26, 35; 24:49; Jn 1:16, 51; Ac 1:8; 2:17, 18, 43; 4:33; 8:16; 10:44; 11:15^{2}; 12:1; 16:15; 19:6; Ro 11:25; 1Co 7:35; 2Co 11:20; Gal 6:16^{2}; Eph 2:20; 1Th 5:3^{2}; Rev 16:18; Tob 1:18; 3:3; 5:17, 19; 6:9^{2}; 11:15; 13:6; Jdt 2:28; 3:8; 8:17, 24^{2}; 9:9; 11:11, 15; 14:1; 15:3, 4, 5, 6; 16:1, 6; AdE 4:8; 9:3, 25, 27^{3}; 10:1; 13:15, 17; 14:16; Wis 3:9; 5:6; 6:5; 7:3; 11:4, 15, 17; 12:22, 27; 14:1, 11; 16:4, 5; 17:14; 18:20, 24; 19:13, 15; Sir 1:8, 9, 10^{2}, 26, 30; 2:10; 3:8, 22; 4:17; 5:7; 10:5, 13; 11:12; 12:17; 16:19, 29; 17:11, 19; 18:11; 22:27; 23:19; 27:27; 30:5, 18^{2}; 33:4, 23; 36:1; 37:24; 40:5; 45:12; 46:5, 16; 47:20, 25; 48:2, 20; Bar 2:7, 9, 20; 3:7, 20; 4:9^{2}, 10, 14, 18, 25^{2}, 27, 29, 35; 5:5; LtJ 6:13, 48, 72; Aza 1:5^{3}, 8; 1Mc 1:11, 30, 64; 2:30; 4:2; 6:13, 46; 2Mc 1:7, 21; 2:14, 24; 3:15, 22, 31; 4:14, 15, 21; 6:9; 8:2; 9:4, 18; 10:17, 26; 12:6, 15, 28, 36; 13:10; 14:34, 41, 45, 46; 15:18, 21, 22; 1Es 1:24; 4:36; 5:49, 61, 72; 6:32, 33; 8:21, 61; 3Mc 1:9, 27; 5:7, 11; 6:1, 3^{2}, 17, 21; 2Es 1:8; 2:5; 3:7, 9, 10^{2}; 6:20; 9:45; 10:9, 15; 11:2, 7; 12:4; 14:17; 15:5, 12, 19, 27, 33^{2}, 40, 49, 50; 16:3, 4, 5, 16, 21, 39, 59; 4Mc 8:18; 9:12; 11:18, 23; 15:4, 20^{3}; 16:20

US (1926)

Ge 1:26; 3:22; 4:8; 5:29; 11:3, 4^{2}, 7; 19:5, 13, 31, 32, 34; 20:9; 23:6^{3}; 24:23, 55, 65; 26:10^{2}, 16^{2}, 22, 28^{2}, 29; 31:14, 15^{2}, 16, 37, 44, 50, 53; 32:11, 18, 20; 33:12; 34:9^{2}, 10, 14, 17, 21^{3}, 22^{2}, 23^{2}; 35:3; 37:8^{2}, 17, 20, 21, 27; 39:14^{2}, 17; 41:12^{2}, 13; 42:2, 21^{2}, 28, 30^{2}, 33; 43:2, 3, 4, 5, 7, 8, 18^{2}, 21, 22; 44:9, 25, 26^{2}, 27, 30, 31; 47:15, 19^{2}; 50:15^{2}; Ex 1:10^{2}; 2:14, 19^{2}; 3:18^{2}; 5:3^{3}, 8, 16, 17, 21^{2}; 8:26, 27; 10:7, 25, 26; 11:8; 13:14, 15, 16; 14:11^{3}, 12^{3}, 25; 16:3, 7, 8; 17:2, 3^{2}, 7, 9; 19:23; 20:19^{2}; 24:14; 32:1^{3}, 23^{3}; 33:15, 16; 34:9^{2}; 36:5; Nu 10:29, 31^{2}, 32^{2}; 11:13, 18; 12:2, 11; 13:27, 30; 14:3^{2}, 4, 8^{3}, 9^{2}; 16:13^{3}, 14^{2}, 34; 17:12; 20:4, 5^{2}, 14, 15, 16, 17, 19; 21:5, 7; 22:4, 14; 27:4; 31:49, 50; 32:5, 19, 32; Dt 1:6, 19, 20, 22^{4}, 25^{3}, 27^{4}, 41; 2:29, 30, 32, 33, 36^{2}; 3:1, 3; 5:2, 3^{2}, 24, 25, 27; 6:21, 23^{3}, 24^{2}, 25; 9:28; 12:8; 13:2^{2}, 6, 13; 21:20; 26:3, 6^{3}, 8, 9^{2}, 15; 29:7, 14, 15, 29; 30:12^{2}, 13^{2}; 31:17; 33:2, 4; Jos 1:16^{2}; 2:9, 11, 14, 17, 18, 20, 24; 4:23; 5:6, 13; 7:7^{2}, 9, 25; 8:5, 6^{2}; 9:6, 7, 11^{2}, 20, 22^{2}, 25; 10:4, 6^{4}; 17:4, 16; 22:19^{2}, 22, 25, 26, 27^{2}, 28^{2}, 29, 31, 34; 24:16, 17^{2}, 18, 27^{2}; Jdg 1:1, 24; 6:13^{6}; 8:1^{2}, 21, 22^{2}; 9:8, 10, 12, 14; 10:15^{2}; 11:8^{2}, 10, 17, 19; 12:1, 2; 13:8^{2}, 15, 23^{3}; 14:13, 15^{3}; 15:10^{2}, 11^{2}; 16:2, 24, 25; 18:9, 19^{2}, 25; 19:11, 13, 19; 20:3, 8^{2}, 18, 32^{2}, 39; 21:1, 22^{2}; 1Sa 4:3^{4}, 7, 8^{2}; 5:7^{2}, 8, 10^{2}, 11; 6:2, 9^{3}; 7:8^{2}, 12; 8:5^{2}, 6^{2}, 19, 20^{2}; 9:5^{2}, 6^{2}, 8, 9, 10, 27; 10:16, 19, 27; 11:1, 3^{2}, 10, 12^{2}, 14; 12:4^{2}, 10, 12; 14:1, 6^{2}, 9, 10^{2}, 12, 17, 36^{3}, 38; 17:9; 20:11, 42; 21:5; 23:19; 25:7, 15, 16, 40; 26:11; 27:11; 29:4^{2}, 9; 30:22, 23^{4}; 2Sa 2:14; 5:2; 10:12; 11:23^{2}; 12:18; 13:25, 26; 15:14^{4}, 19, 20; 16:20; 17:5, 6; 18:3^{5}; 19:6, 9^{2}, 10, 42^{2}, 43; 20:6^{2}; 21:4^{2}, 5^{2}, 6, 17; 24:14; 1Ki 3:18^{2}; 5:6; 8:57^{3}; 12:4, 9, 10; 18:23, 26; 20:23, 31; 22:3; 2Ki 1:6^{2}; 3:10, 13; 4:10^{2}, 13; 6:1, 2^{4}, 11, 16; 7:4^{3}, 6, 9, 12, 13; 9:5, 12; 14:8; 18:26, 30, 32; 19:19; 22:13^{2}; 1Ch 13:2^{2}, 3^{2}; 15:13; 16:35^{2}; 19:13; 2Ch 10:4, 9, 10; 13:10, 12; 14:7^{2}, 11; 20:9, 11^{3}, 12; 25:17; 28:13; 29:10; 32:7, 8^{2}, 11; 34:21; Ezr 4:2^{2}, 3^{2}, 12, 14, 18; 5:11, 17; 8:17, 18^{2}, 22, 31^{2}; 9:8^{3}, 9^{4}, 13^{3}, 14^{2}; 10:3, 13, 14; Ne 2:17, 18, 19, 20; 4:12^{2}, 15, 20^{2}, 22; 5:8, 10, 17^{2}; 6:2, 7, 9, 10^{2}, 16; 9:32, 33, 37; 13:18; Job 9:33^{2}; 15:9; 21:14; 22:17^{2}; 31:15; 34:4^{2}, 37; 35:11^{2}; 37:19; Ps 2:3^{2}; 4:6; 10:13; 12:7^{2}; 20:9; 33:22; 34:3; 37:24; 40:5; 44:1, 7^{2}, 9^{2}, 10, 11^{2}, 13^{2}, 14, 17, 19^{2}, 23, 26; 46:7, 11; 47:3, 4; 54:T; 59:7; 60:1^{2}, 3^{2}, 5, 10, 11; 62:8; 64:5; 65:3, 5; 66:9, 10^{2}, 11, 12; 67:1^{3}, 6, 7; 68:19, 28; 74:1, 9; 78:3; 79:4, 8^{2}, 9^{2}; 80:2, 3, 6, 7, 18, 19; 83:4, 12; 85:4^{2}, 5, 6, 7^{2}; 90:3, 12, 14, 15^{2}, 17^{2}; 95:1^{2}, 2^{2}, 6^{2}; 100:3; 103:10^{2}, 12; 106:47^{2}; 108:11, 12; 115:1^{2}, 12^{2}; 117:2; 118:24, 25^{2}, 27; 122:1; 123:2, 3^{2}; 124:2, 3^{2}, 4^{2}, 5, 6; 126:3; 132:7^{2}; 136:23, 24; 137:3^{2}, 8; Pr 1:11^{3}, 12, 14; 7:18^{2}; Ecc 1:10; 5:18; SS 1:4; 2:15; 5:9; 7:11, 12; Isa 1:9, 18; 2:3^{2}, 5; 4:1; 6:8; 7:6; 8:10; 9:6^{2}; 14:8, 10; 17:14^{2}; 22:13; 25:9^{2}; 26:12^{2}, 13; 28:15; 29:15^{2}; 30:10^{2}, 11; 32:15; 33:2, 14^{2}, 21, 22; 36:11, 15, 18; 37:20; 41:1, 22^{3}, 23; 43:9, 26; 44:7; 50:8; 53:5, 6; 56:12^{2}; 59:9^{2}, 11, 12^{2}; 63:7, 16^{2}, 17; 64:6, 7^{2}, 12; Jer 2:6^{2}, 27; 3:25^{2}; 4:5, 8, 13; 5:12, 19, 24^{2}; 6:4^{2}, 5, 24, 26; 8:8, 14^{3}; 9:18; 11:19^{2}; 14:7, 9^{2}, 19^{2}, 21^{2}; 16:10; 18:12, 18^{3}; 20:10; 21:2^{3}, 13; 26:16; 29:15, 28; 31:6; 35:6, 8, 10, 11; 36:15, 17; 37:3, 9; 38:16, 25^{2}; 40:10; 41:8; 42:2^{2}, 3, 5^{2}, 6, 20^{2}; 43:3^{4}; 44:16; 46:16; 48:2; 51:9, 10; La 3:40, 41, 43, 45, 46, 47; 4:19^{2}; 5:1, 8^{2}, 16, 20^{2}, 21, 22^{2}; Eze 8:12; 11:15; 20:32; 24:19^{2}; 33:10, 24; 35:12; 37:18; Da 1:12; 2:23; 3:17^{2}; 9:7, 8, 10, 11, 12^{2}, 13, 14; Hos 6:1^{3}, 2^{2}, 3^{3}; 10:3, 8^{2}; 14:3; Am 9:10; Ob 1:1; Jnh 1:6, 7^{2}, 8^{2}, 11, 14^{2}; Mic 2:6; 3:11^{2}; 4:2^{2}; 5:1, 6; 7:15, 19; Hab 3:14, 16; Zec 1:6; 8:21, 23; Mal 1:2, 9; 2:10; Mt 1:23; 3:15; 6:11, 12, 13^{2}; 8:25, 29^{2}, 31^{2}; 9:27; 13:28, 36, 56; 15:15, 23; 17:4; 19:7; 20:7, 12, 30, 31; 21:25, 38; 22:17, 25; 24:3; 25:8, 9, 11; 26:17, 46, 63, 68; 27:4, 25, 49; Mk 1:24^{2}, 38; 4:35; 5:12^{2}; 6:3; 9:5^{2}, 22^{2}, 38, 40^{2}; 10:35, 37; 12:7, 19; 13:4; 14:12, 15, 42; 15:36; 16:3; Lk 1:1, 2, 69, 71, 73, 78; 2:15^{2}, 48; 4:34^{3}; 7:5, 16, 20; 8:22; 9:33^{2}, 49, 54; 10:17; 11:1, 3, 4^{3}, 45; 12:41; 13:25; 15:23; 16:26^{2}; 17:13; 19:14; 20:2, 6, 14, 22, 28; 22:8, 9, 12, 67; 23:2, 15, 18, 30^{2}, 39; 24:22, 23, 24, 29, 32^{3}; Jn 1:14, 22^{2}; 2:18; 4:12, 25; 6:30, 34, 52; 8:5; 9:34; 10:24^{2}; 11:7, 15, 16; 14:8, 9, 22, 31; 16:17; 17:21; 19:24; Ac 1:17, 21^{2}, 22^{2}, 24; 2:8, 29, 32; 3:4, 12; 4:17; 5:4, 28; 6:14; 7:27, 38, 40^{3}; 9:38; 10:33, 41, 42; 11:12, 13, 15, 17; 13:26, 33, 47; 14:11; 15:8, 9, 24^{2}, 28, 36; 16:9, 10, 14, 15^{2}, 17, 21, 37^{4}; 17:20, 27; 20:5, 14; 21:5, 11, 16, 17, 18; 24:4; 25:24; 27:4, 6, 7; 28:2^{2}, 7^{2}, 10, 15^{2}; Ro 3:5, 8^{2}; 4:16, 24; 5:5^{2}, 8^{2}; 6:3; 7:6; 8:4, 18, 26, 31^{2}, 32^{2}, 34, 35, 37, 39; 9:24, 29; 12:6; 13:11, 12, 13; 14:12, 13, 19; 15:2; 1Co 1:18, 30; 2:10, 12; 4:1, 6, 8, 9; 5:8; 6:14; 8:1, 6, 8; 10:6, 11; 15:32, 57; 2Co 1:4, 5, 10^{3}, 11^{2}, 14, 21^{2}, 22^{2}; 2:14^{2}; 3:3, 5, 6, 18; 4:7, 12, 14^{2}, 17; 5:5^{2}, 10, 12, 14, 18^{2}, 19, 20; 7:1, 2, 6, 7, 9, 12; 8:4, 5, 19, 20; 9:11; 10:13; Gal 1:4, 23; 2:4; 3:13^{2}; 4:3; 5:1, 25, 26; 6:9, 10; Eph 1:3, 4, 5, 6, 8, 9, 19; 2:3, 4, 5, 6^{2}, 7, 10, 14, 18; 3:20; 4:7, 13, 25; 5:2^{2}; Php 3:15, 16, 17; Col 1:8, 13^{2}; 2:13, 14; 4:3^{2}; 1Th 1:6, 9, 10; 2:8, 13, 15, 16, 17; 3:6^{5}; 4:1, 7; 5:6^{2}, 8, 9, 10, 25; 2Th 1:7; 2:2, 15, 16^{2}; 3:1, 6, 7; 1Ti 5:14; 6:17; 2Ti 1:7, 9^{3}, 14; 2:12; Tit 2:8, 12, 14^{2}; 3:5, 6, 15; Heb 1:2; 2:3; 4:1, 2, 11, 14, 16; 6:1, 18; 10:15, 20, 22, 23, 24; 11:40; 12:1^{3}, 9, 10^{2}, 28; 13:13, 15, 18, 21; Jas 1:18; 3:2, 3; 4:5; 5:17; 1Pe 1:3; 4:17; 2Pe 1:3^{2}, 4; 1Jn 1:2, 3, 7, 8, 9^{2}, 10; 2:19^{5}, 25; 3:1^{2}, 16, 18, 20, 21, 23, 24^{2}; 4:6^{2}, 7, 9, 10, 11, 12^{2}, 13^{2}, 16, 17, 19; 5:11, 14, 15, 20; 2Jn 1:2^{2}, 3, 5; 3Jn 1:10; Rev 1:5^{2}, 6; 6:16^{2}; 19:7; Tob 3:4^{2}, 9; 5:18, 20^{2}, 21; 6:13; 8:4^{2}, 6, 12, 16; 11:3, 17; Jdt 3:2; 5:24; 6:2^{2}; 7:24^{2}, 25^{2}, 27, 28, 30^{3}, 31; 8:11, 15^{3}, 17^{2}, 20, 21, 22, 23, 24^{3}, 25^{2}, 27^{2}, 30^{2}, 31^{2}; 10:15; 11:3; 12:3, 11^{2}, 12, 13, 17; 13:5, 11; 14:5, 13, 18; AdE 4:8^{2}; 10:9; 13:3, 4, 15^{2}; 14:6, 11, 13, 14, 19; 16:12, 14, 16, 23; Wis 2:6, 7^{2}, 8, 9^{2}, 10^{2}, 12^{4}, 14, 15, 17^{2}, 19, 20, 23^{2}; 3:3; 5:6^{2}, 8^{2}; 12:18, 22; 15:2, 4; 18:8^{2}; Sir Pr:T; 2:17; 8:6; 24:23; 36:1, 4^{2}; 37:14; 44:1; 50:22, 23, 24^{2}; Bar 1:12, 13^{2}, 15, 18, 20^{2}, 21, 22; 2:1, 3, 4, 6, 7^{2}, 8, 9^{2}, 10, 13^{2}, 14^{3}, 16, 20, 27; 3:4, 8; Aza 1:5^{2}, 7, 8^{2}, 9, 11, 12, 19^{2}, 20, 66^{4}; Sus 1:13, 20^{2}, 41, 50^{2}; Bel 1:12, 29; 1Mc 1:11^{3}; 2:21, 37^{3}, 40, 41^{3}; 3:20^{3}, 22, 43, 52^{3}, 53, 58^{2}, 59; 4:5, 10^{3}, 17, 18, 36; 5:10^{2}, 12^{2}, 15, 38, 40^{2}, 48, 57^{3}; 6:24^{2}, 25, 57, 58, 59; 7:6, 7, 14, 42; 8:20; 9:8, 9^{2}, 10^{2}, 29, 44, 45^{2}, 58; 10:4^{2}, 20, 23, 26^{2}, 27^{2}, 53, 54, 70^{2}, 71^{2}, 72^{2}; 11:9, 33^{2}, 35^{3}, 50^{2}; 12:3, 10, 13^{3}, 17, 18, 22, 23, 53; 13:6, 9, 16, 40, 46; 14:21, 22^{2}, 28; 15:17, 20; 2Mc 1:7, 20; 2:14, 18^{3}, 26, 29, 32; 6:14, 15, 16^{2}; 7:2, 6^{2}, 9^{2}, 33; 8:18; 11:29; 14:35; 15:4, 23; 1Es 2:18; 3:5, 17; 5:69, 70, 71; 6:13, 22; 8:46, 47, 50, 51, 61^{2}, 78^{2}, 79^{2}, 80^{2}, 81, 86, 87, 88^{2}, 93; 3Mc 2:2, 10, 17^{2}, 20^{2}; 3:14, 18, 19, 21, 23, 24^{2}, 25; 5:40; 6:10^{2}, 12^{2}, 15^{2}, 26; 7:3^{2}, 7; 2Es 1:18^{3}; 4:12, 14^{2}, 15, 25, 38, 39, 45; 5:18, 41; 6:55, 57^{2}, 59; 7:48^{5}, 64, 66, 67, 69, 71, 75, 119^{2}, 120, 121; 8:6^{2}, 17, 31, 32; 9:29, 35; 10:2, 6, 7, 23; 12:41, 42, 43, 44^{2}; 16:52; 4Mc 1:34; 2:6; 3:2^{2}, 3, 4, 19; 5:8, 18, 23^{2}, 24^{2}, 25^{2}, 26^{2}, 27^{3}; 6:17, 34; 8:16, 17, 19, 20, 21, 22, 24, 25, 26^{2}; 9:3^{2}, 5^{2}, 7^{3}, 9; 11:4, 12^{2}, 20, 25^{2}, 26, 27; 13:9^{2}, 10, 13^{3}, 14^{2}, 16, 17^{2}, 18^{2}; 17:7

WAS (5254)

Ge 1:2, 3, 4, 5^{2}, 7, 8^{2}, 9, 10, 11, 12, 13^{2}, 15, 18, 19^{2}, 21, 23^{2}, 24, 25, 30, 31^{3}; 2:5^{2}, 19, 20, 23; 3:1, 6^{4}, 10^{2}, 20, 23; 4:2, 5, 18^{2}, 19, 20, 21^{2}, 22, 26; 5:24, 32; 6:5^{2}, 6, 9, 11^{2}, 12; 7:6, 15, 22, 23^{2}; 8:2, 11, 13, 14; 9:18, 19, 20; 10:8, 9, 10, 25^{3}; 11:9, 10, 27^{2}, 29^{3}, 30; 12:4, 10^{2}, 11, 14, 15, 18; 13:2, 7, 10^{2}; 14:10, 13, 18; 15:12, 17; 16:1, 14, 16; 17:1, 24^{2}, 25^{2}; 18:10, 15; 19:1, 22, 29, 30; 20:6; 21:4, 5^{2}, 8^{2}, 11, 15, 20, 31; 22:20, 24; 23:1, 10, 17^{2}; 24:1, 11, 15^{2}, 16, 29, 30, 33, 36, 45, 62, 67; 25:1, 3, 6, 8, 10, 17, 19, 20, 21, 24, 26^{2}, 27^{2}, 28, 29^{2}, 30; 26:1, 7, 34; 27:1, 5, 33; 28:12, 17, 19; 29:2, 9, 12^{2}, 16^{2}, 17, 25, 31^{2}, 34; 30:35, 36; 31:1, 4, 22, 31, 39, 40; 32:7, 24, 25; 34:3, 19^{2}, 24, 28, 29; 35:4, 7, 8^{2}, 10, 16, 17, 18, 19, 29; 36:12, 22, 39; 37:2^{2}, 3, 24^{2}, 29; 38:1, 2, 5, 6, 7, 10, 12, 13, 14, 16, 21, 24, 25^{2}, 28, 29, 30; 39:1, 2^{2}, 3, 5, 6, 11, 21, 22^{2}, 23^{2}; 40:2, 3, 9, 11, 15, 16, 20; 41:1, 7, 8^{2}, 10, 12, 13^{2}, 14, 17, 24, 46, 48, 49, 54^{2}, 55, 56; 42:1, 6^{2}, 25, 35; 43:1, 7, 12^{2}, 21, 30^{2}, 34; 44:3, 12, 14, 17; 45:8, 16, 26; 47:13^{2}, 15, 18, 20; 48:1, 2, 7, 14^{2}; 49:15^{2}, 26, 33; 50:9, 11, 15, 26; Ex 1:5^{2}, 7, 15; 2:2, 6, 13, 14; 3:1, 2^{2}, 6; 4:6, 7, 14, 26; 6:16, 18, 20, 26, 27; 7:7, 13, 15, 20, 21; 8:15, 19, 24; 9:7^{2}, 18, 24, 25, 26, 31^{2}, 35; 10:15^{2}, 19, 22, 27; 11:3; 12:29, 30^{2}, 34, 39, 40, 42; 13:17; 14:5, 11, 19, 20; 15:23^{2}; 16:6, 13, 14, 15, 20, 31^{2}; 17:1; 18:3, 4, 5, 14; 19:16, 18; 20:21; 21:13, 36^{2}; 22:12, 13, 15^{2}; 24:10, 17, 18; 29:27^{2}; 31:17; 32:12, 16; 33:7; 34:28, 30, 35; 35:21^{2}; 36:2, 6, 7, 9, 12, 13, 15, 21; 37:1, 6, 21, 25^{2}; 38:1^{2}, 17, 18^{2}, 23, 24^{2}, 25, 26, 29^{2}; 39:3, 5, 9^{2}, 10, 23, 32; 40:17, 35, 36, 37^{2}, 38^{2}; Lev 6:4, 28; 7:24; 8:4, 10, 15, 16, 19, 20, 21, 23, 25, 26, 28, 29, 30, 31; 9:8, 15, 20; 10:3, 16, 18; 11:34; 13:35; 14:6, 28, 48; 15:10; 16:27; 18:28; 22:8; 24:10^{2}, 11; 25:27, 28; 27:24; Nu 1:46; 2:32^{2}; 3:16, 22, 25, 31, 32, 34, 35, 36, 38, 39, 43; 4:36, 37, 40, 41, 44, 48; 5:7, 13; 6:12; 7:10, 12, 13, 17, 23, 25, 29, 31, 35, 37, 41, 43, 47, 49, 53, 55, 59, 61, 65, 67, 71, 73, 77, 79, 83, 84^{2}, 88^{2}, 89; 8:4^{3}; 9:15^{2}, 16, 22; 10:14, 15, 16, 17, 18, 19, 20, 21, 22, 23, 24, 25, 26, 27, 28; 11:1, 3, 7^{2}, 8, 10, 18, 25, 32, 33^{3}, 34; 12:3, 9, 10, 15; 13:20, 22, 24; 14:16; 15:24, 25, 26, 34; 16:15, 31, 48, 50; 17:6; 19:13; 20:1, 2; 21:1, 3, 24, 26, 35; 22:3^{2}, 4, 22^{3}, 26, 27; 23:6, 17; 24:10, 20; 25:1, 3, 8, 13, 14^{2}, 15^{3}, 18; 26:7, 18, 22, 27, 29, 34, 37, 41, 46, 47, 50, 51, 58, 59^{2}, 62^{2}, 64, 65; 27:1, 3, 13; 30:8; 31:36, 37, 38, 39, 40, 43, 52; 32:1, 10, 13; 33:14, 39; 35:23, 25; 36:2; Dt 1:4, 34, 37; 2:14, 15, 30, 36; 3:3, 4, 11, 26; 4:11, 12, 21, 35; 5:5, 23; 7:7, 8; 8:2; 9:8^{2}, 15, 18, 19^{2}, 20^{2}, 21, 28; 10:6, 10; 11:2; 19:6; 21:6; 22:20, 27; 25:10; 26:5, 14; 29:27; 32:9, 12, 19, 27, 50; 33:21; 34:6, 7^{2}, 8, 9, 11; Jos 1:5, 17; 2:1, 2, 5, 7, 11, 15; 3:7; 4:10; 5:1, 7, 8, 13; 6:1, 15, 27^{2}; 7:16, 17^{2}, 18, 22; 8:13, 14, 17, 18, 20, 21, 22, 23, 25, 35; 9:12, 24; 10:2^{2}, 17; 11:10, 11, 19, 20, 22; 13:1, 12, 16, 23^{2}, 25, 29; 14:2, 4, 7, 10, 11^{2}, 15^{2}; 15:12, 13, 15; 16:5^{2}; 17:1^{3}, 6; 19:8, 9, 47; 20:5, 6, 9; 21:42; 22:22; 23:1; 24:12; Jdg 1:10, 11, 17, 19, 20, 22, 23; 2:10, 11, 14, 15, 18, 20; 3:2, 7, 8, 12^{2}, 17, 20, 25, 30; 4:1, 2, 4, 12, 16, 17, 21, 22; 5:8^{2}; 6:1, 6, 11, 21, 22, 27, 28^{3}, 32, 38, 40^{2}; 7:1, 6, 8, 13; 8:11, 20^{2}, 26, 28, 31, 32; 9:7, 25, 30, 42, 44, 47, 51, 55; 10:2, 5, 6, 7, 9; 11:1^{2}, 18, 34^{2}; 12:7, 10, 12, 15; 13:1, 2^{3}, 6, 9, 16, 21; 14:4^{2}, 8, 20; 15:2, 17, 18, 19; 16:4, 9, 16, 27; 17:1^{2}, 4, 6^{2}, 7^{2}, 12; 18:1^{2}, 17, 28^{3}, 29^{2}, 31; 19:1, 2, 10, 11, 16^{3}, 26^{2}, 27, 28; 20:4, 27, 34^{2}, 38, 40, 41; 21:9^{2}, 25^{2}; Ru 1:1, 2, 3, 4, 5, 12, 18, 19; 2:1, 3, 5, 6, 14, 17, 18; 3:7, 8^{2}; 4:7^{2}; 1Sa 1:1^{2}, 2, 9, 10, 13^{3}, 18, 24, 26; 2:13, 15^{2}, 17, 18, 22, 25; 3:1^{2}, 2, 3^{2}, 8, 15, 17, 19, 20; 4:2^{2}, 10^{2}, 11, 13, 15, 18^{2}, 19^{2}, 20; 5:3, 4, 6, 9, 11^{2}; 6:1, 4, 14, 15; 7:2, 10, 13, 14, 17; 8:2; 9:1^{2}, 2^{2}, 5, 9, 10, 24, 25; 10:20, 21^{2}, 23, 27; 11:5, 6; 12:12; 13:1, 3, 7, 19, 21, 22; 14:2, 4^{2}, 15, 16, 19, 20^{2}, 25, 26, 27, 33, 35, 39, 42, 43, 49, 50^{2}, 51^{2}, 52; 15:9^{2}, 11, 12, 19, 35; 16:12^{2}; 17:4, 5^{2}, 7, 12^{2}, 14, 20, 28, 29, 39, 40, 42, 50, 51; 18:1, 4, 5, 8, 10, 12^{2}, 14, 16, 19, 20, 26, 28, 29^{2}; 19:7, 8, 9, 16, 19, 21, 23; 20:9, 25, 27, 30, 33, 34, 35; 21:6, 7^{2}, 12; 22:2^{3}, 4, 6, 9, 22; 23:7, 9, 13, 15, 25, 26, 28; 24:1, 3, 5; 25:2^{4}, 3^{4}, 4, 21^{2}, 36^{3}, 39, 44; 26:5^{2}, 12, 16, 21, 24; 27:4, 7, 11; 28:5, 14, 20, 21; 30:6, 19, 27; 31:3, 4^{2}, 5; 2Sa 1:5, 6, 10^{2}, 21, 26; 2:4, 10, 11^{2}, 16, 17, 18, 24, 32; 3:1, 2, 6^{2}, 7, 22, 23^{2}, 35; 4:1, 2, 4^{3}, 5, 7, 10^{2}; 5:2^{2}, 4, 10; 6:3, 7, 8, 9, 10, 12, 14, 21; 7:1, 19; 8:16^{2}, 17, 18; 9:2^{3}, 12, 13; 10:5, 9, 17; 11:2^{2}, 3, 4, 7, 16, 17, 26, 27; 12:3, 4, 5, 18^{2}, 19, 21, 22, 30^{3}; 13:1, 2^{2}, 3^{2}, 8, 15^{2}, 18, 19, 21, 30, 39; 14:1, 6, 19^{2}, 25^{2}, 26, 27^{2}; 15:12, 31^{2}, 32, 37; 16:5, 15, 23^{2}; 17:19, 22, 23^{2}, 25; 18:6, 7, 9^{3}, 14, 24, 29, 33; 19:1, 2, 18^{2}, 32^{2}; 20:8^{2}, 13, 23^{2}, 24^{2}, 25, 26; 21:1, 7, 11, 16, 18, 19^{2}, 20^{3}; 22:8, 10, 11, 19, 24, 42; 23:8, 9^{2}, 11^{2}, 13, 14^{2}, 16, 18, 19, 20, 23; 24:1, 10, 16^{2}, 17, 25; 1Ki 1:1, 4, 6^{2}, 15^{2}, 22, 23, 42, 51; 2:10, 11, 12, 15^{2}, 29, 34, 39, 41, 46; 3:4, 17, 18, 21^{2}, 26, 28; 4:1, 2, 3, 4, 5^{2}, 6^{2}, 19, 21, 22, 31; 5:12, 14; 6:2, 3^{2}, 6^{3}, 7^{3}, 8, 10, 17, 18^{2}, 20, 24^{2}, 26^{2}, 27^{2}, 37, 38^{2}; 7:1, 3, 6, 7, 8, 10, 14^{2}, 15^{2}, 16^{2}, 20, 22^{2}, 23, 24, 25, 26^{2}, 27, 28, 31^{4}, 32, 35, 38, 47, 51; 8:9, 57, 64^{3}; 10:2, 3, 5, 6, 14, 19, 20, 21, 28; 11:4^{3}, 6, 9, 14, 15, 17, 20, 21, 25, 26, 27, 28^{2}, 29, 30, 42, 43; 12:2, 6, 15, 18, 20, 32; 13:1, 5, 6^{2}, 9, 17, 18, 24; 14:8, 20, 21^{2}, 22, 30, 31^{2}; 15:2, 3, 5, 7, 10, 11, 14, 16, 22, 23, 24, 26, 29, 32, 34; 16:6, 9^{2}, 18, 25, 28; 17:7, 10, 11, 16, 17^{2}, 19; 18:2, 3, 4, 7, 26^{2}, 28, 29, 38, 45, 46; 19:3, 6, 11^{4}, 12, 19^{2}; 20:16, 40^{2}; 21:11, 15, 16, 25^{2}; 22:33, 35, 37, 42^{2}, 43, 47^{2}, 49, 50, 52; 2Ki 1:7, 9; 2:1, 8, 14, 17, 23; 3:2, 4, 9, 15, 20, 25, 26, 27; 4:8, 18, 31, 38^{2}, 41; 5:1, 13, 14^{2}; 6:5^{2}, 8, 10, 11, 13, 15, 17, 25, 26, 30, 32, 33; 7:5, 7, 10, 15, 16; 8:4, 5, 6, 7^{2}, 11, 17, 18^{2}, 24, 26^{2}, 27^{2}, 29; 9:16; 10:9, 12, 19, 21^{2}, 26, 30, 31, 36; 11:1, 2, 14, 16, 20, 21; 12:1, 2, 9, 10^{2}, 11, 13, 14, 16, 18, 21^{2}; 13:2, 3, 7, 11, 13, 14, 19, 21^{3}, 23; 14:2^{2}, 3, 5, 12, 16, 20, 21, 24, 25, 26^{2}; 15:2^{2}, 3, 5^{2}, 9, 12, 18, 24, 28, 33^{2}, 34, 38; 16:2^{2}, 10, 14, 20; 17:2, 18^{2}, 23, 26; 18:2^{2}, 3, 4, 5, 7, 9, 10^{2}, 15, 18, 36, 37; 19:2, 37; 20:1, 13^{2}; 21:1^{2}, 2, 16, 18, 19^{2}, 20, 26; 22:1^{2}, 2, 9, 19; 23:11, 23, 25, 26, 31^{2}, 32, 36^{2}, 37; 24:4, 8^{2}, 9, 10, 18^{2}, 19; 25:2, 3, 4, 5, 8, 15^{2}, 16, 17^{3}, 19, 30; 1Ch 1:10, 19^{2}, 39, 43, 46, 50; 2:3, 8, 17, 21, 26^{2}, 29, 34, 42, 45, 49; 3:9, 19; 4:3, 4, 9, 11, 25, 40, 41; 5:1^{2}, 6, 7, 15, 22; 6:10; 7:7, 9, 15^{2}, 16, 24, 25, 31, 40; 8:29, 34, 37; 9:1^{2}, 17, 20^{2}, 21, 31, 35, 36, 40, 43; 10:3, 4^{2}, 5, 13; 11:2^{2}, 7, 9, 11, 12, 13^{2}, 15, 16^{2}, 18, 20, 21, 22, 25; 12:3, 15, 22, 40; 13:10, 11, 12; 14:2; 15:22, 27; 16:5^{2}, 39; 17:13, 17; 18:15^{2}, 16, 17; 19:5, 10, 17; 20:2^{2}, 4, 5^{2}, 6^{3}; 21:6, 7, 15^{2}, 17, 30; 23:1, 3, 11, 13; 25:1; 26:10, 15, 24, 31^{2}; 27:2, 3^{2}, 4^{2}, 5, 6^{2}, 7, 8, 9, 10, 11, 12, 13, 14, 15, 16, 24, 25^{2}, 26, 27^{2}, 28^{2}, 29^{2}, 30^{3}, 32, 33^{2}, 34; 29:2, 27; 2Ch 1:1, 3^{2}, 5, 6, 11; 3:3, 4^{2}, 6, 8^{2}, 9, 12; 4:2, 3, 4, 5^{2}, 6^{2}, 18; 5:1, 10, 13^{3}; 7:7; 8:16^{3}; 9:1, 2, 4, 5, 11, 13, 19, 20, 31; 10:2, 6, 15, 18; 12:1, 13^{2}, 16; 13:2^{2}, 7, 13, 14; 14:2, 14^{2}; 15:3, 4, 5, 8, 9, 15, 17, 19; 16:10^{2}, 12; 17:3, 6, 14; 18:32; 20:3, 30, 31^{2}, 32; 21:1, 3, 4, 5, 6^{2}, 17, 20; 22:2^{2}, 3, 4, 6, 7, 8, 9^{2}, 10, 11; 23:13, 19, 21; 24:1^{2}, 2, 9, 10, 11^{2}, 15, 22; 25:1^{2}, 2, 3, 15, 16, 20, 22, 28; 26:1, 3^{2}, 4, 12, 13, 15, 16, 19, 20, 21^{3}; 27:1^{2}, 2, 8; 28:1^{2}, 5, 9^{3}; 29:1^{2}, 2, 6, 19, 22^{2}, 25, 28, 29, 32, 34, 35^{2}; 30:12, 17, 26, 27; 31:1, 3, 10, 12, 14, 17^{2}, 19, 20; 32:5, 9, 12, 14, 23, 24, 25, 31; 33:1, 2, 12, 13, 21, 22; 34:1, 2, 3, 16, 17, 24, 27; 35:16, 18, 19, 24; 36:2, 5^{2}, 8, 9^{2}, 11, 12, 16; Ezr 1:6, 9, 11; 2:61, 64; 3:6, 11, 13; 4:7, 15^{2}, 23, 24; 5:1, 5^{2}, 7, 11^{2}, 17; 6:2^{3}, 15, 21; 7:6^{2}, 8, 9^{2}, 28; 8:18, 22, 31, 33, 34^{2}, 35; 10:6, 9, 19; Ne 1:1, 11; 2:1, 2, 6, 8, 11, 12, 14^{2}, 16; 4:1, 3, 6, 7, 15, 18; 5:1, 6, 14, 18^{2}; 6:1^{2}, 6, 10, 13, 15, 18; 7:2, 4, 63, 64, 66, 72; 8:2, 5, 9, 17, 18; 10:29; 11:9^{2}, 14, 17, 22, 23^{2}, 24; 12:8, 10, 43, 46, 47^{2}; 13:1, 4^{2}, 6^{2}, 8, 13, 26^{2}, 28; Est 1:7, 8, 10, 11, 12, 13; 2:5^{2}, 7, 8, 11, 12, 13, 14^{2}, 15, 16, 19, 20, 21, 23^{2}; 3:4, 5, 12^{2}, 14, 15^{2}; 4:3, 4, 5; 5:1, 2, 9; 6:2; 7:6, 8; 8:1, 9, 13, 14, 16, 17; 9:4, 11, 14, 17, 26, 27, 32; 10:3^{2}; Job 1:1^{3}, 3, 16, 17, 18; 2:13; 3:3, 16; 4:7, 16^{2}; 8:7; 10:13;

15:19; 16:12; 20:21; 22:16; 29:4[2], 5, 14, 15, 16, 20; 30:25[2]; 31:20, 23, 25; 32:1, 2, 3, 5, 6, 12; 33:6, 27[2]; 36:16[3]; Ps 4:1; 18:7, 9, 18, 23, 41; 22:9, 10; 30:7; 31:21; 32:4[2]; 34:6[2]; 39:2; 50:21; 51:5; 57:6; 63:T; 66:14, 17; 69:20; 71:6; 73:3, 21[2], 22[2]; 76:5, 8; 77:18, 19; 78:8[2], 21[2], 30, 35, 37, 59; 79:3; 87:4, 6; 99:6; 105:17, 18, 37, 38; 106:11, 30, 38, 40; 116:6; 118:13[2]; 119:67, 71; 122:1, 4; 124:1, 2, 3; 126:2[2]; 135:8; 139:13, 15[2]; 142:T; Pr 4:3; 8:23, 24, 25, 27, 30[2]; 23:35; 24:30, 31[3]; Ecc 2:1, 3, 10, 11[2], 17; 3:16[2]; 4:1, 16; 5:6; 7:23; 9:14, 15; 12:7; SS 1:12; 2:3, 4; 3:10; 5:2, 6; 6:12; 8:5[2], 10[2], 11; Isa 1:21; 5:4, 25; 8:11; 9:17, 19; 10:14; 11:16; 16:13; 20:1; 22:13, 25[2]; 23:3, 13; 25:4, 5; 26:16; 33:4; 36:3, 21, 22; 37:2, 38; 38:1, 17; 39:2[2]; 41:25, 26; 42:21, 24; 43:10, 12; 45:12, 21; 47:6; 49:1[2], 21[2]; 50:1, 2, 5; 51:2, 9, 10; 52:14; 53:3[2], 5[2], 7[2], 8[2], 9, 10, 12; 57:17[2]; 59:15, 16[3]; 61:7[2]; 63:3, 4, 5[2], 9; 65:1, 12; 66:4, 7, 8; Jer 2:3; 4:23, 25, 26; 7:12; 11:18, 19[2]; 13:7[2], 20; 15:9; 17:16; 18:3, 4[2]; 20:1, 7, 14; 22:15, 16; 24:1; 25:1; 26:20, 21, 24[2]; 29:2, 3; 31:18, 19[3], 26, 32; 32:1, 2[3], 8, 31; 33:1; 34:7, 15; 35:4; 36:10, 17, 22[3], 23[2], 24; 37:4, 16, 21[2]; 38:1, 6[2], 26, 28; 39:2, 3, 15; 41:9; 46:2; 48:13, 27[2]; 51:7, 59; 52:1[2], 2, 5, 6, 7, 8, 12, 20, 21[4], 22[2], 34; La 1:1[3], 7, 9[2], 12, 21; 2:7, 15; 4:6[2], 13, 14, 15, 16, 20; Eze 1:1, 2, 3, 5[2], 13[2], 16, 20, 21, 22, 26[2], 27, 28[2]; 2:9[2]; 3:3, 13, 22; 4:14; 6:9; 7:19; 8:2[3], 4, 5, 7, 8, 11; 9:2, 8; 10:1, 4[2], 5, 7, 9, 14[2], 17, 19; 11:13, 22; 12:7; 13:16; 14:23; 15:5[2]; 16:3, 4, 13, 14, 19, 34, 36, 45, 49, 56, 57; 17:7[2], 8; 19:2, 4, 5[2], 7, 8, 10, 12[3]; 23:4, 5, 10, 11, 13, 15, 20, 40, 42; 24:18; 25:3[2]; 27:7[2], 32; 28:13, 15, 17; 29:18[2]; 30:22; 31:4, 7, 8, 10, 18; 32:25, 27; 33:22[2], 24; 34:5, 8; 35:10, 15; 36:17, 20, 34[2], 35, 36; 37:1, 7, 8; 40:1[2], 2, 3[2], 5[2], 7[2], 9, 12, 15, 18, 21, 22, 23, 24, 25, 26, 27, 28, 29, 32, 33, 36, 38[2], 43, 47, 48, 49; 41:1, 2, 7, 9, 10, 11[2], 12[3], 16, 17, 18, 21, 25; 42:2[2], 4, 7; 43:2[2], 3, 6, 22; 44:1, 31; 46:19, 21, 23; 47:1[2], 2, 3, 4[2], 5[2]; Da 1:15, 19; 2:1, 13, 19, 26, 31[4], 32, 34, 36, 45; 3:1[2], 19[3], 22[2], 24[2], 27; 4:4, 8, 10[2], 11, 12, 13, 19[2], 20, 21, 26, 29, 33[3], 34, 36[2]; 5:1, 5, 11, 13, 20[4], 21[5], 24[2], 25, 29[3], 30; 6:3, 4, 14[2], 16, 17, 18, 20, 22, 23[3]; 7:4[3], 5[2], 6, 7[3], 8, 9[2], 11[2], 12, 13, 14, 15, 19[2], 21, 22; 8:2[2], 3, 5, 7[2], 8, 12, 18, 22, 27[2]; 9:20[2], 21; 10:1[3], 4, 6, 8, 11, 15[2], 19; 11:29; 12:6, 7; Hos 1:10; 2:3, 7, 8; 5:11; 7:15; 10:11; 11:1, 3, 4; 12:10, 13; 13:1[2], 5, 6; Am 1:1; 2:9[2]; 5:19[2]; 7:1[2], 4[2], 7; Jnh 1:5[2], 10, 11, 17; 2:7; 3:3; 4:1, 2, 6, 8; Mic 1:13; Na 3:9; Hab 3:3, 4, 8; Hag 2:15, 18; Zec 1:2, 8, 10, 11, 15; 3:3, 5; 5:7[2], 9; 7:5, 7, 14[2]; 8:9, 10; 11:11[2], 13; Mal 2:5, 6[2], 14; 3:16; Mt 1:2, 6, 12, 16, 18; 2:1, 3, 4, 9, 15, 16, 17, 18, 22[2]; 3:4; 4:1, 2; 5:21, 27, 31, 33, 38, 43; 6:29; 7:27; 8:2, 3, 10, 13, 17, 24[2], 26, 30; 9:9, 18, 22, 32[2]; 11:2, 26; 12:4, 10, 13, 17, 22, 40, 46; 13:19, 20, 22, 23, 25, 33, 35, 47, 48; 14:9, 11, 15, 20, 23, 24[2]; 15:24, 28, 31; 16:11, 20; 17:2, 5, 13, 18; 18:24; 19:8[2]; 20:17, 30; 21:10, 18, 23, 25, 33, 42, 45; 22:7, 10, 11, 12, 31, 46; 24:1, 3, 15, 43; 25:5, 6, 10, 25, 27, 35[3], 36[3], 37, 38, 39, 42[2], 43, 44; 26:3, 6, 14, 20, 47[2], 58, 63, 69, 71; 27:3, 9, 12, 14, 15, 18, 19, 24, 51, 54, 57[2], 63; 28:1, 2, 3, 5; Mk 1:6, 9, 10, 13[2], 14, 23, 30, 33, 35, 42; 2:1[2], 2[2], 14, 16, 23, 26, 27; 3:1, 5[2], 8, 32; 4:1, 6, 10, 36, 37, 38, 39; 5:5, 11, 14, 18, 20, 21, 25, 26, 29, 35, 40, 42; 6:6, 20[2], 26, 47[2], 49, 55; 7:24, 26, 35; 8:1, 25; 9:2, 26, 27, 31, 32, 33, 34, 38; 10:1, 14, 17, 22, 32[2], 46, 47; 11:11, 12, 13, 17, 18, 27, 30; 12:5, 11, 35, 37; 13:3; 14:1, 3, 4, 10, 17, 43[2], 49, 51, 54, 61, 66; 15:1, 5, 7, 10, 21[2], 25, 33, 38, 39, 41, 42, 43, 45, 47; 16:1, 4, 6, 11, 19; Lk 1:5[3], 7, 8[2], 9, 10, 12, 23, 26, 27[2], 29, 36, 41, 45, 64, 66, 67, 80; 2:2[3], 4, 5[2], 7, 13, 21[3], 25[3], 27, 33, 36[2], 40, 42, 43, 44, 51; 3:1[2], 21[2], 23[3]; 4:1, 2[2], 15, 16, 17[2], 25[2], 26, 27, 29, 31, 33, 38, 40, 41, 43; 5:1[2], 12[2], 17[2], 24, 29; 6:1, 6[2], 10, 15, 49; 7:2, 6, 9, 12[4], 37[2]; 8:5, 20, 23, 24, 29, 32, 33, 42, 43, 49, 53; 9:7[2], 12, 17[2], 18, 29, 31, 34, 36, 42, 43[2], 45, 46, 53; 10:21, 30, 31, 33, 36, 39, 40; 11:1, 14[2], 27, 37, 38; 12:27, 39, 47; 13:10, 11[2], 17[2], 21; 14:1, 2, 30; 15:6, 11, 20[2], 24[2], 25, 26, 32[2]; 16:1[2], 19[2], 22[2], 23; 17:9, 11, 15, 16, 18, 20[2], 26, 28; 18:2, 3, 11, 13, 23, 34[2], 35, 36; 19:1, 2[3], 3[3], 4, 6, 11[2], 21, 22, 37, 47; 20:1, 4, 6; 21:5, 37[2]; 22:1, 3, 6, 24, 37, 39, 47[2], 49, 53, 54, 56, 59, 60; 23:6, 7[2], 8[2], 14, 19, 26, 38, 44, 45, 47, 50, 51, 54[2], 55; 24:6, 10, 18, 19, 21, 23, 26, 30, 32[2], 44, 51[2]; Jn 1:1[3], 2, 4[2], 6[2], 8, 9, 10, 11, 15[2], 17, 28, 30, 35, 39[2], 40, 44; 2:1[2], 13, 17, 21, 22, 23[2], 25; 3:1, 23[2], 26; 4:2, 6[3], 27, 46, 47, 51[2], 53, 54; 5:1, 5, 9[2], 13[2], 15, 16, 18[2], 35; 6:2, 4, 6, 10, 17, 18, 32, 59, 62, 64, 71[2]; 7:2, 12, 28, 37, 39[2], 43, 50; 8:4, 9, 20, 27, 30, 44, 56, 58; 9:2, 3, 14, 17, 19, 20, 25; 10:6, 22, 23, 41; 11:1, 2[2], 6[2], 13, 15, 16, 18, 20, 30, 31, 32, 33, 38[2], 49, 51, 55, 57; 12:2, 3, 4, 5, 6[2], 9, 11, 12, 16, 18, 21, 29, 33, 38; 13:3, 5, 11, 21, 22, 23, 24, 29, 30; 15:25; 16:4; 17:12[2]; 18:1, 4, 5, 9, 10, 13, 14[2], 15, 16[2], 18[2], 25, 28, 32[2], 37, 40; 19:8, 14[2], 20[3], 23, 24, 28, 29, 31[2], 33, 38, 41[3], 42[2]; 20:1, 14, 19, 24[2], 26; 21:4, 7[2], 11, 12, 14[2], 20; Ac 1:2, 9, 10, 17[2], 19, 22, 23, 26; 2:6, 16, 24, 26, 29, 30, 31; 3:2; 4:3, 9, 11, 22, 31, 32, 33, 34[2], 35, 36; 5:4, 8, 36; 6:9, 15; 7:2, 9, 12, 20[3], 21, 22[2], 23, 25, 27, 31, 35, 38, 45, 47; 8:3, 6, 8, 9, 12, 13, 18, 27, 28[2], 32[3], 33, 40; 9:3, 9, 10, 18[2], 19, 22, 26, 31, 33, 36[3], 38[2], 39; 10:1[2], 2, 10, 16, 17, 18[2], 19, 22, 24, 29, 30, 38, 44; 11:5[2], 10, 17, 21, 24, 26[2]; 12:3, 5, 6[2], 9[3], 12, 14[2], 15, 18, 20, 23, 25; 13:1, 7, 12, 25, 29, 36, 45, 46; 14:5, 8, 9, 12, 13, 19; 16:1[3], 2, 3, 13, 14[3], 19, 26, 27; 17:1, 2, 3, 16[3], 18[2]; 18:3, 5[2], 7, 12, 14, 18, 24; 19:1, 4, 17[2], 19[2], 29, 32, 34; 20:3[2], 4, 7, 9[2], 16, 37; 21:3, 30, 31, 33, 35, 37, 40; 22:6, 9, 12, 17, 20[2], 24, 25, 28, 29[2], 30; 23:1, 5, 7, 27[3], 29[2], 30, 34; 24:9, 18, 21, 22, 24, 27; 25:4, 14, 15, 16, 18, 20, 23; 26:9, 11, 12, 19, 24, 26; 27:1, 2, 7, 9, 12[3], 15, 20, 41, 42, 44; 28:1, 2, 3, 6, 16[2], 17, 18, 19, 25; Ro 1:3, 4; 3:26; 4:1, 2, 3, 9, 10[4], 11[2], 12, 18, 19[2], 21, 22, 23, 25[2]; 5:13, 14; 6:4, 6; 7:9, 13; 8:20, 34; 9:12, 25, 26; 11:7; 15:4[2]; 16:5, 7, 25; 1Co 1:13; 7:18[2], 22[2]; 9:10; 10:4, 5; 11:8, 9, 23; 13:11; 15:4[2], 10, 11, 47, 48; 16:12; 2Co 1:15, 17, 19, 23; 2:12; 3:9, 11, 13; 5:15, 19; 7:7, 12[2], 14[2]; 8:9; 11:9[2], 25[3], 33; 12:2, 4, 7, 16; 13:4; Gal 1:11, 12, 13[2], 14, 15[2], 22, 23; 2:2, 3[3], 10[2], 13; 3:1[2], 4, 6, 19[2], 22, 24; 4:13, 23[2], 29[2]; Eph 3:2, 3, 5, 7, 8, 11; 4:7; Php 2:5, 6, 26, 27; 4:14, 16; Col 1:19, 20, 25; 1Th 2:1, 10; 3:5; 2Th 1:10; 2:5; 3:9; 1Ti 1:3, 13; 2:6, 7, 13, 14[2]; 3:16; 4:14; 2Ti 1:9, 11, 16; 4:17; Tit 1:12; Phm 1:11, 15; Heb 2:2, 3[2], 9, 10, 18; 3:2[2], 5, 6, 10, 16, 17[2]; 5:4, 5, 7[2], 8; 7:1, 10, 14, 18, 20, 26; 8:5[3]; 9:2, 3, 18, 23, 25; 10:36; 11:3, 5[4], 8[3], 11[2], 17, 23[2], 24, 26, 38, 39; 12:2, 17, 20, 21; Jas 2:7, 21, 22[2], 23[3], 25; 5:17; 1Pe 1:10, 12, 20[2], 25; 2:22, 23; 3:5, 18; 4:6; 2Pe 1:17; 2:8, 16, 21; 3:5, 6; 1Jn 1:1, 2[3]; 3:5, 8, 12; 4:9; 5:18; 2Jn 1:4; 3Jn 1:3; Jude 1:3, 14; Rev 1:4, 8, 9, 10, 12, 15, 16, 18; 2:8, 13; 4:2, 8; 5:3, 4, 7, 12; 6:2[2], 4[2], 5, 8[2], 14; 7:9; 8:1, 3, 7[2], 8, 11, 12[3]; 9:1, 5, 9, 16, 17, 18; 10:1, 4, 10[2]; 11:1[2], 8, 13, 19[2]; 12:2[2], 4[2], 5, 8, 9[2], 14, 17; 13:2[2], 5[2], 7[2], 8, 15; 14:1, 2, 5, 14[2], 16, 20; 15:5, 8; 16:8, 10, 12, 18, 19, 21; 17:3, 4, 5, 6[2], 8[2], 11; 18:1, 18, 24; 19:11, 20; 20:10, 11, 12, 15[2]; 21:1, 5, 17, 19; Tob 1:2, 4[2], 10, 12, 19[3], 20[3], 22[2]; 2:1, 2, 9, 10, 14; 3:7, 10, 17[2]; 5:4[2]; 6:10, 14, 18[4]; 8:14[2]; 9:5; 11:15, 17; 12:1, 12, 14, 18[2], 19; 14:2[3], 3, 4, 10[2]; Jdt 1:1; 2:1; 4:6, 7; 5:1, 18, 19; 7:19, 21; 8:1, 3, 7[2], 10, 18, 19, 26, 28; 9:1[2], 3[2]; 10:3, 14, 18[2], 21[2]; 11:19[3]; 12:1, 16[2], 20[2]; 13:2[2], 4, 16, 20; 14:10, 11, 14; 15:3, 7; 16:21, 22; AdE 1:1, 2, 5, 6, 7[2], 8, 9, 10, 11; 2:1, 5[2], 7[2], 8[2], 12[2], 15, 19, 20[2]; 3:4[2], 5, 10, 15[2]; 4:2, 3, 4, 11, 14; 5:9, 14; 6:4[2]; 7:6, 7, 10; 8:1[2], 9, 10, 14, 17[2]; 9:11, 22, 26, 28, 32; 10:3[2], 6[2]; 11:1[2], 3, 4[2], 8, 9; 12:6; 13:12, 18; 14:5, 18; 15:5[2], 6[2], 13, 15, 16; 16:11[2]; Wis 3:2; 5:4, 6; 6:3; 7:1, 3[2], 4, 7, 12; 8:19, 21[2]; 9:9; 10:4, 13, 14; 11:4, 13; 12:10, 11; 14:2[2], 8, 10, 12[2], 15, 16, 22; 16:4[2], 7[2], 9, 12, 18, 21, 27[2]; 17:5, 6, 7, 14, 16[2], 20, 21[2]; 18:1, 4, 6, 10, 11, 14, 15, 21[2], 24[2], 25; 19:6, 7; Sir Pr:T[2]; 1:4, 30; 7:15, 28; 10:18; 11:5; 15:11, 12, 14; 23:20[2]; 24:4, 10, 11, 30; 33:10, 16[2]; 38:5, 22; 40:1; 44:16, 17[2], 19, 20; 45:1, 6, 15, 19, 24, 25; 46:1[2], 2, 4, 6[2], 13, 15; 47:2, 6, 21; 48:12[2], 13[2], 16, 22[3], 25; 49:2, 8, 11, 12, 14, 15, 16; 50:1, 3, 5, 12, 19; 51:6, 7[2], 11, 13, 18, 19, 21; Bar 4:6, 12, 33; LtJ 6:43[2]; Sus 1:1[2], 4[2], 15, 16, 21[2], 31, 32, 37, 39, 40, 45, 62, 63; Bel 1:1, 2[2], 8, 21[2], 23, 31, 33[2]; 1Mc 1:3[2], 5, 6, 16, 27, 28, 40, 57, 59; 2:7[2], 24, 25, 31, 52[2], 54, 57, 58, 60, 69, 70; 3:1, 4, 9, 27, 29, 31, 33, 35[2], 41, 45[4]; 4:4, 19, 20, 27, 30, 40, 54, 58[2]; 5:1, 14, 16, 34, 44, 46, 50, 55, 62, 63; 6:1[2], 2, 8, 9, 11, 17, 28, 30, 36, 40, 41, 43[3], 49, 53, 56, 59, 62; 7:2, 8[2], 16, 17, 23, 30, 33, 43[2], 46; 8:4, 6, 18; 9:5, 7[2], 11, 12, 13, 16, 27, 37, 41, 55[4], 57, 68, 69; 10:22, 55, 64, 68, 74, 80, 82, 83; 11:2, 9, 12, 14, 16, 21, 22, 38[2], 39, 52, 55, 70; 12:1, 7[2], 42; 13:7, 12, 14, 18, 23, 34, 41; 14:4[2], 7, 12, 13, 16, 17, 28, 30, 34; 15:3, 15, 32, 36; 16:5, 9, 12, 13, 14, 22; 2Mc 1:19, 23, 24, 31, 32, 33; 2:4, 9; 3:1, 5, 6[2], 7, 9, 12, 14, 16, 18, 21, 25, 28, 30[2], 31, 33, 40; 4:1, 2, 4[2], 7, 13[2], 18, 19, 20[2], 21, 22, 26[2], 28, 30, 37, 41; 5:5[2], 6, 8, 11, 13, 17[4], 20[2], 21; 6:3, 4, 5, 7, 8, 18, 21, 30; 7:5, 9, 10[2], 14, 18, 20, 22, 24[2], 30[2]; 8:1, 3, 8[2], 11, 25, 26; 9:2, 3, 5[2], 7[3], 8, 9, 10, 11[2], 14[2], 18, 24; 10:5, 9[2], 10, 12, 13, 19, 28, 32, 37; 11:1, 4, 5, 6, 7, 13, 16, 18, 27; 12:4, 9, 13[2], 21, 31, 35[3], 38, 40, 45[2]; 13:1, 4, 8, 9, 17, 19[2], 20, 21, 22, 23; 14:3, 5[2], 24, 26, 27, 28, 29, 30[2], 32, 37[3], 38, 43, 46; 15:11, 12[2], 18, 20, 28, 29, 30, 38; 1Es 1:6, 17, 21, 22, 23, 27, 31[2], 32, 34, 39[2], 43[2], 44, 46, 47; 2:13, 22, 23, 30; 3:15; 4:13, 45, 51; 5:38, 39[2], 53, 65; 6:5, 14[3], 22, 23[2]; 7:5, 6; 8:1, 3, 6, 8, 27, 45, 49, 51, 61, 63, 64[2], 91[2]; 9:2, 3, 5, 23, 48; Pm 151:1, 4, 5; 3Mc 1:1, 5, 8, 9, 11[3], 14, 17, 21, 24; 2:22[2], 26; 3:1[2], 2, 6, 14, 20, 30; 4:1[2], 2, 5, 11[2], 14, 15, 16, 18, 19, 21[2]; 5:1, 12[2], 14[2], 15, 17, 19, 26[2], 27, 28, 30, 35, 49; 6:5, 7, 16, 22, 34, 38[2]; 7:4; 2Es 1:3, 7, 13[2]; 2:10, 43[3]; 3:1[2], 3, 5[2], 13, 21, 22[2], 25; 4:1, 16, 17, 30, 50, 52; 5:14, 31, 35; 6:4, 17[2], 29, 36, 37[2], 39[2], 43, 47, 48, 55; 7:1, 11, 30, 92, 109, 118[2], 129; 8:14[2], 19; 9:4, 11, 13, 18[3], 20[2], 27[2], 28, 32, 34[3], 38[2], 43; 10:5, 25[4], 27[3], 28, 29, 32, 45[2], 46, 47, 48, 53, 54; 11:4[2], 6, 13, 14, 24, 26, 29[2]; 12:1, 2, 3[2], 12, 28, 29, 30[2], 51; 13:7, 11[3], 12, 37, 38, 39, 45; 14:1, 31, 39[3], 41[2], 42, 43; 15:39[2]; 16:55[2], 68; 4Mc 1:11; 2:3, 17; 3:10, 15[2]; 4:1[2], 9, 10, 11, 20[2], 21, 22; 5:4[2], 25; 6:5, 6, 10, 24, 26; 7:4, 13; 8:2, 4; 9:10, 13, 19, 20[2]; 10:1, 2, 9; 11:9, 10, 13[2], 18[3]; 12:2, 15; 13:3, 19, 20; 14:9, 20; 16:3[2], 20, 21; 17:1, 11, 12, 13, 14, 15, 21; 18:5[2], 7[2], 9, 10, 11, 20

WE (2326)

Ge 3:2; 11:4; 13:8; 19:2, 5, 9, 13, 32[2], 34; 20:13; 22:5[2]; 24:25, 50, 57; 26:22, 28[2], 29, 32; 29:4, 5, 8[2], 27; 31:15, 49; 32:6; 34:14, 15[2], 16[3], 17; 37:7, 10, 20[2], 26, 32; 38:23; 40:8; 41:11, 12, 38; 42:2, 11[2], 13, 21[4], 31[3], 32; 43:4, 5, 7[2], 8[2], 10[2], 18, 20, 21[3], 22[2]; 44:8[3], 16[5], 20[2], 22, 24[2], 26[4]; 46:34; 47:4[2], 15, 18, 19[4], 25; 50:15, 18; Ex 1:9; 3:18; 8:26[2], 27; 10:9[3], 26[3]; 12:33; 14:5, 12; 15:24; 16:3[2], 7, 8; 19:8; 20:19[2]; 24:3, 7[2], 14; 32:1, 23; 33:16; Lev 25:20[2]; Nu 9:7[2]; 10:29[2], 31, 32; 11:4, 5[2], 18, 20; 12:11; 13:27, 28, 30, 31[2], 32[2], 33[3]; 14:2[2], 7, 40[3]; 16:12, 14; 17:12[2], 13; 20:3, 10, 15, 16[2], 17[3], 18, 19[4]; 21:2, 5, 7, 22[4], 30; 31:50; 32:5, 16, 17[2], 18, 19, 31, 32; Dt 1:19[2], 22[2], 28[3], 41[2]; 2:1, 8[2], 13, 14[2], 33, 34[3], 35[2]; 3:1, 3, 4[2], 6[2], 7, 8, 12, 29; 4:7; 5:24[2], 25[3], 26, 27; 6:21, 25[2]; 12:8; 18:21; 21:7; 26:7; 29:7, 8, 16[2], 19[2]; 30:12, 13; Jos 1:16[2], 17[2]; 2:10, 11, 14, 17, 18, 19[2], 20; 4:23; 6:17; 7:7; 8:5, 6[2]; 9:6, 7, 8, 9, 11, 12[2], 13, 19[2], 20[3], 22, 24, 25; 17:14; 21:2; 22:17[2], 23, 24, 26, 27, 28[2], 29, 31; 24:15, 16, 17[2], 18, 21, 22, 24[2]; Jdg 1:3, 24; 8:6, 15, 25; 9:28[3], 38; 10:10[2], 15; 11:6, 8, 10, 24; 12:1; 13:8, 17, 22[2]; 14:15; 15:10, 12[2], 13[2]; 16:2, 5[3]; 18:5[2], 9; 19:12[2], 18, 19[2], 22, 28; 20:8, 9[2], 10, 13, 23, 28[2]; 21:7[3], 16, 18, 22[2]; Ru 1:10; 4:11; 1Sa 5:8; 6:2[2], 4, 9, 20; 7:6; 8:19, 20; 9:6, 7[3]; 10:14[2]; 11:1, 3[2], 10, 12; 12:10[3], 19[2]; 14:8, 9[3], 10, 12; 15:15; 16:11; 17:9, 10; 23:3[2]; 25:7, 8, 15[4], 16; 30:14[2], 22[2]; 2Sa 5:1; 7:22; 11:23; 12:18[2]; 13:25; 14:7[2], 14[2]; 16:20; 17:6, 12[2], 13; 18:3; 19:10, 42, 43[3]; 20:1; 21:5, 6; 1Ki 3:18; 8:47[2]; 12:4, 9, 16[2]; 17:12; 18:5; 20:23[2], 25[2], 31; 22:3, 7, 8, 15[2]; 2Ki 2:16; 3:8, 11; 6:1, 15, 28[2], 29[2]; 7:3[2], 4[6], 9[3], 10, 12[2]; 10:4, 5[3], 13[2]; 18:22, 26; 1Ch 11:1; 12:18; 13:3; 15:13; 16:35; 17:20; 29:13, 14[2], 15, 16; 2Ch 2:16; 6:37[2]; 10:4, 9, 16[2]; 13:10[2], 11; 14:7[2], 11[2]; 18:3, 5, 6, 7, 14; 20:9, 12[2]; 25:9, 16; 29:18, 19; 31:10[2]; Ezr 4:2[2], 3, 14[2], 16; 5:8, 9, 10[2], 11[2]; 7:24; 8:15, 21, 22, 23, 31, 32; 9:7[2], 9, 10[2], 14, 15[2]; 10:2, 4, 12, 13; Ne 1:6, 7; 2:17[2], 20; 4:1, 4, 6, 9, 10, 11, 15, 19, 21; 5:2[3], 3, 4, 5[2], 8[2], 12[2]; 9:33, 36, 37, 38; 10:30, 31[2], 32, 34, 35, 39; 13:27; Est 5:5; 7:4[2]; Job 2:10; 5:27; 8:9[2]; 9:32; 15:9; 17:16; 18:2, 3[2]; 19:28; 21:14, 15[3]; 26:14; 28:22; 31:31; 32:13; 36:26; 37:5, 19[2], 23; 38:35; Ps 4:6; 10:6[2]; 12:4; 20:5, 8, 9; 21:13; 33:21, 22; 35:25[2]; 36:9; 37:24[2]; 44:1, 5[2], 8[2], 17, 20, 22, 25; 46:2; 48:8[2], 9; 49:10; 55:14; 60:12; 64:6; 65:4; 66:6, 12; 74:8, 9; 75:1[2]; 78:3, 4[2]; 79:4, 8, 13[2]; 80:3, 7, 18[4], 19; 90:7[3], 10[2], 12, 14, 15; 95:7; 100:3[2]; 103:14[2]; 106:6[2], 47; 108:13; 115:18; 118:25[2], 26; 123:3; 124:7[2]; 126:1, 3; 129:8; 132:6[2]; 137:1[3], 2, 4; Pr 1:13[2], 14; 20:24; 24:12; SS 1:4[2], 11; 6:1, 13; 8:8[2], 9[2]; Isa 1:9; 2:3; 4:1; 5:19[2]; 9:10[2]; 14:10; 16:6; 20:6[4]; 22:13; 24:16; 25:9[2]; 26:1, 8, 12, 13, 17, 18[4]; 28:15[4]; 29:11, 12; 30:16[2]; 33:2; 36:7, 11; 38:20; 41:22[2], 23[2], 26[2]; 42:24; 46:5; 51:23; 53:1, 2[2], 3, 4, 5, 6[2]; 58:3; 59:9[2], 10[3], 11[3], 12; 63:17, 19; 64:3, 5[2], 6[2], 8[2], 9; 66:5; Jer 2:31[2]; 3:22, 25[3]; 4:13; 5:12; 6:16, 17, 24; 7:10; 8:8, 14[2], 15, 20; 9:19[3]; 13:12; 14:7, 9, 19, 20[2], 22; 15:2; 16:10; 18:12; 20:10; 26:19; 30:5; 35:6, 8, 9, 10, 11[2]; 36:16; 38:25; 41:8; 42:3[2], 5, 6[3], 13, 14[3], 20; 44:16, 17[4], 18[2], 19[2], 25[2]; 48:14, 29; 50:7; 51:9, 51[2]; La 2:4, 16[3]; 3:42; 4:17, 18, 20[2]; 5:3, 4[3], 5[3], 6, 7, 9, 16, 21; Eze 11:3; 21:10; 33:10[2], 24; 35:10; 37:11; Da 2:4, 7, 23, 36; 3:16, 17, 18[2], 24; 6:5[2]; 9:5, 6, 8, 9, 11, 13, 14, 15[2], 16, 18; Hos 6:2; 8:2; 10:3[2]; 14:2, 3[2]; Am 6:10, 13; 8:5[3]; Ob 1:1; Jnh 1:6, 7, 11, 14; 3:9; Mic 2:4; 4:2, 5; 5:5; Zec 1:11; 8:23; Mal 1:4[2], 6, 7; 2:10[2], 17; 3:7, 8, 13, 14, 15; Mt 2:2; 3:9; 6:12, 31[3]; 7:22; 8:25; 9:14; 11:3, 17[2]; 12:38; 14:17; 15:33; 16:7; 17:19, 27; 19:27[2]; 20:18, 22; 21:25, 26[2], 27; 22:16; 23:30[2]; 25:37, 38, 39, 44; 26:65; 27:42, 63; 28:13, 14; Mk 2:12; 4:30[2], 38; 5:9; 6:37; 8:16; 9:28, 38[2]; 10:28, 33, 35[2], 39; 11:31, 32, 33; 12:14, 15[2]; 14:58, 63; 15:32; Lk 1:71, 74; 3:8, 10, 12, 14[2]; 4:23; 5:5, 26; 7:19, 20, 32[2]; 8:24; 9:12, 13[2], 49[2]; 10:11; 11:4; 13:26; 15:32; 17:10[3]; 18:28, 31; 19:14; 20:5, 6, 21; 22:8, 49, 71[2]; 23:2, 41[3]; 24:21; Jn 1:14, 16, 41, 45; 3:2, 11[3]; 4:22[2], 42[3]; 6:5, 28, 30, 42, 68, 69; 7:27, 35; 8:33, 41[2], 48, 52; 9:4, 20, 21[2], 24, 28, 29[2], 31, 40[2], 41; 10:33; 11:16, 47, 48; 12:21, 34; 13:29; 14:5[2], 8, 23; 16:18, 30[2]; 17:11, 22; 18:30, 31; 19:7, 15; 20:2, 25; 21:3, 24; Ac 2:8, 11, 37; 3:12, 15; 4:9, 12, 16[2], 20[2]; 5:23[3], 28, 29, 32; 6:2, 3, 4, 11, 14; 7:40; 10:39, 47; 11:11, 12, 17; 13:32, 46; 14:15[2], 22; 15:10, 11[2], 19, 20, 24, 25, 27, 36; 16:10, 11, 12, 13[3], 16[2], 28; 17:19, 20, 28[2], 29[2], 32; 19:2, 25, 40[2]; 20:6[3], 7, 8, 13, 14, 15[4], 35; 21:1[2], 2[2], 3[2], 4, 5[2], 6, 7[3], 8[2], 10, 12[2], 14, 15, 16, 17, 23[2], 25; 23:9, 14[2], 15; 24:2, 3, 5, 6, 8; 25:26; 26:14; 27:1, 2, 3, 4, 5[2], 7[2], 8, 15, 16, 18, 26, 27, 29, 37; 28:1[2], 10[2], 11, 12, 13[2], 14[2], 16, 21, 22[2]; Ro 1:5, 12; 2:2; 3:5, 8, 9[2], 19, 28, 31[2]; 4:1, 9; 5:1[2], 2[3], 3, 6, 8, 9[2], 10[3], 11[2]; 6:1[2], 2, 4[2], 5[2], 6[2], 8[3], 9, 15[2]; 7:4, 5, 6[2], 7, 14; 8:12, 15, 16, 17[2], 22, 23[2], 24, 25[3], 26[2], 28, 31, 36[2], 37; 9:14, 29, 30; 10:8; 12:4, 5[2], 6; 13:11; 14:7[2], 8[7], 10; 15:1, 4; 1Co 1:23; 2:6, 7, 12[2], 13, 16; 3:9; 4:8, 9, 10[3], 11[2], 12[3], 13[2]; 6:3; 8:1, 4, 6[2], 8[3]; 9:4, 5, 11[2], 12[3], 25; 10:6, 8, 9, 16[2], 17[2], 22[2]; 11:16, 31[2], 32[3]; 12:13[2], 23[2]; 13:9[2], 12[2]; 15:11, 15[2], 19[2], 30, 32, 49[2], 51[2], 52; 2Co 1:4[2], 6[3], 7, 8[4], 9[3], 10, 12, 13, 14, 19, 20, 24[2]; 2:11[3], 15, 17[2]; 3:1[3], 4, 5, 12[2]; 4:1[2], 2[3], 5[2], 7, 8, 11[2], 13[3], 14, 16, 18; 5:1[3], 2, 3[2], 4[3], 6[4], 7, 8[2], 9[2], 11[3], 12, 13[2], 14, 16[3], 20[2], 21; 6:1[2], 3, 4, 8, 9, 11, 16; 7:1, 2[3], 5[2], 13[2], 14; 8:1, 5, 6, 7, 18, 19, 20[2], 21, 22[2]; 9:4; 10:2, 3[2], 4, 5, 6, 7, 11[2], 12, 13, 14[3], 15, 16; 11:4, 6, 21; 12:18[2], 19[3]; 13:4[2], 6, 7[3], 8, 9[3]; Gal 1:8[2], 9; 2:4, 5, 9, 10, 15, 16[3], 17; 3:14, 23, 24, 25; 4:3[2], 5, 31; 5:5, 25; 6:9[2], 10; Eph 1:7, 11, 12; 2:3, 5, 10; 3:12, 20; 4:14, 15, 25; 5:30; 6:8[3], 22; Php 3:3, 16, 20; Col 1:3, 4, 9[2], 14, 28[2]; 4:3, 8; 1Th 1:2, 4, 5, 8, 9; 2:2[2], 4[2], 5, 6, 7[2], 8[2], 9[3], 11, 13, 17[2], 18; 3:1[2], 2, 3, 4[3], 6, 7, 8, 9[2], 10[2], 12; 4:1, 2, 6, 10, 11, 13, 14, 15[2], 17[2]; 5:5, 8, 10[2], 12, 14; 2Th 1:3, 4, 11; 2:1, 13; 3:2, 4[2], 6, 7[2], 8[3], 9, 10[2], 11, 12, 14; 1Ti 1:8; 2:2; 4:10[2]; 6:7[2], 8[2]; 2Ti 2:11[2], 12[3], 13; Tit 1:4; 2:13; 3:3, 5, 7; Phm 1:6; Heb 2:1[3], 3[2], 5, 8, 9; 3:6[2], 14[2], 19; 4:3, 13, 14, 15[3], 16; 5:11; 6:3, 9[2], 11, 18, 19; 7:19, 26; 8:1[2]; 9:5; 10:10, 19, 21, 26, 30, 39; 11:3; 12:1, 9[3], 10, 25[2], 28[2]; 13:6, 10, 14[2], 18[2]; Jas 1:18; 3:1, 3[2], 9[2]; 4:13, 15; 5:11; 1Pe 2:24; 2Pe 1:16[3], 18[2], 19; 3:13; 1Jn 1:1[4], 2, 3[2], 4, 5, 6[4], 7[2], 8[3], 9, 10[3]; 2:1, 3[3], 5[2], 18, 28; 3:1[2], 2[5], 11, 12, 14[3], 16[2], 19[2], 21, 22[3], 23, 24; 4:6[2], 9, 10, 11, 12, 13[2], 14, 16, 17[2], 19, 21; 5:2[3], 3, 9, 14[2], 15[4], 18, 19[2], 20[3]; 2Jn 1:4, 5, 6, 8; 3Jn 1:8[2], 12, 14; Jude 1:3; Rev 7:3; 11:17; Tob 1:8; 2:13; 3:5, 9; 4:12, 21; 5:3[2], 16; 6:11, 13[6]; 7:3, 4; 8:7, 10, 21; 10:12; 11:2; Jdt 3:2; 5:20[2], 21, 23; 6:3, 4; 7:9, 13, 25, 27[2], 28[2]; 8:17, 20[2], 21, 22[2], 30[2], 31; 9:6; 10:19; 11:8, 9; 12:3, 12[2]; AdE 5:5; 6:3; 7:4[2]; 13:4, 5, 6, 17; 14:6, 7, 8; 16:7, 8, 11, 15; Wis 2:2[3], 16, 19; 5:4[3], 6, 7[3], 13[3]; 7:16; 9:16[2]; 12:22[4]; 15:2[4]; Sir Pr:T[2]; 8:5, 7; 25:11, 24; 31:9; 36:5; 43:24[2], 27, 28; 48:11; 49:11; Bar 1:10, 12[2], 13, 14, 17, 18, 19[2], 21; 2:8, 10, 12[3], 13, 19, 24; 3:2, 3, 6, 7[3], 8, 34; 4:4[2]; LtJ 6:6, 69; Aza 1:6[2], 7[2], 10[2], 14, 15, 16, 17, 18[2]; Sus 1:20, 21, 36, 38[3], 39[3], 40, 41; Bel 1:11, 12, 29; 1Mc 1:11; 2:13, 22, 34[2], 40; 3:17[4], 21, 50[2], 53; 5:11, 19, 40, 41, 48; 6:23, 57[2], 59; 7:15; 8:20, 31, 32; 9:8, 9[2], 30; 10:5, 16[2], 19, 20, 23, 26, 27, 28, 53, 56; 11:31[2], 33, 34[2], 35; 12:9[2], 10[2], 11[2], 12, 14, 15[2], 16, 17, 22, 23[2], 44; 13:9, 15, 16, 37[2], 38, 39; 14:21, 22, 25; 15:9[2], 19, 31, 33, 34[2], 35; 16:2; 2Mc 1:6, 7, 8[3], 11, 10[3]; 2:16[2], 18, 23, 25, 27; 6:17[2]; 7:2, 9, 18, 32; 8:18; 10:10; 11:23, 24, 25, 28[2], 35, 36[2], 37; 1Es 1:26; 2:20, 24; 4:42; 5:68, 69[2], 71; 6:8[2], 11, 12[2], 13; 8:41, 52, 53[2], 61[3], 62, 76, 77, 80, 82[3], 87, 89, 90[2], 92, 93, 95; 9:10, 11[3], 13; 3Mc 2:10[2], 13, 18; 3:15[2], 16[2], 17, 18, 20[3], 21[2], 23, 24[2], 25, 26; 5:40; 6:35; 7:2, 6[4], 7[2], 8, 9[2]; 2Es 4:14, 15, 23, 24[2], 35; 5:41; 6:54, 58, 59; 7:64[3], 67, 69, 75[2], 106, 119, 120, 121, 122, 123, 124, 126[3]; 8:6, 7, 31; 9:36, 45; 10:8[3], 22; 12:41[2], 44, 45; 14:35, 37; 4Mc 1:14, 17, 33[2], 34[2]; 2:9; 3:4; 5:16, 17[2], 18, 19, 23[2], 24[2], 25[3]; 6:15, 17[2], 18, 20, 32, 33; 8:17[2], 18, 19, 21[2], 22, 23, 26[2]; 9:1, 2[2], 3, 4, 6, 8[2]; 10:10, 20; 11:5, 15[2], 20, 24, 27; 12:7; 13:2, 17; 14:9[2]; 15:4

WERE (3182)

Ge 1:7[2], 10; 2:1, 4, 25[2]; 3:7[2], 11, 19; 4:8; 5:2, 4, 5, 8, 11, 14, 17, 20, 23, 27, 31; 6:1, 2, 4[3]; 7:11, 19, 23[2]; 8:1, 2, 7, 9, 13; 9:18, 19, 23, 29; 10:1, 21, 25, 29; 11:32; 12:6; 13:6, 13; 14:5, 13, 17; 17:26, 27; 18:11; 19:11[2], 14; 20:8, 10; 23:17; 24:32, 54; 25:3, 4[2], 24; 27:1, 15, 23, 42; 28:12; 29:2, 3, 17; 30:35[2], 39, 41,

42; **31**:1, 10; **32**:7; **34**:5, 7, 25; **35**:2, 4, 6, 16, 22, 26^2, 28; **36**:5, 7^2, 11, 12, 13^2, 14, 22; **37**:7, 9, 11; **38**:27; **39**:20, 22; **40**:5, 6, 7, 10, 13, 16, 17^2; **41**:5, 21; **42**:5, 35^2; **43**:18^2, 33, 34^2; **44**:3; **45**:3, 16, 24; **46**:12, 20, 22, 26^2, 27^3, 31; **47**:3, 27, 28; **48**:5, 10; **49**:24, 31^2, 32; **50**:4, 8, 23; **Ex 1**:7, 12, 14; **4**:19; **5**:13^2, 14^2, 19^2, 20; **8**:18; **9**:26, 31, 32; **10**:8, 11, 23; **12**:39; **14**:5, 8, 10, 11, 21; **15**:4, 15, 27; **16**:24; **17**:12; **19**:16; **20**:18; **22**:21; **23**:9; **26**:30; **27**:8; **32**:15, 16, 25; **34**:1, 30; **35**:22; **36**:4, 6, 8, 9, 12, 15, 29, 30, 36, 38; **37**:9, 14, 16, 17^2, 18, 20, 22, 25; **38**:2, 9, 10^2, 11^3, 12^2, 14, 15, 16, 17^3, 19^2, 20, 21, 25, 27; **39**:6, 13, 14^2; **Lev 5**:16; **8**:21, 24; **18**:27, 30; **19**:34; **24**:14; **25**:50; **26**:35; **Nu 1**:16, 21, 22, 23, 25, 27, 29, 31, 33, 35, 37, 39, 41, 43, 44, 47; **2**:33; **3**:17, 21, 23, 28, 29, 35, 38^2, 49; **4**:46, 49^2; **7**:2^2, 9; **9**:6^2; **11**:26, 29; **12**:1, 8; **13**:4, 16, 22; **14**:6; **15**:32; **16**:39^2, 49; **19**:18; **21**:32; **22**:3, 18, 22, 34, 40; **25**:6, 9; **26**:4, 20, 21, 33, 40, 60, 62, 63; **27**:1; **31**:5, 8, 38, 39, 40, 48; **32**:39; **33**:4, 9; **34**:29; **35**:23; **36**:12; **Dt 1**:26; **3**:5; **5**:5, 15; **6**:21; **7**:7^2; **8**:3; **9**:10, 15; **10**:2, 19; **15**:15; **16**:12; **21**:7; **23**:7; **24**:18, 22; **25**:18; **28**:60, 62, 67^2; **29**:17; **32**:18, 29; **33**:2, 3; **Jos 2**:10; **3**:14, 15, 16, 17; **4**:7^2; **5**:7, 8, 10; **6**:20; **8**:11, 16^3, 22; **9**:1, 5, 10, 13, 16^2, 17, 24; **10**:1, 2, 11^2, 20; **11**:2, 11, 19; **13**:31; **14**:4, 12; **15**:21, 46; **16**:9; **17**:1, 2^2; **18**:21; **20**:9; **21**:4, 19, 20, 21, 26, 27, 33, 34, 40, 41; **22**:30^2, 33; **24**:32; **Jdg 2**:12, 15; **3**:4, 24, 25; **4**:13; **5**:8, 15, 16; **6**:29, 31, 34, 35; **7**:1, 11, 12, 19^2, 23, 24; **8**:4, 10^2, 18, 19, 21, 24, 26; **9**:29, 44, 45, 47, 48; **10**:8, 17; **11**:33; **12**:1, 2; **14**:10; **15**:14; **16**:2, 9, 12, 17, 25, 27^2, 30^2; **17**:2; **18**:3, 7^2, 22^3, 26, 30; **19**:11, 16, 22; **20**:16^2, 31, 33, 36, 41, 42, 45^3, 46; **21**:13; **Ru 1**:2^2, 13; **4**:11; **1Sa 1**:3; **2**:5^2, 12, 22, 27; **3**:1, 13; **4**:4, 7, 15, 19; **5**:4, 7, 12; **6**:13, 15; **7**:7, 10, 13, 14; **8**:2, 10; **9**:4, 14, 20, 22, 27; **10**:9, 10, 14, 18, 27; **11**:8, 11^2; **13**:2^2, 4, 6^2, 11^2, 15, 16; **14**:2^2, 16, 17^2, 20, 21, 22, 31, 41^2, 49^2; **17**:1, 11, 13, 19, 24, 31; **18**:6, 27; **20**:15; **22**:2, 6^2, 11; **23**:13, 24, 26; **24**:3; **25**:7, 15^3, 16^2; **26**:12; **27**:2, 8; **29**:1, 2^2, 4; **30**:2, 4, 6, 9^2, 16, 20, 21; **31**:7^2; **2Sa 1**:11, 14, 23^3, 26; **2**:3, 15, 17, 18, 30; **3**:2, 5, 19, 20, 31, 34^2; **4**:2; **5**:13, 14, 22; **6**:3, 5; **8**:2^3, 7, 17, 18; **10**:5, 8, 13, 16, 19^2; **11**:16; **12**:1, 18, 19, 31; **13**:18, 30, 31, 33; **14**:27; **15**:4, 11, 14, 22, 30; **16**:6, 14; **17**:17, 22; **18**:1, 7; **19**:6^2, 8, 9, 17, 28, 43^2; **20**:3, 8, 12^2, 15, 25; **21**:2, 9, 22; **22**:16^2, 18, 23, 38; **23**:9, 22, 24; **24**:2, 9^2; **1Ki 1**:41; **3**:2, 16, 18^2; **4**:2, 3, 4, 8, 20^2; **5**:16; **6**:27^2, 31, 34^2; **7**:3, 4, 9, 11, 17, 18, 19^2, 20^2, 24^2, 25, 28, 29^3, 30^2, 31^2, 32^2, 33^2, 34^2, 35, 37, 41^2, 42, 45, 47, 48; **8**:4, 5, 8^2; **9**:20^2, 21^2, 22^2, 23^2, 27; **10**:19, 20, 21^3, 29; **11**:3, 17, 29; **12**:17, 31; **13**:20; **14**:4, 9, 24; **15**:14, 18, 27; **16**:15, 16, 21, 25, 30, 33; **19**:19; **20**:1, 23, 30, 33; **22**:10^2, 12, 43, 46, 48; **2Ki 2**:1, 3, 5, 7, 15; **3**:9, 14, 21^3; **4**:6, 39, 40; **5**:3; **6**:20, 32; **7**:2, 3, 10, 19; **9**:5; **10**:4, 6^2, 11, 17, 29; **11**:2, 9^2, 10, 15; **12**:3, 13, 14; **14**:4, 14; **15**:4, 16, 35; **16**:17; **17**:2, 9, 14, 15; **18**:5, 36; **19**:12, 18^2, 35; **21**:11; **23**:3, 7, 8^2, 13, 19, 20, 24^2; **24**:11; **25**:4, 10, 11, 13^2, 17, 19^2, 25, 26, 28; **1Ch 1**:19, 23, 33, 51; **2**:9, 16, 18, 23, 33, 50; **3**:1, 4, 5, 9; **4**:2, 3, 4, 6, 14, 19, 23, 31, 32, 33^2, 38, 41; **5**:14, 17, 20^2, 23, 24; **6**:33, 44, 48, 60, 61, 62, 63, 67; **7**:4, 5, 8, 11, 12, 16, 17, 19, 21, 28, 40; **8**:6^2, 10, 13, 16, 18, 21, 25, 27, 28, 38, 40^2; **9**:2, 9, 17, 18, 19, 22^3, 23, 24, 25^2, 26^2, 28^2, 29, 33, 34, 44; **10**:7^2; **11**:4, 13, 24, 26; **12**:1, 2^2, 8^2, 14, 21, 31, 34, 38, 39; **13**:7, 8; **14**:12; **15**:2, 19, 20, 21, 23, 24^2, 26, 27^2; **16**:6, 19, 38, 41, 42; **18**:7, 16, 17; **19**:7, 9, 11, 14, 16, 19; **20**:3, 4, 8; **21**:5, 20, 29; **22**:2; **23**:3, 7, 9, 10, 11, 14, 17, 24^3, 27; **24**:1, 4, 5, 30; **25**:5, 6^2, 7^2; **26**:6^2, 7, 8, 17, 18, 19, 22, 25, 26, 28, 29, 31; **27**:2, 4, 5, 7, 8, 9, 10, 11, 12, 13, 14, 15, 22, 31; **29**:15; **2Ch 1**:12, 16, 17; **2**:17^2; **4**:3^2, 4, 6, 12, 13, 19, 22; **5**:5, 6, 9^2, 11, 12; **6**:38; **8**:7^2, 8, 9, 10; **9**:9, 18^2, 19, 20^2, 28; **10**:17; **11**:13; **12**:12, 15; **13**:13, 18; **14**:8, 13; **15**:6, 9, 10, 17; **16**:8; **17**:8, 19; **18**:2, 9^3, 11; **20**:21, 22, 24, 33, 37^2; **21**:2, 13; **22**:4, 11; **23**:8^2, 9, 14; **24**:13, 14, 26; **25**:5, 12, 24; **26**:17; **28**:12, 15^2, 23; **29**:23, 29, 31, 32, 33, 34^2, 35; **30**:7, 8, 14, 15, 17, 21; **31**:1, 13, 15, 18^2, 19^2; **32**:3, 4, 8, 9, 13, 18, 19; **34**:10, 12, 13^2, 14, 31, 32, 33; **35**:3, 7^2, 14, 15^2, 17, 18; **36**:14; **Ezr 1**:11; **2**:1, 58, 59, 62^2, 63, 65; **3**:1, 3, 10; **4**:1, 20; **5**:1, 2, 6, 14; **6**:1, 20; **8**:3, 16^2, 20, 30, 33^2; **10**:18; **Ne 2**:16; **3**:7^2; **4**:1, 7^2, 17; **5**:2, 3, 4, 8^2, 15, 16, 17, 18; **6**:16, 18; **7**:4, 5, 60, 61, 64, 65, 67; **8**:3, 12; **9**:1, 17, 25, 26, 30; **11**:6, 16, 18, 19, 20, 21, 36; **12**:7, 12, 22, 23, 25, 26, 44, 46; **13**:5, 13; **Est 1**:3, 5, 6^2, 7, 13, 14; **2**:8^2, 19, 23; **3**:1, 2, 3, 6, 12, 13; **5**:6; **6**:1, 14; **7**:2; **8**:9, 11, 13; **9**:1, 3, 14, 15, 16, 18, 20, 30; **Job 1**:2, 13, 14^2, 18; **3**:12; **4**:4, 7; **6**:2, 20, 26; **10**:19; **15**:7; **16**:4; **19**:23^2, 24; **20**:4; **22**:16; **26**:13; **29**:2, 5, 6, 10; **32**:4; **34**:36; **38**:4, 6, 21; **39**:16; **41**:9; **42**:15; **Ps 18**:15^2, 17, 22, 37, 38; **22**:5^2; **33**:6; **35**:13; **37**:36; **40**:5; **48**:5^2; **50**:12; **51**:16; **55**:21^2; **76**:5; **77**:16, 19; **78**:29, 37, 39, 53, 57; **80**:10; **81**:6; **83**:10; **85**:1; **87**:5; **90**:2; **99**:6, 8; **102**:20; **103**:14; **105**:12, 18; **106**:7, 16, 33, 42, 43^2; **107**:12, 17, 27, 29, 30; **122**:5; **126**:1; **139**:16^2; **141**:6; **148**:5; **Pr 8**:24^2; **Ecc 1**:16; **2**:7, 9; **5**:13, 14; **7**:10; **8**:10; **SS 1**:6; **2**:6; **6**:11; **8**:1, 3, 10; **Isa 5**:25; **6**:2; **9**:1, 16^2, 20^2, 21; **10**:10, 22; **12**:1; **14**:2, 3, 8, 9^2; **22**:3^3, 7, 9; **23**:3^2, 8^2; **26**:17, 18; **27**:7, 13^2; **36**:21; **37**:12, 19^2, 36; **45**:24; **46**:5; **48**:8; **50**:1; **51**:1^2; **52**:3, 14^2; **58**:2; **59**:10; **64**:5; **Jer 1**:1, 5; **2**:3, 36; **4**:24, 26; **5**:8; **6**:15; **8**:12; **9**:1; **15**:16; **20**:2; **22**:24, 26; **28**:5; **31**:36; **32**:12; **33**:4, 7; **34**:1, 5, 7^2; **36**:12, 28, 32; **37**:5, 15; **39**:9; **40**:1, 6, 11; **41**:3, 8, 10^2, 13^2, 18; **42**:8, 18; **44**:6, 15, 20; **49**:18; **50**:24^2; **52**:7, 14, 15, 17^2, 20, 23, 25^2, 30, 32; **La 1**:7, 14^2; **3**:52; **4**:5, 7^2, 9, 17, 18, 19; **Eze 1**:1, 5, 7^2, 11^2, 18^2, 23; **2**:10; **8**:10, 14, 16; **9**:6, 8; **10**:3, 9, 12, 13, 15, 20^2, 22^2; **11**:1; **14**:14, 16, 18, 20; **16**:3, 4^2, 5^3, 7^2, 8, 13, 20, 22, 27, 28^2, 29, 31, 34^2, 47, 50; **20**:21, 24, 25; **21**:30; **23**:2, 3^2, 11, 20; **27**:8^3, 9^2, 10, 11^2, 15, 19, 21, 25; **28**:12, 13^4, 14, 15^2, 16; **29**:6, 13; **31**:8, 9, 15, 16^2; **32**:27; **34**:5, 6^2; **36**:19, 31; **37**:2^2, 8; **38**:8^2, 12; **40**:4, 6, 10^3, 12, 16, 17, 21, 22, 25, 26, 29^2, 30, 31, 33^2, 36, 39^2, 40^2, 41^2, 42^3, 43, 44, 48, 49; **41**:2, 6^2, 16^2, 19, 20, 21, 22, 25^2, 26; **42**:1, 4, 5, 6^2, 8^2, 10, 11, 12; **43**:8; **46**:22^2; **Da 1**:4, 5, 6, 16, 19; **2**:13, 28, 31, 35, 42; **3**:3, 21^2, 27; **4**:12, 31, 36; **5**:9, 12, 15; **6**:24; **7**:4, 8^2, 9^2, 10, 12, 20; **8**:3, 4; **10**:7; **Hos 2**:9; **8**:7; **10**:14; **13**:6^2; **Am 4**:7, 8, 11; **Ob 1**:11; **Jnh 1**:5, 10; **2**:5; **Mic 1**:13; **2**:11; **4**:7; **Na 3**:9, 10^2; **Hab 1**:5; **3**:6, 9, 14; **Zep 3**:7; **Hag 2**:16^2; **Zec 1**:8; **3**:4; **6**:7; **7**:7^2; **8**:9, 10; **10**:8; **11**:11; **Mt 2**:10, 16, 20; **3**:5, 6, 16; **4**:18, 24; **5**:12; **7**:28; **8**:16^2, 27, 28; **9**:2, 8, 10, 30, 33, 36; **12**:1, 3, 23, 25, 46; **13**:6, 54; **14**:20, 21, 26, 35, 36; **15**:37, 38; **17**:6, 9, 22, 23; **18**:6^2, 31; **19**:8, 13, 25; **20**:24, 29, 30; **21**:9, 11, 12, 20; **22**:8, 22, 25, 33, 41; **23**:37; **24**:37, 38; **25**:2^2, 10, 24; **26**:8, 21, 26, 43, 55, 59, 69; **27**:38, 41, 44, 51, 52^2, 54^2, 55, 56, 61; **28**:11, 13, 15; **Mk 1**:5^2, 16, 19, 22, 27, 32, 34; **2**:6, 8, 12, 15^2, 18, 25; **3**:4, 21; **4**:10, 33, 36, 41; **5**:13, 15, 40, 42; **6**:2, 13, 14, 31, 34, 42, 48, 50, 51, 52, 56; **7**:2, 35, 37; **8**:8, 9; **9**:4, 6, 9, 15, 32, 33, 34, 42; **10**:13, 24, 26, 32^3, 46; **11**:1, 4, 9, 15^2, 18, 32; **12**:17, 20; **14**:1, 4, 11, 18, 22, 35, 40, 48, 53, 55, 67; **15**:31, 32, 40^2, 41, 44; **16**:5, 8, 10, 12, 14; **Lk 1**:2^2, 6, 7, 21, 59, 63, 65; **2**:6, 8, 9, 18, 33, 38, 47, 48, 49; **3**:15^2, 21; **4**:2, 20, 22, 25, 27, 28, 32, 36, 40, 42; **5**:2, 6, 9^2, 10^2, 17, 18, 26, 30; **6**:3, 8, 11, 18^2, 19; **7**:21, 39, 47, 49; **8**:1, 23^2, 25, 35, 37, 40, 52, 56; **9**:14, 17, 31, 32, 33, 34, 43, 45, 57; **11**:14, 17, 29, 52; **12**:49; **13**:1, 2, 4^2, 17, 34; **14**:1, 4, 24, 25; **15**:1, 2, 16; **16**:1, 14, 16; **17**:2^2, 10, 14, 17, 27, 28; **18**:9, 15, 39; **19**:11, 32, 33, 40, 45, 48; **20**:26, 29; **21**:5; **22**:2^2, 5, 49, 52, 63; **23**:5, 27^2, 32^2, 39; **24**:4, 5, 13, 15, 16, 22, 24, 28^2, 31, 32, 34, 36, 37^2, 41, 53; **Jn 1**:13; **2**:6, 16; **3**:19, 23; **4**:27, 30, 31, 43; **5**:18, 35; **6**:11, 12, 15, 19, 21, 24, 42, 61, 62, 64; **7**:1, 10, 11, 12^2, 15, 25, 31, 39; **8**:39, 42; **9**:9^2, 10, 16, 22, 33, 34, 41; **10**:19, 20, 21, 35, 41; **11**:8, 31, 56^2; **12**:11^2, 20; **13**:1; **14**:2; **17**:6; **18**:18, 30, 36; **19**:25; **20**:4, 19, 26^2; **21**:2, 6^2, 8, 11, 18, 25; **Ac 1**:9, 10, 13, 14; **2**:1, 2, 4, 5, 12, 37, 41^2, 43, 44, 47; **3**:1, 7, 10; **4**:1, 2, 6, 13^2, 23, 31^2, 32; **5**:4, 12^2, 14, 16, 17, 24, 26, 33, 36, 37, 39, 41; **6**:1^2; **7**:16, 26, 39, 59; **8**:1, 4, 7^3, 12, 36; **9**:7, 8, 21, 24, 26, 28; **10**:9, 12, 17^2, 38, 41, 45; **11**:1, 11, 18, 19, 20, 24, 26; **12**:6, 11, 12, 16; **13**:1, 2, 42, 45, 48, 52; **14**:4; **15**:1, 2, 3, 4, 30, 32, 33; **16**:3, 4, 5, 15, 16, 25^2, 26^3, 32, 33, 38^2; **17**:4, 5, 8, 11^2; **18**:3, 8, 14; **19**:3, 5, 7, 12, 14, 28, 29, 31, 32; **20**:5, 8^2, 12; **21**:5, 10, 16, 18, 27, 30, 31; **22**:5, 9, 11, 23, 29; **23**:6^2, 13, 20; **24**:19; **25**:3, 14; **26**:10, 31; **27**:1, 4, 15, 16, 17, 18, 27^2, 36, 37, 44; **28**:6, 7, 9, 10, 14, 24, 25; **Ro 1**:21, 27, 29; **3**:2, 3; **4**:23; **5**:6, 8, 10^2, 14, 19; **6**:3, 17, 20^2; **7**:5^2; **8**:24; **9**:3, 25, 27, 32; **11**:7, 17^2, 19, 20, 30; **15**:27; **16**:7^2; **1Co 1**:9, 13, 15, 26^3; **2**:4; **3**:2; **4**:7; **6**:11^3, 20; **7**:7, 20, 21, 23, 24, 30^2; **10**:1, 2, 5, 9, 10, 11; **12**:2^2, 13^2, 17^2, 19; **16**:15; **2Co 1**:8; **3**:14; **7**:5, 9^2; **10**:14^2; **11**:9, 21; **12**:12; **Gal 1**:10, 17; **2**:6^2, 9, 14; **3**:16, 23, 27; **4**:3^2, 5, 8, 20; **5**:7, 13; **Eph 1**:12, 13; **2**:1, 3, 5, 12, 13, 17^2; **4**:4, 11, 21, 22, 30; **5**:8; **Php 4**:10; **Col 1**:16, 21; **2**:7, 11, 12^2, 13; **3**:7, 15; **1Th 2**:7, 17; **3**:4^2; **2Th 2**:15; **3**:7^2, 10; **1Ti 6**:12; **Tit 3**:3; **Heb 2**:15; **3**:16^2, 18, 19; **4**:2, 3; **7**:23^2; **8**:4; **9**:2, 4, 5; **10**:29, 34; **11**:3, 9, 12, 13, 23, 29^2, 31, 35, 37^3, 39; **13**:3^2; **Jas 1**:24; **1Pe 1**:12, 18; **2**:8, 10, 25; **3**:9, 20; **4**:12; **2Pe 1**:18; **3**:4; **1Jn 3**:12; **2Jn 1**:5; **Jude 1**:4; **Rev 1**:14^2, 15; **3**:15; **4**:11; **5**:9; **6**:8, 11^2; **7**:4; **8**:2, 5, 7^2, 9; **9**:2, 3, 4, 5, 7^3, 15, 17, 20; **11**:11, 13^2, 15, 17, 19; **12**:8, 9; **13**:1^2, 2; **14**:1; **15**:8; **16**:5, 9, 18, 20; **18**:23^2; **19**:14, 20, 21^2; **20**:3, 4, 5, 10, 12^2, 13^3, 14; **Tob 2**:1, 10^2; **3**:16; **4**:4, 12; **5**:14; **6**:6; **11**:16, 17, 18^2; **12**:16^2, 19; **Jdt 1**:9, 11; **4**:2^2; **5**:7, 9, 18^3, 19; **6**:15; **7**:4, 20, 21, 22^2, 32; **8**:3, 9, 19, 30; **10**:7, 11; **13**:1, 10, 17; **14**:12, 19; **15**:1, 5, 12, 13; **16**:10, 11, 14, 18, 24; **AdE 1**:6^2, 7, 14; **2**:8, 18, 20, 21^2; **3**:2, 12^3, 13, 14^2; **4**:8, 14; **5**:6; **6**:2, 14; **7**:2; **8**:9, 17; **9**:3, 15, 18, 25, 26, 28; **10**:2, 9; **11**:9, 11; **12**:2, 3; **16**:15; **Wis 2**:2, 21; **3**:4; **4**:10^3, 11, 14; **5**:4^2, 13^2; **9**:18^3; **10**:6, 8, 11, 21; **11**:4, 5, 9^3, 11; **12**:8, 9, 10, 11, 24; **13**:1^3, 2, 4; **14**:6, 16; **15**:8^2, 15; **16**:1^2, 4, 5, 6, 9, 10, 11^2, 16, 18, 22; **17**:3^2, 8, 15^2, 17^3, 21; **18**:2^2, 7, 9, 12, 13, 18, 24; **19**:1, 3^2, 14, 17^2, 19; **Sir 7**:28; **16**:11; **29**:18; **33**:8; **37**:3; **39**:25; **40**:7, 10; **44**:3^2, 4, 7^2, 10, 18; **45**:19; **46**:8; **47**:3^2, 14^2, 16, 19, 20, 24; **48**:4, 9, 11, 14, 15^3, 19^2; **49**:4, 15, 16; **Bar 1**:7; **2**:2, 5; **3**:18, 26^2, 34; **4**:6^2, 26, 28; **LtJ 6**:1, 24, 40; **Aza 1**:17, 25, 27; **Sus 1**:3, 5^3, 6, 10, 11, 15, 16, 18, 33^2, 36, 38, 41, 52, 57; **Bel 1**:10, 13, 18, 28, 30, 32^2, 42; **1Mc 1**:18, 34, 39, 48, 58, 62; **2**:15, 16, 29, 59; **3**:6, 9, 11, 23, 29, 42, 56^4; **4**:2, 7, 8, 9, 14, 20, 21, 35; **5**:4, 5^2, 7, 13, 16^2, 20, 21, 26, 43, 44, 49, 55, 58, 60^2, 63; **6**:18, 23, 35, 37^3, 38, 39, 40, 54; **7**:5, 13, 22, 29; **8**:1^2, 2^2, 10; **9**:5, 6^3, 8, 14, 17, 22, 33, 35, 40, 44, 60, 61; **10**:8, 11, 12, 53, 72, 77, 82; **11**:14, 18, 29, 34, 39, 73; **12**:14, 15^2, 26, 28^3, 34, 52; **13**:2, 17, 47, 49^3; **14**:13, 16, 19, 21, 36^2, 40; **15**:2, 10, 13, 35; **16**:6, 7, 8, 10, 16, 22; **2Mc 1**:8, 13, 19, 21; **2**:1, 2, 8, 11, 22; **3**:1, 10, 19, 22, 24; **4**:3, 9, 14, 18, 28, 35, 40, 41, 43; **5**:14^3, 18; **6**:4, 5, 7^2, 10, 11^2, 12, 21, 29; **7**:1^2, 4, 12; **8**:2, 13, 16, 20, 25, 33, 36; **9**:2; **10**:15^2, 20^3, 29, 30, 31, 33; **11**:8, 9, 13, 17; **12**:3, 7, 8, 11, 14, 19, 22, 27, 28, 36, 37, 44; **13**:8, 10, 25^2; **14**:11, 20, 21, 31, 35, 41^2, 45; **15**:1, 2, 3, 17, 19, 20, 21, 27, 28, 31; **1Es 1**:7^2, 14, 15, 16, 17, 18, 19, 21, 23, 47, 57; **2**:9, 12, 14, 15, 16, 23, 27; **3**:1^2, 2, 3, 16; **4**:44, 47, 49, 54; **5**:1, 3, 35, 38, 39, 41, 42^2, 43, 47, 50^2, 58, 67, 73; **6**:1, 2, 5, 6, 18, 23, 27; **7**:9, 10, 11^2; **8**:44, 50, 62, 63, 72, 77, 80, 88; **9**:17, 18^2, 37, 49, 50, 55; **Pm 151**:5; **3Mc 1**:4, 5, 11, 17, 21, 27; **2**:4, 5, 12, 25; **3**:2, 5, 7^2, 8^2, 10, 18^2; **4**:2, 3, 4, 5, 6^2, 7, 9^2, 10, 17, 18; **5**:3, 6, 7, 14, 20, 24, 26, 29, 31, 32, 39, 49; **6**:15, 29, 34; **7**:21; **2Es 1**:15, 17, 20, 22; **2**:42; **3**:12, 13, 21^2, 23; **4**:18, 42; **5**:21, 40, 54; **6**:1, 2, 3^2, 4^2, 5^3, 6, 8, 26, 44; **7**:12, 22, 69, 87, 94, 112, 139; **8**:41, 56, 60; **9**:4, 38^2; **10**:45; **11**:2, 4, 6, 11, 19, 20, 23, 28, 29^2, 31^2; **12**:3, 24, 36, 40; **13**:5, 8, 11, 13^3, 38, 40^2; **14**:3, 22, 29, 44, 45, 46; **15**:53; **16**:56; **4Mc 3**:9, 10, 20^2; **4**:9, 12, 17, 23, 24, 25, 26; **5**:3^2, 18, 19, 22; **6**:1, 6^2; **8**:2, 3, 15, 28; **9**:13, 20, 21, 26, 27; **10**:7, 8; **11**:10, 15, 19; **12**:11, 13; **13**:5, 18^2, 20, 21, 23, 27; **15**:2, 10, 11, 22; **16**:3, 12, 15, 17, 21; **17**:6, 7, 11, 14, 16, 21; **18**:3^2

WHAT (2117)

Ge 2:19; **3**:13; **4**:10, 23; **9**:24; **11**:6; **12**:18; **14**:24; **15**:2; **18**:17, 19, 25; **19**:25; **20**:9, 10; **21**:17, 29; **23**:15; **25**:32; **26**:10; **27**:37, 45, 46; **28**:15; **29**:15, 25; **30**:31; **31**:1, 26, 28, 32, 36^2, 37, 43; **32**:13, 27; **33**:8, 9; **37**:10, 15, 20, 26; **38**:10, 16, 18, 29; **41**:25, 28, 55; **42**:21, 28; **43**:7; **44**:15, 16^2; **46**:33; **47**:3; **49**:1, 28; **50**:15; **Ex 2**:4; **3**:13^2, 16; **4**:2, 12, 14, 15; **6**:1; **10**:2, 11, 26; **12**:16, 19, 26, 36; **13**:8, 14; **14**:5, 11; **15**:24, 26; **16**:5, 7, 8, 15^2, 16, 23^3, 32; **17**:4; **18**:14, 17; **19**:4; **21**:22; **22**:27; **23**:11, 16; **26**:13; **29**:1, 38; **30**:13; **32**:1, 21, 23; **33**:5; **34**:11, 34; **35**:25; **36**:7; **Lev 3**:10; **6**:4, 16; **7**:16, 17; **8**:5, 32; **9**:5; **10**:3; **17**:2, 15^2; **19**:8; **25**:6, 12, 20, 25, 28; **27**:8; **Nu 4**:31; **6**:21; **9**:8; **13**:18; **15**:34; **16**:11; **22**:19, 20, 28, 35, 38; **23**:5, 11, 12, 16, 17, 23, 26; **24**:13^2, 14; **27**:7; **30**:1; **31**:50; **32**:24; **36**:5, 6; **Dt 3**:24; **4**:2, 3, 7, 8, 25; **6**:18, 20; **7**:18; **8**:2; **9**:18; **10**:12; **11**:4, 5, 6; **12**:25, 28; **13**:18; **16**:4; **17**:2; **18**:16, 17; **21**:9; **24**:9, 20, 21; **25**:9, 17; **29**:24; **31**:21, 29; **32**:20, 21^2, 29; **Jos 2**:10; **4**:6, 21; **5**:14; **7**:8, 9, 19, 20; **9**:3, 20, 26; **14**:6; **15**:18; **22**:16, 24; **24**:5, 7; **Jdg 1**:14; **2**:2, 11; **3**:7, 12^2; **4**:1; **6**:1; **7**:11; **8**:1, 2, 3, 18; **9**:48; **10**:6; **11**:12, 24, 36; **13**:1, 8, 12^2, 17; **14**:6, 18^2; **15**:7, 11; **16**:5, 6, 15; **17**:6; **18**:3^2, 8, 14, 18, 23, 24^2, 27; **20**:9, 12; **21**:7, 11, 16, 25; **Ru 2**:9, 17, 18; **3**:4; **1Sa 1**:23; **2**:14, 35; **3**:17, 18; **4**:6, 14; **5**:8; **6**:2^2, 4; **9**:7^2, 24^2; **10**:2, 8, 11, 15; **11**:5; **12**:24; **13**:11, 14; **14**:40, 43; **15**:2, 14, 16, 19; **16**:3, 4; **17**:26, 29; **18**:8, 24; **20**:1^3, 32; **21**:3; **22**:3; **24**:19; **25**:17, 35; **26**:18^2; **28**:2, 9, 13, 14, 15, 21; **29**:3, 8^2; **30**:23; **31**:11; **2Sa 3**:9, 24; **7**:18, 20; **9**:8; **10**:12; **12**:9, 21; **14**:5; **15**:2, 26; **16**:10, 20; **17**:5, 6; **18**:11, 21, 22, 23, 29; **19**:22, 27, 28, 35^4; **21**:3, 4, 11; **24**:10, 13, 17, 22; **1Ki 1**:16; **2**:5, 9; **3**:5, 11, 13; **8**:15, 39; **9**:13; **10**:13; **11**:6, 10, 22, 33, 38; **12**:9, 16; **13**:4; **14**:3, 22; **15**:5, 11, 26, 34; **16**:5, 25; **17**:18; **18**:13; **19**:9, 13, 20; **20**:22; **21**:4, 20, 25; **22**:43, 52; **2Ki 1**:7; **2**:9; **3**:2, 13; **4**:2^2, 13, 14, 39; **5**:4, 20; **6**:15, 28; **7**:9, 12; **8**:13, 14, 18, 27; **9**:12, 18, 19, 22; **10**:10, 30; **11**:5; **12**:2; **13**:2, 11; **14**:3, 6, 24; **15**:3, 9, 18, 24, 28, 34; **16**:2; **17**:2; **18**:3, 19; **19**:11, 25, 29^2; **20**:3, 8, 14, 15; **21**:2, 15, 16, 20; **22**:2; **23**:17, 32, 37; **24**:9, 19; **25**:15^2; **1Ch 4**:10; **12**:32; **17**:16, 18; **19**:13; **21**:12, 17, 23, 24; **29**:14; **2Ch 1**:7; **4**:6; **6**:4, 15; **8**:15; **9**:12; **10**:9, 16; **13**:9; **14**:2; **19**:6, 7; **20**:12, 32, 37; **21**:6; **22**:4; **23**:4; **24**:2; **25**:2, 4, 9; **26**:4; **27**:2; **28**:1, 10; **29**:2, 6, 36; **30**:12; **31**:20; **32**:10, 13; **33**:2, 22; **34**:2; **35**:21, 26; **36**:5, 8, 9, 12; **Ezr 5**:4; **6**:8, 13; **8**:17; **9**:10; **Ne 2**:4, 8, 12, 16, 19; **4**:2; **7**:72; **13**:17; **Est 1**:15; **2**:1^2, 15; **4**:5, 9, 12; **5**:3^2, 6^2; **6**:3, 6; **7**:2^2; **8**:1; **9**:12^3, 23, 26^2; **Job 1**:5; **3**:25; **6**:11^2, 25; **7**:17, 20; **8**:8; **9**:12, 35; **11**:8^2; **13**:2, 13; **15**:9^2, 14, 17, 18; **16**:3; **20**:26; **21**:15^2, 21, 31; **22**:13, 17, 20; **23**:5^2, 13, 14; **24**:25; **27**:8; **30**:2; **31**:2, 8, 14^2; **32**:9, 11; **33**:3, 27; **34**:4^2, 16, 32, 33; **35**:3, 6^2, 7^2; **36**:16; **37**:19; **38**:6, 24; **40**:4; **42**:3, 7, 8, 9; **Ps 8**:4; **9**:13; **11**:3; **15**:2; **17**:4, 14; **24**:4; **25**:9, 19; **30**:9; **39**:4, 7, 11; **44**:1; **46**:8; **50**:16; **51**:4; **52**:9; **56**:4, 11; **58**:1; **64**:9^2; **66**:5, 16; **69**:4; **77**:13; **78**:11, 29; **85**:8, 12; **89**:47; **94**:2; **105**:19; **106**:15; **116**:12; **118**:6; **119**:121; **120**:3^2; **137**:8; **144**:3; **Pr 4**:19; **8**:6, 15; **10**:24, 32^2; **11**:24; **14**:14^2; **16**:13; **19**:22; **20**:11; **21**:7; **22**:21; **23**:1, 16; **24**:29; **25**:7, 8; **27**:1; **30**:4^2; **31**:5; **Ecc 1**:3, 9^4, 15^2; **2**:2, 3, 12^2, 15, 17, 22; **3**:2, 9, 11, 15, 22; **5**:4, 11, 16, 18; **6**:8^2, 10, 12^2; **7**:13, 27; **8**:4, 7, 17; **9**:7; **10**:14^2; **11**:2; **SS 3**:6; **5**:9^2; **8**:8; **Isa 1**:11; **2**:8, 22; **3**:11, 15; **5**:4, 5; **8**:12; **10**:3, 7, 11; **11**:3^2; **14**:32; **15**:7; **16**:5; **17**:8; **19**:12; **20**:6; **21**:6, 10, 11^2; **22**:1, 16; **30**:10; **33**:13; **36**:4; **37**:11, 26, 30^2; **38**:3, 15, 22; **39**:3, 4; **40**:6, 18; **41**:22^2, 23; **42**:5; **44**:7; **45**:9, 10^2, 19; **47**:13; **50**:11; **52**:5; **53**:1; **55**:2; **56**:1; **59**:6; **61**:11; **65**:12^2, 18; **66**:1^2, 4^3; **Jer 1**:11, 13; **2**:5, 18^2, 23; **3**:6; **4**:30; **5**:15, 31; **6**:18, 20; **7**:12, 14, 17; **8**:6, 9, 13; **9**:7; **11**:15; **13**:21; **15**:4, 19^2; **16**:10^2; **17**:11, 16; **18**:19; **23**:25, 28, 33, 35^2, 37^2; **24**:3; **27**:4; **29**:5, 28; **32**:24; **34**:15; **37**:5, 18; **38**:20, 21, 25^2; **42**:3; **44**:25; **45**:4^2; **48**:19; **49**:9; **51**:6, 12, 44; **52**:2; **La 2**:13^3, 17; **3**:17; **5**:1; **Eze 1**:27^2; **2**:8^2; **3**:1; **4**:14; **5**:9; **7**:13; **8**:2, 6, 12; **10**:22; **11**:5; **12**:9, 22; **17**:12; **18**:2, 5, 18, 19, 21, 27; **19**:2; **20**:29, 32; **21**:13; **23**:39; **24**:19; **33**:14, 15, 16, 19, 30, 32; **34**:19^2; **37**:18; **45**:9; **48**:21; **Da 1**:13; **2**:10, 22, 23^2, 28, 29^2, 45; **4**:10, 35^2; **7**:7, 19, 23; **8**:12, 19, 24; **9**:12; **10**:14, 21; **11**:24, 36; **12**:8; **Hos 5**:9; **6**:4^2; **9**:5, 14; **10**:3; **14**:8; **Joel 1**:4^3; **3**:4; **Am 3**:9^2; **7**:1, 4, 7, 8; **8**:1, 2; **Ob 1**:5; **Jnh 1**:6, 8^3, 10, 11; **2**:9; **3**:10; **4**:2, 5; **Mic 1**:5^2; **6**:1, 3^2, 5^3, 6, 8^2, 14; **7**:3; **Na 2**:11; **Hab 2**:1^2, 6, 18^2; **Zep 2**:15; **3**:4; **Hag 1**:11; **2**:14, 15; **Zec 1**:9^2, 19, 21; **2**:2^2; **4**:2, 4, 5, 7, 11, 12, 13; **5**:2, 5, 6; **6**:4; **9**:17; **11**:9^2; **13**:6; **Mal 1**:13^2, 14; **2**:15; **3**:14; **Mt 1**:22; **2**:15, 17, 23; **4**:14; **5**:46, 47; **6**:3, 8, 25^3, 31^3; **7**:6; **8**:17, 27, 29, 33; **9**:13; **10**:19^2, 27^2; **11**:2, 4, 7, 8, 9, 16; **12**:2, 3, 7, 17, 25; **13**:12, 17^2, 19^2, 20, 22, 23, 35^2, 52^2; **14**:20; **15**:11^2, 12, 18^2, 20; **16**:26^2, 27; **17**:25; **18**:12, 28, 31; **19**:6, 16, 17, 20, 27; **20**:14, 15^2, 21, 22, 32; **21**:4, 16, 21, 23, 24, 27, 28, 40; **22**:15, 17, 31, 42; **23**:3; **24**:3, 17, 42, 43; **25**:25, 27, 29; **26**:13, 15, 39^2, 50, 62, 66, 70, 75; **27**:4, 9, 22, 23, 54, 63; **Mk 1**:24, 27, 38, 44; **2**:24, 25; **4**:24, 25, 30^2; **5**:7, 9, 14, 16, 19, 33, 36; **6**:2^2, 24; **7**:15, 20; **8**:36, 37; **9**:6, 9, 10, 16, 32, 33; **10**:3, 9, 17, 21, 32, 36, 38, 51; **11**:5, 6, 23, 28, 29, 33; **12**:9, 13; **13**:1^2, 4, 11, 37; **14**:8, 9, 36^2, 40, 60, 64, 68; **15**:12, 14, 24; **Lk 1**:25, 29, 45, 62, 66; **2**:17, 18, 24, 27, 33, 50; **3**:10, 12, 14; **4**:34, 36; **5**:25; **6**:2, 3, 8, 11, 23, 26, 32, 33, 34, 46, 47; **7**:22, 24, 25, 26, 31^2, 39; **8**:9, 14, 18, 28, 30, 34, 35, 56; **9**:17, 25, 33; **10**:8, 23, 24^2, 25, 26^2, 39; **11**:17; **12**:3, 11, 12, 17, 22^2, 29^2, 39, 47^2, 48, 50, 57; **13**:18^2, 20; **14**:22, 31; **15**:8, 26; **16**:2, 3, 4, 12^2, 15, 21; **17**:9, 10; **18**:6, 18, 27, 34^2, 36, 41; **19**:15, 21^2, 22^2, 26, 48; **20**:2, 8, 13, 15, 17, 20, 21, 26; **21**:7, 26; **22**:37, 49, 60, 71; **23**:22, 31, 34, 41, 47, 48; **24**:12, 17, 19, 35, 49; **Jn 1**:3, 11, 21, 22, 38; **2**:4, 18, 25; **3**:6^2, 11^2, 21, 27, 32; **4**:18, 22^2, 27, 42; **5**:19, 47^2; **6**:6, 9, 28, 30^2, 62; **7**:36, 51; **8**:5, 22, 26, 29, 33, 38^2, 39, 40, 41, 43; **9**:17, 26; **10**:6, 29; **11**:45, 46, 47, 56; **12**:6, 27, 49^2, 50; **13**:7, 12, 13, 27, 29; **15**:14, 15; **16**:14, 15, 17, 18^2, 19; **18**:21^2, 29, 32, 35, 38; **19**:17, 22, 24, 25; **21**:21, 22, 23; **Ac 1**:4; **2**:12, 14, 16, 22, 37; **3**:6, 10, 18; **4**:7^2, 16, 20, 21, 23, 34; **5**:7, 24, 35; **6**:5; **7**:40, 49^2; **8**:6, 24, 30, 36; **9**:6; **10**:4, 15, 17, 21, 22, 35; **11**:9; **12**:9, 18; **13**:12, 25, 29, 40, 45; **14**:11; **15**:29^2; **16**:14, 30; **17**:18, 19, 20, 23; **19**:3; **20**:22, 38; **21**:13, 22, 23, 24, 25^2, 33; **22**:10, 15, 26, 30; **23**:9, 19, 30, 34; **24**:20; **26**:10, 22; **27**:11; **28**:22, 24; **Ro 1**:19; **2**:14, 15, 18; **3**:1^2, 3, 5, 9, 27^2; **4**:1, 3, 18, 21; **6**:1, 15, 21; **7**:7^2, 13^2, 15, 16, 18, 19, 20, 21; **8**:3, 24, 25, 27, 31; **9**:9, 14, 20, 22, 23, 30; **10**:8, 17^2; **11**:2, 4, 7^2, 15, 24; **12**:2^2, 9^2, 17; **13**:2, 3, 4, 7, 11; **14**:15^2, 19, 20, 22; **15**:18, 28; **16**:19^2; **1Co 1**:12, 27^2, 28; **2**:9^2, 11^3; **3**:5^2, 13, 14; **4**:6, 7, 21; **5**:12; **6**:11; **9**:13, 18; **10**:15, 19, 20; **11**:22^3, 23; **14**:7, 9, 15, 16, 26, 29, 37; **15**:3, 10, 29, 32, 35, 36, 37, 42^2, 50; **2Co 1**:13; **2**:10; **3**:10, 11; **4**:18^4; **5**:4, 10; **6**:14^2, 15^2, 16; **7**:11^7; **8**:12^2, 21; **10**:7, 11; **11**:12^2, 17; **12**:6, 14; **13**:7, 9; **Gal 1**:8, 9,

20; 2:6, 10; 3:2, 5, 22; 4:15, 30; 5:17^{3}; 6:9, 11; Eph 1:18^{2}, 19; 2:10; 3:9, 18; 4:9, 29; 5:10, 12, 17; 6:21; Php 1:10, 12, 18; 3:13^{2}, 16; 4:12^{2}; Col 1:24; 2:17; 1Th 1:5, 9; 2:13, 19; 3:3; 4:2; 5:21; 2Th 2:6, 11; 3:13, 14; 1Ti 1:7; 5:13; 6:20^{2}; 2Ti 1:12; 2:2, 7; 3:11, 14; Tit 1:5, 11; 2:1, 3; Heb 2:1, 6, 18; 5:8; 7:11; 8:1, 13; 10:36; 11:3, 32, 39; 12:7, 13, 27^{2}; 13:5, 6, 16; Jas 1:24; 2:14, 16; 4:3, 14^{2}; 1Pe 2:20; 3:6, 13, 14^{2}; 4:3, 17, 18; 2Pe 2:6, 12; 3:11; 1Jn 1:1^{4}, 3, 6; 2:24^{2}, 25; 3:1^{2}, 2^{2}, 7, 10, 22; 4:5; 5:16; 2Jn 1:8; 3Jn 1:10, 11^{2}; Rev 1:1, 3, 11, 19^{3}; 2:5, 7, 10, 11, 17, 24, 25, 29; 3:2, 3^{2}, 6, 11, 13, 22; 4:1; 6:6; 9:7; 10:4, 6^{3}; 15:2; 16:6; 18:18; 19:1, 6; 20:13; 22:6; Tob 2:12; 4:15, 21; 5:2, 9, 10, 11^{2}, 12; 6:7; 8:21; 12:19; 13:6^{3}; 14:8^{2}, 10, 11^{2}; Jdt 2:12; 5:3^{3}; 6:2, 16, 17; 7:9; 8:11, 26^{2}, 30, 34^{2}; 9:5, 9; 10:12, 16; 11:10, 11; 12:4, 19; 14:8; 15:1, 4, 5, 7; AdE 1:15, 17, 18; 2:1, 11; 4:4, 7, 8, 17; 5:3^{2}, 6; 6:3, 6, 10, 13; 7:2^{3}; 8:7, 8, 14; 9:12, 23, 26^{3}, 29; 11:12; 14:9, 11; 15:9; 16:7, 9; Wis 1:7; 2:11, 17, 20; 4:12, 17^{2}; 5:8^{2}; 6:22; 7:15, 17, 21^{2}; 8:5, 6; 9:9^{2}, 10, 13, 16^{3}, 18; 11:12; 12:12, 21; 13:7; 14:10, 11, 15, 26; 15:17; 16:27; 17:13; 19:4, 18; Sir Pr:T; 2:14; 3:21^{2}, 22^{2}; 5:4, 10, 12; 7:28; 8:18; 9:11, 12; 11:3, 23^{2}, 24; 12:12; 13:6, 17, 18^{2}, 23; 14:3, 4, 15; 15:11; 16:17; 17:26, 31; 18:8^{4}; 19:30; 20:30; 21:25; 22:10, 14^{2}; 29:3, 26; 30:19; 31:13, 16, 27; 33:4; 34:3, 4^{2}, 9, 28, 30, 31; 37:8, 9, 27; 39:4, 8, 15, 17, 21; 40:11; 41:14; 42:1, 15, 19^{2}; 43:2, 24; 48:16, 22, 25; 49:2; Bar 1:22; 2:2; 4:4; LtJ 6:45, 63; Aza 1:7; Sus 1:18, 26, 42, 47, 54, 58; Bel 1:21, 27; 1Mc 2:10, 18, 33, 34; 3:41, 42, 50, 52; 4:20, 44, 46; 5:16; 6:11^{2}, 23, 62; 8:3; 10:23, 27; 11:5, 31, 40; 13:3; 14:22, 27, 44; 16:1; 2Mc 2:29, 32; 3:22, 23, 37; 5:11, 20, 27; 6:17; 7:2, 16, 30; 9:3, 25^{2}; 10:10, 21; 11:1, 18, 31, 35; 12:42; 15:12, 38; 1Es 1:10, 26, 39, 44, 47; 2:22; 3:5, 9, 17, 23; 4:39, 42^{2}, 46; 5:66; 7:6; 8:12, 14^{2}, 82; 9:48; Man 1:10; 3Mc 1:8, 9, 21; 3:22; 4:3^{3}; 5:26, 27, 35; 7:12; 2Es 1:21, 24, 30, 34, 35; 2:3, 4, 8, 9, 37; 3:22, 24, 32, 35; 4:21^{2}, 25, 46^{2}; 5:2^{2}, 19, 41; 6:7; 7:11, 16^{2}, 21^{2}, 42, 46, 58^{2}, 59^{3}, 62, 67, 72, 73, 96^{2}, 100, 117, 118, 119, 120, 126, 128^{2}; 8:8, 9, 11, 14^{2}, 34^{2}; 9:33, 34^{3}, 42; 10:6, 25, 31, 32, 35^{2}, 49, 59; 11:36, 37; 12:41; 13:20, 22, 52; 14:25, 32, 38, 42; 15:20, 28; 16:18, 36, 63, 66, 68; 4Mc 1:14^{2}; 2:14; 3:15; 4:14; 5:11, 26; 7:21; 8:16; 11:4; 14:9, 10, 17; 15:4

WHEN (3693)

Ge 1:1; 2:4, 5; 3:5, 6; 4:8, 12; 5:1, 2, 3, 6, 9, 12, 15, 18, 21, 25, 28; 6:1, 4; 7:6; 8:21; 9:14, 16, 24; 11:10, 12, 14, 16, 18, 20, 22, 24, 26, 31; 12:4, 5, 11, 12, 14, 15; 14:14; 15:11, 17; 16:4, 5, 16; 17:1, 12, 22, 24, 25; 18:2, 33; 19:1, 15, 17, 23, 29^{2}, 33^{2}, 35^{2}; 20:13; 21:4, 5, 15, 25, 32; 22:9; 24:11, 19, 22, 30, 31, 36, 41, 52, 54, 64; 25:20, 24, 26, 27, 29; 26:7, 8, 19, 34; 27:1, 5^{2}, 30, 34, 40; 28:8; 29:3, 10, 13, 25, 31; 30:1, 9, 16, 25, 30, 33, 38; 31:49; 32:2, 17, 19, 25; 33:5; 34:2, 7, 25; 35:1, 7, 9, 16, 17; 37:4, 5, 10, 21, 23, 28, 29; 38:5, 12, 13, 15, 20, 27; 39:11, 13, 15, 19; 40:6, 13, 14, 16; 41:12, 14, 15, 21, 24, 46, 48, 55; 42:1, 7, 21, 27, 29, 35; 43:2, 16, 21, 24^{2}, 26, 33; 44:4^{2}, 6, 24, 25, 30, 31; 45:1, 16, 27^{2}; 46:1, 28, 33; 47:15, 18, 29, 30; 48:2, 7, 8, 17; 49:28, 33; 50:4, 10, 11, 17, 25; Ex 1:16; 2:2, 3, 6, 10, 13, 15, 18; 3:4, 12, 21; 4:6, 7, 14, 21, 31; 5:13, 19; 6:28; 7:4, 5, 7, 9; 8:9, 15; 9:19, 34; 10:13; 11:1; 12:13^{2}, 23, 25, 26, 27; 13:5, 8, 11, 14, 15, 17; 14:5, 18; 15:19, 23; 16:3, 5, 8, 14, 15, 18, 21, 22, 32; 18:11, 14, 16; 19:9^{2}, 13, 20; 20:18; 21:2, 7, 18, 20, 22, 26, 28; 22:1, 4, 5, 6, 7, 10, 14, 16, 23; 23:2, 4, 5, 16, 23; 27:7; 28:4, 29, 30, 35^{3}, 43^{2}; 29:30, 36; 30:7, 8, 12, 15, 20^{2}, 37; 31:18; 32:1, 5, 17, 25, 34; 33:4, 9, 10; 34:15, 24, 30, 33, 34; 39:9, 43; 40:32^{2}; Lev 1:2; 2:1, 4, 8; 4:2, 14, 22, 28; 5:1, 2, 3^{2}, 4^{2}, 5, 15; 6:2, 4, 5, 20, 27; 7:21, 36, 38; 8:4, 33; 9:24; 10:3, 9, 20; 11:31, 32; 12:6; 13:2, 9, 18, 24, 29, 38, 47, 58; 14:34, 57^{2}; 15:2, 13, 19, 23; 16:1, 20, 23; 19:5, 9, 23, 33; 20:4; 21:9; 22:7, 18, 21, 27, 29; 23:10, 12, 22, 39, 43; 24:16; 25:2, 14, 15, 22^{2}, 50; 26:26, 35, 44; 27:2, 21; Nu 1:51^{2}; 3:1, 4, 13; 4:5, 15, 19; 5:6, 21, 27, 29, 30; 6:2, 13, 19; 7:1, 10, 84, 89; 8:2, 10; 9:19, 21^{2}, 22; 10:3, 5, 6, 7, 9, 28, 34; 11:1, 9, 25; 12:6, 10, 12; 14:17, 39; 15:2, 8, 28, 32, 39; 16:4, 42, 50; 17:8; 18:26, 30, 32; 19:14; 20:3, 16, 29; 21:1; 22:25, 27, 36; 23:17; 24:23; 25:7; 26:9, 10^{2}, 61; 27:13, 14; 28:26; 30:2, 3; 32:1, 8, 9; 33:39, 51; 34:2; 35:10, 19, 21; 36:4; Dt 1:24, 34, 45; 2:8, 19, 25, 32; 3:1, 20; 4:6, 10, 15, 19, 25, 30, 45, 46; 5:23, 28; 6:7^{4}, 10, 11, 20; 7:1, 2; 8:12, 13; 9:4, 9, 23, 25; 11:19^{4}, 29, 31^{2}; 12:10^{2}, 20, 29^{2}; 14:24; 15:6, 10, 13, 18; 16:6, 8, 13; 17:14, 18; 18:9, 16; 19:1, 4, 5; 20:1, 9, 10, 13; 21:10, 16, 18, 22; 22:8, 14; 23:9, 11^{2}, 13; 24:5, 10, 19, 20, 21; 25:5, 18, 19; 26:1, 4, 6, 12; 27:3, 4, 12; 28:6^{2}, 19^{2}; 29:7, 25; 30:1, 10; 31:1, 4, 11, 20, 21, 24; 32:8^{2}, 35, 36, 41, 45; 33:5; 34:7; Jos 2:5, 10, 14; 3:3, 8, 13, 14, 15; 4:1, 6, 7, 18, 21; 5:1, 8, 13; 6:5, 16; 7:21; 8:5, 8, 14, 20, 21, 24^{2}; 9:1, 3, 12, 13, 16; 10:1, 12, 14, 20^{2}, 24; 11:1; 14:7; 15:18; 17:13; 19:47, 49; 22:7, 10, 12, 30; 23:1; 24:6, 7, 11; Jdg 1:14, 24, 28; 2:4, 6, 21; 3:9, 15, 18, 24, 25, 27; 4:12; 5:2^{2}, 4^{2}, 8; 6:7, 28, 38; 7:4^{2}, 13, 15, 17, 18, 19, 22; 8:1, 3, 7, 9, 13; 9:7, 16, 26, 30, 33, 35, 36, 42, 43, 46, 55; 11:2, 5, 7, 16, 31, 35; 12:2, 3, 5; 13:12, 17, 20; 14:5, 9, 11; 15:3, 5, 14, 17, 19; 16:9, 15, 18, 20, 24, 25; 17:4; 18:2, 7, 8, 10, 18, 22, 26; 19:1, 3, 7, 9, 11, 17, 27, 29; 20:31, 38, 40, 45; 21:9, 21; Ru 1:1, 4, 18, 19, 21; 2:10, 15; 3:4, 7; 4:8, 13; 1Sa 1:4, 24; 2:13, 19, 27, 31; 4:2, 3, 5, 6^{2}, 13^{2}, 14, 18, 19; 5:1, 3, 4, 7, 10; 6:13, 16, 19; 7:7^{2}; 8:1, 6, 21; 9:5, 17, 25, 27; 10:2, 7, 10, 11, 13, 14, 21, 23; 11:4, 6, 8, 9; 12:8, 12; 13:1, 4, 6, 11; 14:17, 22, 26, 47, 52; 15:2, 6, 13; 16:6, 16; 17:11, 24, 31, 42, 48, 51, 55; 18:1, 6, 15, 19, 26, 28; 19:5, 14, 16, 20, 21; 20:12, 24, 37; 21:5^{2}, 13; 22:1, 8, 22; 23:6, 9, 13, 15, 25^{2}; 24:1, 8, 16, 18; 25:9, 15, 23, 30, 31, 37, 39, 40; 26:3; 27:4, 10; 28:5, 6, 12, 21, 22; 30:1, 3, 12, 16, 21, 26; 31:5, 7, 8, 11; 2Sa 1:1, 2, 7; 2:4, 10, 30; 3:13, 20, 23, 26, 27, 28; 4:1, 4, 10, 11; 5:4, 17, 23, 24; 6:6, 13, 18; 7:1, 12, 14; 8:5, 9, 13; 10:2, 5, 6, 7, 9, 14, 15, 17, 19; 11:1, 2, 7, 10, 19, 26, 27; 12:19, 20, 21; 13:5, 6, 11, 21, 28^{2}, 34; 14:4, 26^{2}; 15:2^{2}, 32; 16:1, 5, 16; 17:6, 9, 20^{2}, 23, 27; 18:5, 24, 29; 19:3, 25; 20:8; 21:11, 21; 22:1; 23:9, 20; 24:8, 11, 16, 17, 20; 1Ki 1:21, 23, 32, 41; 2:1, 7, 8^{2}, 28, 29, 39, 41; 3:21^{2}; 5:1, 7; 7:24; 8:9, 10, 21, 30, 33, 35, 36, 41, 42, 53, 54; 9:1, 12; 10:1, 2, 4; 11:4, 15, 21, 28, 29, 30; 12:2, 7, 16, 18, 20, 21; 13:4, 26, 31; 14:5, 6, 12, 21; 15:21; 16:9, 11, 18; 17:10; 18:4, 10, 12, 13, 17, 39; 19:13, 15; 20:12, 36; 21:27; 22:15, 25, 32, 33, 42; 2Ki 2:1, 9, 12, 14, 15, 17, 18, 24; 3:5, 9, 21, 22, 24, 26; 4:4, 6, 11, 12, 15, 18, 25, 27, 32, 36, 38; 5:6, 7, 8, 13, 18^{2}, 19, 21, 24, 26; 6:4, 6, 8, 15, 18, 21, 30, 32; 7:5, 8, 12, 17, 18; 8:3, 6, 7, 9, 17, 26, 29; 9:2, 11, 15, 22, 25, 27, 30, 35, 36; 10:7, 8, 9, 12, 15, 17; 11:1, 13, 14, 21; 12:17; 13:14, 24; 14:2; 15:2, 33; 16:2, 10, 12; 17:21, 25; 18:2, 17, 18, 24, 32; 19:1, 5, 9, 35; 20:17; 21:1, 19; 22:1, 8, 11, 19; 23:16, 29, 31, 36; 24:8, 18; 25:23; 1Ch 1:44, 45, 46, 47, 48, 49, 50; 2:19, 21; 5:7, 20; 6:15; 9:28; 10:5, 7, 8, 11; 11:13, 22; 12:15, 19; 13:9; 14:8, 14, 15; 16:2, 19; 17:1, 11; 18:5, 9; 19:2, 5, 6, 8, 10, 15, 16, 17^{2}, 19; 20:1, 7; 21:15, 28; 22:12; 23:1; 2Ch 4:3; 5:11, 13; 6:21, 24, 26, 27, 32^{2}; 7:1, 3, 13; 9:1^{2}, 3; 10:2, 16, 18; 11:1; 12:1, 7, 13; 13:7, 14, 15; 15:4, 8, 9; 16:5; 18:14, 24, 31, 32; 20:10, 21, 23, 24, 25, 29, 31; 21:4, 5, 20; 22:2, 6, 7, 8, 10; 23:12, 13; 24:1, 11, 14, 25; 25:1; 26:3, 16, 19, 20; 27:1, 8; 28:1; 29:1, 19, 27, 29; 31:1, 8; 32:2, 11, 21; 33:1, 21; 34:1, 8, 19, 27; 35:10, 20; 36:2, 5, 9, 11; Ezr 1:11; 3:1, 10, 11, 12; 4:1, 23; 9:3; Ne 1:4; 2:1, 3, 6, 10, 19; 4:1, 7, 12, 15; 5:6; 6:1, 10, 16; 7:1; 8:5, 9; 9:18, 28; 10:38; 13:3, 19; Est 1:2, 5, 10, 20; 2:1, 7, 8^{2}, 13, 15, 16, 19, 20, 23; 3:4, 5; 4:1, 4, 12; 5:9; 6:13; 7:8; 9:1^{3}, 25; Job 1:5, 13; 2:11, 12; 3:22; 4:13; 5:21; 6:17; 7:4^{2}, 13; 9:5, 23; 11:3, 11, 12; 13:9; 16:22; 19:7, 18; 21:6, 21, 32; 22:29; 23:10, 15; 24:22; 27:8^{2}, 9; 28:25, 26; 29:2, 3, 4^{2}, 5^{2}, 6, 7^{2}, 11^{2}, 21; 30:24, 26^{2}; 31:13, 14^{2}, 26, 29; 32:5; 33:15; 34:29^{2}; 35:14; 36:13, 20; 37:4, 17, 21^{2}; 38:4, 7, 8, 9, 38, 40, 41; 39:1, 2, 3, 18, 25; 41:25; 42:10; Ps 3:T; 4:1^{2}, 3, 4, 7; 8:3; 9:3; 14:7; 17:15; 18:T; 20:9; 21:9; 22:24; 27:2, 7; 31:21, 22; 34:T, 17; 35:13; 37:23, 33; 38:16; 41:5, 6^{2}; 42:2; 46:5; 48:7; 49:5, 10, 16^{2}, 17, 18; 50:18; 51:T, 4, 5; 52:T; 53:6; 54:T; 56:T, 3, 9; 57:T; 58:10; 59:T; 60:T^{2}; 61:2; 63:T, 6; 65:3; 66:14; 68:7^{2}, 9, 14; 69:10, 11; 71:9, 23; 72:12; 73:16, 20, 21^{2}; 75:3; 76:7, 9, 10; 77:16^{2}; 78:21, 34, 42, 43, 59; 81:5; 88:1; 89:9; 90:4; 91:15; 94:8, 18, 19; 95:9; 101:2; 102:T, 2, 22; 104:20, 22, 28^{2}, 29^{2}, 30; 105:12, 16, 38; 106:4^{2}, 7, 44; 107:39; 109:7, 25; 114:1; 116:6, 10; 119:7, 26, 52, 59, 82, 84; 120:7; 122:1; 124:2, 3; 126:1; 127:5; 133:1; 137:1; 139:2^{2}, 15, 16; 141:1, 6; 142:T, 3; 146:4; 147:9; Pr 1:26, 27^{2}; 3:24, 27, 28, 30; 4:3, 12; 5:11; 6:9, 22^{3}, 30, 34; 8:24^{2}, 26, 27^{2}, 28^{2}, 29^{2}; 9:8; 10:19, 25; 11:2, 7, 10^{2}; 16:7; 17:16, 28; 18:3; 19:7; 21:11^{2}, 15, 27; 22:6; 23:1, 5, 16, 22, 31^{2}, 35; 24:17^{2}; 25:8; 26:25; 27:25; 28:1, 2, 9, 12^{2}, 28^{2}; 29:2^{2}, 16; 30:22^{2}, 23^{2}; 31:21; Ecc 1:12; 5:1, 4, 11; 8:3, 16; 9:12; 10:3, 16, 17; 11:3; 12:1, 3, 4, 5; SS 3:4; 5:6; 8:8; Isa 1:12, 15; 2:19, 21; 5:4; 6:13; 7:2; 8:21; 9:3; 10:12, 18, 24, 26; 11:16; 13:19; 14:3, 9; 16:4, 12^{3}; 17:5^{2}, 6; 18:3^{2}, 5; 19:20; 21:7; 23:1, 5; 24:13^{2}; 25:4; 26:9, 16, 17; 27:9, 11; 28:15, 18, 25; 29:8, 23; 30:19, 21^{2}, 25, 26, 29^{2}, 31; 31:3, 4; 32:7; 33:1^{2}; 34:5; 36:9; 37:1, 5, 9, 36; 39:6; 40:7, 24; 41:17, 28^{2}; 43:2^{2}, 12; 46:4; 48:13, 21; 50:2^{2}; 51:2, 7; 53:10; 54:6; 57:13; 58:7; 64:2, 3; 65:12^{2}; 66:4^{2}; Jer 2:7, 26; 3:16; 5:7, 19, 31; 6:14; 7:13^{2}, 32; 8:4, 8, 11, 12, 13; 9:25; 10:13; 11:4, 7, 14, 15; 12:1; 13:14, 21; 15:2; 16:10, 14; 17:6, 8; 18:22; 19:6, 14; 20:3, 14; 21:1; 22:23; 23:5, 7, 32, 33, 38; 25:5; 26:8, 10, 21^{2}; 27:20, 22; 28:9; 29:10, 12, 13, 19; 30:3; 31:2, 6, 23, 27, 31, 32, 38; 33:14; 34:1, 7, 13, 16, 18; 35:11; 36:3, 11, 13, 16, 25; 37:5, 11, 13; 39:3, 4, 5; 40:1, 7, 11; 41:7, 11, 13; 42:6, 18; 43:1; 45:1; 47:7; 48:12; 49:2, 8, 18; 50:31, 40; 51:2, 16, 33, 39, 47, 52, 59, 61, 63; 52:1; La 1:7; 3:28, 34, 35, 36, 57; Eze 1:17, 19^{2}, 21^{3}, 24^{2}, 25, 28; 2:2; 3:27; 4:6; 5:2, 13, 15, 16^{2}; 6:13; 7:25; 8:8; 10:3, 5, 6, 11, 16^{2}, 17^{2}; 11:18; 12:15; 13:6, 7, 10^{2}, 12, 14, 16; 14:13, 21, 22, 23; 15:4, 5^{2}, 7; 16:22, 50, 61, 63; 17:10^{2}, 17; 18:19, 24, 26, 27; 19:5; 20:5, 28, 31, 41, 42, 44; 21:7; 22:14, 28; 23:16, 18, 19, 21, 39; 24:13, 24, 25; 25:3^{3}, 17; 26:10, 15^{2}, 19^{2}; 27:33; 28:22, 25, 26; 29:7^{2}, 16; 30:4, 8, 18, 25; 31:16; 32:7, 10, 15^{3}, 31; 33:12^{3}, 17, 18, 19, 29, 33; 34:12, 18, 27; 35:11; 36:17, 20, 23; 37:13, 18, 20, 28; 38:14, 16, 18; 39:26, 27, 29; 40:3; 42:14, 15; 43:3, 8, 11, 18, 23, 27; 44:7, 10, 15, 17, 19, 21; 45:1; 46:8, 9, 10^{2}, 12; 47:8; 48:11; Da 2:2; 3:3, 5, 15; 4:34; 5:10, 20; 6:14, 20; 7:8, 22; 8:15, 17, 23; 10:9, 19, 20; 11:2, 12, 34; 12:7; Hos 1:2, 8; 2:13, 15; 4:14^{2}, 18; 5:13; 6:11; 7:1; 8:11; 9:12; 10:10, 14; 11:1, 10; 13:1, 6; Joel 3:1; Am 2:13; 3:4, 5^{2}; 4:2, 7, 11; 7:2; 8:5, 11; 9:13; Jnh 3:6, 10; 4:7, 8; Mic 2:1; 3:5; 5:3, 8; 7:8^{2}, 15; Na 2:3; 3:17; Hab 1:13; 3:8; Zep 3:8, 20^{2}; Hag 1:9; 2:5, 16^{2}; Zec 5:11; 6:7; 7:5, 6^{2}, 7^{2}, 13^{2}; 8:9, 14; 12:4, 10; 13:3, 4; 14:1, 3; Mal 1:8^{2}, 12; 3:2, 15, 17; 4:1, 3; Mt 1:18, 20, 24; 2:3, 7, 8, 9, 10, 16, 19, 22; 3:3, 7, 16; 4:12; 5:1, 11, 23; 6:3, 7, 17; 7:28; 8:1, 5, 10, 14, 18, 23, 28, 34; 9:2, 8, 11, 12, 15, 23, 25, 28, 33, 36; 10:19, 23; 11:1, 2; 12:2, 3, 15, 24, 34, 43, 44; 13:6, 19, 21, 26, 32, 48, 53; 14:6, 13^{2}, 14, 15, 23, 26, 30, 32, 34; 15:7, 12, 31; 16:2, 5, 13; 17:6, 8, 14, 24, 25, 26, 27; 18:15, 24, 31; 19:1, 22, 25, 28; 20:3, 5, 8, 9, 10, 11, 24, 30; 21:1, 10, 15, 18, 20, 23, 34, 38, 40, 45; 22:11, 22, 33, 34; 23:13; 24:3^{2}, 15, 33, 46, 50; 25:3, 31, 37, 38, 39, 44; 26:1, 8, 20, 29, 30, 71; 27:1, 3, 12, 24, 33, 34, 35, 47, 54, 57; 28:17; Mk 1:21, 37; 2:1, 4, 5, 16, 17, 20, 25, 26; 3:21; 4:6, 10, 15, 16, 17, 29, 31, 32, 35; 5:2, 6, 21, 22, 38, 39; 6:16, 20, 21, 22, 29, 35, 38, 47, 48, 49, 53, 54; 7:1, 17; 8:1, 19, 23, 38; 9:8, 14, 15, 20, 25, 28, 33; 10:14, 22, 41, 47; 11:1, 11, 12, 13, 18, 19; 12:2, 12, 20, 25, 34; 13:3, 4, 7, 11, 14, 29, 33, 34, 35, 36; 14:11, 12, 17, 18, 25, 26, 45, 67; 15:25, 33, 35, 39, 41, 42, 45; 16:1, 2, 4, 11; Lk 1:8, 12, 22, 23, 25, 41; 2:15, 17, 22, 27, 39, 42, 43, 45, 48; 3:1, 21^{2}, 23; 4:2, 13, 16, 25, 28, 35, 42; 5:4, 6, 8, 11, 12^{2}, 20, 22, 35; 6:3, 13, 22^{2}, 26, 42, 48, 49; 7:3, 4, 6, 9, 10, 13, 20, 24, 39, 42; 8:4, 8, 13, 15, 28, 34, 35, 40, 45, 47, 50, 51; 9:11, 18, 26, 36, 37, 51, 54; 10:31, 32, 33, 35; 11:2, 14, 21, 22, 24, 25, 29, 36, 45, 53; 12:1, 11, 37, 43, 46, 54, 55, 58; 13:4, 12, 13, 17, 25, 28, 35; 14:1, 7, 8, 10^{2}, 12, 13, 29; 15:5, 6, 9, 14, 17, 25, 30; 16:4, 9; 17:10, 14, 15, 20, 22; 18:8, 15, 22, 23, 36, 40, 43; 19:5, 15, 23, 29, 43; 20:10, 14, 16, 19; 21:5, 6, 7, 9, 20, 28, 31; 22:6, 10, 14, 19, 32, 35, 40, 45, 49, 53, 55, 66; 23:6, 7, 8, 29, 31^{2}, 33, 42, 47, 48; 24:3, 23, 30, 40; Jn 1:19, 38, 47; 2:3, 9, 23; 4:1, 21, 23, 25, 40, 43, 45, 47, 52, 53; 5:6, 7, 25, 28, 44; 6:5, 11, 12, 14, 15, 16, 19, 24, 25^{2}, 60; 7:15, 27, 31, 40; 8:7, 9, 28, 44; 9:4, 6, 14, 35; 10:4; 11:4, 17, 20, 28, 29, 32, 33, 43; 12:9, 16, 17, 32; 13:19, 26^{2}, 31; 14:29; 15:26; 16:2, 4, 8, 13, 19, 21^{2}, 25, 32; 18:6, 22, 32; 19:6, 8, 13, 23, 26, 28, 30, 33; 20:14, 19, 20, 22, 24; 21:7, 9, 15, 18^{2}, 21; Ac 1:2, 6^{2}, 8, 9, 13, 22; 2:1, 37; 3:3, 12, 26; 4:7, 13, 14, 24, 31; 5:5, 10, 21^{2}, 22, 23, 24, 27, 33, 40; 6:1; 7:2, 10, 12, 21, 23, 24, 29, 30, 31, 35, 44, 45, 54, 60; 8:12, 13, 14, 18, 39; 9:26, 30, 37, 39; 10:7, 29, 30; 11:2, 17, 18, 23, 26; 12:4, 10, 13, 16, 18, 19; 13:5, 6, 12, 22, 29, 43, 45, 48; 14:5, 11, 14, 20, 25, 27; 15:4, 30, 31; 16:7, 10, 15, 19, 20, 27, 35, 38, 40; 17:6, 8, 10, 13, 32; 18:5, 6, 12, 19, 20, 22, 26, 27; 19:2, 6, 9, 12, 17, 19, 28, 34, 35, 41; 20:2, 3, 7, 14, 18, 36; 21:1, 2, 5, 7, 12, 17, 20, 26, 27, 32, 35, 40^{2}; 22:2, 25, 26; 23:6, 7, 10, 27, 30, 33, 34, 35; 24:2, 10, 20, 22, 24, 25; 25:7, 15, 17, 18, 21, 25; 26:10, 13, 14; 27:1, 13, 20, 27, 30; 28:3, 4, 10, 15, 16, 17, 18, 19; Ro 2:1, 3, 5, 14, 16; 4:19^{2}; 5:13; 6:20; 7:9, 21; 8:15; 9:10; 11:27; 13:11; 15:24, 28, 29; 1Co 2:1; 3:4; 4:12^{2}, 13; 5:4; 6:1; 7:21, 22; 8:12^{2}; 11:17, 18, 20, 21, 23, 24, 32, 33, 34^{2}; 12:2; 13:10, 11^{2}; 14:26; 15:24, 27, 28, 54; 16:2, 3, 12; 2Co 1:6, 17; 2:3, 12; 3:14, 16; 5:3; 7:5; 10:1^{2}, 2, 6, 11^{2}, 12, 14; 11:9, 20; 12:20, 21; 13:2, 9, 10; Gal 1:15; 2:7, 9, 11, 14; 4:4, 8, 18; 6:11; Eph 1:13, 20; 2:5; 4:8, 9; 6:19; Php 1:26; 4:15, 16; Col 2:12, 13^{2}; 3:4, 7; 4:16; 1Th 2:13, 17; 3:1, 4, 5; 5:3; 2Th 1:7, 10; 2:5, 6; 3:7, 10; 1Ti 1:3; 5:11, 25; 2Ti 1:3, 17; 4:3, 13; Tit 3:4, 12; Phm 1:4, 6; Heb 1:3, 6; 5:4; 6:13, 17; 7:10, 12, 15, 27; 8:5, 8^{2}, 9; 9:11, 19; 10:5, 8, 12, 32, 36; 11:8, 17, 21, 24, 29; 12:5, 17, 25; 13:23; Jas 1:13, 15^{2}; 2:21, 25; 1Pe 1:7, 11, 13; 2:12, 20^{2}, 23^{2}; 3:2, 16, 20; 4:13; 5:4; 2Pe 1:16, 17; 2:4, 5, 12; 1Jn 2:28; 3:2; 5:2; 3Jn 1:3; Jude 1:9; Rev 1:17; 2:27; 5:8; 6:3, 5, 7, 9, 12, 13; 8:1; 9:5; 10:3, 4, 7, 10; 11:7; 12:13; 17:6, 8, 10; 18:9; 20:7; 22:8; Tob 1:4, 9, 15, 18^{2}, 19; 2:2, 3, 4, 5, 7, 12, 13; 3:10; 4:3^{2}, 4, 7; 5:21; 6:2, 10, 13^{2}, 14, 16, 17, 18^{2}; 7:1, 9, 11, 12; 8:1, 4, 11, 21; 9:6; 10:1, 7^{2}; 11:1, 6, 16, 17; 12:1, 11, 12, 13, 18, 22; 14:2^{2}, 3, 5, 12; Jdt 2:4; 4:1; 5:10, 18, 22; 6:1, 12; 7:4, 5; 8:9^{2}; 9:1; 10:1, 7, 10, 14, 16, 22, 23; 11:11, 15, 16, 17; 13:1, 12, 20; 14:6, 7, 9, 10, 12, 15, 17, 19; 15:1, 5, 7, 9; 16:18; AdE 1:2, 4, 10; 2:7, 8, 15, 20; 3:5; 4:1, 4, 8, 12; 5:9; 7:8^{2}; 13:3, 9; 14:16^{2}; 15:1, 6; 16:6; Wis 1:3, 8; 2:1, 3; 3:13; 4:2^{2}, 6, 20; 5:2, 10, 11, 12; 7:3; 8:12^{2}, 15, 16, 17; 9:9; 10:1, 3, 4, 5, 6, 10, 11, 13, 14; 11:4, 9^{2}, 13, 14, 20; 12:17, 22^{2}, 27; 13:17; 14:6, 17; 15:8, 13, 18; 16:3, 5, 27; 17:2; 18:5, 13, 23; 19:11, 14, 17; Sir Pr:T^{3}; 2:1, 14; 3:5, 28, 31; 4:31; 6:7, 8, 11, 18, 19, 27; 7:9, 10, 14; 8:9; 9:10; 10:11, 26^{2}; 11:4, 8, 9, 19; 12:9, 13; 13:6, 8, 9, 21^{2}; 16:19, 26; 18:7^{2}, 21, 24, 27, 33; 19:27, 28, 29; 20:6, 21; 21:7, 15^{2}, 20, 27; 22:13; 23:14; 25:22; 26:6, 10; 27:4^{2}; 28:2; 29:2; 30:4, 20, 21; 31:3, 19, 26; 32:2, 9, 19; 33:7, 24; 34:28, 29; 35:10, 17; 37:2, 6; 38:9, 13, 19, 23^{2}; 39:18, 23, 31; 40:5, 29; 41:9^{2}; 42:7^{2}, 9; 43:2, 7, 16, 30; 44:17, 20; 45:23; 46:2, 5, 16; 47:4, 6, 14; 48:12, 13; 50:11^{2}, 12; 51:10; Bar 1:2, 19, 20; 2:28; LtJ 6:3, 6, 12, 17, 18, 20, 21, 24, 40, 43, 48, 55, 60, 61, 62; Sus 1:7, 14^{2}, 19, 26, 27, 28, 38, 52; Bel 1:1, 12, 28, 40; 1Mc 1:3, 16; 2:7, 23, 24, 39, 52; 3:11, 13, 16, 17, 23, 27, 40, 41; 4:5, 8, 9, 12, 21^{2}, 27, 30, 35, 40; 5:1, 16, 34, 42; 6:1, 8, 17, 28, 39, 47, 62; 7:3, 25, 31, 41, 44; 9:1, 6, 7, 16, 32, 43, 57, 63, 70; 10:2, 8, 22, 46, 64, 68, 74, 77, 88; 11:3, 4, 15, 22, 23, 38, 44, 49, 60, 73; 12:1, 27, 28, 35, 42, 44, 48, 51; 13:7, 16, 23; 14:2, 17, 25, 31; 15:9, 32^{2}; 16:6, 16, 22; 2Mc 1:13, 15, 18, 19, 20^{2}, 21, 22^{2}, 32^{2}, 33; 2:7; 3:7, 9, 24, 27, 37; 4:3, 7, 10, 18, 21, 24, 28, 33, 36, 39^{2}, 41, 44; 5:5^{2}, 11, 20, 25; 6:7, 15, 28, 30; 7:5, 6, 9, 10, 14, 18, 34; 8:8, 12, 19^{2}, 20^{2}, 27, 29; 9:4, 12, 18, 23, 25; 10:4, 11, 14, 18, 21, 27, 29, 38; 11:6; 12:1, 4, 5, 10, 17, 21, 22, 25, 30, 34, 35, 37; 13:4, 10, 12; 14:5, 11, 15, 20, 26, 28^{2}, 31, 32, 38, 41; 15:1, 2, 4, 8, 10, 20, 28, 31; 1Es 1:39, 43; 2:11, 30; 3:3, 9, 13, 22, 23, 24; 4:24, 41, 43, 44, 45, 55, 58; 5:39, 44, 47, 66; 6:8, 15; 8:1, 42, 62, 82; 9:37, 46; 3Mc 1:1, 4, 11, 13, 27; 2:7, 8, 9^{2}, 10, 12, 25; 3:1, 8, 9, 14, 16, 17, 20, 26; 4:11, 12, 20; 5:3, 10, 15, 17, 19, 21, 45, 47, 48, 50; 6:15, 17, 23, 30, 36; 7:13, 17, 19; 2Es 1:17, 20, 22, 25, 26, 31; 2:23, 27, 33; 3:4, 12, 13, 17, 29, 35; 4:11, 32, 33, 35, 36, 40, 48, 49; 5:1, 31, 53; 6:7, 17, 18, 19^{2}, 20, 23, 52; 7:1, 11, 21, 26, 70, 75, 78, 88, 97, 98, 111, 116; 8:2, 9, 36, 56, 63; 9:1, 2, 3, 18, 29^{2}, 34^{2}, 38, 47; 10:1, 3, 27, 29; 11:37; 12:3, 13, 21^{2}, 33, 40; 13:4, 9, 11, 29, 32, 33, 46, 49; 14:3, 26, 35, 40, 45; 15:50, 53, 60; 16:13, 18^{5}, 30, 38^{2}, 50^{2}, 65; 4Mc 1:33, 34; 2:3, 8, 11, 13, 14, 17, 21; 3:8, 12, 18, 20; 4:1, 4, 15, 22, 24, 26; 5:4, 5, 7, 8, 14, 15; 6:1, 24, 26, 34; 7:20; 8:2, 3, 4, 12, 13, 14, 15, 22, 26; 9:10, 12, 13, 16, 25; 10:1, 9, 12, 17; 11:1, 13^{2}, 17; 12:1, 2, 6, 7, 18; 13:21, 23; 15:18^{3}, 19, 20^{2}; 16:11, 15, 20; 17:1, 23; 18:9, 20

WHICH (1284)

Ge 1:21; 2:14; 3:11, 17, 23; 4:11; 6:17; 7:15; 10:14, 30; 11:5; 13:18; 17:10; 19:21, 29; 20:13; 21:2; 23:9, 17; 24:5; 25:18; 27:15, 41; 28:13, 22; 31:10, 39, 51; 32:12; 33:13, 18, 19; 35:6, 20; 38:14; 40:20; 45:6; 50:10, 13; Ex 3:5; 4:17, 28^{2}; 6:4; 10:8, 19; 12:7; 13:3, 5; 16:1, 26, 32; 17:5; 21:13; 22:9; 23:28; 24:12; 25:14, 29, 40; 26:32; 29:27, 33; 30:1, 4; 32:34; 33:1, 7; 34:1, 12; 37:16, 27; 38:21; 40:31; Lev 3:4, 9, 10, 15; 4:7, 9; 5:3, 16; 6:5, 10, 28, 30; 7:4, 25, 38; 9:8, 13, 18; 11:21, 32, 35, 39; 13:43, 54, 57, 58; 14:34, 40; 15:4^{2}, 6, 9, 17, 20^{2}, 22, 23, 24, 26^{2}; 16:9, 10, 16; 18:3, 7; 20:22, 25^{2}; 22:2, 3, 5, 8, 15; 23:4, 15, 37, 38; 27:22, 26; Nu 3:31, 48; 4:9, 14; 5:8, 18; 6:5; 10:29; 13:2, 27; 14:24, 27, 30, 34; 15:2, 18; 18:13, 15, 24; 19:2^{2}, 6; 20:13; 21:16; 22:5, 30; 23:13, 28; 25:18; 28:23; 30:4^{2}, 5, 6, 7, 8^{2}, 9, 11, 14; 31:38, 39, 40, 42; 33:1, 6, 7;

WHO (6635)

WHOM (822)

WHOSE (347)

WILL (7477)

See also the selected listing for "WILL" in the Main Concordance.

51, 61, 62, 63^{4}, 64; **3:**14^{2}, 22, 53, 60; **4:**10, 11; **5:**17, 40^{2}, 41, 48^{2}; **6:**22, 27^{2}; **7:**14, 15, 35; **8:**32; **9:**58; **10:**5, 16, 24, 27, 28, 30, 54^{2}, 56^{2}, 72, 73; **11:**9, 42^{2}, 43^{2}; **12:**45^{2}; **13:**6, 9, 16^{2}; **15:**9^{2}, 31, 35; **2Mc 1:**3; **2:**8^{2}, 16, 18^{2}, 27; **3:**38; **4:**17; **6:**27, 29; **7:**6, 7, 9, 14, 17, 19, 23, 30, 31, 33, 36; **9:**4, 25, 27^{2}; **10:**10^{2}; **11:**19^{2}, 26, 30; **12:**3, 16, 30; **14:**6, 26, 33; **15:**16, 37, 39; **1Es 2:**19^{2}, 22^{2}, 24; **3:**5, 9; **4:**37, 42; **5:**68, 71; **7:**15; **8:**16, 52^{2}, 93; **9:**9, 10, 52; **Man 1:**14^{2}, 15; **Pm 151:**3; **3Mc 2:**17, 26; **3:**26, 27, 28^{2}; **5:**40; **7:**7; **2Es 1:**24^{2}, 25^{2}, 26, 30, 31, 32, 33, 34, 35^{4}, 36, 37, 39; **2:**9, 10, 11^{2}, 13, 16, 18, 19, 23, 24, 26^{2}, 29, 30, 31^{2}, 32, 34^{2}, 35; **3:**8, 34^{2}, 36; **4:**4^{2}, 25, 26^{2}, 27, 29, 30, 32, 33, 35, 37, 43, 47, 51; **5:**11, 32^{2}, 37, 41, 43, 45^{3}, 51, 53, 55, 56; **6:**7^{2}, 13, 15, 16, 20, 31^{2}, 34, 59; **7:**9, 18, 26^{2}, 37, 38, 43, 47, 49^{2}, 52, 54^{2}, 60^{2}, 61, 73^{2}, 75, 76, 77, 86, 100, 102, 104, 111, 113, 115, 122; **8:**2, 5^{2}, 11, 14, 15^{2}, 17, 19, 25^{2}, 29, 32, 36, 37, 38, 39, 41^{3}, 46, 48, 49, 50, 63^{2}; **9:**2, 4, 7^{2}, 8^{2}, 13^{2}, 15^{2}, 23, 25, 36; **10:**4^{2}, 9, 10^{2}, 16^{2}, 18^{3}, 33, 38, 56, 59^{2}; **11:**38, 45; **12:**6, 23, 32^{4}, 33^{2}, 34^{2}, 49; **13:**16, 17, 20, 21^{2}, 23, 26^{2}, 29, 32, 37, 38^{2}, 47, 49, 50, 56^{2}; **14:**20^{4}, 21, 22, 25, 34, 35; **15:**1, 8^{2}, 9^{2}, 10, 11^{3}, 12, 17, 21^{2}, 22^{2}, 25, 26, 27, 29, 49, 56^{3}; **16:**8, 9, 10^{4}, 11^{2}, 13, 17, 20, 21^{2}, 25, 26, 27, 32, 38, 39^{3}, 41^{2}, 42^{2}, 43^{2}, 44, 46, 48, 50, 52^{2}, 53, 64^{2}, 66^{2}, 67, 74; **4Mc 1:**24; **2:**23; **5:**10, 11, 13, 26, 29, 34^{2}, 35^{2}, 37; **6:**15; **8:**7^{2}, 9, 11, 14, 22; **9:**9, 18, 32; **10:**11, 15, 19, 21; **11:**2, 3, 12, 22, 23; **12:**4, 5, 12, 14, 18; **13:**17^{2}; **18:**16, 22

WITH (7619)

Ge 1:11, 12, 21, 29; **2:**21; **3:**6, 12; **4:**1; **5:**22, 24; **6:**7, 9, 11, 13^{2}, 14, 16, 18^{2}, 19, 21; **7:**2, 7, 9, 13, 15, 23; **8:**1, 9, 16, 17^{2}, 18; **9:**4, 8, 9, 10^{3}, 11, 12; **10:**5; **11:**4; **12:**4, 8, 13, 16, 17, 20; **13:**1, 5; **14:**2, 5, 9, 16, 17, 24; **15:**14, 18; **16:**4, 5, 6, 12^{2}; **17:**4, 12, 13, 19, 21, 22, 23, 27^{2}; **18:**3, 11, 16, 23, 25; **19:**1, 9^{2}, 10, 11, 19, 30^{2}, 32, 33, 34^{2}, 35; **20:**16; **21:**1, 6, 9, 10^{2}, 14, 18, 19, 20^{2}, 22^{2}, 23^{6}, 32; **22:**3, 5; **23:**16, 17; **24:**15, 32, 40, 45, 49, 54, 55, 58, 59; **25:**10, 26; **26:**3, 10, 15, 20^{2}, 24, 26, 28^{2}; **27:**15, 34, 37, 41, 44; **28:**4, 15, 20; **29:**6^{2}, 9^{2}, 14, 19, 25; **30:**2, 8^{2}, 15, 16^{2}, 20, 29, 33^{2}, 40; **31:**3, 5, 6, 21, 23^{2}, 25, 27^{2}, 32, 38, 40, 50; **32:**4, 6, 7, 10, 11, 13, 20, 24, 25, 28^{2}; **33:**1, 2^{2}, 5, 8, 10^{2}, 11, 15^{2}; **34:**2, 5, 6, 7, 8, 9, 10, 11, 19, 21, 23, 26; **35:**2, 3, 6, 13, 14, 15, 22; **37:**2, 3, 14^{2}, 23, 25, 32; **38:**26, 30; **39:**2, 3, 6, 7, 8, 10, 12, 14^{2}, 21, 23; **40:**2, 4, 5, 7, 14; **41:**10, 11, 12, 40; **42:**4, 6, 13, 21, 23, 25, 26, 30, 32, 33, 38^{2}; **43:**3, 4, 5, 8, 12^{2}, 15, 16^{2}, 19, 21, 22, 30^{2}, 32^{2}, 34; **44:**1, 2, 3, 9, 10^{2}, 12^{2}, 18, 23, 26^{2}, 30, 31^{2}, 33, 34; **45:**1, 5, 15, 23^{2}; **46:**1, 4, 6, 7^{2}, 15; **47:**1, 9, 12, 17, 19, 29^{2}, 30; **48:**1, 6, 10, 12, 21, 22^{2}; **49:**25, 28, 29; **50:**4, 7, 9, 14^{2}; **Ex 1:**1^{2}, 7, 10, 11, 14, 20; **2:**3, 21, 24; **3:**8, 12, 17, 18, 20, 21; **4:**12, 15^{2}, 17, 25, 28^{2}; **5:**3, 21; **6:**4, 6^{2}; **7:**17; **8:**2, 3, 5, 17, 21; **9:**3, 15, 24; **10:**9^{3}, 10^{2}, 24, 26; **12:**8, 9, 22, 34, 38, 48; **13:**5, 9, 13, 19^{2}; **14:**6, 7, 20, 25; **15:**10, 19, 20^{2}; **16:**3, 18, 20, 31, 32; **17:**2^{2}, 3, 4, 5^{2}, 8, 9^{2}, 10, 13, 16; **18:**3, 6, 11, 12^{2}, 18, 19, 22; **19:**9, 13, 24; **20:**22; **21:**3, 6, 8, 9^{2}, 18, 19, 20, 31; **22:**16, 19, 24, 25, 30^{3}; **23:**1, 2, 11^{2}, 18, 32; **24:**2, 3, 8^{2}, 12, 13, 14; **25:**9, 11, 13, 19, 20, 22, 24, 28^{2}, 29, 31, 33^{2}, 34, 35^{3}, 36; **26:**1^{2}, 6, 24, 25, 29^{2}, 31, 32, 36, 37; **27:**2^{2}, 6, 8, 12, 14, 15, 10^{7}, 17, 18; **28:**1, 3, 11, 21^{2}, 28, 32, 33, 37, 39, 41; **29:**2^{2}, 4, 5, 9, 12, 13, 14, 17, 21, 22, 23, 34, 40^{2}, 41, 42, 43; **30:**2, 3, 4, 5, 6, 10, 18, 19, 20, 26, 28^{2}, 34, 35, 36; **31:**3^{2}, 6, 8, 9^{2}, 18^{2}; **32:**11^{2}, 12, 20; **33:**3, 9, 12, 14, 16, 22; **34:**3, 5, 9, 10, 12, 15, 20, 25, 27^{3}, 28, 29^{2}, 31, 32, 33, 34, 35; **35:**12, 13, 14, 15, 16^{2}, 25, 31^{2}, 35; **36:**1, 8^{3}, 13, 30, 34^{2}, 35, 36, 37, 38^{2}; **37:**2, 4, 8, 9, 11, 15, 16, 17, 19^{2}, 20, 21^{3}, 22, 25, 26, 27, 28; **38:**2^{2}, 6, 7^{2}, 8, 12, 14, 15, 17, 18, 23, 30; **39:**14^{2}, 21, 23, 29, 35, 36, 37, 39; **40:**3, 11, 12, 31; **Lev 1:**8, 9, 12, 13, 16; **2:**2, 4^{2}, 5, 11, 13^{2}, 14, 16; **3:**4^{2}, 5, 10^{2}, 15^{2}; **4:**9^{2}, 20^{3}, 25, 30, 34, 35; **5:**12, 16; **6:**15, 17, 21, 30; **7:**4^{2}, 7, 10, 12^{3}, 13^{2}, 30; **8:**2, 6, 7^{2}, 13, 15, 16, 17, 21, 25, 26, 28, 31, 32; **9:**4, 11, 14; **10:**15, 16; **11:**21, 43^{2}, 44; **13:**31, 33, 57; **14:**6, 10, 11, 12, 16, 21, 27, 31, 37, 49, 51, 52^{4}; **15:**3, 4, 6, 7, 8, 9, 11, 12, 13, 17, 18, 24, 33; **16:**3, 14^{2}, 15^{2}, 16, 19; **17:**13; **18:**20^{2}, 22^{2}, 23^{3}; **19:**15, 19^{2}, 20, 22, 26, 33, 34; **20:**10, 11, 12, 13^{2}, 15, 16, 18, 20, 24, 25; **21:**20; **22:**2, 25, 27, 28; **23:**13^{3}, 17, 18^{2}, 20^{2}, 24; **24:**7; **25:**6, 23, 28, 35, 36, 40^{2}, 41, 43, 45^{2}, 46, 47, 50^{2}, 53, 54; **26:**9^{2}, 42^{3}, 44, 45; **27:**16, 27; **Nu 1:**4, 44, 47, 49; **2:**4, 6, 8, 11, 13, 15, 17, 19, 21, 23, 26, 28, 30; **3:**1, 24, 25, 30, 31, 37; **4:**5, 8, 9^{2}, 10, 11, 12, 19, 25, 26, 31, 32^{2}; **5:**2, 6, 8, 13, 19, 20; **6:**15^{3}, 17, 20, 21^{2}; **7:**1^{2}, 9, 13, 19, 25, 31, 37, 43, 49, 55, 61, 67, 73, 79, 87, 89; **8:**7, 8, 20^{2}, 22, 26; **9:**11; **10:**9, 29, 32, 33; **11:**8, 9, 16, 17^{2}, 21, 33; **12:**7^{2}, 8; **13:**23, 27, 31; **14:**8^{2}, 9, 12, 21, 42, 43; **15:**4, 5, 6, 9^{2}, 12, 14, 16, 24; **16:**1, 10, 13, 14, 18, 22, 27, 30, 32, 33; **17:**4; **18:**1^{3}, 2^{2}, 7, 11, 19; **19:**4, 5, 12, 15; **20:**3, 11, 13, 18, 20; **21:**18^{2}, 34; **22:**3, 7, 8, 9, 12, 13, 14, 20, 21, 22, 23, 24, 27, 31, 35^{2}, 39, 40; **23:**6, 13, 17, 21; **24:**4, 8, 11, 16; **25:**1, 14, 18; **26:**3, 10; **27:**14, 21; **28:**5, 8, 9, 12^{2}, 13, 20, 28, 30, 31; **29:**3, 5, 9, 11, 14, 18^{2}, 21^{2}, 24^{2}, 27^{2}, 30^{2}, 33^{2}, 37; **30:**10; **31:**6^{2}, 8, 14, 17, 18, 23, 35; **32:**19, 29, 30, 32, 33; **34:**12; **35:**5, 7, 16, 17, 18, 21, 24, 25; **Dt 1:**18, 37; **2:**5, 7, 26, 33; **3:**2, 5, 12, 16, 17^{2}, 26; **4:**2, 3, 21, 23, 29, 31, 37, 49; **5:**2, 3^{2}, 4, 15, 16, 22, 23, 29^{2}, 33; **6:**3^{2}, 5^{3}, 10, 11, 15, 18, 21; **7:**2, 3, 5^{2}, 8, 9, 12, 14, 21, 25; **8:**3^{2}, 7^{2}, 15, 16; **9:**8, 9, 10, 20, 21, 26; **10:**3, 7, 9, 12^{2}, 14; **11:**6, 9, 13^{2}; **12:**3, 12^{2}, 18, 23, 25, 28^{2}; **13:**3, 16; **14:**25, 27, 29; **15:**9, 14, 16, 17, 19, 20; **16:**3^{2}, 4; **17:**9, 19; **19:**5, 11, 13, 15; **20:**1, 4, 20; **21:**4, 14; **22:**2, 3^{3}, 6^{3}, 7, 9, 10, 12, 14, 22^{2}, 23, 25^{2}, 28, 29; **23:**4, 11, 13^{2}, 14, 16, 23, 25; **24:**1, 5^{3}; **25:**2, 11; **26:**8^{3}, 9, 11^{2}, 13, 15, 16^{2}; **27:**2, 3, 4, 20, 21, 22, 23; **28:**22^{3}, 27^{2}, 28, 30, 35, 40, 47, 59, 66; **29:**1^{2}, 12, 14^{2}, 15^{2}, 21, 22, 25; **30:**2^{2}, 6^{2}, 10^{2}; **31:**5^{2}, 6, 7, 8, 16^{2}, 20, 23; **32:**5, 12, 13^{3}, 14^{2}, 16^{2}, 21^{4}, 24, 34, 42^{2}, 51; **33:**1, 2, 4, 8, 13, 14, 15, 16, 17, 23; **34:**4; **Jos 1:**5^{2}, 7, 8, 9, 17^{2}; **2:**6, 12^{2}, 14, 19; **3:**1, 7^{2}; **4:**3, 8; **5:**6, 13; **6:**2, 4, 5^{2}, 8, 17, 23, 25, 27; **7:**12, 15^{2}, 21, 22, 24^{4}, 25; **8:**1^{2}, 4, 5, 10, 11^{2}, 24, 26, 33; **9:**2, 4, 5, 6, 7, 11, 15, 16; **10:**1, 4^{2}, 5, 7, 11, 15, 24, 28, 29, 30, 31, 32, 34, 35, 36, 37^{2}, 38, 39^{2}, 43; **11:**4^{2}, 5, 6, 7, 9, 10, 11, 12, 14, 18, 19, 21; **12:**1; **13:**8, 17, 21, 22, 23, 28; **14:**4, 8, 12^{2}; **15:**12, 32, 36, 41, 44, 45, 46, 47, 51, 54, 57, 59, 60, 62, 63; **16:**9^{2}; **17:**4, 6, 10; **18:**4, 24, 28; **19:**6, 7, 8, 15, 16, 22, 23, 30, 31, 38, 39, 48; **20:**4; **21:**2, 11, 13^{2}, 14^{2}, 15^{2}, 16^{3}, 17^{2}, 18^{2}, 19, 21^{2}, 22^{2}, 23^{2}, 24^{2}, 25^{2}, 26, 27^{2}, 28^{2}, 29^{2}, 30^{2}, 31^{2}, 32^{3}, 33, 34^{2}, 35^{2}, 36^{2}, 37^{2}, 38^{2}, 39^{2}, 41, 42; **22:**5^{2}, 8^{5}, 14, 18, 24, 27, 30; **23:**4, 7, 12; **24:**5, 6, 8, 25, 27; **Jdg 1:**3^{3}, 7, 16^{2}, 17, 18^{3}, 19, 22, 24; **2:**1, 2, 18; **3:**13, 16, 21, 27, 31; **4:**7, 8^{2}, 9^{2}, 10, 13, 14, 18, 22; **5:**14, 15, 17, 21, 22; **6:**12, 13, 16, 17^{2}, 26, 38, 39; **7:**1, 2, 4^{3}, 5, 7, 10, 11, 16, 18, 19; **8:**2, 3, 4, 10, 16, 33; **9:**4, 16, 19^{2}, 23, 26, 32, 33^{2}, 34, 35, 38, 39, 44, 45, 48^{2}, 52; **11:**3, 6, 8^{2}, 9, 11, 20, 25^{2}, 34^{2}, 39^{2}; **12:**1, 2, 4; **13:**9, 19; **14:**5, 7, 11, 15, 18; **15:**8, 13, 15, 16^{2}; **16:**4, 7, 8, 11, 12, 13^{2}, 14, 15, 16, 21, 28, 30^{2}; **17:**10, 11; **18:**7, 11, 16, 17^{2}, 19, 20, 23, 28; **19:**2, 3^{2}, 4, 5, 9, 10^{2}, 19^{2}, 22, 27; **21:**11, 12; **Ru 1:**3, 6, 8^{3}, 10, 11, 18, 20, 21, 22^{2}; **2:**4, 6, 10, 19^{2}, 22, 23; **3:**1, 2, 16; **4:**11; **1Sa 1:**18, 24^{2}; **2:**5, 8, 13, 17, 19, 20, 22, 25, 26^{2}, 29, 30, 32; **3:**19; **4:**4, 8, 12^{2}; **5:**6, 7, 8, 12; **6:**2^{2}, 11, 13, 19; **7:**3, 10; **9:**3, 5, 8, 19, 24^{3}; **10:**5, 6, 7, 10, 11, 26; **11:**1, 2, 5; **12:**2, 3, 7, 20, 24; **13:**2^{2}, 5, 15, 16, 22; **14:**2, 3, 7, 13, 17, 18, 20, 21^{3}, 23, 27, 28, 32, 33, 34^{2}, 43, 45; **15:**6, 8, 25, 26, 30; **16:**1, 2, 5, 18, 19, 20, 23; **17:**3, 5, 9, 19, 20, 23, 28, 32, 33, 37, 38^{2}, 39, 41, 43, 45, 50, 51, 52, 57; **18:**3, 6^{3}, 12, 14, 17, 22, 27, 28; **19:**1^{2}, 9, 10, 13, 16, 20; **20:**5, 7, 8^{2}, 13^{2}, 16, 35^{2}, 41^{2}; **21:**1, 2^{3}, 8^{2}; **22:**2, 4^{2}, 6^{2}, 8, 17, 23^{2}; **23:**5, 6, 23^{2}; **24:**8, 18, 19; **25:**7, 13, 15, 16, 25, 26, 31, 41; **26:**2, 5, 6^{2}, 7, 8, 13; **27:**2, 3^{3}, 5; **28:**1, 8, 12, 14, 19^{2}, 20, 23; **29:**2, 3, 4^{3}, 6, 9, 10, 11; **30:**4, 9, 10, 21, 22^{2}, 23; **31:**4, 5; **2Sa 1:**2, 11, 21, 24; **2:**2, 3^{2}, 23; **3:**8, 12, 13, 16, 20^{2}, 21, 22^{3}, 23, 27, 31, 39; **5:**3, 10, 11; **6:**2, 4, 5^{2}, 8, 12, 14^{2}, 15^{2}; **7:**3, 7, 9, 12, 14^{2}, 17^{2}, 22, 29; **8:**2, 10^{2}, 11; **10:**2^{2}, 3, 7, 13, 16, 17, 19; **11:**1^{2}, 4, 9, 11, 13, 17; **12:**3^{2}, 9^{2}, 11, 16, 17, 24, 31; **13:**1, 11, 14, 15, 18, 20, 24, 26^{2}, 27, 28; **14:**2, 6, 17, 19, 22, 32, 33; **15:**11, 12, 14^{2}, 19^{2}, 20^{2}, 22^{2}, 24, 27, 30^{2}, 31, 32, 33, 35, 36; **16:**1, 10, 12, 14, 15, 17, 18, 21; **17:**2, 8, 10^{2}, 12, 16, 22, 24, 29; **18:**1, 2, 5, 14, 27, 28, 29, 32; **19:**4, 5, 7, 16, 17^{2}, 22, 25, 26, 31, 32, 33, 34, 36^{2}, 37, 38, 40, 41; **20:**7, 8, 9^{2}, 22; **21:**15^{2}, 16, 17, 18, 19; **22:**26^{2}, 27^{2}, 33, 40, 44; **23:**5^{2}, 6, 9, 18, 21^{2}; **24:**2, 20; **1Ki 1:**1, 7^{2}, 8, 14, 21, 22, 23, 31, 33, 37^{2}, 40, 41, 44, 51; **2:**4^{2}, 5, 7^{2}, 8^{3}, 9, 10, 14, 32, 43; **3:**1, 13, 18; **4:**13; **5:**3, 17; **6:**4, 7, 9, 10, 12, 15^{3}, 16, 20^{2}, 21^{2}, 22^{2}, 28, 29, 30, 32^{2}, 35, 36; **7:**2, 3, 6, 7, 9, 17, 18^{2}, 20, 30, 34, 35, 36, 37; **8:**5, 9, 15^{2}, 21, 23, 24^{2}, 33, 46, 47, 48, 54, 55, 57^{2}, 59, 62, 65; **9:**4, 11, 27^{3}; **10:**1, 2^{2}, 13, 18, 22, 26; **11:**1, 2^{2}, 9, 17, 18, 21, 22, 29, 38, 43; **12:**6, 8^{2}, 10, 11^{2}, 14^{2}; **13:**7, 8, 15, 16^{3}, 18, 19, 25, 28; **14:**3, 6, 8, 20, 22, 31^{2}; **15:**8, 19, 20, 22^{2}, 24^{2}; **16:**2, 6, 7, 13, 17, 18, 28; **17:**20; **18:**4, 13, 19, 21, 28, 32, 33, 35, 45; **19:**1, 10, 14, 19; **20:**1^{2}, 12, 16, 20, 21, 34, 38; **21:**8^{2}; **22:**4, 11, 13, 19, 31^{2}, 40, 44, 49, 50^{2}; **2Ki 1:**8, 9, 11, 13, 14, 15^{2}; **3:**7^{2}, 9, 12, 13, 17, 19, 20, 26; **4:**10; **5:**1, 3, 5, 7, 9, 23, 26; **6:**3, 4, 8^{2}, 11, 15, 16^{2}, 18^{2}, 22, 32, 33; **7:**2, 15, 19; **8:**1, 2, 4, 6, 8, 9, 12, 21, 24^{2}, 28; **9:**14, 18, 19, 24, 26, 28; **10:**2, 5, 6^{2}, 15, 16, 19, 23, 30^{2}, 31, 35; **11:**3, 4, 8^{2}, 9, 11, 14, 15, 20; **12:**7, 14, 21; **13:**7, 9, 12, 13^{2}, 14, 18, 19, 23; **14:**10^{2}, 15, 16^{2}, 20, 22, 29; **15:**7^{2}, 22, 25^{2}, 38^{2}; **16:**11, 15, 20^{2}; **17:**13, 15, 18, 35, 36^{2}, 38; **18:**7, 17, 23, 27, 31, 37; **19:**1, 2, 6, 23, 24, 32, 37; **20:**3, 12, 21; **21:**6^{2}, 11, 18; **22:**17; **23:**2, 3, 11, 14, 15, 18, 25^{3}, 26; **24:**4, 6; **25:**1, 4, 10, 17, 23, 24, 25^{3}, 28; **1Ch 4:**10, 23, 33; **5:**20; **6:**32, 57^{2}, 58^{2}, 59^{2}, 60^{3}, 64, 67^{2}, 68^{2}, 69^{2}, 70^{2}, 71^{2}, 72^{2}, 73^{2}, 74^{2}, 75^{2}, 76^{3}, 77^{2}, 78^{2}, 79^{2}, 80^{2}, 81^{2}; **7:**4; **8:**12, 32; **9:**20, 25, 38; **10:**4; **11:**3, 9, 10, 13, 20, 23^{2}, 42; **12:**2, 8, 18, 19, 27, 33^{2}, 34^{2}, 37, 38, 39; **13:**1^{2}, 8^{2}, 14; **14:**1; **15:**5, 6, 7, 8, 9, 10, 15, 18, 21, 25, 27, 28; **16:**5, 16, 41, 42; **17:**2, 6, 8, 11, 15, 20; **18:**8, 10, 11; **19:**2^{2}, 7, 14, 16, 17, 19; **20:**3, 4, 5; **21:**7, 20, 21, 26; **22:**11, 14, 16, 18; **23:**5, 29^{2}; **24:**3; **25:**1, 3, 6; **26:**8; **28:**1, 9, 20, 21; **29:**9, 19, 21, 22, 30; **2Ch 1:**1, 3, 14; **2:**2, 3, 7, 8, 12, 13, 14; **3:**4, 5^{2}, 6, 7, 8, 9, 10, 15; **4:**9; **5:**10, 12^{2}, 13^{2}; **6:**4^{2}, 11, 14^{2}, 15^{2}, 18, 23, 24, 36, 37, 38, 41; **7:**3, 6, 8, 18; **8:**5, 18^{2}; **9:**1^{2}, 12, 17, 21, 25, 31; **10:**6, 8, 10, 11^{2}, 14^{3}; **12:**1, 3^{2}, 16; **13:**3, 8, 9, 12, 17, 19^{3}; **14:**1, 7, 8, 9, 13; **15:**2^{2}, 6, 9^{2}, 12^{2}, 14^{4}, 15^{2}; **16:**3, 6^{2}, 8, 10^{2}, 13, 14; **17:**3, 8^{2}, 9, 14, 15, 16, 17^{2}, 18; **18:**1, 2, 3^{3}, 10, 12, 18, 30^{2}; **19:**6, 7, 9, 11; **20:**1, 13, 17, 18, 19, 21, 27^{2}, 28, 35, 37; **21:**1^{2}, 3, 7, 9, 15, 17, 18, 20; **22:**1, 5, 7, 9, 12; **23:**1, 3, 7^{2}, 8, 10, 13, 18^{2}, 21; **24:**14, 24; **25:**2, 7^{2}, 10, 13, 15, 19, 24, 28; **26:**2, 13, 17, 19, 23; **27:**5, 9; **28:**5, 9, 15^{2}, 18^{3}, 27; **29:**8, 10, 24, 25, 26^{2}, 29, 30^{2}; **30:**6, 9, 19, 21, 23; **31:**12, 18, 21^{2}; **32:**3, 7^{3}, 8^{2}, 9, 18, 21, 33; **33:**6^{2}, 11, 20; **34:**12^{2}, 21, 25, 30, 31; **35:**12, 13, 21^{3}, 22, 26; **36:**6, 10, 17, 19, 23; **Ezr 1:**3, 4^{3}, 6^{5}; **2:**2; **3:**2^{2}, 8, 9^{2}, 10^{2}, 11, 12; **4:**2, 3; **5:**2; **6:**4, 12, 13, 16, 22; **7:**13, 16^{2}, 17^{2}, 18, 21, 23, 28; **8:**1, 3, 4, 5, 6, 7, 8, 9, 10, 11, 12, 13, 14, 18, 19^{2}, 24, 33^{2}; **9:**1, 2, 5, 11^{3}, 14^{2}; **10:**2, 3, 4, 12, 14, 44; **Ne 1:**2, 5; **2:**5, 9, 12, 17; **3:**1; **4:**13, 17^{2}; **5:**2, 7, 18; **6:**5, 16; **7:**2, 7, 65; **8:**2, 6, 8, 13; **9:**1^{2}, 4, 6, 8, 12^{2}, 13, 24^{2}, 25, 30; **10:**29, 38; **11:**25; **12:**1, 8, 24, 27^{4}, 35, 36, 38, 40, 41, 42, 43; **13:**2, 9, 11, 17, 25; **Est 1:**6, 10, 17; **2:**6, 9^{2}, 12^{2}, 13, 18; **3:**1, 11, 12; **4:**1, 2, 3; **5:**9, 11, 12^{2}, 14; **6:**8, 12, 14; **7:**1; **8:**3, 8^{3}, 10, 11, 15; **9:**5, 29; **10:**3; **Job 1:**4, 15, 17, 22; **2:**8, 10, 13; **3:**14, 15^{2}; **4:**2, 18; **5:**14, 23^{2}; **6:**16^{2}; **7:**5, 14^{2}; **8:**21^{2}, 22; **9:**3, 14, 17, 18, 30^{2}; **10:**11^{2}, 15; **12:**2, 12, 13, 16; **13:**3, 4, 9, 19; **14:**3; **15:**2^{2}, 3, 4, 11, 26, 27; **16:**5, 10, 16, 21; **17:**3; **19:**2, 4, 16, 22, 24^{2}; **20:**11, 17; **21:**3, 34; **22:**4, 18, 21; **23:**4, 6, 7; **24:**8, 13, 17; **25:**2; **26:**4; **27:**11, 13, 19; **28:**14, 19, 22; **29:**5, 6, 19, 20; **30:**1, 18, 21, 30; **31:**1, 5, 20, 30, 31; **32:**14; **33:**16, 19^{2}, 25, 26, 29; **34:**8^{2}; **35:**4; **36:**2, 4, 7, 17, 32, 33; **37:**4, 5, 11; **38:**8, 32; **39:**10, 16, 19, 24; **40:**2^{2}, 9, 10^{2}, 19, 24^{2}; **41:**1^{2}, 2, 4, 5^{2}, 7^{2}, 15; **42:**8, 11, 15; **Ps 2:**9, 11^{2}; **4:**T; **5:**4, 9, 12^{2}; **6:**T, 2, 3, 6^{3}, 10; **7:**2, 4, 14; **8:**5; **9:**1, 8^{2}; **10:**7; **12:**2, 4; **13:**6; **14:**5; **15:**3; **17:**10, 14; **18:**11, 25^{2}, 26^{2}, 32, 39, 43; **19:**5; **20:**3, 6; **21:**3, 6, 12; **23:**4, 5; **25:**19; **26:**4^{2}, 5, 9^{2}; **27:**6; **28:**3^{3}, 7; **29:**11; **30:**5, 11; **31:**10^{2}, 18; **32:**7, 8, 9; **33:**2^{2}, 3; **34:**3; **35:**1^{2}, 5, 6, 13^{2}, 16, 26; **36:**9; **38:**7, 17; **39:**1, 3; **40:**5; **41:**11; **42:**4^{2}, 8, 10; **43:**4; **44:**1, 2, 9, 19; **45:**1, 7, 8, 12, 13^{2}, 15; **46:**3, 7, 9, 11; **47:**1, 5^{2}, 7; **48:**10; **49:**13; **50:**5, 18^{2}; **51:**7; **54:**T, 6; **55:**T, 12, 14^{2}, 20, 21^{3}; **59:**7^{2}; **60:**T^{2}, 5, 6, 10, 12; **61:**T; **62:**4; **63:**5^{2}; **64:**8; **65:**4, 5, 6, 9, 10, 11^{2}, 12, 13^{2}; **66:**13, 15, 17; **67:**T, 4; **68:**3, 13^{2}, 16, 17, 30; **69:**3^{2}, 10, 13, 30^{2}, 31; **71:**8^{2}, 13, 22^{2}; **72:**2^{2}; **73:**7^{2}, 8, 23, 24^{2}; **74:**5, 6; **75:**2, 3, 5, 8; **76:**T; **77:**6, 15; **78:**9, 14^{2}, 36^{2}, 47^{2}, 58^{2}, 72^{2}; **79:**12; **80:**4, 5, 10^{2}, 16; **81:**2, 16^{2}; **83:**5, 7, 15^{2}, 16; **84:**6; **85:**5; **86:**12; **87:**4; **88:**7; **89:**1, 3, 10, 20, 21, 24, 28, 32^{2}, 39, 45, 51^{2}; **90:**14; **91:**4, 8, 15, 16; **93:**1; **94:**20; **95:**2^{2}; **96:**10, 13^{2}; **98:**5^{2}, 6, 9^{2}; **100:**2^{2}, 4^{2}; **101:**2, 6^{2}; **102:**9; **103:**4, 5, 10; **104:**1, 2, 6^{2}, 13, 28; **105:**9, 18, 25, 30, 37, 43^{2}; **106:**29, 32, 35, 38; **107:**9, 12^{2}, 22; **108:**6, 7, 11, 13; **109:**2, 3, 10, 29, 30; **110:**6; **111:**1, 8; **112:**5^{2}; **113:**8^{2}; **116:**7; **118:**6, 27; **119:**2, 7, 10, 13, 17, 20, 34, 58, 65, 69^{2}, 78, 82, 98, 124, 131, 145, 150, 158; **120:**4; **125:**5; **126:**2^{2}, 5, 6; **127:**5; **128:**2; **129:**7; **130:**4, 7^{2}; **131:**1, 2^{2}; **132:**9, 15, 16, 18; **136:**12; **138:**1; **139:**3, 18, 22; **140:**5; **141:**4^{2}; **142:**1^{2}, 7; **143:**2; **144:**13, 14; **147:**7, 8, 14, 20; **149:**3^{2}, 4, 8^{2}; **150:**3^{2}, 4^{2}, 5^{2}; **Pr 1:**11, 13, 31; **2:**16; **3:**5, 9^{2}, 10^{2}, 15, 28, 30; **4:**3, 23; **5:**17; **6:**3, 12, 14, 22, 25, 29; **7:**1, 5, 13, 16, 17, 18, 20, 21^{2}; **8:**11, 12, 18, 21, 24; **10:**22; **11:**2, 9, 10, 16; **12:**14, 21; **13:**10, 20; **14:**1, 18^{2}; **15:**16^{2}, 17, 19, 22; **16:**7, 8^{2}, 19; **17:**1^{2}; **18:**3; **19:**11, 23; **20:**8, 19; **21:**9, 19, 24, 27; **22:**9, 14, 24^{2}, 27; **23:**1, 13, 14, 21; **24:**1, 4, 28, 31^{2}; **25:**9, 15, 24; **26:**23, 26; **27:**14, 22^{2}; **28:**2, 17, 20, 23; **29:**3, 9, 14; **30:**8, 19, 22; **31:**13, 16, 17, 24, 26; **Ecc 1:**8^{2}, 13; **2:**3^{3}, 9, 21, 22; **3:**10, 18; **4:**1^{2}, 6^{2}, 8; **5:**2, 3^{2}, 7, 10^{2}, 11, 15, 18, 20; **6:**10; **7:**18; **8:**12, 13, 15; **9:**4, 7^{2}, 9, 10, 14; **12:**2; **SS 1:**2, 6, 10^{2}, 11; **2:**3, 5^{3}; **3:**6^{2}, 8^{2}, 10, 11; **4:**8^{2}, 9^{2}, 13^{2}, 14^{2}; **5:**1^{4}, 2^{2}, 5^{2}, 8, 14^{2}; **6:**1, 4, 10; **7:**2; **8:**5, 9; **Isa 1:**4, 6, 7, 13, 22, 25, 31; **2:**6, 7^{2}, 8; **3:**14, 16^{3}, 17; **5:**2, 6, 13, 18^{2}, 30; **6:**2^{3}, 4, 6, 7, 10^{3}; **7:**2, 5, 14, 20^{2}, 24, 25; **8:**10; **9:**3, 7^{2}, 10, 12; **10:**22, 24, 33, 34^{2}; **11:**4^{4}, 6^{2}, 15; **12:**1, 3; **13:**9, 14; **14:**3, 6^{2}, 19, 20, 21, 23; **16:**9^{2}; **18:**5; **19:**16, 21, 23, 24; **20:**4; **21:**3, 14; **22:**6, 21, 23:17; **24:**2^{12}, 4, 9; **25:**5, 6; **26:**17, 18; **27:**1, 5^{2}, 6, 8; **28:**1^{2}, 2, 4, 7^{5}, 8, 11^{2}, 15^{2}, 18^{2}, 27^{3}; **29:**3, 6^{2}, 11, 13^{2}, 14; **30:**22, 23, 24, 25, 27, 28, 30, 31, 32^{2}, 33; **32:**1, 7; **33:**1^{2}, 5, 14^{2}, 21; **34:**3, 6^{4}, 7^{4}, 14, 15, 17; **35:**2, 4^{2}, 10; **36:**2, 8, 12, 16, 22; **37:**1, 2, 6, 24, 25, 33, 38; **38:**3, 14; **39:**1; **40:**9, 10^{2}, 12, 18, 19, 31; **41:**2^{2}, 3, 4, 7^{2}, 10^{2}, 12, 17; **42:**22^{2}; **43:**2, 5, 23^{3}, 24^{4}; **44:**12^{2}, 13^{4}; **45:**9^{2}, 10, 14, 17; **47:**6, 12, 13, 15^{2}; **48:**20; **49:**4^{2}, 23, 25^{2}, 26^{2}; **50:**1, 3, 4, 8; **51:**11, 19, 21; **53:**3, 9^{2}, 10, 12^{3}; **54:**7, 8, 9, 11, 15; **55:**3; **56:**12; **57:**5, 8, 9, 15, 18; **58:**4, 7, 14; **59:**3^{2}, 6, 12, 21; **60:**9, 11, 15; **61:**8, 10^{4}; **62:**11; **63:**3, 11; **65:**4; **66:**10^{2}, 11, 14; **Jer 1:**8, 19; **2:**10, 22, 37; **3:**1, 2^{2}, 8, 9, 10, 15; **4:**4, 10, 30^{2}; **5:**17, 28; **6:**3, 28; **7:**3, 5, 7, 16, 23; **8:**8, 19^{2}; **9:**7, 13, 15, 18^{2}, 24, 26; **10:**3, 4^{2}; **11:**5, 10, 16^{2}, 19; **12:**3, 5^{2}, 6; **13:**12^{2}, 13, 17, 19; **14:**3, 17^{3}, 18, 21; **15:**7, 17, 20; **16:**8, 18^{2}; **17:**1^{2}, 18; **18:**6, 23; **19:**1, 4, 9, 10; **20:**4, 9, 11; **21:**4, 5, 7, 10, 12; **22:**3, 7, 8, 14^{3}, 15, 19; **23:**17, 28; **24:**1, 7; **25:**6, 7, 31; **26:**11, 14, 21, 22, 23, 24; **27:**5, 8^{3}, 10, 15, 18^{2}; **29:**11, 13, 16, 18^{3}, 23; **30:**6, 11; **31:**3, 7, 8, 9^{2}, 14, 24, 27, 31, 32, 33; **32:**4, 8, 21^{3}, 22, 24, 29, 40, 41; **33:**5, 20^{2}, 21^{2}, 25; **34:**2, 3, 8, 13, 22; **35:**2; **36:**18, 23, 27, 31; **37:**8, 10; **38:**10, 11, 17, 18, 20, 23, 25; **39:**3, 12, 14; **40:**1, 2, 4^{2}, 5, 6, 9; **41:**1, 2^{2}, 3, 5, 7, 8, 9, 11, 13^{2}, 15, 16; **42:**6, 8, 11; **43:**1, 6, 13; **44:**8, 13^{3}, 19; **45:**3; **46:**4, 22, 28; **48:**7, 9, 33; **49:**2, 3^{2}, 5; **50:**5, 32, 39; **51:**14, 20^{2}, 21^{2}, 22^{3}, 23^{3}, 28, 32, 34, 58, 59; **52:**4, 14, 15, 22, 32; **La 1:**2^{2}, 3, 9, 16, 21, 22^{2}; **2:**4, 11; **3:**5, 9, 15^{2}, 30, 43, 44, 48; **4:**14; **5:**5, 6, 22; **Eze 1:**4, 20, 21; **2:**1; **3:**3, 10, 22, 24, 25, 27; **4:**7, 16; **5:**2, 5, 11^{2}, 15; **7:**19, 27; **8:**1, 11, 16, 17, 18; **9:**1^{2}, 2^{2}, 6, 7, 11; **10:**2, 4, 17, 19; **11:**6, 13, 22; **12:**7, 12, 18^{3}, 19; **13:**14, 15, 20; **14:**4, 11, 19; **16:**4^{2}, 8, 9^{2}, 10^{3}, 11, 13, 17, 19, 26, 28^{2}, 29^{2}, 36, 37, 40, 43, 46^{2}, 53, 59, 60^{2}, 61, 62; **17:**3, 7, 12, 13, 16, 17, 20; **18:**7, 16; **19:**4, 9, 11; **20:**6, 7, 15, 18, 27, 31, 33^{2}, 34^{2}, 35, 36^{2}, 39, 40, 44; **21:**6, 12, 31; **22:**7, 11, 14, 21, 31; **23:**7, 8, 10, 15^{2}, 17^{2}, 23, 24^{2}, 25, 29, 30^{2}, 33, 37, 40, 41, 42, 43^{2}, 47; **24:**4, 7, 12, 16; **25:**6, 10, 15^{2}, 17; **26:**7, 9, 11, 16, 20^{2}; **27:**6, 9, 12, 13, 15, 16, 17, 18, 20, 21, 22, 23, 24^{3}, 27^{2}, 31, 33, 34; **28:**2, 6, 14, 16, 24, 26; **29:**4, 7; **30:**5, 11^{2}, 21, 24; **31:**3, 8, 9, 11, 14^{2}, 16, 17^{2}, 18^{2}; **32:**2, 4, 5, 6^{2}, 7, 18^{2}, 19, 21, 24, 25^{2}, 27^{2}, 28, 29^{3}, 30^{3}, 32; **33:**25; **34:**3, 4, 6, 14, 16, 18^{2}, 19^{2}, 21^{2}, 25, 29, 30; **35:**8^{2}, 11, 13, 15; **36:**5, 17, 18, 19, 38; **37:**6, 16^{2}, 19, 23^{2}, 26^{2}, 27; **38:**4^{2}, 5^{2}, 6^{2}, 9, 15, 22^{3}; **39:**4, 20^{2}, 23, 24, 26; **40:**3, 16, 38, 42; **41:**7, 13, 15, 16^{2}; **42:**11^{2}, 16; **43:**2, 8, 13, 14^{2}, 17, 22; **44:**7, 18, 19; **45:**2, 16; **46:**5^{3}, 7^{4}, 10, 11^{4}, 14, 23; **47:**3, 17, 22; **48:**1, 8, 10, 20, 21; **Da 1:**4, 8, 10, 13^{2}, 19^{2}; **2:**8, 11, 14, 18, 22, 41, 43^{3}; **3:**19; **4:**8, 9, 15^{3}, 18, 23^{3}, 25^{2}, 27^{2}, 32, 33, 35; **5:**11, 21^{2}; **6:**4, 5, 17^{2}; **7:**7, 11, 13, 19^{2}, 21; **8:**6^{2}, 12, 20, 22; **9:**3, 4, 15, 25, 26, 27; **10:**5, 7, 13, 17, 20, 21; **11:**3, 4, 8^{2}, 11, 13, 17, 23^{2}, 25^{2}, 28, 32, 38^{2}, 39, 40^{2}, 44, 45; **Hos 2:**2, 3, 6, 7, 13, 18; **3:**3^{2}; **4:**3, 4, 5, 14^{2}; **5:**5, 6, 7^{2}; **6:**4^{2}, 7, 8; **7:**5^{2}, 8; **8:**4, 10; **10:**4, 14; **11:**4^{2}, 12^{3}; **12:**1, 3, 4^{2}; **14:**2, 8; **Joel 2:**5, 12^{4}, 24, 26; **3:**2, 18^{2}; **Am 1:**3, 11, 14^{2}; **2:**3, 8; **3:**12; **4:**2^{2}, 9, 10; **5:**2, 6, 14, 20; **6:**6, 10, 12; **7:**7^{2}, 9; **8:**5; **9:**1, 9, 13; **Jnh 1:**3; **2:**9; **3:**6, 8; **Mic 1:**7; **2:**4, 8, 10, 12; **3:**8^{3}, 10^{2}, 11; **5:**1^{2}, 6^{2}, 8; **6:**2^{2}, 6^{3}, 7^{2}, 8, 12, 15; **7:**2, 6, 14; **Na 2:**11, 12^{2}; **3:**6, 8, 12, 18; **Hab 1:**9, 15^{2}; **2:**6^{2}, 14, 16; **3:**9, 14, 15, 19; **Zep 1:**9, 12; **3:**9, 14, 17^{2}, 19; **Hag 1:**6, 12, 13^{2}; **2:**4, 7, 12, 13, 14^{3}, 17; **Zec 1:**2, 6, 9, 12, 13^{2}, 14, 15, 16, 17, 19; **2:**1, 3, 7; **3:**3, 4, 5, 9; **4:**1, 2^{2}, 4, 5; **5:**5, 10; **6:**4, 6, 13; **7:**7, 14; **8:**2^{2}, 4, 11, 23^{2}; **9:**8, 11; **10:**5, 7; **11:**8, 10; **12:**4^{3}; **14:**5, 12; **Mal 1:**4, 8; **2:**4, 5, 6, 13^{3}, 16, 17; **3:**9, 16; **4:**2, 6; **Mt 1:**18, 23, 25; **2:**3, 10, 11; **3:**4, 11^{2}, 12, 17; **4:**10, 21, 24; **5:**22, 23^{2}, 20^{7}, **7:**2; **8:**9, 11, 14, 16^{2}, 29; **9:**8, 10, 11, 15, 19; **10:**5; **11:**15; **12:**10, 18, 30^{2}, 41, 42, 45; **13:**9, 14, 15^{3}, 20, 29, 33, 40, 43, 56; **15:**8, 20, 30, 32; **16:**27; **17:**1, 3, 5, 17^{2}; **18:**9, 16, 23, 25, 26, 29^{2}, 32; **19:**10; **20:**2, 8, 13, 15, 20, 24, 34; **21:**2, 22, 25; **22:**10, 16^{3}, 37^{3}; **23:**7, 30; **24:**30, 31, 49, 51; **25:**3, 4, 10, 16, 19, 22, 27^{2}, 28, 31; **26:**7, 11, 18, 20, 23, 29, 35, 36, 37, 38, 40, 47^{2}, 51, 55, 58, 69, 71, 72; **27:**19, 22, 34, 38, 41, 44, 46, 48, 50, 54, 66; **28:**8, 12, 20; **Mk 1:**6^{2}, 8^{2}, 11, 13, 20, 23, 24, 26, 27, 29, 30, 32, 34, 41; **2:**15, 16^{2}, 19^{2}; **3:**5, 6, 7, 14; **4:**9, 10, 16, 23, 29, 30, 33, 36^{2}, 41; **5:**2, 3, 4, 5, 7, 18, 24, 40, 42; **6:**3, 13, 27, 51; **7:**2, 5, 6; **8:**2, 4, 10, 11, 14, 27, 34, 38; **9:**1, 2, 4^{2}, 8, 12, 14, 15, 16, 19, 34, 47, 49, 50; **10:**30, 38^{2}, 39^{2}, 41; **11:**11, 31; **12:**5, 14^{2}, 28, 30^{4}, 33^{3}, 37, 38; **13:**26, 34; **14:**3, 7, 14, 17, 18, 20, 31, 33, 43^{2}, 48, 49, 54, 58^{2}, 62, 67; **15:**1, 7, 12, 19, 23, 27, 31, 32, 34, 36, 41; **16:**10, 20; **Lk 1:**15, 17, 28, 30, 37, 38, 39, 41, 42, 48, 51, 53, 56, 58, 66, 67; **2:**5, 13, 16, 36, 37, 40, 51; **3:**11, 14, 15, 16^{2}, 17, 18, 22; **4:**14, 28, 32, 33, 34, 36, 40; **5:**9, 10, 12^{2}, 17, 19, 26, 29, 30, 34; **6:**11^{2}, 17^{2}, 18; **7:**6, 8, 11, 12, 29, 36, 38^{3}, 44^{2}, 46^{2},

49; 8:1, 7, 8, 13, 15, 22, 23, 28, 29, 37, 38, 51; 9:10, 18, 28, 32[2], 41[2], 49; 10:17, 27[4], 33; 11:7, 23[2], 31, 32, 36[2], 37, 43, 46, 50; 12:13, 21, 46, 50, 58; 13:1, 11, 21, 26; 14:10, 25, 31[2], 35; 15:2, 6, 9, 16, 20, 28, 29, 30, 31; 16:8, 11, 12, 20, 21, 22, 23; 17:15, 20; 18:9; 19:13, 23, 37; 20:1, 5, 21, 46; 21:5, 27, 34; 22:4, 11, 14, 15, 20, 21, 26, 33, 48, 49, 52, 53, 56, 59; 23:11[2], 12, 18, 23, 32, 33, 43, 46, 55; 24:10, 14, 15, 17, 24, 27, 29[2], 30, 36, 44, 49, 52; Jn 1:1, 2, 26, 31, 33[2], 35, 39; 2:7, 12; 3:8, 22, 26; 4:9, 12, 27[2], 40, 53; 6:3, 22, 66; 7:23, 24, 33; 8:6, 9[2], 29; 9:6, 37; 10:6; 11:2[2], 16, 31, 33, 43, 44, 45, 54; 12:2, 3[2], 8, 17, 35, 40[2]; 13:5, 8, 33; 14:9, 16, 17, 23, 25, 27, 30; 15:27; 16:4, 32; 17:5, 12, 24, 26; 18:1, 2, 3[2], 5, 15, 18, 26; 19:15[2], 18[2], 32, 34, 40; 20:7, 19, 21, 24, 26[2]; 21:3, 9, 13; Ac 1:4, 5[2], 14, 18, 22; 2:4, 13, 14, 22, 28, 29, 30, 36, 40, 46; 3:8, 10; 4:6, 8, 15, 16, 27, 29, 31[2], 33; 5:1, 2, 17[2], 21[2], 26, 28; 6:5, 9, 10; 7:9, 19, 38[2], 45, 46, 48, 55, 57; 8:6, 7, 11, 13, 20[2], 35; 9:7, 17, 19, 29, 38, 39[2], 43; 10:2, 6, 20, 23, 27, 28, 38[3], 41, 45; 11:3, 12, 16[2], 21, 23, 26; 12:2, 6, 9, 17, 20, 25; 13:7, 9, 16, 17, 18, 31, 45, 52[2]; 14:4[2], 5, 17[2], 18, 20, 23, 27, 28; 15:2[2], 4, 15, 22[2], 23, 24, 25, 35, 37, 38, 39; 16:9, 22; 17:2, 5, 17[2], 18, 23, 34; 18:2, 3, 5, 8, 10, 19, 25; 19:4, 9, 16, 25, 26, 29[2], 38, 40; 20:7, 11, 19[2], 28, 31, 34, 36; 21:5, 7, 8, 11, 16, 18, 24, 25, 26, 29, 33, 36; 22:9, 11, 22, 25; 23:1, 9, 15, 23, 27, 29, 32; 24:1, 3, 4, 12, 22, 24, 26; 25:5, 12, 18, 19, 23[2], 24; 26:3, 10, 12[2], 20, 30[2]; 27:7, 8, 10, 19, 24, 39; 28:8, 11, 14, 16, 20[2], 22, 23, 25, 27[3], 31; Ro 1:4, 9, 11, 27[3], 29; 2:2; 3:2; 5:1, 20; 6:4, 5[2], 6, 8[2]; 7:3, 23, 25[2]; 8:3, 16, 17[3], 18, 19, 25, 26, 32; 9:20, 22; 10:9, 10[2], 19; 11:2, 27; 12:3, 10, 15[2], 16[2], 18, 21; 13:6; 15:1, 5[2], 6, 10, 13, 14, 23, 26, 32, 33; 16:3, 7, 14, 15, 16, 20; 1Co 1:2, 17; 2:4[2]; 3:2, 10, 12, 13, 19; 4:3, 8, 21[2]; 5:1, 4, 8[2], 9, 11[2], 12; 6:7, 16, 17, 20; 7:9, 12, 13, 23, 24, 31[2]; 9:17, 19; 10:5, 13, 20, 30; 11:4, 5, 13, 18, 21, 32; 12:12, 23[2], 26[2]; 14:7, 9, 12, 15[4], 16, 19, 36; 15:3, 4, 10, 32[2], 35, 42; 16:3, 6, 7, 11, 12, 16, 19, 20, 21, 23, 24; 2Co 1:4[2], 12, 21, 24; 2:4; 3:3[2], 12, 18; 4:13, 14[2]; 5:1, 2, 8; 6:1, 3, 7, 14, 15[2], 16; 7:4, 7, 8[2], 15; 8:18, 19, 22; 9:4, 8, 12, 13[2]; 10:1, 9, 12[2], 14; 11:1[2], 9, 17, 19, 20, 23[2], 25; 12:10, 12, 18[2]; 13:3, 4[2], 11[2], 12, 13; Gal 1:2, 16, 18; 2:1[2], 2, 3, 5, 7[2], 12, 14, 19; 3:3[2], 5, 9, 27; 4:3, 18, 20, 25, 30; 5:24; 6:6, 18; Eph 1:3, 8, 13, 18; 2:4, 5, 6[2], 15, 19, 20; 3:11, 16, 18, 19; 4:2[3], 16, 24, 28[2], 30[2], 31; 5:6, 7, 18[2], 26; 6:2, 3, 5, 7, 9, 16[2], 19, 23, 24; Php 1:1, 4, 7, 8, 9, 14, 20, 23, 25, 27; 2:6, 12, 17, 18, 22[2], 23, 29; 3:18; 4:3, 6, 9, 11, 15, 21, 23; Col 1:9, 11[2], 29; 2:4, 5, 11, 12[2], 13, 14, 19, 20, 22; 3:1, 3, 4, 9, 10, 12, 13, 14, 16; 4:2, 6, 9, 18[2]; 1Th 1:5, 6; 2:4, 5[2], 8, 11[2], 17; 3:4, 13; 4:5, 11, 14, 16[3], 17[2], 18; 5:10, 14, 26, 28; 2Th 1:6, 7; 2:5, 8; 3:7, 8, 10, 14, 16, 17, 18; 1Ti 1:4, 14, 18; 2:9[2], 10, 11, 15; 3:6, 9; 4:2, 3, 4, 7, 14; 5:2; 6:3[2], 6, 8, 10, 17, 21; 2Ti 1:3, 4, 8, 9, 14; 2:10, 11[2], 12, 22, 23, 25; 3:4; 4:2, 3, 10, 11[2], 13, 22[2]; Tit 1:1, 3, 9[2]; 2:1, 15; 3:10, 15[2]; Phm 1:13, 19, 25; Heb 1:9; 2:7, 9; 3:10, 17; 4:2, 15, 16; 5:2, 7; 7:14, 20, 21; 8:8[3], 9, 10; 9:4, 10, 11, 12[2], 13, 19[2], 21, 22, 23, 25, 28; 10:16, 22[3], 32, 33; 11:7, 9, 25, 31; 12:1, 14, 17, 21, 28; 13:3, 5, 6, 17[2], 22, 23, 25; Jas 1:11[2], 17[2], 21; 2:1, 2, 4, 22; 3:1, 2, 9[2], 13; 4:4[2]; 5:7, 14; 1Pe 1:2, 8, 18, 19; 2:18; 3:4, 9, 16, 22; 4:1[2], 10, 11, 17[2], 19; 5:5[2], 13, 14; 2Pe 1:5[2], 6[3], 7[2], 17, 18; 2:3, 5, 13, 16, 18; 3:6, 8, 9, 10[2], 12, 13, 17; 1Jn 1:1[2], 2, 3[3], 6, 7; 2:1, 19; 4:18; 5:6[2]; 2Jn 1:2, 3, 12; 3Jn 1:2[2], 8, 10, 13; Jude 1:9, 12, 14, 23, 24; Rev 1:7, 9, 13[2], 16; 2:16, 22, 27; 3:4, 20[2], 21[2]; 4:2, 4, 7, 8; 5:1, 2, 12; 6:1, 8[2], 10; 7:2, 3, 9; 8:3[2], 4, 5, 7, 8, 13; 9:2, 9, 10, 19; 10:1; 11:6; 12:1[2], 3, 5, 9, 12, 15, 17; 13:10[2], 18; 14:1, 4, 6, 9, 10, 14, 15, 18; 15:1[2], 2[2], 6[2], 8; 16:8; 17:2[2], 4, 6, 7, 12, 14, 16; 18:1, 2, 3, 8, 9, 16[3], 21; 19:2, 8, 10, 15[2], 17, 19, 20[2], 21; 20:4, 6; 21:3[2], 8, 12, 16, 19; 22:2, 9[2], 12, 16, 21; Tob 1:3, 6, 12, 13, 14; 2:2, 10, 14; 3:1[2], 5, 6, 8, 9, 11, 14, 17; 4:1, 6, 15, 20; 5:3[2], 4[2], 6[2], 7, 9, 10[2], 14[2], 15, 16, 17; 6:1, 2[2], 5, 8, 13, 18[2]; 7:11, 12[2]; 8:7, 15, 16, 20; 9:2[2], 5[3], 6; 10:6, 8, 13; 11:6, 11[2], 13, 16, 17, 18; 12:1, 2, 3, 6, 7, 8[4], 11, 17, 18; 13:6[3], 14[2], 16[6]; 14:2, 8[2], 12, 13; Jdt 1:2, 12[2], 15; 2:2, 5, 7, 8, 15, 19[2], 20; 3:2, 3, 4, 6, 7; 4:9[2], 12, 14, 15[3]; 5:12, 17, 23; 6:4, 8; 7:12, 14, 15, 17, 23, 24, 29; 8:3, 8, 18, 21, 26, 27, 33; 9:1, 3[2], 4, 6, 8, 10[2]; 10:3[2], 5, 6, 21, 22; 11:13, 16, 17, 18; 12:1[2], 2[2], 3, 4, 11, 12, 13, 16, 17, 20; 13:2, 8, 11, 14, 16, 17, 20; 14:14, 15, 16; 15:2[2], 5[2], 9, 10[2], 12, 13[2]; 16:1[2], 3, 4, 6, 7, 8, 15, 20; AdE 1:6[2], 8[2], 12, 19; 2:9[2], 12[2], 13, 20; 3:11, 12; 4:1; 5:9, 12, 14; 6:12, 13; 7:1, 3, 8, 10; 8:8[2], 9, 10[2], 14; 9:17, 18, 29; 10:3, 13; 11:4, 10; 12:1, 6; 13:2[2]; 14:1, 2[2], 8, 13; 15:2, 5[2], 6, 7, 8, 11, 13; 16:2, 5, 9, 13[2], 18, 22, 24; Wis 1:1, 16; 2:8, 19; 3:9; 4:1, 15, 20; 5:1, 2, 15, 16[2], 20, 21; 6:23; 7:2, 4, 8, 11, 14, 15, 28, 29; 8:3, 9, 16[3], 17, 18, 21; 9:5, 9, 11, 16; 10:13, 16, 20; 11:6; 12:18[2], 19, 20, 21; 13:10[2], 11, 13[2], 14, 15, 19; 14:8, 10, 15, 16, 23; 15:4, 8, 9, 11, 15[4], 17; 16:20; 17:4, 8, 17, 19, 20; 18:2, 9, 11, 16; 19:6, 15, 16[2], 17, 18; Sir Pr:T[2]; 1:1, 14, 16, 17[2], 28; 2:16; 3:13, 17; 4:12, 17[2]; 5:6, 14; 6:1, 6, 13, 20, 26[2]; 7:24, 27, 29, 30, 34; 8:1, 2, 3, 8, 15[2], 16[2], 17; 9:4, 9[2], 10, 14, 15; 10:6, 28; 11:9, 10, 17; 12:14, 16; 13:1, 2[2], 5, 7, 13, 16, 17[2]; 14:1, 9, 19; 15:3; 16:4, 11, 13, 14, 29, 30; 17:3, 7, 12, 22; 18:11, 15, 33; 19:2, 8, 10, 11, 16; 20:26; 21:8, 10; 22:13, 18, 23[2]; 23:11, 16, 22[2]; 24:22, 25, 26; 25:8[3], 16[2]; 26:20; 27:9, 17, 23; 28:7, 19, 24, 26; 29:3, 5[2], 6[2], 8, 23; 30:5, 9, 10[2], 20; 31:3, 20, 21, 23, 24; 32:2, 3, 6, 13, 15; 33:31; 34:9, 23; 35:11[2], 15; 36:19[2], 25; 37:3, 10, 11[9], 12[3]; 38:5, 16, 25, 28, 29, 30[2]; 39:1, 3, 6, 15[3], 30, 35; 40:26, 29; 41:22; 42:1, 3[2], 4, 5, 16; 43:12; 44:6, 11[2], 18, 20, 21, 23; 45:7[2], 8, 9[2], 10[2], 11[2], 12[2], 15, 17, 24, 25, 26[2]; 46:5, 8, 9, 11, 17; 47:3[2], 8, 9, 14, 15, 23; 48:9, 11, 12[2], 15, 17; 49:10; 50:9, 10, 12, 18, 20, 22, 28; 51:19, 20, 22, 27; Bar 1:2, 7, 10, 20; 2:2, 7, 11[3], 18, 27, 35; 3:10, 32, 34, 37; 4:11[2], 23[2], 24[2], 25, 28, 29; 5:9[2]; LtJ 6:7, 8, 11, 18, 28, 31, 39, 42, 50, 55, 57, 58, 63, 70, 71; Aza 1:16, 17[2], 18, 19, 20, 23, 26, 28; Sus 1:10, 15, 20[2], 21, 24, 30, 33, 36, 37, 42, 46, 54, 57, 58, 59, 62; Bel 1:1, 5, 10, 11, 14, 15, 16, 36, 41; 1Mc 1:6, 11, 15, 17[3], 20, 24, 28, 29, 31, 33, 56; 2:18, 24, 26, 27[2], 38, 40, 42, 70; 3:13, 15, 16, 39, 40, 41, 50, 58; 4:6, 7, 8, 9, 10, 13, 29, 32, 33[2], 35, 39[2], 40, 46, 54, 57[2], 59[2], 60; 5:5, 6, 7, 14, 18, 19, 23[2], 28, 31, 35, 44[2], 45, 47, 54, 58, 68; 6:6, 7, 10, 31, 35[3], 36, 39, 43, 49, 56[2], 58[3]; 7:1, 9, 10[2], 11, 14, 16, 20, 23, 25, 27, 28, 30, 40; 8:1, 6[2], 12, 20, 22, 23[2], 29; 9:1, 4, 5, 9, 12, 14, 29, 33, 34, 35, 36, 37, 39[3], 43, 44, 45, 48, 50, 59, 60, 62, 65, 67, 68, 70; 10:4[2], 6, 11, 20, 21, 23, 26[3], 27[2], 51, 54[2], 58, 60[2], 63, 64, 71[2], 84, 85, 86, 87[2]; 11:2, 6, 7, 9, 15, 34, 49, 51, 54, 61, 62[2], 63, 70; 12:1, 3, 8, 10, 14, 16, 24, 35, 38, 41, 42, 43, 45[2], 47, 48[2], 50; 13:2, 11, 12[2], 14, 15, 26, 27, 31, 33, 34, 37, 43, 45[4], 47[2], 50, 51[3], 52; 14:10[2], 11, 14, 18[2], 22, 23, 24[2], 40, 46; 15:10, 13, 15, 19, 27, 28, 32; 16:3, 10, 13, 14, 19; 2Mc 1:2, 3, 13, 14, 15, 28, 33, 35; 2:3, 4, 22, 29[2], 30; 3:2, 3, 4, 7, 19, 23, 24[2], 25[2], 28, 30, 32, 35, 36; 4:11, 22[2], 24, 34, 36, 37, 38[2], 39, 40; 5:2, 15, 16[2], 24, 26, 27; 6:4[3], 5, 10, 14, 16, 17, 19[2], 21, 22, 23, 29; 7:1, 7, 12, 20, 21[2], 24[3], 29, 33; 8:8, 9, 15, 18, 20, 21[2], 23, 24, 29, 30, 35; 9:2[2], 4[2], 5[3], 6, 7, 9, 11, 15, 16, 21, 27; 10:4, 6, 12, 20, 25, 29, 30, 35[2], 38; 11:4, 6, 7, 20, 35; 12:3, 10, 11, 12, 13, 16, 20, 23, 24, 25, 27, 28, 33, 37, 39, 42; 13:1, 2[2], 3, 9, 12, 13, 15, 16, 22, 23; 14:1, 2, 9[2], 13, 27, 30, 38, 45, 46; 15:1, 7, 11[2], 12, 16, 17, 20, 24, 25, 26, 27, 28, 37, 39; 1Es 1:5, 12[2], 17, 26, 27[2], 28, 29, 32, 40, 45, 53, 55, 56; 2:5, 6, 7[2], 9[4], 15, 25, 30; 3:6, 22; 4:19, 21[2], 29, 30, 31[2], 36, 39, 46, 47, 52, 63; 5:1, 2[2], 3, 8, 47, 48[2], 49, 56, 58[2], 59[2], 62, 63, 64, 68, 70; 6:2[2], 5, 9, 10, 19, 22, 24, 25, 34; 7:2, 4, 9; 8:5, 10[2], 11, 12, 14[2], 16[2], 27, 28, 30, 31, 32[2], 33, 34, 35, 36, 37, 38, 39, 40, 47, 50, 52, 54, 63[2], 70, 73, 77, 80, 83[2], 85, 87, 88, 93, 95; 9:4, 10, 13, 14, 15, 36, 38; Man 1:2, 3, 10, 13[2]; Pm 151:T, 4, 5; 3Mc 1:1, 2, 4, 7, 16, 18[3], 27; 2:1, 5, 7, 13, 26[2], 27, 29, 30, 31[2], 32; 3:4, 5[2], 14, 15, 17, 20, 21, 23, 25[3], 27[2], 29; 4:1, 3, 4, 5[2], 6, 8, 10, 11[2], 13, 14, 15, 16[3]; 5:1, 2, 3, 7, 8, 10[2], 15, 18, 19, 21, 25, 30[2], 39, 41, 42, 43, 44, 45[2], 46, 47[4], 49, 50; 6:1, 2, 4[3], 5, 6, 14, 15, 16, 17, 19[2], 26, 30, 40; 7:3[2], 5[2], 6, 8, 16, 17, 19, 22[2]; 2Es 1:10, 20, 26, 34, 37[3], 38; 2:3[2], 15, 18, 19[2], 30, 42; 3:11, 15, 21, 22; 4:10, 22; 5:1, 15, 38; 6:21; 7:28[2], 64, 66[2], 68, 71, 72, 74, 76, 77, 87[2], 91, 92[2], 94, 98, 137; 8:8, 14, 30, 33, 34; 9:5, 9, 19, 21, 22, 25, 35, 38, 39, 43, 46; 10:5, 13, 27, 31, 47, 57; 11:4, 5, 19, 30, 31[2], 32, 40[3], 41; 12:5, 28, 32, 45; 13:3, 8[2], 38[2], 52, 56; 14:4, 9[2], 22, 24; 15:11[3], 15, 19, 29, 30[3], 37, 41, 52, 62; 16:12, 31, 48, 77[2]; 4Mc 1:10, 15, 20; 2:6, 8, 17; 3:3, 7, 15; 4:1, 5, 6, 9, 10[2], 11, 25; 5:1[2], 24; 6:2, 11, 13, 18[2], 25; 7:4[2], 7, 8, 11, 18; 8:1, 3, 4, 5, 9, 15, 29; 9:5, 8, 11, 12, 14, 20, 26, 28; 10:5, 7, 21; 11:22[2]; 12:8; 13:13, 26; 14:6, 17, 19; 15:7, 11, 20, 22; 16:10, 12; 17:2, 5[2], 20; 18:9[2], 10, 20, 21, 23

WOULD (884)

Ge 2:6, 19; 4:15; 14:23; 19:9; 21:7[2]; 26:10; 29:3; 30:15; 31:27, 31, 42; 34:14; 38:9[2], 11; 39:10; 41:21; 42:21, 22, 36, 38; 43:7, 10, 25; 44:8, 22, 34; Ex 2:4; 6:9, 30; 7:13, 22; 8:15, 19, 26, 32; 9:7, 12, 15, 35; 10:20; 14:12; 19:19[2]; 23:5, 29[2]; 33:3, 5, 7, 8, 9[2], 10, 11[2]; 34:34, 35[2]; 40:36; Lev 6:4; 7:29; 10:19; Nu 7:89; 9:17[2], 18[3], 19[2], 20[3], 21[3], 22[3], 23[2]; 10:35, 36; 11:9, 29[2]; 12:14; 14:2[2], 3, 31; 16:14; 20:3; 21:9, 23; 22:29, 33; 24:13; Dt 1:39, 43, 45; 3:26; 4:35; 6:15[2]; 7:4[3], 16, 22; 8:2, 20; 9:19; 12:15, 31; 15:9, 22; 23:21; 24:4, 6, 15; 28:68; 32:29[3]; Jos 5:6; 7:7; 11:20; 21:43; 24:10; Jdg 2:18, 19[2], 22; 3:4; 6:3, 4, 5[2]; 7:2; 8:19; 9:29[2]; 11:17[2], 40; 12:3, 5; 13:23; 14:18; 15:1; 16:17[2]; 19:10, 25; 20:13; Ru 1:13[2]; 4:4; 1Sa 1:4, 7; 2:13, 14[2], 15, 16, 20[2], 25; 7:17; 9:9; 10:27[2]; 13:13; 15:9; 16:23[2]; 17:35; 18:2; 20:9; 22:17, 22; 25:34; 26:23; 27:10; 29:4; 30:24; 2Sa 2:21, 27; 5:8; 11:20; 12:8, 17; 13:13, 14, 16, 21, 25; 14:7, 16, 29[2], 32; 15:2, 3, 4, 5; 17:17; 18:11, 12, 13, 33; 19:6; 20:18; 21:16; 23:15, 16, 17; 1Ki 4:33[2]; 5:14; 7:8, 15, 23; 8:12; 12:16; 18:9, 10[2]; 21:4; 22:18; 2Ki 3:14; 4:8, 13; 5:3, 11[2], 13; 8:14, 19; 12:8, 11; 13:19, 23; 14:11, 27; 17:14, 40; 18:7; 23:10; 1Ch 4:10[2]; 9:27; 11:17, 18, 19; 2Ch 4:2; 6:1; 9:8; 10:16; 12:11[2]; 15:13; 18:17; 20:10; 21:7; 24:11, 19; 25:20; 35:22; Ezr 9:14; 10:5; Ne 3:5; 4:3; 6:11; 9:29, 30; Est 2:11; 3:4[2]; 4:4; 6:6; 7:4; 9:1, 27; Job 1:4, 5[2]; 2:10; 3:13[3]; 5:8[2]; 6:3, 8, 9[2], 10[2], 27; 7:15, 16; 9:16, 20[2], 34, 35; 10:18; 11:5, 6; 13:3, 5[2], 19; 14:13[3], 14, 15[3], 16[2], 17[2]; 16:5, 21; 23:4, 5[3], 6[2], 17; 30:1; 31:2, 11[2], 12[2], 28, 36[2], 37[2]; 32:22; 34:15, 36; 41:32; Ps 14:6, 7; 40:5; 44:21; 50:12; 51:16; 52:7; 53:6; 55:6, 7[2], 8; 62:3; 66:18; 69:4; 73:15; 81:8, 11, 13[2], 14, 15[2], 16[2]; 84:10; 94:17; 95:7; 106:23, 26, 27; 109:31; 119:92; 124:3, 4[2], 5; 139:19[2]; Pr 1:25, 30; 11:9; SS 3:4; 8:1[2], 2[2], 7; Isa 1:9; 14:17; 28:12; 40:16; 42:24[2]; 44:10; 48:5, 8, 18, 19[2]; 54:9; 57:16; 64:1[2]; 66:1; Jer 3:1[2], 19[3]; 10:7; 13:11; 15:1; 17:23; 20:17; 22:24; 23:22[2]; 29:19; 30:21; 31:36; 32:33; 33:20, 21, 26; 34:10[2]; 36:23, 25, 31; 37:10, 14; 38:19; 40:14, 15[2]; 49:9[2]; 51:53, 60; Eze 1:12, 20; 3:6; 14:14, 16[3], 18[2], 20[2]; 20:6, 8[2], 13, 15, 21, 23; 22:30[2]; 33:5; 38:17; Da 1:8, 10; 2:16, 29; 6:22; 7:16; 12:7[2]; Hos 6:11; 7:1, 13; 8:7; 12:8; 13:8; Am 4:7[2]; Ob 1:5[2]; Jnh 3:10; 4:5; Mic 2:11; Hab 1:5; Zec 7:13[2]; Mal 1:10[2]; Mt 3:14; 7:12; 11:21, 23; 12:7; 13:15, 29; 18:6, 30, 34; 20:10; 22:3; 23:30; 24:22, 43[2]; 25:27; 26:24, 54, 58; 27:34, 40, 64; Mk 1:34; 3:2, 9; 4:26, 27[2]; 9:42; 11:13, 16; 13:20; 14:21; 15:29; 16:11; Lk 1:45, 71; 2:26; 4:41; 5:15, 16; 6:7, 31; 7:39; 8:29; 10:13; 12:39; 14:9, 12; 15:16; 16:21; 17:2, 6, 7, 8; 18:13; 19:40; 21:37, 38; 22:23; Jn 2:24; 4:10[2]; 5:46; 6:7, 64; 7:13; 8:19, 24, 39, 42, 55[2], 56; 9:22, 27, 41; 11:21, 32, 40; 12:40, 42; 14:2, 28; 15:19, 22, 24; 18:30, 36; 19:11; 21:19, 23[2], 25; Ac 2:30, 45; 3:2, 18; 5:16; 7:6[2], 19, 25; 11:28, 29; 15:7; 16:17; 17:20, 21, 26, 27; 18:4[2], 14; 19:30; 20:38; 21:14, 26; 23:10, 30; 24:26; 25:22; 26:22, 23; 27:17; 28:22, 27; Ro 4:13, 18; 7:7[2]; 9:29; 11:6, 8[2]; 1Co 2:8; 4:21; 5:2, 10; 7:14, 28; 9:3, 15; 11:31; 12:15[2], 16[2], 17[2], 19; 14:5, 19; 15:1, 32; 2Co 1:9; 2:3; 5:8; 9:3, 4; 11:1; 12:8; Gal 1:10; 3:8, 19, 21, 23; 4:15; 5:12; Eph 4:11; Php 2:27; 1Th 3:3; 1Ti 1:16; 5:14; Phm 1:9, 17; Heb 3:5, 18; 4:8; 6:18; 7:11; 8:4, 7; 9:26; 10:2[2], 13; 11:6, 15, 28, 32, 40; 13:17; Jas 1:18; 1Pe 5:2; 2Pe 2:21; 1Jn 2:19, 26; 2Jn 1:12; 3Jn 1:13; Rev 2:14; 6:4, 11; 13:15; 20:3; Tob 1:6, 7[2], 8[3], 17[2], 18; 2:12; 5:6; 6:14; 10:1, 7[3]; 11:5; 12:2, 12; Jdt 1:12[2]; 4:7; 6:17; 7:27; 11:2; 12:12; 13:3; 16:4; AdE 1:12, 22; 2:11; 3:4; 4:4; 6:6; 7:5; 9:27; 13:13; 16:14[2]; Wis 8:9, 21; 11:24, 25[2]; 12:10; 15:19; 16:11; 18:9; 19:2; Sir 16:11; 19:8; 21:24; 25:7, 16; 44:21[2]; Bar 2:24; 3:7, 13; Sus 1:7, 41, 57; Bel 1:32; 1Mc 1:49; 4:45; 7:30; 8:7; 9:71; 12:43, 51; 13:17; 2Mc 2:32; 3:22, 37; 4:6, 47; 5:18; 6:25, 26; 7:24[3], 25; 8:6; 9:13, 15, 16[3], 17[2], 24[2]; 11:14; 12:2, 24, 44[2]; 13:3; 14:14, 40; 15:7, 8, 33[2]; 1Es 1:50; 4:29, 31, 50, 55; 5:44, 45; 8:96; 9:4; 3Mc 1:22; 2:10, 23; 3:8, 11; 4:10; 5:5, 31, 32, 42, 43[2]; 6:34; 7:4, 11; 2Es 1:18, 24; 2:1, 5; 3:15; 4:8, 12, 18; 5:35; 7:63, 69, 99, 116, 135, 137, 140; 10:52; 12:44; 13:41; 15:52; 4Mc 1:10; 2:20; 4:12, 13, 17, 25; 5:6, 18, 19, 26, 27; 6:18, 20, 32, 34; 7:22; 8:2[2], 16, 25; 9:6; 13:2, 12; 15:27; 16:5, 17; 17:7, 8

YOU (16651)

Ge 1:29[2]; 2:16, 17[3]; 3:1, 3[3], 4, 5[2], 9, 10, 11[4], 12, 13, 14[4], 15[2], 16[2], 17[5], 18[2], 19[5]; 4:6, 7[5], 10, 11, 12[3], 14, 23; 6:15, 18[4], 19[2], 20, 21[2]; 7:1[2], 2; 8:16[2], 17[2]; 9:2, 3[3], 4, 7, 9[2], 10[2], 11, 12[2], 15; 12:1, 2[3], 3[3], 11, 12[2], 13[2], 18[2], 19; 13:8, 9[3], 14, 15[2], 17; 14:23; 15:2, 3, 5, 7[2], 15[2]; 16:2, 5[2], 6, 8[2], 11[2], 13; 17:2[2], 4[2], 5, 6[3], 7[4], 8[3], 9[4], 10[4], 11[2], 12, 15, 16, 19[2], 20, 21; 18:3, 5[4], 10, 14, 15, 23, 24, 25[2], 28; 19:2, 5, 7, 8[2], 9, 12[2], 15, 17, 19[2], 21[2], 22, 34; 20:3[2], 4, 6[3], 7[3], 9[4], 10[2], 13, 15[2], 16[2]; 21:12[3], 17, 22[2], 23[4], 26, 29, 30[2]; 22:2[2], 5, 12[2], 16, 17, 18; 23:4[2], 6[2], 8, 11[3], 13, 15; 24:3[2], 5, 6, 7[2], 8[3], 14[2], 23, 31, 37, 38, 40[2], 41[4], 42, 47, 49, 50, 51, 58, 60; 25:23; 26:2, 3[3], 9, 10[2], 16, 24[2], 27[3], 28[3], 29[5]; 27:4, 7, 8, 10[2], 18, 19[2], 20, 21[2], 24, 25, 28, 29[5], 31, 32, 33, 36, 37, 38, 40[4], 42, 45[4]; 28:1, 3[3], 4[5], 6, 13[2], 14[2], 15[6], 22[2]; 29:4, 5, 14, 15[2], 18, 19, 25[3], 27; 30:2, 15[3], 16[2], 26[3], 27[2], 29[2], 30[2], 31[3], 33[2], 34; 31:3, 6, 12, 13, 16, 24, 26[2], 27[2], 28[2], 29[2], 30[3], 31, 32, 35, 36, 37[2], 38, 39[2], 41[2], 42[2], 43, 44[2], 48, 49, 50[3], 51, 52[2]; 32:4, 6, 9, 10, 12[2], 17[5], 18, 19[2], 20, 26[2], 28[2], 29; 33:5, 8, 9, 10[2], 11, 12, 15; 34:10[2], 11[2], 12[2], 15[3], 16[2], 17, 30; 35:1[2], 2, 10, 11[2], 12[2], 17; 37:8[2], 10[2], 13, 15; 38:16[3], 17[3], 18, 23[2], 29; 39:9, 17; 40:13[4], 14, 19[3]; 41:15[3], 39[2], 40[3], 41, 55; 42:1, 7, 9[2], 12, 14[2], 15[2], 16[4], 18, 19[3], 20, 22[2], 33, 34[3], 36[2], 37[3], 38[3]; 43:3[2], 4[2], 5[3], 6[2], 7, 8, 9[3], 12[2], 14, 23, 27, 29[2]; 44:4[3], 5, 8, 10, 15[2], 17, 18, 19, 21, 23[3], 27, 29[2], 32; 45:4, 5[2], 7[3], 8, 10[4], 11[3], 12, 13[2], 18[2], 19; 46:3, 4[2], 30, 33, 34[2]; 47:4, 5, 6[2], 16, 23[2], 24, 25, 29, 30; 48:2, 4[3], 5[2], 6, 20[2], 21[2], 22; 49:1[2], 3, 4[4], 8[2], 9, 25[2]; 50:4, 5, 6, 17[2], 20, 21, 24[2], 25[2]; Ex 1:16, 18, 22[2]; 2:7[2], 9, 13, 14[3], 18, 20; 3:5, 10, 12[5], 13, 14[2], 15[2], 16[2], 17, 18, 19, 20, 21[2], 22[2]; 4:1, 5, 8, 9[3], 10, 12[2], 14[2], 15[3], 16[3], 17, 21[2], 22, 23[2], 25; 5:4, 5, 7, 8, 10, 11, 13, 14[2], 15, 16, 17[2], 18[2], 19, 21[2], 22[2], 23; 6:1, 6[3], 7[3], 8[2], 29; 7:1, 2[2], 4, 9[2], 16[2], 17; 8:2, 4, 9[2], 10[2], 11, 21[2], 22, 28[2], 29; 9:2, 14[2], 15[2], 16[2], 17, 19, 28[2], 29, 30[2]; 10:2[2], 3, 4, 5, 7, 10[3], 11, 16, 24, 25, 28[3], 29; 11:1[3], 7, 8[2], 9; 12:2[2], 5, 6, 10[2], 11[2], 13[4], 14[3], 15[2], 16[2], 17[2], 18, 20[2], 22, 23, 24[2], 25[3], 26[2], 27, 31[2], 32, 46[2], 48, 49; 13:3[2], 4, 5[3], 6, 7, 8, 9[2], 10, 11[3], 12, 13[4], 14[2], 19[3]; 14:2, 11[2], 12, 13[3], 14[2], 15, 16; 15:7[2], 10, 11[2], 12, 13[3], 16, 17[2], 26[3]; 16:3, 4, 6[2], 7[2], 8[2], 12[3], 15, 16, 23[2], 25, 26, 28, 29[4], 32[2]; 17:2[2], 3, 5[2], 6; 18:6, 10, 14[3], 17, 18[5], 19[4], 21, 22[3], 23[3]; 19:3, 4[3], 5[2], 6[2], 9[3], 12, 23, 24; 20:2, 3, 4, 5, 7, 9, 10[2], 12, 13, 14, 15, 16, 17[2], 19, 20[3], 22[3], 23[2], 24[3], 25[3], 26; 21:1, 2, 13, 14, 23; 22:18, 21[2], 22, 23, 24, 25[4], 26[2], 28, 29[2], 30[2], 31[3]; 23:1[2], 2[3], 3, 4[2], 5[4], 6, 8, 9[3], 10, 11[2], 12[2], 13, 14, 15[4], 16[4], 18, 19[2], 20[3], 22, 23[2], 24[2], 25[2], 27[3], 28[2], 29[2], 30[2], 31[3], 32, 33[3]; 24:1, 8, 12, 14[2]; 25:2, 3, 9[2], 11[3], 12, 13, 14, 16[2], 17, 18[2], 19, 21[3], 22[2], 23, 24, 25, 26, 28, 29[2], 30, 31, 37, 40[2]; 26:1[2], 4[2], 5[2], 6, 7[2], 9[2], 10, 11, 14, 15, 17, 18, 19, 22, 23, 26, 29[2], 30[2], 31, 32, 33[2], 34, 35[2], 36, 37[2]; 27:1, 2[2], 3[2], 4[2], 5, 6, 8[2], 9, 20[2]; 28:1, 2, 3, 9, 11[2], 12, 13, 14, 15[3], 17, 22, 23, 24, 25, 26, 27, 30, 31, 33, 36, 37, 39[3], 40[2], 41, 42; 29:1, 2, 3, 4, 5, 6, 7, 8, 9[2], 10, 11, 12, 13, 14, 15, 16, 17, 19, 20, 21, 22, 24, 25, 26, 27, 31, 34, 35[3], 36[3], 37, 38, 39[2], 41, 42[2]; 30:1[2], 3[2], 4[2], 5, 6[2], 9[2], 12, 15, 16, 18[3], 25, 26, 29, 30, 31, 32[2], 36[3], 37[3]; 31:6, 11, 13[5], 14[2]; 32:4, 7, 8, 10, 11, 13, 21[2], 22, 27[2], 29, 30, 32[2], 34[2]; 33:1[2], 2, 3[3], 5[4], 12[6], 13, 14[2], 16, 17[3], 19[2], 20, 21, 22[2], 23; 34:1, 3, 10[2], 11[2], 12[2], 13, 14, 15[3], 16, 17, 18[4], 20[4], 21[3], 22, 24[2], 25, 26[2], 27; 35:1, 2, 3, 5, 10; 40:2, 3[2], 4[2], 5, 6, 8, 9, 10, 11, 12, 13, 14, 15; Lev 1:2[2], 3[2], 4[2], 14; 2:4, 8, 11[2], 12, 13[2], 14[2], 15; 3:1[2], 2, 3, 6, 7[2], 9, 10, 12, 14, 15, 17; 4:27, 28[4], 29, 31, 32[2], 33, 35[3]; 5:1[3], 2[2], 3[3], 4[3], 5[3], 6[2], 7[3], 8, 10[2], 11[4], 12, 13[2], 15[2], 16[3], 17[2], 18[3], 19; 6:2[2], 3, 4[4], 5[4], 6, 7, 21[2], 27; 7:12[2], 13, 14, 15, 16[2], 21[2], 23, 24, 25[2], 26, 27, 29, 30, 32; 8:32, 33[2], 34, 35[2]; 9:4, 6[2]; 10:6, 7[3], 9[3], 10, 11, 13, 14[2], 17[3], 18; 11:2, 3, 4[2], 5, 6, 7, 8[3], 9[2], 10, 11[2], 12, 13, 20, 21, 22, 23, 24, 26, 27, 28, 29, 31, 33, 35, 38, 39, 42, 43[2], 44, 45[2]; 13:55, 57, 58; 14:34[2]; 15:31; 16:29[3], 30[3], 31[2], 34; 17:11, 12[2], 14; 18:3[5], 4[2], 5, 6, 7[2], 8, 9, 10, 11, 12, 13, 14[2], 15[2], 16, 17[2], 18, 19, 20, 21, 22, 23, 24, 26[2], 27, 28[2], 30; 19:2, 3[2], 5, 6, 9[2], 10[2], 11[3], 12, 13[3], 14[2], 15[3], 16[2], 17[3], 18[2], 19[4], 23[3], 25[2], 26[2], 27, 28[2], 30, 32[2], 33[2], 34[5], 35, 36[2], 37; 20:8, 14, 15, 16, 19, 22[3], 23[2], 24[4], 25[3], 26[2]; 21:8[3]; 22:20, 22, 23, 24[2], 25, 28, 29[2], 30, 31, 32[2], 33; 23:2, 3, 4, 6, 7[2], 8[2], 10[4], 11, 12[2], 14[2], 15[2], 16[2], 17, 18, 19, 21[3], 22[3], 24, 25[2], 27[2], 28, 31, 32[3], 35, 36[3], 37, 38, 39[2], 40[2], 41[2], 42; 24:2, 5, 6, 7, 22; 25:2[2], 3[2], 4, 5, 6[3], 8, 9[2], 10[6], 11[2], 12[2], 13[2], 14[2], 15[3], 16[3], 17[2], 18[2], 19, 20, 21, 22[3], 23, 24[2], 35[3], 36, 37, 38[2], 39[3], 40[2], 43, 44[3], 45[3], 46[3], 47; 26:1[2], 2, 3, 4, 5, 6[2], 7[2], 8[3], 9[4], 10[2], 11, 12[2], 13[2], 14, 15[3], 16[3], 17[5], 18[2], 21[2], 22[3], 23, 24[2], 25[4], 26[2], 27, 28[2], 29[2], 30, 33[2], 34, 35, 36, 37, 38[2], 39; Nu 1:3, 4, 5, 49[2], 50; 3:9, 10, 15, 41, 47; 4:18, 19, 23, 27, 29, 30, 32; 5:3, 19[2], 20[3], 21; 6:23[2], 24[2], 25[2], 26[2]; 8:2, 7, 8, 9, 10, 13[2], 14, 15, 26; 9:3[2], 8, 10, 14[2]; 10:2[2], 3, 4, 5, 6, 7[2], 8, 9[4], 10, 29[2], 31[2], 32[2], 35; 11:11[2], 12[2], 15, 16[2], 17[4], 18[4], 19, 20[3], 21, 23[2], 29; 12:4, 6, 8; 13:2, 27; 14:12, 13, 14[3], 15[2], 17[2], 19, 20, 28[2], 30[2], 31[2], 32, 34[3], 41, 42, 43[4]; 15:2[3], 3, 5, 6, 7, 8, 9, 10, 12[2], 14[3], 15[2], 16[2], 18[2], 19[2], 20[3], 21, 22, 23, 29, 39[3], 40[2], 41; 16:3[2], 7, 8, 9[3], 10[3], 11[2], 13[2], 14[2], 16[2], 17[3], 22, 26, 28, 30, 41; 17:4, 5, 10; 18:1[3], 2[5], 3[2], 4[2], 5, 7[2], 8[3], 9, 10[2], 11, 12, 15[2], 16, 17[2], 19[2], 20[2], 26[4], 27, 28[3], 29[2], 30, 31[2], 32[3]; 19:2, 3; 20:4, 5, 8[3], 10[2], 12[2], 14, 18[2], 20, 24; 21:2, 5, 7, 29[2], 34[2]; 22:6[2], 8, 9, 12[2], 13, 16, 17[2], 19, 20[2], 28[2], 29[2], 30[2], 32, 33, 34[2], 35, 37[3], 38; 23:3, 5, 11[3], 13[2], 16, 26, 27[2]; 24:9[2], 10[2], 11[3], 12, 14, 22; 25:5, 18[2]; 26:54[2]; 27:7, 8[2], 9, 10, 11, 13[2], 14[2], 20; 28:2, 3[2], 4[2], 7, 8[2],

YOUR (8109)

11:43^{2}, 45^{5}, 46; 12:7^{2}, 8, 11, 17, 19, 22, 26, 29, 38, 47, 49; 13:14, 25, 27, 39, 48, 54, 55^{2}; 14:8, 13^{2}, 14, 19, 21, 22, 25, 31, 33, 34^{2}, 38, 46; 15:1, 47^{2}, 49, 50, 51, 53, 54, 55^{2}, 57^{3}, 60^{2}, 62^{5}, 63^{3}; 16:2^{2}, 63^{2}, 65^{3}, 66, 67^{2}, 75, 76^{2}; 4Mc 2:5^{2}; 5:7^{2}, 10, 11^{3}, 12, 32, 37; 6:22, 28; 7:6^{2}, 9^{3}; 8:7, 8^{2}, 10^{2}; 9:3, 6, 9, 17, 23, 30; 10:11, 13; 11:12, 24, 25, 26^{2}; 12:3, 4, 11; 15:29, 32^{2}; 16:8, 9, 15^{2}; 17:2^{2}, 3, 5, 6, 7, 19; 18:19^{2}

YOURS (103)

Ge 14:23; 20:7; 31:32; 45:20; 48:6; Ex 10:5; 11:8; Nu 18:6, 9, 11, 13, 14, 15, 18^{2}; Dt 3:24; 11:24; 28:41; Jos 2:14; 17:18; 23:12; Jdg 6:14; 1Sa 15:28; 2Sa 16:4; 1Ki 1:47; 3:22^{2}, 26; 20:4; 2Ki 1:13; 10:15; 18:19; 1Ch 12:18; 21:24; 29:11^{3}; 2Ch 1:10; 20:15; Job 42:2; Ps 71:16; 74:16^{2}; 86:8; 89:11^{2}; 119:94; Isa 36:4; 45:14; Jer 5:19; 32:7, 8; Eze 12:22; Da 2:39; Mal 1:9; Mt 25:25; Mk 11:24; Lk 4:7; 6:20; 15:30, 31, 32; 22:42; Jn 15:20; 17:6, 9, 10^{2}; Ac 8:22; Ro 1:12; 1Co 3:21; 8:9; 16:18; 2Co 6:12; 12:14; Php 4:19; Heb 10:35; 1Pe 1:2, 10; 2Pe 1:2, 8; Jude 1:2; Tob 3:9; 8:21; 10:11; AdE 13:15; Wis 11:26; 15:2^{2}; Sir 8:2; 38:22^{2}; 48:4; 1Mc 15:7; 1Es 4:59; Man 1:15; 2Es 3:7, 24; 7:118; 9:32; 4Mc 5:13; 9:4; 12:13

YOURSELF (323)

Ge 6:14; 13:9; 14:21; 15:15; 30:29; 33:9; 38:29; 39:9; Ex 8:20; 9:13, 14, 17; 10:3; 18:18; 19:23; 20:4; 31:13; 34:2; Lev 7:29; 9:7; 18:20, 23; 19:13, 17, 18, 34; Nu 5:20; 11:17; Dt 5:8, 27; 7:17, 25; 8:14, 17; 9:4; 18:21; 22:7, 12; 23:13; 28:40; Jdg 19:5, 6, 8, 9; Ru 3:3^{2}; 4:6, 8; 1Sa 1:14; 9:27; 19:2; 20:3, 8, 19; 25:26; 2Sa 7:24; 9:7; 14:2; 16:21; 18:13; 20:4; 22:26^{2}, 27^{2}; 1Ki 2:36; 3:11^{2}; 11:31; 14:2, 9; 17:3, 13; 18:1; 20:22, 34, 40; 21:20; 2Ki 2:2, 4, 6; 4:30; 22:19; 1Ch 17:21; 2Ch 1:11; 21:13, 15; 25:8; 34:27^{2}; Ne 9:10; Job 5:27; 15:8; 17:3; 18:4; 22:26; 40:10^{2}; Ps 7:6; 10:1; 18:25^{2}, 26^{2}; 35:23; 44:23; 49:18; 50:21; 55:1; 59:4; 80:17; 89:46; Pr 5:17; 6:1, 3, 5; 9:12; 22:25; 23:4; 25:6; 26:4; 30:32; Ecc 2:1; 7:16, 22; Isa 22:16^{2}; 33:1; 51:17^{2}; 52:2; 57:8; 58:7; 63:14; 64:5, 12; 65:5; Jer 2:17, 22, 28; 4:30^{7}; 13:1; 20:4; 27:2; 31:21^{2}; 32:8, 20, 24; 34:3; 36:6; 38:18, 23; 45:5; 47:6; 50:24; 51:62; La 2:18; 3:43, 44; 4:21; 5:21; Eze 3:24; 4:9; 12:3, 4; 16:16, 17, 24^{2}, 25; 23:30, 40^{2}; 28:4; 32:2; 38:14; Da 5:17, 23; 10:12; Hos 1:2; Am 7:17; Hab 2:16, 19; Mt 4:6; 8:4; 19:19; 21:16; 22:39; 27:4, 40; Mk 1:44; 12:31; 15:30; Lk 4:9, 23; 5:14; 6:42; 7:6; 10:27; 23:37, 39; Jn 1:22; 7:4; 10:33; 14:22; Ac 16:28; 21:24; 24:8; 26:1; Ro 2:1, 3, 5, 17, 21; 12:3; 13:9; 2Co 10:7; Gal 5:14; 1Ti 4:7, 15, 16^{2}; 5:22; 2Ti 2:15; Tit 2:7; Jas 2:8; Tob 4:9, 13, 14^{2}; 5:3, 15; 7:10; 10:7; AdE 4:13; 6:13; 13:16; 14:12; Wis 18:8; Sir 1:30^{2}; 2:1; 3:10, 18; 4:7, 20, 27; 6:32, 34; 7:7, 14, 17, 24, 26; 8:8; 9:2, 6; 10:28^{2}; 11:4, 10; 13:8; 14:11, 14, 16; 18:20, 21, 23; 23:14; 25:26; 29:20; 30:21^{2}, 23; 31:18; 32:1, 12, 23; 33:20, 31; 37:12, 27; 38:21; Bar 2:11; Bel 1:11; 1Mc 12:45; 2Mc 7:18; 3Mc 6:9; 2Es 3:13, 16, 23; 4:31, 34, 50; 5:2, 24^{2}, 25^{2}, 26^{2}, 27; 7:59, 76^{2}, 129; 8:47, 49^{2}, 51; 9:29; 10:15, 20; 13:54; 14:14, 24; 15:47; 4Mc 5:6; 6:14, 15; 10:13

YOURSELVES (245)

Ge 18:4, 5; 34:9; 35:2; 45:5; 47:24; Ex 5:11; 20:22, 23; 30:37; 32:29^{2}; Lev 11:43^{2}, 44^{2}; 16:29, 31; 18:24, 30; 19:4; 20:7, 25; 23:27, 32; 26:1; Nu 11:18; 14:42; 16:3, 21; 18:5; 29:7; 31:18, 19; Dt 4:3, 9, 15, 16, 23, 38; 9:16; 11:23; 14:1; 28:68; 31:14; Jos 2:16; 3:5; 7:13; 8:2; 10:19; 17:15; 22:16, 19^{2}; 23:7; 24:22; Jdg 15:12; 1Sa 2:29; 8:18; 10:19; 12:17; 14:34; 16:5; 17:8; 1Ki 8:61; 18:25; 2Ki 17:35, 36; 1Ch 15:12; 2Ch 13:9; 29:5, 31; 30:8; 35:6; Ezr 10:11; Ne 13:25; Job 19:5; 27:12; 42:8; Isa 1:16^{2}; 8:9^{2}; 26:20; 29:9^{2}; 32:11; 45:20; 49:9; 52:11; 55:2; Jer 4:4; 23:35; 26:15; 34:15; 37:9; 42:20; 44:2, 7^{2}; 47:5; 48:6; 49:3, 14, 29; Eze 18:31; 20:7, 18, 30, 31, 43^{2}; 34:2, 3; 35:13; 36:31; 38:7; 47:22; Hos 10:12; Joel 3:11; Am 3:9; 5:26; Mic 1:10, 16^{2}; 6:15; Na 3:15; Hab 2:6; Hag 1:4, 6; Zec 7:6; Mal 2:15, 16; Mt 3:9; 6:19, 20; 23:13, 15, 31; 25:9; 27:24; Mk 6:31; 9:50; 13:9; Lk 3:8; 11:46, 52; 12:11, 33, 57; 13:28; 16:9, 15; 17:14; 21:30; 22:17; 23:28; Jn 3:28; 6:43; 7:8; 16:19; 18:31; 19:6; Ac 2:22, 40; 6:3; 10:28; 13:46; 15:29; 18:15; 20:18, 28, 34; Ro 1:6; 6:11, 13, 16; 12:19; 15:14; 1Co 3:18; 6:8; 7:5; 10:15; 11:13, 28; 14:9, 12; 16:16; 2Co 3:2; 7:11^{2}; 11:19; 13:5^{2}; Gal 3:27; 5:2, 4; 6:1; Eph 4:24; 5:19; Php 2:3; Col 1:6; 3:10, 12, 14, 23; 4:2, 5; 1Th 2:1; 3:3; 4:9; 5:2, 13; 2Th 3:7; Heb 10:34; 13:3; Jas 1:21; 2:4; 4:7, 10; 1Pe 1:13, 15; 2:1, 5, 12; 3:3; 4:1, 7; 5:5, 6, 8; 1Jn 5:21; Jude 1:20, 21; Jdt 8:12; Sir 51:25; 1Mc 3:58; 13:3; 2Mc 7:23; 1Es 1:4; 9:9; 3Mc 3:14; 2Es 1:27; 4:36; 4Mc 8:10

INDEX TO NRSV FOOTNOTES

FEATURES OF THE INDEX TO NRSV FOOTNOTES

NRSV WORD HEADING
The indexed word as spelled in the NRSV footnotes (see the introduction, page xiv).

FREQUENCY COUNT
Total number of occurrences of the word in this index (see introduction, page xiv).

GOD (83)

NRSV CONTEXT
Locates the footnote within the NRSV text (see the introduction, page xiv).

BRACES { }
Enclose the text of the NRSV footnote (see the introduction, page xiv).

Ex 31: 3 with divine spirit {Or *with the spirit of* ***God***}

BIBLICAL REFERENCE
See the abbreviations the table preceding page 1 of the Main Concordance.

INDEXED WORD
Spelled in full, usually in ***bold italic*** type (see the introduction, page xiv).

ELLIPSES (...)
Used to abridge context or footnote text (see the introduction, page iv).

ABBREVIATIONS
For abbreviations used in NRSV footnotes see the table below.

Dt 30: 16 If ... of the LORD your God {Gk: Heb lacks *If you obey the commandments of the LORD your* ***God***}

PLUS VERSE (+ v.)
Marks the text of a full verse not included in the NRSV (see introduction, p. xiv).

ANGLE BRACKETS < >
Left angle bracket (<) indicates further footnote text *precedes* context; right bracket (>) indicates further text *follows* (see the introduction, page xiv).

Sir 24: 23 + v.24 < *the Lord Almighty alone is* ***God.*** >

ABBREVIATIONS USED IN NRSV FOOTNOTES

CANONICAL BOOKS

1 Chr ...... 1 Chronicles
1 Cor ...... 1 Corinthians
1 Jn .... 1 John
1 Kings .... 1 Kings
1 Pet .... 1 Peter
1 Sam .... 1 Samuel
1 Thess ... 1 Thessalonians
1 Tim .... 1 Timothy
2 Chr ...... 2 Chronicles
2 Cor ...... 2 Corinthians
2 Jn .... 2 John
2 Kings .... 2 Kings
2 Pet .... 2 Peter
2 Sam .... 2 Samuel
2 Thess ... 2 Thessalonians
2 Tim .... 2 Timothy
3 Jn .... 3 John
Acts .... Acts
Am .... Amos
Col .... Colossians
Dan .... Daniel
Deut .... Deuteronomy
Eccl .... Ecclesiastes
Eph .... Ephesians
Esth .... Esther
Ex .... Exodus
Ezek .... Ezekiel
Ezra .... Ezra
Gal .... Galatians
Gen .... Genesis
Hab .... Habakkuk
Hag .... Haggai
Heb .... Hebrews
Hos .... Hosea
Isa .... Isaiah
Jas .... James
Jer .... Jeremiah
Jn .... John
Job .... Job
Joel .... Joel
Jon .... Jonah
Josh .... Joshua
Jude .... Jude
Judg .... Judges
Lam .... Lamentations
Lev .... Leviticus
Lk .... Luke
Mal .... Malachi
Mic .... Micah
Mk .... Mark
Mt .... Matthew
Nah .... Nahum
Neh .... Nehemiah
Num .... Numbers
Ob .... Obadiah
Phil .... Philippians
Philem .... Philemon
Prov .... Proverbs
Ps .... Psalms
Rev .... Revelation
Rom .... Romans
Ruth .... Ruth
Song ..... Song of Songs
Titus .... Titus
Zech .... Zechariah
Zeph .... Zephaniah

APOCRYPHA

1 Esd .... 1 Esdras
1 Macc ..... 1 Maccabees
2 Esd .... 2 Esdras
2 Macc ..... 2 Maccabees
3Macc ..... 3 Maccabees
4Macc ...... 4 Maccabees
Add Esth .... Additions to Esther
Bar .... Baruch
Bel ... Bel and the Dragon
Jdt .... Judith
Let Jer .. Letter of Jeremiah
Pm .... Psalm 151
Pr Man .... Prayer of Manasseh
Sir .... Sirach
Song of Thr .... Prayer of Azariah and the Song of the Three Jews
Sus .... Susanna
Tob .... Tobit
Wis .... Wisdom

OTHER

Ant. . . Josephus, *Antiquities*
Aram .... Aramaic
Ch(s) .... Chapter(s)
Cn .... Correction
Gk ... Greek (Septuagint)
Heb .... Hebrew
MT .... Masoretic Text
Ms(s) ..... Manuscript(s)
OL .... Old Latin
Q Ms(s) .... Qumran manuscipt(s)
Sam ...... Samaritan text
Syr .... Syriac
Syr H ... Syriac version of Origen's Hexapla
Tg .... Targum
Vg .... Latin Vulgate

INDEX TO NRSV FOOTNOTES

A

AARON (2)
Ex 29: 9 gird them with sashes {Gk: Heb *sashes, **Aaron** and his sons*}
Sir 36:22 according to the goodwill toward {Heb and two Gk witnesses: Lat and most Gk witnesses read *according to the blessing of **Aaron** for*}

ABANDONED (1)
Sir 17:20 + v.21 < *has neither left them nor **abandoned** them, but has spared them.*

ABARIM (1)
Eze 39:11 the Valley of the Travelers {Or *of the **Abarim***}

ABIATHAR (1)
2Sa 15:27 you and Abiathar, {Cn: Heb lacks *and **Abiathar***}

ABIDE (2)
2Es 7:*112* [42] the full glory does not remain in it; {Or *the glory does not continuously **abide** in it*}
8:20 who inhabit eternity, {Or *you who **abide** forever*}

ABIDES (1)
Sir 1:20 + v.21 < *and where it **abides**, it will turn away all anger.*

ABOUT (13)
1Sa 11: 1 About a month later, {Q Ms Gk: MT lacks ***About** a month later*}
2Ki 20:13 Hezekiah welcomed them; {Gk Vg Syr: Heb *When Hezekiah heard **about** them*}
Lk 2:49 be in my Father's house?" {Or *be **about** my Father's interests?*}
Jn 6:19 about three or four miles, {Gk ***about** twenty-five or thirty stadia*}
Ac 19:39 anything further {Other ancient authorities read ***about** other matters*} you want to know
27:37 in all two hundred seventy-six {Other ancient authorities read *seventy-six*; others, ***about** seventy-six*} persons
Ro 4: 1 gained by {Other ancient authorities read *say **about***} Abraham
10:17 word of Christ. {Or ***about** Christ*; other ancient authorities read *of God*}
Sir 22:13 an unintelligent person. {Other ancient authorities add *For being without sense he will despise everything **about** you*}
23:12 comparable to death; {Other ancient authorities read *clothed **about** with death*}
36:30 become a fugitive and a wanderer. {Heb: Gk *wander **about** and sigh*}
2Es 9:38 I looked around, {Syr Arab Arm: Lat *I looked **about** me with my eyes*}
15:48 deeds and devices. {Other ancient authorities add *you have followed after that one **about** to gratify her magnates and leaders* >}

ABOVE (5)
Ge 28:13 stood beside him {Or *stood **above** it*}
Dt 33:12 the High God {Heb ***above** him*} surrounds him
Jdt 8:12 the place of {Or ***above***} God
1Es 6:32 things herein written, {Other authorities read *stated **above** or added in writing*}
3Mc 6:26 those of us who from {Or *excelled **above***}

ABRAHAM (1)
1Ch 16:13 his servant Israel, {Another reading is ***Abraham*** (compare Ps 105.6)}

ABRAM (1)
Ge 16:16 when Hagar bore him {Heb ***Abram***} Ishmael.

ABREK (1)
Ge 41:43 "Bow the knee!" {***Abrek***, apparently an Egyptian word similar in sound to the Hebrew word meaning *to kneel*}

ABSALOM (1)
2Sa 13:27 Absalom ... feast. {Gk Compare Q Ms: MT lacks ***Absalom** made a feast like a king's feast*}

ABSHAI (1)
1Ch 11:20 Now Abishai, {Gk Vg Tg Compare 2 Sam 23.18: Heb ***Abshai***} the brother of Joab,

ABUNDANT (2)
Ps 73:10 no fault in them. {Cn: Heb ***abundant** waters are drained by them*}
Sir 1: 6 + v.7 < *And her **abundant** experience—who has understood it?*

ACCEPTANCE (2)
Sir 10:20 + v.21 *The fear of the Lord is the beginning of **acceptance**;* >
19:17 + v.18 < *The fear of the Lord is the beginning of **acceptance**,* >

ACCEPTED (1)
1Ti 3: 1 sure: {< Other ancient authorities read *The saying is commonly **accepted***}

ACCOMPLISH (1)
Wis 19: 5 your people might experience {Other ancient authorities read ***accomplish***}

ACCORDING (10)
Est 1:22 his own house. {Heb adds *and speak **according** to the language of his people*}
Hos 13: 6 when I fed {Cn: Heb ***according** to their pasture*}
Jn 8:15 by human standards; {Gk ***according** to the flesh*}
Ac 24: 6 seized him. {Other ancient authorities add *and we would have judged him **according** to our law.* >}
1Co 1:26 by human standards, {Gk ***according** to the flesh*}
10:18 the people of Israel; {Gk *Israel **according** to the flesh*}
2Co 5:16 from a human point of view; {Gk ***according** to the flesh*}
5:16 from a human point of view, {Gk ***according** to the flesh*}
Man 1: 7 O Lord, ... you may be saved. {Other ancient authorities lack *O Lord, **according** ... be saved*}
2Es 7:*135* [65] he would rather give than take away; {Or *he is ready to give **according** to requests*}

ACCOUNT (3)
Ro 8:11 also through {Other ancient authorities read *on **account** of*} his Spirit
Php 4: 8 think about {Gk *take **account** of*} these things.
2Pe 3: 9 patient with you, {Other ancient authorities read *on your **account***}

ACCOUNTS (1)
Ac 6: 2 wait on tables. {Or *keep **accounts***}

ACCUSER (17)
Job 1: 6 Satan {Or *the **Accuser***; Heb *ha-satan*}
1: 7 Satan, {Or *the **Accuser***; Heb *ha-satan*}
Job 1: 7 Satan {Or *the **Accuser***; Heb *ha-satan*}
1: 8 Satan, {Or *the **Accuser***; Heb *ha-satan*}
1: 9 Satan {Or *the **Accuser***; Heb *ha-satan*}
1:12 Satan, {Or *the **Accuser***; Heb *ha-satan*}
1:12 Satan {Or *the **Accuser***; Heb *ha-satan*}
2: 1 Satan {Or *the **Accuser***; Heb *ha-satan*}
2: 2 Satan, {Or *the **Accuser***; Heb *ha-satan*}
2: 2 Satan {Or *The **Accuser***; Heb *ha-satan*}
2: 3 Satan, {Or *the **Accuser***; Heb *ha-satan*}
2: 4 Satan {Or *the **Accuser***; Heb *ha-satan*}
2: 6 Satan, {Or *the **Accuser***; Heb *ha-satan*}
2: 7 Satan {Or *the **Accuser***; Heb *ha-satan*}
3: 1 Satan {Or *the **Accuser***; Heb *the Adversary*}
3: 2 Satan, {Or *the **Accuser***; Heb *the Adversary*}
3: 2 Satan! {Or *the **Accuser***; Heb *the Adversary*}

ACCUSERS (1)
Ac 24: 6 + v.8 < *commanding his **accusers** to come before you.*

ACQUIRED (1)
Sir 24: 6 I have held sway. {Other ancient authorities read *I have **acquired** a possession*}

ACT (1)
Sir 19:20 + v.21 < *When a slave says to his master, "I will not **act** as you wish,"* >

ACTING (1)
Sir 32:18 fear. {Meaning of Gk uncertain. Other ancient authorities add *and after **acting**,* >}

ACTUALLY (1)
2Pe 2:18 who have just {Other ancient authorities read ***actually***} escaped

ACUB (1)
1Es 5:31 the descendants of Acuph, {Other ancient authorities read ***Acub*** or *Acum*}

ACUM (1)
1Es 5:31 the descendants of Acuph, {Other ancient authorities read *Acub* or ***Acum***}

ADAM (13)
Gen 1:26 "Let us make humankind {Heb ***adam***}
1:27 So God created humankind {Heb ***adam***}
2: 7 formed man ... ground, {Or *formed a man* (Heb ***adam***) *of dust from the ground* (Heb *adamah*)}
2:20 for the man {Or *for **Adam***}
3:17 to the man {Or *to **Adam***}
3:21 for the man {Or *for **Adam***}
5: 1 God created humankind, {Heb ***adam***}
5: 2 named them "Humankind" {Heb ***adam***}
Job 31:33 as others do, {Or *as **Adam** did*}
Ps 8: 4 mortals {Heb *ben **adam***, lit. *son of man*}
Eze 2: 1 O mortal, {Or *son of man*; Heb *ben **adam*** (and so throughout the book >)}
Zec 9: 1 the capital of Aram, {Cn: Heb *of **Adam*** (or *of humankind*)}

Sir 33:10 and humankind {Heb: Gk ***Adam***} was created

ADAMAH (1)

Ge 2: 7 formed man ... ground, {Or *formed a man* (Heb *adam*) *of dust from the ground* (Heb ***adamah***)}

ADDED (2)

1Mc 1:50 He added, {Gk lacks *He **added***}
1Es 6:32 things herein written, {Other authorities read *stated above* or ***added** in writing*}

ADDS (1)

Ge 30:24 Joseph, {That is *He **adds***}

ADMIRE (1)

Sir 22:23 inheritance. {Other ancient authorities add ... *or **admire** a rich person who is stupid.*}

ADORN (1)

Jer 31: 4 you shall take {Or ***adorn** yourself with*}

ADULTERY (2)

Mt 19: 9 except ... adultery." {Other ancient authorities read *except on the ground of unchastity, causes her to commit **adultery***; others add at the end of the verse *and he who marries a divorced woman commits **adultery***}

ADVANCED (1)

4Mc 5: 4 because of his philosophy. {Other ancient authorities read *his **advanced** age*}

ADVERSARY (3)

Zec 3: 1 Satan {Or *the Accuser*; Heb *the **Adversary***}
3: 2 Satan, {Or *the Accuser*; Heb *the **Adversary***}
3: 2 O Satan! {Or *the Accuser*; Heb *the **Adversary***}

AFFECTION (1)

Sir 11:14 + v.15 < ***affection** and the ways of good works come from him.* >

AFFLICT (1)

Tob 13: 9 he afflicted {Other ancient authorities read *will **afflict***} you

AFFLICTED (2)

Ps 22:26 The poor {Or ***afflicted***} shall eat
Tob 13: 5 He will afflict {Other ancient authorities read *He **afflicted***} you

AFFORD (3)

Lev 14:31 afford, [31]one {Gk Syr: Heb ***afford,*** *[31]such as he can **afford**, one*}
Sir 38:11 as much as you can afford. {Heb: Lat lacks *as much as you can **afford***; Meaning of Gk uncertain}

AFFORDING (1)

Sir Pr: 3 I found opportunity for no little instruction. {Other ancient authorities read *I found a copy **affording** no little instruction*}

AFLAME (1)

Ps 57: 4 that greedily devour {Cn: Heb *are **aflame** for*}

AFRAID (1)

Sir 29: 7 Many refuse ... but from fear {Other ancient authorities read *many refuse to lend, therefore, because of such meanness; they are **afraid***}

AFTER (15)

Ne 11: 8 And his brothers {Gk Mss: Heb *And **after** him*}
Ps 49:13 the end of those {Tg: Heb ***after** them*}
Ecc 12: 2 with {Or ***after***; Heb *'ahar*} the rain
Jer 50:21 destroy the last of them, {Tg: Heb *destroy **after** them*}
Zec 6: 6 go toward the west country, {Cn: Heb *go **after** them*}
Jn 5: 3 + v.4 < *whoever stepped in first **after** the stirring of the water* >
6:23 after the Lord had given thanks. {Other ancient authorities lack ***after** the Lord had given thanks*}
Ac 20:15 and {Other ancient authorities add ***after** remaining at Trogyllium*} the day after that
Jude 1: 7 pursued unnatural lust, {Gk *went **after** other flesh*}
Sir 32:18 fear. {Meaning of Gk uncertain. Other ancient authorities add *and **after** acting, with him, without deliberation*}
43: 8 new moon, as its names suggests, renews itself; {Heb: Gk *The month is named **after** the moon*}
2Es 12:18 In the midst of {Syr Arm: Lat ***After***}
14:48 did so. {Syr adds ... *three months and twelve days **after** creation. ... **after** he had written all these things.* >}
15:48 devices. {Other ancient authorities add *you have followed **after** that one about to gratify her magnates and leaders* >}

AFTERNOON (1)

Ac 19: 9 of Tyrannus. {Other ancient authorities read *of a certain Tyrannus, from eleven o'clock in the morning to four in the **afternoon***}

AFTERWARDS (1)

2Es 6: 1 "At the beginning of the circle of the earth, before {< Ethiop: *At first by the Son of Man, and **afterwards** I myself.* >}

AGAIN (1)

Lk 22:16 I will not eat it {Other ancient authorities read *never eat it **again***}

AGAINST (16)

Lev 19:16 shall not profit by the blood {Heb *stand **against** the blood*}
Jos 18:18 of the slope of Beth-arabah {Gk: Heb *to the slope over **against** the Arabah*}
Jdg 19: 2 became angry with {Gk OL: Heb *prostituted herself **against***} him
Ru 1:21 has dealt harshly with {Or *has testified **against***}
1Sa 2:10 the Most High {Cn Heb ***against** him he*}
4: 1 In those ... Israel, {Gk: Heb lacks *In those days the Philistines mustered for war **against** Israel*}
12: 3 Testify against me {Gk: Heb lacks *Testify **against** me*}
2Sa 6: 8 Perez-uzzah, {That is *Bursting Out **Against** Uzzah*}
1Ch 13:11 Perez-uzzah {That is *Bursting Out **Against** Uzzah*}
Ps 53: 5 the bones of the ungodly; {Cn Compare Gk Syr: Heb *him who encamps **against** you*}
64: 8 bring them to ruin; {Cn: Heb *They will bring him to ruin, their tongue being **against** them*}
81: 5 went out over {Or ***against***}
Jer 33: 5 Chaldeans are coming in to fight {Cn: Heb *They are coming in to fight **against** the Chaldeans*}
Mt 18:15 against you, {Other ancient authorities lack ***against** you*}
Sir 10:29 those who condemn {Heb: Gk *sin **against***}
18:33 purse. {Other ancient authorities add *for you will be plotting **against** your own life*}

AGE (5)

Mk 16:14 risen. {Other ancient authorities add, in whole or in part, ... *saying, "This **age** of lawlessness and unbelief is under Satan,* >}
Ro 12: 2 conformed to this world, {Gk ***age***}
Sir 42:18 he sees from of old the things that are to come. {Heb: Gk *he sees the sign(s) of the **age***}
4Mc 5: 4 because of his philosophy. {Other ancient authorities read *his advanced **age***}
12:12 throughout all time {Gk *throughout the whole **age***}

AGES (3)

1Ti 1:17 forever and ever. {Gk *to the **ages** of the **ages***}
Rev 15: 3 King of the nations! {Other ancient authorities read *the **ages***}

AGITATED (1)

Ge 45:24 "Do not quarrel {Or *be **agitated***}

AGO (1)

Jer 31: 3 to him from far away. {Or *to him long **ago***}

AGORA (1)

Ac 17:17 in the marketplace {Or *civic center*; Gk ***agora***}

AGREED (1)

Ex 8:12 the frogs that he had brought upon Pharaoh. {Or *frogs, as he had **agreed** with Pharaoh*}

AHAR (1)

Ecc 12: 2 with {Or *after*; Heb ***'ahar***} the rain

AHASHTARI (1)

1Ch 4: 6 Haahashtari. {Or ***Ahashtari***}

AHASUERUS (2)

Tob 14:15 Cyaxares {Cn: Codex Sinaiticus *Ahikar*; other ancient authorities read *Nebuchadnezzar and **Ahasuerus***}
AdE 9:29 {Verse 30 in Heb is lacking in Gk: *Letters ... to the one hundred twenty-seven provinces of the kingdom of **Ahasuerus,*** >}

AHAZ (1)

1Ch 9:41 and Ahaz; {Compare 8.35: Heb lacks *and **Ahaz***}

AHIKAR (1)

Tob 14:15 Cyaxares {Cn: Codex Sinaiticus ***Ahikar***; >}

AIR (1)

Tob 8: 3 fled to the remotest parts {Or *fled through the **air** to the parts*}

AKAN (1)

1Ch 1:42 and Jaakan. {Or *and **Akan***; See Gen 36.27}

ALEMA (1)

1Mc 5:35 Maapha, {Other ancient authorities read ***Alema***}

ALIEN (2)

Pr 23:27 an adulteress {Heb *an **alien** woman*} is a narrow well.
Sir 32:18 an insolent {Heb: Gk ***alien***} and proud person

ALIENS (2)

Isa 5:17 fatlings and kids {Cn Compare Gk: Heb ***aliens***}
1Mc 5:15 Galilee of the Gentiles, {Gk ***aliens***}

ALIVE (3)

Ps 22:29 and I shall live for him. {Compare Gk Syr Vg: Heb *and he who cannot keep himself **alive***}
Tob 7: 4 "Is he {Other ancient authorities add ***alive** and*} in good health?"
Sir 17:11 life. {Other ancient authorities add *so that they may know that they who are **alive** now are mortal*}

ALL (38)

Dt 2:37 just as {Gk Tg: Heb *and **all***}the LORD
1Sa 1:11 He shall drink neither wine nor intoxicants, {Cn Compare Gk Q Ms 1.22: MT *then I will give him to the LORD **all** the days of his life*}
1:22 I will offer him as a nazirite for all time." {Cn Compare Q Ms: MT lacks *I will offer him as a nazirite for **all** time*}
30: 2 and all {Gk: Heb lacks *and **all***}
Job 10: 8 made me; and now, you turn and destroy me. {Cn Compare Gk Syr: Heb *made me together **all** around, and you destroy me*}
24:24 like the mallow; {Gk: Heb *like **all** others*}
Ps 89:50 bosom the insults of the peoples, {Cn: Heb *bosom **all** of many peoples*}
138: 2 for you have exalted your name and your word above everything. {Cn: Heb *you have exalted your word above **all** your name*}
Pr 28:18 fall into the Pit. {Syr: Heb *fall **all** at once*}
Eze 42:11 with the same exits {Heb *and **all** their exits*}
42:17 Then he turned and measured {Gk: Heb *measuring reed **all** around. He measured*}
42:18 Then he turned and measured {Gk: Heb *measuring reed **all** around. He measured*}
Lk 8:43 and had spent all she had on physicians, {Other ancient authorities lack *and had spent **all** she had on physicians*}
Ac 8:36 baptized?" {Other ancient authorities add all or most of verse 37, *And Philip said, "If you believe with **all** your heart, you may."* >}
15:18 things [18]known from long ago.' {Other ancient authorities read *things.* *[18]Known to God from of old are **all** his works.'* }
18:21 he said, "I {Other ancient authorities read *I must at **all** costs keep the approaching festival in Jerusalem, but I*} will return to you,
Ro 16:23 + v.24 *The grace of our Lord Jesus Christ be with **all** of you. Amen.*
Heb 3: 2 faithful in all {Other ancient authorities lack ***all***}
Rev 22:21 with all the saints. Amen. {Other ancient authorities lack ***all***; >}
Tob 11:14 May his holy name be blessed {Codex Sinaiticus reads *May his great name be upon us and blessed be **all** the angels*}
Jdt 6: 1 Achior {Other ancient authorities add *and to **all** the Moabites*}
AdE 9: 4 + v.5 *So the Jews struck down **all** their enemies* >
9:29 Purim. {Verse 30 in Heb is lacking in Gk: *Letters were sent to **all** the Jews, to the one hundred twenty-seven provinces of the kingdom of Ahasuerus, in words of peace and truth.*}
Sir 1:20 + v.21 < *and where it abides, it will turn away **all** anger.*
13:13 + v.14 < *During **all** your life love the Lord,* >
16: 9 because of their sins; {Other ancient authorities add ***All** these things he did to the hard-hearted nations,* >}
16:21 most of his works are concealed. {Meaning of Gk uncertain: Heb Syr *If I sin, no eye can see me, and if I am disloyal **all** in secret, who is to know?*}
16:22 far off." {Other ancient authorities add *and a scrutiny for **all** comes at the end*}
18: 2 + v.3 < *the span of his hand, **all** things obey his will; for he is king of **all** things by his power,* >
18: 9 one hundred years. {Other ancient authorities add *but the death of each one is beyond the calculation of **all***}
24:17 + v.18 < *I am given to **all** my children, to those who are named by him.*
42:15 and all ... will. {Syr Compare Heb: most Gk witnesses lack *and **all** ... will*}
42:23 to meet a particular need. {Heb: Gk *forever for every need, and **all** are obedient*}
2Es 14:48 did so. {Syr adds ... *after he had written **all** these things.* >}
15: 4 unbelief. {Other ancient authorities add *and **all** who believe shall be saved by their faith*}
4Mc 2: 4 also over every desire. {Or ***all** covetousness*}
18:20 to more {Other ancient authorities read *to **all** his*} tortures,

ALLEGORICALLY (1)

Rev 11: 8 prophetically {Or ***allegorically***; Gk *spiritually*}

ALLOTTING (1)

Sir 17:17 + v.18 < ***allotting** to him the light of his love,* >

ALLOW (1)
Mk 16:14 risen. {Other ancient authorities add ... *who does not **allow** the truth and power of God to prevail* >}

ALLOWED (1)
2Es 8:52 rest is appointed, {Syr Ethiop: Lat ***allowed***}

ALMIGHTY (4)
Sir 24:23 + v.24 < *the Lord **Almighty** alone is God, and besides him there is no savior."*
2Es 1:15 the Lord Almighty: {Other ancient authorities lack ***Almighty***}
1:22 the Lord Almighty: {Other ancient authorities lack ***Almighty***}
1:32 says the Lord. {Other ancient authorities add *Thus says the Lord **Almighty:** Recently you also laid hands on me,* >}

ALONE (1)
Sir 24:23 + v.24 < *the Lord Almighty **alone** is God, and besides him there is no savior."*

ALONG (2)
Joel 2: 7 they do not swerve from {Gk Syr Vg: Heb *they do not take a pledge **along***}
Heb 1: 3 and he sustains {Or *bears **along***} all things

ALOUD (1)
Isa 15: 4 the loins of Moab quiver; {Cn Compare Gk Syr: Heb *the armed men of Moab cry **aloud***}

ALREADY (3)
Ro 4:19 which was already {Other ancient authorities lack ***already***}
3Mc 4: 8 seeing death immediately before them. {Gk *seeing Hades **already** lying at their feet*}
4Mc 7:13 his body no longer being tense and firm, {Gk *the tautness of the body **already** loosed*}

ALTAR (2)
Isa 29: 2 like an Ariel. {Probable meaning, ***altar** hearth*; compare Ezek 43.15}
Sir 50:14 service at the altars, {Other ancient authorities read ***altar***}

ALVAH (1)
1Ch 1:51 Aliah, {Or ***Alvah***; See Gen 36.40}

ALWAYS (1)
Sir 22:23 inheritance. {Other ancient authorities add *For one should not **always** despise restricted circumstances,* >}

AMALEK (1)
Jdg 5:14 set out into the valley, {Gk: Heb *in **Amalek***}

AMANA (1)
2Ki 5:12 Abana {Another reading is ***Amana***}

AMBASSADOR (1)
Phm 1: 9 as an old man, and now also as a prisoner of Christ Jesus. {Or *as an **ambassador** of Christ Jesus, and now also his prisoner*}

AMEN (23)
Mt 6:13 rescue us from the evil one. {< Other ancient authorities add, in some form, *For the kingdom and the power and the glory are yours forever. **Amen.***}
28:20 of the age." {Other ancient authorities add ***Amen***}
Mk 16: 8 proclamation of eternal salvation. {Other ancient authorities add ***Amen***}
16:20 signs that accompanied it. {Other ancient authorities add ***Amen***}
Lk 24:53 in the temple blessing God. {Other ancient authorities add ***Amen***}
Ro 16:23 + v.24 *The grace of our Lord Jesus Christ be with all of you. **Amen.***
1Co 16:24 in Christ Jesus. {Other ancient authorities add ***Amen***}
Eph 6:24 our Lord Jesus Christ. {Other ancient authorities add ***Amen***}
Php 4:23 your spirit. {Other ancient authorities add ***Amen***}
Col 4:18 with you. {Other ancient authorities add ***Amen***}
1Th 5:28 with you. {Other ancient authorities add ***Amen***}
2Th 3:18 all of you. {Other ancient authorities add ***Amen***}
1Ti 6:21 with you. {< Other ancient authorities add ***Amen***}
2Ti 4:22 Grace be with you. {< Other ancient authorities add ***Amen***}
Tit 3:15 all of you. {Other ancient authorities add ***Amen***}
Phm 1:25 your spirit. {Other ancient authorities add ***Amen***}
Heb 13:25 all of you. {Other ancient authorities add ***Amen***}
1Pe 5:14 who are in Christ. {Other ancient authorities add ***Amen***}
2Pe 3:18 Amen. {Other ancient authorities lack ***Amen***}
1Jn 5:21 from idols. {Other ancient authorities add ***Amen***}
2Jn 1:13 greetings. {Other ancient authorities add ***Amen***}
Rev 22:21 with all the saints. Amen. {< others lack ***Amen***}
Tob 14:15 Amen. {Other ancient authorities lack ***Amen***}

AMMONITES (1)
2Ch 20: 1 Meunites, {Compare 26.7: Heb ***Ammonites***}

AMNESTY (1)
Est 2:18 He also granted a holiday {Or *an **amnesty***}

AMON (2)
Mt 1:10 Amos, {Other ancient authorities read ***Amon***}
1:10 Amos {Other ancient authorities read ***Amon***}

AMONG (21)
Ge 41:56 opened all the storehouses, {Gk Vg Compare Syr: Heb *opened all that was in* (or, ***among***) *them*}
Jos 8: 9 night in the camp. {Heb ***among** the people*}
Jdg 5: 2 When the people offer themselves willingly—bless {Or *You who offer yourselves willingly **among** the people, bless*}
1Sa 17:12 advanced in years. {Gk Syr: Heb ***among** men*}
1Ch 11:21 most renowned {Compare 2 Sam 23.19: Heb *more renowned **among** the two*} of the Thirty,
2Ch 20:25 they found livestock {Gk: Heb ***among** them*}
Job 36:14 ends in shame. {Heb *ends **among** the temple prostitutes*}
Ps 68:17 the Lord came from Sinai into the holy place. {Cn: Heb *The Lord **among** them Sinai in the holy* (place)}
Da 11:24 into the richest parts {Or ***among** the richest men*}
Mt 27:35 casting lots; {Other ancient authorities add ... *"They divided my clothes **among** themselves, and for my clothing they cast lots."*}
Mk 15:27 + v.28 < *he was counted **among** the lawless."*
Lk 1:28 with you." {Other ancient authorities add *Blessed are you **among** women*}
Jn 5:42 love of God in {Or ***among***} you.
14:17 he will be in {Or ***among***} you.
17:13 complete in themselves. {Or ***among** themselves*}
21:23 in the community {Gk ***among** the brothers*}
Ac 28:28 + v.29 < *arguing vigorously **among** themselves*
Ro 8:29 within a large family. {Gk ***among** many brothers*}
Col 3: 7 living that life. {Or *living **among** such people*}
Sir 18: 2 + v.3 < *separating **among** them the holy things from the profane.*
2Es 14:33 are farther in the interior. {Syr Ethiop Arm: Lat *are **among** you*}

ANCESTOR (2)
Ge 17: 5 Abram, {That is *exalted **ancestor***}
17: 5 Abraham; {Here taken to mean ***ancestor** of a multitude*}

ANCESTORS (2)
1Sa 12:15 and your king. {Gk: Heb *and your **ancestors***}
Sir 8: 9 learned from their parents; {Or ***ancestors***}

ANCIENT (1)
Ps 139:24 lead me in the way everlasting. {Or *the **ancient** way*. Compare Jer 6.16}

ANEW (3)
2Sa 21:16 was fitted out with new weapons, {Heb *was belted **anew***}
Jn 3: 3 without being born from above." {Or *born **anew***}
3: 7 must be born from above.' {Or ***anew***}

ANGEL (2)
Jn 5: 3 + v.4 < *for an **angel** of the Lord went down at certain seasons* >
Pm 151: 4 he who sent his messenger {Or ***angel***}

ANGELS (6)
Ps 8: 5 a little lower than God, {Or *than the divine beings* or ***angels***: Heb *elohim*}
2Pe 2:10 slander the glorious ones, {Or ***angels***; Gk *glories*}
Jude 1: 8 slander the glorious ones. {Or ***angels***; Gk *glories*}
Tob 11:14 May his holy name be blessed {Codex Sinaiticus reads *May his great name be upon us and blessed be all the **angels***}
2Es 1:32 says the Lord. {Other ancient authorities add ... *let my Father and his **angels** return and judge between you and me;* >}
1:40 the messenger of the Lord. {Other ancient authorities read ... *and twelve **angels** with flowers*}

ANGER (2)
Mk 1:41 Moved with pity, {Other ancient authorities read ***anger***}
Sir 1:20 + v.21 < *it will turn away all **anger**.*

ANGERS (1)
Sir 19:20 + v.21 < *he **angers** the one who supports him.*

ANGRY (2)
Ps 4: 4 when you are disturbed, {Or *are **angry***}
Sir 19:17 take its course. {Other ancient authorities add *and do not be **angry**.* >}

ANGUISH (1)
Isa 63: 9 It was no messenger {Gk: Heb ***anguish***}

ANIMAL (1)
Ge 9:10 came out of the ark. {Gk: Heb adds *every **animal** of the earth*}

ANIMALS (3)
Sir 10:11 maggots and vermin {Heb: Gk *wild **animals***}
1Mc 11:56 Trypho captured the elephants {Gk ***animals***}
2Mc 15:20 the elephants {Gk ***animals***} strategically stationed

ANNA (2)
Tob 1: 9 I married a woman, {Other ancient authorities add ***Anna***}
5:18 But his mother {Other ancient authorities add ***Anna***}

ANNULS (1)
Mt 5:19 whoever breaks {Or ***annuls***} one of the least

ANOINTED (2)
Lk 23: 2 is the Messiah, a king." {Or *is an **anointed** king*}
2Es 12:32 this is the Messiah {Literally ***anointed** one*}

ANOTHER (5)
Mt 27:49 to save him." {Other ancient authorities add *And **another** took a spear and pierced his side,* >}
1Co 4: 7 For who sees anything different in you? {Or *Who makes you different from **another?***}
2Co 13:11 listen to my appeal, {Or *encourage one **another***}
2Es 7:*105* on that ... another; {Syr Ethiop: Lat lacks *on that ... **another***}
13:45 Arzareth. {That is ***Another** Land*}

ANSWER (1)
1Ki 8:35 because you punish {Or *when you **answer***} them,

ANSWERED (4)
1Sa 5: 8 The inhabitants of Gath replied, ... to us." {Gk Compare Q Ms: MT *They **answered,** "Let the ark of the God of Israel be brought around to Gath."*}
2Ki 1:11 He went up {Gk Compare verses 9, 13: Heb *He **answered***}
Ps 22:21 you have rescued {Heb ***answered***}
Da 7: 2 I, {Theodotion: Aram *Daniel **answered** and said, "I*}

ANSWERING (1)
2Sa 22:36 and your help {Q Ms: MT *your **answering***}

ANTICIPATED (1)
Wis 17:11 it has always exaggerated {Other ancient authorities read ***anticipated***} the difficulties.

ANTIOCHIAN (1)
2Mc 6: 1 Athenian {Other ancient authorities read ***Antiochian***}

ANXIOUS (1)
Wis 9:15 burdens the thoughtful {Or ***anxious***} mind

ANY (1)
4Mc 10: 3 + v.4 *So if you have **any** instrument of torture,*

ANYONE (4)
Jdg 18: 7 with Aram. {Symmachus: Heb *with **anyone***}
18:28 with Aram. {Cn Compare verse 7: Heb *with **anyone***}
Mk 7:15 + v.16 *"Let **anyone** with ears to hear listen"*
8:26 village." {Other ancient authorities add *or tell **anyone** in the village*}

ANYTHING (2)
Dt 8: 3 by every word that comes from the mouth of the LORD. {Or *by **anything** that the LORD decrees*}
Ac 25:18 with any of the crimes {Other ancient authorities read *with **anything***}

APART (1)
Heb 2: 9 by the grace of God {Other ancient authorities read ***apart** from God*}

APOSTLE (1)
Php 2:25 your messenger {Gk ***apostle***} and minister

APOSTLES (4)
Mk 3:14 whom he also named apostles, {Other ancient authorities lack *whom he also named **apostles***}
2Co 8:23 they are messengers {Gk ***apostles***}
2Es 1:32 and torn their bodies {Other ancient authorities read *the bodies of the **apostles***}
1:37 I call to gladness ... rejoice with gladness; {Other ancient authorities read *The **apostles** bear witness to the coming people with joy*}

APPEAR (1)
Sir 37:18 it sprouts four branches, {Heb: Gk *As a clue to changes of heart four kinds of destiny **appear***}

APPEARANCE (2)
Eze 1:13 In the middle of {Gk OL: Heb *And the **appearance** of*}
Mt 23:13 + v.14 < *for the sake of **appearance** you make long prayers;* >

APPEARING (1)
2Es 7:26 the city that now is not seen shall appear, {Arm: Lat Syr *that the bride shall appear, even the city **appearing***}

APPEARS (1)
Sir 1:10 love him. {Other ancient authorities add < *to those to whom he **appears** he apportions her,* >}

APPEASED (1)
Sir 16:9 their sins; {Other ancient authorities add < *by the multitude of his holy ones he was not **appeased.*** }

APPLY (1)
4Mc 10:3 + v.4 *So if you have any instrument of torture, **apply** it to my body;* >

APPOINTED (2)
Mic 6:9 O tribe and assembly of the city! {Cn Compare Gk: Heb *tribe, and who has **appointed** it yet?*}
Mk 3:16 So he appointed the twelve: {Other ancient authorities lack *So he **appointed** the twelve*}

APPORTIONING (1)
Sir 17:22 eye. {Other ancient authorities add ***apportioning** repentance to his sons and daughters*}

APPORTIONS (1)
Sir 1:10 love him. {Other ancient authorities add < *to those to whom he appears he **apportions** her,* >}

APPROACHING (1)
Ac 18:21 he said, "I {Other ancient authorities read *I must at all costs keep the **approaching** festival in Jerusalem, but I*} will return

ARABAH (1)
Jos 18:18 north of the slope of Beth-arabah {Gk: Heb *to the slope over against the **Arabah***}

ARAM (5)
2Ki 16:6 the king of Edom {Cn: Heb *King Rezin of **Aram***}
16:6 Edom, {Cn: Heb ***Aram***}
2Ch 20:2 Edom, {One Ms: MT ***Aram***}
Eze 27:16 Edom {Another reading is ***Aram***}
Lk 3:33 son of Arni, {Other ancient authorities read *Amminadab, son of **Aram***; others vary widely}

ARAMAIC (12)
Ezr 4:7 written in Aramaic and translated. {Heb adds *in **Aramaic,*** indicating that 4.8-6.18 is in Aramaic. Another interpretation is *The letter was written in the **Aramaic** script and set forth in the **Aramaic** language*}
Lk 23:38 an inscription over him, {Other ancient authorities add *written in Greek and Latin and Hebrew* (that is, ***Aramaic***)}
Jn 5:2 Hebrew {That is, ***Aramaic***}
19:13 Hebrew {That is, ***Aramaic***}
19:17 Hebrew {That is, ***Aramaic***}
19:20 Hebrew, {That is, ***Aramaic***}
20:16 Hebrew, {That is, ***Aramaic***}
Ac 21:40 Hebrew {That is, ***Aramaic***}
22:2 Hebrew, {That is, ***Aramaic***}
26:14 Hebrew {That is, ***Aramaic***}

ARAMEANS (1)
2Sa 8:13 returned, ... Edomites {Gk: Heb *returned from striking down eighteen thousand **Arameans***}

ARBA (3)
Jos 14:15 Kiriath-arba; {That is *the city of **Arba***}
14:15 this Arba was {Heb lacks *this **Arba** was*}
15:13 Kiriath-arba, {That is *the city of **Arba***}

ARDAB (1)
2Es 9:26 Ardat; {Syr Ethiop *Arpad*; Arm ***Ardab***}

ARGUING (1)
Ac 28:28 + v.29, < *the Jews departed, **arguing** vigorously among themselves*

ARISE (1)
2Es 13:2 As I kept looking the wind made something like the figure of a man come up {Other ancient authorities read *I saw a wind **arise** from the sea and stir up*}

ARM (2)
Isa 9:20 the flesh of their own kindred; {Or *arm*}
3Mc 5:38 Equip {Or ***Arm***} the elephants now

ARMED (2)
Isa 15:4 the loins of Moab quiver; {Cn Compare Gk Syr: Heb *the **armed** men of Moab cry aloud*}
3Mc 5:23 having equipped {Or ***armed***} the animals,

ARMS (2)
Dt 33:27 the forces of old; {Or *the everlasting **arms***}
Eze 31:17 along with its allies, {Heb *its **arms***}

ARMY (5)
Pr 11:14 a nation {Or *an **army***} falls,
Eze 27:11 Men of Arvad and Helech {Or *and your **army***}
Ob 1:20 Israelites who are in Halah {Cn: Heb *in this **army***}
Lk 2:13 a multitude of heavenly host, {Gk ***army***}
2Es 1:16 you still complain. {Other ancient authorities read verse 16, *Your pursuer with his **army** I sank in the sea, but still the people complain also concerning their own destruction.*}

AROER (2)
Isa 17:2 Her towns will be deserted forever; {Cn Compare Gk: Heb *the cities of **Aroer** are deserted*}
Jer 48:6 Be like a wild ass {Gk Aquila: Heb *like **Aroer***}

AROSE (1)
1Sa 9:26 Then at the break of dawn {Gk: Heb *and they **arose** early and at break of dawn*}

AROUND (6)
1Sa 5:8 "Let the ark of God be moved on to us." {Gk Compare Q Ms: MT *They answered, "Let the ark of the God of Israel be brought **around** to Gath."*}
Job 10:8 made me; and now you turn and destroy me. {Cn Compare Gk Syr: Heb *made me together all **around,** and you destroy me*}
11:18 you will be protected {Or *you will look **around***}
Eze 42:17 Then he turned and measured {Gk: Heb *measuring reed all **around.** He measured*}
42:18 Then he turned and measured {Gk: Heb *measuring reed all **around.** He measured*}
2Es 11:2 the clouds were gathered around it. {Syr: Compare Ethiop Arab: Lat lacks *the clouds and **around** it*}

AROUSE (1)
Mal 2:12 any to witness {Cn Compare Gk: Heb ***arouse***}

ARPAD (1)
2Es 9:26 Ardat; {Syr Ethiop ***Arpad***; Arm *Ardab*}

ARRAY (1)
2Mc 1:11 for taking our side against the king, {Cn: Gk *as those who **array** themselves against a king*}

ARROGANT (1)
Ps 138:3 you increased my strength of soul. {Syr Compare Gk Tg: Heb *you made me **arrogant** in my soul with strength*}

ARROWS (1)
Ex 19:13 with arrows; {Heb lacks *with **arrows***}

ARTISANS (1)
1Ch 4:14 Ge-harashim, {That is *Valley of **artisans***}

ASA (2)
Mt 1:7 Asaph, {Other ancient authorities read ***Asa***}
1:8 Asaph {Other ancient authorities read ***Asa***}

ASARELAH (1)
1Ch 25:14 Jesarelah, {Or ***Asarelah***; see 25.2}

ASBASARETH (1)
1Es 5:69 Esar-haddon {Gk ***Asbasareth***}

ASBEBIAS (1)
1Es 8:47 Sherebiah {Gk ***Asbebias***}

ASCENT (1)
2Ch 9:4 offerings {Gk Syr Vg 1 Kings 10.5: Heb ***ascent***}

ASHER (1)
Ge 49:20 Asher's {Gk Vg Syr: Heb *From **Asher***}

ASHERAH (11)
Dt 16:21 sacred pole {Heb ***Asherah***}
Jdg 6:25 sacred pole {Heb ***Asherah***}
6:26 sacred pole {Heb ***Asherah***}
6:28 sacred pole {Heb ***Asherah***}
6:30 sacred pole {Heb ***Asherah***}
1Ki 16:33 sacred pole. {Heb ***Asherah***}
2Ki 13:6 sacred pole {Heb ***Asherah***}
17:16 sacred pole, {Heb ***Asherah***}
18:4 sacred pole. {Heb ***Asherah***}
21:3 sacred pole, {Heb ***Asherah***}
23:15 sacred pole. {Heb ***Asherah***}

ASHERIM (19)
Ex 34:13 sacred poles {Heb ***Asherim***}
Dt 7:5 sacred poles, {Heb ***Asherim***}
12:3 sacred poles {Heb ***Asherim***}
1Ki 14:15 sacred poles, {Heb ***Asherim***}
14:23 sacred poles {Heb ***Asherim***}
2Ki 17:10 sacred poles {Heb ***Asherim***}
23:14 sacred poles, {Heb ***Asherim***}
2Ch 14:3 sacred poles, {Heb ***Asherim***}
17:6 sacred poles {Heb ***Asherim***}
24:18 sacred poles {Heb ***Asherim***}
31:1 sacred poles, {Heb ***Asherim***}
33:19 sacred poles {Heb ***Asherim***}
34:3 sacred poles, {Heb ***Asherim***}
34:4 sacred poles {Heb ***Asherim***}
34:7 sacred poles {Heb ***Asherim***}
Isa 17:8 sacred poles {Heb ***Asherim***}
27:9 sacred poles {Heb ***Asherim***}
Jer 17:2 sacred poles, {Heb ***Asherim***}
Mic 5:14 sacred poles {Heb ***Asherim***}

ASHEROTH (2)
2Ch 19:3 sacred poles {Heb ***Asheroth***}
2Ch 33:3 sacred poles, {Heb ***Asheroth***}

ASHES (1)
3Mc 1:18 dust, {Other ancient authorities add *and **ashes***}

ASIARCHS (1)
Ac 19:31 some officials of the province of Asia, {Gk *some of the **Asiarchs***}

ASIDE (1)
1Sa 22:14 and is quick {Heb *and turns **aside***}

ASK (1)
Isa 45:11 Will you question me {Cn: Heb ***Ask** me of things to come*}

ASKED (1)
1Sa 2:20 for the gift she made to {Q Ms Gk: MT *for the petition that she **asked** of*}

ASKS (1)
Lk 11:11 asks for {Other ancient authorities add *bread, will give a stone; or if your child **asks** for*}

ASLEEP (13)
Ge 41:22 I fell asleep a second time {Gk Syr Vg: Heb lacks *I fell **asleep** a second time*}
Ac 7:60 died. {Gk *fell **asleep***}
13:36 died, {Gk *fell **asleep***}
1Co 7:39 dies, {Gk *falls **asleep***}
11:30 died. {Gk *fallen **asleep***}
15:6 died. {Gk *fallen **asleep***}
15:18 died {Gk *fallen **asleep***}
15:20 died. {Gk *fallen **asleep***}
15:51 die, {Gk *fall **asleep***}
1Th 4:13 died, {Gk *fallen **asleep***}
4:14 died. {Gk *fallen **asleep***}
4:15 died. {Gk *fallen **asleep***}
2Pe 3:4 our ancestors died, {Gk *our fathers fell **asleep***}

ASS (1)
Sir 25:8 and ... ass together. {Heb Syr: Gk lacks *and the one who does not plow with ox and **ass** together*}

ASSEMBLED (1)
3Mc 1:28 cry of the crowds {Other ancient authorities read *vehement cry of the **assembled** crowds*}

ASSIGNED (7)
Ne 3:9 ruler of half the district of {Or *supervisor of half the portion **assigned** to*}
3:12 ruler of half the district of {Or *supervisor of half the portion **assigned** to*}
3:14 ruler of the district of {Or *supervisor of the portion **assigned** to*}
3:15 ruler of the district of {Or *supervisor of the portion **assigned** to*}
3:16 ruler of half the district of {Or *supervisor of half the portion **assigned** to*}
3:17 ruler of half the district of {Or *supervisor of half the portion **assigned** to*}
3:18 ruler of half the district of {Or *supervisor of half the portion **assigned** to*}

ASSOCIATE (2)
Job 24:21 harm {Gk Tg: Heb *feed on* or ***associate** with*}
Pr 24:21 do not disobey either of them; {Gk: Heb *do not **associate** with those who change*}

ASTIN (8)
AdE 1:9 Vashti {Gk ***Astin***}
1:12 Vashti {Gk ***Astin***}
1:13 Vashti {Gk ***Astin***}
1:13 Vashti has answered me. {Gk ***Astin** has said thus and so*}
1:15 Vashti {Gk ***Astin***}
1:16 Vashti {Gk ***Astin***}
2:1 Vashti {Gk ***Astin***}
2:4 Vashti. {Gk ***Astin***}

ASTROLOGERS (4)
Mt 2:1 wise men {Or ***astrologers***; Gk *magi*}
2:7 wise men {Or ***astrologers***; Gk *magi*}
2:16 wise men, {Or ***astrologers***; Gk *magi*}
2:16 wise men. {Or ***astrologers***; Gk *magi*}

ATE (3)
Dt 32:13 and fed him with {Sam Gk Syr Tg: MT *he **ate***}
32:15 Jacob ate his fill; {Q Mss Sam Gk: MT lacks *Jacob **ate** his fill*}
Ob 1:7 those who ate {Cn: Heb lacks *those who **ate***}

ATHA (1)
1Co 16:22 Our Lord, come! {Gk *Marana tha.* These Aramaic words can also be read *Maran* ***atha,*** meaning *Our Lord has come*}

ATONE (1)
Sir 5: 6 he will forgive {Heb: Gk *he* (or *it*) *will **atone** for*}

ATONEMENT (2)
Heb 9: 5 the mercy seat. {Or *the place of **atonement***}
Sir 5: 5 so confident of forgiveness {Heb: Gk ***atonement***}

ATTEMPTING (1)
4Mc 1: 5 Their attempt at argument is ridiculous! {Or *They are **attempting** to make my argument ridiculous!*}

AUTHORITY (1)
Jer 5:31 rule as the prophets direct; {Or *rule by their own **authority***}

AVAIL (1)
1Co 7:21 make use of your present condition now more than ever. {Or ***avail** yourself of the opportunity*}

AVENGED (1)
Jdg 16:28 this one act of revenge ... for my two eyes." {Or *so that I may be **avenged** upon the Philistines for one of my two eyes*}

AWAITS (1)
Ro 8:24 For who hopes {Other ancient authorities read ***awaits***} for what is seen?

AWAKE (1)
Ps 139:18 I come to the end—I {Or *I **awake***}

AWAY (6)
Ps 148: 6 he fixed their bounds, which cannot be passed. {Or *he set a law that cannot pass **away***}
Pr 31: 8 rights of all the destitute. {Heb *all children of passing **away***}
Jer 46:15 Why has Apis fled? {Gk: Heb *Why was it swept **away***}
1Jn 4: 3 that does not confess Jesus {Other ancient authorities read *does **away** with Jesus* (Gk *dissolves Jesus*)}
Sir 1:20 + v.21 *The fear of the Lord drives **away** sins; and where it abides, it will turn **away** all anger.*

AWESOME (1)
Eze 1:22 like crystal, {Gk: Heb *like the **awesome** crystal*}

AX (1)
Isa 44:12 The ironsmith fashions it {Cn: Heb *an **ax***}

AZUBAH (1)
Isa 62: 4 Forsaken, {Heb ***Azubah***}

B

BABBLING (1)
Pr 10:10 but the one who rebukes boldly makes peace. {Gk: Heb *but a **babbling** fool will come to ruin*}

BABEL (2)
Jer 25:26 Sheshach {*Sheshach* is a cryptogram for ***Babel***, Babylon}
51:41 Sheshach {*Sheshach* is a cryptogram for ***Babel***, Babylon}

BABOONS (2)
1Ki 10:22 peacocks. {Or ***baboons***}
2Ch 9:21 peacocks. {Or ***baboons***}

BABYLON (3)
Jer 25:26 Sheshach {*Sheshach* is a cryptogram for *Babel*, ***Babylon***}
50:39 hyenas in Babylon, {Heb lacks *in **Babylon***}
51:41 Sheshach {*Sheshach* is a cryptogram for *Babel*, ***Babylon***}

BACCHURUS (1)
1Es 9:24 Zaccur. {Gk ***Bacchurus***}

BACK (5)
Job 9: 8 trampled the waves of the Sea; {Or *trampled the **back** of the sea dragon*}
Ps 35:13 I prayed with head bowed {Or *My prayer turned **back***}
85: 8 to those who turn to him in their hearts. {Gk: Heb *but let them not turn **back** to folly*}
126: 1 restored the fortunes of Zion, {Or *brought **back** those who returned to Zion*}
Mt 21: 3 And he will send them immediately." {Or *'The Lord needs them and will send them **back** immediately.'*}

BAD (1)
Sir 41:11 virtuous name will never be blotted out. {Heb: Gk *... but the **bad** name of sinners will be blotted out*}

BAGS (1)
2Ki 5:24 he took the bags {Heb lacks *the **bags***}

BALAL (1)
Ge 11: 9 because there the LORD confused {Heb ***balal***, meaning *to confuse*} the language

BALANCE (1)
4Mc 5:24 so that in all our dealings we act impartially, {Or *so that we hold in **balance** all our habitual inclinations*}

BAN (1)
Mal 4: 6 with a curse. {Or *a **ban** of utter destruction*}

BANI (2)
Ezr 8:10 Bani, {Gk 1 Esdras 8.36: Heb lacks ***Bani***}
10:38 Binnui: {Gk: Heb ***Bani***, *Binnui*}

BAPTISM (1)
Mt 20:22 about to drink?" {Other ancient authorities add *or to be baptized with the **baptism** that I am baptized with?*}

BAPTIZED (2)
Mt 20:22 about to drink?" {Other ancient authorities add *or to be **baptized** with the baptism that I am **baptized** with?*}

BAPTIZING (1)
Mk 1: 4 John the baptizer appeared {Other ancient authorities read *John was **baptizing***}

BARE (1)
1Sa 19:22 to the great well that is in Secu; {Gk reads *to the well of the threshing floor on the **bare** height*}

BARLEY (1)
Hos 3: 2 a homer of barley and a measure of wine. {Gk: Heb *a homer of barley and a lethech of **barley***}

BASINS (1)
Jdg 1:15 Gulloth-mayim." {That is ***Basins** of Water*}

BASIS (1)
Ro 11: 6 grace. {Other ancient authorities add *But if it is by works, it is no longer on the **basis** of grace*, >}

BASKET (1)
Lk 11:33 in a cellar, {Other ancient authorities add *or under the bushel **basket***}

BAVVAI (1)
Ne 3:18 Binnui, {Gk Syr ... Heb ***Bavvai***}

BEACHES (1)
Sir 24:14 a palm tree in En-gedi, {Other ancient authorities read *on the **beaches***}

BEAM (1)
Hab 2:11 and the plaster {Or ***beam***} will respond

BEAN (1)
Jnh 4: 6 The LORD God appointed a bush, {Heb *qiqayon*, possibly *the castor **bean** plant*}

BEAR (5)
Eze 39:26 shall forget {Another reading is *They shall **bear***}
Mal 2: 3 and I will put you out of my presence. {Cn Compare Gk Syr: Heb *and he shall **bear** you to it*}
Mt 23: 4 hard to bear, {Other ancient authorities lack *hard to **bear***}
2Es 1:37 I call to witness ... gladness; {Other ancient authorities read *The apostles **bear** witness to the coming people with joy*}
4Mc 15: 5 give birth to many, ... children. {Or *... and the more children they **bear**, the more they are devoted to their children.*}

BEARS (3)
Ro 8:16 that very Spirit bearing witness {Or *... The Spirit itself **bears** witness*}
Heb 1: 3 and he sustains {Or ***bears** along*} all things
2Es 8:23 and whose truth is established {Arab 2: Other authorities read *truth **bears** witness*}

BEAST (1)
Rev 18: 2 a haunt of every foul ... beast. {Other ancient authorities lack *a haunt of every foul **beast*** >}

BEASTS (2)
3Mc 5:29 pointed out that the animals ... purpose." {Other ancient authorities read *pointed to the **beasts*** >}
4Mc 2:14 what has fallen. {Or *the **beasts** that have fallen*}

BEAUTIFUL (2)
Ge 49:21 that bears lovely fawns. {Or *that gives **beautiful** words*}
Sir 24:17 + v.18 *I am the mother of **beautiful** love, of fear, of knowledge*, >

BEAUTY (3)
Eze 26:20 or have a place {Gk: Heb *I will give **beauty***}
Sir 25: 1 I take pleasure ... mortals: {Syr Lat: Gk *In three things I was beautiful and I stood in **beauty** before the Lord and mortals.*}
25:21 desire a woman for her possessions. {Heb Syr: Other Gk authorities read *for her **beauty***}

BEBAI (1)
Jdt 15: 4 Betomasthaim {Other ancient authorities add *and **Bebai***}

BECAUSE (15)
Dt 32:19 he spurned {Cn: Heb *he spurned **because** of provocation*} his sons
Jdg 12: 4 because ... Manasseh." {Meaning of Heb uncertain: Gk omits ***because** ... Manasseh*}
1Sa 6:19 The descendants ... greeted {Gk: Heb *And he killed some of the people of Beth-shemesh, **because** they looked into*}
Ps 56: 9 This I know, that {Or ***because***} God is for me.
60: 4 to rally to it out of bowshot. {Gk Syr Jerome: Heb ***because** of the truth*}
Pr 6:26 for the prostitute's fee is only a loaf of bread, {Cn Compare Gk Syr Vg Tg: Heb *for **because** of a harlot to a piece of bread*}
Isa 10:27 and his yoke will be destroyed from your neck. He has gone up from Rimmon, {Cn: Heb *and his yoke from your neck, and a yoke will be destroyed **because** of fatness*}
Jn 5:13 had disappeared in {Or *had left **because** of*}
Ro 9:28 for the Lord will execute his sentence on the earth quickly and decisively." {Other ancient authorities read *for he will finish his work and cut it short in righteousness, **because** the Lord will make the sentence shortened on the earth*}
Heb 11:23 the king's edict. {Other ancient authorities add *By faith Moses, when he was grown up, killed the Egyptian, **because** he observed the humiliation of his people* (Gk *brothers*)}
11:27 for he preserved as though {Or ***because***} he saw
Sir 31:11 established, {Other ancient authorities add ***because** of this*}
2Es 1:11 I destroyed all nations before them, ... provinces, {Other ancient authorities read *Did I not destroy the city of Bethsaida **because** of you, and to the south burn two cities ... ?*}
16:71 They shall {Other ancient authorities read *For people, **because** of their misfortunes, shall*}
4Mc 3:12 young soldiers, respecting {Or *embarrassed **because** of*} the king's desire,

BECOME (1)
Na 2: 8 a pool whose waters {Cn Compare Gk: Heb *a pool, from the days that she has **become**, and they*} run away.

BED (2)
2Ki 4:34 on the bed {Heb lacks *on the **bed***}
Ps 41: 3 you heal all their infirmities. {Heb *you change all his **bed***}

BEDAN (1)
1Sa 12:11 Barak, {Gk Syr: Heb ***Bedan***}

BEDS (1)
Mk 7: 4 kettles.) {Other ancient authorities add *and **beds***}

BEFORE (16)
1Sa 1: 9 and presented herself before the LORD. {Gk: Heb lacks *and presented herself **before** the LORD*}
1:28 She left him there for {Gk ... MT *And he* (that is, Elkanah) *worshiped there **before***}
29:10 and go to the place ... well before me. {Gk: Heb lacks *and go to the place ... done well **before** me*}
Job 3:24 sighing comes like {Heb ***before***} my bread,
Eze 40:19 from the inner front of {Compare Gk: Heb *from **before***} the lower gate
40:22 on the inside. {Gk: Heb ***before** them*}
40:26 on the inside. {Gk: Heb ***before** them*}
42: 2 on the north side was {Gk: Heb ***before** the length*}
Mic 2: 8 the robe from the peaceful, {Cn: Heb *from **before** a garment*}
Mk 1: 2 messenger ahead of you, {Gk ***before** your face*}
Ac 24: 6 + v.8 < *his accusers to come **before** you.*
2Pe 2:11 from the Lord. {Other ancient authorities read ***before** the Lord*; others lack the phrase}
Sir 25: 1 I take pleasure ... mortals: {Syr Lat: Gk *In three things I was beautiful and I stood in beauty **before** the Lord and mortals.*}
41:19 Be ashamed of breaking an oath or agreement, {Heb: Gk ***before** the truth of God and the covenant*}
42:11 to shame in public gatherings. {Heb: Gk *to shame **before** the great multitude*}
2Es 1:32 says the Lord. {Other ancient authorities add < *crying out **before** the judge's seat for him to deliver me to you.* >}

BEGAN (2)

Ge 1: 1 In the beginning when God created {Or *when God **began** to create* >}

Jn 12:17 with him when he called ... from the dead continued to testify. {Other ancient authorities read *with him **began** to testify that he had called ... from the dead*}

BEGAT (1)

2Es 2: 2 The mother who bore them {Other ancient authorities read *They **begat** for themselves a mother who*}

BEGINNING (11)

Da 7: 1 dream: {Q Ms Theodotion: MT adds *the **beginning** of the words; he said*}

Jn 8:25 "Why do I speak to you at all? {Or *What I have told you from the **beginning***}

2Th 2:13 because God chose you as the first fruits {Other ancient authorities read *from the **beginning***}

Rev 3:14 the origin {Or ***beginning***} of God's creation:

Sir 10:20 + v.21 *The fear of the Lord is the **beginning** of acceptance; obduracy and pride are the **beginning** of rejection.*

19:17 + v.18 < *The fear of the Lord is the **beginning** of acceptance,* >

25:11 + v.12 *The fear of the Lord is the **beginning** of love for him, and faith is the **beginning** of clinging to him.*

2Es 7:*113* [43] and the beginning {Syr Ethiop: Lat lacks *the **beginning***}

12:18 but shall regain its former power. {Ethiop Arab 1 Arm: Lat Syr *its **beginning***}

BEGOT (1)

Dt 32:18 Rock that bore you; {Or *that **begot** you*}

BEGOTTEN (1)

Lk 3:22 "You are my Son, the Beloved; with you I am well pleased." {Other ancient authorities read *You are my Son, today I have **begotten** you*}

BEGUILE (1)

Sir 30:23 Indulge yourself {Other ancient authorities read ***Beguile** yourself*}

BEHIND (1)

2Sa 13:34 coming from the Horonaim road {Cn Compare Gk: Heb *the road **behind** him*}

BEHOLD (1)

Isa 41:27 I first have declared it to Zion, {Cn: Heb *First to Zion—**Behold,** behold them*}

BEING (10)

2Ki 8:16 Ahab of Israel, {Gk Syr: Heb adds *Jehoshaphat **being** king of Judah,*}

Ps 64: 8 Because of their tongue he will bring them to ruin; {Cn: Heb *They will bring him to ruin, their tongue **being** against them*}

Ro 3: 4 and prevail in your judging." {Gk *when you are **being** judged*}

1Co 11:32 But when we are judged by the Lord, we are disciplined {Or *When we are judged, we are **being** disciplined by the Lord*}

2Co 12: 7 to keep me from being too elated. {Other ancient authorities lack *to keep me from **being** too elated*}

1Pe 2: 5 let yourselves be built {Or *you yourselves are **being** built*}

Sir 17:17 + v.18 *whom, **being** his firstborn, he brings up with discipline,* >

22:13 unintelligent person. {Other ancient authorities add *For **being** without sense he will despise everything about you*}

24:17 + v.18 < ***being** eternal, I am given to all my children,* >

31:16 like a well brought-up person, {Heb: Gk *like a human **being***}

BEINGS (4)

Ge 32:28 striven with God and with humans, {Or *with divine and human **beings***}

Ps 8: 5 you have made them a little lower than God, {Or *than the divine **beings** or angels*: Heb *elohim*}

Lk 9:56 Then {Other ancient authorities read *... for the Son of Man has not come to destroy the lives of human **beings** but to save them." Then*}

1Pe 2:13 accept the authority of every human institution, {Or *every institution ordained for human **beings***}

BELIEVE (5)

Jn 10:38 so that you may know and understand {Other ancient authorities lack *and understand*; others read *and **believe***}

Ac 8:36 baptized?" {Other ancient authorities add all or most of verse 37, *And Philip said, "If you **believe** with all your heart, you may." And he replied, "I **believe** that Jesus Christ is the Son of God."*}

2Es 15: 4 their unbelief. {Other ancient authorities add *and all who **believe** shall be saved by their faith*}

16:36 do not disbelieve what the Lord says. {Cn: Lat *do not **believe** the gods of whom the Lord speaks*}

BELIEVERS (1)

Ac 11: 2 the circumcised believers {Gk lacks ***believers***}

BELIEVES (1)

Sir 32:24 who keeps the law preserves himself, {Heb: Gk *who **believes** the law heeds the commandments*}

BELLY (2)

Jn 7:38 'Out of the believer's heart {Gk *out of his **belly***}

Ro 16:18 but their own appetites, {Gk *their own **belly***}

BELONGS (1)

Ge 49:10 until tribute comes to him; {Or *until Shiloh comes* or *until he comes to Shiloh* or (with Syr) *until he comes to whom it **belongs***}

BELOVED (3)

2Sa 12:25 Jedidiah, {That is ***Beloved** of the* LORD}

Lk 9:35 "This my Son, my Chosen; {Other ancient authorities read *my **Beloved***}

1Co 10:14 Therefore, my dear friends, {Gk *my **beloved***}

BELTED (1)

2Sa 21:16 was fitted out with new weapons, {Heb *was **belted** anew*}

BEN (2)

Ps 8: 4 mortals {Heb ***ben** adam*, lit. *son of man*}

Eze 2: 1 O mortal, {Or *son of man*; Heb ***ben** adam* (and so throughout the book when Ezekiel is addressed)}

BEN-HADAD (1)

2Ki 8:14 Ben-hadad, {Heb lacks ***Ben-hadad***}

BEND (1)

Sir 7:23 and make them obedient {Gk ***bend** their necks*}

BENEFICIAL (1)

Phm 1:11 but now he is indeed useful {The name Onesimus means *useful* or (compare verse 20) ***beneficial***}

BENEFIT (2)

Tob 3: 8 have not borne the name of {Other ancient authorities read *have had no **benefit** from*}

4Mc 16: 9 without offspring. {Gk *without **benefit***}

BENEVOLENCE (2)

2Co 9: 9 righteousness {Or ***benevolence***} endures forever."

9:10 harvest of your righteousness. {Or ***benevolence***}

BENJAMIN (2)

1Sa 13:15 went on his way from Gilgal. {Gk: Heb *went up from Gilgal to Gibeah of **Benjamin***}

13:15 The rest ... of Benjamin. {Gk: Heb lacks *The rest ... of **Benjamin***}

BEOR (1)

2Pe 2:15 of Bosor, {Other ancient authorities read ***Beor***}

BERAAH (1)

1Ch 7:23 named him Beriah, because disaster {Heb ***beraah***}

BERITES (1)

2Sa 20:14 Bichrites {Compare Gk Vg: Heb ***Berites***}

BESIDE (3)

AdE 16: 7 matters close at hand. {Gk *matters **beside** (your) feet*}

Sir 18: 2 just. {Other ancient authorities add *and there is no other **beside** him;* >}

24:14 beside water {Other ancient authorities omit ***beside** water*}

BESIDES (3)

Ex 20: 3 no other gods before {Or ***besides***} me.

Dt 5: 7 no other gods before {Or ***besides***} me.

Sir 24:23 + v.24 < *the Lord Almighty alone is God, and **besides** him there is no savior."*

BESIEGING (1)

Jdg 9:31 are stirring up {Cn: Heb *are **besieging***} the city

BETHEL (1)

Ge 35: 7 El-bethel, {That is *God of **Bethel***}

BETHER (1)

SS 2:17 on the cleft mountains. {Or *on the mountains of **Bether***: meaning of Heb uncertain}

BETHESDA (1)

Jn 5: 2 Beth-zatha, {Other ancient authorities read ***Bethesda***, others *Bethsaida*}

BETHLEHEM (1)

Tob 2: 6 against Bethel, {Other ancient authorities read *against **Bethlehem***}

BETHSAIDA (2)

Jn 5: 2 Beth-zatha, {Other ancient authorities read *Bethesda*, others ***Bethsaida***}

2Es 1:11 I destroyed all nations ... provinces, {Other ancient authorities read *Did I not destroy the city of **Bethsaida** because of you,* >}

BETTER (5)

Pr 27: 9 soul is torn by trouble. {Gk: Heb *the sweetness of a friend is **better** than one's own counsel*}

Lk 5:39 'The old is good.' " {Other ancient authorities read ***better***; others lack verse 39}

Sir 18:29 proverbs. {Other ancient authorities add ***Better** is confidence in the one Lord* >}

20:31 + v.32 *Unwearied endurance in seeking the Lord is **better*** >

40:19 but better ... prosperous; {Heb Syr: Gk lacks *but **better** ... prosperous*}

BETWEEN (10)

Lev 23: 5 at twilight, {Heb ***between** the two evenings*}

Nu 9: 3 at twilight, {Heb ***between** the two evenings*}

9: 5 at twilight, {Heb ***between** the two evenings*}

9:11 at twilight, {Heb ***between** the two evenings*}

28: 4 at twilight {Heb ***between** the two evenings*}

28: 8 at twilight {Heb ***between** the two evenings*}

1Sa 14: 4 In the pass, {Heb ***Between** the passes*}

Zec 13: 6 wounds on your chest?" {Heb *wounds **between** your hands*}

2Es 1:32 says the Lord. {Other ancient authorities add *... and judge **between** you and me;* >}

16:58 confined the sea in the midst of the waters; {Other ancient authorities read *confined the world **between** the waters and the waters*}

BEULAH (1)

Isa 62: 4 and your land Married; {Heb ***Beulah***}

BEWARE (1)

Sir 32:22 and give heed to your paths. {Heb Syr: Gk *and **beware** of your children*}

BEYOND (2)

Nu 32:32 this side of {Heb ***beyond***} the Jordan."

Sir 18: 9 one hundred years. {Other ancient authorities add *but the death of each one is **beyond** the calculation of all*}

BIDDEN (1)

4Mc 15:24 this noble mother disregarded these {Other ancient authorities read *having **bidden** them farewell, surrendered them*}

BIND (2)

Job 28:11 they probe; {Gk Vg: Heb ***bind***}

Ps 105:22 to instruct {Gk Syr Jerome: Heb *to **bind***}

BIRD (2)

Jer 12: 9 Is the hyena greedy {Cn: Heb *Is the hyena, the **bird** of prey*}

Rev 18: 2 a haunt of ... beast. {Other ancient authorities lack the words *a haunt of every foul beast* and attach the words *and hateful* to the previous line so as to read *a haunt of every foul and hateful **bird***}

BIRDS (2)

Job 5: 7 just as sparks {Or ***birds***; Heb *sons of Resheph*} fly upward.

Eze 13:20 hands with which you hunt lives; {Gk Syr: Heb *lives for **birds***}

BIRTH (4)

Mt 1: 1 An account of the genealogy {Or ***birth***} of Jesus

Jas 1:23 look at themselves {Gk *at the face of his **birth***}

3: 6 the cycle of nature, {Or *wheel of **birth***}

Sir 22: 6 + v.7 < *conceal the lowly **birth** of their parents.* >

BITTER (1)

Ru 1:20 Mara, {That is ***Bitter***}

BITTERNESS (1)

Ex 15:23 Marah. {That is ***Bitterness***}

BLASPHEMED (3)

Mt 27:39 who passed by derided {Or ***blasphemed***} him,

Mk 15:29 who passed by derided {Or ***blasphemed***} him,

1Pe 4:14 resting on you. {Other ancient authorities add *On their part he is **blasphemed,*** >}

BLASPHEMING (1)

Lk 23:39 kept deriding {Or ***blaspheming***} him and saying,

BLASPHEMY (1)

Jude 1: 9 condemnation of slander {Or *condemnation for **blasphemy***} against him,

BLESS (9)

Ge 12: 3 shall be blessed." {Or *by you all the families of the earth shall **bless** themselves*}

18:18 shall be blessed in him? {Or *and all the nations of the earth shall **bless** themselves by him*}

Ge 28:14 shall be blessed {Or *shall **bless** themselves*}
Job 2: 9 Curse {Heb ***Bless***} God, and die."
Ps 72:17 be blessed in him; {Or ***bless** themselves by him*}
Jer 4: 2 shall be blessed {Or *shall **bless** themselves*
Tob 12:20 now get up from the ground, {Other ancient authorities read *now **bless** the Lord on earth*}
13:15 My soul blesses {Or *O my soul, **bless***} the Lord,
3Mc 6:11 praise their vanities {Or ***bless** their vain gods*}

BLESSED (2)
Eze 3:12 and as the glory of the LORD rose {Cn: Heb *and **blessed** be the glory of the* LORD}
Lk 1:28 with you." {Other ancient authorities add ***Blessed** are you among women*}

BLESSES (1)
1Sa 2: 8 seat of honor. {Gk (Compare Q Ms) adds < *and **blesses** the years of the just*}

BLESSING (2)
2Ch 20:26 Beracah {That is ***Blessing***}
Sir 36:22 according to your goodwill toward {Heb and two Gk witnesses: Lat and most Gk witnesses read *according to the **blessing** of Aaron for*}

BLIND (1)
Mt 15:14 of the blind. {Other ancient authorities lack *of the **blind***}

BLOCK (1)
Eze 18:30 iniquity will be your ruin. {Or *so that they shall not be a stumbling **block** of iniquity to you*}

BLOOD (5)
Eze 19:10 a vine in a vineyard {Cn: Heb *in your **blood***}
Mt 27:49 to save him." {Other ancient authorities add *And another took a spear and pierced his side, and out came water and **blood***}
Lk 22:20 which is given ... in my blood. {Other ancient authorities lack, in whole or in part, verses 19b-20 (*which is given ... in my **blood***)}
Ac 17:26 From one ancestor {Gk *From one*; other ancient authorities read *From one **blood***}
Col 1:14 forgiveness of sins. {Other ancient authorities add *through his **blood***}

BLOWING (1)
Sir 43: 4 A man tending {Other ancient authorities read ***blowing** upon*} a furnace

BOARS (1)
2Es 15:30 like wild boars {Other ancient authorities lack *like wild **boars***}

BOAST (2)
Sir 17: 8 of his works. {Other ancient authorities add *and he gave them to **boast** of his marvels forever*}
3Mc 1:14 to take that as a portent. {Or *to **boast** of this*}

BOASTING (1)
2Co 9: 4 in this undertaking. {Other ancient authorities add *of **boasting***}

BOAT (1)
Mk 5:21 in the boat {Other ancient authorities lack *in the **boat***}

BODIES (2)
Php 3:21 transform the body of our humiliation {Or *our humble **bodies***}
Rev 18:13 chariots, slaves—and human lives. {Or *chariots, and human **bodies** and souls*}

BODY (3)
Heb 13: 3 are being tortured. {Gk *were in the **body***}
Sir 7:24 concerned for their chastity, {Gk ***body***}
4Mc 10: 3 + v.4 < *So if you have any instrument of torture, apply it to my **body**;* >

BOILINGS (1)
Eze 24: 5 boil its pieces, {Two Mss: Heb *its **boilings***}

BOLD (1)
2Es 7:104 The day of judgment is decisive {Lat ***bold***}

BONDMAN (1)
Dt 15:17 slave {Or ***bondman***}

BONDWOMAN (1)
Dt 15:17 slave. {Or ***bondwoman***}

BONES (4)
Isa 66:14 your bodies {Heb ***bones***} shall flourish
Eze 24: 5 pile the logs {Compare verse 10: Heb *the **bones***}
Eph 5:30 of his body. {Other ancient authorities add *of his flesh and of his **bones***}
Heb 11:22 instructions about his burial. {Gk *his **bones***}

BOOKS (1)
Sir Pr: 1 the Prophets and the others {Or *other **books***}

BOORISHLY (1)
Sir 22: 6 + v.8 < *Children who are disdainfully and **boorishly** haughty stain the nobility of their kindred.*

BOOTHS (1)
Ge 33:17 Succoth, {That is ***Booths***}

BORDER (1)
1Sa 13:18 turned toward the mountain {Cn Compare Gk: Heb *toward the **border***}

BORDERS (1)
Jdt 3: 8 demolished all their shrines {Syr: Gk ***borders***}

BORE (1)
1Ch 4:17 she conceived and bore {Heb lacks *and **bore***}

BORN (1)
Zep 2: 2 before you are driven away like the drifting chaff, {Cn Compare Gk Syr: Heb *before a decree is **born**; like chaff a day has passed away*}

BORNE (1)
2Mc 7:27 have taken care of you. {Or *have **borne** the burden of your education*}

BOSOM (3)
Lk 16:22 to be with Abraham. {Gk *to Abraham's **bosom***}
16:23 with Lazarus by his side. {Gk *in his **bosom***}
Jn 1:18 close to the Father's heart, {Gk ***bosom***}

BOTH (2)
Col 2: 2 of God's mystery, that is, Christ himself, {Other ancient authorities read *of the mystery of God, **both** of the Father and of Christ*}
Sir 1:18 flourish. {Other ancient authorities add ***Both** are gifts of God for peace; glory opens out* >}

BOUGEAN (1)
AdE 9:24 the Macedonian, {Other ancient witnesses read *the **Bougean***}

BOUGH (1)
Isa 17: 9 places of the Hivites and the Amorites, {Cn Compare Gk: Heb *places of the wood and the highest **bough***}

BOUGHS (3)
Eze 31: 3 top among the clouds. {Gk: Heb *thick **boughs***}
31:10 top among the clouds, {Gk: Heb *thick **boughs***}
31:14 tops among the clouds, {Gk: Heb *thick **boughs***}

BOUGHT (1)
Jn 12: 7 She bought it {Gk lacks *She **bought** it*}

BOUND (2)
Hos 10:10 When they are punished {Gk: Heb ***bound***}
Ac 20:22 And now, as a captive to the Spirit, {Or *And now, **bound** in the spirit*}

BOUNDARIES (1)
Ge 49:26 the bounties {Cn Compare Gk: Heb *of my progenitors to the **boundaries***}

BOUNDARY (1)
Jos 12: 4 and King Og {Gk: Heb *the **boundary** of King Og*}

BOWS (1)
Isa 22: 3 without the use of a bow. {Or *without their **bows***}

BOXWOOD (1)
Eze 27: 6 your deck of pines {Or ***boxwood***}

BRANCH (1)
Isa 14:19 like loathsome carrion, {Cn Compare Gk: Heb *like a loathed **branch***}

BREACH (1)
Ge 38:29 Perez. {That is *A **breach***}

BREAD (2)
Mk 14:20 who is dipping bread {Gk lacks ***bread***}
Lk 11:11 child asks for {Other ancient authorities add ***bread**, will give a stone; or if your child asks for*}

BREAK (2)
Da 4:27 atone for {Aram ***break** off*} your sins
Hos 2:18 I will abolish {Heb ***break***} the bow,

BREATH (5)
Ps 104:30 send forth your spirit, {Or *your **breath***}
Ecc 8: 8 power over the wind {Or ***breath***} to restrain the wind, {Or ***breath***}
Jdt 16:14 send forth your spirit, {Or ***breath***}
2Es 16:62 the spirit {Or ***breath***} of Almighty God.

BRIDE (2)
Mt 25: 1 the bridegroom. {Other ancient authorities add *and the **bride***}
2Es 7:26 that the city that now is not seen shall appear, {Arm: Lat Syr *that the **bride** shall appear, even the city appearing*}

BRIDLE (1)
Job 41:13 its double coat of mail? {Gk: Heb ***bridle***}

BRIERS (1)
2Es 16:32 fields shall be plowed up, {Other ancient authorities read *be for **briers***}

BRIGHTEN (1)
Job 10:20 that I may find a little comfort {Heb *that I may **brighten** up a little*}

BRIGHTNESS (2)
Ge 38:30 Zerah. {That is ***Brightness***; perhaps alluding to the crimson thread}
2Es 8:29 have gloriously taught your law. {Syr *have received the **brightness** of your law*}

BRING (5)
Ps 90: 9 our years come to an end {Syr: Heb *we **bring** our years to an end*}
Isa 45: 8 that salvation may spring up, {Q Ms: MT *that they may **bring** forth salvation*}
Eze 32: 9 as I carry you captive {Gk: Heb ***bring** your destruction*}
Eph 3: 9 to make everyone see {Other ancient authorities read *to **bring** to light*}
Sir 8:18 what they will divulge. {Or *it will **bring** forth*}

BRINGING (1)
Ro 15:31 that my ministry {Other ancient authorities read *my **bringing** of a gift*} to Jerusalem

BRINGS (1)
Sir 17:17 + v.18 *being his firstborn, he **brings** up with discipline,* >

BROAD (2)
Ge 26:22 Rehoboth, {That is ***Broad** places* or *Room*}
Sir 47:12 lived in security: {Heb: Gk *in a **broad** place*}

BROKEN (2)
Lk 1:78 will break upon {Other ancient authorities read *has **broken** upon*} us,
1Co 11:24 "This is my body that is for {Other ancient authorities read *is **broken** for*} you.

BROTHER (30)
2Sa 6: 3 Uzzah and Ahio, {Or *and his **brother***}
6: 4 and Ahio {Or *and his **brother***} went in front
2Ki 1:17 His brother, {Gk Syr: Heb lacks *His **brother***}
1Ch 13: 7 Uzzah and Ahio {Or *and his **brother***}
Ps 49: 7 no ransom avails for one's life, {Another reading is *no one can ransom a **brother***}
Jer 9: 4 trust in any of your kin; {Heb *in a **brother***} for all your kin {Heb *for every **brother***}
Mt 7: 4 say to your neighbor, {Gk ***brother***}
18:15 If another member of the church {Gk *If your **brother***}
18:15 that one. {Gk *the **brother***}
18:21 if another member of the church {Gk *if my **brother***}
Mk 12:19 the man {Gk *his **brother***} shall marry the widow
Lk 6:42 say to your neighbor, {Gk ***brother***} 'Friend, {Gk ***brother***} let me take out the speck
17: 3 If another disciple {Gk *your **brother***} sins,
20:28 the man {Gk *his **brother***} shall marry the widow
Ac 1:13 James son of {Or *the **brother** of*} Alphaeus,
Ro 14:13 in the way of another. {Gk *of a **brother***}
1Co 6: 5 decide between one believer {Gk ***brother***}
6: 6 but a believer {Gk ***brother***} goes to court against a believer {Gk ***brother***}
7:12 that if any believer {Gk ***brother***} has a wife
8:11 those weak believers ... are destroyed. {Gk *the weak **brother** ... is destroyed*}
8:13 cause one of them {Gk *cause my **brother***} to fall.
2Th 3: 6 from believers who are {Gk *from every **brother** who is*} living in idleness
3:15 warn them as believers. {Gk *a **brother***}
Jas 1: 9 Let the believer {Gk ***brother***} who is lowly
1Jn 3:10 their brothers and sisters. {Gk *his **brother***}
AdE 15: 9 I am your husband. {Gk ***brother***}
2Es 1:38 father, {Other ancient authorities read ***brother***}

BROTHER'S (6)
Mt 7: 3 the speck in your neighbor's {Gk ***brother's***} eye,
7: 5 speck out of your neighbor's {Gk ***brother's***} eye.
14: 3 his brother Philip's wife, {Other ancient authorities read *his **brother's** wife*}
Lk 6:41 the speck in your neighbor's {Gk ***brother's***} eye,
6:42 speck out of your neighbor's {Gk ***brother's***} eye.
1Co 8:13 of their falling, {Gk *my **brother's** falling*}

BROTHERHOOD (2)
1Pe 2:17 Love the family of believers. {Gk *Love the **brotherhood***}

1Pe 5: 9 know that your brothers and sisters {Gk *your* ***brotherhood***}

BROTHERLY (2)

2Pe 1: 7 godliness with mutual {Gk ***brotherly***} affection, and mutual {Gk ***brotherly***} affection with love.

BROTHERS (79)

Hos 2: 1 Say to your brother, {Gk: Heb ***brothers***}
13:15 flourish among rushes, {Or *among* ***brothers***}
Mt 23: 8 you are all students. {Gk ***brothers***}
25:40 these who are members of my family, {Gk *these my* ***brothers***}
Jn 21:23 in the community {Gk *among the* ***brothers***}
Ac 1:15 Peter stood up among the believers {Gk ***brothers***}
1:16 "Friends, {Gk *Men,* ***brothers***}
2:29 "Fellow Israelites, {Gk *Men,* ***brothers***}
3:17 friends, {Gk ***brothers***}
3:22 people {Gk ***brothers***}
6: 3 friends, {Gk ***brothers***}
7:23 his relatives, the Israelites. {Gk *his* ***brothers,*** *the sons of Israel*}
7:37 your own people {Gk *your* ***brothers***}
9:30 believers {Gk ***brothers***}
10:23 believers {Gk ***brothers***}
11: 1 believers {Gk ***brothers***}
11:29 believers {Gk ***brothers***}
12:17 believers." {Gk ***brothers***}
15: 3 believers. {Gk ***brothers***}
15:23 believers {Gk ***brothers***}
15:32 believers. {Gk ***brothers***}
15:33 believers {Gk ***brothers***}
15:36 believers {Gk ***brothers***}
15:40 believers {Gk ***brothers***}
16: 2 believers {Gk ***brothers***}
17: 6 believers {Gk ***brothers***}
17:10 believers {Gk ***brothers***}
17:14 believers {Gk ***brothers***}
18:18 believers {Gk ***brothers***}
18:27 believers {Gk ***brothers***}
21: 7 believers {Gk ***brothers***}
28:14 believers {Gk ***brothers***}
28:15 believers {Gk ***brothers***}
Ro 7: 4 friends, {Gk ***brothers***}
8:29 within a large family. {Gk *among many* ***brothers***}
9: 3 my own people, {Gk *my* ***brothers***}
1Co 6: 8 believers {Gk ***brothers***}
8:12 against members of your family, {Gk *against the* ***brothers***}
14:26 friends? {Gk ***brothers***}
14:39 my friends, {Gk *my* ***brothers***}
15:58 beloved, {Gk *beloved* ***brothers***}
2Co 11: 9 friends {Gk ***brothers***}
Gal 1: 2 all the members of God's family {Gk *all the* ***brothers***}
2: 4 false believers {Gk *false* ***brothers***}
4:12 Friends, {Gk ***Brothers***}
4:28 friends, {Gk ***brothers***}
4:31 friends, {Gk ***brothers***}
5:11 friends, {Gk ***brothers***}
5:13 sisters; {Gk ***brothers***}
6: 1 friends, {Gk ***Brothers***}
Eph 6:23 to the whole community, {Gk *to the* ***brothers***}
Php 1:12 beloved {Gk ***brothers***}
3:13 Beloved, {Gk ***Brothers***}
4: 8 beloved, {Gk ***brothers***}
4:21 friends {Gk ***brothers***}
1Th 4:10 beloved, {Gk ***brothers***}
5: 4 beloved, {Gk ***brothers***}
5:14 beloved, {Gk ***brothers***}
5:25 Beloved, {Gk ***Brothers***}
5:27 to all of them. {Gk *to all the* ***brothers***}
2Th 3: 6 beloved, {Gk ***brothers***}
1Ti 6: 2 are members of the church; {Gk *are* ***brothers***}
Heb 7: 5 kindred, {Gk ***brothers***}
10:19 Therefore, my friends, {Gk *Therefore,* ***brothers***}
11:23 the king's edict. {Other ancient authorities add ... the humiliation of his people (Gk ***brothers***)}
Jas 1:16 my beloved. {Gk *my beloved* ***brothers***}
1:19 my beloved: {Gk *my beloved* ***brothers***}
5: 7 beloved, {Gk ***brothers***}
5: 9 Beloved, {Gk ***Brothers***}
5:10 beloved, {Gk ***brothers***}
5:12 beloved, {Gk ***brothers***}
3Jn 1: 3 friends {Gk ***brothers***}
1: 5 friends, {Gk ***brothers***}
1:10 friends, {Gk ***brothers***}
Rev 12:10 comrades {Gk ***brothers***}
19:10 comrades {Gk ***brothers***}
22: 9 comrades {Gk ***brothers***}
Sir 49:15 like Joseph; {Heb Syr: Gk adds *the leader of his* ***brothers,*** *the support of the people*}
2Es 14:33 people {Lat ***brothers***}

BROUGHT (8)

Jdg 19: 3 he reached {Gk: Heb *she* ***brought*** *him*}
1Sa 5: 8 "Let the ark of God be moved on to us." {Gk Compare Q Ms: MT *They answered, "Let the ark of the God of Israel be* ***brought*** *around to Gath."*}
2Sa 6: 4 with the ark of God; {Compare Gk: Heb *and* ***brought*** *it out of the house of Abinadab, which was on the hill with the ark of God*}
Job 12: 6 who bring their god in their hands. {Or *whom God* ***brought*** *forth by his hand*; Meaning of Heb uncertain}
Ps 126: 1 restored the fortunes of Zion, {Or ***brought*** *back those who returned to Zion*}
Hos 7: 6 they are kindled {Gk Syr: Heb ***brought*** *near*}
Sir 22: 6 + v.7 *Children who are* ***brought*** *up in a good life, conceal the lowly birth of their parents.* >
2Es 8:47 have often compared yourself {Syr Ethiop: Lat ***brought*** *yourself near*}

BRUISE (1)

1Pe 2:24 by his wounds {Gk ***bruise***} you have been healed.

BUILD (1)

Tob 13:12 who revere you. {Other ancient authorities read *who* ***build*** *you up*}

BUILT (1)

4Mc 18: 7 the rib which woman was made. {Gk *the rib that was* ***built***}

BULLS (2)

1Sa 1:24 a three-year old bull, {Q Ms Gk Syr: MT *three* ***bulls***}
Hos 14: 2 the fruit {Gk Syr: Heb ***bulls***} of our lips.

BURDEN (2)

Ecc 12: 5 grasshopper drags itself along {Or *is a* ***burden***}
2Mc 7:27 have taken care of you. {Or *have borne the* ***burden*** *of your education*}

BURIED (1)

Sir 40: 1 they return to {Other Gk and Lat authorities read *are* ***buried*** *in*} the mother

BURN (3)

Jer 34: 5 as spices {Heb *shall* ***burn***} were burned
Sir 28:10 so strife will increase; {Other ancient authorities read ***burn***}
2Es 1:11 I destroyed all nations before them, ... provinces, {Other ancient authorities read *Did I not destroy the city of Bethsaida because of you, and to the south* ***burn*** *two cities ... ?*}

BURNED (3)

1Co 13: 3 body so that I may boast, {Other ancient authorities read *body to be* ***burned***}
2Pe 3:10 will be disclosed. {Other ancient authorities read *will be* ***burned*** *up*}
2Es 13: 4 melted as wax melts {Syr: Lat ***burned*** *as the earth rests*}

BURNING (4)

Nu 11: 3 Taberah, {That is ***Burning***}
Pr 26:23 smooth {Gk: Heb ***burning***} lips with an evil heart.
Jer 34: 5 spices were burned {Heb *as there was* ***burning***}
Am 6:10 who burns the dead, {Or *who makes a* ***burning*** *for him*}

BURNT (1)

Isa 61: 8 I hate robbery and wrongdoing; {Or *robbery with a* ***burnt*** *offering*}

BURSTING (4)

2Sa 5:20 Baal-perazim. {That is *Lord of* ***Bursting*** *Forth*}
6: 8 Perez-uzzah, {That is ***Bursting*** *Out Against Uzzah*}
1Ch 13:11 Perez-uzzah {That is ***Bursting*** *Out Against Uzzah*}
14:11 Baal-perazim. {That is *Lord of* ***Bursting*** *Out*}

BUSH (1)

Dt 33:16 one who dwells on Sinai. {Cn: Heb *in the* ***bush***}

BUSHEL (1)

Lk 11:33 in a cellar, {Other ancient authorities add *or under the* ***bushel*** *basket*}

C

CAIN (1)

Ge 4: 1 I have produced {The verb in Heb resembles the word for ***Cain***}

CAKE (1)

Ps 35:16 they impiously mocked me more and more, {Cn Compare Gk: Heb *like the profanest of mockers of a* ***cake***}

CALCULATION (1)

Sir 18: 9 one hundred years. {Other ancient authorities add *but the death of each one is beyond the* ***calculation*** *of all*}

CALL (3)

Isa 41:25 he was summoned by name. {Cn Compare Q Ms Gk: MT *and he shall* ***call*** *on my name*}
Mk 15:12 the man you call {Other ancient authorities lack *the man you* ***call***}
Sir 13:13 + v.14 < *During all your life love the Lord, and* ***call*** *on him for your salvation.*

CALLED (6)

Jdg 15:19 En-hakkore, {That is *The Spring of the One who* ***Called***}
Eze 23:23 officers and warriors, {Compare verses 6 and 12: Heb *officers and* ***called*** *ones*}
Mt 10: 3 and Thaddaeus; {Other ancient authorities read *Lebbaeus,* or *Lebbaeus* ***called*** *Thaddaeus*}
20:16 will be last." {Other ancient authorities add *for many are* ***called*** *but few are chosen*}
Col 1:12 who has enabled {Other ancient authorities read ***called***} you
2Es 14:48 did so. {Syr adds < *And he was* ***called*** *the scribe of the knowledge of the Most High for ever and ever.*}

CALVE (1)

Ps 29: 9 causes the oaks to whirl, {Or *causes the deer to* ***calve***}

CALVES (1)

Hos 10: 5 calf {Gk Syr: Heb ***calves***}

CAME (11)

Ge 50:18 his brothers also wept, {Cn: Heb *also* ***came***}
Dt 33: 2 With him were myriads of holy ones; {Cn Compare Gk Sam Syr Vg: MT *He* ***came*** *from Ribeboth-kodesh,*}
1Sa 10:10 were going from there {Gk: Heb *they* ***came*** *there*}
10:13 he went home. {Cn: Heb *he* ***came*** *to the shrine*}
1Ki 13:29 and brought it back to the city, {Gk: Heb *he* ***came*** *to the town of the old prophet*}
Isa 66: 2 these things are mine, {Gk Syr: Heb *these things* ***came*** *to be*}
Mt 18:10 + v.11 *For the Son of Man* ***came*** *to save the lost*
27:49 save him." {Other ancient authorities add *And another took a spear and pierced his side, and out* ***came*** *water and blood*}
Ac 24: 6 + v.7 < *But the chief captain Lysias* ***came*** *and with great violence took him out of our hands,* >
Jude 1:14 the Lord is coming {Gk ***came***}
2Es 11:40 You, the fourth that has come, ... deceit. {Syr Arab Arm: Lat Ethiop *The fourth* ***came,*** >}

CAMELS (1)

Tob 9: 5 on the camels. {Other ancient authorities lack *on the* ***camels***}

CAMP (3)

Jdg 18:12 Mahaneh-dan {That is ***Camp*** *of Dan*}
Jdt 12: 7 in the camp. {Other ancient authorities lack *in the* ***camp***}
2Mc 15:17 to carry on a campaign {Or *to remain in* ***camp***}

CAMPS (1)

Ge 32: 2 Mahanaim. {Here taken to mean *Two* ***camps***}

CAN (4)

Lev 14:31 afford, [31]one {Gk Syr: Heb *afford,* [31]*such as he* ***can*** *afford, one*}
Ps 49: 7 no ransom avails for one's life, {Another reading is *no one* ***can*** *ransom a brother*}
Sir 38:11 as much as you can afford. {Heb: Lat lacks *as much as you* ***can*** *afford;* >}
38:32 wherever they live, they will not go hungry. {Syr: Gk *and people* ***can*** *neither live nor walk there*}

CANAANITES (1)

Zec 14:21 no longer be traders {Or ***Canaanites***}

CANNOT (3)

Ps 22:29 and I shall live for him. {Compare Gk Syr Vg: Heb *and he who* ***cannot*** *keep himself alive*}
Man 1:10 so that I am rejected {Other ancient authorities read *so that I* ***cannot*** *lift up my head*}
4Mc 10: 3 + v.4 < *for you* ***cannot*** *touch my soul, even if you wish."*

CANOPIES (2)

Eze 41:26 on the sidewalls of the vestibule. {Cn: Heb *vestibule. And the side chambers of the temple and the* ***canopies***}
3Mc 1:19 the bridal chambers {Or *the* ***canopies***}

CANOPY (1)

3Mc 4: 6 the bridal chamber {Or *the* ***canopy***}

CAPTAIN (1)

Ac 24: 6 + v.7 < *But the chief* ***captain*** *Lysias came and with great violence took him out of our hands,* >

CAPTAINS (1)

1Ch 11:11 chief of the Three; {Compare 2 Sam 23.8: Heb *Thirty* or ***captains***}

CAPTIVE (1)
Eze 21:24 shall be taken in hand. {Or *be taken* ***captive***}

CAPTIVITY (1)
Am 4:10 I carried away your horses; {Heb *with the* ***captivity*** *of your horses*}

CARE (1)
Jude 1:12 without fear, feeding themselves. {Or *without fear. They are shepherds who* ***care*** *only for themselves*}

CARED (1)
Ac 13:18 he put up with {Other ancient authorities read ***cared*** *for*}

CARRIED (3)
1Ch 8:7 Heglam, {Or *he* ***carried*** *them into exile*}
Lk 24:51 and was carried up into heaven. {Other ancient authorities lack *and was* ***carried*** *up into heaven*}
1Pe 2:24 bore our sins in his body on the cross, {Or ***carried*** *up our sins in his body to the tree*}

CAST (3)
Ps 68:4 lift up a song to him who rides up the clouds—{Or ***cast*** *up a highway for him who rides through the deserts*}
Mt 27:35 casting lots; {Other ancient authorities add ... *and for my clothing they* ***cast*** *lots."*}
Lk 6:22 and defame you {Gk ***cast*** *out your name as evil*}

CASTOR (1)
Jnh 4:6 happy about the bush, {Heb *qiqayon*, possibly *the* ***castor*** *bean plant*}

CATCH (1)
Pr 12:12 covet the proceeds of wickedness, {Or *covet the* ***catch*** *of the wicked*}

CAUGHT (1)
2Es 14:48 did so. {Syr adds < *At that time Ezra was* ***caught*** *up, and taken to the place* >}

CAUSE (13)
Ps 55:3 they bring {Cn Compare Gk: Heb *they* ***cause*** *to totter*} trouble
106:27 and would disperse {Syr Compare Ezek 20.23: Heb ***cause*** *to fall*} their descendants
Jer 29:8 the dreams that they dream, {Cn: Heb *your dreams that you* ***cause*** *to dream*}
Am 1:3 revoke the punishment; {Heb ***cause*** *it to return*}
1:6 revoke the punishment; {Heb ***cause*** *it to return*}
1:9 revoke the punishment; {Heb ***cause*** *it to return*}
1:11 revoke the punishment; {Heb ***cause*** *it to return*}
1:13 revoke the punishment; {Heb ***cause*** *it to return*}
2:1 revoke the punishment; {Heb ***cause*** *it to return*}
2:4 revoke the punishment; {Heb ***cause*** *it to return*}
2:6 revoke the punishment; {Heb ***cause*** *it to return*}
Zep 1:3 sea. I will make the wicked stumble. {Cn: Heb *sea, and those who* ***cause*** *the wicked to stumble*}
Mt 5:22 or sister, {Gk *a brother*; other ancient authorities add *without* ***cause***}

CAUSED (3)
Isa 8:2 and have it attested {Q Ms Gk Syr: MT *and I* ***caused*** *to be attested*}
Zec 13:5 for the land has been my possession {Cn: Heb *for humankind has* ***caused*** *me to possess*}
Sir 45:3 he performed swift miracles; {Heb: Gk ***caused*** *signs to cease*}

CAUSES (1)
Mt 19:9 and marries another commits adultery." {Other ancient authorities read *except on the ground of unchastity,* ***causes*** *her to commit adultery;* >}

CEASE (3)
Job 10:20 not the days of my life few? {Cn Compare Gk Syr: Heb *Are not my days few? Let him* ***cease!***}
Sir 24:23 + v.24 *"Do not* ***cease*** *to be strong in the Lord,* >
45:3 he performed swift miracles; {Heb: Gk *caused signs to* ***cease***}

CELEBRATION (1)
Sir 36:19 Fill Zion with your majesty, {Heb Syr: Gk *the* ***celebration*** *of your wondrous deeds*}

CENSUS (1)
Nu 26:4 take a census of the people, {Heb lacks *take a* ***census*** *of the people*: Compare verse 2}

CENTER (1)
Ac 17:17 in the marketplace {Or *civic* ***center***; Gk *agora*}

CERTAIN (3)
Jn 5:3 + v.4 <*for an angel of the Lord went down at* ***certain*** *seasons into the pool,* >
Ac 19:9 the lecture hall of Tyrannus. {Other ancient authorities read *of a* ***certain*** *Tyrannus,* >}
1Ti 6:7 world, so that {Other ancient authorities read *world—it is* ***certain*** *that*}

CHAMBERS (3)
Eze 41:26 on the sidewalls of the vestibule. {Cn: Heb *vestibule. And the side* ***chambers*** *of the temple and the canopies*}
42:3 the chambers rose {Heb lacks *the* ***chambers*** *rose*}
45:5 as their holding for cities to live in. {Gk: Heb *as their holding, twenty* ***chambers***}

CHANGE (4)
Ps 41:3 you heal all their infirmities. {Heb *you* ***change*** *all his bed*}
Pr 24:21 do not disobey either of them; {Gk: Heb *do not associate with those who* ***change***}
Hos 4:7 they changed {Ancient Heb tradition: MT *I will* ***change***} their glory
Heb 12:17 no chance to repent, {Or *no chance to* ***change*** *his father's mind*}

CHANGED (1)
Wis 19:2 had permitted {Other ancient authorities read *had* ***changed*** *their minds to permit*}

CHANGES (2)
Job 10:17 toward me; you bring forth fresh troops against me. {Cn Compare Gk: Heb *toward me;* ***changes*** *and a troop are with me*}
Sir 37:18 it sprouts four branches, {Heb: Gk *As a clue to* ***changes*** *of heart four kinds of destiny appear*}

CHANGING (1)
Wis 19:18 the elements changed {Gk ***changing***} places

CHARIOT (1)
Jdt 11:19 I will set your throne. {Or ***chariot***}

CHARIOTEER (1)
Sir 20:31 + v.32 < *better than a masterless* ***charioteer*** *of one's own life.*

CHARIOTS (1)
Eze 39:20 with horses and charioteers, {Heb ***chariots***}

CHASTISING (1)
Sir 16:10 stubbornness. {Other ancient authorities add ***Chastising,*** *showing mercy, striking, healing, the Lord persisted in mercy and discipline.*}

CHEERFUL (1)
Sir 13:25 for evil. {Other ancient authorities add *and a glad heart makes a* ***cheerful*** *countenance*}

CHEESE (1)
Jdt 10:5 bread; {Other ancient authorities add *and* ***cheese***}

CHELEOUDITES (1)
Jdt 1:6 Chaldeans. {Syr: Gk ***Cheleoudites***}

CHIEF (4)
Ge 36:30 clan by clan {Or ***chief*** *by* ***chief***}
1Ch 24:23 Jeriah the chief, {See 23.19: Heb lacks *the* ***chief***}
Ac 24:6 + v.7 < *But the* ***chief*** *captain Lysias came* >

CHIEFS (18)
Ge 36:15 clans {Or ***chiefs***}
36:15 clans {Or ***chiefs***}
36:16 clans {Or ***chiefs***}
36:17 clans {Or ***chiefs***}
36:17 clans {Or ***chiefs***}
36:18 clans {Or ***chiefs***}
36:18 clans {Or ***chiefs***}
36:19 clans {Or ***chiefs***}
36:21 clans {Or ***chiefs***}
36:29 clans {Or ***chiefs***}
36:29 clans {Or ***chiefs***}
36:30 clans {Or ***chiefs***}
36:40 clans {Or ***chiefs***}
36:40 clans {Or ***chiefs***}
36:43 clans {Or ***chiefs***}
1Ch 1:51 clans {Or ***chiefs***}
1:51 clans {Or ***chiefs***}
1:54 clans {Or ***chiefs***}

CHILD (9)
Pr 8:30 a master worker; {Another reading is *little* ***child***}
Ecc 10:16 your king is servant, {Or *a* ***child***}
Lk 11:11 asks for {Other ancient authorities add *bread, will give a stone; or if your* ***child*** *asks for*}
Ac 3:13 servant {Or ***child***}
3:26 servant, {Or ***child***}
4:25 servant: {Or ***child***}
4:27 servant {Or ***child***}
4:30 servant {Or ***child***}
Sir 7:3 Do {Gk *My* ***child,*** *do*} not sow

CHILDBEARING (1)
4Mc 17:6 For your children were true descendants of father Abraham. {Gk *For your* ***childbearing*** *was from Abraham the father;* >}

CHILDREN (18)
Pr 5:7 my child, {Gk Vg: Heb ***children***} listen to me,
Pr 31:8 all the destitute. {Heb *all* ***children*** *of passing away*}
Isa 49:17 Your builders outdo your destroyers, {Or *Your* ***children*** *come swiftly; your destroyers*}
Mt 11:19 deeds." {Other ancient authorities read ***children***}
Col 3:6 on those who are disobedient. {Other ancient authorities lack *on those who are disobedient* (Gk *the* ***children*** *of disobedience*)}
1Jn 3:9 because God's seed abides in them; {Or *because the* ***children*** *of God abide in him*}
Tob 13:9 the deeds of your hands, {Other ancient authorities read *your* ***children***}
14:12 his wife and children {Codex Sinaiticus lacks *and* ***children***}
Wis 12:7 the servants {Or ***children***} of God.
12:20 enemies of your servants {Or ***children***}
Sir 11:28 by how he ends, a person becomes known. {Heb: Gk *and through his* ***children*** *a person becomes known*}
22:6 + v.7 ***Children*** *who are brought up in a good life, conceal the lowly birth ...* [8]***Children*** *who are disdainfully and boorishly haughty stain the nobility of their kindred.*
24:17 + v.18 *being eternal, I am given to all my* ***children,*** *to those who are named by him.*
32:22 and give good heed to your paths. {Heb Syr: Gk *and beware of your* ***children***}
2Es 1:21 Perizzites, and the Philistines {Other ancient authorities read *Perizzites and their* ***children***}
4Mc 15:5 give birth to many ... children. {Or < *and the more* ***children*** *they bear, the more they are devoted to their* ***children.***}

CHOICE (1)
1Co 11:10 have a symbol of authority on her head, {Or *have freedom of* ***choice*** *regarding her head*}

CHOICEST (2)
Jer 49:19 and I will appoint over it whomever I choose. {Or *and I will single out the* ***choicest*** *of his rams*: Meaning of Heb uncertain}
50:44 and I will appoint over her whomever I choose. {Or *and I will single out the* ***choicest*** *of her rams*: Meaning of Heb uncertain}

CHOSEN (3)
2Sa 21:6 at Gibeon on the mountain of the LORD." {Cn Compare Gk and 21.9: Heb *at Gibeah of Saul, the* ***chosen*** *of the* LORD}
Mt 20:16 will be last." {Other ancient authorities add *for many are called but few are* ***chosen***}
Jn 1:34 this is the Son of God." {Other ancient authorities read *is God's* ***chosen*** *one*}

CHRIST (75)
Mt 1:1 Jesus the Messiah, {Or *Jesus* ***Christ***}
1:16 the Messiah. {Or *the* ***Christ***}
1:17 the Messiah, {Or *the* ***Christ***}
1:18 the Messiah {Or *Jesus* ***Christ***}
2:4 the Messiah {Or *the* ***Christ***}
11:2 the Messiah {Or *the* ***Christ***}
16:16 the Messiah, {Or *the* ***Christ***}
16:20 the Messiah. {Or *the* ***Christ***}
22:42 Messiah? {Or ***Christ***}
23:10 the Messiah. {Or *the* ***Christ***}
24:5 the Messiah!' {Or *the* ***Christ***}
24:23 the Messiah!' {Or *the* ***Christ***}
26:63 the Messiah, {Or ***Christ***}
26:68 Messiah! {Or ***Christ***}
27:17 the Messiah?" {Or *the* ***Christ***}
27:22 the Messiah?" {Or *the* ***Christ***}
Mk 8:29 the Messiah." {Or *the* ***Christ***}
12:35 the Messiah {Or *the* ***Christ***}
13:21 the Messiah!' {Or *the* ***Christ***}
14:61 the Messiah, {Or *the* ***Christ***}
15:32 the Messiah, {Or *the* ***Christ***}
16:14 risen. {Other ancient authorities add, in whole or in part, ... *—thus they spoke to* ***Christ.*** *And* ***Christ*** *replied to them,* >}
Lk 2:11 the Messiah, {Or *the* ***Christ***}
2:26 the Lord's Messiah. {Or *the Lord's* ***Christ***}
3:15 the Messiah, {Or *the* ***Christ***}
4:41 the Messiah. {Or *the* ***Christ***}
9:20 the Messiah {Or *The* ***Christ***}
20:41 the Messiah {Or *the* ***Christ***}
22:67 the Messiah, {Or *the* ***Christ***}
23:35 the Messiah {Or *the* ***Christ***}
23:39 the Messiah? {Or *the* ***Christ***}
24:26 the Messiah {Or *the* ***Christ***}
24:46 the Messiah {Or *the* ***Christ***}
Jn 1:20 the Messiah." {Or *the* ***Christ***}
1:25 the Messiah, {Or *the* ***Christ***}
1:41 translated Anointed). {Or ***Christ***}
3:28 the Messiah, {Or *the* ***Christ***}
4:29 the Messiah, {Or *the* ***Christ***}
6:69 the Holy One of God." {Other ancient authorities read *the* ***Christ,*** *the Son of the living God*}
7:26 the Messiah? {Or *the* ***Christ***}
7:27 the Messiah {Or *the* ***Christ***}
7:31 the Messiah {Or *the* ***Christ***}
7:41 the Messiah." {Or *the* ***Christ***}
7:41 the Messiah {Or *the* ***Christ***}
7:42 the Messiah {Or *the* ***Christ***}
9:22 the Messiah {Or *the* ***Christ***}
10:24 the Messiah, {Or *the* ***Christ***}

Jn 11:27 the Messiah, {Or *the* **Christ**}
12:34 the Messiah {Or *the* **Christ**}
20:31 the Messiah, {Or *the* **Christ**}
Ac 2:31 the Messiah, {Or *the* **Christ**}
2:36 Messiah, {Or **Christ**}
3:18 his Messiah {Or *his* **Christ**}
3:20 the Messiah {Or *the* **Christ**}
4:26 his Messiah.' {Or *his* **Christ**}
5:42 the Messiah. {Or *the* **Christ**}
8: 5 the Messiah {Or *the* **Christ**}
8:36 + v.37 < *And he replied, "I believe that Jesus* ***Christ*** *is the Son of God."*
9:22 the Messiah. {Or *the* **Christ**}
17: 3 the Messiah {Or *the* **Christ**}
17: 3 the Messiah, {Or *the* **Christ**}
18: 5 the Messiah {Or *the* **Christ**}
18:28 the Messiah {Or *the* **Christ**}
26:23 the Messiah {Or *the* **Christ**}
Ro 9: 5 the Messiah, {Or *the* **Christ**}
14:10 of God. {Other ancient authorities read *of* **Christ**}
16:23 + v.24 *The grace of our Lord Jesus* ***Christ*** *be with all of you. Amen.*
Gal 4: 7 an heir, through God. {Other ancient authorities read *an heir of God through* **Christ**}
6:15 For {Other ancient authorities add *in* ***Christ*** *Jesus*} neither circumcision
Eph 3:14 the Father, {Other ancient authorities add *of our Lord Jesus* **Christ**}
Col 3:13 just as the Lord {Other ancient authorities read *just as* **Christ**}
1Ti 2: 7 in faith and truth, {Other ancient authorities add *in* **Christ**}
Rev 11:15 Messiah, {Gk **Christ**}
12:10 Messiah, {Gk **Christ**}

CHRISTS (2)
Mt 24:24 messiahs {Or **christs**}
Mk 13:22 messiahs {Or **christs**}

CHUSI (1)
2Es 1: 3 [1]The book of the prophet Ezra son of Seraiah ... [3]Persians. {Other ancient authorities ... begin the chapter: *The word of the Lord that came to Ezra son of* ***Chusi*** >}

CIRCUMCISED (1)
Ac 15:24 minds, {Other ancient authorities add *saying, 'You must be* ***circumcised*** *and keep the law,'*}

CIRCUMSTANCES (2)
Eph 6:16 With all of these, {Or *In all* **circumstances**}
Sir 22:23 his inheritance. {Other ancient authorities add *For one should not always despise restricted* ***circumstances,*** >}

CITIES (7)
Ge 47:21 he made slaves of them {Sam Gk Compare Vg: MT *He removed them to the* ***cities***}
Jdg 20:42 out of the city {Compare Vg and some Gk Mss: Heb ***cities***}
Isa 17: 2 Her towns will be deserted forever; {Cn Compare Gk: Heb *the* ***cities*** *of Aroer are deserted*}
33: 8 its oaths {Q Ms: MT ***cities***} are despised
Jer 22: 6 an uninhabited city. {Cn: Heb *uninhabited* ***cities***}
Mic 7:12 from Assyria to {One Ms: MT *Assyria and* ***cities*** *of*} Egypt,
2Es 1:11 I destroyed ... peoples of two provinces, {Other ancient authorities read *Did I not destroy the city of Bethsaida because of you, and to the south burn two* ***cities*** *... ?*}

CITIZENS (2)
2Es 9:45 all my neighbors; {Literally *all my* ***citizens***}
10: 2 all my neighbors {Literally *all my* ***citizens***}

CITY (7)
Jos 14:15 Kiriath-arba; {That is *the* ***city*** *of Arba*}
15:13 Kiriath-arba, {That is *the* ***city*** *of Arba*}
2Ki 10: 1 of Jezreel, {Or *of the* ***city***; Vg Compare Gk}
Tob 13:16 be built {Other ancient authorities add *for a* ***city***}
AdE 4: 5 + v.6 *So Hachratheus went out to Mordecai in the street of the* ***city*** *opposite the* ***city*** *gate.*
2Es 1:11 I destroyed all nations before them, ... peoples of two provinces, {Other ancient authorities read *Did I not destroy the* ***city*** *of Bethsaida because of you, and to the south burn two cities ... ?*}

CIVIC (1)
Ac 17:17 in the marketplace {Or ***civic*** *center*; Gk *agora*}

CLANS (1)
Nu 26:50 the Naphtalites {Heb ***clans*** *of Naphtali*}

CLAUDA (1)
Ac 27:16 Cauda {Other ancient authorities read ***Clauda***}

CLEANING (1)
Sir 38:30 firing {Cn: Gk ***cleaning***} the kiln.

CLEANNESS (1)
Ps 89:44 removed the scepter from his hand, {Cn: Heb *removed his* ***cleanness***}

CLEANSE (1)
Lk 11: 2 Your kingdom come. {A few ancient authorities read *Your Holy Spirit come upon us and* ***cleanse*** *us.* >}

CLEVER (1)
Sir 21:20 the wise {Syr Lat: Gk ***clever***} smile quietly.

CLING (1)
Sir 24:23 + v.24 < ***cling*** *to him so that he may strengthen you;* >

CLINGING (2)
Sir 18:29 proverbs. {Other ancient authorities add *Better is confidence in the one Lord than* ***clinging*** *with a dead heart to a dead one.*}
25:11 + v.12 < *faith is the beginning of* ***clinging*** *to him.*

CLOSED (3)
Nu 24: 3 whose eye is clear, {Or ***closed*** or *open*}
24:15 whose eye is clear, {Or ***closed*** or *open*}

CLOTH (1)
2Es 16: 2 cloth of goats' hair, {Other ancient authorities lack ***cloth*** *of goats' hair*}

CLOTHED (2)
2Ch 24:20 took possession of {Heb ***clothed*** *itself with*}
Sir 23:12 comparable to death; {Other ancient authorities read ***clothed*** *about with death*}

CLOTHES (1)
Mt 27:35 casting lots; {Other ancient authorities add < *"They divided my* ***clothes*** *among themselves,* >}

CLOTHING (3)
Ps 45:13 The princess ... with gold-woven robes; {Or ... *All glorious is the princess within, gold embroidery is her* ***clothing***}
Mt 27:35 casting lots; {Other ancient authorities add < *and for my* ***clothing*** *they cast lots."*}
Heb 1:12 and like clothing {Other ancient authorities lack *like* ***clothing***}

CLOUDS (1)
2Es 11: 2 the clouds were gathered around it. {Syr: Compare Ethiop Arab: Lat lacks *the* ***clouds*** *and around it*}

CLUE (1)
Sir 37:18 branches, {Heb: Gk *As a* ***clue*** *to changes of heart four kinds of destiny appear*}

CLUSTER (2)
Nu 13:24 Eshcol, {That is ***Cluster***}
2Es 16:30 Some clusters may be left {Other ancient authorities read *a* ***cluster*** *may remain exposed*}

COALS (1)
Ps 18:13 his voice. {Gk See 2 Sam 22.14: Heb adds *hailstones and* ***coals*** *of fire*}

COAT (1)
Ge 37: 3 a long robe with sleeves. {Traditional rendering (compare Gk): *a* ***coat*** *of many colors*; Meaning of Heb uncertain}

COCK (1)
Mk 14:68 Then the cock crowed. {Other ancient authorities lack *Then the* ***cock*** *crowed*}

COLD (1)
Pr 25:20 Like vinegar on a wound {Gk: Heb *Like one who takes off a garment on a* ***cold*** *day, like vinegar on lye*}

COLORS (1)
Ge 37: 3 a long robe with sleeves. {Traditional rendering (compare Gk): *a coat of many* ***colors***; Meaning of Heb uncertain}

COME (18)
Jdg 9:24 might be avenged {Heb *might* ***come***}
Job 3: 7 joyful cry be heard {Heb ***come***}
Ps 22:31 and {Compare Gk: Heb ... *they will* ***come*** *and*}
71: 3 a strong fortress, {Gk Compare 31.3: Heb *to* ***come*** *continually you have commanded*}
Pr 10:10 but the one who rebukes boldly makes peace. {Gk: Heb *but a babbling fool will* ***come*** *to ruin*}
Isa 41:25 He shall trample {Cn: Heb ***come***}
45:11 Will you question me {Cn: Heb *Ask me of things to* ***come***}
49:17 Your builders outdo your destroyers, {Or *Your children* ***come*** *swiftly; your destroyers*}
Mt 17:20 + v.21 *But this kind does not* ***come*** *out except by prayer and fasting*
Mk 7: 4 they wash it; {Other ancient authorities read *and when they* ***come*** *from the marketplace,* >}
Lk 9:56 Then {Other ancient authorities read *... for the Son of Man has not* ***come*** *to destroy the lives of human beings but to save them." Then*}
Lk 18: 5 by continually coming.' " {Or *so that she may not finally* ***come*** *and slap me in the face*}
Ac 24: 6 + v.8 < *his accusers to* ***come*** *before you.*
1Co 15:24 Then comes the end, {Or *Then* ***come*** *the rest*}
Sir 11:14 + v.15 *Wisdom, understanding, and knowledge of the law* ***come*** *from the Lord; affection and the ways of good works* ***come*** *from him.* >
2Es 13:52 except in the time of his day. {Syr: Ethiop *except when his time and his day have* ***come.*** >}
14:12 the tenth part. {Ethiop *For the world is divided into ten parts, and has* ***come*** *to the tenth,* >}

COMES (3)
Isa 32:19 The forest will disappear completely, {Cn: Heb *And it will hail when the forest* ***comes*** *down*}
Lk 13:35 the time comes when {Other ancient authorities lack *the time* ***comes*** *when*}
Sir 16:22 far off." {Other ancient authorities add *and a scrutiny for all* ***comes*** *at the end*}

COMFORT (1)
Sir 3: 6 those who honor {Heb: Other ancient authorities read ***comfort***} their mother

COMFORTED (1)
Ge 38:12 when Judah's time of mourning was over, {Heb *when Judah was* ***comforted***}

COMING (4)
Ge 24:62 had come from {Syr Tg: Heb *from* ***coming*** *to*}
Mt 11:12 has suffered violence, {Or *has been* ***coming*** *violently*}
25:13 the day nor the hour. {Other ancient authorities add *in which the Son of Man is* ***coming***}
2Es 1:37 I call to witness ... with gladness; {Other ancient authorities read *The apostles bear witness to the* ***coming*** *people with joy*}

COMMAND (2)
3Mc 1: 2 issued to him, {Or *the best of the Ptolemaic soldiers previously put under his* ***command***}
2Es 8:14 will suddenly and quickly {Syr: Lat *will with a light* ***command***} destroy

COMMANDED (5)
Ge 50:16 they approached {Gk Syr: Heb *they* ***commanded***}
Ps 71: 3 a strong fortress, {Gk Compare 31.3: Heb *to come continually you have* ***commanded***}
Mt 15: 4 For God said, {Other ancient authorities read ***commanded,*** *saying*}
2Es 1:31 for I have rejected your {Other ancient authorities read *I have not* ***commanded*** *for you*} festal days
1:32 Lord. {Other ancient authorities add < *if I have not done the things my Father* ***commanded,*** >}

COMMANDER (1)
2Sa 24: 2 to Joab and the commanders of the army, {1 Chr 21.2 Gk: Heb *to Joab the* ***commander*** *of the army*}

COMMANDERS (1)
1Ki 1:25 Joab the commander {Gk: Heb *the* ***commanders***}

COMMANDING (1)
Ac 24: 6 + v.8 < ***commanding*** *his accusers to come before you.*

COMMANDMENT (3)
Mt 15: 6 make void the word {Other ancient authorities read *law*; others, ***commandment***}
Tit 2:15 reprove with all authority. {Gk ***commandment***}
2Es 1:32 says the Lord. {Other ancient authorities add < *if I have not kept the* ***commandment*** *of the Father,* >}

COMMANDMENTS (6)
Dt 11:13 heed his every commandment {Compare Gk: Heb *my* ***commandments***}
30:16 If you obey ... God {Gk: Heb lacks *If you obey the* ***commandments*** *of the* L*ORD* *your God*}
Rev 22:14 who wash their robes, {Other ancient authorities read *do his* ***commandments***}
Sir 1: 4 + v.5 < *her ways are the eternal* ***commandments.***
19:17 + v.19 < *The knowledge of the Lord's* ***commandments*** *is life-giving discipline;* >
32:24 who keeps the law preserves himself, {Heb: Gk *who believes the law heeds the* ***commandments***}

COMMANDS (1)
3Mc 6:27 begging pardon for your former actions! {Other ancient authorities read *revoking your former* ***commands***}

COMMISSIONED (1)
2Es 2:36 I publicly call on my savior to witness. {Other ancient authorities read *I testify that my savior has been* ***commissioned*** *by the Lord*}

COMMIT (1)
Mt 19: 9 except for unchastity, and marries another commits adultery." {Other ancient authorities read *except on the ground of unchastity, causes her to* ***commit*** *adultery;* >

COMMITS (1)
Mt 19: 9 commits adultery." {< others add at the end of the verse *and he who marries a divorced woman **commits** adultery*}

COMMITTED (1)
Ac 14:26 commended to the grace of God for the work {Or ***committed*** *in the grace of God to the work*}

COMMONLY (1)
1Ti 3: 1 The saying is sure: {< Other ancient authorities read *The saying is **commonly** accepted*}

COMMONWEALTH (1)
Php 3:20 Our citizenship {Or ***commonwealth***} is in heaven,

COMPANIES (1)
Jdg 9:44 the company that was {Vg and some Gk Mss: Heb ***companies*** *that were*} with him

COMPANY (1)
Hos 6: 9 are banded together; {Syr: Heb *are a **company***}

COMPARING (1)
1Co 2:13 interpreting spiritual things to those who are spiritual. {< or ***comparing*** *spiritual things with spiritual*}

COMPATRIOT (1)
Ro 16:11 relative {Or ***compatriot***}

COMPATRIOTS (2)
Ro 16: 7 relatives {Or ***compatriots***}
16:21 relatives. {Or ***compatriots***}

COMPENSATION (1)
1Ti 5:17 worthy of double honor, {Or ***compensation***}

COMPLETE (1)
1Th 5:23 be kept sound {Or ***complete***} and blameless

COMPLETELY (3)
1Th 2:16 overtaken them at last. {Or ***completely*** **or** *forever*}
Heb 7:25 able for all time to save {Or *able to save **completely***}
3Mc 6:34 boldness was ignominiously {Other ancient authorities read ***completely***} quenched.

COMPLETION (1)
Sir 47:10 throughout the year, {Gk *to **completion***}

COMPULSION (2)
Sir 20:14 nothing, {Other ancient authorities add *so it is with the envious who give under **compulsion***}
30:20 a girl. {Other ancient authorities add *So is the person who does right under **compulsion***}

CONCEAL (1)
Sir 22: 6 + v.7 < ***conceal*** *the lowly birth of their parents.* >

CONCEALED (1)
Job 23:17 thick darkness would cover my face! {Or *But I am not destroyed by the darkness; he has **concealed** the thick darkness from me*}

CONCEIVE (1)
Heb 11:11 By faith he received power of procreation, ... promised. {Other ancient authorities read *By faith Sarah herself, though barren, received power to **conceive.*** >}

CONCERNING (1)
2Es 1:16 you still complain. {Other ancient authorities read verse 16, ... *but still the people complain also **concerning** their own destruction.*}

CONDEMN (1)
Ex 22: 9 whom God condemns {Or *the judges **condemn***}

CONDEMNATION (2)
Mt 23:13 + v.14 < *therefore you will receive the greater **condemnation***
Jude 1: 9 a condemnation of slander {Or ***condemnation*** *for blasphemy*}

CONDUCT (1)
1Mc 14:35 people saw Simon's faithfulness {Other ancient authorities read ***conduct***}

CONFESS (1)
Ro 14:11 give praise to {Or ***confess***} God.

CONFESSED (1)
1Ti 6:12 you made {Gk ***confessed***} the good confession

CONFIDENCE (2)
Sir 18:29 proverbs. {Other ancient authorities add *Better is **confidence** in the one Lord than clinging with a dead heart to a dead one.*}
Sir 37:26 people will inherit honor, {Other ancient authorities read ***confidence***}

CONFIDENTLY (1)
Sir 41:16 nor is every kind of abashment to be approved. {Heb: Gk *and not everything is **confidently** esteemed by everyone*}

CONFIRM (1)
Sir 6:37 will give insight to {Heb: Gk *will **confirm***}

CONFOUNDED (1)
Jdt 16: 5 hand of a woman. {Other ancient authorities add *he has **confounded** them*}

CONFUSE (1)
Ge 11: 9 Babel, because there the LORD confused {Heb *balal*, meaning *to **confuse***}

CONSECRATED (18)
Nu 6: 2 nazirite, {That is *one separated* or *one **consecrated***}
6: 4 nazirites {That is *those separated* or *those **consecrated***}
6: 8 nazirites {That is *those separated* or *those **consecrated***}
6:12 nazirites, {That is *those separated* or *those **consecrated***}
6:13 nazirites {That is *those separated* or *those **consecrated***}
6:18 nazirites {That is *those separated* or *those **consecrated***}
6:19 nazirites, {That is *those separated* or *those **consecrated***}
6:20 nazirites {That is *those separated* or *those **consecrated***}
6:21 nazirites {That is *those separated* or *those **consecrated***}
6:21 nazirite {That is *one separated* or *one **consecrated***}
Jdg 13: 5 nazirite {That is *one separated* or *one **consecrated***}
13: 7 nazirite {That is *one separated* or *one **consecrated***}
16:17 nazirite {That is *one separated* or *one **consecrated***}
1Sa 1:11 nazirite {That is *one separated* or *one **consecrated***}
1:22 nazirite {That is *one separated* or *one **consecrated***}
Am 2:11 nazirites. {That is, *those separated* or *those **consecrated***}
2:12 nazirites {That is, *those separated* or *those **consecrated***}
1Mc 3:49 nazirites {That is *those separated* or *those **consecrated***}

CONSPIRACY (1)
Eze 22:25 princes {Gk: Heb ... *A **conspiracy** of its prophets*}

CONSTANTLY (1)
1Pe 1:22 love one another deeply {Or ***constantly***}

CONSUME (2)
Ps 74:11 do you keep your hand in {Cn: Heb *do you **consume** your right hand from*} your bosom?
2Th 2: 8 the Lord Jesus will destroy {Other ancient authorities read ***consume***}

CONSUMES (1)
Job 18:13 By disease their skin is consumed, {Cn: Heb *It **consumes** the limbs of his skin*}

CONTAIN (1)
Eze 21:28 Polished to consume, {Cn: Heb *to **contain***}

CONTEMPTS (1)
2Es 7:*139* [69] the multitude of their sins, {Lat ***contempts***}

CONTEND (3)
Hos 5:13 sent to the great king. {Cn: Heb *to a king who will **contend***}
10: 6 tribute to the great king. {Cn: Heb *to a king who will **contend***}
2Es 1:32 says the Lord. {Other ancient authorities add < *I will **contend** in judgment with you, says the Lord.*}

CONTENDED (1)
Dt 33: 7 strengthen his hands for him, {Cn: Heb *with his hands he **contended***}

CONTENTION (1)
Ge 26:20 Esek, {That is ***Contention***}

CONTINUALLY (1)
Ps 71: 3 a strong fortress, {Gk Compare 31.3: Heb *to come **continually** you have commanded*} to save me,

CONTINUE (1)
Jn 20:31 may come to believe {Other ancient authorities read *may **continue** to believe*}

CONTINUED (2)
Ac 21: 7 When we had finished {Or ***continued***} the voyage
2Es 7:29 all who draw human breath. {Arm *all who have **continued** in faith and in patience*}

CONTINUING (1)
Jdg 17: 8 Ephraim to carry on his work. {Or *Ephraim, **continuing** his journey*}

CONTINUOUSLY (1)
2Es 7:*112* [42] the full glory does not remain in it; {Or *the glory does not **continuously** abide in it*}

CONTROLS (1)
Sir 19: 5 + v.6 *One who **controls** the tongue will live without strife,*

CONVICT (1)
Jn 16: 8 prove the world wrong about {Or ***convict*** *the world of*}

CONVICTION (3)
Ro 14: 1 weak in faith, {Or ***conviction***}
14:23 act from faith; {Or ***conviction***}
14:23 proceed from faith {Or ***conviction***}

COPY (1)
Sir Pr: 3 I found opportunity for no little instruction. {Other ancient authorities read *I found a **copy** affording no little instruction*}

CORPSE (1)
Isa 26:19 their corpses {Cn Compare Syr Tg: Heb *my **corpse***} shall rise.

CORRUPTIBLE (1)
2Es 7:*88* separated from their mortal body. {Lat *the **corruptible** vessel*}

COSTS (1)
Ac 18:21 he said, "I {Other ancient authorities read *I must at all **costs** keep the approaching festival in Jerusalem, but I*} will return

COUNSEL (2)
Pr 27: 9 soul is torn by trouble. {Gk: Heb *the sweetness of a friend is better than one's own **counsel***}
Hos 10: 6 ashamed of his idol. {Cn: Heb ***counsel***}

COUNSELS (1)
Ps 13: 2 must I bear pain {Syr: Heb *hold **counsels***}

COUNTED (1)
Mk 15:27 + v.28 *And the scripture was fulfilled that says, "And he was **counted** among the lawless."*

COUNTENANCE (1)
Sir 13:25 for evil. {Other ancient authorities add *and a glad heart makes a cheerful **countenance***}

COUNTRY (1)
AdE 8: 6 my ancestral nation {Gk ***country***}

COURT (3)
Eze 41:15 and the outer {Gk: Heb *of the **court***} vestibule
Mt 5:25 the way to court {Gk lacks *to **court***}
1Mc 13:40 enrolled in our bodyguard, {Or ***court***}

COVENANT (8)
2Ch 5:10 made a covenant {Heb lacks *a **covenant***}
Gal 3:15 a person's will {Or ***covenant*** (as in verse 17)}
Heb 9:16 Where a will {The Greek word used here means both ***covenant*** and *will*} is involved,
9:17 For a will {The Greek word used here means both ***covenant* and *will***} takes effect
Sir 14:12 the decree {Heb Syr: Gk ***covenant***} of Hades
14:17 the decree {Heb: Gk ***covenant***} from of old
16:22 For his decree {Heb *the decree*: Gk *the **covenant***} is far off."
41:19 of breaking an oath or agreement, {Heb: Gk *before the truth of God and the **covenant***}

COVENANTS (1)
Sir 45:17 authority and {Heb: Gk *authority in **covenants** of*}

COVER (29)
Ex 25:17 a mercy seat {Or *a **cover***}
25:18 the mercy seat. {Or *the **cover***}
25:19 the mercy seat {Or *the **cover***}
25:20 the mercy seat {Or *the **cover***}
25:20 the mercy seat. {Or *the **cover***}
25:21 the mercy seat {Or *the **cover***}
25:22 the mercy seat, {Or *the **cover***}
26:34 the mercy seat {Or *the **cover***}
30: 6 the mercy seat {Or *the **cover***}
31: 7 the mercy seat {Or *the **cover***}
35:12 the mercy seat, {Or *the **cover***}
37: 6 a mercy seat {Or *a **cover***}
37: 7 the mercy seat {Or *the **cover***}
37: 8 the mercy seat {Or *the **cover***}
37: 9 the mercy seat {Or *the **cover***}

Ex 37: 9 the mercy seat. {Or *the* ***cover***}
39:35 the mercy seat; {Or *the* ***cover***}
40:20 the mercy seat {Or *the* ***cover***}
Lev 16: 2 the mercy seat {Or *the* ***cover***}
16: 2 the mercy seat {Or *the* ***cover***}
16:13 the mercy seat {Or *the* ***cover***}
16:14 the mercy seat, {Or *the* ***cover***}
16:14 the mercy seat {Or *the* ***cover***}
16:15 the mercy seat {Or *the* ***cover***}
16:15 the mercy seat. {Or *the* ***cover***}
Nu 7:89 the mercy seat {Or *the* ***cover***}
1Sa 24: 3 to relieve himself. {Heb *to* ***cover*** *his feet*}
1Ch 28:11 the mercy seat; {Or *the* ***cover***}
2Es 2:29 My power will protect {Lat *hands will* ***cover***}

COVERING (1)
Jdg 3:24 relieving himself {Heb ***covering*** *his feet*}

COVETOUSLY (1)
Pr 21:26 all day long the wicked covet, {Gk: Heb *all day long one covets* ***covetously***}

COVETOUSNESS (1)
4Mc 2: 4 over every desire. {Or *all* ***covetousness***}

COVETS (1)
Pr 21:26 all day long the wicked covet, {Gk: Heb *all day long one* ***covets*** *covetously*}

CRAVING (1)
Nu 11:34 Kibroth-hattaavah, {That is *Graves of* ***craving***}

CREATE (1)
Ge 1: 1 In the beginning when God created {Or *when God began to* ***create*** >}

CREATED (4)
Jdt 16:14 and it formed them; {Other ancient authorities read *they were* ***created***}
Sir 11:14 + v.16 < *Error and darkness were* ***created*** *with sinners;* >
44: 2 The Lord apportioned to them {Heb: Gk ***created***}
2Es 6: 1 "At the beginning of the circle of the earth, before {<Ethiop: ... *For before the earth and the lands were* ***created,*** *and before*}

CREATION (3)
Sir 16:14 + v.16 *His mercy is manifest to the whole of* ***creation,*** >
2Es 7:60 the judgment {Syr Arab 1: Lat ***creation***}
14:48 did so. {Syr adds < *three months and twelve days after* ***creation.*** *At that time Ezra was caught up,* >

CREATURES (1)
Wis 1:14 the generative forces {Or *the* ***creatures***}

CRIED (2)
La 2:18 Cry aloud {Cn: Heb *Their heart* ***cried***}
Mk 15:39 this way he {Other ancient authorities add ***cried*** *out and*} breathed his last,

CROCODILE (1)
Job 41: 1 Leviathan {Or *the* ***crocodile***}

CROCUS (1)
SS 2: 1 a rose {Heb ***crocus***} of Sharon,

CROSSED (2)
2Sa 19:18 the crossing was taking place, {Cn: Heb *the ford* ***crossed***}
Jdt 2:24 Then he followed {Or ***crossed***} the Euphrates

CROSSING (1)
Isa 23: 2 crossed over the sea {Q Ms: MT ***crossing*** *over the sea, they replenished you*}

CROWDS (1)
Mt 12:15 crowds {Other ancient authorities lack ***crowds***}

CROWED (1)
Mk 14:68 Then the cock crowed. {Other ancient authorities lack *Then the cock* ***crowed***}

CROWN (1)
2Es 5:42 liken my judgment to a circle; {Or ***crown***}

CROWNED (1)
3Mc 3:28 awarded their freedom. {Gk ***crowned*** *with freedom*}

CROWNS (3)
Zec 6:11 make a crown, {Gk Mss Syr Tg: Heb ***crowns***}
6:14 And the crown {Gk Syr: Heb ***crowns***}
Sir 19: 5 condemned, {Other ancient authorities add *but one who withstands pleasures* ***crowns*** *his life.* >}

CRUSHES (1)
Da 2:40 and smashes everything, {Gk Theodotion Syr Vg: Aram adds *and like iron that* ***crushes***}

CRY (1)
Isa 15: 4 the loins of Moab quiver; {Cn Compare Gk Syr: Heb *the armed men of Moab* ***cry*** *aloud*}

CRYING (1)
2Es 1:32 says the Lord. {Other ancient authorities add < *Recently you also laid hands on me,* ***crying*** *out before the judge's seat* >}

CUB (1)
Eze 30: 5 Libya, {Compare Gk Syr Vg: Heb ***Cub***}

CUBIT (3)
Eze 42: 4 one hundred cubits deep, {Gk Syr: Heb *a way of one* ***cubit***}
Mt 6:27 add a single hour to your span of life? {Or *add one* ***cubit*** *to your height*}
Lk 12:25 add a single hour to your span of life? {Or *add a* ***cubit*** *to your stature*}

CUBITS (2)
Eze 41:22 two cubits wide; {Gk: Heb lacks *two* ***cubits*** *wide*}
Jn 21: 8 about a hundred yards {Gk *two hundred* ***cubits***}

CULTIVATE (1)
Ps 104:14 plants for people to use, {Or *to* ***cultivate***}

CUP (2)
Ge 44: 4 Why have you stolen my silver cup? {Gk Compare Vg: Heb lacks *Why have you stolen my silver* ***cup?***}
3Mc 7:18 they celebrated their deliverance, {Gk *they made a* ***cup*** *of deliverance*}

CUSH (21)
2Ki 19: 9 Ethiopia, {Or *Nubia*; Heb ***Cush***}
Est 1: 1 Ethiopia. {Or *Nubia*; Heb ***Cush***}
8: 9 Ethiopia, {Or *Nubia*; Heb ***Cush***}
Job 28:19 Ethiopia {Or *Nubia*; Heb ***Cush***}
Ps 68:31 Ethiopia {Or *Nubia*; Heb ***Cush***}
87: 4 Ethiopia—{Or *Nubia*; Heb ***Cush***}
Isa 11:11 Ethiopia, {Or *Nubia*; Heb ***Cush***}
18: 1 Ethiopia, {Or *Nubia*; Heb ***Cush***}
20: 3 Ethiopia, {Or *Nubia*; Heb ***Cush***}
20: 5 Ethiopia {Or *Nubia*; Heb ***Cush***}
37: 9 Ethiopia, {Or *Nubia*; Heb ***Cush***}
43: 3 Ethiopia {Or *Nubia*; Heb ***Cush***}
45:14 Ethiopia {Or *Nubia*; Heb ***Cush***}
Jer 46: 9 Ethiopia {Or *Nubia*; Heb ***Cush***}
Eze 29:10 Ethiopia. {Or *Nubia*; Heb ***Cush***}
30: 4 Ethiopia, {Or *Nubia*; Heb ***Cush***}
30: 5 Ethiopia, {Or *Nubia*; Heb ***Cush***}
30: 9 Ethiopians; {Or *Nubians*; Heb ***Cush***}
38: 5 Ethiopia, {Or *Nubia*; Heb ***Cush***}
Na 3: 9 Ethiopia {Or *Nubia*; Heb ***Cush***}
Zep 3:10 Ethiopia {Or *Nubia*; Heb ***Cush***}

CUSHITE (5)
2Ch 14: 9 Ethiopian {Or *Nubian*; Heb ***Cushite***}
Jer 38: 7 Ethiopian, {Or *Nubian*; Heb ***Cushite***}
38:10 Ethiopian, {Or *Nubian*; Heb ***Cushite***}
38:12 Ethiopian {Or *Nubian*; Heb ***Cushite***}
39:16 Ethiopian: {Or *Nubian*; Heb ***Cushite***}

CUSHITES (11)
2Ch 12: 3 Ethiopians. {Or *Nubians*; Heb ***Cushites***}
14:12 Ethiopians {Or *Nubians*; Heb ***Cushites***}
14:12 Ethiopians {Or *Nubians*; Heb ***Cushites***}
14:13 Ethiopians {Or *Nubians*; Heb ***Cushites***}
16: 8 Ethiopians {Or *Nubians*; Heb ***Cushites***}
21:16 Ethiopians. {Or *Nubians*; Heb ***Cushites***}
Isa 20: 4 Ethiopians {Or *Nubians*; Heb ***Cushites***}
Jer 13:23 Ethiopians {Or *Nubians*; Heb ***Cushites***}
Da 11:43 Ethiopians {Or *Nubians*; Heb ***Cushites***}
Am 9: 7 Ethiopians {Or *Nubians*; Heb ***Cushites***}
Zep 2:12 Ethiopians, {Or *Nubians*; Heb ***Cushites***}

CUT (4)
Ps 31:22 "I am driven far {Another reading is ***cut*** *off*}
La 3:22 love of the LORD never ceases, {Syr Tg: Heb *LORD, we are not* ***cut*** *off*}
Zep 3: 7 it will not lose sight {Gk Syr: Heb *its dwelling will not be* ***cut*** *off*}
Ro 9:28 for the Lord will execute his sentence on the earth quickly and decisively." {Other ancient authorities read *for he will finish his work and* ***cut*** *it short in righteousness, because the Lord will make the sentence shortened on the earth*}

CYPRESSES (1)
Na 2: 3 the chargers {Cn Compare Gk Syr: Heb ***cypresses***} prance,

CYRUS (1)
1Es 6:21 royal archives of our lord {Other ancient authorities read *of* ***Cyrus***}

D

DAILY (1)
Sir 47: 9 their voices. {Other ancient authorities add *and* ***daily*** *they sing his praises*}

DAN (1)
Jdg 18:12 Mahaneh-dan {That is *Camp of* ***Dan***}

DAN-JAAN (1)
2Sa 24: 6 they came to Dan, and from Dan {Cn Compare Gk: Heb *they came to* ***Dan-jaan*** *and*}

DANCE (1)
3Mc 6:35 the aforementioned choral group {Or ***dance***}

DANCES (1)
3Mc 6:32 they formed choruses {Or ***dances***}

DANEL (3)
Eze 14:14 Daniel, {Or, as otherwise read, ***Danel***}
14:20 Daniel, {Or, as otherwise read, ***Danel***}
28: 3 Daniel; {Or, as otherwise read, ***Danel***}

DARDA (1)
1Ch 2: 6 Dara, {Or ***Darda***; Compare Syr Tg some Gk Mss; See 1 Kings 4.31}

DARIUS (1)
1Mc 12: 7 Arius, {Vg Compare verse 20: Gk ***Darius***}

DARKENED (2)
Lk 23:45 the sun's light failed; {Or *the sun was eclipsed.* Other ancient authorities read *the sun was* ***darkened***}
Wis 17: 3 unobserved behind a dark curtain of forgetfulness, they were scattered terribly {Other ancient authorities read *unobserved, they were* ***darkened*** *behind a dark curtain of forgetfulness, terribly*}

DARKNESS (5)
Job 10:22 gloom {Heb *gloom as* ***darkness,*** *deep* ***darkness***}
Sir 11:14 + v.16 < *Error and* ***darkness*** *were created with sinners;* >
16:14 + v.16 < *and he divided his light and* ***darkness*** *with a plumb line.*
17:26 iniquity, {Other ancient authorities add *for he will lead you out of* ***darkness*** *to the light of health.*}

DATHEMA (1)
1Mc 5:29 of Dathema. {Gk lacks *of* ***Dathema.*** See verse 9}

DAUGHTER (5)
Ge 36: 2 son {Sam Gk Syr: Heb ***daughter***}
36:14 son {Gk Syr: Heb ***daughter***}
Ps 45:12 the richest of the people {Heb ***daughter***}
Isa 23:10 O ships of {Cn Compare Gk: Heb *like the Nile,* ***daughter***} Tarshish;
Tob 7:16 the tears, {Other ancient authorities read *the tears of her* ***daughter***}

DAUGHTERS (3)
Ps 48:11 the towns {Heb ***daughters***} of Judah
97: 8 the towns {Heb ***daughters***} of Judah
Sir 17:22 eye. {Other ancient authorities add *apportioning repentance to his sons and* ***daughters***}

DAVID (3)
2Sa 13:39 And the heart of {Q Ms Gk: MT *And* ***David***}
1Ch 12:33 to help David {Gk: Heb lacks ***David***}
2Ch 17: 3 his father; {Another reading is *his father* ***David***}

DAWNING (1)
Lk 23:54 the sabbath was beginning. {Gk *was* ***dawning***}

DAY (13)
Nu 9:16 covered it by day {Gk Syr Vg: Heb lacks *by* ***day***}
1Sa 14:33 before me here." {Gk: Heb *me this* ***day***}
1Ch 26:17 each day, {Gk: Heb lacks *each* ***day***}
Job 3: 8 curse the Sea, {Cn: Heb ***day***}
Pr 25:20 Like vinegar on a wound {Gk: Heb *Like one who takes off a garment on a cold* ***day,*** *like vinegar on lye*}
Ob 1:12 over {Heb *on the* ***day*** *of*}
Zep 2: 2 before you are driven away like the drifting chaff, {Cn Compare Gk Syr: Heb *before a decree is born; like chaff a* ***day*** *has passed away*}
Lk 7:11 afterwards {Other ancient authorities read *Next* ***day***} he went
17:24 in his day. {Other ancient authorities lack *in his* ***day***}
1Pe 2:12 God when he comes to judge. {Gk *God on the* ***day*** *of visitation*}
Sir 12: 6 ungodly. {Other ancient authorities add *and he is keeping them for the* ***day*** *of their punishment*}

2Es 5: 4 after the third period; {Literally *after the third*; ... Georg *after the third* **day**}
6:31 these, {Syr Ethiop Arab 1 Arm: Lat adds *by* **day**}

DAYS (15)

1Sa 1:11 He shall drink neither wine nor intoxicants, {Cn Compare Gk Q Ms 1.22: MT *then I will give him to the* LORD *all the* **days** *of his life*}
4: 1 In those ... Israel, {Gk: Heb lacks *In those* **days** *the Philistines mustered for war against Israel*}
1Ki 8:65 seven days. {Compare Gk: Heb *seven* **days** *and seven* **days**, *fourteen* **days**}
Ps 23: 6 my whole life long. {Heb *for length of* **days**}
Da 5:26 the days of {Aram lacks *the* **days** *of*}
7: 9 an Ancient One {Aram *an Ancient of* **Days**}
7:13 the Ancient One {Aram *the Ancient of* **Days**}
7:22 the Ancient One {Aram *the Ancient of* **Days**}
Na 2: 8 pool whose waters {Cn Compare Gk: Heb *a pool, from the* **days** *that she has become, and they*}
2Es 1: 3 in the reign of Artaxerxes, king of the Persians. {Other ancient authorities, ... begin the chapter: ... *in the* **days** *of King Nebuchadnezzar*, >}
7:*108* [38] in the days of Saul, {Syr Ethiop Arab 1: Lat Arab 2 Arm lack *in the* **days** *of Saul*}
12:32 of days ... and speak {Syr: Lat lacks *of* **days** ... *and speak*}
14:48 I did so. {Syr adds < *and three months and twelve* **days** *after creation*. >}

DEACON (1)

1Ti 4: 6 a good servant {Or **deacon**} of Christ Jesus,

DEACONS (1)

1Ti 3:11 Women {Or *Their wives*, or *Women* **deacons**}

DEAD (5)

Mt 28: 7 from the dead, {Other ancient authorities lack *from the* **dead**}
Ac 24:15 a resurrection of both {Other ancient authorities read *of the* **dead**, *both of*}
Sir 18:29 proverbs. {Other ancient authorities add *Better is confidence in the one Lord than clinging with a* **dead** *heart to a* **dead** *one*.}
Bar 3: 4 the prayer of the people {Gk **dead**}

DEAL (1)

Dt 29: 9 that you may succeed {Or **deal** *wisely*}

DEATH (10)

Ps 23: 4 the darkest valley, {Or *the valley of the shadow of* **death**}
Pr 14:32 refuge in their integrity. {Gk Syr: Heb *in their* **death**}
Isa 53: 9 and his tomb {Q Ms: MT *and in his* **death**}
Mk 16:14 risen. {Other ancient authorities add, in whole or in part, ... *And for those who have sinned I was handed over to* **death**, >}
Rev 13: 3 but its mortal wound {Gk *the plague of its* **death**}
13:12 mortal wound {Gk *whose plague of its* **death**}
Sir 18: 9 one hundred years. {Other ancient authorities add *but the* **death** *of each one is beyond the calculation of all*}
41:11 The human body is a fleeting thing, ... out. {Heb: Gk *People grieve over the* **death** *of the body*, >}
2Es 1:32 says the Lord. {Other ancient authorities add < *and you delivered me to* **death** *by hanging me on the tree;* >}
8:53 and death {Syr Ethiop Arm: Lat lacks **death**}

DECEIVE (1)

1Sa 15:29 will not recant {Q Ms Gk: MT **deceive**}

DECLARE (3)

1Sa 12: 7 and I will declare to you {Gk: Heb lacks *and I will* **declare** *to you*}
Ps 75: 9 But I will rejoice {Gk: Heb **declare**}
Sir 44:15 The assembly declares {Heb: Gk *Peoples* **declare**}

DECLARED (1)

2Es 14: 5 declared to him {Syr Ethiop Arab Arm: Lat lacks **declared** *to him*}

DECREE (2)

Zep 2: 2 before you are driven away like the drifting chaff, {Cn Compare Gk Syr: Heb *before a* **decree** *is born; like chaff a day has passed away*}
AdE 3:10 seal the decree {Gk lacks *the* **decree**}

DECREES (1)

Dt 8: 3 by every word that comes from the mouth of the LORD. {Or *by anything that the* LORD **decrees**}

DEDANITES (1)

Eze 27:15 The Rhodians {Gk: Heb *The* **Dedanites**}

DEEDS (2)

1Ti 6: 2 since those who benefit by their service are believers and beloved. {Or *since they are believers and beloved, who devote themselves to good* **deeds**}
Sir 36:19 Fill Zion with your majesty, {Heb Syr: Gk *the celebration of your wondrous* **deeds**}

DEEP (3)

Job 10:22 gloom {Heb *gloom as darkness*, **deep** *darkness*}
Eze 40: 6 deep. {Heb **deep**, *and one threshold, one reed* **deep**}

DEER (1)

Ps 29: 9 causes the oaks to whirl, {Or *causes the* **deer** *to calve*}

DEFEATED (1)

1Mc 1: 1 had defeated {Gk adds *and he* **defeated**}

DEFENDER (1)

Isa 34: 8 of vindication by Zion's cause. {Or *of recompense by Zion's* **defender**}

DEFILED (1)

2Es 7:*68* entangled in {Syr **defiled** *with*} iniquities,

DEGREE (1)

4Mc 15: 5 Considering that mothers are the weaker sex ... children. {Or *For to the* **degree** *that mothers are weaker* >}

DELAYED (1)

3Mc 5:17 make the present {Other ancient authorities read **delayed** (Gk *untimely*)} portion

DELIBERATE (1)

Sir 20: 8 hated. {Other ancient authorities add < *for so you will escape* **deliberate** *sin!*}

DELIBERATION (1)

Sir 32:18 deterred by fear. {Meaning of Gk uncertain. Other ancient authorities add *and after acting, with him, without* **deliberation**}

DELIGHT (1)

Pr 23:26 your eyes observe {Another reading is **delight** *in*}

DELIGHTS (1)

SS 7: 6 delectable maiden! {Syr: Heb *in* **delights**}

DELIVER (2)

Jdg 10:11 I not deliver you {Heb lacks *Did I not* **deliver** *you*}
2Es 1:32 says the Lord. {Other ancient authorities add ... *crying out before the judge's seat for him to* **deliver** *me to you*. >}

DELIVERED (1)

2Es 1:32 says the Lord. {Other ancient authorities add ... *and you* **delivered** *me to death by hanging me on the tree;* >}

DEMON (1)

Mt 17:18 and it {Gk *the* **demon**} came out

DENARII (1)

Jn 6: 7 Six months' wages {Gk *Two hundred* **denarii**; the denarius was the usual day's wage for a laborer}

DENARIUS (6)

Mt 20: 2 the usual daily wage, {Gk *a* **denarius**}
20: 9 the usual daily wage. {Gk *a* **denarius**}
20:10 the usual daily wage. {Gk *a* **denarius**}
20:13 the usual daily wage? {Gk *a* **denarius**}
Rev 6: 6 a day's pay, {Gk *a* **denarius**}
6: 6 a day's pay, {Gk *a* **denarius**}

DEPART (3)

Jdg 7: 3 home.' " Thus Gideon sifted them out; {Cn: Heb *home and* **depart** *from Mount Gilead' "*}
2Sa 7:15 But I will not take {Gk Syr Vg 1 Chr 17.13: Heb *shall not* **depart**}
Job 15:30 blossom will be swept away {Cn: Heb *will* **depart**}

DEPARTED (1)

Ac 28:28 + v.29 < *the Jews* **departed**, *arguing vigorously among themselves*

DEPRIVE (1)

Sir 7:19 Do not dismiss {Heb: Gk **deprive** *yourself of*} a wise

DEPTH (1)

Sir 1: 3 the abyss, and wisdom {Other ancient authorities read *the* **depth** *of the abyss*}

DEPUTY (1)

2Ch 35:24 in his second chariot {Or *the chariot of his* **deputy**}

DESCENDANT (1)

Isa 65: 9 I will bring forth descendants {Or *a* **descendant**}

DESCENDANTS (2)

Ge 10: 5 These are the descendants of Japheth {< Heb lacks *These are the* **descendants** *of Japheth*}
Ro 9:29 Lord of hosts had not left survivors {Or **descendants**; Gk *seed*}

DESCENDS (1)

2Es 2: 9 Gomorrah, whose land lies in lumps of pitch and heaps of ashes. {Other ancient authorities read *Gomorrah, whose land* **descends** *to hell*}

DESERTS (1)

Ps 68: 4 lift up a song to him who rides upon the clouds— {Or *cast up a highway for him who rides through the* **deserts**}

DESIRE (1)

Hos 10:10 I will come {Cn Compare Gk: Heb *In my* **desire**}

DESIRES (1)

Wis 15: 5 so that they desire {Gk *and he* **desires**}

DESIRING (1)

2Pe 3:12 waiting for and hastening {Or *earnestly* **desiring**}

DESOLATE (1)

Mt 23:38 desolate. {Other ancient authorities lack **desolate**}

DESOLATION (1)

Zep 2:14 the raven {Gk Vg: Heb **desolation**} croak

DESOLATIONS (1)

Jer 25: 9 and an everlasting disgrace. {Gk Compare Syr: Heb *and everlasting* **desolations**}

DESPAIRING (1)

Lk 6:35 expect nothing in return. {Other ancient authorities read **despairing** *of no one*}

DESPISE (2)

Sir 22:13 unintelligent person. {Other ancient authorities add *For being without sense he will* **despise** *everything about you*}
22:23 his inheritance. {Other ancient authorities add *For one should not always* **despise** *restricted circumstances*, >}

DESTINY (1)

Sir 37:18 it sprouts four branches, {Heb: Gk *As a clue to changes of heart four kinds of* **destiny** *appear*}

DESTITUTE (1)

Pr 11:16 The timid ... destitute, {Gk: Heb lacks *The timid ...* **destitute**}

DESTROY (4)

Jer 6: 2 I will have likened daughter Zion to the loveliest pasture. {Or *I will* **destroy** *daughter Zion, the loveliest pasture*}
Lk 9:56 Then {Other ancient authorities read < *for the Son of Man has not come to* **destroy** *the lives of human beings but to save them." Then*}
2Es 1:11 I destroyed all nations before them, ... provinces, {Other ancient authorities read *Did I not* **destroy** *the city of Bethsaida because of you*, >}
15:44 its fury; {Other ancient authorities add *until they* **destroy** *it to its foundations*}

DESTROYED (1)

Job 23:17 If only I could vanish in darkness, and thick darkness would cover my face! {Or *But I am not* **destroyed** *by the darkness; he has concealed the thick darkness from me*}

DESTROYER (2)

Jer 51: 1 stir up a destructive wind {Or *stir up the spirit of a* **destroyer**}
Rev 9:11 Apollyon. {That is, **Destroyer**}

DESTROYING (1)

AdE 9: 4 + v.5 *So the Jews struck down all their enemies with the sword, killing and* **destroying** *them*, >

DESTRUCTION (10)

Nu 21: 3 Hormah. {Heb **Destruction**}
Jos 6:18 to covet {Gk: Heb *devote to* **destruction** Compare 7.21}
Ps 52: 7 in wealth!" {Syr Tg: Heb *in his* **destruction**}
Eze 32: 9 as I carry you captive {Gk: Heb *bring your* **destruction**}
Mal 4: 6 strike the land with a curse. {Or *a ban of utter* **destruction**}
Jn 17:12 except the one destined to be lost, {Gk *except the son of* **destruction**}
2Pe 2:12 they also will be destroyed, {Gk *in their* **destruction**}
Rev 9:11 Abaddon, {That is, **Destruction**}
Tob 13: 2 from the great abyss, {Gk *from* **destruction**}
Sir 31: 5 pursues money will be led astray {Heb Syr: Gk *pursues* **destruction** *will be filled*}

DEVASTATED (1)

Ps 137: 8 O daughter Babylon, you devastator! {Or *you who are* **devastated**}

DEVOTE (2)
Jos 6:18 devoted to destruction, so as not to covet {Gk: Heb ***devote*** *to destruction* Compare 7.21}
1Ti 6: 2 since those who benefit by their service are believers and beloved. {Or *since they are believers and beloved, who* ***devote*** *themselves to good deeds*}

DEVOUR (1)
Mt 23:13 + v.14 < *For you* ***devour*** *widows' houses and for the sake of appearance you make long prayers;* >

DEVOURER (1)
Mal 3:11 I will rebuke the locust {Heb ***devourer***}

DEVOUT (2)
Nu 12: 3 Moses was very humble, {Or ***devout***}
4Mc 1: 7 reason {Other ancient authorities read ***devout*** *reason*} is dominant

DEW (1)
Job 29:22 like dew. {Heb lacks *like* ***dew***}

DIBLAH (1)
Eze 6:14 Riblah. {Another reading is ***Diblah***}

DID (14)
Jdg 10:11 I not deliver you {Heb lacks ***Did*** *I not deliver you*}
1Sa 2:27 I revealed {Gk Tg Syr: Heb ***Did*** *I reveal*} myself
Job 31:33 as others do, {Or *as Adam* ***did***}
Ps 105:28 they rebelled {Cn Compare Gk Syr: Heb *they* ***did*** *not rebel*} against his words.
Mk 6:20 he was greatly perplexed; {Other ancient authorities read *he* ***did*** *many things*}
Lk 9:54 consume them?" {Other ancient authorities add *as Elijah* ***did***}
Ac 5:28 "We gave you ... name, {Other ancient authorities read ***Did*** *we not give you strict orders* >}
Heb 4: 2 who listened. {Other ancient authorities read *it* ***did*** *not meet with faith in those who listened*}
AdE 9: 4 + v.5 < *and they* ***did*** *as they pleased to those who hated them.*
9:10 they indulged {Other ancient authorities read ***did*** *not indulge*} themselves
Sir 16: 9 their sins; {Other ancient authorities add *All these things he* ***did*** *to the hard-hearted nations,* >}
Sir 16:14 + v.15 *The Lord hardened Pharaoh so that he* ***did*** *not recognize him,* >
2Es 1:11 I destroyed all nations ... provinces, {Other ancient authorities read ***Did*** *I not destroy the city of Bethsaida because of you,* >}
13:57 the wonders that he does {Lat ***did***}

DIDRACHMA (2)
Mt 17:24 the temple tax {Gk ***didrachma***}
17:24 the temple tax?" {Gk ***didrachma***}

DIDYMUS (3)
Jn 11:16 the Twin, {Gk ***Didymus***}
20:24 the Twin), {Gk ***Didymus***}
21: 2 the Twin, {Gk ***Didymus***}

DIE (1)
Jdt 7:27 captured by them. {Other ancient authorities add *than to* ***die*** *of thirst*}

DIED (3)
1Pe 3:18 suffered {Other ancient authorities read ***died***}
Sir 48:11 and were adorned {Other ancient authorities read *and have* ***died***} with your love!
4Mc 9: 6 lived piously {Other ancient authorities read ***died***}

DIES (1)
Sir 14:20 meditates on {Other ancient authorities read ***dies*** *in*} wisdom

DIG (1)
Job 39:21 It paws {Gk Syr Vg: Heb *they* ***dig***} violently,

DIMON (2)
Isa 15: 9 Dibon {Q Ms Vg Compare Syr: MT ***Dimon***}
15: 9 Dibon {Q Ms Vg Compare Syr: MT ***Dimon***}

DIPPING (1)
Sir 31:26 tests the work of the smith, {Heb: Gk *tests the hardening of steel by* ***dipping***}

DISADVANTAGE (1)
Ro 3: 9 Are we any better off? {Or *at any* ***disadvantage?***}

DISASTER (1)
Job 18:12 Their strength is consumed by hunger, {Or ***Disaster*** *is hungry for them*}

DISCIPLES (1)
Mt 26:20 twelve; {Other ancient authorities add ***disciples***}

DISCIPLINE (3)
Sir 16:10 stubbornness. {Other ancient authorities add *Chastising, showing mercy, striking, healing, the Lord persisted in mercy and* ***discipline.***}
Sir 17:17 + v.18 *whom, being his firstborn, he brings up with* ***discipline,*** >
19:17 + v.19 < *The knowledge of the Lord's commandments is life-giving* ***discipline;*** >

DISDAINFULLY (1)
Sir 22: 6 + v.8 < *who are* ***disdainfully*** *and boorishly haughty stain the nobility of their kindred.*

DISEASE (2)
Isa 53:10 crush him with pain. {Or *by* ***disease***; meaning of Heb uncertain}
Jn 5: 3 + v.4 < *in first after the stirring of the water was made well from whatever* ***disease*** *that person had.*

DISFIGURED (1)
Job 30:18 he seizes my garment; {Gk: Heb *my garment is* ***disfigured***}

DISHON (1)
1Ch 1:42 Dishan: {See 1.38: Heb ***Dishon***}

DISLIKES (1)
Sir 21:15 he laughs at {Syr: Gk ***dislikes***} it

DISLOYAL (1)
Sir 16:21 so most of his works are concealed. {Meaning of Gk uncertain: Heb Syr *If I sin, no eye can see me, and if I am* ***disloyal*** *all in secret, who is to know?*}

DISOBEDIENCE (1)
Col 3: 6 on those who are disobedient. {Other ancient authorities lack *on those who are disobedient* (Gk *the children of* ***disobedience***)}

DISOBEDIENT (1)
Col 3: 6 on those who are disobedient. {Other ancient authorities lack *on those who are* ***disobedient*** (Gk *the children of disobedience*)}

DISSOLVES (1)
1Jn 4: 3 does not confess Jesus {Other ancient authorities read *does away with Jesus* (Gk ***dissolves*** *Jesus*)}

DISTILL (1)
Job 36:27 he distills {Cn: Heb *they* ***distill***} his mist

DISTRACTS (1)
Heb 12: 1 sin that clings so closely, {Other ancient authorities read *sin that easily* ***distracts***}

DISTRESS (1)
Tob 14: 4 of God in it will be burned ... a while. {Lat: Other ancient authorities read *of God will be in* ***distress*** *and will be burned for a while*}

DISTRESSED (2)
1Sa 14:24 Now Saul committed a very rash act that day. {Gk: Heb *The Israelites were* ***distressed*** *that day*}
Isa 63: 9 savior [9]in all their distress ... that saved them; {Or *savior.* [9]*In all their distress he was* ***distressed;*** *the angel of his presence saved them;*}

DISTRIBUTED (1)
Sir 17: 4 + v.5 < *he* ***distributed*** *to them the gift of mind,* >

DIVESTED (1)
Col 2:15 He disarmed {Or ***divested*** *himself of*} the rulers

DIVIDED (2)
Mt 27:35 casting lots; {Other ancient authorities add ... *"They* ***divided*** *my clothes among themselves,* >}
Sir 16:14 + v.16 < *and he* ***divided*** *his light and darkness with a plumb line.* >

DIVINE (8)
Ge 32:28 striven with God and with humans, {Or *with* ***divine*** *and human beings*}
Ps 8: 5 a little lower than God, {Or *than the* ***divine*** *beings or angels*: Heb *elohim*}
Da 4: 8 a spirit of the holy gods {Or *a holy,* ***divine*** *spirit*}
4: 9 a spirit of the holy gods {Or *a holy,* ***divine*** *spirit*}
4:18 spirit of the holy gods." {Or *a holy,* ***divine*** *spirit*}
5:11 a spirit of the holy gods. {Or *a holy,* ***divine*** *spirit*}
5:14 a spirit of the gods {Or *a* ***divine*** *spirit*}
4Mc 7: 9 of divine {Other ancient authorities lack ***divine***}

DIVINERS (1)
Isa 2: 6 full of diviners {Cn: Heb lacks *of* ***diviners***}

DIVISION (3)
Ge 10:25 Peleg, {That is ***Division***}
1Sa 23:28 Rock of Escape. {Or *Rock of* ***Division***; Meaning of Heb uncertain}
Sir 17:15 + v.17 *For in the* ***division*** *of the nations of the whole earth, he appointed*

DIVORCED (1)
Mt 19: 9 commits adultery." {< others add at the end of the verse *and he who marries a* ***divorced*** *woman commits adultery*}

DO (16)
2Sa 15:27 said to the priest Zadok, "Look, {Gk: Heb *Are you a seer or* ***Do*** *you see?*}
Ecc 5: 1 keep from doing evil. {Cn: Heb *they* ***do*** *not know how to* ***do*** *evil*}
Isa 42:20 He sees many things, but does {Heb *You see many things but* ***do***}
Ob 1:12 But you should not have gloated {Heb *But* ***do*** *not gloat* (and similarly through verse 14)}
Mk 11:25 + v.26 *"But if you* ***do*** *not forgive, neither will your Father in heaven forgive your trespasses."*
Lk 1:34 since I am a virgin?" {Gk *I* ***do*** *not know a man*}
6: 2 is not lawful {Other ancient authorities add *to* ***do***}
9:56 rebuked them. [56]Then {Other ancient authorities read *rebuked them, and said, "You* ***do*** *not know what spirit you are of,* [56]*for the Son of Man* >}
Jn 8:39 "If you were Abraham's children, you would be doing {Other ancient authorities read *If you are Abraham's children, then* ***do***}
1Pe 5: 2 as God would have you do it {Other ancient authorities lack *as God would have you* ***do*** *it*}
Rev 22:14 who wash their robes, {Other ancient authorities read ***do*** *his commandments*}
Sir 4:23 and do not hide your wisdom. {< Other Gk Mss lack *and* ***do*** *not hide your wisdom*}
19:17 its course. {Other ancient authorities add *and* ***do*** *not be angry,* >}
19:17 + v.19 < *and those who* ***do*** *what is pleasing to him enjoy the fruit of the tree of immortality.*
24:23 + v.24 *"****Do*** *not cease to be strong in the Lord,* >
2Es 4:35 'How long are we to remain here? {Syr Ethiop Arab 2 Georg: Lat *How long* ***do*** *I hope thus?*}

DOBRATH (1)
1Ch 6:72 Daberath {Or ***Dobrath***}

DODANIM (2)
Ge 10: 4 Rodanim. {Heb Mss Sam Gk See 1 Chr 1.7: MT ***Dodanim***}
1Ch 1: 7 Rodanim. {Gen 10.4 ***Dodanim***; See Syr Vg}

DOES (9)
Mt 17:20 + v.21 *But this kind* ***does*** *not come out except by prayer and fasting*
Mk 9:38 "Teacher, we saw someone {Other ancient authorities add *who* ***does*** *not follow us*}
16:14 risen. {Other ancient authorities add, in whole or in part, < *who* ***does*** *not allow the truth and power of God to prevail* >}
Sir 17:17 + v.18 < *and allotting to him the light of his love, he* ***does*** *not neglect him.*
19:20 + v.21 < *"I will not act as you wish," even if later he* ***does*** *it, he angers the one who supports him.*
20:17 how often! {Other ancient authorities add < *and what he* ***does*** *not have is unimportant to him*}
25: 8 and ... together. {Heb Syr: Gk lacks *and the one who* ***does*** *not plow with ox and ass together*}
30:20 a girl. {Other ancient authorities add *So is the person who* ***does*** *right under compulsion*}
4Mc 11: 5 It is because {Other ancient authorities read *Or* ***does*** *it seem evil to you that*}

DOG (1)
Dt 23:18 the wages of a male prostitute {Heb *a* ***dog***}

DOING (2)
Lk 23:34 Then ... doing." {Other ancient authorities lack the sentence *Then Jesus ... what they are* ***doing***}
Jn 7:31 this man has done?" {Other ancient authorities read *is* ***doing***}

DOME (3)
Ps 19: 1 the firmament {Or ***dome***} proclaims
150: 1 in his mighty firmament! {Or ***dome***}
Da 12: 3 the brightness of the sky, {Or ***dome***}

DOMINION (1)
Ps 49:14 to the grave they descend, {Cn: Heb *the upright shall have* ***dominion*** *over them in the morning*}

DONE (5)
1Sa 29:10 and go to ... done well before me. {Gk: Heb lacks *and go to the place ...* ***done*** *well before me*}
Lk 11: 2 kingdom come. {< Other ancient authorities add *Your will be* ***done****, on earth as in heaven*}
2Es 1:32 says the Lord. {Other ancient authorities add ... *these are the things you have* ***done.*** *... if I have not* ***done*** *the things my Father commanded,* >}
16:53 not sinned; {Other ancient authorities add *or the unjust* ***done*** *injustice*}

DONKEY (1)
Lk 14: 5 a child {Other ancient authorities read *a* ***donkey***}

DOOM (1)
Eze 30: 3 a time of doom {Heb lacks *of* ***doom***}

DOOR (1)
Eze 42: 2 on the north side {Gk: Heb ***door***}

DOUBLE (1)
Jer 50:21 land of Merathaim; {Or *of* ***Double*** *Rebellion*}

DOUBLE-TONGUED (1)
Sir 5: 9 every path. {Gk adds *so it is with the **double-tongued** sinner* (see 6.1)}

DOWN (7)
Jdg 11:37 go and wander {Cn: Heb *go **down***}
1Sa 9:25 and he lay down to sleep. {Gk: Heb lacks *and he lay **down** to sleep*}
2Sa 8:13 he killed ... Edomites {Gk: Heb *returned from striking **down** eighteen thousand Arameans*}
Isa 32:19 The forest will disappear completely, {Cn: Heb *And it will hail when the forest comes **down***}
42:10 Let the sea roar {Cn Compare Ps 96.11; 98.7: Heb *Those who go **down** to the sea*}
Jn 5: 3 + v.4 <*for an angel of the Lord went **down** at certain seasons into the pool*, >
AdE 9: 4 + v.5 *So the Jews struck **down** all their enemies with the sword*, >

DOWNFALL (2)
Mic 7:10 see her downfall; {Heb lacks ***downfall***}
Sir 11:30 they observe your weakness; {Heb: Gk ***downfall***}

DRACHMAS (1)
Lk 15: 8 ten silver coins, {Gk ***drachmas***, each worth about a day's wage for a laborer}

DRAGGED (1)
2Mc 6:28 he went {Other ancient authorities read *was **dragged***} at once

DRAGON (2)
Job 9: 8 trampled the waves of the Sea; {Or *trampled the back of the sea **dragon***}
2Es 15:31 And then the dragons, {Cn: Lat ***dragon***}

DRAINED (1)
Ps 73:10 and find no fault in them. {Cn: Heb *abundant waters are **drained** by them*}

DRANK (2)
Jdg 19: 8 and drank. {Gk: Heb lacks *and **drank***}
1Sa 1:18 and drank with her husband, {Gk: Heb lacks *and **drank** with her husband*}

DRAW (1)
Mk 16:14 risen. {Other ancient authorities add, in whole or in part, ... *but other terrible things **draw** near*. >}

DREAMS (1)
Jer 27: 9 your dreamers, {Gk Syr Vg: Heb ***dreams***}

DRINK (3)
Mt 6:25 or what you will drink, {Other ancient authorities lack *or what you will **drink***}
Mk 2:16 he eat {Other ancient authorities add *and **drink***}
Rev 18: 3 For all nations have drunk {Other ancient authorities read *she has made all nations **drink***}

DRIVES (1)
Sir 1:20 + v.21 *The fear of the Lord **drives** away sins*; >

DROSS (1)
Pr 26:23 Like the glaze {Cn: Heb *silver of **dross***}

DROUGHT (1)
1Ki 18: 1 of the drought, {Heb lacks *of the **drought***}

DRUNKARD (1)
Sir 19: 1 The one who does this {Heb: Gk *A worker who is a **drunkard***}

DRY (2)
2Es 15:61 broken down by them like stubble, {Other ancient authorities read *like **dry** straw*}
16: 6 fire in the stubble once it has started to burn? {Other ancient authorities read *fire when **dry** straw has been set on fire*}

DUG (1)
Ps 40: 6 you have given me an open ear. {Heb *ears you have **dug** for me*}

DURING (3)
Ps 127: 2 for he gives sleep to his beloved. {Or *for he provides for his beloved **during** sleep*}
Am 1: 1 two years {Or ***during** two years*} before
Sir 13:13 + v.14 < ***During** all your life love the Lord, and call on him for your salvation*.

DUST (2)
Job 19:25 stand upon the earth; {Heb ***dust***}
Wis 5:14 the ungodly is like thistledown {Other ancient authorities read ***dust***}

DWELLING (5)
Dt 33:27 He subdues the ancient gods, {Or *The eternal God is a **dwelling** place*}
Jer 9: 5 too weary to repent. {Cn Compare Gk: Heb *they weary themselves with iniquity. [6]Your **dwelling***
9: 6 Oppression upon oppression, deceit {Cn: Heb *Your **dwelling** in the midst of deceit*}
Zep 3: 7 it will not lose sight {Gk Syr: Heb *its **dwelling** will not be cut off*}
Ac 28:30 at his own expense {Or *in his own hired **dwelling***}

E

EACH (5)
1Ki 6:10 each story {Heb lacks ***each** story*}
1Ch 26:17 each day, {Gk: Heb lacks ***each** day*}
Jn 8: 8 on the ground. {Other ancient authorities add *the sins of **each** of them*}
Sir 18: 9 years. {Other ancient authorities add *but the death of **each** one is beyond the calculation of all*}
2Mc 4:36 the Jews in the city {Or *in **each** city*}

EAR (1)
Sir 38:28 deafens his ears, {Cn: Gk *renews his **ear***}

EARLY (1)
1Sa 9:26 Then at the break of dawn {Gk: Heb *and they arose **early** and at break of dawn*}

EARNESTLY (1)
2Pe 3:12 waiting for and hastening {Or ***earnestly** desiring*}

EARS (2)
Ps 40: 6 you have given me an open ear. {Heb ***ears** you have dug for me*}
Mk 7:15 + v.16 *"Let anyone with **ears** to hear listen"*

EARTH (10)
Ge 9:10 the ark. {Gk: Heb adds *every animal of the **earth***}
Jer 17:13 recorded in the underworld, {Or *in the **earth***}
Mt 27:45 over the whole land {Or ***earth***}
Mk 15:33 over the whole land {Or ***earth***}
Lk 11: 2 kingdom come. {< Other ancient authorities add *Your will be done, on **earth** as in heaven*}
23:44 over the whole land {Or ***earth***}
1Jn 5: 7 {A few other authorities read (with variations) ... [8]*And there are three that testify on **earth**:*}
Tob 12:20 now get up from the ground, {Other ancient authorities read *now bless the Lord on **earth***}
Sir 17:15 + v.17 < *For in the division of the nations of the whole **earth**, he appointed*
2Es 13: 4 melted as wax melts {Syr: Lat *burned as the **earth** rests*}

EARTH'S (1)
2Es 6:26 heart of the earth's {Syr Compare Ethiop Arab 1 Arm: Lat lacks ***earth's***}

EARTHQUAKES (1)
2Es 6: 3 the powers of movements {Or ***earthquakes***}

EASE (1)
Hos 11: 4 who lift infants to their cheeks. {Or *who **ease** the yoke on their jaws*}

EASIER (1)
2Es 13:20 Yet it is better {Ethiop Compare Arab 2: Lat ***easier***}

EASILY (1)
Heb 12: 1 sin that clings so closely, {Other ancient authorities read *sin that **easily** distracts*}

EAST (4)
Eze 40:19 hundred cubits. {Heb adds *the **east** and the north*}
42:10 on the south {Gk: Heb ***east***} also,
Mt 2: 2 star at its rising, {Or *in the **East***}
2: 9 star at its rising, {Or *in the **East***}

EASTWARD (1)
Ge 11: 2 migrated from the east, {Or *migrated **eastward***}

EAT (1)
Tob 10: 7 and would heed no one. {Other ancient authorities read *and she would **eat** nothing*}

EATEN (1)
Ps 22:29 To him, {Cn: Heb *They have **eaten** and*} indeed,

EATING (3)
Mt 6:19 moth and rust {Gk ***eating***} consume
6:20 moth nor rust {Gk ***eating***} consumes
Ac 1: 4 While staying {Or ***eating***} with them,

ECBATANA (1)
Tob 6: 6 Media. {Other ancient authorities read ***Ecbatana***}

ECLIPSED (1)
Lk 23:45 the sun's light failed; {Or *the sun was **eclipsed**.* >}

EDICT (1)
Ps 110: 4 forever according to the order of Melchizedek." {Or *forever, a rightful king by my **edict***}

EDOM (1)
Eze 16:57 Aram {Another reading is ***Edom***}

EDUCATION (1)
2Mc 7:27 have taken care of you. {Or *have borne the burden of your **education***}

EDUTH (39)
Ex 16:34 covenant, {Or *treaty* or *testimony*; Heb ***eduth***}
25:16 covenant {Or *treaty*, or *testimony*; Heb ***eduth***}
25:21 covenant {Or *treaty*, or *testimony*; Heb ***eduth***}
25:22 covenant {Or *treaty*, or *testimony*; Heb ***eduth***}
26:33 covenant {Or *treaty*, or *testimony*; Heb ***eduth***}
26:34 covenant {Or *treaty*, or *testimony*; Heb ***eduth***}
27:21 covenant {Or *treaty*, or *testimony*; Heb ***eduth***}
30: 6 covenant {Or *treaty*, or *testimony*; Heb ***eduth***}
30: 6 covenant, {Or *treaty*, or *testimony*; Heb ***eduth***}
30:26 covenant, {Or *treaty*, or *testimony*; Heb ***eduth***}
30:36 covenant {Or *treaty*, or *testimony*; Heb ***eduth***}
31: 7 covenant, {Or *treaty*, or *testimony*; Heb ***eduth***}
31:18 covenant, {Or *treaty*, or *testimony*; Heb ***eduth***}
32:15 covenant {Or *treaty*, or *testimony*; Heb ***eduth***}
34:29 covenant {Or *treaty*, or *testimony*; Heb ***eduth***}
38:21 covenant, {Or *treaty*, or *testimony*; Heb ***eduth***}
39:35 covenant {Or *treaty*, or *testimony*; Heb ***eduth***}
40: 3 covenant, {Or *treaty*, or *testimony*; Heb ***eduth***}
40: 5 covenant, {Or *treaty*, or *testimony*; Heb ***eduth***}
40:20 covenant {Or *treaty*, or *testimony*; Heb ***eduth***}
40:21 covenant; {Or *treaty*, or *testimony*; Heb ***eduth***}
Lev 16:13 covenant, {Or *treaty*, or *testament*; Heb ***eduth***}
24: 3 covenant, {Or *treaty*, or *testament*; Heb ***eduth***}
Nu 1:50 covenant, {Or *treaty*, or *testimony*; Heb ***eduth***}
1:53 covenant, {Or *treaty*, or *testimony*; Heb ***eduth***}
1:53 covenant. {Or *treaty*, or *testimony*; Heb ***eduth***}
4: 5 covenant {Or *treaty*, or *testimony*; Heb ***eduth***}
7:89 covenant {Or *treaty*, or *testimony*; Heb ***eduth***}
9:15 covenant; {Or *treaty*, or *testimony*; Heb ***eduth***}
10:11 covenant. {Or *treaty*, or *testimony*; Heb ***eduth***}
17: 4 covenant, {Or *treaty*, or *testimony*; Heb ***eduth***}
17: 7 covenant. {Or *treaty*, or *testimony*; Heb ***eduth***}
17: 8 covenant {Or *treaty*, or *testimony*; Heb ***eduth***}
17:10 covenant, {Or *treaty*, or *testimony*; Heb ***eduth***}
18: 2 covenant. {Or *treaty*, or *testimony*; Heb ***eduth***}
Jos 4:16 covenant, {Or *treaty*, or *testimony*; Heb ***eduth***}
2Ki 11:12 covenant; {Or *treaty* or *testimony*; Heb ***eduth***}
2Ch 23:11 covenant; {Or *treaty*, or *testimony*; Heb ***eduth***}
24: 6 covenant?" {Or *treaty*, or *testimony*; Heb ***eduth***}

EFFECTIVE (1)
Gal 5: 6 faith working {Or *made **effective***} through love.

EFFECTS (1)
2Es 9: 6 end in penalties {Syr: Lat Ethiop *in **effects***}

EGYPT (7)
Ge 50:11 Abel-mizraim; {That is *mourning* (or *meadow*) *of **Egypt***}
2Sa 7:23 before his people nations and their gods? {Cn: Heb *before your people, whom you redeemed for yourself from **Egypt**, nations and its gods*}
Jer 26:22 Jehoiakim sent {Heb adds *men to **Egypt***} Elnathan
Eze 23:21 When the Egyptians {Two Mss: MT *from **Egypt***}
30: 9 the day of Egypt's doom; {Heb *the day of **Egypt***}
47:19 the Wadi of Egypt {Heb lacks *of **Egypt***}
48:28 the Wadi of Egypt {Heb lacks *of **Egypt***}

EGYPTIAN (1)
Heb 11:23 king's edict. {Other ancient authorities add *By faith Moses, when he was grown up, killed the **Egyptian**,* >}

EGYPTIANS (1)
1Sa 12: 8 and the Egyptians oppressed them, {Gk: Heb lacks *and the **Egyptians** oppressed them*}

EHUD (1)
1Ch 8: 3 Abihud, {Or *father of **Ehud***; see 8.6}

EL (13)
Ge 14:18 God Most High. {Heb ***El** Elyon*}
14:19 God Most High, {Heb ***El** Elyon*}
14:20 God Most High, {Heb ***El** Elyon*}
14:22 God Most High, {Heb ***El** Elyon*}
17: 1 God Almighty; {Traditional rendering of Heb ***El** Shaddai*}
21:33 the Everlasting God. {Or *the* LORD, ***El** Olam*}
28: 3 Almighty {Traditional rendering of Heb ***El** Shaddai*}
35:11 God Almighty: {Traditional rendering of Heb ***El** Shaddai*}
43:14 God Almighty {Traditional rendering of Heb ***El** Shaddai*}
48: 3 God Almighty {Traditional rendering of Heb ***El** Shaddai*}
Ex 6: 3 God Almighty, {Traditional rendering of Heb ***El** Shaddai*}
Isa 8:10 for God is with us. {Heb *immanu **el***}
Eze 10: 5 God Almighty {Traditional rendering of Heb ***El** Shaddai*}

ELATED (1)
2Co 12: 7 to keep me from being too elated. {Other ancient authorities lack *to keep me from being too* ***elated***}

ELDER (1)
1Ti 5: 1 an older man, {Or *an* ***elder***, or *a presbyter*}

ELEMENTS (1)
Sir 16:27 their dominion {Or ***elements***} for all generations.

ELEVEN (2)
Eze 40:49 the width twelve {Gk: Heb ***eleven***} cubits;
Ac 19: 9 Tyrannus. {Other ancient authorities read *of a certain Tyrannus, from* ***eleven*** *o'clock in the morning to four in the afternoon*}

ELI (1)
Ex 18: 4 Eliezer {Heb ***Eli***, my God; *ezer*, help}

ELIJAH (2)
Lk 9:54 and consume them?" {Other ancient authorities add *as* ***Elijah*** *did*}
2Es 1:40 and Jacob, and Hosea ... of the Lord. {Other ancient authorities read *and Jacob,* ***Elijah*** >}

ELIZABETH (1)
Lk 1:46 Mary {Other ancient authorities read ***Elizabeth***}

ELOHIM (1)
Ps 8: 5 a little lower than God, {Or *than the divine beings* or *angels*: Heb ***elohim***}

ELSE (1)
Pr 25: 8 for {Cn: Heb *or* ***else***} what will you do

ELYON (6)
Ge 14:18 God Most High. {Heb *El* ***Elyon***}
14:19 God Most High, {Heb *El* ***Elyon***}
14:20 God Most High, {Heb *El* ***Elyon***}
14:22 God Most High, {Heb *El* ***Elyon***}
Nu 24:16 of the Most High, {Or *of* ***Elyon***}
Dt 32: 8 Most High {Traditional rendering of Heb ***Elyon***}

EMBARRASSED (1)
4Mc 3:12 respecting {Or ***embarrassed*** *because of*} the king's desire,

EMBROIDERY (1)
Ps 45:13 The princess is decked in her chamber with gold-woven robes; {Or ... *All glorious is the princess within, gold* ***embroidery*** *is her clothing*}

EMINENT (1)
2Es 15:40 every high and lofty place {Or ***eminent*** *person*}

EMOTIONS (1)
4Mc 1:28 of these plants, {Other ancient authorities read *these* ***emotions***}

EMPTY (1)
2Es 15:19 shall make an assault upon {Cn: Lat *shall* ***empty***}

ENCAMPED (1)
2Sa 24: 5 began from {Gk Mss: Heb ***encamped*** *in Aroer south of*} Aroer

ENCAMPS (1)
Ps 53: 5 scatter the bones of the ungodly; {Cn Compare Gk Syr: Heb *him who* ***encamps*** *against you*}

ENCIRCLED (1)
1Ki 7:15 and a cord of twelve cubits would encircle it; the second pillar was the same. {Cn: Heb *and a cord of twelve cubits* ***encircled*** *the second pillar*; >}

ENCOURAGE (1)
2Co 13:11 listen to my appeal, {Or ***encourage*** *one another*}

END (7)
Jer 8:13 When I wanted to gather them ... there are {Or *I will make an* ***end*** *of them, says the* LORD. *There are*}
Da 11:13 and after some years {Heb *and at the* ***end*** *of the times years*}
12:13 go your way, {Gk Theodotion: Heb adds *to the* ***end***}
Heb 3: 6 if we hold firm {Other ancient authorities add *to the* ***end***}
Sir 16: 3 their numbers; {Other ancient authorities add *For you will groan in untimely mourning, and will know of their sudden* ***end***.}
Sir 16:22 far off." {Other ancient authorities add *and a scrutiny for all comes at the* ***end***}
2Es 6: 1 "At the beginning ... before {Meaning of Lat uncertain: Compare Syr *The beginning by the hand of humankind, but the* ***end*** *by my own* >}

ENDED (1)
Wis 4:16 youth that is quickly perfected {Or ***ended***}

ENDURANCE (1)
Sir 20:31 + v.32 *Unwearied* ***endurance*** *in seeking the Lord is better than a masterless charioteer of one's own life.*

ENDURING (1)
Pr 13:15 faithless is their ruin. {Cn Compare Gk Syr Vg Tg: Heb *is* ***enduring***}

ENEMESSAROS (4)
Tob 1: 2 Shalmaneser {Gk ***Enemessaros***}
1:13 Shalmaneser, {Gk ***Enemessaros***}
1:15 Shalmaneser {Gk ***Enemessaros***}
1:16 Shalmaneser {Gk ***Enemessaros***}

ENEMIES (3)
1Sa 25:22 God do so to David {Gk Compare Syr: Heb *the* ***enemies*** *of David*}
2Sa 12:14 scorned the LORD, {< Heb *scorned the* ***enemies*** *of the* LORD}
AdE 9: 4 + v.5 *So the Jews struck down all their* ***enemies*** >

ENEMY (1)
Sir 46: 7 the congregation, {Other ancient authorities read *the* ***enemy***}

ENEMY'S (1)
Sir 25:15 a woman's {Other ancient authorities read *an* ***enemy's***} wrath

ENJOY (1)
Sir 19:17 + v.19 < *and those who do what is pleasing to him* ***enjoy*** *the fruit of the tree of immortality.*

ENLARGED (2)
Ps 25:17 Relieve the troubles of my heart, and bring me {Or *The troubles of my heart are* ***enlarged***; >}
Isa 60: 5 heart shall thrill and rejoice, {Heb *be* ***enlarged***}

ENMITY (1)
Ge 26:21 Sitnah. {That is ***Enmity***}

ENOCH (3)
2Es 1:40 and Jacob, and Hosea ... Lord. {Other ancient authorities read *and Jacob, Elijah and* ***Enoch***, >}
6:49 Behemoth {Other Lat authorities read ***Enoch***}
6:51 Behemoth {Other Lat authorities read ***Enoch***}

ENTERED (2)
1Sa 10:27 Now Nahash ... entered Jabesh-gilead. {Q Ms Compare Josephus, *Antiquities* VI.v.1 (68-71): MT lacks *Now Nahash ...* ***entered*** *Jabesh-gilead.*}
Eze 41: 6 There were offsets {Gk Compare 1 Kings 6.6: Heb *they* ***entered***}

ENTERS (1)
Sir 36:29 gets his best possession, {Heb: Gk ***enters*** *upon a possession*}

ENTRAILS (1)
Sir 21:14 The mind {Syr Lat: Gk ***entrails***} of a fool

ENTRANCE (1)
Eze 44: 5 who may be admitted to {Cn: Heb *the* ***entrance*** *of*} the temple

ENTRANCES (2)
Mic 5: 6 with the drawn sword; {Cn: Heb *in its* ***entrances***}
2Es 4: 7 of Hades, or which are the entrances {Syr Compare Ethiop Arab 2 Arm: Lat lacks *of Hades, or which are the* ***entrances***}

ENTREATY (1)
Wis 12:20 with great care and indulgence {Other ancient authorities lack *and indulgence*; others read *and* ***entreaty***}

ENVIOUS (1)
Sir 20:14 profit you nothing, {Other ancient authorities add *so it is with the* ***envious*** *who give under compulsion*}

EPHAH (6)
Zec 5: 6 basket {Heb ***ephah***}
5: 7 basket! {Heb ***ephah***}
5: 8 basket, {Heb ***ephah***}
5: 9 basket {Heb ***ephah***}
5:10 basket?" {Heb ***ephah***}
5:11 basket {Heb ***ephah***}

EPHESUS (1)
Eph 1: 1 saints who are in Ephesus and are faithful {Other ancient authorities lack *in* ***Ephesus***, reading *saints who are also faithful*}

EPHOD (2)
1Sa 14:18 the ark {Gk *the* ***ephod***} of God
14:18 the ark {Gk *the* ***ephod***} of God

EPHRAIN (1)
2Ch 13:19 Ephron {Another reading is ***Ephrain***}

EPIPHANY (1)
3Mc 2: 9 by your magnificent manifestation, {Or ***epiphany***}

ERROR (1)
Sir 11:14 + v.16 < ***Error*** *and darkness were created with sinners;* >

ESCAPE (1)
Sir 20: 8 is hated. {Other ancient authorities add *How good it is to show repentance when you are reproved, for so you will* ***escape*** *deliberate sin!*}

ESTABLISH (2)
Pr 21:29 give thoughts to {Another reading is ***establish***} their ways.
Sir 37:13 And heed {Heb: Gk ***establish***} the counsel

ESTABLISHED (3)
2Es 10:27 but a city was being built, {Lat: Syr Ethiop Arab 1 Arab 2 Arm *but there was an* ***established*** *city*}
10:42 a city being built) {Lat: Syr Ethiop Arab 1 Arab 2 Arm *an* ***established*** *city*}
10:44 a city being built. {Cn: Lat *an* ***established*** *city*}

ESTABLISHES (1)
Sir 28: 1 for he keeps a strict account of {Other ancient authorities read *for he firmly* ***establishes***} their sins.

ESTEEMED (1)
Sir 41:16 nor is every kind of abashment to be approved. {Heb: Gk *and not everything is confidently* ***esteemed*** *by everyone*}

ESYELUS (1)
1Es 1: 8 Jehiel, {Gk ***Esyelus***}

ETERNAL (5)
Dt 33:27 He subdues the ancient gods, {Or *The* ***eternal*** *God is a dwelling place*}
Isa 44: 7 from of old the things to come? {Cn: Heb *from my placing an* ***eternal*** *people and things to come*}
Sir 1: 4 + v.5 < *and her ways are the* ***eternal*** *commandments.*
24:17 + v.18 < *being* ***eternal***, *I am given to all my children, to those who are named by him.*
30:17 and eternal sleep {Other ancient authorities lack ***eternal*** *sleep*}

ETHIOPIA (1)
AdE 1: 1 to Ethiopia. {Other ancient authorities lack *to* ***Ethiopia***}

ETHNARCH (1)
2Co 11:32 the governor {Gk ***ethnarch***}

EVENING (1)
3Mc 5:12 deep a sleep {Other ancient authorities add *from* ***evening*** *until the ninth hour*}

EVENINGS (6)
Lev 23: 5 at twilight, {Heb *between the two* ***evenings***}
Nu 9: 3 at twilight, {Heb *between the two* ***evenings***}
9: 5 at twilight, {Heb *between the two* ***evenings***}
9:11 at twilight, {Heb *between the two* ***evenings***}
28: 4 at twilight {Heb *between the two* ***evenings***}
28: 8 at twilight {Heb *between the two* ***evenings***}

EVER (2)
2Es 14:48 did so. {Syr adds < *And he was called the scribe of the knowledge of the Most High for* ***ever*** *and* ***ever***. >}

EVERLASTING (2)
Dt 33:27 the forces of old; {Or *the* ***everlasting*** *arms*}
Sir 2: 9 joy and mercy. {Other ancient authorities add *For his reward is an* ***everlasting*** *gift with joy.*}

EVERY (8)
Ge 9:10 out of the ark. {Gk: Heb adds ***every*** *animal of the earth*}
Jer 9: 4 for all your kin {Heb *for* ***every*** *brother*}
Mk 9:49 "For everyone will be salted with fire. {Other ancient authorities either add or substitute *and* ***every*** *sacrifice will be salted with salt*}
2Th 3: 6 from believers who are {Gk *from* ***every*** *brother who is*}
2Ti 3:16 All scripture is inspired by God and is {Or ***Every*** *scripture inspired by God is also*}
Rev 18: 2 a haunt of every foul and hateful beast. {Other ancient authorities lack *a haunt of* ***every*** *foul beast* and attach the words *and hateful* to the previous line so as to read *a haunt of* ***every*** *foul and hateful bird*}
Sir 42:23 preserved to meet a particular need. {Heb: Gk *forever for* ***every*** *need, and all are obedient*}

EVERYONE (2)
Isa 33: 8 its obligation {Or ***everyone***} is disregarded.
Sir 41:16 nor is every kind of abashment to be approved. {Heb: Gk *and not everything is confidently esteemed by* ***everyone***}

EVERYTHING (4)
Ecc 9: 2 is vanity, {Syr Compare Gk: Heb ... *is* ***everything***}
Sir 22:13 unintelligent person. {Other ancient authorities add ... *he will despise* ***everything*** *about you*}
41:16 nor is every kind of abashment to be approved. {Heb: Gk *and not* ***everything*** *is confidently esteemed by everyone*}
Pm 151: 3 he who hears. {Other ancient authorities add ***everything***; >}

EVIL (10)
Pr 6:24 the wife of another, {Gk: MT *the* ***evil*** *woman*}
Ecc 9: 2 and the evil, {Gk Syr Vg: Heb lacks *and the* ***evil***}
Mt 20:15 are you envious because I am generous?' {Gk *is your eye* ***evil*** *because I am good?*}
Lk 6:22 and defame you {Gk *cast out your name as* ***evil***}
11: 4 to the time of trial." {< Other ancient authorities add *but rescue us from the* ***evil*** *one* (*or from* ***evil***)}
Sir 11:14 + v.16 < ***evil*** *grows old with those who take pride in malice.*
17:15 + v.16 *Their ways from youth tend toward* ***evil,*** >
2Es 8:53 The root of evil {Lat lacks *of* ***evil***}
4Mc 11: 5 Is it because {Other ancient authorities read *Or does it seem* ***evil*** *to you that*} we revere

EXALTED (3)
Ge 17: 5 Abram, {That is ***exalted*** *ancestor*}
Ps 89:16 extol {Cn: Heb *are* ***exalted*** *in*} your righteousness.
140: 8 their evil plot. {Heb adds *they are* ***exalted***}

EXALTS (1)
Sir 4:11 Wisdom teaches {Heb Syr: Gk ***exalts***}

EXAMINATION (1)
Wis 4: 6 God examines them. {Gk *at their* ***examination***}

EXCEEDINGLY (1)
Ps 31:11 a horror {Cn: Heb ***exceedingly***} to my neighbors,

EXCELLED (1)
3Mc 6:26 differed from {Or ***excelled*** *above*} all nations

EXCELLENCY (1)
Ac 24: 2 Your Excellency, {Gk lacks *Your* ***Excellency***}

EXCEPT (2)
Mt 17:20 + v.21 *But this kind does not come out* ***except*** *by prayer and fasting*
Jn 13:10 except for the feet, {Other ancient authorities lack ***except*** *for the feet*}

EXCHANGE (1)
Sir 44:17 Kept the race alive; {Heb: Gk *was taken in* ***exchange***}

EXCLAIMED (1)
Jdg 5:28 gazed {Gk Compare Tg: Heb ***exclaimed***} through

EXCUSED (1)
Mk 16:14 risen. {Other ancient authorities add, in whole or in part, *And they* ***excused*** *themselves, saying,* >}

EXERCISING (1)
1Pe 5: 2 exercising the oversight, {Other ancient authorities lack ***exercising*** *the oversight*}

EXILE (1)
1Ch 8: 7 Heglam, {Or *he carried them into* ***exile***}

EXIST (1)
2Mc 7:28 God did not make them out of things that existed. {Or *God made them out of things that did not* ***exist***}

EXISTED (1)
2Es 6: 1 "At the beginning ... before {< Compare Syr: ... *For as before the land of the world* ***existed*** *there, and before;* >}

EXPECTATION (1)
Sir 7:17 the punishment of the ungodly is fire and worms. {Heb *for the* ***expectation*** *of mortals is worms*}

EXPERIENCE (1)
Sir 1: 6 + v.7 < *And her abundant* ***experience***—*who has understood it?*

EXPOSED (1)
2Es 16:30 some clusters may be left {Other ancient authorities read *a cluster may remain* ***exposed***}

EXTENT (1)
Eze 11:16 for a little while {Or *to some* ***extent***}

EXTINCTION (1)
2Pe 2: 6 condemned them to extinction {Other ancient authorities lack *to* ***extinction***}

EXTINGUISHED (1)
Ps 118:12 blazed {Gk: Heb *were* ***extinguished***} like a fire

EXULT (1)
Hos 10: 5 idolatrous priests shall wail {Cn: Heb ***exult***}

EXULTATION (1)
Hos 9: 1 Do not exult {Gk: Heb *To* ***exultation***}

EYE (5)
Zec 5: 6 their iniquity {Gk Compare Syr: Heb *their* ***eye***}
9: 1 the capital {Heb ***eye***} of Aram,
Mt 20:15 are you envious because I am generous?' {Gk *is your* ***eye*** *evil because I am good?*}
Sir 16:21 Like a tempest that no one can see, ... concealed. {Meaning of Gk uncertain: Heb Syr *If I sin, no* ***eye*** *can see me, and if I am disloyal* >}
17: 8 He put the fear of him into {Other ancient authorities read *He set his* ***eye*** *upon*}

EYES (3)
Job 40:24 take it with hooks {Cn: Heb *in his* ***eyes***}
Sir 20:14 he looks for recompense sevenfold. {Syr: Gk *he has many* ***eyes*** *instead of one*}
2Es 9:38 I looked around, {Syr Arab Arm: Lat *I looked about me with my* ***eyes***}

EYING (1)
AdE 13:15 for the eyes of our foes are upon us {Gk *for they are* ***eying*** *us*}

EZER (1)
Ex 18: 4 Eliezer {Heb *Eli*, my God; ***ezer***, help}

EZRA (5)
Ne 9: 6 And Ezra said: {Gk: Heb lacks *And* ***Ezra*** *said*}
1Es 8:25 Then Ezra the scribe said, {Other ancient authorities lack *Then* ***Ezra*** *the scribe said*}
8:95 Rise up {Other ancient authorities read ... *rose and said to* ***Ezra,*** *"Rise up*}
2Es 7:49 "Listen to me, Ezra, {Syr Arab 1 Georg: Lat Ethiop lack ***Ezra***}
14:48 {Syr adds < *At that time* ***Ezra*** *was caught up,* >}

F

FACE (8)
Ge 32:30 Peniel, {That is *The* ***face*** *of God*}
Pr 27:17 one person sharpens the wits {Heb ***face***}
Isa 1:12 come to appear before me, {Or *see my* ***face***}
53: 3 as one from whom others hide their faces {Or *as one who hides his* ***face*** *from us*}
Mk 1: 2 messenger ahead of you, {Gk *before your* ***face***}
Lk 18: 5 by continually coming.' " {Or *so that she may not finally come and slap me in the* ***face***}
Jas 1:23 look at themselves {Gk *at the* ***face*** *of his birth*}
2Es 15:32 and shall turn and flee. {Other ancient authorities read *turn their* ***face*** *to the north*}

FACES (2)
Eze 1:15 of the four of them. {Heb *of their* ***faces***}
2Es 13:13 Then many people {Lat Syr Arab 2 literally *the* ***faces*** *of many people*}

FACING (1)
Eze 40:13 from wall to wall. {Heb *opening* ***facing*** *opening*}

FACTORY (1)
3Mc 4:20 both the paper {Or *paper* ***factory***} and the pens

FACULTIES (2)
Sir 17: 4 + v.5 *They obtained the use of the five* ***faculties*** *of the Lord; ... and as seventh, reason, the interpreter of one's* ***faculties.***

FAITH (7)
Ro 5: 2 have obtained access {Other ancient authorities add *by* ***faith***}
Eph 4:29 useful for building up, {Other ancient authorities read *building up* ***faith***}
Heb 11:23 king's edict. {Other ancient authorities add *By* ***faith*** *Moses, when he was grown up, killed the* >}
Jas 2: 1 do you with your acts of favoritism really believe in our glorious Lord Jesus Christ? {Or *hold the* ***faith*** *of our glorious Lord Jesus Christ without acts of favoritism*}
Sir 25:11 + v.12 < ***faith*** *is the beginning of clinging to him.*
2Es 7:29 all who draw human breath. {Arm *all who have continued in* ***faith*** *and in patience*}
2Es 15: 4 in their unbelief. {Other ancient authorities add *and all who believe shall be saved by their* ***faith***}

FAITHFUL (1)
Sir 4:17 until she dreads them, {Or *until they remain* ***faithful*** *in their heart*}

FAITHFULNESS (1)
Hab 2: 4 righteous live by their faith. {Or ***faithfulness***}

FALL (5)
Ps 106:27 would disperse {Syr Compare Ezek 20.23: Heb *cause to* ***fall***} their descendants
Pr 11:28 trust in their riches will wither, {Cn: Heb ***fall***}
1Co 15:51 We will not all die, {Gk ***fall*** *asleep*}
Sir 38:15 will be defiant toward the physician. {Heb: Gk *may he* ***fall*** *into the hands of the physician*}
LtJ 6:27 if any of these gods falls {Gk *if they* ***fall***}

FALLEN (10)
Eze 24: 6 piece, making no choice at all. {Heb *piece, no lot has* ***fallen*** *on it*}
Ac 8:16 the Spirit had not yet come {Gk ***fallen***}
1Co 11:30 died. {Gk ***fallen*** *asleep*}
15: 6 died. {Gk ***fallen*** *asleep*}
15:18 died {Gk ***fallen*** *asleep*}
15:20 died. {Gk ***fallen*** *asleep*}
1Th 4:13 died, {Gk ***fallen*** *asleep*}
4:14 died. {Gk ***fallen*** *asleep*}
4:15 died. {Gk ***fallen*** *asleep*}
2Mc 7:36 have drunk {Cn: Gk ***fallen***} of everflowing life,

FALLS (1)
1Co 7:39 if the husband dies, {Gk ***falls*** *asleep*}

FALSELY (2)
Zec 5: 3 falsely {The word ***falsely*** added from verse 4}
Mt 5:11 falsely {Other ancient authorities lack ***falsely***}

FALTERED (1)
2Mc 13:19 was turned back, attacked again, {Or ***faltered***}

FAMILY (1)
Sir 29:23 reproach for being a guest. {Lat: Gk *reproach from your* ***family***; other ancient authorities lack this line}

FAR (1)
Isa 14:13 heights of Zaphon; {Or *assembly in the* ***far*** *north*}

FAREWELL (5)
Ac 23:30 him." {Other ancient authorities add ***Farewell***}
Php 3: 1 rejoice {Or ***farewell***} in the Lord.
4: 4 Rejoice {Or ***Farewell***} in the Lord always; again I will say, Rejoice. {Or ***Farewell***}
4Mc 15:24 all these {Other ancient authorities read *having bidden them* ***farewell,*** *surrendered them*}

FASHIONED (1)
Ex 32: 4 formed it in a mold, {Or ***fashioned*** *it with a graving tool*; Meaning of Heb uncertain}

FAST (9)
Lev 16:29 you shall deny yourselves, {Or *shall* ***fast***}
16:31 you shall deny yourselves; {Or *shall* ***fast***}
23:27 you shall deny yourselves {Or *shall* ***fast***}
23:29 does not practice self-denial {Or *does not* ***fast***}
23:32 you shall deny yourselves; {Or *shall* ***fast***}
Nu 29: 7 and deny yourselves; {Or *and* ***fast***}
30:13 to deny herself, {Or *to* ***fast***}
Ezr 8:21 that we might deny ourselves {Or *might* ***fast***}
2Es 3:18 shook {Syr Ethiop Arab 1 Georg: Lat *set* ***fast***}

FASTING (2)
Mt 17:20 + v.21 *But this kind does not come out except by prayer and* ***fasting***
Mk 9:29 out only through prayer." {Other ancient authorities add *and* ***fasting***}

FAT (2)
Ps 22:29 all who sleep in {Cn: Heb *all the* ***fat*** *ones*}
63: 5 with a rich feast, {Heb *with* ***fat*** *and fatness*}

FATE (1)
4Mc 8:24 Let us not struggle against compulsion {Or ***fate***}

FATHER (17)
1Ch 4: 3 sons {Gk Compare Vg: Heb *the* ***father***}
8: 3 Abihud, {Or ***father*** *of Ehud*; see 8.6}
Pr 13: 1 A wise child loves discipline, {Cn: Heb *A wise child the discipline of his* ***father***}
Da 5:11 and diviners, {Aram adds *the king your* ***father***}
Mk 11:25 + v.26 < *neither will your* ***Father*** *in heaven forgive your trespasses."*
14:36 "Abba, {Aramaic for ***Father***}
Jn 16:27 I came from God. {Other ancient authorities read *the* ***Father***}
Ro 8:15 "Abba! {Aramaic for ***Father***}
Gal 4: 6 "Abba! {Aramaic for ***Father***}
Col 2: 2 of God's mystery, that is, Christ himself, {Other ancient authorities read *of the mystery of God, both of the* ***Father*** *and of Christ*}

1Jn 5: 7 that testify: {A few other authorities read (with variations) [7]*There are three that testify in heaven, the **Father**, the Word, and the Holy Spirit,* >}
Wis 11:10 tested them as a parent {Gk *a **father***}
Sir 3: 7 they will serve their parents as their masters. {In other ancient authorities this line is preceded by *Those who fear the Lord honor their **father**,*}
2Es 1:32 says the Lord. {Other ancient authorities add ... *not as a **father** who freed you from slavery, ... let my **Father** and his angels return and judge ... if I have not kept the commandment of the commandment of the **Father**, ... if I have not done the things my **Father** commanded,* >}

FATHER'S (3)
Dt 13: 6 your father's son or {Sam Gk Compare Tg: MT lacks *your **father's** son or*}
Jn 1:14 a father's only son, {Or *the **Father's** only Son*}
Heb 12:17 he found no chance to repent, {Or *no chance to change his **father's** mind*}

FATHERHOOD (1)
Eph 3:15 from whom every family {Gk ***fatherhood***}

FATHERS (3)
Ps 109:14 the iniquity of his father {Cn: Heb ***fathers***}
Isa 14:21 of their father. {Syr Compare Gk: Heb ***fathers***}
2Pe 3: 4 our ancestors died, {Gk *our **fathers** fell asleep*}

FATNESS (2)
Ps 63: 5 with a rich feast, {Heb *with fat and **fatness***}
Isa 10:27 and his yoke will be destroyed from your neck. He has gone up from Rimmon, {Cn: Heb ... *and a yoke will be destroyed because of **fatness***}

FAVOR (2)
Tob 7:16 joy {Other ancient authorities read ***favor***}
Sir 8:19 or you may drive away your happiness. {Heb: Gk *and let him not return a **favor** to you*}

FEAR (8)
Ps 72: 5 May he live {Gk: Heb *may they **fear** you*}
Sir 1:12 and long life. {Other ancient authorities add *The **fear** of the Lord is a gift from the Lord;* >}
1:20 + v.21 *The **fear** of the Lord drives away sins;* >
3: 7 they will serve their parents as their masters. {In other ancient authorities this line is preceded by *Those who **fear** the Lord honor their father,*}
10:20 + v.21 *The **fear** of the Lord is the beginning of acceptance;* >
19:17 + v.18 < *The **fear** of the Lord is the beginning of acceptance,* >
24:17 + v.18 *I am the mother of beautiful love, of **fear**, of knowledge, and of holy hope;* >
25:11 + v.12 *The **fear** of the Lord is the beginning of love for him,* >

FEARED (1)
Jdt 16:11 my weak people cried out, {Other ancient authorities read ***feared***}

FEARS (1)
Sir 32:14 who seeks God {Heb: Gk *who **fears** the Lord*}

FEAST (3)
2Sa 13:27 Absalom made a feast like a king's feast. {Gk Compare Q Ms: MT lacks *Absalom made a **feast** like a king's **feast***}
AdE 1: 5 at the end of the festivity {Gk *marriage **feast***}

FEASTS (1)
2Pe 2:13 reveling in their dissipation {Other ancient authorities read *love **feasts***}

FEED (1)
Job 24:21 They harm {Gk Tg: Heb ***feed** on* or *associate with*} the childless woman,

FEEDING (9)
Ecc 1:14 chasing after wind. {Or *a **feeding** on wind.* >}
1:17 chasing after wind. {Or *a **feeding** on wind.* >}
2:11 chasing after wind. {Or *a **feeding** on wind.* >}
2:17 chasing after wind. {Or *a **feeding** on wind.* >}
2:26 chasing after wind. {Or *a **feeding** on wind.* >}
4: 4 chasing after wind. {Or *a **feeding** on wind.* >}
4: 6 chasing after wind. {Or *a **feeding** on wind.* >}
4:16 chasing after wind. {Or *a **feeding** on wind.* >}
6: 9 chasing after wind. {Or *a **feeding** on wind.* >}

FEELINGS (1)
4Mc 11: 6 + v.7 *If you but understood human **feelings*** >

FEET (6)
Jdg 3:24 relieving himself {Heb *covering his **feet***}
1Sa 24: 3 to relieve himself. {Heb *to cover his **feet***}
Jn 12: 3 wiped them {Gk *his **feet***} with her hair.
13:10 except for the feet, {Other ancient authorities lack *except for the **feet***}
AdE 16: 7 matters close at hand. {Gk *matters beside* (your) ***feet***}
3Mc 4: 8 seeing death immediately before them. {Gk *seeing Hades already lying at their **feet***}

FELL (5)
Ge 25:18 he settled down {Heb *he **fell***}
41:22 I fell asleep a second time {Gk Syr Vg: Heb lacks *I **fell** asleep a second time*}
Ac 7:60 died. {Gk ***fell** asleep*}
13:36 died, {Gk ***fell** asleep*}
2Pe 3: 4 our ancestors died, {Gk *our fathers **fell** asleep*}

FESTIVAL (2)
Lk 23:16 + v.17 *Now he was obliged to release someone for them at the **festival***
Ac 18:21 he said, "I {Other ancient authorities read *I must at all costs keep the approaching **festival** in Jerusalem, but I*} will return to you,

FEW (2)
Mt 20:16 will be last." {Other ancient authorities add *for many are called but **few** are chosen*}
Lk 10:42 need of only one thing. {Other ancient authorities read ***few** things are necessary, or only one*}

FIELD (5)
Ge 4: 8 "Let us go out to the field." {Sam Gk Syr Compare Vg: MT lacks *Let us go out to the **field***}
2Sa 2:16 Helkath-hazzurim, {That is ***Field** of Sword-edges*}
Isa 37:27 blighted {With 2 Kings 19.26: Heb ***field***}
Jer 18:14 the crags of Sirion? {Cn: Heb *of the **field***}
Lk 17:35 + v.36 *"Two will be in the **field**; one will be taken and the other left."*

FIERY (4)
Nu 21: 6 poisonous {Or ***fiery***; Heb *seraphim*} serpents
Nu 21: 8 poisonous {Or ***fiery***; Heb *seraph*} serpent
Dt 8:15 poisonous {Or ***fiery***; Heb *seraph*} snakes
4Mc 7:11 fiery {Other ancient authorities lack ***fiery***} angel,

FIFTEEN (1)
Jn 11:18 some two miles {Gk ***fifteen** stadia*} away,

FIFTEENTH (1)
AdE 10:13 and fifteenth {Other ancient authorities lack *and **fifteenth***} of that month,

FIFTY (4)
1Sa 6:19 killed seventy men of them. {Heb *killed seventy men, **fifty** thousand men*}
Tob 1:21 not forty {Other ancient authorities read either *forty-five* or ***fifty***} days passed
2Mc 12:17 they had gone ninety-five miles {Gk *seven hundred **fifty** stadia*}
Pm 151: T *outside the number),* {Other ancient authorities add *of the one hundred **fifty*** (psalms)}

FIFTY-EIGHT (1)
Tob 14: 2 He was sixty-two {Other ancient authorities read ***fifty-eight***} years old

FILL (2)
Dt 32:15 Jacob ate his fill; {Q Mss Sam Gk: MT lacks *Jacob ate his **fill***}
Jer 4: 5 shout aloud {Or *shout, take your weapons*: Heb *shout, **fill*** (your hand)}

FILLED (1)
Sir 31: 5 pursues money will be led astray {Heb Syr: Gk *pursues destruction will be **filled***}

FILTHY (1)
Col 3: 8 abusive {Or ***filthy***} language from your mouth.

FINALLY (2)
1Sa 10:21 Finally ... man by man, {Gk: Heb lacks ***Finally** ... man by man*}
Lk 18: 5 by continually coming.' " {Or *so that she may not **finally** come and slap me in the face*}

FINDING (1)
Ps 32: 6 at a time of distress, {Cn: Heb *at a time of **finding** only*}

FINDS (1)
SS 8:10 as one who brings {Or ***finds***} peace,

FINISH (1)
Ro 9:28 for the Lord will execute ... decisively." {Other ancient authorities read *for he will **finish** his work and cut it short in righteousness,* >}

FIR-TREES (1)
2Sa 6: 5 with songs {Q Ms Gk 1 Chr 13.8: Heb ***fir-trees***} and lyres

FIRE (5)
Ps 18:13 his voice. {Gk See 2 Sam 22.14: Heb adds *hailstones and coals of **fire***}
Eze 8: 2 looked like a human being; {Gk: Heb *like **fire***}
2Es 16: 6 fire in the stubble ... to burn? {Other ancient authorities read ***fire** when dry straw has been set on **fire***}
4Mc 11:18 he was roasted {Other ancient authorities add *by **fire***}

FIRM (1)
Sir 1:12 and long life. {Other ancient authorities add ... *also for love he makes **firm** paths.*}

FIRMLY (1)
Sir 28: 1 for he keeps a strict account of {Other ancient authorities read *for he **firmly** establishes*}

FIRST (13)
Jer 16:18 And {Gk: Heb *And **first***} I will doubly repay
Eze 32:17 in ... month, {Gk: Heb lacks *in the **first** month*}
Lk 6: 1 One sabbath {Other ancient authorities read *On the second **first** sabbath*} while Jesus was going
Jn 5: 3 + v.4 < *whoever stepped in **first** after the stirring of the water was made well* >
Ac 16:12 a leading city of the district {Other authorities read *a city of the **first** district*}
Eph 4: 9 descended {Other ancient authorities add ***first***}
1Mc 10:65 among his chief {Gk ***first***} Friends.
11:27 among his chief {Gk ***first***} Friends.
2Mc 8: 9 one of the king's chief {Gk *one of the **first***}
1Es 8: 2 son of Aaron the high {Gk *the **first***} priest.
2Es 6: 1 "At the beginning ... before; {< Ethiop: *At **first** by the Son of Man, and afterwards I myself.* >}
6:55 you created this world. {Syr Ethiop Arab 2: Lat *the firstborn world* Compare Arab 1 ***first** world*}
4Mc 5: 4 leader of the flock, was brought {Or *was the **first** of the flock to be brought*}

FIRSTBORN (4)
2Sa 13:21 but he would not punish ... firstborn. {Q Ms Gk: MT lacks *but he would not punish ... **firstborn***}
Mt 1:25 she had borne a son; {Other ancient authorities read *her **firstborn** son*}
Sir 17:17 + v.18 *whom, being his **firstborn**, he brings up with discipline,* >
2Es 6:55 you created this world. {Syr Ethiop Arab 2: Lat *the **firstborn** world* Compare Arab 1 *first world*}

FIVE (2)
Sir 17: 4 + v.5 *They obtained the use of the **five** faculties* >
2Es 14:48 did so. {Syr adds < ***five** thousand years and three months and twelve days after creation.* >}

FLAMES (1)
Hos 8: 6 be broken to pieces. {Or *shall go up in **flames***}

FLED (1)
2Ki 25: 4 the king with all the soldiers fled {Gk Compare Jer 39.4; 52.7: Heb lacks *the king* and lacks ***fled***}

FLESH (29)
Lev 15: 2 discharge from his member, {Heb ***flesh***}
15: 3 whether his member {Heb ***flesh***} flows ... or his member {Heb ***flesh***} is stopped
Jn 8:15 by human standards; {Gk *according to the **flesh***}
17: 2 authority over all people, {Gk ***flesh***}
Ro 6:19 your natural limitations. {Gk *the weakness of your **flesh***}
11:14 to make my own people {Gk *my **flesh***} jealous,
1Co 1:26 by human standards, {Gk *according to the **flesh***}
1:29 that no one {Gk *no **flesh***} might boast
7:28 distress in this life, {Gk *in the **flesh***}
10:18 Consider the people of Israel; {Gk *Israel according to the **flesh***}
2Co 1:17 according to ordinary human standards, {Gk *according to the **flesh***}
5:16 from a human point of view; {Gk *according to the **flesh***} ... knew Christ from a human point of view, {Gk *according to the **flesh***}
10: 2 according to human standards. {Gk *according to the **flesh***}
10: 3 as human beings, {Gk *in the **flesh***} ... according to human standards; {Gk *according to the **flesh***}
11:18 according to human standards, {Gk *according to the **flesh***}
Gal 5:13 an opportunity for self-indulgence, {Gk *the **flesh***}
Eph 2:11 Gentiles by birth, {Gk *in the **flesh***}
5:30 members of his body. {Other ancient authorities add *of his **flesh** and of his bones*}
Col 1:22 in his fleshly body {Gk *in the body of his **flesh***}
2:18 by a human way of thinking, {Gk *by the mind of his **flesh***}
2:23 are of no value in checking self-indulgence. {Or *are of no value, serving only to indulge the **flesh***}
1Pe 4: 2 rest of your earthly life {Gk *rest of the time in the **flesh***}
Jude 1: 7 unnatural lust, {Gk *went after other **flesh***}
1:23 defiled by their bodies. {Gk *by the **flesh**.* >}
Sir 17:15 + v.16 < *they are unable to make for themselves hearts of **flesh** in place of their stony hearts.* >
2Es 1:31 of the flesh. {Other ancient authorities lack *of the **flesh***}

FLESHLY (1)
2Co 10: 4 not merely human, {Gk ***fleshly***}

FLOCKS (1)
2Ch 32:28 and sheepfolds. {Gk Vg: Heb ***flocks** for folds*}

FLOOR (1)
1Sa 19:22 to the great well that is in Secu; {Gk reads *to the well of the threshing **floor** on the bare height*}

FLOWERS (1)
2Es 1:40 the messenger of the Lord. {Other ancient authorities read *... and twelve angels with **flowers***}

FOLDS (1)
2Ch 32:28 and sheepfolds. {Gk Vg: Heb *flocks for **folds***}

FOLLOW (2)
Mk 9:38 we saw someone {Other ancient authorities add *who does not **follow** us*}
Sir 23:27 + v.28 *It is a great honor to **follow** God, and to be received by him is long life.*

FOLLOWED (1)
2Es 15:48 deed and devices. {Other ancient authorities add *you have **followed** after that one about to gratify her magnates and leaders* >}

FOLLY (3)
Ps 85: 8 who turn to him in their hearts. {Gk: Heb *but let them not turn back to **folly***}
Pr 14:24 is the garland {Cn: Heb *is the **folly***} of fools.
Sir 13: 8 then you are enjoying yourself. {Other ancient authorities read *in your **folly***}

FOOD (1)
AdE 2: 9 her portion of food, {Gk lacks *of **food***}

FOODS (1)
Heb 13: 9 not by regulations about food, {Gk *not by **foods***}

FOOL (2)
1Sa 25:25 Nabal {That is ***Fool***}
Pr 10:10 but the one who rebukes boldly makes peace. {Gk: Heb *but a babbling **fool** will come to ruin*}

FOOLISH (1)
Sir 20:22 because of human respect. {Other ancient authorities read *his **foolish** look*}

FOOLS (2)
Ps 107:17 Some were sick {Cn: Heb ***fools***}
Pr 12:23 the mind of a fool {Heb *the heart of **fools***}

FOOT (1)
2Sa 10:18 forty thousand horsemen, {1 Chr 19.18 and some Gk Mss read ***foot** soldiers*}

FOOTSTOOL (1)
Jas 2: 3 "Sit at my feet," {Gk *Sit under my **footstool***}

FORD (1)
2Sa 19:18 the crossing was taking place, {Cn: Heb *the **ford** crossed*}

FOREHEAD (1)
Nu 24:17 crush the borderlands {Or ***forehead***} of Moab,

FOREIGN (2)
Pr 27:13 for foreigners. {Vg and 20.16: Heb *for a **foreign** woman*}
Jer 18:14 Do the mountain {Cn: Heb ***foreign***} waters

FOREIGNER (1)
Pm 151: 6 meet the Philistine, {Or ***foreigner***}

FOREIGNERS (1)
Eze 44: 8 have appointed foreigners {Heb lacks ***foreigners***}

FORESKINS (1)
Jos 5: 3 Gibeath-haaraloth. {That is *the Hill of the **Foreskins***}

FOREVER (6)
Mt 6:13 from the evil one. {< Other ancient authorities add, in some form, *For the kingdom and the power and the glory are yours **forever**. Amen.*}
1Th 2:16 overtaken them at last. {Or *completely* or ***forever***}
Tob 3: 2 judge the world. {Other ancient authorities read *you render true and righteous judgment **forever***}
Sir 17: 8 of his works. {Other ancient authorities add *and he gave them to boast of his marvels **forever***}
2Es 8:20 who inhabit eternity, {Or *you who abide **forever***}
4Mc 9:23 leave your post in my struggle {Other ancient authorities read *post **forever***}

FORGET (2)
Ge 41:51 Manasseh, {That is *Making to **forget***}
Jer 23:39 lift you up {Heb Mss Gk Vg: MT ***forget** you*}

FORGIVE (2)
Mk 11:25 + v.26 *"But if you do not **forgive**, neither will your Father in heaven **forgive** your trespasses."*

FORM (1)
2Es 8:22 they are changed to wind and fire, {Syr: Lat *they whose service takes the **form** of wind and fire*}

FORMED (3)
Sir 17:20 + v.21 *But the Lord, who is gracious and knows how they are **formed**,* >
2Es 3: 4 planted {Other ancient authorities read ***formed***}
8: 8 the womb {Lat *what you have **formed***} endures

FORNICATIONS (1)
2Es 15:48 deeds and devices. {Other ancient authorities add < *so that you may be made proud and be pleased by her **fornications***}

FORSAKEN (1)
2Es 3:31 your way may be comprehended. {Syr; compare Ethiop: Lat *how this way should be **forsaken***}

FORTH (7)
2Sa 5:20 Baal-perazim. {That is *Lord of Bursting **Forth***}
18: 2 divided the army into three groups: {Gk: Heb *sent **forth** the army*}
Ezr 4: 7 written in Aramaic and translated. {< Another interpretation is *The letter was written in the Aramaic script and set **forth** in the Aramaic language*}
Job 12: 6 who bring their god in their hands. {Or *whom God brought **forth** by his hand*; Meaning of Heb uncertain}
38:14 and it is dyed {Cn: Heb *and they stand **forth***}
Isa 45: 8 that salvation may spring up, {Q Ms: MT *that they may bring **forth** salvation*}
Sir 8:18 what they will divulge. {Or *it will bring **forth***}

FORTRESS (5)
1Ch 29: 1 the temple {Heb ***fortress***} will not be for mortals
29:19 he may build the temple {Heb ***fortress***}
Ps 46: 7 the God of Jacob is our refuge. {Or ***fortress***}
46:11 the God of Jacob is our refuge. {Or ***fortress***}
Jer 6:27 a refiner {Or *a **fortress***} among my people

FORTUNE (1)
Ge 30:11 Gad. {That is ***Fortune***}

FORTY (2)
2Sa 15: 7 And the end of four {Gk Syr: Heb ***forty***} years
2Mc 12: 9 thirty miles {Gk *two hundred **forty** stadia*} distant.

FORTY-FIVE (2)
Ne 7:68 They had ... forty-five mules, {Ezra 2.66 and the margins of some Hebrew Mss: MT lacks *They had ... **forty-five** mules*}
Tob 1:21 But not forty {Other ancient authorities read either ***forty-five*** or *fifty*} days passed

FOUL (2)
Rev 18: 2 a haunt of every foul and hateful beast. {Other ancient authorities lack *a haunt of every **foul** beast* and attach the words *and hateful* to the previous line so as to read *a haunt of every **foul** and hateful bird*}

FOUND (1)
Dt 32:10 sustained {Sam Gk Compare Tg: MT ***found***} him

FOUNDATIONS (2)
2Ch 3: 3 These are Solomon's measurements {Syr: Heb ***foundations***}
2Es 15:44 all its fury; {Other ancient authorities add *until they destroy it to its **foundations***}

FOUNDED (1)
Lk 6:48 because it had been well built. {Other ancient authorities read ***founded** upon the rock*}

FOUNDING (1)
2Ch 24:27 rebuilding {Heb ***founding***} of the house of God

FOUNTAIN (1)
Dt 33:28 untroubled is Jacob's abode {Or ***fountain***}

FOUR (3)
1Sa 17: 4 whose height was six {MT: Q Ms Gk ***four***} cubits
Ac 19: 9 of Tyrannus. {Other ancient authorities read *of a certain Tyrannus, from eleven o'clock in the morning to **four** in the afternoon*}
Rev 9:13 the four {Other ancient authorities lack ***four***}

FOURTEEN (1)
1Ki 8:65 seven days. {Compare Gk: Heb *seven days and seven days, **fourteen** days*}

FOURTH (1)
Nu 23:10 number the dust-cloud {Or ***fourth** part*}

FREE (3)
Lk 24:21 the one to redeem Israel. {Or *to set Israel **free***}
Sir 23:10 he cleansed {Syr *be **free***} from sin.
2Es 10:22 our children {Ethiop ***free** men*} have suffered

FREED (1)
2Es 1:32 says the Lord. {Other ancient authorities add ... *You took me as a sinner, not as a father who **freed** you from slavery,* >}

FREEDOM (1)
1Co 11:10 have a symbol of authority on her head, {Or *have **freedom** of choice regarding her head*}

FRESH (1)
Mk 2:22 but one puts new wine into fresh wineskins." {Other ancient authorities lack *but one puts new wine into **fresh** wineskins*}

FRIEND (1)
Pr 27: 9 the soul is torn by trouble. {Gk: Heb *the sweetness of a **friend** is better than one's own counsel*}

FRONTLET (3)
Ex 13:16 as an emblem {Or *as a **frontlet***; Meaning of Heb uncertain}
Dt 6: 8 as an emblem {Or *as a **frontlet***}
11:18 as an emblem {Or *as a **frontlet***}

FRUIT (4)
Hos 14: 8 your faithfulness {Heb *your **fruit***} comes from me
Mal 1:12 the food for it {Compare Syr Tg: Heb *its **fruit**, its food*}
Ro 15:28 have delivered to them what has been collected, {Gk *have sealed to them this **fruit***}
Sir 19:17 + v.19 < *and those who do what is pleasing to him enjoy the **fruit** of the tree of immortality.*

FRUITFUL (1)
Ge 41:52 Ephraim, {From a Hebrew word meaning *to be **fruitful***}

FRUITS (1)
Ro 16: 5 the first convert {Gk *first **fruits***} in Asia

FUGITIVES (1)
Eze 17:21 All the pick {Another reading is ***fugitives***}

FULFILLED (3)
Mt 27:35 casting lots; {Other ancient authorities add *in order that what had been spoken through the prophet might be **fulfilled**,* >}
Mk 15:27 + v.28 *And the scripture was **fulfilled** that says, "And he was counted among the lawless."*
16:14 risen. {Other ancient authorities add, in whole or in part, *... of Satan's power has been **fulfilled**,* >}

FULL (1)
2Sa 8: 2 put to death, and one length {Heb *one **full** length*}

FULLER (1)
Mk 9: 3 such as no one {Gk *no **fuller***} on earth

FULLNESS (1)
2Es 7:96 the straits and toil {Syr Ethiop: Lat ***fullness***}

FULLY (1)
Lk 9:32 but since they had stayed awake, {Or *but when they were **fully** awake*}

FUTURE (1)
Jer 12: 4 blind to our ways." {Gk: Heb *to our **future***}

G

GADARENES (3)
Mk 5: 1 Gerasenes. {Other ancient authorities read *Gergesenes*; others, ***Gadarenes***}
Lk 8:26 Gerasenes, {Other ancient authorities read ***Gadarenes***; others, *Gergesenes*}
8:37 Gerasenes {Other ancient authorities read ***Gadarenes***; others, *Gergesenes*}

GADFLY (1)
4Mc 2: 3 he nullified the frenzy {Or ***gadfly***}

GAI (1)
1Sa 17:52 Gath {Gk Syr: Heb ***Gai***}

GAIN (1)
Sir 51:28 you will acquire silver and gold. {Syr Compare Heb: Gk *... and you will **gain** by it much gold.*}

GALAL (1)
Jos 5: 9 Gilgal {Related to Heb ***galal*** to roll}

GALATIAN (1)
Ac 18:23 the region of Galatia {Gk *the **Galatian** region*}

GALATIANS (1)
2Mc 8:20 Galatians {Gk lacks ***Galatians***}

GALILEE (2)
Lk 4:44 of Judea. {Other ancient authorities read ***Galilee***}
Jn 6: 1 the Sea of Tiberias. {Gk *of* ***Galilee*** *of Tiberius*}

GARMENT (3)
Dt 24:12 the garment given you as {Heb lacks *the* ***garment*** *given you as*}
Pr 25:20 vinegar on a wound {Gk: Heb *Like one who takes off a* ***garment*** *on a cold day, like vinegar on lye*}
Mic 2: 8 you strip the robe from the peaceful, {Cn: Heb *from before a* ***garment***}

GARRISONS (1)
1Ch 18: 6 garrisons {< Heb lacks ***garrisons***}

GASHMU (1)
Ne 6: 6 Geshem {Heb ***Gashmu***}

GATE (4)
Da 8: 2 by the river Ulai. {Or *the Ulai* ***Gate***}
8: 3 standing beside the river. {Or ***gate***}
8: 6 standing beside the river, {Or ***gate***}
AdE 4: 5 + v.6 *So Hachratheus went out to Mordecai in the street of the city opposite the city* ***gate.***

GATES (1)
Eze 40:38 in the vestibule of the gate, {Cn: Heb *at the pilasters of the* ***gates***}

GATEWAY (1)
Mk 14:68 And he went out into the forecourt. {Or ***gateway***}

GATH (3)
1Sa 5: 8 "Let the ark of God be moved on to us." {Gk Compare Q Ms: MT *They answered, "Let the ark of the God of Israel be brought around to* ***Gath."***}
5: 8 to Gath. {Gk: Heb lacks *to* ***Gath***}
5: 9 to Gath, {Q Ms: MT lacks *to* ***Gath***}

GATHER (1)
2Es 7:33 shall be withdrawn. {Lat *shall* ***gather*** *together*}

GAUL (1)
2Ti 4:10 Galatia, {Other ancient authorities read ***Gaul***}

GAVE (4)
Mt 27:50 and breathed his last. {Or ***gave*** *up his spirit*}
Sir 17: 8 of his works. {Other ancient authorities add *and he* ***gave*** *them to boast of his marvels forever*}
4Mc 12:19 and so ended his life. {Gk *and so* ***gave*** *up*; other ancient authorities read ***gave*** *up his spirit* or *his soul*}

GAZA (1)
1Mc 13:43 Gazara {Cn: Gk ***Gaza***}

GAZELLE (1)
Ac 9:36 Dorcas. {The name Tabitha in Aramaic and the name Dorcas in Greek mean *a* ***gazelle***}

GEDALIAH (1)
Jer 41: 9 he had struck down was the large cistern {Gk: Heb *whom he had killed by the hand of* ***Gedaliah***}

GEHENNA (14)
Mt 5:22 hell {Gk ***Gehenna***}
5:29 hell. {Gk ***Gehenna***}
5:30 hell. {Gk ***Gehenna***}
10:28 hell. {Gk ***Gehenna***}
18: 9 hell {Gk ***Gehenna***}
23:15 hell {Gk ***Gehenna***}
23:33 hell? {Gk ***Gehenna***}
Mk 9:43 hell, {Gk ***Gehenna***}
9:45 hell. {Verses {Gk ***Gehenna***}
9:47 hell, {Gk ***Gehenna***}
Lk 12: 5 hell. {Gk ***Gehenna***}
Jas 3: 6 hell. {Gk ***Gehenna***}
2Es 2:29 hell. {Lat ***Gehenna***}
7:36 hell {Lat Syr Ethiop ***Gehenna***}

GELILOTH (2)
Jos 22:10 to the region {Or *to* ***Geliloth***} near the Jordan
22:11 in the region {Or *at* ***Geliloth***} near the Jordan,

GENERATION (1)
Ps 71:18 to all the generations to come. {Gk Compare Syr: Heb *to a* ***generation,*** *to all that come*}

GENEROUS (1)
Ps 51:12 sustain in me a willing {Or ***generous***} spirit.

GENTILES (2)
2Ti 1:11 and a teacher, {Other ancient authorities add *of the* ***Gentiles***}
3Jn 1: 7 no support from non-believers. {Gk *the* ***Gentiles***}

GENTLENESS (1)
Ps 18:35 your help {Or ***gentleness***} has made me great.

GER (2)
Ex 2:22 an alien {Heb ***ger***}
18: 3 an alien {Heb ***ger***}

GERASENES (1)
Mt 8:28 Gadarenes, {Other ancient authorities read *Gergesenes*; others, ***Gerasenes***}

GERGESENES (4)
Mt 8:28 Gadarenes, {Other ancient authorities read ***Gergesenes***; others, *Gerasenes*}
Mk 5: 1 Gerasenes. {Other ancient authorities read ***Gergesenes***; others, *Gadarenes*}
Lk 8:26 Gerasenes, {Other ancient authorities read *Gadarenes*; others, ***Gergesenes***}
8:37 Gerasenes {Other ancient authorities read *Gadarenes*; others, ***Gergesenes***}

GERON (1)
2Mc 6: 1 sent an Athenian senator {Or ***Geron*** *an Athenian*}

GERSHOM (3)
Ex 6:16 Gershon, {Also spelled ***Gershom***; see 2.22}
6:17 Gershon: {Also spelled ***Gershom***; see 2.22}
1Ch 23: 6 Gershon, {Or ***Gershom***; See 1 Chr 6.1, note, >}

GERSHON (1)
1Ch 6: 1 Gershom, {Heb ***Gershon,*** variant of *Gershom*; >}

GERSHONITE (1)
1Ch 23: 7 The sons of Gershon {Vg Compare Gk Syr: Heb *to the* ***Gershonite***}

GET (1)
Sir 51:28 Hear but a little of my instruction, ... gold. {Syr Compare Heb: Gk ***Get*** *instruction with a large sum of silver,* >}

GIBEAH (2)
1Sa 13:15 went on his way from Gilgal. {Gk: Heb *went up from Gilgal to* ***Gibeah*** *of Benjamin*}
2Sa 21: 6 at Gibeon on the mountain of the LORD." {Cn Compare Gk and 21.9: Heb *at* ***Gibeah*** *of Saul, the chosen of the LORD*}

GIBEATH (1)
Jos 18:28 Gibeah {Heb ***Gibeath***}

GIFT (4)
Ro 15:31 that my ministry {Other ancient authorities read *my bringing of a* ***gift***}
Sir 1:12 long life. {Other ancient authorities add *The fear of the Lord is a* ***gift*** *from the Lord;* >}
2: 9 mercy. {Other ancient authorities add *For his reward is an everlasting* ***gift*** *with joy.*}
17: 4 + v.5 < *he distributed to them the* ***gift*** *of mind,* >

GIFTS (1)
Sir 1:18 flourish. {Other ancient authorities add *Both are* ***gifts*** *of God for peace; glory opens out* >}

GILEAD (1)
Jdg 7: 3 home.'" Thus Gideon sifted them out; {Cn: Heb *home, and depart from Mount* ***Gilead***' "}

GILGAL (1)
Jos 12:23 Galilee, {Gk: Heb ***Gilgal***}

GIRD (2)
Isa 50:11 you are kindlers of fire, lighters of firebrands. {Syr: Heb *you* ***gird*** *yourselves with firebrands*}
1Pe 1:13 prepare your minds for action; {Gk ***gird*** *up the loins of your mind*}

GIVE (10)
Dt 33: 8 Give to Levi {Q Ms Gk: MT lacks ***Give*** *to Levi*}
1Sa 1:11 then I will set him ... neither wine nor intoxicants, {Cn Compare Gk Q Ms 1.22: MT *then I will* ***give*** *him to the LORD all the days of his life*}
2:20 "May the LORD repay {Q Ms Gk: MT ***give***}
Eze 26:20 you will not be inhabited or have a place {Gk: Heb *I will* ***give*** *beauty*}
37:26 and I will bless {Tg: Heb ***give***}
Lk 11:11 child asks for {Other ancient authorities add *bread, will* ***give*** *a stone; or if your child asks for*}
Ac 5:28 We gave you strict orders not to teach in this name, {Other ancient authorities read *Did we not* ***give*** *you strict orders not to teach in this name?*}
Ro 12:16 but associate with the lowly; {Or ***give*** *yourselves to humble tasks*}
Tob 4: 6 + v.19 < *the Lord will* ***give*** *good counsel.* >
Sir 20:14 nothing, {Other ancient authorities add *so it is with the envious who* ***give*** *under compulsion*}

GIVEN (7)
Dt 24:12 the garment given you as {Heb lacks *the garment* ***given*** *you as*}
Ps 55:22 Cast your burden {Or *Cast what he has* ***given*** *you*}
La 5: 6 have made a pact with {Heb *have* ***given*** *the hand to*} Egypt
Lk 22:20 which is given ... in my blood. {Other ancient authorities lack, in whole or in part, verses 19b-20 (*which is* ***given*** *... in my blood*)}
Jn 6:23 after the Lord had given thanks. {Other ancient authorities lack *after the Lord had* ***given*** *thanks*}
7:39 for as yet there was no Spirit, {Other ancient authorities read *for as yet the Spirit* (others, *Holy Spirit*) *had not been* ***given***}
Sir 24:17 + v.18 < *I am* ***given*** *to all my children,* >

GIVES (1)
Ge 49:21 that bears lovely fawns. {Or *that* ***gives*** *beautiful words*}

GLAD (1)
Sir 13:25 for evil. {Other ancient authorities add *and a* ***glad*** *heart makes a cheerful countenance*}

GLADNESS (1)
Sir 6:31 a splendid crown. {Heb: Gk *crown of* ***gladness***}

GLOAT (1)
Ob 1:12 But you should not have gloated {Heb *But do not* ***gloat*** (and similarly through verse 14)}

GLORIES (2)
2Pe 2:10 the glorious ones, {Or *angels*; Gk ***glories***}
Jude 1: 8 the glorious ones. {Or *angels*; Gk ***glories***}

GLORIFIED (2)
Jn 13:32 If God has been glorified in him, {Other ancient authorities lack *If God has been* ***glorified*** *in him*}
1Pe 4:14 you. {Other ancient authorities add *On their part he is blasphemed, but on your part he is* ***glorified***}

GLORIFY (1)
2Es 2:47 to praise those who had stood valiantly for the name of the Lord. {Other ancient authorities read *to praise and* ***glorify*** *the Lord*}

GLORIOUS (3)
Ps 45:13 with all kinds of wealth. The princess is decked ... with gold-woven robes; {Or *... All* ***glorious*** *is the princess within, gold embroidery is her clothing*}
Php 3:21 the body of his glory, {Or *his* ***glorious*** *body*}
Sir 1:10 who love him. {Other ancient authorities add *Love of the Lord is* ***glorious*** *wisdom;* >}

GLORY (8)
Ps 30:12 so that my soul {Heb *that* ***glory***} may praise
73:24 receive me with honor. {Or *to* ***glory***}
Mt 6:13 evil one. {Or *from evil.* Other ancient authorities add, in some form, *For the kingdom and the power and the* ***glory*** *are yours forever. Amen.*}
Mk 16:14 risen. {Other ancient authorities add, in whole or in part, *... that they may inherit the spiritual and imperishable* ***glory*** *of righteousness* >}
1Co 11: 7 he is the image and reflection {Or ***glory***} of God; but woman is the reflection {Or ***glory***} of man.
Sir 1:18 flourish. {Other ancient authorities add *Both are gifts of God for peace;* ***glory*** *opens out for those who love him.* >}
45:26 who ... glory. {Heb: Gk lacks *who ...* ***glory***}

GO (12)
Ge 4: 8 "Let us go out to the field." {Sam Gk Syr Compare Vg: MT lacks *Let us* ***go*** *out to the field*}
Jdg 20: 9 we will go up {Gk: Heb lacks *we will* ***go*** *up*}
1Sa 29:10 and go to the place ... done well before me. {Gk: Heb lacks *and* ***go*** *to the place ... done well before me*}
Ps 30: 3 from among those gone down to the Pit. {Or *that I should not* ***go*** *down to the Pit*}
Isa 42:10 Let the sea roar {Cn Compare Ps 96.11; 98.7: Heb *Those who* ***go*** *down to the sea*}
Eze 47: 9 Wherever the river goes, {Gk Syr Vg Tg: Heb *the two rivers* ***go***}
Hos 8: 6 shall be broken to pieces. {Or *shall* ***go*** *up in flames*}
Rev 6: 1 "Come!" {Or ***"Go!"***}
6: 3 "Come!" {Or ***"Go!"***}
6: 5 "Come!" {Or ***"Go!"***}
6: 7 "Come!" {Or ***"Go!"***}
Wis 1:11 is without result, {Or *will* ***go*** *unpunished*}

GOATS (2)
Zec 10: 3 I will punish the leaders; {Or *male* ***goats***}
Heb 9:19 and goats, {Other ancient authorities lack *and* ***goats***}

GOD (83)
Ge 28:19 Bethel; {That is *House of* ***God***}
32:28 Israel, {That is *The one who strives with* ***God*** or ***God*** *strives*}
32:30 Peniel, {That is *The face of* ***God***}
33:20 El-Elohe-Israel. {That is ***God,*** *the* ***God*** *of Israel*}
35: 7 El-bethel, {That is ***God*** *of Bethel*}
Ex 18: 4 Eliezer {Heb *Eli,* my ***God;*** *ezer,* help}
31: 3 with divine spirit, {Or *with the spirit of* ***God***}
35:31 filled him with divine spirit, {Or *the spirit of* ***God***}
Dt 10:13 your God {Q Ms Gk Syr: MT lacks *your* ***God***}
30:16 If ... of the LORD your God {Gk: Heb lacks *If you obey the commandments of the LORD your* ***God***}

Dt 33:27 He subdues the ancient gods, {Or *The eternal **God** is a dwelling place*}
1Sa 2:25 another, someone can intercede for the sinner with the LORD; {Gk Compare Q Ms: MT *another, **God** will mediate for him*}
4: 7 "Gods have {Or *A **god** has*} come into the camp."
10: 5 Gibeath-elohim, {Or *the Hill of **God***}
23:14 but the LORD {Q Ms Gk: MT ***God***} did not give
23:16 through the LORD. {Compare Q Ms Gk: MT ***God***}
28:13 "I see a divine being {Or *a **god***; or ***gods***}
Ezr 9: 8 he {Heb ***our God***} may brighten our eyes
Job 1: 6 the heavenly beings {Heb ***sons of God***}
2: 1 the heavenly beings {Heb ***sons of God***}
12: 6 who bring their god in their hands. {Or *whom **God** brought forth by his hand*; Meaning of Heb uncertain}
27:22 It {Or *He* (that is **God**)} hurls at them
27:23 It {Or *He* (that is **God**)} claps its hands
32: 3 declared Job to be in the wrong. {Another ancient tradition reads *answer, and had put **God** in the wrong*}
38: 7 all the heavenly beings {Heb ***sons of God***}
Ps 52: 1 mischief done against the godly? {Cn Compare Syr: Heb *the kindness of **God***}
Isa 7:14 Immanuel. {That is ***God** is with us*}
Hos 1: 4 Jezreel; {That is ***God** sows*}
2:22 Jezreel; {That is ***God** sows*}
Mt 6:33 of God {Other ancient authorities lack *of **God***}
21:12 the temple {Other ancient authorities add *of **God***}
22:30 like angels {Other ancient authorities add *of **God***}
27:54 this man was God's Son!" {Or *a son of **God***}
Mk 1: 1 the Son of God. {Other ancient authorities lack *the Son of **God***}
7:11 an offering to God)—{Gk lacks *to **God***}
15:39 this man was God's Son!" {Or *a son of **God***}
16:14 had risen. {Other ancient authorities add, in whole or in part, *< who does not allow the truth and power of **God** to prevail >*}
Lk 19:44 visitation from God." {Gk lacks *from **God***}
Jn 9:35 the Son of Man?" {Other ancient authorities read *the Son of **God***}
13:32 If God has been glorified in him, {Other ancient authorities lack *If **God** has been glorified in him*}
Ac 7:46 for the house of Jacob. {Other ancient authorities read *for the **God** of Jacob*}
8:36 + v.37 *< And he replied, "I believe that Jesus Christ is the Son of **God**."*
13:44 the Lord. {Other ancient authorities read ***God***}
15:18 things [18]known from long ago.' {Other ancient authorities read *things. [18]Known to **God** from of old are all his works.'*}
16:32 the word of the Lord {Other ancient authorities read *word of **God***}
Ro 10:17 the word of Christ. {Or *about Christ*; other ancient authorities read *of **God***}
11:28 enemies of God {Gk lacks *of **God***}
14: 4 the Lord {Other ancient authorities read *for **God***}
14:12 to God. {Other ancient authorities lack *to **God***}
2Co 11: 7 God's good news {Gk *the gospel of **God***}
Php 1:14 dare to speak the word {Other ancient authorities read *word of **God***}
Col 2: 2 knowledge of God's mystery, that is, Christ himself, {Other ancient authorities read *of the mystery of **God**, both of the Father and of Christ*}
3:16 the word of Christ {Other ancient authorities read *of **God***, or *of the Lord*}
1Ti 3:16 He {Gk *Who*; other ancient authorities read ***God***; others, *Which*} was revealed in flesh,
Jas 1:12 Lord {Gk *he*; other ancient authorities read ***God***}
1Pe 5: 2 as God would have you do it— {Other ancient authorities lack *as **God** would have you do it*}
1Jn 3: 9 because God's seed abides in them; {Or *because the children of **God** abide in him*}
4:19 We love {Other ancient authorities add *him*; others add ***God***} because he first loved us.
5:20 know him who is true; {Other ancient authorities read *know the true **God***}
Rev 20: 9 fire came down from heaven {Other ancient authorities read *from **God**, out of heaven*, or *out of heaven from **God***}
21: 3 as their God; {Other ancient authorities lack *as their **God***} ... and God himself will be with them; {Other ancient authorities add *and be their **God***}
Sir 1:18 flourish. {Other ancient authorities add *Both are gifts of **God** for peace; >*}
20:15 to God and humans. {Other ancient authorities lack *to **God** and humans*}
23:27 + v.28 *It is a great honor to follow **God**, >*
24:23 + v.24 *< the Lord Almighty alone is **God**, >*
41:19 of breaking an oath or agreement, {Heb: Gk *before the truth of **God** and the covenant*}
1Mc 14:28 Asaramel, {This word resembles the Hebrew words for *the court of the people of **God*** or *the prince of the people of **God***}
2Es 7:19 better judge than the Lord, {Other ancient authorities read ***God**; >*}
7:21 For the Lord {Other ancient authorities read ***God***} strictly commanded
7:28 For my son the Messiah {< Arm *the Messiah of **God***; Lat *my son Jesus*}
15:24 the Lord; {Other ancient authorities read ***God***}
16:54 Lord {Other ancient authorities read *Lord **God***}
16:71 fear the Lord. {Other ancient authorities read *fear **God***}
4Mc 11: 6 + v.7 *If you but understood human feelings and had hope of salvation from **God**—[8]but, as it is, you are a stranger to **God** >*
15: 3 according to God's promise. {Gk *according to **God***}
17:20 for the sake of God, {Other ancient authorities lack *for the sake of **God***}

GOD'S (5)

Lk 12:31 for his {Other ancient authorities read ***God's***}
Jn 1:34 this is the Son of God." {Other ancient authorities read *is **God's** chosen one*}
1Co 16:12 he was not at all willing {Or *it was not at all **God's** will for him*}
2Ti 2:26 by him to do his will. {Or *by him, to do his* (that is, **God's**) *will*}
Sir 1: 4 + v.5 *The source of wisdom is **God's** word >*

GOD-HATED (1)

Ro 1:30 God-haters, {Or ***God-hated***}

GODDESS (1)

2Mc 1:13 the priests of the goddess {Gk lacks *the **goddess***}

GODS (10)

Ge 3: 5 you will be like God, {Or ***gods***}
1Sa 28:13 "I see a divine being {Or *a god*; or ***gods***}
2Ki 23:24 teraphim, {Or *household **gods***}
Ps 29: 1 O heavenly beings, {Heb *sons of **gods***}
Eze 21:21 teraphim, {Or *the household **gods***}
Da 1: 2 the land of Shinar, {Gk Theodotion: Heb adds *to the house of his own **gods***}
3:25 appearance of a god." {Aram *a son of the **gods***}
Zec 10: 2 teraphim {Or *household **gods***}
3Mc 6:11 praise their vanities {Or *bless their vain **gods***}
2Es 16:36 do not disbelieve what the Lord says. {Cn: Lat *do not believe the **gods** of whom the Lord speaks*}

GOES (3)

1Sa 1:23 the LORD establish his word." {MT: Q Ms Gk Compare Syr *that which **goes** out of your mouth*}
Jer 48: 5 they go {Cn: Heb *he **goes***} up weeping
Eze 40:40 the outside of the vestibule {Cn: Heb *to him who **goes** up*}

GOG (2)

Eze 39:11 Hamon-gog. {That is, *the Horde of **Gog***}
39:15 Hamon-gog. {That is, *the Horde of **Gog***}

GOING (1)

Eze 31: 4 making its rivers flow {Gk: Heb *rivers **going***}

GOLD (3)

Ps 45:13 with all kinds of wealth. The princess ... with gold-woven robes; {Or ... *All glorious is the princess within, **gold** embroidery is her clothing*}
Zec 4:12 pour out the oil {Cn: Heb ***gold***}
6:10 silver and gold {Cn Compare verse 11: Heb lacks *silver and **gold***}

GOOD (11)

1Ki 9:13 Cabul {Perhaps meaning *a land **good** for nothing*}
Pr 15: 2 The tongue of the wise dispenses knowledge, {Cn: Heb *makes knowledge **good***}
Da 3:15 well and good. {Aram lacks *well and **good***}
Mt 20:15 are you envious because I am generous?' {Gk *is your eye evil because I am **good**?*}
Ac 15:33 + v.34 *But it seemed **good** to Silas to remain there*
1Ti 6: 2 since those who benefit ... are believers and beloved. {Or *since they are believers and beloved, who devote themselves to **good** deeds*}
Tob 4: 6 + v.19 *< the Lord will give **good** counsel. >*
Sir 11:14 + v.15 *< affection and the ways of **good** works come from him. >*
20: 8 hated. {Other ancient authorities add *How **good** it is to show repentance when you are reproved, >*}
22: 6 + v.7 *Children who are brought up in a **good** life conceal the lowly birth of their parents. >*
25: 9 who finds a friend, {Lat Syr: Gk ***good** sense*}

GOODWILL (1)

Lk 2:14 peace among those whom he favors!" {Other ancient authorities read *peace, **goodwill** among people*}

GOSPEL (21)

Mt 4:23 good news {Gk ***gospel***}
24:14 good news {Or ***gospel***}
26:13 good news {Or ***gospel***}
Mk 1: 1 good news {Or ***gospel***}
1:14 good news {Or ***gospel***}
1:15 good news." {Or ***gospel***}
10:29 good news, {Or ***gospel***}
13:10 good news {Gk ***gospel***}
14: 9 good news {Or ***gospel***}
16:15 good news {Or ***gospel***}
Ro 10:16 good news; {Or ***gospel***}
15:19 good news {Or ***gospel***}
15:20 good news, {Or ***gospel***}
15:29 of the blessing {Other ancient authorities add *of the **gospel***}
1Co 15: 1 good news {Or ***gospel***}
2Co 8:18 the good news; {Or *the **gospel***}
10:14 the good news {Or *the **gospel***}
10:16 the good news {Or *the **gospel***}
11: 7 God's good news {Gk *the **gospel** of God*}
Eph 6:19 of the gospel, {Other ancient authorities lack *of the **gospel***}
2Th 2:14 through our proclamation of the good news, {Or *through our **gospel***}

GOVERNOR (2)

1Es 5:40 Attharias {Or *the **governor***}
9:49 Attharates {Or *the **governor***}

GRACE (7)

Ro 11: 6 grace. {Other ancient authorities add ... *it is no longer on the basis of **grace**, >*}
16:23 + v.24 *The **grace** of our Lord Jesus Christ be with all of you. Amen.*
2Co 8: 4 for the privilege {Gk ***grace***} of sharing
8: 6 this generous undertaking {Gk *this **grace***}
8: 7 in this generous undertaking. {Gk *this **grace***}
8: 9 know the generous act {Gk *the **grace***}
8:19 this generous undertaking {Gk *this **grace***}

GRACIOUS (1)

Sir 17:20 + v.21 *But the Lord, who is **gracious** and knows how they are formed, >*

GRAIN (4)

2Sa 17:28 lentils, {Heb *and lentils and parched **grain***}
Hos 14: 7 they shall flourish as a garden; {Cn: Heb *they shall grow **grain***}
Mt 17:20 faith the size of a {Gk *faith as a **grain** of*}
Lk 17: 6 faith the size of a {Gk *faith as a **grain** of*}

GRANTS (1)

1Sa 2: 8 honor. {Gk (Compare Q Ms) adds *He **grants** the vow of the one who vows, >*}

GRASP (1)

Jer 46: 9 the Ludim, who draw {Cn: Heb *who **grasp**, who draw*}

GRATIFY (1)

2Es 15:48 and devices. {Other ancient authorities add *you have followed after that one about to **gratify** her magnates and leaders >*}

GRATITUDE (1)

Sir 37:11 a miser about generosity {Heb: Gk ***gratitude***}

GRAVES (1)

Nu 11:34 Kibroth-hattaavah, {That is ***Graves** of craving*}

GRAVING (1)

Ex 32: 4 formed it in a mold, {Or *fashioned it with a **graving** tool*; Meaning of Heb uncertain}

GREAT (4)

Jer 5: 5 go to the rich {Or *the **great***}
Ac 24: 6 + v.7 *But the chief captain Lysias came and with **great** violence took him out of our hands, >*
Sir 23:27 + v.28 *It is a **great** honor to follow God, and to be received by him is long life.*
42:11 to shame in public gatherings. {Heb: Gk *to shame before the **great** multitude*}

GREATER (3)

Mt 23:13 + v.14 *< therefore you will receive the **greater** condemnation*
Heb 11: 4 to God a more acceptable {Gk ***greater***} sacrifice
2Es 7:87 worse {Lat Syr Ethiop ***greater***} than all the ways

GREATEST (8)

AdE 16:16 God, most high, most mighty, {Gk ***greatest***}
2Mc 14:13 high priest of the great {Gk ***greatest***} temple.
14:31 went to the great {Gk ***greatest***} and holy temple
3Mc 1: 9 to the supreme God {Gk *the **greatest** God*}
1:16 entreated the supreme God {Gk *the **greatest** God*}
3:11 might of the supreme God, {Gk *the **greatest** God*}
4:16 against the supreme God. {Gk *the **greatest** God*}
5:25 implored the supreme God {Gk *the **greatest** God*}

GREATLY (1)

Ps 89: 7 great and awesome {Gk Syr: Heb ***greatly** awesome*}

GREEK (1)

Lk 23:38 inscription over him, {Other ancient authorities add *written in **Greek** and Latin and Hebrew* (that is, *Aramaic*)}

GREEKS (2)

Ac 11:20 spoke to the Hellenists {Other ancient authorities read ***Greeks***}
18:17 Then all of them {Other ancient authorities read *all the **Greeks***}

GREW (1)

2Es 13: 3 I saw that this man flew {Syr Ethiop Arab Arm: Lat ***grew** strong*}

GRIEF (1)

Tob 7: 7 noble father!" {Other ancient authorities add ... *he was stricken with **grief** and wept. Then he said,*}

GRIEVE (1)
Sir 41:11 The human body is a fleeting thing, ... blotted out. {Heb: Gk *People* ***grieve*** *over the death of the body, ... blotted out*}

GRIEVED (1)
Sir 12: 9 One's enemies are friendly {Heb: Gk ***grieved***}

GROAN (1)
Sir 16: 3 numbers; {Other ancient authorities add *For you will* ***groan*** *in untimely mourning,* >}

GROUND (3)
Isa 50: 2 and die of thirst. {Or *die on the thirsty* ***ground***}
Mt 19: 9 except for unchastity, and marries another commits adultery." {Other ancient authorities read *except on the* ***ground*** *of unchastity, causes her to commit adultery;* >}
Sir 32:20 stumble at an obstacle twice. {Heb: Gk *stumble on stony* ***ground***}

GROW (2)
Hos 14: 7 they shall flourish as a garden; {Cn: Heb *they shall* ***grow*** *grain*}
2Es 15:13 to grow {Lat lacks *to* ***grow***}

GROWN (1)
Heb 11:23 king's edict. {Other ancient authorities add *By faith Moses, when he was* ***grown*** *up, killed the* >}

GROWS (1)
Sir 11:14 + v.16 < *evil* ***grows*** *old with those who take pride in malice.*

GUESTS (1)
Ac 11:26 they met with {Or *were* ***guests*** *of*} the church

GUIDED (1)
2Ch 32:22 he gave them rest {Gk Vg: Heb ***guided*** *them*}

GUILTY (1)
Eze 6: 6 and ruined, {Syr Vg Tg: Heb *and be made* ***guilty***}

H

HA-SATAN (14)
Job 1: 6 Satan {Or *the Accuser*; Heb ***ha-satan***}
1: 7 Satan, {Or *the Accuser*; Heb ***ha-satan***}
1: 7 Satan {Or *the Accuser*; Heb ***ha-satan***}
1: 8 Satan, {Or *the Accuser*; Heb ***ha-satan***}
1: 9 Satan {Or *the Accuser*; Heb ***ha-satan***}
1:12 Satan, {Or *the Accuser*; Heb ***ha-satan***}
1:12 Satan {Or *the Accuser*; Heb ***ha-satan***}
2: 1 Satan {Or *the Accuser*; Heb ***ha-satan***}
2: 2 Satan, {Or *the Accuser*; Heb ***ha-satan***}
2: 2 Satan {Or *The Accuser*; Heb ***ha-satan***}
2: 3 Satan, {Or *the Accuser*; Heb ***ha-satan***}
2: 4 Satan {Or *the Accuser*; Heb ***ha-satan***}
2: 6 Satan, {Or *the Accuser*; Heb ***ha-satan***}
2: 7 Satan {Or *the Accuser*; Heb ***ha-satan***}

HABITUAL (1)
4Mc 5:24 so that in all our dealings we act impartially, {Or *so that we hold in balance all our* ***habitual*** *inclinations*}

HACHMONITE (1)
1Ch 11:11 son of Hachmoni, {Or *a* ***Hachmonite***}

HACHRATHEUS (1)
AdE 4: 5 + v.6 *So* ***Hachratheus*** *went out to Mordecai* >

HAD (6)
Ne 7:68 They had ... forty-five mules, {Ezra 2.66 and the margins of some Hebrew Mss: MT lacks *They* ***had*** *... forty-five mules*}
Lk 8:43 and ... on physicians, {Other ancient authorities lack *and had spent all she* ***had*** *on physicians*}
Jn 5: 3 + v.4 < *was made well from whatever disease that person* ***had.***
Tob 3: 8 have not borne the name of {Other ancient authorities read *have* ***had*** *no benefit from*}
1Mc 2:10 has not inherited her palaces {Other ancient authorities read *has not* ***had*** *a part in her kingdom*}
4Mc 11: 6 + v.7 *If you but understood human feelings and* ***had*** *hope of salvation from God*—>

HADES (5)
3Mc 4: 8 seeing death immediately before them. {Gk *seeing* ***Hades*** *already lying at their feet*}
5:42 death {Gk ***Hades***}
5:51 death. {Gk ***Hades***}
6:31 death, {Gk ***Hades***}
2Es 4: 7 of Hades, or which are the entrances {Syr Compare Ethiop Arab 2 Arm: Lat lacks *of* ***Hades,*** *or which are the entrances*}

HAIL (1)
Isa 32:19 The forest will disappear completely, {Cn: Heb *And it will* ***hail*** *when the forest comes down*}

HAILSTONES (1)
Ps 18:13 his voice. {Gk See 2 Sam 22.14: Heb adds ***hailstones*** *and coals of fire*}

HAIR (1)
2Es 16: 2 cloth of goats' hair, {Other ancient authorities lack *cloth of goats'* ***hair***}

HALF (1)
2Es 13:40 these are the nine {Other Lat Mss *ten*; Syr Ethiop Arab 1 Arm *nine and a* ***half***} tribes

HAMATH (1)
Eze 47:15 on to Zedad, {Gk: Heb *Lebo-zedad,* [16]***Hamath***}

HAMMIPHKAD (1)
Ne 3:31 the Muster Gate, {Or ***Hammiphkad*** *Gate*}

HANANAEL (1)
Tob 1:21 Hanael {Other authorities read ***Hananael***}

HANANIEL (1)
Tob 1: 8 Tobiel, {Lat: Gk ***Hananiel***}

HAND (25)
Ge 35:18 Benjamin. {That is *Son of the right* ***hand*** or *Son of the South*}
Nu 11:23 "Is the LORD's power limited? {Heb *LORD's* ***hand*** *too short?*}
1Sa 23:11 And now, will {Q Ms Compare Gk: MT *Will the men of Keilah surrender me into his* ***hand?*** *Will*}
Job 12: 6 who bring their god in their hands. {Or *whom God brought forth by his* ***hand***; Meaning of Heb uncertain}
21:16 their own achievement? {Heb *in their* ***hand***}
Pr 6: 5 from the hunter, {Cn: Heb *from the* ***hand***}
Isa 57: 8 their nakedness. {Or *their phallus*; Heb *the* ***hand***}
Jer 41: 9 filled that cistern {Gk: Heb *whom he had killed by the* ***hand*** *of Gedaliah*} with those whom had had killed.
La 5: 6 made a pact with {Heb *have given the* ***hand*** *to*}
Mt 3: 2 has come near." {Or *is at* ***hand***}
4:17 has come near." {Or *is at* ***hand***}
10: 7 has come near.' {Or *is at* ***hand***}
Mk 1:15 has come near; {Or *is at* ***hand***}
Lk 10: 9 has come near to you.' {Or *is at* ***hand*** *for you*}
10:11 has come near.' {Or *is at* ***hand***}
21: 8 'The time is near!' {Or *at* ***hand***}
21:20 has come near. {Or *is at* ***hand***}
Jas 5: 8 the coming of the Lord is near. {Or *is at* ***hand***}
1Pe 4: 7 The end of all things is near; {Or *is at* ***hand***}
Sir 18: 2 + v.3 < *he steers the world with the span of his* ***hand,*** >
31:18 do not help yourself {Gk *reach out your* ***hand***}
49: 6 as Jeremiah had foretold. {Gk *by the* ***hand*** *of Jeremiah*}
Aza 1:66 from the power {Gk ***hand***} of death,
3Mc 5:40 your decree in the matter? {Other ancient authorities read *when the matter is in* ***hand***}
2Es 6: 1 "At the beginning ... before {< Compare Syr *The beginning by the* ***hand*** *of humankind, but the end by my own hands.* >}

HANDED (1)
Mk 16:14 risen. {Other ancient authorities add, in whole or in part, *... And for those who have sinned I was* ***handed*** *over to death,* >}

HANDS (15)
Ge 49:24 and his arms {Heb *the arms of his* ***hands***}
1Sa 21:13 mad when in their presence. {Heb *in their* ***hands***}
Est 2:21 conspired to assassinate {Heb *to lay* ***hands*** *on*}
6: 2 conspired to assassinate {Heb *to lay* ***hands*** *on*}
Eze 23:42 put bracelets on the arms {Heb ***hands***}
Zec 13: 6 these wounds on your chest?" {Heb *wounds between your* ***hands***}
Mk 16:18 in their hands, {Other ancient authorities lack *in their* ***hands***}
Ac 24: 6 + v.7 *But the chief captain Lysias came and with great violence took him out of our* ***hands,*** >
Col 2:11 circumcised with a spiritual circumcision, {Gk *a circumcision made without* ***hands***}
1Ti 5:22 Do not ordain {Gk *Do not lay* ***hands*** *on*} anyone
Heb 2: 7 glory and honor, {Other ancient authorities add *and set them over the works of your* ***hands***}
Sir 38:15 will be defiant toward the physician. {Heb: Gk *may he fall into the* ***hands*** *of the physician*}
2Es 1:32 Lord. {Other ancient authorities add *Thus says the Lord Almighty: Recently you also laid* ***hands*** *on me,* >}
2:29 My power will protect {Lat ***hands*** *will cover*}
6: 1 "At the beginning ... before {Meaning of Lat uncertain: Compare Syr *The beginning by the hand of humankind, but the end by my own* ***hands.*** >}

HANGING (1)
2Es 1:32 says the Lord. {Other ancient authorities add *... and you delivered me to death by* ***hanging*** *me on the tree;* >}

HANNA (1)
Lk 2:36 Anna {Gk ***Hanna***}

HAPPY (1)
Ge 30:13 Asher. {That is ***Happy***}

HARD (1)
Mt 23: 4 hard to bear, {Other ancient authorities lack ***hard*** *to bear*}

HARD-HEARTED (1)
Sir 16: 9 their sins; {Other ancient authorities add *All these things he did to the* ***hard-hearted*** *nations,* >}

HARDENED (1)
Sir 16:14 + v.15 *The Lord* ***hardened*** *Pharaoh so that he did not recognize him,* >

HARDENING (1)
Sir 31:26 test the work of the smith, {Heb: Gk *tests the* ***hardening*** *of steel by dipping*}

HARLOT (1)
Pr 6:26 for a prostitute's fee is only a loaf of bread, {Cn Compare Gk Syr Vg Tg: Heb *for because of a* ***harlot*** *to a piece of bread*}

HARORITE (1)
1Ch 11:27 Shammoth of Harod, {Compare 2 Sam 23.25: Heb *the* ***Harorite***}

HAS (4)
Job 2: 4 All that people have they will give to save their lives. {Or *All that the man* ***has*** *he will give for his life*}
Hos 14: 8 O Ephraim, what have I {Or *What more* ***has*** *Ephraim*}
Sir 20:14 for he looks for recompense sevenfold. {Syr: Gk *he* ***has*** *many eyes instead of one*}
20:17 how often! {Other ancient authorities add *for he has not honestly received what he* ***has,*** >}

HASTENS (1)
Isa 8: 1 Maher-shalal-hash-baz," {That is *The spoil speeds, the prey* ***hastens***}

HATE (1)
2Sa 5: 8 those whom David hates." {Another reading is *those who* ***hate*** *David*}

HATED (1)
AdE 9: 4 + v.5 < *and they did as they pleased to those who* ***hated*** *them.*

HATEFUL (2)
Rev 18: 2 a haunt of every foul and hateful beast. {Other ancient authorities lack the words *a haunt of every foul beast* and attach the words *and* ***hateful*** to the previous line so as to read *a haunt of every foul and* ***hateful*** *bird*}

HATES (1)
Mal 2:16 For I hate {Cn: Heb *he* ***hates***} divorce,

HAUGHTY (1)
Sir 22: 6 + v.8 < *who are disdainfully and boorishly* ***haughty*** *stain the nobility of their kindred.*

HAUNT (1)
Rev 18: 2 a haunt of every foul and hateful beast. {Other ancient authorities lack the words *a* ***haunt*** *of every foul beast* >}

HAVE (5)
Ps 49:14 to the grave they descend, {Cn: Heb *the upright shall* ***have*** *dominion over them in the morning*}
Php 2: 5 that was {Or *that you* ***have***} in Christ Jesus,
1Pe 5: 2 as God would have you do it— {Other ancient authorities lack *as God would* ***have*** *you do it*}
Sir 20:17 how often! {Other ancient authorities add *... and what he does not* ***have*** *is unimportant to him*}
4Mc 10: 3 + v.4 *So if you* ***have*** *any instrument of torture,* >

HAYAH (1)
Ex 3:15 LORD, {The word "LORD" when spelled with capital letters stands for the divine name, *YHWH*, which is here connected with the verb ***hayah***, "to be"}

HEAD (6)
2Sa 23:13 three of the thirty {Heb adds ***head***} chiefs
Ps 44:14 a laughingstock {Heb *a shaking of the* ***head***}
140: 9 Those who surround me lift up their heads; {Cn Compare Gk: Heb *those who surround me are uplifted in* ***head***; >}

Sir 25:15 no venom {Syr: Gk ***head***}
25:15 a snake's venom, {Syr: Gk ***head***}
Man 1:10 so that I am rejected {Other ancient authorities read *so that I cannot lift up my* ***head***}

HEALING (1)
Sir 16:10 stubbornness. {Other ancient authorities add *Chastising, showing mercy, striking,* ***healing,*** *the Lord persisted in mercy and discipline.*}

HEALTH (1)
Sir 17:26 iniquity, {Other ancient authorities add *for he will lead you out of darkness to the light of* ***health.***}

HEAP (2)
Ge 31:47 Jegar-sahadutha: {In Aramaic *The* ***heap*** *of witness*}
31:47 Galeed. {In Hebrew *The* ***heap*** *of witness*}

HEAR (6)
Mt 11:15 with ears {Other ancient authorities add *to* ***hear***}
13: 9 with ears {Other ancient authorities add *to* ***hear***}
13:43 with ears {Other ancient authorities add *to* ***hear***}
Mk 7:15 + v.16 *"Let anyone with ears to* ***hear*** *listen"*
Sir 13:13 + v.14 *When you* ***hear*** *these things in your sleep,* >
Pm 151: 3 he who hears. {Other ancient authorities read ... *who will* ***hear*** *me*}

HEARD (4)
2Ki 20:13 Hezekiah welcomed them; {Gk Vg Syr: Heb *When Hezekiah* ***heard*** *about them*}
Mt 21:15 and heard {Gk lacks ***heard***}
Tob 7: 7 father!" {Other ancient authorities add *When he* ***heard*** *that Tobit had lost his sight,* >}
2Es 10:35 I hear {Other ancient authorities read *have* ***heard***} what I do not understand

HEARING (1)
Mk 5:36 But overhearing {< other ancient authorities read ***hearing***} what they said,

HEARS (1)
Ge 16:11 Ishmael, {That is *God* ***hears***}

HEART (19)
2Ki 10:15 "Is your heart true to mine as mine is to yours?" {Gk: Heb *Is it right with your* ***heart,*** *as my* ***heart*** *is with your* ***heart?***}
2Ch 29:34 conscientious {Heb *upright in* ***heart***}
Job 34:14 take back his spirit {Heb *his* ***heart*** *his spirit*}
Ps 108: 1 my heart is steadfast; {Heb Mss Gk Syr: MT lacks *my* ***heart*** *is steadfast*}
Pr 12:23 but the mind of a fool {Heb *the* ***heart*** *of fools*}
25:20 Like a moth ... human heart. {Gk Syr Tg: Heb lacks *Like a moth ... human* ***heart***}
La 2:18 Cry aloud {Cn: Heb *Their* ***heart*** *cried*}
Eze 11:21 whose heart goes after ... abominations, {Cn: Heb *And to the* ***heart*** *of their detestable things and their abominations their* ***heart*** *goes*}
Ac 8:36 + v.37 *And Philip said, "If you believe with all your* ***heart,*** >
Sir 4:17 until she trusts them, {Or *until they remain faithful in their* ***heart***}
13:25 evil. {Other ancient authorities add *and a glad* ***heart*** *makes a cheerful countenance*}
18:29 proverbs. {Other ancient authorities add ... *than clinging with a dead* ***heart*** *to a dead one.*}
19: 5 One who rejoices in wickedness {Other ancient authorities read ***heart***}
25:18 Her husband sits {Heb Syr: Gk *loses* ***heart***}
37: 6 during the battle, {Heb: Gk *in your* ***heart***}
37:18 it sprouts four branches, {Heb: Gk *As a clue to changes of* ***heart*** *four kinds of destiny appear*}

HEARTH (1)
Isa 29: 2 Ariel. {Probable meaning, *altar* ***hearth***; >}

HEARTS (3)
2Co 7: 2 in your hearts {Gk lacks *in your* ***hearts***}
Sir 17:15 + v.16 < ***hearts*** *of flesh in place of their stony* ***hearts.*** >

HEAVEN (11)
Dt 30: 4 the ends of the world, {Heb *of* ***heaven***}
Mk 11:25 + v.26 < *neither will your Father in* ***heaven*** *forgive your trespasses."*
16:14 risen. {Other ancient authorities add, in whole or in part, ... *of righteousness that is in* ***heaven."***}
Lk 11: 2 "When you pray, say: Father, {Other ancient authorities read *Our Father in* ***heaven***} ... Your kingdom come. {< Other ancient authorities add *Your will be done, on earth as in* ***heaven***}
11:13 the heavenly Father give the Holy Spirit {Other ancient authorities read *the Father give the Holy Spirit from* ***heaven***}
24:51 and was carried up into heaven. {Other ancient authorities lack *and was carried up into* ***heaven***}
Jn 3:13 the Son of Man. {Other ancient authorities add *who is in* ***heaven***}
1Jn 5: 7 There are three that testify: {A few other authorities read (with variations) [7]*There are three that testify in* ***heaven,*** *the Father, the Word, and the Holy Spirit,* >}

Sir 1: 4 + v.5 *The source of wisdom is God's word in the highest* ***heaven,*** >
16:14 + v.15 < *in order that his works might be known under* ***heaven.*** >

HEAVENS (1)
2Es 8:20 whose eyes are exalted {Another Lat text reads *whose are the highest* ***heavens***}

HEBREW (1)
Lk 23:38 over him, {Other ancient authorities add *written in Greek and Latin and* ***Hebrew*** (that is, *Aramaic*)}

HEBREWS (1)
Ex 1:22 to the Hebrews {Sam Gk Tg: Heb lacks *to the* ***Hebrews***}

HEBRON (2)
2Sa 15: 8 in Hebron." {Gk Mss: Heb lacks *in* ***Hebron***}
1Ch 24:23 Hebron: {See 23.19: Heb lacks ***Hebron***}

HEED (1)
Sir 34: 2 who believes in {Syr: Gk *pays* ***heed*** *to*} dreams.

HEEDS (1)
Sir 32:24 who keeps the law preserves himself, {Heb: Gk *who believes the law* ***heeds*** *the commandments*}

HEEL (2)
Ge 25:26 Jacob. {That is *He takes by the* ***heel*** or *He supplants*}
27:36 Jacob? {That is *He supplants* or *He takes by the* ***heel***}

HEIFER (2)
Tob 1: 5 sacrificed to the calf {Other ancient authorities read ***heifer***}

HEIGHT (3)
1Sa 19:22 to the great well that is in Secu; {Gk reads *to the well of the threshing floor on the bare* ***height***}
Eze 32: 5 fill the valleys with your carcass. {Symmachus Syr Vg: Heb *your* ***height***}
Mt 6:27 add a single hour to your span of life? {Or *add one cubit to your* ***height***}

HEIGHTS (1)
Job 11: 8 It is higher than heaven—what {Heb *The* ***heights*** *of heaven*}

HELD (1)
Joel 3:21 I will avenge their blood, and I will not clear the guilty, {Gk Syr: Heb *I will hold innocent their blood that I have not* ***held*** *innocent*}

HELEM (1)
Zec 6:14 Heldai, {Syr Compare verse 10: Heb ***Helem***}

HELL (1)
2Es 2: 9 Gomorrah, whose land lies in lumps of pitch and heaps of ashes. {Other ancient authorities read *Gomorrah, whose land descends to* ***hell***}

HELP (3)
Ex 18: 4 Eliezer {Heb *Eli*, my God; *ezer*, **help**}
1Sa 7:12 Ebenezer; {That is *Stone of* ***Help***}
Ps 89:19 "I have set the crown {Cn: Heb ***help***}

HELPER (4)
Jn 14:16 Advocate, {Or ***Helper***}
14:26 Advocate, {Or ***Helper***}
15:26 Advocate {Or ***Helper***}
16: 7 Advocate {Or ***Helper***}

HELPERS (1)
Php 1: 1 with the bishops and deacons: {Or *overseers and* ***helpers***}

HELPS (2)
Job 30:13 no one restrains {Cn: Heb ***helps***} them.
Ac 27:17 they took measures {Gk ***helps***}

HEN (1)
Zec 6:14 Josiah {Syr Compare verse 10: Heb ***Hen***}

HEPHZIBAH (1)
Isa 62: 4 Her, {Heb ***Hephzibah***}

HERE (2)
Ps 73:10 the people turn and praise them, {Cn: Heb *his people return* ***here***}
Lk 24: 5 He is not here, but has risen. {Other ancient authorities lack *He is not* ***here,*** *but has risen*}

HERITAGE (1)
Eph 1:11 also obtained an inheritance, {Or *been made a* ***heritage***}

HERODIANS (1)
Mk 8:15 and the yeast of Herod." {Other ancient authorities read *the* ***Herodians***}

HEROES (1)
4Mc 17: 8 as a reminder to the people of our nation: {Or *as a memorial to the* ***heroes*** *of our people*}

HESITATE (1)
Ac 11:12 not to make a distinction between them and us. {Or *not to* ***hesitate***}

HEZRAI (1)
2Sa 23:35 Hezro {Another reading is ***Hezrai***}

HID (2)
Mt 13:33 mixed in with {Gk ***hid in***}
Lk 13:21 mixed in with {Gk ***hid in***}

HIDDEN (2)
Job 40:13 faces in the world below. {Heb *the* ***hidden*** *place*}
Ps 143: 9 I have fled to you for refuge. {One Heb Ms Gk: MT *to you I have* ***hidden***}

HIDE (1)
Sir 4:23 and do not hide your wisdom. {So some Gk Mss and Heb Syr Lat: Other Gk Mss lack *and do not* ***hide*** *your wisdom*}

HIGH (8)
2Sa 23: 1 whom God exalted, {Q Ms: MT *who was raised on* ***high***}
1Ki 9: 8 will become a heap of ruins; {Syr Old Latin: Heb *will become* ***high***}
Jer 17: 3 spoil as the price of your sin {Cn: Heb *spoil your* ***high*** *places for sin*}
Eze 20:29 Bamah {That is ***High*** *Place*}
43: 7 at their death. {Or *on their* ***high*** *places*}
43:13 one cubit high, {Gk: Heb lacks ***high***}
2Es 14:48 did so. {Syr adds ... *And he was called the scribe of the knowledge of the Most* ***High*** *for ever and ever.* >}
4Mc 4:20 constructed at the very citadel {Or ***high*** *place*}

HIGHEST (3)
Isa 17: 9 places of the Hivites and the Amorites, {Cn Compare Gk: Heb *places of the wood and the* ***highest*** *bough*}
Sir 1: 4 + v.5 *The source of wisdom is God's word in the* ***highest*** *heaven,* >
2Es 8:20 whose eyes are exalted {Another Lat text reads *whose are the* ***highest*** *heavens*}

HIGHLANDS (1)
2Es 15:58 and highlands {Gk: Lat omits *and* ***highlands***}

HIGHWAY (1)
Ps 68: 4 lift up a song to him who rides upon the clouds—{Or *cast up a* ***highway*** *for him who rides through the deserts*}

HILEZ (1)
1Ch 6:58 Hilen {Other readings ***Hilez,*** *Holon*; See Josh 21.15}

HILL (6)
Jos 5: 3 Gibeath-haaraloth. {That is *the* ***Hill*** *of the Foreskins*}
Jdg 15:17 Ramath-lehi. {That is *The* ***Hill*** *of the Jawbone*}
1Sa 10: 5 Gibeath-elohim, {Or *the* ***Hill*** *of God*}
10:10 Gibeah, {Or *the* ***hill***}
2Sa 6: 4 with the ark of God; {Compare Gk: Heb *and brought it out of the house of Abinadab, which was on the* ***hill*** *with the ark of God*}
Jdt 6:12 town saw them, {Other ancient authorities add *on the top of the* ***hill***}

HIRED (2)
Lk 15:21 your son.' {Other ancient authorities add *treat me as one of your* ***hired*** *servants*}
Ac 28:30 at his own expense {Or *in his own* ***hired*** *dwelling*}

HOBAB (1)
Jdg 1:16 Hobab {Gk: Heb lacks ***Hobab***}

HODAH (1)
Ge 29:35 praise {Heb ***hodah***}

HOLD (5)
2Sa 24:12 Three things I offer {Or ***hold*** *over*} you;
Ps 13: 2 must I bear pain {Syr: Heb ***hold*** *counsels*}
Joel 3:21 and I will not clear the guilty, {Gk Syr: Heb *I will* ***hold*** *innocent their blood that I have not held innocent*}
Jas 2: 1 do you ... really believe in our glorious Lord Jesus Christ? {Or ***hold*** *the faith of our glorious Lord Jesus Christ without acts of favoritism*}
4Mc 5:24 so that in all our dealings we act impartially, {Or *so that we* ***hold*** *in balance all our habitual inclinations*}

HOLINESS (3)
Ps 60: 6 promised in his sanctuary: {Or *by his **holiness***}
108: 7 promised in his sanctuary: {Or *by his **holiness***}
2Co 1:12 in the world with frankness {Other ancient authorities read ***holiness***}

HOLON (1)
1Ch 6:58 Hilen {Other readings *Hilez, **Holon***; See Josh 21.15}

HOLY (13)
Eze 36:38 Like the flock for sacrifices, {Heb *flock of **holy** things*}
Lk 11: 2 Your kingdom come. {A few ancient authorities read *Your **Holy** Spirit come upon us and cleanse us.* >}
Jn 7:39 for as yet there was no Spirit, {Other ancient authorities read *for as yet the Spirit* (others, ***Holy** Spirit*) *had not been given*}
Ro 15:19 by the power of the Spirit of God, {Other ancient authorities read *of the Spirit* or *of the **Holy** Spirit*}
Heb 9:14 through the eternal Spirit {Other ancient authorities read ***Holy** Spirit*}
1Jn 5: 7 testify: {A few other authorities read (with variations) [7]*There are three that testify in heaven, the Father, the Word, and the **Holy** Spirit,* >}
Sir 16: 9 their sins; {Other ancient authorities add < *and by the multitude of his **holy** ones he was not appeased.*}
18: 2 + v.3 < *separating among them the **holy** things from the profane.*
24:17 + v.18 *I am the mother of beautiful love, of fear, of knowledge, and of **holy** hope;* >
36:18 the city of your sanctuary, {Or *on your **holy** city*}
3Mc 7:16 the eternal Savior {Other ancient authorities read *the **holy** Savior*; others, *the **holy** one*}
2Es 4:25 do for his {Ethiop adds ***holy***} name

HOME (1)
Jn 1:11 to what was his own, {Or *to his own **home***}

HOMER (1)
Eze 45:14 (the cor, {Vg: Heb ***homer***} like the homer,

HONESTLY (1)
Sir 20:17 how often! {Other ancient authorities add *for he has not **honestly** received what he has,* >}

HONOR (3)
Wis 4: 2 people imitate {Other ancient authorities read ***honor***} it,
Sir 3: 7 they will serve their parents as their masters. {In other ancient authorities this line is preceded by *Those who fear the Lord **honor** their father,*}
23:27 + v.28 *It is a great **honor** to follow God, and to be received by him is long life.*

HOPE (5)
Jdt 13:19 Your praise {Other ancient authorities read ***hope***}
Sir 23: 3 over me. {Other ancient authorities add *From them the **hope** of your mercy is remote*}
24:17 + v.18 *I am the mother of beautiful love, of fear, of knowledge, and of holy **hope;*** >
2Es 4:35 'How long are we to remain here? {Syr Ethiop Arab 2 Georg: Lat *How long do I **hope** thus?*}
4Mc 11: 6 + v.7 *If you but understood human feelings and had **hope** of salvation from God—*>

HOPES (1)
Wis 15: 6 such objects of hope {Gk *such **hopes***}

HORDE (3)
Eze 39:11 Hamon-gog. {That is, *the **Horde** of Gog*}
39:15 Hamon-gog. {That is, *the **Horde** of Gog*}
39:16 Hamonah {That is *The **Horde***}

HORN (5)
Lk 1:69 a mighty savior {Gk *a **horn** of salvation*}
Jdt 9: 8 to break off the horns {Syr: Gk ***horn***}
Sir 47: 5 to exalt the power {Gk ***horn***}
47: 7 he crushed their power {Gk ***horn***}
47:11 and exalted his power {Gk ***horn***}

HORNETS (3)
Ex 23:28 I will send the pestilence {Or ***hornets***: Meaning of Heb uncertain}
Dt 7:20 God will send pestilence {Or ***hornets***: Meaning of Heb uncertain}
Wis 12: 8 sent wasps {Or ***hornets***} as forerunners

HORNS (1)
Am 6:13 Karnaim {Or ***horns***}

HOSHEA (1)
Dt 32:44 Joshua {Sam Gk Syr Vg: MT ***Hoshea***}

HOSTILITY (1)
Ps 39:10 I am worn down by the blows {Heb ***hostility***}

HOTHAM (1)
1Ch 7:35 Helem {Or ***Hotham***; see 7.32}

HOUR (2)
Mt 24:42 do not know on what day {Other ancient authorities read *at what **hour***}
3Mc 5:12 deep a sleep {Other ancient authorities add *from evening until the ninth **hour***}

HOUSE (17)
Ge 28:19 Bethel; {That is ***House** of God*}
Jdg 19:18 going to my home. {Gk Compare 19.29. Heb *to the **house** of the* LORD}
2Sa 6: 4 ark of God; {Compare Gk: Heb *and brought it out of the **house** of Abinadab, which was on the hill with the ark of God*}
19:11 to the king. {Gk: Heb *to the king, to his **house***}
1Ki 12:31 He also made houses {Gk Vg Compare 13.32: Heb *a **house***}
Pr 2:18 for her way {Cn: Heb ***house*** leads down to death,
Isa 15: 2 Dibon {Cn: Heb *the **house** and Dibon*} has gone
Eze 44: 6 the rebellious house, {Gk: Heb lacks ***house***}
Da 1: 2 land of Shinar, {Gk Theodotion: Heb adds *to the **house** of his own gods*}
Am 5: 3 ten left. {Heb adds *to the **house** of Israel*}
Ac 2:46 at home {Or *from **house** to **house***}
5:42 the temple and at home {Or *from **house** to **house***}
Sir 42:11 See ... house. {Heb: Gk lacks *See ... **house***}
50:18 in sweet and full-toned melody. {Other ancient authorities read *in sweet melody throughout the **house***}
1Mc 10:41 the service of the temple. {Gk ***house***}

HOUSEHOLD (4)
2Ki 23:24 teraphim, {Or ***household** gods*}
Eze 21:21 teraphim, {Or *the **household** gods*}
Zec 10: 2 teraphim {Or ***household** gods*}
Sir 29:28 scolding about lodging {Or *scolding from the **household***}

HOUSES (2)
Isa 23: 1 for your fortress is destroyed. {Cn Compare verse 14: Heb *for it is destroyed, without **houses***}
Mt 23:13 + v.14 < *For you devour widows' **houses** and for the sake of appearance you make long prayers;* >

HOW (4)
Isa 51:19 who will comfort you? {Q Ms Gk Syr Vg: MT ***how** may I comfort you?*}
Mt 27:65 as secure as you can." {Gk *you know **how***}
Sir 17:20 + v.21 *But the Lord, who is gracious and knows **how** they are formed,* >
20: 8 hated. {Other ancient authorities add ***How** good it is to show repentance when you are reproved,* >}

HOWEVER (1)
2Es 11:40 the fourth that has come, ... deceit. {Syr Arab Arm: Lat Ethiop *The fourth came, **however,*** >}

HOZAI (1)
2Ch 33:19 records of the seers. {One Ms Gk: MT *of **Hozai***}

HU (1)
Ex 16:15 "What is it?" {Or *"It is manna"* (Heb *man **hu***, see verse 31)}

HUMAN (7)
Ge 32:28 striven with God and with humans, {Or *with divine and **human** beings*}
Pr 25:20 Like a moth ... human heart. {Gk Syr Tg: Heb lacks *Like a moth ... **human** heart*}
29:25 The fear of others {Or ***human** fear*}
Da 2:43 mix with one another in marriage, {Aram *by **human** seed*}
Lk 9:56 Then {Other ancient authorities read *... for the Son of Man has not come to destroy the lives of **human** beings but to save them." Then*}
Sir 31:16 like a well brought-up person, {Heb: Gk *like a **human** being*}
4Mc 11: 6 + v.7 *If you but understood **human** feelings and had hope of salvation from God—*>

HUMANKIND (5)
Ps 90: 3 You turn us {Heb ***humankind***}
94:11 knows our thoughts, {Heb *the thoughts of **humankind***}
Zec 9: 1 the capital of Aram, {Cn: Heb *of Adam* (or *of **humankind***)}
13: 5 for the land has been my possession {Cn: Heb *for **humankind** has caused me to possess*}
2Es 6: 1 "At the beginning ... before {Meaning of Lat uncertain: Compare Syr *The beginning by the hand of **humankind**, but the end by my own* >}

HUMANS (1)
Sir 20:15 to God and humans. {Other ancient authorities lack *to God and **humans***}

HUMBLE (4)
Pr 6: 3 go, hurry, {Or ***humble** yourself*} and plead
Ro 12:16 but associate with the lowly; {Or *give yourselves to **humble** tasks*}
Php 3:21 body of our humiliation {Or *our **humble** bodies*}
Sir 3:18 + v.19 *Many are lofty and renowned, but to the **humble** he reveals his secrets.*

HUMBLED (1)
Isa 51:21 you who are wounded, {Or ***humbled***}

HUMBLES (1)
Hos 7:10 Israel's pride testifies against {Or ***humbles***}

HUMILIATION (1)
Heb 11:23 kings' edict. {Other ancient authorities add ... *because he observed the **humiliation** of his people* (Gk *brothers*)}

HUNDRED (7)
Lk 24:13 about seven miles {Gk *sixty stadia;* other ancient authorities read *a **hundred** sixty stadia*}
Jn 6: 7 Six months' wages {Gk *Two **hundred** denarii;* >}
AdE 9:29 + v.30 ... *to the one **hundred** twenty-seven provinces of the kingdom of Ahasuerus,* >
2Mc 12: 9 thirty miles {Gk *two **hundred** forty stadia*}
12:17 ninety-five miles {Gk *seven **hundred** fifty stadia*}
12:29 seventy-five miles {Gk *six **hundred** stadia*}
Pm 151: T outside the number), {Other ancient authorities add *of the one **hundred** fifty* (psalms)}

HUNGRY (1)
Job 18:12 Their strength is consumed by hunger, {Or *Disaster is **hungry** for them*}

HURRIED (1)
4Mc 3: 8 When evening fell, he {Other ancient authorities read *he **hurried** and*} came,

HURRYING (1)
Nu 32:17 take up arms as a vanguard {Cn: Heb ***hurrying***}

HURTFUL (1)
Ps 139:24 if there is any wicked {Heb ***hurtful***} way

HUSBAND (6)
1Sa 1:18 and drank with her husband, {Gk: Heb lacks *and drank with her **husband***}
1Ti 2:12 authority over a man; {Or *her **husband***}
3: 2 married only once, {Gk *the **husband** of one wife*}
5: 9 married only once; {Gk *the wife of one **husband***}
Tit 1: 6 married only once, {Gk ***husband** of one wife*}
Sir 40:23 but a sensible wife {Heb Compare Syr: Gk *wife with her **husband***}

HUSBANDS (1)
1Ti 3:12 married only once, {Gk *be **husbands** of one wife*}

HUSHIM (1)
Ge 46:23 Hashum. {Gk: Heb ***Hushim***}

HYACINTH (1)
Rev 9:17 sapphire {Gk ***hyacinth***}

HYPOCRITES (1)
Mt 23:13 + v.14 *Woe to you, scribes and Pharisees, **hypocrites!** For you devour widows' houses* >

I

IDLE (1)
2Es 15:60 crush the hateful {Another reading is ***idle*** or *unprofitable*} city,

IF (19)
Lev 20:10 if a man ... with the wife of {Heb repeats ***if** a man commits adultery with the wife of*}
Dt 30:16 If you obey the commandments of the LORD your God {Gk: Heb lacks ***If** you obey the commandments of the LORD your God*}
Mk 11:22 "Have {Other ancient authorities read ***"If** you have*} faith in God.
11:25 + v.26 *"But **if** you do not forgive, neither will your Father in heaven forgive your trespasses."*
Lk 11:11 child asks for {Other ancient authorities add *bread, will give a stone; or **if** your child asks for*}
Jn 13:32 If God has been glorified in him, {Other ancient authorities lack ***If** God has been glorified in him*}
Ac 8:36 + v.37 *And Philip said, "**If** you believe with all your heart, you may."* >
Ro 11: 6 grace. {Other ancient authorities add *But **if** it is by works, it is no longer on the basis of grace,* >}
AdE 8: 7 Now that I {Gk ***If** I*} have granted
Sir 16:21 Like a tempest ... concealed. {Meaning of Gk uncertain: Heb Syr ***If** I sin, no eye can see me, and **if** I am disloyal all in secret, who is to know?*}
Sir 19:20 + v.21 < *"I will not act as you wish," even **if** later he does it,* >
2Es 1:32 says the Lord. {Other ancient authorities add ***if** I have not kept the commandment of the Father, **if** I have not nourished you, **if** I have not done the things my Father commanded,* >

2Es 5:45 If ... one time {Lat lacks *If ... one time*}
4Mc 10: 3 + v.4 *So* ***if*** *you have any instrument of torture, apply it to my body; for you cannot touch my soul, even* ***if*** *you wish."*
11: 6 + v.7 ***If*** *you but understood human feelings and had hope of salvation from God—* >

IGNORANT (1)
Sir 5:15 cause no harm, {Heb Syr: Gk *be* ***ignorant***}

IGNORING (1)
Mk 5:36 But overhearing {Or ***ignoring***; >} what they said,

IMAGE (1)
2Ki 23: 6 image of {Heb lacks ***image*** *of*}

IMMANU (1)
Isa 8:10 God is with us. {Heb ***immanu*** *el*}

IMMORTALITY (1)
Sir 19:17 + v.19 < *and those who do what is pleasing to him enjoy the fruit of the tree of* ***immortality.***

IMPERISHABLE (1)
Mk 16:14 risen. {Other ancient authorities add, in whole or in part, ... *inherit the spiritual and* ***imperishable*** *glory of righteousness that is in heaven."* }

IMPRISONED (1)
2Mc 5: 8 Accused {Cn: Gk ***Imprisoned***} before Aretas

INCLINATIONS (1)
4Mc 5:24 in all our dealings we act impartially, {Or *so that we hold in balance all our habitual* ***inclinations***}

INCORRUPTIBLE (1)
2Es 4:11 the corrupt world understand incorruption?" {Syr Ethiop *the way of the* ***incorruptible?***}

INDULGE (2)
Col 2:23 are of no value in checking self-indulgence. {Or *are of no value, serving only to* ***indulge*** *the flesh*}
AdE 9:10 and they indulged {Other ancient authorities read *did not* ***indulge***}

INDULGENCE (1)
Wis 12:20 and indulgence {Other ancient authorities lack *and* ***indulgence***; others read *and entreaty*}

INDUSTRIOUS (1)
Sir 31:22 be moderate, {Heb Syr: Gk ***industrious***}

INFANTS (1)
1Th 2: 7 gentle {Other ancient authorities read ***infants***}

INHABITANT (1)
Isa 12: 6 O royal {Or *O* ***inhabitant*** *of*} Zion,

INHABITANTS (1)
Eze 26:17 on all the mainland! {Cn: Heb *its* ***inhabitants***}

INHABITED (1)
Eze 26:17 have vanished {Gk OL Aquila: Heb *have vanished, O* ***inhabited*** *one,*} from the seas,

INHERIT (3)
Job 13:26 make me reap {Heb ***inherit***} the iniquities
Pr 14:18 The simple are adorned with {Or ***inherit***} folly,
Mk 16:14 risen. {Other ancient authorities add, in whole or in part, ... ***inherit*** *the spiritual and imperishable glory of righteousness that is in heaven."* }

INHERITOR (1)
Isa 65: 9 inheritors {Or *an* ***inheritor***} of my mountains;

INIQUITIES (2)
Eze 32:27 shields {Cn: Heb ***iniquities***} are upon their bones;
2Es 1:36 their former state. {Other ancient authorities read *their* ***iniquities***}

INIQUITY (3)
2Sa 16:12 look on my distress, {Gk Vg: Heb ***iniquity***}
Ps 31:10 because of my misery, {Gk Syr: Heb *my* ***iniquity***}
La 4: 6 For the chastisement {Or ***iniquity***} of my people

INJUSTICE (1)
2Es 16:53 not sinned; {Other ancient authorities add *or the unjust done* ***injustice***}

INNER (1)
2Ch 3:16 encircling {Cn: Heb *in the* ***inner*** *sanctuary*}

INNERMOST (1)
Ps 28: 2 your most holy sanctuary. {Heb *your* ***innermost*** *sanctuary*}

INNOCENT (2)
Joel 3:21 the guilty, {Gk Syr: Heb *I will hold* ***innocent*** *their blood that I have not held* ***innocent***}

INSTEAD (2)
Heb 12: 2 who for the sake of {Or *who* ***instead*** *of*}
Sir 20:14 he looks for recompense sevenfold. {Syr: Gk *he has many eyes* ***instead*** *of one*}

INSTRUCTION (1)
Pr 9: 9 Give instruction {Heb lacks ***instruction***}

INSTRUMENT (1)
4Mc 10: 3 + v.4 *So if you have any* ***instrument*** *of torture,* >

INTELLIGENT (1)
Wis 13:13 with skill gained in idleness; {Other ancient authorities read *with* ***intelligent*** *skill*}

INTERESTS (1)
Lk 2:49 I must be in my Father's house?" {Or *be about my Father's* ***interests?***}

INTERPRETER (1)
Sir 17: 4 + v.5 < *reason, the* ***interpreter*** *of one's faculties.*

INVITED (1)
1Sa 9:24 it is set ... eat with the guests." {Cn: Heb *it was kept for you, saying, I have* ***invited*** *the people*}

INWARD (1)
Ps 49:11 Their graves {Gk Syr Compare Tg: Heb *their* ***inward*** (thought)} are their homes

IOB (1)
Ge 46:13 Jashub, {Compare Sam Gk Num 26.24 1 Chr 7.1: MT ***Iob***}

IOTA (1)
Mt 5:18 not one letter, {Gk *one* ***iota***}

IRON (1)
Da 2:40 smashes everything, {Gk Theodotion Syr Vg: Aram adds *and like* ***iron*** *that crushes*}

ISAAC (1)
Ge 21: 9 with her son Isaac. {Gk Vg: Heb lacks *with her son* ***Isaac***}

ISAIAH (2)
Mt 13:35 spoken through the prophet: {Other ancient authorities read *the prophet* ***Isaiah***}
27: 9 spoken through the prophet Jeremiah, {Other ancient authorities read *Zechariah* or ***Isaiah***}

ISH (1)
Ge 2:23 Man {Heb ***ish***}

ISH-BOSHETH (11)
2Sa 2: 8 Ishbaal {Gk Compare 1 Chr 8.33; 9.39: Heb ***Ish-bosheth***, "man of shame"}
2:10 Ishbaal, {Gk Compare 1 Chr 8.33; 9.39: Heb ***Ish-bosheth***, "man of shame"}
2:12 Ishbaal {Gk Compare 1 Chr 8.33; 9.39: Heb ***Ish-bosheth***, "man of shame"}
2:15 Ishbaal {Gk Compare 1 Chr 8.33; 9.39: Heb ***Ish-bosheth***, "man of shame"}
3: 8 Ishbaal {Gk Compare 1 Chr 8.33; 9.39: Heb ***Ish-bosheth***, "man of shame"}
3:14 Ishbaal, {Heb ***Ish-bosheth***}
3:15 Ishbaal {Heb ***Ish-bosheth***}
4: 5 Ishbaal, {Heb ***Ish-bosheth***}
4: 8 Ishbaal {Heb ***Ish-bosheth***}
4: 8 Ishbaal, {Heb ***Ish-bosheth***}
4:12 Ishbaal {Heb ***Ish-bosheth***}

ISH-HAI (1)
2Sa 23:20 a valiant warrior {Another reading is *the son of* ***Ish-hai***}

ISHBAAL (1)
2Sa 4: 1 Ishbaal {Heb lacks ***Ishbaal***}

ISHSHAH (1)
Ge 2:23 Woman, {Heb ***ishshah***}

ISRAEL (18)
Ge 33:20 El-Elohe-Israel. {That is *God, the God of* ***Israel***}
48: 2 he {Heb ***Israel***} summoned his strength
Nu 22:41 the people of Israel. {Heb lacks *of* ***Israel***}
1Sa 4: 1 In those days ... against Israel, {Gk: Heb lacks *In those days the Philistines mustered for war against* ***Israel***}
5: 8 "Let the ark of God ... to us." {Gk Compare Q Ms: MT *They answered, "Let the ark of the God of* ***Israel*** *be brought around to Gath."* }
5:10 the God of Israel {Q Ms Gk: MT lacks *of* ***Israel***}
10: 1 over his people ... ruler {Gk: Heb lacks *over his people* ***Israel.*** *You shall ... anointed you ruler*}
10:18 and said to them, {Heb *to the people of* ***Israel***}
2Sa 16:15 all the Israelites {Gk: Heb *all the people, the men of* ***Israel***}
1Ki 20:34 The king of Israel responded, {Heb lacks *The king of* ***Israel*** *responded*}
2Ch 21: 2 Judah. {Gk Syr: Heb ***Israel***}
Ps 73: 1 good to the upright, {Or *good to* ***Israel***}
105: 6 offspring of his servant Abraham, {Another reading is ***Israel*** (compare 1 Chr 16.13)}
Hos 5: 5 Ephraim {Heb ***Israel*** *and Ephraim*} stumbles
Am 5: 3 ten left. {Heb adds *to the house of* ***Israel***}
Ac 7:23 his relatives, the Israelites. {Gk *his brothers, the sons of* ***Israel***}
Ro 11:23 of Israel, {Gk lacks *of* ***Israel***}
3Mc 6:32 praising God, their Savior and worker of wonders. {Other ancient authorities read *praising* ***Israel*** *and the wonder-working God;* >}

ISRAEL'S (1)
3Mc 6:32 praising God, their Savior and worker of wonders. {Other ancient authorities read ... *praising* ***Israel's*** *Savior, the wonder-working God*}

ISRAELITE (1)
2Sa 17:25 Ishmaelite, {1 Chr 2.17: Heb ***Israelite***}

ISRAELITES (2)
Dt 32: 8 the number of the gods; {Q Ms Compare Gk Tg: MT *the* ***Israelites***}
1Sa 14:24 Now Saul committed a very rash act on that day. {Gk: Heb *The* ***Israelites*** *were distressed that day*}

J

JABESH-GILEAD (1)
1Sa 10:27 Now Nahash ... entered Jabesh-gilead. {< MT lacks *Now Nahash ... entered* ***Jabesh-gilead.***}

JABIN (1)
1Sa 12: 9 Jabin king of {Gk: Heb lacks ***Jabin*** *king of*}

JACOB (1)
Dt 32:15 Jacob ate his fill; {Q Mss Sam Gk: MT lacks ***Jacob*** *ate his fill*}

JAIR (2)
Nu 32:41 Havvoth-jair. {That is *the villages of* ***Jair***}
Dt 3:14 Havvoth-jair, {That is *Settlement of* ***Jair***}

JAPHETH (1)
Ge 10: 5 These ... of Japheth {Compare verses 20, 31. Heb lacks *These are the descendants of* ***Japheth***}

JASHUBI-LAHEM (1)
1Ch 4:22 but returned to Lehem {Vg Compare Gk: Heb *and* ***Jashubi-lahem***}

JATHAN (1)
Tob 5:14 Nathan, {Other ancient authorities read ***Jathan*** or *Nathamiah*}

JAWBONE (1)
Jdg 15:17 Ramath-lehi. {That is *The Hill of the* ***Jawbone***}

JAWS (1)
Hos 11: 4 who lift infants to their cheeks. {Or *who ease the yoke on their* ***jaws***}

JEALOUS (1)
Dt 32:19 was jealous {Q Mss Gk: MT lacks *was* ***jealous***}

JEBUSITE (1)
Jos 18:28 Jebus {Gk Syr Vg: Heb *the* ***Jebusite***}

JEHOAHAZ (1)
1Es 1:34 Jeconiah {2 Kings 23.30; 2 Chr 36.1 ***Jehoahaz***}

JEHOIAKIM (2)
Jer 27: 1 Zedekiah {Another reading is ***Jehoiakim***}
1Es 1:43 Jehoiachin {Gk ***Jehoiakim***}

JEHOSHAPHAT (1)
2Ki 8:16 Ahab of Israel, {Gk Syr: Heb adds ***Jehoshaphat*** *being king of Judah,*}

JEHOVAH (1)
Ge 22:14 "The LORD will provide"; {Or *will see*; Heb traditionally transliterated ***Jehovah*** *Jireh*}

JEHU (1)
2Ki 10:15 Jehu said, {Gk: Heb lacks ***Jehu*** *said*}

JEIEL (1)
1Ch 8:29 Jeiel {Compare 9.35: Heb lacks ***Jeiel***}

JERUBBESHETH (1)
2Sa 11:21 Jerubbaal? {Gk Syr Judg 7.1: Heb ***Jerubbesheth***}

JERUSALEM (3)
Ezr 2:70 lived in ... its vicinity; {1 Esdras 5.46: Heb lacks *lived in **Jerusalem** and its vicinity*}
Jer 8:5 has this people {One Ms Gk: MT *this people, **Jerusalem,***} turned away
Ac 18:21 "I {Other ancient authorities read *I must at all costs keep the approaching festival in **Jerusalem**, but I*} will return

JESHIMON (2)
Nu 21:20 overlooks the wasteland. {Or ***Jeshimon***}
23:28 overlooks the wasteland. {Or *overlooks **Jeshimon***}

JESUS (15)
Mt 16:20 that he was {Other ancient authorities add ***Jesus***} the Messiah
27:16 called Jesus {Other ancient authorities lack ***Jesus***} Barabbas.
27:17 Jesus {Other ancient authorities lack ***Jesus***} Barabbas
Lk 23:34 Then Jesus ... what they are doing." {Other ancient authorities lack the sentence *Then **Jesus** ... what they are doing*}
24:3 find the body. {Other ancient authorities add *of the Lord **Jesus***}
Ac 8:36 + v.37 < *And he replied, "I believe that **Jesus** Christ is the Son of God."*
Ro 8:11 he who raised Christ {Other ancient authorities read *the Christ* or *Christ **Jesus*** or ***Jesus** Christ*}
16:23 + v.24 *The grace of our Lord **Jesus** Christ be with all of you. Amen.*
1Co 5:5 day of the Lord. {Other ancient authorities add ***Jesus***}
Gal 6:15 For {Other ancient authorities add *in Christ **Jesus***} neither circumcision
Eph 3:14 before the Father, {Other ancient authorities add *of our Lord **Jesus** Christ*}
2Th 2:8 Lord Jesus {Other ancient authorities lack ***Jesus***}
Jude 1:5 though you are ... for all saved {Other ancient authorities read *though you were once for all fully informed, that **Jesus** (or Joshua) who saved*}
2Es 7:28 For my son the Messiah {< Lat *my son **Jesus***}

JEWS (5)
Jn 3:25 a Jew. {Other ancient authorities read *the **Jews***}
Ac 28:28 + v.29 *And when he had said these words, the **Jews** departed, arguing vigorously among* >
AdE 9:4 + v.5 *So the **Jews** struck down all their enemies with the sword,* >
9:29 + v.30 *Letters were sent to all the **Jews**,* >
2Mc 8:20 Jews {Gk lacks ***Jews***}

JEZANIAH (1)
Jer 42:1 Azariah {Gk: Heb ***Jezaniah***}

JIREH (1)
Ge 22:14 "The LORD will provide"; {Or *will see*; Heb traditionally transliterated *Jehovah **Jireh***}

JOASH (1)
2Ki 11:21 Jehoash {Another spelling is ***Joash***; see verse 19}

JOEL (1)
1Ch 6:28 Joel {Gk Syr Compare verse 33 and 1 Sam 8.2: Heb lacks ***Joel***}

JOINED (1)
Mk 10:7 and be joined to his wife, {Other ancient authorities lack *and be **joined** to his wife*}

JONATHAN (1)
Ac 4:6 John, {Other ancient authorities read ***Jonathan***}

JORDAN (1)
2Sa 16:14 at the Jordan; {Gk: Heb lacks *at the **Jordan***}

JOSHUA (1)
Jude 1:5 though you are ... for all saved {Other ancient authorities read *though you were once for all fully informed, that Jesus* (or ***Joshua***) *who saved*}

JOURNEY (1)
Jdg 17:8 Ephraim to carry on his work. {Or *Ephraim, continuing his **journey***}

JOY (3)
Jer 49:25 the joyful town! {Syr Vg Tg: Heb *the town of my **joy***}
Sir 2:9 joy and mercy. {Other ancient authorities add *For his reward is an everlasting gift with **joy**.*}
2Es 1:37 I call to witness ... rejoice with gladness; {Other ancient authorities read *The apostles bear witness to the coming people with **joy***}

JUDAH (4)
Ge 38:12 when Judah's time of mourning was over, {Heb *when **Judah** was comforted*}
2Ki 8:16 Ahab of Israel, {Gk Syr: Heb adds *Jehoshaphat being king of **Judah**,*}
Ezr 3:9 Hodaviah {Compare 2.40; Neh 7.43; 1 Esdras 5.58: Heb *sons of **Judah***}
1Mc 14:4 The land {Other ancient authorities add *of **Judah***} had rest

JUDAS (1)
Jude 1:1 Jude, {Gk ***Judas***}

JUDGE (1)
2Es 1:32 says the Lord. {Other ancient authorities add ... *let my Father and his angels return and **judge** between you and me;* >}

JUDGE'S (1)
2Es 1:32 says the Lord. {Other ancient authorities add ... *crying out before the **judge's** seat for him to deliver me to you.* >}

JUDGED (5)
Ge 30:6 Dan. {That is *He **judged***}
Ac 24:6 seized him. {Other ancient authorities add *and we would have **judged** him according to our law.* >}
Ro 3:4 and prevail in your judging." {Gk *when you are being **judged***}
Sir 16:26 the Lord created {Heb: Gk ***judged***} his works

JUDGES (4)
Ex 21:6 bring him before God. {Or *to the **judges***}
22:8 brought before God, {Or *before the **judges***}
22:9 come before God; {Or *before the **judges***} the one whom God condemns {Or *the **judges** condemn*}

JUDGMENT (5)
Am 7:4 for a shower of fire, {Or *for a **judgment** by fire*}
Tob 3:2 you judge the world. {Other ancient authorities read *you render true and righteous **judgment** forever*}
2Es 1:32 says the Lord. {Other ancient authorities add ... *I will contend in **judgment** with you, says the Lord.*}
6:20 my judgment {Syr: Lat lacks *my **judgment***}
4Mc 1:6 courage, and self-control; {Other ancient authorities add *and rational **judgment***}

JULIA (1)
Ro 16:7 Junia, {Or *Junias*; other ancient authorities read ***Julia***}

JUNIAS (1)
Ro 16:7 Junia, {Or ***Junias***; other ancient authorities read *Julia*}

JUST (2)
1Sa 2:8 seat of honor. {Gk (Compare Q Ms) adds < *and blesses the years of the **just***}
Col 3:13 just as the Lord {Other ancient authorities read ***just** as Christ*} has forgiven

JUSTIFIED (1)
1Ti 3:16 vindicated {Or ***justified***} in spirit,

K

KAIN (1)
Jdg 4:11 from the other Kenites, {Heb *from the **Kain***}

KARYOT (2)
Jn 6:71 Judas son of Simon Iscariot, {Other ancient authorities read < *Judas son of Simon from **Karyot*** (Kerioth)}
13:26 Judas son of Simon Iscariot. {Other ancient authorities read < *Judas son of Simon from **Karyot*** (Kerioth)}

KASDIM (1)
Jer 51:1 Leb-qamai; {*Leb-qamai* is a cryptogram for ***Kasdim***, Chaldea}

KEEP (5)
Ps 22:29 and I shall live for him. {Compare Gk Syr Vg: Heb *and he who cannot **keep** himself alive*}
Ac 6:2 to wait on tables. {Or ***keep** accounts*}
15:24 minds, {Other ancient authorities add *saying, 'You must be circumcised and **keep** the law,'*}
18:21 "I {Other ancient authorities read *I must at all costs **keep** the approaching festival in Jerusalem, but I*} will return
2Co 12:7 to keep me from being too elated. {Other ancient authorities lack *to **keep** me from being too elated*}

KEEPING (1)
Sir 12:6 ungodly. {Other ancient authorities add *and he is **keeping** them for the day of their punishment*}

KEEPS (1)
Rev 16:15 awake and is clothed, {Gk *and **keeps** his robes*}

KEILAH (1)
1Sa 23:11 will {Q Ms Compare Gk: MT *Will the men of **Keilah** surrender me into his hand? Will*}

KEPHA (1)
Jn 1:42 Cephas" (which is translated Peter). {From the word for *rock* in Aramaic (***kepha***) and Greek (*petra*), respectively}

KEPT (1)
2Es 1:32 the Lord. {Other ancient authorities add ... *if I have not **kept** the commandment of the Father,* >}

KERIOTH (3)
Jer 48:41 the towns {Or ***Kerioth***} shall be taken
Jn 6:71 Judas son of Simon Iscariot, {Other ancient authorities read < *Judas son of Simon from Karyot* (**Kerioth**)}
13:26 Judas son of Simon Iscariot. {Other ancient authorities read < *Judas son of Simon from Karyot* (**Kerioth**)}

KEYSTONE (5)
Mt 21:42 cornerstone; {Or ***keystone***}
Mk 12:10 cornerstone; {Or ***keystone***}
Lk 20:17 cornerstone'? {Or ***keystone***}
Ac 4:11 cornerstone.' {Or ***keystone***}
Eph 2:20 cornerstone. {Or ***keystone***}

KICK (2)
1Sa 2:29 look with greedy eye {Q Ms Gk: MT *then **kick***}
2:32 look with greedy eye {Q Ms Gk: MT *will **kick***}

KILL (2)
Ex 20:13 You shall not murder. {Or ***kill***}
Dt 5:17 You shall not murder. {Or ***kill***}

KILLED (3)
1Sa 6:19 The descendants ... when they greeted {Gk: Heb *And he **killed** some of the people of Beth-shemesh, because they looked into*}
Jer 41:9 whom he had struck down was the large cistern {Gk: Heb *whom he had **killed** by the hand of Gedaliah*}
Heb 11:23 king's edict. {Other ancient authorities add *By faith Moses, when he was grown up, **killed** the Egyptian,* >}

KILLING (1)
AdE 9:4 + v.5 *So the Jews struck down all their enemies with the sword, **killing** and destroying them,* >

KIND (1)
Mt 17:20 + v.21 *But this **kind** does not come out except by prayer and fasting*

KINDNESS (2)
Ps 23:6 Surely goodness and mercy {Or ***kindness***}
52:1 mischief done against the godly? {Cn Compare Syr: Heb *the **kindness** of God*}

KINDRED (3)
Ps 22:22 to my brothers and sisters; {Or ***kindred***}
Eze 11:15 your fellow exiles, {Gk Syr: Heb *people of your **kindred***}
Sir 22:6 + v.8 < *Children who are disdainfully and boorishly haughty stain the nobility of their **kindred**.*

KINDS (1)
Sir 37:18 it sprouts four branches, {Heb: Gk *As a clue to changes of heart four **kinds** of destiny appear*}

KING (16)
1Sa 12:9 Jabin king of {Gk: Heb lacks *Jabin **king** of*}
1Ki 20:34 The king of Israel responded, {Heb lacks *The **king** of Israel responded*}
2Ki 8:16 Ahab of Israel, {Gk Syr: Heb adds *Jehoshaphat being **king** of Judah,*}
11:7 the house of the LORD {Heb *the LORD to the **king***}
25:4 the king with all the soldiers fled {Gk Compare Jer 39.4; 52.7: Heb lacks *the **king*** and lacks *fled*}
1Ch 20:2 took the crown of Milcom {Gk Vg See 1 Kings 11.5, 33: MT *of their **king***}
Ps 45:16 O king, {Heb lacks *O **king***}
110:4 forever according to the order of Melchizedek." {Or *forever, a rightful **king** by my edict*}
Isa 57:9 You journeyed to Molech {Or *the **king***}
Da 5:11 and diviners, {Aram adds *the **king** your father*}
Zep 1:5 Milcom; {Gk Mss Syr Vg: Heb *Malcam* (or, *their **king***)}
Ac 26:7 for this hope, your Excellency, {Gk *O **king***}
26:13 along the road, your Excellency, {Gk *O **king***}
Sir 18:2 + v.3 < *for he is **king** of all things by his power,* >
2Es 1:3 king of the Persians. {Other ancient authorities ... begin the chapter: ... *in the days of **King** Nebuchadnezzar, saying, "Go,*}
4Mc 5:36 O king, {Gk lacks *O **king***}

KING'S (3)
2Sa 13:27 Absalom ... king's feast. {Gk Compare Q Ms: MT lacks *Absalom made a feast like a **king's** feast*}

2Sa 18:29 Joab sent your servant, {Heb *the **king's** servant, your servant*}

Ps 99: 4 Mighty King, {Cn: Heb *And a **king's** strength*}

KINGDOM (4)

Mt 6:13 evil one. {Or *from evil.* Other ancient authorities add, in some form, *For the **kingdom** and the power and the glory are yours forever. Amen.*}

Mk 1:14 the good news of God, {Other ancient authorities read *of the **kingdom***}

AdE 9:29 + v.30 < *to the one hundred twenty-seven provinces of the **kingdom** of Ahasuerus,* >

1Mc 2:10 has not inherited her palaces {Other ancient authorities read *has not had a part in her **kingdom***}

KINGDOMS (1)

2Es 12:23 raise up three kings, {Syr Ethiop Arab Arm: Lat ***kingdoms***}

KINGS (3)

2Sa 12:30 took the crown of Milcom {Gk See 1 Kings 11.5, 33: Heb *their **kings***}

2Ch 28:16 sent to the king {Gk Syr Vg Compare 2 Kings 16.7: Heb ***kings***} of Assyria

Da 10:13 I left him there with the prince of the kingdom of Persia, {Gk Theodotion: Heb *I was left there with the **kings** of Persia*}

KINSFOLK (1)

Nu 22: 5 the land of Amaw, {Or *land of his **kinsfolk***}

KIRIATH (1)

Jos 18:28 Kiriath-jearim—fourteen {Gk: Heb ***Kiriath***}

KITTIM (1)

1Mc 8: 5 Macedonians, {Or ***Kittim***}

KNEEL (1)

Ge 41:43 "Bow the knee!" {*Abrek*, apparently an Egyptian word similar in sound to the Hebrew word meaning *to **kneel***}

KNEELING (1)

Mk 1:40 kneeling {Other ancient authorities lack ***kneeling***}

KNEW (1)

Hos 13: 5 It was I who fed {Gk Syr: Heb ***knew***} you

KNOW (15)

Pr 4: 1 that you may gain {Heb ***know***} insight;

Isa 66:18 For I know {Gk Syr: Heb lacks ***know***}

Eze 38:14 you will rouse yourself {Gk: Heb *will you not **know**?*}

Hos 9: 7 Israel cries, {Cn Compare Gk: Heb *shall **know***} "The prophet

Mt 27:65 as secure as you can." {Gk *you **know** how*}

Lk 1:34 since I am a virgin?" {Gk *I do not **know** a man*}

9:56 rebuked them. [56]Then {Other ancient authorities read *rebuked them, and said, "You do not **know** what spirit you are of, [56]for ... to save them."*}

Jn 7:15 this man have such learning, {Or *this man **know** his letters*}

14: 4 you know the way ... going." {Other ancient authorities read *Where I am going you **know**, and the way you **know***}

1Jn 2:20 all of you have knowledge. {Other ancient authorities read *you **know** all things*}

Sir 16: 3 their numbers; {Other ancient authorities add *For you will groan in untimely mourning, and will **know** of their sudden end.*}

16:21 Like a tempest ... so most of his works are concealed. {Meaning of Gk uncertain: Heb Syr *If I sin, no eye can see me, and if I am disloyal all in secret, who is to **know**?*}

17:11 law of life. {Other ancient authorities add *so that they may **know** that they who are alive now are mortal*}

2Es 16:46 for in captivity ... produce their children. {Other ancient authorities read *therefore those who are married may **know** that they will produce children for captivity and famine*}

KNOWLEDGE (8)

Da 12: 4 and evil {Cn Compare Gk: Heb ***knowledge***} shall increase."

Sir 1: 6 + v.7 *The **knowledge** of wisdom—to whom was it manifested?* >

11:14 + v.15 *Wisdom, understanding, and **knowledge** of the law come from the Lord;* >

19:17 + v.19 < *The **knowledge** of the Lord's commandments is life-giving discipline;* >

19:20 of the law. {Other ancient authorities add *and the **knowledge** of his omnipotence.* >}

24:17 + v.18 *I am the mother of beautiful love, of fear, of **knowledge**, and of holy hope;* >

2Es 14:48 so. {Syr adds *And he was called the scribe of the **knowledge** of the Most High for ever and ever.*}

4Mc 9: 2 obedience to the law and to Moses {Other ancient authorities read ***knowledge***}

KNOWN (7)

Ge 18:19 No, for I have chosen {Heb ***known***} him,

1Sa 6: 3 healed and will be ransomed; {Q Ms Gk: MT *and it will be **known** to you*}

Jn 14: 7 From now on you do know {Other ancient authorities read *If you had **known** me, you would have **known***}

1Pe 1: 8 Although you have not seen {Other ancient authorities read ***known***} him,

Sir 16:14 + v.15 < *in order that his works might be **known** under heaven.* >

2Es 5: 7 fish; ... hear his voice. {Cn: Lat *fish; and it shall make its voice heard by night, which the many have not **known**, but all shall hear its voice.*}

KNOWS (1)

Sir 17:20 + v.21 *But the Lord, who is gracious and **knows** how they are formed,* >

L

LACHISH (1)

Sir 48:18 sent his commander {Other ancient authorities add *from **Lachish***}

LAID (1)

2Es 1:32 says the Lord. {Other ancient authorities add *Thus says the Lord Almighty: Recently you also **laid** hands on me,* >}

LAND (10)

Nu 22: 5 the land of Amaw, {Or ***land** of his kinsfolk*}

1Sa 14:25 All the troops {Heb ***land***} came upon

2Sa 7:23 by driving out {Gk 1 Chr 17.21: Heb *for your **land***} before his people

24: 6 in the land of the Hittites; {Gk: Heb *to the **land** of Tahtim-hodshi*}

1Ki 8:37 in any {Gk Syr: Heb *in the **land***} of their cities;

9:13 Cabul {Perhaps meaning *a **land** good for nothing*}

Isa 10:23 in all the earth. {Or ***land***}

Da 12: 2 in the dust of the earth {Or *the **land** of dust*}

2Es 6: 1 "At the beginning ... before {< Syr ... *For as before the **land** of the world existed there, and before;* >}

2Es 13:45 Arzareth. {That is *Another **Land***}

LANDS (1)

2Es 6: 1 "At the beginning ... before {< Ethiop: *For before the earth and the **lands** were created, and before*}

LANGUAGE (3)

Ezr 4: 7 the letter was written in Aramaic and translated. {< Another interpretation is *The letter was written in the Aramaic script and set forth in the Aramaic **language***}

Est 1:22 his own house. {Heb adds *and speak according to the **language** of his people*}

1Co 2:13 interpreting spiritual things to those who are spiritual. {Or *interpreting spiritual things in spiritual **language**,* >}

LAPIS (10)

Ex 28:18 sapphire {Or ***lapis** lazuli*}

39:11 sapphire, {Or ***lapis** lazuli*}

Job 28: 6 sapphires, {Or ***lapis** lazuli*}

28:16 sapphire. {Or ***lapis** lazuli*}

SS 5:14 sapphires. {Heb ***lapis** lazuli*}

Isa 54:11 sapphires. {Or ***lapis** lazuli*}

La 4: 7 sapphire. {Or ***lapis** lazuli*}

Eze 1:26 sapphire; {Or ***lapis** lazuli*}

10: 1 sapphire, {Or ***lapis** lazuli*}

28:13 sapphire, {Or ***lapis** lazuli*}

LARGE (2)

Sir 51:28 Hear but a little of my instruction, ... acquire silver and gold. {Syr Compare Heb: Gk *Get instruction with a **large** sum of silver, and you will gain by it much gold.*}

3Mc 7:22 with extreme fear. {Other ancient authorities read *with a very **large** supplement*}

LASHES (1)

Ac 22:25 tied him up with thongs, {Or *up for the **lashes***}

LAST (2)

Job 19:25 at the last he {Or *that he the **Last***} will stand

1Ti 4: 1 in later {Or *the **last***} times some will renounce

LATER (2)

1Sa 11: 1 About a month later, {Q Ms Gk: MT lacks *About a month **later***}

Sir 19:20 + v.21 < *even if **later** he does it, he angers the one who supports him.*

LATIN (1)

Lk 23:38 over him, {Other ancient authorities add *written in Greek and **Latin** and Hebrew* >}

LAUGHS (1)

Ge 17:19 Isaac. {That is *he **laughs***}

LAW (7)

Ps 148: 6 he fixed their bounds, which cannot be passed. {Or *he set a **law** that cannot pass away*}

Mt 15: 6 void the word {Other ancient authorities read ***law***; others, *commandment*} of God.

Ac 15:24 minds, {Other ancient authorities add *saying, 'You must be circumcised and keep the **law**,'*}

24: 6 accuse him. {Other ancient authorities add *and we would have judged him according to our **law**.* >}

Sir 11:14 + v.15 *Wisdom, understanding, and knowledge of the **law** come from the Lord;* >

1Es 9:48 of the Lord, {Other ancient authorities add *and read the **law** of the Lord to the multitude*}

2Es 9:19 and an inexhaustible pasture, {Cn: Lat ***law***}

LAWAH (1)

Ge 29:34 joined {Heb ***lawah***}

LAWLESS (1)

Mk 15:27 + v.28 *And the scripture was fulfilled that says, "And he was counted among the **lawless**."*

LAWLESSNESS (2)

Mk 16:14 risen. {Other ancient authorities add, in whole or in part, *And they excused themselves, saying, "This age of **lawlessness** and unbelief is under Satan,* >}

2Th 2: 3 the lawless one {Gk *the man of **lawlessness**;* >}

LAY (5)

Nu 12:11 do not punish us {Heb *do not **lay** sin upon us*}

1Sa 9:25 and he lay down to sleep. {Gk: Heb lacks *and he **lay** down to sleep*}

Est 2:21 conspired to assassinate {Heb *to **lay** hands on*}

6: 2 conspired to assassinate {Heb *to **lay** hands on*}

1Ti 5:22 Do not ordain {Gk *Do not **lay** hands on*} anyone hastily,

LAZULI (10)

Ex 28:18 sapphire {Or *lapis **lazuli***}

39:11 sapphire, {Or *lapis **lazuli***}

Job 28: 6 sapphires, {Or *lapis **lazuli***}

28:16 sapphire. {Or *lapis **lazuli***}

SS 5:14 sapphires. {Heb *lapis **lazuli***}

Isa 54:11 sapphires. {Or *lapis **lazuli***}

La 4: 7 sapphire. {Or *lapis **lazuli***}

Eze 1:26 sapphire; {Or *lapis **lazuli***}

10: 1 sapphire, {Or *lapis **lazuli***}

28:13 sapphire. {Or *lapis **lazuli***}

LEAD (1)

Sir 17:26 iniquity, {Other ancient authorities add *for he will **lead** you out of darkness to the light of health.*}

LEADER (2)

Hab 3:14 the head {Or ***leader***} of his warriors,

Sir 49:15 like Joseph; {Heb Syr: Gk adds *the **leader** of his brothers, the support of the people*}

LEADERS (1)

2Es 15:48 deeds and devices. {Other ancient authorities add *you have followed after that one about to gratify her magnates and **leaders*** >}

LEADING (1)

Wis 18: 9 dangers; and already ... ancestors. {Other ancient authorities read *dangers, the ancestors already **leading** the songs of praise*}

LEBBAEUS (2)

Mt 10: 3 Thaddaeus; {Other ancient authorities read ***Lebbaeus***, or ***Lebbaeus** called Thaddaeus*}

LEBO-ZEDAD (1)

Eze 47:15 on to Zedad, {Gk: Heb ***Lebo-zedad**, [16]Hamath*}

LEFT (4)

Lk 17:35 + v.36 *"Two will be in the field; one will be taken and the other **left**."*

Jn 5:13 Jesus had disappeared in {Or *had **left** because of*} the crowd

Sir 17:20 + v.21 < *has neither **left** them nor abandoned them, but has spared them.*

2Es 11:20 on the right {Some Ethiop Mss read ***left***} side,

LEGS (1)

Ps 147:10 speed of a runner; {Heb ***legs** of a person*}

LENGTH (2)

Ps 23: 6 my whole life long. {Heb *for **length** of days*}

Eze 41:22 its corners, its base, {Gk: Heb ***length***}

LET (14)

Ge 4: 8 "Let us go out to the field." {Sam Gk Syr Compare Vg: MT lacks ***Let** us go out to the field*}

Ps 20: 9 Give victory ... answer us when we call. {Gk: Heb *give victory, O* LORD*; **let** the King answer us when we call*}

Ps 85: 8 to those who turn to him in their hearts. {Gk: Heb *but **let** them not turn back to folly*}
Eze 16:15 any passer-by. {Heb adds ***let** it be his*}
Mk 7:15 + v.16 *"**Let** anyone with ears to hear listen"*
Ro 5: 1 we {Other ancient authorities read ***let** us*} have peace with God
5: 2 we {Or ***let** us*} boast in our hope
5: 3 we {Or ***let** us*} also boast in our sufferings
1Co 15:49 we will {Other ancient authorities read ***let** us*} also bear the image
Heb 6: 3 And we will do {Other ancient authorities read ***let** us do*} this,
Sir 8:19 or you may drive away your happiness. {Heb: Gk *and **let** him not return a favor to you*}
36: 5 Then they will know, {Heb: Gk *And **let** them know you*}
2Es 1:32 says the Lord. {Other ancient authorities add *Therefore, says the Lord, **let** my Father and his angels return and judge between you and me;* >}
14:19 Let me speak {Most Lat Mss lack ***Let** me speak*}

LETHECH (1)
Hos 3: 2 a homer of barley and a measure of wine. {Gk: Heb *a homer of barley and a **lethech** of barley*}

LETTERS (2)
Jn 7:15 this man have such learning, {Or *this man know his **letters***}
AdE 9:29 + v.30 ***Letters** were sent to all the Jews,* >

LEVI (1)
Dt 33: 8 Give to Levi {Q Ms Gk: MT lacks *Give to **Levi***}

LEVITAS (1)
AdE 11: 1 a priest and a Levite, {Or *priest, and **Levitas***}

LEVITE (1)
Jdg 17:10 your living." {Heb *living, and the **Levite** went*}

LIBERTY (1)
Jn 7: 1 He did not wish {Other ancient authorities read *was not at **liberty***} to go

LICENSE (1)
Jer 6: 6 the city that must be punished; {Or *the city of **license***}

LIDEBIR (1)
Jos 13:26 Debir, {Gk Syr Vg: Heb ***Lidebir***}

LIE (1)
Pr 3:24 sit down, {Gk: Heb ***lie** down*}

LIFE (11)
1Sa 1:11 then I will set ... neither wine nor intoxicants, {Cn Compare Gk Q Ms 1.22: MT *then I will give him to the LORD all the days of his **life***}
Job 2: 4 All that people have ... to save their lives. {Or *All that the man has he will give for his **life***}
Ps 23: 3 he restores my soul. {Or ***life***}
Jn 11:25 and the life. {Other ancient authorities lack *and the **life***}
Sir 10:29 honor those who dishonor themselves? {Heb Lat: Gk *their own **life***}
13:13 + v.14 < *During all your **life** love the Lord, and call on him for your salvation.*
18:33 your purse. {Other ancient authorities add *for you will be plotting against your own **life***}
19: 5 condemned, {Other ancient authorities add *but one who withstands pleasures crowns his **life**.* >}
20:31 + v.32 < *better than a masterless charioteer of one's own **life**.*
22: 6 + v.7 *Children who are brought up in a good **life**, conceal the lowly birth of their parents.* >
23:27 + v.28 *It is a great honor to follow God, and to be received by him is long **life**.*

LIFE-GIVING (1)
Sir 19:17 + v.19 *The knowledge of the Lord's commandments is **life-giving** discipline;* >

LIFT (1)
Man 1:10 so that I am rejected {Other ancient authorities read *so that I cannot **lift** up my head*}

LIGHT (11)
Job 31:26 looked at the sun {Heb *the **light***}
Ps 74:16 established the luminaries {Or *moon*; Heb ***light***}
Isa 53:11 shall see light; {Q Mss: MT lacks ***light***}
Zec 14: 6 there shall not be {Cn: Heb *there shall not be **light***} either cold
Eph 3: 9 to make everyone see {Other ancient authorities read *to bring to **light***}
Sir 16:14 + v.16 < *His mercy is manifest to the whole of creation, and he divided his **light** and darkness with a plumb line.*
17:17 + v.18 < *and allotting to him the **light** of his love, he does not neglect him.*
17:26 from iniquity, {Other ancient authorities add *for he will lead you out of darkness to the **light** of health.*}
24:27 It pours forth instruction like the Nile, {Syr: Gk *It makes instruction shine forth like **light***}
Sir 50:29 for the fear {Heb: Other ancient authorities read ***light***} of the Lord
2Es 8:14 will suddenly and quickly {Syr: Lat *will with a **light** command*} destroy

LIGHTED (1)
Job 33:30 so that they may see the light of life. {Syr: Heb *to be **lighted** with the light of life*}

LIKE (20)
1Sa 2:33 shall die by the sword. {Q Ms See Gk: MT *die **like** mortals*}
2Sa 13:27 Absalom made a feast like a king's feast. {Gk Compare Q Ms: MT lacks *Absalom made a feast **like** a king's feast*}
17: 3 seek the life of only one man, {Gk: Heb ***like** the return of the whole (is) the man whom you seek*}
Job 29:22 like dew. {Heb lacks ***like** dew*}
30:18 grasps me by {Heb ***like***} the collar
Ps 35:16 they impiously mocked me more and more, {Cn Compare Gk: Heb ***like** the profanest of mockers of a cake*}
Pr 25:20 Like vinegar on a wound {Gk: Heb ***Like** one who takes off a garment on a cold day, **like** vinegar on lye*}
25:20 Like a moth ... human heart. {Gk Syr Tg: Heb lacks ***Like** a moth ... human heart*}
Isa 23:10 O ships of {Cn Compare Gk: Heb ***like** the Nile, daughter*} Tarshish;
Jer 34:18 I will make like {Cn: Heb lacks ***like***}
48:11 like wine {Heb lacks ***like** wine*}
Eze 27:32 was ever destroyed {Tg Vg: Heb ***like** silence*}
43: 3 The {Gk: Heb ***Like** the vision*} vision
Da 2:40 everything, {Gk Theodotion Syr Vg: Aram adds *and **like** iron that crushes*}
Hos 6: 7 But at {Cn: Heb ***like***} Adam
Zec 14:20 shall be as {Heb *shall be **like***} holy
Heb 1:12 like clothing {Other ancient authorities lack ***like** clothing*}
2Es 14:48 did so. {Syr adds *... and taken to the place of those who are **like** him, after he had written all these things.* >}
15:30 like wild boars {Other ancient authorities lack ***like** wild boars*}

LIKENED (1)
Sir 36:17 you have named {Other ancient authorities read *you have **likened** to*}

LIMBS (1)
Job 18:13 By disease their skin is consumed, {Cn: Heb *It consumes the **limbs** of his skin*}

LINE (2)
Ps 19: 4 their voice {Gk Jerome Compare Syr: Heb ***line***}
Sir 16:14 + v.16 < *and he divided his light and darkness with a plumb **line**.*

LINGER (1)
Jdg 19: 8 So they lingered {Cn: Heb ***Linger***} until the day

LION (1)
Isa 21: 8 Then the watcher {Q Ms: MT *a **lion***} called out:

LIONS (1)
Eze 38:13 all its young warriors {Heb *young **lions***}

LIPS (2)
Ex 6:12 poor speaker that I am?" {Heb *me? I am uncircumcised of **lips***}
6:30 I am a poor speaker, {Heb *am uncircumcised of **lips***; see 6.12}

LISTEN (1)
Mk 7:15 + v.16 *"Let anyone with ears to hear **listen**"*

LISTENING (1)
Sir 25:18 and he cannot help sighing {Other ancient authorities read *and **listening** he sighs*}

LITTLE (3)
Ge 19:22 Zoar. {That is ***Little***}
Pr 8:30 a master worker; {Another reading is ***little** child*}
2Es 11:20 wings that followed {Syr Arab 2 *the **little** wings*}

LIVE (3)
Ps 72: 9 May his foes {Cn: Heb *those who **live** in the wilderness*} bow down
Sir 19: 5 + v.6 < *One who controls the tongue will **live** without strife,*
2Es 8:41 will come up {Syr Ethiop *will **live***; Lat *will be saved*} in due season,

LIVED (2)
1Ki 12: 2 Jeroboam returned from {Gk Vg Compare 2 Chr 10.2: Heb ***lived** in*} Egypt.
Ezr 2:70 lived in ... its vicinity; {1 Esdras 5.46: Heb lacks ***lived** in Jerusalem and its vicinity*}

LIVES (1)
Lk 9:56 Then {Other ancient authorities read *... for the Son of Man has not come to destroy the **lives** of* >}

LIVING (5)
Ge 3:20 Eve, {In Heb *Eve* resembles the word for ***living***}
16:14 Beer-lahai-roi; {That is *the Well of the **Living** One who sees me*}
Ps 38:19 my foes without cause {Q Ms: MT *my **living** foes*}
Mt 17:22 gathering {Other ancient authorities read ***living***}
Jn 6:69 the Holy One of God." {Other ancient authorities read *the Christ, the Son of the **living** God*}

LOATHED (2)
Isa 14:19 like loathsome carrion, {Cn Compare Gk: Heb *like a **loathed** branch*}
Wis 16: 3 might lose the least remnant of appetite {Gk ***loathed** the necessary appetite*}

LOAVES (1)
Heb 9: 2 the bread of the Presence; {Gk *the presentation of the **loaves***}

LOFTY (1)
Sir 3:18 + v.19 *Many are **lofty** and renowned, but to the humble he reveals his secrets.*

LOINS (2)
1Pe 1:13 prepare your minds for action; {Gk *gird up the **loins** of your mind*}
4Mc 11:10 they twisted his back {Gk ***loins***}

LONG (5)
Isa 57:11 kept silent and closed my eyes, {Gk Vg: Heb *silent even for a **long** time*}
Jer 31: 3 to him from far away. {Or *to him **long** ago*}
Mt 23:13 + v.14 *For you devour widows' houses and for the sake of appearance you make **long** prayers;* >
Lk 1: 3 from the very first, {Or *for a **long** time*}
Sir 23:27 + v.28 *It is a great honor to follow God, and to be received by him is **long** life.*

LONGER (2)
Ro 11: 6 grace. {Other ancient authorities add *But if it is by works, it is no **longer** on the basis of grace, otherwise work would no **longer** be work*}

LOOK (4)
Job 11:18 you will be protected {Or *you will **look** around*}
SS 4: 8 Depart {Or ***Look***} from the peak
Jn 20:11 to look {Gk lacks *to **look***}
Sir 20:22 lose it because of human respect. {Other ancient authorities read *his foolish **look***}

LOOKED (2)
Jdg 13:19 wonders. {Heb *wonders, while Manoah and his wife **looked** on*}
1Sa 6:19 The descendants ... when they greeted {Gk: Heb *And he killed some of the people of Beth-shemesh, because they **looked** into*}

LOOKING (1)
Da 8: 2 In the vision ... Elam, {Gk Theodotion: MT Q Ms repeat *in the vision I was **looking***}

LOOSED (2)
Jdt 9: 2 torn off a virgin's clothing {Cn: Gk ***loosed** her womb*}
4Mc 7:13 his body no longer tense and firm, {Gk *the tautness of the body already **loosed***}

*LORD (62)
2Sa 5:20 Baal-perazim. {That is ***Lord** of Bursting Forth*}
1Ch 14:11 Baal-perazim. {That is ***Lord** of Bursting Out*}
Ps 73:20 They are {Cn: Heb ***Lord***} like a dream
Mt 20:30 "Lord, {Other ancient authorities lack ***Lord***}
28: 6 he {Other ancient authorities read *the **Lord***} lay.
Mk 7:28 "Sir, {Or ***Lord***; other ancient authorities prefix *Yes*}
Lk 24: 3 find the body. {Other ancient authorities add *of the **Lord** Jesus*}
Jn 4: 1 Now when Jesus {Other ancient authorities read *the **Lord***} learned
5: 3 + v.4 < *for an angel of the **Lord** went down at certain seasons into the pool,* >
6:23 after the Lord had given thanks. {Other ancient authorities lack *after the **Lord** had given thanks*}
8:11 "No one, sir." {Or ***Lord***}
9:36 sir? {*Sir* and ***Lord*** translate the same Greek word}
Ac 17:27 for God {Other ancient authorities read *the **Lord***}
20:28 God {Other ancient authorities read *of the **Lord***}
Ro 16:23 + v.24 *The grace of our **Lord** Jesus Christ be with all of you. Amen.*
1Co 10: 9 We must not put Christ {Other ancient authorities read *the **Lord***} to the test,
15:47 the second man is {Other ancient authorities add *the **Lord***} from heaven.
Eph 3:14 the Father, {Other ancient authorities add *of our **Lord** Jesus Christ*}
Eph 6: 1 in the Lord, {Other ancient authorities lack *in the **Lord***}
Php 2:30 for the work of Christ, {Other ancient authorities read *of the **Lord***}
Col 3:16 Let the word of Christ {Other ancient authorities read *of God*, or *of the **Lord***}
3:16 songs to God. {Other ancient authorities read *to the **Lord***}

***LORD** distinguishes words translated "Lord" and "lord" from the proper name of God, *Yahweh*, rendered LORD in the NRSV and indexed under the heading †**LORD** on page 29.

Col 3:22 obey your earthly masters {In Greek the same word is used for *master* and ***Lord***}
2Ti 2:14 and warn them before God {Other ancient authorities read *the **Lord***}
2Jn 1:3 and from {Other ancient authorities add *the **Lord***} Jesus Christ,
Tob 3:12 Lord, {Other ancient authorities lack ***Lord***}
11:4 And the dog {Codex Sinaiticus reads *And the **Lord***} went along
12:20 now get up from the ground, {Other ancient authorities read *now bless the **Lord** on earth*}
Sir 1:10 love him. {Other ancient authorities add *Love of the **Lord** is glorious wisdom;* >}
1:12 long life. {Other ancient authorities add *The fear of the **Lord** is a gift from the **Lord**; also for love he makes firm paths.*}
1:20 + v.21 *The fear of the **Lord** drives away sins; and where it abides, it will turn away all anger.*
3:7 they will serve their parents as their masters. {In other ancient authorities this line is preceded by *Those who fear the **Lord** honor their father,*}
10:20 + v.21 *The fear of the **Lord** is the beginning of acceptance;* >
11:14 + v.15 *Wisdom, understanding, and knowledge of the law come from the **Lord**;* >
13:13 + v.14 < *During all your life love the **Lord**, and call on him for your salvation.*
16:10 stubbornness. {Other ancient authorities add *Chastising, showing mercy, striking, healing, the **Lord** persisted in mercy and discipline.*}
16:14 + v.15 *The **Lord** hardened Pharaoh so that he did not recognize him,* >
17:4 + v.5 *They obtained the use of the five faculties of the **Lord**;* >
17:20 + v.21 *But the **Lord**, who is gracious and knows how they are formed,* >
18:29 proverbs. {Other ancient authorities add *Better is confidence in the one **Lord** than clinging with a dead heart to a dead one.*}
19:17 + v.18 < *The fear of the **Lord** is the beginning of acceptance, and wisdom obtains his love.* >
20:31 + v.32 *Unwearied endurance in seeking the **Lord** is better than a masterless charioteer of one's own life.*
24:23 + v.24 *"Do not cease to be strong in the **Lord**, cling to him so that he may strengthen you; the **Lord** Almighty alone is God, and besides him there is no savior."*
25:1 beautiful in the sight of God and of mortals: {Syr Lat: Gk *In three things I was beautiful and I stood in beauty before the **Lord** and mortals.*}
25:11 + v.12 *The fear of the **Lord** is the beginning of love for him,* >
32:14 who seeks God {Heb: Gk *who fears the **Lord***}
1Es 9:48 of the Lord, {Other ancient authorities add *and read the law of the **Lord** to the multitude*}
Man 1:7 O Lord, according ... be saved. {Other ancient authorities lack *O **Lord**, according ... be saved*}
2Es 1:32 says the Lord. {Other ancient authorities add *Thus says the **Lord** Almighty: ... Therefore, says the **Lord**, ... in judgment with you, says the **Lord**.*}
2:36 I publicly call on my savior to witness. {Other ancient authorities read *I testify that my savior has been commissioned by the **Lord***}
8:45 O Lord {Ethiop Arab Compare Syr: Lat lacks *O **Lord***}
15:26 For God {Other ancient authorities read *the **Lord***}
15:27 God {Other ancient authorities read *the **Lord***}
15:48 God {Other ancient authorities read *the **Lord***}
16:62 the spirit of Almighty God, {Other ancient authorities read *of the **Lord** Almighty*}
16:67 God {Other ancient authorities read *the **Lord***} is the judge; ... so God {Other ancient authorities read *the **Lord***} will lead you forth
16:75 for God {Other ancient authorities read *the **Lord***}

†LORD (12)

Dt 1:8 the land that I {Sam Gk: MT *the **Lord***} swore
30:16 If ... the LORD your God {Gk: Heb lacks *If you obey the commandments of the **Lord** your God*}
Jdg 19:18 and I am going home. {Gk Compare 19.29. Heb *to the house of the **Lord***}
1Sa 1:9 and presented herself before the LORD. {Gk: Heb lacks *and presented herself before the **Lord***}
1:11 then I will set him ... neither wine nor intoxicants, {Cn Compare Gk Q Ms1.22: MT *then I will give him to the **Lord** all the days of his life*}
1Sa 2:1 exalted in my God. {Gk: Heb *the **Lord***}
5:11 there was a deathly panic {Q Ms reads *a panic from the **Lord***}
20:8 a sacred covenant {Heb *a covenant of the **Lord***}
2Sa 12:25 Jedidiah, {That is *Beloved of the **Lord***}
15:20 may the LORD show {Gk Compare 2.6: Heb lacks *may the **Lord** show*}
Jer 10:16 the LORD, {Heb lacks *the **Lord***}
51:19 the LORD, {Heb lacks *the **Lord***}

LORD'S (3)

Da 9:17 for your own sake, Lord, {Theodotion Vg Compare Syr: Heb *for the **Lord's** sake*}
1Co 11:29 without discerning the body, {Other ancient authorities read *the **Lord's** body*}
Sir 19:17 + v.19 < *The knowledge of the **Lord's** commandments is life-giving discipline;* >

LORDS (3)

Nu 21:28 and swallowed up {Gk: Heb *and the **lords** of*} the heights
Ne 3:5 the work of their Lord. {Or ***lords***}
Ps 58:1 what is right, you gods? {Or *mighty **lords***}

LOSES (1)

Sir 25:18 Her husband sits {Heb Syr: Gk ***loses** heart*}

LOST (2)

Mt 18:10 + v.11 *For the Son of Man came to save the **lost***
Tob 7:7 father!" {Other ancient authorities add *When he heard that Tobit had **lost** his sight,* >}

LOT (2)

Eze 24:6 piece, making no choice at all. {Heb *piece, no **lot** has fallen on it*}
AdE 9:24 made a decree and cast lots {Gk *a **lot***}

LOTS (1)

Mt 27:35 casting lots; {Other ancient authorities add ... *"They divided my clothes among themselves, and for my clothing they cast **lots**."*}

LOVE (12)

Ps 97:10 The LORD loves those who hate {Cn: Heb *You who **love** the LORD hate*}
144:2 my rock {With 18.2 and 2 Sam 22.2: Heb *my steadfast **love***} and my fortress,
Eph 1:15 and your love {Other ancient authorities lack *and your **love***}
2Pe 2:13 reveling in their dissipation {Other ancient authorities read ***love** feasts*}
Sir 1:10 love him. {Other ancient authorities add ***Love** of the Lord is glorious wisdom;* >}
1:12 long life. {Other ancient authorities add *The fear of the Lord is a gift from the Lord; also for **love** he makes firm paths.*}
1:18 flourish. {Other ancient authorities add < *glory opens out for those who **love** him.* >}
13:13 + v.14 < *During all your life **love** the Lord, and call on him for your salvation.*
17:17 + v.18 < *and allotting to him the light of his **love**, he does not neglect him.*
19:17 + v.18 *The fear of the Lord is the beginning of acceptance, and wisdom obtains his **love**.* >
24:17 + v.18 *I am the mother of beautiful **love**, of fear, of knowledge, and of holy hope;* >
25:11 + v.12 *The fear of the Lord is the beginning of **love** for him,* >

LOVED (1)

Isa 38:17 but you have held back {Cn Compare Gk Vg: Heb ***loved***}

LOVER (2)

Dt 33:3 O favorite among {Or *O **lover** of the*} the peoples,
SS 7:9 goes down {Heb *down for my **lover***} smoothly,

LOVES (1)

Sir 10:8 wealth. {Other ancient authorities add here or after verse 9a, *Nothing is more wicked than one who **loves** money,* >}

LOW (1)

Isa 2:12 lifted up and high; {Cn Compare Gk: Heb ***low***}

LOWLY (1)

Sir 22:6 + v.7 *Children who are brought up in a good life, conceal the **lowly** birth of their parents.* >

LOYALTY (1)

Pr 20:28 upheld by righteousness. {Gk: Heb ***loyalty***}

LYE (1)

Pr 25:20 Like vinegar on a wound {Gk: Heb *Like one who takes off a garment on a cold day, like vinegar on **lye***}

LYING (1)

3Mc 4:8 seeing death immediately before them. {Gk *seeing Hades already **lying** at their feet*}

LYSIAS (1)

Ac 24:6 + v.7 *But the chief captain **Lysias** came* >

M

MADE (27)

1Sa 23:7 "God has given {Gk Tg: Heb ***made** a stranger of*}
2Sa 13:27 Absalom ... king's feast. {Gk Compare Q Ms: MT lacks *Absalom **made** a feast like a king's feast*}
Ps 69:10 When I humbled my soul with fasting, {Gk Syr: Heb < *I **made** my soul mourn with fasting*}
Ps 80:15 planted. {Heb adds from verse 17 *and upon the one whom you **made** strong for yourself*}
138:3 you increased my strength of soul. {Syr Compare Gk Tg: Heb *you **made** me arrogant in my soul with strength*}
Isa 12:5 let this be known {Or *this is **made** known*}
Jer 18:15 they have stumbled {Gk Syr Vg: Heb *they **made** them stumble*}
Eze 6:6 will be waste and ruined, {Syr Vg Tg: Heb *and be **made** guilty*}
16:7 Live! [17]and grow up {Gk Syr: Heb *Live! I **made** you a myriad*}
40:14 He measured {Heb ***made***} also the vestibule,
Da 9:22 He came {Gk Syr: Heb *He **made** to understand*} and said to me,
11:35 purified, and cleansed, {Heb ***made** them white*}
Mic 6:13 Therefore, I have begun {Gk Syr Vg: Heb *have **made** sick*} to strike you down,
Mal 2:15 Did not one God make her? {Or *Has he not **made** one?*}
Mk 15:34 why have you forsaken me?" {Other ancient authorities read ***made** me a reproach*}
Jn 5:3 + v.4 < *whoever stepped in first after the stirring of the water was **made** well* >
Gal 5:6 faith working {Or ***made** effective*} through love
Eph 1:11 also obtained an inheritance, {Or *been **made** a heritage*}
Php 3:12 have already reached the goal; {Or *have already been **made** perfect*}
Col 2:11 with a spiritual circumcision, {Gk *a circumcision **made** without hands*}
Rev 18:3 For all nations have drunk {Other ancient authorities read *she has **made** all nations drink*}
Wis 16:25 those who had need, {Or *who **made** supplication*}
Sir 34:21 the offering is blemished; {Other ancient authorities read *is **made** in mockery*}
2Mc 7:28 God did not make them out of things that existed. {Or *God **made** them out of things that did not exist*}
3Mc 7:18 There they celebrated their deliverance, {Gk *they **made** a cup of deliverance*}
2Es 1:20 I clothed you with the leaves of trees. {Other ancient authorities read *I **made** for you trees with leaves*}
15:48 deeds and devices. {Other ancient authorities add < *so that you may be **made** proud and be pleased by her fornications*}

MAGDALA (2)

Mt 15:39 Magadan. {Other ancient authorities read ***Magdala** or Magdalan*}
Mk 8:10 Dalmanutha. {Other ancient authorities read *Mageda* or ***Magdala***}

MAGDALAN (1)

Mt 15:39 Magadan. {Other ancient authorities read *Magdala* or ***Magdalan***}

MAGEDA (1)

Mk 8:10 Dalmanutha. {Other ancient authorities read ***Mageda** or Magdala*}

MAGI (4)

Mt 2:1 wise men {Or *astrologers*; Gk ***magi***}
2:7 wise men {Or *astrologers*; Gk ***magi***}
2:16 wise men, {Or *astrologers*; Gk ***magi***}
2:16 wise men. {Or *astrologers*; Gk ***magi***}

MAGNATES (1)

2Es 15:48 deeds and devices. {Other ancient authorities add *you have followed after that one about to gratify her **magnates** and leaders* >}

MAHANAIM (1)

SS 6:13 dance before two armies? {Or *dance of **Mahanaim***}

MAKE (11)

Lev 26:34 the land shall enjoy {Or ***make** up for*} its sabbath years ... and enjoy {Or ***make** up for*} its sabbath years.
26:43 and enjoy {Or ***make** up for*} its sabbath years
Jos 22:19 or rebel against us {Or ***make** rebels of us*}
Jdg 16:14 and make it tight ... into the web, {Compare Gk: in verses 13-14, Heb lacks *and **make** it tight ... into the web*}
Ps 50:14 offer to God a sacrifice of thanksgiving, {Or ***make** thanksgiving your sacrifice to God*}
Jer 8:13 When I wanted to gather them, says the LORD, there are {Or *I will **make** an end of them, says the LORD. There are*}
Mt 23:13 + v.14 < *for the sake of appearance you **make** long prayers;* >
Ro 9:28 for the Lord will execute his sentence quickly and decisively." {Other ancient authorities read *for he will ... because the Lord will **make** the sentence shortened on the earth*}
Sir 17:15 + v.16 < *they are unable to **make** for themselves hearts of flesh in place of their stony hearts.* >
4Mc 1:5 Their attempt at argument is ridiculous! {Or *They are attempting to **make** my argument ridiculous!*}

MAKERS (1)

Isa 1:31 and their work {Or *its **makers***} like a spark;

†**LORD** distinguishes the proper name of God, *Yahweh*, rendered LORD in the NRSV, from words translated "Lord" and "lord," indexed under the heading ***LORD** on pages 28-29.

MAKES (7)
Pr 15: 2 The tongue of the wise dispenses knowledge, {Cn: Heb ***makes*** *knowledge good*}
Am 6:10 one who burns the dead, {Or *who* ***makes*** *a burning for him*}
Ro 8:28 We know that all things work together for good {Other ancient authorities read *God* ***makes*** *all things work together for good,* >}
1Co 4: 7 For who sees anything different in you? {Or *Who* ***makes*** *you different from another?*}
Sir 1:12 long life. {Other ancient authorities add *The fear of the Lord is a gift from the Lord; also for love he* ***makes*** *firm paths.*}
13:25 or for evil. {Other ancient authorities add *and a glad heart* ***makes*** *a cheerful countenance*}
24:27 It pours forth instruction like the Nile, {Syr: Gk *It* ***makes*** *instruction shine forth like light*}

MAKING (1)
Ge 41:51 Manasseh, {That is ***Making*** *to forget*}

MALCAM (1)
Zep 1: 5 Milcom; {Gk Mss Syr Vg: Heb ***Malcam*** (or, *their king*)}

MALCHIJAH (1)
Ezr 10:25 Hashabiah, {1 Esdras 9.26 Gk: Heb ***Malchijah***}

MALE (1)
Zec 10: 3 I will punish the leaders; {Or ***male*** *goats*}

MALICE (1)
Sir 11:14 + v.16 < *evil grows old with those who take pride in* ***malice.***

MALIGN (1)
1Pe 4: 4 and so they blaspheme. {Or *they* ***malign*** *you*}

MAMMON (4)
Mt 6:24 wealth. {Gk ***mammon***}
Lk 16: 9 wealth {Gk ***mammon***}
16:11 wealth, {Gk ***mammon***}
16:13 wealth." {Gk ***mammon***}

MAN (36)
Ge 43:24 When the steward {Heb *the* ***man***} had brought
Ex 16:15 "What is it?" {Or *"It is manna"* (Heb ***man*** *hu*, see verse 31)}
Lev 20:10 if a man commits adultery with the wife of {Heb repeats *if a* ***man*** *commits adultery with the wife of*}
Jos 7:17 family by family, {Mss Syr: MT ***man*** *by* ***man***}
1Sa 10:21 Finally ... man by man, {Gk: Heb lacks *Finally ...* ***man*** *by* ***man***}
2Sa 2: 8 Ishbaal {Gk Compare 1 Chr 8.33; 9.39: Heb *Ish-bosheth,* "***man*** of shame"}
2:10 Ishbaal, {Gk Compare 1 Chr 8.33; 9.39: Heb *Ish-bosheth,* "***man*** of shame"}
2:12 Ishbaal {Gk Compare 1 Chr 8.33; 9.39: Heb *Ish-bosheth,* "***man*** of shame"}
2:15 Ishbaal {Gk Compare 1 Chr 8.33; 9.39: Heb *Ish-bosheth,* "***man*** of shame"}
3: 8 Ishbaal {Gk Compare 1 Chr 8.33; 9.39: Heb *Ish-bosheth,* "***man*** of shame"}
Job 2: 4 All that people have they will give to save their lives. {Or *All that the* ***man*** *has he will give for his life*}
Ps 8: 4 mortals {Heb *ben adam*, lit. *son of* ***man***}
82: 7 fall like any prince." {Or *fall as one* ***man,*** *O princes*}
Pr 11:30 but violence {Cn Compare Gk Syr: Heb *a wise* ***man***} takes lives away.
18:24 Some {Syr Tg: Heb *A* ***man*** *of*} friends play at friendship
24: 5 Wise warriors are mightier than strong ones, {Gk Compare Syr Tg: Heb *A wise* ***man*** *is strength*}
Eze 2: 1 O mortal, {Or *son of* ***man***; Heb *ben adam* (and so throughout the book when Ezekiel is addressed)}
Da 7:13 I saw one like a human being {Aram *one like a son of* ***man***}
8:17 O mortal, {Heb *son of* ***man***}
Mt 18:10 + v.11 *For the Son of* ***Man*** *came to save the lost*
25:13 hour. {Other ancient authorities add *in which the Son of* ***Man*** *is coming*}
Mk 15:12 the man you call {Other ancient authorities lack *the* ***man*** *you call*}
Lk 1:34 Since I am a virgin?" {Gk *I do not know a* ***man***}
5:20 "Friend, {Gk ***Man***} your sins are forgiven
9:56 Then {Other ancient authorities read *for the Son of* ***Man*** *has not come to destroy the lives* >}
2Th 2: 3 the lawless one {Gk *the* ***man*** *of lawlessness*; other ancient authorities read *the* ***man*** *of sin*}
1Ti 5:16 believing woman {Other ancient authorities read *believing* ***man*** *or woman*; others, *believing* ***man***}
Heb 2: 6 human beings ... of them, {Gk *What is* ***man*** *that you are mindful of him?*} or mortals, that you care for them? {Gk *or the son of* ***man*** *that you care for him?* In the Hebrew of Psalm 8.4-6 both ***man*** and *son of* ***man*** refer to all humankind}
2Es 6: 1 "At the beginning ... before {< Ethiop: *At first by the Son of* ***Man,*** *and afterwards I myself.* >}

MAN'S (1)
Ps 37:23 Our steps {Heb *a* ***man's*** *steps*} are made firm

MANASSEH (2)
Jdg 12: 4 because ... Manasseh." {Meaning of Heb uncertain: Gk omits *because ...* ***Manasseh***}
18:30 Moses, {Another reading is *son of* ***Manasseh***}

MANASSES (1)
Tob 14:10 Ahikar {Gk *he*; other ancient authorities read ***Manasses***}

MANIFEST (1)
Sir 16:14 + v.16 < *His mercy is* ***manifest*** *to the whole of creation,* >

MANIFESTATION (1)
1Es 5:40 Urim and Thummim. {Gk ***Manifestation*** *and Truth*}

MANIFESTED (1)
Sir 1: 6 + v.7 *The knowledge of wisdom—to whom was it* ***manifested?*** >

MANIFOLD (1)
Mt 19:29 will receive a hundredfold, {Other ancient authorities read ***manifold***}

MANNA (1)
Ex 16:15 "What is it?" {Or *"It is* ***manna****"* (Heb *man hu*, see verse 31)}

MANNER (2)
Isa 51: 6 Will die like gnats; {Or *in like* ***manner***}
1Co 11:29 eat and drink {Other ancient authorities add *in an unworthy* ***manner,***}

MANOAH (1)
Jdg 13:19 wonders. {Heb *wonders, while* ***Manoah*** *and his wife looked on*}

MANY (12)
Ge 37: 3 a long robe with sleeves. {Traditional rendering (compare Gk): *a coat of* ***many*** *colors*; Meaning of Heb uncertain}
Ex 5: 5 "Now they are more numerous than the people of the land {Sam: Heb *The people of the land are now* ***many***}
Job 32: 9 It is not the old {Gk Syr Vg: Heb ***many***}
Ps 89:50 the insults of the peoples, {Cn: Heb *bosom all of* ***many*** *peoples*}
Jer 11:15 Can vows {Gk: Heb *Can* ***many***} and sacrificial
Am 3:15 the great houses {Or ***many*** *houses*} shall come
Mt 20:16 will be last." {Other ancient authorities add *for* ***many*** *are called but few are chosen*}
Mk 6:20 he was greatly perplexed; {Other ancient authorities read *he did* ***many*** *things*}
Ro 8:29 within a large family. {Gk *among* ***many*** *brothers*}
Sir 3:18 + v.19 ***Many*** *are lofty and renowned, but to the humble he reveals his secrets.*
20:14 for he looks for recompense sevenfold. {Syr: Gk *he has* ***many*** *eyes instead of one*}
2Es 6:17 the sound of mighty {Lat ***many***} waters.

MARAN (1)
1Co 16:22 Our Lord, come! {Gk *Marana tha*. These Aramaic words can also be read ***Maran*** *atha*, meaning *Our Lord has come*}

MARANA (1)
1Co 16:22 Our Lord, come! {Gk ***Marana*** *tha*. These Aramaic words can also be read *Maran atha*, meaning *Our Lord has come*}

MARBLE (1)
LtJ 6:72 From the purple and linen {Cn: Gk ***marble***, Syr *silk*}

MARESHAH (1)
1Ch 2:42 Mesha {Gk reads ***Mareshah***}

MARKET (1)
Eze 27:24 in these they traded with you. {Cn: Heb *in your* ***market***}

MARKETPLACE (1)
Mk 7: 4 and they do not eat anything from the market ... it; {Other ancient authorities read *and when they come from the* ***marketplace,*** *they do not eat* >}

MARRIAGE (1)
AdE 1: 5 the end of the festivity {Gk ***marriage*** *feast*}

MARRIED (1)
2Es 16:46 for in captivity and famine they will produce their children. {Other ancient authorities read *therefore those who are* ***married*** *may know that they will produce children for captivity and famine*}

MARRIES (1)
Mt 19: 9 commits adultery." {< others add at the end of the verse *and he who* ***marries*** *a divorced woman commits adultery*}

MARRY (2)
Lev 18:17 you shall not take {Or ***marry***}
18:18 you shall not take {Or ***marry***}

MARVELS (1)
Sir 17: 8 of his works. {Other ancient authorities add *and he gave them to boast of his* ***marvels*** *forever*}

MASH (1)
1Ch 1:17 Meshech. {***Mash*** in Gen 10.23}

MASHAH (1)
Ex 2:10 "I drew him out {Heb ***mashah***}

MASKIL (1)
Ps 47: 7 psalm. {Heb ***Maskil***}

MASTER (6)
Jer 31:32 though I was their husband, {Or ***master***}
Hos 2:16 "My Baal." {That is, *"My* ***master****"*}
Col 3:22 obey your earthly masters {In Greek the same word is used for ***master*** and *Lord*} ... fearing the Lord. {In Greek the same word is used for ***master*** and *Lord*}
Sir 19:20 + v.21 *When a slave says to his* ***master,*** *"I will not act as you wish,"* >
36: 1 Have mercy upon us, O God {Heb: Gk *O* ***Master,*** *the God*}

MASTERLESS (1)
Sir 20:31 + v.32 < *better than a* ***masterless*** *charioteer of one's own life.*

MATTATHIAS (1)
2Es 1:40 the messenger of the Lord. {Other ancient authorities read ... *Mattia* (or ***Mattathias***), *Habakkuk, and twelve angels with flowers*}

MATTERS (2)
1Ch 4:22 now the records {Or ***matters***} are ancient.
Ac 19:39 If there is anything further {Other ancient authorities read *about other* ***matters***}

MATTIA (1)
2Es 1:40 the messenger of the Lord. {Other ancient authorities read ... ***Mattia*** (or *Mattathias*), *Habakkuk, and twelve angels with flowers*}

MATURITY (1)
Heb 6: 1 let us go toward perfection, {Or *toward* ***maturity***}

MEADOW (1)
Ge 50:11 Abel-mizraim; {That is *mourning* (or ***meadow***) *of Egypt*}

MEASURE (3)
Eze 47:18 Tamar. {Compare Syr: Heb *you shall* ***measure***}
Sir 1:18 flourish. {Other ancient authorities add < *those who love him. He saw her and took her* ***measure.***}
2Es 4: 5 a blast {Syr Ethiop Arab 1 Arab 2 Georg *a* ***measure***} of wind,

MEASURES (1)
Eze 41:17 there was a pattern. {Heb ***measures***}

MEDIATE (1)
1Sa 2:25 another, someone can intercede for the sinner with the LORD; {Gk Compare Q Ms: MT *another, God will* ***mediate*** *for him*}

MEEKNESS (2)
Ps 45: 4 and to defend {Cn: Heb *and the* ***meekness*** *of*} the right;
Sir 3:17 perform your tasks with humility; {Heb: Gk ***meekness***}

MEET (1)
Heb 4: 2 they were not united by faith with those who listened. {Other ancient authorities read *it did not* ***meet*** *with faith in those who listened*}

MEHEBEL (1)
Jos 19:29 Mahalab, {Cn Compare Gk: Heb ***Mehebel***}

MELTED (2)
Isa 64: 7 delivered {Gk Syr Old Latin Tg: Heb ***melted***}
Wis 19:21 nor did they melt {Cn: Gk *nor could be* ***melted***}

MEMORIAL (1)
4Mc 17: 8 as a reminder to the people of our nation: {Or *as a* ***memorial*** *to the heroes of our people*}

MEMORY (1)
Sir 49: 1 The name {Heb: Gk ***memory***} of Josiah

MEN (33)

Jos 9:14 So the leaders {Gk: Heb **men**} partook
1Sa 6:19 killed seventy men of them. {Heb *killed seventy **men**, fifty thousand **men***}
8:16 the best of your cattle {Gk: Heb *young **men***}
17:12 and advanced in years. {Gk Syr: Heb *among **men***}
23:11 will {Q Ms Compare Gk: MT *Will the **men** of Keilah surrender me into his hand? Will*}
2Sa 16:15 all the Israelites {Gk: Heb *all the people, the **men** of Israel*}
1Ki 10: 8 Happy are your wives! {Gk Syr: Heb **men**}
Isa 15: 4 the loins of Moab quiver; {Cn Compare Gk Syr: Heb *the armed **men** of Moab cry aloud*}
41:14 you insect {Syr: Heb ***men** of*} Israel!
Jer 26:22 King Jehoiakim sent {Heb adds **men** *to Egypt*}
Eze 24:17 eat the bread of mourners. {Vg Tg: Heb *of **men***}
24:22 eat the bread of mourners. {Vg Tg: Heb *of **men***}
Da 11:24 into the richest parts {Or *among the richest **men***}
Jn 6:10 so they {Gk *the **men***} sat down,
Ac 1:16 "Friends, {Gk ***Men**, brothers*}
2:22 Israelites, {Gk ***Men**, Israelites*}
2:29 Israelites, {Gk ***Men**, brothers*}
2:37 "Brothers, {Gk ***Men**, brothers*}
3:12 Israelites, {Gk ***Men**, Israelites*}
5: 4 you did not lie to us {Gk *to **men***}
5:29 rather than any human authority. {Gk *than **men***}
5:35 Israelites, {Gk ***Men**, Israelites*}
7: 2 "Brothers {Gk ***Men**, brothers*}
13:16 Israelites, {Gk ***Men**, Israelites*}
14:15 "Friends, {Gk ***Men***}
15: 7 brothers, {Gk ***Men**, brothers*}
15:13 brothers, {Gk ***Men**, brothers*}
15:25 to choose representatives {Gk ***men***}
23: 1 "Brothers, {Gk ***Men**, brothers*}
Col 3:23 masters, {Gk *not for **men***}
2Ti 3: 9 two men, {Gk lacks *two **men***}
2Es 10:22 our children {Ethiop *free **men***} have suffered

MEONOTHAI (1)

1Ch 4:13 and Meonothai. {Gk Vg: Heb lacks *and **Meonothai***}

MERCIFULLY (1)

3Mc 6: 8 watched over and restored {Other ancient authorities read *rescued and restored*; others, ***mercifully** restored*}

MERCY (5)

Tit 1: 4 Grace {Other ancient authorities read *Grace, **mercy**,*} and peace from God
Sir 16:10 stubbornness. {Other ancient authorities add *Chastising, showing **mercy**, striking, healing, the Lord persisted in **mercy** and discipline.*}
16:14 + v.16 *His **mercy** is manifest to the whole of creation,* >
23: 3 rejoice over me. {Other ancient authorities add *From them the hope of your **mercy** is remote*}

MERIB-BAAL (14)

2Sa 4: 4 Mephibosheth. {In 1 Chr 8.34 and 9.40, ***Merib-baal***}
9: 6 Mephibosheth {Or ***Merib-baal***: See 4.4 note}
9: 6 "Mephibosheth!" {Or ***Merib-baal***: See 4.4 note}
9:10 Mephibosheth {Or ***Merib-baal***: See 4.4 note}
9:11 Mephibosheth {Or ***Merib-baal***: See 4.4 note}
9:12 Mephibosheth {Or ***Merib-baal***: See 4.4 note}
9:13 Mephibosheth {Or ***Merib-baal***: See 4.4 note}
16: 1 Mephibosheth {Or ***Merib-baal***: See 4.4 note}
16: 4 Mephibosheth {Or ***Merib-baal***: See 4.4 note}
19:24 Mephibosheth {Or ***Merib-baal***: See 4.4 note}
19:25 Mephibosheth?" {Or ***Merib-baal***: See 4.4 note}
19:30 Mephibosheth {Or ***Merib-baal***: See 4.4 note}
21: 7 Mephibosheth, {Or ***Merib-baal***: See 4.4 note}
21: 8 Mephibosheth; {Or ***Merib-baal***: See 4.4 note}

MERIB-BAAL'S (1)

2Sa 9:12 Mephibosheth's {Or ***Merib-baal's***: See 4.4 note}

MESSENGER (3)

2Ki 6:33 the king {See 7.2: Heb **messenger**} came down
Mal 1: 1 by Malachi. {Or *by my **messenger***}
Gal 1: 8 an angel {Or *a **messenger***} from heaven

MESSIAH (3)

Heb 11:26 suffered for the Christ {Or *the **Messiah***}
1Jn 2:22 denies that Jesus is the Christ? {Or *the **Messiah***}
5: 1 believes that Jesus is the Christ {Or *the **Messiah***}

MICHAL (1)

2Sa 21: 8 Merab {Two Heb Mss Syr Compare Gk: MT ***Michal***}

MIDST (2)

Jer 9: 6 oppression upon oppression, deceit upon deceit {Cn: Heb *Your dwelling in the **midst** of deceit*}
Lk 5:19 into the middle of the crowd {Gk *into the **midst***}

MIGHT (2)

Mt 27:35 casting lots; {Other ancient authorities add *in order that what had been spoken through the prophet **might** be fulfilled,* >}
Sir 16:14 + v.15 *in order that his works **might** be known under heaven.* >

MIGHTILY (1)

Sir 39:28 can dislodge mountains; {Heb Syr: Gk *can scourge **mightily***}

MIGHTY (2)

Ge 1: 2 while a wind from God {Or *while the spirit of God* or *while a **mighty** wind*}
Ps 58: 1 what is right, you gods? {Or ***mighty** lords*}

MIND (4)

Col 2:18 by a human way of thinking, {Gk *by the **mind** of his flesh*}
Heb 12:17 found no chance to repent, {Or *no chance to change his father's **mind***}
1Pe 1:13 prepare your minds for action; {Gk *gird up the loins of your **mind***}
Sir 17: 4 + v.5 < *as sixth he distributed to them the gift of **mind**, and as seventh, reason,* >

MINDS (2)

Wis 19: 2 though they themselves had permitted {Other ancient authorities read *had changed their **minds** to permit*}
4Mc 14: 2 O reason, {Or *O **minds***} more loyal than kings

MINE (3)

1Sa 14: 7 so is mine." {Gk: Heb lacks *so is **mine***}
Mk 8:38 ashamed of me and of my words {Other ancient authorities read *and of **mine***}
Sir 38:22 yesterday it was his, {Heb: Gk ***mine***}

MINISTER (1)

Ro 16: 1 deacon {Or ***minister***}

MISFORTUNES (1)

2Es 16:71 They shall {Other ancient authorities read *For people, because of their **misfortunes**, shall*}

MIXING (1)

2Mc 14: 3 the times of separation, {Other ancient authorities read *of **mixing***}

MOABITES (1)

Jdt 6: 1 to Achior {Other ancient authorities add *and to all the **Moabites***}

MOCKERIES (1)

Sir 34:22 the gifts {Other ancient authorities read ***mockeries***} of the lawless

MOCKERS (1)

Ps 35:16 they impiously mocked me more and more, {Cn Compare Gk: Heb *like the profanest of **mockers** of a cake*}

MOCKERY (1)

Sir 34:21 the offering is blemished; {Other ancient authorities read *is made in **mockery***}

MOLECH (12)

Isa 30:33 ready for the king, {Or ***Molech***}

MONEY (4)

Mt 19:21 the money {Gk lacks *the **money***}
Mk 10:21 the money {Gk lacks *the **money***}
Lk 18:22 the money {Gk lacks *the **money***}
Sir 10: 8 wealth. {Other ancient authorities add here or after verse 9a, *Nothing is more wicked than one who loves **money**,* >}

MONTH (4)

1Sa 11: 1 About a month later, {Q Ms Gk: MT lacks *About a **month** later*}
Est 3: 7 on the thirteenth day {Cn Compare Gk and verse 13 below: Heb *the twelfth **month***}
Eze 32:17 in the first month {Gk: Heb lacks *in the first **month***}
Sir 43: 8 new moon, as its name suggests, renews itself; {Heb: Gk *The **month** is named after the moon*}

MONTHS (2)

2Es 5: 4 after the third period; {Literally *after the third*; Ethiop *after three **months***; >}
14:48 did so. {Syr adds *... five thousand years and three **months** and twelve days after creation.* >}

MOON (2)

Dt 16: 1 observe the month {Or *new **moon***} of Abib
Ps 74:16 established the luminaries {Or ***moon***; Heb *light*}

MORDECAI (1)

AdE 4: 5 + v.6 *So Hachratheus went out to **Mordecai** in the street of the city opposite the city gate.*

MORE (9)

1Ch 11:21 He was the most renowned {Compare 2 Sam 23.19: Heb ***more** renowned among the two*}
Job 4:17 'Can mortals be righteous before {Or ***more** than*} God? Can human beings be pure before {Or ***more** than*} their Maker?
Hos 14: 8 O Ephraim, what have I {Or *What **more** has Ephraim*}
Mk 16:14 risen. {Other ancient authorities add, in whole or in part, *... that they may return to the truth and sin no **more**,* >}
Heb 9:11 the greater and perfect {Gk ***more** perfect*} tent
Sir 10: 8 wealth. {Other ancient authorities add here or after verse 9a, *Nothing is **more** wicked than one who loves money,* >}
4Mc 15: 5 give birth to many, ... children. {Or *... and the **more** children they bear, the **more** they are devoted to their children.*}

MORNING (2)

Ps 49:14 straight to the grave they descend, {Cn: Heb *the upright shall have dominion over them in the **morning***}
Ac 19: 9 of Tyrannus. {Other ancient authorities read *of a certain Tyrannus, from eleven o'clock in the **morning** to four in the afternoon*}

MORTAL (1)

Sir 17:11 law of life. {Other ancient authorities add *so that they may know that they who are alive now are **mortal***}

MORTALS (2)

1Sa 2:33 shall die by the sword. {Q Ms See Gk: MT *die like **mortals***}
Sir 7:17 the punishment of the ungodly is fire and worms. {Heb *for the expectation of **mortals** is worms*}

MOSES (1)

Heb 11:23 king's edict. {Other ancient authorities add *By faith **Moses**, when he was grown up, killed the* >}

MOSHEH (1)

Ex 2:10 Moses, {Heb ***Mosheh***}

MOST (2)

Mt 21: 8 A very large crowd {Or ***Most** of the crowd*}
2Es 14:48 did so. {Other ancient authorities add, in whole or in part, *... And he was called the scribe of the knowledge of the **Most** High for ever and ever.* >}

MOTH (1)

Pr 25:20 Like a moth ... human heart. {Gk Syr Tg: Heb lacks *Like a **moth** ... human heart*}

MOTHER (2)

Mt 15: 5 honor the father. {Other ancient authorities add *or the **mother***}
Sir 24:17 + v.18 *I am the **mother** of beautiful love, of fear, of knowledge, and of holy hope;* >

MOTHER-IN-LAW (1)

Tob 10:12 Then ... mother-in-law, {Other ancient authorities lack parts of *Then ... **mother-in-law***}

MOUNT (1)

Jdg 7: 3 home.' " Thus Gideon sifted them out; {Cn: Heb *home, and depart from **Mount** Gilead*' "}

MOUNTAIN (6)

Ge 48:22 one portion {Or ***mountain** slope* (Heb *shekem*, a play on the name of the town and district of Shechem)}
48:22 the portion {Or ***mountain** slope* (Heb *shekem*, a play on the name of the town and district of Shechem)}
Ps 11: 1 "Flee like a bird to the mountains; {Gk Syr Jerome Tg: Heb *flee to your **mountain**, O bird*}
Gal 4:25 Now Hagar is Mount Sinai in Arabia {Other ancient authorities read *For Sinai is a **mountain** in Arabia*}
Heb 12:18 You have not come to something {Other ancient authorities read *a **mountain***}
Sir 50:26 Those who live in Seir, {Heb Compare Lat: Gk *on the **mountain** of Samaria*}

MOUNTAINS (3)

Ps 50:11 the birds of the air, {Gk Syr Tg: Heb ***mountains***}
Am 3: 9 "Assemble yourselves on Mount {Gk Syr: Heb *the **mountains** of*}
Zec 14: 5 the LORD's mountain, {Heb *my **mountains***}

MOURN (1)

Ps 69:10 When I humbled my soul with fasting, {Gk Syr: Heb *... I made my soul **mourn** with fasting*}

MOURNING (2)

Ge 50:11 Abel-mizraim; {That is ***mourning*** (or *meadow*) *of Egypt*}
Sir 16: 3 numbers; {Other ancient authorities add *For you will groan in untimely **mourning**, and will know of their sudden end.*}

MOUTH (7)

Jdg 9:38 "Where is your boast {Heb ***mouth***} now,
1Sa 1:23 the LORD establish his word." {MT: Q Ms Gk Compare Syr *that which goes out of your **mouth***}
Job 15:30 their blossom {Gk: Heb ***mouth***} will be swept

Pr 6: 2 the utterance of your lips, {Cn Compare Gk Syr: Heb *the words of your **mouth***}
Lk 21:15 I will give you words {Gk *a **mouth***}
AdE 13:17 do not destroy the lips {Gk ***mouth***}
Sir 48:12 He performed ... mouth. {Heb: Gk lacks *He performed ... **mouth***}

MOUTHS (1)

Dt 18:18 my words in the mouth of the prophet, {Or ***mouths** of the prophets*}

MOVED (1)

Jos 10:21 my words in the mouth of the speak {Heb ***moved** his tongue*}

MUCH (3)

Sir 38:11 as much as you can afford. {Heb: Lat lacks *as **much** as you can afford*; Meaning of Gk uncertain}
51:28 Hear but a little ... acquire silver and gold. {Syr Compare Heb: Gk *Get instruction with a large sum of silver, and you will gain by it **much** gold.*}
4Mc 16:10 alone, with many sorrows. {Or ***much** to be pitied*}

MULES (1)

Ne 7:68 They had ... mules, {Ezra 2.66 and the margins of some Hebrew Mss: MT lacks *They had ... forty-five **mules***}

MULTITUDE (6)

Ge 17: 5 Abraham; {Here taken to mean *ancestor of a **multitude***}
Am 4: 9 I laid waste {Cn: Heb *the **multitude** of*}
Wis 18:22 He conquered the wrath {Cn: Gk ***multitude***}
Sir 16: 9 their sins; {Other ancient authorities add < *and by the **multitude** of his holy ones he was not appeased.*}
42:11 put you to shame in public gatherings. {Heb: Gk *to shame before the great **multitude***}
1Es 9:48 law of the Lord, {Other ancient authorities add *and read the law of the Lord to the **multitude***}

MURDER (2)

Gal 5:21 envy, {Other ancient authorities add ***murder***}
Jas 4: 2 And you covet {Or *you **murder** and you covet*}

MUSIC (1)

Ps 77: 6 I commune {Gk Syr: Heb *My **music***} with my

MUST (2)

Ac 15:24 minds, {Other ancient authorities add *saying, 'You **must** be circumcised and keep the law,'*}
18:21 he said, "I {Other ancient authorities read *I **must** at all costs keep the approaching festival in Jerusalem, but I*} will return

MUSTERED (1)

1Sa 4: 1 In those ... Israel, {Gk: Heb lacks *In those days the Philistines **mustered** for war against Israel*}

MUTILATION (1)

Php 3: 2 those who mutilate the flesh! {Gk *the **mutilation***}

MYRA (1)

Ac 21: 1 there to Patara. {Other ancient authorities add *and **Myra***}

MYRIAD (1)

Eze 16: 7 Live! [7]and grow up {Gk Syr: Heb *Live! I made you a **myriad***}

MYSTERIES (2)

Mt 13:11 to know the secrets {Or ***mysteries***} of the kingdom
Lk 8:10 to know the secrets {Or ***mysteries***} of the kingdom

MYSTERY (1)

Mk 4:11 the secret {Or ***mystery***} of the kingdom

N

NAHASH (1)

1Sa 10:27 Now Nahash ... entered Jabesh-gilead. {Q Ms Compare Josephus, *Antiquities* VI.v.1 (68-71): MT lacks *Now **Nahash** ... entered Jabesh-gilead.*}

NAME (4)

Lk 6:22 and defame you {Gk *cast out your **name** as evil*}
Heb 6:10 showed for his sake {Gk *for his **name***}
3Jn 1: 7 the sake of Christ, {Gk *for the sake of the **name***}
Wis 18:12 by the one form {Gk ***name***} of death,

NAMED (4)

Mk 3:14 whom he also named apostles, {Other ancient authorities lack *whom he also **named** apostles*}
Sir 24:17 + v.18 < *being eternal, I am given to all my children, to those who are **named** by him.*
43: 8 new moon, as its name suggests, renews itself; {Heb: Gk *The month is **named** after the moon*}
2Es 10:57 have been called to be with {Or *been **named** by*}

NAMELY (1)

Ro 10: 9 because {Or ***namely**, that*} if you confess

NAPHTALI (1)

Nu 26:50 These are the Naphtalites {Heb *clans of **Naphtali***}

NATHAMIAH (1)

Tob 5:14 Nathan, {Other ancient authorities read *Jathan* or ***Nathamiah***}

NATION (2)

Zep 2:14 every wild animal; {Tg Compare Gk: Heb ***nation***}
3Mc 2:27 on the Jewish community, {Gk *the **nation***}

NATIONS (4)

Dt 32:43 O heavens, {Q Ms Gk: MT ***nations***} his people,
Eze 2: 3 to a nation {Syr: Heb *to **nations***} of rebels
Sir 16: 9 their sins; {Other ancient authorities add *All these things he did to the hard-hearted **nations**,* >}
17:15 + v.17 < *For in the division of the **nations** of the whole earth, he appointed*

NATURAL (1)

1Co 2:14 Those who are unspiritual {Or ***natural***} do not

NATURALLY (1)

Nu 19:16 who died naturally, {Heb lacks ***naturally***}

NATURE (2)

Wis 2:23 the image of his own eternity, {Other ancient authorities read ***nature***}
12:10 unaware that their origin {Or ***nature***} was evil

NAVEL (1)

Eze 38:12 live at the center {Heb ***navel***} of the earth.

NAZIRITE (1)

1Sa 1:22 I will offer ... time." {Cn Compare Q Ms: MT lacks *I will offer him as a **nazirite** for all time*}

NAZOREAN (12)

Mt 26:71 Jesus of Nazareth." {Gk *the **Nazorean***}
Lk 18:37 "Jesus of Nazareth {Gk *the **Nazorean***}
24:19 Jesus of Nazareth, {Other ancient authorities read *Jesus the **Nazorean***}
Jn 18: 5 "Jesus of Nazareth." {Gk *the **Nazorean***}
18: 7 "Jesus of Nazareth." {Gk *the **Nazorean***}
19:19 "Jesus of Nazareth, {Gk *the **Nazorean***}
Ac 2:22 Jesus of Nazareth, {Gk *the **Nazorean***}
3: 6 Jesus Christ of Nazareth, {Gk *the **Nazorean***}
4:10 Jesus Christ of Nazareth, {Gk *the **Nazorean***}
6:14 Jesus of Nazareth {Gk *the **Nazorean***}
22: 8 Jesus of Nazareth {Gk *the **Nazorean***}
26: 9 Jesus of Nazareth. {Gk *the **Nazorean***}

NAZOREANS (1)

Ac 24: 5 the sect of the Nazarenes. {Gk ***Nazoreans***}

NEAR (3)

Hos 7: 6 For they are kindled {Gk Syr: Heb *brought **near***}
Mk 16:14 risen. {Other ancient authorities add, in whole or in part, ... *term of years of Satan's power has been fulfilled, but other terrible things draw **near**.* >}
2Es 8:47 But you have often compared yourself {Syr Ethiop: Lat *brought yourself **near***}

NEBUCHADNEZZAR (2)

Tob 14:15 Cyaxares {Cn: Codex Sinaiticus *Ahikar*; other ancient authorities read ***Nebuchadnezzar** and Ahasuerus*}
2Es 1: 3 Artaxerxes, king of the Persians. {Other ancient authorities, ... begin the chapter: < *in the days of King **Nebuchadnezzar**, saying, "Go,*}

NECESSARY (2)

Lk 10:42 for only one thing. {Other ancient authorities read *few things are **necessary**, or only one*}
Wis 16: 3 lost the remnant of appetite {Gk *loathed the **necessary** appetite*}

NECKS (2)

Sir 7:23 make them obedient {Gk *bend their **necks***}
3Mc 5:49 falling into one another's arms— {Gk *falling upon their **necks***}

NEGLECT (1)

Sir 17:17 + v.18 < *and allotting to him the light of his love, he does not **neglect** him.*

NEITHER (4)

Mk 11:25 + v.26 *"But if you do not forgive, **neither** will your Father in heaven forgive your trespasses."*
Ro 11:21 perhaps he will not spare you. {Other ancient authorities read ***neither** will he spare you*}
Sir 17:20 + v.21 < *knows how they are formed, has **neither** left them nor abandoned them,* >
38:32 and wherever they live, they will not go hungry. {Syr: Gk *and people can **neither** live nor walk there*}

NEPHTHAI (1)

2Mc 1:36 naphtha. {Gk ***nephthai***}

NER (1)

1Ch 8:30 Baal, {Gk Ms adds ***Ner***; Compare 8.33 and 9.36}

NEST (1)

Sir 1:15 made {Gk *made as a **nest***} among human beings

NET (2)

1Ki 7:17 seven {Heb: Gk *a **net***} for the one capital, and seven {Heb: Gk *a **net***} for the other capital.

NEVER (1)

Lk 22:16 will not eat it {Other ancient authorities read ***never** eat it again*}

NEW (5)

Dt 16: 1 Observe the month {Or ***new** moon*} of Abib
Eze 11:19 give them one {Another reading is *a **new***} heart,
Mt 26:28 my blood of the {Other ancient authorities add ***new***} covenant,
Mk 2:22 but one puts new wine into fresh wineskins." {Other ancient authorities lack *but one puts **new** wine into fresh wineskins*}
14:24 my blood of the {Other ancient authorities add ***new***} covenant,

NEXT (2)

Nu 30:14 from day to day, {Or *from that day to the **next***}
Lk 7:11 Soon afterwards {Other ancient authorities read ***Next** day*}

NIGHT (1)

Isa 60:19 by night; {Q Ms Gk Old Latin Tg: MT lacks *by **night***}

NILE (1)

Isa 23:10 O ships of {Cn Compare Gk: Heb *like the **Nile**, daughter*} Tarshish;

NINE (1)

2Mc 12:10 more than a mile {Gk ***nine** stadia*}

NINTH (1)

3Mc 5:12 deep a sleep {Other ancient authorities add *from evening until the **ninth** hour*}

NIPHTAL (1)

Ge 30: 8 I have wrestled {Heb ***niphtal***}

NO-AMON (1)

Na 3: 8 Thebes {Heb ***No-amon***}

NOBILITY (1)

Sir 22: 6 + v.8 < *who are disdainfully and boorishly haughty stain the **nobility** of their kindred.*

NOBLE (1)

Pr 17: 7 false speech to a ruler. {Or *a **noble** person*}

NON (1)

1Ch 7:27 Nun {Here spelled ***Non***; see Ex 33.11}

NOON (1)

Ac 8:26 go toward the south {Or *go at **noon***}

NORTH (4)

Job 26: 7 stretches out Zaphon {Or *the **North***}
Isa 14:13 assembly on the heights of Zaphon; {Or *assembly in the far **north***}
Eze 40:19 hundred cubits. {Heb adds *the east and the **north***}
2Es 15:32 and shall turn and flee. {Other ancient authorities read *turn their face to the **north***}

NOTHING (4)

1Ki 9:13 the land of Cabul {Perhaps meaning *a land good for **nothing***}
Pr 10:22 and he adds no sorrow with it. {Or *and toil adds **nothing** to it*}
Tob 10: 7 and would heed no one. {Other ancient authorities read *and she would eat **nothing***}
Sir 10: 8 and wealth. {Other ancient authorities add here or after verse 9a, ***Nothing** is more wicked than one who loves money,* >}

NOTHINGNESS (1)

Am 6:13 in Lo-debar, {Or *in a thing of **nothingness***}

NOURISH (1)

2Es 1: 5 so that they may tell {Other ancient authorities read ***nourish***}

NOURISHED (1)

2Es 1:32 says the Lord. {Other ancient authorities add < *if I have not **nourished** you, if I have not done* >}

NOW (7)

1Sa 10:27 Now Nahash ... entered Jabesh-gilead. {Q Ms Compare Josephus, *Antiquities* VI.v.1 (68-71): MT lacks *Now Nahash ... entered Jabesh-gilead.*}
2Sa 18: 3 But you are worth ten thousand of us; {Gk Vg Symmachus: Heb *for **now** there are ten thousand such as we*}
Da 10:17 For I am shaking, {Gk: Heb *from **now***}
Mk 16:14 risen. {Other ancient authorities add, in whole or in part, < *Therefore reveal your righteousness **now**"—thus they spoke to Christ.* >}
Lk 23:16 + v.17 ***Now** he was obliged to release someone for them at the festival*
Ro 11:31 may now {Other ancient authorities lack ***now***} receive mercy.
Sir 17:11 of life. {Other ancient authorities add *so that they may know that they who are alive **now** are mortal*}

NUBIA (20)

2Ki 19: 9 Ethiopia, {Or ***Nubia***; Heb *Cush*}
Est 1: 1 Ethiopia. {Or ***Nubia***; Heb *Cush*}
8: 9 Ethiopia, {Or ***Nubia***; Heb *Cush*}
Job 28:19 Ethiopia {Or ***Nubia***; Heb *Cush*}
Ps 68:31 Ethiopia {Or ***Nubia***; Heb *Cush*}
87: 4 Ethiopia— {Or ***Nubia***; Heb *Cush*}
Isa 11:11 Ethiopia, {Or ***Nubia***; Heb *Cush*}
18: 1 Ethiopia, {Or ***Nubia***; Heb *Cush*}
20: 3 Ethiopia, {Or ***Nubia***; Heb *Cush*}
20: 5 Ethiopia {Or ***Nubia***; Heb *Cush*}
37: 9 Ethiopia, {Or ***Nubia***; Heb *Cush*}
43: 3 Ethiopia {Or ***Nubia***; Heb *Cush*}
45:14 Ethiopia, {Or ***Nubia***; Heb *Cush*}
Jer 46: 9 Ethiopia {Or ***Nubia***; Heb *Cush*}
Eze 29:10 Ethiopia. {Or ***Nubia***; Heb *Cush*}
30: 4 Ethiopia, {Or ***Nubia***; Heb *Cush*}
30: 5 Ethiopia, {Or ***Nubia***; Heb *Cush*}
38: 5 Ethiopia, {Or ***Nubia***; Heb *Cush*}
Na 3: 9 Ethiopia {Or ***Nubia***; Heb *Cush*}
Zep 3:10 Ethiopia {Or ***Nubia***; Heb *Cush*}

NUBIAN (5)

2Ch 14: 9 Ethiopian {Or ***Nubian***; Heb *Cushite*}
Jer 38: 7 Ethiopian, {Or ***Nubian***; Heb *Cushite*}
38:10 Ethiopian, {Or ***Nubian***; Heb *Cushite*}
38:12 Ethiopian {Or ***Nubian***; Heb *Cushite*}
39:16 Ethiopian: {Or ***Nubian***; Heb *Cushite*}

NUBIANS (12)

2Ch 12: 3 Ethiopians. {Or ***Nubians***; Heb *Cushites*}
14:12 Ethiopians {Or ***Nubians***; Heb *Cushites*}
14:12 Ethiopians {Or ***Nubians***; Heb *Cushites*}
14:13 Ethiopians {Or ***Nubians***; Heb *Cushites*}
16: 8 Ethiopians {Or ***Nubians***; Heb *Cushites*}
21:16 Ethiopians. {Or ***Nubians***; Heb *Cushites*}
Isa 20: 4 Ethiopians {Or ***Nubians***; Heb *Cushites*}
Jer 13:23 Ethiopians {Or ***Nubians***; Heb *Cushites*}
Eze 30: 9 Ethiopians; {Or ***Nubians***; Heb *Cush*}
Da 11:43 Ethiopians {Or ***Nubians***; Heb *Cushites*}
Am 9: 7 Ethiopians {Or ***Nubians***; Heb *Cushites*}
Zep 2:12 O Ethiopians, {Or ***Nubians***; Heb *Cushites*}

O

O'CLOCK (1)

Ac 19: 9 of Tyrannus. {Other ancient authorities read *of a certain Tyrannus, from eleven **o'clock** in the morning to four in the afternoon*}

OAK (2)

Ge 35: 8 Allon-bacuth. {That is ***Oak** of weeping*}
Jdg 9:37 Elon-meonenim." {That is *Diviners' **Oak***}

OAKS (1)

Dt 11:30 beside the oak {Gk Syr: Compare Gen 12.6; Heb ***oaks*** or *terebinths*} of Moreh.

OATH (4)

Ge 21:31 Beer-sheba; {That is *Well of seven* or *Well of the **oath***}
26:33 Shibah; {A word resembling the word for ***oath***}
26:33 Beer-sheba {That is *Well of the **oath*** **or** *Well of seven*}
Sir 36:10 remember the appointed time, {Other ancient authorities read *remember your **oath***}

OATHS (2)

Hab 3: 9 sated {Cn: Heb ***oaths***} were the arrows
Wis 14:31 things by which people swear, {Or *of the **oaths** people swear*}

OBDURACY (1)

Sir 10:20 + v.21 < ***obduracy** and pride are the beginning of rejection.*

OBEDIENT (1)

Sir 42:23 to meet a particular need. {Heb: Gk *forever for every need, and all are **obedient***}

OBEY (2)

Dt 30:16 If you ... your God {Gk: Heb lacks *If you **obey** the commandments of the* LORD *your God*}
Sir 18: 2 + v.3 < *and all things **obey** his will; for he is king of all things by his power,* >

OBEYED (1)

1Es 8:95 Rise up {Other ancient authorities read ... *And all who **obeyed** the law of the Lord rose and said to Ezra, "Rise up*}

OBLIGED (1)

Lk 23:16 + v.17 *Now he was **obliged** to release someone for them at the festival*

OBLIVION (1)

2Es 8:53 Hades has fled and corruption has been forgotten; {Syr: Lat *Hades and corruption have fled into **oblivion***; >}

OBSERVED (1)

Heb 11:23 king's edict. {Other ancient authorities add < *killed the Egyptian, because he **observed** the humiliation of his people* (Gk *brothers*)}

OBTAINED (2)

Lk 22:31 Satan has demanded {Or *has **obtained** permission*} to sift
Sir 17: 4 + v.5 *They **obtained** the use of the five faculties of the Lord;* >

OBTAINS (1)

Sir 19:17 + v.18 < *The fear of the Lord is the beginning of acceptance, and wisdom **obtains** his love.* >

OFF (9)

Ps 31:22 "I am driven far {Another reading is *cut **off***}
Pr 25:20 vinegar on a wound {Gk: Heb *Like one who takes **off** a garment on a cold day, like vinegar on lye*}
La 3:22 love of the LORD never ceases, {Syr Tg: Heb LORD, *we are not cut **off***}
Da 4:27 atone for {Aram *break **off***} your sins
Zep 3: 7 it will not lose sight {Gk Syr: Heb *its dwelling will not be cut **off***}
Mt 24:51 cut him in pieces {Or *cut him **off***}
Lk 12:46 cut him in pieces, {Or *cut him **off***}
2Pe 1:14 my death {Gk *the putting **off** of my tent*}
4Mc 10: 7 they abandoned the instruments {Other ancient authorities read *they tore **off** his skin*}

OFFER (1)

1Sa 1:22 I will offer him as a nazirite for all time." {Cn Compare Q Ms: MT lacks *I will **offer** him as a nazirite for all time*}

OFFERING (3)

Isa 61: 8 I hate robbery and wrongdoing; {Or *robbery with a burnt **offering***}
Mt 15: 5 is given to God,' {Or *is an **offering***}
Ro 8: 3 and to deal with sin, {Or *and as a sin **offering***}

OFFICERS (1)

1Ch 12:21 against the band of raiders, {Or *as **officers** of his troops*}

OFFICIALS (1)

Jer 17:25 kings {Cn: Heb *kings and **officials***} who sit on the throne

OFTEN (1)

Mt 9:14 Pharisees fast often, {Other ancient authorities lack ***often***}

OIL (3)

Pr 21:20 Precious treasure remains {Gk: Heb *and **oil***}
Eze 45:14 oil, {Cn: Heb ***oil**, the bath the **oil***}

OLAM (1)

Ge 21:33 the LORD, the Everlasting God. {Or *the* LORD, *El **Olam***}

OLD (5)

1Sa 27: 8 from Telam {Compare Gk 15.4: Heb *from of **old***}
1Ki 13:29 and brought it back to the city, {Gk: Heb *he came to the town of the **old** prophet*}
2Ki 25:26 all the people high and low {Or *young and **old***}
Ac 15:18 known from long ago.' {Other ancient authorities read ... *Known to God from of **old** are all his works.'*}
Sir 11:14 + v.16 < *evil grows **old** with those who take pride in malice.*

OLDER (1)

1Pe 5: 5 of the elders. {Or *of those who are **older***}

OMNIPOTENCE (1)

Sir 19:20 of the law. {Other ancient authorities add *and the knowledge of his **omnipotence**.* >}

ONCE (1)

Pr 28:18 fall into the Pit. {Syr: Heb *fall all at **once***}

ONE (89)

Ge 16:14 Beer-lahai-roi; {That is *the Well of the Living **One** who sees me*}
32:28 Israel, {That is *The **one** who strives with God* or *God strives*}
Nu 6: 2 nazirite, {That is ***one** separated* or ***one** consecrated*}
6:21 nazirite {That is ***one** separated* or ***one** consecrated*}
Dt 6: 4 The LORD is our God, the LORD alone. {Or *The* LORD *our God is **one*** LORD, or *The* LORD *our God, the* LORD *is **one***, or *The* LORD *is our God, the* LORD *is **one***}
Jdg 13: 5 nazirite {That is ***one** separated* or ***one** consecrated*}
13: 7 nazirite {That is ***one** separated* or ***one** consecrated*}
15:19 En-hakkore, {That is *The Spring of the **One** who Called*}
16:17 nazirite {That is ***one** separated* or ***one** consecrated*}
Ru 3: 9 next-of-kin." {Or ***one** with the right to redeem*}
3:13 next-of-kin {Or ***one** with the right to redeem*}
3:13 next-of-kin {Or ***one** with the right to redeem*}
3:13 next-of-kin {Or ***one** with the right to redeem*}
4: 1 next-of-kin, {Or ***one** with the right to redeem*}
4: 3 next-of-kin, {Or ***one** with the right to redeem*}
4: 6 next-of-kin {Or ***one** with the right to redeem*}
4: 8 next-of-kin {Or ***one** with the right to redeem*}
4:14 next-of-kin; {Or ***one** with the right to redeem*}
1Sa 1:11 nazirite {That is ***one** separated* or ***one** consecrated*}
1:22 nazirite {That is ***one** separated* or ***one** consecrated*}
2: 8 honor. {Gk (Compare Q Ms) adds *He grants the vow of the **one** who vows, and blesses the years of the just*}
2Sa 7:23 Is there another {Gk: Heb ***one***} nation
Job 41: 9 were not even the gods {Cn Compare Symmachus Syr: Heb ***one** is*} overwhelmed
Ps 22:20 my life {Heb *my only **one***}
49: 7 no ransom avails for one's life, {Another reading is *no **one** can ransom a brother*}
80:15 planted. {Heb adds from verse 17 *and upon the **one** whom you made strong for yourself*}
82: 7 and fall like any prince." {Or *fall as **one** man, O princes*}
Pr 21:26 All day long the wicked covet, {Gk: Heb *all day long **one** covets covetously*}
25:20 vinegar on a wound {Gk: Heb *Like **one** who takes off a garment on a cold day, like vinegar on lye*}
30: 3 knowledge of the holy ones. {Or *Holy **One***}
Isa 10:34 Lebanon with its majestic trees {Cn Compare Gk Vg: Heb *with a majestic **one***}
Jer 51:60 Jeremiah wrote in a {Or ***one***} scroll
Eze 26:17 How you have vanished {Gk OL Aquila: Heb *have vanished, O inhabited **one,***}
40: 6 one reed deep. {Heb *deep, and **one** threshold, **one** reed deep*}
40:44 court, one {Heb lacks ***one***} at the side
Da 8: 5 The goat had a horn {Theodotion: Gk ***one** horn*; Heb *a horn of vision*}
8: 9 another {Cn Compare 7.8: Heb ***one***}
9:24 to anoint a most holy place. {Or *thing* or ***one***}
Mt 6:27 add a single hour to your span of life? {Or *add **one** cubit to your height*}
27: 9 the price of the one on whom a price had been set, {Or *the price of the precious **One***}
Mk 2:22 but one puts new wine into fresh wineskins." {Other ancient authorities lack *but **one** puts new wine into fresh wineskins*}
Lk 6:35 expecting nothing in return. {Other ancient authorities read *despairing of no **one***}
11: 4 trial." {< Other ancient authorities add *but rescue us from the evil **one*** (or *from evil*)}
15:21 son.' {Other ancient authorities add *treat me as **one** of your hired servants*}
17:35 + v.36 *"Two will be in the field; **one** will be taken and the other left."*
Jn 1:34 this is the Son of God." {Other ancient authorities read *is God's chosen **one***}
5:19 what he sees the Father {Gk *that **one***} doing;
17:21 may they also be in us, {Other ancient authorities read *be **one** in us*}
19:35 and he knows {Or *there is **one** who knows*} that he tells
Ro 8:27 And God, {Gk *the **one***} who searches
16:25 Now to God {Gk *the **one***} who is able
2Co 13:11 listen to my appeal, {Or *encourage **one** another*}
1Ti 3: 2 married only once, {Gk *the husband of **one** wife*}
3:12 married only once, {Gk *be husbands of **one** wife*}
5: 9 married only once; {Gk *the wife of **one** husband*}
Tit 1: 6 married only once, {Gk *husband of **one** wife*}
Heb 3: 3 Yet Jesus {Gk *this **one***} is worthy
10:12 But when Christ {Gk *this **one***} had offered

1Jn 5: 7 There are three that testify: {Other ancient authorities read (with variations) [7]*There are three that testify ... these three are* ***one.*** >}
Rev 14:20 about two hundred miles. {Gk ***one*** *thousand six hundred stadia*}
AdE 9:29 + v.30 *Letters were sent to all the Jews, to the* ***one*** *hundred twenty-seven provinces of the kingdom* >
Sir 10: 8 wealth. {Other ancient authorities add here or after verse 9a, *Nothing is more wicked than* ***one*** *who loves money,* >}
18: 9 years. {Other ancient authorities add *but the death of each* ***one*** *is beyond the calculation of all*}
18:29 proverbs. {Other ancient authorities add *Better is confidence in the* ***one*** *Lord than clinging with a dead heart to a dead* ***one.***}
19: 5 condemned, {Other ancient authorities add *but* ***one*** *who withstands pleasures crowns his life.* [6]***One*** *who controls the tongue will live without strife,*}
19:20 + v.21 < *even if later he does it, he angers the* ***one*** *who supports him.*
20:14 he looks for recompense sevenfold. {Syr: Gk *he has many eyes instead of* ***one***}
22:23 inheritance. {Other ancient authorities add *For* ***one*** *should not always despise restricted circumstances,* >}
25: 8 and the one who does not plow with ox and ass together. {Heb Syr: Gk lacks *and the* ***one*** *who does not plow with ox and ass together*}
Sir 49:14 Few have {Heb Syr: Gk *No* ***one*** *has*} ever been created
Pm 151: T outside the number), {Other ancient authorities add *of the* ***one*** *hundred fifty* (psalms)}
3Mc 1: 3 vengeance meant for the king. {Gk *that* ***one***}
7:16 the eternal Savior {Other ancient authorities read *the holy Savior;* others, *the holy* ***one***} of Israel,
2Es 5:45 If one ... time {Lat lacks *If* ... ***one*** *time*}
7:19 better judge than the Lord, {Other ancient authorities read *God;* Ethiop Georg *the only* ***One***}
12:32 Messiah {Literally *anointed* ***one***}
15:48 devices. {Other ancient authorities add *you have followed after that* ***one*** *about to gratify her magnates and leaders* >}

ONE'S (3)

Pr 27: 9 soul is torn by trouble. {Gk: Heb *the sweetness of a friend is better than* ***one's*** *own counsel*}
Sir 17: 4 + v.5 < *reason, the interpreter of* ***one's*** *faculties.*
20:31 + v.32 *Unwearied endurance in seeking the Lord is better than a masterless charioteer of* ***one's*** *own life.*

ONES (5)

Ps 22:29 all who sleep in {Cn: Heb *all the fat* ***ones***}
Isa 56: 8 besides those already gathered. {Heb *besides his gathered* ***ones***}
Eze 23:23 officers and warriors, {Compare verses 6 and 12: Heb *officers and called* ***ones***}
Da 11:17 kingdom, and he shall bring peace {Gk: Heb *kingdom, and upright* ***ones*** *with him*}
Sir 16: 9 their sins; {Other ancient authorities add ... *by the multitude of his holy* ***ones*** *he was not appeased.*}

ONLY (9)

Ps 22:20 my life {Heb *my* ***only*** *one*} from the power
23: 6 Surely {Or ***Only***} goodness and mercy
32: 6 at a time of distress, {Cn: Heb *at a time of finding* ***only***}
Ro 16:27 to whom {< The verse then reads, *to the* ***only*** *wise God be the glory through Jesus Christ forever. Amen.*}
Col 2:23 are of no value in checking self-indulgence. {Or *are of no value, serving* ***only*** *to indulge the flesh*}
Heb 2: 7 them for a little while lower {Or *them* ***only*** *a little lower*}
Jude 1:12 without fear, feeding themselves. {Or *without fear. They are shepherds who care* ***only*** *for themselves*}
2Mc 9:12 not think that they are equal God." {Or *not think thoughts proper* ***only*** *to God*}
2Es 7:19 better judge than the Lord, {Other ancient authorities read *God;* Ethiop Georg *the* ***only*** *One*}

OPEN (2)

Nu 24: 3 whose eye is clear, {Or *closed* or ***open***}
24:15 whose eye is clear, {Or *closed* or ***open***}

OPENED (1)

2Es 10:49 happened. {Most Lat Mss and Arab 1 add *these were the things to be* ***opened*** *to you*}

OPENING (2)

Eze 40:13 from wall to wall. {Heb ***opening*** *facing* ***opening***}

OPENLY (3)

Mt 6: 4 reward you. {Other ancient authorities add ***openly***}
6: 6 reward you. {Other ancient authorities add ***openly***}
6:18 reward you. {Other ancient authorities add ***openly***}

OPENS (1)

Sir 1:18 flourish. {Other ancient authorities add ... *glory* ***opens*** *out for those who love him.* >}

OPPORTUNE (1)

Ro 12:11 serve the Lord. {Other ancient authorities read *serve the* ***opportune*** *time*}

OPPORTUNITY (2)

1Co 7:21 make use of your present condition now more than ever. {Or *avail yourself of the* ***opportunity***}
Col 4: 5 making the most of the time. {Or ***opportunity***}

OPPOSITE (3)

Ne 12:38 went to the left, {Cn: Heb ***opposite***}
AdE 4: 5 + v.6 *So Hachratheus went out to Mordecai in the street of the city* ***opposite*** *the city gate.*
1Mc 4:34 they fell in action. {Or *and some fell on the* ***opposite*** *side*}

OPPOSITION (1)

Ge 25:18 he settle down alongside of {Or *down in* ***opposition*** *to*}

OPPRESSED (2)

Jdg 12: 2 who oppressed us {Gk OL, Syr H: Heb lacks *who* ***oppressed*** *us*}
1Sa 12: 8 and the Egyptians oppressed them, {Gk: Heb lacks *and the Egyptians* ***oppressed*** *them*}

ORDAIN (1)

Ex 32:29 Today you have ordained yourselves {Gk Vg Compare Tg: Heb *Today* ***ordain*** *yourselves*}

ORDAINED (1)

1Pe 2:13 the authority of every human institution, {Or *every institution* ***ordained*** *for human beings*}

ORDER (2)

Mt 27:35 casting lots; {Other ancient authorities add *in* ***order*** *that what had been spoken through the prophet might be fulfilled,* >}
Sir 16:14 + v.15 < *in* ***order*** *that his works might be known under heaven.* >

ORNAMENT (1)

Eze 16: 7 arrived at full womanhood; {Cn: Heb ***ornament*** *of ornaments*}

ORNAMENTS (1)

Eze 16: 7 arrived at full womanhood; {Cn: Heb *ornament of* ***ornaments***}

OTHER (8)

2Ch 23: 6 all the other {Heb lacks ***other***} people
Mk 16:14 risen. {Other ancient authorities add, in whole or in part, ... *term of years of Satan's power has been fulfilled, but* ***other*** *terrible things draw near.* >}
Lk 17:35 + v.36 *"Two will be in the field; one will be taken and the* ***other*** *left."*
Ac 19:39 If there is anything further {Other ancient authorities read *about* ***other*** *matters*}
Heb 7:27 the other {Gk lacks ***other***} high priests
Jude 1: 7 pursued unnatural lust, {Gk *went after* ***other*** *flesh*}
Sir Pr: 1 and the others {Or ***other*** *books*} that followed
18: 2 alone is just. {Other ancient authorities add *and there is no* ***other*** *beside him;* >}

OTHERS (3)

Job 24:24 fade like the mallow; {Gk: Heb *like all* ***others***}
Eze 40:36 were of the same size as the others; {One Ms: Compare verses 29 and 33: MT lacks *were of the same size as the* ***others***}
2Co 2:17 like so many; {Other ancient authorities read *like the* ***others***}

OTHERWISE (1)

Ro 11: 6 grace. {Other ancient authorities add ... *on the basis of grace,* ***otherwise*** *work would no longer be work*}

OUGHT (1)

Sir 15:11 he does not do {Heb: Gk *you* ***ought*** *not do*}

OUTER (1)

Eze 42: 6 of the outer {Gk: Heb lacks ***outer***} court;

OVER (14)

Lev 18:21 your offspring to sacrifice them {Heb *to pass them* ***over***}
Jos 18:18 to the north of the slope of Beth-arabah {Gk: Heb *to the slope* ***over*** *against the Arabah*}
1Sa 10: 1 over ... anointed you ruler {Gk: Heb lacks ***over*** *his people Israel. You shall ... anointed you ruler*}
2Sa 8:18 was over {Syr Tg Vg 20.23; 1 Chr 18.17: Heb lacks *was* ***over***}
24:12 Three things I offer {Or *hold* ***over***}
Ps 49:14 straight to the grave they descend, {Cn: Heb *the upright shall have dominion* ***over*** *them in the morning*}
Isa 9:17 the Lord did not have pity on {Q Ms: MT *rejoice* ***over***}
34:11 over {Heb lacks ***over***} its nobles.
Mk 16:14 risen. {Other ancient authorities add, in whole or in part, ... *allow the truth and power of God to prevail* ***over*** *the unclean things of the spirits. ... And for those who have sinned I was handed* ***over*** *to death,* >}
Heb 2: 7 glory and honor, {Other ancient authorities add *and set them* ***over*** *the works of your hands*}
Sir 41:11 The human body ... be blotted out. {Heb: Gk *People grieve* ***over*** *the death of the body, but the bad name of sinners will be blotted out*}
1Mc 6:28 and those in authority. {Gk *those* ***over*** *the reins*}
14:47 to be protector of them all. {Or *to preside* ***over*** *them all*}
1Es 3:12 but above all things truth is victor." {Or *but truth is victor* ***over*** *all things*}

OVERSEER (3)

1Ti 3: 1 bishop {Or ***overseer***}
3: 2 a bishop {Or *an* ***overseer***}
Tit 1: 7 a bishop, {Or *an* ***overseer***}

OVERSEERS (2)

Php 1: 1 bishops {Or ***overseers***}
1: 1 bishops and deacons: {Or ***overseers*** *and helpers*}

OVERSIGHT (1)

1Pe 5: 2 exercising the oversight, {Other ancient authorities lack *exercising the* ***oversight***}

OVERWHELM (1)

2Es 7:*115* [45] or to harm {Syr Ethiop: Lat ***overwhelm***}

OWN (13)

Pr 27: 9 soul is torn by trouble. {Gk: Heb *the sweetness of a friend is better than one's* ***own*** *counsel*}
Jer 5:31 rule as the prophets direct; {Or *rule by their* ***own*** *authority*}
Da 1: 2 land of Shinar, {Gk Theodotion: Heb adds *to the house of his* ***own*** *gods*}
Ac 4:23 they went to their friends {Gk *their* ***own***}
20:28 with the blood of his own Son. {< Gk *with the blood of his* ***Own***}
1Th 2:15 both the Lord Jesus and the prophets, {Other ancient authorities read *their* ***own*** *prophets*}
AdE 11: 9 the evils that threatened them, {Gk *their* ***own*** *evils*}
Sir 10: 8 wealth. {Other ancient authorities add here or after verse 9a, ... *for such a person puts his* ***own*** *soul up for sale.*}
10:29 those who dishonor themselves? {Heb Lat: Gk *their* ***own*** *life*}
18:33 purse. {Other ancient authorities add *for you will be plotting against your* ***own*** *life*}
20:31 + v.32 *Unwearied endurance in seeking the Lord is better than a masterless charioteer of one's* ***own*** *life.*
2Es 1:16 you still complain. {Other ancient authorities read verse 16, ... *complain also concerning their* ***own*** *destruction.*}
6: 1 "At the beginning ... before {< Compare Syr *The beginning by the hand of humankind, but the end by my* ***own*** *hands.* >}

OWNERS (1)

Pr 3:27 from those whom it is due, {Heb *from its* ***owners***}

OX (1)

Sir 25: 8 and ... together. {Heb Syr: Gk lacks *and the one who does not plow with* ***ox*** *and ass together*}

P

PAIN (1)

Ps 69:26 they attack still more. {Gk Syr: Heb *recount the* ***pain*** *of*}

PAINS (2)

Ac 2:24 freed him from death, {Gk *the* ***pains*** *of death*}
Sir 30:13 make his yoke heavy, {Heb: Gk *take* ***pains*** *with him*}

PALACE (2)

Am 8: 3 The songs of the temple {Or ***palace***}
Wis 1:14 the dominion {Or ***palace***} of Hades

PALACES (2)

Joel 3: 5 treasures into your temples. {Or ***palaces***}
Mic 5: 5 and tread upon our soil, {Gk: Heb *in our* ***palaces***}

PALATE (1)

SS 7: 9 and your kisses {Heb ***palate***} like the best wine

PARABLE (1)
Heb 9: 9 a symbol {Gk ***parable***} of the present time,

PARABLES (1)
Sir 38:33 found among the rulers. {Cn: Gk *among **parables***}

PARAH (4)
Jer 13: 4 to the Euphrates, {Or *to **Parah***; Heb *perath*}
13: 5 by the Euphrates, {Or *by **Parah***; Heb *perath*}
13: 6 to the Euphrates, {Or *to **Parah***; Heb *perath*}
13: 7 to the Euphrates, {Or *to **Parah***; Heb *perath*}

PARAZ (2)
2Sa 5:20 burst forth against {Heb ***paraz***}
1Ch 14:11 "God has burst out {Heb ***paraz***}

PARBAR (2)
1Ch 26:18 colonnade {Heb ***parbar***: meaning uncertain}
26:18 colonnade. {Heb ***parbar***: meaning uncertain}

PARCHED (1)
2Sa 17:28 lentils, {Heb *and lentils and **parched** grain*}

PARENTS (1)
Sir 22: 6 + v.7 *Children who are brought up in a good life, conceal the lowly birth of their **parents.*** >

PARSIN (1)
Da 5:28 PERES, {The singular of ***Parsin***}

PART (4)
Nu 23:10 number the dust-cloud {Or *fourth **part***} of Israel?
1Pe 4:14 resting on you. {Other ancient authorities add *On their **part** he is blasphemed, but on your **part** he is glorified*}
1Mc 2:10 has not inherited her palaces {Other ancient authorities read *has not had a **part** in her kingdom*}

PARTNERS (1)
3Mc 3:21 participants in our regular religious rites. {Other ancient authorities read ***partners** of our regular priests*}

PASS (3)
Lev 18:21 sacrifice them {Heb *to **pass** them over*} to Molech,
Ps 148: 6 he fixed their bounds, which cannot be passed. {Or *he set a law that cannot **pass** away*}
Isa 35: 8 shall not travel on it, {Or ***pass** it by*}

PASSAGE (2)
Eze 42:10 of the passage {Heb lacks *of the **passage***}
1Es 6:23 scroll {Other authorities read ***passage***} was found

PASSED (1)
Zep 2: 2 before you are driven away like the drifting chaff, {Cn Compare Gk Syr: Heb *before a decree is born; like chaff a day has **passed** away*}

PASSES (1)
1Sa 14: 4 In the pass, {Heb *Between the **passes***}

PASSING (1)
Pr 31: 8 all the destitute. {Heb *all children of **passing** away*}

PAST (2)
1Sa 15:32 "Surely this is the bitterness of death." {Q Ms Gk: MT *Surely the bitterness of death is **past***}
Sir 16:18 visitation! {Other ancient authorities add *The whole world **past** and present is in his will.*}

PASTURE (2)
Hos 13: 6 When I fed {Cn: Heb *according to their **pasture***} them,
Na 2:11 the cave {Cn: Heb ***pasture***} of the young lions,

PATHS (1)
Sir 1:12 long life. {Other ancient authorities add *The fear of the Lord is a gift from the Lord; also for love he makes firm **paths.***}

PATIENCE (1)
2Es 7:29 all who draw human breath. {Arm *all who have continued in faith and in **patience***}

PAYS (1)
Sir 34: 2 who believes in {Syr: Gk ***pays** heed to*} dreams.

PEACE (4)
Lk 24:36 and said ... with you." {Other ancient authorities lack *and said to them, "**Peace** be with you."*}
AdE 9:29 + v.30 < *to the one hundred twenty-seven provinces of the kingdom of Ahasuerus, in words of **peace** and truth.*
Sir 1:18 flourish. {Other ancient authorities add *Both are gifts of God for **peace**; glory opens out* >}
38: 8 from him health {Or ***peace***} spreads

PEBBLES (1)
Sir 22:18 Fences {Other ancient authorities read ***Pebbles***} set on a high place

PELICAN (2)
Lev 11:18 the desert owl, {Or ***pelican***}
Dt 14:17 the desert owl, {Or ***pelican***}

PENTAPOLIS (1)
Wis 10: 6 descended on the Five Cities. {Or *on **Pentapolis***}

PEOPLE (42)
Nu 20:26 to his people, {Heb lacks *to his **people***}
26: 4 take a census of the people, {Heb lacks *take a census of the **people***: Compare verse 2}
Jos 8: 9 that night in the camp. {Heb *among the **people***}
Jdg 1:16 the Amalekites. {See 1 Sam 15.6: Heb ***people***}
7: 8 So he took jars ... from their hands, {Cn: Heb *So the **people** took provisions in their hands*}
1Sa 9:24 was kept ... eat with the guests." {Cn: Heb *it was kept for you, saying, I have invited the **people***}
10: 1 over his people Israel. You shall ... anointed you ruler {Gk: Heb lacks *over his **people** Israel. You shall ... anointed you ruler*}
10:18 and said to them, {Heb *to the **people** of Israel*}
2Sa 16:15 Absalom and all the Israelites {Gk: Heb *all the **people**, the men of Israel*}
22:44 from strife with the peoples; {Gk: Heb *from strife with my **people***}
Est 1:22 his own house. {Heb adds *and speak according to the language of his **people***}
Job 12:24 from the leaders {Heb adds *of the **people***}
Ps 18:43 from strife with the peoples; {Gk Tg: Heb ***people***}
74:14 as food {Heb *food for the **people***} for the creatures
144: 2 who subdues the peoples {Heb Mss Syr Aquila Jerome: MT *my **people***}
Isa 44: 7 from of old things to come? {Cn: Heb *from my placing an eternal **people** and things to come*}
63:11 of Moses his servant. {Cn: Heb *his **people***}
Eze 11:15 your fellow exiles, {Gk Syr: Heb ***people** of your kindred*}
34:31 the sheep of my pasture {Gk OL: Heb *pasture, you are **people***}
Hos 1: 9 Lo-ammi, {That is *Not my **people***}
2: 1 Ammi, {That is *My **People***}
2:23 Lo-ammi, {That is *Not my **people***}
Lk 2:14 peace among those whom he favors!" {Other ancient authorities read *peace, goodwill among **people***}
Col 3: 7 living that life. {Or *living among such **people***}
1Ti 6: 5 means of gain. {Other ancient authorities add *Withdraw yourself from such **people***}
Heb 11:23 king's edict. {Other ancient authorities add ... *because he observed the humiliation of his **people*** (Gk *brothers*)}
Rev 21: 3 they will be his peoples, {Other ancient authorities read ***people***}
Jdt 6: 6 the spear {Lat Syr: Gk ***people***} of my servants
Sir 36:19 your temple {Heb Syr: Gk Lat ***people***}
38:32 they will not go hungry. {Syr: Gk *and **people** can neither live nor walk there*}
41:11 The human body ... be blotted out. {Heb: Gk ***People** grieve over the death of the body, but the bad name of sinners will be blotted out*}
46:18 the leaders of the enemy {Heb: Gk *leaders of the **people** of Tyre*}
49:12 and raised a temple {Other ancient authorities read ***people***}
49:15 born like Joseph; {Heb Syr: Gk adds *the leader of his brothers, the support of the **people***}
49:16 Shem and Seth and Enosh were honored, {Heb: Gk *Shem and Seth were honored by **people***}
1Mc 2:66 battle against the peoples. {Or *of the **people***}
14:28 Asaramel, {This word resembles the Hebrew words for *the court of the **people** of God* or *the prince of the **people** of God*}
2Mc 4:48 spoken for the city and the villages {Other ancient authorities read *the **people***}
2Es 1:16 you still complain. {Other ancient authorities read verse 16, ... *but still the **people** complain also concerning their own destruction.*}
3: 4 and commanded the dust {Syr Ethiop: Lat ***people** or world*}
16:71 They shall {Other ancient authorities read ***For people**, because of their misfortunes, shall*} be like maniacs,

PEOPLE'S (1)
Sir 47:23 broad in {Heb (with a play on the name Rehoboam) Syr: Gk *the **people's***} folly

PEOPLES (1)
Sir 44:15 The assembly declares {Heb: Gk ***Peoples** declare*} their wisdom,

PERATH (4)
Jer 13: 4 to the Euphrates, {Or *to Parah*; Heb ***perath***}
13: 5 by the Euphrates, {Or *by Parah*; Heb ***perath***}
13: 6 to the Euphrates, {Or *to Parah*; Heb ***perath***}
13: 7 to the Euphrates, {Or *to Parah*; Heb ***perath***}

PERFECT (2)
Ezr 7:12 Peace. {Syr Vg 1 Esdras 8.9: Aram ***Perfect***}
Php 3:12 have already reached the goal; {Or *have already been made **perfect***}

PERFORMED (1)
Sir 48:12 He performed ... mouth. {Heb: Gk lacks *He **performed** ... mouth*}

PERMISSION (1)
Lk 22:31 Satan has demanded {Or *has obtained **permission***} to sift

PERMIT (1)
Wis 19: 2 had permitted {Other ancient authorities read *had changed their minds to **permit***}

PERSECUTE (1)
4Mc 11: 6 + v.8 < *but, as it is, you are a stranger to God and **persecute** those who serve him."*

PERSECUTED (1)
Rev 12:13 he pursued {Or ***persecuted***} the woman

PERSIA (1)
Eze 27:10 Paras {Or ***Persia***}

PERSISTED (1)
Sir 16:10 stubbornness. {Other ancient authorities add *Chastising, showing mercy, striking, healing, the Lord **persisted** in mercy and discipline.*}

PERSON (10)
Ps 147:10 in the speed of a runner; {Heb *legs of a **person***}
Pr 17: 7 is false speech to a ruler. {Or *a noble **person***}
28: 3 A ruler {Cn: Heb *A poor **person***} who oppresses
Isa 49:24 the captives of a tyrant {Q Ms Syr Vg: MT *of a righteous **person***}
53: 9 his tomb with the rich, {Cn: Heb *with a rich **person***}
Jn 5: 3 + v.4 < *after the stirring of the water was made well from whatever disease that **person** had.*
Sir 10: 8 wealth. {Other ancient authorities add here or after verse 9a, <*for such a **person** puts his own soul up for sale.*}
22:23 inheritance. {Other ancient authorities add < *or admire a rich **person** who is stupid.*}
30:20 girl. {Other ancient authorities add *So is the **person** who does right under compulsion*}
2Es 15:40 every high and lofty place {Or *eminent **person***}

PERSONS (2)
1Co 12: 1 concerning spiritual gifts, {Or *spiritual **persons***}
Wis 18: 4 For their enemies {Gk *those **persons***} deserved

PERSUADE (1)
Ac 26:28 "Are you so quickly persuading me to become a Christian?" {Or *Quickly you will **persuade** me to play the Christian*}

PERSUASIVENESS (1)
1Co 2: 4 with plausible words of wisdom, {Other ancient authorities read *the **persuasiveness** of wisdom*}

PESTILENCES (1)
Mt 24: 7 there will be famines {Other ancient authorities add *and **pestilences***}

PETITION (2)
1Sa 2:20 for the gift that she made to {Q Ms Gk: MT *for the **petition** that she asked of*}
2Mc 4: 8 promising the king at an interview {Or *by a **petition***}

PETRA (2)
Mt 16:18 rock {Gk ***petra***}
Jn 1:42 is translated Peter). {From the word for *rock* in Aramaic (*kepha*) and Greek (*petra*), respectively}

PETROS (1)
Mt 16:18 Peter, {Gk ***Petros***}

PHALLUS (1)
Isa 57: 8 their nakedness. {Or *their **phallus***; Heb *the hand*}

PHARAOH (1)
Sir 16:14 + v.15 *The Lord hardened **Pharaoh** so that he did not recognize him,* >

PHARISEES (1)
Mt 23:13 + v.14 *Woe to you, scribes and **Pharisees**, hypocrites! For you devour widows' houses* >

PHILIP (1)
Ac 8:36 + v.37 *And **Philip** said, "If you believe with all your heart, you may."* >

PHILISTINES (2)
1Sa 4: 1 In those ... Israel, {Gk: Heb lacks *In those days the **Philistines** mustered for war against Israel*}
1Sa 4: 1 against them; {Gk: Heb *against the **Philistines***}

PHYSICIANS (1)

Lk 8:43 and had spent all she had on physicians, {Other ancient authorities lack *and had spent all she had on **physicians***}

PIECE (1)

Pr 6:26 for a prostitute's fee is only a loaf of bread, {Cn Compare Gk Syr Vg Tg: Heb *for because of a harlot to a **piece** of bread*}

PIERCED (2)

Mt 27:49 save him." {Other ancient authorities add *And another took a spear and **pierced** his side, and out came water and blood*}

3Mc 2:22 since he was smitten {Other ancient authorities read ***pierced***}

PILASTERS (1)

Eze 40:37 Its vestibule {Gk Vg Compare verses 26, 31, 34: Heb ***pilasters***}

40:38 in the vestibule of the gate, {Cn: Heb *at the **pilasters** of the gates*}

PILLAR (1)

Ge 31:49 the pillar {Compare Sam: MT lacks *the **pillar***}

PILLARS (1)

2Ki 10:26 the pillar {Gk Vg Syr Tg: Heb ***pillars***}

PIM (1)

1Sa 13:21 was two-thirds of a shekel {Heb *was a **pim***}

PIT (3)

Ps 35: 7 they hid their net {Heb *a **pit**, their net*}

49: 9 never see the grave. {Heb *the **pit***}

2Es 5:24 chosen for yourself one region, {Ethiop: Lat ***pit***}

PITIED (5)

Jer 22:23 you will groan {Gk Vg Syr: Heb *will be **pitied***}

Hos 1: 6 Lo-ruhamah, {That is *Not **pitied***}

2: 1 Ruhamah. {That is ***Pitied***}

2:23 Lo-ruhamah, {That is *Not **pitied***}

4Mc 16:10 alone, with many sorrows. {Or *much to be **pitied***}

PITS (1)

2Pe 2: 4 to chains {Other ancient authorities read ***pits***}

PLACE (18)

Dt 33:27 He subdues the ancient gods, {Or *The eternal God is a dwelling **place***}

Jdg 20:43 they pursued them from Nohah {Gk: Heb *pursued them at their resting **place***}

1Sa 29:10 and go to the place ... well before me. {Gk: Heb lacks *and go to the **place** ... done well before me*}

Job 40:13 faces in the world below. {Heb *the hidden **place***}

Isa 35: 7 the haunt of jackals shall become a swamp, {Cn: Heb *in the haunt of jackals is her resting **place***}

Eze 20:29 Bamah {That is *High **Place***}

Na 1: 8 end of his adversaries, {Gk: Heb *of her **place***}

Ac 27:41 But striking a reef, {Gk ***place** of two seas*}

Ro 3:25 as a sacrifice of atonement {Or *a **place** of atonement*}

Heb 9: 5 the mercy seat. {Or *the **place** of atonement*}

Sir 17:15 + v.16 < *they are unable to make for themselves hearts of flesh in **place** of their stony hearts.* >

47:12 lived in security: {Heb: Gk *in a broad **place***}

Bel 1:23 in that place {Other ancient authorities lack *in that **place***}

1Mc 11:34 Samaria. To all those ... granted release from {Or *Samaria, for all those who offer sacrifice in Jerusalem, in **place** of*}

2Es 7:36 The pit {Syr Ethiop: Lat ***place***} of torment

8: 6 mortal who bears the likeness {Syr: Lat ***place***}

14:48 did so. {Other ancient authorities add < *At that time Ezra was caught up, and taken to the **place** of those who are like him,* >}

4Mc 4:20 constructed at the very citadel {Or *high **place***}

PLACES (7)

Ge 26:22 Rehoboth, {That is *Broad **places*** or *Room*}

Isa 17: 9 places of the Hivites and the Amorites, {Cn Compare Gk: Heb ***places** of the wood and the highest bough*}

Jer 7:31 building the high place {Gk Tg: Heb *high **places***}

17: 3 spoil as the price of your sin {Cn: Heb *spoil your high **places** for sin*}

Eze 43: 7 kings at their death. {Or *on their high **places***}

Mic 1: 5 what is the high place {Heb *what are the high **places***}

2Es 7:*124* [54] lived in perverse ways? {Cn: Lat Syr ***places***}

PLACING (1)

Isa 44: 7 from of old the things to come? {Cn: Heb *from my **placing** an eternal people and things to come*}

PLAGUE (3)

Rev 13: 3 its mortal wound {Gk *the **plague** of its death*}

13:12 whose mortal wound {Gk *whose **plague** of its death*}

13:14 that has been wounded by the sword {Or *that had received the **plague** of the sword*}

PLAIN (1)

Jdg 20:33 rushed out of their place west {Gk Vg: Heb *in the **plain***}

PLAN (2)

Pr 16:30 One who winks the eyes plans {Gk Syr Vg Tg: Heb *to **plan***}

1Ti 1: 4 rather than the divine training {Or ***plan***}

PLANT (1)

Jnh 4: 6 the bush, {Heb *qiqayon*, possibly *the castor bean **plant***}

PLANTING (1)

Isa 51:16 stretching out {Syr: Heb ***planting***} the heavens

PLATE (1)

Mt 23:26 inside of the cup, {Other ancient authorities add *and of the **plate***}

PLAY (1)

Ac 26:28 "Are you so quickly persuading me to become a Christian?" {Or *Quickly you will persuade me to **play** the Christian*}

PLAYS (1)

Isa 57: 3 an adulterer and a whore. {Heb *an adulterer and she **plays** the whore*}

PLEASANT (1)

Ru 1:20 Naomi, {That is ***Pleasant***}

PLEASED (2)

AdE 9: 4 + v.5 < *killing and destroying them, and they did as they **pleased** to those who hated them.*

2Es 15:48 deeds and devices. {Other ancient authorities add *... so that you may be made proud and be **pleased** by her fornications*}

PLEASES (1)

Sir 7:26 who pleases you? {Heb Syr lack *who **pleases** you*}

PLEASING (1)

Sir 19:17 + v.19 < *and those who do what is **pleasing** to him enjoy the fruit of the tree of immortality.*

PLEASURE (1)

2Co 1:15 you might have a double favor; {Other ancient authorities read ***pleasure***}

PLEASURES (1)

Sir 19: 5 condemned, {Other ancient authorities add *but one who withstands **pleasures** crowns his life.* >}

PLEDGE (2)

Joel 2: 7 they do not swerve from {Gk Syr Vg: Heb *they do not take a **pledge** along*}

1Pe 3:21 as an appeal to God for {Or *a **pledge** to God from*}

PLOTTING (1)

Sir 18:33 your purse. {Other ancient authorities add *for you will be **plotting** against your own life*}

PLOW (2)

Sir 7:12 Do not devise {Heb: Gk ***plow***} a lie

25: 8 and ... together. {Heb Syr: Gk lacks *and the one who does not **plow** with ox and ass together*}

PLOWSHARE (1)

1Sa 13:20 aves, or sickles; {Gk: Heb ***plowshare***}

PLUCKED (1)

Jer 18:14 Do the mountain waters run dry, {Cn: Heb *Are ... **plucked** up?*}

PLUMB (1)

Sir 16:14 + v.16 < *and he divided his light and darkness with a **plumb** line.*

POISON (1)

Hab 2:15 pouring out your wrath {Or ***poison***}

POLITARCHS (1)

Ac 17: 6 the city authorities, {Gk ***politarchs***}

POOL (1)

Jn 5: 3 + v.4 < *for an angel of the Lord went down at certain seasons into the **pool**,* >

POOR (4)

Pr 28: 3 A ruler {Cn: Heb *A **poor** person*}

Jer 9: 7 do with my sinful people? {Or *my **poor** people*}

Eze 18:17 his hand from iniquity, {Gk: Heb *the **poor***}

Sir 13:21 the humble {Other ancient authorities read ***poor***}

POPLARS (1)

Ps 137: 2 On the willows {Or ***poplars***} there

PORTION (7)

Ne 3: 9 ruler of half the district of {Or *supervisor of half the **portion** assigned to*} Jerusalem,

3:12 ruler of half the district of {Or *supervisor of half the **portion** assigned to*} Jerusalem,

3:14 ruler of the district of {Or *supervisor of the **portion** assigned to*} Bethhaccherem,

3:15 ruler of the district of {Or *supervisor of the **portion** assigned to*} Mizpah,

3:16 ruler of half the district of {Or *supervisor of half the **portion** assigned to*} Bethzur,

3:17 ruler of half the district of {Or *supervisor of half the **portion** assigned to*} Keilah,

3:18 ruler of half the district of {Or *supervisor of half the **portion** assigned to*} Keilah;

POSSESS (1)

Zec 13: 5 for the land has been my possession {Cn: Heb *for humankind has caused me to **possess***}

POSSESSION (2)

1Pe 2: 9 God's own people, {Gk *a people for his **possession***}

Sir 24: 6 I have held sway. {Other ancient authorities read *I have acquired a **possession***}

POTSHERDS (1)

Isa 45: 9 earthen vessels with the potter! {Cn: Heb *with the **potsherds**,* or *with the potters*}

POTTER (2)

Zec 11:13 "Throw it into the treasury"— {Syr: Heb *it to the **potter***} ... and threw them into the treasury {Syr: Heb *it to the **potter***}

POTTERS (1)

Isa 45: 9 vessels with the potter! {Cn: Heb *with the potsherds*, or *with the **potters***}

POUND (1)

Lk 19:13 ten pounds, {The mina, rendered here by ***pound***, was about three months' wages for a laborer}

POURED (1)

2Sa 13: 9 and set them {Heb *and **poured***} out

POVERTY (1)

Sir 2: 5 humiliation. {Other ancient authorities add *in sickness and **poverty** put your trust in him*}

POWER (8)

Da 8:24 but not with his power, {Theodotion and one Gk Ms: Heb repeats (from 8.22) *but not with his **power***}

Mt 6:13 the evil one. {< Other ancient authorities add, in some form, *For the kingdom and the **power** and the glory are yours forever. Amen.*}

Mk 16:14 risen. {Other ancient authorities add, in whole or in part, *... who does not allow the truth and **power** of God to prevail over the unclean things of the spirits. ... "The term of years of Satan's **power** has been fulfilled, but other terrible things draw near.* >}

Lk 12: 5 has authority {Or ***power***} to cast into hell.

1Pe 4:14 the spirit of glory, {Other ancient authorities add *and of **power***}

Sir 18: 2 + v.3 < *for he is king of all things by his **power**, separating among them the holy things from the profane.*

Bel 1:36 with the speed of the wind {Or *by the **power** of his spirit*}

PRAETORIUM (8)

Mt 27:27 the governor's headquarters, {Gk *the **praetorium***}

Mk 15:16 governor's headquarters); {Gk *the **praetorium***}

Jn 18:28 to Pilate's headquarters. {Gk *the **praetorium***}

18:28 the headquarters, {Gk *the **praetorium***}

18:33 the headquarters {Gk *the **praetorium***}

19: 9 his headquarters {Gk *the **praetorium***}

Ac 23:35 Herod's headquarters. {Gk ***praetorium***}

Php 1:13 the whole imperial guard {Gk *whole **praetorium***}

PRAISE (4)

Mt 11:25 "I thank {Or ***praise***} you, Father,

Lk 10:21 "I thank {Or ***praise***} you, Father,

Jdt 16: 1 Raise to him a new psalm; {Other ancient authorities read *a psalm and **praise***}

Wis 18: 9 dangers; and already they were ancestors. {Other ancient authorities read *dangers, the ancestors already leading the songs of **praise***}

PRAISED (1)

Lk 7:29 acknowledge the justice of God, {Or ***praised** God*}

PRAISES (1)

Sir 47: 9 their voices. {Other ancient authorities add *and daily they sing his **praises***}

PRAY (1)

Mk 13:33 keep alert; {Other ancient authorities add *and **pray***}

PRAYER (3)
Ps 35:13 I prayed with head bowed {Or *My **prayer** turned back*}
Mt 17:20 + v.21 *But this kind does not come out except by **prayer** and fasting*
Sir 38:34 their concern is for {Syr: Gk ***prayer** is in*}

PRAYERS (1)
Mt 23:13 + v.14 < *For you devour widows' houses and for the sake of appearance you make long **prayers;*** >

PREACHER (7)
Ecc 1: 1 Teacher, {Heb *Qoheleth*, traditionally rendered ***Preacher***}
1: 2 Teacher, {Heb *Qoheleth*, traditionally rendered ***Preacher***}
1:12 Teacher, {Heb *Qoheleth*, traditionally rendered ***Preacher***}
7:27 Teacher, {*Qoheleth*, traditionally rendered ***Preacher***}
12: 8 Teacher; {*Qoheleth*, traditionally rendered ***Preacher***}
12: 9 Teacher {*Qoheleth*, traditionally rendered ***Preacher***}
12:10 Teacher {*Qoheleth*, traditionally rendered ***Preacher***}

PRECINCTS (1)
3Mc 1:13 entered every other temple, {Or *entered the temple **precincts***}

PRECIOUS (1)
Mt 27: 9 a price had been set, {Or *the price of the **precious** One*}

PREPARE (1)
Dt 19: 3 shall calculate the distances {Or ***prepare** roads to them*}

PREPARED (1)
2Es 5:28 and dishonored {Syr Ethiop Arab: Lat ***prepared***} the one root

PRESBYTER (1)
1Ti 5: 1 speak harshly to an older man, {Or *an elder*, or *a **presbyter***}

PRESBYTERY (1)
1Ti 4:14 by the council of elders. {Gk *by the **presbytery***}

PRESENT (3)
Lk 5:17 was with him to heal. {Other ancient authorities read *was **present** to heal them*}
1Co 7:26 in view of the impending {Or ***present***} crisis,
Sir 16:18 visitation! {Other ancient authorities add *The whole world past and **present** is in his will.*}

PRESENTATION (1)
Heb 9: 2 the bread of the Presence; {Gk *the **presentation** of the loaves*}

PRESENTED (1)
1Sa 1: 9 and presented herself before the LORD. {Gk: Heb lacks *and **presented** herself before the LORD*}

PRESIDE (1)
1Mc 14:47 to be protector of them all. {Or *to **preside** over them all*}

PREVAIL (1)
Mk 16:14 risen. {Other ancient authorities add, in whole or in part, ... *who does not allow the truth and power of God to **prevail** over the unclean things of the spirits.* >}

PREVENTED (1)
1Mc 7:24 and preventing those in the city {Gk *and they were **prevented***}

PREY (3)
Ps 76: 4 more majestic than the everlasting mountains. {Gk: Heb *the mountains of **prey***}
Isa 8: 1 Maher-shalal-hash-baz," {That is *The spoil speeds, the **prey** hastens*}
Jer 12: 9 Is the hyena greedy {Cn: Heb *Is the hyena, the bird of **prey***}

PRICE (1)
Job 28:13 the way to it, {Gk: Heb *its **price***}

PRIDE (5)
Job 41:15 Its back {Cn Compare Gk Vg: Heb ***pride***} is made of shields
Ps 90:10 their span {Cn Compare Gk Syr Jerome Tg: Heb ***pride***} is only toil
Pr 14: 3 is a rod for their backs, {Cn: Heb *a rod of **pride***}
Sir 10:20 + v.21 < *obduracy and **pride** are the beginning of rejection.*
11:14 + v.16 < *evil grows old with those who take **pride** in malice.*

PRIESTLY (1)
1Es 4:54 vestments which {Gk *in what **priestly** vestments*}

PRIESTS (4)
Zep 1: 4 the idolatrous priests; {Compare Gk: Heb *the idolatrous **priests** with the **priests***}
3Mc 1:23 restrained by the old men and the elders, {Other ancient authorities read ***priests***}
3:21 participants in our regular religious rites. {Other ancient authorities read *partners of our regular **priests***}

PRINCE (1)
1Mc 14:28 Asaramel, {This word resembles the Hebrew words for *the court of the people of God* or *the **prince** of the people of God*}

PRINCES (1)
Ps 82: 7 and fall like any prince." {Or *fall as one man, O **princes***}

PROCLAIMING (1)
1Th 3: 2 in proclaiming {Gk lacks ***proclaiming***} the gospel

PROFANE (1)
Sir 18: 2 + v.3 < *separating among them the holy things from the **profane.***

PROFANEST (1)
Ps 35:16 they impiously mocked me more and more, {Cn Compare Gk: Heb *like the **profanest** of mockers of a cake*}

PROGENITORS (1)
Ge 49:26 of the eternal mountains, the bounties {Cn Compare Gk: Heb *of my **progenitors** to the boundaries*}

PROMPTLY (1)
2Ti 1:17 he eagerly {Or ***promptly***} searched for me

PROPER (2)
Sir 17: 3 strength like his own, {Lat: Gk ***proper** to them*}
2Mc 9:12 not think that they are equal to God." {Or *not think thoughts **proper** only to God*}

PROPHECIES (1)
1Th 5:20 despise the words of prophets, {Gk *despise **prophecies***}

PROPHET (4)
1Ki 13:29 brought it back to the city, {Gk: Heb *he came to the town of the old **prophet***}
2Ch 15: 8 the prophecy of Azariah son of Oded, {Compare Syr Vg: Heb *the prophecy, the **prophet** Obed*}
Ezr 5: 1 Haggai {Aram adds *the **prophet***}
Mt 27:35 casting lots; {Other ancient authorities add *in order that what had been spoken through the **prophet** might be fulfilled,* >}

PROPHETS (6)
Dt 18:15 raise up for you a prophet {Or ***prophets***} ... heed such a prophet. {Or *such **prophets***}
18:18 raise up for them a prophet {Or ***prophets***} ... in the mouth of the prophet, {Or *mouths of the **prophets***}
Eze 22:25 indignation. [25]Its princes {Gk: Heb *indignation.* [25]*A conspiracy of its **prophets***}
Mk 1: 2 written in the prophet Isaiah, {Other ancient authorities read *in the **prophets***}

PROSPERITY (1)
Ps 147:14 He grants peace {Or ***prosperity***} within your borders;

PROSPEROUS (1)
Sir 40:19 but better ... prosperous; {Heb Syr: Gk lacks *but better ... **prosperous***}

PROSTITUTED (1)
Jdg 19: 2 became angry with {Gk OL: Heb ***prostituted** herself against*}

PROSTITUTES (1)
Job 36:14 ends in shame. {Heb *ends among the temple **prostitutes***}

PROTECTED (1)
Jn 17:11 protect them in your name that {Other ancient authorities read ***protected** in your name those whom*}

PROTECTION (1)
3Mc 4:11 claim to be inside the circuit of the city. {Or *claim **protection** of the walls*; meaning of Gk uncertain}

PROUD (3)
Ps 19:13 also from the insolent; {Or *from **proud** thoughts*}
Sir 10:15 plucks up the roots of the nations, {Other ancient authorities read ***proud** nations*}
2Es 15:48 device. {Other ancient authorities add *so that you may be made **proud** and be pleased by her fornications*}

PROVED (1)
Ps 46: 1 a very present {Or *well **proved***} help in trouble.

PROVIDES (1)
Ps 127: 2 for he gives sleep to his beloved. {Or *for he **provides** for his beloved during sleep*}

PROVINCES (1)
AdE 9:29 + v.30 < *to the one hundred twenty-seven **provinces** of the kingdom of Ahasuerus,* >

PROVISIONS (1)
Jdg 7: 8 So he took the jars ... from their hands, {Cn: Heb *So the people took **provisions** in their hands*}

PROVOCATION (1)
Dt 32:19 he spurned {Cn: Heb *he spurned because of **provocation***} his sons and daughters.

PTOLEMIES (1)
2Mc 6: 8 suggestion of the people of Ptolemais {Cn: Gk *suggestion of the **Ptolemies*** (or *of Ptolemy*)}

PTOLEMY (1)
2Mc 6: 8 suggestion of the people of Ptolemais {Cn: Gk *suggestion of the Ptolemies* (or *of **Ptolemy***)}

PUL (1)
Isa 66:19 Put, {Gk: Heb ***Pul***}

PUNISH (3)
2Sa 13:21 but he would not punish ... firstborn. {Q Ms Gk: MT lacks *but he would not **punish** ... firstborn*}
Isa 66: 4 choose to mock {Or *to **punish***} them
Wis 5:17 to repel {Or ***punish***} them;

PUNISHED (1)
Sir 12: 8 A friend is not known {Other ancient authorities read ***punished***}

PUNISHMENT (2)
Jer 50:21 inhabitants of Pekod {Or *of **Punishment***}
Sir 12: 6 on the ungodly. {Other ancient authorities add *and he is keeping them for the day of their **punishment***}

PURE (2)
2Co 11: 3 and pure {Other ancient authorities lack *and **pure***}
1Pe 1:22 love one another deeply from the heart. {Other ancient authorities read *a **pure** heart*}

PURIFY (1)
Mk 7: 4 and they do not eat ... unless they wash it; {Other ancient authorities read *and when they come from the marketplace, they do not eat unless they **purify** themselves*}

PURPOSE (1)
2Es 10:34 die before my time. {Syr Ethiop Arab: Lat *die to no **purpose***}

PURSUED (1)
Ecc 3:15 what has gone by. {Heb *what is **pursued***}

PURSUER (1)
2Es 1:16 You have not exulted ... you still complain. {Other ancient authorities read verse 16, *Your **pursuer** with his army ... complain also concerning their own destruction.*}

PURSUING (1)
Jdg 8: 4 with him, exhausted and famished. {Gk: Heb ***pursuing***}

PUT (6)
2Sa 18: 9 he was left hanging {Gk Syr Tg: Heb *was **put***}
2Ki 11: 2 she put {With 2 Chr 22.11: Heb lacks *she **put***}
Job 32: 3 answer, though they had declared Job to be in the wrong. {Another ancient tradition reads *answer, and had **put** God in the wrong*}
2Co 5: 3 when we have taken it off {Other ancient authorities read ***put** it on*}
Sir 2: 5 humiliation. {Other ancient authorities add *in sickness and poverty **put** your trust in him*}
3Mc 1: 2 the best ... had been issued to him, {Or *the best of the Ptolemaic soldiers previously **put** under his command*}

PUTS (3)
Job 28: 3 Miners put {Heb *He **puts***} and end to darkness,
Mk 2:22 but one ... wineskins." {Other ancient authorities lack *but one **puts** new wine into fresh wineskins*}
Sir 10: 8 wealth. {Other ancient authorities add here or after verse 9a, ... *for such a person **puts** his own soul up for sale.*}

PUTTING (1)
2Pe 1:14 that my death {Gk *the* ***putting*** *off of my tent*}

Q

QAYITS (2)
Am 8: 1 a basket of summer fruit. {Heb ***qayits***}
8: 2 "A basket of summer fruit." {Heb ***qayits***}

QESITAH (3)
Ge 33:19 one hundred pieces of money {Heb *one hundred* ***qesitah***}
Jos 24:32 one hundred pieces of money; {Heb *one hundred* ***qesitah***}
42:11 a piece of money {Heb *a* ***qesitah***}

QETS (1)
Am 8: 2 The end {Heb ***qets***} has come

QIQAYON (1)
Jnh 4: 6 bush, {Heb ***qiqayon***, possibly *the castor bean plant*}

QOHELETH (7)
Ecc 1: 1 Teacher, {Heb ***Qoheleth***, traditionally rendered *Preacher*}
1: 2 Teacher, {Heb ***Qoheleth***, traditionally rendered *Preacher*}
1:12 Teacher, {Heb ***Qoheleth***, traditionally rendered *Preacher*}
7:27 Teacher, {***Qoheleth***, traditionally rendered *Preacher*}
12: 8 Teacher; {***Qoheleth***, traditionally rendered *Preacher*}
12: 9 Teacher {***Qoheleth***, traditionally rendered *Preacher*}
12:10 Teacher {***Qoheleth***, traditionally rendered *Preacher*}

QUARREL (2)
Ex 17: 7 Meribah, {That is ***Quarrel***}
Nu 20:13 Meribah, {That is ***Quarrel***}

QUESTION (1)
Jn 16:23 will ask nothing of me. {Or *will ask me no* ***question***}

QUIVERING (1)
4Mc 15:15 fingers scattered {Or ***quivering***} on the ground,

R

RABBOUNI (1)
Mk 10:51 teacher, {Aramaic ***Rabbouni***}

RACA (1)
Mt 5:22 if you insult {Gk *say* ***Raca*** *to* (an obscure term of abuse)}

RACE (1)
4Mc 12:17 be merciful to our nation; {Other ancient authorities read *my* ***race***}

RAGES (1)
Tob 6:10 Ecbatana, {Other ancient authorities read ***Rages***}

RAGUEL (1)
Tob 1: 1 son of Raphael {Other ancient authorities lack *son of Raphael son of* ***Raguel***}

RAISED (1)
2Sa 23: 1 whom God exalted, {Q Ms: MT *who was* ***raised*** *on high*}

RAMATHAIM-ZOPHIM (1)
1Sa 1: 1 of Ramathaim, a Zuphite {Compare Gk and 1 Chr 6.35-36: Heb ***Ramathaim-zophim***}

RAMP (1)
Ge 28:12 he dreamed that there was a ladder {Or *stairway* or ***ramp***}

RAMS (2)
Jer 49:19 and I will appoint over it whomever I choose. {Or *and I will single out the choicest of his* ***rams***: Meaning of Heb uncertain}
Jer 50:44 and I will appoint over it whomever I choose. {Or *and I will single out the choicest of her* ***rams***: Meaning of Heb uncertain}

RAPHAEL (1)
Tob 1: 1 son of Raphael {Other ancient authorities lack *son of* ***Raphael*** *son of Raguel*}

RATIONAL (1)
4Mc 1: 6 self-control; {Other ancient authorities add *and* ***rational*** *judgment*}

REACH (1)
Sir 31:18 do not help yourself {Gk ***reach*** *out your hand*}

READ (2)
Tob 12:12 and read {Lat: Gk lacks *and* ***read***}
1Es 9:48 Lord, {Other ancient authorities add *and* ***read*** *the law of the Lord to the multitude*}

READY (1)
2Es 7:*135* [65] he would rather give than take away; {Or *he is* ***ready*** *to give according to requests*}

REASON (1)
Sir 17: 4 + v.5 < ***reason***, *the interpreter of one's faculties.*

REASONABLE (1)
Ro 12: 1 which is your spiritual {Or ***reasonable***} worship.

REASONING (1)
4Mc 2: 2 by mental effort {Other ancient authorities add *in* ***reasoning***}

REBEL (1)
Ps 105:28 they rebelled {Cn Compare Gk Syr: Heb *they did not* ***rebel***} against his words.

REBELLION (1)
Jer 50:21 the land of Merathaim; {Or *of Double* ***Rebellion***}

REBELLIOUS (2)
Job 23: 2 complaint is bitter; {Syr Vg Tg: Heb ***rebellious***}
Mic 2: 4 Among our captors {Cn: Heb *the* ***rebellious***}

REBELS (1)
Jos 22:19 rebel against us {Or *make* ***rebels*** *of us*}

RECEIVE (2)
Mt 23:13 + v.14 < *therefore you will* ***receive*** *the greater condemnation*
2Es 8:59 that I have predicted await {Syr: Lat *will* ***receive***}

RECEIVED (6)
2Ch 30:16 that they received {Heb lacks *that they* ***received***}
35:11 that they received {Heb lacks *that they* ***received***}
Rev 13:14 that had been wounded by the sword {Or *that had* ***received*** *the plague of the sword*}
Sir 20:17 how often! {Other ancient authorities add *for he has not honestly* ***received*** *what he has*, >}
23:27 + v.28 *It is a great honor to follow God, and to be* ***received*** *by him is long life.*
2Es 8:29 have gloriously taught your law. {Syr *have* ***received*** *the brightness of your law*}

RECEIVING (2)
Mk 11:24 believe that you have received {Other ancient authorities read *are* ***receiving***}
2Pe 2:13 suffering {Other ancient authorities read ***receiving***} the penalty for doing wrong

RECENTLY (1)
2Es 1:32 says the Lord. {Other ancient authorities add *Thus says the Lord Almighty:* ***Recently*** *you also laid hands on me*, >}

RECKONED (1)
Gal 2:16 we might be justified {Or ***reckoned*** as righteous; and so elsewhere} by faith

RECLINED (2)
Mt 9:10 as he sat at dinner {Gk ***reclined***}
Mk 2:15 as he sat at dinner {Gk ***reclined***}

RECLINING (3)
Mt 9:10 and were sitting {Gk *were* ***reclining***}
Mk 2:15 sinners were also sitting {Gk ***reclining***}
Lk 5:29 others sitting at the table {Gk ***reclining***}

RECOGNIZE (1)
Sir 16:14 + v.15 *The Lord hardened Pharaoh so that he did not* ***recognize*** *him*, >

RECOMPENSE (1)
Isa 34: 8 of vindication by Zion's cause. {Or *of* ***recompense*** *by Zion's defender*}

RECOUNT (1)
Ps 69:26 attack still more. {Gk Syr: Heb ***recount*** *the pain of*}

RECOVERED (1)
Jer 41:16 whom Ishmael son of Nethaniah had carried away captive {Cn: Heb *whom he* ***recovered*** *from Ishmael son of Nethaniah*}

RED (1)
Ge 25:30 he was called Edom.) {That is ***Red***}

REDEEM (10)
Ru 2:20 nearest kin." {Or *one with the right to* ***redeem***}
3: 9 next-of-kin." {Or *one with the right to* ***redeem***}
3:13 next-of-kin {Or *one with the right to* ***redeem***}
3:13 next-of-kin {Or *one with the right to* ***redeem***}
3:13 next-of-kin {Or *one with the right to* ***redeem***}
4: 1 next-of-kin, {Or *one with the right to* ***redeem***}
4: 3 next-of-kin, {Or *one with the right to* ***redeem***}
4: 6 next-of-kin {Or *one with the right to* ***redeem***}
4: 8 next-of-kin {Or *one with the right to* ***redeem***}
4:14 next-of-kin; {Or *one with the right to* ***redeem***}

REDEEMED (1)
2Sa 7:23 before his people nations and their gods? {Cn: Heb *before your people, whom you* ***redeemed*** *for yourself from Egypt, nations and its gods*}

REDEMPTION (1)
Ex 8:23 I will make a distinction {Gk Vg: Heb *will set* ***redemption***}

REEDS (24)
Ex 10:19 the Red Sea; {Or *Sea of* ***Reeds***}
13:18 the Red Sea. {Or *Sea of* ***Reeds***}
15: 4 the Red Sea. {Or *Sea of* ***Reeds***}
15:22 the Red Sea, {Or *Sea of* ***Reeds***}
23:31 the Red Sea {Or *Sea of* ***Reeds***}
Nu 14:25 the Red Sea." {Or *Sea of* ***Reeds***}
21: 4 the Red Sea, {Or *Sea of* ***Reeds***}
33:10 the Red Sea. {Or *Sea of* ***Reeds***}
33:11 the Red Sea {Or *Sea of* ***Reeds***}
Dt 1:40 the Red Sea." {Or *Sea of* ***Reeds***}
2: 1 the Red Sea, {Or *Sea of* ***Reeds***}
11: 4 the Red Sea {Or *Sea of* ***Reeds***}
Jos 2:10 the Red Sea {Or *Sea of* ***Reeds***}
4:23 the Red Sea, {Or *Sea of* ***Reeds***}
24: 6 the Red Sea. {Or *Sea of* ***Reeds***}
Jdg 11:16 the Red Sea {Or *Sea of* ***Reeds***}
1Ki 9:26 the Red Sea, {Or *Sea of* ***Reeds***}
Ne 9: 9 the Red Sea. {Or *Sea of* ***Reeds***}
Ps 106: 7 the Red Sea. {Or *Sea of* ***Reeds***}
106: 9 the Red Sea, {Or *Sea of* ***Reeds***}
106:22 the Red Sea. {Or *Sea of* ***Reeds***}
136:13 the Red Sea {Or *Sea of* ***Reeds***}
136:15 the Red Sea, {Or *Sea of* ***Reeds***}
Jer 49:21 the Red Sea. {Or *Sea of* ***Reeds***}

REEFS (1)
Jude 1:12 are blemishes {Or ***reefs***} on your love-feasts,

REFUGE (3)
2Sa 22:33 girded me with strength {Q Ms Gk Syr Vg Compare Ps 18.32: MT *God is my strong* ***refuge***}
Ps 27: 1 The LORD is the stronghold {Or ***refuge***}
90: 1 our place {Another reading is *our* ***refuge***}

REGARDING (1)
1Co 11:10 have a symbol of authority on her head, {Or *have freedom of choice* ***regarding*** *her head*}

REGIMENTS (1)
Nu 2:31 set out last, by companies. {Compare verses 9, 16, 24: Heb *by their* ***regiments***}

REINS (1)
1Mc 6:28 those in authority. {Gk *those over the* ***reins***}

REJECTION (1)
Sir 10:20 + v.21 < *obduracy and pride are the beginning of* ***rejection.***

REJOICE (2)
Isa 9:17 did not have pity on {Q Ms: MT ***rejoice*** *over*}
2Co 13:11 Finally, brothers and sisters, farewell. {Or ***rejoice***}

REJOICED (2)
1Sa 6:13 rejoicing to meet it. {Gk: Heb ***rejoiced*** *to see it*}
Php 4:10 I rejoice {Gk *I* ***rejoiced***} in the Lord

RELEASE (2)
Lk 23:16 + v.17 *Now he was obliged to* ***release*** *someone for them at the festival*
2Es 8: 4 "Then drink your fill of understanding, {Syr: Lat *Then* ***release*** *understanding*}

REMAIN (4)
Ac 15:33 + v.34 *But it seemed good to Silas to* ***remain*** *there*
Sir 4:17 until she trusts them, {Or *until they* ***remain*** *faithful in their heart*}
2Mc 15:17 to carry on a campaign {Or *to* ***remain*** *in camp*}
2Es 16:30 some clusters may be left {Other ancient authorities read *a cluster may* ***remain*** *exposed*}

REMAINING (1)

Ac 20:15 at Samos, and {Other ancient authorities add *after **remaining** at Trogyllium*}

REMAINS (1)

2Es 14:12 For the age ... half of the tenth part. {Syr lacks verses 11, 12: Ethiop *For the world is divided into ten parts, and has come to the tenth, and half of the tenth **remains.** Now ...* }

REMNANT (2)

Isa 7: 3 Shear-jashub, {That is *A **remnant** shall return*}

Mal 2:15 Both flesh and spirit are his. {Cn: Heb *and a **remnant** of spirit was his*}

REMOTE (1)

Sir 23: 3 rejoice over me. {Other ancient authorities add *From them the hope of your mercy is **remote***}

REMOVED (3)

Ge 47:21 he made slaves of them {Sam Gk Compare Vg: MT *He **removed** them to the cities*}

Ex 14:25 He clogged {Sam Gk Syr: MT ***removed***} their chariot

Ecc 12: 6 before the silver cord is snapped, {Syr Vg Compare Gk: Heb *is **removed***}

RENDER (1)

Tob 3: 2 you judge the world. {Other ancient authorities read *you **render** true and righteous judgment forever*}

RENEWS (1)

Sir 38:28 deafens his ears, {Cn: Gk ***renews** his ear*}

RENOWNED (1)

Sir 3:18 + v.19 *Many are lofty and **renowned,** but to the humble he reveals his secrets.*

REPAY (1)

Job 41:11 and be safe? {Gk: Heb *that I shall **repay***}

REPENTANCE (2)

Sir 17:22 eye. {Other ancient authorities add *apportioning **repentance** to his sons and daughters*}

20: 8 hated. {Other ancient authorities add *How good it is to show **repentance** when you are reproved,* >}

REPLENISHED (1)

Isa 23: 2 crossed over the sea {Q Ms: MT *crossing over the sea, they **replenished** you*}

REPLIED (2)

Mk 16:14 risen. {Other ancient authorities add, in whole or in part, ... *And Christ **replied** to them, "The term of years of Satan's power has been fulfilled,* >}

Ac 8:36 + v.37 < *And he **replied,** "I believe that Jesus Christ is the Son of God."*

REPROACH (2)

Mk 15:34 why have you forsaken me?" {Other ancient authorities read *made me a **reproach***}

1Ti 4:10 we toil and struggle, {Other ancient authorities read *suffer **reproach***}

REPROOFS (1)

Sir 48:10 you are destined {Heb: Gk *are for **reproofs***}

REPROVED (1)

Sir 20: 8 hated. {Other ancient authorities add *How good it is to show repentance when you are **reproved,*** >}

REQUESTS (1)

2Es 7:*135* [65] he would rather give than take away; {Or *he is ready to give according to **requests***}

RESCUE (2)

Ps 56: 7 so repay {Cn: Heb ***rescue***} them for their crime;

Lk 11: 4 the time of trial." {< Other ancient authorities add *but **rescue** us from the evil one* (or *from evil*)}

RESCUED (1)

3Mc 6: 8 watched over and restored {Other ancient authorities read ***rescued** and restored*; others, *mercifully restored*}

RESHEPH (1)

Job 5: 7 just as sparks {Or *birds*; Heb *sons of **Resheph***} fly upward.

RESOURCES (1)

Rev 18: 3 grown rich from the power {Or ***resources***}

RESPECT (1)

1Pe 3:16 do it with gentleness and reverence. {Or ***respect***}

RESPONDED (1)

1Ki 20:34 The king of Israel responded, {Heb lacks *The king of Israel **responded***}

REST (7)

1Sa 13:15 The rest ... of Benjamin. {Gk: Heb lacks *The **rest** ... of Benjamin*}

Ps 23: 2 leads me beside still waters; {Heb *waters of **rest***}

1Co 15:24 Then comes the end, {Or *Then come the **rest***}

Sir 36:18 the place of your dwelling. {Heb: Gk *your **rest***}

36:29 and a pillar of support. {Heb: Gk ***rest***}

38:14 grant them success in diagnosis {Heb: Gk ***rest***}

Sus 1:50 rest of the {Gk lacks ***rest** of the*}

RESTING (2)

Jdg 20:43 pursued them from Nohah {Gk: Heb *pursued them at their **resting** place*}

Isa 35: 7 the haunt of jackals shall become a swamp, {Cn: Heb *in the haunt of jackals is her **resting** place*}

RESTORE (1)

Mk 9:50 how can you season it? {Or *how can you **restore** its saltiness?*}

RESTRAINT (1)

Isa 23:10 this is a harbor {Cn: Heb ***restraint***} no more.

RESTRICTED (1)

Sir 22:23 inheritance. {Other ancient authorities add *For one should not always despise **restricted** circumstances,* >}

RESTS (1)

2Es 13: 4 melted as wax melts {Syr: Lat *burned as the earth **rests***}

RETURN (17)

2Sa 17: 3 seek the life of only one man, {Gk: Heb *like the **return** of the whole (is) the man whom you seek*}

Ne 4:12 the places where they live {Cn: Heb *you **return***}

Ps 7: 7 take your seat {Cn: Heb ***return***} on high.

73:10 the people turn and praise them, {Cn: Heb *his people **return** here*}

Isa 7: 3 Shear-jashub, {That is *A remnant shall **return***}

Am 1: 3 revoke the punishment; {Heb *cause it to **return***}

1: 6 revoke the punishment; {Heb *cause it to **return***}

1: 9 revoke the punishment; {Heb *cause it to **return***}

1:11 revoke the punishment; {Heb *cause it to **return***}

1:13 revoke the punishment; {Heb *cause it to **return***}

2: 1 revoke the punishment; {Heb *cause it to **return***}

2: 4 revoke the punishment; {Heb *cause it to **return***}

2: 6 revoke the punishment; {Heb *cause it to **return***}

Mk 16:14 risen. {Other ancient authorities add, in whole or in part, ... *that they may **return** to the truth and sin no more,* >}

Tob 5:16 and {Other ancient authorities add *when you **return** safely*} I will add

Sir 8:19 or you may drive away your happiness. {Heb: Gk *and let him not **return** a favor to you*}

2Es 1:32 says the Lord. {Other ancient authorities add ... *let my Father and his angels **return** and judge between you and me;* >}

RETURNED (1)

Ps 126: 1 restored the fortunes of Zion, {Or *brought back those who **returned** to Zion*}

REVEAL (2)

1Sa 2:27 'I revealed {Gk Tg Syr: Heb *Did I **reveal***} myself to the family

Mk 16:14 risen. {Other ancient authorities add, in whole or in part, ... *Therefore **reveal** your righteousness now"—thus they spoke to Christ.* >}

REVEALS (1)

Sir 3:18 + v.19 *Many are lofty and renowned, but to the humble he **reveals** his secrets.*

REVELER (1)

Sir 21:15 When a fool {Syr: Gk ***reveler***} hears it,

REVOKING (1)

3Mc 6:27 begging pardon for your former actions! {Other ancient authorities read ***revoking** your former commands*}

REWARD (1)

Sir 2: 9 joy and mercy. {Other ancient authorities add *For his **reward** is an everlasting gift with joy.*}

REZIN (2)

2Ki 16: 6 the king of Edom {Cn: Heb *King **Rezin** of Aram*}

Isa 9:11 So the LORD raised adversaries {Cn: Heb *the adversaries of **Rezin***}

RIBEBOTH-KODESH (1)

Dt 33: 2 With him were myriads of holy ones; {Cn Compare Gk Sam Syr Vg: MT *He came from **Ribeboth-kodesh,***}

RIBS (1)

Da 7: 5 had three tusks {Or ***ribs***} in its mouth

RICH (1)

Sir 22:23 inheritance. {Other ancient authorities add ... *or admire a **rich** person who is stupid.*}

RICHES (2)

Pr 14:24 The crown of the wise is their wisdom, {Cn Compare Gk: Heb ***riches***}

Mk 10:24 hard it is {Other ancient authorities add *for those who trust in **riches***}

RICHNESS (1)

Ro 11:17 to share the rich root {Other ancient authorities read *the **richness***}

RIDDLE (1)

1Co 13:12 For now we see in a mirror, dimly, {Gk *in a **riddle***}

RIGHT (17)

Ge 35:18 Benjamin. {That is *Son of the **right** hand* or *Son of the South*}

Ru 2:20 nearest kin." {Or *one with the **right** to redeem*}

3: 9 next-of-kin." {Or *one with the **right** to redeem*}

3:13 next-of-kin {Or *one with the **right** to redeem*}

3:13 next-of-kin {Or *one with the **right** to redeem*}

3:13 next-of-kin {Or *one with the **right** to redeem*}

4: 1 next-of-kin, {Or *one with the **right** to redeem*}

4: 3 next-of-kin, {Or *one with the **right** to redeem*}

4: 6 next-of-kin {Or *one with the **right** to redeem*}

4: 8 next-of-kin {Or *one with the **right** to redeem*}

4:14 next-of-kin; {Or *one with the **right** to redeem*}

2Ki 10:15 "Is your heart as true to mine as mine is to yours?" {Gk: Heb *Is it **right** with your heart, as my heart is with your heart?*}

Job 9:15 appeal for mercy to my accuser. {Or *for my **right***}

Ps 74:11 why do you keep your hand in {Cn: Heb *do you consume your **right** hand from*}

Mal 3: 3 present offerings to the LORD in righteousness. {Or ***right** offerings to the LORD*}

Wis 3:10 those who disregard righteous {Or *what is **right***}

Sir 30:20 girl. {Other ancient authorities add *So is the person who does **right** under compulsion*}

RIGHTEOUS (7)

Isa 49:24 the captives of a tyrant {Q Ms Syr Vg: MT *of a **righteous** person*}

Mt 27: 4 sinned by betraying innocent {Other ancient authorities read ***righteous***} blood."

27:24 "I am innocent of this man's blood; {Other ancient authorities read *this **righteous** blood*, or *this **righteous** man's blood*}

Lk 23:47 this man was innocent." {Or ***righteous***}

Gal 2:16 a person is justified {Or *reckoned as **righteous;*** and so elsewhere}

Tob 3: 2 you judge the world. {Other ancient authorities read *you render true and **righteous** judgment forever*}

RIGHTEOUSNESS (7)

Ps 23: 3 He leads me in right paths {Or *paths of **righteousness***}

Pr 21:21 will find life {Gk: Heb *life and **righteousness***}

Mk 16:14 risen. {Other ancient authorities add, in whole or in part, ... *Therefore reveal your **righteousness** now"—thus they spoke to Christ. ... that they may inherit the spiritual and imperishable glory of **righteousness** that is in heaven."* }

Ro 5:21 exercise dominion through justification {Or ***righteousness***}

9:28 for the Lord will execute his sentence on the earth quickly and decisively." {Other ancient authorities read *for he will finish his work and cut it short in **righteousness,** ... on the earth*}

Gal 2:21 for if justification {Or ***righteousness***} comes through the law,

RIGHTFUL (1)

Ps 110: 4 forever according to the order of Melchizedek." {Or *forever, a **rightful** king by my edict*}

RIPATH (1)

1Ch 1: 6 Diphath, {Gen 10.3 ***Ripath***; See Gk Vg}

RISE (2)

Hos 1:11 they shall take possession of {Heb ***rise** up from*} the land,

Mk 12:23 In the resurrection {Other ancient authorities add *when they **rise***}

RISEN (2)

Ps 109:28 Let my assailants be put to shame; {Gk: Heb *They have **risen** up and have been put to shame*}

Lk 24: 5 He is not here, but has risen. {Other ancient authorities lack *He is not here, but has **risen***}

RISING (2)

2Ki 19:27 rising {Gk Compare Isa 37.27 Q Ms: MT lacks ***rising***}

Isa 37:28 your rising up {Q Ms Gk: MT lacks *your **rising** up*}

RISK (1)
2Sa 18:13 dealt treacherously against his life {Another reading is *at the **risk** of my life*}

RIVER (5)
Ge 31:21 he crossed the Euphrates, {Heb *the **river***}
Hab 3: 8 wrath against the rivers, {Or *against **River***} O LORD? Or your anger against the rivers, {Or *against **River***}
Sir 44:21 from the Euphrates {Syr: Heb Gk ***River***}
47:14 overflowed like the Nile {Heb: Gk *a **river***}

RIVERS (1)
Eze 47: 9 where the river goes, {Gk Syr Vg Tg: Heb *the two **rivers** go*}

ROADS (1)
Dt 19: 3 calculate the distances {Or *prepare **roads** to them*}

ROAMS (1)
Hos 11:12 Judah still walks {Heb ***roams*** or *rules*} with God,

ROBES (2)
2Sa 13:18 were clothed in earlier times.) {Cn: Heb *were clothed in **robes***}
Rev 16:15 and is clothed, {Gk *and keeps his **robes***}

ROCK (4)
1Sa 23:28 the Rock of Escape. {Or ***Rock** of Division*; Meaning of Heb uncertain}
Ps 73:26 God is the strength {Heb ***rock***} of my heart
Lk 6:48 it had been well built. {Other ancient authorities read *founded upon the **rock***}
Jn 1:42 Peter). {From the word for ***rock*** in Aramaic (*kepha*) and Greek (*petra*), respectively}

RODS (1)
Est 1: 6 to silver rings {Or ***rods***}

ROOF (2)
Eze 40:13 measured the gate from the back {Gk: Heb ***roof***} of the one recess to the back {Gk: Heb ***roof***}

ROOM (1)
Ge 26:22 Rehoboth, {That is *Broad places* or ***Room***}

ROOT (1)
Jdg 5:14 From Ephraim they set out {Cn: Heb *From Ephraim their **root***}

ROSE (3)
Eze 42: 3 the chambers rose {Heb lacks *the chambers **rose***}
Mic 2: 8 But you rise up against my people {Cn: Heb *But yesterday my people **rose***}
2Es 12: 2 rose up and {Ethiop: Lat lacks ***rose** up and*}

RUDIMENTS (4)
Gal 4: 3 the elemental spirits {Or *the **rudiments***}
4: 9 beggarly elemental spirits? {Or *beggarly **rudiments***}
Col 2: 8 the elemental spirits of the universe, {Or *the **rudiments** of the world*}
2:20 the elemental spirits of the universe, {Or *the **rudiments** of the world*}

RUIN (2)
Job 30:24 turn against the needy, {Heb ***ruin***}
Pr 10:10 but the one who rebukes boldly makes peace. {Gk: Heb *but a babbling fool will come to **ruin***}

RULE (1)
Mt 2: 6 who is to shepherd {Or ***rule***}

RULER (1)
1Sa 10: 1 over ... anointed you ruler {Gk: Heb lacks *over his people Israel. You shall ... anointed you **ruler***}

RULES (1)
Hos 11:12 Judah still walks {Heb *roams* or ***rules***} with God,

RUNS (1)
Job 7: 6 come to their end without hope. {Or *as the thread **runs** out*}

S

SABANNUS (1)
1Es 8:63 Binnui, {Gk ***Sabannus***}

SABBATHS (1)
Lev 25: 8 count off seven weeks {Or ***sabbaths***}

SACHERDONOS (3)
Tob 1:21 Esar-haddon {Gk ***Sacherdonos***}
1:22 Esar-haddon {Gk ***Sacherdonos***}
2: 1 Esar-haddon {Gk ***Sacherdonos***}

SACRIFICE (1)
Mk 9:49 "For everyone will be salted with fire. {Other ancient authorities either add or substitute *and every **sacrifice** will be salted with salt*}

SACRIFICES (2)
Hos 4:19 because of their altars. {Gk Syr: Heb ***sacrifices***}
13: 2 "Sacrifice to these," they say. {Cn Compare Gk: Heb *To these they say **sacrifices** of people*}

SAFELY (1)
Tob 5:16 and {Other ancient authorities add *when you return **safely***} I will add

SAID (16)
Jdg 9:29 I would say {Gk: Heb *and he **said***} to him,
19:30 "Thus shall you say ... such a thing ever happened {Compare Gk: Heb *[30]And all who saw it **said**, "Such a thing has not happened or been seen*}
2Ki 10:15 Jehu said, {Gk: Heb lacks *Jehu **said***}
Ne 9: 6 And Ezra said: {Gk: Heb lacks *And Ezra **said***}
Jer 44:19 And the women said, {Compare Syr: Heb lacks *And the women **said***}
Da 7: 1 dream: {Q Ms Theodotion: MT adds *the beginning of the words; he **said***}
7: 2 I, {Theodotion: Aram *Daniel answered and **said**, "I*}
Lk 9:56 rebuked them. [56]Then {Other ancient authorities read *rebuked them, and **said**, "You do not know* >}
24:36 and said ... with you." {Other ancient authorities lack *and **said** to them, "Peace be with you."*}
Ac 8:36 + v.37 *And Philip **said**, "If you believe with all your heart, you may."* >
28:28 + v.29 *And when he had **said** these words, the Jews departed, arguing vigorously among themselves*
Tob 7: 7 noble father!" {Other ancient authorities add < *he was stricken with grief and wept. Then he **said**,*}
8:20 Tobias and swore on oath to him in these words: {Other ancient authorities read *Tobias and **said** to him*}
AdE 1:13 This is how Vashti answered me. {Gk *Astin has **said** thus and so*}
1Es 8:25 Then Ezra the scribe said, {Other ancient authorities lack *Then Ezra the scribe **said***}
8:95 as seems good to you ... Rise up {Other ancient authorities read *as seems good to you." ... the Lord rose and **said** to Ezra, "Rise up*}

SAINTS (3)
2Pe 1:21 but men and women moved by the Holy Spirit spoke from God. {Other ancient authorities read *but moved by the Holy Spirit **saints** of God spoke*}
Rev 22:21 all the saints. Amen. {Other ancient authorities lack *... the **saints**;* >}
3Mc 6: 9 to those of the nation of Israel—who {Other ancient authorities read *to the **saints** of Israel*}

SAKAR (1)
Ge 30:18 "God has given me my hire {Heb ***sakar***}

SAKE (3)
Eze 23:21 fondled your bosom and caressed {Cn: Heb *for the **sake** of*}
Mt 23:13 + v.14 < *For you devour widows' houses and for the **sake** of appearance you make long prayers;* >
4Mc 17:20 for the sake of God, {Other ancient authorities lack *for the **sake** of God*}

SALATHIEL (1)
Lk 3:27 Shealtiel, {Gk ***Salathiel***}

SALE (1)
Sir 10: 8 wealth. {Other ancient authorities add here or after verse 9a, < *for such a person puts his own soul up for **sale**.*}

SALMON (1)
Lk 3:32 Sala, {Other ancient authorities read ***Salmon***}

SALT (10)
Ge 14: 3 Dead Sea). {Heb ***Salt** Sea*}
Nu 34: 3 Dead Sea {Heb ***Salt** Sea*}
34:12 Dead Sea. {Heb ***Salt** Sea*}
Dt 3:17 Dead Sea, {Heb ***Salt** Sea*}
Jos 3:16 Dead Sea, {Heb ***Salt** Sea*}
12: 3 Dead Sea, {Heb ***Salt** Sea*}
15: 2 Dead Sea, {Heb ***Salt** Sea*}
15: 5 Dead Sea, {Heb ***Salt** Sea*}
18:19 Dead Sea, {Heb ***Salt** Sea*}
Mk 9:49 "For everyone will be salted with fire. {Other ancient authorities either add or substitute *and every sacrifice will be salted with **salt***}

SALTINESS (1)
Mk 9:50 how can you season it? {Or *how can you restore its **saltiness**?*}

SALVATION (4)
Lk 1:69 a mighty savior {Gk *a horn of **salvation***}
Sir 4:23 speaking at the proper moment, {Heb: Gk *at a time of **salvation***}
13:13 + v.14 < *During all your life love the Lord, and call on him for your **salvation.***
4Mc 11: 6 + v.7 *If you but understood human feelings and had hope of **salvation** from God—*>

SAMARIA (2)
Sir 50:26 Those who live in Seir, {Heb Compare Lat: Gk *on the mountain of **Samaria***}
1Mc 5:66 Marisa. {Other ancient authorities read ***Samaria***}

SAME (2)
Eze 40:36 were of the same size as the others; {One Ms: Compare verses 29 and 33: MT lacks *were of the **same** size as the others*}
Mk 14:20 dipping bread into the bowl {Other ancient authorities read ***same** bowl*}

SAMUEL (1)
1Sa 12:11 Samson, {Gk: Heb ***Samuel***}

SANABASSAROS (1)
1Es 2:12 Sheshbazzar, {Gk ***Sanabassaros***}

SANABASSARUS (1)
1Es 6:18 Sheshbazzar {Gk ***Sanabassarus***}

SANCTIFIED (1)
Jude 1: 1 who are beloved {Other ancient authorities read ***sanctified***} in God

SANCTIFY (1)
Joel 3: 9 Prepare war, {Heb ***sanctify** war*}

SANCTUARY (3)
2Ch 3:16 encircling {Cn: Heb *in the inner **sanctuary***}
1Co 6:19 your body is a temple {Or ***sanctuary***}
1Mc 6:53 they had no food in storage, {Other ancient authorities read *in the **sanctuary***}

SAND (2)
Job 29:18 multiply my days like the phoenix; {Or *like **sand***}
Jdt 2:20 like the dust {Gk ***sand***} of the earth

SANK (1)
2Es 1:16 you still complain. {Other ancient authorities read verse 16, *Your pursuer with his army I **sank** in the sea,* >}

SATAN (2)
Mk 16:14 risen. {Other ancient authorities add, in whole or in part, ... *"This age of lawlessness and unbelief is under **Satan**,* >}
Sir 21:27 an ungodly person curses an adversary, {Or *curses **Satan***}

SATAN'S (1)
Mk 16:14 risen. {Other ancient authorities add, in whole or in part, ... *And Christ replied to them, "The term of years of **Satan's** power has been fulfilled,* >}

SATURATION (1)
Ps 66:12 out to a spacious place. {Cn Compare Gk Syr Jerome Tg: Heb *to a **saturation***}

SAUL (8)
Ge 46:10 Shaul, {Or ***Saul***}
Ex 6:15 Shaul, {Or ***Saul***}
Nu 6:23 Shaul ... Shaulites. {Or ***Saul** ... Saulites*}
2Sa 21: 6 at Gibeon on the mountain of the LORD." {Cn Compare Gk and 21.9: Heb *at Gibeah of **Saul**, the chosen of the* LORD}
1Ch 1:48 Shaul {Or ***Saul***}
1:49 Shaul {Or ***Saul***}
4:24 Shaul; {Or ***Saul***}
2Es 7:*108* [38] in the days of Saul, {Syr Ethiop Arab 1: Lat Arab 2 Arm lack *in the days of **Saul***}

SAULITES (1)
Nu 26:13 Shaul ... Shaulites. {Or *Saul ... **Saulites***}

SAVE (2)
Mt 18:10 + v.11 *For the Son of Man came to **save** the lost*
Lk 9:56 Then {Other ancient authorities read ... *the Son of Man has not ... but to **save** them." Then*}

SAVED (4)
Man 1: 7 O Lord, according ... be saved. {Other ancient authorities lack *O Lord, according ... be **saved***}
2Es 8:41 sown will come up {Syr Ethiop *will live*; Lat *will be **saved***}
13:48 shall be saved. {Syr: Lat lacks *shall be **saved***}
15: 4 unbelief. {Other ancient authorities add *and all who believe shall be **saved** by their faith*}

SAVIOR (1)
Sir 24:23 + v.24 < *the Lord Almighty alone is God, and besides him there is no **savior**."*

SAVIORS (1)
Ob 1:21 Those who have been saved {Or ***Saviors***}

SAW (9)
Ex 20:18 they were afraid {Sam Gk Syr Vg: MT *they* ***saw***}
Jdg 19:30 "Thus you shall say ... such a thing ever happened {Compare Gk: Heb [30]*And all who* ***saw*** *it said, "Such a thing has not happened or been seen*}
1Sa 23:15 when he learned that {Or ***saw*** *that*}
Ne 6:16 were afraid {Another reading is ***saw***}
Tob 11:13 saw his son and {Other ancient authorities lack ***saw*** *his son and*}
14:15 Before he died he heard {Codex Sinaiticus reads ***saw*** *and heard*}
Sir 1:18 flourish. {Other ancient authorities add < *those who love him. He* ***saw*** *her and took her measure.*}
2Es 13:2 a wind arose from the sea and stirred up {Other ancient authorities read *I* ***saw*** *a wind arise from the sea and stir up*}
13:3 saw {Syr: Lat lacks *the wind ... I* ***saw***}

SAWED (1)
1Ch 20:3 and set them to work {Compare 2 Sam 12.31: Heb *and he* ***sawed***} with saws

SAWS (1)
1Ch 20:3 axes. {Compare 2 Sam 12.31: Heb ***saws***}

SAY (6)
Ps 109:6 They say, {Heb lacks *They* ***say***}
Pr 23:35 you will say, {Gk Syr Vg Tg: Heb lacks *you will* ***say***}
Mt 5:22 and if you insult {Gk ***say*** *Raca to* (an obscure term of abuse)}
22:23 saying there is no resurrection; {Other ancient authorities read *who* ***say*** *that there is no resurrection*}
Ro 2:2 You say, {Gk lacks *You* ***say***}
2Es 7:*128* [58] receive what I have said. {Syr Ethiop Arab 1: Lat *what I* ***say***}

SAYING (6)
1Sa 9:24 "See ... eat with the guests." {Cn: Heb *it was kept for you,* ***saying,*** *I have invited the people*}
Jer 3:1 If {Q Ms Gk Syr: MT ***Saying,*** *If*} a man divorces
Mt 15:4 For God said, {Other ancient authorities read *commanded,* ***saying***} 'Honor your father
Mk 16:14 risen. {Other ancient authorities add, in whole or in part, *And they excused themselves,* ***saying,*** *"This age of lawlessness and unbelief* >}
Ac 15:24 minds, {Other ancient authorities add ***saying,*** *'You must be circumcised and keep the law,'* }
3Mc 5:29 pointed out that ... purpose." {Other ancient authorities read *pointed to the beasts and the armed forces,* ***saying,*** *"They are ready,* >}

SAYS (5)
Mk 15:27 + v.28 *And the scripture was fulfilled that* ***says,*** *"And he was counted among the lawless."*
Sir 19:20 + v.21 *When a slave* ***says*** *to his master, "I will not act as you wish,"* >
2Es 1:32 says the Lord. {Other ancient authorities add *Thus* ***says*** *the Lord Almighty: Recently you also laid hands on me, ... Therefore,* ***says*** *the Lord, let my Father and his angels return ... I will contend in judgment with you,* ***says*** *the Lord.*}

SCAPEGOAT (4)
Lev 16:8 Azazel. {Traditionally rendered *a* ***scapegoat***}
16:10 Azazel. {Traditionally rendered *a* ***scapegoat***}
16:10 Azazel. {Traditionally rendered *a* ***scapegoat***}
16:26 Azazel {Traditionally rendered *a* ***scapegoat***}

SCATTERER (1)
Na 2:1 A shatterer {Cn: Heb ***scatterer***} has come up

SCEPTERS (1)
Eze 19:11 Its strongest stem became a ruler's scepter; {Heb *Its strongest stems became rulers'* ***scepters***}

SCOURGE (1)
Sir 39:28 they can dislodge mountains; {Heb Syr: Gk *can* ***scourge*** *mightily*}

SCOUTS (1)
1Ki 20:17 scouts, {Heb lacks ***scouts***}

SCRIBE (3)
Sir 10:5 honor upon the lawgiver. {Heb: Gk ***scribe***}
1Es 8:25 Then Ezra the scribe said, {Other ancient authorities lack *Then Ezra the* ***scribe*** *said*}
2Es 14:48 so. {Syr adds ... *he was called the* ***scribe*** *of the knowledge of the Most High for ever and ever.* >}

SCRIBES (2)
Mt 23:13 + v.14 *Woe to you,* ***scribes*** *and Pharisees,* >
1Mc 5:42 he stationed the officers {Or ***scribes***}

SCRIPT (1)
Ezr 4:7 Aramaic and translated. {< Another interpretation is *The letter was written in the Aramaic* ***script*** *and set forth in the Aramaic language*}

SCRIPTURE (1)
Mk 15:27 + v.28 *And the* ***scripture*** *was fulfilled that says, "And he was counted among the lawless."*

SCRUTINY (1)
Sir 16:22 far off." {Other ancient authorities add *and a* ***scrutiny*** *for all comes at the end*}

SEA (8)
Ps 106:7 rebelled against the Most High {Cn Compare 78.17, 56: Heb *rebelled at the* ***sea***}
107:3 and from the south. {Cn: Heb ***sea***}
Jer 48:32 as far as Jazer; {Two Mss and Isa 16.8: MT *the* ***sea*** *of Jazer*}
Hab 3:8 rage against the sea, {Or *against* ***Sea***}
Mt 14:24 was far from the land, {Other ancient authorities read *was out on the* ***sea***}
Sir 40:11 from above returns above. {Heb Syr: Gk Lat *from the waters returns to the* ***sea***}
2Es 1:16 + v.16 *Your pursuer with his army I sank in the* ***sea,*** >
13:32 from the sea. {Syr and most Lat Mss lack *from the* ***sea***}

SEAHS (1)
Ge 18:6 three measures {Heb ***seahs***} of choice flour,

SEAL (2)
Jn 3:33 accepted his testimony has certified {Gk *set a* ***seal*** *to*} this,
2Es 2:23 commit them to the grave and mark it, {Or ***seal*** *it; or mark them and commit them to the grave*}

SEALED (1)
Ro 15:28 delivered to them what has been collected, {Gk *have* ***sealed*** *to them this fruit*}

SEARCHES (1)
Ps 77:6 search my spirit: {Syr Jerome: Heb *my spirit* ***searches***}

SEAS (1)
Ac 27:41 But striking a reef, {Gk *place of two* ***seas***}

SEASONING (1)
Lk 14:34 how can its saltiness be restored? {Or *how can it be used for* ***seasoning?***}

SEASONS (1)
Jn 5:3 + v.4 <*for an angel of the Lord went down at certain* ***seasons*** *into the pool,* >

SEAT (1)
2Es 1:32 says the Lord. {Other ancient authorities add ... *crying out before the judge's* ***seat*** *for him to deliver me to you.* >}

SEATED (1)
Jn 19:13 and sat {Or ***seated*** *him*} on the judge's bench

SECOND (5)
Ge 41:22 I fell asleep a second time {Gk Syr Vg: Heb lacks *I fell asleep a* ***second*** *time*}
Est 2:19 gathered together, {Heb adds *a* ***second*** *time*}
Ecc 4:15 follow that {Heb *the* ***second***} youth
Lk 6:1 One sabbath {Other ancient authorities read *On the* ***second*** *first sabbath*} while Jesus was going
2Es 1:1 The book {Other ancient authorities read *The* ***second*** *book*} of the prophet Ezra

SECRET (3)
Eze 7:22 profane my treasured {Or ***secret***} place;
Sir 16:21 Like a tempest ... works are concealed. {Meaning of Gk uncertain: Heb Syr *If I sin, ... disloyal all in* ***secret,*** *who is to know?*}
3Mc 2:5 notorious for their vices; {Other ancient authorities read ***secret*** *in their vices*}

SECRETS (1)
Sir 3:18 + v.19 *Many are lofty and renowned, but to the humble he reveals his* ***secrets.***

SEE (10)
Ge 22:14 "The LORD will provide"; {Or *will* ***see***; Heb traditionally transliterated *Jehovah Jireh*}
29:32 Reuben; {That is ***See,*** *a son*}
1Sa 6:13 they went with rejoicing to meet it. {Gk: Heb *rejoiced to* ***see*** *it*}
2Sa 15:27 the priest Zadok, "Look, {Gk: Heb *Are you a seer* or *Do you* ***see?***}
Isa 1:12 come to appear before me, {Or ***see*** *my face*}
42:20 He sees many things, but does {Heb *You* ***see*** *many things but do*}
Php 2:26 for he has been longing for {Other ancient authorities read *longing to* ***see***}
Sir 1:10 him. {Other ancient authorities add ... *to those to whom he appears he apportions her, that they may* ***see*** *him.*}
42:11 See ... house. {Heb: Gk lacks ***See*** *... house*}
2Es 5:37 travail that you ask to understand." {Lat ***see***}

SEED (10)
Ge 12:7 offspring {Heb ***seed***}
13:15 offspring {Heb ***seed***}
17:7 offspring {Heb ***seed***}
Da 2:43 in marriage, {Aram *by human* ***seed***}
Ro 9:29 left survivors {Or *descendants*; Gk ***seed***}
Gal 3:16 offspring; {Gk ***seed***}
3:16 offspring," {Gk ***seed***}
3:19 offspring {Gk ***seed***}
3:29 offspring, {Gk ***seed***}
2Es 16:77 its path {Other ancient authorities read ***seed***}

SEEDS (2)
Gal 3:16 say, "And to offsprings," {Gk ***seeds***}
2Es 4:36 number of those like yourselves is completed; {Syr Ethiop Arab 2: Lat *number of* ***seeds*** *is completed for you*}

SEEING (2)
Ge 16:13 El-roi"; {Perhaps *God of* ***seeing*** or *God who sees*}
Nu 35:23 unintentionally {Heb *without* ***seeing***}

SEEK (3)
Ps 109:10 they be driven out of {Gk: Heb *and* ***seek***}
Sir 32:14 to seek him {Other ancient authorities lack *to* ***seek*** *him*}
2Es 2:13 Go {Other ancient authorities read ***Seek***} and you will receive;

SEEKERS (1)
Pr 21:6 and a snare {Gk: Heb ***seekers***} of death.

SEEKING (1)
Sir 20:31 + v.32 *Unwearied endurance in* ***seeking*** *the Lord is better* >

SEEM (1)
4Mc 11:5 because {Other ancient authorities read *Or does it* ***seem*** *evil to you that*} we revere the Creator

SEEMED (1)
Ac 15:33 + v.34 *But it* ***seemed*** *good to Silas to remain there*

SEEN (2)
Ge 22:14 it shall be provided." {Or *he shall be* ***seen***}
Jdg 19:30 Then he commanded ... a thing ever happened {Compare Gk: Heb [30]*And all who saw it said, "Such a thing has not happened or been* ***seen***}

SEER (1)
2Sa 15:27 priest Zadok, "Look, {Gk: Heb *Are you a* ***seer*** or *Do you see?*}

SEERS (1)
2Es 10:22 our righteous men {Syr *our* ***seers***}

SEES (2)
Ge 16:13 El-roi"; {Perhaps *God of seeing* or *God who* ***sees***}
16:14 Beer-lahai-roi; {That is *the Well of the Living One who* ***sees*** *me*}

SEIR (1)
Eze 25:8 Moab {Gk Old Latin: Heb *Moab and* ***Seir***} said,

SELA (2)
Jer 49:16 the clefts of the rock, {Or *of* ***Sela***}
Ob 1:3 the clefts of the rock, {Or *clefts of* ***Sela***}

SELF-RELIANT (1)
Sir 40:18 Wealth and wages make life sweet, {Heb: Gk *Life is sweet for the* ***self-reliant*** *worker*}

SELLS (2)
Dt 15:12 is sold {Or ***sells*** *himself or herself*} to you
Na 3:4 who enslaves {Heb ***sells***} nations

SEMEIOS (2)
AdE 11:2 Shimei {Gk ***Semeios***}
2:5 Shimei {Gk ***Semeios***}

SENDING (1)
1Co 4:17 I sent {Or *am* ***sending***} you Timothy,

SENSE (2)
Sir 22:13 person. {Other ancient authorities add *For being without* ***sense*** *he will despise everything about you*}
25:9 one who finds a friend, {Lat Syr: Gk *good* ***sense***}

SENT (2)
2Sa 18:2 divided the army into three groups: {Gk: Heb ***sent*** *forth the army*}
AdE 9:29 + v.30 *Letters were* ***sent*** *to all the Jews, to the one hundred twenty-seven provinces* >

SEPARATED (18)
Nu 6:2 nazirite, {That is *one* ***separated*** or *one consecrated*}
6:4 nazirites {That is *those* ***separated*** or *those consecrated*}

Nu 6: 8 nazirites {That is *those* **separated** *or those consecrated*}
6:12 nazirites, {That is *those* **separated** or *those consecrated*}
6:13 nazirites {That is *those* **separated** or *those consecrated*}
6:18 nazirites {That is *those* **separated** or *those consecrated*}
6:19 nazirites, {That is *those* **separated** or *those consecrated*}
6:20 nazirites {That is *those* **separated** or *those consecrated*}
6:21 nazirites {That is *those* **separated** or *those consecrated*}
6:21 nazirite {That is *one* **separated** or *one consecrated*}
Jdg 13: 5 nazirite {That is *one* **separated** or *one consecrated*}
13: 7 nazirite {That is *one* **separated** or *one consecrated*}
16:17 nazirite {That is *one* **separated** or *one consecrated*}
1Sa 1:11 nazirite {That is *one* **separated** or *one consecrated*}
1:22 nazirite {That is *one* **separated** or *one consecrated*}
Am 2:11 nazirites. {That is, *those* **separated** or *those consecrated*}
2:12 nazirites {That is, *those* **separated** or *those consecrated*}
1Mc 3:49 nazirites {That is *those* **separated** or *those consecrated*}

SEPARATING (1)

Sir 18: 2 + v.3 < ***separating*** *among them the holy things from the profane.*

SERAPH (2)

Nu 21: 8 a poisonous {Or *fiery*; Heb ***seraph***} serpent,
Dt 8:15 with poisonous {Or *fiery*; Heb ***seraph***} snakes

SERAPHIM (1)

Nu 21: 6 sent poisonous {Or *fiery*; Heb ***seraphim***} serpents

SERVANT (4)

2Sa 18:29 your servant, {Heb *the king's* ***servant,*** *your* ***servant***}
Wis 2:13 calls himself a child {Or ***servant***} of the Lord.
4Mc 17: 6 For ... of father Abraham. {< other ancient authorities read *For ... Abraham the* ***servant***}

SERVANTS (3)

Dt 32:43 of his children, {Q Ms Gk: MT *his* ***servants***}
Lk 15:21 son.' {Other ancient authorities add *treat me as one of your hired* ***servants***}
Wis 19: 6 your children {Or ***servants***} might be kept

SERVE (1)

4Mc 11: 6 + v.8 < *you are a stranger to God and persecute those who* ***serve*** *him."*

SERVICE (2)

Nu 18: 7 priesthood as a gift; {Heb *as a* ***service*** *of gift*}
2Es 8:22 they are changed to wind and fire, {Syr: Lat *they whose* ***service*** *takes the form of wind and fire*}

SERVING (1)

Col 2:23 are of no value in checking self-indulgence. {Or *are of no value,* ***serving*** *only to indulge the flesh*}

SET (10)

Ex 8:23 Thus I will make a distinction {Gk Vg: Heb *will* ***set*** *redemption*}
Ezr 4: 7 the letter was written in Aramaic and translated. {< Another interpretation is *The letter was written in the Aramaic script and* ***set*** *forth in the Aramaic language*}
Ps 50:23 those who get the right way {Heb *who* ***set*** *a way*}
148: 6 he fixed their bounds, which cannot be passed. {Or *he* ***set*** *a law that cannot pass away*}
Lk 24:21 the one to redeem Israel. {Or *to* ***set*** *Israel free*}
Jn 3:33 Whoever ... has certified {Gk ***set*** *a seal to*} this,
Heb 2: 7 and honor, {Other ancient authorities add *and* ***set*** *them over the works of your hands*}
Sir 17: 8 He put the fear of him into {Other ancient authorities read *He* ***set*** *his eye upon*}
2Es 3:18 and shook {Syr Ethiop Arab 1 Georg: Lat ***set*** *fast*} the earth,
16: 6 fire in the stubble once it has started to burn? {Other ancient authorities read *fire when dry straw has been* ***set*** *on fire*}

SETH (1)

Ge 4:25 "God has appointed {The verb in Heb resembles the word for ***Seth***}

SETTLEMENT (1)

Dt 3:14 Havvoth-jair, {That is ***Settlement*** *of Jair*}

SETTLEMENTS (1)

Eze 37:23 from all the apostasies into which they have fallen, {Another reading is *from all the* ***settlements*** *in which they have sinned*}

SETTLERS (1)

1Ki 17: 1 of Tishbe {Gk: Heb *of the* ***settlers***} in Gilead,

SEVEN (8)

Ge 21:31 Beer-sheba; {That is *Well of* ***seven*** *or Well of the oath*}
26:33 Beer-sheba {That is *Well of the oath or Well of* ***seven***}
2Sa 24:13 "Shall three {1 Chr 21.12 Gk: Heb ***seven***} years
1Ki 8:65 seven days. {Compare Gk: Heb ***seven*** *days and* ***seven*** *days, fourteen days*}
Mt 18:22 seventy-seven {Or *seventy times* ***seven***} times.
Tob 14: 3 and the seven sons of Tobias {Lat: Gk lacks *and the* ***seven*** *sons of Tobias*}
2Mc 12:17 ninety-five miles {Gk ***seven*** *hundred fifty stadia*}

SEVENTH (3)

Jdg 14:15 on the fourth {Gk Syr: Heb ***seventh***} day
Sir 17: 4 + v.5 < *and as* ***seventh,*** *reason, the interpreter of one's faculties.*
2Es 14:48 did so. {Syr adds *in the* ***seventh*** *year of the sixth week, five thousand years and three months* >}

SEVENTY (1)

Mt 18:22 I tell you, seventy-seven {Or ***seventy*** *times seven*}

SEVENTY-TWO (2)

Lk 10: 1 the Lord appointed seventy {Other ancient authorities read ***seventy-two***} others
10:17 The seventy {Other ancient authorities read ***seventy-two***} returned with joy,

SHADDAI (48)

Ge 17: 1 God Almighty; {Traditional rendering of Heb *El* ***Shaddai***}
28: 3 God Almighty {Traditional rendering of Heb *El* ***Shaddai***}
35:11 God Almighty: {Traditional rendering of Heb *El* ***Shaddai***}
43:14 God Almighty {Traditional rendering of Heb *El* ***Shaddai***}
48: 3 God Almighty {Traditional rendering of Heb *El* ***Shaddai***}
49:25 Almighty {Traditional rendering of Heb ***Shaddai***}
Ex 6: 3 God Almighty, {Traditional rendering of Heb *El* ***Shaddai***}
Nu 24: 4 Almighty, {Traditional rendering of Heb ***Shaddai***}
24:16 Almighty, {Traditional rendering of Heb ***Shaddai***}
Ru 1:20 Almighty {Traditional rendering of Heb ***Shaddai***}
1:21 Almighty {Traditional rendering of Heb ***Shaddai***}
Job 5:17 Almighty. {Traditional rendering of Heb ***Shaddai***}
6: 4 Almighty {Traditional rendering of Heb ***Shaddai***}
6:14 Almighty. {Traditional rendering of Heb ***Shaddai***}
8: 3 Almighty {Traditional rendering of Heb ***Shaddai***}
8: 5 Almighty, {Traditional rendering of Heb ***Shaddai***}
11: 7 Almighty? {Traditional rendering of Heb ***Shaddai***}
13: 3 Almighty, {Traditional rendering of Heb ***Shaddai***}
15:25 Almighty, {Traditional rendering of Heb ***Shaddai***}
21:15 Almighty, {Traditional rendering of Heb ***Shaddai***}
21:20 Almighty. {Traditional rendering of Heb ***Shaddai***}
22: 3 Almighty {Traditional rendering of Heb ***Shaddai***}
22:17 Almighty {Traditional rendering of Heb ***Shaddai***}
22:23 Almighty, {Traditional rendering of Heb ***Shaddai***}
22:25 Almighty {Traditional rendering of Heb ***Shaddai***}
22:26 Almighty, {Traditional rendering of Heb ***Shaddai***}
23:16 Almighty {Traditional rendering of Heb ***Shaddai***}
24: 1 Almighty, {Traditional rendering of Heb ***Shaddai***}
27: 2 Almighty, {Traditional rendering of Heb ***Shaddai***}
27:10 Almighty? {Traditional rendering of Heb ***Shaddai***}
27:11 Almighty {Traditional rendering of Heb ***Shaddai***}
27:13 Almighty: {Traditional rendering of Heb ***Shaddai***}
29: 5 Almighty {Traditional rendering of Heb ***Shaddai***}
31: 2 Almighty {Traditional rendering of Heb ***Shaddai***}
31:35 Almighty {Traditional rendering of Heb ***Shaddai***}
32: 8 Almighty, {Traditional rendering of Heb ***Shaddai***}
33: 4 Almighty {Traditional rendering of Heb ***Shaddai***}
34:10 Almighty {Traditional rendering of Heb ***Shaddai***}
34:12 Almighty {Traditional rendering of Heb ***Shaddai***}
35:13 Almighty {Traditional rendering of Heb ***Shaddai***}
37:23 Almighty {Traditional rendering of Heb ***Shaddai***}
40: 2 Almighty? {Traditional rendering of Heb ***Shaddai***}
Ps 68:14 Almighty {Traditional rendering of Heb ***Shaddai***}
91: 1 Almighty, {Traditional rendering of Heb ***Shaddai***}
Isa 13: 6 Almighty! {Traditional rendering of Heb ***Shaddai***}
Eze 1:24 Almighty, {Traditional rendering of Heb ***Shaddai***}
10: 5 God Almighty {Traditional rendering of Heb *El* ***Shaddai***}
Joel 1:15 Almighty {Traditional rendering of Heb ***Shaddai***}

SHADES (2)

Pr 9:18 the dead {Heb ***shades***} are there
Isa 26:19 to those long dead. {Heb *to the* ***shades***}

SHADOW (2)

Ps 23: 4 walk through the darkest valley, {Or *the valley of the* ***shadow*** *of death*}
Bar 1:12 live under the protection {Gk *in the* ***shadow***}

SHAGGY (1)

Da 8:21 The male goat {Or ***shaggy*** *male goat*} is the king

SHAKE (1)

2Es 1: 8 and hurl {Other ancient authorities read *and* ***shake*** *out*} all evils

SHAKING (1)

Ps 44:14 a laughingstock {Heb *a* ***shaking*** *of the head*}

SHALOM (1)

1Ch 22: 9 I will give him peace {Heb ***shalom***}

SHAMA (1)

Ge 29:33 "Because the LORD has heard {Heb ***shama***}

SHAME (7)

2Sa 2: 8 Ishbaal {Gk Compare 1 Chr 8.33; 9.39: Heb *Ish-bosheth*, "man of **shame**"}
2:10 Ishbaal, {Gk Compare 1 Chr 8.33; 9.39: Heb *Ish-bosheth*, "man of **shame**"}
2:12 Ishbaal {Gk Compare 1 Chr 8.33; 9.39: Heb *Ish-bosheth*, "man of **shame**"}
2:15 Ishbaal {Gk Compare 1 Chr 8.33; 9.39: Heb *Ish-bosheth*, "man of **shame**"}
3: 8 Ishbaal {Gk Compare 1 Chr 8.33; 9.39: Heb *Ish-bosheth*, "man of **shame**"}
Pr 11:16 but she ... shame. {Compare Gk Syr: Heb lacks *but she ...* ***shame***}
Isa 3:24 shame. {Q Ms: MT lacks ***shame***}

SHAON (1)

Jer 48:45 the scalp of the people of tumult. {Or *of* ***Shaon***}

SHAQED (1)

Jer 1:11 branch of an almond tree." {Heb ***shaqed***}

SHARE (1)

Ac 1:25 go to his own place {Other ancient authorities read *the* ***share***}

SHARING (1)

2Co 13:13 and the communion of {Or *and the* ***sharing*** *in*}

SHATTER (1)

Ps 68:23 may bathe {Gk Syr Tg: Heb ***shatter***} your feet

SHAUL (2)

1Ch 8:33 Saul, {Or ***Shaul***}
8:33 Saul {Or ***Shaul***}

SHEATH (1)

Da 7:15 troubled within me, {Aram *troubled in its* ***sheath***}

SHEDDING (1)

2Sa 3:27 shedding {Heb lacks ***shedding***}

SHEEP (1)

Hos 12:12 sheep. {Heb lacks ***sheep***}

SHEEPFOLDS (1)

Jdt 3: 3 all our encampments {Gk *all the* ***sheepfolds*** *of our tents*}

SHEKEM (2)

Ge 48:22 one portion {Or *mountain slope* (Heb ***shekem***, a play on the name of the town and district of Shechem)}
48:22 the portion {Or *mountain slope* (Heb ***shekem***, a play on the name of the town and district of Shechem)}

SHELOMITH (1)

1Ch 26:28 Shelomoth {Gk Compare 26.28: Heb ***Shelomith***}

SHELOMOH (1)

1Ch 22: 9 Solomon, {Heb ***Shelomoh***}

SHEMAIAH (1)

Tob 5:14 Shemeliah, {Other ancient authorities read ***Shemaiah***}

SHEMAMAH (1)

Isa 62: 4 Desolate; {Heb ***Shemamah***}

SHEN (1)
1Sa 7:12 Jeshanah, {Gk Syr: Heb ***Shen***}

SHEPHERD (3)
Rev 2:27 to rule {Or *to* ***shepherd***} them with an iron rod
12: 5 who is to rule {Or *to* ***shepherd***}
19:15 he will rule {Or *will* ***shepherd***}

SHEPHERDS (2)
Jer 2: 8 rulers {Heb ***shepherds***} transgressed against me;
Jude 1:12 without fear, feeding themselves. {Or *without fear. They are* ***shepherds*** *who care only for themselves*}

SHILOH (2)
Ge 49:10 until tribute comes to him; {Or *until* ***Shiloh*** *comes* or *until he comes to* ***Shiloh*** or (with Syr) *until he comes to whom it belongs*}

SHIMEI (1)
1Ch 25: 3 Shimei, {One Ms: Gk: MT lacks ***Shimei***}

SHINE (1)
Sir 24:27 It pours forth instruction like the Nile, {Syr: Gk *It makes instruction* ***shine*** *forth like light*}

SHOOTING (1)
Ps 78: 9 armed with {Heb *armed with* ***shooting***} the bow,

SHOQED (1)
Jer 1:12 for I am watching {Heb ***shoqed***}

SHORT (2)
Nu 11:23 "Is the LORD's power limited? {Heb *LORD's hand too* ***short?***}
Ro 9:28 for the Lord will execute his sentence on the earth quickly and decisively." {Other ancient authorities read *for he will finish his work and cut it* ***short*** *... on the earth*}

SHORTENED (1)
Ro 9:28 for the Lord will execute his sentence on the earth quickly and decisively." {Other ancient authorities read *for he will finish his work ... the sentence* ***shortened*** *on the earth*}

SHOT (2)
Nu 21:30 So their prosperity perished from Heshbon {Gk: Heb *we have* ***shot*** *at them; Heshbon has perished*}
2Ki 9:27 and they shot him {Syr Vg Compare Gk: Heb lacks *and they* ***shot*** *him*}

SHOW (3)
2Sa 15:20 may the LORD show {Gk Compare 2.6: Heb lacks *may the LORD* ***show***}
Php 4:10 to show it. {Gk lacks *to* ***show*** *it*}
Sir 20: 8 hated. {Other ancient authorities add *How good it is to* ***show*** *repentance when you are reproved,* >}

SHOWING (1)
Sir 16:10 stubbornness. {Other ancient authorities add *Chastising,* ***showing*** *mercy, striking, healing, the Lord persisted in mercy and discipline.*}

SHREDS (1)
4Mc 9:27 they heard his noble decision. {Other ancient authorities read *having heard his noble decision, they tore him to* ***shreds***}

SHRINE (1)
1Sa 10:13 he went home. {Cn: Heb *he came to the* ***shrine***}

SICK (1)
Mic 6:13 have begun {Gk Syr Vg: Heb *have made* ***sick***} to strike

SICKNESS (1)
Sir 2: 5 humiliation. {Other ancient authorities add *in* ***sickness*** *and poverty put your trust in him*}

SICKNESSES (1)
Jer 14:18 look—those sick with {Heb *look—the* ***sicknesses*** *of*} famine!

SIDE (4)
Eze 41:26 vestibule. {Cn: Heb *vestibule. And the* ***side*** *chambers of the temple and the canopies*}
48: 1 on the Hethlon road, {Compare 47.15: Heb *by the* ***side*** *of the way*}
Mt 27:49 save him." {Other ancient authorities add *And another took a spear and pierced his* ***side,*** *and out came water and blood*}
1Mc 4:34 they fell in action. {Or *and some fell on the opposite* ***side***}

SIDES (1)
Jdg 2: 3 they shall become adversaries {OL Vg Compare Gk: Heb ***sides***}

SIDON (1)
Mk 7:24 region of Tyre. {Other ancient authorities add *and* ***Sidon***}

SIGH (1)
Sir 36:30 become a fugitive and a wanderer. {Heb: Gk *wander about and* ***sigh***}

SIGHS (1)
Sir 25:18 and he cannot help sighing {Other ancient authorities read *and listening he* ***sighs***}

SIGHT (3)
Mt 11:26 for such was your gracious will. {Or *for so it was well-pleasing in your* ***sight***}
Lk 10:21 for such was your gracious will. {Or *for so it was well-pleasing in your* ***sight***}
Tob 7: 7 father!" {Other ancient authorities add *When he heard that Tobit had lost his* ***sight,*** >}

SIGN (2)
Tob 5: 2 What evidence {Gk ***sign***} am I to give
Sir 42:18 he sees from old the things that are to come. {Heb: Gk *he sees the* ***sign(s)*** *of the age*}

SIGNS (1)
Sir 45: 3 he performed swift miracles; {Heb: Gk *caused* ***signs*** *to cease*}

SILAS (1)
Ac 15:33 + v.34 *But it seemed good to* ***Silas*** *to remain there*

SILENCE (1)
Eze 27:32 was ever destroyed {Tg Vg: Heb *like* ***silence***}

SILENT (2)
Jer 48: 2 brought to silence; {The place-name *Madmen* sounds like the Hebrew verb *to be* ***silent***}
Zep 3:17 he will renew you {Gk Syr: Heb *he will be* ***silent***}

SILK (1)
LtJ 6:72 the purple and linen {Cn: Gk *marble,* Syr ***silk***}

SILVER (4)
Ge 44: 4 Why ... my silver cup? {Gk Compare Vg: Heb lacks *Why have you stolen my* ***silver*** *cup?*}
Pr 26:23 Like the glaze {Cn: Heb ***silver*** *of dross*} covering
Da 5: 3 and silver {Theodotion Vg: Aram lacks *and* ***silver***}
Zec 6:10 silver and gold {Cn Compare verse 11: Heb lacks ***silver*** *and gold*}

SIMON (1)
2Pe 1: 1 Simeon {Other ancient authorities read ***Simon***}

SIMPLENESS (1)
Pr 9: 6 Lay aside immaturity, {Or ***simpleness***}

SIN (8)
Ex 5:16 beaten! You are unjust to your own people." {Gk Compare Syr Vg: Heb *beaten, and the* ***sin*** *of your people*}
Nu 12:11 do not punish us {Heb *do not lay* ***sin*** *upon us*}
La 4: 6 than the punishment {Or ***sin***} of Sodom,
Mk 16:14 risen. {Other ancient authorities add, in whole or in part, *that they may return to the truth and* ***sin*** *no more,* >}
2Th 2: 3 the lawless one {< other ancient authorities read *the man of* ***sin***}
Sir 10:29 acquit those who condemn {Heb: Gk ***sin*** *against*}
16:21 Like a tempest ... concealed. {Meaning of Gk uncertain: Heb Syr *If I* ***sin,*** *no eye can see me, ... who is to know?*}
20: 8 hated. {Other ancient authorities add *... for so you will escape deliberate* ***sin!***}

SINCE (2)
Hag 2:16 how did you fare? {Gk: Heb ***since*** *they were*}
Jas 5: 3 will eat your flesh like fire. You have laid up treasure {Or *will eat your flesh,* ***since*** *you have stored up fire*}

SINCERE (1)
Ac 2:46 with glad and generous {Or ***sincere***} hearts,

SINCERITY (1)
Tob 12: 8 Prayer with fasting {Codex Sinaiticus *with* ***sincerity***}

SING (1)
Sir 47: 9 voices. {Other ancient authorities add *and daily they* ***sing*** *his praises*}

SINGLE (2)
Jer 49:19 and I will appoint over it whomever I choose. {Or *and I will* ***single*** *out the choicest of his rams:* Meaning of Heb uncertain}
50:44 and I will appoint over it whomever I choose. {Or *and I will* ***single*** *out the choicest of her rams:* Meaning of Heb uncertain}

SINIM (1)
Isa 49:12 Syene. {Q Ms: MT ***Sinim***}

SINNED (2)
Eze 37:23 from all the apostasies into which they have fallen, {Another reading is *from all the settlements in which they have* ***sinned***}
Mk 16:14 risen. {Other ancient authorities add, in whole or in part, < *And for those who have* ***sinned*** *I was handed over to death,* >}

SINNER (2)
Sir 5: 9 path. {Gk adds *so it is with the double-tongued* ***sinner*** (see 6.1)}
2Es 1:32 says the Lord. {Other ancient authorities add < *You took me as a* ***sinner,*** *not as a father who freed you from slavery,* >}

SINNERS (2)
Sir 11:14 + v.16 < *Error and darkness were created with* ***sinners;*** >}
41:11 The human body ... be blotted out. {Heb: Gk *People grieve over the death of the body, but the bad name of* ***sinners*** *will be blotted out*}

SINS (2)
Jn 8: 8 ground. {Other ancient authorities add *the* ***sins*** *of each of them*}
Sir 1:20 + v.21 *The fear of the Lord drives away* ***sins;*** >

SION (1)
Dt 4:48 Sirion {Syr: Heb ***Sion***}

SIR (2)
Jn 9:36 sir? {***Sir*** and *Lord* translate the same Greek word}
9:38 "Lord, {***Sir*** and *Lord* translate the same Greek word}

SISTER (8)
1Co 9: 5 by a believing wife, {Gk *a* ***sister*** *as wife*}
Tob 6:18 kinswoman, {Gk ***sister***}
7: 9 kinswoman {Gk ***sister***}
7:11 kinswoman; {Gk ***sister***}
8:21 as to your wife {Gk ***sister***}
10: 6 dear; {Gk ***sister***}
10: 6 dear; {Gk ***sister***}
10:12 Sarah is your beloved wife. {Gk ***sister***}

SISTERS (2)
Hos 2: 1 and to your sister, {Gk Vg: Heb ***sisters***}
Mk 3:32 and sisters {Other ancient authorities lack *and* ***sisters***}

SIT (2)
Isa 52: 2 rise up, O captive {Cn: Heb *rise up,* ***sit***}
Rev 14: 6 proclaim to those who live {Gk ***sit***}

SITTING (1)
2Sa 23: 7 consumed in fire on the spot. {Heb *in* ***sitting***}

SIX (2)
Rev 14:20 about two hundred miles. {Gk *one thousand* ***six*** *hundred stadia*}
2Mc 12:29 seventy-five miles {Gk ***six*** *hundred stadia*}

SIXTEEN (1)
Rev 13:18 Its number is six hundred sixty-six. {Other ancient authorities read *six hundred* ***sixteen***}

SIXTH (2)
Sir 17: 4 + v.5 < *as* ***sixth*** *he distributed to them the gift of mind,* >
2Es 14:48 did so. {Syr adds *in the seventh year of the* ***sixth*** *week five thousand years* >}

SIXTY (2)
Lk 24:13 about seven miles {Gk ***sixty*** *stadia;* other ancient authorities read *a hundred* ***sixty*** *stadia*}

SIZE (1)
Eze 40:36 were of the same size as the others; {< MT lacks *were of the same* ***size*** *as the others*}

SKILL (1)
Wis 13:13 skill gained in idleness; {Other ancient authorities read *with intelligent* ***skill***}

SKIN (1)
4Mc 10: 7 they abandoned the instruments {Other ancient authorities read *they tore off his* ***skin***}

SKIRT (2)
Dt 22:30 violating his father's rights. {Heb *uncovering his father's* ***skirt***}
27:20 violated his father's rights." {Heb *uncovered his father's* ***skirt***}

SKULL (1)
Nu 24:17 the territory {Some Mss read ***skull***} of all the Shethites.

SLAIN (1)
1Sa 31: 1 and many fell {Heb *and they fell **slain***}

SLANDERER (2)
AdE 8: 1 property of the persecutor {Gk ***slanderer***} Haman.
Sir 5:14 to the double-tongued {Heb: Gk *a **slanderer***}

SLAP (1)
Lk 18: 5 by continually coming.' " {Or *so that she may not finally come and **slap** me in the face*}

SLAUGHTER (1)
Ge 22:10 took the knife to kill {Or *to **slaughter***} his son.

SLAUGHTERERS (1)
Wis 12: 5 their merciless slaughter {Gk ***slaughterers***}

SLAVE (19)
Lk 2:29 servant {Gk ***slave***}
Jn 15:15 servant {Gk ***slave***}
Ro 1: 1 servant {Gk ***slave***}
Gal 1:10 servant {Gk ***slave***}
Col 1: 7 servant. {Gk ***slave***}
4: 7 servant {Gk ***slave***}
4:12 servant {Gk ***slave***}
2Ti 2:24 servant {Gk ***slave***}
Tit 1: 1 servant {Gk ***slave***}
Jas 1: 1 servant {Gk ***slave***}
2Pe 1: 1 servant {Gk ***slave***}
Jude 1: 1 servant {Gk ***slave***}
Rev 1: 1 servant {Gk ***slave***}
15: 3 servant {Gk ***slave***}
19:10 servant {Gk ***slave***}
22: 9 servant {Gk ***slave***}
Wis 9: 5 servant {Gk ***slave***}
Sir 7:21 slaves; {Heb *Love a wise **slave** as yourself*}
19:20 + v.21 < *When a **slave** says to his master, "I will not act as you wish,"* >

SLAVERY (1)
2Es 1:32 says the Lord. {Other ancient authorities add < *not as a father who freed you from **slavery**,* >}

SLAVES (24)
1Sa 2:27 slaves {Q Ms Gk: MT lacks ***slaves***}
Jn 13:16 servants {Gk ***slaves***}
15:15 servants {Gk ***slaves***}
15:20 'Servants {Gk ***Slaves***}
Ac 4:29 servants {Gk ***slaves***}
Php 1: 1 servants {Gk ***slaves***}
Col 3:24 you serve {Or *you are **slaves** of*, or *be **slaves** of*} the Lord Christ.
1Pe 2:16 servants {Gk ***slaves***}
Rev 1: 1 servants {Gk ***slaves***}
2:20 servants {Gk ***slaves***}
6:11 servants {Gk ***slaves***}
7: 3 servants {Gk ***slaves***}
10: 7 servants {Gk ***slaves***}
11:18 servants, {Gk ***slaves***}
19: 2 servants." {Gk ***slaves***}
19: 5 servants, {Gk ***slaves***}
22: 3 servants {Gk ***slaves***}
22: 6 servants {Gk ***slaves***}
1Mc 3:41 fetters, {Syr: Gk Mss, Vg ***slaves***}
2Mc 7: 6 servants.' " {Gk ***slaves***}
7:33 servants. {Gk ***slaves***}
8:29 servants. {Gk ***slaves***}
2Es 2:26 servants {Or ***slaves***}

SLEEP (3)
1Sa 9:25 and he lay down to sleep. {Gk: Heb lacks *and he lay down to **sleep***}
Sir 13:13 + v.14 *When you hear these things in your **sleep**, wake up!* >
30:17 eternal sleep {Other ancient authorities lack *eternal **sleep***}

SLEEPERS (1)
SS 7: 9 gliding over lips and teeth. {Gk Syr Vg: Heb *lips of **sleepers***}

SLINGSTONES (1)
Zec 9:15 tread down the slingers; {Cn: Heb *the **slingstones***}

SLOPE (2)
Ge 48:22 one portion {Or *mountain **slope*** (Heb *shekem*, a play on the name of the town and district of Shechem)}
48:22 the portion {Or *mountain **slope*** (Heb *shekem*, a play on the name of the town and district of Shechem)}

SLOWLY (2)
Isa 38:15 All my sleep has fled {Cn Compare Syr: Heb *I will walk **slowly** all my years*}
2Mc 14:17 had been temporarily {Other ancient authorities read ***slowly***} checked

SNARE (1)
Job 5: 5 and the thirsty {Aquila Symmachus Syr Vg: Heb ***snare***} pant

SODOM (1)
2Es 5: 7 the Dead Sea {Lat *Sea of **Sodom***}

SOLDIERS (2)
2Sa 10:18 and forty thousand horsemen, {1 Chr 19.18 and some Gk Mss read *foot **soldiers***}
3Mc 1: 2 the best of the Ptolemaic arms ... issued to him, {Or *the best of the Ptolemaic **soldiers** previously put under his command*}

SOME (3)
1Sa 6:19 The descendants ... when they greeted {Gk: Heb *And he killed **some** of the people of Beth-shemesh, because they looked into*}
Eze 11:16 to them for a little while {Or *to **some** extent*}
1Mc 4:34 they fell in action. {Or *and **some** fell on the opposite side*}

SOMEONE (1)
Lk 23:16 + v.17 *Now he was obliged to release **someone** for them at the festival*

SON (36)
Ge 21: 9 with her son Isaac. {Gk Vg: Heb lacks *with her **son** Isaac*}
29:32 Reuben; {That is *See, a **son***}
35:18 Ben-oni; {That is ***Son** of my sorrow*}
35:18 Benjamin. {That is ***Son** of the right hand* or ***Son** of the South*}
Dt 13: 6 your father's son or {Sam Gk Compare Tg: MT lacks *your father's **son** or*}
2Sa 23:20 a valiant warrior {Another reading is *the **son** of Ish-hai*}
23:33 son of {Gk: Heb lacks ***son** of*}
1Ch 2:50 The sons {Gk Vg: Heb ***son***} of Hur
11:22 a valiant man {Syr: Heb *the **son** of a valiant man*}
24:26 Beno. {Or *his **son***: Meaning of Heb uncertain}
24:27 Beno, {Or *his **son***: Meaning of Heb uncertain}
Ps 8: 4 mortals {Heb *ben adam*, lit. ***son** of man*}
Eze 2: 1 O mortal, {Or ***son** of man*; Heb *ben adam* (and so throughout the book when Ezekiel is addressed)}
Da 3:25 appearance of a god." {Aram *a **son** of the gods*}
7:13 one like a human being {Aram *one like a **son** of man*}
8:17 O mortal, {Heb ***son** of man*}
Mt 18:10 + v.11 *For the **Son** of Man came to save the lost*
24:36 nor the Son, {Other ancient authorities lack *nor the **Son***}
25:13 hour. {Other ancient authorities add *in which the **Son** of Man is coming*}
27:54 this man was God's Son!" {Or *a **son** of God*}
Mk 1: 1 the Son of God. {Other ancient authorities lack *the **Son** of God*}
15:39 this man was God's Son!" {Or *a **son** of God*}
Lk 9:56 Then {Other ancient authorities read *... for the **Son** of Man has not come to destroy the lives of human beings but to save them." Then*}
Jn 1:14 a father's only son, {Or *the Father's only **Son***}
6:69 the Holy One of God." {Other ancient authorities read *the Christ, the **Son** of the living God*}
17:12 except the one destined to be lost, {Gk *except the **son** of destruction*}
Ac 8:36 + v.37 < *And he replied, "I believe that Jesus Christ is the **Son** of God."*
2Th 2: 3 the one destined for destruction. {Gk *the **son** of destruction*}
Heb 2: 6 "What are human beings that you are mindful of them? {Gk *or the **son** of man that you care for him?* In the Hebrew of Psalm 8.4-6 both *man* and ***son** of man* refer to all humankind}
Tob 1: 1 son of Raphael {Other ancient authorities lack ***son** of Raphael **son** of Raguel*}
11:13 saw his son and {Other ancient authorities lack *saw his **son** and*}
2Mc 3: 5 he went to Apollonius of Tarsus, {Gk *Apollonius **son** of Tharseas*}
2Es 6: 1 "At the beginning ... before {< Ethiop: *At first by the **Son** of Man, and afterwards I myself.* >}

SONG (2)
Ex 15: 2 The LORD is my strength and my might, {Or ***song***}
Eze 33:32 like a singer of love songs, {Cn: Heb *like a love **song***}

SONGS (1)
Wis 18: 9 and already ... praises of the ancestors. {Other ancient authorities read *dangers, the ancestors already leading the **songs** of praise*}

SONS (41)
Ex 29: 9 with sashes {Gk: Heb *sashes, Aaron and his **sons***}
2Sa 23:20 sons of Ariel {Gk: Heb lacks ***sons** of*}
1Ki 20:35 member of a company of prophets {Heb *of the **sons** of the prophets*}
2Ki 2: 3 company of prophets {Heb ***sons** of the prophets*}
2: 5 company of prophets {Heb ***sons** of the prophets*}
2: 7 company of prophets {Heb ***sons** of the prophets*}
2:15 company of prophets {Heb ***sons** of the prophets*}
4: 1 company of prophets {Heb *the **sons** of the prophets*}
4:38 company of prophets was {Heb ***sons** of the prophets were*}
4:38 company of prophets." {Heb ***sons** of the prophets*}
5:22 a company of prophets {Heb ***sons** of the prophets*}
6: 1 company of prophets {Heb ***sons** of the prophets*}
9: 1 company of prophets {Heb ***sons** of the prophets*}
10: 1 of the sons of {Gk: Heb lacks *of the **sons** of*}
1Ch 2:31 son {Heb ***sons***}
2:31 son {Heb ***sons***}
2:31 son {Heb ***sons***}
3:21 son {Gk Compare Syr Vg: Heb ***sons** of*}
3:21 son {Gk Compare Syr Vg: Heb ***sons** of*}
3:21 son {Gk Compare Syr Vg: Heb ***sons** of*}
3:21 son {Gk Compare Syr Vg: Heb ***sons** of*}
3:22 son {Heb ***sons***}
4:15 son {Heb ***sons***}
7: 3 son {Heb ***sons***}
7:12 son {Heb ***sons***}
7:17 son {Heb ***sons***}
11:22 sons of {See 2 Sam 23.20: Heb lacks ***sons** of*}
11:34 Hashem {Compare Gk and 2 Sam 23.32: Heb *the **sons** of Hashem*}
2Ch 24:25 son {Gk Vg: Heb ***sons***}
Ezr 3: 9 Hodaviah {Compare 2.40; Neh 7.43; 1 Esdras 5.58: Heb ***sons** of Judah*}
Job 1: 6 the heavenly beings {Heb ***sons** of God*}
2: 1 the heavenly beings {Heb ***sons** of God*}
5: 7 just as sparks {Or *birds*; Heb ***sons** of Resheph*}
38: 7 the heavenly beings {Heb ***sons** of God*}
Ps 29: 1 O heavenly beings, {Heb ***sons** of gods*}
Isa 62: 5 your builder {Cn: Heb *your **sons***} marry you,
Mt 12:27 your own exorcists {Gk ***sons***} cast them out?
Lk 11:19 your exorcists {Gk ***sons***} cast them out?
Ac 7:23 his relatives, the Israelites. {Gk *his brothers, the **sons** of Israel*}
Tob 14: 3 and the seven sons of Tobias {Lat: Gk lacks *and the seven **sons** of Tobias*}
Sir 17:22 eye. {Other ancient authorities add *apportioning repentance to his **sons** and daughters*}

SORROW (1)
Ge 35:18 Ben-oni; {That is *Son of my **sorrow***}

SORROWS (1)
Isa 53: 3 a man of suffering {Or *a man of **sorrows***}

SOUL (4)
Jer 4:19 beating wildly; I {Another reading is *for you, O my **soul**,*} cannot
Sir 10: 8 wealth. {Other ancient authorities add here or after verse 9a, *... for such a person puts his own **soul** up for sale.*}
4Mc 10: 3 + v.4 <*for you cannot touch my **soul**, even if you wish."*
12:19 and so ended his life. {< other ancient authorities read *gave up his spirit* or *his **soul***}

SOULS (4)
Rev 18:13 chariots, slaves—and human lives. {Or *chariots, and human bodies and **souls***}
2Es 6:49 two living creatures; {Syr Ethiop: Lat *two **souls***}
4Mc 5:26 suitable for our lives, {Or ***souls***}
13:13 gave us our lives, {Or ***souls***}

SOURCE (1)
Sir 1: 4 + v.5 *The **source** of wisdom is God's word in the highest heaven,* >

SOURCES (1)
4Mc 1:20 types {Or ***sources***} of the emotions

SOUTH (4)
Ge 35:18 Benjamin. {That is *Son of the right hand* or *Son of the **South***}
1Sa 20:41 from beside the stone heap {Gk: Heb *from beside the **south***}
2Sa 24: 5 and began from {Gk Mss: Heb *encamped in Aroer **south** of*} Aroer and from
2Es 1:11 I destroyed all ... peoples of two provinces, {Other ancient authorities read *Did I not destroy ... and to the **south** burn two cities ... ?*}

SOWN (1)
Ps 97:11 Light dawns {Gk Syr Jerome: Heb *is **sown***} for the righteous,

SOWS (2)
Hos 1: 4 Jezreel; {That is *God **sows***}
2:22 Jezreel; {That is *God **sows***}

SPAN (1)
Sir 18: 2 + v.3 *he steers the world with the **span** of his hand,* >

SPARED (1)
Sir 17:20 + v.21 < *has neither left them nor abandoned them, but has **spared** them.*

SPEAK (5)
Est 1:22 house. {Heb adds *and **speak** according to the language of his people*}
Job 12: 8 ask the plants of the earth, {Or ***speak** to the earth*}
Lk 8:10 I speak {Gk lacks *I **speak***}
2Es 12:32 of days ... and speak {Syr: Lat lacks *of days ... and **speak***}
14:19 Let me speak {Most Lat Mss lack *Let me **speak***}

SPEAKING (1)
Isa 58:13 or pursuing your own affairs; {Heb *or* ***speaking*** *words*}

SPEAKS (1)
2Es 16:36 do not disbelieve what the Lord says. {Cn: Lat *do not believe the gods of whom the Lord* ***speaks***}

SPEAR (1)
Mt 27:49 save him." {Other ancient authorities add *And another took a* ***spear*** *and pierced his side, and out came water and blood*}

SPEEDS (1)
Isa 8: 1 Maher-shalal-hash-baz," {That is *The spoil* ***speeds,*** *the prey hastens*}

SPENT (2)
Pr 30: 1 How can I prevail? {Or *I am* ***spent***. Meaning of Heb uncertain}
Lk 8:43 and had spent all she had on physicians, {Other ancient authorities lack *and had* ***spent*** *all she had on physicians*}

SPIDER (1)
Pr 30:28 the lizard {Or ***spider***} can be grasped

SPIDER'S (1)
Wis 5:14 like a light frost {Other ancient authorities read ***spider's*** *web*}

SPIRIT (38)
Ge 1: 2 while a wind from God {Or *while the* ***spirit*** *of God* or *while a mighty wind*}
Ecc 12: 7 the breath {Or *the* ***spirit***} returns to God
Jer 51: 1 stir up a destructive wind {Or *stir up the* ***spirit*** *of a destroyer*}
Eze 37: 5 cause breath {Or ***spirit***} to enter you,
37: 6 put breath {Or ***spirit***} in you,
37: 9 say to the breath: {Or *wind* or ***spirit***}
37: 9 O breath, {Or *wind* or ***spirit***}
Mt 22:43 David by the Spirit {Gk *in* ***spirit***}
27:50 and breathed his last. {Or *gave up his* ***spirit***}
Lk 9:56 rebuked them. [56]Then {Other ancient authorities read *rebuked them, and said, "You do not know what* ***spirit*** *you are of,* >}
10:21 rejoiced in the Holy Spirit {Other authorities read *in the* ***spirit***}
11: 2 Your kingdom come. {A few ancient authorities read *Your Holy* ***Spirit*** *come upon us and cleanse us.* >}
Jn 3: 8 The wind {The same Greek word means both *wind* and ***spirit***} blows
Ac 6:10 the Spirit {Or ***spirit***} with which he spoke.
20:22 And now, as a captive to the Spirit, {Or *And now, bound in the* ***spirit***}
Ro 1: 4 according to the spirit {Or ***Spirit***}
8: 2 Spirit {Or ***spirit***}
8: 4 Spirit. {Or ***spirit***}
8: 5 Spirit {Or ***spirit***}
8: 5 Spirit. {Or ***spirit***}
8: 6 Spirit {Or ***spirit***}
8: 9 Spirit, {Or ***spirit***}
8:10 Spirit {Or ***spirit***}
Eph 2:22 are built together spiritually {Gk *in the* ***Spirit***}
Php 3: 3 worship in the Spirit of God {Other ancient authorities read *worship God in* ***spirit***}
1Ti 3:16 vindicated in spirit, {Or *by the* ***Spirit***}
1Pe 1:22 to the truth {Other ancient authorities add *through the* ***Spirit***}
1Jn 5: 7 There are three that testify: {A few other authorities read (with variations) *[7]There are three that testify in heaven, the Father, the Word, and the Holy* ***Spirit,*** >}
Rev 1:10 in the spirit {Or *in the* ***Spirit***}
4: 2 in the spirit, {Or *in the* ***Spirit***}
11:11 the breath {Or *the* ***spirit***}
13:15 to give breath {Or ***spirit***}
17: 3 in the spirit {Or *in the* ***Spirit***}
21:10 in the spirit {Or *in the* ***Spirit***}
AdE 16:12 and our life, {Gk *our* ***spirit***}
Sir 9: 9 and in blood {Heb: Gk *by your* ***spirit***}
Bel 1:36 with the speed of the wind {Or *by the power of his* ***spirit***}
4Mc 12:19 and so ended his life. {< other ancient authorities read *gave up his* ***spirit*** or *his soul*}

SPIRITS (2)
Zec 6: 5 "These are the four winds {Or ***spirits***}
Mk 16:14 risen. {Other ancient authorities add, in whole or in part, *... truth and power of God to prevail over the unclean things of the* ***spirits.*** >}

SPIRITUAL (1)
Mk 16:14 risen. {Other ancient authorities add, in whole or in part, *... that they may inherit the* ***spiritual*** *and imperishable glory of righteousness that is in heaven."*}

SPIRITUALLY (1)
Rev 11: 8 is prophetically {Or *allegorically*; Gk ***spiritually***}

SPLENDOR (1)
Ps 110: 3 on the holy mountains. {Another reading is *in holy* ***splendor***}

SPOIL (1)
Isa 8: 1 Maher-shalal-hash-baz," {That is *The* ***spoil*** *speeds, the prey hastens*}

SPOKE (3)
Dt 31: 1 When Moses had finished speaking all {Q Ms Gk: MT *Moses went and* ***spoke***}
1Sa 9:25 a bed was spread for Saul {Gk: Heb *and he* ***spoke*** *with Saul*}
Mk 16:14 risen. {Other ancient authorities add, in whole or in part, *... Therefore reveal your righteousness now"—thus they* ***spoke*** *to Christ.* >}

SPOKEN (1)
Mt 27:35 casting lots; {Other ancient authorities add *in order that what had been* ***spoken*** *through the prophet might be fulfilled,* >}

SPRING (1)
Jdg 15:19 En-hakkore, {That is *The* ***Spring*** *of the One who Called*}

SPRINKLED (1)
Rev 19:13 dipped in {Other ancient authorities read ***sprinkled*** *with*} blood,

SQUARE (1)
Tob 2: 4 from the square {Other ancient authorities lack *from the* ***square***}

STADIA (11)
Lk 24:13 seven miles {Gk *sixty* ***stadia;*** other ancient authorities read *a hundred sixty* ***stadia***}
Jn 6:19 about three or four miles, {Gk *about twenty-five or thirty* ***stadia***}
11:18 two miles {Gk *fifteen* ***stadia***}
Rev 14:20 two hundred miles. {Gk *one thousand six hundred* ***stadia***}
21:16 fifteen hundred miles; {Gk *twelve thousand* ***stadia***}
2Mc 12: 9 thirty miles {Gk *two hundred forty* ***stadia***}
12:10 a mile {Gk *nine* ***stadia***}
12:16 a quarter of a mile {Gk *two* ***stadia***}
12:17 ninety-five miles {Gk *seven hundred fifty* ***stadia***}
12:29 seventy-five miles {Gk *six hundred* ***stadia***}

STAIN (1)
Sir 22: 6 + v.8 < *Children who are disdainfully and boorishly haughty* ***stain*** *the nobility of their kindred.*

STAIRWAY (1)
Ge 28:12 dreamed that there was a ladder {Or ***stairway*** **or** *ramp*}

STAND (3)
Lev 19:16 not profit by the blood {Heb ***stand*** *against the blood*}
Job 38:14 and it is dyed {Cn: Heb *and they* ***stand*** *forth*}
Eze 29: 7 made all their legs unsteady. {Syr: Heb ***stand***}

STATE (1)
1Es 6:32 any of the things herein written, {Other authorities read ***stated*** *above* or *added in writing*}

STATER (1)
Mt 17:27 coin; {Gk ***stater***; the stater was worth two didrachmas}

STATURE (3)
SS 7: 7 You are stately {Heb *This your* ***stature*** *is*}
Lk 2:52 Jesus increased in wisdom and in years, {Or *in* ***stature***}
12:25 add a single hour to your span of life? {Or *add a cubit to your* ***stature***}

STEADFAST (3)
Ps 51:10 put a new and right {Or ***steadfast***} spirit
108: 1 my heart is steadfast; {Heb Mss Gk Syr: MT lacks *my heart is* ***steadfast***}
144: 2 my rock {With 18.2 and 2 Sam 22.2: Heb *my* ***steadfast*** *love*} and my fortress,

STEEL (1)
Sir 31:26 tests the work of the smith, {Heb: Gk *tests the hardening of* ***steel*** *by dipping*}

STEERS (1)
Sir 18: 2 + v.3 *he* ***steers*** *the world with the span of his hand,* >

STELE (1)
3Mc 2:27 set up a stone {Gk ***stele***}

STEMS (1)
Eze 19:11 Its strongest stem became a ruler's scepter; {Heb *Its strongest* ***stems*** *became rulers' scepters*}

STEPPED (1)
Jn 5: 3 + v.4 < *whoever* ***stepped*** *in first after the stirring of the water was made well* >

STEPS (1)
Ps 17:11 They track me down; {One Ms Compare Syr: MT *Our* ***steps***}

STILL (1)
2Es 1:16 complain. {Other ancient authorities read verse 16, *... but* ***still*** *the people complain also concerning their own destruction.*

STIR (1)
2Es 13: 2 As I kept looking ... the figure of a man come up {Other ancient authorities read *I saw a wind arise from the sea and* ***stir*** *up*}

STIRRED (1)
Jn 5: 3 + v.4 < *an angel of the Lord went down at certain seasons into the pool, and* ***stirred*** *up the water;* >

STIRRING (2)
Jn 5: 3 paralyzed. {Other ancient authorities add, wholly or in part, *waiting for the* ***stirring*** *of the water; [4]for ... whoever stepped in first after the* ***stirring*** *of the water was made well* >}

STOLEN (1)
Ge 44: 4 Why ... my silver cup? {Gk Compare Vg: Heb lacks *Why have you* ***stolen*** *my silver cup?* }

STOMACH (1)
Lk 15:16 filled himself with {Other ancient authorities read *filled his* ***stomach*** *with*}

STONE (3)
1Sa 7:12 Ebenezer; {That is ***Stone*** *of Help*}
Lk 11:11 child asks for {Other ancient authorities add *bread, will give a* ***stone;*** *or if your child asks for*}
Rev 15: 6 pure bright linen, {Other ancient authorities read ***stone***}

STONES (1)
2Co 3: 7 letters on stone tablets, {Gk *on* ***stones***}

STONY (2)
Sir 17:15 + v.16 < *to make for themselves hearts of flesh in place of their* ***stony*** *hearts.* >
32:20 stumble at an obstacle twice. {Heb: Gk *stumble on* ***stony*** *ground*}

STOOD (2)
Rev 12:18 Then the dragon {< other ancient authorities read *Then I* ***stood***} took his stand
Sir 25: 1 I take pleasure ... the sight of God and of mortals: {Syr Lat: Gk *In three things I was beautiful and I* ***stood*** *in beauty before the Lord and mortals.*}

STOPS (1)
2Es 13:47 the Most High will stop {Syr: Lat ***stops***} the channels

STORED (1)
Jas 5: 3 will eat your flesh like fire. You have laid up treasure {Or *will eat your flesh, since you have* ***stored*** *up fire*}

STORM (1)
2Es 7:*41* or heat or winter {Or ***storm***}

STORY (1)
1Ki 6:10 each story {Heb lacks *each* ***story***}

STRANGE (4)
Pr 2:16 the loose {Heb ***strange***} woman
5: 3 a loose {Heb ***strange***} woman
7: 5 the loose {Heb ***strange***} woman
22:14 a loose {Heb ***strange***} woman

STRANGER (3)
1Sa 23: 7 "God has given {Gk Tg: Heb *made a* ***stranger*** *of*}
Pr 6: 1 bound yourself to another, {Or *a* ***stranger***}
4Mc 11: 6 + v.8 < *you are a* ***stranger*** *to God and persecute those who serve him."*

STRANGERS (2)
Isa 29: 5 But the multitude of your foes {Cn: Heb ***strangers***}
Sir 21:25 babblers speak of what is not their concern. {Other ancient authorities read *of* ***strangers*** *speak of these things*}

STRANGLE (1)
4Mc 10: 7 to break his spirit, {Gk *to* ***strangle*** *him*}

STRANGLED (3)
Ac 15:20 and from whatever has been strangled {Other ancient authorities lack *and from whatever has been* ***strangled***}

Ac 15:29 and from what is strangled {Other ancient authorities lack *and from what is **strangled***}
21:25 and from what is strangled {Other ancient authorities lack *and from what is **strangled***}

STRANGLES (1)
Tob 3: 8 the one who kills {Other ancient authorities read ***strangles***} your husbands!

STRAW (2)
2Es 15:61 broken down by them like stubble, {Other ancient authorities read *like dry **straw***}
16: 6 fire in the stubble once is has started to burn? {Other ancient authorities read *fire when dry **straw** has been set on fire*}

STREET (1)
AdE 4: 5 + v.6 *So Hachratheus went out to Mordecai in the **street** of the city opposite the city gate.*

STRENGTH (3)
Ps 22:15 my mouth {Cn: Heb ***strength***} is dried up
99: 4 Mighty King, {Cn: Heb *And a king's **strength***}
Pr 24: 5 Wise warriors ar mightier than strong ones, {Gk Compare Syr Tg: Heb *A wise man is **strength***}

STRENGTHEN (1)
Sir 24:23 + v.24 < *cling to him so that he may **strengthen** you;* >

STRICKEN (1)
Tob 7: 7 father!" {Other ancient authorities add *When he heard that Tobit had lost his sight, he was **stricken** with grief and wept. Then he said,*}

STRIFE (2)
Ps 80: 6 You make us the scorn {Syr: Heb ***strife***}
Sir 19: 5 + v.6 < *One who controls the tongue will live without **strife,***

STRIKE (1)
Jer 18:18 bring charges against him, {Heb ***strike** him with the tongue*}

STRIKING (2)
2Sa 8:13 he killed ... Edomites {Gk: Heb *returned from **striking** down eighteen thousand Arameans*}
Sir 16:10 stubbornness. {Other ancient authorities add *Chastising, showing mercy, **striking,** healing, the Lord persisted in mercy and discipline.*}

STRIVES (2)
Ge 32:28 Israel, {That is *The one who **strives** with God* or *God **strives***}

STRONG (4)
2Sa 22:33 The God who has girded me with strength {Q Ms Gk Syr Vg Compare Ps 18.32: MT *God is my **strong** refuge*}
Ps 80:15 planted. {Heb adds from verse 17 *and upon the one whom you made **strong** for yourself*}
Sir 24:23 + v.24 *"Do not cease to be **strong** in the Lord,* >
2Es 13: 3 I saw that this man flew {Syr Ethiop Arab Arm: Lat *grew **strong***}

STRONGLY (1)
Lk 16:16 everyone tries to enter it by force. {Or *everyone is **strongly** urged to enter it*}

STRUCK (1)
AdE 9: 4 + v.5 *So the Jews **struck** down all their enemies with the sword,* >

STRUCTURE (1)
1Ki 6: 6 The lowest story {Gk: Heb ***structure***}

STUMBLE (3)
Jer 18:15 they have stumbled {Gk Syr Vg: Heb *they made them **stumble***}
Mt 24:10 many will fall away, {Or ***stumble***}
Mk 4:17 immediately they fall away. {Or ***stumble***}

STUMBLED (1)
Mk 6: 3 And they took offense {Or ***stumbled***}

STUMBLES (2)
Ps 37:24 though we stumble, {Heb *he **stumbles***}
Mt 13:21 immediately falls away. {Gk ***stumbles***}

STUMBLING (1)
Eze 18:30 iniquity will be your ruin. {Or *so that they shall not be a **stumbling** block of iniquity to you*}

STUPID (1)
Sir 22:23 inheritance. {Other ancient authorities add < *or admire a rich person who is **stupid.***}

SUCCOTH (13)
Lev 23:34 booths {Or *tabernacles*: Heb ***succoth***}
Dt 16:13 booths {Or *tabernacles*; Heb ***succoth***}
16:16 booths. {Or *tabernacles*; Heb ***succoth***}
Dt 31:10 booths, {Or *tabernacles*; Heb ***succoth***}
2Sa 11:11 remain in booths; {Or *at **Succoth***}
Ezr 3: 4 booths, {Or *tabernacles*; Heb ***succoth***}
Ne 8:14 booths {Or *tabernacles*; Heb ***succoth***}
8:15 booths, {Or *tabernacles*; Heb ***succoth***}
8:16 booths {Or *tabernacles*; Heb ***succoth***}
8:17 booths {Or *tabernacles*; Heb ***succoth***}
Zec 14:16 booths. {Or *tabernacles*; Heb ***succoth***}
14:18 booths. {Or *tabernacles*; Heb ***succoth***}
14:19 booths. {Or *tabernacles*; Heb ***succoth***}

SUCH (6)
Lev 14:31 afford, [31]one {Gk Syr: Heb *afford,* [31]***such** as he can afford, one*}
2Sa 18: 3 But you are worth ten thousand of us; {Gk Vg Symmachus: Heb *for now there are ten thousand **such** as we*}
Col 3: 7 when you were living that life. {Or *living among **such** people*}
1Ti 6: 5 gain. {Other ancient authorities add *Withdraw yourself from **such** people*}
Sir 10: 8 wealth. {Other ancient authorities add here or after verse 9a, *... for **such** a person puts his own soul up for sale.*}
29: 7 Many refuse to lend, not because of meanness, but from fear {Other ancient authorities read *many refuse to lend, therefore, because of **such** meanness; they are afraid*}

SUDDEN (2)
Isa 65:23 bear children for calamity; {Or ***sudden** terror*}
Sir 16: 3 numbers; {Other ancient authorities add *For you will groan in untimely mourning, and will know of their **sudden** end.*}

SUFFER (2)
1Ti 4:10 we tail and struggle, {Other ancient authorities read ***suffer** reproach*}
4Mc 13:17 For if we so die, {Other ancient authorities read ***suffer***}

SUFFERING (1)
1Sa 9:16 the suffering of {Gk: Heb lacks *the **suffering** of*}

SUM (1)
Sir 51:28 Hear but a little ... acquire silver and gold. {Syr Compare Heb: Gk *Get instruction with a large **sum** of silver, and you will gain by it much gold.*}

SUN (3)
Hab 3:11 the moon {Heb ***sun,** moon*} stood still
Lk 23:45 the sun's light failed; {Or *the **sun** was eclipsed.* Other ancient authorities read *the **sun** was darkened*}

SUPERVISOR (8)
Ne 3: 9 ruler of half the district of {Or ***supervisor** of half the portion assigned to*}
3:12 ruler of half the district of {Or ***supervisor** of half the portion assigned to*}
3:14 ruler of the district of {Or ***supervisor** of the portion assigned to*}
3:15 ruler of half the district of {Or ***supervisor** of the portion assigned to*}
3:16 ruler of half the district of {Or ***supervisor** of half the portion assigned to*}
3:17 ruler of half the district of {Or ***supervisor** of half the portion assigned to*}
3:18 ruler of half the district of {Or ***supervisor** of half the portion assigned to*}
3:19 ruler {Or ***supervisor***}

SUPPER (1)
Jn 13: 4 got up from the table, {Gk *from **supper***}

SUPPLANTS (2)
Ge 25:26 Jacob. {That is *He takes by the heel* or *He **supplants***}
27:36 Jacob? {That is *He **supplants*** or *He takes by the heel*}

SUPPLEMENT (1)
3Mc 7:22 with extreme fear. {Other ancient authorities read *with a very large **supplement***}

SUPPLICATION (1)
Wis 16:25 who had need, {Or *who made **supplication***}

SUPPLICATIONS (1)
Jer 31: 9 and with consolations {Gk Compare Vg Tg: Heb ***supplications***}

SUPPORT (1)
Sir 49:15 Joseph; {Heb Syr: Gk adds *the leader of his brothers, the **support** of the people*}

SUPPORTS (1)
Sir 19:20 + v.21 < *even if later he does it, he angers the one who **supports** him.*

SURELY (1)
Jnh 2: 4 how {Theodotion: Heb ***surely***} shall I look again

SURRENDER (1)
1Sa 23:11 And now, will {Q Ms Compare Gk: MT *Will the men of Keilah **surrender** me into his hand? Will*}

SURRENDERED (1)
4Mc 15:24 disregarded all these {Other ancient authorities read *having bidden them farewell, **surrendered** them*}

SURROUNDED (1)
Eze 41: 7 The passageway {Cn: Heb *it was **surrounded***} of the side chambers

SURROUNDING (1)
Jdg 20:43 and trod them down {Gk: Heb ***Surrounding***}

SURVIVE (1)
2Es 13:22 and ... not survive, {Syr Arab 1: Lat lacks *and ... not **survive***}

SWEETNESS (1)
Pr 27: 9 soul is torn by trouble. {Gk: Heb *the **sweetness** of a friend is better than one's own counsel*}

SWELLING (1)
Ac 1:18 and falling headlong, {Or ***swelling** up*}

SWELLINGS (1)
Isa 45: 2 and level the mountains, {Q Ms Gk: MT *the **swellings***}

SWEPT (1)
Jer 46:15 Why has Apis fled? {Gk: Heb *Why was it **swept** away*}

SWIFTLY (1)
Isa 49:17 Your builders outdo your destroyers, {Or *Your children come **swiftly;** your destroyers*}

SWORD (4)
Jdg 4:15 into a panic {Heb adds *to the **sword***; compare verse 16}
Jer 50:38 A drought {Another reading is *A **sword***} against her waters,
AdE 9: 4 + v.5 *So the Jews struck down all their enemies with the **sword,*** >
4Mc 16:20 wielding a knife {Gk ***sword***}

SWORD-EDGES (1)
2Sa 2:16 Helkath-hazzurim, {That is *Field of **Sword-edges***}

SWORDS (1)
Ps 59: 7 with sharp words {Heb *with **swords***}

SYMBOL (1)
1Co 11:10 a symbol of {Gk lacks *a **symbol** of*}

SYMEON (2)
Lk 2:25 Simeon; {Gk ***Symeon***}
2:34 Simeon {Gk ***Symeon***}

SYNAGOGUE (1)
Mt 9:18 of the synagogue {Gk lacks *of the **synagogue***}

SYZYGUS (1)
Php 4: 3 my loyal companion, {Or *loyal **Syzygus***}

T

TABERNACLE (13)
Heb 8: 2 tent {Or ***tabernacle***}
8: 5 tent, {Or ***tabernacle***}
9: 2 tent {Or ***tabernacle***}
9: 3 tent {Or ***tabernacle***}
9: 6 tent {Or ***tabernacle***}
9: 8 tent {Or ***tabernacle***}
9:11 tent {Or ***tabernacle***}
9:21 tent {Or ***tabernacle***}
13:10 tent {Or ***tabernacle***}
Rev 15: 5 tent {Or ***tabernacle***}
21: 3 home {Gk ***tabernacle***}
21: 3 dwell {Gk ***tabernacle***}
Tob 13:10 tent {Or ***tabernacle***}

TABERNACLES (14)
Lev 23:34 booths {Or ***tabernacles***: Heb *succoth*}
Dt 16:13 booths {Or ***tabernacles***; Heb *succoth*}
16:16 booths. {Or ***tabernacles***; Heb *succoth*}
31:10 booths, {Or ***tabernacles***; Heb *succoth*}
Ezr 3: 4 booths, {Or ***tabernacles***; Heb *succoth*}
Ne 8:14 booths {Or ***tabernacles***; Heb *succoth*}
8:15 booths, {Or ***tabernacles***; Heb *succoth*}
8:16 booths {Or ***tabernacles***; Heb *succoth*}

Ne 8:17 booths {Or *tabernacles*; Heb *succoth*}
Zec 14:16 booths. {Or *tabernacles*; Heb *succoth*}
14:18 booths. {Or *tabernacles*; Heb *succoth*}
14:19 booths. {Or *tabernacles*; Heb *succoth*}
Jn 7: 2 Booths {Or ***Tabernacles***}
1Mc 10:21 booths, {Or ***tabernacles***}

TAHTIM-HODSHI (1)

2Sa 24: 6 to the land of the Hittites; {Gk: Heb *to the land of* ***Tahtim-hodshi***}

TAKE (9)

Nu 26: 4 take a census of the people, {Heb lacks ***take*** *a census of the people*: Compare verse 2}
Jer 4: 5 shout aloud {Or *shout,* ***take*** *your weapons*: Heb *shout, fill* (your hand)}
19: 1 take with you {Syr Tg Compare Gk: Heb lacks ***take*** *with you*}
Joel 2: 7 they do not swerve from {Gk Syr Vg: Heb *they do not* ***take*** *a pledge along*}
Mt 27:65 "You have a guard {Or ***Take*** *a guard*}
Php 4: 8 think about {Gk ***take*** *account of*} these things
1Th 4: 4 how to control your own body {Or *how to* ***take*** *a wife for himself*}
Sir 11:14 + v.16 < *evil grows old with those who* ***take*** *pride in malice.*
30:13 make his yoke heavy, {Heb: Gk ***take*** *pains with him*}

TAKEN (4)

Lk 17:35 + v.36 *"Two will be in the field; one will be* ***taken*** *and the other left."*
Jn 10:18 No one takes {Other ancient authorities read *has* ***taken***} it from me,
Sir 44:17 he kept the race alive; {Heb: Gk *was* ***taken*** *in exchange*}
2Es 14:48 did so. {Syr adds < *At that time Ezra was caught up, and* ***taken*** *to the place* >

TAKES (4)

Ge 25:26 Jacob. {That is *He* ***takes*** *by the heel* or *He supplants*}
27:36 Jacob? {That is *He supplants* or *He* ***takes*** *by the heel*}
Pr 25:20 Like vinegar on a wound {Gk: Heb *Like one who* ***takes*** *off a garment on a cold day, like vinegar on lye*}
2Es 8:22 at whose command they are changed to wind and fire, {Syr: Lat *they whose service* ***takes*** *the form of wind and fire*}

TALENT (1)

Rev 16:21 weighing about a hundred pounds, {Gk *weighing about a* ***talent***}

TALENTS (1)

1Es 3:21 makes everyone talk in millions. {Gk ***talents***}

TARTAROS (1)

2Pe 2: 4 cast them into hell {Gk ***Tartaros***}

TASKS (1)

Ro 12:16 associate with the lowly; {Or *give yourselves to humble* ***tasks***}

TAUGHT (2)

Jdg 8:16 he trampled {With verse 7, Compare Gk: Heb *he* ***taught***} the people of Succcoth.
Isa 50: 4 the tongue of a teacher, {Cn: Heb *of those who are* ***taught***}

TAUTNESS (1)

4Mc 7:13 his body no longer tense and firm, {Gk *the* ***tautness*** *of the body already loosed*}

TEACH (1)

SS 8: 2 the one who bore me. {Gk Syr: Heb *my mother; she* (or *you*) *will* ***teach*** *me*}

TEACHING (1)

Job 11: 4 'My conduct {Gk: Heb ***teaching***} is pure,

TEARS (1)

Mk 9:24 cried out, {Other ancient authorities add *with* ***tears***}

TELL (2)

Est 1:18 will rebel against {Cn: Heb *will* ***tell***} the king's officials,
Mk 8:26 village." {Other ancient authorities add *or* ***tell*** *anyone in the village*}

TEMPLE (4)

Job 36:14 life ends in shame. {Heb *ends among the* ***temple*** *prostitutes*}
Eze 41:26 sidewalls of the vestibule. {Cn: Heb *vestibule. And the side chambers of the* ***temple*** *and the canopies*}
Mal 1:10 shut the temple {Heb lacks ***temple***} doors,
Jn 11:48 destroy both our holy place {Or *our* ***temple***; Greek *our place*}

TEMPTATION (6)

Mt 6:13 us to the time of trial, {Or *us into* ***temptation***}
26:41 into the time of trial; {Or *into* ***temptation***}
Mk 14:38 into the time of trial; {Or *into* ***temptation***}
Lk 11: 4 us to the time of trial." {Or *us into* ***temptation***. >}
22:40 into the time of trial." {Or *into* ***temptation***}
22:46 into the time of trial." {Or *into* ***temptation***}

TEMPTED (2)

Heb 4:15 has been tested {Or ***tempted***} as we are,
11:37 sawn in two, {Other ancient authorities add *they were* ***tempted***}

TEN (6)

Eze 45: 1 and twenty {Gk: Heb ***ten***} thousand cubits wide;
48: 9 and twenty {Compare 45.1: Heb ***ten***} thousand
48:13 the width twenty {Gk: Heb ***ten***} thousand.
2Es 13:40 these are the nine {Other Lat Mss ***ten***; >} tribes
14:11 and nine {Cn: Lat Ethiop ***ten***} of its parts
14:12 For the age is divided into twelve parts, ... part. {Syr lacks verses 11, 12: Ethiop *For the world is divided into* ***ten*** *parts,* >}

TEND (1)

Sir 17:15 + v.16 *Their ways from youth* ***tend*** *toward evil,* >

TENT (5)

1Ch 17: 5 but I have lived in a tent and a tabernacle. {Gk 2 Sam 7.6: Heb *but I have been from* ***tent*** *to* ***tent*** *and from tabernacle*}
Eze 41: 1 the pilasters. {Compare Gk: Heb ***tent***}
2Pe 1:13 I am in this body, {Gk ***tent***}
1:14 my death {Gk *the putting off of my* ***tent***}

TENTH (2)

Heb 7: 5 to collect tithes {Or *a* ***tenth***}
7: 6 collected tithes {Or *a* ***tenth***}

TENTS (5)

Mt 17: 4 dwellings {Or ***tents***}
Mk 9: 5 dwellings, {Or ***tents***}
Lk 9:33 dwellings, {Or ***tents***}
16: 9 homes. {Gk ***tents***}
Jdt 3: 3 and all our encampments {Gk *all the sheepfolds of our* ***tents***}

TERAPHIM (2)

1Sa 19:13 Michal took an idol {Heb *took the* ***teraphim***}
19:16 the idol {Heb *the* ***teraphim***} was in the bed,

TEREBINTH (1)

Ge 12: 6 oak {Or ***terebinth***}

TEREBINTHS (4)

Ge 13:18 oaks {Or ***terebinths***}
14:13 oaks {Or ***terebinths***}
18: 1 oaks {Or ***terebinths***}
Dt 11:30 oak {Gk Syr: Compare Gen 12.6; Heb *oaks* or ***terebinths***}

TERM (1)

Mk 16:14 risen. {Other ancient authorities add, in whole or in part, < *And Christ replied to them, "The* ***term*** *of years of Satan's power has been fulfilled,* >}

TERRIBLE (1)

Mk 16:14 risen. {Other ancient authorities add, in whole or in part, ... *term of years of Satan's power has been fulfilled, but other* ***terrible*** *things draw near.* >}

TERRIFIED (1)

2Es 10:25 I was too ... terrified. While {Syr Ethiop Arab 1: Lat lacks *I was too ...* ***terrified.*** *While*}

TERRITORY (1)

2Ch 16: 1 the territory of {Heb lacks *the* ***territory*** *of*}

TERROR (1)

Isa 65:23 bear children for calamity; {Or *sudden* ***terror***}

TEST (1)

Ex 17: 7 Massah {That is ***Test***}

TESTAMENT (2)

Lev 16:13 covenant, {Or *treaty*, or ***testament***; Heb *eduth*}
24: 3 covenant, {Or *treaty*, or ***testament***; Heb *eduth*}

TESTED (1)

Pr 27:21 is tested {Heb lacks *is* ***tested***}

TESTIFIED (1)

Ru 1:21 has dealt harshly with {Or *has* ***testified*** *against*}

TESTIFY (4)

1Sa 12: 3 Testify against me {Gk: Heb lacks ***Testify*** *against me*}
1Jn 5: 7 There are three that testify: {A few other authorities read (with variations) *[7]There are three that* ***testify*** *in heaven, ... [8]And there are three that* ***testify*** *on earth:*}
2Es 2:36 I publicly call on my savior to witness. {Other ancient authorities read *I* ***testify*** *that my savior has been commissioned by the Lord*}

TESTIMONY (38)

Ex 16:34 covenant, {Or *treaty* or ***testimony***; Heb *eduth*}
25:16 covenant {Or *treaty*, or ***testimony***; Heb *eduth*}
25:21 covenant {Or *treaty*, or ***testimony***; Heb *eduth*}
25:22 covenant, {Or *treaty*, or ***testimony***; Heb *eduth*}
26:33 covenant {Or *treaty*, or ***testimony***; Heb *eduth*}
26:34 covenant {Or *treaty*, or ***testimony***; Heb *eduth*}
27:21 covenant, {Or *treaty*, or ***testimony***; Heb *eduth*}
30: 6 covenant, {Or *treaty*, or ***testimony***; Heb *eduth*}
30: 6 covenant, {Or *treaty*, or ***testimony***; Heb *eduth*}
30:26 covenant, {Or *treaty*, or ***testimony***; Heb *eduth*}
30:36 covenant {Or *treaty*, or ***testimony***; Heb *eduth*}
31: 7 covenant, {Or *treaty*, or ***testimony***; Heb *eduth*}
31:18 covenant, {Or *treaty*, or ***testimony***; Heb *eduth*}
32:15 covenant, {Or *treaty*, or ***testimony***; Heb *eduth*}
34:29 covenant {Or *treaty*, or ***testimony***; Heb *eduth*}
38:21 covenant, {Or *treaty*, or ***testimony***; Heb *eduth*}
39:35 covenant {Or *treaty*, or ***testimony***; Heb *eduth*}
40: 3 covenant, {Or *treaty*, or ***testimony***; Heb *eduth*}
40: 5 covenant, {Or *treaty*, or ***testimony***; Heb *eduth*}
40:20 covenant {Or *treaty*, or ***testimony***; Heb *eduth*}
40:21 covenant; {Or *treaty*, or ***testimony***; Heb *eduth*}
Nu 1:50 covenant, {Or *treaty*, or ***testimony***; Heb *eduth*}
1:53 covenant, {Or *treaty*, or ***testimony***; Heb *eduth*}
1:53 covenant. {Or *treaty*, or ***testimony***; Heb *eduth*}
4: 5 covenant {Or *treaty*, or ***testimony***; Heb *eduth*}
7:89 covenant {Or *treaty*, or ***testimony***; Heb *eduth*}
9:15 covenant; {Or *treaty*, or ***testimony***; Heb *eduth*}
10:11 covenant. {Or *treaty*, or ***testimony***; Heb *eduth*}
17: 4 covenant, {Or *treaty*, or ***testimony***; Heb *eduth*}
17: 7 covenant. {Or *treaty*, or ***testimony***; Heb *eduth*}
17: 8 covenant {Or *treaty*, or ***testimony***; Heb *eduth*}
17:10 covenant, {Or *treaty*, or ***testimony***; Heb *eduth*}
18: 2 covenant. {Or *treaty*, or ***testimony***; Heb *eduth*}
Jos 4:16 covenant, {Or *treaty*, or ***testimony***; Heb *eduth*}
2Ki 11:12 covenant; {Or *treaty* or ***testimony***; Heb *eduth*}
2Ch 23:11 covenant; {Or *treaty*, or ***testimony***; Heb *eduth*}
24: 6 covenant?" {Or *treaty*, or ***testimony***; Heb *eduth*}
1Co 2: 1 mystery {Other ancient authorities read ***testimony***}

TETRARCH (7)

Mt 14: 1 ruler {Gk ***tetrarch***}
Lk 3: 1 ruler {Gk ***tetrarch***}
3: 1 ruler {Gk ***tetrarch***}
3: 1 ruler {Gk ***tetrarch***}
3:19 ruler, {Gk ***tetrarch***}
9: 7 ruler {Gk ***tetrarch***}
Ac 13: 1 ruler, {Gk ***tetrarch***}

THA (1)

1Co 16:22 Our Lord, come! {Gk *Marana* ***tha***. >}

THAN (7)

Job 4:17 righteous before {Or *more* ***than***} God? ... pure before {Or *more* ***than***} their Maker?
Pr 27: 9 but the soul is torn by trouble. {Gk: Heb *the sweetness of a friend is better* ***than*** *one's own counsel*}
Jdt 7:27 captured by them. {Other ancient authorities add ***than*** *to die of thirst*}
Sir 10: 8 wealth. {Other ancient authorities add here or after verse 9a, *Nothing is more wicked* ***than*** *one who loves money,* >}
18:29 proverbs. {Other ancient authorities add *Better is confidence in the one Lord* ***than*** *clinging with a dead heart to a dead one.*}
20:31 + v.32 < *better* ***than*** *a masterless charioteer of one's own life.*

THANK (1)

Ro 15: 9 I will confess {Or ***thank***} you

THANKFUL (1)

1Co 1:14 I thank God {Other ancient authorities read *I am* ***thankful***}

THANKS (1)

Jn 6:23 after the Lord had given thanks. {Other ancient authorities lack *after the Lord had given* ***thanks***}

THARSEAS (1)

2Mc 3: 5 Apollonius of Tarsus, {Gk *Apollonius son of* ***Tharseas***}

THEREFORE (7)

Ge 4:15 "Not so! {Gk Syr Vg: Heb ***Therefore***}
Mt 23:13 + v.14 < *you make long prayers;* ***therefore*** *you will receive the greater condemnation*
Mk 16:14 risen. {Other ancient authorities add, in whole or in part, ... ***Therefore*** *reveal your righteousness now"—thus they spoke to Christ.* >}
Sir 29: 7 Many refuse to lend, ... from fear {Other ancient authorities read *many refuse to lend,* ***therefore,*** *because of such meanness; they are afraid*}
2Mc 7:18 Therefore {Lat: Other ancient authorities lack ***Therefore***} astounding things
2Es 1:32 says the Lord. {Other ancient authorities add ... ***Therefore,*** *says the Lord, let my Father and his angels return* >}

2Es 16:46 for in captivity and famine they will produce their children. {Other ancient authorities read ***therefore*** *those who are married may know that they will produce children for captivity and famine*}

THICK (3)

Eze 31: 3 among the clouds. {Gk: Heb ***thick*** *boughs*}

31:10 among the clouds, {Gk: Heb ***thick*** *boughs*}

31:14 among the clouds, {Gk: Heb ***thick*** *boughs*}

THICKEN (1)

Zep 1:12 who rest complacently {Heb *who* ***thicken***}

THING (2)

Da 9:24 anoint a most holy place. {Or ***thing*** **or** *one*}

Am 6:13 in Lo-debar, {Or *in a* ***thing*** *of nothingness*}

THINGS (23)

2Ki 23:16 proclaimed, {Gk: Heb *proclaimed, who had predicted these* ***things***} when Jeroboam stood

Isa 45:11 Will you question me {Cn: Heb *Ask me of* ***things*** *to come*}

Eze 36:38 the flock for sacrifices, {Heb *flock of holy* ***things***}

Mk 6:20 he was greatly perplexed; {Other ancient authorities read *he did many* ***things***}

Mk 16:14 risen. {Other ancient authorities add, in whole or in part, *... the truth and power of God to prevail over the unclean* ***things*** *of the spirits. ... but other terrible* ***things*** *draw near.* >}

Lk 10:42 need of only one thing. {Other ancient authorities read *few* ***things*** *are necessary, or only one*}

Jn 12:32 who draw all people {Other ancient authorities read *all* ***things***}

Ro 15:18 speak of anything except what Christ has accomplished {Gk *speak of those* ***things*** *that Christ has not accomplished*}

1Jn 2:20 all of you have knowledge. {Other ancient authorities read *you know all* ***things***}

Wis 12:13 care is for all people, {Or *all* ***things***}

Sir Pr: 1 also with his book {Gk *with these* ***things***}

13:13 + v.14 *When you hear these* ***things*** *in your sleep, wake up!* >

16: 9 sins; {Other ancient authorities add *All these* ***things*** *he did to the hard-hearted nations,* >}

18: 2 + v.3 <*for he is king of all* ***things*** *by his power, separating among them the holy* ***things*** *by his power, separating among them the holy* ***things*** *from the profane.*

Sir 21:25 babblers speak of what is not their concern. {Other ancient authorities read *of strangers speak of these* ***things***}

LtJ 6:63 But these idols {Gk *these* ***things***}

2Es 1:32 says the Lord. {Other ancient authorities add ... *these are the* ***things*** *you have done. ... if I have not done the* ***things*** *my Father commanded,* >}

2Es 10:49 happened. {Most Lat Mss and Arab 1 add *these were the* ***things*** *to be opened to you*}

14:48 did so. {Syr adds < *who are like him, after he had written all these* ***things.*** >}

THINK (1)

Ps 59: 7 they think, {Heb lacks *they* ***think***}

THIRD (2)

Sir 28:14 Slander {Gk *A* ***third*** *tongue*} has shaken many,

28:15 Slander {Gk *a* ***third*** *tongue*} has driven

THIRST (1)

Jdt 7:27 captured by them. {Other ancient authorities add *than to die of* ***thirst***}

THIRSTY (1)

Isa 50: 2 and die of thirst. {Or *die on the* ***thirsty*** *ground*}

THIRTEENTH (1)

AdE 3: 7 The lot fell on the fourteenth {Other ancient witnesses read ***thirteenth***; see 8.12} day

THIRTIETH (1)

2Es 3:29 during these thirty years. {Ethiop Arab 1 Arm: Lat Syr *in this* ***thirtieth*** *year*}

THIRTY (4)

1Sa 11: 8 from Judah seventy {Q Ms Gk: MT ***thirty***} thousand.

1Ch 11:11 was chief of the Three; {Compare 2 Sam 23.8: Heb ***Thirty*** or *captains*}

Jn 6:19 about three or four miles, {Gk *about twenty-five or* ***thirty*** *stadia*}

1Mc 6:37 on each were four {Cn: Some authorities read ***thirty***; >} armed men

THIRTY-TWO (1)

1Mc 6:37 on each were four {Cn: Some authorities read *thirty*; others ***thirty-two***} armed men

THOCANOS (1)

1Es 9:14 Tikvah {Gk ***Thocanos***}

THOUGH (2)

Job 13:15 See, he will kill me; I have no hope; {Or ***Though*** *he kill me, yet I will trust in him*}

3Mc 4: 6 as they were torn by the harsh treatment of the heathen. {Other ancient authorities read *as* ***though*** *torn by heathen whelps*}

THOUGHTS (2)

Ps 19:13 also from the insolent; {Or *from proud* ***thoughts***}

2Mc 9:12 not think that they are equal to God." {Or *not think* ***thoughts*** *proper only to God*}

THOUSAND (4)

1Sa 6:19 he killed seventy men of them. {Heb *killed seventy men, fifty* ***thousand*** *men*}

Rev 14:20 about two hundred miles. {Gk *one* ***thousand*** *six hundred stadia*}

21:16 fifteen hundred miles; {Gk *twelve* ***thousand*** *stadia*}

2Es 14:48 did so. {Syr adds *in the seventh year of the sixth week, five* ***thousand*** *years and three months* >}

THOUSANDS (4)

Ex 20: 6 to the thousandth generation {Or *to* ***thousands***}

34: 7 for the thousandth generation, {Or *for* ***thousands***}

Dt 5:10 to the thousandth generation {Or *to* ***thousands***}

Jer 32:18 to the thousandth generation, {Or *to* ***thousands***}

THREAD (1)

Job 7: 6 come to the end without hope. {Or *as the* ***thread*** *runs out*}

THREE (7)

1Sa 1:24 a three-year-old bull, {Q Ms Gk Syr: MT ***three*** *bulls*}

2Sa 23:18 the Thirty. {Two Heb Mss Syr: MT ***Three***}

23:19 renowned of the Thirty, {Syr Compare 1 Chr 11.25: Heb *Was he the most renowned of the* ***Three?***}

1Ch 11:20 was chief of the Thirty. {Syr: Heb ***Three***}

11:21 renowned of the Thirty, {Syr: Heb ***Three***}

2Es 5: 4 after the third period; {Literally *after the third*; Ethiop *after* ***three*** *months*; >}

14:48 did so. {Syr adds *... five thousand years and* ***three*** *months and twelve days after creation.* >}

THREE-STRINGED (1)

1Sa 18: 6 with musical instruments. {Or *triangles*, or ***three-stringed*** *instruments*}

THRESHING (1)

1Sa 19:22 to the great well that is in Secu; {Gk reads *to the well of the* ***threshing*** *floor on the bare height*}

THRESHOLD (1)

Eze 40: 6 deep. {Heb *deep, and one* ***threshold,*** *one reed deep*}

THRESHOLDS (1)

Eze 41:16 the temple was paneled, {Gk: Heb *the* ***thresholds***}

THREW (1)

Jer 41: 7 and threw them {Syr: Heb lacks *and* ***threw*** *them*; compare verse 9}

THRIVES (1)

Job 8:16 The wicked thrive {Heb *He* ***thrives***} before the sun,

THRONES (1)

Wis 9:12 worthy of the throne {Gk ***thrones***} of my father.

THROUGH (11)

Ps 68: 4 lift up a song to him who rides upon the clouds— {Or *cast up a highway for him who rides* ***through*** *the deserts*}

Mt 27:35 casting lots; {Other ancient authorities add *in order that what had been spoken* ***through*** *the prophet might be fulfilled,* >}

Ro 1:17 "The one who is righteous will live by faith." {Or *The one who is righteous* ***through*** *faith will live*}

Gal 3:11 "The one who is righteous will live by faith." {Or *The one who is righteous* ***through*** *faith will live*}

6:14 by which {Or ***through*** *whom*} the world has been crucified

Col 1:14 forgiveness of sins. {Other ancient authorities add ***through*** *his blood*}

1Pe 1:22 to the truth {Other ancient authorities add ***through*** *the Spirit*}

2Pe 1: 3 who called us by {Other ancient authorities read ***through***}

Tob 8: 3 fled to the remotest parts {Or *fled* ***through*** *the air to the parts*}

Sir 11:28 by how he ends, a person becomes known. {Heb: Gk *and* ***through*** *his children a person becomes known*}

4Mc 2:15 evident that reason rules even {Other ancient authorities read ***through***}

THROUGHOUT (1)

Sir 50:18 in sweet and full-toned melody. {Other ancient authorities read *in sweet melody* ***throughout*** *the house*}

THUS (4)

Mk 16:14 risen. {Other ancient authorities add, in whole or in part, *... Therefore reveal your righteousness now"—****thus*** *they spoke to Christ.* >}

AdE 1:13 "This is how Vashti has answered me. {Gk *Astin has said* ***thus*** *and so*}

2Es 1:32 says the Lord. {Other ancient authorities add ***Thus*** *says the Lord Almighty: Recently you also laid hands on me,* >}

4:35 'How long are we to remain here? {Syr Ethiop Arab 2 Georg: Lat *How long do I hope* ***thus?***}

TIBERIUS (1)

Jn 6: 1 of Galilee, also called the Sea of Tiberias. {Gk *of Galilee of* ***Tiberius***}

TIGHT (1)

Jdg 16:14 and make it tight ... into the web, {Compare Gk: in verses 13-14, Heb lacks *and make it* ***tight*** *... into the web*}

TIME (13)

Ge 41:22 I fell asleep a second time {Gk Syr Vg: Heb lacks *I fell asleep a second* ***time***}

1Sa 1:22 I will offer him as a nazirite for all time." {Cn Compare Q Ms: MT lacks *I will offer him as a nazirite for all* ***time***}

Est 2:19 together, {Heb adds *a second* ***time***}

Isa 57:11 kept silent and closed my eyes, {Gk Vg: Heb *silent even for a long* ***time***}

Lk 1: 3 from the very first, {Or *for a long* ***time***}

13:35 the time comes when {Other ancient authorities lack *the* ***time*** *comes when*}

Ro 12:11 serve the Lord. {Other ancient authorities read *serve the opportune* ***time***}

1Pe 4: 2 the rest of your earthly life {Gk *rest of the* ***time*** *in the flesh*}

Sir 4:23 speaking at the proper moment, {Heb: Gk *at a* ***time*** *of salvation*}

3Mc 1:29 at that time {Other ancient authorities lack *at that* ***time***}

2Es 5:45 If ... one time {Lat lacks *If ... one* ***time***}

14:48 did so. {Syr adds *... At that* ***time*** *Ezra was caught up, and taken to the place* >}

4Mc 1:10 On this anniversary {Gk *At this* ***time***}

TIMES (3)

Est 1:13 sages who knew the laws {Cn: Heb ***times***}

Da 11:13 and after some years {Heb *and at the end of the* ***times*** *years*}

Mt 16: 3 When it is ... of the times. {Other ancient authorities lack [2]*When it is ... of the* ***times***}

TIMID (1)

Pr 11:16 The timid ... destitute, {Gk: Heb lacks *The* ***timid*** *... destitute*}

TITUS (1)

Ac 18: 7 Titius {Other ancient authorities read ***Titus***}

TOBIAS (1)

Tob 14: 3 and the seven sons of Tobias {Lat: Gk lacks *and the seven sons of* ***Tobias***}

TOBIT (1)

Tob 7: 7 father!" {Other ancient authorities add *When he heard that* ***Tobit*** *had lost his sight,* >}

TODAY (3)

Ge 25:33 "Swear to me first." {Heb ***today***}

Dt 12:28 I command you today, {Gk Sam Syr: MT lacks ***today***}

Lk 3:22 "You are my Son, the Beloved; with you I am well pleased." {Other ancient authorities read *You are my Son,* ***today*** *I have begotten you*}

TOGETHER (4)

Dt 33:17 the peoples, driving them to {Cn: Heb *the peoples,* ***together***}

Job 10: 8 made me; and now you turn and destroy me. {Cn Compare Gk Syr: Heb *made me* ***together*** *all around, and you destroy me*}

Sir 25: 8 and the one who does not plow with ox and ass together. {Heb Syr: Gk lacks *and the one who does not plow with ox and ass* ***together***}

2Es 7:33 shall be withdrawn. {Lat *shall gather* ***together***}

TOIL (1)

Pr 10:22 and he adds no sorrow with it. {Or *and* ***toil*** *adds nothing to it*}

TOLBANES (1)

1Es 9:25 Telem. {Gk ***Tolbanes***}

TOLD (2)

Jdg 16: 2 were told, {Gk: Heb lacks *were* ***told***}

Jn 8:25 "Why do I speak to you at all? {Or *What I have* ***told*** *you from the beginning*}

TOMORROW (2)

Mt 6:11 our daily bread. {Or *our bread for* ***tomorrow***}

Lk 11: 3 our daily bread. {Or *our bread for* ***tomorrow***}

TONGUE (5)
Jos 10:21 no one dared to speak {Heb *moved his **tongue***}
Jer 18:18 bring charges against him, {Heb *strike him with the **tongue***}
Sir 19: 5 + v.6 < *One who controls the **tongue** will live without strife,*
28:14 Slander {Gk *A third **tongue***} has shaken many
28:15 Slander {Gk *a third **tongue***} has driven

TOOK (4)
Mt 27:49 save him." {Other ancient authorities add *And another **took** a spear and pierced his side, and out came water and blood*}
Ac 24: 6 + v.7 < *But the chief captain Lysias came and with great violence **took** him out of our hands,* >
Sir 1:18 flourish. {Other ancient authorities add ... *He saw her and **took** her measure.*}
2Es 1:32 says the Lord. {Other ancient authorities add ... *You **took** me as a sinner, not as a father who freed you from slavery,* >}

TOOL (1)
Ex 32: 4 formed it in a mold, {Or *fashioned it with a graving **tool***; Meaning of Heb uncertain}

TOP (1)
Jdt 6:12 saw them, {Other ancient authorities add *on the **top** of the hill*}

TOPHETH (1)
Isa 30:33 For his burning place {Or ***Topheth***}

TORE (3)
Am 1:11 he maintained his anger perpetually, {Syr Vg: Heb *and his anger **tore** perpetually*}
4Mc 9:27 and they heard his noble decision. {Other ancient authorities read *having heard his noble decision, they **tore** him to shreds*}
10: 7 they abandoned the instruments {Other ancient authorities read *they **tore** off his skin*}

TORMAH (1)
Jdg 9:31 Arumah, {Cn See 9.41. Heb ***Tormah***}

TORMENT (1)
Jdg 16:19 He began to weaken, {Gk: Heb *She began to **torment** him*}

TORTURE (1)
4Mc 10: 3 + v.4 *So if you have any instrument of **torture**, apply it to my body;* >

TOTTER (1)
Ps 55: 3 For they bring {Cn Compare Gk: Heb *they cause to **totter***} trouble upon me,

TOUCH (1)
4Mc 10: 3 + v.4 < *for you cannot **touch** my soul, even if you wish."*

TOWARD (1)
Sir 17:15 + v.16 *Their ways from youth tend **toward** evil,* >

TOWN (1)
1Ki 13:29 and brought it back to the city, {Gk: Heb *he came to the **town** of the old prophet*}

TOWNS (3)
Jdg 12: 7 in his town in Gilead. {Gk: Heb *in the **towns** of Gilead*}
Eze 25: 9 from the towns {Heb ***towns** from its **towns***}

TRAILS (8)
Isa 41:18 the bare heights, {Or ***trails***}
49: 9 the bare heights {Or *the **trails***}
Jer 3: 2 the bare heights, {Or *the **trails***}
3:21 the bare heights {Or *the **trails***}
4:11 the bare heights {Or *the **trails***}
7:29 the bare heights, {Or *the **trails***}
12:12 the bare heights {Or *the **trails***}
14: 6 the bare heights, {Or *the **trails***}

TRAMPLING (1)
Ps 68:30 Trample {Cn: Heb ***Trampling***} under foot

TRANSGRESSION (2)
Ro 11:11 through their stumbling {Gk ***transgression***}
11:12 Now if their stumbling {Gk ***transgression***}

TRAVELED (1)
Sir 34: 9 An educated {Other ancient authorities read *A **traveled***} person knows

TRAVELERS (2)
Eze 39:14 and bury any invaders {Heb ***travelers***}
39:15 As the searchers {Heb ***travelers***} pass through

TREAT (1)
Lk 15:21 called your son.' {Other ancient authorities add ***treat** me as one of your hired servants*}

TREATY (39)
Ex 16:34 covenant, {Or ***treaty*** or *testimony*; Heb *eduth*}
25:16 covenant {Or ***treaty***, or *testimony*; Heb *eduth*}
25:21 covenant {Or ***treaty***, or *testimony*; Heb *eduth*}
25:22 covenant, {Or ***treaty***, or *testimony*; Heb *eduth*}
26:33 covenant {Or ***treaty***, or *testimony*; Heb *eduth*}
26:34 covenant {Or ***treaty***, or *testimony*; Heb *eduth*}
27:21 covenant, {Or ***treaty***, or *testimony*; Heb *eduth*}
30: 6 covenant, {Or ***treaty***, or *testimony*; Heb *eduth*}
30: 6 covenant, {Or ***treaty***, or *testimony*; Heb *eduth*}
30:26 covenant, {Or ***treaty***, or *testimony*; Heb *eduth*}
30:36 covenant {Or ***treaty***, or *testimony*; Heb *eduth*}
31: 7 covenant, {Or ***treaty***, or *testimony*; Heb *eduth*}
31:18 covenant, {Or ***treaty***, or *testimony*; Heb *eduth*}
32:15 covenant, {Or ***treaty***, or *testimony*; Heb *eduth*}
34:29 covenant {Or ***treaty***, or *testimony*; Heb *eduth*}
38:21 covenant, {Or ***treaty***, or *testimony*; Heb *eduth*}
39:35 covenant {Or ***treaty***, or *testimony*; Heb *eduth*}
40: 3 covenant, {Or ***treaty***, or *testimony*; Heb *eduth*}
40: 5 covenant, {Or ***treaty***, or *testimony*; Heb *eduth*}
40:20 covenant {Or ***treaty***, or *testimony*; Heb *eduth*}
40:21 covenant; {Or ***treaty***, or *testimony*; Heb *eduth*}
Lev 16:13 covenant, {Or ***treaty***, or *testament*; Heb *eduth*}
24: 3 covenant, {Or ***treaty***, or *testament*; Heb *eduth*}
Nu 1:50 covenant, {Or ***treaty***, or *testimony*; Heb *eduth*}
1:53 covenant, {Or ***treaty***, or *testimony*; Heb *eduth*}
1:53 covenant. {Or ***treaty***, or *testimony*; Heb *eduth*}
4: 5 covenant, {Or ***treaty***, or *testimony*; Heb *eduth*}
7:89 covenant {Or ***treaty***, or *testimony*; Heb *eduth*}
9:15 covenant; {Or ***treaty***, or *testimony*; Heb *eduth*}
10:11 covenant. {Or ***treaty***, or *testimony*; Heb *eduth*}
17: 4 covenant, {Or ***treaty***, or *testimony*; Heb *eduth*}
17: 7 covenant. {Or ***treaty***, or *testimony*; Heb *eduth*}
17: 8 covenant {Or ***treaty***, or *testimony*; Heb *eduth*}
17:10 covenant, {Or ***treaty***, or *testimony*; Heb *eduth*}
18: 2 covenant. {Or ***treaty***, or *testimony*; Heb *eduth*}
Jos 4:16 covenant, {Or ***treaty***, or *testimony*; Heb *eduth*}
2Ki 11:12 covenant; {Or ***treaty*** **or** *testimony*; Heb *eduth*}
2Ch 23:11 covenant; {Or ***treaty***, or *testimony*; Heb *eduth*}
24: 6 covenant?" {Or ***treaty***, or *testimony*; Heb *eduth*}

TREE (4)
Ex 15:25 a piece of wood; {Or *a **tree***}
1Pe 2:24 bore our sins in his body on the cross, {Or *carried up our sins in his body to the **tree***}
Sir 19:17 + v.19 < *and those who do what is pleasing to him enjoy the fruit of the **tree** of immortality.*
2Es 1:32 Lord. {Other ancient authorities add ... *and you delivered me to death by hanging me on the **tree**;* >}

TREMBLING (1)
2Es 4:24 our life is like a mist, {Syr Ethiop Arab Georg: Lat *a **trembling***}

TRESPASSES (1)
Mk 11:25 + v.26 < *neither will your Father in heaven forgive your **trespasses**."*

TRIALS (1)
Sir 2: 1 prepare yourself for testing. {Or ***trials***}

TRIANGLES (1)
1Sa 18: 6 with musical instruments. {Or ***triangles***, or *three-stringed instruments*}

TRIBE (1)
2Es 9:21 out of a great forest. {Syr Ethiop Arab 1: Lat ***tribe***}

TRIBES (1)
2Sa 7: 7 any of the tribal leaders {Or *any of the **tribes***}

TRIFLE (1)
Sir 27: 1 committed sin for gain, {Other ancient authorities read *a **trifle***}

TROGYLLIUM (1)
Ac 20:15 at Samos, and {Other ancient authorities add *after remaining at **Trogyllium***}

TROOP (1)
Job 10:17 toward me; you bring fresh troops against me. {Cn Compare Gk: Heb *toward me; changes and a **troop** are with me*}

TROOPS (1)
1Ch 12:21 against the band of raiders, {Or *as officers of his **troops***}

TROUBLE (2)
Jos 7:26 Achor. {That is ***Trouble***}
Jer 49:23 they are troubled like the sea {Cn: Heb *there is **trouble** in the sea*}

TRUE (3)
Tob 3: 2 you judge the world. {Other ancient authorities read *you render **true** and righteous judgment forever*}
2Mc 4:13 and no true {Gk lacks ***true***} high priest
4Mc 17:16 athletes of the divine {Other ancient authorities read ***true***} legislation?

TRUNK (1)
1Sa 5: 4 the trunk of {Heb lacks *the **trunk** of*}

TRUST (4)
Job 13:15 See, he will kill me, I have no hope; {Or *Though he kill me, yet I will **trust** in him*}
Mk 10:24 how hard it is {Other ancient authorities add *for those who **trust** in riches*}
Sir 2: 5 humiliation. {Other ancient authorities add *in sickness and poverty put your **trust** in him*}
32:23 Guard {Heb Syr: Gk ***Trust***} yourself in every act,

TRUSTS (1)
Ro 9:33 whoever believes in him {Or ***trusts** in it*}

TRUSTWORTHY (1)
Sir 37:22 the fruits of his good sense will be praiseworthy. {Other ancient witnesses read ***trustworthy***}

TRUTH (6)
Ps 60: 4 to rally to it out of bowshot. {Gk Syr Jerome: Heb *because of the **truth***}
Mk 16:14 risen. {Other ancient authorities add, in whole or in part, ... *who does not allow the **truth** and power of God to prevail ... that they may return to the **truth** and sin no more,* >}
AdE 9:29 + v.30 < *provinces of the kingdom of Ahasuerus, in words of peace and **truth**.*
Sir 41:19 breaking an oath or agreement, {Heb: Gk *before the **truth** of God and the covenant*}
1Es 5:40 Urim and Thummim. {Gk *Manifestation and **Truth***}

TUMBLEWEED (1)
Ps 83:13 make them like whirling dust, {Or *a **tumbleweed***}

TUMULT (1)
Ps 40: 2 from the desolate pit, {Cn: Heb *pit of **tumult***}

TURN (2)
1Sa 14: 7 "Do all that your mind inclines to. {Gk: Heb *Do all that is in your mind. **Turn***}
Sir 1:20 + v.21 < *and where it abides, it will **turn** away all anger.*

TURNED (1)
Ps 35:13 I prayed with my head bowed {Or *My prayer **turned** back*}

TURNING (1)
Jas 1:17 variation or shadow due to change. {Other ancient authorities read *variation due to a shadow of **turning***}

TURNS (2)
1Sa 22:14 and is quick {Heb *and **turns** aside*} to do your bidding,
Job 23: 9 I turn {Syr Vg: Heb *he **turns***} to the right,

TWELFTH (1)
Est 3: 7 the thirteenth day {Cn Compare Gk and verse 13 below: Heb *the **twelfth** month*}

TWELVE (4)
Mk 3:16 So he appointed the twelve: {Other ancient authorities lack *So he appointed the **twelve***}
Rev 21:16 fifteen hundred miles; {Gk ***twelve** thousand stadia*}
2Es 1:40 and Jacob, ... messenger of the Lord. {Other ancient authorities read *and Jacob, ... and **twelve** angels with flowers*}
14:48 did so. {Syr adds ... *five thousand years and three months and **twelve** days after creation* >}

TWENTY (1)
Eze 45: 5 as their holding for cities to live in. {Gk: Heb *as their holding, **twenty** chambers*}

TWENTY-FIVE (1)
Jn 6:19 about three or four miles, {Gk *about **twenty-five** or thirty stadia*}

TWENTY-FOUR (1)
2Es 14:45 twenty-four {Syr Arab 1: Lat lacks ***twenty-four***}

TWENTY-SEVEN (1)
AdE 9:29 + v.30 *Letters were sent to all the Jews, to the one hundred **twenty-seven** provinces* >

TWO (21)
Ge 32: 2 Mahanaim. {Here taken to mean ***Two** camps*}
Lev 23: 5 at twilight, {Heb *between the **two** evenings*}
Nu 9: 3 at twilight, {Heb *between the **two** evenings*}
9: 5 at twilight, {Heb *between the **two** evenings*}
9:11 at twilight, {Heb *between the **two** evenings*}
28: 4 at twilight {Heb *between the **two** evenings*}
28: 8 at twilight {Heb *between the **two** evenings*}
1Sa 18:21 to David a second time, {Heb *by **two***}
1Sa 18:27 and killed one hundred {Gk Compare 2 Sam 3.14: Heb ***two** hundred*}

1Ch 11:21 He was the most renowned {Compare 2 Sam 23.19: Heb *more renowned among the **two***}
Eze 41:22 two cubits wide; {Gk: Heb lacks ***two** cubits wide*}
47: 9 live where the river goes, {Gk Syr Vg Tg: Heb *the **two** rivers go*}
Mt 11: 2 sent word by his {Other ancient authorities read ***two** of his*} disciples
Lk 17:35 + v.36 *"**Two** will be in the field; one will be taken and the other left."*
Jn 6: 7 Six months' wages {Gk ***Two** hundred denarii*; the denarius was the usual day's wage for a laborer}
21: 8 about a hundred yards {Gk ***two** hundred cubits*}
Ac 10:19 "Look, three {One ancient authority reads ***two***; >} men are searching
27:41 But striking a reef, {Gk *place of **two** seas*}
2Ti 3: 9 case of those two men, {Gk lacks ***two** men*}
2Mc 12: 9 thirty miles {Gk ***two** hundred forty stadia*} distant.
12:16 a quarter of a mile {Gk ***two** stadia*} wide,

TWO-THIRDS (1)
Dt 21:17 a double portion {Heb ***two-thirds***}

TYRE (2)
Eze 27: 8 skilled men of Zemer {Cn Compare Gen 10.18: Heb *your skilled men, O **Tyre***}
Sir 46:18 the leaders of the enemy {Heb: Gk *leaders of the people of **Tyre***}

U

UNABLE (2)
Mt 27:42 he cannot save himself. {Or *is he **unable** to save himself?*}
Sir 17:15 + v.16 < *and they are **unable** to make for themselves hearts of flesh in place of their stony hearts.* >

UNBELIEF (1)
Mk 16:14 risen. {Other ancient authorities add, in whole or in part,< *"This age of lawlessness and **unbelief** is under Satan,* >}

UNBELIEVING (2)
Heb 11:31 who were disobedient, {Or ***unbelieving***}
Rev 21: 8 the cowardly, the faithless, {Or *the **unbelieving***}

UNCIRCUMCISED (5)
Ex 6:12 me, poor speaker that I am?" {Heb *me? I am **uncircumcised** of lips*}
6:30 I am a poor speaker, {Heb *am **uncircumcised** of lips*; see 6.12}
Jer 6:10 their ears are closed, {Heb *are **uncircumcised***}
Eze 32:27 fallen warriors of long ago {Gk Old Latin: Heb *of the **uncircumcised***}
Hab 2:16 Drink, and you yourself, stagger! {Q Ms Gk: MT *be **uncircumcised***}

UNCIRCUMCISION (2)
Lev 19:23 regard their fruit as forbidden; {Heb *as their **uncircumcision***} three years it shall be forbidden {Heb ***uncircumcision***}

UNCLEAN (1)
Mk 16:14 risen. {Other ancient authorities add, in whole or in part, ... *the truth and power of God to prevail over the **unclean** things of the spirits.* >}

UNCOVERED (1)
Dt 27:20 violated his father's rights." {Heb ***uncovered** his father's skirt*}

UNCOVERING (1)
Dt 22:30 violating his father's rights. {Heb ***uncovering** his father's skirt*}

UNDER (8)
Jer 38:11 went to the house of {Cn: Heb *to **under***} the king,
Mk 16:14 risen. {Other ancient authorities add, in whole or in part, ... *saying, "This age of lawlessness and unbelief is **under** Satan,* >}
Lk 11:33 cellar, {Other ancient authorities add *or **under** the bushel basket*}
Jas 2: 3 "Sit at my feet," {Gk *Sit **under** my footstool*}
Sir 16:14 + v.15 < *in order that his works might be known **under** heaven.* >
20:14 profit you nothing, {Other ancient authorities add *so it is with the envious who give **under** compulsion*}
30:20 girl. {Other ancient authorities add *So is the person who does right **under** compulsion*}
3Mc 1: 2 the best of the Ptolemaic arms that had been previously issued to him, {Or *the best of the Ptolemaic soldiers previously put **under** his command*}

UNDERNEATH (1)
Dt 33:27 shatters {Cn: Heb *from **underneath***} the forces

UNDERSTAND (3)
Da 9:22 He came {Gk Syr: Heb *He made to **understand***}
Jn 10:38 and understand {Other ancient authorities lack *and **understand***; others read *and believe*}
2Es 7:*104* to be ill {Syr Ethiop Arm: Lat *to **understand***}

UNDERSTANDING (1)
Sir 11:14 + v.15 *Wisdom, **understanding,** and knowledge of the law come from the Lord;* >

UNDERSTOOD (2)
Sir 1: 6 + v.7 < *And her abundant experience—who has **understood** it?*
4Mc 11: 6 + v.7 *If you but **understood** human feelings and had hope of salvation from God*—>

UNDERWINGS (4)
2Es 11:25 little wings {Syr: Lat ***underwings***}
11:31 little wings {Syr: Lat ***underwings***}
12:19 little wings {Syr: Lat ***underwings***}
12:29 little wings {Arab 1: Lat ***underwings***}

UNEXPLORED (1)
Sir 32:21 on a smooth {Or *an **unexplored***} road,

UNIMPORTANT (1)
Sir 20:17 how often! {Other ancient authorities add < *and what he does not have is **unimportant** to him*}

UNIVERSE (1)
Wis 15: 1 ruling all things {Or *ruling the **universe***}

UNJUST (1)
2Es 16:53 sinned; {Other ancient authorities add *or the **unjust** done injustice*}

UNPROFITABLE (2)
Sir 16: 1 a multitude of worthless {Heb: Gk ***unprofitable***}
2Es 15:60 hateful {Another reading is *idle* or ***unprofitable***}

UNPUNISHED (1)
Wis 1:11 is without result, {Or *will go **unpunished***}

UNTIL (2)
3Mc 5:12 deep a sleep {Other ancient authorities add *from evening **until** the ninth hour*}
2Es 15:44 all its fury; {Other ancient authorities add ***until** they destroy it to its foundations*}

UNTIMELY (2)
Sir 16: 3 numbers; {Other ancient authorities add *For you will groan in **untimely** mourning, and will know of their sudden end.*}
3Mc 5:17 to make the present {Other ancient authorities read *delayed* (Gk ***untimely***)} portion

UNWEARIED (1)
Sir 20:31 + v.32 ***Unwearied** endurance in seeking the Lord is better than a masterless charioteer of one's own life.*

UNWORTHY (1)
1Co 11:29 drink {Other ancient authorities add *in an **unworthy** manner,*}

UP (31)
Lev 26:34 enjoy {Or *make **up** for*}
26:34 enjoy {Or *make **up** for*}
26:43 enjoy {Or *make **up** for*}
Jdg 20: 9 we will go up {Gk: Heb lacks *we will go **up***}
1Sa 13:15 on his way from Gilgal. {Gk: Heb *went **up** from Gilgal to Gibeah of Benjamin*}
Job 10:20 that I may find a little comfort {Heb *that I may brighten **up** a little*}
Ps 109:28 Let my assailants be put to shame; {Gk: Heb *They have risen **up** and have been put to shame*}
Isa 37:28 your rising up {Q Ms Gk: MT lacks *your rising **up***}
Jer 18:14 Do the mountains run dry, {Cn: Heb *Are ... plucked **up**?*}
Eze 21:15 it is polished {Tg: Heb *wrapped **up***} for slaughter.
40:40 on the outside of the vestibule {Cn: Heb *to him who goes **up***}
Hos 1:11 they shall take possession of {Heb *rise **up** from*}
8: 6 shall be broken to pieces. {Or *shall go **up** in flames*}
Mt 27:50 and breathed his last. {Or *gave **up** his spirit*}
Lk 24:51 and was carried up into heaven. {Other ancient authorities lack *and was carried **up** into heaven*}
Jn 5: 3 + v.4 < *went down at certain seasons into the pool, and stirred **up** the water;* >
Ac 1:18 and falling headlong, {Or *swelling **up***}
Heb 11:23 king's edict. {Other ancient authorities add *By faith Moses, when he was grown **up**, killed the Egyptian,* >}
1Pe 1:13 prepare your mind for action; {Gk *gird **up** the loins of your mind*}
2:24 bore our sins in his body on the cross, {Or *carried **up** our sins in his body to the tree*}
2Pe 3:10 done on it will be disclosed. {Other ancient authorities read *will be burned **up***}
Tob 13:12 all who revere you. {Other ancient authorities read *who build you **up***}
Sir 10: 8 wealth. {Other ancient authorities add here or after verse 9a, ... *for such a person puts his own soul **up** for sale.*}
13:13 + v.14 *When you hear these things in your sleep, wake **up**!* >
17:17 + v.18 *whom, being his firstborn, he brings **up** with discipline,* >
22: 6 + v.7 *Children who are brought **up** in a good life, conceal the lowly birth of their parents.* >
Man 1:10 so that I am rejected {Other ancient authorities read *so that I cannot lift **up** my head*}
2Es 12: 2 rose up and {Ethiop: Lat lacks *rose **up** and*}
14:48 did so. {Syr adds ... *At that time Ezra was caught **up**, and taken to the place* >}
4Mc 12:19 and so ended his life. {Gk *and so gave **up***; other ancient authorities read *gave **up** his spirit* or *his soul*}

UPHOLD (2)
Ps 54: 4 is the upholder of {Gk Syr Jerome: Heb *is of those who **uphold*** or *is with those who **uphold***}

UPLIFTED (1)
Ps 140: 9 Those who surround me lift up their heads; {Cn Compare Gk: Heb *those who surround me are **uplifted** in head*; >}

UPRIGHT (3)
2Ch 29:34 for the Levites were more conscientious {Heb ***upright** in heart*}
Ps 49:14 straight to the grave they descend, {Cn: Heb *the **upright** shall have dominion over them in the morning*}
Da 11:17 kingdom, and he shall bring terms of peace {Gk: Heb *kingdom, and **upright** ones with him*}

UPROOTED (1)
Sir 21: 4 will be laid waste. {Other ancient authorities read ***uprooted***}

UPSET (1)
Ro 14:21 stumble. {Other ancient authorities add *or be **upset** or be weakened*}

UPWARD (1)
Php 3:14 the prize of the heavenly {Gk ***upward***} call

URGED (1)
Lk 16:16 everyone tries to enter it by force. {Or *everyone is strongly **urged** to enter it*}

USE (1)
Sir 17: 4 + v.5 *They obtained the **use** of the five faculties of the Lord;* >

USED (1)
Lk 14:34 how can its saltiness be restored? {Or *how can it be **used** for seasoning?*}

UTTER (1)
Mal 4: 6 strike the land with a curse. {Or *a ban of **utter** destruction*}

UZZAH (2)
2Sa 6: 8 Perez-uzzah, {That is *Bursting Out Against **Uzzah***}
1Ch 13:11 Perez-uzzah {That is *Bursting Out Against **Uzzah***}

UZZIAH (1)
Jdt 8:10 Uzziah and {Other ancient authorities lack ***Uzziah** and* (see verses 28 and 35)}

V

VAIN (2)
3Mc 6:11 vain-minded praise their vanities {Or *bless their **vain** gods*}
2Es 4:17 was in vain, {Lat lacks *was in **vain***}

VALLEY (2)
1Ch 4:14 Ge-harashim, {That is ***Valley** of artisans*}
Jer 47: 5 O remnant of their power! {Gk: Heb *their **valley***}

VANITY (1)
Pr 13:11 Wealth hastily gotten {Gk Vg: Heb *from **vanity***}

VASHNI (1)
1Ch 6:28 the second Abijah. {Heb reads ***Vashni,** and Abijah* for *the second Abijah*, taking *the second* as a proper name}

VERY (1)
3Mc 7:22 with extreme fear. {Other ancient authorities read *with a **very** large supplement*}

VESSEL (2)
1Pe 3: 7 woman as the weaker sex, {Gk ***vessel***}
2Es 7:*88* separated from their mortal body. {Lat *the corruptible **vessel***}

VESTMENTS (1)
1Es 4:54 in which {Gk *in what priestly **vestments***}

VICINITY (1)
Ezr 2:70 lived in ... its vicinity; {1 Esdras 5.46: Heb lacks *lived in Jerusalem and its **vicinity***}

VICTORIOUS (1)
4Mc 18:23 received pure and immortal {Other ancient authorities read ***victorious***}

VIGILANT (1)
1Pe 5: 8 keep alert. {Or *be **vigilant***}

VIGOROUSLY (1)
Ac 28:28 + v.29 < *the Jews departed, arguing **vigorously** among themselves*

VILLAGE (1)
Mk 8:26 village." {Other ancient authorities add *or tell anyone in the **village***}

VILLAGES (2)
Nu 32:41 Havvoth-jair. {That is *the **villages** of Jair*}
Jer 49: 3 O daughters {Or ***villages***} of Rabbah!

VINDICATION (1)
Isa 58: 8 your vindicator {Or ***vindication***} shall go before

VINDICATOR (1)
Job 19:25 that my Redeemer {Or ***Vindicator***} lives,

VIOLENCE (1)
Ac 24: 6 + v.7 < *But the chief captain Lysias came and with great **violence** took him out of our hands,* >

VIOLENTLY (1)
Mt 11:12 the kingdom of heaven has suffered violence, {Or *has been coming **violently***}

VIRGIN (5)
Isa 7:14 the young woman {Gk *the **virgin***} is with child
1Co 7:36 fiancée, {Gk ***virgin***}
7:37 fiancée, {Gk ***virgin***}
7:38 fiancée {Gk ***virgin***}
1Es 1:53 or young woman, {Gk ***virgin***}

VIRGINS (4)
Mt 25: 1 bridesmaids {Gk ***virgins***}
25: 7 bridesmaids {Gk ***virgins***}
25:11 bridesmaids {Gk ***virgins***}
Ac 21: 9 He had four unmarried daughters {Gk *four daughters, **virgins,***}

VIRTUE (1)
4Mc 17:17 marveled at their {Other ancient authorities add ***virtue** and*} endurance.

VISION (3)
Da 8: 5 The goat had a horn {Theodotion: Gk *one horn*; Heb *a horn of **vision***}
Ac 9:12 in a vision {Other ancient authorities lack *in a **vision***}
2Es 5: 4 after the third period; {< Arm *after the third **vision***; Georg *after the third day*}

VISIONS (2)
Eze 43: 3 destroy the city, and {Syr: Heb *and the **visions***}
Da 4: 9 Hear {Theodotion: Aram *The **visions** of*} the dream that I saw;

VISITATION (1)
1Pe 2:12 God when he comes to judge. {Gk *God on the day of **visitation***}

VOICE (1)
Zep 2:14 the owl {Cn: Heb *a **voice***} shall hoot

VOICES (1)
AdE 11: 5 Noises {Or ***Voices***} and confusion,

VOW (1)
1Sa 2: 8 honor. {Gk (Compare Q Ms) adds *He grants the **vow** of the one who vows, and blesses the years of the just*}

VOWED (1)
1Es 4:44 when he began {Cn: Gk ***vowed***} to destroy Babylon,

VOWS (1)
1Sa 2: 8 honor. {Gk (Compare Q Ms) adds *He grants the vow of the one who **vows**, and blesses the years of the just*}

W

WAIT (1)
Ps 52: 9 I will proclaim {Cn: Heb ***wait** for*}

WAITING (1)
Jn 5: 3 paralyzed. {Other ancient authorities add, wholly or in part, ***waiting** for the stirring of the water;* >}

WAKE (1)
Sir 13:13 + v.14 *When you hear these things in your sleep, **wake** up!* >

WALK (6)
Isa 38:15 All my sleep has fled {Cn Compare Syr: Heb *I will **walk** slowly all my years*}
Mk 7: 5 your disciples not live {Gk ***walk***} according
Lk 24:17 They stood still, looking sad. {Other ancient authorities read ***walk** along, looking sad?"*}
Col 2: 6 continue to live your lives {Gk *to **walk***}
Sir 38:32 and wherever they live, they will not go hungry. {Syr: Gk *and people can neither live nor **walk** there*}
2Es 10:10 almost all go {Literally ***walk***} to perdition,

WALL (3)
1Ki 11:27 in the wall {Heb lacks *in the **wall***}
2Ki 25: 4 in the city wall; {Heb lacks ***wall***}
Jer 52: 7 in the city wall; {Heb lacks ***wall***}

WALLS (2)
Ps 144:14 in the walls, {Heb lacks *in the **walls***}
3Mc 4:11 claim to be inside the circuit of the city. {Or *claim protection of the **walls***; meaning of Gk uncertain}

WANDER (1)
Sir 36:30 a fugitive and a wanderer. {Heb: Gk ***wander** about and sigh*}

WANDERING (1)
Ge 4:16 Nod, {That is ***Wandering***}

WANTED (1)
2Co 11:32 in order to {Other ancient authorities read *and **wanted** to*} seize me,

WAR (2)
Nu 31: 6 priest, {Gk: Heb adds *to the **war***}
1Sa 4: 1 In those days the Philistines mustered for war against Israel, {Gk: Heb lacks *In those days the Philistines mustered for **war** against Israel*}

WASHED (1)
Rev 1: 5 and freed {Other ancient authorities read ***washed***} us from our sins

WASHING (1)
Tit 3: 5 through the water {Gk ***washing***} of rebirth

WASTELAND (2)
1Sa 26: 1 opposite Jeshimon." {Or *opposite the **wasteland***}
26: 3 opposite Jeshimon {Or *opposite the **wasteland***}

WATCHED (1)
Lk 12:39 thief was coming, he {Other ancient authorities add *would have **watched** and*}

WATCHPOST (1)
Ge 31:49 Mizpah, {That is ***Watchpost***}

WATER (7)
Jdg 1:15 Gulloth-mayim." {That is *Basins of **Water***}
Ne 4:23 each kept his weapon in his right hand. {Cn: Heb *each his weapon the **water***}
Mt 27:49 save him." {Other ancient authorities add *And another took a spear and pierced his side, and out came **water** and blood*}
Jn 5: 3 paralyzed. {Other ancient authorities add, wholly or in part, *waiting for the stirring of the **water**;* [4]*for an angel ... and stirred up the **water**; whoever stepped in first after the stirring of the **water** was made well* >}
Sir 24:14 beside water {Other ancient authorities omit *beside **water***}

WATERS (5)
Ps 73:10 and find no fault in them. {Cn: Heb *abundant **waters** are drained by them*}
Isa 48: 1 from the loins {Cn: Heb ***waters***} of Judah;
Sir 40:11 what is from above returns above. {Heb Syr: Gk Lat *from the **waters** returns to the sea*}
2Es 16:58 confined the sea in the midst of the waters; {Other ancient authorities read *confined the world between the **waters** and the **waters***}

WAVE (1)
Zec 2: 9 I am going to raise {Or ***wave***} my hand

WAY (8)
1Sa 1:18 went to her quarters, {Gk: Heb *went her **way***}
Job 19:12 have thrown up siegeworks {Cn: Heb *their **way***}
Pr 8:22 the beginning of his work, {Heb ***way***}
Eze 42: 4 and one hundred cubits deep, {Gk Syr: Heb *a **way** of one cubit*}
48: 1 on the Hethlon road, {Compare 47.15: Heb *by the side of the **way***}
3Mc 4:18 and some at the place; {Other ancient authorities read *on the **way***}
7: 8 in any place {Other ancient authorities read ***way***}
2Es 4:11 the corrupt world understand incorruption?" {Syr Ethiop *the **way** of the incorruptible?*}

WAYS (6)
Pr 1:19 Such is the end {Gk: Heb ***ways***} of all
14:12 end is the way to death. {Heb ***ways** of death*}
Isa 2: 6 forsaken the ways of {Heb lacks *the **ways** of*}
Sir 1: 4 + v.5 < *her **ways** are the eternal commandments.*
11:14 + v.15 < *affection and the **ways** of good works come from him.* >
17:15 + v.16 *Their **ways** from youth tend toward evil,* >

WEAK (1)
Ps 41: 1 those who consider the poor; {Or ***weak***}

WEAKENED (1)
Ro 14:21 stumble. {Other ancient authorities add *or be upset or be **weakened***}

WEAKNESS (1)
Ro 6:19 your natural limitations. {Gk *the **weakness** of your flesh*}

WEALTH (1)
Sir 37: 6 him when you distribute your spoils. {Heb: Gk *him in your **wealth***}

WEAPONS (3)
Jer 4: 5 shout aloud {Or *shout, take your **weapons***: Heb *shout, fill* (your hand)}
Ro 6:13 as instruments {Or ***weapons***} of wickedness
6:13 as instruments {Or ***weapons***} of wickedness.

WEARY (1)
Jer 51:64 I am bringing on her.' " {Gk: Heb *on her. And they shall **weary** themselves*}

WEAVE (2)
Mic 7: 3 thus they pervert justice. {Cn: Heb *they **weave** it*}
Lk 12:27 Consider the lilies, ... they neither toil nor spin; {Other ancient authorities read *Consider the lilies; they neither spin nor **weave***}

WEB (2)
Jdg 16:14 and make it tight ... into the web, {Compare Gk: in verses 13-14, Heb lacks *and make it tight ... into the **web***}
Wis 5:14 like a light frost {Other ancient authorities read *spider's **web***}

WEDDINGS (1)
AdE 9:22 a time for feasting {Gk *of **weddings***} and gladness

WEEK (1)
2Es 14:48 did so. {Syr adds *in the seventh year of the sixth **week**, five thousand years and* >}

WEEPERS (1)
Jdg 2: 5 Bochim, {That is ***Weepers***}

WEEPING (1)
Ge 35: 8 Allon-bacuth. {That is *Oak of **weeping***}

WEIGHT (1)
Sir 16:25 impart discipline precisely {Gk *by **weight***}

WELL (10)
Ge 16:14 Beer-lahai-roi; {That is *the **Well** of the Living One who sees me*}
21:31 Beer-sheba; {That is ***Well** of seven* or ***Well** of the oath*}
26:33 Beer-sheba {That is ***Well** of the oath* or ***Well** of seven*}
Nu 21:16 Beer; {That is ***Well***}
1Sa 29:10 and go to the place ... well before me. {Gk: Heb lacks *and go to the place ... done **well** before me*}
Ps 46: 1 a very present {Or ***well** proved*} help in trouble.

Da 3:15 well and good. {Aram lacks *well and good*}
Jn 5: 3 + v.4 < *whoever stepped in first after the stirring of the water was made* ***well*** >

WELL-PLEASING (2)

Mt 11:26 for such was your gracious will. {Or *for so it was* ***well-pleasing*** *in your sight*}
Lk 10:21 for such was your gracious will. {Or *for so it was* ***well-pleasing*** *in your sight*}

WELLS (1)

Dt 10: 6 Beeroth Bene-jaakan {Or *the* ***wells*** *of the Bene-jaakan*}

WENT (10)

Dt 31: 1 When Moses had finished speaking all {Q Ms Gk: MT *Moses* ***went*** *and spoke*}
Jdg 17:10 and your living." {Heb *living, and the Levite* ***went***} [11]The Levite agreed
1Sa 14:16 the multitude was searching back and forth. {Gk: Heb *they* ***went*** *and there*}
1Ki 12:30 before the other as far as Dan. {Compare Gk: Heb ***went*** *to the one as far as Dan*}
Ezr 10: 6 where he spent the night. {1 Esdras 9.2: Heb *where he* ***went***}
Eze 40:49 ten steps led up {Gk: Heb *and by steps that* ***went*** *up*}
Jn 5: 3 + v.4 *for an angel of the Lord* ***went*** *down at certain seasons into the pool,* >
Jude 1: 7 pursued unnatural lust, {Gk ***went*** *after other flesh*}
Rev 6: 4 And out came {Or ***went***} another horse,
AdE 4: 5 + v.6 *So Hachratheus* ***went*** *out to Mordecai in the street of the city opposite the city gate.*

WEPT (2)

Ps 69:10 When I humbled my soul with fasting, {Gk Syr: Heb ***I wept,*** *with fasting my soul,* >}
Tob 7: 7 father!" {Other ancient authorities add *When he heard that Tobit had lost his sight, he was stricken with grief and* ***wept.*** *Then he said,*}

WESTWARD (1)

Jos 18:15 from there to Ephron, {Cn See 15.9. Heb ***westward***}

WHATEVER (2)

Jn 5: 3 + v.4 < *after the stirring of the water was made well from* ***whatever*** *disease that person had.*
Ac 15:20 and from whatever has been strangled {Other ancient authorities lack *and from* ***whatever*** *has been strangled*}

WHEEL (1)

Jas 3: 6 the cycle of nature, {Or ***wheel*** *of birth*}

WHELPS (1)

3Mc 4: 6 as they were torn by the harsh treatment of the heathen. {Other ancient authorities read *as though torn by heathen* ***whelps***}

WHERE (6)

2Sa 3:12 sent messengers to David at Hebron, {Gk: Heb ***where*** *he was*}
Pr 31: 4 for rulers to desire {Cn: Heb ***where***} strong drink;
Eze 3:15 who lived by the river Chebar. {Two Mss Syr: Heb *Chebar, and to* ***where*** *they lived.* Another reading is *Chebar, and I sat* ***where*** *they sat*}
Col 3:11 its creator. [11]In that renewal {Gk *its creator,* [11]***where***}
Sir 1:20 + v.21 < *and* ***where*** *it abides, it will turn away all anger.*

WHITE (1)

Da 11:35 purified, and cleansed, {Heb *made them* ***white***}

WHOEVER (1)

Jn 5: 3 + v.4 < ***whoever*** *stepped in first after the stirring of the water was made well* >

WHOLE (8)

Dt 27: 6 build the alter ... of unhewn {Heb ***whole***} stones.
Jos 8:31 an alter of unhewn {Heb ***whole***} stones,
2Sa 17: 3 seek the life of only one man, {Gk: Heb *like the return of the* ***whole*** *(is) the man whom you seek*}
Sir 16:14 + v.16 *His mercy is manifest to the* ***whole*** *of creation,* >
16:18 visitation! {Other ancient authorities add *The* ***whole*** *world past and present is in his will.*}
17:15 + v.17 < *For in the division of the nations of the* ***whole*** *earth, he appointed*
1Mc 4:47 Then they took unhewn {Gk ***whole***} stones,
4Mc 12:12 throughout all time {Gk *throughout the* ***whole*** *age*}

WHY (6)

Ge 44: 4 Why ... my silver cup? {Gk Compare Vg: Heb lacks ***Why*** *have you stolen my silver cup?*}
1Sa 5:10 "Why {Q Ms Gk: MT lacks ***Why***} have they brought
Job 13:14 I will take ... in my hand. {Gk: Heb ***Why*** *should I take ... in my hand?*}
Mt 11: 8 What then did you go out to see? Someone {Or ***Why*** *then did you go out? To see someone*}
Mt 11: 9 What then did you go out to see? A prophet? {Other ancient authorities read ***Why*** *then did you go out? To see a prophet?*}
Lk 7:25 What then did you go out to see? Someone {Or ***Why*** *then did you go out? To see someone*}

WICKED (2)

Pr 12:12 covet the proceeds of wickedness, {Or *covet the catch of the* ***wicked***}
Sir 10: 8 wealth. {Other ancient authorities add here or after verse 9a, *Nothing is more* ***wicked*** *than one who loves money,* >}

WIDE (1)

Eze 41:22 two cubits wide; {Gk: Heb lacks *two cubits* ***wide***}

WIDOWS (1)

Eze 19: 7 he ravaged their strongholds, {Heb *his* ***widows***}

WIDTH (2)

Eze 40:48 the sidewalls of the gate were three cubits {Gk: Heb *and the* ***width*** *of the gate was three cubits*}
41: 3 and the sidewalls {Gk: Heb ***width***}

WIFE (10)

Lev 20:10 if a man commits adultery with the wife of {Heb repeats *if a man commits adultery with the* ***wife*** *of*}
Jdg 13:19 to him who works wonders. {Heb *wonders, while Manoah and his* ***wife*** *looked on*}
Mk 10: 7 and be joined to his wife, {Other ancient authorities lack *and be joined to his* ***wife***}
1Th 4: 4 how to control your own body {Or *how to take a* ***wife*** *for himself*}
1Ti 2:11 Let a woman {Or ***wife***} learn
2:12 I permit no woman {Or ***wife***}
3: 2 married only once, {Gk *the husband of one* ***wife***}
3:12 married only once, {Gk *be husbands of one* ***wife***}
5: 9 married only once; {Gk *the* ***wife*** *of one husband*}
Tit 1: 6 married only once, {Gk *husband of one* ***wife***}

WILD (2)

Sir 10:11 inherits maggots and vermin {Heb: Gk ***wild*** *animals*}
2Es 15:30 like wild boars {Other ancient authorities lack *like* ***wild*** *boars*}

WILDERNESS (1)

Ps 72: 9 May his foes {Cn: Heb *those who live in the* ***wilderness***} bow down before him,

WILL (5)

Lk 11: 2 come. {< Other ancient authorities add *Your* ***will*** *be done, on earth as in heaven*}
1Co 16:12 but he was not at all willing {Or *it was not at all God's* ***will*** *for him*}
Heb 9:15 under the first covenant. {The Greek word used here means both *covenant* and ***will***}
Sir 16:18 visitation! {Other ancient authorities add *The whole world past and present is in his* ***will.***}
18: 2 + v.3 < *he steers the world with the span of his hand, and all things obey his* ***will;*** >

WIND (4)

Eze 37: 9 "Prophecy to the breath: {Or ***wind*** or *spirit*} ... O breath, {Or ***wind*** or *spirit*}
Jn 3: 6 born of the Spirit is spirit. {The same Greek word means both ***wind*** and *spirit*}
2Es 13: 3 the wind ... I saw {Syr: Lat lacks *the* ***wind*** *... I saw*}

WINDOW (1)

Ge 6:16 Make a roof {Or ***window***} for the ark,

WINDS (1)

Wis 7:20 the powers of spirits {Or ***winds***}

WINE (3)

Jer 48:11 settled like wine {Heb lacks *like* ***wine***}
Hab 2: 5 wealth {Other Heb Mss read ***wine***} is treacherous;
Mk 2:22 but ... wineskins." {Other ancient authorities lack *but one puts new* ***wine*** *into fresh wineskins*}

WINESKINS (1)

Mk 2:22 but one puts new wine into fresh wineskins." {Other ancient authorities lack *but one puts new wine into fresh* ***wineskins***}

WINTER (1)

Sir 21: 8 for his burial mound. {Other ancient authorities read *for the* ***winter***}

WISDOM (9)

Pr 14: 1 The wise woman {Heb ***Wisdom*** *of women*} builds
Sir 1: 4 + v.5 *The source of* ***wisdom*** *is God's word in the highest heaven,* >
1: 6 + v.7 *The knowledge of* ***wisdom****—to whom was it manifested?* >
1:10 love him. {Other ancient authorities add *Love of the Lord is glorious* ***wisdom;*** >}
4:23 and do not hide your wisdom. {< Other Gk Mss lack *and do not hide your* ***wisdom***}
Sir 11:14 + v.15 ***Wisdom,*** *understanding, and knowledge of the law come from the Lord;* >
19:17 + v.18 < *the beginning of acceptance, and* ***wisdom*** *obtains his love.* >
40:20 but the love of friends {Heb: Gk ***wisdom***}
51:25 Acquire wisdom {Heb: Gk lacks ***wisdom***}

WISE (4)

Pr 11:30 but violence {Cn Compare Gk Syr: Heb *a* ***wise*** *man*} takes lives away.
22:17 Incline your ear and hear my words, {Cn Compare Gk: Heb *Incline your ear, and hear the words of the* ***wise***}
Sir 7:21 Let your soul love intelligent slaves; {Heb *Love a* ***wise*** *slave as yourself*}
2Es 14:13 and ... wise. {Lat lacks *and ...* ***wise***}

WISELY (1)

Dt 29: 9 in order that you may succeed {Or *deal* ***wisely***}

WISH (2)

Sir 19:20 + v.21 *When a slave says to his master, "I will not act as you* ***wish,***" >
4Mc 10: 3 + v.4 < *apply it to my body; for you cannot touch my soul, even if you* ***wish.***"

WITHDRAW (2)

Eze 5:11 I will cut you down; {Another reading is *I will* ***withdraw***}
1Ti 6: 5 gain. {Other ancient authorities add ***Withdraw*** *yourself from such people*}

WITHDREW (1)

1Mc 12:28 and withdrew. {Other ancient authorities omit *and* ***withdrew***}

WITHIN (4)

Ps 45:13 with all kinds ... gold-woven robes; {Or *... All glorious is the princess* ***within,*** *gold embroidery is her clothing*}
131: 2 my soul is like the weaned child that is with me. {Or *my soul* ***within*** *me is like a weaned child*}
Lk 17:21 the kingdom of God is among {Or ***within***} you."
24:32 burning within us {Other ancient authorities lack ***within*** *us*}

WITHOUT (9)

Nu 35:23 unintentionally {Heb ***without*** *seeing*}
Job 19:26 then in {Or ***without***} my flesh
Isa 23: 1 for your fortress is destroyed. {Cn Compare verse 14: Heb *for it is destroyed,* ***without*** *houses*}
Mt 5:22 brother or sister, {< other ancient authorities add ***without*** *cause*}
Col 2:11 circumcised with a spiritual circumcision, {Gk *a circumcision made* ***without*** *hands*}
Jas 2: 1 do you with your acts of favoritism really believe in our glorious Lord Jesus Christ? {Or *hold the faith of our glorious Lord Jesus Christ* ***without*** *acts of favoritism*}
Sir 19: 5 + v.6 < *One who controls the tongue will live* ***without*** *strife,*
22:13 person. {Other ancient authorities add *For being* ***without*** *sense he will despise everything about you*}
32:18 fear. {Meaning of Gk uncertain. Other ancient authorities add *and after acting, with him,* ***without*** *deliberation*}

WITHSTANDS (1)

Sir 19: 5 condemned, {Other ancient authorities add *but one who* ***withstands*** *pleasures crowns his life.* >}

WITNESS (7)

Ge 31:47 Jegar-sahadutha: {In Aramaic *The heap of* ***witness***}
31:47 Galeed. {In Hebrew *The heap of* ***witness***}
Jos 22:34 called the alter Witness; {Cn Compare Syr: Heb lacks ***Witness***}
1Sa 12: 6 is witness, who {Gk: Heb lacks *is* ***witness,*** *who*}
20:23 the LORD is witness {Gk: Heb lacks ***witness***}
2Es 8:23 whose truth is established {Arab 2: Other authorities read *truth bears* ***witness***}
4Mc 12:16 not desert the excellent example {Other ancient authorities read *the* ***witness***}

WIVES (2)

1Ti 3:11 Women {Or *Their* ***wives,*** or *Women deacons*}
1Es 1:32 women, {Or *their* ***wives***}

WOE (1)

Mt 23:13 + v.14 ***Woe*** *to you, scribes and Pharisees, hypocrites!* >

WOMAN (5)

Pr 6:24 the wife of another, {Gk: MT *the evil* ***woman***}
23:27 an adulteress {Heb *an alien* ***woman***} is a narrow well.
27:13 as surely for foreigners. {Vg and 20.16: Heb *for a foreign* ***woman***}
Mt 19: 9 commits adultery " {< others add at the end of the verse *and he who marries a divorced* ***woman*** *commits adultery*}
1Co 11: 3 the head of his wife, {Or *head of the* ***woman***}

WOMB (1)
Jdt 9: 2 torn off a virgin's clothing {Cn: Gk *loosed her **womb***}

WOMEN (4)
Ps 68:11 the company of those {Or *company of the **women***}
Pr 14: 1 The wise woman {Heb *Wisdom of **women***} builds
Jer 44:19 And the women said, {Compare Syr: Heb lacks *And the **women** said*}
Lk 1:28 is with you." {Other ancient authorities add *Blessed are you among **women***}

WONDER-WORKING (2)
3Mc 6:32 praising God, their Savior and worker of wonders. {Other ancient authorities read *praising Israel and the **wonder-working** God*; or *praising Israel's Savior, the **wonder-working** God*}

WONDROUS (1)
Sir 36:19 Fill Zion with your majesty, {Heb Syr: Gk *the celebration of your **wondrous** deeds*}

WOOD (1)
Isa 17: 9 places of the Hivites and the Amorites, {Cn Compare Gk: Heb *places of the **wood** and the highest bough*}

WORD (5)
Dt 5: 5 declare to you the words {Q Mss Sam Gk Syr Vg Tg: MT ***word***}
2Sa 16:23 consulted the oracle {Heb ***word***}
1Jn 5: 7 There are three that testify: {Other ancient authorities read (with variations) [7]*There are three that testify in heaven, the Father, the **Word**, and the Holy Spirit*, >}
Sir 1: 4 + v.5 *The source of wisdom is God's **word** in the highest heaven*, >
2Es 9: 5 the beginning is evident, {Syr: Ethiop *is in the **word***; Meaning of Lat uncertain}

WORDS (12)
Ge 49:21 that bears lovely fawns. {Or *that gives beautiful **words***}
Ex 34:28 the ten commandments. {Heb ***words***}
Dt 4:13 the ten commandments; {Heb *the ten **words***}
10: 4 the ten commandments {Heb *the ten **words***}
Pr 6: 2 the utterance of your lips, {Cn Compare Gk Syr: Heb *the **words** of your mouth*}
Ecc 1: 8 All things {Or ***words***} are wearisome;
Isa 58:13 or pursuing your own affairs; {Heb *or speaking **words***}
Da 7: 1 dream: {Q Ms Theodotion: MT adds *the beginning of the **words**; he said*}
Ac 28:28 + v.29 *And when he had said these **words**, the Jews departed*, >
Tob 12: 6 the deeds {Gk ***words***; other ancient authorities read ***words** of the deeds*} of God.
AdE 9:29 + v.30 <*provinces of the kingdom of Ahasuerus, in **words** of peace and truth*.

WORE (1)
Lk 8:27 a man of the city ... he had worn {Other ancient authorities read *a man of the city who had had demons for a long time met him. He **wore***}

WORK (5)
Mic 2: 1 and evil deeds {Cn: Heb ***work** evil*} on their beds!
Ro 9:28 the Lord will execute his sentence ... decisively." {Other ancient authorities read *for he will finish his **work** and cut it short in righteousness*, >}
11: 6 grace. {Other ancient authorities add *But if it is by works, it is no longer on the basis of grace, otherwise **work** would no longer be **work***}
Sir 51: 8 and your kindness {Other ancient authorities read ***work***} from of old,

WORKER (1)
Sir 19: 1 The one who does this {Heb: Gk *A **worker** who is a drunkard*}
40:18 Wealth and wages make life sweet, {Heb: Gk *Life is sweet for the self-reliant **worker***}

WORKING (1)
Jdg 13:19 to him who works {Gk Vg: Heb *and **working***} wonders.

WORKS (7)
Jer 48: 7 you trusted in your strongholds {Gk: Heb ***works***}
Ac 15:18 things [18]known from long ago.' {Other ancient authorities read *things*. [18]*Known to God from of old are all his **works**.'*}
Ro 8:28 all things work together for good {Other ancient authorities read ... *in all things God **works** for good*}
11: 6 grace. {Other ancient authorities add *But if it is by **works**, it is no longer on the basis of grace*, >}
Heb 2: 7 honor, {Other ancient authorities add *and set them over the **works** of your hands*}
Sir 11:14 + v.15 < *affection and the ways of good **works** come from him*. >
16:14 + v.15 < *in order that his **works** might be known under heaven*. >

WORLD (8)
Mt 13:35 foundation of the world." {Other ancient authorities lack *of the **world***}
Col 2: 8 the elemental spirits of the universe, {Or *the rudiments of the **world***}
2:20 the elemental spirits of the universe, {Or *the rudiments of the **world***}
Sir 16:18 visitation! {Other ancient authorities add *The whole **world** past and present is in his will*.}
18: 2 + v.3 < *he steers the **world** with the span of his hand*, >
2Es 3: 4 commanded the dust {Syr Ethiop: Lat *people* or ***world***}
14:12 For the age is divided into ten parts ... part. {Syr lacks verses 11, 12: Ethiop *For the **world** is divided into ten parts*, >}
16:58 confined the sea in the midst of the waters; {Other ancient authorities read *confined the **world** between the waters and the waters*}

WORSHIPED (2)
1Sa 1:28 she left him there for {Gk (Compare Q Ms) and Gk at 2.11: MT *And he* (that is, Elkanah) ***worshiped** there before*}
Lk 24:52 worshiped him, and {Other ancient authorities lack ***worshiped** him, and*}

WORST (1)
2Mc 13: 9 things far worse than those that had been done {Or *the **worst** of the things that had been done*}

WORTHILY (1)
Tob 13:10 Lord, for he is good, {Other ancient authorities read *Lord **worthily***}

WORTHLESSNESS (1)
2Sa 23: 6 But the godless are {Heb *But **worthlessness***}

WORTHY (1)
AdE 7: 4 brings shame on {Gk *is not **worthy** of*}

WOUNDS (1)
Mic 1: 9 For her wound {Gk Syr Vg: Heb ***wounds***} is incurable.

WRAPPED (1)
Eze 21:15 it is polished {Tg: Heb ***wrapped** up*} for slaughter.

WRITING (2)
Ro 16:22 I, Tertius, the writer of the letter, greet you in the Lord. {Or *I Tertius, **writing** this letter in the Lord, greet you*}
1Es 6:32 any of the things herein written, {Other authorities read *stated above* or *added in **writing***}

WRITTEN (2)
Lk 23:38 over him, {Other ancient authorities add ***written** in Greek and Latin and Hebrew* (that is, *Aramaic*)}
2Es 14:48 did so. {Syr adds ... *of those who are like him, after he had **written** all these things*. >}

Y

YAH (2)
Isa 12: 2 the LORD GOD {Heb *for **Yah**, the LORD*}
26: 4 the LORD GOD {Heb *in **Yah**, the LORD*}

YAMIN (1)
Ps 89:12 The north and the south {Or *Zaphon and **Yamin***}

YAPHT (1)
Ge 9:27 make space for {Heb ***yapht***, a play on *Japheth*}

YEAR (2)
2Es 3:29 during these thirty years. {Ethiop Arab 1 Arm: Lat Syr *in this thirtieth **year***}
14:48 did so. {Syr adds *in the seventh **year** of the sixth week, five thousand years* >}

YEARS (4)
1Sa 2: 8 honor. {Gk (Compare Q Ms) adds *He grants the vow of the one who vows, and blesses the **years** of the just*}
Isa 38:15 All my sleep has fled {Cn Compare Syr: Heb *I will walk slowly all my **years***}
Mk 16:14 risen. {Other ancient authorities add, in whole or in part, ... *The term of the **years** of Satan's power has been fulfilled*, >}
2Es 14:48 did so. {Syr adds <*five thousand **years** and three months and twelve days after creation*. >}

YES (1)
Mk 7:28 "Sir, {Or *Lord*; other ancient authorities prefix ***Yes***}

YESTERDAY (1)
Mic 2: 8 But you rise up against my people {Cn: Heb *But **yesterday** my people rose*}

YET (6)
1Sa 10:22 "Did the man come here?" {Gk: Heb *Is there **yet** a man to come here?*}
Job 13:15 See, he will kill me; I have no hope; {Or *Though he kill me, **yet** I will trust in him*}
34:23 not appointed a time {Cn: Heb ***yet***}
Mic 6: 9 O tribe and assembly of the city! {Cn Compare Gk: Heb *tribe, and who has appointed it **yet**?*}
Jn 7: 8 I am not {Other ancient authorities add ***yet***} going
Php 3:13 I have made it my own; {Other ancient authorities read *my own **yet***}

YHWH (4)
Ex 3:15 LORD, {The word "LORD" when spelled with capital letters stands for the divine name, ***YHWH***, which is here connected with the verb *hayah*, "to be"}
6: 3 LORD' {Heb ***YHWH***; see note at 3.15}
33:19 LORD'; {Heb ***YHWH***; see note at 3.15}
34: 5 LORD." {Heb ***YHWH***; see note at 3.15}

YOKE (5)
1Sa 14:14 in an acre {Heb ***yoke***} of land.
Isa 10:27 and his yoke will be destroyed ... Rimmon, {Cn: Heb *and his **yoke** from your neck, and a **yoke** will be destroyed because of fatness*}
La 5: 5 With a yoke {Symmachus: Heb lacks *With a **yoke***}
Hos 11: 4 who lift infants to their cheeks. {Or *who ease the **yoke** on their jaws*}

YOUNG (2)
1Sa 8:16 the best of your cattle {Gk: Heb ***young** men*}
2Ki 25:26 people, high and low {Or ***young** and old*}

YOUTH (4)
Nu 11:28 of Moses, one of his chosen men, {Or *of Moses from his **youth***}
Zec 11:16 or seek the wandering, {Syr Compare Gk Vg: Heb *the **youth***}
Mt 19:20 kept all these; {Other ancient authorities add *from my **youth***}
Sir 17:15 + v.16 *Their ways from **youth** tend toward evil*, >

Z

ZABAL (1)
Ge 30:20 honor {Heb ***zabal***}

ZAPHON (1)
Ps 89:12 The north and the south {Or ***Zaphon** and Yamin*}

ZATTU (1)
Ezr 8: 5 of Zattu, {Gk 1 Esdras 8.32: Heb lacks *of **Zattu***}

ZEALOUS (1)
1Es 8:72 who were ever moved at {Or ***zealous** for*}

ZECHARIAH (1)
Mt 27: 9 Jeremiah, {Other ancient authorities read ***Zechariah*** or *Isaiah*}

ZEREDAH (1)
Jdg 7:22 Zererah, {Another reading is ***Zeredah***}

ZEUS-OUTSIDE-THE-CITY (1)
Ac 14:13 The priest of Zeus, whose temple was just outside the city, {Or *The priest of **Zeus-Outside-the-City***}

ZION (1)
Ps 84: 5 to Zion. {Heb lacks *to **Zion***}

ZOHAR (1)
1Ch 4: 7 Izhar, {Another reading is ***Zohar***}

TOPICAL INDEX TO THE NRSV

Compiled by Verlyn D. Verbrugge

FEATURES OF THE TOPICAL INDEX TO THE NRSV

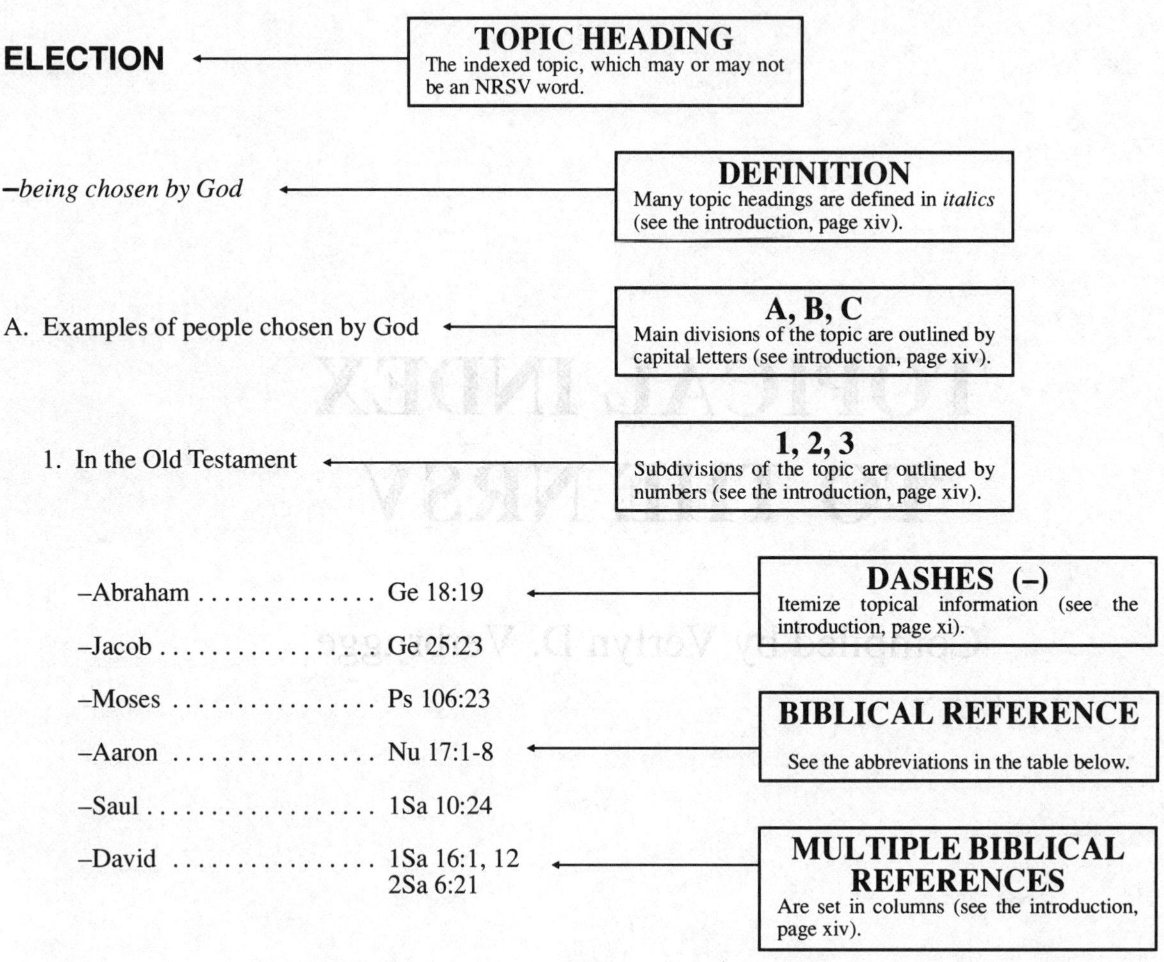

ELECTION
TOPIC HEADING
The indexed topic, which may or may not be an NRSV word.
–being chosen by God
DEFINITION
Many topic headings are defined in italics (see the introduction, page xiv).
A. Examples of people chosen by God
A, B, C
Main divisions of the topic are outlined by capital letters (see introduction, page xiv).
1. In the Old Testament
1, 2, 3
Subdivisions of the topic are outlined by numbers (see the introduction, page xiv).
–Abraham . . . . Ge 18:19
DASHES (–)
Itemize topical information (see the introduction, page xi).
–Jacob . . . . Ge 25:23
–Moses . . . . Ps 106:23
BIBLICAL REFERENCE
–Aaron . . . . Nu 17:1-8
See the abbreviations in the table below.
–Saul 1Sa 10:24
–David 1Sa 16:1, 12
2Sa 6:21
MULTIPLE BIBLICAL REFERENCES
Are set in columns (see the introduction, page xiv).

ABBREVIATIONS FOR THE BOOKS OF THE BIBLE

CANONICAL BOOKS

1Ch . . . . 1 Chronicles
1Co . . . 1 Corinthians
1Jn . . . . 1 John
1Ki . . . . 1 Kings
1Pe . . . . 1 Peter
1Sa . . . . 1 Samuel
1Th . 1 Thessalonians
1Ti . . . . . . 1 Timothy
2Ch . . . . 2 Chronicles
2Co . . . 2 Corinthians
2Jn . . . . 2 John
2Ki . . . . 2 Kings
2Pe . . . . 2 Peter
2Sa . . . . 2 Samuel
2Th . . 2 Thessalonians
2Ti . . . . . . 2 Timothy
3Jn . . . . 3 John
Ac . . . . Acts
Am . . . . Amos
Col . . . . . . Colossians
Da . . . . Daniel
Dt . . . . Deuteronomy
Ecc . . . . . Ecclesiastes
Eph . . . . . . Ephesians
Est . . . . Esther
Ex . . . . Exodus
Eze . . . . Ezekiel
Ezr . . . . Ezra
Gal . . . . Galatians
Ge . . . . Genesis
Hab . . . . . . Habakkuk
Hag . . . . Haggai
Heb . . . . . . Hebrews
Hos . . . . Hosea
Isa . . . . Isaiah
Jas . . . . James
Jdg . . . . Judges
Jer . . . . Jeremiah
Jn . . . . John
Jnh . . . . Jonah
Job . . . . Job
Joel . . . . Joel
Jos . . . . Joshua
Jude . . . . Jude
La . . . . Lamentations
Lev . . . . Leviticus
Lk . . . . Luke
Mal . . . . Malachi
Mic . . . . Micah
Mk . . . . Mark
Mt . . . . Matthew
Na . . . . Nahum
Ne . . . . . . Nehemiah
Nu . . . . Numbers
Ob . . . . Obadiah
Phm . . . . . . Philemon
Php . . . . . Philippians
Pr . . . . Proverbs
Ps . . . . Psalms
Rev . . . . . Revelation
Ro . . . . Romans
Ru . . . . Ruth
SS . . . Song of Songs
Tit . . . . Titus
Zec . . . . . . Zechariah
Zep . . . . . Zephaniah

APOCRYPHA

1Es . . . . 1 Esdras
1Mc . . . 1 Maccabees
2Es . . . . 2 Esdras
2Mc . . . 2 Maccabees
3Mc . . . 3 Maccabees
4Mc . . . 4 Maccabees
AdE . . . . Additions to Esther
Aza . . . . . . Prayer of Azariah
Bar . . . . Baruch
Bel . . . . Bel and the Dragon
Jdt . . . . Judith
LtJ . . . . Letter of Jeremiah
Man . . . . . . Prayer of Manasseh
Pm . . . . . . Psalm 151
Sir . . . . Sirach
Sus . . . . Susanna
Tob . . . . Tobit
Wis . . . . Wisdom

OTHER

S . . . Shorter Ending of Mark
T . . . . . . Psalm Titles
Pr: . . Sirach Prologue

TOPICAL INDEX TO THE NRSV

AARON

A. Family data
- –Genealogy ... Ex 6:16–20; 1Ch 6:3–15
- –Son of Amram and Jochebed ... Ex 6:20
- –Older brother of Moses ... Ex 7:1,7
- –Brother of Miriam ... Nu 26:59
- –Married Elisheba ... Ex 6:23
- –Four children ... Ex 6:23; Lev 10:1,6

B. His priesthood
1. His garments ... Ex 28:1–43; Ex 39:1–31
2. His consecration ... Ex 29:1–46
3. His ordination ... Lev 8:1–36
4. His duties
   - –To teach God's decrees ... Lev 10:8–11
   - –To offer prescribed sacrifices ... Lev 6:9–13
   - –To officiate on the Day of Atonement ... Heb 9:7
   - –To make atonement in special situations ... Nu 16:46–47
5. Hereditary high priesthood ... Nu 20:25–26
6. Established the house of Aaron ... 2Ch 29:21; Ps 115:10,12; Lk 1:5

C. Significant events
- –Spokesman for Moses ... Ex 4:14–16, 27–31; Ex 7:1–2
- –Supported Moses' hands ... Ex 17:8–13
- –Built golden calf ... Ex 32:1–24
- –Saved through Moses' prayer ... Dt 9:20
- –With Miriam, criticized Moses ... Nu 12:1 16
- –His staff budded ... Nu 17:1–11
- –Forbidden to enter Canaan ... Nu 20:1–12
- –His death ... Nu 20:22–29; Nu 33:38–39

ABEDNEGO

- –Hebrew deported to Babylon ... Da 1:1–6
- –Name changed from Azariah ... Da 1:7
- –Refused to be defiled by food ... Da 1:8–20
- –Was appointed administrator over Babylon ... Da 2:49
- –Refused to worship idols ... Da 3:1–12
- –Saved from fiery furnace ... Da 3:13–30

ABEL

- –Second son of Adam ... Ge 4:2
- –The first shepherd ... Ge 4:2
- –Offered proper sacrifice ... Ge 4:4; Heb 11:4
- –Considered righteous ... Mt 23:35
- –Murdered by Cain ... Ge 4:8; 1Jn 3:12
- –Christ's blood superior to his ... Heb 12:24
- –His place taken by Seth ... Ge 4:25

ABIATHAR

- –High priest in days of Saul and David ... Mk 2:26
- –Escaped Saul's slaughter ... 1Sa 22:18–23
- –Became high priest under David ... 1Sa 23:6,9
- –Joint high priest with Zadok ... 2Sa 19:11
- –Supported David against Absalom ... 2Sa 15:24–29
- –Supported Adonijah ... 1Ki 1:7–42
- –Deposed by Solomon ... 1Ki 2:22–35

ABIGAIL

A. Stepsister of David ... 2Sa 17:25; 1Ch 2:16–17
- –Married Jether ... 2Sa 17:25
- –Mother of Amasa, Absalom's commander ... 2Sa 17:25
- –Aunt of Joab, David's commander ... 2Sa 17:25

B. Wife of Nabal ... 1Sa 25:3
- –Begged David to spare Nabal's life ... 1Sa 25:23–35
- –Became David's wife after Nabal's death ... 1Sa 25:36–42
- –Captured and rescued ... 1Sa 30:5,18
- –Gave birth to Kileab ... 2Sa 3:3

ABIHU

- –Son of Aaron ... Ex 6:23
- –Went up Mount Sinai ... Ex 24:1,9
- –Consecrated as priest ... Ex 28:1
- –Killed for offering unauthorized fire ... Lev 10:1–2; Nu 3:2–4
- –Had no sons ... 1Ch 24:2

ABIJAH

A. Second son of Samuel ... 1Ch 6:28
- –A corrupt judge ... 1Sa 8:1–5

B. An Aaronic priest ... 1Ch 24:10
- –Ancestor of Zechariah ... Lk 1:5

C. Son of Jeroboam I of Israel ... 1Ki 14:1
- –Died as Ahijah prophesied ... 1Ki 14:1–18

D. King of Judah; son of Rehoboam ... 1Ki 14:31; Mt 1:7
- –Reigned three years ... 1Ki 15:1–2
- –Fought against Jeroboam ... 2Ch 13:1–22
- –A wicked king ... 1Ki 15:3

ABIMELECH

A. King of Gerar
- –Took Abraham's wife Sarah ... Ge 20:1–2
- –Warned by God in a dream ... Ge 20:3–7
- –Angry with Abraham ... Ge 20:8–16
- –Healed by God ... Ge 20:17–18
- –Made a covenant with Abraham ... Ge 21:22–33

B. Another king of Gerar
- –Discovered truth about Rebekah ... Ge 26:1–11
- –Controversy with Isaac over wells ... Ge 26:12–22
- –Made a covenant with Isaac ... Ge 26:26–31

C. Son of Gideon ... Jdg 8:31
- –Attempted to make himself king ... Jdg 9:1–49
- –His death ... Jdg 9:50–57

ABISHAG

- –Shunammite virgin who attended David ... 1Ki 1:1–4
- –Adonijah killed for wanting to marry her ... 1Ki 2:13–25

ABISHAI

- –Son of Zeruiah, David's sister ... 1Ch 2:16
- –Brother of Joab ... 1Sa 26:6
- –One of David's chief warriors ... 1Ch 11:15–21
- –Wanted to kill Saul ... 1Sa 26:6–9
- –Fought against Edomites ... 1Ch 18:12–13
- –Killed Abner ... 2Sa 2:18–27
- –Fought against Ammonites ... 2Sa 10:9–10
- –Wanted to kill Shimei ... 2Sa 16:5–12
- –Fought against Absalom ... 2Sa 18:2,5,12
- –Fought against Sheba ... 2Sa 20:1–6,10
- –Fought against Philistines ... 2Sa 21:15–17

ABNER

- –Cousin of Saul ... 1Sa 14:50
- –Commander of Saul's army ... 1Sa 17:55–57
- –Chided by David for carelessness ... 1Sa 26:5–16
- –Made Ish-Bosheth king after Saul ... 2Sa 2:8–10
- –Defeated by David's men ... 2Sa 2:12–17
- –Defected to David ... 2Sa 3:8–21
- –Killed by Joab and Abishai ... 2Sa 3:22–39

ABORTION

A. Law regarding accidental loss of a child ... Ex 21:22

B. What is said about a fetus
- –It is called a child ... Mt 1:20
- –It has conscious awareness ... Lk 1:36,41,44
- –Sinful nature is present at conception ... Ps 51:5

C. How God relates to a fetus
- –God cares for a conceived child ... Isa 46:3
- –God forms a child ... Ps 139:13–15; Isa 44:2,24
- –God plans a child's life ... Ps 139:16; Isa 49:1; Jer 1:5; Gal 1:15

ABRAHAM

A. Family data
- –Line of Shem ... 1Ch 1:24–27
- –Son of Terah ... Ge 11:26–27
- –Original name: Abram ... Ge 11:27
- –Husband of Sarai ... Ge 11:29
- –Father of Ishmael with Hagar ... Ge 16:1–4, 15–16
- –Father of Isaac with Sarah ... Ge 21:1–3
- –Father of many children with Keturah ... Ge 25:1–4
- –Died at 175 years old ... Ge 25:7–8

B. Covenant with the Lord
1. Called while in Ur ... Ge 12:1–3; Ac 7:2–4
2. Received promises
   - –Land and descendants ... Ge 13:14–17; Ge 15:18–21; Ge 22:15–18
   - –A son by Sarah ... Ge 17:16; Ge 18:9–15
3. Given circumcision as a sign ... Ge 17:1–14, 23–27; Ro 4:9–12
4. Declared righteous through faith ... Ge 15:6; Ro 4:3,20–24; Gal 3:6–9
5. Covenant sealed by sacrifice ... Ge 15:8–21
6. Name changed to Abraham ... Ge 17:5; Ne 9:7
7. Covenant remembered ... Lk 1:68–75; Heb 6:13–15

C. Travels and significant events
- –Left Ur ... Ge 11:31
- –Went to Canaan ... Ge 12:1–6; Ac 7:2–4
- –Deceived Pharaoh about Sarai ... Ge 12:10–20
- –Divided land with Lot, settled in Hebron ... Ge 13:1–18
- –Rescued Lot from four kings ... Ge 14:1–16
- –Blessed by Melchizedek ... Ge 14:17–20; Heb 7:1–7
- –Declared righteous through faith ... Ge 15:6

–Fathered Ishmael with Hagar ... Ge 16:1–16
–Entertained three visitors ... Ge 18:1–15
–Interceded for the city of Sodom ... Ge 18:16–33
–Deceived Abimelech about Sarah ... Ge 20:1–10
–Fathered Isaac with Sarah ... Ge 21:1–3
–Sent Hagar and Ishmael away ... Ge 21:8–21
Gal 4:22–30
–Made a covenant with Abimelech ... Ge 21:22–32
–Tested by command to sacrifice Isaac ... Ge 22:1–18
Heb 11:17–19
–Bought field for Sarah's burial ... Ge 23:1–20
–Secured wife for Isaac . Ge 24:1–67
–Fathered children with Keturah ... Ge 25:1–6
–Died ... Ge 25:7–11
D. Titles ascribed to him
–Mighty prince ... Ge 23:5–6
–Servant of God ... Ge 26:24
–Friend of God ... Isa 41:8
Jas 2:23
–Prophet ... Ge 20:7
–Father of Israel ... Ex 3:15
Mt 3:9
–Father of all believers .. Ro 4:11–12,16
Gal 3:7
E. Significance in New Testament
–Jesus is a son of Abraham ... Mt 1:1
–His true offspring is Christ ... Gal 3:15–16,29
–Jesus preceded him ... Jn 8:57–58
–Rejoiced to see Jesus' day ... Jn 8:56
–Showed greatness of Christ by giving a tithe to Melchizedek ... Heb 7:4–10
–Lived by faith ... Heb 11:8–12,17–19
–Believed in the power of the resurrection ... Ro 4:17–21
–Became the father of believers ... Ro 4:11–12
Gal 3:7
–His faith preceded the law ... Ro 4:9–11,13–16
Gal 3:17–19
–Cast out the sons of the law ... Gal 4:21–31
–Demonstrated faith by works ... Jas 2:20–24

ABSALOM

–Son of David by Maacah .. 2Sa 3:3
1Ch 3:2
–Killed Amnon for rape of Tamar ... 2Sa 13:23–33
–Fled to Geshur ... 2Sa 13:36–38
–Allowed by David to return ... 2Sa 14:1–24
–Reconciled with David ... 2Sa 14:28–33
–Rebelled against David ... 2Sa 15:1–12
–David fled from him ... 2Sa 15:13–37
–Accepted the advice of Hushai ... 2Sa 16:15—17:23
–Fought against David's men ... 2Sa 18:1–8
–Killed by Joab ... 2Sa 18:9–18
–Mourned by David ... 2Sa 18:19—19:8

ACCESS TO GOD

A. The command to approach God
–In the Old Testament .. Isa 55:6
Am 5:4,6
–In the New Testament .. Mt 7:7
Lk 11:9
Jas 4:8
B. How can we approach God?
1. From God's standpoint
–The Father draws us to himself ... Jn 6:44
–Jesus is the way to the Father ... Jn 14:6
Ro 5:2
Eph 3:12
1Pe 3:18
–The Spirit enables us to come near ... Eph 2:18
2. From our standpoint
–We must believe ... Ro 5:2
Heb 11:6
–We must live clean, obedient lives ... Ps 24:3–5
Mt 5:8
–We must pray to the Father ... Mt 6:6
–We must call upon God's name ... Ps 145:18
C. Promises to those who approach God
–We will find God ... Dt 4:29
2Ch 15:2
–God will listen to us ... 2Ki 13:4
–God will forgive us ... 2Ch 7:14
–God will make a covenant with us ... Isa 55:3
–God will bless us ... Ps 65:4
–We can have confidence before God ... Eph 3:12
Heb 4:16
1Jn 5:14

See also PRAYER

ACHAN

–Son of Carmi, of tribe of Judah ... Jos 7:1
–Stole things from Jericho ... Jos 7:1
–His sin caused defeat at Ai Jos 7:3–12
–His sin revealed ... Jos 7:13–23
–Stoned to death ... Jos 7:24–26
–A lesson for Israel ... Jos 22:18–20

ACHISH

–King of Gath before whom David feigned insanity ... 1Sa 21:10–15
–Gave David town of Ziklag ... 1Sa 27:1–7
–Trusted David ... 1Sa 27:10–12
–Philistines asked him to expel David ... 1Sa 29:1–11
–Still king in time of Solomon ... 1Ki 2:39–40

ADAM

A. The first Adam
1. The creation of Adam
–Made in God's image ... Ge 1:26–27
–Made from dust of the earth ... Ge 2:7
–Became a living being ... Ge 2:7
1Co 15:45
–Woman was created from him ... Ge 2:21–23
2. The work of Adam
–Was placed in Eden . Ge 2:8
–Took care of Eden .. Ge 2:15
–Named the animals .. Ge 2:19–20
–Work cursed after the fall ... Ge 3:17–19
–Was banished from Eden ... Ge 3:23–24
3. Marriage of Adam and Eve
–Was established by God ... Ge 2:23–24
–Eve tempted her husband ... Ge 3:6
1Ti 2:14
–Adam blamed Eve .. Ge 3:12
–Adam and Eve had children ... Ge 4:1–2
Ge 4:25—5:4
4. Temptation and fall of Adam
–God warned Adam not to sin ... Ge 2:16–17
–Adam disobeyed God ... Ge 3:1–6
–God pronounced punishment ... Ge 3:16–19
–Adam died ... Ge 5:5
–Sin and death passed on to all humans ... Ro 5:12,15–17,19
–God condemns us for Adam's sin ... Ro 5:16,18
B. The second Adam (Christ) ... 1Co 15:45
1. Prophecy concerning him in Eden ... Ge 3:15
2. Christ as the second Adam
–Descended from the first Adam ... Lk 3:23–38
–Obedient to God's will ... Ro 5:19
–Victorious over the devil ... Mt 4:1–11
1Jn 3:8
3. Results for believers
–They receive righteousness and life ... Ro 5:15–18
1Co 15:22
–They will receive new bodies like his . 1Co 15:46–49
Php 3:20–21

ADONIJAH

–Son of David by Haggith .. 2Sa 3:4
1Ch 3:2
–Attempted to be king after David ... 1Ki 1:5–27
–David made Solomon king instead ... 1Ki 1:28–53
–Wanted Abishag as wife ... 1Ki 2:13–22
–Killed at Solomon's command ... 1Ki 2:23–25

ADOPTION

–Becoming someone's child by a legal act
A. In human relationships
–Abram wants to adopt .. Ge 15:2–4
–Pharaoh's daughter adopts Moses ... Ex 2:10
–Mordecai adopts Esther ... Est 2:7
–A wife adopts a maid's son ... Ge 16:1–3
Ge 30:1–5
Ge 30:9–12
B. In the God-man relationship
1. It is rooted in God's eternal love ... Eph 1:4–5
Ro 8:29
1Jn 3:1
2. Israel is God's adopted son ... Ex 4:22–23
Dt 14:2
Jer 31:9
Hos 11:1
Ro 9:4
3. Christians are God's adopted children
–We become children by God's grace ... Eph 1:5–6
–We become children through faith in Christ ... Jn 1:12–13
Gal 3:26
–We can call God Father ... Mt 6:9
Ro 8:15
Gal 4:6–7
–We become siblings of Christ ... Mk 3:34–35
Heb 2:11–12
–We are united as one body in Christ ... Eph 2:11–13,19
Eph 3:6
–Our adoption is completed only at the resurrection ... Ro 8:19,23
1Jn 3:2
4. Results of being God's children
–We receive the rights of inheritance ... Ro 8:17
Gal 4:7
–We must walk in light ... Jn 12:35–36
Eph 5:8–10
1Th 5:4–5
–We must live as obedient children ... 1Pe 1:14–16
–We must live in peace ... Mt 5:9
Eph 2:17–19
–We must live in love ... Mt 5:44–45
Lk 6:35
–We must separate ourselves from evil .. 2Co 6:17–18
Php 2:15
–We are subject to God's discipline ... Heb 12:5–11
–We can expect suffering ... Ro 8:18,22

ADULLAM

–A city in southwest Judah .. Jos 15:21,33,35
–Judah married a woman from there ... Ge 38:1–2
–David hid his followers in a cave near it ... 1Sa 22:1–2
–David's men risked getting water from Bethlehem ... 2Sa 23:13–17
1Ch 11:15–19
–Fortified by Rehoboam ... 2Ch 11:5–10
–Judgment prophesied against it ... Mic 1:15
–Established again after the exile ... Ne 11:30

ADULTERY

–Sexual unfaithfulness to one's spouse
A. Old Testament perspective
1. Laws against adultery
–In the Ten Commandments ... Ex 20:14
Dt 5:18
–Various laws on adultery ... Lev 20:10
Nu 5:12–31
Dt 22:22–24
2. Examples of adultery
–Judah and Tamar ... Ge 38:15–18
–David and Bathsheba ... 2Sa 11:2–5
–Others in Judah ... Jer 5:7–9
Jer 29:23
3. Characteristics of adultery
–Is a sin against one's spouse and God ... Ge 39:7–9
2Sa 12:13
Ps 51:4
–Is personally dangerous ... Pr 2:16–19
Pr 6:25–29,32
–Pollutes a whole nation ... Jer 3:1
Jer 23:10–15
Eze 33:26
B. New Testament perspective
1. The sin of adultery
–Starts in a sinful heart ... Mt 15:19
–Considered a sinful action ... Ro 7:2–3
Jas 2:11
2Pe 2:14
–Sinful even in thought ... Mt 5:27–28
–Remarriage as adultery ... Mt 5:31–32
Mt 19:8–9
2. Results of adultery
–Leads to God's judgment ... Heb 13:4
–Leads to exclusion from the kingdom ... Gal 5:19–21
1Co 6:9
Rev 22:15
3. Pardon promised for adulterers ... Jn 8:3–11
1Co 6:11
C. Spiritual adultery
–References in the Old Testament ... Jer 3:6–10,20
Eze 16:32–35
Hos 1:2
–References in the New Testament ... Mt 12:39
Jas 4:4
–God judges spiritual adultery ... Jer 5:11–17
Eze 16:37–42
Mk 8:38
–God desires faithfulness to Christ ... 2Co 11:2

See also MARRIAGE

AFFLICTION

See PAIN

AGABUS

–A prophet in the early church ... Ac 11:27–28
–Predicted a severe famine for the world ... Ac 11:28

–Predicted Paul's arrest in Jerusalem .... Ac 21:10–11

AGAG

–King of Amalekites; spared by Saul 1Sa 15:7–9, 20
–Killed by Samuel 1Sa 15:32–33

AGRIPPA

–King who visited Festus .... Ac 25:13–22
–Paul spoke before him .... Ac 25:23—26:23
–Paul invited him to believe .... Ac 26:25–27
–Rejected the gospel .... Ac 26:28
–Declared Paul innocent .... Ac 26:31–32

AHAB

A. Personal data
–Son of Omri; king of Israel 1Ki 16:28–29
–Husband of Jezebel 1Ki 16:31
B. Significant events
–Promoted Baal worship 1Ki 16:31–33
–Opposed by Elijah 1Ki 17:1
–Contest on Mount Carmel 1Ki 18:16–39
–Defeated Ben-Hadad 1Ki 20:1–34
–Coveted Naboth's vineyard 1Ki 21:1–16
–Fought against king of Aram 1Ki 22:29–30
–Accidentally killed in battle 1Ki 22:34–38
C. Prophesied against
–By an unnamed prophet 1Ki 20:35–43
–By Elijah 1Ki 21:17–29
–By Micaiah 1Ki 22:9–28
D. Subsequent history
–Elisha told Jehu to destroy Ahab's family 2Ki 9:6–10
–House of Ahab destroyed 2Ki 10:1–17
–Name became a symbol of wickedness .... 2Ch 21:6,13; 2Ch 22:3–4; Mic 6:16

AHAZ

–Son of Jotham; king of Judah 2Ki 16:1; 2Ch 28:1
–Worshiped idols 2Ki 16:1–4, 10–18; 2Ch 28:1–4, 22–25
–Fought against Aram and Israel .... 2Ki 16:5–6; Isa 7:1
–Defeated by Aram and Israel 2Ch 28:5–15
–Fought against Edom and Philistia 2Ch 28:16–19
–Sought help from Assyria 2Ki 16:7–9
–Refused a sign from the Lord .... Isa 7:2–17
–His death 2Ki 16:19–20

AHAZIAH

A. Son of Ahab; king of Israel 1Ki 22:51
–Worshiped idols 1Ki 22:52–53
–Made an alliance with Jehoshaphat 2Ch 20:36–37
–Died while seeking advice from Baal 2Ki 1:1–17
B. Son of Jehoram; king of Judah 2Ki 8:25–26; 2Ch 22:1–2
–Worshiped idols 2Ki 8:27; 2Ch 22:3–4
–Allied with Joram, king of Israel 2Ki 8:28–29
–Killed by Jehu while visiting Joram 2Ki 9:14–29; 2Ch 22:1–9

–Only surviving son was Joash 2Ki 11:1–3

AHIMELECH

A. Priest at Nob during Saul's time 1Sa 21:1
–Gave David consecrated bread 1Sa 21:2–6
–Gave David Goliath's sword 1Sa 21:8–9
–Betrayed to Saul by Doeg 1Sa 22:9–16
–Killed by Doeg with other priests 1Sa 22:17–19
–Son Abiathar escaped to join David 1Sa 22:20–23
B. Grandson of Ahimelech 2Sa 8:17
–Co-priest with Zadok during David's reign 1Ch 18:16; 1Ch 24:6,31
C. One of David's warriors 1Sa 26:6

AHITHOPHEL

–A counselor of David 2Sa 15:12
–Joined Absalom against David 2Sa 15:31–37
–Advised Absalom 2Sa 16:15–23
–Absalom rejected his counsel 2Sa 17:1–14
–Committed suicide 2Sa 17:23

AI

–A city in Palestine, east of Bethel .... Jos 7:2
–Abram built an altar near there .... Ge 12:8
–Joshua's troops were initially defeated there .... Jos 7:3–5
–After Achan's death, Ai was destroyed .... Jos 8:1–29
–Later rebuilt, with Israelites settling there .... Ezr 2:2,28

ALCOHOL

A. Terms used in the Bible
–Drink and strong drink .... 1Sa 1:15; Pr 31:4,6
–Wine vinegar .... Nu 6:3
–Mixed wine .... Pr 9:2; Pr 23:30
–Old wine and new wine .... Lk 5:37–39
B. Various uses for alcohol
–In family meals .... Ge 27:25
–In public feasting .... Est 1:7–8,10; Da 5:1–4
–At weddings .... Jn 2:3
–As an offering to God .... Ex 29:38,40; Lev 23:12–13
–As a tithe .... Dt 12:17; Ne 13:5
–In barter exchange 2Ch 2:10
–As a commodity for commerce .... Eze 27:18
–As medicine .... Lk 10:34; 1Ti 5:23
–As a drug for pain .... Pr 31:6; Mk 15:23
–As a means to become drunk .... Ge 9:20–21
C. Positive aspects of alcohol
–A blessing from God .... Joel 2:19
–Can help one celebrate .... Jn 2:1–11
–Can give enjoyment .... Ps 104:15; Zec 9:17
–Can aid in happiness .... Ecc 10:19
–Can help to refresh someone 2Sa 16:2
–Can help one's health 1Ti 5:23
D. Dangers of using alcohol
–Loosens morals .... Ge 9:21–22
–Inflames an individual .... Isa 5:11–12
–Destroys health 1Sa 25:36–37
–Impairs judgment .... Pr 31:4–5; Isa 28:7
–Raises tempers .... Pr 20:1
–Leads to poverty .... Pr 23:21
–Leads to sorrow .... Pr 23:29–30
–Creates disunity in the church 1Co 11:18–21
E. Drunkenness forbidden .... Isa 5:11–12, 22; Ro 13:13; 1Co 5:11; 1Co 6:9–10; Eph 5:18
F. Symbolic uses of alcohol
–Symbolizes the blood of Christ .... Mt 26:27–29
–Symbolizes the gospel of salvation .... Isa 55:1
–Symbolizes the judgment of God .... Ps 75:8; Jer 25:15–16; Rev 14:10
–Symbolizes the sins of the antichrist .... Rev 17:2; Rev 18:3

ALIEN

–A citizen of one country residing in another

A. Aliens within the nation of Israel
1. Who were they?
–Those leaving Egypt with Israelites .... Ex 12:38
–Unconquered nations in Canaan .... Jos 9:26–27; 1Ki 9:20–21
–Captives taken in war .... Dt 21:10–11
–Slaves purchased .... Lev 25:44–46
–Foreigners hired in Israel 1Ki 9:27
–Foreigners attracted to Israel 2Ch 6:32–33
2. How were they to be treated?
–God had a special love for them .... Dt 10:18; Ps 146:9
–They were not to be oppressed .... Ex 22:21; Ex 23:9; Lev 19:33–34
–They enjoyed equal protection .... Lev 24:22; Lev 25:35; Dt 1:16–17; Dt 24:17–21
–They shared equal responsibility .... Ex 20:8–10; Nu 15:14–16
–Israel condemned for oppressing them .... Ps 94:6; Eze 22:7,29
B. God's people as aliens
1. In the Old Testament
–Abraham in Canaan .... Ge 17:8; Ge 23:4
–Jacob in Canaan .... Ge 28:4
–Moses in Midian .... Ex 18:3
–Israelites in Egypt .... Ge 15:13; Ex 23:9
–Israelites in Canaan .... Lev 25:23; 1Ch 29:15; Ps 39:12; Ps 119:19
–Israelites in Babylon .... La 5:2
–Their true homeland was elsewhere .... Heb 11:13–15
2. In the New Testament
–We are called aliens 1Pe 2:11
–We are not part of this world .... Jn 17:14,16
–Our true home is heaven .... Php 3:20–21; Col 3:1,3; Heb 11:16
–We must not love the world .... Ro 12:2; 1Jn 2:15–17
–We may not alienate people in the church .... Eph 2:19–22; Heb 13:1–2

ALTAR

A. Altars used in heathen religions
1. Such altars built .... Ex 32:5; 1Ki 16:32–33; 1Ki 18:26; Ac 17:23
2. Such altars destroyed
–At God's command .... Ex 34:13; Dt 7:5
–By Moses .... Ex 32:20
–By Gideon .... Jdg 6:25–28
–By all the Israelites 2Ki 11:18; 2Ch 31:1
–By various kings 2Ki 18:4; 2Ki 23:12; 2Ch 14:3,5
–By the Lord himself .... Hos 10:2
B. Altars used in the worship of the Lord
1. Such altars built or rebuilt by:
–Noah .... Ge 8:20
–Abram .... Ge 12:7–8; Ge 13:18
–Isaac .... Ge 26:25
–Jacob .... Ge 35:6–7
–Moses .... Ex 17:15
–Joshua .... Jos 8:30
–Gideon .... Jdg 6:24
–Samuel 1Sa 7:17
–Saul 1Sa 14:35
–David 2Sa 24:25
–Solomon 2Ch 8:12
–Asa 2Ch 15:8
–Elijah 1Ki 18:30–32
–Hezekiah's men 2Ch 29:18
–Manasseh 2Ch 33:16
–Jeshua and Zerubbabel .... Ezr 3:2–3
2. Altars located in
–The tabernacle .... Ex 37:25—38:7
–Solomon's temple 2Ch 4:1,19
–The second temple .... Ezr 7:17
–Ezekiel's temple .... Eze 43:13–27
–Herod's temple .... Lk 1:11
3. Purpose of altars to the Lord
–To sacrifice to the Lord .... Ge 8:20; Ge 12:7–8
–To make atonement for God's people .... Lev 16:18–20
–To burn incense to the Lord .... Ex 30:1–10
–To function as memorials .... Ex 17:15; Jos 22:26–27
4. Altars in the Christian religion
–Christ's cross is our altar .... Heb 13:10–12
–No need for sacrifice after Christ came .... Heb 9:6–15, 23–28; Heb 10:1–18
–The heavenly altar of incense .... Rev 6:9; Rev 8:3–5

AMALEKITES

A. Their identity
–The descendants of Amalek, grandson of Esau .... Ge 36:15–16
–Lived in the Negeb (south Canaan) .... Nu 13:29
B. Their wars
–Defeated by Chedorlaomer and his allies .... Ge 14:5–7
–Defeated by Israelites in the desert .... Ex 17:8–13
–Defeated the disobedient Israelites .... Nu 14:41–45
–Allied with Eglon against Israelites .... Jdg 3:12–13
–Allied with Midianites against Israelites .... Jdg 6:3,33
–Defeated by Gideon .... Jdg 7:12,22–24
–Defeated by King Saul 1Sa 14:47–48; 1Sa 15:1–9
–King Agag killed by Samuel 1Sa 15:32–33
–Defeated by David 1Sa 27:8–9; 1Sa 30:1–19
–An Amalekite soldier killed King Saul 2Sa 1:4–15
C. Important data concerning them
–They had no fear of God .... Dt 25:17–18
–Moses prophesied their complete destruction .... Ex 17:14; Dt 25:17–19
–Balaam predicted their destruction .... Nu 24:20

–Destruction completed by the Simeonites 1Ch 4:42–43

AMASA

–Nephew of David 1Ch 2:17
–Commander of Absalom's forces 2Sa 17:25
–Came back to David 2Sa 19:13
–Killed by Joab 2Sa 20:4–13

AMAZIAH

A. Son of Joash; king of Judah 2Ki 14:1–2
–Killed his father's assassins 2Ki 14:5–6
–Raised a large army ... 2Ch 25:5–6
–Defeated Edom 2Ki 14:7; 2Ch 25:7–13
–Worshiped Edom's gods 2Ch 25:14
–Rebuked by a prophet .. 2Ch 25:15–16
–Defeated by Israel 2Ki 14:8–14; 2Ch 25:17–24
–Killed by conspirators .. 2Ch 25:27
B. Idolatrous priest who opposed Amos ...... Am 7:10–17

AMBITION

–A goal one sets in life

A. Examples of proper ambitions
–Witnessing to unbelievers ...... Ro 15:20
–Being fully devoted to the Lord 1Co 7:32,34
–Desiring the greater gifts, especially love ... 1Co 12:31—13:7
–Pleasing God in everything 2Co 5:9
–Striving for perfection, unity and peace 2Co 13:11
–Forging ahead in service to Christ ...... Php 3:12–14
–Leading a quiet, diligent life 1Th 4:11
–Pursuing righteousness and godliness 1Ti 6:11; 2Ti 2:22
B. Examples of improper ambitions
–Competing with others in the kingdom ...... Mk 10:35–45; Php 1:15,17
–Serving one's own selfish wants ...... Php 2:3; Jas 2:14–16
–Seeking riches ...... 1Ki 3:7–12; Lk 12:13–21; 1Ti 6:9–10
–Attempting to glorify oneself ...... Ge 11:3–4; Da 4:28–30
–Attempting to displace God ...... Eze 28:2; 2Th 2:3–4

See also PRIDE

AMMONITES

A. Their identity
–Descendants of Benammi, son of Lot ...... Ge 19:38
–Related to the Moabites ...... Ge 19:36–38
–Given land east of the Jordan ...... Dt 2:19; Dt 3:16
–Served the god Molech . 1Ki 11:7,33
B. Significant Ammonites
–Nahash: besieged Jabesh 1Sa 11:1–2
–Hanun: opposed David . 2Sa 10:1–4
–Zelek: one of David's mighty men 1Ch 11:39
–Naamah: the mother of Rehoboam 1Ki 14:21,31
–Zabad: conspired against Joash 2Ch 24:26
–Tobiah: opposed Nehemiah ...... Ne 2:10,19; Ne 4:3,7–8
C. Their wars
–Allied with Eglon against Israelites ...... Jdg 3:12–13
–Allied with Philistines against Israelites ...... Jdg 10:7–9, 17–18
–Defeated by Jephthah .. Jdg 11:4–33
–Defeated by Saul 1Sa 11:1–11; 1Sa 14:47
–Defeated by David's army 2Sa 10:1–14; 2Sa 12:26–31; 1Ch 19:1–15; 1Ch 20:1
–Allied with Moabites against Jehoshaphat 2Ch 20:1
–They and Moabites destroyed each other 2Ch 20:22–24
–Defeated by Uzziah 2Ch 26:8
–Defeated by Jotham 2Ch 27:5
–Allied against Jehoiakim 2Ki 24:1–2
–Plotted against rebuilding of Jerusalem ...... Ne 2:19; Ne 4:1–3, 7–8
D. Important data concerning them
1. During the time of Moses and Joshua
–Not attacked by the Israelites ...... Dt 2:19,37
–Refused to give food to Israelites ...... Dt 23:4
–Not allowed to join the Israelites ...... Dt 23:4; Ne 13:1–8
–Half of their land given to Gad ...... Jos 13:25
2. During the time of the kings
–Israelites worshiped their gods ...... Jdg 10:6; 1Ki 11:5,7
–David used them to kill Uriah 2Sa 12:9
–Solomon intermarried with them 1Ki 11:1; 1Ki 14:21
3. Numerous Jews intermarried with them ... Ezr 9:1; Ne 13:23–27
4. Prophecies concerning their destruction ...... Isa 11:12–14; Jer 49:1–5; Eze 21:28–32; Eze 25:1–7; Am 1:13–15; Zep 2:8–11

AMNON

–Firstborn of David 2Sa 3:2
–Raped Tamar 2Sa 13:1–19
–Killed by Absalom 2Sa 13:20–29
–David mourned for him 2Sa 13:37

AMON

A. Son of Manasseh; king of Judah 2Ki 21:18–19
–Promoted idolatry 2Ki 21:20–22
–Assassinated 2Ki 21:23–24
B. Ruler of city of Samaria under Ahab 1Ki 22:26; 2Ch 18:25

AMORITES

A. Their identity
–Descendants of Canaan, grandson of Noah ...... Ge 10:6,15–16
–One of the Canaanite nations ...... Ex 33:2
–Lived in hill country, east of the Jordan ...... Nu 13:29; Jos 2:10
–Boundaries given ...... Jos 12:2–5
B. Significant Amorites
–Mamre, Eshcol, Aner: friends of Abram ...... Ge 14:13
–Sihon and Og: fought against Israelites ...... Nu 21:21,33; Dt 4:46–47
C. Their wars
–Defeated by Chedorlaomer and his allies ...... Ge 14:5–7
–Sihon and Og defeated by the Israelites ...... Nu 21:21–31
–They defeated disobedient Israelites ...... Dt 1:42–45
–Five Amorite kings defeated by Joshua ..... Jos 10:5–26
D. Important data concerning them
1. Exceptionally sinful .. Ge 15:16; 2Ki 21:11
2. God promised their land to the Israelites .. Ex 3:8,17; Ex 34:11
3. Political relationship with Israelites
–Land given to tribe of Reuben ...... Jos 13:15,21
–Israelites told to destroy them ...... Dt 7:1–6; Dt 20:16–18
–Israelites did not destroy them ...... Jos 13:2,4; Jdg 1:34–36
–Amorites and Israelites at peace 1Sa 7:14
–Became slaves of Israelites 1Ki 9:20–21; 2Ch 8:7–8
4. Religious relationship with Israelites
–Israelites must not worship their gods .. Jos 24:14–15
–Israelites worshiped their gods ...... Jdg 6:10
5. Intermarried with the Israelites ...... Jdg 3:5–6; Ezr 9:1–2

AMOS

A. Prophet from Tekoa ..... Am 1:1
–Originally a farmer and shepherd ...... Am 7:14
–Confronted the prophet Amaziah ...... Am 7:10–17
B. Ancestor of Jesus ...... Lk 3:25

ANANIAS

A. Husband of Sapphira .... Ac 5:1
–Kept back part of their money ...... Ac 5:2
–Died for lying to God .. Ac 5:3–10
B. Disciple in Damascus who baptized Saul/Paul .. Ac 9:10–17
–Commissioned Paul .... Ac 22:12–16
C. High priest at Paul's arrest ...... Ac 23:2; Ac 24:1

ANCESTRY

–Those from whom one has descended

A. Physical ancestry of the Israelites
–Genealogies were important ...... Ge 5:1–32; Ge 46:8–26; 1Ch 1:1—9:44; Ezr 2:3–61; Mt 1:1–17; Lk 3:23–38
–Priests had to prove ancestry ...... Ezr 2:62; Ne 7:64
–Israelites proud of Abraham as father ...... Isa 41:8; Isa 51:2; Lk 3:8; Jn 8:31–33
B. Ancestry of Jesus
–A descendant of Adam . Lk 3:38
–A descendant of Abraham ...... Mt 1:1; Ro 9:5
–A descendant of David . Mt 1:1; Ro 1:3
C. Spiritual ancestry of God's people
1. Physical ancestry insufficient to be saved ...... Ro 9:6–7
2. Requirements for becoming true children of Abraham
–We must be chosen by God ...... Ro 9:10–13
–We must believe in Jesus ...... Ro 4:11,16; Gal 3:7,26–29
–We must do God's will ...... Jn 8:39–40
3. True children of Abraham
–Are heirs of God ... Ro 8:17; Gal 3:29
–Include both Jews and Gentiles ...... Ro 4:16–17; Eph 3:6

ANDREW

–Brother of Simon Peter .... Mt 4:18
–Fisherman ...... Mk 1:16–18
–Disciple of John the Baptist ...... Jn 1:35–40
–Introduced Peter to Jesus ... Jn 1:41–42
–Became a disciple of Jesus . Mt 4:18
–Introduced little boy to Jesus ...... Jn 6:8
–Introduced Greeks to Jesus . Jn 12:21–22
–Asked Jesus about destruction of temple ...... Mk 13:3
–One of the apostles ...... Ac 1:13

ANGEL

–Spiritual beings created by God

A. Their origin and nature
–They are spirits ...... Heb 1:14
–They were created by God ...... Ps 148:2,5; Col 1:16
–They were created early in creation ...... Job 38:6–7
–They were created good ...... Ge 1:31
–They are not to be worshiped ...... Col 2:18; Rev 19:10
–They do not marry or die ...... Lk 20:35–36
–Some angels rebelled against God 2Pe 2:4
B. Names and ranks of good angels
–Michael ...... Da 12:1; Jude 9; Rev 12:7
–Gabriel ...... Da 9:21; Lk 1:19,26
–Archangels 1Th 4:16
–Seraphs ...... Isa 6:2
–Cherubim ...... Eze 10:1–3
–Rulers and authorities .. Eph 3:10; Col 1:16
–Thrones and powers ... Col 1:16
–There are numerous angels ...... Rev 5:11
C. Duties of good angels
1. General duties
–They revealed the law ...... Ac 7:38; Gal 3:19; Heb 2:2
–They bring messages from God ...... Zec 1:14–17; Ac 10:3–6
–They praise and worship God ...... Heb 1:6; Rev 5:11–12
–They provide for God's people ...... 1Ki 19:5–8; Mt 4:11; Heb 1:14
–They protect God's people ...... Ps 91:11; Da 6:22; Ac 12:7–10
–Some serve as guardian angels ...... Mt 18:10; Ac 12:15
–They give guidance to God's people ..... Ac 8:26; Ac 27:23–24
–They interpret God's will ...... Da 7:16; Zec 1:9,13–14
–They carry out God's will ...... Nu 22:22; Ps 103:20–21; Mt 28:2
–They punish God's enemies ...... 2Ki 19:35; Ac 12:23; Rev 14:17—16:21
2. Duties connected with Christ
–Gabriel announced conception to Mary . Lk 1:26–38
–An angel announced conception to Joseph ...... Mt 1:20–21
–An angel announced his birth ...... Lk 2:9–12
–Angels sang at his birth ...... Lk 2:13–14
–An angel warned Joseph to flee to Egypt ...... Mt 2:13
–An angel told Joseph to return ...... Mt 2:19–20

–Angels strengthened Christ — Mt 4:11; Lk 22:43
–Angels were available to help him — Mt 26:53
–An angel rolled away the stone — Mt 28:2
–Angels announced his resurrection — Mt 28:5–7; Lk 24:23; Jn 20:11–13
–Angels were present at his ascension — Ac 1:11
–Angels will return with Christ — Mt 25:31; 2Th 1:7

D. Evil angels
1. Satan is their leader — Job 1:6; Zec 3:1; Mt 4:10
2. Duties
–They oppose good angels — Rev 12:7–9
–They work through false teachers — 2Th 2:9–10; 1Ti 4:1–2
–They try to separate believers from God — Ro 8:38–39
–They oppose Christ and his church — Rev 12:3–6, 13–17
–They do evil to humans — Job 2:6–8; Mt 13:38–39; Lk 13:11,16
–They tempt humans to sin — Mt 4:3; 1Pe 5:8
–They accuse us before God — Zec 3:1

ANGEL OF THE LORD

A. To whom did he appear?
–To Hagar — Ge 16:7; Ge 21:17
–To Abraham — Ge 22:11,15
–To Jacob — Ge 31:11–13
–To Moses — Ex 3:2
–To the Israelites in the exodus — Ex 14:19
–To Balaam — Nu 22:22–36
–To Joshua — Jdg 2:1,4
–To Gideon — Jdg 6:11
–To Samson's parents — Jdg 13:21–22
–To David — 1Ch 21:16
–To Elijah — 2Ki 1:3–6
–To Daniel — Da 6:22

B. What tasks did he perform?
–Delivered messages from the Lord — Ge 22:15–18
–Protected God's people — 2Ki 19:34–35
–Redeemed God's people — Isa 63:9
–Punished God's people — 2Sa 24:16–17
–Destroyed God's enemies — Ex 23:23

C. How can we identify him as God (Jesus)?
–He uses I'' when he brings a message — Ge 16:10; Ge 22:16–17; Ge 31:13; Ex 3:6; Jdg 6:14
–He describes himself as holy — Ex 3:2,5
–He carries out God's judgment — 2Sa 24:16; 2Ki 19:35
–God's name is in him — Ex 23:20–23
–He takes on a human appearance — Jos 5:13–15; Jdg 13:6,10, 21

ANGER

A. Human anger
1. Expressed by such people as:
–Cain — Ge 4:5–6
–Jacob — Ge 30:2
–Moses — Ex 11:8
–Saul — 1Sa 20:30
–David — 2Sa 6:8
–Naaman — 2Ki 5:11
–Nehemiah — Ne 5:6
–Jonah — Jnh 4:1,9
2. Control of our anger
–We must refrain from anger — Ps 37:8; Eph 4:31
–We must be slow to anger — Jas 1:19–20
–We must keep our temper in check — Pr 16:32
–In our anger we must not sin — Ps 4:4; Eph 4:26–27
3. Anger puts us in danger of hell — Mt 5:21–22
4. We must let God avenge sin — Ps 94:1; Ro 12:19; 2Th 1:6–8

B. The anger of Jesus
–At injustice — Mk 3:5; Mk 10:14
–At the misuse of God's house — Jn 2:12–17
–In the final judgment — Rev 6:16–17

C. The anger of God
1. God's anger is righteous — Ro 3:5–6; Rev 16:5–6
2. Reasons for his anger
–The worship of idols — 1Ki 14:9,15, 22; 2Ch 34:25
–Sin — Dt 9:7; 2Ki 22:13; Ro 1:18
–Unbelief — Ps 78:21–22; Jn 3:36
–Unjust treatment of others — Isa 10:1–4; Am 2:6–7
–Refusal to repent — Isa 9:13,17; Ro 2:5
3. Expressions of his anger
–In temporal judgments — Nu 11:1,33; Isa 10:5; La 1:12
–In the day of the Lord — Ps 110:5; Zep 1:15,18; Ro 2:5,8; Rev 11:18
4. God's control of his anger
–God is slow to anger — Ex 34:6; Ps 103:8
–God's mercy overshadows his anger — Ps 30:5; Isa 54:8; Hos 11:8–11
–God will turn away his anger — Ps 78:38; Isa 48:9; Da 9:16
–Believers are spared from God's anger — Ro 5:9; 1Th 1:10; 1Th 5:9

ANIMALS

A. Animals mentioned in the Bible
–Antelope — Dt 14:5
–Ape — 1Ki 10:22
–Baboon — 1Ki 10:22
–Bear — 1Sa 17:34–37
–Behemoth — Job 40:15–24
–Camel — Lev 11:4
–Cattle (bull, cow, calf) — 1Sa 6:7; Ps 68:30
–Deer — Ps 42:1
–Dog — Mt 15:26–27
–Donkey — Mt 21:2,5
–Fish — Jn 21:3–11
–Fox — Mt 8:20
–Gazelle — Dt 14:5
–Goat — Ge 30:35
–Hare — Lev 11:6
–Horse — Ge 47:17
–Hyena — Isa 13:22
–Ibex — Dt 14:5
–Jackal — Isa 13:22
–Leopard — Isa 11:6
–Leviathan — Job 41:1
–Lion — Ge 49:9
–Mole — Isa 2:20
–Mouse — Lev 11:29
–Mule — 2Sa 18:9
–Ox — Ex 22:1,4
–Pig — Lev 11:7
–Rock badger — Lev 11:5
–Rodent — Isa 66:17
–Sheep (ram, ewe, lamb) — Ge 32:14; 2Sa 12:1–4
–Weasel — Lev 11:29
–Wolf — Isa 11:6

B. Animals used as symbols
1. Behemoth: symbolizes power — Job 40:15–24
2. Deer
–Symbolizes the thirsty soul — Ps 42:1
–Symbolizes the joy of the redeemed — Isa 35:6; Hab 3:19
3. Dog
–Symbolizes God's judgment — 1Ki 21:19, 23–24; Rev 22:15
–Symbolizes a fool — Pr 26:11
–Symbolizes an enemy — Ps 22:16,20
4. Donkey: symbolizes gentleness — Zec 9:9
5. Fish
See FISH
6. Fox
–Symbolizes that which threatens us — SS 2:15
–Symbolizes slyness — Lk 13:32
7. Horse
See HORSE
8. Lamb
See LAMB
9. Lion
See LION
10. Ox: symbolizes faithfulness — Isa 1:3
11. Wolf: symbolizes a false prophet — Mt 7:15; Ac 20:29

See also BIRDS
INSECTS
REPTILES

ANNA

–A prophetess from the tribe of Asher — Lk 2:36
–Elderly widow — Lk 2:36–37
–Witnessed to others about baby Jesus — Lk 2:28

ANNAS

–High priest when John the Baptist ministered — Lk 3:2
–Father-in-law of Caiaphas, the high priest — Jn 18:13
–Jesus on trial before him — Jn 18:13,19–23
–Sent Jesus to Caiaphas — Jn 18:24
–Peter and John on trial before him — Ac 4:5–7

ANOINTING

–Pouring oil on God's servants

A. Purposes of anointing with oil
1. For beautifying oneself — Ru 3:3; Ps 104:15
2. For healing — Lk 10:34; Jas 5:14
3. For dedicating officials to God — Ex 29:7; 1Sa 10:1; 1Ki 19:16
4. For dedicating things to God
–Jacob's stone pillow — Ge 28:18
–The tabernacle and its utensils — Ex 40:9–11

B. Which officials received an anointing?
1. In the Old Testament
a. Prophets — 1Ki 19:16; Ps 105:15
b. Priests — Ex 29:1,7; Lev 8:12
c. Kings
–Specific examples — 1Sa 10:1; 1Sa 16:1,13; 1Ki 19:16
–Kings called the Lord's anointed'' — 1Sa 12:3; 1Sa 26:9; 2Ch 6:42
2. In the New Testament
a. Jesus, anointed by the Holy Spirit
–Prophesied — Ps 2:2; Isa 61:1; Da 9:25–26
–Performed at his baptism — Mt 3:16; Jn 1:32–33
b. Christians, anointed by the Holy Spirit — 2Co 1:21; 1Jn 2:20,27

ANTICHRIST

A. Anyone who opposes Christ
–Called an antichrist — 1Jn 2:18,22; 1Jn 4:3; 2Jn 7
–Called a false Christ — Mt 24:24; Mk 13:22

B. *The* antichrist
1. Given the title the antichrist'' — 1Jn 2:18
2. Symbols of the antichrist
–Daniel's little horn — Da 7:8,24–26
–The king who exalts himself — Da 11:36–45
–The desolating sacrilege — Mk 13:14
–The lawless one — 2Th 2:3–4, 8–10
–The beast — Rev 11:7; Rev 13:1,11
3. Characteristics of the antichrist
–He is controlled by Satan — 2Th 2:9; Rev 13:2
–He opposes God — Da 7:25; Da 11:36; 2Th 2:4; Rev 13:6
–He teaches false views of Christ — 1Jn 2:22; 1Jn 4:3; 2Jn 7
–He lies and deceives humanity — 1Jn 2:22; 2Jn 7
–He performs counterfeit miracles — 2Th 2:9; Rev 13:3; Rev 19:20
–He persecutes Christians — Rev 13:7
–He gains political control of the world — Da 7:25; Da 11:40–45; Rev 13:7
–He gains economic control of the world — Rev 13:16–17
–He gains religious control of the world — 2Th 2:4; Rev 13:11–14
4. The end of the antichrist
–He is now being restrained — 2Th 2:6–7
–He will be destroyed at Christ's return — 2Th 2:8
–He will be thrown into the lake of fire — Rev 19:20; Rev 20:10

ANTIOCH

A. The capital of Syria
1. Important Christian events at Antioch
–First Gentile church located there — Ac 11:19–21
–Barnabas sent there — Ac 11:22–24
–Paul brought there by Barnabas — Ac 11:25–26
–Disciples first called Christians there — Ac 11:26
–Agabus prophesied there — Ac 11:27
–Peter and Paul had conflict there — Gal 2:11–14
–Sent delegates to council in Jerusalem — Ac 15:1–3
–Church heard report of the council — Ac 15:22–31
2. Antioch as a missionary church
–Church sent out Paul and Barnabas — Ac 13:1–3
–Paul and Barnabas reported to them — Ac 14:26–27
–Paul's second journey began from there — Ac 15:35–40
–Paul returned there after second journey — Ac 18:22

–Paul's third journey began from there .... Ac 18:23
B. An important town in Pisidia
–Paul preached the gospel there .... Ac 13:14–48
–Word spread from there throughout region ...... Ac 13:49
–Antioch Jews ran Paul out of town .... Ac 13:50–51
–Paul made brief return visit .... Ac 14:21–23
–Paul recalled persecution that occurred there 2Ti 3:11

ANXIETY

–The experience of worry and concern

A. The experience of anxiety
1. Appropriate concern
–For other family members .... 1Sa 10:2; Lk 2:48
–At the thought of having sinned .... Ps 139:23–24
–For not being able to understand a vision .. Da 7:15
–For the welfare of other Christians ...... 2Co 11:28–29; Php 2:20,26,28
2. Inappropriate anxiety
–For life's basic necessities .... Ecc 2:22–23; Eze 4:16–17; Mt 6:25–34; Lk 12:22–31
–For trivial, unnecessary things .... Lk 10:41
–For the cares of this life .... Mk 4:18–19
3. Anxiety weighs us down .... Pr 12:25
B. The cure for anxiety
–We must not be anxious .... Ecc 11:10; Mt 6:31; 1Co 7:32
–God promises to remove anxiety .... Ps 94:19
–God promises to take care of us .... Mt 6:34; 1Pe 5:7
–We must rely on Jesus . Lk 21:14–15
–We must pray .... Php 4:6

See also PROVIDENCE

APOLLOS

–Jewish Christian from Alexandria .... Ac 18:24–25
–Instructed by Aquila and Priscilla .... Ac 18:26
–Ministered at Corinth ...... Ac 18:27–28; Ac 19:1; 1Co 3:4–9
–Urged to revisit Corinth 1Co 16:12
–Messenger for Paul to Titus .... Tit 3:13

APOSTASY

–Falling away from the truth

See FALLING AWAY

APOSTLE

–Someone sent out on an official commission

A. Jesus was an apostle, sent out by God .... Heb 3:1
B. Apostles sent out by Jesus
1. The twelve disciples as apostles
–Commissioned before his resurrection ..... Mt 10:5–10
–Commissioned after his resurrection ..... Mt 28:19; Ac 1:8
2. Paul as an apostle
–His call from the risen Christ .... Ac 9:5–6; Ac 22:8–10,18; Ac 26:15–18
–His defense of his apostleship .... 1Co 9:1–2; 2Co 10:1–11:33; 2Co 12:11–13; Gal 1:1–2:10
–His calling as apostle to the Gentiles ...... Ro 11:13; Ro 15:16; Gal 2:8–9
3. Others called apostles
–Barnabas, with Paul . Ac 14:4
–James, the Lord's brother .... Gal 1:19
–Andronicus and Junias .... Ro 16:7
–Silas and Timothy, with Paul 1Th 2:6
C. The duties of Christ's apostles
–Apostleship is one of God's gifts .... 1Co 12:28; Eph 4:11
–Forming the foundation of the church .... Eph 2:20; Rev 21:14
–Witnessing about Christ .... Ac 1:8
–Teaching true doctrine . Ac 2:42
–Ministering the word of God .... Ac 6:2,4
–Making important decisions for the church .... Ac 15:1–2; Gal 2:1–3,7–10
D. The signs of apostleship
–Having seen the risen Christ .... Ac 1:21–22; 1Co 9:1
–Performing signs, wonders and miracles 2Co 12:12
–Being persecuted for the Lord .... Ac 5:40–41; 2Co 11:22–33

AQUILA

–Husband of Priscilla; tentmakers .... Ac 18:1–3
–Invited Paul to live with them .... Ac 18:3
–Traveled with Paul to Ephesus .... Ac 18:18–19
–Instructed Apollos .... Ac 18:26
–Paul considered him a fellow worker .... Ro 16:3
–Church met in their house .. Ro 16:4

ARAM, ARAMEANS

See DAMASCUS

ARK OF THE COVENANT

A. Its construction
–Made of acacia wood, overlaid with gold ..... Ex 25:10–11; Ex 37:1–2
–Had gold rings for poles .... Ex 25:12–15; Ex 37:3–5
–Its lid was the mercy seat .... Ex 25:17–21; Ex 37:6–9
B. Its contents
–A pot of manna .... Ex 16:32–34
–Aaron's staff that had budded .... Nu 17:10–11
–The Ten Commandments .... Dt 10:1–2; 1Ki 8:9
–All three mentioned together .... Heb 9:4
C. Its symbolism
–Symbolized God's presence among his people . Ex 30:6
–Symbolized the power of God .... Nu 10:35–36; Ps 132:8
–Sprinkled blood symbolized forgiveness of sin . Lev 16:15–16
D. Its history
1. During the time of Moses and Joshua
–Placed in the Most Holy Place of tabernacle .... Ex 26:34
–Went before the Israelites on journey .... Nu 10:33
–Instrumental in crossing the Jordan ...... Jos 3:1–3, 14–17
–Instrumental in the capture of Jericho ... Jos 6:4–11
–Joshua prayed before the ark after Ai ..... Jos 7:6
–Present at covenant renewal at Mount Ebal .... Jos 8:30–33
2. During the time of the judges
–Placed at Shiloh during Eli's time 1Sa 3:3,21
–Taken by Israelites into battle 1Sa 4:3–5
–Captured by Philistines 1Sa 4:11,17
–Returned by Philistines 1Sa 5:1–6:16
–Ark desecrated at Beth-shemesh 1Sa 6:19–20
–Ark sent to Kiriath-jearim 1Sa 6:21–7:2
3. During the time of David and Solomon
–Uzzah touched the ark and was killed .. 2Sa 6:1–8; 1Ch 13:1–10
–Ark stationed at the house of Obed-edom 2Sa 6:10–11; 1Ch 13:13–14
–David brought it to Jerusalem 2Sa 6:12–17; 1Ch 15:1–16:1
–Temporarily removed under Absalom 2Sa 15:24–29
–Placed in the Most Holy Place of the temple 1Ki 8:3–9; 2Ch 5:2–10

See also TABERNACLE

ARMAGEDDON

See MEGIDDO

ARTAXERXES

–Permitted Ezra and his group to go to Canaan ..... Ezr 7:1,11–26
–Employed Nehemiah as cupbearer .... Ne 2:1
–Issued order to stop rebuilding Jerusalem .... Ezr 4:7–23
–Sent Nehemiah to rebuild walls of Jerusalem .... Ne 2:1–9
–Appointed Nehemiah as governor .... Ne 5:14

ASA

–Son of Abijah; king of Judah 1Ki 14:31; 1Ki 15:8–10
–A godly reformer 1Ki 15:11–12; 2Ch 15:1–19
–Removed grandmother as queen 1Ki 15:13
–Increased strength of Judah . 2Ch 14:7–8
–Defeated Cushites 2Ch 14:9–15
–Waged war with Israel 1Ki 15:16–17
–Made alliance with Ben-Hadad 1Ki 15:18–21; 2Ch 16:2–6
–Hanani prophesied against him 2Ch 16:7–9
–Punished by God in his death 2Ch 16:11–14

ASAHEL

–Nephew of David 1Ch 2:16
–One of David's warriors ... 1Ch 11:26
–One of David's twelve commanders 1Ch 27:7
–Pursued Abner 2Sa 2:18–22
–Killed by Abner 2Sa 2:23
–Death avenged by Joab 2Sa 3:22–27

ASAPH

A. Father of Hezekiah's recorder .... 2Ki 18:18,37; Isa 36:3,22
B. A Levite musician 1Ch 15:19; 1Ch 16:4–7, 37
–Called a seer 2Ch 29:30
–His descendants were singers .... 1Ch 25:1–2,6; Ezr 2:41; Ne 11:22–23
–Wrote various psalms .. 2Ch 29:30; Ps 50; Ps 73–83

ASCENSION

–The return of Jesus to heaven

A. The event
–Prophesied in the Old Testament .... Ps 24:7–11; Ps 68:18; Ps 110:1
–Prophesied by Jesus .... Jn 7:33; Jn 13:1,3; Jn 20:17
–Recorded in the New Testament .... Mk 16:19; Lk 24:51; Ac 1:9
–Occurred forty days after the resurrection ... Ac 1:3
B. Activities of the ascended Christ
–He sat at God's right hand .... Ac 2:33; Ac 5:31; Heb 1:3
–He stood at God's right hand .... Ac 7:55–56
–He brought his atoning blood to God .... Heb 9:12
–He sent forth his Spirit . Jn 16:7; Ac 1:4–5; Ac 2:33
–He gave gifts to humans .... Eph 4:8–10
–He is now enthroned in power .... Eph 1:20–21; Php 2:9–11; 1Pe 3:22; Rev 1:5
–He is crowned with glory and honor .... 1Ti 3:16; Heb 2:9
–He is praised by multitudes in heaven .... Rev 5:6–14; Rev 7:9–12
–He is destroying God's enemies .... 1Co 15:24–26; Heb 10:12–13
–He is interceding for us .... Ro 8:34; Heb 7:25–26; 1Jn 2:1
–He is preparing a place for us .... Jn 14:2–3
–He is preparing for us to reign with him ...... 2Ti 2:12; Rev 20:5–6
–He is planning his return .... Jn 14:18,28; Ac 1:11
C. Activities of the ascended Christ on earth
–He identifies himself with believers .... Mt 25:40; Jn 17:21–23; Ac 9:4–5
–He draws believers to himself .... Eph 2:6; Col 3:1–4
–He is with Christians gathered in his name ... Mt 18:20
–He is with us always ... Mt 28:20
–He protects Christians .. Ac 18:9–10
–He directs Christians ... Ac 22:17–21

ASHER

A. Son of Jacob by Zilpah . Ge 35:26
–Name means happy" ... Ge 30:12–13
–Went to Egypt with family .... Ge 46:8,17
–Father of five sons ..... Ge 46:17
–Blessed by Jacob .... Ge 49:20
B. Tribe descended from Asher
–Blessed by Moses ..... Dt 33:24–25
–Numbered .... Nu 1:40–41; Nu 26:44–47
–Allotted land in Canaan .... Jos 19:24–31; Eze 48:2
–Failed to possess land .. Jdg 1:31–32
–Failed to support Deborah .... Jdg 5:17

–Supported Gideon ...... Jdg 6:35; Jdg 7:23
–Supported David 1Ch 12:36
–Supported Hezekiah 2Ch 30:10–11
–Anna from the tribe of Asher .... Lk 2:36
–One of the tribes of the 144,000 .... Rev 7:6

ASIA

–Area east of the Aegean Sea (present-day Turkey)

A. The Jews of Asia
 –Were in Jerusalem at Pentecost .... Ac 2:7–9
 –Opposed Stephen .... Ac 6:9
 –Incited riot against Paul in Jerusalem .... Ac 21:27–31
B. The church in Asia
 1. Churches established there
  –Ephesus .... Eph 1:1; Rev 2:1
  –Colossae .... Col 1:1
  –Laodicea .... Col 4:16; Rev 3:14
  –Troas .... Ac 20:6–12
  –Smyrna .... Rev 2:8
  –Pergamum .... Rev 2:12
  –Thyatira .... Rev 2:18
  –Sardis .... Rev 3:1
  –Philadelphia .... Rev 3:7
 2. Events
  –Paul's first convert was Epenetus .... Ro 16:5
  –Paul ministered in Ephesus .... Ac 19:8–10, 22; Ac 20:17–18
  –Gospel went through Asia from Ephesus .. Ac 19:10,26
  –Paul suffered greatly there 2Co 1:8–9
  –Paul addressed letters to them .... Eph 1:1; Col 1:2; Col 4:16
  –Peter addressed his letter to them 1Pe 1:1
  –Timothy ministered in Ephesus 1Ti 1:3
  –John wrote to seven churches there .... Rev 1:4

ASSURANCE

–Being certain of our salvation

A. Of what can we be sure?
 –Our calling and election 2Pe 1:10
 –God's abiding love .... Ro 8:38–39
 –Being God's children ... Ro 8:16
 –Our salvation at the last day .... Php 1:6; 2Ti 1:12
 –Our inheritance from God .... Heb 6:11–12
 –Our resurrection at the last day .... Job 19:25–26
 –Seeing our ascended Lord 1Jn 3:2
 –Receiving a crown of righteousness 2Ti 4:8
 –Having eternal life 1Jn 5:13
B. How do we obtain assurance?
 –By believing God's word 1Jn 5:13
 –By accepting God's promises .... Jn 3:16,36; Jn 6:39–40; 1Jn 5:12–13
C. On what is our assurance founded?
 –On God's choosing of us .... Eph 1:4–8; 1Th 1:4
 –On God's keeping us safe .... Jn 6:39; Jn 10:28–30
 –On God's powerful love .... Ro 8:35–39
D. What assures us of our salvation?
 –The Spirit living within us .... Ro 8:14–16; Gal 4:6
 –Our faith .... Ac 13:48; Ro 3:22,30; Ro 10:9–10; Eph 2:8
 –Our hope .... Heb 6:11, 18–19
 –Our life of love and good works .... Mt 7:20; Gal 5:19–24; 2Pe 1:5–8,10; 1Jn 3:10–14
E. Examples of those who experienced assurance
 –David .... Ps 23:6
 –Old Testament saints ... Isa 32:17
 –Paul 2Ti 1:12; 2Ti 4:7–8,18
 –Christians in general ... 1Jn 2:12–14
F. Assurance is compatible with
 –Doubt .... Mk 9:23–24
 –Sin in our lives .... Gal 6:1; 1Jn 1:8–10
 –Partial understanding of God's truth 1Co 13:8–12

ASSYRIANS

A. Their identity
 –Descendants of Cush, grandson of Noah ...... Ge 10:6,8–11
 –Capital city is Nineveh . Ge 10:11
  See NINEVEH
 –Located by the Euphrates River .... Isa 27:12–13; Jer 2:18
B. Kings of Assyria (in chronological order)
 –Pul 2Ki 15:19
 –Tiglath-pileser 2Ki 15:29
 –Shalmaneser 2Ki 17:3–4
 –Sargon .... Isa 20:1
 –Sennacherib 2Ki 18:13
 –Esar-haddon 2Ki 19:37
 –Osnappar .... Ezr 4:10
C. Campaigns against God's people
 1. Against the northern kingdom
  –First invasion 2Ki 15:19
  –Received tribute money and withdrew 2Ki 15:19–20
  –Second invasion 2Ki 15:29
  –Territories annexed and people deported . 2Ki 15:29
  –Hoshea refused to submit 2Ki 17:3–4
  –Three-year siege of Samaria 2Ki 17:5; 2Ki 18:9
  –Samaria captured and people deported 2Ki 17:6; 2Ki 18:10–11
  –Other people settled in Samaria 2Ki 17:24
 2. Against the southern kingdom
  –King Ahaz allied with Assyria 2Ki 16:7–9; 2Ch 28:16–18
  –Assyria did not help Ahaz 2Ch 28:19–21
  –Hezekiah refused to pay tribute 2Ki 18:7
  –Sennacherib attacked cities of Judah 2Ki 18:13
  –Hezekiah paid tribute from temple riches .. 2Ki 18:14–16
  –Sennacherib attacked Jerusalem .... 2Ki 18:17—19:13; 2Ch 32:9–19; Isa 36:1—37:13
  –Hezekiah prayed for deliverance .... 2Ki 19:14–19; Isa 37:14–20
  –Isaiah prophesied the fall of Assyria ...... 2Ki 19:20–34; Isa 37:21–35
  –The defeat of Assyria and Sennacherib .... 2Ki 19:35–36; 2Ch 32:20–21; Isa 37:36–38
D. Important data concerning them
 1. Garden of Eden in vicinity of Asshur .... Ge 2:14
 2. Country of Assyria was beautiful .... Eze 31:3–9
 3. Character of the Assyrians
  –A godless nation .... Isa 10:6
  –A powerful nation .. 2Ki 19:11,17; Isa 28:2
  –A proud nation ..... 2Ki 19:23–24; Isa 10:12; Eze 31:3,10
  –A cruel nation ...... Na 3:1–4
 4. God used Assyrians to punish Israelites ...... 2Ki 17:7–17; Isa 7:17–25; Isa 10:5–6
 5. Prophecies concerning them
  –Assyrians to be destroyed .... Isa 10:5,12–19; Isa 30:31–33; Na 2:1–13; Zep 2:13–15
  –Israelites to be called back from Assyria .. Isa 11:11–16; Isa 27:12–13; Hos 11:11; Mic 7:11–12; Zec 10:8–12
  –Assyrians to worship the Lord someday ... Isa 19:23–25

ATHALIAH

–Daughter of Ahab 2Ki 8:26
–Wife of Jehoram and mother of Ahaziah 2Ki 8:18,26; 2Ch 22:2
–Made herself queen by killing Ahaziah's sons 2Ki 11:1–2; 2Ch 22:10–12
–Ruled for six years 2Ki 11:3
–Killed when Joash was made king 2Ki 11:4–16; 2Ch 23:1–15

ATHLETICS

A. References to athletic activities in the Bible
 –Wrestling .... Ge 32:24–25
 –Slinging .... Jdg 20:16
 –Archery 1Sa 20:18–22,35–40
 –Running 2Sa 18:19–26
 –Boxing 1Co 9:26
 –Competing in the games 1Co 9:25
B. Athletics used in symbolic ways
 1. Archery: Job felt like God's target .... Job 16:12–13
 2. Ball-throwing: symbol of God's judgment ... Isa 22:17–18
 3. Running races
  –Running in the path of God's commands . Ps 119:32
  –Running the Christian race .... Heb 12:1–2
  –Not running in vain . Gal 2:2; Php 2:16
 4. Wrestling: symbol of struggling with Satan . Eph 6:12
 5. The games
  –The necessity of strict training 1Co 9:24–27
  –Competing according to the rules 2Ti 2:5
 6. The crown or prize awaiting believers .... 1Co 9:25; Php 3:13–14; 2Ti 2:5; 2Ti 4:8; 1Pe 5:4

ATONEMENT

–Procedure of reconciling sinners to God

A. Elements involved in atonement
 –Sin of humanity .... Isa 6:7; Isa 27:9; Da 9:24; Jn 1:29
 –Blood must be shed .... Lev 16:14, 18; Heb 9:19–22
 –Substitutionary sacrifice is offered .... Lev 4:13–20; Lev 5:5–10; Isa 53:4–7; 1Jn 2:2
 –Guilt is transferred to the substitute .... Lev 1:3–4; Lev 16:21–22; 2Co 5:21
 –Forgiveness is granted .. Lev 4:26,31, 35; Ro 3:23–25
B. Old Testament day of atonement
 –Description of the day of atonement .... Lev 16:2–34; Lev 23:26–32; Nu 29:7–11
 –Involved only the high priest .... Heb 9:7
 –Performed in the most holy place .... Lev 16:2, 16–20; Heb 9:8,25
 –Done once a year ...... Ex 30:10; Lev 16:34; Heb 9:7
 –Year of jubilee began on day of atonement ... Lev 25:9
C. Atonement accomplished by Christ
 1. Symbolized in Old Testament sacrifices
  –The passover lamb .. Ex 12:1–7, 12–13; 1Co 5:7
  –A lamb that takes away sin .... Isa 53:7; Jn 1:29,36; 1Pe 1:18–19; Rev 5:6
  –The day of atonement .... Heb 9:7–14, 23–28
 2. Fulfilled in the New Testament
  –Sacrifice of Christ atones for sin .... Ro 3:25; 1Co 5:7; Heb 9:28; 1Jn 2:2; 1Jn 4:10
  –Christ presented his blood to God .... Heb 9:12,14
 3. The results of Christ's atoning blood
  –Our sins are forgiven .... Eph 1:7
  –We are purified from sin 1Jn 1:7
  –We are freed from sin .... Rev 1:5
  –We are redeemed ... Ro 3:24–25; 1Pe 1:18
  –We are saved .... Ro 5:9
  –We are reconciled with God .... Ro 5:10; Col 1:20
  –We have peace with God .... Col 1:20
  –We are made holy ... Heb 13:12
  –We are reconciled to other Christians ..... Eph 2:14–17
  –The power of the devil is destroyed ... Col 2:15; Heb 2:14

AUTHORITY

–The ability to exercise power over others

A. Human authority
 1. Given as a gift from God and Christ
  –To humans for ruling creation .... Ge 1:28; Ps 8:6–8
  –To kings for ruling people .... Ps 72:1; Ro 13:1–5
  –To prophets for speaking .... Dt 18:18
  –To disciples for casting out demons ..... Mk 6:7,13
  –To apostles for forgiving sins .... Jn 20:22–23
  –To apostles for founding the church . Mt 16:19; Mt 18:18
  –To church leaders for building the church .. 2Co 10:8; 2Co 13:10; Eph 4:11–13; Tit 2:15
  –To saints for judging the world 1Co 6:2–3
 2. Exercised by humans

–Often done by exerting power ... Mt 20:25; Mk 10:42; Lk 22:25
–Christian authority defined by service ... Mt 20:26–28; Mk 10:43–45; Lk 22:26–27
See SERVANT

3. Misused by humans
–In ascribing power to ourselves, not God ... Dt 8:10–18
–In depending on ourselves, not God ... Ps 147:10–11
–In oppressing the poor ... Ps 10:2–11
–In exalting power rather than wisdom ... Ecc 9:12–18

B. Divine authority
1. Authority of God
–Power and authority ascribed to him ... 2Ch 20:6; Ps 66:3,5–7; Jude 25
–His authority may not be questioned ... Ro 9:20–21
–Even Satan under his control ... Job 1:6–12; Job 2:1–7

2. Authority of Jesus
a. While on earth
–To cast out evil spirits ... Mk 1:34
–To preach the word ... Mt 7:28–29
–To forgive sins ... Mk 2:5–12
–To give eternal life ... Jn 17:2
–To control nature ... Mk 4:39–41
–To raise the dead ... Jn 10:17–18; Jn 11:23–27, 38–44
–To judge ... Jn 5:27–30
b. Now in heaven
–All authority given to him ... Mt 28:18; Php 2:9–11
–Has authority at God's right hand ... Eph 1:20–23; Col 2:9–10
–Controls history ... Rev 5:1–5
–Is ruler of the kings of the earth ... Rev 1:5
–Is King of kings and Lord of lords ... Rev 17:14; Rev 19:16

AWE

–Reverence for the Lord
See FEAR

BAASHA

–Killed Nadab to become king of Israel ... 1Ki 15:27–28
–Killed rest of Jeroboam's family ... 1Ki 15:29–30
–Fought against Asa of Judah ... 1Ki 15:16–22,32
–Evil reign for twenty-four years ... 1Ki 15:33–34
–Jehu prophesied against him ... 1Ki 16:1–4
–Family killed by Zimri ... 1Ki 16:9–13

BABYLON

A. Identity and early history of the city
–Descendants of Ham ... Ge 10:6,8–10
–City is built by Nimrod ... Ge 10:8–10
–Rebellion against God at the Tower of Babel ... Ge 11:1–9

B. The nation of Babylon
1. Significant Babylonians
–Merodach-baladan: paid visit to Hezekiah ... 2Ki 20:12–13
–Nebuchadnezzar ... 2Ki 24:1
See NEBUCHADNEZZAR
–Nebuzaradan: commander of army ... 2Ki 25:8
–Evil-merodach: released Jehoiachin ... 2Ki 25:27
–Belshazzar: saw handwriting on the wall ... Da 5:1

2. Chronological history
–Under the control of Assyria ... 2Ki 17:24
–Envoys visited Hezekiah ... 2Ki 20:12–18
–Invaded Judah during Jehoiakim's reign ... 2Ki 24:1–2
–Exiles deported with Jehoiachin ... 2Ki 24:10–16
–Nebuchadnezzar's dream ... Da 2:1–49
–Nebuchadnezzar's image and fiery furnace ... Da 3:1–30
–King Zedekiah's revolt ... 2Ch 36:13
–Nebuchadnezzar marched on Jerusalem ... Jer 52:4–5
–Jerusalem totally destroyed ... 2Ki 25:4,8–10; Jer 52:12–14
–A second group deported ... 2Ki 25:11; 2Ch 36:20
–Nebuchadnezzar's madness and restoration ... Da 4:1–37
–A third group deported ... Jer 52:24–27
–King Belshazzar's banquet ... Da 5:1–4
–Medes took over Babylon ... Da 5:30–31

3. Jews in Babylon
–Three waves of exiles ... Jer 52:28–30
–Daniel and friends in royal service ... Da 1:1–21
–Ezekiel saw visions ... Eze 1:1–28
–Jews encouraged to settle there ... Jer 29:1–7
–Seventy years of exile ... Jer 25:11; 2Ch 36:21
–Jews experienced grief ... Ps 137:1–6
–Jews allowed to return under Persians ... 2Ch 36:22–23; Ezr 1:1–4; Ezr 7:1–8:36

4. Characteristics of the Babylonians
a. A powerful nation
–A naval power ... Isa 43:14
–A military power ... Jer 5:15–17; Jer 51:34
–A worldwide kingdom ... Da 2:37–38; Da 4:22
–A glorious nation ... Da 4:28–30, 36
–A wealthy people ... Jer 51:13
b. A wicked nation
–They trusted in wickedness ... Isa 47:10
–They were idolatrous ... Jer 50:38
–They engaged in sacrilegious feasting ... Da 5:1–3
–They were cruel ... Isa 14:4,16–17; Hab 1:6–7
–They showed arrogance against God ... Isa 14:13–14

5. Prophecies concerning Babylon
–They will conquer the world ... Jer 21:3–10; Jer 27:1–11; Eze 21:18–23; Eze 29:19
–They will be destroyed ... Isa 13:1–14:23; Isa 14:3–22; Isa 21:1–10; Isa 47:1–15; Jer 50:1–51:58

C. New Testament references to Babylon
1. As a symbol of the Roman empire ... 1Pe 5:13
2. As a symbol of the power of the antichrist
–Inspires people to sin ... Rev 14:8; Rev 18:2–5
–Persecutes the church ... Rev 17:5–6; Rev 18:24
–Makes war with the Lamb ... Rev 17:9–18
–Will be destroyed completely ... Rev 18:2–10,16–24

BALAAM

A. Personal data
–Son of Beor ... Nu 22:5
–Lived in Mesopotamia ... Dt 23:4
–Considered a prophet ... 2Pe 2:16
–Killed by Israelites ... Nu 31:8; Jos 13:22

B. His history
–Asked by Balak to curse Israelites ... Nu 22:4–8
–Commanded by God not to go ... Nu 22:9–13
–Asked by Balak a second time ... Nu 22:15–17
–Permitted to go ... Nu 22:18–20
–Met by an angel on the way ... Nu 22:21–35
–Uttered blessings instead of curses ... Nu 23:1–24:10
–Prophesied about Christ ... Nu 24:15–19
–Advised Balak to intermarry with Israelites ... Nu 31:15–16
–Returned home ... Nu 24:25

C. New Testament references
–Considered an example of greed ... 2Pe 2:14–15; Jude 11
–Considered a teacher of immorality ... Rev 2:14

BALAK

–Moabite king, frightened by Israelites ... Nu 22:1–4
–Hired Balaam to curse Israelites ... Nu 22:4–20; Jos 24:9
–Encouraged Moabites to marry Israelites ... Rev 2:14

BANNER

–A flag or insignia

A. How banners were used
–To designate different families ... Nu 2:2
–To rally troops ... SS 6:4
–To send messages ... Isa 13:2; Isa 18:3

B. The banner used as a symbol
–The Lord as our banner ... Ex 17:15
–Jesus Christ as a banner for all nations ... Isa 11:10
–God rallies us to his banner ... Ps 60:4
–God rallies all nations to his banner ... Isa 11:12; Isa 49:22–23
–We lift up victory banners ... Ps 20:5
–We raise a banner for the nations ... Isa 62:10–11
–God rallies armies to use in judgment ... Isa 5:26–29; Isa 13:2

BAPTISM

–The sacrament of initiation

A. Baptism of John the Baptist
–Where John baptized ... Jn 1:28; Jn 3:23
–He baptized many people ... Mt 3:5–6
–He baptized Jesus ... Mt 3:13–15
–His baptism symbolized repentance ... Mt 3:11
–His baptism meant to reveal Jesus ... Jn 1:31
–His baptism looked ahead to Spirit baptism ... Lk 3:16

B. Baptism by Jesus' disciples ... Jn 3:22; Jn 4:1–2

C. Christian baptism
1. It was commanded by Jesus ... Mt 28:19–20; Mk 16:16
2. It was done in the name
–Of the Father, the Son, the Holy Spirit ... Mt 28:19
–Of Jesus Christ ... Ac 2:38; Ac 10:48
–Of the Lord Jesus ... Ac 19:5
3. It was typified in the Old Testament
–In the story of the flood ... 1Pe 3:19–21
–In the rite of circumcision ... Col 2:11–12
–In the crossing of the Red Sea ... 1Co 10:2
4. Occurrences of Christian baptism
–Three thousand on Pentecost ... Ac 2:41
–New believers in Samaria ... Ac 8:12
–Ethiopian eunuch ... Ac 8:36–38
–Saul at his conversion ... Ac 9:18
–Cornelius and his friends ... Ac 10:48
–Lydia and her household ... Ac 16:15
–Philippian jailer and his household ... Ac 16:33
–New believers in Corinth ... Ac 18:8
–Gaius, Crispus, household of Stephanas ... 1Co 1:14–16
–New believers at Ephesus ... Ac 19:1–7
5. Symbolism of Christian baptism
–Forgiveness of sins ... Ac 2:38
–Washing away of sin ... Ac 22:16
–Spiritual rebirth ... Tit 3:5
–Salvation ... 1Pe 3:21
–Dying with Christ ... Ro 6:3–4; Col 2:12
–Spiritual circumcision ... Col 2:11–12
–Inclusion in the body of Christ ... 1Co 12:13
–Unity in the body of Christ ... Eph 4:3–6
–Being clothed with Christ ... Gal 3:27
6. Characteristics of Christian baptism
–Only one baptism ... Eph 4:5
–Done with water ... Ac 8:36–38; Ac 10:47
–Faith is essential ... Mk 16:16; Ac 8:12; Ac 16:31–34
–Repentance is essential ... Ac 2:38
–Linked with receiving the Holy Spirit ... Ac 2:38; Ac 10:44–48; Ac 19:2–6
–Separated from receiving the Spirit ... Ac 8:14–17
–Administered to households ... Ac 16:15,33; 1Co 1:16

BAPTISM OF THE HOLY SPIRIT

A. Jesus was baptized with the Holy Spirit ... Mt 3:16; Jn 1:32–33

B. Jesus baptized with the Holy Spirit
–Prophesied by John ... Mt 3:11; Lk 3:16
–Prophesied by Jesus ... Ac 1:5
–Fulfilled at Pentecost ... Ac 2:1–4

C. Relationship to water baptism
–Water baptism linked with Spirit baptism ... Ac 2:38–39; Ac 9:17–18; Ac 10:44–48; Ac 19:1–6

–Water baptism separated from Spirit baptism .... Ac 8:12,14–17
–Born of water and the Spirit .... Jn 3:5
–Baptized by one Spirit into one body 1Co 12:13
–Washing of rebirth and renewal by Spirit .... Tit 3:5

BARABBAS
–Prisoner at the time of Jesus .... Mt 27:16
–Committed murder and insurrection .... Mk 15:7; Jn 18:40
–Received freedom in place of Jesus .... Mt 27:17–26; Ac 3:13–14

BARAK
–Warrior who fought with Deborah against Sisera .... Jdg 4:6–16
–Sang song with Deborah .... Jdg 5:1–31
–Considered an example of faith .... Heb 11:32

BARNABAS
A. Personal data
–Originally named Joseph .... Ac 4:36
–Full of the Holy Spirit and faith .... Ac 11:24
–Sold property, brought proceeds to the church .... Ac 4:37
–Considered a prophet and teacher .... Ac 13:1
–Considered an apostle .... Ac 14:14
B. Relationship with Paul
–Brought Paul to the apostles .... Ac 9:27
–Brought Paul to Antioch .... Ac 11:25–26
–Brought gift with Paul to Jerusalem .... Ac 11:28–29
–Accompanied Paul on missionary journey .... Ac 13—14
–Went to Jerusalem for conference .... Ac 15:1–2,12; Gal 2:1–9
–Conflict with Paul over John Mark .... Ac 15:36–40
–Conflict with Paul over eating with Gentiles .... Gal 2:11–13
–Fellow worker with Paul .... 1Co 9:6; Col 4:10

BARTHOLOMEW
–Disciple of Jesus .... Mk 3:18
–One of the apostles .... Mt 10:3; Ac 1:13
–Probably also known as Nathanael .... Jn 1:45–49

BARUCH
–Son of Neriah .... Jer 32:12
–Jeremiah's secretary and friend .... Jer 32:12–16; Jer 36:4–32
–Forced to go to Egypt .... Jer 43:1–7
–Received comforting message from Jeremiah .... Jer 45:1–5

BARZILLAI
–Gileadite who aided David 2Sa 17:27–29
–Unable to go with David because of age 2Sa 19:31–39

BATHSHEBA
–Wife of Uriah 2Sa 11:3
–Committed adultery with David 2Sa 11:4
–Sent message she was pregnant 2Sa 11:5
–Became wife of David after Uriah was killed 2Sa 11:27
–First child died 2Sa 12:13–23
–Mother of Solomon 2Sa 12:24
–Influenced David to make Solomon king 1Ki 1:11–31
–Pleaded with Solomon for Adonijah 1Ki 2:13–25

BEER-SHEBA
A. History of Beer-sheba
–Southernmost city in the land of Israel .... Jdg 20:1
–Hagar fled there from Sarah .... Ge 21:14–19
–Abraham made a treaty with Abimelech there .... Ge 21:22–31
–Abraham lived there a while .... Ge 22:19
–Isaac made a treaty with Abimelech there .... Ge 26:23–33
–Jacob stopped there on the way to Egypt .... Ge 46:1–5
–Allotted to tribe of Judah .... Jos 15:21,28
–Later allotted to tribe of Simeon .... Jos 19:1–2
–Samuel's sons served as judges there 1Sa 8:1–3
–Elijah escaped there from Jezebel 1Ki 19:3
–Became a center of idolatry .... 2Ki 23:8; Am 8:14
–Resettled after the exile .... Ne 11:27,30
B. Appearances of God there
–To Hagar, to give her water .... Ge 21:17–19
–To Isaac, to bless him .... Ge 26:23–25
–To Jacob, to reassure him .... Ge 46:1–4
–To Elijah, to strengthen him 1Ki 19:3–7

BELSHAZZAR
–King of Babylon .... Da 7:1
–Gave a huge feast .... Da 5:1–4
–Saw handwriting on the wall .... Da 5:5–29
–Killed by the Medes .... Da 5:30–31

BENEVOLENCE
See THE RICH AND THE POOR; STEWARDSHIP

BEN-HADAD
A. King of Damascus 1Ki 15:18
–Made treaty with Asa 1Ki 15:18–19
–Fought against Israelite cities 1Ki 15:20–21
B. Another king of Damascus 1Ki 20:1
–Fought against Ahab 1Ki 20:2–12
–Defeated by Ahab 1Ki 20:13–21
–Fought Israel again the next year 1Ki 20:26–28
–Again defeated by Ahab 1Ki 20:29–30
–Made peace with Israelites 1Ki 20:31–34
–Later besieged Samaria 2Ki 6:24
–Siege miraculously lifted 2Ki 7:5–7
–Killed by Hazael 2Ki 8:7–15
C. Another king of Damascus 2Ki 13:24
–Son of Hazael 2Ki 13:24
–Defeated by Jehoash three times 2Ki 13:25
–Amos prophesied against him .... Am 1:3–5

BENJAMIN
A. Twelfth son of Jacob, second of Rachel .... Ge 35:16–24
–Name means "son of my right hand" .... Ge 35:16–18
–Favored by Jacob .... Ge 42:4
–Accompanied brothers to Egypt .... Ge 43:1–15
–Royal cup found in his sack .... Ge 44:1–13
–Judah interceded for him .... Ge 44:18–34
–Moved to Egypt with his family .... Ge 46:8,19
–Father of ten sons .... Ge 46:21
–Blessed by Jacob .... Ge 49:27
B. Tribe descended from Benjamin
–Blessed by Moses .... Dt 33:12
–Numbered .... Nu 1:36–37; Nu 26:38–41
–Allotted land .... Jos 18:11–28
–Failed to possess land fully .... Jdg 1:21
–Nearly obliterated .... Jdg 20—21
–King Saul from this tribe 1Sa 10:20–24
–Sided with Ishbaal after Saul's death 2Sa 2:8–11
–Turned to David 1Ch 12:23,29
–The apostle Paul was from this tribe .... Ro 11:1; Php 3:5
–One of the tribes of the 144,000 .... Rev 7:8

BETHANY
–A town on the Mount of Olives .... Lk 19:29
–Less than two miles from Jerusalem .... Jn 11:18
–The hometown of Mary, Martha and Lazarus .... Jn 11:1
–Jesus stayed there after triumphal entry .... Mk 11:11
–Jesus anointed by Mary there .... Mt 26:6–13; Mk 14:3–9; Jn 12:1–8
–Jesus ascended into heaven from there .... Lk 24:50–51

BETHEL
A. Identity of Bethel
–Originally called Luz .... Ge 28:19
–Close to Ai .... Jos 12:9
–On the border between Ephraim and Benjamin .... Jos 16:1–2; Jos 18:11–13
–Originally given to Benjamin .... Jos 18:21–22
–Later belonged to Ephraim .... Jdg 4:5; 1Ch 7:20,28
–Southernmost city of northern kingdom 1Ki 12:26–29
B. History of Bethel
–Abram built an altar near there .... Ge 12:8; Ge 13:3
–Jacob had a dream there .... Ge 28:10–17
–Jacob returned there with his family .... Ge 35:1–7
–Ephraim attacked the city and took it .... Jdg 1:22–26
–Samuel served as judge there 1Sa 7:15–16
–Prophet spoke against Jeroboam there 1Ki 13:1–6
–Abijah captured it from Jeroboam 2Ch 13:19–20
–Youths mocked Elisha and were killed 2Ki 2:23–24
–Amos prophesied against Israel there .... Am 7:10–13
–Josiah destroyed Jeroboam's altars 2Ki 23:15
–Resettled after exile .... Ne 11:31
C. Religious importance of Bethel
–God appeared to Jacob there .... Ge 28:10–19; Ge 35:9–15
–God was "the God of Bethel" .... Ge 31:13
–People inquired of the Lord there .... Jdg 20:18; Jdg 21:2–3
–The ark was kept there for a while .... Jdg 20:26–27
–Jeroboam set up golden calf there 1Ki 12:28–32
–A company of prophets lived there 2Ki 2:2–3,23
–Became known for its idolatry .... Am 4:4
–Prophesied against because of idolatry .... Hos 10:15; Am 3:14; Am 5:5–6

BETHLEHEM
A. Identity of Bethlehem
–Originally called Ephrath .... Ge 35:19
–A city given to Judah .... Ru 1:1
–Known as "the city of David" .... Lk 2:4,11
B. Important events at Bethlehem
–Rachel buried there .... Ge 35:19–20
–Ibzan judged there .... Jdg 12:8–10
–Home of Elimelech and Naomi .... Ru 1:1,19–22
–Ruth married Boaz there .... Ru 4:11–13
–David anointed king there 1Sa 16:4–13
–Philistines controlled it for a while 2Sa 23:14–17
–Rehoboam fortified it 2Ch 11:5–6
C. Jesus and Bethlehem
–Micah prophesied Messiah to be born there .... Mic 5:2; Mt 2:3–6; Jn 7:42
–Jesus was born in Bethlehem .... Mt 2:1; Lk 2:1–7
–Herod killed babies there .... Mt 2:16–18

BETHSAIDA
–A town in Galilee .... Jn 12:21
–Three of the disciples came from there .... Jn 1:44
–Feeding of five thousand occurred there .... Lk 9:10–17
–Jesus healed a blind man there .... Mk 8:22–26
–Jesus denounced it for unbelief .... Mt 11:20–22; Lk 10:13–14

BEZALEL
–Craftsman filled with God's Spirit .... Ex 31:1–3; Ex 35:30–31
–Supervised building of the tabernacle .... Ex 31:4–11; Ex 36:1–5

BILDAD
–One of Job's friends who tried to comfort him .... Job 2:11–13
–His first speech .... Job 8:1–22
–His second speech .... Job 18:1–21
–His third speech .... Job 25:1–6
–Offered sacrifices to God after Job's restoration .... Job 42:7–9

BILHAH
–Servant of Rachel .... Ge 29:29
–Mother of Dan and Naphtali .... Ge 30:1–7; Ge 35:25
–Reuben slept with her .... Ge 35:22

BIRDS
A. Birds mentioned in the Bible
–Bat .... Lev 11:19
–Birds of prey .... Ge 15:11
–Carrion birds .... Lev 11:19
–Chicken .... Mt 23:37
–Cormorant .... Lev 11:17
–Crane .... Jer 8:7
–Dove .... Gen 8:8
–Eagle .... Jer 49:16
–Gull .... Lev 11:16
–Hawk .... Lev 11:16
–Heron .... Lev 11:19
–Hoopoe .... Lev 11:19
–Kite (various types) .... Lev 11:14
–Mourning dove .... Isa 38:14
–Ostrich .... Job 39:13–18
–Owl (various types) .... Isa 34:11
–Partridge 1Sa 26:20
–Pigeon .... Lev 5:7,11
–Quail .... Nu 11:31–32
–Raven .... Ge 8:7
–Rooster (cock) .... Mt 26:74
–Sparrow .... Ps 84:3
–Stork .... Lev 11:19
–Swallow .... Pr 26:2
–Turtledove .... SS 2:12,14
–Vulture (various types) .... Lev 11:13

B. Birds used as symbols
1. The dove
–Symbolizes mourning .... Isa 38:14; Isa 59:11
–Symbolizes renewal . Ge 8:10–12
–Symbolizes the Holy Spirit .... Mt 3:16
–Symbolizes innocence .... Mt 10:16
2. The eagle
–Symbolizes deliverance .... Ex 19:4; Rev 12:14
–Symbolizes power ... Jer 4:13; Eze 17:3,7
–Symbolizes youthfulness .... Ps 103:5; Isa 40:31
3. The sparrow
–Symbolizes God's protecting care ...... Ps 84:3; Mt 10:29–31

BLASPHEMY

–Bringing reproach against God

A. How can one blaspheme God?
–By speaking against God .... Lev 24:11, 16; Mt 26:64–65; Ac 6:11
–By speaking against God's word .... Ac 6:11
–By engaging in idolatry .... Ne 9:18,26; Eze 20:27–28
–By persecuting the church 1Ti 1:13
–By oppressing the poor . Jas 2:2–7
–By bearing a sacrilegious name .... Rev 13:1
B. Regulations concerning blasphemy
–Prohibited by the law of God .... Ex 20:7; Ex 22:28
–Punishable by death .... Lev 24:13–16,23; Mt 26:65–66
C. Jesus is charged with blasphemy
–For claiming to forgive sins .... Mt 9:2–3; Mk 2:7
–For claiming to be Son of Man .... Mt 26:64–65
–For claiming to be God .... Jn 10:33
D. Blasphemy against Holy Spirit
–Linked with calling Jesus an agent of Satan .... Mt 12:24–27; Mk 3:22–26
–Considered an unforgivable sin .... Mt 12:31–32; Mk 3:29; Lk 12:10

BLESSING

A. Human blessings
1. Blessing sacred things
–Sacrifices 1Sa 9:13
–The cup in the Lord's Supper 1Co 10:16
2. Blessing other human beings
–A father blesses his sons .... Ge 27:1–40; Ge 48:15–16
–A family blesses a daughter leaving .... Ge 24:60
–Moses blesses the Israelites .... Dt 33
–Leaders bless the people .... Ex 39:43; Jos 22:6–7; 2Sa 6:18; 1Ki 8:14; 2Ch 31:8
–Priests bless the people .... Nu 6:24–26; 1Sa 2:20; 2Ch 30:27
–A prophet blesses the people .... Nu 23:11, 25–26
–The people bless the king 1Ki 8:66
–A blessing used as a greeting .... Ru 2:4; 1Sa 15:13
–Children bless their mother .... Pr 31:28
–The command to bless one's enemies .. Lk 6:28; Ro 12:14
B. Divine blessings
1. What/whom does God bless?
–Nature .... Ge 1:22
–The Sabbath .... Ex 20:11
–The work of his people .... Dt 28:8,12
–Humanity in general . Ge 1:28
–His covenant people . Ge 9:1; Ge 24:1; Dt 2:7
–God-fearing individuals .... Ps 1:1–3; Pr 3:13; Pr 16:20
–Those who live by godly principles ..... Ps 41:1; Pr 14:21; Mt 5:3–11
–The home of the righteous .... Pr 3:33
–Nations other than Israel .... Ge 39:5; Isa 19:25; Jer 4:2
2. What are God's blessings?
a. Material blessings given to us
–General statements .... Dt 7:13–14; Dt 28:2–14
–Peace and prosperity .... Eze 34:26
–Health, happiness and long life ..... Ps 21:3–5
–Children and a happy home ..... Ps 128:1–6
–Abundant crops and food .... Ps 67:6–7; Mal 3:10–12; Ac 14:17
–Showers of blessing .... Eze 34:26–30
b. Spiritual blessings given to us
–General statements .... Jn 1:16–17; 1Co 9:23; Eph 1:3
–God's favor and grace .... Ps 5:12
–Forgiveness of sins .... Ps 32:1–2; Ro 4:7–8
–Salvation .... Ro 10:12–13
–Being part of God's people .... Ro 15:27
–Eternal joy .... Ps 21:6
–Spiritual strength and peace .... Ps 29:11
–Having God as a shepherd .... Ps 28:9
c. The blessing of Abraham
–First mentioned to Abram .... Ge 12:2–3
–Repeated to Abraham .... Ge 22:17–18
–Repeated to Isaac .... Ge 26:3–5
–Repeated to Jacob .... Ge 28:13–15
–Repeated regarding David's line ..... Ps 72:17
–Fulfilled in Christ for the Jews ...... Ac 3:24–26
–Fulfilled in Christ for the Gentiles .. Gal 3:8–9,14
3. Who are blessed by the Lord?
–Those who avoid sin .... Ps 1:1
–Those who take refuge in the Lord ..... Ps 2:12
–Those whose sins are forgiven .... Ps 32:1
–Those who trust in the Lord .... Ps 40:4
–Those who show concern for the weak .... Ps 41:1
–Those chosen by the Lord .... Ps 65:4
–Those who dwell in God's house .... Ps 84:4
–Those disciplined by the Lord .... Ps 94:12
–Those who fear the Lord .... Ps 112:1
–Those who walk according to God's law .... Ps 119:1–2
–Those who find wisdom in the Lord .... Pr 3:13
–Those who wait for the Lord .... Isa 30:18
–Those who follow the way of Jesus .... Mt 5:3–12; Lk 6:20–22
–Those who confess Jesus as God's Son . Mt 16:16–17
–Those who hear and obey God's word ... Lk 11:28
–Those who persevere in their faith .... Jas 1:12
–Those who die in the Lord .... Rev 14:13
–Those invited to Christ's marriage feast .... Rev 19:9

BLOOD

A. Blood referred to literally
–In a human being 2Sa 20:12
–In an animal .... Ge 9:4
B. Blood used as a symbol
1. Blood symbolizes life
–Abel's blood meant his life .... Ge 4:10
–Eating blood means eating life .... Dt 12:23
–"Shedding blood" means taking a life .. Ge 9:5; Hab 2:8,17; Mt 27:24
–"Being innocent of blood" means not being responsible for physical death ...... Mt 27:24
–"Being innocent of blood" means not being responsible for spiritual death ...... Eze 3:17–19; Ac 18:6
2. Blood used in Old Testament sacrifices
–Examples .... Lev 1:5,11; Lev 3:2,8,13; Lev 16:14–16
–Shed blood symbolized forgiveness ..... Lev 17:11; Heb 9:22
3. The blood shed by Christ
a. What happened to it
–It flowed from the cross .... Jn 19:34
–It was presented to God in heaven ... Heb 9:12, 24–28
b. What it accomplishes
–Our forgiveness .. Eph 1:7; Heb 9:22; Rev 1:5
–Our redemption .. Ac 20:28; Heb 9:12; 1Pe 1:18–19
–Our atonement ... Ro 3:25
–Our justification .. Ro 5:9
–Our reconciliation .... Eph 2:13–16
–Our cleansing .... Heb 9:14; 1Jn 1:7; Rev 7:14
–Our holiness ..... Heb 10:29; Heb 13:12
–Our new life ..... Jn 6:53–56
–Establishment of the new covenant . Lk 22:20; 1Co 11:25
–Power over Satan .... Rev 12:11

BOASTING

See PRIDE

BOAZ

–Bethlehemite .... Ru 2:1
–Acted kindly to Ruth ...... Ru 2:8–16
–Married Ruth .... Ru 4:1–13
–Became ancestor of David . Ru 4:18–22; 1Ch 2:12–15
–Became ancestor of Jesus .. Mt 1:5–16; Lk 3:23–32

BODY

A. The human body
1. Refers to the physical body
–Originally fashioned by God .... Ge 2:7,22
–Now formed in the womb .... Ps 139:13, 15–16; Isa 44:2
–Refers to one's outward appearance .... Ge 25:25; SS 5:10–16
–We clothe the body . Mt 6:25
–Refers to the sexual side of humans 1Co 7:4
–The body must be controlled .... 1Th 4:4; Jas 3:2
–The body can be healthy .... Pr 3:8
–The body can become ill .... Ps 38:3,7
–The body can suffer . 1Pe 4:1
–The body remains behind at death 1Sa 31:10; 1Ki 13:24–25
2. Refers to the whole human person
–It experiences life and peace .... Pr 14:30
–It experiences freedom .... Mk 5:29
–We can discipline it . 1Co 9:27
–We can love or hate it .... Eph 5:29
–It can be washed by God .... Heb 10:22
–It can yearn for God .... Ps 63:1
–It can please God ... Ro 12:1
–It can reveal the living Jesus .... 2Co 4:10; Php 1:20
3. Effects of sin on the human body/person
–It becomes an instrument of sin .... Ro 6:12–13, 19; Ro 7:5
–It becomes subject to death .... Ge 3:19; Ps 90:3–5; Ro 8:10
4. Effects of salvation on the human body/person
–It receives new life .. Ro 8:11
–It becomes a member of Christ 1Co 6:15
–It becomes a temple of the Spirit 1Co 6:19
–It seeks to do God's will .... Ro 6:13,19
–It must honor God ... Ro 12:1; 1Co 5:20; Php 1:20
5. The future of the Christian's body
–Our bodies will be resurrected .... Jn 5:28–29; Jn 11:23–24; 1Co 15:42–44
–Our bodies will be redeemed .... Ro 8:23
–We will receive new bodies, like Jesus ... 1Co 15:52–54; Php 3:21
B. The body of Christ
1. His physical body
–Jesus came in a human body 1Ti 3:16; 1Jn 4:2–3
–Jesus was conceived by the Holy Spirit .. Lk 1:35
–Jesus suffered in his body 1Pe 4:1
–Jesus sacrificed himself in his body ..... Heb 10:10
–Jesus died in his body .... Ro 7:4; 1Pe 3:18
–Jesus' body was buried .... Mt 27:58–60; Jn 19:38–40
–Jesus' body was raised to life .... Ac 2:31–32
–Jesus received a glorified body .... Php 3:21
2. Spiritual significance of his body
a. His body symbolized by bread in the

Lord's supper ..... Mt 26:26; 1Co 10:16; 1Co 11:24
b. The church as the body of Christ
–Identified as such ..... Col 1:24
–Christ as the head of his body ..... Eph 1:22–23; Col 1:18
–Christ as Savior of his body ..... Eph 5:23
–Emphasis on one body ..... Ro 12:4–5; 1Co 10:16–17
–Emphasis on unity in the body ..... 1Co 12:25–26; Eph 2:14–16; Eph 4:3–4, 12–13
–Each member in the body important 1Co 12:14–24

BOLDNESS

See COURAGE

BOOK

A. In the Old Testament
1. Books of the law and prophecy
–The book(s) of God ..... Ex 32:32–33; Ps 139:16; Da 7:10
–The book of the covenant ..... Ex 24:7
–The book of the law ..... Dt 28:61; Ne 8:1,3,8, 18
–The book of Moses ..... Ezr 6:18
–The book of Jeremiah's prophecies ..... Jer 25:13; Jer 30:2–3
–The book of the vision of Nahum ..... Na 1:1
–The book of truth ..... Da 10:21
2. Books of history and poetry
–The Book of the Wars of the LORD ..... Nu 21:14
–The Book of Jashar ..... Jos 10:12–13
–The book of the Annals of King David 1Ch 27:24
–The Book of the Acts of Solomon 1Ki 11:41
–The Book of the Annals of the kings 1Ki 14:19,29
–The book of Jeremiah's Laments 2Ch 35:25
–The book of the annals of Persian kings ..... Est 2:23
3. No end to the making of books ..... Ecc 12:12

B. In the New Testament
1. References to parts of the Old Testament
–The book of Moses ..... Mk 12:26
–The book of the law ..... Gal 3:10
–The book of the prophets ..... Ac 7:42
–The book of Isaiah ..... Lk 3:4; Ac 8:28
–The book of Psalms ..... Lk 20:42; Ac 1:20
2. References to parts of the New Testament
–The Gospel of Luke ..... Ac 1:1
–The Gospel of John ..... Jn 20:30
–The Revelation of John ..... Rev 22:7, 18–19
3. God's special books
–The scroll of history ..... Rev 5:1–5
–The book of life ..... Php 4:3; Rev 3:5; Rev 21:27
–The books opened on the judgment day ..... Rev 20:12

BORN AGAIN

–Spiritual rebirth by the power of Jesus

A. Why is spiritual birth necessary?
–Because we are dead in sin ..... Eph 2:1,4–5; Col 2:13
–Because we need the Spirit ..... Jn 3:3–6

B. How does spiritual birth take place?
–By a decision of God ..... Jn 1:13
–By a decision of Jesus, the Son of God ..... Jn 5:21
–By an act of God through Christ ..... Col 2:13
–By the Holy Spirit ..... Jn 3:6; Tit 3:5
–Through the word of God ..... Jas 1:18; 1Pe 1:23
–Through believing in Jesus 1Jn 5:1

C. What does spiritual birth result in?
–Salvation and new life ..... Tit 3:5
–Entrance into God's kingdom ..... Jn 3:3
–Being a new creation ..... 2Co 5:17; Eph 4:24
–Victory over a sinful life ..... Ro 6:4–7; 1Jn 3:9; 1Jn 5:4,18
–Ability to do what is right 1Jn 2:29
–Ability to love one another 1Jn 4:7
–Safety from the evil one 1Jn 5:18

BREAD

A. Physical bread
1. Bread as a food
–Bread is eaten ..... Ge 14:18; 1Ki 17:6; Mt 14:16–17
–Bread stands for life's necessities ..... Dt 8:3; Ps 37:25; Pr 30:8; Mt 6:11
2. God's use of bread
–God tested Israel by giving only manna ..... Dt 8:3
–God tested Israel by a lack of bread ..... Nu 21:5
–God punished Israel by cutting off bread ..... Lev 26:26; La 1:11

B. Bread in Old Testament worship
1. Used in fellowship offerings ..... Lev 7:11–13
2. Used in Aaron's ordination ..... Lev 8:2,26, 31–32
3. The Bread of the Presence
–Placed in tabernacle ..... Ex 25:30
–Placed in the temple 2Ch 4:19
–Twelve loaves for twelve tribes ..... Lev 24:5–8
–David was given this bread ..... 1Sa 21:3–6; Mt 12:3–4
4. First bread each harvest offered to God ..... Nu 15:19–21
5. The Festival of Unleavened Bread
–A reminder of bread used in the exodus ..... Ex 12:8–20
–Regulations given ..... Lev 23:6; Dt 16:3–4
–Celebrated in Israel's history ..... Jos 5:11; 2Ch 30:21–27; 2Ch 35:17–19; Ezr 6:22
–Celebrated at the time of Jesus ..... Mt 26:17
–Celebrated in the early church ..... Ac 20:6

C. Bread related to Jesus
1. Physical bread
–Feeding of the five thousand ..... Mt 14:13–21; Mk 6:35–44; Lk 9:12–17; Jn 6:5–13
–Feeding of the four thousand ..... Mt 15:29–38; Mk 8:1–9
–A parable on bread ..... Lk 11:5–8
–Jesus served bread in the upper room ..... Mt 26:26
2. Bread used symbolically
–Jesus as bread of life ..... Jn 6:35,41, 48,51
–"This [bread] is my body" ..... Mk 14:22; Lk 22:19; 1Co 11:23–24
–Participating in the body of Christ 1Co 10:16
–Being one body in Christ 1Co 10:17

BROTHERS AND SISTERS

A. Natural use of brother and sister
1. People with the same parents ..... Ge 4:2,8; Ge 34:13–15
2. People with the same father ..... Ge 20:12; Ge 37:2,4,8
3. Any relative
–Members of the same tribe 2Sa 19:11–12
–Members of the Israelite nation ..... Dt 1:16; Dt 18:15; Isa 66:20; Hos 2:1; Ro 9:3–4
–People with same ancestors (Esau/Jacob) ..... Nu 20:14; Dt 2:8

B. Brothers and sisters of Jesus
1. Names
–James ..... Mt 13:55; Gal 1:19
–Joseph ..... Mt 13:55
–Simon ..... Mt 13:55
–Judas ..... Mt 13:55; Jude 1
2. Relationship to Jesus
–Wanted to see Jesus ..... Mt 12:46–47
–Gave advice to Jesus ..... Jn 7:3
–Did not believe in Jesus ..... Jn 7:5
–Later became disciples of Jesus ..... Ac 1:14
–Went on missionary excursions 1Co 9:5
–James became a leader of the church ..... Ac 15:13–21; Gal 2:9

C. Spiritual use of brother and sister
–Christ is our brother ..... Ro 8:29; Heb 2:11
–We are brothers and sisters of Christ ..... Mt 12:50
–Christians are brothers and sisters of one another ..... Mt 23:8; 1Co 6:6; Phm 16
–Specific references to sisters ..... Ro 16:1; Phm 2; Jas 2:15; 2Jn 13

D. Living as Christian brothers and sisters
–Be concerned about a brother or sister in need ..... Jas 2:15; 1Jn 3:17
–Forgive each other ..... Mt 5:23–24; Mt 18:15, 21–22
–Love each other ..... Ro 12:10; 1Th 4:9–10; Heb 13:1; 1Pe 1:22; 1Pe 2:17; 1Jn 4:20–21
–Overlook social differences ..... Phm 15–16; Gal 3:28
–Discipline an errant brother or sister 1Co 5:11; 2Th 3:6,14–15
–Do not judge each other ..... Ro 14:10,13; 1Co 6:5–7; Jas 4:11
–Do not destroy each other 1Co 8:9–13

BUILDING

A. Building in a physical sense
1. Things built to honor the Lord
–Altars ..... Ge 12:8; Ge 35:1
–The tabernacle ..... Ex 35:8–38:20
–The temple 1Ki 6:1–38
2. Things built against God's will
–The tower of Babel ..... Ge 11:4
–Altars to pagan gods ..... Ex 32:5; 1Ki 12:26–31

B. Building in a spiritual sense
1. Christians as builders
–Of their own lives on Christ and his words ..... Mt 7:24–27; 1Co 3:12–15; Col 2:7
–Of themselves in the faith ..... Jude 20
–Of the church into a unified body ..... Eph 2:21; Eph 4:16
–Of other Christians in love ..... Ro 15:2; 1Co 8:1; 1Th 5:11
2. The Lord as a builder
–Of Jerusalem ..... Ps 147:2
–Of the house of David 2Sa 7:27; 1Ki 11:38
–Of the nation of Judah ..... Jer 31:4
–Of our homes ..... Ps 127:1
–Of the church ..... Mt 16:18
–Of a place in heaven for his people ..... Jn 14:1–2; 2Co 5:1
–Of the new Jerusalem ..... Heb 11:10
–Christ is the cornerstone ..... Ps 118:22–23; 1Pe 2:6

CAESAREA

–A seacoast city ..... Ac 9:30; Ac 18:22
–Roman capital of Palestine ..... Ac 12:19–20; Ac 23:23–24
–Philip's home and headquarters for preaching ..... Ac 8:40; Ac 21:8
–Cornelius stationed there ..... Ac 10:1
–Peter preached to Cornelius there ..... Ac 10:23–48
–Paul imprisoned for two years there ..... Ac 24:1,27
–Paul on trial before Felix there ..... Ac 24:1–21
–Paul appealed to Caesar there ..... Ac 25:6–12
–Paul spoke to Agrippa there ..... Ac 25:13–26:32

CAIAPHAS

–A high priest at the time of John the Baptist ..... Lk 3:2
–Son-in-law of Annas, the high priest ..... Jn 18:13
–Spoke prophetically about Jesus ..... Jn 11:49–53
–Jesus on trial before him ..... Mt 26:57–67; Jn 18:24
–Peter and John on trial before him ..... Ac 4:5–7

CAIN

A. History in the Old Testament
–Firstborn son of Adam ..... Ge 4:1
–The first farmer ..... Ge 4:2
–Offered an unsatisfactory offering ..... Ge 4:3,5
–Murdered his brother Abel ..... Ge 4:8; 1Jn 3:12
–Became a wanderer ..... Ge 4:10–16
–His marriage and family ..... Ge 4:17–18

B. Significance in the New Testament
–Considered a symbol of evil ..... Jude 11
–Did not offer a sacrifice in faith ..... Heb 11:4

–Serves as warning not to hate others 1Jn 3:11–13

CALEB

–Son of Jephunneh; of tribe of Judah .... Nu 13:6
–One of the chosen spies of Canaan .... Nu 13:1–2,6
–Gave a positive report ..... Nu 13:30
–Pled with Israelites to have faith .... Nu 14:6–9
–Allowed to enter Canaan ... Nu 14:30–32
–Given city of Hebron ...... Jos 14:6–15; Jdg 1:20
–Gave daughter to be wife of Othniel .... Jdg 1:12–15

CALENDAR

See MONTH

CALL, CALLING

–God's summoning us to himself

A. Basic meanings of "call"
 –To summon to a conference .... Ge 3:9; Ac 4:18
 –To pray to the Lord ... Ge 4:26; Ro 10:13
 –To name something/someone .... Ge 2:19; Lk 1:60
 –To make someone one's own .... Isa 43:1; 1Pe 2:9
 –To appoint someone to service .... Ex 3:4–5; Mk 1:19–20
B. The call to become God's children
 1. What is its nature?
  –It is heavenward .... Php 3:14; Heb 3:1
  –It is irrevocable ..... Ro 11:29
  –It is linked to our election .... Ro 8:30; 2Th 2:13–14
  –More are called than chosen .... Mt 22:14
 2. What must we do?
  –We must repent ..... Lk 5:32; Ac 2:38–39; Ac 17:30
  –We must call on God's name .... Ac 9:21; Ro 10:12
  –We must confirm God's call by our lives 2Pe 1:5–10
 3. What are its results?
  –We are justified and glorified .... Ro 8:28–30
  –We have fellowship with Jesus 1Co 1:9
  –We enter God's kingdom 1Th 2:12; 2Pe 1:9–10
  –We enter God's light 1Pe 2:9
  –We enter Christ's glory 2Th 2:14
  –We have Christian hope .... Eph 4:4
  –We receive our inheritance .... Heb 9:15
  –We will conquer along with the Lamb .... Rev 17:14
C. The call to live a holy life
 1. Basic call .... Eph 4:1; 1Th 1:4; 2Ti 1:9
 2. What that call involves
  –Patient suffering 1Pe 2:20–21
  –Working for peace .. 1Co 7:15; Col 3:15
  –Serving one another . Gal 5:13
  –Working as an apostle .... Ro 1:1
  –Working as missionaries ...... Ac 13:2
D. The means used by God to call us
 –The Holy Spirit 1Th 1:5
 –Grace .... Gal 1:15
 –The message of the gospel .... 2Th 2:14; Ro 10:14

CANAAN, CANAANITES

A. Identity
 –Canaanites were descendants of Ham .... Ge 10:6,15–17
 –Various Canaanite nations .... Ge 15:19–21; Ex 3:8; Nu 13:29; Dt 7:1
 –Borders of Canaan given .... Ge 10:18–19
B. Relationship to God's people
 1. Land promised to Abraham and descendants .... Ge 15:18–21; Ge 17:8; Ex 6:4; Ps 105:11
 2. Brief history of God's people in Canaan
  –Abraham wandered there .... Ge 17:8
  –Isaac lived there .... Ge 26:1–6
  –Jacob left Canaan for Egypt .... Ge 46:5–6
  –Under Joshua, Israelites conquered Canaan .... Jos 12:1–24
  –Land divided out to the twelve tribes .... Jos 14:1–5
  –Northern tribes removed from Canaan 2Ki 17:18, 22–23
  –People of Judah exiled into Babylon . 2Ki 24:14
  –Jews returned to Canaan .... Ezr 1:1–5
 3. The destruction of the Canaanites
  –God promised to destroy them .... Ex 23:23, 27–31; Ex 34:11
  –God ordered Israelites to destroy them ..... Nu 33:51–53; Dt 20:16–17
  –Israelites to make no alliance with them .. Ex 23:32; Dt 7:2–4
  –Canaan was never fully taken .... Jos 13:1–5; Jdg 1:27–36
  –Some still existed at time of Jesus .... Mt 15:22
C. Significance of Canaan
 –Promised inheritance for Israelites .... Nu 26:52–56
  See INHERITANCE
 –A symbol of God's final land of rest .... Heb 4:1–11

CAPERNAUM

A. Jesus' ministry at Capernaum
 –Headquarters of Jesus' Galilean ministry ...... Mt 4:13–17; Jn 2:12
 –Jesus taught there ...... Mk 1:21–22; Lk 4:31–32
 –Jesus spoke about the bread of life there ..... Jn 6:24–59
B. Miracles of Jesus at Capernaum
 –Demon cast out .... Mk 1:21–27; Lk 4:31–37
 –Healing of Peter's mother-in-law .... Mk 1:29–31; Lk 4:38–39
 –Healing of official's son .... Jn 4:46–54
 –Healing of paralytic man .... Mk 2:1–12
 –Healing of centurion's servant .... Mt 8:5–13; Lk 7:1–10
 –Healing of many people .... Mk 1:32–34; Lk 4:40–41
 –Paying temple tax from a fish .... Mt 17:24–27
C. Jesus denounced Capernaum for unbelief .... Mt 11:23–24; Lk 10:15

CASTING LOTS

A. Occasions for casting lots
 1. Decisions of God's people through casting lots
  –Choosing a goat on Day of Atonement .. Lev 16:8
  –Dividing Canaan for the tribes of Israel .. Jos 18:6–10
  –Determining a guilty party 1Sa 14:40–44
  –Assigning duties to priests and Levites .. 1Ch 24:5,31; 1Ch 26:13–16; Lk 1:5–9
  –Deciding who would live in Jerusalem .... Ne 11:1
  –Choosing a replacement for Judas ...... Ac 1:26
 2. Decisions by heathens through casting lots
  –Haman's choice of a day for killing Jews . Est 3:7
  –Detection of Jonah by sailors .... Jnh 1:7
  –Owners of conquered Israelites .... Joel 3:3; Ob 11; Na 3:10
  –Recipient of Jesus' garment .... Mt 27:35
B. God controls the casting of lots .... Pr 16:33
C. Urim and Thummim likely a form of casting lots . Ex 28:30; Lev 8:8; Nu 27:21; Dt 33:8; 1Sa 28:6

CEPHAS

See PETER

CHARIOT

A. Uses for the chariot
 1. For royalty to ride in . Ge 41:43; 1Ki 18:44
 2. For important officials to ride in .... 2Ki 5:21; Ac 8:28–30
 3. For use in war
  –The Egyptians ...... Ex 14:7
  –The Canaanites ..... Jos 11:4,6,9
  –The Philistines 1Sa 13:5
  –The Arameans 1Ki 22:31–33
  –The Assyrians 2Ki 19:23
  –The Israelites 1Ch 18:4
  –The Cushites 2Ch 14:9
  –The Babylonians .... Eze 23:15, 23–24
 4. For use in pagan worship 2Ki 23:11
B. The chariot referred to symbolically
 –Elijah's ascension in a fiery chariot 2Ki 2:11–12
 –The clouds are God's chariot .... Ps 104:3
 –God's heavenly host are charioteers .... 2Ki 6:15–17; Ps 68:17
 –God executes judgment by his chariots .... Isa 66:15–16

CHASTISEMENT

See DISCIPLINE

CHILDREN

A. Proper opinion of children
 –A gift from God .... Ge 4:1; Ge 33:5
 –A heritage from the Lord .... Ps 127:3–5
 –A blessing from God ... Lk 1:42
 –A crown to the aged ... Pr 17:6
B. Familiar stories involving children
 –Abraham's willingness to sacrifice Isaac ...... Ge 22:1–19
 –The baby Moses .... Ex 2:1–10
 –Jephthah's daughter ...... Jdg 11:29–40
 –The call of Samuel 1Sa 3:1–18
 –David anointed king ... 1Sa 16:1–13
 –David killed a lion and a bear 1Sa 17:34–37
 –Elijah raised a dead boy 1Ki 17:17–24
 –Elisha raised a dead boy 2Ki 4:8–37
 –Joash became king at seven years 2Ki 11:4–12, 21; 2Ch 23:1–11; 2Ch 24:1
 –Josiah became king at eight years 2Ki 22:1–2; 2Ch 34:1–2
 –Jesus raised a girl from the dead .... Mt 9:22–25; Mk 5:35–43; Lk 8:49–56
 –Jesus raised a boy from the dead .... Lk 7:11–15
 –Jesus used a boy's lunch to feed a crowd .... Jn 6:1–13
 –Jesus called children to come to him .... Mt 19:13–15; Mk 10:13–16; Lk 18:15–17
C. God's relationship to children
 1. Blesses barren women with children .... Ps 113:9
  –Sarah .... Ge 21:1–3
  –Rebekah .... Ge 25:21–22
  –Rachel .... Ge 30:1–2
  –Hannah 1Sa 1:6–8
  –Elizabeth .... Lk 1:7,24–25
 2. Forms children in the womb .... Ps 139:13–16
 3. Knows children even before birth .... Jer 1:5; Gal 1:15
 4. Includes children in his covenant .... Ge 17:7; Ac 2:39
 5. Considers children of believers holy 1Co 7:14
 6. Shows concern for orphans .... Dt 10:18; Ps 10:14; Hos 14:3; Jas 1:27
D. Jesus and children
 1. His own childhood
  –His conception ...... Mt 1:18; Lk 1:26–38
  –His birth .... Mt 1:25; Lk 2:1–7
  –His circumcision and dedication .... Lk 2:21–38
  –His flight into Egypt .... Mt 2:14–15
  –His visit to the temple at twelve years .. Lk 2:41–50
  –Summary of his boyhood .... Lk 2:51–52
 2. His feelings about children
  –He wanted children to come to him ..... Mt 19:13–15; Mk 10:13–16; Lk 18:15–17
  –He used them to teach disciples humility .... Mt 18:1–4; Mk 9:36–37; Lk 9:46–48
  –He used them in parables .... Mt 11:16–17
  –He raised them from the dead .... Mt 9:22–25; Mk 5:35–43; Lk 7:11–15; Lk 8:49–56
E. Relationship between parents and children
 1. Parents' duties to children
  –Give them names ... Ge 21:3; Ge 29:31—30:24; Mt 1:25; Lk 1:59–63
  –Care for their physical needs 1Sa 1:22–24
  –Educate them .... Dt 6:6–7
   See EDUCATION
  –Discipline them ..... Pr 23:13–14
   See DISCIPLINE
  –Lay up inheritance for them 2Co 12:14
 2. Children's duties to parents
  –Obey them .... Pr 6:20; Eph 6:1; Col 3:20
  –Listen to and follow their instruction ..... Pr 1:8–9; Pr 3:1–2
  –Honor them .... Ex 20:12; Lev 19:3; Dt 5:16
  –Respect them in their old age .... Pr 23:22
  –Care for them 1Ti 5:4

F. Symbolic use of "children"
–Jesus' term for his disciples .... Mk 10:24
–A term for all believers .... Ro 8:16–17
See ADOPTION
–An elderly pastor's term for his church 1Jn 2:1,18
–Paul's term for those he led to Christ .... 1Co 4:14–17; 1Ti 1:2; Tit 1:4

See also FATHER
MOTHER
YOUTH

CHOOSING
See ELECTION

CHRIST
See JESUS CHRIST

CHRISTIAN
A. References in the New Testament
–Disciples first called Christians at Antioch ... Ac 11:26
–Paul wanted Agrippa to become a Christian .... Ac 26:28
–Christians need not be ashamed 1Pe 4:16
B. Other titles for Christians
–Aliens in the world 1Pe 2:11
See ALIEN
–Believers .... Ac 2:44
See FAITH
–Brothers and sisters .... Jas 2:15
See BROTHERS AND SISTERS
–Children of God .... Ro 8:16
See CHILDREN
–Children of light .... Eph 5:8
See LIGHT
–Disciples of the Lord .. Ac 9:1
See DISCIPLES
–The elect of God 1Pe 1:1
See ELECTION
–Friends of Christ .... Jn 15:14
See FRIENDSHIP
–Heirs of God .... Ro 8:17
See INHERITANCE
–Members of the body of Christ .... Ro 12:4–5
See BODY
–Priests .... Rev 1:6
See PRIEST
–Those sanctified in Christ 1Co 1:2
See SANCTIFICATION
–Saints 2Co 1:1
See SANCTIFICATION
–Servants of God 1Pe 2:16
See SERVANT

CHURCH
–God's called-out people
A. Definition of church
1. Church as a local group of believers
–In Jerusalem .... Ac 8:1
–In Antioch .... Ac 13:1
–In Caesarea .... Ac 18:22
–In Ephesus .... Ac 20:17
–In Cenchrea .... Ro 16:1
–In Corinth 1Co 1:2
–In Laodicea .... Col 4:16
–In Thessalonica 1Th 1:1
–Several in Galatia ... Gal 1:2
–Seven in Asia Minor .... Rev 2—3
2. Church as one world-wide church .... Mt 16:18; 1Co 10:32; Eph 5:25; Col 1:18
B. Titles ascribed to the church
–God's building 1Co 3:9
–God's field 1Co 3:9
–The temple of the Holy Spirit 1Co 6:19
–The church of God 2Co 1:1
–A chaste virgin 2Co 11:2
–The Jerusalem that is above .... Gal 4:26
–The Israel of God .... Gal 6:16
–The body of Christ .... Eph 1:22–23
–A holy temple .... Eph 2:21
–The bride of Christ .... Eph 5:25–28
–A chosen people 1Pe 2:9
–A royal priesthood 1Pe 2:9
–A holy nation 1Pe 2:9
–God's own people 1Pe 2:9
–The flock of God 1Pe 5:2
–The wife of the Lamb .. Rev 21:9–10
C. Characteristics of the New Testament church
1. Saved by Christ's blood .... Ac 20:28; Eph 5:25–27
2. Usually met in homes .... Ro 16:5; Col 4:15; Phm 2
3. Held worship services .... Ac 20:7–11; 1Co 14:26–28; Heb 10:25
4. Shared in the sacraments
–Baptism .... Ac 18:8; 1Co 12:13
–Lord's Supper (breaking bread) .... Ac 2:42; Ac 20:7; 1Co 11:23–33
5. Experienced unity
–Into one body .... Ro 12:5; Eph 4:13
–As one flock with one shepherd .... Jn 10:16
6. Enjoyed fellowship .. Ac 2:42; 1Jn 1:3–7
7. Helped each other .. Ac 4:32–37; 2Co 8:1–5
8. Evangelized others .. Ro 1:8; 1Th 1:8–10
9. Grew .... Ac 4:4; Ac 5:14; Ac 16:5
10. Was organized .... Ac 14:23; Php 1:1; 1Ti 3:1–13; Tit 1:5–9
11. Had problems .... 1Co 1:11–12; 1Co 11:17–22; Gal 3:1–5
12. Had to exercise discipline .... Mt 18:15–17; 1Co 5:1–5; 2Th 3:11–15; Tit 3:10–11
13. Experienced persecution .... Ac 8:1–3; Ac 17:5–9; 1Th 2:14–15

See also BROTHERS AND SISTERS
DEACON
ELDER
FELLOWSHIP
GROWTH
MISSION
SACRAMENT
UNITY
WORSHIP

CIRCUMCISION
–The cutting off of the foreskin
A. Occurrences of circumcision
–Abraham and his household .... Ge 17:23–27
–Isaac .... Ge 21:4; Ac 7:8
–All males in the city of Shechem .... Ge 34:24
–Moses' son .... Ex 4:24–25
–The Israelites at Gilgal . Jos 5:2–3
–John the Baptist .... Lk 1:59
–Jesus .... Lk 2:21
–The apostle Paul .... Php 3:5
–Timothy .... Ac 16:3
B. Circumcision in the Old Testament
–Done at eight days .... Ge 17:12
–A sign of the covenant . Ge 17:9–14
–A sign of Abraham's faith .... Ro 4:11
–Must be accompanied by heart circumcision .. Dt 10:16; Dt 30:6; Jer 4:4
C. Circumcision in the New Testament
1. Controversy in early church
–A circumcision party in the church .... Ac 11:2–3; Gal 2:12; Gal 6:12–13; Tit 1:10
–Discussed by leaders in Jerusalem .... Ac 15:1–22; Gal 2:4
–Decision: circumcision unnecessary .. Ac 15:6–29; Gal 2:1–3, 15–16
2. Discussion in Paul's letters
–Physical circumcision means nothing .... 1Co 7:19; Gal 5:6; Col 3:11
–Circumcision not needed for salvation . Ro 4:9–12; Gal 2:2–3; 1Co 7:18
–True circumcision involves obedience .. Ro 2:25
–True circumcision is of the heart .... Ro 2:28–29
–True worshipers are true circumcision .... Php 3:3
–Christians are circumcised in baptism .... Col 2:11–12

CITY
A. Major cities mentioned in the Bible
–Antioch .... Ac 11:19–20
–Athens .... Ac 17:15
–Babel/Babylon .... Ge 11:9; Da 4:30
–Caesarea .... Ac 23:23
–Corinth .... Ac 18:1
–Damascus 2Sa 8:6
–Ephesus .... Ac 19:1
–Jericho .... Jos 6:1
–Jerusalem 2Sa 5:6–7
–Nineveh .... Jnh 1:2
–Philippi .... Ac 16:12
–Rome .... Ac 28:14
–Samaria 1Ki 16:24
–Sodom and Gomorrah .. Ge 18:20
B. Types of Israelite cities
–The capital city 2Sa 5:6–9; 1Ki 16:24
–Cities for defense 2Ch 11:5–12
–Chariot cities 2Ch 1:14
–Cities for storage 2Ch 8:4,6
–Cities for the Levites .. Nu 35:1–5,7
–Cities of refuge .... Nu 35:6–15; Dt 19:1–3; Jos 20:1–9
C. Critical importance of cities
1. Defense of cities
–Usually fortified with walls .... Nu 13:28; Dt 3:5; Jos 6:5; 2Ch 11:5–13
–Besieged by armies . 1Ki 20:1; 2Ki 16:5
–Kingdom fell when the city was entered . 2Ki 17:5–6; 2Ki 25:1–7
2. Cities as centers for missions
a. Jonah sent to Nineveh .... Jnh 1:2
b. Disciples evangelized cities .... Mt 10:23
c. Paul preached in cities
–Antioch .... Ac 11:25–26
–Paphos on Cyprus .... Ac 13:6–12
–Antioch of Pisidia .... Ac 13:14–49
–Philippi .... Ac 16:12–40
–Thessalonica 1Th 1:7–10
–Corinth .... Ac 18:1–17
–Ephesus .... Ac 19:1–41
D. The city used as a symbol
–Of total rebellion against God .... Rev 18:1–24
See BABYLON
–Of the church and of heaven .... Heb 12:22–23; Rev 21:1–4

See JERUSALEM

CLEANNESS
A. The Old Testament regarding clean/unclean
1. How did one become unclean?
–By eating unclean foods .... Lev 11:1–23
–Through childbirth .. Lev 12:1–8
–Through skin diseases .... Lev 13:1—14:57
–Through discharges from the body .... Lev 15:1–33
–By touching a dead body .... Nu 5:2
–By worshiping false gods .... Jer 13:25–27; Hos 8:5
–Through a life of sin .... Isa 64:5–7
2. How could one become clean?
–By washing self and clothes .... Ex 19:10–14; Ex 30:18–21; Lev 22:6
–By certain sacrifices and ceremonies .... Lev 12:6–8; Lev 14:1–11
–By turning to the Lord .... Ps 51:2,7; Isa 4:4; Isa 6:5–7
B. Inward cleansing from sin
1. The need for such cleansing .... Mt 23:25–28
2. God's promise for such cleansing .... Jer 33:8; Eze 36:25,33
3. The process of such cleansing
–The believer must ask for it .... Ps 51:2,7; 1Jn 1:9
–It takes place in the heart .... Ps 24:3–4; Mk 7:18–23
–It occurs through Christ's blood .... Heb 9:14; Heb 10:19–22; 1Jn 1:7
–It occurs through the word of God .... Eph 5:25–27
4. The results of such cleansing
–It leads to a life of holiness 2Co 7:1
–It leads to a life of purity 1Jn 3:3
–It leads to a life of love 1Pe 1:22

CLOTHING
A. Purposes and uses of clothing
1. Clothing for natural uses
–To cover nakedness . Ge 3:7,21
–To keep warm .... Pr 31:21
–To trade in business . Pr 31:24; Ac 16:14
2. Clothing for religious purposes
–To use in special service to God .... Ex 28:1–5
–To symbolize a message from God 1Ki 11:29–32
–To appoint a prophet as successor 1Ki 19:19; 2Ki 2:13–14
3. Clothing used for display
–Special favor to a child .... Ge 37:3–4
–Honor to a citizen .. Est 6:11
–One's wealth .... Mt 11:8
–One's power .... Ac 12:21
–One's position as ruler .... Ge 41:42
–One's self-righteousness ... Mt 23:5
–Mourning .... Ge 37:34; 2Sa 3:31; Job 1:20
–Sorrow for sin .... Ezr 9:3
–Shock .... Mk 14:63; Ac 14:14
B. Significant garments in the Bible
–Garments sewn by God for Adam and Eve .... Ge 3:21
–The robe of Joseph from his father .... Ge 37:3–4
–The garments stolen by Achan .... Jos 7:20–21
–The purple robe put on Jesus .... Mk 15:17
–The seamless garment of Jesus at the cross .... Mt 27:35; Mk 15:24; Jn 19:23–24
C. Clothing used as a symbol
–Taking off a garment means putting off sin .. Eph 4:22; Col 3:9

–Putting on a garment means putting on Jesus . . . Ro 13:14; Gal 3:27
–Receiving a new garment symbolizes forgiveness . . . Zec 3:3–5; Mt 22:11–13; Rev 3:5
–Being clothed with white robes in heaven . . . Rev 7:9,13–14

COMFORT

–Consolation and strength in a time of need

A. People who need comfort
–Those grieving . . . Ge 37:33–35; Job 2:11; Isa 61:2; Mt 5:4
–Those in a new country . . . Ru 2:13
–Those facing troubles . . . Ps 71:21; Isa 51:19
–Those downcast . . . 2Co 7:6
–Those being punished for sin . . . Isa 40:1; La 1:9,17; 2Co 2:6–7

B. Sources of comfort
1. Human comfort given by
–Spouses . . . Ge 24:67; 2Sa 12:24
–Children . . . Ge 37:33–35
–Friends . . . Job 2:11–13; Jn 11:19
–Prophets . . . Isa 40:1–2; 1Co 14:3
–Preachers . . . Isa 61:1–2; 2Co 1:4–6; 1Th 2:11–12
–Any Christian . . . 2Co 2:6–7; Col 4:11
2. Divine comfort given through
–God . . . Isa 51:3,12; Isa 57:18; Isa 66:13; Zec 1:17
–The God of all comfort . . . Jer 8:18; 2Co 1:3
–God's rod and staff . . . Ps 23:4
–God's promises . . . Ps 119:50,76
–Jesus Christ . . . Jn 14:27; Jn 16:33
–Christ's love . . . Php 2:1
–The Holy Spirit as Counselor . . . Jn 14:16,26; Jn 15:5–7

COMPASSION

–Deep feeling of concern for suffering and needy people

A. Human compassion commanded
–In the Old Testament . . . Mic 6:8; Zec 7:9
–In the New Testament . . . Gal 6:2; Eph 4:32; Col 3:12; 1Pe 3:8

B. The compassion of Christ
–To people without leaders . . . Mt 9:36; Mk 6:34
–To sick people . . . Mt 14:14; Mt 20:34; Mk 1:41
–To hungry people . . . Mt 15:32; Mk 8:2
–To a grieving widow . . . Lk 7:13
–To all of us in our weaknesses . . . Heb 4:15

C. The compassion of God
1. A chief characteristic of God
–God is the God of compassion . . . 2Co 1:3
–He is compassionate . . . Ex 34:6; Ps 103:8; Jnh 4:2
–He is full of compassion . . . Ps 116:5; Jas 5:11
–His compassions never fail . . . La 3:22
2. His expressions of compassion
–To Adam and Eve when they sinned . . . Ge 3:15
–To the Israelites in Egypt . . . Ex 3:7
–To the Israelites in the desert . . . Ne 9:17–21
–To the Israelites groaning under enemies . . . Jdg 2:18
–To the Israelites in exile . . . Isa 54:7–8; Jer 42:11–12
–To all of us as sinners . . . Ps 51:1; Ps 103:8–12; Mic 7:19
–To aliens and the oppressed . . . Ex 22:27; Dt 10:18–19

See also MERCY

CONFESSION

A. Confession of sin before God
1. Examples of people confessing sin
–Aaron . . . Nu 12:11
–David . . . 2Sa 12:13; Ps 32:5; Ps 38:18; Ps 51:1–5
–Nehemiah . . . Ne 1:6–7
–Isaiah . . . Isa 6:5
–Peter . . . Lk 5:8
–A tax collector . . . Lk 18:13
2. Those who may confess sin
–Individual sinners . . . Lev 5:5; Mt 6:12
–Priests on behalf of the people . . . Lev 16:21; Ezr 9:5–10:1
–Prophets on behalf of the people . . . Isa 6:5; Isa 59:12–15; Jer 14:7,20–21; Da 9:7–11
3. The results of confessing sin
–We receive God's mercy . . . Pr 28:13
–We receive God's forgiveness . . . Ps 32:5; 1Jn 1:9
–We are justified . . . Lk 18:13–14
–We receive healing . . . Jas 5:16
–We become purified . . . 1Jn 1:9

B. Confession of faith in Jesus Christ
1. Such confession is necessary to be saved . . . Mt 10:32–33; Ro 10:9–10
2. Earliest confessions of faith
–"Jesus is Lord" . . . Jn 20:28; Ro 10:9; 1Co 12:3; Php 2:11
–"Jesus is the Christ" . . . Mt 16:16; Jn 20:31; Ac 17:2–3; 1Jn 2:22
–"Jesus is the Son of God" . . . Mt 16:16; Mt 27:54; Jn 20:31; 1Jn 4:15
3. Other elements added to confessions
–Certain teachings about Christ . . . 1Jn 4:2–3; 2Jn 7
–Trustworthy sayings . . . 1Ti 1:15; 1Ti 4:9–10; 2Ti 2:11; Tit 3:8
4. Brief creeds in the New Testament . . . 1Co 15:3–5; 1Ti 3:16; 2Ti 2:11–13; Tit 3:4–7

CONFIDENCE

See ASSURANCE

CONSCIENCE

–An inner voice defining right and wrong

A. Everyone has a conscience . . . Ro 2:14–15

B. Our conscience and sin
–It helps us do what is right . . . Ro 2:15; 2Co 1:12
–It accuses us of sin . . . 2Sa 24:10; Ac 2:37; 1Co 8:7
–It can be distorted . . . Pr 30:20; Eph 4:19; 1Ti 4:2
–A good conscience can be rejected . . . 1Ti 1:19

C. Our conscience and Christ
–It becomes cleansed through Christ . . . Heb 9:14; Heb 10:19, 22
–It inspires us to love others . . . 1Ti 1:5
–It inspires us to obey God's law . . . 1Jn 3:21–22
–We must hold a clear conscience . . . Ac 24:16; 1Ti 3:9; Heb 13:18

C. Our conscience and other Christians
–A weak Christian has a weak conscience . . . 1Co 8:7,10; 1Co 10:27–29
–A weak Christian's faith can be destroyed . . . Ro 14:14–15; 1Co 8:11
–We must protect a weak Christian . . . Ro 14:13,15, 19–21; 1Co 8:9–13; 1Co 10:27–32
–We must not judge another's conscience . . . Ro 14:1–13; 1Co 10:29

CONTENTMENT

See COVETING

CONVERSION

See REPENTANCE

CORINTH

A. Events of the church in Corinth
–Paul preached there for one and a half years . . . Ac 18:1–11
–Paul's trial before Gallio . . . Ac 18:12–17
–Apollos sent there . . . Ac 18:27–19:1
–First (lost) letter of Paul to them . . . 1Co 5:9–10
–Paul's second letter to them . . . 1Co 1:1–2
–Timothy sent there . . . 1Co 4:17; 1Co 16:10–11
–Paul's third (lost) letter to them . . . 2Co 2:3–4; 2Co 7:8–12
–Titus sent there . . . 2Co 7:5–7
–Paul's fourth letter to them . . . 2Co 1:1
–Titus sent there again . . . 2Co 8:16–24
–Paul's visit there for three months . . . Ac 20:2–3
–Paul's collection among them . . . Ro 15:25–27; 1Co 16:1–4; 2Co 8:6–15; 2Co 9:1–15

B. Character of the church in Corinth
–Most held to the teachings of Paul . . . 1Co 11:2; 1Co 15:1–2
–Disunified . . . 1Co 1:11–12
–Spiritually immature . . . 1Co 3:1–2; 1Co 14:20
–Proud; tolerated sinners . . . 1Co 5:1–2
–Lack of concern for weak Christians . . . 1Co 8:9–13
–Lack of love for each other . . . 1Co 11:17–22
–Trouble over speaking in tongues . . . 1Co 14:1–20
–Some denied the resurrection . . . 1Co 15:12
–Some challenged Paul's leadership . . . 2Co 10:1–11; 2Co 11:13–21

CORNELIUS

–Roman centurion who feared God . . . Ac 10:1–2
–Received vision from God . . . Ac 10:3–8
–Peter preached to him . . . Ac 10:23–43
–Received Holy Spirit . . . Ac 10:44–46
–Became a baptized Christian . . . Ac 10:47–48

COUNSELOR

–One who gives advice and direction for life

A. Human counselors
1. A class of people called counselors . . . Isa 3:3
2. Wise counsel
–Good counsel is necessary . . . Pr 15:22; Pr 22:20–21
–Wisdom counsels us . . . Pr 8:12–16
–God's law counsels us . . . Ps 119:24
–David had wise counselors . . . 1Ch 27:32–33
–Jeremiah was a good counselor . . . Jer 38:14–27
3. Foolish counsel
–Wicked counselors must be rejected . . . Job 21:16; Ps 1:1
–Rehoboam followed foolish counselors . . . 1Ki 12:1–15
–The Babylonians had poor counselors . . . Isa 47:13

B. God as counselor
–The Lord as counselor . . . Ps 16:7; Ps 73:24; Isa 28:29
–Christ, the Wonderful Counselor . . . Isa 9:6
–The Holy Spirit as Counselor (Advocate) . . . Isa 11:2; Jn 14:16,26; Jn 15:26; Jn 16:7

COURAGE

–The ability to face danger without fear

A. Remarkable stories of courage
–Moses and Aaron confronting Pharaoh . . . Ex 5:1–4; Ex 10:24–29
–Ehud killing Eglon . . . Jdg 3:15–30
–Gideon against the Midianites . . . Jdg 7:1–24
–Jonathan against the Philistines . . . 1Sa 14:1–14
–David against Goliath . . . 1Sa 17:26–50
–Elijah on Mount Carmel . . . 1Ki 18:1–40
–Esther approaching King Xerxes . . . Est 5:1–8
–Daniel's three friends and the fiery furnace . . . Da 3:1–30
–Daniel and the lions' den . . . Da 6:1–23
–The apostles facing the Sanhedrin . . . Ac 4:1–22; Ac 5:17–41
–Saul (Paul) preaching in Damascus . . . Ac 9:20–25
–Paul heading to Jerusalem . . . Ac 21:10–14

B. The command to be courageous
–To the Israelites from Moses . . . Dt 31:6
–To the Israelites from Joshua . . . Jos 10:25
–To Joshua from Moses . . . Dt 31:7,23
–To Joshua from the Lord . . . Jos 1:6–9,18
–To Solomon from David . . . 1Ch 22:13; 1Ch 28:20
–To judges from King Jehoshaphat . . . 2Ch 19:11
–To the Israelites from Hezekiah . . . 2Ch 32:7
–To Peter from Jesus . . . Mt 14:27
–To the disciples from Jesus . . . Mk 6:50
–To Paul from the Lord . . . Ac 23:11
–To all of us . . . 1Co 16:13; Heb 3:6

C. Aspects of courage
1. When do we need courage?
–As we face dangers and difficulties . . . Jos 1:6–9; 1Co 16:13
–As we face the future . . . Ro 8:37–39; 2Co 5:1–7

2. Who is our source of courage?
 –God — Ge 26:24; Jos 1:9; Ps 18:29–50; Ps 46:1–2
 –Christ — Php 4:13; Col 1:11; Rev 1:17–18
 –The Holy Spirit — Ac 4:8–13

COVENANT

–An agreement established between two parties

A. Covenants between humans
 1. Examples of human covenants
  –Between Isaac and Abimelech — Ge 26:26–31
  –Between Jacob and Laban — Ge 31:43–54
  –Between Joshua and the Gibeonites — Jos 9:3–15
  –Between David and Jonathan — 1Sa 18:3
  –Between David and Abner — 2Sa 3:12–16
  –Between Jehoiada and the guards — 2Ki 11:4–12
  –Between Joash and the people — 2Ki 11:17
  –Between Zedekiah and the people — Jer 34:8–10
 2. Elements in a covenant
  –Promises — 1Sa 20:14–17
  –Stipulations — 2Sa 3:13
  –Oaths — Ge 31:53
  –Responsibilities — 2Ki 12:8
  –Witnesses — Ge 31:45–48; 1Sa 20:42
  –Implied threats — Ge 31:53

B. Covenants between God and humans
 1. Examples of such covenants
  –With Adam before the fall — Ge 2:15–17
  –With Adam after the fall — Ge 3:14–19
  –With Noah — Ge 9:1–19
  –With Abram — Ge 12:1–3
  –With Israel at Sinai — Ex 19:5–8
  –With Israel before entering Palestine — Dt 29—30
  –With Israel in the promised land — Jos 24:1–27
  –With David — 2Sa 7:14–17
  –With the returned exiles — Ne 9:38—10:39
  –Future covenant of peace — Eze 34:25–31
  –The new covenant — Jer 31:33–34
 2. The covenants with Adam
  a. First covenant (before the fall)
   –Requirement was obedience — Ge 2:16–17
   –Promise was life — Ge 3:22
   –Penalty was death — Ge 2:17
   –Adam and Eve disobeyed — Ge 3:1–6
   –God pronounced punishment — Ge 3:14–19
   –Christ perfectly obeyed God's will — Jn 6:38; Ro 5:18–19; 2Co 5:21; Heb 4:15
   –Christ's death reversed Adam's — Ro 5:15–19
  b. Second covenant (after the fall)
   –Conflict between Satan and humans — Ge 3:15
   –God promised Satan's defeat — Ge 3:15
   –Fulfilled in Satan's defeat by Christ — Ro 16:20; Heb 2:14; 1Jn 3:8
 3. The covenant with Abraham
  a. Where is it mentioned?
   –First mentioned to Abram — Ge 12:2–3
   –Repeated to Abraham — Ge 22:17–18
   –Repeated to Isaac — Ge 26:3–5
   –Repeated to Jacob — Ge 28:13–15
   –Repeated to Moses — Ex 6:2–4
   –Celebrated by the psalmists — Ps 105:7–11
   –Acknowledged by the returned exiles — Ne 9:7–8
  b. What are its elements?
   –Several promises — Ge 12:2–3
   –No conditions attached — Ge 12:2–3
   –Faith came later — Ge 15:6
   –Law of circumcision followed faith — Ge 17:3–14
  c. How was it fulfilled in Christ?
   –John the Baptist began fulfillment — Lk 1:72–75
   –Peter preached its fulfillment — Ac 3:25
   –Its center is faith in Christ — Gal 3:6–9
   –The law follows faith — Ro 4:9–13
 4. The covenant of the law made at Mount Sinai
  a. Where is it mentioned?
   –First made at Mount Sinai — Ex 19:3–6
   –Confirmed by the Israelites — Ex 24:1–8
   –Renewed at the border of Canaan — Dt 29
   –Renewed at Mount Ebal — Jos 8:30–35
   –Renewed at Shechem — Jos 24:1–27
   –Rejected by the ten tribes — 2Ki 17:7–20
   –Renewed under Josiah — 2Ch 34:29–33
   –Broken by the nation of Judah — Jer 31:32
   –Renewed by the returned exiles — Ne 9:38–10:39
  b. What are its elements?
   –Centered on the law of God — Ex 34:27–28; Dt 4:13–14
   –Required obedience — Ex 24:7; Ex 34:10–11; Dt 29:9
   –Linked with blessings and curses — Dt 28; Jos 8:34–35
   –Did not annul covenant with Abraham — Gal 3:15–17
   –Pointed out human sin — Ro 3:20,23; Gal 3:19
   –Increased sin — Ro 5:20
   –Prepared for the coming of Christ — Gal 3:23–25
  c. How was it fulfilled in Christ?
   –He fulfilled the law — Mt 5:17
   –He perfectly obeyed the law — Ro 5:18–19; 2Co 5:21; Heb 4:15
   –He died the death of a curse — Gal 3:10–13
   –His death removed the curse from us — Gal 3:13–14
 5. The covenant with David
  a. Where is it mentioned?
   –First promised to David — 2Sa 7:4–17
   –Celebrated by David — 2Sa 23:5
   –Mentioned to Solomon — 1Ki 2:2–4
   –Celebrated by Solomon — 1Ki 8:22–26
   –Mentioned to Jeroboam — 1Ki 11:34–36
   –Reaffirmed during Jehoram's reign — 2Ki 8:19
   –Celebrated by psalmists — Ps 89:3; Ps 132:10–12
   –Reaffirmed by Isaiah — Isa 9:6–7
   –Reaffirmed by Ezekiel — Eze 37:24–25
  b. What are its elements?
   –Several promises — 2Sa 7:9–16
   –No conditions attached — 2Sa 7:15–16
  c. How was it fulfilled in Christ?
   –Mentioned by Gabriel to Mary — Lk 1:32–33
   –Preached by Paul — Ac 13:22–23,34
   –Hinted at in book of Hebrews — Heb 1:8
   –Jesus is the Son of David — Mt 1:1; Ro 1:3
   –Jesus is a king who rules — Jn 18:33–37; 1Co 15:24–25; Rev 19:16
 6. The new covenant
  a. Where is it promised?
   –Through Jeremiah — Jer 31:33–34; Jer 32:38–40
   –Through Ezekiel — Eze 16:60–62; Eze 34:25–31
   –Through Hosea — Hos 2:18–20
  b. What are its elements?
   –Several promises — Jer 31:33–34
   –No conditions attached — Jer 31:33–34
  c. How was it fulfilled in Christ?
   –Asserted by Christ in the upper room — Lk 22:20; 1Co 11:25
   –Mentioned by Paul — 2Co 3:6
   –Explained in book of Hebrews — Heb 8:6–13; Heb 9:15–28; Heb 10:11–18; Heb 12:22–24
 7. God's relationship to his covenants
  –He establishes his covenant — Ge 6:18; Ge 17:7; Ex 6:4; Eze 16:60–62
  –He is faithful to his covenant — Dt 7:9; 1Ki 8:23; Ne 9:32; Da 9:4
  –He remembers his covenant — Ex 2:24; Ps 105:8; Ps 111:5; Eze 16:60; Lk 1:72

COVETING

–The sinful desire for what belongs to someone else; greed

A. The command against coveting
 –In the Old Testament — Ex 20:17; Dt 5:21; Dt 7:25
 –In the New Testament — Ro 7:7–11; Eph 5:3; Col 3:5

B. Coveting often leads to other sins — 1Ti 6:10; 1Jn 2:15–16
 –To deceit (Jacob) — Ge 27:18–26
 –To adultery (David) — 2Sa 11:1–5
 –To disobedience to God (Achan) — Jos 7:20–21
 –To hypocritical worship (Saul) — 1Sa 15:9–23
 –To murder (Ahab) — 1Ki 21:1–14
 –To theft (Gehazi) — 2Ki 5:20–24
 –To family disharmony — Pr 15:27
 –To lying (Ananias and Sapphira) — Ac 5:1–10

C. Contentment as the answer to coveting
 –The command to be content — Lk 3:14; 1Ti 6:8; Heb 13:5
 –The experience of Paul — Php 4:11–12

CREATION

A. The work of creation
 –Accounts of creation — Ge 1:1—2:3; Ge 2:4–24; Job 38:4–38; Ps 104:1–26
 –Done out of nothing — Heb 11:3
 –Done in six days — Ge 1:3–31; Ex 20:11; Ex 31:17

B. Creation as the work of God
 –God as the creator — Ge 1:1; Isa 44:24; Ac 4:24
 –Accomplished through Christ — Jn 1:3,10; Col 1:16; Heb 1:2
 –The Holy Spirit involved in creation — Job 33:4; Ps 104:30

C. Creation reveals God
 –His glory — Ps 19:1
 –His power — Isa 40:26,28
 –His divine nature — Ro 1:20
 –His wisdom — Ps 104:24
 –His love — Ps 33:5–6

D. Creation after Adam and Eve sinned
 –Was cursed by God — Ge 3:14,17–19
 –Was subjected to frustration — Ro 8:20
 –Praises God — Ps 145:10; Ps 148:1–5; Isa 55:12
 –Eagerly awaits redemption — Ro 8:19
 –Will someday be liberated — Ro 8:21
 –Will someday be recreated — Isa 65:17; 2Pe 3:10–13; Rev 21:1

E. Humans commanded to rule creation — Ge 1:26,28; Ps 8:6–8; Ps 115:16

CREED

See CONFESSION

CROSS

A. Jesus and the cross
 1. What it involved
  –The means to bring about Jesus' death — Jn 19:17–18; Ac 5:30
  –Was the death of a curse — Gal 3:13
  –Planned by God — Lk 24:26–27; Ac 2:23
  –Carried out by humans — Ac 2:23; Ac 5:30
  –Showed Jesus' obedience — Php 2:8
 2. What it accomplished
  –Redeemed us from the curse of God — Gal 3:10,13
  –Took away our sins — Col 2:13–14; 1Pe 2:24
  –Reconciled us with God — Eph 2:16; Col 1:20
  –Gave us eternal life — Jn 3:14–15
  –Brought about victory over Christ's enemies — Col 2:15

B. The message of the cross
 –Was preached by the apostles — Ac 2:23; Ac 8:32–35; Ac 13:28–29; 1Co 1:23; 1Co 2:1–2
 –Was a stumbling block to Jews — 1Co 1:23
 –Was foolishness to Gentiles — 1Co 1:18,23

C. Believers and the cross
 –They are crucified with Christ — Gal 2:20
 –Their sinful nature is put to death — Ro 6:6; Gal 5:24; 1Pe 2:24
 –They are crucified to the world — Gal 6:14
 –They must carry their cross — Mt 10:38

CROWN

A. Examples of those who wore a crown
- –Priests ... Lev 8:9; Zec 6:9–11
- –Kings ... 2Sa 12:30; SS 3:11
- –Queens ... Est 1:11; Est 2:17
- –Christ with a crown of thorns ... Mt 27:29; Jn 19:2,5
- –Christ with a royal crown ... Rev 14:14; Rev 19:12

B. Crowns used as a symbol
1. In the present life
   - –God crowns humans with glory and honor ... Ps 8:5
   - –God crowns us with salvation ... Ps 149:4
   - –God crowns us with love ... Ps 103:4
   - –God crowns us with blessings ... Pr 10:6
   - –A good wife is her husband's crown ... Pr 12:4
   - –Gray hair is a crown of splendor ... Pr 16:31
   - –Grandchildren are a crown to the aged ... Pr 17:6
   - –Christians are a crown to Paul ... 1Th 2:19; Php 4:1
2. In the life hereafter
   - –God will be a glorious crown for us ... Isa 28:5
   - –Christians will be a crown for God ... Isa 62:3
   - –Everlasting joy will crown us ... Isa 35:10
   - –We receive an everlasting crown ... 1Co 9:25
   - –We receive a crown of righteousness ... 2Ti 4:8
   - –We receive a crown of life ... Jas 1:12; Rev 2:10
   - –We receive a crown of glory ... 1Pe 5:4

CURSE, CURSING

A. The curse as a result of sin
1. Warnings of the curse
   - –Principle stated ... Dt 11:26–28; Pr 3:33; Jer 11:3
   - –Extended list of curses ... Dt 27:15–26; Dt 28:15–68
2. Expressions of the curse
   a. In the Old Testament
   - –On the serpent ... Ge 3:14
   - –On Cain ... Ge 4:9–12
   - –On Canaan ... Ge 9:25
   - –On Simeon and Levi ... Ge 49:7–9
   - –On any who disobey the law ... Dt 27:26
   - –On those who dishonor God ... Mal 2:2
   - –On the land ... Ge 3:17; Isa 24:6; Jer 23:10; Jer 44:22; Mal 4:6

   b. In the New Testament
   - –On those not kind to the needy ... Mt 25:41–46
   - –On those who refuse the gospel ... Gal 1:8–9
   - –On those who do not love the Lord ... 1Co 16:22
   - –On those who fall away from Christ ... Heb 6:4–8
   - –On all sinners ... Gal 3:10
3. Removal of the curse by Christ's cross ... Gal 3:13

B. Human cursing
1. Cursing God
   - –Humans may not curse God ... Ex 20:7; Dt 5:11; 1Co 12:3
   - –Penalty for cursing God was death ... Lev 24:10–16; 1Ki 21:13; Job 2:9

   See also BLASPHEMY
2. Cursing other humans
   a. Examples
   - –Balak's desire to curse Israel ... Nu 23:11,25
   - –Joshua cursed rebuilders of Jericho ... Jos 6:26
   - –Citizens of Shechem cursed Abimelech ... Jdg 9:26–27
   - –Goliath cursed David ... 1Sa 17:43
   - –Shimei cursed David ... 2Sa 16:5–7
   - –Curses on greedy people ... Pr 11:26
   - –Non-Christians curse Christians ... 1Co 4:12

   b. The command not to curse other humans ... Ex 21:17; Pr 20:20; Pr 30:10–11; Jas 3:10–12

   c. We must bless instead of curse ... Lk 6:28; Ro 12:14

CYRUS

- –Persian king ... 2Ch 36:22; Da 6:28
- –Allowed Israel to return from exile ... 2Ch 36:23
- –Commanded rebuilding of the temple ... Ezr 1:1–4
- –His decree recalled ... Ezr 6:1–5
- –Called shepherd of the Lord ... Isa 44:28
- –Called anointed of the Lord ... Isa 45:1–13

DAMASCUS

A. Identity and location
- –Capital city of the Arameans or Syrians ... 1Ki 15:18; Isa 7:8
- –Arameans were descendants of Shem ... Ge 10:22–23

B. Significant Arameans
- –Eliezer: servant of Abram ... Ge 15:2
- –Three kings called Ben-hadad
  See BEN-HADAD
- –Naaman: the leprous commander ... 2Ki 5:1
  See NAAMAN
- –Hazael: king after Ben-Hadad ... 2Ki 8:15
  See HAZAEL
- –Rezin: allied with Israel against Ahaz ... Isa 7:1–9

C. Significant events of Damascus/Syria
1. Old Testament
   - –Abram passed through it ... Ge 14:15
   - –David conquered it ... 2Sa 8:5–6; 1Ch 18:5–6
   - –Twenty thousand Aramean soldiers defeated by Joab ... 2Sa 10:6–19
   - –Asa made a treaty with its king ... 1Ki 15:18–20; 2Ch 16:2
   - –Elisha prophesied there ... 2Ki 8:7–13
   - –Jeroboam II conquered it ... 2Ki 14:28
   - –Joash defeated by the Arameans ... 2Ch 24:23–25
   - –Israel allied with it against Judah ... 2Ki 16:5; Isa 7:1–2
   - –Ahaz defeated by the Arameans ... 2Ch 28:5
   - –Assyria captured it ... 2Ki 16:9; Isa 8:3–7
2. New Testament
   - –News of Jesus went to Syria ... Mt 4:24
   - –Saul went there to persecute Christians ... Ac 9:1–2
   - –Saul converted near there ... Ac 9:3–9
   - –Saul/Paul preached there ... Ac 9:19–22; Gal 1:17–18
   - –Paul escaped from there in a basket ... Ac 9:23–25; 2Co 11:32–33
   - –Paul traveled through Syria ... Ac 15:41; Gal 1:21

D. Prophecies against Damascus ... Isa 17:1–14; Jer 49:23–27; Am 1:3–5; Zec 9:1

DAN

A. Son of Jacob by Bilhah ... Ge 35:25
- –Name means "vindicated" ... Ge 30:4–6
- –Went to Egypt with family ... Ge 46:8,23
- –Father of one son ... Ge 46:23
- –Blessed by Jacob ... Ge 49:16–17

B. Tribe descended from Dan ... Nu 26:42
- –Blessed by Moses ... Dt 33:22
- –Numbered ... Nu 1:38–39; Nu 26:43
- –Allotted land ... Jos 19:40–48; Eze 48:1
- –Failed to possess the land fully ... Jdg 1:34–35
- –Failed to support Deborah ... Jdg 5:17
- –Samson was a Danite ... Jdg 13:2,24–25
- –Stole Micah's priest ... Jdg 18:1–26

C. A city in Israel ... Ge 14:14
- –At one time called Leshem ... Jos 19:47
- –Also called Laish ... Jdg 18:27–31
- –Northernmost city in land of Israel ... Jdg 20:1
- –Jeroboam set up golden calf there ... 1Ki 12:25–30
- –Conquered by Ben-Hadad ... 1Ki 15:20

DANCING

A. There is a time to dance ... Ecc 3:4

B. Occasions for dancing
1. Appropriate
   - –To praise and worship God ... Ex 15:20–21; Ps 68:24–25; Ps 149:3; Ps 150:4
   - –To express human elation ... 1Sa 18:6–7; 2Sa 6:16; Jer 31:4
2. Inappropriate
   - –In pagan worship ... Ex 32:5–6, 19; 1Ki 18:26–29; 1Co 10:7
   - –Herodias before Herod ... Mt 14:6
3. Dancing ceases at a time of sorrow ... La 5:15; Mt 11:17

C. God's blessing turns sorrow into dancing ... Ps 30:11

DANIEL

A. Hebrew exile to Babylon ... Da 1:6
- –Educated in Babylonia ... Da 1:3–5
- –Name changed to Belteshazzar ... Da 1:7
- –Refused non-Jewish food ... Da 1:8–21
- –Interpreted dreams of Nebuchadnezzar ... Da 2:24–47; Da 4:4–27
- –Interpreted handwriting on the wall ... Da 5:1–28
- –Survived the lions' den ... Da 6:1–23
- –Recorded visions ... Da 7:1–12:13
- –Jesus referred to his prophecy ... Mt 24:15

B. Son of David and Abigail ... 1Ch 3:1

DARIUS

A. King of the Medes; conquered Babylon ... Da 5:31
- –Son of Xerxes ... Da 9:1

B. A later king of Persia ... Ezr 4:5; Hag 1:1,15
- –Asked to order rebuilding of temple to stop ... Ezr 5:3–17
- –Allowed rebuilding of temple ... Ezr 6:1–12

DARKNESS

A. Physical darkness
- –Created by God ... Isa 45:7
- –Originally covered the earth ... Ge 1:2
- –Separated from light ... Ge 1:4
- –Called night ... Ge 1:5
- –Comes when the sun sets ... Ge 15:17
- –God can see things in the dark ... Ps 139:11–12; Da 2:22

B. Darkness as a symbol
1. For the mysteriousness of God ... Ex 20:21; Ps 18:9; Ps 97:2
2. For afflictions ... Job 18:6,18; Isa 59:9; La 3:1–2
3. For ignorance about God ... Job 37:19; Isa 60:2; 1Jn 2:8
4. For sin and evil
   - –Sinful deeds are deeds of darkness ... Ro 13:12; Eph 5:11
   - –The way of the wicked is darkness ... Pr 2:13; Pr 4:19; 1Th 5:4–5
   - –Living in sin is walking in darkness ... Jn 3:19; 1Jn 1:6; 1Jn 2:9,11
5. For judgment from God ... Joel 2:2; Am 5:18,20; Rev 16:10
6. For the realm of Satan ... Lk 22:53; Eph 6:12; Col 1:13
7. For hell as a place of punishment ... Mt 8:12; 2Pe 2:17; Jude 13

C. Antidotes to darkness as evil
1. God
   - –His first act was to dispel darkness ... Ge 1:2–3
   - –He surrounds himself with light ... Ps 104:1–2; 1Ti 6:16
   - –He is the God of light ... 1Jn 1:5
2. Jesus
   - –Jesus came to dispel darkness ... Jn 1:4–9; Jn 3:19–21; Jn 12:46
   - –Jesus is the light of the world ... Jn 8:12; Jn 9:5
3. Heaven
   - –God's light permeates heaven ... Isa 60:19–20; Rev 21:23
   - –Heaven has no night ... Zec 14:7; Rev 22:5

See also LIGHT

DAVID

A. Personal data
1. Ancestry
   - –Son of Jesse ... Ru 4:17–22; 1Ch 2:13–15
   - –Youngest in the family ... 1Sa 16:10–13
2. Wives
   - –Michal, daughter of Saul ... 1Sa 18:2–27
   - –Abigail, widow of Nabal ... 1Sa 25:39–44
   - –Bathsheba, widow of Uriah ... 2Sa 11

–Many wives and concubines 2Sa 5:13–15
3. Descendants
–Solomon 2Sa 12:24
–Amnon 2Sa 13:1
–Absalom 2Sa 13:1
–Adonijah 1Ki 1:5–6
–Many sons 2Sa 3:2–5; 1Ch 3:1–9
–Jesus was the Son of David .... Mt 1:1–17; Lk 3:31
4. Occupations
–A shepherd 1Sa 16:11; 1Sa 17:20, 34–37
–A musician 1Sa 16:14–23; 2Sa 23:1
–A psalmist .... 1Ch 16:7; Ps 3—34, etc.; Lk 20:42
–A prophet .... 2Sa 23:1–2; Ac 2:25–31
–A king 2Sa 5:3–4

B. David's life during Saul's reign
1. His anointing as future king 1Sa 16:1–13
2. His work in Saul's service
–Played music for Saul 1Sa 16:14–23; 1Sa 18:10
–Killed Goliath 1Sa 17:4–51
–Became a mighty warrior 1Sa 18:2–7
3. Saul's reaction to David
–Was jealous of him . 1Sa 18:6–9, 12,29
–Tried to kill him 1Sa 18:10–11; 1Sa 19:1–18
4. David's flights
–To Nob 1Sa 21:1
–To Gath 1Sa 21:10
–To the cave of Adullam 1Sa 22:1
–To Keilah 1Sa 23:7
–To desert strongholds 1Sa 23:14–24
–To the land of the Philistines 1Sa 27:1–3
–David spared Saul's life 1Sa 24:1–21; 1Sa 26:1–25
5. His military victories
–Killed two hundred Philistines 1Sa 18:24–27
–Saved town of Keilah 1Sa 23:1–6
–Defeated Amalekites 1Sa 30:1–31
–Not allowed to fight on side of Philistines 1Sa 29:1–11
6. His covenant with Jonathan 1Sa 18:1–4; 1Sa 20:16–17; 1Sa 23:15–18
7. His lament over Saul and Jonathan 2Sa 1:17–27

C. David's life as king
1. His fight to become king
–Became king of Judah 2Sa 2:1–11
–Fought with Saul's supporters .... 2Sa 2:8—4:12
–Became king of all Israel 2Sa 5:1–4; 1Ch 11:1–3
2. His military accomplishments
–Conquered Jerusalem 2Sa 5:6–10; 1Ch 11:4–9
–Conquered Philistines 2Sa 5:17–25; 2Sa 21:15–22; 1Ch 14:8–17
–Conquered Ammonites 2Sa 10:1–19; 1Ch 19:1–19
–Conquered many others 2Sa 8:1–14; 1Ch 18:1–13
–Avenged the Gibeonites 2Sa 21:1–14
–Organized army and government 1Ch 27:1–34
–Had many mighty men .... 2Sa 23:8–39; 1Ch 11—12
–Numbered his army; angered the Lord 2Sa 24:1–17; 1Ch 21:1–19
3. His involvement in Israel's worship
–Brought ark to Jerusalem 2Sa 6:1–19
–Planned the temple .. 1Ch 22:1–19; 1Ch 28:8—29:9
–Organized Israel's worship .... 1Ch 15:16—16:43
–Organized priests and Levites 1Ch 23:26
4. God's covenant with him 2Sa 7:1–17
See COVENANT
5. David's sin and its consequences
–His sin with Bathsheba 2Sa 11:1–5
–Attempt at cover-up . 2Sa 11:6–27
–Sin exposed by Nathan 2Sa 12:1–14
–Death of his son 2Sa 12:15–23
–Absalom's revolt .... 2Sa 14:1—18:8
–Death of Absalom .. 2Sa 18:9–18
–David mourned Absalom's death .... 2Sa 18:33—19:4
–Return to Jerusalem . 2Sa 19:9–43
–Sheba's revolt 2Sa 20:1–22
6. His last days
–Abishag took care of him 1Ki 1:1–4
–Appointed Solomon king .... 1Ki 1:28—2:9
–Gave charge to Solomon 1Ki 2:1–9
–His last words 2Sa 23:1–7
–His death 1Ki 2:10–12

D. His spiritual life
1. Positive qualities
–Depended on the Lord .... 1Sa 17:45–47; Ps 27:1–6
–Trusted in the Lord . Ps 25:1–5
–Praised God .... 1Ch 16:7–10; Ps 9:1–2
–Was concerned about God's house 1Ch 17:1–2; 1Ch 22:5
–Respected those in authority 1Sa 24:5; 1Sa 26:9–11
–Was faithful to his promises 2Sa 9:1–13
–Repented of his sin . 2Sa 12:13; Ps 32:3–5
2. Negative qualities
–Took pride in his military power 2Sa 24:1–10
–Committed adultery with Bathsheba 2Sa 11:1–5
–Committed a murder indirectly 2Sa 11:14–17

E. New Testament significance
–Jesus is David's Son ... Mt 1:1; 2Ti 2:8
–Jesus is the Root of David .... Rev 5:5; Rev 22:16
–Jesus sat on David's throne .... Lk 1:30–33
–David confessed Jesus to be Lord .... Mt 22:42–43
–David was not a legalist .... Lk 6:1–5
–David prophesied the resurrection .... Ac 2:25–31
–David believed righteousness came through faith .... Ro 4:6–8
–David was a hero of faith .... Heb 11:32–33
–God spoke through David .... Heb 4:7

DAY

A. Meanings of the word "day"
1. The period of light after the night
–Light called "day" by God .... Ge 1:5
–"Day and night" ... Ge 8:22; Est 4:16; Jn 9:4–5
–Divided into twelve hours .... Mt 20:1–12; Jn 11:9
2. The time period of twenty-four hours .... Ge 1:5,13,19; Ge 8:4–5, 13–14; Ex 2:11,13
3. A synonym for "time"
–The day of creation . Dt 4:32
–The day of the exodus 1Ki 8:16
–The day of the giving of the law .... Nu 15:23
–A day of disaster .... Dt 32:35
–To the present day .. Jos 4:9
–The day of one's death .... Jdg 13:7
–The day Jerusalem was built .... Jer 32:31
–The day the temple was built .... Hag 2:18
–The day of salvation 2Co 6:2

B. The day of the Lord
1. In the Old Testament, it can refer to:
–The time of God's judgment .... Joel 1:15; Am 5:18; Am 8:11–14; Zep 1:14–17
–The time of Israel's restoration .... Isa 10:20; Isa 11:10–11; Zec 9:16
–The first coming of Christ .... Mal 3:1–3
–The outpouring of the Spirit .... Joel 2:28–31
–The kingdom of Christ .... Isa 4:2–6; Mic 4:1–7
–The end of the world .... Isa 24:21–23; Isa 27:12–13; Zec 14:1–3
2. In the New Testament, it can refer to:
–The day of the final battle .... Rev 16:14
–The day of Christ's return .... Mk 13:24–27; 1Co 1:7–8; 2Co 1:14
–The day of judgment 1Co 3:12–15; 1Th 5:2–3; 2Pe 3:12
–The day of God's wrath .... Ro 2:5–6
–The day of blessing for Christians . 1Co 1:8; 2Ti 4:8

DEACON

A. Often translated "servant"
–Used of Jesus .... Ro 15:8
–Used of Paul 1Co 3:5
–Used of Timothy 1Ti 4:6
–Used of any follower of Christ .... Jn 12:26
B. An office in the New Testament church .... Php 1:1
–Assistants to apostles .. Ac 6:1–4
–Qualifications given .... Ac 6:3; 1Ti 3:8–13
–Possibly women were deacons .... Ro 16:1; 1Ti 3:11

DEATH

A. Physical death
1. Phrases used
–Dying .... Ge 5:5,8,11, 24
–Returning to the dust .... Ge 3:19; Ecc 12:7
–Lying down in the dust .... Job 7:21
–Going to one's ancestors .... Ge 15:15
–Resting with one's ancestors .... Dt 31:16; 2Sa 7:12
–Being gathered to one's people .... Ge 25:8; Ge 49:29
–Breathing one's last . Ge 35:29; Lk 23:46
–Going down to Sheol .... Ge 37:35; 1Ki 2:6,9
–Falling asleep .... Jn 11:11; Ac 7:60
–Being asleep .... Ps 76:5; Da 12:2
–Being away from the body 2Co 5:8
–Departing .... Php 1:23; 2Ti 4:6; 2Pe 1:15
2. All human beings die . Ecc 8:8; Heb 9:27
–First examples ...... Ge 4:8; Ge 5:5–20, 25–31
–Two exceptions: Enoch and Elijah ... Ge 5:21–24; 2Ki 2:11–12
3. Death came as a result of sin
–A result of Adam's sin .... Ge 2:17; Ro 5:12; 1Co 15:21–22
–The wages of sin for everyone .... Ro 6:23
4. Death was conquered by Christ
–He was raised from the dead .... Ro 6:9
–He holds the keys of death .... Rev 1:18
–He releases us from fear of death .... Heb 2:15
–He will destroy death completely 1Co 15:26, 53–57
5. What is death for believers?
–Falling asleep in Christ 1Co 15:18; 1Th 4:14
–Gain .... Php 1:21
–Precious to God .... Ps 116:15; Rev 14:13
–The entrance into peace .... Isa 57:1–2
–The entrance into glory .... Ps 73:24
–Clothes us with our heavenly dwelling ... 2Co 5:4
–Prepares us to receive a crown .... 2Ti 4:8; Rev 2:10
6. What is death for the wicked?
–Without salvation ... Eze 3:19; Jn 8:21
–Without hope .... Job 8:13; Pr 11:7
–A judgment from God .... Nu 16:29–30; Lk 12:20
–The pathway to hell . Lk 16:22–23; Ac 1:25
–Not pleasurable to God .... Eze 18:23,32
–Something for them to fear .... Job 27:19–21; Pr 10:24

B. Spiritual death
1. Its origin
–Came as a result of sin .... Ge 2:17; Ro 5:12; Ro 6:23
–Is part of the sinful human nature .... Ro 8:6
2. Who are spiritually dead?
–Everyone who does not have Christ ..... Eph 2:1,5; Col 2:13; 1Jn 5:12
–Those seeking personal pleasure ...... Eph 4:17–19; 1Ti 5:6

–Those not serving God by good works . Heb 6:1; Heb 9:14; Rev 3:1–2
3. How can one overcome spiritual death?
–Through faith in Christ .... Eph 2:4–5; Eph 5:14; 1Jn 5:12
–By repenting and turning to God ...... Lk 15:17–24; Rev 3:1–3

C. Eternal death
1. Phrases used to describe eternal death
–Eternal punishment .. Mt 25:46
–Hell .... Mt 5:29–30
–The eternal fire ..... Mt 25:41
–The lake of burning sulfur .... Rev 19:20
–The lake of fire ..... Rev 20:15
–Shut out from God's presence 2Th 1:9
–The outer darkness .. Mt 25:30
–The deepest darkness .... Jude 13
–The second death ... Rev 20:6
–The coming wrath .. 1Th 1:10
2. What is its origin?
–Came as a result of sin .... Ge 2:17; Ro 5:12; Ro 6:23; Jas 1:15
–Symbolized by removal from Eden .. Ge 3:22–24
3. Who are subject to eternal death?
–The devil and his angels .... 2Pe 2:4; Rev 20:10
–The antichrist .... 2Th 2:8; Rev 19:20
–Those who worship the beast .... Rev 14:9–11
–Those who choose the broad road ...... Mt 7:13
–Those who live a wicked life .... Ro 1:28–31
–Those who do not love the needy ...... Mt 25:41–46
–Those who do not believe in Jesus ..... Jn 3:36
–False teachers in the church 2Pe 2:1–17
–Godless, greedy people in the church .... Jude 4,8–13
4. Jesus conquered eternal death 1Co 15:20, 54–57; 2Ti 1:10
5. Who will escape eternal death?
–Those who believe in Jesus .... Jn 3:16,18, 36; Jn 11:25–26
–Those who are raised with Christ .... Ro 6:5–11
–Those who keep the word of God .... Jn 8:51
–Those who choose the narrow road ..... Mt 7:14
–Those who are kind to the needy .... Mt 25:34–40
–Those who do not worship the beast ... Rev 20:4–6

DEBORAH
A. Rebekah's nurse .... Ge 35:8
B. A prophetess .... Jdg 4:4
–Judged Israel .... Jdg 4:5
–Fought Sisera's army with Barak .... Jdg 4:6–10, 14–16
–Deborah's song of triumph .... Jdg 5:1–31

DEBT
–What is owed to another person
A. Financial debts
1. Regulated by Old Testament laws
–No interest to be charged .... Ex 22:25; Lev 25:36–37; Dt 15:8; Dt 23:19–20
–Security to be returned .... Ex 22:26–27; Dt 24:10–13
–The seventh year for canceling debts ..... Dt 15:1–6
–The year of jubilee for canceling debts .. Lev 25:8–54
2. Examples of oppressed debtors
–Numerous people in David's time 1Sa 22:2
–A widow in Elisha's day 2Ki 4:1–7
–The poor in Amos's day .... Am 2:6–8
–Many Israelites in Nehemiah's day ..... Ne 5:1–13
3. Warnings against co-signing for a debt . Pr 6:1–5; Pr 11:15; Pr 17:18; Pr 22:26–27
4. Debts in the New Testament world
–Borrowing was common .... Lk 6:34
–Jesus used imagery of debt in parables .. Mt 18:23–35; Lk 7:41–42; Lk 11:5–8; Lk 16:1–9
–Jesus used imagery of interest in parables .... Mt 25:14–30; Lk 19:12–27
–We must lend without expecting return . Lk 6:35
–We must pay what is owed .... Ro 13:7
B. Debts used as a symbol
1. Debt symbolizes sin .. Mt 6:12–15; Mt 18:23–35; Lk 7:41–48
2. Debt symbolizes our Christian obligations
–Paul's debt to preach the gospel .... Ro 1:14; 1Co 9:16
–Our debt to love others .... Ro 13:8
–The Gentile debt to Jews .... Ro 15:25–27

DEMETRIUS
–Silversmith in Ephesus ..... Ac 19:24
–Incited a riot over evangelism there .... Ac 19:25–29
–Told to work through legal channels .... Ac 19:38–40

DEMONS
–Evil spirits that can afflict humans
A. The characteristics of demons
1. Their identity
–They are related to false gods .... Dt 32:17; Ps 106:37; 1Co 10:20; Rev 9:20
–They are also called evil spirits .... Mk 5:12–13; 1Ti 4:1
2. Their behavior
–Insane raving .... Mk 1:23–24; Mk 5:2–5
–Self-destructive behavior .... Mk 5:5; Mk 9:22
–Convulsions .... Mk 9:18,20
–Could cause physical ailments .... Mt 12:22
–Could speak .... Mk 1:34; Mk 5:12
–Could perform miracles .... Rev 16:13–14
B. The relationship of demons to Jesus
1. They recognized Jesus .... Mt 8:28–29; Mk 1:23–24; Ac 19:13–16
2. They were driven out in the name of Jesus
–By Jesus himself .... Mk 1:23–24, 32–34; Mk 5:1–13; Mk 9:14–27
–By the followers of Jesus .... Mk 16:17; Lk 10:17; Ac 5:16; Ac 16:16–18
3. Jesus' power over demons demonstrates
–That he was not influenced by Beelzebub .... Mt 12:25–29; Mk 3:23–27; Lk 11:17–22
–That the kingdom of God worked in Jesus .... Mt 12:28; Lk 11:20

DEPRAVITY
See SIN

DEPRESSION
–The feeling of despair over life's problems
A. Examples of depressed people
–Moses .... Nu 11:10–15
–Elijah 1Ki 19:1–4
–Job .... Job 3:1–26
–The psalmist .... Ps 42:1–11
–The Teacher .... Ecc 2:20
–Jonah .... Jnh 4:3
B. Perspectives for depressed people
–Being reminded of God's presence 1Ki 19:11–13
–Experiencing the Holy Spirit .... Isa 61:1–3; Jn 16:6–7
–Placing hope and trust in God .... Ps 31:24; Ps 42:5,11; Heb 6:18–19
–Casting anxiety on God 1Pe 5:7
–Receiving the support of believers .... 1Sa 20:41–42; Job 2:11–13; Job 42:10–11; 1Th 5:11

DESPAIR
See DEPRESSION

DEVIL
See SATAN

DEVOTION
See MEDITATION

DINAH
–Daughter of Jacob .... Ge 30:21; Ge 46:15
–Raped by Shechem .... Ge 34:1–4
–Avenged by Simeon and Levi .... Ge 34:25–29

DISCIPLESHIP
–Following the lifestyle outlined by Jesus
A. Who are called disciples?
–Twelve chosen followers of Jesus .... Mk 3:16–19
–Believers in Jesus ...... Ac 6:7; Ac 9:1; Ac 11:26
B. What is expected of disciples?
–Commitment to Jesus .. Mt 8:19–22; Mk 1:17–18; Lk 14:26–27
–Humble service .... Mk 10:43–44
–Following teachings of the Sermon on the Mount .... Mt 5:1—7:27
–Doing the will of God .. Mt 12:49–50
–Loving one another ..... Jn 13:34–35; Jn 15:9–17
–Sharing with one another .... Ac 4:32–37; Ac 11:28–29
–Making disciples of all nations .... Mt 28:19
C. What happens to Jesus' disciples?
–They receive eternal life .... Mk 10:29–30
–Jesus teaches them ..... Lk 11:2–4
–Jesus acknowledges them before his Father . Mt 10:32
–They are called Christians .... Ac 11:26
–They may have to suffer .... Jn 15:20; 2Ti 3:12
–They may experience rejection .... Mt 10:22, 34–35; Jn 15:18,21; Jn 17:14
–They need strengthening .... Ac 14:21–22; Ac 18:23

DISCIPLINE
–Measures taken to ensure conformity to the accepted standard
A. Methods of discipline
1. Human discipline
–By instruction and warning .... Pr 1:2–4,8–10; 2Ti 4:2; Tit 2:15
–By the rod .... Pr 13:24; Pr 22:15
2. God's discipline of us
–By instruction and warning .... Jer 7:27–28; Jer 17:23
–By adversity and affliction .... Lev 26:23–26; Job 33:19; Ps 39:10–11; Jer 2:30
B. Motives of discipline
–Love .... 2Sa 7:14–15; Pr 3:12; Heb 12:6; Rev 3:19
–Desire for another's growth and improvement .... Job 5:17; Pr 25:12; Pr 29:15; Heb 12:10
C. Types of discipline
1. Self-discipline .... Ro 6:12–14; Ro 8:13; 1Co 9:26–27
2. Discipline in the home .... Pr 13:24; Pr 15:5; Pr 19:18
3. Mutual discipline
–Between friends ...... Pr 17:10; Pr 27:5–6; Pr 28:23
–Among believers .... Lk 17:3; 1Th 5:11, 14–15; 2Th 3:15
4. Church discipline
a. Done through preaching the word .... 2Ti 3:16–17; 2Ti 4:2; Tit 2:15
b. Done through direct measures
–Rebuke sinners publicly .... 1Ti 5:20; Tit 1:13
–Have nothing to do with sinners .. Ro 16:17; 1Co 5:9–11; 2Th 3:6,14; Tit 3:10
–Remove sinners from the church .. 1Co 5:1–5, 13; 1Ti 1:20

DIVORCE
–The breaking of the marital bond
A. Physical divorce
1. Divorce in the Old Testament
–Not part of God's original plan .... Ge 2:24; Mt 19:8
–Allowed and regulated .... Dt 22:13–19, 28–29; Dt 24:1–4
–Evidence of human stubbornness .... Mt 19:8
–Priests not to marry divorcees .... Lev 21:7,14
–Hated by God ...... Mal 2:16
–Defiled the land ..... Jer 3:1–2
–Required for those with idolatrous wives .... Ezr 10:2–17
2. Divorce in the New Testament

–Marriage considered binding ... Mt 19:3–6; Ro 7:2–3
–Permitted by Jesus for unfaithfulness ... Mt 5:31–33; Mt 19:9
–Permitted by Paul in mixed marriages ... 1Co 7:12–15
–Divorce was a pardonable sin ... Jn 4:17–18, 39–42

B. Spiritual divorce
1. A result of sin and idolatry ... Isa 50:1; Jer 3:2
2. Northern kingdom: divorced by God ... Jer 3:8
3. Southern kingdom of Judah
–Equally as adulterous as Israel ... Jer 3:8–11
–Temporary separation through the exile ... Isa 50:1; Isa 54:7
–Taken back by God as spouse ... Isa 54:6–8; Isa 62:4–5

See also ADULTERY, MARRIAGE

DOCTRINE

–True teachings concerning faith and life

A. The importance of knowing doctrine
–Stressed in the Old Testament ... Ps 78:1–8; Pr 7:1–5; Pr 13:14
–Stressed in the New Testament ... 1Co 11:2; 2Th 2:15; 2Ti 1:13; Tit 1:9; Tit 2:1

See also CONFESSION, EDUCATION

B. Concern over false doctrine
1. The identity of false teachers
–The teachers of the law ... Mt 23:2–4, 16–22; Mk 12:38–40; Lk 20:46–47; 1Ti 1:6–7
–Teachers of unsound doctrine ... 1Ti 4:1–3; 2Ti 4:3–4; Tit 1:9–11
–Teachers who distort the truth ... Ac 20:29–30; 2Ti 2:17–18
–Teachers who introduce heresies ... 2Pe 2:1; 2Jn 7
–Teachers who cause divisions ... Ro 16:17; 1Ti 6:3–5
–Teachers who promote immorality ... 2Ti 3:6–8; Rev 2:14,20
2. Commands concerning false teachers
–Watch out for them ... Mk 12:38; Lk 20:46; Ac 20:31; 2Jn 8
–Command them to stop teaching ... 1Ti 1:3–4; Tit 1:10–11, 13–14
–Withdraw from them ... Ro 16:17; 2Ti 2:16–18; 2Jn 10–11

DOEG

–An Edomite; Saul's head shepherd ... 1Sa 21:7
–Reported to Saul about priests of Nob ... 1Sa 22:9–10
–Killed the priests of Nob for Saul ... 1Sa 22:18–19
–David wrote a psalm about the incident ... Ps 52:1–9

DOG

See ANIMALS

DORCAS

–Disciple in Joppa who died . Ac 9:36–37
–Raised to life by Peter ... Ac 9:38–41

DOUBT

–A questioning of one's faith

A. Examples of believers who doubted
–Abram ... Ge 12:10–20; Ge 15:2–3; Ge 16:1–4; Ge 20:1–13
–Moses ... Ex 33:15–19
–Gideon ... Jdg 6:36–37, 39
–John the Baptist ... Mt 11:2–3
–Peter ... Mt 14:28–31
–Martha ... Jn 11:39
–Some disciples ... Mt 28:17
–Thomas ... Jn 20:24–25

B. Ending doubt
1. How doubts were ended
–Abram, by believing God's word ... Ge 15:6
–Moses, by seeing God's glory ... Ex 33:21–23
–Gideon, by throwing out the fleece ... Jdg 6:36–40
–John, by seeing Christ's miracles ... Mt 11:4–6
–Peter, by reaching out to Christ ... Mt 14:30–31
–Thomas, by seeing the risen Christ ... Jn 20:26–29
2. God wants us to overcome doubt ... Mk 11:22–24; Jas 1:6; Jude 22

DOVE

See BIRDS

DREAMS AND VISIONS

A. Dreams and visions in general
–Closely related ... Da 7:1–2
–Used by God for revelation ... Nu 12:6
–Authenticity must be tested ... Dt 13:1–5
–God alone can interpret dreams ... Ge 40:8; Ge 41:16; Da 2:27–28

B. Examples of dreams and visions used for revelation
1. Dreams
–Jacob ... Ge 28:12–16
–Joseph ... Ge 37:5–9
–Pharaoh, interpreted by Joseph ... Ge 41:1–36
–Solomon ... 1Ki 3:5
–Nebuchadnezzar, interpreted by Daniel ... Da 2:24–47; Da 4:4–27
–Joseph, husband of Mary ... Mt 1:20–21
2. Visions
–Abram ... Ge 15:1
–Jacob ... Ge 46:2
–Samuel ... 1Sa 3:10–15
–Various prophets ... Isa 1:1; Da 7:1; Ob 1; Mic 1:1; Na 1:1
–Cornelius ... Ac 10:3–6
–Peter ... Ac 10:9–17
–Paul ... Ac 18:9

C. Warnings against those who feign dreams ... Jer 23:25–28; Eze 13:3–9; Zec 10:2; Jude 8

DROUGHT

See HUNGER AND THIRST

DRUGS

See ALCOHOL

DRUNKENNESS

See ALCOHOL

DUST

A. Humans are creatures of dust
–Created from the dust of the ground ... Ge 2:7; Ecc 3:20; 1Co 15:47
–Pictures human frailty ... Ps 103:14
–Will return to the dust ... Ge 3:19; Ps 104:29; Ecc 12:7

B. Dust used as a symbol
–Dust symbolizes a large number ... Ge 13:16; Nu 23:10
–Rain turned into dust as God's judgment ... Dt 28:24
–Dust on the head expresses grief ... Job 2:12; Isa 47:1
–Sitting in dust expresses repentance ... Jnh 3:6
–Lying in dust expresses humiliation ... Ps 44:25; Ps 113:7
–Lying down in dust means death ... Job 7:21; Ps 7:5
–Enemies licking the dust means defeat ... Ps 72:9; Mic 7:17
–Shaking dust off the feet means rejection ... Mt 10:14; Ac 13:51
–Throwing dust in the air expresses shock ... Ac 22:23

EAGLE

See BIRDS

EAR

A. The human ear
1. Uses for the human ear
–To hear ... 2Sa 7:22
–To acquire wisdom and knowledge ... Pr 2:2; Pr 18:15
–To wear earrings ... Ge 35:4
–To designate, by piercing, a permanent servant ... Ex 21:6
2. Types of human ears
–The ear eager to listen to Jesus ... Mt 11:15
–The ear eager to listen to the Spirit ... Rev 2:7,11, 17,29
–The understanding ear ... Job 13:1
–The deaf ear ... Isa 43:8
–The closed ear ... Jer 6:10
–The uncircumcised ear ... Ac 7:51
–The ear itching to hear falsehood ... 2Ti 4:3

B. The ears of God
–His ears are attentive to our prayers ... Ps 34:15; 1Pe 3:12
–His ears hear the cries of the oppressed ... Jas 5:4
–His ear is not dull ... Isa 59:1
–His ears hear insolence . 2Ki 19:28
–He closes his ears to sinners ... Eze 8:18
–We can ask God to give ear to us ... Ps 5:1; Ps 17:1,6; Ps 130:2

EARTH

A. God and the earth
1. His actions regarding it
–He created it ... Ge 1:1
–He laid its foundations ... Heb 1:10
–He suspended it in space ... Job 26:7
–He called forth plants from it ... Ge 1:11
–He called forth animals from it ... Ge 1:24
–He made people from it ... Ge 2:7
–He filled it with his creatures ... Ps 104:24
–He holds it firmly ... Ps 75:3
–He governs it ... Job 34:12–15
–He will judge it ... Ps 96:13

See also CREATION, PROVIDENCE

2. His relationship to it
–He owns it ... Ps 24:1; 1Co 10:26
–He is King over all of it ... Ps 47:2,7,9
–He loves it ... Ps 33:5
–His glory fills it ... Isa 6:3
–His knowledge will fill it ... Isa 11:9; Hab 2:14
–It is his footstool ... Isa 66:1; Mt 5:35

B. Humans and the earth
–Made from the earth ... Ge 2:7; 1Co 15:47
–It is given to humans .. Ps 115:16
–Humans must fill and rule it ... Ge 1:28; Ge 9:7; Ps 8:6–8
–Believers shall inherit it ... Mt 5:5; Ro 4:13

C. The earth and sin
–Ground cursed after Adam's sin ... Ge 3:17–19
–Earth groans as a result of sin ... Ro 8:22
–Earth became the domain for Satan ... Rev 12:9
–Earth waits for redemption ... Ro 8:20–21
–God will someday make a new earth ... Isa 65:17; 2Pe 3:13; Rev 21:1

EARTHQUAKE

–At the Lord's appearance to Elijah ... 1Ki 19:11–12
–At the Lord's judgment of Jerusalem ... Isa 29:5–6
–During the reign of Uzziah . Am 1:1; Zec 14:5
–After the death of Christ ... Mt 27:54
–At the resurrection of Christ ... Mt 28:2
–During Paul's imprisonment in Philippi ... Ac 16:26
–As a sign of Christ's coming ... Mt 24:4–8; Mk 13:3–8; Lk 21:7–11
–In the great tribulation ... Rev 6:12; Rev 11:13
–In God's final judgment ... Rev 16:17–18

EDOMITES

A. Their identity
–The descendants of Esau (Edom) ... Ge 25:30; Ge 36:8–9
–Lived in hill country, southeast of Israel ... Ge 36:9
–Country also called Mount Seir ... Ge 32:3
–Territory bordered on Judah ... Jos 15:21

B. Significant Edomites
–Numerous kings listed .. Ge 36:31–39; 1Ch 1:43–50
–Doeg: head shepherd of King Saul ... 1Sa 21:7; 1Sa 22:9,18–19
–Hadad: fought against Solomon ... 1Ki 11:14–22

C. Their wars
–Defeated by King Saul . 1Sa 14:47
–Defeated by David ... 2Sa 8:11–14; 1Ch 18:11–13
–Defeated Moab with Israel and Judah ... 2Ki 3:1–27
–Allied with Moab against Jehoshaphat ... 2Ch 20:1,10
–Their warriors killed by Moabites and Ammonites ... 2Ch 20:22–24
–Defeated Jehoram of Judah ... 2Ki 8:20–22; 2Ch 21:8–10
–Defeated by King Amaziah ... 2Ki 14:7; 2Ch 25:10–12
–Defeated King Ahaz of Judah ... 2Ch 28:17

D. Important data concerning them
- –Refused passage to Israelites in desert ... Nu 20:14–21
- –Israelites passed around their country ... Nu 21:4; Jdg 11:17–18
- –Solomon intermarried with them ... 1Ki 11:1
- –Prophecies concerning their destruction ... Isa 34:4–15; Jer 49:7–22; Eze 25:12–14; Eze 35:1–15; Am 1:11–12; Ob 1–21

EDUCATION

A. People as educators
1. Primary educators: parents
   - –A never-ending task . Dt 4:9; Dt 6:4–7; Pr 1:8; Pr 6:20
   - –Usually done by fathers ... Ge 18:19; Ps 44:1; Eph 6:4
   - –Could be done by mothers ... Pr 6:20; 2Ti 1:5; 2Ti 3:15
2. Officials authorized by a government ... Ezr 7:6,10; 2Ch 17:7–9; Ne 8:7–8; Ac 7:22
3. Authorized religious officials ... Mk 12:28; Jn 3:10; Ac 22:3
4. The apostles ... Mt 28:20; Ac 2:42; Ac 4:2
5. People gifted by the Spirit ... 1Co 12:28–29; Eph 4:11
6. Any mature Christian . Heb 5:11–14

B. The content of education
- –The law of God ... Dt 6:6–7; Dt 33:10
- –The praiseworthy deeds of God ... Ps 78:4–6
- –The holy Scriptures ... 2Ti 3:14–17
- –General knowledge and wisdom ... Da 1:17; Col 2:3

C. The foundation of education
- –The fear of God ... Ps 111:10; Pr 1:7; Pr 9:10
- –Knowing the Lord Jesus Christ ... 1Co 1:30; Col 2:3

D. Purpose of education
- –To impart information .. Ps 78:4–6
- –To inspire trust and obedience ... Ps 78:7–8; Pr 22:19
- –To inspire wisdom ... Pr 4:5–8
- –To attain skill in holy living ... Ge 18:19; Pr 1:2–4; 2Ti 3:17
- –To prepare for adulthood ... Pr 22:6

EGLON

A. City in Canaan ... Jos 10:3
- –Its king joined others against city of Gibeon .. Jos 10:3–8
- –Defeated by Joshua ... Jos 10:9–14

B. King of Moab ... Jdg 3:12–14
- –Killed by Ehud ... Jdg 3:16–23

EGYPT

A. Names and geography
1. Other terms for Egypt
   - –The land of Ham ... Ps 105:23
   - –The land of slavery . Ex 20:2
   - –The South ... Da 11:5
   - –Rahab ... Isa 51:9–10
2. Areas of Egypt
   - –Upper and Lower Egypt ... Isa 11:11
   - –The Nile River ... Eze 29:3
   - –The land of Goshen . Ge 47:6
   - –Rameses, a district in Goshen ... Ge 47:11
   - –Pithom and Rameses: built by Israelites ... Ex 1:11
   - –Memphis, the capital city ... Hos 9:6
   - –Thebes ... Eze 30:14
   - –Tahpanhes, the city to which Jews fled .. Jer 43:8; Jer 44:1

B. Important Egyptians
- –Their kings were called Pharaohs *See* PHARAOH
- –Hagar: servant of Sarai . Ge 16:1
- –Potiphar: owner of Joseph ... Ge 39:1
- –Shishak: ransacked the temple ... 1Ki 14:25–26

C. Interaction with God's people
1. During the time of the patriarchs
   - –Abram went to Egypt during famine ... Ge 12:10–20
   - –Joseph sold there by merchants ... Ge 37:28
   - –Joseph became governor of Egypt ... Ge 41:33–45
   - –Joseph's brothers bought grain there .. Ge 42:1–26; Ge 43:1–44:3
   - –Jacob and his sons moved there ... Ge 46:1–47:12
2. At the time of the exodus *See* EXODUS
3. During the time of the kings
   - –Solomon intermarried with them ... 1Ki 3:1
   - –Solomon ruled territory to its border ... 1Ki 4:21
   - –Solomon traded with them ... 1Ki 10:28–29; 2Ch 1:16–17
   - –Enemies of Solomon fled there ... 1Ki 11:14–18; 1Ki 11:40
   - –Gained victory over Rehoboam ... 1Ki 14:25–26; 2Ch 12:1–12
   - –Hoshea allied with them against Syria .. 2Ki 17:4
   - –Josiah killed in a battle against them ... 2Ki 23:29–30; 2Ch 35:20–24
   - –Jehoahaz deposed by king of Egypt ... 2Ki 23:33–35; 2Ch 36:2–4
   - –Jews fled there after death of Gedaliah ... 2Ki 25:25–26
   - –Jeremiah forced to go there ... Jer 43:4–7
4. In the New Testament
   - –Jesus and his parents fled there ... Mt 2:13–15
   - –Egyptian Jews in Jerusalem on Pentecost ... Ac 2:10

D. Prophecies concerning Egypt
- –God's people to be enslaved there ... Ge 15:13
- –God's people to be freed ... Ge 15:14; Ex 3:7–10
- –Judgment against Egypt ... Isa 19:1–17; Jer 46:2–26; Eze 29:3–30:26
- –Judgment on those who seek help from Egypt .. Isa 30:1–3; Isa 31:1–4; Jer 2:18–19, 36–37; Jer 42:7–22; Hos 7:11–16
- –God will call his people back from Egypt ... Isa 11:10–11; Isa 27:12–13
- –God will call his Son from Egypt ... Hos 11:1; Mt 2:15
- –Egyptians will someday worship the Lord ... Isa 19:18–25; Isa 45:14; Mic 7:11–13

EHUD

- –Left-handed judge of Israel . Jdg 3:15
- –Killed Eglon ... Jdg 3:16–23
- –Led Israelites against Moabites ... Jdg 3:26–30

ELAH

- –Son of Baasha ... 1Ki 16:6
- –Became king of Israel ... 1Ki 16:6,8
- –Murdered by Zimri ... 1Ki 16:9–10

ELDER

A. Elders in the Old Testament
- –Assisted in government . Nu 11:16–17
- –Advised kings ... 1Ki 12:6–7
- –Judged the people ... Dt 22:13–19
- –Witnessed legal matters ... Ru 4:2–11
- –Performed religious rituals ... Ex 12:21
- –Represented the tribes .. 1Ki 8:1–3
- –Helped educate the people ... Ex 19:7

B. Elders in the New Testament
1. In Jewish society
   - –Leaders of the people ... Mt 27:12; Ac 24:1
   - –Established religious tradition ... Mt 15:2
2. In the church
   - –Synonymous with "bishop" ... Tit 1:6–7
   - –Appointed by the apostles ... Ac 14:23; Tit 1:5
   - –Qualifications given . 1Ti 3:1–7; Tit 1:5–9
   - –Directed the affairs of church ... 1Ti 5:17
   - –Preached and taught the truth ... 1Ti 3:2; 1Ti 5:17
   - –Guarded against false teaching ... Ac 20:29–31; Tit 1:9
   - –Served as pastors ... Ac 20:28; Jas 5:14; 1Pe 5:1–3
   - –Church members should submit to them ... 1Th 5:12; Heb 13:7,17
3. Twenty-four elders in heaven
   - –They are seated on thrones ... Rev 4:4; Rev 11:16
   - –They worship God .. Rev 4:10; Rev 5:8–14; Rev 7:11–12; Rev 19:4

ELEAZAR

- –Son of Aaron ... Ex 6:23–25
- –Became high priest after Aaron ... Nu 20:26–28; Dt 10:6
- –Took census with Moses ... Nu 26:1–4
- –Aided Joshua in dividing up Canaan ... Jos 14:1
- –His death ... Jos 24:33

ELECTION

–Being chosen by God

A. Examples of people chosen by God
1. In the Old Testament
   - –Abraham ... Ge 18:19
   - –Jacob ... Ge 25:23
   - –Moses ... Ps 106:23
   - –Aaron ... Nu 17:1–8
   - –Saul ... 1Sa 10:24
   - –David ... 1Sa 16:1,12; 2Sa 6:21
   - –People of Israel ... Isa 41:8–9
   - –Servant of the Lord . Isa 42:1
2. In the New Testament
   - –Jesus, God's Son ... Lk 9:35
   - –The disciples ... Jn 15:16
   - –Paul ... Ac 9:15; Gal 1:15
   - –The church ... 1Pe 2:9
   - –Individual Christians ... Eph 1:4; 1Pe 1:2

B. The basis of election
- –God's love ... Dt 10:14–15; Eph 1:4; 2Ti 1:9
- –God's grace ... Ro 11:5–6
- –God's faithfulness to his promises ... Dt 7:7–8
- –God's decision to fulfill his purposes ... Ro 9:11
- –God's foreknowledge ... Ro 8:29; 1Pe 1:2
- –Not based on human works ... Ro 9:11–12

C. The purposes of election
1. For God
   - –To show his grace .. Ro 11:5–6; Eph 1:7
   - –To redeem his children ... Eph 1:5,7; 2Th 2:13
2. For the elect
   - –To come to faith ... Ac 13:48; 2Th 2:13
   - –To assure us of salvation ... Isa 41:9–10; Ro 8:33–34; 2Pe 1:10
   - –To praise God ... Eph 1:11–12
   - –To become like Christ ... Ro 8:29
   - –To do good works .. Eph 2:10; Col 3:12
   - –To bear fruit ... Jn 15:16
   - –To witness to others . Isa 42:1,6–7; Ac 9:15

ELI

- –High priest ... 1Sa 1:9
- –Blessed Hannah ... 1Sa 1:12–18
- –Raised Samuel ... 1Sa 2:11–21
- –Grieved over his sons' wickedness ... 1Sa 2:22–25
- –Did not restrain his sons ... 1Sa 3:13
- –Prophet spoke against him . 1Sa 2:27–36
- –His death ... 1Sa 4:12–22

ELIHU

- –Younger friend of Job ... Job 32:4
- –Angry with Job and his friends ... Job 32:2–3
- –Gave a lengthy speech ... Job 32:6–37:24

ELIJAH

A. His life as a prophet of God
- –Predicted drought in Israel ... 1Ki 17:1; Jas 5:17
- –Fed by ravens ... 1Ki 17:2–6
- –Stayed with a widow in Zarephath ... 1Ki 17:7–16
- –Raised the widow's dead son ... 1Ki 17:17–24
- –Challenged Baal's prophets to a contest ... 1Ki 18:19–26
- –Prayed for fire from heaven ... 1Ki 18:30–39
- –Killed the prophets of Baal ... 1Ki 18:40
- –Prayed for rain ... 1Ki 18:41–45
- –Fled from Jezebel ... 1Ki 19:1–3
- –Prayed that he might die ... 1Ki 19:4–5
- –Strengthened by the Lord ... 1Ki 19:6–18
- –Anointed Elisha as successor ... 1Ki 19:19–21
- –Confronted Ahab after death of Naboth ... 1Ki 21:17–29
- –Prophesied death of Azariah ... 2Ki 1:3–17
- –Taken to heaven without dying ... 2Ki 2:11–12

B. Later references
- –Malachi prophesied his return ... Mal 4:5–6
- –John the Baptist likened to him ... Mt 17:9–13; Mk 9:9–13
- –Jesus compared to him . Mt 16:14
- –Jesus compared his rejection to Elijah's ... Lk 4:24–26

–Appeared to Jesus in the transfiguration .... Mt 17:1–8; Mk 9:1–8
–Paul recalled a remnant in Elijah's day .... Ro 11:2–5
–His prayers are an example for us .... Jas 5:17–18

ELIMELECH
–Husband of Naomi .... Ru 1:2
–Fled to Moab during famine .... Ru 1:1
–Died in Moab .... Ru 1:3

ELIPHAZ
A. Firstborn son of Esau ... Ge 36:4,10
B. One of Job's friends who tried to comfort him .... Job 2:11
 –His first speech .... Job 4:1–5:27
 –His second speech ..... Job 15:1–35
 –His third speech .... Job 22:1–30
 –Offered sacrifices to God after Job's restoration .... Job 42:7–9

ELISHA
A. His association with Elijah
 –Anointed by Elijah as successor 1Ki 19:16–21
 –Accompanied Elijah on his last day 2Ki 2:1–8
 –Inherited Elijah's cloak . 2Ki 2:9–13
 –Divided the Jordan with Elijah's cloak 2Ki 2:14
B. His ministry
 –Purified bad water 2Ki 2:19–22
 –Pronounced a curse on mocking young men 2Ki 2:23–25
 –Aided Israelites in the defeat of Moab 2Ki 3:11–20
 –Increased widow's oil .. 2Ki 4:1–7
 –Raised Shunammite's son 2Ki 4:8–37
 –Purified food by a miracle 2Ki 4:38–41
 –Fed a hundred men by a miracle 2Ki 4:42–44
 –Healed Naaman's leprosy 2Ki 5:1–19
 –Caused axhead to float . 2Ki 6:1–7
 –Captured Arameans 2Ki 6:8–23
 –Advised king of Israel . 2Ki 6:24–8:6
 –Prophesied end to siege of Arameans 2Ki 7:1–2
 –Prophesied Ben-hadad's death 2Ki 8:7–15
 –Anointed Jehu as king of Israel 2Ki 9:1–3
 –Prophesied victory for Jehoash 2Ki 13:14–17
 –His death 2Ki 13:20
C. Later references
 –His dead body raised another one to life 2Ki 13:20–21
 –Jesus compared his rejection to Elisha's .... Lk 4:24,27

ELIZABETH
–Wife of Zechariah; barren .. Lk 1:5–7
–Relative of the virgin Mary .... Lk 1:36
–Gave birth to John the Baptist .... Lk 1:11–23, 57–58
–Visited by Mary .... Lk 1:39–45

ELKANAH
–Husband of Hannah and Peninnah 1Sa 1:1–2
–Worshiped every year at Shiloh 1Sa 1:3–8
–Father of Samuel 1Sa 1:19–20

ENCOURAGEMENT
–Giving support and inspiration
A. Human encouragement
 1. Those who need encouragement
  –Leaders .... Dt 1:38; Dt 3:28
  –The oppressed ...... Isa 1:17
  –The persecuted ..... Ac 14:21–22; 1Th 3:1–3
  –All Christians .... Ac 20:1; Heb 3:13
 2. Those who do the encouraging
  –Kings 2Sa 19:7; 2Ch 32:6–8
  –Prophets .... Ac 15:32
  –Apostles .... Ac 16:40; Ac 20:2; 1Th 2:11–12
  –Church pastors ...... Col 4:7–8; 2Ti 4:2; Tit 2:15; 1Pe 5:12
  –Specially gifted Christians .... Ro 12:6,8
  –All Christians to each other .... Ro 1:12; 1Th 4:18; Heb 10:25
B. Divine encouragement
 –God encourages us ..... Ps 10:17; 2Th 2:16–17; Heb 6:17–18
 –Christ encourages us ... Php 2:1; 2Th 2:16–17
 –The Holy Spirit encourages us .... Ac 9:31
 –The Scriptures encourage us .... Ro 15:4; Heb 12:5

ENEMY
A. Types of enemies
 –Heathen nations .... Jos 5:13; 1Sa 4:3; Jer 12:7
 –Personal adversaries .... 2Sa 4:8; 1Ki 21:20; Est 7:6; Pr 16:7
 –Spiritual forces .... Eph 6:12; 1Pe 5:8
 –Death 1Co 15:26
B. Reactions to one's enemies
 1. In Israelite history
  –Destroyed in war
   See WARFARE
  –Occasionally treated kindly 1Sa 26:7–12
 2. In the psalms
  –Prayers for deliverance from them ..... Ps 59:1; Ps 64:1–2; Ps 143:9
  –Prayers for God to judge them .... Ps 35:4–8,26; Ps 58:6–9; Ps 69:22–28; Ps 109:6–15
 3. In the New Testament
  –Jesus prayed for them .... Lk 23:34
  –Stephen prayed for them .... Ac 7:60
C. Commands from God regarding enemies
 –Treat them with kindness .... Pr 25:21–22; Ro 12:19–21
 –Pray for them .... Mt 5:44
 –Love them .... Mt 5:44; Lk 6:27,35

ENOCH
A. Son of Cain .... Ge 4:17–18
B. Descendant of Seth ..... Ge 5:19–20
 –Walked with God .... Ge 5:22–24
 –Taken by God to heaven without dying .... Ge 5:24
 –An example of faith ... Heb 11:5

ENVY
–Intense feeling of ill will or malice
A. In the Old Testament
 –Examples of envy ..... Ge 37:11; Nu 16:1–3; Ps 106:16–18
 –The command not to envy .... Pr 3:31; Pr 23:17; Pr 24:1
B. In the New Testament
 –Examples of envy ..... Mt 27:18; Mk 15:10; Php 1:15,17
 –Negative effects of envy .... Mk 7:20–23; Jas 3:14,16
 –A positive result from envy .... Ro 11:13–14
 –Envy in a list of vices . Ro 1:29; Gal 5:21; 1Pe 2:1
 –Love does not envy 1Co 13:4

EPHESUS
–Paul left Priscilla and Aquila there .... Ac 18:19
–Apollos learned about Christ there .... Ac 18:24–26
–Paul converted some disciples of John there .... Ac 19:1–7
–Paul spent two years there . Ac 19:8–22
–Riot over Paul's evangelism there .... Ac 19:23–41
–Paul wrote letter to the church there .... Eph 1:1
–Timothy ministered there ... 1Ti 1:3
–Tychicus ministered there .. 2Ti 4:12
–Church there lost its first love .... Rev 2:1–7

EPHRAIM
A. Second son of Joseph ... Ge 41:52; Ge 46:20
 –Name means "twice fruitful" .... Ge 41:52
 –Blessed by Jacob ahead of Manasseh .... Ge 48:12–20
B. Tribe descended from Ephraim
 –Numbered .... Nu 1:33; Nu 26:37
 –Blessed by Moses ..... Dt 33:17
 –Allotted land in Canaan .... Jos 16:4–9; Eze 48:5
 –Failed to possess the land .... Jos 16:10; Jdg 1:29
 –Quarreled with Gideon . Jdg 8:1–3
 –Quarreled with Jephthah .... Jdg 12:1–6
 –Many joined kingdom of Judah during Asa's reform 2Ch 15:8–9
C. A synonym for the northern kingdom .... Isa 7:17; Hos 5:5

ESAU
A. His birth
 –Firstborn of Isaac ...... Ge 25:25
 –Twin with Jacob .... Ge 25:26
 –Also called Edom ...... Ge 25:30
B. Significant events
 –Became a hunter ...... Ge 25:27
 –Sold his birthright ..... Ge 25:29–34
 –His blessing stolen by Jacob .... Ge 27:1–40
 –Wanted to kill Jacob ... Ge 27:41
 –Married pagan women . Ge 26:34; Ge 28:6–9
 –Reconciled to Jacob .... Ge 33:1–17
 –With Jacob, buried Isaac .... Ge 35:29
C. His descendants .... Ge 36:1–43
 See EDOMITES
D. Later significance of Esau
 –Descendants to be obliterated .... Ob 1–21; Jer 49:7–22
 –Jacob chosen over him . Mal 1:2–3
 –Demonstrates God's purpose of election .... Ro 9:11–13
 –His rejection for not repenting .... Heb 12:16–17

ESTHER
–Daughter of Abihail .... Est 2:15
–Cousin of Mordecai .... Est 2:7
–Chosen queen by Xerxes ... Est 2:8–18
–Objected to appearing before Xerxes .... Est 4:10–11
–Asked for a fast .... Est 4:15–16
–Risked her life by approaching Xerxes .... Est 5:1–2
–Foiled Haman's plan to kill Jews .... Est 7:1–8
–Caused Haman's execution . Est 7:9–10
–Her plan preserved the Jews .... Est 8:1–9:17
–Decreed celebration of Purim .... Est 9:18–32

ETERNAL
–Without end in time
A. Eternity related to humans
 1. The human body does not live forever ...... Ecc 12:7
  See DEATH
 2. Eternal life for believers
  –Jesus came to give eternal life .... Jn 11:25–26; 2Ti 1:10; 1Jn 5:11–12
  –We receive eternal life through faith .... Jn 3:16,36; 1Jn 5:13
  –We receive eternal salvation through Christ .... Heb 5:9; Heb 9:12
  –We have an eternal house in heaven 2Co 5:1
  –We are called into God's eternal glory .. 1Pe 5:10
  –We enter an eternal kingdom 2Pe 1:11
  –We receive an eternal inheritance .... Heb 9:15
 3. Eternal punishment for the wicked .... Mt 25:46; 2Th 1:9; Rev 21:8
B. Eternity related to God
 1. His being and person
  –God is the eternal God .... Dt 33:27
  –God is the eternal Rock .... Isa 26:4
  –God is from everlasting to everlasting ...... Ps 90:2
  –God lives forever ... Isa 57:15
  –God's name endures forever .... Ps 135:13
  –God is not bound by time .... Ps 90:4; 2Pe 3:8; Rev 1:8
 2. His attributes
  –He does not change . Ps 102:27; Mal 3:6; Heb 13:8
  –His love endures forever .... 2Ch 7:3,6; Ps 136:1–26
  –His righteousness endures forever ..... Ps 111:3; 2Co 9:9
  –His faithfulness endures forever ..... Ps 100:5; Ps 117:2
  –His purpose for humanity is eternal .. Eph 3:11
  –His power is eternal . Ro 1:20
 3. His kingdom
  –God is the eternal King 1Ti 1:17
  –His kingdom is eternal .... Ps 145:13; Da 4:3,34
  –Christ reigns forever and ever .... Rev 11:15
 4. His everlasting covenant
  –With Abraham, Isaac, Jacob .... Ge 17:7–8; 1Ch 16:17
  –With David 2Sa 7:13–16; 2Sa 23:5
  –With us in the new covenant .... Isa 55:3; Jer 32:40; Eze 37:26
 5. God's word is eternal .... Ps 119:89; Isa 40:8; 1Pe 1:24–25

EUPHRATES
–One of the rivers of Eden .. Ge 2:14
–Abraham came from beyond it .... Jos 24:2–3
–Israel's borders to expand there .... Ge 15:18; Dt 11:22–25
–Hittites controlled it .... Jos 1:4
–David expanded kingdom to it 2Sa 8:3; 1Ch 18:3
–Solomon's kingdom bordered on it .... 1Ki 4:21; Ps 72:8
–Assyrians controlled it ..... 2Ki 23:29; Isa 8:7–8

–Babylon controlled it ...... 2Ki 24:1; Jer 46:2
–Christ's kingdom to reach to it ...... Zec 9:9–10
–Army of the final battle to come from there ...... Rev 9:14; Rev 16:12

EVANGELISM

See MISSION

EVE

A. Eve in the Old Testament
1. Her history
–Made in God's image ...... Ge 1:27; Ge 5:1–2
–Made from Adam's rib ...... Ge 2:22
–Became Adam's wife ...... Ge 2:23–24
–Entered conversation with serpent ...... Ge 3:1–5
–Ate forbidden fruit with Adam ...... Ge 3:6
–Tried to hide from God ...... Ge 3:8
–Blamed serpent for her sin ...... Ge 3:13
–Received curse from God ...... Ge 3:16
–Banished with Adam from Eden ...... Ge 3:23
–Mother of Cain, Abel and Seth ...... Ge 4:1–2,25
2. Her significance as mother of all humans . Ge 3:20
B. Eve in the New Testament
–Significance of Eve being created after Adam 1Co 11:8; 1Ti 2:13
–Significance of Eve deceived by serpent 2Co 11:3

EXAMPLE

A. Old Testament people as examples
1. As warnings 1Co 10:6–11; 2Ti 3:8
2. As models for Christian behavior
–Job in his perseverance ...... Jas 5:10–11
–Elijah in his prayers . Jas 5:16–18
–Numerous saints in their faith ...... Heb 11:4–40
B. Christ as an example
–His humility ...... Php 2:5–8
–His love ...... Jn 15:12–13; Eph 5:2
–His service ...... Jn 13:14–15
–His gentleness ...... Mt 11:29
–His consideration of others ...... Ro 15:2–3
–His grace of giving 2Co 8:7–9
–His forgiveness ...... Col 3:13
–His purity 1Jn 3:3
–His unjust suffering 1Pe 2:20–23
–His obedience to the Father ...... Jn 15:10
–His general walk of life 1Jn 2:6
C. Paul as an example
–Thessalonians followed his example 1Th 1:6
–Churches encouraged to imitate him ...... 1Co 4:16; 1Co 11:1; Php 3:17; 2Th 3:7,9
D. Christians as examples
–The Thessalonians were examples 1Th 1:7
–Church leaders must be examples ...... 1Ti 4:12; Tit 2:7; 1Pe 5:3
–We must all be examples ...... Mt 5:16; Php 2:14–15; 1Pe 2:12

EXHORTATION

See ENCOURAGEMENT

EXILE

–The captivity of the people of Judah by the Babylonians
A. Judah carried away into Babylon
1. The story of the exile told 2Ki 24:11–16; 2Ki 25:11
2. Three waves of exiles ...... Jer 52:28–30
–Daniel in the first ... Da 1:1–6
–Ezekiel in the second ...... Eze 1:1–3
–Remainder of the people in the third .. 2Ch 36:20
3. Reasons for the exile
–Because of the sins of Manasseh ...... 2Ki 21:10–15; Jer 15:1–4
–Because of Judah's idolatry ...... Dt 28:45–52; Isa 40:2; Jer 5:7–17; Eze 6:1–8
–Because Judah failed to heed prophets 2Ch 36:15–20
4. Lessons the Jews learned in the exile
–That God was everywhere ...... Eze 11:16
–That God was Redeemer ...... Isa 59:12–20
–That God still loved them ...... Jer 30:10–11,18–22; Eze 34:20–31
–That the Law was important ...... Ezr 7:10; Ne 8:1–9
B. The return from exile
–Occurred after seventy years ...... Jer 25:11
–God remembered his promises ...... Jer 29:10
–God remembered his covenant ...... Eze 16:60
–Cyrus decreed the Jews could return ...... 2Ch 36:23; Ezr 1:2–4
–The Jews returned in two groups ...... Ezr 1:5–6; Ezr 7:1–9

EXODUS

–The escape of the Israelites from Egypt
A. Jacob and his sons in Egypt
–Moved to Egypt ...... Ge 46:1–27
–Became slaves of the Egyptians ...... Ex 1:8–14
B. God's deliverance of his people from Egypt
1. God's choosing of a deliverer
–Moses preserved at birth ...... Ex 2:1–10
–Moses called as deliverer ...... Ex 3:7–22
–Aaron appointed to assist Moses ...... Ex 4:13–17, 27–31
2. The process of deliverance
–Signs given to Moses ...... Ex 4:1–9
–The first appearance before Pharaoh ...... Ex 5:1–5
–The second appearance before Pharaoh . Ex 7:10–13
–The first nine plagues ...... Ex 7:14—10:29
–The preparation for the tenth plague ...... Ex 11:1—12:28
–The slaying of the firstborn in Egypt ... Ex 12:29–30
–The escape from Egypt ...... Ex 12:31–39
–The pursuit of the Israelites ...... Ex 14:5–9
–The crossing of the Red Sea ...... Ex 14:10–22,29
–The drowning of the Egyptians ...... Ex 14:23–28
3. God's motive in the exodus
–Faithfulness to his promises ...... Ge 15:13–16; Dt 7:8–9
–His love for his people ...... Dt 7:8–9; Hos 11:1
C. Israelite remembrance of the exodus
–Sung after crossing the Red Sea ...... Ex 15:1–21
–Celebrated annually in the Passover ...... Ex 13:3–16
–Recalled in the Ten Commandments ...... Ex 20:2; Dt 5:6
–Celebrated by psalmists ...... Ps 66:5–6; Ps 78:12–14; Ps 105:26–39; Ps 106:8–12
–Taught by prophets .... Isa 43:16–21; Isa 63:11–14; Hos 12:9,13; Na 1:4
D. The exodus in the New Testament
–As an affirmation of God's power ...... Ac 13:17; Ro 9:17
–As a picture of salvation in Christ 1Co 10:1–4
–As an example of God's care ...... Jn 6:31–33
–As an example of human faith ...... Heb 11:29
–As a warning against disobedience ...... Heb 3:7—4:2; Jude 5

EYE

A. The human eye
1. The physical eyes
–Leah's weak eyes ... Ge 29:17
–Lovers' eyes ...... SS 1:15; SS 7:4
–Cruelty in eyes being gouged out ...... Jdg 16:21; 2Ki 25:7
2. Figurative use of eyes
–Enlightened eyes symbolize knowledge ...... Ps 19:8; Eph 1:18
–Opened eyes symbolize knowledge ...... Ge 3:5,7
–Bright eyes symbolize well-being 1Sa 14:27
–Dim eyes symbolize grief ...... Job 17:7
–Winking eyes express mockery ...... Ps 35:19
–Winking eyes plot perversity ...... Pr 16:30
–Dissatisfied eyes express greed ...... Pr 27:20
–Closed eyes express spiritual blindness ... Isa 6:10; Mt 13:15
–Lustful eyes 1Jn 2:16
–Eyes full of adultery 2Pe 2:14
–Haughty eyes ...... Ps 18:27
–A jealous eye 1Sa 18:9
B. The eye of God
–Symbolizes God's all-knowing nature ...... Ps 139:16; Pr 15:3
–Symbolizes God's holiness ...... Hab 1:13
–Symbolizes God watching over us ...... Ezr 5:5; Ps 33:18
–Symbolizes Christ's control of history ...... Rev 5:6

EZEKIEL

A. Family background and history
–A priest ...... Eze 1:3
–Carried into exile ...... Eze 1:1
–Called to be prophet ...... Eze 2:1—3:11
–Married; wife died ...... Eze 24:18
B. His symbolic actions as a prophet
–City of Jerusalem on a clay tablet ...... Eze 4:1–3
–Lying immobile for more than a year ...... Eze 4:4–8
–Strange diet during the "siege" of Jerusalem .. Eze 4:9–17
–A strange haircut ...... Eze 5:1–4
–Packing his belongings for exile ...... Eze 12:1–16
–Shuddering while eating his food ...... Eze 12:17–20
–Groaning in public ...... Eze 20:6–7
–Not mourning when his wife died ...... Eze 24:15–24
–A prophecy using sticks ...... Eze 37:15–28
C. His parables as a prophet
–The parable of the useless vine ...... Eze 15:1–8
–The parable of the wife turned prostitute ...... Eze 16:1–63
–The parable of two eagles and a vine ...... Eze 17:1–24
–The parable of the lion . Eze 19:1–9
–The parable of the two adulterous sisters ...... Eze 23:1–49

EZRA

–A priest ...... Ezr 7:1–5
–A teacher of the Law ...... Ezr 7:6–10
–Led exiles back to Jerusalem ...... Ezr 8:15–36
–Concerned about intermarriage ...... Ezr 9:1–4
–Prayed about intermarriage problem ...... Ezr 9:5–15
–Corrected intermarriage problem ...... Ezr 10:1–17
–Read Law at the festival of tabernacles ...... Ne 8:1–8
–Participated in dedication of wall of Jerusalem ...... Ne 12:31–36

FACE

A. The human face
1. Significance of the human face
–Seeing a face means meeting a person .... Ge 43:3,5; 2Sa 14:28,32
–Talking face to face . 2Jn 12; 3Jn 14
–A radiant face means closeness to God .... Ex 34:29–30
–One can slap a face in anger 1Ki 22:24
–One can spit in a face in disgust ...... Mt 26:67
2. Emotions expressed by the face
–The cheerful face ... Pr 15:13
–The face bowed down in respect ...... Ge 48:12; 1Sa 25:23
–The downcast face .. Ge 4:5–6; Lk 24:17
–The sad face ...... Ne 2:3–4
–The face hidden in fear ...... Ex 3:6
–The terrified face ... Da 5:6,9
–The face bowed down in grief ...... Jos 7:10
–The face turned away in grief 2Ki 20:2
–The face turned away in shame ...... Ezr 9:6
–The face covered with shame ...... Ps 69:7
B. The face of God
–God's face synonymous with himself ...... Hos 5:15
–God's glory seen in the face of Christ 2Co 4:6
–Seeing God face to face ...... Ge 32:30; 1Co 13:12
–Seeking God's face in prayer ...... Ps 24:6; Ps 27:8
–God's face shining on us in blessing ...... Nu 6:24–26; Ps 4:6
–God's face hidden from our sins ...... Ps 51:9
–God's face hidden in judgment ...... Dt 31:17–18; Ps 13:1–2
–God's face set against evildoers ...... Lev 20:3,5; Ps 34:16; Eze 15:7; 1Pe 3:12

FAITH

–Belief in a person or a teaching
A. What are the basic elements of faith?
1. Trust in God and commitment to Christ .... Ge 15:6; Pr 3:5; Ro 3:22; Heb 11:1
2. True knowledge of God and Christ
–Truths of the faith are important 1Ti 3:9; 1Ti 4:1

–They must be based on God's word 2Ti 3:16
–They are worth fighting for ..... Jude 3

B. What must we believe?

1. We must believe *in*:
–God ..... Ex 14:31; Jn 14:1
–Christ ..... Jn 2:11; Ac 16:31
–The name of the Son of God 1Jn 3:23
–The prophets ..... Ex 14:31; 2Ch 20:20

2. We must believe

a. What God has said
–The commandments of God ..... Ps 119:66
–The writings of the Old Testament ..... Lk 24:25; Jn 5:46–47; Ac 26:27
–The gospel ..... Mk 1:15; 1Co 15:1–2
–The holy Scriptures 2Ti 3:14–15
–The promises of God ..... Ro 4:20–21
–Things God has said to us ..... Ge 15:6

b. What God teaches about Jesus
–That Jesus is the Christ ..... Jn 20:31; 1Jn 5:1
–That Jesus is God's Son 1Jn 5:5
–That Jesus was raised from the dead ..... Ro 10:9
–Summary creed 1Co 15:3–11

See also CONFESSION
DOCTRINE

C. Where does faith come from?
–From God, as a gift ..... Eph 2:8; Php 1:29
–From the Father and the Son ..... Eph 6:23
–From the power of God in us 1Co 2:5
–From the Holy Spirit 1Co 12:9
–From hearing the gospel ..... Jn 17:20; Ac 15:7; Ro 10:14,17
–From reading the Scriptures ..... Jn 20:31; 1Jn 5:13

D. What happens when we believe?
–We receive forgiveness of sin ..... Ac 10:43
–We are justified ..... Ro 3:28; Gal 2:16
–We are saved ..... Ac 16:30–31; Ro 10:9
–We receive eternal life ..... Jn 3:14–16
–We become free from condemnation ..... Jn 3:17
–We become free from spiritual death ..... Jn 11:25–26
–We become God's children ..... Jn 1:12; Gal 3:26
–We become children of light ..... Jn 12:36
–We gain access to God ..... Eph 3:12
–We enter God's rest ..... Heb 4:3
–Our hearts are purified ..... Ac 15:9
–We are sanctified ..... Ac 26:18
–The word of God goes to work in us 1Th 2:13
–We receive peace with God ..... Ro 5:1
–We experience joy ..... Ac 16:34
–We gain security in God's power 1Pe 1:5

E. What must we do as believers?
–Live by faith ..... 2Co 5:7; Gal 2:20
–Walk by faith ..... Ro 4:12
–Face everything by faith ..... Heb 11:33–39
–Remain true to the faith ..... Ac 14:22
–Continue in the faith ..... Col 1:23
–Stand firm in the faith 1Co 16:13; 1Pe 5:9
–Fight for the faith ..... 1Ti 6:12; Jude 3
–Increase our faith ..... Lk 17:5
–Grow in faith ..... 2Th 1:3; Jude 20
–Please God by our faith ..... Heb 11:6
–Combine faith with hope and love ..... 1Co 13:2,13; Gal 5:6; 1Th 1:3
–Do everything by faith ..... Ro 14:22–23
–Pray in faith ..... Jas 1:5–6
–Tell others about our faith 2Co 4:13–14
–Demonstrate faith by good works ..... Jas 2:14–26
–Overcome sin by our faith 1Jn 5:4–5
–Fight the devil by our faith ..... Eph 6:16

G. Striking examples of faith
–Abraham ..... Ro 4:1–3,9–21
–Numerous Old Testament people ..... Heb 11:4–40
–Daniel's three friends ..... Da 3:16–18
–Daniel ..... Da 6:1–11
–A centurion ..... Mt 8:5–10
–A sick woman ..... Mt 9:20–22
–A Canaanite woman ..... Mt 15:22–28
–Blind Bartimaeus ..... Mk 10:46–52
–A sinful woman ..... Lk 7:36–50
–Martha ..... Jn 11:21–27
–Thomas ..... Jn 20:24–29
–Philippian jailer ..... Ac 16:29–34
–Lois, Eunice, and Timothy 2Ti 1:5
–Paul 2Ti 1:12

FAITHFULNESS

–Remaining steadfast to one's commitments

A. Human faithfulness

1. Faithfulness is an aspect of the fruit of the Spirit ..... Gal 5:22

2. Examples of those who were faithful
–Abraham ..... Ne 9:8
–Moses ..... Nu 12:7
–Hezekiah 2Ch 31:20
–The Zadokite priests ..... Eze 48:11
–Timothy 1Co 4:17
–Epaphras ..... Col 1:7
–Onesimus ..... Col 4:9
–Silas 1Pe 5:12

3. We must be faithful
–In obeying God's commands ..... Dt 11:13
–In our walk before God 1Ki 2:4
–In serving God 2Ch 19:9
–In our prayer life ..... Ro 12:12
–In the use of our gifts 1Pe 4:10
–In persevering until death ..... Rev 2:10

4. God's promises to those who are faithful
–He is faithful to them ..... Ps 18:25
–His eyes are on them ..... Ps 101:6
–He preserves them ..... Ps 31:23
–He guards their lives ..... Ps 97:10
–He protects them ..... Pr 2:8
–He blesses them ..... Dt 11:13–15
–He rewards them ..... Mt 25:21–23
–He does not forsake them ..... Ps 37:28
–He guarantees them life ..... Eze 18:9

B. God's faithfulness

1. God is faithful in himself
–He is the faithful God ..... Dt 7:9; Heb 10:23
–He abounds in faithfulness ..... Ps 86:15
–His faithfulness is great ..... La 3:23
–He will remain faithful 2Ti 2:13

2. God is faithful in his actions
–He is faithful in all he does ..... Ps 33:4; Ps 111:7–8
–He is faithful to his covenant ..... Ps 78:24–28
–He keeps all his promises ..... Ge 21:1–2; 1Ki 8:20; Ac 13:23, 32–33
–Christ fulfills all God's promises 2Co 1:18,20

3. God is faithful in his relationship to us
–In his love for us ..... Ps 89:24; Ps 143:1
–In helping us 1Co 10:13
–In protecting us ..... Ps 91:4; 2Th 3:3
–In forgiving us 1Jn 1:9

4. God's word is faithful ..... 2Sa 7:28; Ps 19:7; Rev 21:5

FALLING AWAY

–Falling away from the faith, backsliding, apostasy

A. Falling away in the Old Testament

1. Examples
–At Mount Sinai ..... Ex 32:1–35
–During the time of the judges ..... Jdg 2:10–12
–In Israel 1Ki 16:30–33
–In Judah 2Ch 24:17–19
–A regular pattern ..... Ps 106:6–47

2. Causes
–Mixed marriages ..... Nu 25:1–3; Ne 13:26–27
–Poor examples of kings 1Ki 16:29–33; 2Ki 21:1–11

3. Judgment for those who fall away ..... Dt 13:13–18; 2Ki 21:12–15

B. Falling away in the New Testament

1. Examples
–At the time of Jesus ..... Jn 6:66
–In the early church 1Ti 1:19–20; 2Ti 2:17–18; 2Pe 2:20–21
–Future severe apostasy ..... Mt 24:12; 2Th 2:3; 2Ti 3:1,5

2. Causes
–Influence of deceiving spirits 1Ti 4:1
–False teachers ..... Ac 20:29–30; Rev 2:14–15
–Human desires 2Ti 4:3–4
–Love of world 2Ti 4:10
–Hardened hearts ..... Ac 7:51–52; Ac 28:26–27
–Persecution ..... Mt 24:9–10
–A time of testing ..... Lk 8:13

3. Judgment for those who fell away
–Judgment from God ..... Heb 10:26–31; Jude 11–15
–Removal from God's kingdom ..... Rev 2:5
–Impossible to renew to repentance ..... Heb 6:4–8

4. The antidote to falling away
–Heed the warning not to fall away ..... Heb 3:12; 2Pe 3:17
–Depend on God ..... Ro 8:35–39; 1Co 10:13; Jude 24
–Remain steadfast in faith ..... Heb 6:11–12; Jude 20–21
–Continue reading God's word 2Ti 3:14–17
–Keep growing in Christian character 2Pe 1:5–10
–Associate with other believers ..... Heb 3:13; Heb 10:24

FAMILY

A. The establishment of the family
–Marriage begun in the Garden of Eden ..... Ge 2:18–24
–The first children, given by God ..... Ge 4:1–2
–The family built by God ..... Ps 127:1–6
–The family blessed by God ..... Ps 128:1–6
–The central unit in God's covenant ..... Ge 17:7; Jos 24:15

B. Responsibilities in the family

1. The father as head
–Head of the family ..... Ex 6:14
–Head of the wife ..... Eph 5:23–24
–Must love his wife ..... Eph 5:25–33; 1Pe 3:7
–Must supervise religious observances ..... Ge 35:1–7; Ex 12:3; 1Sa 1:21
–Must supervise education of children ..... Ps 44:1; Ps 78:3; Eph 6:4
–Must care for the children's needs ..... 2Co 12:14; Col 3:21

2. The role of the mother
–Subject to her husband ..... Eph 5:24; 1Pe 3:1–6
–Assist in training of children ..... Pr 1:8; Pr 6:20
–Could take an important role in home ..... 1Sa 1:9–28; Pr 31:10–31; 2Ti 1:5

3. The place of children
–A blessing from the Lord ..... Ps 127:3–5
–Must honor parents ..... Ex 20:12; Lev 19:3
–Must obey parents ..... Dt 21:18–21; Eph 6:1–3; Col 3:20

C. Things that disturb or destroy the family
–Jealousy and hatred ..... Ge 4:3–8
–Lack of respect toward parents ..... Ge 9:21–22
–Parents picking favorites ..... Ge 25:27–28
–Rivalry and selfishness ..... Ge 27:1–41
–Polygamy ..... Ge 30:1–2; 1Sa 1:1–6
–Lack of discipline 1Sa 2:22–25
–Lust and incest 2Sa 13:1–21
–Personal ambition ..... Jdg 9:1–5; 2Sa 15:1–17
–Mixed marriages ..... Ne 13:23–27
–Materialism 1Ti 6:6–10
–False teaching ..... Tit 1:10–11

D. New Testament teachings on the family
–Salvation took place in households ..... Ac 16:15, 31–34; Ac 18:8; 1Co 1:16; 1Co 16:15
–Children of believers are holy 1Co 7:14
–A well-ordered family was important ..... 1Ti 3:4–5,12; Tit 1:6
–Care for members in the family circle 1Ti 5:4,8,16

E. The family used figuratively
–As a picture of the nation of Israel ..... Ps 115:9–12
–As a picture of the church ..... Gal 6:10; Eph 2:19; Heb 2:11; 1Pe 4:17

See also CHILDREN
FATHER
MARRIAGE
MOTHER

FAMINE

See HUNGER AND THIRST

FASTING

–Voluntarily depriving oneself of food

A. In the Old Testament

1. Occasions for fasting
–To prepare to receive God's law ..... Ex 34:28; Dt 9:9,18
–To prepare for the Day of Atonement ..... Lev 16:29, 31

–To show sorrow at time of death 1Sa 31:13; 2Sa 1:12
–To show sorrow for sin 1Ki 21:27; Ne 9:1; Jnh 3:6–9
–To show humility Ps 35:13
–To pray in time of national need 2Ch 20:3; Ezr 8:21; Est 4:16; Joel 2:15–17
–To accompany deep personal prayer 2Sa 12:16,21; Ne 1:4; Da 9:3–4
2. Prophets criticized fasting as outward show Isa 58:3–7; Jer 14:12; Zec 7:4–10

B. In the New Testament
1. Occasions for fasting
–A regular pattern for many Jews Mt 9:14; Lk 2:37; Ac 23:12–14
–Paul after his conversion Ac 9:9
–To prepare for mission work Ac 13:2–3; Ac 14:23
–Not done by Jesus' disciples Mt 9:14
2. Jesus criticized fasting as outward show Mt 6:16–18; Lk 18:9–14

FATHER

A. Various meanings of father
–Creator Jas 1:17
–Caretaker Job 29:16
–Counselor Ge 45:8
–A respected prophet 2Ki 6:21
–A respected priest Jdg 17:10
–One's male parent Ge 4:18
–One's grandfather Ge 28:13
–One's great-grandfather 1Ki 15:11

B. The father in the family
1. Duties of a father
–Supervise religious observances Ge 35:1–7; Ex 12:3; 1Sa 1:21
–Responsible for education of children Ge 18:19; Dt 4:9–10; Eph 6:5
–Responsible for discipline of children Dt 8:4; Pr 3:11–12
–Care for his children's needs 2Co 12:14; Col 3:21
–Give blessing to his children Ge 27:27–29,39–40; Ge 49:1–28
2. Responsibility of children
–Respect their fathers Ex 20:12; Lev 19:3
–Obey their fathers Ex 20:12; Eph 6:1; Col 3:20

C. Spiritual use of father
–Abraham as the father (ancestor) of believers Ro 4:11,16–17; Gal 3:7
–Paul as the father of his churches 1Co 4:15; 1Th 2:11–12
–God as Father of Jesus Christ Jn 17:1,5; Eph 1:3
–God as Father of everyone Mal 2:10; Ac 17:28–29
–God as Father of his chosen people Isa 63:16; Jer 31:9
–God as Father of believers in Jesus Mt 6:9; Jn 1:12–13; Gal 1:1,4
–Christians can call God "Abba" (Father) Ro 8:15; Gal 4:6
–The devil as father of the ungodly Jn 8:44; 1Jn 3:10–12

FEAR

–One's apprehension in a frightening situation; reverence

A. Fear as being afraid
1. Why did people experience fear?
–Fear of seeing God Ex 3:6
–Fear of a vision of angels Mt 28:4; Lk 2:8–9
–Fear of the unknown Lk 9:34,45
–Fear of punishment for sin Ge 3:8–10; Ge 18:15; Ac 24:25
–Fear of danger Ac 27:17,29
–Fear of being killed Ge 26:7; 1Ki 19:3
–Fear of losing one's life Jnh 1:5; Mt 14:30
–Fear of losing one's loved ones Ge 31:31; Ge 42:4
–Fear of bringing unpleasant news 1Sa 3:15; 2Sa 12:18
–Fear of an enemy 1Sa 28:5; Jn 20:19
–Fear of a person in authority Ne 2:2
–Fear of what another person might do 1Sa 18:12,15
–Fear of what others might say Gal 2:12
–Fear of the future Ge 21:17
2. The command not to be afraid
–Given by God Ge 21:17; Ge 26:24; Isa 41:10; Ac 18:9
–Given by Moses Ex 14:13; Ex 20:20
–Given by Joshua Jos 10:25
–Given by Samuel 1Sa 12:20
–Given by Elijah 1Ki 17:13
–Given by David 1Ch 22:13
–Given by the prophet Jahaziel 2Ch 20:15,17
–Given by Hezekiah 2Ch 32:7
–Given by Isaiah Isa 44:2,8
–Given by Jeremiah Jer 42:11
–Given by Jesus Mt 14:27; Mk 5:36; Lk 12:4,7,32; Jn 6:20
–Given by an angel Lk 1:13,30; Lk 2:10; Ac 27:23–24
3. How to conquer fear
–By trusting in God Ps 3:3–6; Ps 56:4,11
–By believing in Jesus Mk 5:36
–By knowing God is with us Ge 26:24; Dt 31:6,8; Ps 23:4; Isa 43:5
–By knowing Jesus is with us Jn 6:20; Ac 18:9–10
–By knowing God is our Savior Ps 27:1,3
–By knowing God is our refuge Ps 46:1–2; Ps 91:1–6; Heb 13:6
–By knowing God will fight for us Dt 3:22; Dt 20:3–4; 2Ch 20:15–17
–By obeying the Lord 1Sa 12:20–21; 1Ch 22:12–13
4. Courage as the answer to fear
See COURAGE

B. Fear as reverence for the Lord
1. The command to fear the Lord Dt 6:13; Jos 24:14; 2Ch 19:7; Ps 33:8; Pr 3:7; Ecc 12:13
2. Examples of those who feared the Lord
–Noah Heb 11:7
–Abraham Ge 22:12
–Joseph Ge 42:18
–Job Job 1:1
–David Ps 5:7
–Hezekiah Jer 26:19
–Nehemiah Ne 5:15
–The early church Ac 9:31
3. Reasons for fearing the Lord
–His awesome power Ex 20:18–20
–His glory Lk 2:9
–His holiness Rev 15:4
–His majesty Ps 96:4–6
–His greatness 1Sa 12:24
–His forgiveness Ps 130:4
–His faithfulness Ps 119:38
4. Benefits of fearing God
–A way to praise God Ps 22:23
–A way to serve God Ps 2:11
–A way to obey God Ecc 12:13
–A way to fight evil Pr 8:13; Pr 16:6
–A way to become wise Ps 111:10; Pr 1:7
–A way to lengthen life Pr 10:27
–God loves those who fear him Ps 103:11,13,17
–God saves those who fear him Ps 85:9
–God protects those who fear him Ps 60:4; Pr 14:26–27
–God blesses those who fear him Ps 115:12–13
–God provides for those who fear him Ps 34:9; Ps 111:5

FELIX

–Governor of Judea Ac 23:24
–Letter addressed to him Ac 23:26–30
–Paul on trial before him Ac 24:1–21
–Sought personal interview with Paul Ac 24:24–26
–Kept Paul in prison to please the Jews Ac 24:27
–Replaced by Festus Ac 24:27

FELLOWSHIP

–A sharing together between persons

A. Human fellowship among God's people Ge 2:18
1. Basis of such fellowship
–Fellowship with God 1Jn 1:3,7
–The presence of Christ Mt 18:20
–The word of God Ac 2:42
2. The expression of such fellowship
–Prayed for by Christ Jn 17:20–23
–Sung by the psalmists Ps 133:1–2
–Demonstrated by mutual sharing Ac 2:44–45; Ac 4:32–35
–Demonstrated by prayers for each other Ac 1:14; Ac 4:24–31; Ro 15:30–32
–Symbolized in the Lord's Supper Ac 2:46–47; 1Co 10:16–17
–Exercised among church leaders Gal 2:9
3. "One another" commands
–Be devoted to one another Ro 12:10
–Live in harmony with one another Ro 12:16; 1Pe 3:8
–Accept one another Ro 15:7
–Instruct one another Ro 15:14
–Use your gifts for one another 1Co 12:7; 1Pe 4:10
–Share with one another 2Co 8:7,13–15
–Greet one another 2Co 13:12
–Serve one another in love Gal 5:13
–Bear one another's burdens Gal 6:2
–Be kind to one another Eph 4:32; 1Th 5:15
–Forgive one another Eph 4:32
–Look to the interest of others Php 2:3–4
–Bear with one another Col 3:13
–Love one another Col 3:14; 1Jn 4:11–12
–Admonish one another Col 3:16
–Encourage one another 1Th 5:11; Heb 10.25
–Build up one another 1Th 5:11
–Live in peace with one another 1Th 5:13
–Spur one another to good works Heb 10:24
–Confess your sins to each other Jas 5:16
–Pray for one another Jas 5:16
–Be hospitable to one another 1Pe 4:9
4. We may have no fellowship with the ungodly 1Co 5:1–2; 2Co 6:14–16; Eph 5:5–7,11

B. Fellowship with God
1. Fellowship with the Triune God
–With God the Father 1Jn 1:3
–With God the Son Jn 15:3–4; 1Co 1:9
–With God the Holy Spirit 2Co 13:14; Php 2:1
2. Developing such fellowship
–By desiring it Ps 42:1; Ps 63:1
–By believing in Jesus, God's Son 1Jn 1:2–3
–By meditating on God's word Ps 1:2; Ps 119:10–15; 2Pe 1:4
–By praying to God Mk 1:35; Lk 5:16
–By thinking wholesome thoughts Php 4:8–9
–By living a holy life Ps 15:1–5; 2Co 6:14–18
–By participating in the Lord's Supper 1Co 10:16; 1Co 11:23–26
3. Examples of such fellowship
–Enoch Ge 5:22–24
–Noah Ge 6:9
–Abraham Ge 18:17–19
–Jacob Ge 48:15
–Moses Ex 33:1
–David Ps 23
–Jesus Mt 26:39–42
–Paul Ac 22:17–21; 2Co 12:1–4

FESTIVALS

A. Religious festivals
1. Commanded in the Old Testament
–Passover Ex 12:1–14; Lev 23:5; Nu 9:1–14; Dt 16:1–7
–Unleavened bread Ex 12:15–20; Ex 13:3–10; Lev 23:6–8; Nu 28:17–25; Dt 16:3–4,8
–First fruits Lev 23:9–14

–Weeks (harvest, Pentecost) .... Ex 23:16
Lev 23:15–21
Nu 28:26–31
Dt 16:9–12
–Trumpets .... Lev 23:23–25
Nu 29:1–6
–Day of atonement ... Lev 16:1–34
Nu 29:7–11
–Tabernacles (Ingathering, Booths) .... Ex 23:16
Lev 23:33–43
Nu 29:12–34
Dt 16:13–15
–Sacred assembly .... Lev 23:36
Nu 29:35–38
–Purim .... Est 9:27–28
2. Celebrations in the Old Testament
–Passover .... Jos 5:10
2Ki 23:21–23
2Ch 30:1–20
2Ch 35:1–17
Ezr 6:19–21
–Unleavened bread ... Jos 5:11
2Ch 30:21–27
2Ch 35:17–19
Ezr 6:22
–Day of atonement ... Ne 9:1–38
–Tabernacles (Booths) .... Ezr 3:4
Ne 8:13–18
–Purim .... Est 9:18–32
3. Celebrations in the New Testament
–Passover .... Mt 26:1–2, 17–29
Mk 14:12–25
Lk 22:7–38
Jn 2:13–25
Jn 11:55–56
Jn 13:1–30
–Unleavened bread ... Mt 26:17
Mk 14:1,12
Lk 22:1,7
–Weeks (Pentecost) .. Ac 2:1–41
–Tabernacles (Booths) .... Jn 7:2–36
–Sacred assembly .... Jn 7:37–44
–Dedication (Hanukkah) .... Jn 10:22–39
–The Lord's Supper .. Mt 26:26–29
Mk 14:22–25
Lk 22:17–20
1Co 11:17–26
4. Criticism when festivals became empty rituals
–In the Old Testament .... Isa 1:14
Isa 5:12
Hos 2:11
Am 5:21–23
–In the New Testament 2Pe 2:13
Jude 12

B. Non-religious occasions for feasting
–At weanings .... Ge 21:8
–At the signing of a treaty .... Ge 26:30
–At marriages .... Ge 29:21–22
Jdg 14:10
–At a coronation 1Ki 1:41
–At a family celebration . Lk 15:23

FESTUS

–Succeeded Felix as governor .... Ac 24:27
–Visited Jerusalem authorities .... Ac 25:1–5
–Convened court to deal with Paul .... Ac 25:6–12
–Paul appealed to Caesar before him .... Ac 25:12
–Consulted Agrippa about Paul .... Ac 25:13–22
–Arranged an audience for Agrippa with Paul .... Ac 25:23–26:29

FIRE

A. Human uses of fire
1. Domestic uses
–For cooking .... Isa 44:15–16
Jn 21:9
–For warmth .... Isa 44:15–16
Mk 14:54
–For metalworking ... Ex 32:24
2. Military uses
–For destroying a city .... Jos 6:24
1Sa 30:1
2Ch 36:19
–For destroying crops 2Sa 14:30
3. Religious uses
–For sacrifices .... Ge 8:20
Lev 1:9
Nu 18:17
–For burning incense . Ex 30:7–8
1Ki 9:25
Lk 1:9
–For burning unclean substances .... Lev 13:52,55
–Unholy fire could not be used .... Lev 10:1–2

B. God's use of fire
1. God is a consuming fire .... Dt 4:24
Heb 12:29
2. Positive uses of fire
a. To represent his presence
–To Moses in the burning bush ..... Ex 3:1–4
–To Israel in the pillar of fire ..... Ex 13:21–22
Ex 14:24
–To Israel on Mount Sinai ..... Ex 19:18
–To Elijah going into heaven 2Ki 2:11
–To the disciples on Pentecost ..... Ac 2:3
b. To burn sacrifices prepared for him .. Ge 15:17
1Ki 18:38–39
2Ch 7:1
c. To purify his people .... Isa 48:10
Mal 3:3
3. Negative uses of fire
–To express his wrath .... Dt 32:22
Ps 89:46
–To judge sinners on earth .... Ge 19:24–25
Lev 10:2
Nu 11:1–2
2Ki 1:10,12
–To punish eternally in hell .... Mt 5:22
2Th 1:7–8
Jas 3:6
Rev 18:17–18

FIRST FRUITS

A. First fruits in the Old Testament
1. First fruits to be dedicated to God
–Firstborn son .... Ex 13:1–2
–Firstborn of livestock .... Ex 13:1–2
–First fruits of the crops .... Ex 23:16
Lev 23:9
–First fruits of grain, wine, oil, wool ..... Dt 18:4
2Ch 31:5
–First fruits of fruit trees .... Lev 19:23–24
–First fruits of everything grown .... Dt 26:2
Pr 3:9
2. Rules and regulations
a. General
–In the laws of Moses .... Lev 2:11–16
Lev 23:9–14
Dt 26:1–15
–After the exile ... Ne 10:35
Ne 12:44
–In the new temple .... Eze 44:30
b. Must be brought to the Lord's house .. Ex 23:19
Ex 34:26
c. Must precede eating of harvested crops . Lev 23:14

B. First fruits as symbol in the New Testament
–Christ as the first fruits of those raised 1Co 15:20,23
–The Holy Spirit as our first blessing .... Ro 8:23
–The Holy Spirit as a guaranteed deposit 2Co 1:22
2Co 5:5
Eph 1:14
–Early Christians as first fruits of others .... Jas 1:18

FISH

A. Fish in the Old Testament
–A food for humans .... Nu 11:5
Ne 13:16
–Humans given dominion over fish .... Ge 1:26,28
Ps 8:6–8
–The great fish that swallowed Jonah .... Jnh 1:17
Mt 12:40

B. Fish in the New Testament
1. Several disciples were fishermen .... Mt 4:18–21
Jn 21:1–3
2. Miracles with fish
–Miraculous catch of fish .... Lk 5:4–7
Jn 21:4–11
–Feeding the multitude with two fish .... Mk 6:37–44
Jn 6:1–11
–Tax money in the mouth of a fish ..... Mt 17:24–27
3. Parable concerning fish and net .... Mt 13:47–48

FOLLY

A. Characteristics of the fool
–Begins with a denial of God .... Ps 14:1
–Does not trust in God .. 2Ch 16:7–9
–Trusts in self .... Pr 28:26
–Has no desire to get wisdom .... Pr 1:7,22
Pr 17:16
–Spurns discipline ...... Pr 15:5
–Finds pleasure in evil .. Pr 10:23
Tit 3:3
–Is rebellious .... Ps 107:17
–Engages in senseless merriment .... Ecc 7:4–6
–Loves to quarrel .... Pr 20:3
–Does not control anger . Pr 29:9,11
–Comes to ruin .... Pr 10:8,10,14

See also WISDOM

B. Special aspects of foolishness in the New Testament
–The foolishness of preaching 1Co 1:21–24
–The foolishness of God is wiser than human wisdom 1Co 1:25
–Being fools for Christ's sake 1Co 3:18
1Co 4:10
–Paul's speech of the fool 2Co 11:16–12:13

FOOL

See FOLLY

FOOT

A. The human foot
1. Symbolic uses of the human foot
–Washing feet in ceremonial cleansing .... Ex 30:17–21
–Washing feet as a sign of courtesy ..... Ge 18:4
–Washing feet as a sign of repentance .. Lk 7:37–48
–Washing feet as a sign of servanthood . Jn 13:3–15
–Cutting off feet as a punishment 2Sa 4:12
2. Metaphors concerning the foot
a. Dominion: everything under our feet .... Ps 8:6
b. Security: feet on solid rock .... Ps 40:2
c. Gratitude: falling down at one's feet . Lk 17:16
d. Victory
–Trampling underfoot .... Mic 7:10
–Placing feet on the neck .... Jos 10:24
–Enemies as one's footstool .... Ps 110:1
Ac 2:35
e. Submission: falling down at one's feet . 1Sa 25:24
2Sa 22:40
Rev 19:10
f. Rejection: shaking dust off one's feet . Mt 10:14
Ac 13:51
g. Sin
–Straying feet ..... Ps 44:18
–Stumbling feet ... Ps 116:8
h. Miscellaneous
–Beautiful feet of gospel preachers .. Isa 52:7
Ro 10:15
–God's word as a lamp to our feet .. Ps 119:105

B. The feet of God
–Bowing down at his feet in submission .... Dt 33:3
–The earth as God's footstool .... Isa 66:1
Mt 5:35
–The ark as God's footstool 1Ch 28:2

FORGET

A. Human forgetting
1. What we ought to forget
–Our troubles .... Ge 41:51
Isa 65:16
–The trials of the past .... Isa 43:18
Php 3:13
–Our sin and the shame it brings ..... Isa 54:4
Eze 39:26
2. What we ought not to forget
–The Lord .... Dt 6:12
Isa 17:10
Jer 2:32
–God's mighty acts .. Dt 4:9
Ps 78:7,11
–God's covenant with us .... Dt 4:23,31
2Ki 17:38
–God's law .... Ps 119:61,83,109
–God's patience with us 2Pe 3:9–10
–God's benefits to us . Ps 103:2
–The teachings of our parents .... Pr 3:6
Pr 4:5

B. Divine forgetting
1. What God forgets
–The sins of those who repent .... Isa 43:25
Jer 31:34
Heb 8:12
–Those who persistently refuse to believe .... Jer 23:39–40
2. What God does not forget
–His people .... Isa 44:21
Isa 49:21
–Our good deeds and love .... Heb 6:10
–Even the smallest of his creatures .... Lk 12:6
–The sins of those who refuse to repent .... Am 8:7
3. Praying that God will not forget
–Us .... Ps 13:1
–The helpless .... Ps 10:12
–Those who are afflicted .... Ps 74:19

See also REMEMBER

FORGIVENESS

–Pardon for human sins and shortcomings

A. Human forgiveness of others
1. Examples
–Esau of his brother Jacob .... Ge 33:4
–Joseph of his brothers .... Ge 50:15–21
–The father of his wayward son .... Lk 15:17–24
–Jesus of his enemies .... Lk 23:34
–Stephen of his enemies .... Ac 7:60

–Paul of those deserting him ... 2Ti 4:16
2. Required of Christians ... Mt 18:35; Lk 11:4; Eph 4:32; Col 3:13
B. God's forgiveness of us
1. Why does God forgive?
–Because of his compassion ... Ex 34:6–7; Mic 7:19
–Because of his love . Ps 51:1
–Because of his grace ... Ps 103:8
–Because of his mercy ... Isa 55:7
2. How does God forgive?
–Always by shedding of blood ... Heb 9:22
–Foreshadowed by Old Testament sacrifice .. Lev 4:1–5:13
–Fulfilled by the blood of Christ ... Col 1:14; Col 2:13–14; Heb 9:14,28
–Jesus can forgive sins ... Mk 2:1–11
3. What happens to our sins?
–They go out of sight ... Isa 38:17
–They go out of reach ... Ps 103:12; Mic 7:19
–They go out of mind ... Isa 43:25; Jer 31:34
–They go out of existence ... Ps 51:1–2, 7,9; Isa 44:22; Ac 3:19
4. How do we receive forgiveness?
–We must confess our sins ... Ps 32:5; 1Jn 1:9
–We must repent of our sins ... Ac 2:38; Ac 3:19
–We must believe in Christ ... Lk 24:47; Ac 10:43; Ac 13:38

FORNICATION
See SEXUAL STANDARDS

FREEDOM
–Being liberated from bondage
A. Freedom from human slavery
1. In the Old Testament
–God delivered his enslaved people ... Ex 1:11; Ex 6:6–7; Ex 20:2
–God forbade slavery among Hebrews ... Ex 21:2; Dt 15:12–15; Jer 34:8–17
–Prophets spoke against slavery ... 2Ki 4:1–7; Ne 5:4–8
2. In the New Testament
–Apostles accepted slavery ... Eph 6:5–8; Col 3:22–25; 1Pe 2:18–19
–Slaves were to be treated as brothers and sisters ... Phm 15–16
See also SLAVERY
B. Spiritual freedom
1. Who sets us free?
–God ... Ro 6:17–18
–Christ ... Jn 8:34–36; Gal 2:4; Gal 5:1
–The Holy Spirit ... Ro 8:15; 2Co 3:17
2. From what are we set free?
–From sin ... Jn 8:36; Ro 6:7
–From sin and death . Ro 8:2
–From fear of death .. Heb 2:15
–From fear ... Ro 8:15
–From the law ... Ro 7:6; Gal 3:23–25; Jas 1:25
–From the curse of the law ... Gal 3:13–14
–From bondage to decay ... Ro 8:21
–From the basic principles of the world .. Gal 4:3–4; Col 2:20–22
3. How are we set free?
–By hearing and believing the truth .. Jn 8:32
–By participating in Christ's death ... Ro 6:6–14; Ro 7:4
–By the power of the Holy Spirit ... Ro 7:6; Ro 8:15
4. Our response to being free
–We must thank God . Ps 116:16–17
–We must glorify God ... 1Co 10:31
–We must walk in freedom ... Ps 119:45
–We must serve others ... 1Co 9:19–23; 1Co 10:32–33
–We must not hurt other Christians ... Ro 14:13–21; 1Co 8:9–12
–We must not use freedom as excuse to sin ... Gal 5:1,13; 1Pe 2:16

FRIENDSHIP
A. Human friendship
1. Examples of human friendship
–Ruth and Naomi ... Ru 1:15–18
–David and Jonathan . 1Sa 18:1–4; 1Sa 20:41–42
–Job and three friends ... Job 2:11
2. Characteristics of true friendship
–Loyalty ... Ps 41:9; Pr 17:17; Pr 27:6
–Love and support ... Pr 17:17; Pr 18:24; Ecc 4:10; Ac 24:23
–Comfort in sorrow .. Job 2:11; Jn 11:33–36
–Encouragement ... 3Jn 5; Jude 17,20
3. Dangers of bad friendships
–Can give bad advice ... 1Ki 12:8–14
–Can double-cross us . Ps 41:9; Pr 16:28; Pr 17:9; Ps 109:4–5
–Can desert us ... Ps 38:11
–Can lead us away from the Lord ... Dt 13:6–9; Pr 22:24–25; Jas 4:4
B. Friendship with God
1. Examples of God's friends
–Moses ... Ex 33:11
–Abraham ... 2Ch 20:7; Jas 2:23
–Job ... Job 29:4
2. Friendship with Jesus
–Calls his disciples friends ... Jn 15:14–15
–Calls tax collectors and sinners friends .. Mt 11:19
–Emphasizes sacrificial love ... Jn 15:13
–Emphasizes obedience ... Jn 15:14

FRUIT OF THE SPIRIT
–Specific listing of aspects of the Spirit's fruit ... Gal 5:22–23
–Other listings of these aspects ... Ro 14:17; Eph 3:15–16; Eph 4:2–3; Col 3:12–15; 2Pe 1:5–7
See also entries for each aspect

GABRIEL
–An angel ... Lk 1:19
–Interpreted Daniel's visions . Da 8:16–26; Da 9:20–27
–Announced birth of John the Baptist ... Lk 1:11–20
–Announced birth of Jesus to Mary ... Lk 1:26–38

GAD
A. Son of Jacob by Zilpah . Ge 35:26
–Name means "good fortune" ... Ge 30:11
–Went to Egypt with family ... Ge 46:8,16
–Father of seven sons ... Ge 46:16
–Blessed by Jacob ... Ge 49:19
B. Tribe descended from Asher
–Blessed by Moses ... Dt 33:20–21
–Numbered ... Nu 1:25; Nu 26:18
–Asked to settle east of the Jordan ... Nu 32:1–27
–Allotted land on east side of the Jordan ... Nu 32:31–38; Jos 18:7
–Allotted land on west side of the Jordan ... Eze 48:27–28
–One of the tribes of the 144,000 ... Rev 7:5
C. A prophet ... 1Sa 22:5
–A seer of David ... 2Sa 24:11–19
–Recorded events of David's reign ... 1Ch 29:29

GALATIA
–Paul preached the gospel there ... Ac 16:6; Ac 18:23
–Paul collected money there . 1Co 16:1–2
–Paul wrote a letter to churches there ... Gal 1:2
–Peter wrote a letter to Christians there ... 1Pe 1:1

GALILEE
A. In the the Old Testament
–Land belonging to the tribe of Naphtali ... Jos 20:7
–Key city: Kadesh ... Jos 21:32
–Twenty towns given to Hiram of Tyre ... 1Ki 9:11
–Tiglath-pileser took that land ... 2Ki 15:29
–Future blessing for Galilee promised ... Isa 9:1–7
B. In the New Testament
1. A district governed by Herod ... Lk 3:1; Lk 23:5–7
2. Important towns in Galilee
–Nazareth ... Mt 2:22–23
–Capernaum ... Lk 4:31
–Cana ... Jn 2:1
–Bethsaida ... Jn 12:21
3. The Sea of Galilee
–Disciples used to fish there ... Mt 4:18–22; Mk 1:16–20
–Jesus taught from a boat ... Lk 5:3
–Jesus taught on its shore ... Jn 6:1–3
–Jesus stilled a storm on it ... Mt 8:23–27; Mk 4:36–41; Lk 8:22–26
–Jesus walked on it .. Mt 14:25–33; Jn 6:16–21
–Disciples met the risen Christ there ... Jn 21:1–14
4. Jesus and Galilee
–Joseph and Mary were from there ... Lk 1:26; Lk 2:4
–Jesus grew up in Nazareth ... Mt 2:22; Mk 1:9; Lk 2:39
–Jesus called "Jesus of Galilee" ... Mt 26:69
–Jesus fulfilled Isaiah's prophecy ... Mt 4:12–17
–Jesus had extensive ministry there ... Mt 4:23–25; Mt 11:1; Mk 1:14,39; Lk 4:14–15; Jn 7:1
–Great Commission given in Galilee ... Mt 28:16–20
–Church spread through Galilee ... Ac 9:31

GAMBLING
See STEALING; STEWARDSHIP

GATH
–One of the five great Philistine cities ... Jos 13:3
–Giants (including Goliath) came from there ... 1Sa 17:4; 2Sa 21:19–22
–David fled there from Saul . 1Sa 21:10–11; 1Sa 27:2–4
–David feigned insanity there ... 1Sa 21:12–15
–King David conquered it ... 1Ch 18:1
–Rehoboam fortified it ... 2Ch 11:5,8
–Hazael king of Aram took it from Joash ... 2Ki 12:17
–Uzziah captured it back ... 2Ch 26:6

GAZA
–Originally a Canaanite city . Ge 10:19
–One of the five great Philistine cities ... 1Sa 6:17–18
–Given to tribe of Judah ... Jos 15:47
–Taken by the men of Judah ... Jdg 1:18
–Samson carried away its gates ... Jdg 16:1–3
–Samson died there ... Jdg 16:21–30
–Solomon ruled over it ... 1Ki 4:24
–Hezekiah conquered it ... 2Ki 18:7–8
–Prophecies against it ... Am 1:6–7; Jer 47:1–7; Zep 2:4; Zec 9:5
–Gospel preached on the road to Gaza ... Ac 8:26–39

GEDALIAH
–Governor of Judah, appointed by Nebuchadnezzar ... 2Ki 25:22–23
–Encouraged settling down in Babylon ... 2Ki 25:24
–Became guardian of Jeremiah ... Jer 39:14
–Warned of an assassination plot ... Jer 40:13–16
–Assassinated by Ishmael ... 2Ki 25:25; Jer 41:1–3

GEHAZI
–Servant of Elisha ... 2Ki 4:12
–Unable to raise Shunammite's son from the dead ... 2Ki 4:29–31
–Sought reward from Naaman ... 2Ki 5:20–25
–Inflicted with leprosy ... 2Ki 5:26–27
–Told the king about the Shunammite ... 2Ki 8:4–6

GENEALOGY
See ANCESTRY

GENTILES
See NATIONS

GENTLENESS
See MEEKNESS

GIBEON
–A city of the Hivites ... Jos 11:19
–Tricked Joshua into making a treaty ... Jos 9:1–27
–Joshua protected it from five kings ... Jos 10:1–14
–Given to the tribe of Benjamin ... Jos 18:21,25; 1Ch 6:60
–Saul and David battled there ... 2Sa 2:12–28
–David defeated Philistines there ... 2Sa 5:25
–Tabernacle kept there for a while ... 1Ch 16:39–42
–Solomon offered sacrifices there ... 1Ki 3:4; 2Ch 1:3–6

–Solomon asked for wisdom there 1Ki 3:5–15; 2Ch 1:7–13
–Gedaliah's assassin fled there .... Jer 41:11–15
–City rebuilt after the exile .. Ne 3:7

GIDEON

A. His background and call as judge
- –Youngest son of Joash . Jdg 6:11,15
- –Also called Jerubbaal .. Jdg 7:1
- –Angel called him ..... Jdg 6:11–24
- –Prepared sacrifice ...... Jdg 6:19–22
- –Supported by his father .... Jdg 6:25–32
- –Needed assurance through throwing out a fleece .... Jdg 6:36–40
- –Had many wives ...... Jdg 8:30–31

B. His war against Midianites
- –Gathered an army ...... Jdg 6:34–35
- –Reduced size of army to three hundred .... Jdg 7:2–8
- –Developed battle plan .. Jdg 7:15–21
- –Achieved victory ...... Jdg 7:22–25

C. Subsequent events
- –Took revenge on men of Succoth .... Jdg 8:4–21
- –Refused to be king .... Jdg 8:22–23
- –Made an idol for worship .... Jdg 8:24–27
- –Served as judge for forty years .... Jdg 8:28
- –His death .... Jdg 8:32
- –Called a hero of faith .. Heb 11:32

GIFTS OF THE SPIRIT

A. Types of gifts
- –Speaking in tongues ... Ac 10:46; Ac 19:6; 1Co 12:10, 28,30; 1Co 14:2,6–11
- –Interpreting tongues 1Co 12:10, 30; 1Co 14:13, 27–28
- –Prophecy .... Ro 12:6; 1Co 12:10, 28–29; 1Co 14:3–5, 22–25
- –Serving .... Ro 12:7; 1Pe 4:11
- –Teaching .... Ro 12:7; 1Co 12:28–29
- –Being an apostle .... 1Co 12:28–29; Eph 4:11
- –Contributing to others .. Ro 12:8
- –Exercising leadership ... Ro 12:8
- –Showing mercy .... Ro 12:8
- –Encouraging others .... Ro 12:8
- –Being single 1Co 7:7–8
- –Wisdom 1Co 12:8
- –Knowledge 1Co 12:8
- –Faith 1Co 12:9
- –Healing 1Co 12:9,28, 30
- –Miraculous powers 1Co 12:10, 28–29
- –Distinguishing between spirits 1Co 12:10
- –Helping others 1Co 12:28
- –Administration 1Co 12:28
- –Doing evangelism ...... Eph 4:11
- –Being a pastor .... Eph 4:11
- –Speaking in public 1Pe 4:11
- –Skill and knowledge in crafts .... Ex 31:1–5

B. The purposes of gifts
- –To be enjoyed privately 1Co 14:4
- –To witness to Christ ... 1Co 12:1–3
- –To build up the church . 1Co 12:7; 1Co 14:3,5, 12,26; 1Pe 4:10
- –To demonstrate God's grace in us .... Ro 12:6
- –To praise God 1Co 14:24–25; 1Pe 4:11

C. Gifts are subordinate to love
- –The greatest way is the way of love 1Co 12:31–13:3
- –Gifts will disappear 1Co 13:8–10
- –Love will always remain 1Co 13:13

D. Warning against gifts that deceive
- –False prophets can do wonders and signs ..... Mt 24:24
- –The antichrist will do counterfeit signs .... 2Th 2:9; Rev 13:13–14
- –We must test the spirits 1Jn 4:1

GLORY

–The grandeur and majesty of God

A. God and his glory
1. Glory belongs to God .... 1Ch 29:11; Ps 29:1,3; Ps 96:7; Ro 11:36
2. God dwells in awesome majesty .... Job 37:22; Ps 93:1; Ps 145:5
3. God's name is glorious .... Dt 28:58; 1Ch 29:13; Ps 8:1; Ps 79:9
4. God reveals his glory
   - –In Jesus Christ ...... Isa 40:5; Jn 1:14
   - –In the Tent of Meeting .... Ex 40:34–35
   - –In the temple .... 2Ch 5:14; Eze 10:4; Eze 43:5
   - –In his works .... Ps 19:1; Ps 111:3
   - –Through Moses ..... Ex 34:29–35
   - –On Mount Sinai .... Ex 24:15–17
   - –To Isaiah .... Isa 6:3
   - –To his people through his redemption .... Isa 44:23; Isa 46:13
   - –To Ezekiel .... Eze 1:28
   - –To the shepherds of Bethlehem .... Lk 2:9
   - –To Stephen .... Ac 7:55
   - –To the whole world . Ps 97:6; Isa 66:18; Hab 2:14

B. Jesus and his glory
1. He is the Lord of glory .... 1Co 2:8; Jas 2:1
2. He has God's glory
   - –Had it from the beginning .... Jn 17:5
   - –Surpassed glory of the Old Testament .. 2Co 3:7–11
   - –Now exalted in glory .... 1Ti 3:16; Rev 5:12–13
   - –Will return in glory . Mt 24:30; Mt 25:31
3. He revealed God's glory
   - –In human flesh ...... Jn 1:14; Heb 1:3
   - –In his actions .... Jn 2:11; Jn 11:40–44
   - –In his transfiguration ...... Lk 9:29–30; 2Pe 1:16–19
   - –In his death .... Jn 12:23–24
   - –In the resurrection .. Lk 24:26; Php 3:21

C. The Spirit and his glory
- –Called the Spirit of glory 1Pe 4:14
- –His ministry is glorious 2Co 3:8

D. Believers and the glory of God
1. The present
   - –We fall short of his glory .... Ro 3:23
   - –Christ came to bring us to glory .... Lk 2:29–32; Col 1:27
   - –We receive God's glory through Christ . Jn 17:22; 2Co 4:6
   - –We receive the Spirit of glory 1Pe 4:14
   - –We must reflect his glory 1Co 10:31; 2Co 3:18
   - –We must pray that his glory will endure .... Ps 104:31
2. The future
   - –We will be brought into his glory .... Heb 2:10; Jude 24
   - –We will share in Christ's glory .... Ro 8:17–18; 1Pe 5:10
   - –Our new bodies will bear his glory ...... 1Co 15:42–43; Php 3:21
   - –We will receive a crown of glory 1Pe 5:4

GOD

A. The being of God
   See HOLY SPIRIT; JESUS CHRIST; TRINITY

B. Names of God
- –God .... Ge 1:1
- –LORD .... Ge 4:1,4
- –LORD God .... Ge 2:4
- –God Most High .... Ge 14:18–20
- –The Lord GOD .... Ge 15:2
- –God Almighty .... Ge 17:1
- –The Everlasting God .... Ge 21:33
- –The God of Bethel ..... Ge 31:13
- –God of Abraham, Isaac, Jacob .... Ex 3:6
- –I AM WHO I AM .... Ex 3:14
- –The God of the Hebrews .... Ex 3:18
- –Jealous .... Ex 34:14
- –The God of Israel 1Sa 1:17
- –God, the Rock 2Sa 22:47
- –The LORD, the God of heaven .... Ezr 1:2
- –The mighty one, God, the LORD .... Ps 50:1
- –God the King .... Ps 145:1
- –The Holy One of Israel .... Isa 1:4
- –The Mighty One of Israel .... Isa 1:24

C. Characteristics of God
1. Divine characteristics
   - –Holy .... Lev 11:44
   - –Eternal .... Ps 90:2
   - –Infinite 1Ki 8:27
   - –Immortal 1Ti 1:17
   - –Invisible .... Jn 1:18
   - –All-knowing .... Ps 147:5
   - –Everywhere present . Ps 139:7–21
   - –All-powerful .... Isa 40:6–7
   - –Unchanging .... Mal 3:6
   - –Incomparable .... Isa 40:18,25
   - –Righteous .... Ps 145:17
   - –Perfect .... Mt 5:48
   - –Awesome and majestic .... Ex 15:11
   - –Gracious .... Ex 34:6
   - –Spirit .... Jn 4:24
2. Human characteristics ascribed to him
   - a. Physical characteristics
     - –Face of God ..... Nu 6:25–26 (*See* FACE)
     - –Ears of God ..... Ne 1:6 (*See* EAR)
     - –Eyes of God ..... 2Ch 16:9 (*See* EYE)
     - –Nostrils of God .. Ex 15:8
     - –Mouth of God ... Dt 8:3 (*See* MOUTH)
     - –Voice of God .... Ex 15:26 (*See* VOICE)
     - –Hands of God .... Ezr 7:9 (*See* HAND)
     - –Fingers of God ... Ps 8:3
     - –Arms of God .... Dt 33:27
     - –Shoulders of God .... Dt 33:12
     - –Back of God ..... Ex 33:21–22
     - –Feet of God ..... Ps 18:9 (*See* FOOT)
   - b. Physical actions
     - –God sits .... Ps 102:12
     - –God stands ...... Ge 28:13
     - –God walks .... Ge 3:8
     - –God comes down . Ge 11:5
     - –God goes up ..... Ge 17:22
     - –God marches ..... Zec 9:14
     - –God rides .... Ps 68:33
     - –God soars 2Sa 22:11
     - –God shoots arrows 2Sa 22:15
     - –God reaches down 2Sa 22:17
     - –God rests .... Ge 2:2
     - –God sleeps ...... Ps 44:23
   - c. Emotional characteristics
     - –God loves .... Ex 34:6; 1Jn 4:8–10
     - –God is compassionate .... Ex 3:7
     - –God is patient 2Pe 3:9
     - –God laughs ...... Ps 2:4
     - –God becomes angry .... Dt 9:7
     - –God grieves ..... Ge 6:6
     - –God is jealous ... Ex 34:14
     - –God fears .... Dt 32:26–27
     - –God hates .... Ps 5:5

D. Our response to God
- –We should trust in him . Jn 14:1 (*See* TRUST)
- –We should hope in him .... Ps 131:3 (*See* HOPE)
- –We should believe him . Ge 15:6 (*See* FAITH)
- –We should fear him .... Dt 6:13 (*See* FEAR)
- –We should praise him .. Ps 150:1–6 (*See* PRAISE)
- –We should worship him .... Ps 96:9 (*See* WORSHIP)
- –We should stand in awe of him .... Hab 3:2
- –We should honor him .. Pr 3:9
- –We should glorify him . Ps 34:3
- –We should thirst for him .... Ps 42:2

GOLD

A. Uses for gold
1. In Israelite worship
   - –The tabernacle structure .... Ex 26:29,32
   - –The tabernacle furniture .... Ex 25:10–40; Ex 30:3–5
   - –Priestly garments .... Ex 28:11–36
   - –The temple structure 2Ch 3:4–6
   - –The temple furniture 2Ch 4:7–8, 20–22
2. In pagan worship
   - –The golden calf in the desert .... Ex 32:1–4
   - –The golden calves of Jeroboam 1Ki 12:26–30
   - –Other idols .... Isa 2:20; Hos 8:4
3. For personal wealth .. 2Ch 9:13; Ecc 2:8; Mt 10:9
4. For gifts .... 2Ch 9:9; Ezr 2:69; Mt 2:11
5. For jewelry .... Ge 24:22; Ex 32:2; Jdg 8:24,26
6. For royal display ..... 2Ch 9:15–16; Est 1:6–7

B. Value of gold for God's people
1. Positive: a blessing from God .... Ge 13:2; Isa 60:6,17
2. Negative
   - –Spiritual values worth more than gold ..... Ps 19:10; Pr 3:13–14; 1Pe 1:7
   - –Gold valueless in redemption 1Pe 1:18

C. Gold as a symbol
- –For saints surviving God's testing .... Job 23:10
- –For trustworthy spiritual values .... 1Co 3:12–13; Rev 3:18
- –For the new heaven .... Rev 21:18, 21

GOLIATH

- –A Philistine giant 1Sa 17:4–7
- –Taunted the Israelite army .. 1Sa 17:8–11
- –David offered to fight him . 1Sa 17:32–37
- –David killed him 1Sa 17:48–51

–David obtained his sword .. 1Sa 21:9

GOMORRAH

See SODOM AND GOMORRAH

GOSPEL

–The good news of salvation for humanity

A. Terms used to describe the gospel
- –The gospel of God ..... Ro 1:1
- –The glorious gospel of God 1Ti 1:11
- –The gospel of God's grace ..... Ac 20:24
- –The gospel of God's Son ..... Ro 1:9
- –The gospel of our Lord Jesus 2Th 1:8
- –The gospel of Christ ... Ro 15:19
- –The gospel of the glory of Christ 2Co 4:4
- –The good news about Jesus Christ ..... Mk 1:1
- –The good news of the kingdom ..... Mt 24:14
- –The gospel of salvation ..... Eph 1:13
- –The gospel of peace ... Eph 6:15
- –The eternal gospel ..... Rev 14:6

B. The gospel in the Old Testament
- –First revealed to Adam and Eve ..... Ge 3:15
- –Revealed to Abraham .. Ge 12:2–3; Ge 18:18; Ge 22:18; Gal 3:8
- –Revealed to Israel through prophets ..... Isa 40:9; Isa 52:7–10; Isa 61:6; Ro 1:1–2

C. The gospel in the New Testament
1. The proclaimers of the gospel
   - –The angel at Christ's birth ..... Lk 2:10
   - –John the Baptist .... Lk 3:18
   - –Jesus Christ ..... Mk 1:14–15; Lk 4:43
   - –The twelve disciples . Lk 9:6
   - –The twelve apostles . Ac 5:42
   - –Peter and John ..... Ac 8:25; Ac 15:7
   - –Philip ..... Ac 8:12,40
   - –Paul ..... Ac 14:7; Ro 15:19
   - –Unnamed missionaries 1Pe 1:12
   - –Our responsibility ... Mt 24:14; Mt 28:19
2. The content of the gospel (good news)
   - –The basic story about Jesus ..... Mk 1:1; 1Co 15:1–8, 11
   - –Jesus is the Christ .. Ac 5:42
   - –Humans should repent ..... Mk 1:15
   - –Salvation is by faith in Jesus ..... Ro 1:16–17
   - –God gives us his grace ..... Ac 20:24
   - –Both Jew and Gentile can be saved ..... Eph 3:6–7
   - –Jesus will return as judge ..... Ro 2:16
   - –How believers should live ..... Php 1:27
3. The characteristics of the gospel
   - –It reveals the glory of Christ 2Co 4:4
   - –It is eternal ..... 1Pe 1:25; Rev 14:6
   - –It demonstrates God's power ..... Ro 1:16
   - –It calls us 2Th 2:14
   - –It saves us 1Co 15:2
   - –It gives us peace ..... Eph 6:15
   - –It gives us hope .... Col 1:23
   - –It gives us life 2Ti 1:10
   - –It grows and bears fruit ..... Col 1:6
   - –It tolerates no rival .. Gal 1:6–9
4. The response to the gospel
   - –We should believe it ..... Heb 4:2
   - –We should obey it .. 2Co 9:13; 2Th 1:8; Heb 4:6
   - –We should not be ashamed of it ..... Ro 1:16
   - –We should live in line with its truth ... Gal 2:14; Php 1:27
   - –We should serve it .. 2Co 8:18
   - –We should continue in it ..... Col 1:23
   - –We should promote it 1Co 9:16
   - –We should defend it . Php 1:7,16; Jude 3
   - –We should preach it . Mk 16:15; Ac 8:4; Ro 15:19–20; 1Co 9:16
   - –We may have to suffer for it 2Ti 1:8; 2Ti 2:8–9

GOVERNMENT

–The rule of humans by other humans

A. Phases of civil government among the Israelites/Jews
1. Rule by the fathers (patriarchs)
   - –Abram ..... Ge 14:13–16
   - –Isaac ..... Ge 26:26–32
   - –Jacob ..... Ge 34:5,30–31; Ge 46:5–27
2. Rule by God's chosen leader
   - –Moses ..... Ex 3:7–12; Ex 18:13–26
   - –Moses and Aaron ... Nu 17:1–13
   - –Joshua ..... Dt 31:1–8; Jos 1:1–11
3. Rule by God's chosen judges
   See JUDGE, JUDGMENT
4. Rule through God's chosen kings
   - –Israel asked for a king 1Sa 8:4–22
   - –Israel's first king, Saul 1Sa 10:20–26
   - –David anointed as king 1Sa 16:1–13
   - –David's line to be the royal line 2Sa 7:8–16
   See KING
5. Rule by foreign kings
   - –The Babylonians .... 2Ch 36:15–21; Da 1:1–6
   - –The Persians ..... Ezr 1:1–4; Isa 44:28–45:6
   - –The Herods of Idumea ..... Mt 2:1–8, 16–22
   - –The Romans ..... Mt 27:11–14; Jn 18:28–40

B. Principles of government
1. God and human government
   - –God is the real ruler ..... Dt 33:5; Jdg 8:23; 1Ch 29:23; Ps 29:10–11; Isa 33:22
   - –God rules through anointed servants .... Ps 45:6–7; Isa 45:1
2. Humans in the government
   - –They derive authority from God ..... Da 4:17; Jn 19:11; Ro 13:1,4
   - –God's people may serve pagan governments ..... Ne 2:1–9; Ne 5:14–18; Est 8:1–2; Da 1:17–21

C. Our responsibility to government
- –We must respect it 1Sa 14:6–7; 1Sa 26:7–11; 1Pe 2:17
- –We must submit to it .. Ro 13:1,5; Tit 3:1; 1Pe 2:13–14
- –We must support it with taxes ..... Mt 22:15–21; Ro 13:6–7
- –We must pray for it ... 1Ti 2:1–2
- –Occasionally we may have to disobey it ..... Ac 5:29

GRACE

–God's free and undeserved favor

A. Grace comes as a gift
- –From God ..... Eph 2:8; 1Pe 5:10
- –From the Father ..... Ps 84:11; Jas 1:17
- –From Christ, the Son .. Jn 1:17; 1Co 1:4
- –From the Holy Spirit ... Zec 12:10; Heb 10:29

B. How can we receive grace?
- –We must accept Christ . Jn 1:14,16; 2Co 8:9; Eph 1:6–7
- –We must be humble ... Pr 3:34; Jas 4:6
- –We cannot earn it by good works ..... Ro 11:6; 2Ti 1:9
- –We cannot earn it by keeping the law ..... Ro 6:14; Gal 2:16

C. Examples of those who received grace
- –Abraham ..... Gal 3:18
- –Paul ..... Eph 3:2; 1Ti 1:12–16
- –All believers ..... Eph 1:7–8

D. What happens to believers through grace?
- –They are chosen ..... Ro 11:5
- –They are called ..... Gal 1:15
- –They believe ..... Ac 18:27
- –They are justified ..... Ro 3:24; Tit 3:7
- –They receive righteousness ..... Ro 5:17
- –They are saved ..... Ac 15:11; Tit 2:11
- –They are redeemed .... Ro 3:24
- –They are forgiven ..... Eph 1:7
- –They receive many good things ..... Ro 8:32; Jas 1:17
- –They receive spiritual gifts ..... Ro 12:6; Eph 4:7–12
- –They receive encouragement 2Th 2:16
- –They receive help in time of need ..... Heb 4:16
- –They are able to bear up under suffering 2Co 12:9
- –They have hope 2Th 2:16
- –They are glorified in Christ 2Th 1:12

E. Relationship of believers to grace
- –They are under grace .. Ro 6:14
- –They stand in grace .... Ro 5:2
- –They are what they are by grace 1Co 15:10
- –They abound in grace .. 2Co 9:8; 1Ti 1:14
- –They share in God's grace ..... Php 1:7
- –They may approach God's throne of grace .. Heb 4:16
- –They are strengthened by grace ..... Heb 13:9
- –They must grow in grace 2Pe 3:18
- –They must not receive grace in vain 2Co 6:1
- –They can fall away from grace ..... Gal 5:4; Heb 6:4–6

F. The wicked experience grace ..... Isa 26:10; Mt 5:45; Ac 14:17

GRAVE (SHEOL)

*–***Sheol** *is a Hebrew word of uncertain meaning*

A. Where everyone goes at death ..... Isa 14:9–11
- –The righteous ..... Ge 37:35; Ps 88:3–5
- –The wicked ..... Nu 16:30; Eze 32:21,27

B. Characteristics
- –A place of darkness and corruption ..... Job 17:13–16
- –A place of inactivity ... Ps 6:5; Ps 31:17; Ecc 9:10; Isa 38:18
- –The opposite of the heavens ..... Ps 139:8; Am 9:2
- –The opposite of life .... Pr 15:24
- –It is never satisfied .... Pr 27:20; Isa 5:14; Hab 2:5

C. Resurrection takes place from there ..... Ps 16:10–11; Ps 49:14–15

GREAT TRIBULATION

–A time of intense distress at the end of the world

A. General tribulation
   See PAIN

B. The Great Tribulation
- –Great ordeal ..... Rev 7:14
- –A time of great distress ..... Isa 24:1–20; Da 12:1; Mt 24:15–28
- –The time is limited .... Da 9:24–27
- –Dominated by the antichrist ..... Rev 13:11–17
- –Ends with the destruction of Babylon ..... Rev 14:8; Rev 18:1–24
- –Shortened for the sake of the elect ..... Mt 24:22

GREECE, GREEK

–A Roman province, south of Macedonia

A. Paul's ministry in Greece
1. Greece is also called Achaia ..... Ac 18:12,27; Ro 15:26; 1Co 16:15
2. Ministry in Athens
   - –Paul preached to Jews and Greeks there ..... Ac 17:16–17
   - –Altar to unknown god located there ... Ac 17:22–23
   - –Paul's sermon to the Areopagus ..... Ac 17:22–31
3. Ministry in Corinth
   See CORINTH

B. The Greeks
- –Greeks wanted to speak with Jesus ..... Jn 12:20–21
- –God-fearing Greeks joined with Jews ..... Ac 17:4,17
- –Grecian Jews in the early church ..... Ac 6:1; Ac 9:29
- –Paul preached to Jews and Greeks ..... Ac 18:4; Ac 20:21
- –"Greek" sometimes meant any non-Jew .... 1Co 1:22–24; Gal 2:3; Col 3:11
- –In the church, neither Jew nor Greek ..... Gal 3:28; Col 3:11

GREED

See THE RICH AND THE POOR

GRIEF

A. Human grief
1. Occasions for human grief
   - –Death of a loved one ..... Ge 37:34–35; 2Sa 18:33
   - –A loved one likely to die soon ..... 2Sa 12:15–17; Mt 17:23
   - –A loved one departing ..... Jn 16:19–20
   - –Experiencing pain and suffering ..... Ps 10:12–13; Ps 31:9–13; 1Pe 1:6
   - –Seeing the pain of others ..... Job 30:25; Jer 48:36
   - –Feeling sorrow for sin ..... Ne 8:8–11; Jas 4:8–9
   - –Being punished for sin ..... La 1:4–5; 2Co 2:5–7
   - –Seeing the sin of others 1Sa 16:1
   - –Not being able to bear children 1Sa 1:10–11, 15–16
   - –Children marrying outside the faith .... Ge 26:34–35
   - –Children choosing the way of folly ..... Pr 10:1; Pr 17:21

–One's relatives not receiving Christ ..... Ro 9:2–3, 2Co 12:21
2. The answer to human grief
–Receiving comfort from friends .... Job 2:11–13, Jn 11:19, Ro 12:15
–Receiving comfort from the Lord ...... Ps 23:4, Isa 61:2, Mt 5:4
–Seeing the risen Christ .... Jn 20:20, 1Th 4:13–14
–Experiencing salvation 2Co 7:9–10, 1Pe 1:5–6
–Knowing that God does not reject us ... La 3:31–33
–Knowing that God turns grief into joy .. Isa 61:3, Jer 31:13, Jn 16:20
–Knowing that God will wipe away all tears .... Isa 25:8, Rev 21:4

B. Divine grief
1. The grief of the Triune God
–Grief of the Father .. Ge 6:6–7, 1Sa 15:10–11
–Grief of the Son .... Lk 19:41–44, Jn 11:33–35
–Grief of the Holy Spirit .... Isa 63:10, Eph 4:30
2. Occasions for divine grief
–Grief because of human sin .... Ge 3:6–7, 1Sa 15:10–11, Eze 6:9–10
–Grief because of punishment for sin ..... 2Sa 24:16, Jer 42:10, Lk 19:41–44

GROWTH

A. Natural growth
–Of plants .... Ps 90:5–6
–Of human beings ...... Lk 1:80, Lk 2:40
–Of political power 2Sa 3:1

B. Numerical growth of the church
1. Parables of growth
–Parable of the sower .... Mt 13:3–9, 18–23
–Parable of the weeds .... Mt 13:24–30,36–43
–Parable of the mustard seed .... Mt 13:31–32
–Parable of the yeast . Mt 13:33
2. Growth of the New Testament church .... Ac 4:4, Ac 5:14, Ac 6:7, Ac 9:31, Ac 16:5

C. Spiritual growth of Christians
1. What shows lack of growth?
–Inadequate knowledge of God's truth ...... Ac 18:24–28, Ac 19:1–6
–Lack of doctrinal soundness .... Eph 4:14
–Jealousy and quarreling 1Co 3:1–3
–Living a life of evil . 1Co 14:20
–Inability to understand deeper truths .. Heb 5:12–14
2. How does growth takes place?
–By study of God's word 1Pe 2:1–3
–By increasing our knowledge of God .. Col 1:10
–By deepening our faith .... Eph 4:13
–By showing love .... Eph 4:15–16
–By developing Christian character 2Pe 1:5–8
3. God wants us to grow and bear fruit .... Ps 1:1–3, Ps 92:12–15, Jn 15:2,4–5, 16

GUILT

–The condition of one who breaks the law

A. Guilt in the Old Testament
1. Standing guilty before God
–Because of deliberate sin .... Lev 6:1–4
–Because of unintentional sin .... Lev 5:2–4, 14–17
–Guilty even before birth .... Ps 51:5
–Dressed in dirty clothes .... Isa 64:6, Zec 3:3–4
–God knows our guilt .... Ps 69:5
–God does not leave guilt unpunished .... Ex 34:7, Na 1:3
2. Feeling guilty because of sin .... 2Sa 24:10, Ezr 9:5–7,15, Ps 38:4
3. Resolving guilt before God
–The call to acknowledge guilt .... Jer 3:13, Hos 5:15
–The guilt offering ... Lev 5:14–6:7, Lev 7:1–6
–Confession and forgiveness .... Ps 32:5, Isa 6:5–7

B. Guilt in the New Testament
1. The reality of guilt
–Christ's coming convicts us of guilt ..... Jn 15:22,24
–The Spirit convicts us of guilt .... Jn 16:7–8
–One sin makes us guilty of breaking the whole law .... Jas 2:10
–All stand guilty before God .... Ro 3:19,23
–All are guilty because of Adam's sin ...... Ro 5:12–14
2. The resolution of guilt
–We must confess our sins 1Jn 1:9
–We must draw near to God in faith ..... Heb 10:22
–We become free of guilt through Christ . Ro 5:15–18

See also CONFESSION, FORGIVENESS, SIN

HAGAR

–Egyptian servant of Sarai .. Ge 16:1
–Given to Abram to conceive a child .... Ge 16:3
–Driven away by Sarai while pregnant .... Ge 16:5–16
–Gave birth to Ishmael ...... Ge 25:12
–Driven away after birth of Isaac .... Ge 21:9–21
–Story interpreted by Paul ... Gal 4:21–31

HAGGAI

–A post-exilic prophet ...... Ezr 5:1
–Encouraged rebuilding of temple .... Ezr 6:14, Hag 1:12–13
–Warned God's people of dangers of selfishness ...... Hag 1:3–11

HAM

–Son of Noah .... Ge 5:32, 1Ch 1:4
–Laughed at Noah's nakedness .... Ge 9:20–27
–Father of Canaan .... Ge 9:18, 1Ch 1:8–16

HAMAN

–Agagite noble honored by Xerxes .... Est 3:1–2
–Angry when Mordecai would not bow down ...... Est 3:2–5
–Plotted to execute Jews .... Est 3:6–15
–Built gallows to hang Mordecai .... Est 5:9–14
–Forced to honor Mordecai .. Est 6:1–13
–Plot exposed by Esther .... Est 7:1–8
–Hanged on his own gallows .... Est 7:9–10

HAND

A. The human hand
1. What the human hand does
–Works .... Ps 90:17
–Holds .... Rev 7:9
–Writes .... Gal 6:11
–Touches 1Jn 1:1
–Claps .... Ps 47:1
–Fights .... Ps 18:34
–Blesses .... Lev 9:22
–Lifts up in prayer ... 1Ti 2:8
–Lifts up in praise ... Ps 134:2
–Takes oath before God .... Ge 14:22
2. Significance of the right hand
–Place of honor ...... Ps 45:9
–Position of power ... 1Ki 2:19
–Used to confirm an agreement .... Gal 2:9
3. Laying on of hands
a. In the Old Testament
–Ordained Levites . Nu 8:10
–Ordained leaders . Nu 27:18, 22–23
–Transferred guilt . Lev 16:20–21
b. In the New Testament
–Conferred healing .... Mk 6:5, Lk 4:40, Ac 28:8
–Transferred the Holy Spirit ...... Ac 8:17, Ac 9:17, Ac 19:6
–Ordained missionaries ..... Ac 13:3
–Ordained church officers .... Ac 6:6, 1Ti 4:14, 2Ti 1:6

B. The hand of God
1. What it does
–It saves us .... Ex 6:1, Dt 5:15
–It guides us .... Ezr 7:9
–It provides for us .... Ps 104:28
–It protects us .... Ps 139:10
–It receives our spirits .... Ps 31:5
–It pleads with us .... Isa 65:2
–It chastises us ...... Ps 32:4
–It punishes unbelievers .... Ex 7:5
2. Significance of the right hand of God
–His hand of power .. Ps 17:7, Ps 73:23, Ps 118:15–16
–Sitting at his right hand as ruler .... Ps 110:1, Ac 2:33, Eph 1:20, Heb 1:3

HANNAH

–Wife of Elkanah 1Sa 1:1–2
–Prayed to have a child 1Sa 1:9–18
–Gave birth to Samuel 1Sa 1:19–20
–Dedicated Samuel to the Lord's work 1Sa 1:24–28
–Prayed at Samuel's dedication 1Sa 2:1–10
–Blessed by Eli 1Sa 2:18–20
–Gave birth to other children 1Sa 2:21

HARAN

A. The father of Lot .... Ge 11:27
–Died in Ur .... Ge 11:28

B. A city in Mesopotamia
–Terah, Abram and Lot emigrated there .... Ge 11:31, Ac 7:4
–Abram set out from there for Canaan .... Ge 12:4
–Abraham sent there to find a wife for Isaac ... Ge 24:1–4
–Jacob fled there .... Ge 28:10
–Home of Laban, Leah and Rachel .... Ge 29:4–6
–Jacob lived there twenty years .... Ge 31:41
–Belonged to Assyrian empire 2Ki 19:12

HARVEST

A. The importance of harvests
1. Events were calculated by harvest times ..... Ge 30:14, Jdg 15:1, Ru 1:22
2. Israelite festivals centered around harvest
–Festival of the first fruits .... Lev 23:9–14
–Festival of weeks ... Lev 23:15–21
–Festival of tabernacles .... Lev 23:33–43
3. Provision made for the poor at harvesttime .... Lev 19:9–10, Dt 24:19–22, Ru 2:1–9

B. God's use of harvests
–Abundant harvest demonstrated his love ...... Dt 8:7–9, Ps 23:1, Ps 144:12–15
–God chastised by means of crop failure and famine .... Isa 17:10–11, Joel 1:8–12, Hag 1:5–6

C. Harvesting used as a metaphor
1. To picture mission work
–Pray for workers in God's harvest .... Mt 9:37–38
–The fields ripe for harvest .... Jn 4:35–36
2. To picture God's judgment .... Isa 17:1–5, Jer 51:33
3. To picture the end of the world
–Gathering the saints . Mt 13:24–30,36–43
–Judging God's enemies .... Rev 14:14–19, Joel 3:12–13
4. The law of the harvest
–Reaping what we sow .... 2Co 9:6, Gal 6:7
–Sowing evil and reaping trouble ..... Job 4:8, Pr 22:8, Hos 10:13
–Sowing good and reaping blessing ..... Hos 10:12, Gal 6:8–9

HAZAEL

–A servant of King Ben-hadad of Aram 2Ki 8:7–8
–Anointed by Elijah as king over Aram 1Ki 19:15
–Asked Elisha about Ben-hadad 2Ki 8:8–9
–Murdered Ben-hadad 2Ki 8:14–15
–Became king of Aram 2Ki 8:15
–Fought against Israel and Judah 2Ki 8:28, 2Ch 22:5–6
–Conquered part of Israel ... 2Ki 10:32–33, 2Ki 13:22
–Gained power over Joash .. 2Ki 12:17–18
–Succeeded by son Ben-hadad 2Ki 13:24
–Judgment prophesied against him .... Am 1:3–5

HEAD

A. The human head
1. Literal use
–Hand put on the head in blessing .... Ge 48:14–18
–People were anointed on the head .... Ex 29:7, 1Sa 10:1
–Anointing head with oil meant blessings .. Ps 23:5
–Crowns were put on the head .... 1Ch 20:2, Est 2:17
–No razor on the head of a Nazirite .... Nu 6:5–6, Jdg 13:5
–Cutting off the head, a sign of victory 1Sa 17:51, 1Sa 31:9
–Woman's covered head showed submission 1Co 11:5,10

–A bowed head showed reverence ... Ge 24:26 Ge 43:28 Ex 4:31
–A bowed head showed grief ... Ps 35:14
–Dust on one's head showed sorrow ... 1Sa 4:12
–Pulling hair from the head showed sorrow . Ezr 9:3
–Shaving hair from the head showed grief .. Job 1:20 Isa 15:2
–Ashes on one's head showed shame ... 2Sa 13:19
–Shaking the head showed disdain ... Job 16:4 Ps 22:7 Mt 27:39
2. Figurative use
–Blessings crown the head ... Pr 10:6
–Joy crowns the head ... Isa 35:10 Isa 51:11
–Blood on one's head meant guilt ... 2Sa 1:15–16 Eze 33:4
–Lifting up one's head meant pride ... Ps 83:2
–From head to foot meant the whole body ... Dt 28:35 Isa 1:6
–The Lord gives grace by lifting a head ... Ps 3:3 Ps 27:5–6
–Heaping coals of fire on the head ... Pr 25:22 Ro 12:20
–Jesus had nowhere to lay his head ... Mt 8:20
B. Head as a symbolic word
1. Political leadership
–Heads as leaders of the clans of Israel ... Nu 1:16 Jos 14:1
–Heads as leaders of the tribes ... Nu 30:1
–Heads as leaders of families ... 2Ch 1:2 Ezr 2:68
–A head as the king of a country ... Isa 7:8–9
2. Husband as the head of his wife ... 1Co 11:3,8–10 Eph 5:23
3. Christ as the head
–Head of all creation . Eph 1:10
–Head of every man .. 1Co 11:3
–Head of the church .. Eph 5:23 Col 1:18 Col 2:19

HEALING

A. Roles in healing
1. God is the ultimate healer ... Dt 32:39 Ps 103:3 Jer 30:17
2. Human elements that play a role
–Faith ... Mt 13:58 Mk 5:34 Lk 18:42
–Prayer ... Jas 5:14–16
–Intercession ... Nu 12:10–15 1Ki 13:6
–A cheerful heart ... Pr 17:22
–Positive words ... Pr 16:24
B. Physical healing of the body
1. Medical care used ... 2Ki 20:7 Lk 10:34–35 1Ti 5:23
2. Miracles performed
–Directly by God ... Ge 20:17
–By prophets ... 1Ki 17:17–24 2Ki 5:1–14
–By Jesus ... Mt 4:24
–By followers of Jesus ... Ac 5:15–16 Ac 28:8
–By agents of Satan .. 2Th 2:9 Rev 13:3
3. Spiritual gifts of miracles and healing ... 1Co 12:9–10,28
C. Spiritual healing
–Received by the land ... 2Ch 7:13–14
–Received by people ... 2Ch 30:18–20 Hos 14:4 1Pe 2:24
–Performed by Jesus with physical healing ... Mk 2:5–11

See also MIRACLE

HEART

–The center of the human being

A. Basic concept of the heart
1. The wellspring of all life ... Pr 4:23 Lk 6:45
2. Combined with other basic human elements
–The heart and soul .. Dt 6:5 1Sa 14:7 Mt 22:37
–The heart and body . Ps 16:9
–The heart and mind . Ps 26:2 Mt 22:37 Rev 2:23
–The heart and spirit . Ps 51:10,17 Eze 18:31
–The heart and flesh . Ps 73:26 Ps 84:2
–The heart and thoughts ... Ps 139:23
B. What the heart controls
1. Human emotions
–The glad heart ... Ex 4:14 Ac 2:26
–The singing heart ... Eph 5:19
–The heart that loves . Dt 6:5 SS 3:1–3
–The heart that takes delight ... Ecc 2:10 Jer 15:16
–The excited heart ... Lk 24:32
–The courageous heart ... 1Sa 10:26 Ps 27:14
–The heart that is encouraged ... Col 2:2 2Th 2:17
–The thankful heart .. Col 3:16
–The repentant heart .. Ps 51:17
–The humble heart ... Mt 11:29
–The compassionate heart ... Lk 7:13
–The anxious heart ... Pr 12:25
–The discouraged heart ... Jos 2:11
–The troubled heart .. Jn 12:27
–The grieving heart .. 1Sa 2:33 La 2:18
–The tormented heart . La 2:11
–The broken heart ... Eze 21:6
–The heavy heart ... Pr 25:20
–The anguished heart . Isa 65:14 Jer 4:19 Ro 9:2
–The fearful heart ... Dt 28:67 Jos 5:1
–The angry heart ... Ps 39:3 Pr 19:3
2. The human will
–To do according to one's heart ... 1Sa 2:35 1Ch 28:2
–To decide in the heart ... 2Ch 6:7
–To devote the heart . 1Ch 22:19
–To direct the heart .. 2Th 3:5
–To turn the heart ... 1Ki 8:58 Ps 119:36
–To incline the heart . Dt 5:29
–To win over the heart ... 2Sa 19:14
–To yield the heart ... Jos 24:23
–To agree with one heart ... Jer 32:39 Ac 4:32
–To be moved in the heart ... Ex 35:21
–The purposes of the heart ... Jer 23:20
–The motives of the heart ... 1Co 4:5
–The desires of the heart ... Ps 21:2 Ro 10:1
–The willing heart ... 2Ch 29:31
–The unrepentant heart ... Ro 2:5
–The hardened heart .. Ex 4:21 Pr 28:14
3. The human intelligence
–To acknowledge in the heart ... Dt 4:39
–To know in the heart ... Dt 8:5
–To take something to heart ... Ex 7:23 Ecc 7:2
–To fix words in the heart ... Dt 11:18
–To lay up words in the heart ... Job 22:22 Pr 4:21
–To search the heart .. Ps 4:4
–To say in the heart .. Ro 10:6
–To muse in the heart ... Ps 77:6
–To ponder in the heart ... Lk 2:19
–To think in the heart ... Mk 2:8
–To understand in the heart ... Pr 2:2
–To meditate in the heart ... Ps 19:14
–To pray in the heart . Ge 24:45 1Sa 1:13
–To believe in the heart ... Ro 10:9
–To be wise in the heart ... Pr 2:10 Pr 10:8
–To doubt in the heart ... Mk 11:23
–To harbor deceit in the heart ... Pr 26:24 Jer 17:9
–To devise evil in the heart ... Ps 140:2
–The thoughts of the heart ... Ge 6:5 Lk 2:35
C. Key elements in the human heart
1. Characteristics of the unregenerate heart
–Proud ... Pr 18:12
–Foolish ... Pr 12:23
–Deceitful ... Jer 17:9
–Rebellious ... Jer 5:23
–Perverse ... Pr 11:20
–Evil ... Ge 6:5
–Wicked ... Pr 6:18
–Callous ... Ps 119:70
–Malicious ... Ps 28:3
–Hardened ... Eph 4:18
–Darkened ... Ro 1:21
–Deluded ... Isa 44:20
–Unrepentant ... Ro 2:5
–Unbelieving ... Heb 3:12
–Gone astray ... Ps 95:10
–Devoted to idols ... Eze 11:21
–Filled with schemes to do wrong ... Ecc 8:11
–Filled with madness . Ecc 9:3
–Far from God ... Isa 29:13 Mk 7:6
2. What the regenerate heart does
–Cries out for the living God ... Ps 84:2
–Seeks God ... Ps 119:2,10
–Responds to God ... 2Ki 22:19
–Trusts in the Lord .. Pr 3:5
–Loves the Lord ... Dt 6:5 Mt 22:37
–Praises the Lord ... Ps 9:1
–Sings to the Lord ... Ps 30:12
–Rejoices in the Lord ... 1Sa 2:1
–Rejoices in salvation ... Ps 13:5
–Is grateful to God ... Col 3:16
–Obeys God's law ... Ps 119:34,69,112 Eph 6:6
–Hides God's word within ... Ps 119:11
–Is on fire for God's word ... Jer 20:9
–Meditates on God and his word ... Ps 19:14
–Is upright ... Ps 7:10
–Speaks the truth ... Ps 15:2
–Is steadfast and secure ... Ps 57:7 Ps 112:7–8
–Is pure ... Ps 24:4 Mt 5:8
–Is wise ... Pr 10:8
–Is sincere ... Ac 2:46 Heb 10:22
–Is unafraid and courageous ... Ps 27:3,14
–Is contrite ... Ps 51:17
–Is circumcised ... Dt 10:16 Ro 2:29
–Walks blamelessly .. Ps 101:2
–Loves others ... 1Pe 1:22
D. God's relationship to the human heart
–He knows it ... 1Sa 16:7
–He searches it ... Ps 7:9 Jer 17:10
–He tests it ... 1Ch 29:17 1Th 2:4
–He influences it ... Ezr 7:27
–He directs it ... Pr 21:1
–He opens it ... Ac 16:14
–He touches it ... 1Sa 10:26
–He makes light shine in it ... 2Co 4:6
–He cleanses it ... Heb 10:22
–He writes his law on it . Jer 31:33
–He strengthens it ... 1Th 3:13
–He keeps it loyal ... 1Ch 29:18
–He gives a new heart .. Ps 51:10 Eze 11:19

HEAVEN

A. What is heaven?
1. Part of God's creation ... Ge 1:1
–A component of the universe ... Ex 20:4 Php 2:10
–Where God placed sun, moon and stars . Ge 1:14–18 Dt 4:19
–Where precipitation comes from ... Ge 8:2 Job 38:29 Isa 55:10
2. The place where God dwells
–His dwelling place .. 1Ki 8:30 Mt 6:9
–His sanctuary ... Ps 102:19
–Where his throne is . Ps 2:4 Isa 63:15
–Where Christ ascended ... Lk 24:51 Heb 9:24
B. What does God do from heaven?
1. Actions in Bible history
–God talked to his people ... Ge 22:11,15
–God made the Israelites hear him ... Dt 4:36
–God heard his people when they prayed ... Ne 9:27–28
–God sent bread ... Ex 16:4,13–15 Ne 9:15
–God sent fire of judgment ... 2Ki 1:12
–God sent fire for sacrifice ... 1Ch 21:26
–God revealed mysteries ... Da 2:18–19 Ac 10:10–16
2. Continuing actions
–God reigns ... Ps 99:1–2
–God observes human actions ... Ps 14:2 Ps 102:19
–God blesses his people ... Dt 26:15
–God hears our prayers ... 2Ch 6:21,23,25,27
–God saves us ... Ps 57:3
–God sends his Holy Spirit ... 1Pe 1:12
–God reveals his wrath ... Ro 1:18
–Christ prepares a place for us ... Jn 14:2–3
–Christ will return from heaven ... 1Th 4:16
C. Our relationship to heaven
1. How can we enter heaven?
–We must be chosen and called ... 2Pe 1:10–11
–We must be born again ... Jn 3:5
–We must trust in God and in Jesus ... Jn 14:1–2
–We must have our names recorded there ... Lk 10:20
–We must be righteous ... Mt 5:19–20

–We must live holy lives — Rev 22:14–15
–We must do the will of God — Mt 7:21
–We must be humble — Mt 18:3–4
–We must be poor in spirit — Mt 5:3
–We must overcome — Rev 2:7; Rev 21:7
–We must receive new bodies — 1Co 15:50–54

2. What should our attitude be toward heaven?
–We should lay up treasures there — Mt 6:20
–We should sacrifice everything for it — Mt 13:44–46
–We should long for it — 2Co 5:2
–We should eagerly look for it — 2Pe 3:13
–We should hope for it — Col 1:5
–In spirit we are already there — Eph 2:6; Php 3:20; Col 3:1

D. Aspects of the present heaven
1. Positive
–God dwells there — 1Ki 8:30
–Christ dwells there at God's right hand — Ac 7:55–56; Eph 1:20
–Christ intercedes for us there — Heb 9:24
–There is joy there — Lk 15:7,10
–There is comfort there — Lk 16:22–25
–Satan has been cast out of there — Rev 12:7–9
2. Negative
–God reveals his wrath from there — 1Sa 2:10; Ro 1:18
–Powers of evil intrude there — Job 1:6–7; Eph 6:12
–Wars occur there — Rev 12:7
–Saints cry out from there — Rev 6:9–11
–Saints do not yet have new bodies — 1Co 15:48–54
–It must be destroyed and renewed — 2Pe 3:7,10, 12–13; Rev 21:1

E. What the new heaven will be like
1. It will be free from:
–Death — Lk 20:35–36; Rev 21:4
–Pain, sorrow and crying — Isa 65:19–23; Rev 21:4
–Night — Rev 22:5
–Hunger and thirst — Rev 7:16
–The curse of God — Rev 22:3
–Wicked people — Rev 22:15
2. For believers, it will be:
–Eternal — 2Co 5:1
–A place of eternal light — Rev 22:5
–The home of righteousness — 2Pe 3:13
–The place of harmony and unity — Isa 65:25
–The place of eternal praise to God — Rev 7:15
–The place of exquisite beauty — Rev 21:10–21
–The place of purity — Rev 21:27
–The place of the tree of life — Rev 22:1–2

HEBRON
–A city, originally called Kiriath Arba — Jos 14:15
–Also called Mamre — Ge 23:19
–Abram built an altar and lived there — Ge 13:18
–Abraham and Sarah's burial plot located there — Ge 23:1–19
–Allied with other cities against Gibeonites — Jos 10:1–5
–Defeated by Joshua — Jos 10:6–26; Jos 11:21
–Given to Caleb — Jos 14:13–15; Jdg 1:9–10, 20
–Later given to Kohathites — 1Ch 6:54–56
–David ruled from there for seven years — 2Sa 2:1–4; 1Ki 2:11
–Soldiers joined David there — 1Ch 12:23–40
–David anointed king of all Israel there — 2Sa 5:1–3; 1Ch 11:1–3
–Absalom crowned king there — 2Sa 15:7–10

HEIR
See INHERITANCE

HELL
A. A place of punishment
–For fallen angels — 2Pe 2:4
–For the devil and his angels — Mt 25:41
–For the beast and the false prophet — Rev 19:20
–For those who worship the beast — Rev 14:9–11
–For wicked humans — Rev 21:8
–For those who reject the gospel — Mt 10:11–15

B. Hints of hell in the Old Testament
–The wicked perish in death — Ps 49:10–15
–There will be judgment for the wicked — Job 24:21–24
–There will be eternal punishment — Isa 66:24; Da 12:2

C. Description of hell in the New Testament
–A place of separation from God — 2Th 1:9
–The second death — Rev 21:8
–The place of condemnation — Mt 23:33
–The place of torment — Lk 16:23
–The place of weeping and the gnashing of teeth — Mt 8:12; Mt 25:30
–The place where body and soul is destroyed — Mt 10:28
–Eternal punishment — Mt 25:46
–Everlasting destruction — 2Th 1:9
–Everlasting chains — Jude 6
–Eternal fire — Mt 18:8; Jude 7
–The lake of fire — Rev 20:15
–The deepest darkness — Jude 13

HERESY
See DOCTRINE

HEROD
A. Herod the Great
–King of Judea at time of Jesus' birth — Mt 2:1; Lk 1:5
–Magi contacted him — Mt 2:1–8
–Ordered babies in Bethlehem killed — Mt 2:16

B. Herod Antipas
–Tetrarch of Galilee — Mt 14:1; Lk 3:1
–Beheaded John the Baptist — Mt 14:3–12
–Worried about Jesus — Lk 9:7–9
–Jesus called him a fox — Lk 13:31–32
–Participated in trial of Jesus — Lk 23:6–15

C. Herod Agrippa
–Persecuted the early church — Ac 12:1
–Killed James — Ac 12:2
–Arrested Peter — Ac 12:3–19
–Died a miserable death from God — Ac 12:19–23

HERODIAS
–Wife of Herod Antipas — Mt 14:3–4; Mk 6:17
–Told daughter to ask for John's severed head — Mt 14:6–11; Mk 6:21–27

HEZEKIAH
–King of Judah — 2Ch 29:1
–Purified the temple — 2Ch 29:3–19
–Restored proper sacrifices — 2Ch 29:20–36
–Celebrated the Passover for two weeks — 2Ch 30:1–27
–Cleansed land of idols — 2Ch 31:1
–Organized priests and Levites — 2Ch 31:2–19
–Collected Solomon's proverbs — Pr 25:1
–Sought the Lord for help against Assyria — 2Ch 32:1–20; Isa 36:1–37:20
–Witnessed the destruction of Sennacherib — 2Ch 32:21–23; Isa 37:36–37
–Had fatal illness — 2Ki 20:1
–Illness healed by God through prayer — 2Ki 20:2–11; Isa 38:2–8
–Sang a song after his recovery — Isa 38:9–20
–Judged for sin of pride — 2Ki 20:12–21; Isa 39:1–8

HILKIAH
–High priest during time of Josiah — 2Ki 22:4
–Reported his finding of the book of the law — 2Ki 22:8; 2Ch 34:14–15
–Questioned Huldah about the law — 2Ki 22:14; 2Ch 34:22
–Ordered by Josiah to cleanse the temple — 2Ki 23:4; 2Ch 34:9–11
–Became administrator of the temple — 2Ch 35:8

HIRAM
–King of Tyre — 2Sa 5:11
–Helped David build his palace — 2Sa 5:11–12; 1Ch 14:1
–Helped Solomon build the temple — 1Ki 5:1–12; 2Ch 2:3–18
–Scorned towns that Solomon gave him — 1Ki 9:10–13
–Helped build Solomon's navy — 1Ki 9:26–28; 2Ch 8:17–18
–Engaged in extensive trade — 1Ki 10:11–12

HITTITES
A. Their identity
–Descendants of Canaan, grandson of Noah — Ge 10:6,15
–One of the seven Canaanite nations — Ex 33:2

B. Significant Hittites
–Ephron: sold Abraham a burial plot — Ge 23:10–20
–Judith and Basemath: wives of Esau — Ge 26:34
–Ahimelech: a soldier with David — 1Sa 26:6
–Uriah: husband of Bathsheba — 2Sa 11:3–24; 1Ki 15:5

C. Their wars
–Allied with others against Joshua — Jos 11:1–5
–Defeated by Joshua — Jos 12:7–8

D. Important data concerning them
–Controlled much land in Moses' time — Nu 13:27–29; Jos 1:4
–God promised their land to his people — Ex 3:8,17; Ex 34:11
–Israelites told to destroy them completely — Dt 7:1–6; Dt 20:17
–Israelites did not destroy them completely — Jdg 3:5
–Solomon traded with them — 1Ki 10:29
–Many became Solomon's slaves — 1Ki 9:20–21; 2Ch 8:7–8
–Intermarried with the Israelites — Jdg 3:5–6; 1Ki 11:1; Ezr 9:1–2

HOLINESS
–Being set apart from sin; purity

A. The holiness of God
1. In the Old Testament
–He is holy — Ps 99:3,5,9
–He is called the Holy One of Israel — Ps 22:3; Isa 30:11–12,15
–His Spirit is holy — Isa 63:10
–His name is holy — Ps 111:9
–His throne is holy — Ps 47:8
–He is majestic in holiness — Ex 15:11
–His holiness has splendor — 1Ch 16:29
–He is surrounded by holiness — Isa 6:3
–He is unique in his holiness — 1Sa 2:2
–He swears by his holiness — Am 4:2
–He will show himself holy — Isa 5:16
–His words are holy — Jer 23:9
–His arm is holy — Isa 52:10
2. In the New Testament
–The Father is holy — Mt 6:9; Jn 17:11
–The Son is holy — Lk 1:35; Ac 4:27,30
–The Spirit is holy — Ac 2:4; Ro 1:4

B. The holiness of God's people
1. Israel in the Old Testament
–They were holy to the Lord — Jer 2:3
–They were a holy people — Ex 19:6; Dt 7:6
–They formed a holy race — Ezr 9:2
–They were expected to be holy — Lev 11:44–45; Lev 19:12
–The priests were holy — Lev 21:5–6
2. Christians in the New Testament
–They are a holy people — Col 3:12; 1Pe 2:9
–They are a holy temple — Eph 2:21
–They are saints (holy ones) — 2Co 1:1; Eph 1:1
–They are sanctified (made holy) — 1Co 6:11
–They are chosen to be holy — Eph 1:4
–They are called to a holy life — 1Th 4:7
–They must live holy lives — Heb 12:14; 1Pe 1:15–16
–They are to serve God in holiness — Lk 1:74–75
–They must purify themselves in holiness — 2Co 7:1
–They will be presented to God as holy — Col 1:22

C. The holiness of special things
1. Referred to in the Old Testament
–The ground where one meets God — Ex 3:4–5
–The holy place and the most holy place — Ex 26:33
–The altar in the tabernacle — Ex 29:37
–The garments of the priests — Ex 28:2–4
–The turban of the priest — Ex 39:30–31
–The furnishings used by the priests — Nu 4:15
–The guilt offering — Lev 7:1
–Anything given to the Lord — Lev 27:9,14, 21,28
–The camp of the Israelites — Dt 23:14
–The temple — Hab 2:20
–The Sabbath — Ex 16:23

–The Year of Jubilee . Lev 25:12
–Mount Zion in Jerusalem .... Ps 2:6; Isa 27:13
–The city of Jerusalem .... Ne 11:1
2. Referred to in the New Testament
–The angels .... Ac 10:22; 1Th 3:13
–The city of Jerusalem .... Mt 4:5
–The Scriptures ...... Ro 1:2; 2Ti 3:15
–The law of God .... Ro 7:12
–A Christian's faith .. Jude 20
–A Christian's hands in prayer 1Ti 2:8
–The kiss of greeting among Christians ... 1Co 16:20; 1Th 5:26

See also SANCTIFICATION

HOLY SPIRIT

A. The Spirit's divine nature
1. Called God .... Lk 1:32,35; Ac 5:3–4
2. United with the Father and Son .... Mt 28:19; 2Co 13:14
3. Has characteristics of God
–Eternal .... Heb 9:14
–Everywhere present . Ps 139:7–10
–All-knowing 1Co 2:10–11
–Has great power .... Ac 1:8; Ro 15:19
–Raised Christ from the dead 1Pe 3:18
–Performs miracles ... Mt 12:28; Ro 15:19
–Involved in creation . Ge 1:2
–Gives spiritual life to us .... Jn 3:3–8

B. The Spirit as a person
–He teaches .... Jn 14:26
–He hears and speaks ... Jn 16:13
–He testifies about Christ .... Jn 15:26
–He encourages .... Ac 9:31
–He counsels .... Jn 14:16
–He convicts people of sin .... Jn 16:8
–He prays for us .... Ro 8:27
–He sends people out ... Ac 13:4
–He experiences grief ... Eph 4:30
–He can be resisted ..... Ac 7:51
–He can be tested ...... Ac 5:9

C. The Spirit's work
1. In the Old Testament
–Involved in creation . Ge 1:2
–Gave life to God's creatures .... Ps 104:30
–Guided God's people .... Isa 63:11–13
–Instructed God's people .... Ne 9:20
–Led God's people in the right way .... Ps 143:10
–Inspired God's people to do right .... Ps 51:10–12
–Admonished God's people .... Ne 9:30
–Reacted to human evil .... Ge 6:3
–Gave artistic ability to individuals .... Ex 31:2–3
–Gave his power to Israel's leaders ...... Jdg 6:34; 1Sa 16:13; Zec 4:6
–Lived among God's people .... Hag 2:5
–Inspired the prophets .... Nu 11:29; Mic 3:8; Zec 7:12; 2Pe 1:21
–Spoke through the psalmists .... 2Sa 23:2; Ac 1:16,20; Heb 3:7–11
–Old Testament prophecies on the Spirit .. Isa 11:1–3; Isa 32:15; Isa 42:1; Isa 44:3; Isa 61:1–3; Eze 36:26–27; Joel 2:28–32

2. In the life of Jesus Christ
–Jesus was conceived by the Spirit .... Lk 1:34–35
–He received the Spirit at his baptism ...... Lk 3:21–22
–He was filled with the Spirit .... Lk 4:1
–He ministered in the power of the Spirit .. Mt 12:15–21; Lk 4:18–21
–He cast out demons by the Spirit .... Mt 12:28
–He offered himself to God through the Spirit .... Heb 9:14
–He was raised by the Spirit .... Ro 8:11; 1Ti 3:16; 1Pe 3:18
–He promised to send the Spirit .... Jn 15:26
–He sent the Spirit on Pentecost .... Ac 2:33
–The Spirit is the Spirit of Jesus ...... Ac 16:7; Ro 8:9; Gal 4:6

3. In the church
–The Spirit came at Pentecost .... Ac 2:1–4
–He dwells in the church .... 1Co 3:16–17; Eph 2:22
–He appoints officers for the church ...... Ac 20:28
–He directs decisions of the church .... Ac 15:28
–He chooses missionaries .... Ac 13:2
–He sends out missionaries .... Ac 13:4
–He directs the mission enterprise ...... Ac 8:29,39; Ac 16:6–7

4. In individuals
–The Spirit dwells in us .... Jn 14:16–17; Ro 8:11; 1Co 6:19
–He convicts us of sin .... Jn 16:7–11
–He gives us new life .... Jn 3:5–6; Tit 3:5
–He makes us realize God's love .... Ro 5:5
–He gives us power to witness .... Ac 1:8; Ac 6:9–10
–He teaches us what to say .... Lk 12:12
–He reveals God's secrets to us 1Co 2:10–16
–He brings Christ's presence to us ...... Jn 14:16–18
–He keeps us in touch with God .... Ro 8:26; Jude 20
–He teaches us about Christ .... Jn 14:26; Jn 15:26
–He enables us to find the truth .... Jn 16:13; 1Jn 4:1–6
–He encourages us ... Ac 9:31
–He controls us ...... Ro 8:9
–He gives us joy and peace .... Ro 14:17
–He draws us into fellowship .... 2Co 13:14; Php 2:1
–He enables us to live the Christian life .... Ro 8:5–9
–He works his fruit in us .... Gal 5:16–25
–He sanctifies us ..... Ro 15:16; 2Th 2:13
–He gives us gifts 1Co 12:4–11

See GIFTS OF THE SPIRIT

–He gives us his sword to fight Satan . Eph 6:17
–He prays for us in times of crisis ...... Ro 8:26
–He will raise us from the dead .... Ro 8:11

D. The Spirit in our life
1. How to receive the Spirit
–We must repent of our sins .... Ac 2:37–38
–We must believe in Jesus .... Ac 11:15–17; Ro 8:9; Gal 3:2–3,14; Eph 1:13
–We must be baptized in Jesus' name ...... Ac 2:38; Ac 19:1–6
–We must pray to receive him .... Lk 11:13; Ac 8:15
2. Being filled with the Holy Spirit
a. His filling is a gift for all believers
–Old Testament promise .... Joel 2:28–29
–New Testament fulfillment .... Ac 2:17–18
–New Testament promise to us .... Ac 2:38; Ro 8:9
b. Persons *filled* with the Holy Spirit
–Bezalel .... Ex 31:2–5
–Samson .... Jdg 14:19
–Saul 1Sa 10:10
–John the Baptist .. Lk 1:15
–Elizabeth .... Lk 1:47
–Zechariah .... Lk 1:67
–The disciples on Pentecost .... Ac 2:4
–Peter before the Jewish council ... Ac 4:8
–The early Christians at prayer ... Ac 4:31
–Paul in his preaching .... Ac 13:9
–New Christians ... Ac 13:52
c. Persons *full* of the Holy Spirit
–Jesus .... Lk 4:1
–The first deacons . Ac 6:3
–Stephen .... Ac 6:5
–Barnabas .... Ac 11:24
d. The command to be filled with the Spirit
–To Paul at his conversion .... Ac 9:17
–To all Christians . Eph 5:18
3. Being sealed with the Spirit .... 2Co 1:21–22; 2Co 5:5; Eph 1:13–14
4. Baptized with the Spirit

See BAPTISM OF THE SPIRIT

HOME

See FAMILY

HOMOSEXUALITY

See SEXUAL STANDARDS

HONESTY

See INTEGRITY

HOPE

–Certainty in the present and firm expectation for the future

A. The nature of hope
1. Basic concept of hope
–It is linked with faith .... 1Co 13:13; Heb 11:1
–It is linked with trust .... Ps 33:20–21; Ro 15:13
–It is linked with expectation .... Ro 4:18–19; Tit 1:2
2. In whom/what do we hope?
–In God .... Ps 42:5,11; Ps 130:7; 1Ti 6:17
–In Jesus Christ ...... Ro 15:12; 1Co 15:19; Eph 1:12; Php 2:19
–In the name of God . Ps 52:9
–In the word of God . Ps 119:74; Ps 130:5
–In the promises of God .... Ac 26:6
–In the resurrection of the dead .... Ac 23:6
3. For what do we hope?
–God's righteousness . Gal 5:5
–Salvation .... Ro 8:24–25; 1Th 5:8
–God's saving arm ... Isa 51:5
–Liberation from bondage to decay ... Ro 8:20–21
–The resurrection .... Ac 2:26; Ac 26:7
–The glory of God ... Ro 5:2; 2Co 3:11–12
–Our glorious inheritance .... Eph 1:18; Col 1:5
–The appearance of Jesus Christ .... Tit 2:13; 1Jn 3:2–3
–A crown of righteousness 2Ti 4:8
–A crown of glory 1Pe 5:4
–A crown of life ..... Rev 2:10
–Eternal life .... Tit 1:2; Tit 3:7

B. Jesus Christ and our hope
1. He is called our hope
–He is our hope 1Ti 1:1
–He is the hope of Israel .... Ac 28:20
–He is the hope of glory .... Col 1:27
2. He fulfilled the hope of the Old Testament
–Jesus confirms the promises of God .... Ac 26:6–7; Ro 15:8
–All promises of God fulfilled in him 2Co 1:20

C. Hope in the Christian life
1. The choice we face
–Hope in humans or in God .... Ps 33:16–19
–Hope in riches or in God 1Ti 6:17
–Without God, there is no hope .... Eph 2:12; 1Th 4:13
2. Attaining hope
–We are called to only one hope .... Eph 1:18; Eph 4:4
–We must set our hope fully on Jesus . 1Pe 1:13
–We must believe the resurrection 1Pe 1:3
–We must abound in hope .... Ro 15:13; 1Co 13:13
–We must never lose our hope .... Ps 25:5
3. The benefits of hope
–Causes us to praise God .... Ps 71:14
–Causes us to rejoice . Ro 5:2; Ro 12:12
–Renews our strength . Isa 40:31
–Inspires us to a life of purity 1Jn 3:3
–Inspires us to persevere 1Th 1:3
–Cures the downcast soul .... Ps 42:5,11; La 3:20–21
–Will never disappoint us .... Isa 49:23; Ro 5:5
–Our hope is like a stabilizing anchor ... Heb 6:18–19
4. We should defend our hope 1Pe 3:15

HOPHNI

–Son of Eli, brother of Phinehas 1Sa 1:3
–A wicked priest 1Sa 2:12–17
–Scorned his father's rebuke . 1Sa 2:22–25
–His death prophesied as a sign 1Sa 2:30–34
–Brought the ark into battle . 1Sa 4:4
–Killed in the battle 1Sa 4:11,17

HOREB

See SINAI

HORSE

A. Literal uses of horses
1. Military
–Description of the war-horse .... Job 39:19–25
–Pharaoh's horses .... Ex 14:9,23
–Canaanite horses .... Jos 11:4
–Solomon's horses ... 2Ch 1:14–16
–Syrian horses 2Ki 6:14–15
2. Non-military uses
–Horses used to reinforce royal power ... 2Sa 15:1; 1Ki 1:5

–Horse riding to honor a person .... Est 6:6–11
–Horses as livestock .. Ge 47:17
–Horses used in farm labor .... Isa 28:28
–Horses used for transportation .... Isa 66:20
–Horses used to bring messages .... Est 8:10
3. Relying on horses
–They cannot bring victory .... Ps 33:16–17
–Trust in God instead of horses .... Ps 20:7; Isa 31:1
B. Figurative use of horses
–Horses of fire carried Elijah to heaven 2Ki 2:11
–God's people becoming like the proud horse ... Zec 10:3
–God's angels using horses and chariots 2Ki 6:17
–God's power symbolized in his horses .... Hab 3:8,15
–The returning Lord riding a white horse ...... Rev 19:11–13

HOSEA
–A prophet, son of Beeri .... Hos 1:1
–His wife pictured unfaithful Israel .... Hos 1:2–11
–Became reconciled with his wife .... Hos 3:1–3

HOSHEA
A. Original name of Joshua . Nu 13:16
B. Last king of Israel 2Ki 17:1
–Murdered Pekah to get throne 2Ki 15:30
–Captured and deported by Assyria 2Ki 17:2–6

HOSPITALITY
See KINDNESS

HULDAH
–A prophetess 2Ki 22:14
–Visited by Hilkiah during Josiah's reign 2Ki 22:12–20; 2Ch 34:19–28

HUMILITY
–Lowliness; freedom from pride
A. What humility involves
–A childlike attitude .... Mt 18:1–4
–Repentance .... Isa 66:2; Lk 18:13–14
–Submission before God . 2Ch 34:27; Da 5:22–23
–Seeking God's face in prayer 2Ch 7:14
–Fasting .... Ezr 8:21; Ps 35:13
–Following God's laws .. Jer 44:10; Zep 2:3
–Working for justice and mercy .... Mic 6:8
–Opposite of pride ...... Pr 3:34; Da 4:37; 1Pe 5:5
B. Humility in our lives
1. The command to be humble
–We must humble ourselves .... Eph 4:2; 1Pe 5:6
–We must walk humbly with God ...... Mic 6:8
–We must clothe ourselves with humility . Col 3:12; 1Pe 5:5
–We must consider others better than ourselves .... Php 2:3
–We must avoid false humility .... Col 2:18,23
2. The benefits of humility
–God saves the humble .... Ps 18:27; 1Co 1:26–29
–God gives the humble grace .... Pr 3:34; Jas 4:6
–God raises the lowly .... Job 5:11; Mt 23:12; Lk 1:52
–God revives the lowly .... Isa 57:15
–God honors the humble .... Pr 15:33; Pr 18:12
–God rewards the humble .... Pr 22:4
–God blesses the humble 2Ch 7:14
–God holds the humble in esteem .... Isa 66:2
–God guides and teaches the humble .. Ps 25:9
–With humility comes wisdom .... Pr 11:2
C. Examples of humility
1. The supreme example: Jesus Christ
–In his coming to earth 2Co 8:9
–In his lowliness ..... Mt 11:29
–In his life of service .... Lk 22:27
–In his submission to God's will .... Jn 6:38
–In his sufferings .... Isa 53:1–9
–In his washing of the disciples' feet .... Jn 13:4–5
–In his triumphal entry .... Mt 21:5,7
–In his death on the cross .... Php 2:5–8
2. Other examples
–The Israelites in the desert .... Dt 8:3
–Ahab 1Ki 21:29
–Josiah 2Ki 22:19
–Rehoboam and his people 2Ch 12:5–12
–Job .... Job 42:2–6
–Isaiah .... Isa 6:1–6
–John the Baptist .... Jn 3:27–30
–Peter .... Lk 5:8–9
–Paul .... Ac 20:19

HUNGER AND THIRST
A. Examples of famines and droughts
–Worldwide famine in Joseph's day .... Ge 41:53
–Famine in Bethlehem .. Ru 1:1
–Famine in David's time 2Sa 21:1
–Drought and famine in Elijah's day 1Ki 17:1
–Famine in Elisha's day . 2Ki 6:25; 2Ki 8:1
–Famine in Jerusalem ... 2Ki 25:3
–Famine in Nehemiah's day .... Ne 5:3
–Famine predicted by Agabus .... Ac 11:27–28
B. How times of hunger and thirst were used:
1. By God
–To fulfill his plan for his people .... Ge 15:13–14; Ge 41:56–42:3; Ge 46:3–4
–To humble and teach the Israelites .... Ex 16:2–3; Dt 8:2–3
–To get people to look to God for help ..... Jdg 6:3–6; Ps 107:4–9
–To punish stubborn disobedience .... Dt 28:47–48; Isa 65:11–13
–To bring judgment on sinners .... Isa 9:18–21; Am 4:6,9
2. By Jesus
–To demonstrate his compassion .... Mk 6:34–44; Mk 8:1–9
–To show he was bread from heaven .. Jn 6:33,48–51
3. By the church
–To show kindness to the needy .... Ac 11:28–30; 2Co 8:13–15
–To show church unity .... Ro 15:25–27
C. Spiritual hunger and thirst
1. The reality of such hunger and thirst
–Physical bread cannot satisfy .... Dt 8:3; Mt 4:4
–Prediction of a famine of God's word .. Am 8:11–12
2. Satisfying such hunger and thirst
–God promises to satisfy .... Isa 55:1–3; Mt 5:6
–Jesus is the bread of life .... Jn 6:35,48–58; 1Co 10:16
–Jesus is the water of life .... Jn 4:13–14; Jn 7:37–38

HUR
–A chief magistrate of the Israelites .... Ex 24:14
–With Aaron, supported Moses' hand .... Ex 17:10–12

HUSHAI
–Friend of David 2Sa 15:37
–Conspired with David to outwit Absalom 2Sa 15:32–37
–Foiled Absalom's revolt by giving poor advice 2Sa 16:15–17:16

HYPOCRISY
–Open display of religion without genuine commitment
A. Description of hypocrisy
–Displaying religion with no love for God .... Isa 29:13; Mt 6:2–6, 16–18; Mt 23:5–7
–Claiming love for God, mistreating others ...... Mk 12:38–40; 1Jn 3:17; 1Jn 4:20
–Not practicing what one preaches .... Mt 23:3; Ro 2:17–24
–Sticking only to the letter of the law .... Mt 23:16–23; Lk 13:15–16
–Criticizing another for one's own sins .... Mt 7:3–5; Mk 7:6–13
–Being outwardly beautiful but inwardly rotten . Mt 23:27–28
–Having only an outward form of godliness 2Co 11:13–15; 2Ti 3:5
–Lying to make oneself look good .... Ac 5:1–10
B. God and human hypocrisy
1. God's reaction to hypocrites
–Is angry with them .. Lk 13:14–15
–Has no reward for them .... Mt 6:2,5,16
–Pronounces woe to them .... Mt 23:13–16,23–29
–Has punishment in store for them ...... Lk 20:46–47
–Condemns them to hell .... Mt 23:33
2. God's will for his people
–Wants us to avoid hypocrites 2Ti 3:5
–Warns us against hypocrisy 1Pe 2:1
–Wants us to express our faith by works .. Jas 2:14–17; 1Jn 3:17–19
–Wants us to show genuine love .... Ro 12:9; 1Pe 1:22
–Wants us to exercise a sincere faith 1Ti 1:5; 2Ti 1:5

ICHABOD
–Son born to Phinehas's wife after his death 1Sa 4:19–22
–Name means "no glory" .. 1Sa 4:21

IDOLATRY
–The worship of false gods
A. Idols mentioned in the Bible
–Adrammelech 2Ki 17:31
–Anammelech 2Ki 17:31
–Artemis .... Ac 19:24, 27–28
–Asherah 1Ki 14:15
–Ashima 2Ki 17:30
–Astarte 1Sa 31:10
–Baal 1Ki 16:31–32
–Baal-berith .... Jdg 8:33
–Baal-zebub 2Ki 1:3
–Bel .... Isa 46:1
–Chemosh 1Ki 11:7,33
–Dagon 1Sa 5:2–4
–Golden calf 1Ki 12:28
–Hermes .... Ac 14:12
–Ishtar (Queen of Heaven) .... Jer 7:18
–Molech 1Ki 11:5,7
–Merodach .... Jer 50:2
–Nergal 2Ki 17:30
–Nebo .... Isa 46:1
–Nibhaz 2Ki 17:31
–Nisroch 2Ki 19:37
–Rephan .... Ac 7:43
–Rimmon 2Ki 5:18
–Succoth-benoth 2Ki 17:30
–Tammuz .... Eze 8:14
–Tartak 2Ki 17:31
–Zeus .... Ac 14:12
B. Principles concerning idols
–They have no real existence 1Co 8:4
–They cannot save ...... Ps 115:4–8; Ps 135:14–18; Isa 46:1–7; Da 5:23
–The worship of idols is mocked .... 1Ki 18:27; Isa 44:9–20; Jer 10:3–5
C. God's perspective concerning idolatry
1. In the Old Testament
–Israel may not worship idols .... Ex 20:3–4; 2Ki 17:35; Ex 34:14,17
–Israel must destroy idols in Canaan ..... Ex 23:24; Ex 34:13; Dt 7:5
2. In the New Testament
–Idolaters do not inherit the kingdom . 1Co 6:9–10; Gal 5:20–21
–We must flee from idolatry 1Co 10:14; 1Jn 5:21
–Greed condemned as idolatry .... Col 3:5
–Money considered a false god .... Mt 6:24

IMAGE OF GOD
A. Humans created in God's image .... Ge 1:26–27; Ge 5:1; 1Co 11:7
B. The image and humanity's fall into sin
1. The image was lost
–Sin pervades everyone .... Ro 3:23; Ro 5:12–14
–We need to be restored in God's image .... Ro 8:29; Col 3:10
2. The image was partially retained
–All humans are in touch with God ..... Ac 17:27–28
–God's image in us rules out murder .... Ge 9:6
–God's image in us rules out cursing .... Jas 3:9
C. Christ and the image of God
1. He bears God's perfect image
–He is the image of God *par excellence* .. 2Co 4:4; Col 1:15; Heb 1:3
–We see God in Christ .... Jn 1:18; Jn 12:45; Jn 14:9
2. He works in fallen, but redeemed humans
–To restore us to God's image .... Ro 8:29; 2Co 3:18
–To renew us in knowledge .... Col 3:10

–To renew us in righteousness .... Eph 4:24
–To renew us in holiness .... Eph 4:24
–Some day he will completely restore us 1Co 15:49; 1Jn 3:2

D. Our responsibility as image-bearers of God
–We must rule creation wisely .... Ge 1:28; Ps 8:6–8
–We may not worship images created by humans .... Ex 20:4; Ac 17:29
–We may not murder another person .... Ge 9:6
–We may not curse another person .... Jas 3:9

INCARNATION

See JESUS CHRIST

INCENSE

A. Incense burned
1. To pagan gods .... 1Ki 11:7–8; 2Ki 17:9–12; Jer 11:12
2. To the Lord God
a. Two incense offerings
–Daily burning on altar of incense .. Ex 30:1–8; 2Ch 2:4
–Incense on the day of atonement ..... Lev 16:12–13; 1Ch 6:49
b. Regulations concerning incense .... Ex 30:9,34–38; Lev 10:1–2; Nu 16:35–38
c. Continued in the New Testament ... Lk 1:8–9
d. Incense detestable if insincere .... Isa 1:13; Jer 6:20

B. Incense as symbolic of prayer .... Ps 141:2; Lk 1:10; Rev 5:8; Rev 8:3–4

INHERITANCE

A. Inheritance in the Old Testament
1. Family inheritance
–Firstborn son received birthright ... Ge 25:29–34; Dt 21:15–17
–Firstborn son received double share .... Dt 21:17
–If no sons, daughters inherit .... Nu 27:1–8
–If no children, next of kin inherit .... Nu 27:9
–Land had to stay within the tribe ..... Nu 36:7; 1Ki 21:3
–Each allotted land was an inheritance .. Nu 26:53,56
2. Israel's inheritance
–Canaan: the land of God's inheritance ... Dt 4:21; 1Ki 8:36; Ps 78:55
–Promised to Abram . Ge 12:7; Ge 15:18–21
–Land divided as inheritance to Israelites .... Jos 11:23
–To remain an heir required obedience .. Dt 4:25–27; 2Ki 21:12–15
–Inheritance lost in the exile .... Ps 79:1–8
–Inheritance regained in the return .... Ne 11:20; Isa 65:8–9; Eze 36:12
3. Spiritualizing the inheritance
–The Lord as the people's inheritance ... Ps 73:26; Ps 142:5
–The people as the Lord's inheritance ... Dt 4:20; Isa 47:6
–God's inheritance to include Gentiles ..... Ps 2:8; Jer 10:16

B. Inheritance in the New Testament
1. Jesus is the heir ..... Heb 1:2
2. We become heirs
–When we become sons of God .... Gal 4:7
–When we believe in Jesus .... Ro 4:13; Heb 6:12
–When we receive God's grace .... Gal 3:18
–We become joint heirs with Christ .... Ro 8:17
3. What we are to inherit
–The earth .... Mt 5:5
–The kingdom of light .... Col 1:12
–The kingdom of heaven .... Mt 25:34
–The kingdom of God 1Co 6:9
–Eternal life .... Mt 19:29; Tit 3:7
–Everything .... Rev 21:7
4. The nature of our inheritance
–It is given by God and his word .... Ac 20:32
–It is received as a reward .... Col 3:24
–It is kept in heaven for us 1Pe 1:4
–It is imperishable ... 1Co 15:50–53; 1Pe 1:4
–It is eternal .... Heb 9:15
–It is guaranteed by the Spirit .... Eph 1:13–14
–It can be lost through disobedience .... Mt 25:41–46; Heb 4:6,11

INSECTS

A. Insects and other small creatures mentioned in Bible
–Ant .... Pr 6:6
–Bee .... Jdg 14:8
–Cricket .... Lev 11:22
–Flea 1Sa 24:14
–Fly .... Ex 8:21–24
–Gadfly .... Jer 46:20
–Gnat .... Ex 8:16–18
–Grasshopper .... Lev 11:22
–Hornet .... Jos 24:12
–Leech .... Pr 30:15
–Locust .... Joel 1:4
–Moth .... Mt 6:20
–Scorpion .... Dt 8:15
–Spider .... Job 8:14
–Worm .... Jnh 4:7

B. God's use of insects
–Some suitable for food, some not .... Lev 11:21–24
–Sometimes used as a judgment .... Ex 8:16–32; Joel 1:2–12
–Ants used to teach us lessons .... Pr 6:6–8
–Moths used as a symbol of destruction .... Mt 6:19–20
–Honey used as a symbol of God's blessing ...... Dt 11:9

INSPIRATION OF SCRIPTURE

–The Bible as God's written word

A. Scripture is inspired by God
1. Basic statement 2Ti 3:16; 2Pe 1:21
2. Affirmations in the Old Testament
–God put words in prophets' mouths .... Dt 18:18; Isa 51:16; Jer 1:9
–The Spirit spoke through David 2Sa 23:2
–"Thus says the LORD" .... Isa 43:1; Jer 6:16
–"The word of the LORD came to . . ." .... 1Ki 17:2; Eze 1:3
3. Affirmations in the New Testament
–David spoke by the Holy Spirit .... Mk 12:36; Ac 4:25
–God speaks in the Old Testament ...... Heb 4:3,7; Heb 8:8
–The Spirit speaks in the Old Testament .. Ac 28:25; Heb 3:7
–In the Old Testament, "It is written" .... Mt 4:4,6,10; 1Co 1:19,31
–The Scriptures cannot be broken .... Jn 10:35
–The Scriptures must be fulfilled .... Mt 5:18; Mt 24:35; Lk 24:44

B. Characteristics of the inspired word of God
–Trustworthy .... 2Sa 7:28; Ps 111:7–8; Jn 17:17
–Eternally fixed .... Ps 119:89; Isa 40:8
–Unbreakable .... Mt 5:18; Jn 10:35
–A sure guide for life ... Ps 119:105; 2Ti 3:16–17
–Effective in its purposes .... Jer 23:29; Heb 4:12

C. How Bible writers received their material
–In various ways .... Heb 1:1
–By direct speech from God .... Ex 34:27–28; Nu 12:8; Jer 30:1–2
–By angels .... Zec 1:12–17; Ac 7:53
–By visions .... Ge 15:1; Mic 1:1
–By dreams .... Da 7:1
See DREAMS AND VISIONS
–By an inner impulse from God .... Jer 20:9; 2Pe 1:21
–By eyewitness accounts .... Lk 1:2; 1Jn 1:1–4
–By careful research .... Lk 1:3–4

INTEGRITY

–Honesty in life and adherence to moral principle

A. Examples of those showing integrity
–Job .... Job 2:3
–David .... 1Ch 29:17; Ps 78:72
–Financial officials of the temple 2Ki 12:9–15
–Hananiah .... Ne 7:2
–Jesus .... Mt 22:16

B. Expectation of living in integrity and honesty
–Linked with observing all God's commands ... 1Ki 9:4
–Preferred above wealth . Pr 28:6
–Expected of the upright .... Pr 11:3
–Expected of Christian leaders .... Tit 2:7
–Required in business dealings .... Lev 19:36; Dt 25:15; Pr 16:11

C. Blessings of living in integrity and honesty
–We please God 1Ch 29:17
–We gain a good reputation .... Pr 16:13
–We receive God's protection .... Pr 2:7
–We gain security for ourselves .... Ps 25:21; Pr 10:9
–We gain security for future generations 1Ki 9:4–5

See also TRUTH

INTERCESSION

–The prayer of one person for another

A. Human intercession
1. Examples of intercession by officials
–By leaders .... Ex 32:11–14; Nu 14:13–19; Jos 7:6–9
–By priests .... Lev 5:10; Lev 16:21; Ezr 9:5–15
–By prophets .... 1Sa 7:5–6; 1Ki 13:6; Da 9:3–19; Jas 5:17–18
–By kings 2Sa 24:17; 1Ki 8:33–51
–By apostles .... Ac 8:15; Eph 3:14–19; Php 1:9–11; Col 1:9–12
–By elders .... Jas 5:14
2. Examples of intercession by individuals
a. In the Old Testament
–Abraham for Lot . Ge 18:23–32
–David for his sick child 2Sa 12:16
–David for Solomon 1Ch 29:19
–Job for his children .... Job 1:5
–A psalmist for the people .... Ps 20:1–5; Ps 25:22
–A psalmist for all nations .... Ps 67:3–5
b. In the New Testament
–Stephen for his persecutors ...... Ac 7:60
–Peter for Dorcas .. Ac 9:40
–Paul for a sick man .... Ac 28:8
–Paul for Timothy . 2Ti 1:3
–Paul for Philemon .... Phm 4
–Christians for their persecutors ...... Mt 5:44
–The church for Peter .... Ac 12:5,12
–The church for missionaries ..... Mt 9:38; Ac 13:3; Heb 13:18
–The church for Paul .... Ro 15:31–32; Eph 6:19–20
–The church for each other .... Jas 5:16
–The church for all people 1Ti 2:1–2
3. The purposes of human intercession
–For averting judgment .... Ge 18:23–32; Nu 14:13–19
–For escape from danger .... Ac 12:5,12; Ro 15:31
–For God's blessings . Nu 6:24–26; 1Ki 18:41–45
–For the Holy Spirit's power .... Ac 8:15–17; Eph 3:14–17
–For healing .... 1Ki 17:20–21; Ac 28:8; Jas 5:14–16
–For forgiveness ..... Ezr 9:5–15; Ac 7:60
–For the ability to rule well 1Ch 29:19; 1Ti 2:2
–For Christian growth .... Php 1:9–11; Col 1:10–11
–For effective pastors . 2Ti 1:3–7
–For effective mission work .... Mt 9:38; Eph 6:19–20
–For the salvation of others .... Ro 10:1–4
–For others to praise God .... Ps 67:3–5

B. Divine intercession
1. The intercession of Christ
–For his followers ..... Lk 22:32; Jn 14:16; Jn 17:6–26
–For his enemies ..... Lk 23:34
–Continual intercession for us .... Ro 8:34; Heb 7:24; Heb 9:24; 1Jn 2:1
2. The Spirit as intercessor .... Ro 8:26–27

INTEREST

See DEBT

ISAAC

A. History of Isaac
–Promised son of Abraham and Sarah .... Ge 17:19
1Ch 1:28
–His birth .... Ge 21:1–3
–His circumcision .... Ge 21:4
–Party at his weaning ... Ge 21:8–13
–Offered up by Abraham .... Ge 22:1–14
Heb 11:17–19
–Took Rebekah as wife . Ge 24:1–67
–Inherited Abraham's estate .... Ge 25:5
–With Ishmael, buried Abraham .... Ge 25:7–11
–Fathered Esau and Jacob .... Ge 25:19–26
1Ch 1:34
–Lied to Abimelech about Rebekah .... Ge 26:1–11
–Became very wealthy .. Ge 26:12–13
–Made a covenant with Abimelech .... Ge 26:14–31
–Tricked into blessing Jacob .... Ge 27:1–40
–Sent Jacob away to find a wife .... Ge 28:1–5
–His death .... Ge 35:27–29

B. Significance of Isaac
–Perpetuated Abrahamic covenant .... Ge 17:21
Ge 26:2–5
–Shows grace and faithfulness of God .... Ge 21:1
–Shows who are true children of Abraham ... Ro 9:7–9
Gal 4:21–31
–Shows God's purpose in election .... Ro 9:10–13
–Is an example of true faith .... Heb 11:20

ISAIAH

–A prophet in Judah and Jerusalem .... Isa 1:1
–Called by God .... Isa 6:1–13
–Announced judgment to Ahaz .... Isa 7:1–25
–Married a prophetess and fathered children .... Isa 8:1–4
–Prophesied Hezekiah's death 2Ki 20:1
Isa 38:1
–Prophesied fifteen more years of life for Hezekiah .. 2Ki 20:4–6
Isa 38:4–8
–Prophesied Sennacherib's fall 2Ki 19:20–34
Isa 37:21–35
–Prophesied coming victory of Babylon 2Ki 20:14–18
Isa 39:3–7
–Wrote down Judah's history 2Ch 26:22
2Ch 32:32

ISCARIOT

See JUDAS

ISHBAAL

–Son of Saul 1Ch 8:33
–Tried to succeed Saul as king 2Sa 2:8–11
–Had conflict with his general, Abner 2Sa 3:6–11
–Murdered by two supporters of David 2Sa 4:1–12

ISHMAEL

–Son of Abram by Hagar ... Ge 16:15–16
1Ch 1:28
–Blessed, but not the son of the covenant .... Ge 17:18–21
Gal 4:21–31
–Teased Isaac at Isaac's weaning .... Ge 21:8–9
–Sent away with his mother by Sarah .... Ge 21:8–21
–With Isaac, buried Abraham .... Ge 25:9–11
–Married and fathered children .... Ge 25:12–16
1Ch 1:29–31
–His death .... Ge 25:17

ISRAEL

A. Israel in the Old Testament
1. Name God gave Jacob
–Given after wrestling with God .... Ge 32:28
–His sons called the sons of Israel .... Ge 46:8
See JACOB
2. The nation of God's people
–Each son became a tribe .... Ge 49:28
–Together became known as Israelites .. Ex 1:9
–Called the house of Israel .... Ex 40:38
–Called Israel .... Jdg 2:7
Ps 14:7
Isa 43:1,22, 28
–Specifically, the northern kingdom ... 1Ki 12:16–17
–Israel (northern kingdom) destroyed 2Ki 17:18
–Thereupon Judah was called Israel 2Ch 29:24
–Returned exiles called Israel .... Ezr 2:2,70
Ne 12:47

B. Israel in the New Testament
1. The Jewish nation .... Mt 10:6
Jn 3:10
Php 3:5
2. Spiritual use of Israel
–Spiritual descendants of Abraham .... Ro 9:6–8
–Jewish Christians as true Israel .... Eph 3:6
–The church is true Israel .... Gal 6:16
–The total sum of God's people ...... Ro 11:26

ISSACHAR

A. Son of Jacob by Leah ... Ge 35:23
1Ch 2:1
–Name means "reward" .... Ge 30:18
–Went to Egypt with family .... Ge 46:8,13
–Father of four sons .... Ge 46:13
–Blessed by Jacob ...... Ge 49:14–15

B. Tribe descended from Issachar
–Blessed by Moses ..... Dt 33:18–19
–Numbered .... Nu 1:29
Nu 26:25
–Allotted land .... Jos 19:17–23
Eze 48:25
–Assisted Deborah ...... Jdg 5:15
–One of the tribes of the 144,000 .... Rev 7:7

ITHAMAR

–Son of Aaron .... Ex 6:23
1Ch 6:3
–Had duties at tabernacle .... Ex 38:21
–Served as priest during lifetime of Aaron .... Nu 3:4
–Supervised Gershonites and Merarites .... Nu 4:22,33
–Founded one of the Levitical families 1Ch 24:4–6

JACOB

A. Family data
–Second son of Isaac and Rebekah .... Ge 25:26
–Twin brother of Esau .. Ge 25:24–25
–Married Leah and Rachel .... Ge 29:16–30
–Father of twelve sons and one daughter ...... Ge 29:31–30:24
Ge 35:16–18,23–26
Ge 46:8–27
1Ch 2:1–2

B. History of his life
1. Before his arrival in Haran
–A quiet man who stayed at home ..... Ge 25:27
–Bought Esau's birthright .... Ge 25:29–34
–Tricked Isaac into blessing him .... Ge 27:1–37
–Fled to Haran because of Esau's anger .... Ge 27:41
Ge 28:1–5
–Had dream at Bethel .... Ge 28:10–22
–God renewed Abraham's covenant with him .... Ge 28:13–15
2. At Haran
–Arrived in Haran .... Ge 29:1–8
–Met and stayed at Uncle Laban's ...... Ge 29:9–14
–Served Laban for Leah and Rachel .... Ge 29:16–30
–Became father of many children ...... Ge 29:31–30:24
–Worked for wages to be paid in goats .... Ge 30:25–43
–Decided to return to Canaan .... Ge 31:1–21
–Pursued by Laban ... Ge 31:22–55
3. Upon return to Canaan
–Devised scheme to make peace with Esau .... Ge 32:1–21
–Wrestled with God .. Ge 32:22–26
–Name changed to Israel .... Ge 32:27–30
–Reconciled with Esau .... Ge 33:1–17
–Settled in Shechem .. Ge 33:18–20
–Returned to Bethel .. Ge 35:1–15
–Grieved over disappearance of Joseph .. Ge 37:31–35
–Sent sons to Egypt during famine ...... Ge 42:1–5
Ge 43:1–15
4. In Egypt
–Moved to Egypt .... Ge 46:1–7
–Met Pharaoh .... Ge 47:7–11
–Blessed Ephraim and Manasseh .... Ge 48:1–20
–Blessed each of his sons .... Ge 49:1–28
Heb 11:21
–His death .... Ge 49:29–33
–Buried back in Canaan .... Ge 50:1–14

C. Significance in the New Testament
–Samaritans considered Jacob their father ...... Jn 4:7–12
–Demonstrates God's purpose in election ...... Ro 9:11–13
–Is an example of faith .. Heb 11:21

D. Name became a synonym for all Israelites .... Nu 23:7
Ps 14:7
Isa 43:1,22, 28
Ro 11:26

JAEL

–Woman who killed Sisera .. Jdg 4:17–22
–Praised by Deborah .... Jdg 5:24–27

JAIR

–Judge from Gilead .... Jdg 10:3–5

JAIRUS

–Synagogue ruler whose daughter Jesus raised ...... Mk 5:22–43
Lk 8:41–56

JAMES

A. A disciple of Jesus
–Son of Zebedee and brother of John .... Mt 4:21–22
Mk 3:17
–Originally a fisherman . Mt 4:21
–Wanted hostile Samaritans killed .... Lk 9:52–55
–Observed the transfiguration .... Mt 17:1–13
Mk 9:1–13
–Sought top place in Jesus' kingdom .... Mk 10:35–45
–Accompanied Jesus to Gethsemane .... Mt 26:36–46
–One of the apostles .... Ac 1:13
–Killed by Herod .... Ac 12:2

B. Another disciple of Jesus
–Son of Alphaeus .... Mt 10:3
Mk 3:18
–One of the apostles .... Ac 1:13

C. Son of Joseph and Mary .... Mt 13:55
–A brother of the Lord Jesus .... Gal 1:19
–Brother of Jude .... Jude 1
–Did not believe in Jesus .... Jn 7:3–5
–Met the risen Lord 1Co 15:7
–Stayed with believers before Pentecost .... Ac 1:13
–Became leader of the Jerusalem church ...... Ac 12:17
Gal 2:9,12
–Proposed solution at the council in Jerusalem ... Ac 15:12–21
–Visited by Paul .... Ac 21:18
Gal 1:19
–Wrote the letter of James .... Jas 1:1

JAPHETH

–Son of Noah .... Ge 5:32
1Ch 1:4–5
–With Shem, covered his father with a garment ...... Ge 9:23
–Blessed by Noah .... Ge 9:27
–Sons listed .... Ge 10:2–5

JEALOUSY

–An emotion expressing possessiveness; related to zeal

A. Jealousy as a positive emotion
1. In humans
–Jealous for the things of the Lord .... Nu 25:11–13
1Ki 19:10,14
–Jealous for faithfulness in marriage .... Pr 6:34
SS 8:6
–Jealous for the purity of the church 2Co 11:2
2. In God
–He is jealous for his people .... Joel 2:18
Zec 1:14
Zec 8:2
–He jealously tolerates no rivals .... Ex 20:5
Jos 24:19
1Co 10:21–22
–Sin arouses him to jealousy .... Ps 78:58
Na 1:2
–His name is Jealous . Ex 34:14

B. Jealousy as a negative emotion
1. Sins that it leads to
–To envy .... Ge 37:11
Ps 106:16–18
–To discontent .... Ge 30:1
–To quarreling 1Co 3:3–4
–To verbal abuse ..... Ac 13:45
–To intense anger .... Pr 27:4
–To persecution ...... Ac 5:17–18
2. The command to get rid of jealousy .... Ro 13:13
2Co 12:20
Gal 5:20

JECONIAH

See JEHOIACHIN

JEHOAHAZ

A. Son of Jehu; king of Israel 2Ki 13:1–9

B. Son of Josiah; king of Judah 2Ki 23:31–34
2Ch 36:1–4

JEHOASH

A. A king of Judah
See JOASH

B. Son of Jehoahaz; king of Israel 2Ki 13:10–11
–Defeated Arameans three times 2Ki 13:14–25
–Defeated Amaziah, king of Judah 2Ki 14:1–16
2Ch 25:17–24

JEHOIACHIN

–Son of Jehoiakim; king of Judah 2Ki 24:8–9
2Ch 36:8–9
–Brought to Babylon by Nebuchadnezzar 2Ki 24:10–15
2Ch 36:10
Jer 24:1

–Freed from prison in Babylon 2Ki 25:27–30
Jer 52:31–34

JEHOIADA
–A priest during Athaliah's reign 2Ki 11:1–4
–Son-in-law of King Jehoram 2Ch 22:11
–Helped hide Joash for six years in temple 2Ch 22:11–12
–Arranged for crowning of Joash as king 2Ki 11:5–16
2Ch 23:1–15
–Decided to rid the land of idols 2Ki 11:17–20
2Ch 23:16–17
–Managed the temple 2Ch 23:18–21
–Advised Joash 2Ki 12:2
2Ch 24:2
–With Joash, repaired the temple 2Ki 12:4–16
2Ch 24:3–14
–His death 2Ch 24:15–16

JEHOIAKIM
–Son of Josiah; king of Judah 2Ki 23:34
–Had conflict with Nebuchadnezzar 2Ki 24:1–6
2Ch 36:5–8
–Killed the prophet Uriah Jer 26:20–23
–Burned scroll of Jeremiah's prophecies Jer 36:16–26

JEHORAM
A. Son of Jehoshaphat; king of Judah 2Ki 8:16–19
2Ch 21:4–7
–Warred against Edom 2Ki 8:20–22
–Prophesied against by Elijah 2Ch 21:12–15
–Warred against the Philistines 2Ch 21:16–17
–Killed by the Lord 2Ch 21:18–19
B. A king of Israel
See JORAM

JEHOSHAPHAT
–Son of Asa; king of Judah 1Ki 22:41–44
2Ch 17:1
–Strengthened his kingdom 2Ch 17:2–19
–Joined with Ahab of Israel against Aram 1Ki 22:1–33
2Ch 18:1–32
–Appointed judges 2Ch 19:4–11
–Joined with Joram of Israel against Moab 2Ki 3:5–27
–Miraculously delivered from Moab and Ammon 2Ch 20:1–26
–Prayed intensely to the Lord 2Ch 20:5–12
–Punished for alliance with Israel 2Ch 20:35–37

JEHU
A. Prophet who spoke against Baasha 1Ki 16:1–4, 12
B. King of Israel 2Ki 9:6
–Elijah told to anoint him king 1Ki 19:16
–Anointed by servant of Elisha 2Ki 9:1–13
–Appointed to obliterate house of Ahab 2Ki 9:6–10
–Killed Joram and Ahaziah 2Ki 9:14–29
2Ch 22:7–9
–Killed Jezebel 2Ki 9:30–37
–Killed relatives of Ahab 2Ki 10:1–17
–Killed ministers of Baal 2Ki 10:18–29
–His death 2Ki 10:30–36

JEPHTHAH
–Judge from Gilead Jdg 11:1–3
–Delivered Israel from Ammon Jdg 11:4–33
–Made a rash vow affecting his daughter Jdg 11:30–40
–Punished the Ephraimites Jdg 12:1–6
–His death Jdg 12:7

JEREMIAH
–Prophet to kingdom of Judah Jer 1:1–3
–Called by the Lord Jer 1:4–19
–Composed laments at Josiah's death 2Ch 35:25
–His life threatened for continuing to prophesy Jer 11:18–23
Jer 26:1–16
–Put in stocks Jer 20:1–3
–Opposed by Hananiah Jer 28:1–17
–Wrote scroll that was burned by king Jer 36:1–26
–Rewrote the scroll Jer 36:27–32
–Imprisoned; Zedekiah sought his advice Jer 37:1–21
–Charged with treason and thrown into cistern Jer 38:1–13
–Zedekiah sought his advice again Jer 38:14–27
–Purchased field just before Jerusalem destroyed Jer 32:1–15
–Taken with some of the people to Egypt Jer 43:1–7

JERICHO
A. Identity
–Located in a valley Dt 34:3
–Near the Jordan River Nu 33:50
–Called "City of the Palms" Dt 34:3
B. History of the city
1. In the Old Testament
–Rahab lived there Jos 2:1
–Israelites spied it out Jos 2:1–21
–Israelites camped opposite it Jos 3:16
–Israelites marched around it Jos 6:1–15
–Its walls collapsed Jos 6:20
–All except Rahab destroyed Jos 6:21–25
–Joshua pronounced curse on rebuilding it Jos 6:26
–Curse fulfilled when Hiel rebuilt it 1Ki 16:34
–A company of prophets stationed there 2Ki 2:5
–It was reinhabited 2Ch 28:15
Ne 3:2
2. In the New Testament
–Good Samaritan headed towards it Lk 10:30–35
–Jesus healed Bartimaeus there Mk 10:46–52
Lk 18:35–43
–Jesus healed two blind men there Mt 20:29–34
–Zacchaeus lived there Lk 19:1–10

JEROBOAM
A. First king of the northern kingdom
–An official of king Solomon 1Ki 11:26–28
–Ahijah prophesied he would be king 1Ki 11:29–39
–Fled to Egypt 1Ki 11:40
–Led rebellion against Rehoboam 1Ki 12:18–19
–Became king of the northern kingdom 1Ki 12:20
–Instituted idolatry 1Ki 12:25–33
–Judged for idolatry 1Ki 13:1–6
1Ki 14:1–18
–His death 1Ki 14:19–20
B. Son of Jehoash; king of Israel 2Ki 14:23–29
–Denounced by Amos Am 7:10–11

JERUBBAAL
See GIDEON

JERUSALEM
A. Important names for this city
–Salem Ge 14:18
Ps 76:2
–Jebus 1Ch 11:4
–Jerusalem 2Sa 5:6
–Zion 2Sa 5:7
Ps 48:12
–The city of David 2Sa 6:12,16
1Ki 2:10
–The city of the great King Ps 48:2
–The city of God Ps 46:4
Ps 87:3
–The city of the LORD Isa 60:14
–The city of righteousness Isa 1:26
–The faithful city Zec 8:3
–The holy city Ne 11:1,18
Isa 48:2
–The LORD is there Eze 48:35
–Moriah Ge 22:1–2
2Ch 3:1
–Ariel Isa 29:1
B. Significant historical events of Jerusalem
–Abraham's "sacrifice" of Isaac Ge 22:1–18
–King of Jerusalem conquered by Joshua Jos 10:1–14
–City given to the tribe of Benjamin Jos 18:28
–Conquered by David; became his capital 2Sa 5:6–10
–Temple built there 2Ch 3:1
–Became capital of the southern kingdom 1Ki 14:21
–Destroyed by Nebuchadnezzar 2Ch 36:19
–The center of Jewish life after exile Ezr 1:5
Mt 2:1,3
–Jesus entered it as king Mt 21:9–10
–Jesus was crucified there Lk 9:31
Lk 24:18
–Holy Spirit poured out there Ac 2:1–5
–Gospel spread out from there Lk 24:47
Ac 1:8
–First council of the church held there Ac 15:1–2
Gal 2:1–5
–Jesus predicted its destruction Lk 19:42–44
Lk 21:20–24
C. Spiritual significance of Jerusalem
–The city chosen by God 1Ki 11:13
–The place where God put his Name Dt 12:11
1Ki 14:21
–The city that Jews prayed towards 1Ki 8:44
Da 6:10
–The place from which God's word comes Isa 2:3
–The place from which God rules Ps 48:1–3, 12–14
Ps 99:1–2
–The place from which the Messiah rules Isa 9:6–7
–The site of history's final battle Zec 14:1–5
Rev 20:7–10
–A symbol of the church Gal 4:26
Heb 12:22
–Heaven as the new Jerusalem Rev 3:12
Rev 21:2, 10–27

JESSE
–Grandson of Boaz and Ruth; father of David Ru 4:17–22
–Visited by Samuel 1Sa 16:1–13
–Had eight sons 1Sa 16:8–11
1Sa 17:12
–Sent David to enter Saul's service 1Sa 16:18–20
–Sent David to visit his brothers at battle 1Sa 17:17–19

JESUS CHRIST
A. His divine nature
1. Preexistence with God
–Asserted in the Old Testament Isa 9:6–7
Mic 5:2
–Asserted in the New Testament Jn 1:1
Php 2:6
Col 1:15–17
Rev 1:4,8
2. Divine names ascribed to him
–God Jn 1:1
Heb 1:8
1Jn 5:20
–God over all Ro 9:5
–God with us Isa 7:14
Mt 1:23
–Our God and Savior Tit 2:13
2Pe 1:1
–Lord Ac 2:36
Ro 10:9
Php 2:11
Col 2:6
–Lord of all Ac 10:36
–Lord and God Jn 20:28
–Lord and Savior 2Pe 1:11
2Pe 2:20
2Pe 3:18
–Lord of glory 1Co 2:8
–Lord of lords Rev 17:14
Rev 19:16
–Alpha and Omega Rev 1:8
Rev 21:5–6
–The living one Rev 1:18
–The Holy One of God Mk 1:24
–The Holy and Righteous One Ac 3:14
–The "I am" Jn 8:58
3. His relationship with the Father
–Equal with the Father Jn 5:18
Jn 10:33
Php 2:6
–One with the Father Jn 10:33
Jn 17:22
4. Divine qualities ascribed to him
–Has the fullness of God Col 2:9
–Was involved in creation Jn 1:3
Col 1:16
Heb 1:2
–Has the glory of God Jn 1:14
Heb 1:3
–Preserves creation Col 1:17
Heb 1:3
–Is present everywhere Mt 28:20
–Is all-powerful Mt 28:18
Php 3:21
–Knows everything Jn 2:24–25
Jn 6:61,64
–Is unchanging Heb 1:12
Heb 13:8
–Has the power to forgive sins Mk 2:5–11
Lk 7:48
–Receives worship from people Mt 2:11
Rev 5:11–14
–Receives worship from angels Heb 1:6
–We must believe in him as we do in God Jn 14:1
Ac 16:31–34
B. His human nature
1. Had a human genealogy Mt 1:1–17
Lk 3:23–28
2. His birth and childhood
–Conceived in Mary's womb Mt 1:20
Lk 1:26–37
–His human birth Mt 1:25
Lk 2:1–7
–Circumcised on the eighth day Lk 2:21
–Visited the temple as a boy Lk 2:41–51
–Grew as anyone else does Lk 2:52
3. His suffering, death and burial

–Bloody sweat in the garden .... Lk 22:44
–Death on the cross .... Mt 27:50; Jn 19:33; Php 2:7–8
–Blood and water flowed from his wound .... Jn 19:34–35
–Body taken down from the cross .... Lk 23:53
–Body prepared and laid in a tomb .... Jn 19:39–41
–Burial clothes used .... Jn 20:6–7

4. His resurrection and ascension
–His resurrection on Easter Sunday .... Mt 28:1–15; Lk 24:1–8
–His appearances for forty days .... Lk 24:9–49; Jn 20:1–29; Ac 1:1–5
–His body still a human body .... Lk 24:40–43; Jn 20:24–29
–His ascension into heaven .... Lk 24:50–51; Ac 1:9–11

5. He had human characteristics
–Could be touched .... Mk 5:27–32; Jn 20:27; 1Jn 1:1
–Became hungry .... Mt 4:2; Mt 21:18
–Became thirsty .... Jn 19:28
–Became tired .... Jn 4:6
–Needed sleep .... Mt 8:20; Mk 4:38
–Showed compassion .... Mt 9:36; Mk 8:2
–Showed anger and indignation .... Mk 10:14; Jn 2:13–16
–Wept .... Lk 19:41; Jn 11:35

6. His human nature specifically mentioned
–He became flesh .... Jn 1:14
–He shared our humanity .... Heb 2:14
–He is like us in all things=mexcept sin .... Heb 2:17; Heb 4:15
–We must acknowledge that Jesus came in the flesh 1Jn 4:2; 2Jn 7

C. His most important names
–Jesus, our Savior .... Mt 1:21
–Immanuel .... Mt 1:23
–Christ, the Messiah .... Mt 16:16; Ac 17:3
–The Son of God .... Mk 1:1; Jn 20:31
–The Holy One of God .... Mk 1:24
–The capstone .... Mk 12:10
–The Word of God .... Jn 1:1; Rev 19:13
–The Lamb of God .... Jn 1:36
–The bridegroom of the church .... Jn 3:29
–The Prophet .... Jn 6:14
–The bread of life .... Jn 6:48
–The light of the world .... Jn 8:12
–The good shepherd .... Jn 10:11; Heb 13:20; 1Pe 5:4
–The resurrection and the life .... Jn 11:25
–The King of Israel .... Jn 12:13
–The way, the truth, the life .... Jn 14:6
–King of the Jews .... Jn 19:19–21
–The author of life .... Ac 3:15
–Leader and Savior .... Ac 5:31
–Son of Man .... Ac 7:56
–Judge of the living and the dead .... Ac 10:42
–Lord .... Ro 10:9; Php 2:11
–The Lord of glory 1Co 2:8
–Our Passover lamb 1Co 5:8
–The second Adam 1Co 15:45–47
–Husband of the church 2Co 11:2
–Head of the church .... Col 1:18
–The mediator 1Ti 2:5
–The righteous Judge 2Ti 4:8
–Great high priest .... Heb 4:14
–Alpha and Omega .... Rev 1:8
–The lion of the tribe of Judah .... Rev 5:5
–Lord of lords .... Rev 17:14
–The Root and descendant of David .... Rev 22:16
–The bright morning star .... Rev 22:16

D. His work on earth and in heaven

1. His work on earth
–Did his Father's will .... Mt 26:39; Jn 4:34; Jn 6:38
–Fulfilled the Old Testament .... Mt 5:17
–Came to seek and save the lost .... Lk 19:10
–Came to give us eternal life .... Jn 10:10,28
–Gave his life as a ransom for many .... Mk 10:45
–Made an atoning sacrifice .... Ro 3:25; 1Jn 2:2
–Died for our sins .... 1Co 15:3; Gal 1:4; 1Pe 3:18
–Reconciled us to God .... 2Co 5:18–19; Eph 2:14–17
–Rose again for our justification .... Ro 4:25
–Destroyed the works of Satan .... Heb 2:14; 1Jn 3:8

2. His work as God's Anointed One
–Called the anointed one .... Ps 2:2; Ac 4:26
–His anointing as prophet .... Jn 6:14; Ac 3:21–23; Heb 1:1
–His anointing as priest .... Heb 6:20; Heb 9:11–14,23–28
–His anointing as king .... Jn 12:13; Rev 19:13–16

3. His work as the exalted Lord in heaven
–Sent out the Spirit .... Jn 15:26; Ac 2:32–33
–Rules the world at God's right hand .... 1Co 15:25; Heb 1:3–4
–Rules the church at God's right hand .... Eph 1:20–22; Col 1:18
–Makes intercession for us .... Ro 8:34; Heb 7:25
–Will overcome all his enemies .... 1Co 15:26–28; Rev 17:14; Rev 19:11–21
–Will come again to take us to himself 1Th 5:16–17
–Will come again to judge humanity .... Ac 10:42; 2Co 5:10; 2Ti 4:1

See also TRINITY

JETHRO

–Father-in-law of Moses; priest of Midian .... Ex 3:1
–Also called Reuel .... Nu 10:29
–Owned flocks of sheep .... Ex 2:16–20
–Permitted Moses to return to Egypt from Midian .... Ex 4:18
–Brought wife and sons to Moses in desert .... Ex 18:1–7
–Acknowledged power of the Lord .... Ex 18:9–12
–Advised Moses to appoint judges for Israel .... Ex 18:13–27

JEW

A. Their identity
–Name given to God's people in Babylon .... Est 3:4–6; Est 8:9; Jer 32:12; Jer 44:1
–Jews returned to Jerusalem .... Ezr 5:1,5; Ne 4:1–2
–Jews lived all over the world .... Zec 8:23; Ac 24:5

B. The Jews in the New Testament

1. Their history
–Many opposed Jesus .... Jn 5:15–16; Jn 9:22
–They asked for Jesus' death .... Jn 19:4–12; 1Th 2:14–16
–First Christians were Jews .... Ac 2:5–14
–Jews continued to become believers .... Ac 14:1; Ac 17:4,12
–The Jews persecuted the apostles .... Ac 9:23; Ac 13:50; Ac 17:5–9, 13

2. Paul and the Jews
–Paul was proud to be a Jew .... Php 3:4–5
–His message was to the Jew first .... Ac 13:46; Ro 1:16
–Jews were as sinful as Gentiles .... Ro 2:9–10
–Christ is Savior of Jew and Gentile .... Ro 10:12–13; 1Co 1:24
–True Jew is marked by inner regeneration .... Ro 2:28–29
–Paul's sorrow over Jews rejecting Jesus .... Ro 9:1–5
–Salvation of Gentiles would arouse Jews .... Ro 11:13–15

JEZEBEL

–Sidonian wife of Ahab 1Ki 16:31
–Promoted Baal worship 1Ki 16:32–33
–Killed prophets of the Lord 1Ki 18:4,13
–Opposed Elijah 1Ki 19:1–2
–Had Naboth killed 1Ki 21:1–15
–Death prophesied 1Ki 21:23
–Killed by Jehu 2Ki 9:30–37
–Became a symbol of wickedness .... Rev 2:20

JOAB

–Nephew of David 1Ch 2:16
–Commander of David's army 2Sa 8:16
–Defeated Ishbaal and his army 2Sa 2:10–32
–Killed Abner 2Sa 3:22–27
–Captured the city of Jerusalem 1Ch 11:6
–Defeated Ammon 2Sa 10:7–19; 1Ch 19:8–19
–Put Uriah in front line of battle 2Sa 11:16–24
–Defeated Rabbah 1Ch 20:1–3
–Devised plan to reconcile David and Absalom 2Sa 14:1–24
–Killed Absalom 2Sa 18:9–15
–Rebuked David's grief over Absalom's death 2Sa 19:1–8
–Put down Sheba's revolt 2Sa 20:1–22
–Tried to convince David not to number his men 2Sa 24:1–4
–Numbered David's men 2Sa 24:9
–Supported Adonijah over Solomon 1Ki 1:7
–Killed under Solomon's orders 1Ki 2:28–34

JOASH

–Son of Ahaziah; king of Judah 2Ki 11:2
–Sheltered from Athaliah 2Ki 11:2–3; 2Ch 22:11–12
–Proclaimed king by Jehoiada at seven years of age 2Ki 11:4–12, 21; 2Ch 23:1–11
–Repaired the temple 2Ki 12:1–16; 2Ch 24:1–14
–Gave temple objects to king of Aram 2Ki 12:17–18
–Later led the people into idolatry 2Ch 24:17–19
–Assassinated 2Ki 12:20; 2Ch 24:23–25

JOB

–A God-fearing man from Uz .... Job 1:1
–Very wealthy .... Job 1:1–3
–His righteousness tested by disaster .... Job 1:6–22
–His righteousness tested by affliction .... Job 2:7–8
–His three friends tried to comfort him .... Job 2:11–13
–Cursed the day of his birth .... Job 3:1–26
–Gave rebuttals to Eliphaz .... Job 6:1—7:21; Job 16:1—17:16; Job 23:1—24:25
–Gave rebuttals to Bildad .... Job 9:1—10:22; Job 19:1–29; Job 26:1—31:40
–Gave rebuttals to Zophar .... Job 12:1—13:28; Job 21:1–34
–Repented .... Job 42:1–6
–Prayed for his friends .... Job 42:10
–Was made prosperous again .... Job 42:10–17
–Considered an example of righteousness .... Eze 14:14,20
–Considered an example of perseverance .... Jas 5:11

JOCHEBED

–Mother of Moses and Aaron .... Ex 6:20; Nu 26:59
–Hid Moses from the Egyptians .... Ex 2:1–2
–Hid Moses among the reeds .... Ex 2:3–4
–Was asked to take care of Moses .... Ex 2:7–10
–Considered an example of faith .... Heb 11:23

JOHN

A. John the Baptist
–His birth announced to his father Zechariah .... Lk 1:11–20
–Mother Elizabeth conceived .... Lk 1:23–25
–His birth .... Lk 1:57–66
–Ministered in the wilderness of Judea .... Mt 3:1–12; Mk 1:2–8
–Preached a baptism of repentance .... Lk 3:7–14; Ac 13:24; Ac 19:3–4
–Witnessed concerning Jesus .... Mt 3:11–12; Mk 1:7–8; Jn 1:29–36
–Said Jesus must become greater .... Jn 3:25–30
–Baptized Jesus .... Mt 3:13–17; Lk 3:21–22
–Expressed doubts about Jesus .... Mt 11:2–6; Lk 7:18–23
–Arrested by Herod .... Mt 4:12; Mk 1:14
–Beheaded by Herod .... Mt 14:1–12; Mk 6:14–29
–Fulfilled prophecy about Elijah .... Mt 11:7–19; Mk 9:11–13

B. A disciple of Jesus

1. Events during Jesus' lifetime
–Son of Zebedee and brother of James .... Mt 4:21–22; Mk 3:17
–Originally a fisherman .... Mt 4:21
–Uneducated .... Ac 4:13
–Wanted hostile Samaritans killed .... Lk 9:52–55
–Observed the transfiguration .... Mt 17:1–13; Mk 9:2–13

–Sought top place in Jesus' kingdom ..... Mk 10:35–45
–With Peter, prepared for the Passover .... Lk 22:8
–Accompanied Jesus to Gethsemane ...... Mt 26:36–45
–Was called the disciple whom Jesus loved .... Jn 13:23; Jn 19:26; Jn 20:2; Jn 21:7,20
–Jesus committed his mother to him ...... Jn 19:26–27
–Ran to the tomb on Easter Sunday ...... Jn 20:2–8
–Breakfast with Jesus after resurrection .... Jn 21:1–14
2. Events after Jesus' ascension
–One of the apostles . Ac 1:13
–Healed a lame man with Peter .... Ac 3:1–8
–Arrested with Peter .. Ac 4:1–3
–Questioned before the Sanhedrin .... Ac 4:7–21
–Sent to new Christians in Samaria ...... Ac 8:14–17
–Involved in the council at Jerusalem ...... Gal 2:9
–Wrote letters as "the elder" 2Jn 1; 3Jn 1
–Exiled to Patmos .... Rev 1:9
–The prophet who wrote Revelation .... Rev 1:1–33; Rev 22:8

C. Cousin of Barnabas *See* MARK

JONAH
–Prophet in the days of Jeroboam II 2Ki 14:25
–Called to preach to city of Nineveh .... Jnh 1:1–2
–Fled to Tarshish .... Jnh 1:3
–His flight caused a storm .. Jnh 1:4–12
–Thrown overboard .... Jnh 1:13–16
–Swallowed by fish .... Jnh 1:17
–Prayed while inside the fish .... Jnh 2:1–9
–Called a second time to preach to Nineveh .... Jnh 3:1–4
–Reproved by the Lord ...... Jnh 4:1–11
–His life considered a sign of resurrection .... Mt 12:39–41; Lk 11:29–32

JONATHAN
–Oldest son of King Saul ... 1Sa 14:49
–Attacked Philistines 1Sa 13:3–4; 1Sa 14:1–14
–Ate honey in disobedience to Saul 1Sa 14:24–45
–Became David's best friend 1Sa 18:1
–Made covenant with David . 1Sa 18:3–4; 1Sa 20:16–17; 1Sa 23:16–18
–Informed David of Saul's plans 1Sa 19:1–3
–Interceded for David 1Sa 19:4–6
–Warned David to flee 1Sa 20:18–42
–Killed in battle 1Sa 31:2

JORAM
A. Son of Ahab; king of Israel 2Ki 1:17; 2Ki 3:1–3
–Fought with Jehoshaphat against Moab 2Ki 3:4–27
–Wounded in battle against Hazael 2Ki 8:25–29; 2Ch 22:5–6
–Killed by Jehu 2Ki 9:14–26; 2Ch 22:7–8

B. King of Judah *See* JEHORAM

JORDAN
–The river flowing from the Sea of Galilee to the Dead Sea

A. In the time of the patriarchs
–Well-watered plain where Lot settled ...... Ge 13:10–11
–Jacob crossed it, going to Haran .... Ge 32:10
–Jacob's sons mourned Jacob's death there ..... Ge 50:10–11

B. In the time of Moses and Joshua
–Israelites camped along it .... Nu 22:1
–A census taken there ... Nu 26:1–4
–Some Israelites given land east of the Jordan . Nu 32:1–33; Nu 34:10–15
–Israelites crossed the Jordan .... Jos 3:1–17; Ps 114:3,5
–Twelve stones from the Jordan formed a memorial .... Jos 4:1–9
–Canaanites afraid because of the crossing . Jos 5:1

C. In the time of the judges and kings
–Controlling the Jordan important in war .... Jdg 3:28; Jdg 7:24–25; Jdg 12:5–6
–David fled from Absalom across the Jordan .. 2Sa 17:21–22
–Elijah miraculously crossed the Jordan 2Ki 2:7–8
–Elisha miraculously crossed the Jordan 2Ki 2:13–14
–Naaman cured by washing in the Jordan 2Ki 5:9–14
–Axhead floated in the Jordan 2Ki 6:1–7

D. In the New Testament
–John the Baptist baptized there .... Mt 3:6; Mk 1:5; Lk 3:3
–Jesus was baptized in the Jordan .... Mt 3:13–17; Mk 1:9–11; Lk 3:21–22
–Jesus ministered across the Jordan .... Mt 19:1; Mk 10:1; Jn 10:40–42

JOSEPH
A. Son of Jacob by Rachel
1. His life in Canaan
–His birth .... Ge 30:24
–Name means "may he add" .... Ge 30:24
–Favored by Jacob, hated by brothers ... Ge 37:3–4
–His dreams .... Ge 37:5–11
–Sold by brothers to Midianites .... Ge 37:12–36
2. His life in Egypt
–Served under Potiphar .... Ge 39:1–19
–Put into prison ...... Ge 39:20–23
–Interpreted dreams of Pharaoh's servants .. Ge 40:1–19
–Interpreted dreams of Pharaoh .... Ge 41:14–40
–Was appointed ruler in Egypt .... Ge 41:41–57
–Father of two sons .. Ge 41:50–52
–Treated brothers harshly during famine .... Ge 42:6–24
–Ordered return of money to his brothers .... Ge 42:25–28
–Had meal with all his brothers .... Ge 43:26–34
–Ordered silver cup put in Benjamin's sack .... Ge 44:1–13
–Revealed himself to his brothers .... Ge 45:1–15
–Invited his family to live in Egypt ...... Ge 45:16–28
–Brought Jacob and sons to Egypt .... Ge 46:1–47:12
–Joseph's administration ...... Ge 47:13–26
–Had Jacob bless Ephraim and Manasseh .... Ge 48:1–22
–Blessed by Jacob ... Ge 49:22–26
–His death .... Ge 50:22–26; Heb 11:22
–Bones taken back to Canaan .... Jos 24:32
3. Tribe divided into Ephraim and Manasseh .... Dt 33:13–17
See EPHRAIM MANASSEH
–One of the tribes of the 144,000 .... Rev 7:8

B. Husband of Mary, mother of Jesus .... Mt 1:16; Lk 1:27
–Considered not marrying Mary .... Mt 1:18–19
–Visited by angel .... Mt 1:20–24
–Went to Bethlehem during census .... Lk 2:1–5
–Gave name "Jesus" to Mary's son .... Mt 1:25
–Circumcised Jesus; presented him in the temple .... Lk 2:21–24
–Took Mary and Jesus to Egypt .... Mt 2:13–15
–Returned and settled in Nazareth .... Mt 2:19–23
–Went to Jerusalem for Passover .... Lk 2:41–51

C. A rich man from Arimathea .... Mt 27:57
–A member of the Jewish Council .... Mk 15:43
–Had not consented to Jesus' crucifixion ...... Lk 23:51
–A secret disciple of Jesus .... Jn 19:38
–With Nicodemus, prepared Jesus' body ...... Jn 19:39–40
–Buried Jesus in Joseph's own tomb .... Mt 27:58–60; Mk 15:43–46; Jn 19:41–42

D. A companion of Paul *See* BARNABAS

JOSHUA
A. Son of Nun; name changed from Hoshea ... Nu 13:8,16; 1Ch 7:27
1. Ministry under Moses
–Fought Amalekites .. Ex 17:9–14
–Accompanied Moses on Mount Sinai ..... Ex 24:13; Ex 32:17
–Spied out Canaan .... Nu 13:8,16–25
–Encouraged Israelites to enter Canaan ..... Nu 14:6–9
–Allowed to enter land .... Nu 14:30
–Appointed as Moses' successor .... Nu 27:12–23; Dt 31:1–8
2. Leader of Israelites into Canaan
–Encouraged by the Lord as leader ...... Jos 1:1–9
–Charged Israel to conquer Canaan ..... Jos 1:10–16
–Led Israelites through the Jordan .... Jos 3:1–17
–Had stone memorial built at the Jordan .. Jos 4:1–9
–Circumcised Israelites .... Jos 5:1–9
–Visited by commander of the Lord ...... Jos 5:13–15
–Conquered Jericho .. Jos 6:1–25
–Defeated at Ai ...... Jos 7:1–5
–Conquered Ai ...... Jos 8:1–28
–Deceived by Gibeonites .... Jos 9:1–27
–Conquered five kings at Gibeon .... Jos 10:1–28
–Conquered southern Canaan .... Jos 10:29–43
–Conquered northern Canaan .... Jos 11:1–12:24
–Renewed covenant .. Jos 8:30–35; Jos 24:1–27
–Divided land among tribes .... Jos 14:1–5
–His farewell .... Jos 23:1–16
–His death .... Jos 24:28–31

B. High priest during time of Zerubbabel .... Hag 1:1,12,14
–Also called Jeshua ..... Ezr 3:2
–Rebuilt the altar of the Lord .... Ezr 3:2–6
–Helped rebuild the temple .... Ezr 5:2
–Zechariah's vision of Joshua's trial in heaven .... Zec 3:1–9
–A crown for him ...... Zec 6:9–15

JOSIAH
–Son of Amon; king of Judah 2Ki 21:24; 2Ch 33:25
–Began reign when eight years old 2Ki 22:1; 2Ch 34:1
–Purged the land of idolatry . 2Ki 23:4–20, 24–25; 2Ch 34:3–7
–A prophecy concerning his reign 1Ki 13:2
–Repaired the temple 2Ki 22:3–7; 2Ch 34:8–13
–Book of Law discovered ... 2Ki 22:8–20; 2Ch 34:14–28
–Renewed the covenant 2Ki 23:1–3; 2Ch 34:29–32
–Celebrated the Passover 2Ki 23:21–23; 2Ch 35:1–19
–Killed by Pharaoh Neco 2Ki 23:29–30; 2Ch 35:20–27

JOTHAM
A. Youngest son of Gideon . Jdg 9:5
–Spoke to Shechemites against Abimelech ..... Jdg 9:7–20
–Fled to Beer .... Jdg 9:21

B. Son of Uzziah; king of Judah 2Ki 15:32–38
–Reigned while Uzziah had leprosy 2Ch 26:21
–Repaired temple and walls of Jerusalem 2Ch 27:1–4
–Defeated Ammonites ... 2Ch 27:5–6
–His death 2Ch 27:8–9

JOY
A. The nature of true joy
1. It centers in God
–In the Father .... Ps 32:11; Ro 5:11
–In the Son .... Jn 15:11; Php 4:4
–In the Holy Spirit ..... Ro 14:17; Ro 15:13; Gal 5:22
2. It can be experienced even while suffering .. Mt 5:11–12; Ac 5:41; Ro 5:3; Col 1:24; Jas 1:2–3; 1Pe 4:13
3. One aspect of the fruit of the Spirit .... Gal 5:22
4. Our joy should never end .... Php 4:4; 1Th 5:16

B. Reasons for joy
1. Expressed in the Old Testament
a. Personal joy
–For salvation ..... Isa 12:3; Isa 52:8–9
–For forgiveness .. Ps 51:7–8
–For personal well-being .... Dt 12:17–18; 1Ch 12:40
–For God's protection .... Ps 5:11–12; Ps 31:7–8
–For life in the presence of God .. Ps 16:11; Ps 21:6
–For a happy home .... Pr 5:18; Pr 23:24–25
b. National joy
–At religious festivals .... 2Ch 30:23–25; Ne 8:12,17; Est 8:16–17
–At coronations ... 1Sa 11:15; 1Ki 1:39–40
–At the dedication of the temple .... 1Ki 8:65–66; Ezr 3:10–13

–For all that the Lord does .... Ps 98:1–9; Ps 100:1–2
–For victory over enemies 1Sa 18:6–7; 2Ch 20:27–28
–For the return from exile .... Ps 126:1–3; Jer 31:10–13

2. In the New Testament
–For the birth of Jesus .... Mt 2:10; Lk 2:10,20
–For the resurrection of Jesus .... Mt 28:8; Lk 24:41,52
–For salvation .... Ac 13:48; 1Pe 1:8–9
–For our names in the book of life .... Lk 10:20
–For miraculous healing .... Ac 8:7–8
–For privilege of preaching about Christ .... Php 1:18
–For one sinner who repents .... Lk 15:7,10
–For the wedding of the Lamb .... Rev 19:7

JUDAH

A. Son of Jacob by Leah ... Ge 35:23; 1Ch 2:1
–Name means "praise" . Ge 29:35
–Spoke against killing brother Joseph .... Ge 37:25–27
–Married a woman from Adullam .... Ge 38:1–5
–Engaged in illicit sex with Tamar .... Ge 38:12–24
–Fathered Perez and Zerah by Tamar .... Ge 38:27–30
–Promised to be security for Benjamin .... Ge 43:8–10
–Interceded for Benjamin before Joseph .... Ge 44:18–34
–Went to Egypt with family .... Ge 46:8,12
–Father of five sons ..... Ge 46:12
–Blessed by Jacob ...... Ge 49:8–12

B. Tribe of Judah
–Blessed by Moses ..... Dt 33:7
–Numbered .... Nu 1:27; Nu 26:22
–Allotted land .... Jos 15; Eze 48:7
–Failed to fully possess the land .... Jos 15:63; Jdg 1:1–20
–David was from this tribe .... 1Ch 28:2–4; Mt 1:2–6
–David ruled this tribe first 2Sa 2:1–4
–Became the name for the southern kingdom .. 1Ki 12:21–22; 1Ki 14:21–22
–Taken captive to Babylon 2Ki 24:1–16
–Returned from exile .... Ezr 1:1–5
–One of the tribes of the 144,000 .... Rev 7:5

JUDAS

A. Disciple of Jesus, called Iscariot .... Mt 10:4; Mk 3:19
–Criticized Mary for wastefulness .... Jn 12:4–5
–Treasurer of disciples; pilfered money .... Jn 12:6
–Satan entered into him . Lk 22:3; Jn 13:27
–Agreed with Jews to betray Jesus .... Mt 26:14–16; Mk 14:10–11
–Identified as betrayer in upper room .... Mt 26:25; Jn 13:21–30
–Betrayed Jesus with a kiss .... Mt 26:47–49; Mk 14:43–45; Lk 22:47–48
–Returned money to the Jews .... Mt 27:3–5
–Committed suicide ..... Mt 27:5
–Died a horrible death .. Ac 1:18–19
–Better not to have been born .... Mk 14:21
–Called a devil .... Jn 6:70–71
–Jesus said he was doomed to destruction .. Jn 17:12
–Replaced by Matthias .. Ac 1:15–26

B. Another disciple of Jesus; son of James .... Lk 6:16; Jn 14:22
–Probably also called Thaddaeus .... Mt 10:3; Mk 3:18
–One of the apostles .... Ac 1:13

C. Brother of Jesus and James .... Mt 13:55; Mk 6:3
–Also called Jude .... Jude 1

D. A Christian prophet ...... Ac 15:22–32
–Also called Barsabbas .. Ac 15:22

JUDE

See JUDAS

JUDEA

A. A district governed by the Romans
–Located west of the Jordan River .... Mt 19:1
–Ruled by King Herod at birth of Jesus .... Mt 2:1–3; Lk 1:5
–Ruled by Herod's son Archelaus .... Mt 2:22
–Governed by Pilate .... Lk 3:1
–Ruled by Herod Agrippa .... Ac 12:1–3,19

B. Important towns in Judea
–Jerusalem .... Mt 2:1; Ac 26:20
–Bethlehem .... Mt 2:1; Lk 2:4
–Arimathea .... Lk 23:51

C. John the Baptist preached in wilderness of Judea ... Mt 3:1

D. Jesus and Judea
–Born in Bethlehem of Judea .... Mt 2:1–6
–Preached in synagogues of Judea .... Lk 4:44
–Ministered in Judean countryside .... Jn 3:22
–News about Jesus spread throughout Judea ...... Lk 7:17; Lk 23:5
–Many from Judea followed Jesus .... Mt 4:25; Mk 3:8; Lk 6:17
–Jesus crucified in Judea 1Th 2:14–15

E. The apostles and Judea
–Gospel was to spread throughout Judea ...... Ac 1:8
–Residents of Judea present on Pentecost ... Ac 2:5–9
–Christians scattered throughout Judea ...... Ac 8:1
–Famine aid for Christians in Judea .... Ac 11:29; Ro 15:25–26
–Christians there suffered persecution 1Th 2:14–16

JUDGE, JUDGMENT

A. Judgment done by humans
1. Official judgment
a. In the political realm
–God raised up judges for his people .... Jdg 2:16
–Ehud as judge .... Jdg 3:12–30
–Deborah as judge . Jdg 4:4–16
–Gideon as judge .. Jdg 6:11—8:32
–Jephthah as judge .... Jdg 10:6—12:7
–Samson as judge . Jdg 13:1—16:31
–Eli as judge 1Sa 4:18
–Samuel as judge .. 1Sa 7:15–17

b. In the legal realm
–Judges set up by Moses .... Ex 18:13–26; Dt 16:18–20
–Approved transactions regarding Ruth .... Ru 4:1–12
–Judges set up by Jehoshaphat 2Ch 19:5–7
–Judges set up by Ezra .... Ezr 8:25–27
–Pilate was a judge .... Mt 27:19; Jn 19:13
–Paul on trial before Gallio ..... Ac 18:12–16
–Paul on trial before Felix ..... Ac 24:1–23
–Paul on trial before Festus .... Ac 25:6–12
–Lawsuits among believers 1Co 6:1–8
–Lawsuits often instituted by the rich .... Jas 2:6–7

c. In the religious realm
–Sanhedrin against Jesus .... Mt 26:57–66
–Sanhedrin against followers of Jesus .... Jn 9:22,28–34
–Sanhedrin against Christians .... Ac 4:5–21; Ac 5:21–40; Ac 22:30—23:7
–Judgment done by the church .... 1Co 5:1–5; 1Ti 1:20; Tit 3:10–11

d. Standards for official judgment
–Two or three witnesses needed .... Dt 19:15; Mt 26:60
–Must be impartial .... Dt 1:17; Dt 16:19; Pr 24:23
–Must be fair and just .... Dt 1:16; Dt 16:20; Isa 56:1
–Oath could be required .... Ex 22:11; Heb 6:16
–Decisions made before witnesses .. Ru 4:9–11
–Casting lots sometimes used .... Pr 18:18

2. The judging attitude
–We must not judge others .... Mt 7:1–5; Ro 14:1–4,13; 1Co 4:5; 1Co 10:29; Jas 4:11–12
–We must judge ourselves .... Mt 7:3–5; Gal 6:1,4

3. Human participation in the final judgment .... Mt 19:28; Lk 22:30; 1Co 6:2–3

B. Judgment done by God
1. God described as a judge
–God as judge of all the earth .... Ge 18:25; Ps 94:2
–Christ as judge ..... Jn 5:22; Ac 10:42; 2Ti 4:1
–His judgment is always right .... Dt 32:4; Job 34:10; 2Th 1:5

2. Temporal judgments
a. Examples of those whom God judged
–The world in the flood .... Ge 7:17–23
–Sodom and Gomorrah .... Ge 19:24–26
–The firstborn in Egypt .... Ex 12:29–30
–Pharaoh and his army .... Ex 14:23–28
–The Israelites in the desert .... Nu 14:26–35
–Korah and his men .... Nu 16:31–35
–The Israelites during the judges .... Jdg 2:14–15
–Ahab and his family 2Ki 9:6–10
–The city of Samaria 2Ki 17:16–18
–The Jews in exile 2Ki 24:1–4
–Proud Nebuchadnezzar .. Da 4:29–33
–King Belshazzar .. Da 5:25–30
–The city of Jerusalem .... Lk 19:41–44
–King Herod ...... Ac 12:21–23
–The magician Elymas .... Ac 13:9–11

b. Types of temporal judgments
–Drought 1Ki 17:1
–Famine .... La 2:11–12
–Fire from heaven . 2Ki 1:10,12
–Flood .... Ge 7:17–23
–An invasion of locusts .... Joel 1:2–7
–Earthquake ...... Isa 24:18–20
–Plague 2Sa 24:15–16
–Blight and mildew .... Am 4:9
–Severe storms .... Jos 10:10–11
–Destruction of property .... Eze 33:23–29
–Exile 2Ch 36:20
–Famine of hearing God's word ...... Am 8:11
–Death 2Ki 9:8–10, 30–33

c. Purposes of temporal judgments
–To punish sin .... Ge 6:5–7; Hos 5:1,8–11
–To reveal himself as God .... Ex 9:14–16; Eze 5:13
–To purify his people .... Mal 3:2–4; Jn 15:2
–To drive his people to repentance . Am 5:6,15; Lk 13:2–5

3. The final judgment
a. Names for the final judgment
–The day of judgment 2Pe 2:9
–The day of the Lord 1Th 5:2
–The day of God's wrath .... Ro 2:5–6
–The great Day ... Jude 6
–The Day 1Co 3:13

b. The judges of the final judgment
–God as the judge . Ps 96:13; Ecc 3:17
–Administration given to Christ ... Jn 5:22; Ac 10:42; Ro 2:16

c. Those who are to be judged
–The living and the dead .... Ac 10:42
–All nations ...... Mt 25:31–32
–All people .... 2Co 5:10; Heb 9:27; Rev 20:11–14

d. Time of the final judgment: unknown .... Mt 24:36–42; Lk 12:40; 1Th 5:1–3

e. The basis of the final judgment
–Our faith in Jesus .... Jn 3:16–18; Jn 5:24–26
–Our sincere commitment to Jesus . Mt 7:22–23
–Our being heirs of God .... Mt 25:34
–Our names being in the book of life .... Rev 20:15
–Our adherence to God's law .... Ro 2:12–16; Jas 2:12
–What we've done with God's gifts .. Lk 12:48
–Our actions ...... Ecc 12:14; Mt 25:35–46; 1Co 3:12–15; 2Co 5:10
–Our words .... Mt 12:36–37; Jas 3:1–2

–Our inner thoughts ... 1Co 4:5
–Our perseverance to the end ... Mt 24:13
–In God mercy triumphs over judgment ... Jas 2:13
f. The results of the final judgment
–Unbelievers will be punished ... Ro 2:5; 2Th 1:8–9; Rev 20:15
–Believers will receive eternal life ... Jn 3:16; 1Jn 5:11–12
–Believers will receive salvation . Ro 13:11; Heb 9:27–28
–Believers will receive redemption ... Lk 21:28; Eph 4:30
–Believers will receive a crown .. 2Ti 4:8; Jas 1:12
g. Attitude towards the final judgment
–Be on your guard ... Mk 13:23,33
–Be alert ... 1Th 5:6
–Watch ... Mt 25:13

JUSTICE

–Fairness in the treatment of others

A. Human justice
1. Israelites commanded to exercise justice ... Ex 23:1–3,6; Lev 19:15; Dt 1:17; Dt 16:18–20
2. The prophets and justice
–They called the people to justice ... Jer 22:3; Hos 12:6; Am 5:24; Mic 6:8
–They spoke against injustice ... Isa 3:15; Am 2:6–8; Mic 3:1–3
3. Christians called to exercise justice ... Mt 23:23; Col 4:1; Jas 2:1–4
B. The justice of God
1. God is just ... 2Th 1:6
–His ways are just ... Dt 32:4; Da 4:37; Rev 15:3
–He loves justice ... Ps 11:7; Ps 33:5
–He does no wrong .. Zep 3:5
–He judges justly ... 1Pe 2:23; Rev 16:5,7
2. The nature of God's justice
–He is impartial ... 2Ch 19:7; Job 34:19; Ro 2:11
–He champions victims of injustice ... Ps 10:17–18; Ps 103:6
3. Expressions of God's justice
–Requires death for sin ... Ge 2:17; Ro 6:23
–Is expressed in his forgiveness ... 1Jn 1:9

See also RIGHTEOUSNESS

JUSTIFICATION

–Being declared right with God; acceptance by God

A. The basis of justification
–Christ as our righteousness ... 1Co 1:30
–Christ's perfect obedience ... Ro 5:19; 2Co 5:21; Heb 4:15; 1Pe 2:22
–Christ's death on the cross ... Ro 3:24–25; Ro 5:9
–Christ's resurrection ... Ro 4:25
B. The manner of justification
–We cannot earn it by obedience ... Ro 3:28; Ro 9:31–32; Gal 2:16; Gal 3:11; Php 3:9
–We receive it as a gift of God's grace ... Ro 3:24; Ro 4:16; Ro 5:15–17; Gal 2:21
–We receive it by repenting ... Lk 18:13–14
–We receive it through faith ... Ac 13:39; Ro 3:22,26–28; Ro 4:10–12; Gal 2:16; Gal 5:5; Php 3:9
–Faith must be a living faith ... Jas 2:14–26
C. The results of justification
–We become children of Abraham ... Ro 4:11–12, 16–17; Gal 3:6–7
–We are redeemed ... Ro 3:24
–We receive forgiveness of sins ... Ac 13:38–39
–We receive the gift of eternal life ... Ro 5:17–18; Ro 8:10; Tit 3:7
–We are saved from God's wrath ... Ro 5:9
–We become free from condemnation ... Ro 8:1,33–34
–We have peace with God ... Ro 5:1
–We are blessed by God ... Ro 4:6–9; Gal 3:9,14
–We are considered to have kept God's law ... Ro 8:3–4; 2Co 5:21
–We become free from the law ... Gal 5:1
–We share in Christ's sufferings ... Php 3:10
–We go on to live a life of holiness ... Ro 6:19,22; Gal 2:17–19
–We will someday be glorified ... Ro 8:30

KADESH, KADESH-BARNEA

–City bordering on Edom ... Nu 20:14–16
–God appeared to Hagar near there ... Ge 16:7–14
–Abraham lived near there .. Ge 20:1
–Moses sent out spies from there ... Nu 13:1–2, 26; Dt 1:19–25; Jos 14:6–7
–Israelites rebelled against the Lord there ... Nu 14:1–45; Dt 1:26–45; Dt 9:23–24
–Israelites camped there again for many days ... Dt 1:46; Jdg 11:16–17
–Miriam died there ... Nu 20:1
–Moses struck the rock there to get water ... Nu 20:2–12
–Joshua conquered that area . Jos 10:41
–Became southernmost town of Judah ... Jos 15:3; Eze 47:19

KETURAH

–Wife of Abraham after Sarah ... Ge 25:1
–Also called Abraham's concubine ... 1Ch 1:32
–Mother of six sons ... Ge 25:2

KINDNESS

–A hospitable, friendly attitude towards others

A. Human kindness
1. Expected of Christians
–Commanded ... 2Co 6:6; Gal 5:22; Col 3:12; 2Pe 1:7
–One aspect of the fruit of the Spirit ... Gal 5:22
2. Expressions of kindness
–Showing forgiveness ... Ge 50:21
–Sparing someone's life ... Jos 2:12–13
–Healing the sick ... Ac 4:9
–Helping the needy .. 2Sa 9:1–7; Pr 14:21,31; Pr 19:17
–Helping victims of injustice ... Ge 40:14
–Helping strangers ... Ac 28:2; Heb 13:1–2; 3Jn 5–8
B. Kindness of God
–In giving us salvation .. Tit 3:4
–In being faithful to his promises ... 1Ki 3:6
–In watching over us ... Job 10:12
–In showing compassion to us ... Isa 54:8
–In providing for needs . Ge 32:10; Ru 2:20; Hos 11:4; Ac 14:17
–In helping us in various life situations ... Ge 39:21; Ezr 9:9

See also MERCY

KING

A. Human kings
1. Examples of non-Israelite kings
–Four kings warring against five ... Ge 14:8–11
–Melchizedek, king of Salem ... Ge 14:18
–List of the kings of Edom ... Ge 36:32–39
–Pharaoh, king of Egypt ... Ex 1:8,15–22
–Sihon and Og defeated ... Nu 21:21–35
–Various kings in Canaan defeated ... Jos 8:1–2; Jos 10:1–3, 16–42; Jos 12
–David defeated various kings ... 2Sa 8:1–14
–The king of Assyria took Israel ... 2Ki 17:3–6
–King Nebuchadnezzar took Judah ... 2Ki 25:1–7
–King Cyrus allowed return to Judah ... Ezr 1:1–4
–Nehemiah served King Artaxerxes ... Ne 2:1
–Esther became wife of King Xerxes ... Est 2:1,17–18
–Caesar as king ... Jn 19:12,15
–The kings of the earth ... Ps 2:2; Ps 102:15; Ps 138:4
2. The kings of Israel and Judah
a. The beginning of kingship
–The people asked for a king ... 1Sa 8:4–5
–Samuel warned them ... 1Sa 8:10–18
–Saul anointed as first king ... 1Sa 10:20–24; 1Sa 11:14–15
b. Kings of the united kingdom
–Saul (42 years) ... 1Sa 13:1
See SAUL
–David (40 years) . 1Ki 2:11
See DAVID
–Solomon (40 years) ... 1Ki 11:42
See SOLOMON
c. The kings of Israel (in chronological order)
–Jeroboam (22 years) ... 1Ki 12:25—14:20
–Nadab (2 years) .. 1Ki 15:25–31
–Baasha (24 years) ... 1Ki 15:32—16:7
–Elah (2 years) ... 1Ki 16:8–14
–Zimri (7 days) ... 1Ki 16:15–20
–Tibni (with Omri) ... 1Ki 16:21–22
–Omri (12 years) .. 1Ki 16:23–28
–Ahab (22 years) .. 1Ki 16:29—22:40; 2Ch 18:1–34
–Ahaziah (2 years) ... 1Ki 22:51–53; 2Ki 1:1–18
–Joram (12 years) . 2Ki 3:1–8:15
–Jehu (28 years) .. 2Ki 9:6—10:36
–Jehoahaz (17 years) ... 2Ki 13:1–9
–Jehoash (16 years) ... 2Ki 13:10–25
–Jeroboam II (41 years) ... 2Ki 14:23–29
–Zechariah (6 months) ... 2Ki 15:8–12
–Shallum (1 month) ... 2Ki 15:13–15
–Menahem (10 years) ... 2Ki 15:16–22
–Pekahiah (2 years) ... 2Ki 15:23–26
–Pekah (20 years) . 2Ki 15:27–31
–Hoshea (9 years) . 2Ki 17:1–6

See also entries for each of these kings

d. The kings of Judah (in chronological order)
–Rehoboam (17 years) ... 1Ki 12:1–24; 1Ki 14:21–31; 2Ch 10:1—12:16
–Abijah (3 years) .. 1Ki 15:1–8; 2Ch 13:1—14:1
–Asa (41 years) ... 1Ki 15:9–24; 2Ch 14:2—16:14
–Jehoshaphat (25 years) ... 1Ki 22:41–50; 2Ch 17:1—21:3
–Jehoram (8 years) ... 2Ki 8:16–24; 2Ch 21:4–20
–Ahaziah (1 year) . 2Ki 8:25–29; 2Ch 22:1–9
–Athaliah (7 years) ... 2Ki 11:1–21; 2Ch 22:10—23:21
–Joash (40 years) .. 2Ki 12:1–21; 2Ch 24:1–27
–Amaziah (29 years) ... 2Ki 14:1–22; 2Ch 25:1–28
–Azariah or Uzziah (52 years) ... 2Ki 15:1–7; 2Ch 26:1–23
–Jotham (16 years) ... 2Ki 15:32–38; 2Ch 27:1–8
–Ahaz (16 years) .. 2Ki 16:1–20; 2Ch 28:1–27
–Hezekiah (29 years) ... 2Ki 18:1—20:21; 2Ch 29:1—32:33; Isa 36:1—39:8
–Manasseh (55 years) ... 2Ki 21:1–18; 2Ch 33:1–20

- –Amon (2 years) .. 2Ki 21:19–26; 2Ch 33:21–25
- –Josiah (31 years) . 2Ki 22:1–23:30; 2Ch 34:1–35:27
- –Jehoahaz (3 months) 2Ki 23:31–33; 2Ch 36:1–4
- –Jehoiakim (11 years) 2Ki 23:24–24:7; 2Ch 36:5–8
- –Jehoiachin (3 months) 2Ki 24:8–17; 2Ch 36:9–10
- –Zedekiah (11 years) 2Ki 24:18–25:26; 2Ch 36:11–21

See also entries for each of these kings

B. God as a king
  1. God called a king
    - –The King of heaven . Ps 95:3; Da 4:37
    - –The King of glory .. Ps 24:10
    - –The eternal, immortal King 1Ti 1:17
    - –The great King ..... Ps 47:2
    - –He rules over all the earth .... 2Ch 20:6; Ps 99:1–2; Isa 52:7
    - –He rules from his throne .... 1Ki 22:19; Ps 9:4,7–8; Isa 6:1–3
  2. Christ is a king
    a. Prophesied in the Old Testament
      - –The coming one will have a scepter .... Ge 49:10; Nu 24:17
      - –He will rule on David's throne ... Ps 132:11–12; Isa 9:6–7; Jer 33:17
      - –He will rule at God's right hand . Ps 110:1
      - –He will rule eternally .... Da 2:44–45
      - –He will rule with authority .... Da 7:13–14
      - –He will rule as a shepherd .... Isa 40:10–11; Eze 34:23–24; Mic 5:2–4
      - –He will rule wisely .... Isa 52:13; Jer 23:5
      - –He will rule with justice .... Isa 32:1; Jer 33:15–16
      - –He will rule humbly .... Zec 9:9
      - –He will function as a priest .... Ps 110:4; Zec 6:12–13
    b. Fulfilled in the New Testament
      - –He is the king of the Jews .... Mt 2:2; Jn 19:19–21
      - –He is the king of Israel .... Jn 1:49
      - –He claimed kingship .... Mt 27:11; Jn 18:37
      - –He entered Jerusalem as king ...... Mt 21:1–9
      - –He came to rule on David's throne .... Lk 1:32–33; Ac 2:29–33
      - –He now rules at God's right hand . Eph 1:20–23; Heb 1:3–8
      - –He is ruling over his enemies 1Co 15:25–27
      - –He will sit as a King who judges . Mt 25:31–34

KINGDOM

–The rule of humans or God over others

A. Human kingdoms
  1. General kingdoms of Bible history
    - –Kingdom of Bashan . Nu 32:33
    - –Kingdom of the Amorites .... Nu 32:33
    - –The Aramean kingdom 1Ch 18:6
    - –The kingdom of Babylon .... Da 1:20; Da 4:36
    - –The kingdom of Media and Persia ... Est 1:2–4; Da 5:28,30
    - –Four kingdoms in Nebuchadnezzar's dream .... Da 2:36–43
    - –All the kingdoms of the earth .... Dt 28:25; 2Ki 19:15,19; Jer 15:4; Mt 4:8
  2. The kingdom(s) of Israel and Judah
    - –The kingdom taken away from Saul 1Sa 13:13–14
    - –The kingdom united under David 2Sa 5:1–5,12
    - –The kingdom expanded under David 2Sa 8:11–14
    - –The kingdom given to Solomon 1Ki 1:28–40
    - –The kingdom to be divided after Solomon 1Ki 11:9–13
    - –The kingdom divided under Rehoboam 1Ki 12:16–24
    - –The kingdom of Israel destroyed 2Ki 17:7–23
    - –The kingdom of Judah destroyed 2Ki 25:1–21

B. Kingdom of God
  1. When and where is that kingdom?
    a. The kingdom is present in Jesus
      - –John preached it was near .... Mt 3:2
      - –Jesus preached it was near .... Mk 1:15
      - –Jesus preached the gospel of the kingdom .... Mt 4:23
      - –Some parables describe its life .. Mt 13:11–52
      - –Jesus' miracles proved its presence .... Lk 7:18–22
      - –Casting out demons proved it . Lk 11:20
      - –"The kingdom of God is among you" .... Lk 17:20–21
      - –It comes through Jesus' death ..... Lk 23:42–43
      - –It comes through Jesus' resurrection 1Co 15:20–25
      - –The apostles preached the kingdom .... Ac 8:12; Ac 19:8; Ac 28:23,28
      - –Christ brings us into his kingdom . Col 1:12–13
    b. The kingdom is yet to come
      - –Jesus prayed, "Your kingdom come" .... Mt 6:10
      - –Some parables describe it as future .... Mt 25:1–34
      - –It comes with the return of Jesus ... 2Ti 4:1
      - –It is something we will inherit ...... Mt 25:34; 1Co 15:50; Jas 2:5
      - –It is a heavenly kingdom .... 2Ti 4:18; Heb 12:26–28
      - –It is a kingdom we will receive .. 2Pe 1:11
      - –The millennial kingdom .... Rev 20:1–6
  2. How can we enter the kingdom?
    - –By experiencing new birth .... Jn 3:3
    - –By receiving it as a gift from Jesus ..... Lk 22:29
    - –By responding to God's call 1Th 2:12
    - –By repenting of our sins .... Mk 1:15
    - –By being redeemed through Christ ...... Col 1:12–14
    - –By accepting Christ's righteousness .... Mt 5:20
    - –By following Jesus .. Mt 19:21–24; Lk 9:61–62
    - –By loving God ..... Jas 2:5
    - –By persevering in the faith .... Ac 14:22; 2Th 1:4–5
    - –By doing the will of God .... Mt 7:21–23
  3. What is life in the kingdom like?
    - –Described in the Sermon on the Mount .. Mt 5:1–7:27
    - –Described in the Sermon on the Plain ... Lk 6:17–49
    - –Described in many parables of Jesus .... Mt 13:11–52; Mt 18:23–35; Mt 20:1–16; Mt 21:28–22:14
    - –A life of childlike humility .... Mt 18:1–4
    - –A life of joy and peace .... Ro 14:17
    - –A life free from sin's control .... 1Co 6:9–11; Gal 5:16–21; Eph 5:3–5
    - –A life of producing the fruit of the Spirit .... Gal 5:21–23
  4. How must we relate to the kingdom?
    - –We must pray for it . Mt 6:10
    - –We must seek it first .... Mt 6:33
    - –We must preach it .. Ac 8:22; Ac 28:31
    - –We must work for it .... Col 4:11
    - –We may have to suffer for it .... Ac 14:22; 2Ti 4:16–18

KISS

A. Legitimate uses
  - –To say hello .... Ge 29:13; Ge 33:4
  - –To say good-bye ...... Ge 31:55; Ru 1:9; 1Sa 20:41
  - –To accompany a blessing .... Ge 27:26–27
  - –To express deep affection 1Sa 20:41
  - –To express sexual love . SS 1:2
  - –To express grief .... Ge 50:1; Ac 20:37
  - –To demonstrate forgiveness .... Ge 33:4; Ge 45:15; Lk 15:20
  - –To show honor and respect .... 1Sa 10:1; Lk 7:38
  - –To express submission . Ps 2:12
  - –To show Christian love .... Ro 16:16; 1Pe 5:14

B. Pagan use: kissing idols . 1Ki 19:18; Job 31:26–27; Hos 13:2

C. Hypocritical uses
  - –Absalom trying to gain popularity 2Sa 15:5
  - –Joab when he killed Amasa 2Sa 20:9
  - –Judas when he betrayed Jesus .... Mt 26:48–49; Mk 14:44–45; Lk 22:47–48
  - –A prostitute seducing a man .... Pr 7:13
  - –Can be used by any enemy .... Pr 27:6

KNOWLEDGE

A. Human knowledge of God and his ways
  1. Source of our knowledge
    - –God himself .... Pr 2:6; Jer 9:23–24
    - –Christ .... Col 2:3,8
    - –The Holy Spirit 1Co 2:9–16
    - –The world around us .... Ps 19:1; Ro 1:19–20
    - –God's word .... Pr 2:1–5; Jn 17:17; 2Ti 3:15–16
    - –God's mighty acts for his people .... Ex 6:6–7; Eze 37:13–14
  2. Corruption of human knowledge of God
    - –First sin: seeking knowledge apart from God .... Ge 3:4–7
    - –Humans suppress the truth about God ..... Ro 1:18; 2Ti 3:7; Tit 1:16
    - –Idolatry is evidence of this .... Ro 1:21–23
  3. Proper attitude to the knowledge of God
    - –We must know God . Jer 9:24
    - –To know God is to do his will .... Jer 22:15–16
    - –We must know Christ .... Php 3:8,10
    - –We must pray for knowledge .... Ps 119:66
    - –We must grow in knowledge .... Eph 4:13; Heb 5:12–6:1; 2Pe 1:5–8; 2Pe 3:18
    - –We must recognize its limitations 1Co 13:8–12
    - –We must realize love surpasses it .... 1Co 8:1; Eph 3:19
    - –We must not become proud of it 1Co 8:1
    - –We must not wander away from it 1Ti 6:20–21
  4. Benefits of the knowledge of God
    - –Gives stability to life .... Pr 24:3–6
    - –Enables us to know the love of God 1Jn 3:1
    - –Enables us to fight sin and evil 2Pe 1:3–4
    - –Keeps us from destruction by God .. Hos 4:6
    - –Essential to eternal life .... Jn 17:3

B. Knowledge possessed by God
  - –God is all-knowing .... Ps 139:1–6; Isa 46:10; 1Jn 3:20
  - –God's knowledge of us precedes our birth ..... Ps 139:15–16; Jer 1:5
  - –God knows what is inside us .... 1Sa 16:7; Ps 44:21
  - –God knows our needs .. Ps 103:13–14; Mt 6:31–32
  - –Little things do not escape his notice ...... Mt 10:29–30
  - –God cannot be taught by humans .... Job 21:22; Isa 40:12–14
  - –Jesus knew God's will for him .... Lk 18:31–33; Jn 13:1
  - –Jesus knows us completely .... Jn 2:25; Jn 4:16–18; Jn 6:64
  - –All knowledge is hidden in Christ .... Col 2:3

KORAH

- –A descendant of Levi ...... Ex 6:19,21,24
- –Led a rebellion against Moses .... Nu 16:1–3
- –Killed by the Lord for this rebellion .... Nu 16:4–35

–His descendants became temple gatekeepers 1Ch 9:17,19; 1Ch 26:1
–His descendants became temple musicians 1Ch 6:31–32,37; 2Ch 20:19
–Sons of Korah wrote various psalms .... Ps 44–49, 85–88
–His rebellion illustrates God's judgment .... Jude 11

LABAN

–Son of Bethuel .... Ge 24:24
–Brother of Rebekah .... Ge 24:29
–Father of Leah and Rachel . Ge 29:16
–Deceived Jacob into marrying Leah .... Ge 29:22–27
–Became Jacob's boss ...... Ge 29:18–20; Ge 30:25–34
–Became jealous of Jacob's prosperity .... Ge 31:1–2
–Disinherited his daughters .. Ge 31:14–16
–Pursued the fleeing Jacob .. Ge 31:22–25
–Made a covenant with Jacob .... Ge 31:43–55

LAMB

A. Uses for lambs
–For food .... Dt 32:14; Am 6:4
–For clothing .... Pr 27:26
–For sealing a treaty .... Ge 21:27–31
–For the payment of tribute 2Ki 3:4
–For a sacrifice in place of Isaac .... Ge 22:8,13
–For a regular burnt offering .... Ex 29:38–42
–For offerings at special feasts .... Nu 28:27; Nu 29:2
–For the Passover .... Ex 12:3–6; Nu 28:16–19

B. The lamb as a symbol
–Of extraordinary joy ... Ps 114:1–4
–Of innocence 2Sa 12:1–4
–Of weak people .... Isa 40:11; Jn 21:15
–Of peace-loving missionaries .... Lk 10:3
–Of the age of peace .... Isa 11:6; Isa 65:25

C. Jesus as the Lamb of God
–Prophesied by Isaiah ... Isa 53:4–7
–Fulfilled in Jesus ...... Ac 8:32–35
–Called the Lamb of God .... Jn 1:29,36
–Called the passover lamb 1Co 5:7
–Shed his blood as a lamb without blemish .. 1Pe 1:19
–Receives praise as the slain Lamb .... Rev 5:6–13; Rev 7:9–11
–Celebrates with his 144,000 .... Rev 14:1–5
–Conquers the antichrist . Rev 17:14
–Marries the church as a bride .... Rev 19:7,9; Rev 21:9

LANGUAGE

A. Languages mentioned in the Bible
–Hebrew .... Jn 19:20
–Chaldean .... Da 1:4
–Aramaic .... Ezr 4:7
–Ashdod .... Ne 13:23–24
–Lycaonian .... Ac 14:11
–Latin .... Jn 19:20
–Greek .... Ac 21:37
–Numerous languages ... Ge 10:5,20, 31; Ac 2:5–11

B. Language barriers begun at Babel .... Ge 11:1–9

C. Language barriers removed
–At Pentecost .... Ac 2:4–11
–Through gift of tongues .... Ac 10:46; Ac 19:6; 1Co 12:10, 28–30; 1Co 13:1
–Through the interpretation of tongues 1Co 12:10, 30; 1Co 14:5,13, 27

–In heaven .... Rev 5:9; Rev 7:9

LAW

A. Meanings of the word "law"
–A general principle .... Ro 7:23
–Rules of conduct in the conscience .... Ro 2:14
–Edicts made by human governments .... Da 6:12
–Rules revealed by God through Moses .... Ex 21:1; Ro 5:13; Ac 15:5
–The first five books of the Bible .... Gal 3:10
–The whole Old Testament .... Jn 15:25; 1Co 14:21

B. The law of God
1. Characteristics
–True .... Ps 119:142, 151
–Perfect .... Ps 19:7; Jas 1:25
–Trustworthy .... Ps 19:7; Ps 119:86, 138
–Enduring .... Ps 119:91, 160; Mt 5:18
–Right and righteous . Ps 19:8; Ps 119:75, 137; Ro 7:12
–Holy .... Ro 7:12
–Good .... Ro 7:12,16; 1Ti 1:8
–Spiritual .... Ro 7:14
–Love is its summary .... Mt 22:37–40; Ro 13:8–10; Gal 5:14
2. Brief history of God's law revealed to Moses
–Spoken directly by God .... Ex 20:1,18–19; Dt 5:4,22
–Spoken by Moses to the Israelites .... Ex 20:22
–Written on tablets of stone .... Ex 24:12; Ex 31:18
–Tablets broken by Moses .... Ex 32:15–19
–Written on tablets a second time .... Ex 34:1–5, 27–28
–Repeated in Deuteronomy .... Dt 4:44–46
–Placed in the ark of the covenant .... Dt 31:24–26
–Repeated by Joshua . Jos 24:25–26
–Honored by David .. 1Ch 16:40
–Disobeyed by God's people 2Ki 17:12–20
–Taught by Jehoshaphat 2Ch 17:9; 2Ch 19:8
–Honored during Joash's reign 2Ch 23:18–19
–Honored during Hezekiah's reign 2Ch 31:3–4, 21
–Rediscovered during Josiah's reign 2Ch 34:14–18
–Studied by Ezra ..... Ezr 7:10
–Reintroduced by Ezra to the people .... Ne 8:1–18
–Read in the synagogues .... Ac 15:21
–Fulfilled by Jesus Christ .... Mt 5:17–18
3. Purpose of the law of God
–To show the way to life .... Lev 18:4–5; Dt 30:15–20; Gal 3:12
–To point out our sin . Ro 3:20; Gal 3:19
–To increase sin ..... Ro 5:20
–To show that we lie under its curse ...... Gal 3:10,13
–To lead us to Christ . Gal 3:24
4. The Israelites and the law of God
–Must know it .... Ex 33:12–13
–Must fix it in their hearts .... Dt 11:18; Ps 119:11
–Must teach it .... Dt 4:9–10; Dt 11:19–21
–Must observe it ..... Dt 4:1,6; Dt 29:9
–Must remember it ... Nu 15:38–40; Mal 4:4
–Must love it .... Ps 119:47,97
–Must delight in it ... Ps 1:2; Ps 112:1
5. Jesus Christ and the law of God
–Came to fulfill it .... Mt 5:17–18
–Born under it .... Gal 4:4
–Circumcised according to it .... Lk 2:21
–Consecrated according to it .... Lk 2:22–24
–Attended feasts prescribed in it .... Mk 14:12–16; Jn 2:23
–Perfectly obeyed it .. 2Co 5:21; Heb 4:15; 1Pe 2:22–23
–Completed what it pointed to .... Heb 8:5–6; Heb 9:11–15,23–28
–Bore its curse on the cross .... Gal 3:13
–Ended its burden .... Ro 7:4–6; Ro 10:1–5; Gal 3:24–25
–Gave us freedom from it .... Jn 8:31–36; Gal 5:1
6. Christians and the law of God
–Cannot keep it perfectly .... Ro 3:19–20, 23; Ro 7:4–5
–Cannot be justified through it .... Ro 3:20,28; Gal 3:11
–Have met its requirements .... Ro 8:4
–Are free from its condemnation .... Ro 8:2
–Are free from its curse .... Gal 3:13–14
–Are free from its burden .... Gal 2:1–5; Gal 5:1
–Have it written on their hearts .... Heb 8:10–13
–Are under the law of Christ .... Jn 14:15; 1Co 9:21; Gal 6:2
–Must keep the law of love .... Jn 13:34–35; Ro 13:8–10; Gal 5:13–14; 1Jn 3:11–18
–Must keep the Ten Commandments ..... Eph 6:2; Jas 2:8–11
7. The Spirit and the law
–Sets us free from it . Ro 8:2,13; 2Co 3:17
–Enables us to keep its spirit .... Ro 7:6; 2Co 3:6; Gal 5:16–17, 22–25

LAZARUS

A. Poor man in Jesus' parable .... Lk 16:19–31

B. Brother of Mary and Martha .... Jn 11:1
–Became sick and died .. Jn 11:2–15
–Raised from the dead .. Jn 11:38–44
–Present at a meal with Jesus .... Jn 12:2
–His resurrection caused a stir .... Jn 12:17–19

LEADER

A. Types of leaders
–Moses as God's chosen leader .... Nu 33:1; Mic 6:4
–Joshua as Moses' successor .... Dt 1:38; Jos 1:6
–Tribal leaders .... Nu 2:3,5,7, 10; Nu 7:2
–Judges .... Jdg 4:4; Jdg 12:7–14
–Kings 1Sa 8:5–6,20; 1Ch 11:2; 2Ch 1:10
–Priests .... Ne 9:38
–The shepherds of Israel .... Jer 25:34–36
–Church officials .... Ac 15:22; Heb 13:7,17, 24

B. Principles of leadership
1. Positive principles
–Depend on the Lord's strength .... Jos 1:6
–Obey the law of God .... Jos 1:7–8
–Use wisdom and knowledge from God .... 2Ch 1:10; Jer 3:15
–Exercise justice ..... Mic 3:1–3
–Live an exemplary life 1Ti 4:12; 1Pe 5:3
–Serve the people selflessly .... Mt 20:26; Lk 22:26–27; 1Pe 5:2
–Govern diligently ... Ro 12:8
2. Negative principles
–Do not be rebellious against God .... Jer 2:8–9; Hos 9:15–17
–Do not lead the people astray .... Isa 3:12–15; Jer 23:30–32; 1Jn 3:7
–Do not be a poor example .... Ezr 9:1–2
–Do not exert power . Mt 20:25–26; 1Pe 5:3
–Do not seek your own needs and wants first .... Eze 34:1–6; Am 5:11–13

See also KING; SHEPHERD

C. God as leader of his people
–God the Father as leader .... Ex 15:13; Dt 8:2,15; 2Ch 13:12; Ps 23:1–3; Ps 139:23–24
–Jesus the Son as leader . Jn 10:2–3, 10–14; Jn 13:12–15
–The Holy Spirit as leader .... Ro 8:14; Gal 5:18

LEAH

–Older daughter of Laban ... Ge 29:16
–First wife of Jacob .... Ge 29:22–27
–Not loved by Jacob .... Ge 29:31
–Bore six sons and one daughter .... Ge 29:31–35; Ge 30:17–21; Ge 35:23
–Buried with Abraham and Sarah .... Ge 49:31

LEAVEN

See YEAST

LEBANON

A. Location of Lebanon
–Northeast part of the promised land .... Dt 11:24; Jos 13:5–6
–Land of mountains and valleys .... Jos 12:7; Jdg 3:3
–Contained Mount Hermon .... Jos 11:17

B. Importance of Lebanon to Israelites
–Never totally occupied by Israelites .... Jos 13:5–6
–Its wood used in the first temple 1Ki 5:6–10
–Its wood used in Solomon's palace 1Ki 7:2–3
–Its wood used in the second temple .... Ezr 3:7

C. Lebanon used as a symbol
- –Of the majesty of the Creator ... Ps 104:16
- –Of the power of the Creator ... Ps 29:4–6
- –Of the fruitfulness of God's people ... Ps 72:16; Ps 92:12–14
- –Of the new world of the redeemed ... Isa 35:1–2; Isa 60:13
- –Of one's beauty and majesty ... SS 3:6–9; SS 5:15
- –Of the importance of the royal house ... Jer 22:6–7
- –Of the arrogance of humanity ... Isa 2:12–18

LEGALISM

See FREEDOM

LEISURE

See REST

LEVI, LEVITE

A. Son of Jacob by Leah ... Ge 35:23; 1Ch 2:1
- –Name means "attached" ... Ge 29:34
- –With Simeon, avenged rape of sister Dinah ... Ge 34:25–31
- –Went to Egypt with family ... Ge 46:8,11
- –Father of three sons ... Ge 46:11
- –Blessed by Jacob ... Ge 49:5–7

B. Tribe descended from Levi

1. History of the tribe
   - –Moses and Aaron from that tribe ... Ex 2:1
   - –Tribe blessed by Moses ... Dt 33:8–11
   - –Tribe chosen to serve as priests ... Nu 3:1–4:49
   - –Made ceremonially clean ... Nu 8:5–26
   - –Numbered ... Nu 3:39; Nu 26:62
   - –Allotted cities, but not land ... Nu 18:20,24; Nu 35:1–5
   - –Allotted land ... Eze 48:8–22
   - –One of the tribes of the 144,000 ... Rev 7:7
2. Duties
   - –Belonged to the Lord ... Nu 3:11–13
   - –Were Israel's religious leaders ... Dt 10:8
   - –Were in charge of the tabernacle ... Nu 1:50–53; Nu 4:1–33
   - –Assisted Aaron ... Nu 3:5–9; Nu 18:1–7
   - –Prepared the sacrifices ... 2Ch 35:10–14; Ezr 6:19–21
   - –Gathered tithes and offerings ... Nu 18:20–24; Dt 18:1–2; Ne 10:37–39
   - –Served as judges of the people ... Dt 17:8–9; 1Ch 23:3–4; 1Ch 26:29
   - –Recited the curses of God ... Dt 27:14–26
   - –Supervised the work of the temple ... 1Ch 23:3–4, 28–32; 1Ch 26:20–28
   - –Instructed the people in the law ... Ne 8:7–9
   - –Some were gatekeepers ... 1Ch 23:3–5; 1Ch 26:1–19
   - –Some were musicians ... 1Ch 23:3–5; 1Ch 25:1–31; Ne 12:24, 27–43

C. One of Jesus' disciples
See MATTHEW

LIFE

A. God and life
- –God is a living God ... Dt 5:26; Ps 42:2; 1Th 1:9
- –God has life in himself ... Jn 5:26
- –Jesus is the living one ... Rev 1:18
- –Jesus is the life ... Jn 11:25; Jn 14:6; 1Jn 1:1–2
- –Jesus has life in himself ... Jn 1:4
- –The Spirit of life ... Ro 8:2

B. Physical life

1. Plant and animal life
   - –Created by God ... Ge 1:11–12, 20–25; Ps 104:24–25,30
   - –Preserved by God ... Ps 104:21, 24–28; Ps 145:15–16; Ps 147:8–9
2. Human life
   - –God is its source ... Ge 2:7; Job 33:4; Isa 42:5; Ac 17:26,28
   - –God preserves it ... Job 12:10; Ps 138:7
   - –God removes it as punishment for sin ... Ge 3:19; Ro 5:12
   - –Human life should be reproduced ... Ge 1:28; Ge 9:1,7
   - –Human life is fleeting and fragile ... Job 20:4–11; Ps 90:3–10; Ps 103:14–16
   - –God's kingdom is more important ... Mt 6:25–34; Mt 10:38–39; Jn 12:25
   - –Taking a human life is forbidden ... Ge 9:5–6; Ex 20:13; Ro 13:9–10

C. Spiritual life

1. The source of spiritual life
   - –God, the Father ... Eph 2:4–5; Col 2:13
   - –Jesus Christ, God's Son ... Jn 1:4; Jn 10:10; Ac 3:15
   - –The Holy Spirit ... Eze 37:14; Jn 3:5–6; Ro 8:2,11
   - –The word of God ... Jas 1:18; 1Pe 1:23
2. Phrases describing spiritual life
   - –Being born from above ... Jn 3:3–8
   - –Being crucified with Christ ... Gal 2:20; Ro 6:8–10
   - –Being raised with Christ ... Ro 6:4; Eph 2:5–6; Col 3:1–3
   - –Being a new creation ... 2Co 5:17
   - –Living by the Spirit ... Gal 5:16,25
   - –Having names in the book of life ... Lk 10:20; Php 4:3
   - –Already having eternal life ... Jn 3:36; Jn 6:47; 1Jn 5:11–13
   - –Not being subject to the second death ... Rev 20:6
3. How to obtain spiritual life
   - –We must choose it ... Dt 30:19–20
   - –We must hear the word of God ... Ac 16:14; Ro 10:13–14
   - –We must be called by God ... 2Th 2:13–14
   - –We must repent of our sins ... Ac 2:38
   - –We must believe in Jesus ... Jn 3:15–16; Jn 20:31
4. Stages of spiritual life
   - –The time of birth ... Jn 3:3–8; 1Pe 1:23
   - –Being babes in Christ ... 1Co 3:1; 1Pe 2:2
   - –Growth must take place ... Eph 4:14–16; Col 1:10; 1Pe 2:2
   - –Becoming mature Christians ... 1Co 2:6; Eph 4:13; Heb 5:14–6:1; Jas 1:4
   - –We must not slip back ... Php 3:13–16; Heb 5:12–14

See also GROWTH

D. Eternal life

1. How can we receive eternal life?
   - –By being appointed to it by God ... Ac 13:48
   - –By being called to it ... 1Ti 6:12
   - –By reading the Scriptures ... Jn 5:39
   - –By receiving it as a gift from God ... Ro 6:23
   - –By receiving it as a gift from Jesus ... Jn 5:40; Jn 10:28
   - –By taking hold of it ... 1Ti 6:12,19
   - –By realizing Jesus is eternal life ... 1Jn 1:2; 1Jn 5:20
   - –By believing in Jesus ... Jn 3:15–16
   - –By trusting in Jesus ... Jn 14:1–3
   - –By drinking of Jesus as water of life ... Jn 4:13–14
   - –By eating of Jesus as bread of life ... Jn 6:48–51
   - –By eating of the tree of life ... Ge 3:22; Rev 2:7
   - –By dying with Christ ... 2Ti 2:11
   - –By knowing God ... Jn 17:3
   - –By being righteous ... Mt 25:46
   - –By obeying the commands of God ... Jn 12:50
   - –By pleasing the Spirit ... Gal 6:8
2. Eternal life begins now
   - –We have eternal life ... Jn 3:36; Jn 5:24
   - –We are already with Christ in heaven ... Eph 2:6; Col 3:3
3. Eternal life is still in the future
   - –We have been promised it ... 1Ti 4:8
   - –We have hope of it ... Tit 1:2; Tit 3:7
   - –We will rise again to receive it ... Jn 5:28–29
   - –We will receive it as a crown ... 1Pe 5:4
   - –We will inherit it ... Mt 19:29
   - –We will reap it ... Gal 6:8
   - –We will reign in it ... Ro 5:17
   - –Jesus will bring us to it ... Jude 21
   - –We will someday be in paradise ... Lk 23:43; Rev 2:7

LIGHT

A. God and light
- –God is light ... 1Jn 1:5
- –He created light ... Ge 1:3; Isa 45:7
- –He is the Father of lights ... Jas 1:17
- –He lives in light ... Ps 104:2; 1Ti 6:16
- –Jesus reflects the Father's light ... Heb 1:3
- –Jesus is the light of the world ... Jn 1:9; Jn 8:12; Jn 9:5

B. God's word as a light
- –God's word is a light ... Ps 119:105; Pr 6:23; 2Pe 1:19
- –God's word gives light ... Ps 119:130
- –The gospel proclaims light ... Ac 26:18,23; 2Co 4:4
- –In God's light we see light ... Ps 19:8; Ps 36:9
- –God's light guides us ... Ps 43:3; Isa 51:4

C. Believers and the light of God
- –We are enlightened ... Heb 6:4; Heb 10:32
- –We are children of the light ... 1Th 5:5; Mt 5:14
- –We are called into God's light ... 1Pe 2:9
- –We confess that the Lord is our light ... Ps 27:1; Mic 7:8–9
- –We walk in the light ... Isa 2:5; 1Jn 1:5,7
- –Our path gets ever brighter ... Pr 4:18
- –We put on the armor of light ... Ro 13:12
- –We live as children of light ... Eph 5:8–11
- –We must be light to the world ... Mt 5:14–16; Php 2:15
- –We shall someday enter the kingdom of light ... Col 1:12–13
- –We look for a new heaven of only light ... Isa 60:19; Rev 21:23; Rev 22:5
- –We have no fellowship with darkness ... Lk 11:35; 2Co 6:14; Eph 5:11

See DARKNESS

LION

A. Lion stories in the Bible
- –Samson killed a lion ... Jdg 14:5–6
- –David killed a lion ... 1Sa 17:34–35
- –A lion killed a prophet ... 1Ki 13:24; 1Ki 20:36
- –Settlers in Samaria killed by lions ... 2Ki 17:25–26
- –Daniel in the lions' den ... Da 6:16–24

B. The lion as a symbol

1. Characteristics that stand out
   - –Majestic ... Pr 30:29–30
   - –Fierce ... Am 3:8
   - –Stealthy ... Job 10:16
   - –Mean when hungry ... Ps 17:12
2. As a symbol of evil
   - –Of the devil ... 1Pe 5:8
   - –Of enemies attacking God's people ... Isa 5:29
   - –Of cruel rulers of the people ... Zep 3:3
   - –Of one's persecutors ... Ps 17:10–12; Ps 22:13,21; 2Ti 4:17
3. As a symbol of God and good
   - –Of Christ, the triumphant Ruler ... Rev 5:5
   - –Of the protecting power of God ... Isa 31:4–5
   - –Of the anger of God against sin ... Hos 5:14; Hos 13:8
   - –Of the powerful Israelites ... Nu 24:9
   - –Of the tribe of Judah ... Ge 49:9; Mic 5:8
   - –Of the bravery of humans ... 2Sa 1:23
   - –Of the boldness of believers ... Pr 28:1
   - –Of the victory of believers ... Ps 91:13
   - –The lion lies peacefully with the lamb ... Isa 11:6–9; Isa 65:25

LORD

A. Human lords
- –Used to refer to someone in authority ... Ge 44:16,18; 2Sa 24:3
- –Used as a title of respect ... Ge 23:15; Jdg 4:18; 1Sa 1:15

B. God as the Lord

1. The God of Israel

–First revealed as LORD to Moses ..... Ex 3:13–14; Ex 6:2–8
–Called the Lord of lords ..... Dt 10:17; Ps 136:3; 1Ti 6:15
–Reigns in majesty and strength ..... Ps 93:1; Ps 96:6
–Expects trust and reverence as Lord ..... Dt 28:58; Ps 96:4; Pr 3:5–6

2. Jesus as Lord
–The Lord Jesus Christ 2Co 13:14; 2Th 1:2
–Our Lord Jesus Christ ..... 1Th 5:9; Eph 6:24
–Jesus Christ our Lord 1Co 1:9; 1Ti 1:2
–Designated Lord through his resurrection ..... Ro 10:9; Php 2:8–11
–He is the Old Testament "Lord" ..... Ac 2:21; Ro 10:13; 2Ti 2:19
–He is Lord of all ..... Ac 10:36; Ro 14:9
–He is the Lord of lords ..... Rev 17:14; Rev 19:13–16
–He is the only Lord ..... 1Co 8:6; Eph 4:5

3. Believers confess Jesus as Lord
–Confession of Thomas ..... Jn 20:28
–Confession of early Christians ..... Ac 2:36; 1Co 1:2; 1Co 12:3; Col 2:6
–Confession commanded of us ..... Ro 10:9; Php 2:11

LORD'S SUPPER

–The sacramental meal of God's people

A. Titles for this feast
–The Lord's Supper 1Co 11:20
–The breaking of bread ..... Ac 2:42; Ac 20:7
–Participation in body and blood of Christ 1Co 10:16

B. Celebration of this feast
–Commanded by Christ ..... Lk 22:17–20; 1Co 11:23–24
–Done frequently in the early church ..... Ac 2:42,46–47; Ac 20:7,11
–Sometimes done in the wrong spirit 1Co 11:20–22

C. Purpose of this feast
–To remember the death of Christ ..... Lk 22:19; 1Co 11:24–25
–To symbolize Christ's body and blood ..... Mt 26:26,28; Jn 6:51–56; 1Co 10:16
–To participate in Christ's body and blood 1Co 10:16
–To proclaim the death of Christ 1Co 11:26
–To recall eating with the risen Lord ..... Lk 24:30,35,41–43; Jn 21:13; Ac 1:4
–To introduce the new covenant ..... Mt 26:28; 1Co 11:25
–To have fellowship with one another ..... Ac 2:42,46–47; 1Co 10:16–17
–To anticipate Christ's return ..... Mt 26:29; 1Co 11:26

LOT

A. Nephew of Abram ..... Ge 11:27
–Went with Abram to Canaan ..... Ge 12:5
–Chose to live in Sodom ..... Ge 13:5–12
–Rescued from four kings ..... Ge 14:11–16
–Rescued from Sodom ..... Ge 19:1–29; 2Pe 2:7
–His wife killed while fleeing Sodom ..... Ge 19:26; Lk 17:32
–Fathered Moab and Ammon by his daughters ..... Ge 19:30–38

B. Casting the lot
See CASTING LOTS

LOVE

A. Human love

1. Love for God

a. Expressions of this love
–Expressed by the psalmist ..... Ps 18:1; Ps 116:1
–Commanded in the Old Testament ..... Dt 6:5; Ps 31:23
–The first and great commandment ..... Mt 22:37–38

b. What we receive through this love
–God's love ..... Ex 20:6; Ps 119:132
–God's protecting care ..... Ps 91:14; Ps 145:20; Ro 8:28
–Blessing from God ..... Dt 11:13–15
–A life of joy ..... Ps 5:11
–Life in the promised land ..... Ps 69:35–36
–The kingdom as inheritance ..... Jas 2:5
–A crown of life ..... Jas 1:12

c. What we do through this love
–Love others 1Jn 4:20–21
–Obey God's law ..... Dt 13:3–4; 1Jn 5:2–3
–Hate evil ..... Ps 97:10

2. Love for Christ

a. Expressing this love
–Should be foremost in our lives ..... Mt 10:37
–Should be a permanent love ..... Eph 6:24
–Linked with faith in Christ 1Pe 1:8
–Linked with love for God ..... Jn 8:42; 1Jn 5:1
–Linked with obedience to God ..... Jn 14:21,23
–Expressed by loving others ..... Mt 25:40

b. Results of this love
–Results in God's love for us ..... Jn 14:21; Jn 16:27
–Results in a call to care for the church ..... Jn 21:15–17
–Lack of such love strongly rebuked 1Co 16:22

3. Love for other Christians

a. The command for such love
–Commanded by God 1Jn 4:21; 2Jn 6
–Commanded by Jesus ..... Jn 13:34–35; Jn 15:12,17; 1Jn 3:11,23
–Commanded by Paul ..... Ro 12:9–10; Gal 5:13; Eph 5:2; Php 2:2–4; Col 3:14; 1Th 4:9–10; 1Ti 1:5
–Commanded in Hebrews ..... Heb 10:24; Heb 13:1
–Commanded by Peter 1Pe 1:22; 1Pe 2:17; 1Pe 4:8; 2Pe 1:7
–Encouraged by John 1Jn 3:18; 1Jn 4:7,11–12; 2Jn 5
–We should pray for it to increase ..... Php 1:9; 1Th 3:12

b. Expressions of this love
–An aspect of the fruit of the Spirit ..... Gal 5:22; Col 1:8
–Linked with faith and hope ..... 1Co 13:13; Col 1:4–5
–Expresses itself in self-sacrifice ..... Jn 15:13; 1Co 13:4–7
–Involves concern for the weak ..... Ro 14:1,13–16
–Involves caring for the needy ..... 2Co 8:7–8; Phm 9–10
–No fear in such love 1Jn 4:18

c. Results of this love
–Demonstrates we are true disciples ..... Jn 13:35
–Assures us of eternal life 1Jn 3:14–15
–Builds the church ..... 1Co 8:1; Eph 4:15–16

4. Love for all humans

a. Love your neighbor as yourself
–Commanded in the Old Testament ..... Lev 19:18
–Commanded by Jesus ..... Mt 22:39
–Commanded by the apostles ..... Ro 13:9; Gal 5:14; Jas 2:8

b. Love for strangers ..... Lev 19:34; Dt 10:19; Heb 13:2

c. Do good to all humans ..... Gal 6:10

d. Love even for enemies
–Commanded in the Old Testament ..... Ex 23:4–5; Pr 25:21–22
–Commanded by Jesus ..... Mt 5:43–45
–Commanded by Paul ..... Ro 12:20–21
–Commanded by Peter 1Pe 3:9

5. The song of love 1Co 13
–Highest of all Christian virtues 1Co 13:13
–Everything valueless without it 1Co 13:1–3
–Central nature is selflessness 1Co 13:4–7
–Endures throughout eternity 1Co 13:8–13

B. Love of Christ

1. Love of Christ for the Father ..... Jn 14:31

2. Love of Christ for his people
–His love for Mary, Martha, Lazarus ..... Jn 11:3,5,36
–His love for his disciples ..... Jn 13:1,34; Jn 15:9,12
–The disciple whom Jesus loved ..... Jn 13:23; Jn 19:26; Jn 20:2; Jn 21:7,20
–His love for the church ..... Eph 5:25
–His love expressed by his sacrifice ..... Jn 15:13; Gal 2:20; Eph 5:2,25

3. Our relationship to this love
–We must realize how extensive it is ..... Eph 3:17–19
–We must remain in it ..... Jn 15:9–10
–Nothing can separate us from it ..... Ro 8:35–37
–It motivates us to love others ..... Jn 13:34; Jn 15:12; Eph 5:2
–It serves as a pattern for husbands ..... Eph 5:25–28
–It motivates us to mission work 2Co 5:14

C. Love of God

1. God is love 1Jn 4:8,16

2. God loves the Son
–Prophesied in the Old Testament ..... Isa 42:1; Mt 12:18
–Expressed at Jesus' baptism ..... Mt 3:17
–Expressed at the transfiguration ..... Mt 17:5; 2Pe 1:17
–Acknowledged by Jesus ..... Jn 5:20; Jn 10:17; Jn 15:9–10; Jn 17:23–24,26

3. God loves the sinful world
–His love for the world stated ..... Jn 3:16
–His love in spite of sin ..... Ro 5:8; Tit 3:3–4
–His love expressed in sending his Son ..... Jn 3:16; 1Jn 4:9–10

4. God expresses a special love for his people
–In his love for Jesus ..... Jn 16:27; Jn 17:23
–In our election ..... Eph 1:4; 1Th 1:4
–In our being called ..... Ro 1:7; Jude 1
–In our receiving his grace 2Th 2:16
–In our adoption 1Jn 3:1
–In our salvation ..... 2Th 2:13; Tit 3:4–5
–In our redemption ..... Dt 7:8; Isa 63:9
–In our forgiveness ..... Isa 38:17
–In our being made alive with Christ ..... Eph 2:4–5
–In our receiving the Holy Spirit ..... Ro 5:5
–In our being disciplined ..... Heb 12:5–7
–In our obedience 1Jn 2:5
–In our love for others 1Jn 3:17; 1Jn 4:12
–In our receiving eternal life ..... Jude 21

5. Our relationship to this love
–It is everlasting ..... Jer 31:3
–We must be directed into it 2Th 3:5
–We must keep ourselves in it ..... Jude 21
–Nothing can separate us from it ..... Ro 8:35–39

LUKE

–The beloved doctor ..... Col 4:14
–Co-worker with Paul ..... 2Ti 4:11; Phm 24
–Likely a travel companion with Paul ..... Ac 16:10–17; Ac 20:5–21:18; Ac 27:1–28:16

LUST

See SEXUAL STANDARDS

LYDIA

–Seller of cloth from Thyatira ..... Ac 16:14
–Responded to Paul's preaching ..... Ac 16:14
–Invited Paul to stay at her house in Philippi ..... Ac 16:15
–Church met in her house ..... Ac 16:40

LYING

–Misrepresenting or falsifying the truth

A. Perspectives on lying
–God does not lie ..... Tit 1:2

–Denying that Jesus is the Christ is lying 1Jn 2:22; 1Jn 5:10
–Hypocrites are liars .... Ps 62:4; 1Jn 4:20
–The antichrist deceives humanity 2Th 2:9–10
–Satan is the father of lies .... Jn 8:44; Ac 13:10
–Lying will be exposed . Pr 12:19

B. The prohibition against lying
–Ninth commandment prohibits lying .... Ex 20:16; Dt 5:20
–Other laws prohibit lying .... Lev 19:11; Eph 4:25; Col 3:9
–Lying is detestable to God .... Pr 6:16–17
–Pray to be kept from lying .... Pr 30:8

C. The punishment for lying
–Severe punishment for false witnesses .... Dt 19:16–19; Pr 19:5
–God silences liars ...... Ps 63:11
–God punishes liars ..... Ps 120:3–4
–God destroys liars ..... Ps 5:6; Mic 6:12–13
–God excludes liars from heaven .... Rev 21:8,27

D. Examples of lying in the Bible
1. Sinful lying
–Satan in the Garden of Eden .... Ge 3:4
–Cain to God .... Ge 4:9
–Abram about Sarai .. Ge 12:10–20
–Sarah to God .... Ge 18:15
–Jacob to his father .. Ge 27:14–25
–Joseph's brothers to Jacob .... Ge 37:31–33
–Gibeonites to Joshua .... Jos 9:1–13
–Saul to Samuel 1Sa 15:1–3, 13–22
–False witnesses about Naboth 1Ki 21:11–12
–Lying prophets to Ahab 1Ki 22:6,19–28
–Gehazi to Naaman .. 2Ki 5:20–24
–False prophets to the people .... Eze 13:1–9
–False witnesses about Jesus .... Mt 26:59–62
–Peter about Jesus ... Mt 26:69–74
–Ananias and Sapphira to God .... Ac 5:1–10
2. Lying with God's approval
–Midwives lie to spare babies .... Ex 1:15–21
–Rahab lies to save the spies .... Jos 2:1–14
–Ehud deceives King Eglon .... Jdg 3:15–18
–Jael deceives Sisera . Jdg 4:17–21; Jdg 5:24–27

See also HYPOCRISY; TRUTH

MACEDONIA

–A Roman province, north of Achaia (Greece)

A. Paul in the main cities of Macedonia
–Paul's vision of man of Macedonia .... Ac 16:9
–Philippi .... Ac 16:12–40
–Thessalonica .... Ac 17:1–9
–Berea .... Ac 17:10–15

See also PAUL

B. Christians in Macedonia
–Suffered persecution ... Ac 17:5–8, 13; 1Th 1:6
–Were dedicated believers 1Th 1:7–10; 2Co 8:1,5
–Were poor 2Co 8:1–2
–Gave generously to the poor .... Ro 15:25–26; 2Co 8:2–4
–Helped Paul financially . 2Co 11:7–9; Php 4:14–18

MACHPELAH

–Cave purchased by Abraham from Ephron .... Ge 23:7–18
–Sarah buried there .... Ge 23:19
–Abraham buried there ...... Ge 25:9–10
–Isaac, Rebekah and Leah buried there .... Ge 49:29–31
–Jacob buried there .... Ge 50:12–13

MAGIC, WITCHCRAFT AND SORCERY

A. Terms used
–Divination .... Dt 18:10
–Sorcery .... Dt 18:10
–Soothsaying .... Dt 18:10
–Augury .... Dt 18:10
–Casting spells .... Dt 18:11
–Mediums and spiritists . Dt 18:11
–Consulting the dead 1Sa 28:3–19
–Magic .... Eze 13:18,20

B. Purpose of magic and sorcery
–To determine the future .... Ge 44:15; 1Sa 28:5–7; Da 2:2,27
–To control the future ... Ge 30:14; Nu 23:23

C. Warnings against magic and sorcery
–In the law .... Ex 22:18; Lev 19:26, 31; Lev 20:6,27; Dt 18:10–12, 20–21
–In the prophets .... Isa 2:6; Isa 47:10–14; Jer 27:9; Mic 5:12; Mal 3:5
–In the early church .... Ac 8:9–24; Ac 13:6–12; Ac 16:16–18; Ac 19:13–19; Gal 5:20; Rev 21:8

MANASSEH

A. Firstborn of Joseph ..... Ge 41:51; Ge 46:20
–Name means "forget" . Ge 41:51
–Blessed by Jacob, but not as firstborn .... Ge 48:12–20

B. Tribe descended from Manasseh
–Blessed by Moses ..... Dt 33:17
–Numbered .... Nu 1:35; Nu 26:34
–Allotted land east of the Jordan .... Nu 32:33, 39–42; Jos 13:8–33
–Allotted land west of the Jordan .... Jos 17:1–11; Eze 48:4
–Failed to fully possess the land .... Jos 17:12–13; Jdg 1:27
–One of the tribes of the 144,000 .... Rev 7:6

C. Son of Hezekiah; king of Judah 2Ki 20:21; 2Ch 32:33
–Judah's most wicked king 2Ki 21:1–11; 2Ch 33:1–10
–Captured by Assyrians . 2Ch 33:11
–Repented of his sins ... 2Ch 33:12–13
–Began to clear land of idols 2Ch 33:15–16
–Judah exiled for his sins 2Ki 21:10–15

MARK

–Jewish name is John .... Ac 12:25
–A cousin of Barnabas ...... Col 4:10
–A close friend of Peter 1Pe 5:13
–Believers gathered at his home to pray .... Ac 12:12
–Went to Antioch with Barnabas and Saul .... Ac 12:25
–Did mission work with Barnabas and Saul .... Ac 13:4–5
–Deserted Paul in Pamphylia .... Ac 15:37–38
–Returned with Barnabas to Cyprus .... Ac 15:39
–Later became fellow worker with Paul again .... Phm 24; 2Ti 4:11

MARRIAGE

A. God and marriage
1. God honors marriage
–Established it in Garden of Eden .... Ge 2:18,21–24
–Command repeated in New Testament ..... Mt 19:5; Eph 5:31
–Regulated it by Old Testament laws ..... Lev 20:10–21; Nu 36:1–12; Dt 25:5–10
–Jesus attended a wedding .... Jn 2:1–2
–Marriage must be honored .... Mal 2:15; Heb 13:4
2. Monogamy versus polygamy
–Ideal is monogamy .. Ge 2:24; 1Ti 3:2,12
–Polygamy practiced in Old Testament ... Ge 29:16–30; 1Sa 1:1–2; 1Sa 25:42–43; 1Ki 11:1–3
–Polygamy often caused friction ...... Ge 30:1; Lev 18:18; 1Sa 1:3–8
3. Adultery
–In all cases forbidden .... Ex 20:14; Lev 18:20
–Excludes one from the kingdom of God . Gal 5:19–21; 1Co 6:9

See ADULTERY

4. Marriage with unbelievers forbidden
–In the Old Testament law .... Ex 34:15–16; Dt 7:3–4
–By Old Testament examples .... Jdg 16:4–21; 1Ki 11:1–8; Ezr 9:1–5, 10–15; Ne 13:23–27
–In the New Testament 1Co 7:12–16; 2Co 6:14–18
5. Permanency of marriage
–Marriage is union for life .... Mt 19:3–6,9; Ro 7:2–3; 1Co 7:39
–God hates divorce ... Mal 2:16
–Divorce allowed for hardness of heart .... Dt 24:1–4; Mt 19:7–8

See DIVORCE

B. Being single and being married
1. Remaining single is an option
–It is a gift from God 1Co 7:7–8
–It is preferable in times of crisis 1Co 7:25–28
–It frees one to serve God totally 1Co 7:32–35
2. Purposes of marriage
–To inspire human happiness .... Ge 2:18
–To express love intimately .... Pr 5:15–20; SS 2:3–7; SS 8:5–7
–To have children .... Ge 1:27–28; Mal 2:15; 1Ti 5:14
–To prevent immorality 1Co 7:2,8–9

C. Weddings in the Bible
–The wedding of Isaac .. Ge 24:62–67
–The weddings of Jacob . Ge 29:21–28
–The wedding of Samson .... Jdg 14:10–19
–The wedding of a king . Ps 45:1–17
–Jesus at a wedding in Cana .... Jn 2:1–11
–Wedding parables of Jesus .... Mt 22:1–14; Mt 25:1–13; Lk 14:8–11

D. Duties of marriage partners
–Husband to be devoted to his wife's good ..... Eph 5:25; Col 3:19; 1Pe 3:7
–Wife to be subject to her husband .... Eph 5:22; Col 3:18; 1Pe 3:1
–Equal responsibility 1Co 7:1–5, 32–35

E. Marriage as a symbol
–God as the husband of Israel .... Isa 54:5; Jer 3:14; Hos 2:16, 19–20
–Christ as the bridegroom of the church .... Mk 2:19–20; Jn 3:29
–Christ as the husband of the church .... 2Co 11:2; Eph 5:22–32
–Church as the bride of Christ .... Eph 5:22–24; Rev 21:2,9–10
–Heaven begins with a wedding .... Mt 22:1–10; Mt 25:1–10; Rev 19:7,9

MARTHA

–Sister of Mary and Lazarus . Lk 10:38–39; Jn 11:1
–Kept busy in the kitchen ... Lk 10:40
–Rebuked by Jesus .... Lk 10:41–42
–Went to meet Jesus after Lazarus died .... Jn 11:20
–Confessed the resurrection .. Jn 11:20–27
–Objected to opening Lazarus's tomb .... Jn 11:38–40

MARY

A. Mother of Jesus .... Mt 1:16
–Angel announced her pregnancy .... Lk 1:26–38
–Visited cousin Elizabeth .... Lk 1:39–40
–Sang a song .... Lk 1:46–55
–Her virgin birth announced to Joseph ... Mt 1:18–25
–Gave birth to Jesus in Bethlehem .... Lk 2:1–7
–Presented Jesus in the temple .... Lk 2:21–24
–Fled with Joseph and baby to Egypt .... Mt 2:13–15
–Returned and settled in Nazareth .... Mt 2:19–23
–With twelve-year-old Jesus in temple .... Lk 2:41–52
–Had other children ..... Mk 6:3
–Went to a wedding in Cana .... Jn 2:1–5
–Questioned Jesus' sanity .... Mk 3:21
–Observed Jesus' crucifixion .... Mt 27:55–56
–Entrusted to John at the cross .... Jn 19:25–27
–Among the disciples after ascension .... Ac 1:14

B. Mary Magdalene
–Former demoniac ...... Lk 8:2
–Helped support Jesus' ministry .... Lk 8:1–3
–Present at the cross .... Mt 27:56; Mk 15:40
–Present at Jesus' burial . Mt 27:61; Mk 15:47
–Went to the tomb early on Easter Sunday ...... Mt 28:1
–Saw angel after the resurrection .... Mt 28:2–10; Mk 16:1–8
–Saw Jesus after the resurrection .... Mk 16:9; Jn 20:1–2, 10–18

C. Sister of Martha and Lazarus
–Jesus visited them ..... Lk 10:38–39
–Went to meet Jesus after Lazarus died .... Jn 11:28–32
–Listened to Jesus' teaching .... Lk 10:39
–Washed Jesus' feet .... Jn 11:2; Jn 12:1–8
–Commended by Jesus .. Mt 26:6–13; Lk 10:41–42

MATTHEW

–A disciple of Jesus .... Mt 10:3; Mk 3:18
–A tax collector, called by Jesus to follow him .... Mt 9:9
–Also called Levi .... Mk 2:14–17; Lk 5:27–32
–Held dinner for Jesus ...... Mt 9:10–13
–One of the apostles .... Ac 1:13

MATTHIAS

–Apostle, chosen to replace Judas .... Ac 1:26

MEDES AND PERSIANS

A. Two related nations ..... Est 1:14; Da 6:8,12,15; Da 8:20
B. Significance for God's people
 –Northern kingdom deported there 2Ki 17:6; 2Ki 18:11
 –Defeated Babylonians .. Isa 13:17; Jer 51:11,28; Da 5:28,30–31
 –Allowed Jews to rebuild Palestine 2Ch 36:20–23
C. Kings of the Medes and Persians, in chronological order
 –Darius the Mede .... Da 5:31
 –Cyrus .... Ezr 1:1–2
 –Darius the Persian ..... Ezr 4:5,24
 –Xerxes .... Est 1:1
 –Artaxerxes .... Ezr 7:1; Ne 2:1

–See entries for each individual king

MEDIATOR

–Someone who helps bring reconciliation between two parties

A. Human mediators at work
 –Judah spoke to Joseph for Benjamin .... Ge 44:18–34
 –Moses spoke to Pharaoh for the Israelites .... Ex 5:1–5
 –Jonathan spoke to Saul for David 1Sa 19:1–7
 –Abigail spoke to David for her husband 1Sa 25:14–35
 –Esther spoke to the king for her people .... Est 7:1–6
B. Mediators between God and humans
 1. The need for a mediator
  –Israelites desired one at Mount Sinai ..... Ex 20:18–19
  –Job cried out for one .... Job 9:33
  –Job knew one existed .... Job 16:19–21
  –The task of a mediator .... 1Sa 2:25; Job 33:23–25; Gal 3:20
 2. Human mediators between God and his people
  –Moses .... Ex 32:7–14; Nu 14:11–20; Dt 5:5; Gal 3:19
  –Prophets .... 1Ki 21:17–19; Jer 23:21–22; Da 9:3–19; Heb 1:1
  –Priests .... Lev 16:20–21; Nu 6:22–27; Ezr 9:3–15
  –Kings 1Ki 8:22–53; 1Ch 21:16–17
 3. Jesus as mediator between us and God
  a. Described as a mediator
   –Our chief mediator with God .... Heb 8:6; Heb 9:15; Heb 12:24
   –The only one needed 1Ti 2:5
  b. His qualifications as a mediator
   –He is fully God .. Jn 1:1; Heb 1:3; 1Jn 5:20
   –He is fully human .... Jn 1:14; Php 2:6–8; Heb 2:14,17; 1Jn 4:2
  c. His tasks as our mediator
   –Isaiah prophesied Jesus' task .... Isa 53:3–12
   –Reversed consequences of Adam's sin ...... Ro 5:15–19; 1Co 15:21–22
   –Reconciled us to God through death .... 2Co 5:18–21; Col 1:21–22
   –Intercedes with God on our behalf .... Jn 17:6–26; Ro 8:34; Heb 7:25; 1Jn 2:1
   –Brings messages from God to us .. Jn 12:49–50; Heb 1:1–2

MEDITATION

–Reflecting on God and his word

A. On what are we to meditate?
 –On God .... Ps 63:6
 –On God's law .... Ps 1:2; Ps 119:15, 48,97
 –On God's promises .... Ps 119:148
 –On God's unfailing love .... Ps 48:9
 –On God's works .... Ps 77:12; Ps 143:5; Ps 145:5
B. What does meditation accomplish?
 –Gives us a sense of peace .... Php 4:6–9
 –Develops close relationship with God .... Ps 63:6–8
 –Prepares us for important decisions .... Lk 6:12–13
 –Gives us strength for Christian living .... Ps 1:2–3; 2Co 12:7–9
 –Helps give us direction for life .... Ac 22:17–21
C. When did people meditate?
 –In the morning .... Ps 5:1–3; Mk 1:35
 –All day long .... Ps 119:97
 –Day and night .... Jos 1:8; Ps 1:2
 –In the evening .... Ge 24:63
 –Through the watches of the night .... Ps 119:148
D. Examples of those who meditated
 –Isaac .... Ge 24:63
 –Psalmists .... Ps 48:9; Ps 119:48, 97,148; Ps 143:5
 –Jesus .... Mt 14:23; Mk 1:35; Lk 5:16
 –Jesus' followers .... Ac 9:11–12; Ac 10:2,9–16; Ac 22:17–18

MEEKNESS

–The quality of a gentle spirit

A. Human meekness
 1. Meekness is required of us
  –A Christian quality .. Col 3:12; 1Ti 6:11
  –An aspect of the fruit of the Spirit .... Gal 5:22–23
  –We must act with gentleness .... Eph 4:2; Php 4:5; 1Pe 3:15
 2. Meekness is a powerful force
  –A gentle tongue is persuasive .... Pr 25:15
  –A gentle answer turns away anger .... Pr 15:1
  –A gentle spirit wins people to Christ 1Pe 3:1–4
 3. The meek are blessed .... Ps 37:11; Mt 5:5

See also HUMILITY

B. God's meekness
 –The gentle whisper of God 1Ki 19:12
 –The meekness and gentleness of Christ .... Zec 9:9; Mt 21:5; 2Co 10:1

MEGIDDO

–Its king defeated by Joshua . Jos 12:21
–A city given to Manasseh .. Jos 17:11
–Manasseh did not conquer it .... Jdg 1:27
–Deborah and Barak fought there .... Jdg 5:19
–Solomon built it up 1Ki 9:15
–King Ahaziah died there ... 2Ki 9:27
–Josiah was killed there 2Ki 23:29–30; 2Ch 35:20–27
–Final battle at Armageddon ("hill of Megiddo") .... Rev 16:14–16

MELCHIZEDEK

–King of Salem; priest of God Most High .... Ge 14:18
–Blessed Abram .... Ge 14:19–20
–Called a high priest forever .... Ps 110:4
–His priesthood prophetic of Jesus .... Heb 5:6; Heb 6:20
–His priesthood explained ... Heb 7:1–28

MENAHEM

–King of Israel 2Ki 15:17–22
–Assassinated Shallum to become king 2Ki 15:14
–Extremely cruel 2Ki 15:16

MEPHIBOSHETH

–Son of Jonathan 2Sa 4:4
–Shown kindness by David .. 2Sa 9:1–13
–Accused by Ziba of siding with Absalom 2Sa 16:1–4
–Explained his story to David 2Sa 19:24–30
–Spared from death 2Sa 21:7

MERCY

–Undeserved kindness and compassion

A. Human mercy
 1. The command to be merciful
  –Be merciful .... Lk 6:36; Ro 12:8; Jude 22
  –Mercy is more important than sacrifice .... Hos 6:6; Mic 6:6–8; Mt 9:13
 2. Expressions of human mercy
  –Being forgiving ..... Mt 18:23–35
  –Being kind to the hurting .... Lk 10:30–37
  –Being kind to the poor .... Lk 16:19–26
B. The mercy of God
 1. A part of his nature
  –God is merciful ..... Dt 4:31; Ne 9:31; Lk 6:36
  –God exercises mercy freely .... Ex 33:19; Ro 9:15–18
  –Mercy triumphs over judgment .... Jas 2:13
 2. Expressions of his mercy
  –Forgiving our sins .. Ps 51:1–2; Da 9:9; 1Ti 1:13–16
  –Saving us in Christ .. Eph 2:4–5; Tit 3:4–5; 1Pe 1:3–4
  –Being faithful to his covenant .... Dt 4:31; Dt 13:17–18; Ne 9:31
  –Receiving us back to himself .... Jer 3:12–13
  –Healing us when ill . Php 2:27
  –Sparing his own from destruction .... Ge 19:16; Ps 116:1–6
  –Keeping us safe from the enemy .... Ps 6:9–10; Ps 28:6–7
 3. Praying for God's mercy
  –"Be gracious to me" .... Ps 4:1; Ps 9:13
  –"Hear my cry for help" .... Ps 28:2; Ps 86:6,16
  –"Be mindful of your mercy" .... Ps 25:6
  –"Be merciful to me, a sinner" .... Lk 18:13
  –"Jesus, have mercy on us" .... Mt 9:27; Mt 20:30–31

See also GRACE; COMPASSION

MESHACH

–Hebrew deported to Babylon .... Da 1:1–6
–Name changed from Mishael .... Da 1:7
–Refused to be defiled by food .... Da 1:8–20
–Appointed administrator over Babylon .... Da 2:49
–Refused to worship idols ... Da 3:1–12
–Saved from the fiery furnace .... Da 3:13–30

MESSIAH

See JESUS CHRIST

METHUSELAH

–Son of Enoch, father of Lamech .... Ge 5:21–27
–Lived 969 years .... Ge 5:27

MICAIAH

–Prophet of the Lord 1Ki 22:7–8
–Warned Ahab of disaster ... 1Ki 22:9–28; 2Ch 18:1–27

MICHAEL

–An archangel .... Jude 9
–Stood against the forces of evil .... Da 10:13,21
–Conducted war in heaven against Satan .... Rev 12:7

MICHAL

–Daughter of Saul 1Sa 14:49
–Became wife of David 1Sa 18:20–28
–Warned David of Saul's plot 1Sa 19:11–17
–Given by Saul to Paltiel ... 1Sa 25:44
–Retrieved by David 2Sa 3:13–16
–Criticized David for dancing before the ark 2Sa 6:16–23; 1Ch 15:29

MIDIANITES

A. Their identity
 –Descendants of Abraham through Keturah .... Ge 25:1–4
 –Very wealthy .... Jdg 8:24–26
B. Important Midianites
 –Jethro: priest of Midian .... Ex 3:1
 –Zipporah: Moses' wife . Ex 2:21
 –Cozbi: killed for marrying an Israelite .... Nu 25:14–15
 –Oreb and Zeeb: kings killed by Gideon ...... Jdg 7:25–26
 –Zeba and Zalmunna: kings killed by Gideon . Jdg 8:12,21
C. Their interactions with God's people
 –Brought Joseph to Egypt .... Ge 37:36
 –Allied with Moabites against Israelites .... Nu 22:4,7
 –Intermarried with the Israelites .... Nu 25:6
 –Were considered enemies of Israel .... Nu 25:16–18
 –Defeated by Moses .... Nu 31:1–12
 –Oppressed the Israelites .... Jdg 6:1–6
 –Defeated by Gideon .... Jdg 7:1–25

MILK

A. Sources of milk
 –Cattle .... Dt 32:14

–Held land east of the Jordan ... Nu 33:48–49; Dt 2:9
–Served the god Chemosh ... 1Ki 11:7

B. Important Moabites
–Balak: hired Balaam to curse them ... Nu 22:2–24:25
–Eglon: killed by Ehud ... Jdg 3:12,15–23
–Ruth: married Boaz ... Ru 1:22
See RUTH

C. Their wars against Israelites
–Allied with Midianites against Israel ... Nu 22:4,7
–Allied with Ammonites against Israel ... Jdg 3:12–13
–Defeated by Israelites under Ehud ... Jdg 3:28–30
–Defeated by King Saul ... 1Sa 14:47
–Defeated by David ... 2Sa 8:11–12; 1Ch 18:11
–Rebelled against Israel ... 2Ki 3:5
–Defeated by Joram and Jehoshaphat ... 2Ki 3:6–25
–Allied with Ammonites against Judah ... 2Ch 20:1
–They and Ammonites destroyed each other ... 2Ch 20:22–24
–Raided the land of Israel ... 2Ki 13:20
–Allied against Jehoiakim ... 2Ki 24:1–2

D. Important data concerning them
1. Before the time of the kings
–Intermarried with Israelites ... Nu 25:1–3
–Israelites did not pass through Moab ... Jdg 11:17–18
–Not allowed to join Israelites ... Dt 23:3; Ne 13:1–3
–Moses died on Mount Pisgah in Moab ... Dt 34:1–5
–Elimelech and Naomi lived there ... Ru 1:1–5
2. During the time of the kings
–David brought his parents there ... 1Sa 22:3–4
–Solomon intermarried with them ... 1Ki 11:1
–Israelites worshiped their gods ... 1Ki 11:7
–Paid tribute to Ahab ... 2Ki 3:4
3. Numerous Jews intermarried with them ... Ezr 9:1; Ne 13:23–27
4. Prophecies concerning their destruction ... Isa 15:1–16:14; Jer 48:1–47; Eze 25:8–11; Am 2:1–3; Zep 2:8–11

MONEY

See THE RICH AND THE POOR
STEWARDSHIP

MONTH

–*Twelve time segments per year, based on the moon*
–Abib or Nisan, the first month ... Ex 13:4; Ne 2:1
–Ziv or Iyyar, the second month ... 1Ki 6:1
–Sivan, the third month ... Est 8:9
–Tammuz, the fourth month ... Jer 52:6
–Ab, the fifth month ... Nu 33:38
–Elul, the sixth month ... Ne 6:15
–Ethanim or Tishri, the seventh month ... 1Ki 8:2
–Bul or Heshvan, the eighth month ... 1Ki 6:38
–Chislev, the ninth month ... Zec 7:1
–Tebeth, the tenth month ... Est 2:16
–Shebat, the eleventh month ... Zec 1:7
–Adar, the twelfth month ... Ezr 6:15

MOON

A. Data concerning the moon
–Created by God ... Ge 1:16; Ps 8:3
–Controlled by God ... Jos 10:12–13; Jer 31:35
–Governs the night ... Ge 1:16; Ps 136:9
–Marks off the seasons ... Ge 1:14; Ps 104:19
–New moon festivals ... Nu 10:10; 1Sa 20:5,18,24; Am 8:5
–Involved in the blessing of productive land ... Dt 33:13–14
–Must praise God ... Ps 148:3
–Believed to cause mental illness ... Ps 121:6
–Worshiped by the heathen ... 2Ki 23:5; Jer 8:2
–No moon needed in heaven ... Isa 60:19–20; Rev 21:23

B. The moon used in a symbolic way
–Of stability and endurance ... Ps 72:5,7
–Of judgment at the end of time ... Isa 13:10–11; Mt 24:29; Rev 6:12

MORDECAI

–Benjamite exile who brought up Esther ... Est 2:5–10
–Exposed plot to kill Xerxes ... Est 2:19–23
–Refused to honor Haman ... Est 3:1–6; Est 5:9–14
–Gallows made for him ... Est 5:14
–Begged Esther to foil Haman's plot ... Est 4:1–17
–Haman forced to honor him ... Est 6:1–11
–Exalted by the king ... Est 8:1–2,15; Est 9:3–4
–With Esther, established Purim ... Est 9:18–32

MORIAH

–Region where Abraham went to "sacrifice" Isaac ... Ge 22:1–18
–Mountain on which temple was built ... 2Ch 3:1–2

MOSES

A. Family data
–Son of Amram and Jochebed ... Ex 6:20; 1Ch 6:3
–Tribe of Levi ... Ex 2:1
–Brother of Aaron ... Ex 4:14
–Name means "drawn out" ... Ex 2:10
–Married Zipporah ... Ex 2:21
–Father of Gershom and Eliezer ... Ex 2:22; Ex 18:2–4

B. His history
1. His youth
–Hid by his parents for three months ... Ex 2:2; Heb 11:23
–Hid in a basket in the Nile ... Ex 2:3–4
–Discovered by Pharaoh's daughter ... Ex 2:5–9
–Brought up by Pharaoh's daughter ... Ex 2:10
–Killed an Egyptian ... Ex 2:11–12
–Fled to Midian ... Ex 2:13–15
–Became a shepherd ... Ex 3:1
2. Delivered Israel from Egypt
–Called by God ... Ex 3:2—4:17
–Explained his call to Israelites ... Ex 4:29–31
–Made demands to Pharaoh ... Ex 5:1–5
–The ten plagues ... Ex 7:14—11:9
–Arranged the Passover ... Ex 12:1–28
–Led Israelites out of Egypt ... Ex 12:29–42
–Led them to the border of the Red Sea ... Ex 13:17—14:4
–Led them across the Red Sea ... Ex 14:21–31
–Sang song of deliverance ... Ex 15:1–21
3. Led Israel to Mount Sinai
–Water at Marah and Elim ... Ex 15:22–27
–Asked God for food; received manna ... Ex 16:1–16
–Brought water from the rock ... Ex 17:1–7
–Raised hands to defeat Amalekites ... Ex 17:8–16
–Delegated judges ... Ex 18:13–27; Dt 1:9–18
–Received law at Mount Sinai ... Ex 19:3–25; Ex 24:12–18; Jn 1:17
–Announced law to Israel ... Ex 24:3–7
–Broke tablets because of golden calf ... Ex 32:19–20; Dt 9:7–17
–Received law a second time ... Ex 34:1–4, 27–28
–Saw glory of the Lord ... Ex 33:18–23
–His face reflected glory of God ... Ex 34:29–35
–Supervised building of tabernacle ... Ex 35:4—36:7
–Set apart Aaron and priests ... Lev 8:1—9:24
–Numbered tribes ... Nu 1:1—4:49
4. From Sinai to the border of Canaan
–Left Sinai ... Nu 10:11–13
–Handled the people's complaints ... Nu 11:1–34
–Opposed by Aaron and Miriam ... Nu 12:1–15
–Sent spies into Canaan ... Nu 13:1–33
–Prayed for the rebellious people ... Nu 14:1–25
–Announced forty years of wandering ... Nu 14:26–40
–Opposed by Korah ... Nu 16:1–50
–Struck rock; forbidden to enter Canaan ... Nu 20:1–13; Dt 1:37
–Put bronze snake on a pole for healing ... Nu 21:4–9; Jn 3:14
–Defeated kings in battle ... Nu 21:1–3, 21–31
–Numbered tribes a second time ... Nu 26:1–65
–Designated Joshua as successor ... Nu 27:12–23; Dt 34:9
–Gave final address (Deuteronomy) ... Dt 1:5
–Sang a song ... Dt 31:30—32:43
–Blessed the twelve tribes ... Dt 33:1–29
–Saw the promised land ... Dt 34:1–4
–His death ... Dt 34:5–8

C. Titles ascribed to him
–The man of God ... Ezr 3:2
–God's chosen one ... Ps 106:23
–The servant of the Lord ... 2Ch 24:6,9; Ps 105:26
–The lawgiver ... Jn 1:17
–Prophet of the Lord ... Dt 18:15,18
–Intimate friend of God ... Ex 33:11
–Leader of God's people ... Mic 6:4
–Shepherd of God's people ... Ps 77:20

D. Moses in the New Testament
–Appeared to Jesus at the transfiguration ... Mt 17:2–4
–Respected for giving the Law ... Mt 19:7–8; Jn 7:19,23
–Exemplified true faith ... Heb 11:24–28
–Foreshadowed Jesus as the Prophet ... Ac 3:21–23
–His writings prophetic of Jesus ... Jn 1:45
–His lifting up of snake pictured Jesus' death ... Jn 3:14–15
–Crossing the Red Sea pictured baptism ... 1Co 10:1–2
–His veil symbolized the old covenant ... 2Co 3:7–16
–His faithfulness foreshadowed that of Jesus ... Heb 3:1–6
–God, not Moses, gave manna ... Jn 6:30–33

MOTHER

A. Motherhood in the Bible
1. The experience of motherhood
–It is a gift from God ... Ps 113:9; Ps 127:3
–It can be painful ... Ge 3:16; Isa 13:8; Jn 16:21
–Infertility can cause frustration ... Ge 25:21; Ge 30:1; 1Sa 1:1–20
2. Women saved through childbearing ... 1Ti 2:15
3. Significant experiences of motherhood
–Eve, the mother of the living ... Ge 3:20; Ge 4:1–2,25
–Sarah ... Ge 21:1–5
–Rebekah ... Ge 25:21–26
–Leah ... Ge 29:31–35; Ge 30:17–21
–Rachel ... Ge 30:1–3, 22–23; Ge 35:16–18
–Jochebed (Moses' mother) ... Ex 2:1–10
–Samson's mother ... Jdg 13:1–24
–Ruth ... Ru 4:13–15
–Hannah ... 1Sa 1:1–20
–Bathsheba ... 2Sa 12:24–25
–Isaiah's wife ... Isa 8:3–4
–Hosea's wife ... Hos 1:2–9
–Elizabeth ... Lk 1:24–25, 39–44
–The virgin Mary ... Lk 1:26–38; Lk 2:4–7

B. The mother in the family
1. Duties of a mother to her children
–Loves them ... 1Ki 3:26; Isa 49:15
–Comforts and cares for them ... Ru 4:16; Isa 66:13; 1Th 2:13
–Protects them ... Ex 2:1–3; Heb 11:23
–With their husbands, educates them ... Pr 1:8; Pr 31:1,26
–Educates them alone, if necessary ... 2Ti 1:5; 2Ti 3:15
–Watches over their affairs ... Ge 27:5–17; 1Ki 1:11–31; Pr 31:15,27
2. Responsibility of children to mothers
–Obey them ... Dt 21:18; Eph 6:1–2
–Respect them ... Ex 20:12; Lev 19:3; Pr 23:22
–Listen to them ... Pr 1:8; Pr 6:20

C. Mother used as a symbol
–God compared to a mother ... Isa 49:15; Isa 66:13
–The church as mother ... Isa 66:10–11; Gal 4:26

MOUNTAIN

A. Mountains mentioned in the Bible
–Mount Ararat ... Ge 8:4
–Mount Baalah ... Jos 15:11
–Mount Carmel ... 1Ki 18:19
–Mount Ebal ... Dt 11:29
–Mount Ephron ... Jos 15:9
–Mount Gaash ... Jos 24:30
–Mount Gerizim ... Dt 11:29
–Mount Gilboa ... 1Sa 31:1
–Mount Gilead ... Jdg 7:3
–Mount Halak ... Jos 11:17
–Mount Heres ... Jdg 1:35
–Mount Hermon ... Dt 3:8
–Mount Hor ... Nu 20:22
–Mount Horeb ... Ex 33:6
–Mount Jearim ... Jos 15:10

–Mount Mizar ... Ps 42:6
–Mount Moriah ... 2Ch 3:1
–Mount Nebo ... Dt 32:49
–Mount of Olives ... Zec 14:4
See OLIVES, MOUNT OF
–Mount Paran ... Dt 33:2
–Mount Perazim ... Isa 28:21
–Mount Pisgah ... Jos 12:3
–Mount Samaria ... Am 4:1
–Mount Seir ... Dt 1:2
–Mount Shepher ... Nu 33:23
–Mount Sinai ... Ex 19:11
See SINAI
–Mount Sirion ... Dt 4:48
–Mount Tabor ... Jdg 4:6
–Mount Zalmon ... Jdg 9:48
–Mount Zemaraim ... 2Ch 13:4
–Mount Zion ... Ps 48:2
See ZION
B. Mountains used in illustrations
–Of God's creative power ... Am 4:13
–Of God's continuing power ... Ps 65:5–7
–Of God's redemptive power ... Isa 40:4–5
–Of the power of God's judgment ... Rev 6:14–16
–Of God's righteousness . Ps 36:6
–Of God's glory in the new age ... Isa 2:2–3
–Of prosperity for God's people ... Ps 72:3; Am 9:13
–Of the strength of human faith ... Mt 17:20–21
–Of the joy of the redeemed ... Isa 44:23

MOUTH

A. The human mouth
1. Appropriate functions of our mouths
–To praise God ... Ps 63:5
–To sing to the Lord . Ps 40:3
–To testify concerning God ... Ps 89:1
–To confess Jesus as Lord ... Ro 10:9–10
–To reveal God's word ... Dt 18:18
–To reveal what is in the heart ... Mt 12:34–35
–To speak words ... Ps 19:14
–To laugh with joy ... Ps 126:2
–To eat ... 1Sa 14:26–27
–To drink ... Jdg 7:6
–To kiss ... SS 1:2
2. Responsibilities to our mouths
a. Negative
–Keep them from sin ... Ecc 5:6
–Keep them from perversity ... Pr 4:24
–Keep them from flattery ... Pr 26:28
–Keep them from arrogance ... 1Sa 2:3
–Keep them from lies ... Rev 14:5
–Keep them from unwholesome talk ... Eph 4:29
–Keep them from cursing ... Jas 3:9–10
b. Positive
–Speak what is true and just ... Pr 8:7–8
–Speak what is wise ... Ps 37:30
–Guide them properly ... Pr 16:23
–Guard them properly ... Pr 21:23
B. The mouth of God
–God created with his mouth ... Ps 33:6
–God gave his law with his mouth ... Ps 119:13,72
–God gives promises with his mouth ... Isa 40:3–5
–God teaches with his mouth ... Dt 8:3
–God pronounces judgment with his mouth ... Isa 1:20
–God rejects by spitting us out of his mouth ... Rev 3:16
–God destroys with his mouth ... Ps 18:8
–Jesus destroys with a sword in his mouth ... Rev 2:16; Rev 19:15

MURDER

–The deliberate killing of another human
A. The command against murder
–The sixth commandment ... Ex 20:13; Dt 5:17; Jas 2:10–11
–Anger as the root of murder ... Mt 5:21–22
–Hatred as the root of murder ... 1Jn 3:15
–Murder roots out of a sinful heart ... Mt 15:18–19
B. What happens after a murder
–One can be cursed by God ... Ge 4:11
–One can be excluded from heaven ... 1Jn 3:15; Rev 22:15
–One is subject to capital punishment ... Ge 9:5–6; Ex 21:12–14,23
–More than one witness required ... Nu 35:30; Dt 19:15
–Cities of refuge in Israel ... Nu 35:16–32; Dt 19:1–14
–Murderers can be forgiven ... Lk 23:34; Ac 7:60
C. Examples of murder in the Bible
–Cain killed Abel ... Ge 4:8
–Moses killed an Egyptian ... Ex 2:11–12
–Abimelech killed his brothers ... Jdg 9:5
–David killed Uriah ... 2Sa 12:9
–Absalom killed Ammon ... 2Sa 13:28–33
–Jezebel killed Naboth .. 1Ki 21:8–14
–Hazael killed Ben-hadad ... 2Ki 8:14–15
–Athaliah killed the royal family ... 2Ki 11:1
–Herod killed the babies in Bethlehem ... Mt 2:16
–Herod killed John the Baptist ... Mt 14:6–11
–The Jews killed Jesus .. Ac 2:23; 1Th 2:15
–The Jews killed Stephen ... Ac 7:57–60
–Herod killed James ... Ac 12:2

MUSIC AND SONG

A. Musical instruments
1. Begun by Jubal ... Ge 4:21
2. Types of instruments in the Bible
–Bells ... Ex 28:33–35
–Castanets ... 2Sa 6:5
–Cymbals ... 2Sa 6:5
–Drum ... Da 3:5
–Harp ... Ge 4:21
–Horn ... Da 3:5,10,15
–Lute ... 1Sa 18:6
–Lyre ... 2Sa 6:5
–Pipe ... Da 3:5,10,15
–Tambourine ... 2Sa 6:5
–Trigon ... Da 3:5,10,15
–Trumpet ... Nu 10:2
3. Used in Israelite worship
–Organized by David . 1Ch 25:1,6; 2Ch 7:6
–Mentioned in the psalms ... Ps 47:6; Ps 98:5–6; Ps 150:4–5
4. Used when Jesus returns ... 1Co 15:52; 1Th 4:16
B. Songs
1. In the Old Testament
a. Occasions for singing
–In sacred processions ... 2Sa 6:5; 1Ch 13:8
–At dedications ... 2Ch 5:12–13; Ezr 3:10–11; Ne 12:27–28,40
–On feast days ... 2Ch 30:21
–At coronations ... 2Ch 23:13
–To celebrate victories ... Ex 15:1–18; Nu 21:17; Jdg 5:1–31
b. The psalmist's intention to sing ... Ps 27:6; Ps 57:7,9; Ps 61:8; Ps 101:1; Ps 104:33
c. Instructions to sing ... Ps 30:4; Ps 68:32; Ps 98:1; Ps 149:1
d. All creation should sing ... Ps 148:1–12; Isa 44:23; Isa 49:13
2. In the New Testament
–Songs at the birth of Jesus ... Lk 1:46–55, 68–79; Lk 2:14,29–32
–Songs in the worshiping church ... 1Co 14:15; Eph 5:19; Col 3:16; Jas 5:13
–Songs in heaven ... Rev 5:9–10, 12–13; Rev 7:10,12, 15–17; Rev 15:3–4; Rev 19:1–8

MYSTERY

–Secret truths revealed by God
A. God and his secret truths
1. God discloses mysteries
–To his prophets ... Ge 40:8; Isa 48:6; Am 3:7; Da 2:18,27–28; Ro 16:25–26
–To his apostles ... Mk 4:10–12; Eph 3:4–5; Rev 1:19–20
2. Only believers understand mysteries ... Mk 4:10–12; 1Co 2:6–11; 2Co 4:3–6
B. Mysteries revealed to God's people
1. In the Old Testament
–Future events revealed to Joseph .. Ge 40:8–22; Ge 41:1–32
–Future events revealed to Daniel .. Da 2:24–47; Da 4:19–27
2. In the New Testament
–Basic teachings about Christ ... 1Ti 3:16
–Basic message of the gospel ... Col 4:3
–All wisdom hidden in Christ ... Col 2:2–3
–The nature of the kingdom of God ... Lk 8:10–15
–The union of Christ and his church ... Eph 5:29–32
–Christ's care for his church ... Rev 1:19–20
–What happens at Christ's return ... 1Co 15:51–52
–Inclusion of Gentiles in the kingdom ... Eph 3:6; Col 1:26
–Plan to reach the Jews with gospel ... Ro 11:25–26
C. Love is preferable to knowing mysteries ... 1Co 13:2

NAAMAN

–Aramean general afflicted with leprosy ... 2Ki 5:1
–Cured by Elisha ... 2Ki 5:2–14
–Took Israelite soil back to Damascus ... 2Ki 5:15–19
–His cure mentioned by Jesus ... Lk 4:27

NABAL

–Wealthy Carmelite; husband of Abigail ... 1Sa 25:1–3
–Name means "fool" ... 1Sa 25:25
–Refused to help David ... 1Sa 25:4–13
–Abigail pleaded for his life . 1Sa 25:14–25
–His death ... 1Sa 25:36–38

NABOTH

–Owner of a vineyard in Jezreel ... 1Ki 21:1
–Refused to sell vineyard to King Ahab ... 1Ki 21:2–3
–Killed by Jezebel ... 1Ki 21:4–14
–Ahab's family destroyed for this ... 1Ki 21:17–24
–Joram killed in Naboth's vineyard ... 2Ki 9:21–26

NADAB

A. Firstborn of Aaron ... Ex 6:23
–Went up Mount Sinai .. Ex 24:1,9
–Consecrated as priest ... Ex 28:1
–Killed for offering unauthorized fire ... Lev 10:1–3; Nu 3:2–4
–Had no sons ... 1Ch 24:2
B. Son of Jeroboam I; king of Israel ... 1Ki 15:25
–Killed all his brothers .. 1Ki 15:29
–Killed by Baasha ... 1Ki 15:27–28

NAME

A. Human names
1. Giving a name implied authority ... Ge 2:19; Ge 41:45; 2Ki 23:34; Da 1:7
2. Bible names could express
–The feelings of the mother at birth ... Ge 4:1,25; Ge 29:31–35; Ge 30:4–24
–The feelings of the father at birth ... Ge 35:16–18; Ge 41:51–52
–Circumstances of the child's conception ... Ge 17:17,19; 1Sa 1:20
–Circumstances of the child's birth ... Ge 25:24–26; Ge 38:27–30; Ex 2:10
–Historical situation at time of birth ... 1Sa 4:19–22; Isa 8:1–4; Hos 1:6–9
–How a person's life would develop ... Ge 3:20; Ge 27:36; 1Sa 25:25; 1Ch 22:9; Mt 1:21
–A name directly given by God ... Lk 1:13,60
3. A name change meant a new role
–From Abram to Abraham ... Ge 17:5–6
–From Sarai to Sarah . Ge 17:15–16
–From Jacob to Israel ... Ge 32:28
–From Simon to Peter ... Jn 1:42
–Promise of new names for us ... Isa 62:2; Rev 2:17
4. The names of believers
–Are called Christians ... Ac 11:26
–Are known by Christ ... Jn 10:3–4
–Are acknowledged before the Father ... Mt 10:32; Rev 3:5
–Are entered into the book of life ... Lk 10:20; Php 4:3; Rev 20:15
B. The name of God and Christ
1. God's name describes him
–It is identical with himself ... 2Sa 7:5,13; Ps 99:6
–It defines his nature . Isa 9:6
–It defines his power . Heb 1:4
2. God's name has power
–It delivers us ... Ex 3:13–15

–It saves us .... Ps 54:1
Mt 1:21,23
Ac 4:12
–It gives us life .... Jn 20:31
–It justifies us 1Co 6:11
–It sanctifies us 1Co 6:11
–It protects us .... Pr 18:10
–It helps us .... Ps 116:3–4
Jn 14:13–14
3. Our attitude towards God's name
–Praise it .... Ps 68:4
Ps 99:3
–Glorify it .... Ps 86:12
Ps 105:3
–Exalt it .... Ps 34:3
–Hallow it .... Mt 6:9
–Rejoice in it .... Ps 89:16
–Love it .... Isa 56:6
–Give thanks to it .... Ps 106:47
–Trust in it .... Ps 33:21
–Hope in it .... Ps 52:9
–Fear it .... Ps 86:11
Isa 59:19
–Call on it .... Ps 116:4,13,17
Joel 2:32
–Declare it .... Ps 22:22
–Live to reflect it .... Dt 28:9–10
Ro 2:21–24
–Don't misuse it .... Ex 20:7
Mal 1:6
4. Our attitude towards Christ's name
–Bow before it .... Php 2:10–11
–Believe in it .... Jn 2:23
1Jn 3:23
–Confess it .... Ro 10:9
Heb 13:15
–Be baptized into it .... Ac 10:48
–Call on it 1Co 1:2
–Pray in it .... Jn 14:13–14
Jn 16:23–24
–Give thanks in it .... Eph 5:20
–Assemble in it 1Co 5:4
–Preach it .... Ac 8:12
Ac 9:27–28
–Live to reflect it 2Th 1:12
–Do miracles in it .... Mk 16:17
Ac 3:16
Ac 4:30
–May have to suffer for it .... Ac 5:40–41
Ac 9:16
Rev 2:3

NAOMI
–Wife of Elimelech; mother-in-law of Ruth .... Ru 1:2,4
–Left Bethlehem for Moab during famine .... Ru 1:1
–Returned as a widow with Ruth .... Ru 1:6–22
–Advised Ruth to seek marriage with Boaz .... Ru 2:17–3:4
–Cared for Ruth's son Obed .... Ru 4:13–17

NAPHTALI
A. Son of Jacob by Bilhah .... Ge 35:25
1Ch 2:2
–Name means "my struggle" .... Ge 30:7–8
–Went to Egypt with family .... Ge 46:8,24
–Father of four sons .... Ge 46:24
–Blessed by Jacob .... Ge 49:21
B. Tribe descended from Naphtali
–Blessed by Moses .... Dt 33:23
–Numbered .... Nu 1:43
Nu 26:50
–Allotted land .... Jos 19:32–39
Eze 48:3
–Failed to fully possess the land .... Jdg 1:33
–Supported Deborah .... Jdg 4:10
Jdg 5:18
–Supported David 1Ch 12:34
–One of the tribes of the 144,000 .... Rev 7:6

NATHAN
–A prophet and chronicler 1Ch 29:29
2Ch 9:29
–Announced God's covenant with David 2Sa 7:1–17
1Ch 17:1–15
–Denounced David's sin with Bathsheba 2Sa 12:1–15
–Revealed Adonijah's plot to David 1Ki 1:10–27
–Participated in Solomon's coronation 1Ki 1:28–40

NATHANAEL
–One of Jesus' disciples .... Jn 1:45–51
Jn 21:2
–Probably also called Bartholomew .... Mt 10:3
Ac 1:13

NATIONS
A. The origin of nations
–Came from one family .... Ac 17:26
–Began after the flood .... Ge 10:1–32
–God divided up the nations .... Dt 32:8
B. God's intentions for the nations
1. God is king over all nations 2Ch 20:6
Ps 47:2
Jer 10:7,10
2. God chose a special nation
–Began with God's choice of Abram .... Ge 12:2
–Israelites were a holy, chosen nation .... Ex 19:5–6
Am 3:1–2
–Israelites commanded to remain separate .... Ex 34:15–16
Dt 7:1–6
–God's choice intended to bless all nations .... Ge 12:3
Ge 18:18
Ge 22:18
3. God prophesied salvation for all nations .... Ps 22:27–28
Ps 67:2
Isa 45:22–23
Isa 52:10
Zec 8:20–23
4. The nations are called to salvation
–Called by Jonah in the Old Testament .... Jnh 3:1–10
–Gospel to be preached to all nations .... Mt 24:14
Mt 28:19
Mk 16:15
Lk 24:47
Ac 1:8
–Apostles preached to all nations .... Ac 2:5–14
Ac 10:34–35
Ro 1:16
Ro 15:8–12,19
–Church composed of all nations .... Eph 2:11–22
Rev 5:9
Rev 7:9

NATURE
See CREATION

NAZARETH
–A Galilean town .... Mt 4:13
–Had a poor reputation .... Jn 1:46
–Gabriel appeared to Mary there .... Lk 1:26–38
–Jesus grew up there .... Mt 2:23
Lk 2:39,51–52
–Jesus called "Jesus of Nazareth" .... Jn 18:5,7
Jn 19:19
Ac 2:22
–Jesus was rejected by the town .... Mt 13:54–58
Mk 6:1–6
Lk 4:16–30

NEBUCHADNEZZAR
–Babylonian king 2Ki 24:1
–Campaigned against Judah 2Ki 24:1–4,10–16
2Ch 36:6–10
–Destroyed Jerusalem and the temple 2Ki 25:1–17
2Ch 36:15–21
Jer 39:1–10
–Was kind to Jeremiah .... Jer 39:11–14
–Was impressed with Daniel and his friends .... Da 1:18–20
–Dreams interpreted by Daniel .... Da 2:14–47
Da 4:9–27
–Put Daniel's three friends in fiery furnace .... Da 3:1–27
–Lived seven years like an animal .... Da 4:28–33
–Worshiped God .... Da 3:28–29
Da 4:34–37

NECO
See PHARAOH

NEEDY
See THE RICH AND THE POOR

NEHEMIAH
–Cupbearer for Artaxerxes .... Ne 1:11
–Became sad over condition of the exiles .... Ne 1:2–11
–Became governor of Jews .... Ne 8:9
–Inspected walls of Jerusalem .... Ne 2:11–20
–Rebuilt walls of Jerusalem .... Ne 3:1–4:23
Ne 6:15–19
–Showed concern for the poor .... Ne 5:1–13
–With Ezra, reestablished true worship .... Ne 8:1–12
–Signed a renewed covenant with the Lord .... Ne 9:38–10:1
–Dedicated walls of Jerusalem .... Ne 12:27–47
–Made a later visit to Jerusalem .... Ne 13:1–30

NEIGHBOR
–Anyone near you; any fellow human being
A. How not to treat your neighbors
–Do not give false testimony against them .... Ex 20:16
–Do not covet what is theirs .... Ex 20:17
–Do not deceive them .... Lev 6:2
–Do not rob them .... Lev 19:13
–Do not kill them .... Dt 22:26
–Do not plot harm against them .... Pr 3:29
–Do not despise them .... Pr 14:21
–Do not deceive them .... Pr 26:19
–Do not flatter them .... Pr 29:5
–Do not judge them .... Jas 4:12
–Do not commit adultery with neighbor's wife .... Lev 20:10
B. How to treat your neighbors
–Love them as yourself .... Lev 19:18
Mt 22:39
Ro 13:9
Jas 2:8
–Be kind to them .... Lk 10:29–37
–Speak the truth to them .... Eph 4:25

NICODEMUS
–Pharisee who visited Jesus at night .... Jn 3:1–21
–Argued for fair treatment of Jesus .... Jn 7:50–52
–With Joseph, prepared Jesus for burial .... Jn 19:38–42

NIGHT
See DARKNESS

NINEVEH
–A city founded by Nimrod .... Ge 10:11–12
–The capital of Assyria 2Ki 19:36
Isa 37:37
–Jonah told to preach against it .... Jnh 1:1–2
Jnh 3:1–3
–The people of Nineveh repented .... Jnh 3:5–10
–The people of Nineveh condemn unbelievers .... Mt 12:41
Lk 11:32
–Prophecies concerning its destruction .... Na 1:8–3:19
Zep 2:13–15

NOAH
–A righteous man .... Eze 14:14,20
–Called to build the ark .... Ge 6:11–22
–Entered the ark .... Ge 7:1–9
–Survived the flood .... Ge 8:15–19
–Worshiped the Lord after the flood .... Ge 8:20–22
–God made covenant with him .... Ge 9:1–17
–Became drunk .... Ge 9:18–23
–Blessed Shem and Japheth and cursed Canaan .... Ge 9:24–27

NUMBERS
A. Numbers used as a literary device
–In poetry .... Ps 62:11
Pr 6:16–19
Pr 30:15–29
–In prophecy .... Am 1:3–2:6
Mic 5:5
–In genealogies .... Mt 1:17
B. Numbers used in a symbolic fashion
1. The number "one"
–One God .... Dt 6:4
1Co 8:6
Eph 4:6
Jas 2:19
–One Lord 1Co 8:6
Eph 4:5
–One Spirit 1Co 12:13
Eph 4:4
–Father and Son are one .... Jn 10:30
–One body .... Ro 12:4–5
Eph 4:4
–One in Christ .... Jn 17:11,21
Gal 3:28
Eph 2:14–15
–One hope .... Eph 4:4
–One faith and one baptism .... Eph 4:5
–One father of the human race, Adam .... Ac 17:26
Ro 5:12
1Co 15:21–22
–One flesh in marriage .... Ge 2:24
Eph 5:31
2. The number "two"
–Two ways to choose .... Jos 24:15
1Ki 18:21
Mt 7:13–14
–The two-edged sword .... Heb 4:12
Rev 1:16
–Male and female .... Ge 1:27
–Two by two into the ark .... Ge 7:8–9,15–16
–Two tablets of the law .... Ex 32:15
Dt 9:10
–Disciples sent out two by two .... Mk 6:7
–Two witnesses .... Nu 35:30
Jn 8:17–18
2Co 13:1
3. The number "three"
–Father, Son, Holy Spirit .... Mt 28:19
2Co 13:14
See TRINITY
–Three annual festivals in Israel .... Ex 23:14–17
–Threefold benediction by priests .... Nu 6:24–26
–Job's three friends .... Job 2:11
–Jonah's three days in the fish .... Jnh 1:17
Mt 12:40
–Three temptations of Jesus .... Mt 4:3–10
–Three prayers in Gethsemane .... Mt 26:39–44
–Three denials of Peter .... Mt 26:34,69–75
–Jesus' resurrection on the third day .... Mt 16:21
Lk 24:46
1Co 15:4
–Three questions for Peter .... Jn 21:15–17
–Peter's three visions .... Ac 10:10–16
–Faith, hope, love 1Co 13:13
4. The number "four"
–The four rivers in Eden .... Ge 2:10–14
–The four winds .... Jer 49:36
–The four corners of the earth .... Eze 7:2
–Series of fours in Zechariah's visions .... Zec 1:8,18–21

–Four creatures around God's throne .... Eze 1:4–14
Rev 4:6–8
–Four kingdoms seen in a vision .... Da 2:36–43
Da 7:2–7,17

5. The number "seven"
–Creation in seven days .... Ge 1:1—2:3
–The Sabbath on the seventh day .... Ex 20:8–11
–The sabbath year .... Lev 25:1–7
–The Year of Jubilee . Lev 25:8–12
–Seven lamps on the lampstand .... Ex 25:37
–Festival of unleavened bread for seven days .... Ex 34:18
–Festival of tabernacles for seven days .. Lev 23:34
–Seven sprinklings for a cleansed leper ..... Lev 14:7,16
–Seven dippings for leper Naaman 2Ki 5:10,14
–Seven days marching around Jericho ...... Jos 6:1–16
–Seven deacons ...... Ac 6:3–5
–Numerous series of sevens in Revelation .... Rev 1:12–20
Rev 5:1
Rev 8:1–2
Rev 15:1, 6–8

6. The number "ten"
–Ten righteous men to save Sodom .... Ge 18:32
–The ten plagues ..... Ex 7:14—12:36
–The Ten Commandments ..... Ex 34:28
–Ten testings of the Israelites .... Nu 14:22
–The tithe (a tenth) .. Ge 14:20
See TITHES AND OFFERINGS
–Ten virgins in Jesus' parable .... Mt 25:1–13
–Ten horns and crowns on a beast ... Rev 13:1

7. The number "twelve"
–Twelve sons of Jacob .... Ge 35:22–26
–Twelve tribes .... Ex 24:4
–Twelve stones from the Jordan .... Jos 4:9
–Twelve stones in Elijah's altar 1Ki 18:31
–Twelve disciples of Jesus .... Mt 10:1–5
–Twelve hours of daylight .... Jn 11:9
–A crown of twelve stars .... Rev 12:1
–Twelve apostles ..... Ac 1:26
–Several twelves in the new Jerusalem .. Rev 21:12–14,21

8. The number "forty"
–Rain for forty days and nights .... Ge 7:12
–Moses for forty days on Mount Sinai ..... Ex 24:18
–Forty years wandering in the desert .... Nu 14:33–34
–Moses' life divided into three forties .... Ac 7:23,30, 36
–David's reign of forty years 1Ki 2:11
–Solomon's reign of forty years 1Ki 11:42
–Elijah for forty days on the mountain 1Ki 19:8
–Jesus for forty days in the desert .... Mt 4:2
–Jesus ascended after forty days .... Ac 1:3

9. The number "seventy"
–Seventy people came to Egypt .... Ge 46:27
–Seventy elders in Israel .... Ex 24:1,9
–Seventy years of exile .... Jer 25:11–12
–Seventy "sevens" in Daniel's visions ..... Da 9:20–27
–Forgiving seventy-seven times .... Mt 18:22
–The sending of the seventy-two .... Lk 10:1,17

10. "Thousands"
–One thousand years (the Millennium) ..... Rev 20:1–7
–A thousand years as one day .... Ps 90:4
2Pe 3:8
–Three thousand converts on Pentecost ... Ac 2:41
–Feeding the four thousand .... Mt 15:29–38
–Feeding the five thousand .... Mt 14:13–21
–Seven thousand not bowing to Baal 1Ki 19:18
Ro 11:4
–Thousands who love and obey the Lord .. Ex 20:6
–Thousands of thousands of chariots .... Ps 68:17
–Thousands and thousands before God ... Da 7:10
–Thousands and thousands praising God .. Heb 12:22
Rev 5:11
–One hundred forty-four thousand .... Rev 7:4–8
Rev 14:1–3

11. Mysterious numbers
–Forty-two months ... Rev 11:2
Rev 13:5
–One thousand, two hundred sixty days .. Rev 11:3
Rev 12:6
–Six hundred sixty-six .... Rev 13:18

OATH

A. The human oath
1. Expressions of the oath
–"May God . . . judge between us" .. Ge 31:53
–"As surely as the LORD lives" .... Ru 3:13
–"May God do so to you" 1Sa 3:17
–"As your soul lives" 1Sa 17:55
–"The LORD is witness between you and me" 1Sa 20:23,42
–"I am telling the truth, I am not lying" 1Ti 2:7
–"God . . . is my witness" .... Ro 1:9
–"I am speaking the truth in Christ" ..... Ro 9:1
2. Features of the oath
a. Purposes
–To settle an issue .... Ex 22:10–11
–To confirm an agreement with someone .... Ge 31:45–54
–To confirm a covenant with a people .... Jos 9:3–15
–To confirm a covenant with God .. 2Ch 15:12–15
–To ensure obedience to a master . Ge 24:1–4
–To ensure obedience to a king ... Ecc 8:2
–To ensure obedience to the Lord . Ne 10:29
b. Other aspects of the oath
–Must be fulfilled . Nu 30:1–2
–Could bind future generations ...... Ge 50:24–25
–Conditions sometimes attached .... Jos 2:12–21
–Not necessary for Christians .... Mt 5:33–37
Jas 5:12
–Christ responded to an oath .... Mt 26:63–64

B. God's oath
1. Content of God's oaths
–To give Canaan to Abraham's descendants .... Ge 22:15–18
Ge 50:24
–To keep someone on David's throne 2Sa 7:10–16
–To set up a priesthood like Melchizedek's ...... Ps 110:4
2. Character of God's oaths
–He swears by himself .... Ge 22:16
Heb 6:13–15
–God does not lie .... Nu 23:19
Heb 6:16–18
–God fulfills his oaths .... Ps 105:42–43
Lk 1:69–75
Lk 1:32–33
Heb 6:19—7:22

See also CURSE
VOW

OBADIAH

A. Servant of King Ahab ... 1Ki 18:3
–Sheltered one hundred prophets from Jezebel .. 1Ki 18:4
–Notified Ahab of Elijah's return 1Ki 18:7–16
B. Prophet against Edom ... Ob 1

OBEDIENCE

A. Obedience in the Old Testament
1. Relationships of obedience
–Israelites obey the Lord their God ..... Ex 19:5
Dt 4:30
–Israelites obey the law of God .... Ex 34:11
Dt 11:13,27, 32
–Citizens obey the king 1Ki 2:43
Ecc 8:2
–Children obey parents .... Ex 20:12
Pr 1:8–9
Pr 6:20–21
2. Rewards for obedience .... Ex 19:5–6
Dt 28:1–14
Jos 1:7–8
3. Punishment for disobedience .... Dt 28:15–68
1Sa 12:15
2Ki 17:7–20
Jer 11:1–3
4. Obedience more important than outward ritual 1Sa 15:22
Ps 40:6–8
Pr 21:3
Jer 7:22–23

B. Obedience in the New Testament
1. Relationships of obedience
–Christians obey God . Heb 12:9
Jas 4:7
1Jn 5:3
–Christians obey Christ .... Jn 14:13,23
Ro 1:5
1Co 9:21
Gal 6:2
Heb 5:9
–Citizens obey government authorities ...... Ro 13:1–5
1Pe 2:13–14
–Christians obey church leaders ...... Heb 13:17
–Servants obey masters .... Eph 6:5–8
Col 3:22
–Children obey parents .... Eph 6:1
Col 3:20
2. Obeying God precedes obeying humans ..... Ac 4:19–20
Ac 5:29

OCCULT

See MAGIC, WITCHCRAFT AND SORCERY

OFFERINGS

See TITHES AND OFFERINGS

OG

–King of Bashan .... Nu 21:33
Dt 1:4
–Destroyed by the Israelites . Nu 21:34–35
Dt 3:1–11
–Victory sung by the Israelites .... Ps 136:20

OLIVES, MOUNT OF

–A hill east of Jerusalem .... Eze 11:23
Zec 14:4
–David climbed it while fleeing from Absalom 2Sa 15:30
–Jesus often went there ..... Lk 22:39
Jn 8:1
–Triumphal entry began from there .... Mt 21:1–9
Mk 11:1–10
Lk 19:29–40
–Jesus predicted destruction of Jerusalem there .... Mt 24:3–34
Mk 13:3–31
–Gethsemane located there .. Mt 26:30,36
Mk 14:26,32
–Jesus ascended into heaven from there .... Ac 1:9–12

OMRI

–King of Israel 1Ki 16:21–28
–Father of Ahab 1Ki 16:28

ORDER

A. For the Israelites in the desert .... Nu 2:1–34
B. In Christian worship 1Co 14:40
–In the Christian life .... Col 2:5
–In presenting the truth about Christ .... Lk 1:3

See also CHURCH
DEACON
ELDER

ORPAH

–Moabitess; daughter-in-law of Naomi .... Ru 1:3–5
–Remained in Moab .... Ru 1:14

OTHNIEL

–Nephew of Caleb; married Caleb's daughter .... Jos 15:15–19
Jdg 1:12–15
–Became a judge .... Jdg 3:10
–Freed Israelites from Arameans .... Jdg 3:7–11

PAIN

–Various types of suffering experienced in our lives

A. Pain and suffering as a universal experience
1. In humans
–The righteous .... Ps 22:1–2, 12–18
–The wicked .... Pr 10:16
Pr 12:21
2. In creation as a whole .... Ro 8:20–22

B. The problem of pain and suffering for God's people
1. Examples of those who experienced pain
–Joseph .... Ge 39:11–20
–The Israelites in Egypt .... Ex 1:8–14
–The poor .... Ne 5:1–5
Am 2:6–7
–Job .... Job 7:7–13
–David .... Ps 22:1–18
–Asaph .... Ps 73:2–14
–Daniel's three friends .... Da 3:13–23
–Daniel .... Da 6:16–17
–Peter and John ...... Ac 5:40–41
–Paul .... Ac 14:19
2Co 11:23–26
–The Hebrew Christians .... Heb 10:33–34
–Other Christians 1Th 2:14–15
1Pe 2:19–21
–Christians in Smyrna .... Rev 2:9–10
–Saints in John's vision .... Rev 6:9–10
2. Christian attitude toward pain
–We must expect it .. Mt 24:9
Jn 16:1–4,33
2Ti 3:12
–We may have to endure it 2Ti 2:3
2Ti 4:5
–We must realize not all are delivered .... Heb 11:35–38

- –We must be patient in it ... Ro 12:12; 1Pe 2:20–21
- –We can rejoice in it . Ro 5:3; Col 1:24; Jas 1:2–3; 1Pe 4:12–14
- –We must overcome it ... Ro 8:35–37; Rev 2:10–11
- –We must not become discouraged ... Eph 3:13
- –We must not lose heart ... 2Co 4:7–10, 16–17; 1Th 3:3
- –We do complain against it ... Job 3:3–26; Ps 74:1,10–11; 2Co 12:7–8

3. Why does God allow such pain?
   - –To punish sins ... 2Sa 12:9–18; 2Ch 33:10–11
   - –To test us ... Dt 8:2; Job 2:1–6; Isa 48:10
   - –To teach us his will . Ps 119:71,75
   - –To teach us patience ... Ro 5:3; Jas 1:3
   - –To humble us ... Dt 8:3; 2Ch 7:13–14
   - –To discipline us in love ... Heb 12:4–11
   - –To drive us to repentance ... Jdg 6:1–6; Ps 107:4–6, 10–13; Hos 5:15
   - –To get us to rely on his grace ... 2Co 12:7–10
   - –To purify us ... Zec 13:7–9; Mal 3:2–3; Jn 15:2
   - –To promote his glory ... Jn 9:1–3
   - –To further the gospel ... Ac 8:3–4; 2Ti 4:16–17
4. How does God relate to pain?
   - –He is in control ... Job 1:6–12; Ro 8:38–39
   - –He causes good to triumph ... Ps 49:13–15; Ps 73:16–20; Ro 8:28
   - –He is a refuge for believers ... Ps 16:1,8; Ps 46:1; Isa 25:4
   - –He shares our pain .. Isa 53:2–4; Isa 63:9
   - –He walks with us through pain ... Ps 23:4; Ps 46:7,11; Isa 43:2
   - –He comforts us ... Isa 49:13; Zec 1:17; 2Co 1:4–5; Mt 11:28–30
   - –He will terminate pain at Christ's return ... 2Th 1:4–7; Rev 21:1–4
5. How should believers relate to those in pain?
   - –We should pray for them ... Ac 12:5; Ro 15:30–31; 2Co 1:10–11; Jas 5:13–16
   - –We should comfort them ... Job 2:11–13; 2Co 1:6–8
   - –We should share their burdens ... Job 30:25; Ro 12:15; Gal 6:2; Heb 13:3
   - –We should encourage them ... 1Th 4:18; 1Th 5:11
   - –We should give them help ... Isa 58:7; Lk 10:30–37; Php 4:14; 1Jn 3:17–18

PARABLE

–Stories that illustrate spiritual truths

A. The purposes of parables
   - –To teach things to children ... Ps 78:2–4; Pr 1:1–6
   - –To make an important point ... Jdg 9:7–20; 1Sa 12:1–7
   - –To give a prophetic message ... Isa 5:1–7; Eze 17:1–18; Hos 12:10
   - –To teach us about the kingdom ... Mk 4:2,10
   - –To obscure teaching from unbelievers ... Mt 13:11–15

B. Parables and fables in the Old Testament
   - –The fable of Jotham to Abimelech ... Jdg 9:7–15
   - –The parable of Nathan to David ... 2Sa 12:1–6
   - –The fable of Jehoash to Amaziah ... 2Ki 14:9
   - –The parable of Isaiah to the people ... Isa 5:1–7
   - –The parables of Ezekiel to the people ... Eze 17:1–8, 22–24; Eze 20:45–49; Eze 24:1–5

C. Jesus' use of parables
   - –He used them regularly ... Mk 4:33–34
   - –He explained things to the disciples alone ... Mt 13:10–13; Mk 4:3–8, 14–20; Lk 8:9–10
   - –He taught about the kingdom of God ... Mk 4:11,26, 30–32

D. Parables of Jesus
   - –Lamp under a bowl ... Mt 5:14–15; Mk 4:21–22; Lk 8:16
   - –Wise and foolish builders ... Mt 7:24–27; Lk 6:47–49
   - –New cloth on an old garment ... Mt 9:16; Mk 2:21; Lk 5:36
   - –New wine in old wineskins ... Mt 9:17; Mk 2:22; Lk 5:37–38
   - –Sower ... Mt 13:3–23; Mk 4:3–25; Lk 8:5–15
   - –Seed's growth ... Mk 4:25–29
   - –Wheat and weeds ... Mt 13:24–30,36–43
   - –Mustard seed ... Mt 13:31–32; Mk 4:30–32; Lk 13:18–19
   - –Yeast ... Mt 13:33; Lk 13:20–21
   - –Hidden treasure ... Mt 13:43
   - –Valuable pearl ... Mt 13:45–46
   - –Net ... Mt 13:47–51
   - –House owner ... Mt 13:52
   - –Good Samaritan ... Lk 10:25–37
   - –Lost sheep ... Mt 18:10–14; Lk 15:3–7
   - –Lost coin ... Lk 15:8–10
   - –Lost son ... Lk 15:11–32
   - –Unmerciful servant ... Mt 18:15–35
   - –Dishonest manager ... Lk 16:1–9
   - –Rich man and Lazarus . Lk 16:19–31
   - –Persistent widow ... Lk 18:1–8
   - –Pharisee and tax collector ... Lk 18:9–14
   - –Payment of workers ... Mt 20:1–16
   - –Two sons ... Mt 21:28–32
   - –Tenants and the vineyard ... Mt 21:33–46; Mk 12:1–6; Lk 20:9–18
   - –Wedding banquet ... Mt 22:1–14
   - –Faithful servant ... Mt 24:45–51; Lk 12:42–48
   - –Ten virgins ... Mt 25:1–13
   - –Talents ... Mt 25:14–30; Lk 19:12–27
   - –Sheep and goats ... Mt 25:31–46

PATIENCE

–Long-suffering, perseverance

A. Human patience
   1. The command to be patient
      - –Be patient ... Ro 12:12; 1Th 5:14; Heb 12:1; Jas 5:7–8
      - –Bear with others' shortcomings ... Eph 4:2; Col 3:12–13
   2. The manner of achieving patience
      - –By dependence on God ... Ro 15:5; Col 1:11
      - –Through hope in Christ ... 1Th 1:3; Jas 5:7
      - –As part of the fruit of the Spirit ... Gal 5:22
   3. Examples of patience
      - –Abraham ... Heb 6:15
      - –Job ... Jas 5:11
      - –The prophets ... Jas 5:10
      - –Paul ... 2Ti 3:10
      - –John ... Rev 1:9

   See also PERSEVERANCE

B. Patience of God
   1. Statements of God's patience
      - –God is slow to anger ... Ex 34:6; Nu 14:18; Ps 30:5; Ps 78:38
      - –Jesus is patient with us ... 1Ti 1:16
   2. Purpose: to call humans to repentance . Ro 2:4; 2Pe 3:9,15
   3. God's patience at time of Noah ... 1Pe 3:20

PAUL

A. His background
   - –Originally called Saul .. Ac 13:9
   - –From Tarsus ... Ac 9:11; Ac 21:39
   - –From the tribe of Benjamin ... Php 3:5
   - –A Pharisee ... Php 3:5
   - –Educated by Gamaliel .. Ac 22:3
   - –Unmarried ... 1Co 7:8

B. His life as a persecutor of Christians
   - –Assisted in stoning of Stephen ... Ac 7:58; Ac 8:1
   - –Zealously persecuted church ... Ac 9:1; Gal 1:13–14; Php 3:6
   - –Cast vote against Christians ... Ac 26:9–10
   - –Went to Damascus to persecute ... Ac 9:2; Ac 22:4–5
   - –Converted on the way to Damascus ... Ac 9:3–19; Ac 22:6–21; Ac 26:12–18

C. His life as an apostle
   1. From conversion to first missionary journey
      - –Called as missionary to Gentiles ... Ac 22:17–21; Ac 26:16–18
      - –Went to Arabia ... Gal 1:17
      - –Preached in Damascus; escaped in basket ... Ac 9:19–25; 2Co 11:32–33
      - –Went to Jerusalem .. Ac 9:26–29
      - –Went to Tarsus ... Ac 9:30
      - –Brought to Antioch by Barnabas ... Ac 11:22–26
      - –Brought offering to Jerusalem ... Ac 11:29–30
      - –Returned to Antioch . Ac 12:25
   2. First missionary journey
      - –Called by God ... Ac 13:2–4
      - –Preached throughout Cyprus ... Ac 13:5–12
      - –Preached in Antioch in Pisidia ... Ac 13:14–52
      - –Was persecuted in Iconium ... Ac 14:1–7
      - –Preached and stoned at Lystra ... Ac 14:8–20
      - –Preached at Derbe .. Ac 14:20–21
      - –Returned to Antioch . Ac 14:21–28
   3. The Jerusalem council
      - –Sent to Jerusalem ... Ac 15:1–4; Gal 2:1–2
      - –Discussed circumcision privately ... Gal 2:3–10
      - –Open meeting on circumcision issue ... Ac 15:5–22
      - –Letter drafted and sent with them ... Ac 15:23–31
      - –Friction developed with Peter ... Gal 2:11–14
   4. Second missionary journey
      - –Split with Barnabas over John Mark ... Ac 15:36–41
      - –Took Silas along ... Ac 15:40
      - –Visited previous churches ... Ac 15:41
      - –Added Timothy to his group ... Ac 16:1–4
      - –At Troas, called to Macedonia ... Ac 16:6–10
      - –Preached to women at Philippi ... Ac 16:13–15
      - –Imprisoned and freed in Philippi ... Ac 16:16–40
      - –Ministered in Thessalonica ... Ac 17:1–9
      - –Ministered in Berea . Ac 17:10–15
      - –Preached in Athens .. Ac 17:16–33
      - –Ministered in Corinth for eighteen months . Ac 18:1–11
      - –Attacked by Jews ... Ac 18:12–17
      - –Left Corinth and returned to Antioch . Ac 18:18–22
   5. Third missionary journey
      - –Arrived at Ephesus in Asia ... Ac 19:1
      - –Ministered for two years there ... Ac 19:2–22
      - –Suffered many hardships there ... 2Co 1:3–10
      - –Visited with leaders from Corinth ... 1Co 16:17–18
      - –Riot in Ephesus ... Ac 19:23–41
      - –Left for Macedonia .. Ac 20:1
      - –Met Titus in Macedonia ... 2Co 7:5–7
      - –Gathered money for Jerusalem ... 2Co 8:1–5; Ro 15:26
      - –Arrived in Greece ... Ac 20:2–3
      - –Gathered more money for Jerusalem ... Ro 15:26
      - –Left Greece for Jerusalem ... Ac 20:3–6; Ro 15:25
      - –Spoke all night at Troas ... Ac 20:7–12
      - –Said farewell to elders of Ephesus ... Ac 20:17–38
      - –Sailed for Jerusalem . Ac 21:1–6
      - –Traveled to Jerusalem ... Ac 21:7–17
      - –Reported to Jerusalem leaders ... Ac 21:17–25
   6. Paul's period of imprisonment
      - –Attacked and beaten by Jews from Asia .. Ac 21:27–32
      - –Arrested by Roman commander ... Ac 21:33–35
      - –Addressed the Jewish crowd ... Ac 22:1–21
      - –Addressed Sanhedrin ... Ac 23:1–11
      - –Transferred to Caesarea ... Ac 23:12–35
      - –On trial before Felix ... Ac 24:1–21
      - –Kept in prison in Caesarea ... Ac 24:22–27
      - –On trial before Festus ... Ac 25:1–12
      - –Appealed to Caesar . Ac 25:12
      - –Spoke before Agrippa ... Ac 25:13–26:32
      - –Sailed for Rome; shipwrecked ... Ac 27:1–44
      - –Stranded on island of Malta ... Ac 28:1–10
      - –Arrived in Rome ... Ac 28:11–16
      - –Preached to Jews of Rome ... Ac 28:17–28
      - –Remained two years in Rome ... Ac 28:30–31
      - –Freed after trial before emperor ... 2Ti 4:16–17
   7. Travels after release from imprison-

ment
- –In Macedonia ... 1Ti 1:3
- –In Crete ... Tit 1:5
- –In Nicopolis ... Tit 3:12
- –In Miletus ... 2Ti 4:20
- –In Troas ... 2Ti 4:13
- –Imprisoned again ... 2Ti 2:8–9
- –Probably killed this time ... 2Ti 4:6–8

D. Significant issues in Paul's letters
- –His apostleship ... 1Co 9:1–3; 2Co 11:4—12:13; Gal 1:1—2:14
- –Salvation possible only in the name of Jesus ... Ro 3:21–26; Ro 5:1–2; Ro 10:3–13; 2Co 5:18–21; Gal 3:10–14, 24–29; Eph 2:1–22; Php 3:7–14; Col 1:13–23; 1Ti 1:12–16
- –Salvation through faith alone ... Ro 3:21—5:1; Gal 2:15–21; Eph 2:8–9; Php 3:9
- –Circumcision not necessary for salvation ... Ro 4:9–12; Gal 2:3; Gal 5:1–6; Col 2:11–12
- –Christian freedom ... Ro 14:1—15:13; 1Co 8:1–13; 1Co 11:23–33; Gal 4:31—5:13
- –Concern for the salvation of Jews ... Ro 9:1–5; Ro 10:1–4
- –Proper use of spiritual gifts ... Ro 12:3–8; 1Co 12:1—14:40
- –Life led by the Spirit of God ... Ro 8:1–17; Gal 5:16–26
- –Proper order needed in the church ... 1Co 11:17–34; 1Co 14:26–40; 1Ti 2:1—3:15; Tit 1:5–2:15

PEACE

–Wholeness and well-being in all areas of life

A. Basic meanings of peace
1. Peace ("Shalom") is a basic greeting
   - –Hello ... Da 10:19; Jn 20:19; Gal 1:3
   - –Good-bye ... 1Sa 25:35; 2Sa 15:9; 1Pe 5:14; 3Jn 14
2. Peace in a political sense
   - –On the international scene ... 1Sa 7:14; 1Ki 4:24; Ac 24:2
   - –On the national scene ... 2Sa 3:21–23; 1Ki 22:44; 2Ch 14:1
3. Peace in human relationships
   - –In relationships with others ... Ro 12:18; Heb 12:14; 1Pe 3:11
   - –Among the Israelite people ... Ps 34:14; Ps 122:6–7
   - –In relationships in the church ... Ac 9:31; Ro 14:19; 2Co 13:11; Eph 2:14–17
   - –In relationships in the home ... Ge 44:17; Pr 17:1; Pr 29:17; 1Co 7:15
4. Personal sense of peace
   - –In relationship with oneself ... Ps 4:8; Pr 14:30; 2Co 2:13
   - –In relationship with God ... Nu 6:26; Isa 26:3; Ro 5:1; Php 4:7–9; Col 1:20

B. The source of peace
1. It comes as a divine gift
   - –From God the Father ... Ro 1:7; Ro 15:33; Php 4:7
   - –From the Lord Jesus Christ ... Isa 9:6–7; Lk 2:14; Jn 14:27; Ro 1:7; Eph 2:14; 2Th 3:16
   - –From the Holy Spirit ... Ro 14:17; Gal 5:22; Eph 4:3
   - –God promises a covenant of peace ... Isa 54:10; Eze 34:25; Eze 37:26
   - –We must pray to God for peace ... Ps 122:6–7; Jer 29:7; 1Ti 2:1
2. It comes through human effort
   - –We must let peace rule in us ... Col 3:15
   - –We must live in peace ... 2Co 13:11; 1Th 5:13
   - –We must seek peace ... Ps 34:14; 1Pe 3:11
   - –We must try to live in peace ... Ro 12:18; Ro 14:19; Heb 12:14
   - –We must pursue peace ... Ps 34:14; 2Ti 2:22
   - –We must obey God to receive peace ... Lev 26:3,6

C. Jesus and our peace
- –Prophesied to be the Prince of Peace ... Isa 9:6
- –Peace proclaimed at his birth ... Lk 2:14
- –Peace promised to his disciples ... Jn 14:27; Jn 16:33
- –Peace achieved on the cross ... Isa 53:5; Col 1:20
- –Began the good news of peace ... Isa 52:7; Ac 10:36
- –He is our peace ... Eph 2:14
- –Enables us to have peace with God ... Ro 5:1
- –Establishes peace within the church ... Eph 2:15
- –Guides us in the way of peace ... Lk 1:79
- –Blesses us with peace ... Nu 6:24–26; Ps 29:11; 1Co 1:3
- –Enables us to die in peace ... Lk 2:29–31

D. The wicked and peace
- –They proclaim a false peace ... Jer 6:14; Eze 13:10
- –They do not know the way of peace ... Isa 59:8; Lk 19:42
- –They hate peace ... Ps 120:6–7
- –They have no peace ... Isa 48:18,22; Isa 57:21

PEKAH

- –King of Israel ... 2Ki 15:27–31
- –Assassinated Pekahiah to become king ... 2Ki 15:25
- –Allied with Syria against Judah ... 2Ki 15:37; Isa 7:1–2
- –Inflicted much destruction on Judah ... 2Ch 28:5–8
- –Destruction of the alliance foretold ... Isa 7:3–9
- –Failed in attempt to take Jerusalem ... 2Ki 16:5–6

PEKAHIAH

- –King of Israel ... 2Ki 15:23–26
- –Assassinated by Pekah, an officer ... 2Ki 15:25

PERFECTION

–Complete and without sin or error

A. Perfection as a human goal
1. The goal stated ... Mt 5:48; 2Co 13:9,11
2. Perfection possible only in the Lord
   - –Animal sacrifice cannot make us perfect ... Heb 10:1
   - –The law cannot make us perfect ... Ro 3:20; Heb 7:11,19
   - –God makes our way perfect ... 2Sa 22:33
   - –God's strength makes us perfect ... 2Co 12:7–10
   - –Jesus is the perfecter of our faith ... Heb 12:2
   - –Jesus makes us perfect by his sacrifice ... Heb 10:14
   - –The Spirit helps us attain perfection ... Gal 3:3
3. Perfection requires various human actions
   - –Learning God's wisdom ... Col 1:28
   - –Knowing God's word ... 2Ti 3:14–17
   - –Pressing forward in faith ... Php 3:12–14
   - –Self-sacrifice ... Mt 19:21
   - –Love ... Col 3:14
   - –Purifying ourselves ... 2Co 7:1
   - –Controlling what we say ... Jas 3:2
   - –Not being afraid ... 1Jn 4:18
4. Perfection attained only in the hereafter ... 1Co 13:8–10; Heb 12:22–23

See also HOLINESS; SANCTIFICATION

B. Perfection as the nature of God
1. God the Father
   - –He is perfect ... Mt 5:48
   - –His works are perfect ... Dt 32:4
   - –His way is perfect ... 2Sa 22:31
   - –His law is perfect ... Ps 19:7; Jas 1:25
   - –His will is perfect ... Ro 12:2
   - –He is perfect in knowledge ... Job 37:16
   - –He is perfect in faithfulness ... Isa 25:1
2. Christ the Son
   - –He is without sin ... 2Co 5:21; Heb 7:26; 1Jn 3:5
   - –He was made perfect through suffering ... Heb 2:10; Heb 5:8–9; Heb 7:28

PERSECUTION

–Oppression because of one's faith

A. Examples of persecution
1. The prophets
   - –Prophets in general ... 2Ch 36:15–16; Mt 5:12; Mt 23:31,37; Ac 7:52
   - –Elijah ... 1Ki 19:1–3
   - –Micaiah ... 1Ki 22:9–28
   - –Jeremiah ... Jer 26:1–19; Jer 37:11—38:13
   - –Uriah son of Shemaiah ... Jer 26:20–22
2. The apostles
   - –Persecution prophesied ... Mt 24:9; Jn 15:18–21; Jn 16:1–4
   - –The apostles as a group ... Ac 5:27,40
   - –James ... Ac 12:1–2
   - –Peter ... Ac 12:3–5
   - –Paul ... Ac 14:5–6, 19–20; Ac 16:22–24; Ac 22:27–36; 2Co 11:23–26
   - –John ... Rev 1:9
3. Christians in general
   - –Stephen ... Ac 7:57–60
   - –Christians in Judea ... Ac 8:1–3; 1Th 2:14–15
   - –Christians outside Judea ... Ac 9:1–2; Ac 26:11
   - –Christians in Thessalonica ... 1Th 2:14–15
   - –Christians in Smyrna ... Rev 2:9–10
   - –To be expected for all ... 2Ti 3:12

B. Attitudes in relationship to persecution
- –Commit yourself to God ... 1Pe 4:19
- –Persevere under it ... Mk 13:13; Heb 10:32–36; Jas 1:12; Rev 2:10
- –Rejoice in it ... Mt 5:12; Ac 5:41; Php 2:17; Col 1:24
- –Flee from it ... Mt 10:23; Ac 14:6
- –Do not be ashamed ... 1Pe 4:16
- –Pray for persecutors ... Mt 5:44; Lk 23:34; Ac 7:60

PERSEVERANCE

–Remaining firm in our faith

A. God preserves us in our faith
- –He draws us firmly to himself ... Jn 6:37
- –He holds us in his hand ... Ps 37:24; Jn 10:27–29
- –He keeps us in his love ... Ro 8:35–39
- –He watches over us ... Ps 121:3–8; Ps 145:20
- –He protects us from the evil one ... 2Th 3:3; 1Jn 5:18
- –He keeps our commitment firm ... 1Co 1:8; 2Ti 1:12
- –He will keep us until the final day ... Php 1:6; 1Pe 1:4–5

B. We must persevere in our faith
- –The command to persevere ... Heb 10:35–36; Heb 12:2; Jas 1:12
- –The command to use spiritual armor ... Eph 6:10–17; 1Th 5:8
- –The warning not to turn away from God ... Heb 3:12; Heb 6:1–6; Heb 10:26–31; Rev 2:4–5
- –The possibility of rejecting the faith ... 1Ti 1:19–20; 1Ti 6:20–21; 2Ti 2:17–18; Heb 3:16–18

PERSIA

See MEDES AND PERSIANS

PETER

A. Background information
- –Father's name was John ... Jn 1:42
- –Given name: Simon ... Jn 1:42
- –Brother of Andrew ... Mt 10:2
- –A native of Bethsaida ... Jn 1:44

–Originally a fisherman . Lk 5:1–5
–Uneducated .... Ac 4:13
–Married .... Mk 1:30; 1Co 9:5

B. Events during Jesus' public ministry
–Let Jesus use his boat to speak from .... Lk 5:3
–Caught numerous fish at Jesus' command .... Lk 5:5–7
–Given the name Cephas (Peter) .... Mt 16:17–18; Jn 1:42
–Called by Jesus to be fisher of men .... Mt 4:18–20; Mk 1:16–18
–Witnessed raising of Jairus's daughter .... Mk 5:37–41
–Walked on water at Jesus' bidding .... Mt 14:28–31
–Confessed Christ as Son of God .... Mt 16:13–16; Mk 8:27–30; Lk 9:18–20
–Rebuked by Jesus ...... Mt 16:21–23; Mk 8:31–33
–Observed the transfiguration .... Mt 17:1–8; Mk 9:2–8
–Caught fish that had coin in its mouth .... Mt 17:24–27
–Inquired about limits of forgiveness .... Mt 18:21
–Did not want Jesus to wash his feet .... Jn 13:6–10
–Jesus prayed for him ... Lk 22:31–32
–His denial of Jesus predicted .... Mt 26:31–35; Mk 14:27–31; Lk 22:33–34
–Accompanied Jesus to Gethsemane .... Mt 26:36–45; Mk 14:32–42
–Cut off ear of the high priest's servant .... Jn 18:10–11
–Denied Jesus three times .... Mt 26:69–75; Mk 14:66–72; Lk 22:54–62; Jn 18:15–18, 25–27

C. Events between resurrection and Pentecost
–Ran to tomb on Easter Sunday .... Lk 24:12; Jn 20:2–8
–Jesus appeared to him .. Lk 24:33–34; 1Co 15:5
–Decided to go fishing .. Jn 21:3
–Had breakfast with Jesus .... Jn 21:4–14
–Was asked three times, "Do you love me?" ... Jn 21:15–17
–One of the apostles in upper room .... Ac 1:13
–Suggested that Judas's vacancy be filled ...... Ac 1:15–22

D. Events after Pentecost
–Preached a sermon on Pentecost Sunday ...... Ac 2:14–36
–Called the people to repent .... Ac 2:37–40
–With John, healed a lame man .... Ac 3:1–8
–Preached in the temple . Ac 3:11–26
–Arrested with John ..... Ac 4:1–3
–Questioned before the Sanhedrin .... Ac 4:7–21; Ac 5:27–32
–Spoke judgment against Ananias and Sapphira .. Ac 5:1–10
–His shadow healed people .... Ac 5:15–16
–Was sent to new Christians in Samaria .... Ac 8:14–17
–Through a vision, was sent to Cornelius ...... Ac 10:9–48
–Explained how God was saving Gentiles .... Ac 11:1–18
–Imprisoned by Herod ... Ac 12:3–5
–Freed from prison by an angel .... Ac 12:6–11
–Left Jerusalem .... Ac 12:17
–Did missionary work among the Jews .... 1Co 9:5; Gal 2:9
–Had conflict with Paul at Antioch .... Gal 2:11–14
–Spoke at council in Jerusalem .... Ac 15:7–11

E. His character and significance
1. Often spoke impulsively
–Asked to come to Jesus on the water .. Mt 14:28
–Rebuked Jesus ...... Mt 16:22
–Said he was willing to die with Jesus .... Lk 22:33
–Claimed he would never deny Jesus .... Mt 26:33–35
–Did not want Jesus to wash his feet ...... Jn 13:6–9
2. A leader among the disciples
–His name always mentioned first ..... Mt 10:2; Mk 3:16; Lk 6:14; Ac 1:13
–Often the spokesman for the rest .... Mt 16:16; Mt 26:33–35; Ac 2:14; Ac 4:29
3. One of the major leaders of the church
–Called "rock" by Jesus .... Mt 16:18–19
–Led the church in Jerusalem .... Ac 5:1–9
–Paul met specifically with him .... Gal 1:18
–Spoke at Jerusalem council .... Ac 15:7–11
–Called a "pillar" ... Gal 2:9
–A party at Corinth called by his name .. 1Co 1:12
–Wrote two letters .. 1Pe 1:1; 2Pe 1:1

PETITION

–Asking God for personal things in prayer

A. Why must we ask?
–God commands it ...... Mt 7:7–9
–We have needs .... Php 4:19
–We follow the example of the saints .... 1Ch 16:4; Da 6:11; Da 9:17–18

B. How must we ask?
–In faith .... Mk 11:24; Jn 14:12–14
–With thanksgiving ..... Php 4:6
–In Christ's name .... Jn 14:6,13; Jn 15:16; Jn 16:23–24; Ro 5:2
–Without worry .... Mt 6:25–34; Lk 12:22–31

C. For what may we ask?
–For daily bread .... Mt 6:11
–For forgiveness .... Da 9:19; Mt 6:12
–For freedom from temptation .... Mt 6:13
–For the Holy Spirit ..... Lk 11:13
–For the ability to witness with boldness ..... Ac 4:29–30
–For safety in travel .... Ezr 8:21–23
–For healing .... Isa 38:2; Mk 1:40
–For a child 1Sa 1:11
–For anything .... Jn 14:14

PHARAOH

–The title given to the king of Egypt

A. Pharaohs mentioned in the Bible
1. The Pharaoh at the time of Abram
–Sarai taken into his palace .... Ge 12:14–15
–Diseases inflicted on his household .... Ge 12:17
–Expelled Abram from Egypt .... Ge 12:18–20
2. The Pharaoh at the time of Joseph
–Put butler and baker in prison .... Ge 40:1–4
–Had dreams, interpreted by Joseph .... Ge 41:1–32
–Made Joseph second in command .... Ge 41:37–43
–Gave Joseph a wife .. Ge 41:44–45
–Invited Jacob to live in Egypt .... Ge 45:16–20
–Greeted Jacob and his family .... Ge 47:1–10
–Settled Jacob and family in Goshen ... Ge 47:5–6
–Allowed Joseph to bury Jacob in Canaan .... Ge 50:4–6
3. The Pharaoh at the time of the exodus
a. Oppression of the Israelites
–Did not know about Joseph ..... Ex 1:8
–Turned the Israelites into slaves ... Ex 1:9–11
–Ordered the death of baby boys ..... Ex 1:15–22
–Tried to kill Moses .... Ex 2:15
–Increased burden of slavery .... Ex 5:1–18
b. Interaction with Moses and Aaron
–First appearance before him .... Ex 5:1–5
–Second appearance, first miracles .... Ex 7:10–21
–Asked for plagues to be stopped .... Ex 8:8,28; Ex 9:27–28; Ex 10:16–17
–Agreed to let Israelites worship .... Ex 8:25–29; Ex 9:27–28; Ex 10:8–10, 24
–Hardened his heart .... Ex 7:13,22; Ex 8:15,32; Ex 9:7,12, 34–35; Ex 10:1,20, 27
c. The exodus
–His firstborn son killed .... Ex 12:29–30
–Ordered Israelites to leave .... Ex 12:31–32
–Changed mind and pursued Israelites . Ex 14:5–9
–Followed Israelites into the sea ...... Ex 14:23–25
–Drowned .... Ex 14:26–28; Ps 106:10–11
4. The Pharaoh at the time of Solomon
–Alliance between him and Solomon 1Ki 3:1
–Solomon married his daughter 1Ki 3:1; 1Ki 11:1
–Conquered Gezer and gave it to Solomon .. 1Ki 9:16
5. Shishak, at the end of Solomon's reign
–Befriended Hadad, adversary of Solomon 1Ki 11:14–22
–Befriended Jeroboam 1Ki 11:40
–Attacked and defeated Rehoboam 1Ki 14:25–26; 2Ch 12:1–11
6. The Pharaoh in Hoshea's time
–Possibly called So .. 2Ki 17:4
–Hoshea made alliance with him 2Ki 17:4
7. The Pharaoh in Hezekiah's time
–Made alliance with Hezekiah .... Isa 30:1–2
–Advanced against Sennacherib 2Ki 19:9
–A weak Pharaoh .... 2Ki 18:21; Isa 36:6
–Unable to save Judah .... Isa 30:3–5; Isa 31:1–3
8. Pharaoh Neco
–Allied with Assyria against Babylon 2Ki 23:29; 2Ch 35:20
–Fought and defeated Josiah 2Ki 23:29–30; 2Ch 35:20–24
–Deposed Jehoahaz ... 2Ki 23:33; 2Ch 36:3
–Made Jehoiakim king 2Ki 23:34–35; 2Ch 36:4
–Defeated by the Babylonians .... Jer 46:2
9. Hophra, at the time of the exile
–Zedekiah asked his help against Babylon .... Eze 17:15
–Marched against the Babylonians .... Jer 37:5
–Deserted Zedekiah .. Jer 37:7
–His defeat to Nebuchadnezzar prophesied .... Jer 44:30; Eze 29:19–20

B. Prophecies against Pharaoh
–By Jeremiah .... Jer 44:30; Jer 46:14–19
–By Ezekiel .... Eze 29:1–5; Eze 32:1–15

PHARISEES

–A Jewish party, prominent at the time of Jesus

A. Major characteristics
–Political leaders of the Jews .... Mt 27:62–64
–Members of the Sanhedrin (Jewish council) ... Ac 23:6
–Leaders of the synagogue .... Jn 9:13–16, 22
–Official interpreters of the law .... Mt 23:2
–Strict observers of the law of God .... Mt 12:2,8–14; Mt 23:23
–Strict adherents of Jewish traditions .... Mk 7:2–3; Gal 1:14
–Believed circumcision was necessary .... Ac 15:5
–Believed in the resurrection and in angels ..... Ac 23:8
–Tried to remain separate from sinners .... Mt 9:11
–Promoted Judaism throughout the world ... Mt 23:15

B. Prominent Pharisees in the Bible
–Nicodemus .... Jn 3:1
–Gamaliel .... Ac 5:34
–Paul .... Ac 23:6; Php 3:5

C. The Pharisees and Jesus
1. Regularly questioned and tested Jesus ...... Lk 11:53–54
–About eating with sinners .... Mt 9:11; Mk 2:16; Lk 5:30
–About fasting .... Mt 9:14; Mk 2:18; Lk 5:33
–About failing to keep the Sabbath .... Mt 12:2; Mk 2:24; Lk 6:2
–About not keeping traditions .... Mt 15:1–2; Mk 7:5
–About marriage and divorce .... Mt 19:3; Mk 10:2
–About a woman taken in adultery ...... Jn 8:1–6
–About paying taxes to Caesar .... Mt 22:15–17; Mk 12:13–15
–About the most important commandment ...... Mt 22:34–36
–About the kingdom of God .... Lk 17:20–21
–About the validity of Jesus' testimony .... Jn 8:12–13
–About their own blindness .... Jn 8:40
–Asked for a miraculous sign .... Mt 12:38
–Asked for a sign from heaven .... Mt 16:1; Mk 8:11
2. Criticized Jesus
–Said he was controlled by a demon .. Mt 9:34; Mt 12:24
–Said he spoke blasphemy .... Lk 5:21

–Said he failed to keep the Sabbath .... Lk 6:6–7
–Criticized his association with sinners .... Lk 7:36–39; Lk 15:1–2
–Criticized his acceptance of praise ...... Lk 19:38–39
3. Desired to get rid of Jesus
–Tried to arrest him .. Jn 7:32; Jn 18:1–3
–Sought to kill him .. Mt 12:14; Mk 3:6; Jn 11:46–50
–Asked for soldiers to guard the tomb ..... Mt 27:62–64
4. Some secretly believed in Jesus .... Jn 12:42–43
D. Jesus criticized the Pharisees
–For their lack of true righteousness .... Mt 5:20
–For their questionable teachings .... Mt 16:6,11–12
–For persecuting God's messengers .... Mt 21:33–46; Mt 23:33–36
–For failing to understand Scripture .... Mt 22:41–45
–For their hypocrisy .... Mt 23:1–32; Lk 11:37–44; Lk 18:9–14
–For their lack of concern for people .... Lk 14:1–14
–For their love of money .... Lk 16:14–15

PHILIP

A. Disciple of Jesus .... Mt 10:3; Mk 3:18
–Brought Nathanael to Jesus .... Jn 1:44–46
–Jesus tested him at feeding of five thousand ... Jn 6:5–7
–Introduced Greeks to Jesus .... Jn 12:20–22
–Wanted to see the Father .... Jn 14:8–9
–One of the apostles .... Ac 1:13
B. One of the seven deacons .... Ac 6:1–7
–Became an evangelist in Samaria .... Ac 8:5–13
–Witnessed to and baptized Ethiopian eunuch . Ac 8:26–39
–Continued preaching the gospel .... Ac 8:40
–Had four daughters who prophesied .... Ac 21:9

PHILISTINES

A. Their identity
–Descendants of Mizraim, son of Ham .. Ge 10:6,13–14
–Came from Caphtor (Crete) .... Am 9:7
–Five main cities .... Jos 13:3; 1Sa 6:17
–Advanced in culture and war techniques 1Sa 13:5–7, 19–21
–Their land not fully taken over by Joshua ..... Jos 13:2; Jdg 3:1–3
B. Prominent Philistines
–Abimelech: wanted Rebekah as wife .... Ge 26:1,7–11
–Delilah: Samson's lover and deceiver .... Jdg 16:4–20
–Goliath: giant killed by David 1Sa 17:4,41–49
–Achish: king of Gath, friend of David 1Sa 21:10–15; 1Sa 27:1–7
C. Their wars
1. The period of the judges
a. Defeated by Shamgar .... Jdg 3:31
b. Fought Israel at time of Jephthah .. Jdg 10:7–9
c. Fought Israel at time of Samson ... Jdg 13:1,5
See SAMSON
d. Fought Israel at time of Samuel
–Captured the ark in battle 1Sa 4:1–11
–Returned the ark . 1Sa 6:1–12
–Defeated by Samuel at Mizpah 1Sa 7:2–14
2. The period of the kings
a. During Saul's reign
–Attacked by Jonathan 1Sa 13:3–7
–Defeated by Jonathan and troops .. 1Sa 14:1–47
–Defeated after death of Goliath .. 1Sa 17:1–53
–Two hundred killed by David .. 1Sa 18:24–27
–Defeated by David 1Sa 19:8; 1Sa 23:1–5
–Attacked King Saul 1Sa 28:1,4–5
–Defeated Israelites; Saul died 1Sa 31:1–7; 1Ch 10:1–7
b. During David's reign
–God promised to defeat them 2Sa 3:18
–David's victories over them 2Sa 5:17–25; 2Sa 8:1; 2Sa 21:15–22; 1Ch 14:8–17; 1Ch 18:1; 1Ch 20:4–8
–Exploits of David's mighty men .. 2Sa 23:9–17; 1Ch 11:12–19
c. Solomon ruled them 1Ki 4:21; 2Ch 9:26
d. Jehoshaphat ruled them 2Ch 17:10–11
e. They defeated Jehoram 2Ch 21:16–17
f. Uzziah defeated them 2Ch 26:6–7
g. They defeated Ahaz 2Ch 28:18
h. Hezekiah defeated them 2Ki 18:8
D. Important data concerning them
–Isaac made treaty with Abimelech .... Ge 26:26–31
–David hid from Saul among them 1Sa 27:1–7; 1Sa 29:1–11
–Prophecies against them .... Isa 14:28–32; Jer 47:1–7; Eze 25:15–17; Am 1:6–8; Zep 2:4–7; Zec 9:5–7
–Promise concerning their salvation .... Ps 87:4

PHINEHAS

A. Son of Eleazar and grandson of Aaron ...... Ex 6:25
–Killed Zimri and Cozbi to end plague .... Nu 25:6–15
–Investigated an altar across the Jordan ...... Jos 22:13–31
B. Son of Eli, brother of Hophni 1Sa 1:3
–A wicked priest 1Sa 2:12–17
–Scorned his father's rebuke 1Sa 2:22–25
–His death prophesied as a sign to Eli 1Sa 2:30–34
–Brought the ark into battle 1Sa 4:4
–Killed in the battle 1Sa 4:11,17

PHOEBE

–Christian from Cenchrea commended by Paul .... Ro 16:1–2

PIETY

See MEDITATION
SPIRITUALITY

PILATE

–Governor of Judea .... Jn 18:28–29
–Presided over Jesus' trial ... Mt 27:11–26; Mk 15:1–15; Lk 23:1–5, 13–25; Jn 18:28–19:16
–Sent Jesus to Herod .... Lk 23:6–12
–Washed his hands as sign of innocence .... Mt 27:24–25
–Consented to Jesus' crucifixion .... Mt 27:15–26; Mk 15:6–15
–Gave body of Jesus to Joseph and Nicodemus ..... Mt 27:57–60; Jn 19:38–42
–Authorized a guard at the tomb .... Mt 27:62–66
–His name forever associated with Jesus' death .... Ac 3:13; Ac 4:27; Ac 13:28; 1Ti 6:13

PITY

See COMPASSION
MERCY

POTIPHAR

–Egyptian official who bought Joseph .... Ge 37:36
–Put Joseph in charge of his household .... Ge 39:1–6
–Sent Joseph to prison, unjustly .... Ge 39:7–20

POVERTY

See THE RICH AND THE POOR

POWER

See AUTHORITY

PRAISE

A. Praising God is a command
1. Commanded throughout the Bible
–In the law of God .. Dt 8:10
–In the prophets ..... 1Ch 29:20; Isa 61:11; Jer 20:13; Joel 2:26
–In the psalms .... Ps 103:1; Ps 104:1; Ps 145–150
–In the New Testament .... Eph 1:3,6, 12,14; 1Pe 1:3,7; Rev 19:5
2. Praise is commanded of:
–God's people .... Ps 30:4; Ps 135:1–2, 19–21
–Children .... Ps 8:2; Mt 21:16
–The nations .... Ps 67:3–5; Ps 117:1; Ro 15:11
–The angels .... Ps 103:20; Ps 148:2
–Everything that breathes .... Ps 150:6
–All creation .... Ps 98:8; Ps 148:3–12; Isa 44:23
B. Reasons for praise
–God's greatness .... Ps 145:3
–God's splendor and majesty .... Ps 96:4–6
–God's glory .... Ps 66:1–2
–God's holiness .... Ps 99:3; Isa 6:3
–God's love and faithfulness .... Ps 57:9–10; Ps 89:1–2
–God's acts of power ... Ps 150:2
–God's marvelous deeds . Isa 25:1
–God's glorious grace .... Eph 1:6
–God's salvation .... Ps 106:1–5; Lk 1:68–75; Lk 2:14,20
–God's benefits to his people .... Ps 103:1–18; Ps 111:1–10; Isa 63:7
–God's deliverance of us .... Ps 40:1–3; Ps 124:6–8
C. Methods of praise
–By public worship ..... Ps 100:4
–By singing .... Ps 146:1; Ps 147:1
–By musical instruments . Ps 150:3–5
–By speaking .... Ps 51:15; Heb 13:15
–By dancing .... Ps 149:3
–By witnessing to unbelievers 1Pe 2:9

PRAYER

–Communication with God
A. What is prayer?
–Calling on the name of the Lord .... Ge 4:26; Ge 12:8; Zep 3:9
–Calling to God .... Ps 4:1,3; Ps 17:6
–Seeking God's face .... 2Ch 7:14; Ps 27:8
–Seeking the Lord ...... Ps 34:4; Isa 55:6
–Crying out to God ..... Ps 3:4; Ps 66:1
–Lifting up the soul to God .... Ps 25:1; Ps 86:4
–Lifting up one's hands to God .... Ps 28:2; Ps 141:2
–Approaching God's throne of grace .... Heb 4:16
–Drawing near to God .. Heb 10:22
B. To whom should we pray?
–To God .... 2Ch 20:5–6; Ezr 9:6; Ac 4:24
–To the Father .... Eph 1:17; Eph 3:14; Col 1:3
–To the Lord .... 2Ch 20:5–6; Ac 4:24; 2Co 12:8
–To Jesus Christ .... Lk 23:42; Ac 7:59
C. What are the elements of prayer?
–Praise .... Ps 150; Mt 11:25–26
See PRAISE
–Thanksgiving .... Ps 136; Php 4:6
See THANKSGIVING
–Confession .... Ps 51; Mt 6:12
See CONFESSION
–Intercession .... Ps 122:6–9; Jn 17:6–26
See INTERCESSION
–Petition .... Ps 27:7–12; Mt 26:39,42
See PETITION
D. How should we pray?
1. Divine elements
–Through Jesus Christ .... Ro 1:8; Col 3:17
–In the name of Jesus Christ .... Jn 14:13–14; Eph 5:20
–In the Holy Spirit .... Eph 6:18; Jude 20
2. Human elements
–In the fear of the Lord .... Ps 145:19; Pr 1:28–29
–In faith .... Mk 11:24; Jas 1:6; Jas 5:15
–In humility 2Ch 7:14; 2Ch 33:12–13
–In repentance .... 2Ch 6:37; Ac 3:19
–With all our heart ... Dt 4:29; Jer 29:13
–With a heart free from sin .... Ps 66:18–19; Isa 1:15–16; Jn 9:31
–With a life free from selfishness .... Lk 18:9–14; Jas 4:3
–With a heart free from doubt .... Mt 21:21; Jas 1:5–7
–With a forgiving spirit .... Mt 6:14–15; Mk 11:25

–With confidence .... Eph 3:12; Heb 10:19, 35; 1Jn 3:21–22
–With persistence .... Lk 11:5–10; Lk 18:1–7; 1Th 5:17
–With sincerity and simplicity .... Mt 6:5–8; Mk 12:38–40
–In accordance with God's will .... Mt 26:42; 1Jn 5:14
–By accompanying prayer with obedience 1Jn 3:22

E. Does God answer the prayers of his people?
1. Remarkable answers to prayers
–Abraham's servant for a wife for Isaac . Ge 24:12–27
–Moses for the defeat of Amalek .... Ex 17:8–13
–Gideon and his fleece .... Jdg 6:36–40
Samson for strength . Jdg 16:25–30
–Hannah for a child .. 1Sa 1:9–20
–Elijah for return to life of a dead boy 1Ki 17:19–23
–Elijah for fire from heaven 1Ki 18:30–38
–Elijah for rain ...... 1Ki 18:41–45; Jas 5:17–18
–Elisha for return to life of a dead boy ... 2Ki 4:32–35
–Hezekiah for healing 2Ki 20:1–7
–Daniel for safety in the lions' den .... Da 6:10,16–22
–Zechariah for a child .... Lk 1:7,11–17
–The thief on the cross for salvation .. Lk 23:42–43
–Early Christians for Peter in prison ...... Ac 12:3–11
–Paul and Silas in prison .... Ac 16:25–26
2. God's promises to answer us
–In the Old Testament .... Ps 86:7; Isa 30:19; Isa 58:9
–In the words of Jesus .... Mt 7:7–11; Jn 14:13–14
–In New Testament letters .... Jas 1:5–8; 1Jn 5:14–15
3. The basis of God's answers
–God's glory .... Nu 14:13–16; Jn 17:1–5
–God's grace .... Ex 32:31–32; Nu 14:17–19; Isa 30:19; 2Co 12:8–9
–God's faithfulness to his word .... Ex 32:12–13; 2Ch 20:7–9
4. The manner of God's answers
–Sometimes immediately .... Nu 14:20; 1Ki 17:20–21; Lk 23:43
–Sometimes after a delay .... Lk 18:1–7
–Sometimes more than asked for .... 1Ki 18:24, 36–38; Eph 3:20
–Sometimes different from the request 1Ki 19:1–9; 2Co 12:7–9
–Sometimes "No" ... 2Sa 12:15–20
–God requires action on our part .... Ne 4:9

F. Various aspects of prayer
1. Postures of prayer
–Standing .... 1Ki 8:22; Ne 9:4–5
–Sitting .... 1Ch 17:16; Lk 10:13
–Kneeling .... Ezr 9:5; Da 6:10; Ac 20:36
–Bowing down ...... Ex 34:8; Ps 5:7; Ps 95:6
–Lying on the ground .... 2Sa 12:16; Mt 26:39
–Lifting up hands .... Ps 28:2; Isa 1:15; 1Ti 2:8
2. Manner of prayer
–Alone, silently 1Sa 1:18
–Alone, aloud .... Eze 11:13
–With two or three ... Mt 18:19
–In a larger group .... Ps 35:18
3. Time of prayer
–In the morning ...... Ps 5:1–3; Mk 1:35
–In the evening ...... Ge 24:63
–At fixed times ...... Ps 55:17; Da 6:10
–Always .... Lk 18:1; Ro 1:10; 1Th 5:17
4. Possible places of prayer
–In secret .... Mt 6:6
–In bed .... Ps 63:6
–In a family setting .. Ac 10:1–2
–Out in the open ..... Ge 24:11–12
–In the battlefield .... Jos 10:12–13
–By the riverside ..... Ac 16:13
–In the temple 2Ki 19:14
–In the church gathered together .... Ac 4:23–24, 31
–Anywhere 1Ti 2:8

PREACHING

A. Preachers in the Bible
1. Old Testament saints who preached
–Noah 2Pe 2:5
–Jonah .... Jnh 1:2; Jnh 3:2
–Isaiah .... Isa 61:1
–Ezekiel .... Eze 21:2
–Amos .... Am 7:16
–Haggai and Zechariah .... Ezr 6:14
2. New Testament saints who preached
–John the Baptist .... Mt 3:1
–Jesus .... Mt 4:17
–Peter and John ...... Ac 8:25
–Philip .... Ac 8:40
–Paul .... Ac 9:27; 1Co 9:16
–Timothy 1Ti 4:13
–Numerous believers . Ac 8:4; Ac 15:35
–All Christians .... Mt 28:19; Mk 16:15

B. The content of preaching
1. In the Old Testament
–A message of judgment .... Eze 20:46; Eze 21:2; Am 7:16; Jnh 3:4
–A message of hope .. Isa 40:1–2,9; Isa 52:7–10; Am 9:11–15
2. In the New Testament
–The good news of the kingdom .... Lk 9:2; Lk 16:16; Ac 20:25
–The good news of salvation 1Co 1:21; 1Co 15:1–2
–The cross of Christ .. 1Co 2:1–2
–The resurrection of Christ .... Ac 17:18,31; 1Co 15:12–14
–Jesus Christ is Lord . 2Co 4:5
–Fulfillment of the Scriptures in Christ .. Ac 2:14–36; Ac 4:12–26; Ac 13:16–41; 1Co 15:3–5
–The coming judgment .... Ac 10:42; Ac 17:31
–The call to repent and believe .... Mk 1:15; Ac 2:38; Ac 10:43; Ac 26:20

PREDESTINATION

See ELECTION; PROVIDENCE

PRIDE

A. Legitimate pride
1. Occasions for such pride
–Boasting in the Lord .... Ps 34:2; Ps 44:8; Jer 9:24; 1Co 1:31
–Boasting in the cross of Christ .... Gal 6:14
–Boasting about God-fearing churches .... 2Co 1:14; 2Co 7:4; Php 2:16
2. The glory of such pride
–Must be in God's grace 2Co 1:12
–Must be in Jesus Christ .... Ro 15:17–18
–Must be in the Holy Spirit .... Ro 15:18–19

B. Sinful pride
1. Characteristics of a proud person
–Tries to be like God .... Ge 3:5–6
–Thinks himself or herself better than others .... Lk 18:10–12
–Boasts about ancestry .... Lk 3:8; Jn 8:33
–Takes pride in the temple .... Jer 7:4
–Takes pride in self-accomplishment . Isa 10:12–15; Eze 28:1–7; 1Co 4:7
2. Notable examples
–Adam and Eve ..... Ge 3:5–6
–David 1Ch 21:1–7
–Uzziah 2Ch 26:16
–Hezekiah 2Ch 32:25
–Nebuchadnezzar ..... Da 4:30
–Herod .... Ac 12:21–23
3. Results of such pride
–Deceives the heart ... Jer 49:16
–Hardens the heart ... Da 5:20
–Produces quarrels ... Pr 13:10
–Brings disgrace ..... Pr 11:2
–Leads to destruction . Pr 16:18
–Brings opposition from God .... Pr 3:34; Jas 4:6
–Brings judgment from God .... Lev 26:18–20; Zep 2:10–11; Mal 4:1
4. Warnings against such pride .... Pr 8:13; Pr 16:5,18; Pr 21:4,24; Lk 18:9; Ro 12:16; 1Jn 2:16

See also HUMILITY

PRIEST

A. Basic requirements for being priests
–Must belong to the tribe of Levi .... Ex 29:9,44; Ezr 2:61–62
–Had to follow special marriage laws .... Lev 21:7–9, 13–15
–Had to remain unshaven .... Lev 21:5–6
–Had to honor proper procedures .... Lev 10:1–7
–Non-priests punished for doing priestly work .... Nu 18:7; 1Sa 13:8–14; 2Ch 26:16–21

B. Basic tasks of the priests (including Levites)
–Presented needs of the people to God .... Heb 5:1–3
–Made atonement for sin .... Lev 16:1–22
–Sprinkled blood of the sacrifices .... Lev 1:5,11; Lev 17:11
–Offered sacrifices on the altar .... Lev 6:8–9
–Kept fire burning on the altar .... Lev 6:13
–Burned incense on the altar .... Ex 30:7–9; Lk 1:5–9
–Took care of the sanctuary .... Nu 3:38
–Responsible for the treasury 1Ch 26:20
–Supervised the work of the temple 1Ch 23:4
–Carried the ark .... Nu 4:15
–Led the people in music .... Ne 12:27–43
–Blessed the people ..... Nu 6:23–27
–Prayed for the people .. Lev 16:20–21; Ezr 9:5–15
–Made diagnosis regarding leprosy .... Lev 13:1–8
–Taught the law .... Ne 8:7–8; Mal 2:7
–Made judgments according to the law .... Dt 21:5; 1Ch 23:4

C. Christ fulfilled the Old Testament priesthood
–Compared to a high priest .... Heb 8:1–6
–Sacrificed himself ...... Heb 9:26,28; Heb 10:12; 1Jn 2:2
–Brought his blood into heaven .... Heb 9:12
–Justifies us .... Ro 3:24–28
–Reconciles us to God .. 2Co 5:18–19
–Continues to pray for us .... Ro 8:34; Heb 7:25; 1Jn 2:1

D. Priesthood of all believers
–Believers are called a holy priesthood .... 1Pe 2:5,9; Rev 1:6
–We can approach God directly through Christ . Jn 14:6; Ro 5:2; Eph 2:18
–We can confess sins directly to God .... Mt 6:12; Lk 18:13; Ac 2:37–38; Ac 17:30
–Our lives must be spiritual sacrifices .... Ro 12:1; Heb 13:15–16; 1Pe 2:5

PRISCILLA

–Wife of Aquila; tentmakers . Ac 18:1–3
–Invited Paul to live with them .... Ac 18:3
–Traveled with Paul to Ephesus .... Ac 18:18–19
–Instructed Apollos .... Ac 18:26
–Paul considered her a fellow worker .... Ro 16:3
–Church met in their house .. Ro 16:4

PROMISE

–God's pledge for the future

A. Major promises of God
1. Concerning Christ
–Coming offspring of the woman .... Ge 3:15
–Abraham as a father of many .... Ge 12:1–3
–Scepter to come from Judah .... Ge 49:10
–Star to come from Jacob .... Nu 24:17
–Prophet like Moses .. Dt 18:15,18
–David's throne to be established forever .. 2Sa 7:16
–The virgin birth ..... Isa 7:14
–The coming Prince of Peace .... Isa 9:6–7
–The suffering servant of God .... Isa 53:1–12
–The new covenant .. Jer 31:31–34
–The coming shepherd .... Eze 34:23
–The coming Holy Spirit .... Joel 2:28–32
–A king born in Bethlehem .... Mic 5:2–4
–Jesus riding into Jerusalem .... Zec 9:9

–The forerunner of the Messiah .... Mal 3:1
2. Concerning believers
–God will forgive sin . 1Jn 1:9
–God will give us peace .... Ps 85:8
–God will bless us ... Ps 67:6–7
–God will lead us .... Ps 23:1–6
–God will never leave us .... Heb 13:5
–Jesus will never leave us .... Mt 28:20
–God will answer prayer 1Jn 5:14–15
–Jesus will answer prayer .... Jn 14:13–14
–God will help us overcome temptation 1Co 10:13
–God will protect us from Satan 2Th 3:3
–God will give us eternal life 1Jn 2:25
–God will give us the kingdom .... Jas 2:5
–God will make us his heirs .... Gal 3:29

B. God's attitude to his promises
–Gives us many promises 2Pe 1:4
–Confirms his promises by an oath .... Heb 6:13–20
–Remembers his promises .... Ps 105:42
–Keeps his promises .... Jos 23:15; Isa 38:7; Ac 13:23, 32–33; 2Pe 3:9
–Is faithful to his promises .... 1Th 5:24; Heb 10:23
–Fulfills all his promises in Christ 2Co 1:18,20
–God's promises never fail 1Ki 8:56

C. Believers and God's promises
–We have them from God 2Co 7:1
–We must believe them . Ps 106:12,24; Ro 4:16–21
–We must share in them .... Eph 3:6
–We must rejoice in them .... Ps 119:162
–We must meditate on them .... Ps 119:148
–We must not fall short of them .... Heb 4:1

PROPHET

A. How did one become a prophet?
–Called directly by God . Isa 6:8; Jer 1:4–5; Am 7:14–15
–Inspired by God to prophesy 1Sa 10:6,9–11; 1Sa 19:23–24
–Appointed by another prophet 1Ki 19:19–21
–Some joined the company of the prophets 2Ki 2:3,5,7; 2Ki 6:1–4

B. What did a prophet do?
1. Spoke messages from God to the people
–God commanded them to speak ...... Dt 18:18; Jnh 3:2
–The Spirit moved them to speak 2Pe 1:21
–They said, "Thus says the LORD" ..... Isa 44:6; Jer 6:16
2. Served as watchmen for the people .... Jer 6:16–17; Eze 3:16–21
3. Pointed out the sins of kings 2Sa 12:1–12; 1Ki 18:18–19
4. Pronounced judgment on the people .... 1Ki 21:20–24; Isa 2:6–21; Jer 4:5–18
5. Predicted the future .. 1Sa 9:9
–The near future ..... 1Ki 17:1; Ac 11:28
–The distant future ... Isa 65:17–25; Joel 2:28–32; Mic 5:2–5; Lk 24:25–27
6. Called the people to repentance .... 2Ki 17:13; Jer 18:11; Am 5:4–6, 14–15
7. Gave hope to the people .... Jer 23:3–8; Am 9:11–15; Zep 3:9–17
8. Interpreted dreams ... Da 2:17–45; Da 3:9–28
9. Wrote down messages from God .... Jer 30:2; Hab 2:2; Rev 1:11,19

C. Tests for determining the true prophet
–Does the prophecy come true? .... Dt 18:21–22; Jer 28:1–17
–Does it correspond with God's word? .... Dt 13:1–3; 1Ki 22:17–28,37; 1Jn 4:1–3
–Does the prophet live a God-fearing life? ...... Jer 23:9–18; 2Pe 2:1–3, 13–18

D. Responses to the prophets
1. Positive
–They were to be heeded .... Dt 18:15
–They were to be trusted 2Ch 20:20
2. Negative
–They were often persecuted .... 2Ch 36:16; Ac 7:52
–They were sometimes put in prison .... 2Ch 18:25–26; Jer 37:15–16
–They were even killed .... 1Ki 19:10; Mt 21:35–36; 1Th 2:15

E. Jesus Christ as God's final prophet
–He fulfilled God's promise of a prophet ... Dt 18:15,18; Ac 3:21–23; Ac 7:37
–He fulfilled all Old Testament prophecies ...... Mt 5:17; 2Co 1:20; 1Pe 1:10–11
–He is called "The prophet" .... Jn 6:14–15; Jn 7:40
–He called himself a prophet .... Mt 13:57; Lk 13:33
–He perfectly spoke God's word .... Jn 7:16; Jn 12:49–50; Heb 1:1–2
–He is the Word of God in human flesh .... Jn 1:14

F. Prophets in the New Testament church
1. Names
–Agabus .... Ac 11:28; Ac 21:10
–Judas and Silas ..... Ac 15:32
–Twelve men in Ephesus .... Ac 19:6
–Daughters of Philip . Ac 21:9
–Paul 1Co 13:2; 1Th 4:13–17
–Peter 2Pe 3:10–13
–John .... Rev 1:1
2. Prophecy as a gift of the Spirit
–Mentioned by Peter on Pentecost .... Ac 2:17
–Mentioned by Paul .. 1Co 12:10; 1Co 14:1; Eph 4:11
–Distinct from the gift of teaching .... Ac 13:1; 1Co 12:28; Eph 4:11
3. Function of prophets in the church
–Served as foundation of the church .... Eph 2:20
–Their gift preferred to tongues 1Co 14:1–5
–Message must edify the church 1Co 14:4–5, 12
–Message must reach unbelievers 1Co 14:23–25
–Message must be tested by other prophets 1Co 14:29–32; 1Th 5:19–20; 1Jn 4:1

PROVIDENCE

–God's care over creation and his control of history

A. God's care for his whole creation
1. Aspects of God's providence
–Cares for all his creatures .... Ps 145:9; Mt 10:29
–Provides food for his creatures .... Ps 104:14, 27–28; Ps 145:16; Mt 6:26
–Preserves his creatures .... Ne 9:6; Ps 36:6
–Determines the events of history .... Ge 50:20; Ps 33:10–11; Ac 2:22–23
–Determines the ways of humans .... Pr 16:1,9; Pr 19:21
–Controls everything that happens .... Isa 40:22–26; Da 4:35; Ac 17:26; Eph 1:11
–Controls the weather .... Ps 68:9; Mt 5:45; Ac 14:15–17
–Controls the smallest details .... Mt 10:29–30
–Controls evil .... Job 2:1–8; Isa 14:24–27; Isa 45:7; Am 3:6
2. Means of God's control
–By his powerful word .... Ps 29:3–9; Heb 1:3
–By Jesus Christ ..... Col 1:17

B. God's special care for his own people
1. General statements ... Ps 91:1–16; Isa 31:5; Ro 8:35–39; 1Pe 3:12
2. Specific statements
–Opens hearts to believe the gospel ... Lk 24:45; Ac 16:14
–Controls specific events .... Ge 22:8,13–14; Ps 105:5–44; Ps 136:10–24; Isa 38:17
–Works for good of those who love him . Ge 50:20; Ro 8:28

C. Our response to God's providence
–Acknowledge it 1Sa 2:6–10; 1Ch 29:11–12
–Rejoice in it .... Ps 4:7–8; Ps 16:7–11
–Trust in it .... Ps 13:6; Ps 28:7
–Humble ourselves in the face of it .... Dt 8:2–3; Job 1:20–22; Job 42:1–6
–Do not worry about tomorrow .... Mt 6:25–34; Mt 10:28–31

PUNISHMENT

–Penalty inflicted because of sin

A. Human punishment through law
1. Principles of punishment
–Power to punish given to government ... Ro 13:4
–Eye for eye, tooth for tooth .... Ex 21:23–25; Lev 24:19–20; Dt 19:21
–Restitution to be made .... Ex 22:1–9; Nu 5:5–8
–Must be impartial ... Lev 24:22; Dt 1:16–17
–Innocent must be acquitted .... Dt 25:1
2. Methods of punishment
a. Non-capital punishments
–Fines .... Ex 21:22; Am 2:8
–Confiscation of property .... Ezr 7:26
–Beating .... Dt 25:2–3; 2Co 11:23–25
–Gouging out eyes .... Jdg 16:21
–Imprisonment .... 1Ki 22:27; Ac 12:4
–Confinement in a dungeon .... Jer 38:6
–Chains .... 2Ki 23:33; Php 1:7,13
–Banishment ...... Ezr 7:26; Rev 1:9
–Excommunication from synagogue .. Jn 9:22; Jn 16:2
b. Capital punishment
–Stoning .... Dt 22:24; Ac 7:59
–Burning .... Lev 20:14
–The sword .... Ac 12:2; Heb 11:37
–Hanging .... Est 7:9–10
–Crucifixion ...... Mk 15:20,24
–Beheading .... Ge 40:19
–Cutting in pieces . Heb 11:37
–Throwing to wild beasts .... Da 6:16,24

B. God's punishment
1. Basic reasons for God's punishment
–Human sin .... Am 1:3—2:16; Ro 6:23
–Idolatry .... 2Ki 17:14–20; Jer 2:9–13
–Disobedience to God's law .... Dt 28:15–68; Ne 9:26–27
2. Methods of God's punishments
a. Temporal
–Sickness 2Ch 26:19–20
–Death of a loved one 2Sa 12:14
–Drought 1Ki 17:1
–Famine .... La 2:11–12
–Violent storms ... Jnh 1:4
–Plagues .... Joel 1:2–11
–Defeat by foreign armies .... Jdg 2:10–15
–Exile 2Ch 36:15–20
b. Eternal punishment
See HELL

QUEEN

A. Queen of Sheba
–Came to visit Solomon . 1Ki 10:1–2; 2Ch 9:1
–Overwhelmed at Solomon's wisdom 1Ki 10:3–9; 2Ch 9:2–8
–Gave Solomon many gifts 1Ki 10:10; 2Ch 9:9
–Received gifts from Solomon 1Ki 10:13; 2Ch 9:12
–Jesus used her as an example .... Mt 12:42; Lk 11:31

B. Queen Athaliah
See ATHALIAH

C. Queen Vashti
See VASHTI

D. Queen Esther
See ESTHER

E. Queen of Heaven (goddess Ishtar) .... Jer 7:18; Jer 44:17–19,25

F. Babylon pictured as a queen ... Isa 47:5–8; Rev 18:7

RACHEL
–Younger daughter of Laban ... Ge 29:16
–Second wife of Jacob ... Ge 29:28
–Loved by Jacob more than Leah ... Ge 29:30
–Bore two sons ... Ge 30:22–24; Ge 35:16–18,24
–Stole Laban's gods ... Ge 31:19, 32–35
–Her death ... Ge 35:19–20
–Prophecy concerning her ... Jer 31:15
–Prophecy fulfilled at the birth of Jesus ... Mt 2:16–18

RAHAB
–Prostitute at Jericho who hid spies ... Jos 2:1–21
–Spared when Jericho was destroyed ... Jos 6:22–25
–Mother of Boaz ... Mt 1:5
–An example of true faith ... Heb 11:31; Jas 2:25–26

RAIN
See WEATHER

RANSOM
See REDEMPTION

REBEKAH
–Sister of Laban ... Ge 24:29
–Secured as bride for Isaac .. Ge 24:34–61
–Mother of Esau and Jacob . Ge 25:19–26
–Abimelech discovered that she was Isaac's wife ... Ge 26:1–11
–Helped Jacob deceitfully get Isaac's blessing ... Ge 27:1–17
–Convinced Isaac that Jacob should leave ... Ge 27:42–28:4
–Buried in cave of Machpelah ... Ge 49:29–31

RECONCILIATION
–Establishing harmony between conflicting parties

A. The need for reconciliation
 1. Between humans
  –Adam and Eve argued in Eden ... Ge 3:12–13
  –Abram and Lot could not agree ... Ge 13:5–11
  –Sarai and Hagar could not get along . Ge 16:3–6
  –Jacob fled from Esau ... Ge 27:41–45
  –There will always be conflicts ... Mt 24:6
 2. Between God and humans
  –Adam and Eve hid from God ... Ge 3:8
  –Sinners are hostile to God ... Ro 8:7; Col 1:21
  –Sinners cannot stand in God's presence ... Ps 5:5–6
  –Isaiah fearful of God's presence ... Isa 6:5
 3. Between God and nature
  –Nature cursed by God ... Ge 3:14–18
  –Nature groans because of sin ... Ro 8:20,22
B. The process of reconciliation
 1. Only God can reconcile us to himself
  –God took the initiative ... 2Co 5:18
  –God reconciles sinners to himself ... 2Co 5:19; Col 1:22
  –He reconciles all things to himself ... Eph 1:10; Col 1:20
 2. Accomplished through the cross ... Ro 5:10; 2Co 5:18–19; Col 1:22; Heb 2:17
 3. Reconciliation among humans rooted in Christ
  –Christ is our peace .. Eph 2:14–17
  –We are one in Christ ... Jn 17:11,22–23; Gal 3:28; Col 3:11
  –Harmony experienced in the early church .. Ac 2:44–45; Ac 4:32–35
C. Believers and reconciliation
 1. Reconciliation with God
  –We must be reconciled to God ... 2Co 5:20
  –We must proclaim reconciliation ... 2Co 5:19–20
 2. Reconciliation among believers
  –Conflicts resolved in the early church ... Ac 15:1–29; Gal 2:1–10
  –We may show no partiality in the church ... Jas 2:1–4,9; 1Pe 1:17
  –There may be no divisions in the church ... 1Co 1:10–13; 1Co 11:18–22
  –We must work for harmony in the church ... Gal 6:1–2; Eph 4:29–32; Php 2:1–5
  –We must end personal conflicts ... Mt 5:23–24; Mt 18:15–16; 1Co 6:1–8; Php 4:2–3

REDEMPTION
–Freedom obtained through a price paid

A. Redemption among humans
 1. Redemption of an Israelite slave
  –Slave could redeem himself ... Lev 25:49
  –Slave could be redeemed by relatives ... Lev 25:48–49
  –Slave released in year of jubilee ... Lev 25:54
 2. Redemption of property
  –A person could redeem his own land ... Lev 25:26–27
  –A relative could redeem the land ... Lev 25:25, 48–53
  –Land returned in the year of jubilee ... Lev 25:28, 39–43
  –Land could be redeemed through marriage ... Ru 4:1–12
B. Redemption by God
 1. Natural redemption for Israelites
  –Israelites were slaves in Egypt ... Ge 15:13; Ex 1:11–14; Dt 5:15
  –Israelites redeemed through the exodus .. Ex 6:6; 2Sa 7:22–24; Ps 106:8–10; Mic 6:4
  –Price paid was the destruction of Egypt . Isa 43:3
  –Judah redeemed from Babylon ... Isa 54:5–8; Jer 31:10–11; Mic 4:10
 2. Spiritual redemption from sin
  a. We need redemption
   –We are all slaves to sin ... Jn 8:34; Ro 6:17
   –Humans cannot redeem themselves ... Ps 49:7–8
  b. God redeemed the Israelites ... Ps 130:8; Isa 44:21–22; Lk 1:68–71
  c. Christ redeems us
   –Redemption accomplished in Christ ... Ro 3:24; Col 1:13–14
   –The ransom paid was his blood ... Eph 1:7; 1Pe 1:19; Rev 5:9
   –The ransom paid was his death ... Mk 10:45; Heb 9:15; 1Ti 2:6
  d. The purpose of redemption
   –To justify us before God ... Ro 3:24
   –To free us from wickedness ... Ro 6:7,22; Tit 2:14
   –To free us from the law ... Gal 4:5
   –To free us from the curse ... Gal 3:13
   –To free us from an empty way of life ... 1Pe 1:18
  e. The results of redemption
   –We are forgiven .. Eph 1:7; Col 1:14
   –We can now live free lives ... Gal 5:1,13
   –We can now serve God ... 1Pe 2:16
   –We await our final redemption ... Lk 21:27–28; Ro 8:23; Eph 1:14

REGENERATION
See BORN AGAIN

REHOBOAM
–Son of Solomon; king of Judah ... 1Ki 11:43; 1Ch 3:10
–Had various wives ... 2Ch 11:18–21
–Was asked to lighten Israelite yoke ... 1Ki 12:1–4; 2Ch 10:1–4
–Refused to ease the Israelites' burden ... 1Ki 12:5–15; 2Ch 10:5–15
–Caused division in the kingdom ... 1Ki 12:16–24; 2Ch 10:16–19
–Told not to fight to regain ten tribes ... 2Ch 11:1–4
–Built up defenses of Judah . 2Ch 11:5–12
–Supported by Levites from Israel ... 2Ch 11:13–17
–Led Judah into idolatry ... 1Ki 14:21–24; 2Ch 12:1,14
–Fought with Shishak of Egypt ... 1Ki 14:25–28; 2Ch 12:2–11
–Humbled himself ... 2Ch 12:12
–His death ... 1Ki 14:31; 2Ch 12:16

REJOICE
See JOY

REMEMBER
A. Human remembrance
 1. Examples of what humans must remember
  –The day of the exodus ... Ex 13:3
  –The Sabbath day ... Ex 20:8
  –God's care during forty years in wilderness ... Dt 8:2
  –Rebellion against God ... Dt 9:7
  –The power of God .. Ne 4:14
  –The miracles of God ... Ps 77:11
  –The name of God ... Ps 119:55
  –The creator ... Ecc 12:1,6
  –The body and blood of the Lord ... 1Co 11:24–25
  –The poor ... Gal 2:10
  –The stranger ... Heb 13:2
 2. What do humans do when they remember?
  –They celebrate the passover ... Ex 13:3–10
  –They keep the Sabbath holy ... Ex 20:8
  –They trust God ... Dt 8:17–18
  –They obey and serve God ... Dt 10:12–13
  –They fight for the Lord ... Ne 4:14
  –They meditate on God and his mighty acts ... Ps 77:11–20
  –They keep God's law ... Ps 119:55
  –They fear God and obey his commandments ... Ecc 12:13
  –They celebrate the Lord's Supper ... 1Co 11:26–29
  –They give on behalf of the poor ... Gal 2:10
  –They show hospitality ... Heb 13:2
B. Divine remembrance
 1. Examples of what/whom God remembers
  –His covenant with Noah ... Ge 9:14–15
  –His covenant with Abraham ... Ex 2:23–25; Ps 105:8
  –His promises ... Ps 105:42
  –His love and faithfulness ... Ps 98:3
  –Noah ... Ge 8:1
  –Abraham ... Ge 19:29
  –Rachel ... Ge 30:22
  –Hannah ... 1Sa 1:19–20
  –The wickedness of his people ... Jer 14:10; Hos 8:13
 2. What does God do when he remembers?
  –He spares the world from a flood ... Ge 9:14–15
  –He rescues his people from Egypt ... Ex 3:7–9; Ps 105:43–44
  –He saves his people . Ps 98:3
  –He dries up the earth ... Ge 8:1
  –He brings Lot out of Sodom ... Ge 19:29
  –He gives children to barren women ... Ge 30:22–24; 1Sa 1:20
  –He punishes sin ... Jer 14:10; Hos 8:13

See also FORGET

REMNANT
–A small but faithful number of God's people preserved

A. Basis of God's promise to keep a remnant
  –The honor of his name . 1Sa 12:22
  –His promise to Abraham ... Ge 17:7
  –His promise to David .. 1Ki 6:13
B. God kept his promise to preserve a remnant
  –Remnant kept at the time of Elijah ... 1Ki 19:18; Ro 11:4
  –A remnant of Israel joined with Judah ... 2Ch 30:25; 2Ch 34:9; Isa 10:20–22; Ro 9:27–29
  –The entire nation of Judah was a remnant ... 2Ki 17:18; Hos 1:7
  –Remnant preserved from Assyria ... 2Ki 19:4,29–31; Mic 5:6–8
  –Remnant kept after Jerusalem was destroyed ... 2Ch 36:20; Jer 40:11; Jer 42:2; Eze 11:13
  –Remnant returned from the exile ... Ezr 9:8,13–15; Ne 1:2; Jer 23:3; Eze 34:12–14; Hag 1:12,14

–Believing Jews were a remnant of Israel ...... Ro 11:5
C. God's promise to preserve the church
–Promise of Jesus to Peter .... Mt 16:18
–Promise of Jesus for the end times .... Mt 24:21–22
–Remnant preserved in Thyatira .... Rev 2:24–25
–Remnant preserved in Sardis .... Rev 3:4–5

REPENTANCE

–Sorrow for sin and turning to God

A. The command to repent
–God calls all people to repent .... Jer 18:11; Eze 18:30–32; Ac 17:30; 2Pe 3:9
–Christ calls people to repent .... Mk 1:14–15; Lk 13:1–5; Rev 2:5,16; Rev 3:3
–John the Baptist called people to repent ...... Mt 3:2
–The apostles called people to repent .... Mk 6:12; Ac 2:38; Ac 3:19–20; Ac 26:20
–The call must go out today .... Lk 24:46–48

B. Essential aspects of repentance
–Acknowledging we are lost .... Lk 15:3–7
–Expressing sorrow for sin .... Lk 5:32; Ac 2:37–38; Ac 8:22; 2Co 7:9–10
–Returning to the Father . Lk 15:17–20
–Believing in Jesus Christ .... Mk 1:15; Ac 20:21; Rev 3:19–20
–Doing good works ..... Jer 18:11–12; Mt 3:8; Ac 26:20; Rev 2:4–5

C. The results of repentance
–Escape from disaster ... Jer 18:7–8
–Forgiveness .... 1Ki 8:46–50; Ac 2:38
–Salvation 2Co 7:10
–A new heart and spirit . Eze 18:30–31
–A knowledge of the truth 2Ti 2:25
–Eternal life .... Ac 11:18
–Regret without repentance brings death ..... Mt 27:3–5; 2Co 7:10

REPTILES

A. Reptiles mentioned in the Bible
–Adder .... Ps 58:4
–Chameleon .... Lev 11:30
–Cobra .... Isa 11:8
–Crocodile .... Lev 11:30
–Frog .... Ex 8:2–13
–Gecko .... Lev 11:30
–Lizard .... Lev 11:29–30
–Serpent .... Job 26:13
–Snake .... Mt 7:10
–Viper .... Ac 28:3
–Worm .... Jnh 4:7

B. Serpents and snakes used symbolically
–As a symbol of healing .... Nu 21:8–9; Jn 3:14–15
–As a symbol of shrewdness .... Mt 10:16
–As a symbol of alcohol's effects .... Pr 23:31–32
–As a symbol of hypocrites .... Mt 23:23; Lk 3:7–8
–As a symbol of evil people .... Dt 32:33; Ps 140:1–3
–As a symbol of God's judgment .... Nu 21:6–7; Isa 14:28–29
–As a symbol of Satan .. Ge 3:1–5; Rev 12:9; Rev 20:2

REST

A. Types of rest
–The Sabbath day ...... Ex 20:8–11
–Sleep .... Pr 3:23–24
–Life in the land of Canaan .... Jos 1:13
–Absence of war 1Ch 22:9
–Getting away from trouble .... Ps 55:6–8
–Getting away from people .... Mk 6:31
–Death 1Ki 2:10; 1Th 4:13,15
–Heaven as the land of rest .... Heb 4:8–11; Rev 14:13

B. The human need for rest
–Because of six days of work .... Ex 20:8–10
–Because of fatigue ..... Mt 8:24; Mt 26:43
–Because of overwork ... Mk 6:30–31
–Because of depression .. 1Ki 19:3–6
–Because of anxiety ..... Ecc 2:22–23; 2Co 2:13
–Because of the storms of life .... Job 3:20–26; Ps 55:4–8

C. The realization of true rest
–Through trusting in God .... Ps 37:3–7; Ps 91:1–2
–Through resting in God .... Ps 23:1–3; Ps 62:1,5
–Through experiencing God's presence .... Ex 33:14; Ps 31:19–20
–Through coming to Jesus .... Mt 11:28–29; Jn 16:33
–Through the Spirit of God .... Isa 63:14

RESURRECTION

–Resuscitation of a dead body

A. The resurrection of Christ
1. Prophecies of Christ's resurrection
a. The Old Testament in general .... Lk 24:25–26,44–46; Jn 20:9; 1Co 15:4
b. Specific prophecies in the Old Testament
–David .... Ps 16:3–11; Ac 2:24–32
–Isaiah .... Isa 55:3; Ac 13:34
–Jonah .... Jnh 1:17; Mt 12:39–40
c. Prophesied by Jesus before his death .... Mk 8:31; Mk 9:9,31; Mk 10:33–34; Jn 2:19–22
2. The event of Christ's resurrection .... Mt 28:1–7; Mk 16:1–8; Lk 24:1–8; Jn 20:1–8
3. The power used to raise Christ
–The power of God .. Ac 2:24; Eph 1:19–20; Col 2:12
–Christ's own power . Jn 10:18
–Jesus is *the* resurrection .... Jn 11:25–26
–The power of the Spirit .... Ro 8:11; 1Pe 3:18
4. The nature of Christ's resurrected body
a. The same body that died was raised ... Lk 24:39–40; Jn 20:27
b. It was a physical body
–He ate .... Lk 24:41–43; Jn 21:12–13; Ac 10:40–41
–He could be touched .... Jn 20:27; 1Jn 1:1
c. It was a glorified body .... 1Co 15:42–44; Php 3:21
–He passed through locked doors ..... Jn 20:19,26
–He ascended into heaven .... Ac 1:9
5. The appearances of the risen Christ
–To Mary Magdalene . Mk 16:9; Jn 20:10–18
–To several women .. Mt 28:8–10
–To Peter .... Lk 24:34; 1Co 15:5
–To two disciples going to Emmaus ... Lk 24:13–31
–To a group of disciples .... Lk 24:36–44
–To the disciples, minus Thomas ...... Jn 20:19–25
–To the disciples, with Thomas .... Jn 20:26–29; 1Co 15:5
–To disciples at the Sea of Tiberias ..... Jn 21:1–14
–To the disciples in Galilee .... Mt 28:16–20
–To a group of five hundred 1Co 15:6
–To James 1Co 15:7
–To all the apostles in Jerusalem .... Ac 1:4–9; 1Co 15:7
–To Paul .... Ac 9:3–6; 1Co 15:8
–Jesus gave many convincing proofs ...... Ac 1:3
6. The significance of Christ's resurrection
–Declares his deity .. Ro 1:4
–Declares his Lordship .... Ro 10:9
–Justifies us .... Ro 4:25
–Forgives us 1Co 15:17
–Saves us .... Ro 10:9; 1Pe 3:21
–Gives us living hope 1Co 15:18–19; 1Pe 1:3
–Gives us victory over death .... Ro 6:9–11; 1Co 15:57
–Guarantees our resurrection .... 1Co 15:20, 23; Php 3:10–11
–Guarantees the coming judgment .... Ac 17:31
7. The proclamation of Christ's resurrection
–Proclaimed by angels .... Mt 28:5–7; Lk 24:3–7
–Acknowledged by Christ's enemies .... Mt 28:11–15
–Preached by Peter .... Ac 2:24–32; Ac 10:40–41
–Preached by Paul .... Ac 13:30–37; Ac 17:31; 1Co 15:3–5

B. The resurrection of humans
1. Resurrection miracles
a. In the Old Testament
–By Elijah 1Ki 17:17–23
–By Elisha 2Ki 4:19–37; 2Ki 13:21
b. In the New Testament
–By Jesus .... Mk 5:38–42; Lk 7:11–15; Jn 11:38–44
–At Jesus' death .. Mt 27:52–53
–By Peter .... Ac 9:32–35
–By Paul .... Ac 20:9–10
–In Hebrews ...... Heb 11:35
2. The resurrection at the last day
a. Affirmed in the Old Testament .... Job 19:26; Ps 16:10; Isa 26:19; Da 12:2
b. Affirmed in the New Testament
–Believed by the Jews .... Jn 11:24; Ac 23:6; Ac 24:15
–Denied by the Sadducees .... Mt 22:23; Ac 23:7–8
–Prophesied by Jesus .... Mk 12:26–27; Jn 5:28–29; Jn 5:39,44
–Proclaimed by the apostles .... Ac 24:14–15; Ro 2:7–8; Ro 8:11; 1Co 15:50–57; 1Th 4:13–17; Rev 20:4–5, 12–13
3. The nature of the resurrection
a. For believers
–Have already risen to a new life ..... Ro 6:3–4; Eph 2:6; Col 2:12
–Will rise first ..... 1Th 4:6; Rev 20:4–5
–Will receive bodies like Christ's .. Php 3:21; 1Jn 3:2
–Will receive imperishable bodies 1Co 15:42
–Will receive glorious bodies 1Co 15:43
–Will receive spiritual bodies 1Co 15:44
b. For unbelievers
–Will go to everlasting contempt .. Da 12:2
–Will be condemned ...... Jn 5:28–29
–Will be judged ... Rev 20:14–15

REUBEN

A. Firstborn of Jacob by Leah .... Ge 35:23; 1Ch 2:1
–Name means "He has seen my misery" ..... Ge 29:32
–Slept with his father's concubine .... Ge 35:22; Ge 49:4
–Attempted to rescue Joseph .... Ge 37:21–30
–Went to Egypt with family .... Ge 46:8–9
–Father of four sons .... Ge 46:9
–Blessed by Jacob ...... Ge 49:3–4

B. Tribe descended from Reuben
–Blessed by Moses ..... Dt 33:6
–Numbered .... Nu 1:21; Nu 26:7
–Allotted land east of the Jordan .... Nu 32:1–33; Nu 34:14
–Allotted land west of the Jordan .... Eze 48:6
–Failed to help Deborah . Jdg 5:15–16
–Supported David 1Ch 12:37
–One of the tribes of the 144,000 .... Rev 7:5

REVELATION

–God's disclosure of himself and his truth

A. God's revelation in nature
–It reveals God's glory .. Ps 19:1–6
–It reveals God's kindness .... Ac 14:17
–It proclaims his majesty .... Ps 8:1
–It proclaims his righteousness .... Ps 50:6; Ps 97:6
–It proclaims his eternal power .... Ro 1:19–20

B. God's special revelation to his people
1. Direct revelation
–By speaking .... Ge 17:1–2; Ex 33:11; Rev 1:10–11
–By dreams .... Ge 20:3; Nu 12:6
–By visions .... Ge 15:1; Job 33:14–15; 2Co 12:1–4
2. Revelation in events of Bible history .... Dt 3:24; Eze 6:13–14; Eze 37:13–14
3. Revelation in his written word
–God revealed to prophets 2Ti 3:15–16; 2Pe 1:21

–God revealed to apostles ... 1Co 2:10; 2Co 12:7; 2Pe 3:15
4. His key revelation is Jesus Christ
–Jesus reveals the Father ... Jn 1:18; Jn 14:9; Heb 1:1–2
–Jesus is the Word of God ... Jn 1:1,14; Rev 19:11–13

C. God's continuing revelation to the church
–Revelation is a gift of the Spirit ... 1Co 14:26; Eph 1:17
–Revelations must witness to Christ ... 1Co 12:3
–Revelations must be evaluated by the church ... 1Co 14:29–32

See also DREAMS AND VISIONS; WORD OF GOD

REWARD

–What God has in store for humans

A. In the Old Testament
1. Rewarded according to one's deeds
–Stated in the law ... Lev 26:3–39; Dt 28:1–68
–Stated in the psalms . Ps 19:11; Ps 28:4; Ps 62:12
–Stated in Proverbs .. Pr 1:29–31; Pr 12:14; Pr 14:14
–Stated in the prophets ... Isa 59:18; Isa 66:6; Jer 17:10; Jer 21:13–14; Eze 9:9–10
2. Cannot always be applied to this life ... Job 1:1—2:10; Job 9:21–22; Ps 73:1–14; Ecc 9:1–12
3. God does not treat us as our sin deserves ... Ezr 9:13; Job 33:26–28; Ps 103:8–10
4. God's final reward is in the world to come . Ps 73:16–20; Ecc 12:13–14

B. In the New Testament
1. Whom does God reward with good?
–Those who receive God's grace ... Ro 6:23; Ro 11:6
–Those who believe in Jesus ... Jn 14:1–3; Ro 4:5,16
–Those who have an obedient faith ... Lk 14:12–14; 1Co 3:8,12–14; Eph 6:8; Col 3:23–24; Jas 2:14–24
–Those persecuted for Jesus' sake ... Mt 5:11–12
2. Do we earn our reward?
–We *inherit* our reward ... Mt 25:34; Ac 20:32; Col 1:12; Rev 21:7
–Good works are not done for rewards ... Mt 6:1–6, 16–18; Lk 17:7–10
3. What is our reward?
–A crown of righteousness ... 2Ti 4:8
–A crown of glory ... 1Pe 5:4
–A crown of life ... Jas 1:12
–A crown that lasts forever ... 1Co 9:25
–The kingdom prepared for us ... Mt 25:34
–A place in heaven .. Jn 14:2–3; 2Co 5:1; 2Ti 4:8
–Eternal life ... Ro 2:7; Gal 6:8
–Eternal glory ... 2Co 4:17
4. Judgment in store for the disobedient ... Ro 1:18; Ro 2:8–9; Rev 21:8; Rev 22:14–15

THE RICH AND THE POOR

A. God is the source of all wealth
–He owns everything ... Ex 19:5; Ps 24:1; Hag 2:8; 1Co 10:26
–He gives wealth ... Ge 26:12–13; Dt 8:16–18; 1Co 4:7
–He decides who is rich or poor ... 1Sa 2:7; Pr 10:22; Pr 22:2

B. Riches
1. Examples of wealthy people
–Abraham ... Ge 24:34–35
–Isaac ... Ge 26:12–14
–Esau ... Ge 36:7
–Laban ... Ge 30:29–30
–Jacob ... Ge 30:43
–Nabal ... 1Sa 25:2–3
–David ... 2Sa 5:9–13
–Solomon ... 1Ki 10:14–29
–Jehoshaphat ... 2Ch 17:5
–Job ... Job 1:1–3
–Joseph of Arimathea ... Mt 27:57
2. Means of gaining wealth
–Prosperity as God's reward to righteous .. Ps 25:12–13; Ps 112:1–3; Pr 10:22
–The wicked can also be wealthy ... Job 21:7–13; Ps 73:3,12; Jer 12:1–2
–Wealth gained by taking bribes ... Isa 1:23; Eze 22:12; Am 5:12
–Wealth gained by usury and extortion .. Ne 5:1–7; Pr 28:8; Jer 22:17; Eze 22:12
–Wealth gained by exploiting the poor .. Isa 3:14–15; Jer 2:34; Am 2:6–8; Jas 2:6
3. Reactions of the rich to their wealth
a. Unwholesome reactions
–Hoard it up for themselves ... Ecc 5:13; Lk 12:16–19; Jas 5:3
–Become greedy and fall into sin .. Pr 15:27; 1Ti 6:9–10
–Trust in it ... Job 31:24–28; Ps 49:5–6; Ps 52:7; 1Ti 6:17
–Become proud because of it ... Eze 28:5; Hos 12:8; Rev 3:17
–Reject God because of it ... Dt 8:12–14; Dt 32:15; Ne 9:25–26; Mt 19:16–22
b. Wholesome reactions
–Use it to help the poor ... Ne 5:14–19; Job 29:11–17; Lk 19:8–9; Ac 4:34–37; 2Co 8:1–4
–Use it to help bring about peace ... Ge 32:13–21; Ge 43:11–15; 1Sa 25:18–35; Pr 18:16
4. God's commands concerning wealth
–We must acknowledge God as the source ... Dt 8:18; 1Ch 29:12; Hos 2:8
–We must use wealth in God's service ... Ex 35:4–9; 1Ch 29:3; Mal 3:8–10
–We must help the poor ... Ps 82:3–4; Mt 19:16–21; Eph 4:28; 1Ti 6:18
–We must not store up treasures on earth ... Mt 6:19–21
–We should not trust in wealth ... Ps 62:10; 1Ti 6:17
–We should not be greedy ... Eph 5:3; Col 3:5; 1Pe 5:2
–We cannot serve God and Money ... Mt 6:24–25
5. Riches are considered
–Fleeting ... Pr 23:5; Pr 27:24
–Corruptible ... Mt 6:19; Jas 5:2–3
–Perishable ... 1Pe 1:18
–Uncertain ... 1Ti 6:17
–Unsatisfying ... Ecc 4:8; Ecc 5:10
–Deceitful ... Mt 13:22
–Spiritually dangerous ... Lk 18:18–25
6. Judgments often spoken against the rich
–In the Old Testament ... Isa 1:23–25; Jer 17:11; Am 4:1–3; Mic 2:1–5; Hab 2:6–8; Zec 7:8–14
–In the New Testament ... Lk 6:24–25; Lk 16:13–15; Ac 8:20–23; Jas 5:1–6; 2Pe 2:3,14–15
7. True riches are spiritual
–Having Jesus is worth everything ... Mt 13:44–47; Php 3:7–8; Heb 10:34
–Believing in Jesus brings true wealth ... 1Pe 1:7; Rev 3:17–18
–God's grace brings spiritual riches ... Eph 1:7,18; Eph 3:8,16; Col 1:27
–All things are ours in Christ ... 1Co 3:21–23
–We should store up treasures in heaven .. Mt 6:20; 1Ti 6:19

C. Poverty
1. Examples of poor people
–Lot ... Ge 19:23–30
–Naomi and Ruth ... Ru 1:20–2:2
–Widow of Zarephath ... 1Ki 17:10–12
–Jesus ... Mt 8:20; 2Co 8:9
–Lazarus ... Lk 16:20
–Paul (on occasion) .. Php 4:12
2. Reasons for becoming poor
a. God's choice for us ... 1Sa 2:7
b. Exploitation by the rich ... Isa 3:14–15; Jer 2:34; Am 2:6–8; Mic 3:1–3; Jas 2:6
c. The result of
–Laziness ... Pr 6:9–11
–Haste ... Pr 21:5
–Alcohol ... Pr 23:21
–Greed ... Pr 22:16
3. Laws given to protect the poor
–There must be no poor ... Dt 15:4
–Poor must not be taken advantage of .. Ex 22:22–23
–The poor must be paid daily ... Dt 24:14–15
–Poor allowed to glean in fields ... Lev 19:10; Dt 24:19–21
–Laws regarding security on loans ... Dt 24:10–13
–No interest may be charged to the poor . Ex 22:25; Lev 25:36
–The year for canceling debts ... Dt 15:1–11
–The Year of Jubilee . Lev 25:5–55
–Equal justice for rich and poor ... Ex 23:2–3,6; Dt 1:17; Pr 31:9
4. Blessings for those who show kindness to the poor
–Their throne will be secure ... Ps 72:1–5; Pr 29:14
–Their righteousness endures forever ... Ps 112:9; Isa 58:6–8
–God will answer their prayers ... Isa 58:6–7,9
–They will be rewarded by God ... Pr 14:21; Pr 19:17; Pr 22:9; Pr 28:27
–They will have treasure in heaven ... Mt 19:21; Lk 12:33; Lk 19:8–9
5. God as the hope of the poor
–He is their refuge ... Ps 14:6; Isa 25:4
–He is their protector . Ps 12:5
–He is their deliverer . 1Sa 2:8; Ps 34:6; Ps 113:7
–He is their helper ... Ps 40:17; Ps 70:5; Isa 41:17
–He is their provider . Ps 132:15; Isa 61:1–3; Lk 4:18–19

RIGHTEOUSNESS

–The state of being perfect and without sin

A. The righteousness of humans
1. In themselves humans are unrighteous
–No one is righteous . Ps 14:1–3; Ps 53:1–3; Ro 3:10–12, 23
–Our righteous acts are like filthy rags .. Isa 64:6
–We deserve God's wrath ... Ro 1:18; Eph 2:3
2. God gives us righteousness
a. Experienced in the Old Testament
–By Abram ... Ge 15:6
–By David ... Ps 32:1–2; Ps 103:17
–By Isaiah ... Isa 45:8,24; Isa 46:13; Isa 61:10
b. Experienced by believers in Christ
–God declares us righteous ... Ro 3:21–22; Ro 4:1–8; Gal 3:21–22; Php 3:8–9
–God credits us with Christ's righteousness ... Ro 4:11,22–24
–His righteousness is a gift ... Ro 5:17
–We become God's righteousness ... 2Co 5:21
3. Believers are called "the righteous"
–In the Old Testament ... Ps 1:5–6; Pr 10:3,6–7, 20–22; Isa 26:7; Hos 14:9; Am 2:6
–In the New Testament ... Mt 25:37,46; Heb 12:23; Jas 5:16
4. Responsibilities regarding a righteous way of life

–Be servants of righteousness ... Ro 6:13,18–19
–Long for righteousness ... Mt 5:6
–Perform righteousness ... Am 5:24; Mt 5:20
–Pursue righteousness ... Isa 51:1; 1Ti 6:11; 2Ti 2:22
–Put on righteousness ... Eph 4:24; Eph 6:14
–Seek righteousness ... Mt 6:33
–Bring forth fruits of righteousness ... Hos 10:12; 2Co 9:10; Heb 12:11
–Live for righteousness ... 1Pe 2:24
–Do what is right ... 1Jn 2:29; 1Jn 3:7
–Shun wickedness ... 2Co 6:14–15
5. God's word teaches how to be righteous ... 2Ti 3:16–17
6. Our final righteousness
–Heaven is the home of righteousness ... 2Pe 3:13
–We receive a crown of righteousness ... 2Ti 4:8
See also JUSTIFICATION
B. The righteousness of God
1. God the Father
–God is righteous ... Ps 7:9; Isa 45:21; Jer 12:1; Jn 17:25
–He always acts righteously ... 1Sa 12:7; Ps 145:17; Jer 9:24; Mic 6:5
–He judges righteously ... Ps 9:4; Ps 98:9; Jer 11:20
–His commandments are righteous ... Ps 19:9; Ps 119:138, 160; Ro 1:32; Ro 7:12
–His righteousness endures forever ... Ps 111:3; Ps 112:3
2. Jesus is righteous
a. Old Testament prophecies
–His name is "The LORD Our Righteousness" ... Jer 23:6; Jer 33:16
–He is the righteous servant ... Isa 53:11
–He is the sun of righteousness ... Mal 4:2
–He is clothed in righteousness ... Isa 11:5; Isa 59:16–17
–He loves righteousness ... Ps 45:7
–He judges in righteousness ... Ps 72:2; Isa 11:4
–He reigns in righteousness ... Isa 32:1; Zec 9:9
b. New Testament assertions
–He is the Righteous One ... Ac 3:14; Ac 7:52; 1Jn 2:1
–He fulfilled all righteousness ... Mt 3:15
–He lived a righteous life ... Ro 5:18; 2Co 5:21; 1Pe 3:18
–He is our righteousness ... 1Co 1:30
–He loves righteousness ... Heb 1:8–9
–He is the righteous Judge ... 2Ti 4:8
3. Believers and God's righteousness
–They acknowledge it ... Ezr 9:15; Da 9:7
–They see it ... Mic 7:9
–They speak of it ... Ps 35:28
–They proclaim it ... Ps 22:31; Ps 71:15–16
–They sing of it ... Ps 51:14
–They exult in it ... Ps 89:16
–They give thanks for it ... Ps 7:17
–They are led in it ... Ps 5:8
–They are upheld by it ... Isa 41:10
–They pray for it ... Ps 31:1; Ps 143:11

RIVER
A. Rivers and streams mentioned in the Bible
–Abana ... 2Ki 5:12
–Ahava ... Ezr 8:15,21
–Arnon ... Nu 21:13,24
–Besor ... 1Sa 30:9,21
–Cherith ... 1Ki 17:3–5
–Egypt ... Ge 15:18
–Euphrates ... Dt 1:7
See EUPHRATES
–Gihon ... 1Ki 1:33,38
–Gozan ... 1Ch 5:26
–Jabbok ... Ge 32:22
–Jordan ... Ge 13:10
See JORDAN
–Kanah ... Jos 16:8
–Kebar ... Eze 10:15
–Kidron ... Jn 18:1
–Kishon ... Jdg 4:7,13
–Nile ... Ge 41:1,3,17
–Pharpar ... 2Ki 5:12
–Pishon ... Ge 2:11
–Shihor ... Jos 13:3
–Tigris ... Ge 2:14
–Ulai ... Da 8:2
–Zered ... Dt 2:13–14
B. How were rivers and streams used?
1. Literally
–For drinking ... 1Ki 17:3–4
–For bathing ... Ex 2:5
–For irrigation ... Ge 2:10
–For transportation ... Isa 23:3
–For fishing ... Lev 11:9–10
–For healing ... 2Ki 5:14
–For baptism ... Mk 1:5
2. As a symbol
–Of an enemy's strength ... Ps 124:1–4
–Of God's judgment ... Ps 88:16–17; Isa 42:15
–Of God's blessings ... Ps 36:8; Isa 41:17–18
–Of God's peace ... Isa 48:18; Isa 66:12
–Of wisdom ... Pr 18:4
–Of life in the Spirit ... Jn 7:38–39
–Of healing, life-giving power ... Eze 47:1–12; Rev 22:1–2

ROCK
A. Uses for rocks
–As a pillow ... Ge 28:11
–As an altar ... Jdg 6:20–21
–As a landmark ... Jdg 15:8
–As a memorial ... Jos 4:1–9
–As a habitat for animals ... Ps 104:18
–As a hiding place ... 1Sa 13:6
–As a tomb ... Mt 27:60
–As a place from which water flowed ... Ex 17:6; Nu 20:8–11
B. The rock as a symbol
1. Of Simon, named Peter ... Mt 16:18; Jn 1:42
2. Of the apostles as the church's foundation ... Eph 2:20; Rev 21:14
3. Of Christ
–The rock in the wilderness ... 1Co 10:4
–The foundation of the church ... 1Co 3:11
–The cornerstone of the church ... Eph 2:20; 1Pe 2:6
–A stone over which people stumble ... Ro 9:33; 1Pe 2:8
4. Of God who protects and saves ... Dt 32:4,15; Ps 18:2; Isa 26:4; Hab 1:12

ROME
–The capital city of the New Testament world
A. The government of Rome
–Ruled the world at the time of Christ ... Lk 2:1; Jn 18:28; Ac 16:12
–Expelled Jews from the city ... Ac 18:2
–Gave privileges to Roman citizens ... Ac 16:37–38; Ac 22:25–29
B. Christianity and Rome
1. Jews from Rome in Jerusalem at Pentecost ... Ac 2:10
2. Paul and Rome
–Paul wrote to the church in Rome ... Ro 1:7
–Paul wanted to go to Rome ... Ro 1:15; Ro 15:23–24
–Paul arrived in Rome as a prisoner ... Ac 28:14–16
–Paul visited with Christians of Rome ... Ac 28:15
–Paul preached in Rome ... Ac 28:23–31; Php 1:12–13
–Paul was probably killed in Rome ... 2Ti 4:6–8
3. Peter may have referred to Rome as Babylon ... 1Pe 5:13

RUTH
–Moabitess; widowed daughter-in-law of Naomi ... Ru 1:3–5
–Went with Naomi to Bethlehem ... Ru 1:22
–Gleaned in field of Boaz ... Ru 2:2–17
–Proposed marriage to Boaz ... Ru 3:1–14
–Married Boaz ... Ru 4:1–13
–Gave birth to Obed ... Ru 4:13–17
–Ancestor of David ... Ru 4:17–22
–Ancestor of Jesus ... Mt 1:5

SABBATH
–Seventh day of the week, the day of rest
A. The Sabbath in the Old Testament
1. The Sabbath day of rest
a. God rested on the Sabbath ... Ge 2:2–3
b. Israel observed it before law was given ... Ex 16:23,25
c. Laws concerning the Sabbath
–The fourth commandment ... Ex 20:8–11
–No work to be done ... Ex 31:14–15; Ex 35:2–3
–A day of sacred assembly ... Lev 23:2–3
–A day for special offerings ... Nu 28:9–10
2. Purposes of the Sabbath
–To be a sign of the covenant ... Ex 31:16–17; Isa 56:6; Eze 20:12,20
–To honor God ... Isa 58:13
–To worship God ... Lev 23:3
–To remember God's salvation ... Dt 5:15
–To rest from work ... Dt 5:12–14
3. The sabbath year ... Lev 25:1–7; Eze 46:3
4. The Israelites and the Sabbath
–Disobeyed the Sabbath ... Jer 17:20–23
–Desecrated the Sabbath ... Eze 20:21,24; Eze 22:8; Eze 23:38–39
–Couldn't wait for Sabbath to be over ... Am 8:4–5
–Wanted to work on Sabbath ... Ne 13:20–21
–Nehemiah reinstituted Sabbath laws ... Ne 13:15–22
B. In the New Testament
1. The Jews and the Sabbath
–Worshiped regularly on that day ... Lk 4:16,31; Ac 13:14–15; Ac 17:2
–Used it as a focal point for legalism ... Mt 12:2,10; Lk 13:14; Jn 9:13–16
2. Jesus and the Sabbath
–Is Lord of the Sabbath ... Mt 12:8; Mk 2:28
–Tried to restore its proper spirit ... Lk 13:10–16; Lk 14:1–6; Jn 5:16–18
–Taught Sabbath was for our good ... Mk 2:27
3. Symbolism of the Sabbath
–Symbolizes the rest God wants for us ... Heb 4:3–4
–Symbolizes the eternal Sabbath ... Heb 4:8–11
4. The day of worship in the early church
a. The Sabbath ... Ac 13:14; Ac 17:2; Ac 18:4
b. The first day of the week
–Christ's resurrection on that day ... Lk 24:1–7; Jn 20:1,19
–Pentecost on that day ... Ac 2:1
–Worship on that day ... Ac 20:7
–Offerings set aside on that day ... 1Co 16:2
–John's vision on the Lord's Day ... Rev 1:10

SACRIFICE
A. Sacrifices in the Old Testament
1. Persons performing them
–Cain and Abel ... Ge 4:3–5
–Noah ... Ge 8:20–21
–Abram ... Ge 12:7–8; Ge 15:9–11
–Jacob ... Ge 31:54; Ge 46:1
–Job ... Job 1:5
–Regular duties of priests ... Lev 1:3–17
2. Types of sacrifices
a. According to substance used
–Various animal sacrifices ... Lev 1:2–17; Lev 3:1–4:35
–Grain sacrifices ... Lev 2:1–16; Lev 6:14–23
b. According to time performed
–Daily sacrifices ... Ex 29:38–41; Nu 28:1–8
–Weekly sacrifices ... Nu 28:9–10
–Monthly sacrifices ... Nu 28:11–15
–Annual sacrifices ... Nu 28:16–29:38
3. Purpose of sacrifices
a. As cleansing for sin
–Burnt offerings ... Lev 1:3–17
–Sin offerings ... Lev 4:1–5:13
–Guilt offerings ... Lev 5:14–6:7
b. As thanksgiving to God
–Grain offerings ... Lev 2:1–16
–Offerings of well-being ... Lev 3:1–16
4. The insufficiency of sacrifices alone
a. Had to be accompanied by
–A true faith ... Heb 11:4
–A humble heart ... Ps 51:17; Isa 66:2–3
–A repentant heart ... Isa 1:11–16
–A life of obedience ... 1Sa 15:22; Ps 40:6–8
–A life of justice ... Mic 6:6–8
–A desire to give one's best ... Mal 1:6–14
b. Despised if offered by unjust people ... Isa 1:11–15; Am 5:21–24
B. Sacrifice in the New Testament
1. View of Old Testament sacrifices
–They cannot take away sin ... Heb 9:9–10, 23; Heb 10:1–4, 11

–They point to the sacrifice of Christ ... Heb 9:11–14,24–26
2. The sacrifice of Christ
–He is the lamb who was sacrificed ... Jn 1:29; 1Co 5:7; Rev 5:6
–He is the atoning sacrifice ... Ro 3:25; Heb 7:27; Heb 9:28; 1Jn 4:10
3. Sacrifices expected of the Christian
–Total commitment to Christ ... Mt 16:24–25
See SELF-DENIAL
–Lives of service to God ... Ro 12:1; 1Pe 2:5
–Praising and confessing God ... Heb 13:15
–Deeds of kindness ... Heb 13:16
–Gifts of money for use in God's work ... Php 4:18

SADDUCEES

–A Jewish party, prominent at the time of Jesus

A. Major characteristics
–Members of the Sanhedrin (Jewish council) ... Ac 23:6
–Did not believe in the resurrection of the dead ... Mt 22:23; Ac 23:8
B. The Sadducees and Jesus
1. The Sadducees questioned and tested Jesus
–About a sign from heaven ... Mt 16:1; Mk 8:11
–About the resurrection of the dead ... Mt 22:23–27; Mk 12:18–23; Lk 20:27–33
2. Jesus criticized the Sadducees ... Mt 16:6,11–12
B. The Sadducees and the early church
–Persecuted the church ... Ac 4:1–3; Ac 5:17–18
–Put the apostles on trial ... Ac 5:21–32
–Put Paul on trial ... Ac 22:30—23:6

SALOME

–The mother of James and John, sons of Zebedee ... Mt 27:56; Mk 15:40
–Wanted a high position for her sons ... Mt 20:20–23
–Watched Jesus die on the cross ... Mk 15:40
–Went to the empty tomb ... Mk 16:1

SALT

A. Uses for salt
–For seasoning food ... Job 6:6
–For seasoning sacrifices ... Lev 2:13; Eze 43:24
–For ratifying a covenant ... Nu 18:19; 2Ch 13:5
–For rubbing a newborn child ... Eze 16:4
B. Symbolism of salt
–Symbol of judgment ... Ge 19:26; Jer 48:9
–Symbol of permanency of covenant ... Nu 18:19
–Symbol of preservation ... Mt 5:13
–Symbol of peace ... Mk 9:50; Col 4:6

SALVATION

A. Definition of salvation
1. "Save" translated as "heal" ... Mk 6:56; Ac 14:9
2. "Save" as rescue from physical danger ... Da 6:27; Mt 8:25; Lk 23:39; Ac 27:20,31; Heb 5:7
3. "Save" as rescue from personal enemies ... Ps 18:3–6; Ps 59:2
4. "Save" as deliverance from political oppression
–Salvation from Egypt ... Ex 14:13,30; Ps 106:8–11
–Salvation from enemies invading Canaan ... Jdg 3:9,31; Jdg 8:22; 2Ki 14:27
5. "Save" as deliverance from sin
a. In the Old Testament
–Asking for salvation from sin ... Ps 39:8; Ps 51:14
–Promise of salvation through Messiah ... Jer 23:5–6; Eze 37:23–25
b. In the New Testament, it embraces
–The past: "have been saved" ... Eph 2:5,8; 2Ti 1:9; Tit 3:5
–The present: "are being saved" ... Ac 2:47; 1Co 1:18; 2Co 2:15
–The future: "will be saved" ... Ro 5:9–10; Ro 13:11; 1Pe 1:5,9
B. God as the source of salvation
1. Israel's God in the Old Testament
a. He is called "Savior" ... Isa 43:11; Isa 45:15,21
b. He is Israel's salvation ... Ex 15:1–2; Ps 27:1; Isa 12:2; Jnh 2:9
c. He promised worldwide salvation ... Ps 67:2; Isa 49:6; Isa 52:10
2. Christ as Savior
–Salvation is in his name alone ... Ac 4:12; Ac 10:43; Ro 10:13
–He is called Savior ... Lk 2:11; Eph 5:23; Tit 1:4
–He saves his people from sin ... Mt 1:21; Ac 5:31; Tit 2:13–14
–He saves the lost ... Lk 15:3–10; Lk 19:10
–He saves the world ... Jn 3:16–17; Jn 12:47; 1Jn 4:14
C. The process of salvation
1. Salvation required the work of Christ
–His coming to this earth ... 2Co 8:9; Php 2:6–8
–His death on the cross ... Jn 3:14–15; 1Co 1:18; 1Co 15:2–3
–The shedding of his blood ... 1Pe 1:18–19; Rev 5:9
–His resurrection from the dead ... Ro 10:9; 1Pe 1:3–5
–His ascension into heaven ... Ac 5:31
2. Salvation comes as a gift from God
–A gift of his love ... Ro 5:8–9; Tit 3:5; 1Jn 4:9–10
–A gift of his grace ... Eph 2:5,8; Tit 2:11
–A gift of his mercy ... Tit 3:4–5; 1Pe 1:3
3. Requirements for salvation
–Read the Scriptures ... 2Ti 3:15
–Believe in Jesus Christ ... Jn 3:16; Ac 16:30–31; Eph 2:8
–Repent of our sins ... Isa 30:15; Ac 2:37–38; Ac 3:19; 2Co 7:10
–Accept salvation as a free gift ... Isa 55:1; Rev 21:6
–Realize we can do nothing to earn salvation ... Eph 2:8–9; 2Ti 1:9; Tit 3:5
–Give our all in response to salvation ... Mt 13:44–46; Lk 14:33; Php 3:7–8
D. Our relationship to God's salvation
–We long for it ... Ps 119:81,174
–We wait for it ... La 3:26
–We hope for it ... 1Th 5:8–9
–We pray for it ... Ps 54:1; Ps 85:7; Jer 31:7
–We realize that it is *now* ... 2Co 6:2
–We must count its cost ... Lk 14:25–33
–We are clothed with it ... 2Ch 6:41; Isa 61:10
–We rejoice in it ... Ps 9:14; Isa 25:9
–We delight in it ... Ps 35:9
–We love it ... Ps 40:16
–We make it known ... Ps 67:2
–We proclaim it ... 1Ch 16:23; Ps 96:2
–We grow in it ... 1Pe 2:2
–We work it out ... Php 2:12
E. Pictures of salvation
–Horn of salvation ... 2Sa 22:3; Ps 18:2
–Cup of salvation ... Ps 116:13
–Crown of salvation ... Ps 149:4
–Wells of salvation ... Isa 12:3
–A abundance of salvation ... Isa 33:6
–Springs of salvation ... Isa 45:8
–Helmet of salvation ... Isa 59:17; Eph 6:17
–Garments of salvation ... Isa 61:10
–Torch of salvation ... Isa 62:1
–Gospel of salvation ... Eph 1:13

SAMARIA

A. Identity of Samaria
–City built by Omri, king of Israel ... 1Ki 16:23–24
–Became capital of northern kingdom ... 1Ki 16:29,32; 1Ki 21:18
–Became synonymous with the northern kingdom ... 1Ki 21:1; Hos 7:1
B. History in the Old Testament
–Besieged by Ben-hadad ... 2Ki 6:24–25
–Besieged by Assyria ... 2Ki 17:5
–City taken; people deported ... 2Ki 17:6; 2Ki 18:10–12
–City plundered ... Isa 8:4
–Other people settled in the region ... 2Ki 17:24
–Capital city of Trans-Euphrates province ... Ezr 4:17; Ne 4:1–2
C. History in the New Testament
–Jesus visited it ... Lk 17:11; Jn 4:4–6
–Gospel must be preached there ... Ac 1:8
–Gospel spread there ... Ac 8:1
–Philip preached there ... Ac 8:5–7
–Holy Spirit was poured out there ... Ac 8:14–17
–Simon the magician lived there ... Ac 8:9–13, 18–24
–Paul traveled through there ... Ac 15:3

SAMARITANS

A. In the Old Testament
–A mixed race resettled in Samaria ... 2Ki 17:24
–Had a polytheistic religion ... 2Ki 17:25–33
–Wanted to help rebuild the temple ... Ezr 4:1–2
–Offer to rebuild the temple refused ... Ezr 4:3
–Tried to frustrate rebuilding of the temple ... Ezr 4:4–5,24; Ezr 5:3–17
–Tried to frustrate rebuilding of Jerusalem ... Ezr 4:7–23; Ne 4:1–23; Ne 6:1–14
B. In the New Testament
–Jews and Samaritans did not associate ... Jn 4:9
–Jesus told parable of Good Samaritan ... Lk 10:30–35
–A Samaritan leper returned to thank Jesus ... Lk 17:11–19
–A Samaritan town rejected Jesus ... Lk 9:52–53
–James and John wanted to destroy the town ... Lk 9:54–55
–Jesus talked with a Samaritan woman ... Jn 4:7–26
–Many Samaritans believed in Jesus ... Jn 4:39–42; Ac 8:5,12

SAMSON

A. History of his life
–Judge from the tribe of Dan ... Jdg 13:2,24–25
–Birth promised ... Jdg 13:2–14
–Married Philistine woman ... Jdg 14:1–18
–Took revenge on Philistines ... Jdg 15:1–20
–Betrayed by Delilah ... Jdg 16:1–20
–Captured and eyes gouged out ... Jdg 16:21–22
–His death ... Jdg 16:23–31
B. Feats of strength
–Killed a lion ... Jdg 14:6
–Killed thirty Philistines ... Jdg 14:19
–Killed a thousand Philistines with jawbone ... Jdg 15:13–17
–Carried off gates of Gaza ... Jdg 16:3
–Pushed down temple of Dagon, at cost of his life ... Jdg 16:25–30
C. An example of faith ... Heb 11:32

SAMUEL

A. Early life
–Hannah prayed that God would give her a son ... 1Sa 1:10–18
–Dedicated to God's service ... 1Sa 1:21–28
–Raised by Eli ... 1Sa 2:11,18–26
–Called by God to be a prophet ... 1Sa 3:1–20
B. His life as prophet and judge
–Judged Israel many years ... 1Sa 7:15–17
–Functioned as prophet ... 1Sa 9:9,19
–Led Israel to victory over Philistines ... 1Sa 7:2–14
–Israelites asked him to anoint a king ... 1Sa 8:1–22
–Anointed Saul as king ... 1Sa 10:1,17–24; Ac 13:20–21
–Gave farewell speech as Israel's leader ... 1Sa 12:1–25
–Rebuked Saul for offering a sacrifice ... 1Sa 13:8–14
–Rebuked Saul for disobedience ... 1Sa 15:12–23
–Announced God's rejection of Saul ... 1Sa 15:24–29
–Anointed David as king ... 1Sa 16:1–13; Ac 13:22
–David fled to him for protection ... 1Sa 19:18–24

–Wrote about the events of his day ... 1Ch 29:29
–His death ... 1Sa 25:1
C. Importance after his death
–Summoned by a witch to speak to Saul ... 1Sa 25:5–20
–Seen as a prophet who spoke of Jesus ... Ac 3:24
–Considered an example of faith ... Ps 99:6; Heb 11:32

SANBALLAT

–Chief political opponent of Nehemiah ... Ne 2:10
–Ridiculed rebuilding of Jerusalem ... Ne 2:19; Ne 4:1–2
–Opposed rebuilding of Jerusalem ... Ne 4:7–12
–Schemed to harm Nehemiah ... Ne 6:1–14
–His daughter married high priest's son ... Ne 13:28

SANCTIFICATION

–Being holy and becoming holy

A. Christians have been sanctified
–Sanctified in Christ ... 1Co 1:2; 1Co 6:11
–Sanctified through Christ's blood ... Heb 10:29
–Sanctified by the Holy Spirit ... Ro 15:16
–Sanctified by faith ... Ac 26:18
–Christians are called saints ... Ps 16:3; Ac 9:13; Ro 15:25–26,31
B. Christians are being sanctified ... Ac 20:32
–Through the word of God ... Jn 17:17–19
–Through the work of God ... 1Th 5:23
–Through the work of the Holy Spirit ... 2Th 2:13; 1Pe 1:2
–Through resisting sin ... 1Th 4:3–7
See also HOLINESS

SANHEDRIN

–The Jewish political and religious council

A. Its structure
1. Members
–Elders, chief priests, scribes ... Mt 16:21; Mt 27:41
–Chief priests and Pharisees ... Jn 11:47
–Pharisees and Sadducees ... Ac 23:6
2. Led by high priest ... Mt 26:59, 62–66
B. Meetings and decisions mentioned in the Bible
1. Concerning Jesus
–Decided that he should be put to death ... Jn 11:47–50
–Made agreement with Judas to betray him ... Mt 26:14–16; Mk 14:10–11; Lk 22:3–6
–Condemned him to death ... Mt 26:57–66; Mk 14:53–64; Jn 18:12–14, 19–24
–Asked Pilate for a guard at the tomb ... Mt 27:62–65
2. Concerning the apostles
–Interviewed Peter and John ... Ac 4:5–17
–Ordered them not to preach about Jesus ... Ac 4:18–21
–Interviewed them a second time ... Ac 5:27–40
–Flogged the apostles ... Ac 5:40–41
–Brought Stephen before their assembly ... Ac 6:12–7:56
–Decided to kill Stephen ... Ac 7:57–58
–Voted to kill numerous believers ... Ac 26:10
–Authorized Saul to persecute believers in Damascus ... Ac 9:1–2
–Interviewed Paul in Jerusalem ... Ac 22:30–23:9
–Prosecuted Paul before Felix ... Ac 24:1–9
–Prosecuted Paul before Festus ... Ac 25:6–7

SAPPHIRA

–Wife of Ananias ... Ac 5:1
–Deceitfully kept back part of their money ... Ac 5:2
–Died for lying to God ... Ac 5:7–10

SARAH

A. Her life
–Original name: Sarai ... Ge 11:29
–Wife of Abram; barren ... Ge 11:29–30
–Went with Abram to Canaan ... Ge 12:4–5
–Taken by Pharaoh to be Abram's sister ... Ge 12:10–20
–Gave Hagar to Abram as concubine ... Ge 16:3
–Mistreated Hagar so that Hagar ran away ... Ge 16:4–6
–Name changed to Sarah ... Ge 17:15
–Birth of Isaac promised ... Ge 17:16–21
–Laughed about a possible pregnancy ... Ge 18:10–15
–Thought by Abimelech to be Abraham's sister ... Ge 20:1–18
–Isaac born ... Ge 21:1–7
–Wanted Abraham to send Hagar and Ishmael away ... Ge 21:8–21
–Her death and burial ... Ge 23:1–19
B. Significance of Sarah
–Mother of the Israelites ... Isa 51:2
–Birth of Isaac shows God's election ... Ro 9:6–9
–Sending Hagar away illustrates our freedom ... Gal 4:21–31
–An example of true faith with Abraham ... Heb 11:11–13
–An example of a submissive wife ... 1Pe 3:5–6

SATAN

–An angel who became the archenemy of God

A. Terms for Satan
–The accuser ... Zec 3:1; Rev 12:10
–The devil ... Mt 4:1; Rev 12:9
–The tempter ... Mt 4:3; 1Th 3:5
–The evil one ... Mt 6:13; 1Jn 2:13–14
–Beelzebul ... Mt 12:24
–Beliar ... 2Co 6:15
–A murderer from the beginning ... Jn 8:44
–The father of lies ... Jn 8:44
–The ruler of this world ... Jn 12:31; Jn 14:30
–The god of this age ... 2Co 4:4
–Leader of the kingdom of evil ... Eph 2:2
–The angel of the Abyss ... Rev 9:11
–Abaddon or Apollyon ... Rev 9:11
–The ancient serpent ... Rev 12:9
B. Activities of Satan
1. Activities in the past
–Originally created as good ... Ge 1:31
–Led revolt of angels in heaven ... 2Pe 2:4; Rev 12:7–8
–Tempted Adam and Eve ... Ge 3:1–7
–Incited David to sin ... 1Ch 21:1–2
–Afflicted Job ... Job 1:6–19; Job 2:1–10
–Tempted Jesus ... Mt 4:1–11
–Involved in effort to put Jesus to death ... Lk 22:3; Jn 14:30–31
2. Activities in the present
–Rules a kingdom opposed to God ... Mt 12:25–26; Mt 25:41
–Controls the present sinful world ... 1Jn 5:19; Rev 12:9
–Afflicts people with illness ... Job 2:7; Lk 13:16; Ac 10:38; 2Co 12:7
–Tempts believers to sin ... 1Ch 21:1; Mt 16:23; Ac 5:3; 1Th 3:5
–Tries to keep people from true worship ... Mt 13:19; 1Pe 5:8–9
–Thwarts the spread of the gospel ... Mt 13:19; 2Co 4:3–4; 1Th 2:18
–Wants people to worship him ... Mt 4:9
–Masquerades as an angel of light ... 2Co 11:14
–Uses many schemes ... 2Co 2:11; Eph 6:11
–Persecutes the church ... Rev 2:10; Rev 12:13–17
–Holds the power of death ... Heb 2:14–15
3. Future activities
–Will be bound in the Millennium ... Rev 20:2–3
–Will be set free during the Great Tribulation ... Rev 20:7–9
–Will empower the antichrist ... 2Th 2:9; Rev 13:2–4
C. Victory over Satan
1. God has power over him ... Job 1:6–12; Job 2:1–6; Lk 22:31–32
2. Christ has disarmed him
–Prophesied in Eden ... Ge 3:15
–Christ came to destroy him ... 1Jn 3:8
–Demonstrated in Christ's victory over temptation ... Mt 4:1–11
–Demonstrated by casting out demons ... Lk 10:18; Lk 11:20
–The cross of Christ sealed his defeat ... Jn 12:31–33; Col 2:15; Rev 12:11
3. Believers must fight against him
–We must pray for deliverance ... Mt 6:13
–We must keep busy for the Lord ... 1Ti 5:13–15
–We must resist his temptations ... 1Co 7:5; Jas 4:7
–We must extinguish his flaming arrows by our faith ... Eph 6:16
–We must overcome him ... 1Jn 2:13; Rev 2:10–11; Rev 12:10–11
–Christ prays for the victory of our faith ... Lk 22:31–32
4. Final defeat of Satan
–Prophesied by Paul ... Ro 16:20
–Satan bound in the Millennium ... Rev 20:2–3
–Final victory at Christ's return ... Mt 25:31,41; Rev 20:10, 14

SAUL

A. First king of Israel
1. Family data and early life
–A member of the tribe of Benjamin ... 1Sa 9:1–2
–Son of Kish ... 1Sa 9:1–2
–His family ... 1Sa 14:49–50; 1Ch 8:33
–Searched for his father's donkeys ... 1Sa 9:3–4
–Consulted Samuel ... 1Sa 9:5–20
–Anointed king by Samuel ... 1Sa 10:1
–Prophesied ... 1Sa 10:9–13; 1Sa 19:23–24
–Chosen as king at Mizpah ... 1Sa 10:20–26
2. Early events as king
–Defeated Ammonites at Jabesh-gilead ... 1Sa 11:1–11
–Confirmed as king ... 1Sa 11:12–15
–Fought the Philistines ... 1Sa 13:1–7, 16–22
–Did not wait for Samuel to offer sacrifice ... 1Sa 13:8–14
–Disobeyed God regarding Amalekites ... 1Sa 15:1–23
–Repented ... 1Sa 15:24–31
3. His interaction with David
–Employed David as musician ... 1Sa 16:14–23
–Approved David's offer to fight Goliath ... 1Sa 17:31–39
–Became jealous of David ... 1Sa 18:1–9
–Tried to kill David, who was playing music ... 1Sa 18:10–11
–Gave David his daughter Michal as wife ... 1Sa 18:20–28
–Again tried to kill David ... 1Sa 19:1–17
–Angry at Jonathan for befriending David ... 1Sa 20:26–34
–Pursued David; killed priests at Nob ... 1Sa 22:6–19
–Went to Keilah and Ziph ... 1Sa 23:7–28
–Spared by David in a cave at En-gedi ... 1Sa 24:1–21
–Spared by David while sleeping in camp ... 1Sa 26:1–25
4. Saul's death
–Sought Samuel's advice through a witch ... 1Sa 28:1–14
–Rebuked by Samuel's spirit ... 1Sa 28:15–20
–Wounded by Philistines; killed himself ... 1Sa 31:1–6; 1Ch 10:1–6
–His death lamented by David ... 2Sa 1:17–27
B. One of Christ's apostles
See PAUL

SEA

A. Seas mentioned in the Bible
1. The Mediterranean Sea
–The Sea ... Nu 34:5
–The Great Sea ... Nu 34:6–7
–The sea of the Philistines ... Ex 23:31
–The western sea ... Dt 11:24
2. The Red Sea ... Ac 7:36
–The Sea of Reeds (NRSV text note) ... Ex 10:19
–The sea of Egypt ... Isa 11:15
3. The Sea of Galilee ... Mt 4:18
–The Sea of Chinnereth ... Nu 34:11
–The Sea of Tiberias ... Jn 6:1
4. The Dead Sea
–The Salt Sea (NRSV note) ... Ge 14:3
–The sea of the Arabah ... Dt 3:17
–The eastern sea ... Zec 14:8
5. The Adriatic Sea ... Ac 27:27
B. The sea used as a symbol
1. Negative

–Of human sin and restlessness ... Ge 49:4; Isa 57:20; Eph 4:14
–Of human instability ... Jas 1:6
–Of the lifestyle of heretics ... Jude 13
–Of God's judgment .. Jer 49:23–24; La 2:13
–Of the abode of satanic powers ... Da 7:2–3; Rev 13:1
–No sea in heaven ... Rev 21:1

2. Positive
–Of the vast mysteries of God ... Job 11:7–9
–Of God's presence everywhere ... Ps 139:9
–Of the wide expanse of a kingdom ... Ps 72:8
–Of God's great forgiveness ... Mic 7:19
–Of God's promise of righteousness ... Isa 48:18
–Of the extension of the gospel ... Isa 11:9; Hab 2:14

See also WATER

SEAL

A. Literal uses of the seal
–A plate on the high priest's turban ... Ex 39:30–31
–An item for personal identification ... Ge 38:18,25
–A mark for identifying correspondence ... 1Ki 21:8
–A governmental mark warning people ... Mt 27:66
–A mark securing a title deed ... Jer 32:9–14

B. Figurative use of the seal
–Circumcision: a seal of the covenant ... Ro 4:11
–Zerubbabel: a seal of the coming Messiah ... Hag 2:23
–The Holy Spirit: a seal of salvation ... 2Co 1:22; Eph 1:14; Eph 4:30
–Christians: a seal of apostleship ... 1Co 9:2
–God's word: a seal for the church ... 2Ti 2:19
–The seven seals: Jesus' control of history ... Rev 5:1–6:17
–The sealed 144,000: God's elect ... Rev 7:1–8
–The sealed Abyss: God's control of Satan . Rev 20:3

SECOND COMING

–The return of Jesus at the end of history

A. Terms for the second coming
–The day of the Lord ... 1Co 1:8; Php 1:6,10; 1Th 5:2
–The day of God ... 2Pe 3:12
–The last day ... Jn 12:48
–The Day ... 1Co 3:13; Heb 10:25
–The last time ... 1Pe 1:5
–The manifestation of Jesus Christ ... Tit 2:13

B. Prophecies of his second coming
–By Jesus before the crucifixion ... Mt 24:30–31; Mt 26:64; Jn 14:3
–By Jesus after the resurrection ... Jn 21:22
–By two angels at Jesus' ascension ... Ac 1:10–11
–By the apostles in their preaching ... Ac 3:20; Ac 17:31
–By the apostles in their writings ... Php 3:20; 1Th 4:14–17; 1Ti 6:14; Tit 2:13

C. The event of the second coming
1. Time of the return
–It is unknown ... Mk 13:32
–It will be sudden ... Mt 24:27; Mk 13:36
–It will be unexpected ... Lk 12:40; 2Pe 3:10
–It will be after the great ordeal ... Mt 24:29–31; 2Th 2:2–3

2. Characteristics of the return
–It will be on the clouds ... Mt 24:30; Mk 14:62; 1Th 4:17
–It will be visible ... Rev 1:7
–It will be a bodily return ... Ac 1:11
–It will be with his angels ... Mt 16:27; 2Th 1:7
–It will be with great glory ... Mt 16:27; Mt 25:31; 2Th 2:8
–It will be with power ... Mt 24:30
–It will be with a great noise ... 1Co 15:51–52; 1Th 4:16

D. The purposes of the second coming
–That he might be glorified in his people ... 2Th 1:10
–That he might deliver the kingdom to God ... 1Co 15:24
–That he might reign over all ... Rev 11:15
–That he might expose the secrets of human hearts ... 1Co 4:5
–That he might judge the human race ... Mt 25:31–46; Ac 10:42; 2Ti 4:1; 1Pe 4:5
–That he might complete salvation for believers .. Heb 9:28
–That he might take his people to be with him .. Jn 14:3
–That he might gather the elect ... Mk 13:27

E. Believers and the second coming
1. The attitude of believers towards it
–Should live holy lives until that day ... 2Pe 3:11–12
–Should long for it ... 2Ti 4:8
–Should watch for it . Mk 13:35–37; Lk 12:35–40
–Should wait for it ... 1Co 1:7; Php 3:20; Tit 2:13
–Should look forward to it ... 2Pe 3:12–13
–Should be patient until it ... Jas 5:7–8
–Should persevere until it ... Rev 2:10–11; Rev 3:11–12
–Should pray for its fulfillment ... 1Co 16:22; Rev 22:20

2. Promises for believers when it occurs
–We will be preserved by Christ ... Php 1:6; Jude 24
–We will be found blameless ... 1Co 1:8; 1Th 3:13
–We will be clothed anew by God ... 2Co 5:4–5
–We will receive new bodies ... 1Co 15:42–53
–We will be made like Christ ... 1Co 15:49; Php 3:20–21; 1Jn 3:2
–We will receive a crown ... 1Co 9:25; 2Ti 4:8; 1Pe 5:4; Jas 1:12; Rev 2:10
–We will reign with Christ ... 2Ti 2:12; Rev 22:5
–We will be incredibly happy ... 1Pe 4:13

SELF-CONTROL

–Control of one's body and emotions

A. Self-control as a Christian trait
–Expressed negatively ... Pr 25:28; 2Ti 3:3
–Expressed positively ... 1Ti 3:2; Tit 2:2,5–6,12; 2Pe 1:6
–An aspect of the Spirit's fruit ... Gal 5:22–23

B. Reasons for self-control
–To control anger ... Pr 16:32; Pr 29:11
–To control sexual sins .. 1Co 7:3–5; 1Th 4:3–4
–To prepare for Christ's return ... 1Th 5:6–8
–To enable us to pray properly ... 1Pe 4:7
–To show resistance to Satan ... 1Pe 5:8–9

SELF-DENIAL

–Rejection of a self-centered life

A. Jesus exemplified self-denial
–In coming to this earth . 2Co 8:9; Php 2:6–7
–In resisting temptations of Satan ... Mt 4:3–4,8–10
–In doing his Father's will ... Jn 6:38; Mt 26:39,42
–In washing his disciples' feet ... Jn 13:4–5,12–15
–In dying on the cross .. Mk 10:45; 1Pe 2:21–24

B. Christians called to self-denial
–The call to self-denial .. Mt 16:24–26; Mk 8:34–37; Lk 9:23–25
–The priority of love for Jesus ... Mt 10:37–39; Lk 14:25–33
–Giving of ourselves to others ... Mt 5:38–42; 1Co 10:24
–The necessity of being a servant ... Mk 10:42–44; Lk 22:25–27; Jn 12:24–26

See SERVANT

–Renouncing selfish desires ... Gal 5:24; Tit 2:12
–The life of self-sacrifice ... Ro 12:2; 2Co 4:10–11

SELFISHNESS

See SELF-DENIAL

SENNACHERIB

–An Assyrian king ... 2Ki 18:13
–Attempted siege of Jerusalem ... 2Ki 18:13–37; 2Ch 32:1–19; Isa 36:1–22
–His army destroyed by the angel of the Lord ... 2Ki 19:35–36; 2Ch 32:21; Isa 37:36–37
–His death by murder ... 2Ki 19:37; 2Ch 32:21; Isa 37:38

SERVANT

A. Essential qualities of a servant
–Must have only one master ... Lk 16:13
–Must be submissive to a master's will ... Ps 123:2; Eph 6:5; 1Pe 2:18
–Must be faithful to a master ... 1Co 4:2

B. Servants on a human level
1. Servants in the home
–Hagar ... Ge 16:1
–Abraham's servant (Eliezer) ... Ge 24:1–2
–Zilpah ... Ge 29:24
–Bilhah ... Ge 29:29
–Joseph ... Ge 39:1–4

2. Servants in the economic realm
–Laws concerning servants and slaves ... Ex 21:2–11; Lev 25:39–46
–Hired servants ... 2Ch 24:12; Mt 20:1–15; Lk 15:17–19

3. Servants on a political level
–Servants of a king .. 1Sa 16:16,18; 2Sa 12:18–19; 2Ki 9:28
–The king's children are called servants .. 2Sa 13:24; 1Ki 1:17
–The king as servant of the people ... 1Ki 12:7
–A king as servant to another king ... 2Ki 16:7; 2Ki 24:1

C. Believers as servants of one another
–We are called to serve as Jesus did ... Jn 13:14–16; 1Pe 2:21
–We are commanded to serve others ... Gal 5:13; Eph 5:21
–Paul as a servant of others ... 1Co 9:19–23; 2Co 4:5

D. Servants of the Lord
1. Examples of servants of the Lord
–Abraham, Isaac and Jacob ... Ex 32:13
–Moses ... Nu 12:7
–Joshua ... Jdg 2:8
–Samson ... Jdg 15:18
–David ... 2Sa 7:5
–Elijah ... 1Ki 18:36
–The prophets ... 2Ki 9:7; Zec 1:6; Rev 10:7
–The apostles ... 1Co 4:1; 2Co 6:4; Php 1:1
–All Christians ... Ro 6:22; Eph 6:6; 1Pe 2:16
–The 144,000 ... Rev 7:4

2. Isaiah's servant songs ... Isa 42:1–4; Isa 49:1–6; Isa 50:4–9; Isa 52:13–53:12

3. Jesus as the servant of the Lord
–Fulfilled the servant songs of Isaiah ... Mt 12:17–21; Ac 8:32–35; 1Pe 2:22–25
–Took the nature of a servant ... Php 2:7
–Called himself a servant ... Mk 10:45; Lk 22:27
–Compared himself to a servant ... Lk 12:37
–Demonstrated servanthood by washing feet ... Jn 13:4–11
–Demonstrated servanthood by his cross ... Isa 53:4–6; Php 2:7–8
–Exalted as servant ... Isa 52:13

SETH

–Third son of Adam and Eve ... Ge 4:25
–Took the place of Abel ... Ge 4:25
–Made in Adam's image ... Ge 5:3
–His family ... Ge 5:6–8
–An ancestor of Jesus ... Lk 3:38

SEXUAL STANDARDS

A. Sexual sins condemned in the Bible
–Adultery ... Ex 20:14; Pr 5:1–23
–Incest ... Lev 20:19–21
–Sex with animals ... Lev 20:15–16
–Loss of virginity before marriage ... Dt 22:20–21
–Prostitution ... Dt 23:17–18; Pr 7:10–27
–Homosexuality ... Ro 1:26–27; 1Co 6:9

–Obscenity .... Eph 5:4
–Lust .... Mt 5:27–28
1Th 4:5
B. God's will regarding sexual standards
1. In negative terms
–Laws against illicit sexual behavior ..... Ex 20:14
Lev 20:10–21
Dt 23:17–18
–The command to flee immorality 1Co 6:18
Eph 5:3
Col 3:5
1Th 4:3
–Sexual sin excludes one from the kingdom 1Co 6:9–10
Gal 5:19–21
Eph 5:3–5
Rev 22:15
2. In positive terms
–Strive for purity 1Th 4:4,7
1Pe 3:2
–Be faithful in marriage 1Co 7:2–4
–Exercise self-control . 1Co 7:8–9
Gal 5:23
1Th 4:4

See also MARRIAGE
ADULTERY
DIVORCE

SHADRACH
–Hebrew deported to Babylon .... Da 1:6
–Name changed from Hananiah .... Da 1:7
–Refused to be defiled by food .... Da 1:8–20
–Appointed administrator over Babylon .... Da 2:49
–Refused to worship idols ... Da 3:1–18
–Saved from fiery furnace ... Da 3:19–30

SHALLUM
–King of Israel 2Ki 15:10–15
–Assassinated by Menahem .. 2Ki 15:14

SHAME
A. Reasons for feeling ashamed
–Being naked .... Ge 3:7
Eze 23:29
–Experiencing defeat .... Ps 6:10
Isa 29:22–23
–Being humiliated ...... Eze 16:63
Zec 13:3–5
1Co 1:27–29
–Experiencing sin .... Ezr 9:6
Jer 22:22
2Th 3:14
–Being taunted by one's enemies .... Ps 44:15–16
–Having an undisciplined child .... Pr 19:26
–Falsely accusing someone .... Pr 25:8–10
1Pe 3:16
–Giving less than poorer people 2Co 9:3–4
–Being inconsistent with one's principles .... Ezr 8:22
B. When the Christian need not be ashamed
–When looking to the Lord .... Ps 34:5
–When hoping in the Lord .... Ps 25:3
–When taking refuge in the Lord .... Ps 25:20
–When trusting in the Lord .... Ro 9:33
1Pe 2:6
–When believing in Christ .... Mk 8:38
2Ti 1:12
–When believing Christ and his word .... Mk 8:38
Lk 9:26
–When preaching the gospel .... Ro 1:16
2Ti 1:8
–When suffering for Christ's sake 1Pe 4:16
–When obeying God's law .... Ps 119:5–6
–When doing one's best for the Lord 2Ti 2:15

–When the Lord returns . 1Jn 2:28

SHAMGAR
–Judge; killed six hundred Philistines .... Jdg 3:31

SHAPHAN
–Secretary during Josiah's reign 2Ki 22:3
–Supervised finances for temple repairs 2Ki 22:3–7
2Ch 34:8–13,16–17
–Brought newly discovered law to Josiah 2Ki 22:8–10
2Ch 34:14–17
–Read the law to Josiah 2Ki 22:10
2Ch 34:18
–With others, visited prophetess Huldah 2Ki 22:14–20
2Ch 34:20–28

SHECHEM
A. A man who raped Jacob's daughter Dinah .. Ge 34:1–4
–Agreed to circumcision and marriage .... Ge 34:11–24
–Killed by Simeon and Levi .... Ge 34:25–29
B. A city in Canaan
–The Lord appeared to Abram there .... Ge 12:6–7
–Jacob purchased land there .... Ge 33:18–19
–Pillaged by the sons of Jacob .... Ge 34:26–29
–Joseph went there to find his brothers .... Ge 37:14–17
–One of the cities of refuge .... Jos 20:7
–Joshua renewed the covenant there .... Jos 24:1–27
–Gideon's son Abimelech was crowned its king .. Jdg 9:1–6
–Civil war between Abimelech and Shechem .... Jdg 9:22–57
–Rehoboam was made king there 1Ki 12:1
–Jeroboam fortified it as his capital 1Ki 12:25
–In New Testament, Shechem is Sychar .... Jn 4:5

SHEEP
See LAMB

SHEM
–Son of Noah .... Ge 5:32
1Ch 1:4
–With Japheth, covered his father with a garment ...... Ge 9:23
–Blessed by Noah .... Ge 9:26
–Sons listed .... Ge 10:21–31
–Abram came from his line Ge 11:10–26

SHEOL
See GRAVE

SHEPHERD
A. The shepherd as an human occupation
1. Examples of shepherds .... Ge 4:2
Ge 29:9
1Sa 16:11
Lk 2:8
2. Responsibilities of shepherds
–Find pasture for flocks .... Eze 34:2,13–14 Provide water for flocks... Ge 29:2–8
Ex 2:16
–Protect the flocks ... 1Sa 17:34–36
Lk 2:8
–Seek lost sheep ..... Eze 34:16
Mt 18:10–13
–Care for injured sheep .... Mt 12:11
–Regularly account for the sheep .... Jn 10:2–5
–Know what happens to the sheep .... Ge 31:38–39

–Shear the sheep ..... Ge 38:12
1Sa 25:2,7
B. Figurative use of shepherd
1. Leaders of God's people as shepherds
a. Old Testament leaders
–Joshua .... Nu 27:15–18
–David 2Sa 5:2
Ps 78:70–72
–Cyrus .... Isa 44:28
–Selfish shepherds . Isa 56:10–11
Jer 10:21
Eze 34:2–6
Zec 10:2–3
b. Church leaders .... Jn 21:15–17
Ac 20:28–31
1Pe 5:2–3
2. God as a shepherd
–God is called a shepherd .... Ps 23:1
Ps 80:1
–We are his sheep ... Ps 95:7
Ps 100:3
–God acted as a shepherd in the exodus .. Ps 77:20
Ps 78:52
Isa 63:11
–God cares for us like a shepherd .... Isa 40:11
Eze 34:11–16
Mic 7:14
3. Jesus Christ as a shepherd
a. He is called a shepherd
–The good shepherd .... Jn 10:11,14
–The great shepherd .... Heb 13:20
–The chief shepherd 1Pe 5:4
–The shepherd and guardian of souls . 1Pe 2:25
b. He acts as a shepherd
–Old Testament prophecies .... Isa 40:11
Eze 34:23
Mic 5:2–4
Zec 13:7
–He died for the sheep .... Jn 10:15
–He has compassion for the sheep .... Mt 9:36
–He knows his sheep .... Jn 10:3–4,14
–He searches for lost sheep .... Mt 18:12–14
Lk 15:3–7
–He will judge like a shepherd .... Mt 25:32

SHILOH
–Located in Ephraim, near Bethel .... Jdg 21:19
–The first religious center in Canaan .... Jos 18:1
Jdg 18:31
–Joshua's political center .... Jos 21:1–2
–Joshua divided the land there .... Jos 18:9
–Benjamites seized women there .... Jdg 21:19–23
–Hannah asked for a son there 1Sa 1:3–18
–Eli and sons ministered there 1Sa 2:12–14
–God appeared to Samuel there 1Sa 3:21
–Ark taken into battle from there 1Sa 4:3–6
Ps 78:60–61
–Eli died there 1Sa 4:12–18
–Prophet Ahijah ministered there 1Ki 11:29
1Ki 14:2
–City lay in ruins in Jeremiah's day .... Jer 7:12–14
Jer 26:9

SHIMEI
–A Benjamite who cursed David 2Sa 16:5–14
–Spared from execution 2Sa 19:16–23
–Killed on Solomon's orders 1Ki 2:8–9, 36–46

SIDON
A. Identity and location
–A chief city of Phoenicia .... Isa 23:11–12
–A seacoast city .... Ac 27:3
–Often linked with Tyre . Isa 23:1–2
Mt 15:21
–Sidonians were descendants of Ham .... Ge 10:6,15
–A peaceful, prosperous people .... Jdg 18:7
–Skillful in felling timber 1Ki 5:6
1Ch 22:4
Zec 9:2
–Served the goddess Ashtoreth 1Ki 11:5,33
B. Significance of Sidon
1. In the Old Testament
–Territory given to tribe of Asher ...... Jos 19:24,28
–Asher did not drive out its inhabitants ... Jdg 1:31
–Cut timber for the temple 1Ki 5:6
–Solomon intermarried with them 1Ki 11:1
–Ahab married Jezebel, a Sidonian .. 1Ki 16:31
–Elijah stayed with a Sidonian widow 1Ki 17:9–16
–Prophecies against them .... Isa 23:2,4, 11–12
Eze 28:20–23
Joel 3:4–8
2. In the New Testament
–Jesus ministered there .... Mt 15:21–28
Mk 7:24–30
–Paul spent a night there .... Ac 27:3

SIDONIANS
See SIDON

SIGN
–An outward event with a spiritual significance
A. Miracles as signs
1. In the Old Testament
–Signs for Israel ..... Ex 4:29–31
Nu 14:11
–Signs for Pharaoh ... Ex 10:1–2
–Signs for Gideon .... Jdg 6:17–24, 36–40
–Signs for Saul 1Sa 10:7,9
–A sign for Jeroboam 1Ki 13:3–5
–A sign for Ahaz .... Isa 7:11–14
2. In the New Testament
–Jesus' miracles were signs .... Jn 2:11,23
Jn 12:37
Jn 20:30
–The Jews wanted miraculous signs .... Mt 12:38–40
Mt 16:1–4
Jn 2:18
1Co 1:22
–The apostles performed signs .... Ac 4:16,30
Ac 8:6
Ac 14:3
B. Signs of the covenant
1. In the Old Testament
–The rainbow with Noah .... Ge 9:12–16
–Circumcision with Abraham .... Ge 17:11
Ro 4:11
–The blood of the Passover at the exodus .... Ex 12:13
–The Sabbath at Mount Sinai .... Ex 31:12–17
–The altar at the crossing of the Jordan .... Jos 4:5–7
2. In the New Testament
–The water of baptism .... Mt 28:19
1Pe 3:21
–Bread and wine of the Lord's Supper ... 1Co 11:23–26
C. Signs of the end times
1. Jesus is asked to

reveal these signs .... Mk 13:1–4
2. Listing of these signs
–Wars and rumors of wars .... Mk 13:7–8
–Persecution of Christians .... Mk 13:9; Jn 15:18–21
–False teachers and false Christs .... Mk 13:6,22; 1Jn 2:18–19
–The worldwide spread of the gospel . Mt 24:14; Rev 7:9–10
–The antichrist .... 2Th 2:3–4,8; Rev 13:1–9
–The great ordeal .... Mk 13:14–20; Rev 7:14
–Signs in the heavens .... Lk 21:11,25
D. The purpose of signs
–To bring about faith in God .... Nu 14:11; Jn 20:30
–To strengthen faith in God .... Jos 24:16–17; Ro 4:11
–To confirm a message from God .... 2Ki 19:28–29; Lk 2:12,16–20
–To protect God's people from danger .... Ex 12:13
–To bring to mind God's care and promises .... Ge 9:12–16; Ex 13:7–9; 1Co 11:23–26

SIHON

–King of the Amorites .... Nu 21:21; Dt 1:4
–Marched out against Israelites .... Nu 21:23
–Destroyed by Israelites .... Nu 21:24–31; Dt 2:32–36
–Victory sung by the Israelites .... Nu 21:27–30; Ps 136:19

SILAS

–A prophet of the early church .... Ac 15:32
–Delegated to report on council in Jerusalem .... Ac 15:22
–Traveled with Paul on second missionary journey .... Ac 15:40
–With Paul in prison at Philippi .... Ac 16:19–36
–With Paul in Thessalonica and Berea .... Ac 17:1–10
–Stayed behind in Berea .... Ac 17:14
–Came to Paul in Corinth ... Ac 18:5
–Preached with Paul in Corinth 2Co 1:19
–Co-writer with Paul 1Th 1:1; 2Th 1:1
–Co-writer with Peter 1Pe 5:12

SILVER

A. Uses for silver
1. In Israelite worship
–The tabernacle furniture .... Ex 26:19–25; Ex 27:9–11,17
–Offerings .... Nu 7:13,19,25; Ezr 1:4,6,9–11
–The temple building . 1Ch 29:2–5
–The temple furniture 1Ch 28:14–17
2. In crafting idol gods .. Isa 2:20; Hos 8:4; Ac 19:24
3. For personal wealth .. Ge 13:2; Ecc 2:8
4. For gifts .... 1Ki 15:18–19; Ezr 2:69
5. For payment as money .... Ge 42:25–27; Jdg 9:4; Mt 26:15
6. For jewelry .... Ge 24:53; Eze 16:17
7. For royal display .... Ge 44:2; Est 1:6–7
B. Value of silver for God's people
1. Positive: a blessing from God .... Ge 13:2; Isa 60:9,17
2. Negative
–Wisdom worth more than silver .... Job 28:12–15; Pr 3:13–14; Pr 16:16
–Silver valueless in redemption 1Pe 1:18
C. Silver as a symbol
–For saints surviving God's testing .... Isa 48:10; Zec 13:9
–For God's dependable word .... Ps 12:6
–For trustworthy spiritual values 1Co 3:12–13

SIMEON

A. Son of Jacob by Leah ... Ge 35:23; 1Ch 2:1
–Name means "one who hears" .... Ge 29:33
–With Levi, avenged rape of Dinah .... Ge 34:25–31
–Held hostage by Joseph in Egypt .... Ge 42:24–43:23
–Went to Egypt with family .... Ge 46:8,10
–Father of six sons .... Ge 46:10
–Blessed by Jacob .... Ge 49:5–7
B. Tribe descended from Simeon
–Numbered .... Nu 1:23; Nu 26:14
–Allotted land .... Jos 19:1–9; Eze 48:24
–One of the tribes of the 144,000 .... Rev 7:7
C. A righteous man who blessed Jesus .... Lk 2:25–35
–Sang a song .... Lk 2:29–32

SIMON

A. One of Jesus' disciples
See PETER
B. Another disciple of Jesus
–Called the Zealot .... Mt 10:4; Mk 3:18
–One of the apostles .... Ac 1:13
C. A Samaritan sorcerer .... Ac 8:9–11
–Baptized as a Christian . Ac 8:12
–Offered Peter money for power to impart the Holy Spirit .... Ac 8:18–19
–Severely rebuked by Peter .... Ac 8:20–23

SIN

A. Words for sin
–Transgression .... Ps 32:1,5
–Iniquity .... Ps 51:2,9
–Wickedness .... Ge 6:5
–Evil .... Ge 8:21
–Rebellion .... Jer 29:32
–Uncleanness .... Lev 16:16
–Disobedience .... Ro 5:19
–Wrongdoing 1Sa 26:21
–Guilt .... Ps 25:11
–Unrighteousness 1Jn 1:9
–Lawlessness 1Jn 3:4
–Corruption 2Pe 2:19
–Faults .... Ps 19:12
B. The origin and extent of sin
1. Original sin
–Adam and Eve disobeyed God's command .... Ge 3:1–7
–Their sin passed down to all humans . Ro 5:12,15; 1Co 15:22
2. Present extent of sin
–There is sin in everyone .... Ps 14:2–3; Ro 3:10–20,23
–Present already at conception .... Ps 51:5
–Permeates to the heart of people .... Ge 6:5; Jer 17:9; Mt 15:18–20
–Christ alone was without sin .... 2Co 5:21; Heb 4:15; 1Pe 2:22; 1Jn 3:5
C. God and human sin
1. His negative reaction
–He is grieved over sin .... Ge 6:6
–He is angry over sin .... Ps 78:19–21,56–59; Jn 3:36; Ro 1:18
–He hates sin .... Ps 5:5; Pr 6:16–19
–He punishes sin .... Ge 3:15–19; Isa 3:11–26; Am 3:2
2. His positive reaction
–He sent his Son to die for sinners .... Jn 3:16; Ro 5:8; 1Jn 4:10
–He forgives sin .... Ex 34:6–7; 1Jn 1:9
–He removes sin far away .... Ps 103:8–12
–He sweeps away sin . Isa 44:22
–He casts sin away ... Mic 7:19
–He puts sin behind his back .... Isa 38:17
–He no longer remembers our sin .... Jer 31:34
D. Christ and human sin
–He was sinless .... 2Co 5:21; Heb 4:15; Heb 7:26; 1Pe 2:22; 1Jn 3:5
–He paid the penalty for sin .... Ro 4:25; Ro 8:3; Col 2:13–14; 1Pe 2:24
–He forgives sin .... Mk 2:5–12; Lk 7:48; Col 1:13–14
–His blood redeems us from sin .... Eph 1:7
–His blood cleanses us from sin 1Jn 1:7
–He takes away the sin of the world .... Jn 1:29; 1Jn 2:2
E. Humans and their sin
1. How has sin affected us?
–We are responsible for our sin .... Eze 18:10–18
–We are accountable to God for sin .... Jer 17:10; 2Co 5:10; Rev 20:12
–We are subject to death because of sin . Ge 2:17; Ro 6:23; Jas 1:15
–We cannot atone for our own sin .... Ps 49:7; Mt 16:26
2. What should we do with our sin?
–We should confess it .... Ps 32:1–5; Pr 28:13; 1Jn 1:9
–We should repent of it .... Eze 18:30–31; Ac 3:19–20
–We should turn from it .... Ps 34:14; Isa 1:16; 3Jn 11
–We should hate it ... Ps 97:10; Am 5:15; Ro 12:9
–We should throw it off .... Heb 12:1
–We should fight against it .... Eph 6:12–13; Heb 12:4
3. What are the blessings after confession?
–We are forgiven our sin .... Ps 32:5; Ac 2:38; Ac 10:43; Col 2:13
–God considers us righteous .... Ro 4:5–8; Php 3:9
–We are purified from sin 1Jn 1:9
–We are freed from sin .... Ro 6:7,18,22; Rev 1:5
–We are no longer slaves to sin .... Ro 6:6,17
–We do not continue a life of sin 1Jn 3:6,9; 1Jn 5:18
–We are dead to sin .. Ro 6:2,11
–We pass from death to life .... Ro 6:23

SINAI

A. A desert area where the Israelites camped .... Ex 19:1–2
–Census taken there .... Nu 1:1–4,19
–Passover celebrated there .... Nu 9:1–5
–Israelites stayed there nearly a year .... Nu 10:12
B. Mount Sinai, in the above area
1. Identity
–Called Mount Horeb .... Ex 33:6
–Called the mountain of God .... Ex 3:1; Ex 24:13
–God came down from Mount Sinai .... Dt 33:2
–God is the God of Mount Sinai .... Ps 68:8
2. History and significance
–God appeared to Moses there .... Ex 3:1–6
–God spoke his law from there .... Ex 19:20–20:17; Dt 5:4–21
–Israelites frightened at the mountain .... Ex 20:18–19; Dt 5:5,22–27
–Moses received the law there .... Ex 24:15–18; Dt 9:9–11
–Israelites worshiped golden calf there .... Ex 32:1–20; Dt 9:8–17; Ps 106:19–23
–Moses received the law a second time .. Ex 34:1–32; Lev 7:38; Dt 10:1–5,10
–Elijah talked with God there 1Ki 19:8–18

SINGLES

See MARRIAGE

SISERA

–Canaanite commander .... Jdg 4:2
–Fought against Deborah and Barak .... Jdg 4:12–16
–Killed by Jael .... Jdg 4:21; Jdg 5:24–30

SISTER

See BROTHERS AND SISTERS

SLAVERY

A. Slavery in the Old Testament
1. Slavery common
–Abraham had slaves . Ge 20:14; Ge 21:10
–Israelites were slaves in Egypt .... Ex 1:11; Dt 6:20–21
–David had slaves 2Sa 6:20,22
–Solomon conscripted slaves 1Ki 9:20–22
–The Teacher had slaves .... Ecc 2:7
–Sons were made slaves to pay debts .. 2Ki 4:1
–Israelites were slaves to Babylon .... La 1:1
–Israelites were slaves to Persia .... Ne 9:36
–There were slaves among returning Jews .... Ne 5:5
2. God and human slavery
a. Delivered Israelites

from slavery ...... Ex 13:3; Ex 20:2
- b. Regulated slavery in Israel
  - –Treatment of slaves .... Ex 21:5–11, 20–21; Dt 15:12–18; Dt 23:15–16
  - –Release in the year of jubilee ... Lev 25:39–55
- c. Gave rights to slaves
  - –Were members of the covenant ..... Ge 17:12–13
  - –Rested on the Sabbath .... Ex 20:10; Dt 5:12–15
  - –Included in religious meals ...... Ex 12:44; Dt 16:11,14
  - –Could expect equal justice ...... Job 31:13
  - –Could become an heir .... Ge 15:2–3

B. Slavery in the New Testament
1. Common in Roman society .... Ac 16:16,19; 1Co 7:21; 1Ti 1:10
2. Messages for Christian slaves
   - –Slave and master are equal in Christ ...... 1Co 12:13; Gal 3:28; Col 3:11; Phm 15–16
   - –Slaves must respect their masters 1Ti 6:1–2
   - –Slaves must submit to their masters ..... Tit 2:9–10; 1Pe 2:18
   - –Slaves must obey their masters .... Eph 6:5–8; Col 3:22–25
   - –If possible, try to gain freedom 1Co 7:21
3. Messages given to Christian masters
   - –Masters must treat slaves kindly .... Eph 6:9; Phm 17
   - –Masters must treat slaves justly .... Col 4:1

C. Slavery as a symbol
- –By nature we are slaves to sin .... Jn 8:34; Ro 6:16–17; Ro 7:14; 2Pe 2:19
- –The Old Testament era saw slavery to the law . Gal 4:3–5; Gal 5:1
- –We must become slaves to righteousness .... Ro 6:18
- –We must become slaves to God and Christ ..... Ro 6:22; 1Co 7:22; Eph 6:6

SNOW
See WEATHER

SODOM AND GOMORRAH
A. Their identity and location
- –Wealthy cities in the Jordan plain .... Ge 13:10
- –Extremely wicked inhabitants .... Ge 13:13; Ge 18:20–21

B. History of Sodom and Gomorrah
- –Lot went to live there .. Ge 13:11–12
- –Cities defeated by four kings .... Ge 14:8–12
- –Abram rescued the cities .... Ge 14:13–16
- –Abraham interceded for the cities .... Ge 18:23–33
- –Sodom and Gomorrah destroyed .... Ge 19:1–29
- –God's promise of restoration .... Eze 16:53–57

C. Sodom and Gomorrah used as symbols
- –A symbol of total wickedness .... Isa 3:9; Jer 23:14; Eze 16:46–50; Mt 10:15
- –A symbol of evil Jerusalem .... Rev 11:8
- –A symbol of God's judgment .... Isa 13:19; Jer 49:18; Am 4:11; Zep 2:9
- –A symbol of eternal punishment .... 2Pe 2:6; Jude 7

SOLOMON
A. Family data
- –Son of David by Bathsheba 2Sa 12:24; 1Ch 3:5
- –Married Pharaoh's daughter 1Ki 3:1
- –Later married numerous pagan women 1Ki 11:1–3

B. His early life as king
- –Appointed as king by David 1Ki 1:11–53
- –Given parting charge ... 1Ki 2:1–9
- –Had Adonijah and his supporters killed 1Ki 2:13–46
- –Asked for wisdom 1Ki 3:4–15; 2Ch 1:2–13
- –Judged between two prostitutes 1Ki 3:16–28
- –Known widely for his wisdom 1Ki 4:29–31, 34
- –Wrote three thousand proverbs .... 1Ki 4:32; Pr 1:1
- –Wrote one thousand and five songs .... 1Ki 4:32; SS 1:1
- –Built temple 1Ki 5:1–6:38; 2Ch 2:1–3:17
- –Built palace 1Ki 7:1–12
- –Furnished the temple ... 1Ki 7:13–51; 2Ch 4:1–5:1
- –Brought ark into the temple 1Ki 8:1–11; 2Ch 5:2–14
- –Offered prayer of dedication for temple 1Ki 8:22–53; 2Ch 6:14–42
- –Dedicated the temple with sacrifices 1Ki 8:62–66; 2Ch 7:1–10
- –God made promises to Solomon 1Ki 9:1–9; 2Ch 7:11–22
- –Administrated his kingdom 1Ki 9:10–28; 2Ch 8:1–18
- –Visited by Queen of Sheba 1Ki 10:1–13; 2Ch 9:1–12
- –Had a glorious kingdom 1Ki 10:14–29; 2Ch 9:13–28

C. His later life as king
- –Wives turned his heart from God 1Ki 11:1–13
- –Hadad and Rezon rebelled against him ... 1Ki 11:14–25
- –Jeroboam rebelled against him 1Ki 11:26–40
- –His death 1Ki 11:41–43; 2Ch 9:29–31

D. Solomon remembered after his death
- –For his organization of temple service .... 2Ch 35:3–4; Ne 12:45
- –For marrying idolatrous wives .... Ne 13:26
- –For his splendor .... Mt 6:29
- –For his wisdom .... Mt 12:42
- –For his building of the temple .... Ac 7:47

SON OF MAN
A. Phrase translated as
- –"Human being" .... Nu 23:19
- –"Mere mortal" .... Ps 8:4; Isa 51:12
- –Ezekiel called "Mortal" .... Eze 2:1; Eze 3:1

B. Jesus as the Son of Man
- –Prophesied in the Old Testament .... Da 7:13–14
- –Identified himself as such .... Mk 2:10; Lk 7:34; Lk 9:58; Jn 9:35–37
- –Died and rose again ... Mk 8:31; Mk 9:31; Mk 10:33–34; Jn 3:14–15
- –Is in heaven .... Mt 26:64; Ac 7:56; Rev 1:13
- –Will return .... Mt 13:41; Mk 13:26; Mk 14:62
- –We must feed on him .. Jn 6:53

SONG
See MUSIC AND SONG

SORROW
See GRIEF

SOUL
–The non-physical element in humans

A. Defining the soul
1. Basic concepts
   - –Humans were created as whole people .... Ge 2:7
   - –Soul referred to in the context of death . Ecc 12:7; Mt 10:28; Rev 6:9
2. Soul often synonymous with:
   - –Spirit .... Ecc 12:7; Lk 1:46–47
   - –Heart .... Ps 19:7–8; Ps 84:2
   - –Life .... Ps 26:9; Ps 88:3
   - –One's whole being .. Ps 35:9–10
   - –I (i.e., one's person) .... Ps 130:5
3. Sometimes soul appears distinct from:
   - –Heart .... Dt 4:29; Dt 6:5
   - –Spirit .... 1Th 5:23; Heb 4:12

B. What does the soul do?
1. Expresses human emotions
   - –Peace .... Ps 23:3
   - –Refreshment .... Ps 19:7
   - –Joy .... Ps 35:9
   - –Courage .... Jdg 5:21
   - –Support 1Sa 14:7
   - –Grief .... 1Sa 1:10,15; Job 30:25
   - –Sorrow .... Mt 26:38
   - –Bitterness .... Job 7:11
   - –Anguish .... Ps 6:3
   - –Depression .... Ps 42:5,11; La 3:20
2. Has spiritual desires
   - –Thirsts for God ..... Ps 42:1–2
   - –Yearns for God ..... Ps 84:2
   - –Seeks God .... Dt 4:29; 2Ch 15:12
   - –Finds rest in God ... Ps 62:1,5
   - –Waits for God ...... Ps 130:5–6
   - –Turns to God .... Dt 30:10; 1Ki 8:48
   - –Takes refuge in God .... Ps 57:1
   - –Loves God .... Dt 6:5; Dt 13:3
   - –Serves God .... Dt 10:12; Jos 22:5
   - –Obeys God .... Dt 30:2; 2Ki 23:3
   - –Boasts in God ...... Ps 34:2
   - –Praises God .... Ps 103:1–2, 22
   - –Cries out to God .... Rev 6:9–10

C. What does God do for the soul?
- –He redeems the soul ... Ps 49:15
- –He delivers the soul ... Ps 56:13
- –He saves the soul 1Pe 1:9
- –Gives hope as an anchor for the soul .... Heb 4:12

SPIRIT
–An immaterial being

A. The human spirit
1. Defining the spirit
   See SOUL
2. What does the spirit do?
   - a. Involved with the emotions
     - –The compelled spirit .... Job 32:18–20
     - –The stirred-up spirit 1Ch 5:26
     - –The revived spirit .... Ge 45:27
     - –The stubborn spirit .... Dt 2:30
     - –The bitter spirit .. 1Sa 30:6
     - –The fainting spirit .... Ps 142:3
     - –The longing spirit 2Sa 13:39
     - –The broken spirit . Ps 51:17
     - –The troubled spirit .... Jn 13:21
     - –The anguished spirit .... Job 7:11
     - –The crushed spirit .... Ps 34:18
     - –The provoked spirit .... Ecc 7:9
     - –The proud spirit .. Pr 16:18
     - –The lowly spirit .. Isa 57:15
     - –The contrite spirit .... Isa 66:2
     - –The joyful spirit .. Lk 1:47
     - –The gentle, quiet spirit 1Pe 3:4
   - b. Involved with the will
     - –The spirit that follows God .... Nu 14:24
     - –The spirit that follows itself .... Eze 13:3
     - –The spirit that guards itself ..... Mal 2:15
     - –The spirit of power and love 2Ti 1:7
     - –The steadfast spirit .... Ps 51:10
     - –The willing spirit . Ps 51:12
     - –The worshiping spirit .... Jn 4:24
     - –The unified spirit . Php 1:27
   - c. Involved with the intellect
     - –The inquiring spirit .... Ps 77:6
     - –The understanding spirit .... Isa 29:24
3. What does God do for the spirit?
   - –He can stir it up .... Jer 51:1; Hag 1:14
   - –He searches it ...... Pr 20:27
   - –He gives us a new one .... Eze 36:26
   - –He gives it new birth .... Jn 3:6
   - –He testifies with our spirit .... Ro 8:16
   - –It returns to him .... Ecc 12:7
   - –He receives it ...... Ps 31:5

B. The Holy Spirit
See HOLY SPIRIT

C. Spirit beings
1. God sends out spirits
   - –Angels are spirits he sends out .... Heb 1:14
     See ANGEL
   - –A reporting spirit sent to Sennacherib . Isa 37:7
   - –An evil spirit sent to Abimelech .... Jdg 9:23
   - –An evil spirit sent to Saul 1Sa 16:14–15,23
   - –A lying spirit sent to false prophets 1Ki 22:19–23
2. Evil spirits
   - –Have influence over humans .... 1Ti 4:1; Rev 16:13–14
   - –Were cast out by Jesus .... Mt 8:16; Mk 1:23–27
   - –Were cast out by the apostles .... Ac 5:16; Ac 16:16–18

SPIRITUALITY
See HOLINESS; MEDITATION

STARS

A. Data concerning the stars
–Created by God ... Ge 1:16
Ps 8:3
–Controlled by God ... Ps 147:4
Jer 31:35
–Show God's power ... Isa 40:26
–Must praise God ... Ps 148:3
–Were worshiped by the heathen ... 2Ki 21:3
Jer 19:13
Ac 7:43
B. Stars and constellations mentioned in the Bible
–The Bear ... Job 9:9
–Orion ... Job 9:9
–Pleiades ... Am 5:8
–The Star of Bethlehem . Mt 2:2,9
C. Stars used as symbols
–Of Jesus the Messiah .. Nu 24:17
Rev 22:16
–Of an innumerable number ... Ge 22:17
Ne 9:23
–Of Christians as witnesses ... Php 2:15–16
–Of the saints in heaven . Da 12:3
–Of angels ... Rev 1:16,20
–Of heretics ... Jude 13
–Of judgment at the end of time ... Isa 13:10–11
Mt 24:29
Rev 6:12

STEADFASTNESS

See PERSEVERANCE

STEALING

–Taking what belongs to someone else
A. The command against stealing
–The eighth commandment ... Ex 20:15
Dt 5:19
Mt 19:17–18
–Fraud and dishonest weights outlawed ... Lev 19:13
Pr 20:10,23
–Theft prohibited in Paul's writings ... Ro 13:8–9
Eph 4:28
–Theft profanes the name of God ... Lev 19:11–12
Jer 7:9–11
–Theft often accompanied by greed ... Ps 62:10
B. The punishment for thieves
–Expected to make restitution ... Ex 22:1–9
Nu 5:5–8
–Are subject to God's judgment ... Hab 2:6
–Can be excluded from the kingdom of God ... 1Co 6:9–10
C. Examples of stealing in the Bible
–Rachel and the household gods ... Ge 31:19, 30–32
–Achan and goods from Jericho ... Jos 7:11
–Micah and eleven hundred shekels of silver .. Jdg 17:2
–Ahab and Naboth's vineyard ... 1Ki 21:16,19
See also THE RICH AND THE POOR
D. Theft used as a metaphor
–For gaining admiration (stealing hearts) ... 2Sa 15:6
–For withholding tithes (robbing God) ... Mal 3:8–9
–For claiming to speak God's word (stealing words from others) ... Jer 23:30
–For the unexpectedness of Christ's return ... Lk 12:39–40
1Th 5:2
2Pe 3:10
Rev 3:3

STEPHEN

–One of the seven deacons .. Ac 6:5
–Spoke eloquently ... Ac 6:8–10
–Arrested by the Jews ... Ac 6:11–15
–Gave powerful speech to the Sanhedrin ... Ac 7:1–53
–Stoned to death ... Ac 7:54–60
Ac 22:20

STEWARDSHIP

–How one handles what God has given
A. God's relationship to what we have
1. God owns everything . Ex 19:5
Ps 24:1
Hag 2:8
2. God is the source of everything
–All our wealth ... Ge 26:12–13
1Co 4:7
–Our personal talents . Ro 12:3,6
1Co 12:7–11
–Our ability to work . Dt 8:17–18
Ecc 2:24–25
–Every moment of our lives ... Ps 39:4–5
Mt 6:27
–Everything we have . Job 1:21
Jn 3:27
B. Our relationship to what we have
1. Our gifts and talents
–Must use them faithfully ... Mt 25:14–27
1Co 4:2
–Must be trustworthy with them ... Lk 16:10–12
–Must use them for God's glory ... 1Sa 17:45–46
Ro 14:7–8
1Co 10:31
1Pe 4:11
–Must use them to serve others ... Ro 14:19
1Co 12:7
1Co 14:12
1Pe 4:10
2. Our time
–Recognize the brevity of time ... Job 7:7
Ps 89:47
Ecc 9:11–12
–Must be faithful in use of time ... Ps 90:12,17
Eph 5:15–16
3. Our wealth and possessions
a. Basic attitude
–Must believe that God will provide . Mt 6:25–34
Php 4:19
–Cannot take credit for what we have ... Da 4:28–35
1Co 4:7
–Must be content with what we have ... Php 4:11–12
1Ti 6:6–8
Heb 13:5
b. Principles of giving to the Lord
–Giving should be proportionate ... Pr 3:9
Mal 3:8–10
1Co 16:1–2
–Giving should be willing ... Ex 25:1–2
1Ch 29:6–9
2Co 8:1–5, 11–12
–Giving should be spontaneous ... 2Co 9:2–5
–Giving should be cheerful ... 2Ch 24:10
2Co 9:7
–Giving should be generous ... 2Co 8:2
2Co 9:5,11, 13
c. Blessings await a giver
–On earth ... Dt 15:4
Ac 20:35
2Co 9:6,10
–In heaven ... Mt 19:21
1Ti 6:19

STRANGERS

See ALIEN

SUFFERING

See PAIN

SUN

A. Data concerning the sun
–Created by God ... Ge 1:16
Ps 74:16
–Governs the day ... Ge 1:16
Ps 136:8
–Controlled by God ... Jos 10:12–13
Ps 19:4–6
Jer 31:35
–Needed for crops ... Dt 33:13–14
–Needed for warmth ... Ps 19:6
–Must praise God ... Ps 148:3
–Can harm a person ... Ps 121:6
–Worshiped by the heathen ... 2Ki 23:5,11
Jer 8:2
–No sun needed in heaven ... Isa 60:19–20
Rev 21:23
B. The sun used as a symbol
–Of God ... Ps 84:11
–Of God's glory ... Ps 19:1–6
–Of Christ ... Mal 4:2
–Of Christ's glory ... Mt 17:2
Ac 26:13–15
Rev 1:16
–Of the future glory of believers ... Mt 13:43
–Of stability and endurance ... Ps 72:5,17
–Of judgment at the end of time ... Isa 13:10–11
Mt 24:29
Rev 6:12

SWEARING

See CURSE

SYMPATHY

See COMPASSION

SYRIA, SYRIANS

See DAMASCUS

TABERNACLE

A. Also called "the tent of meeting" ... Nu 4:25
Nu 9:17–18
B. The building of the tabernacle
1. Planning the tabernacle
–Extensive plans outlined by God ... Ex 25:8—30:38
–Based on pattern of heaven ... Heb 8:5
Heb 9:24
2. Building the tabernacle
–Material collected ... Ex 35:4–29
Ex 36:3–7
–Supervisers chosen .. Ex 35:30—36:2
–Work performed ... Ex 36:8—39:31
–Inspected by Moses . Ex 39:32–43
–The completed tabernacle set up ... Ex 40:1–33
3. Structure of the tabernacle
a. Contents of the courtyard
–Its construction ... Ex 38:9–20
–Altar of burnt offering ... Ex 38:1–7
–Basin for washing ... Ex 38:8
b. Contents of the holy place
–Table for bread of the Presence ... Ex 25:23–30
–Golden lampstand ... Ex 37:17–24
–Altar of incense .. Ex 37:25–29
c. Contents of the most holy place ... Ex 37:1–9
Heb 9:4
See ARK OF THE COVENANT
d. Two parts separated by a curtain ... Ex 26:33
Heb 9:3
C. History of the tent of meeting
–God talked with Moses there ... Lev 1:1
Nu 7:89
–Aaron and his sons were consecrated there ... Ex 29:1–4, 10–11
–Filled with God's glory at dedication ... Ex 40:34–35
–Covered by the cloud .. Nu 9:15–23
–Used in Israelite sacrifices ... Lev 1:3–5
Lev 3:2,8
–Placed in the center of the camp ... Nu 2:1–2,17
–Joshua was commissioned there ... Dt 31:14–15, 23
–Set up at Shiloh in Canaan ... Jos 18:1
Jdg 18:31
1Sa 2:14,22
–Located at Nob during Saul's time ... 1Sa 21:1–6
–Located at Gibeon during David's time ... 1Ch 16:37–40
–Brought to Jerusalem during David's reign ... 1Ch 23:25–26,32
2Ch 1:4,13
–Solomon replaced it with the temple ... 2Ch 5:4–6
D. Symbolism of the tabernacle
1. Symbol of God's presence among the people ... Ex 25:8
Ex 29:43
Ex 40:34–35
2. Its contents symbolized Christ
–He is the tabernacle dwelling among men ... Jn 1:14
–His death is the atoning sacrifice ... 1Jn 4:10
–His body is sacred bread ... Jn 6:27–59
–His body is the curtain ... Heb 10:20
–His blood washes and purifies us ... 1Jn 1:7

TAMAR

A. Wife of Judah's sons Er and Onan ... Ge 38:1–10
–Tricked Judah into fathering children ... Ge 38:11–26
–Gave birth to twins ... Ge 38:27–30
–An ancestor of Jesus ... Mt 1:3
B. Daughter of David, sister of Absalom ... 2Sa 13:1
–Raped by half-brother Amnon ... 2Sa 13:2–21
–Rape avenged by Absalom ... 2Sa 13:23–33

TEACHING

See DOCTRINE
EDUCATION

TEMPLE

A. The first temple
1. Its construction
–The idea conceived by David ... 2Sa 7:1–2
–David not allowed to construct it ... 2Sa 7:4–13
–Planned by David ... 1Ch 28:11–19
–Gifts collected by David ... 1Ch 29:1–9
–Built by Solomon ... 2Ch 3:1—5:1
2. Its structure based on the tabernacle
–Contained the most holy place ... 2Ch 3:8–14
–Its parts separated by a curtain ... 2Ch 3:14
Mt 27:51
3. Its history
–Ark brought into it .. 2Ch 5:2–10
–Filled with the glory of God ... 2Ch 5:13–14
2Ch 7:1–3
–Dedicated by Solomon ... 2Ch 6:1–13
2Ch 7:4–7
–Ransacked by Shishak of Egypt ... 2Ch 12:9
–Refurbished by Asa . 2Ch 15:8,18
–Joash hidden there .. 2Ch 22:12
–Restored by Joash ... 2Ch 24:4–14
–Furnishings sent by Ahaz to Assyria ... 2Ch 28:21, 24
–Purified by Hezekiah ... 2Ch 29:3–19
–Desecrated by Manasseh ... 2Ch 33:3–7
–Purified by Josiah ... 2Ch 34:8–11
–Ransacked by Nebuchadnezzar ... 2Ch 36:7
–Destroyed by Nebuchadnezzar ... 2Ch 36:18–19
B. The second temple
1. Its construction
–Cyrus ordered its rebuilding ... Ezr 1:1–4

–Rebuilding begun under Zerubbabel ... Ezr 3:7–13
–Opposition to its rebuilding ... Ezr 4:1–4
–Work resumed ... Ezr 5:1–2
–Completed ... Ezr 6:13–15
–Dedicated ... Ezr 6:16–18
–Repaired and beautified by Herod ... Jn 2:20
2. New Testament events in the temple
–Zechariah met by an angel there ... Lk 1:8–20
–Jesus presented there ... Lk 2:22,27
–Jesus there at twelve years old ... Lk 2:42–50
–Jesus taught there ... Mt 26:55; Mk 12:35; Jn 7:14,28
–Jesus drove out money changers ... Mt 21:12–13; Jn 2:14–17
–Curtain torn at Jesus' death ... Mt 27:51
–Early Christians worshiped there ... Ac 2:46
–Apostles taught there ... Ac 3:1–4:2; Ac 5:21,42
–Paul arrested there ... Ac 21:27–33; Ac 26:21

C. Prophecies regarding the temple
1. Temple may not give false sense of security
–Jeremiah ... Jer 7:2–8
–Micah ... Mic 3:9–12
–Stephen ... Ac 7:47–50
2. Predictions of its destruction
–The first temple ... Jer 7:14; Eze 24:20–21
–The second temple ... Mk 13:1–2
3. Prophets bemoaned its destruction ... Isa 64:10–11; La 1:9–10
4. Prophets stirred up the people to rebuild ... Ezr 5:1; Ezr 6:14; Hag 1:2–15; Zec 4:8–9
5. Predictions of its future glory ... Isa 60:7,13; Hag 2:3,7–9
6. Ezekiel's new temple ... Eze 40:1–43:27; Eze 47:1–12
7. The new Jerusalem has no temple ... Rev 21:22

D. Symbolism of the temple
1. Symbol in the Old Testament
–Of God dwelling with his people ... 2Ch 6:20,33; Ps 18:6
–Of God's favor to his people ... Ps 65:4
2. Symbol in the New Testament
–Jesus Christ as a temple ... Jn 2:19–22
–The church as a temple ... 1Co 3:16–17; 2Co 6:16; Eph 2:21–22; Heb 3:6
–The human body as a temple ... 1Co 6:19

TEMPTATION

–Enticing one to sin against God

A. The source of temptation
1. God does not tempt us to sin ... Jas 1:13
2. Satan entices us to sin
–Adam and Eve ... Ge 3:1–4
–David ... 1Ch 21:1
–Job ... Job 1:6–12
–Jesus ... Mt 4:1–11
–Ananias and Sapphira ... Ac 5:1–3
3. Situations tempt us to sin
–Taking the easy way ... Mt 7:13–14; Mt 16:21–23
–The things of the world ... Mt 18:7–9
–Weakness of faith ... Lk 22:31–32
–Sexual desire ... 1Co 7:3–5
–Pride in one's own strength ... Gal 6:1
–Persecution ... 1Th 3:4–5
–Riches ... 1Ti 6:9
–Evil desires ... Jas 1:14–15

B. The fight against temptation
–We must beware of the devil's schemes ... 2Co 2:11; Eph 6:11
–We must watch out for temptation ... Mt 26:41; Lk 22:40,46; 1Pe 5:8
–God helps us overcome temptation ... 1Co 10:13
–Christ helps us overcome temptation ... Heb 2:17–18; Heb 4:15–16
–We must pray for help against temptation ... Mt 6:13

TEN COMMANDMENTS

–Given by God from Mount Sinai ... Ex 20:1–17; Ex 34:28; Dt 5:7–21
–Written on stone tablets ... Ex 34:1; Dt 4:13; Dt 10:4
–Stored in the ark of the covenant ... Dt 10:1–2; 1Ki 8:9
–Summary of commandments is love ... Mt 22:37–40; Ro 13:9–10
–Ten individual commandments ... Ex 34:28; Dt 4:13

See ADULTERY
CHILDREN
COVETING
CURSE
IDOLATRY
LYING
MURDER
SABBATH
SEXUAL STANDARDS
STEALING
WORSHIP

TESTAMENT

See COVENANT

TESTING

A. Humans' testing
1. Testing God
a. Positive examples
–Gideon testing God's call ... Jdg 6:36–40
–Ahaz invited to test God ... Isa 7:10–12
–Israelites invited to test God ... Mal 3:10
b. Negative examples
–Grumbling over water ... Ex 17:1–2,7; Dt 33:8; Ps 95:9
–Grumbling over food ... Ps 78:17–18; Ps 106:14–15
–Many times of testing ... Nu 14:22; Ps 78:41
–Pharisees tested Jesus ... Mt 16:1; Mt 19:3; Mk 8:11
–Ananias and Sapphira test the Spirit ... Ac 5:1–10
c. The command not to test God ... Dt 6:16; Mt 4:7; 1Co 10:9
2. The testing of ourselves
–The Teacher tests himself ... Ecc 2:1–11
–We must test our faith ... 2Co 13:5–7
–We must test our actions ... Gal 6:4
–We must test everything ... 1Th 5:21
–We must test the spirits ... 1Jn 4:1

B. God's testing of humans
1. God as a testing God
–God tests our hearts ... 1Ch 29:17; Pr 17:3; Jer 11:20; 1Th 2:4
–His testing refines us ... Ps 66:10; Isa 48:10; Jer 9:7
–We may ask God to test us ... Ps 26:2; Ps 139:23
2. Examples of God's testing
–Abraham, with sacrifice of Isaac ... Ge 22:1; Heb 11:17
–The Israelites, with lack of water ... Ex 15:22–26
–The Israelites, with rules on manna ... Ex 16:4–5; Dt 8:2–3,16
–The Israelites, with thunder on Mount Sinai ... Ex 20:18–20
–The Israelites, with false prophets ... Dt 13:1–3
–The Israelites, with heathen nations ... Jdg 2:20–3:4
–Hezekiah, with envoys from Babylon ... 2Ch 32:31
–Job, with suffering ... Job 23:10
–Christians, with trials and suffering ... Jas 1:2–3,12; Rev 3:10
3. Purpose of God's testing
–To humble us ... Dt 8:2–3
–To see if we will love him ... Dt 13:3
–To see if we will fear him ... Ex 20:18–20
–To see if we will obey him ... Ge 22:1; Ex 16:4–5
–To see if we will persevere in our faith ... Jas 1:2–3; Rev 3:10–11

THADDAEUS

–Disciple of Jesus ... Mt 10:3; Mk 3:18
–Probably also known as Judas son of James ... Lk 6:16; Jn 14:22
–One of the apostles ... Ac 1:13

THANKSGIVING

A. Thanksgiving is a command
–A command in the psalms ... Ps 75:1; Ps 107:1; Ps 118:1; Ps 136:1–3
–A command in the prophets ... Isa 12:4; Jer 33:11
–A command in the New Testament ... Eph 5:20; Php 4:6; Col 3:15,17; 1Th 5:18
–The command to give thank offerings ... Lev 7:12–15; 2Ch 29:31; Ps 107:22
–The duty of certain Levites to give thanks ... 1Ch 16:4–7; 1Ch 23:28–30

B. Reasons for thanksgiving
–For God's goodness and love ... 1Ch 16:34; 2Ch 20:21; Ps 118:29
–For God's wonderful deeds ... Ps 75:1; Ps 107:8,15,21,31
–For God's protection ... Ps 56:12–13
–For salvation ... 1Ch 16:35; Ps 118:21; Ro 7:24–25
–For daily provisions ... Mt 14:19; 2Co 9:12; 1Ti 4:3–5
–For faith, hope and love ... Ro 1:8; Col 1:3–5; 1Th 1:2–4; 2Th 1:3–4
–For God's grace ... 1Co 1:4
–For healing ... Lk 17:16
–For victory over sin and death ... 1Co 15:57
–For all people ... 1Ti 2:1
–For everything ... Eph 5:20; 1Th 5:18

C. Methods of thanksgiving
–By singing ... Ps 28:7; Ne 12:27,31,40; Col 3:16–17
–By playing musical instruments ... 1Ch 25:1
–By praying ... Ro 1:8–10; 1Co 1:4–9
–By giving offerings ... Lev 7:12–15; Ps 56:12; 2Co 9:12–15
–By worshiping God ... Ps 100:2–4; Heb 12:28
–By speaking about Jesus ... Lk 2:38
–By living holy lives ... Ro 12:1; 1Co 6:20

THEFT

See STEALING

THIRST

See HUNGER AND THIRST

THOMAS

–Disciple of Jesus ... Mt 10:3; Mk 3:18
–Ready to die with Christ ... Jn 11:16
–Asked where Jesus was going ... Jn 14:5
–Doubted Jesus' resurrection ... Jn 20:24–25
–Convinced of Jesus' resurrection ... Jn 20:26–27
–Confessed Jesus as Lord and God ... Jn 20:28–29

THRONE

A. The human throne
1. Examples
–The throne of Pharaoh ... Ge 41:40
–The throne of David ... 2Sa 3:10
–The throne of Solomon ... 1Ki 2:12
–The throne of Elah ... 1Ki 16:11
–The thrones of Ahab and Jehoshaphat ... 1Ki 22:10
–The throne of Xerxes ... Est 1:2
–The throne of Nebuchadnezzar ... Da 4:36
–The throne of Herod ... Ac 12:21
2. God and human thrones
–All thrones established by God ... 2Sa 7:13; Ps 47:7–8
–Those on thrones must rule righteously ... 2Ch 9:8; Pr 16:12; Isa 16:5
–David's throne is the Lord's throne ... 1Ch 29:23
–God can destroy thrones ... Jer 22:2–5; Hag 2:20–22

B. The throne of Christ
–He came to sit on David's throne ... Lk 1:32–33; Ac 2:30
–He sits on his heavenly throne ... Mt 19:28; Heb 8:1; Heb 12:2
–His throne lasts forever ... Heb 1:8
–His throne is one of righteousness ... Mt 25:31–46; Heb 1:8
–We will someday sit with him on his throne ... Rev 3:21

C. The throne of God
–His throne is in heaven ... Ps 11:4; Ps 103:19
–His throne is a throne of grace ... Heb 4:16
–His throne is glorious ... Isa 6:1; Eze 1:26–28
–His throne is eternal ... Ps 45:6; Ps 93:2

–His throne is one of righteousness .... Ps 9:4; Ps 45:6–7
–His throne is surrounded by praise .... Rev 4:2–11; Rev 7:9–17

TIME

A. Time as chronological time
1. God and time
–Time created by God "in the beginning" .. Ge 1:1
–God is above time .. Ps 90:4; 2Pe 3:8
2. Human division of time
–Hours .... Mt 20:1–12; Jn 11:9; Ac 5:7
–Days and seasons ... Ge 8:22; Ex 34:21
–Weeks .... Dt 16:9; Ac 28:14
–Months .... Ex 12:2; Lk 1:24,56
–Years .... Ge 1:14; Ge 15:13
3. Phrases used in God's timetable of history
–"The time is fulfilled" .... Mk 1:15
–"When the fullness of time had come" .. Gal 4:4
–"The times of the Gentiles" .... Lk 21:24
–"In the last days" .. Ac 2:17; 2Ti 3:1
–"On the last day" .. Jn 12:48
4. The end of time
–Time is moving toward final victory .. Ac 1:6–7
–Time ends at Christ's return .... Mt 16:27; Ac 1:11; 1Th 4:15–17
–Time ends with final judgment .... Rev 20:11–15

B. Time as opportunity
–A time for everything .. Ecc 3:1–8,17; Ecc 8:6
–Our times are in God's hands .... Ps 31:15
–We must make proper use of time .... Ps 90:12; 1Co 7:29–31; Eph 5:15; Col 4:5

TIMOTHY

A. Early life
–From Lystra .... Ac 16:1–2
–From a mixed marriage; uncircumcised .... Ac 16:1,3
–Brought up as a good Jewish boy 2Ti 3:15
–Taught by mother and grandmother 2Ti 1:5
–Became a believer through Paul 1Co 4:17; 1Ti 1:1
–Circumcised by Paul ... Ac 16:3
–A young man 1Ti 4:12

B. His life as co-worker with Paul
–Went with Paul on second missionary journey .. Ac 16:3–4
–Stayed in Berea with Silas .... Ac 17:14
–Sent to Thessalonica ... 1Th 3:2
–Came to Paul in Corinth .... Ac 18:5; 1Th 3:6
–Sent to Macedonia .... Ac 19:22
–Sent to settle problems at Corinth 1Co 4:17; 1Co 16:10
–Accompanied Paul as he headed to Jerusalem ... Ac 20:1–4
–Co-writer with Paul .... 2Co 1:1; Col 1:1; 1Th 1:1
–Ministered to Paul in Philippi .... Php 2:19–24
–Led church at Ephesus . 1Ti 1:3
–A pastor responsible for worship 1Ti 2:1–10; 2Ti 4:2–5
–Spent some time in prison .... Heb 13:23

C. His character
–A hard worker for the Lord .... Php 2:19–24; 2Ti 2:15; 2Ti 4:5
–A good follower of Paul .... 1Co 4:17; Php 2:22; 2Ti 1:13–14
–Somewhat timid 2Ti 1:6–7
–Needed encouragement . 1Ti 4:11–16; 1Ti 6:11–14,20
–Tendency to get sick ... 1Ti 5:23

TITHES AND OFFERINGS

A. Tithes
1. In the Old Testament
–Tithing commanded . Lev 27:30–33; Dt 12:6–7; 2Ch 31:4–8
–A tenth of everything required .... Ge 14:20; Ge 28:22; Dt 14:23
–Tithes used to support Levites .... Nu 18:21–24; Dt 14:22–27
–Israelites stopped tithing .... Ne 13:10–12; Mal 3:8–10
2. In the New Testament
–Tithing became hypocritical .... Mt 23:23; Lk 11:42
–Tithers were self-righteous .... Lk 18:9–12

B. Offerings
1. In the Old Testament
a. The burnt offering . Lev 1:1–17; Lev 6:8–13; Lev 8:18–21
b. The grain offering . Lev 2:1–16; Lev 6:14–23
c. The offering of well-being .... Lev 3:1–17; Lev 7:11–34
d. The sin offering ... Lev 4:1–5:13; Lev 6:24–30; Lev 8:14–17
e. The guilt offering . Lev 5:14–6:7; Lev 7:1–6
f. Freewill offerings
–For the tabernacle .... Ex 25:1–7; Ex 35:4–9,29
–For the first temple 1Ch 29:6–9; 2Ch 24:8–11
–For the second temple .... Ezr 2:68
–In the festival of weeks .... Dt 16:10
g. Offerings sometimes given hypocritically .... Isa 1:11–13; Hag 2:14; Mal 1:6–14; Mal 3:8–9
2. Freewill offerings in the New Testament
–Given for the poor .. Lk 19:8; Ac 11:28–30; Ro 15:25–27
–Given to support Paul .... 2Co 11:8–9; Php 4:15–18
3. Principles of giving offerings
–Freely .... Mt 10:8
–Joyfully 2Co 9:7
–In proportion to income .... Dt 16:17; Pr 3:9; 1Co 16:2
–Generously .... Ps 37:26; 2Co 9:5–6; 1Ti 6:18

See also THE RICH AND THE POOR; SACRIFICE; STEWARDSHIP

TITUS

–A Christian led by Paul to the Lord .... Tit 1:4
–Gentile co-worker of Paul .. 2Co 8:23; Gal 2:1–3
–Sent to Corinth 2Co 2:13; 2Co 8:6,16–18; 2Co 12:18
–Sent to Crete .... Tit 1:4–5
–Sent to Dalmatia 2Ti 4:10

TONGUES

See GIFTS OF THE SPIRIT; LANGUAGE

TRADITION

–Teachings and religious observances handed down

A. Teachings passed down
–By parents to children ... Ps 78:3–6; Pr 1:7
–By the Jewish elders ... Mk 7:3,5
–By the apostles 1Co 11:2,23–26; 1Co 15:3–7; 2Th 2:15

B. Dangers of traditions
–Can obscure God's word .... Mt 15:1–9; Mk 7:1–13
–Can misdirect a person's life .... Mic 6:16; Gal 1:14

C. Reactions to traditions
–Consider bad ones to be rubbish .... Php 3:4–8
–Hold fast to good ones . 1Co 15:1–5; 2Th 2:15

TREE

A. Kinds of trees mentioned in the Bible
–Acacia .... Ex 25:5
–Algum 2Ch 2:8
–Almond .... Ge 30:37
–Apple .... SS 2:3
–Balsam 2Sa 5:23
–Broom 1Ki 19:4
–Cedar 1Ki 4:33
–Cypress .... Ge 6:14
–Ebony .... Eze 27:15
–Fig .... Mt 21:19
–Myrtle .... Ne 8:15
–Nut .... SS 6:11
–Oak .... Ge 35:4
–Olive .... Jdg 9:8
–Palm .... Ex 15:27
–Pine .... Isa 41:19
–Plane .... Ge 30:37
–Pomegranate 1Sa 14:2
–Poplar .... Ps 137:2
–Sycamore .... Lk 19:4
–Tamarisk .... Ge 21:33
–Terebinth .... Hos 4:13
–Willow .... Eze 17:5

B. Trees used in a symbolic way
1. Significant trees
–The tree of knowledge of good and evil .... Ge 2:17
–The tree of life .... Ge 3:22,24; Rev 22:2
–The tree of the cross .... Ac 5:30; Gal 3:13; 1Pe 2:24
2. Comparison to trees
–The righteous are like a tree .... Ps 1:3; Ps 92:12–15; Isa 61:3
–Wisdom is like a tree .... Pr 3:18
–The branch is a symbol of Christ .... Isa 11:1; Jer 23:5–6
3. Illustrations connected with trees
–Parable of the trees and bramble .... Jdg 9:7–20
–Parable of the coming new tree .... Eze 17:22–24
–Parable of the tree and its fruit .... Mt 7:17–19
–Parable of the mustard seed .... Mt 13:31–32
–Parable of the barren fig tree .... Lk 13:6–9
–Cursing of the fig tree .... Mk 11:12–14, 20–21
–A lesson from the fig tree .... Mt 24:32–33
–Parable of the two olive trees .... Ro 11:17–24

TRIBULATION

See GREAT TRIBULATION; PAIN

TRINITY

–One God in three persons–Father, Son and Holy Spirit

A. There is only one God
–Expressed in the Old Testament .... Dt 4:35,39; Dt 6:4; Isa 45:21
–Expressed in the New Testament .... 1Co 8:5–6; Eph 4:6; 1Ti 2:5; Jas 2:19

B. Hints of a plurality in God in the Old Testament
–God speaks of himself as "us" .... Ge 1:26–27; Ge 3:22; Ge 11:7; Isa 6:8
–Someone coming from God is God .... Isa 7:14; Isa 9:6
–The Angel of the Lord speaks as God; *See* ANGEL OF THE LORD

C. The Son as God; *See* JESUS CHRIST

D. The Holy Spirit as God; *See* HOLY SPIRIT

E. Father, Son and Spirit together
–One name for the three .... Mt 28:19
–The three persons mentioned together .... Mt 3:16–17; Jn 15:26; Ro 5:5–6; Ro 8:11,16–17; 1Co 12:4–6; 2Co 13:14; Gal 4:4–6; Eph 4:4–6; 1Th 1:2–5; 2Th 2:13; Tit 3:4–6; 1Pe 1:2; 1Jn 4:2; Jude 20–21

F. Similar divine characteristics for all three
1. Holiness
–Of the Father .... Jn 17:11
–Of the Son 1Co 1:30
–Of the Spirit .... Ro 1:4
2. Eternity
–Of the Father 1Ti 1:17
–Of the Son .... Heb 1:2–3,8
–Of the Spirit .... Heb 9:14
3. All-knowing
–Of the Father .... Mt 6:8,32
–Of the Son .... Jn 2:24–25
–Of the Spirit 1Co 2:10–11
4. All-powerful
–Of the Father .... Ps 135:5–7
–Of the Son 1Co 15:24–27
–Of the Spirit .... Ro 15:13,19
5. Everywhere present
–Of the Father .... Jer 23:24
–Of the Son .... Mt 28:20
–Of the Spirit .... Ps 139:7–10

G. Similar divine activities for all three
1. Creating
–By the Father .... Ge 1:1
–By the Son .... Jn 1:3
–By the Spirit .... Ps 104:30
2. Giving of spiritual life
–By the Father .... Eph 2:4–5
–By the Son .... Jn 10:10
–By the Spirit .... Eze 37:14
3. Performing miracles
–By the Father 1Ki 18:38
–By the Son .... Mt 4:23–24
–By the Spirit .... Ro 15:19
4. Teaching
–By the Father .... Ps 71:17; Isa 48:17
–By the Son .... Jn 13:13
–By the Spirit .... Jn 14:26
5. Experiencing grief because of sin
–By the Father .... Ge 6:6
–By the Son .... Lk 19:41–44

–By the Spirit .... Eph 4:30

TRUST

–Confidence put in someone or something

A. In whom/what must we trust?
- –In God .... Ps 25:2; Ps 56:3–4,11; Ps 91:2
- –In the Lord .... Ps 4:5; Pr 3:5; Na 1:7; Ac 14:23
- –In Christ .... Jn 14:1; Ro 10:11; 1Pe 2:6
- –In the name of the Lord .... Ps 20:7; Isa 50:10; Zep 3:12
- –In the word of God .... Ps 119:42
- –In God's unfailing love .... Ps 9:10; Ps 52:8

B. What are the results of trusting in God?
- –We become righteous and just .... Ps 37:5–6
- –We are saved .... Isa 25:9
- –We are blessed .... Ps 40:4
- –We experience joy ..... Ps 33:21
- –We are released from fear .... Ps 56:3–4
- –We receive direction from the Lord .... Pr 3:5–6
- –We stand firm .... Ps 20:7–8
- –We prosper .... Pr 28:25
- –God keeps us safe ..... Jer 39:17–18
- –God delivers us .... Ps 22:4
- –God cares for us ...... Na 1:7
- –God surrounds us with his love .... Ps 32:10
- –Jesus prepares a place for us .... Jn 14:1–2

C. In what ought we *not* trust?
- –In idols .... 2Ki 17:14–15; Isa 42:17; Jer 13:25
- –In other people .... Ps 118:8–9; Ps 146:3; Jer 17:5–7
- –In ourselves .... Pr 28:26
- –In fortified cities ...... Jer 5:17
- –In horses and chariots .. Ps 20:7; Isa 31:1–3
- –In weapons .... Ps 44:6
- –In riches .... Job 31:24–28; Ps 52:7; Lk 12:13–21; 1Ti 6:17

TRUTH

–What is accurate and agrees with reality

A. Of whom/what is truth characteristic?
1. God
   - –The Father .... Ps 31:5; Isa 65:16
   - –Jesus .... Jn 1:14; Jn 14:6
   - –The Spirit .... Jn 14:17; 1Jn 5:6
2. God's revelation
   - –God's law .... Ps 119:43
   - –God's word .... 2Sa 7:28; Isa 45:19; Jn 17:17
   - –The testimony of Jesus .... Jn 8:45–46; Jn 18:37
   - –The word of the prophets .... 1Ki 18:24; 1Ki 22:16; Jer 26:15
   - –The gospel proclaimed by the apostles .... 2Co 4:2; Gal 2:5,14; Eph 1:13
3. The church, the pillar of truth 1Ti 3:15

B. How must believers relate to the truth?
- –Must know it .... Ps 51:6; 1Ti 2:4
- –Must come to a knowledge of it .... 2Ti 2:25; Tit 1:1; Heb 10:26
- –Must seek it .... Jer 5:1
- –Must choose it .... Ps 119:30
- –Must buy it .... Pr 23:23
- –Must believe it 2Th 2:13
- –Must love it .... Zec 8:19
- –Must walk in it .... Ps 26:3; 3Jn 3–5
- –Must live by it .... Jn 3:21; 1Jn 1:6
- –Must obey it .... Gal 5:7
- –Must worship in it ..... Jn 4:23–24
- –Must speak it .... Ps 15:2; Zec 8:16; Eph 4:25

C. What does the truth do for us?
- –Protects us .... Ps 40:11
- –Guides us .... Ps 43:3
- –Sets us free .... Jn 8:31–32
- –Sanctifies us .... Jn 17:17,19
- –Purifies us 1Pe 1:22

D. What do the wicked do with respect to truth?
- –Reject it .... Isa 59:14–15; Ro 2:8
- –Do not speak it .... Jer 9:5
- –Distort it .... Ac 20:30
- –Suppress it .... Ro 1:18
- –Exchange it for a lie ... Ro 1:25
- –Wander away from it .. 2Ti 2:18
- –Oppose it 2Ti 3:8
- –Turn away from it 2Ti 4:4

TYRE

A. Identity and location
- –A merchant city .... Ne 13:16
- –A seacoast city .... Lk 6:17
- –Often linked with Sidon .... Isa 23:1–2; Mt 15:21

See SIDON

B. Significance of Tyre
1. In the Old Testament
   - –Territory given to tribe of Asher ...... Jos 19:24,29
   - –King Hiram sent wood for David's palace 2Sa 5:11–12; 1Ch 14:1–2
   - –King Hiram sent wood for the temple . 1Ki 5:7–12; 2Ch 2:11–16
   - –Huram of Tyre was a temple craftsman 1Ki 7:13–14
   - –Prophecies against them .... Isa 23:1–18; Eze 26:1—28:19; Joel 3:4–8; Am 1:9–10
2. In the New Testament
   - –Jesus ministered there .... Mt 15:21–28; Mk 7:24–30
   - –Paul spent seven days there .... Ac 21:3–6

UNION WITH CHRIST

A. Christians are:
- –In Christ 1Th 2:14
- –New creation in Christ . 2Co 5:17
- –The faithful in Christ .. Eph 1:1

B. Our participation in events of Christ's life
- –We suffer with him .... Ro 8:17; Php 3:10; 1Pe 4:13
- –We share in his broken body 1Co 10:16–17
- –We share in his shed blood 1Co 10:16–17
- –We are crucified with him .... Ro 6:6,8; Col 2:20
- –We are buried with him .... Ro 6:4; Col 2:12
- –We are raised with him .... Eph 2:6; Col 2:12; Col 3:1
- –We sit at God's right hand with him .... Eph 2:6; Col 3:1
- –We will return with him 1Th 4:14
- –We will share in his glory .... Ro 8:17
- –We will reign with him 2Ti 2:12

C. Our involvement in Christ
- –We are chosen in him .. Eph 1:4,11
- –We are justified in him .... Gal 2:17
- –We who are in him are free from condemnation .... Ro 8:1
- –We are baptized into him .... Gal 3:27; Col 2:11–13
- –We are babes in him ... 1Co 3:1
- –We are found in him ... Php 3:9
- –We are one with him .. Jn 14:20; Jn 17:21,23; 1Co 6:17
- –We must remain in him .... Jn 15:4–5,7
- –We live in him 1Jn 3:24
- –Our way of life is in him 1Co 4:17
- –We grow in him .... Eph 4:16
- –We pray in him .... Eph 2:18; Eph 3:12
- –We are blessed in him . Eph 1:3
- –We are sanctified in him 1Co 1:2
- –We fall asleep (die) in him 1Th 4:14,16; 1Co 15:18
- –We will be made alive in him 1Co 15:22

D. Pictures of union with Christ
- –Vine and branches ..... Jn 15:1–7
- –Foundation and building .... 1Co 3:10–11; Eph 2:20–21
- –Head and members of the body .... Ro 12:4–5; 1Co 12:14–27
- –Husband and wife ..... Eph 5:23–32
- –Shepherd and sheep .... Jn 10:11,14–16

UNITY

A. Expressions of the unity of the church
- –One nation and people . 1Pe 2:9–10
- –One body .... Ro 12:4–5; 1Co 12:13, 27
- –One family .... Eph 2:19
- –One bride/spouse ...... 2Co 11:2; Eph 5:23–30
- –One temple 1Co 3:16–17
- –One building with one foundation .... 1Co 3:9–11; Eph 2:20–21
- –One spiritual house 1Pe 2:5
- –One field/vineyard ..... Jn 15:5; 1Co 3:9
- –One flock .... Jn 10:16
- –One city .... Heb 12:22–23

B. The basis of unity
- –Christ's unity with the Father .... Jn 17:20–23
- –Christ's death on the cross .... Eph 2:14–16
- –Our unity with Christ .. Gal 3:26–28
- –The one Holy Spirit ... Eph 4:3–4
- –Our common faith and hope .... Eph 4:4–5, 13

C. Demonstrations of unity
- –The life of the early church .... Ac 2:42–47; Ac 4:32
- –The Lord's supper 1Co 10:16–17

D. Important elements of unity
- –Unity is good and pleasant .... Ps 133:1
- –Unity makes God's people fruitful .... Ps 133:3
- –Unity is a challenge we must strive to achieve .. Eph 4:12–16; Php 1:27; Php 2:1–3; 1Th 5:13; 1Pe 3:8
- –Unity requires that we love one another .... Eph 4:15–16
- –Diversity in gifts is consistent with unity ...... Ro 12:4–8; 1Co 12:7–30
- –Diversity in thinking is consistent with unity ... Ro 14:1–6

E. Causes of disunity
- –Quarreling .... Ac 15:36–39; 1Co 3:3
- –Favoritism .... Jas 2:1–4
- –Spiritual immaturity 1Co 1:10–12; 1Co 3:1–2
- –Hypocrisy .... Gal 2:11–14; 1Pe 2:1

URIAH

- –Hittite husband of Bathsheba 2Sa 11:2–3
- –One of David's brave warriors 2Sa 23:39
- –Devoted to duty 2Sa 11:8–13
- –Killed on David's orders ... 2Sa 11:16–25

URIM AND THUMMIM

See CASTING LOTS

USURY

See DEBT

UZZIAH

- –Son of Amaziah; king of Judah 2Ch 26:1–5
- –Also called Azariah 2Ki 15:1
- –An effective and powerful king 2Ch 26:6–15
- –Became proud and unlawfully burnt incense 2Ch 26:16–19
- –Punished with leprosy 2Ki 15:5; 2Ch 26:20–21

VASHTI

- –Wife of Xerxes; Queen of Persia .... Est 1:9
- –Refused to display her beauty .... Est 1:10–12
- –Deposed as queen .... Est 1:15–21
- –Replaced by Esther .... Est 2:17

VICTORY

See WARFARE

VINEYARD

A. Significant vineyards in the Bible
- –Noah's .... Ge 9:20
- –Those in Canaan ...... Nu 13:23–24; Dt 8:8
- –Naboth's 1Ki 21:1–16
- –Vineyards in Jesus' parables .... Mt 20:1–15; Mt 21:28–31,33–40

B. Design and care of vineyards
1. The design
   - –Had protecting walls .... Nu 22:24; Pr 24:30–31
   - –Had a tower for watchmen .... Isa 5:1–2; Mt 21:33
   - –Had a wine press in it .... Isa 5:2; Mt 21:33
2. The care
   - –Clearing the field ... Isa 5:2
   - –Planting .... Ps 107:37; Ecc 2:4; Isa 5:2
   - –Cultivating .... Dt 28:39; Isa 7:25
   - –Pruning .... Lev 25:3; Jn 15:2
   - –Harvesting .... Lev 19:10; Jdg 9:27
   - –Treading the wine press .... Isa 16:10

C. Vineyards used as a symbol
1. A symbol of prosperity and security
   - –To sit in one's vineyard meant security . 1Ki 4:25; Mic 4:4
   - –To eat from one's vineyard meant prosperity .... 2Ki 18:31; Ps 107:37–38; Isa 36:16
2. Spiritual symbols
   - –A symbol of the Israelite nation .... Ps 80:8–11; Isa 5:7; Jer 2:21; Hos 10:1
   - –A symbol of the followers of Jesus ..... Jn 15:1–6

–A symbol of the kingdom of heaven .. Mt 20:1–15; Mt 21:28–33

VISION

See DREAMS AND VISIONS

VOICE

A. The human voice
1. Uses of the human voice
–Ordinary communication 1Sa 24:16
–Recognizing a person ..... Ge 27:22; 1Sa 26:17; Ac 12:14
–Expressing unity (one voice) ..... Ex 24:3
–Praying ..... Ps 66:19
–Requesting a favor .. Lk 17:13
–Preaching ..... Ac 2:14
2. Expressions of the human voice
–The praising voice .. 2Ch 20:19; Lk 17:15
–The shouting voice .. Isa 40:9
–The complaining voice ..... Ps 64:1
–The weeping voice .. Jer 31:15–16
B. The voice of God
1. Expressions of God's voice
a. People called by his voice
–Moses ..... Ex 3:4–6; Ac 7:31–32
–Samuel 1Sa 3:1–14
–Isaiah ..... Isa 6:8–10
b. The power of his voice
–Accompanied by fire ..... Dt 4:33
–Sounds like thunder ..... 2Sa 22:14; Job 37:4–5; Ps 29:3–4
–Accomplishes great things ..... Ps 29:5–9; Ps 46:6
–Can come as a gentle whisper ... 1Ki 19:12–13
c. Messages of his voice
–His law from Mount Sinai ..... Dt 5:22–26
–Affirmation of Jesus as his Son .. Mt 3:17; Lk 9:35–36
–Glorification of Jesus ..... Jn 12:28–30
2. The voice of Jesus
–Jesus proclaimed with a loud voice ..... Jn 7:37–38
–Jesus cried out with a loud voice ..... Mt 27:46,50
–His voice raised Lazarus ..... Jn 11:43
–His voice called Paul to be an apostle ..... Ac 9:4–6
–His voice revealed things to John ..... Rev 1:10–13
–His voice calls his sheep ..... Jn 10:16,27
–His voice will raise the dead ..... Jn 5:25,28
3. Our response to God's voice
–We must recognize his voice ..... Jn 10:3–5
–We must listen to his voice ..... Ex 15:26; Dt 30:20
–We must obey his voice ..... 1Sa 15:22; Hag 1:12

VOW

–A solemn promise made to God

A. Significant vows in the Bible
–Jacob's vow at Bethel .. Ge 28:20–22
–The nazirite vow ..... Nu 6:1–21
–Jephthah's vow ..... Jdg 11:30–31
–Nazirite vow required for Samson ..... Jdg 13:1–7
–Hannah's vow regarding Samuel 1Sa 1:11
–David's vow regarding a temple for the Lord ..... Ps 132:1–5
–Paul's nazirite vow ..... Ac 18:18
B. The nature of the vow
–Often arose in times of distress ..... Ge 28:20–22; Nu 21:1–2; Ps 66:13–14; Ps 116:7–14
–Made only to God ..... Lev 27:2,9; Dt 23:21–23; Isa 19:21
–Was completely voluntary ..... Dt 23:22; Ecc 5:5
–Had to be fulfilled ..... Dt 23:21,23; Ecc 5:4,6
–Should not be made rashly ..... Pr 20:25
–Rules for redeeming vows ..... Lev 27:1–33
–Could be abused at times ..... Mk 7:9–13

WALK OF LIFE

–The Christian way of life

A. What the Christian walk is not
–Not walking according to the sinful nature ..... Ro 8:4; Gal 5:16–21
–Not walking in the ways of evildoers ..... 1Ki 15:26,34; Pr 4:14
–Not walking in dark ways ..... Pr 2:13
–Not walking in darkness ..... Jn 8:12; 1Jn 1:6; 1Jn 2:11
–Not walking in the counsel of the wicked .. Ps 1:1
–Not walking in pride ... Da 4:37; Mic 2:3
B. What the Christian walk is
–Walking with God ..... Ps 56:13; Mic 6:8; Rev 3:4
–Walking in God's ways ..... Dt 5:33; Dt 10:12; Jos 22:5
–Walking before God ... 1Ki 2:4; 2Ch 7:17
–Walking in truth ..... Ps 26:3; 3Jn 3–4
–Walking in the light ... Ps 89:15; Isa 2:5; 1Jn 1:7
–Walking in the name of God ..... Mic 4:5
–Walking in the fear of God ..... Ne 5:9
–Walking in the law of God ..... Ps 119:1
–Walking in love and obedience 2Jn 6
–Walking in the Spirit ... Ro 8:4
–Walking in the paths of the righteous ..... Pr 2:20
–Walking as Jesus walked 1Jn 2:6
C. Examples of those who walked with God
–Enoch ..... Ge 5:22–24
–Noah ..... Ge 6:9
–Abraham ..... Ge 24:40
–Isaac ..... Ge 48:15
–Levi ..... Mal 2:4–6
–Jotham 2Ch 27:6
–Hezekiah ..... Isa 38:3
D. God's promise to walk with us ..... Lev 26:12; 2Co 6:16

WARFARE

A. Physical Warfare
1. Wars in the Bible
a. First recorded war Ge 14:1–17
b. Israelite wars on the way to Canaan ..... Ex 17:8–13; Nu 21:1–3, 21–35
c. Wars of Joshua
–The battle against Jericho ..... Jos 6:1–25
–The battle against Ai ..... Jos 7:3–5; Jos 8:1–29
–The battle against five kings ..... Jos 10:1–28
–The southern cities defeated ..... Jos 10:29–43
–The northern cities defeated ..... Jos 11:1–23
d. Wars in the period of the judges
–Deborah and Barak ..... Jdg 4:12–23
–Gideon ..... Jdg 7:1–25
–Jephthah ..... Jdg 11:4–33
–During Eli's judgeship 1Sa 4:1–10; 1Sa 7:2–14
e. Wars during the time of Saul
–Saul rescued the city of Jabesh 1Sa 11:1–11
–Against the Philistines 1Sa 13:2–7; 1Sa 14:1–46; 1Sa 17:1–54; 1Sa 31:1–7
–Against the Amalekites 1Sa 15:4–9; 1Sa 30:1–20
f. Wars during the time of David
–Gained control of all Israel ..... 2Sa 2:8—4:12
–Against the Philistines 2Sa 5:17–25; 2Sa 21:15–22
–Against the Ammonites 2Sa 10:1–14
–Against the Arameans 2Sa 10:15–19
–Civil war against Absalom ..... 2Sa 15:1—18:18
–Summary of wars 2Sa 8:1–14
g. Wars of the northern kingdom
–Against the southern kingdom 1Ki 15:16–17,32; 2Ki 13:12; 2Ki 14:9–14; 2Ki 16:5–6
–Against the Philistines 1Ki 16:15–17
–Against the Arameans 1Ki 20:1–34; 1Ki 22:1–37; 2Ki 6:8–7:11; 2Ki 8:28–29; 2Ki 13:3–7
–Against Assyria .. 2Ki 15:19–20,29–30; 2Ki 16:7–10; 2Ki 17:1–6
h. Wars of the southern kingdom
–Against the Egyptians 1Ki 14:25–26
–Against the Edomites 2Ki 8:20–22; 2Ki 14:7
–Against the Ammonites and Moabites 2Ch 20:1–26
–Against Assyria .. 2Ch 32:1–22; 2Ch 33:10–11
–Against Babylon . 2Ki 24:1–4, 10–16; 2Ki 25:1–21
2. Victory for God's people
a. God is the source of victory ..... Nu 21:3; Dt 20:1–4; Jos 11:7–8; 2Ch 20:15–17; Ps 18:29,34–43; Pr 21:31
b. Principles of victory
–Success when faithful to the Lord ..... Jdg 7:1–25; 1Sa 17:41–50; 2Ch 20:20
–Defeat when unfaithful 2Ki 17:5–20; 2Ki 21:10–15
c. God controls foreign armies ..... Isa 13:3–5; Jer 25:8–9; Eze 21:18–22
B. Spiritual warfare
1. God is at war with Satan
–At the time of Job ..... Job 1:6–12; Job 26:6–13
–In the days of Israel . Isa 27:1
–At the time of Christ ..... Mt 4:1–11; Lk 10:18
–In heaven ..... Rev 12:7–9
2. Christians are at war
–With the devil ..... Ge 3:1–15; 2Co 2:11; 1Pe 5:8
–With the powers of darkness ..... Eph 6:12
–With the world ..... Jn 15:18–19; 1Jn 2:15–17
–With the old self .... Ro 6:6,12
–With the sinful nature ..... Ro 8:5–9; Gal 5:16–25
–With sinful desires .. Ro 7:15–20; 1Pe 2:11
–With death ..... 1Co 15:26; Heb 2:14–15
3. How Christians ought to fight
–By depending on God ..... 2Sa 22:33–49; Ps 18:29,32; Ps 27:1–2
–By being dedicated to Jesus Christ 2Ti 2:4; 1Pe 5:10
–By standing firm in the Lord ..... Eph 6:10–14
–By holding on to the faith 1Ti 1:18–19; 1Jn 5:4–5
–By laying hold of eternal life 1Ti 6:12
–By being good soldiers 2Ti 2:3
–By enduring hardship 2Ti 2:3
–By exercising self-denial 1Co 9:26–27
–By praying ..... Eph 6:18
–By resisting the devil 1Pe 5:8–9
4. Protection provided by the Lord
–The full armor of God ..... Eph 6:11,13
–The armor of light .. Ro 13:12
–God as our shield ... Ge 15:1; Dt 33:29; Ps 115:9–11
–The shield of faith .. Eph 6:16
–The belt of righteousness ..... Isa 11:5
–The belt of truth .... Eph 6:14
–The breastplate of righteousness ..... Isa 59:17; Eph 6:14
–The breastplate of faith and love 1Th 5:8
–Feet ready to run to bring the good news ..... Isa 52:7; Eph 6:15
–The helmet of salvation ..... Eph 6:17; 1Th 5:8
–The sword of the Spirit, the word of God ..... Eph 6:17; Heb 4:12
5. Victory is certain
a. Accomplished by Christ
–On the cross ..... Jn 12:31–33; Col 2:15; Heb 2:14
–In his ascension .. Eph 1:20–21; Php 2:9–11
–In his return ..... 1Co 15:24–28; Rev 19:11–16
b. Our victory given through Christ
–God gives us the victory ..... Ro 7:25; 1Co 15:55–57
–We can do all things in Christ .. Php 4:13
–God will crush Satan under our feet ..... Ro 16:20
c. Victory over sin through the Spirit .. Ro 8:9–13; Gal 5:16–18

WATCHFULNESS

A. God watches over people
- –His protective watch ... Ge 31:49; Ps 121:3–8; Isa 27:2–3; Jer 31:10
- –His watch over good and evil ... Job 7:17–21; Job 13:27; Pr 15:3; Jer 31:28

B. God's people must be watchful
1. What we must watch
   - –Ourselves and our manner of life ... Dt 4:9; Dt 4:15; Ps 39:1; 1Ti 4:16
   - –For false teachers ... Mk 13:5–6; Ac 20:28–31; Php 3:2–3; 2Jn 8
   - –For those who divide the church ... Ro 16:17
   - –For hypocrites ... Mk 12:38–40
   - –For the second coming of Jesus ... Mt 25:13; 1Th 5:5–6; Rev 16:15
2. How we must watch
   - –With prayer ... Mk 14:38; Eph 6:18
   - –With alertness ... Mk 13:33; 1Th 5:6
   - –With care not to fall into temptation ... Mk 14:38; Gal 6:1
   - –With care not to forget what God has done ... Dt 4:9
   - –With hope ... Mic 7:7
   - –With thankfulness ... Col 4:2

WATER

A. Uses of water
1. Water for washing
   a. Simple cleansing
   - –Washing body ... Ru 3:3
   - –Washing face ... Ge 43:31
   - –Washing feet ... Ge 18:4; 2Sa 11:8; Jn 13:4–5

   b. Ritual cleansing
   - –Washing clothes at Mount Sinai ... Ex 19:10,14
   - –Washing necessary for priests ... Ex 30:17–21
   - –Washing necessary for Levites ... Nu 8:5–7
   - –Washing parts of a sacrifice ... Lev 1:9,13
   - –Washing after a skin disease ... Lev 14:8–9
   - –Washing after uncleanness ... Lev 15:5–13,21–22; Nu 19:11–13
   - –Various Jewish washing rituals ... Mt 23:25–26; Mk 7:3–4
2. Water for drinking
   a. Water drunk by humans and animals ... Ge 24:11–19; Jdg 7:4–5; Mt 10:42

   b. God provided water for his people
   - –Hagar ... Ge 21:15–19
   - –The Israelites in the desert ... Ex 17:1–6; Nu 20:1–11; Ps 78:20
   - –The Israelites in the time of Elisha ... 2Ki 3:15–20

B. God and water
1. God is the source of living water ... Ps 23:2; Isa 55:1; Jer 2:13
2. Christ is the source of living water ... Jn 4:10–14; Jn 7:37–38; Rev 21:6; Rev 22:1–2
3. Water used in judgment by God
   - –The flood ... Ge 7:17–24; 1Pe 3:20
   - –The destruction of the Egyptians ... Ex 14:26–30; Ps 106:9–11
   - –The destruction of the Philistines ... Jer 47:2–5
   - –The storm in the story of Jonah ... Jnh 1:3–15
   - –Sea storms in general ... Ps 107:23–30

C. Water used as a symbol
1. As a symbol of evil people ... Ge 49:4; Isa 57:20; Jude 13
2. As a symbol of personal affliction
   - –Waters overwhelming someone ... Ps 42:7; Ps 69:1–2, 14–15; Jer 49:23
   - –God protects his people from the waters ... Ps 18:16–17; Ps 124:1–5; Isa 43:2
   - –Heaven has no sea ... Rev 21:1
3. As a symbol of cleansing from sin ... Isa 1:16; Eze 36:25; Eph 5:26; Heb 10:22
4. As a cleansing symbol in baptism ... Ac 8:36; Ac 22:16; 1Pe 3:21
5. As a symbol of the Holy Spirit ... Isa 44:3; Jn 7:38–39
6. As a symbol of heavenly peace ... Isa 35:6–7; Isa 43:19–21; Jer 31:11–12; Zec 14:6–9; Rev 22:1–2

WEALTH

See THE RICH AND THE POOR

WEATHER

A. God and the weather
1. God controls the weather
   - –He sends sunshine ... Ps 19:4–6; Mt 5:45
   - –He sends rain and snow ... Job 5:10; Job 38:22–30; Ps 147:16–17
   - –He sends wind ... Ex 10:13; Ps 78:26; Ps 147:18
   - –He sends storms ... Ps 107:25–26; Jnh 1:4; Eze 13:13
2. God uses weather elements
   a. To exhibit his power ... Ex 19:16

   b. To bless his people ... Dt 11:13–15; Ps 65:9–11; Ps 147:7–9

   c. To help his people in battle ... Jos 10:11–14; 1Sa 7:10; 2Sa 22:13–15

   d. To judge people
   - –By withholding rain ... Lev 26:18–20; 1Ki 17:1; Am 4:7
   - –By sending floods ... Ge 7:11–24; Isa 8:6–8; Na 1:8
   - –By sending violent storms ... Ex 9:22–26; Ps 107:25–27; Na 1:3–4; Hag 2:17

B. Weather elements used as symbols
1. The sun
   See SUN
2. Clouds
   - –God's presence among his people ... Ex 13:21–22; Ps 104:3
   - –The mystery of God . Ps 97:2
   - –Sin and forgiveness ... Isa 44:22
   - –Departed Christians who surround us as witnesses ... Heb 12:1
   - –God's judgment ... Joel 2:2
   - –An advancing army . Jer 4:13
3. Wind
   - –God's presence around us ... Ps 104:3
   - –The Holy Spirit ... Jn 3:8; Ac 2:2
   - –Meaninglessness ... Ecc 1:6,14
   - –False teaching ... Eph 4:14
4. Gentle rain showers
   - –The word of God ... Isa 55:10–12
   - –God's blessings ... Eze 34:26; Hos 6:3
5. Snow
   - –Forgiveness ... Ps 51:7; Isa 1:18
   - –Leprosy ... Nu 12:10
   - –God's wonders ... Job 38:22
   - –Brightness ... Mt 28:3
   - –Glory of Christ ... Rev 1:14
6. Hail
   - –God's wonders ... Job 38:22
   - –God's power and majesty ... Ps 18:12
   - –God's judgment ... Rev 8:7
7. Thunder
   - –God's voice ... Ps 18:13; Ps 29:3–7; Ps 68:32–33
   - –God's majesty ... Rev 4:5
8. Lightning
   - –Christ's return ... Mt 24:27; Lk 17:24
   - –Satan's fall ... Lk 10:18
9. Violent storms, as God's final judgment ... Eze.38:22...; Rev 11:19; Rev 16:18–21

See also HUNGER AND THIRST WATER

WICKEDNESS

See SIN

WILL OF GOD

A. God's will: what God wants us to do
1. What does God's will include?
   - –His law in general .. Ro 2:18; 1Pe 4:2–3
   - –His word in general . Ac 20:27
   - –Doing what is good . 1Pe 2:15
   - –Avoiding sexual immorality ... 1Th 4:3
   - –Giving thanks in all circumstances ... 1Th 5:18
2. How did Jesus relate to God's will?
   - –He came to do God's will ... Jn 4:34; Jn 6:38; Heb 10:5,7
   - –He was obedient to God's will ... Php 2:7–8
   - –He submitted to God's will for him .. Mt 26:39,42
3. How must we relate to God's will
   - –We must know his will ... Col 1:9
   - –We must understand his will ... Eph 5:17
   - –We must choose to do his will ... Jn 7:17
   - –We must do his will ... Ps 40:8; Ps 143:10; Mt 12:50
   - –We must approve his will by obedience ... Ro 12:2
   - –We must stand firm in his will ... Col 4:12

B. God's will: what God plans in history
1. Aspects of God's will
   - –God does whatever he pleases ... Ps 115:3; Ps 135:6; Da 4:35; Ro 9:18–21
   - –Everything occurs according to his will ... Eph 1:11
2. What can we know about God's plan?
   a. His plan may be kept secret
   - –Hidden in the Old Testament ... Eph 1:9; Eph 3:4–5
   - –Hidden from learned people ... Mt 11:25–26
   - –Even now we may not understand it . Ro 9:18–24

   b. Some parts of his plan are revealed
   - –That salvation is in Christ ... Gal 1:4
   - –That God saves both Jew and Gentile ... Eph 3:6
   - –That everyone should be saved .. 1Ti 2:4; 2Pe 3:9
   - –That all God's children come to him ... Mt 18:14; Jn 6:39–40
   - –That Paul was called as apostle .. 1Co 1:1
3. God's will and human suffering
   - –His will may include suffering ... Job 1:6–22; 1Pe 3:17; 1Pe 4:19
   - –God works for his people's good ... Ge 50:20; Jer 29:11; Ro 8:28

   See also PAIN
4. Our relationship to God's plan for us
   - –Pray that God's will be done ... Mt 6:10
   - –Pray that things happen by God's will .. Ac 18:21; Ro 15:31–32; 1Co 16:7; Jas 4:13–15
   - –Submit to God's plan for us ... Ac 21:14

WIND

See WEATHER

WINE

See ALCOHOL

WISDOM

–Comprehensive knowledge that is put into practice

A. Human wisdom
1. Source of wisdom
   - –Received as a gift from God ... 1Ki 3:11–12; Pr 2:6; Ecc 2:26; Da 2:21; Jas 1:5
   - –Received as a gift from the Spirit ... 1Co 12:8; Eph 1:17
   - –Starts with the fear of the Lord ... Job 28:28; Ps 111:10; Pr 9:10
   - –Comes from listening to the wise ... Pr 1:2; Pr 4:1–11; Pr 13:20
   - –Comes from research and education ... Ecc 1:13,17; Ecc 7:25
   - –Comes from discipline ... Pr 29:15
   - –Comes from admonishing one another .. Col 3:16
2. Expressions of wisdom
   - –Serving as craftsman ... Ex 28:3
   - –Following God's law ... Dt 4:6; Hos 14:9; Mt 7:24–26
   - –Writing proverbs and songs ... 1Ki 4:29,32
   - –Studying God's creation ... 1Ki 4:29,33
   - –Administering justice ... 1Ki 3:16–28; 1Ki 10:8–9
   - –Avoiding evil ... Pr 5:1–6
   - –Taking advice ... Pr 13:10
   - –Giving advice ... Da 1:20
   - –Interpreting visions and dreams ... Da 2:23,30

–Preparing for the future .... Mt 25:1–13
–Exercising patience .. Pr 19:11
–Living the Christian lifestyle .... Pr 2:20–21; Jas 3:17
–Defending the gospel .... Ac 6:3,10
3. Benefits of wisdom
–Makes us blessed ... Pr 3:13
–Leads to a long life . Pr 3:16
–Preserves our lives .. Ecc 7:12
–Protects us .... Pr 4:6
–Exalts us .... Pr 4:8–9
–Brings us joy .... Pr 29:3; Pr 27:11
–Gives us strength ... Ecc 7:19
–Brings us healing ... Pr 12:18
–Saves us from evil ways .... Pr 2:12–19
B. Divine wisdom
1. True wisdom centers in God
–God has wisdom .... Job 12:13; Job 28:20–24; Da 2:20
–Christ is the wisdom of God .... 1Co 1:24,30; Col 2:3
–The Spirit is the Spirit of wisdom .... Isa 11:2; Eph 1:17
2. The nature of God's wisdom
–Profound .... Job 9:4
–Precious .... Pr 8:18–19
–Deep and rich .... Ro 11:33
–Magnificent .... Isa 28:29
–Manifold .... Eph 3:10
–Unsurpassable .... Jer 10:7
3. Activities of God's wisdom
–Operative in creation .... Ps 104:24; Pr 3:19; Pr 8:22–31; Jer 10:12
–Controls nature .... Job 26:12; Job 39:26
–Controls history .... Isa 10:12–13
–Counsels rulers .... Pr 8:14–16

WITCHCRAFT

See MAGIC, WITCHCRAFT AND SORCERY

WITNESS

–One who bears testimony to something or someone
A. Types of witnesses
–God as a witness .... Ge 31:50; Jdg 11:10
–People as witnesses .... Jos 24:22; Ru 4:9–11; Jer 32:12
–Things as witnesses .... Dt 31:19–21; Jos 24:27; Isa 19:19–20
B. Legal witnesses
–Two or three necessary to convict someone .... Dt 17:6; Mt 26:60–61; 2Co 13:1
–No false testimony to be given .... Ex 20:16; Dt 19:16–18; Pr 24:28–29
C. Witnesses to God's truth and salvation
–Israel as witnesses .... Isa 43:10–12; Isa 44:8
–The prophets as witnesses .... Ac 10:43; Ac 26:22–23
–John the Baptist as witness .... Jn 1:7,15, 32–34; Jn 5:33–34
–Jesus Christ as the faithful witness .... Jn 8:18; Jn 18:37; Rev 1:5–6
–The Holy Spirit as witness .... Jn 15:26; Ac 5:30–32; Ro 8:16
–Signs and wonders as witnesses .... Jn 2:11; Jn 20:30–31; Heb 2:3–4
–Jesus' followers as witnesses .... Lk 1:2; Ac 1:8; Ac 3:15–16; Ac 5:30–32; Ac 10:41–42

WOMEN

A. Status of women
1. In creation
–Created in the image of God .... Ge 1:27
–Equal responsibility and blessing .... Ge 1:26,28–30
–Created as a companion for man .... Ge 2:18,20
–Created second, from man .... Ge 2:21–22; 1Co 11:3,7–8,12
2. In and after the fall
–Eve was tempted and sinned first .... Ge 3:1–6; 2Co 11:3; 1Ti 2:14
–Were subordinated to husbands .... Ge 3:16
–Were considered weak and insecure .. Isa 19:16; Jer 50:37; 1Pe 3:7
3. In the covenant of the Old Testament
–Circumcision only for males .... Ge 17:10–14
–Only males instructed to appear before Lord .... Ex 23:17
–Value of woman was less than that of a man .... Lev 27:1–8
–Sons had priority over daughters .... Nu 36:1–9; Ps 127:3–4
–Women served in the worship of God .... Ex 15:20; Ex 38:8; Ezr 2:65
–Women also expected to keep the festivals . Dt 16:9–15
4. Jesus' attitude to women
–Healed women as well as men .... Mk 1:30–31; Mk 5:25–34; Lk 13:10–17
–Used women as examples in parables .... Lk 13:20–21; Lk 15:8–10; Lk 17:35; Lk 18:1–8
–Was supported by women .... Lk 8:1–3
–Affirmed women eager to learn .... Lk 10:38–42; Jn 4:7–26
–Forgave an adulteress .... Jn 8:1–11
–Praised a poor widow and her gift .... Lk 21:1–4
–Praised Martha's confession .... Jn 11:24–27
–Women were first witnesses to resurrection .... Mt 28:1–10; Mk 16:1–8; Lk 24:1–11; Jn 20:1–2, 10–18
5. In the redemption won by Christ
–In Christ no male or female .... Gal 3:28
–Salvation came through woman .... Gal 4:4–5
–Woman saved through childbearing . 1Ti 2:15
–Spirit poured out on sons and daughters .. Joel 2:28–29; Ac 2:17–18
–Women filled with the Holy Spirit .... Lk 1:41–45; Ac 2:1–4
–Women and men both saved .... Ac 9:36–39; Ac 17:4,12
–Women prayed and prophesied .... Ac 1:14; 1Co 11:5
–Women were to be silent in the churches 1Co 14:33–35; 1Ti 2:11–12
B. Roles and occupations of women
–Wife
See MARRIAGE
–Mother
See MOTHER
–Shepherd .... Ge 29:6; Ex 2:16
–Businesswoman .... Pr 31:13–19; Ac 16:14
–Judge .... Jdg 4:4–5
–Prophetess .... 2Ki 22:14–20; Ac 21:8–9
–Teacher .... Ac 18:26
–Workers in the church . Ro 16:1–2; Php 4:2–3
C. Prominent women in the Bible
–Abigail 1Sa 25:3
–Anna .... Lk 2:36
–Athaliah 2Ki 11:1
–Bathsheba 2Sa 11:3
–Deborah .... Jdg 4:4
–Dorcas .... Ac 9:36
–Elizabeth .... Lk 1:5
–Esther .... Est 2:7
–Eve .... Ge 3:20
–Hagar .... Ge 16:1
–Hannah 1Sa 1:2
–Huldah 2Ki 22:14
–Jael .... Jdg 4:17
–Jezebel 1Ki 16:31
–Leah .... Ge 29:16
–Lydia .... Ac 16:14
–Mary the mother of Jesus .... Lk 1:27
–Mary Magdalene .... Lk 8:2
–Mary and Martha .... Lk 10:38–39
–Miriam .... Ex 15:20
–Phoebe .... Ro 16:1
–Priscilla .... Ac 18:2
–Rachel .... Ge 29:16
–Rahab .... Jos 2:3
–Rebekah .... Ge 24:29
–Ruth .... Ru 1:4
–Salome .... Mk 15:40
–Sapphira .... Ac 5:1
–Sarah .... Ge 12:5
–Tamar .... Ge 38:6
See also entries for each of these women

WORD OF GOD

A. What is the word of God?
–The word God spoke in creation .... Ps 33:6–9
–The word God spoke to the prophets .... 1Ki 17:2,8; Jer 1:2,4,11–13; Eze 6:1–3
–The Old Testament revelation .... Jn 10:34–45
–The word spoken by Jesus .... Lk 5:1
–Jesus himself as the Word become flesh .... Jn 1:1,14
–The word spoken by the apostles .... Ac 13:44; 1Th 2:13; 1Pe 1:25
–Instructions given by pastors .... Gal 6:6; 2Ti 4:2
B. What power does the word of God have?
–The power to create .... Ps 33:6; Heb 11:3; 2Pe 3:5
–The power to sustain all of creation .... Ps 147:15–18; Heb 1:3
–The power to heal .... Ps 107:20; Mt 8:8
–The power to judge our hearts .... Heb 4:12
–The power to give us new birth .... Jas 1:18; 1Pe 1:23
–The power to lead us to faith .... Ro 10:17
–The power to save us .. 2Ti 3:15
–The power to make us holy .... Eph 5:26
–The power to fight against Satan .... Eph 6:17; Rev 19:13–15
–The power to destroy the world 2Pe 3:7
C. Characteristics of God's word
–It is reliable 2Sa 7:28
–It is true .... 1Ki 17:24; Jn 17:17
–It is flawless .... Pr 30:5
–It is alive and active ... Heb 4:12
–It is eternal .... Ps 119:89
–It will endure .... Isa 40:8; Mt 5:18; Mt 24:35
–It will not return empty .... Isa 55:11
D. Our reaction to the word of God
–We must hear it .... Isa 1:10; Jer 7:1–2
–We must understand it . Mt 13:23
–We must accept it .... Mk 4:20; Ac 2:41; 1Th 2:13
–We must hide it in our hearts .... Ps 119:11
–We must retain it .... Lk 8:15
–We must let it dwell in us .... Col 3:16
–We must trust in it .... Ps 119:42
–We must hope in it .... Ps 119:74, 81,114; Ps 130:5
–We must praise it .... Ps 56:4,10
–We must live according to it .... Ps 119:9
–We must obey it .... Ps 119:17,67; Jas 1:22–24
–We must handle it correctly 2Ti 2:15
–We must preach it .... Ac 8:4
E. Pictures used for the word of God
–Lamp and light .... Ps 119:105
–Rain producing fruit ... Isa 55:10–11
–Consuming fire .... Jer 5:14
–Destroying hammer .... Jer 23:29
–Seed .... Mk 4:14
–Sword .... Eph 6:17; Heb 4:12
F. Scripture as the word of God
See INSPIRATION OF SCRIPTURE
G. Jesus as the Word of God
–He is the Word of God .... Jn 1:1
–He is the creative Word .... Jn 1:3
–He is the Word become flesh .... Jn 1:14
–He is the Word of life . 1Jn 1:2
–He is the victorious Word .... Rev 19:13–16

WORK

A. The work of humans
1. Humans in general
a. Nature of work
–Required of Adam before the fall .... Ge 1:28; Ge 2:15,19–20
–Required of humans after the fall .... Ex 20:9; Eph 4:28; 1Th 4:11
–Became hard work .... Ge 3:17–19; Ecc 3:9–10
–Can seem meaningless .... Ecc 1:14; Ecc 2:11,17
b. God's relationship to human work
–He commands it .. Dt 5:13
–He expects it .... Ps 104:23
–He blesses honest toil .... Pr 14:23; Pr 27:23–27
–He speaks against laziness .... Pr 6:6–11; Pr 10:4–5
2. Daily work for Christians
–We must earn our daily bread 2Th 3:10
–We must pray for God to establish it .. Ps 90:17
–We must depend on God in it .... Ps 127:1–2; Isa 26:12

–We must bring glory to God's name through it .... 1Co 10:31; Col 3:17
–We must accompany it with prayer .... Ne 4:6–9
–Our work is not in vain 1Co 15:58

B. The work of God
1. Aspects of his work
–Created the world ... Ge 1:1–2:3; Ps 8:3
–Preserves the world .. Ps 36:6
–Governs the world .. Ac 17:26; Eph 1:11
–Redeems the world .. Jn 3:16–17; Jn 12:47
–Always at work in the world .... Jn 5:17
2. His works described as:
–Manifold .... Ps 104:24
–Great .... Ps 92:5
–Awesome .... Ps 66:5
–Amazing .... Rev 15:3
–Wonderful .... Ps 139:14
–Faithful .... Ps 111:7
3. Our reaction to God's works
–We should see them . Ps 46:8; Ps 66:5
–We should have regard for them ..... Ps 28:5
–We should consider them .... Ps 8:3
–We should meditate on them .... Ps 77:12; Ps 143:5
–We should sing for joy at them .... Ps 92:4
–We should praise them .... Job 36:24
–We should tell others about them .... Ps 107:21–22; Ps 145:4–6

WORLD

A. Meaning of the word "world"
–The entire created universe .... Jer 10:12
–All men and women on earth .... Ge 11:1,9; 1Sa 17:46; Isa 12:5; Jn 3:16
–People opposed to God . Jn 14:30–31; 1Jn 5:19
–Natural life as opposed to spiritual life 1Co 7:33

B. God's relationship to the sinful world
1. God the Father
–He loves it .... Jn 3:16
–He sent Jesus to save it .... Jn 3:16–17; Jn 17:18,23
–He reconciled it through Christ 2Co 5:19
–He holds it accountable to him .... Ro 3:19
–He will judge it ..... Ps 96:13; Ps 98:9
2. Jesus the Son
–He is its light ...... Jn 3:19; Jn 8:12; Jn 9:5
–He takes away its sin .... Jn 1:29
–He is its Savior ..... Lk 2:10–11; Jn 4:42; 1Ti 1:15; 1Jn 4:14
–He gives it life ..... Jn 6:33,51
–He has overcome it . Jn 16:33
–He will judge it ..... Ac 17:31

C. Our relationship to the sinful world
1. How we relate to the world
–We are in it .... Jn 17:15; 2Co 10:3
–We are strangers in it 1Pe 2:11
–We are not of it .... Jn 15:19; Jn 17:14,16; Jas 4:4
–We may not adopt its standards .... Ro 12:2; Tit 2:12; Jas 1:27
–We must not love it . 2Ti 4:10; 1Jn 2:15–16
–We must be crucified to it .... Ro 6:6; Gal 6:14
–We must overcome it .... Jn 16:33; 1Jn 5:4–5
–We must proclaim the gospel to it ..... Mt 24:14; Mt 28:19; Mk 16:15
–We will judge it 1Co 6:2
2. How the world relates to us
–The world hates us .. Jn 15:18; Jn 17:14; 1Jn 3:13
–The world persecutes us .... Jn 15:20–21; 2Ti 3:12
–The world has false prophets 1Jn 4:1,3; 2Jn 7

WORSHIP

A. The call to worship
1. Commanded by God . 2Ki 17:35–39; Ps 29:2; Ps 96:9
2. Affirmed by believers .... Ps 95:6; Ps 100:1–2; Ps 132:6–7; Heb 10:25

B. Examples of people at worship
1. The formal worship of God
–Cain and Abel ...... Ge 4:3–4
–Noah .... Ge 8:20
–Abraham .... Ge 22:5
–Isaac .... Ge 26:23–25
–Jacob .... Ge 35:1–7
–The Israelites under Moses .... Ex 24:1–8
–The Israelites under David 1Ch 23:28–31
–Daniel .... Da 6:10
–The returned exiles .. Ezr 3:10–11; Ne 8:2–18
–Jesus .... Lk 4:15–27
–The apostles .... Ac 3:1
–The early church .... Ac 2:42,46–47; Ac 20:7–11
–The hosts of heaven . Rev 5:8–14; Rev 7:9–17
2. The worship of Christ
–The wise men ...... Mt 2:11
–Christ's disciples .... Mt 14:33; Mt 28:17; Lk 24:52
–A blind man who received his sight ... Jn 9:38
–The heavenly hosts .. Rev 5:8–14

C. The day for worship
See SABBATH

D. Characteristics of true worship
1. Principles to follow
–Worship God alone . Ex 20:4–5; Ex 23:24–25; Mt 4:10
–Love God with all your heart .... Dt 6:4–6; Dt 10:12–13
–Be humble in heart .. Ps 51:17; Isa 66:2; Mic 6:6–8
–Depend on the Holy Spirit .... Jn 4:20–24; Php 3:3
–Formal ritual alone is insufficient .... Isa 1:11–15; Am 5:21–24
2. Specific elements in Christian worship
–Reading Scripture ... 1Ti 4:13
–Preaching .... Ac 20:7; 2Ti 4:2
See PREACHING
–Praying 1Ti 2:1,8
See PRAYER
–Singing .... Col 3:16
See MUSIC AND SONG
–Giving an offering .. 1Co 16:1–2
See TITHES AND OFFERINGS
–Exercising spiritual gifts 1Co 14:26–33
See GIFTS OF THE SPIRIT
–Celebrating the sacraments .... Ac 2:41–42; 1Co 11:18–29
See BAPTISM; LORD'S SUPPER

WRATH

See ANGER

XERXES

–King of Persia .... Est 1:1–2
–Deposed Queen Vashti ..... Est 1:15–21
–Made Esther queen .... Est 2:17
–Signed edict to annihilate the Jews .... Est 3:12–15
–Received Esther without having summoned her ...... Est 5:1–8
–Honored Mordecai .... Est 6:1–11
–Furious at Haman .... Est 7:1–8
–Hanged Haman .... Est 7:9–10
–Signed edict allowing Jews to defend themselves ...... Est 8:3–14
–Exalted Mordecai .... Est 8:1–2,15; Est 9:4

YEAR OF JUBILEE

See THE RICH AND THE POOR; SLAVERY

YEAST

–A leavening substance for bread

A. Yeast and bread
–Allowed in some offerings .... Lev 7:13; Lev 23:17
–Not allowed in other offerings .... Ex 23:15–16; Lev 2:11; Dt 16:1–8
–The festival of unleavened bread
See FESTIVALS

B. Yeast as a symbol
–A symbol of corruption and evil .... Mt 16:6,12; Gal 5:7–9; 1Co 5:6–8
–A symbol of the penetrating influence of the kingdom .... Mt 13:33; Lk 13:21

YOKE

A. Uses for the yoke
–To use on animals at work 1Ki 19:19–21
–To control slaves 1Ti 6:1
–To wear as a prophetic symbol .... Jer 27:2

B. The yoke as a symbol
1. Positive
–A symbol of service to God's law .... Jer 2:20
–A symbol of discipleship .... Mt 11:28–30
2. Negative
–A symbol of oppression .... 1Ki 12:4,9–11; Jer 28:10–14
–A symbol of bondage to sin .... La 1:14
–A symbol of legalism .... Ac 15:10; Gal 5:1
–A symbol of union with unbelievers 2Co 6:14

YOUTH

A. Characteristics of youth
–Strong .... Pr 20:29; Isa 40:30; 1Jn 2:14
–Devoted and zealous ... 1Ki 18:12; Jer 2:2; Gal 1:13–14
–Inexperienced .... 1Sa 17:33; 1Ch 22:5; Jer 1:6
–Sinful and foolish ...... Job 13:26; 1Sa 2:17; 1Ki 12:8–15; Ps 25:7; 2Ti 2:22
–Lacking in knowledge and judgment .... Ge 37:2–11; Pr 1:4; Pr 7:7

B. Encouragement to youth
–To commit their lives to God .... Ps 119:9; Ecc 12:1; La 3:27
–To seek knowledge from God 1Ki 3:7–9
–To enjoy life .... Pr 5:18; Ecc 11:9
–To see visions and to prophesy .... Joel 2:28; Ac 2:17
–To exercise self-control .... Tit 2:6

C. Familiar stories involving youths
–Joseph sold into Egypt . Ge 37:12–28
–Joseph serving faithfully in Egypt .... Ge 39:1–12
–Gideon called to be military leader .... Jdg 6:15–16
–David killing Goliath ... 1Sa 17:26–50
–Joash repairing the temple 2Ch 24:4–14
–Josiah purifying the land and the temple 2Ch 34:3–13
–Jeremiah called to serve as prophet .... Jer 1:4–19
–James and John following Jesus .... Mk 1:19–20
–Timothy accompanying Paul .... Ac 16:1–3
–Timothy serving as pastor 1Ti 4:12

ZACCHAEUS

–Tax collector .... Lk 19:1–2
–Climbed a tree to see Jesus .... Lk 19:3–4
–Welcomed Jesus into his house .... Lk 19:5–7
–Saved by Jesus .... Lk 19:8–9

ZADOK

–A priest in the time of David 2Sa 8:17
–Ministered in Hebron after Saul's death 1Ch 12:23–28
–Helped bring the ark to Jerusalem 1Ch 15:11–13
–Became David's priest 1Ch 16:39–40; 1Ch 24:6
–Loyal to David during Absalom's rebellion 2Sa 15:24–36; 2Sa 17:15, 17–21
–Loyal to David during Adonijah's rebellion 1Ki 1:8
–Anointed Solomon king 1Ki 1:32–40
–Became Solomon's priest .. 1Ki 2:35; 1Ki 4:4; 1Ch 29:22

ZEAL

See JEALOUS

ZEBULUN

A. Son of Jacob by Leah ... Ge 35:23; 1Ch 2:1
–Name means "honor" . Ge 30:20
–Went to Egypt with family .... Ge 46:8,14
–Father of three sons .... Ge 46:14
–Blessed by Jacob ...... Ge 49:13

B. Tribe descended from Zebulun
–Blessed by Moses ..... Dt 33:18–19
–Numbered .... Nu 1:31; Nu 26:27
–Allotted land .... Jos 19:10–16; Eze 48:26
–Failed to fully possess the land .... Jdg 1:30
–Supported Deborah .... Jdg 4:6–10; Jdg 5:14,18
–Supported David 1Ch 12:33
–One of the tribes of the 144,000 .... Rev 7:8

ZECHARIAH

A. Son of Jeroboam II; king of Israel 2Ki 15:8–9

–Assassinated by Shallum 2Ki 15:10
B. A post-exilic prophet
–Encouraged rebuilding of temple .... Ezr 5:1; Ezr 6:14
–Received various visions and prophecies .... Zec 1:1,7; Zec 7:1,8
C. Father of John the Baptist
–Took his turn as priest in temple .... Lk 1:5,8–10
–Received announcement of the birth of a son ... Lk 1:11–20
–Could not speak for nine months .... Lk 1:20–22
–Gave name "John" to his son .... Lk 1:59–63
–Praised God with a song .... Lk 1:64–79

ZEDEKIAH
A. A false prophet 1Ki 22:11; 2Ch 18:10
–Slapped true prophet Micaiah in the face 1Ki 22:24; 2Ch 18:23
B. Son of Josiah 1Ch 3:15
–Also called Mattaniah .. 2Ki 24:17
–Made king of Judah by Nebuchadnezzar 2Ki 24:17–20; 2Ch 36:10
–Asked Jeremiah to pray for Jerusalem .... Jer 37:3
–Consulted with Jeremiah .... Jer 38:14–27
–Rebelled against Nebuchadnezzar 2Ki 24:20; 2Ch 36:13
–Jerusalem destroyed during his time 2Ki 25:1–17; 2Ch 36:15–19
–Saw his sons killed .... Jer 39:5–6
–Blinded and taken to Babylon .... Jer 39:7

ZERUBBABEL
–Descendant of David ...... 1Ch 3:19; Mt 1:3
–Led return of Jews from exile .... Ezr 2:2; Ne 7:7
–Restored worship in Judah . Ezr 3:1–8
–Helped rebuild temple ..... Ezr 3:8–13; Hag 1:1–12; Zec 4:1–9
–Handled opposition to rebuilding .... Ezr 4:1–5

ZILPAH
–Servant of Leah .... Ge 29:24
–Mother of Gad and Asher .. Ge 30:9–12; Ge 35:26

ZIMRI
–King of Israel 1Ki 16:9–20
–Gained throne by assassination 1Ki 16:9–10
–Committed suicide 1Ki 16:18

ZION
A. Zion as an earthly place
–The Jebusite city captured by David 2Sa 5:6–7
–The place where David built his palace 2Ch 5:2
–The temple of the Lord .... Ps 20:2; Isa 18:7
–The holy mountain of God in Jerusalem ...... Ps 74:2; Joel 3:17,21
–The whole city of Jerusalem .... 2Ki 19:31; Ps 48:1–2; Isa 33:20; Am 1:2
–The whole nation of Judah .... Ps 78:68; Isa 51:16
B. Zion as a symbolic place
–The heavenly throne of God .... Ps 9:7,11; Mic 4:7
–The prophetic kingdom of Jesus .... Ps 2:6; Ps 110:2; Isa 28:16; Isa 59:20
–The heavenly Jerusalem .... Heb 12:22
–The place from which Christ rules .... Rev 14:1

ZIPPORAH
–Daughter of Reuel; wife of Moses .... Ex 2:18,21–22
–Moved with Moses back to Egypt .... Ex 4:20
–Had two sons .... Ex 18:2–4
–Circumcised her son .... Ex 4:24–26
–Visited Moses in the desert . Ex 18:5–6

ZOPHAR
–One of Job's friends who tried to comfort him .... Job 2:11–13
–His first speech .... Job 11:1–20
–His second speech .... Job 20:1–29
–Offered sacrifices to God after Job's restoration ...... Job 42:7–9

Colophon

The New Revised Standard Version database is copyrighted by the National Council of Churches
and maintained by Auto-Graphics Inc. of Pomona, California.

The Main Concordance was produced with original software created by Dennis Thomas for the AT&T UnixPC.
The Index of Articles Etc. and the Index to NRSV Footnotes were generated with
WordCruncher 4.0 from the Electronic Text Corporation.

The Main Concordance and the Index to NRSV Footnotes were typeset by
John R. Kohlenberger III, using Xerox Ventura Publisher 3.0;
the Index of Articles Etc. was also edited and typeset by
John R. Kohlenberger III, using WordPerfect 5.0.

The Topical Index to the NRSV was compiled by Verlyn D. Verbrugge
and typeset at Auto-Graphics Inc. of Pomona, California.

The database was edited and typeset on a Leading Edge D3/25 computer
with a Cornerstone XL single-page monitor.
Page proofs were produced on an NEC Silentwriter2 290 laser printer.

Final camera-ready pages were produced on a Linotype Linotronic P200
at the facilities of Multnomah Graphics in Portland, Oregon.

The NRSV Concordance Unabridged was designed and edited by
John R. Kohlenberger III and Ed M. van der Maas.